A Greek-English Lexicon of the New Testament and Other Early Christian Literature

A Greek-English Lexicon *of the* New Testament *and other* Early Christian Literature

—— THIRD EDITION ——

(BDAG)

revised and edited by

Frederick William Danker

based on

WALTER BAUER'S

Griechisch-deutsches Wörterbuch zu den Schriften des Neuen Testaments und der frühchristlichen Literatur, sixth edition, ed. Kurt Aland and Barbara Aland, with Viktor Reichmann and on previous English editions by W. F. Arndt, F. W. Gingrich, and F. W. Danker

THE UNIVERSITY OF CHICAGO PRESS | CHICAGO AND LONDON

First edition, 1957, translated and adapted by William F. Arndt and F. Wilbur Gingrich from the fourth edition of Walter Bauer's lexicon.

Second edition, 1979, revised and augmented by F. W. Gingrich and F. W. Danker from W. Bauer's fifth edition.

Frederick William Danker is Christ Seminary-Seminex Professor Emeritus of New Testament at the Lutheran School of Theology, Chicago, Illinois.

The University of Chicago Press, Chicago 60637
The University of Chicago Press, Ltd., London

Printed in the United States of America
09 08 07 06 05 04 03 02 01   2 3 4 5

ISBN: 0-226-03933-1 (cloth)

Library of Congress Cataloging-in-Publication Data

Danker, Frederick W.
A Greek-English lexicon of the New Testament and other early Christian Literature / revised and edited by Frederick William Danker.—3rd. ed.
p.   cm.
"Based on Walter Bauer's Griechisch-deutsches Wörterbuch zu den Schriften des Neuen Testaments und der frühchristlichen Literatur, sixth edition, ed. Kurt Aland and Barbara Aland, with Viktor Reichmann and on previous English editions by W. F. Arndt, F. W. Gingrich, and F. W. Danker."
Includes bibliographical references.
ISBN 0-226-03933-1 (acid-free paper)
1. Greek language, Biblical—Dictionaries—English. 2. Bible. N.T.—Dictionaries—English. I. Bauer, Walter, 1877–1960. Griechisch-deutsches Wörterbuch zu den Schriften des Neuen Testaments und der frühchristlichen Literatur. II. Title

PA881 .D27   2000
487′.4—dc21

00-026844

The paper used in this publication meets the minimum requirements of the American National Standard for Information Sciences—Permanence of Paper for Printed Library Materials, ANSI Z39.48-1992.

Foreword to the Revised Edition

Much of the historical material in forewords to the earlier editions of this lexicon is here included in condensed form.

The history of dictionaries specifically designed for the Greek New Testament opens with a Greek-Latin glossary of seventy-five unnumbered pages in the first volume of the Complutensian Polyglot of 1522, including the words of the New Testament, Ecclesiasticus, and the Wisdom of Solomon. The incompleteness, inaccuracy, and elementary character of this glossary reflect the low state of Greek studies at the time it was published, but it was the first in a long and useful succession of New Testament lexical works.

More in keeping with scholarly demands was the *Lexicon Graeco-Latinum in Novum Domini nostri Jesu Christi Testamentum* by Georg Pasor, published in 1619 at Herborn in Nassau. Pasor listed words alphabetically according to their roots, a procedure also adopted by Francis Brown, Samuel R. Driver, and Charles A. Briggs in their Hebrew-Aramaic lexicon of 1907. In 1640 (Basel), Ludovicus Lucius put out his *Dictionarium Novi Testamenti* with words arranged for the first time in strict alphabetic order instead of by word-roots.

Many faults of contemporary NT lexicons were pointed out by Johann F. Fischer in his *Prolusiones de vitiis lexicorum Novi Testamenti* (Leipzig, 1791). Among these defects were neglect of the smaller words, whose frequent use makes them extremely difficult to analyze and classify, and insufficient attention to the background of New Testament words in Hebrew, the LXX, and general Greek literature.

Among the works that showed the effect of Fischer's criticism was Christian A. Wahl's Greek-Latin lexicon of 1822 (Leipzig). This was translated into English in 1825 by Edwin Robinson, an eminent American biblical scholar. Robinson brought out his own Greek-English dictionary of the NT in 1836 (Boston).

Up to this time it was customary for dictionaries intended for scholars to provide definitions in Latin, though Edward Leigh in his *Critica Sacra* (London, 1639) had made a partial and apologetic attempt to give them in English, and John Parkhurst had published a Greek-English lexicon in 1769.

Karl Ludwig Wilibald Grimm published in 1868 (Leipzig) a thorough revision of Christian G. Wilke's Greek-Latin *Clavis Novi Testamenti philologica* (1839; 2d ed. 1851). Four years earlier, through special arrangement with Grimm's publisher, Joseph H. Thayer of Harvard University began the augmented translation of Grimm's book, published in 1886 as *Greek-English Lexicon of the New Testament* (New York and Edinburgh).

The first dictionary to appear after the epoch-making discoveries (especially of papyri) near the end of the nineteenth century was Erwin Preuschen's Greek-German lexicon of 1910.

Unfortunately, it failed to make much use of the newfound material, which was of little interest to some scholars because of its documentary banality compared to the purity of Plato's tongue. But Preuschen's work did include for the first time the words of the Apostolic Fathers.

Upon Preuschen's untimely death in 1920, the revision of his lexicon was entrusted to Walter Bauer of Göttingen (b. 8 August 1877, d. 17 November 1960). When his revision appeared in 1928 (Giessen) as the second edition of Preuschen, it was hailed as the best thing in its field. A third edition, thoroughly revised and reset, came out in 1937 (Berlin), with Bauer's name alone on the title page.

For the fourth edition, Bauer undertook a systematic search in Greek literature down to Byzantine times for parallels to the language of the New Testament. Hans von Campenhausen acknowledged the magnitude of this task, when he reviewed its first three fascicles (TLZ 75, 1950, 349): We are here dealing with a work "which, when considered as the performance of one man, strikes one as almost fabulous. Not only was there a gigantic amount of material to be mastered, involving the most minute acquaintance with the whole body of Christian literature, but this task required at the same time the gift of combining and relating facts, and of preserving an adequate scholarly alertness which is granted to but few people; one thinks of the difficulty of immediately recognizing parallels in the respective authors and making proper use of them. This art is all the more admirable because its achievements manifest themselves only in the apparently insignificant form of articles in a lexicon, which purposely are kept as brief and factual as possible. Most of the readers will normally not become aware of what has been accomplished." F. Wilbur Gingrich echoed the accolade (NTS 9, 1962–63, 3–10).

On this fourth edition of Bauer's *Griechisch-deutsches Wörterbuch zu den Schriften des Neuen Testaments und der übrigen urchristlichen Literatur* (Berlin, 1949–52), William F. Arndt (b. 1 December 1880, d. 25 February 1957) and F. Wilbur Gingrich (b. 27 September 1901, d. 19 October 1993) based *A Greek-English Lexicon of the New Testament and Other Early Christian Literature* (also known as BAG, for Bauer-Arndt-Gingrich). It was not their purpose to make a literal translation, which would indeed have been impossible; and they did not hesitate to recommend recourse to Bauer's original German to determine "exactly what Bauer says about any word." Their own contribution to the work was considerable, to judge from the list of over ninety entries cited as representative of "more or less significant adaptations or additions" in their 1957 edition.

In the course of making slight adjustments in the arrangement of entries, as well as correction of typographical and other errors in the original, Arndt and Gingrich added a few new words drawn especially from Papias and the apparatus in later editions of the NT text, not to speak of an interesting conjecture, ἀπαρτί, included for the first time in a NT lexicon. In addition to Bauer's bibliographical notices, the American team called attention to the contributions of James Hope Moulton and George Milligan's *Vocabulary of the Greek Testament* (M-M) and Carl D. Buck's *Dictionary of Selected Synonyms in the Principal Indo-European Languages*. The latter partially made up for the paucity of etymological information deplored by Bauer in the foreword to his third edition of 1937. References were likewise given to all the words treated by Edgar J. Goodspeed in his *Problems of New Testament Translation*, and to some from Frederick Field's *Notes on the Translation of the New Testament*. Frequent reference was also made to the NT grammars of James Hope Moulton (2d vol. completed by Wilbert F. Howard) and Archibald T. Robertson. Still remaining to be probed in depth is the phenomenon of similar semantic transference in languages whose users are separated by centuries, but Arndt and Gingrich offered some stimulus through exploration here and there of the *New (Oxford) English Dictionary*.

In their preface, Arndt and Gingrich sketched a brief history of their own endeavor: "When in 1947 the Lutheran Church Missouri Synod observed its centennial, a part of the thank offering gathered was set aside as a fund for scholarly research. The Lutheran Academy of Scholarship, Dr. M. H. Scharlemann president, had a prominent part in the discussions that led to this decision. The committee, appointed by Dr. J. W. Behnken, the president of the church, to administer the fund, resolved to have Bauer's *Wörterbuch* done into English with such adaptations and additions as would be required. Since the University of Chicago Press had been negotiating with Dr. Bauer on this subject, the committee turned to this publishing house and enlisted its co-operation and services. The translation rights were duly obtained. Professor F. W. Gingrich of Albright College, Reading, Pa., was engaged to give his full time to the undertaking, having been granted a leave of absence in September 1949. Professor W. F. Arndt of Concordia Seminary, St. Louis, Mo., an institution of the Lutheran Church–Missouri Synod, was appointed to be the director of the venture. The manuscript was finished in January 1955. This dictionary in its English dress constitutes a gift of the Lutheran Church–Missouri Synod to the English-speaking world, presented in the hope that the work may assist in the interpretation and dissemination of the Divine Word which lives and abides forever."

Yet, even as the first volumes were coming off the press, plans for a revised edition began to take shape. When the English translation of Walter Bauer's *Wörterbuch* was published on 29 January 1957, Prof. Bauer was completing work on the fifth edition of his book, which came out in nine fascicles during 1957 and 1958. Upon the death of Prof. Arndt, my revered teacher, I was asked to serve with Prof. Gingrich in the preparation of the new edition, which was to contain the new material in Bauer's work and a vast amount of reference to studies that postdated it. The number of such and other supplemental references to scholarly literature ran into four figures (apart from Bauer's own additions). More important, the standard ancient Greek texts, as well as papyri and inscriptions, yielded additional formal and semantic parallels, in some cases necessitating rearrangement of patterns of definition. References to the literature of Qumran and to texts of portions of the New Testament published since the first edition were frequent. Indeed, the number of new words and other variants that were incorporated reflects the contribution made especially by the Bodmer Papyri to the study of the New Testament. Without the encouragement and support of the Committee for Scholarly Research of the Lutheran Church–Missouri Synod, the project could not have been undertaken, and the editors accorded their warmest thanks to Prof. Lorman M. Petersen of Concordia Theological Seminary (located at that time in Springfield, Illinois) for providing the necessary leadership. This second edition of BAG was published in 1979 and became known as BAGD (Bauer-Arndt-Gingrich-Danker). The present edition (BDAG: Bauer-Danker-Arndt-Gingrich) builds on traditions established in these earlier editions and the more recent publication of a sixth edition of Walter Bauer's work (*Griechisch-deutsches Wörterbuch* [Walter de Gruyter: Berlin, New York, 1988]), a "völlig neu bearbeitete Auflage" by Kurt Aland (d. 13 April 1994) and Barbara Aland, with substantial assistance from Viktor Reichmann (therefore known as BAAR). Through the guidance of Dr. Walter L. Rosin, the Committee for Scholarly Research of the Lutheran Church–Missouri Synod has again demonstrated its fervent support of New Testament lexical study.

As already indicated, any lexicographic endeavor worth its name must evolve in a context of new discoveries and constantly changing theoretical structures. Yet the claims of tradition are strong, and some balance must be maintained between contemporary demand and vision of what the future must inevitably require. In any event, judgments relating to a variety of approaches and modes of presentation of data will inevitably differ, as the publication of any new lexicon creates a crop of instant lexicographers. And this is as it should be. "Every other author may aspire to praise; the lexicographer can only hope to escape reproach, and even this negative recompense has been yet granted to very few." So wrote Samuel Johnson in a preface to his Dictionary.

This revision makes a primary departure in the use of bold roman typeface to highlight the meanings of words or their functional usage. Traditionally, lexicons have shown a preference for definition of a word in the source language with a corresponding word or phrase in the receptor language. A series of words or glosses is then offered to cover a variety of possibilities for translation. But these alleged meanings are for the most part mere formal equivalents, and in the case of words that occur very frequently in a language they run the hazard of being devoid of semantic value. Even worse, an unwary reader may think that a given word bears all the content expressed by a series of synonyms. Not to speak of the student whose primary language is not English and who therefore may not understand distinctions between the English synonyms that supposedly define a given Greek term. In an effort to overcome this problem, this revision builds on and expands Bauer's use of extended definition. This approach permits readers to explore the semantic structures of their own native language for adequate interpretation without the need of first deciphering the meaning of various glosses or synonyms. In this lexicon an arabic numeral at the head of a classification signifies that all the passages contained in that classification share a given meaning structure. Numerous entries therefore variously modify some older classifications that were based on mere grammatical or theological distinctions. Subsets of a meaning or collections of data relating to it—such as Bauer's valuable collections of grammatical or theological association—are indicated, as needed, through the traditional use of lettering a, b, α, β, and א, ב. Some words, such as ἀχαριστέω or γαμέω, do not require multiple classifications: in such instances no arabic numeral is used and any subsets follow the pattern cited above. Extended definitions are given in bold roman and may be followed by one or more formal equivalents in bold italics. The user of the lexicon can explore such equivalents for translation of passages that follow, but within the boundaries of the definition. When a formal equivalent is sufficient to convey the meaning, as *marry* in the entry γαμέω, this meaning stands in bold italics without extended definition. Normal italic type is used for suggested translation equivalents. In short, pains have been taken to provide readers with ample resources to form an independent critical judgment.

One of the more noteworthy developments in biblical studies in the latter third of the twentieth century relates to appreciation of ancient documents as literary monuments in their own right, an awareness that had been exhibited by students of Homer, Plato, et al. for a far longer period of time. Such awareness, together with increased emphasis on the relevance of anthropological and sociological studies for interpretation of ancient texts, places new demands on the lexicographer, and the current revision endeavors to reflect developments in this area. Also of concern are respect for inclusiveness and tolerance. But a scientific work dare not become a reservoir for ideological pleading, and culture-bound expressions must be given their due lest history be denied its day in court. It is an undeniable fact that God is primarily viewed patriarchally in the Bible, but translation must avoid exaggeration of the datum. "Brother" is a legitimate rendering of many instances of the term ἀδελφός, but when it appears that the term in the plural includes women (as in a letter to a congregation) some functional equivalent, such as "brothers and sisters", is required. A special problem relates to the use of "Jew" as a formal equivalent for Ἰουδαῖος. Much acrimonious debate has been needlessly engendered by use of an English term that bears an historical burden calculated to distort understanding of the term as used in New Testament texts. In the interest of more scientific discussion of texts, this revision resorts to the loanword "Judean" to render Ἰουδαῖος, but uses the term "Jew" in historical observations. Problems of a related nature involve terms that have experienced ecclesiastical evolution. To translate διάκονος or ἐπίσκοπος respectively as "deacon" and "bishop" would contaminate the rendering of ancient texts with associations made in later periods in which the English terms have taken on a technical sense that cannot be established for the original biblical terms. Frequently time-honored expressions are therefore given parenthetical status. In a related vein, a lexicographer is not obligated to celebrate opaqueness as a virtue in translation, when such opaqueness would suggest an opaqueness not present in the original. The fact that a given word or phrase has become a subject of intense debate during centuries of special theological or dogmatic pleading ought not automatically impose a judgment of unclarity or ambiguity on the original text.

A signal contribution of the German sixth edition of Walter Bauer's lexicon is the generous account taken of intertestamental resources. The broader coverage of early Christian literature includes especially apocryphal material associated with the name of Paul, and notably the Acts of Paul in various papyrus fragments. Also welcome is the vastly increased use of early Christian apologists (esp. Aristides, Athenagoras, Justin, and Tatian) for the understanding of NT diction. Among other frequent visitors from the past are Irenaeus and Origen. The present revision incorporates the new material, sometimes in updated and corrected form, as is apparent, e.g., from entries based on AcPl BMM (s. Abbreviation List 1). To assist the user in more ready location of early Christian material formerly found in generally inaccessible German publications, use is made of Prof. Kurt Aland's *Synopsis Quattuor Evangeliorum*[13] 1988 by citation of section number and line for such items as GPt and GNaass. Bauer received some criticism for proliferation of references to Greek literature, but contemporary biblical study endorses his judgment, and the present edition increases the coverage, in part to reinforce Bauer's awareness of the role of non-verbal linguistic components relating especially to socio-cultural perspectives. Indeed, in some instances the heaping of references is necessary to discourage risky assumptions of literary dependency on a single alleged source. Also, where Semitic influence appears to be strong, parallel Hellenic usage indicates that the Semitic cast may not be barbarous, as noted in G. H. R. Horsley's study on bilingualism in *New Documents* 5 (1989) 5–40. The latter work, now in eight volumes, has also been mined for papyrological and epigraphical references, which supplement material derived from Moulton-Milligan (M-M), *Vocabulary of the Greek Testament*. In this connection it is necessary to note that some entries in the *Vocabulary* are, in the absence of papyrus evidence, sources only for literary data or exegetical observations. For detailed etymological observations the reader is urged to note the acronym "DELG", with occasional reference to "Frisk" (s. List 6 for both).

To meet one of the major criticisms of previous editions, this revision offers a total overhaul of the lists of abbreviations. Users have complained that many references were in such abbreviated form that it was difficult to trace the sources. As partial remedy, the abbreviation lists cite many names and titles that appeared in earlier editions but were left undefined. From the listing of these new works one ought not therefore infer that all the new names result from an increase in the bibliographic base. A by-product of this procedure is the avoidance of multiplication of data in the main text, especially chronological, e.g. in connection with *Fragmente der Griechischen Historiker* (FGrH/Jac.) and numerous poets and dramatists. No apologies are here offered for preservation of Bauer's bibliographical data. The editors of BAAR excised much of it, but numerous lemmata in their edition now record cross-references to excised material. Indeed, it would be inappropriate to delete titles that provided a large amount of data for Bauer's entries, and it would be necessary first to determine which titles could be safely jettisoned without loss of carefully garnered data and well-pondered intepretations that are not to be had elsewhere. The fact that many subsequent discussions, including especially commentaries, fail to take account of numerous important books and articles referenced by Bauer makes their preservation all the more urgent. Inclusion of additional bibliography in certain entries in the present edition will give the reader access to other lines of inquiry. Scholars known for a commentary on a specific NT book are, in keeping with Bauer's practice, ordinarily noted only by surname in connection with NT references. Inasmuch as previous abbreviation lists were erroneously interpreted by some users as bibliographies for the entire work, it is important to note that the lists serve to interpret short titles or abbreviations and do not take notice of studies for which sufficient data are included in the main text. With a few exceptions, no attempt has been made to record the dates of reprints of older works. It also proved impossible, given the enormity of the task, to check more than a small percentage of Bauer's citations of ancient authors against the vast number of newer editions. This editor therefore welcomes, for inclusion in another publication, any contributions derived from such effort that might affect lexicographic judgment.

For the most part, the abbreviations follow generally recognized standards, including the *Checklist of Editions of Greek and Latin Papyri, Ostraca and Tablets* (Bulletin of the American Society of Papyrologists, Suppl. 7, 1992) and "Instructions for Contributors", published periodically in the *Journal of Biblical Literature*. In support of the efforts of Australian scholars G. H. R. Horsley and John A. Lee to standardize epigraphic abbreviations, references to epigraphs in List 3 generally follow their pattern. Since BDAG is of interest to scholars in numerous disciplines, some abbreviations may vary from standard practice, as, e.g., "ClB", whose abbreviation ordinarily is "CB". Similarly, Bauer's abbreviation "Pauly-W." (Pauly-Wissowa) departs from the standard "RE", which is applied in biblical circles to a different "Realencyklopädie". Some users might wish that such variations had been multiplied, but that would have defeated the objective of substantial standardization. Some items appear in more than one abbreviated form, but in some cases the lack of standardized forms in titles, or simply the fact that the source language is different from English—e.g., Henoch (German) = En—requires such variation. As an antidote to annoyance created by the liberal use of abbreviations, readers may console themselves with the fact that the bulk and therefore price of the lexicon are substantially reduced by such procedure. Out of courtesy to readers, the publishers have also encouraged the inclusion of a composite listing of all the abbreviations from the various lists. Instead of wandering through six lists for the identity of some ZYX, the reader will find its resolution in the composite list or be directed to a specific list.

The principal New Testament textual base is Nestle-Aland^{27} (s. N. at the beginning of List 1). Some of the words appearing in BDAG are not noted in the apparatus of that edition. Frequent account is taken of variant readings which are not recorded in the Nestle-Aland apparatus. Thus the word γενέθλιος appears Mk 6:21 in codex D, and is so noted in BAAR, but not in the Nestle-Aland apparatus. Although some words, such as ἀκαθάρτης or νάρκη, would not ordinarily merit attention, either because they are editorial inventions which have wormed their way into respected editions without strict accounting (e.g., some Erasmian readings) or are the result of erroneous restoration of a fragmentary text, their appearance in learned discussions requires identification with cautionary notice in this lexicon. Since little advantage is to be gained by cluttering the lexicon with an unscientific collection of selected manuscript sigla, users of the lexicon are encouraged to find the sources for such variants in earlier editions of Nestle, in Tischendorf (s. Tdf. at the beginning of List 1), or in other critical editions. For related reasons I have not included in citation of text the brackets used in many passages in Nestle-Aland.

The proliferation of papyri and new editions of early Christian literature suggests caution about certainty respecting completeness of citation. The use of asterisks (indicating completeness of citation, either of the NT or the Apostolic Fathers or both) at the end of entries has therefore been abandoned. But students can count on completeness of citation of all except the most common words appearing in the main text of the 27th edition of Nestle.

Future revisions of this lexicon will probably feature inclusion of lexemes from early Christian pseudepigrapha that are not found in the present text. Apart from fragmentary papyri, limited references are presently made to the Apocryphal Acts of the Apostles (Aa). Increased acquaintance especially with lectionaries will also provide a fund of terms that can enrich the vocabulary base. A major development will most certainly be the bestowal of greater attention on idiomatic usage.

Preparation of this lexicon has required the rereading of many ancient texts, renewed assessment of countless NT texts, and the scrutiny of all early Christian material not used in earlier editions of the lexicon. Much of the inquiry called for reams of out-of-print material, copies of which were made available through the following assistants: Dawn Hass, Jan Harbough, Linda Kersten, Michelle Ports, Nancy Werner, and Crysta Wille. To the Rev. Ms. Dawn Hass I owe thanks also for proofreading of a substantial portion of the text, and to the Rev. Mr. David Householder for scrutinizing select portions. For acute observations, solid suggestions, and careful reading of at least five hundred pages of laser printouts I am especially indebted to Prof. James Voelz, who has challenged old perceptions with his seminal philological work. Many of the references to contemporary studies in periodicals owe their presence to the careful industry of Prof. Mikeal C. Parsons, whose work on literary analysis of New Testament writings has broken new ground. In earlier editions scholars were invited to communicate suggestions and corrections. Prof. Dr. Rykle Borger, of Göttingen, has been extraordinarily helpful in the refining process through various studies and reviews, including especially "Zum Stande der neutestamentlichen Lexicographie", GGA 241 (1989) 103–46; and "NA[26] und die neutestamentliche Textkritik", TRu 52 (1987) 1–58 and 326. Although the present work is necessarily of a different order from that of Johannes P. Louw and Eugene A. Nida (*Greek-English Lexicon of the New Testament Based on Semantic Domains*, 2 vols., 1988), their forward linguistic thrust has left its mark, along with generously shared verbal echoes, and I am delighted to recommend their lexicon to all students who are serious about rendering the Greek of the New Testament into idiom that is translatable beyond narrow national borders. Responses to requests in previous editions for suggestions and corrections came from all ends of the planet, and many of the changes introduced in this revision attest their impact. Besides Prof. Borger, those who responded especially bountifully include H. Braunert, D. J. Georgacas, and Peter Katz (Rev. Dr. W. P. M. Walters). The same request therefore goes forth with this revision. For notice especially of cut-and-paste errors or related computer glitches I will be grateful. In the preparation of copy I have used SoftQuad's Author/Editor program, adapted especially for this project at Dallas Theological Seminary by Steve de Rosa, Hal Thompson, and their assistants. Electronics expert Thomas Thomas looked constantly after the health of my computer. To the staff responsible for production at the University of Chicago, I cannot express warm enough thanks. Bruce Barton used his electronic wizardry in solution of numerous technical problems. For their discerning scrutiny and preparation of my manuscript I commend the following assistants at the University of Chicago Press editorial offices: Mieke Holkeboer, Jessica Vande Vusse, and Michael Lee. No words can possibly express gratitude commensurate with the contributions of copy editor Kathryn Krug. Her constant stream of stimulating queries, critical observations, and encouraging sense of humor turned what can be at times sheer drudgery into exciting enterprise. I can think of no better term than the Greek word ἀρετή to characterize the Press's associate director, Penelope Kaiserlian, and her cohorts. They are truly people of "exceptional excellence". With the completion of this foreword I am also able to keep a promise made to Lois, my wife. For more than five years she has been surrounded by stacks of boxes and done without a dining room table. It is now hers again, and friends, some of whom may have lost all hope, can be invited back.

Finally, to the One whose Word surpasses all other words, I say εὐχαριστῶ, in full awareness that numerous lexicons remain unfinished as monuments to human fragility. As my predecessors concluded their foreword to the first edition:

SOLI DEO GLORIA

Frederick William Danker

An Introduction to the Lexicon of the Greek New Testament

Walter Bauer

[The translation by W. F. Arndt and F. W. Gingrich of Walter Bauer's essay and notes is here reproduced without comment from the second English edition, but with a few formal alterations relating especially to abbreviations and addition in brackets of classification in BDAG. The timeless value of much of the essay will be apparent to discerning readers, who will form their own judgments from a comparison of Bauer's data with developments in New Testament lexicography since publication of this remarkable essay.—F.W.D.]

The second edition of the *Griechisch-deutsches Wörterbuch zu den Schriften des Neuen Testaments und der übrigen urchristlichen Literatur* of 1928, which reached its fourth edition in 1952, contained in its opening pages a short 'introduction' to its use. The exigencies of space and the desire to keep the price of the book as reasonable as possible caused the omission of these pages in later editions. This was deplored by certain scholars whose judgment on the lexicon was favorable, among them A. Deissmann in the *Deutsche Literaturzeitung* (1937), p. 520. Their ranks were joined by A. Fridrichsen, the editor of the series 'Coniectanea Neotestamentica,' who declared himself ready to give the introduction a new home in his series. The publishers also gave their consent, for which they deserve our gratitude. Accordingly, it is here presented once more, with some corrections and a supplement.

The earliest Christian literature, with which this book deals, is made up of a number of writings which were composed in the Greek language. It is not the Greek of more ancient times, least of all that of the Golden Age of Athens which is now taught in the institutions of higher learning and occupies the most prominent place in the dictionaries used in them. A comparison reveals, on the contrary, differences in phonology and morphology, in syntax and style, and, not least of all, in the vocabulary as well. These divergences are too plain to have remained unnoticed. When in the seventeenth century the learned controversy about the purity of New Testament Greek arose, the so-called 'Hebraists' tried to explain the peculiarities of this Greek as due to the influence of the Hebrew. Although they shot wide of the mark in some of their conclusions, their recognition of the special character of the New Testament language constituted a strong impetus in the right direction, when compared with the conception of their opponents, the 'purists,' whose attempt to demonstrate that the Holy Spirit inspired the New Testament writers with as fine and pure a Greek as any classical author ever wrote could not maintain itself indefinitely.

However, neither did the Hebraists achieve a real grasp of the situation. This was due largely to the fact that philology at that time knew the Greek language only from its literature and

[The German original was published as No. XV of 'Coniectanea Neotestamentica,' 1955, under the title *Zur Einführung in das Wörterbuch zum Neuen Testament*. Translated and published . . . with the permission of the author, the editor, Harald Riesenfeld, and the publishers, C. W. K. Gleerup, Lund and Ejnar Munksgaard, Copenhagen.—AG]

consequently fell into the error of equating Greek with the literary language. In addition, the writings contemporaneous with the New Testament, upon which they based their judgments, were deeply colored by Atticism, an artificial revival of the classical language. This prevented recognition of the truth that Greek had been developing since the days of the Attic orators and Plato, as any living language must.

This judgment, one-sided to say the least, was destined to hold the field as long as formal literature was almost the only source of our knowledge. But the situation took a decided change when, in the 1890s, there began to appear in great abundance those volumes which make available to the learned world the Greek papyri found in Egypt. As a result, interest was awakened, too, in the earlier isolated publications of similar nature, and it spread to other non-literary sources: the ostraca (fragments of broken pottery which served as cheap writing materials) and inscriptions. In all of them we have witnesses of the speech of daily life, especially in its colloquial form, in so far as they avoid the influence of custom, formula, and school—and infinitely many do just that! Here, at length, was discovered the proper background for a truly scientific view of the language of the oldest Christian literature. The honor of having been discoverer and pathfinder in this field belongs to Adolf Deissmann, who, beginning in 1895, demonstrated to us more and more clearly—both in numerous single investigations and in comprehensive works—that our literature on the whole represents the late Greek colloquial language, which, to be sure, some authors used with more literary polish, others with less. The upper and lower limits of our literature in this respect are marked by Hb, MPol, and Dg on the literary side, and Rv on the colloquial.*

While theology in particular became interested in these discoveries, so recently made or appreciated, because they provided the possibility of arriving at a better understanding of the language of the Greek Bible, this newly discovered field appeared no less attractive to classical philology as well. As a matter of fact, philologists now had the opportunity—of which they made good use—to investigate thoroughly what was known even in ancient times as the 'Koine,' ἡ κοινὴ διάλεκτος, 'the common language.'

This 'common language' was formed from the old dialects (Ionic, Attic, Doric, Aeolic) by a mixture to which, as one might expect, the Attic made the greatest contribution. Then, in almost complete homogeneity, it conquered the Hellenistic world.

Peculiarities characteristic of the Koine are met first in the fifth century BC. Perhaps, indeed, we may speak of a Koine, or at least its beginnings, in this early period when, in the time of the first Athenian maritime empire, the need was felt of a common Greek language for purposes of communication. Complete development and displacement of the dialects, however, were not achieved by the common language until toward the end of the fourth century BC, when, through the agency of Alexander the Great of Macedonia, not Attic, nor Ionic, but Greek conquered the Eastern world. In the kingdoms of the Diadochi it expanded and confirmed its domain, while the Romans, their successors in the rule of the East, preserved it carefully and made it serve their own interests. Furthermore, the Romans did not need to visit this part of the world to learn the nature and significance of Greek. This language had been used in Greek colonies in the West for centuries; it was heard a great deal in the capital city itself and was quite generally spoken there by the educated classes (cp. H. Lietzmann, 'Das Problem der Spätantike,' SBBerlAk [1927], p. 347).†

The writings of our literature arose in this period, when the Greek language ruled over the East and many parts of the West. They were written by men who spoke the common language of

*Cp. J. Ros, *De studie van het Bijbelgrieksch van Hugo Grotius tot Adolf Deissmann* (1940). Of course, Deissmann's methods are capable of further refinement, and the investigations which he inspired attempt to go beyond his own achievements.

†[The abbreviations here and in what follows are those of the present lexicon.—F.W.D.]

communication in their day more or less colloquially. Hence, in order to understand their works, we must make ourselves familiar with that stage in the development of the Greek language which we call the 'Koine.' The sources from which we gain our knowledge are, in the first place, the afore-mentioned non-literary evidences (papyri, ostraca, inscriptions). But in addition to these there are a number of authors who were more or less able to avoid the spell of antiquarianism which we know as 'Atticism' (Polybius, Diodorus Siculus, Strabo, Plutarch, Epictetus, Artemidorus, Pseudo-Apollodorus, Vettius Valens, et al.). The representatives of Jewish Hellenism are especially important for the investigation of our literature because of the close similarity in the content of their works; included here are Philo, Josephus, the Epistle of Aristeas, and, above all, the Septuagint, which not only contains original Greek words of the late period but also uses the contemporary tongue even when it translates. Ancient Christian writings, too, outside the scope of our literature, like the Apocryphal Acts of the Apostles and old legends,* are valuable as witnesses of the colloquial common speech. Finally, the contribution of medieval and modern Greek is not to be neglected, because the Koine finds in them its lineal descendants (cp. G. N. Hatzidakis, *Einleitung in die neugriechische Grammatik* [1892]; A. Thumb, *Handbuch der neugriechischen Volkssprache* [1895; 2d ed., 1910]; A. N. Jannaris, *An Historical Greek Grammar* [1897]).

On the basis of these sources, what conception can we gain of this common speech? Even though we recognize the Attic dialect as the main factor in its origin, that dialect had to sacrifice much to the common cause—so much, in fact, that some investigators are not willing to regard it as the main element (cp. P. Kretschmer, 'Die Entstehung der Κοινή,' SBWienAk 143 [1900]. For the opposite view, see Mlt. 33f). In this connection we need not chiefly call to mind the classical writers, nor regretfully note the absence of their elegance in periodic sentence structure, in the use of particles, in the employment of the moods, in the change of prepositions or negatives. The Attic had to give up the characteristics which differentiated it from all or most of the other dialects, e.g. ττ instead of σσ (cp. B-D-F §34, 1), ρρ instead of ρσ (cp. B-D-F §34, 2 and see ἄρσην, θαρρέω and θαρσέω), ξυν instead of συν (cp. B-D-F §34, 4). It gave up the dual altogether and used the optative very modestly. The Attic second declension ekes out a miserable existence, represented in the New Testament only by ἵλεως (q.v.); the Attic future is in process of dying out and maintains itself in the New Testament only in the case of several verbs in -ίζω, even there predominantly in quotations from the LXX (B-D-F §74, 1). The Attic ἕνεκα (q.v.) is attested unanimously only in one New Testament passage. Where, as in this case, the tradition is divided, it is impossible to escape the suspicion that scribes under the influence of Atticism have subsequently restored to classical Greek what, according to their view, presumably belonged to it [i.e., was its appropriate form, F.W.D.]. In this way the Attic future has got into some manuscripts (B-D-F §74, 1), or, for instance, the Attic forms πανδοκεῖον and πανδοκεύς force their way into the text of Lk 10:34, 35 (s. πανδοχεῖον, πανδοχεύς). Cp. W. Michaelis, 'Der Attizismus und das NT', ZNW, XXII [1923], 91–121.

Just as noticeable as the losses suffered by Attic are the influences taken over from other dialects. Of Doric origin are: ἀμφιάζω (q.v.), which, together with the similarly Hellenistic form ἀμφιέζω, takes the place of the older ἀμφιέννυμι (B-D-F §73), πιάζω (q.v.) and προσαχέω (q.v.). Likewise ἀλέκτωρ (Ion-Att. ἀλεκτρυών), βουνός (q.v.), ἔναντι as well as ἀπέναντι and κατέναντι (B-D-F §214, 4), ἐνδιδύσκω (?B-D-F §73), λαός and ναός (for Att. λεώς and νεώς; cp. B-D-F §44, 1), μοιχάομαι, μαρυκάομαι (q.v.), οἰκοδομή (q.v.), ὁρκίζω (E. Fraenkel, *Geschichte der griechischen* nomina agentis *auf* -τήρ, -τωρ, -της, I [1910], 180), ὁρκωμοσία (q.v.), ὄρνιξ (q.v.). On the pass. ἐγενήθην as the aor. of γίνομαι s. that entry.

*See especially those edited by H. Usener, of St. Pelagia (1879), St. Marina and St. Christopher (1886), St. Tychon (1907); also G. Björck, *Der Fluch des Christen Sabinus, Papyrus Upsaliensis 8* (1938).

Ionic, as the dialect most closely related to Attic, offers a richer contribution. Here belong uncontracted noun forms like νεομηνία (q.v.) and ἐπαοιδός; on the other side, contractions like ἱερωσύνη (Att. ἱερεωσύνη); the disappearance of the vowel before another vowel in νοσσός (for νεοσσός); [consonantal changes in] βαθμός (Att. βασμός) and κλίβανος (q.v.; Att. κρίβανος). Likewise the forms τέσσερα and τεσσεράκοντα (for τέσσαρα [q.v.] and τεσσαράκοντα [q.v.]), ἔσω (Att. εἴσω), ἕνεκεν as well as εἵνεκεν (Att. ἕνεκα), εἶτεν (Att. εἶτα, q.v. end). Further, Hellenistic Greek shares a number of verbal forms with the Ionic, e.g.: ἐλεύσομαι as future of ἔρχομαι (Att. εἶμι); ἔζησα (Att. ἐβίων); ἐκέρδησα (Att. ἐκέρδανα and ἐκέρδηνα); ἐπόθησα (Att. ἐπόθεσα); τέτευχα (Att. τετύχηκα). The Ionic may also be responsible for the inflection of -μι verbs in -ω or in -ῶ (cp. Mlt. 33). Cp. γογγύζω (q.v.); πρὶν ἤ (s. πρίν).

Most of the peculiarities of the Koine in comparison with the classical languages can be referred to no definite dialect. So it is when forms appear like εἶδα, εἴδαμεν, εἴδατε, εἶδαν (s. εἶδον); ἤνεγκα with the ptc. ἐνέγκας (s. φέρω); ἔπεσα beside ἔπεσον (s. πίπτω), in which the two aorists are mingled. Further, the imperfect with endings of the first aorist: εἴχαμεν, εἶχαν (s. ἔχω); ἔλεγαν (s. λέγω). Perf. with aorist endings (inscr. and pap. since II BC): ἔγνωκαν (s. γινώσκω); τετήρηκαν (J 17:6); γέγοναν (s. γίνομαι); εἴρηκαν (s. εἶπον); πέπτωκαν (s. πίπτω). The ending -σαν expands its territory and is especially noticeable in the imperfect and second aorist: εἴχοσαν (s. ἔχω); παρελάβοσαν (s. παραλαμβάνω); ἐξήλθοσαν (Mk 8:11 D). Or the types of inflection in -ᾶν and -εῖν become confused (cp. ἐλλογέω). While among Attic writers many active verbs form a middle future—at least as the regular form—the Koine insists on the active, although not quite inflexibly: ἀκούσω (s. ἀκούω); ἁμαρτήσω (Mt 18:21; cp. Hm 4, 1, 1; 2); ἀπαντήσω (Mk 14:13) and συναντήσω (Lk 22:10; Ac 20:22); ἁρπάσω (J 10:28); γελάσω (s. γελάω); κλαύσω (s. κλαίω); ῥεύσω (J 7:38). Correspondingly, it prefers the 'regular' first aorist to the second aorist, which was formerly the favorite: ἡμάρτησα (s. ἁμαρτάνω); ἐβίωσα (s. βιόω); ἐβλάστησα (s. βλαστάνω); ἔκραξα (s. κράζω). In deponents the common dialect values the aor. and fut. passive more highly than the middle: ἀπεκρίθην (s. ἀποκρίνομαι) and διεκρίθην (as aor. of the mid. διακρίνομαι; s. διακρίνω 2, mid. [= 5–6]); ἐθαυμάσθην and θαυμασθήσομαι (s. θαυμάζω 2). Yet it also uses middle forms where the Attic dialect has the passive: ἠρνησάμην (s. ἀρνέομαι); διελεξάμην (s. διαλέγομαι).

Far more than its grammatical structure, the vocabulary and use of words in the Greek language suffered radical changes in the course of centuries. Instead of classical middles or deponents, the common speech employs the corresponding actives: ἀτενίζω (q.v.); εὐαγγελίζω (q.v.). Above all, however, it resorts to new formations (s. the respective articles in the lexicon), which in part take the place of related forms in more ancient times:

Of verbs in -ίζω: αἱρετίζω, αἰχμαλωτίζω, ἀνακαθίζω, ἀνεμίζω (Att. ἀνεμόω), ἀπελπίζω, ἀποθησαυρίζω, ἀποκεφαλίζω, ἀσφαλίζομαι, γαμίζω, διασκορπίζω and σκορπίζω, διαφημίζω, ἐξαρτίζω, ἐξερίζω, ἐξυπνίζω, εὐνουχίζω, ἰουδαΐζω, καθαρίζω (for καθαίρω), κατασοφίζομαι, κατοπτρίζω, κλυδωνίζομαι, ὀξίζω, παρορίζω and προορίζω, πελεκίζω, προελπίζω, προσεγγίζω, ῥαντίζω (for ῥαίνω), σκοτίζω, συμμερίζω.— -ιάζω: ἁγιάζω (for ἁγίζω), ἐνταφιάζω, καυστηριάζω, νηπιάζω, σεληνιάζομαι, σινιάζω.— -ματίζω (from neuters in -μα): ἀναθεματίζω and καταθεματίζω, δειγματίζω and παραδειγματίζω, δογματίζω, ἱματίζω, καυματίζω.— -άζω: ἀνετάζω, ἀποσκευάζομαι, διαυγάζω, ἑδράζω, ἐκθαυμάζω, ἐξαγοράζω, μονάζω (from μόνος), στυγνάζω (from στυγνός).— -όω: ἀκυρόω, ἀναστατόω, ἁπλόω, ἀποδεκατόω, ἀφιερόω (religious t.t.), ἀφυπνόω, ἀχρειόω, βεβηλόω, δυναμόω, ἐκριζόω, ἑνόω, ἐντυπόω, ἐξαπλόω, καθηλόω, κατιόω, καυσόω, κραταιόω (class. κρατύνω), μεταμορφόω and μορφόω, νεκρόω, προδηλόω, προσκληρόω, σαρόω (class. σαίρω), σημειόω, σπιλόω, χαριτόω.— -έω: ἀθετέω, ἀναθεωρέω, ἀναισθητέω, ἀναντλέω, ἀνομέω, ἀντιλοιδορέω, ἀντιμετρέω, ἀντοφθαλμέω, ἀποκυέω, ἀπολαλέω, ἀστοχέω, αὐθεντέω (together with αὐθέντης and αὐθεντικός), ἀφυστερέω, ἐγκακέω, εἰσκαλέομαι, ἐκδικέω, ἐκζητέω, ἐκκακέω, ἐλλογέω (commercial t.t.), ἐνειλέω, ἐξαπορέομαι, ἐξουδενέω, ἐπιχορηγέω, κατηχέω, λατομέω, συγγνωμονέω, συγκρατέω, συλλαλέω, συνομιλέω.— -άω: ἀναζάω, ἀροτριάω (for ἀρόω), δειλιάω, (ἐξ)εραυνάω (for [ἐξ]ερευνάω), λικμάω, μηνιάω, ξυράω (q.v.), προσδαπανάω, σπαταλάω, στρηνιάω, συγχράομαι.— -εύω: αἰχμαλωτεύω, ἀκριβεύομαι, γυμνιτεύω, ἐγκρατεύομαι, ἱερατεύω, κατακυριεύω, κατασκοπεύω, κυκλεύω (for κυκλόω), μαθητεύω, μεθοδεύω, μεσιτεύω, ὀλοθρεύω, παραβολεύομαι, παροδεύω, περπερεύομαι, συμβασιλεύω, συνοδεύω, σωρεύω and ἐπισωρεύω.—Cp. also ἀνακυλίω and ἀποκυλίω, ἀναζώννυμι, ἀναθάλλω, ἀνατάσσομαι, ἀπολείχω, ἀποτάσσομαι (mid.), ἐκπλέκω, ἐπιφώσκω, καμμύω, κνήθω, κρύβω (for κρύπτω), ὁμείρομαι, ὀπτάνομαι, περιλάμπω, περιπείρω, προαμαρτάνω, προβλέπω, στήκω, χύν(ν)ω (present for χέω; B-D-F §73).

Of substantives in -μός: ἁγνισμός, ἀπαρτισμός, ἁρπαγμός, ἀφανισμός, βαπτισμός, γογγυσμός, διαλογισμός, ἐνταφιασμός, ἱλασμός, ἱματισμός, καθαρισμός, καταρτισμός, κυλισμός, μιασμός, μολυσμός, ὀνειδισμός, πειρασμός, πλατυσμός, πορισμός, συγκλεισμός, σωφρονισμός, ψιθυρισμός.— -μα (the Ionic shows a marked preference for this form): ἁγίασμα, ἀγνόημα, αἰτίωμα (for αἰτίαμα), ἀνόμημα, ἄντλημα, ἀπαύγασμα, ἀπόκριμα, γένημα, διάταγμα, ἔκτρωμα, ἐλάττωμα, ἕλιγμα, ἐνέργημα, ἔνταλμα, ἐξέραμα, θέλημα, κατάκριμα and πρόκριμα, κατάλυμα, καταπέτασμα, κατάχυμα, κατόρθωμα, κένωμα, κτίσμα, παράπτωμα, περίσσευμα, πρόσκομμα, ῥάντισμα, ῥάπισμα, σέβασμα, χόρτασμα. If the ending of the stem before the suffixes -σις and -της (-τος) is short, the Koine introduces the short ending of the stem in the corresponding forms in -μα as well (B-D-F §109, 3): δόμα, θέμα, ἀνάθεμα (for the class. ἀνάθημα) and κατάθεμα, κλίμα, κρίμα, πόμα (as early as Pindar and Hdt.; the classic writers used πῶμα); see also s.v. εὕρημα and κατάστημα.— -σις: ἀθέτησις, ἄθλησις, ἀνάδειξις, ἀνάχυσις, ἀνάψυξις, ἀπάντησις, ἀποκάλυψις, ἀπολύτρωσις and λύτρωσις (technical business terms), ἀπόχρησις, βίωσις, διάταξις, ἐκδίκησις, ἐκπέτασις, ἐκπλήρωσις, ἔλεγξις, ἔλευσις, ἐξομολόγησις and ὁμολόγησις, ἐρήμωσις, θέλησις, θλῖψις, κατάκρισις, κατάνυξις, κατάρτισις, κατασκήνωσις, καύχησις, μείωσις, μόρφωσις, νέκρωσις, ὅρασις, παρατήρησις, πεποίθησις, περίθεσις, περιποίησις, προσκαρτέρησις, πρόσκλισις, σημείωσις, συζήτησις, συνείδησις, συνέλευσις.— -ότης: ἀγαθότης, ἁγιότης, ἁγνότης, ἀδελφότης, ἀδηλότης, ἁδρότης, ἀφελότης, γυμνότης, δολιότης, εἰκαιότης, θειότης, θεότης, ἱλαρότης, ἰσχυρότης, ματαιότης, μεγαλειότης, ποσότης.— -σύνη: ἀκεραιοσύνη, ἐλεημοσύνη; with lengthening of the ο after a short syllable ἁγιωσύνη, μεγαλωσύνη.— -ία: ἀβροχία, αἰχμαλωσία, ἀμεριμνία, ἀνοδία, ἀποστασία (class. ἀπόστασις), ἀποτομία, ἀφειδία, ἀφθαρσία, ἐλαφρία, ἐπιχορηγία, ἑτοιμασία, κατοικία, λυχνία (for λυχνεῖον), μετοικεσία, ὀπτασία, παραχειμασία, πρωΐα, σκοτία (for σκότος), συνοδία.— -εία: ἐριθεία, ἱερατεία, λογεία, μαθητεία, μεθοδεία, περισσεία, προφητεία.— -εια: ἀπώλεια, ἀρέσκεια, ἐκτένεια.— -ή: ἁρμογή, βροχή and ἐμβροχή, διαταγή and ἐπιταγή, ἐγκοπή, κοπή, προκοπή, προσκοπή and συγκοπή, κατ᾽ ἐξοχήν, ἐπισκοπή, μηλωτή, ὀφειλή, πεισμονή, περιοχή, προσευχή.— -της (agent nouns): ἀποστάτης, βαπτιστής, βιαστής, γνώστης, διωγμίτης, ἐξορκιστής, καθηγητής, καταφρονητής, μεριστής, μεσίτης, προσαίτης, προσκυνητής, σαλπιστής, στασιαστής, συμμύστης, χρεώστης, ψιθυριστής.— -ωρ: ἀντιλήπτωρ, κατήγωρ, κτήτωρ.— -ων: ἀμπελών, ἐλαιών, καύσων, κοιτών, λαμπηδών, νυμφών, πυλών.— -τήριον: ἁγνευτήριον, ἀκροατήριον, ἱλαστήριον (religious t.t.).—The feminine forms βασίλισσα (q.v.) and Συροφοινίκισσα are Hellenistic, also μοιχαλίς, συγγενίς, μαθήτρια and some diminutives, whose actual diminutive force is no longer felt in many cases; animals: ἐρίφιον, ὀνάριον (ἀρνίον, ἰχθύδιον, κυνάριον, προβάτιον are taken over from the older language); parts of the body: ὠτίον and ὠτάριον. Cp. ἀγρίδιον, βιβλίδιον (βιβλαρίδιον and βιβλιδάριον), κλινίδιον (κλινάριον is older), κοράσιον, νησίον, πτερύγιον, ῥαβδίον, ψωμίον.—Formations in -ιον that are not diminutive: γεώργιον, δοκίμιον, δυσεντέριον, ὀψώνιον, προαύλιον, προσφάγιον, συμβούλιον, τελώνιον, ὑποπόδιον.—Finally, a large group of nouns, like ἀγάπη, ἄρκος (for ἄρκτος), βασιλίσκος, βραβεῖον, βυρσεύς, γρόνθος, καταγγελεύς, καταιγίς, κειρία, κρύπτη, κύθρα, λατόμος, λειτουργός, ληνός, μάμμη, μύλος (for μύλη), νῖκος (for νίκη), ὁδηγός, περικεφαλαία, πινακίς, πλήμμυρα, πολιά, ῥομφαία, σαγήνη, σκύβαλον, σπίλος, στρῆνος, συγκληρονόμος (legal t.t.), συμπολίτης (in one passage in Euripides), σύνοδος, ταμεῖον (for ταμιεῖον).

Of adjectives in -ιος: ἐπιθανάτιος, ἐπιούσιος (q.v.), μετακόσμιος, παρόδιος, περιούσιος, σεβάσμιος.— -ικός (-ιακός): ἀγγελικός, αἱρετικός, ἀνατολικός, ἀρσενικός, ἀρχοντικός, αὐθεντικός, δαιμονικός, διδακτικός, ἐθνικός, καθολικός, κυριακός, λαϊκός, λειτουργικός, λογικός (a philosophical t.t. Aristot.+), νεωτερικός, οἰκιακός, ὀνικός, προβατικός, προφητικός, σαρκικός, σηρικός, χοϊκός.— -ινος: ἀμαράντινος, δερμάτινος, καθημερινός, καρπάσινος, κόκκινος, μύλινος, ὀρθρινός, ὀστράκινος, πρωϊνός, ταχινός.— -τος: ἀρκετός, δεκτός, διαβόητος, ἔκπληκτος, ἐπήλυτος, ἐπιπόθητος and ποθητός, κατάκριτος, οἰκοδομητός, παθητός, σεβαστός, σιτιστός.—Cp. also γραώδης, ἔγγραφος, ἔκτρομος and ἔντρομος, ἐνάρετος (Stoic t.t.), ἔξυπνος, ἐπάλληλος, ἐπίμονος, ἤρεμος, θηλυκός, πρόσκαιρος, σύμμορφος, σύμψυχος, σύνδενδρος, ὕπανδρος.—Double comparison for the purpose of attaining greater clarity is occasionally found in classical times (Kühner-Bl. I 373), and becomes very popular with Hellenistic writers (B-D-F §61, 2; Mlt. 236; Mayser I 301, 1; Crönert 190): διπλότερος (s. διπλοῦς), ἐλαχιστότερος (s. ἐλάχιστος, beg.), μειζότερος (s. μέγας, beg.).

In general, it becomes a very common custom to put new life into certain forms that show the wear and tear of time—that is, have become indistinct in meaning—by compounding them with other words. This explains in part the preference of the Koine for compounds, of which the previous lists exhibit a considerable number, even in the simplest speech. Where the older language does very well with a simple form, Hellenistic Greek likes to prefix a preposition (cp. G. B. Winer's five reports [Programme], *De verborum cum praepos. compositorum in Novo Testamento usu* [Leipzig, 1834–43]): ἀνανήφω and ἐκνήφω, ἀνατρέφομαι, ἀποδεκατεύω, ἀποτυφλόω, ἀποφθέγγομαι, διανεύω, διανυκτερεύω, διερμηνεύω and μεθερμηνεύω, ἐγκαυχάομαι, ἐγχρίω, ἐκλιπαρέω, ἐκπειράζω, ἐναγκαλίζομαι, ἐνδοξάζομαι, ἐνορκίζω, ἐξακολουθέω and κατακολουθέω, ἐξηχέω, ἐξισχύω, ἐξομολογέω, ἐπαγωνίζομαι, ἐπαθροίζω, ἐπιβαρέω and καταβαρέω, ἐπιπορεύομαι, ἐπισκηνόω, ἐπισπουδάζω (?q.v.), ἐπισφραγίζω, καταντάω, καταπιστεύω, παραβιάζομαι, προσεγγίζω, προσονομάζω.—ἐπίγνωσις.—ἀπόκενος, περίπικρος.—ἔκπαλαι, ἐπαύριον, ὑπεράγαν, ὑπεράνω, ὑπερεκπερισσοῦ, ὑπερλίαν, ὑπερπερισσῶς.

Compare also the great number of multiple compounds, by which the classical store of such forms is increased (cp. A. Rieder, 'Die mit mehr als einer Präposition zusammengesetzten Verba [und überhaupt Wörter] des N [und A] T,' *Programm Gumbinnen* [1876]): ἀντιδιατίθημι, ἀντιπαρέρχομαι, ἀπεκδέχομαι, ἀπεκδύομαι, ἐμπεριπατέω, ἐπαναπαύομαι, ἐπανατρέχω, ἐπενδύομαι, ἐπιδιορθόω, ἐπισυνάγω, καταδιαιρέω, παρεισέρχομαι, παρεκφέρω, παρενθυμέομαι, παρεπιδημέω, προεπαγγέλλω and προκαταγγέλλω, συγκατανέυω, συγκαταψηφίζομαι, συναντιλαμβάνομαι, συνεπέρχομαι, συνεπιμαρτυρέω, συνυποκρίνομαι.—διαπαρατριβή, ἐγκατάλειμμα, ἐπισυναγωγή, ἐπισύστασις, συγκατάθεσις.—ἐπικατάρατος, παρείσακτος, παρεπίδημος, συνέκδημος.

But the common speech uses various other combinations as well. Verbal adjectives, with α- privative prefixed: ἀδιάκριτος, ἀδιάλειπτος, ἀκατάγνωστος, ἀκατακάλυπτος, ἀκατάληπτος, ἀκατάλυτος, ἀκατάπαυστος, ἀκατάστατος (also ἀκαταστατέω and ἀκαταστασία), ἀκατάσχετος, ἀλάλητος, ἀμάραντος, ἀμετάθετος, ἀμετανόητος, ἀναντίρρητος, ἀναπάρτιστος, ἀναπολόγητος, ἀνεκλάλητος, ἀνέκλειπτος, ἀνεξιχνίαστος, ἀνεπαίσχυντος, ἀνυπόκριτος, ἀνυπότακτος, ἀπαράβατος, ἀπερινόητος, ἀπερίσπαστος, ἀπρόσιτος, ἄσκυλτος, ἀστήρικτος, ἀστομάχητος, ἀσύγκριτος, ἄτρεπτος, ἄφθαρτος, ἄψευστος, ἀψηλάφητος (cp. also ἀδρανής, ἄθεσμος, ἀμέριμνος, ἀπροσδεής, ἀπρόσκοπος, ἄσπιλος, ἄτονος);—with δυσ- prefixed: δυσβάστακτος, δυσερμήνευτος, δυσνόητος;—with εὐ- prefixed: εὐάρεστος (also εὐαρεστέω and εὐαρέστησις), εὐλογητός, εὐμετάδοτος, εὐοικονόμητος, εὐπρόσδεκτος, εὐσυνείδητος (cp. other combinations with εὐ- in the Koine: εὐδοκέω and συνευδοκέω, εὐδόκησις, εὐδοκία, εὐκαιρέω, εὔκοπος, εὔλαλος, εὐποιΐα, εὐπροσωπέω, εὐστάθεια, εὐσταθέω, εὐψυχέω);—with a noun prefixed: θεόπνευστος, πατροπαράδοτος, ποταμοφόρητος.

Compounds of various other kinds: ἀγαθοποιέω and ἀγαθοποιός, ἀλεκτοροφωνία, ἀλλογενής, ἀμνησίκακος, ἀνθρωπόμορφος, ἀργυροκόπος, ἀρσενοκοίτης, ἀρτιγέννητος, ἀρχάγγελος, ἀρχέγονος, ἀρχιποίμην, ἀρχισυνάγωγος, ἀρχιτρίκλινος, αὐτοκατάκριτος, γαζοφυλάκιον, γονυπετέω, δεσμοφύλαξ, διετία, διθάλασσος, δικαιοκρισία, δικαιοπραγία, δωροφορία, ἐθνάρχης, ἑτερόγλωσσος, ἑτερογνώμων, ἡδύοσμον, ἡμιθανής, ἡμίξηρος, θεομάχος (θεομαχέω is older), θεοπρεπής, θεοσεβέω (θεοσέβεια and θεοσεβής are older), θυμομαχέω, ἱερουργέω, ἰσάγγελος, ἰσότιμος, ἰσχυροποιέω, κακουχέω, καλοποιέω, κενοδοξέω, κενοδοξία and κενόδοξος, κενόσπουδος, κενοφωνία, κοινωφελής, κοσμοκράτωρ, κωμόπολις, λειποτακτέω, λιθοβολέω, μακροθυμία, μακροθυμέω and μακρόθυμος, μακροχρόνιος, ματαιολογία and ματαιολόγος, ματαιοπονία, μεγαλο(ρ)ρημονέω and μεγαλο(ρ)ρημοσύνη, μεσουράνημα, μετριοπαθέω, μογιλάλος, νεκροφόρος, νυχθήμερον, οἰκοδεσπότης and οἰκοδεσποτέω, οἰνόμελι, ὁλοκληρία (ὁλόκληρος is older), ὁλοτελής, ὁροθεσία, πανάρετος, πάνσεμνος, παντεπόπτης, παντοκράτωρ, πληροφορία (πληροφορέω is earlier, in isolated cases), πολιτάρχης, πολύτιμος, πρωτότοκος, ῥᾳδιούργημα, σαρδόνυξ, σιτομέτριον, στενοχωρέω, συλαγωγέω, υἱοθεσία, φιλαργυρέω (also ἀφιλάργυρος, whereas φιλάργυρος is attested even earlier), φίλαυτος, φιλήδονος, φιλόθεος, φιλοπρωτεύω, φρεναπάτης, χειραγωγέω and χειραγωγός, χειρόγραφον, χρεοφειλέτης. Cp. also the contractions κἀκεῖ, κἀκεῖθεν, κἀκεῖνος, κἀκεῖσε.

Adverbs of Hellenistic Greek: ἀντιπέρα; ἀπέναντι, ἔναντι and κατέναντι (Doric; see p. xv above); ἐνώπιον, ἐξάπινα, ἐφάπαξ, καθά, καθώς, καθεξῆς, μακρόθεν, παιδιόθεν, παμπληθεί, πανοικεί, πάντοτε, ῥητῶς, ῥοιζηδόν, ὑπέρ (q.v. 3 [= C]).—Adjectival comparison of adverbs: ἐξώτερος, ἐσώτερος, κατώτερος.

Another way in which a language can be made more expressive is by adopting foreign words. The Koine had demonstrably incorporated many such terms, now found in our literature, before the New Testament period: ἀγγαρεύω, ἀσσάριον, βαΐον, βύσσος, γάζα, δηνάριον, εὐρακύλων, θριαμβεύω, Καῖσαρ, καλάνδαι, καμάρα, κεντυρίων, κερβικάριον, κῆνσος, κολωνία, κουστωδία, κράβαττος, κύμινον, λεγιών, λέντιον, λιβερτῖνος, λίτρα, μάκελλον [but see this entry, AG], μίλιον, μόδιος, νάρδος, ξέστης (?), πραιτώριον, σάκκος, σάπφειρος, στατίων, συκάμινος, φαιλόνης [but see this entry also, AG]. The same may confidently be assumed of not a few others: ἄκκεπτα, δεπόσιτα, δεσέρτωρ, ἐξεμπλάριον, ζιζάνιον, καροῦχα, κοδράντης, κομφέκτωρ, μεμβράνα, ῥέδη, σικάριος, σιμικίνθιον, σουδάριον, σπεκουλάτωρ, συμψέλιον, τίτλος, φραγέλλιον and φραγελλόω, χῶρος (q.v. II).

The words quoted above are clearly shown by secular witnesses to be a part of the Hellenistic vocabulary (s. B-D-F §5, 1). Naturally, it is possible that some of them were used in more ancient times, as in the case of θριαμβεύω, used by Ctesias.

A language improves not only through new formations and the appropriation of foreign words but also through the process by which terms which have long been available develop new possibilities of usage. Much-used words acquire a new meaning beside the older one and sometimes repress the earlier meaning or even exclude it altogether. The change often consists in the rise of specialized or technical terms: ἀδελφός as a member of a religious community (s. ἀδελφός 2); ἀνακλίνω = to cause to recline at table (s. ἀνακλίνω 1b [= 2]); ἀναπίπτω = lie down, viz. at a meal (s. ἀναπίπτω 1); ἀναστροφή (q.v.) = way of life; ἀντιλαμβάνεσθαι = notice (q.v. 2 [= 3]); ἀντιλέγω = oppose (q.v. 2); ἀντίλημψις = help (q.v.); ἀπαρτίζω = accomplish (q.v.); ἀπέχω as a commercial t.t. (q.v. 1); ἀποκόπτω = emasculate (q.v. 2 [= a]); ἀποτάσσω in the middle (q.v. 1; 2); ἀρετή = a demonstration of divine power, miracle (q.v. 3 [= 2]); ἄριστον = noon meal, or meal in general (q.v. 2); ἄρτι of the present time in general (q.v. 3); τὴν ἀρχήν = at all (s. ἀρχή 1b [= 1a]); αὐτάρκεια = contentment, a t.t. of the Cynic-Stoic teaching concerning virtue (q.v. 2); βαρύτιμος = very expensive; βίος = way of life (q.v. 2 [=1]); γενέσια = birthday celebration (q.v.); δαιμόνιον and δαίμων = evil spirit; δαιμονίζομαι = be possessed by an evil spirit; διαθήκη exclusively = last will and testament; διάκονος as a cult t.t.; διαπονέομαι = be angry; δύναμις = personal supernatural being (q.v. 6 [= 5]); δῶμα = roof; ἐμβατεύω as a t.t. of the mystery religions (q.v. 4); ἐμβλέπω = observe with the eyes of the spirit (q.v. 2); ἐμβριμάομαι = scold (q.v.); ἐπαγγελία = promise; ἐπιθυμητής in the bad sense; ἐπιστρέφομαι = be converted (s. ἐπιστρέφω 2b [= 4b]); ἐπιτιμάω = punish (q.v. 2); ἐπιφάνεια, of the process by which the hidden divinity becomes visible; ἐπόπτης as a t.t. of the mysteries; ἐρεύγομαι = proclaim; ἐρωτάω = request; εὐαγγέλιον = good news, occasionally with a religious tinge (s. εὐαγγέλιον and cp. εὐαγγελιστής); εὐσχήμων = distinguished, of high repute; εὐχαριστέω = give thanks, sometimes to a deity (q.v. 2); θυρεός = a shield (large as a door); κεφαλίς = book in the form of a scroll; κοίμησις of death (q.v. 2); κρύσταλλος = rock crystal; λαλιά no longer exclusively in the bad sense; λειτουργέω and derivatives, of religious service; μάρμαρος = marble; μέθυσος of males; μνημεῖον = grave (q.v. 2); νήφω in the metaphorical sense; ὀψάριον = fish; παρακαλέω = request (q.v. 3); παρουσία in the technical sense (q.v. 2b); παρρησία = frankness, joyousness (q.v. 3ab); περισπάω = occupy fully (q.v. 2); πήρα = beggar's knapsack (q.v.); πλῆθος = community (q.v. 2bδ); πνεῦμα and ψυχή as contrasting terms (s. πνευματικός 2αγ); ποιμήν as a religious t.t. (q.v. 2bγ); πρεσβύτερος as the designation of an official (q.v. 2b); πτῶμα = corpse; πύργος = farm or business building (q.v. 2); ῥύμη = street; σεβάζομαι of religious reverence; σταυρόω = crucify; στέγω = endure; στενοχωρία in the metaphorical sense; στόμαχος = stomach; συνίστημι = show, prove (q.v. I 1c [=A3]); σχολή = school; φθάνω = arrive (q.v. 2).

A considerable number of older words have been appropriated as technical terms from the Roman civil and military administration: ἀπογραφή = census; ἑκατόνταρχος (ἑκατοντάρχης) = centurio; ἔπαρχος = praefectus; ἐπίτροπος = procurator; ἡγεμών and ἡγεμονεύειν of the imperial governor; ῥαβδοῦχος = lictor; σεβαστός = Augustus; σπεῖρα = cohors; στρατηγοί = duumviri coloniae; στρατόπεδον = legio; χιλίαρχος = tribunus militum; κράτιστος = vir egregius; τὸ ἱκανὸν ποιεῖν τινι = satisfacere alicui; λαμβάνειν τὸ ἱκανόν = satis accipere (s. ἱκανός 1c [= 1]). Other terms of this kind appear for the first time in the Hellenistic period: ἀνθύπατος = proconsul (cp. ἀνθυπατεύειν); ἐπαρχεία and ἡ ἐπάρχειος = provincia (from the older ἔπαρχος).

We have yet to consider those words which our literature, primarily the New Testament, either shares with the LXX alone, or for which it is the only witness, and which for this reason play a unique role as 'voces biblicae' in the philology of the Greek Bible. Before the systematic investigation of the popular speech, their number was much larger. The fact that the advances in our knowledge have freed one after another of these words from their isolation and demonstrated that they were part of the living language forces upon us the conclusion that the great mass of biblical words for which we do not yet have secular evidence also belong to that language.* Of course, there are some formations

*The following lists have become noticeably shorter when compared with those of 1928. The words that have been omitted are now demonstrably part of the common language; we need no longer rely on conjecture.

with regard to which it is not only possible, but in some instances very probable, that the translators of the Old Testament formed them for their own purposes and then handed them on to the composers of our literature, while the latter, in turn, created other terms to satisfy their own needs. The Hellenistic spirit, however, makes itself felt even in these cases through the fact that those forms are preferred for which we have been able to establish a preference in the common speech. Here belong, for instance, ἀγαλλιάομαι and ἀγαλλίασις,* ἁγιασμός, αἴνεσις, ἀλίσγημα, ἀλλοτριεπίσκοπος, ἀνθρωπαρεσκέω and ἀνθρωπάρεσκος, ἀνταπόδομα and ἀνταποδότης, ἀντιμισθία, ἀξιαγάπητος and other combinations with ἄξιος in Ignatius, ἀποκαταλλάσσω, ἐθελοθρησκία, ἑτεροδιδασκαλέω, ἑτεροζυγέω, θεοδρόμος, θεομακάριστος, θεομακαρίτης, θεοπρεσβευτής, θυσιαστήριον, κακοδιδασκαλία, καλοδιδάσκαλος, καρδιογνώστης, κατακληρονομέω, λυτρωτής, μισθαποδοσία and μισθαποδότης, νομοδιδάσκαλος, ὀλιγοπιστία and ὀλιγόπιστος, ὀλοθρευτής, ὀφθαλμοδουλία, πατριάρχης, πολυσπλαγχνία and πολύσπλαγχνος, πρεσβυτέριον, πρωτοκαθεδρίτης, σκανδαλίζω and σκάνδαλον, σκληροκαρδία, σπλαγχνίζομαι, ψευδάδελφος, ψευδοδιδασκαλία and ψευδοδιδάσκαλος, ψευδοπροφήτης.

Likewise it is certain that there are specific expressions for biblical or Jewish or primitive Christian things which, like the things they denote, are limited to the Old Testament (and Jewish writers influenced by it) and our literature (together with the Christian writings dependent on it): ἀκροβυστία and ἀκρόβυστος, ἀντίχριστος, ἀπερίτμητος, ἀποσυνάγωγος, βάπτισμα, ἐγκαίνια, εἰδωλεῖον, εἰδωλόθυτος; εἰδωλολατρία, εἰδωλολατρέω, εἰδωλολάτρης; κατείδωλος, μοσχοποιέω, ὁλοκαύτωμα, χριστέμπορος, χριστομαθία, χριστόνομος, ψευδαπόστολος, ψευδόχριστος.

In the case of most of the words found only in the LXX and our literature, it is highly improbable that they originated in Jewish or early Christian circles. This is, at any rate, a totally unwarranted assumption when secular speech exhibits closely related forms and there is nothing specifically Jewish or early Christian or even religious about these 'biblical' words. Due allowance must be made for the chance which has preserved one word while allowing another to disappear. It is pure accident that προσευχή = prayer, so common in the LXX and our literature, has come to light in only one pagan papyrus. If this had not turned up, we would have had another 'vox biblica.' Why should παροικία be 'biblical' when πάροικος in the same sense is quite common? Who would be so rash as to deduce a rule from the fact that καταλιθάζω is found only in Christian writers, while in the LXX it is καταλιθοβολέω, and in secular writers καταλιθόω?

In my judgment, the following 'biblical words,' for example, belong to the common language: ἀγαθωσύνη, ἀδιαφθορία, ἀκρογωνιαῖος, ἀνακαίνωσις, ἀπάρτισμα, ἀπελεγμός, ἀποδεκατόω, ἀποκαραδοκία, ἀφθορία, ἀφιλάγαθος, γόγγυσος and γογγυστής, διενθυμέομαι, διώκτης, ἑδραίωμα, εἰρηνοποιέω, ἐκμυκτηρίζω, ἐλεγμός, ἐμπαιγμονή and ἐμπαίκτης, ἐπιδιατάσσομαι, ἐπικαταλλάσσομαι, ἐπιπόθησις [q.v.] and ἐπιποθία, εὐνουχία, ἥττημα, ἱεράτευμα, καταλαλιά, κατοικητήριον, κερματιστής, κρυσταλλίζω, λαξευτός, λογομαχέω, ματαίωμα, μέθυσμα, ὀξυχολία, ὀρθοποδέω, ὀρθοτομέω, ὀχλοποιέω, παγιδεύω, παιδοφθορέω, παραπικραίνω and παραπικρασμός, παραφρονία, παροργισμός, προενάρχομαι, πρόσχυσις, ῥαντισμός, σινιάζω, συζητητής, φρεναπατάω, φυλακίζω.

*There are no secular occurrences of ἀγαλλίασις. The reference to Ps.-Callisthenes in Liddell-Scott is based on the inadequate edition of C. Müller (1846), where it is found at the end of 2, 22. In the oldest form attainable of the Historia Alex. Mag. of Ps.-Callisthenes, prepared by W. Kroll in 1926, the word is found nowhere, not even in the apparatus. It belongs, evidently, to one of the many later reworkings of the original text of Ps.-Callisthenes. But this reworking obviously took place under biblical influence. In addition to other things, 2, 42 (which also is omitted in Kroll) has Alexander say: εἰς τὴν Ἰουδαίαν παρήμην γῆν. Οἵτινες (οἱ ἐκεῖσε) ζῶντι θεῷ ἔδοξαν λατρεύειν, ὃς ἐμὲ ἐποίησε πρὸς αὐτοὺς ἀγαθὴν ἔχειν γνώμην, καὶ ὅλη μου ἡ ψυχὴ πρὸς αὐτὸν ἦν. . . . Κἀκεῖσε [in Alexandria] πάντας τοὺς θεοὺς ἐξουθένισα, ὡς οὐκ ὄντας θεούς. τὸν δὲ ἐπὶ τῶν Σεραφὶμ θεὸν ἀνεκήρυξα.

More important than the appearance of newly formed words is the fact that our literature, sometimes following the LXX, sometimes apart from it, uses many words of the older or even of the common Greek in new meanings: τὰ ἄζυμα (s. ἄζυμος 1 [= 2]); ἀνάθεμα (q.v. 2); ἀναφέρω as a t.t. of sacrificial practice (q.v. 2 [= 3]); ἀπαρχή of a first convert (q.v. 2 [= 1bα]); ἀποκαλύπτω of divine revelations of every possible kind; ἀπόστολος as t.t. (q.v. 3 [= 2c]); βαπτίζω = baptize (q.v. 2); δέησις exclusively = prayer; διάβολος = devil (q.v. 2); διασπορά (q.v.); ἐπισκέπτομαι of a visitation of divine grace (q.v. 3); ἐπισκοπή = visitation and = office of overseer (q.v. 2 and 3 [= 1 and 2]); εὐλογέω and εὐλογία in the sense of 'blessing' and 'consecrating'; κιβωτός = ark and = ark of the covenant; μάρτυς = martyr (q.v. 3); μετάνοια with definite religious coloring; παιδεύω = discipline, punish (q.v. 2); παράδεισος (q.v.); παρασκευή = day of preparation; παρουσία of the coming of Christ (q.v. 2b); πεντηκοστή = Pentecost; προσήλυτος as a t.t.; σκηνή (τοῦ μαρτυρίου); φυλακτήριον = phylactery; χήρα as a t.t. (q.v. 2 [= b]).—Cp. also the words used by Christian piety with a connotation of its own, like δικαιόω and πιστεύω together with their derivatives; πνεῦμα, χάρις and the like.*

Sometimes it is plainly Hebrew influence which gives special meaning to words and expressions in the LXX and our literature. τὰ ἔθνη = 'the heathen, Gentiles' comes about when that plural form is used to translate גּוֹיִם, a rendering that was more natural for the translators of the LXX, because among the Greeks it had become customary to call foreigners ἔθνη (s. ἔθνος 2). πρόσωπον λαμβάνειν is נָשָׂא פָּנִים, and there are found in our literature in addition to this expression (borrowed from the LXX) the forms προσωπολημπτέω, προσωπολήμπτης, and προσωπολημψία (s. πρόσωπον 1b and cp. there under b–e [= a and b] still other OT expressions using πρόσωπον). Cp. ῥῆμα = thing (q.v. 2); ῥίζα = root-shoot, sprout (q.v. 2); σάκκος = mourning garment; πᾶσα σάρξ (s. σάρξ 3 [= 3a]); στόμα μαχαίρης (s. στόμα 2 [= 4]); υἱός with a genitive of the thing, like υἱός γεέννης (s. υἱός 1cδ [= 2cβ). Cp. also τέκνον (q.v. 2f [= 5]).

The Semitic coloring is especially plain where Hebrew and Aramaic words or expressions, Hellenized or not, appear as a foreign element: ἀλληλούϊα, ἀμήν, βάτος = bath [Hebrew measure], γέεννα, κόρος, μάννα, πάσχα, Σαβαώθ, σάββατον, σατάν and σατανᾶς, σάτον, σίκερα, ὕσσωπος, ὡσαννά.

A special place must be accorded those expressions which originated not in the Old Testament but in the Aramaic basis of the gospel tradition or from the religious language of the primitive community: ἀββᾶ, ἐλωΐ, ἐφφαθά, κορβᾶν and κορβανᾶς, λαμά, μαμωνᾶς, μαρὰν ἀθά, ῥαββί, ῥαββουνί, ῥαβιθά (q.v.), ῥακά, σαβαχθάνι, ταλιθὰ κούμ.

Spoken Jewish-Greek as an entity to be clearly differentiated from the language of the people in general is something that can rarely be established, though more often suspected (cp. B-D-F §4, 3). As for the influence of the LXX, every page of this lexicon shows that it outweighs all other influences on our literature. In the body of the work will also be found references to the important recent literature for lexicographical investigations, as occasion requires. Cp. also U. von Wilamowitz[-Moellendorff], *Geschichte der griechischen Sprache* (1928).

It is the purpose of this lexicon to facilitate the understanding of the texts that were composed in the late Greek described above. This kind of Greek was the mother-tongue of those who wrote them (C. C. Torrey, *The Four Gospels* [1933], 243; G. Björck, Ην Διδασκων [1940], 123f), no matter how well they may have been acquainted with Semitic idiom. Likewise, those who heard and read their messages spoke the same kind of Greek. They, at least, were no longer conscious of Semitic

*[See F. W. Gingrich, 'Prolegomena to a study of the Christian Element in the Vocabulary of the NT and Apost. Fathers,' in *Search the Scriptures,* memorial vol. for R. T. Stamm, Leiden, '69, 173–78.—AG]

originals upon which, in one form or another, some of those writings were based. With regard to the authors, too, we do well to maintain a cautious reserve on this question, since the solution of the problem of Semitic influence* is burdened with so much uncertainty at the present time (s. Björck, loc. cit.).† We shall do well to have recourse to Semitic originals only in cases where the Greek of our literature either cannot be understood from the background of the contemporary language at all or at least not sufficiently well.

In the Greek world to which the early Christian writings belong there were not only gentile literary men, but Jewish authors as well; this fact militates against the unity of later Greek literature at a point that is important for its understanding. We are incomparably better informed concerning the language of Hellenistic Judaism than we are about its gentile counterpart. How easy it is, comparatively speaking, to gain a conception of the language of the LXX, Philo, and the Epistle of Aristeas, of the Greek Enoch and the Testaments of the 12 Patriarchs! Because of the work already done, we can learn a good deal about Ps.-Phocylides and Josephus without too great an expenditure of time. These works comprise the greater part of the available sources. On the other hand, for gentile writers we must depend on chance references in the lexicons, on sections from the ancient gatherers of annotations that have survived in literature, and what modern studies** have contributed to New Testament philology or to the Koine. This means that we are comparing two entities, which, when viewed together, must present a distorted picture; only the one can be seen in its proper dimensions, while the other has been woefully retarded in its development. It is all too easy to yield to the inclination to assume that Jewish influence is present, when, in reality, a typical Greek sentiment may be expressed in a Jewish-Greek source. In this case we can bring about a greater degree of equality by giving gentile Greek literature more of a chance to speak for itself than it has had in the past.

This will serve to indicate the general direction in which the third and fourth editions [of Bauer's *Wörterbuch*] have departed from the second. Yet, as is easy to understand, only a beginning has been made so far. Systematic, connected reading of secular Greek literature can and must bring to light with still greater clarity its relation to Greek used by the earliest Christians. A few observations, made while the fourth edition was in process of being published, but too late to be included in it, may serve to demonstrate how far even the latest edition is from being exhaustive in this respect, and how far removed it is from forcing upon a (possible) collaborator the unwanted role of mere gleaner in this wide field. This or that item submitted here may contribute a little to an understanding of pertinent facts. Yet how important is this result, too, when we wish to know what effect our literature produced on people who were thoroughly steeped in pagan thought, feeling, and custom!

The following linguistic phenomena, not included in the fourth edition, are to be found in non-Christian Greek literature:

αἰσχρολογία = 'obscene speech,' Diod. S. 5, 4, 7; αἰσχρός = 'obscene,' Ps.-Demetr., Eloc. 151.

βιβλίδιον = 'letter,' Polyaenus 7, 33, 1.

γένος (1 at Rv 22:16) τινός of a single offspring: Hom.; Soph., Ant. 1117; esp. Epimenides [VI BC] no. 457 fgm. 3 Jac. ἐγὼ (Musaeus) γένος εἰμὶ Σελήνης.

ἐγείρω (1aγ [= 10] τὸν λίθον = 'lift' or 'move a stone from its place': Seleucus of Alexandria [I AD] no. 341 fgm. 4 Jac.

*For references on this subject see B-D-F §4.

†Especially the handling of the problem of whether and to what extent are we able to recover the living speech of Jesus which was behind the Greek reports of his teaching must be left to the daring and the specialized work of the small group of those really qualified to do it.

**Because of their fragmentary character, these studies are only partly available even to those who industriously seek them out.

εἰμί (I 5 [= 5]) the short clause of J 10:22 is like Polyaenus 7, 44, 2 πόλεμος ἦν.
ἐκλείπω Lk 22:32 of faith: 'fail, die out.' So Plut., Lyc. 31, 8 of a race of men.
ἐλπίζω (1 [= 1a]) τὰ ἐλπιζόμενα: Polyaenus 3, 9, 11.
θηρεύω 'go on a hunting expedition' after statements of someone, in order to use them against him: Pla., Gorg. 489b ὀνόματα θηρεύειν . . . ἐάν τις ῥήματι ἁμάρτῃ.
ἴδε (4 [= 4a]) 'hear': schol. on Pla. 130c Ἀλκιβιάδης, ἴδε, τί λέγει.
καταπατέω (1b on Lk 12:1) Polyaenus 4, 3, 21 ὑπ᾽ ἀλλήλων καταπατούμενοι.
κέραμος (2 on Lk 5:19) = 'roof-tile': Pausanias 1, 13, 8.
κρίνω (4aα [= 5aα]) κρίνομαι ἐπί τινος = 'be judged before someone': schol. on Hes., Op. 9.
μαρτυρία (2c, end [= 3]) God's 'good testimony': Dio Chrys. 16 [33], 12 τῆς μεγίστης ἔτυχε μαρτυρίας παρὰ τοῦ δαιμονίου.
μάρτυς (2c) of a man as a witness for a divine message: Epict. 3, 24, 112f; 3, 26, 28.
ὁμολογέω (5 [= 4c]) τινί 'praise someone': Dio Chrys. 10 [11], 147.
πόσος (1) πόσῳ foll. by comp.: Polyaenus 3, 9, 25 πόσῳ ἡμεῖς ἐκείνοις φοβερώτεροι;
ῥιζόω (end) ῥιζοῦσθαι ἐν = 'be firmly rooted in': Nicander, Theriaca 183.
ὑδρία λιθίνη J 2:6: Athen. 13, 589b.
χωλός symbolically: Pla., Leg. 1, 634a; Plut., Cim. 16, 10.

Other characteristics which appeared in the fourth edition as Jewish peculiarities have now been found in pagan sources:

ἅγιος (1bα [= 1aβℵ]) of a pagan: Ramsay, CB I/2, 386 no. 232, 8 Γάϊος, ὡς ἅγιος, ὡς ἀγαθός.
ἀθλητής fig. as early as Gorgias (E. Scheel, *De Gorgianae disciplinae vestigiis* [diss., Rostock, 1890], p. 13). Also Dio Chrys. 2, 18.
ἀκοῇ (1b [= 2]) ἀκούω occurs in the New Testament only as a quot. from the Old Testament but can hardly be called a 'reproduction of the Hebrew,' since it is also found in Polyaenus, Exc. 55, 2.
ἀποχωρέω = 'fall away, desert': Sb 7835 [I BC] the cult brotherhood of Zeus Hypsistos forbids its members to desert the (monarchic) ἡγούμενος, to whom they all owe obedience, and thus to cause σχίσματα.
ἀρνέομαι (3d [= 3e]) = 'deny, reject,' with a thing as object: Lycophron 348.
διάκονος (2 [= 1 and 2]) as fem.: Epict. 3, 7, 28; 2, 23, 8.
εἰσακούω (2a) = 'hear, grant' of God: Quintus Smyrnaeus 12, 154.
ἐκχέω (1 [= 1b], at Ac 1:18) of the entrails: Quintus Smyrnaeus 8, 302; 9, 190.
ἐξέρχομαι ἔξω τινός (s.v. ἔξω 2b) Polyaenus 3, 7, 3.
ἐπιστρέφεσθαι (2b [= 4b]) πρός τινα = 'turn to someone': Diog. L. 3, 25.
ἡσυχάζω (4 [= 3]) ='have rest': Diog. L. 3, 21.
κάμνω (3) ='die': Crinagoras [I BC–I AD] 25, 1 [ed. M. Rubensohn (1888)] καμοῦσιν ὡς ζωοῖς 'for dead as well as for living'; Dionys. Byz. [200 AD] §109; 110 [ed. R. Güngerich (1927)]; Kaibel 321, 8.
καρδία (1bβ) as the seat of the intellect, as early as an 'ancient poet,' perhaps Hesiod: fgm. 247 Rzach.
κρίμα (2) ='decree': *Explor. arch. de la Galatie* etc. [= IGal], G. Perrot et al. I [1872], inscr. no. 25 [II AD].
λύτρον ὑπέρ τινος Lucian, Dial. Deor. 4, 2.
λύω (2a) τι ἀπό τινος at Lk 13:15: Quintus Smyrnaeus 4, 373.
μανθάνω (1) w. inf. foll.: Aristoxenus [300 BC] fgm. 96 [ed. F. Wehrli (1945)].

μανθάνω (4 [= 3]) at Hb 5:8: schol. on Pla. 222b ἐὰν μὴ πάθῃς, οὐ μὴ μάθῃς.
μέμφομαι (end) at Ro 9:19 'find fault, complain': Ps.-Pla., Axiochus 7, 368a.
νεφέλη as a medium for snatching a person away as Ac 1:9; 1 Th 4:17; better parallels than those quoted from Josephus are to be found: Dosiadas [III BC] no. 458 fgm. 5 Jac. νέφος ἥρπασεν αὐτὸν (Ganymede) εἰς οὐρανόν; Ps.-Apollodorus 2, 7, 7, 12 (Heracles).
οἰκία (3) = 'household' at Phil 4:22: Diog. L. 5, 75 on Demetrius of Phalerum ἦν ἐκ τῆς Κόνωνος οἰκίας.
ὁράω (1aβ, end [= A1b]) = 'perceive' in the sense 'hear': Polyaenus 7, 14, 2; schol. on Nicander, Ther. 165 ὁρῶ οἷα λέγεις.
πειράζω (2 [= 2b]) of God putting men to the test: Ps.-Apollodorus 3, 7, 7, 4.
πληρόω (4a) of the fulfilment of divine prophecy: Polyaenus 1, 18 τοῦ λογίου πεπληρωμένου.
ποιέω of God as the Creator of the universe (s.v. κόσμος 2, end [= 3]): Epict. 4, 7, 6. As far as I know, the same meaning cannot be quoted for κτίζω from secular sources today. But it certainly is not insignificant that κτίστης in this sense was used of pagan divinities even in pre-Christian times.
φεύγω (5 [= 4]) ἀπὸ τοῦ προσώπου at Rv 20:11: Ctesias, Pers. 2 φυγεῖν ἀπὸ προσώπου Κυρίου; schol. on Nicander, Ther. 377. Herodas the writer of mimes 8, 59 has, in a passage inaccurately cited by this scholion, ἔρρ' ἐκ προσώπου 'get out of my sight.'
φρονέω (1) ἄλλο = 'have a different opinion': Hdt. 7, 205, 3.

The closer Judaism and Hellenism approach each other in relation to the understanding of early Christianity, the more insistent becomes the question of how we may give proper credit to both of them. The use of the same words here and there does not mean that the language is identical. Both sides present their own challenge, and the author of a lexicon that seeks to shed light on primitive Christianity from the Greek world should have an ear for both. He must reckon with the possibility that what, for instance, Paul said, conditioned as he was by his Jewish past, was not always understood in the same terms by his gentile Christian hearers, who were also unable to dissociate themselves entirely from their previous ways of thought. Certainly, speaker and hearer were better attuned to each other when Paul addressed himself to Christians among whom he had worked, and the apostle was more certain to be understood correctly under these circumstances than when he wrote to people who did not know him personally. Yet even in Corinth, where Paul worked so long, there was a notable lack of understanding. It was not only that the old immorality lived on uncontrolled in some circles. The state of 'being long accustomed to idols' (1 Cor 8:7) had not yet died out for some of them. In general, there is much in 1 Cor that we can begin to understand only after we have made an effort to form some conception of pagan Greek life and thought.

When Paul speaks of sacrifice, of the wrath of God, or of the δικαιοσύνη θεοῦ, it is quite correct to understand his words from the standpoint of Judaism. But what about his public, who have heard these words before, but with different connotations [concepts, F.W.D.] and associations? His hearers certainly did not feel themselves challenged to make an eschatological decision as often as the apostle summoned them to it. With this in mind we might conclude that sometimes there are two meanings for the same passage, one from the standpoint of the writer and another which becomes evident when one puts one's self in the place of the recipient, intellectually and spiritually; the lexicographer naturally feels an obligation to draw the proper conclusions. The way a passage is understood by its first readers has an immediate effect upon its later interpretation. We know how hard it was to understand Paul's letters (2 Pt 3:15, 16), and in what manifold and sometimes contradictory fashion they have been interpreted.

I give herewith a few examples (not found in the fourth edition) to illustrate that different meanings have been associated with similar words:

On πολίτευμα Phil 3:20: Epict. 2, 23, 38; 39 'you have gone on a journey to return thither where you were born, and where you are a πολίτης' (39 = εἰς τὴν πατρίδα 38). Olympiodorus in Platonis Phaedonem [ed. W. Norvin (1913)] p. 122, 8 says of the wise man συμπολιτεύεσθαι τοῖς θεοῖς καὶ συνοικονομεῖν.

On κρίνω (4bβ [= 5bβ]) 1 Cor 6:2, on the saints as fellow-rulers with God: Epict., Ench. 15; Sallustius 21 p. 36, 14 [ed. A. D. Nock (1926)] τὸν ὅλον κόσμον συνδιοικοῦσιν ἐκείνοις (the pious with the gods).

On εἰρήνη (3 [= 2b]) τοῦ θεοῦ: Epict. 3, 13, 12 εἰρήνη ὑπὸ τοῦ θεοῦ κεκηρυγμένη διὰ τοῦ λόγου (= philosophy).

On 1 Cor 7:34f: Epict. 3, 22, 69 ἀπερίσπαστον εἶναι δεῖ τὸν Κυνικὸν ὅλον πρὸς τῇ διακονίᾳ τοῦ θεοῦ, coupled with an exhortation to keep one's self free from marriage and other earthly bonds. In such a case would a Greek not feel himself deeply moved by the apostle's preaching? Would he not receive its words with connotations familiar to him, and so pass them on to others?

Sometimes one gets the distinct impression that the Greek must have failed to understand the basic meaning of a New Testament author. He may have been led in another direction by his own background and have lacked a knowledge of Jewish and Old Testament matters which the author took for granted:

On Mt 1:17, a better parallel than can be found in rabbinic literature may be pointed out in the numerological statements found as early as Hellanicus [400 BC] with γενεαί (no. 323a fgm. 22a Jac.): ἐννέα γενεαῖς ὕστερον ... ἓξ γενεαῖς ὕστερον ... τρισὶ γενεαῖς ὕστερον....

Βοανηργές Mk 3:17 has less light shed on it by the unsatisfactory explanations of the word's meaning than by the fact that, among the Greeks, pairs of brothers or sisters are often referred to by a special name: Apollodorus no. 244 fgm. 210 Jac. Σταγόνιον καὶ Ἄνθις ἀδελφαί· αὗται Ἀφύαι ἐκαλοῦντο, ὅτι λευκαὶ κ.τ.λ. In Diog. L. 2, 52 Gryllus and Diodorus, the two sons of Xenophon, Διόσκουροι ἐπεκαλοῦντο. In schol. on Pla. 118e Ξάνθιππος καὶ Πάραλος οἱ Περικλέους υἱοί, οὓς καὶ βλιττομάμμας ἐκάλουν.

On Mt 15:27=Mk 7:28: Aelius Dionysius [II AD] α, 159 [ed. H. Erbse (1950)] ψωμὸς εἰς ὃν ἐκματτόμενοι τὰς χεῖρας μετὰ τὸ δεῖπνον ἐρρίπτουν τοῖς κυσίν.

On Lk 6:15; Ac 1:13: the word ζηλωτής as a surname of the second Simon may have been meant by the author to have the sense 'zealot'; his readers were much more likely to understand it as meaning 'enthusiastic adherent,' which it has so often meant (Polyaenus 5, 2, 22; Diog. L. 2, 113, al.).

At Mt 18:22 the number ἑβδομηκοντάκις ἑπτά probably comes from Gen 4:24. But Gentiles did not need to know this in order to understand that Mt means to indicate a number that is large out of all proportion. In a story taken from older accounts, Plut., Mor. 245d uses the number 7,777 for the same purpose (cp. Polyaenus 8, 33).

On Ro 13:1b: here Paul was possibly thinking of Wisdom 6:3 and similar Jewish sayings. But the Roman Christians were probably more impressed and encouraged by the 'old saying' (Artemidorus 2, 36 p. 135, 24, also 2, 69 p. 161, 17) τὸ κρατοῦν δύναμιν ἔχει θεοῦ 'the government derives its power from God.' Similar sentiments are found as early as Hesiod, Theogony 96. This was an old Greek belief (H. Fränkel, *Dichtung und Philosophie des frühen Griechentums* [1951], 141, 5).

On 1 Cor 9:9: the apostle quotes the Law of Moses. But in connection with the words immediately following, the Greeks might easily think of their own proverb τῶν δ' ὄνων οὔ μοι μέλει (Aelius Dionysius τ, 35).

On 1 Cor 15:32: the writer certainly has Is 22:13 in mind, but it is just as certain that his readers are reminded of a very common and primitive piece of worldly wisdom brought to their attention by the tombs along the road (e.g., *Explor.* etc. [=IGal], Perrot et al. [see p. xxiv above], inscr. no. 78, 11).

The writer of the Revelation, too, is no exception: When in his vision (10:9f) he swallows a book that 'makes' his stomach 'bitter,' the concept comes without doubt from Ezk 2:8; 3:1–3. But would the gentile Christians of Asia Minor not rather be reminded of the dream-books that interpreted ἐσθίειν βιβλία to mean an early death (Artem. of Ephesus 2, 45 p. 149, 6)?

And in connection with Babylon the Harlot (Rv 17:4) would they not think of something like the image portrayed on the painting of Cebes [I AD] 5, 1? Sitting on the throne is the beautifully adorned woman Ἀπάτη, ἣ ἐν τῇ χειρὶ ἔχει ποτήριόν τι. She gives men wine to drink (ποτίζει Cebes 5, 2 as Rv 14:8) and thus leads them astray (πλανάω as Rv 18:23).

Artemidorus 2, 70 p. 167, 25 asks the readers of his books μήτε προσθεῖναι μήτε τι τῶν ὄντων ἀφελεῖν, and in 168, 2ff he commends his work to the protection of Apollo, who commissioned him to write it and who helped him carry it to completion. Is this not a pagan commentary on Rv 22:18, 19 (and 1:9ff), and is it not worth more for a living understanding of these passages than the Old Testament parallels printed in heavy type in the editions?

What we can learn here and there about communal meals among the Greeks will, perhaps, shed some light on the observance of the Lord's Supper in Corinth. The references that we have come from the vicinity of that city, and they illuminate both the observance and the words used in connection with it. In order to gain a proper insight into this point it seems to me that we must do more than point out that rabbinical literature permits us to trace a Hebrew expression for 'sacred cup' back to about 300 AD:*

Diog. L. 8, 35 has Pythagoras say that the εἷς ἄρτος (cp. 1 Cor 10:17) had served as a symbol of the bond between φίλοι. Theopompus (in Athen. 4, 31, 149d) tells us about banquets in Arcadia at which the diners gathered about *one* table on which the food for all of them was set; likewise, they all drank from the same jar. κοινωνία with the genitive (1 Cor 10:16) is the common possession or enjoyment of something (Diog. L. 7, 124 al.). The eating together of the *one* loaf, which means the body of Christ (11:24), brings the many together in *one* body (10:17). We read of communal meals in Crete in the historian Pyrgion (Hellenistic times; no. 467 fgm. 1 Jac.) that they were consecrated by the offering of a libation with prayer (μετ' εὐφημίας) at the beginning of them. When the offering has been made, the food is distributed to all present. The νεώτατοι waited on the tables.

Is it too bold to look upon the Corinthian sacral meal as a Christianized communal dinner at which the consecration was brought about by a calling to mind of what had happened on the last evening of Jesus' life? The unseemly conduct that Paul condemned (11:17–22) had a strong 'heathen' tone to it. And similar occurrences were a cause for concern to serious-minded Greeks long before this time. Dicaearchus [300 BC] fgm. 59 [ed. F. Wehrli (1944)] complains of carelessness and encroachment upon the rights of others at common meals, which should really serve to make brothers of those who eat together. Eratosthenes [III BC] no. 241 fgm. 16 Jac. waxes bitter over the fact that at the festival of the Lagynophoria each one eats what he has brought along and drinks from his own (ἴδιος as 1 Cor 11:21) bottle, which he has brought with him. His judgment is as severe as that of the apostle: 'such a festal meeting is a dirty thing [mob affair, F.W.D.], ἀνάγκη γὰρ τὴν σύνοδον γίνεσθαι παμμιγοῦς ὄχλου.'

*Similarly, the importance of the word in the services of the church at Corinth cannot be understood from the viewpoint of the synagogue (W. Bauer, *Der Wortgottesdienst der ältesten Christen* [1930], pp. 19ff). On the other hand, it is from 1 Cor that we learn how tolerant Paul could be of heathen customs (eating meat offered to idols, baptism for the dead). And the same letter proclaims as one of the basic principles of his mission to the Gentiles: 'To those who do not know the Mosaic law I became as one who does not concern himself about it, in order to win them' (9:21).

There is at least something comparable to the unworthy partaking of the Eucharist and its results (1 Cor 11:29f). Simplicius in Epict. p. 93, 51–53 Düb. tells in detail how the divine power (ἐνέργεια) passes over to first-fruits that are offered with a pure heart. Someone, so he says, has asserted that he was cured of his epilepsy by eating such first-fruits. With the unseemly conduct described by Paul we may contrast the conduct ἀπὸ ζωῆς καθαρᾶς in Simplicius line 49. Just as the eating of the consecrated food, laden with divine power, can bring healing when it is accompanied by a pure life, so in Corinth participation in the Lord's Supper, coupled with the wrong kind of conduct, can bring illness or even death.

Finally, one more proposal, which may possibly illuminate the meaning ἀγάπη (II [= 2]) 'love-feast.' Scholia on Pla. 122b: the common meals of the Lacedaemonians καλεῖται φιλίτια, ἐπεὶ φιλίας συναγωγά ἐστιν. If it is permissible to see in ἀγάπη a transfer of φιλία into the Christian realm, this passage can shed light on the custom as well as the vocabulary of the Christians.

At times the information in the fourth edition [of Bauer's *Wörterbuch*] seems in need of correction or supplementation:

On ἁρπάζω (2b, end) τι Mt 11:12. The meaning 'plunder, pillage something thoroughly' is also possible: Libanius, Or. 1 p. 147, 4F. κώμας ἁρπάζειν; Polyaenus 8, 11 τῆς πόλεως ἁρπαγή.

On ἱκανός (1c [= 1]) Mk 15:15 τὸ ἱκανὸν ποιεῖν τινι better: 'do someone a favor' Diog. L. 4, 50.

On καρτερέω Hb 11:27. The translation 'endure, hold out' is hardly correct. This is apart from the question whether this quality is particularly characteristic of Moses. The participle with καρτερεῖν does not express an accompanying circumstance, but the respect in which someone is 'enduring' or 'constant.' Diod. Sic. 14, 65, 4 μέχρι τίνος καρτερήσομεν ταῦτα πάσχοντες; 'how long will we continue to endure this?' Arrian, Anab. 7, 8, 3 οὔκουν σιγῇ ἔχοντες ἐκαρτέρησαν = 'they therefore continued in silence.' Ps.-Dicaearchus, Βίος Ἑλλάδος [ed. M. Fuhr (1841), p. 141, line 11 = C. Müller, GGM I (1855) p. 99 I] ἀκούων καρτ. = 'keep on listening.' So in Hb 11:27, giving the reason for his fearlessness: 'for he kept his eyes constantly upon him who is unseen.'

On ῥύομαι 2 Cor 1:10a. ῥ. ἐκ τοῦ θανάτου does not mean 'preserve from death' in general, but 'rescue from a(n actual) situation in which death was threatened': Aristoxenus [300 BC] fgm. 113 [ed. F. Wehrli (1945)] ῥύεσθαι καὶ ἐρύεσθαι διαφορὰν ἔχει πρὸς ἄλληλα. τὸ μὲν γὰρ ῥύεσθαι ἐκ θανάτου ἕλκειν, τὸ δὲ ἐρύεσθαι φυλάττειν.

On λυπέω (1) abs.: in 2 Cor 2:5 it is more than 'vex' or 'cause grief.' Polyaenus 8, 47 uses it of the severe humiliation felt by a king whose subjects have deposed him.

On πῶλος I have presented material which I hope is significant and more to the point in a study that appeared in JBL 72 (1953), 220–29.

In the case of certain entries, new and better examples have turned up:

On ἀδελφός (1). There is no longer any doubt in my mind that ἀδελφοί can mean 'brothers and sisters' in any number. There are passages that scarcely permit any other interpretation. Ptolemaeus, Apotelesm. 3, 5 has as its subject περὶ γονέων and 3, 6 περὶ ἀδελφῶν, divided into male and female. The meaning is so clear that F. E. Robbins [1948] rightly translates the second title 'Of Brothers and Sisters.' Likewise Diog. L. 7, 108; 120 al.

On ἀπό (II 3a [= 2ca]) Jd 14: Diog. L. 3, 1 in the list of descendants Plato is ἕκτος ἀπὸ Σόλωνος.

On σὺ εἶπας (εἶπον 1 [= 1a]) Mt 26:25, 64: schol. on Pla. 112e Socrates says in declining or yielding: σὺ ταῦτα εἶπες, οὐκ ἐγώ.

εὐνουχίζω (literally) as early as Clearchus IV/III BC fgm. 49 [ed. F. Wehrli (1948)].

φαντάζομαι of a theophany (Athena) in Ps-Aristotle, Mirabilia 108.

φωτισμός in Strato of Lampsakos [300 BC] fgm. 76 [ed. F. Wehrli (1950)].

I shall add some passages here in which the subject is of interest, as well as the words themselves:

On ἀναγινώσκω (2 [= b]): at the end of the sixth letter of Plato we read ταύτην τὴν ἐπιστολὴν πάντας ὑμᾶς ἀναγνῶναι χρή, just as 1 Th 5:27.

On Γαλατία: for Memnon of Asia Minor, a slightly older contemporary of Paul, the Galatians (of whom he speaks now and again: no. 434 fgm. 1, 11ff Jac.) are the people who came from Europe to Asia Minor, with a very definite national composition and tone. He would certainly never address Lycaonians as Γαλάται. For him, Γαλατία is the land of these particular people (e.g., fgm. 1, 20, 2).

On ἐγώ εἰμί J 8:58. Ammonius Hermiae (Comm. in Aristot. IV 5 ed. A. Busse [1897]) c. 9 p. 136, 20f: in the Timaeus (37e) it is written that one should not say of the gods τὸ ἦν, ἢ τὸ ἔσται, μεταβολῆς τινος ὄντα σημαντικά, μόνον δὲ τὸ ἔστι.

On ἐξέλκω Js 1:14: Pla., Ep. 7, 325b εἷλκεν δέ με ἡ ἐπιθυμία.

On ἱλάσκομαι Lk 18:13: Sb 8511, 7 ἵλαθί μοι, Μανδοῦλι (a divinity), σῶζέ με.

On κεράτιον Lk 15:16: fodder for swine as Lycophron, Al. 675–78.

On πᾶσα Ἱεροσόλυμα Mt 2:3: of the inhabitants as Pla., Ep. 7, 348a πᾶσα Σικελία; Demosth. 18,18 ἡ Πελοπόννησος ἅπασα.

On Ac 9:1: Saul breathing out murder has a parallel in Theocr. 22, 82: the two opponents φόνον ἀλλήλοισι πνέοντες.

The parallel in language can be absent entirely, and yet there may be significant similarities in subject matter. This is especially true of some passages from Diogenes Laërtius:

Diog. L. 2, 14 has a story of Hieronymus of Rhodes concerning the trial of Anaxagoras. Pericles puts on a scene with the latter, his teacher, in order to arouse the sympathy of the judges. In Nicol. Dam. no. 90 fgm. 68, 4 Jac., in connection with the fall of Croesus, Cyrus lets a woeful spectacle take its course βουλόμενος καὶ τοὺς Πέρσας οἶκτόν τινα λαβεῖν αὐτοῦ. Compare the Ecce Homo J 19:5.

Diog. L. 2, 48 Socrates stops Xenophon at their first meeting and says: 'ἕπου καὶ μάνθανε.' καὶ τοὐντεῦθεν ἀκροατὴς Σωκράτους ἦν. Cp. ἀκολουθέω (3).

Diog. L. 2, 127 Menedemus the philosopher [300 BC], in whose presence someone has acted in an unseemly manner, διέγραφεν εἰς τοὔδαφος. By doing this he shames him. Cp. J 8:6, 8.

Diog. L. 3, 19 Plato awaits a verdict before the popular assembly on the island of Aegina that could mean death, but says not a word (μηδ' ὁτιοῦν φθέγξασθαι). Cp. Mt 26:63; Mk 14:61, and σιωπάω (1).

Diog. L. 6, 97 Crates the Cynic goes about with his like-minded wife, seeking adherents for his cause. Cp. 1 Cor 9:5.

Now and then everything is clear from a linguistic point of view, but the subject matter poses questions for which an answer should at least be sought among the Greeks:

Why does Mt (13:55) say of Jesus τοῦ τέκτονος υἱός for Mark's ὁ τέκτων (6:3)? Aristoxenus [300 BC] fgm. 115 (ed. F. Wehrli [1945]) describes Sophillus, the father of Sophocles, as τέκτων. The Vita Sophoclis 1 rejects this and will only admit that he owned τέκτονες as slaves.

Why do we read in 1 Cor 15:5 of οἱ δώδεκα, when Judas the traitor has disappeared from the scene? The variant ἕνδεκα shows that the problem was felt. 'The Twelve' is a fixed expression, like οἱ τριάκοντα in Athens. Xenophon, Hell. still refers to them in these terms in 2, 4, 23, despite the fact 2, 4, 19 tells of the deaths of Critias and Hippomachus.

These examples must suffice. They represent a small sampling from the work of gathering parallels during the years 1951 and 1952. No one need fear that the task is almost finished and that there are no more parallels to be found. One who gives himself to this task with any devotion at all cannot escape the feeling thus expressed: how great is the ocean, and how tiny the shell with which we dip!

Abbreviations

1. The New Testament, the Apostolic Fathers, and Selected Apocrypha

The basic text for the NT is Nestle-Aland, Novum Testamentum Graece[27] 1993; the sigla S/Sin. and Vat. are frequently used in reference to the manuscripts Sinaiticus and Vaticanus. For the Apostolic Fathers and related witnesses the basic text is KBihlmeyer (ed.), Die Apostolischen Väter: Neubearbeitung der Funckschen Ausgabe, I, 2d ed. 1956 (supersedes OGebhardt/AHarnack/TZahn [G-H-Z], Patrum Apostolicorum Opera 1920), but s. also JFischer, Die apostolischen Väter 1959; KWengst, Didache (Apostellehre), Barnabasbrief, Zweiter Klemensbrief, Schrift an Diognet 1984; for the apocryphal Gospel texts: KAland, Synopsis Quattuor Evangeliorum[13] (ASyn.), 1985 (s. pp. 584–86 index). Readings not received into the text of these editions are treated as either variants or conjectures.

Editors/Editions of New Testament Texts

Bov. JMBover, 1943; 5th ed. 1968
GNT The Greek New Testament (United Bible Societies), 1st ed. 1966; 2d ed. 1968; 3d ed. 1975 (corrected 1983); 4th ed. 1993
GNT-MT The Greek New Testament according to the Majority Text, ed. ZCHodges/ALFarstad 1982
L. KLachmann, 1842–50
M. AMerk, 1933; 10th ed. 1984
N. Nestle-Aland[27] 1993; except that earlier edd. are indicated by superscripts
Sod. HvSoden, 1913
Tdf. CvTischendorf, editio octava critica maior, 1869–72. This edition should be consulted for variants not included in the Nestle apparatus
Vog. HJVogels, 1922; 4th ed. 1955
W-H. BFWestcott-FJAHort, 1881

Apocryphal texts relating to the NT and drawn primarily from papyri are frequently cited. Some of this literature, especially AcPlHa, is quite fragmentary, and the user of this lexicon will be able to determine much of the actual state of the more damaged texts from the standard notations used in recording papyrological data (s. List 7); esp. useful is AdeSantosOtero, Los Evangelios apocrifos (2d ed. 1963). Canonical books are marked with an asterisk (*).

***Ac** = Acts of the Apostles
AcPl Ant = Acta Pauli, PAntinoopolis 13 in The Antinoopolis Papyri I, ed. CRoberts 1950, 26–28
AcPl BMM = the text of PMich 1317+ PBerlin 13893, with PMich 3788 recto, 1–9 following PMich 1317 recto 30, and 3788 verso joining the text of PMich 1317 at line 32, thereby providing a recto page of 38 lines and a verso of 40 lines. Text is cited by line according to WRordorf, Les Actes de Paul sur papyrus: problèmes liés aux PMich. inv. 1317 et 3788, in ProcXVIIICongPap (1986) I, 1988, 453–61. For earlier ed. of PMich inv. 1317 s. esp. HSanders, HTR 31, 1938, 73–90; for PMich inv. 3788 s. Sanders, ibid. 36, 1943, 166–67 and ed. by GKilpatrick and CRoberts, JTS 47, 1946, 196–99. S. also Ox 1602=AcPl Ha 8, 9–16. On the history of the restoration s. Borger, GGA 116–18.
AcPlCor = PBodmer X: Correspondance apocryphe des Corinthiens et de l'apôtre Paul, ed. MTestuz 1959 (for tr. and bibl. s. EHennecke, NT Apokryphen[3] II, 1964, ed. WSchneemelcher, 258ff; Eng. tr. RMcLWilson, 1964, 374ff)

AcPl Ha = CSchmidt/WSchubart, Πράξεις Παύλου, Acta Pauli: Nach dem Papyrus der Hamburger Staats- und Universitätsbibliothek 1936
AcPl M1 = PMich 1317 and PBerlin 13893. HASanders, A Fgm. of the Acta Pauli, HTR 31, 1938, 73–90
AcPl M2 = Acta Pauli, PMich 3788. GDKilpatrick/CHRoberts, JTS 47, 1946, 196–99
AcPl Ox 6 = Acta Pauli, POxy 6
AcPl Ox 1602 = Acta Pauli, POxy 1602
AcPt Ox 849 = Acta Petri, POxy 849
Agr = Agraphon (EPreuschen, Antilegomena[2] 1905, 26–31: Herrenlose Herrnworte [non-canonical sayings ascribed to Jesus])
ApcPt = Apocalypse of Peter (Kl. T. 3, 1908 [reprinted EKlostermann, Apokrypha I 1933]) 8–13; cited by ch. and vs.
ApcPt Bodl. = Bodleian Apocalypse of Peter, in MRJames, Additional Notes on the Apocalypse of Peter, JTS 12, 1910–11, 157; also 367–69
ApcPt Rainer = MRJames, The Rainer Fgm. of the Apocalypse of Peter, JTS 32, 1931, 270–79
Apolog(ists), s. EJGoodspeed, Die ältesten Apologeten 1914; Index Apologeticum 1912
ASyn. = KAland, Synopsis Quattuor Evangeliorum[13] 1988
B = Barnabas (the Letter of), except in series of uncial witnesses, in which case B refers to Codex Vaticanus (s. also Vat.). When the abbr. B is ambiguous, Vat. is used. Bihlmeyer 10–34; s. also PPrigent/RKraft, Épître de Barnabé 1971; KWengst, in Schriften des Urchristentums II 1984, 101–202
1 Cl = 1 Clement. Bihlmeyer 35–70; s. also AJaubert, Épître aux Corinthiens, Clément de Rome 1971
2 Cl = 2 Clement. Bihlmeyer 71–81
***Col** = Colossians
***1 Cor** = 1 Corinthians
***2 Cor** = 2 Corinthians
D = Didache, except that in a list of manuscripts or as textual variant D refers to Codex Bezae. Bihlmeyer 1–9; s. also KWengst, in Schriften des Urchristentums II 1984, 1–100; WRordorf/ATuillier, La doctrine de douze apôtres 1978
Dg = Diognetus. Bihlmeyer 141–49; also KWengst, in Schriften des Urchristentums II 1984, 281–348; EBlakeney, The Ep. to Dg. 1943; HMarrou, A Diognète, 2d ed., 1965
***Eph** = Ephesians
EpilMosq = Epilogus Mosquensis to the Martyrdom of Polycarp. Bihlmeyer 132
***Gal** = Galatians
GEb = Gospel of the Ebionites, cited by no. and line of ASyn.
GEg = Gospel according to the Egyptians, cited by no. and line of ASyn.
GHb = Gospel according to the Hebrews, cited by no. and line of ASyn.
GJs = Gospel of James (Protevangelium Jacobi): Papyrus Bodmer V (Nativité de Marie, ed. MTestuz, 1958); also cited: ÉdeStrycker, La forme la plus ancienne du protévangile de Jacques 1961; KTischendorf, Evangelia apocrypha, 2d ed. 1876. The notation "not pap." indicates that a term in texts of GJs is not found in this papyrus.
GMary 463 = The Gospel of Mary [Magdalene]. CHRoberts, Catalogue of the Greek and Latin Papyri in the John Rylands Library, Manchester, III (1938) 18–23; cited by number (463) and line.
GMary Ox 3525 = Gospel of Mary, POxy 3525
GNaass = Gospel of the Naassenes, cited by no. and line of ASyn.
GPt = Gospel of Peter (Kl. Texte 3, 4–8), cited by no. and line of ASyn.
GTh = Gospel of Thomas in Coptic or in Oxy. documents, cited by no. in ASyn. appendix; s. Ox 1, Ox 654, Ox 655 below
H = Hermas, MWhittaker, Der Hirt des Hermas, in GCS, Die Apostolischen Väter I 1956; 2d ed. 1967; also cited: RJoly, Hermas, Le Pasteur[2] 1968; MLeutzsch, Hirt des Hermas, in UKörtner/ML.: Papias Fragmente, Hirt des Hermas 1998, 105–497. Text is cited acc. to Whittaker, but divisions of the text are in the traditional form also given by Whittaker, Joly, and Leutzsch; reff. to PMich 129–30 of Hermas are cited as Bonner.
  m = Mandates
  s = Similitudes
  v = Visions
***Hb** = Hebrews
I = Ignatius as author
IEph = Ignatius to the Ephesians. Bihlmeyer 82–88
IMg = Ignatius to the Magnesians. Bihlmeyer 88–92
IPhld = Ignatius to the Philadelphians. Bihlmeyer 102–5
IPol = Ignatius to Polycarp. Bihlmeyer 110–13
IRo = Ignatius to the Romans. Bihlmeyer 96–101
ISm = Ignatius to the Smyrneans. Bihlmeyer 105–10
ITr = Ignatius to the Trallians. Bihlmeyer 92–96
***J** = John (Gospel of)
***1J** = 1 John
***2J** = 2 John
***3J** = 3 John
***Jd** = Jude
Jeremias, Unknown Sayings, s. Unknown Sayings
***Js** = James
Judaicon = remnants of an early Judean/Christian gospel edition; s. list of passages in ASyn. p. 585
***Lk** = Luke
***Mk** = Mark
MPol = Martyrdom of Polycarp. Bihlmeyer 120–32
***Mt** = Matthew
Ox 1 = POxy 1 = (in varying degrees) GTh 26, 27, 28, 29, 30+77, 31, 32, 33. This pap. contains 8 logia or sayings, but we note only line, not specific logion, in our citations; JAFitzmyer, The Oxyrhynchus Logoi and the Coptic Gospel According to Thomas: TS 20, 1959, 529–43; in earlier editions of Bauer cited as LJ (Logia Jesu: Kl. Texte 8[3], 19–22).
Ox 6 = POxy 6 = fgm. Acts of Paul and Thecla
Ox 654 = POxy 654 = GTh prologue, 2, 3, 4, 5, 6; Fitzmyer (s. Ox 1) 511–29
Ox 655 = POxy 655 = fragment of a lost gospel = GTh 36, 37, 38, 39; Fitzmyer (s. Ox 1) 543–51
Ox 840 = POxy 840 = gospel fragment = Kl. T., ed. HLietzmann, 31, 1908 (repr. 1924), 4f
Ox 847 = POxy 847 (J 2:11–22)
Ox 849 = POxy 849; s. AcPt Ox 849
Ox 1081 = POxy 1081; AdeSantosOtero, Los Evangelios apocrifos (2d ed. 1963) 82–83; s. also SJCh for the Coptic text
Ox 1224 = POxy 1224; non-canonical gospel fragment, IV AD

Ox 1596 = POxy 1596 (J 6:18–22)
Ox 1602 = AcPl Ha 8, 9–26, with variations
Ox 3525 = POxy 3525; s. GMary Ox 3525
P[66] = Papyrus Bodmer II, Evangile de Jean chap. 1–14, ed. VMartin 1956; Supplément, Jean chap. 14–21, ed. VMartin/JBarns 1962
P[72] = Papyrus Bodmer VII–IX: VII L'Épître de Jude; VIII Les deux Épîtres de Pierre; IX Les Psaumes 33 et 34, ed. MTestuz, 1959
P[74] = Papyrus Bodmer XVII: Actes des Apôtres, Épîtres de Jacques, Pierre, Jean et Jude, ed. RKasser 1961
P[75] = Papyrus Bodmer XIV: Evangile de Luc chap. 3–24, ed. VMartin/RKasser 1961; PBodmer XV: Ev. de Jean chap. 1–15, 1961
Papias = Fragmenta, cited according to Bihlmeyer 133–40, with ref. in parentheses; s. also FPreuschen, Antilegomena 1905, 91–99; JKürzinger, Papias von Hierapolis und die Evangelien des NT 1983
PEg[2] = Papyrus Egerton No. 2, in HIBell/TCSkeat, Fragments of an Unknown Gospel 1935, pp. 8–15, cited by line
***Phil** = Philippians
***Phlm** = Philemon (Letter to)
Pol = Polycarp to the Philippians. Bihlmeyer 114–20
***1 Pt** = 1 Peter
***2 Pt** = 2 Peter
PtK = Petruskerygma (Preaching of Peter): EKlostermann, Apokrypha I (Kl. T. 3) 1933 pp. 13–16 (by p. and line)
Qua = Quadratus fragment: Die Ältesten Apologeten, ed. EJGoodspeed 1911, p. 1; Bihlmeyer, p. 140
***Ro** = Romans
***Rv** = (Book of) Revelation
SJCh = Sophia Jesu Christi, in TU 60/5/5: Die gnostischen Schriften des Koptischen Papyrus, Berolinensis 8502, ed. WCTill, 1955, 216–21; 2d ed. HMSchenke 1972, 216–21. Substantially = Ox (POxy) 1081; s. AdeSantosOtero, Los Evangelios apocrifos (2d ed. 1963) 82–83.
***1 Th** = 1 Thessalonians
***2 Th** = 2 Thessalonians
***1 Ti** = 1 Timothy
***2 Ti** = 2 Timothy
***Tit** = Titus (Letter to)
Unknown Sayings = JJeremias, Unknown Sayings of Jesus, Eng. tr. (orig.: Jesusworte) RFuller, 1957

2. The Old Testament and Intertestamental/ Pseudepigraphical Literature

The Old Testament literature is cited according to the LXX in the edition of ARahlfs (1935; freq. reprinted), unless it is expressly stated that the quotation is from the translation of Aq(uila), Sym(machus), or Theod(otion). Occasionally reference is made to HSwete, The Old Testament in Greek, 3 vols. var. edd. 1887–1912. The following codices are sometimes cited in ref. to LXX readings: A (=Alexandrinus), B or Vat. (=Vaticanus [not Barnabas, in whose case the abbr. B is clear from the context]), S/Sin. (=Sinaiticus or א). Unless otherwise specified, all divisions of the OT text follow Rahlfs. For discrepancies in the numbering of portions of the OT see FDanker, Multipurpose Tools for Bible Study, rev. ed. 1993, 77f. In addition to pseudepigrapha cited below, reference is freq. made to 'Denis' = Fragmenta pseudepigraphorum quae supersunt Graeca, ed. AMDenis 1970. Books included in the Rahlfs ed. are noted with an asterisk (*).

***Am** = Amos
ApcEl = Apocalypse of Elijah, PSI I, 7 pp. 16f; also ed. Denis 103f
ApcEsdr = Apocalypse of Esdras, ed. OWahl 1977; Tdf.=KTischendorf, Apocalypses Apocryphae 1866; repr. 1966. Not to be confused with 4 Esdras.
Apc4Esdr = Apocalypse of Fourth Esdras, ed. Denis 130–32; s. also 4(6) Esdras
ApcMos = Apocalypse of Moses (=Life of Adam and Eve ['revealed to Moses', according to the prologue]), ed. KTischendorf (Tdf.), Apocalypses Apocryphae 1866, pp. 1–23; cited by page and line
ApcrEzk = Apocryphon Ezechiel, ed. Denis, 121–28. For Papyrus Chester Beatty no. 185, s. pp. 125–28.
ApcSed = Apocalypse of Sedrach, ed. OWahl 1977; Harris = JRHarris, The Rest of the Words of Baruch 1889; Ja. = MRJames, Apocrypha Anecdota 1893; also Tdf.= KTischendorf, Apocalypses Apocryphae 1866, pp. 24–31
ApcZeph = Apocalypse of Zephaniah (Apocalypsis Sophoniae), ed. Denis 129
AscIs = Ascension of Isaiah: PAmh I, pp. 1–22 (2:4–4:4); also cited: Martyrium Isaiae, Denis 105–14; s. also RHCharles, The Ascension of Isaiah 1900 (includes Ethiopic version)
AssMos = Assumptio Mosis, ed. Denis 63–67; JTromp, The Assumption of Moses 1993 (the Gk. portions: 272–85)
***Bar** = Baruch
***Bel** = Bel and the Dragon
***1 Ch** = 1 Chronicles (Paralipomena I)
***2 Ch** = 2 Chronicles (Paralipomena II)
***Da** = Daniel
***Dt** = Deuteronomy
***Eccl** = Ecclesiastes (Qoheleth)
En = I Enoch: MBlack, Pseudepigrapha Veteris Testamenti Graece III 1970. Chapters 1–32; 89:42–49, ed. LRadermacher 1901; chapters 97:6–104:13; 106f, ed. CBonner 1937

***EpJer** = Epistle of Jeremiah
***1 Esdr** = 1 Esdras (apocryphal book = Lat. 3 Esdras). Rahlfs I 873
***2 Esdr** = 2 Esdras (chs. 1–10 = MT Ezra; 11–23 = MT Nehemiah). Rahlfs I 903
4 (6) Esdr = POxy 1010 (15:57–59). Otherwise extant only in Lat.; tr. NRSV under 2 Esdras. See also Apc4Esdr above for other Gk. fragments of this work.
***Esth** = Esther
***Ex** = Exodus
***Ezk** = Ezekiel
***Gen** = Genesis
GrBar = Apocalypsis Baruchi Graece, ed. J-CPicard 1967; also ed. by MRJames (Ja.) 1897. Also known as 3 Baruch.
***Hab** = Habbakuk
***Hg** = Haggai
***Hos** = Hosea
***Is** = Isaiah
***Jdth** = Judith
***Jer** = Jeremiah; s. also Bar, La, and EpJer
***Jo** = Joel
***Job** (unabbreviated)
***Jon** = Jonah
JosAs = Joseph and Aseneth, ed. MPhilonenko 1968; PBat(iffol) 1889; MIstrin 1888 (cod. B and Vat. Pal. 364)
***Josh** = Joshua
***Judg** = Judges
***1 Km** = 1 Kingdoms (Heb. 1 Samuel)
***2 Km** = 2 Kingdoms (Heb. 2 Samuel)
***3 Km** = 3 Kingdoms (Heb. 1 Kings)
***4 Km** = 4 Kingdoms (Heb. 2 Kings)
***La** = Lamentations
***Lev** = Leviticus
***1 Macc** = 1 Maccabees
***2 Macc** = 2 Maccabees
***3 Macc** = 3 Maccabees
***4 Macc** = 4 Maccabees
***Mal** = Malachi
***Mi** = Micah
***Na** = Nahum
***Nehemiah,** s. 2 Esdr
***Num** = Numbers
***Ob** = Obadiah
***Ode(s)** = Odai (Rahlfs II 164–83), songs or hymnodic prayers, for the most part drawn from OT writings and functioning as part of the Psalter in liturgical usage of the Greek Church. Especially notable is the Prayer of Manasseh (no. 12).
OdeSol = Ode(s) of Solomon: Greek Ode of Solomon 11, ed. MTestuz, PBodmer XI, 1959. Probably a translation of a Syriac original. For the Syriac corpus (prob. a Christian composition, c. 100 AD) see JRHarris, The Odes and Psalms of Solomon: Now First Published from the Syriac Version 1909.
ParJer = Paraleipomena Jeremiou, ed. AEPurintun/RAKraft 1972; also JRHarris, The Rest of the Words of Baruch 1889. Also known as 4 Baruch.
***Pr** = Proverbs
***Ps(s)** = Psalms, Book of
***PsSol** = Psalms of Solomon
Qumran texts, s. end of this list
***Ruth** (unabbreviated)
***Sir** = Jesus Sirach (Ecclesiasticus)
***SSol** = Song of Solomon (Canticles)
***Sus** = Susanna
SyrBar = Apocalypsis Syriaca Baruch [12–14], ed. Denis 118–20; variants cited from POxy 403. Also known as 2 Baruch.
TestAbr = Testament of Abraham, ed. MRJames, Texts and Studies II 1892 (recensions A and B), cited by ch., p., and line; MEStone, Missoula 1972, cited only by p. if lineation is identical.
TestJob = Testamentum Iobi, ed. SPBrock 1967
Test12Patr = Testaments of the Twelve Patriarchs: MdeJonge, 1978; RHCharles 1908 (repr. 3d ed. 1966)
- **TestAsh** = Testament of Asher
- **TestBenj** = Testament of Benjamin
- **TestDan** = Testament of Dan
- **TestGad** = Testament of Gad
- **TestIss** = Testament of Issachar
- **TestJos** = Testament of Joseph
- **TestJud** = Testament of Judah
- **TestLevi** = Testament of Levi
- **TestNapht** = Testament of Naphtali
- **TestReub** = Testament of Reuben
- **TestSim** = Testament of Simeon
- **TestZeb** = Testament of Zebulun

TestSol = Testament of Solomon, ed. CHMcCown 1922 (recensions A, B, C, etc.); Pap. Vindob(onensis), ed. KPreisdendanz, Eos 48, 3 (1956) 161–67 (prol. = prologus, Sig = sigilla)
***Tob** = Tobit
Vi, s. next entry
ViIs, ViJer, ViEzk, etc. = Vita of Isaiah, Vita of Jeremiah, Vita of Ezekiel, etc.: CCutler Torrey, The Lives of the Prophets 1946; TSch(ermann), Prophetarum vitae fabulosae 1907
***Wsd** = Wisdom of Solomon
***Zech** = Zechariah
***Zeph** = Zephaniah

Selected Qumran and Related Literature

See for all the following (except IQIs[a]) ELohse, Die Texte aus Qumran, Hebräisch und deutsch, mit masoretischer Punktation: Übersetzung, Einführung und Anmerkungen 1962.

CD = Cairo (Genizah text of the) Damascus (Document), a.k.a. Zadokite Document or Damascus Rule
1QH = Hôdāyôt: Psalms of Thanksgiving
1QIs[a] = St. Mark's Isaiah Scroll: MBurrows, with JTrever/WBrownlee, The Dead Sea Scrolls of St. Mark's Monastery I 1950
1QM = War (Milḥama) of the Sons of Light and the Sons of Darkness
1QpHab = Pesher Habakkuk: The Habakkuk Commentary
1QS = The Manual of Discipline

3. Inscriptions

Aberciusins. = Aberciusinschrift, ed. TKlauser, RAC I 1950, 13
Benndorf-Niemann = OB./GN., s. IAsMinLyk
BMI, s. IBM
Boffo, Iscrizioni = LB., Iscrizioni greche e latine per lo studio della bibbia 1994
Breccia, Iscrizioni, s. IAlexandriaMus
CB, s. Ramsay
Choix, s. IDelosChoix
ChronLind = Die Lindische Tempelchronik, ed. CBlinkenberg, Kleine Texte 131, 1915; s. also FGrH IIB no. 240 (Xenagoras) pp. 1005–10
CIA = Corpus Inscriptionum Atticarum, ed. WDittenberger et al., 4 vols. 1873–97
CIG = Corpus Inscriptionum Graecarum, ed. ABoeckh et al. 1828–77
CIJ = Corpus Inscriptionum Iudaicarum, ed. JFrey 1936–52
CIL = Corpus Inscriptionum Latinarum, begun by TMommsen, 1863ff
CIMRM = Corpus Inscriptionum et Monumentorum Religionis Mithraicae, ed. MVermaseren, 2 vols. 1956–60
CPJ III Inscr = "The Jewish Inscriptions of Egypt," ed. DLewis in CPJ (s. List 4) III, 1964, 138–96
CRAI = Comptes-rendus de l'Academie des Inscriptions et Belles Lettres, ser. 4
Cyr. Ins. = Cyrene Inscription (Augustus), ed. JStroux/LWenger, in ABayAW 34/2 1928, 1–145; SEG IX, 8; Ehrenberg/Jones no. 311
DocsAugTib = Documents Illustrating the Reigns of Augustus and Tiberius, ed. VEhrenberg/AHMJones, 2d ed. 1955; repr. with addenda 1976
DocsGaius = Documents Illustrating the Principates of Gaius, Claudius, and Nero, ed. ESmallwood 1967
DocsNerva = Documents Illustrating the Principates of Nerva, Trajan, and Hadrian, ed. ESmallwood 1966
EA, s. EpigrAnat
Ehrenberg-Jones, s. DocsAugTib
EphemEpigr = Ephemeris Epigraphica 1872ff
EpigrAnat = Epigraphica Anatolica 1983ff
Epigraphica = Textus Minores 31, 1964 (Epigraphica I, Texts on the Economic History of the Greek World); 41, 1969 (Epigr. II, Texts on the Social History of the Greek World), both ed. HPleket; 47, 1976 (Epigr. III, Texts on Bankers, Banking and Credit in the Greek World), ed. RBogaert
EpigraphicaRiv = Epigraphica: Rivista italiana di epigraphia 1937ff
Epigr. Gr., s. Kaibel
FD = Fouilles de Delphes III: Épigraphie fasc. 1–6, 1929ff
Ferguson = WF., The Legal Terms Common to the Macedonian Inscriptions and the NT 1913
FX, s. IXanthos.
GDI = Sammlung der griechischen Dialekt-Inschriften, ed. HCollitz/FBechtel 4 vols. 1884–1915
Guarducci = Epigrafia greca, ed. MGuarducci 4 vols. 1967–78
GVI = Griechische Vers-inschriften I: Die Grabepigramma, ed. WPeek 1955. Of the more than 2,000 inscriptions, 486 are available in Peek, Griechische Grabgedichte 1960
Hatch = WH., Some Illustrations of NT Usage from Greek Inscriptions of Asia Minor: JBL 27, 1908, 134–46
Hauser = KH., Grammatik der griechischen Inschriften Lykiens, diss. Zurich 1916
Hicks-Hill = EH./GH., A Manual of Greek Historical Inscriptions 1901
IAlexandriaMus = EBreccia, Catalogue général des antiquités égyptiennes du Musée d'Alexandrie, nos. 1–568: Iscrizioni greche e latine 1911 (=IGA II)
IAndrosIsis = Der Isishymnus von Andros und verwandte Texte, ed. WPeek 1930, text fr. Andros pp. 15–22
  Cyrene = text fr. Cyrene, p. 129
  Ios = text fr. Ios, pp. 123, 125
  Kyme = text fr. Kyme, pp. 122, 124
  Mesomedes = Isis hymn of Mesomedes, p. 145
IArsameia = FDörner/TGoell, Arsameia am Nymphaios 1963
IAsMinLyk = Reisen im südwestlichen Kleinasien, I: Reisen in Lykien und Karien, ed. OBenndorf/GNiemann 1884; II: Lykien, Milyas und Kibyratis, ed. EPetersen/FvonLuschan 1889
IAsMinSW = Bericht über zwei Reisen im südwestlichen Kleinasien, ed. RHeberdey/EKalinka 1896
IBildhauer = Inschriften griechischer Bildhauer, ed. ELoewy 1885
IBM (BMI) = Ancient Greek Inscriptions in the British Museum, 4 vols., ed. EHicks et al. 1874–1916
ICypr = Cyprian Inscriptions, in OHoffmann, Die griechische Dialekte I 1891
IDefixAudollent = Defixionum tabellae quotquot innotuerant tam in Graecis Orientis quam in totius Occidentis partibus praeter Atticas in C. I. A. editas, ed. AAudollent 1904
IDefixWünsch = Antike Fluchtafeln, ed. RWünsch, 2d ed. 1912
IDelosChoix = Choix d'inscriptions de Délos, ed. FDurrbach 1921–23
IEgChr = Recueil des inscriptions grecques-chrétiennes d'Egypte, ed. GLefebvre 1907 (IGA V)
IEphes = Die Inschriften von Ephesos, ed. HWankel et al., 7 vols. and index vol., 1974–84
IG = Inscriptiones Graecae 1873ff
IG^2 = Inscriptiones Graecae, ed. minor 1913ff
IGA = Inscriptiones Graecae Aegypti, s. IAlexandriaMus; IEgChr
IGal = GPerrot et al., Exploration archéologique de la Galatie et de la Bithynie I 1872
IGDial = Inscriptiones graecae ad illustrandas dialectos selectae, ed. FSolmsen; 4th ed. EFräenkel 1930
IGerasaWelles = "The Inscriptions", ed. CWelles, in Gerasa (City of the Decapolis), ed. CKraeling 1938, 355–494
IGLSyria = Inscriptions grecques et latines de la Syrie, ed. LJalabert/RMoutarde et al., 1929ff
IGolanHeights = RGregg/DUrman, Jews, Pagans, and Christians in the Golan Heights: Greek and Other Inscriptions 1996
IGR = Inscriptiones Graecae ad res Romanas pertinentes, ed. RCagnat et al. I 1911; III 1906; IV 1927
IGUR = Inscriptiones Graecae Urbis Romae, ed. LMoretti 1968ff

IHierap, s. IHierapJ
IHierapJ = "Inschriften," ed. WJudeich, in Altertümer von Hierapolis: Jahrbuch des kaiserlich deutschen archäologischen Instituts 4, 1898, 67–180 nos. 1–363
IK = Inschriften griechischer Städte aus Kleinasien (freq. followed by name of archeological site, e.g. Nikaia) 1972ff
IKosPH = The Inscriptions of Cos, ed. WPaton/EHicks 1891
IKourion = The Inscriptions of Kourion, ed. TMitford 1971
IKret = Inscriptiones Creticae, ed. MGuarducci, 4 vols. 1935–50
IKyme = Die Inschriften von Kyme (=IKV), ed. HEngelmann 1976
IKymeIsis, s. IAndrosIsis, Kyme
ILegesSacr = Leges Graecorum sacrae e titulis collectae, ed. JvonPrott/LZiehen, 2 vols. 1896–1906
ILegGort = Leges Gortyniae, in Buck, Dialects 314–22 no. 117; IGDial (q.v.) 40; RWillets, The Law Code of Gortyn (Kadmos Suppl. I) 1967
ILS = Inscriptiones Latinae Selectae, ed. HDessau, 3 vols. 1892–1916
ILydiaKP = JKeil/AvPremerstein, Berichte über eine Reise in Lydien 1908–14
IMagnMai = Die Inschriften von Magnesia am Mäander, ed. OKern 1900
IMagnSip = Die Inschriften von Magnesia am Sipylos (=IK VIII), ed. TIhnken 1978
IMakedD = Ἡ Μακεδονία κ.τ.λ., ed. MDimitsas, 2 vols. 1896
IMaronIsis = Une nouvelle arétalogie d'Isis à Maronée, ed. YGrandjean 1975
InsCos, s. IKosPH
Inscr. Gr. Sic. et It. = IG XIV, ed. GKaibel 1890
InsGal, s. IGal
Ins. gr., s. Michel
InsOenoand = Inscriptio Oenoandensis, s. IOenoandaDiog
Ins. of Sinuri = LRobert, Le sanctuaire de Sinuri près de Mylasa: Pt. I, Les inscriptions grecques 1945
InsSyr, s. ISyriaW
IOenoandaDiog = Diogenes Oenoandensis, Fragmenta, ed. CChilton 1967; s. also Diogenes of Oenoanda: The Epicurean Inscription, ed. MFSmith 1993
IPaidesEpit = Παῖδες ἄωροι, Poésie funéraire, ed. A-MVérilhac, 2 vols. 1978–82
IPE, s. IPontEux
IPergamon = Die Inschriften von Pergamon, ed. MFränkel 1890; 1895
IPontEux = Inscriptiones antiquae orae septentrionalis Ponti Euxini Graecae et Latinae, ed. BLatyschev: I (1885), 2d ed. 1916; II 1890; IV 1901 (III not published)
IPriene = Die Inschriften von Priene, ed. HvonGaertringen 1906
IReisenKN = Kommagenischen Denkmäler, in KHumann/OPuchstein, Reisen in Kleinasien und Nordsyrien 1890, 209–412
ISardGauthier = Nouvelles inscriptions de Sardes II, ed. PGauthier, 1989
ISardRobert = Nouvelles inscriptions de Sardes I, ed. LRobert, 1964
Isishymnus von Andros, s. IAndrosIsis
ISmyrnaMcCabe = Smyrna Inscriptions, Texts and List (Princeton Epigraphic Project), ed. DMcCabe/TBrennan/RElliott, 1988
ISyriaW = Inscriptions grecques et latines de la Syrie (nos. 1826–2724, continuation of LBW), ed. WWaddington 1870
IXanthos = Fouilles de Xanthos VII, 1981
Kaibel = Epigrammata Graeca ex Lapidibus Conlecta, ed. GKaibel 1878
Keil-Premerstein = JK./AvP., s. ILydiaKP
Larfeld = WL., Handbuch der griechischen Epigraphik, I 1907; II 1902
Laum = BL., ed., Stiftungen in der griechischen und römischen Antike: Ein Beitrag zur antiken Kulturgeschichte 2 vols. 1914
LBW = PLeBas/WWaddington, edd., Inscriptions grecques et latines recueilies en Asie Mineure (nos. 1–1825) 1870
Lind. Tempelchr. = Die Lindische Tempelchronik, s. ChronLind
LJ = Logia Jesus, s. Ox 1, List 1
MAI = Mitteilungen des Deutschen Archäologischen Instituts, Athenische Abteilung 1876ff
MAMA = Monumenta Asiae Minoris Antiqua, var. edd. 1928ff
Marm(or) Par(ium) = Marmor Parium, ed. FJacoby 1904; also no. 239 Jac (an inscribed marble stele set up at Paros, a.k.a. Parian Chronicle)
Meisterhans-Schw(yzer) = KM., Grammatik der attischen Inschriften; 3d ed. ES. 1900
Michel = CM., Recueil d'inscriptions grecques 1900; Supplément 1912
Muratori = Novus thesaurus veterum inscriptionum in praecipuis earundem collectionibus hactenus praetermissarum, collectore Ludovico Antonio Muratorio 4 vols. 1739–42
Nachmanson = EN., Laute und Formen der Magnetischen Inschriften 1903
Neugebauer-Hösen = ON./HvanH., Greek Horoscopes 1959
New Docs = New Documents Illustrating Early Christianity, ed. GHorsley, vols. 1–5 1980/81–89; SLlewelyn, vols. 6–8 1992–98
NouvChoix = Nouveau choix d'inscriptions grecques 1971
OGI = Orientis Graeci Inscriptiones Selectae, ed. WDittenberger 2 vols. 1903–1905
Pfuhl-Möbius = EP./HM., edd., Die ostgriechischen Grabreliefs, 2 vols, 1977–79
Pleket, s. TextMin 31 and 41
Prott-Ziehen, s. ILegesSacr
Ramsay = WR.
—, **Bearing** = The Bearing of Recent Discovery on the Trustworthiness of the NT 1915
—, **CB** = The Cities and Bishoprics of Phrygia I/1–2 (vol. II not produced) 1895–97
—, **Church** = The Church in the Roman Empire before AD 170^5 1897
—, **Cities of St. Paul** = The Cities of St. Paul: Their Influence on His Life and Thought 1907
—, **Hist. Geogr.** = The Historical Geography of Asia Minor 1890
—, **Letters** = The Letters to the Seven Churches of Asia and Their Place in the Plan of the Apocalypse 1904
Res Gestae Augusti = Res Gestae divi Augusti, ed. JGagé 1935
RevÉpigr = Revue Épigraphique, ed. AReinach 2 vols. 1913–14

Rouffiac = JR., Recherches sur les caractères du Grec dans le NT d'après les inscriptions de Priène 1911
Sb = Sammelbuch griechischer Urkunden aus Aegypten, begun by FPreisigke 1915
Schlageter = JS., Wortschatz der ausserhalb Attikas gefundenen attischen Inschriften, diss. Freiburg im Breisgau 1911
Schweizer = ESch., Grammatik der pergamenischen Inschriften 1898
SEG = Supplementum Epigraphicum Graecum, begun by JHondius 1923
Sherk = RS., Roman Documents from the Greek East 1969
SIG = Sylloge Inscriptionum Graecarum^3, ed. WDittenberger 4 vols. 1915–24 (superscript omitted in text)
SIG^2 = Sylloge Inscriptionum Graecarum^2, ed. WDittenberger, 3 vols 1898–1901 (used when an item from this ed. was not taken over into the 3d ed.)
TAM = Tituli Asiae Minoris, var. edd. 1920ff
TextMin 31 = Textus Minores 31: Epigraphica I, Texts on the Economic History of the Greek World, ed. HPleket 1964
TextMin 41 = Textus Minores 41: Epigraphica II, Texts on the Social History of the Greek World, ed. HPleket 1969
TextMin 47 = Textus Minores 47: Epigraphica III, Texts on Bankers, Banking and Credit in the Greek World, ed. RBogaert 1976
Thieme = GT., Die Inschriften von Magnesia am Mäander und das NT, diss. Heildelberg 1905
Threatte = LT., The Grammar of Attic Inscriptions, I: Phonology 1980; II: Morphology 1996
Tituli Lyciae =TAM II
T. Kellis 22 = RJenkins, The Prayer of the Emanations in Greek from Kellis: Le Muséon 108/3–4, 243–63, 1995
Tod, GkHIns = MTod, A Selection of Greek Historical Inscriptions (VI BC–323 BC): I, 2d ed. 1946; II 1948 (reprint with tables of concordance 1985)
Wadd. = WWaddington, s. ISyriaW
Welles = CW., Royal Correspondence in the Hellenistic Period 1943
Witkowski = SW., Epistulae privatae Graecae quae in papyris aetatis Lagidarum servantur^2 1911
Wuthnow = HW., Die semitischen Menschennamen in griechischen Inschriften und Papyri des vorderen Orients 1930
Ziemann = FZ., De epistularum Graecarum formulis solemnibus quaestiones selectae, diss. Halle 1911
ZPE = Zeitschrift für Papyrologie und Epigraphik 1967ff

4. Papyri/Parchments and Ostraca

AcPl Ant = Acts of Paul, PAntinoopolis 13 in The Antinoopolis Papyri I, ed. CRoberts 1950, 26–28
AcPl BMM, s. List 1
AcPl Ha = Acts of Paul, PHamb, s. List 1
AcPl M1 = Acts of Paul, PMich 1317 and PBerlin 13893, s. List 1
AcPl M2 = Acts of Paul, PMich 3788, s. List 1
AcPl Ox 6 = Acts of Paul, POxy 6, s. List 1
AcPl Ox 1602 = Acts of Paul, POxy 1602, s. List 1
AcPt Ox 849 = Acts of Peter, POxy 849, s. List 1
ApcPt Rainer = Rainer Fgm. of the Apocalypse of Peter, s. List 1
APF = Archiv für Papyrusforschung und verwandte Gebiete 1901ff
Arch. Abinn., s. PAbinn
AscIs = Ascension of Isaiah, s. List 2
ASP = American Studies in Papyrology 1966ff
BASP = Bulletin of the American Society of Papyrologists 1963ff
BGU = Aegyptische Urkunden aus den Königlichen (later, Staatlichen) Museen zu Berlin, Griechische Urkunden 1895ff
BKT = Berl(iner) Klassikertexte 7 vols. 1904–39
Bodm(er) = Bodmer Papyri (first publication in the series: Homère, Iliad chants 5 et 6 [grec] 1954)
CGFPR = Comicorum Graecorum fragmenta in papyris reperta, ed. CAustin 1973
CPJ = Corpus Papyrorum Judaicarum, ed. VTcherikover et al., I–III 1957–64
CPR = Corpus Papyrorum Raineri, esp. I–III, 1895ff. Not to be confused with MPER (q.v.). Freq. cited are: I, Griechische Texte I, Rechtsurkunden, ed. CWessely 1895 nos. 1–247 (cited by Bauer as PRainer); V, Griechische Texte II, ed. JRea/PSipjesteijn 1976, nos. 1–25 + PVindob G 38947 (=no. 26)
Crönert = WC., Memoriae Graecae Herculanensis 1903
Crum = WC., Coptic Ostraca from the Collections of the Egypt Exploration Fund, the Cairo Museum and Others 1902
DocsAugTib, s. Ehrenberg-Jones
Dssm., LO, s. List 6
Eg^2, s. PEg^2, List 1
Ehrenberg-Jones = VE./AHMJ., Documents Illustrating the Reigns of Augustus and Tiberius^2 1955 (repr. with addenda 1976)
Enteux., s. PEnteux
Fitzmyer, Oxy, s. Ox 1 in List 1
Gignac = FGignac, A Grammar of the Greek Papyri of the Roman and Byzantine Periods, I: Phonology 1976; II: Morphology 1981
GMary 463 = The Gospel of Mary (Magdalene), Roberts catalogue no. 463, s. List 1
GMary Ox 3525 = Gospel of Mary, POxy 3525
Gnomon (BGU V) = Der Gnomon des Idios Logos: BGU V/1, Text, ed. WSchubart 1919; V/2, Kommentar, WGyllenband 1934
GPt = Gospel of Peter, s. List 1
Grae(cus) Venet(us), s. Atumano, List 5
Hell. Oxy = VBartoletti, Hellenica Oxyrhynchia 1959
Hunt-Edgar = AH./CE., Select Papyri, 2 vols. 1923–36
JJP = Journal of Juristic Papyrology 1946ff
Jur. Pap. = P(aul)Meyer, Juristische Papyri 1920
Kuhring = WK., De praepositionum Graecarum in chartis Aegyptiis usu quaestiones selectae, diss. Bonn 1906
Ltzm. Pap. = HLietzmann, Griechische Papyri, Kleine Texte 14, 2d ed. 1910

Maspero, s. PCairMasp
Mayser = EM., Grammatik der griechischen Papyri aus der Ptolemäerzeit, 2 vols. The first vol. is indicated without reference to the volume number.
Mitt-Wilck. = LMitteis/UWilcken, Grundzüge und Chrestomathie der Papyruskunde 1912. I Historischer Teil: 1 Grundzüge, 2 Chrestomathie, ed. UWilcken; II Juristischer Teil: 1 Grundzüge, 2 Chrestomathie, ed. LMitteis; cited by no. and line, unless otherwise specified
M-M = JMoulton/GMilligan, The Vocabulary of the Greek Testament Illustrated from the Papyri and Other Non-literary Sources 1914–30 (one-vol. ed. 1930)
Moses, 8th Book of = ADieterich, Abraxas 1891, 167–205 = PGM (q.v.) 13
MPER = Mittheilungen aus der Sammlung der Papyrus Erzherzog Rainer, ed. JKarabacek, I–VI 1887–97
MPER N.S. = Mitteilungen aus der Papyrussammlung der Österreichischen Nationalbibliothek in Wien (Papyrus Erzherzog Rainer), n.s. 1932ff
Neugebauer-Hösen = ON./HvanH., Greek Horoscopes 1959
New Docs = New Documents Illustrating Early Christianity, ed. GHorsley, vols. 1–5, 1980/81–89; ed. SLlewelyn, vols. 6–8, 1992–98
O. Amst = Ostraca in Amsterdam Collection, ed. RBagnall/PSijpesteijn/KWorp 1976
O. Bodl = Greek Ostraca in the Bodleian Library at Oxford and Various Other Collections, ed. JTait/CPréaux et al., 3 vols. 1930–64
O. Fay = Ostraca Fayum 1900, numbered separately 1–50 in PFay
O. Joach = Die Prinz-Joachim Ostraka, ed. FPreisigke/WSpiegelberg 1914
Olsson = BO., Papyrusbriefe aus der frühen Römerzeit 1925
Ostr. = Ostraca
O. Theb = Theban Ostraca, ed. AGardiner/HThompson/JMilne 1913
O. Wilck = Griechische Ostraka aus Aegypten u. Nubien, ed. UWilcken, 2 vols. 1899 (I contains commentary, II texts; reprint with addenda by PSijpesteijn 1970); for the papyri in this corpus s. PFay
Ox = POxy (Papyrus Oxyrhynchus), but refers to fragments of documents esp. relating to the lexical data base; s. List 1
P^{66} = Papyrus Bodmer II, s. List 1
P^{72} = Papyrus Bodmer VII–IX, s. List 1
P^{74} = Papyrus Bodmer XVII, s. List 1
P^{75} = Papyrus Bodmer XIV, XV, s. List 1
PAberd = Catalogue of Greek and Latin Papyri and Ostraca in the Possession of the University of Aberdeen, ed. EGTurner 1939
PAbinn = The Abinnaeus Archive: Papers of a Roman Officer in the Reign of Constantius II, ed. HBell et al. 1962
PAchm = Les Papyrus grecs d'Achmîm à la Bibliothèque Nationale de Paris, ed. PCollart 1930
PAdl = The Adler Papyri, Greek texts 1939
PAmh = The Amherst Papyri, ed. BGrenfell/AHunt, I–II 1901f
PAmulett = Ein christliches Amulett auf Papyrus, ed. SEitrem/AFridrichsen 1921
PAnt = The Antinoopolis Papyri, ed. CRoberts et al., I–III 1950–67
PapHeid I = Die Septuaginta-Papyri und andere alttestamentliche Texte der Heidelberger Papyrussammlung, ed. ADeissmann 1905
Papyrus de Magdôla, ed. JLesquier 1912 = PLille II and a reediting by OGuéraud in PEnteux, nos. 1–42
PAthen = Papyri Societatis Archaeologicae Atheniensis, ed. GPetropoulos 1939
PBabatha, s. PYadin
PBad = Veröffentlichungen aus der badischen Papyrussammlungen, var. editors, I–VI 1923–38
PBas = Papyrusurkunden der öffentlichen Bibliothek der Universität zu Basel, Pt. I ed. ERabel 1917
PBeatty = Chester Beatty Biblical Papyri, ed. FKenyon, I–VIII 1933–41; for no. 185 s. ApcrEzk (List 2)
PBerlin 5025 = PGM no. 1
PBerlin 5026 = PGM no. 2
PBerlin 11710, in ZNW 22, 1923, 153f
PBerlSchubart = WS., Griechische literarische Papyri: SBLeipzAk 97/5, '50
PBerlZill = Vierzehn Berliner griechische Papyri, ed. HZilliacus 1941
PBilabel = FBilabel, ed., Die kleineren Historikerfragmente auf Papyrus 1922
PBodm = Papyrus Bodmer, s. also P^{66}; P^{72}; P^{74}; P^{75}, List 1
PBon = Papyri Bononienses, ed. OMontovecchi 1953
PBour = Les Papyrus Bouriant, a parchment named after Urbain B., ed. PCollart 1926
PBrem = Die Bremer Papyri, ed. UWilcken 1936
PCairCat = Greek Papyri, Catalogue général des antiquités égyptiennes du Musée du Caire, nos. 10001–10869, ed. BGrenfell/AHunt 1903
PCairGoodsp = Greek Papyri from the Cairo Museum (Decennial Publications of the University of Chicago, ser. 1/V) 1902, ed. EGoodspeed 1902
PCairIsid = The Archive of Aurelius Isidorus in the Egyptian Museum, Cairo, and the U. of Michigan, ed. ABoack/HYoutie 1960
PCairMasp = Papyrus grecs d'époque byzantine, ed. JMaspero, I–III 1911–16
PCairPreis = Griechische Urkunden des Ägyptischen Museums zu Cairo, ed. FPreisigke 1911
PCairZen = Zenon Papyri, Catalogue général des antiquités égyptiennes du Musée du Caire, ed. CEdgar, I–V (nos. 59001–59853; the first two digits are omitted in citation) 1925–40
PCatt = Papyrus Cattaoui [=BGU 114], in APF 3, 1906, 55–67, ed. BGrenfell/AHunt
PChBeatty = Chester Beatty Biblical Papyri, ed. FKenyon, I–VIII 1933–41
PChic = Chicago Literary Papyri, ed. EGoodspeed 1908
PCol 123 = WWestermann/ASchiller, Apokrimata: Decisions of Septimius Severus on Legal Matters 1954, later treated as Columbia Papyri VI, no. 123
PCollYoutie = Collectanea Papyrologica: Texts Published in Honor of HCYoutie, ed. AHanson 1976
PColZen = Columbia Papyri: Zenon Papyri, Business Papers of the Third Century B.C. Dealing with Palestine and Egypt III, nos. 2–59, ed. WWestermann/EHasenoerhl 1934; IV (PColZen II, nos. 60–122), ed. WW./HLiebesny 1940
PCorn = Greek Papyri in the Library of Cornell University, ed. WWestermann/CKraemer, Jr. 1926

PDidot, cited in FSandbach, Menandri Reliquiae Selectae 1990, 328–30; s. Menand. in List 5

PEdfou = papyri relating to Tell Edfou published in Fouilles Franco-Polonaises I–III, var. editors 1937–39

PEdg(ar) = Selected Papyri from the Archives of Zenon, nos. 1–111, in Annales du Service des Antiquités de l'Égypte, ed. CEdgar 1918–24

PEg^2, s. List 1

PEleph = Elephantine-Papyri, ed. ORubensohn 1907

PEnteux = ΕΝΤΕΥΞΕΙΣ: Requêtes et plaintes addressées au Roi d'Égypte au IIIe siècle avant J.C., ed. OGuéraud 1931, nos. 1–113 and appendix of 4 texts; nos. 1–42=PLille II (PMagd)

PErl = Die Papyri der Universitätsbibliothek Erlangen, ed. WSchubart 1942

PFamTeb = A Family Archive from Tebtunis, ed. BvanGroningen 1950

PFay = Fayûm Towns and Their Papyri, ed. BGrenfell/AHunt/DHogarth 1900; ostraca are numbered separately, 1–50

PFlor = Papiri Fiorentini I–III, var. editors 1906–15

PFouad = Les Papyrus Fouad I, var. editors 1939

PFrankf = Griechische Papyri aus . . . Frankfurt, ed. HLewald 1920

PFreib = Mitteilungen aus der Freiburger Papyrussammlung I–IV, var. editors 1914–86

PFuad I Univ = Fuad I University Papyri, ed. DCrawford 1949

PGen = Les Papyrus de Genève I nos. 1–81, ed. JNicole 1896–1906; II nos. 82–117, ed. CWehrli 1986

PGenLat = Archives militaires du I[e] siècle; texte inédit du Papyrus latin de Genève no. 1, ed. JNicole/CMorel 1900

PGiss = Griechische Papyri im Museum des oberhessischen Geschichtsvereins zu Giessen, ed. OEger/EKornemann/ PMeyer 1910–12

PGissUniv = Mitteilungen aus der Papyrussammlung der Giessener Universitätsbibliothek I–VI, var. editors 1924–39

PGM = Papyri Graecae Magicae: Die griechischen Zauberpapyri, I 1928, II 1931, ed. KPreisendanz; 2d ed. AHenrichs 1973–74; III, with index, ed. KP. with EDiehl/SEitrem 1941; esp. significant are nos. 1 and 2 (=PBerlin 5025; 5026), 3 (PMimaut), 4 (Paris Magic Pap.), 5 (PLond 46), 7 (PLond 121), 12 (PLeid V), 13 (PLeid W), 36 (POslo 1). For details s. HBetz, ed., The Greek Magical Papyri in Translation Including the Demotic Spells 1986, p. xliv.

PGoodspCair, s. PCairGoodsp

PGot = Papyrus grecs de la Bibliothèque municipale de Gothembourg, ed. HFrisk 1929

PGrad = Griechische Papyri der Sammlung Gradenwitz, ed. GPlaumann 1914

PGrenf I = BGrenfell, An Alexandrian Erotic Fragment and Other Greek Papyri Chiefly Ptolemaic 1896

PGrenf II = BGrenfell/AHunt, New Classical Fragments and Other Greek and Latin Papyri 1897

PGron = Papyri Groninganae, ed. ARoos 1933

PGronAmst 1 and 2 = the two Amsterdam papyri in PGron, pp. 53–58

PGurob = Greek Papyri from Gurob, ed. JSmyly 1921

PHal = Dikaiomata, in a papyrus published by the Graeca Halensis 1913

PHamb = Griechische Papyrusurkunden der Hamburger Staats- und Universitätsbibliothek, ed. PMeyer I 1911–24

PHarr = The Rendell Harris Papyri of Woodbrooke College, Birmingham, ed. JPowell 1936

PHeid = PHeid III

PHeid III = Griechische Papyrusurkunden und Ostraka d. Heidelberger Papyrussammlung, ed. PSattler 1963

PHercul 182 = Papyrus from Herculaneum no. 182, ed. KWilke, Philodemi De Ara Liber 1914

PHerm = Papyri from Hermopolis and Other Documents of the Byzantine Period, ed. BRees 1964

PHermWess = Corpus Papyrorum Hermopolitanorum . . . ed. CWessely 1905

PHib = The Hibeh Papyri I, ed. BGrenfell/AHunt 1906; II, ed. ETurner/MLenger 1955

Phileas = Papyrus Bodmer XX, Apologie de Philéas, ed. VMartin 1964

PHolm = Papyrus Graecus Holmiensis, Recepte für Silber, Steine und Purpur, ed. OLagercrantz 1913

PIand = Papyri Iandanae I–VIII, CKalbfleisch et al. 1912–38

PJena = Jenäer Papyrus-Urkunden, ed. FZucker/FSchneider 1926; fragments of Irenaeus 5, 3, 2–5, 13, 1 (Harvey II pp. 326–55) in HLietzmann, NAWG, Ph. 1912, 292–320 = idem, Kleine Schriften I 1958, 370–409

PJews = PLondon VI, nos. 1912–1929, but first published separately, Jews and Christians in Egypt: The Jewish Troubles in Alexandria and the Athanasian Controversy, ed. HBell 1924; s. PLond 1912

PKöln = Köllner Papyri, var. editors 1976ff

PKöln VI, 245 = Ptocheia or Odysseus in Disguise at Troy (P. Köln VI 245), ed. MParca 1990 (ASP 31)

PKroll = Eine Ptolemäische Königsurkunde (Papyrus Kroll), ed. LKoenen 1957

PLaur = Dai Papiri della Biblioteca Medicea Laurenziana, I–IV, ed. RPintaudi 1976ff

PLeid = Papyri Graeci Musei Antiquarii Publici Lugduni-Batavi, I–II, ed. CLeemans 1843–85

PLille = Papyrus grecs (Institut Papyrologique de l'Université Lille) I, in 4 fascicles 1907, 1908, 1923, 1928; II, Papyrus de Magdôla (s. PEnteux), ed. JLesquier 1912

PLips = Griechische Urkunden der Papyrussammlung zu Leipzig, ed. LMitteis 1906

PLond = PLondon = Greek Papyri in the British Museum I–VII, var. editors 1893–1974. Especially notable is PJews (q.v.).

PLond 1912 = PLondon VI no. 1912, Letter of Claudius to the Alexandrians, in Jews and Christians in Egypt: The Jewish Trouble in Alexandria and the Athanasian Controversy, ed. HBell 1924, 1–37 (text pp. 23–26); CPJ II no. 153

PLond 1913–1917 = PLondon VI nos. 1913–1917 relating to the Meletian Schism (s. PJews)

PLund = Aus der Papyrussammlung der Universitätsbibliothek in Lund I–VI, var. edd. 1934–52

PMagd = Papyrus de Magdôla, ed. JLesquier 1912 = PLille II, reedited by OGuéraud in PEnteux (q.v.) nos. 1–42

PMert = A Descriptive Catalogue of the Greek Papyri in the Collection of Wilfred Merton I–III, var. editors, 1948–67

PMeyer = Papyrus edited by PM.: Griechische Texte aus Ägypten I–II 1916

PMich = Michigan Papyri, var. editors, 1931ff (vol. I is also known as PMichZen, q.v.)

PMich 1317 = Michigan Papyri inv. 1317
PMichZen = Zenon Papyri or PMich I (nos. 1–120), ed. CEdgar 1931
PMichael = Papyri Michaelidae, being a Catalogue of the Greek and Latin Papyri, Tablets and Ostraca in the Library of Mr. GAMichaïlidis of Cairo, ed. DCrawford 1955
PMilVogl = Papiri della Università degli Studie Milano, I ed. AVogliano 1937; II–IV 1961–67
PMimaut = PGM no. 3 = papyrus inventory (Louvre) no. 2391, named after JMimaut, an earlier owner
PMonac = Byzantinische Papyri in der Königlichen Hof- und Staatsbibliothek zu München, ed. AHeisenberg/LWenger 1914
POslo = Papyri Osloenses I–III, ed. SEitrem/LAmundsen 1925–36; s. PGM
POxf = Some Oxford Papyri, ed. EWegener 1942
POxy = (The) Oxyrhynchus Papyri, numbered consecutively, 1898ff
POxyHels = Fifty Oxyrhynchus Papyri, ed. HZilliacus et al. (Helsinki) 1979
PParis = Notices et textes des papyrus du Musée du Louvre et de la Bibliothèque Impériale, ed. ALetronne/WdePresle/EEgger, 1865
PPetr = The Flinders Petrie Papyri I–III, ed. JMahaffy/JSmyly 1891–1905
PPrinc = Papyri in the Princeton University Collections I–III, AJohnson/HBvanHoesen et al., 1931–42
PRainer, s. CPR
PRein I = Papyrus Reinach I: Papyrus grecs et démotiques recueilles en Égypte, ed. TReinach/WSpiegelberg/SdeRicci 1905
PRein II = Papyrus Reinach II: Les Papyrus Théodore Reinach, ed. PCollart 1940
Preis. = FPreisigke, Wörterbuch der griechischen Papyrusurkunden, mit Einschluss der griechischen Inschriften, Aufschriften, Ostraka, Mumienschilder usw aus Ägypten, ed. FPreisigke/EKiessling I–IV and supplements 1925ff
Preisigke = FP.
—, Fachwörter 1915
—, Namenbuch 1922
—, Sb. = Sammelbuch griechischer Urkunden aus Aegypten, begun by FP., 1915ff
—, Wörterbuch = Preis. (q.v.)
PRev = Revenue Laws of Ptolemy Philadelphus, ed. BGrenfell 1896; reedited JBingen, in SB Beiheft 1, 1952
ProcXVIIICongPap = Proceedings of the 18th International Congress of Papyrologists (Athens, 25–31 May, 1986), 2 vols., ed. BMandilaras 1988
ProcXXCongPap = Proceedings of the 20th International Congress of Papyrologists (Copenhagen, 23–29 August, 1992), collected by ABülow-Jacobsen 1994
PRossGeorg = Papyri russischer u. georgischer Sammlungen I–V, ed. GZereteli et al. 1925–35
PRyl = Catalogue of the Greek Papyri in the John Rylands Library Manchester I–IV, ed. AHunt et al. 1911–52
PSI = Papiri greci e latini: Pubblicazioni della Società Italiana per la Ricerca dei Papiri Greci e Latini in Egitto 1912ff
PStras = Griechische Papyrus der kaiserlichen Universitäts- und Landesbibliothek zu Strassburg, ed. FPreisigke et al. 1912ff
PTebt = The Tebtunis Papyri 1–IV, ed. BGrenfell/AHunt/GSmyly et al. 1902–76
PThéad = Papyrus de Théadelphie, ed. PJouguet 1911
PThmouis 1 = Le Papyrus Thmouis 1, colonnes 68–160, ed. SKambitsis 1985
PTor, s. PTurin
PTurin = Papyri graeci Regii Taurinensis Musei Aegyptii, ed. APeyron, in Reale Accademia di Torino, 2 parts 1827–29; republished in UPZ
PUps 8 = Der Fluch des Christen Sabinus, Papyrus Upsaliensis 8, ed. GBjörk 1938
PVat A = PVaticanus A = Witkowski no. 36
PVindobBosw = Einige Wiener Papyri, ed. EBoswinkel 1942
PWarr = The Warren Papyri, ed. MDavid/BvanGroningen/JvanOven 1941
PWisc = The Wisconsin Papyri I–II, ed. PSijpesteijn 1967, 1977
PWürzb = Mitteilungen aus der Würzburger Papyrussammlung, ed. UWilken 1934
PYadin = The Documents from the Bar Kokhba Period in the Cave of Letters, Greek Papyri, ed. NLewis 1989 (named after YYadin, leader of the expedition that found the letters); a.k.a. PBabatha
PYale = Yale Papyri in the Beinecke Rare Book and Manuscript Library I–II, var. edd. 1967, 1984
Rossberg = CR., De praepositionum Graecarum in chartis Aegyptiis Ptolemaeorum aetatis usu, diss. Jena 1909
Sb = Sammelbuch griechischer Urkunden aus Aegypten, begun by FPreisigke 1915
StudPal = Studien zur Paläographie und Papyrusurkunde, ed. CWessely 1901–24; some revisions
Taubenschlag = RT.
—, Law^2 = The Law of Greco-Roman Egypt in the Light of the Papyri^2 1955
—, OpMin = Opera Minora, 2 vols. 1959
UPZ = Urkunden der Ptolemäerzeit (Ältere Funde), ed. UWilcken, I 1927 (nos. 1–150); II 1935–57 (nos. 151–229)
VBP, s. PBad
White, LAL = JW., Light from Ancient Letters 1986
Witkowski = SW., Epistulae privatae Graecae quae in papyris aetatis Lagidarum servantur^2 1911
Wuthnow = HW., Die semitischen Menschennamen in griechischen Inschriften und Papyri des vorderen Orients 1930
Ziemann = FZ., De Epistularum Graecarum Formulis Solemnibus Quaestiones Selectae, diss. Halle 1911
ZPE = Zeitschrift für Papyrologie und Epigraphik 1967ff
ZPWess = Neue Griechische Zauberpapyri, ed. CWessely (Denkschrift Akad. Wien 42) 1893

5. Writers and Writings of Antiquity

Aa = Acta apostolorum apocrypha, ed. RLipsius/MBonnet I, II/1–2, III 1891–1903 (repr. 1959) cited by volume, page, and line. Acts of Andrew, John, Peter, Thomas, and Paul are said to have been published outside the Christian mainstream by a Leukios (Lucius?) Charinos.

AcAnd = (Fragmenta) ex Actis Andreae: Aa II/1 38–45 **uncertain**

AcAnd/Mat = Acta Andreae et Matthiae: Aa II/1 65–116 **uncertain**

Achilles Tat(ius), s. Erotici; ed. EVilborg 1955 **II AD**

Achmes, Oneirocriton, a Gr-Rom. text reworked from a Christian viewpoint, ed. FDrexl 1925, cited by page and line **c. 900 AD**

AcJ = Acta Ioannis: Aa II/1 151–216 **II/III AD**

AcJ (Prochorus) = Acta Ioannis (attributed to the legendary Prochorus), ed. TZahn 1880 **uncertain**

AcPh = Acta Philippi: Aa II/2 1–98 **II/III AD**

AcPlMart = Acta Pauli, Martyrium Pauli: Aa I 104–17 **II/III AD**

AcPtPl = Acta Petri et Pauli: Aa I 178–222 **II/III AD**

AcPlTh = Acta Pauli et Theclae: Aa I 235–71 **II/III AD**

Acta Alex. = HMusurillo, Acta Alexandrinorum: De mortibus Alexandriae nobilium fragmenta papyracea Graeca 1961 **II/III AD**

Acta Pilati = Ea (Tdf.) 210–32 **uncertain**

AcThom = Acta Thomae: Aa II/2 99–291 **II/III AD**

Ael. Aristid. = Aelius Aristides, orations 17–53, ed. BKeil 1898 (only vol. II published), 2d ed. 1958; the rest ed. WDindorf 1829; s. also FLenz/CBehr 1976– **II AD**

Ael. Dion. = Aelius Dionysius and Pausanias, Two Atticists, ed. HErbse, Untersuchungen zu den attizistischen Lexika 1950, pp. 95–151; 152–221 **II AD**

Aelian(us), ed. RHercher 1864–66; NA=De Natura Animalium; VH=Varia Historia, ed. MDilts 1974 **II AD**

Aeneas Tact(icus), ed. RSchöne 1911, cited by prose lines **IV BC**

Aeschin(es), ed. FBlass/USchindel 1978 **IV BC**

—, spurious letters, ed. EDrerup 1904 **II AD**

Aeschrion, s. AnthLG **IV BC**

Aeschyl(us), ed. DPage 1972; Fragments: HMette 1959 **V BC**

Aesop, cited editions of writings associated with Aesop (VI BC) include: Aesopica, ed. BPerry 1952 (Vitae Aesopi, Sententiae, Proverbia, Fabulae); Vitae Aes., ed. Eberhard 1872 (s. Vi. Aes. below); and other editions of the fables: CHalm (H.) 1854; AChambry (Ch.) 1925; AHausrath/HHunger (H-H.), Corpus Fabularum Aesopicarum I/1 1970, I/2 1959. Synt.=Syntipas, referring to a collection of fables (date uncertain) associated with a philosopher of that name in a Sinbad-type of story, prob. of Persian origin.

Aëtius, Treatment of Diseases of the Eye (Augenheilkunde), ed. JHirschberg 1899; AOlivieri 1935–50 **VI AD**

Agatharchides of Cnidus, ed. CMüller, GGM I 1855; no. 86 Jac. **II BC**

Agathias, ed. WDindorf, HGM II 1871; RKeydell, Agathiae Myrinaei historiarum libri quinque 1967 **VI AD**

Albinus Phil., Introductio in Platonem, ed. KHermann, Platonis dialogi secundum Thrasylii tetralogias dispositi, vol. 6, 1853 **II AD**

Alcaeus, s. AnthLG, ed. EDiehl[2] 1936–42; ELobel/DPage (L-P.) 1955 **VII–VI BC**

Alcidamas, ed. FBlass 1892 **IV BC**

Alciphr(on), ed. MSchepers 1905; ABenner/FFobes 1962 **c. 200 AD**

Alcmaeonis Epic., for fragments associated with this name s. Epici **VII BC**

Alcman, s. AnthLG **VII BC**

Alex(ander) Aphr(odisiensis), Scripta Minora = Supplementum Aristotelicum II/1 and 2 1887; 1892: (De) An(ima), Mant(issa), Quaest(iones), (De) Fat(o), (De) Mixt(ione) **c. 200 AD**

Alex(andri) Ep(istolae), in Die Quellen des griechischen Alexanderromans, ed. RMerkelbach, Zetemata 9, 1954, 195f **uncertain**

Alexis Com(icus), s. Com. **IV/III BC**

Ammonius, phil., of Alexandria, son of Hermaias and Aidesia: Vi. Aristot., ed. AWestermann 1845 (s. Biogr.); In Int.=Ammonius in Aristotelis de interpretatione commentariis, ed. A Busse 1897 **V AD**

Ammonius Gr(ammaticus), a.k.a. Ammonius Hist., of uncertain identity: De adfinium vocabulorum differentia, ed. ENickau 1966; also ed. LValckenaer (Valck.) 1822 **I/II? AD**

Amphis Com(icus), s. Com. **IV BC**

Anacr(eon), s. AnthLG **VI BC**

Anacreontea Carmina, poetry associated with the name of Anacreon, ed. CPreis(endanz) 1912; MWest 1984; DCampbell, Greek Lyric II 1988, 162–247 **post-Christian**

Ananius, s. AnthLG **VI BC**

AnaphoraPilatiA, Ea 435–42 **uncertain**

Anaxagoras, Vorsokr. no. 59 **V BC**

Anaxandrides Com(icus), s. Com. **IV BC**

Anaximander, Vorsokr. no. 12 **VII–VI BC**

Andoc(ides), ed. FBlass, CFuhr 1913; KMaidment 2d ed. 1953 **V–IV BC**

Anecd(ota) Gr(aecae), ed. IBekker 1814–16; the two vols. are paginated consecutively

Anna Comn(ena), Alexias (hist. work covering period 1069–1118), ed. AReiffenscheid 1884; BLeib 1937–45 **1148 AD**

An. Ox. = Anecdota Graeca e codd. manuscriptis Bibliothecarum Oxoniensium, ed. JCramer, 4 vols., 1835–37 **uncertain**

AnthLG = Anthologia Lyrica Graeca, ed. EDiehl[2] 1936–42; EDiehl/EBeutler[3] 1949–52; ELobel/DPage (L-P.), Poetarum Lesbiorum Fragmenta 1955; DPage, Poetae Melici Graeci 1962 (repr. w. corr. 1967; rev. ed. MDavies, Poetarum Melicorum Graecorum Fragmenta: PMGF I 1991, incl. conversion lists); MWest, Iambi et Elegi Graeci II 1972; DCampbell, Greek Lyric (Loeb Cl. Lib.) I 1982, II 1988, IV 1992, V 1993; JEdmonds, Greek Elegy and Iambus (Loeb) 2 vols. 1931, Lyra Graeca (Loeb) III 1927 (rev. 1940)

Anth. Pal. = Anthologia Palatina, ed. FDübner 1864–72; PWaltz et al. 1928ff

Anth. Plan. = Anthologia Planudea, included in Anth. Pal.

'Anti-Atticist' = ΑΝΤΙΑΤΤΙΚΙΣΤΗΣ, title of a grammatical work, in Anecd. Gr. I 75–116 **uncertain**

Antig. Car. = Antigonus of Carystus, ed. OKeller: Rerum Naturalium Scriptores Graeci Minores 187; PGR 1965 pp. 32–106 **III BC**

Antilegomena, Die Reste der ausserkanonischen Evangelien und urchristlichen Überliefungen, ed. EPreuschen 1905

Antipater of Tarsus, ed. J(H)vArnim, Stoic. III 1903 **II BC**

Antiphanes Com(icus), s. Com. IV BC

Antiphon (the Orator), Antiphon (the Sophist), prob. identical; ed. TThalheim 1914; HDiels/WKrantz (D-K.), no. 87; also LGernet, Antiphon 1923 V BC

Anton(inus) Lib(eralis), ed. EMartini 1896; MPapathomopoulos 1968 II? AD

ApcEl Apocalypse of Elijah, PSI I, 7 p. 16f; also ed. Denis 103f uncertain

ApcEsdr = Apocalypse of Esdras, ed. OWahl 1977; Tdf.=KTischendorf, Apocalypses Apocryphae 1866, repr. 1966; not to be confused with 4 Esdras uncertain

Apc4Esdr = Apocalypse of 4 Esdras, ed. OWahl 1977; Tdf.=KTischendorf, Apocalypses Apocryphae 1866 uncertain

ApcMos = Apocalypse of Moses (=Life of Adam and Eve ['revealed to Moses', according to the prologue]), ed. KTischendorf (Tdf.), Apocalypses Apocryphae 1866, pp. 1–23; cited by page and line uncertain

ApcPl = Apocalypse of Paul, ed. KTischendorf (Tdf.), Apocalypses Apocryphae 1866, pp. 34–69; cited by page and line uncertain

ApcPt = Apocalypse of Peter (Kl. T. [s. List 6] 3, 1908 [repr. EKlostermann, Apokrypha I 1933] 8–13); cited by ch. and no. uncertain

ApcrEzk = Apocryphon Ezekiel, ed. Denis 121–28

ApcSed = Apocalypse of Sedrach, ed. OWahl 1977; JRHarris, The Rest of the Words of Baruch 1889; MRJames (Ja.), Apocrypha Anecdota 1893; also KTischendorf (Tdf.), Apocalypses Apocryphae 1866, pp. 24–31 uncertain

ApcZeph = Apocalypse of Zephaniah (Apocalypsis Sophoniae), ed. Denis 129 uncertain

Apollod. Com. = Apollodorus (of Carystus) Com., s. Com. IV–III BC

Apollodorus of Athens, no. 244 Jac. II BC

Apollon(ius) Dysc(olus) = Grammatici Graeci II/1, 2, 3, ed. RSchneider/GUhlig 1878–1910 (repr. 1965); Synt.=Syntaxi, cited by IBekker's line, w. Uhlig's page number in brackets II AD

Apollon(ius) Paradox(ographus), ed. OKeller (s. Antig. Car.) II? BC

Apollon(ius) Rhod(ius) = Apollonius of Rhodes, ed. GMooney 1964 III BC

Apolog(ists) = EGoodspeed, Die ältesten Apologeten 1914, Index Apologeticum 1912

Apost(olic) Const(itutions), s. Const(itutiones) Apost(olorum)

Apostolius (Apostoles), Michael, paroemiogr., s. Paroem. Gr. II 233–744 XV AD

Appian = Appianus, ed. PViereck/ARoos I 1936; II 1905 (repr. corr. EGabba 1962) I/II AD

Apuleius = Ap(p)uleius of Madaura in Africa, Latin writer: Apologia, Metamorphoses (Golden Ass) II AD

Aq. = Aquila; for fragments of his version of the OT in Greek s. Orig., Hexapla; s. also JReider, An Index to Aquila (rev. NTurner) 1966 II AD

Ar. = Aristides, ed. EGoodspeed, Die Ältesten Apologeten 1914, 2–23; POxy 1778; HMilne, A New Fragment of the Apology of Aristides, JTS 25 (1924), 73–77 (cited as Milne by page and line) II AD

Arat(us), of Soli in Cilicia, ed. EMaass 1893 (repr. 1955) IV–III BC

Archestr(atus), parod., Paradorum epicorum Graecorum et Archistrati reliquiae, ed. PBrandt 1888 IV BC

Archilochus Lyr(icus), s. AnthLG VII BC

Archinus, ed. JBaiter/HSauppe, Oratores Attici, 2 vols. in 1 (1839–50), 166–67 after IV? BC

Aretaeus, ed. CHude: CMG II 1923; 2 ed. 1958 II AD

Aristaen(etus), s. Ep.; ed. OMazal 1971 V AD

Aristarch(us of) Sam(os), astronomer, ed. THeath 1913 IV–III BC

Aristippus, for letters attributed to him, s. Ep. uncertain

Aristobul(us Judaeus), ed. Denis pp. 217–28; also CHolladay, in Fragments from Hellenistic Jewish Authors III: Aristobulus 1985, by page and line II BC

Aristodem(us), hist. and gramm., no. 383 FGrH II BC

Ariston of Ceos, ed. FWehrli 1952 III BC

Aristonous, fragments in Coll. Alex. 162–65 III BC

Aristoph(anes), ed. VCoulon 1923–30 V–IV BC

Aristophon Com(icus), s. Com. IV BC

Aristot(le), ed. IBekker, Prussian Royal Academy, 2 ed. (OGignon et al.) 1960; for fragments: VRose, ed., Aristotelis qui ferebantur librorum fragmenta 1886 IV BC

- **De Mundo** (spurious), ed. WLorimer 1933 I AD
- **EN** = Ethica Nichomachea
- **GA** = De Generatione Animalium
- **HA** = Historia Animalia

Aristoxenus, mus., ed. FWehrli 1945 IV BC

Arrian(us) = Flavius Arrianus, ed. ARoos I 1907, II 1928 (repr. corr. GWirth 1967–68) I–II AD

Artapanus, no. 726 Jac. II BC

Artem(idorus), onir., ed. RHercher 1864; RPack 1963 II AD

Asclepiod(otus), Tact(ica), ed. COldfather/WOldfather, Aeneas Tacticus, Asclepiodotus, Onasander 1923 I BC

Astrampsychus, Magus, before IV BC; later works associated with his name: Oraculorum decades ciii, ed. RHercher 1863, probably Christian, but containing Gr-Rom. material uncertain

Ath. = Athenagoras, ed. EGoodspeed, Die ältesten Apologeten 1914; R.=De Resurrectione, ed. ESchwartz, TU 4, 21891; WSchoedel, Athenagoras: Legatio and De Resurrectione 1972 II AD

Athanasius of Alexandria, ed. HGOpitz 1934ff IV AD

Athen(aeus), ed. GKaibel I–III (1887–1890; repr. 1961) III AD

Atumano = Simon Atumano, a Gk. humanist and prelate of the Western rite. His 'Graecus Venetus' ms. in the St. Mark library at Venice contains his tr. of the OT into Gk. but has no text-critical value. GMercati, Se la versione dall' ebraico del Codice veneto greco VII sia di Simone Atumano 1916 XIV AD

Babrius, ed. BPerry (P.) 1965; OCrusius (C.) 1897; Tetrasticha Iambici, Crusius pp. 264–96; Babrius: Mythiambae Aesopi, ed. MLuzzatto/ALaPenna (L-P.) c. 200 AD

Bacchylides, ed. BSnell 1949; 8th ed. 1961 V BC

Basilica (τὰ βασίλικα 'the imperial laws', based on the Justinian legal corpus) = Basilicorum libri LX, Text 8 vols.; Scholia 9 vols., ed. HScheltema/NvanderWal/DHolwerda 1953–88 IX AD

Basilius = St. Basil: Lettres, ed. YCourtonne, 3 vols. 1957–66 IV AD

Batr(achomyomachia) ('Battle of the Frogs', attributed to the Carian Pigres), ed. ALudwich 1896; WAllen 1912, corr. 1946 prob. not before I AD

Berosus, no. 680 Jac. IV–III BC

Biogr. = Βιογραφοι. Vitarum scriptores Graeci minores, ed. AWestermann 1845 (cited by page)

Bion Bucol(icus), ed. UWilamowitz-Moellendorf[2] 1911; AGow, Bucolici Graeci 1952 II BC

Buc(oloci) Gr(aeci), ed. AGow 1952; 2d ed. 1958. Includes Bion, Moschus, Theocritus.
Caecil(ius) Calac(tinus), ed. EOfenloch 1907 **I BC–I AD**
CAG = Commentaria in Aristotelem Graeca 23 vols. +3 suppl. 1882–1909
CALG = Collection des anciens alchimistes grecs, ed. MBertholet/CRuelle 1888; in three sections: Introduction, Texte Grec, Traduction
Callim(achus), ed. RPfeiffer 1949–53 **III BC**
Callinus, s. Poet. Eleg.; AnthLG **VII BC**
Callisth(enes), no. 124 Jac. **IV BC**
Callixenus, Hist., no. 627 Jac. **III–II BC**
Carmina Pop. = DPage, Poetae Melici Graeci 1962 (corrected ed. 1967), fragments pp. 450–70; also AnthLG, Diehl²
Cass(ius) Dio, ed. UBoissevain 1895–1901 **II–III AD**
Cat(alogus) Cod(icum) Astr(ologorum Graecorum)/CCAG, 12 vols. 1898–1953
Cebes, ed. KPraechter 1893 **I AD**
Cecaumen(us), author of a Byzantine work on pursuit of a military career: Strategikon, ed. Wassiliewsky/VJernstedt 1896 **XI AD**
Celsus, in Origen/Origenes, Contra Celsum, ed. PKoetschau 1899; MBorret 1967–69 **II AD**
Cephalion, no. 93 Jac. **II AD**
Cercidas, s. AnthLG; Coll. Alex. 201–19; AKnox, Herodes, Cercidas etc. 1929, 190–217 **III BC**
CGFPR = CAustin, Comicorum Graecorum fragmenta in papyris reperta 1973
Chaeremon (Historicus), ed. HSchwyzer 1932; also PvanderHorst 1987 **I AD**
Charax of Pergamum, no. 103 Jac. **II? AD**
Chariton, ed. RHercher 1859; WBlake 1938; s. also GMolinié 1989 **I–II AD**
Charon of Naucratis, no. 612 Jac. (testimonium) **after IV? BC**
Chion, epistolographer (IV BC), s. Ep. for letters attributed to him; s. also IDüring, Chion of Heraclea 1951 **I AD**
Choerilus, s. Epici **V BC**
Choniates, Niketas, MPG CXXXIX 1101–1140 **d. 1217 AD**
Chron(icon) Pasch(ale), ed. LDindorf, 2 vols. 1832 **VII AD**
Chrysipp(us), phil., ed. J(H)vArnim, Stoicorum veterum fragmenta II 1903 **III BC**
Chrysost. = Joannes Chrysostomus **IV–V AD**
Cleanthes, s. Stoic. **IV–III BC**
Clearch(us), ed. FWehrli 1948; 2d ed. 1969 **IV–III BC**
Clem(ent of) Al(exandria), ed. OStählin 1905ff; OS./UTreu/ LFrüchtel 1960ff. Strom.=Stromata **II–III AD**
Cleom(edes Astronomus), ed. HZiegler 1891 **II AD**
Cleopatra = texts alleging conversations of a queen named Cleopatra with philosophers (alchemists), ed. RReitzenstein, Zur Geschichte der Alchemie und des Mystizismus, Nachrichten von der Königlichen Gesellschaft der Wissenschaften zu Göttingen, Philologisch-historische Klasse 1919, 1–37; Gk. text cited by page and line. The Gr.-Rom. material in it dates from III AD.
CMG = Corpus Medicorum Graecorum appearing since 1908; quoted by vol., page, line
Codex Iustin(ianus), ed. PKrüger (in Corpus Iuris Civilis, vol. 2) 1877 **534 AD**
Coll(ectanea) Alex(andrina), ed. JPowell 1925
Com. = Comicorum Atticorum fragmenta, ed. TKock, 3 vols. 1880–88; Fragmenta comicorum Graecorum, ed. AMeineke, 5 vols. in 7, 1839–57; CAustin, Comicorum Graecorum fragmenta in papyris reperta 1973; cp. JEdmonds 1957–61; RKassel/CAustin, Poetae comici Graeci 1983ff; WArnott, Alexis, the Fragments: A Commentary 1996
Com(icorum) Graec(orum) Frag(menta), ed. GKaibel 1899; cp. CAustin, CGFPR; also Meineke (s. prec. entry)
Commentaria in Aristot., s. CAG
Comp(aratio Menandri et Philistionis), ed. SJaekel, Menandri Sententiae 1964 **uncertain**
Constant(inus) Manasses, Byzantine poet and hist.: Chronike Synopsis; also H. = RHercher, Erotici Scriptores Graeci, 1858–59 **XII AD**
Const(itutiones) Apost(olorum), ed. FFunk 1905 **IV AD**
Corinna, s. AnthLG **V/III? BC**
Cornutus, Theologiae Graecae Compendium, ed. CLang 1881; ND=Natura Deorum **I AD**
Cos(mas) and Dam(ian), ed. LDeubner 1907; ERupprecht 1935 **IV AD**
Crates, for letters attributed to the poet-philosopher C. (IV–III) s. Ep.
Cratinus Com(icus), s. Com. **V BC**
Cratinus Jun. = Cratinus the Younger, s. Com. **IV BC**
Crinagoras, ed. MRubensohn 1888 **I BC–I AD**
Critias, Vorsokr. no. 88 **V BC**
CSHB = Corpus Scriptorum Historiae Byzantinae, begun by BNiebuhr, 50 vols. 1828–97
Ctesias, ed. CMüller 1844 (ed. after Herodotus by GDindorf); no. 688 Jac. **V–IV BC**
Cyprian, ed. AWilliams 1935 **III AD**
Cyr. Al. = Cyril of Alexandria, MPG LXVIII–LXXVII **IV–V AD**
Cyranides = Les Cyranides, in FdeMély, Les lapidaires de l'antiquité et du Moyen Age, II (1898): Les lapidaires Grecs, Texte, ed. CRuelle, pp. 3–124; a compilation on magical healing properties of stones, plants, and animals. attributed to Cyranus (Cyrus?), king of Persia, and Harpocration (Medicus); cp. DKaimakis, Die Kyraniden 1976 **perh. antedating I/II AD**
Cyr. Scyth. = Cyril of Scythopolis, ed. ESchwartz 1939 (=TU 49, 2) **VI AD**
Damascius, Vita Isidori, s. Biogr.; De Princ., ed CRuelle 1889 **V–VI AD**
Damianus of Larissa, ed. RSchöne 1897 **IV AD**
Delph(ic) Orac(le), ed. HParke/DWormell, 2 vols. 1956
Demades, no. 227 Jac.; ed. FBlass 1888; VdeFalco, 2d ed. 1955 **IV BC**
Demetr(ius Iudaeus), no. 722 Jac. **III BC**
Demetr(ius of) Phaler(on), ed. FWehrli 1949; also no. 228 Jac.—Form(ae) Ep(istolicae), s. Ps.-Demetrius **IV–III BC**
Demochares, no. 75 Jac. **IV–III BC**
Democr(itus), phil., Vorsokr. no. 68 **V/IV BC**
Demophilus, gnom., author or collector of alleged Pythagorean sayings, ed. JOrelli, Opuscula graecorum veterum sentensiosa et moralia 1819; HSchenkl, WienStud 8, 1886, 262–81; AElter, Gnomica homoeomata, in Program zur Feier des Geburtstages seiner Majestät des Kaisers und Königs 1904; cp. FPhGr I, 486–96 **II–III AD**
Demosth(enes), ed. SButcher/WRennie 1903–31 **IV BC**
Denis = AD., Fragmenta pseudepigraphorum quae supersunt Graeca (Pseudepigrapha Veteris Testamenti Graece 3) 1970
Dexippus of Athens, no. 100 Jac. **III AD**
Dicaearchus, ed. FWehrli 1944; 2 ed. 1967. The writings

wrongly attributed to him are found in MFuhr, Dicaearchi Messenii quae supersunt composita 1841 **IV BC**

Did. = Didymus Caecus, Kommentar zu Gen., ed. PNautin/LDoutreleau 1976–78; Komm. zu Hiob, ed. AHenrichs/UHagedorn/LKoenen 1968 **IV AD**

Didymus, gramm. = Claudius Didymus Junior (Chalcenterus or Bronze-guts) fragments, ed. MSchmidt 1854 **I BC–I AD**

Dig. Just. = Digest of Justinian, part of the Corpus Juris Civilis, Latin text ed. TMommsen/PKrueger (2 vols. 1870), w. Eng. tr. by AWatson, 4 vols. 1985 **VI AD**

Dinarchus, Orator, ed FBlass 1888 (repr. 1967); NConomis 1975 **IV–III BC**

Dio Cassius, s. Cassius Dio **II–III AD**

Dio Chrys(ostom), ed. GdeBudé 1916–19; J(H)vArnim 1893–96 (repr. 1962) **I–II AD**

Diocles, med., Die Fragmente der sikelischen Ärzte Akron, Philistion, Diokles von Karystos, ed. MWellmann 1901 **IV BC**

Diocles Com(icus), s. Com. **V BC**

Diod(orus) S(iculus), ed. [LDindorf,] FVogel, CFischer [1866ff] 1888ff; COldfather 1933ff **I BC**

Diogenes, of Sinope; for letters attributed to this philosopher s. Ep. **uncertain**

Diogenian(us) Epicureus, ed. AGercke, Jahrbuch für classische Philologie, Suppl. 14, 1885, 748–55; s. also JHammerstaedt, JAC 36, 1993, 24–32 **II? AD**

Diog. L. = Diogenes Laertius, ed. CCobet 1850; HLong 1964 **III AD**

Diog. Oen. = Diogenes Oenoandensis, fragments, ed. JWilliam 1907; CChilton 1967; s. also IOenoandaDiog in List 3 **II AD or earlier**

Dionys(ius) Areop(agita), pseudonymous wr., MPG III **V–VI AD**

Dionys(ius) Byz(antius), geog., Anaplus Bospori, ed. RGüngerich 1927, 2nd ed. 1958; cited by §§ **c. 200 AD**

Dionys(ius) Hal(icarnassensis), Opuscula, ed. HUsener/LRademacher 1899–1929; Antiquitates, ed. CJacoby 1885–1925; ECary 1937–50. De Thu. Jud.=On Thucydides, a critical essay on T. as historian **I BC**

Dionys(ius) Perieg(eta), ed. CMüller, GGM II 1861 **II AD**

Dionys(ius) Soph(ista), for letters attributed to him s. Ep. **VI AD**

Diosc(orides) or Dioscurides (I AD), med., ed. KSprengel 1830; De Materia Medica, ed. MWellmann, 3 vols. 1906–14; some pseudonymous after I AD

Diphilus Com(icus), s. Com. **IV–III BC**

Dositheus, Ars Grammatica (a bilingual work for Greeks interested in learning Latin), ed. JTolkiehn 1913 **IV(?) AD**

Doukas (Dukas), Byzantine historian **XV AD**

Doxogr(aphi) Gr(aeci), coll. HDiels 1879

Doxopatres, Joannes, Prolegomenon sylloge (Rhetores Graeci 14), ed. HRabe 1931; s. also Rhetores Graeci 2 and 6 **XI AD**

Ea = Evangelia apocrypha, ed. KvTischendorf 1876 (repr. 1966)

Emped(ocles), Vorsokr. no. 31 **V BC**

En = I Enoch, ed. MBlack, Pseudepigrapha Veteris Testamenti Graece III 1970; s. also for ch. 1–32; 89:42–49: LRadermacher 1901; for ch. 97:6–104:13; 106f: CBonner 1937 **II–I BC**

Ep. = Epistola/Epistula: letters associated esp. w. Aeschines, Alciphron, Apollonius of Tyana, Brutus, Crates, Demosthenes, Dionysius Sophista, Epicurus, Heraclitus, Julian, Philostratus, Phalaris, Plato, Procopius, Pythagoras, Socrates; unless otherwise specified, the letter is found in the Epistolographi Graeci, ed. RHercher 1873; some are reprinted in AMalherbe, The Cynic Epistles 1977

EpArist = Epistle of Aristeas, ed. PWendland 1900; MHadas 1951 **II BC**

Ephippus, hist., no. 126 Jac. **IV/III BC**

Ephorus Cumaeus, hist., no. 70 Jac. **IV BC**

Epicharm(us) Com(icus), Vorsokr. 23 and Com. Graec. Frag. (Kaibel) pp. 88–147ff; CAustin, Comicorum Graecorum fragmenta in papyris reperta, pp. 52–83, nos. 81–91 **V BC**

Epici = Epicorum Graecorum Fragmenta, ed. GKinkel 1877; Poetae Epici Graeci I, ed. ABernabé 1988

Epict(etus), ed. HSchenkl 1894; 2d ed. 1916. The name alone refers to Arrian's Dissertationes or Discourses **I–II AD**

Enchir(idion), ed. Schenkl, op. cit.

Gnomol(ogion), fr. Stobaeus bks. 3–4, ed. Schenkl, op. cit.

Epicurus, PvdMühll 1922; GArighetti[2] 1973; also ed. HUsener, Epicurea 1887 **IV–III BC**

Epicus, of an epic poet; also in ref. to poets cited in Epicorum Graecorum Fragmenta, s. Epici.

Epimenides, Vorsokr. no. 3 **VI BC**

Epiph(anius) (same as next entry, freq. cited as source of fragments), s. Denis index; also KHoll in GCS vol. 25 **IV–V AD**

Epiph(anius) Const(antiensis), bishop of Constantia (Salamis) in Cyprus, MPG XLI–XLIII **IV–V AD**

Epist(ula) Apost(olorum), in a Coptic version, ed. CSchmidt, TU no. 43, 1919 **II AD**

Eratosth(enes), ed. AOlivieri 1897 **III BC**

Erotian, ed. ENachmanson 1918 **I AD**

Erotici (Scriptores Graeci), ed. RHercher, Leipzig 1858–59

Eth(ica) Epic(urea), ed. WSchmid 1939 = Studia Herculanensia 1

Etym(ologicum) Gud(ianum), ed. EAloysius de Stefani I 1909; II 1920 **XII AD**

Etym(ologicum) Mag(num), ed. TGaisford 1848 (repr. 1962) **XII AD**

Euagrius Ponticus, s. Evagrius Ponticus

Eubul(us) Com(icus), ed. RHunter 1983 **IV BC**

Euhem(erus), no. 63 Jac. **IV–III BC**

Eunap(ius), Vi(tae) Soph(istarum), ed. JBoissonade 1822, cited by page; GGiangrande 1956 **IV–V AD**

Eupolem(us Judaeus) Hist(oricus), no. 723 Jac. **II BC**

Eupolis Com(icus), s. Com. **V BC**

Eur(ipides), ed. GMurray 1937–47; for fragments TGF (Nauck) or TrGF **V BC**

Eus. = Eusebius of Caesarea, ed. ESchwartz et al. 1902ff (DE=Demonstratio Evangelica; HE=Historia Ecclesiastica, PE=Praeparatio Evangelica) **IV AD**

Eus(ebius of) Alex(andria), or Ps.-Eus., MPG LXXXVI, 288–462 **VI? AD**

Eustath(ius), comm. on Hom. et al. **XII AD**

Eustath(ius) Macrembolites, or Eumathius, ed. RHercher, Erotici scriptores Graeci II 1859, 159–86 **XI/XII AD**

Eutecnius, on (Ps.-)Oppian's Cynegetica, ed. OTüselmann: GGAbh, n.s. IV/1, 1900 **uncertain**

Euthymius Zig(abenus), MPG CXXIX **XII AD**

Evagrius Ponticus, Sententiae, ed. IHausherr, Orientalia Christiana 5, 1939, 7–71 **IV AD**

Ezk. Trag. = Ezekiel the Tragedian; ed. BSnell, TrGF I 1971 (s. also JWieneke, diss. Münster 1931); cited by line; cp. Denis pp. 207–16 **II BC**

FGrH = FJacoby, Die Fragmente der griechischen Historiker 1923ff

FHG = Fragmenta Historicorum Graecorum, ed. KMüller, 5 vols. 1841–70

Form(ae) Ep(istolicae), ed. VWeichert 1910; s. Ps.-Demetrius

FPhGr = Fragmenta Philosophorum Graecorum, ed. FMullach, 3 vols. 1860–81; freq. ref. is made to Philosoph(ical) Max(ims) and Hierocles in vol. I

Galen, ed. CKühn 1821–33; KKoch, GHelmreich, et al. 1923 **II AD**

Inst(itutio) log(ica), ed. CKalbfleisch 1896

Protr(eptici quae supersunt), ed. GKaibel 1894; also Γαλήνου Προτρέπτικος ἐπ' ἰατρικήν, ed. w. German tr. by WJohn; also JMarquardt, Scripta Minora I 1884

GCS = Die griechischen christlichen Schriftsteller der ersten drei Jahrhunderte 1897ff

Geogr. Graec. Minor., s. GGM

Geopon(ica), ed. HBeckh 1895, a coll. of older material **X AD**

Georg(ius) Mon(achus) (surnamed Hamartolus), Georgii Monachi Chronikon, ed. CdeBoor, 2 vols. 1904 **IX AD**

Georg(ius) Syncell(ius) = Georg the Synkellos ('cell-mate' of the patriarch Tarasios), Ecloga Chronographica, ed. AMosshammer 1984 **VIII–IX AD**

GGM = Geographi Graeci Minores, ed. CMüller, 1855–61

G-H-Z, s. List 1, beg.

Glykas = Michael Glykas, Annales, ed. IBekker 1836 **XII AD**

GNicod(emus), s. Acta Pilati, Tdf.

GNT = The Greek NT (United Bible Societies), 1st ed. 1966; 2d ed. 1968; 3d ed. 1975 (corrected 1983); 4th ed. 1993

GNT-MT = The Greek NT According to the Majority Text, ed. ZHodges/AFarstad 1982

Goodsp., Apol. = EJGoodspeed, Die ältesten Apologeten 1914

Gorgias of Leontini, Vorsokr. no. 82 **V–IV BC**

Grae(cus) Venet(us), s. Atumano

Gramm. Gr. = Grammatici Graeci, 4 vols. in 6, ed. GUhlig/AHilgard/ALentz 1867–1910 (repr. 1965)

Gregor(ius) Cypr(ius) = Paroemiae, ed. EvonLeutsch/FSchneidewin, Corpus Paroemiographorum Graecorum I 1839 **XIII AD**

Gregor(ius) Naz(ianzenus), MPG CXXXV–CXXXVIII **IV AD**

GThGk = Gospel of Thomas in Greek (not papyrus), Ea (Tdf.) 140–63 **uncertain**

Hanno, Periplus, s. GGM; also AOikonomides (Oik.), Hanno the Carthaginian: Periplus 1977, 24–28; cited by line **V/IV BC**

Harpocration, ed. WDindorf 1853 II **II AD**

Hdt. = Herodotus of Halicarnassus, ed. CHude[3] 1927 (repr. 1941–47) **V BC**

Heath, Aristarchus = TH., Aristarchus of Samos 1913 **IV–III BC**

Hecataeus (Abderita), no. 264 Jac. **IV–III BC**

Hecataeus Mil(esius), no. 1 Jac. **VI–V BC**

Heliod(orus Eroticus), Aethiopica, ed. RRattenbury/TLumb/JMaillon 1935–43; 2d ed. 1960 **III? AD**

Heliod(orus) Phil(osophus), of Prusa, credited with a pseudepigraphical work: Heliodori in ethica Nicomachea paraphrasis, ed. GHeylbut 1889 **uncertain**

Hell(enica) Oxy(rhynchia), VBartoletti, 1959; also cited is the Oxf. ed. by BGrenfell/AHunt (G-H.) 1909

Henioch(us) Com(icus, s. Com. **IV BC**

Henoch, s. En(och)

Heph. Astr. = Hephaestion of Thebes, astrol., s. Cat. Cod. Astr., also DPingree, ed. of Apotelismatica 1973 **IV AD**

Heraclid(es Criticus/Creticus), perieg., s. GGM I 97ff; ed. FPfister, SBWienAk 227, 2 (1951) **III–II BC**

Heraclid(es) Lembus, (Excerpta) Pol(itiarum), FHG III 167ff; MDilts 1971; Aristot. Fgm., ed. VRose 1886, 370ff **II BC**

Heraclid(es) Miles(ius), gramm, Fragmenta, ed. LCohn 1884 **I/II AD**

Heraclid(es) Pont(icus), ed. FWehrli 1953 **IV BC**

Heraclit., Ep. = Heraclitus of Ephesus (VI–V BC), Epistulae, all of later origin; 'The Epistles of Heraclitus': The Cynic Epistles, ed. AMalherbe (SBLSBS 12) pp. 186–215, 1977; also available in Ep. (Hercher)

Heraclit. Sto. = Heraclitus Stoicus, author of Homeric allegories, Quaestiones Homericae, ed. Societas Philologa Bonnensis 1910; FBuffière 1962 **I BC–I AD**

Heraclitus, phil., Vorsokr. no. 22; s. also MMarcovich, Heraclitus: Greek Text w. a Short Commentary, ed. maior 1967 **VI–V BC**

Hermagoras (Minor), ed. DMatthes 1962, 59–65 **I/II AD**

Hermagoras (Rhetor), student of Theodorus of Gadara, ed. DMatthes 1962, 56ff **I BC–I AD**

Hermagoras Temnites, ed. DMatthes 1962, 1ff **II BC**

Hermippus Com(icus), s. Com. **V BC**

Hermogenes Rhet(or), ed. HRabe 1913. De Inv.=Περὶ εὑρέσεως. **II–III AD**

Herm. Wr. = Hermetic Writings, ed. WScott: Hermetica I–IV 1924–36 (vol. IV completed by ASFerguson); ADNock and A-JFestugière 1945–54 **imperial times**

Hero Alex. = Hero(n) of Alexandria, ed. WSchmidt et al.; vols. I–V 1899–1914 **I? BC/I AD**

Herodas (Herondas), writer of mimiambi or literary mimes in a form of iambic trimeter (scazon, choliambus), ed. OCrusius[5] 1914; ADKnox/WHeadlam 1966; ICunningham (C.) 1971, w. papyrus fragments of mimes nos. 1–15, pp. 36–61 **III BC**

Herodian = Herodianus Historicus, ed. KStavenhagen 1921 **III AD**

Herodian(us) Gramm(aticus), ed. ALentz 1867–70; Philet.=Philetaerus: ADain, Le 'Philétairos,' attribué à Hérodien 1954 **II AD**

Hes(iod), ed. FSolmsen, RMerkelbach/MWest[2] 1983; also ARzach (Rz), 1913. Op.=Opera (Works and Days) **uncertain, perh. before VI BC**

Hesych(ius Lexicographus), ed. MSchmidt 1858–68; KLatte I [A–Δ] 1953 and II [E–O] 1966, with a text that differs widely **V AD**

Hesych(ius) Miles(ius), no. 390 Jac. **VI AD**

Hexapla, s. Orig.

HGM = Historici Graecae Minores, ed. LDindorf, 2 vols. 1870–71

Hierocles, phil., Commentarius in aureum carmen, FPhGr I 1860 pp. 416–84, cited by paragr. and page; FKoehler 1974 **V AD**

Himerius, Declamationes et orationes, ed. AColonna 1951. The earlier method of citation (from the time of FDübner 1849), when it differs, is given in brackets. Ecl.=Eclogae; Or.=Orationes **IV AD**

Hippiatr. = Corpus Hippiatricorum Graecorum, ed. EOder and CHoppe I 1924; II 1927 **IX AD**

Hippocr(ates) = Corpus Hippocraticum, ed. ELittré 1839–61; also Hippocratis Opera, ed. HKuehlewein/JIlberg 2 vols. 1894, 1902 **V–IV BC**

Hippol(ytus), Ref(utatio omnium haeresium), ed. PWendland et al. 1897ff.; MMarcovich 1987 **II–III AD**
Hipponax, s. AnthLG: Diehl and West; EDegani, 2d ed. 1991 **VI BC**
Hist. Gr. Min, s. HGM
Hom(er), ed. DMonro/TAllen: Homeri Opera[5], 5 vols. 1958–61. Il.=Iliad; Od.=Odyssey; Epigr.=Epigrammata. Freq. Il. and Od. are cited without ref. to Hom. **VIII BC**
Hom(eric) Hymns, s. Hom. **fr. VII BC**
Horapollo, Hieroglyphica, ed. CLeemans 1835; FSbordone 1940 **IV/V? AD**
Hyperid(es), ed. CJensen 1917 **IV BC**
Iambl(ichus), phil., De Myst., ed. GParthey 1857. Protrepticus, ed. HPistelli 1888. Vi(ta) Pyth(agorica), ed. ANauck 1884; LDeubner 1937 **III–IV AD**
Iambl(ichus) Erot(icus), ed. RHercher 1858; EHabrich 1960 **II AD**
Il. = Iliad, s. Hom.
Ion of Chios, s. AnthLG (West); TrGF I 96–114; Aloisius Leurini 1992 **V BC**
Iren. = Irenaeus, Haereses, ed. ARousseau, LDoutreleau 1979–82, cited according to Massuet's divisions; WHarvey (Harv.), cited by vol., page, and line after Massuet's divisions 1857 (reprint 1965) **II AD**
Isaeus, ed. TThalheim 1903 **V–IV BC**
Isid(orus) Pelus(iota), presbyter and monk in a monastery near Pelousion on the Nile, noted for a large epistolary production (pseudonymous?) MPG LXXVIII **IV/V AD**
Isocr(ates), ed. GBenseler/FBlass 1878–79; GMathieu/EBrémond 1929–62 **IV BC**
Isyllus, fragments, Coll. Alex. 132–35 **III BC**
Jac(oby) = Die Fragmente der griech. historiker, ed. FJacoby 1923ff (cited by number of author and number and line of fragment, occasionally with Jac.'s vol. and page)
Joannes Sar(dianus), identity uncertain, Commentarium in Aphthonii Progymnasmata, ed. HRabe 1928 **VIII–IX (Rabe: X) AD**
Jo. Lydus, s. Lydus
Jo. Philopon. = Joannes Philoponus, CAG, vols. 13–17, 1897–1909 **VI AD**
Jos. = Josephus, ed. BNiese 1887–95 (repr. 1955); HThackeray/RMarcus/HFeldman 1926–65; some references made to edition of SNaber 1888–96. This abbr. used when book and sec. are cited., otherwise Joseph. **I AD**
JosAs = Joseph and Aseneth, ed. MPhilonenko 1968; PBat(iffol) 1889; MIstrin 1888 (cod. B and Vat. Pal. 364) **uncertain**
Joseph(us), s. Jos.
Jubilees = Book of J.: Denis 70–102
Julian (Imperator), Letters, ed. JBidez 1922, 2d ed. 1960. Or.=Oratio. Caes.=Caesares, ed. CLacombrade 1964 **IV AD**
Just(in), ed. EGoodspeed, Die ältesten Apologeten (A I= Apology, pp. 26–77; A II=Second Apology or Appendix, pp. 78–89; D.=Dialogue, Trypho, pp. 90–265) 1914 **II AD**
Justin., Nov. = (Flavius) Justinianus Imperator, Novellae, ed. RSchöll/WKroll, Corpus Iuris Civilis, vol. 3 (4th ed.) **VI AD**
Kephal(aia) = Manichäische Hss. der Staatlichen Museen, Berlin, ed. CSchmidt et al. 1935ff
Kleopatra, s. Cleopatra
Kock, s. Com.
Kyraniden, s. Cyranides
Laud(atio) Therap(ontis), in LDeubner, De Incubatione 1900, 120–34 **VII AD**
Leo. = Leonis imperatoris strategemata, an appendix to the edition of Polyaenus (q.v.), JMelber 1887, pp. 505–40 (a very close connection with Polyaenus is unmistakable) **V AD**
Leonidas Tarent(inus), ed. JGeffcken, 1896; DPage, Epigrammata Graeca 1975 **IV–III BC**
Leontius (of Naples), Life of St. John the Merciful, ed. HGelzer 1893 **VII AD**
Les Lapidaires, s. Cyranides
Lex. Cantabr. = Lexicon Rhetoricum Cantabrigiense, ed. ANauck/PDobree 1867; also EHoutsma 1870 in Lexica Graeca Minora, ed. KLatte/HErbse 1965, 61–139; text 69–86 **uncertain**
LexGrMin = Lexica Graeca Minora, ed. KLatte/HErbse 1965
Lex. Vind. = Lexicon Vindobenense, ed. ANauck 1867 **uncertain**
Libanius, ed. RFörster, 12 vols. 1903–23; RF./ERichtsteig 1963 **IV AD**
Lob. = CLobeck, s. Phryn.
Longus, ed. GDalmeyda, 2d ed. 1960; also OSchönberger 1960, 4th ed. 1989 **II AD**
L-P. = ELobel/DPage, s. AnthLG
Lucian, ed. CJacobitz 1836–41 (repr. 1966); MMacleod 1974–87 **II AD**
LXX, s. List 2, beg.
Lycon (of Troas), phil., ed. FWehrli 1952 **III BC**
Lycophron (Tragicus), ed. EScheer 1881; LMascialino 1964 **IV–III BC**
Lycurgus, ed. FBlass 1899; 2d ed. FDurrbach 1956 **IV BC**
Lydus = Joannes Laurentius L. **VI AD**
  Mag. = De Magistratibus Populi Romani, ed. RWünsch 1903 (1967)
  Men. = De Mensibus, ed. RWünsch 1898
Lysias, ed. CHude 1912; UAlbini 1955 **V–IV BC**
Lysippus Com., s. Com., Kock **V BC**
Lysis, for material attributed to him s. Vorsokr. no. 46 **IV–II BC**
Machon (Comicus), s. Com.; ed. AGow 1965 **III BC**
Macrembolites, Eustathius, writer of the romance De Hysmenes et Hysmineae amoribus libri XI, ed. IHilberg 1876 **XI/XII AD**
Malalas = John Malalas, Chronographia, ed. LDindorf 1831 **VI AD**
Manetho, hist., no. 609 Jac. (as cited in Jos., C. Ap.); ed. WWaddell 1948 **III BC**
Manetho, Apot. = Manetho (astrol.), Apotelesmatica, ed. AKöchly 1858 **IV? AD**
M(arcus) Ant(oninus) = Marcus Aurelius, ed. HSchenkl 1913; JDalfen 1979; also ed. FBoissonade 1814 **II AD**
Marcus Diaconus, ed. Societatis Philologiae Bonnensis sodales 1897; cp. Marc le Diacre, ed. HGregoire/MKugener 1930 **V AD**
Marinus, Vi. Procli = RMasullo, Marino di Neapoli, Vita di Proclo 1985 **V AD**
Mart. = Martyrium (of var. saints, Carpus, Papylus, Agathonica), HMusurillo, The Acts of the Christian Martyrs 1972 **II AD**
MartAndrPrius = Martyrium Andreae Prius (1 of 2 accounts), in Aa II/1 46–57 **uncertain**
MartMt = Martyrium Matthaei Aa II/1 217–62 **uncertain**
MartPl = Martyrium Pauli: Aa I 104–17 **uncertain**
MartPt = Martyrium Petri: Aa I 78–103 **uncertain**
MartPtPl = Martyrium Petri et Pauli: Aa I 118–77 **uncertain**

Μαρτύριον τῆς ἁγίας Αἰκατερίνας (martyrdom of St. Catherine)=Passions des Saints Écaterine et Pierre d'Alexandrie, Barbara et Anysia, ed. JViteau 1897, 4–65; cp. MPG CXVI, 275–302 **uncertain**

Max(imus) Conf(essor), Opusc(ula), MPG XCI **VI–VII AD**

Maximus Tyr(ius), soph., Philosophumena, ed. HHobein 1910 **II AD**

Meineke = AM., ed., Fragmenta comicorum Graecorum, 5 vols., 1839–57; s. also Com.

Mel. = Melito of Sardis. HE=Melito in Euseb., HE; P=Paschal Homily, ed. OPerler 1966; SHall 1979. Fgm. fr. ancient sources in Goodsp., Apologists pp. 303–13. Ch.=PBeatty VIII 1941; Bodm.=PBodmer XIII **II AD**

Mel. chor. = Melici choriambici; for lyric poets using choriambic meter; s. AnthLG

Memnon, perh. fr. Heraclea Pontica, no. 434 Jac. **I BC–I? AD**

Menand(er of Athens Comicus), ed. CJensen 1929; AKörte/AThierfelder (Kö.) 1957–59; also cited are Meineke (q.v.); Kock (s. Com.); FSandbach (S.), Menandri reliquiae selectae 1972 **IV–III BC**

- **Aspis,** PBodm XXVI ed. RKasser/CAustin 1969
- **Dist(icha),** s. Com.
- **Dys(colus)** = PBodm IV ed. Victor Martin, 1958; some corrections: PBodm XXVI ed. RKasser/CAustin 1969, 48–49
- **Epitr(epontes),** Sandbach 97–130
- **Mis(umenus),** Sandbach 181–95
- **Monost(icha),** ed. AMeineke, Com. Graec. IV 340ff; SJaekel 1964
- **Peric(omene),** Sandbach 199–221
- **Perinth(ia),** Sandbach 225–28
- **Samian** = The Samian: PBodm XXV ed. RKasser 1969

Menand(er of) Ephes(us), hist., no. 783 Jac. **before II BC**

Menand(er) Protector, hist., ed. LDindorf, HGM II **VI AD**

Menand(er) Rhet(or), ed. LSpengel, Rhetores Graeci vol. III pp. 329ff; also DRussell/NWilson 1981 **III/IV AD**

Mesomedes, Hymnen, ed. KHorna (SBWienAk 207/1) 1928; EHeitsch, GGAbh ser. 3., no. 49, 2d ed. 1963 **II AD**

Metrodorus Philos(ophus), ed. AKörte, Jahrb. klass. Phil. Suppl. XVII 1890 **IV–III BC**

Mich. Glykas, s. Glykas

Mich. Psellus, s. Psellus

Mimnermus, s. AnthLG; ed. MWest 1972 **VII/VI BC**

Minucius Felix, author of Octavius, ed. CHalm, in Corpus Scriptorum Ecclesiasticorum Latinorum II 1867, 1–71, cited by ch. **II–III AD**

Mishnah = HDanby, The Mishnah, tr. fr. the Hebrew 1933

Moeris, attic., ed. JPierson 1759; JP./GKoch 1830–31 (repr. 1969) **II AD**

Molpis, no. 590 Jac. **II–I BC**

Moschus, bucol., ed. AGow 1952 **II BC**

Moses (Alchem.), 8th Book of, ed. ADieterich, Abraxas 1891, 167–205; PGM 13 **uncertain**

MPG = JPMigne, Patrologia Graeca, 161 vols., 1857–66

MPL = JPMigne, Patrologia Latina, 221 vols., 1844–64

Mu(llach) = WM., s. FPhGr

Musaeus, phil., for wr. attributed to him s. Vorsokr. **uncertain**

Musaeus (Gramm.), Hero and Leander, ed. ALudwich = Kleine Texte 98, ed. HLietzmann 1929; HLivrea/PEleuteri 1982 **V/VI AD**

Musonius (Rufus), ed. OHense 1905 **I AD**

Musurillo, Ac. Chr. M. = HM., The Acts of the Christian Martyrs 1972, esp. Martyrium Carpi, Papyli et Agathonicae, pp. 22–28 **II AD**

Nauck = AN., s. TGF

Neophron (Tragicus), TrGF I 92–94, fgm. 1–3 **V BC**

Nepualius (or Neptunalius/Neptunianus), phil., ed. WGemoll 1884 **II? AD**

Nicander, ed. OSchneider 1856; AGow/AScholfield 1953; Scholia: OSchneider; ACrugnola 1971; MGeymonat 1974 **III/II BC**

Nicetas Eugen(ianus), s. Erotici II **XII AD**

Nicol(aus) Com(icus), s. Com. **IV? BC**

Nicol(aus) Dam(ascenus), no. 90 Jac. **I BC**

Nicomachus Gerasenus, math., ed. RHoche 1866 **II AD**

Nicostr(atus) Com(icus), s. Com. **IV BC**

Nonnus (Epicus), Dionys(iaca), ed. ALudwich 1909, 1911; RKeydell 1959 **IV/V AD**

Numenius (of Apamea), phil., ed. ELeemans 1937; ÉdesPlaces 1973 **II AD**

Nymphis, no. 432 Jac. **IV–III BC**

Ocellus Luc(anus), ed. RHarder 1926 (repr. 1966) **II? BC**

Od. = Odyssey, s. Hom.

Oenomaus (Cynicus), ed. PValette 1908, as cited by Eus., PE 5, 18, 6–5, 36, 4; 6, 7, 1–6, 7, 42 **II AD (reign of Hadrian)**

Olympiodor(us), ed. WNorvin 1913; LWesterink 1976 **VI AD**

Onosander, ed. WOldfather 1923 **I AD**

Oppian (of Apamea) = Oppianus of Apamea, Cynegetica, s. Ps.-Oppian **II–III AD**

Or(atores) Att(ici), ed. GBeiter/HSauppe 1850

Oribasius, ed. JRaeder, CMG VI, 1926–31 **IV AD**

Orig(enes) **II–III AD**

- **C(ontra) Cels(um),** ed. MBorret 1967–69
- **De Or(atione),** ed. PKoetschau 1899
- **Hexapla,** ed. FField 1875

Orph(ica), ed. EAbel 1885, includes Lithiaca; GDottin 1930; the Hymns, ed. WQuandt 1941, 3d ed. 1962. Fgm., K.=Fragmenta, ed. OKern 1922 (Arg.=Argonautica), cited by page and no. See also Ps-Orph.

Orph. Hymns, s. Orphica

Or. Sib. = Oracula Sibyllina, s. SibOr

Otero = AdeSantosOtero, Los Evangelios apocrifos, 2d ed. 1963

Palaeph(atus), ed. NFesta 1902 **uncertain**

Palladius, of Helenopolis, Hist(oria) Laus(iaca), ed. CButler, 2 vols., 1898–1904; based on a later textual tradition is MPG XXXIV, 997ff **IV–V AD**

Παραδοξόγραφοι, Scriptores rerum mirabilium Graeci, ed. AWestermann 1839

Paradoxogr. Flor. = Paradoxographi Florentini Anonymi Opusculum de Aquis Mirabilibus, ed. HÖhler (diss. Tübingen) 1913; AGiannini, PGR 1965 pp. 316–28 **II? AD**

Paradoxogr. Vat. = Paradoxographus Vaticanus; includes fragments attributed to Antig. Car.; ed. AGiannini, PGR 1965, 332–50 **II? AD**

Parmenides, Vorsokr. no. 28; ed. DGallop 1984 **VI–V BC**

Paroem(iographi) Gr(aeci), ed. EvLeutsch/FSchneidewin 1839–51

Parthenius, ed. EMartini 1902; s. AnthLG **I BC**

PassPtPl = Passio Petri et Pauli, s. MartPtPl **uncertain**

Pass. Scilit. = Passio Scilitanorum, ed. OvGebhardt 1902 **II AD**

Paul. Aeg. = Paulus Aegineta (Med.): CMG IX/1 and 2 **VII AD**

Paus(anias Periegeta), Graeciae descriptio, ed. HHitzig/HBluemner 1896–1907; MRocha-Perreira 1973–81 **II AD**

Paus. Attic. = Pausanias the Atticist, s. Ael. Dion. **II AD**

Pel(agia)-Leg(enden) = Legenden der heiligen Pelagia, ed. HUsener 1879 **V? AD**
Per. et Felic. = Perpetua et Felicitas, ed. IvanBeek 1936 **III AD**
Peripl(us Maris) Eryth(raei), ed. HFrisk 1927 **after II AD**
Periplus Maris Magni, s. Stadiasmus
Περὶ ὕψους (De Sublimitate, attributed to Longinus) ed. JVahlen 1910; also WRoberts, Longinus on the Sublime, 2d ed. 1907; APrickard (OxfT) 1906 **I AD**
Petosiris (and Nechepso), astrolog. writings are associated with their names. Collection of fragments by ERiess, Philol. Suppl. VI 1891/93, pp. 327–94 **before II BC**
PGR = Paradoxographorum Graecorum Reliquiae, ed. AGiannini 1965
Phalaris, for letters attributed to P., s. Ep. **II? AD**
Pherecr(ates Comicus), s. Com. **V BC**
Pherecyd. = Pherecydes of Syros, ed. HSchibli 1990; also Vorsokr. no 7 **VI BC**
Pherecydes of Athens, no. 3 Jac. **V BC**
Phileas = Apologie de Philéas (Papyrus Bodmer XX), ed. VMartin **ca. 307 AD**
Philemon Com(icus), s. Com. (a few of the verses associated with this name belong to Comp.; s. Pauly-W. 19, 2144–45) **IV–III BC**
Philistion, alleged composer of mimes, ed. AEberhard 1869; AThierfelder 1968 (probably all pseudonymous) **I AD**
Philistion Med. = P., physician from Locri, s. Diocles **V–IV BC**
Philo = P. of Alexandria, ed. LCohn/PWendland/SReiter 1896–1915. Vol. VII 1930 contains the indexes by JLeisegang. **I BC–I AD**
Philo Bybl. = P. of Byblos; fragments of his Τὰ φοίνικα are transcribed in Eus., PE; no. 790 Jac.; also HAttridge/ROden, Philo of Byblos: CBQ Monograph Ser. 9, 1981, 28–71 **c. 100 AD**
Philochorus, no. 328 Jac. **IV–III BC**
Philod(emus), on Hom., ed. AOlivieri 1909; Vit.=περὶ κακίων ι', ed. CJensen 1911; Ira=περὶ ὀργῆς, ed. KWilke 1914. Also cited: SSudhaus, Volumina Rhetorica, 2 vols. 1892, 1896, by vol. and page; σημ.=περὶ σημείων καὶ σημειώσεων, ed. TGomperz, Herkulanische Studien I 1965. Philod. Herc.=Herculanensium voluminum quae supersunt collectio altera 1862–76, cited acc. to the nos. of the papyri. **I BC**
Philod. Herc., s. Philod.
Philo Mech(anicus), ed. RSchöne 1893 **III–II BC**
Philopon. = Joannes Philoponus, commentator on Arist., De anima, ed. MHayduck 1897, De generatione animalium 1903 **VI AD**
Philosoph(ical) Max(ims), fr. var. sources, in FPhGr I 485–509 (by page and number)
Philostorg(ius), Historia Ecclesiastica, ed. JBidez, in GCS 21, 1913 **V AD**
Philostrat(us) = Flavius Philostratus, the Sophist, ed. KKayser, I 1870–71 **II–III AD**
Philostrat(us) Jun(ior) = Philostratus the Younger, Imagines, ed. KKayser, II 1871 **III AD**
Philumen(us), ed. MWellmann, CMG XI/1, 1908 **II AD**
Phlegon, no. 257 Jac. **II (time of Hadrian) AD**
Phoenicides Com(icus), s. Com. **III BC**
Phoenix (of) Colophon, Coll. Alex. pp. 231–36 **III BC**
Phot(ius), ed. SNaber 1864–65; CTheodoridis 1982ff; one of his chief works: Bibl(iotheca), ed. IBekker 1824–25 **IX AD**
Phryn(ichus), the Atticist, signifying his Eclogae, ed. CLobeck (Lob.) 1820; EFischer 1974. The abbr. Lob. precedes Phryn. when Lobeck's comments are cited. **II AD**
—, Praep. Soph., ed. JdeBorries 1911
Physiogn. = Scriptores Physiognomici, ed. RFörster 1893
Pind(ar), ed. CBowra (OxfT) 1935; OSchröder 1900, 3d ed. 1930; BSnell 1955, 2d ed. HMaehler 1984. Odes: O.=Olympian; P.=Pythian; N.=Nemean; I.=Isthmian **V BC**
Pirke (Pirque) Aboth, Mishnah (q.v.) 446–61
Pla(to), ed. JBurnet 1900–1907 and often; for spurious wr. s. Ps.-Plato **V–IV BC**
Pla(to) Com(icus), s. Com. **V–IV BC**
Pliny the Elder, ed. KMayhoff 1892–1909. NH=Naturalis Historia **I AD**
Pliny the Younger, Epistulae, ed. MSchuster/RHanslik, 3d ed. 1958 **I–II AD**
Plotinus, ed. PHenry/HSchwyzer 1964–82 **III AD**
Plut(arch), Mor(alia), ed. WPaton et al. 1925–78; Vi(tae) ed. CLindskog/KZiegler 1914–39, 2d ed. 1957–80 **I–II AD**
PMG = Poetae Melici Graeci, ed. DPage 1962; s. AnthLG
PMGF = Poetarum Melicorum Graecorum Fragmenta I, ed. MDavies 1991; s. AnthLG
Poeta de Herbis = an anonymous poet, author of Carmina de viribus herbarum, in Poetae Bucolici et Didactici, ed. FLehrs 1851 **uncertain**
Poetae Melici Graeci, s. AnthLG
Poet. Eleg. = Poetae Elegiaci, ed. BGentili/CPrato I 1979, 2d ed. 1988; II 1985
Poet. Philos. = Poetarum Philosophorum Fragmenta, ed. HDiels 1901
Polemo/Polemon Soph., ed. HHinck 1873; WReader/AChvala-Smith, The Severed Hand and the Upright Corpse: The Declamations of Marcus Antonius Polemo 1996. Decl.=Declamations. The two speeches are cited as nos. 1 and 2, and ed. is noted only in case of variant **I–II AD (time of Trajan)**
Pollux, ed. EBethe 1900–1937 **II AD**
Polyaen(us Rhetor), ed. JMelber 1887; unless exc(erpta) accompanies the ref., the main work, Strategemata, is meant **II AD**
Polyb(ius), ed. TBüttner-Wobst 1882–1904 **III–II BC**
Polycrates, no. 588 Jac. **I BC**
Polystrat(us Epicureus), ed. CWilke 1905 **III–II BC**
Porph(yry), ed. ANauck 1886; specific works include De Abstinentia, ed. Nauck; Ep. ad Anebonem, ed. ASodono 1958; Vi(ta) Plot(ini) ed. PHenry/HSchwyzer, Plotini Opera 1951 **III AD**
Posidippus Com(icus), s. Com. **III BC**
Posidippus, Epigrams, ed. PSchott, 1905; AGow/DPage 1965. This writer of epigrams may be identical with P. the historian, no. 447 Jac. **III BC**
Posidon(ius Apamensis), no. 87 Jac.; ed. WTheiler 1982 **II–I BC**
Proclus (Diadochus), his (Institutio) Theol(ogica) = Στοιχείωσις θεολογική, ed. EDodds 1933, 2d ed. 1963; In Platonis Timaeum Commentaria, ed. EDiehl, 3 vols. 1903–6; In Platonis Rem Publicam Commentarii, ed. WKroll, 2 vols. 1899, 1901; on Cratylus, ed. GPasquali 1908 **V AD**
Procop(ius) Gaz(aeus) = Procop. Soph. **V–VI AD**
Procop(ius) Hist., ed. JHaury 1905–13 (repr. [GWirth] 1962–64) **VI AD**
Procop(ius) Soph(ista) = Procop. Gaz., s. Ep. **V–VI AD**
Prodicus, Vorsokr. no. 84 **V–IV BC**
Proleg(omenon) Syllog(e), ed. HRabe: Rhetores Graeci XIV 1931 **uncertain**

Protagoras, Vorsokr. no. 80 **V BC**
Ps.-Aeschin(es), s. Aeschin(es)
Ps.-Apollod(orus), ed. RWagner 1894, 2 ed. 1926 **I/II AD**
Ps.-Aristot., s. Aristot(le)
Ps.-Caesarius (of Nazianzus), MPG XXXVIII **VI AD**
Ps.-Callisth(enes), Historia Alexandri Magni, ed. WKroll 1926 (repr. 1958); cp. LBergson 1965 for recension B **II–III? AD**
Ps.-Clemens, Hom(iliae), ed. BRehm 1953; 2d ed. BRehm/JIrmscher/FPaschke 1969 **III AD**
Ps.-Crates = letters attributed to the poet-philosopher Crates, s. Ep. **IV–III BC**
Ps.-Demetr., De Eloc. = Ps.-Demetrius, De Elocutione, ed. LRadermacher 1901 **I BC–II? AD**
Ps.-Demetrius = Ps.-Demetrius, Formae Epistolicae, cited according to: Demetrii et Libanii qui feruntur Τύποι ἐπιστολικοί et Ἐπιστολιμαῖοι Χαρακτῆρες, ed. VWeichert 1910 (by page and line) **uncertain**
Ps.-Dicaearchus, s. Dicaearchus
Ps.-Diogenes = letters attributed to Diogenes of Sinope (IV BC), s. Ep. **uncertain**
Psellus, History, ed. CSathas 1899; ERenauld 1926–28; cited according to Sathas unless otherwise noted; also cited is Περὶ λίθων δυνάμεων, in Les Lapidaires (s. Cyranides) 201–204 **XI AD**
Ps.-Hecataeus, historical accounts attributed to Hecataeus of Abdera, no. 264 Jac. **uncertain**
Ps.-Heraclitus, letters attributed to Heraclitus of Ephesus (VI–V BC), s. Ep. **uncertain**
Ps.-Libanius, ed. RFörster (F.), Characteres Epistolici in Libanii Opera IX (1927, repr. 1963) pp. 27–47; Epistulae Pseudepigraphae, vol. XI 1922. See also Ps.-Demetrius. **uncertain**
Ps.-Lucian, ed. CJacobitz 1836–41 (repr. 1966); MMacLeod 1967. The works include Asinus, Amores, Calumn(iae), Charid(emus), Cyn(icus), Dem(osthenes Encomium), Epig(ramma), Halc(yon), Nero, Ocy(pus), Phil(opatris), Salt.=De Saltatione, Trag(odopodagra), et al. **after II AD**
Ps.-Oppian = Oppian of Apamea, Cyn(egetica), ed. AMair 1928 **II–III AD**
Ps.-Orph(eus), fragments, Denis 1970 pp. 163–67; also s. Orphica
Ps.-Philo = the pseud. Liber antiquitatum biblicarum (Biblical Antiquities)=Pseudo-Philon, Les antiquités bibliques I (Sources Chrétiennes no. 229), ed. DHarrington 1976 **I AD**
Ps.-Phoc(ylides), s. AnthLG; ed. DYoung^2 1971; PvanderHorst, The Sentences of Pseudo-Phocylides 1978 **I/II AD**
Ps.-Plato, including Alcibiades I (?) and II, Amatores, Axiochus, Definitiones, Hipparchus, Minos, Theages, Timaeus of Locri et al., ed. JBurnet 1900–1907 **uncertain**
Ps.-Plut(arch), Vi(ta) Hom(eri), s. Homer, ed. Monro/Allen V 239–45
Ps.-Polemon, Physiognom. = Pseudo-P., ed. RFoerster, Scriptores physiognomonici Graeci et Latini I 427–31 **II AD**
Ps.-Scylax = a compilation in the name of the explorer Scylax and titled Periplus: GGM I 15–96; s. also FGrH no. 709 **V/IV BC**
Ps.-Socrates, for letters attributed to the philosopher Socrates s. Ep. **uncertain**
Ps.-Sotades, poems attributed to Sotades (iambographus), Coll. Alex. esp. nos. 6–14, pp. 240–42; s. Sotades **uncertain**
Ps.-X(enophon), s. X.
Ptolem(aeus), math.: Apotelesmatica, ed. FBoll/EBoer 1940 **II AD**
Pythag(oras), for letters attributed to the philosopher P. (VI–V BC) s. Ep. **uncertain**
Quint(us) Smyrn(aeus), ed. AZimmermann 1891; FVian, 3 vols. 1963–69 **IV AD**
Rhet(ores) Gr(aeci), ed. CWalz 1832–36 (a mixture of Gr-Rom. and Christian works). The collection of the Rhet. Gr. put out since 1853 by LSpengel et al. is cited according to ancient authors and modern editors.
Rhinthon (Comicus), s. Com.; ed. AOlivieri 1947 **III BC**
Sallust(ius), Περὶ θεῶν κ. κόσμου, ed. ANock 1926; GRochefort 1960 **IV AD**
Sappho, s. AnthLG; ed. ELobel/DPage (L-P.) 1955, 2d ed. 1963; EVoigt 1975; DCampbell, Greek Lyric I: Sappho and Alcaeus 1982 **VII–VI BC**
Sch. = TSchermann, Prophetarum vitae fabulosae 1907
Schol(ia), all from var. times
  on Aeschyl(us), ed. WDindorf 1851; OSmith 1976–82
  on Apollon(ius of) Rhod(es), ed. KWendel 1935
  on Aratus, ed. EMaass 1898; JMartin 1974
  on Aristoph(anes), ed. WDindorf 1838; WKoster/DHolwerda 1960ff
  on Eur(ipides), ed. ESchwartz, 2 vols. 1887–91
  on Lucian, ed. HRabe 1906
  on Pind(ar), ed. ADrachmann, 3 vols. 1903–27
  on Pla(to), ed. GGreene 1938
  on Soph(ocles), ed. PPapageorgius 1888
Scr. Erot., s. Erotici
Scylax, s. Ps.-Scylax
Scymnus Chius, geogr. I BC; the account attributed to him, GGM I 196ff, was prob. written II/I BC
Secundus, Athenian philosopher, Sententiae, FPhGr I 512–17; BPerry, Secundus the Silent Philosopher, APAPM 22, 1964, 78–90 (Sententiae) **II AD**
Semonides of Amorgos, ed. MWest 1972, 2d ed. 1992; s. AnthLG **VII BC**
Serap(ion) of Thmuis, Euchologium, ed. GWobbermin, TU 5/2, 3b 1898; ADimitrijewskij 1894 **IV AD**
Sext(us) Emp(iricus), ed. HMutschmann et al. 1911–54; 2 ed. 1957ff **II–III AD**
Sextus (Pythagoras) = Sententiae, a Christian reworking of a Gr-Rom. original, ed. AElter, Academica Bonn 1891–92; HChadwick 1959; also in The Sentences of Sextus, ed. REdwards/RWild 1981 **end of II AD**
SibOr = Oracula Sibyllina, ed. JGeffcken 1902; AKurfess 1951 **II–III AD**
Simmias (of Rhodes), s. AnthLG; Coll. Alex. 109–20 **IV–III BC**
Simonid(es of Ceos), s. AnthLG; DPage, PMG **VI–V BC**
Simplicius, Commentarius in Epict(eti Enchiridion), ed. FDübner 1840; cited by page and line **VI AD**
Slav. En. = Slavonic Book of Enoch (II Enoch), a pseudepigraphical apocalyptic work attested only in Slavonic **uncertain**
Socrat(es), Ep., letters attributed to the philosopher Socrates: Die Briefe des Sokrates und der Sokratiker, by Liselotte Köhler: Philologus Suppl. 20/2, 1928; freq. cited: AMalherbe, The Cynic Epistles 1977 **uncertain**
Socrates HE = Socrates (Scholasticus Hist.): Historia Ecclesiastica, ed. WBright^2 1893 **IV–V AD**
Socratics = letters attributed to followers of Socrates: AMalherbe, The Cynic Epistles 1977, 244–305
Solon, s. AnthLG; MWest 1972 **VII–VI BC**

Soph(ocles), ed. APearson 1924; RDawe 1975–79; HLloydJones/NWilson 1990 **V BC**

Soranus, ed. JIlberg: CMG IV 1927 **I–II AD**

Sostratus, gramm., no. 23 Jac. **I BC**

Sotades (Maronita), AnthLG; also Coll. Alex. pp. 238–40 **III BC**

Sotion, paradoxogr., in Scriptores rerum mirabilium Graeci, ed. AWestermann 1839 **I AD**

Stadiasmus = S. sive periplus Maris Magni, ed. KMüller, GGM I 427–514 **uncertain**

Stephan(us) Byz(antius), ed. AMeineke 1849 (repr. 1956) **V–VI AD**

Stesichorus, s. AnthLG; also PMG 1936–42 **VII–VI BC**

Stob(aeus), ed. CWachsmuth/OHense, 5 vols. 1884–1912; Sch.=Scholia, ed. AHeeren, Stobaeus 1792–1801 **V AD**

Stoic(orum Veterum Fragmenta), coll. J(H)vArnim I–IV 1903–24

Strabo, ed. AMeineke 1877; FLassere et al. 1966ff **I BC–I AD**

Straton (of Lampsacus), phil., ed. FWehrli 1950, 2d ed. 1969 **III BC**

Straton (of Sardis), epigr., Anth. Pal. (s. index) **II AD**

Suda (ἡ Σοῦδα), "The Fortress" or "Stronghold," a lexical work (freq. cited as Suidas in handbooks), ed. AAdler, 4 vols. 1928–35 **X AD**

Sym. = Symmachus; for fragments of his version of the OT in Greek s. Orig., Hexapla **II AD**

Synes(ius), with no work specified, signifies the letters: Epistolographi Gr. [s. Ep.]; the Opuscula, ed. NTerzaghi 1944; Calvit.=Calvitii Encomium; chapter numerals are those of Terzaghi, and DPetau's pagination is cited in the margin **IV–V AD**

Syntipas = the pseudonymous Book of the Philosopher Syntipas, a Greek translation fr. Syriac by Michael Andreopoulos, ed. VJernstedt/PNikition: Mémoires de l'Acad. impériale des sciences hist.-phil. tome XI 8me série, 1912 pp. 1–200 (by page and line); also Perry (P.) 511–50 (s. Aesop) **before XI AD**

Tat(ian), ed. ESchwartz 1888; EGoodspeed (s. Just.) 1914 **II AD**

Teles, ed. OHense[2] 1909 (repr. 1969) **III BC**

Telestes, s. AnthLG **V/IV BC**

Tert(tullian), Opera, ed. EDekkers et al., 2 vols. 1954 **II–III AD**

TestAbr = Testament of Abraham, ed. MJames 1892, cited by page and line; repr. MStone 1972 **I BC/I AD**

TestAdam = Testament of Adam, ed. SRobinson 1982; the Syriac text II/III AD, the Gk. portion (the Horarium) in Byzantine form X? AD

Tetras(ticha) iamb(ica), s. Babrius, ed. OCrusius pp. 264–96

TGF = Tragicorum Graecorum Fragmenta, ed. ANauck 1899 (repr. w. Suppl. by BSnell 1964)

Thales, Vorsokr. no. 11 **VI BC**

Themist(ius), Orationes, ed. WDindorf 1832 (repr. 1961); HSchenkl/GDowney/ANorman 1965–71 **IV AD**

Theocr(itus Bucolicus), ed. HAhrens 1897; AGow in Bucolici Graeci[2] 1958; these edd. include the spurious poems **IV–III BC**

Theod. = Theodotion; for fragments of his version of the OT in Greek, s. Orig., Hexapla **II AD**

Theodoret (of Cyrrhus), ed. JSchultze/JNoesselt I–V 1769–74; MPG LXXX–LXXXIV **IV–V AD**

Theodor(us) Prodr(omus of Constantinople), s. Erotici II 287ff **XII AD**

Theodos(ius) Melitenus, ed. GTafel, in Monumenta saecularia (=centennial Festschrift of ABayAW, III Classe/1) 1859 **X AD**

Theodotus (Judaeus Epic.), s. Denis 204–7; no. 732 Jac. **before I BC**

Theognis, s. AnthLG, ed. DYoung[2] 1971; MWest, Iambi et Elegi Graeci ante Alexandrum Cantati I[2] 1989 **VI BC**

Theognost(us Grammaticus), author of On Orthography, in Anecdota graeca . . . , ed. JCramer II 1835–37 **IX AD**

Theon Smyrn(aeus), De utilitate mathematicae, in EHiller, ed., Theonis Smyrnaei philosophi Platonici expositio 1878 **II AD**

Theophanes Conf(essor), ed. CdeBoor, 2 vols. 1883–85; also JClassen/IBekker 1839–41 **VIII–IX AD**

Theoph. Ant. = Theophilus Antiochenus, ed. GBardy 1948 **II AD**

Theophilus Antecessor, ed. OReitz 1751; JZepos/PZepos 1931 **VI AD**

Theophr(astus), ed. FWimmer 1854–62; HP=Historia Plantarum; Char.=Characteres; CP=De Curis Plantarum **IV–III BC**

Theophyl(actus) Sim(ocatta), MPG CXXIII; Ep(istulae), ed. GZanetto 1985 **VII AD**

Theopomp(us), no. 115 Jac. **IV BC**

Theosophien = Fragmente griechischer Theosophien, ed. HErbse (diss. Hamburg) 1941

Thom(as) Mag(ister), ed. FRitschl 1832 **XIII–XIV AD**

Thrasymachus, rhet./soph., Vorsokr. no. 85 **V BC**

Thu(cydides), ed. HJones/JPowell 1900–1901, 2 ed. 1942 **V BC**

Timaeus, hist., of Tauromenion, no. 566 Jac. **IV–III BC**

Tim. Locr. = Timaeus (hist.) Locrus, a late work passed under the name of Timaeus of Locri (III/II BC), a speaker in Plato's Timaeus, ed. CHerman 1852; WMarg 1972 **I? AD**

Timochares, no. 165 Jac. **II BC**

Timon, s. Poet(arum) Philos(ophorum Fragmenta), pp. 173ff **IV–III BC**

TrGF = Tragicorum Graecorum Fragmenta: I, ed. BSnell 1971 (Tragici minores); II, ed. RKannicht/BSnell 1981 (adespota); III, ed. SRadt 1985 (Aischyl.); IV, ed. SRadt 1977 (Soph.)

Trypho = Trypho of Alexandria, s. Gramm. Gr. **I BC**

Tyrtaeus, s. AnthLG **VII BC**

Vett(ius) Val(ens), ed. WKroll 1908; cited by page and line **II AD**

Vi. Aesopi = Vitae Aesopi, ed. AEberhard: Fabulae Romanenses Graece Conscriptae (Vita P1) I 1872; BPerry, ed. Aesopica (Vita G) I 1952 **I AD**

Vi. Homeri et Hesiodi = Vitae H. et H., ed. UvWilamowitz = Kleine Texte 137 (repr. 1929); s. Homer, Allen vol. 5

VIs, ViJer, ViEzk, et al. = Vita of Isaiah, Vita of Jeremiah, Vita of Ezekiel, et al.: CTorrey, The Lives of the Prophets 1946; TSchermann (Sch.), Prophetarum vitae fabulosae 1907; Rec. Dor.=recension of Dorotheos

Vi(ta) Philonidis (Epicurei), ed. WCrönert 1900 **II/I BC**

Vi(ta) Pol(ycarpi), ed. FFunk, FDiekamp[3] 1913 **c. 400 AD**

Vi(ta) Sophoclis, in Sophoclis Fabulae, ed. APearson 1923, xviii–xxi (because of its historical deficiencies not reprinted in the ed. of 1990, s. Soph.) **uncertain**

Vi(ta) Thu(cydidis), ed. CHude 1898; also HJones/JPowell (Oxf. Text) 1942 **uncertain**

Vorsokr. = Vorsokratiker, fragments ed. by HDiels, 5th ed. by WKranz 3 vols. 1934–37; 6th ed. 1951ff. The term

Pre-Socratic(s) is used when no specific ref. is made to the German ed.
West = MWest, ed. Iambi et Elegi Graeci ante Alexandrum Cantati, 2 vols., 2d ed. I 1989, II 1992
X. = Xenophon, ed. EMarchant 1900–1920 **V–IV BC**
Cyn. = Cynegetica
Cyr. = Cyropaedia
HG = Historia Graeca
spurious: Constitution of Athens
Xenophanes, s. AnthLG and Vorsokr. no. 21 **VI–V BC**
X. Eph. = Xenophon of Ephesus, ed. RHercher 1858; APapanikolaou 1973 **II/III AD**
Zeno, the Stoic, ed. J(H)vArnim, Stoicorum Veterum Fragmenta I 1905 **IV–III BC**
Zenob(ius) Soph(ista), in Corpus Paroemiographorum Graecorum I 1839 1–175 **II AD**
Zonaras = Zonarae Lexicon (inaccurately ascribed to John Zonaras), ed. JTittmann, 2 vols., 1808 **XII AD**
Zosimus = Z. alchem., when cited in Rtzst., Poim.; Herm. Wr. (Hermetica, Hermet.); and MBerthelot, CALG **III/IV AD**
Zosimus, Hist. = Zosimi Historia nova, ed. LMendelssohn 1887; FPaschoud 1971–86 **V? AD**

6. Periodicals, Collections, Modern Authors and Literature

Abbreviations following a virgule designate an alternate form used in Theologische Realenzyklopädie, 2d ed., ed. SSchwertner.

AAWW/AnzAWW = Anzeiger der (Kaiserlichen) Akademie der Wissenschaften (in Wien), Philosophisch-historische Klasse 1864ff; Anzeiger der philosophisch-historische Klasse der Österreichischen Akademie der Wissenschaften 1947ff
ABA/AAWB = Abhandlungen der Königlichen Akademie der Wissenschaften zu Berlin, Philosophisch-historische Klasse 1804ff; continuation as APAW (q.v.)
ABayAW/ABAW = Abhandlungen der Philosophisch-philologischen Klasse der (Königlich) Bayerischen Akademie der Wissenschaften 1835ff; Philosophisch-philologische und historische Klasse 1909ff; Philosophisch-historische Abteilung 1929ff; Philosophisch-historische Klasse 1947ff
ABD = Anchor Bible Dictionary, 6 vols. 1992
Abel = FA., Grammaire du Grec biblique 1927
AC/AuC = FDölger, Antike und Christentum, Kultur- und religionsgeschichtliche Studien, I–VI 1929–50
ActNTUps, s. ASNU
Aeg = Aegyptus, Rivista Italiana di Egittologia e di papirologia 1920ff
AGG, s. GGAbh
AGWG, s. GGAbh
AJA = American Journal of Archaeology 1885ff (var. ser.)
AJP = American Journal of Philology 1880ff
AJSL = American Journal of Semitic Languages and Literature 1884–1941, then JNES 1942ff
AJT = American Journal of Theology 1897–1920
Amicitiae Corolla, A Volume of Essays Presented to James Rendell Harris, ed. HWood 1953
AnalBoll/AnBoll = Analecta Bollandiana 1882ff
Analecta Biblica, 1952ff
AnnBSA = Annual of the British School at Athens 1894ff
ANRW = Aufstieg und Niedergang der römischen Welt: Geschichte und Kultur Roms im Spiegel der neueren Forschung, ed. HTemporini/WHaase 1972ff. I: Von den Anfängen Roms bis zum Ausgang der Republik 1, 1972ff. II: Principat 1, 1974ff
AntCl/AnCl = L'Antiquité classique 1932ff
Anz = HA., Subsidia ad recognoscendum Graecorum sermonem Bulgarem e Pentateuchi versione Alexandrina repetita: diss. Philolog. Halenses XII 1894, 259–387
APAPM = American Philological Association Philological Monographs 1931ff
APAW = Abhandlungen der (Königlich) Preussischen Akademie der Wissenschaften zu Berlin, Philosophisch-historische Klasse 1901ff; s. ABA
APF = Archiv für Papyrusforschung und verwandte Gebiete 1900ff
APOT = Apocrypha and Pseudepigrapha of the Old Testament, 2 vols., ed. RHCharles 1913; s. also The Old Testament Pseudepigrapha, ed. JCharlesworth, 2 vols. 1983–85
Ar = Archaeologia (London) 1770, 1888ff
Ἀρχαιολογικὴ Ἐφημερίς/ArchEph, 1837ff (var. ser., including the variant title Ἐφημερὶς Ἀρχαιολογική)
Arnott, Alexis, s. Com. in List 5
ARW = Archiv für Religionswissenschaft 1–37, 1898–1941/42
ASAW, s. ASG(Leipz)
ASG(Leipz)/ASGW = Abhandlungen der (Königlich) Sächsischen Gesellschaft der Wissenschaften, Philologisch-historische Klasse 1850ff; then ASAW=Abhandlungen der Sächsischen Akademie der Wissenschaften, Philologisch-historische Klasse (Leipzig) 1916ff
ASNU = Acta Seminarii Neotestamentici Upsaliensis 1936ff
ASP = American Studies in Papyrology 1966ff
ASTI = Annual of the Swedish Theological Institute (in Jerusalem) 1962ff
ASyn. = KAland Synopsis Quattuor Evangeliorum[13] 1988, cited by no. and line, unless otherwise specified.
Athen. Mitt., s. MAI
ATR/AthR = Anglican Theological Review 1918ff
B. = CBuck, A Dictionary of Selected Synonyms in the Principal Indo-European Languages: A Contribution to the History of Ideas 1949
BA = Biblical Archaeologist 1938ff
BAAR = WBauer, KAland, BAland, VReichmann, Griechisch-deutsches Wörterbuch zu den Schriften des

Neuen Testaments und der frühchristlichen Literatur, 6th ed. 1988

Baedeker = KB., Palästina u. Syrien[7] 1910.

BAFCS = The Book of Acts in Its First Century Setting, series ed. BWinter, 6 vols., 1993ff

BAR/BArR = Biblical Archaeology Review 1975ff

BASOR = Bulletin of the American Schools of Oriental Research 1919ff

BASP = Bulletin of the American Society of Papyrologists 1963ff

BCH = Bulletin de correspondance hellénique 1877ff

B-D-F = FBlass, Grammatik des neutestamentlichen Griechisch, ed. ADebrunner[9] (Bl-D.) 1954; translation (with some modifications and additions based on unpublished work by Debrunner) by RFunk, A Greek Grammar of the New Testament and Other Early Christian Literature 1961; ordinarily cited by paragraph

B-D-R = FBlass, ADebrunner, Grammatik des neutestamentlichen Griechisch[16], ed. FRehkopf 1984

Bechtel = FB., Die historischen Personennamen des griechischen bis zur Kaiserzeit 1917

Beginn. = The Beginnings of Christianity, ed. FJFoakesJackson and KLake, Part I, 5 vols. (Acts) 1920–33

Bengel = JB., Gnomon Novi Testamenti 1742 (many editions)

Berl. Kopt. Urk./ÄgU.K = Aegyptische Urkunden aus der Königlichen Museum zu Berlin: Koptische Urkunden I 1904; II/2 1901; then Aegyptische Urkunden aus der Staatlichen Museen Berlin, Koptische Urkunden III 1908

BETL/BEThL = Bibliotheca Ephemeridum Theologicarum Lovaniensium 1947ff

Betz = HB.

—, Gal. = Galatians (Hermeneia) 1979

—, SM = The Sermon on the Mount (Hermeneia) 1995

Beyer, Syntax = KBeyer, Semitische Syntax im Neuen Testament 1962

BFCT = Beiträge zur Förderung christlicher Theologie 1897ff

BHHW/BHH = Biblisch-historisches Handwörterbuch I–IV, ed. BReicke/LRost 1962–79

Bibel-Lexikon, ed. DSchenkel, 5 vols., 1869–75

Bibelwörterbuch = Kurzes Bibelw., ed. HGuthe 1903

Biblica (unabbr.) 1920ff

BiblSacra/BS = Bibliotheca Sacra, A Theological Quarterly 1844ff

Bihlmeyer = KB., Die Apostolischen Väter: Neubearbeitung der Funkschen Ausgabe, Pt I, 2d ed. 1956

Billerb. = (HLStrack and) PBillerbeck, Kommentar zum NT aus Talmud und Midrasch, 4 vols. 1922–28; 2 Index vols. 1956–61

BIOSCS = Bulletin of the International Organization for Septuagint and Cognate Studies 1968ff

BJRL, Bulletin of the John Rylands Library 1903ff

BK/BiKi, Bibel und Kirche 1946ff

Black, Aramaic Approach = MB., An Aramaic Approach to the Gospels and the Acts[2] 1953; 3d ed. 1967

Bl-D. = FBlass/ADebrunner; this abbr. occasionally used when B-D-F (q.v.) differs.

Boisacq = ÉBoisacq, Dictionnaire étymologique de la Langue Grecque 1916

Boll = FB., Aus der Offenbarung Johannis 1914

—, Sternglaube = FBoll/CBezold/WGundel, Sternglaube und Sterndeutung, Die Geschichte und das Wesen der Astrologie[4] 1931 (reprint as 5th ed. 1966)

Borger, GGA = RB., Göttingische Gelehrte Anzeigen 241, Heft 1/2, 1989, 103–46

Bousset, Rel. = WB., Die Religion des Judentums im neutestamentlichen Zeitalter[3] 1926, reprinted with bibliographic updating by ELohse 1966

BPhW/BPhWs = Berliner Philologische Wochenschrift 1884–1920; formerly Philolog. Woch. 1881–83

BR = Biblical Research 1956ff

Breusing = AB., Die Nautik der Alten 1886

BRev = Bible Review 1985ff

Brown, Death = RB., The Death of the Messiah, 2 vols. 1994

Bruce, Acts = FB., The Acts of the Apostles: Greek Text w. Introduction and Commentary 1990

BS, s. Dssm., BS

BSA/ABSA = Annual of the British School at Athens 1894ff

BSac, s. BiblSacra

BSG(Leipz)/BSGW/BSAW = Berichte über die Verhandlungen der (Königlich) Sächsischen Gesellschaft der Wissenschaften zu Leipzig 1846ff; then BSAW=Berichte über die Verhandlungen der (Königlich) Sächsischen Gesellschaft/Akademie der Wissenschaften, Philologisch-historische Klasse 1919ff

BT/BiTr = The Bible Translator 1950ff

BTB = Biblical Theology Bulletin 1971ff

Buck = CB.

—, Dialects = The Greek Dialects 1955

—, Reverse Index = CB./WPetersen, A Reverse Index of Greek Nouns and Adjectives 1944

Buhl = FB., Geographie von Palästina 1896

Bultmann = RB., commentator on NT, esp. John

Burton, MT = EB., Syntax of the Moods and Tenses in New Testament Greek[2] 1893; also s. Zwaan (some revision of Burton, MT)

Buttmann = AB., Grammatik des neutestamentlichen Sprachgebrauchs 1859

Byzantion, revue internationale des études byzantines 1924ff

ByzZ/ByZ = Byzantinische Zeitschrift 1892ff

BZ = Biblische Zeitschrift 1903ff (var. ser.)

BZNW = Beihefte zur Zeitschrift für die neutestamentliche Wissenschaft 1923ff

CAD = The Assyrian Dictionary of the Oriental Institute of the University of Chicago, ed. AOppenheim et al. 1956ff

Cadbury, Style = HC., The Style and Literary Method of Luke (Harvard Theological Studies VI), 1920

CB, s. Ramsay, CB

CBQ = Catholic Biblical Quarterly 1939ff

CCD = Confraternity of Christian Doctrine, sponsors of The NT Translated from the Latin Vulgate 1941

Charles = RC., Revelation (ICC), 2 vols. 1920

ChQR, s. CQR

ClAnt/ClA = Classical Antiquity 1982ff

ClBull = Classical Bulletin (St. Louis, Mo.) 1925–88

Clemen = CC., Religionsgeschichtliche Erklärung des Neuen Testaments[2] 1924

ClJ/CJ = Classical Journal (Chicago) 1905ff

ClPh/CP = Classical Philology 1906ff

ClQ/CQ = Clasical Quarterly 1907ff

ClR = Classical Review 1887ff

ClW = Classical Weekly 1907–57
CMRDM = Corpus Monumentorum Religionis Dei Menis, 4 vols. 1971–78
ConcJour/ConJ = Concordia Journal 1975ff
Congr. d'Hist. du Christ. = Congrès d'Histoire du Christianisme, Jubilé ALoisy, 3 vols. 1928
ConNeot/CNT = Coniectanea Neotestamentica, ed. AFridrichsen et al. 1935ff
Contemp. Rev. = Contemporary Review 1866ff
CQR = Church Quarterly Review 1875ff
CRAI = Comptes-rendus des séances de l'Académie des Inscriptions et Belles Lettres 1857ff (var. ser.)
CRINT = Compendia Rerum Iudaicarum ad Novum Testamentum 1974ff
CSHB = Corpus Scriptorum Historiae Byzantinae, 50 vols. 1828–97
CTM = Concordia Theological Monthly 1930–72; continued as CTM (unabbreviated) 1973–74 (XLIV/1 January '73–XLV/1 January '74); then CurTM (q.v.)
Cumont = FC., Die orientalische Religionen im römischen Heidentum[3] 1931
—, **Lux Perpetua** 1949
CurTM = Currents in Theology and Mission 1974 (I/1 August) ff; s. CTM
DACL = Dictionnaire d'archéologie chrétienne et de liturgie, ed. FCabrol, HLeclercq, I–XV 1903–53
Dalman = GD.
—, **Arbeit** = Arbeit und Sitte in Palästina, 7 vols. 1928–42
—, **Gramm.** = Grammatik des jüdisch-palästinischen Aramäisch[2] 1905
—, **Jesus** = Jesus-Jeschua 1922, tr. Jesus-Jeshua, PLevertoff 1929
—, **Orte** = Orte u. Wege Jesu[3] 1924, tr. Sacred Sites and Ways PLevertoff 1935
—, **Worte** = D. Worte Jesu 1898, tr. DMKay, 1902; 2d German ed. 1930
Dana and Mantey = HD./JRM., A Manual Grammar of the Greek NT 1927
Danker, Benefactor = FD., Benefactor: Epigraphic Study of a Graeco-Roman and New Testament Semantic Field 1982
Daremberg-Saglio/DAGR = CVDaremberg/ESaglio, Dictionnaire des antiquités grecques et romaines d'après les textes et les monuments, 5 vols. and index 1877–1919
DBS = Dictionnaire de la Bible (ed. by LVigouroux, 5 vols. 1895–1912), Supplement, ed. LPirot 1928ff
DDD = Dictionary of Deities and Demons in the Bible, ed. KToorn/BBecking/PvanderHorst 1995
DeJonge, Studies = MdeJonge, Studies on the Testaments of the Twelve Patriarchs 1975
DELG = PChantraine, Dictionnaire étymologique langue grecque: histoire des mots, 4 vols. 1968–80
Delph(ic) Orac(le), ed. HWParke/DEWormell, 2 vols. 1956
Denis = AD., Fragmenta Pseudepigraphorum quae supersunt Graeca (Pseudepigrapha Veteris Testamenti Graece 3) 1970
—, **Conc.** = Concordance grecque des pseudépigraphes d'ancien testament 1987
Denniston = JD., The Greek Particles[2] 1950 (9th impression 1987)
DeutscheTheol(ogie)/DTh, s. DTh
DGE = Diccionario Griego-Español, ed. FAdrados et al., 1989ff
Dibelius, Geisterwelt = MD., Die Geisterwelt im Glauben des Paulus 1909
Dict. d'Arch., s. DACL
Dict(ionnaire) de la Bible/DB(V) = Dictionnaire de la Bible, ed. LVigouroux, 5 vols. 1895–1912; Supplement (DBS), ed. LPirot 1928ff
Div. Thomas/DT = Divus Thomas, Jahrbuch für Philosophie und spekulative Theologie 1914–54, superseded by Freiburger Zeitschrift für Philosophie und Theologie 1954ff
Div. Thomas Piac./DT(P) = Divus Thomas, Commentarium de philosophia et theologia (Piacenza, Italy) 1880ff (var. ser.)
DLNT = Dictionary of the Later NT and Its Developments, ed. RMartin/PDavids 1997
DNP = Der Neue Pauly: Enzyklopädie der Antike, ed. HCancik/HSchneider 1996ff (without much of the detail in Pauly-W.)
Dodd = CHD., The Bible and the Greeks 1935
Dssm. = ADeissmann
—, **B** = Bibelstudien 1895
—, **BS** = Bible Studies, tr. of Dssm. B and Dssm. NB by AGrieve 1901
—, **LO** = Licht vom Osten[4] 1923 = LAE (Light from the Ancient East, tr. by LStrachan[2] 1927)
—, **NB** = Neue Bibelstudien 1897
DTh = Deutsche Theologie, Monatschrift für die deutsche evangelische Kirche 1934–43; then merger w. TRu 1944
DTT = Dansk Teologisk Tidsskrift 1938ff
Ea = Evangelia Apocrypha, ed. KTischendorf (Tdf.)[2] 1876
ExclRev/EcR/AEcR = Ecclesiastical Review 1889ff
EDNT = Exegetical Dictionary of the New Testament, ed. HBalz/HSchneider, 3 vols. 1990–93 (a tr. of Exegetisches Wörterbuch zum Neuen Testament [EWNT] 1978–83)
Elbogen = IE., Der jüdische Gottesdienst[2] 1924; [3]1931
Ἑλληνικά: ἱστόρικον περιόδικον δημοσίευμα 1928ff
EncBibl/EB(C) = Encyclopaedia Biblica, ed. TCheyne and JBlack, 4 vols. 1899–1903
EncJud/EJ = Encyclopaedia Judaica, ed. CRoth, 16 vols. 1971–72, and supplements
EncRel/EncRel(E) = Encyclopedia of Religion, ed. Mircea Eliade, 16 vols. 1987
EncRelEth/ERE = Encyclopaedia of Religion and Ethics, ed. JHastings, JSelbie et al., 13 vols. 1908–26.
EphemEpigr = Ephemeris Epigraphica, 9 vols. 1872–1913
EphemeridesTL, s. ETL
EpigrAnat = Epigraphica Anatolica 1983ff
Epigraphica = Epigraphica: Revista italiana di epigrafia 1939ff
ÉPRO = Études préliminaires aux religions orientales dans l'empire romain 1961ff
Eranos/Er, Acta Philologica Suecana 1896ff
EstBíbl = Estudios Bíblicos; 1st ser. 1929–36; 2d ser. 1941ff
ET = Expository Times 1889ff
ETL = Ephemerides Theologicae Lovanienses 1924ff
ÉTR = Études théologiques et religieuses 1926ff
EvQ = Evangelical Quarterly 1929ff
EvTh = Evangelische Theologie (Munich) 1934ff
EWNT, s. EDNT
Exp. = Expositor (London) 1875ff
Field = FF.
—, **Hexapla** = H.: Origenis hexaplorum quae supersunt . . . fragmenta, 2 vols. 1875

—, **Notes** = N. on the Translation of the NT 1899
Filología neotestamentaria, unabbr. 1988ff
Fitzmyer = JF.
—, **Essays** = Essays on the Semitic Background of the NT 1971
—, **Oxy,** s. Ox 1 in List 1 for details
Frisk = HF., Griechisches etymologisches Wörterbuch, 3 vols., 1960–72
FRLANT = Forschungen zur Religion und Literatur des Alten und Neuen Testaments 1903ff
Funk = RF., s. B-D-F
FZPhT/FZPhTh = Freiburger Zeitschrift für Philolosophie und Theologie, 4th ser., 1954ff
GCS = Die griechischen christlichen Schriftsteller der ersten drei Jahrhunderte 1897ff
GereformTT/GThT = Gereformeerd Theologisch Tijdschrift 1900ff
GGA = Göttingische Gelehrte Anzeigen 1801ff (earlier series 1739ff)
GGAbh/AGWG/AAWG = Abhandlungen der (Königlichen) Gesellschaft/Akademie der Wissenschaften zu Göttingen, Philologisch-historische Klasse 1838ff (Akademie, ser. 3, 1942ff: AAWG)
Gignac = FGignac, A Grammar of the Greek Papyri of the Roman and Byzantine Periods, I: Phonology 1976; II: Morphology 1981
Gildersleeve, Syntax = BG./CMiller, Syntax of Classical Greek, Pt. I 1900, Pt. II 1911 (no other parts published)
Gingrich Festschr. = Festschrift to Honor F. Wilbur Gingrich, ed. EHBarth/RECocroft, 1972
Gnomon, Kritische Zeitschrift für die gesamte klassische Altertumswissenschaft 1925ff
Goodsp. = EGoodspeed. With no title specified this abbr. refers to The NT: An American Translation 1923 (republished in the Goodspeed Parallel NT 1943)
—, **Probs.** = Problems of NT Translation 1945
Goodwin = WG., Syntax of the Moods and Tenses of the Greek Verb, rewritten and enlarged 1890
Haenchen = EH., Commentary on Acts (16th Ger. ed. 1977); Eng. tr. of the 14th ed. (1965) by BNoble/GShinn 1971
Hahn = LH., Rom und Romanismus im griechischen-römischen Osten 1906
Handwörterbuch des Bibl. Altertums, ed. ERiehm, 2 vols., 2d ed. 1893f
Hansa, Verkehrs- und Hafenblatt 1863ff
Harnack, Studien = AH., Studien zur Geschichte des Neuen Testaments und der alten Kirche 1931
HastDAC = Dictionary of the Apostolic Church, 2 vols., ed. JHastings 1915; 1918
HastDB/DB(H) = Dictionary of the Bible, 4 vols, and extra vol., ed. JHastings 1898–1904
HastDCG/DCG = Dictionary of Christ and the Gospels, 2 vols., ed. JHastings 1906; 1908
Hatch and Redpath = EH./HR., A Concordance to the Septuagint and the Other Greek Versions of the OT, 2 vols. and supplement 1892–1906; EdosSantos, An Expanded Hebrew Index for the Hatch-Redpath Concordance to the Septuagint 1973
Hdb. = Handbuch, in reference to various series of reference works in German; s. HNT
Helbing = RH., Grammatik der LXX: Laut- und Wortlehre 1907
—, **Kasussyntax** = Die Kasussyntax der Verba bei den LXX 1928
Hemer, Acts = CH., The Book of Acts in the Setting of Hellenistic History 1990
Hengel, Judaism = MH., Judaism and Hellenism 1974, tr. by JBowden of Judentum und Hellenismus 1966
Hennecke-Schneemelcher (Wils.) = EH., New Testament Apocrypha, ed. WS., I rev. ed. tr. RWilson 1991; II tr. RW. 1965
Her = Hermes, Zeitschrift für klassische Philologie 1866ff
Hermeneia = commentary series 1971ff
HistZeitschr/HZ = Historische Zeitschrift 1859ff
HNT = Handbuch zum Neuen Testament, a series founded by HLietzmann (1875–1942), published since 1906
Hobart, = WH., The Medical Language of St. Luke 1882
Hollander-DeJonge = HWH./MdeJ., The Testaments of the Twelve Patriarchs: A Commentary 1985
HSCP = Harvard Studies in Classical Philology 1890ff
HTR/HThR = Harvard Theological Review 1908ff
HUCA = Hebrew Union College Annual 1924ff
ICC = International Critical Commentary 1895ff
IDB = Interpreter's Dictionary of the Bible 1962
IJCT = International Journal of the Classical Tradition 1994
IndogF/IGF = Indogermanische Forschungen 1891ff
Int = Interpretation 1947ff
IOSCS = International Organization for Septuagint and Cognate Studies
ISBE = International Standard Bible Encyclopedia, rev. ed., 4 vols. 1979–88
JAC = Jahrbuch für Antike und Christentum 1958ff
Jac. = Die Fragmente der griechischen historiker, ed. FJacoby 1923ff; cited by number of author and number and line of fragment (occasionally with Jac.'s vol. and page)
Jahrb. klass. Phil. = Jahrbücher für klassische Philologie
Jannaris = ANJ., An Historical Greek Grammar, London 1897
JAOS = Journal of the American Oriental Society 1843ff
JB = Jerusalem Bible, ed. AJones 1966
JBL = Journal of Biblical Literature 1881ff
JDAI/JDI = Jahrbuch des (Königlich) Deutschen Archäologischen Instituts 1886ff
JEA = Journal of Egyptian Archaeology 1914ff
JECS = Journal of Early Christian Studies 1993ff
JETS = Journal of the Evangelical Theological Society 1958ff
JHS = Journal of Hellenic Studies 1880ff
JJP = Journal of Juristic Papyrology 1946ff
JJS = Journal of Jewish Studies 1948ff
JNES = Journal of Near Eastern Studies 1942ff (successor to AJSL)
JÖAI = Jahreshefte des Österreichischen Archäologischen Institutes in Wien 1898ff
Johannessohn = MJ.
—, **Kasus** = Der Gebrauch des Kasus in LXX, diss., Berlin 1910
—, **Präp.** = Der Gebrauch der Präpositionen in LXX: NGG, Beiheft 1926
Jos. Lex. = A Lexicon to Josephus, begun by HSJThackeray/RMarcus, but not completed 1930ff
JournAsiat/JA = Journal Asiatique 1822 (var. ser.)
JPh/JP = Journal of Philology 1868–1920
JPOS = Journal of the Palestine-Oriental Society 1920ff
JQR = Jewish Quarterly Review 1888–1908; 1910ff

JR = Journal of Religion 1921ff
JRS = Journal of Roman Studies 1911ff
JSNT = Journal for the Study of the NT 1978ff
JSOR = Journal of the Society of Oriental Research 1917–32
JSS = Journal of Semitic Studies, 1956ff
JTS = Journal of Theological Studies 1899ff
Jülicher, Gleichn. = AJ., Die Gleichnisreden Jesu 1899
Kalt = EK., Biblisches Reallexikon, 2 vols. 1931; 2d ed. 1938ff
KEK = Kritisch-exegetischer Kommentar über das NT, begun by HMeyer, 1829ff
KJV = King James version, originally 1611; text generally cited is the one standardized since BBlayney 1769
Kl. Pauly/KP = Der Kleine Pauly: Lexikon der Antike, I–V 1964–75
Kl. T./KlT = Kleine Texte 1902ff, ed. HLietzmann, also KAland
Krüger = KWK., Griechische Sprachlehre[5] 1875–79
Kühner-Bl. and Kühner-G. = RK., Ausführliche Grammatik der griechischen Sprache, 3d ed. by FBlass and BGerth 1890–1904 (reprint 1966) (cited by vol. and page)
Kuhring = WK., De praepositionum Graecarum in chartis Aegypticis usu quaestiones selectae 1906
Κυπρ. = Τα Κυπριακα, ed. ASakellarios, I–II 1890–91
LAE, s. Dssm LO
Lampe = GL., ed., A Patristic Greek Lexicon 1961–68 (a project initiated in 1906)
L'AntCl/AnCl = L'Antiquité classique 1932ff
Larfeld = WL., Handbuch der griechischen Epigraphik, 2 vols. 1902–7
Laum = BL., ed., Stiftungen in der griechischen und römischen Antike: Ein Beitrag zur antiken Kulturgechichte, 2 vols. 1914
LexThK/LThK = Lexikon für Theologie und Kirche, ed. MBuchberger, 10 vols. 1930–38; 2d ed. JHöfer/KRahner, 11 vols. 1957–67; 3d ed. 1993ff
LfgrE = Lexicon des frühgriechischen Epos, ed. BSnell, HJMette, et al. 1955–
LGPN = A Lexicon of Greek Personal Names, I: The Aegean Islands, Cyprus, Cyrenaica, ed. PFraser/EMatthews 1987
LO = Licht vom Osten, s. Dssm., LO
Lob. = ALobeck, s. Phryn(ichus) in List 5
L-S-J-M = HGLiddell and RScott, A Greek-English Lexicon, New Edition by HSJones and RMcKenzie, 2 vols. 1925–40 (later publ. as one volume); suppl., ed. EABarber et al. 1968; rev. suppl. PGlare/AThompson 1996
MAAR = Memoirs of the American Academy in Rome 1917ff
Magie = DM., De Romanorum Juris Publici Sacrique Vocabulis Sollemnibus in Graecum Sermonem Conversis 1905
MAI/MDAI. A = Mitteilungen des deutschen Archäologischen Instituts, Athenische Abteilung 1876ff
Mason = HM., Greek Terms for Roman Institutions 1974
Masson = EM., Recherches sur les plus anciens emprunts sémitiques en grec 1967
Mausberger = AM., Polybios-Lexikon 1956ff
Mayser = EM., Grammatik der griechischen Papyri aus der Ptolemäerzeit, 2 vols. 1906–34. The first vol. is indicated without reference to the volume number.
M'Clintock-Strong = JM./JS., Cyclopaedia of Biblical, Theological, and Ecclesiastical Literature, 10 vols. 1867–81; 2-vol. suppl. 1885–87
Μέγα Λέξικον τῆς Ἑλληνικῆς Γλώσσης, (JSZerbos), 9 vols. 1950
Meisterhans-Schw. = KM., Grammatik der Attischen Inschriften, 3d ed. ESchwyzer 1900; cp. Threatte, below
Metzger = BM., A Textual Commentary of the Greek New Testament 1971
Meyer = EM., Ursprung und Anfänge des Christentums, 3 vols. 1921–23
Mft. = JMoffatt, The Bible: A New Translation 1926
Mishnah = HDanby, The Mishnah 1933
Mitt-Wilck. = LMitteis/UWilcken, Grundzüge und Chrestomathie der Papyruskunde 1912. I Historischer Teil: 1 Grundzüge, 2 Chrestomathie, ed. UW.; II Juristischer Teil: 1 Grundzüge, 2 Chrestomathie, ed. LM.
Mlt. = JMoulton; with page number alone specified, this abbr. refers to A Grammar of NT Greek, I: Prolegomena 1908
Mlt-H. = JMoulton, in turn WHoward, A Grammar of NT Greek, II: Accidence and Word-Formation, w. an appendix on Semitisms 1919–29; cited by page
Mlt-Turner = JMoulton, in turn NTurner, A Grammar of NT Greek, III: Syntax 1963; IV: Style, by Turner, 1976
M-M. = JMoulton/GMilligan, The Vocabulary of the Greek Testament Illustrated from the Papyri and Other Non-Literary Sources 1914–30
Moore = GMoore, Judaism in the First Centuries of the Christian Era, 3 vols. 1927–30
Murray = JM. et al., A New English Dictionary on Historical Principles, 10 vols. and Supplement 1888–1933, s. OED
MusHelv/MH = Museum Helveticum 1944ff
Mussies = GM., The Morphology of Koine Greek as Used in the Apocalypse of St. John 1971
NAB = New American Bible 1970 (includes textual notes, not included in later editions, on OT readings)
NABRev = New American Bible with Revised New Testament 1986
Nachmanson = EN., Laute und Formen der Magnetischen Inschriften 1903
Nägeli = TN., Der Wortschatz des Apostels Paulus 1905
NAWG, Ph. (NAG) = Nachrichten der Akademie der Wissenschaften Göttingen, Philologisch-historische Klasse 1941ff
NEB = New English Bible 1970; also s. REB
NedTTs/NedThT = Nederlands theologisch Tijdschrift 1946ff (supersedes NThT)
Neophilol/NP = Neophilologus 1915ff
Neot/Neotest = Neotestamentica 1967ff
New Life = The New Life Testament, tr. by GLedyard 1969
NGG/NGWG = Nachrichten der Gesellschaft der Wissenschaften zu/in Göttingen, Philologisch-historische Klasse 1884ff
NJklA/NJKA = Neue Jahrbücher für das klassische Altertum 1898ff (var. ser.)
NKZ = Neue Kirchliche Zeitschrift 1890–1933
Nock = AN., Essays on Religion and the Ancient World, 2 vols. 1972
Norden, Agn. Th. = EN., Agnostos Theos 1913
NorTT = Norsk teologisk tidsskrift 1900ff
NouvRT/NRTh = Nouvelle revue théologique 1869ff
NovT = Novum Testamentum 1956ff
NRSV = New Revised Standard Version of the NT 1990
NThSt/NThS = Nieuwe theologische Studiën 1918–42

NThT = Nieuw Theologisch Tijdschrift 1912–46; superseded by NedTTs
NTS = New Testament Studies 1954ff
OEANE = Oxford Encyclopedia of Archaeology in the Near East, ed. EMeyers, 5 vols. 1997
OED = Oxford English Dictionary, 2d ed., JSimpson/EWeiner, 20 vols. 1989. For earlier ed. see Murray.
ÖJh, s. JÖAI
OLD = Oxford Latin Dictionary, ed.. PGlare 1968–82
OLZ = Orientalische Literaturzeitung 1898ff
Orientalia Christiana = Orientalia Christiana Periodica (=OCP), 1935ff
Pape-Benseler = WP./FB., Wörterbuch der griechischen Eigennamen 1875
PASA = Papers of the American School of Classical Studies at Athens 1–4, 1882–88
Passow = FP., Handwörterbuch der griechischen Sprache, 5th ed. by VRost, FPalm, et al., 2 vols. in 4 parts 1841–57. Completely rev. by WCrönert, only 3 fascicles 1912; 1913.
PatrOr/PO = Patrologia Orientalis (Paris) 1907ff
Pauly-W(issowa)/RECA/PRE = APauly, Real-Encyclopädie der klassischen Altertumswissenschaft, I–VI 1839–52. New revision in progress since 1892 by GWissowa, then by WKroll, KMittelhaus, KZiegler, et al. 1894ff; s. also DNP, above
PECS = Princeton Encyclopedia of Classical Sites, ed. RStillwell/WMacDonald/MMcAllister 1976
PEF/PEFQSt = Palestine Exploration Fund (Quarterly Statement) 1869–1936; then Palestine Exploration Quarterly/PEQ 1937ff
Philol(ogus), Zeitschrift für das klassische Altertum 1846ff
PhilolWoch/PhWS = Philologische Wochenschrift 1881ff (variations in title)
PJ = Preussische Jahrbücher 1858–1935
Pj = Palästinajahrbuch des Deutschen Evangelischen Instituts für Altertumswissenschaft des Heiligen Landes zu Jerusalem 1905–41
PM/PrM = Protestantische Monatshefte 1854–1921
Poland = FP., Geschichte des griechischen Vereinswesen 1909
Preis. = FPreisigke, Wörterbuch der griechischen Papyrusurkunden, mit Einschluss der griechischen Inschriften, Aufschriften, Ostraka, Mumienschilder u.s.w. aus Ägypten (finished by EKiessling), 4 vols. and supplements 1925ff
Preisigke = FP.
—, **Fachwörter** = Fachwörter des öffentlichen Verwaltungsdienstes Ägyptens in den griechischen Papyrusurkunden der ptolemäisch-römischen Zeit 1915
—, **Namenbuch** = Namenbuch 1922
—, **Sb** = Sammelbuch griechischer Urkunden aus Ägypten, begun by FP., 1915ff
—, **Wörterbuch** = Preis.
Preuschen, Antilegomena = EP., Antilegomena, Die Reste der ausserkanonischen Evangelien und urchristlichen Überliefungen 1905
PrJ, s. PJ
ProBib = Protokolle zur Bibel 1992ff
Prümm = KP., Religionsgeschichtliches Handbuch für den Raum der altchristlichen Umwelt 1943
Psaltes, Grammatik = SP., Grammatik der Byzantinischen Chroniken (Forschungen zur griechischen und lateinischen Grammatik 2) 1913
PTR = Princeton Theological Review 1903ff
QDAP = Quarterly of the Department of Antiquities in Palestine 1931–50
RAC = Reallexikon für Antike und Christentum, begun by FDölger, ed. TKlauser et al. 1950ff
Ramsay = WR.
—, **Bearing** = The Bearing of Recent Discovery on the Trustworthiness of the NT 1915
—, **CB** = The Cities and Bishoprics of Phrygia, vol. I in two parts 1895–97, second vol. not published (by page and no.)
—, **Church** = The Church in the Roman Empire[5] 1897
—, **Cities of St. Paul** 1907
—, **Hist. Geogr.** = The Historical Geography of Asia Minor 1890
—, **Letters** = The Letters to the Seven Churches of Asia 1904
RB = Revue Biblique 1892ff (var. ser.; s. also Vivre et Penser)
Rdm. = LRadermacher, Neutestamentliche Grammatik[2] 1925
RE = Realencyclopädie für protestantische Theologie und Kirche, 3d ed., 24 vols., ed. AHauck 1896–1913
REA = Revue des études anciennes 1899ff
Reader, Polemo, s. Polemo, List 5
Reallexikon der Vorgeschichte, 15 vols., ed. MEbert 1924–32
REB = The Revised English Bible with the Apocrypha 1989
RechScRel, s. RSR
Rehkopf, s. B-D-R
Reinhold = HR., De graecitate patrum apostolicorum librorumque apocryphorum NTi quaestiones grammaticae, Diss. Phil. Hal. XIV/11898, 1–115
REJ = Revue des études juives 1880ff
Renehan = RR., Greek Lexicographical Notes, A Critical Supplement to the Greek-English Lexicon of Liddell-Scott-Jones (Hypomnemata 45) 1975; Second Series (Hypomnemata 74) 1982
RevArch/RAr = Revue archéologique 1844ff
RevÉpigr = Revue épigraphique, new ser., 2 vols., 1913–14
RevÉtGr/REG = Revue des études grecques 1888–1939
RevExp/RExp = Review and Expositor 1904ff
RevHistEccl, s. RHE
RevPhilol = Revue de philologie, de littérature et d'histoire anciennes 1845ff (var. ser.)
RevQ = Revue de Qumran 1958ff
RevSém = Revue Sémitique d'epigraphie et d'histoire ancienne 1893–1914
Revue de philol., s. RevPhilol
RGG = Die Religion in Geschichte und Gegenwart, 5 vols. and index vol., 2d ed. 1927–32; 6 vols., 3d ed. 1957–62; 4th ed. vol. 1, 1998
RHE = Revue d'histoire ecclésiastique (Louvain) 1900ff
RhM = Rheinisches Museum für Philologie 1827ff (var. ser.)
RHPR/RHPhR = Revue d'histoire et de philosophie religieuses 1921ff
RHR = Revue de l'histoire des religions 1880ff
RivBib = Rivista Biblica 1953ff
RivFil/RFIC = Rivista di filologia e d'istruzione classica 1873ff (var. ser.)
Rob. = ATRobertson, A Grammar of the Greek NT in the Light of Historical Research[4] 1923
Rohde, Psyche = ER., Psyche, 9th and 10th ed., 2 vols. 1925

Roscher = WR., Ausführliches Lexikon der griechischen und römischen Mythologie, 6 vols. and 4 suppl. 1884–1937, concluded by KZiegler

Rossberg = CR., De praepositionum Graecarum in chartis Aegyptiis Ptolemaeorum aetatis usu, diss. Jena 1909

RSPT/RSPhTh = Revue des sciences philosophiques et théologiques 1907ff

RSR = Recherches de science religieuse 1910ff

RSV = The Revised Standard Version of the NT (1946, and reprinted with some modifications)

RThAM = Recherches de théologie ancienne et médiéviale 1929f

RTP/RThPh = Revue de théologie et de philosophie 1868ff (var. ser.)

RTQR/RThQR = Revue de théologie et des questions religieuses 1891–1915

Rtzst. = RReitzenstein

—, **Erlösungsmyst.** = Das iranische Erlösungsmysterium 1921

—, **Herr der Grösse** = Das mandäische Buch des Herrn der Grösse 1919

—, **Hist. Mon.** = Historia Monachorum und Historia Lausiaca 1916

—, **Mysterienrel.** = Die hellenistischen Mysterienreligionen[3] 1927

—, **Poim.** = Poimandres 1904

—, **Taufe** = Die Vorgeschichte der christl. Taufe 1929

RVV = Religionsgeschichtliche Versuche und Vorarbeiten 1903ff

Rydbeck = LR., Fachprosa, vermeintliche Volkssprache und Neues Testament 1967

SAB, s. SBBerlAk

Safrai-Stern, Jewish People = SS./MS., The Jewish People in the First Century, 2 vols. 1974–76

SAH, s. SBHeidAk

SAWien, s. SBWienAk

SBBayAk/SBAW = Sitzungsberichte der (Königlich) Bayerischen Akademie der Wissenschaften (zu München) 1860–70; . . . Philosophisch-philologische und Historische Klasse 1871–1923; . . . Philosophisch-historische Abteilung 1931ff; . . . Philosophisch-historische Klasse 1944ff

SBBerlAk/SPAW = Sitzungsberichte der Preussischen Akademie der Wissenschaften 1882–1921; Philosophisch-historische Klasse 1922ff; Sitzungsberichte der Deutschen Akademie der Wissenschaften (SDAW) 1948ff (several classes)

SBHeidAk/SHAW = Sitzungsberichte der Heidelberger Akademie der Wissenschaften, Philolosophisch-historische Klasse 1910–38; 1953ff

SBLDS = Society of Biblical Literature Dissertation Series

SBLeipzAk/SSAW = Sitzungsberichte der Sächsischen Akademie der Wissenschaften zu Leipzig, Philosophisch-historische Klasse 1962ff

SBLSBS = Society of Biblical Literature Sources for Biblical Study

SBLSP = Society of Biblical Literature Seminar Papers 1973ff

SBMünAk, s. SBBayAk

SBWienAk/SAWW/SÖAW = Sitzungsberichte der (Kaiserlichen) Akademie der Wissenschaften in Wien, Philosophisch-historische Klasse 1848ff; SÖAW: Sitzungsberichte der Österreichischen Akademie der Wissenschaften in Wien, Philosophisch-historische Klasse 1947ff

Schmid = WS., Der Atticismus in seinen Hauptvertretern, 5 vols. in 3, 1887–97

Schmidt, Joseph. = WS., De Flavii Iosephi elocutione: Jahrbücher für klass. Philol., Suppl. XX 1894, pp. 341–550

Schmidt, Syn. = JS., Synonymik der griechischen Sprache, 4 vols., 1876–86

SchTZ = Schweizerische Theologische Zeitschrift 1884–1920

Schürer = ES., The History of the Jewish People in the Age of Jesus Christ (175 BC–AD 135), a new and revised English version by GVermes/FMiller/MBlack/MGoodman of Geschichte des jüdischen Volkes[4] (3 vols. and index vol. 1901–11): 3 vols. in 4, 1973–87

Schweizer = ES., Grammatik der pergamenischen Inschriften 1898

Schwyzer = ES., Griechische Grammatik, 3 vols. 1950–53

SEÅ = Svensk Exegetisk Årsbok 1936ff

Sherk = RS., Roman Documents from the Greek East 1969

SJT/SJTh = Scottish Journal of Theology 1948ff

SÖAW, s. SBWienAk

Soph(ocles) Lex. = ES., Greek Lexicon of the Roman and Byzantine Periods (From BC 146 to AD 1100), corrected printing of 2d impression, 2 vols. 1887

Spicq = CS., Lexique théologique du Nouveau Testament[2] 1991; tr. JErnest, Theological Lexicon of the NT, 3 vols. 1994

Steinleitner = FS., Die Beicht im Zusammenhange mit der sakralen Rechtspflege in der Antike: Ein Beitrag zur näheren Kenntnis kleinasiatisch-orientalischer Kulte der Kaiserzeit 1913

StKr = Theologische Studien und Kritiken 1828ff

Straub = WS., Die Bildersprache des Apostels Paulus 1937

StTh = Studia Theologica, Internordisk tidskrift for teologi og religionsvidenskab (Lund) 1947ff

StThR(iga) = Studia Theologica (Riga) 1935ff

STZ = Schweizerische Theologische Zeitschrift 1884ff; s. TZS

Sv (at the end of entries) = HJSieben, Voces: Eine Bibliographie zu Wörtern und Begriffen aus der Patristik (1918–78), 1980

SvExÅrsb, s. SEÅ

SvTK = Svensk Teologisk Kvartalskrift 1925ff

SymbBU(ps)/SyBu = Symbolae Biblicae Upsalienses 1943ff (=Suppl. to SEÅ)

SymbOsl/SO = Symbolae Osloenses 1923ff (as Symbolae Arctoae 1922)

Syn. = KAland, Synopsis Quattuor Evangeliorum[13] 1988, cited by no. and line

TAPA/TPAPA = Transactions of the American Philological Association 1869ff

Taubenschlag = RT.

—, **Law**[2] = The Law of Greco-Roman Egypt in the Light of the Papyri[2] 1955

—, **OpMin** = Opera Minora I–II 1959.

TBl/ThBl = Theologische Blätter 1922–42

TGl = Theologie und Glaube 1908ff

Thackeray = HT., A Grammar of the OT in Greek according to the Septuagint, vol. I 1909

ThBl, s. TBl

TheolRev/ThRv = Theologische Revue 1902ff

TheolViat, s. ThViat

Thesaurus-Onomasticon = Thesaurus Linguae Latinae (TLL), Onomasticon II
ThGl, s. TGl
Threatte = LT., The Grammar of Attic Inscriptions I: Phonology 1980; II: Morphology 1996
ThStud, s. TSt
Thumb = AT., Die griechische Sprache im Zeitalter des Hellenismus 1901
ThViat = Theologia Viatorum, Jahrbuch der kirchlichen Hochschule Berlin 1948/49–1979/80
TLL = Thesaurus Linguae Latinae 1900ff
TLZ = Theologische Literaturzeitung 1876ff
TQ = Theologische Quartalschrift 1819ff
TRE = Theologische Realenzyklopädie, ed. GKrause/GMüller, et al. 1977ff
TRu = Theologische Rundschau 1879ff (var. ser.)
TS = Theological Studies 1940ff
TSt/ThSt = Theologische Studiën (Utrecht) 1883–1917 (then NThSt [q.v.] 1918–42)
TT = T(h)eologisch Tijdskrift 1867ff
TTK = Tidsskrift for Teologi og Kirke (Oslo) 1930ff
TU = Texte und Untersuchungen zur Geschichte der altchristlichen Literatur 1882ff (var. ser.)
TW = Theologisches Wörterbuch zum NT, ed. GKittel (d. 1948), GFriedrich 11 vols. 1933–79; tr. GWBromiley, Theological Dictionary of the NT I–IX 1964–74; index vol. RPitkin 1976 (cited only by roman numerals at the end of entries)
Twentieth Century NT = Twentieth Century New Testament 1900
TZ/ThZ = Theologische Zeitschrift (Basel) 1945ff
TZS/ThZS = Theologische Zeitschrift aus der Schweiz (=STZ after vol. 16, 1899)
Unknown Sayings = JJeremias, Unknown Sayings of Jesus, Eng. tr. RFuller 1957
UPZ = Urkunden der Ptolemäerzeit, ed. UWilcken I–II 1927–57
Ursing = UU., Studien zur griechischen Fabel; diss. Lund 1930
VD = Verbum Domini 1921ff
Verb. Dom., s. VD
VetusT = Vetus Testamentum 1951ff
VigChr = Vigiliae Christianae 1947ff
Vivre et Penser = RB 1941–44
Vorsokr. = Vorsokratiker, their fragments, ed. by HDiels, 5th ed. by WKranz 3 vols. 1934–37; 6th ed. 1951ff. The term Pre-Socratic(s) is used when no specific ref. is made to the German ed.
Wahl, Clavis = CAW., Clavis librorum VT apocryphorum philologica, 1853, bound w. JBBauer, Index verborum in libris pseudepigraphis usurpatorum, 1972
Warnecke, Romfahrt = HW., Die tatsächliche Romfahrt des Apostels Paulus 1987(?)
WBC = Word Biblical Commentary, general edd. DHubbard/GBarker 1982ff
Welles = CBWelles, Royal Correspondence in the Hellenistic Period 1934
Wendland = PW., Die hellenistisch-römische Kultur in ihren Beziehungen zu Judentum und Christentum: Die urchristlichen Literaturformen, 2d and 3d ed. 1912
Wet(t)stein = JJW., Novum Testamentum Graecum, 2 vols. 1751–52
White, LAL = JW., Light from Ancient Letters 1986
Wien(er)Stud = Wiener Studien 1879ff
Winer, Gramm. = GW., Grammatik des neutestamentlichen Sprachidioms[7] 1867
Wlh. = JWellhausen, Einleitung in die drei ersten Evangelien[2] 1911
W-S. = Winer, Gramm., 8th ed. by PSchmiedel 1894ff; cited by §§
WTJ = Westminster Theological Journal 1938ff
Wuthnow = HW., Die semitischen Menschennamen in griechischen Inschriften und Papyri des vorderen Orients 1930
Zahn = TZ.
—, AG. = Apostelgeschichte (commentary)
—, Einl. = Einleitung in das Neue Testament[3], 2 vols. 1906f; Eng. tr. 3 vols. repr. 1953
—, Forsch. = Forschungen zur Geschichte des neutestamentlichen Kanons 1881ff
—, GK. = Geschichte des neutestamentlichen Kanons I–II 1888–92
ZASA/ZÄS = Zeitschrift für ägyptische Sprache und Altertumskunde 1863ff
ZAszMyst/ZAM = Zeitschrift für Aszese und Mystik (1926–46); superseded by Geist und Leben (1947ff)
ZAW = Zeitschrift für die Alttestamentliche Wissenschaft 1881ff
ZDMG = Zeitschrift der Deutschen Morgenländischen Gesellschaft 1847ff
ZDPV = Zeitschrift des Deutschen Palästina-Vereins 1878ff
ZKG = Zeitschrift für Kirchengeschichte 1876ff
ZKT = Zeitschrift für katholische Theologie 1876ff
ZMRW = Zeitschrift für Missionskunde und Religionswissenschaft 1886–1939
ZNW = Zeitschrift für die neutestamentliche Wissenschaft 1900ff
Zohary = MZ.
—, Geobot. = Geobotanical Foundations of the Middle East 2 vols. 1973
—, Plants = Plants of the Bible: A Complete Handbook 1982
Zorell = FZ., Novi Testamenti Lexicon Graecum[2] 1931
ZPE = Zeitschrift für Papyrologie und Epigraphik 1967ff
ZSavRG/ZSRG = Zeitschrift der Savigny-Stiftung für Rechtsgeschichte 1880ff
ZST/ZSTh = Zeitschrift für systematische Theologie 1923ff
ZTK/ZThK = Zeitschrift für Theologie und Kirche 1891ff (var. ser.)
ZVS/ZVSF = Zeitschrift für vergleichende Sprachforschung auf dem Gebiete der indogermanischen Sprache 1852ff
Zwaan = Johannes de Z., Syntaxis der Wijzen en Tijden in het Grieksche Nieuwe Testament: E. W. Burton's 'Syntax of New Testament Moods and Tenses' voor het Nederlandsch Taaleigen bewerkt (note: incorporates papyrological data with other improvements) 1906
ZWT/ZWTh = Zeitschrift für Wissenschaftliche Theologie 1858ff

7. Sigla

+ when used at the beginning of entries indicates that the lexeme is found not only in the first document cited, but also in inscriptions, papyri, LXX (Septuagint), pseudepigrapha, Philo, Josephus, and one or more apologists. Occasionally the + is followed by a more complete listing because of special philological considerations.

Textual Sigla: These are for the most part used only in connection with very damaged texts, or when traditional restorations or supplements invite renewed examination. Note, e.g., the contrast between readings in AcPlBMM and POxy 1081.

α̣β̣, letters of which sufficient traces remain to print as text, but not to the exclusion of other possible readings
. . . . , letters missing, up to the number noted by the editor
- - - - , lost or illegible letters of an uncertain number
[α β], letters lost from document and restored by editor
α′ or α̅, letter stands for a numerical equivalent
|, marker of line division
//, marker of a duplicate document, as in some AcPlHa references
[[α β]], letter(s) which the scribe or corrector added
(α β), letters which fill out an abbreviation in the text
‹αβ›, letters omitted by scribe and added by editor (not to be confused with [αβ])
recto, the front of a writing sheet
verso, the back of a writing sheet

8. Composite List of Abbreviations (Except List 7, Sigla)

A = Codex Alexandrinus—List 2, beg.
Aa = Acta apostolorum apocrypha—List 5
AAWW = Anzeiger der Akademie der Wissenschaften in Wien, Philosophisch-historische Klasse—List 6
AB = Anchor Bible
ABA/AAWB = Abhandlungen der Berliner Akademie der Wissenschaften, Philosophisch-historische Klasse—List 6
ABayAW/ABAW = Abhandlungen der Bayerischen Akademie der Wissenschaften, Munich—List 6
abbr. = abbreviation
ABD = Anchor Bible Dictionary—List 6
Abel = FA., Grammaire du Grec biblique—List 6
Aberciusins. = Aberciusinschrift—List 3
abs. = absolute
abstr. (pro concreto) = abstractum pro concreto (abstract for the concrete)
AC = FDölger, Antike und Christentum—List 6
Ac = Acts of the Apostles—List 1
AcAnd = Acts of Andrew—List 5
AcAnd/Mt = Acts of Andrew and Matthew—List 5
acc. = accusative
acc. to = according to
Achilles Tat(ius), II AD—List 5
Achmes, Oneirocriton, c. 900 AD—List 5
AcJ = Acts of John—List 5
AcJ (Prochorus) = Acts of John, attributed to Prochorus—List 5
AcPh = Acts of Philip—List 5
AcPl Ant = Acts of Paul, PAntinoopolis 13—Lists 1, 4
AcPl BMM = Acts of Paul, as reconstructed in part from various papyri, Berlin and Michigan—List 1
AcPlCor = Acts of Paul: correspondence with Corinthians (a.k.a. Third Corinthians), text according to PBodmer X—List 1
AcPl Ha = Acts of Paul, PHamb—List 1
AcPl M1 = Acts of Paul, PMich 1317 and PBerlin 13893—List 1
AcPl M2 = Acts of Paul, PMich 3788—List 1
AcPlMart = Acts of Paul: Martyrdom—List 5
AcPl Ox 6 = Acts of Paul, POxy 6—List 1
AcPl Ox 1602 = Acts of Paul, POxy 1602—List 1
AcPlTh = Acts of Paul and Thecla—List 5
AcPt Ox 849 = Acts of Peter, POxy 849—List 1
AcPtPl = Acts of Peter and Paul—List 5
act. = active
Acta Alex. = Acta Alexandrinorum—List 5
Acta Pilati —List 5
AcThom = Acts of Thomas—List 5
ActNTUps, s. ASNU—List 6
AD = Anno Domini
add. = additional
adesp. = adespotum (author unknown)
adj. = adjective
ad loc. = ad locum (to or at the place under consideration)
admin. = administrative
adv. = adverb, adverbially
Aeg. = Aegyptus—List 6
Ael. Aristid. = Aelius Aristides, II AD—List 5
Ael. Dion. = Aelius Dionysius, II AD—List 5
Aelian(us), II AD—List 5
Aeneas Tact(icus), IV BC—List 5
Aeschin(es), IV BC; spurious letters II AD—List 5
Aeschrion, lyric poet, IV BC—List 5
Aeschyl(us), V BC—List 5
Aesop = a calque for a variety of lit. associated with the name of Aesop—List 5
Aëtius, med., VI AD—List 5
AG = Apostelgeschichte (in German titles relating to Acts)

Agatharchides, of Cnidus, II BC—List 5
Agathias, VI AD—List 5
AGG, s. GGAbh.—List 6
Agr = Agraphon (non-canonical sayings of Jesus)—List 1
AGWG, s. GGAbh.—List 6
AJA = American Journal of Archaeology—List 6
AJP = American Journal of Philology—List 6
AJSL = American Journal of Semitic Languages and Literature—List 6
AJT = American Journal of Theology—List 6
Ak. = Akademie
a.k.a. = alias, also known as
al. = alibi (elsewhere), aliter (otherwise), alii (others)
Albinus, II AD—List 5
Alcaeus, lyric poet, VII–VI BC—List 5
alchem. = alchemista, alchemist
Alcidamas, IV BC—List 5
Alciphr(on), c. 200 AD—List 5
Alcmaeonis, an epic title, VII BC—List 5
Alcman, VII BC—List 5
Alex(ander) Aphr(odisiensis), c. 200 AD—List 5
Alex. Ep. = Alexandri Epistolae, correspondence associated with Alexander the Great, date uncertain—List 5
Alexis Com(icus), IV/III BC—List 5
alt. = alternate expression, alternately
AM, s. MAI—List 6
Am = Amos—List 2
Amicitiae Corolla = JRHarris Festschrift—List 6
Ammonius, phil., V AD—List 5
Ammonius Gr(ammaticus), a.k.a. Ammonius Hist., of uncertain identity, I/II? AD—List 5
Amphis Com(icus), IV BC—List 5
Anacr(eon), VI BC—List 5
Anacreontea Carmina = poetry associated with the name of Anacreon, I?–VI AD—List 5
AnalBoll = Analecta Bollandiana—List 6
Analecta Biblica—List 6
Ananius, VI BC—List 5
Anaphora Pilati A—List 5
Anaxagoras (Phil.), V BC—List 5
Anaxandrides Com(icus), IV BC—List 5
Anaximander, phil., VII–VI BC—List 5
Andoc(ides), V–IV BC—List 5
Anecd(ota) Gr(aeca) —List 5
Anna Comn(ena), Alexias, 1148 AD—List 5
AnnBSA = Annual of the British School at Athens—List 6
anon. = anonymous
An. Ox. = Anecdota Graeca, ed. JCramer, fr. Oxford mss.—List 5
ANRW = Aufstieg und Niedergang der Römischen Welt—List 6
AntCl/AnCl = L'Antiquité classique—List 6
AnthLG = Anthologia Lyrica Graeca—List 5
Anth. Lyr. Gr., s. prec.—List 5
Anth(ologia) Pal(atina)—List 5
Anth(ologia) Plan(udea), included in Anth. Pal.—List 5
'Anti-Atticist' = ΑΝΤΙΑΤΤΙΚΙΣΤΗΣ, the title of a grammatical work in Anecd. Gr., date uncertain—List 5
Antig(onus of) Car(ystus), III BC—List 5
Antilegomena, non-canonical gospel and other sayings—List 5
Antipater of Tarsus, II BC—List 5
Antiphanes Com(icus), IV BC—List 5
Antiphon (the Orator) and Antiphon Soph. (the Sophist), both V BC—List 5
Anton(inus) Lib(eralis), II? AD—List 5
Anz = HA., Subsidia—List 6
aor. = aorist
APAPM = APA Philological Monographs—List 6
APAW = Abhandlungen der (Königlich) Preussischen Akademie der Wissenschaften zu Berlin, Philosophisch-historische Klasse 1901ff, s. ABA
Apc = Apocalypse, but Rv is used for the last book of NT
apc. = apocalypse
ApcEl = Apocalypse of Elijah—List 2
ApcEsdr = Apocalypse of Esdras—List 2
Apc4Esdr = Apocalypse of Fourth Esdras—List 2
ApcMos = Apocalypse of Moses—List 2
ApcPl = Apocalypse of Paul, date uncertain—List 5
ApcPt = Apocalypse of Peter—List 1
ApcPt Bodl. = Apocalypse of Peter, Bodleian—List 1
ApcPt Rainer = Rainer Fgm. of the Apocalypse of Peter—List 1
apcr. = apocryphal, apocryphon
ApcrEzk = Apocryphon Ezechiel—List 2
ApcSed = Apocalypse of Sedrach—List 2
ApcZeph = Apocalypse of Zephaniah (Sophonia)—List 2
APF = Archiv für Papyrusforschung—Lists 4, 6
Apollod. Com. = Apollodorus (of Carystus) Comicus, IV–III BC—List 5
Apollodorus of Athens, II BC—List 5
Apollon(ius) Dysc(olus), II AD—List 5
Apollon(ius) Paradox(ographus), II? BC—List 5
Apollon(ius) Rhod(ius), III BC—List 5
Apolog(ists)—Lists 1, 5
apolog. = apologist(s)
Apost(olic) Const(itutions), s. Const(itutiones) Apost(olorum)—List 5
Apostolius (Apostoles), Michael, XV AD—List 5
APOT = Apocrypha and Pseudepigrapha of the Old Testament—List 6
app. = appendix, apparatus (when ref. to marginal text-critical information, esp. in N.)
Appian, I–II AD—List 5
approx. = approximately
Apuleius, wr. in Latin, II AD—List 5
Aq(uila), II AD—List 5
Ar = Archaeologia—List 6
Ar. = Aristides, apologist, II AD—List 5
Arat(us) of Soli in Cilicia, IV–III BC—List 5
Arch. Abinn. = The Abinnaeus Archive—s. PAbinn, List 4
Ἀρχαιολογικὴ Ἐφημερίς—List 6
Archestr(atus), parod., IV BC—List 5
Archilochus Lyr(icus), VII BC—List 5
Archinus, ed. JGBaiter/HSauppe, Oratores Attici, after IV? BC—List 5
Aretaeus, II AD—List 5
Aristaen(etus), epistologr., V AD—List 5
Aristarch(us of) Sam(os), IV–III BC—List 5
Aristippus, Ep. = letters atttributed to the Socratic Aristippus, date uncertain—List 5
Aristobul(us Judaeus), II BC—List 5
Aristodem(us), hist. and gramm., II BC—List 5

Ariston of Ceos, III BC—List 5
Aristonous, III BC—List 5
Aristoph(anes Comicus), V–IV BC—List 5
Aristophon Com(icus), IV BC—List 5
Aristot(le), various works, IV BC—List 5
Aristoxenus, mus., IV BC—List 5
Armen. = Armenian
Arnott, Alexis = GArnott (ed.), Alexis Com.; s. Com.—List 5
Arrian = Flavius Arrianus, I–II AD—List 5
art. = article
Artapanus, II BC—List 5
Artem(idorus), onir., II AD—List 5
ARW = Archiv für Religionswissenschaft—List 6
ASAW, s. ASG(Leipz)
AscIs = Ascension of Isaiah—List 2
Asclepiodot(us), Tact(ica), I BC—List 5
ASG s. next entry
ASG(Leipz) = Abhandlungen der Sächsischen Gesellschaft der Wissenschaften, Leipzig—List 6
ASNU = Acta Seminarii Neotestamentici Upsaliensis—List 6
ASP = American Studies in Papyrology—Lists 4, 6
AssMos = Assumption of Moses—List 2
ASTI = Annual of the Swedish Theological Institute—List 6
astr., astrol. = astrological, astrologer
Astrampsychus (Magus), before IV BC; later works associated with his name, date uncertain—List 5
ASyn. = KAland, Synopsis Quattuor Evangeliorum[13]—Lists 1, 6
Ath. = Athenagoras, II AD—List 5
Athanasius of Alexandria, IV AD—List 5
Athen(aeus), III AD—List 5
Athen. Mitt., s. MAI
atl. = alttestamentlich(e) (relating to the OT)
ATR = Anglican Theological Review—List 6
Att. = Attic, esp. in ref. to dialect
attic. = atticista, atticist
attrib. = attribute, attributive
Atumano = Simon Atumano, tr. of OT into Gk., XIV AD—List 5
Audollent, Defix. Tab., s. IDefixAudollent—List 3
augm. = augment
B = Barnabas (the Letter of), II AD, except in series of uncial witnesses, in which case B refers to Codex Vaticanus (s. also Vat.). When the abbr. B would be ambiguous, Vat. is used for the codex.—List 1
B. = CDBuck, A Dictionary of Selected Synonyms—List 6
BA = Biblical Archaeologist—List 6
BAAR = WBauer, KAland, BAland, VReichmann, Wörterbuch zum NT—List 6
Babrius, c. 200 AD—List 5
Bacchylides, V BC—List 5
Baedeker = KB., Palästina u. Syrien—List 6
BAFCS = The Book of Acts in Its First Century Setting—List 6
BAR = Biblical Archaeology Review—List 6
Bar = Baruch—List 2
Basilica, imperial legislation, IX AD—List 5
Basilius of Caesarea, IV AD—List 5
BASOR = Bulletin of the American Schools of Oriental Research—List 6
BASP = Bulletin of the American Society of Papyrologists—Lists 4, 6
Bat. = PBatiffol, s. JosAs—List 5
Batr(achomyomachia), prob. not before I AD—List 5
BayAW, s. ABayAW
BC = before Christ
BCH = Bulletin de correspondance hellénique—List 6
B-D-F = FBlass, ADebrunner, RFunk, A Greek Grammar of the New Testament and Other Early Christian Literature—List 6
B-D-R = FBlass, ADebrunner, FRehkopf, Grammatik des neutestamentlichen Griechisch—List 6
Bechtel = FB., Die historischen Personennamen des griechischen bis zur Kaiserzeit—List 6
beg. = beginning
Beginn. = The Beginnings of Christianity, ed. FJFoakesJackson and KLake—List 6
Bel = Bel and the Dragon—List 2
Bengel =JB., Gnomon Novi Testamenti—List 6
Benndorf-Niemann = OB./GN., Reisen in Lykien und Karien, s. IAsMinLyk—List 3
Berl(iner) Klassikertexte, s. BKT—List 4
Berl. Kopt. Urk. = Koptische Urkunden, Berlin—List 6
Berosus, IV–III BC—List 5
BETL = Bibliotheca Ephemeridum Theologicarum Lovaniensium—List 6
betw. = between
Betz = HB.—List 6
—, Gal. = Galatians (Hermeneia)
—, SM = The Sermon on the Mount (Hermeneia)—List 6
Beyer, Syntax = KB., Semitische Syntax im NT—List 6
BFCT = Beiträge zur Förderung christlicher Theologie—List 6
BGU = Aegyptische Urkunden aus den Museen zu Berlin: Griechische Urkunden—List 4
BHHW = Biblisch-historisches Handwörterbuch—List 6
Bibel-Lexikon, ed. DSchenkel—List 6
Bibelwörterbuch = Kurzes Bibelw., ed. HGuthe—List 6
bibl. = biblical
Biblica (unabbr.)—List 6
bibliog. = bibliography
BiblSacra = Bibliotheca Sacra, A Theological Quarterly—List 6
Bihlmeyer = KB., Die Apostolischen Väter—List 6
Billerb. = (HLStrack and) PBillerbeck, Kommentar z. NT aus Talmud u. Midrasch—List 6
Biogr. = Βιογραφοι, Vitarum scriptores Gr. minores—List 5
Bion Bucol(icus), II BC—List 5
BIOSCS = Bulletin of the International Organization for Septuagint and Cognate Studies—List 6
BJRL = Bulletin of the John Rylands Library—List 6
BK = Bibel und Kirche—List 6
bk. = book
BKT = Berliner Klassikertexte—List 4
Black, Aramaic Approach = MB., An Aramaic Approach to the Gospels and the Acts—List 6
Bl-D. = FBlass/ADebrunner—List 6
BMI = Inscriptions of the British Museum, s. IBM—List 3
Bodm(er) = Bodmer Papyri—List 4
Boffo, Iscrizioni = LB., Iscrizioni greche e latine—List 3
Bogaert = RB., s. Epigraphica (III)—List 3
Boisacq = ÉB., Dictionnaire étymologique de la Langue Grecque—List 6
Boll = FB., Aus der Offenb. Johannis—List 6

—, Sternglaube = FBoll/CBezold/WGundel, Sternglaube und Sterndeutung—List 6
Bonner = CB., s. H (=Hermas)—List 1
Borger, GGA = RB., Göttingische Gelehrte Anzeigen—List 6
Bousset, Rel. = WB., D. Religion des Judentums im neutestamentlichen Zeitalter—List 6
Bov = JBover, ed. of the Greek NT—List 1, beg.
BPhW = Berliner Philologische Wochenschrift—List 6
BR = Biblical Research—List 6
Breccia, Iscr. = EB., Iscrizioni greche e latine; s. IAlexandriaMus—List 3
Breusing = AB., D. Nautik d. Alten—List 6
BRev = Bible Review—List 6
Brown, Death = RB., The Death of the Messiah—List 6
Bruce, Acts = FB., The Acts of the Apostles: Greek Text w. Introduction and Commentary—List 6
BS, s. Dssm., BS—List 6
BSA = Annual of the British School of Athens—List 6
BSac = Bibliotheca Sacra, s. BiblSacra—List 6
BSGLeipz = Berichte über die Verhandlungen der Sächsischen Gesellschaft der Wissenschaften, Leipzig—List 6
BT = Bible Translator—List 6
BTB = Biblical Theology Bulletin—List 6
Buc. Gr. = Bucoloci Graeci—List 5
Buck = CB.—List 6
—, Dialects = The Greek Dialects
—, Reverse Index = Reverse Index of Greek Nouns and Adjectives
bucol. = bucolicus, writer of pastoral lit.
Buhl = FB., Geographie v. Palästina—List 6
Bultmann = RB., in var. contexts—List 6
Burton, MT = EB., Syntax of the Moods and Tenses in New Testament Greek—List 6
Buttmann = AB., Grammatik des neutestamentlichen Sprachgebrauchs—List 6
Byz. = Byzantine, esp. in ref. to papyri
Byzantion, revue internationale—List 6
ByzZ = Byzantinische Zeitschrift—List 6
BZ = Biblische Zeitschrift—List 6
BZNW = Beihefte zur Zeitschr. für die neutestamentliche Wissenschaft—List 6
c. = circa (about), or capitulum (late Latin for chapter, used esp. in connection w. Aesop)
CAD = Chicago Assyrian Dictionary—List 6
Cadbury, Style = HC., The Style and Literary Method of Luke—List 6
Caecil(ius) Calac(tinus), I BC–I AD—List 5
CAG = Commentaria in Aristotelem Graeca—List 5
CALG = Collection des anciens alchimistes Grecs—List 5
Callim(achus), III BC—List 5
Callinus, VII BC—List 5
Callisth(enes), IV BC—List 5
Callixenus, Hist., III–II BC—List 5
Cant(icles) = SSol (Song of Solomon)—List 2
Carmina Pop(ularia), included in PMG—List 5
Cass(ius) Dio, II–III AD—List 5
Cat(alogus) Cod(icum) Astr(ologorum Graecorum)—List 5
CB, s. Ramsay, CB—Lists 3, 6
CBQ = Catholic Biblical Quarterly—List 6
CCD = Confraternity of Christian Doctrine, sponsors of The NT, Translated from the Latin Vulgate—List 6
CD = Cairo (Genizah text of the) Damascus (Document), a.k.a. Zadokite Document or Damascus Rule—List 2, end
Cebes, prominent in Platonic dialogues; ref. is to a dialogue associated with his name, I AD—List 5
Cecaumen(us), XI AD—List 5
Celsus, in Origen, Contra Celsum, II AD—List 5
Cephalion, II AD—List 5
Cercidas, III BC—List 5
CGFPR = Comicorum Graecorum fragmenta in papyris reperta; s. also Com(icorum) Graec(orum) Frag(menta)—Lists 4, 5
ch. = chapter(s)
1 Ch = 1 Chronicles—List 2
2 Ch = 2 Chronicles—List 2
Chaeremon (Historicus), I AD—List 5
Chantraine = PC.; s. DELG—List 6
Charax of Pergamum, II? AD—List 5
Chariton, scriptor eroticus (writer of romances) I–II AD—List 5
Charles = RC., Revelation (ICC); also used in connection with Test12Patr—Lists 2, 6
Charon (of Naucratis), after IV BC? BC—List 5
chem. = chemical
Chion, IV BC; for letters attributed to him, I AD, s. Ep.—List 5
Choerilus, V BC; s. Epici—List 5
Choix, s. IDelosChoix—List 3
Choniates, Niketas, Byz. hist. and theologian, d. 1217—List 5
ChQR, s. CQR
Christ. = Christian
ChronLind = Die Lindische Tempelchronik—List 3
Chron. Pasch. = Chronicon Paschale, VII AD—List 5
Chrysipp(us), phil., III BC—List 5
Chrysost. = Joannes Chrysostomus, IV–V AD—List 5
CIA = Corpus Inscriptionum Atticarum—List 3
CIG = Corpus Inscriptionum Graecarum—List 3
CIJ = Corpus Inscriptionum Iudaicarum—List 3
CIL = Corpus Inscriptionum Latinarum—List 3
CIMRM = Corpus Inscriptionum et Monumentorum Religionis Mithraicae—List 3
cj. = conjecture(d by)
1 Cl = 1 Clement—List 1
2 Cl = 2 Clement—List 1
ClAnt = Classical Antiquity—List 6
class. = classical
ClBull = Classical Bulletin—List 6
Cleanthes, IV–III BC—List 5
Clearch(us), phil., IV–III BC—List 5
Clem. Al. = Clement of Alexandria, II–III AD—List 5
Clemen = CC., Religionsgeschichtliche Erklärung des NT—List 6
Cleom(edes Astronomus), II AD—List 5
Cleopatra = conversations alleged between a queen Cleopatra and philosophers (alchemists), date uncertain—List 5
ClJ = Classical Journal (Chicago)—List 6
ClPh = Classical Philology—List 6
ClQ = Classical Quarterly—List 6
ClR = Classical Review—List 6
ClW = Classical Weekly—List 6
CMG = Corpus Medicorum Graecorum—List 5
CMRDM = Corpus Monumentorum Religionis Dei Menis—List 6

cod., codd. = codex, codices, usually with name of codex, as cod. A, B, Sin. etc.
Codex Iustin(ianus)—List 5
Col = Colossians—List 1
col. = column
coll. = collection, collected
Coll(ectanea) Alex(andrina)—List 5
colloq. = colloquial
Com. = Comicorum Atticorum fragmenta (TKock) and related collections of comedy fragments as noted in text; various dates—List 5
combin. = combination
Com(icorum) Graec(orum) Frag(menta)—List 5
comm. = commentary, -aries, commentator(s)
Commentaria in Aristot., s. CAG—List 5
comp. = comparative(ly)
Comp(aratio Menandri et Philistionis) date uncertain—List 5
ConcJour = Concordia Journal—List 6
concr. = concrete(ly), cp. abstr.
Congr. d'Hist. du Christ. = Congrès d'Histoire du Christianisme—List 6
conj. = conjunction
conjug. = conjugation
ConNeot = Coniectanea Neotestamentica—List 6
connot. = connotation
Constant(inus) Manasses, Byz. poet and hist., XII AD—List 5
Const(itutiones) Apost(olorum), IV AD—List 5
constr. = construction
Contemp(orary) Rev(iew)—List 6
contr. = contracted, -action
Copt. = Coptic
1 Cor = 1 Corinthians—List 1
2 Cor = 2 Corinthians—List 1
Corinna, s. AnthLG; V/III? BC—List 5
Cornutus, I AD—List 5
correl. = correlative(ly)
corresp. = corresponding(ly)
Cos(mas) and Dam(ian), IV AD—List 5
cp. = compare, freq. in ref. to citation fr. ancient texts
cpd. = compound
CPJ = Corpus Papyrorum Judaicarum—List 4
CPJ III Inscr = "The Jewish Inscriptions," CPJ III—List 3
CPR = Corpus Papyrorum Raineri—List 4
CQR = Church Quarterly Review—List 6
CRAI = Comptes-rendus de l'Academie des Inscriptions et Belles-lettres—Lists 3, 6
Crates, letters attributed to the poet-philosopher C.; date uncertain—List 5
Cratinus Com(icus), V BC—List 5
Cratinus Jun. = Cratinus the Younger, IV BC—List 5
Crinagoras, I BC–I AD—List 5
CRINT = Compendia Rerum Iudaicarum ad Novum Testamentum—List 6
Critias, s. Vorsokr.; V BC—List 5
Crönert = WC., Memoria Graecae Herculanensis—List 4
Crum, Copt. Ostr. = WC., Coptic Ostraca—List 4
CSHB = Corpus Scriptorum Historiae Byzantinae—Lists 5, 6
Ctesias, V–IV BC—List 5
CTM = Concordia Theological Monthly, then CTM; s. also CurTM—List 6
Cumont = FC., Die orientalische Religionen im römischen Heidentum—List 6
—, Lux Perpetua—List 6
CurTM = Currents in Theology and Mission—List 6
Cyprian, III AD—List 5
Cyr. Al. = Cyril of Alexandria, IV–V AD—List 5
Cyranides, a compilation relating to magical properties of stones, plants, and animals; perh. antedating I/II AD—List 5
Cyr. Ins. = Cyrene Inscription (Augustus)—List 3
Cyr. Scyth. = Cyril of Scythopolis, VI AD—List 5
D = Didache, except that in a list of manuscripts or as textual variant D refers to Codex Bezae—List 1
Da = Daniel—List 2
DACL = Dictionnaire d'Archéologie chrétienne et de Liturgie—List 6
Dalman = GD., various works—List 6
Damascius, Vita Isidori, V–VI AD—List 5
Damianus of Larissa, IV AD—List 5
Dana and Mantey = HD./JM., A Manual Grammar of the Greek NT—List 6
Danker, Benefactor = FD., Benefactor: Epigraphic Study—List 6
Daremberg-Saglio = CD./ES., Dictionnaire des antiquités grecques et romaines—List 6
dat. = dative
DBS = Dictionnaire de la Bible, Supplements—List 6
DDD = Dictionary of Deities and Demons in the Bible—List 6
def. = definition
DeJonge, Studies = MdeJonge, Studies on the Testaments of the Twelve Patriarchs—List 6
DELG = PChantraine, Dictionnaire étymologique de la langue grecque—List 6
Delph(ic) Orac(le)—Lists 5, 6
Demades, IV BC—List 5
Demetr(ius Iudaeus), III BC—List 5
Demetr(ius of) Phaler(on), IV–III BC—List 5
Demochares, IV–III BC—List 5
Democr(itus), phil., V/IV BC—List 5
demonstr. = demonstrative
Demophilus, gnom., II–III AD—List 5
Demosth(enes), IV BC—List 5
Denis = AD., Fragmenta pseudepigraphorum quae supersunt Graeca—Lists 2 beg., 5, 6
—, Conc. = Concordance grecque des pseudépigraphes d'ancien testament—List 6
Denniston = JD., The Greek Particles—List 6
denom. = denominative
dep. = deponent
deriv. = derived, -ation, -ative (fr.)
descr. = description (of inventoried papyrus)
desig. = designation
Dessau, s. ILS—List 3
deStrycker = ÉdeStrycker; s. GJs—List 1
Deutsche Theol., s. DTh—List 6
Dexippus of Athens, III AD—List 5
Dg = Letter of Diognetus, attributed to an unidentifiable apologist; II AD—List 1
DGE = Diccionario Griego-Español—List 6
Dialekt-Inschr., s. GDI—List 3
Dibelius, Geisterwelt = MD., D. Geisterw. im Glauben des Paulus—List 6

Dicaearchus, IV BC—List 5
Dict. d'Arch., s. DACL—List 6
Dict(ionnaire) de la Bible —List 6
Did. = Didymus Caecus (the Blind), commentator on OT books, IV AD—List 5
Didymus = Claudius Didymus Junior (Chalcenterus or Bronze-guts), gramm., I BC–I AD—List 5
Diehl, ed., s. AnthLG—List 5
difft. = different(ly)
Dig. Just. = Digest of Justinian, VI AD—List 5
dim. = diminutive
Dinarchus, orator, IV–III BC—List 5
Dio Cassius, s. Cass. Dio; II–III AD—List 5
Dio Chrys(ostom), I–II AD—List 5
Diocles of Carystus, med., IV BC—List 5
Diocles Com(icus), V BC—List 5
Diod(orus) S(iculus), I BC—List 5
Diogenes = letters attributed to the philosopher D. of Sinope; date uncertain—List 5
Diogenian(us) Epicureus, II? AD—List 5
Diog. L. = Diogenes Laertius, III AD—List 5
Diog. Oen. = Diogenes Oenoandensis, Epicurean phil., II AD or earlier—List 5
Dionys(ius) Areop(agita), pseud. of an author of theological works, V–VI AD—List 5
Dionys(ius) Byz(antius), c. 200 AD—List 5
Dionys(ius of) Hal(icarnassus), I BC—List 5
Dionys(ius) Perieg(eta), II AD—List 5
Dionys(ius) Soph(ista) = letters attributed to Dionys. Soph., VI AD—List 5
Diosc(orides), or Dioscurides, I AD physician, also Ps.-Dioscorides after I AD—List 5
Diphilus Com., IV–III BC—List 5
dir. = direct
diss. = dissertation
dist. = distinct, distinguished
Div. Thomas = Divus Thomas 1914–54; superseded by Freiburger Zeitschrift für Philosophie und Theologie 1954ff—List 6
Div. Thomas Piac. = Divus Thomas: Commentarium de philosophia et theologia (Piacenza)—List 6
D-K = HDiels/WKranz, s. Vorsokr.—List 6
DLNT = Dictionary of the Later NT and Its Developments—List 6
DNP = Der Neue Pauly—List 6
DocsAugTib = Documents Illustrating the Reigns of Augustus and Tiberius—Lists 3, 4
DocsGaius = Documents Illustrating the Principates of Gaius, Claudius, and Nero—List 3
DocsNerva = Documents Illustrating the Principates of Nerva, Trajan, and Hadrian—List 3
Dodd = CD., The Bible and the Greeks—List 6
Dositheus, gramm., noted for a bilingual work: Ars Grammatica, IV? AD—List 5
Doukas (Dukas), Byz. hist., XV AD—List 5
Doxogr(aphi) Gr(aeci), ed. HDiels; various dates—List 5
Doxopatres, Joannes, XI AD—List 5
Dssm. = ADeissmann, various works—List 6
Dt = Deuteronomy—List 2
DTh = Deutsche Theologie, Monatschrift—List 6
DTT = Dansk Teologisk Tidsskrift—List 6
dub. l. = dubia lectio (questionable rdg.)
EA, s. EpigrAnat—List 3
Ea = Evangelia apocrypha—List 5
Eccl = Ecclesiastes (Qoheleth)—List 2
eccl. = ecclesiastical
EcclRev = Ecclesiastical Review—List 6
ed. = edited (by), edition
edd. = editions, editors
EDNT = Exegetical Dictionary of the NT—List 6
ed. pr. = editio princeps (first publication)
Eg², s. PEg²—List 1
e.g. = exempli gratia (for example)
Ehrenberg-Jones = VE./AHMJ, Documents . . . Reigns of Augustus and Tiberius (DocsAugTib)—Lists 3, 4
Elbogen = IE., Der jüd. Gottesdienst—List 6
Ἑλληνικα: ἱστόρικον περιόδικον δημοσίευμα—List 6
ellipt. = elliptical(ly)
elsew. = elsewhere
emend. = emendation
Empedocles, V BC—List 5
En = I Enoch—List 2
EncBibl = Encyclopaedia Biblica—List 6
EncJud = Encyclopaedia Judaica—List 6
encl. = enclitic
EncRel = Encyclopedia of Religion—List 6
EncRelEth = Encyclopaedia of Religion and Ethics—List 6
Engl. = English
Eng. tr. = English translation
Enteux, s. PEnteux—List 4
Ep. = Epistola/Epistula, when applied to letters mostly pseudonymous—List 5
ep. = epistle
EpArist = Epistle of Aristeas, II BC—List 5
epex. = epexegetical
Eph = Ephesians—List 1
EphemEpigr = Ephemeris Epigraphica—Lists 3, 6
EphemeridesTL, s. ETL—List 6
Ephippus, hist., IV/III BC—List 5
Ephorus Cumaeus, hist., IV BC—List 5
Epic. = Epicus, of an epic poet, s. Epici
Epicharm(us Comicus), V BC—List 5
Epici = fragments of Greek epic, various editions; V BC—List 5
Epict(etus), various works, I–II AD—List 5
Epicurus, IV–III BC—List 5
Epicus = of an epic poet
EpigrAnat = Epigraphica Anatolica—List 3
Epigraphica (I, II, III) = epigraphic texts in series Textus Minores—List 3
Epigraphica (Riv) = Epigraphica: Rivista italiana di epigraphia—Lists 3, 6
Epigr. Gr., s. Kaibel—List 3
EpilMosq = Epilogus Mosquensis—List 1
Epimenides, VI BC—List 5
Epiph(anius), IV–V AD—List 5
Epiph(anius) Const(antiensis), IV–V AD—List 5
Epist. Apost. = Epistula Apostolorum, II AD—List 5
epistologr. = epistolographus, in ref. to ancient letter writers
EpJer = Epistle of Jeremiah—List 2
ÉPRO = Études préliminaires aux religions orientales dans l'empire romain—List 6
equiv. = equivalent

Eranos, Acta Philologica Suecana—List 6
Eratosth(enes), III BC—List 5
Erotian, I AD—List 5
Erotici (Scriptores)—List 5
eschat. = eschatological, eschatology
1 Esdr = 1 Esdras (apocryphal book)—List 2
2 Esdr = 2 Esdras—List 2
4 (6) Esdr = POxy 1010 (15:57–59)—List 2
esp. = especially
EstBíbl = Estudios Bíblicos—List 6
Esth = Esther—List 2
ET = Expository Times—List 6
et al. = et alii (and others)
eth. = ethics and related forms
Eth(ica) Epic(urea)—List 5
ETL = Ephemerides Theologicae Lovanienses—List 6
ÉTR = Études théologiques et religieuses—List 6
etym. = etymology, -ical
Etym(ologicum) Gud(ianum)—List 5
Etym(ologicum) Mag(num)—List 5
Euagrius Ponticus, s. Evagrius Ponticus; IV AD—List 5
Eubul(us) Com(icus), IV BC—List 5
Euhem(erus), IV–III BC—List 5
Eunap(ius), IV–V AD—List 5
euphem. = euphemism
Eupolem(us Judaeus) Hist(oricus) II BC; also Ps.-Eupolemus II? BC—List 5
Eupolis Com(icus), V BC—List 5
Eur(ipides), V BC—List 5
Eus. = Eusebius of Caesarea, various works; IV AD—List 5
Eus(ebius of) Alex(andria), or Ps.-Eusebius, VI? AD—List 5
Eustath(ius), XII AD—List 5
Eustath(ius) Macrembolites, or Eumathius, XI/XII AD—List 5
Eutecnius, date uncertain—List 5
Euthymius Zig(abenus), XII AD—List 5
Evagrius Pont(icus), IV AD—List 5
EvQ = Evangelical Quarterly—List 6
EvTh = Evangelische Theologie—List 6
EWNT = Exegetisches Wörterbuch zum NT, s. EDNT—List 6
Ex = Exodus—List 2
ex. = example
exc. = except
excl. = exclamation
Exp. = Expositor—List 6
expl. = explanation, explained
expr. = expression
ext. = extension
exx. = examples
Ezk = Ezekiel—List 2
Ezk. Trag. = Ezekiel the Tragedian, II BC—List 5
f = (and) following
FD = Fouilles de Delphes, III: Épigraphie—List 3
fem. = feminine
Ferguson = WF., The Legal Terms Common to the Macedonian Inscriptions and the NT—List 3
Festschr. = Festschrift, in ref. to any honorary publication
ff = (and) following
Fgm., fgm. = fragment, fragmentary
FGrH = FJacoby, Die Fragmente der griechischen Historiker—List 5
FHG = Fragmenta Historicorum Graecorum—List 5
Field = FF.—List 6
—, Hexapla = Origenis hexaplorum quae supersunt . . . fragmenta
—, Notes = Notes on the Translation of the NT
Filología Neotestamentaria—List 6
Fitzmyer = JF.
—Essays = Essays on the Semitic Background of the NT—List 6
—Oxy, s. Ox 1 in List 1 for details
f.l. = falsa lectio (spurious rdg.)
Fluchtaf. = Fluchtafel(n), s. IDefixAudollent and IDefixWünsch—List 3
fol. = folio
foll. = followed, following
foreg. = foregoing
Form(ae) Ep(istolicae), ed. VWeichert, date uncertain—List 5
FPhGr = Fragmenta Philosophorum Graecorum—List 5
fr. = from
freq. = frequent(ly)
Frisk = HF., Griechisches etymologisches Wörterbuch—List 6
FRLANT = Forschungen z. Rel. u. Lit. des A u. NT—List 6
func. = function(ing)
Funk, s. B-D-F—List 6
fut. = fut.
FX, s. IXanthos—List 3
FZPhT = Freiburger Zeitschrift für Philolosophie und Theologie—List 6
Gal = Galatians—List 1
Galen, II AD—List 5
  Inst. Log. = Institutio Logica
  Protr. = Protreptici quae supersunt
Gbh. = OvGebhardt, s. G-H-Z—List 1, beg.
GCS = Die griechischen christlichen Schriftsteller der ersten drei Jahrhunderte—Lists 5, 6
GDI = Sammlung der griechischen Dialekt-Inschriften—List 3
GEb = Gospel of the Ebionites—List 1
GEg = Gospel according to the Egyptians—List 1
Gen = Genesis—List 2
gen. = genitive
gener. = generally
geogr. = geographus, geographer
Geogr. Graec. Minor., s. GGM—List 5
Geopon(ica), a collection of older material, X AD—List 5
Georg(ius) Mon(achus), surnamed Hamartolus, IX AD—List 5
Georg(ius) Syncell(ius) = George the Synkellos ('cell-mate' of the patriarch Tarasios), VIII–IX AD—List 5
Ger. = German
GereformTT = Gereformeerd theologisch Tijdschrift—List 6
GGA = Göttingische Gelehrte Anzeigen—List 6
GGAbh = Abhandlungen der Gesellschaft der Wissenschaften zu Göttingen—List 6
GGM = Geographi Graeci Minores—List 5
GHb = Gospel according to the Hebrews—List 1
G-H-Z = Patrum Apostolicorum Opera, ed. OGebhardt/ AHarnack/TZahn—List 1, beg.
Gignac = FG., Grammar of Greek Papyri—Lists 4, 6
Gildersleeve, Syntax = BG./CMiller, Syntax of Classical Greek—List 6
Gingrich Festschr. = Festschrift to Honor F. Wilbur Gingrich—List 6
GJs = Gospel of James (Protevangelium Jacobi), II AD—List 1

Gk. = Greek
GkBar, s. GrBar—List 2
Glykas = Michael G., Annales, XII AD—List 5
GMary 463 = The Gospel of Mary (Magdalene), Roberts catalogue no. 463, II AD—List 1
GMary Ox 3525 = Gospel of Mary, POxy 3525, II AD—List 1
GNaass = Gospel of the Naassenes, II AD—List 1
GNicod(emus), s. Acta Pilati, Tdf.—List 5
gnom. = gnomologus, gnomologist (writer/collector of maxims)
Gnomon, periodical—List 6
Gnomon (BGU V), papyrus—List 4
GNT = The Greek NT (United Bible Societies)—Lists 1, beg.; 5
GNT-MT = The Greek NT according to the Majority Text—Lists 1, beg.; 5
Goodsp. = EGoodspeed; with no title specified, this abbr. refers to The New Testament: An American Translation—List 6
—, Apol. = Die ältesten Apologeten—List 5
—, Probs. = Problems of NT Translation—List 6
Goodwin = WG., Syntax of the Moods and Tenses of the Greek Verb—List 6
Gorgias of Leontini, V–IV BC—List 5
gov. = governed
GPt = Gospel of Peter—List 1
Grae(cus) Venet(us), s. Atumano; XIV AD—List 5
gramm. (after a personal name) = grammaticus, grammarian
Gramm. Gr. = Grammatici Graeci—List 5
GrBar = Greek Baruch (Apocalypsis Baruchi Graece)—List 2
Gregor(ius) Cypr(ius), XIII AD—List 5
Gregor(ius) Naz(ianzenus), IV AD—List 5
Gr-Rom. = Greco-Roman (gener. in contrast to Israelite/ Christian tradition)
GTh = Gospel of Thomas in Coptic or in Oxy. documents —List 1
GThGk = Gospel of Thomas in Greek (not pap.), date uncertain—List 5
Guarducci = Epigrafia greca, ed. MGuarducci—List 3
GVI = Griechische Vers-inschriften I: Die Grabepigramma —List 3
H = Hermas; cited, unless otherwise noted, according to MWhittaker; II AD—List 1
  m = Mandates
  s = Similitudes
  v = Visions
H. = FHort, s. W-H.—List 1, beg.
Hab = Habbakuk—List 2
Haenchen = EH., Commentary on Acts—List 6
Hahn = LH., Rom und Romanismus im griechischen-römischen Osten—List 6
Handwörterbuch des Bibl(ischen) Altertums —List 6
Hanno, Periplus, V/IV BC—List 5
Hansa, periodical—List 6
hapax leg. = hapax legomenon (occurring only once)
Harnack, Studien = AH., Studien zur Geschichte des Neuen Testaments—List 6
Harpocration, gramm./lexicographer, II AD—List 5
Harv. = WHarvey; s. Iren.—List 5
HastDAC = JHastings, Dictionary of the Apostolic Church—List 6
HastDB = JHastings, Dictionary of the Bible—List 6
HastDCG = JHastings, Dictionary of Christ and the Gospels—List 6
Hatch = WH.—List 3
Hatch and Redpath = EH./HR., A Concordance to the Septuagint and the Other Greek Versions of the OT—List 6
Hauser = KH., Grammatik der griechischen Inschriften Lykiens—List 3
Hb = Hebrews—List 1
Hb. = Hebrew
HDB, s. HastDB—List 6
Hdb. = Handbuch (in connection with a specific NT book, the ref. is to a commentary in the series Handbuch zum Neuen Testament, founded by HLietzmann)—List 6
Hdt. = Herodotus, V BC—List 5
HE/H.E. = Historia Ecclesiastica, used with Eusebius and Melito
Heath, Aristarchus = TH., Aristarchus of Samos—List 5
Heb. = Hebrew
Hebraist. = Hebraistically
Hecataeus (Abderita), IV–III BC—List 5
Hecataeus Mil(esius), VI–V BC—List 5
Helbing = RH.—List 6
Heliod(orus Eroticus), III? AD—List 5
Heliod(orus) Phil(osophus), date uncertain—List 5
Hellen. = Hellenistic. Not to be confused with the use of "Hellenic" as a national epithet.
Hell(enica) Oxy(rhynchia)—Lists 4, 5
Hemer, Acts = CH., The Book of Acts in the Setting of Hellenistic History—List 6
Hengel, Judaism = MH., Judaism and Hellenism—List 6
Henioch(us) Com(icus), s. Com.; IV BC—List 5
Hennecke-Schneemelcher (Wils.) = EH., New Testament Apocrypha, ed. WS., tr. RWilson—List 6
Henoch, s. En—List 2
Heph(aestion of Thebes,) Astr(ologus), IV AD—List 5
Her = Hermes, Zeitschrift für klassische Philologie—List 6
Heraclid(es Criticus/Creticus), perieg., III–II BC—List 5
Heraclid(es) Lembus, hist., II BC—List 5
Heraclid(es) Miles(ius), gramm., I/II AD—List 5
Heraclid(es) Pont(icus), phil., IV BC—List 5
Heraclit., Ep(istulae) = letters attributed to the philosopher Heraclitus, date uncertain—List 5
Heraclit. Sto. = Heraclitus the Stoic, I BC–I AD—List 5
Heraclitus, phil., V BC—List 5
Hermagoras (Minor), I/II AD—List 5
Hermagoras (Rhetor), I BC–I AD—List 5
Hermagoras Temnites, II BC—List 5
Hermas, s. H—List 1
Hermeneia = commentary series—List 6
Hermet., s. Herm. Wr.
Hermetica, s. Herm. Wr.
Hermippus Com(icus), V BC—List 5
Hermogenes Rhet(or), II–III AD—List 5
Herm. Wr. = Hermetic Writings—List 5
Hero Alex. = Hero(n) of Alexandria, I? BC/I AD—List 5
Herodas, a.k.a. Herondas, III BC—List 5
Herodian = Herodianus Historicus, III AD—List 5
Herodian(us) Gramm(aticus), II AD—List 5
Hes(iod), date uncertain, perh. before VI BC—List 5
Hesych(ius Lexicographus), V AD—List 5
Hesych(ius) Miles(ius) = Hesychius of Miletus, hist., VI AD—List 5

Hexapla, s. Orig(enes) II–III AD—List 5
Hg = Haggai—List 2
H. Gk. = Hellenistic Greek
HGM = Historici Graecae Minores—List 5
Hicks-Hill = EH./GH., A Manual of Greek Historical Inscriptions—List 3
Hierocles, Commentarius in aureum carmen, V AD—List 5
Himerius, IV AD—List 5
Hippiatr. = Corpus hippiatricorum Graecorum, IX AD—List 5
Hippocr(ates) = Corpus Hippocraticum, V–IV BC—List 5
Hippol(ytus), II–III AD—List 5
Hipponax, VI BC—List 5
Hist. (after a personal name) = historicus, historian
hist. = historian, historical
Hist. Gr. Min., s. HGM—List 5
Hist. Zeitschr. = Historische Zeitschrift—List 6
Hm = Hermas, Mandates—List 1
HNT = Handbuch zum Neuen Testament—List 6
Hobart = WH., Medical Language of St. Luke—List 6
Hollander-DeJonge = HH./MdeJ., The Testaments of the Twelve Patriarchs: A Commentary—List 6
Hom(er), VIII BC—List 5
Hom(eric) Hymns (Hymni Homerici), fr. VII BC—List 5
Horapollo, IV/V? AD—List 5
Horst = PvanderHorst, s. Ps.-Phocyl(ides)—List 5
Hos = Hosea—List 2
Hs = Hermas, Similitudes—List 1
HSCP = Harvard Studies in Classical Philology—List 6
HTR = Harvard Theological Review—List 6
HUCA = Hebrew Union College Annual—List 6
Hunt-Edgar = AH./CE., Select Papyri—List 4
Hv = Hermas, Visions—List 1
Hyperid(es), IV BC—List 5
hypoth. = hypothetical
I = Ignatius (always followed by abbr. of an epistle), I–II AD—List 1
IAlexandriaMus = Iscrizioni greche e latine (in the Museum of Alexandria)—List 3
Iambl(ichus), phil., III–IV AD—List 5
Iambl(ichus) Erot(icus), II AD—List 5
IAndrosIsis = Der Isishymnus von Andros und verwandte Texte—List 3
  Cyrene = text fr. Cyrene
  Ios = text fr. Ios
  Kyme = text fr. Kyme
  Mesomedes = Isis hymn of Mesomedes
IArsameia = inscription from Arsameia (on the river Nymphaios)—List 3
IAsMinLyk = inscriptions from Asia Minor: Lycia etc.—List 3
IAsMinSW = inscriptions fr. southwest Asia Minor—List 3
ibid. = ibidem (in the same book or passage)
IBildhauer = Inschriften griechischer Bildhauer—List 3
IBM = Ancient Greek Inscriptions in the British Museum—List 3
ICC = International Critical Commentary—List 6
ICypr = Cyprian Inscriptions—List 3
IDB = Interpreter's Dictionary of the Bible—List 6
IDefixAudollent = Defixionum tabellae, ed. AA.—List 3
IDefixWünsch = Antike Fluchtafeln, ed. RWünsch—List 3
IDelosChoix = Choix d'inscriptions de Délos—List 3
idem = the same (in ref. to the person just mentioned)
I.-E. Indo-European
i.e. = id est (that is)
IEgChr = Recueil des inscriptions grecques-chrétiennes d'Egypte—List 3
IEph = Ignatius to the Ephesians—List 1
IEphes = Die Inschriften von Ephesos—List 3
IG = Inscriptiones Graecae—List 3
IG² = Inscriptiones Graecae, ed. minor—List 3
IGA = Inscriptiones Graecae Aegypti—List 3
IGal = Exploration archéol. de la Galatie et de la Bithynie—List 3
IGDial = Inscriptiones graecae ad illustrandas dialectos selectae—List 3
IGerasaWelles = "The Inscriptions", ed. CWelles—List 3
IGLSyria = Inscriptions grecques et latines de la Syrie—List 3
Ign. = Ignatius; always simply I. when cited with one of his epistles
IGolanHeights = Jews, Pagans, and Christians in the Golan Heights: Greek and Other Inscriptions—List 3
IGR = Inscriptiones Graecae ad res Romanas pertinentes—List 3
IGUR = Inscriptiones Graecae Urbis Romae—List 3
IHierap, s. IHierapJ
IHierapJ = "Inschriften", ed. WJudeich, in Altertümer von Hierapolis—List 3
IJCT = International Journal of the Classical Tradition—List 6
IK = Inschriften griechischer Städte aus Kleinasien—List 3
IKosPH = The Inscriptions of Cos, ed. WPaton/EHicks—List 3
IKourion = The Inscriptions of Kourion—List 3
IKret = Inscriptiones Creticae—List 3
IKyme = Die Inschriften von Kyme—List 3
Il. = Iliad, s. Hom.—List 5
ILegesSacr = Leges Graecorum sacrae e titulis collectae—List 3
ILegGort = Leges Gortyniae—List 3
ill. = illustration
ILS = Inscriptiones Latinae Selectae—List 3
ILydiaKP = JKeil/AvPremerstein, Berichte über eine Reise in Lydien—List 3
IMagnMai = Die Inschriften von Magnesia am Mäander—List 3
IMagnSip = Die Inschriften von Magnesia am Sipylos—List 3
IMakedD = Ἡ Μακεδονία κ.τ.λ., ed. MDimitsas—List 3
IMaronIsis = Une nouvelle arétalogie d'Isis à Maronée—List 3
IMg = Ignatius to the Magnesians—List 1
imp. = imperial
impers. = impersonal(ly)
impf. = imperfect
impv. = imperative
incl. = including
ind. = index
indecl. = indeclinable
indef. = indefinite
indic. = indicative
indir. = indirect
IndogF = Indogermanische Forschungen—List 6
inf. = infinitive
infl. = influence(d)
Ins, ins = Inscription, Inschrift, inscription(s). Without a period, esp. in lists, as at the beginning of entries; the capitalized

form is used in titles. In conjunction with literary works this abbr. refers to the title or description of contents.
InsCos = The Inscriptions of Cos, s. IKosPH—List 3
Inscr. Gr. Sic. et It. = IG XIV—List 3
InsGal, s. IGal—List 3
Ins. gr., s. Michel—List 3
InsOenoand, s. IOenoandaDiog—List 3
Ins. of Sinuri = Inscription of Sinuri—List 3
InsSyr, s. ISyriaW—List 3
instr. = instrumental
Int = Interpretation—List 6
interpol. = interpolated
interpr. = interpreted, interpretation
interrog. = interrogative
intertest. = intertestamental (lit.), s. also pseudepigr. and List 2, beg.
intr. = intransitive
introd. = introduction
inv. = inventory (usually of numbers of papyri as inventoried)
IOenoandaDiog = Diogenes Oenoandensis, Fragmenta—List 3
Ion of Chios, V BC—List 5
IOSCS, s. BIOSCS
IPaidesEpit = Παῖδες ἄωροι—List 3
IPE, s. IPont Eux—List 3
IPergamon = Die Inschriften von Pergamon—List 3
IPhld = Ignatius to the Philadelphians—List 1
IPol = Ignatius to Polycarp—List 1
IPontEux = Inscriptiones antiquae orae septentrionalis Ponti Euxini Graecae et Latinae—List 3
IPriene = Die Inschriften von Priene—List 3
IReisenKN = Reisen in Kleinasien und Nordsyrien—List 3
Iren. = Irenaeus, Haereses, II AD—List 5
IRo = Ignatius to the Romans—List 1
irreg. = irregular
Is = Isaiah—List 2
Isaeus, V–IV BC—List 5
ISardGauthier = Nouvelles inscriptions de Sardes II, ed. PGauthier—List 3
ISardRobert = Nouvelles inscriptions de Sardes I, ed. LRobert—List 3
ISBE = International Standard Bible Encyclopedia, rev. ed.—List 6
Isid(orus) Pelus(iota), IV/V AD—List 5
Isishymnus von Andros, s. IAndrosIsis
ISm = Ignatius to the Smyrnaeans, I–II AD—List 1
ISmyrnaMcCabe = Smyrna Inscriptions, Texts and List, prepared by DMcCabe et al.—List 3
Isocr(ates), IV BC—List 5
Israelite/Christian = Israelite or Christian or both in contrast to Gr-Rom
Isyllus, III BC—List 5
ISyriaW = Inscriptions grecques et latines de la Syrie, ed. WWaddington, continuation of LBW—List 3
It. = Itala, early version of the NT in Latin
ITr = Ignatius to the Trallians—List 1
IXanthos = Fouilles de Xanthos VII—List 3
J = John (Gospel of)—List 1
1J = 1 John—List 1
2J = 2 John—List 1
3J = 3 John—List 1
JAC = Jahrbuch für Antike und Christentum—List 6
Jac. = Die Fragmente der griechischen Historiker, ed. FJacoby—Lists 5, 6
Jahrb. klass./class. Phil = Jahrbücher für classische Philologie—List 6
Jannaris = AJ., Historical Grammar—List 6
JAOS = Journal of the American Oriental Society—List 6
JB = Jerusalem Bible—List 6
JBL = Journal of Biblical Literature—List 6
Jc = Jacobus (James), s. Js
Jd = Jude—List 1
JDAI = Jahrbuch des deutschen archäologischen Instituts—List 6
Jdth = Judith—List 2
JEA = The Journal of Egyptian Archaeology—List 6
Jer = Jeremiah—List 2
Jeremias, Unknown Sayings, s. Unknown Sayings
JETS = Journal of the Evangelical Theological Society—List 6
JHS = Journal of Hellenic Studies—List 6
JJP = Journal of Juristic Papyrology—Lists 4, 6
JJS = Journal of Jewish Studies—List 6
JNES = Journal of Near Eastern Studies—List 6
Jo = Joel—List 2
Joannes Sar(dianus), VIII–IX (Rabe: X) AD—List 5
Job (Book of)—List 2
JÖAI = Jahreshefte des Österreichischen Archäologischen Institutes in Wien—List 6
Joh. = Johannine
Johannessohn = MJ.—List 6
—, Kasus = Der Gebrauch des Kasus in LXX
—, Präp. = Der Gebrauch der Präpositionen in LXX
Joly = Hermas, Le Pasteur; s. H—List 1
Jo. Lydus, s. Lydus—List 5
Jon = Jonah—List 2
Jo. Philopon. = Joannes Philoponus, VI AD—List 5
Jos. = Josephus. This abbr. used when followed by title; I AD—List 5
JosAs = Joseph and Aseneth—Lists 2, 5
Joseph(us) This abbr. used when no specific texts are cited (s. Jos.); I AD—List 5
Josh = Joshua—List 2
Jos. Lex. = A Lexicon to Josephus, incomplete—List 6
JournAsiat(ique) —List 6
JPh = Journal of Philology—List 6
JPOS = Journal of the Palestine-Oriental Society—List 6
JQR = Jewish Quarterly Review—List 6
JR = Journal of Religion—List 6
JRS = Journal of Roman Studies—List 6
Js = James—List 1
JSNT = Journal for the Study of the NT—List 6
JSOR = Journal of the Society of Oriental Research—List 6
JSS = Journal of Semitic Studies—List 6
JTS = Journal of Theological Studies—List 6
Jubilees = Book of J.—List 5
Judaicon = remnants of an early Judean/Christian gospel edition; s. list of passages in ASyn. p. 585—List 1
Judg = Judges—List 2
Jülicher, Gleichn. = AJ., D. Gleichnisreden Jesu—List 6
Julian (Imperator), various works; IV AD—List 5
Jur(istische) Pap(yri)—List 4
Just(in), II AD—List 5
Justinus, Nov. = Justinianus Imperator, Novellae, VI AD—List 5

Kaibel = Epigrammata Graeca ex Lapidibus Conlecta, ed. GK.—List 3
Kalt = EK., Biblisches Reallexikon—List 6
Keil-Premerstein = JK./AvP., s. ILydiaKP—List 3
KEK = Kritisch-exegetischer Kommentar über das NT—List 6
Kephal(aia) = Manichäische Handschriften der Staatlichen Museen Berlin, date uncertain—List 5
kgdm. = kingdom
KJV = King James version of the Bible—List 6
Kleopatra, s. Cleopatra; III AD—List 5
Kl. Pauly = Der Kleine Pauly: Lexikon der Antike—List 6
Kl. T. = Kleine Texte, ed. HLietzmann, also KAland—List 6
1 Km = 1 Kingdoms—List 2
2 Km = 2 Kingdoms—List 2
3 Km = 3 Kingdoms—List 2
4 Km = 4 Kingdoms—List 2
km. = kilometer
Kock, s. Com.—List 5
Kö. = AKörte, s. Menand.—List 5
Krüger = KK., Griechische Sprachlehre—List 6
κτλ. = καὶ τὰ λοῖπα (=etc.)
Kühner-Bl. and Kühner-G. = RK., Ausführliche Grammatik der griechischen Sprache[3]—List 6
Kuhring = WK., De praepositionum Graecarum in chartis Aegyptis usu quaestiones selectae—Lists 4, 6
Κυπρ. = Τα Κυπριακα, ed. ASakellarios—List 6
Kyraniden, s. Cyranides—List 5
L. = KLachmann, editor of the Greek NT (1842–50)—List 1, beg.
La = Lamentations—List 2
Lachmann = KLachmann. This abbreviation used when no other editors of the Gk. NT are mentioned.
LAE, s. Dssm., LO—List 6
Lampe = GL., ed., A Patristic Greek Lexicon—List 6
Larfeld = WL., Handbuch der griechischen Epigraphik—Lists 3, 6
Lat. = Latin
Lat. Vulg. = Latin Vulgate
Laud(atio) Therap(ontis), in LDeubner, De Incubatione, VII AD—List 5
Laum = BL., ed., Stiftungen in der griechischen und römischen Antike—List 6
LBW = PLeBas/WWaddington, edd., Inscriptions grecques et latines (nos. 1–1825)—List 3
l.c. = loco citato (in the place already cited)
Leipz. = Leipzig
Leo = Leonis imperatoris strategemata, V AD—List 5
Leonidas Tarent(inus), IV–III BC—List 5
Leontius (of Naples), Life of St. John the Merciful, VII AD—List 5
Les Lapidaires, s. Cyranides—List 5
Leutzsch, Hermas = MLeutzsch, Hirt des Hermas—List 1 (s. H)
Lev = Leviticus—List 2
Lex. Cantabr. = Lexicon Rhetoricum Cantabrigiense—List 5
LexGrMin = Lexica Graeca Minora—List 5
Lexicog(raphus) = lexicographer
LexThK = Lexikon für Theologie und Kirche—List 6
Lex. Vind. = Lexicon Vindobenense—List 5
LfgrE = Lexicon des frühgriechischen Epos—List 6
Lghtf. = JBLightfoot
LGPN = A Lexicon of Greek Personal Names—List 6
Libanius, IV AD—List 5
likew. = likewise
Lind. Tempelchr. = Die Lindische Tempelchronik, s. ChronLind—List 3
lit. = literal(ly); literature (ancient writing other than "documentary"; refererences to [scholarly] literature)
LJ = Logia Jesus, s. Ox 1 in List 1
Lk = Luke—List 1
ln. = line
LO = Licht vom Osten—s. Dssm., LO in List 6
loanw. = loanword
Lob. = CLobeck, s. Phryn.—List 5
loc. cit = loco citato (in the place already cited)
Longus, II? AD—List 5
L-P. = ELobel/DPage; s. AnthLG—List 5
L-S-J-M = (L-S-J) HLiddell/RScott, A Greek-English Lexicon; New Edition by HSJones/RMcKenzie—List 6
Ltzm. = HLietzmann, commentator and editor of various works
Ltzm. Pap. = HLietzmann, Griechische Papyri—List 4
Lucian, II AD—List 5
LXX = Septuaginta, ed. ARahlfs, unless otherwise specified—List 2, beg.
Lyc. = Lycian
Lycon, of Troas, III BC—List 5
Lycophron, trag., IV–III BC—List 5
Lycurgus, IV BC—List 5
Lydus = Joannes Laurentius Lydus, VI AD—List 5
  Mag. = De Magistratibus Populi Romani
  Men. = De Mensibus
Lyric. = lyricus, lyric poet
LyricPoets, s. AnthLG—List 5
Lysias, V–IV BC—List 5
Lysippus Com(icus), s. Com.; V BC—List 5
Lysis, V BC; for writings attributed to him, IV–II BC, s. Vorsokr. 46—List 5
M. = AMerk, ed. of Greek NT—List 1, beg.
m. = masculine
MAAR = Memoirs of the American Academy in Rome—List 6
1 Macc = 1 Maccabees—List 2
2 Macc = 2 Maccabees—List 2
3 Macc = 3 Maccabees—List 2
4 Macc = 4 Maccabees—List 2
Machon, III BC—List 5
Macrembolites, Eustathius, De Hysmenes et Hysmineae Amoribus, XI/XII AD—List 5
mag. = magic(al)
Magie = DM., De Romanorum . . . Vocabulis Sollemnibus etc.—List 6
MAI = Mitteilungen des Deutschen Archäologischen Instituts—Lists 3, 6
Mal = Malachi—List 2
Malalas = John Malalas, Chronographia, VI AD—List 5
Malherbe = AM., various works
MAMA = Monumenta Asiae Minoris Antiqua—List 3
Manetho, hist., III BC—List 5
Manetho Apot(elesmatica), astrol., IV? AD—List 5
M. Ant. = Marcus Aurelius Antoninus, II AD—List 5
Marc. Diac. = Marcus Diaconus, V AD—List 5

Marinus, Vi. Procli = Marinus the phil., Vita Procli, V AD—List 5
Marm(or) Par(ium)—List 3
Mart = Martyrium, martyrdom; of various saints (Carpus, Papylus, Agathonica), ed. HMusurillo, The Acts of the Christian Martyrs—List 5
MartAndrPrius = Martyrium Andreae I—List 5
MartIs = Martyrium Isaeae, s. AscIs in List 2
MartMt = Martyrium Matthaei—List 5
MartPl = Martyrium Pauli—List 5
MartPt = Martyrium Petri—List 5
MartPtPl = Martyrium Petri et Pauli—List 5
Μαρτύριον τῆς ἁγίας Αἰκατερίνας (martyrdom of St. Catherine), date uncertain—List 5
masc. = masculine
Mason = HMason, Greek Terms for Roman Institutions—List 6
Maspero, s. PCairMasp—List 4
Masson = EM., Recherches sur les plus anciens emprunts sémitiques en grec—List 6
Math(ematicus) = mathematician
Mausberger = AM., Polybios-Lexikon—List 6
Max(imus) Conf(essor), VI–VII AD—List 5
Maximus Tyr(ius), II AD—List 5
Mayser = EM., Grammatik der griechischen Papyri aus der Ptolemäerzeit—Lists 4, 6
M'Clintock-Strong = JM./JS., Cyclopaedia of Biblical, Theological, and Ecclesiastical Literature—List 6
M.D. = Doctor of Medicine
Mechan. = mechanicus, engineer
med. = medicus (medical writer), medical
Μέγα Λέξικον τῆς Ἑλληνικῆς Γλώσσης—List 6
Meineke = AM., ed. Fragmenta comicorum Graecorum—List 5
Meisterhans-Schw(yzer) = KM./ES., Grammatik der attischen Inschriften—Lists 3, 6
Mel. = Melito of Sardis, II AD—List 5
Mel(ici) chor(iambici)—List 5
mem. = memorial
Memnon (of Heracleon?), I BC–I? AD—List 5
Menand(er of Athens Comicus), various dramas cited; IV–III BC—List 5
Menand(er of) Ephes(us), hist., II BC—List 5
Menand(er) Protector, VI AD—List 5
Menand(er) Rhet(or), III/IV AD—List 5
Merk = AM., ed. Greek NT, s. M. in List 1
Mesomedes, hymns, II AD—List 5
metaph. = metaphor(ically)
Metrodorus Philos(ophus), IV–III BC—List 5
Metzger = BM., A Textual Commentary of the Greek NT—List 6
Meyer = EM., Ursprung und Anfänge des Christentums—List 6
Mft. = JMoffatt, The Bible, A New Translation—List 6
mg. = margin
Mi = Micah—List 2
Michel = CM., Recueil d'inscriptions grecques—List 3
Mich. Glykas, s. Glykas—List 5
mil. = military
Mimiambi, used of mimes written in a special iambic meter, s. Herodas—List 5
Mimnermus (Elegiacus), s. AnthLG; VII/VI BC—List 5
min. = minuscule
Minucius Felix, Marcus, Rom. lawyer and apologist, II/III AD—List 5
Mishnah = HDanby, The Mishnah—Lists 5, 6
Mitt-Wilck. = LMitteis/UWilcken, Grundzüge und Chrestomathie der Papyruskunde—Lists 4, 6
Mk = Mark—List 1
Mlt. = JMoulton; with page number alone specified, this abbr. refers to A Grammar of NT Greek I: Prolegomena—List 6
Mlt-H. = JMoulton, in turn WHoward, A Grammar of NT Greek II: Accidence and Word-formation—List 6
Mlt-Turner = JMoulton, in turn NTurner, A Grammar of NT Greek III: Syntax; IV: Style, by Turner—List 6
M-M = JMoulton/GMilligan, The Vocabulary of the Greek Testament—Lists 4, 6
mng(s). = meaning(s)
mod. = modern
Mod. Gk. = Modern Greek
Moeris, attic., II AD—List 5
Moffatt, s. Mft.—List 6
Molpis, II–I BC—List 5
Moore, Judaism = GFM., Judaism—List 6
Moschus, bucol., II BC—List 5
Moses, 8th Book of, alchem., date uncertain—Lists 4, 5
MPER = Mittheilungen aus der Sammlung der Papyrus Erzherzog Rainer—List 4
MPER N.S. = Mitteilungen aus der Papyrussammlung der Österreichischen Nationalbibliothek in Wien (Papyrus Erzherzog Rainer), n.s.—List 4
MPG = Migne, Patrologia Graeca—List 5
MPL = Migne, Patrologia Latina—List 5
MPol = Martyrdom of Polycarp; after II AD—List 1
ms(s). = manuscript(s)
MT = Masoretic Text
Mt = Matthew—List 1
Mu(llach) = WM., s. FPhGr—List 5
Muratori = Novus thesaurus veterum inscriptionum . . . collectore Ludovico Antonio Muratorio—List 3
Murray = JM. et al., A New English Dictionary on Historical Principles—List 6
mus. = musicus, writer on music
Musaeus, phil., date uncertain—List 5
Musaeus (Gramm.), Hero and Leander, V/VI AD—List 5
MusHelv = Museum Helveticum—List 6
Musonius (Rufus) = Gaius Musonius Rufus, I AD—List 5
Mussies = GM., The Morphology of Koine Greek—List 6
Musurillo, Ac. Chr. M. = HMusurillo, The Acts of the Christian Martyrs—List 5
myth. = mythographus, writer on myths/mythology
N. = Nestle/Aland, Novum Testamentum Graece, 27th ed. Other editions are indicated by a superscript—List 1, beg.
n. = neuter; note (in bibliographical references)
Na = Nahum—List 2
NAB = New American Bible—List 6
NABRev = New American Bible with Revised New Testament—List 6
Nachmanson = EN., Laute und Formen der Magnetischen Inschriften—Lists 3, 6
Nägeli = TN., Der Wortschatz des Apostels Paulus—List 6
Nauck = AN., s. TGF—List 5
NAWG, Ph. = Nachrichten der Akademie der Wissenschaften in Göttingen, Philosophisch-historische Klasse—List 6

NEB = New English Bible—List 6
nec. = necessary, -ily
NedTTs = Nederlands theologisch Tijdschrift—List 6
neg. = negative
Nehemiah, s. on 2 Esdr in List 2
Neophilol = Neophilologus—List 6
Neophron (Tragicus), V BC—List 5
Neot = Neotestamentica—List 6
Nepualius (or Neptunalius/Neptunianus) II? AD—List 5
Neugebauer-Hösen = ON./HvanH., Greek Horoscopes—Lists 3, 4
neut. = neuter (used when "n." would be ambiguous)
New Docs = New Documents Illustrating Early Christianity—Lists 3, 4
New Life = The New Life Testament—List 6
N.F. = Neue Folge (new series)
NGG = Nachrichten der Gesellschaft der Wissenschaften zu/in Göttingen, Philologisch-historische Klasse—List 6
Nicander (Colophonius Epicus/Historicus), III/II BC—List 5
Nicetas Eugen(ianus), XII AD—List 5
Nicol(aus) Com(icus), IV? BC—List 5
Nicol(aus) Dam(ascenus), I BC—List 5
Nicomachus Gerasenus, II AD—List 5
Nicostr(atus) Com(icus), IV BC—List 5
NJklA = Neue Jahrbücher für das klassische Altertum—List 6
NKZ = Neue Kirchliche Zeitschrift—List 6
Nock = AN., Essays on Religion and the Ancient World—List 6
non-bibl. Gk. = Greek usage outside biblical and related or eccl. lit.
non-bibl. wr. = all Gk. lit. outside writings within biblical tradition or related belief systems
non-lit. = non-literal, not literally
Nonnus, Dionys(iaca), IV/V AD—List 5
Norden, Agn. Th. = EN., Agnostos Theos—List 6
NorTT = Norsk Teologisk Tidsskrift—List 6
NouvChoix = Nouveau choix d'inscriptions grecques—List 3
NouvRT = Nouvelle revue théologique—List 6
NovT = Novum Testamentum (periodical)—List 6
n. pr. f. = nomen proprium femininum (feminine proper name)
n. pr. m. = nomen proprium masculinum (masculine proper name)
NRSV = New Revised Standard Version of the NT—List 6
n.s. = new series (also used to render Neue Folge)
NT = New Testament
NThSt = Nieuwe Theologische Studiën—List 6
NThT = Nieuw Theologisch Tijdschrift—List 6
NTS = New Testament Studies—List 6
Num = Numbers—List 2
num. = numeral
Numenius (of Apamea), II AD—List 5
Nymphis, IV–III BC—List 5
O. Amst = Ostraca in Amsterdam Collection—List 4
Ob = Obadiah—List 2
obj. = object, objective
O. Bodl = Greek Ostraca in the Bodleian Library at Oxford and Various Other Collections—List 4
occas. = occasionally
Ocellus (of) Luc(ania), II? BC—List 5
Od(yssey), s. Hom.; VIII? BC—List 5
Odes = the 14 Odes in Rahlfs, Septuaginta II, date uncertain—List 2
OdeSol = Gk. Ode of Solomon 11: PBodmer XI; III AD—List 2
OdesSol = Odes of Solomon, the Syriac corpus; I–II AD; s. OdeSol in List 2
OEANE = Oxford Encyclopedia of Archaeology in the Near East—List 6
OED = Oxford English Dictionary—List 6
ÖJh, s. JÖAI—List 6
Oenomaus (Cynicus), II AD—List 5
O. Fay = Ostraca Fayum—List 4
oft. = often
OGI = Orientis Graeci Inscriptiones Selectae—List 3
O. Joach = Die Prinz-Joachim Ostraka—List 4
OLD = Oxford Latin Dictionary—List 6
Olsson = BO., Papyrusbriefe aus d. frühen Römerzeit—List 4
Olympiodor(us), VI AD—List 5
OLZ = Orientalische Literaturzeitung—List 6
om. = omits, omitted in
onir. = onirocriticus, one versed in dreams and their interpretation
Onosander (Onasander), I AD—List 5
op. cit. = opere citato (in the work already cited)
opp. = opposed to, opposite
Oppian (of Apamea), s. Ps.-Oppian, II–III AD—List 5
opt. = optative
Or(atores) Att(ici)—List 5
Oribasius, IV AD—List 5
Orientalia Christiana—List 6
orig. = original(ly)
Orig(enes), var. works, II–III AD—List 5
Orph. = Orphica—List 5
Orph. Hymns = Orphic Hymns, s. Orph.
Or. Sib. = Oracula Sibyllina, s. SibOr—List 5
ostr. = ostraca
OT = Old Testament
Otero = AdeSantosO., Los Evangelios Apocrifos—List 5
O. Theb = Theban Ostraca—List 4
otherw. = otherwise
O. Wilck = UWilcken, ed., Griechische Ostraka aus Aegypten und Nubien—List 4
Ox = POxy, but refers to fragments of documents esp. relating to the lexical data base—List 1
OxfT = Oxford Text
P freqently = Papyrus, and is readily identifiable in connection with abbreviations that are included in List 4
P^{66} = Papyrus Bodmer II—List 1
P^{72} = Papyrus Bodmer VII–IX—List 1
P^{74} = Papyrus Bodmer XVII—List 1
P^{75} = Papyrus Bodmer XIV, XV, s. List 1
p. = page
PAberd = Catalogue of Greek and Latin Papyri and Ostraca in the Possession of the University of Aberdeen—List 4
PAbinn = The Abinnaeus Archive—List 4
PAchm = Les Papyrus grecs d'Achmîm—List 4
PAdl = The Adler Papyri, Greek texts—List 4
Page = DP., s. AnthLG—List 5
Palaeph(atus Mythographus), date uncertain—List 5
Palladius, Historia Lausiaca, IV–V AD—List 5
PAmh = The Amherst Papyri I–II—List 4

PAmulett = Ein christliches Amulett auf Papyrus—List 4
PAnt = The Antinoopolis Papyri I–III—List 4
pap = papyrus, -yri
Pape-Benseler = WP./FB., Wörterbuch der griechischen Eigennamen—List 6
PapHeid I = Die Septuaginta-Papyri und andere alttestamentliche Texte der Heidelberger Papyrussammlung—List 4
Papias, early Christian writer, II AD—List 1
Papyrus de Magdôla—List 4
par. = parallel
paradoxogr. = paradoxographus, writer on marvels
Παραδοξόγραφοι, writers on marvels—List 5
Paradoxogr(aphus) Flor(entinus), anon. compiler of marvels, II? AD—List 5
Paradoxogr(aphus) Vat(icanus), anon. compiler of marvels, II? AD—List 5
ParJer = Paraleipomena Jeremiou, II? AD—List 2
Parmenides, Pre-Socratic, VI–V BC—List 5
parod. = parodus, parodist
Paroem. Gr. = Paroemiographi Graeci—List 5
paroemiogr. = paroemiographus, writer/collector of proverbs or maxims
Parthenius, I BC—List 5
partic. = particular(ly)
PASA = Papers of the American School of Classical Studies at Athens—List 6
pass. = passive (either of grammatical form or of passive experience); also used in reference to literary portion = passage
Passow = FP., Handwörterbuch der griech. Sprache, var. edd.—List 6
PassPtPl = Passio Petri et Pauli; s. MartPtPl—List 5
Pass. Scilit. = Passio Scilitanorum, II AD—List 5
PAthen = Papyri Societatis Archaeologicae Atheniensis—List 4
patr. = patristic, patristic writings
PatrOr = Patrologia Orientalis—List 6
Paul. = Pauline
Paul(us) Aeg(ineta), med., VII AD—List 5
Pauly-W(issowa) = AP./GW., Real-Encyclopädie der klassischen Altertumswissenschaft—List 6
Paus(anias), perieg., II AD—List 5
Paus(anias) Attic(ist), s. Ael. Dion.; II AD—List 5
PBabatha, s. PYadin—List 4
PBad = Veröffentlichungen aus der badischen Papyrussammlungen—List 4
PBas = Papyrusurkunden der öffentlichen Bibliothek der Universität zu Basel—List 4
PBeatty = The Chester Beatty Biblical Papyri—List 4
PBerlin 5025 = PGM 1—List 4
PBerlin 5026 = PGM 2—List 4
PBerlin 11710—List 4
PBerlZill = Vierzehn Berliner griechische Papyri, ed. HZilliacus—List 4
PBilabel = FBilabel, ed., Die kleineren Historikerfragmente auf Papyrus—List 4
PBodm = Papyrus Bodmer, s. also P^{66}; P^{72}; P^{74}; P^{75}—List 1
PBon = Papyri Bononienses—List 4
PBour = Les Papyrus Bouriant—List 4
PBrem = Die Bremer Papyri—List 4
PCairCat = Greek Papyri, Catalogue général des antiquités égyptiennes du Musée du Caire, nos. 10001–10869—List 4
PCairGoodsp = EJGoodspeed, ed., Greek Papyri from the Cairo Museum—List 4
PCairIsid = The Archive of Aurelius Isidorus in the Egyptian Museum, Cairo, and the University of Michigan—List 4
PCairMasp = JMaspero, Papyrus grecs d'époque byzantine—List 4
PCairPreis = Griechische Urkunden des Ägyptischen Museums zu Cairo, ed. FPreisigke—List 4
PCairZen = Zenon Papyri, Catalogue général . . . du Musée du Caire—List 4
PCatt = Papyrus Cattaoui—List 4
PChBeatty = Chester Beatty Biblical Papyri—List 4
PChic = Chicago Literary Papyri—List 4
PCol 123 = Columbia Papyri VI: Apokrimata—List 4
PCollYoutie = Collectanea Papyrologica: Texts Published in Honor of HCYoutie—List 4
PColZen = Columbia Papyri III, IV: Zenon Papyri—List 4
PCorn = Greek Papyri in the Library of Cornell University—List 4
PDidot, cited in FSandbach, Menandri Reliquiae Selectae; s. Menand.—List 5
PECS = Princeton Encyclopedia of Classical Sites—List 6
pecul. = peculiar
PEdfou = papyri relating to Tell Edfou—List 4
PEdg(ar) = CE., Selected Papyri—List 4
PEF = Palestine Exploration Fund—List 6
PEg² = Papyrus Egerton No. 2—List 1
PEleph = Elephantine-Papyri—List 4
Pel.-Leg. = Legenden der heiligen Pelagia, V? AD—List 5
PEnteux = Papyrus Enteuxeis—List 4
per. = period
Per. et Felic. = Perpetua and Felicity, III AD—List 5
perf. = perfect
perh. = perhaps
perieg. = periegeta, traveler/writer of travels
Peripl(us Maris) Eryth(raei), after II AD—List 5
Periplus Maris Magni, s. Stadiasmus—List 5
Περὶ ὕψους (De Sublimitate), attributed to Longinus, I AD—List 5
PErl = Die Papyri der Universitätsbibliothek Erlangen—List 4
pers. = person(s)
personif. = personified
pert. = pertaining (to)
Petosiris (and Nechepso) = astrolog. writings attributed to P. and N.: collection of fragments; before II BC—List 5
pf. = perfect
PFamTeb = A Family Archive from Tebtunis—List 4
PFay = Fayûm Towns and Their Papyri—List 4
PFlor = Papiri Fiorentini—List 4
PFouad = Les Papyrus Fouad I—List 4
PFrankf = Griechische Papyri aus . . . Frankfurt—List 4
PFreib = Mitteilungen aus der Freiburger Papyrussammlung—List 4
PFuad I Univ = Fuad I University Papyri—List 4
Pfuhl-Möbius = EP./HM., Die ostgriechischen Grabreliefs—List 3
PGen = Les Papyrus de Genève—List 4
PGenLat = Papyrus latin de Genève no. 1—List 4
PGiss = Griechische Papyri . . . zu Giessen—List 4

PGissUniv = Mitteilungen aus der Papyrussammlung der Giessener Universitätsbibliothek—List 4
PGM = Papyri Graecae Magicae—List 4
PGoodspCair, s. PCairGoodsp—List 4
PGot = Papyrus grecs de la Bibliothèque municipale de Gothembourg—List 4
PGR = Paradoxographorum Graecorum Reliquiae—List 5
PGrad = Griechische Papyri der Sammlung Gradenwitz—List 4
PGrenf I = BGrenfell, An Alexandrian Erotic Fragment, etc.—List 4
PGrenf II = BGrenfell/AHunt, New Classical Fragments—List 4
PGron = Papyri Groninganae—List 4
PGronAmst 1 and 2 = the two Amsterdam papyri in PGron—List 4
PGurob = Greek Papyri from Gurob—List 4
PHal = Dikaiomata: in a papyrus published by the Graeca Halensis—List 4
Phalaris, tyrant of Acragas (VI BC), in whose name letters were written centuries later, II? AD—List 5
PHamb = Griechische Papyrusurkunden der Hamburger Staats- und Universitätsbibliothek—List 4
PHarr = The Rendell Harris Papyri of Woodbrooke College—List 4
PHeid = PHeid III
PHeid III = Griechische Papyrusurkunden und Ostraka der Heidelberger Papyrussammlung—List 4
PHercul 182 = Papyrus from Herculaneum no. 182—List 4
Pherecr(ates Comicus), s. Com.; V BC—List 5
Pherecyd. = Pherecydes of Syros, VI BC—List 5
Pherecydes of Athens, V BC—List 5
PHerm = Papyri from Hermopolis and Other Documents of the Byzantine Period—List 4
PHermWess = Corpus Papyrorum Hermopolitanorum . . . ed. CWessely—List 4
PHib = The Hibeh Papyri I–II—List 4
Phil = Philippians—List 1
phil. = philosophus, philosopher
Phileas = Papyrus Bodmer XX: Apologie de Philéas—Lists 4, 5
Philemon Com(icus), IV–III BC (a few of the verses included here belong to Comp., q.v.)—List 5
Philistion, composer of mimes, I AD—List 5
Philistion Med(icus) = P. of Locri, s. Diocles; V–IV BC—List 5
Philo = P. of Alexandria, I BC–I AD—List 5
Philo Bybl. = P. of Byblos, hist., c. 100 AD—List 5
Philochorus, IV–III BC—List 5
Philod(emus), I BC—List 5
Philod. Herc., s. Philod.
Philol(ogus), Zeitschrift für das klassische Altertum—List 6
PhilolWoch = Philologische Wochenschrift—List 6
Philo Mech(anicus), III–II BC—List 5
Philopon. = Joannes Philoponus, commentator on Aristotle, VI AD—List 5
Philosoph(ical) Max(ims) fr. var. sources, in FPhGr I—List 5
Philostorg(ius), V AD—List 5
Philostrat(us) = Flavius Philostratus, the Sophist II–III AD—List 5
Philostrat(us) Jun(ior) = Philostratus the Younger, Imagines, III AD—List 5
Philumen(us), II AD—List 5
Phlegon, II AD—List 5
Phlm = Philemon (Letter to)—List 1
Phoenicides Com(icus), s. Com.; III BC—List 5
Phoenix (of) Col(ophon), III BC—List 5
PHolm = Papyrus Graecus Holmiensis—List 4
Phot(ius), IX AD—List 5
phr. = phrase
Phryn(ichus), the Atticist, signifying his Eclogae, II AD—List 5
—, Praep. Soph. = Praeparatio Sophistica
Physiogn. = Scriptores Physiognomici—List 5
PIand = Papyri Iandanae—List 4
Pind(ar), V BC—List 5
Pirke (Pirque) Aboth, Mishnah (q.v.) 446–61, date uncertain—List 5
PJ = Preussische Jahrbücher—List 6
Pj = Palästinajahrbuch—List 6
PJena = Jenäer Papyrus-Urkunden; fragments of Irenaeus 5 in HLietzmann, Kleine Schriften—List 4
PJews, s. PLondon 1912—List 4
PKöln = Köllner Papyri—List 4
PKöln VI, 245 = Ptocheia or Odysseus in Disguise at Troy—List 4
PKroll = Eine Ptolemäische Königsurkunde (Papyrus Kroll)—List 4
pl. = plural
Pla(to), V–IV BC; s. also Ps.-Plato—List 5
Pla(to) Com(icus), V–IV BC—List 5
PLaur = Dai Papiri della Biblioteca Medicea Laurenziana —List 4
PLeid = Papyri Graeci Musei Antiquarii Publici Lugduni-Batavi—List 4
Pleket = HP., Epigraphica (II)—List 3
PLille = Papyrus grecs de Lille—List 4
Pliny the Elder (NH=Naturalis Historia), I AD—List 5
Pliny the Younger (Letters), I–II AD—List 5
PLips = Griech. Urkunden der Papyrussammlung zu Leipzig—List 4
PLond = PLondon = Greek Papyri in the British Museum—List 4
PLond 1912 = Letter of Claudius to the Alexandrians—List 4
PLond 1913–1917 = PLondon nos. 1913–1917 relating to the Meletian Schism—List 4
Plotinus, III AD—List 5
plpf. = pluperfect
Pls. = Paulus (Paul, in German titles)
PLund = Aus der Papyrussammlung der Universitätsbibliothek in Lund—List 4
Plut(arch), I–II AD—List 5
PM = Protestantische Monatshefte—List 6
PMagd = Papyrus de Magdôla—List 4
PMert = A Descriptive Catalogue of the Greek Papyri in the Collection of Wilford Merton—List 4
PMeyer = Papyrus edited by PM.: Griechische Texte aus Ägypten—List 4
PMG = Poetae Melici Graeci—List 5
PMGF = Poetarum Melicorum Graecorum Fragmenta—List 5
PMich = Michigan Papyri—List 4
PMich 1317 = Michigan Papyri inv. 1317—List 4
PMichael = Papyri Michaelidae, a collection by GAMichaïlidis of Cairo—List 4

PMichZen = Zenon Papyri in the Univ. of Michigan Collection—List 4
PMilVogl = Papiri della Università degli Studie Milano, ed. AVogliano—List 4
PMimaut = PGM no. 3 = papyrus inventory (Louvre) no. 2391, named after JMimaut—List 4
PMonac = Byzantinische Papyri (Munich)—List 4
Poeta de Herbis = an anonymous poet, author of Carmina de viribus herbarum—List 5
Poetae Melici Graeci, s. AnthLG—List 5
Poet. Eleg. = Poetae Elegiaci—List 5
Poet. Philos. = Poetarum Philosophorum fragmenta—List 5
Pol = Polycarp to the Philippians—List 1
Poland = FP., Geschichte des griechischen Vereinswesen—List 6
Polemo/Polemon Soph(ista), I–II AD (time of Trajan)—List 5
Pollux, II AD—List 5
Polyaen(us Rhetor), II AD—List 5
Polyb(ius), III–II BC—List 5
Polycrates, hist., before I BC—List 5
Polystrat(us Epicureus), III–II BC—List 5
polyth. = polytheist, polytheism, polytheistic
Porph(yry), phil., III AD—List 5
pos. = positive
Posidippus Com(icus), s. Com.; III BC—List 5
Posidippus, Epigrams, III BC—List 5
Posidon(ius Apamensis), II–I BC—List 5
POslo = Papyri Osloenses—List 4
poss. = possible
possess. = possessive
POxf = Some Oxford Papyri—List 4
POxy = Oxyrhynchus Papyri—List 4
POxyHels = Fifty Oxyrhynchus Papyri (Helsinki)—List 4
pp. = pages
PParis = Notices et textes des papyrus (Paris)—List 4
PPetr = The Flinders Petrie Papyri—List 4
PPrinc = Papyri in the Princeton University Collections—List 4
Pr = Proverbs—List 2
PRainer = Papyrus Rainer (Archduke of Austria), s. CPR—List 4
prec. = preceding
pred. = predicate
predom. = predominant(ly)
pref. = prefix
PRein I = Papyrus Reinach I—List 4
PRein II = Papyrus Reinach II—List 4
Preis. = FPreisigke, Wörterbuch der griech. Papyrusurkunden—Lists 4, 6
Preisigke = FP.—Lists 4, 6
—, Fachwörter
—, Namenbuch
—, Sb. = Sammelbuch griechischer Urkunden aus Aegypten, begun by FP.
—, Wörterbuch = Preis.
prep. = preposition(al)
Pre-Soc. = Pre-Socratics, s. Vorsokr(atiker)—List 5
pres. = present
Preuschen, Antilegomena = EP., Antilegomena; s. Antilegomena in List 5
PRev = Revenue Laws of Ptolemy Philadelphus—List 4
prim. = primarily
priv. = privativum (in grammar: privative, w. negating force)
PrJ, s. PJ
prob. = probable, probably
ProBib = Protokolle zur Bibel—List 6
Prochorus, s. AcJ (Prochorus)—List 5
Proclus (Diadochus): his work, (Institutio) Theol(ogica)=Στοιχείωσις θεολογική, V AD—List 5
Procop(ius) Gaz(aeus), s. Procop. Soph., V–VI AD—List 5
Procop(ius) Hist., VI AD—List 5
Procop(ius) Soph(ista), a.k.a. Procopius Gazaeus, V–VI AD—List 5
ProcXVIIICongPap = Proceedings of the 18th International Congress of Papyrologists—List 4
ProcXXCongPap = Proceedings of the 20th International Congress of Papyrologists—List 4
Prodicus, V–IV BC—List 5
prol. = prologus (prolog, prologue)
Proleg(omenon) Syllog(e), date uncertain—List 5
pron. = pronoun
prop. = properly
PRossGeorg = Papyri russischer und georgischer Sammlungen—List 4
Protagoras, V BC—List 5
Prott-Ziehen, s. ILegesSacr—List 3
prov. = proverbial(ly)
Prümm = KP., Religionsgeschichtliches Handbuch für den Raum der altchristlichen Umwelt—List 6
PRyl = Catalogue of the Greek Papyri in the John Rylands Library—List 4
Ps = (Book of) Psalms—List 2
Ps. = pseudo, pseudonymous
Ps.-Aeschin(es), s. Aeschines—List 5
Psaltes, Grammatik = SP., Grammatik der Byzantinischen Chroniken—List 6
Ps.-Apollod(orus), myth., I/II AD—List 5
Ps.-Aristot(le), s. Aristot.—List 5
Ps.-Caesarius (of Nazianzus), VI AD—List 5
Ps.-Callisth(enes), Historia Alexandri Magni, II–III? AD—List 5
Ps.-Clem(ens), Hom(iliae), III AD—List 5
Ps.-Crates, letters attributed to the poet-philosopher C. (IV–III BC), date uncertain—List 5
Ps.-Demetr., De Eloc. = Ps.-Demetrius, De Elocutione, I BC–II? AD—List 5
Ps.-Demetrius = Ps.-Demetrius, Formae Epistolicae, date uncertain—List 5
Ps.-Dicaearchus, s. Dicaearchus—List 5
Ps.-Diogenes = letters attributed to Diogenes of Sinope (IV BC), s. Ep.; date uncertain—List 5
Psellus, History, XI AD—List 5
pseudepigr. = pseudepigraphon, pseudepigrapha
Ps.-Eupolemus, s. Eupolem. Hist.—List 5
Ps.-Hecataeus = historical accounts attributed to Hecataeus of Abdera, date uncertain—List 5
Ps.-Heraclitus = letters attributed to Heraclitus of Ephesus (VI–V BC), date uncertain—List 5
PSI = Papiri greci e latini: Pubblicazioni della Società Italiana—List 4
Ps.-Libanius, date uncertain—List 5

Ps.-Lucian, after II AD—List 5
Ps.-Oppian = Oppian of Apamea, imitator of Oppian of Anazorbos in Cilicia, II–III AD—List 5
Ps.-Orph(eus)—List 5
Ps.-Philo = the pseud. Liber antiquitatum biblicarum (Biblical Antiquities), I AD—List 5
Ps.-Phoc(ylides), I/II AD—List 5
Ps.-Plato—List 5
Ps.-Plut(arch), Vi(ta) Hom(eri), II AD—List 5
Ps.-Polemon, Physiognom(ica), II AD—List 5
Ps.-Scylax/Ps. Skylax, V/IV BC—List 5
Ps.-Socrates = letters attributed to the philosopher Socrates; s. Ep.; date uncertain—List 5
PsSol = Psalms of Solomon—List 2
Ps.-Sotades, date uncertain—List 5
PStras = Griechische Papyrus der kaiserlichen Universitäts- und Landesbibliothek zu Strassburg—List 4
Ps.-X(enophon), s. X.—List 5
pt. = part
1 Pt = 1 Peter—List 1
2 Pt = 2 Peter—List 1
ptc. = participle
PTebt = The Tebtunis Papyri—List 4
PThéad = Papyrus de Théadelphie—List 4
PThmouis 1 = Le Papyrus Thmouis 1—List 4
PtK = Petruskerygma (Preaching of Peter)—List 1
Ptolem(aeus), math., II AD—List 5
PTor, s. PTurin
PTR = Princeton Theological Review—List 6
PTurin = APeyron, Papyri graecae . . . Taurinensis—List 4
PUps 8 = PUpsaliensis 8—List 4
PVat A = PVaticanus A = Witkowski no. 36—List 4
PVindobBosw = Einige Wiener Papyri, ed. EBoswinkel—List 4
PWarr = The Warren Papyri—List 4
PWisc = The Wisconsin Papyri—List 4
PWürzb = Mitteilungen aus der Würzburger Papyrussammlung —List 4
PYadin = The Documents from the Bar Kokhba Period named in honor of YYadin (a.k.a. PBabatha)—List 4
PYale = Yale Papyri—List 4
Pythag(oras) = letters attributed to the phil. Pythagoras (VI–V BC); s. Ep.; date uncertain—List 5
Q = Qumran, cited with numbers indicating cave of origin—List 2, end
QDAP = Quarterly of the Department of Antiquities in Palestine—List 6
1QH = Psalms of Thanksgiving (Hôdāyôt)—List 2, end
1QIs[a] = St. Mark's Isaiah Scroll—List 2, end
1QM = War of the Sons of Light and the Sons of Darkness—List 2, end
1QpHab = The Habakkuk Commentary—List 2, end
1QS = The Manual of Discipline—List 2, end
Qua = Quadratus fragment, II AD—List 1
quest. = question
Quint(us) Smyrn(aeus), IV AD—List 5
quot. = quotation
q.v. = quod vide (which see, see that which has just been mentioned)
rabb. = rabbinical (literature etc.)
RAC = Reallexikon für Antike u. Christentum—List 6
Rahlfs = AR., ed. of LXX (1935; freq. reprinted)—List 2, beg.
Ramsay = WR.—Lists 3, 6
—, Bearing = The Bearing of Recent Discovery on the Trustworthiness of the NT
—, CB = The Cities and Bishoprics of Phrygia
—, Church = The Church in the Roman Empire
—, Cities of St. Paul
—, Hist. Geogr. = The Historical Geography of Asia Minor
—, Letters = The Letters to the Seven Churches of Asia
RB = Revue Biblique—List 6
rdg(s). = reading(s)
Rdm. = LRadermacher, Neutestamentliche Grammatik—List 6
RE = Realencyclopädie für protestantische Theologie und Kirche—List 6
REA = Revue des études anciennes—List 6
Reader, Polemo, s. Polemo—List 5
Reallexikon der Vorgeschichte —List 6
REB = Revised English Bible—List 6
rec. = recension
RechScRel, s. RSR—List 6
reconst. = reconstruction, reconstructed
ref(f). = reference(s)
reflex. = reflexive
regul. = regular(ly)
Reinhold = HR., De graecitate patrum apostolicorum librorum apocryphorum novi testamenti etc.—List 6
REJ = Revue des études Juives—List 6
rel., relat. = relative
relig. = religious
Renehan = RR., Greek Lexicographical Notes—List 6
repres. = represents, -enting
Res Gestae Augusti—List 3
rest. = restored, restoration
rev. = review
RevArch = Revue Archéologique—List 6
RevÉpigr = Revue Épigraphique—Lists 3, 6
RevÉtGr = Revue des Études grecques—List 6
RevExp = Review and Expositor—List 6
RevHistEccl, s. RHE—List 6
Rev. Laws, s. PRev—List 4
RevPhilol = Revue de philologie—List 6
RevQ = Revue de Qumran—List 6
RevSém = Revue Sémitique—List 6
Revue de philol(ogie), s. RevPhilol—List 6
RGG = Die Religion in Geschichte und Gegenwart—List 6
RHE = Revue d'histoire ecclésiastique—List 6
rhet. = rhetor, rhetorica, rhetorician, rhetorical
Rhet(ores) Gr(aeci)—List 5
Rhinthon (Comicus), III BC—List 5
RhM = Rheinisches Museum für Philologie—List 6
RHPR = Revue d'histoire et de philosophie religieuses—List 6
RHR = Revue de l'histoire des religions—List 6
rit. = ritual
RivBib = Rivista Biblica—List 6
RivFil = Rivista di Filologia e d'istruzione classica, n.s.—List 6
Ro = Romans—List 1
Rob. = ATRobertson, A Grammar of the Greek NT in the Light of Historical Research—List 6
Rohde, Psyche = ER., Psyche—List 6

Roscher = WR., Ausfürhliches Lexikon der . . . Mythologie —List 6
Rossberg = CR., De praepositionum Graecarum in chartis Aegyptiis Ptolemaeorum aetatis etc.—Lists 4, 6
Rouffiac = JR., Recherches sur les caractères du Grec dans le NT d'après les inscriptions de Priène—List 3
RSPT = Revue des sciences philosophiques et théologiques—List 6
RSR = Recherches de science religieuse—List 6
RSV = The Revised Standard Version of the NT—List 6
RThAM = Recherches de théologie ancienne et médiéviale—List 6
RTP = Revue de théologie et de philosophie—List 6
RTQR = Revue de théologie et des questions religieuses—List 6
Rtzst. = RReitzenstein—List 6
—, Erlösungsmyst. = Das iranische Erlösungsmysterium
—, Herr der Grösse = Das mandäische Buch des Herrn der Grösse
—, Hist. Mon. = Historia Monachorum und Historia Lausiaca
—, Mysterienrel. = Die hellenistischen Mysterienreligionen
—, Poim. = Poimandres
—, Taufe = Die Vorgeschichte der christlichen Taufe
Ruth—List 2
Rv = (Book of) Revelation—List 1
RVV = Religionsgesch. Versuche und Vorarbeiten—List 6
Rydbeck = LR., Fachprosa, vermeintliche Volkssprache und Neues Testament—List 6
S = Codex Sinaiticus (א), as used in Rahlfs, Septuaginta; cp. Sin/Sin. below—List 2, beg.
S. = HvonSoden, s. Sod. in List 1, beg.
s. = see
SAB, s. SBBerlAk—List 6
Safrai-Stern, Jewish People = SS./MS., The Jewish People in the First Century (CRINT)—List 6
SAH, s. SBHeidAk—List 6
Sallust(ius), IV AD—List 5
Sappho, VII–VI BC—List 5
SAWien, s. SBWeinAk—List 6
Sb = Sammelbuch griechischer Urkunden aus Aegypten—Lists 3, 4
SBBayAk/SBAW = Sitzungsberichte der (Königlich) Bayerischen Akademie der Wissenschaften—List 6
SBBerlAk/SPAW = Sitzungsberichte der Preussischen Akademie der Wissenschaften (Berlin)—List 6
SBHeidAk/SHAW = Sitzungsberichte der Heidelberger Akademie der Wissenschaften—List 6
SBLDS = Society of Biblical Literature Dissertation Series—List 6
SBLeipzAk/SSAW = Sitzungsberichte der Sächsischen Akademie der Wissenschaften (Leipzig)—List 6
SBLSBS = Society of Biblical Literature Sources for Biblical Study—List 6
SBLSP = Society of Biblical Literature Seminar Papers—List 6
SBMünAk, s. SBBayAk—List 6
SBWienAk/SAWW/SÖAW = Sitzungsber. der (Kaiserlichen) Österreichischen Akademie der Wissenschaften in Wien (Phil.-hist. Klasse)—List 6
sc. = scilicet (one may understand, supply)
Sch. = TSchermann, Prophetarum vitae fabulosae—List 5
Schlageter = JS., Wortschatz der ausserhalb Attikas gefundenen attischen Inschriften—List 3
Schmid = WS., Der Atticismus in seinen Hauptvertretern —List 6
Schmidt, Joseph. = WS., De Flavii Iosephi elocutione—List 6
Schmidt, Syn. = JS., Synonymik—List 6
schol. = scholion, scholia, scholiast
Schol(ia), on various authors—List 5
SchTZ = Schweizerische Theologische Zeitschrift—List 6
Schürer = ES., The History of the Jewish People in the Age of Jesus Christ (175 BC–AD 135)—List 6
Schweizer = ES., Grammatik der pergamenischen Inschriften—Lists 3, 6
Schwyzer = ES., Griechische Grammatik—List 6
Scr. Erot., s. Erotici—List 5
Scylax, s. Ps.-Scylax; V–IV BC—List 5
Scymnus Chius, geogr., I BC; the account attributed to him was prob. written II/I BC—List 5
SEÅ = Svensk Exegetisk Årsbok—List 6
Secundus, Athenian phil., Sententiae, II AD—List 5
SEG = Supplementum Epigraphicum Graecum—List 3
Semonides of Amorgos, VII BC—List 5
ser. = series
Serap(ion) of Thmuis, IV AD—List 5
Sext. Emp. = Sextus Empiricus, II–III AD—List 5
Sextus (Pythagoricus), end of II AD—List 5
sg. = singular
Sherk = RS., Roman Documents from the Greek East—Lists 3, 6
SibOr = Oracula Sibyllina, II–III AD—List 5
sic = so, thus (indicating an error or extraordinary form transcribed from the original)
SIG = Sylloge Inscriptionum Graecarum^3; superscript omitted in text—List 3
SIG^2 = Sylloge Inscriptionum Graecarum^2—List 3
signf. = signification
sim. = similarly
Simmias (of Rhodes), IV–III BC—List 5
Simonid(es of Ceos), VI–V BC—List 5
Simplicius, VI AD—List 5
Sin/Sin. = Codex Sinaiticus (א), in textual-critical references; cp. S above
sing. = singular
Sir = Jesus Sirach—List 2
SJCh = Sophia Jesu Christi—List 1
SJT = Scottish Journal of Theology—List 6
Slav. En. = Slavonic Book of Enoch or II Enoch—List 5
Socrat(es), Ep. = letters attributed to the philosopher Socrates, date uncertain—List 5
Socrates HE = Socrates hist., Historia Ecclesiastica, IV–V AD—List 5
Socratics, letters attributed to disciples of the phil. Socrates —List 5
Sod. = HvSoden, ed. Gk. NT—List 1, beg.
SÖAW, s. SBWienAk—List 6
Solon, VII–VI BC—List 5
somet. = sometimes
someth. = something
soph. = sophistes, sophist
Soph(ocles), V BC—List 5
Soph(ocles) Lex. = ES., Greek Lexicon of the Roman and Byzantine Periods—List 6
Soranus, I–II AD—List 5
Sostratus, gramm., I BC—List 5

Sotades (Maronita), s. AnthLG; III BC—List 5
Sotion, paradoxogr., I AD—List 5
sp. = spelling
specif. = specifically
Spicq = CS., Lexique théologique du Nouveau Testament—List 6
SSol = Song of Solomon—List 2
Stadiasmus (Maris Magni) (a.k.a. Periplus Maris Magni) —List 5
Steinleitner = FS., Die Beicht im Zusammenhange mit der sakralen Rechtspflege in der Antike—List 6
Stephan(us) Byz(antius), V–VI AD—List 5
Stesichorus, VII–VI BC—List 5
StKr = Theologische Studiën und Kritiken—List 6
Stob(aeus), V AD—List 5
Stoic(orum Veterum Fragmenta), various dates—List 5
Strabo, I BC–I AD—List 5
Straton (of Lampsacus), phil., III BC—List 5
Straton (of Sardis), epigr., II AD—List 5
Straub = WS., Die Bildersprache des Apostels Paulus—List 6
Strycker = ÉdeStrycker, s. GJs in List 1
StTh = Studia Theologica (Lund)—List 6
StThR(iga) = Studia Theologica, Riga—List 6
StudPal = CWessely, Studien zur Paläographie und Papyrusurkunden—List 4
STZ = Schweizerische Theologische Zeitschrift—List 6
subj. = subjunctive; subject
subscr. = subscription
subst. = substantive(ly)
Suda = a lexical work (freq. cited as Suidas in handbooks); X AD—List 5
suf. = suffix
superl. = superlative
superscr. = superscription
Suppl. = Supplement (to serials)
suppl. = supplement, supplied (in grammatical references)
Sus = Susanna—List 2
susp. = suspect
Sv (at the end of entries) = HSieben, Voces—List 6
s.v. = sub voce (under the word, look up the word)
SvExÅrsb = Svensk Exegetisk Årsbok, s. SEÅ—List 6
SvTK = Svensk Teologisk Kvartalskrift—List 6
Swete = HS., editor of the Greek OT—List 2, beg.
syll. = syllable
Sym. = Symmachus, Greek version of the OT—List 2, beg., 5
SymbBU(ps) = Symbolae Biblicae Upsalienses—List 6
SymbOsl = Symbolae Osloenses—List 6
Syn. = KAland, Synopsis Quattuor Evangeliorum—List 6
syn. = synopsis, synoptic
Synes(ius), IV–V AD—List 5
synon. = synonym, synonymous
Syntipas, a collection of fables under the name of Syntapis; before XI AD—List 5
Syr. = Syriac
SyrBar = Apocalypsis Syriaca Baruch—List 2
T = Theological, Theology, Theologisch(e)
TAM = Tituli Asiae Minoris—List 3
TAPA = Transactions of the American Philological Association—List 6
Tat(ian), II AD—List 5
Taubenschlag = RT.—Lists 4, 6
—, Law² = Law of Graeco-Rom. Egypt in Light of Papyri
—, OpMin = Opera Minora
TBl = Theologische Blätter—List 6
Tdf. = CvTischendorf, ed. of Gk NT and other works—List 1, beg.
Teles, III BC—List 5
Telestes, s. AnthLG; V/IV BC—List 5
temp. = temporally
Tert(tullian), II–III AD—List 5
test. = testimonies or biographical data, as distinguished from fragments (fgm.) as cited in a corpus, such as Jac. (=FGrH)
TestAbr = Testament of Abraham, with some interpolations; I BC/I AD—Lists 2, 5
TestAdam = Testament of Adam, II–III AD—List 5
TestAsh = Testament of Asher, s. Test12Patr—List 2
TestBenj = Testament of Benjamin, s. Test12Patr—List 2
TestDan = Testament of Dan, s. Test12Patr—List 2
TestGad = Testament of Gad, s. Test12Patr—List 2
TestIss = Testament of Issachar, s. Test12Patr—List 2
TestJob = Testament of Job—List 2
TestJos = Testament of Joseph, s. Test12Patr—List 2
TestJud = Testament of Judah, s. Test12Patr—List 2
TestLevi = Testament of Levi, s. Test12Patr—List 2
TestNapht = Testament of Naphthali, s. Test12Patr—List 2
Test12Patr = Testaments of the Twelve Patriarchs, with interpolations II BC–III AD—List 2
TestReub = Testament of Reuben, s. Test12Patr—List 2
TestSim = Testament of Simeon, s. Test12Patr—List 2
TestSol = Testament of Solomon, I–III AD—List 2
TestZeb = Testament of Zebulun, s. Test12Patr—List 2
Tetrast(icha) Iamb(ica) = Babrius (q.v.); date uncertain—List 5
TextMin 31 = Textus Minores 31: Epigraphica I, Texts on the Economic History of the Greek World—List 3
TextMin 41 = Textus Minores 41: Epigraphica II, Texts on the Social History of the Greek World—List 3
TextMin 47 = Textus Minores 47: Epigraphica III, Texts on Bankers, etc.—List 3
TGF = Tragicorum Graecorum Fragmenta—List 5
TGl = Theologie u. Glaube—List 6
1 Th = 1 Thessalonians—List 1
2 Th = 2 Thessalonians—List 1
Thackeray = HT., A Grammar of the OT in Greek according to the Septuagint—List 6
Thales, s. Vorsokr.; VI BC—List 5
ThBl, s. TBl—List 6
Themist(ius), IV AD—List 5
Theocr(itus Bucolicus), IV–III BC—List 5
Theod. = Theodotion, revision of Greek OT, II AD—List 2, beg.
Theodoret, of Cyrrhus, IV–V AD—List 5
Theodor(us) Prodr(omus), s. Erotici; XII AD—List 5
Theodos(ius) Melitenus, X AD—List 5
Theodotus (Judaeus), before I BC—List 5
Theognis, VI BC—List 5
Theognost(us Grammaticus), IX AD—List 5
theol. = theology, theological
TheolRev = Theologische Revue—List 6
Theol. Viat, s. ThViat—List 6
Theon Smyrn(aeus), II AD—List 5
Theophanes Conf(essor), VIII–IX AD—List 5

Theoph. Ant. = Theophilus Antiochenus, II AD—List 5
Theophilus Antecessor, VI AD—List 5
Theophr(astus), IV–III BC—List 5
Theophyl(actus) Sim(ocatta), VII AD—List 5
Theopomp(us), hist., IV BC—List 5
Theosophien = Fragmente griechischer Theosophien, dates uncertain—List 5
Thesaurus-Onomasticon = Thesaurus Linguae Latinae (TLL), Onomasticon II—List 6
ThGl, s. TGl
Thieme = GT., Die Inschriften von Magnesia am Mäander und das NT—List 3
Thom(as) Mag(ister), XIII–XIV AD—List 5
thr. = through
Thrasymachus, rhet./soph., V BC—List 5
Threatte = LT., The Grammar of Attic Inscriptions I: Phonology; II: Morphology—List 6
ThStud, s. TSt—List 6
Thu(cydides), V BC—List 5
Thumb = ATh., Die griechische Sprache im Zeitalter des Hellenismus—List 6
ThViat = Theologia Viatorum—List 6
1 Ti = 1 Timothy—List 1
2 Ti = 2 Timothy—List 1
Timaeus (Historicus), IV–III BC—List 5
Tim(aeus) Locr(us), I? AD—List 5
Timochares, II BC—List 5
Timon, IV–III BC—List 5
Tit = Titus (Letter to)—List 1
tit. = titulus, heading, introductory inscription
Tituli Lyciae, s. TAM (II)—List 3
T. Kellis 22 = RJenkins, The Prayer of the Emanations in Greek from Kellis (inscribed on a tablet)—List 3
TLL = Thesaurus Linguae Latinae—List 6
TLZ = Theolog. Literaturzeitung—List 6
Tob = Tobit—List 2
Tod, GkHIns = MTod, Greek Historical Inscriptions—List 3
TQ = Theologische Quartalschrift—List 6
tr. = translate, etc.
t.r. = textus receptus
trad. = tradition
Trag. = writer(s) of tragedy
trag. = tragedy, writer(s) of tragedy
trans. = transitive
transf. = transferred
transl. = translate, translation
translit. = transliteration, transliterated
TRE = Theologische Realenzyklopädie—List 6
TrGF I, II, III, IV = Tragicorum Graecorum Fragmenta—List 5
Tromp, s. AssMos—List 2
TRu = Theologische Rundschau—List 6
Trypho (Alexandrinus), s. Gramm. Gr.; I BC—List 5
TS = Theological Studies (Washington, D.C.)—List 6
TSt = Theologische Studiën—List 6
TT = Theologisch Tijdskrift—List 6
t.t. = terminus technicus (termini technici), technical term(s)
TTK = Tidsskrift for Teologi og Kirke (Oslo)—List 6
TU = Texte und Untersuchungen—List 6
TW = Theologisches Wörterbuch zum NT; tr. GBromiley, Theological Dictionary of the NT—List 6
Twentieth Century NT—List 6
Tyrtaeus, s. AnthLG; VII BC—List 5
TZ = Theologische Zeitschrift—List 6
TZS = Theologische Zeitschrift aus der Schweiz—List 6
Unknown Sayings = JJeremias, Unknown Sayings of Jesus—List 6
UPZ = Urkunden der Ptolemäerzeit—Lists 4, 6
Ursing = UU., Studien zur griechischen Fabel—List 6
usu. = usually
var. = various(ly)
Vat/Vat. = Codex Vaticanus—List 1, beg. and 2, beg.
VBP = Veröffentlichungen aus den Badischen Papyrussammlungen—List 4
VD = Verbum Domini—List 6
Verb. Dom., s. VD
vernac. = vernacular
vers. = version(s)
Vett(ius) Val(ens), II AD—List 5
VetusT = Vetus Testamentum—List 6
Vi. = Vita, Vitae
Vi. Aesopi, = Vitae Aesopi, I AD—List 5
ViEzk, s. ViIs
VigChr = Vigiliae Christianae—List 6
ViHab, s. ViIs
Vi. Homeri et Hesiodi = Vitae H. et. H., dates uncertain—List 5
ViIs, ViEzk, ViHab, ViJer, et al. = Vita of Isaiah, Ezkiel, Habakkuk, Jeremiah et al.—Lists 2, 5
ViJer, s. ViIs
Vi(ta) Philonidis (Epicurei), II/I BC—List 5
Vi(ta) Pol(ycarpi), c. 400 AD—List 5
Vi(ta) Sophoclis, date uncertain—List 5
Vi(ta) Thu(cydidis), date uncertain—List 5
Vivre et Penser—List 6
viz. = videlicet (namely)
v.l. = varia lectio (variant reading)
voc. = vocative
Vog. = HVogels, editor of the Greek NT—List 1, beg.
vol. = volume
Vorsokr. = Vorsokratiker, their fragments, ed. by HDiels/WKranz (the term Pre-Socratic[s] is used when no specific ref. is made to the German ed.)—Lists 5, 6
vs., vss. = verse(s)
Vulg. = Vulgate
vv.ll. = variae lectiones (variant readings)
w. = with
Wadd., s. ISyriaW—List 3
Wahl, Clavis = CW., Clavis librorum Veteris Testamenti apocryphorum philologica—List 6
Warnecke, Romfahrt = HW., Die tatsächliche Romfahrt des Apostels Paulus—List 6
WBC = Word Bible Commentary—List 6
Wel. = JWellhausen, in various contexts (also Wlh.)
Welles = CW., Royal Correspondence in the Hellenistic Period—Lists 3, 6
Wendland, Kultur = PW., Die hellenistisch-römische Kultur—List 6
West = MWest, Iambi et Elegi Graeci—List 5
Wet(t)stein = JJW., Novum Testamentum Graecum—List 6
W-H. = BWestcott/FHort, editors of Gk. NT—List 1, beg.
White, LAL = JW., Light from Ancient Letters—Lists 4, 6

Whittaker = MW.; s. H—List 1
Wien(er)Stud = Wiener Studien—List 6
Wilcken, Ostr., s. O. Wilck
Winer, Gramm. = GW., Grammatik des neutestamentlichen Sprachidioms—List 6
Wiss. Abhdl. = Wissenschaftliche Abhandlung(en): scholarly proceedings or reports
Witkowski = SW., Epistulae Privatae Graecae—Lists 3, 4
Wlh. = JWellhausen, Einleitung—List 6
wr. = writers, writings
W-S. = GWiner, Grammatik des neutestamentlichen Sprachidioms, ed. PSchmiedel—List 6
Wsd = Wisdom of Solomon—List 2
WTJ = Westminster Theological Journal—List 6
WUNT = Wissenschaftliche Untersuchungen zum NT
Wuthnow = HW., Die semitischen Menschennamen—List 6
X. = Xenophon, V–IV BC—List 5
Xenophanes, VI–V BC—List 5
X. Eph. = Xenophon of Ephesus, II/III AD
Z = Zeitschrift
Zahn = TZ., various works—List 6
ZASA = Zeitschrift für ägyptische Sprache und Altertumskunde—List 6
ZAszMyst = Zeitschrift für Aszese und Mystik—List 6
ZAW = Zeitschrift für die Alttestamentliche Wissenschaft—List 6
ZDMG = Zeitschrift der Deutschen Morgenländischen Gesellschaft—List 6
ZDPV = Zeitschrift der Deutschen Palästina-Vereins—List 6
Zech = Zechariah—List 2
Zeitschr. = Zeitschrift
Zeno, the Stoic, IV–III BC—List 5
Zenob(ius) Soph(ista), paroemiogr., II AD—List 5
Zeph = Zephaniah—List 2
Ziemann = FZ., De Epistularum Graecarum Formulis Solemnibus Quaestiones Selectae—Lists 3, 4
ZKG = Zeitschrift für Kirchengeschichte—List 6
ZKT = Zeitschrift für katholische Theologie—List 6
ZMRW = Zeitschrift für Missionskunde und Religionswissenschaft—List 6
ZNW = Zeitschrift für die ntl. Wissenschaft—List 6
Zohary = MZ., various works—List 6
Zonaras = Zonarae Lexicon (inaccurately ascribed to John Zonaras), XII AD—List 5
Zorell = FZ., Novi Testamenti Lexicon Graecum—List 6
Zosimus = Z. alchem, III/IV AD—List 5
Zosimus, Hist(oricus), V? AD—List 5
ZPE = Zeitschrift für Papyrologie und Epigraphik—Lists 3, 4, 6
ZPWess = Neue Griechische Zauberpapyri, ed. CWessely—List 4
ZSavRG = Zeitschrift der Savigny-Stiftung für Rechtsgeschichte—List 6
ZST = Zeitschrift für systematische Theologie—List 6
ZTK = Zeitschrift für Theologie und Kirche—List 6
Zts. = Zeitschrift
ZVS = Zeitschrift für vergleichende Sprachforschung—List 6
Zwaan = Johannes de Z., Syntaxis—List 6
ZWT = Zeitschrift für Wissenschaftliche Theologie—List 6

A
Greek-English Lexicon
of the
New Testament
and other Early Christian Literature

A

Α, α, τό indecl. (s. ἄλφα) **first letter of the Gk. alphabet,** ***alpha*** (cp. SibOr 5, 15) hence as numeral α′ = 1 (*one* εἷς or *first* πρῶτος e.g. TestSol, PVindobBosw at 18:34; oft. in pap): πρώτη (or πρωτέρα?, in pap freq. = πρότερον, q.v.) in titles of letters ἐπιστολή: 1 Cor; 1 Th; 1 Ti; 1 Pt; 1J; 1 Cl; ἐντολή Hm 1, title. As a symbolic letter A signifies the beginning, Ω the end (FBoll, Sphaera 1903, 469ff). The two came to designate the universe and every kind of divine and superhuman power. S. Rtzst., Poim. 256ff, Erlösungsmyst. 244; FBoll, Aus d. Offb. Joh. 1914, 26f. The Sator-anagram of Pompeii (JDaniélou, Primitive Christian Symbols, tr. DAttwater ’64, 99–101) offers the earliest Christian usage. In the expr. ἐγώ εἰμι τὸ ἄλφα καὶ τὸ ὦ the letters are explained as *beginning* and *end* Rv 1:8 v.l.; 21:6 (s. OWeinreich, ARW 19, 1919, 180f); as *first* and *last* **1:11 v.l.;** and as both **22:13** (cp. Mel., P. 105, 812 [B]). Is. 44:6 offers precedent for the πρῶτος/ἔσχατος in this and related rabbinic symbolism.—S. on Ω and FCabrol, Dict. d’Arch. I, 1, 1–25; FDornseiff, D. Alphabet in Mystik u. Magie[2] 1925, 17f; 122ff; RCharles, HDB I 70.—TW.

Ἀαρών, ὁ indecl. (אַהֲרוֹן) (LXX, Philo.—In Jos. Ἀαρών, ῶνος [Ant. 3, 54]; Just.) ***Aaron*** brother of Miriam (Ex 15:20) and of Moses (Ex 4:14) **Ac 7:40** (Ex 32:1). Embodies the (high) priesthood (Ex 28:1; Num 3:10) **Hb 5:4; 7:11;** θυγατέρες Ἀ. **Lk 1:5** (Just.).—GEb 13, 75. The strife of Aaron and Miriam w. Moses (Num 12; also Demetrius: 722 fgm. 2, 3 Jac.) 1 Cl 4:11; the test of the rods (Num 17) 43:5; **Hb 9:4.**—New Docs. 1, 66f. TW.

Ἀβαδδών, ὁ indecl. (אֲבַדּוֹן Pr 15:11; Ps 87:12; Theod. Job 26:6; 28:22 = ἀπώλεια LXX) ***Abaddon,*** name of the ruling angel in hell **Rv 9:11,** explained as Ἀπολλύων *Destroyer* (cp. אָבַד). This name for the ἄγγελος τῆς ἀβύσσου and its transl. are based on the OT passages above, in which ἀπώλεια is parallel to ᾅδης = שְׁאוֹל Job 26:6 Theod.; Pr 15:11 and to τάφος Ps 87:12. In Theod. Job 28:22 it is personified, together with θάνατος; cp. the derivation of Apollo, source of plagues, from ἀπόλλυμι.—TW.

ἀβαναύσως adv. of uncertain mng.; **not in narrow-minded fashion,** ***unselfishly, nobly*** prob. do justice to the term; λειτουργεῖν ἀ. beside ἀμέμπτως, μετὰ ταπεινοφροσύνης and ἡσύχως 1 Cl 44:3. The adj. ἀβάναυσος stands betw. εὔσπλαγχνος and ἀγαπητικός Const. Apost. 2, 3, 3 and is understood by the Syrian of the Didasc. Apost. Syr. (p. 35 Lewis) as תַּנָּן *kind;* cp. Clem. Al., Paed. 3, 34 φιλανθρώπως, οὐ βαναύσως.—DELG. s.v. βάναυσος.

ἀβαρής, ές, gen. οῦς (Aristot. et al.; s. Nägeli 38) lit. ‘light in weight’, only fig. ***not burdensome*** (CIG 5361, 15 [I BC] ἀ. ἑαυτὸν παρέσχηται; BGU 248, 26 [II AD] ἐάν σοι ἀβαρὲς ᾖ; 1080, 17; POxy 933, 29 et al.) ἀβαρῆ ἐμαυτὸν ὑμῖν ἐτήρησα *I kept myself fr. being a burden to you* **2 Cor 11:9.**—DELG. s.v. βαρύς. M-M.

ἀββα (accented ἀββά in W-H. and N.[25]; others ἀββᾶ; Aram. אַבָּא vocative form, orig. a term of endearment, later used as title and personal name; rarely used in ref. to God) ***father,*** translit. ***abba,*** Aram. form used in prayer (Dalman, Worte 157) and in the family circle, taken over by Greek-speaking Christians as a liturgical formula (Ltzm., Hdb. on Ro 8:15), transl. ὁ πατήρ (= voc., s. s.v. πατήρ) **Mk 14:36; Ro 8:15; Gal 4:6.** Not found in patristic lit.—CFabricius, RSeeberg Festschr. 1929, I 21–41; SMcCasland, JBL 72, ’53, 79–91; JJeremias, Abba ’66, 15–67 (Central Message of the NT ’65, 9–30); against him, JGreig, Studia Evangelica 5, ’68, 5–10.—TW. Sv.

Ἀβ(ε)ιρών, ὁ indecl. (אֲבִירָם) (LXX.—In Joseph. Ἀβίραμος, ου [Ant. 4, 19]) ***Abiram,*** son of Eliab, w. Dathan and On leader of a rebellion of the sons of Reuben against Moses and Aaron (Num 16); ex. of fatal jealousy 1 Cl 4:12; GJs 9:2.

Ἄβελ, ὁ indecl. (Ἅβελ edd.—הֶבֶל, in pause הָבֶל) (LXX, En, TestAbr, Test12Patr, ApcMos, Philo; Mel., P. 59, 430; 69, 498.—In Joseph. Ἄβελος, ου [Ant. 1, 67]), ***Abel,*** son of Adam (Gen 4); Abel's blood **Mt 23:35; Lk 11:51; Hb 12:24** (En 22:7); his sacrifice **11:4;** 1 Cl 4:1f; cp. 6.—VAptowitzer, Kain u. Abel 1922.—TW.

Ἀβιά, ὁ indecl. (אֲבִיָּה) *Abijah,* B-D-F §3—❶ Son of Rehoboam (1 Ch 3:10), an ancestor of Jesus **Mt 1:7ab.**

❷ Founder of the class of priests to which Zacharias belonged (1 Ch 24:10; 2 Esdr 22:16f; the name Zacharias occurs in the latter pass.) **Lk 1:5.** S. ἐφημερία, Ζαχαρίας.

Ἀβιαθάρ, ὁ (Ἀβιάθαρ edd.) indecl. (אֶבְיָתָר) (in Joseph. Ἀβιάθαρος, ου [Ant. 7, 110]) ***Abiathar,*** priest at Nob (1 Km 22:20ff), son of Ahimelech (1 Km 21:2, 7) **Mk 2:26,** where he is mentioned in place of his father.

Ἀβιληνή, ῆς, ἡ (Ἀβειλ W-H.) *Abilene,* the territory around the city of Abila (τὰ Ἄβιλα) at the southern end of the Anti-Lebanon range, northwest of Damascus; administered by Lysanias the tetrarch. **Lk 3:1.**—S. lit. on Λυσανίας.

Ἀβιούδ, ὁ indecl. (אֲבִיהוּד) (Philo.—In Joseph. Ἀβιοῦς) ***Abiud,*** son of Zerubbabel (not mentioned in 1 Ch 3:19; 8:3 the name occurs as that of a member of a Benjamite family), in genealogy of Jesus **Mt 1:13ab; Lk 3:23ff** D.

Ἀβραάμ, ὁ indecl. (אַבְרָהָם 'father of a multitude') (LXX; TestSol 18:22 P; TestAbr, Test12Patr, ParJer; ApcSed 14:6; ApcEsdr; ApcrEzk P 1 recto, 10; SibOr 2, 246; Philo, Just.; Mel., P. 83 [B], 625 and fgm.; PGM 7, 315; 13, 817 δύναμιν τοῦ Ἀβραάμ, Ἰσὰκ καὶ τοῦ Ἰακώβ; 35, 14 τοῦ θεοῦ τοῦ Ἀβρὰμ καὶ Ἰσακὰ καὶ Ἰακώβ. Indecl. also in Apollonius Molon [I BC], an opponent of the Jews: 728 fgm. 1, 2 and 3 Jac. [Eus., PE 9, 19, 2; 3].—In the Jew Artapanus [II BC]: 726 fgm. 1 Jac. [Eus. 9, 18, 1]; in Ps.-Hecataeus: 264 fgm. 24 Jac. in a work Κατ' Ἄβραμον καὶ τοὺς Αἰγυπτίους; and in Joseph. Ἄβραμος, ου [Ant. 1, 148]; cp. EpArist 49; BGU 585 II, 3 [212 AD]; Damasc., Vi. Isid. 141.—Nicol. Dam. [I BC]: 90 fgm. 52 Jac. [Jos., Ant. 1, 159f] Ἀβράμης, ου. Charax of Pergam. [II AD]: 103 fgm. 52 Jac. ἀπὸ Ἀβράμωνος.—Hesychius 1, 81 has Ἀβραμίας, obviously a Hellenized form of Abraham, as the name of a throw in dice-playing. Personal names were frequently used for this purpose: Eubulus, Com. fgm. 57K. Dssm., NB 15 [BS 187]; B-D-F §260, 2). In the NT receives mention second to Moses. ***Abraham*** (husband of Sarah Gen 18:10f), in the genealogy of Jesus **Mt 1:1, 2, 17; Lk 3:34;** progenitor of the Israelite nation (Jos., Ant. 1, 158 ὁ πατὴρ ἡμῶν Ἀ.), and of the Christians, as authentically Israel **Mt 3:9; Lk 1:73; 3:8; J 8:39, 53, 56; Ac 7:2; Ro 4:1; Js 2:21.** Hence the people of Israel are called A.'s seed (e.g. PsSol 9:9; 18:3) **J 8:33, 37; Ro 9:7; 11:1; 2 Cor 11:22; Gal 3:29; Hb 2:16.**—A. as bearer of the promise **Ac 3:25; 7:17; Ro 4:13; Gal 3:8, 14, 16, 18; Hb 6:13.** His faith **Ro 4:3** (Gen 15:6), **9, 12, 16; Gal 3:6** (Gen 15:6), **9;** 1 Cl 10:6 (Gen 15:6); **Js 2:23.** Here and 1 Cl 10:1; 17:2 called a friend of God (cp. Is 41:8; 2 Ch 20:7; Da 3:35. But only Is 41:8 Sym. and, indirectly, Ex 33:11 use the word φίλος [as TestAbr A 1 78, 6=Stone p. 4]. LXX Is 41:8 and the other passages use a form of ἀγαπάω; s. EPeterson, ZKG 42, 1923, 172ff. Philo quotes Gen 18:17 φίλος μου Sobr. 56 [s. PKatz, Philo's Bible, '50, 85; on use of the name, 154ff]; cp. Wsd 7:27; Book of Jubilees 19:9; 30:20); like Isaac, Jacob, and the prophets **Lk 13:28,** A. occupies a prominent place in the next life **16:22ff** (s. on κόλπος 1). God is designated as God of Abraham, Isaac, and Jacob (Ex 3:6.—MRist, The God of A., I., and J.: JBL 57, '38, 289–303) **Mt 22:32; Mk 12:26; Lk 20:37; Ac 3:13; 7:32;** B 6:8. W. Isaac and Jacob at the banquet in the Kingdom **Mt 8:11;** listed among the great people of God (cp. SibOr 2, 245–48) B 8:4; IPhld 9:1 (on the triad s. above and s.v. Ἰακώβ). Points typologically to Jesus B 9:7f.—OSchmitz, Abr. im Spätjudent. u. im Urchristent.: ASchlatter Festschr. 1922, 99–123; Billerb. (s. index of persons and things: IV 1213); MColacci, Il Semen Abrahae alla luce del V e del NT: Biblica 21, '40, 1–27.—M-M. TW.

ἀβροχία, ας, ἡ ***drought*** (OGI 56, 15 [III BC]; pap since 238 BC [Mayser I^2/3, p. 27, 39 ; Mitt-Wilck. I/1, index b]; SWaszynski, D. Bodenpacht 1905, 130ff; LXX; SibOr 3, 540) ἀ. γίνεται *a drought comes* Hs 2:8. S. βρέχω.

ἄβρωτος, ον (Ctesias, Menand. et al.; Pr 24:22e; Philo, Spec. Leg. 3, 144; Jos., Ant. 5, 219; loanw. in rabb.) of wood ***not eaten*** by worms (Theophr., HP 5, 1, 2) ῥάβδοι Hs 8, 4, 6. S. βιβρώσκω.

ἄβυσσος, ου, ἡ (orig. adj., Aeschyl., Hdt.+; so also Dt 33:13. The fem. sg. is used freq. in LXX, w. art. or adj. Gen 1:2; Job 41:23; Ps 77:15; Am 7:4; also En passim; TestSol 2:8 BC; TestJob 33:6; TestLevi 3:9 v.l.; JosAs 12:3, 10; 4 Esdr 8:23 fgm. c; ApcEsdr 4:21 p. 28, 24 Tdf.; Just. A I, 60, 9 [for ᾅδου Dt 32:22]; without art. or adj. LXX; Mel., P. 28, 614. Fem. pl. w. art. or adj. Ps 134:6; 148:7; Prov 8:24; TestLevi 3:9; without art. or adj. freq. LXX; PsSol 17:19) lit. 'deep hole', hence: 'immense depth' (Diog. L. 4, 5, 27; Iambl., Myst. 6, 5 p. 245, 15 Parthey; Herm. Wr. 3, 1; 16, 5; PGM 1, 343; 3, 554; 4, 1148; 1350; 2835; 7, 261; 517; PWarr 21, 29; 31; LXX; En 21:7; Philo, Op. M. 29; SibOr 1, 223).

❶ **an immensely deep space, *depth, abyss,*** gener., contrasted w. sky and earth (Did., Gen. 30, 8) 1 Cl 28:3 (pl. as Dt 8:7; Ps 32:7; 76:17 al.; TestLevi 3:9; Cat. Cod. Astr. VIII/2 p. 173, 29); Dg 7:2. Dark (Gen 1:2), hence unfathomable to the human eye 1 Cl 20:5, and discernible only by God 59:3 (Theoph. Ant. 1, 6, p. 70, 23; cp. Da 3:55 Theod.).

❷ **a transcendent place associated with the dead and hostile powers, *netherworld, abyss,*** esp. the abode of the dead **Ro 10:7** (Ps 106:26) and of demons **Lk 8:31;** dungeon where the devil is kept **Rv 20:3;** abode of the θηρίον, the Antichrist **11:7; 17:8;** of Ἀβαδδών (q.v.), the angel of the underworld **9:11** (cp. PGM 13, 169 and s. Ael. Aristid. 38 p. 724 D. on Philip: ἀνὴρ ὑβριστὴς ἐκ τοῦ βαράθρου τ. γῆς ὁρμώμενος κακῇ μοίρᾳ τ. Ἑλλήνων); φρέαρ τῆς ἀ. **9:1f;** capable of being sealed **9:1; 20:1, 3.**—JKroll, Gott u. Hölle '32; KSchneider, RAC I 60–62.—DELG. s.v. βυθός. M-M. TW. Sv.

Ἄγαβος, ου, ὁ (N. and Bov. Ac 11:28; others accent Ἀγ.) (s. B-D-F §53, 2a.) ***Agabus*** (a Palmyrene ins [Répert. d'épigraphie sémitique II 1907–1914, no. 1086] has ᶜAgaba [עגבא] as a woman's name), a Christian prophet fr. Judea **Ac 11:28; 21:10.**

ἀγαγεῖν s. ἄγω.

ἀγαθά, ῶν, τά subst. neut. of ἀγαθός (q.v. 1b).

ἀγαθοεργέω (Pythag., Ep. 10 p. 607; contr. ἀγαθουργέω **Ac 14:17;** except for use in patristic lit., the verb is quite rare, but ἀγαθουργός and ἀγαθουργίη go back to Hdt. [B-D-F §119, 1]) **to do that which benefits others, *do good, confer benefits:*** of the rich **1 Ti 6:18;** of God **Ac 14:17.**—TW.

ἀγαθοεργός, όν (Plut., Mor. 370e; 1015e; Physiogn. I 364, 13; Julian, Or. 4, 144d; Proclus on Pla., Tim. III p. 313, 17 Diehl, Theol. 122 p. 108, 21) ***doing good,*** subst. (opp. ὁ κακός) **Ro 13:3 v.l.** (WLorimer, NTS 12, '66, 389f).

ἀγαθόν, οῦ, τό subst. neut. of ἀγαθός (q.v. 1b).

ἀγαθοποιέω 1 aor. ἠγαθοποίησεν Judg 17:13, inf. ἀγαθοποιῆσαι. W. antonym ἁμαρτάνειν **1 Pt 2:20,** κακοποιέω **Mk 3:4 v.l.; Lk 6:9; 1 Pt 2:14; 3J 11;** πονηρεύεσθαι Hs 9, 18, 1f; Dg 5:16 (πονηρία Hs 3, 5, 4).

❶ **to do that which is beneficial to another,** ***do good, be benevolent, be helpful*** (Sext. Emp., Math. 11, 70; Aesop 66 H.; LXX; EpArist 242; TestBenj 5:2.—B-D-F §119, 1) **Mk 3:4 vl.; Lk 6:9; Ac 14:17** D. W. pers. obj. ἀ. τινά *do good to someone* (Tob 12:13 BA) **Lk 6:33;** abs. (Zeph 1:12) **6:35.**

❷ **to meet a high level of exemplary conduct,** ***do what is right, be a good citizen*** **1 Pt 2:15** (cp. the adj. vs. 14), **20; 3:17; 3J 11;** Hs 9, 18, 1f; Dg 5:16; 2 Cl 10:2; Hv 3, 5, 4; 3, 9, 5; cp. **1 Pt 3:6** of exemplary wives.—M-M. TW. Spicq.

ἀγαθοποίησις, εως, ἡ *doing good* Hm 8:10; προθυμίαν ἔχειν τῆς ἀ. *be zealous to do good* Hs 5, 3, 4 (rare term, used by Eustratius [XI–XII AD] in a comm. on Aristot. EN, s. DGE s.v.).

ἀγαθοποιΐα, ας, ἡ (Ptolem., Apotel. 1, 18, 4 ed. FBoll-EBoer '40; Vett. Val. 164, 17; Vi. Aesopi III p. 309, 8) **engagement in doing what is good,** ***doing good*** (TestJos 18:2 v.l. B-D-F §119, 1); together with other ἀγαθ- terms, ἀ. is part of the semantic field relating to the esteem in which Gr-Rom. persons of exceptional merit were held. κτίστῃ παρατίθεσθαι τὰς ψυχὰς ἐν ἀγαθοποιΐᾳ (v.l.ἀγαθοποιΐαις) *entrust their souls to the creator while* (or *by*) *doing good,* which can be taken gener. or as meaning specif. acts (so, if pl.) **1 Pt 4:19;** πόθος εἰς ἀ. *a longing to do good* 1 Cl 2:2—cp. 2:7; 33:1; πρόθυμος εἰς ἀ. *eager to do good* 34:2.—TW. Spicq. Sv.

ἀγαθοποιός, όν (besides use in passages cited below, this late word appears, e.g., Ath. 26, 2, R. 35, 7; Sext. Emp., Math. 5, 29f; PGM 4, 2678; 5, 48), ***beneficent, doing good, upright*** (Plut., Mor. 368a; Physiogn. II 342, 31 al.; Sir 42:14); subst. ὁ ἀ. (StudPal XX, 293 verso, 7f [Byz.]) *one who does good, is a good citizen* **1 Pt 2:14** (a 'benefactor', opp. κακοποιός 'malefactor', as Artem. 4, 59 p. 238; 9, 11; Porphyr., Ep. ad Aneb. [GParthey, Iambl. De Myst. Lb. 1857 pp. xxix–xlv] c. 6; PGM 4, 2872; 13, 1028 and 1033).—M-M. TW. Spicq. Sv.

Ἀγαθόπους, ποδος, ὁ, acc. **Ἀγαθόπουν** (-ποδα longer Gk. recension) ***Agathopus,*** epithet of Ῥέος (q.v.) IPhld 11:1; I Sm 10:1. Freq. as name of slaves and freedpersons, s. Hdb. ad loc.; Preisigke, Namenbuch 1922; ins in RevArch 5, sér. 22, 1925, p. 363 no. 97, 2; Clem. Al., Strom. III 7, 59, 3.

ἀγαθός, ή, όν (Hom.+) Comp. ἀμείνων (not in NT, but e.g. PGM 5, 50; 6, 2; Jos., Bell. 5, 19, Ant. 11, 296) 1 Cl 57:2; IEph 13:2; 15:1; βελτίων, also κρείσσων, colloq. ἀγαθώτερος (Diod. S. 8 fgm. 12, 8; Judg 11:25 B; 15:2 B) Hm 8:9, 11. Superl. ἄριστος (Jos., C. Ap. 2, 156, Ant. 16, 142; Ath., R. 72, 8); colloq. ἀγαθώτατος (Diod. S. 16, 85, 7; Philo Bybl. [c. 100 AD] s. below 2aα; Heliod. 5, 15, 2; Synes., Ep. 143; Jos., Bell. 2, 277) Hv 1, 2, 3.—Ael. Dion. α, 10 rejects the forms ἀγαθώτερος, -τατος as wholly foreign to Greek (B-D-F §61, 1). When used of pers., freq. in ref. to good citizenship or acceptance of communal responsibility (cp. the def. in Cleanthes 3 [Coll. Alex. p. 229]).

❶ **pert. to meeting a relatively high standard of quality,** of things.—ⓐ adj. ***useful, beneficial*** καρποί (Procop. Soph., Ep. 27; Sir 6:19; Da 4:12 LXX) **Js 3:17.** δένδρον **Mt 7:17f.** γῆ *productive, fertile soil* (X., Oec. 16, 7 γῆ ἀ.—γῆ κακή; Diod. S. 5, 41, 6; Arrian, Anab. 4, 28, 3; Jos., Ant. 5, 178) **Lk 8:8;** B 6:8, 10. δόματα *beneficial* (Sir 18:17) **Mt 7:11; Lk 11:13.** δόσις **Js 1:17;** λόγος ἀ. πρὸς οἰκοδομήν *useful for edification* **Eph 4:29** (cp. X., Mem. 4, 6, 11; Chion, Ep. 3, 6 πρὸς ἀνδρείαν ἀμείνους; Isocr. 15, 284 ἄριστα πρὸς ἀρετήν); γνώμη ἀ. *a gracious declaration* 1 Cl 8:2; ἡμέραι ἀ. *happy* (Cass. Dio 51, 19; PGen 61, 10; Sir 14:14; 1 Macc 10:55) **1 Pt 3:10;** 1 Cl 22:2 (both Ps 33:13; 34:12); cp. 50:4.

ⓑ used as a pure subst.: sg. (Hom. et al.; ins, pap, LXX), **ἀγαθόν, οῦ, τό** *the good* (Diog. L. 1, 105 ἀγαθόν τε καὶ φαῦλον=a good and bad thing at the same time. TestAbr A 4, p. 80, 32 [Stone p. 8] of food); opp. (τὸ) κακόν Did., Gen. 21, 5; pl. ***ἀγαθά, ὧν, τά good things, possessions.***

α. quite gener. τὰ ἀγαθά σου **Lk 16:25** (cp. Job 21:13; En 103:3; PsSol 1:6, 5, 18; 17:44; 18:6; the opp. of τὰ κακά as Ephorus of Cyme [IV BC] περὶ ἀγαθῶν κ. κακῶν: 70 test. 1 Jac.; Diod. S. 18, 53, 1 ἀγαθῶν τε καὶ κακῶν μεταλαμβάνων; Job 2:10; s. SAalen NTS 13, '66, 5 on En 98:9); τοιαῦτα ἀ. *such fine things* Hs 9, 10, 1.—ποιῆσαι ταῦτα κ. περισσότερα ἀ. μεθ' ἡμῶν *to do these and far better things for us* 1 Cl 61:3.

β. *possessions, treasures* (Hdt. 2, 172 et al.; PRyl 28, 182 δεσπότης πολλῶν ἀγαθῶν κ. κτημάτων; Sir 14:4; Wsd 7:11; TestJob 4:8; SibOr 3, 660; 750) **Lk 1:53** (Ps 106:9.—Amphis Com. fgm. 28 [IV BC], in Athen. 3, 56, 100a, χορτάζομαι ἐν ἅπασιν ἀγαθοῖς; Sb 7517, 4 [211/12 AD] ἀγαθῶν πεπληρῶσθαι); **Gal 6:6;** Hv 3, 9, 6; τὰ ἀ. τῆς γῆς 1 Cl 8:4 (Is 1:19; cp. TestAbr A 4 p. 81, 18 [Stone p. 10] ἀ. τῶν ἐπιγείων); esp. of crops (Diod. S. 3, 46, 1 τὰ ἀ.='the good gifts', specifically 'products of nature'; likewise 19, 26, 3. Even more generally Synes., Kingship 16 p. 17d τὰ ἀ.=food; Philo, Op. M. 16, Mos. 1, 6) **Lk 12:18f.**

γ. possessions of a higher order (Dio Chrys. 64 [14], 1 ἐλευθερία as μέγιστον τ. ἀγαθῶν; Ael. Aristid. 24, 4 K.=44 p. 825 D.: ὁμόνοια as μέγ. τῶν ἀ.; 45, 18 K.=8 p. 89 D.: τὰ τῆς ψυχῆς ἀγ. Diog. L. 6, 4 the priest promises the initiate into the Orphic mysteries πολλὰ ἐν ᾅδου ἀγαθά) **Ro 3:8; 10:15** (Is 52:7).—**Hb 9:11; 10:1;** 2 Cl 6:6; 15:5.

❷ **pert. to meeting a high standard of worth and merit,** ***good***—ⓐ as adj.—α. of humans and deities (the primary focus is on usefulness to humans and society in general, so Pind.+, s. AAdkins Merit and Responsibility '60, 189f) *beneficent,* of God (Dio Chrys. 80 [30], 26 οἱ θεοί; Zoroaster in Philo Bybl.: 790 fgm. 4, 52 Jac. [Eus. PE 1, 10, 52] God is ἀγαθῶν ἀγαθώτατος. Sallust. 1 πᾶς θεὸς ἀγαθός; contrast Did., Gen. 109, 3 ὁ διάβολος οὐ φύσει κακός . . . ἐστίν, ἀλλὰ . . . ἀγαθὸς γέγονεν.—Cp. IKosPH 92, 6f which calls Nero ἀ. θεός, ἀγαθὸς δαίμων [OGI 666, 3; POxy 1021, 8, both referring to Nero; POxy 1449, 4; s. also JKroll, D. Lehren d. Hermes Trismeg. 1914, 90; Rtzst., Erlösungsmyst. 189; 191ff] and Sb 349 θεῷ ἀγαθῷ Διὶ Ἡλίῳ; Philo, Leg. All. 1, 47 al.; Celsus 4, 14) **Mt 19:17b** (in Cleanthes, Stoic. I 127, 3ff [Eus. PE 13, 13, 37], a description of God follows the question τἀγαθὸν ἐρωτᾷς μ' οἷόν ἐστ'; cp. Orig., C.Cels. 3, 70, 9; Did., Gen. 98, 28); **Mk 10:18**b (Unknown Sayings 33–36); **Lk 18:19b;** Dg 8:8 (on these passages cp. Simonid., fgm. 4, 6f χαλεπὸν ἐσθλὸν [=ἀγαθός ln. 10] ἔμμεναι; 7 θεὸς ἂν μόνος τοῦτ' ἔχοι γέρας); μόνος ἀ. ἐστιν ibid.; πατὴρ ἀ. 1 Cl 56:16 (Philo, Op. M. 21 ἀ. εἶναι τὸν πατέρα κ. ποιητήν); ἀ. ἐν τ. ὁρωμένοις *good in the visible world* 60:1.—Of Christ **Mk 10:17, 18a** (DomGMurray, Downside Review 103, '85, 144–46, w. ref. to Pirke Aboth 6, 3); **Lk 18:18, 19a** (WWagner, ZNW 8, 1907, 143–61; FSpitta, ibid. 9, 1908, 12–20; BWarfield, PTR 12, 1914, 177–228; WCaspari, Christent. u. Wissensch. 8, '32, 218–31.—Cp. also the saying of Pythagoras in Diog. L., Prooem. 12, who does not wish to be called σοφός because μηδένα εἶναι σοφὸν ἀλλ' ἢ θεόν);

J 7:12.—Of humans, other than Jesus **Mt 12:35; Ro 5:7;** D 3:8; νομοθέται B 21:4; πονηροί τε καὶ ἀ. *good and bad* designating a motley crowd **Mt 22:10.** Same contrast **5:45** (cp. Jos., Ant. 8, 314). βελτίονα ποιεῖν *make better* 1 Cl 19:1; βελτίω γενέσθαι *become better* Dg 1; *kind, generous* (X., Cyr. 3, 3, 4; CIG 37, 49) **Mt 20:15** (in **Mk 10:17f=Lk 18:18** [s. above] it is understood as *kind* by JWellhausen, EKlostermann, Billerb., Wagner, Spitta, Dalman [Worte 277], EHirsch [D. Werden des Mk '41, 246]); δεσπόται *benevolent* **1 Pt 2:18** (cp. PLips 40 II, 19, where a slave says ὁ ἀγαθὸς δεσπότης μου). δοῦλος (Heraclitus, Ep. 9, 3 [p. 212, 4 Malherbe]) **Mt 25:21, 23; Lk 19:17.** ἀνήρ (Teles p. 16, 6; Diod. S. 20, 58, 1; Epict. 3, 24, 51 al.; PLond I, 113/1, 8 p. 201; 2 Macc 15:12; 4 Macc 4:1; Jos., Bell. 5, 413, Ant. 18, 117; JGerlach, ΑΝΗΡ ΑΓΑΘΟΣ, diss. Munich '32) **Lk 23:50; Ac 11:24;** νέαι **Tit 2:5.** ἀπόστολοι *superb* 1 Cl 5:3.

β. of things characterized esp. in terms of social significance and worth, πνεῦμα **Lk 11:13 v.l.;** ἐντολή **Ro 7:12** (Ps.-Archytas [IV BC] in Stob., Ecl. 4, 138, IV 85, 17 H. νόμος ἀ. καὶ καλός); ἀγγελία (Pr 25:25) Hv 3, 13, 2; παιδεία s 6, 3, 6; μνεία ἀ. *kindly remembrance* **1 Th 3:6** (2 Macc 7:20 μνήμη ἀ.); ἐλπίς *dependable* (Pla., Rep. 331a; Chariton 7, 5, 10; Jos., Ant. 14, 96) **2 Th 2:16;** μερὶς ἀ. *the better part* **Lk 10:42;** πρᾶξις (Democr. 177 πρῆξις; Did., Gen. 69, 7) 1 Cl 30:7; συνείδησις *clear* **Ac 23:1; 1 Ti 1:5, 19; 1 Pt 2:19 v.l.; 3:16, 21;** 1 Cl 41:1; διάνοια Hm 5, 2, 7; ἐπιθυμία (Pr 11:23; 13:12) *pure* (i.e. directed toward pure things) *desire* m 12, 1, 1f; 2:4f; 3:1; γνώμη ἀ. *good intention* B 21:2; ἀ. ἐν Χριστῷ ἀναστροφή *admirable Christian conduct* **1 Pt 3:16;** ἀ. θησαυρός **Mt 12:35; Lk 6:45;** καρδία καλὴ καὶ ἀ. **8:15;** ἔργον (Thu. 5, 63, 3; PCairMasp 151, 237) *a good deed* **2 Cor 9:8; Col 1:10; 1 Ti 5:10; 2 Ti 2:21; 3:17; Tit 1:16; 3:1;** 1 Cl 2:7; 33:1; 34:4. Pl. ἔργα ἀ. (Empedocles [V BC] 112, 2) **1 Ti 2:10;** also specif. of benefactions (w. ἐλεημοσύναι) **Ac 9:36;** 1 Cl 33:7; ἐν παντὶ ἔργῳ κ. λόγῳ ἀ. (for this Hellenic formulation cp. Lk 24:19; Ac 7:22; for the simple λόγος ἀ. s. 3Km 8:56; 4 Km 20:19; Is 39:8) **2 Th 2:17;** ὑπομονὴ ἔργου ἀ. *persistency in doing right* **Ro 2:7.**

ⓑ as subst., sg. (s. 1b). Opp. (τὸ) κακόν Did., Gen. 21, 5; 27, 5.—**α.** that which is beneficial or helpful ἐργάζεσθαι τὸ ἀ. *do what is good* **Ro 2:10;** Hm 4, 2, 2; 7:4; also specif. of benefaction **Gal 6:10** and of socially acceptable work **Eph 4:28;** Hm 2:4; τὸ ἀ. ποιεῖν (cp. Jos., Bell. 1, 392) **Ro 13:3b;** Hm 8:12; cp. 6, 2, 8.—**Mt 19:17a; Ro 7:13; 12:9; 16:19; 1 Th 5:15; 1 Pt 3:13;** 1 Cl 21:6; 2 Cl 13:1; Hm 8:2, 7.

β. τὰ ἀ. (ἀληθινὰ ἀ. Orig., C. Cels 7, 21, 10) *good deeds* **J 5:29;** cp. Hm 10, 3, 1 (TestAbr A 9 p. 87, 28 [Stone p. 22] ἀγαθά τε καὶ πονηρά).—B. 1176. DELG. M-M. TW. Sv.

ἀγαθότης, ητος, ἡ *goodness* (s. prec. ἀγαθ- entries; Philo, Leg. All. 1, 59 ἡ γενικωτάτη ἀρετή, ἥν τινες ἀγαθότητα καλοῦσιν; Albinus, Didasc, 10 p. 165, 8) of God (Sallust. 3 p. 4, 4; 7 p. 14, 1 al.; Themist., Or. 1, p. 8, 28 D; Procl. on Pla., Rep. I p. 27, 10; 28, 4 al. WKroll; Simplicius in Epict. p. 12, 7; Cat. Cod. Astr. VIII/2 p. 156, 16; Sb 2034, 7; Wsd 7:26; 12:22; TestAbr A 14 p. 94, 29 [Stone p. 36]; ParJer 6:13; ApcEsdr 5, 18; Philo, Deus Imm. 73 al.) and of humans (Wsd 1:1; Sir 45:23; TestAsh 3:1; TestBenj 8:1), as 2 Cl 13:4; Hm 8:10 v.l.

ἀγαθουργέω Ac 14:17, s. ἀγαθοεργέω.

ἀγαθωσύνη, ης, ἡ (LXX; TestAbr A 1 p. 78, 4 [Stone p. 4]; Thom. Mag. p. 391, 12; for the formation s. W-S §16b note 14; Rob. 201) as human characteristic (2 Ch 24:16; Ps 51:5; TestAbr A 1; Hippol. Ref. 4, 15, 5; Physiogn. II 342, 17 ἀγαθοσύνη) **positive moral quality characterized esp. by interest in the welfare of others.**

ⓐ in gener. ***goodness*** **Ro 15:14; Eph 5:9; 2 Th 1:11.**

ⓑ ***generosity*** **Gal 5:22.** Of God (2 Esdr 19:25, 35) ἀ. τοῦ πατρὸς ἡμῶν B 2:9.—M-M. TW. Spicq.

ἀγαλλίασις, εως, ἡ (s. ἀγαλλιάω; only in Bibl. [incl. En 5:9; PsSol 5:1; Test12Patr] and eccl. wr. [s. Bauer's Introduction in this lexicon, p. xxi, note]; freq. in Ps.) **a piercing exclamation, *exultation*** ἦν πολλὴ ἀ. **Ac 11:28** D; w. χαρά **Lk 1:14;** 1 Cl 63:2; MPol 18:3; w. εὐφροσύνη 1 Cl 18:8; B 1:6; ἐν ἀ. *full of exultation, joy* **Lk 1:44; Ac 2:46; Jd 24;** MPol 18:3. ἔλαιον ἀγαλλιάσεως *oil of gladness* **Hb 1:9** (Ps 44:8 שֶׁמֶן שָׂשׂוֹן i.e. the oil w. which people anointed themselves at festivals). ἀπόδος μοι τὴν ἀ. τοῦ σωτηρίου σου *restore to me the joy of your salvation* 1 Cl 18:12 (Ps 50:14).—BReicke, Diakonie, Festfreude u. Zelos, etc. '51, 165–229.—TW.

ἀγαλλιάω (new formation in H. Gk. from ἀγάλλω, found only in Bibl. and eccl. wr.) seldom act. (B-D-F §101; Mlt-H. 225f): ἀγαλλιᾶτε **1 Pt 1:8 v.l.** (for ἀγαλλιᾶσθε); **Rv 19:7** ἀγαλλιῶμεν (v.l. ἀγαλλιώμεθα); ἀγαλλιῶντα GJs 17:2; ἀγαλλιῶντες ApcPt Rainer. 1 aor. (as POxy 1592, 4 [IV AD]) ἠγαλλίασεν **Lk 1:47** (ἐπὶ τ. θεῷ, cp. Hab 3:18 v.l.); usu. dep. ἀγαλλιάομαι (Syntipas p. 75, 28); fut. ἀγαλλιάσομαι (LXX); 1 aor. mid. ἠγαλλιασάμην or pass. ἠγαλλιάθην (v.l. ἠγαλλιάσθην; B-D-F §78; Mlt-H. 225) **to be exceedingly joyful, *exult, be glad, overjoyed*** (LXX; En 104:13; TestSol 19:1 P; TestAbr A 7 p. 84, 2f [Stone p. 16]; TestJob; ParJer 6:20; ApcrEzk P 1 recto 1; Test12Patr; Mel., P. 80, 586) abs. **1 Pt 1:6** (ἀγαλλιάσαντες P^{72}); 1 Cl 18:8 (Ps 50:10); IMg 1:1; Hm 5, 1, 2; 5, 2, 3; s 1:6; MPol 19:2; GJs 17:2; ApcPt Rainer; *my tongue exults* **Ac 2:26** (Ps 15:9); as here w. εὐφραίνεσθαι (Ps 30:8; 31:11; Is 25:9) Hm 5, 1, 2; s 9, 18, 4; χαίρειν καὶ ἀ. (Tob 13:15 BA; TestJob 43:15) **Mt 5:12; Rv 19:7;** cp. ἵνα χαρῆτε ἀγαλλιώμενοι *that you might shout for joy* **1 Pt 4:13;** ἀγαλλιώμενοι προσηύχοντο AcPl Ha 1, 32; ἀγαλλιώμενος ἐσκίρτησεν 3, 17; ἀ. . . . καὶ κλαίειν *weep for joy* 6, 2. W. complementary ptc. (B-D-F §415) ἠγαλλιάσατο πεπιστευκώς *he was overjoyed because he had become a believer* **Ac 16:34.** ἠγαλλιάσοντο μεγάλως μηνύ[οντες] AcPl Ha 8, 5 (ἠγαλλι[ᾶτο] μηνύων BMM recto 3f). W. ἵνα foll. (s. ἵνα 2aα): ἀ., ἵνα ἴδῃ *he was overjoyed that he was to see* **J 8:56** (B-D-F §392, 1). The one who causes the joy is given in the dat. ἀ. τῷ πνεύματι τῷ ἁγίῳ **Lk 10:21 v.l.;** w. ἐν and dat. ibid.—W. dat. of cause ἀ. χαρᾷ ἀνεκλαλήτῳ *exult w. unspeakable joy* **1 Pt 1:8.** οἷς ἀγαλλιῶμαι *I rejoice in this* IEph 9:2 (cp. Quint. Smyrn. 9, 118 παισὶν ἀγαλλόμενος=rejoicing aloud over his sons). The object of the joy is indicated by ἐπί τινι (Ps 9:15; 20:2; Sir 30:3 al.; B-D-F §196): 1Cl 33:2; Hs 8, 1, 18; 9, 24, 2. Also ἔν τινι (Ps 88:17) **J 5:35;** ἀ. ἐν τῷ πάθει *rejoice in the Passion* IPhld ins; the acc. occurs once ἀ. τὴν δικαιοσύνην *rejoice in righteousness* 1 Cl 18:15 (Ps 50:16).—[ἀγαλ]λ[ι]ῶσιν a prob. restoration AcPl BMM verso 20f.—Goodsp., Probs. 192–94; WNauck, Freude im Leiden, ZNW 46, '55, 68–80.—DELG s.v. ἀγάλλομαι. TW.

ἀγάλλομαι (Hom.+; Jos., Ant. 18, 66; SibOr 3, 785; TestAbr A 11 p. 89, 17 [Stone p. 26] al.; ParJer 6:6 ἀγάλλου) ***be glad, take pleasure*** ἐπί τινι *in someth.* (Thu. 3, 82, 7; Polemon Soph., Decl. 2, 17 p. 22, 1; Aesop., Fab. 74 P.=128 H.; Philo, Somn. 2, 211; Jos., Ant. 17, 112) 1 Cl 33:2 v.l. (the text ἀγαλλιᾶται, q.v.).—DELG.

ἄγαμος, ου, ὁ and **ἡ** (Hom. et al.; pap freq; Ath. 33:1) ***an unmarried man/woman,*** of both **1 Cor 7:8** (opp. γεγαμηκότες vs. 10 as X., Symp. 9, 7). Of men vs. **32;** Agr 18; of women (Aeschyl. Suppl. 143; Hyperid. 2, 12 et al.) **1 Cor 7:34;** ApcPt 11:26 (Klostermann notes Gebhardt's restoration: ἄ[γαμοι τὰ βρέφη τεκο]ῦσαι, but in the text reads the adv. ἀγάμως); of divorced women **1 Cor 7:11.** There is a curious usage in **Mt 22:10 v.l.** in ms. C.—DELG s.v. γαμέω. M-M. TW.

ἀγανακτέω (Aristoph. Vesp. 287+; Thu. 8, 43, 4; ins, pap; LXX, ApcrEzk [Epiph. 70, 70]) fut. 3 sg. ἀγανακτήσει Wsd 5:22; 1 aor. ἠγανάκτησα (s. ἀγανάκτησις) **be indignant against what is assumed to be wrong, *be aroused, indignant, angry*** (Bel 28 Theod.; Jos., Ant. 2, 284) **Mt 21:15; 26:8; Mk 10:14;** 2 Cl 19:2; Ox 1224 fgm. 2, II, 3. W. the pers. mentioned ἀ. περί τινος *at someone* **Mt 20:24; Mk 10:41** (cp. Pla., Ep. 7, 349d; Jos., Ant. 14, 182; B-D-F §229, 2). ἀ. ἐπί τινι (Lysias 1, 1; Isocr. 16, 49; PLond I, 44, 20 p. 34 [II BC]=UPZ 8, 20 ἀγανακτοῦντα ἐφ᾽ οἷς διετελοῦντο ἐν τοιούτῳ ἱερῷ; Wsd 12:27) *at someone* GPt 4:14; *at someth.* (Diod. S. 4, 63, 3 ἐπὶ τῷ γεγονότι; Appian, Macedon. 1, 3) 1 Cl 56:2; **Mk 14:4** ἦσαν δέ τινες ἀγανακτοῦντες πρὸς ἑαυτούς is difficult; perh. *some expressed their displeasure to each other* (but elsewh. πρός introduces the one against whom the displeasure is directed: Dio Chrys. 13 [7], 43 ὁ ἄρχων ἠγανάκτησε πρός με; Socrat., Ep. 6, 7.—D reads οἱ δὲ μαθηταὶ αὐτοῦ διεπονοῦντο καὶ ἔλεγον). A reason for displeasure is added w. ὅτι (Herodian 3, 2, 3) **Lk 13:14.**—DELG. M-M. Spicq.

ἀγανάκτησις, εως, ἡ (Thu. 2, 41, 3 et al.; Appian, Bell. Civ. 1, 10 §39; 4, 124 §521; PGrenf II, 82, 17f; Esth 8:12i v.l.; Jos., Bell. 4, 342) ***indignation*** **2 Cor 7:11.**—M-M. TW. Spicq.

ἀγαπάω impf. ἠγάπων; fut. ἀγαπήσω; 1 aor. ἠγάπησα; pf. ἠγάπηκα, ptc. ἠγαπηκώς; plpf. 3 sg. ἠγαπήκει Is. 2:25. Pass.: 1 fut. ἀγαπηθήσομαι; 1 aor. 2 sg. ἠγαπήθης Sir 47:16; pf. ptc. ἠγαπημένος (in var. mngs. Hom.+.—STromp de Ruiter, Gebruik en beteekenis van ἀγαπᾶν in de Grieksche Litteratuur 1930; CRichardson, Love: Gk. and Christian, JR 23, '43, 173–85).

❶ to have a warm regard for and interest in another, *cherish, have affection for, love*—ⓐ by human beings (Pind., Pla. et al.)—**α.** to a broad range of persons, apart from recipients of special devotion, for which see β; w. obj. given γυναῖκας **Eph 5:25, 28, 33** (on proper attitude of the husband cp. Plut., Mor. 142e); **Col 3:19;** ὡς ἀδελφήν Hv 1, 1, 1. τὸν πλησίον **Mt 5:43; 19:19; 22:39; Mk 12:31, 33** (on 33b s. Aristaen., Ep. 2, 13, end φιλῶ σε ὡς ἐμαυτήν); **Ro 13:9; Gal 5:14; Js 2:8;** B 19:5 (all quots. fr. Lev 19:18); s. πλησίον 2; τὸν ἕτερον **Ro 13:8.** τὸν ἀδελφόν **1J 2:10; 3:10; 4:20f.** τοὺς ἀδελφοὺς **3:14.** τὰ τέκνα τοῦ θεοῦ **5:2.** ἀλλήλους **J 13:34; 15:12, 17; 1J 3:11, 23; 4:7, 11f; 2J 5; Ro 13:8; 1 Th 4:9.** τοὺς ἀγαπῶντας **Mt 5:46; Lk 6:32.** τὸ ἔθνος ἡμῶν **7:5.** τοὺς ἐχθρούς **Mt 5:44; Lk 6:27, 35;** s. WvanUnnik, NovT 8, '66, 284–300, and s. ἐχθρός 2bβ; ἀ. τινα ὑπὲρ τὴν ψυχήν *love someone more than one's own life* B 1:4; 4:6; 19:5; D 2:7 (cp. Philo, Rer. Div. Her. 42 ὑπερφυῶς ἀ.; Kaibel 716, 5 φίλους ὑπὲρ ἁτὸν [=αὑτὸν] ἐτίμα). εἰ περισσοτέρως ὑμᾶς ἀγαπῶ, ἧσσον ἀγαπῶμαι; *if I love you the more, am I to be loved less?* **2 Cor 12:15;** ἀ. πολύ, ὀλίγον *show much* or *little affection* **Lk 7:47;** cp. πλεῖον ἀγαπήσει αὐτόν *will love him more* vs. **42** (on the love-hate pair s. AFridrichsen, Svensk Exegetisk Årsbok 5, '40, 152–62.—The meaning *be grateful* is suggested for **Lk 7:42** by HWood, ET 66, '55, 319, after JJeremias. See Jos., Bell. 1, 392 and Ps 114:1 LXX). Abs. ἡμεῖς ἀγαπῶμεν **1J 4:19.** πᾶς ὁ ἀγαπῶν vs. **7.** ὁ μὴ ἀγαπῶν vs. **8.** W. indication of the kind of affection: ἀ. ἐν Ἰησοῦ Χρ. I Mg 6:2. Opp. μισεῖν (Dt 21:15–17) **Mt 6:24; Lk 16:13.**

β. to transcendent recipients of special devotion: to Jesus **1 Pt 1:8.** Esp. in **J: 8:42; 14:15, 21, 23f; 21:15f** (always spoken by Jesus).—On the last passage s. AFridrichsen, SymbOsl 14, '35, 46–49; EMcDowell, RevExp 32, '35, 422–41; Goodsp., Probs. 116–18; JScott, ClW 39, '45–'46, 71f; 40, '46–'47, 60f; M-EBoismard, RB 54, '47, 486f.—ἀ. and φιλέω may be used interchangeably here (cp. the freq. interchange of synonyms elsewh. in the same chapter [βόσκειν–ποιμαίνειν, ἀρνία–προβάτια, ἑλκύειν–σύρειν], but s. KMcKay, NovT 27, '85, 319–33; also φιλέω).—To God (Dio Chrys. 11 [12], 61; Sextus 442; 444; ParJer 6:6; LXX; Philo, Post. Caini 69; Jos., Ant. 7, 269; TestBenj 3:1; 4:5) **Mt 22:37; Mk 12:30, 33; Lk 10:27** (all Dt 6:5); **Ro 8:28; 1 Cor 2:9; 8:3.** Of affection for the Creator B 19:2.

ⓑ of the affection of transcendent beings—**α.** for ordinary human beings (Dio Chrys. 3, 60 ἀγαπώμενος ὑπὸ θεῶν; 79 [28], 13; CIG 5159 Βρουτταρᾶτος, ὃν ἀγαπᾷ ἡ Φαρία Ἶσις; Norden, Agn. Th. 225 ὃν Ἄμμων ἀγαπᾷ; 226 [= OGI 90, 4]; s. β below; LXX; Jos., Ant. 8, 173; 314; TestNapht 8:4, 10) **Ro 8:37; 9:13** (Mal 1:2); **2 Th 2:16; Hb 12:6** (Pr 3:12); **J 14:21** (τηρηθήσεται P^{75}); **1J 4:10, 19;** 1 Cl 56:4 (Pr 3:12). ἱλαρὸν δότην **2 Cor 9:7.**—Jesus' affection for people Ἰ. ἠγάπησεν αὐτον *J. liked him* or *was fond of him* **Mk 10:21** (*displayed affection, caressed him* has also been suggested; cp. X., Cyr. 7, 5, 50; Plut., Pericl. 152 [1, 1] al.).—**Gal 2:20; Eph 5:2; J 11:5; 15:9;** B 1:1. Of the beloved disciple **J 13:23; 19:26; 21:7, 20;** s. Hdb.[3] on **J 13:23,** also JMaynard, JSOR 13, 1929, 155–59; Bultmann ad loc. et al.; AKragerud, Der Lieblingsjünger im Johannesevangelium, '59; LJohnson, ET 77, '66, 157f; see also μαθητής 2bα.—W. pf. pass. ptc. (cp. β) ἀδελφοὶ ἠ. ὑπὸ τ. θεοῦ (cp. Sir 45:1; 46:13) **1 Th 1:4; 2 Th 2:13;** ἅγιοι καὶ ἠ. **Col 3:12;** τοῖς ἐν θεῷ πατρὶ ἠγαπημένοις **Jd 1;** ἐκκλησία ἠ. ITr ins; IRo ins.—**Ro 9:25** (Hos 2:25 v.l.).

β. for other transcendent beings: God's love for Jesus **J 3:35; 10:17; 17:26,** from before creation **17:24.** Here belongs also the pf. pass. ptc. *the one loved* by God (cp. Dt 32:15; 33:5, 26; Is 44:2) as designation of Jesus (cp. ParJer 3:11; AscIs 3:4; TestAbr A 1 p. 78, 6 [Stone p. 4] Ἀβραὰμ τὸν ἠ. μου φίλον; OGI 90, 4 [II BC] an Egyptian king is ἠγαπημένος ὑπό τοῦ Φθᾶ; Mitt-Wilck. I/2, 109, 12 [III BC] a king ἠγαπημένος ὑπὸ τ. Ἴσιδος) **Eph 1:6;** B 3:6; 4:3, 8. ἠγαπημένος παῖς αὐτοῦ 1 Cl 59:2f; υἱὸς ἠ. Hs 9, 12, 5. Of Jerusalem τὴν πόλιν τὴν ἠ. (Sir 24:11) **Rv 20:9.**—S. the lit. on φιλέω 1a.—Jesus' love for God **J 14:31.**

❷ to have high esteem for or satisfaction with someth., *take pleasure in* (Aesop, Fab. 156 P.)—Appian, Mithrid. 57 §230 τὰ προτεινόμενα=the proffered terms. PsSol 14:6 ἡμέραν ἐν μετοχῇ ἁμαρτίας αὐτῶν day of partnership in their sin. Also striving after someth. (Theopomp. [IV BC]: 115 fgm. 124 Jac. τιμήν; Diod. S 11, 46, 2 τ. πλοῦτον; Appian, Bell. Civ. 1, 49 §215 citizenship; SIG 1268 I, 9 [III BC] φιλίαν ἀγάπα='value friendship'; pap of early Ptolemaic times in WCrönert, NGG 1922, 31; Ps 39:17; Sir 3:26) τὴν πρωτοκαθεδρίαν καὶ τοὺς ἀσπασμούς **Lk 11:43.** μισθὸν ἀδικίας **2 Pt 2:15.** τὸν κόσμον **1J 2:15.** τὸν νῦν αἰῶνα **2 Ti 4:10;** Pol 9:2. δικαιοσύνην (Wsd 1:1; Orig., C. Cels. 6, 79, 22) **Hb 1:9** (Ps 44:8). σεμνότητα Hm 5, 2, 8. τὴν ἀλήθειαν (Jos., C. Ap. 2, 296; TestReub 3:9) 1 Cl 18:6 (Ps 50:8); Hm 3:1. Opp. ἀ. ψεύδη B 20:2. ὅρκον ψευδῆ 2:8 (Zech 8:17). μᾶλλον τὸ σκότος ἢ τὸ φῶς **J 3:19** (on ἀγ. μᾶλλον w. acc. cp. Jos., Ant. 5, 350 and see μᾶλλον 3c); ἀ. τὴν δόξαν τ. ἀνθρώπων μᾶλλον ἤπερ τ. δ. τοῦ θεοῦ *value the approval of human beings more highly than that of God* **12:43** (cp. Pla. Phdr. 257e). ζωήν *enjoy life* (Sir 4:12) **1 Pt 3:10;** also τὴν ψυχήν (Sir 30:23 v.l.) **Rv 12:11.**—Hence *long for* τὶ *someth.* (Ps

39:17) τὴν ἐπιφάνειαν αὐτοῦ *his appearing* **2 Ti 4:8.** W. inf. fol. *wish* (Anton. Lib. 40, 1 ἠγάπησεν ἀεὶ παρθένος εἶναι) ἀ. ἡμέρας ἰδεῖν ἀγαθάς *to see good days* 1 Cl 22:2 (Ps 33:13). τὸ παθεῖν *wish for martyrdom* ITr 4:2.—ἀγάπην ἀ. (2 Km 13:15) *show love* **J 17:26; Eph 2:4;** *show one's admiration* τὰ δεσμά *for my bonds* i.e. they were not embarrassed by them IPol 2:3 (not *kiss;* there is so far no evidence for that mng. of ἀ.).—ISm 7:1 the context seems to require for ἀ. the sense ἀγάπην ποιεῖν (8:2) = *hold a love-feast,* but so far this mng. cannot be confirmed lexically. But since the noun ἀγάπη is used absolutely in 6:2 in the sense 'concern for' someone, it may be that ἀγαπᾶν in 7:1 refers to *acts of kindness.*

❸ **to practice/express love,** ***prove one's love*** **J 13:1, 34** (perh. an allusion to the agape or love-feast, s. ἀγάπη 2). Abs. w. indication of the means μὴ ἀγαπῶμεν λόγῳ μηδὲ τῇ γλώσσῃ ἀλλὰ ἐν ἔργῳ *let us show our love with deeds as well as w. word or tongue* (TestGad 6:1 ἀγαπήσατε ἀλλήλους ἐν ἔργῳ) **1J 3:18;** cp. ἀ. τῷ στόματι *love w. the mouth* 1 Cl 15:4 (Ps 77:36 Swete; ed. Rahlfs '31 v.l.).—RJoly, Le vocabulaire chretien de l'amour est-il original? '68.—B. 1110. DELG. M-M. TW. Spicq. Sv.

ἀγάπη, ης, ἡ (this term has left little trace in polytheistic Gk. lit. A sepulchral ins, prob. honoring a polytheistic army officer, who is held in 'high esteem' by his country [SEG VIII, 11, 6 (III AD)] sheds light on an ex. such as Philod., παρρ. col. 13a, 3 Oliv., but s. Söding [below] 294. The restorations in POxy 1380, 28 and 109f [II AD] are in dispute: s. New Docs 4, 259 [lit.]; Söding [end] 294f, n. 68 [lit.]. For other exx. from the Gr-Rom. world s. Ltzm., exc. after 1 Cor 13; L-S-J-M; ACeresa-Gastaldo, Ἀγάπη nei documenti anteriori al NT: Aegyptus 31, '51, 269–306, has a new pap and a new ins ex. fr. III AD secular sources; in RivFil 31, '53, 347–56 the same author shows it restored in an ins of 27 BC, but against C-G. s. lit. Söding 293, n. 57. In Jewish sources: LXX, esp. SSol, also pseudepigr., Philo, Deus Imm. 69; Just., D. 93, 4. Cp. ACarr, ET 10, 1899, 321–30. Its paucity in gener. Gk. lit. may be due to a presumed colloq. flavor of the noun (but s. IPontEux I, 359, 6 as parallel to 2 Cor 8:8 below). No such stigma attached to the use of the verb ἀγαπαω (q.v.).

❶ **the quality of warm regard for and interest in another,** ***esteem, affection, regard, love*** (without limitation to very intimate relationships, and very seldom in general Greek of sexual attraction).

ⓐ of human love—**α.** without indication of the pers. who is the object of interest (cp. Eccl 9:1, 6; Sir 48:11 v.l.): ἀ. as subj. ἡ ἀ. οἰκοδομεῖ **1 Cor 8:1.**—13:4, 8 (on **1 Cor 13** see the comm. [Maxim Tyr. 20:2 praise of ἔρως what it is not and what it is; s. AHarnack, SBBerlAk 1911, 132–63, esp. 152f; ELehmann and AFridrichsen, 1 Cor 13 e. christl.-stoische Diatribe: StKr Sonderheft 1922, 55–95]; EHoffmann, Pauli Hymnus auf d. Liebe: Dtsche Vierteljahrsschrift für Literaturwiss. u. Geistesgesch. 4, 1926, 58–73; NLund, JBL 50, '31, 266–76; GRudberg, Hellas och Nya Testamentet '34, 149f; HRiesenfeld, ConNeot 5, '41, 1–32, Nuntius 6, '52, 47f); **Phil 1:9.** ἡ ἀ. κακὸν οὐκ ἐργάζεται **Ro 13:10;** πλήρωμα νόμου ἡ ἀ. ibid.; ψυγήσεται ἡ ἀ. τ. πολλῶν **Mt 24:12;** ἡ ἀ. ἀνυπόκριτος *let love be genuine* **Ro 12:9,** cp. **2 Cor 6:6.** As predicate **1 Ti 1:5; 1J 4:16b** (cp. bα). As obj. ἀγάπην ἔχειν (Did., Gen. 221, 30) **1 Cor 13:1–3; Phil 2:2** φιλίαν ἢ ἀγάπην ἔχοντες Just., D. 93, 4; διώκειν **1 Cor 14:1; 1 Ti 6:11; 2 Ti 2:22;** ἐνδύσασθαι τὴν ἀ. **Col 3:14.** ἀφιέναι **Rv 2:4.—2 Pt 1:7; Col 1:8.** ἐμαρτύρησάν σου τῇ ἀ. **3J 6.** Attributively in gen. case ὁ κόπος τῆς ἀ. **1 Th 1:3;** τὸ τ. ὑμετέρας ἀ. γνήσιον *the genuineness of your love* **2 Cor 8:8.** ἔνδειξις τῆς ἀ. vs. **24;** cp. πᾶσαν ἐνδεικνυμένους ἀ. **Tit 2:10 v.l.—Hb 10:24; Phil 2:1; 1 Pt 5:14;** 1 Cl 49:2.—In prep. phrases ἐξ ἀγάπης *out of love* **Phil 1:16;** παράκλησις ἐπὶ τῇ ἀ. σου *comfort from your love* **Phlm 7;** περιπατεῖν κατὰ ἀ., ἐν ἀ. **Ro 14:15; Eph 5:2;** ἐν ἀ. ἔρχεσθαι (opp. ἐν ῥάβδῳ) **1 Cor 4:21;** ἀληθεύειν ἐν ἀ. **Eph 4:15.** Other verbal combinations w. ἐν ἀ., **1 Cor 16:14; Eph 3:17; 4:2; Col 2:2; 1 Th 5:13;** cp. **Eph 4:16** (on **Eph 1:4** s. bα). ἐν τῇ ἀ. **1J 4:16b, 18.** διὰ τῆς ἀ. δουλεύετε ἀλλήλοις **Gal 5:13.** πίστις δι' ἀγάπης ἐνεργουμένη **5:6.** διὰ τὴν ἀ. παρακαλῶ *for love's sake I appeal* **Phlm 9.** μετὰ ἀγάπης πολιτεύεσθαι *live in love* 1 Cl 51:2.—W. ἀλήθεια **2J 3;** πίστις **1 Th 3:6; 5:8; 1 Ti 1:14; 2 Ti 1:13; Phlm 5;** B 11:8; IEph 1:1; 9:1; 14:1 al. W. πίστις and other concepts on the same plane **Eph 6:23; 1 Ti 2:15; 4:12; 6:11; 2 Ti 2:22; 3:10; Tit 2:2; Rv 2:19;** Hm 8:9; cp. v 3, 8, 2–5. The triad πίστις, ἐλπίς, ἀγάπη **1 Cor 13:13;** s. also **Col 1:4f; 1 Th 1:3; 5:8;** B 1:4 (cp. Porphyr., Ad Marcellam 24 τέσσαρα στοιχεῖα μάλιστα κεκρατύνθω περὶ θεοῦ· πίστις, ἀλήθεια, ἔρως, ἐλπίς and s. Rtzst., Hist. Mon. 1916, 242ff, NGG 1916, 367ff; 1917, 130ff, Hist. Zeitschr. 116, 1916, 189ff; AHarnack, PJ 164, 1916, 5ff = Aus d. Friedens- u. Kriegsarbeit 1916, 1ff; PCorssen, Sokrates 7, 1919, 18ff; ABrieger, D. urchr. Trias Gl., Lbe, Hoff., diss. Heidelb. 1925; WTheiler, D. Vorbereitung d. Neuplatonismus 1930, 148f). W. δύναμις and σωφρονισμός **2 Ti 1:7.** Cp. B 1:6.—Attributes of love: ἀνυπόκριτος **Ro 12:9; 2 Cor 6:6.** γνησία 1 Cl 62:2. φιλόθεος and φιλάνθρωπος Agr 7. σύμφωνος IEph 4:1 ἄοκνος IPol 7:2. ἐκτενής **1 Pt 4:8.** It is a *fruit of the Spirit* καρπὸς τοῦ πνεύματος **Gal 5:22,** and takes first rank among the fruits. ἀ. τοῦ πνεύματος **Ro 15:30;** cp. **Col 1:8.** Since the term denotes concern for another, the sense *alms, charity* ISm 6:2 is readily apparent (cp. ἀ. λαμβάνειν 'receive alms' PGen 14, 7).—ἀσπάζεται ὑμᾶς ἡ ἀγάπη τῶν ἀδελφῶν *the members greet you with love* IPhld 11:2; ISm 12:1, cp. ITr 13:1; IRo 9:3. In these passages the object of the love is often made plain by the context; in others it is

β. expressly mentioned—**א.** impers. ἀ. τῆς ἀληθείας **2 Th 2:10;** ἀ. τῆς πατρίδος *love for the homeland* 1 Cl 55:5.

ב. human beings ἀ. εἴς τινα *love for someone* εἰς πάντας τοὺς ἁγίους **Eph 1:15; Col 1:4.** εἰς ἀλλήλους καὶ εἰς πάντας **1 Th 3:12; 2 Th 1:3;** cp. **2 Cor 2:4, 8; 1 Pt 4:8; 2J 6.** ἐν ἀλλήλοις **J 13:35.** ἐξ ἡμῶν ἐν ὑμῖν **2 Cor 8:7;** ἡ ἀ. μου μετὰ ὑμῶν **1 Cor 16:24.**

ג. God or Christ (πρὸς τὸν θεόν Orig., C. Cels. 3, 15, 12) ἀ. τοῦ θεοῦ *love toward God* (but in many cases the gen. may be subjective) **Lk 11:42; J 5:42; 2 Th 3:5; 1J 2:5, 15; 3:17; 4:12; 5:3; 2 Cor 7:1** P 46 (for φόβος); ἀ. εἰς θεὸν καὶ Χριστὸν καὶ εἰς τὸν πλησίον Pol 3:3; ἀ. εἰς τὸ ὄνομα θεοῦ **Hb 6:10.**

ⓑ of the love of God and Christ—**α.** to humans. Of God (cp. Wsd 3:9): **1J 4:10;** ἐν ἡμῖν **1J 4:9, 16.** εἰς ἡμᾶς **Ro 5:8,** cp. vs. **5.** τετελείωται ἡ ἀ. μεθ' ἡμῶν **1J 4:17** (s. HPreisker app. to HWindisch Comm. 167); ἀπὸ τῆς ἀ. τοῦ θεοῦ τῆς ἐν χριστῷ Ἰησοῦ **Ro 8:39.** ἀγάπην διδόναι *bestow love* **1J 3:1;** ἐν ἀ. προορίσας ἡμᾶς εἰς υἱοθεσίαν **Eph 1:4f:** the rhythm of the passage suggests the believers as agents for ἀ. in vs. **4** (cp. vs. **15**), but **2:4** favors God; s. the comm.—**2 Cor 13:13; Jd 2** and **21.** God is the source of love **1J 4:7,** the θεὸς τῆς ἀ. **2 Cor 13:11,** and therefore *God is love* **1J 4:8, 16.** Christians, embraced by God's love, are τέκνα ἀγάπης B 9:7; 21:9.—Of Jesus' love **J 15:9, 10a, 13** (s. MDibelius, Joh 15:13: Deissmann Festschr. 1927, 168–86); **1J 3:16.—Ro 8:35; 2 Cor 5:14;** cp. **Eph 3:19.** Perh. the ἀληθὴς ἀγάπη of Pol 1:1 is a designation of Jesus or his exemplary concern for others.

β. of the relation betw. God and Christ **J 15:10b; 17:26** (on the constr. cp. Pel.-Leg. 12, 21 ὁ πλοῦτος ὅν με ἐπλούτισεν ὁ σατανᾶς). τοῦ υἱοῦ τῆς ἀ. αὐτοῦ *of the son of (God's) love,* i.e. *of (God's) beloved son* **Col 1:13** (s. PsSol 13:9 υἱὸς ἀγαπήσεως).—WLütgert, D. L. im NT 1905; BWarfield, PTR 16, 1918, 1–45; 153–203; JMoffatt, Love in the NT 1929;

HPreisker, StKr 95, 1924, 272–94, D. urchr. Botschaft v. der L. Gottes 1930; RSchütz, D. Vorgeschichte der joh. Formel ὁ θεὸς ἀγ. ἐστίν diss. Kiel 1917; CBowen, Love in the Fourth Gosp.: JR 13, '33, 39–49; GEichholz, Glaube u. L. im 1 J: EvTh '37, 411–37. On ἔρως and ἀ. s. Harnack, SBBerlAk 1918, 81–94; ANygren, Eros u. Agape I 1930, II '37 (Eng. tr. Agape and Eros, AHebert and PWatson '32, '39; on this JRobinson, Theology 48, '45, 98–104); LGrünhut, Eros u. Ag. '31. Cp. CTarelli, Ἀγάπη: JTS n.s. 1, '50, 64–67; ELee, Love and Righteousness: ET 62, '50/51, 28–31; AŠuštar, Verbum Domini 28, '50, 110–19; 122–40; 193–213; 257–70; 321–40; TOhm, D. Liebe zu Gott in d. nichtchristl. Religionen, '50; WHarrelson, The Idea of Agape: JR 31, '51, 169–82; VWarnach, Agape: Die Liebe als Grundmotiv der ntl. Theol. 1951; JSteinmueller, Ἐρᾶν, Φιλεῖν, Ἀγαπᾶν in Extrabiblical and Bibl. Sources: Studia Anselmiana 27f, '51, 404–23.—Full bibliog. in HRiesenfeld, Étude bibliographique sur la notion biblique d' ἀγάπη, surtout dans 1 Cor 13: ConNeot 5, '41, 1–32; s. also EDNT.

❷ **a common meal eaten by early Christians in connection with their worship, for the purpose of fostering and expressing mutual affection and concern, *fellowship meal, a love-feast*** (the details are not discussed in the NT, although Paul implicitly refers to it 1 Cor 11:17ff; cp. D 9–10; s. also Pliny ep. 10, 96, 7; AcPlTh 25 [Aa I 252]; Clem. Al., Paed. 2, 1, 4, Strom. 3, 2, 10; Pass. Perp. et Felic. 17, 1; Tertull., Apolog. 39, De Jejun. 17; Minucius Felix 31) **Jd 12** (v.l. ἀπάταις; in **2 Pt 2:13** ἀγάπαις is v.l. for ἀπάταις; the same v.l. Eccl 9:6, where ἀπάτη in ms. S is meaningless: s. RSchütz, ZNW 18, 1918, 224; s. ἀγαπάω 3 on **J 13:1, 34**). ἀγάπη ἄφθαρτος IRo 7:3. ἀγάπην ποιεῖν *hold a love-feast* ISm 8:2, in both pass. w. prob. ref. to the eucharist (s. ἀγαπάω 2 and 3).—Meals accompanied by religious rites and in a religious context were conducted by various social groups among the Greeks from early times (s. Bauer's Introduction, pp. xxvii–viii, above). A scholion on Pla. 122b says of such meals among the Lacedaemonians that they were called φιλίτια, because they φιλίας συναγωγά ἐστιν. Is ἀγ. perhaps a translation of φιλία into Christian terminology?—JKeating, The Ag. and the Eucharist in the Early Church 1901; HLeclercq, Dict. d'Arch. I 1903, 775–848; FFunk, Kirchengesch. Abhdlgen. 3, 1907, 1–41; EBaumgartner, Eucharistie u. Ag. im Urchr. 1909; RCole, Love Feasts, a History of the Christian Ag. 1916; GWetter, Altchr. Liturgien II 1921; HLietzmann, Messe u. Herrenmahl 1926 (on this ALoisy, Congr. d'Hist. du Christ. I 1928, 77–95); KVölker, Mysterium u. Ag. 1927; DTambolleo, Le Agapi '31; BReicke, Diakonie, Festfreude u. Zelos in Verbindung mit der altchristlichen Agapenfeier, '51.—TSöding, Das Wortfeld der Liebe im paganen und biblischen Griechisch: ETL 68, '92, 284–330.—DELG s.v. ἀγαπάω. M-M. TW. Spicq. TRE s.v. Liebe.

ἀγαπητός, ή, όν (verbal adj. of ἀγαπάω, fixed as an adj. B-D-F §65, 3; Rob. 1096) 'beloved.'

❶ **pert. to one who is in a very special relationship with another, *only, only beloved,*** in ref. to an only son (common Hom.+; Pollux 3, 19 καλοῖτο ἂν υἱὸς ἀγ. ὁ μόνος ὢν πατρί; LXX [יָחִיד] Gen 22:2, 12, 16 al.; ParJer 7:24 [Baruch]; AscIs 3:13, 17, 18; 4:3; 7:24 [Baruch]; subst. ὁ ἀγαπητός. Philo, Ebr. 30 μόνος κ. ἀγ. υἱός). Of Christ's (cp. the interpolation in TestBenj 11:2) relationship to God ὁ υἱός μου ὁ ἀ. **Mt 3:17** (BBacon, Jesus' Voice fr. Heaven: AJT 9, 1905, 451–73) = GEb 18, 39; **Mt 17:5; Mk 1:11** = GEb 18, 37; **Mk 9:7,** cp. **12:6** (CTurner, JTS 27, 1926, 113–29; 28, 1927, 362 would translate *only;* s. ASouter, ibid. 28, 1927, 59f); **Lk 3:22; 9:35 v.l.;** cp. **20:13; 2 Pt 1:17.—Mt 12:18;** MPol 14:1, 3; Dg 8:11.

❷ **pert. to one who is dearly loved, *dear, beloved, prized, valued*** (pap, LXX; pseudepigr.; Jos., Bell. 1, 240, Ant. 15, 15; Mel., P. 2, 7) indicating a close relationship, esp. that betw. parent and child υἱός (TestAbr A 83, 31f [Stone p. 14]; Artem. 5, 37) Hs 5, 2, 6. W. τέκνον **1 Cor 4:17,** τέκνα vs. **14; Eph 5:1;** ἀδελφός **Phlm 16.** W. proper names (POxy 235, 2 [I BC] Τρύφων ἀγαπητέ) **Ro 16:12; Phlm 1; Ac 15:25; 3J 1;** w. proper names and ἀδελφός **Eph 6:21; Col 4:7, 9; 2 Pt 3:15;** w. σύνδουλος **Col 1:7;** w. τέκνον **2 Ti 1:2;** w. ἰατρός **Col 4:14;** w. gen. of the pers. pron. and a proper name Ἐπαίνετον τὸν ἀ. μου **Ro 16:5;** cp. vs. **8f;** IPol 8:2.—Oft. in dir. address (Hippol., Ref. 4, 50, 1) ἀγαπητέ *dear friend* **3J 2, 5, 11** (cp. Tob 10:13); mostly pl. ἀγαπητοί **Ro 12:19; 2 Cor 7:1; 12:19; Hb 6:9; 1 Pt 2:11; 4:12; 2 Pt 3:1, 8, 14, 17; 1J 2:7; 3:2, 21; 4:1, 7, 11; Jd 3, 17, 20;** 1 Cl 1:1; 7:1; 12:8; 21:1; 24:1f al.; ἀ. μου **1 Cor 10:14; Phil 2:12;** IMg 11:1. ἄνδρες ἀγαπητοί *dear people* 1 Cl 16:17. ἀδελφοί μου ἀ. **1 Cor 15:58; Js 1:16, 19; 2:5;** ἀδελφοί μου ἀ. καὶ ἐπιπόθητοι **Phil 4:1.**—Of members of a Christian group ἀ. θεοῦ **Ro 1:7** (cp. Ps 59:7; 107:7; ApcEsdr 1:1 p. 24, 3 [Ezra]). (Παῦλον) τὸν ἀγαπητόν τοῦ κυρίου AcPl Ha 8, 2. The Israelites are κατὰ τὴν ἐκλογὴν ἀ. **Ro 11:28.** Of the prophets IPhld 9:2.—ἀγαπητοὶ ἡμῖν ἐγενήθητε *you have become dear to us* **1 Th 2:8;** cp. **1 Ti 6:2** (perh. = *worthy of love,* as X., Mem. 3, 10, 5); ἀ. λίαν ἔχειν τινά *hold someone very dear* IPol 7:2.—EHvanLeeuwen, Ἀγαπητοί: ThStud 21, 1903, 139–51.—New Docs 4, 252. M-M. TW.

Ἁγάρ, ἡ (Bov., N.; Ἀγάρ M.; Ἄγαρ t.r., Tdf., S., Vog.; Ἅγαρ W-H.—הָגָר) indecl. (LXX, Philo.—In Jos. Ἀγάρη, ης [Ant. 1, 215]) ***Hagar,*** a concubine of Abraham, mother of Ishmael (Gen 16); taken allegorically by Paul as a type of Judaism **Gal 4:24.** In vs. **25** τὸ δὲ Ἁγὰρ Σινᾶ ὄρος ἐστὶν ἐν τῇ Ἀραβίᾳ the ms. readings vary considerably (Zahn, Gal exc. II p. 296–99). Perh. this is a play on names, since Arab. 'hajar' (or ḥadschar, ḥağar) means 'stone', and names compounded w. it are found on the Sinai peninsula. The sense is: Hagar is a type of the Mosaic law, since Ἁγάρ = Σινᾶ.—TW.

ἀγγαρεύω fut. ἀγγαρεύσω; 1 aor. ἠγγάρευσα (cogn. ἄγγαρος Persian [s. RSchmitt, Glotta 49, '71, 97ff; B-D-F §6] term for royal messengers [Nicol. Dam.: 90, 4 Jac. II A p. 333, 27ff] later of mounted national postal couriers [= ἀγγαρήιον Hdt 8, 98]; loanw. in Aeschyl., Ag. 282; Hdt 3, 126, with derivation of the verb in H. Gk.: Menand. fgm. 373 Kö. = Sicyon fgm. 4 S. p. 285; pap since 257 BC [Mayser I^1 p. 42 and I^2, 3 p. 139, 3; also PCairZen 509, 5]; OGI 665, 24; Jos., Ant. 13, 52. For the v.l. ἐγγαρεύω s. B-D-F §42, 2; Mlt-H. 67. Also in rabbin. lit. [PFiebig, ZNW 18, 1920, 64–72], and in Lat. as 'angariare': Ulpian, Dig. XLIX 18, 4) ***requisition*** (orig. of the official post in the Hellenistic period), *press into service,* and so *force, compel* w. obj. τοῦτον ἠγγάρευσαν, ἵνα ἄρῃ τὸν σταυρὸν *they pressed him into service, to carry the cross* **Mt 27:32;** cp. **Mk 15:21.** ὅστις σε ἀγγαρεύσει μίλιον ἕν (sc. ὑπάγειν) *whoever forces you to go one mile* **Mt 5:41;** D 1:4.—FOertel, Die Liturgie 1917, 24ff.; HPflaum, Essai sur le cursus publicus, Mém. Acad. Insc. et Bell. Lettr. 14, '40, 1ff. MRostovtzeff, Klio 6, 1906, 249ff; Wilcken, Grundzüge 372ff, APF 4, 1908, 228; FZucker SBBerlAk 1911, 803ff; FPreisigke, Klio 7, 1907, 241ff, Fachwörter 1915; SMitchell, JRS 66, '76, 106–31 (new ins fr. Pisidia).—DELG s.v. ἄγγαρος. New Docs 1, 42; 2, 77. M-M. Spicq.

ἀγγεῖον, ου, τό (Hdt.+; ins, pap, LXX) ***vessel, flask, container*** e.g. for oil (PColZen 21, 2 [III BC]; BGU 248, 40 [I AD]; Num 4:9; Philo; Jos., Bell. 3, 272, Ant. 9, 48) **Mt 25:4.** Of containers for fish (cp. PSI 553, 11 [III BC] for edible snails) **13:48 v.l.** for ἄγγη. Fig., of the body (Hippocr. et al.; Dio Chrys. 11 [12], 59; M. Ant. 3, 3, 6; Stob. I 414, 9; Philo, Post. Cain. 137,

Migr. Abr. 193; 197) as the home of spirits (w. ἄγγος) Hm 5, 2, 5. S. ἄγγος.—DELG s.v. ἄγγος. M-M.

ἀγγελία, ας, ἡ (Hom. et al.; LXX).—❶ ***message*** (Jos., Ant. 17, 332, Vi. 380; TestNapht 2:1) gener. ἀ. ἀγαθή (Pr 12:25; 25:25) *good news* Hv 3, 13, 2; of the gospel **1J 1:5,** with content indicated by a ὅτι-clause.

❷ ***instruction, directive*** to love one's fellow-members in Christ **3:11,** w. ἵνα foll.—DELG s.v. ἄγγελος. M-M. TW.

ἀγγελικός, ή, όν (Pollux 4, 103) **pertaining to a heavenly messenger, *angelic*** (τῇ ἀ. διαλέκτῳ TestJob 48:3; τῆς ἀ. στρατιᾶς Just., A I, 52, 3; Theosophien 14 p. 170, 11; Hierocles 2, 423; Proclus on Pla., Rep., index Kroll; schol. on Pla. 216a; Simplicius in Epict. p. 42, 53 ἀρεταὶ ἀγγελικαί; 45, 54; 80, 7) τοποθεσίαι ἀ. *places of the angels* ITr 5:2. φοβοῦμαι μήπως ἀγγελικόν ‹ἐστιν τὸ› ἐν ἑαυτῇ *I fear lest that which is in her is of angelic parentage* GJs 14:1 deStrycker (cp. Gen 6:1, 4; En 106:6, 12; Jubilees 5:1–12).—JBartlet's restoration Ox 1081, 34 is untenable (SJCh 90, 12 reads ἀγένητος [s. ἀγέννητος]).

ἀγγέλλω 1 aor. ἤγγειλα (Hom.+; ins, pap [seldom], LXX in several pass., e.g. Jer 4:15 as v.l.; Jos., Vi. 301 al.; Just.) ***announce*** τινί *to someone,* of the Easter message brought by Mary Magdalene **J 20:18; 4:51 v.l.** (for λέγοντες, also w. v.l. ἀπ- and v.l. ἀν-) followed by ὅτι; GJs 6:3.—S. also ἀναγγέλλω 1 end, and ἀπαγγέλλω. AcPl Ha 2, 15: καὶ ἀπελθοῦ||[σα ἤγγει]λεν τῷ Παύλῳ.—B. 1278. DELG s.v. ἄγγελος. M-M. TW.

ἄγγελος, ου, ὁ (Hom.+) 'messenger'.—❶ **a human messenger serving as an envoy, *an envoy, one who is sent***—ⓐ by humans (Hom.+; ins, pap; Gen 32:4, 7; Jdth 1:11; 3:1; 1 Macc 1:44; 7:10; Jos., Ant. 14, 451, Vi. 89): in his earthly ministry Jesus ἀπέστειλεν ἀγγέλους (Diod. S. 2,18,1 the king of India to Semiramis; 4, 65, 4) **Lk 9:52;** of John the Baptist's disciples **7:24;** of Joshua's scouts **Js 2:25** (cp. Josh 7:22).

ⓑ by God (prophets Hg 1:13; Mal subscr.; a priest Mal 2:7.—1 Esdr 1:48f. S. also Theognis 1, 769, where the poet is Μουσέων ἄγγελος; Epict. 3, 22, 23; 38; Ael. Aristid. 37 K.=1 p. 15 D.; Maximus Tyr. 11, 9c Plato, as the one who brings us information about God, is called ὁ ἐξ Ἀκαδημίας ἄγγ.; Oenomaus in Eus., PE 5, 20, 3; 5 Carnus the soothsayer is ἄγγ. of the gods) of John the Baptist as forerunner **Mt 11:10; Mk 1:2; Lk 7:27** (all Mal 3:1; cp. Ex 23:20).

❷ **a transcendent power who carries out various missions or tasks, *messenger, angel*** (ἄ. as a spirit-being, oft. connected w. the nether world in Gr-Rom. sources [EZiebarth, Neue attische Fluchtafeln: NGG 1899, 127ff no. 24; IG XII/3, 933–74. Other material in Dibelius, Geisterwelt 209ff. S. also the oracles: Theosophien 13 p. 169, 31; Ps.-Callisth. 1, 1, 3 ἐπεκαλεῖτο τοὺς ἀγγέλους καὶ θεὸν Ἄμμωνα; 2, 25, 1; Porphyr., Ad Marcellam 21 ἄγγελοι θεῖοί τε κ. ἀγαθοὶ δαίμονες; Hierocles 3, 424; 23, 468.—ἀ. w. θεοί and δαίμονες Damascius (V/VI AD) 183 Ruelle; ἀ. w. δαίμονες and ἥρωες Proclus, Rep. II 243 Kroll, Tim. III 109 Diehl.—FCumont, RHR 72, 1915, 159–82; FAndres, D. Engellehre d. griech. Apologeten 1914 and in Pauly-W. Suppl. III 1918, 101ff; Rtzst., Myst. 171, 2; Bousset, ARW 18, 1915, 170ff] and as a transcendent power in Judaism [LXX; En 10:7; 20:1; 99:3 al.; Essenes in Jos., Bell. 2, 142; Philo, cp. Schürer III 881–85 (on Philo) w. lit.; Joseph.; Test12Patr; prayers for vengeance fr. Rheneia (I BC) 9f κύριε ὁ πάντα ἐφορῶν καὶ οἱ ἄνγελοι θεοῦ; on this Dssm. LO 353f; 357=LAE 414; 418f; SIG 1181 w. note 2; PFouad 203, 3f (I AD); on this PBenoit, RB 58, '51, 549–65; PKatz, TZ 10, '54, 228–31. Loanw. in rabb.—Bousset, Rel. 320ff; J-BFrey, L'Angélologie juive au temps de J-Chr.: RSPT 5, 1911, 75–110; HKuhn, JBL 67, '48, 217–32 Jewish apocalypses], likewise in the magical pap, w. their mixture of gentile and Jewish infl. [PGM 1, 76 an ἄ. as a star fr. heaven; 4, 570ff; 998; 1112; 13, 329; 585; 609; 744]. Cp. the ins APF 3, 1906, 445 no. 67; 451 no. 94. The more common term in polytheistic lit. for beings intermediate between gods and humans is δαίμων [q.v.], which monotheistic writers reserved for reference to a realm hostile to God's interests, while retaining the term ἄ. for intermediate beings, either those loyal to God or those in rebellion [s. c].)

ⓐ as messengers of God, *angels* (LXX; Philo, Somn. 1, 190; transcendent messengers of the gods in Hom. are not intermediate beings. Yet the description of Hermes, the κῆρυξ τῶν θεῶν, as their ἄγγελος ἄριστος [Diod. S. 5, 75, 2] may have made it easier for Gr-Romans in general to understand ἄ. as God's heavenly messenger; cp. the messenger of the god Men: EA 18, '91 p. 92f, no. 2, 5f [lit.]) mostly w. gen.: κυρίου (Gen 16:10f al.) **Mt 1:20; 2:13, 19; Lk 1:11; 2:9; Ac 5:19; 12:7, 23.** τοῦ θεοῦ (Gen 31:11; 32:2 al.; Philo, Deus Imm. 1; Jos., Bell. 5, 388) **Lk 12:8f; 15:10; J 1:51** (HWindisch, ZNW 30, '31, 215–33; also s. below on **Lk. 2:15**). ἄ. θεοῦ (Gen 21:17 A; Judg 13:6 B; Jos., Ant. 1, 73; Orig., C. Cels. 8, 31, 18) **Gal 4:14; Hb 1:6** (Ps 96:7; Dt 32:43); 1 Cl 29:2 (Dt 32:8). Abs. (Num 20:16; Judg 13:11; Tob 6:4ff al.) **Lk 1:13, 18, 38; 2:10, 13, 15, 21; J 20:12; Ac 7:53; 1 Ti 3:16; 1 Pt 1:12** (in wordplay on the superiority of human beings to angels s. Sextus 32; on their status and classification s. also Orig., C. Cels. 4, 29, 16) al. ἅγιοι ἄ. (PGM 4, 1934, 1938) **Mk 8:38; Lk 9:26; Ac 10:22; Rv 14:10;** 1 Cl 39:7 (Job 5:1); Hv 2, 2, 7; ἐκλεκτοὶ ἄ. **1 Ti 5:21** (ἄ. as witnesses so TestLevi 19:3 and SIG 1181, 10=Dssm. LO 351–62 [LAE 413–24]; cp. Jos., Bell. 2, 401); ἄ. ἰσχυρός (cp. Da 4:13; Ps 102:20) **Rv 5:2; 18:21.** Their abode is heaven, and so they are ἄ. τῶν οὐρανῶν **Mt 24:36** (unless οὐρ.=θεοῦ); ἄ. ἐν τοῖς οὐρανοῖς **Mk 12:25;** ἄ. ἐν οὐρανῷ **13:32;** ἄ. ἐξ οὐρανοῦ **Gal 1:8,** cp. **Mt 22:30; 28:2; Lk 22:43.** They return to heaven when they have fulfilled their mission on earth **2:15.** Hence ἄ. φωτός (cp. SJCh 78, 17) **2 Cor 11:14;** ἄ. φωταγωγοί B 18:1. There the good are united w. them after death Hv 2, 2, 7; s 9, 27, 3. They appear in dazzling light **Lk 2:9; Ac 7:30** (Ex 3:2); ISm 6:1; cp. the 'shining face' of **Ac 6:15;** or in white garments **J 20:12;** cp. Mt 28:3; Lk 24:4. Called πνεύματα **Hb 1:7;** 1 Cl 36:3 (both after Ps 103:4). πνεύματα λειτουργικά *serving spirits* **Hb 1:14.** Their voice is like thunder **J 12:29;** γλῶσσαι τῶν ἀ. *language of angels* **1 Cor 13:1** (after the analogy of the languages of the gods, Plato in Clem. Al., Strom. 1, 143; cp. 2 Cor 12:4; Rv 14:2f; TestJob 48–50; GSteindorff, Apk. d. Elias: TU 17, 3a, 1899, 153). They bring messages fr. God to men **Lk 1:11f; Mt 28:2ff,** and were also active in the giving of the law νόμος διαταγεὶς δι' ἀγγέλων **Gal 3:19;** cp. **Ac 7:38, 53; Hb 2:2** (Jos., Ant. 15, 136 τῶν ἐν τοῖς νόμοις δι' ἀγγέλων παρὰ τ. θεοῦ μαθόντων; cp. Did., Gen. 110, 15 κἂν γὰρ διὰ ὑπουργῶν ἀγγέλων ποιῇ ἃ βούλεται θεός). As guardian angels of individuals (Tob 5:6, 22; cp. PGM 1, 172ff; Ael. Aristid. 50, 57 K.=26 p. 519 D.: ὁ σὸς Ἑρμῆς ἐστιν, to whom Aristid. has been entrusted since his birth) **Mt 18:10** (PBarry, ET 23, 1912, 182); **Ac 12:15** (JMoulton, JTS 3, 1902, 514–27, ET 14, 1903, 5ff); **Lk 4:10** (Ps 90:11); Hv 5:1f. They conduct the blessed dead into heaven **Lk 16:22** (Hermes does this acc. to Pythag. [Diog. L. 8, 31]); instruct humans to do good Hv 3, 5, 4; δικαιοσύνης m 6, 2, 1 (ParJer 8:12); rejoice at the repentance of a sinner **Lk 15:10;** cp. the ἄ. τῆς μετανοίας Hm 12, 4, 7; 12, 6, 1 al. They preside over various realms ἄ. ὁ ἔχων ἐξουσίαν ἐπὶ τοῦ πυρός **Rv 14:18;** ἄ. τῶν ὑδάτων **16:5;** the four winds **7:1.** God assigns them διακόσμησις γῆς Pa (4) (cp. ἄγγελοι ἐπὶ τῶν ἐξουσιῶν GrBar 12:3). An angel, Thegri, rules the animal world Hv 4, 2, 4 (Synes., Ep. 57 p. 192b δαίμονες as leaders of the grasshoppers). ἄ. τοῦ πνεύματος τοῦ προφητικοῦ m 11:9; τὸν ἄ. τὸν τιμωρητήν s 7:6; cp. ὁ ἄ. ὁ μέγας Hs 8, 4, 1.—As creator of the world AcPlCor 1:15. On ἄ. τῶν ἐκκλησιῶν **Rv 1:20,** cp. **2:1, 8, 12, 18; 3:1, 7, 14** (on the textual problems associated w. these vss. s. RCharles, ICC Comm. 1920, I, clvii; clxf; II 244; RBorger, TRu 52, '87, 42f) and s. on ἀστήρ.—Subordinate to Christ **Mt 4:11; 13:41; 16:27; Hb 1:4ff** (Ps 96:7; B-D-F §254, 2); **1 Pt 3:22; Rv 5:11f;** glorify him **J 1:51** (JFritsch ". . . videbitis . . . angelos Dei ascendentes . . .," VD 37, '59, 1–11). δώδεκα λεγιῶνας ἀ. **Mt 26:53;** μυριάσιν ἀ. **Hb 12:22;** cp. **Rv 5:11.** Seven principal angels (Tob 12:15) **Rv 8:2, 6; 15:1, 6; 16:1; 17:1; 21:9** (GDix, The Seven Archangels and the Seven Spirits: JTS 28, 1927, 233–50). Six angels, created first, to whom the management of all creation is entrusted Hv 3, 4, 1. Angels at the Parousia **Mt 24:31; 2 Th 1:7.** Μιχαὴλ καὶ οἱ ἄ. αὐτοῦ **Rv 12:7.** Revered by people (Celsus 1, 26 'Ιουδαίους σέβειν ἀγγέλους; 5, 6) θρησκείᾳ τῶν ἀ. *worship of angels* **Col 2:18;** λατρεύειν ἀγγέλοις as a sign of Jewish piety PtK 2 p. 14, 26=Clem. Al., Strom. 6, 41 p. 452, 9. Christ as σεμνότατος ἄ. Hv 5:2; m 5, 1, 7; cp. ὁ ἅγιος ἄ. s 5, 4, 4 v.l.; ὁ ἔνδοξος ἄ. s 5, 4, 4; 7:1ff; 8, 1, 2. ὁ ἄ. κυρίου s 7:5; 8, 1, 2ff; called Michael in s 8, 3, 3, where it is to be noted that Michael was the guardian angel of God's people (WLueken, D. Erzengel Michael 1900; MDibelius, Hdb. exc. on Hs 5, 6, 8 p. 575f).

ⓑ intermediate beings gener., w. no ref. to their relation to God (opp. ἄνθρωποι; s. 2 above immediately before a) **1 Cor 4:9** (cp. TestJos 19:9 ἔχαιρον ἐπ' αὐτῷ οἱ ἄγγελοι κ. οἱ ἄνθρωποι κ. πᾶσα ἡ γῆ).—**Ro 8:38** ἄ. as serving spirit-powers seem to be differentiated fr. the ἀρχαί, who rule.

ⓒ evil spirits (Lactant., Inst. 2, 15, 8 daemonas Trismegistus ἀγγέλους πονηρούς appellat. Cp. also Job 1:6; 2:1; Philo, Gig. 16; TestAsh 6:4; PGM 4, 2701; αἱ πονηραὶ δυνάμεις, διάβολος καὶ οἱ ἄγγελοι αὐτοῦ Did., Gen. 45, 5; ADieterich, Nekyia 1893, 60f) τῷ διαβόλῳ καὶ τοῖς ἀγγέλοις αὐτοῦ **Mt 25:41;** cp. **Rv 12:9.** ὁ δράκων καὶ οἱ ἄ. αὐτοῦ vs. **7;** ἄ. τῆς ἀβύσσου **9:11** (s. Ἀβαδδών); ἄ. πονηρός B 9:4; ἄ. τῆς πονηρίας in contrast to guardian angels Hm 6, 2, 1; ἄ. Σατανᾶ, which causes physical pain **2 Cor 12:7;** esp. called ἄ. τρυφῆς καὶ ἀπάτης Hs 6, 2, 1f; leading men into evil B 18:1. Of the angels' fall and their punishment (cp., in the opinion of many, Gen 6:2; En 6ff; 54; Book of Jubilees 5; SyrBar 56:13; LJung, Fallen Angels in Jewish, Christian, and Mohammedan Lit. 1926; ALods, Congr. d'Hist. du Christ. I 29–54) ὁ θεὸς ἀγγέλων ἁμαρτησάντων οὐκ ἐφείσατο **2 Pt 2:4;** ἀ. τοὺς μὴ τηρήσαντας τὴν ἑαυτῶν ἀρχήν *who did not keep to their proper domain* (s. ἀρχή 7) **Jd 6.** From the pass. already quoted above w. Gen. 6:2 (cp. also TestReub 5:3; Jos., Ant. 1, 73 ἄγγελοι θεοῦ γυναιξὶ συνιόντες; and polytheists' concept of erotic desires of transcendent beings: HUsener, Weihnachtsfest[2] 1911, 74f; Rtzst., Poim. 228ff. Herr der Grösse 14f; and GJs 14:1) some conclude that the angels were subject to erotic desires; this is held to explain the regulation that women are to wear a veil in church services, since angels are present (cp. Origen, Orat. 31 and Ps 137:1 ἐναντίον ἀγγέλων ψαλῶ σοι) **1 Cor 11:10** (for another view and for the lit. s. ἐξουσία 7; s. also JFitzmyer, [Qumran angelology] NTS 4, '57/58, 48–58; LJervis, JBL 112, '93, 243–45: angels mediate God's presence). In **6:3** οὐκ οἴδατε, ὅτι ἀγγέλους κρινοῦμεν; it is not certain whether only fallen angels are meant; θρησκείᾳ τῶν ἀ. worship of angels **Col 2:18** polemicizes against what appears to be a type of gnostic reverence for angels. (On Qumran angelology s. Fitzmyer, cited above.)—OEverling, D. paulinische Angelologie u. Dämonologie 1888; Dibelius, Geisterwelt 1909; GKurze, D. Engels- u. Teufels-glaube d. Ap. Pls 1915; MJones, St Paul and the Angels: Exp. 8th ser., 16, 1921, 356–70; 412–25; EPeterson, D. Buch von den Engeln '35; JMichl, D. Engelvorstellungen in Apk I '37; ELangton, The Angel Teaching of the NT '37; JBernardin, JBL 57, '38, 273–79; ESchick, D. Botschaft der Engel im NT '40; WMichaelis, Z. Engelchristol. im Urchristent. '42; GHatzidakis, Ἄγγελος u. Verwandtes: SB-WienAk 173, 1914.—B. 1486. DELG. DDD 81–96 (lit.). M-M. New Docs 5, 72f. TW. Sv.

ἄγγος, ους, τό (Hom. et al.; CIG 3573; Michel 1361, 5; LXX; Philo, Post. Cai. 130; Jos., Ant. 8, 322) **a container primarily for liquids or wet objects,** ***vessel, container*** B 8:1. Of containers for fish **Mt 13:48** (v.l. ἀγγεῖα, q.v.). Fig., of the body as the home of evil spirits Hm 5, 2, 5 (w. ἀγγεῖον). On the v.l., s. GKilpatrick, Style and Text in the Gk. NT: Studies and Docs. 29, '67, 156.—DELG. M-M., s.v. ἀγγεῖον.

ἄγε present impv. of ἄγω, used as an interjection (since Hom., w. sg. or pl.; LXX; SibOr 3, 562; B-D-F §144. ἄγε μέν) ***come!*** ἄγε νῦν (esp. oft. in comedy) w. impv. foll. (Hom.) **Js 5:1;** w. anacoluthon foll. **4:13;** ἄ. δή (Aeschyl. et al.) *come then* Dg 2:1.

ἀγέλη, ης, ἡ (Hom.et al.) *herd* of swine (Hes. Scutum 168; Eudoxus Rhod. [II BC] in Aelian, NA 10, 16) **Mt 8:30–32; Mk 5:11, 13; Lk 8:32f.**—DELG. M-M.

ἀγενεαλόγητος, ον *without genealogy,* of Melchizedek (w. ἀπάτωρ and ἀμήτωρ) **Hb 7:3** (found elsewh. only w. ref. to this pass.).—M-M.

ἀγενής, ές gen. οῦς ***not of noble birth*** (ignobilis; opp. Γ εὐγενής; in this sense since X., Pla.; POxy 33 V, 5 [II AD]=Acta Alex. XI, B col. V, 5; Jos., Bell. 4, 148; ἀγεννής Just. A II, 3, 3) but also in the more general sense ***base, low, insignificant*** (Soph., fgm. 84 Pears., opp. ἀγαθός; Philo, Conf. Lingu. 43; POxy 79, 3; SIG[2] 855, 11; 862, 22) which is most probably its mng. in **1 Cor 1:28.**—DELG s.v. γίγνομαι 223. M-M.

ἀγέννητος, ον (Soph. et al.) **pert. to one who exists without having gone through the process of being born,** ***unborn,*** lit. 'unbegotten' (so of God, Herm. Wr. 2, 4; 5, 2; 14, 2 al.; TestSol; ParJer 9:6; Philo, Mos. 2, 171 v.l. [for ἀγένητος]; Just. Written ἀγένητος: Thales fgm. A 1, 35=Diog. L. 1, 35; Zoroaster in Philo Bybl. [c. 100 AD]: 790 fgm. 4, 52 Jac. [Eus., PE 1, 10, 52]; PGM 13, 842; Philo; Jos., C. Ap. 2, 167; SibOr, fgm. 1, 7; 17; Ath. [ἀγένν.—codex A]; Theoph. Ant. 1, 4, p. 64, 3) w. γεννητός, of Christ (cp. AcPh 141 [Aa II/2, 76, 27]) IEph 7:2 (v.l. ἀγένητος); cp. Lghtf., Apost. Fath. II/2[2] 1889, p. 90–94. This term is to be restored Ox 1081, 34 ἀγ[εννή]ṭου π̅ρ̅ς̅ *unbegotten father;* sim. ln. 48 (both on the basis of the Coptic text ἀγένητος SJCh 90, 12; 91, 13)—PStiegele, D. Agennesiebegriff in d. griech. Theol. d. 4 Jh. 1913; LPrestige, JTS 24, 1923, 486–96; JLebreton, Ἀγέννητος dans la Tradition philos. et dans la Litt. chrét. du IIe siècle: RSR 16, 1926, 431–43; GDelling, Jüd. Lehre u. Frömmigkeit, Berlin '67, 36ff.—DELG s.v. γίγνομαι 223. Sv.

ἅγια, ων s. ἅγιος 2b.

ἁγιάζω 1 aor. ἡγίασα, impv. ἁγίασον; pf. ἡγίακα 2 Ch 7:16; Jer 1:5. Pass.: 1 fut. ἁγιασθήσομαι; 1 aor. ἡγιάσθην, impv. ἁγιασθήτω; pf. ἡγίασμαι, ptc. ἡγιασμένος 1 Cl 46:2 (LXX; Philo, Leg. All. 1, 18, Spec. Leg. 1, 67. Quite rare in extra-Bibl. usage, where ἁγίζω is the usual form; but s. PGM 4, 522 ἁγιασθείς; Cat. Cod. Astr. VII 178, 1; 27; Anecd. Gr. p. 328, 1ff and Herm. Wr. 1, 32 συναγιάζειν. Cp. also καθαγιάζειν under 3 below).

❶ **set aside someth. or make it suitable for ritual purposes,** ***consecrate, dedicate*** of things: (Ex 29:27, 37, 44 al.) ἁ. τὸ δῶρον *the sacrifice* **Mt 23:19; 1 Ti 4:5** (AcThom 79 [Aa II/2, 194, 11] τὴν προσφορὰν ἁ.); of profane things *make holy* by contact w. someth. holy ἁ. τὸν χρυσόν *the gold* in the temple **Mt 23:17.**

❷ **include a pers. in the inner circle of what is holy, in both cultic and moral associations of the word, *consecrate, dedicate, sanctify*** (cp. Ex 28:41; Sir 33:12; 45:4; Zeph 1:7). So of Christians, who are consecrated by baptism (cp. Orig., C. Cels. 8, 33, 26 on the Eucharist ἄρτους ἐσθίομεν, σῶμα γενομένους . . . ἁγιάζον τοὺς μετὰ ὑγιοῦς προθέσεως αὐτῷ χρωμένους); w. ἀπολούσασθαι **1 Cor 6:11.** Of the Christian community or church ἵνα αὐτὴν ἁγιάσῃ καθαρίσας τῷ λουτρῷ τοῦ ὕδατος **Eph 5:26;** *sanctify* by the blood of a sacrifice, i.e. atone for sins **Hb 9:13.** Of Christ ἵνα ἁγιάσῃ διὰ τοῦ ἰδίου αἵματος τὸν λαόν **13:12** (ἁ. τὸν λαόν Josh 7:13; Ezk 46:20; λαὸς ἡγιασμένος PsSol 17, 26. ἁ. by blood Ex 29:21); cp. **2:11; 10:10, 29;** *consecrate, sanctify* by contact w. what is holy: unbelievers by a Christian marriage **1 Cor 7:14.** Hence Christians are ἡγιασμένοι (cp. Dt 33:3; 4 Macc 17:19) **Hb 10:14; Ac 20:32; 26:18;** IEph 2:2; ἡ. ἐν Χριστῷ Ἰησοῦ **1 Cor 1:2;** ἡ. ἐν ἀληθείᾳ **J 17:19b** (cp. Sir 45:4 ἐν πίστει); of Gentile Christians ἐν πνεύματι ἁγίῳ **Ro 15:16;** the church ἁγιασθεῖσα = ἁγία D 10:5; κλητοὶ ἡ. 1 Cl ins; of an individual σκεῦος ἡγιασμένον **2 Ti 2:21;** Paul ἡγιασμένος IEph 12:2. God consecrates his own, incl. Christ **J 10:36** (s. Hdb.[3] ad loc.), and Christians (cp. schol. on Apollon. Rhod. 3, 62 ἐλεήσας αὐτὸν ὁ Ζεὺς ἁγνίζει = Zeus absolves him, takes away his guilt) **17:17; 1 Th 5:23;** the latter through Christ 1 Cl 59:3. Of Jesus ὑπὲρ αὐτῶν (ἐγὼ) ἁγιάζω ἐμαυτόν *I dedicate myself for them* (the disciples) as an offering **J 17:19a** (ἁ. of an offering Ex 13:2; Dt 15:19).

❸ **to treat as holy, *reverence*** of pers. κύριον δὲ τὸν Χριστὸν ἁγιάσατε **1 Pt 3:15** (Is 8:13); of things: ἁγιασθήτω τὸ ὄνομά σου *may thy name be held in reverence* (cp. Is 29:23; Ezk 36:23; Ps.-Clem., Hom. 13, 4; also gnostic ἁγιασθήτω τὸ θέλημά σου PPrinc 107, 14; PGM 4, 1191f τὸ ὄνομα τὸ ἅγιον τὸ καθηγιασμένον ὑπὸ τ. ἀγγέλων πάντων; 1, 206) **Mt 6:9; Lk 11:2;** D 8:2 (AFridrichsen, Geheiligt werde dein Name: TT 8, 1917, 1–16; LBrun, Harnack Festschr. 1921, 22–31; RAsting, D. Heiligkeit im Urchristentum 1930, 75–85 w. lit.). τὸ σάββατον B 15:1, 3, 6f (Ex 20:8–11). ἁγιασθῆναι *keep oneself holy* **Rv 22:11.**

❹ **to eliminate that which is incompatible with holiness, *purify*** (Num 6:11 al.) ἁ. ἀπὸ πάσης πονηρίας καὶ ἀπὸ πάσης σκολιότητος Hv 3, 9, 1. This mng. is also prob. in such pass. as **Ro 15:16; 1 Cor 1:2; 1 Th 5:23.**—V.l. for ἠγαπημένη IRo ins—DELG s.v. ἅζομαι. M-M. TW.

ἁγίασμα, ατος, τό (almost excl. Bibl. and Christian, but also Philo, Plant. 50; PGM 4, 522) **a space set aside for devotion, *sanctuary*** (1 Macc 1:21, 36ff; 5:1; Sir 36:12; 49:6; 50:11; TestDan 5:9. Holiness: En 12:4; PsSol) τὰ δεξιὰ μέρη τοῦ ἁ. Hv 3, 2, 1. ἐποίησεν ἁ. ἐν τῷ κοιτῶνι αὐτῆς *(Anna) dedicated a place for prayer in (Mary's) bedroom* GJs 6:1; cp. 6:3; 8:2.—Of a structure in the temple where the altar was located 24:2.—DELG s.v. ἅζομαι. TW.

ἁγιασμός, οῦ, ὁ (LXX; PsSol 17:30; Test12Patr.—Diod. S. 4, 39, 1 has ἁγισμός) **personal dedication to the interests of the deity, *holiness, consecration, sanctification;*** the use in a moral sense for a process or, more often, its result (the state of being made holy) is peculiar to our lit. (cp. Jer 6:16 v.l.; TestBenj 10:11) εἰς ἁγιασμόν *for consecration* (opp. εἰς ἀνομίαν) **Ro 6:19, 22** (AcThom 121 [Aa II/2, 230, 23]). Opp. ἀκαθαρσία **1 Th 4:7;** w. τιμή vs. **4,** cp. vs. **3;** w. πίστις and ἀγάπη **1 Ti 2:15;** w. εἰρήνη **Hb 12:14.** ἐν ἁ. πνεύματος *in consecration through the Spirit* **2 Th 2:13; 1 Pt 1:2** (TestLevi 18:7 πνεῦμα ἁγιασμοῦ). Christ described as ἁ. w. δικαιοσύνη and ἀπολύτρωσις (abstr. for concr. *author of holiness;* cp. the triad in Did., Gen. 221, 15) **1 Cor 1:30.** ποιεῖν τὰ τοῦ ἁ. πάντα *do everything that belongs to holiness* 1 Cl 30:1; ἐγκράτεια ἐν ἁ. *self-control with consecration* 35:2.—EGaugler, D. Heiligung in d. Ethik des Ap. Pls: Internat. kirchl. Ztschr. 15, 1925, 100–120; MEnslin, The Ethics of Paul 1930; SDjukanovič, Heiligkt u. Heilgg b. Pls, diss. Bern '39.—DELG s.v. ἅζομαι. TW.

ἅγιοι, ων, οἱ s. ἅγιος 2d.

ἅγιον, ου, τό s. ἅγιος 2a.

ἁγιοπρεπής, ές **fitting/proper for one who is holy, *holy*** λόγοι ἁ. *holy words* 1 Cl 13:3; δεσμοὶ ἁ. *bonds fitting for a saint* Pol 1:1.

ἅγιος, ία, ον orig. a cultic concept, of the quality possessed by things and persons that could approach a divinity (so among the trag. poets only Thespis, fgm. 4 p. 833 Nauck[2] βωμῶν ἁγίων, but found since V BC as a cultic term in Ion. and Att., e.g. ἱρόν Hdt. 2, 41; 44; Pla., Critias 116c, τόπος Leg. 904e; τελεταί Aristoph., Nub. 304 and Demosth. 25, 11 [ἁγιώταται τ.]; above all in the mysteries [GWobbermin, Rel. gesch. Studien 1896, 59ff, cp. OGI 721, 1 τῶν ἁγιωτάτων, Ἐλευσῖνι μυστηρίων]; LXX [HGehman, VetusT 4, '54, 337–48]; LXX, pseudepigr., Philo, Joseph., apolog.)

❶ as adj. **pert. to being dedicated or consecrated to the service of God—ⓐ** in the cultic sense ***dedicated to God, holy, sacred,*** i.e. reserved for God and God's service:

α. of things ἁ. πόλις of Jerusalem (Appian, Syr. 50, §250: Jerus. is called the ἁγιωτάτη πόλις of the Jews; also Mithrid. 106 §498; Is 48:2; 52:1; 66:20; 2 Esdr 21:1; Da 3:28; 1 Macc 2:7 al.; B-D-F §474, 1) **Mt 4:5; 27:53; Rv 11:2;** of the heavenly Jerusalem **21:2, 10; 22:19;** τόπος ἁ. of the temple (2 Macc 2:18; 8:17; 3 Macc 2:14) **Mt 24:15; Ac 6:13; 21:28,** but of the next life 1 Cl 5:7, like ὁ ἁ. αἰών *the holy age* = αἰὼν μέλλων (cp. in the addition to the Lat. transl. of Sir 17:27 'aevum sanctum') B 10:11; γῆ ἁ. (2 Macc 1:7; TestJob 33:5) **Ac 7:33** (Ex 3:5); ὄρος ἅ. (Wsd 9:8; Ps 14:1; 42:3 al.—Appian, Bell. Civ. 1, 1 §2 τὸ ὄρος τὸ ἀπὸ τοῦδε [i.e. something extremely significant occurred] κληζόμενον ἱερόν) of the mountain of Transfiguration **2 Pt 1:18;** σκεύη (1 Esdr 8:57; 1 Macc 4:49) Ox 840, 14; 21; 29 (ASyn. 150, 112; 114; 116); σκηνή **Hb 9:2** (JSwetnam, CBQ 32, '70, 205–21, defends the Vulgate transl.). διαθήκη (Da 11:28ff Theod.; 1 Macc 1:15) **Lk 1:72;** γραφαί **Ro 1:2** (cp. 1 Macc 12:9; Philo, Rer. Div. Her. 159); εὐαγγέλιον AcPlCor 2:36. λόγος 1 Cl 13:3; 56:3; Dg 7:2 (cp. Herm. Wr. 1:18 ὁ θεὸς εἶπεν ἁγίῳ λόγῳ). Since Christians are called 'holy ones' (s. 2dβ), their κλῆσις is also ἁ. **2 Ti 1:9;** so also of the ἐντολή given them **2 Pt 2:21.** Their community forms an ἐκκλησία ἁ. ITr ins; Hv 1, 1, 6; 1, 3, 4; cp. 4, 1, 3, as well as a ἱεράτευμα ἅ. **1 Pt 2:5** and an ἔθνος ἅ. (Wsd 17:2) vs. **9.** For φίλημα ἅ. s. φίλημα.—πίστις is ἁγιωτάτη *most holy* **Jd 20** (for the superl. cp. Pla., Leg. 729e; Diod. S. 3, 44, 2 ἱερὸν ἁγιώτατον = an exceptionally holy temple; SIG 339, 14; 768, 16 [31 BC]; Jos., Ant. 16, 115; ἁγιώτατος θεός: OGI 755, 1; 756, 3; cp. PGM 4, 668. Of the synagogue CIJ 754; 781; 867).

β. of humans and transcendent beings**—ℵ.** of human beings *consecrated to God, holy, pure, reverent* (Ramsay, CB I/2, 386 no.

232, 8 [early III AD] of a gentile: Γάϊός, ὡς ἅγιος, ὡς ἀγαθός) prophets (Wsd 11:1; cp. ἅ. Ἀβράμ Did., Gen. 228, 23) **Lk 1:70; Ac 3:21; 2 Pt 3:2.** John the Baptist (w. δίκαιος) **Mk 6:20;** apostles **Eph 3:5;** of Polycarp, in EpilMosq 1; 3; 5; αἱ ἅ. γυναῖκες **1 Pt 3:5.** Israel a λαὸς ἅ. (Is 62:12; Sir 49:12 v.l.; Da 7:27; PsSol 17) 1 Cl 8:3; cp. B 14:6; πᾶν ἄρσεν τῷ κυρίῳ **Lk 2:23.**—The Christians (Orig., C. Cels 3, 60, 16) ἅ. ἔσεσθε **1 Pt 1:16a** (Lev 19:2). Charismatics (?; so EKäsemann, Beiträge zur hist. Theol. 9, '33, 146, n. 5) **Col 1:26.** ἀδελφοὶ ἅ. **Hb 3:1;** their children **1 Cor 7:14** (GDelling, Studien zum NT, '70, 270–80, 281–87=Festschrift Fascher, 84–93; JBlinzler in Festschrift Schmid, '63, 23–41; KAland, Die Stellung d. Kinder in d. frühen christl. Gemeinden u. ihre Taufe, '67, 13–17). Presbyters IMg 3:1. W. ἄμωμος **Eph 1:4; 5:27; Col 1:22;** ἅ. ἐν ἀναστροφῇ **1 Pt 1:15,** cp. D 10:6.

ב. of angels *holy* (Job 5:1; Tob 11:14; 12:15; cp. Bousset, Rel.[3] 321; Cat. Cod. Astr. VIII/2 p. 176, 19; cp. PGM 4, 668; AscIs 3, 16) **Mk 8:38; Lk 9:26; Ac 10:22; Rv 14:10;** 1 Cl 39:7; Hv 2, 2, 7; 3, 4, 1f; ἐν ἁ. μυριάσιν αὐτοῦ *w. his holy myriads* **Jd 14** (w. ἄγγελος P^{72}; cp. En 1:9).

ג. of Christ *holy* τὸν ἅγιον παῖδά σου **Ac 4:27, 30;** τὸ γεννώμενον ἅ. κληθήσεται **Lk 1:35;** GJs 11:3 (ἅ. belongs to the pred.).

ד. of God (Aristoph., Av. 522; Pla., Soph. 249a; OGI 262, 25; 378, 1 [19 AD] θεῷ ἁγίῳ ὑψίστῳ; 590, 1; 620, 2 [98 AD]; UPZ 79, 22 [159 BC] of Isis; likew. POxy 1380, 34; 36; 89; IDefixWünsch 4, 10 τὸν ἅ. Ἑρμῆν; Herm. Wr. 1, 31; PGM 1, 198; 3, 312; 4, 851; 2093. Further exx. in Wobbermin 70; Cumont[3] 266.—LXX; Philo, Sacr. Abel. 101; SibOr 3, 478) *holy* **J 17:11; 1 Pt 1:16b** (Lev 19:2); **Rv 4:8** (Is 6:3; TestAbr A 3, p. 79, 19 [Stone p. 6]; ParJer 9:3.—The threefold ἅγιος serves to emphasize the idea, as the twofold καλὸν καλόν=indescribably beautiful Theocr. 8, 73); **6:10.** Of God's name (LXX; PGM 4, 1190; 13, 638) **Lk 1:49;** 1 Cl 64.

ה. of spirit τὸ πνεῦμα τὸ ἅγιον or τὸ ἅγιον πνεῦμα or πν. ἅ., s. πνεῦμα 5c.

ⓑ shading over into the sense ***holy = pure, perfect, worthy of God*** (Stephan. Byz. s.v. Παλική: ὅρκος ἅγιος) θυσία **Ro 12:1.** ἀναστροφαί **2 Pt 3:11.** Of the divine law **Ro 7:12;** ἀπαρχή (cp. Ezk 48:9ff) **11:16**a; ναός (Ps 10:4; 17:7 al.; Jos., Bell. 7, 379; cp. ἱερὸν ἅ.: Hdt. 2, 41; Diod. S. 5, 72, 3; 15, 14, 3; Paus., 10, 32, 13) **1 Cor 3:17; Eph 2:21.**

❷ used as a pure subst. **the holy (thing, pers.)—ⓐ ἅγιον, ου, τό** ***that which is holy*—α.** concrete *sacrificial meat* (Lev 22:14.—Also concr. θύειν τὸ ἱερόν: 67th letter of Apollon. of Ty. [Philostrat. I 363, 30 K.]) μὴ δῶτε τὸ ἅ. τοῖς κυσίν **Mt 7:6;** cp. D 9:5. Cp. 1QS 9:17.

β. *sanctuary* (OGI 56, 59 [239 BC]; UPZ 119, 12 [156 BC]; Num 3:38; Ezk 45:18; 1 Esdr 1:5 v.l.; 1 Macc 10:42; Philo, Leg. All. 3, 125; Jos., Ant. 3, 125) τὸ ἅ. κοσμικόν **Hb 9:1.**

ⓑ **ἅγια, ων, τά** ***sanctuary*** (Jdth 4:12; 16:20; 1 Macc 3:43, 59 al.; Philo, Fuga 93 οἷς [sc. ἡ Λευιτικὴ φύλη] ἡ τῶν ἁγίων ἀνάκειται λειτουργία; Jos., Bell. 2, 341) **Hb 8:2; 9:24f; 13:11.** Also the front, or outer part of the temple, *the holy place* (3 Km 8:8; Philo, Rer. Div. Her. 226) **Hb 9:2.** τὰ ἅ. of the heavenly sanctuary (SibOr 3, 308) vs. **12; 10:19.**—(τὰ) ἅγια (τῶν) ἁγίων *the holy of holies* (3 Km 8:6; 2 Ch 4:22; 5:7; GrBar ins 2; Philo, Leg. All. 2, 56. Cp. Polyb. 16, 12, 7 τὸ τοῦ Διὸς ἄβατον.—Formed like κακὰ κακῶν Soph., Oed. C. 1238, ἄρρητ' ἀρρήτων Oed. R. 465; ἔσχατα ἐσχάτων Ael. Aristid. 46 p. 260 D.; B-D-F §141, 8; 245, 2) **Hb 9:3;** IPhld 9:1; GJs 8:3; 13:2; 15:3. Of Christians 1 Cl 29:3 (cp. 2 Ch 31:14; Ezk 48:12).

ⓒ **ἅγιος, ου, ὁ** ***the holy one*—α.** of God (En 14:1; 97: 6; 98:6; 104:9) **1J 2:20** (β is also prob. [s. OPiper, JBL 66, '47, 437–51]).

β. of Christ ὁ ἅ. **Rv 3:7;** 1 Cl 23:5; Dg 9:2; ὁ ἅ. καὶ δίκαιος **Ac 3:14.** ὁ ἅ. τοῦ θεοῦ **Mk 1:24; Lk 4:34; J 6:69** (cp. Ps 105:16 ὁ ἅ. κυρίου of Aaron).

γ. of the martyr Polycarp EpilMosq 2 (of psalmists Did., Gen. 60, 18).

ⓓ **ἅγιοι, ων, οἱ** ***the holy ones*—α.** of angels (Zech 14:5; Ps 88:6; En 1:9; PsSol 17:43; PGM 1, 198; 4, 1345; 1347). For **1 Th 3:13; 2 Th 1:10;** D 16, 7; **Col 1:12** (cp. 1QS 11:7f), β is also prob.

β. *believers, loyal followers, saints* of Christians as consecrated to God (cp. Is 4:3; Tob 8:15; Ps 33:10; Da 7:18, 21) **Ac 9:13, 32; Ro 8:27; 12:13; 15:25** (Ltzm., exc. ad loc. on the early community in Jerusalem); **1 Cor 6:1f; 2 Cor 1:1; Eph 2:19; 3:8; Phil 4:22; Col 1:4; 1 Ti 5:10; Hb 6:10; Rv 22:21 v.l.** (s. RBorger, TRu 52, '87, 56f); D 16:7 perh.; 1 Cl 46:2; Hv 1, 1, 9 al.; κλητοὶ ἅ. **Ro 1:7; 1 Cor 1:2;** οἱ ἅ. αὐτοῦ **Col 1:26;** cp. **Ac 9:13;** Hv 3, 8, 8; οἱ ἅ. καὶ πιστοὶ αὐτοῦ ISm 1:2.

γ. of other people esp. close to God (Dionys. Soph., Ep. 70 σωφροσύνη … προσήγαγέ σε θεῷ … τοῖς ἁγίοις παρέστησεν) **Mt 27:52;** cp. **Rv 18:20, 24; Eph 2:19.**—FJDölger, ΙΧΘΥΣ 1910, 180–83; WLink, De vocis 'sanctus' usu pagano, diss. Königsb. 1910; AFridrichsen, Hagios-Qadoš 1916; EWilliger, Hagios 1922; JDillersberger, Das Heilige im NT 1926; HDelehaye, Sanctus 1927[2]; '33; RAsting, D. Heiligkeit im Urchristentum 1930; UBunzel, D. Begriff der Heiligkeit im AT, diss. Breslau 1914; JHänel, D. Religion d. Heiligkeit '31; PChantraine/OMasson, Debrunner Festschr., '54, 85–107; FNötscher, Vom Alten zum NT, '62, 126–74 (Qumran). SWoodward, JETS 24, '81, 107–16 (Qumran displays transition from association of the term for 'saints' with celestial beings to human beings, s. 1QS 5:6f; 8:5 and 8).—B. 1475. EDNT. DDD 1359–64. New Docs 4, 111. DELG s.v. ἅζομαι. M-M. TW. Sv.

ἁγιότης, ητος, ἡ ***holiness*** (schol. Aristoph., Plut. 682; 2 Macc 15:2; Ps 28:2 in one transl. of the Hexapla; TestLevi 3:4 ὑπεράνω πάσης ἁγιότητος; Did., Gen. 211, 18; Byz. honorary title, cp. Preis. III 183) μεταλαβεῖν τῆς ἁ. *share in his holy character* **Hb 12:10.** Of moral purity w. εἰλικρίνεια **2 Cor 1:12 v.l.** (for ἁπλότης) Hv 3, 7, 3 v.l. (for ἁγνότης).—DELG s.v. ἅζομαι. M-M.

ἁγιοφόρος, ον ***bearing holy things*** (cultic vessels in processions) of persons (ἁγιαφόρος IG III, 162 of pers. engaged in Isis-worship); in Christian use only fig. (cp. Plut., Mor. 352b: the ἱεραφόροι in the Isis cult are those who bear the teaching about the gods, purified from all superstition, in their souls as in a cabinet, or as an adornment) w. ναοφόροι et al. IEph 9:2. Of the church ISm ins, cp. Lghtf. ad loc.—DELG s.v. φέρω A, 1189.

ἁγιωσύνη, ης, ἡ (also ἁγιοσύνη) ***holiness*** (Herodian. Gr. I 335; 18; schol. [Plato] Axioch. 371d; LXX Ps and 2 Macc 3:12; Pel.-Leg. p. 10, 2; AcThom 58; 97; 104 al. [Aa II/2, 175, 15; 210, 10; 217, 5] Byz. honorary title Preis. III 183; PMeyer 24, 2) of Christ κατὰ πνεῦμα ἁγιωσύνης (πνεῦμα ἅγιον as TestLevi 18:11; cp. 1QS 4:21; 9:3), intensified πνεῦμα ἅγιον (opp. κατὰ σάρκα [Semitic idiom, BSchneider, Biblica 48, '67, 380]) **Ro 1:4.** Of Christians ἐπιτελεῖν ἁγιωσύνην *to perfect holiness*=become perfectly holy **2 Cor 7:1.** ἐν ἁγιωσύνῃ *in holiness* (AcThom 85; 86 [Aa II/2, 201, 14f; 202, 6]) **1 Th 3:13.**—DELG s.v. ἅζομαι §2. M-M. s. ἁγιότης. TW.

ἀγκάλη, ης, ἡ (trag., Hdt. et al.; ins, pap, LXX, mostly pl.) **the arm bent as to receive someth.,** *arm* δέξασθαι εἰς τὰς ἀ. *take into one's arms* (Jos., Ant. 8, 28 τὸ παιδίον . . . εἰς τὰς ἀ. μου τίθησι; OGI 56, 60 of a cult image τὶς τῶν ἱερέων οἴσει ἐν ταῖς ἀγκάλαις) **Lk 2:28** (Mk 9:36 uses ἐναγκαλίσασθαι).—DELG s.v. ἀγκ-. M-M.

ἄγκιστρον, ου, τό (Hom. et al.; LXX, e.g. Is 19:8) ***fishhook*** ⓐ lit. βάλλειν ἄ. εἰς θάλασσαν **Mt 17:27.**—ⓑ fig. (Polyaenus, Exc. 1 p. 431, 10 χρυσοῖς ἀγκίστροις [to fish] w. golden fishhooks) ἐμπεσεῖν εἰς τὰ ἄ. τῆς κενοδοξίας *be caught on the fishhooks of error* IMg 11.—B. 897; 899. DELG s.v. ἀγκ-.

ἄγκυρα, ας, ἡ (nautical term, lit. and fig.: Alcaeus et al.; SIG[2] 588, 168; 171; PCairZen 782a V, 64 [III BC]; PColZen 43, 6 [III BC]; PLond III, 1164h, 9 p. 164; V, 1714, 2; Jos., Vi. 167.—Jer 52:18 Sym. in special mng.) **a ship's anchor,** ***anchor***

ⓐ lit. ῥίπτειν ἀ. *let go* or *drop an anchor* **Ac 27:29.** ἀ. ἐκτείνειν *lay out an anchor* vs. **30** (Breusing 195; LCasson, Ships and Seamanship in the Anc. World, '71, 256). ἀ. περιαιρεῖν vs. **40** (s. περιαιρέω 1).

ⓑ fig. (Eur., Hec. 80 ἄ. οἴκων; Soph., fgm. 623 ἄ. βίου; Heliod. 7, 25, 4 πᾶσα ἐλπίδος ἄ.; IG XII, VII 123b, 3 ἄ. γήρως) of hope (Marinus, Vi. Procli 29) ἣν ὡς ἄγκυραν ἔχομεν τῆς ψυχῆς **Hb 6:19** (s. PStumpf, RAC I 440–43; CSpicq, StTh 3, '49, 185–87).—B. 737. DELG s.v. ἀγκ-. M-M.

ἀγκών, ῶνος, ὁ (Hom. et al.; pap, LXX; Jos., Ant. 17, 187; TestSol 4:5 P and other mss; Jos., Ant. 17, 187) **the bent arm,** ***arm*** αἴρειν τινὰ τῶν ἀ. *take someone by the arms* Hv 1, 4, 3.—B. 238. DELG s.v. ἀγκ-.

ἄγναφος, ον (Peripl. Eryth. c. 6; Moeris p. 31 under ἄκναπτον; Thom. Mag. p. 12, 14; PCairZen 92, 16 [III BC]; PHamb 10, 32. κιτῶνα [χιτῶνα] ἄγναφον: BGU 1666, 13 [I AD]; PLond II, 193 verso, 22 p. 246 [II AD]) **pert. to cloth fresh from the weaver's loom,** ***not fulled, unshrunken, unsized, new*** (s. PMeyer on the Hamb. pap above) ἐπίβλημα ῥάκους ἀγνάφου *a patch of new cloth* (not to be transl. 'unbleached') **Mt 9:16; Mk 2:21.**—DELG s.v. κνάπτω. M-M.

ἁγνεία, ας, ἡ (Soph., Oed. R. 864 ἁ. λόγων ἔργων τε πάντων; Pla.; ins [e.g. fr. Epidaurus in Theophr., De Pietate 9, 11, and Porphyr., Abst. 2, 19 ἁγνὸν χρὴ ναοῖο θυώδεος ἐντὸς ἰόντα ἔμμεναι· ἁγνεία δ' ἐστὶ φρονεῖν ὅσια; ISyriaW 2034; 2203]; pap; LXX [of cultic purity]; TestJos 10:2; AscIs 3:21; EpArist, Philo, Joseph.; Mel., P. 49, 350) **the quality of moral purity,** ***purity;*** of a pure mind (s. ins fr. Epidaurus above; Jos., Ant. 19, 331) specif. ***chastity*** (Diod. S. 10, 21, 2 ἁγνεία τ. σώματος; Philo, Abr. 98 ἁ. τῆς γυναικός; Jos., Ant. 3, 78) ἐν πάσῃ ἁ, *w. all propriety* **1 Ti 5:2.** W. πίστις and ἀγάπη Pol 4:2. W. δικαιοσύνη (so also ISmyrnaMcCabe 1, 15) Hs 9, 16, 7. W. σεμνότης (Diod. S. 4, 24, 5) Hs 5, 6, 5. W. σωφροσύνη (TestJos 10:2) IEph 10:3. W. other virtues **1 Ti 4:12;** 1 Cl 21:7; 64; Hs 9, 15, 2; Hm 6, 2, 3 (AcJ 29 [Aa II/1, 166, 24]; AcPh 3 [Aa II/2, 2, 30]; 37 [p. 18, 16]; AcThom 104 [Aa II/2, 217, 15]). As first duty of youth Pol 5:3; ἐν ἁ. μένειν *remain chaste* IPol 5:2 (AcPhil 119 [Aa II/2, 49, 3]). ἐν ἁ. κατοικεῖν Hm 4, 3, 2 (cp. AcThom 131 [Aa II/2, 239, 2]); ἁ. φυλάσσειν (cp. Philo, Vi. Cont. 68) 4, 1, 1= ἁ. τηρεῖν 4, 4, 3.—JMüller, D. Keuschheitsideen in ihrer gesch. Entwicklung 1897; EFehrle, D. kult. Keuschh. im Altertum 1910, 42ff.—DELG s.v. ἅζομαι. M-M. TW. Sv.

ἁγνευτήριον, ου, τό (s. ἁγνεύω; Chaeremon Hist. [I AD]: 618 fgm. 6, p. 150, 9 Jac.=Porphyr., De Abst. 4, 6) lit. 'place of purification', perh. ***sanctuary,*** of the part of the temple precinct in which the ἅγια σκεύη were kept Ox 840, 8; 13 (s. Unknown Sayings 37 n. 2; 41–43: 'inner court, court of the Israelites').—DELG s.v. ἅζομαι. M-M s.v. ἁγνεία.

ἁγνεύω fut. ἁγνεύσω (Aeschyl., Hdt. et al.; ins; PRein 94, 22; PTebt 298, 68 [both II AD]; Philo; Jos., Bell. 5, 227, Ant. 14, 285) ***be pure*** ὑπὲρ τῆς ψυχῆς *for your soul's sake* B 19:8 (cp. Diod. S. 10, 9, 6 [Exc. De Virt. II 201 Vogel] τ. ψυχὴν ἁγνεύουσαν; Philo, Mut. Nom. 44).

ἁγνίζω 1 aor. ἥγνισα; pf. ptc. ἡγνικώς. Pass.: 1 aor. impv. ἁγνίσθητι, ptc. ἁγνισθείς; pf. ptc. ἡγνισμένος (trag., Hdt. et al.; LXX; TestSol C 12:5; Joseph.; SibOr 3, 592; Just., D. 86, 6).

❶ **to purify or cleanse and so make acceptable for cultic use,** ***purify***—ⓐ act. of lustrations and rites of atonement (so in trag., also ChronLind D 74; Plut., Mor. 263e τὸ πῦρ καθαίρει κ. τὸ ὕδωρ ἁγνίζει), of the Judeans before Passover **J 11:55** (cp. Ex 19:10; 2 Chr 31:17f; Jos., Bell. 6, 425, Ant. 12, 145).

ⓑ mid. *purify oneself* (Plut., Mor. 1105b; Josh 3:5; Hippol., Ref. 9, 21, 2) of the lustrations with the Nazirite oath (cp. Num 6:3) **Ac 21:24, 26; 24:18** (cp. B-D-F §314).

❷ **to cause to be morally pure,** ***purify,*** fig. ext. of 1: καρδίας **Js 4:8;** ψυχάς **1 Pt 1:22;** ἑαυτόν **1J 3:3.** Pass. ἁ. τῇ ἀφέσει τ. ἁμαρτιῶν *become pure through forgiveness of sins* B 5:1. Also ἁ. ἀπὸ τῶν ἁμαρτιῶν 8:1.

❸ mid. (w. pass. aor.) **to set oneself apart in dedication,** ***to dedicate oneself*** i.e. *give oneself up as a propitiation* ὑπὲρ ὑμῶν *for you* IEph 8:1. ἁγνίζεται ὑπὲρ ὑμῶν τὸ ἐμὸν πνεῦμα *my spirit dedicates itself for you* ITr 13:3.—DELG s.v. ἅζομαι. M-M.

ἁγνισμός, οῦ, ὁ (Dionys. Hal. 3, 22; Plut., Mor. 418b al.; SIG 1219, 19)

❶ **the process of making someth. cultically acceptable,** ***purification,*** of the purification customs when a vow was accomplished τῶν ἡμερῶν τοῦ ἁ. **Ac 21:26** (πᾶσαι αἱ ἡμέραι τοῦ ἁ. Num 6:5).

❷ **the process of being morally purified,** ***purification,*** fig. ext. of 1 (s. ἁγνίζω 2) ὁ ἁ. τῆς καρδίας B 8:3, w. forgiveness of sins.—DELG s.v. ἅζομαι. M-M. TW.

ἀγνοέω impf. ἠγνόουν; 1 aor. ἠγνόησα; pf. ἠγνόηκα LXX; ptc. ἠγνοηκώς 3 Macc 3:9. Pass.: 1 fut. 3 sg. ἀγνοηθήσεται (Ath., R. 50, 34); plpf. 3 sg. ἠγνόητο (Ath., R. 50, 30). On the philological history s. FLindemann, SymbOsl 38, '63, 69–75. (Hom.+)

❶ **to be uninformed about,** ***not to know, be ignorant (of)***

ⓐ w. ὅτι foll. (Περὶ ὕψους 33, 3 [οὐδὲ ἐκεῖνο ἀγνοῶ ὅτι=nor do I fail to recognize this, namely that . . .]; PGiss 11, 17 [118 AD]) **Ro 2:4; 6:3; 7:1;** MPol 17:2. A favorite of Paul's is the formula οὐ θέλω ὑμᾶς ἀγνοεῖν (cp. Theophr., CP 2, 4, 8; 3, 9, 5; PTebt 314, 3 [II AD] πιστεύω σε μὴ ἀγνοεῖν; Philo, Opif. M. 87 χρὴ μηδ' ἐκεῖνο ἀγνοεῖν ὅτι; Jos., Ant. 13, 354 οὐ γὰρ ἀγνοεῖν βούλομαί σε) *I want you to know* w. ὅτι foll. **Ro 1:13; 1 Cor 10:1;** cp. 2 Cl 14:2; w. περί τινος **1 Cor 12:1; 1 Th 4:13;** w. ὑπέρ τινος and ὅτι foll. **2 Cor 1:8;** w. acc. foll. **Ro 11:25;** cp. οὐ γὰρ αὐτοῦ τὰ νοήματα ἀγνοοῦμεν *we are well aware of (Satan's) designs* **2 Cor 2:11** (cp. Diod. S. 3, 66, 4; Appian, Samn. 4 §14 [sim. Just., D. 33, 1] οὐκ ἀγνοεῖν ὅτι=know very well that; Athen. 4, 73, 172f οὐκ ἀγνοῶ . . . ἅ.; Wsd 12:10; Jos., Bell. 1, 608, Ant. 6, 253; 7, 217; PGM 7, 245 οὐκ ἀγνοοῦμεν); w. indir. question foll. 2 Cl 10:4; MPol 10:1. Abs. ἀγνοῶν ἐποίησα *I did it in ignorance* **1 Ti 1:13** (TestJud 12:5; s. 4 below).

ⓑ *not to know* w. acc. of pers. (PGiss 69, 4 Χαιρήμονα οὐκ ἀγνοεῖς; PPetr III, 53n, 4 [III BC]; Herm. Wr. 11, 21b ἀ. τὸν θεόν [codd. τὸ θεῖον]) or thing (SIG 336, 9 ἀ. τοὺς τῆς πόλεως νόμους; 881, 3–4; Mitt-Wilck. I/2, 57, 6 [II BC]; Jos., Vi. 107) τοῦτον ἀγνοήσαντες **Ac 13:27.** τὴν τοῦ θεοῦ δικαιοσύνην **Ro 10:3** (here perh.=*disregard,* s. 2 below). παράπτωμα Hm 9:7. τὸ χάρισμα IEph 17:2; cp. MPol 11:2. Abs. ὅ ἀγνοοῦντες εὐσεβεῖτε *what you worship without knowing it* (on the subject matter Maximus Tyr. 11, 5e: all sorts of philosophers ἴσασιν οὐκ ἑκόντες καὶ λέγουσιν ἄκοντες sc. τὸ θεῖον=they know and name God without intending to do so) **Ac 17:23;** cp. ISm 5:1. ὁ ἀγνοῶν *the person who does not know it* ITr 6:2. Pass. (Jos., Ant. 1, 286) ἀγνοοῦνται (the Christians) *are not well known* Dg 5:12; ἀγνοούμενοι (opp. ἐπιγινωσκόμενοι) **2 Cor 6:9;** ἀγνοούμενος τῷ προσώπῳ ταῖς ἐκκλησίαις *unknown to the congregations by face* (=personally, dat. of relation B-D-F §197; manner, Rob. 530) **Gal 1:22.**

❷ **to pay little or no attention to,** ***not to recognize, disregard, ignore*** (cp. **Ro 10:3** above) εἴ τις ἀγνοεῖ, ἀγνοεῖται *anyone who disregards (it), is disregarded (by God)* **1 Cor 14:38** (v.l. ἀγνοείτω *let that person remain ignorant.*—For the juxtaposition of act. and pass. s. Alex. Aphr., Fat. 31, II/2 p. 202, 18 ἀγνοῶν καὶ ἀγνοούμενος).

❸ **to fail to understand, w. implication of lack of capacity or ability,** ***not to understand*** w. acc. τὸ ῥῆμα **Mk 9:32; Lk 9:45.** ἐν οἷς (=ἐν τούτοις, ἅ) ἀγνοοῦσιν βλασφημοῦντες *deriding what they do not understand* **2 Pt 2:12** (cp. PTebt 43, 25 [118 BC] ὑφ᾽ ἡμῶν ἔν τισιν ἠγνοηκότων).

❹ **to be unaware about one's wrongdoing,** ***lapse/do wrong/sin unintentionally*** (Isocr., X. et al.; Polyb. 1, 67, 5; Diod. S. 1, 70, 7 ὑπὲρ τῶν ἀγνοουμένων; 11, 16, 1 τὰ ἠγνοημένα=lapses; 17, 73, 6; Sir 5:15; 2 Macc 11:31; PTebt 23, 12 [II BC] τὰ προηγνοημένα the former sins; s. ἄγνοια 2 beg.) w. πλανᾶσθαι **Hb 5:2** (Moffatt: 'err through ignorance'; s. next entry and μετριοπαθέω).—LCerfaux, RAC I 186–88.—DELG s.v. γιγνώσκω 225. M-M. TW. Sv.

ἀγνόημα, ατος, τό (s. ἀγνοέω; since Gorgias [V BC], 11 [Helena] 19; s. FZucker, Semantica ABA 38, '63, 51f) ***sin committed in ignorance/unintentionally*** (Diod. S. 1, 71, 3 ἐλάχιστα ἀ.; 13, 90, 7; OGI 116, 2; UPZ 111, 3 [163 BC]; PTebt 5, 3 [118 BC] ἀγνοήματα, ἁμαρτήματα, ἐνκλήματα, καταγνώσματα [Taubenschlag, Law^2 430; APF 2, 1903, 483ff; Jur. Pap. no. 69; KLatte, ARW 20, 1921, p. 287, 1]; BGU 1185, 7; 1 Macc 13:39; Tob 3:3; Sir 23:2; JosAs 13 [p. 57, 20 Bat.] Cod. A; Eus., DemEv 4, 10.—Soph. Oed. R. is devoted to dramatic exposition of the theme of such ἅ.) **Hb 9:7** (s. ἄγνοια 2 beg.; REB: 'inadvertent sins'; NRSV: 'sins committed unintentionally'). Forgiven by God Hs 5, 7, 3f.—DELG s.v. γιγνώσκω 225. M-M. TW.

ἄγνοια, ας, ἡ (since Aeschyl. and Thu. 8, 92, 11; ins, pap, LXX, Test12Patr, JosAs; EpArist 130; Philo; Jos., Bell. 4, 29, Ant. 18, 335, C. Ap. 1, 73; Just.; Tat. 7, 3; ἀγνοιῶν14, 1; Ath.; Mel. HE 4, 26, 10)

❶ in a gener. sense **lack of information about someth.,** ***ignorance*** (Aeschyl. et al.) as v.l. for ἀγνωσία=*ignorant talk* **1 Pt 2:15** P^{72}. But this may belong equally in 2.

❷ spec. **lack of information that may result in reprehensible conduct,** ***ignorance, unawareness, lack of discernment*** (opp. συνείδησις, γνῶσις, ἐπιστήμη, σοφία). In our lit., of unawareness in relation to deity or of unintentional or involuntary (as opposed to deliberate [cp. Jos., Ant. 11, 130; Philo, Leg. All. 1, 35]) moral lapses. (Cp. Steinleitner ins 14, 3 of one who was unaware that the grove in which he felled trees was sacred to deities; for an OT perspective s. Ps. 18:12 and cp. TestGad 5:7 μετάνοια ἀναιρεῖ τὴν ἄ.).

ⓐ of those who condemned Jesus κατὰ ἄγνοιαν ἐπράξατε *you acted in ignorance*=you were unaware of what you were doing **Ac 3:17** (Polyb. 12, 12, 4; κατ᾽ ἄ. παραπαίειν; Parthenius 9, 8; Plut., Mor. 551e; POxy 237 VIII, 36; BGU 619, 4) ἄχρι τῆς ἀγνοίας *as long as he knows nothing of it* Hm 4, 1, 5; PtK 2 p. 14, 11; 3 p. 15, 26.—**1 Pt 2:15** P^{72} (s. 1 above).

ⓑ almost=*sin* (so LXX, e.g. Sir 23:3 [in parallelism with ἁμαρτίαι]; 28:7; PsSol 3:8; TestLevi 3:5; TestZeb 1:5; Philo, Ebr. 154ff; cp. Pla., Tht. 176c; Stoic. III, p. 65, 20; Diod. S. 14, 1, 3 τ. ἰδίαν ἄγνοιαν=one's own mistaken conduct; Epict. 1, 26, 6; Herm. Wr. 13, 8; 11, 21 ἡ τελεία κακία τὸ ἀγνοεῖν τὸ θεῖον, also 10, 9; PTebt 24, 33 [II BC] of evildoers: λήγοντες τῆς ἀγνοίας.—Diod. S. 4, 11, 2 ἄ. is the "delusion" that drove Heracles to commit murder) IEph 19:3. Of the times when people did not know God τοὺς χρόνους τῆς ἀγνοίας **Ac 17:30** (TestGad 5:7 μετάνοια ἀναιρεῖ τὴν ἄ). διὰ τὴν ἄγνοιαν (Diod. S. 11, 10, 2; SIG 904, 6; cp. Alex. Aphr., Fat. 19, II/2 p. 189, 16 δι᾽ ἄγνοιαν ἁμαρτάνειν); **Eph 4:18.** ἐν τῇ ἀγνοίᾳ ὑμῶν **1 Pt 1:14** (some find gnostic usage in the three NT passages cited); **2:15 v.l.** (for ἀγνωσία). ἄ. προτέρα Hs 5, 7, 3. The pl. as v.l. for ἀπάταις **2 Pt 2:13.**—LCerfaux, RAC I, 186–88. DELG s.v. γιγνώσκω 225. M-M. TW. Sv.

ἁγνός, ή, όν (Hom.+) ***pure, holy,*** cultic word, orig. an attribute of the divinity and everything belonging to it; cp. ἅζομαι 'stand in awe of' DELG s.v. ἅζομαι (Hom. et al.; ἁ. θεαὶ Demeter and Persephone IG 14, 204; SEG VIII, 550, 2 [I BC] Ἶσι, ἁγνή, ἁγία; PUps 8 no. 14 [pre-Christian] τῇ Ἁγνῇ Θεᾷ s. LMoulinier, Le pur et l'impur dans la pensée des Grecs, '52) then transf. to moral sense (Clem. Al., Strom. defines it 7, 27, 2 πᾶς ἁ. ἐστιν ὁ μηδὲν ἑαυτῷ κακὸν συνειδώς).

ⓐ of pers. (Diog. L. 7, 119: acc. to the Stoics wise people are ἁγνοί, ὅσιοι, δίκαιοι; POxy 41, 29f ἁγνοὶ πιστοὶ σύνδικοι; Sb 4117; PHarr 55, 24 magic formula) of Christ **1J 3:3** (SibOr 3, 49 of the Messiah); of the apostles τῶν ἁγνῶν ἀνδρῶν AcPl Ha 1, 16; σεαυτὸν ἁ. τήρει *keep yourself pure* (fr. sins) **1 Ti 5:22;** ἁ. ἐν τῇ σαρκί 1 Cl 38:2; ἁ. ἐν ἔργοις 48:5.—*Innocent* (Pla., Leg. 6, 759c ἁ. τοῦ φόνου) συνεστήσατε ἑαυτοὺς ἁγνοὺς εἶναι *you have shown that you were innocent* **2 Cor 7:11,** where τῷ πράγματι is to be connected w. ἁγνούς.—Esp. of women *chaste, pure* (since Aeschyl., fgm. 420 [238 N.]; Pla., Leg. 840d; SIG 985, 35; Sb 2481, 1f Ἰουλία ἁγνή; PGM 36, 289) παρθένος (Herodian 1, 11, 4; SIG 797, 20 [37 AD]; Aberciusins. 14; 4 Macc 18:7; Philo, Spec. Leg. 1, 107) **2 Cor 11:2;** cp. **Tit 2:5.**

ⓑ of things ὅσα ἁγνά *everything that is pure* **Phil 4:8;** ἔργα ἁ. (Pr 21:8) Hv 3, 8, 7; μερίς (Dt 3:9) 1 Cl 30:1; χεῖρες (Eur., Hipp. 316f, Or. 1604) 1 Cl 29:1; ἁ. ἀναστροφή **1 Pt 3:2.** ἀγωγή 1 Cl 48:1. συνείδησις *clear conscience* (w. ἄμωμος, σεμνός) 1:3; Pol 5:3; ἀγάπη *holy love* 1 Cl 21:8. Of one's person (cp. Herm. Wr. 1, 31 θυσίας ἁ.): (w. ἀμίαντον) τὸ βάπτισμα ἁ. τηρεῖν *keep oneself pure after baptism* 2 Cl 6:9. τὴν σάρκα ἁ. τηρεῖν keep the body pure 8:4; 6. Of the wisdom from above **Js 3:17.**—EWilliger, Hagios 1922.—M-M. TW. Sv.

ἁγνότης, ητος, ἡ ***purity, sincerity*** (s. ἁγνός; Cornutus 32 p. 67, 2; IG IV, 588, 15 [II AD] δικαιοσύνης ἕνεκεν καὶ ἁγνότητος) ἐν ἁγνότητι **2 Cor 6:6;** in **11:3** (w. ἁπλότης) it is a questioned reading, though w. very ancient attestation. ἁ. τῆς ἀληθείας *true purity* Hv 3, 7, 3; πορεύεσθαι ἐν ἁ. *lead a pure life* m 4, 4, 4.—M-M. TW.

ἁγνῶς (Hes. et al.; OGI 485, 13; 524, 6; SIG 986, 8; 16; EpArist 317; PGM 4, 2639; 12, 38 ἁ. καὶ καθαρῶς) adv. fr. ἅγνος *purely, sincerely* μένειν *abide in purity* B 2:3. πολιτεύεσθαι *lead a pure life* Hs 5, 6, 6. Also ἀναστρέφεσθαι s 9, 27, 2. διακονεῖν *in sincerity* v 3, 5, 1; cp. s 9, 26, 2. διδάσκειν σεμνῶς καὶ ἁ. *teach seriously and sincerely* s 9, 25, 2; τὸν Χριστὸν καταγγέλλουσιν οὐχ ἁ. *not from pure motives* **Phil 1:17.**—EDNT.

ἀγνωσία, ας, ἡ (Eur., Thu. et al.; pap, LXX; Test12Patr) ***ignorance,*** not predominantly in the intellectual sense but, as in the speech of the mysteries (Herm. Wr. 1, 27 ἀ. τοῦ θεοῦ; 7, 1; 10, 8; Kore Kosmu 53 [s. HBetz, ZTK 63, '66, 179; 187]), a lack of religious experience or *lack of spiritual discernment* (s. Rtzst., Mysterienrel.[3] 292f) ἀγνωσίαν θεοῦ τινες ἔχουσιν *some have no knowledge of God* (cp. Wsd 13:1; APF 5, 1913, 383) **1 Cor 15:34.** καλεῖν ἀπὸ ἀ. εἰς ἐπίγνωσιν δόξης ὀνόματος αὐτοῦ 1 Cl 59:2; φιμοῦν τὴν τῶν ἀφρόνων ἀνθρώπων ἀ. *silence the ignorant talk of foolish men* **1 Pt 2:15** (ἄγνοια P^{72}).—DELG s.v. γιγνώσκω 224. M-M. TW.

ἄγνωστος, ον (Hom.+; pap [PGiss 3, 2f [117 AD] ἥκω σοι, ὦ δῆμε, οὐκ ἄγνωστος Φοῖβος θεός]; LXX; ApcSed 11, 4; Iren. 1, 20, 3 [Harv. I 180, 12]; 21, 3 [Harv. I 183, 9] al.; Philo; Jos., C. Ap. 2, 167 [of God's οὐσία] al.; Just.) **pert. to that which is unknown because of lack of information, *unknown*** in the ins on an altar in Athens ἀγνώστῳ θεῷ **Ac 17:23** (this phrase is found neither in the Hebrew Bible nor in the LXX; cp. Paus. 1, 1, 4: ἐπὶ τῇ Φαλερῷ . . . Ἀθηνᾶς ναός ἐστιν . . . βωμοὶ θεῶν τε ὀνομαζομένων ἀγνώστων καὶ ἡρώων; cp. 5, 14, 8 and a Pergamene ins [HHepding, MAI 35, 1910, 454–57]). Cp. also Diog. L. 1, 110 ἔτι καὶ νῦν ἔστι εὑρεῖν κατὰ τοὺς δήμους τ. Ἀθηναίων βωμοὺς ἀνωνύμους. Norden, Agn. Th. 1913, 115–25 thinks that this expr. comes fr. a speech by Apollonius of Tyana (cp. Philostrat., Vi. Apoll. 6, 3, 5 ἀγνώστων δαιμόνων βωμοὶ ἵδρυνται). On the problem s. Clemen 290–300; REgger, Von Römern, Juden, Christen u. Barbaren: SBWienAk 247, 3 '65; WGöber, Pauly-W. 2d ser. V '34, 1988–94; AHarnack, TU 39, 1, 1913, 1–46; Rtzst., NJklA 31, 1913, 146ff; 393ff; PCorssen, ZNW 14, 1913, 309ff; FBurkitt, JTS 15, 1914, 455–64; TBirt, RhM 69, 1914, 342ff; OWeinreich, De Dis Ignotis: ARW 18, 1915, 1–52; AWikenhauser, D. Apostelgesch. 1921, 369–94; Meyer III 1923, 96–98; Dssm., Paulus[2] 1925, 226–29 (Eng. tr. Paul 1926, 287–91); KLake: Beginn. I/5, '33, 240–46; MDibelius, Pls. auf d. Areopag '39=ch. 2 in Studies in the Acts, ed. HGreeven, '56. BGärtner, The Areopagus Speech and Natural Revelation, '55, 242–47 (lit.); PvanderHorst, in: Knowledge of God in the Graeco-Roman World '88, 19–42. For further lit. see s.v. Ἄρειος πάγος.—DELG s.v. γιγνώσκω 224. M-M. TW.

ἀγορά, ᾶς, ἡ (Hom.+; ins, pap, LXX; TestJob 22:3; ParJer 6:19 τῶν ἐθνῶν; Jos., Bell. 5, 513 al.; Ath.; loanw. in rabb.) ***market place*** as a place for children to play **Mt 11:16; Lk 7:32.** Place for people seeking work and for idlers (Harpocration, s.v. Κολωνέτας: the μισθωτοί are standing in the marketplace) **Mt 20:3;** cp. **23:7; Mk 12:38; Lk 11:43; 20:46.** Scene of public events, incl. the healings of Jesus ἐν ταῖς ἀ. ἐτίθεσαν τοὺς ἀσθενοῦντας **Mk 6:56.** Scene of a lawsuit (so as early as Hom.; cp. Demosth. 43, 36 τῶν ἀρχόντων) against Paul **Ac 16:19, 35** D. Of the Agora in Athens (in the Ceramicus), the center of public life **17:17** (s. ECurtius, Paulus in Athen: SBBerlAk 1893, 925ff; SHalstead, Paul in the Agora: Quantulacumque [KLake Festschr.] '37, 139–43; RMartin, Recherches sur l'Agora greque '51). ἀπ' ἀγορᾶς (+ὅταν ἔλθωσιν [D it] is the correct interpr.) ἐὰν μὴ ῥαντίσωνται οὐκ ἐσθίουσιν *when they return fr. the market place they do not eat unless they wash themselves* (pregnant constr. as Vi. Aesopi G 40 P. πιεῖν ἀπὸ τοῦ βαλανείου=after returning from the bath; PHolm 20, 26 μετὰ τὴν κάμινον=after burning in the oven; Epict. 3, 19, 5 φαγεῖν ἐκ βαλανείου; Sir 34:25 βαπτιζόμενος ἀπὸ νεκροῦ) **Mk 7:4.** Since the mid. form ῥαντ. expresses someth. about the persons of those who eat, the words ἀπ' ἀ. prob. refer to them, too, and so the interpr. of ἀπ' ἀ.='(of) the things sold in the market', though linguistically poss. (ἀ. in this sense X. et al.; simply='food': Memnon [I BC/I AD]: 434 fgm. 1, 29, 9 p. 359, 12 Jac.; Appian, Sicil. 2 §10 and 4; Polyaenus 3, 10, 10; 5, 2, 10; Jos., Bell. 1, 308, Ant. 14, 472; pap in Preis.) is untenable.—B. 822. DELG. M-M.

ἀγοράζω impf. ἠγόραζον; 1 pl fut. ἀγοράσομεν Gen 43:4; 1 aor. ἠγόρασα, pass. ἠγοράσθην.

❶ **to acquire things or services in exchange for money, *buy, purchase*** (so, trans., Aristoph. et al.; ins, pap, LXX; Jos., Ant. 12, 175; Test12Patr), w. acc. of thing (X., An. 1, 5, 10; Gen 42:7; 2 Ch 34:11) τὸν ἀγρὸν ἐκεῖνον **Mt 13:44; Lk 14:18;** αὐτόν (i.e. μαργαρίτην) **Mt 13:46;** σινδόνα **Mk 15:46;** ἀρώματα **16:1;** μάχαιραν **Lk 22:36;** cp. **14:19; J 4:8; 6:5.** τὸν γόμον αὐτῶν **Rv 18:11.** W. rel. clause as obj.: ἀ. ὧν χρείαν ἔχομεν *what we need* **J 13:29.** Of fields and fig. of souls=*win* Hs 1:8 f. W. dat. of pers. and acc. of thing (Gen 43:4; 44:25) ἑαυτοῖς βρώματα **Mt 14:15;** cp. **Mk 6:36.** W. dat. of pers. only **Mt 25:9.** ἀ. τι εἴς τινα *someth. for someone* **Lk 9:13.** Abs. (Gen 42:5; 2 Ch 1:16) **Mt 25:10; 1 Cor 7:30.** W. πωλεῖν (Aristoph., Ach. 625; SIG 330, 19; Is 24:2; 1 Macc 13:49; Jos., Bell. 2, 127) **Rv 13:17;** cp. **Mt 21:12; Mk 11:15; Lk 17:28; 19:45 v.l.** W. price given in genit. (UPZ 93, 6=PParis 59, 6; Dt 2:6; Bar 1:10; s. B-D-F §179; Rob. 510f) δηναρίων διακοσίων ἄρτους *buy 200 denarii worth of bread* **Mk 6:37.** Also ἐκ (pap in Kuhring [s. ἀνά beg.] 27f; EpJer 24) ἠγόρασαν ἐξ αὐτῶν (i.e. w. the 30 shekels of silver) τὸν ἀγρόν **Mt 27:7.** W. the seller mentioned παρά τινος (Isocr. 2, 54; PCairZen 25, 25 [III BC]; PLond III, 882, 24 p. 14; 1208, 10 p. 19; POxy 1149, 5; Dt 2:6; 2 Esdr 20:32) ἀ. παρ' ἐμοῦ χρυσίον **Rv 3:18.**

❷ **to secure the rights to someone by paying a price, *buy, acquire as property,*** fig. ext. of 1, of believers, for whom Christ has paid the price w. his blood: w. gen. of price ἠγοράσθητε τιμῆς *you were bought for a price* **1 Cor 6:20; 7:23** (s. τιμή 1). τινά **2 Pt 2:1.** W. dat. of possessor and ἐν of price (B-D-F §219, 3; cp. 1 Ch 21:24): ἠγόρασας τῷ θεῷ ἐν τῷ αἵματί σου **Rv 5:9.** W. ἀπό τινος to indicate from whom or from what the purchase separates: ἠγορασμένοι ἀπὸ τῆς γῆς **Rv 14:3;** cp. vs. **4.**—Since Deissmann (LO 271–81) it has been fashionable to understand esp. St. Paul's statements from the perspective of religious law which in reality bestowed freedom on a slave purchased by a divinity (ἀ. of the purchase of a slave SIG[2] 844, 9; OGI 338, 23; PGissUniv 20, 14 [II AD]; POxy 1149, 5f. SIG 845, 1 has ἐπρίατο in a manumission; s. LMitteis, Reichsrecht u. Volksrecht 1891, 374ff; Dssm. LO 275, n. 9 [LAE 322ff]). For arguments against the traditional application of Deissmann's data, see WElert, TLZ 72, '47, 265–70; FBonner, Untersuchungen über die Religion der Sklaven in Griechenland und Rom '57; SLyonnet, Biblica 42, '61, 85–89. The normal practice of slave-purchase can account for the NT formulation (cp. HKraft, Hdb. ad loc.) but whatever the writers' intentions, sacral imagery would occur to some of their Gr-Rom. publics.—B. 818. DELG s.v. ἀγορά. M-M. TW. Spicq. Sv.

ἀγοραῖος, ον (Aeschyl., Hdt.+; ins, pap) 'pertaining to a market', in our lit. used only as subst.

❶ οἱ ἀ. ***market people,*** specif. *the crowd in the market place,* and so *rabble* (Gramm. Ammonius ἀγοραῖος σημαίνει τ. πονηρόν, τὸν ἐν ἀγορᾷ τεθραμμένον, cp. Aristoph., Ran.

1015; Pla., Prot. 347c; Theophr., Char. 6, 2; Dio Chrys. 49 [66], 25; Plut., Aemil. Paul. 38, 4 ἀνθρώπους ἀγεννεῖς καὶ δεδουλευκότας, ἀγοραίους δὲ καὶ δυναμένους ὄχλον συναγαγεῖν al.) **Ac 17:5.**

❷ αἱ ἀγοραῖοι (sc. ἡμέραι or σύνοδοι) ***court days/sessions*** ἀ. ἄγονται *the courts are in session* **Ac 19:38** (Jos., Ant. 14, 245 ἄγειν τὴν ἀγοραῖον; EphemEpigr VII 436, no. 44, 10 [II AD] ἡ ἀγοραῖος ἤχθη; Strabo 13, 4, 12 τὰς ἀ. ποιεῖσθαι=Lat. conventus forenses agere; B-D-F §5, 3b).—DELG s.v. ἀγορά 12. M-M.

ἄγρα, ας, ἡ (Hom. et al.; Jos., Ant. 8, 40)—❶ **the act of catching, *catching*** (Ctesias 688 [Ind. 24]: fgm. 45g p. 494, 13 Jac.; Alciphron 1, 15, 1; Aesop, Fab. 21 P.//24 H.; 191 P.//260 H.=154 III H-H.) εἰς ἄ. *to catch someth.* (Eur., Suppl. 885 ἐς ἄγρας ἰέναι) **Lk 5:4;** likew. vs. **9** ἐπὶ τῇ ἄγρᾳ τῶν ἰχθύων, ὧν συνέλαβον.

❷ **that which is caught, *a catch*** (Solon 23, 3 Diehl[2]; X., Cyr. 2, 4, 19; Lycophron 665; Appian, Bell. Civ. 4, 129 §545; Iambl. Erot. 34; TestZeb 6:6; POxy 3269, 1 [III AD]) ἣ = ἣν συνέλαβον v.l. in **Lk 5:9.**—DELG. New Docs 3, 17f.

ἀγράμματος, ον 'unable to write' (X., Mem. 4, 2, 20; Epict. 2, 2, 22; BGU 118; 152; POxy 71; 133; 134; 137; 139 al.—EMajer-Leonhard, Ἀγράμματοι, diss. Marb. 1913; RCalderini, Aeg. 30, '50, 14–41), also ***uneducated, illiterate*** (Pla., Tim. 23b; ἄνθρωποι Epicurus in Philod., Rhet. 1, 141; Philo, Omn. Prob. Lib. 51) of Peter and John ἄνθρωποι ἀ. καὶ ἰδιῶται **Ac 4:13** (WWuellner, The Mng. of 'Fishers of Men' '67, 45–63 ἀγράμ.=lacking in legal proficiency).—DELG s.v. γράφω. New Docs 5, 12f. M-M.

ἀγραυλέω ***live out of doors*** (Aristot. et al.; Plut., Num. 61 [4, 1]. Of shepherds Bryso in Stob. 4, 28, 15; Parthenius 29, 1; cp. Hom., Il. 18, 162 ποιμένες ἄγραυλοι. TestAbr A 10 p. 87, 23 [Stone p. 22]; ParJer) **Lk 2:8.**—S. DELG ἀγρός and αὐλή.

ἀγρεύω 1 aor. ἤγρευσα 'catch' (Soph., Hdt.et al.; pap, LXX) in NT only as fig. ext. ***catch unawares*** (Soph., TGF fgm. 510; Pr 5:22; 6:25f) ἵνα αὐτὸν ἀγρεύσωσιν λόγῳ *that they might catch him in a(n unguarded) statement* **Mk 12:13** (cp. Aen. Tact. 22, 11 οὕτως γὰρ ἂν . . . ἥκιστα ὑπό τινων ἀγρευθεῖεν λάθρᾳ προσελθόντων=for so they would least of all be caught off guard by any hostile forces approaching them in stealth.—DELG s.v. ἄγρα. M-M.

ἀγρίδιον, ου, τό (Diod. S. 13, 84, 4; Epict. 2, 22, 10 al.; M. Ant. 4, 3, 9; Sb 5230, 28 [I AD]) **a small land-holding in the country, *a little farm*** or ***country house*** MPol 5:1; 6:1.

ἀγριέλαιος, ον (growing) ***from a wild olive tree*** really an adj. (B-D-F §120, 3; Rob. 168, cp. 166) and so perh. **Ro 11:17** (as Erycius in Anth. Pal. 9, 237; Ps.-Theocr., Idyll 25, 257). But it may also be taken as a subst., as we say 'oak' of a piece of furniture (see next).—DELG s.v. ἀγρός. M-M.

ἀγριέλαιος, ου, ἡ ***wild olive tree*** (Theophr., HP 2, 2, 5; Theocr. 7, 18; Nicol. Dam.: 90 fgm. 66, 40 Jac.; PCairZen 184, 7=PEdgar 100 [=Sb 6815], 7 [255 BC]. As masc. in schol. on Apollon. Rhod. 2, 843, 848–50a; B-D-F §241, 6) fig. of the gentiles **Ro 11:17, 24** (if subst., but s. preceding entry; opp. καλλιέλαιος).—TFischer, D. Ölbaum 1904; WRamsay, The Olive-Tree and the Wild-Olive: Exp. 6th ser., 11, 1905, 16–34; 152–60; EFickendey, D. Ölbaum in Kleinasien 1922; SLinder, D. Pfropfen m. wilden Ölzweigen (Ro 11:17): Pj 26, 1930, 40–43; FJBruijel, De Olijfboom: GereformTT 35, '35, 273–80.—M-M.

ἄγριος, ία, ον (Hom.+; loanw. in rabb.)—❶ **pert. to being in a natural state or condition, *wild,*** of plants in the open field (Diod. S. 5, 2, 4; Artem. 4, 57; Jos., Bell. 5, 437; PSI 816, 3 [II BC]) Hs 9, 26, 4. Of animals (so Diod. S. 4, 17, 4 ζῷα; 4, 17, 5 θηρία; Arrian, Ind. 11, 11; 13, 1; PSI 406, 42; 409, 18 [III BC]; BGU 1252, 4; as a rule LXX; Jos., C. Ap. 2, 139) 1 Cl 56:11f (Job 5:22f); μέλι ἄ. *honey fr. wild bees* (Iambl. Erot. p. 222, 16 μέλιτται ἄγριαι w. their μέλι; Cat. Cod. Astr. X 86b, 6 ἀγριομέλισσα.—Others think of a plant product; cp. Ps.-Aristot., Mirab. 19 ἐν Λυδίᾳ ἀπὸ τῶν δένδρων τὸ μέλι συλλέγεσθαι πολύ; Diod. S. 19, 94, 10 φύεται παρ' αὐτοῖς [i.e. the Nabataeans] ἀπὸ τ. δένδρων μέλι πολὺ τὸ καλούμενον ἄγριον, ᾧ χρῶνται ποτῷ μεθ' ὕδατος; Jos., Bell. 4, 468) **Mt 3:4; Mk 1:6;** GEb 13, 79. By fig. ext., of persons *wild in appearance:* of women in black w. flowing hair Hs 9, 9, 5; more completely ἄ. τῇ ἰδέᾳ of a shepherd 6, 2, 5.

❷ **pert. to being untamed or running one's own course, *uncontrolled,*** fig. ext. of 1, of desires *savage, fierce* (Pla., Rep. 572b) Hm 12, 1, 2; cp. 12, 4, 6. τὸ ἄγριον *cruelty* (Pla., Rep. 571c et al.; Herm. Wr. 486, 38; 492, 4 Sc.) IEph 10:2 (opp. ἥμερος). Of natural phenomena *stormy* (Aeschyl., Hdt. et al.) κύματα ἄ. θαλάσσης (Wsd 14:1; SibOr 3, 778) **Jd 13.**—DELG s.v. ἀγρός. M-M.

ἀγριότης, ητος, ἡ (X. et al.; 2 Macc 15:21; TestAbr A 16 p. 97, 1 [Stone p. 42]; 17 p. 99, 4 [Stone p. 46] al.; Philo; Jos., Ant. 16, 363 θυμὸς καὶ ἀ.) ***wildness, savagery*** of desires Hm 12, 1, 2.—DELG s.v. ἀγρός.

ἀγριόω ('make wild' trag., X. et al.; 3 Macc 5:2 ἀγριωθέντας; TestSol 13:5 ἠγριωμέναι). Pass. in act. sense, fig., ***become wild/uncontrolled*** of humans Hs 9, 26, 4 (Diod. S. 19, 6, 6; Appian, Iber. 96 §417; the act.= 'cause to become wild' TestSim 4:8 ἀγριοῖ τοῦτο τ. ψυχήν).—DELG s.v. ἀγρός.

Ἀγρίππας, α, ὁ name of various political figures: ***Agrippa*** (lit. [Diod. S. 12, 30, 1; ParJer 3:14; 21:5; 22; GrBar ins 2; Philo, Joseph.]; ins, pap, coins B-D-F §54; 55, 1)

❶ ***Herod Agrippa I*** (10 BC–44 AD), son of Aristobulus, grandson of Herod the Great; ruler first (37) of Gaulanitis, Trachonitis, Batanaea, Panias, then (39) also of Abilene, Galilee, and Perea, finally (41) also of Judea and Samaria; called Herod in **Ac 12:1ff.**—Schürer I 442–54 (sources and lit.); ESchwartz, NGG 1907, 263ff; Rosenberg in Pauly-W. X/1, 1917, 143–46; Meyer III 42f; 167f; 541f.

❷ ***Herod Agrippa II*** (28–92/93 AD), son of 1, ruled over the tetrarchy of Philip fr. 53 to his death. For his part in Paul's trial s. **Ac 25:13ff** (he is mentioned **25:13, 22–24, 26; 26:1f, 7 v.l., 19, 27f, 32**).—Schürer I 471–83 (sources and lit.); ESchwartz, NGG 1907, 263ff; HTajra, The Trial of St. Paul '89, 152–71; Rosenberg in Pauly-W. X/1, 1917, 146–50.—On both s. WOtto and HWillrich on Ἡρῴδης, beg.

❸ Name of Rom. governor AcPt Ox 849 recto, 25f.

ἀγρός, οῦ, ὁ (cp. ἄγω: DELG s.v. ἀγρός; Hom.+) ***field, land, countryside.***

❶ **open country as opposed to city or village, *countryside, land, field*** Hv 2, 1, 4; 9:3 al. ἐν (τῷ) ἀγρῷ *in the field* (PAmh 134, 5; '[like a gazelle] in open country' 2 Km 2:18; 10:8 al.) **Mt 24:18; Lk 17:31;** εἰς τὸν ἀγρόν *in the field* **Mk 13:16;** εἶναι ἐν (τῷ) ἀ. **Mt 24:40; Lk 15:25; 17:35 v.l.;** ἔρχεσθαι εἰς τὸν ἀ. *go (out) into the country* Hv 3, 1, 2; πορεύεσθαι εἰς ἀ. (Timaeus Hist. [IV/III BC]: 566 fgm. 48, 2 Jac. [Athen. 12, 15, 518d]; Ruth 2:2) **Mt 24:18; Mk 16:12** or ὑπάγειν εἰς ἀ. Hv 4, 1, 2; περιπατεῖν εἰς τὸν ἀ. s 2:1. ἔρχεσθαι ἀπ' ἀγροῦ *come in* *fr. the country* **Mk 15:21; Lk 23:26;** εἰσέρχεσθαι ἐκ τοῦ ἀ. (cp. PEleph 13, 6 οὔπω εἰσελήλυθεν ἐξ ἀγροῦ; Gen 30:16; Jos., Ant. 5, 141) **Lk 17:7** (s. B-D-F §255; Mlt. 82); cp. πάρεστιν ἀπ' ἀγροῦ **11:6** D.—B. 1304.

❷ freq. in pl. **property that is used for farming purposes,** ***farm, estate*** (cp. Lat. ager=estate.—X., Mem. 3, 9, 11; SIG 914, 39; OGI 235, 2; 1 Km 8:14; 22:7 al.; cp. Josh 19:6; Jos., Ant. 17, 193) **Mt 19:29; 22:5; Mk 10:29f; 14:18** (but s. 3); **Lk 15:15.** W. πόλις: ἀπήγγειλαν εἰς τὴν πόλιν καὶ εἰς τοὺς ἀγρούς *among the farms* **Mk 5:14; Lk 8:34;** w. κῶμαι (Dio Chrys. 13 [7], 42) **Mk 6:36; Lk 9:12;** w. κῶμαι and πόλεις **Mk 6:56.**

❸ **land put under cultivation,** ***arable land, field*** (X., Mem. 1, 1, 8) **Mt 13:24, 27, 31, 38; Lk 14:18** (s. 2); **Ac 4:37;** Hv 3, 1, 3. In it grow τὰ κρίνα τοῦ ἀ. *wild lilies* **Mt 6:28;** χόρτος τοῦ ἀ. (Gen 3:18; 4 Km 19:26) vs. **30;** ζιζάνια τοῦ ἀ. *weeds in the field* **13:36;** παμβότανον τοῦ ἀ. 1 Cl 56:14 (Job 5:25).—Used to hide treasure **Mt 13:44;** ἀ. τοῦ κεραμέως *potter's field* **27:7f, 10** (s. GStrecker, Der Weg der Gerechtigkeit '62, 76–82). KDieterich, RhM 59, 1904, 226ff.—M-M. TW.

ἀγρυπνέω (Theognis et al.; pap, LXX; JosAs 25:3; Philo, Aet. M. 70; Tat. 11, 2: lit. 'to keep oneself awake, be awake') in our lit. fig.

❶ **to be vigilant in awareness of threatening peril,** ***be alert,*** *be on the alert, keep watch over someth., be on guard:* ἀγρυπνεῖτε **Mk 13:33; Lk 21:36** (cp. 1 Esdr 8:58; 2 Esdr 8:29).

❷ **to be alertly concerned about,** ***look after, care for*** (Plut., Mor. 337b; OGI 521, 6; Da 9:14 ἀ. ἐπὶ τὰ κακά; En 100:8 ἀ. νοῆσαι τὸ κακόν); ἀ. ὑπὲρ τῶν ψυχῶν **Hb 13:17;** εἰς αὐτό **Eph 6:18;** ἀ. οὐκ εἰς τὸ ἀγαθὸν ἀλλ' εἰς τὸ πονηρόν D 5:2; οὐκ εἰς φόβον θεοῦ ἀλλὰ ἐπὶ τὸ πονηρόν B 20:2.—GTheissen, Sociology of Early Christianity, tr. JBowden, '78. DELG s.v. ἀγρός. M-M. TW.

ἀγρυπνία, ας, ἡ (s. ἀγρυπνέω; Hdt. et al.; BGU 1764, 9 [I BC]; Sir 31:2; 38:26 al.; 2 Macc 2:26; TestSol 18:32; Jos., Bell. 3, 318)

❶ **the state of remaining awake because one is unable to go to sleep,** ***sleeplessness*** lit., only pl. (SIG 1169, 50) ἐν ἀγρυπνίαις *with sleepless nights* (and other hardships, as X., Mem. 4, 5, 9; Plut., Mor. 135e, Sertor. 574 [13, 2] πόνοι, ὁδοιπορίαι, ἀγρυπνίαι, Sulla 470 [28, 14] ἀγρυπνίαι κ. κόποι) **2 Cor 6:5; 11:27.** (On the rhetorical figure "peristasis" s. AFridrichsen, SymbOsl 7, 1928, 25–29; 8, 1929, 78–82; K. Hum. Vetensk.-Samfundet i. Upps. Årsbok '43, 31–34; Danker, Benefactor 363–64, Augsburg Comm.: 2 Cor '89, 89–91.)

❷ **the state of being alertly concerned,** ***care*** fig. ext. of 1 (SEG VIII, 548, 30 [I BC]; Sir 42:9 to the extent of causing loss of sleep) B 21:7 (w. ἐπιθυμία; but there is no suggestion of sleeplessness in the context).—M-M. TW. Sv.

ἄγω fut. ἄξω; 2 aor. ἤγαγον; also 3 pl. ἤγαγαν (GJs 10:1); ἠγάγοσαν LXX; pf. ἀγήοχα LXX. Pass.: impf. ἠγόμην; 1 fut. ἀχθήσομαι; 1 aor. ἤχθην; pf. 3 sg. ἦκται Is 23:1. See the pres. act. impv. ἄγε as a separate entry (Hom.+).

❶ **to direct the movement of an object from one position to another—ⓐ** ***lead, bring, lead off, lead away*** w. acc. τὴν ὄνον καὶ τὸν πῶλον **Mt 21:7** (cp. Just., A I, 32, 6; 54, 7); γυναῖκα **J 8:3;** παῖδα **Ac 20:12.** ἄγαγε αὐτήν *bring her here!* AcPl Ha 2, 15f. θέλεις χαλκέα ἄγωμεν; *Do you wish us to fetch a locksmith?* 3, 5. W. acc. and indication of the goal πρὸς αὐτόν **Lk 4:40; 18:40;** cp. **19:35; J 9:13; Ac 9:27; 23:18.** πρὸς τὸ συμψέλιον Hv 3, 1, 7. εἰς τὴν ἔρημον B 7:8. ἐπὶ σφαγήν *to be slaughtered* **Ac 8:32;** 1 Cl 16:7; B 5:2 (all three Is 53:7). ἔξω **J 19:4, 13;** ὧδε **Lk 19:27.** W. dat. of pers. (1 Macc 7:2) ἀγάγετέ μοι *bring it to me* **Mt 21:2.** τινὰ σύν τινι (cp. PGM 1, 179) **1 Th 4:14.** Pass. τὸ πλοῖον ἀγόμενον εἰς Μακεδονίαν *the ship sailing for Macedonia* AcPl Ha 5, 15.—In transf. sense, of Jesus as shepherd **J 10:16;** ὁ θεὸς ἤγαγεν τῷ Ἰσραὴλ σωτῆρα Ἰησοῦν *God brought Jesus as savior to Israel* **Ac 13:23.**

ⓑ ***bring/take along*** (Jos., Ant. 10, 179) εἰς Ἀντιόχειαν **Ac 11:26.** ἕως Ἀθηνῶν **17:15.** ἐπὶ τὸν Ἄρειον πάγον vs. **19;** ἄγοντες παρ' ᾧ ξενισθῶμεν Μνάσωνι (=πρὸς Μνάσωνα) ἵνα παρ' αὐτῷ ξενισθῶμεν **21:16;** s. on this ξενίζω and B-D-F §294, 5; Rob. 719). ἄγε μετὰ σεαυτοῦ *bring (him) along* **2 Ti 4:11** (PPetr II, 32 [2a], 13 ἄγων μεθ' αὐτοῦ).

❷ **to take into custody,** ***lead away, arrest,*** legal t.t. w. acc. **Mk 13:11; Lk 22:54; J 7:45; Ac 5:26.** ὅπως δεδεμένους ἀγάγῃ εἰς Ἰερουσαλήμ **9:2;** cp. **22:5.** Of arraignment and trial w. ἐπί and acc. (BGU 22, 34ff; PTebt 331, 16f; Just., A II, 2, 12) ἐπὶ ἡγεμόνας **Mt 10:18.** ἐπὶ τὸ βῆμα **Ac 18:12.** ἐπ' ἐξουσίαν Hs 9, 28, 4. εἰς τὸ συνέδριον **Ac 6:12.** [εἰς τὸ συμ]β[ο]ύλιον AcPl BMM verso 20 (cp. Just. A II, 10, 4 εἰς δικαστήριον). Abs. **Ac 25:6, 17, 23.** Of the transport of a prisoner **23:31; J 18:28.** εἰς τὴν παρεμβολήν *take away to the barracks* **Ac 21:34; 23:10.** Of leading away to execution (cp. Diod. S. 13, 102, 1; Appian, Bell. Civ. 5, 9 §36; Lucian, Syr. Dea 25; 2 Macc 6:29; 7:18) **Lk 23:32; J 19:16 v.l.;** s. entry ἀπάγω 2c.

❸ **to lead/guide morally or spiritually,** ***lead, encourage (in the direction of)*** (X., Mem. 1, 6, 14 ἐπὶ καλοκἀγαθίαν; Demosth. 25, 76 εἰς ἔλεον; 18, 316 εἰς ἀχαριστίαν; Pr 18:6; Jos., Ant. 2, 174; εἰς πίστιν Just., A I, 10, 4; εἰς ἐπίστασιν καὶ ἀνάμνησιν 44, 11) τινὰ εἰς μετάνοιαν **Ro 2:4** (Polyb. 5, 16, 2 εἰς μετάνοιαν ἄξειν τ. βασιλέα; EpArist 188; Jos., Ant. 4, 144); εἰς δόξαν **Hb 2:10.** Of jealousy ἀ. εἰς θάνατον 1 Cl 9:1. γυναικάρια ἀγόμενα ἐπιθυμίαις ποικίλαις **2 Ti 3:6** (Aristot., EN 7, 3, 10, 1147a, 34 ἡ ἐπιθυμία ἄγει. Cp. Eur., Med. 310 σε θυμὸς ἦγεν; Pla., Prot. 355a ὑπὸ τ. ἡδονῶν ἀγόμενος; Demosth. 18, 9 τοῖς ἔξωθεν λόγοις ἠγμένος; Parthenius 29, 2 ἄγειν εἰς ἐπιθυμίαν=entice to desire; ἤγοντο εἰς τοὺς χώρους τῶν ἐπιθυμιῶν Mel., P. 50, 359). Freq. of the working of the Spirit on human beings: pass. *be led, allow oneself to be led* πνεύματι θεοῦ ἄγεσθαι **Ro 8:14;** cp. **Gal 5:18; Lk 4:1, 9** (on the "permissive pass." s. Gildersleeve, Syntax I §167).—**1 Cor 12:2** is difficult: ὅτι πρὸς τὰ εἴδωλα τὰ ἄφωνα ὡς ἂν ἤγεσθε ἀπαγόμενοι may be transl. *how you were attracted, carried away again and again to mute idols,* where ἄν denotes repetition, and ὡς takes up the preceding ὅτι; for another expl., presupposing the rdg. ὡς ἀνήγεσθε, s. JWeiss ad loc.; s. also ICC ad loc. (Psellus p. 96, 33 offers a choice between ἂν ἀγάγοι and ἀναγάγοι; Herodas 6, 73 ἂν εὑρήσεις RHerzog or ἀνευρήσεις AKnox; Ramsay, CB I/2, 390 no. 248 ὃς ἂν ὀρύξει or ὃς ἀνορύξει). [τ]ὰς ἐπὶ τὴν ἀπάτην ἀγούσας *(paths) that lead to deceit* AcPl Ha 1, 13.

❹ **to make use of time for a specific purpose,** ***spend, observe*** (Eur., Hdt.+; Aberciusins 18; LXX) ἀ. τὴν ἡμέραν τὴν ὀγδόην εἰς εὐφροσύνην *celebrate the eighth day as a festival of joy* B 15:9 (cp. OGI 90, 47 [196 BC] ἄγειν τὰς ἡμέρας ταύτας ἑορτάς; PCairGoodsp 3, 18 [III BC] ἡμέραν καλὴν ἤγαγον; freq. in PCairZen, s. Preis. IV). Perh. impers. τρίτην ταύτην ἡμέραν ἄγει *this is the third day* **Lk 24:21;** but, since this expr. cannot be found elsewhere, it is prob. better to supply Ἰησοῦς as subj. (B-D-F §129) lit. *Jesus is spending the third day* (cp. Galen XIII 581 Kühn τετάρτην ἡμέραν ἄγων ἀνώδυνος ἦν, ad Glauc. de med. meth. 1, 16 XI 65 K. πόστην ἄγει τὴν ἀπὸ τοῦ νοσεῖν ἡμέραν ὁ ἄνθρωπος). Of festivals *celebrate, observe* (Hdt.+; Aesop, Fab. 389 P. γενέθλιον ἄγειν; PCairZen 541, 5 [III BC] Jos., Ant 11, 77, cp. 1 Esdr 5:50; ἄγοντα ἑορτάς Ar. 10, 8; μυστήρια ἄγετε Just., A I, 25, 1; Ath. 1, 1) γενέσια **Mt 14:6 v.l.;** τὸ σάββατον PtK 2 p. 14, 28; νεομηνίαν ibid.

ln. 29. Of meetings (like Lat. agere) συμβούλιον ἄγειν hold a meeting IPol 7:2. Pass. ἀγοραῖοι ἄγονται (s. ἀγοραῖος 2) **Ac 19:38.**

❺ **to move away from a position,** ***go,*** intr. (X. et al.) ἄγωμεν *let us go* (so Vi. Aesopi G 77 P.; loanw. in rabb.; B-D-F §308) **Mt 26:46; Mk 14:42; J 11:16.** W. the goal given (Ael. Aristid. 51, 28 K.=27 p. 541 D.: εἰς τὸ ἱερόν; Epict. 3, 22, 55 ἄγωμεν ἐπὶ τ. ἀνθύπατον) εἰς τὰς κωμοπόλεις **Mk 1:38.** εἰς τὴν 'Ιουδαίαν **J 11:7.** εἰς τὸ ὄρος ApcPt 2:4. εἰς ἀγρόν Hs 6, 1, 5; ἐπὶ τὴν θεωρίαν AcPl Ha 4, 7; πρὸς αὐτόν **J 11:15.** παρὰ τὸν πύργον Hs 9, 5, 6. ἄγωμεν ἴδωμεν τὸν ἔχοντα τὸν θεὸν θηριομαχοῦντα *let us go and see this man, who possesses divinity, fight with the beasts* AcPl Ha 4, 7. W. the point of departure given ἐντεῦθεν **J 14:31.** JFitzmyer, The Use of Agein and Pherein in the Synoptics: Gingrich Festschr. 147–60.—B. 711; 713. DELG. M-M.

ἀγωγή, ῆς, ἡ (Aeschyl., Hdt. et al.; ins, pap, LXX) 'leading' (Orig. C. Cels. 3, 73, 12) then ***way of life, conduct*** (so X., Eq. 3, 4; Polyb. 4, 74, 1; 4 ἀ. τοῦ βίου; Diod. S. 13, 82, 7; M. Ant. 1, 6; IMagnMai 164, 3 ἤθει καὶ ἀγωγῇ κόσμιον; OGI 223, 15 [III BC]; 474, 9; 485, 3; UPZ 113, 12 [156 BC]; PTebt 24, 57 [117 BC]; SB 9050 V, 11f. ἡ τοῦ βίου ἀ. [s. AKränzlein, JJP 6, '52, 232]; Horoscope in PPrinc 75, 5; Esth 2:20; 2 Macc 11:24; EpArist, Philo, Jos., Ant. 14, 195; Iren. 4, 38, 1 [Harv. II 292, 9]; Orig. C. Cels. 3, 51, 16; s. Nägeli 34) **2 Ti 3:10.** ἡ ἐν Χριστῷ ἀ. *the Christian way of life* 1 Cl 47:6 (v.l. ἀγάπε). σεμνὴ . . . ἁγνὴ ἀ. 48:1.—DELG s.v. ἄγω 18. TW. Sv.

ἀγών, ἀγῶνος, ὁ (w. many mngs. Hom.+; ins, pap, LXX; EpArist 14; Philo; Jos., Ant. 17, 92; 185 al.; Just., D. 142, 2; Tat. 12, 4; loanw. in rabb.) in our lit. only fig.

❶ the sense 'athletic competition' transfers to the moral and spiritual realm **a competition,** ***contest, race*** (cp. Wsd 4:2) τρέχωμεν τὸν προκείμενον ἡμῖν ἀγῶνα *let us run the race that lies before us* **Hb 12:1** (cp. Eur., Or. 847; Hdt. 9, 60, 1 ἀγῶνος μεγίστου προκειμένου, cp. 7, 11, 3; Lucian, Anach. 15; Epict. 3, 25, 3.—Hdt. 8, 102, 3 πολλοὺς ἀγῶνας δραμέονται οἱ Ἕλληνες; Dionys. Hal. 7, 48). Cp. 1 Cl 7:1; GJs 20:1 (not pap).

❷ gener. **a struggle against opposition,** ***struggle, fight*** (Iren. 5, 29, 1 [Harv. II 404, 16]; Hippol., Ref. 9, 6; Orig., C. Cels., 1, 22, 18; Did., Gen. 250, 29) for the gospel **Phil 1:30,** and struggle in its service ἐν πολλῷ ἀ. *under a great strain* or *in the face of great opposition* **1 Th 2:2.** ἀ. ἀγωνίζομαι (Socrat., Ep. 14, 4; Epict. 1, 9, 12; Appian, Bell. Civ. 1, 110 §515; SIG 434/5, 10; IBM III, 604, 7f ἠγωνίσατο ἀ. τρεῖς, ἐστέφθη δύω; Philo; Herm. Wr. 10, 19a) *fight a fight, engage in a contest* **1 Ti 6:12; 2 Ti 4:7** (cp. Thu. 7, 68, 3 καλὸς ὁ ἀ.; Synes., Ad. Paeon. 3, 309c ὡς ἀγῶνα καλὸν ὑπὲρ ἡμῶν ἀγωνίζῃ=that you fight . . .; s. JBarton, Bonum certamen certavi, Biblica 40, '59, 878–84); ὁ τῆς ἀφθαρσίας ἀ. 2 Cl 7:5. Also ἄφθαρτος ἀ. vs. 3; opp. φθαρτὸς ἀ. vs. 1 (s. καταπλέω), 4.—*Anxiety, concern* (Eur., Phoen. 1350; Thu. 7, 71, 1; Polyb. 4, 56, 4; Plut., Tit. Flamin. 378 [16, 1] ἀγῶνα καὶ πόνον; PHeid 228, 14 [III BC]; BGU 1139, 17; Is 7:13) ὑπέρ τινος **Col 2:1;** cp. 1 Cl 2:4.—FDölger, AC II 1930, 294ff; III '32, 177ff; JJüthner, RAC I, 188f; VPfitzner, Paul and the Agon Motif, athletic imagery in the Pauline lit., '67.—DELG s.v. ἄγω. M-M. TW. Spicq. Sv.

ἀγωνία, ας, ἡ (Pind., Hdt. and other ancient writers=ἀγών; so also δι' ὅπλων ἀγωνίας Ath. 35, 1) in later times (ἀγωνιάω underwent a similar change) **apprehensiveness of mind, esp. when faced with impending ills,** ***distress, anguish*** (anxiety varying in degree of intensity: Hyperid., fgm. 203; Demosth. 18, 33 φόβος καὶ ἀ.; PHib 186, 31: πόνος καὶ ἀγωνία. Esp. Stoic. as a species of φόβος; w. λύπη as expr. of ἀληγδών Chrysipp.: Stoic. II 248, 16; Epict. 2, 13, 10; schol. on Apollon. Rhod. 3, 471 ἐτετάρακτο καὶ ἐν ἀγωνίᾳ ἦν; BGU 884 I, 6; PTebt 423, 13f: εἰς ἀ. γενέσθαι; 2 Macc 3:14, 16; Philo; Jos., Bell. 4, 90, Ant. 11, 326 ἦν ἐν ἀγωνίᾳ κ. δέει; Iren. 1, 4, 4 [Harv. I 37, 9]) γενόμενος ἐν ἀ. *being in anguish* **Lk 22:44.**—JNeyrey, Biblica 61, '80, 159–65 (ἀ. as victorious struggle). Field, Notes 77f.—DELG s.v. ἄγω. M-M. TW.

ἀγωνιάω impf. ἠγωνίων; 1 aor. ptc. ἀγωνιάσας (Esth 5:1e); inf. ἀγωνιᾶσαι (Just., A I, 4, 2) ***be anxious, be distressed*** (so in later writers, including Dio Chrys. 4, 55 [w. μή foll.]; ins, pap [s. Preis.; Witkowski index], LXX; Jos., Ant. 9, 32) ἀγωνιῶντες μεγάλως (PGiss 19, 3; 2 Macc 3:21; cp. συναγωνιάω 'be in fearful suspense' Polyb. 3, 43, 7 and 8) *full of great anxiety* GPt 11:45; w. indir. quest. foll. μήποτε (UPZ 62, 30 [161/160 BC]; w. μή Just., A I, 4, 2) 5:15. W. gen. abs. foll. οὐ γὰρ μικρῶς ἀγωνιῶ τοιούτου σου ὄντος *I am quite worried seeing you like this* (in reaction to the disturbed countenance of Jesus) AcPl Ha 7, 31.—DELG s.v. ἄγω.

ἀγωνίζομαι impf. ἠγωνιζόμην; fut. ἀγωνίσομαι (Just., D. 65, 2) and ἀγωνιοῦμαι (68, 3); 1 aor. ἠγωνισάμην; pf. ἠγώνισμαι (Eur., Hdt.+).

❶ of a(n athletic) contest, lit. and fig. ***engage in a contest*** πᾶς ὁ ἀγωνιζόμενος **1 Cor 9:25** (AEhrhardt, ZNW 48, '57, 101–10); cp. 2 Cl 7:1ff.

❷ gener. ***to fight, struggle***—ⓐ lit., w. weapons (Polyb. 1, 45, 9; Plut., Marcell. 303 [10, 4]; 2 Macc 8:16) ἠγωνίζοντο ἄν, ἵνα μὴ παραδοθῶ **J 18:36.**

ⓑ fig. of any struggle (περὶ τῆς ἀληθείας Orig., C. Cels. 1, 62, 63) κοπιῶ ἀγωνιζόμενος *I labor, striving* **Col 1:29;** cp. **1 Ti 4:10.** Of wrestling in prayer (ἀ. δὲ διὰ τῶν πρὸς θεὸν εὐχῶν ὑπὲρ τῶν δικαίως στρατευομένων Orig., C. Cels. 8, 73, 24) ἀ. ὑπὲρ ὑμῶν **Col 4:12** (ἀ. ὑπέρ τινος: Diod. S. 13, 14, 3; SIG 317, 20; 386, 19; 409, 33; Jos., Ant. 13, 193). ἀ. ἀγῶνα (s. ἀγών 2) **1 Ti 6:12; 2 Ti 4:7** (JBarton, Biblica 40, '59, 878–84). W. inf. foll. (Thu. 8, 89, 4 ἠγωνίζετο εἷς ἕκαστος αὐτὸς πρῶτος προστάτης τοῦ δήμου γενέσθαι; Diod. S. 31, 19, 8 ὥστε ὁ πατὴρ ἐξίστασθαι τῆς ὅλης ἀρχῆς ἠγωνίζετο τῷ παιδί; PLond 1338.—ἀγ. simply='take pains, exert oneself': Just., D. 38, 2; 65, 2 al.; Alex. Aphr., Fat. 31, II 2 p. 203, 9; Sb 6997, 9 [III BC]) ἀγωνίζεσθε εἰσελθεῖν *strain every nerve to enter* **Lk 13:24;** cp. 1 Cl 35:4; B 4:11.—DELG s.v. ἄγω. M-M. TW.

'Αδάμ, ὁ indecl. (אָדָם) (LXX, pseudepigr., Philo, Just.; Mel., P. 83.—In Joseph. Ἄδαμος, ου [Ant. 1, 66]) ***Adam,*** the first human being **1 Ti 2:13;** B 6:9 (cp. Gen 1:27ff). Ancestor of humanity **Ro 5:14; Jd 14;** 1 Cl 50:3. Hence πατὴρ ἡμῶν 6:3; people are υἱοὶ Ἀ. 29:2 (cp. Dt 32:8). In the genealogy of Jesus **Lk 3:38.** His fall **Ro 5:14; 1 Ti 2:14.** While A. was praying, Eve was seduced by the serpent GJs 13:1 (ApcMos 17). Some hold there existed the conception that at the end of the world the initial events will repeat themselves, and that hence Adam, who destroys all, is contrasted w. Christ, who gives life to all **1 Cor 15:22** (HGunkel, Schöpfung u. Chaos 1895). The parallel betw. Adam and Christ and the designation of Christ as future **Ro 5:14** is well known. It is debatable whether the well-known (gnostic) myth of the first human being as a redeemer-god directly influenced Paul or whether he arrived at his view through Jewish perceptions (s. Bousset, Kyrios Christos 2, 1921, 140–45; Rtzst., Erlösungsmyst. 107ff and s. on ἄνθρωπος 1d). On the debate stimulated by KBarth, Christus u. Adam nach Römer 5, '52, s.

RBultmann, Adam u. Christus nach Röm. 5, ZNW 50, '59, 145–68; EBrandenburger, Adam u. Christus, '62; EJüngel, ZTK 60, '63, 42–74.—BMurmelstein, Adam. E. Beitrag z. Messiaslehre: Wiener Ztschr. f. d. Kunde d. Morgenlandes 35, 1928, 242–75; 36, 1929, 51–86; Ltzm., exc. on 1 Cor 15:45–49; AVitti, Christus-Adam: Biblica 7, 1926, 121–45; 270–85; 384–401; ARawlinson, The NT Doctrine of the Christ 1926, 124ff; CKraeling, Anthropos and the Son of Man, 1927; AMarmorstein, ZNW 30, '31, 271–77; OKuss, Ro 5:12–21. D. Adam-Christusparallele, diss. Bresl. 1930; GWestberg, The Two Adams: BiblSacra 94, '37, 37–50; ARöder, D. Gesch.-philos. des Ap. Pls., diss. Frb. '38; SHanson, Unity of the Church in the NT, '46, 66–73; RScroggs, The Last Adam, '66 (bibliog. 123–28); JFitzmyer, ABComm Ro 423–28 (lit.).—EDNT. TW.

ἀδάπανος, ον (Aristoph., Pax 593; Teles 7, 8 al.; Michel 1006, 21=CIG 3065 [II BC] ἀδάπανον τὴν συμμορίαν καθιστάνει) ***free of charge*** typical of many Greco-Roman benefactors (Danker, Benefactor 332–36) ἵνα ἀ. θήσω τὸ εὐαγγέλιον *that I might offer the gospel free of charge* **1 Cor 9:18.** —DELG s.v. δάπτω. M-M.

Ἀδδί, ὁ indecl. ***Addi*** in the genealogy of Jesus **Lk 3:28** (Ἀδδει Tdf.; W-H., S., Vog.).

ἀδελφή, ῆς, ἡ (Aeschyl.+)—❶ **a female who comes from the same womb as the reference pers.,** ***sister*** lit. **Mt 19:29; Mk 10:29f; Lk 10:39f; 14:26; J 11:1, 3, 5, 28, 39; 19:25; Ro 16:15; 1 Ti 5:2.** Of Jesus' *sisters* (s. on ἀδελφός 1) **Mt 13:56; Mk 3:32; 6:3.** Paul's sister **Ac 23:16.**

❷ **a pers. or thing viewed as a sister in relation to another entity,** ***sister*** metaph.—ⓐ of a female who shares beliefs of the reference person or of others in a community of faith, *sister.* Used by Jesus of a spiritual, rather than a natural relationship **Mt 12:50; Mk 3:35.** Sim. ἀγαπᾶν ὡς ἀ. Hv 1, 1, 1; ἐντρέπεσθαι ὡς ἀ. v 1, 1, 7. Of relationship in community: *sister* in the faith (as Hebr. אָחוֹת; sister=countrywoman Num 25:18; s. ἀδελφός 2 and cp. PGM 4, 1135–37 χαίρετε, οἷς τὸ χαίρειν ἐν εὐλογίᾳ δίδοται, ἀδελφοῖς καὶ ἀδελφαῖς, ὁσίοις καὶ ὁσίαις) **Ro 16:1; 1 Cor 7:15; 9:5; Phlm 2; Js 2:15;** IPol 5:1; 2 Cl 12:5; Hv 2, 2, 3; 2, 3, 1; Ox 3525, 15. In address w. ἀδελφοί 2 Cl 19:1; 20:2.

ⓑ of a close relationship of similar communities (OGI 536, 5) **2J 13** (s. κυρία). Hm 9:9 v.l. (for θυγάτηρ).

ⓒ of a condition or circumstance, grief: ἀδελφή ἐστιν τῆς διψυχίας *is a sister of doubt* Hm 10, 1, 1f (Alcaeus 142 Diehl [364 L.-P.]: poverty and helplessness as sisters; Paroem. Gr. Append. 3, 12 ἡ μωρία ἀ. πονηρίας; Pla., Rep. 3, 404b; Cebes 16, 2 ἐγκράτεια and καρτερία as ἀδελφαί; Herm. Wr. 9, 1c ἡ νόησις ἀ. τοῦ λόγου).—DELG s.v. ἀδελφός. M-M. TW.

ἀδελφοκτονία, ας, ἡ (Philo, De Jos. 13; Jos., Bell. 1, 606, Ant. 17, 60; 91; Tat. 34, 1) ***fratricide*** of Cain (Philo, Agric. 21) 1 Cl 4:7.

ἀδελφός, οῦ, ὁ (Hom. [ἀδελφεός]+; accord. to B-D-F §13; Schwyzer I 555; Mlt-H. II 58; PKatz, TLZ 83, '58, 315f vocative ἄδελφε should be accented on the antepenult in **Ac 9:17; 21:20** contrary to the practice of the editions; also GPt 2:5.)

❶ **a male from the same womb as the reference pers.,** ***brother,*** **Mt 1:2, 11; 4:18, 21** al.; τὸν ἀ. τ. ἴδιον **J 1:41** (s. Jos., Ant. 11, 300). Of Jesus' brothers (passages like Gen 13:8; 14:14; 24:48; 29:12; Lev 10:4; 1 Ch 9:6 do not establish the mng. 'cousin' for ἀ.; they only show that in rendering the Hebr. אָח ἀ. is used loosely in isolated cases to designate masc. relatives of various degrees. The case of ἀδελφή [q.v. 1] is similar Gen 24:59f; Tob 8:4, 7 [cp. 7:15]; Jos., Ant. 1, 211 [ἀδελφή = ἀδελφοῦ παῖς]. Sim. M. Ant., who [1, 14, 1] uses ἀ. for his brother-in-law Severus; the same use is found occas. in the pap: JCollins, TS 5, '44, 484–94; s. VTscherikover HTR '42, 25–44) **Mt 12:46f; 13:55; Mk 3:31f; J 2:12; 7:3, 5; Ac 1:14; 1 Cor 9:5.** James ὁ ἀδελφὸς τοῦ κυρίου **Gal 1:19.** The pl. can also mean ***brothers and sisters*** (Eur., El. 536; Andoc. 1, 47 ἡ μήτηρ ἡ ἐκείνου κ. ὁ πατὴρ ὁ ἐμὸς ἀδελφοί; Anton. Diog. 3 [Erot. Gr. I 233, 23; 26 Hercher]; POxy 713, 21f [97 AD] ἀδελφοῖς μου Διοδώρῳ κ. Θαΐδι; schol. on Nicander, Ther. 11 [p. 5, 9] δύο ἐγένοντο ἀδελφοί, Φάλαγξ μὲν ἄρσην, θήλεια δὲ Ἀράχνη τοὔνομα. The θεοὶ Ἀδελφοί, a married couple consisting of brother and sister on the throne of the Ptolemies: OGI 50, 2 [III BC] and pap [Mitt-Wilck. I/1, 99; I/2, 103–7, III BC]). In all these cases only *one* brother and *one* sister are involved. Yet there are also passages in which ἀδελφοί means *brothers and sisters,* and in whatever sequence the writer chooses (Polyb. 10, 18, 15 ποιήσεσθαι πρόνοιαν ὡς ἰδίων ἀδελφῶν καὶ τέκνων; Epict. 1, 12, 20 ἀδ. beside γονεῖς, τέκνα, γείτονες; 1, 22, 10; 4, 1, 111; Artem. 3, 31; Ptolem., Apotel. 3, 6; Diog. L. 7, 108; 120; 10, 18. In PMich 214, 12 [296 AD] οἱ ἀδελφοί σου seems to be even more general='your relatives'). Hence there is no doubt that in **Lk 21:16** ἀδελφοί=*brothers and sisters,* but there is some room for uncertainty in the case of the ἀδελφοί of Jesus in **Mt 12:46f; Mk 3:31; J 2:12; 7:3, 5; Ac 1:14.**

❷ **a pers. viewed as a brother in terms of a close affinity,** ***brother, fellow member, member, associate*** fig. ext. of 1.

ⓐ one who shares beliefs (for an associated duality, s. Did., Gen. 127, 6 ἀ. ἐστι τοῦ φαινομένου ἔξω ἀνθρώπου ὁ κρυπτὸς καὶ ἐν διανοίᾳ ἄνθρωπος=brother to the man as he appears from without is the man who is hidden in thought): Jesus calls everyone who is devoted to him *brother* **Mt 12:50; Mk 3:35,** esp. his disciples **Mt 28:10; J 20:17.** Hence gener. for those in such spiritual communion **Mt 25:40; Hb 2:12** (Ps 21:23), **17** al. Of a relationship w. a woman other than that of husband Hs 9, 11, 3 al.; 2 Cl 12:5.—Of the members of a relig. community (PParis 20 [II BC] al. of the hermits at the Serapeum in Memphis; UPZ 162 I, 20 [117 BC] ἀδελφοὶ οἱ τὰς λειτουργίας ἐν ταῖς νεκρίαις παρεχόμενοι; IG XIV, 956 B, 11f. ἀ.=member of the ἱερὰ ξυστικὴ σύνοδος; IPontEux II, 449f εἰσποιητοὶ ἀ. σεβόμενοι θεὸν Ὕψιστον [Ltzm. ZWT 55, 1913, 121]. Mystery pap [III AD]: APF 13, '39, 212. Essenes in Jos., Bell. 2, 122. Vett. Val. 172, 31; Cleopatra ln. 94. See GMilligan 1908 on 1 Th 1:4; Ltzm. Hdb. on Ro 1:13 [lit.]; Dssm. B 82f, 140 [BS 87f, 142]; Nägeli 38; Cumont[3] 276). Hence used by Christians in their relations w. each other **Ro 8:29, 1 Cor 5:11; Eph 6:23; 1 Ti 6:2; Ac 6:3; 9:30; 10:23; Rv 1:9; 12:10;** IEph 10:3; ISm 12:1 al. So esp. w. proper names (for ἀδ. in a figurative sense used with a name, cp. the address of a letter PMich 162 verso [II AD] ἀπὸ Ἀπλωναρίου ἀδελφοῦ) to indicate membership in the Christian community **Ro 16:23; 1 Cor 1:1; 16:12; 2 Cor 1:1; Phil 2:25; Col 1:1; 4:7, 9; 1 Th 3:2; Phlm 1; 1 Pt 5:12; 2 Pt 3:15;** AcPl Ha 1, 30 al. Completely ἀδελφὸς ἐν κυρίῳ **Phil 1:14.** Oft. in direct address 1 Cl 1:1 (cod. A); 4:7; 13:1; 33:1; 2 Cl 20:2 al.; B 2:10; 3:6 al.; IRo 6:2; Hv 2, 4, 1; 3, 1, 1; 4; AcPl Ha 7, 4; 8, 21; AcPlCor 1:16. ἀδελφοί μου B 4:14; 5:5; 6:15; IEph 16:1; ἄνδρες ἀ. **Ac 1:16** (rabb. par. in EStauffer, TLZ 77, '52, 202); **15:7, 13;** 1 Cl 14:1; 37:1; 43:4; 62:1. To interpret ἀ. in **Ac 15:23** as 'colleague' (e.g. PGaechter, Petrus u. seine Zeit, '58, 141f) is speculative; and the interpretation of ἀ. in **3J 5** and **10** as itinerant preachers (AKragerud, D. Lieblingsjünger im Johannesevangelium, '59, 105) is based entirely on the context.

ⓑ a *compatriot* (cp. Pla., Menex. 239a ἡμεῖς δὲ καὶ οἱ ἡμέτεροι, μιᾶς μητρὸς πάντες ἀδελφοὶ φύντες; Lev 10:4; Dt

15:3, 12; 17:15 al.; Philo, Spec. Leg. 2, 79f 'ἀ.' τὸν ὁμόφυλον εἶπεν he termed a compatriot 'brother'; Jos., Ant. 10, 201; 7, 371 after 1 Ch 28:2) **Ac 2:29; 3:17, 22** (Dt 18:15); **7:2, 23** (Ex 2:11), **25f** al.; **Ro 9:3.**

ⓒ without ref. to a common nationality or faith *neighbor* (of an intimate friend X., An. 7, 2, 25; 38. Specif. in the sense 'neighbor' Gen 9:5; Lev 19:17 al.) **Mt 5:22ff; 7:3ff; 18:15, 21, 35; Lk 6:41f; 17:3;** B 19:4; Hm 2:2 al.

ⓓ Form of address used by a king to persons in very high position (OGI 138, 3; 168, 26; 36 [both II BC]; Jos., Ant. 13, 45; 126) Herod says ἀδελφὲ Πιλᾶτε GPt 2:5.—JO'Callaghan, El vocativo sing. de ἀδελφός, Biblica 52, '71, 217–25.—B. 107. DELG. M-M. EDNT. TW. Sv.

ἀδελφότης, ητος, ἡ (B-D-F §110, 1; Mlt-H. 367; DELG s.v. ἀδελφός)

❶ **a group of fellow-believers,** ***a fellowship*** (cp. 4 Macc 9:23; 10:3, 15; Phryg. ins [III AD, in Harnack, Mission[4] 1924, 773 n.] εἰρήνη πᾶσι τ. ἀδελφοῖς, εἰρήνη πάσῃ τ. ἀδελφότητι) of the Christian community, whose members are ἀδελφοί and ἀδελφαί **1 Pt 5:9;** 1 Cl 2:4. τὴν ἀ. ἀγαπᾶν **1 Pt 2:17** (on the social significance s. JElliott, A Home for the Homeless '81 [w. new introd. '90])

❷ **mutual affection such as brothers or sisters have for one another,** ***familial affection*** (Dio Chrys. 21 [38], 15; Vett. Val. p. 2, 28; 4, 5; 1 Macc 12:10, 17; 4 Macc 13:27) ἀ. συντηρεῖν Hm 8:10 (v.l. ἀγαθότητα cod. Athous).—M-M. TW. Sv.

ἀδεῶς adv. (Hdt.+; Aristoph., Vesp. 359; Manetho: 609 fgm. 9, 100. Also IG IV, 597; PMich 425, 20 [both II AD]; 3 Macc 2:32; Philo, Cherub. 99; Jos., Ant. 6, 313; 18, 370; Just., A II, 12, 5) ***without fear/disturbance*** προσεύχεσθαι MPol 7:2; λαμβάνειν ITr 6:2.—DELG s.v. δείδω.

ἄδηλος, ον (Hes. et al.; ins; PLond 940, 23; POxy 118, 5f; PLips 37, 23; PGM 4, 3048; LXX, Philo; Jos., Bell. 7, 115, Ant. 1, 268; 13, 151; Ath. 5, 2).

❶ **pert. to not being readily apparent,** ***not clear, latent, unseen*** (Soph. et al.; OGI 218, 129 [III BC]) τὰ μνημεῖα τὰ ἄ. *graves that are (hazardously) latent* **Lk 11:44.** τὰ ἄ. δηλοῦν *reveal what is unseen* 1 Cl 18:6 (Ps 50:8). πῶς ἡ πίστις εὑρετέα τῶν ἀδήλων ἡ φαινομένη τοῦ ἀγεννήτου πατρός *how faith in the unseen is to be found, namely in connection with the unbegotten Father* (reconstruction of POxy 1081, 32–34 based on the Coptic SJCh 90, 12).

❷ **pert. to not being clearly defined,** ***indistinct*** (Polyb. 8, 1, 2 ἄ. ἐλπίδες=vague hopes; likew. Maximus Tyr. 36, 4a) of a trumpet ἄ. φωνὴν διδόναι *give out an indistinct sound,* so that the signal cannot be recognized **1 Cor 14:8.**—DELG s.v. δῆλος. M-M.

ἀδηλότης, ητος, ἡ ***uncertainty*** (Protagoras [V BC] et al.; Polyb., Plut., Philo al.) ἐλπίζειν ἐπὶ πλούτου ἀδηλότητι *to rest one's hope in such an uncertain thing as wealth* **1 Ti 6:17** (Dio Chrys. 16, 8; B-D-F §165). S. δῆλος.

ἀδήλως adv. fr. ἄδηλος (Thu. et al.; Plut.; Aelian, VH 1, 21 p. 10, 4; Philo, Conf. Lingu. 119) ***uncertainly*** (Ps.-Phocyl. 25; 117) of a race οὕτως τρέχω ὡς οὐκ ἀδήλως *not aimlessly,* i.e. not as one who has no fixed goal **1 Cor 9:26** (cp. Ps.-Phocyl. 28 ἄδηλος πλοῦς). PEg[2] 61 (context fragmentary).

ἀδημονέω (Hippocr. et al.; Pla., X.; TestAbr A 7, p. 84, 9 [Stone p. 16]; Jos., Ant 15, 211; 388; POxy 298, 45 [I AD] λίαν ἀδημονοῦμεν χάριν τῆς θρεπτῆς Σαραποῦτος; Job 18:20 Aq.; Sym. Ps 60:3 al.) ***be in anxiety, be distressed, troubled*** w. λυπεῖσθαι **Mt 26:37;** w. ἐκθαμβεῖσθαι **Mk 14:33;** foll. by διότι *because* **Phil 2:26.**—MHarl, La Bible et les Pères, '71, 257.—DELG. M-M.

ᾅδης, ου, ὁ (w. var. spellings Hom.+)—❶ Orig. proper noun, god of the nether world, 'Hades', then ***the nether world, Hades*** as place of the dead, **Ac 2:27, 31** (Ps 15:10; Eccl 9:10; PGM 1, 179; 16, 8; Philo, Mos. 1, 195; Jos., Bell. 1, 596, Ant. 6, 332). Of Jonah's fish ἐκ τοῦ κατωτάτου ᾅδου. In the depths, contrasted w. heaven ἕως (τοῦ) ᾅδου **Mt 11:23; Lk 10:15** (PsSol 15:10; cp.; Is 14:11, 15); ἐν τῷ ᾅδῃ **16:23;** ἐν Ἅιδου ApcPt Rainer. Accessible by gates (but the pl. is also used [e.g. Hom., X., Ael. Aristid. 47, 20 K.=23 p. 450 D.] when only one gate is meant), hence πύλαι ᾅδου (Il. 5, 646; Is 38:10; Wsd 16:13; 3 Macc 5:51; PsSol 16:2.—Lucian, Menipp. 6 the magicians can open τοῦ Ἅιδου τὰς πύλας and conduct people in and out safely) **Mt 16:18** (s. on πέτρα 1b and πύλη a); locked ἔχω τὰς κλεῖς τοῦ θανάτου καὶ τοῦ ᾅδου **Rv 1:18** (the genitives are either obj. [Ps.-Apollod. 3, 12, 6, 10 Aeacus, the son of Zeus holds the κλεῖς τοῦ Ἅιδου; SEG VIII, 574, 3 (III AD) τῷ τὰς κλεῖδας ἔχοντι τῶν καθ' Ἅιδου (restored)] or possess.; in the latter case death and Hades are personif.; s. 2). ὠδῖνες τοῦ ᾅδου (Ps 17:6) Pol 1:2; **Ac 2:24 v.l.** (for θανάτου). εἰς ᾅδου (sc. δόμους B-D-F §162, 8; Hom. et al.; Bar 3:11, 19; Tob 3:10; En 102:5; 103:7; Ar. 11, 3) **Ac 2:31 v.l.;** 1 Cl 4:12; 51:4 (Just., D. 99, 3 ἐν ᾅδου μένειν; Mel., fgm. 8b, 44 τοῖς ἐν ᾅδου νεκροῖς; Iambl., Vi. Pyth. 30, 179 ἐν ᾅδου κεῖσθαι τὴν κρίσιν; Hierocles 14, 451 τὰ ἐν ᾅδου κολαστήρια; Simplicius in Epict. p. 108, 14 punishments for sinners ἐν ᾅδου).

❷ ***Hades*** personif. (perh. derived fr. OT usage, cp. מוּת, s. JHealey, Mot: DDD 1121–32), w. θάνατος (cp. Is 28:15; Job 38:17; Mel., P. 102, 782 ἐγὼ … ὁ καταπατήσας τὸν ᾅδην) **Rv 6:8; 20:13f; 1 Cor 15:55 v.l.**—GBeer, D. bibl. Hades: HHoltzmann Festschr. 1902, 1–30; ERohde, Psyche[4] I 54ff; 309ff; ADieterich, Nekyia 1893; Bousset, Rel.[3] 285f; 293ff; Billerb. IV 1016–29; AHeidel, The Gilgamesh Epic and OT Parallels[2], '49, 173–91; LSullivan, Theological Studies (Woodstock, Md.) 10, '49, 62ff; JBremmer, DDD 725f. S. also s.v. πνεῦμα 2 and 4c.—B. 1485. Frisk s.v. Ἀιδης. M-M. TW.

ἀδιάκριτος, ον (Hippocr. et al.; Polyb. 15, 12, 9; OGI 509, 8; LXX Pr 25:1; Gen 1:2 Sym.; Philo, Spec. Leg. 3, 57 al.; var. mngs. in Lghtf. on IEph 3:2.—As a human virtue also in Ptolem., Apotel. 3, 14, 29.)

❶ **pert. to not being judgmental or divisive,** ***nonjudgmental, not divisive, impartial*** (Anecd. Gr. 213, 22) **Js 3:17** (the literary structure, with climax 4:11f, points strongly in this direction; cp. NRSV 'without a trace of partiality'; Dibelius-Greeven, Hermeneia comm. '64, 214, w. ref. to usage in Ignatius: 'simple' or 'harmonious'). Sim. IEph 3:2; IMg 15. Some prefer

❷ **pert. to not being uncertain,** ***unwavering*** **Js 3:17** (cp. 1:6; s. JMayor, comm. ad loc.: 'single-minded', 'unhesitating'; RSV 'without uncertainty'; but s. 1 above); ἐν ὑπομονῇ ITr 1:1.— DELG s.v. κρίνω. M-M. TW.

ἀδιακρίτως adv. (Anecd. Gr. 352; Proclus on Pla., Crat. p. 91, 13; schol. on Apollon. Rhod. 2, 62; Philo, fgm. 105 Harris [1886]; TestZeb 7:2; POxy 715, 36 [131 AD]=Wilcken, APF 4, 1908, 254) ***without wavering*** IRo ins; IPhld ins (s. ἀδιάκριτος).

ἀδιάλειπτος, ον (Ps.-Pla., Tim. Locr. 98e al.; SIG 1104, 35; PTebt 27, 45 [113 BC]; PGM 8, 32; EpArist 84; Jos., Bell. 2, 155; 5, 31) ***unceasing, constant*** ὀδύνη **Ro 9:2;** μνεία **2 Ti 1:3;** προσευχαί IPol 1:3; ἀ. ἔχειν ὕδωρ *without failing* Hs 2:8; ἵνα ἀ. γένηται ἐν τῇ ζωῇ αὐτοῦ *that he might lack nothing in his life* 2:6 (s. MDibelius ad loc.).—M-M.

ἀδιαλείπτως adv. (since Metrodorus Philos. [IV/III BC]: PHercul 831, 8; Polyb. 9, 3, 8; SIG 1104, 15; 1171, 4; pap fr. II BC on [Mayser 458]; 1, 2, 3 Macc; EpArist 92; 294; Aristobulus in Eus., PE 13, 12, 4; TestLevi 13:2; TestSol 3:7; Jos., Bell. 3, 164; 241; Just., D. 133, 6) ***constantly, unceasingly*** μνείαν ποιεῖσθαι **Ro 1:9; 1 Th 1:2.** εὐχαριστεῖν **2:13.** προσεύχεσθαι **5:17;** IEph 10:1; Hs 9, 11, 7; cp. Pol 4:3. προσκαρτερεῖν τῇ ἐλπίδι Pol 8:1. διδόναι (of God) Hs 5, 4, 4 v.l. (for ἀδιστάκτως). σκεπάζειν s 9, 27, 2.—DELG s.v. λείπω.

ἀδιαφθορία, ας, ἡ (the subst. is not found elsewhere before Just., A II, 3, 7; but ἀδιάφθορος is common enough Plato et al.; Philo; ApcEsdr 1:20 p. 25, 14 Tdf.; Just., A I, 18, 3; Ath. 2, 3) ***sincerity, integrity*** **Tit 2:7 v.l.** (for ἀφθορία, q.v.).—DELG s.v. φθείρω. M-M. s.v.ἀδιάφθορος.

ἀδιήγητος, ον ***indescribable*** (so X. et al.; Ael. Aristid. 33, 30 K.=51 p. 581 D.; PGM 1, 164; EpArist 89; 99; Just., D. 32, 2 [cp. Is 53:8=Ac 8:33]) ὁ ἐν ἀγάπῃ ἀ. *a man of inexpressible love* IEph 1:3.—DELG s.v. ἡγέομαι.

ἀδικέω fut. ἀδικήσω; 1 aor. ἠδίκησα; pf. ἠδίκηκα. Pass.: 1 fut. 3 sg. ἀδικηθήσεται (Pr 17:8 v.l.); 1 aor. ἠδικήθην; pf. ptc. ἠδικημένος LXX (Hom. Hymns+).

❶ **to act in an unjust manner, *do wrong*—ⓐ** intr. of violation of human or divine law (defined Aristot., Rhet. 1, 10: ἔστι τὸ ἀδικεῖν τὸ βλάπτειν ἑκόντα παρὰ τὸν νόμον; Philo, Dec. 66; Hippol., Ref. 9, 15, 6) ὁ ἀδικῶν *the evildoer* (SIG 635, 22) ὁ ἀδικῶν ἀδικησάτω ἔτι, i.e. such a one is now beyond redemption **Rv 22:11.** Cp. **Col 3:25** (the part.); also the 3 sg. κομίσεται ὃ ἠδίκησεν *will reap the reward of wrongdoing* (BGU 1138, 13 ὃ ἠδίκησεν ἐμαρτύρησεν; cp. Diod. S. 8, 15, 1 οὓς ἀδικοῦντας οὐκ ἂν εἴη δυνατὸν οὔτε λαθεῖν οὔτε διαφυγεῖν [sin against deities] whom the evildoers would be unable to elude or escape).

ⓑ intr. *be in the wrong* (Ex 2:13) εἰ ἀδικῶ **Ac 25:11** (B-D-F §322).—ⓒ trans. *do wrong* (τινά) *to someone, treat someone unjustly* (58th letter of Apollonius of Tyana [Philostrat. I 361, 25 K.] τὸν υἱόν) οὐκ ἀδικῶ σε *I am not cheating you* **Mt 20:13** (PSI 417, 10, 27 [III BC] οὐ σὲ ἀδικεῖ Ἐτέαρχος). ἱνατί ἀδικεῖτε ἀλλήλους; **Ac 7:26.** τὸν πλησίον vs. **27;** οὐδένα **2 Cor 7:2;** ἀδελφούς **1 Cor 6:8;** νηπίους 1 Cl 57:7 (Pr 1:32). W. acc. to be supplied **2 Cor 7:12a.** W. double acc. (Demosth. 21, 129; Epict. 3, 24, 81; Jos., Ant. 2, 138; Lev 5:21; Pr 24:29) οὐδέν με ἠδικήσατε *you have done me no wrong* **Gal 4:12;** cp. **Ac 25:10;** MPol 9:3.—Pass. (B-D-F §314; Rob. 808; 816) *be wronged, be unjustly treated* (Ael. Aristid. 45 p. 81 D.: ἀδικεῖσθαι βέλτιον ἢ ἀδικεῖν; Jos., Bell. 5, 377) 1 Cl 8:4 (Is 1:17); Dg 6:5. ἰδών τινα ἀδικούμενον **Ac 7:24.** ὁ ἀδικηθείς **2 Cor 7:12b.** τίς πλέον ἀδικηθῇ; *who has suffered more injustice?* IEph 10:3; *let oneself be wronged* **1 Cor 6:7.**

❷ **to cause damage to or mistreat, *injure*** (Thu., Antiphon et al.; Tob 6:15; Jdth 11:4; s. Renehan '75, 13 s.v.) w. acc. of pers. (Jos., Ant. 17, 109) με (Appian, Bell. Civ. 4, 69 §291 ἀδικεῖν με) IRo 1:2. τοὺς ἀνθρώπους (EpArist 146) **Rv 9:10.** αὐτούς **11:5.** W. acc. of thing (Dio Chrys. 14 [31], 54 τὸν τόπον; BCH 26, 1902, 217 ἐάν τις τὴν στήλην ἀδικήσει; SIG 635, 8; 9) *damage, spoil* τὴν γῆν **Rv 7:2f;** τὸν χόρτον τῆς γῆς **9:4;** τὸ ἔλαιον καὶ τὸν οἶνον **6:6.** W. double acc. (Demosth., Ep. 2, 16 οὔτε ἠδίκηχ' ὑμᾶς οὐδέν) οὐδὲν ὑμᾶς οὐ μὴ ἀδικήσῃ **Lk 10:19** (in case οὐδέν is not the subj.—B-D-F §431, 3); *if he has caused you any loss* **Phlm 18** (PMich 8, 492, 21f). W. ἐν of the means by which the harm results ἐν αὐταῖς (i.e. οὐραῖς) ἀδικοῦσιν **Rv 9:19.**—Pass. foll. by ἐκ of the source fr. which the harm comes οὐ μὴ ἀδικηθῇ ἐκ τοῦ θανάτου τοῦ δευτέρου *will not be harmed by the second death* **Rv 2:11.** ἀδικούμενοι μισθὸν ἀδικίας *damaged in respect to* (i.e. *cheated out of*) *the reward of unrighteousness* **2 Pt 2:13** (the readings vary [s. κομίζω 3] and the text is uncertain; B-D-F §351, 2; PSkehan, Biblica 41, '60, 69–71, takes ἀδικούμενοι with the phrase that precedes).—DELG s.v. δίκη. M-M. TW.

ἀδίκημα, ατος, τό (Hdt.+; ins, pap, LXX, En; TestJob 37:6; Philo, Joseph., Just., Ath.; Mel., P. 73, 534; 81, 597)

❶ **a violation of norms of justice, *a wrong, crime, misdeed*** (Aristot., EN 5, 7 τὸ ἄδικον . . . ὅταν πραχθῇ, ἀ. ἐστιν; Appian, Bell. Civ. 4, 69 §292; Jos., Ant. 3, 321; 5, 234) **Ac 18:14; 24:20; Rv 18:5.**

❷ **that which causes harm or injury, *mistreatment,*** pl. (En 13:2; Diod. S. 14, 2, 2; PHal 1, 193) IRo 5:1.—DELG s.v. δίκη. M-M. TW.

ἀδικία, ας, ἡ (Anaximander, Hdt.+).—❶ **an act that violates standards of right conduct, *wrongdoing*** (opp. δικαιοσύνη, as Aristot., Cat. 10b, 13 and 20) **Hb 1:9 v.l.** (Ps 44:8 v.l.); 2 Cl 19:2. W. ἀνομία (Epict. 2, 16, 44; Is 33:15) 1 Cl 35:5 v.l.; χαρίσασθέ μοι τὴν ἀδικίαν ταύτην *pardon me for this wrong* (ironic) **2 Cor 12:13;** ἀπέχεσθαι πάσης ἀ. Pol 2:2. Pl. *misdeeds* (Sir 17:20; Bar 3:8; Tob 13:5 al.; En 9:6; 99:16; Philo, Conf. Lingu. 21, Migr. Abr. 60; Jos., Bell. 7, 260) **Hb 8:12** (Jer 38 [31]:34). W. ἀνομίαι et al. 1 Cl 60:1.

❷ **the quality of injustice, *unrighteousness, wickedness, injustice*** (Isocr. 8, 35; Herm. Wr. 13, 9; LXX; Jos., C. Ap. 2, 291 [opp. δικαιοσύνη] Hippol., Ref. 4, 43, 12; Did., Gen. 20, 27; Iren. 5, 29, 2 [Harv. II 405, 12; w. ἀποστασία and πονηρία]) Dg 9:1f. Said to be sin **1J 5:17** (but 1 is also poss.), hence impossible in God **Ro 9:14** and at enmity w. truth ἐπὶ ἀδικίαν ἀνθρώπων τῶν τὴν ἀλήθειαν ἐν ἀ. κατεχόντων **1:18;** the same contrast betw. ἀ. and ἀληθής (cp. 1 Esdr 4:37) **J 7:18;** cp. also πείθεσθαι τῇ ἀ. *follow the wrong* **Ro 2:8;** χαίρειν ἐπὶ τῇ ἀ. **1 Cor 13:6;** εὐδοκεῖν τῇ ἀ. *take pleasure in wickedness* **2 Th 2:12;** ἀφιστάναι ἀπὸ ἀ. (Sir 35:3; TestDan 6:10) **2 Ti 2:19.** καθαρίζειν ἡμᾶς ἀπὸ πάσης ἀ. **1J 1:9;** πεπληρωμένος πάσῃ ἀ. **Ro 1:29;** cp. **3:5.** ἐν πάσῃ ἀπάτῃ ἀδικίας lit. *with every kind of deception of wickedness* i.e. w. all the arts of deception that the wicked one can devise **2 Th 2:10.** ὅπλα ἀδικίας *weapons of unrighteousness* **Ro 6:13.**—The gen. is oft. found as in Sem. lang. (cp. 2 Km 3:34; 7:10; Hos 12:8), but also in nonbiblical Gk. (ENachmanson, Eranos 9, 1909, 63–66; Mlt. 73f; Rdm. 108f.—Polyaenus 1, 19 στρατήγημα τῆς ἀπάτης 'deceitful military stratagem') in place of the adj. μισθὸς ἀ. *iniquitous reward* **2 Pt 2:13, 15;** but in **Ac 1:18** ἐκ μισθοῦ τῆς ἀ. means that Judas paid the fee for the *field purchased with the fee paid him for his crime* (of a single misdeed: Arrian, Anab. 3, 25, 8, a murder; cp. Ezk 14:4 κόλασις τ. ἀδικίας). οἰκονόμος τῆς ἀ. **Lk 16:8;** κριτὴς τῆς ἀ. **18:6;** μαμωνᾶς τῆς ἀ. **16:9** (also μ. ἄδικος vs. **11**); s. NSchlögl, BZ 14, 1917, 41–43; GCamps and MUbach, Un sentido biblico de ἄδικος, ἀδικία; Estudios biblicos 25, '66, 75–82 (emphasizes opp. to ἀλήθεια: s. above on **Rom 1:18**). In a broader sense ἀ. can refer to the essence of the evil world (HKosmala, The Parable of the Unjust Steward, ASTI 3, '64, 115); in such case the gen. signifies one's allegiance or subjugation to it; s. the foll. passages cited above: **Lk 16:8, 9; 18:6.** On κόσμος τῆς ἀ. **Js 3:6** s. κόσμος 8, on σύνδεσμος ἀ. **Ac 8:23** s. σύνδεσμος; also B 3:3 (Is 58:6). In ἐργάται ἀ. (cp. 1 Macc 3:6 ἐργάται τ. ἀνομίας) the gen. represents the obj. acc.= ἐργαζόμενοι τὴν ἀ. *evildoers* **Lk 13:27** (1 Macc 9:23; cp. Ps 6:9; 13:4).—BvanGroningen,

Ἀδικία: Mnemosyne, n.s. 55, 1927, 260–62.—DELG s.v. δίκη. M-M. TW. Sv.

ἀδικοκρίτης, ου, ὁ (opp. δικαιοκρίτης 2 Macc 12:41; PRyl 113, 35 [II AD]; ἀδικοκρισία in Heph. Astr. [IV AD] 3, 34: Cat. Cod. Astr. V 3 p. 81, 7) ***an unjust judge*** **Tit 1:9 v.l.**—DELG s.v. δίκη and κρίνω.

ἄδικος, ον (Hes.+) 'unjust'.—**❶ pert. to acting in a way that is contrary to what is right, *unjust, crooked*** of pers.: opp. δίκαιος model citizen (Aristot., Cat. 10b, 15 al.; Epict. 2, 11, 5; Aesop, Fab. 173 P.=308 H.; Philo, Abr. 33; Jos., Bell. 2, 139; 5, 407) **Mt 5:45; Ac 24:15; 1 Pt 3:18;** Dg 9:2; Hm 6, 1, 1f. W. ἄνομος (X., Mem. 4, 4, 13) 1 Cl 56:11 (Job 5:22). W. ἅρπαγες and μοιχοί **Lk 18:11.** Negative of God **Ro 3:5; Hb 6:10.** The ἄ. is excluded fr. the Kingdom **1 Cor 6:9;** ἄ. become rich 2 Cl 20:1. In a statement critical not of secular judges but, as the opp. term ἅγιοι indicates, of the litigious conduct of Paul's addressees κρίνεσθαι ἐπὶ τῶν ἄ. *go to law before the unjust* (that is, 'those who are from your Christian perspective impious unbelievers') **1 Cor 6:1** (Maximus Tyr. 3, 4c ὡς ἐπὶ δικαστῶν; ἀλλὰ ἄδικοι). In MPol 19:2 a proconsul's judgment is declared to be unjust. Opp. εὐσεβής **2 Pt 2:9** (Diod. S. 4, 2, 6 ἀδίκους κ. ἀσεβεῖς; Jos., Ant. 8, 251 ἄδ. κ. ἀσεβής); *dishonest, untrustworthy* (opp. πιστός) ὁ ἐν ἐλαχίστῳ ἄ. καὶ ἐν πολλῷ ἄ. ἐστιν **Lk 16:10.** Of Satan AcPlCor 2:11 (s. ἄρχων 1c).

❷ pert. to being associated w. injustice, *unjust* of things (Phalaris, Ep. 70 κέρδος ἄ.; Pr 15:26; Jos., Vi. 299) μαμωνᾶς **Lk 16:9** D, **11** (s. ἀδικία 2.—πλοῦτος ἄ. of ill-gotten gains: Chariton 3, 3, 11; Philo, Spec. Leg. 4, 158 and the opp. πλοῦτος δίκαιος SibOr 3, 783); κρίσις ἄ. (TestJos 14:1) Pol 6:1; ἄ. βίος (w. ἄνομος) MPol 3:1; ζῆλος ἄ. 1 Cl 3:4; 5:4; 45:4; ἄ. συγγραφή B 3:3 (Is 58:6). οὐδὲν ἄ. 1 Cl 45:3.—Lit. s.v. ἀδικία.—DELG s.v. δίκη. M-M. TW.

ἀδίκως adv. of ἄδικος (Aeschyl., Hdt.+) ***unjustly*** (opp. δικαίως as Menand., Sam. 311 διαφέρει οὐδὲ γρῦ ἀδίκως παθεῖν ταῦτ' ἢ δικαίως; Ael. Aristid. 46 p. 223 D.) B 5:4 (Pr 1:17); μισεῖν τινα ἀ. 1 Cl 60:3 (cp. Just., A I, 1, 1; 14, 3 al.) ***undeservedly*** (Plut., Mor. 216d; ἀ. πάσχειν Jos., Ant. 10, 115. Opp. δικαίως πάσχειν Ael. Aristid. 35 p. 671 D.; TestSim 4:3) πάσχων ἀ. **1 Pt 2:19** (cp. Plut., Mor. 609c of slaves unjustly treated). Vs. **23** has the v.l. τῷ κρίνοντι ἀδίκως (applied to Pilate; defended by Harnack, Beiträge VII 1916 p. 89f. See UHolzmeister, Comm. p. 270ff; ESelwyn, 1 Pt '58 ad loc.).—TW.

ἀδιστάκτως adv. of ἀδίστακτος 'undoubted'.—**❶** act. ***without doubting, without hesitating*** (Philod., Rhet I 133 Sudh.) αἰτεῖσθαι *ask confidently* Hm 9:2, 4, 6. ἐπιχορηγεῖν πάντα τῷ πένητι *provide everything for the poor without hesitating*=without giving it a second thought s 2:5, cp. 7; cp. 9, 24, 2 (w. ἀνονειδίστως). παρέχεσθαι τῷ πένητι s 2:7. τοῖς αἰτουμένοις διδόναι s 5, 4, 4 (v.l. ἀδιαλείπτως). μετανοεῖν *repent without delay* s 8, 10, 3.

❷ pass. ***beyond doubt, surely*** (Apollon. Dysc.: Gramm. Graeci II 2 p. 213, 5 U.; Anth. Pal. 12, 151; PGM 4, 2511) οἵ τοιοῦτοι οὖν ἀ. κατοικήσουσιν ἐν τῇ βασιλείᾳ τοῦ θεοῦ=*such people will unquestionably be able to inhabit God's kingdom* s 9, 29, 2.—DELG s.v. δίς.

Ἀδμίν, ὁ indecl. ***Admin,*** son of Arni, in the genealogy of Jesus **Lk 3:33** (the name is lacking, either through omission or substitution, in vv.ll.).

ἀδόκιμος, ον (Democr. et al.; also Polyb. 6, 25, 8; 16, 14, 9; ins, pap; Pr 25:4; Is 1:22) 'not standing the test', then ***unqualified, worthless, base*** of pers. (X., De Rep. Lac. 3, 3; Plut., Mor. 4c ἀνθρώποις ἀδοκίμοις ἐγχειρίζουσι τ. παῖδας; Herodian 7, 7, 5; Jos., C. Ap. 2, 236 ἀ. σοφισταί; Did., Gen. 122, 6) **1 Cor 9:27;** ITr 12:3. **2 Cor 13:5–7** (on the self-affirmation cp. Demosth. 18, 111); ἀνὴρ ἀ. ἀπείραστος *a man who is not tempted is unproved* Agr 21. W. indication of the respect in which the test is not met ἀδόκιμοι περὶ τὴν πίστιν **2 Ti 3:8;** πρὸς πᾶν ἔργον ἀγαθὸν ἀ. *unfit for any good deed* **Tit 1:16.**—Of things (Philo, Conf. Lingu. 198; PCairZen 176, 64 [III BC] of money) barren soil **Hb 6:8.** Of the gentile νοῦς in a play on words w. οὐ δοκιμάζειν **Ro 1:28.**—DELG s.v. δοκάω. TW. Spicq.

ἄδολος, ον 'without deceit' (Pind. et al., but mostly act., 'honest', so also as adv. Wsd 7:13 and Jos., Ant. 1, 212; Just., D. 125, 1 ἀδόλως) pass. ***unadulterated*** (esp. in pap and ins since III BC; e.g. PHib 85, 16f [261 BC]; 98, 19 [261 BC]; POxy 729, 19; BGU 290, 13; 1005, 5; 1015, 13; PTebt 105; SIG 736, 100; Philo, Rer. Div. Her. 95) of milk **1 Pt 2:2.**—FDölger, AC I 1929, p. 170, 39.—DELG s.v. δόλος. M-M.

ἄδοξος, ον ***without reputation, obscure*** (so TGF p. 921, adespota no. 423; X.+; OGI 5, 63f [311 BC]; POxy 79 II, 4 [II AD]; Sir 10:31; Jos., Vi. 278; Just.) 1 Cl 3:3; MPol 8:1 (both times as opp. of ἔνδοξος, as Just., D. 32, 1; Ael. Aristid. 26, 39 K.=14 p. 338 D.; Diog. L. 7, 117).—DELG s.v. δοκάω.

Ἀδραμυττηνός, ή, όν (Ἀδραμυντηνός W-H.; for the spelling s. Stephan. Byz. s.v. Ἀδραμύττειον; B-D-F §42, 3; Rob. 210; 223) ***of Adramyttium*** (Ἀτραμύττειον Hdt. 7, 42 et al., later Ἀδραμύττειον. The adj. e.g. Strabo 13, 1, 61; 62; Plut., Cic. 862 [4, 5]; OGI 238, 4), a seaport in Mysia (n.w. Asia Minor) on the Aegean Sea **Ac 27:2.** See RHarris, Adramyttium (Ac 27:2): Contemp. Rev. 128, 1925, 194–202.

ἀδρανής, ές (δραίνω=be ready to do, have strength; Posidippus [c. 280 BC]; Anth. Pal. 9. 359; Plut.; Dio Chrys. 11 [12], 31; Philostrat., Vi. Apoll. 3, 39; Wsd 13:19) ***powerless*** (w. ἀδύνατος; cp. Proclus, Theol. 149 p. 130, 25) πνεύματα ἐπίγεια ἀ. Hm 11:19.—DELG s.v. 1. δράω.

Ἀδρίας, ου, ὁ (Hdt. et al.; ins since 325 BC Meisterhans³-Schw.; B-D-F §261, 8) ***the Adriatic Sea*** (the sea betw. Crete and Sicily is included in it: Eudoxus [III BC]: 79 fgm. 1 Jac.; Ptolem. 3, 4, 1; 17, 1; Ael. Aristid. 48, 66 K.=24 p. 483 D.; Jos., Vi. 15) **Ac 27:27.** Warnecke, Romfahrt 69–74.

ἁδρότης, ητος, ἡ (Il. 24, 6; Theophr. and Epicurus [Diog. L. 10, 83]) ***abundance*** ἐν τῇ ἁ. ταύτῃ *in this lavish gift* (the collection that was made in behalf of Jerusalem) **2 Cor 8:20.**—DELG s.v. ἅδην. M-M.

ἀδυνατέω fut. ἀδυνατήσω lit. 'be powerless, be disabled' (so since Epicharmus [? c. 480 BC], fgm. 266, who uses it personally [Vorsokrat.⁵ 23 B, 23 ἀδυνατεῖ δ' οὐδὲν θεός]; also PEnteux 26, 3 [III BC]; UPZ 110, 13 and 89 [164 BC] 6, 36 [163 BC] al.; Herm. Wr. 10, 18; Philo; Jos., Ant. 15, 211; Ar. 3, 2; Tat. 16, 2; Ath. 21, 2; R. 57, 27); in NT only impers. (Philod., Ira p. 98 W.; Job 10:13; 42:2; 2 Ch 14:10; Wsd 13:16) ***it is impossible***

οὐδὲν ἀδυνατήσει ὑμῖν **Mt 17:20;** οὐκ ἀδ. παρὰ τοῦ θεοῦ (v.l. π. τῷ θεῷ) πᾶν ῥῆμα *nothing will be impossible w. God (as far as God is concerned)* **Lk 1:37** (Gen 18:14; Dt 17:8.—The idea that nothing is impossible for gods is also found among Greeks from early times: Od. 16, 211f; Hes., Works 5f; Alcaeus 78, 7 Diehl [34, 7 L.-P.]).—DELG s.v. δύναμαι. M-M. TW.

ἀδύνατος, ον—❶ pert. to lacking capability in functioning adequately, ***powerless, impotent*** (since Epicharmus).

ⓐ adj., of spirit beings Hm 11:19c. W. dat. ἀνὴρ ἀ. τοῖς ποσίν **Ac 14:8** (cp. PLond 678, 6 [99/98 BC] ἀ. ὄμμασι, also PStras 81, 17 [II BC]; PAdl Gk. 17, 5 [I BC]; Tob S 2:10; 5:10).

ⓑ subst. οἱ ἀδύνατοι (Hyperid. 2, 10 contrasted w. δυνάμενοι εἰπεῖν, those who cannot speak; TestJob 45:2 [w. πτωχοί in a gener. sense]) of those weak in faith (opp. οἱ δυνατοί) **Ro 15:1.**—τὰ ἀδύνατα *what is powerless* Dg 9:6b.—τὸ ἀδύνατον *inability* εἰς τὸ τυχεῖν 6a; τὸ καθ' ἑαυτοὺς ἀδύνατον εἰσελθεῖν *our own inability to enter* 9:1. Cp. δύναμαι w. neg.

❷ incapable of happening or being done, ***impossible*** (Pind., Hdt. et al.; LXX, Philo, Joseph.; Ar. 5, 2; Just.; Tat. 20, 2; Ath.).

ⓐ adj. ἀ. w. and without ἐστίν (B-D-F §127, 2) *it is impossible* Hm 11:19ab; παρὰ ἀνθρώποις τοῦτο ἀ. ἐστιν **Mt 19:26; Mk 10:27** (cp. Philo, Spec. Leg. 1, 282; Jos., Ant. 10, 196; PCairZen 31, 8 [III BC]; dedicatory ins fr. Phrygia in Steinleitner 59, no. 31, 4f: Μητρὶ Λητῷ ὅτι ἐξ ἀδυνάτων δυνατὰ ποιεῖ.—Ps.-Lucian, Halc. 3 ἀδύνατος and δυνατός of that which God cannot and can do); οὐδὲν ἀ. παρὰ τῷ θεῷ 1 Cl 27:2 (cp. Pind., P. 10, 48–50); cp. **Lk 18:27.** W. inf. foll. and acc. w. the inf. (Wsd 16:15; 2 Macc 4:6; Jos., Ant. 5, 109; Ar., Just., Ath.) **Hb 6:4, 18; 10:4; 11:6;** Hs 9, 26, 6; MPol 6:1. οὐκ ἔστιν ἀ. ὑπὲρ ὀνόματος θεοῦ (sc. τοῦτο ποιεῖν) IPhld 10:2.

ⓑ subst. (B-D-F §263, 2; Rob. 372; Mitt-Wilck. II/2, 372 V, 24: ἐπιχειρεῖς τοῖς ἀδυνάτοις; Jos., Ant. 11, 195; Tat. 20, 2 τὸ ἀ. τῆς θεορίας; Ath. 23, 5; 30, 1) τὸ ἀ. τοῦ νόμου *what was impossible for the law* (God has done) **Ro 8:3.**—M-M. TW. Spicq. S. ἀδυνατέω.

ἀδυσβάστακτος (hapax leg.) ***not too difficult to bear*** **Mt 23:4** D* (prob. in error for δυσβάστακτος). S. βαστάζω.

ᾄδω (since Hom., but there in the uncontracted form ἀείδω; ins, pap, LXX; TestSol 8:2 D; TestAbr B, 3, p. 107, 8 [Stone p. 62]; ParJer 7:34; Just., D. 74, 3; Tat.) fut. ᾄσω and ᾄσομαι LXX; 1 aor. ᾖσα (LXX; Mel. [?], PBodm 12) ***sing (in praise)*** abs. (w. χορεύειν, ὀρχεῖσθαι) Hs 9, 11, 5. W. dat. of pers. (LXX; Philostrat., Imag. 1, 11, 780; Heliod. 5, 15, 3 ἐμβατήρια ᾄδ. τ. Διονύσῳ; cp. Diod. S. 2, 47, 3 ὕμνους λέγειν τῷ θεῷ; Nägeli 42f) ᾄ. διὰ Ἰ. Χρ. τῷ πατρί IEph 4:2; τῷ πατρὶ ἐν Χρ. Ἰ. IRo 2:2; ᾄ. ἐν ταῖς καρδίαις ὑμῶν τ. θεῷ **Col 3:16;** ᾄδοντες καὶ ψάλλοντες (+ ἐν v.l.) τῇ καρδίᾳ ὑμῶν τῷ κυρίῳ *singing and playing (instrumentally) heartily to the Lord (praise the Lord heartily with words and music* Mft.) **Eph 5:19** (difft. NRSV; VMatthews, ABD IV 934; for Qumran s. Schürer II 290f. Cp. Rv 5:8; 14:2f; 15:2f). W. acc. foll., of the song that is sung (Polycrates: 588 fgm. 1 Jac.; Jos., Ant. 3, 64 ὕμνους) ᾠδὴν καινήν (Ps 143:9; cp. Philo, Mos. 1, 255 ᾄ. ᾆσμα καινόν) **Rv 5:9.** ὡς ᾠδὴν καινήν **14:3.** τὴν ᾠδὴν Μωυσέως **15:3** (Dt 31:30; cp. Ex 15:1); αἴσω ᾠδὴν ἁγίαν Κυρίῳ τῷ θεῷ μου GJs 6:3. Pass. Ἰησοῦς Χριστὸς ᾄδεται (praise of) *Jesus Christ is being sung* IEph 4:1. ᾄδω τὰς ἐκκλησίας *I sing (the praise of) the churches* IMg 1:2. φόβος νόμου ᾄδεται *the fear of the law is sung* Dg 11:6 (but s. Philo, Sacr. Abel. 131 λόγος ᾄδεται=a teaching is presented; Aelian, NA 17, 5 Φύλαρχος ᾄδει [=says] τοιαῦτα; Arrian, Anab. 4, 9, 5 'proclaim'. Likewise Epict., Gnomolog. 26 [fgm. Stob.] ᾄδειν τὰ λόγια; Plut., Thes. 8 [19, 1]; Maximus Tyr. 32, 1b).—JKroll, D. christl. Hymnodik bis zu Klemens v. Al.: Beigabe z. Vorlesungsverz. v. Braunsberg SS. 1921 and WS. 1921/22; VMatthews (above, w. lit.).—B. 1249. DELG s.v. ἀείδω. M-M. TW.

ἀεί adv. (since Hom.+; ins, pap [Mayser 103f], LXX; TestSol 22:5 Q; TestAbr B 14, p. 119, 4 [Stone p. 86]; SyrBar 13, 1; GrBar; JosAs 7:6 [A]; ApcEsdr 7, 16, p. 33, 5 Tdf.; ApcMos 43; EpArist; Jos., Vi. 87 al.; Just., Tat., Ath.—The form αἰεί is used by Philo.)

❶ duration of time as continuous, ***always*** ἀ. χαίροντες **2 Cor 6:10;** ἕτοιμοι ἀ. πρὸς ἀπολογίαν *always prepared to make a defense* **1 Pt 3:15;** cp. Dg 8:8; 12:8; IEph 11:2; Pol 6:1 (cp. Pr 3:4); οὗτος ὁ ἀεί he (the Logos) is forever Dg 11:5; εἰς ἀ. *forever* (Dio Chrys. 21 [38], 51; Ael. Aristid. 43, 9 K.=1 p. 3 D.; BGU 180, 24; 316, 22; POxy 67, 22; 2133, 28; PLips 4, 24; Jos., C. Ap. 2, 156; Ath. R. 66, 26) IPol 2:2. τοῦ δὲ σωτῆρος ἡμῶν τὰ ἔργα ἀεὶ παρῆν, ἀληθῆ γὰρ ἦν (i.e. 'reality') Qua. w. ἀεὶ παρόντες foll. in ref. to those who are healed and resurrected.

❷ duration of time as episodic, of a freq. recurring action or situation ***continually, constantly*** (Diod. S. 19, 39, 1 allies were coming on 'from time to time'; Appian, Bell. Civ. §2, 139, 579; PRyl 114, 26 ἐμὲ τὴν χήραν ἀ. ἀποστερεῖν; EpArist 196; Just., A II, 7, 9; D. 27, 2; 28, 1 al.; Tat. 6, 1; Ath. 11, 2) ἀ. εἰς θάνατον παραδιδόμεθα **2 Cor 4:11;** ἀ. τῷ πνεύματι τῷ ἁγίῳ ἀντιπίπτετε **Ac 7:51;** ἀ. ὑμᾶς ὑπομιμνῄσκειν *from time to time* **2 Pt 1:12;** ἀ. πλανῶνται **Hb 3:10** (Ps 94:10). καθὼς ἀ. ἐποίει *as he was accustomed to do* **Mk 15:8 v.l.** διὰ τὸ ἀεὶ ἕκαστον τῶν πιστῶν σπουδάζειν = *for each of the believers was eagerly awaiting a turn to touch Polycarp's body* MPol 13:2.—B. 985. DELG s.v. αἰών. M-M.

ἀέναος, ον (in var. spellings [mostly w. one ν; on the etym. s. Boisacq.] Hes., Hdt.+; ins, pap, LXX. Adv. ἀεννάως ApcEsdr p. 33, 3 Tdf.).

❶ lit. ***ever-flowing*** of springs (Hes., Opera 595; Simonides fgm. 48 Diehl [581, 2 Page] in Diog. L. 1, 90; Epict., Gnomol. 2 [p. 463 Sch.] fr. Stob.; M. Ant. 8, 51; Wsd 11:6; Philo, Spec. Leg. 1, 303; Jos., Bell. 3, 45, Ant. 3, 258; SibOr 4, 15) 1 Cl 20:10.

❷ fig. ***eternal*** (Pind. et al.; UPZ 14, 33 [II BC]; LXX; SibOr 3, 698; Herm. Wr. 18, 14a; PGM 13, 842) God (Sb 8141, 22 [ins I BC] θεοῦ μεγάλου ἔκγονος ἀενάου) PtK 2. τὴν ἀ. τοῦ κόσμου σύστασιν *the everlasting constitution of the universe* 1 Cl 60:1 (cp. OGI 56, 48 εἰς τὸν ἀ. κόσμον).—DELG s.v. αἰών.

ἀετός, οῦ, ὁ (since Hom., who, as do many after him, writes αἰετός early Attic [cp. Jos., Bell. 5, 48]; ins, pap, LXX; Test12Patr, ParJer; ApcMos 33; Jos., Bell. 1, 650f, Ant. 17, 151; Tat. 10, 1f; DELG s.v. αἰετός) ***eagle*** symbol of swiftness **Rv 12:14** (s. Ezk 17:3, 7); cp. **4:7; 8:13** (s. Boll 37f; 113f—ἀ. πετόμενος as Job 9:26). Eating carrion, in the proverb (cp. Job 39:30) ἐκεῖ (ἐπι)συναχθήσονται οἱ ἀ. **Mt 24:28; Lk 17:37** (where ***vulture*** is meant; Aristot., HA 9, 32, 592b, 1ff, and Pliny, Hist. Nat. 10, 3 also class the vulture among the eagles; TManson, Sayings of Jesus '54, 147, emphasizes the swiftness of the coming of the Day of the Son of Man). Moses forbade eating of its flesh B 10:1, 4 (Dt 14:12; Lev 11:13).—M-M.

Ἀζαρίας, ου, ὁ (Joseph.; Just., A I, 46, 3) ***Azariah,*** in Da 1:6f; 3:23ff one of the three youths in the fiery furnace 1 Cl 45:7 (cp. TSchneider/EStemplinger, RAC I, 87–94).

ἄζυμος, ον 'without fermentation' (Pla., Tim. 74d σάρξ unfermented=firm, solid, of sinews; ἄρτος 'made without leaven, unleavened': Hippocr., περὶ διαίτης [Vict.] 2, 42; 3, 79; Trypho of Alex. [I BC] fgm. 117 [Athen. 3, 109b] ἄρτοι ἄζυμοι; Galen: CMG V 4, 2 p. 220, 1; 3 of peasants who ἑορτάζοντες make loaves of bread which they call ἄζυμοι; Pollux 6, 32; LXX; Just., D. 12, 3; 14, 2; Mel., P. 93, 697)

❶ subst. ***unleavened bread*** in the form of flat cakes, *matzoth* (מַצּוֹת; [the Gk. word μάζα, ἡ='dough, bread' Hdt. et al.; Harmodius, III BC: 319 fgm. 1 Jac. p. 32, 21 μάζας καὶ ἄρτους; Antig. Car. 173]; τὰ ἄ. Ex 12:8, 15 al.; 23:15; Philo, Congr. Erud. Gr. 161; Jos., Ant. 3, 249b; 17, 213; λάγανα 'flat cakes' Lev 2:4; Num 6:15, as ἄρτοι ἄ. Ex 29:2; Lev 2:5; Jos., Ant. 3, 142; Mel., P. 93, 697 ἔδεσθε ἄζυμα) eaten by Israel at Passover. In the NT only fig., ἑορτάζειν ἐν ἀ. εἰλικρινείας καὶ ἀληθείας *celebrate the festival w. the unleavened bread of purity and truth,* i.e. w. a pure and true life **1 Cor 5:8.**—As subst. and fig. ext. of the prec., of people in whom sin has been overcome in principle καθώς ἐστε ἄ. *even as you are a batch of unleavened dough* **1 Cor 5:7.**

❷ subst. τὰ ἄζυμα ***festival of unleavened bread*** (s. πάσχα 1; GBeer, Pesachim 1912 [p. 1, 1 lit.]. On the pl. s. B-D-F §141, 3) PtK 2 p. 14, 29; w. πάσχα (1 Esdr 1:17; cp. Jos., Ant. 14, 21 κατὰ τὸν καιρὸν τῆς τ. ἀζύμων ἑορτῆς, ἣν πάσχα λέγομεν; 18, 29 and **Lk 22:7** s. below) **Mk 14:1;** ἡ ἑορτὴ τῶν ἀ. (Ex 23:15; 34:18; Dt 16:16; Jos., Ant. 2, 317; 14, 21 s. above; IHierapJ 342, 6; Mel., P. 93, 697) **Lk 2:42** D; **22:1;** ἡ ἡμέρα τῶν ἀ., ᾗ ἔδει θύεσθαι τὸ πάσχα vs. **7** (s. above); αἱ ἡμέραι τῶν ἀ. **Ac 12:3; 20:6** (s. FStrobel, NovT 2, '58, 216, note 2). τῇ πρώτῃ ἡμέρᾳ τῶν ἀ. **Mk 14:12;** cp. **Mt 26:17** (LDieu, ETL14, '38, 657–67). πρὸ μιᾶς τῶν ἀ. *one day before the festival of unleavened bread* GPt 2:5 (ASyn. 341, 21; on this use s. WSchulze, Graeca Latina 1901, 14f; B-D-F §213; Mlt. 100f).—DELG s.v. ζύμη. M-M. TW.

Ἀζώρ, ὁ indecl. ***Azor,*** in the genealogy of Jesus **Mt 1:13f; Lk 3:23ff** D.

Ἄζωτος, ου, ἡ (since Hdt. 2, 157; also Diod. S. 19, 85, 1; LXX; Joseph., index Niese) ***Azotus,*** the OT (Is 20:1) *Ashdod,* one of the five Philistine cities, on the coast of S. Palestine **Ac 8:40.**—Schürer II, 108f (lit.).

ἀηδής, ές (ἀ- + ἦδος 'delight') gen. οῦς (Hippocr., Hdt. et al.; also PCairZen 638, 11; Gen 48:17 and 1 Km 29:7 [both Sym.]; TestSol, Philo, Joseph.) ***unpleasant, odious.*** ὡς ... μηδὲν ἀηδές ... ὑπομείναντος *how (Justus) ... had experienced no ill effects (despite drinking poison)* Papias (2:9). Comp. ἀηδέστερος, α, ον *more loathsome* (of the illness that befell Judas and affected his genitals) Papias (3:2). S. adv. ἀηδῶς below.—DELG s.v. ἥδομαι.

ἀηδία, ας, ἡ lit. 'unpleasantness' (so Demosth. et al.; UPZ 72, 8 [152 BC]; 119, 23; BGU 22, 14ff [s. further Preis. IV]; LXX Pr 23:29; Aq. Sym. Jer 15:10; Philo; Jos., Ant. 17, 307; TestDan 4:3) ***displeasure,*** ὄντες ἐν ἀηδίᾳ *being at odds* **Lk 23:12** D (ἐν ἀ. εἶναι Ael. Aristid. 47, 10 K.=23 p. 447 D.).—DELG s.v. ἥδομαι. M-M.

ἀηδῶς adv. 'unwillingly, reluctantly' i.e. 'without pleasure to oneself' (so X., Pla. et al.; BGU 801, 4 λίαν ἀηδῶς; TestSol 2:9ff D; Jos., Ant. 11, 149; 12, 174; Just., D. 80, 4) ἀ. ἔχειν (Demosth. 20, 142; 37, 11; BGU 665 III, 10f [I AD] ἀηδῶς ἔσχον περὶ τοῦ ἵππου; PGiss 20, 9; PRossGeorg III, 2, 2; PIand 117, 3) ***be displeased*** (w. ἀγανακτεῖν) 2 Cl 19:2. S. ἀηδής.

ἀήρ, έρος, ὁ (Hom. [where, as in Hes., it is fem. in the sense 'mist, haze'; fr. Hdt. downwards it is masc. and in various senses] +; loanw. in rabb.)

❶ **the atmosphere immediately above the earth's surface,** ***air,*** w. the sun **Rv 9:2;** as an element w. fire and water (PGM 12, 251; 17b, 15) Dg 7:2. To indicate the direction 'up' (Achilles Tat. 7, 15, 3 ἐξάλλομαι εἰς ἀέρα; PParis 21b, 16 ἀπὸ ἐδάφους μέχρι ἀέρος; sim. PLond III, 991, 10 p. 258; PGM 13, 832 εἰς ἀέρα βλέπων; Jos., Ant. 7, 327) GJs 18:2 codd., not pap; βάλλειν εἰς τὸν ἀ. *throw into the air* **Ac 22:23;** ἁρπάζεσθαι εἰς ἀ. **1 Th 4:17** (cp. PGM 1, 179); ἐκχέειν ἐπὶ τὸν ἀ. **Rv 16:17.** In figures of speech: ἀέρα δέρειν *beat the air* fr. the language of the arena, of a gladiator who misses a stroke **1 Cor 9:26** (s. δέρω; Vergil, Aen. 5, 377 verberat ictibus auras; 6, 294; sim. Quint. Smyrn. 9, 259f ἐς κενεὴν τύψας ἠέρα); proverb. (AOtto, D. Sprichwörter d. Röm. 1890, 364) εἰς ἀ. λαλεῖν *talk to the wind* **14:9** (Ovid, Am. 1, 6, 42 dare verba in ventos; Lucret. 4, 931).

❷ **the space above the earth,** ***sky, space, air***—ⓐ of space as locale of celestial bodies or phenomena (Artem. 2, 8 p. 91, 10ff; 2, 36 p. 138, 2 οἱ ὑπὲρ ἀέρα ἀστέρες; Cyranides p. 49, 7 τὰ ἐν οὐρανῷ κ. ἐν ἀέρι) πετεινὰ τ. ἀέρος PtK 2 p. 14, 17; rainbow ἶρις ἐν ἀ. ApcPt 3:10.

ⓑ of the political domain of transcendent beings or powers (Ocellus Luc. 40: gods live in heaven, people on earth, δαίμονες in the ἀέριος τόπος; Diog. L. 8, 32 after Pythagoras εἶναι τε πάντα τὸν ἀέρα ψυχῶν ἔμπλεον, καὶ τούτους δαίμονάς τε καὶ ἥρωας νομίζεσθαι; Plut., Mor. 274b; Celsus 8, 35; PGM 13, 278 πνεῦμα ἐν ἀέρι φοιτώμενον; 4, 1134; 2699; 3042 ἀέριον 'air-spirit'; likew. 7, 314.—1, 129 a transcendent being as μόνος κύριος τοῦ ἀέρος; IDefixWünsch 4, 37 p. 19 ἀέρος τὴν ἐξουσίαν ἔχοντα Ωη Ἰαω; cp. pap SEitrem and AFridrichsen, E. christl. Amulett auf Pap. 1921, p. 31, 5; p. 13f; Philo, Plant. 14, Gig. 6f, Conf. Lingu. 174 al.) ὁ ἄρχων τῆς ἐξουσίας τοῦ ἀ. *the ruler of the kingdom of the air* i.e. Satan, **Eph 2:2** (cp. AscIs 11, 23; Slav. En. 31; TestBenj 3:4 ἀέριον πνεῦμα τοῦ Βελίαρ).—FPfister, Philol. 69, 1910, 416ff; Cumont[3] 289, 55.—B. 63. DELG. M-M. TW. Sv.

ἀθᾶ s. μαρὰν ἀθᾶ.

ἀθανασία, ας, ἡ (Isocr., Pla.+; Vett. Val. 221; 330; SIG 798, 4; Sb 4127, 14; PGM 4, 477; Wsd, 4 Macc; JosAs 8:5; 15:4; Philo; Jos., Bell. 7, 348, Ant. 17, 354; SibOr 2, 41; 150; Just., Tat.; Orig., C. Cels. 3 , 81, 2 al.; loanw. in rabb.) ***immortality*** (w. γνῶσις, πίστις) D 10:2. ἐνδύσασθαι ἀ. *put on immortality*=be clothed w. an immortal body **1 Cor 15:53f;** God ὁ μόνος ἔχων ἀ. **1 Ti 6:16;** ζωὴ ἐν ἀ. 1 Cl 35:2. In accord w. widespread medical terminology (TSchermann, TQ 92, 1910, 6ff) the Lord's Supper is called a φάρμακον ἀθανασίας (syn. ἀντίδοτος τοῦ μὴ ἀποθανεῖν) *medicine of immortality* IEph 20:2 (Diod. S. 1, 25 τὸ τῆς ἀ. φάρμακον; Lucian, Dial. Deor. 10, 5 πίνειν τῆς ἀ.).—DELG s.v. θάνατος. M-M. TW. Sv.

ἀθάνατος, ον (Hom.+; ins, pap, LXX; pseudepigr.; Jos., Ant. 11, 56, C. Ap. 2, 277; apolog.) **pert. to not being subject to death,** ***immortal*** of God (Philo, Aet. M. 44; SibOr 3, 276; 582; TestAbr A 17 p. 98, 20 [Stone p. 44]; οἱ ἀ. Hom. et al.) **1 Ti 1:17 v.l.** Of the soul (acc. to Diog. L. 1, 24 since Thales and Choerilus Ep. [V BC]; s. further Pla., Ep. 7, 335a; Diod. S. 5, 28, 6; Paus. 4, 32, 4; Herm. Wr. 8, 1; Vett. Val. 242, 16; Iambl., Vi. Pyth. 30, 173; Philo, Op. M. 119.—MNilsson, The Immortality of the Soul in Gk. Rel.: Eranos 39, '41, 1–16) Dg 6:8. Of γνῶσις (cp. the combin. w. χάρις Demosth., Ep. 4, 9; SIG 798, 7; w. κρίσις OGI 383, 207) 1 Cl 36:2. τὸν ἀ. τῆς ἀναστάσεως καρπὸν τρυγᾶν 2 Cl 19:3. Subst. of Jesus ὁ ἀ. Dg 9:2 (opp. οἱ θνητοί); τὸ ἀ. *that which is immortal* (opp. τὸ θνητόν, like Philo, Rer. Div. Her. 265) D 4:8 (cp. Alexis 158 τὸ ἀ. in contrast to σῶμα). As name of a horseman **Rv 6:8 v.l.**—MTreu Griechische Ewigkeitsworter, Glotta 43, '65, 7.—DELG s.v. θάνατος. TW. Sv.

ἀθέμιστος Dg 4:2 s. the foll.

ἀθέμιτος, ον (Hom. and other early wr. ἀθέμιστος; since Antiphon, more and more commonly in the Koine, incl. LXX; TestSol 10:2 P; 20:4 and Jos. [e.g. Bell. 4, 562, Vi. 26]; Just., A I, 9, 5; UPZ 162 II, 22 [117 BC] ἀθέμιτος). This term refers prim. not to what is forbidden by ordinance but to violation of tradition or common recognition of what is seemly or proper.

❶ **pert. to not being sanctioned, *not allowed, forbidden*** ἀθέμιτόν ἐστιν *it is forbidden* w. inf. foll. (Plut., Mor. 150f; Jos., Bell. 1, 650) **Ac 10:28.**

❷ **pert. to violating canons of decency, *wanton, disgusting, unseemly,*** εἰδωλολατρίαι **1 Pt 4:3.** ὀργή 1 Cl 63:2. πῶς οὐκ ἀθέμιστον; Dg 4:2.—Subst. ἀ. ποιεῖν (X., Mem. 1, 1, 9) *commit lawless acts* D 16:4.—DELG s.v. θέμις. M-M. TW.

ἄθεος, ον (Aeschyl.+; Diog. L. 7, 119; Stoic. III 157, 606; Vett. Val. ind.; PGM 36, 319; 337; Cat. Cod. Astr. II 98, 15; 108, 3; 109, 12; Philo, Leg. All. 1, 49 al.; Just.; Tat. 6, 2 [ἄθλιος Wilamowitz]; Ath.; Iren. 1, 6, 4 [Harv. I 56, 13].—PLond 1915, 8; 27) 'without God, godless'.

❶ **pert. to being without a relationship to God, *without God,*** expressed without censure (Artem. 1, 8 p. 14, 4 οὐδὲν ἔθνος ἄθεον; Maximus Tyr. 30, 2d δι' ἀμαθίαν ἄθεοι of those who, through no fault of their own, have never heard of gods), of those who had been polytheists ἄ. ἐν τῷ κόσμῳ **Eph 2:12.** So also, if with Blass it is correctly restored [οὐκ] ε[ἰσὶ]ν ἄθεοι, Ox 1 recto, 3=GTh 30; Fitzmyer Oxy 539 reconstructs ε[ἰσὶ]ν θεοί (text cited ASyn. 171, 4).

❷ **one who disdains or denies God or the gods and their laws, *god-denier, atheist*** (Euhemerus and other Gk. thinkers are so termed in Sext. Emp., Math. 9, 50 and 9, 17; Diogenes, Epicurus et al. in Aelian, VH 2, 31.—Nicol. Dam.: 90 fgm. 16 Jac. p. 341, 2 οἷα ἀθέους ἐπόντωσεν; Ptolem., Apotel. 3, 14, 28 in a catalogue of vices).

ⓐ in the mouth of polytheists against Christians (also Jews: Jos., C. Ap. 2, 148) αἶρε τοὺς ἀ. *away w. the atheists!* MPol 3:2; 9:2a (cp. Just., A I, 6, 1; 13, 1 al.; OGI 569, 22; TMommsen, Hist. Ztschr. 64, 1890, 407; ADrachmann, Atheism in Pagan Antiquity 1922. The charge was especially volatile, since the security of the state depended on proper relationships with the gods.).

ⓑ in the mouth of Christians, w. ref. to polytheists MPol 9:2b (likew. SibOr 8, 395; Ps.-Clem., Hom. 15, 4; Clem. Al., Paed. 3, 11, 80). Of heterodox Christians ITr 10 and hence prob. also 3:2 (cp. AcPlCor 2:37).—M-M. TW.

ἄθεσμος, ον (Diod. S. 1, 14; Plut., Caes. 712 [10, 5]; POxy 129, 8; PLond 1678, 5 [VI AD]; PGM 4, 2607; 2670; TestSol; Philo, Mos. 2, 198; Jos., Bell. 7, 264; 3 Macc 5:12; 6:26; Just., D. 10, 1; Ath. 34, 1) **pert. to being unprincipled, *unseemly, disgraceful, lawless*** (opp. δίκαιος). Subst. ὁ ἄ. *the disgraceful/lawless person* (Philo, Praem. 126; SibOr 5, 177) **2 Pt 2:7; 3:17** (s. ἀθέμιτος 2). —DELG s.v. θεσμός. M-M. TW.

ἀθετέω fut. ἀθετήσω; 1 aor. ἠθέτησα; pf. ἠθέτηκα Is 27:4 (Polyb. et al.; ins, pap, LXX, Jos. [but only Ant. 15, 26 v.l.]; Test12Patr; Just., D. 16, 4; Hippol., Ref. 9, 15, 6)

❶ **to reject someth. as invalid, *declare invalid, nullify, ignore*** (BGU 1123, 11 [I BC]; Ps 88:35; 1 Macc 11:36; 2 Macc 13:25 al.) a will **Gal 3:15.** τὴν ἐντολὴν τοῦ θεοῦ **Mk 7:9** (cp. AcPh 142 [Aa II/2, p. 80, 8; 20]). τὴν βουλὴν τοῦ θεοῦ **Lk 7:30** (cp. Ps 32:10). νόμον Μωϋσέως **Hb 10:28** (cp. Ezk 22:26; τὴν παλαιάν [διαθήκην] Did., Gen. 156, 8f). τὴν χάριν τοῦ θεοῦ **Gal 2:21.** τὴν πρώτην πίστιν *break their first pledge* **1 Ti 5:12** (πίστιν ἀ. Polyb. 8, 2, 5; 11, 29, 3; Diod. S. 21, 20 al.); *thwart, confound* (Ps 32:10) τὴν σύνεσιν τῶν συνετῶν **1 Cor 1:19.**

❷ **to reject by not recognizing someth. or someone, *reject, not recognize, disallow*** (POxy 1120, 8; PGiss 34, 8) Christ **J 12:48** (cp. AcPlCor 2:3 κύριος Χρ. ἀθετούμενος); God **1 Th 4:8** (cp. AcJ 3; 41 [Aa II/1, 152, 15; 170, 33]; Theoph. Ant. 2, 34 [p. 186, 21]); both, together w. the apostles **Lk 10:16.** κυριότητα **Jd 8.** τὸν κύριον Hm 3:2. Gener. *disallow:* οὐκ ἠθέλησεν ἀθετῆσαι αὐτήν *he did not want to refuse* (prob. *break faith w., go back on his word to, renege on his promise to* [Is 1:2]; Polyb. 3, 29, 2) *her* **Mk 6:26.**—Pass. of Christians τίς ἀθετηθῇ IEph 10:3 (s. Lghtf.; difft. Bihlmeyer).

❸ **to make of no account, *be insolent /offensive,*** intr. (so oft. LXX; PCairMasp 151, 251) *commit an offense* εἰς τὸν θεόν Hv 2, 2, 2 (cp. 3 Km 12:19; Ezk 39:23).—DELG s.v. τίθημι. M-M. TW. Spicq. Sv.

ἀθέτησις, εως, ἡ (Cicero, Ad Att. 6, 9, 3; Diog. L. 3, 39, 66 al.; pap, LXX).

❶ **a refusal to recognize the validity of someth., *annulment*** legal t.t. (BGU 44, 16 [102 AD]; 196, 21; 281, 18 al.) ἀ. γίνεται προαγούσης ἐντολῆς *a former commandment is annulled* **Hb 7:18.**

❷ gener. **the process of causing someth. to be set aside, *removal*** (Sext. Emp., Math. 8, 142 w. ἀναίρεσις) εἰς ἀ. τῆς ἁμαρτίας **Hb 9:26.**—Dssm., NB 55f [BS 228f].—M-M. TW. Spicq. S. ἀθετέω.

Ἀθῆναι, ῶν, αἱ (Hom. et al.; Philo, Joseph.) ***Athens,*** capital of Attica **Ac 17:15f; 18:1; 1 Th 3:1** (also in **subscr.** to **1 and 2 Th** and **Hb**). Cp. Haenchen on Ac 17:15 (lit.); OBroneer, BA 21, '58, 2–28.—DDD s.v. Athena.

Ἀθηναῖος, α, ον (Hom. et al.; Philo, Joseph.; Ar. ins; Tat.; Mel., HE 4, 26, 10; Ath.) ***Athenian;*** subst. ὁ Ἀ. *the Athenian* **Ac 17:21;** in dir. address: ἄνδρες Ἀθηναῖοι *gentlemen of Athens* (Demosth. 8, 35; 18, 27; Diod. S. 13, 102, 2 al.) vs. **22.**—DDD s.v. Athena.

ἄθικτος, ον *inviolable, sacred* (so trag. et al.; SIG 569, 16; Sb 7202, 68 [III BC]; BGU 1773, 13 [I BC]; Sym. Lev 8:9; 21:12; JosAs 14:13 [στολή 'untouched', 'pure', with the connotation 'never before worn']) τὰ ἄ. ἀρχεῖα IPhld 8:2.—DELG s.v. θιγγάνω.

ἀθλέω 1 aor. ἤθλησα (specialized word since Homer; Philo; Tat. 3, 2; Orig., C. Cels. 8, 70, 19) **to compete in a contest, *compete,*** of athletic contests in the arena **2 Ti 2:5;** νομίμως *according to the rules, properly qualified* ibid. (Epict. 3, 10, 8; Galen, In Hippocratis de victu acutorum commentaria 4, 15, 464 οἱ γυμνασταί, καὶ οἵ γε νομίμως ἀθλοῦντες *athletes, in any case those who qualify for competition*). Metaph. of the apostles ἕως θανάτου ἤθλησαν *they contended to the death* 1 Cl 5:2. Gener. θεοῦ ζῶντος πεῖραν ἀ. (w. γυμνάζεσθαι) *we are competing in a contest of a living God* 2 Cl 20:2.—DELG s.v. ἄεθλος. TW.

ἄθλησις, εως, ἡ (since Polyb. 5, 64, 6; Sb 6997, 12; 16, 24 [III BC]: BCH 23, 1899, 557 [II BC]; IG XIV, 1102 [II AD]; SIG 1073, 24; StudPal 5, 119 verso, III, 13=PHerm 119b III, 13; Philo; 'contest', esp. of athletes) ***contest,*** in NT only fig. of temptations and suffering that, so to speak, fight against people: πολλὴν ἄ. ὑπεμείνατε παθημάτων *you have had to endure a hard struggle w. suffering* **Hb 10:32** (perh. *challenge*).—M-M. TW. S. ἀθλέω.

ἀθλητής, οῦ, ὁ (since Pind. [ἀεθλητής]; ins, pap, 4 Macc, TestJob, Philo; Jos., Ant. 13, 327; 17, 259; loanw. in rabb.) ***contender, athlete,*** in our lit. only fig. (since Gorgias [EScheel, De Gorgianae Disciplinae Vestigiis, diss. Rostock 1890, 13], also Diod. S. 9, 1, 1 ἀ. πάσης ἀρετῆς; Dio Chrys. 2, 18; 4 Macc 6:10; 17:15f) of the martyrs οἱ ἔγγιστα γενόμενοι ἀ. 1 Cl 5:1. Of one practiced in suffering τέλειος ἀ. *master athlete* IPol 1:3; μέγας ἀ. 3:1; θεοῦ ἀ. 2:3. S. ἀθλέω.

ἄθραυστος, ον (Eur. et al.; SIG 970, 15; Sb 8960, 20 ἄ. βίος) ***unbroken*** ἄ. διαφυλάσσειν τὸν ἀριθμὸν τῶν ἐκλεκτῶν *to preserve unbroken the number of the elect* 1 Cl 59:2.—DELG s.v. θραύω.

ἀθροίζω fut. ἀθροίσω, 1 aor. ἤθροισα LXX. Pass.: 1 aor. 2 and 3 pl. ἠθροίσθητε, -θησαν LXX; pf. ptc. ἠθροισμένος (denominative fr. ἀθρόος 'in crowds'; trag., Hdt. et al.; OGI 764, 9; UPZ 12, 42 [158 BC]; LXX; Philo, De Jos. 158; Jos., Ant. 3, 300 Μωϋσῆς εἰς ἐκκλησίαν ἀθροίζει τὸ πλῆθος; Just., D. 109, 3 [ἀθροίσω for εἰσδέξομαι Mi 4:6]) **to cause to be together in a group, *collect, gather,*** pass. in act. sense *assemble* **Lk 24:33.**—DELG s.v. ἀθρόος. M-M.

ἀθυμέω 1 aor. 3 sg. ἠθύμησεν LXX (since Aeschyl., Thu. 5, 91, 1; PAmh 37, 7; 10 [II BC]; PGiss 79 III, 11; LXX, Philo; Jos., Bell. 6, 94, Ant. 9, 87; Just., D. 107, 3) **to become disheartened to the extent of losing motivation, *be discouraged, lose heart, become dispirited,*** of children (Hyperid., fgm. 144) ἵνα μὴ ἀθυμῶσιν *that they may not lose heart* **Col 3:21.**—DELG s.v. θυμός. M-M.

ἀθυμία, ας, ἡ (Soph., Hdt. et al.; UPZ 19, 14 [163 BC]; LXX; TestSol 1:3 L; TestAbr A 20, p. 103, 4 [Stone p. 54] of loss of energy; Philo; Jos., Bell. 3, 182, Ant. 12, 35, C. Ap. 1, 236) **disheartenment to the extent of loss of motivation, *discouragement*** εἰς ἀ. βάλλειν τινά *plunge someone into disc.* 1 Cl 46:9 (cp. Aeschin. 3, 177 εἰς τὴν ἐσχάτην ἀ. ἐμβαλεῖν). S. ἀθυμέω.

ἀθῷος, ον (cp. θωή 'penalty'; Eur.+; SIG 1157, 59; 1217, 6; PTebt 44, 28; 800, 38 [both II BC]; LXX, Philo; Jos., Ant. 4, 271; 8, 15; Just.; Mel., P. 74, 542) ***innocent*** αἷμα ἀ. (oft. LXX e.g. Dt 27:25; Philo, Spec. Leg. 1, 204; TestLevi 16:3; TestZeb 2:2; Mel., P. 73) **Mt 27:4;** GJs 14:1; 23:3. Of pers.: ἀ. εἶναι ἀπό τινος (B-D-F §182, 3; cp. Gen 24:41; Num 5:19, 31) *be innocent of* **Mt 27:24;** 1 Cl 59:2. μετὰ ἀνδρὸς ἀθῴου ἀ. ἔσῃ 1 Cl 46:3 (Ps 17:26). W. δίκαιος vs. 4 (cp. Ex 23:7); *guiltless* of the almsgiver, so far as he has fulfilled the commandment D 1:5; Hm 2:6.—B. 1446. DELG s.v. θωή. M-M.

αἴγειος, εία, ειον (αἴξ 'goat'; Hom. et al.; ins, pap, LXX; Jos., Ant. 3, 102) ***of a goat;*** of the clothing of the prophets: ἐν αἰγείοις δέρμασιν (PCairZen 60, 8 [III BC]; PFay 107, 2f, al. δέρμα αἴγειον) *in goatskins* **Hb 11:37;** 1 Cl 17:1 (w. μηλωταί). Of the clothing of the angel of punishment Hs 6, 2, 5; of the shepherd Hv 5:1.—M-M.

αἰγιαλός, οῦ, ὁ ***shore, beach*** (Hom. et al., mostly of the sea, as OGI 199, 21; Judg 5:17 A; Philo, Aet. M. 42; Jos., Ant. 14, 292; TestZeb 6:3, TestSol 2:5; but also of lakes: e.g. PTebt 79 [148 BC]; 82; 83; PFay 82, 3; Jos., Bell. 3, 521 [Lake Gennesaret]) gener. ἑστάναι ἐπὶ τὸν αἰ. **Mt 13:2;** ἑστάναι εἰς τὸν αἰ. **J 21:4;** ἀναβιβάζειν ἐπὶ τὸν αἰ. **Mt 13:48;** cp. **Ac 21:5.** Suitable for beaching ships κόλπον ἔχοντα αἰ. *a bay with a (fine) beach* **27:39** (cp. X., An. 6, 4, 4 λιμὴν αἰγιαλὸν ἔχων); κατέχειν εἰς τ. αἰ. *to head for the beach* (s. κατέχω 7) vs. **40.**—B. 32. DELG. M-M.

Αἰγύπτιος, ία, ιον (Hom.+) ***Egyptian*** τὸ Αἰ. εὐαγγέλιον Kl. T. 8[3], p. 15, 8.—Subst. only as a national name ***the Egyptian*** **Ac 7:24; Hb 11:23** D (both Ex 2:12; cp. Ezk. Trag. 93 [Eus., PE 9, 28]); **Ac 7:28;** 1 Cl 4:10 (both Ex 2:14). Their wisdom **Ac 7:22.** Of a certain unnamed Egyptian **21:38** (cp. Jos., Ant. 20, 171; 172). οἱ Αἰγύπτιοι of the Pharaoh of the Exodus and his army **Hb 11:29.** Of the nation as a whole B 9:6; τὸ κατ' Αἰγυπτίους εὐαγγ. Kl. T. 8[3], p. 4, 14; 15, 19; 16, 5; 9.—M-M.

Αἴγυπτος, ου, ἡ (Hom.+; except for **Ac 7:11;** 1 Cl 25:3; Just., D. 131, 3; Mel., P. 11, 74; 60, 439 [in both Bodm. against Ch.]., always without the art. [W-S. §18, 5d; B-D-F §261, 7]) ***Egypt*** **Mt 2:13f, 15** (Hos 11:1), **19; Ac 2:10; 7:9ff, 34** (Ex 3:7, 10), **39; Hb 3:16; 11:26f;** 1 Cl 4:10; 25:3; 51:5. More fully **Ac 7:36** (Ex 7:3), **40; 13:17; Hb 8:9** (Jer 38:32); **Jd 5;** 1 Cl 51:5 v.l.; 53:2; B 4:8; 14:3 (the last three Ex 32:7; Dt 9:12); B 2:7 (Jer 7:22). Country by metonymy for its people 1 Cl 17:5.—As symbolic name (w. Sodom) of a city; the addition of ὅπου καὶ ὁ κύριος αὐτῶν ἐσταυρώθη shows that Jerusalem is meant **Rv 11:8.**

αἰδέομαι 1 aor. ᾐδέσθην (Hom.+; s. Nägeli 57) 1 aor. mid. ᾐδέσατο (Jdth 9:3 'be ashamed'), mid.-pass. ᾐδέσθην ***respect*** τινά *someone* (Callinus [VII BC], fgm. 1, 2 Diehl[2]; Apollon. Rhod. 4, 796 ἐμέ=me, i.e. Hera; Diod. S. 5, 31, 5 Ἄρης αἰδεῖται τὰς Μούσας) τοὺς προηγουμένους 1 Cl 21:6; *have regard for* (PGissUniv 21, 8; Appian, Maced. 9 §6; Dio Chrys. 71 [21], 13) αἰδέσθητί σου τὴν ἡλικίαν *have some regard for your age* MPol 9:2 (cp. 4 Macc 5:7; Philo, Spec. Leg. 2, 238).—DELG s.v. αἴδομαι. M-M. s.v. αἰδώς.

ἀΐδιος, ον (ἀεί 'always'; Hom. Hymns, Hes. et al.; ins; PSI 1422, 16; Wsd 7:26; 4 Macc 10:15; a favorite w. Philo: Jos., Ant. 4, 178; 17, 152; Just., A II, 11, 5; Tat. 14, 2; Ath.; Mel., P. 2f, 20) ***eternal*** ἡ ἀ. αὐτοῦ (of God) δύναμις **Ro 1:20** (Zoroaster in Philo Bybl.: 790 fgm. 4, 52 Jac. [Eus., PE 1, 10, 52]; 58th letter of Apollonius of Tyana [Philostrat. I 360, 29 K.]; SibOr 5, 66 θεὸς ἀ.). ζωή (Philo, Fug. 97; Tat.14, 2) IEph 19:3; δεσμοῖς ἀ. **Jd 6** (PGM 4, 1466 πυλωρὲ κλείθρων ἀϊδίων).—DELG s.v. αἰών. M-M. TW.

αἰδοῖον, ου, τό (s. αἰδώς; subst. fr. adj. αἰδοῖος, α, ον Hom. et al.; PSI 1180, 53 [II AD]; Ezk 23:20; Tat. 8:2; Ath. Sing. Hdt. et al.; UPZ 77 col. 2, 29 [II BC]; Jos.) ***private part(s)*** Papias (3:2) (s. entry ἀηδής).

αἰδώς, οῦς, ἡ (etym. s. end of entry in DGE; Hom.+; Epict.; OGI 507, 8; PCairMasp 295 III, 22 [V AD]; LXX; TestJud 14:7; Jos., Bell. 2, 325; SibOr 1, 35; Ath. 30, 2). This term expresses the opposite of considering or treating someth. in a common or ordinary manner; a respect for convention.

❶ ***modesty*** of women (Diod. S. 13, 55, 4). With σωφροσύνη: μετὰ αἰ. **1 Ti 2:9** (cp. Jos., Ant. 2, 52; AcPl Ox 6 [Aa I 241, 15]).

❷ *reverence, respect* (Pind. et al.; Plut., Timol. 238 [7, 1]; Jos., Ant. 6, 262; Iren. 1, 8, 2 [Harv. I 70, 1] w. εὐλάβεια [as Philo, Leg. ad Gai. 352; Ath. 30, 2]) **Hb 12:28 v.l.** (cp. Appian, Bell. Civ. 1, 71 §331 αἰδὼς θεῶν).—RSchultz, ΑΙΔΩΣ, diss. Rostock 1910; CEvErffa, ΑΙΔΩΣ: Philol. Suppl. 30, 2, '37; DCairns, Aidōs '93.—B. 1141. DELG s.v. αἴδομαι. M-M (no pap). TW. Spicq.

Αἰθίοψ, οπος, ὁ (Hom.+; ins, pap, LXX; ParJer 3:12; ApcMos 35; Philo, Deus Imm. 174; Joseph.; EpArist 13; SibOr) ***Ethiopian*** (s. Hdt., OxfT index s.v. Αἰθίοπες; on complexion s. Hdt. 2, 22, 3) βασίλισσα Αἰθιόπων **Ac 8:27;** as adj. w. ἀνήρ (Stephan. Byz. s.v. Αἰθίοψ acc. to Favorinus) ibid.; ethnicity is the primary component, cp. ἀνὴρ Ἰουδαῖος **Ac 22:3.**—For lit. s. Κανδάκη.

αἴθριος (Hom., Hymns Apollo 433; Heraclitus fgm. 120 Diels; Hdt., LXX; TestJob 24:3; Joseph.) ***clear, bright*** αἰθρίου ὄντος τοῦ ἀέρος *although the sky was clear* AcPl Ha 5, 6.—DELG s.v. αἴθω.

αἰκία, ίας, ἡ (also -εία, w. var. spellings Aeschyl. et al.; pap; 2 and 3 Macc; Joseph.; Just., D. 34, 8; Ath., R. 71, 9 al.) ***mistreatment, torture,*** w. painful death (Andoc. 1, 138; Polyb. 1, 85, 2; Ps.-Pla., Axioch 372a) 1 Cl 6:1 (w. βάσανος; cp. Jos., Bell. 3, 321). εἰς αἰ. περιβαλεῖν (Lghtf. cj. παραβαλεῖν) *torture* 45:7 (cp. 3 Macc 6:26; EpArist 208). αἰκίαις περιπίπτειν *be tortured, tormented* 51:2.—Frisk s.v. ἀϊκής.

αἴκισμα, ατος, τό (trag. et al.; Lysias 6, 26; Pollux 6, 183) ***mistreatment, torment*** 1 Cl 6:2; (w. μάστιγες) 17:5.—Frisk s.v. ἀϊκής.

αἰκισμός, οῦ, ὁ (since Ctesias [400 BC]; Pollux 8, 79; pap, LXX; Just., A II, 12, 4) ***mistreatment*** (PHal 1, 118 [III BC]; 2 and 4 Macc) (w. κόλασις) *punishment* (Plut., Mor. 8f) εἰς αἰ. τιθέναι=αἰκίζειν *punish* 1 Cl 11:1.—Frisk s.v. ἀϊκής.

Αἰλαμίτης s. Ἐλαμίτης

αἴλουρος, ου, ὁ, ἡ (since Hdt. 2, 66 [αἰέλουρος]) ***cat*** (Hdt., Aristot., Diod. S. 20, 58, 2; Ptolem., Apotel. 3, 9, 2 κυνῶν ἢ αἰλούρων; Aelian; Plut., Mor. 144c; Cyranides p. 59, 13 αἴ. ἤτοι κάττα; EpJer 21) PtK 2 p. 14, 19.—DELG s.v. αἰέλουρος.

αἷμα, ατος, τό (Hom.+)—❶ lit. **blood as basic component of an organism, *blood***—ⓐ of human blood **J 19:34** (PHaupt, Blood and Water: AJP 45, 1924, 53–55; FDölger, AC II 1930, 117ff). ὅταν ἐκ ξύλου αἷ. στάξῃ *when blood drips from a tree* B 12:1 (cp. 4 Esdr 5:5). ῥύσις αἵματος *hemorrhage* (cp. Lev 15:25; 20:18) as a woman's malady **Mk 5:25; Lk 8:43f;** πηγὴ τοῦ αἵ. **Mk 5:29;** θρόμβοι αἵματος **Lk 22:44;** ὕδωρ καὶ αἷμα **J 19:34;** ἱμάτιον βεβαμμένον αἵματι **Rv 19:13.**—Esp. as a principal component of the human body, w. σάρξ; σὰρξ καὶ αἷμα=*human being,* w. strong emphasis on ephemeral character, shortsightedness, and moral weakness (Sir 14:18; 17:31; TestAbr B 13, p. 117, 26 [Stone p. 82]; Philo, Rer. Div. Her. 57. Freq. in rabb. as בָּשָׂר וָדָם, s. Billerb. I 730f; Polyaenus 3, 11, 1 of human beings in contrast to gods: αἷμα καὶ σάρκας ἔχοντες; Herm. fgm. 25, 8b in Stob., Floril. I 461, 12 W.=510, 27 Sc. of souls σαρκὶ καὶ αἵμ. βεβαπτισμέναι) **Mt 16:17; 1 Cor 15:50; Gal 1:16; Eph 6:12.** κοινωνεῖν αἵματος καὶ σαρκός *share in (the) human nature* (of their parents) **Hb 2:14.**—Pl. τὰ αἵματα (pl. in trag.; Polyb. 15, 33, 1; LXX; EpArist 88; 90; Ar. 4, 3; Just., Tat.; Mel., P. 50, 368; B-D-F §141, 6) *descent* ἐξ αἱμάτων γεννηθῆναι (w. ἐκ θελήματος σαρκός, opp. ἐκ θεοῦ)=owe one's descent to the physical nature **J 1:13** (cp. Aeschyl., Choëph. 284 ἐκ τ. πατρῴων αἱμάτων; Lycophron 1249 τῶν Ἡρακλείων ἐκγεγῶτες αἱμάτων; ins [Ramsay, CB I/2, 537 no. 394, 4 τέκνα ἐκ τ. αἵματός μου, cp. p. 472 no. 315 ἀπὸ τοῦ αἵ.]; PLips 28, 16ff [381 AD] υἱὸν ἐξ ἰδίου αἵματος γεννηθέντα. See HCadbury, The Ancient Physiological Notions Underlying J 1:13a, Hb 11:11: Exp. 9th ser., 2, 1924, 430–39). ἐξ ἑνὸς αἵματος *fr. the blood of one person* **Ac 17:26 v.l.** (cp. Musonius, Ep. 1, 10 ἐξ αἵματος; Jos., Ant. 20, 226).

ⓑ of animals **Hb 9:7, 18, 21f, 25.** αἷ. τράγων (cp. Is 1:11) vs. **12, 19;** ταύρων vs. **13;** both in **10:4** and B 2:5; μόσχων **Hb 9:12, 19;** ζῴων τὸ αἷ. **13:11;** πρόσχυσις τοῦ αἵ. **11:28;** cp. αἵματι ῥαντισμοῦ **12:24** (αἵ. ἐξεχεῖν; s. 2a) of the blood offering at the altar (Ex 29:12; Lev 4:17ff; 8:15; 9:9). Its use as food is forbidden (cp. Lev 3:17; 7:26f; 17:10) in the Jerusalem decree **Ac 15:20, 29; 21:25** (representatives of this point of view in Haenchen on Ac 15:21; s. HSchoeps, Theol. u. Gesch. d. Judenchristent. '49, 191–93; others [e.g. GResch; Harnack; Six; Zahn, Ac II 546ff; lit. s.v. πνικτός] on the basis of a 'western' rdg. interpret ἀπέχεσθαι τ. αἵματος as a command not to shed blood; αἷ. act. *shedding of blood* in Paus. Attic. μ, 14; Maximus Tyr. 24, 4k w. σφαγή; Herodian 2, 6, 14; Wsd 14:25 αἷμα κ. φόνος).

❷ fig. ext. of 1: **blood as constituting the life of an individual, *life-blood, blood***—ⓐ the seat of life (Lev 17:11; Wsd 7:2; Jos., Ant. 1, 102) αἷ. ἐκχύννειν or ἐκχέειν *shed blood = kill* (Aeschyl.; Gen 9:6; 37:22; Lev 17:4, 13; 1 Km 25:31 al.; prayers for vengeance fr. Rheneia: Dssm., LO 351ff [LAE 423ff] and SIG 1181, 5f) **Lk 11:50; Ac 22:20; Ro 3:15** (Ps 13:3; Is 59:7); **Rv 16:6;** AcPl Ha 11, 7. αἷ. Ἅβελ, Ζαχαρίου **Mt 23:35; Lk 11:51;** the Galileans **Lk 13:1;** τῶν προφητῶν **Mt 23:30.** ἁγίων καὶ προφητῶν **Rv 16:6; 18:24;** ἁγίων κ. μαρτύρων **17:6.** τῶν δούλων αὐτοῦ **19:2** (4 Km 9:7); cp. **6:10;** Pol 2:1; αἷ. ἀθῷον **Mt 27:4, 24;** GJs 14:1; 23:3 (s. ἀθῷος). αἷ. δίκαιον **Mt 23:35;** AcPl Ha 11, 7. οὔπω μέχρις αἵματος ἀντικατέστητε *you have not yet resisted as far as blood* i.e. so that your blood was shed **Hb 12:4** (cp. Heliod. 7, 8, 2 τῆς μέχρις αἵματος στάσεως). τιμὴ αἵματος *the reward for a bloody deed* (αἷ.=bloody deed, murder Diod. S. 18, 56, 4; Paroem. Gr. I p. 18: Zenobius 1, 47 Αἰσώπειον αἷμα=the murder of Aesop; Pr 1:11) **Mt 27:6** (cp. TestZeb 3:3; UPZ 77 II, 9 λάβε τοὺς χαλκοὺς τοῦ αἵματος). ἀγρὸς αἵματος *a field bought with blood-money* vs. **8;** difft. **Ac 1:19** χωρίον αἵ.=a field soaked w. blood. αἷ. ἐκζητεῖν (oft. LXX) *demand the blood* **Lk 11:50.** ἐκδικεῖν (Dt 32:43; 4 Km 9:7; prayers for vengeance fr. Rheneia, s. above) **Rv 6:10; 19:2.** τὸ αἷμα αὐτοῦ ἐφ' ἡμᾶς **Mt 27:25;** cp. **23:35; Ac 5:28; 18:6** (2 Km 1:16; TestLevi 16:3 τὸ ἀθῷον αἷ. ἐπὶ τῆς κεφαλῆς ὑμῶν ἀναδεχόμενοι.—For a judgment on one's head [**Ac 18:6**] and children [**Mt 27:25;** FLovsky, ETR 62, '87, 343–62; FMatera, The Bible Today 27, '89, 345–50; RSmith, CurTM 17, '90, 421–28; TCargal, NTS 37, '91, 101–12: a double literary sense that recalls Mt 1:21] cp. 2 Km 1:16; Ezk 33:4 and the saying of the Pythia in Aelian, VH 3, 43 ἀλλ' αὐτῶν κεφαλῇσι και ἐν σφετέροισι τέκεσσιν εἰλεῖται); αἷμα αὐτοῖς δέδωκας πιεῖν **Rv 16:6.** καθαρὸς ἀπὸ τοῦ αἵ. πάντων (Sus 46 Theod.) **Ac 20:26.** Also αἵματα 1 Cl 18:14 (Ps 50:16).

ⓑ blood and life as an expiatory sacrifice 1 Cl 55:1.—Esp. of the blood of Jesus (cp. Orig., C. Cels. 1, 66, 12 τὸ ἐπὶ σταυρῷ προχυθὲν αἷ. Ἰη. Χρ.) as a means of expiation ἱλαστήριον … ἐν τῷ αὐτοῦ αἵ. **Ro 3:25.** ἀπολύτρωσις διὰ τοῦ αἵ. αὐτοῦ **Eph 1:7** (**Col 1:14 v.l.**). Of the high-priestly sacrifice of Jesus **Hb 9:12, 14; 10:19;** cp. **13:12; 1J 1:7; Rv 1:5; 5:9;** B 5:1; ῥαντισμὸς αἵ. *sprinkling w. blood* **1 Pt 1:2;** αἷ. τοῦ ἀρνίου **Rv**

7:14; 12:11. ἀμνοῦ **1 Pt 1:19.** As the means of freeing from guilt **Ro 5:9;** 1 Cl 7:4; 12:7; 21:6; 49:6. Hence πιστεύειν εἰς τὸ αἷ. Χρ. ISm 6:1; αἷ. τῆς διαθήκης **Hb 9:20** (Ex 24:8); **10:29; 13:20** (TestBenj 3:8; cp. Ex 24:8). Esp. in the words of institution of the Eucharist (s. διαθήκη 2 and end) **Mt 26:28; Mk 14:24; Lk 22:20; 1 Cor 11:25;** cp. **10:16; J 6:53–55; 1J 5:6, 8;** τοῦ αἵ. τοῦ κυρίου **1 Cor 11:27.** Of association in the Eucharist ποτήριον εἰς ἕνωσιν τοῦ αἵ. αὐτοῦ IPhld 4. Described as bringing about a Christian assembly or congregation **Ac 20:28** (the blood appears to be that of Jesus, God's prized possession, and therefore an expression of superb generosity; on αἵ. τοῦ ἰδίου in this pass. s. Danker, Benefactor 335–36; difft. CDeVine, The Blood of God: CBQ 9, '47, 381–408; s. also JLambrecht, Paul's Farewell-Address at Miletus [Acts 20:17–38], in Les Actes des Apôtres, ed. JKremer '79, 322 n. 54); **Eph 2:13;** cp. εἰρηνοποιήσας διὰ τοῦ αἵ. τοῦ σταυροῦ αὐτοῦ **Col 1:20.** Love descr. as the blood of Jesus ITr 8:1; IRo 7:3, cp. ISm 1:1; αἷ. θεοῦ IEph 1:1 (s. Hdb., and on **Ac 20:28** above).—FRüsche, Blut, Leben u. Seele 1930; AAnwander, D. Blut in rel.-gesch. Schau: TGl 26, '34, 414–27; OSchmitz, D. Opferanschauung d. späteren Judentums u. d. Opferaussagen d. NT 1910; AScott, Christianity acc. to St. Paul 1927, 85ff; JSchneider, D. Passionsmystik d. Pls 1929, 28ff; 120ff; HWindisch, Hdb. Exc. on Hb 9:22 (2d ed. '31; lit. here and JWaszink, RAC II 459–73).

❸ **the (apocalyptic) red color, whose appearance in heaven indicates disaster,** ***blood*** (s. MMüller, ZNW 8, 1907, 290ff; EWunderlich, D. Bed. d. roten Farbe im Kult d. Griechen u. Römer 1925): w. fire and smoke **Ac 2:19** (Jo 3:3). So the world will end δι' αἵματος καὶ πυρός Hv 4, 3, 3. W. fire and hail **Rv 8:7.** Of the color of water vs. **8; 11:6** (Jos., Ant. 3, 17, the water turned to blood is not potable); cp. **16:3f.** Of the color of the moon **Ac 2:20** (Jo 3:4); **Rv 6:12.** The figure 'blood of the grape' (Gen 49:11; Dt 32:14; Sir 39:26) used apocalyptically ἐξῆλθεν αἷ. ἐκ τῆς ληνοῦ **14:20** (cp. Is 63:1–3). On the role of blood with other frightful portents, cp. Appian, Bell. Civ. 2, 36 §144; 4, 4 §14.—On the whole LMorris, JTS n.s. 3, '52, 216–27; LDewar, ibid. 4, '53, 204–8.—B. 206. DELG. M-M. TW. Sv.

αἱματεκχυσία, ας, ἡ (fr. αἷμα and ἐκχέω, s. αἷμα 2a) ***the shedding*** or ***pouring out of blood*** (found only in Christian wr., e.g. Tat. 23, 2; Byz. Chroniclers in Psaltes p. 349, but cp. ἔκχυσις αἵματος 3 Km 18:28; Sir 27:15; Charax of Pergamum [II/III AD]: 103 fgm. 5 Jac.) χωρὶς αἱ. οὐ γίνεται ἄφεσις *without the shedding of blood there is no forgiveness* **Hb 9:22** (blood offered at the altar is the referent; s. TThornton, JTS n.s. 15, '64, 63–65, w. ref. to such passages as Lev 4:7, 18, 25 al.)—TW.

αἱματώδης, ες (αἷμα + -ώδης; Thu. et al.) ***blood-red*** (schol. on Nicander, Ther. 228; Cat. Cod. Astr. VIII/2 p. 174, 3 Ἄρες αἱ.), i.e. dark red Hv 4, 1, 10 (as apocal. color w. black, yellow, and white; s. αἷμα 3); w. πυροειδής (q.v.) *red as fire,* i.e. light red 4, 3, 3.

αἱμορροέω (Hippocr. et al.; Lev 15:33) **to experience a loss of blood,** ***bleed, suffer with hemorrhage*** **Mt 9:20;** AcPl BMM verso 17; Acta Pilati Ea 7 (ASyn. 95, 90).—DELG s.v. ῥέω 971. M-M.

Αἰνέας, ου, ὁ (lit.; ins [e.g. ISyriaW 1929; 2238, also fr. Palestine: SEG VIII, 255—112/111 BC]; pap [Preisigke, Namenbuch]) ***Aeneas*** at Lydia cured of palsy **Ac 9:33f.**—DDD s.v. Aeneas.

αἴνεσις, εως, ἡ (Philod., παρρ. col. 8a, p. 48 [10 Oliv.]; LXX; Philo, Spec. Leg. 1, 224; Iren. 1, 14, 8 [Harv. I 143, 10]) ***praise*** ἀναφέρειν θυσίαν αἰνέσεως *offer a sacrifice of praise* **Hb 13:15** (cp. זֶבַח תּוֹדָה Lev 7:12, 13, 15); cp. 1 Cl 35:12 (Ps 49:23); 52:3 (Ps 49:14); ἀναγγέλλειν τὴν αἴ. τινος *proclaim the praise of someone* 1 Cl 18:15 (Ps 50:17). S. αἰνέω.

αἰνέω fut. αἰνέσω, 1 aor. ᾔνεσα LXX ***to praise*** (so Hom. et al.; LXX; TestSol 12:5; TestAbr, Just. The primary idea: 'express approval' cp. IG IX/1, 119, 8.) in our lit. used only of the praise of God (Diog. L. 1, 39; very oft. LXX; TestAbr B 14, p. 119, 2 [Stone p. 86]; Just., A I, 13, 1, D. 106, 1; PGM 4, 1146) αἰ. τὸν θεόν **Lk 2:13, 20; 19:37; 24:53** D; **Ac 2:47; 3:8f;** cp. MPol 14:3. τὸν κύριον **Ro 15:11** (Ps 116:1). τῷ θεῷ ἡμῶν **Rv 19:5** (the dat. corresp. to לְ w. הוֹדָה and הִלֵּל LXX e.g. Jer 20:13; 1 Ch 16:36; 2 Ch 5:13; B-D-F §187, 4); cp. B 7:1. W. εὐλογεῖν (Da 5:23) **Lk 24:53 v.l.** (s. GKilpatrick in Essays in Memory of GHCMacgregor '65, 19). Of praise of gods by polytheists Dg 2:7 (cp. Judg 16:24 A; Da 5:23). Cp. αἶνος.—M-M. TW.

αἴνιγμα, ατος, τό (Pind., Aeschyl. et al.; LXX, Philo; Jos., C. Ap. 1, 114f; SibOr 3, 812)

❶ lit. **that which requires special acumen to understand because it is expressed in puzzling fashion,** ***riddle*** PtK 4 p. 15, 31. This sense is preferred by some for **1 Cor 13:12:** βλέπομεν δι' ἐσόπτρου ἐν αἰνίγματι (ἐν αἰν. as Athen. 452a; REB: *puzzling reflections;* NRSV *dimly* [= indistinctly] but mg. *in a riddle*). Hugedé may offer the better explanation (see 2 below, at end).

❷ **indirect mode of communication.** In the context of mirror imagery α. signifies *indirect image,* and ἐν αἰνίγματι functions as an idiom meaning ***indirectly.*** βλέπομεν δι' ἐσόπτρου ἐν αἰνίγματι then gives the sense *we see by reflection as in a mirror* with emphasis on anticipation of direct personal encounter (cp. Num 12:8 of direct as opp. to oblique communication; Plut., Mor. 382a αἴ. τοῦ θείου refers to inanimate or incorporeal things such as numerals as 'mirrors' or 'models' for understanding divine matters. Cp. Mor. 12d of Pythagorean maxims, which communicate αἰνίγμασιν=speak in circumlocutions, i.e. 'ambiguously' or with 'double sense'; 370f contrasts Plato's earlier presentations δι' αἰνιγμῶν οὐδὲ συμβολικῶς w. his later use of κύρια ὀνόματα 'plain terms'. On the mirror imagery cp. Mor. 672e.—αἴνιγμα=intimation: Sallust. c. 6 p. 12, 10).—NHugedé, La Métaphore du miroir dans 1 et 2 Cor '57; other lit. s.v. ἀγάπη 1aα and ἔσοπτρον.—DELG s.v. αἶνος. TW. Sv.

αἶνος, ου, ὁ (Hom. et al.; ins, LXX [PsSol 3:1 for καινός]. In var. senses, incl. 'story, decree, eulogy'; cp. αἰνέω.) ***praise*** αἶνον διδόναι τῷ θεῷ *to praise God* **Lk 18:43;** 2 Cl 1:5; 9:10. καταρτίζεσθαι αἶνον *bring praise* for oneself **Mt 21:16** (Ps 8:3).—DELG. M-M. TW. Sv.

Αἰνών, ἡ indecl. ***Aenon*** place where John the Baptist was baptizing **J 3:23.** Ancient church tradition (Eus., Onom. p. 41) places it in the Jordan valley ca. 13 km south of Scythopolis (Bethshan).—TZahn, NKZ 18, 1907, 593–608; CKopp, Holy Places of the Gospels, '63, 129–37; and s. Σαλίμ.

αἴξ, αἰγός, ὁ, ἡ ***goat*** (Hom.+; ins, pap, LXX; TestJob 15:4 ἐρίφους αἰγῶν; GrBar 2:3; Philo, Omn. Prob. Lib. 30; Jos., Ant. 6, 217; 295; TestZeb 4:9; SibOr 3, 627; Just.) ἔριφος ἐξ αἰγῶν (Gen 38:20) **Lk 15:29** D.—B. 165. DELG.

αἵρεσις, έσεως, ἡ (Aeschyl., Hdt. et al.; a term used in H. Gk. esp. in ref. to political preference or group loyalty as in SIG 675, 28 [II BC], where αἵ. is used in bonam partem, common in diplomatic correspondence: γίνωνται δὲ καὶ ἄλλοι ζηλωταὶ τῆς αὐτῆς αἱρέσεως).

❶ **a group that holds tenets distinctive to it,** ***sect, party, school, faction*** (of schools of philos. Diod. S. 2, 29, 6; Dionys.

Hal., Comp. Verb. 2 τ. Στωϊκῆς αἱ.; Diog. L. 1, 18 and 19, al.; Iambl., Vi. Pyth. 34, 241; Orig., C. Cels. 4, 45, 32; HDiels, Doxographi Graeci 1879, index; Aristobulus in Eus., PE 13, 12, 10=Denis 224, col. 1, 13; Holladay 196; s. Nägeli 51; Poland 154).

ⓐ of the Sadducees, as *sect* **Ac 5:17** (Jos., Ant. 13, 171; 20, 199). Of the Pharisees **15:5** (Jos., Vi. 10; 12; 191 al.). The latter described as ἡ ἀκριβεστάτη αἵ. τῆς ἡμετέρας θρησκείας *the strictest sect of our religion* **26:5.** Of the Christians αἵρεσις τῶν Ναζωραίων **24:5;** cp. vs. **14** and **28:22.** The last three exx. incline toward sense b.

ⓑ in the later sense, *heretical sect* (Iren. 1, 11, 1 [Harv. I 98, 5]; Orig., C. Cels. 5, 54, 9) IEph 6:2; ITr 6:1; Epil Mosq 1. Cp. also the agraphon from Justin, Trypho 35 in JJeremias, Unknown Sayings 59–61. In general, WBauer, Rechtgläubigkeit u. Ketzerei im Aeltesten Christentum '34, 2d ed. w. supplement, GStrecker, '64; MMeinertz, Σχίσμα und αἵρεσις im NT: BZ 1, '57, 114–18.

ⓒ w. negative connotation, *dissension, a faction* **1 Cor 11:19; Gal 5:20.**

❷ **that which distinguishes a group's thinking, *opinion, dogma*** (Philo, Plant. 151 κυνικὴ αἵ.) αἱ. ἀπωλείας *destructive opinions* **2 Pt 2:1** (perh. also in sense 1b).—*Way of thinking* (UPZ 20, 26 [163 BC]; 144, 10 al.) αἵ. ἔχειν *hold to a way of thinking* Hs 9, 23, 5 (*inclination* is also possible: GDI 2746, 14; 2800, 7, both from Delphi).—DELG s.v. αἱρέω. M-M. TW. Sv.

αἱρετίζω fut. αἱρετιῶ LXX; 1 aor. ᾑρέτισα; pf. ᾑρέτικα LXX (Hippocr. et al.; SIG 1042, 2; UPZ 109, 4 [98 BC] perh. Babrius 61, 5 [L-P.]) act. ***choose*** **Mt 12:18** (Hg 2:23; perh. in the specif. sense 'adopt' as 1 Ch 28:6; Mal 3:17; Kaibel 252).—Mid. (since Ctesias: 688 fgm. 13, 10 Jac.; LXX) *choose for oneself* w. inf. foll. (1 Macc 9:30) 2 Cl 14:1.—DELG s.v. αἱρέω. M-M. TW.

αἱρετικός, ή, όν (in Ps.-Pla., Definit. 412a; Aelian, NA 6, 59; Hierocles Stoic. [I/II AD] Eth. 9, 5; here 7 and Diog. L. 7, 126 also the adv.; subst. pl. οἱ αἱ. Iren. 5, 13, 2 [Harv. II 356, 8] al.) **pert. to causing divisions, *factious, division-making.*** ἄνθρωπος αἱ. *division-maker* **Tit 3:10** (s. αἵρεσις 1b, c).—TW.

αἱρετός, ή, όν comp. αἱρετώτερος ***desirable*** (so Hdt. et al.; LXX; Ath. R. 75, 23; Sb 6996, 25 [II AD]) αἱρετώτερον ἦν αὐτοῖς w. inf. foll. (X., Cyr. 3, 3, 51; Diod. S. 14, 45, 3; Polyaenus 4, 6, 6; Aesop, Fab. 261 P.=273 H.; 168 H-H.; 223 Ch.; cp. Sextus 362) *it would have been better for them* Hv 4, 2, 6.—DELG s.v. αἱρέω.

αἱρέω fut. mid. αἱρήσομαι; 2 aor. εἱλόμην and εἱλάμην **2 Th 2:13;** Hs 5, 6, 6; α-forms in Tdf., W-H, M., Bov., N.; o-forms in V., t.r.; s. also ἀν-, ἐξαιρέω (Hom.+).

❶ act. ***take*** καρπὸν αἱρῶν *if you pick fruit* Dg 12:8 (text uncertain; s. Bihlmeyer ad loc.).

❷ mid. (so exclus. in NT, Tat., Ath.) ***choose*** (s. Nägeli 19f) w. double acc. (Hdt. 1, 96; Jos., Ant. 9, 106) Hs 5, 6, 6. τινὰ εἴς τι *someone for someth.* **2 Th 2:13.** W. acc. *prefer* (Diod. S. 17, 29, 3; 17, 48, 2; Jos., Bell. 6, 330) **Phil 1:22;** likew. μᾶλλον αἱ. w. inf. foll. and ἤ w. inf. (Pla., Ap. 38e; Diod. S. 11, 11, 1 μᾶλλον εἵλοντο τελευτᾶν ἢ ζῆν; Περὶ ὕψους 33, 5; Appian, Bell. Civ. 4, 117 §491) **Hb 11:25.**—B. 743. DELG. M-M. TW.

αἴρω fut. ἀρῶ; 1 aor. ἦρα (ἧρα v.l.; TestAbr; GrBar); pf. ἦρκα **Col 2:14.** Pass.: 1 fut. ἀρθήσομαι; 1 aor. ἤρθην; pf. ἦρμαι **J 20:1;** Hs 9, 5, 4 (Hom.+; he, like some later wr., has ἀείρω).

❶ **to raise to a higher place or position, *lift up, take up, pick up***—ⓐ lit., of stones (Dio Chrys. 12 [13], 2) **J 8:59** (cp. Jos., Vi. 303); **Rv 18:21;** Hs 9, 4, 7. Fish **Mt 17:27;** coffin 1 Cl 25:3; hand (X., An. 7, 3, 6) **Rv 10:5** (Dt 32:40). Hands, in prayer 1 Cl 29:1 (Ael. Aristid. 24, 50 K.=44 p. 840 D.; 54 p. 691; PUps 8 p. 30 no. 14 [pre-Christian] Θεογένης αἴρει τὰς χεῖρας τῷ Ἡλίῳ; Sb 1323 [II AD] θεῷ ὑψίστῳ καὶ πάντων ἐπόπτῃ καὶ Ἡλίῳ καὶ Νεμέσεσι αἴρει Ἀρσεινόη ἄωρος τὰς χεῖρας). But αἴ. τὴν χεῖρα ἀπό τινος *withdraw one's hand fr. someone=renounce* or *withdraw fr. someone* B 19:5; D 4:9. Of snakes *pick up* **Mk 16:18.** κλίνην **Mt 9:6.** κλινίδιον **Lk 5:24.** κράβαττον **Mk 2:9, 11f; J 5:8–12.** Of a boat that is pulled on board **Ac 27:17.** Of a spirit that carries a person away Hv 2, 1, 1 (cp. TestAbr B 10 p. 115, 11 [Stone p. 78] of angels). Take up a corpse to carry it away AcPt Ox 849 verso, 8 (cp. TestAbr A 20 p.103, 20 [Stone p. 54]). αἴ. σύσσημον *raise a standard* ISm 1:2 (Is 5:26); αἴ. τινὰ τῶν ἀγκώνων *take someone by one's arms* Hv 1, 4, 3. For **Ac 27:13** s. 6 below.—Pass. 2 Cl 7:4. ἄρθητι (of mountains) *arise* **Mt 21:21; Mk 11:23.** ἤρθη νεκρός **Ac 20:9.**

ⓑ fig. αἴ. τοὺς ὀφθαλμοὺς ἄνω *look upward* (in prayer, as Ps 122:1; Is 51:6 al.) **J 11:41.** For **10:24** s. 5 below. αἴ. φωνήν *raise one's voice, cry out loudly* (1 Km 11:4; 30:4; 2 Km 3:32 al.) **Lk 17:13.** πρός τινα **Ac 4:24.**

❷ **to lift up and move from one place to another**

ⓐ ***take/carry (along)*** lit. w. obj. acc. σταυρόν **Mt 16:24; 27:32; Mk 8:34; 15:21; Lk 9:23.** ζυγόν (La 3:27) **Mt 11:29.** τινὰ ἐπὶ χειρῶν **4:6; Lk 4:11** (both Ps 90:12). Pass. **Mk 2:3.** αἴ. τι εἰς ὁδόν *take someth. along for the journey* **6:8; Lk 9:3,** cp. **22:36.** Of a gambler's winnings **Mk 15:24.**—Fig. δόξαν ἐφ' ἑαυτὸν αἴ. *claim honor for oneself* B 19:3.

ⓑ ***carry away, remove*** lit. ταῦτα ἐντεῦθεν **J 2:16** (ins [218 BC]: ΕΛΛΗΝΙΚΑ 7, '34, p. 179, 15 ταῦτα αἱρέσθω; Just., D. 56, 3 σκευῶν ἀρθέντων). Crucified body of Jesus **19:38;** cp. **vs. 31; 20:2, 13, 15;** of John the Baptist **Mt 14:12; Mk 6:29.** A stone from a grave-opening **J 11:39, 41;** pass. **20:1.** οἱ αἴροντες οὐκ ἀνέφερον *those who took something* (a mouthful) *brought nothing* (to their mouth) GJs 18:2 (not pap). τὸ περισσεῦον *the remainder* **Mt 14:20; 15:37;** cp. **Lk 9:17.** περισσεύματα **Mk 8:8.** κλάσματα *fragments* **6:43;** *baskets* **8:19f.** ζώνην *take off* **Ac 21:11;** *take:* τὸ σόν *what belongs to you* **Mt 20:14;** τὰ ἀρκοῦντα *what was sufficient for him* Hs 5, 2, 9. αἴ. τι ἐκ τῆς οἰκίας *get someth. fr. the house* **Mk 13:15;** cp. vs.**16** and **Mt 24:17;** cp. **24:18; Lk 17:31;** take (a body) from a tomb **J 20:2, 13, 15;** *take* τινὰ ἐκ τοῦ κόσμου **17:15.**

❸ **to take away, remove, or seize control without suggestion of lifting up, *take away, remove.*** By force, even by killing: abs. ἆρον, ἆρον *away, away* (with him)! **J 19:15** (cp. POxy 119, 10 [Dssm., LO 168; LAE 188 n. 22]; Philo, In Flacc. 144; ἆρον twice also La 2:19 v.l., in different sense). W. obj. αἶρε τοῦτον **Lk 23:18;** cp. **Ac 21:36; 22:22.** ἆραι τὸν μάγον AcPl Ha 4, 35f; αἶρε τοὺς ἀθέους (s. ἄθεος 2a) MPol 3:2; 9:2 (twice); *sweep away* **Mt 24:39;** ὡς μελλούσης τῆς πόλεως αἴρεσθαι *as though the city were about to be destroyed* AcPl Ha 5, 17; cp. κόσμος ἔρεται (=αἴρεται) ἐμ πυρί 2, 26f. W. the connot. of force or injustice or both (Epict. 1, 18, 13; PTebt 278, 27; 35; 38 [I AD]; SSol 5:7): τὸ ἱμάτιον **Lk 6:29;** cp. vs. **30;** D 1:4. τὴν πανοπλίαν *all his weapons* **Lk 11:22;** τάλαντον **Mt 25:28;** cp. **Lk 19:24.** Fig. τὴν κλεῖδα τῆς γνώσεως **11:52.** Pass.: **Mt 13:12; Mk 4:25; Lk 8:18; 19:26.** *Conquer, take over* (Diod. S. 11, 65, 3 πόλιν) τόπον, ἔθνος **J 11:48.** For **Lk 19:21f** s. 4 below. αἴ. τὴν ψυχὴν ἀπό τινος **J 10:18** (cp. EFascher, Deutsche Theol. '41, 37–66).—Pass. ἀπὸ τῆς γῆς **Ac 8:33b** (Is 53:8; Just., D. 110, 6). ἀφ' ὑμῶν ἡ βασιλεία **Mt 21:43.**—Of Satan τὸν λόγον τὸν ἐσπαρμένον εἰς αὐτούς **Mk 4:15;** cp. **Lk 8:12.** τὴν χαρὰν ὑμῶν οὐδεὶς αἴρει ἀφ' ὑμῶν *no one will deprive you of your joy* **J 16:22.** ἐξ ὑμῶν πᾶσαν ὑπόκρισιν *rid ourselves of all pretension* B 21:4; ἀπὸ τῆς καρδίας τὰς διψυχίας αἴ. *put away* *doubt fr. their heart* Hv 2, 2, 4. αἴ. ἀφ' ἑαυτοῦ *put away fr. oneself* Hm 9:1; 10, 1, 1; 10, 2, 5; 12, 1, 1. αἴ. ἐκ (τοῦ) μέσου *remove, expel* (fr. among) (Epict. 3, 3, 15; Plut., Mor. 519d; BGU 388 II, 23 ἆρον ταῦτα ἐκ τοῦ μέσου; PHib 73, 14; Is 57:2) **1 Cor 5:2** (v.l. ἐξαρθῇ); a bond, note, certificate of indebtedness αἴ. ἐκ τοῦ μέσου *destroy* **Col 2:14.** Of branches *cut off* **J 15:2.** Prob. not intrans., since other exx. are lacking, but w. 'something' supplied αἴρει τὸ πλήρωμα ἀπὸ τοῦ ἱματίου *the patch takes someth. away fr. the garment* **Mt 9:16;** cp. **Mk 2:21.** *Remove, take away, blot out* (Eur., El. 942 κακά; Hippocr., Epid. 5, 49, p. 236 pain; cp. Job 6:2; IG II, 467, 81 ζημίας; Epict. 1, 7, 5 τὰ ψευδῆ; SIG 578, 42 τ. νόμον; Pr 1:12; EpArist 215; Just., D. 117, 3) τὴν ἁμαρτίαν τ. κόσμου **J 1:29, 36 v.l.; 1 J 3:5** (Is 53:12 Aq., s. PKatz, VetusT 8, '58, 272; cp. 1 Km 15:25; 25:28). Pass. **Ac 8:33a** (Is 53:8); **Eph 4:31.** Fig. *take,* in order to make someth. out of the obj. **1 Cor 6:15.**

❹ **to make a withdrawal in a commercial sense,** ***withdraw, take,*** ext. of 2 αἴρεις ὃ οὐκ ἔθηκας **Lk 19:21f** (banking t.t.: JBernays, Ges. Abh. I 1885, 272f; JSmith, JTS 29, 1928, 158).

❺ **to keep in a state of uncertainty about an outcome,** ***keep someone in suspense,*** fig. ext. of 1 αἴ. τὴν ψυχήν τινος **J 10:24** (Nicetas, De Manuele Comm. 3, 5 [MPG CXXXIX 460a]: ἕως τίνος αἴρεις, Σαρακηνέ, τὰς ψυχὰς ἡμῶν; The expr. αἴ. τὴν ψυχήν w. different mng. Ps 24:1; 85:4; 142:8; Jos., Ant. 3, 48).

❻ **to raise a ship's anchor for departure,** ***weigh anchor, depart,*** ext. of 1, abs. (cp. Thu. et al.; Philo, Mos. 1, 85; Jos., Ant. 7, 97; 9, 229; 13, 86 ἄρας ἀπὸ τῆς Κρήτης κατέπλευσεν εἰς Κιλίκιαν) **Ac 27:13.**—Rydbeck 155f; B. 669f. DELG s.v. 1 ἀείρω. M-M. TW.

αἰσθάνομαι fut. αἰσθήσῃ Pr 24:14, αἰσθηθήσεσθε Is 33:11, αἰσθανθήσεται 49:26; 2 aor. ᾐσθόμην, subj. αἴσθωμαι (Aeschyl.+).

❶ **to be aware of someth. by means of the senses,** ***notice*** (Cleanthes [s. 2, end]; Appian, Liby. 120 §568; TestJud 15:1; Tat. 17, 4) Dg 2:8 (cp. EpJer 19; 23).

❷ **to have the capacity to discern and therefore understand what is not readily comprehensible,** ***understand*** (X., Cyr. 1, 5, 4 al.; Pr 17:10; 24:14; Ar.; Iren. 1, 4, 1 [Harv. I 32, 7]) ῥῆμα **Lk 9:45** (opp. ἀγνοέω). γνώμην B 2:9. W. ὅτι foll. (Ar. 12, 8; Dio Chrys. 52 [69], 2; Is 49:26) 6:18. αἰσθάνεσθε *(you) notice* w. indir. quest. foll. (Epict. 1, 6, 41; 3, 23, 16) 11:8; cp. 13:3.—Both meanings are included by Cleanthes [IV/III BC] Stoic. 1, p. 136, 1 (in Diog. L. 7, 172) in wordplay when he says to his pupil: οὐκ αἰσθάνομαι, ὅτι αἰσθάνῃ; '(Why, then, do) I not apprehend that you comprehend?'—B. 1020. DELG s.v. 1. ἀΐω. M-M. TW. Sv.

αἴσθησις, εως, ἡ (Pre-Socr., Eur. et al.; Epict., Herm. Wr.; LXX, esp. Pr; Philo; Jos., Bell. 7, 69, C. Ap. 2, 178; Test12Patr; SibOr fgm. 3, 23; Just.; Mel., fgm. 2; Ath., R. 56, 17 al.)

❶ **capability of being affected by external stimuli,** ***perception, sensation*** (EpArist 213) Dg 2:9 (w. λογισμός 'reasoning').

❷ **capacity to understand,** ***discernment*** (cp. Iren. 1, 15, 2 [Harv. I 149, 3]) denoting moral understanding (cp. αἰσθητήριον and ABonhöffer, Epikt. u. d. NT 1911, 105), beside ἐπίγνωσις, 'insight': περισσεύειν ἐν . . . πάσῃ αἰσθήσει εἰς τὸ . . . *abound in insight and thorough discernment, so that . . .* **Phil 1:9.**—B 1020. DELG s.v. 1. ἀΐω. M-M. TW. Sv.

αἰσθητήριον, ου, τό (Hippocr. et al.; Herm. Wr. 7, 3; Jer 4:19; 4 Macc 2:22; Philo) lit. 'organ of sense'; fig. **capacity for discernment,** ***faculty,*** of the ability to make moral decisions (s. PLinde, De Epicuri Vocab., Bresl. Philol. Abh. X/3, 1906, 32) τὰ αἰσθητήρια γεγυμνασμένα ἔχειν πρὸς διάκρισιν καλοῦ τε και κακοῦ *have one's faculties trained to distinguish betw. good and evil* **Hb 5:14** (cp. Galen, De Dign. Puls. 3, 2 vol. VIII 892 K. αἰσθητήριον ἔχειν γεγυμνασμένον; Iren. 4, 38, 2 [Harv. II 294, 12] appears to have **Hb 5:14** in mind).—DELG s.v. 1. ἀΐω. TW.

αἰσχροκερδής, ές (since Eur., And. 451, Hdt. 1, 187; Philo, Sacr. Abel. 32 end; TestJud 16:1) **shamelessly greedy for money,** ***avaricious, fond of dishonest gain*** (cp. Lysias 12, 19) **1 Ti 3:8** (vs. **3 v.l.**); **Tit 1:7** (also in a catalogue of vices Ptolem., Apotel. 3, 14, 15).—DELG s.v. αἶσχος. Spicq.

αἰσχροκερδῶς adv. fr. αἰσχροκερδής ***in fondness for dishonest gain, greedily*** (opp. προθύμως) **1 Pt 5:2.**

αἰσχρολογία, ας, ἡ (X. et al.; Polyb., Diod. S., Plut., Epict.; POxy 410, 77) **speech of a kind that is generally considered in poor taste,** ***obscene speech, dirty talk*** (Aristot., EN 4, 8 [1128a], contrasts the preference for obscenity in older drama with the more refined taste of later times and argues that αἰ., obscenity, can be expected from those of servile nature but not from a cultured gentleman. Clem. Al., Paed. 2, 6, 52 αἰ. εἰκότως ἂν καλοῖτο ἡ περὶ τῶν τῆς κακίας ἔργων λογοποιία, οἷον τὸ περὶ μοιχείας διαλέγεσθαι ἢ παιδεραστίας = αἰ. might properly be defined as story-telling involving such unseemly deeds as adultery or pederasty. αἰσχρός=obscene: Ps.-Demetr. Eloc. 151). Obscene expressions would also be used to flavor derogatory remarks (s. Aristot. above); hence the rendering *scurrilous talk* (Polyb. 8, 11, 8; 31, 6, 4; BGU 909, 11f) is pertinent **Col 3:8,** esp. since βλασφημία (='defamation', s. βλ. a) immediately precedes. The gener. sense *dirty talk* fits D 5:1, which could apply to ribald stories as well as scurrilous talk.—AWikenhauser, BZ 8, 1910, 270. DELG s.v. αἶσχος. M-M. Sv.

αἰσχρολόγος, ου, ὁ (Pollux 6, 123; 8, 80f) ***a foulmouthed person*** (s. αἰσχρολογία) D 3:3.—M-M. s.v. αἰσχρολογία.

αἰσχρός, ά, όν (in var. senses from 'ugly' in an external sense to 'base' as in moral deformity Hom.+; also αἰσχρότερα Ar. 11, 7; αἴσχιστον Just., A II, 7, 3; αἰσχρῶς Just., A I, 27, 1; D. 90, 1. A term esp. significant in honor-shame oriented society; gener. in ref. to that which fails to meet expected moral and cultural standards [opp. καλός]) **pert. to being socially or morally unacceptable,** ***shameful, base*** αἰσχρὸν κέρδος *dishonest gain* **Tit 1:11** (Theognis 466; Polyb. 6, 46, 3; s. αἰσχροκερδής, -ῶς). ῥῆμα (PFlor 309, 4) Hv 1, 1, 7. Neut. in the expr. αἰσχρόν ἐστί τινι w. inf. foll. *it is disgraceful for someone* (cp. 4 Macc 16:17; Jdth 12:12): for a woman to cut her hair **1 Cor 11:6;** to speak in a meeting **14:35.** Without the person **Eph 5:12.** Also the pl. αἰσχρά (sc. ἐστιν) 1 Cl 47:6 (for the doubling cp. Demosth. 25, 28 μιαρόν, μιαρὸν τὸ θηρίον; Caecil. Calact., fgm. 61 p. 42f; Maximus Tyr. 41, 3a; B-D-F §493, 1; Rob. 1200).—B. 1195. DELG s.v. αἶσχος. M-M. TW. Sv.

αἰσχρότης, ητος, ἡ (range of sense like αἰσχρός: Pla., Gorg. 525a; Artem. 4, 2 p. 204, 8) **behavior that flouts social and moral standards,** ***shamefulness, obscenity,*** abstr. for concr.= αἰσχρολογία (q.v.) **Eph 5:4** (KKuhn, NTS 7, '61, 339 [Qumran]).—TW.

αἰσχύνη, ης, ἡ (Theognis, Aeschyl. et al.; pap, LXX; En 13:5; PsSol 9:6; TestLevi 15:2; Ar. 13:5; Just., A I, 16, 3; Ath. 1, 4; Mel., P. 68, 483).

❶ **a sensitivity respecting possibility of dishonor,** ***modesty, shame*** a feeling that one has (Aristoxenus, fgm. 42a; Diod. S. 2,

4, 3; Plut., Mor. 248b; UPZ 70, 25 [II BC]; PGM 17a, 8; PsSol 9:6; En 13:5 ἀπὸ αἰ.; Jos., Ant. 5, 147) τὸ τῆς αἰσχύνης ἔνδυμα πατεῖν prob. to throw off and *tread under foot the garment of shame* (which men have worn since the awakening of modesty, i.e. the fall, Gen 3:7, cp. 2:25) GEg 252, 57 (cp. Mel., P. 68, 483 τὸν θάνατον ἐνδύσας αἴσχύνην). τὰ κρυπτὰ τῆς αἰ. *what one conceals fr. a feeling of shame* **2 Cor 4:2.** *Modesty, reverence* (w. φόβος) of slaves toward masters D 4:11; B 19:7 (cp. X., Cyr. 6, 1, 35; Soph, Ajax 1079; Demosth. 25, 24).

❷ **an experience of ignominy that comes to someone,** ***shame, disgrace*** (Ath. 1:4; Diod. S. 2, 23, 2; Appian, Samn. 4 §11; PEleph 1, 6; PTebt 104, 30; POxy 471, 78; Sir 25:22; EpArist 206; Philo; TestLevi 15:2): ἡ αἰ. τῆς γυμνότητος *shameful nakedness* **Rv 3:18.** καταφρονεῖν αἰσχύνης *disdain the shame* **Hb 12:2.** ἡ δόξα ἐν τῇ αἰσχύνῃ αὐτῶν *they find their glory in that which causes them shame* **Phil 3:19.** μετὰ αἰσχύνης *in disgrace* (Demosth. 20, 16; Polyb. 3, 81, 6; 1 Esdr 8:74; Philo, Det. Pot. Ins. 51; Jos., Ant. 12, 179) **Lk 14:9.**

❸ **commission of someth. shameful,** ***a shameful deed,*** pl. (Eur., Herc. 1423; Isocr. 14, 50; Aeschin. 1, 154; Jos., Ant. 4, 260) ἐπαφρίζειν τὰς αἰ. *casting up their shameful deeds like* (waves casting up) *foam* **Jd 13.**—MKlopfenstein, Scham u. Schande nach d. AT, ’72.—B. 1141. DELG s.v. αἶσχος. M-M. TW.

αἰσχυντηρός, ά, όν (Pla. et al.; Sir 26:15; 32:10; 41:27) **pert. to having regard for decency,** ***modest*** (w. τρυφερός, πραΰς, ἡσύχιος) of the righteous angel Hm 6, 2, 3.—DELG s.v. αἶσχος.

αἰσχύνω in our lit. only mid. and pass.; impf. ᾐσχυνόμην; 1 fut. αἰσχυνθήσομαι; 1 aor. pass. ᾐσχύνθην LXX, subj. αἰσχυνθῶ (Hom.+; ins, pap, LXX, Test12Patr; w. ptc. foll. Just., D. 123, 4).

❶ **to have a sense of shame,** ***be ashamed*** (SIG 1168, 122; UPZ 62, 27 [161 BC] οὐκέτι ἥκει πρὸς ἐμὲ αἰσχυνθείς; Philo, Spec. Leg. 1, 321; Did., Gen. 84, 28) w. inf. foll. (Aeschyl., Hdt.; UPZ 62, 24; Sir 4:26; 22:25; Sus 11 Theod.; Jos., Ant. 13, 327) ἐπαιτεῖν **Lk 16:3.** μετ’ αὐτῶν μένειν Hs 9, 11, 3. ἐξ αὐτῶν λέγεσθαι *be called one of them* IRo 9:2. Abs. (Gen 2:25) **1 Pt 3:16** P[72]; **4:16;** IEph 11:1 (perh. *be reverent*). αἰσχύ(ν)|θω[μεν] *let us be ashamed* (of criticizing Mary) GMary 463, 25–26. ὅταν ἐκδύσησθε καὶ μὴ αἰσχυνθῆτε *when you shall be stripped and not be ashamed* Ox 655, 22f (ASyn. 67, 35).

❷ **to experience shame,** ***be put to shame, be disgraced*** i.e. (as LXX for בּוֹשׁ) be disappointed in a hope (opp. παρρησία) **Phil 1:20; 2 Cor 10:8.** ἀπό τινος (Is 1:29 v.l.; Jer 12:13; cp. Sir 41:17) *before someone* **1J 2:28.**—DELG s.v. αἶσχος. M-M. s.v. αἰσχύνομαι. TW.

αἰτέω impv. αἴτει IPol 2:2; fut. αἰτήσω; 1 aor. ᾔτησα; pf. ᾔτηκα **1J 5:15.** Mid.: impv. αἰτοῦ IPol 1:3; impf. ᾐτούμην; fut. αἰτήσομαι; 1 aor. ᾐτησάμην, impv. αἴτησαι (Hom.+) **to ask for, with a claim on receipt of an answer,** ***ask, ask for, demand*** (without any real distinction betw. act. and mid.: the distinc. betw. act. ['ask' outright] and mid. ['ask' as a loan] found by ancient grammarians has only very limited validity for our lit. [B-D-F §316, 2; Mlt. 160f]; cp. **Js 4:2f,** where they seem to be used interchangeably) w. acc. of person or thing asked for (Lucian, Dial. Mer. 7, 2 αἰ. τὸ δίδραχμον) ἰχθύν **Mt 7:10;** τὸ σῶμα τοῦ Ἰησοῦ **27:58** (Appian, Syr. 63 §335 αἰτήσας τὸ σῶμα, i.e. for burial); **Mk 15:43; Lk 23:52;** πινακίδιον **Lk 1:63;** εἰρήνην **Ac 12:20;** φῶτα **16:29;** σημεῖα **1 Cor 1:22.** τὸν Βαραββᾶν **Mt 27:20** (Appian, Bell. Civ. 4, 18 §71 and 72; Synes., Provid. 2, 3 p. 121c Ὄσιριν ᾔτουν=they asked for O.); cp. **Mk 15:6 v.l.** (s. παραιτέομαι 1a); βασιλέα (Jos., Ant. 6, 88) **Ac 13:21.** Gener. τί **Mk 6:24; 10:38; Mt 20:22.** ὅ **1J 3:22.** αἰτῆσαι τὴν κεφαλὴν Ἰωάννου **Mk 6:24 v.l.** πράγματος οὗ ἐὰν αἰτήσωνται (w. attraction of the relative) *for which they wish to ask* **Mt 18:19,** cp. **Eph 3:20** (s. Judg 8:26). W. acc. of the thing and indication of the purpose αἰ. τι πρός τι: αἰ. τὸ σῶμα τοῦ κυρίου πρὸς ταφήν GPt 2:3; τινί τι αἰ. *pray for someth. for someone* IRo 3:2. W. acc. of the pers. who is asked **Mt 5:42; 6:8; 7:11; Lk 6:30; 11:13; J 4:10; Ac 13:28.** W. double acc. *ask someone for someth.* (Hom. et al.; Diod. S. 14, 108, 1; Eunap., Vi. Soph. p. 31 αἰ. τοὺς θεούς τι; PFay 109, 12; PGM 4, 777; Josh 14:12; 1 Esdr 6:11; Jos., Ant. 12, 24; Just., A I, 61, 2, D. 105, 3) **Mk 6:22f** (Diog. L. 6, 38 αἴτησόν με ὃ θέλεις [Alex. to Diogenes]; Aesop, Fab. 287b H.=235b Ch. αὐτῇ δοῦναι, ὃ ἂν αἰτήσῃ); **10:35; J 11:22; 15:16; 16:23; Mt 7:9; Lk 11:11;** cp. vs. **12;** ApcPt Rainer (s. παρέχω end). αἰ. τινὰ λόγον *demand an accounting fr. someone, call someone to account* (Pla., Pol. 285e; cp. BGU 747, 21) **1 Pt 3:15.** τὶ ἀπό τινος *request someth. fr. someone* (Plut., Galba 1062 [20, 6]) **Mt 20:20; 1J 5:15** (both w. παρά as v.l.); cp. **Lk 12:20 v.l.** τὶ παρά τινος (Appian, Bell. Civ. 3, 7 §23; Apollon. Paradox. 5; Paradoxogr. Vat. 43 αἰτεῖται παρὰ τῶν θεῶν οὐδέν; PFay 121, 12ff; PGM 12, 277; oft. LXX; Jos., Ant. 13, 63; Just., A I, 12, 5) *alms* **Ac 3:2.** Abs. αἴτησαι παρ’ ἐμοῦ *ask me* **13:33** D; 1 Cl 36:4 (both Ps 2:8); Hs 5, 4, 5; cp. Hm 9:1 (text uncertain), 2, 4; **J 4:9; Ac 9:2; Js 1:5.** αἰ. χάριν *ask a favor* B 21:7; αἰτούμενοι χάριν κατ’ αὐτοῦ *they requested a favor against him* i.e. one directed against him (Paul) **Ac 25:3;** αἰτούμενοι κατ’ αὐτοῦ καταδίκην *asking for his conviction* vs. **15.** αἰ. περί τινος *pray for someone* IRo 8:3. W. the manner of asking more exactly described: κακῶς **Js 4:3b;** ἐν τῇ προσευχῇ **Mt 21:22.** Also δεήσεσιν αἰ. τὸν θεόν *beseech God w. supplications* Pol 7:2 (cp. SIG 1168, 11; 13; 17); in the same sense ὅσα προσεύχεσθε κ. αἰτεῖσθε *whatever you request in prayer* **Mk 11:24;** ἐν πίστει **Js 1:6.** ἐν τῷ ὀνόματί μου **J 14:13f; 15:16; 16:24, 26.** τὶ κατὰ τὸ θέλημα αὐτοῦ *someth. in accord w. God's will* **1J 5:14.** Elliptically: αἰτεῖσθαι καθὼς ἐποίει αὐτοῖς *ask* (*to do*) *as he was accustomed to do for them* **Mk 15:8.** Foll. by acc. and inf. (SIG 1168, 11; 3 Km 19:4; Just., D. 105, 3; 5 al.) αὐτὸν σταυρωθῆναι **Lk 23:23;** cp. **Ac 3:14.** W. inf. (Aristoph., Plut. 240; X., An. 2, 3, 18; Appian, Liby. 82, §386) πεῖν αἰτεῖς **J 4:9** (Nic. Dam.: 90 fgm. 4 p. 332, 7f Jac. πιεῖν ᾔτει; Jos., Ant. 18, 192). ᾐτήσατο εὑρεῖν σκήνωμα *he asked to be permitted to find an abode* **Ac 7:46.** αἰ. θεοῦ ἐπιτυχεῖν *ask to reach the presence of God* ITr 12:2; cp. IRo 1:1. Neg. αἰτοῦμαι μὴ ἐγκακεῖν **Eph 3:13.** W. ἵνα foll. (w. προσεύχεσθαι) **Col 1:9** (cp. Polyb 31, 4, 3 αἰτεῖσθαι ἵνα; Ps.-Apollod. 1, 106; Just., D. 30, 2). Abs. (Arrian, Anab. 2, 14, 8 αἴτει καὶ λάμβανε; Ath. 11, 3 τοῖς αἰτοῦσιν διδόναι) **Mt 7:7f; Lk 11:9f; J 16:24; Js 4:3; 1J 5:16.** Mid. **Mk 6:25.**—B. 1270f. DELG. M-M. TW.

αἴτημα, τος, τό ***request*** (so Pla. et al.; POxy 1273, 28 [III AD]; LXX; PsSol 6:6; Philo, Spec. Leg. 1, 43; Jos., Ant. 8, 24; CPJ 153, 52 [41 AD]) Hm 9:4. τὰ αἰ. γνωριζέσθω πρὸς τὸν θεόν *let your requests be made known to God* **Phil 4:6.** αἰτεῖσθαι τὸ αἴ. (Judg 8:24 B; 1 Km 1:27) *make a request* Hm 9:7, 8. ἐπέκρινεν τὸ αἴτημα γενέσθαι Pilate *decided that their demand should be granted* **Lk 23:24;** ἔχειν τὰ αἰ. *obtain the requests* **1J 5:15;** λαμβάνεσθαι τὰ αἰ. *receive what one requests* Hs 4:6; cp. m 9:5, 7. τὸ αἴ. τῆς ψυχῆς σου πληροφορήσει *(the Lord) will fulfill the petition of your soul* Hm 9:2 (πληροφορεῖν=πληροῦν, Ps 19:5).—DELG s.v. αἰτέω. M-M. TW. Sv.

αἴτησις, εως, ἡ ***request*** (Hdt.+; Aristaen., Ep. 2, 7 p. 162: τὴν αἴτησιν ἐπλήρου; ins, pap, LXX; TestAbr A 9 p. 87, 1 [Stone p. 22] al.; ApcSed 12; Philo; Jos., Ant. 10, 27; 17, 232) πληρῶσαι τὴν αἰ. ITr 13:3 (TestAbr A 15 p. 96, 3 [Stone p. 40]); cp. IPol 7:1 v.l. S. αἰτέω.

αἰτία, ας, ἡ (s. αἴτιος; Pind.+; ins, pap, LXX; En 21:4; TestSol 11:2 'illness'; GrBar, Philo, Joseph., Just., Tat., Ath., Mel., P. 56, 411).

❶ **that which is responsible for a condition, *cause, reason*** Dg 5:17; gov. by διά: διὰ ταύτην τὴν αἰτίαν *for this reason* (Iambl., Vi. Pyth. 10, 52; 2 Macc 12:40; Jos., Ant. 3, 279; Just., D. 4, 6; Mel., P. 56, 411; SIG 700, 15; 826G, 21; Michel 456, 14 διὰ ταύτας τὰς αἰτίας; BGU 1243, 6 [III BC]) **Ac 28:20;** cp. **10:21;** 1 Cl 44:2; 2 Cl 10:3; Hs 9, 8, 3. οὐ δι' ἄλλην τινὰ αἰ. . . . ἀλλά *for no other reason . . . than* 1 Cl 51:5. δι' ἣν αἰτίαν (SIG 630, 6f; PEnteux 84, 14 [III BC]; 1 Esdr 2:17; Wsd 18:18; oft. 2 Macc) in indir. quest. *why* **Lk 8:47; Ac 22:24;** at beg. of a sentence as causal conj. (B-D-F §456, 4) *for this reason, therefore* (Diod. S. 4, 80, 4; 13, 11, 2; 2 Macc 4:28; Philo, Op. M. 100; Jos., Ant. 17, 202) **2 Ti 1:6, 12; Tit 1:13; Hb 2:11.** κατὰ πᾶσαν αἰτίαν *for any and every cause* (Appian, Bell. Civ. 3, 25 §94 κατὰ μηδεμίαν αἰτίαν; BGU 136, 26 [II AD] κατὰ ταύτην τ. αἰτίαν; Jos., Ant. 4, 249; 253) **Mt 19:3.**

❷ **the actual state of affairs, *case, circumstance, relationship*** (Latinism=causa B-D-F §5, 3b; cp. PRyl 63, 2f τίς δὲ ἡ αἰ. τούτων τῶν εἰδώλων;) εἰ οὕτως ἐστὶν ἡ αἰ. τοῦ ἀνθρώπου μετὰ τῆς γυναικός *if the relationship of a man with his wife is like this* **Mt 19:10.**

❸ **a basis for legal action,** legal t.t.—ⓐ ***charge, ground for complaint*** (PKroll I, 3 ἐγγενέσθαι αἰτίαις) **Ac 23:28.** αἰ. εὑρίσκειν (ἔν τινι) *find a basis for a charge (in his case)* **J 18:38; 19:4, 6** (Pilate states that he has no 'case'). αἰτία θανάτου=Lat. causa capitalis, *reason/grounds for capital punishment* **Ac 13:28; 28:18.** The charge specified **Mt 27:37; Mk 15:26.**

ⓑ ***accusation*** (Ath. 2, 3; 31, 1; Diod. S. 20, 62, 5 ἐν αἰτίαις ἔχειν τινά=lay charges against someone; Athen. 12, 542e) αἰτίαν φέρειν (v.l. ἐπιφέρειν q.v. 5) *bring an accusation* **Ac 25:18** (Jos., Ant. 20, 47). αἱ κατ' αὐτοῦ αἰ. *the (formal) charges against him* vs. **27.**—B. 1183; 1244. DELG s.v. αἴτιος. M-M.

αἰτίαμα, τος, τό (s. αἰτίωμα) Ac 25:7 v.l.

αἰτιάομαι fut. αἰτιάσομαι LXX; 1 aor. 3 pl. ᾐτιάσαντο (Tat. 20, 2) (Hom. et al.; OGI 484, 30; PTebt 35, 19; Philo, Decal. 87; Jos., Ant. 14, 44; LXX; Just., A I, 22, 3; Tat. 20, 2; Ath., R.) ***blame, accuse*** w. acc. of pers. (Hom. et al.; SIG 1236, 5f; PLips 37, 7; Jos., Ant. 15, 31) σεαυτόν Hm 9:8. τὸν κύριον Hs 6, 3, 5 (cp. Libanius, Or. 6 p. 354, 6 F. αἰτιᾶται τὴν θεόν; Pr 19:3).—*To charge* w. acc. and inf. foll. (as Just. A I, 22, 3; Ath. 34, 8) **Ro 3:9 v.l.**—DELG s.v. αἴτιος. M-M.

αἰτίζω 1 aor. pass. ᾐτίσθην (Hom. et al.) ***beg*** φοβούμενοι μή τι αἰτισθῶσιν ὑπ' αὐτῶν *afraid that they might be begged for someth. by them* Hs 9, 20, 2.—DELG s.v. αἰτέω.

αἴτιος, ία, ον (Hom.+)—❶ **pert. to being the cause of someth.,** in our lit. only subst.—ⓐ ὁ αἴ. one who is ***the cause, source*** αἴ. σωτηρίας **Hb 5:9** (Hdt. et al.; Diod. S. 4, 82 αἴ. ἐγένετο τῆς σωτηρίας; SIG 1109, 80; Philo, Agr. 96, Spec. Leg. 1, 252 θεὸν τ. σωτηρίας αἴτιον al.; Jos., Ant. 14, 136; Bel 42; 2 Macc 4:47; 13:4; EpArist 205; Just., D. 3, 5; 4, 1; Tat., Ath.).

ⓑ neut. ***cause, reason*** (Hdt., Thu. et al.; PHib 73, 18 [243/242 BC]; BGU 1121, 27; 29; Philo; Jos., Ant. 7, 75; 12, 84; Just., D. 5, 6; Tat.; Ath. 19, 2) μηδενὸς αἰ. ὑπάρχοντος i.e. the crowd will be unable to explain its action **Ac 19:40.**

❷ **ground for legal action.** τὸ αἴτ.=αἰτία 3a in a legal expr. ***ground for complaint, basis for a charge*** αἴ. εὑρίσκειν ἔν τινι **Lk 23:4, 14.** οὐδὲν αἴ. θανάτου *no ground for capital punishment* vs. **22.**—DELG. M-M. Sv.

αἰτίωμα, τος, τό (PFay 111, 8 [95 AD]=αἰτίαμα Aeschyl., Thu.; W-S. §5, 21d; Mlt-H. 354) ***charge, complaint*** αἰ. καταφέρειν *bring charges* **Ac 25:7.**—DELG s.v. αἴτιος. M-M.

αἰφνίδιος, ον (Aeschyl., Thu.+; ins; PFay 123, 21, here as adv.; Wsd 17:14; 2 Macc 14:17; 3 Macc 3:24; TestSol 20:17 [Q for ἐξάπινα]; Jos., Ant. 3, 207, Vi. 253; Just., D. 107, 3) ***sudden*** **Lk 21:34; 1 Th 5:3.** αἰ. συμφοραί 1 Cl 1:1 (cp. SIG 730, 20). S. also εὐθέως.—DDaube, The Sudden in the Scripture '64, 28.—DELG s.v. αἶψα. M-M. Spicq.

αἰχμαλωσία, ας, ἡ (Polyb. 5, 102, 5; Diod. S., Plut., Vett. Val.; Michel 965, 6; LXX; PsSol 2:6; TestSol 10:36 C; Test12Patr, ParJer 6:19; GrBar ins 2; AscIs 3:2; Joseph.; Ar 8, 6).

❶ **state of captivity, *captivity,*** mostly in war (Am 1:15; Jos., Ant. 10, 68; Ar. 8, 6) 2 Cl 6:8. W. πόλεμος 1 Cl 3:2. εἴ τις εἰς αἰ. εἰς αἰ. ὑπάγει *anyone who is allotted for capt. goes into capt.* **Rv 13:10** (cp. Jer 15:2); if the addition ἀπάγει (v.l.) is read: *one who leads into captivity goes into captivity.*

❷ abstr. for concr. **a captured military force, *prisoners of war, captives*** (Diod. S. 17, 70, 6; Num 31:12; Jdth 2:9; 1 Esdr 6:5, 8; 1 Macc 9:70, 72; 2 Macc 8:10; Jos., Ant. 11, 1) **Hb 7:1 v.l.;** αἰχμαλωτεύειν αἰ. **Eph 4:8** (Ps 67:19).—TW.

αἰχμαλωτεύω 1 aor. ᾐχμαλώτευσα. Pass. aor. ᾐχμαλωτεύθην LXX; pf. 3 sg. ᾐχμαλώτευται Gen. 14:4 (Ps.-Callisth. 1, 43, 1; 2, 4, 3; Phryn. p. 442 Lob.; LXX; EpArist 23; TestZeb 9:6; TestJob 17:6; ParJer; Tat. 18:2; Suda II p. 187, 387; Etym. Gud. 59, 10) **to capture in war, *capture, take captive,*** fig. **2 Ti 3:6 v.l;** αἰχμαλωσίαν αἰ. **Eph 4:8** (Ps 67:19). Cp. the addition to GJs 13:1 in var. codd., w. the meaning 'alienate/seduce' as w. αἰχμαλωτίζω 2.—DELG s.v. αἰχμή. TW.

αἰχμαλωτίζω 1 aor. ᾐχμαλώτισα LXX; pf. 3 pl. ᾐχμαλωτίκασιν 1 Macc 5:13. Pass.: 1 fut. αἰχμαλωτισθήσομαι; 1 aor. ᾐχμαλωτίσθην; pf. 3 sg. ᾐχμαλώτισται (TestJob 16:5) (s. αἰχμάλωτος; since Diod. S. 14, 37; Plut., Mor. 233c; Epict. 1, 28, 26; Ps.-Callisth. 2, 4, 3; 2, 6, 5 [pass.]; 3, 4, 6 [pass.]; SIG 763, 7; 10 [64 BC]; LXX; TestJob 16:5; EpArist 12; Test12Patr; AscIs 3:2; Jos., Bell. 1, 433 [mid.], Ant. 10, 153 [pass.]; Theoph. Ant. 3, 25 [p. 256, 27] s. Nägeli 29).

❶ **to cause someone to become a prisoner of war**—ⓐ lit. ***take captive*** εἰς τὰ ἔθνη πάντα *be scattered as captives among all nations* **Lk 21:24** (αἰ. εἰς as Tob 1:10; 1 Macc 10:33).

ⓑ fig. (so Dio Chrys. 15 [32], 90 αἰχμάλωτος and αἰχμαλωσία) ***make captive*** of the ἕτερος νόμος: αἰκμαλωτίζοντά με ἐν τῷ νόμῳ τῆς ἁμαρτίας *makes me a prisoner to the law of sin* **Ro 7:23.** αἰχμαλωτίζοντες πᾶν νόημα εἰς τὴν ὑπακοὴν τοῦ Χριστοῦ *we take every thought captive and make it obey Christ* **2 Cor 10:5.** Of the devil μὴ αἰχμαλωτίσῃ ὑμᾶς ἐκ τοῦ προκειμένου ζῆν *lest he lead you captive from the life which lies before you* IEph 17:1.

❷ the military aspect may give way to the more gener. sense **gain control of,** in which case αἰ. connotes *carry away*=***mislead, deceive*** (Jdth 16:9 αἰ. ψυχήν; Iren. 1, praef. 1 [Harv. I 2, 4]) αἰ. γυναικάρια **2 Ti 3:6** (αἰχμαλωτεύοντες v.l.); τινά τινι αἰ. *mislead someone w. someth.* IPhld 2:2 (w. dat., and acc. to be supplied TestReub 5:3). ἵνα μὴ αἰχμαλωτισθήσεται ἡ καρδία αὐτῆς ἐκ ναοῦ κυρίου *so that her heart be not enticed away from the Lord's temple* GJs 7:2.—DELG s.v. αἰχμή. M-M. TW.

αἰχμαλωτισμός, οῦ, ὁ (s. αἰχμάλωτος; Simplicius in Epict. p. 35, 31; schol. on Aristoph., Nub. 186) ***captivity*** (w. θάνατος) αἰ. ἑαυτῷ ἐπισπᾶσθαι *bring captivity on oneself* Hv 1, 1, 8.

αἰχμάλωτος, ώτου, ὁ ***captive*** (fr. αἰχμή 'spear' + ἁλωτός 'captured'; Aeschyl.+) with beggars, the blind, and oppressed as examples of misery **Lk 4:18;** B 14:9 (both Is 61:1).—TPietro, Συναιχμαλῶτος, AnalectaBiblica 17–18, '63, 418f.—B. 1414. DELG s.v. αἰχμή. M-M. TW.

αἰών, ῶνος, ὁ (Hom.+; gener. 'an extended period of time', in var. senses)

❶ **a long period of time, without ref. to beginning or end,—ⓐ** of time gone by, ***the past, earliest times,*** readily suggesting a venerable or awesome eld οἱ ἅγιοι ἀπ᾽ αἰῶνος προφῆται *the holy prophets fr. time immemorial* (cp. Hes., Theog. 609; Περὶ ὕψους 34, 4 τοὺς ἀπ᾽ αἰ. ῥήτορας; Cass. Dio 63, 20 τῶν ἀπὸ τοῦ αἰ. Ῥωμαίων; IMagnMai 180, 4; SIG index; Gen 6:4; Tob 4:12; Sir 14:17; 51:8; En 14:1; 99:14; Jos., Bell. 1, 12; Just., D. 11, 1) **Lk 1:70; Ac 3:21;** *make known from of old* **Ac 15:18;** πρὸ παντὸς τ. αἰ. *before time began* **Jd 25a** (for the combination with πᾶς cp. Sallust. 20 p. 36, 5 τὸν πάντα αἰῶνα=through all eternity); pl. πρὸ τῶν αἰ. **1 Cor 2:7** (cp. Ps 54:20 θεὸς ὁ ὑπάρχων πρὸ τῶν αἰ. [PGM 4, 3067 ἀπὸ τ. ἱερῶν αἰώνων]); ἐξ αἰ. *since the beginning* D 16:4 (Diod. S. 1, 6, 3; 3, 20, 2; 4, 83, 3; 5, 2, 3; Sext. Emp., Math. 9, 62; OGI 669, 61; Philo, Somn. 1, 19; Jos., Bell. 5, 442; Sir 1:4; SibOr fgm. 1, 16 of God μόνος εἰς αἰῶνα κ. ἐξ αἰῶνος). W. neg. foll. ἐκ τοῦ αἰῶνος οὐκ ἠκούσθη *never has it been heard* **J 9:32.**

ⓑ of time to come which, if it has no end, is also known as ***eternity*** (so commonly in Gk. lit. Pla. et al.); εἰς τὸν αἰῶνα (since Isocr. 10, 62, also Diod. S. 1, 56, 1 εἰς τ. αἰ.=εἰς ἅπαντα τ. χρόνον; 4, 1, 4; SIG 814, 49 and OGI index VIII; POxy 41, 30='Long live the Caesars'; PGM 8, 33; 4, 1051 [εἰς αἰ.]; LXX; En 12:6; 102:3; PsSol 2:34, 37; ParJer 8:5; JosAs 15:3 εἰς τὸν αἰῶνα χρόνον 4:10 al. Jos., Ant. 7, 356 [εἰς αἰ.]) *to eternity, eternally, in perpetuity:* live **J 6:51, 58;** B 6:3; remain **J 8:35ab; 12:34; 2 Cor 9:9** (Ps. 111:9); **1 Pt 1:23 v.l., 25** (Is 40:8); **1J 2:17; 2J 2;** be with someone **J 14:16.** Be priest **Hb 5:6; 6:20; 7:17, 21, 24, 28** (each Ps 109:4). Darkness reserved **Jd 13.** W. neg.=*never, not at all, never again* (Ps 124:1; Ezk 27:36 al.) **Mt 21:19; Mk 3:29; 11:14; 1 Cor 8:13.** ἕως αἰῶνος (LXX) 1 Cl 10:4 (Gen 13:15); Hv 2, 3, 3; s 9, 24, 4. In Johannine usage the term is used formulaically without emphasis on eternity (Lackeit [s. 4 below] 32f): never again thirst **J 4:14;** never see death **8:51f;** cp. **11:26;** never be lost **10:28;** never (= by no means) **13:8.** εἰς τὸν αἰ. τοῦ αἰῶνος (Ps 44:18; 82:18 al.) **Hb 1:8** (Ps 44:7). ἕως αἰῶνος (LXX; PsSol 18:11) **Lk 1:55 v.l.** (for εἰς τὸν αἰ.); εἰς ἡμέραν αἰῶνος **2 Pt 3:18.**—The pl. is also used (Emped., fgm. 129, 6 αἰῶνες=generations; Theocr. 16, 43 μακροὺς αἰῶνας=long periods of time; Philod. περὶ θεῶν 3 fgm. 84; Sext. Emp., Phys. 1, 62 εἰς αἰῶνας διαμένει; SibOr 3, 767; LXX, En; TestAbr B 7 p. 112, 3 [Stone p. 72].—B-D-F §141, 1), esp. in doxologies: εἰς τοὺς αἰῶνας (Ps 60:5; 76:8) **Mt 6:13 v.l.; Lk 1:33** (cp. Wsd 3:8); **Hb 13:8.** εἰς πάντας τοὺς αἰ. (Tob 13:4; Da 3:52b; En 9:4; SibOr 3, 50) **Jd 25b.** εὐλογητὸς εἰς τοὺς αἰῶνας *to all eternity* (cp. Ps 88:53) **Ro 1:25; 9:5; 2 Cor 11:31.** αὐτῷ ἡ δόξα εἰς τοὺς αἰ. **Ro 11:36;** ᾧ κτλ. **16:27** (v.l. αὐτῷ). τὸ κράτος εἰς τοὺς αἰ. **1 Pt 5:11;** more fully εἰς τοὺς αἰ. τῶν αἰώνων (Ps 83:5; GrBar 17:4; PGM 4, 1038; 22b, 15) *for evermore* in doxologies **Ro 16:27 v.l.; Gal 1:5; Phil 4:20; 1 Ti 1:17; 2 Ti 4:18; Hb 13:21; 1 Pt 4:11; 5:11 v.l.; Rv 1:6, 18; 5:13; 7:12; 11:15** al. 1 Cl 20:12; 32:4; 38:4; 43:6; εἰς πάσας τὰς γενεὰς τοῦ αἰῶνος τῶν αἰ. **Eph 3:21** (cp. Tob 1:4; 13:12; En 103:4; 104:5). Of God ὁ ζῶν εἰς τοὺς αἰ. (cp. Tob 13:2; Sir 18:1; Da 6:27 Theod.) **Rv 4:9f; 10:6; 15:7;** formulaically=*eternal* **14:11; 19:3; 20:10; 22:5.**—κατὰ πρόθεσιν τῶν αἰώνων *according to the eternal purpose* **Eph 3:11.** All-inclusive ἀπὸ αἰώνων καὶ εἰς τ. αἰῶνας *from* (past) *eternity to* (future) *eternity* B 18:2 (cp. Ps 40:14 and Ps.-Aristot., De Mundo 7, 401a, 16 ἐξ αἰῶνος ἀτέρμονος εἰς ἕτερον αἰῶνα; M. Ant. 9, 28, 1 ἐξ αἰῶνος εἰς αἰῶνα; SibOr fgm. 1, 16 of God μόνος εἰς αἰῶνα κ. ἐξ αἰῶνος).

❷ **a segment of time as a particular unit of history, *age***

ⓐ ὁ αἰὼν οὗτος (הָעוֹלָם הַזֶּה) ***the present age*** (nearing its end) (Orig., C. Cels. 1, 13, 15, in ref. to **1 Cor 3:18;** s. Bousset, Rel. 243ff; Dalman, Worte 120ff; Schürer II 537f; NMessel, D. Einheitlichkeit d. jüd. Eschatol. 1915, 44–60) contrasted w. the age to come (Philo and Joseph. do not have the two aeons) **Mt 12:32.** A time of sin and misery Hv 1, 1, 8; s 3:1ff; ending of Mk in the Freer ms. 2; ἡ μέριμνα τοῦ αἰ. (v.l. + τούτου) *the cares of the present age* **Mt 13:22;** pl. cp. **Mk 4:19.** πλοῦτος *earthly riches* Hv 3, 6, 5. ματαιώματα *vain, futile things* Hm 9:4; s 5, 3, 6. πραγματεῖαι m 10, 1, 4. ἐπιθυμία m 11:8; s 6, 2, 3; 7:2; 8, 11, 3. πονηρία s 6, 1, 4. ἀπάται s 6, 3, 3 v.l. οἱ υἱοὶ τοῦ αἰ. τούτου *the children of this age, the people of the world* (opp. children of light, enlightened ones) **Lk 16:8; 20:34.**—The earthly kingdoms βασιλεῖαι τοῦ αἰ. τούτου IRo 6:1. συσχηματίζεσθαι τῷ αἰ. τούτῳ *be conformed to this world* **Ro 12:2.** As well as everything non-Christian, it includes the striving after worldly wisdom: συζητητὴς τοῦ αἰ. τούτου *searcher after the wisdom of this world* **1 Cor 1:20.** σοφία τοῦ αἰ. τούτου **2:6.** ἐν τῷ αἰ. τούτῳ **3:18** prob. belongs to what precedes=*those who consider themselves wise in this age must become fools (in the estimation of this age).* The ruler of this age is the devil: ὁ θεὸς τοῦ αἰ. τούτου **2 Cor 4:4** (θεός 5). ἄρχων τοῦ αἰ. τούτου IEph 17:1; 19:1; IMg 1:3; ITr 4:2; IRo 7:1; IPhld 6:2; his subordinate spirits are the ἄρχοντες τοῦ αἰ. τούτου **1 Cor 2:6, 8** (ἄρχων 1c).—Also ὁ νῦν αἰών (Did., Gen. 148, 21): πλούσιοι ἐν τῷ νῦν αἰ. **1 Ti 6:17;** ἀγαπᾶν τὸν νῦν αἰ. **2 Ti 4:10;** Pol 9:2. Cp. **Tit 2:12.** Or (Orig., C. Cels. 2, 42, 30) ὁ αἰ. ὁ ἐνεστώς *the present age* **Gal 1:4** (cp. SIG 797, 9 [37 AD] αἰῶνος νῦν ἐνεστῶτος). The end of this period (cp. SibOr 3, 756 μέχρι τέρματος αἰῶνος) συντέλεια (τοῦ) αἰ. **Mt 13:39f, 49; 24:3; 28:20** (cp. TestJob 4:6; TestBenj 11:3; JRobinson, Texts and Studies V introd. 86). συντέλεια τῶν αἰ. **Hb 9:26;** on GMary 463, 1 s. καιρός end.

ⓑ ὁ αἰὼν μέλλων (הָעוֹלָם הַבָּא) ***the age to come,*** the Messianic period (on the expr. cp. Demosth. 18, 199; Hippocr., Ep. 10, 6 ὁ μ. αἰ.=the future, all future time; Ael. Aristid. 46 p. 310 D.: ἡ τοῦ παρελθόντος χρόνου μνεία κ. ὁ τοῦ μέλλοντος αἰῶνος λόγος; Jos., Ant. 18, 287; Ar. 15, 3; Orig., C. Cels. 8, 24, 20; Did., Gen. 164, 2) in 2 Cl 6:3, cp. Hs 4:2ff, opposed to the αἰὼν οὗτος both in time and quality, cp. **Mt 12:32; Eph 1:21;** δυνάμεις μέλλοντος αἰ. **Hb 6:5.** Also αἰ. ἐκεῖνος: τοῦ αἰ. ἐκείνου τυχεῖν *take part in the age to come* **Lk 20:35.** ὁ αἰ. ὁ ἐρχόμενος **Mk 10:30; Lk 18:30;** Hs 4:2, 8. ὁ αἰ. ὁ ἐπερχόμενος Hv 4, 3, 5: pl. ἐν τοῖς αἰῶσιν τοῖς ἐπερχομένοις *in the ages to come* **Eph 2:7.** As a holy age ὁ ἅγιος αἰ. (opp. οὗτος ὁ κόσμος; cp. εἰς τὸν μείζονα αἰ. TestJob 47:3) B 10:11 and as a time of perfection αἰ. ἀλύπητος *an age free from sorrow* 2 Cl 19:4 (cp. αἰ. . . . τοῦ ἀπαραλλάκτου TestJob 33:5), while the present αἰών is an 'aeon of pain' (Slav. Enoch 65, 8).—The plurals **1 Cor 10:11** have been explained by some as referring to both ages, i.e. the end-point of the first and beginning of the second; this view urges that the earliest Christians believed that the two ages came together during their own lifetimes: *we, upon whom the* *ends of the ages have come* (JWeiss. A Greek would not refer to the beginning as τέλος. The Gordian knot has οὔτε τέλος οὔτε ἀρχή: Arrian, Anab. 2, 3, 7). But since τὰ τέλη can also mean 'end' in the singular (Ael. Aristid. 44, 17 K.=17 p. 406 D.: σώματος ἀρχαὶ κ. τέλη='beginning and end'; 39 p. 737 D.: τὰ τέλη ... δράματος; Longus 1, 23, 1 ms. ἦρος τέλη; Vi. Thu. 2, 2 [=OxfT ΘΟΥΚΥΔΙΔΟΥ ΒΙΟΣ 2] τέλη τοῦ πολέμου; Aëtius, Eye Diseases p. 120, 25 Hirschb. after Galen: τὰ τέλη τ. λόγου=the close of the section; Philo, Virt. 182) and, on the other hand, the pl. αἰῶνες is often purely formal (s. above 1a and b, 2a at end) τὰ τέλη τῶν αἰ. can perh. be regarded as equal to τέλος αἰώνων (SibOr 8, 311)=*the end of the age(s)*. Cp. TestLevi 14:1 ἐπὶ τὰ τέλη τῶν αἰώνων.—For the essential equivalence of sing. and pl. cp. Maximus Tyr. 14, 8b τὰ τῆς κολακείας τέλη beside τέλος τῆς σπουδῆς. Cp. also τέλος 5.

❸ **the world as a spatial concept,** ***the world*** (αἰ. in sg. and pl. [B-D-F §141, 1]: Hippocr., Ep. 17, 34; Diod. S. 1, 1, 3 God rules ἅπαντα τὸν αἰῶνα; Ael. Aristid. 20, 13 K.=21 p. 434 D.: ἐκ τοῦ παντὸς αἰῶνος; Maximus Tyr. 11, 5e; IAndrosIsis, Cyrene 4 [103 AD] P. p. 129]; Ps 65:7; Ex 15:18 [cp. Philo, Plant. 47; 51]; Wsd 13:9; 14:6; 18:4; αἰῶνες οἱ κρείττονες Tat. 20:2) ApcPt 4:14. Created by God through the Son **Hb 1:2;** through God's word **11:3.** Hence God is βασιλεὺς τῶν αἰ. **1 Ti 1:17; Rv 15:3** (v.l. for ἐθνῶν); 1 Cl 61:2 (cp. PGM 12, 247 αἰώνων βασιλεῦ; Tob 13:7, 11, cp. AcPh 2 and 11 [Aa II/2, 2, 20 and 6, 9]); πατὴρ τῶν αἰ. 35:3 (cp. Just., A I, 41, 2; AcPh 144 [Aa II/2, 84, 9]); θεὸς τῶν αἰ. 55:6 (cp. Sir 36:17; ὁ θεὸς τοῦ αἰ.; En 1:4; PGM 4, 1163; TSchermann, Griech. Zauber-pap 1909, 23; AcJ 82 [Aa II/1, 191, 24f]). But many of these pass. may belong under 2.

❹ **the Aeon as a person,** ***the Aeon*** (Rtzst., Erlösungsmyst. 268 index under Aion, Taufe 391 index; Epict. 2, 5, 13 οὐ γάρ εἰμι αἰών, ἀλλ' ἄνθρωπος=I am not a being that lasts forever, but a human being [and therefore I know that whatever is must pass away]; Mesomedes 1, 17=Coll. Alex. p. 197, 17; Simplicius in Epict. p. 81, 15 οἱ αἰῶνες beside the μήτηρ τῆς ζωῆς and the δημιουργός; En 9:4 κύριος τ. κυρίων καὶ θεὸς τ. θεῶν κ. βασιλεὺς τ. αἰώνων; PGM 4, 520; 1169; 2198; 2314; 3168; 5, 468; AcPh 132 [Aa II/2, 63, 5]; Kephal. I p. 24, 6; 45, 7) ὁ αἰ. τοῦ κόσμου τούτου **Eph 2:2.** The secret hidden from the Aeons **Col 1:26; Eph 3:9** (Rtzst., Erlösungsmyst. 235f); IEph 19:2 (Rtzst. 86, 3); cp. 8:1 (Rtzst. 236, 2). Various other meanings have been suggested for these passages.—CLackeit, Aion I, diss. Königsbg. 1916; EBurton, ICC Gal 1921, 426–32; HJunker, Iran. Quellen d. hellenist. Aionvorstellung: Vortr. d. Bibl. Warburg I 1923, 125ff; ENorden, D. Geburt des Kindes 1924; MZepf, D. Gott Αιων in d. hellenist. Theologie: ARW 25, 1927, 225–44; ANock, HTR 27, 1934, 78–99=Essays I, '72, 377–96; RLöwe, Kosmos u. Aion '35; EOwen, αἰών and αἰώνιος: JTS 37, '36, 265–83; 390–404; EJenni, Das Wort ᶜōlām im AT: ZAW 64, '52, 197–248; 65, '53, 1–35; KDeichgräber, RGG I[3] 193–95; HSasse, RAC I 193–204; MNilsson, Die Rel. in den gr. Zauberpapyri, K. humanist. Vetenskapssamfundets Lund II '47/48, 81f; GJennings, A Survey of αιων and αιωνιος and their meaning in the NT, '48; GStadtmüller, Aion: Saeculum 2, '51, 315–20 (lit.); EDegani, ΑΙΩΝ da Omero ad Aristotele '61 (s. Classen, Gnomon 34, '62, 366–70; D.'s reply in RivFil 91, '63, 104–10); MTreu, Griech. Ewigkeitswörter, Glotta 43, '65, 1–24; JBarr, Biblical Words for Time[2] '69; OCullman, Christus u. die Zeit[3] '62.—B. 13. EDNT. DDD s.v. Aion. DELG. M-M. TW. Sv.

αἰώνιος (ία Pla., Tim. 38b; Jer 39:40; Ezk 37:26; OdeSol 11:22; TestAbr A; JosAs 8:11 cod. A; **2 Th 2:16; Hb 9:12;** mss. **Ac 13:48; 2 Pt 1:11;** AcPl BMM recto 27=Ox 1602, 29; Just., A I, 8, 4 al.; B-D-F §59, 2; Mlt-H. 157), **ον** *eternal* (since Hyperid. 6, 27; Pla.; ins, pap, LXX, En, TestSol, TestAbr A, Test12Patr; JosAs 12:12; GrBar 4:16; ApcEsdr; ApcMos 29; Ps.-Phocyl. 112; Just.; Tat. 17, 1; Ath., Mel.; standard epithet for princely, esp. imperial, power: OGI index VIII; BGU 176, 12; 303, 2; 309, 4; Sb 7517, 5 [211/12 AD] κύριος αἰ.; al. in pap; Jos., Ant. 7, 352).

❶ **pert. to a long period of time,** ***long ago*** χρόνοις αἰ. *long ages ago* **Ro 16:25;** πρὸ χρόνων αἰ. *before time began* **2 Ti 1:9; Tit 1:2** (in these two last pass. the prep. bears the semantic content of priority; on χρόνος αἰ. cp. OGI 248, 54; 383, 10).

❷ **pert. to a period of time without beginning or end,** ***eternal*** of God (Ps.-Pla., Tim. Locr. 96c θεὸν τ. αἰώνιον; IBM 894, 2 αἰ. κ. ἀθάνατος τοῦ παντὸς φύσις; Gen 21:33; Is 26:4; 40:28; Bar 4:8 al.; Philo, Plant. 8; 74; SibOr fgm. 3, 17 and 4; PGM 1, 309; 13, 280) **Ro 16:26;** of the Holy Spirit in Christ **Hb 9:14.** θρόνος αἰ. 1 Cl 65:2 (cp. 1 Macc 2:57).

❸ **pert. to a period of unending duration,** ***without end*** (Diod. S. 1, 1, 5; 5, 73, 1; 15, 66, 1 δόξα αἰ. everlasting fame; in Diod. S. 1, 93, 1 the Egyptian dead are said to have passed to their αἰ. οἴκησις; Arrian, Peripl. 1, 4 ἐς μνήμην αἰ.; Jos., Bell. 4, 461 αἰ. χάρις=a benefaction for all future time; OGI 383, 10 [I BC] εἰς χρόνον αἰ.; EOwen, οἶκος αἰ.: JTS 38, '37, 248–50; EStommel, Domus Aeterna: RAC IV 109–28) of the next life σκηναὶ αἰ. **Lk 16:9** (cp. En 39:5). οἰκία, contrasted w. the οἰκία ἐπίγειος, of the glorified body **2 Cor 5:1.** διαθήκη (Gen 9:16; 17:7; Lev 24:8; 2 Km 23:5 al.; PsSol 10:4 al.) **Hb 13:20.** εὐαγγέλιον **Rv 14:6;** κράτος in a doxolog. formula (=εἰς τοὺς αἰῶνας) **1 Ti 6:16.** παράκλησις **2 Th 2:16.** λύτρωσις **Hb 9:12.** κληρονομία (Esth 4:17m) vs. **15;** AcPl Ha 8, 21. αἰ. ἀπέχειν τινά (opp. πρὸς ὥραν) *keep someone forever* **Phlm 15** (cp. Job 40:28). Very often of God's judgment (Diod. S. 4, 63, 4 διὰ τὴν ἀσέβειαν ἐν ᾅδου διατελεῖν τιμωρίας αἰωνίου τυγχάνοντα; similarly 4, 69, 5; Jer 23:40; Da 12:2; Ps 76:6; 4 Macc 9:9; 13:15) κόλασις αἰ. (TestReub 5:5) **Mt 25:46;** 2 Cl 6:7; κρίμα αἰ. **Hb 6:2** (cp. κρίσις αἰ. En 104:5). θάνατος B 20:1. ὄλεθρον (4 Macc 10:15) **2 Th 1:9.** πῦρ (4 Macc 12:12; GrBar 4:16.—SibOr 8, 401 φῶς αἰ.) **Mt 18:8; 25:41; Jd 7;** Dg 10:7 (cp. 1QS 2:8). ἁμάρτημα **Mk 3:29** (v.l. κρίσεως, κολάσεως, and ἁμαρτίας). On the other hand, of *eternal life* (Maximus Tyr. 6, 1d θεοῦ ζωὴ αἰ.; Diod. S. 8, 15, 3 life μετὰ τὸν θάνατον lasts εἰς ἅπαντα αἰῶνα; Da 12:2; 4 Macc 15:3; PsSol 3, 12; OdeSol 11:16c; JosAs 8:11 cod. A [p. 50, 2 Bat.]; Philo, Fuga 78; Jos., Bell. 1, 650; SibOr 2, 336) in the Reign of God: ζωὴ αἰ. (Orig., C. Cels. 2, 77, 3) **Mt 19:16, 29; 25:46; Mk 10:17, 30; Lk 10:25; 18:18, 30; J 3:15f, 36; 4:14, 36; 5:24, 39; 6:27, 40, 47, 54, 68; 10:28; 12:25, 50; 17:2f; Ac 13:46, 48; Ro 2:7; 5:21; 6:22f; Gal 6:8; 1 Ti 1:16; 6:12; Tit 1:2; 3:7; 1J 1:2; 2:25; 3:15; 5:11, 13, 20; Jd 21;** D 10:3; 2 Cl 5:5; 8:4, 6; IEph 18:1; Hv 2, 3, 2; 3, 8, 4 al. Also βασιλεία αἰ. **2 Pt 1:11** (ApcPt Rainer 9; cp. Da 4:3; 7:27; Philo, Somn. 2, 285; Mel., P. 68, 493; OGI 569, 24 ὑπὲρ τῆς αἰωνίου καὶ ἀφθάρτου βασιλείας ὑμῶν; Dssm. B 279f, BS 363). Of the glory in the next life δόξα αἰ. **2 Ti 2:10; 1 Pt 5:10** (cp. Wsd 10:14; Jos., Ant. 15, 376.—SibOr 8, 410 φῶς αἰώνιον). αἰώνιον βάρος δόξης **2 Cor 4:17;** σωτηρία αἰ. (Is 45:17; Ps.-Clem., Hom. 1, 19) **Hb 5:9;** short ending of Mk. Of unseen glory in contrast to the transitory world of the senses τὰ μὴ βλεπόμενα αἰώνια **2 Cor 4:18.**—χαρά IPhld ins; δοξάζεσθαι αἰωνίῳ ἔργῳ *be glorified by an everlasting deed* IPol 8:1. DHill, Gk. Words and Hebr. Mngs. '67, 186–201; JvanderWatt, NovT 31, '89, 217–28 (J).—DELG s.v. αἰών. M-M. TW. Sv.

ἀκαθαρσία, ας, ἡ (Hippocr., Pla. et al.; pap, LXX, En, TestAbr A 17 p. 99, 16 [Stone p. 46]; Test12Patr; Ar. 15, 6; Hippol., Ref. 5, 19, 20; in var. senses of something that is not clean)

❶ lit. **any substance that is filthy or dirty,** ***refuse*** (UPZ 20, 70 [II BC]; BGU 1117, 27 [13 BC]; POxy 912, 26; 1128, 25 [173 AD]) of the contents of graves, causing ceremonial impurity **Mt 23:27** (cp. Num 19:13).

❷ fig. **a state of moral corruption** (Epict. 4, 11, 5; 8; Pr 6:16; 24:9; Wsd 2:16; 3 Macc 2:17; 1 Esdr 1:40; EpArist 166; En 10:20; Philo, Leg. All. 2, 29) ***immorality, vileness*** esp. of sexual sins (Vett. Val. p. 2, 19; En 10:11; Ar. 15, 6; Orig., C. Cels. 7, 48, 4) w. πορνεία **2 Cor 12:21; Gal 5:19; Col 3:5; Eph 5:3.** Opp. ἁγιασμός **1 Th 4:7; Ro 6:19.** Of unnatural vices: παραδιδόναι εἰς ἀ. *give over to vileness* **Ro 1:24.** δι' ἀκαθαρσίαν *with immoral intent* B 10:8. εἰς ἐργασίαν ἀκαθαρσίας πάσης *to the practice of every kind of immorality* **Eph 4:19.** Of impure motive (Demosth. 21, 119; BGU 393, 16 [168 AD]; Did., Gen. 196, 17) **1 Th 2:3** (w. πλάνη and δόλος). ἐν ἀ. τινῶν B 19:4 is uncertain; prob. *in the presence of impure people.*—DELG s.v. καθαρός. M-M. TW.

ἀκαθάρτης, ητος, ἡ ***uncleanness*** τ. πορνείας **Rv 17:4** t.r., a reading composed by Erasmus. The word does not otherwise exist (s. ἀκάθαρτος 2).—RBorger, TRu 52, '87, 57.

ἀκάθαρτος, ον (Soph., Hippocr.+; ins; except for mag. pap perh. PTebt 1043, 42 [II BC], LXX, TestSol, Test12Patr, EpArist, Philo, Joseph., Just.)

❶ **pert. to that which may not be brought into contact w. the divinity,** ***impure, unclean*** (the cultic sense, mostly LXX, also Jos., C. Ap. 1, 307; SIG 1042, 3; Just., D. 20, 4): of foods (Orig., C. Cels. 3, 11, 9) w. κοινός: πᾶν κοινὸν καὶ ἀ. *anything common or unclean* **Ac 10:14, 11:8;** GJs 6:1; w. μεμισημένος of birds (and other animals Lev 11:4ff; Dt 14:7ff; Did., Gen. 52, 22) **Rv 18:2;** (τὸ) ἀ. *what is unclean* **2 Cor 6:17** (Is 52:11; Hippol., Ref. 9, 12, 23).—Esp. of everything connected w. polytheism, which defiles whatever it touches (Am 7:17; Is 52:1 ἀπερίτμητος κ. ἀ.; SibOr 5, 264) of gentiles ἄνθρωπος κοινὸς ἢ ἀ. **Ac 10:28;** τέκνα ἀ (opp. ἅγια) **1 Cor 7:14** (on the question of child baptism s. τέκνον 1a). As the ceremonial mng. fades, the moral sense becomes predominant.

❷ **pert. to moral impurity** (since Pla., Leg. 4, 716e; Is 6:5; 64:5; Sir 51:5; Pr 3:32 al.; Philo, Deus Imm. 132, Spec. Leg. 3, 209; Jos., Bell. 4, 562; Just., D. 141, 3) ***unclean, impure*** (s. ἀκαθαρσία 2) B 10:8. W. πόρνος (Plut., Oth. 1067b [2, 2] ἐν γυναιξὶ πόρναις κ. ἀκαθάρτοις. Cp. Vett. Val. 76, 1), πλεονέκτης and εἰδωλολάτρης **Eph 5:5.**—τὰ ἀ. (w. πονηρά) *impure things* Hv 1, 1, 7. τὰ ἀ. τῆς πορνείας *the impurities of fornication* **Rv 17:4** (ἀ. of actions, such as adultery, that defile one TestJos 4:6; on the constr. s. B-D-F §136, 1).—Esp. of evil spirits πνεῦμα, πνευματα ἀ. (cp. Zech 13:2; TestBenj 5:2; Cat. Cod. Astr. X 179, 19; 181, 5; Just., D. 7, 3 al.) **Mt 10:1; 12:43; Mk 1:23, 26f; 3:11, 30; 5:2, 8, 13; 6:7; 7:25; 9:25.** Ending of Mk in Freer ms. 3; **Lk 4:36; 6:18; 8:29; 9:42; 11:24; Ac 5:16; 8:7; Rv 16:13; 18:2.** πνεῦμα δαιμονίου ἀκαθάρτου **Lk 4:33** (cp. PGM 4, 1238). On ἐν πνεύματι ἀ. s. GBjörck, ConNeot 7, '42, 1–3.—B. 1081. DELG s.v. καθαρός. M-M. TW.

ἀκαιρέομαι impf. ἠκαιρούμην; 1 aor. ἠκαιρέθην (act. Diod. S. 10, 7, 3; PEnteux 45, 5 [222 BC]; pass., Corpus Glossariorum Lat. 2, 137) **to lack an opportune time for doing someth.,** ***have no opportunity, have no time*** abs. ἠκαιρεῖσθε *you had no opportunity* to show your love to me **Phil 4:10.** μικρὸν ἔχω ἀκαιρεθῆναι *I am busy for a little while* Hs 9, 10, 5 (B-D-F §30; Mlt-H. 390).—DELG s.v. καιρός. TW.

ἄκαιρος, ον (Aeschyl. et al.; Thu. 5, 65, 2; SIG 1102, 12 [II BC]; Sir 20:19; 22:6; TestSol 4:8; Agatharchides: 86 fgm. 20b Jac. [cited in Jos., Ant. 12, 6] of inapposite religiosity) ***untimely, ill-timed*** εὔνοια ἄ. *an ill-timed kindness* (prov. expr. ἄκαιρος εὔνοι' οὐδὲν ἔχθρας διαφέρει 'untimely goodwill does not differ from hostility' Zenob., Paroem. 1, 50), which becomes burdensome or dangerous IRo 4:1 (s. Lghtf. ad loc.).—TW. S. καιρός.

ἀκαίρως adv. fr. ἄκαιρος (Aeschyl. et al.; BGU 846, 14 [II AD]; Sir 32:4; Philo, Mos. 2, 206; Jos., Ant. 6, 137) ***untimely*** in a play on words εὐκαίρως ἀ. *in season, out of season* (i.e. whether or not the preaching comes at a convenient time for the hearers) **2 Ti 4:2** (AMalherbe, JBL 103, '84, 235–43); s. also εὐκαίρως.—M-M. TW.

ἀκακία, ας, ἡ **state of not being inclined to that which is base,** ***innocence, guilelessness*** (Aristot. et al.; Diog. L. 4, 19; LXX) 1 Cl 14:5 (Ps 36:37) ἀ. ἀσκεῖν Papias (8); w. ἁπλότης (Philo, Op. M. 156; 170; TestIss 5:1) Hv 1, 2, 4; 2, 3, 2; 3, 9, 1. ἐνδύσασθαι ἀκακίαν *put on innocence* (opp. αἴρειν τ. πονηρίαν) s 9, 29, 3; personif. as a Christian virtue v 3, 8, 5; 7; s 9, 15, 2.

ἄκακος, ον ***innocent, guileless*** (so Aeschyl. et al.; Polyb., Diod. S., Plut., LXX; Philo, Spec. Leg. 3, 119; Just., D. 72, 2f; Mel., P. 63, 454 [both Jer. 11:19]) 1 Cl 14:4 (Pr 2:21); Hs 9, 30, 2. ἄκακον γίνεσθαι m 2:1. τὰς καρδίας τῶν ἀ. ἐξαπατᾶν *deceive the hearts of the unsuspecting* **Ro 16:18;** (w. μακρόθυμος, ἐλεήμων et al.) D 3:8; Dg 9:2; (w. ἁπλοῦς [Diod. S. 13, 76, 2 ἄ. καὶ τὴν ψυχὴν ἁπλοῦς; cp. Philo on ἀκακία], μακάριος) Hs 9, 24, 2; (w. καθαρός, ἀμίαντος) m 2:7; cp. 9, 30, 3; of Christ (w. ὅσιος, ἀμίαντος) **Hb 7:26.**—DELG s.v. κακός. M-M. TW. Spicq.

ἄκανθα, ης, ἡ ***thorn-plant*** (since Od. 5, 328; pap, LXX; ApcMos 24; ApcrEzk P 1 verso 5; Jos., Bell. 5, 51; Just., D. 28, 3 [Jer. 4, 3]; Mel., P. 79, 575; 93, 708) of such plants in general, esp. the common weed Ononis spinosa, cammock (s. LFonck, Streifzüge durch d. bibl. Flora 1900, 195) in contrast to useful plants (w. τρίβολος, cp. Gen 3:18; Hos 10:8) **Mt 7:16; Lk 6:44** (cp. Jer 12:13). It is found on cultivated land and is thus harmful to the grain (GDalman, Pj 22, 1926, 126ff) **Mt 13:7, 22; Mk 4:7, 18; Lk 8:7, 14** (on the interpr. of the ἄκανθαι s. Philo, Leg. All. 3, 248); B 9:5 (Jer 4:3).—στέφανος ἐξ ἀ. *crown of thorns* **Mt 27:29; J 19:2** (cp. Mel., P. 79, 575; 93, 708; Fonck 51; 99; FLundgreen, D. Bäume im NT: NKZ 27, 1916, 827–42; EHa-Reubéni, RB 42, '33, 230–34. S. also ἀκάνθινος).—W. thistles (τρίβολοι, s. above) as signs of a neglected field **Hb 6:8;** Hs 6, 2, 6f; 9, 1, 5; 9, 20, 1. W. other weeds Hm 10, 1, 5.—In description of the rites of atonement B 7:11 ἄ. means the *thornbush* on which the wool was placed, s. ῥάχος, ῥαχία.—S. βάτος. DELG. M-M.

ἀκάνθινος, η, ον (Hdt. et al.; pap) ***thorny*** (so Is 34:13) ἀ. στέφανος **Mk 15:17; J 19:5;** GPt 3:8. S. HStJHart, JTS n.s. 3, '52, 66–75; CBonner, HTR 46, '53, 47f; EGoodenough and CWelles, ibid. 46, '53, 241f.

ἀκανθώδης, ες (ἄκανθα, -ώδης; since Hdt. 1, 126, also Agathocles [III BC]: 472, fgm. 4 Jac p. 431, 21–22; Just., D. 20, 3) ***thorny, covered w. thornbushes*** ὁδός Hm 6, 1, 3f; τόπος Hs 6, 2, 6.

ἄκαρπος, ον (Aeschyl. et al.; ins, pap, LXX; TestNaphth 3:5; ParJer 9:16; Jos., Ant. 2, 213; 15, 300; Just., D. 120, 2)

❶ lit. **pert. to not bearing fruit, *unfruitful, fruitless.*** πτελέα ξύλον ἄ. *the elm is an unfruitful* (i.e. bearing no edible fruit, s. Pollux I 234) *tree* Hs 2:3. δένδρα ἄ. (Theophyl. Sim., Ep. 11) *unfruitful trees* (w. φθινοπωρινά) as a type of dissident teachers **Jd 12**, cp. Hs 4:4. Of a mountain, on which nothing grows (Jos., Bell. 4, 452) ὄρος ἄ. *unfruitful, barren* Hs 9, 19, 2.

❷ fig. **pert. to being useless, *useless, unproductive*** (IPriene 112, 16; Jos., Bell. 6, 36) of seed (preaching) **Mt 13:22; Mk 4:19** (Pla., Phdr. 277a λόγοι ἄ; Synes., Dion 3 p. 39c λόγος ἄ.). Of deeds ἔργα ἄ. τοῦ σκότους *useless deeds of darkness* **Eph 5:11.** Of people who do no good deeds (Philostrat., Gymn. 42 p. 284, 11) **Tit 3:14; 2 Pt 1:8** (cp. OdeSol 11:23). Of speaking in tongues νοῦς ἄ. ἐστιν *(my) mind is unproductive,* because it is not active **1 Cor 14:14.**—DELG s.v. 1. καρπός. M-M. TW. Spicq.

ἀκατάγνωστος, ον (Rhet. Gr. I 597; Syntipas p. 129, 12; exx. fr. ins and pap in Nägeli 47) **pert. to not being considered blameworthy, *not condemned*** (2 Macc 4:47), ***beyond reproach*** λόγον ἀ. *preaching that is beyond repr.* **Tit 2:8.**—DELG s.v. γιγνώσκω. M-M. TW. Spicq.

ἀκατακάλυπτος, ον (Polyb. 15, 27, 2; Lev 13:45; AcPhil 60 [Aa II/2, 25, 13]) ***uncovered*** ἀ. τῇ κεφαλῇ (Philo, Spec. Leg. 3, 60) *with unc. head* (of praying women; cp. SIG 999, 10 and 736, 22; Philostrat. Jun. [III AD]: APF 14, '41, p. 8; 19 ln. 60f: γυναῖκες ἀκάλυπτοι in a solemn procession) **1 Cor 11:5.** Concisely γυναῖκα ἀ. *a woman without head-covering* vs. **13.**—JJeremias, TLZ 91,'66,431; JMurphy-O'Connor, CBQ 42, '80, 482–500. DELG s.v. καλύπτω.

ἀκατάκριτος, ον (Corpus Gloss. Lat. 2, 80) **pert. to not undergoing a proper legal process, *uncondemned, without due process*** **Ac 16:37; 22:25.**—DELG s.v. κρίνω. M-M. TW.

ἀκατάληπτος, ον (Aristot. et al.; Jos., Bell. 3, 159) ***incomprehensible*** (so Diog. L. 7, 46; 9, 91; Plut., Mor 1056e; Epict., fgm. 1 Schenkl; EpArist 160; Philo, Spec. Leg. 1, 47, Mut. Nom. 10; Ath. 10:1; τέλος ἀ. Mel., P. 105, 813 [B]) of God's wisdom σύνεσις 1 Cl 33:3. Simply of God PtK 2 (Ath. 10, 1).—DELG s.v. λαμβάνω. Sv.

ἀκατάλυτος, ον (καταλύω 'dissolve, break up' etc.) **pert. to being indestructible, *endless*** (Dionys. Hal. 10, 31, 5; Chion, Ep. 14, 1; 4 Macc 10:11) ζωή **Hb 7:16.**—DELG s.v. λύω. TW.

ἀκατάπαστος s. next. M-M.

ἀκατάπαυστος, ον (Polyb. 4, 17, 4; Diod. S. 11, 67; Plut., Caes. 734 [57, 1], Mor. 114f; Heliod. 1, 13, 5; PSI 28, 52; New Docs 2, 45, no. 11, 12f; PGM 4, 2364) ***unceasing, restless*** w. gen. (B-D-F §182, 3; s. Rob. 503f) ὀφθαλμοὶ ἀ. ἁμαρτίας *eyes unceasingly looking for sin* **2 Pt 2:14** (v.l. ἀκαταπάστους, which cannot be explained w. certainty [perh.='insatiable'] and may be due to a scribal error).—DELG s.v. παύω. M-M. s.v. ἀκατάπαστος.

ἀκαταστασία, ας, ἡ (opp. κατάστασις q.v., cp. στάσις and DELG on the latter; Polyb. 7, 4, 8; 14, 9, 6; Diog. L. 7, 110; Epict. 3, 19, 3; Vett. Val. index; PGrenf I, 1, 4 [173 BC]; Astrol. Pap. I fr. Munich: APF 1, 1901, 494, 26; Tob 4:13; Pr 26:28; ApcMos 24).

❶ **unsettled state of affairs, *disturbance, tumult*** (schol. on Apollon. Rhod. 1, 916, 18b) Hs 6, 3, 4. Pl. (Dionys. Hal. 6, 31) **2 Cor 6:5** prob. of mob action; 2 Cl 11:4 (quot. of unknown orig.).

❷ **opposition to established authority, *disorder, unruliness*** (Nicol. Dam.: 90 fgm. 130, 110 p. 413, 27 Jac. ἐν ἀ. πραγμάτων; Cat. Cod. Astr. VIII/3, 182, 8; 187, 2) 1 Cl 14:1 (w. ἀλαζονεία); cp. 3:2; 43:6; (w. φαῦλον πρᾶγμα) **Js 3:16;** (opp. εἰρήνη) **1 Cor 14:33** (EKäsemann, NTS 1, '54/55, 248–60). Pl. (Cat. Cod. Astr. VII 126, 13; VIII/3, 175, 9) **2 Cor 12:20;** (w. πόλεμος) *insurrections* (PCairMasp 4, 6) **Lk 21:9.**—Boll 130f. M-M. TW.

ἀκαταστατέω (Epict. 2, 1, 12; Vett. Val. index; Cat. Cod. Astr. VII 134, 18; 138, 25; Tob 1:15 BA; Gen 4:12 Aq.) **to be mentally or behaviorally erratic, *be unsettled/vacillating,*** the man possessed by evil spirits is unsettled Hm 5, 2, 7. W. dat. ἀ. ταῖς βουλαῖς *be vacillating in their purposes* Hs 6, 3, 5.

ἀκατάστατος, ον (Hippocr. et al.; Polyb. 7, 4, 6; Plut., Mor. 437d; IDefixAudollent 4b, 12; SibOr 1, 164; Is 54:11 LXX; Gen 4:12 and La 4:14 Sym.; TestJob 36:3f) ***unstable, restless,*** of vacillating persons ἀ. ἐν πάσαις ταῖς ὁδοῖς αὐτοῦ one who is *unstable in all actions* **Js 1:8.** Of the tongue ἀ. κακόν *a restless evil* **3:8** (v.l. ἀκατάσχετον). Of slander personified ἀκατάστατον δαιμόνιον *a restless demon* Hm 2:3.—M-M. TW.

ἀκατάσχετος, ον (κατέχω 'hold back, control'; Hipparch. in Stob. 4, 44, 81; Diod. S. 17, 38; Plut., Mar. 432 [44, 10]; Aelian, NA 4, 48 ἀ. ὁρμῇ; Xenophon Eph. 1, 3, 4 ἔρως; POxy 684, 19 [restored]; Philo, Det. Pot. Ins. 110, Deus Imm. 138, Somn. 2, 275; Jos., Bell. 2, 407; Ps.-Phoc. 96; Job 31:11; 3 Macc 6:17) ***uncontrollable*** ἀκατασχέτῳ θυμῷ *w. uncontr. anger* MPol 12:2; **Js 3:8 v.l.** (s. ἀκατάστατος).

ἀκαυχησία, ας, ἡ (hapax leg.; καυχάομαι 'boast') ***freedom fr. boasting*** ἐν ἀ. *without boasting* IPol 5:2.

Ἀκελδαμάχ (v.l. Ακελδαιμαχ, Ακελδαμα, Ακελδαμακ, Αχελδαμαχ), Aram. חֲקֵל דְּמָא (=field of blood; cp. חקיל Dalman, Grammar[2] 137; חקלא MLidzbarski, Handbuch d. nordsem. Epigr. I [1898] 279) ***Akeldama,*** expl. as χωρίον αἵματος (**Mt 27:8** ἀγρὸς αἵματος) ***Field of Blood,*** of the field bought w. Judas' money **Ac 1:19** (formerly called [for this type of formulation cp. Diod. S. 4, 9, 6] the potter's field **Mt 27:7;** cp. Papias [3:3]); located by tradition south of the valley of Hinnom. Cp. EKautzsch, Gramm. d. Bibl.-Aramäischen 1884, 8; Dalman, Gramm.[2] 137, 1; 202, 2; JSickenberger, Judas als Stifter des Blutackers: BZ 18, 1929, 69–71; MWilcox, The Semitisms of Ac, '65, 87–89.

ἀκέραιος, ον (Eur., Hdt. et al.; ins, pap, EpArist; Jos., Bell. 1, 621, Ant. 1, 61; 5, 47) lit. 'unmixed'; in our lit. only fig. ***pure, innocent*** (cp. Pla., Rep. 3, 409a ἀ. κακῶν ἠθῶν; Epict. 3, 23, 15; Esth 8:12f; EpArist 31; 264) (w. φρόνιμος) **Mt 10:16,** quoted IPol 2:2; (w. σοφὸς εἰς τὸ ἀγαθόν) ἀ. εἰς τὸ κακόν *innocent as far as evil is concerned* **Ro 16:19;** (w. ἄμεμπτος) **Phil 2:15;** (w. εἰλικρινής) 1 Cl 2:5. τὸ ἀ. τῆς πραΰτητος βούλημα *the pure purpose of meekness* 1 Cl 21:7.—DELG and Frisk s.v. ἀκήρατος. M-M.

ἀκεραιοσύνη, ης, ἡ (only in Suda) ***purity*** ἐν ἀ. πιστεύειν *believe in all purity* (of heart) B 3:6. ἐν ἀ. περιπατεῖν 10:4.

ἀκηδεμονέω (hapax leg.) for ἀδημονέω (q.v.) **Mk 14:33** D.

ἀκηδία, ας, ἡ (κῆδος 'care', κήδομαι 'care for'; Hippocr. et al.; LXX; TestJob 25:10 al.) lit. 'indifference', then (cp. Ps

118:28; MHarl, La Bible et les pères '71, 256–59) ***apathy, melancholy*** (pl.=sing. B-D-F §142; Rob. 408) παραδιδόναι ἑαυτὸν εἰς τὰς ἀ. *give oneself over to apathy* Hv 3, 11, 39 (s. AVögtle, RAC I 62f).—DELG s.v. κήδω. Sv.

ἀκίνητος, ον (κινέω 'move'; Parmenides, Pind.+; ins, pap, LXX, TestJob 10:1; 25:5; TestSim 2:4; ApcSed 11:13 p. 134, 32 Ja; Philo; Jos., Ant. 15, 364; 399; Ath. 22, 5; 23, 1) 'without movement'.

❶ lit. **pert. to being in a fixed position—ⓐ** ***immovable*** πέτρα ἀ. IPol 1:1.—ⓑ of cult images ***unable to move*** Dg 2:4.

❷ fig. **pert. to being inwardly firm,** ***unwavering, steadfast*** of πίστις (because nailed at the cross) ISm 1:1; *unmoved* (by passions) τὸ ἀκίνητον (Dionys. Byz. §23 p. 10, 5; Philo, Op. M. 101) *steadfast character* IPhld 1:2.

ἄκκεπτα, ων, τά Lat. loanw. 'accepta' ***savings, back pay,*** t.t. of military finance: a sum credited to a Roman soldier and paid upon his discharge IPol 6:2 (s. δεπόσιτα).

ἀκλινής, ές (κλίνω 'lean'; Pla. et al.; Meleager [I BC]: Anth. Pal. 12, 158, 4 φιλία; Lucian, Encom. Demosth. 33 ἀ. τὴν ψυχήν; Aelian, VH 12, 64; POxy 904, 9; Philo, Mos. 1, 30, Virtut. 158, Spec. Leg. 2, 2 ὅρκος ἀ.; 4 Macc 6:7; 7:3; Ath. 31, 3; ὁ τὸν κανόνα τῆς ἀληθείας ἀκλινῆ ἐν ἑαυτῷ κατέχω Iren. 1, 9, 4 [Harv. I 88, 1]; 'bending to neither side') ***without wavering*** τὴν ὁμολογίαν ἀ. κατέχειν *hold fast the confession without wavering* **Hb 10:23.**—M-M. Spicq.

ἀκμάζω 1 aor. ἤκμασα; pf. inf. ἠκμακέναι Tat 31, 2 (Aeschyl. [impers. 'it is time' for someth.], Hdt. et al.; SIG 814, 17; 4 Macc 2:3; Philo, Aet. M. 63; 73; Jos., Ant. 13, 2, C. Ap. 2, 253; Tat. 31, 2f; Mel., HE 4, 26, 7) ***to bloom*** (fig. of the best time of life Iren. 3, 4, 3 [Harv. II 17, 1]) also (so since Thu. 2, 19, 1; SIG 866, 21f; PGM 5, 231; fig. of pers. Iren. 5, 36, 1 [Harv. II 427, 7]) *become ripe* of grapes (Plut., Mor. 671d) **Rv 14:18.**—DELG s.v. ἀκ- 45. M-M.

ἀκμήν adverbial acc. (*ak in Indo-Europ. expresses the idea of 'point', DELG s.v. ἀκ-; B-D-F §160; Rob. 294; 487f; KKrumbacher, ZVS 27, 1885, 498–521; 29, 1888, 188f) **extension of time up to and beyond a certain point,** ***even yet, still*** **Mt 15:16; Hb 5:13 v.l.** (Hyperid., fgm. 116; X., An. 4, 3, 26; Polyb. 1, 13, 12; 4, 36, 8; Plut., Mor. 346c; OGI 201, 13; PGen 14, 13 al.; TestJob 7:11 al.; Jos., Ant. 19, 118; Just., D. 89, 2; Phryn. p. 123 Lob.).—M-M.

ἄκμων, ονος, ὁ (Hom. et al.; PMich II, 123 recto VII, 10; PCairGoodsp 30, col. 22, 11; 18) ***anvil,*** type of firmness (Aeschyl., Pers. 51; Aristophon [IV BC] 4 K. ὑπομένειν πληγὰς ἄκμων; Job 41:16) ἀ. τυπτόμενος *an anvil when it is beaten* IPol 3:1.—B. 607. DELG.

ἀκοή, ῆς, ἡ (in form ἀκουή as early as Hom.; freq., incl. ins, pap, LXX; PsSol 8:5; ApcSed; ApcMos 8; EpArist, Test12Patr, Philo, Joseph., Just.; Ath. [1, 2]).

❶ **the faculty of hearing,** ***hearing*** (Philo, Rer. Div. Her. 12 of images οἷς ὦτα μέν ἐστιν, ἀκοαὶ δ' οὐκ ἔνεισιν; given by God Did., Gen. 162, 21) **1 Cor 12:17;** but mng. 3 is also prob.

❷ **the act of hearing,** ***listening*** (Pla., Theaet. 142d λόγος ἄξιος ἀκοῆς; Antig. Car. 129 ἀκοῆς ἄξια; BGU 1080, 6; EpArist 142 w. ὅρασις; Jos., Ant. 8, 171; w. ὄψις 172) w. βλέμμα **2 Pt 2:8** (cp. New Docs 3, 61). ἀκοῇ ἀκούειν (Polyaenus, Exc. 55, 2; LXX) **Mt 13:14; Ac 28:26** (both Is 6:9); B 9:2 (cp. Ex 15:26). εἰς ἀ. ὠτίου ὑπακούειν *obey upon hearing with the ear,* i.e. *as soon as one hears* B 9:1 (Ps 17:45; cp. 2 Km 22:45). ἀ. πίστεως *hearing of faith* (=that 'hearing' which Christians call faith) **Gal 3:2, 5** (SWilliams, NTS 35, '89, 82–93, but most prefer mng. 4b).

❸ **the organ w. which one hears,** ***ear*** (Sappho et al.; POxy 129, 4; PGM 4, 306; 323; 2 Macc 15:39; EpArist 166) esp. pl. (Dio Chrys. 15 [32], 11; Aelian, VH 3, 1 p. 39, 21; oft. Philo; Jos., Ant. 8, 172; SibOr 4, 172; Just., D. 131, 4; Orig., C. Cels. 1, 48, 33) αἱ ἀκοαί **Mk 7:35.** εἰσφέρειν εἰς τὰς ἀ. *bring to someone's ears* **Ac 17:20** (cp. Soph., Ajax 147). εἰς τὰς ἀ. τινος *in someone's ears* **Lk 7:1.** νωθρὸς (q.v.) ταῖς ἀ. **Hb 5:11.** κνήθεσθαι τὴν ἀ. *have itching ears* (i.e. they like to have them tickled) **2 Ti 4:3,** cp. vs. **4.** Fig. περιτέμνειν τὰς ἀ. *circumcise the ears*=make someone attentive B 9:4; 10:12.

❹ **that which is heard—ⓐ** ***fame, report, rumor*** (Hom. et al.; Sb 7205, 8; 1 Km 2:24; 2 Km 13:30; 3 Km 2:28; 10:7) **Mt 4:24; 14:1; 24:6; Mk 1:28; 13:7;** 1 Cl 47:7.

ⓑ ***account, report, message*** (Thu. 1, 20, 1 ἀκοὴν δέχεσθαι of things recounted by others in the past; Just., D. 8, 4 ματαίαν ἀ. παραδεξάμενοι) πιστεύειν τῇ ἀ. (cp. Jos., C. Ap. 2, 14; Just., D. 8, 4 [Is 53:1]; Did., Gen. 218, 2) **J 12:38; Ro 10:16f;** 1 Cl 16:3 (all three Is 53:1). ἐξ ἀ. πίστεως *as the result of a message (proclamation) which elicited (only) faith* **Gal 3:2, 5** (difft. Williams, 2 above). λόγος τῆς ἀκοῆς *the word of proclamation (preaching)* **Hb 4:2.** λόγος ἀκοῆς παρ' ἡμῶν τοῦ θεοῦ *the word of divine proclamation that goes out from us* **1 Th 2:13** (RSchippers, NovT 8, '66, 223–34 *tradition*).—AOepke, Die Missionspredigt d. Ap. Pls. 1920, 40ff.—DELG s.v. ἀκούω. M-M. TW. Sv.

ἀκοίμητος, ον (κοιμάω 'put to sleep'; since Aeschyl., Pr. 139; Aelian, NA 11, 3 πῦρ ἄσβεστον καὶ ἀ.; POxy 1468, 7; Wsd 7:10; ApcEsdr 4:20 p. 28, 22 Tdf. [σκώληξ]; Philo; SibOr 2, 181; Mel., fgm. 8b 31 ἀκοίμητον ἔχων τὸ πῦρ) **not to be put to sleep,** ***always active*** σκώληκες ἀ. *restless worms* ApcPt 12:27; ἀ. πνεῦμα IPol 1:3.—DELG s.v. κεῖμαι.

ἀκολουθέω impv. ἀκολούθει; impf. ἠκολούθουν; fut. ἀκολουθήσω; 1 aor. ἠκολούθησα; pf. ἠκολούθηκα **Mk 10:28** (denom. fr. ἀκόλουθος; Thu., Aristoph.+; Did., Gen. 49, 17 restored) prim. 'follow'.

❶ lit. **to move behind someone in the same direction,** ***come after*** abs. (Diod. S. 13, 75, 7) οἱ προάγοντες κ. οἱ ἀκολουθοῦντες **Mt 21:9; Mk 11:9;** cp. **J 21:20; Ac 21:36; 1 Cor 10:4; Rv 14:8.** W. dat. of pers. (X., Hell. 5, 2, 26; Herodian 6, 7, 8; PEnteux 48, 3 [III BC]) **Mt 9:19; 26:58; Mk 14:13; Lk 22:10; J 10:4f; 11:31;** IPhld 11:1; Hv 3, 8, 4; 7. ἠκολούθει τῷ Ἰησοῦ Σίμων Πέτρος κ. ἄλλος μαθητής **J 18:15** (more than one subject with a verb in the sing. as Appian, Bell. Civ. 3, 72 §296 ὑπερόψεταί με Λέπιδος κ. Πλάγκος).

❷ **to follow or accompany someone who takes the lead,** ***accompany, go along with,*** oft. of the crowd following Jesus ἠκολούθησαν αὐτῷ ὄχλοι πολλοί (s. ὄχλος 1a) **Mt 4:25; 8:1; 12:15; 14:13; Mk 5:24; Lk 7:9; 9:11; J 6:2.** μετά τινος *someone* (Thu. 7, 57, 9; Phryn. 353 Lob.; B-D-F §193, 1) **Rv 6:8** (**Lk 9:49** οὐκ ἀκολουθεῖ [sc. σοι] μεθ' ἡμῶν is different, *he does not follow* as your disciple *with us*). For this we have Hebraistically ὀπίσω τινός (3 Km 19:20; Is 45:14; Ezk 29:16) **Mt 10:38; Mk 8:34.**—Of the deeds that follow one into the next world **Rv 14:13** τὰ ἔργα αὐτῶν ἀκολουθεῖ μετ' αὐτῶν *the record of their deeds goes with them* (REB) (cp. Diod. S. 13, 105 νομίσαντες . . . ἑαυτοῖς τὴν μέμψιν ἀκολουθήσειν).

❸ w. transition to the fig. mng. **to follow someone as a disciple,** ***be a disciple, follow*** (Diog. L. 9, 21 of Parmenides: ἀκούσας Ξενοφάνους οὐκ ἠκολούθησεν αὐτῷ; Palaeph. 2 p.

6, 16; Just., D. 8, 3 ἀνθρώποις ἀκολουθῆσαι οὐδενὸς ἀξίοις) ἀκολούθει μοι *follow me =be my disciple* **Mt 9:9** (in Diog. L. 2, 48 Socrates stops Xenophon at their first meeting and says: "ἕπου καὶ μάνθανε". καὶ τοὐντεῦθεν ἀκροατὴς Σωκράτους ἦν); cp. **8:19; 19:21** (Aristoxenus, fgm. 17: Simichos the tyrant hears Pythagoras, divests himself of his kingly power, disposes of his χρήματα [Mt 19:22 v.l.], and attaches himself to him; Sextus 264a ἀφεὶς ἃ κέκτησαι ἀκολούθει τῷ ὀρθῷ λόγῳ); **27f; Mk 1:18** (on the call of a disciple directly fr. his work s. Jos., Ant. 8, 354 εὐθέως … καταλιπὼν τ. βόας ἠκολούθησεν Ἠλίᾳ … μαθητής [after 3 Km 19:20f]); **Mk 2:14; 8:34; Lk 5:11, 27f** al. The transition may be observed in **J 1,** where ἀ. has sense 2 in vss. **37f,** but sense 3 in vss. **40, 43** (OCullmann, TZ 4, '48, 367).—TArvedson, SvTK 7, '31, 134–61; ESchweizer, Lordship and Discipleship, '60; ASchulz, Nachfolgen u. Nachahmen, '62; GKilpatrick, BT 7, '56, 5f; RThysman, L'ethique de l'imitation du Christ dans le NT: ETL 42, '66, 138–75; TAerts, Suivre Jésus, ibid., 475–512.

❹ gener. **to comply with, *follow, obey*** (Thu. 3, 38, 6 γνώμῃ; Ps.-Andoc. 4, 19; Demosth. 26, 5; CPJ II, 152 [=BGU 1079], 10f ἀκολούθει Πτολλαρίωνι πᾶσαν ὥραν; μᾶλλον ἀκολουθῶν αὐτῷ ln. 26f; 2 Macc 8:36 νόμοις; cp. Jdth 2:3.—M. Ant. 7, 31 θεῷ; Jdth 5:7 τοῖς θεοῖς. Just., A I, 3, 2 εὐσεβείᾳ καὶ φιλοσοφίᾳ) τοῖς ἔθεσιν *customs* Dg 5:4. τοῖς νομίμοις τ. δεσπότου *obey the statutes of the Master* 1 Cl 40:4. τῇ ὁδῷ τῆς ἀληθείας 35:5 (cp. TestAsh 6:1 ἀ. τῇ ἀληθείᾳ); the bishop ISm 8:1; a schismatic IPhld 3:3.—Hm 6, 2, 9.

❺ **to come after someth. else in sequence, *follow,*** of things τῶν λοιπῶν τῶν ἀκολουθούντων πάντων *all other persons and things that follow* (in the parable) Hs 5, 5, 1; τινί **Mk 16:17 v.l.** (s. παρακολουθέω 2).—B. 699. DELG s.v. ἀκόλουθος. EDNT. M-M. TW. Sv.

ἀκόλουθος, ον (Bacchylides, Soph.+) **pert. to coming after someth. else in sequence, *following*** (so Demosth. et al.; 2 Macc 4:17) καὶ τῶν λοιπῶν τῶν ἀκολούθων πάντων *and of all the other things that followed* Hs 5, 5, 1 (cod. A). W. gen. (Ps.-Demosth. 59, 8 τὰ ἀ. αὐτῶν; Just., D. 101, 1 τὰ ἀ. τοῦ ψαλμοῦ) τὰ ἀ. τούτων *what follows them* Hm 8:4, 10; cp. s 9, 15, 3. W. dat. (Lucian, Herm. 74; Ps.-Lucian: Anth. Pal. 11, 401, 4) τὰ τούτοις ἀ. (1 Esdr 8:14; Jos., Ant. 14, 1) *and so forth* MPol 8:2; 9:2.—Abs. ἀ. ἐστιν *they follow* from them (OGI 669, 32; PTebt 296, 14) IEph 14:1; *it is suitable* (Demosth. 46, 17; Ael. Aristid. 13 p. 172 D. al.; PTebt 304, 18 τὸ ἀ. 'what is suitable') ὅπου καὶ ἀ. ἦν *where it was suitable=at a suitable place* MPol 18:1.—DELG.

ἀκοντίζω 1 aor. pass. ἠκοντίσθην (ἄκων 'javelin', s. DELG s.v. ἀκ-; Hom., Hdt. et al.; LXX; TestSol 7:8; Test12Patr, JosAs; GrBar 5:3, Joseph.) lit. 'cast a spear' then gener. ***throw, cast*** χάλαζα … ἠκοντίσθη ἀπ' οὐρανοῦ AcPl Ha 5, 7.

ἀκόρεστος, ον (κόρος 'satiety', s. DELG s.v. κορε-; Aeschyl. et al.—in Hom. ἀκόρητος; PCairMasp 89 III, 6; Mel) ***insatiable*** fig. (X., Symp. 8, 15 φιλία; Philo, Somn. 1, 50 ἵμερος, Ebr. 4; Mel., P. 20, 143 θάνατος; 50, 361 ἡδοναί) πόθος *desire* (to do good) 1 Cl 2:2.

ἀκουστός, ή, όν *audible* (Hom. Hymns et al.; LXX; TestSol 22:1 B ἀκουστὸν γέγονεν; Philo) ἀκουστὸν ἐγένετο τοῖς ἀποστόλοις ὅτι *it came to the apostles' ears that* **Ac 11:1** D (ἀ. γίνεσθαι as Isocr. 3, 49; Gen 45:2; Dt 4:36; Is 48:20).—DELG s.v. ἀκούω.

ἀκουτίζω fut. ἀκουτιῶ; 1 aor. ἠκούτισα (LXX; Syntipas p. 73, 1; Aesop. mss. [Ursing 78f]; Suda s.v. δογματίζω; Etym. Mag. p. 51, 32; Etym. Gud. 71, 5; Anecd. Gr. p. 366, 3) ***cause to hear*** ἀ. με ἀγαλλίασιν 1 Cl 18:8 (Ps 50:10).—DELG s.v. ἀκούω.

ἀκούω fut. ἀκούσω SibOr 4, 175; **Mt 12:19; 13:14** (Is 6:9); **J 5:25, 28; 10:16,** ἀκούσομαι EpArist 5; **Ac 3:22** (Dt 18:15); **28:28** (freq. w. vv.ll.); 1 aor. ἤκουσα; pf. ἀκήκοα; ptc. ἠκουκώς Hs 5, 4, 2. Pass.: fut. ἀκουσθήσομαι; 1 aor. ἠκούσθην; pf. 3 sg. ἤκουσται Dt 4:32 (Hom.+) 'hear', as a passive respondent to λέγω.

❶ lit. **to have or exercise the faculty of hearing, *hear***

ⓐ abs. τὰ ὦτα ἀκούουσιν **Mt 13:16;** κωφοὶ ἀ. **11:5;** cp. **Mk 7:37; Lk 7:22;** τοῖς ὠσὶν βαρέως ἀ. *be hard of hearing* **Mt 13:15** (Is 6:10); ἀκοῇ ἀ. **Mt 13:14; Ac 28:26** (both Is 6:9). ἀκούοντες οὐκ ἀκούουσιν *they hear and yet do not hear* **Mt 13:13** (s. Aeschyl., Prom. 448 κλύοντες οὐκ ἤκουον; Demosth. 25 [Against Aristogeiton 1], 89, citing the maxim ὁρῶντας μὴ ὁρᾶν καὶ ἀκούοντας μὴ ἀκούειν), cp. **Mk 8:18** (Ezk 12:2) and s. 7 below. In the protasis of a challenge to hearers, by which their attention is drawn to a special difficulty: ὁ ἔχων ὦτα (οὖς) ἀκούειν ἀκουέτω, w. variations (Arrian, Ind. 5, 1 ὅστις ἐθέλει φράζειν …, φραζέτω) **Mt 11:15 v.l.; 13:9 v.l., 43 v.l.; Mk 4:9, 23; 7:15 [16] v.l.; Lk 8:8; 14:35** (EBishop, BT 7, '56, 38–40); **Rv 2:7, 11, 17, 29; 3:6, 13, 22; 13:9.** Cp. Ox 1081 verso, 6–8; s. 7 below for the restored text. For the sense of the impv. in these challenges also s. 7. S. οὖς 2.

ⓑ w. obj. (on the syntax B-D-F §173; 416, 1; Rob. 506f; on the LXX s. Johannessohn, Kasus, 36; Helbing, Kasussyntax 150ff).

α. foll. by a thing as obj. in acc. (Diod. S. 8, 32, 1 τὶ something) **Mt 11:4; 13:17ff; Lk 7:22; 1J 1:1, 3.** τὴν φωνήν (UPZ 77 I, 25) **Mt 12:19; J 3:8; Ac 22:9** (but see 7 below); 1 Cl 39:3 (Job 4:16); (pass. **Mt 2:18** [Jer 38:15]; **Rv 18:22**). τὸν λόγον **Mt 13:20ff; J 5:24.** τοὺς λόγους, τὰ ῥήματα **Mt 10:14; J 8:47** s. 4 below; **Ac 2:22.** πολέμους καὶ ἀκοὰς πολέμων **Mt 24:6.** τὴν βλασφημίαν **26:65.** τὸν ἀσπασμόν **Lk 1:41.** ἄρρητα ῥήματα **2 Cor 12:4.** τὸν ἀριθμόν **Rv 9:16.** τὴν ἀποκάλυψιν Hv 3, 12, 2. Pass. τὰ ἀκουσθέντα *what has been heard* i.e. the message **Hb 2:1.** ἠκούσθη ὁ λόγος εἰς τὰ ὦτα τῆς ἐκκλησίας … ἐν Ἰερουσαλήμ *the report reached the ears of the church in Jerusalem* **Ac 11:22.** Oft. the obj. is to be supplied fr. context **Mt 13:17; Mk 4:15; J 6:60a; Ac 2:37; 8:30; 9:21; Ro 10:14.** καθὼς ἀκούω = ἃ ἀ. **J 5:30.**

β. τί τινος *hear someth. fr. someone* τὴν ἐπαγγελίαν, ἣν ἠκούσατέ μου *the promise which you heard from me* **Ac 1:4.** Still other constrs. occur, which are also poss. when the hearing is not directly fr. the mouth of the informant, but involves a report which one has received fr. the pers. in any way at all (s. below 3d). τὶ ἔκ τινος (Od. 15, 374; Hdt. 3, 62 ἐκ τοῦ κήρυκος) **2 Cor 12:6.** τὶ παρά τινος (Soph., Oed. R. 7 παρ' ἀγγέλων; Pla., Rep. 6, 506d; Demosth. 6, 26; Jer 30:8; Jos., Bell. 1, 529) **J 8:26, 40** (τὴν ἀλήθειαν ἀ. as Diod. S. 16, 50, 2); **15:15; Ac 10:22; 28:22; 2 Ti 2:2;** w. attraction of the relative λόγων ὧν παρ' ἐμοῦ ἤκουσας *teachings which you have heard from me* **1:13;** τὶ ἀπό τινος (Thu. 1, 125, 1) **1J 1:5.** Hebraistically ἀπὸ τ. στόματός τινος **Lk 22:71** (cp. ἐκ τ. στόμ. τ. Ex 23:13; Ezk 3:17; 33:7).

γ. foll. by a thing as obj. in gen. (Hdt. 8, 135; X., Cyr. 3, 1, 8; Demosth. 18, 3; B-D-F §173, 2; Rob. 507) *hear someth.* τῆς βλασφημίας (= τὴν βλ. **Mt 26:65**) **Mk 14:64.** συμφωνίας καὶ χορῶν **Lk 15:25;** τῆς φωνῆς (BGU 1007, 11 [III BC] ἀκούσαντες φωνῆς) **J 5:25, 28; Ac 9:7** (on the experience of Paul and his companions cp. Maximus Tyr. 9, 7d–f: some see a divine figure, others see nothing but hear a voice, still others both see and hear); **11:7; 22:7** (HMoehring, NovT 3, '59, 80–99; s. Rob. 506). τῶν λόγων **Lk 6:47.** τῶν ῥημάτων **J 12:47.**

ⓒ *hear, listen to* w. gen. of the pers. and a ptc. (Pla., Prot. 320b; X., Symp. 3, 13; Herm. Wr. 12, 8; Jos., Ant. 10, 105 ἤκουσε τοῦ προφήτου ταῦτα λέγοντος): ἠκούσαμεν αὐτοῦ λέγοντος *we have heard him say* **Mk 14:58;** ἀκοῦσαι προσευχομένου Παύλου AcPl Ha 2, 12. ἤκουον εἷς ἕκαστος . . . λαλούντων αὐτῶν *each one heard them speaking* **Ac 2:6, 11; Rv 16:5, 7** (in vs. 7 the altar speaks); Hv 1, 3, 3. W. acc. instead of gen. πᾶν κτίσμα . . . καὶ τὰ ἐν αὐτοῖς πάντα ἤκουσα λέγοντας (v.l. λέγοντα) **Rv 5:13.** Used without ptc. w. pronoun only: μου (Dio Chrys. 79 [28], 14) **Mk 7:14; Ac 26:3.** αὐτῶν **Lk 2:46.** αὐτοῦ vs. **47; 15:1; 19:48; 21:38; J 3:29** etc. ἡμῶν **Ac 24:4.**—ἀ. τινὸς περί τινος (since Hdt. 7, 209; IG II, 168 [338 BC]) *hear someone* (speak) *about someth.* **Ac 17:32.** ἤκουσεν αὐτοῦ περὶ τῆς . . . πίστεως *he heard him speak about faith* **Ac 24:24,** cp. Hm 11:7.—W. ὅτι foll. (X., Cyr. 3, 3, 18) **J 14:28; Ac 22:2.**—Abs. οἱ ἀκούοντες *the hearers* (Diod. S. 4, 7, 4) **Lk 6:27;** MPol 7:3. Esp. impv. ἄκουε *listen!* **Mk 12:29** (Dt 6:4); Hs 5, 1, 3; pl. **Mk 4:3.** ἀκούσατε **Ac 7:2; 13:16;** AcPl Ha 8, 10. W. συνίετε *listen and try to understand* **Mt 15:10.**

❷ legal t.t. **to hear a legal case,** ***grant a hearing*** to someone (X., Hell. 1, 7, 9 al.; PAmh 135, 14; PIand 9, 10; 15; BGU 511 II, 2; POxy 1032, 59) w. παρά τινος: ἐὰν μὴ ἀκούσῃ πρῶτον παρ' αὐτοῦ *without first giving him a hearing* **J 7:51** (SPancaro, Biblica 53, '72, 340–61).—**Ac 25:22.**

❸ **to receive news or information about someth.,** ***learn about*** someth.—ⓐ abs. ἀκούσας δὲ ὁ Ἰησοῦς *when Jesus learned about it* (the death of J. Bapt.) **Mt 14:13.**—**Mk 3:21; 6:14** (s. HLjungvik, ZNW 33, '34, 90–92); **Ro 10:18.** W. ἀναγγέλλειν **15:21** (Is 52:15).

ⓑ w. gen. of person οὗ οὐκ ἤκουσαν *of whom they have not heard* **Ro 10:14a.**—W. acc. of thing (X., Cyr. 1, 1, 4; Diod. S. 19, 8, 4; Chion, Ep. 12 ἀκ. τὴν τυραννίδα; Herodian 4, 4, 8) *learn of* τὴν ἀγάπην **Phlm 5.** τὴν ἀναστροφήν **Gal 1:13.** τὰ ἔργα τοῦ Χριστοῦ **Mt 11:2.** τὴν ἐνέδραν *the ambush* **Ac 23:16:** Χριστιανισμὸν ἀ. *hear Christianity* IPhld 6:1; τὴν οἰκονομίαν **Eph 3:2.** τὴν πίστιν **1:15; Col 1:4.** τὴν ὑπομονήν **Js 5:11.**—Pass. ἀκούεται ἐν ὑμῖν πορνεία *it is reported that there is immorality among you* **1 Cor 5:1** (schol. on Nicander, Ther. 139 τοῦτο ἐξακούεται=this report is heard). ἐὰν ἀκουσθῇ τοῦτο ἐπὶ τοῦ ἡγεμόνος *if this should come to the prefect's ears* **Mt 28:14.**

ⓒ ἀ. τι περί τινος (since Hdt. 2, 43) *learn someth. about someone* **Lk 9:9; 16:2.**—ἀ. περί τινος (Jos., Vi. 246) **Lk 7:3.**

ⓓ w. prep., to denote the author or source of the information (s. 1bβ) ἀ. τι παρά τινος: τῶν ἀκουσάντων παρὰ Ἰωάννου *who had learned fr. John* (who Jesus was) **J 1:40,** cp. **6:45** (Simplicius in Epict. p. 110, 35 τὸ ἀκοῦσαι παρὰ θεοῦ, ὅτι ἀθάνατός ἐστιν ἡ ψυχή); ἀ. τι ἔκ τινος: ἠκούσαμεν ἐκ τοῦ νόμου *we have heard from the law* (when it was read in the synagogue) **J 12:34,** where ἀ. approaches the technical sense *learn* (a body of authoritative teaching), as **1J 1:5** (s. above); **2:7, 24** et al. (OPiper, JBL 66, '47, 437 n. 1). ἀ. ἀπό τινος περί τινος **Ac 9:13.**

ⓔ w. ὅτι foll. (SIG 370, 21; PTebt 416, 8; BGU 246, 19; Josh l0:1; Da 5:14 Theod.; 1 Macc 6:55; 4 Macc 4:22; cp. the constr. ἀ. τινὰ ὅτι Od. 3, 193; X., Mem. 4, 2, 33) **Mt 2:22; 4:12** al.—Pass. ἠκούσθη ὅτι ἐν οἴκῳ ἐστίν *it became known that he was in the house* **Mk 2:1** (s. B-D-F §405, 2). οὐκ ἠκούσθη ὅτι *it is unheard of that* **J 9:32.**

ⓕ w. acc. and inf. foll. (Hom. et al.; Jos., Ant. 11, 165; 13, 292) **J 12:18; 1 Cor 11:18.** W. acc. and ptc. (X., Cyr. 2, 4, 12; Herodian 2, 12, 4) **Ac 7:12; 3J 4.**

❹ **to give careful attention to,** ***listen to, heed*** ἀ. τινός *someone* (Hom. et al.) ἀκούετε αὐτοῦ **Mt 17:5; Lk 9:35; Ac 3:22** (all three Dt 18:15); cp. **Mt 18:15; Lk 16:29, 31; J 10:8; Ac 4:19.** W. acc. of thing **J 8:47** (s. 1bα); PEg[2] 53f (restored).—Abs. (PsSol 2:8) *obey, listen* αὐτοὶ καὶ ἀκούσονται **Ac 28:28;** cp. **Mt 18:16; J 5:25b;** *agree* **9:27a.**

❺ **to pay attention to by listening,** ***listen to*** ἀ. τινός *someone/someth.* (Mitt-Wilck. I/2, 14 I, 18; 461, 6) **Mk 6:11; J 6:60b.** Of God (Hom.+) **Ac 7:34** (Ex 3:7); **J 9:31; 11:41f; 1J 5:14f;** AcPt Ox 849, 27.—Abs. καθὼς ἠδύναντο ἀ. *as they were able to listen* **Mk 4:33** (EMolland, SymbOsl 8, 1929, 83–91; s. also 7 below).

❻ **to be given a nickname or other identifying label,** ***be called*** (Demosth. 18, 46 κόλακες ἀκούουσι; Diog. L. 2, 111 a derisive nickname; 2, 140) ἤκουσαν προδόται γονέων *they were called betrayers of their parents* Hv 2, 2, 2.

❼ **to hear and understand a message,** ***understand*** (Teles p. 47, 12; Galen: CMG Suppl. I p. 12, 29; Aelian, VH 13, 46; Apollon. Dysc., Syntax p. 295, 25 [Gramm. Gr. II/2 p. 424, 5 U.] ἀκούειν=συνιέναι τῶν ἠκουσμένων; Sext. Emp., Math. 1, 37 τὸ μὴ πάντας πάντων ἀκούειν; Julian, Orat. 4 p. 147a; PGM 3, 453 ἀκούσεις τὰ ὄρνεα λαλοῦντα; Philo, Leg. All. 2, 35) abs. (Is 36:11) **1 Cor 14:2.** Perh. also **Mk 4:33** (s. 5 above, and cp. Epict. 1, 29, 66 τ. δυναμένοις αὐτὰ ἀκοῦσαι). On the form of **Lk 6:27a** cp. Cleopatra 16, 57 ὑμῖν δὲ λέγω τοῖς εὖ φρονοῦσιν. W. acc. τὸν νόμον *understand the law* **Gal 4:21;** perh. **Ac 22:9; 26:14** (s. 1bα above) belong here. Cp. also the play on words (1a above) ἀκούοντες οὐκ ἀκούουσιν **Mt 13:13;** cp. **Mk 8:18.** Here belong also the imperatives in **Mt 11:15; 13:9, 43; Mk 4:9, 23; 7:15 [16] v.l.; Lk 8:8; 14:35; Rv 2:7, 11, 17, 29; 3:6, 13, 22; 13:9;** also ὁ ἔχων ὦ[τ]α τ[ῶν ἀ]|περάντων [ἀ]κο[ύει?]ν ἀ|κουέτω *one who has ears to hear the things that are without limits let him hear* Ox 1081, 6–8, rev. on the basis of the Coptic, s. SJCh 89, 5f; cp. Borger, GGA 122.—ἀκούω is occasionally used as a perfective present: *I hear=I have heard* (so as early as Il. 24, 543; Aristoph., Frogs 426; X., An. 2, 5, 13, Mem. 2, 4, 1; 3, 5, 26; Pla., Rep. 583d; Theocr. 15, 23) **Lk 9:9; 1 Cor 11:18; 2 Th 3:11.** B-D-F §322.—B. 1037; 1339. DELG. M-M. TW. Sv.

ἀκρασία, ας, ἡ (s. DELG s.v. κεράννυμι, cp. κράτος; PreSocr. et al.;=ἀκράτεια Phryn. 524f Lob.) ***lack of self-control, self-indulgence*** (so in X. et al.; Philo; Jos., Bell. 1, 34; SibOr 1, 35; Tat. 2:1); w. ref. to sexual activity (X., Symp. 8, 27; Diod. S. 3, 65, 2; 19, 33, 2 δι' ἀκρασίαν; Musonius p. 66 H.; PsSol 4:3 ἐν ἀκρασίαις; Jos., Ant. 8, 191 τ. ἀφροδισίων ἀκ.; Tat. 8, 4; 33, 4 μοιχείαις καί ἀ. βραβεῖον; 34, 1) ἵνα μὴ πειράζῃ ὑμᾶς ὁ σατανᾶς διὰ τὴν ἀ. ὑμῶν *because of your lack of self-control* (cp. Jos., C. Ap. 1, 319; 2, 244) **1 Cor 7:5; Mt 23:25** (the vv.ll. ἀκαθαρσίας, ἀδικίας, πλεονεξίας, πονηρίας do not go well w. ἁρπαγῆς, but 'intemperance' corresponds to the 'cup'). Personif. as a vice Hs 9, 15, 3.—TW. Spicq. Sv.

ἀκρατής, ές (Aesch., Thu. et al.; Vett. Val. 39, 33; ins; Pr 27:20a; EpArist 277; Philo; Jos., Ant. 16, 399; Just.; Tat. 9, 1) ***without self-control, dissolute*** (opp. ἐγκρατής Aristot., EN 7, 4, 1146b, 9f) **2 Ti 3:3** (in a list of vices).—M-M. TW.

ἄκρατος, ον (κεράννυμι; since Hom., who has ἄκρητος; LXX; PsSol 8:14; TestSol 18:31; Philo; Jos., Ant. 17, 103) ***unmixed*** οἶνος (Od. 24, 73; Hdt. 1, 207; Posidon.: 87 fgm. 15, 4 Jac. 22; 3 Macc 5:2) fig. (cp. POxy 237 VII, 40 ἄκρατος τῶν νόμων ἀποτομία) of God's anger *in full strength* **Rv 14:10** (cp. Jer 32:15; Ps 74:9; PsSol 8, 14. On 'mixed/unmixed' wine s. BBandstra, Wine: ISBE IV 1070 and 1072 [bibl.]; s. also RCharles, ICC

Rv ad loc. ἀκρ. is found w. ὀργή Aeschyl., Prom. 678; Alcidamas [IV BC] in Aristot., Rhet. 1406a, 10; Jos., Ant. 5, 150; 17, 148).—DELG s.v. κεράννυμι. M-M.

ἀκρίβεια, ας, ἡ strict conformity to a norm or standard, *exactness, precision* (so Thu. et al. [s. Renehan '75, 19]; pap since III BC: e.g. UPZ 110, 46 [164 BC]; POxy 471, 11ff [I AD]; 237 VIII, 39 [II AD]; also s. Preis.; LXX; En 106:12; EpArist 103; Philo; Jos., Ant. 4, 309; 9, 208 al.; Tat.; Mel., HE 4, 26, 13) πεπαιδευμένος κατὰ ἀ. τοῦ πατρῴου νόμου *educated strictly according to our ancestral law* **Ac 22:3** (Isocr. 7, 40 ἀ. νόμων; Jos., Vi. 191). ABaumgarten, The Name of the Pharisees: JBL 102, '83, 411–28.—DELG s.v. ἀκριβής. M-M. Sv.

ἀκριβεύομαι (περί τινος Sext. Emp., Math. 1, 71; pass. PAmh 154, 7 [VI AD]) in act. sense ***pay strict attention*** περὶ τῆς σωτηρίας B 2:10.—DELG s.v. ἀκριβής.

ἀκριβής, ές (Heraclitus+; ins, pap, LXX; TestSol 4:1 D; Philo; Jos., Ant. 2, 60; Just., Tat., Ath.; Iren. 5, 2, 3 [Harv. II 324, 3]) ***exact, strict*** κατὰ τὴν ἀκριβεστάτην αἵρεσιν *according to the strictest sect* **Ac 26:5.**—DELG. M-M.

ἀκριβόω 1 aor. ἠκρίβωσα (since Eur., X., Pla.; Aristot., Gen. Anim. 5, 1, 780b of inability to distinguish colors; Aq. Is 30:8 and 49:16; Philo; Mel. [?], fgm. 12, 4; Ath.) **make detailed inquiry about someth., *ascertain precisely/exactly*** (Vett. Val. 265, 3; Philo, Op. M. 77; Jos., Bell. 1, 648 of careful study, Vi. 365 of care exercised in writing) τὶ παρά τινος: παρ' αὐτῶν τὸν χρόνον i.e. Herod pressed the Magi for the precise time **Mt 2:7;** cp. vs. **16.**—Frisk s.v. ἀκριβής. M-M.

ἀκριβῶς adv. (Aeschyl., Hdt.+; ins, pap, LXX; TestSol 10:6; 24:2; TestJob 31:1; EpArist, Philo, Joseph., Just.; Ath. 11:1, R. 454, 4; Mel., HE 4, 26, 14; freq. in historical writers, but also medical s. Hobart 251; Alexander [s. below] 131) **pert. to strict conformity to a standard or norm, w. focus on careful attention, *accurately, carefully, well*** βλέπειν (POxy 1381, 111f [I/II]) **Eph 5:15.** ἀκούειν (Thu. 1, 134, 1) Hm 3:4; 4, 3, 7. προσέχειν *pay close attention* B 7:4. γινώσκειν (Antiphanes 196, 15 Kock al.; Diod. S. 11, 41, 5 et al.) Hs 9, 5, 5. κατανοεῖν (Herm. Wr. 11, 6b) s 9, 6, 3. εἰδέναι (Aeschyl., Pr. 328 et al.; Epict. 1, 27, 17; 2, 22, 36; PPetr II, 15 [1], 11) **1 Th 5:2.** διδάσκειν **Ac 18:25;** Pol 3:2. γράφειν Papias 2:15. ἐξετάζειν (Isocr. 7, 63; Demosth. 6, 37; Galen ed. Kühn XIV, 210; Dt 19:18; Jos., Ant. 3, 70) **Mt 2:8;** Hs 9, 13, 6. γράφειν *conscientiously write/record* Papias (2:15). παρακολουθεῖν *follow carefully* **Lk 1:3** (cp. Herodian 1, 1, 3 μετὰ πάσης ἀκριβείας ἤθροισα ἐς συγγραφήν; Stephan. Byz. s.v. Χαράκμωβα: Οὐράνιος ἐν τοῖς 'Αραβικοῖς—ἀξιόπιστος δ' ἀνὴρ ... σπουδὴν γὰρ ἔθετο ἱστορῆσαι ἀκριβῶς ...).—Comp. ἀκριβέστερον *more exactly* (POxy 1102, 12; BGU 388 II, 41; Philo, Joseph.; Tat. 15, 2; Ath. 9, 2) ἀ. ἐκτίθεσθαι *explain more exactly* **Ac 18:26,** cp. **23:15, 20;** also *more accurately* (PPetr II, 16, 13 [205 BC]; Epict. 1, 24, 10) **24:22.** ἀ. αὐτὰ γνωσόμεθα *we will find it out more exactly* Hv 3, 10, 10. ἰδεῖν (v.l. μανθάνειν [Herm. Wr. 10, 25; Jos., Ant. 8, 402]) s 9, 1, 3.—LAlexander, The Preface to Luke's Gospel '93.—DELG s.v. ἀκριβής. M-M.

ἀκρίς, ίδος, ἡ (Hom. et al.; PTebt 772, 2 [236 BC]; PColZen 114 m, 6; LXX, TestSol; GrBar 16:3; Philo; Jos., Ant. 2, 306; SibOr 5, 454) **the desert locust: 'Schistocerca gregaria'; *locust,*** a migratory phase of the grasshopper, of the family Acrididae, even today commonly eaten by the poorer people in Arabia, Africa, and Syria (cp. Aristoph., Ach. 1116; Diod. S. 3, 29, 1f; Strabo 16, 4, 12; Theophyl. Sim., Ep. 14; Pliny the Elder 6, 35; Lev 11:22): used as food by John the Baptist (other, less prob., interpr. of ἀ. in ELohmeyer, Joh. d. T. '32, p. 50, 4) **Mt 3:4; Mk 1:6;** the widespread notion that the ἀ. were carob pods (St. John's-bread; so TKCheyne, EncBibl s.v. 'husks') is supported neither by good linguistic evidence nor by probability (s. HastDB s.v. 'husks' and 'locust'); s. also ἐγκρίς. They appear at the fifth trumpet **Rv 9:3, 7.** Fiery locusts (in an apocalyptic vision) Hv 4, 1, 6.—SKrauss, Z. Kenntnis d. Heuschrecken in Palästina: ZDPV 50, 1927, 244–49; HGrégoire, Les Sauterelles de St Jean: Byzantion 5, 1930, 109–28; FAndersen, The Diet of John the Baptist: Abr-Nahrain 3, '63, 60–74; GKeown, ISBE 3:149–50.—On Rv: Boll 68–77; 145f; against him JFreundorfer, D. Apk. d. Ap. J. u. d. hellenist. Kosmologie u. Astrologie 1929.—DELG.

ἀκροατήριον, ου, τό *audience hall* (Lat. auditorium) of the procurator, in which hearings were held and justice was privately dispensed (Mommsen, Röm. Strafrecht 1899, 362) *hall of justice* **Ac 25:23.** Otherwise gener. *auditorium, chamber, lecture-hall* (Philo, Congr. Erud. Grat. 64; Tat. 22, 2; Dio Chrys. 15 [32], 8; Plut., Mor. 45f; Epict. 3, 23, 8).—DELG s.v. ἀκροάομαι.

ἀκροατής, οῦ, ὁ (Thu. et al.; PLond I, 46, 177 [IV AD] p. 70; Is 3:3; Sir 3:29; EpArist 266; Just.; Tat. 22, 3; Ath. 2, 2) ***a hearer*** Dg 2:1. ἀ. λόγου (cp. Philo, Congr. Erud. Grat. 70) **Js 1:23;** pl. (Diod. S. 4, 7, 4) vs. **22** (Thu., 3, 38, 4 a similar reproach directed against the θεαταὶ μὲν τῶν λόγων, ἀκροαταὶ δὲ τῶν ἔργων). ἀ. νόμου **Ro 2:13** (cp. Jos., Ant. 5, 107; 132 νόμων ἀκροαταί). ἀ. ἐπιλησμονῆς *a forgetful hearer* **Js 1:25.** γενοῦ ἀ. *listen!* Hv 1, 3, 3. ἀκροατὴν καὶ αὐτόπτην *hearer and eye-witness* Papias (2:2)—DELG s.v. ἀκροάομαι. M-M.

ἀκροβυστία, ας, ἡ (prob. from ἀκροποσθία [Hippocrates, Aph. 6, 19; Aristot., HA 1, 13, 493a, 29], connected by popular etymology w. βύειν; B-D-F §120, 4; Mlt-H. 277; found only in Bibl. and eccl. Gk.; Etym. Magn. p. 53, 47; Lampe).

❶ lit. *prepuce, foreskin* (opp. περιτομή). ἄνδρες ἀ. ἔχοντες *uncircumcised people* (=gentiles; cp. Gen 34:14) **Ac 11:3.—1 Cor 7:18f.** ἀπερίτμητος ἀκροβυστίᾳ *w. uncircumcised foreskin* B 9:5.

❷ fig. ***uncircumcision*** as a state of being **Ro 2:25ff; Gal 5:6; 6:15.** πιστεύειν δι' ἀκροβυστίας *to believe as an uncircumcised man,* i.e. *as a non-Judean* or *gentile* **Ro 4:11;** B 13:7; cp. **Ro 4:10–12.** W. ref. to the sins of the gentile world νεκροὶ ... τῇ ἀ. τῆς σαρκὸς ὑμῶν *dead through your uncircumcised* (i.e. full of vice, in the gentile manner) *flesh* **Col 2:13** (cp. Gen 17:11 σὰρξ τῆς ἀ.).

❸ abstr. for concr. ***noncircumcised, gentiles*** i.e. *non-Judeans* (beside περιτομή) **Ro 3:30; 4:9; Col 3:11; Eph 2:11.** τὸ εὐαγγέλιον τῆς ἀ. *the gospel for the gentile world* (*gospel of/about uncircumcision* is less prob., for the corresponding statement about Peter would call for an unlikely emphasis on circumcision by Peter, and vs. 8 balances ἔθνη against περιτομή) **Gal 2:7.**—DELG s.v. ἀκ- 44. M-M (no pap examples). TW.

ἀκρόβυστος, ου, ὁ (not LXX, but used by other translators of the OT; Just., D. 19, 3 οὐκ ἂν ἀ. ὁ θεὸς ἔπλασε τὸν 'Αδάμ; Mel., P. 76, 555 [Ch., so also Perler]; 92, 691) ***an uncircumcised pers.*** IPhld 6:1 (non-Judean Christians).

ἀκρογωνιαῖος, α, ον (purely biblical; TestSol) **lying at the extreme corner** ἀ. λίθος ***cornerstone*** (this meaning is defended by JArmitage Robinson, Eph; ESelwyn, 1 Pt; TAbbott, ICC Eph-Col; JPfammater, Die Kirche als Bau: Analecta Gregoriana 110, '60, 140–51; KSchäfer, Lapis summus angulari:

Festschr. HLützeler '62, 9–29; ibid. Zur Deutung von ἀ. Eph 2:20: Festschr. JSchmid '63, 218–24) or ***capstone*** (TestSol 22:7–23:4; s. κεφαλή 2b; rejected by RMcKelvey who defends *cornerstone,* NTS 8, '61/62, 352–59), only fig., of Christ **Eph 2:20;** w. ref. to the preciousness of the material λίθον ἐκλεκτὸν ἀ. ἔντιμον **1 Pt 2:6** (s. comm.); B 6:2 (both Is 28:16); s. lit. on κεφαλή 2b.—Cp. pap and ins cited DGE s.v. γωνιαῖος. KSchelkle, RAC I, 233f. EDNT. M-M. TW.

ἀκροθίνιον, ου, τό (oft. pl. and usu. 'topmost/best part of the heap'; hence 'first-fruits of the field, booty' reserved for the divinity Eumelus: Epici p. 193 K. [fgm. 11, 1]=p. 113 B. [fgm. 12]; Pind., N. 7, 41; Hdt. 1, 86; Thu. 1, 132, 2 al.; SIG 23; 605a 5) the general sense ***booty, spoils*** is prob. for **Hb 7:4.**—Renehan '82, 17. DELG s.v. ἀκ- 44. M-M.

ἄκρον, ου, τό (Hom.+; really neut. of ἄκρος W-S. §20, 12c; Rob. 775) ***high point, top*** ὄρους *of a mountain* (Ex 34:2) Hs 9, 1, 4; ἐπ᾽ ἄκρον ὄρους ὑψηλοῦ[ς] *on the top of a high mountain* (Is 28:4) Ox 1 recto, 16 (ASyn. 53, 22; cp. GTh 32). τὸ ἄ. τῆς ῥάβδου *the top of his staff* **Hb 11:21** (Gen 47:31). τὸ ἀ. τοῦ δακτύλου (schol. on Nicander, Ther. 383 τὰ ἄκρα τῶν δακτύλων; cp. 4 Macc 10:7; Philo, De Prov. in Eus., PE 8, 14, 65; Jos., Ant. 11, 234; Just., D. 91, 2 of the arms of the cross) *a finger tip* **Lk 16:24;** of the *tip* of a stick Hs 8, 1, 14; 8, 10, 1.—*Extreme limit, end* (Pla., Phd. 109d ἄ. τῆς θαλάσσης; POxy 43 verso I, 17; PThéad 19, 12; En 26:4; Jos., Ant. 14, 299; τὰ ἀ. τῆς γῆς Theoph. Ant. 2, 35 [p. 188, 10]): ἀπ᾽ ἄ. οὐρανῶν ἕως ἄ. αὐτῶν *from one end of heaven to the other* **Mt 24:31** (Dt 30:4; Ps 18:7; cp. Dt 4:32; Jos., Ant. 19, 6 ἀπ᾽ ἄκρων ἐπ᾽ ἄκρα; Just., D. 64, 7 ἀπ᾽ ἄκρων τῶν οὐρανῶν). The expr. found in the OT pass. mentioned is mixed w. the one found in Dt 13:8 and Jer 12:12 (cp. PsSol 17:31) in ἀπ᾽ ἄ. γῆς ἕως ἄ. οὐρανοῦ **Mk 13:27.**—B. 854; 856. DELG s.v. ἀκ-. M-M s.v. ἄκρος.

ἀκτίν (so Herodian Gr. index Lentz; Corp. Gloss. Lat. 3, 278; Kephal. I, 166, 4; 165, 30) ApcPt 3:7 (B-D-F §46, 4; s. Mlt-H. 135 ὠδίν); s. the foll.

ἀκτίς, ῖνος, ἡ (Hom.+; ins [e.g. IAndrosIsis 8]; LXX, En, TestAbr AB; TestJob; TestNapht 5:4; JosAs 5:6; 14:4 cod. A [p. 59, 5 Bat.]; SyrBar 12:3; GrBar; SibOr 3, 803; later form ἀκτίν, s. the foregoing) ***ray, beam*** of the sun (Straton of Lamps. [300 BC], fgm. 65a Wehrli ['50] τοῦ ἡλίου ἀκτῖνες; Ps.-Pla., Axioch. 13, 371d; Diod. S. 3, 48, 3; Wsd 2:4; 16:27; Sir 43:4; Philo, Conf. Lingu. 157; Jos., Ant. 19, 344; Herm. Wr. 10, 4b; Ath. 10, 3) B 5:10; ApcPt 5:15. Of the heavenly radiance of angels ApcPt 3:7 Funk (cp. En 106:5, 10 ἀκτῖνες τοῦ ἡλίου). ἐξ αὐ[τῶν ἀκτῖν]ες πυρός 11, 26 (restored by Diels), [φλόγ]ες James (s. Klostermann mg. ad loc.).—DELG.

Ἀκύλας, acc. **-αν, ὁ** ***Aquila*** (Brutus, Ep. 61; 63; 64; Philostrat., Vi. Soph. 2, 11, 1; OGI 533, 84; 544, 9; PGiss 73, 5; BGU 71, 21; 484, 6; Jos., Ant. 19, 110; 283 [Dssm., NB 15; BS 187]—B-D-F §54; 55, 1) a Jewish artisan (s. σκηνοποιός), husband of Priscilla (s. Πρίσκα), from Pontus (an Aq. fr. Pontus in an ins of Sinope: AJP 27, 1906, p. 269), friend of Paul, who esteemed him and his wife highly, **Ac 18:2, 18, 21 v.l., 26; Ro 16:3; 1 Cor 16:19; 2 Ti 4:19.** S. FBruce, The Pauline Circle '85, 44–51; also RSchumacher, Aquila u. Priscilla: ThGl 12, 1920, 86–99; FPölzl, D. Mitarbeiter des Weltap. Pls 1911, 371–81; Billerb. III 486–93; AHarnack, SBBerlAk 1900, 2–13=Studien I '31, 48–61; on this FSchiele, ZMR 15, 1900, 353–60.—M-M.

ἄκυρος, ον (Thu.+; ins, pap, Pr, Philo; Jos., Ant. 13, 262; 16, 38) ***void, of no effect*** ἄκυρον ποιεῖν *disregard* (Pla., Prot. 356d et al.; Pr 5:7; Theoph. Ant. 3, 3 [p. 210, 6]) τὰς βουλάς 1 Cl 57:4 (Pr 1:25).—DELG s.v. κύριος.

ἀκυρόω 1 aor. ἠκύρωσα ***make void*** (so Dinarchus 1, 63; Diod. S. 16, 24 al. [Nägeli 29]; SIG 742, 30 [86 BC]; BGU 944, 11; 1167, 26; LXX; En 98:14 [emend. Bonner]; Philo, Ebr. 197, Conf. Lingu. 193; Jos., Ant. 18, 304 ἐντολάς; 20, 183; Ath., R. 79, 2) τὸν λόγον τοῦ θεοῦ **Mt 15:6; Mk 7:13.** As legal t.t. (OEger, ZNW 18, 1918, 92f) διαθήκην (POxy 491 [126 AD]; 494, 4; 495, 3) **Gal 3:17.** ὁ θεὸς . . . μὴ βουλόμενος ἀκυρῶσαι τὸ ἴδιον πλάσμα *God . . . who was unwilling to reject his very own creation* AcPlCor 2:12.—DELG s.v. κύριος. M-M. TW.

ἀκωλύτως adv. (Pla. [Cra. 415d] +; freq. in pap as legal t.t.: POxy 502; BGU 917, 14; PLips 26, 11; 30, 9; Job 34:31 Sym.; TestAbr B 9 p. 113, 21 [Stone p. 74]; TestJob 45:4; JosAs 14:12 cod. A [p. 60, 2 Bat.]; Jos., Ant. 12, 104; 16, 41 ἀ. τὴν πάτριον εὐσέβειαν διαφυλάττειν) ***without hindrance*** διδάσκειν ἀ. **Ac 28:31** (GDelling NovT. 15, '73, 196–204).—M-M.

ἄκων, ἄκουσα, ἆκον (since Hom., who has ἀέκων; ins, pap; 4 Macc 11:12; TestSol 12:6 C; Jos., Bell. 2, 123, Ant. 16, 256) ***unwilling;*** to be transl. as adv. *unwillingly* πράσσειν **1 Cor 9:17** (cp. Philo, Omn. Prob. Lib. 61 ἄ. ποιεῖν). ἄ. ἁμαρτάνειν *sin inadvertently* (Soph., fgm. 604 TGF 'one who sins inadvertently is not a bad pers.'; Pla., Rep. 336e ἄκοντες ἡμαρτάνομεν; Dio Chrys. 17 [34], 13; Ael. Aristid. 34, 5 K.=50 p. 547 D.—See also Ps.-Callisth. 1, 9, 2 ἁμαρτήσασα οὐχ ἥμαρτες) 1 Cl 2:3 (cp. Job 14:17). See IRo 5:2 v.l.—DELG s.v. ἑκών. M-M. TW.

ἅλα s. ἅλας.

ἀλάβαστρος, ου, ὁ and **ἡ,** also **ἀλάβαστρον, τό** (s. **Mk 14:3** w. its variants; cp. Theocr. 15, 114; Delian ins [III BC]: IG XI/2, 161b, 9; 4 Km 21:13 with v.l. and B-D-F §49, 1; Mlt-H. 122; fem. gender in Pollux 7, 177; 10, 121; the earlier Attic form ἀλάβαστος or -ον [SEG XIII, 12, 234] does not appear in the biblical lit.) **a vase for holding perfume/ointment,** often made of alabaster, hence ***alabaster vase,*** a vessel w. a rather long neck which was broken off when the contents were used; a container for spikenard ointment (so Hdt. et al.; also a loanword in Lat.: Pliny, NH 13, 3 unguenta optime servantur in alabastris) **Mt 26:7; Lk 7:37;** τὴν ἀ. **Mk 14:3** (vv.ll. τὸ ἀ. and τὸν ἀ.; ἀλ. μύρου as Hdt. 3, 20; Lucian, Dial. Mer. 14, 2; Dionys. Hal. 7, 9; PSI 333, 6; 628, 8).—AvanVeldhuizen, De alabasten flesch: TSt 24, 1906, 170–72.—DELG s.v. ἀλάβαστος. M-M.

ἀλαζονεία, ας, ἡ (also -ία; s. ἀλαζών; Aristoph., Pla.+; Wsd 5:8; 4 Macc 1:26; 2:15; 8:19; TestJos 17:8; TestJob 21:3; JosAs 4:16; Philo, Virt. 162ff; Jos., Ant. 6, 179; 14, 111; Tat.; pap [PLond 1927 (IV AD) Christ., 32]; on the spelling s. Kühner-Bl. II p. 275; Rob. 196f; for def. s. Theophr., Char. 23; Pla., Def. 416) ***pretension, arrogance*** in word and deed καυχᾶσθαι ἐν ταῖς ἀλαζονείαις *boast in arrogance, make arrogant boasts* **Js 4:16.** ἐγκαυχᾶσθαι ἐν ἀ. τοῦ λόγου *boast w. arrogant words* 1 Cl 21:5. ἀποτίθεσθαι ἀ. (w. τῦφος [as Ep. 3 of Apollonius of Tyana: Philostrat. I 345, 22 K.], ἀφροσύνη, ὀργαί) 13:1; (w. ἀκαταστασία) 14:1; (w. ὑπερηφανία) 16:2. W. other vices 35:5; Hm 6, 2, 5; 8:5; D 5:1. Of Judean pride Dg 4:1, 6. ἡ ἀ. τοῦ βίου *pride in one's possessions* **1J 2:16** (cp. X., Hell. 7, 1, 38; Polyb. 6, 57, 6 ἀ. περὶ τοὺς βίους; Wsd 5:8).—PJoüon, RSR 28, '38, 311–14.—DELG s.v. ἀλαζών. M-M. TW. Spicq.

ἀλαζονεύομαι (ἀλαζών; Aristoph., Lysias et al.; Philo, Fug. 33; Jos., Bell. 4, 122) ***boast, be boastful*** w. acc. *about someth.* (Aeschin. 3, 218; Herodian 2, 7, 2 χρήματα; Wsd 2:16) μηδέν 1 Cl 2:1. τὴν μείωσιν τῆς σαρκός Dg 4:4. Abs. (Timaeus Hist. [IV–III BC]: 566 fgm. 132 Jac.; Dio Chrys. 26 [43], 2) 1 Cl 38:2.

ἀλαζών, όνος, ὁ and **ἡ** (Cratinus, Aristoph.+; Job 28:8; JosAs 2:1 cod. A and Pal. 364 [p. 40, 21 Bat.]; Philo, Mos. 2, 240; Theoph. Ant. 1, 2 [p. 60, 28]) ***boaster, braggart*** **Ro 1:30; 2 Ti 3:2.** γύναι . . . ἡ τῶν ἱματίων ἀλαζών *O woman, you boast about your clothes!* AcPl Ha 2, 20.—Also (as in Hdt. 6, 12; Philostrat., Vi. Soph. 2, 9, 2 p. 87, 11; Hab 2:5; Jos., Ant. 8, 264; Plut., Mor. 523e) as adj. (w. ὑπερήφανος, as Syntipas p. 126, 9) ἡ ἀ. αὐθάδεια *boastful presumption* 1 Cl 57:2.—ORibbeck, Alazon 1882.—DELG. TW. Spicq.

ἀλαλάζω fut. ἀλαλάξω, 1 aor. ἠλαλάξα LXX (denom. fr. ἀλαλά 'violent outcry'; Pind. et al.; LXX; TestSol 1:2 L and 6:9; Jos., Ant. 5, 225; 6, 191 al.; Just., D. 53, 3 [Zech 9:9 difft. LXX])

❶ **to cry out loudly in wailing,** of people over one who has died ἀ. πολλά (w. κλαίειν) ***wail loudly*** **Mk 5:38** (cp. Eur., El. 483; Jer 32:34.—EReiner, Die Rituelle Totenklage der Griechen '38; EMartino, Morte e pianto rituale nel mondo antico '58; PHeinisch, D. Trauergebräuche b. d. Israeliten '31; FHvidberg, Weeping and Laughter in the OT '62).

❷ Gener. of shrill tones (Nonnus, Dionys. 12, 354 of the screeching sound of the wine-press) κύμβαλον ἀλαλάζον *a clashing cymbal* **1 Cor 13:1** (Ps 150:5 ἐν κυμβάλοις ἀλαλαγμοῦ). Goodsp., Probs. 160f.—S. κύμβαλον.—DELG s.v. ἀλαλά. TW.

ἀλάλητος, ον (s. λαλέω; Philod. in Anth. Pal. 5, 4; Cyranides p. 19, 19) ***unexpressed, wordless*** στεναγμοὶ ἀ. *sighs too deep for words* (so the Syr. and Armen. tr.; the Vulgate renders it 'inenarrabilis', *inexpressible*) **Ro 8:26.** JSchniewind, Nachgelassene Reden u. Aufsätze, ed. EKähler '52, 86; EKäsemann, Der gottesdienstliche Schrei nach der Freiheit: Apophoreta, EHaenchen Festschr. Beih. ZNW 30 '64, 149–50 (both for the meaning 'inexpressible').

ἄλαλος, ον (s. λαλέω; Aeschyl. et al., also IG XIV, 1627, 9; LXX; SibOr 4, 7), ***mute, unable to speak,*** ἄ. γίνεσθαι *be struck mute* of deceitful lips 1 Cl 15:5 (Ps 30:19); πνεῦμα ἄ. (Plut., Mor. 438b of the Pythia: ἀλάλου καὶ κακοῦ πνεύματος πλήρης. Paris ms. 2316 leaf 318 in Rtzst., Poim. 293, 1 πνεῦμα . . . ἄλαλον) *a mute spirit,* which robs pers. of their speech **Mk 9:17;** acc. to vs. **25** the πν. ἄ. is also deaf (ἄ. w. κωφός Alex. Aphr., Probl. 1, 138; Artem. 1, 76; Ps 37:14).—ὁ ἄ. *a mute person* (Ps 37:14): ποιεῖ ἀ. λαλεῖν **7:37.**

ἅλας, ατος, τό (Aristot. et al.; pap since III BC [Mayser 286; Nägeli 58, 1]; LXX [Helbing 49; Thackeray 152]; TestSol 18:34 [cp. PVindobBosw]; TestLevi 9:14. For the v.l. ἅλα **Mk 9:50; Lk 14:34** [Sb 8030, 21 (47 AD), prob. a back-formation fr. ἅλατ- on the model of σῶμα, ατος] s. W-S. §9, n. 7; B-D-F §47, 4; Mlt-H. 132f. From the class. form ἅλς only ἁλί [cp. Lev 2:13] as v.l. in **Mk 9:49** and ἁλός 1 Cl 11:2 [Gen 19:26]) **salt**

ⓐ lit. as seasoning for food or as fertilizer **Mt 5:13b; Mk 9:50ab; Lk 14:34** (EDeatrick, Biblical Archaeologist 25, '62, 41–48).

ⓑ fig., of the spiritual qualities of the disciples (cp. Diogenes 4 p. 94, 13 Malherbe, of the men at Athens) τὸ ἅ. τῆς γῆς **Mt 5:13a;** cp. **Mk 9:50c** and s. the comm. Of speech that is winsome or witty (Plut., Mor. 514ef; 685a: life seasoned with words) ὁ λόγος ἅλατι ἠρτυμένος (sc. ἔστω) *let your speech be seasoned w. salt* **Col 4:6.** (Diog. L. 4, 67: Timon [III BC] says the speech of the Academics is ἀνάλιστος, 'dry').—B. 382. DELG s.v. ἅλς M-M. TW.

Ἄλασσα Ac 27:8 v.l.; s. Λασαία.

ἀλατόμητος, ον *uncut* Hs 9, 16, 7.

ἀλγέω fut. ἀλγήσω, 1 aor. ἤλγησα LXX (denom. fr. ἄλγος 'pain'; Hom. et al.; ins, pap, LXX; TestSol; Philo, Leg. All. 3, 200; 211; Jos., Ant. 15, 58) ***feel pain*** ἀλγεῖν ποιεῖ *causes pain*=sends suffering 1 Cl 56:6 (Job 5:18). ὁ ἀλγῶν σάρκα *one who is ill in body* B 8:6 (cp. Pla., Rep. 7, 515e τὰ ὄμματα; Artem. 4, 24 p. 218, 7 τὴν κεφαλήν; Jos., Vi. 420 τὴν ψυχήν).—DELG s.v. ἄλγος.

ἁλεεῖς, οἱ s. ἁλιεύς.

ἀλείφω fut. 2 sg. ἀλείψεις Ex 40:15, 1 aor. ἤλειψα, pf. inf. ἀληλιφέναι (Just., D. 86, 2). Mid.: fut. ἀλείψομαι 4 Km 4:2; 1 aor. impv. ἄλειψαι; pf. ptc. ἠλειμμένοι Num 3:3 (Hom.+)

❶ lit. **to anoint by applying a liquid such as oil or perfume,** ***anoint*** (Diod. S. 17, 90, 2) τοὺς πόδας μύρῳ *anoint his feet w. perfume* **Lk 7:38, 46** (KWeiss, ZNW 46, '55, 241–45; WClarke, ClJ 87, '91/92, 257–63); **J 12:3;** cp. **11:2.** Those who were ill were anointed w. oil (household remedy; cp. Cat. Cod. Astr. VII p. 178, 3; 28; TestAdam p. 122, 7; cp. 116, 10) **Mk 6:13; Js 5:14** (MMeinertz, D. Krankensalbung Jk 5:14f: BZ 20, '32, 23–36; CArmerding, BiblSacra 95, '38, 195–201; HFriesenhahn, BZ 24, '40, 185–90. S. ἔλαιον 1a and κάμνω 2 and 3). Of the dead, w. spices **Mk 16:1.** Mid. *anoint oneself* (Jos., Bell. 5, 565) τὴν κεφαλήν **Mt 6:17** (w. washing of the face as Plut., Mor. 142a).

❷ **to besmear with someth. undesirable,** ***besmear*** fig. (Philo, Conf. Lingu. 91, Mos. 1, 298) pass. (on the permissive pass. s. Gildersleeve, Syntax I §167) ἀ. δυσωδίαν *let oneself be besmeared w. filth* of accepting false doctrine IEph 17:1 (ἀ. w. acc. of that which one applies, as 2 Km 14:2; Mi 6:15 al.). S. χρίω.—DELG. M-M. TW.

ἀλεκτοροφωνία, ας, ἡ (Strabo 7, 35; Aesop., Fab. 55 P. [difft. 110 H.]; Phryn. 229 Lob.; B-D-F §123, 1; Mlt-H. 271) ***crowing of a cock*** ἀλεκτοροφωνίας *at cockcrow* (=*dawn*) name of the third watch of the night (12–3 a.m.) **Mt 26:34 v.l.; 26:75 v.l.** (on these variants s. PKatz, TLZ 80, '55, 737; GZuntz, Chronique d' Égypte 26, '51, 205f); **Mk 13:35** (on the gen. s. B-D-F §186, 2; Rob. 471).—On chickens in Judea and Jerusalem s. KRengstorf on Tosefta Yebamoth 3, 4 (Rabb. Texte I 3, '33, p. 36f).—Dalman, Arbeit VII (s. οἰκία 1a); TMartin, Biblical Research 38, '93, 59–69.

ἀλεκτρυών, όνος, ὁ a male chicken, ***cock, rooster*** (on the formation s. DELG s.v. ἀλέξω Thème II p. 50; since Theognis 864; Cratinus 108, κοκκύζει 311; POxy 1207, 8; Michel 692, 5 [I AD]; SIG 1173, 16; 3 Macc 5:23; PGM 3, 693; 701) Gospel fgm. from the Fayum (Kl. T. 8³, p. 23, 10, cp. **Mk 14:26–31** and par.).—B. 174.

ἀλέκτωρ, ορος, ὁ ***cock, rooster*** as prec. entry (for class. times s. WRutherford, New Phryn., 1881, 307; Lycophron 1094; Batr. 192; pap, e.g. PTebt 140 [72 BC]; PFay 119, 29 [c. 100 AD]; BGU 269, 4; 1067, 11; PGM 2, 73; 4, 2190; Pr 30:31) φωνεῖ (GrBar) **Mt 26:34, 74f; Mk 14:30, 68, 72; Lk 22:34, 60f; J 13:38; 18:27.**—M-M.

Ἀλεξανδρεύς, έως, ὁ ***an Alexandrian*** (Plut., Pomp. 645 [49, 6]; SEG XXXVIII, 219, 2; OGI index II; 3 Macc 2:30; 3:21; Philo, Joseph., SibOr; s. Preis. III 264 s.v.) of Apollos **Ac**

18:24 (on Jews as Ἀ. s. Jos., C. Ap. 2, 38, as in pap CPJ I p. 4). συναγωγὴ Ἀ. (Schürer II 76; 428, 445; III 92–94; 127–29) **6:9.**

Ἀλεξανδρῖνος, η, ον (edd. -ινός; on the accent s. Kühner-Bl. II 296; Mlt-H. 359.—Polyb. 34, 8, 7; BGU 142, 5; 143, 3; 741, 4 κλάσῃ Ἀλεξανδρίνῃ=Lat. classis Alexandrina; s. Mitt-Wilck. I/1, 379; Preis. III 264 s.v.) ***Alexandrian*** πλοῖον Ἀ. **Ac 27:6; 28:11.**—Subst. **6:9 v.l.,** s. N[25].

Ἀλέξανδρος, ου, ὁ ***Alexander*** a favorite name w. Jews as well as gentiles (on the origin of this name s. DELG s.v. ἀνήρ p. 88; cp. pap and ins; CPJ I 29; Joseph.—ET 10, 1899, 527).

❶ son of Simon of Cyrene **Mk 15:21.**—❷ a member of Jerusalem's high priestly family **Ac 4:6.**—❸ a Judean of Ephesus **19:33.**—❹ an apostate **1 Ti 1:20,** presumably the smith of **2 Ti 4:14.**

ἀλεσμός, οῦ, ὁ (ἀλέω 'grind') lit. 'grinding' (Jos., Ant. 3, 252 v.l.; s. DELG s.v. ἀλέω), in our lit. only fig. in ref. to torture ἀλεσμοὶ ὅλου τοῦ σώματος ***grinding*** (s. 4:1) *of the whole body* of torture in martyrdom IRo 5:3 (s. Lghtf. ad loc.—Of a partic. kind of torture, Eunap., Vi. Soph. 59 cod.; cp. 312).

ἄλευρον, ου, τό (Hdt. et al.; PGM 7, 539 and elsewh. in pap; LXX; Jos., Ant. 3, 142; 8, 322; SibOr 8, 14; DELG s.v. ἀλέω) ***wheat flour*** used for making bread **Mt 13:33; Lk 13:21.**—B. 361. M-M.

ἀλήθεια, ας, ἡ (cp. λανθάνω 'escape notice' s. DELG s.v. λανθάνω; Schwyzer I 469; Hom. +) prim. 'hiding nothing'.

❶ **the quality of being in accord with what is true, *truthfulness, dependability, uprightness*** in thought and deed (Alcaeus 57 [366 L.-P.]; Mimnermus 8 al.) of God (Gen 24:27 al.) **Ro 3:7; 15:8.** Of people (Pittacus in Diog. L. 1, 78; Arrian, Anab. 7, 30, 3; Lucian, Dial. Mort. 11, 6; 4 Km 20:3; Judg 9:15f al.; EpArist 206) ἐν ἀ. λαλεῖν *speak truthfully* **2 Cor 7:14;** (w. εἰλικρίνεια) **1 Cor 5:8;** (w. ἀγαθωσύνη and δικαιοσύνη) **Eph 5:9;** 1 Cl 19:1; 31:2; 35:2; Pol 2:1; ἐν πάσῃ ἀ. *w. perfect fidelity* 4:2.—Hm 8:9; 12, 3, 1; s 9, 15, 2.

❷ **the content of what is true, *truth*** (opp. ψεῦδος)

ⓐ gener. ἀ. λαλεῖν *tell the truth* (Zech 8:16) **Eph 4:25;** Hm 3:5; 2 Cl 12:3. ἀ. λέγειν (Hdt. 2, 115 al.; PGiss 84, 14 [II AD] τὴν ἀ. εἰπεῖν) **Ro 9:1; 1 Ti 2:7.** Fut. ἀ. ἐρῶ **2 Cor 12:6.** ἀ. ἀγαπᾶν Hm 3:1. Opp. ψεύδεσθαι κατὰ τῆς ἀ. *lie against the truth* **Js 3:14;** εἶπεν αὐτῷ πᾶσαν τὴν ἀ. *she told him the whole truth* **Mk 5:33** (cp. Hdt. 9, 89; Thu. 6, 87, 1 al.; Cleopatra ln. 88; POxy 283, 13f [45 AD] γνωσθῆναι πᾶσαν τὴν ἀ.; Jos., Bell. 7, 31 πυθόμενος παρ᾽ αὐτοῦ πᾶσαν τὴν ἀ.). ἐν λόγῳ ἀληθείας *by truthful speech* **2 Cor 6:7;** ῥήματα ἀληθείας **Ac 26:25;** μόρφωσις τῆς γνώσεως καὶ τῆς ἀ. *embodiment of knowledge and truth* **Ro 2:20;** ἡ ἁγνότης τῆς ἀ. *the purity that belongs to truth* Hv 3, 7, 3. ἔξωθεν τῆς ἀ.=ψευδής 3, 4, 3.

ⓑ esp. of the content of Christianity as the ultimate truth (cp. Plut., Mor. 351e ἀ. περὶ θεῶν; Philo, Spec. Leg. 4, 178, the proselyte is a μεταναστὰς εἰς ἀ.) **Eph 4:21** (CScott, Exp. 8th ser. 3, 1912, 178–85; FBriggs, ET 39, 1928, 526). ὁ λόγος τῆς ἀ. *the word of truth* **Eph 1:13; 2 Ti 2:15; Js 1:18.** ὁ λόγος τῆς ἀ. τοῦ εὐαγγελίου τοῦ παρόντος εἰς ὑμᾶς **Col 1:5;** cp. **2 Pt 1:12.** ἡ ἀ. τοῦ εὐαγγελίου **Gal 2:5, 14.** ἔστιν ἀ. Χριστοῦ ἐν ἐμοί **2 Cor 11:10.** ὁ περὶ ἀ. λόγος Pol 3:2; πείθεσθαι τῇ ἀ. **Gal 5:7;** πιστεύειν τῇ ἀ. **2 Th 2:12;** hence πίστει ἀληθείας *belief in the truth* vs. **13;** δύνασθαί τι κατὰ τῆς ἀ. . . . ὑπὲρ τῆς ἀ. **2 Cor 13:8;** περιπατεῖν ἐν ἀ. **2J 4; 3J 3f** (cp. 4 Km 20:3); ζῆν κατὰ ἀ. IEph 6:2; πορεύεσθαι κατὰ τὴν ἀ. Pol 5:2; ἐν ἀ. (3 Km 2:4) Hm 3:4; gird oneself w. truth **Eph 6:14;** cp. Hm 11:4.—Truth expresses itself in virtues like righteousness and holiness, **Eph 4:24** (Nicol. Dam.: 90 fgm. 67, 1 Jac. δικαιοσύνην κ. ἀλ.). Hence it is contrasted w. ἀδικία **1 Cor 13:6; Ro 1:18; 2:8.** In the last-named passage a negative attitude toward the truth is called ἀπειθεῖν τῇ ἀ. Also πλανᾶσθαι ἀπὸ τῆς ἀ. *wander from the truth* **Js 5:19;** ἀστοχεῖν περὶ τὴν ἀ. **2 Ti 2:18;** καταστρέφειν ἀπὸ τῆς ἀ. Hs 6, 2, 1, cp. 4; ἀποστρέφειν τὴν ἀκοὴν ἀπὸ τῆς ἀ. **2 Ti 4:4** opp. μῦθοι, cp. ἀποστρέφεσθαι **Tit 1:14;** ἀποστερεῖσθαι τῆς ἀ. **1 Ti 6:5;** ἐρευνᾶν περὶ τῆς ἀ. *make inquiries about the truth* Hm 10, 1, 4; 6; ἀνθίστασθαι τῇ ἀ. *oppose the truth* (i.e. the gospel) **2 Ti 3:8.** Opp. μῦθοι **4:4.** Truth can be communicated (cp. Did., Gen. 86, 21): φανερώσει τῆς ἀ. *by a clear statement of the truth* **2 Cor 4:2** (sim. in later Christian prayer POxy 925, 4f φανέρωσόν μοι τὴν παρὰ σοὶ ἀλ.); is taught D 11:10; recognized **1 Ti 4:3;** Hv 3, 6, 2; cp. ἐπίγνωσις τῆς ἀληθείας (Alex. Aphr., Quaest. 3, 12, II 2 p. 102, 3 γνῶσις τ. ἀληθείας) **1 Ti 2:4; 2 Ti 2:25; 3:7; Tit 1:1; Hb 10:26;** ἑδραίωμα τῆς ἀ. **1 Ti 3:15;** ὁδὸς τῆς ἀ. **2 Pt 2:2;** 1 Cl 35:5 (cp. Pind., P. 3, 103; Eur., fgm. 289; Gen 24:48 al.; En 104:13; OdeSol 11:3); ὑπακοὴ τῆς ἀ. **1 Pt 1:22;** ἀγάπη τῆς ἀ. **2 Th 2:10.** God is πατὴρ τῆς ἀ. 2 Cl 3:1; 20:5; φῶς ἀληθείας IPhld 2:1 (cp. Ps 42:3); θεὸς τῆς ἀ. (1 Esdr 4:40) 2 Cl 19:1; cp. 1 Cl 60:2. The reverse genitival constr. in ἀ. τοῦ θεοῦ **Ro 1:25,** is best rendered *truth about God* (so Twentieth Century NT, NRSV) as opp. to the deception of polytheists, who in effect lie about God despite their better knowledge described vss. 19–21 (REB et al.: *truth of God*).—Ἀ. is a favorite word of the Joh. lit., and plays a major role in it. God's word is truth **J 17:17** (Ps 118:142). Truth w. χάρις **1:14, 17;** w. πνεῦμα **4:23f;** cp. ἐν ἔργῳ καὶ ἀ. **1J 3:18** (opp. λόγῳ, γλώσσῃ). W. ἀγάπη **2J 3.** The Spirit leads into truth **J 16:13;** hence πνεῦμα τῆς ἀ. **14:17; 15:26; 16:13; 1J 4:6** (cp. Hm 3:4). πνεῦμα is identified w. ἀ. **1J 5:6;** it is mediated through Christ **J 1:17,** who calls himself truth **14:6** (cp. PGM 5, 148 ἐγώ εἰμι ἡ ἀλήθεια, on the other hand POxy 1380, 63 [early II AD] Isis is called ἀ.; Apollonaretal. Berl. Gr. Pap. 11517 [II AD]: Her 55, 1920, 188–95 ln. 52 Apollo as the ἀψευδὴς ἀ.; M. Ant., 9, 1, 2 God=Nature ἀλήθεια ὀνομάζεται; Lucian, Hist. Conscr. 61 says of a good history-writer: ἦν ἀλήθεια ἐπὶ πᾶσι); hence as source of praise for a Christian Δημητρίῳ μεμαρτύρηται . . . ὑπ᾽ αὐτῆς τῆς ἀ. **3J 12.** One who possesses Christ knows truth (γινώσκ. τὴν ἀ. as Jos., Ant. 13, 291; Tat. 13, 1; ἀληθείας γνῶσις: Maximus Tyr. 26, 5b; Did., Gen. 116, 17) **J 8:32;** (cp. 1QS 5:10); **2J 1;** does the truth **J 3:21,** cp. **1J 1:6** (ποιεῖν τὴν ἀ. Gen 32:11; 47:29; Is 26:10 al.; TestReub 6:9; TestBenj 10:3; ἔλεος καὶ ἀ. PsSol 17:15); stands in the truth **J 8:44;** is of the truth **18:37;** cp. **1J 2:21; 3:19** (ἐκ τῆς ἀληθείας=corresponding to the truth PTurin I, 6, 13). The truth sets one free **J 8:32,** but is not present in those who deny the fact of sin in their lives **1J 1:8** or do not heed Christ's commands. Christ proclaims this truth: λέγειν (Jos., Ant. 10, 124) **J 8:45f; 16:7;** λαλεῖν **8:40** (also λαλεῖν ἐν ἀ. IEph 6:2); μαρτυρεῖν τῇ ἀ. **18:37.** As John the Baptist witnesses to Jesus, he witnesses to the truth **5:33;** cp. μαρτυρούντων σου τῇ ἀληθείᾳ *bear witness to your (fidelity to the) truth* **3J 3;** ἵνα συνεργοὶ γινώμεθα τῇ ἀ. vs. **8.** In Pilate's question τί ἐστιν ἀ.; **J 18:38** the worldling speaks (cp. 4 Macc 5:10). Opp. θάνατος ISm 5:1.—Mlt-Turner 177f.

❸ **an actual event or state, *reality*** (Diogenes 21 p. 114, 10 al. Malherbe; Mel., P. 4, 33; 42, 289 [opp. τύπος] Diod. S. 2, 8, 4) as opposed to mere appearance (opp. πρόφασις) **Phil 1:18.** κατὰ ἀλήθειαν *rightly* **Ro 2:2** (cp. Diod. S. 4, 64, 2 οἱ κατ᾽ ἀλήθειαν γονεῖς; M. Ant. 2, 11, 3; 4, 11; Damianus of Larissa p. 20, 2 [ed. Schöne 1897]; PCairZen 202, 7 [254 BC]; EpArist 140; 4 Macc 5:18; Just. A I, 2, 1; Ath., R. 66, 11; Orig., C. Cels. 2, 13, 84; PGM 12, 235). ἐν ἀληθείᾳ *indeed, truly* (Jer 33:15; ἀγαπᾶν PsSol 6:6; 10:3; 14:1 al.) **Mt 22:16; J 17:19;** 1 Cl 63:1 (s. also 2b on **1J 3:18**). ἐπιγινώσκειν τὴν χάριν ἐν ἀλ. **Col 1:6;** οὓς ἐγὼ ἀγαπῶ ἐν ἀλ. **2J 1,** cp. **3J 1,** belongs here (like the epist. formulas PFay 118, 26; 119, 26 [100–110 AD] τοὺς φιλοῦντας ἡμᾶς πρὸς ἀ.='really and truly'). ἐπ' ἀληθείας *in accordance w. the truth, truly* (Demosth. 18, 17; SIG 495, 174 [III BC]; PAmh 68, 33; POxy 480, 9; Job, Da; Philo, Leg. ad Gai. 60; 248): διδάσκειν **Mk 12:14; Lk 20:21;** εἰπεῖν **Mk 12:32;** λέγειν **Lk 4:25;** συνάγεσθαι **Ac 4:27;** καταλαμβάνεσθαι **10:34;** τελειοῦν 1 Cl 23:5; ἐπιστέλλειν 47:3; ἐπ' ἀ. καὶ οὗτος μετ' αὐτοῦ ἦν *certainly this fellow* (s. οὗτος 1aα) *was with him, too* **Lk 22:59.**—GStorz, Gebr. u. Bedeutungsentwicklg v. ἀλήθεια u. begriffsverwandten Wörtern, diss. Tüb. 1922; WLuther, 'Wahrheit' u. 'Lüge' im ältest. Griechentum '35; HBraun, Qumran und d. NT II '66, 118–44; I de la Potterie, TU 73, '59, 277–94 (John); BJackayya, CTM 41, '70, 171–75 (John); RBultmann, Untersuchungen z. J. Ἀλήθεια: ZNW 27, 1928, 113–63.—EDNT. M-M. TW. Spicq. Sv.

ἀληθεύω fut. 3 sg. ἀληθεύσει Sir 34:4, 1 aor. impv. ἀλήθευσον Gen. 20:16 (Pre-Socr., Aeschyl.+; Pfuhl-Möbius, I, 69, 3 [IV BC]: s. New Docs 4, 145; POxy 2342, 12; PAmh 142, 1; LXX; Jos., C. Ap. 1, 223; Just.; Tat. 31, 4; Ath., R. 50, 13) ***be truthful, tell the truth*** τινί *to someone* (Philo, Cher. 15) **Gal 4:16.** Abs. (Solon : Vorsokr. 10 fgm. 3 β 6 [=Stob. III p. 114, 10 H.]; Philostrat., Vi. Apoll. 4, 16 p. 135, 2; 8, 26 p. 339, 27; Jos., Bell. 3, 322, Vi. 132) ἀληθεύοντες ἐν ἀγάπῃ, i.e. in such a way that the spirit of love is maintained **Eph 4:15** (cp. Pr 21:3).—M-M. TW. Spicq.

ἀληθής, ές (Hom.+.) *true*—❶ **pert. to being truthful and honest, *truthful, righteous, honest*** of pers. (Aeschyl., Thu.; IG XIV, 1071, 8; BGU 1024 VI., 17; 2 Esdr 17:2; Wsd 1:6; Jos., Ant. 8, 234) of Jesus **Mt 22:16; Mk 12:14; J 7:18.** Of God (Wsd 15:1; Philo, Spec. Leg. 1, 36; Jos., Bell. 7, 323; SibOr fgm. 1, 10; 5, 499) **J 3:33; 7:28 v.l.; 8:26; Ro 3:4;** Dg 8:8. Gener. (opp. πλάνοι) **2 Cor 6:8.** Of overseers and assistants D 15:1.

❷ **pert. to being in accordance with fact, *true*** of things, esp. that which is spoken: ῥῆμα (Gen 41:32; ParJer 2:9; 3:3) Hm 3:3f; 11:3. παροιμία (Soph., Ajax 664) **2 Pt 2:22.** λόγος (Pind., O. 1, 28; Galen, in Hippocratis De Natura Hom., 29 p. 17, 26f Mewaldt; Dt 13:15; Jdth 11:10; Wsd 2:17; Philo; Just., A I, 3, 1) Dg 12:7. (τὰ) ἀληθῆ λέγειν (Soph., Ph. 345; Ps.-Demosth. 7, 43; POxy 37, 12 [I AD]; PStras 41, 18 [c. 250 AD]; 3 Macc 7:12; Jos., Vi. 286; Just., A II, 3, 5) **J 19:35;** GJs15:4; 23:2. τοῦτο ἀληθὲς (v.l. ἀληθῶς) εἴρηκας *you have said this truly* (lit., 'as someth. true'; cp. Pla.; Ps.-Demosth. 59, 34 ταῦτ' ἀληθῆ λέγω; Lucian, Fugit. 1) **J 4:18;** cp. **10:41** (πάντα ὅσα . . . ἀλ. like Jos., Ant. 8, 242). οὐδὲν ἀληθές **Ac 14:19 v.l.** (Oenomaus the Cynic in Eus., PE 5, 26, 4 says that in the oracles there is μηδὲν ἀληθὲς ἢ ἔνθεον). τἀληθῆ διδάσκειν Papias (2:3). γραφαί 1 Cl 45:2. *Dependable* μαρτυρία (PHal 1, 227 ἀληθῆ μαρτυρεῖν; Jos., Ant. 4, 219 μαρτυρία) **J 5:31f; 8:13f, 17; 21:24; 3J 12; Tit 1:13.**—κρίσις **J 8:16 v.l.;** γνῶσις Dg 12:6. As quest. τοῦτο ἀληθές; GJs 19:1, not pap. ὅσα ἐστὶν ἀληθῆ **Phil 4:8.** ἀληθές ἐστιν καὶ οὐκ ἔστιν ψεῦδος (the contrast as Pla., Ep. 7 p. 344b; Philo, Rer. Div. Her. 132) **1J 2:27,** cp. vs. **8;** Hv 3, 4, 3.

❸ **pert. to being real, *real, genuine, not imaginary*** (Thu. et al.; PTebt 285, 3; 293, 17; Pr 1:3; Wsd 12:27; Mel., P. 37 τῷ φύσει ἀληθεῖ) ἀγάπη Pol 1:1; MPol 1:2. χάρις **1 Pt 5:12.** ζωή (Philo, Poster. Cai. 45) Dg 12:4. βρῶσις, πόσις of the body and blood of Jesus **J 6:55.** ἵνα τὸ πνεῦμα ἀληθὲς εὑρεθῇ Hm 3:1. ἀ. ἐστιν τὸ γινόμενον διὰ τ. ἀγγέλου *what was done by the angel is a reality* **Ac 12:9.** ἔργα Qua (s. ἀεί 1 end). On μαθητὴς ἀ. IRo 4:2 s. ἀληθῶς b.—B. 1169. DELG s.v. λανθάνω. M-M. TW. Spicq. Sv.

ἀληθινός, ή, όν (Heraclitus, X., Pla. et al.; ins, pap, LXX, En; TestSol 13:8 C [-ῶς]; TestAbr A 4 p. 81, 4 [Stone p. 10]; TestJob, Test12Patr; JosAs 11 [cod. A p. 54, 6 Bat. and cod. Pal. 364]; ParJer 9:3; ApcSed 1:4; Philo, Joseph.; Ar. 15, 7; Just.) 'true'.

❶ **pert. to being in accord with what is true, *true, trustworthy*** (X., An. 1, 9, 17; LXX) of God (Ex 34:6; Num 14:18; 1 Esdr 8:86; 3 Macc 2:11; Jos., Ant. 11, 55) (w. ἅγιος) **Rv 6:10** (v.l. ἀληθής); (w. ἀψευδής) MPol 14:2. More exactly defined ὁ κύριος ἀ. ἐν παντὶ ῥήματι Hm 3:1 (opp. ψεῦδος). Of Christ, the judge of the world, w. ἅγιος **Rv 3:7;** w. πιστός **3:14; 19:11.** Of Job 1 Cl 17:3 (Job 1:1). ἀ. καρδία (Is 38:3; TestDan 5:3) **Hb 10:22.** ὁ πέμψας με='the one who sent me can guarantee my credentials' **J 7:28** (difft. 3 below).

❷ **pert. to being in accordance with fact, *true*** Hm 3:5. λόγος (Pla., Rep. 7, 522a et al.; 3 Km 10:6; 2 Ch 9:5; Da 6:13 and 10:1 Theod.) **J 4:37.** λόγοι (2 Km 7:28; En 99:2) **Rv 19:9;** (w. πιστός) **21:5; 22:6.** μαρτυρία *reliable* **J 19:35;** κρίσις ἀ. (Tob 3:2 BA; Is 59:4; En 27:3) *judgment,* by which the truth is brought to light **8:16** (ἀληθής v.l.); pl. (w. δίκαιος) **Rv 16:7; 19:2.** ὁδοί **15:3;** cp. Hv 3, 7, 1.

❸ **pert. to being real, *genuine, authentic, real*—ⓐ** gener. (Socrates 6 p. 232, 27 Malherbe; X., Oec. 10, 3; Pla., Rep. 6, 499c; Dio Chrys. 47 [64], 21 αἷμα ἀ.; POxy 465, 108 ἄγαλμα κυάνου ἀ.=a statue of genuine lapis lazuli; PGM 8, 20; 41; 43 οἶδά σου καὶ τ. βαρβαρικὰ ὀνόματα . . . τὸ δὲ ἀ. ὄνομά σου; also IDefixWünsch p. 19f; PGM 4, 278; 5, 115) ἀ. πορφύρα GJs 10:1. Of Jesus' deeds Qua.

ⓑ freq. of Christian perspectives ἀ. φῶς (ParJer.; Ael. Aristid. 23, 15 K.=42 p. 772 D. [Asclep.]; Plotinus, Enn. 6, 9, 4) **J 1:9; 1J 2:8;** ἀ. τ. θεοῦ δύναμις (an emendation for ἀλήθειαν) ending of Mk in the Freer ms. 3f; ἄμπελος **J 15:1.** ἄρτος *the real bread* of the Eucharist **6:32.** ζωή (Philo, Leg. All. 1, 32) IEph 7:2; cp. 11:1; ITr 9:2; ISm 4:1. Of God in contrast to other deities, who are not *real* (PGM 7, 634f πέμψον μοι τὸν ἀ. Ἀσκληπιὸν δίχα τινὸς ἀντιθέου πλανοδαίμονος; Philo, Leg. ad Gai. 366; SibOr fgm. 1, 20; Is 65:16; 3 Macc 6:18; Just., A I, 53, 6) **J 17:3** (s. μόνος 1aδ); **1J 5:20** (s. AHarnack, SBBerlAk 1915, 538f=Studien I '31, 110f); **1 Th 1:9** (only ref. in Paul); 1 Cl 43:6; ἀ. ὁ πέμψας με *someone who is very real has sent me* (Goodsp.; but s. 1 above) **J 7:28.** Of human beings (Demosth. 9, 12; 53, 8; 12 ἀ. φίλος; Polyb. 1, 6, 5; 1, 80, 2; 3, 12, 6; Epict. 4, 1, 154; 172; Ar. 15, 7 ἐπὶ ἀδελφῷ ἀ.; Just., A II, 2, 14 τῷ ἀ. χριστιανῷ; PHamb 37, 6 ὁ ἀ. φιλόσοφος; PGiss 40 II, 27 ἀ. Αἰγύπτιοι) προσκυνηταί **J 4:23.** προφῆται in contrast to false prophets D 11:11; cp. 13:1. διδάσκαλος in contrast to false teachers D 13:2.—πάθος *the real suffering* (opp. Docetism) IEph ins; *true* in the sense of the reality possessed only by the archetype, not by its copies (X., Mem. 3, 10, 7; Pla., Leg. 1 p. 643c of toys ὄργανα σμικρά, τῶν ἀ. μιμήματα. Of the real body in contrast to its artistic representation: Alcidamas [IV BC], Soph. 28 Blass; Theocr., Epigr. no. 18 Gow=Anth. Pal. 9, 600; Athen. 6, 253e): σκηνὴ ἀ. *the true tabernacle,* the heavenly sanctuary **Hb 8:2;** the temple ἀντίτυπα τῶν ἀ. *copy of the true sanctuary* **9:24.**—τὸ ἀ. *what is really good* (contrasted w. the supposed good, the ἄδικος μαμωνᾶς) πιστεύειν τὸ ἀ. *entrust the true (riches)* **Lk 16:11** (cp. Philo, Praem. 104 ὁ ἀ. πλοῦτος ἐν οὐρανῷ).—DELG s.v. λανθάνω. M-M. TW. Spicq.

ἀλήθω (Hippocr.; Theophr. 4, 12, 13; Diod. S. 3, 13, 2; POxy 908, 26; 34 [II AD]; PGM 4, 3097; LXX; Jos., Ant. 3, 270 and Is

47:2 [1 aor. ἤλεσα] use ἀλέω, which acc. to Phryn. p. 151 Lob. is Att. for ἀλήθω; DELG s.v. ἀλέω) ***grind*** ἐν τῷ μύλῳ (Num 11:8 impf. ἤληθον) *with the hand-mill* **Mt 24:41** (on the ptc. s. HRiesenfeld, ConNeot 13, '49, 12–16). Also ἀ. ἐπὶ τὸ αὐτό *g. at the same place* since the mills are usu. operated by two women **Lk 17:35.** Used fig. of martyrdom by Ign., who would like to be ground as God's wheat by the teeth of wild beasts IRo 4:1.—B. 362.

ἀληθῶς adv. (Aeschyl., Hdt.+) **corresponding to what is really so, *truly, in truth, really, actually.***

ⓐ in modification of a verb λέγειν *tell truly* (Dio Chrys. 33 [50], 7; PFay 123, 24; Just., D. 94, 4) **Lk 9:27;** IRo 8:2; λαλεῖν ibid.; γινώσκειν *really acknowledge, recognize* **J 7:26; 17:8;** *really perceive, know* εἰδέναι **Ac 12:11.** ἀ. τετελείωται *is truly perfected* **1J 2:5.** κτᾶσθαι IEph 15:2. πέμπειν 17:2. πράσσειν IMg 11. ἐγείρεσθαι ITr 9:2; cp. vs. 1. ἐκλέγεσθαι Pol 1:1. φρονεῖν (w. καλῶς) Hm 3:4. βλέπειν B 1:3. κατοικεῖν 16:8. ζῆν (Chariton 8, 6, 8) Dg 10:7. καθὼς ἀ. ἐστιν (otherw. ὡς ἀ.; cp. 4 Macc 6:5) *as it really is* **1 Th 2:13.** ἀ. καθηλωμένος *in truth nailed* ISm 1:2. ἀ. θεοῦ υἱὸς εἶ *you are really God's Son* (cp. Aeschyl., Suppl. 585) **Mt 14:33;** cp. **27:54.—26:73; Mk 11:32** D; **14:70; 15:39; J 1:49 v.l.; 4:42; 6:14; 7:40;** GPt 11:45; B 7:9; Dg 7:2; I Sm 1:1; 2:1. εἰ ἄρα ἀληθῶς ἀπέθανεν AcPt Ox 849, 3. As a formula of affirmation w. λέγω (s. ἀμήν 2), *truly, I tell you* **Lk 12:44; 21:3.**

ⓑ in attributive relation w. substantives (Pla., Phd. 129e ἐκεῖνός ἐστιν ὁ ἀληθῶς οὐρανός; Plut., Mor. 352c; SIG 834, 6; Ruth 3:12 ἀληθῶς ἀγχιστεὺς ἐγώ εἰμι; 4 Macc 11:23; Jos., Ant. 9, 256 ὁ ἀ. θεός) ἴδε ἀ. Ἰσραηλίτης *here is a real Israelite* (lit. 'really an Is.') **J 1:47;** ἀ. μαθηταί μού ἐστε *you are real disciples of mine* **8:31;** cp. IRo 4:2, where μαθητὴς ἀληθῶς Ἰησοῦ Χριστοῦ (so Bihlmeyer) is to be read (s. ἀληθής 3). ὅτι ἀ. νεκρός ἐστιν *that he is really dead* AcPt Ox 849, 4f.—ἀ. οἰκοδομητὸς ναὸς διὰ χειρός *a temple really built w. hands* B 16:7. καθὼς ἀ. ἐστιν (for which ὡς ἀ. is also found, cp. 4 Macc 6:5) *as it really is* **1 Th 2:13.**—B 16, 7.—DELG s.v. λανθάνω. Spicq.

ἁλιεύς, έως, ὁ (cp. the disused loc. form ἁλί [ἅλς] Schwyzer I 476 and cp. 549; on the form ἁλεεῖς, found also Arrian, Anab. 6, 23, 3 [with ἁλεέας twice as v.l.]; PFlor 127, 15 [256 AD]; BGU 1035, 6; Is 19:8; Ezk 47:10, and as v.l. in all NT passages, s. B-D-F §29, 5; W.-S. §5, 20a; Mlt-H. 76; 142; DELG s.v. ἅλς) **one whose occupation is catching fish, *fisher*** (Hom.+) lit. **Mt 4:18; Mk 1:16; Lk 5:2.** Fig., of the disciples ποιήσω ὑμᾶς ἁ. ἀνθρώπων *I will make you fish for people* **Mt 4:19; Mk 1:17** (CSmith, HTR 52, '59, 187–203), allegorically connecting their present and future vocations (Lk 5:10 has for this ἀνθρώπους ἔσῃ ζωγρῶν, s. ζωγρέω). The figure and expr. are also found in ancient wr. (RhM n.s. 35, 1880, 413 no. 12.—See also Diog. L. 4, 16, 17 θηράω=hunt down, in the sense 'catch someone for one's point of view'. In 8, 36 Diog. L. has Timon [fgm. 58 Diels] say of Pythagoras that he went out θήρῃ ἐπ' ἀνθρώπων=on a hunt for people).—WWuellner, The Mng. of 'Fishers of Men' '67. S. also the lit. s.v. ἀμφιβάλλω.—B. 184. M-M.

ἁλιεύω (as act. IG XII, 5, 126 [II/I BC]; Plut., Ant. 929 [29, 5] al.; PFlor 275, 24; Jer 16:16; TestZeb 6:3, 7, 8. As mid. Philo, Agr. 24, Plant. 102) ***to fish*** ὑπάγω ἁλιεύειν *I am going fishing* **J 21:3.**—DELG s.v. ἅλς. M-M.

ἁλίζω pass.: 1 fut. ἁλισθήσομαι; 1 aor. ἡλίσθην; pf. ptc. ἡλισμένον Tob 6:5 S (Aristot. et al.; LXX; TestLevi 9:14; DELG s.v. ἅλς) ***to salt*** ἐν τίνι ἁλισθήσεται; *how will it* (the salt) *be made salty again?* **Mt 5:13** (but s. on ἐν 5b). In **Mk 9:49** the ms. trad. is uncertain and the mng. obscure; there are 3 rdgs.: 1. πᾶς γὰρ πυρὶ ἁλισθήσεται. 2. πᾶσα γὰρ θυσία ἁλὶ ἁλισθ. (D). 3. πᾶς γὰρ πυρὶ ἁλισθ. καὶ πᾶσα θυσία (ἁλὶ) ἁλισθ. Of these, 2=3b is an OT requirement for sacrifice (Lev 2:13), in 1=3a the fire serves as a symbol of the suffering and sacrifice by which the disciple is tested (difft. WFields, Grace Theological Journal 6, '85, 299–304). S. lit. on ἅλας b and πῦρ c. Of similar apocalyptic obscurity is the saying of Heraclitus fgm. 66 πάντα τὸ πῦρ ἐπελθὸν κρινεῖ καὶ καταλήψεται. Also fig. ἁλίζεσθαι ἐν αὐτῷ (Χριστῷ) *be salted by him,* i.e. appropriate his power to prevent corruption IMg 10:2.

ἀλισγέω (etym. unknown, s. DELG; LXX) ***defile, pollute,*** fut. pass. ἀλισγηθήσεται **Mk 9:49 v.l.;** s. ἁλίζω.

ἀλίσγημα, ατος, τό (cp. Anecd. Gr. p. 377, 1; Hesych.; Suda; from ἀλισγέω 'make ceremonially impure' LXX) ***pollution*** ἀπέχεσθαι τῶν ἀ. τῶν εἰδώλων *avoid pollution* (pl. denotes separate acts) *by images (of deities)* **Ac 15:20** (ἀπέχεσθαι ἐκ τῶν ἀλισγημάτων τῶν ἐθνῶν τῆς Βαβυλῶνος ParJer 7:37 [=7:32 H.]).

Ἄλκη, ης, ἡ *Alce* (Isaeus 6, 19; 20; 55; Diod. S. 5, 49, 3; CIG 3268 [Smyrna]; 7064; Lat. Alce is more freq. [CIL III 2477; VI 20852; IX 3201 al.]) a woman of Smyrna ISm 13:2; IPol 8:3; MPol 17:2.

ἀλλά (Hom.+; DELG s.v. ἄλλος; Schwyzer II 578) gener. adversative particle (orig. neut. pl. of ἄλλος, 'otherwise') indicating a difference with or contrast to what precedes, in the case of individual clauses as well as whole sentences

❶ after a negative or after μέν **on the contrary, *but, yet, rather*—ⓐ** introducing a contrast οὐκ ἦλθον καταλῦσαι, ἀλλὰ πληρῶσαι **Mt 5:17.** οὐ πᾶς ὁ λέγων . . . ἀλλ' ὁ ποιῶν **7:21.** οὐκ ἀπέθανεν, ἀλλὰ καθεύδει **Mk 5:39.** οὐκέτι οὐδένα εἶδον, ἀλλὰ τὸν Ἰησοῦν μόνον **9:8** (v.l. εἰ μὴ τ. Ἰ.). οὐ . . . σαρκὶ ἀλλὰ μόνῳ πνεύματι AcPl Ant 13 (μόνον Aa I 237, 3). οὐκ ἔστι θεὸς νεκρῶν ἀλλὰ ζώντων **Mt 22:32; Mk 12:27; Lk 20:38.** ἀλλὰ καθὼς γέγραπται **Ro 15:21** introduces a statement about a procedure that contrasts with what precedes.—W. ascensive force (B-D-F §448; Rob. 1187) οὐ μόνον . . . ἀλλὰ καί *not only . . . , but also* (EpArist oft.; TestJob 47:2f; Jos., Bell. 3, 102; Just., A I, 5, 4): οὐ μόνον δεθῆναι, ἀλλὰ καὶ ἀποθανεῖν **Ac 21:13.** οὐ μόνον σὲ ἀλλὰ καὶ πάντας τοὺς ἀκούοντας **26:29;** cp. **27:10; Ro 1:32; 4:12, 16; 9:24; 13:5; 2 Cor 8:10, 21; 9:12; Eph 1:21; Phil 1:29; 1 Th 1:5; 2:8; Hb 12:26; 1 Pt 2:18.** W. the first member shortened (cp. TestJob 35:1) οὐ μόνον δέ, ἀλλὰ καί *not only this* (is the case), *but also:* οὐ μόνον δέ (sc. καυχώμεθα ἐπὶ τούτῳ), ἀλλὰ καὶ καυχώμεθα ἐν ταῖς θλίψεσιν **Ro 5:3,** cp. vs. **11; 8:23; 9:10; 2 Cor 8:19.**—Introducing the main point after a question expressed or implied, which has been answered in the negative οὐχί, ἀλλὰ κληθήσεται Ἰωάννης *no; rather his name shall be John* **Lk 1:60.** οὐχί, λέγω ὑμῖν, ἀλλὰ ἐὰν μὴ μετανοῆτε *no! I tell you; rather, if you do not repent* **13:3, 5;** cp. **16:30; J 7:12; Ac 16:37; Ro 3:27** (TestAbr A 5 p. 82, 5; 31f [Stone p. 12]; JosAs 4:15 al.; ApcMos 6) after μὴ γένοιτο, which serves as a strong negation **3:31; 7:7, 13;** cp. **1 Cor 7:21.** The neg. answer is omitted as obvious: *(no,) instead of that* **6:6** (as a declaration). Instead of ἀ.: ἀλλ' ἤ **Lk 12:51;** B 2:8. Also after a negative and ἄλλος, as in Pla., X. et al. (Kühner-G. II 284f; IG IV, 951, 76 [320 BC]; PPetr II, 46a, 5 [200 BC]; Just., A II, 4, 2 al.; in rhetorical quest. PsSol 5:12; B-D-F §448, 8): *except* οὐ γὰρ ἄλλα γράφομεν ὑμῖν ἀλλ' ἢ ἃ ἀναγινώσκετε *for we write you nothing (else) except what you can understand* **2 Cor 1:13.** This construction οὐκ ἄλλος ἀλλ' ἤ is a combination of οὐκ ἄλλος . . . , ἀλλά (PTebt 104, 19 [92 BC] μὴ ἐξέστω Φιλίσκωνι γυναῖκα ἄλλην ἐπαγαγέσθαι, ἀλλὰ Ἀπολλωνίαν) 1 Cl 51:5, and οὐκ ἄλλος ἤ . . . (Ps.-Clem., Hom. 16, 20).

ⓑ within the same clause, used to contrast single words (Just., A I, 15, 7 οὐ τούς δικαίους . . . ἀλλὰ τούς ἀσεβεῖς, D. 48, 1): οὐ . . . δικαίους ἀλλ' ἁμαρτωλούς **Mt 9:13; Lk 5:32.** οὐκ ἐμὲ δέχεται ἀλλὰ τὸν ἀποστείλαντά με **Mk 9:37.** ἀλλ' οὐ τί ἐγὼ θέλω ἀλλὰ τί σύ **14:36,** cp. **J 5:30; 6:38.** ἡ ἐμὴ διδαχὴ οὐκ ἔστιν ἐμὴ ἀλλὰ τοῦ πέμψαντός με **7:16.** οὐκ ἐγὼ ἀλλὰ ὁ κύριος **1 Cor 7:10.** οὐ τῇ πορνείᾳ, ἀλλὰ τῷ κυρίῳ **6:13.** οὐκ εἰς τὸ κρεῖσσον ἀλλὰ εἰς τὸ ἧσσον **11:17.** οὐκ ἔστιν ἓν μέλος ἀλλὰ πολλά **12:14.** οὐκ εἰς τὸ ἀγαθὸν ἀλλ' εἰς τὸ πονηρόν D 5:2. οὐχ ὡς διδάσκαλος ἀλλ' ὡς εἷς ἐξ ὑμῶν B 1:8 al. In **Mt 20:23,** οὐκ ἔστιν ἐμὸν τοῦτο δοῦναι, ἀλλ' οἷς ἡτοίμασται ὑπὸ τοῦ πατρός μου has been shortened from οὐκ ἐμὸν . . . ἀλλὰ τοῦ πατρός, ὅς δώσει οἷς ἡτοίμασται ὑπ' αὐτοῦ.—But s. WBeck, CTM 21, '50, 606–10 for the mng. *except* for **Mt 20:23=Mk 10:40,** and **Mk 4:22,** also **9:8 v.l.** (for εἰ μή); D 9:5. So also B-D-F §448, 8; Mlt-Turner 330; MBlack, An Aramaic Approach[3], '67, 113f.—After μὲν, to indicate that a limiting phrase is to follow πάντα μὲν καθαρά, ἀλλὰ κακὸν τῷ ἀνθρώπῳ **Ro 14:20.** σὺ μὲν γὰρ καλῶς εὐχαριστεῖς, ἀλλ' ὁ ἕτερος οὐκ οἰκοδομεῖται **1 Cor 14:17.**—The use of ἀλλά in the Johannine lit. is noteworthy, in that the parts contrasted are not always of equal standing grammatically: οὐκ ἦν ἐκεῖνος τὸ φῶς ἀλλ' ἵνα μαρτυρήσῃ περὶ τοῦ φωτός=ἀλλὰ μαρτυρῶν π. τ. φ. **J 1:8;** οὐκ ᾔδειν αὐτόν ἀλλ' . . . ἦλθον *although I did not know him, yet I came* vs. **31.** εἶπον [ὅτι] οὐκ εἰμὶ ἐγὼ ὁ Χριστός, ἀλλ' ὅτι *I said, 'I am not the Christ; rather, I was sent before him'* **3:28.** οὔτε οὗτος ἥμαρτεν οὔτε οἱ γονεῖς αὐτοῦ, ἀλλ' ἵνα φανερωθῇ *neither this man has sinned, nor his parents, but* (he was born blind) *that . . . might be revealed* **9:3.**

❷ when whole clauses are compared, ἀλλά can indicate a transition to someth. different or contrasted: **the other side of a matter or issue,** ***but, yet.*** δεῖ γὰρ γενέσθαι, ἀλλ' οὔπω ἐστὶν τὸ τέλος **Mt 24:6,** cp. **Lk 21:9.** κεκοίμηται· ἀλλὰ πορεύομαι ἵνα ἐξυπνίσω αὐτόν **J 11:11,** cp. vs. **15; 16:20; Lk 22:36; J 4:23; 6:36, 64; 8:37; Ac 9:6; Ro 10:18f.** ἁμαρτία οὐκ ἐλλογεῖται . . . ἀλλὰ . . . *sin is not charged; nevertheless . . .* **5:13f.** Introducing an objection, ἀλλὰ ἐρεῖ τις (Jos., Bell. 7, 363 and Just., A I, 7, 1 ἀλλὰ φήσει τις) probably colloq. = 'well', someone will say: **1 Cor 15:35; Js 2:18** (difft. DWatson, NTS 39 '93, 94–121). Taking back or limiting a preceding statement παρένεγκε τὸ ποτήριον τοῦτο ἀπ' ἐμοῦ· ἀλλ' οὐ τί ἐγὼ θέλω **Mk 14:36.** ἀλλ' οὐχ ὡς τὸ παράπτωμα, οὕτως καὶ τὸ χάρισμα **Ro 5:15.** ἀλλ' οὐκ ἐχρησάμεθα τῇ ἐξουσίᾳ ταύτῃ **1 Cor 9:12.** ἀλλὰ ἕκαστος ἴδιον ἔχει χάρισμα **7:7.** ἀλλὰ καὶ περὶ τούτου δὲ εἴρηται D 1:6.—In ἀλλ', οὐ πάντες οἱ ἐξελθόντες . . . ; in **Hb 3:16** ἀλλ', in the opinion of some, seems to owe its origin solely to a misunderstanding of the preceding τίνες as τινές by an early copyist (B-D-F §448, 4), but here ἀλλά may convey strong asseveration *surely* (so REB). See 3 below.

❸ before independent clauses, to indicate that the preceding is to be regarded as a settled matter, thus forming a transition to someth. new (Just., A I, 3; 10, 1) **other matter for additional consideration,** ***but*** ἀλλὰ ὁ ὄχλος οὗτος . . . ἐπάρατοί εἰσιν *but this rabble . . . is accursed* **J 7:49.** ἀλλ' ἐν τούτοις πᾶσιν ὑπερνικῶμεν (no, not at all!) *but in all these we are more than conquerors* **Ro 8:37.** ἀλλ' ὅτι ἃ θύουσιν, δαιμονίοις . . . θύουσιν (no!) *but they* (the gentiles) *offer what they sacrifice to inferior deities* **1 Cor 10:20** (their second-rate status is Paul's connotation). Cp. **Gal 2:3** and **Mt 11:7f** ἀλλὰ τί ἐξήλθατε ἰδεῖν; (you could not have wanted to see that;) *but what did you go out to see?* Also to be explained elliptically is the ascensive ἀλλὰ καί (and not only this,) *but also* **Lk 12:7; 16:21; 24:22; Phil 1:18** (Ath. 21, 4); negative ἀλλ' οὐδέ **Lk 23:15; Ac 19:2; 1 Cor 3:2; 4:3** (Ar. 9:1); strengthened ἀλλά γε καί *indeed* **Lk 24:21;** ἀλλὰ μὲν οὖν γε καί **Phil 3:8; Hb 3:16** (s. 2 above) may well be rendered (as NEB) *all those, surely, whom Moses had led out of Egypt* (cp. Dio Chrys. 33, 36; 47, 3).

❹ **for strong alternative/additional consideration—**ⓐ in the apodosis of conditional sentences, ***yet, certainly, at least*** εἰ καὶ πάντες σκανδαλισθήσονται, ἀλλ' οὐκ ἐγώ *certainly I will not* **Mk 14:29;** cp. **1 Cor 8:6; 2 Cor 4:16; 5:16; 11:6;** strengthened ἀλλὰ καί: εἰ γὰρ σύμφυτοι γεγόναμεν . . . , ἀλλὰ καὶ τῆς ἀναστάσεως (sc. σύμφυτοι) ἐσόμεθα *we shall certainly be united w. him in his resurrection* **Ro 6:5;** limited by γε (ἀλλ' οὖν γε Just., D. 76, 6; 93, 1): εἰ ἄλλοις οὐκ εἰμὶ ἀπόστολος, ἀλλά γε ὑμῖν εἰμι *at least I am one to you* **1 Cor 9:2** (cp. X., Cyr. 1, 3, 6; B-D-F §439, 2). ἐὰν γὰρ μυρίους παιδαγωγοὺς ἔχητε ἐν Χριστῷ, ἀλλ' οὐ πολλοὺς πατέρας *certainly not many fathers* **1 Cor 4:15.**

ⓑ rhetorically ascensive: (not only this,) ***but rather*** πόσην κατειργάσατο ὑμῖν σπουδήν, ἀ. ἀπολογίαν, ἀ. ἀγανάκτησιν, ἀ. φόβον, ἀ. ἐπιπόθησιν, ἀ. ζῆλον, ἀ. ἐκδίκησιν *even, yes indeed* **2 Cor 7:11.** On **Eph 5:24** s. 5 below.

❺ w. an impv. to strengthen the command: ***now, then*** (Arrian, Anab. 5, 26, 4 ἀλλὰ παραμείνατε=so hold on! JosAs 13:9; ApcMos 3; SibOr 3, 624; 632; Jos., Ant. 4, 145): ἀλλὰ ἐλθὼν ἐπίθες τὴν χεῖρά σου *now come and lay your hand on her* **Mt 9:18.** ἀλλ' εἴ τι δύνῃ, βοήθησον *now help me, if you can* (in any way) **Mk 9:22.** ἀλλὰ ὑπάγετε εἴπατε *now go and tell* **16:7.** ἀλλὰ ἀναστὰς κατάβηθι **Ac 10:20.** ἀλλὰ ἀνάστηθι **26:16** (JosAs 14:11).—In same sense w. subjunctive ἀλλ' . . . ἀπειλησώμεθα αὐτοῖς μηκέτι λαλεῖν *now let us warn them not to speak any longer* **4:17.** ἀλλ' ὥσπερ ἐν παντὶ περισσεύετε . . . ἵνα καὶ ἐν ταύτῃ τῇ χάριτι περισσεύητε **2 Cor 8:7.** Unless **Eph 5:24** is to be placed in 4b, it is prob. to be understood as an ellipsis, and can be expanded thus: *then just as the church is subject to Christ, wives should also be subject to their husbands.* Yet ἀλλά is also used to introduce an inference from what precedes: *so, therefore, accordingly* (e.g. Aristoph., Ach. 1189 ὁδὶ δὲ καὐτός. Ἀλλ' ἄνοιγε τὴν θύραν='here he is in person. So open the door', Birds 1718; Herodas 7, 89; Artem. 4, 27 p. 219, 22; cp. AMoorehouse, ClQ 46, '52, 100–104 on 'progressive' ἀλλά as Od. 3, 388).—M-M.

ἀλλαγή, ῆς, ἡ (Aeschyl. et al.; pap; Wsd 7:18; Just., A I, 23, 2; Ath. 22, 3; Theoph. Ant. 1, 6 [p. 70, 1]; DELG I 64 s.v. ἄλλος) ***a change*** τὰς τῶν καιρῶν ἀλλαγὰς καταδιαιρεῖν *make a distinction betw. the changes of the seasons* Dg 4:5 (cp. Wsd 7:18; SibOr 2, 257).

ἀλλάσσω (ἄλλος) fut. ἀλλάξω; 1 aor. ἤλλαξα; 2 fut. pass. ἀλλαγήσομαι (Aeschyl.+; DELG I 64 s.v. ἄλλος).

❶ **to make someth. other or different,** ***change, alter*** τὴν φωνήν μου *change my tone* **Gal 4:20** (Artem. 2, 20 of ravens πολλάκις ἀλλάσσειν τ. φωνήν; TestJos 14:2 ἀλλ. τὸν λόγον; Just., A I, 9, 2 τὸ σχῆμα). Of the hyena τὴν φύσιν *change its nature* B 10:7 (s. Windisch, Hdb. ad loc.). τὰς χρόας *change colors* of stones Hs 9, 4, 5; 8. Of Jesus on the day of final judgment ἀλλάξει τὸν ἥλιον καὶ τὴν σελήνην καὶ τοὺς ἀστέρας *he will change the sun, the moon, and the stars,* so that they lose their radiance B 15:5. τὰ ἔθη *change the customs* **Ac 6:14** (Diod. S. 1, 73, 3 τὰς τῶν θεῶν τιμὰς ἀλλάττειν).—Pass. (Dionys., Perieg. [GGM II, p. 127, 392]; Herm. Wr. 1, 4; 13, 5; Jos., Ant. 2, 97 v.l.;

SibOr 3, 638; 5, 273 ἕως κόσμος ἀλλαγῇ of the last times; Ar. 5, 1 ὕδωρ . . . ἀλλασσόμενον χρώμασι): of the change in the bodily condition of Christians on the Last Day *be changed* **1 Cor 15:51f** (s. MDahl, The Resurrection of the Body '62, 103–5); of the change to be wrought by Christ in the heavens when the world is destroyed **Hb 1:12** (Ps 101:27).

❷ **to exchange one thing for another,** ***exchange*** (Aeschyl. et al.; POxy 729, 43; BGU 1141, 41; 44; Jer 2:11; Jos., Ant. 18, 237) ἤλλαξαν (v.l. ἠλλάξαντο, as in Attic usage) τὴν δόξαν τοῦ ἀφθάρτου θεοῦ ἐν ὁμοιώματι εἰκόνος *they exchanged the glory of the immortal God for . . .* **Ro 1:23** (ἀ. ἔν τινι after Ps 105:20, where it renders הֵמִיר בְּ; but s. ἐν 5b). Of bad stones in a bldg. (cp. PMich I, 41, 10): Hs 9, 5, 2. Of changing clothes (Appian, Bell. Civ. 5, 122 §504 τὴν ἐσθῆτα ἤλλαξεν; Gen 35:2; 2 Km 12:20) Ox 840, 19 (ASyn. 150, 113).—B. 913. M-M. TW.

ἀλλαχόθεν adv. of place (since Antiphon 3, 4, 3; Appian, Liby. 126 §604; Plut., Fab. 178 [6, 9], Mor. 1086d; 1129e; Jos., Ant. 2, 198; 4, 236; 18, 316; CPR 232, 28; POxy 237 V, 15 [186 AD]; 2410, 7 [120 AD] 4 Macc 1:7; Just., D. 92, 3 οὐδαμόθεν . . . ἀ.) ***from another place*** ἀναβαίνειν *climb over at some other place* (opp. εἰσέρχεσθαι διὰ τῆς θύρας) **J 10:1.**—DELG s.v. ἄλλος. M-M.

ἀλλαχοῦ adv. of place ***elsewhere*** (so Soph., X. et al.; Just., A I, 37, 3 in citation, al.), also *in another direction* (Epict. 3, 23, 22; 3, 26, 4; Dio Chrys. 21 [38], 15; Polyaenus 1, 12; 1, 46; 4, 2, 21; SIG 888, 38 [238 AD]; Phryn., 43f Lob.; TestAbr A 10 p. 87, 23; 25 [Stone p. 22]) ἀ. ἄγειν εἰς τὰς ἐχομένας κωμοπόλεις *go in another direction to . . .* **Mk 1:38.**—DELG s.v. ἄλλος. M-M.

ἀλληγορέω (ἀγορεύω 'speak'; Athen. 2 p. 69c; Plut., Mor. 363d; Porphyr., Vi. Pyth. 12 Nauck; schol. on Pind., O. 10, 13a; Philo, Cher. 25, Somn. 2, 31, Vi. Cont. 28; Jos., Ant. 1, 24; Did., Gen. 119, 2; Orig., C. Cels. 1, 17, 4 [w. τροπολογέω]; Tat 21, 2 τοὺς θεούς 'allegorically interpret the gods') **to use analogy or likeness to express someth.,** ***speak allegorically*** ἅτινά ἐστιν ἀλληγορούμενα **Gal 4:24.** (Cp. Plut. Mor. 19f.)—FWehrli, Z. Gesch. der allegor. Deutung Homers, diss. Basel 1928: this kind of interpretation was practiced w. ref. to myths at least as early as the 5th cent. BC. On allegorical interpretation among Greeks and Jews cp. Heraclit. Sto., Allegoriae=Quaestiones Homericae and, of course, Philo of Alexandria.—RHanson, Allegory and Event '59; NWalter, Der Thoraausleger Aristobulos, in TU 86 '64, 60f.—DELG s.v. ἀγορά. EDNT. M-M. TW. Sv.

ἀλληλουϊά (also ἀλ- or -λούϊα for הַלְלוּ־יָהּ) Hb. loanword lit. ***praise Yahweh,*** transliterated ***hallelujah,*** liturg. formula of Israelite (Ps; Tob 13:18; 3 Macc 7:13) and then of Christian worship. Used as such **Rv 19:1, 3, 6;** w. ἀμήν (cp. the Hebr. of Ps 106:48; OdeSol 11:24; PGM 7, 271; a Christian amulet PBerol 6096 in Wilcken, APF 1, 1901, 430; ESchaefer in PIand I p. 29) vs. **4.**—HEngberding, RAC I 293–99.—M-M. TW.

ἀλλήλων gen. of the reciprocal pron.; dat. ἀλλήλοις; acc. ἀλλήλους (Hom.+; Schwyzer I 446, n. 8) ***each other, one another, mutually,*** ἀλλήλων μέλη *members of one another* **Ro 12:5; Eph 4:25;** 1 Cl 46:7. ἀ. τὰ βάρη **Gal 6:2.** καταλαλεῖν ἀ. *slander each other* **Js 4:11;** ἀνέχεσθαι ἀ. **Col 3:13;** ἀπ' ἀ. **Mt 25:32; Ac 15:39;** κατ' ἀ. (Appian, Bell. Civ. 5, 24 §95) **Js 5:9;** μετ' ἀ. **J 6:43; 11:56; 16:19;** ITr 12:2; μεταξὺ ἀ. **Ro 2:15;** παρὰ ἀ. **J 5:44;** ὑπὲρ ἀ. **1 Cor 12:25; Js 5:16** ὑπ' ἀ. (Appian, Bell. Civ. 5, 22 §89) **Gal 5:15.**—ἀλλήλοις ἀντίκειται **Gal 5:17;** ἐγκαλεῖν ἀ. **Ac 19:38;** ἐν ἀ. (Jos., Bell. 2, 127, Ant. 9, 240; Just., D. 101, 3): εἰρηνεύειν **Mk 9:50;** cp. **J 13:35; Ro 15:5.**—ἀλλήλους: ἀγαπᾶν ἀ. **J 13:34; Ro 13:8; 1 Th 4:9; 1J 3:11; 2J 5;** 2 Cl 9:6; παραδιδόναι ἀ. **Mt 24:10;** πρὸς ἀ. (Ael. Aristid. 46 p. 404 D.; En 6:2; Jos., Ant. 2, 108; Just., A I, 61, 10) **Mk 4:41; 8:16;** εἰς ἀ. **J 13:22; Ro 12:10** (cp. ἑαυτούς **1 Pt 4:8**).—DELG s.v. ἄλλος.

ἀλλογενής, ές (OGI 598 [I AD], the famous Jerus. temple ins μηδένα ἀλλογενῆ εἰσπορεύεσθαι; see Schürer II, 285 n. 57; Sb 6235, 6; LXX; PsSol 17:28; JosAs 4:12; Philo; Jos., Bell. 2, 417; Just.) ***foreign*** of the grateful Samaritan εἰ μὴ ὁ ἀ. οὗτος *except this foreigner* **Lk 17:18.**—M-M. TW.

ἀλλοιόω fut. 3 sg. ἀλλοιώσει Sir. 12:18; 1 aor. ἠλλοίωσα. Pass.: fut. ἀλλοιωθήσομαι LXX; aor. ἠλλοιώθην; pf. ἠλλοίωμαι Mal. 3:6 (ἀλλοιος; Pre-Socr. et al.; PEnteux 51, 6 [III BC]; En, TestSol, TestJob, Test12Patr; Ar. 4, 1) **to cause to be different,** ***to change*** τὸ ῥηθέν *the word* (Gen 2:23), so that it becomes null and void 1 Cl 6:3. Of the earth μηδὲ ἀλλοιοῦσά τι τῶν δεδογματισμένων ὑπ' αὐτοῦ *changing none of the things he ordained* 20:4 (cp. Da 2:21; 6:9 both LXX and Theod.; En 2:1; 104:11).—Pass. *be changed* (Thu. 2, 59, 1; Antig. Car. 25, 164; Polyb. 8, 27, 2; Dio Chrys. 35 [52], 13; En 2:2; Ar.; Just.; Ath. 22, 5) **Lk 9:29** D. ἠλλοιώθη ἡ ἰδέα αὐτοῦ Hv 5:4. ἡ μορφὴ αὐτοῦ ἠλλοιώθη Hm 12, 4, 1 (cp. Da 5:6; 7:28 both Theod.).—Hs 8, 5, 1.—DELG s.v. ἄλλος. TW.

ἅλλομαι fut. ἁλοῦμαι, 1 aor. ἡλάμην (Hom. et al.; LXX; Jos., Bell. 5, 330, Ant. 20, 61; Just., D. 69, 6 [s. Is 35:6]).

❶ lit. **to make a quick leaping movement,** ***leap, spring up*** (PRyl 138, 15): of the lame man when healed (Is 35:6) περιπατῶν καὶ ἁλλόμενος *walking and leaping* i.e. showing by slow and fast movement that he was really healed **Ac 3:8.** ἥλατο καὶ περιεπάτει *he leaped up and could walk* **14:10.**

❷ fig., of the quick movement of inanimate things (since Il. 4, 125 an arrow): **to spring up from a source,** of water ***well up, bubble up*** (as Lat. salire Vergil, Ecl. 5, 47; Suet., Octav. 82) πηγὴ ὕδατος ἁλλομένου *a spring of water welling up* **J 4:14.**—DELG. M-M.

ἄλλος, η, ο (Hom.+) adj. and subst.—❶ **pert. to that which is other than some other entity,** ***other***—ⓐ distinguished fr. the subject who is speaking or who is logically understood μήπως ἄλλοις κηρύξας αὐτὸς ἀδόκιμος γένωμαι *lest after preaching to others I myself should be disqualified* **1 Cor 9:27.** ἀ. ἐστὶν ὁ μαρτυρῶν **J 5:32** (ἄλλος of God as Epict. 3, 13, 13). ἄλλη συνείδησις (=ἄλλου συν.) *another's conscientious scruples* **1 Cor 10:29.** ἄλλους ἔσωσεν, ἑαυτὸν οὐ δύναται σῶσαι *others he saved, himself he cannot save* **Mt 27:42; Mk 15:31,** cp. **Lk 23:35.**

ⓑ distinguished fr.—**α.** a previously mentioned subj. or obj. ἄλλα δὲ ἔπεσεν ἐπὶ κτλ. **Mt 13:5, 7f.** ἄλλην παραβολήν vss. **24, 31, 33; 21:33.** ἄλλους ἑστῶτας **20:3, 6.**—Freq. the subj. or obj. is not expressly mentioned, but can be supplied fr. what precedes δι' ἄλλης ὁδοῦ ἀνεχώρησαν **2:12** (cp. 3 Km 13:10) al.

β. different fr. the subj. in a following contrasting phrase ἄλλοι κεκοπιάκασιν, καὶ ὑμεῖς εἰς τὸν κόπον αὐτῶν εἰσεληλύθατε **J 4:38** (JATRobinson, TU 73, '59, 510–15 [identity]).

ⓒ used correlatively in contrast οἱ μὲν . . . ἄλλοι (δέ) *some . . . others* **J 7:12.** Indefinite τινὲς . . . ἄλλοι **9:16.** Also ὁ ὄχλος . . . ἄλλοι *the crowd . . . others* **12:29.** ὁ πλεῖστος ὄχλος . . . ἄλλοι δέ **Mt 21:8.** With no mention of the first part, and the other parts introd. by ἄλλοι . . . ἄλλοι **Mk 6:15; 8:28; Lk 9:19; J 9:9.**—In enumerations, w. ὁ μέν in the first part, continued by ἄλλος δέ (somet. ἕτερος takes the place of ἄλλος Libanius, Or. 32, p. 155, 18 F. ἄλλοι . . . ἕτεροι; Ath. 26, 2; Ps.-Clem., Hom. 19, 9; UPZ 42, 32f [162 BC]; s. 2 below) **1 Cor 12:8ff.** οἱ πέντε

... ὁ εἷς ... ὁ ἄλλος=*the last one* **Rv 17:10.** οἱ ἄλλοι w. a noun expressed or understood (X., Cyr. 3, 3, 4; Herodian 2, 4, 4) *the other(s), the rest* (Ps.-Callisth. 3, 35 τὰ ἄλλα λ' [ἔτη]=the rest of the thirty years) **J 20:25; 21:8; 1 Cor 14:29;** AcPlCor 1:4; τὰ ἄλλα θηρία AcPl Ha 5, 9; τῶν ἄλλων σπερμάτων AcPlCor 2:26.—Various cases of ἄ. in juxtapos. (Epictetus index Schenkl; Hippocr., Ep. 17, 31 ἀλλὰ ἄλλος ἄλλου; Maximus Tyr., 3, 1d ἀλλὰ ἄλλον ἄλλο; 21, 7b; Sallust. 4 p. 6, 19; Jos., Bell. 7, 389; 396, Ant. 7, 325; Ath. 1, 1 al) ἄ. πρὸς ἄ. λέγοντες *one said to the other* **Ac 2:12.** ἄλλοι μὲν οὖν ἄλλο τι ἔκραζον *now some were shouting one thing, some another* (X., An. 2, 1, 15 ἄλλος ἄλλα λέγει; Nicol. Dam.: 90 fgm. 130, 25 p. 409, 25 Jac. ἄλλοι δὲ ἄλλα ὑπελάμβανον) **19:32;** cp. **21:34.**

ⓓ ἄλλος τις *some other, any other* μήτε ἄλλον τινὰ ὅρκον **Js 5:12.** ἄ. τις διϊσχυρίζετο *another man maintained* **Lk 22:59.** εἰ δέ τι ἄλλο παραδέχεσθε AcPlCor 2:34. Esp. εἴ τις ἄ. (1 Macc 13:39) **1 Cor 1:16; Phil 3:4.**—οὐδεὶς ἄλλος *no one else* (cp. Jos., Vi. 196) **J 15:24.**

❷ **pert. to that which is different in type or kind from other entities** in comparisons ***another, different*** (from, compared with).

ⓐ *different in kind* **1 Cor 15:39ff; 2 Cor 11:4** (interchanging w. ἕτερος; s. b, below **Gal 1:7** and 1c, above; cp. B-D-F §306).

ⓑ *another* (except, besides) οὐκ ἔστιν ἄ. πλὴν αὐτοῦ *there is none* (i.e. no other God) *but (the Lord your God)* **Mk 12:32** (cp. Ex 8:6; Is 45:21; Pr 7:1a). ὅτι ... εἷς Χριστὸς Ἰησοῦς καὶ ἄ. οὐχ ὑπάρχει *that ... there is only one Messiah, Jesus, and there will be no other* AcPl Ha 1, 18. W. ἀλλά foll. 1 Cl 51:5; ἀλλ' ἤ **2 Cor 1:13;** εἰ μή **J 6:22;** παρά w. acc. (Philostrat., Vi. Apoll. 5, 30 p. 188, 30; Just., A I, 19, 5; 58, 1) **1 Cor 3:11. Gal 1:6, 7** (B-D-F §306, 4; Mlt. 80 n. 1; 246; EBurton, ICC Gal., 420–22) belongs in this section (s. ἕτερος 1bγ).

ⓒ ἄλλος ἐστὶν ὁ σπείρων καὶ ἄλλος ὁ θερίζων *one sows, another reaps* **J 4:37.**

ⓓ ἄλλος καὶ ἄλλος *each one a different,* or simply *different* (Appian, Iber. 62 §260) Hs 9, 1, 4; 10; 9, 17, 1; 2; 9, 28, 1.

❸ **pert. to being in addition, *more*** (Pla., Leg. 5, 745a ἄλλο τοσοῦτον μέρος) w. cardinal numerals (Stephan. Byz. s.v. Ἐορδαῖαι: ἄλλαι δύο χῶραι; Diog. L. 1, 115 Ἐπιμενίδαι ἄλλοι δύο; Gen 41:3, 6, 23; Jos., Ant. 1, 92) ἄ. δύο ἀδελφούς *two more brothers* **Mt 4:21;** ἄ. πέντε τάλαντα (cp. SIG 201, 17 [356 BC] ἄλλας τριάκοντα μνᾶς; PBour 23, 7 [II AD]; 1 Esdr 4:52; 1 Macc 15:31) **25:20,** cp. vs. **22.** μετ' αὐτοῦ ἄ. δύο **J 19:18.**

❹ w. art. **pert. to being the remaining one of two or more, *the other*** of the two (Soph., El. 739; Eur., Iph. T. 962f; Pla., Leg. 1, 629d; SIG 736, 91 [92 BC]; UPZ 162 VIII, 34 [117 BC]; BGU 456, 10ff; CPR 22, 15 [II AD] τὸ ἄλλο ἥμισυ, also Tob 8:21 S; cp. also 1 Km 14:4. The strictly correct word would be ἕτερος. TestJob 9:8): the healed hand is ὑγιὴς ὡς ἡ ἄλλη **Mt 12:13.** ἡ ἄ. Μαρία (to differentiate her fr. Mary Magdalene, as Appian, Basil. 1a §4 Αἰνείας ἄλλος; Arrian, Anab. 5, 21, 3; 5 ὁ ἄλλος Πῶρος) **27:61; 28:1.** στρέψον αὐτῷ καὶ τὴν ἄ. *turn the other* (i.e. the left cheek) *to him, too* **Mt 5:39;** cp. **Lk 6:29.** ὁ μαθητὴς ὁ ἄλλος **J 18:16** (cp. **20:2ff**); τοῦ ἄ. τοῦ συσταυρωθέντος **19:32.**—S. adv. ἄλλως. DELG. M-M. TW. Sv.

ἀλλοτριεπίσκοπος (v.l. ἀλλοτριοεπίσκοπος, s. Mlt-H. 272; B-D-F §124), **ου, ὁ** (elsewh. only Dionys. Areop., Ep. 8: MPG III 1089c ἀλλοτριοεπίσκοπος; cp. Epiphanius of Constantia [Salamis], Ancoratus 12; s. Lampe s.v.) a word whose meaning has not yet been determined w. certainty; w. φονεύς, κλέπτης, κακοποιός **1 Pt 4:15.** EZeller, SBBerlAK 1893, 129ff, referring to the claim by Cynic preachers to be overseers (ἐπίσκοποι) of all men (Epict. 3, 22, 97 οὐ τὰ ἀλλότρια πολυπραγμονεῖ ὅταν τὰ ἀνθρώπινα ἐπισκοπῇ ἀλλὰ τὰ ἴδια), interprets the word as mng. ***one who meddles in things that do not concern the pers., a busybody*** (sim. REB. NRSV: *mischief maker;* s. PWendland, Kultur[2] 1912, 82, 1; Zahn, Einl. II 39f; ESelwyn, Comm. '46 ad loc. Cp. ἀλλοτρίοις ἐπίσκοπος **1 Pt 4:15** P^{72}, 'meddling in other people's affairs'=Lat. 'alienis custos'.). But it is questionable whether such behavior would merit the kind of reprisal suggested by the context. Therefore a more serious type of crime has been suggested, and the proximity of κλέπτης has led to the conjecture ***concealer of stolen goods.*** For ***spy, informer*** (Lat. delator) s. AHilgenfeld, Einl. 1875, 630. Dssm., NB 51, 5=BS 224, 4 (BGU 531 II, 22 [II AD] οὔτε εἰμὶ ἄδικος οὔτε ἀλλοτρίων ἐπιθυμητής) suggests ***revolutionist*** (s. A Bischoff, ZNW 7, 1906, 271–74; 9, 1908, 171; PSchmidt, ZWT 50, 1908, 26ff). KErbes, ZNW 19, 1920, 39–44; 20, 1921, 249 considers it a Christian coinage, aimed at neglectful bishops. Tertullian, Scorp. 12 'alieni speculator'. Cyprian, Test. 3, 37 'curas alienas agens'. Vulg. 'alienorum adpetitor'.—JBauer, BZ n.s. 22, '78, 109–15.—DELG. M-M. TW.

ἀλλότριος, ία, ον (ἄλλος; Hom.+; DELG I 64 s.v. ἄλλος)

❶ **pert. to what belongs to another, *not one's own, strange*** (opp. ἴδιος; Περὶ ὕψους 4, 1; Epict. 2, 4, 10; 3, 24, 3f; Proverb. Aesopi 114 P.; SIG 982, 5f; pap since III BC, e.g. BGU 1121, 22 [5 BC] μήτε ἴδια μήτ' ἀλλότρια; 15, 15; Jos., Ant. 18, 46; 19, 305).

ⓐ adj. ἀ. οἰκέτης *another's slave* (Dio Chrys. 14 [31], 34 ἀλλ. οἰκ.; Jos., Ant. 18, 47.—ἀ. δοῦλος as early as Pla., Leg. 9, 9, 868a; cp. Diod. S. 36, 2, 2) **Ro 14:4;** γυνὴ ἀ. (Chariton 6, 3, 7; POxy 1067, 6ff) Hm 4, 1, 1; 12, 2, 1. καυχᾶσθαι ἐν ἀ. κόποις *boast about work done by others* **2 Cor 10:15** (cp. Epict. 1, 28, 23 ἀλλότριον ἔργον=another's deed; Tat. 26, 1 λόγους ἀ. 'words of others'); κοινωνεῖν ἁμαρτίαις ἀ. *participate in other people's sins* **1 Ti 5:22.** ἐν ἀ. κανόνι καυχᾶσθαι *boast* (of work already done) *in another's field* **2 Cor 10:16.** πάντα ἀ. εἰσι (w. ὑπ' ἐξουσίαν ἑτέρου) Hs 1:3. ἀ. αἷμα **Hb 9:25.** θεμέλιον **Ro 15:20.** ἀλλοτρίας σάρκας καταφαγεῖν B 10:4b. τὰς ἀ. ἐντολὰς (opp. παρὰ τοῦ κυρίου δεδομένας) Papias (2:3). Of lands (Isis aretalogy SEG VIII, 548, 31 [I BC]) *strange, foreign* πάροικον ἐν γῇ ἀ. **Ac 7:6** (Ex 2:22; ParJer 7:34). παροικεῖν εἰς γῆν ... ὡς ἀ. *sojourn in a land as if it were foreign* **Hb 11:9.** ἀ. τοῦ θεοῦ ὄντες *aliens to God* 1 Cl 7:7 (cp. PsSol 17:13 ἀπὸ τοῦ θεοῦ; Herm. Wr. 2, 16; Just., D. 8, 2 ἀλλοτρίῳ τοῦ πράγματος; B-D-F §182, 3); so τὰ κοσμικὰ ὡς ἀ. ἡγεῖσθαι, i.e. to look on them as someth. that does not concern Christians 2 Cl 5:6.

ⓑ subst.**—α.** τὸ ἀ. *other people's property* (Epict. 2, 6, 8; Jos., C. Ap. 2, 216) B 10:4a. ἐν τῷ ἀ. πιστοί *faithful w. what belongs to another* **Lk 16:12** (the wealth of this world is foreign to the Christian, cp. Epict. 4, 5, 15 of temporal goods: οὐδὲν ἴδιον τῷ ἀνθρώπῳ ἐστίν, ἀλλὰ πάντα ἀλλότρια; also 2, 6, 8; 24.—S. ἡμέτερος). ἀλλοτρίοις ἐπίσκοπος **1 Pt 4:15** P^{72}, 'meddling in other people's affairs'=Lat. 'alienis custos', but s. prec. entry τοῦ ἀ. ἅψασθαι Hs 1:11; ἀλλοτρίων ἐπιθυμεῖν ibid. (cp. Ar. 15, 4 οὐκ ἐπιθυμοῦσι ... τὰ ἀ.).

β. ὁ ἀ. *the stranger* (='one who is unknown' cp. Sir 8:18) **J 10:5a.** οἱ ἀλλότριοι *strange people* vs. **5b;** specif. *aliens* (LXX; Jos., Bell. 7, 266) **Mt 17:25f** (opp. οἱ υἱοί).

❷ **pert. to being outside one's customary experience or practice, *alien, unsuitable*** (cp. UPZ 113, 11 [II BC]; POxy 282, 9) στάσις ἀ., explained by ξένη τοῖς ἐκλεκτοῖς τοῦ θεοῦ 1 Cl 1:1. ἀ. γνώμη *strange*=false (cp. θεὸς ἀλλότριος Ps 80:10; ParJer 7:30) *viewpoint* IPhld 3:3; ἀ. βοτάνη ITr 6:1; χρῶμα IRo ins.

❸ **pert. to being different and therefore in opposition, *hostile,*** as subst. ***enemy*** (Hom. et al.; Polyb. 27, 15, 13; Diod. S. 11,

27 et al.; 1 Macc 1:38; 2:7; cp. OGI 90, 91) παρεμβολὰς κλίνειν ἀλλοτρίων **Hb 11:34.**—M-M. TW.

ἀλλόφυλος, ον (Aeschyl., Thu. et al.; BGU 34; 411; 419; 858; LXX; Philo, Leg. ad Gai. 200; Jos., Bell. 5, 194, Ant. 1, 338 al.; Test12Patr; TestSol 6:4 P; Mel., P. 76, 554; 92, 692) ***alien, foreign,*** hence fr. the Judean viewpoint=*gentiles, outsiders;* subst. *a gentile* (opp. ἀνὴρ Ἰουδαῖος; cp. Jos., Ant. 4, 183) κολλᾶσθαι ἢ προσέρχεσθαι ἀ. *associate w. or approach a gentile* **Ac 10:28;** cp. **13:19** D. Esp. (as LXX) of the Philistines 1 Cl 4:13; or Amalekites B 12:2; or Canaanites AcPl Ha 8, 13; 15. ἡ παρεμβολὴ τῶν ἀ. *the camp of the 'aliens'* 1 Cl 55:4 (cp. Jdth 6:1 of the Assyrians and their allies). Of Christians (some of whom would be Israelites/Jews) in relation to Judeans Dg 5:17.—M-M. TW.

ἄλλως adv. fr. ἄλλος (Hom.+; also TestLevi 6:6) **pert. to difference in manner or condition, *otherwise, in another way*** Hs 7:3; 9, 12, 5f; 9, 13, 2; 9, 16, 2. Of recognition of good works τὰ ἄ. ἔχοντα κρυβῆναι οὐ δύνανται *if they are not* (evident) *they cannot* (in the end) *remain hidden* **1 Ti 5:25.** S. ἄλλος.—M-M.

ἀλοάω fut. ἀλοήσω, 1 aor. ἠλόησα; fut. 3 pl. pass. ἀλοηθήσονται (Aristoph., Pla., X.+) ***thresh*** (so Pla., X.; Theocr. 10, 48; PFrankf 2, 27; 70 [III BC]; PLond I, 131, 502 p. 185 and ln. 576 p. 187 al. [78 AD]; LXX) mostly done w. oxen, which were driven over the threshing-floor **1 Cor 9:9; 1 Ti 5:18** (both Dt 25:4); on this s. IBenzinger, Hebr. Archäologie[2] 1907, §30, 2; GDalman, Arbeit u. Sitte in Palästina III: Von der Ernte z. Mehl usw. '33. ὁ ἀλοῶν (sc. ἀλοᾷ) ἐπ' ἐλπίδι τοῦ μετέχειν *one who threshes,* (does so) *in hope of a share in the crop* **1 Cor 9:10.**—DELG s.v. ἀλωή. M-M.

ἄλογος, ον (Pre-Socr.+; pap, LXX; PsSol 16:10; TestSol 10:8 C; TestZeb 5:1; ApcEsdr 1:22 p. 25, 17 Tdf.; ApcSed 7:9; Philo, Joseph.)

❶ **pert. to lack of reasoning capacity, *without reason*** of animals (Crates 11 p. 62, 16 Malherbe) ὡς ἄ. ζῷα *like unreasoning animals* **2 Pt 2:12; Jd 10;** GJs 3:2 (so Democr. fgm. A 116; B 164; X., Hiero 7, 3 et al.; Herm. Wr. 1, 11; 10, 19; 22 al.; Wsd 11:15; 4 Macc 14:14, 18; Philo, Leg. All. 3, 30 al.; Jos., C. Ap. 2, 213, Ant. 10, 262; Plut., Mor. 493d; Ar. 12:1; Mel., P. 26, 188).

❷ **pert. to lack of a basis or cause, *contrary to reason*** (Thu.+; PsSol 16:10 ὀργὴν καὶ θυμὸν ἄλογον; Jos., Ant. 1, 24 al.) ἄλογόν μοι δοκεῖ *it seems absurd to me* **Ac 25:27** (cp. BGU 74, 8; OGI 519, 15).—M-M. TW.

ἀλόη, ης, ἡ (Plut., Mor. 141f; 693c; Diosc. 3, 22 et al.; PGM 7, 434; PLeid II, X, 12 and 36; PSI 1180,76; SSol 4:14 v.l. [αλωθ in text as rendering of אֲהָלוֹת cp. Ps 45:9; Pr 7:17 both MT and here prob. product of the eaglewood or 'Aqualaria agallocha'—ἀγάλλοχον or 'A. mallacensis']) ***aloes.*** In **J 19:39** ἀλόη prob. refers to the strong aromatic, quick-drying juice of the 'aloe vera' or 'aloe succotrina', here mixed w. myrrh (ἀ. w. σμύρνα PGM 7, 434; SSol 4:14) and used for embalming (Ps.-Callisth. 3, 34, 4 ἀλόη and μύρρα [sic] are used to embalm Alexander's corpse, but in his case a choice variety, such as Aquilaria ovata, would prob. have been used).—M'Clintock-Strong and ISBE, both s.v. 'Aloes', present options. S. also DELG.

ἅλς, ἁλός, ὁ (Hom. et al.; Lev 2:13; TestSol 18:34; Philo, Spec. Leg. 1, 289 al.; Jos., Ant. 3, 227; s. ἅλας; DELG ἅλς) ***salt*** πᾶσα θυσία ἁλὶ ἁλισθήσεται **Mk 9:49 v.l.** (s. ἁλίζω). στήλη ἁλός *a pillar of salt* 1 Cl 11:2 (Gen 19:26). On Mk 9:50b, s. ἅλας.—DELG.

ἁλυκός, ή, όν (Aristoph., Hippocr. et al.; BGU 14 IV, 22; LXX; DELG 65 ἅλς) ***salty;*** of salty water **Js 3:11 v.l.** (s. N. app. and s.v. πικρός); in οὔτε ἁλυκὸν γλυκὺ ποιῆσαι ὕδωρ **3:12** ἁ. is usu. understood as *salt spring* (so ἁλυκίς Strabo 4, 1, 7): *nor can a salt spring give sweet water* (so also the v.l.); but perh. the text is defective (HWindisch and MDibelius ad loc.—Theophr., HP 4, 3, 5 contrasts ἁλ. ὕδωρ w. ὕδωρ γλυκύ. Lycus Hist. [IV–III BC]: 570 fgm. 8 Jac. of the River Himera in Sicily: τὸν δὲ Ἱμέραν ἐκ μιᾶς πηγῆς σχιζόμενον τὸ μὲν ἁλυκὸν τῶν ῥείθρων ἔχειν, τὸ δὲ πότιμον).—DELG s.v. ἅλς. M-M.

ἀλύπητος, ον ***without sorrow*** (s. λύπη; Soph.; Theopomp. [IV BC]: 115 fgm. 399 Jac. 'a synonym for ἄλυπος') εὐφρανθήσεται εἰς τὸν ἀ. αἰῶνα *(the devout person) will rejoice through an eternity free from sorrow* 2 Cl 19:4 (cp. Soph., Trach. 168 τὸ λοιπὸν ἤδη ζῆν ἀλυπήτῳ βίῳ).

ἄλυπος, ον s. λύπη; pass. ***free from anxiety*** (so Soph. et al.; X., Hiero 9, 9; Epict.; Lucian; Herm. Wr. fgm. 23, 44 [482, 9 Sc.]; Crates 35 p. 88, 16 Malherbe; ISyriaW 1835; 1851 al.; PPetr II, xiii, 19, 14 [c. 250 BC]; BGU 246, 17 [II/III AD]; TestAbr A 9 p. 87, 6 [Stone p. 22]; Philo, Cher. 86; Just., D. 117, 3; Ath., R. 78, 1) ἵνα κἀγὼ ἀλυπότερος ὦ *so that I might be less anxious* (than now=*free from all anxiety*) **Phil 2:28.**—M-M. TW.

ἅλυσις, εως, ἡ (α- priv. + λύω; for the breathing s. W-S. §5, 10e; Mlt-H. 100).

❶ lit. ***chain*** (Hdt. et al.; SIG[2] 586, 86; 588, 32; PSI 240, 12; PGM 4, 3092; 13, 294; TestSol 15:7; Philo, Leg. All. 1, 28; Jos., Ant. 3, 170), esp. *handcuffs* **Ac 28:20.** δῆσαί τινα ἁλύσει (since Thu. 4, 100, 2; Wsd 17:16; Jos., Ant. 19, 294) *bind someone w. chains,* of a possessed pers. **Mk 5:3,** cp. vs. **4.** δεσμεύειν ἁλύσεσιν (w. πέδαις, as Polyb. 3, 82, 8; Dionys. Hal. 6, 26, 2; 6, 27, 3; **Mk 5:4) Lk 8:29.** Double chains **Ac 12:6f; 21:33.** At the beginning of the 'Thousand Years' Satan will be bound w. a chain **Rv 20:1f.** Of eternal punishment κ[ρατο]ῦντες ἁλύ[σ]εις *who held chains* ApcPt Bodl.

❷ gener. of ***imprisonment*** πρεσβεύω ἐν ἁλύσει *in chains* =as a prisoner **Eph 6:20;** causing disgrace **2 Ti 1:16.**—DELG. M-M.

ἀλυσιτελής, ές (Socrates 1, 8 p. 22, 21 Malherbe; Hippocr., Pla., X. et al.; PSI 441, 21; PCairZen 481, 2 [both III BC] PTebt 68, 31 [117/116 BC]; Philo; LStraub, Philol 70, 1911, 157–60; a commercial t.t. 'not covering one's expenses'; s. DELG s.v. λύω and τέλος) ***unprofitable*** ἀλυσιτελὲς ὑμῖν τοῦτο *that would be of no help to you* **Hb 13:17;** but ἀ. can also be used positively, *harmful* (Polyb. 11, 4, 7; 28, 6, 4 al.; Philo, Spec. Leg. 1, 100 ἡ οἴνου χρῆσις ἀ.).—M-M.

ἄλφα, τό indecl. (Pla., Cratyl. 431e; Aeneas Tact. 1500; 1505; Herodas 3, 22; PCairZen 269, 41; TestSol; PVindobBosw 18, 38; Just., D. 113, 2) ***alpha*** s. entry A.

Ἁλφαῖος, ου, ὁ (Ἀ other edd.; Hebr. חַלְפַי, cp. Syr.; MLidzbarski, Handb. d. nordsem. Epigraphik 1898, 275; TNöldeke, Beiträge z. semit. Sprachwissenschaft 1904, 98; Procop. Gaz., Ep. 99) ***Alphaeus.***

❶ father of Levi the tax-collector Λευὶν τὸν τοῦ Ἁ. **Mk 2:14; Lk 5:27** D; GPt 14:60.—❷ father of one of the 12 disciples, who is called Ἰάκωβος ὁ τοῦ Ἁ. to distinguish him from the son of Zebedee **Mt 10:3; Mk 3:18,** also simply Ἰ. Ἁλφαίου **Lk 6:15; Ac 1:13.**—On him, and the attempts to equate 2 w. Clopas, as well as 1 w. 2, s. Zahn, Forsch. 6, 1900, 323f; JChapman, JTS 7, 1906, 412ff; FMaier, BZ 4, 1906, 164ff; 255ff.

ἅλων, ωνος, ἡ (a by-form, found since Aristot., also in pap [Mayser 287; Crönert p. ix]; LXX; GrBar 6:7; Jos. [Ant. 20, 181] for Att. [since Aeschyl.] ἅλως, gen. ἅλω or ἅλωος, found 1 Cl 29:3 [prob. after LXX] and in ins [SIG 631, 7; 671A, 9], pap [Mayser 258f; PGM 4, 2746], LXX and Jos., Ant. 4, 281; s. W-S. §8, 13; B-D-F §44, 1; 52; Mlt-H. 121; 127).

❶ lit. **a surface for the threshing of grain, *threshing floor.*** γεννήματα ληνοῦ καὶ ἅλωνος *products of wine-press and threshing floor* D 13:3 (cp. Num 18:30). θημωνιὰ ἅλωνος *a heap on the threshing floor* 1 Cl 56:15 (Job 5:26).

❷ fig. **threshed grain still lying on the threshing floor, *threshed grain*** (PRyl 122, 10; 20 [II AD]; Job 39:12) διακαθαίρειν τὴν ἅλωνα *cleanse (winnow) what he has threshed* **Mt 3:12; Lk 3:17** (Just., D. 49, 3).—DELG. M-M.

ἀλώπηξ, εκος, ἡ (since Archilochus [VII BC], Hdt.; Pla., Rep. 365c; Theocr. 5, 112; graffito Sb 7223, 6 [II BC]; LXX; En 89; Jos., Ant. 5, 295 [after Judg 15:4]; SibOr 8, 41)

❶ lit. ***fox.*** αἱ ἀ. φωλεοὺς ἔχουσιν **Mt 8:20; Lk 9:58.**

❷ metaph., with craftiness of the fox in the foreground (Alcaeus [VII–VI BC] 42, 6 Diehl[2] [69, 6 L.-P]; Theocr. 5, 112; of the trail left by a fox Plut., Solon 95e [30, 2]=Solon fgm. 8, 5, Diehl[3]=West 11, 5; Sulla 469e [28, 5]; Epict. 1, 3, 7; Artem. 2, 12 p. 104, 9.; cp. the simile Pind., P. 2, 77 'like foxes in disposition'.—Billerb. II 678) thus suggesting ***a crafty pers.*** of Herod Antipas εἴπατε τῇ ἀλώπεκι ταύτῃ *tell that fox* **Lk 13:32** (cp. Lam 5:18).—B. 186. DELG.

ἅλως s. ἅλων.

ἅλωσις, εως, ἡ (cp. ἁλίσκομαι 'be taken'; Pind., Hdt. et al.; Jer 27:46; Jos., Ant. 2, 250; 5, 261; SibOr 4, 89; Tat.; Mel., P. 26, 181; 56, 408) ***capture, catching*** of animals for food (so Aristot., HA 593a, 20; 600a, 3; Epict. 4, 1, 29) γεγεννημένα εἰς ἅ. καὶ φθοράν *born to be caught and killed* **2 Pt 2:12.**—DELG s.v. ἁλίσκομαι.

ἅμα (Hom.+)—❶ adv. **marker of simultaneous occurrence, *at the same time,*** denoting the coincidence of two actions in time (B-D-F §425, 2; Rob. index) *at the same time, together* B 8:6; w. ptc. (Is 41:7; Jos., Bell. 3, 497; Just., D. 1, 1; 98, 1) ἅ. ἀνέντες τὰς ζευκτηρίας *while at the same time* **Ac 27:40;** cp. **16:4** D. W. finite verb *everything at once* Dg 8:11. ἅ. (δὲ) καί *(but) at the same time also, besides* ἅ. καὶ ἐλπίζων **Ac 24:26** (Jos., Ant. 18, 246 ἅ. καὶ ἀγόμενος). ἅ. δὲ καὶ ἀργαὶ μανθάνουσιν **1 Ti 5:13** (s. μανθάνω 3). ἅ. δὲ καὶ ἑτοίμαζε **Phlm 22.**—In correspondence ἅμα … ἅμα καί *partly … partly* ἅμα διὰ τὴν ὑποψίαν τὴν πρὸς τὴν γυναῖκα, ἅμα καὶ διὰ τό μὴ φυγεῖν αὐτόν AcPl Ha 4, 8f.—Postpositive προσευχόμενοι ἅμα καὶ περὶ ἡμῶν **Col 4:3.**

❷ **marker of association, *together***—ⓐ as adv. denoting association in someth. (cp. ἠφάνισαν νέον καὶ πρεσβύτην καὶ τέκνα αὐτῶν ἅμα PsSol 17:11) *together* ἅ. ἠχρεώθησαν (like יַחְדָּו) **Ro 3:12** (Ps 13:3; 52:4).

ⓑ used as prep. w. dat. *together with* (Hom. et al.; SIG 958, 21f; 1168, 6; PRein 26, 14; POxy 975; 658, 13; 975; PFlor 21, 15; Wsd 18:11; 1 Esdr 1:43 al.; TestAbr A 10 p. 88, 5 [Stone p. 24]; TestJob 29:1; GrBar 17:1; Just., A I, 4, 9 al.; Ath.) ἐκριζώσητε ἅ. αὐτοῖς **Mt 13:29.** ἅ. Ῥέῳ IPhld 11:1; cp. IEph 2:1; 19:2; IMg 15 al. Apparently pleonastic w. σύν (cp. Alex. Aphr., An. 83, 19 ἅ. αἰσθομένη σὺν αὐτῷ; En 9:7; Jos., Ant. 4, 309; cp. SIG 705, 57 ἅμα μετ' αὐτῶν) to denote what belongs together in time and place (about like Lat. una cum): ἅ. σὺν αὐτοῖς ἁρπαγησόμεθα **1 Th 4:17.** ἅ. σὺν αὐτῷ ζήσωμεν **5:10.**—Also w. adv. of time (POxy 1025, 16 [III AD] ἅμ' αὔριον; cp. Jos., Ant. 6, 40 ἅ. ἕῳ) ἅ. πρωΐ *early in the morning* **Mt 20:1** (Theophanes Continuatus 719, 7 [IBekker 1838]; cp. EpArist 304 ἅ. τῇ πρωΐᾳ).—DELG. M-M.

ἀμαθής, ές (Hdt., Eur., Aristoph. et al.; PMert 82, 21 [II AD] Epict., Ench. 48, 3; Ps 48:11 Sym.; Philo; Jos., Ant. 12, 191; Tat. 35, 2; Ath.; Iren. 3, 11, 9 [Harv. II 50, 12]) ***ignorant*** (w. ἀστήρικτος) of incompetent interpreters **2 Pt 3:16** (cp. Plut., Mor. 25c ἐν πᾶσιν ἁμαρτωλὸν εἶναι τὸν ἀμαθῆ).—DELG s.v. μανθάνω. M-M.

Ἀμάθιος, ου (אֲמִתַּי Αμαθι Jon 1:1) ***Amathios,*** father of Jonah AcPlCor 2:29.

Ἀμαλήκ, ὁ indecl. (LXX, Philo; TestSim 6:3; SibOr 8, 252; Just.—In Joseph. Ἀμάληκος, ου [Ant. 2, 6]) ***Amalek,*** a Semitic tribe in the Sinai desert (cp. Ex 17:8ff) B 12:9.

ἅμαξα, ης, ἡ (ἅμα + ἄξων 'axle', of simultaneous action on an axle; Hom. et al.; ins, pap, LXX; TestSol 5:4; Joseph.; Just., D. 132, 2) ***wagon*** Papias (3:2).

ἀμαράντινος, η, ον (μαραίνω 'to wither') ***unfading*** in our lit. only fig. of eternal life τὸν ἀ. τῆς δόξης στέφανον *the unfading crown of glory* (στεφ. ἀ. also Philostrat., Her. 19, 14 p. 208, 18; perh. CIG 155, 39) **1 Pt 5:4.** Possibly a wreath of amaranths (Diosc. 4, 57 and Aesop, Fab. 384 H.=369 P. τὸ ἀμάραντον or Artem. 1, 77 p. 70, 19 ὁ ἀμάραντος the flower that μέχρι παντὸς διαφυλάττει), or strawflowers (everlastings) is meant; its unfading quality may typify eternal glory. S. next entry.

ἀμάραντος, ον (Diosc. 4, 57; Lucian, Dom. 9; schol. on Apollon. Rhod. 2, 399–401a; burial ins fr. II BC APF 1, 1901, 220; CIG II 2942c, 4 p. 1124; Wsd 6:12). **pert. to not losing pristine quality or character, *unfading***

ⓐ lit. ἀ. ἄνθη *unfading flowers* (as they bloom in the next world) ApcPt 5, 15.—ⓑ fig. (w. ἄφθαρτος and ἀμίαντος) of eternal bliss ἀ. κληρονομία **1 Pt 1:4** (cp. SibOr 8, 411 ζωὴ ἀ.).—DELG s.v. μαραίνω. M-M.

ἁμαρτάνω fut. ἁμαρτήσω **Mt 18:21,** cp. Hm 4, 1, 1f (W-S. §13, 8; Mlt-H. 227); 2 aor. (Theognis, Pind. et al.) ἥμαρτον, subj. ἁμάρτω **Lk 17:3;** 1 aor. (H. Gk.) ἡμάρτησα, subj. ἁμαρτήσω **Mt 18:15; Lk 17:4; Ro 6:15,** ptc. ἁμαρτήσας **Ro 5:14** (cp. ἐπί, 6ac) **16; Hb 3:17; 2 Pt 2:4;** pf. ἡμάρτηκα LXX, 1 pl. ἡμαρτήκαμεν **1J 1:10;** pf. pass. ptc. neut. ἡμαρτημένα (Just.; Ath., R. 76, 10; s. B-D-F §75; 77; Mlt-H. 214; on the LXX forms s. Thackeray 259) **to commit a wrong, *to sin*** (in the sense 'transgress' against divinity, custom, or law since Hom., esp. LXX, also pseudepigr., Philo, Joseph., Herm. Wr., Just., Ath.; in gen. sense 'miss the mark, err, do wrong' Hom. et al.; also Diogenes 37, 7 p. 158, 11 Malherbe; cp. Papias [2:15] of Mark's compilation).

ⓐ abs. (Menand., fgm. 499 K. ἄνθρωπος ὢν ἥμαρτον; Herodas 5, 27; Diogenes 15 p. 108, 17 Malherbe; Orig., C. Cels. 1, 7, 7; Hippol., Ref. 9, 15, 6) **Mt 18:15; Lk 17:3; J 5:14; 8:11; 9:2f** (cp. Hdt. 1, 138 for related line of thought); **Ro 3:23; 5:12** (s. the lit. on ἁμαρτία 3b); **1 Cor 7:28, 36; 15:34; Eph 4:26** (Ps 4:5); **1 Ti 5:20; Tit 3:11; 1 Pt 2:20; 1J 1:10; 2:1; 3:6, 9; 5:18;** 1 Cl 4:4 (Gen 4:7); 56:13 (Job 5:24); 2 Cl 1:2; B 10:10; Hv 3, 5, 5; m 4, 1, 4f; 8; 4, 2, 2 al. Of sinning angels (En 106:14; cp. 7:5; 20:6) **2 Pt 2:4.** Of the devil **1J 3:8.**

ⓑ w. fuller indication of that in which the mistake or moral failure consists, by means of a supplementary ptc. (B-D-F §414, 5; cp. Hipponax [VI BC] 70 Diehl οὐχ ἁμαρτάνω κόπτων=I don't miss when I strike; Jos., Ant. 3, 174; cp. Papias [2:15] cited above) ἥμαρτον παραδοὺς αἷμα ἀθῷον *I have committed a sin by handing over innocent blood* **Mt 27:4.**

ⓒ w. indication of the manner of sinning (μέχρι ἐννοίας καὶ λόγου ἁ. Iren. 1, 6, 4 [Harv. I 56, 15]) ἀνόμως ἁ. **Ro 2:12;** opp. ἐν νόμῳ ἁ. ibid.; ἑκουσίως ἁ. (cp. Job 31:33) **Hb 10:26.** Opp. εἴ τι ἄκοντες ἡμάρτετε 1 Cl 2:3 (s. ἄκων). Also w. acc. (epigr. in Demosth. 18, 289 μηδὲν ἁμαρτεῖν ἐστι θεῶν) ἁ. ἁμαρτίαν (=חָטָא חֲטָאָה; Ex 32:30f al.; cp. Soph., Phil. 1249; Pla., Phd. 113e) *commit a sin* **1J 5:16a;** ἁμαρτίας ἁ. Hv 2, 2, 4; also τοσαῦτα Hm 9:1 (Cornutus 10 τοιαῦτα ἁ.).—ὑπὸ χεῖρα ἁ. *sin repeatedly* Hm 4, 3, 6 (B-D-F §232, 1).

ⓓ w. indication of the one against whom the sin is committed

α. in the dat. (M. Ant. 4, 26; 9, 4 ἑαυτῷ ἁμαρτάνει; Ps 77:17; Bar 1:13; 2:5; ApcSed 15:8) σοὶ μόνῳ ἥμαρτον *against you only* 1 Cl 18:4 (Ps 50:6).

β. other constructions: ἁ. εἴς τινα (Hdt. 1, 138 εἰς τὸν ἥλιον; Soph., fgm. 21 εἰς θεούς; likew. X., Hell. 1, 7, 19; Pla., Phdr. 242c εἰς τὸ θεῖον; Jdth 5:20; 11:10; Sir 7:7; EpJer 12; ApcMos 32; Jos., Ant. 7, 320 εἰς τ. θεόν) **Mt 18:21; Lk 17:4.** εἰς Χριστόν **1 Cor 8:12.** εἰς τοὺς ἀδελφούς ibid. (cp. Heraclitus 3 p. 188, 28 Malherbe). εἰς τὸ ἴδιον σῶμα **1 Cor 6:18** (cp. Aeschin. 1, 22).—εἰς τὸν οὐρανόν *against God* **Lk 15:18, 21.** ἁ. εἴς τινά τι (M. Ant. 7, 26; BGU 1141, 14ff [13 BC] ἡμάρτηκά τι εἰς σέ) **Ac 25:8.**

γ. ἁ. ἐνώπιόν τινος (1 Km 7:6; 20:1; Tob 3:3; TestJob 15:6; JosAs 7:5; B-D-F §214, 6): ἐνώπιόν σου **Lk 15:18, 21.**

ⓔ w. indication of the result ἁ. μὴ πρὸς θάνατον *commit a sin that does not lead to death* (like חָטָא לָמוּת Num 18:22 λαβεῖν ἁμαρτίαν θανατηφόρον; Dt 22:26 ἁμάρτημα θανάτου) **1J 5:16b** (RSeeberg, LIhmels Festschr. 1928, 19–31; OBauernfeind, VSchultze Festschr. '31, 43–54).—EBurton, ICC Gal., 436–43; OHey, Ἁμαρτία: Philol. 83, 1928, 1–17; 137–63; FSteinleitner, D. Beicht 1913; KLatte, Schuld u. Sünde in d. griech. Rel.: ARW 20, 1921, 254–98.—DELG. M-M. TW. Sv.

ἁμάρτημα, τος, τό (w. mngs. ranging fr. involuntary mistake to serious moral default: Arist., EN 1135b; Pre-Socr., Soph. et al.; Diod. S. 14, 76, 4 εἰς θεοὺς ἁμαρτήματα; POxy 34 III, 13; PTebt 5, 3 [s. ἀγνόημα]; PParis 63 XIII, 2ff; BGU 1141, 8; 1185, 7; LXX; En; PsSol 17:8; TestSol D; TestAbr A 14 p. 94, 22 [Stone, p. 36]; ParJer 2:2; ApcEsdr, ApcMos; EpArist 297; Philo; Jos., Bell. 4, 348, Ant. 1, 22, 3:221 al.; Mel., P. 103, 788 [B; ἁμαρτιῶν Ch.]; fgm. 12, 9; Theoph. Ant. 1, 2 [p. 60, 20]) as an individual act ***sin, transgression*** (as moral default Pla., Phd. 113e) **Ro 5:16 v.l.;** αἰώνιον ἁ. *an everlasting sin* **Mk 3:29;** τὰ προγεγονότα ἁμαρτήματα **Ro 3:25** (s. Eunap. p. 76 [B.] τὰ προγεγενημένα τῶν ἁμαρτημάτων); cp. τῶν πάλαι αὐτοῦ ἁμαρτημάτων **2 Pt 1:9 v.l.;** ἐξαλείφειν τὰ πρότερα ἁ. *wipe out our former sins* 2 Cl 13:1; καθαρίζεσθαι ἀπὸ τῶν ἁ. *be cleansed fr. sins* Hv 3, 2, 2; ποιεῖν ἁ. (Hdt. 7, 194, 2; Jdth 11:17; 13:16) **1 Cor 6:18.** κρύπτειν τὸ ἁ. GJs 14:1; φανεροῦν τὸ ἁ. 16:1, 3. ἀφιέναι τινὶ τὰ ἁ. (1 Macc 13:39) *forgive someone's sins* **Mk 3:28;** PtK 3 p. 15, 27; GJs 5:1; for this ἰᾶσθαι τὰ ἁ. (Pla., Gorg. 525b ἰάσιμα ἁμαρτήματα ἁμαρτάνειν) Hv 1, 1, 9; s 9, 23, 5; ποιεῖν ἴασιν τοῖς προτέροις ἁ. m 12, 6, 2; σῴζειν ἐκ τῶν ἁ. GJs 14:2. τελειοῦν τὰ ἁ. GPt 5:17=ASyn. 347, 60. ἵνα κἀκεῖνοι τελειωθῶσιν τοῖς ἁ. *in order that they might be perfected in their sins = that the measure of their* (i.e. the rebellious Israelites at the time of Moses) *sins might be filled* B 14:5. μετανοεῖν ἐπὶ τοῖς ἁ. *repent of sins* 1 Cl 7:7 (Wsd 12:19 ἐπὶ ἁμαρτήμασιν μετάνοια. Cp. Appian, Bell. Civ. 2, 63 §261f ἐπὶ μετάνοιαν … τὸ ἁμάρτημα). ἐφήδεσθαι τοῖς ἁ. *delight in sins* Dg 9:1. OHey, Philol 83, 1928, 1–17, 137–63.—DELG s.v. ἁμαρτάνω. M-M. TW.

ἁμάρτησις, εως, ἡ ***the activity of sinning, sin*** ἐὰν … ἔτι ἁ. γένηται *if there is any more sinning* Hv 2, 2, 5.

ἁμαρτία, ίας, ἡ (w. mngs. ranging fr. involuntary mistake/error to serious offenses against a deity: Aeschyl., Antiphon, Democr.+; ins fr. Cyzicus JHS 27, 1907, p. 63 [III BC] ἁμαρτίαν μετανόει; PLips 119 recto, 3; POxy 1119, 11; LXX; En, TestSol, TestAbr, TestJob, Test12Patr; JosAs 12:14; ParJer, ApcEsdr, ApcSed, ApcMos; EpArist 192; Philo; Jos., Ant. 13, 69 al.; Ar. [Milne 76, 42]; Just., A I, 61, 6; 10; 66, 1, D. 13, 1 al.; Tat. 14, 1f; 20, 1; Mel., P. 50, 359; 55, 400; s. ClR 24, 1910, 88; 234; 25, 1911, 195–97).

❶ **a departure fr. either human or divine standards of uprightness—ⓐ** ***sin*** (w. context ordinarily suggesting the level of heinousness), the action itself (ἁμάρτησις s. prec.), as well as its result (ἁμάρτημα), πᾶσα ἀδικία ἁ. ἐστίν **1J 5:17** (cp. Eur., Or. 649; Gen 50:17). ἁ. w. ἀνομήματα Hv 1, 3, 1; descr. as ἀνομία (cp. Ps 58:3; TestJob 43:17) **1J 3:4;** but one who loves is far from sin Pol 3:3, cp. **Js 5:20; 1 Pt 4:8,** 1 Cl 49:5; Agr 13. ἀναπληρῶσαι τὰς ἁ. *fill up the measure of sins* (Gen 15:16) **1 Th 2:16.** κοινωνεῖν ἁ. ἀλλοτρίαις **1 Ti 5:22.** ποιεῖν ἁ. *commit a sin* (Tob 12:10; 14:7S; Dt 9:21) **2 Cor 11:7; 1 Pt 2:22; Js 5:15; 1J 3:4, 8.** For this ἁμαρτάνειν ἁ. (Ex 32:30; La 1:8) **1J 5:16;** ἐργάζεσθαι ἁ. **Js 2:9;** Hm 4, 1, 2 (LXX oft. ἐργάζ. ἀδικίαν or ἀνομίαν). μεγάλην ἁ. ἐργάζεσθαι *commit a great sin* m 4, 1, 1; 8:2. Pl. (cp. Pla., Ep. 7, 335a τὰ μεγάλα ἁμαρτήματα κ. ἀδικήματα) s 7:2. ἐπιφέρειν ἁ. τινί Hv 1, 2, 4. ἑαυτῷ ἁ. ἐπιφέρειν *bring sin upon oneself* m 11:4; for this ἁ. ἐπισπᾶσθαί τινι m 4, 1, 8 (cp. Is 5:18). προστιθέναι ταῖς ἁ. *add to one's sins* (cp. προσέθηκεν ἁμαρτίας ἐφ' ἁμαρτίας PsSol 3:10) Hv 5:7; m 4, 3, 7; s 6, 2, 3; 8, 11, 3; φέρειν ἁ. 1 Cl 16:4 (Is 53:4). ἀναφέρειν vs. 14 (Is 53:12). γέμειν ἁμαρτιῶν B 11:11. εἶναι ἐν ταῖς ἁμαρτίαις **1 Cor 15:17** (cp. Alex. Aphr., Eth. Probl. 9 II 2 p. 129, 13 ἐν ἁμαρτήμασιν εἶναι).—Sin viewed from the perspective of God's or Christ's response: ἀφιέναι τὰς ἁ. *let go = forgive sins* (Lev 4:20 al.) **Mt 9:2, 5f; Mk 2:5, 7, 9f; Lk 5:20ff;** Hv 2, 2, 4; 1 Cl 50:5; 53:5 (Ex 32:32) al. (ἀφίημι 2); hence ἄφεσις (τῶν) ἁμαρτιῶν (Iren. 1, 21, 2 [Harv. I 182, 4]) *forgiveness of sins* **Mt 26:28; Mk 1:4; Lk 1:77; 3:3; 24:47; Ac 2:38; 5:31; 10:43; 13:38;** Hm 4, 3, 2; B 5:1; 6:11; 8:3; 11:1; 16:8. διδόναι ἄφεσιν ἁ. AcPl Ha 2, 30; λαβεῖν ἄφεσιν ἁ. *receive forgiveness of sins* **Ac 26:18** (Just., D. 54 al); καθαρίζειν τὰς ἁ. *cleanse the sins* (thought of as a stain) Hs 5, 6, 3; καθαρίζειν ἀπὸ ἁ. 1 Cl 18:3 (Ps 50:4; cp. Sir 23:10; PsSol 10:1); also καθαρισμὸν ποιεῖσθαι τῶν ἁ. **Hb 1:3;** ἀπολούεσθαι τὰς ἁ. **Ac 22:16** ([w. βαπτίζειν] Just., D. 13, 1 al.). λύτρον ἁ. *ransom for sins* B 19:10.—αἴρειν **J 1:29;** περιελεῖν ἁ. **Hb 10:11;** ἀφαιρεῖν (Ex 34:9; Is 27; 9) vs. **4;** Hs 9, 28, 3; ῥυσθῆναι ἀπὸ ἁ. 1 Cl 60:3; ἀπὸ τῶν ἁ. ἀποσπασθῆναι AcPlCor 2:9. Sin as a burden αἱ ἁ. κατεβάρησαν Hs 9, 28, 6; as a disease ἰᾶσθαι s 9, 28, 5 (cp. Dt 30:3); s. also the verbs in question.—Looked upon as an entry in a ledger; hence ἐξαλείφεται ἡ ἁ. *wiped away, cancelled* (Ps 108:14; Jer 18:23; Is 43:25) **Ac 3:19.**—Opp. στῆσαι τὴν ἁ. **7:60;** λογίζεσθαι ἁ. *take account of sin* (as a debt; cp. the commercial metaphor **Ro 4:6** and s. FDanker, Gingrich Festschr. 104, n. 2) **Ro 4:8** (Ps 31:2); 1 Cl 60:2 (Just., D. 141, 3). Pass. ἁ. οὐκ ἐλλογεῖται *is not entered in the account* **Ro 5:13** (GFriedrich, TLZ 77, '52, 523–28). Of sinners ὀφειλέτης ἁ. Pol 6:1 (cp. SIG 1042, 14–16 [II AD] ὃς ἂν δὲ πολυπραγμονήσῃ τὰ τοῦ θεοῦ ἢ περιεργάσηται, ἁμαρτίαν ὀφιλέτω Μηνὶ Τυράννωι, ἣν οὐ μὴ δύνηται ἐξειλάσασθαι).—γινώσκειν ἁ. (cp. Num 32:23) **Ro 7:7;** Hm 4, 1, 5. ἐπίγνωσις ἁμαρτίας **Ro 3:20;** ὁμολογεῖν τὰς ἁ. **1J 1:9;** ἐξομολογεῖσθε ἐπὶ ταῖς ἁ. B 19:12; ἐξομολογεῖσθαι τὰς ἁ. **Mt 3:6; Mk 1:5;** Hv 3, 1, 5f; s 9,

23, 4; ἐξομολογεῖσθε ἀλλήλοις τὰς ἁ. *confess your sins to each other* **Js 5:16.**—ἐλέγχειν τινὰ περὶ ἁ. *convict someone of sin* **J 8:46;** cp. ἵνα σου τὰς ἁ. ἐλέγξω πρὸς τὸν κύριον *that I might reveal your sins before the Lord* Hv 1, 1, 5.—σεσωρευμένος ἁμαρτίαις *loaded down w. sins* **2 Ti 3:6;** cp. ἐπισωρεύειν ταῖς ἁ. B 4:6; ἔνοχος τῆς ἁ. *involved in the sin* Hm 2:2; 4, 1, 5. μέτοχος τῆς ἁ. m 4, 1, 9.—In Hb sin is atoned for (ἱλάσκεσθαι τὰς ἁ. **2:17**) by sacrifices θυσίαι ὑπὲρ ἁ. **5:1** (cp. 1 Cl 41:2). προσφορὰ περὶ ἁ. sin-offering **10:18;** also simply περὶ ἁ. (Lev 5:11; 7:37) vss. **6, 8** (both Ps 39:7; cp. **1 Pt 3:18**); προσφέρειν περὶ ἁ. *bring a sin-offering* **Hb 5:3;** cp. **10:12; 13:11.** Christ has made the perfect sacrifice for sin **9:23ff;** συνείδησις ἁ. *consciousness* of sin **10:2;** ἀνάμνησις ἁ. *a reminder of sins* of the feast of atonement vs. **3.**

ⓑ special sins (ἁ. τῆς ἀποστασίας Iren. 5, 26, 2 [Harv. II 397, 4]): πρὸς θάνατον *that leads to death* **1J 5:16b** (ἁμαρτάνω e); opp. οὐ πρὸς θάνατον vs. **17.** μεγάλη ἁ. *a great sin* Hv 1, 1, 8 al. (Gen 20:9; Ex 32:30 al.; cp. Schol. on Pla., Tht. 189d ἁμαρτήματα μεγάλα). μείζων ἁ. m 11:4; ἥττων 1 Cl 47:4. μεγάλη κ. ἀνίατος Hm 5, 2, 4; τέλειαι ἁ. Hv 1, 2, 1; B 8:1, cp. τὸ τέλειον τῶν ἁ. 5:11 (Philo, Mos. 1, 96 κατὰ τῶν τέλεια ἡμαρτηκότων); ἡ προτέρα ἁ. (Arrian, Anab. 7, 23, 8 εἴ τι πρότερον ἡμάρτηκας) sin committed before baptism Hm 4, 1, 11; 4, 3, 3; s 8, 11, 3; cp. v 2, 1, 2.

❷ **a state of being sinful,** ***sinfulness,*** a prominent feature in Johannine thought, and opposed to ἀλήθεια; hence ἁ. ἔχειν **J 9:41; 15:24; 1J 1:8.** μείζονα ἁ. ἔχειν **J 19:11;** ἁ. μένει **9:41.** γεννᾶσθαι ἐν ἁμαρτίαις *be born in sin* **9:34** (ἐν ἁμαρτίᾳ v.l.); opp. ἐν ἁ. ἀποθανεῖν *die in* sin **8:21, 24;** AcPl Ha 1, 16. ἁ. ἐν αὐτῷ οὐκ ἔστιν **1J 3:5.**

❸ **a destructive evil power,** ***sin*—ⓐ** Paul thinks of sin almost in pers. terms (cp. Sir 27:10; Mel., P. 50, 359; PGM 4, 1448 w. other divinities of the nether world, also Ἁμαρτίαι χθόνιαι; Dibelius, Geisterwelt 119ff) as a ruling power that invades the world. Sin came into the world **Ro 5:12** (JFreundorfer, Erbsünde u. Erbtod b. Ap. Pls 1927; ELohmeyer, ZNW 29, 1930, 1–59; JSchnitzer, D. Erbsünde im Lichte d. Religionsgesch. '31; ROtto, Sünde u. Urschuld '32; FDanker, Ro 5:12: Sin under Law: NTS 14, '67/68, 424–39), reigns there vs. **21; 6:14;** everything was subject to it **Gal 3:22;** people serve it **Ro 6:6;** are its slaves vss. **17, 20;** are sold into its service **7:14** or set free from it **6:22;** it has its law **7:23; 8:2;** it revives (ἀνέζησεν) **Ro 7:9** or is dead vs. **8;** it pays its wages, viz., death **6:23,** cp. **5:12** (see lit. s.v. ἐπί 6c). As a pers. principle it dwells in humans **Ro 7:17, 20,** viz., in the flesh (s. σάρξ 2cα) **8:3;** cp. vs. **2; 7:25.** The earthly body is hence a σῶμα τῆς ἁ. **6:6 (Col 2:11 v.l.).**—As abstr. for concr. τὸν μὴ γνόντα ἁ. ὑπὲρ ἡμῶν ἁμαρτίαν ἐποίησεν (God) *made him, who never sinned, to be sin* (i.e. the guilty one) *for our sakes* **2 Cor 5:21.**

ⓑ In Hb (as in OT) sin appears as the power that deceives humanity and leads it to destruction, whose influence and activity can be ended only by sacrifices (s. 1a end): ἀπάτη τῆς ἁ. **Hb 3:13.**—On the whole word s. ἁμαρτάνω, end. GMoore, Judaism I 445–52; ABüchler, Studies in Sin and Atonement in the Rabb. Lit. of the I Cent. 1928; WKnuth, D. Begriff der Sünde b. Philon v. Alex., diss. Jena '34; EThomas, The Problem of Sin in the NT 1927; Dodd 76–81; DDaube, Sin, Ignorance and Forgiveness in the Bible, '61; AGelin and ADescamps, Sin in the Bible, '65.—On the special question 'The Christian and Sin' see PWernle 1897; HWindisch 1908; EHedström 1911; RBultmann, ZNW 23, 1924, 123–40; Windisch, ibid. 265–81; RSchulz, D. Frage nach der Selbsttätigkt. d. Menschen im sittl. Leben b. Pls., diss. Hdlb. '40.—JAddison, ATR 33, '51, 137–48; KKuhn, πειρασμός ἁμαρτία σάρξ im NT: ZTK 49, '52, 200–222; JBremer, Hamartia '69 (Gk. views).—B. 1182. EDNT. DELG s.v. ἁμαρτάνω. M-M. TW.

ἀμάρτυρος, ον (since Thu. 2, 41, 4, also Callim., fgm. 612 [442 Schn.] ἀμάρτυρον οὐδὲν ἀείδω=I announce nothing that is not attested; Herodian 1, 1, 3; Ins. Ariassi 58, 8 [BCH 16, 1892, p. 428]; CPR 232, 30; PFlor 59, 13 [III AD] ἵνα μὴ ἀμάρτυρον ᾖ; POxy 2187, 10; Philo, Sacr. Abel. 34; Jos., Ant. 14, 111; Ath. 24, 5 ὥστε μηδὲν ἡμᾶς ἀμάρτυρον λέγειν; Iren. 1, 8, 1 [Harv. I 67, 2]) ***without witness;*** of God οὐκ ἀμάρτυρον αὐτὸν ἀφῆκεν *God has not left himself without witness*=plainly revealed (as a benefactor, s. FDanker, Benefactor, '82, 442–47 and s.v. μαρτυρέω, μαρτυρία) **Ac 14:17** (Philostrat., Vi. Apoll. 6, 1 p. 204, 3 ἀμ. means simply 'unknown' of unexplored territory).—DELG s.v. μάρτυς. M-M.

ἁμαρτωλός, όν pert. to behavior or activity that does not measure up to standard moral or cultic expectations (being considered an outsider because of failure to conform to certain standards is a freq. semantic component. Persons engaged in certain occupations, e.g. herding and tanning, that jeopardized cultic purity, would be considered by some as 'sinners', a term tantamount to 'outsider'. Non-Israelites were esp. considered out of bounds [cp. Ac 10:28 and s. b, below]).

ⓐ as adj. (Aristoph., Th. 1111; Aristot., EN 2, 9, 1109a 33; Philod., Ira p. 73 W.; Plut., Mor. 25c; LXX; TestAbr A 9 p. 86, 22 [Stone p. 20]; Just., A I, 15, 5, D. 43, 3 al.) ***sinful*** ἐν τῇ γενεᾷ ταύτῃ τῇ μοιχαλίδι καὶ ἁ. *in this adulterous* (=unfaithful) *and sinful generation* **Mk 8:38.** ἵνα γένηται καθ' ὑπερβολὴν ἁ. ἡ ἁμαρτία *that sin might become sinful in the extreme* **Ro 7:13.**—With focus on cultic nonconformity ἀνὴρ ἁ. (Sir 15:12; 27:30; 1 Macc 2:62) *a sinner* **Lk 5:8; 19:7;** ἄνθρωπος ἁ. (Sir 11:32; 32:17) **J 9:16;** pl. (Num 32:14; Just., D. 23, 2) **Lk 24:7.**

ⓑ as subst.**—α.** ὁ ἁ. ***the sinner,*** gener. w. focus on wrongdoing as such (ins from Lycia ἁ. θεοῖς 'sinner against the gods' [IAsMinLyk I, 30, no. 7; CIG 4307; Lyc. ins: ARW 19, 1919, 284] or ἁ. θεῶν [IAsMinLyk II, 36, no. 58; OGI 55, 31f; CIG 4259, 6]; other ins: Steinleitner [see ἁμαρτάνω, end] p. 84f; LXX, En, TestAbr, ApcEsdr, ApcSed, ApcMos, Test12Patr; Just., A I, 15, 8 al.) ἁ. παρὰ πάντας τοὺς Γαλιλαίους *greater sinners than all the other Galileans* **Lk 13:2;** (opp. δίκαιος as En 104:6) οὐκ ἦλθον καλέσαι δικαίους, ἀλλὰ ἁ. **Mt 9:13; Mk 2:17; Lk 5:32;** 2 Cl 2:4; B 5:9; cp. Hs 3:2f; 4:2ff. W. ἀσεβής (En 5:6) **1 Ti 1:9; 1 Pt 4:18** (Pr 11:31); B 11:7 (Ps 1:5); w. πονηρός (Gen 13:13) 4:2; w. ἄπιστος **Rv 21:8 v.l.;** ἁ. εἰμι Hm 4, 2, 3. οὗτος ὁ ἄνθρωπος ἁ. ἐστιν **J 9:24;** cp. vs. **25.** ἁ. μετανοῶν *a sinner who repents* **Lk 15:7, 10.** μετάνοια τῶν ἁ. Hs 8, 6, 6. ἁμαρτωλοὺς προσδέχεσθαι **Lk 15:2.** ἁ. σῶσαι **1 Ti 1:15;** ἐπιστρέφειν ἁ. **Js 5:20;** ἱλάσθητί μοι τῷ ἁ. **Lk 18:13.** ἁμαρτωλῶν οὐκ ἀκούει of God **J 9:31.** ἡ ἁμαρτωλός *the sinful woman* **Lk 7:37, 39** (PJoüon, RSR 29, '39, 615–19). In rhetorical address **Js 4:8.**

β. with focus on status of *outsider*—w. τελώνης (IAbrahams, Publicans and Sinners: Stud. in Pharisaism and the Gospels I 1917, 54ff; JJeremias, ZNW 30, '31, 293–300; WRaney, JR 10, 1930, 578–91; Goodsp., Probs. 28f) ***irreligious,*** *unobservant people, outsiders* of those who did not observe the Law in detail and therefore were shunned by observers of traditional precepts **Mt 9:10f; 11:19; Mk 2:15f; Lk 5:30; 7:34; 15:1.**—**Lk 6:32** has ἁ., whereas its parallel **Mt 5:46** has τελώνης. W. ἔθνη Hs 4:4; more precisely ἡμεῖς οὐκ ἐξ ἐθνῶν ἁμαρτωλοί, which means, in the usage of Judeans and Judean Christians, *no 'sinners' of gentile descent* **Gal 2:15.** Gener. a favorite term for non-Israelites (Is 14:5; Tob 13:8; 1 Macc 1:34 al.); hence the irony in ὁ υἱὸς τ. ἀνθρώπου παραδίδοται εἰς (τὰς) χεῖρας (τῶν) ἁ. (the Israelite Jesus delivered to the 'outsiders', gentiles) **Mt 26:45; Mk 14:41** (on χεὶρ. ἁ. cp. Ps 70:4; 81:4; 96:10); cp. **Lk 6:32ff,** whose parallel **Mt 5:47** has ἐθνικός. (ἡ) ὁδὸς ἁμαρτωλῶν *the way of sinners* B 10:10 (Ps 1:1). Its adj. character is wholly lost in **Jd 15,** where it is itself modif. by ἀσεβεῖς (En 1:9).—Of the state of a person who is not yet reconciled ἔτι ἁ. ὄντων ἡμῶν **Ro 5:8.** ἁ. κατεστάθησαν οἱ πολλοί *the many* (i.e. 'humanity'; opp., 'the one', Adam) *were constituted sinners* (=were exposed to being treated as sinners; s. καθίστημι 3) **5:19.** ὡς ἁμαρτωλὸς κρίνομαι **Ro 3:7.** εὑρέθημεν ἁμαρτωλοί **Gal 2:17.** Opp. κεχωρισμένος ἀπὸ τῶν ἁ. *separated from sinners* of Jesus **Hb 7:26.** ὑπό τῶν ἁ. . . . ἀντιλογίαν **12:3.**—ESjöberg, Gott u. die Sünder im paläst. Judentum '38.—DELG s.v. ἁμαρτάνω. M-M. TW.

Ἀμασίας, ου, ὁ (אֲמַצְיָה) *Amaziah,* king in Jerusalem (2 Ch 25:1; 4 Km 14:1; Jos., Ant. 9, 186) in genealogy of Jesus **Lk 3:23ff** D; cp. Mt 1:8 sy[c].

ἀμαύρωσις, εως, ἡ ***darkening, dimness*** (ἀμαυρός 'hardly seen, scarcely visible' as Od. 4, 824 and 835 of a phantom; Hippocr. et al.; Plut., Anton. 949 [71, 8]; Vett. Val. 109, 31; 110, 36; Herm. Wr. 3, 4), in our lit. only fig. of perception (Aristot., De Anima 408b, 20 of mental dullness.—W. ἀχλύς as Jos., Ant. 9, 57) of polytheists ἀμαύρωσιν περικείμενοι *afflicted w. dimness of sight* 2Cl 1:6.—DELG s.v. ἀμαυρός.

ἄμαχος, ον act. (as X. et al.; Jos., Ant. 15, 115) ***peaceable*** (so Kaibel 387, 6 ἄ. ἐβίωσα μετὰ φίλων; IKosPH 325, 9. The adv. ἀμάχως Sir 19:6 v.l.) of Christians gener. **Tit 3:2;** of congregational overseers **1 Ti 3:3.**—M-M. TW.

ἀμάω fut. 2 pl. ἀμήσετε (Lev 25:11); 1 aor. impv. 2 pl. ἀμήσατε (Is 37:30), ptc. ἀμήσας (Hom. et al.; Philostrat., Gymn. 43 p. 285, 2; PHib 47, 12 [256 BC] θερίζειν δὲ καὶ ἀμᾶν; PStras 35, 14; LXX; Jos., Ant. 4, 231) ***mow*** fields **Js 5:4.**—B. 506. DELG 1 ἀμάω. M-M.

ἀμβλύνω 1 aor. ptc. ἀμβλύνας (Emped. fgm. 2, 2 Diels; Trag., Thu.; Gen. 127:1; Joseph.) prim. 'make blunt' e.g. a sharp instrument, in our lit. only metaph. ***make dim*** ἀστέρα . . . λάμψαντα ἐν τοῖς ἄστροις τούτοις καὶ ἀμβλύναντα αὐτούς *a star that shined among these stars and dimmed their light* GJs 21:2 (codd.).—DELG s.v. ἀμβλύς.

ἀμβλυωπέω impf. ἠμβλυώπουν LXX (Hippocr., X. et al.; Plut., Mor. 53f; PRein II, 113, 9f; 3 Km 12:24i.—PGM 7, 245 ἀμβλυωπός) ***be dim-sighted*** (opp. ὀξυωπεῖν Theophr., Sens. 8) in our lit. only fig., ἐν τῇ πίστει *see poorly in the things of faith* 1 Cl 3:4.—DELG s.v. ἀμβλύς.

ἀμέθυσος s. ἀμέθυστος

ἀμεθύστινος, ου (Lucian, Ver. Hist. 2, 11) ***of amethyst*** **Rv 21:20 v.l.** S. ἀμέθυστος.

ἀμέθυστος, ου, ἡ (verbal adj. derived fr. μεθύω; Pliny, HN 37, 121; Plut., Mor. 15b) or **ὁ** (PHolm δ 3) ***amethyst*** (Ex 28:19; Ezk 28:13; Jos., Bell. 5, 234 [ἀμέθυστος; ἀμέθυσος v.l.], Ant. 3, 168 [ἀμέθυσος; so also Psellus, in Les Lapidaires p. 201, 18]; AClausing, Glotta 20, '32, 292: has the color of wine that is mixed w. water and does not make one drunk) **Rv 21:20** (vv.ll. ἀμέθυσος, ἀμεθύστινος).—MBauer, Edelsteinkunde (3d ed. by KSchlossmacher) '32; EJourdain, The Twelve Stones in the Apc.: ET 22, 1911, 448–50; JMyres, Precious Stones: EncBibl IV 4799–812; CCooper, The Precious Stones of the Bible 1925.—DELG s.v. μέθυ.

ἀμείβομαι fut. ἀμείψομαι (Hom. et al.; ins, pap; 2 Km 1:6 Sym.; Pr 11:17 Aq., Theod.; Just.; Ath. 34, 2 ἀμείβειν) ***to reward,*** w. acc. of pers. (12th letter of Apollonius of Tyana: Philostrat. I 348, 32; Jos., Ant. 12, 139; SIG 898, 23; 902, 15) ISm 12:1. On 9:2 s. ἀμοιβή.—DELG s.v. ἀμείβω. B. 913.

ἀμείνων, ον comp. of ἀγαθός, q.v.—DELG.

ἀμέλεια, ας, ἡ (ἀμελής, ἀμελέω [μέλω 'care for']; Eur., Thu.+; SIG 784, 7; 837, 14; pap since III BC, e.g. POxy 62, 9; 1220; Ps 89:8 Sym.; EpArist 248; Jos., Ant. 6, 316; 12, 164; Theoph. Ant. 2, 27 [p. 164, 24]) ***neglect*** ἄμπελος ἀμελείας τυγχάνουσα *a vine that meets w. neglect* Hs 9, 26, 4; cp. m 10, 1, 5.—DELG s.v. μέλω.

ἀμελέω fut. ἀμελήσω **2 Pt 1:12 v.l.** for διὸ μελλήσω; 1 aor. ἠμέλησα, pass. impv. ἀμελείσθω (s. prec. entry; Hom.+, ins, pap, LXX; TestSol 1:9 H; ParJer 7:24; Just.; Ath. 24, 5, R. 64, 18) **to have no care for, *to neglect, be unconcerned*** τινός *about someone* or *someth.* (Il.; trag.; Appian, fgm. [I p. 532–36 Viereck-R.] 21; UPZ 81 col. 3, 4 τοῦ ἱεροῦ; Wsd 3:10; 2 Macc 4:14; Philo, Exs. 156; Jos., Ant. 4, 67; Just.) κἀγὼ ἠμέλησα αὐτῶν **Hb 8:9** (Jer 38:32); οὐκ ἀμελήσω ἀεὶ ὑμᾶς ὑπομιμνήσκειν **2 Pt 1:12 v.l.;** χήρας Pol 6:1; w. the same noun in pass. *be neglected* IPol 4:1. τηλικαύτης ἀμελήσαντες σωτηρίας *if we disregard so great a salvation* **Hb 2:3.** μὴ ἀμέλει τοῦ ἐν σοὶ χαρίσματος *do not neglect the (spiritual) gift that is in you* **1 Ti 4:14.** ἀμελήσαντες τῆς ἐντολῆς τοῦ θεοῦ *who cared nothing for God's command* ApcPt 15:30. ἁ. ἡμῶν ἐδόκει (w. ἀφρονιστεῖν) Dg 8:10.—Abs. (Epict. 3, 24, 113; PTebt 37, 23ff [73 BC]; POxy 742, 14 [2 BC]; PGiss 13, 22f; Jos., Bell. 4, 168; Ath. 24, 5) ἀμελήσαντες ἀπῆλθον *they paid no attention and went away* **Mt 22:5.**—DELG s.v. μέλω. M-M. Spicq.

ἀμελής, ές ***careless, negligent*** (so Aristoph., X., Pla. et al.; Epict. 2, 6, 2; Plut., Mor. 34d; 64f; PGiss 79 II, 9; Jos., Ant. 11, 20) οὐχ εὑρεθήσομαι ἀ. Hs 8, 2, 7; κἀγὼ ἀ. δόξω εἶναι 9, 7, 6.—DELG s.v. μέλω.

ἄμεμπτος, ον (μέμφομαι 'to blame'; since trag., Pla., X.; freq. in ins and pap [Nägeli 54], LXX, Philo; Jos., Ant. 3, 278; 4, 230) ***blameless, faultless*** of the Mosaic covenant **Hb 8:7.** Of hearts ἄ. ἐν ἁγιωσύνῃ *blameless in holiness* **1 Th 3:13.** Otherw. only of pers. of exceptional merit (Ael. Aristid. 33 p. 637 D.; 45 p. 91 παρὰ θεοῖς ἄ. 46 p. 319) γενόμενος ἄ. **Phil 3:6** (cp. Gen 17:1—MGoguel, JBL 53, '34, 257–67). πορευόμενοι . . . ἄμεμπτοι (for ἀμέμπτως, s. B-D-F. §243; Rob. 659) **Lk 1:6.** W. ἀκέραιος **Phil 2:15;** w. δίκαιος of Job 1 Cl 17:3 (Job 1:1). ἄ. ἀπὸ τῶν ἔργων *blameless in* (lit. *because of*) *his works* (s. B-D-F §210, 1; Rob. 579f) 39:4 (Job 4:17). Of eccl. assistants Pol 5:2; ἄ. ἐν πᾶσιν *in all respects* 5:3.—DELG s.v. μέμφομαι. M-M. TW.

ἀμέμπτως adv. fr. ἄμεμπτος (Aeschyl. et al.; ins, pap; Esth 3:13d; Philo, Migr. Abr. 129; Just., D. 8, 3) used esp. in the Gr-Rom. world of people of extraordinary civic consciousness ***blamelessly*** (w. ὁσίως and δικαίως) γενηθῆναι *comport oneself blamelessly* **1 Th 2:10;** ἀ. τηρεῖσθαι *be kept blameless* **5:23;** ἀναστρέφεσθαι ἀ. *conduct oneself blamelessly* 1 Cl 63:3; δουλεύειν τῷ κυρίῳ ἀ. Hv 4, 2, 5; δουλεύειν τῷ πνεύματι ἀ. s 5, 6, 7 (text restored). λειτουργεῖν ἀ. (UPZ 20, 62 [163 BC]) 1 Cl 44:3; προσφέρειν ἀ. 44:4; μετάγειν ἐκ τῆς ἀ. αὐτοῖς τετιμημένης λειτουργίας *remove them from the office which they filled blamelessly* 44:6 (on the text see Knopf, Hdb.). **1 Th 3:13 v.l.**—Danker, Benefactor 354f; New Docs 4, 141 (ins and pap).—DELG s.v. μέμφομαι.

ἀμεριμνία, ας, ἡ (μέριμνα 'solicitude', μεριμνάω 'care for'; Plut., Mor. 830a; Appian, Liby. 65 §290; Secundus [II AD], Sententiae 8b of a wife ἀμεριμνίας ἐμπόδιον 'an impediment to freedom fr. care'; Herodian 2, 4, 6; ins and pap in many mngs., incl. t.t.) ***freedom from care = confidence*** (Appian, Syr. 61 §321; Jos., Bell. 1, 627.—Ps 107:10 Sym. has ἀ. for ἐλπίς LXX) ἐν ἀ. θεοῦ *w. God-given freedom fr. care* IPol 7:1.—DELG s.v. μέριμνα.

ἀμέριμνος, ον (s. prec.) ***free from care*** (so since the new comedy Philemon Com. 114; Menand., fgm. 1083; Posidippus or Pla. Com. in Anth. Pal. 9, 359, 5; Comp. II 12ff; 137ff; also grave ins: Eranos 13, 1913, 87, no. 9, 5ff; pap; Wsd 6:15; 7:23; s. Nägeli 37, 1)

ⓐ of pers. θέλω ὑμᾶς ἀ. εἶναι *I want you to be free from care* (Appian, Maced. 19, §3 ἀμέριμνός εἰμι; Vett. Val. 355, 34 w. ἀλύπητος; Sext. Emp., Adv. Ethic. 11, 117 syn. χωρὶς ταραχῆς) **1 Cor 7:32** (cp. Theophr. [Jerome, Adv. Jovin. 1, 47=Seneca, fgm. 13, 47 Haase], who recommends celibacy because it makes one free for contemplation; PFay 117, 22 [108 AD] ἵνα ἀ. ἦς; on the topic also cp. Epict. 3, 22, 69). ἀμέριμνον ποιεῖν τινα *keep someone out of trouble* (cp. PMich 211, 8 [c. 200 AD]; on Stoic ideas s. DBalch, JBL 102, '83, 429–39; s. ἀπερισπάστως) **Mt 28:14.**

ⓑ of personal characteristics μακροθυμία Hm 5, 2, 3.—DELG s.v. μέριμνα. M-M.

ἀμέριστος, ον (since Pla., Tim. 35a; PRyl 585, 3; 10 [II BC] also Philo; Ar. [Milne 74, 11]; Ath. 18, 2 mostly = 'indivisible') ***undivided*** (SIG 783, 35f. of a married couple: παρ' ἀμφοτέροις ἀμέριστος ὁμόνοια) ἀγαπᾶν ἐν ἀ. καρδίᾳ *to love w. undivided heart* ITr 13:2; cp. IPhld 6:2.—DELG s.v. μείρομαι.

ἀμετάθετος, ον—❶ ***unalterable, unchangeable*** (μετατίθημι 'change'; since the Stoics Zeno and Chrysippus, also Polyb. 2, 32, 5; 30, 19, 2 al.; Diod. S. 1, 23, 8 et al.; OGI 331, 58 [II BC]; 335, 73 [II/I BC]; POxy 75, 15; 482, 35; 636, 12 [of a will]; 3 Macc 5:1, 12; TestAbr A 13 p. 92, 13 [Stone p. 32]; Jos., C. Ap. 2, 189; Just., D. 120, 5) πράγματα ἀ. **Hb 6:18.**—The neut. as subst. τὸ ἀ. τῆς βουλῆς αὐτοῦ *the unchangeableness of his purpose* **Hb 6:17** (cp. PGM 4, 527f κατὰ δόγμα θεοῦ ἀμετάθετον).

❷ ***impossible*** MPol 11:1 (in wordplay w. μετάνοια, i.e. 'a change of mind from better to worse is not a change that is an option for us').—DELG s.v. τίθημι. M-M.

ἀμετακίνητος, ον (μετακινέω 'shift, change'; Pla., Ep. 7, 343a; Dionys. Hal. 8, 74; ins fr. Nazareth [RB 40, '31, 544, 5 = SEG VIII, 13, 5; Boffo, Iscrizioni no. 39, I AD]; PFamTebt 23, 18; PHamb 62, 18 [123 AD]; Jos., C. Ap. 2, 169; 234; 254, Ant. 1, 8) ***immovable*** (w. ἑδραῖος) γίνεσθε ἀ. **1 Cor 15:58.**—DELG s.v. κινέω. M-M.

ἀμεταμέλητος, ον—❶ pass. ***not to be regretted, without regret*** (μεταμέλομαι 'feel regret'; Pla., Tim. 59d; Polyb. 21, 11, 11; 23, 16, 11; Diod. S. 10, 15, 3; Dionys. Hal. 11, 13; Plut., Mor. 137b) μετάνοια ἀ. *a repentance not to be regretted* **2 Cor 7:10;** πολιτεία ἀ. 1 Cl 54:4. ἔσται ἀμεταμέλητα ὑμῖν *you will have nothing to regret* 58:2. Hence also *irrevocable,* of someth. one does not take back (ὀργὴ ἀ.: PLond 1912, col. 4, 78 [41 AD]; so in Byzantine wills Mitt-Wilck. II/2, 319, 4 [VI AD]; OEger, ZNW 18, 1918, 91, 1; CSpicq, RB 67, '60, 210–19). χαρίσματα, κλῆσις τ. θεοῦ **Ro 11:29.**

❷ act., ***feeling no remorse, having no regret*** (Aristot., EN 7, 7, 1150a 22; 9, 4, 1166a 29) 1 Cl 2:7.—DELG s.v. μέλω. M-M. TW. Spicq.

ἀμεταμελήτως adv. fr. ἀμεταμέλητος (s. prec.; Aesop, Fab. 40d, 7 Ch.; Themist., Or. 19 p. 281, 14) ***without feeling regret*** 1 Cl 58:2 (cp. IPriene 114, 8 [I BC]).

ἀμετανόητος, ον (s. μετανοέω; mostly [Lucian, Vett. Val., Plotinus] pass. 'irrevocable', so also in pap) act. ***unrepentant*** **Ro 2:5** (cp. TestGad 7:5; Epict., fgm. 25 Sch.).—DELG s.v. νόος. M-M.

ἄμετρος, ον (s. μέτρον; Pla., Xen. et al.; TestAbr A 17 p. 98, 27 [Stone p. 44] τὸ ἄ. πέλαγος; OGI 669, 51; Philo; Jos., Bell. 4, 350; Just., D. 47, 5 τὸ ἄ. πέλαγος) ***immeasurable*** εἰς τὰ ἄ. καυχᾶσθαι *boast beyond limits, illimitably* **2 Cor 10:13, 15** (Epict., Ench. 33, 14 ἀμέτρως of self-praise).—DELG s.v. μέτρον. M-M. TW.

ἀμήν (LXX occas. for אָמֵן, usu. transl. by γένοιτο; taken over by Christians; in pap symbol. expressed by the number 99 [α=1 + μ=40 + η=8 + ν=50; ESchaefer, PIand I 29], but also as ἀμήν [POxy 1058, 5]. Ins: ISyriaW 1918; MvOppenheim-HLucas, ByzZ 14, 1905, p. 34ff, nos. 36, 39, 46, 84)

❶ strong affirmation of what is stated—ⓐ as expression of faith ***let it be so, truly, amen*** liturgical formula at the end of the liturgy, spoken by the congregation (cp. 1 Ch 16:36; 2 Esdr 15:13; 18:6; TestSol, TestAbr; TestJob 53:8; GrBar 17:4; ApcEsdr 7 end; ApcMos); hence τὸ ἀ. λέγειν **1 Cor 14:16,** cp. **Rv 5:14.** At the end of a doxology (cp. 3 Macc 7:23; 4 Macc 18:24; Mel., P. 45, 323; 65, 466) **Mt 6:13 v.l.; Ro 1:25; 9:5; 11:36; 15:33; 16:24 v.l., 27; Gal 1:5; 6:18; Eph 3:21; Phil 4:20, 23 v.l.; 1 Ti 1:17; 6:16; 2 Ti 4:18; Hb 13:21, 25 v.l.; 1 Pt 4:11; 5:11; Jd 25; Rv 1:6; 7:12;** 1 Cl 20:12; 32:4; 38:4; 43:6; 45:8; 50:7; 58:2; 61:3; 65:2; 2 Cl 20:5; AcPl Ha 2, 34. W. ναί as transl.: ναί, ἀ., *yes (so shall it be), amen* **Rv 1:7.** Sim. γένοιτο, ἀμήν GJs 6:2, cp. ἀμήν 7:1 (pap, some mss. ἀ. γένοιτο as TestAbr A 2 p.79, 14 [Stone p. 6]; Just., A I, 65, 4, τὸ Ἀμὴν . . . Γένοιτο σημαίνει = 'Amen' means 'May it be so').—Accord. to later custom (cp. Tob; 3 and 4 Macc; ApcSed 16:10 p. 137, 19 Ja.; Cyranides p. 124, 18 Ἀμήν· τέλος· ἀμήν· ἀμήν) ἀ. was almost always put at the end of books, but not in the older mss. (and hence v.l.) **Mt 28:20; Mk 16:20; Lk 24:53; J 21:25; Ac 28:31; 1 Cor 16:24; 2 Cor 13:13; Hb 13:25;** GJs 25:2 al. The liturg. formula is extended to ἀ. ἀλληλουϊά (q.v.) after the doxology **Rv 19:4;** to ἀ., ἔρχου κύριε Ἰησοῦ (cp. μαρὰν ἀθᾶ) **22:20** or μαρὰν ἀθᾶ ἀ. D 10:6.—At beginning and end of a doxology **Rv 7:12.**—τὸ ἀ. (w. τὸ ναί): διὸ καὶ δι' αὐτοῦ τὸ ἀ. τῷ θεῷ πρὸς δόξαν *therefore the 'amen' is spoken through him to God's glory* (w. ref. to the liturgical use of 'amen') **2 Cor 1:20;** s. **1 Cor 14:16,** above.—Hence

ⓑ asseverative particle, ***truly,*** always w. λέγω, beginning a solemn declaration but used only by Jesus (*I assure you that, I solemnly tell you*) **Mt 5:18, 26; 6:2, 5, 16; 8:10** al. **Mk 3:28; 8:12; 9:1** al. **Lk 4:24; 12:37; vs. 44 v.l.; 18:17** al. (JO'Neill, JTS 10, '59, 1–9). For this J always has ἀμὴν ἀμὴν λέγω (OT אָמֵן אָמֵן [Num 5:22; 2 Esdr 18:6; Ps 41:14; 72:19], Gk. mostly γένοιτο, γένοιτο, but 2 Esdr 18:6 ἀμήν and in the corresp. passage 1 Esdr 9:47 likew., w. the v.l. ἀμ. ἀμ. [as in PGM 22b, 21; 25], only to strengthen a preceding statement) **1:51; 3:3, 5, 11; 5:19, 24f** al. On the emphatic force of repetition s. Rdm.[2] 68, 1. Cp. Aristaen., Ep. 1, 24 εὐθὺς εὐ.; 2, 13 οἶδα οἶ.

❷ Christ as the ultimate affirmation, *the Amen,* ὁ ἀ., only in the enigmatic lang. of Rv, explained as ὁ μάρτυς ὁ πιστὸς κ. ἀληθινός **3:14** (Ps 88:38); LGillet, ET 56, '44/45, 134–36; LSilbermann, JBL 82, '63, 213–15.—On the word gener. Dalman, Worte 185; Jesus 27f (Eng. tr. 30); PGlaue, Amen: ZKG, n.F. 7, 1925, 184–98; EPeterson, Εἷς θεός, 1926, index; DDaube

JTS 45, '44, 27–31; Goodsp., Probs., 96–98; FSchilling, ATR 38, '56, 175–81; AStuiber, JAC 1, '58, 153–59; JGreig, Studia Evangelica 5, '68, 10–13; KBerger, Die Amen-Worte Jesu, '70, ZNW 63, '72, 45–75; STalmon, Textus 7, '69, 124–29; JStrugnell, HTR 67, 177–82; PGlaue, RAC I 378–80.—M-M. TW.

ἀμήτωρ, ορος (since Pre-Socr., trag., Hdt. in var. mngs.; denotes origin without a mother in Ps.-Oppian, Cyneg. 2, 567 ἀμήτορα φῦλα [fish, originating fr. slime]; Philostrat., Vi. Apoll. 2, 14 p. 57, 32 [of vipers]; Pla., Symp. 180d [of the heavenly Aphrodite]; Eur., Phoen. 666; Philo, Op. M. 100, Leg. All. 1, 15, Mos. 2, 210; Tat. 8, 3 and Celsus 6, 42 [of Pallas Ath.]; Jo. Lydus, De Mens. 2, 11; oracle of Apollo: Theosophien §13 p. 169=Lactant., Inst. 1, 7, 1, also 4, 13, 2 [of God]; Philo, Ebr. 61 [of Sara]. Cp. ἀπάτωρ) ***without a mother*** (w. ἀπάτωρ [as in Eur., Ion 109; Nonnus, Dionys. 41; 53] and ἀγενεαλόγητος) of Melchizedek, either to indicate that his genealogy is not given in the OT, or to ascribe to him heavenly origin **Hb 7:3.**—DELG s.v. μήτηρ. M-M.

ἀμίαντος, ον (μιαίνω 'to defile'; Pind. et al.; Wsd.; TestJos 4:6; JosAs 15:14 cod. A [p. 62, 17 Bat.]; 2 Macc., Philo; PGM 4, 289) ***undefiled*** only fig. (Pla., Leg. 6, 777e; Plut., 529 [Nic. 9, 5] al.), ***pure*** in relig. and moral sense.

ⓐ of things κοίτη ἀ. (parall. τίμιος γάμος; cp. Kaibel 204, 13 [I BC]; Plut., Numa 66 [9, 5]; Wsd 3:13) **Hb 13:4;** w. καθαρός (Cornutus 20 p. 36, 9; Plut., Per. 173 [39, 2], Mor. 383b; 395e; Jos., Bell. 6, 99; TestJos 4:6): θρησκεία ἀ. **Js 1:27** (cp. Wsd 4:2). σάρξ Hs 5, 7, 1 (cp. Wsd 8:20 σῶμα ἀ.); w. ἁγνός: βάπτισμα 2 Cl 6:9; χεῖρες ἀ. 1 Cl 29:1; w. καθαρός, ἄκακος: μετάνοια Hm 2:7; w. ἄσπιλος: σάρξ Hs 5, 6, 7; w. ἄφθαρτος and ἀμάραντος: κληρονομία **1 Pt 1:4.**—Subst. ὁ ἀμίαντος *asbestos* (cp. deStrycker p. 112, n. 4).

ⓑ of pers.: w. ὅσιος, ἄκακος of Christ **Hb 7:26.** τὰς θυγατέρας τῶν Ἑβραίων τὰς ἀ. GJs 6:1; 7:2; τὰς παρθένους τὰς ἀ. 10:1; of Mary ἀ. τῷ θεῷ 10:1.—DELG s.v. μιαίνω. M-M. TW.

Ἀμιναδάβ, ὁ indecl. (עַמִּינָדָב) (Philo, Poster. Cai. 76 Ἀμιναδάμ.—In Joseph. Ἀμινάδαβος, ου [Ant. 6, 18]) ***Amminadab,*** son of Aram (Lk. Admin), father of Nahshon; in the genealogy of Jesus (cp. Ex 6:23; Num 1:7; 1 Ch 2:10; Ruth 4:19f) **Mt 1:4; Lk 3:33.**

ἄμμον, ου, τό ***sand*** τὸ ἄ. τῆς θαλάσσης **Ro 4:18 v.l.** Cp. next entry.

ἄμμος, ου, ἡ (cp. the epic form ἄμαθος Il. 5, 587; Pla., X. et al.; pap; LXX, pseudepigr., Philo, Apolog.) ***sand*** ἡ ἄ. τῆς θαλάσσης=seashore **Rv 12:18.** Of a sandy subsoil **Mt 7:26.** Cp. **Ac 7:24** D.—Mostly fig., of things that cannot be counted (LXX; Philo, Somn. 1, 175) **Ro 9:27** (Is 10:22); **Rv 20:8.** More specif. ἡ ἄ. ἡ παρὰ τὸ χεῖλος τῆς θ. (Gen 22:17; Da 3:36; 1 Macc 11:1) *the sand on the seashore* **Hb 11:12;** in same sense ἄ. τῆς γῆς 1 Cl 10:5 (Gen 13:16).—B. 22. DELG s.v. ἄμαθος. M-M.

ἀμνάς, άδος, ἡ (Theocr. 8, 35 [Gow]; LXX; TestSol 1:10 D; TestJob 44:4f; Joseph.; Mel., P. 71, 513) ***lamb*** GJs 4:3. S. ἀμνός.

ἀμνησίκακος, ον (μνησικακέω 'remember past injury'; Philo, De Jos. 246.—Nicol. Dam.: 90 fgm. 130, 59 p. 402, 19 Jac. μνησίκακος; 130, 117 p. 415, 25 ἀμνησικακεῖν) **pert. to not recollecting any evil done to one, *bearing no malice, forgiving*** (w. εἰλικρινής, ἀκέραιος) εἰς ἀλλήλους *bearing no malice toward each other* 1 Cl 2:5. ἀμνησίκακον εἶναι Hm 8:10; of God 9:3.—DELG s.v. μιμνήσκω.

ἀμνησικάκως adv. (Diod. S. 31, 8) ***without bearing malice*** ὁμονοεῖν ἀ. 1 Cl 62:2.

ἀμνός, οῦ, ὁ (Soph., Aristoph.+) ***lamb*** (acc. to Istros [III BC]: 334 fgm. 23 Jac., a sheep one year old; acc. to a schol. on Nicander, Alexiph. 151 ὁ μηδέπω κέρατα ἔχων. Acc. to Ex 12:5 the passover lamb must be one year old; Hippol., Ref. 4, 30, 1) ὁ λέων . . . ὡς ἄμνὸς εὐδίδακτος *the lion as well-trained as the lamb* AcPl Ha 4, 30; otherw. in our lit. used only of Christ or referring to him (so also the Christian addition to TestJos 19). Sacrificial lamb without blemish **1 Pt 1:19.** ὁ ἀ. τοῦ θεοῦ **J 1:29, 36** (JJeremias, ZNW 34, '35, 115–23; PJoüon, NouvRT 67, '40, 318–21; CBarrett, NTS 1, '54/55, 210–18; FGryglewicz, D. Lamm Gottes, NTS 13, '66/67, 133–46). Symbol of patience ἀ. ἐναντίον τοῦ κείροντος **Ac 8:32;** 1 Cl 16:7; B 5:2 (all Is 53:7).—B. 159. DELG. M-M. TW.

ἀμοιβή, ῆς, ἡ (ἀμείβω 'exchange'; Hom. et al.; ins, pap, Aq., Sym.; Philo, Aet. M. 108; Just.; Tat. 32, 1) ***a return, recompense*** (so freq. in honorary ins, e.g. IPriene 119, 27; 113, 120; 112, 17; s. also Jos., Ant. 4, 266) ἀμοιβὰς ἀποδιδόναι τοῖς προγόνοις *make a return to those who brought them up* **1 Ti 5:4** (ἀ. ἀποδιδόναι Democr. B 92; PLond V, 1729, 22; Jos., Ant. 5, 13). ἀμοιβή is also to be read ISm 9:2, with the new pap (the Christian letter BKT VI p. 7, ln. 79).—DELG s.v. ἀμείβω. M-M. Spicq.

ἄμορφος, ον (cp. μορφή, which expresses someth. that is in principle harmonious, as Pind., I. 4, 57) ***misshapen, ugly*** (so Eur., Hdt. et al.; Aelian, NA 16, 24 p. 402, 10; Ps.-Apollod. 1, 4, 2, 1; Philo; TestSol 18:1; Just., A I, 10, 2; 59, 1 ὕλη ἄ.; Ath. R. 51, 16 ἀ. οὐσίαν) of εἴδωλα **1 Cor 12:2 v.l.**

ἄμπελος, ου, ἡ (Hom.+; ins, pap, LXX; En 32:4; JosAs, GrBar, EpArist, Philo; Jos., Ant. 12, 75 κλήματα ἀμπέλων σὺν βότρυσιν; Just.; Ath. 22:6f; Did., Gen. 31, 27; s. Frisk s.v. on futile attempts to establish I-E. or Semitic origin) ***vine, grapevine***

ⓐ lit. 1 Cl 23:4=2 Cl 11:3 (quot. of unknown orig.); Hs 5, 2, 5; 5, 2; 9, 26, 4. τὸ γένημα τῆς ἀ. (cp. Is 32:12) **Mt 26:29; Mk 14:25; Lk 22:18.** μὴ δύναται ποιῆσαι ἄ. σῦκα; *can a grapevine yield figs?* **Js 3:12** (Plut., Mor. 472e τὴν ἄμπελον σῦκα φέρειν οὐκ ἀξιοῦμεν; Epict. 2, 20, 18 πῶς δύναται ἄμπελος μὴ ἀμπελικῶς κινεῖσθαι, ἀλλ' ἐλαϊκῶς κτλ.;). Trained on elm trees Hs 2:1ff. τρυγᾶν τοὺς βότρυας τῆς ἀ. τῆς γῆς *to harvest the grapes fr. the vine of the earth* (i.e. fr. the earth, symbol. repr. as a grapevine) **Rv 14:18f;** but ἀ may be taking on the meaning of ἀμπελών, as oft. in pap, possibly PHib 70b, 2 [III BC]; PTebt 24, 3; PAmh 79, 56; PFlor 50, 2; Greek Parchments fr. Avroman in Medina (JHS 34, 1914); Aelian, NA 11, 32 p. 286, 12 Hercher acc. to the mss. (see p. xl); Themistius 21 p. 245d; Aesop mss. (Ursing 77f). In the endtime: dies, in quibus vineae nascentur, singulae decem milia palmitum habentes Papias (1:2; cp. En 10:19).—Lit. on οἶνος 1 and συκῆ. HLutz, Viticulture . . . in the Ancient Orient 1922; ILöw, D. Flora d. Juden I 1928, 48–189.

ⓑ fig. of Christ and his disciples: he is the vine, they the branches **J 15:1, 4f** (cp. Cornutus 27 p. 51, 3, where the pleasant state for the ἀμπ. is τὸ πολυφόρον κ. καθαρόν; Sir 24:17 of wisdom: ἐγὼ ὡς ἀ. ἐβλάστησα χάριν; Did., Gen. 86, 11 ἡ ψυχὴ ποτὲ μὲν ἄμπελος, ποτὲ δὲ πρόβατον, ποτὲ νύμφη . . . λέγεται). The words of the eucharistic prayer over the cup in D 9:2 cannot be explained w. certainty εὐχαριστοῦμέν σοι . . . ὑπὲρ τῆς ἁγίας ἀ. Δαυὶδ τοῦ παιδός σου, ἧς ἐγνώρισας ἡμῖν διὰ Ἰησοῦ τοῦ παιδός σου (s. AHarnack, TU II 1f, 1884 ad loc.; 6, 225ff; RKnopf, Hdb. ad loc.)—M-M. TW.

ἀμπελουργός, οῦ, ὁ (Aristoph., Hippocr. et al.; Lucian, Philops. 11; ins, pap, LXX; Philo, Plant. 1) ***vinedresser, gardener*** **Lk 13:7.**—DELG s.v. ἄμπελος. M-M.

ἀμπελών, ῶνος, ὁ (Theophr., HP 9, 10, 3; PEleph 14, 2; PHib 151; PPetr II, 140 [III BC] and later, also LXX; TestLevi 2:12; ParJer 3:14; GrBar 1:2; Philo; Jos., Ant. 8, 359) ***vineyard*** φυτεύειν ἀ. (Gen 9:20 al.; Philo, Virt. 28, Exs. 128; PCairZen 300, 1) *plant a vineyard* **1 Cor 9:7** (cp. Dt 20:6); Hs 5, 2, 2; 5, 6, 2; ἀ. καλοί *well-cultivated v.* m 10, 1, 5; χαρακοῦν ἀ. *fence a v.* s 5, 2, 3; cp. 5, 4, 1ff; σκάπτειν ἀ. (Diod. S. 4, 31, 7) *spade up a v.* 5, 2, 4. In the parables: **Mt 20:1ff; 21:28ff; Mk 12:1ff** (WKümmel, MGoguel Festschr., '50, 120–31; MHengel, ZNW 59, '68, 1–39); **Lk 20:9ff** (BvanIersel, 'D. Sohn' in den synopt. Jesusworten '64[2], 124–45; JDerrett, Law in the NT, '70, 286–312). Cp. **13:6,** where it may mean *orchard.* Symbol of the Christian people Hs 5, 5, 3.—DELG s.v. ἄμπελος. M-M.

Ἀμπλιᾶτος, ου, ὁ (also -ίατος; by-form Ἀμπλιάς [**Ro 16:8** as v.l.], more correctly accented Ἀμπλιᾶς; s. W-S. §6, 7g; B-D-F §125, 1 and 2) ***Ampliatus*** (common slave name: CIL II, 3771 [Spain]; VI, 14918; 15509 [Rome]; IV, 1182; 1183 [Pompeii]; IG III, 1161, 8; 1892 [Athens]; CIL III, 436 [Ephesus]) recipient of a greeting, designated as ἀγαπητὸς ἐν κυρίῳ **Ro 16:8** (s. Lghtf., Phil. 1891, 172; Rouffiac 90; Ltzm., Hdb. ad loc.).—M-M. s.v. Ἀμπλίας.

ἀμύνομαι fut. 3 sg. ἀμυνεῖται Tat. 17:4, 1 aor. ἠμυνάμην (Hom.+; LXX, JosAs, ApcrEzk [Epiph. 70, 8]; but here just as rare as in the ins [e.g. SIG 780, 35; IAndrosIsis, Kyme 37 p. 124 P.] and the pap [e.g. APF 3, 1906, p. 418, 71]—Jos., Bell. 1, 319; 5, 129, Ant. 9, 9 al.; Tat. 17, 2; 4) **to help by coming to the aid of, *help, assist, defend*** someone (Is 59:16; JosAs 23:11 cod. A [p. 75, 9 Bat.]) abs. w. ἐκδίκησιν ποιεῖν of Moses, who killed an Egyptian **Ac 7:24** (for Att. ἀμύνω B-D-F §316, 1). This mng. is perh. preferable to *retaliate* (as Epict. 4, 13, 7; JosAs 24:7).—DELG s.v. ἀμύνω. M-M.

ἀμφιάζω (Hellen. for ἀμφιέννυμι, s. Schwyzer I 244; Plut., C. Gracch. 835 [2, 3 Z.] v.l.; Vett. Val. 64, 9; Alciphron 3, 6, 3; OGI 200, 24; Sb 6949, 24; PIand 62, 14; LXX; Jos., Bell. 7, 131, Ant. 10, 11; AcThom 7 [Aa II/2, 110, 13]; Mel., P. 47, 330 ὁ κύριος . . . τὸν πάσχοντα ἀμφιασάμενος) by-form with ἀμφιέζω (q.v.) ***clothe*** **Lk 12:28 v.l.** [N.[25] in text].—DELG. M-M.

ἀμφιβάλλω (βάλλω 'cast'; in var. mngs. Hom. et al.; pap; Hab 1:17; TestJob 29:3; Just. D. 51, 2; 123, 7; Ath. R. 48, 21 ['doubt, hesitate']) ***cast,*** a t.t. for the throwing out of the circular casting-net (δίκτυον Geopon. 20, 12; ἀμφίβληστρον Hab 1:17); abs. εἶδεν Σίμωνα κ. Ἀνδρέαν ἀμφιβάλλοντας ἐν τῇ θαλάσσῃ *he saw them casting their net(s) in the sea* **Mk 1:16** (cp. PFlor 119, 3 [254 AD] οἱ ἁλιεῖς . . . ἀμφιβάλλουσι, but the words indicated by dots cannot be restored w. certainty, and hence it remains doubtful whether the word is used abs.; s. also ἀμφιβολεύω PSI 901, 13; 22 [46 AD] sim. ἀμφιβολεύς PCorn 46, 6, par. to Jer 19:8).—Dalman, Arbeit VI: Zeltleben, Vieh- u. Milchwirtschaft, Jagd, Fischfang '39; LBunsmann, De piscatorum in Graec. atque Rom. litteris usu, diss. Münst. 1910.—DELG s.v. βάλλω. M-M. TW.

ἀμφίβληστρον, ου, τό (Hes., Hdt. et al.; Artem. 2, 14 p. 107, 13; LXX; DELG s.v. βάλλω p. 63e) **a circular casting-net used in fishing, *casting-net.*** βάλλειν ἀ. *throw out a casting-net* (Aesop., Fab. 11 P., H-H.=27 H. βάλλειν τὸ ἀμφ.) **Mt 4:18; Mk 1:16 v.l.;** s. ἀμφιβάλλω.

ἀμφιβολία, ας, ἡ (cp. ἀμφιβάλλω; Hdt. et al. in var. mngs.; Aristot.; SIG 827 Tit. F col. V, 6; PLond 1716, 8 [VI AD]; Jos., Bell. 3, 434; Ath. 11, 2, R. 60, 15) ***a quarrel*** ἀ. ἔχειν μετά τινος D 14:2. B. 1244.

ἀμφιέζω (Hellen. by-form w. ἀμφιάζω q.v. [s. also ἀμφιέννυμι]; An. Ox. II 338 τὸ μὲν ἀμφιέζω ἐστὶ κοινῶς, τὸ δὲ ἀμφιάζω δωρικόν='ἀμφιέζω' is used in the vernacular, and 'ἀμφιάζω' is Doric) ***clothe*** **Lk 12:28** (the mss. vary betw. ἀ., ἀμφιέζει, ἀμφιέννυσιν). Cp. B-D-F §29, 2; 73; 101; W-S. §15; Mlt-H. 68; 228; Rdm. 44; 225.

ἀμφιέννυμι 1 aor. ἠμφιέσαντο 4 Km 17:9; pf. pass 1 pl. ἠμφιέσμεθα (Just., D. 116, 1); ptc. ἠμφιεσμένος (POxy 850 [AcJ], 26f restored) (ἕννυμι 'to clothe'; Aelian, NA 4, 46 p. 102, 17; Jos., Ant. 8, 186; Just., D. 116, 1 [Zech 3:3 ἐνδέδυμένος] ἠμφιέσμεθα; cp. W-S. §12, 6; B-D-F §69, 1; Mlt-H. 192) (Hom. et al.; ins; PFouad 10, 8; BGU 388, 41) ***clothe, dress*** w. acc. of what is clothed τὸν χόρτον **Mt 6:30.** Pass. (Jos., Bell. 4, 473, Ant. 15, 403) ἐν μαλακοῖς (ἱματίοις) ἠ. *dressed in soft garments* **Mt 11:8; Lk 7:25; 12:28 v.l.** (on the construction B-D-F §159, 1); of seeds AcPlCor 2:26; cp. **1 Cor 15:37f.** On **Lk 12:28** s. ἀμφιάζω.—DELG s.v. ἕννυμι. M-M.

Ἀμφίπολις, εως, ἡ ***Amphipolis,*** capital of southeast Macedonia, so called because the Strymon R. flows around it (Thu. 4, 102, 4; Appian, Bell. Civ. 4, 104 §437; 4, 107 §447), a military post on the Via Egnatia, the main road from Rome to Asia. Paul went through Ἀ. on a journey from Philippi to Thessalonica **Ac 17:1.**—OHirschfeld in Pauly-W. I 1949ff; PECS 51f (lit.).

ἄμφοδον, ου, τό (Aristoph.; Hyperid., fgm. 137; ins [SIG 961 w. note, OGI 483, 80] and pap [UPZ 77 I, 6 (163 BC); PLond II, 208, 7 p. 67; 225, 4 p. 8 al.; s. Preisigke, Fachwörter] since II BC; Jer 17:27; 30:33; JosAs 2:13) 'a city quarter', surrounded and crossed by streets, then ***street*** (Hesych. explains ἄμφοδα· αἱ ῥῦμαι. ἀγυιαί. δίοδοι) ἔξω ἐπὶ τοῦ ἀ. *outside, in the street* **Mk 11:4** (exx. for ἐπὶ τοῦ ἀ. in pap in Mayser 261, 1). τρέχειν εἰς τὸ ἀ. *run into the street* **Ac 19:28** D; cp. AcPlTh (Aa I 243, 6).—M-M.

ἀμφότεροι, αι, α (DELG s.v. ἄμφω; Hom.+)—❶ ***both*** (Jos., Ant. 16, 125; Just.; Tat. 1, 2; Ath., R. 64, 30 al.) Dg 9:6. ἀ. συντηροῦνται *both* (i.e. wine and skins) *are preserved* **Mt 9:17; Lk 5:38 v.l.;** ἀ. εἰς βόθυνον (ἐμ-)πεσοῦνται *both* (the guide and the one whom he leads) *will fall into the pit* **Mt 15:14; Lk 6:39.** Cp. **Mt 13:30.**—ἦσαν δίκαιοι ἀ. **Lk 1:6;** cp. vs. 7 (the masc. form for a married couple, Ammonius, Vi. Aristot. p. 10, 6 Westerm.). ἀμφοτέροις ἐχαρίσατο **7:42;** κατέβησαν ἀ. **Ac 8:38;** ἀ. οἱ νεανίσκοι GPt 9:37; ἀ. τὰ πλοῖα **Lk 5:7;** τὸν ἐπ' ἀμφοτέροις θεόν *God who is over both* B 19:7; D 4:10.—οἱ ἀ. *both together* (Lat. utrimque; οἱ δύο 'each . . . of the two' [regarded severally], Lat. uterque, s. B-D-F §275, 8) ἀποκαταλλάσσειν τοὺς ἀ. τῷ θεῷ *to reconcile both of them w. God* **Eph 2:16.** οἱ ἀ. ἐν ἑνὶ πνεύματι vs. **18;** τὰ ἀ. ἓν ποιεῖν vs. **14.** *Either* D 7:3.

❷ ***all,*** even when more than two are involved (Diod. S. 1, 75, 1 πρὸς ἀμφότερα=for everything, in every respect; PThéad 26, 4 [296 AD]; PGen 67, 5; 69, 4) **Ac 19:16.** Φαρισαῖοι ὁμολογοῦσιν τὰ ἀ. *believe in them all* **23:8.** JBury, ClR 11, 1897, 393ff; 15, 1901, 440, ByzZ 7, 1898, 469; 11, 1902, 111; Mlt. 80; Rdm. 77f.—M-M.

ἀμώμητος, ον (μωμάομαι 'blame'; Hom. et al.; Diod. S. 33, 7, 3; Plut., Mor. 489a; EpArist 93; Philo, Aet. M. 41; ISyriaW 2007; Sb 332; 367; PGM 13, 89; 603) ***blameless, unblemished,*** of Christians **2 Pt 3:14** (w. ἄσπιλος); **Phil 2:15 v.l.**—M-M. TW.

ἄμωμον, ου, τό (Hippocr. et al.; Theophr., HP 9, 7, 2; Diosc. 1, 15; PGM 4, 1311; Jos., Ant. 20, 25; DELG s.v. ἄμωμον Oriental loanw.) ***amomum,*** an Indian spice-plant, w. κιννάμωμον, θυμιάματα, μύρον and other spices **Rv 18:13.**—RAC I 395.

ἄμωμος, ον (Hes.+; Arrian: 156 fgm. 121 Jac.; CIG 1974; ins of Herod: APF 1, 1901, 220; LXX; Test12Patr; TestAbr A; GrBar 1:2; Philo, Congr. Erud. Grat. 106; Jos., Bell. 5, 229 al.; Just.; Mel.).

❶ pert. to being without defect or blemish, ***unblemished*** of the absence of defects in sacrificial animals (Num 6:14; 19:2 al.; TestAbr A; Philo, Sacr. Abel. 51, Somn. 1, 62; Mel., P.) ἀμνάδας ἀσπίλους καὶ ἀ. GJs 4:3; hence of Christ as sacrificial lamb ὡς ἀμνοῦ ἀ. καὶ ἀσπίλου **1 Pt 1:19** (Mel., P. 12, 78). Cp. ἑαυτὸν προσήνεγκεν ἄ. τῷ θεῷ *presented himself as an offering without blemish to God* **Hb 9:14.**

❷ pert. to being without fault and therefore morally blameless, ***blameless*** (Semonides 4; Aeschyl., Pers. 185; Hdt. 2, 177; Theocr. 18, 25; 2 Km 22:24; Ps 14:2; 17:24 al.).

ⓐ of pers. (Sb 625; Sir 31:8; 40:19; Philo, Mut. Nom 60; Jos., Ant. 3, 279 w. καθαρός Just., D 17, 1, 3; 35, 8; Mel., P. 44, 312 of Christ): of the Christian community (w. ἅγιος) **Eph 1:4; 5:27;** (w. ἅγιος, ἀνέγκλητος) **Col 1:22;** (w. ἄσπιλος) **2 Pt 3:14 v.l.;** τέκνα θεοῦ ἄ. **Phil 2:15** (cp. ἀμώμητος); ἄ. εἰσιν **Rv 14:5;** cp. **Jd 24;** 1 Cl 50:2; ITr 13:3.

ⓑ of characteristics (Jos., Ant. 3, 27f δίαιτα=way of life): βούλησις 1 Cl 35:5. ὄψις 36:2. πρόσωπον IPol 1:1. χεῖρες (w. ἱεραί) 1 Cl 33:4. διάνοια ITr 1:1. καρδία (w. καθαρά) Hv 4, 2, 5 (cp. Ps 118:80). πρόθεσις (w. ὅσιος) 1 Cl 45:7. συνείδησις (w. σεμνός, ἁγνός) 1:3; cp. Pol 5:3. χαρά IEph ins; IMg 7:1. πνεῦμα ISm ins (not the Holy Spirit, for the greeting parallels IEph ins and the use of ἄμωμος IRo; cp. ITrall 1, IPol 1); ἑνότης IEph 4:2; προστάγματα 1 Cl 37:1.—ἄμωμον παθεῖν *suffer as a blameless person* (of Christ) MPol 17:2.—DELG s.v. μῶμος. M-M. TW.

ἀμώμως adv. fr. ἄμωμος ***blamelessly,*** *without blame* χαίρειν IRo ins.

Ἀμών, ὁ indecl. (אָמוֹן) (in Jos., Ant. 10, 46–48 Ἀμμών, ῶνα) ***Amon,*** in genealogy of Jesus **Mt 1:10 v.l.** (text has Ἀμώς, q.v. 2), son of Manasseh, father of Josiah (cp. 1 Ch 3:14 and 4 Km 21:18–26 w. the vv.ll.).

Ἀμώς, ὁ indecl. (on the corresp. Hebr. name s. EbNestle, ZNW 4, 1903, 188) ***Amos*** in genealogy of Jesus.

❶ father of Mattathias, son of Nahum **Lk 3:25.—❷** son of Manasseh, father of Josiah **Mt 1:10** (v.l. Ἀμών, q.v.); **Lk 3:23ff** D.

I. ἄν (after relatives ἐάν [q.v.] is oft. used for ἄν, but the mss. vary greatly, s. B-D-F §107; 377; Mlt. 42ff, 165ff; Mayser 152f; Crönert 130f; Thackeray 67; Dssm., NB 30ff [BS 202ff]).

A particle peculiar to Gk. (Hom.+) denoting **aspect of contingency,** incapable of translation by a single English word; it denotes that the action of the verb is dependent on some circumstance or condition; the effect of ἄν upon the meaning of its clause depends on the mood and tense/aspect of the verb w. which it is used. The NT use of ἄν corresponds in the main to older Gk., although the rich variety of its employment is limited, as is generally the case in later Greek. In certain constructions (s. aβ) an aspect of certainty is indicated, suggesting the gloss ***would.*** In most other instances aspects of varying possibility or conditionality find expression in ways that can be rendered ***ever,*** but with other glosses required when ἄν is used in conjunction with other particles.

ⓐ ἄν w. aor. or impf. indic.**—α.** denoting repeated action in past time, but only under certain given conditions, esp. after relatives (B-D-F §367; Rob. index): aor. (Gen 30:42; Num 9:17; 1 Km 14:47; Ezk 10:11) ὅσοι ἂν ἥψαντο αὐτοῦ, ἐσῴζοντο *whoever touched him was cured* **Mk 6:56.** Impf. (Ezk 1:20; 1 Macc 13:20; Tob 7:11) ὅπου ἂν εἰσεπορεύετο εἰς κώμας *wherever he went* (as he was accustomed to do—ADebrunner, D. hellenist. Nebensatziterativpräteritum mit ἄν: Glotta 11, 1920, 1–28) *into villages* **Mk 6:56.** καθότι ἄν τις χρείαν εἶχεν *as anyone was in need* **Ac 2:45; 4:35.** Similarly ὡς ἂν ἤγεσθε (v.l. ἀνήγεσθε) **1 Cor 12:2.** Cp. also ὅταν 1bγ and δ.

β. in the apodosis of a contrary to fact (unreal) condition w. εἰ (B-D-F §360; but ἄν is not always used [s. the vv.ll. **J 18:36**]: §360, 1; Mlt. 199ff; PMelcher, De sermone Epicteteo 1905, 75); it is found

א. w. impf. (4 Macc 17:7; Bar 3:13; ParJer 5:20; GrBar 6:6; ApcMos 39) οὗτος εἰ ἦν προφήτης, ἐγίνωσκεν ἄν *if he were a prophet, he would* (now) *know* (but he does not) **Lk 7:39.** εἰ ἔχετε πίστιν . . . , ἐλέγετε ἄν *if you had faith . . . , you would say* **17:6.** εἰ ἐπιστεύετε Μωϋσεῖ, ἐπιστεύετε ἂν ἐμοί **J 5:46.** εἰ ἐμὲ ᾔδειτε, καὶ τὸν πατέρα μου ἂν ᾔδειτε **8:19;** cp. vs. **42; 9:41; 15:19.** εἰ ἔτι ἀνθρώποις ἤρεσκον, Χριστοῦ δοῦλος οὐκ ἂν ἤμην **Gal 1:10;** cp. **3:21.** εἰ ἑαυτοὺς διεκρίνομεν, οὐκ ἂν ἐκρινόμεθα **1 Cor 11:31.** εἰ ἦν ἐπὶ γῆς, οὐδ' ἂν ἦν ἱερεύς *if he were on earth, he would not even be a priest* **Hb 8:4;** cp. **4:8; 8:7; 11:15.**

ב. w. aor., placing the assumption in the past (Gen 30:27; Wsd 11:25; Jdth 11:2; 4 Macc 2:20; TestJob 7:9 al.; ParJer 5:5; GrBar 8:7; PGiss 47, 17) εἰ ἐγένοντο αἱ δυνάμεις, πάλαι ἂν . . . μετενόησαν *if the miracles had been performed, they would long ago have repented* **Mt 11:21.** εἰ ἔγνωσαν, οὐκ ἂν ἐσταύρωσαν **1 Cor 2:8;** cp. **Ro 9:29** (Is 1:9). εἰ ἐγνώκειτε, οὐκ ἂν κατεδικάσατε *if you had recognized, you would not have condemned* **Mt 12:7.** εἰ ἠγαπᾶτέ με, ἐχάρητε ἄν *if you loved me, you would have rejoiced* **J 14:28;** cp. **11:21.** The plpf. for aor. indic. (PGiss 79 II, 6 εἰ δυνατόν μοι ἦν, οὐκ ἂν ὠκνήκειν; BGU 1141, 27f) εἰ ἦσαν, μεμενήκεισαν ἄν **1J 2:19;** cp. **J 11:21 v.l.**—In κἀγὼ ἐλθὼν σὺν τόκῳ ἂν αὐτὸ ἔπραξα **Lk 19:23,** ἐλθών functions as an unreal-temporal protasis (B-D-F §360, 2); cp. καὶ ἐλθὼν ἐγὼ ἐκομισάμην ἂν τὸ ἐμόν **Mt 25:27.** Sim. ἐπεὶ οὐκ ἂν ἐπαύσαντο προσφερόμεναι; where ἐπεί functions as protasis, *otherwise* (i.e. if the sacrifices had really brought about a lasting atonement) *would they not have ceased to offer sacrifices?* **Hb 10:2.**

ⓑ ἄν w. subjunc. after relatives, the rel. clause forming virtually the protasis of a conditional sentence (B-D-F §380, 1) of the future more vivid or present general type.

α. w. fut. or impf. in apodosis, to show that the condition and its results are thought of as in the future, of single and repeated action (IG XIV, 865 [VI BC] ὃς δ' ἄν με κλέψῃ, τυφλὸς ἔσται; TestAbr B 4 p. 109, 10 [Stone p. 66]). ὃς δ' ἂν ποιήσῃ καὶ διδάξῃ, οὗτος μέγας κληθήσεται *but whoever does and teaches*=if a person does and teaches it **Mt 5:19.** ὃς ἂν ἐσθίῃ . . . , ἔνοχος ἔσται **1 Cor 11:27.** οὓς ἐὰν (v.l. ἂν) δοκιμάσητε, τούτους πέμψω **16:3—Mt 10:11; 1 Cor 16:2.**

β. w. pres. in apodosis, to show that the condition and its results involve repeated action, regardless of the time element: ἃ ἂν ἐκεῖνος ποιῇ, ταῦτα καὶ ὁ υἱὸς ὁμοίως ποιεῖ *whatever he does, the Son does likewise* **J 5:19.** ὅπου ἐὰν (v.l. ἄν) αὐτὸν καταλάβῃ, ῥήσσει αὐτόν *wherever it seizes him* **Mk 9:18.** ὑμῖν ἐστιν ἡ ἐπαγγελία ... , ὅσους ἂν προσκαλέσηται κύριος **Ac 2:39.** ὃς ἐὰν (v.l. ἂν) βουληθῇ φίλος εἶναι τοῦ κόσμου, ἐχθρὸς τοῦ θεοῦ καθίσταται *whoever wishes to be a friend of the world* **Js 4:4.** Cp. ὅπου ἂν **3:4 v.l.**—Where ὅς or ὅστις appears w. subj. without ἄν (but cp. IG XII/1, 671 ὃς ἀνασπαράξῃ τ. τάφον; CPR I, 24, 33; 25, 19; AcThom 93 [Aa II/2, 206], 19; Is 7:2; 31:4), the reading that gives the fut. ind. is prob. the right one: ὅστις τηρήσῃ (v.l. -σει) **Js 2:10.** ὅσοι (without ἄν PPetr I, 13, 3;5; CPR I, 237, 3; IPergamon 249, 26 ὅσοι ... ἐγλίπωσι τὴν πόλιν; Vett. Val. 125, 16): ὅσοι μετανοήσωσιν καὶ καθαρίσωσιν Hs 8, 11, 3 (s. W. and Joly app. for the textual tradition). See Reinhold 108; B-D-F §380, 4.

ⓒ In temporal clauses ἄν is found w. the subjunct. when an event is to be described which can and will occur, but whose occurrence cannot yet be assumed w. certainty. So

α. ὅταν (=ὅτε ἄν; s. ὅταν) w. pres. subjunct. to indicate regularly recurring action (Wsd 12:18): ὅταν ἄρτον ἐσθίωσιν *whenever they eat bread* **Mt 15:2.** ὅταν λαλῇ τὸ ψεῦδος *whenever he tells a lie* **J 8:44.** ὅταν λέγῃ τις *whenever anyone says* **1 Cor 3:4.**—W. aor. subjunct. to express action in the future which is thought of as already completed (Sir Prol. ln. 22; Tob 8:21) ὅταν ποιήσητε πάντα *when you have done* **Lk 17:10.** ὅταν ἔλθῃ ὁ κύριος *when the owner has come* **Mt 21:40;** ὅταν ἔλθῃ ἐν τῇ δόξῃ **Mk 8:38;** cp. **J 4:25; 16:13; Ac 23:35.** ὅταν πάλιν εἰσαγάγῃ τὸν πρωτότοκον **Hb 1:6.**

β. ἡνίκα ἄν *every time that* (Ex 1:10; 33:22; 34:24 al.; POxy 104, 26 [96 AD]; PTebt 317, 18 [174/75] ἡνίκα ἐὰν εἰς τὸν νόμον παραγένηται). ἡνίκα ἂν (also ἐάν mss.) ἀναγινώσκηται Μωϋσῆς *every time that Moses is read aloud* **2 Cor 3:15;** cp. vs. **16.**

γ. ὁσάκις ἐάν as often as: ὁσάκις ἐὰν (also ἄν mss.) πίνητε **1 Cor 11:25.** ὁσάκις ἐὰν (also ἄν mss.) ἐσθίητε vs. **26.**

δ. ὡς ἄν *as soon as* (PHib 59, 2 [c. 245 BC] ὡς ἂν λάβῃς; 66, 4; PEleph 9, 3 [III BC]; PParis 46, 18 [143 BC]; BGU 1209, 13 [23 BC]; Josh 2:14; Jdth 11:15; 1 Macc 15:9): ὡς ἂν πορεύωμαι *as soon as I travel* **Ro 15:24.** ὡς ἂν ἔλθω *as soon as I come* **1 Cor 11:34.** ὡς ἂν ἀφίδω τὰ περὶ ἐμέ *as soon as I see how it will go with me* **Phil 2:23.** ὡς ἐάν (PFay 111, 16 [95/96]) Hv 3, 8, 9; 3, 13, 2.—ἀφ᾽ οὗ ἄν *after* **Lk 13:25.**—In the case of temporal particles indicating a goal, viz. ἕως οὗ, ἄχρις (οὗ), μέχρις (οὗ), the mss. show considerable variation; the addition of ἄν is prob. correct only in rare cases (see B-D-F §383, 2). Only ἕως ἄν (PPetr II, 40a, 28 [III BC] ἕως ἂν ὑγιαίνοντας ὑμᾶς ἴδωμεν; Gen 24:14, 19; 49:10; Ex 23:30 al.) has certain attestation: μείνατε ἕως ἂν ἐξέλθητε *stay until you go away* **Mt 10:11.** ἕως ἂν ἴδωσιν τὴν βασιλείαν τοῦ θεοῦ **Lk 9:27.—Mt 2:13; 5:26.** ἕως ἂν λάβῃ **Js 5:7 v.l.**—ἄχρις οὗ (+ ἄν v.l.) ἔλθῃ **1 Cor 11:26.** ἄχρις οὗ (+ ἄν v.l.) θῇ **15:25;** ἄχρις οὗ ἂν ἥξω **Rv 2:25** (v.l. ἄχρι). ἄχρις ἂν ἔλθῃ (cp. BGU 830, 13 [I AD] ἄχρις ἄν σοι ἔλθω) **Gal 3:19 v.l.**—πρὶν ἄν: πρὶν ἢ ἂν (vv.ll. πρὶν ἄν, πρὶν ἤ, only πρίν or ἕως ἄν) ἴδῃ τὸν Χριστόν **Lk 2:26** (B-D-F §383, 3).

ⓓ In purpose clauses the Attic (EHermann, Griech. Forschungen I, 1912, 267f; JKnuenz, De enuntiatis Graec. finalibus 1913, 13ff; 26ff) ὅπως ἄν, esp. freq. in earlier ins (Meisterhans[3]-Schw. 254), has become quite rare (LXX still rather often: Gen 18:19; 50:20; Ex 33:13; Jer 7:23 al.) ὅπως ἂν ἀποκαλυφθῶσιν διαλογισμοί **Lk 2:35.** ὅπως ἂν ἔλθωσιν καιροί **Ac 3:20.—15:17** (Am 9:12 v.l.); **Ro 3:4** (Ps 50:6); **Mt 6:5 v.l.**

ⓔ The opt. w. ἄν in a main clause (potential opt.) has almost wholly disappeared; a rare ex. is εὐξαίμην (v.l. εὐξάμην) ἂν **Ac 26:29** in Paul's speech before Agrippa (literary usage; s. B-D-F §385, 1; also Rob. 938; Themist. 6 p. 80 D.—On the rarity of the potential opt. in pap, LXX, Apost. Fathers see CHarsing, De Optat. in Chartis Aeg. Usu, diss. Bonn 1910, 28; Reinhold 111). Cp.—also in the literary lang. of Lk—direct rhetor. questions (Gen 23:15; Job 19:23; Sir 25:3; 4 Macc 7:22; 14:10 v.l.; TestJob 13:5 τίς ἂν δώῃ 35:5) πῶς γὰρ ἂν δυναίμην; **Ac 8:31.** τί ἂν θέλοι οὗτος λέγειν; **17:18.** Dg has also preserved the opt. as a mark of elegant style (2:3, 10; 3:3f; 4:5; 7:2f; 8:3). MPol 2:2 has τίς οὐκ ἂν θαυμάσειεν;—More freq. in an indirect question, after an impf. or histor. pres. (B-D-F §386, 1; Rob. 938f) τὸ τί ἂν θέλοι καλεῖσθαι αὐτό *what he wanted the child's name to be* **Lk 1:62.** τίς ἂν εἴη περὶ οὗ λέγει **J 13:24.** τὸ τίς ἂν εἴη μείζων αὐτῶν *which of them was the greatest* **Lk 9:46;** cp. **18:36 v.l.** τί ἂν ποιήσαιεν τῷ Ἰησοῦ *what they should do to Jesus* **6:11.** τί ἂν γένοιτο τοῦτο **Ac 5:24.** τί ἂν εἴη τὸ ὅραμα **10:17.** (IMagnMai 215 [I AD] ἐπερωτᾷ ... τί ἂν ποιήσας ... ἀδεῶς διατελοίη; Esth 3:13c πυθομένου δέ μου ... πῶς ἂν ἀχθείη τοῦτο.)

ⓕ The use of ἄν w. inf. and ptc., freq. in earlier Gk., is not found in the NT at all (B-D-F §396); ἵνα μὴ δόξω ὡς ἂν (or ὡσάν, q.v.) ἐκφοβεῖν ὑμᾶς **2 Cor 10:9** is surely to be expl. in such a way that ὡς ἄν=Lat. quasi: *I would not want it to appear as if I were frightening you;* s. B-D-F §453, 3; Mlt. 167.—On εἰ μήτι ἂν (sc. γένηται) ἐκ συμφώνου *except perhaps by agreement* **1 Cor 7:5** s. B-D-F §376; Mlt. 169.—M-M.

II. ἄν for ἐάν is rare in Hellen. Gk. (B-D-F §107; Mlt. 43 n. 2; cp. Hyperid. 4, 5; 5, 15; Teles p. 31, 6; Plut., Mor. 547a; Epict., index Schenkl; pap [Mayser 152]; ins, esp. of the Aegean Sea [Rdm.[2] 198, 3; s. also SIG index IV 204]; 1 Esdr 2:16; 4 Macc 16:11; Jos., Ant. 4, 70; 219; Test12Patr; Mel. fgm. 8b 24), but appears **J 13:20; 16:23; 20:23;** as v.l. **5:19; 9:22; 12:32; 19:12; Ac 9:2;** and IMg 10:1.—Mlt. 63, 1.—M-M.

ἀνά prep. w. acc. (Hom.+), lit. 'up, up to'; rare in later Gk.

❶ ἀνὰ μέσον **in a position in the middle** (Aristot. et al.; Polyb., Diod. S., ins, pap, LXX, En; TestAbr B 8, p. 112, 21 al.; JosAs 4:5f; ApcMos; EpArist [ELohmeyer, Diatheke 1913, 86, 1; Nägeli 30; Rossberg 34; Johannessohn, Präp. 170–73, esp. 170, 6]; Just., D. 107, 4 [on Jon 4:11]) w. gen.

ⓐ of position in an area ***among, in the midst of*** (PGM 36, 302) ἀ. μ. τοῦ σίτου **Mt 13:25;** ἀ. μ. τῶν ὁρίων Δεκαπόλεως *into the (midst of the) district of Decapolis* **Mk 7:31;** ἤλθωσιν ἀνὰ μέσον τῆς ὁδοῦ *they had gone half way on their journey* GJs 17:3.

ⓑ of pers. ***(in the middle) between*** (Diod. S. 11, 90, 3 ἀνὰ μέσον ποταμῶν δυοῖν; 12, 9, 2; 14, 80, 2; 17, 52, 1; Strabo 4, 4, 2; En 13:9) διαστεῖλαι ἀνὰ μέσον δικαίου καὶ ἁμαρτωλοῦ PsSol 2:34; cp. ἀνὰ μέσον τῶν δύο πυλῶν TestAbr B 8, p. 112, 21 [Stone p. 72]) GPt 4:10=ASyn. 344, 73; Hs 9, 2, 3; 9, 15, 2. With breviloquence—if the text is undamaged, which Mlt. 99 doubts—διακρῖναι ἀ. μ. τοῦ ἀδελφοῦ αὐτοῦ *decide (a case) between members* **1 Cor 6:5** (on the shortening cp. Sir 25:18 v.l. ἀ. μ. τοῦ πλησίον αὐτοῦ ἀναπεσεῖται ὁ ἀνήρ. S. also μέσος 1b beg.—Lawsuits ἀ. μ. Ἑλλήνων: SEG IX, 8, 64; JosAs 28:6 κρινεῖ κύριος ἀνὰ μέσον ἐμοῦ καὶ ὑμῶν); *in the midst of* (non-Attic.: IBekker, Anecd. I 1814, 80, 24 ἀ. μέσον· ἀντὶ τοῦ ἐν μέσῳ. Cp. Diod. S. 1, 30, 4 ἀνὰ μ. τῆς Κοίλης Συρίας; PPetr III, 37a II, 18; Ex 26:28; Josh 16:9; 19:1) τὸ ἀρνίον τὸ ἀ. μ. τοῦ θρόνου *in the center of the throne* **Rv 7:17.** ἀ. μ. ἐκκλησίας *in the midst of the congregation* B 6:16.

❷ ἀνὰ μέρος lit. 'up to a part' or 'according to a part' **following in sequence, *in turn*** (Aristot., Pol. 1287a, 17; Polyb. 4, 20, 10 ἀνὰ μέρος ᾄδειν; Appian, Iber. 82 §357, Mithrid. 22 §83, Bell. Civ. 3, 44 §183; SEG IX, 8, 122) **1 Cor 14:27.**

❸ distributive, w. numbers, ***each, apiece*** (Aristoph., Ran. 554f; X., An. 4, 6, 4; SEG IX, 8, 27; PAmh II, 88 [128 AD]; POxy 819 [I AD] al.; Gen 24:22; 3 Km 18:13; 1 Ch 15:26; En 10:19; TestJob 44:5; JosAs; Jos., Ant. 8, 179; 17, 172; Rdm. 20) ἀνὰ δηνάριον *a denarius apiece* **Mt 20:9f.** ἀνὰ λαμπάδα *a lamp apiece* GJs 7:2. ἀνὰ ῥάβδον *a staff apiece* 8:3 (not pap). ἀπέστειλεν αὐτοὺς ἀνὰ δύο *he sent them out two by two* **Lk 10:1.** κλισίας ὡσεὶ ἀνὰ πεντήκοντα *by fifties* **9:14;** ἀνὰ μετρητὰς δύο ἢ τρεῖς *two or three measures apiece* **J 2:6** (Diod. S. 3, 13, 2 ἀνὰ τρεῖς ἢ δύο). ἀνὰ ἑκατὸν καὶ ἀνὰ πεντήκοντα **Mk 6:40 v.l. Lk 9:3; Rv 4:8;** GPt 9:35=ASyn. 353, 81. ἀνὰ μέσον αὐτῶν ἀνὰ δύο παρθένοι *between them* (the maidens at the four corners) *two maidens apiece* Hs 9, 2, 3 (see MDibelius, Hdb. ad loc.).—In ἀνὰ δύο παρθένοι ἀ. has become fixed as an adverb. Likew. ἀνὰ εἷς ἕκαστος τῶν πυλώνων **Rv 21:21** (B-D-F §204; 305; Rob. 571). On ἀνὰ δύο δύο **Lk 10:1;** cp. AcPh 142 (Aa II/2, 79, 6) and δύο b.—Special lit. on prepositions: B-D-F §203–40; Rdm.[2] p. 137–46; Mlt-H. 292–332; Rob. 553–649; Mayser II/2, p. 152–68; 337–543.—MJohannessohn, D. Gebrauch d. Präpositionen in LXX: NGG, Beiheft 1926.—PRegard, Contribution à l'Étude des Prépositions dans la langue du NT 1919.—FKrebs, D. Präpositionen b. Polybius, diss. Würzb. 1882; FKrumbholz, De praepos. usu Appianeo, diss. Jena 1885; PMelcher, De sermone Epict. (Diss. philol. Halenses 17, 1) 1905; JKäser, D. Präpos. b. Dionys. Hal., diss. Erl. 1915; HTeykowski, D. Präpositions-gebr. b. Menander, diss. Bonn '40.—RGünther, D. Präpos. in d. griech. Dialektinschriften: IndogF 20, 1906, 1–163; ENachmanson, Eranos 9, 1909, 66ff.—The works of Kuhring and Rossberg on usage in pap.—GRudberg, Ad usum circumscribentem praepositionum graec.: Eranos 19, 1922, 173–206.—DELG. M-M.

ἀναβαθμός, οῦ, ὁ (Hdt. et al.; Aelian, NA 6, 61; 11, 31; Cass. Dio 65, 21; 68, 5; Philo, Leg. ad Gai. 77; PSI 546, 3; LXX; DELG s.v. βαίνω p. 157) *step,* pl. ***flight of stairs.*** Of the stairs that led fr. the temple court to the tower Antonia: ὅτε ἐγένετο ἐπὶ τοὺς ἀ. *when he came to the steps* **Ac 21:35;** ἑστὼς ἐπὶ τῶν ἀ. (cp. 2 Ch 9:19) vs. **40.** Schürer I 366.—M-M. TW.

ἀναβαίνω fut. ἀναβήσομαι; 2 aor. ἀνέβην, impv. ἀνάβα **Rv 4:1,** pl. ἀνάβατε **11:12** (ἀνάβητε v.l.; s. W-S. §13, 22; Mlt-H. 209f); pf. ἀναβέβηκα (Hom.+)

❶ **to be in motion upward,** ***go up, ascend***—ⓐ of living beings—α. of movement in a direction without special focus on making an ascent: εἰς τὸ ὑπερῷον (cp. Jos., Vi. 146) **Ac 1:13;** εἰς τὸ ὄρος (Ex 19:3, 12 al.; Jos., C. Ap. 2, 25; Iren. 1, 14, 6 [Harv. I 139, 8]) **Mt 5:1; 14:23; 15:29; Mk 3:13; Lk 9:28.** Esp. of the road to Jerusalem, located on high ground (like עָלָה; cp. 2 Esdr 1:3; 1 Esdr 2:5; 1 Macc 13:2; Jos., Bell. 2, 40, Ant. 14, 270) **Mt 20:17f; Mk 10:32f; Lk 18:31; 19:28; J 2:13; 5:1; 11:55; Ac 11:2; 21:12, 15; 24:11; 25:1, 9; Gal 2:1.** εἰς τὸ ἱερόν, since the temple lies on a height (UPZ 41, 5; 42, 4 [162 BC] ἀ. εἰς τὸ ἱερὸν θυσιάσαι; 70, 19f [152/51 BC]; Is 37:1, 14 v.l.; 38:22; Jos., Ant. 12, 164f ἀναβὰς εἰς τὸ ἱερὸν . . . καταβὰς ἐκ τ. ἱεροῦ) **Lk 18:10; J 7:14; Ac 3:1.**—ἐν ναῷ GJs 7:2; ἐν τῇ ὀρινῇ 22, 3.—ἀ. εἰς τὴν ἑορτήν *go up to the festival* **J 7:8, 10;** cp. **12:20** (cp. BGU 48, 19 [III AD] ἐὰν ἀναβῇς τῇ ἑορτῇ; Sb 7994, 21).—W. ἐπί τι (X., Cyr. 6, 4, 9; PsSol 2:2; Jos., Bell. 6, 285; Just., A II, 12, 7) ἐπὶ τὸ δῶμα (Josh 2:8; Judg 9:51) **Lk 5:19; Ac 10:9.**—πρός τινα (UPZ 62, 31 [161 BC]) πρὸς τοὺς ἀποστόλους καὶ πρεσβυτέρους εἰς Ἰερουσαλὴμ περὶ τοῦ ζητήματος τούτου **Ac 15:2.** W. indication of the place from which one goes up ἀπό τινος (X., Hell. 6, 5, 26; Polyb. 10, 4, 6; Dio Chrys. 79 [28], 1) ἀπὸ τοῦ ὕδατος in baptism **Mt 3:16** (Just. D. 103, 6 ἀπὸ τοῦ ποταμοῦ); for this ἔκ τινος (X., Hell. 5, 4, 58): ἐκ τοῦ ὕδατος **Mk 1:10; Ac 8:39.** δι' ὕδατος Hs 9, 16, 2. Of the journey to Judea ἀπὸ τῆς Γαλιλαίας εἰς τὴν Ἰουδαίαν **Lk 2:4.** Gener. ἀλλαχόθεν **J 10:1.** Of ships, *embark, get (into)* (Appian, Bell. Civ. 2, 85 §358 v.l. ἀ. ἐς τὸ σκάφος) εἰς τὸ πλοῖον (Jon 1:3 v.l.) **Mt 14:32; Mk 6:51; Lk 8:22 v.l.; J 6:24 v.l.; Ac 21:6** (also ἐνέβησαν, ἐπέβησαν); AcPl Ha 5, 15.—Abs. ἀναβάς *he went up* again to the third story **Ac 20:11;** to Jerusalem (Sir 48:18; 1 Esdr 1:38; 5:1; 1 Macc 3:15; sim. ἀ. of a journey to the capital Epict. 3, 7, 13; POxy 935, 13; 1157, lines 7, 25f; BGU 1097, 3) **18:22.**

β. of any upward movement *ascend, go up* εἰς (τοὺς) οὐρανούς or εἰς τ. οὐρανόν (Chariton 3, 2, 5 to Zeus; Polyaenus 7, 22 to Hera; Artem. 4, 72 τὸ ἀ. εἰς οὐρανόν means the ὑπερβάλλουσα εὐδαιμονία; En 14:5; Just., D. 36, 5; 85, 2 al.; Diogenes, Ep. 33, 4 p. 142, 5 Malherbe ἀ. ἐπὶ τὸν οὐ.; Herm. Wr. 10, 25; 11, 21a; PGM 4, 546; SibOr 5, 72; cp. AscIs 2:16=PAmh 1) **Ac 2:34; Ro 10:6** (Dt 30:12); **J 3:13; Rv 11:12;** B 15:9; for this εἰς ὕψος **Eph 4:8f** (Ps 67:19; Just., D. 39, 5); ὑπεράνω πάντων τῶν οὐρανῶν vs. **10;** paraphrased ἀ. ὅπου ἦν τὸ πρότερον **J 6:62;** ὧδε **Rv 4:1; 11:12;** ἐπὶ τὸ πλάτος τῆς γῆς **20:9.** W. indication of the place from which ἐκ τῆς ἀβύσσου **11:7; 17:8;** ἐκ τῆς θαλάσσης (cp. Da 7:3) **13:1;** ἐκ τῆς γῆς vs. **11.** Abs. of angels (Orig., C. Cels. 5, 4, 9; cp. Iren. 1, 9, 3 [Harv. I 84, 6; of the Logos]) ἀγγέλους τοῦ θεοῦ ἀναβαίνοντας καὶ καταβαίνοντας **J 1:51** (cp. Gen 28:12 and see ἄγγελος 2, also WThüsing s.v. δόξα end; JDavies, He Ascended into Heaven, '58).—*Climb up* ἐπὶ συκομορέαν **Lk 19:4** (Diod. S. 3, 24, 2 ἐπὶ τὰ δένδρα; Aesop, Fab. 32 P.=48 H.; SIG 1168, 91 ἐπὶ δένδρον ἀ.).—Repres. a passive (Wlh., Einl.[2] 19.—Synes., Ep. 67 p. 215d a burden 'is laid' ἐπί τι) τὸν ἀναβάντα πρῶτον ἰχθύν *the first fish that you catch* **Mt 17:27** (B-D-F §315).

ⓑ of things: smoke (Ex 19:18; Josh 8:21; Is 34:10) **Rv 8:4; 9:2; 19:3;** rocks ἐκ τοῦ πεδίου Hs 9, 2, 1; stones ἐκ βυθοῦ 9, 3, 3; of vines that cling to elm trees *climb up* Hs 2:3. Of plants also *come up* (Theophr., HP 8, 3, 2): thorn bushes (cp. Is 5:6; 32:13) **Mt 13:7; Mk 4:7.** ὅταν σπαρῇ ἀναβαίνει vs. **32;** w. αὐξάνεσθαι vs. **8.** Trees *grow up* B 11:10.—Prayers *ascend* to heaven (Ex 2:23; 1 Macc 5:31; 3 Macc 5:9; En 9:10 στεναγμός; Proverbia Aesopi 79 P.: ἀγαθῷ θεῷ λίβανος οὐκ ἀναβαίνει) **Ac 10:4.**—Fig. ἀνέβη φάσις τῷ χιλιάρχῳ *a report came up to the tribune* **Ac 21:31.** ἀνέβη ὁ κλῆρος ἐπὶ Συμεών (i.e. the priesthood went to Simeon) GJs 24:4 (sim. of kingdom Hdt. 1, 109 ἐς τὴν θυγατέρα; 7, 205 ἐς Λεωνίδην).

❷ Semitism (4 Km 12:5; Jer 3:16; 51:21; Is 65:16; MWilcox, The Semitisms of Acts. '65, 63) ἀ. ἐπὶ καρδίαν lit. 'to arise in the heart' ***enter one's mind*** (i.e. one begins to think about someth.) οὐκ ἀ. ἐπὶ καρδίαν *it has never entered our minds,* since the heart was regarded as the organ of thinking (=עָלָה עַל לֵב.—The Greek said ἐπὶ νοῦν ἀναβαίνει [Synes., Ep. 44 p. 182c] or ἦλθεν [Marinus, Vi. Procli 17 Boiss.]) **1 Cor 2:9** (MPhilonenko, TZ 15, '59, 51f); Hv 1, 1, 8; 3, 7, 2 al. (s. καρδία 1bβ). Also ἀ. ἐν τῇ καρδίᾳ s 5, 1, 5. διαλογισμοὶ ἀναβαίνουσιν ἐν τῇ καρδίᾳ *doubts arise in (your) hearts* **Lk 24:38.**—M-M.

ἀναβάλλω (s. βάλλω; Hom.+ in var. mngs.; LXX; Ath. 13, 2 [for ἐξήνεγκεν Gen 1:12) 2 aor. act. ἀνέβαλον LXX, mid. ἀνεβαλόμην LXX; pf. ptc. ἀναβεβλημένος ('wearing' a cloak) act. and mid. 'put off' (mid.: Hes., Works 410 one should not ἀναβάλλεσθαι anything ἐς αὔριον; Nicol. Dam.: 90 fgm. 130, 43 Jac.; Diod. Sic. 14, 100, 1 εἰς ἕτερον καιρὸν ἀνεβάλετο; Syntipas p. 52, 2; Jos., Ant. 4, 288; 14, 28; PCairZen 412, 13); mid. in the only instance in our lit., and as legal t.t. ***adjourn*** a trial, etc. (Hdt., Demosth. et al.; PTebt 22, 9 [112 BC] 'refer matters';

Jos., Ant. 14, 177) τινά *remand someone, adjourn (his trial)* (like ampliare alqm. Cicero, Verr. 1, 29) ἀνεβάλετο αὐτοὺς ὁ Φῆλιξ **Ac 24:22.**—M-M.

ἀναβάτης, ου, ὁ (Pla., X. et. al.; LXX; PsSol 17:33; DELG s.v. βαίνω p. 157) ἅρματα καὶ ἀναβάται αὐτῶν leaves the question open whether αὐτῶν refers to ἅρματα, in which case ἀ. would mean ***drivers*** (of the chariots), or to the Egyptians. In the latter case ἀ. would retain its usu. mng. ***rider,*** which it has in the OT pass. (Ex 14:23, 26, 28) forming the basis for 1 Cl 51:5.

ἀναβιβάζω fut. ἀναβιβάσω LXX, ἀναβιβῶ Am 8:10, and ἀναβάσω ApcSed 2:2; 1 aor. ἀνεβίβασα LXX (Hdt. et al.; TestSol 25:7 [PQ]; rec. C 10:2; TestJob 52:10; PCairZen 736, 36 [III BC]; POxy 513, 27; Philo, De Jos. 120; Jos., Ant. 20, 60; Tat. 10:2; DELG s.v. βαίνω p. 156, 3) ***bring up*** of a net ἀναβιβάσαντες ἐπὶ τὸν αἰγιαλόν *they pulled it up on the shore* **Mt 13:48** (cp. Maximus Tyr. 29, 6a ἀναβ. ἐπὶ ἵππους ἱππέας=cause riders to mount horses; X., Hell. 1, 1, 2 πρὸς τ. γῆν ἀνεβίβαζε τὰς τριήρεις).—M-M.

ἀναβιόω (Aristoph., Andoc., Pla. et al., also Artapanus: 726 fgm. 3, 25 Jac. [in Eus., PE 9, 27, 25]) *come to life again* (Artem. 2, 62; 4, 82; Palaeph. p. 60, 6; Philostrat., Vi. Apoll. 1, 1, 1; 8, 7 p. 324, 27, Heroicus 1, 4; Jos., Ant. 18, 14) 2 Cl 19:4.—DELG s.v. βίος.

ἀναβλέπω fut. 3 sg. ἀναβλέψει Tob 11:8 S and 3 pl. ἀναβλέψονται Is 8:21; aor. ἀνέβλεψα, impv. ἀνάβλεψον (PreSocr., Hdt., Eur.+; pap, LXX; TestAbr B 12 p. 116, 19 [Stone p. 80] al.; TestJob 40:3; TestJos 6:2; JosAs, ParJer, ApcMos; ApcrEzk P 2 recto, 9; Jos., Ant. 10, 270; Just., A I, 48, 2 [on Is 61:1 and **Mt 11:5**?])

❶ **to direct one's vision upward, *look up,*** lit. ἀ. εἰς τὸν οὐρανόν *look up to heaven* (X., Cyr. 6, 4, 9; Ps.-Pla., Axioch. 370b; Chariton 8, 7, 2 εἰς τ. οὐρανόν ἀναβλέψας εὐφήμει τ. θεούς; Dt 4:19; Job 35:5; Jos., Ant. 11, 64) **Mt 14:19; Mk 6:41; 7:34; Lk 9:16;** 1 Cl 10:6 (Gen 15:5); MPol 9:2; 14:1; εἰς τὸν πόλον GJs 18:2 (not pap).—*Look up* **Mk 8:24.** ἀ. τοῖς ὀφθαλμοῖς 1 Cl 10:4 (Gen 13:14; cp. X., Hell. 7, 1, 30 ἀν. ὀρθοῖς ὄμμασιν); MPol 2:3 v.l. ἀναβλέψασαι θεωροῦσιν *when they looked up, they saw* **Mk 16:4; Lk 19:5; 21:1.** ἀνάβλεψον *look up* **Ac 22:13a.** W. εἰς αὐτόν to show the direction of the glance (Jos., Ant. 12, 24) **22:13b;** but perh. this vs. belongs under 2a.

❷ **to gain sight, whether for the first time or again, *regain sight, gain sight***—ⓐ lit.—**α.** of blind persons, who were formerly able to see, ***regain sight*** (Hdt. 2, 111; Aristoph., Plut. 126; Pla., Phdr. 234b; Ps.-Apollod. 1, 4, 3, 3; SIG 1173, 4 and 17 [138 AD]; Tob 14:2; Philo, Cher. 62) **Ac 9:12, 17f.** The full force of ἀνά is not so clear, but quite prob. in the following pass.: **Mt 11:5; Lk 7:22;** εὐθέως ἀνέβλεψαν *they regained their sight at once* **Mt 20:34;** cp. **Mk 10:52.** (θέλω), ἵνα ἀναβλέψω *I want to regain my sight* **Mk 10:51; Lk 18:41ff.** On **Ac 22:13b** s. 1.

β. w. total loss of the force of ἀνά *again* (s. ἀναζάω 2; Aristoph., Plut. 95; 117 πάλιν ἀν.; Philostrat., Vi. Soph. 2, 1, 2) of one born blind *receive sight, become able to see* (Paus. 4, 12, [7] 10 συνέβη τὸν Ὀφιονέα … τὸν ἐκ γενετῆς τυφλὸν ἀναβλέψαι) **J 9:11, 15, 18.**

ⓑ fig., of inward sight (Herm. Wr. 7, 3; 1a) ἐν τίνι ἀνεβλέψατε; *in what (state) did you receive sight?* 2 Cl 9:2; cp. 1:6.—M-M.

ἀνάβλεψις, εως, ἡ (Aristot. et al.) ***recovery of sight*** κηρῦξαι τυφλοῖς ἀνάβλεψιν **Lk 4:18;** B 14:9 (both Is 61:1).

ἀναβοάω 1 aor. ἀνεβόησα (Aeschyl., Hdt. et al.; Antig. Car. 1; LXX; TestJob 19:3; Jos., Bell. 5, 120, Ant. 19, 345; Just., A II, 12, 7; Mel., P. 24, 166; rare in pap: POxy 33 III, 7f; PGM 36, 141) ***cry out*** **Mk 15:8 v.l.; Lk 9:38 v.l.;** GJs 19:2. ἀ. φωνῇ μεγάλῃ (1 Km 28:12; Jdth 7:23; Bel 41 Theod.; 3 Macc 5:51) **Mt 27:46; Lk 1:42 v.l.** ἀνεβόησε λέγων (Jos., Ant. 9, 10) GPt 5:19.—DELG s.v. βοή. M-M.

ἀναβολή, ῆς, ἡ (Hdt. et al. in various mngs.: ins, pap, LXX) 'delay' (Hdt. et al.; SIG 546, 22 [III BC]; PAmh 3a II, 7; POxy 888, 5; PTebt 24, 22; Jos., Bell. 7, 69, Ant. 17, 75; ἀ. ποιεῖσθαι: Thu. 2, 42, 4; Dionys. Hal. 11, 33; Plut., Camill. 147 [35, 3]; Jos., Ant. 19, 70) legal t.t. ***postponement*** (PAmh 34d, 5 [c. 157 BC]) ἀ. μηδεμίαν ποιησάμενος *I did not postpone the matter* **Ac 25:17;** s. ἀναβάλλω.—DELG s.v. βάλλω. M-M.

ἀνάγαιον, ου, τό (ἄνω; γαῖα [γῆ] 'someth. raised fr. the ground') ***a room upstairs*** (Varro, De Lingua Lat. 5, 162; PParis 21c, 19; PSI 709, 17 [both VI AD]) **Mk 14:15; Lk 22:12** (both places have the Doric forms ἀνώγαιον, and ἀνώγεον [as in PParis cited above] as v.l.; cp. Phryn. 297f Lob.; Schwyzer I 632; II 537). Cp. B-D-F §25; 35, 2; 44, 1; W.-S. §5, 18; Mlt-H. 70; 76; 296.—M-M.

ἀναγγέλλω fut. ἀναγγελῶ; 1 aor. ἀνήγγειλα, inf. ἀναγγεῖλαι; pf. ἀνήγγελκα 1 Km 3:13. Pass.: fut. 3 sg. ἀναγγελήσεται Ps 21:31; 2 aor. ἀνηγγέλην (B-D-F §76, 1; Mlt-H. 226); s. Anz 283f on the history of this word (Aeschyl., Thu.+)

❶ w. full force of ἀνά, **to carry back information, *to report,*** of pers. returning fr. a place (X., An. 1, 3, 21; Gen 9:22; Jdth 11:15) **Mk 5:14 v.l.** τινί τι: **Mt 28:11 v.l.;** ἀναγγέλλων ἡμῖν τὴν ὑμῶν ἐπιπόθησιν **2 Cor 7:7;** ἀ. ὅσα ἐποίησεν ὁ θεός *they reported what God had done* **Ac 14:27;** cp. **15:4.** μὴ ἀναγγείλῃς ὅσα εἶδες GJs 20:4. ταῦτα 23:2 (twice). ἃ εἶδεν 24:2. W. ὅτι foll. **J 4:51f v.l.;** GJs 24:3.

❷ gener. **to provide information, *disclose, announce, proclaim, teach*** (=Att. ἀπαγγέλλω, a common usage in ins and pap, but found as early as Aeschyl., Prom. 661, X., et al. On the LXX s. Anz 283f) αἴνεσιν *the praise of God* 1 Cl 18:15 (Ps 50:17). ποίησιν χειρῶν *the work of God's hands* 27:7 (Ps 18:2). τινί τι (En 13:10; Jos., Bell. 1, 663, Ant. 5, 114) ἀ. ταῦτα τοῖς ἐκλεκτοῖς Hv 2, 1, 3; cp. 3, 3, 1. ἀ. τοῖς λοιποῖς τὰ γενόμενα MPol 15:1.—W. ἐξομολογεῖσθαι: ἀ. τὰς πράξεις αὐτῶν *make their deeds known* **Ac 19:18.**—Of a report to officials **Mt 28:11 v.l.; J 5:15** (v.l. ἀπήγγειλεν; s. Anz 283).—Of proclamation of what is to come in the future (Is 41:22f; Tat. 13:3 πνεῦμα … διὰ προαγορεύσεων … το κεκρυμμένον ἀνήγγειλε) through the Spirit τὰ ἐρχόμενα ἀ. ὑμῖν *he will proclaim to you what is to come* **J 16:13,** cp. vss. **14f, 4:25** (PJoüon, RSR 28, '38, 234f: ἀ.=report what one has heard).—Of Jesus **J 16:25 v.l.**—Of didactic speaking: *preach* w. διδάσκειν **Ac 20:20;** cp. ἀ. πᾶσαν τὴν βουλὴν τοῦ θεοῦ vs. **27** (cp. Dt 24:8 τὸν νόμον). ἃ νῦν ἀνηγγέλη ὑμῖν *which have now been proclaimed to you* **1 Pt 1:12; 1J 1:5.** ἀνηγγείλαμεν ἐναντίον αὐτοῦ *we proclaimed before him* 1 Cl 16:3 (Is 53:2); cp. GEb 121, 29. περί τινος **Ro 15:21** (Is 52:15); 2 Cl 17:5.—M-M. TW.

ἀναγεννάω 1 aor. ἀνεγέννησα; pass. ἀνεγεννήθην (Just., Tat.); pf. pass. ptc. ἀναγεγεννημένος (Philod., Ira p. 18 W.; Sir Prol. ln. 28 v.l.) ***beget again, cause to be born again*** fig. of the spiritual rebirth of Christians.—Of God ὁ ἀναγεννήσας ἡμᾶς εἰς ἐλπίδα ζῶσαν *who has given us a new birth for a living hope* **1 Pt 1:3.** ἀναγεγεννημένοι οὐκ ἐκ σπορᾶς φθαρτῆς *born again not of perishable seed* vs. **23** (in Herm. Wr. 13, 1 Sc. ἀγνοῶ, ὦ τρισμέγιστε, ἐξ οἵας μήτρας ἄνθρωπος ἀναγεννηθείη ἄν, σπορᾶς δὲ ποίας the rdg. ἀναγ. is not certain, but Sallust. 4 p. 8, 24=FPhGr III, 33, col. 2, 6 uses the word in describing mysteries γάλακτος τροφή, ὥσπερ ἀναγεννωμένων).—Cp. RPerdelwitz, D. Mysterienreligion u. d. Problem des 1 Pt 1911, 37ff; HWindisch, Hdb. Exc. on 1 Pt 2:2 and the entry παλιγγενεσία.—DELG s.v. γίγνομαι 222. M-M. TW. Sv.

ἀναγι(γ)νώσκω (older Gk. -γιγν-, DELG s.v. γιγνώσκω) fut. ἀναγνώσομαι; 2 aor. ἀνέγνων, inf. ἀναγνῶναι **Lk 4:16,** ptc. ἀναγνούς. Pass.: fut. 3 pl. ἀναγνωσθήσονται (En 97:6); 1 aor. ἀνεγνώσθην; pf. 3 sg. ἀνέγνωσται (Mel., P. 1), ptc. ἀνεγνωσμένος LXX (Hom.+) lit. of written characters 'to know (them) again', **to read someth. that is written or inscribed,** ***read,*** normally done aloud.

ⓐ gener. (Pind., Thu. et al.; PEleph 9, 3 [222 BC]; 13, 3; BGU 1079, 6ff [I AD]; s. Preis.; SIG 785, 1f [I AD]; LXX; Philo, Spec. Leg. 4, 160; 161; Jos., Ant. 11, 98; Just., D. 10, 3; 11, 3 al.) w. indication of that *in* which one reads ἐν τῇ βίβλῳ (TestDan 5:6) **Mk 12:26;** ἐν τῷ νόμῳ **Mt 12:5;** ἐν ταῖς γραφαῖς **21:42.** W. acc. (Jos., Ant. 20, 44 τὸν νόμον; TestLevi 13:2) τὸ ῥηθέν **Mt 22:31;** τὴν γραφὴν ταύτην **Mk 12:10;** cp. **Ac 8:32;** τὸν τίτλον *the inscription* (Lat. titulus) on the cross **J 19:20;** 'Ησαΐαν **Ac 8:28, 30** (the eunuch read aloud to himself); ἐπιστολήν (Diod. S. 15, 8, 4 ἀναγνοὺς τὴν ἐπιστολήν; Jos., Vi. 227) **Col 4:16;** τοῦτο **Lk 6:3.**—βιβλαρίδιον Hv 2, 1, 3.—W. ὅτι foll. **Mt 19:4; 21:16.**—W. question foll. ἀ. τί ἐποίησεν Δαυίδ **Mt 12:3; Mk 2:25.**—πῶς ἀναγινώσκεις; **Lk 10:26.**—Plays on words (cp. Pla., Ep. 2, 312d ἵνα ὁ ἀναγνοὺς μὴ γνῷ; Polyb. 23, 11, 1 μὴ μόνον ἀναγινώσκειν τὰς τραγῳδίας … ἀλλὰ καὶ γινώσκειν; POxy 1062, 13 [II AD] αὐτὴν δέ σοι τὴν ἐπιστολὴν πέμψω διὰ Σύρου, ἵνα αὐτὴν ἀναγνοῖς νήφων καὶ σαυτοῦ καταγνοῖς) γινώσκεις ἃ ἀναγινώσκεις; *do you understand what you are reading?* **Ac 8:30;** ἐπιστολὴ γινωσκομένη καὶ ἀναγινωσκομένη ὑπὸ πάντων ἀνθρώπων *known and read by everybody* **2 Cor 3:2;** cp. **1:13.**—Abs. ὁ ἀναγινώσκων (so Socratics p. 274, 26 Malherbe; PFay 20, 23; Sb 1019; 1020 al.; Sir Prol. ln. 4) νοείτω *let the reader consider (this)* **Mt 24:15, Mk 13:14** (b is also poss. here and in **Rv 1:3,** μακάριος ὁ ἀ. *blessed is the reader* [of this book]). εἰρήνη τῷ γράψαντι καὶ τῷ ἀναγινώσκοντι *peace to the writer and the reader* GJs 25:2. The obj. is usu. easy to supply: ἀναγνόντες (i.e. τὴν ἐπιστολήν) ἐχάρησαν **Ac 15:31.** ἀναγνοὺς (i.e. τὴν ἐπιστολήν) καὶ ἐπερωτήσας **23:34.** δύνασθε ἀναγινώσκοντες (i.e. ἃ προέγραψα) νοῆσαι **Eph 3:4.** ἵνα καὶ ὑμεῖς ἀναγνῶτε (i.e. τὴν ἐπιστολήν) **Col 4:16.**

ⓑ *read aloud* for public hearing (X., Cyr. 4, 5, 26 al.; PGrenf I, 37, 15 [II BC]; POxy 59, 8; PCairGoodsp 29 III, 1 a will; SIG 883, 27; 789, 48; LXX; En 13:4; EpArist 310; Jos., Ant. 4, 209 ἀ. τοὺς νόμους ἅπασι, cp. 12, 52; Just., D. 67, 3f; Mel., P. 1, 1; 11, 72) of scripture reading in the services of synagogue and Christian assembly (cp. Sb 7336, 29 [III AD] ἀναγνώστῃ=for the reader at a Sarapis festival, who prob. read accounts of Sarapis-miracles [Ael. Aristid. 45, 29fK.]). Of Jesus ἀνέστη ἀναγνῶναι *he stood up to read the scripture* (GDalman, Jesus-Jeshua, Eng. tr. 1929, 38–55; s. also Billerb. IV, 1, 153–88) **Lk 4:16.** Μωϋσῆς κατὰ πᾶν σάββατον ἀναγινωσκόμενος *read aloud every Sabbath* **Ac 15:21;** cp. **13:27.** ἡνίκα ἂν ἀναγινώσκηται Μωϋσῆς *whenever Moses is read* **2 Cor 3:15.** Letters of the apostles were read in Christian meetings at an early period (cp. Diod. S. 15, 10, 2 τὴν ἐπιστολὴν ἀναγνόντες=after they had read the letter aloud; cp. POxy 2787, 14 and 15 [II AD]) **Col 4:16; 1 Th 5:27** (the close of the 6th letter of Plato [323c] makes this request: ταύτην τ. ἐπιστολὴν πάντας ὑμᾶς ἀναγνῶναι χρή). ἀναγινώσκω ὑμῖν ἔντευξιν 2 Cl 19:1; παραβολάς Hv 5:5 (sense a above is also prob. here). Abs. v 1, 3, 3; 2, 4, 3. ἐτέλεσεν ἀναγινώσκουσα *she stopped reading (aloud)* v 1, 4, 1. Prob. **Mk 13:14** and **Rv 1:3** also belong here (s. a).—PGlaue, Die Vorlesung hl. Schriften im Gottesdienste I 1907.—B. 1284. M-M. TW. Sv.

ἀναγκάζω (denom. fr. ἀνάγκη) impf. ἠνάγκαζον; fut. ἀναγκάσω LXX; 1 aor. ἠνάγκασα, impv. ἀνάγκασον. Pass.: 1 aor. pass. ἠναγκάσθην; pf. pass. ptc. ἠναγκασμένη 4 Macc 15:7 (Soph., Hdt., Thu.+; ins, pap, LXX, TestSol; TestJob 12:2; EpArist; Philo, Aet. M. 136; Joseph.; Just.; POxy 1778 [Ar.] 14f).

❶ **to compel someone to act in a particular manner,** ***compel, force,*** of inner and outer compulsion; w. inf. foll. (Ps.-Pla., Sisyphus 1 p. 387b ξυμβουλεύειν αὐτοῖς ἠνάγκαζόν με=they tried to compel me to make common cause with them; Jos., Ant. 12, 384f; Crates p. 56, 12 Malherbe) 1 Cl 4:10. ἠνάγκαζον βλασφημεῖν *I tried to force them to blaspheme* **Ac 26:11.** τὰ ἔθνη ἀ. ἰουδαΐζειν *compel the Gentiles to live in the Judean manner* **Gal 2:14.** οὐκ ἠναγκάσθη περιτμηθῆναι *he was not compelled to be circumcised* **2:3** (see Jos., Vi. 113); cp. **6:12,** where mng. 2 is prob. ἠναγκάσθην ἐπικαλέσασθαι Καίσαρα *I was obliged to appeal to Caesar* **Ac 28:19** (cp. Mel., P. 94, 720 λέγειν ἀναγκάζομαι; BGU 180, 16). ἀ. αὐτοὺς πεισθῆναι σοι *I will compel them to obey you* Hm 12, 3, 3. W. εἴς τι for the inf. ἀναγκάζομαι εἰς τοῦτο *I am forced to do this* B 1:4. W. inf. understood **2 Cor 12:11.**

❷ weakened **strongly urge/invite,** ***urge upon, press*** (POxy 1069, 2; 20; cp. HPernot, Études sur la langue des Évang. 1927; ET 38, 1927, 103–8) w. acc. and inf. (Diog. L. 1, 26 τ. μητρὸς ἀναγκαζούσης αὐτὸν γῆμαι) ἠνάγκασεν τ. μαθητὰς ἐμβῆναι *he pressed the disciples to embark* **Mt 14:22; Mk 6:45.** W. acc. supplied **Lk 14:23.**—M-M. TW.

ἀναγκαῖος, α, ον (Hom. et al., in var. mngs.)—❶ ***necessary*** (as meeting need) τὰ μέλη τοῦ σώματος ἀ. ἐστιν *the members of the body are nec.* **1 Cor 12:22;** cp. 1 Cl 37:5; αἱ ἀ. χρεῖαι (Diod. S. 1, 34; IPriene 108, 80 [c. 129 BC]; POxy 56, 6; 1068, 16; Philo, Omn. Prob. Lib. 76; Ath. 22, 4 τῶν ἀναγκαίων 'genitals') *pressing needs* **Tit 3:14.**—Neut. ἀναγκαῖόν ἐστιν *it is necessary* w. inf. (and acc.) foll. (PFlor 132, 11 ὅπερ ἀναγκαῖόν σε ἦν γνῶναι. Philo, Migr. Abr. 82; Jos., Vi. 413; Just., D. 68, 4) **Ac 13:46.** ἀ. ἡγοῦμαι (PFay 111, 19; SIG 867, 9 ἀναγκαῖον ἡγησάμην … φανερὸν ποιῆσαι; 2 Macc 9:21) *I consider it necessary* **2 Cor 9:5; Phil 2:25.** ἀ. ἐστιν, μηδὲν πράσσειν ὑμᾶς ITr 2:2. ὅθεν ἀναγκαῖον (w. ἐστίν to be supplied, as EpArist 197; 205) ἔχειν τι τοῦτον *so this one must have someth.* **Hb 8:3.**—Comp. (PLond I, 42, 31 p. 31; Witkowski 36, 21) ἀναγκαιότερόν ἐστιν *it is more necessary* **Phil 1:24.**—Subst. of defecation δι' αὐτῶν μόνων τῶν ἀ. Papias (3:2).

❷ ***intimate,*** as Lat. necessarius of relatives and friends τοὺς ἀ. φίλους *close friends* **Ac 10:24** (cp. Eur., Andr. 671; Dio Chrys. 3, 120; SIG 1109, 51; POslo 60, 5 [II AD]; PFlor 142, 2; BGU 625, 26; Jos., Ant. 7, 350; 11, 254).—EDNT. M-M. TW. Spicq. Sv.

ἀναγκαστῶς (s. ἀναγκάζω; Ps.-Pla., Axioch. 366a) adv. fr. ἀναγκαστός (Hdt. et al.; Jos., Ant. 18, 37) ***by compulsion*** (opp. ἑκουσίως) ποιμαίνειν **1 Pt 5:2** (the model of the volunteering civic-minded pers. underlies the line of thought).—M-M.

ἀνάγκη, ης, ἡ (Hom.+; ins, pap, LXX, En; PsSol 5:6; TestJob 12:3; TestJos 2:4; ApcSed 10:4; ApcMos 25; Philo, Joseph., Ar., Just.; Mel. fgm. 6, 5; Ath.) never in NT in the exceptional sense of 'fate' (e.g. Eur., Ph. 1000).

❶ **necessity or constraint as inherent in the nature of things, *necessity, pressure*** of any kind, a divine dispensation, some hoped-for advantage, custom, duty, etc. (Appian, Bell. Civ. 5, 17 §68 ἀ. νόμων; Musaeus 289 of love; Crates p. 54, 15 al. Malherbe; SibOr 3, 101; 296; Just., D. 44, 11) ἄνευ ζυγοῦ ἀνάγκης *without the yoke of necessity* B 2:6. ἀνάγκη (sc. ἐστὶν) *it is necessary, inevitable, one must* w. inf., or acc. and inf. (Hdt. 2, 35; SIG 888, 79; BGU 665 II, 16; Just., A I, 21, 4 al.; Ath. 17, 1 al.; Did., Gen. 104, 29) ἀ. (ἐστὶν [v.l.]) ἐλθεῖν τὰ σκάνδαλα *temptations must come* **Mt 18:7.** διὸ ἀ. (sc. ἐστὶν) *therefore it is nec. (for you) to be subject* **Ro 13:5.** θάνατον ἀ. (sc. ἐστὶν) φέρεσθαι τοῦ διαθεμένου *the death of the testator must be announced* **Hb 9:16;** cp. vs. **23.** W. ἐστί and without inf. εἰ ἀ. ἐστί Hs 9, 9, 3. ἐὰν ᾖ ἀ. D 12:2—ἀ. ἔχω w. inf. (Plut., Cato Min. 24, 6; Jos., Ant. 16, 290, Vi. 171 et al.; TestJob 10:3; 12:3 al.; POxy 1061, 4 [22 BC]; PFlor 278 IV, 23; cp. New Docs 1, 45) *I must* ἰδεῖν αὐτόν **Lk 14:18;** ἀπολύειν **23:16 [17] v.l;** γράψαι ὑμῖν **Jd 3;** θυσίας ἀναφέρειν **Hb 7:27;** αἰτεῖσθαι Hs 5, 4, 5; ἐρωτᾶν 9, 14, 4; cp. 9, 16, 2. Without inf. μὴ ἔχων ἀ. **1 Cor 7:37.**—ἀ. μοι ἐπίκειται (Il. 6, 458) *I am under obligation* **9:16.**—W. prep. ἐξ ἀνάγκης *under pressure* (trag., Thu.; Epict. 2, 20, 1; Jos., Bell. 5, 568; Ath., R. 66, 17; Did., Gen. 75, 21; POxy 237 IV, 33; PIand 19, 1) **2 Cor 9:7;** *necessarily* (logically) (Diod. S. 1, 80, 3; Dio Chrys. 21 [38], 31; 34; Philo, Aet. M. 21; 52) **Hb 7:12;** Hs 7:3. For this pleonastically δεῖ ἐξ ἀ. m 6, 2, 8; s 9, 9, 2. ὡς κατὰ ἀνάγκην (opp. κατὰ ἑκούσιον) *as it were, by pressure* **Phlm 14** (cp. X., Cyr. 4, 3, 7; Artem. 5, 23; EpArist 104; 2 Macc 15:2; Jos., Ant. 3, 223; Ar.; Just., A I, 30, 1; Ath. 24, 2; PCairMasp 66, 2).

❷ **a state of distress or trouble, *distress, calamity, pressure*** (characteristic of later Gk.: Diod. S. 10, 4, 6 [mortal danger]; Appian, Bell. Civ. 5, 40 §167 ἐσχάτη ἀ.; LXX; Jos., Bell. 5, 571; Ant. 2, 67. So as loanw. in rabb.) of distress in the last days ἀ. μεγάλη **Lk 21:23.** ἡ ἐνεστῶσα ἀ. *the present distress* **1 Cor 7:26** (the expr. 'present distress' is found in Epict. 3, 26, 7; 3 Macc 1:16 v.l. and PGM 4, 526f. In Antiphon 6, 25 the present coercion is called ἡ παροῦσα ἀνάγκη.—See KBenz, TGl 10, 1918, 388ff; PTischleder, ibid. 12, 1920, 225ff). W. θλῖψις (like Job 15:24) **1 Th 3:7.** Pl. *pressures* (Antiphon 6, 25; Herodas 5, 59; Diod. S. 4, 43, 5; 10, 17, 1; SIG 521, 23 [III BC]; Cat. Cod. Astr. VII 143, 23; VIII/3, 182, 17; 185, 27; LXX; Philo, Rer. Div. Her. 41; Jos., Ant. 16, 253; TestJos 2:4) w. θλίψεις, στενοχωρίαι et al. **2 Cor 6:4;** w. διωγμοί and στενοχωρίαι **12:10** (but see 3 below). In Paul's recitals of woe there surfaces the theme of the endangered benefactor who risks much for his public (s. AFridrichsen, Zum Stil des Paulinischen Peristasenkatalogs: SymbOsl 7, 1928, 25–29; Danker, Benefactor 363–64). ἐξ ἀναγκῶν ἐξαιρεῖσθαι *rescue from calamities* 1 Cl 56:8 (Job 5:19). For this ἐξ ἀναγκῶν λυτροῦσθαι τοὺς δούλους τοῦ θεοῦ Hm 8:10.

❸ concr. for abstr. **compulsion by forcible means, *torture*** (ref. in AFridrichsen, ConNeot 9, '44, 28f and L-S-J-M s.v. 3); this mng. is prob. in some passages, e.g. **2 Cor 12:10** (s. 2 above).—HSchreckenburg, Ananke, '64.—B. 638. DELG. DDD s.v. Ananke. M-M. TW. Sv.

ἄναγνος, ον (ἁγνός 'pure'; trag. et al.; Ramsay, CB I/1, 149 no. 41 [=ritually unclean]; Philo, Cher. 94; Jos., C. Ap. 1, 306; SibOr 3, 496f) ***unchaste*** (w. μιαρός as Antiphon, Tetral. 1, 1, 10 Blass μιαρὸν κἄναγνον) συμπλοκαί *embraces* in sexual intercourse 1 Cl 30:1 (cp. Ptolem., Apotel. 3, 14, 17 τὰς συνουσίας ἀνάγνους).—DELG s.v. ἅζομαι.

ἀναγνωρίζω 1 aor. mid. ἀνεγνωρισάμην (γνωρίζω 'make known'; Pla., Polit. 258a; Herm. Wr. 1, 18; Gen. 45:1) **learn to know again, *become reacquainted*** *see again* ταύτην Hv 1, 1, 1. *Be recognized* ἀνεγνωρίσθη Ἰωσὴφ τ. ἀδελφοῖς αὐτοῦ **Ac 7:13** (Gen 45:1).—DELG s.v. γιγνώσκω 225.

ἀνάγνωσις, εως, ἡ (Hdt. et al.; Sir Prol. 10, 17; EpArist, Philo; Jos., C. Ap. 2, 147) prim. sense 'knowing again'; then 'reading'.

❶ **the process of reading someth. written, *reading*** (s. ἀναγι(γ)ώσκω) of public reading (Pla.; SIG 695, 81; pap, LXX [1 Esdr 9:48; 2 Esdr 18:8]; EpArist 127; 283; 305) of the reading of the law and prophets in the synagogue (cp. the synag. ins in Jerusalem, SEG VIII, 170, 4 συναγωγὴν εἰς ἀνάγνωσιν νόμου) μετὰ τὴν ἀ. τ. νόμου καὶ τ. προφητῶν **Ac 13:15.** ἡ ἀ. τῆς παλαιᾶς διαθήκης *the public reading of the OT* **2 Cor 3:14.** The Christians also knew public reading πρόσεχε τῇ ἀ., τῇ παρακλήσει, τῇ διδασκαλίᾳ *devote yourself to (public) reading, exhorting, teaching* **1 Ti 4:13.** Cp. WBauer, D. Wortgottesdienst d. ältesten Christen 1930, 39–54.

❷ **the content of what is read, *reading*** ἤρεσέν σοι ἡ ἀ. μου; *did my reading* (=what I read) *please you?* Hv 1, 4, 2.—M-M. TW.

ἀναγραφή, ῆς, ἡ (γραφή 'writing'; Pla., X. et al.; ins, pap, EpArist, Philo; Tat. 31, 4) 'that which is written up', pl. ***public records*** (Polyb.; Diod. S. 1, 31, 7 ἐν ταῖς ἱεραῖς ἀναγραφαῖς; Plut.; Jos., C. Ap. 1, 28; 2 Macc 2, 13; GDI 1743, 10) ἐπισκέπτεσθαι τὰς ἀ. τῶν χρόνων *examine the records of the dates* 1 Cl 25:5 (Diod. S. 16, 51, 2 of the ancient documents in Egyptian temples, a t.t. for official publications; s. AWilhelm, Sd.-Schrift österr. Archäol. Inst. 7, 1909, 271ff).

ἀναγράφω fut. 1 pl. ἀναγράψομεν (Tat. 41, 3); 1 aor. ἀνέγραψα. Pass.: 2 aor. ἀνεγράφην (Just., Tat.); pf. 3 sg. ἀναγέγραπται (Hdt.+) **to make an official record, *record, register*** (legal t.t. SIG 679, 19) εἰ αὕτη μοι ἡ ἁμαρτία ἀναγράφεται *if this sin is recorded against me* (in the judgment book—Aesop, Fab. 317, 17 P.=Babrius 75 L-P. of recording in books in the underworld) Hv 1, 2, 1.—ἀναγραφῖσα for ἀνατραφῖσα: transcriptional error in GJs 13:2; 15:3.

ἀνάγω fut. ἀνάξω LXX; 2 aor. ἀνήγαγον; 1 aor. pass. ἀνήχθην (Hom.+; ins, pap, LXX, En 28:3; TestSol, TestAbr, Test12Patr, Philo, Joseph., Just.; Mel., fgm. 9, 6; Ath. 11, 2 ἐπὶ παρρησίαν ἀναγαγεῖν 'raise [my voice] to a pitch of boldness').

❶ **to lead or bring from a lower to a higher point, *lead, bring up*** **Lk 4:5** (εἰς ὄρος ὑψηλόν v.l.); **Mt 17:1** D; εἰς Ἱεροσόλυμα **Lk 2:22** (Jos., Bell. 1, 96). ἀνήχθη εἰς τὴν ἔρημον *he was led up into the desert,* from the Jordan (below sea level) into the highland **Mt 4:1,** unless it be thought that he was 'snatched away'; cp. **1 Cor 12:2 v.l.** ὡς ἀνήγεσθε (Mel., P. 103, 798 εἰς τὰ ὑψηλὰ τῶν οὐρανῶν). εἰς τὸ ὑπερῷον *to the room upstairs* **Ac 9:39.** εἰς τὸν οἶκον *into the house* proper, since the rooms in the cellar served as the prison **16:34.** ἐν ναῷ *in the temple* GJs 7:1.—ἀ. ἐκ νεκρῶν *bring up from the (realm of the) dead,* represented as subterranean **Ro 10:7; Hb 13:20** (cp. Lucian, Dial. Mort. 23, 6; 1 Km 2:6; 28:11; Tob 13:2; Ps 29:4; Just., D. 32, 3 ἀνάγοντα αὐτὸν [Christ] ἀπὸ τῆς γῆς).—Fig. (with εἴς τι, as Joannes Sard., Comm. in Aphth. p. 4, 10 Rabe [1928]) of love τὸ ὕψος εἰς ὃ ἀνάγει ἡ ἀγάπη 1 Cl 49:4.

❷ **bring up for judicial process, *bring before,*** legal t.t. (X., Hell. 3, 3, 11; Polyb. 40, 4, 2; SIG 799, 24 [38 AD] ἀναχθέντα εἰς τ. δῆμον; OGI 483, 185 [Pergamum]; PMagd 33, 8; PTebt 43, 19; TestAbr A 15 p. 95, 9 [Stone p. 38]) τινά τινι (Jos., Ant. 12, 390) **Ac 12:4.**

❸ **to bring an offering, *offer up,*** ἀ. θυσίαν (a festive procedure is suggested by the use of this term, cp. Hdt. 2, 60; 6, 111;

OGI 764, 47 [c. 127 BC] ἀναγαγὼν . . . ταύρους δύο; 3 Km 3:15; Philo, Agr. 127, Mos. 2, 73 al.) **Ac 7:41.**

❹ as a nautical t.t. (ἀ. τὴν ναῦν put a ship to sea), mid. or pass. ἀνάγεσθαι **to begin to go by boat,** ***put out to sea*** (Hdt., Demosth., also Polyb. 1, 21, 4; 1, 23, 3 al.; pap [Mayser 380]; Jos., Bell. 3, 502): ἀνήχθημεν ἐν πλοίῳ *we put to sea in a ship* **Ac 28:11.** ἀ. ἀπὸ τῆς Πάφου (cp. Epict. 3, 21, 12 ἀ. ἀπὸ λιμένος) *put out from Paphos* **Ac 13:13;** cp. **16:11; 18:21; 27:21.** ἐκεῖθεν (Jos., Ant. 14, 377) **27:4, 12.** W. the course given εἰς τὴν Συρίαν **20:3** (cp. BGU 1200, 14 [I BC] ἀ. εἰς Ἰταλίαν). ἐπὶ τὴν Ἆσσον vs. **13.** Abs. ἀνήχθησαν *they set sail* **Lk 8:22,** cp. **Ac 21:1f; 27:2; 28:10;** AcPl Ha 7, 13 (Just., D. 142, 2).

❺ **to put back into a former state or condition,** ***restore, bring back*** fig. (in pap of improvement of the soil) τοὺς ἀσθενοῦντας περὶ τὸ ἀγαθόν *restore those who are weak in goodness* 2 Cl 17:2.—M-M. TW.

ἀναγωγεύς, έως, ὁ (on the form ἀγωγεύς s. DELG s.v. ἄγω 18) (lit. 'that which brings up', so of straps for holding a sandal in place Ael., VH 9, 11; Athen. 543f) ***one who leads upward*** (Proclus, on Pla., Tim. I p. 34, 20 Diehl, of Hermes; Hymni 1, 34 [Orphica p. 277 Abel], of Helios ψυχῶν ἀναγωγεύς), only fig. ἡ πίστις ὑμῶν ἀ. ὑμῶν IEph 9:1 (s. Hdb. ad loc.) the 'windlass' of Lghtf. et al. seems unlikely.—TW.

ἀναδείκνυμι fut. ἀναδείξω LXX; 1 aor. ἀνέδειξα; pf. ἀναδέδειχα LXX. Pass.: fut. ἀναδειχθήσομαι; 1 aor. ἀνεδείχθην; perf. ptc. ἀναδεδειγμένος (all these pass. LXX) (Soph., Hdt. et al.; ins, LXX; TestJos 2:7; Philo, Sacr. Abel. 35; Joseph., Tat.) 'show forth'.

❶ **to make someth. known by clear indication,** ***show clearly, reveal someth. hidden*** (cp. IAndrosIsis, Ios 19 Peek p. 123; 2 Macc 2:8; SibOr 3, 15) τινά **Ac 1:24;** πῶς Ox 1081, 31f (SJCh 90, 70f). W. ἐν *exhibit, display someth. in someth.* ἵνα δικαιοσύνης ναὸν ἐν τῷ τοίῳ σώματι ἀναδείξῃ *so as to display the temple of uprightness in that selfsame body* AcPlCor 2:17.

❷ **to assign to a task or position,** ***appoint, commission*** (freq. as administrative term [s. next entry]; Polyb. 4, 48, 3; 4, 51, 3; Diod. S. 1, 66, 1; 13, 98, 1; Plut., Caes. 725 [37, 2]; OGI 625, 7; PErl 18, 19; Da 1:11, 20; 1 Esdr 8:23; 2 Macc 9:23, 25 al.; Jos., Ant. 14, 280; 20, 227; Tat. 7, 2 θεόν as God) ἀνέδειξεν (ἐνέδ. P^{75}) ὁ κύριος ἑτέρους ἑβδομήκοντα **Lk 10:1.**—EPeterson, Deissmann Festschr. 1927, 320–26.—M-M. TW.

ἀνάδειξις, εως, ἡ (Polyb. et al.; ERoberts and EGardner, Introd. to Gk. Epigraphy II 1905, 119; SB 7346, 8 [?]; Sir 43:6) ***commissioning, installation*** (t.t. in ref. to public recognition of an appointed official Polyb. 15, 26, 7; Plut., Mar. 804 [8, 5]; s. ἀναδείκνυμι 2) ἕως ἡμέρας ἀναδείξεως αὐτοῦ πρὸς τὸν Ἰσραήλ *until the day when he was commissioned before Israel* as forerunner of the Messiah (cp. Lk 3:2; Diod. S. 1, 85 of Osiris) **Lk 1:80.**—EBickerman, Ἀνάδειξις: Mélanges EBoisacq I '37, 117–24. DELG s.v. δείκνυμι. TW. Spicq. Sv.

ἀναδέχομαι 1 aor. ἀνεδεξάμην (Hom.+).—❶ **to experience someth. by being accepting,** ***accept, receive*** (SIG 962, 65 [IV BC]; PEleph 29, 12 [III BC]; PTebt 329, 19; BGU 194, 11 al.; 2 Macc 6:19; 8:36; TestLevi 16:3) τὰς ἐπαγγελίας **Hb 11:17.** *Take* a burden *upon oneself* (Diod. S. 15, 51, 1 ἀ. τ. πόλεμον, cp. Polyb. 1, 88, 12; Plut., Eumen. 586 [6, 3]; Epict. 3, 24, 64; SIG 685, 30 [139 BC] ἀ. πᾶσαν κακοπαθίαν; IXanthos 7, 67, 25f ἀναδεξάμενος τὴν φροντίδα; SB 7738, 13 πόνον ἀ.; Jos., Bell. 3, 4; 14; Just., D. 95, 2 τὰς πάντων κατάρας) τὸ βάρος Dg 10:6; τὰς ἁμαρτίας 9:2 (cp. Demosth. 19, 36 ἁμαρτήματα).

❷ **to extend hospitality to,** ***receive, welcome*** of guests (oft. in diplomatic parlance, expressive of the Gr-Rom. reciprocity system e.g. OGI 339, 20 [II BC] τάς τε πρεσβείας ἀνεδέχετο προθύμως; 441, 9) **Ac 28:7.**—DELG s.v. δέχομαι. M-M. TW. Spicq.

ἀναδίδωμι fut. 3 sg. ἀναδώσει Sir 1:22; 2 aor. ἀνέδωκα Just.; 2 aor. ptc. ἀναδούς; pf. 3 sg. ἀναδέδωκε Just., A II, 2, 8 (Pind. et al.; ins, pap; Sir 1:23; Joseph., Just.) ***deliver, hand over*** τινί τι (Philo, Aet. M. 62; Jos., Ant. 1, 249; βιβλίδιον Just., A I, 29, 2; A II, 2, 8) ἀ. τὴν ἐπιστολὴν τῷ ἡγεμόνι **Ac 23:33** (the same bureaucratese in Polyb. 29, 10, 7; Diod. S. 11, 45, 3; IG XIV, 830, 22; PTebt 448; PFay 130, 15). Of the transmission of an apology to Hadrian Qua (1).—M-M.

ἀναζάω 1 aor. ἀνέζησα (Nicander [II BC] in epic form -ζώω fgm. 70, 8 [Athen. 4, 11 p. 133d]; Chariton 3, 8, 9; Artem. 4, 82; Paradox. Flor. 6; CIG 2566, 2; JosAs 19:3 cod. A for ἀνεζωοπύρησαν; Dssm., LO 75f [LAE 94ff]; Nägeli 47; DELG s.v. ζώω) 'come (back) to life'.

❶ **to come to life out of a condition of death**—ⓐ lit. ***be resurrected*** (so in the places cited above) of the dead **Rv 20:5** t.r., an Erasmian rdg. without known ms. evidence; s. RBorger, TRu 52, '87, 57 (ParJer 7:18); of Christ **Ro 14:9 v.l.**

ⓑ fig. ***be alive again,*** of one morally and spiritually dead ὁ υἱός μου νεκρὸς ἦν καὶ ἀνέζησεν **Lk 15:24** (v.l. ἔζησεν); **32 v.l.** (ἔζησεν in the text).

❷ **to function after being dormant,** ***spring into life*** (with loss of the force of ἀνά; s. ἀναβλέπω 2aβ) ἡ ἁμαρτία ἀνέζησεν *sin became alive* **Ro 7:9.**—M-M. TW.

ἀναζέω (ζέω 'boil, seethe') intr. (so Soph., Hippocr. et al.; Περὶ ὕψους p. 67, 5 V.=44, 4 [206 verso]; Plut., Art. 1019 [16, 6], Mor. 728b; Ex 9:9, 10; 2 Macc 9:9) ***boil up*** of mud, etc., in the netherworld ApcPt 16, 31.

ἀναζητέω (ζητέω 'search') impf. ἀνεζήτουν, 1 aor. ἀνεζήτησα LXX, pass. 3 sg. ἀνεζητήθη 2 Macc 13:21 (Hdt. 1, 137; Thu. 2, 8, 3; ins, pap, LXX; TestSol 12:1 C; TestAbr B 113, 26 [Stone p. 74]; Philo, Somn. 2, 61; Joseph.; Just., D. 5, 6; Tat. 15, 1) **to try to locate by search,** ***look, search*** τινά ***for someone*** (in pap of criminals and fugitive slaves: PHib 71, 9 [245/244 BC]; PCairZen 310, 4 [III BC], PRein 17, 13; PFlor 83, 12; also 2 Macc 13:21; Jos., Bell, 3, 340, Ant. 9, 134) Σαῦλον **Ac 11:25.** ἀνεζήτουν αὐτόν **Lk 2:44;** cp. **45** (in the latter passage v.l. ζητοῦντες). A lost work of literature MPol 22:3.—M-M.

ἀναζώννυμι (ζώννυμι 'to gird') 1 aor. mid. ἀνεζωσάμην (Didym. Gramm. [I BC/I AD] in Athen. 4, 17, 139e; Pr 31:17 τὴν ὀσφύν; Judg 18:16 B; Philo, Leg. All. 2, 28; 3, 153) ***bind up, gird up,*** lit. of long garments to facilitate work or walking (Dio Chrys. 55 [72], 2 ἀνεζωσμένοι; Achilles Tat. 8, 12, 1; Judg 18:16 cod. B ἀνεζωσμένοι; Lat. alte praecinctus), then fig. ἀναζωσάμενοι τὰς ὀσφύας τῆς διανοίας ὑμῶν *when you have girded the loins of your mind,* i.e. prepared for action **1 Pt 1:13;** Pol 2:1.

ἀναζωοπυρέω 2 Ti 1:6 cod. D and JosAs 19:3. S. next entry.

ἀναζωπυρέω (ζωπυρέω 'kindle into flame') 1 aor. ἀνεζωπύρησα; lit. 'cause to blaze again'; usu. fig., and in our lit. only so.

❶ trans. (Pla., X. et al.) **to cause to begin again,** ***rekindle*** τὶ someth. (Plut., Per. 152 [1, 4], Pomp. 645 [49, 5]; Iambl., Vi. Pyth. 16, 70; PGM 13, 739; Jos., Bell. 1, 444 [pass. ὁ ἔρως], Ant. 8, 234; Iren. 3, 11, 8 [Harv II 47, 6]) τὸ χάρισμα τοῦ θεοῦ *rekindle the gift of God* **2 Ti 1:6.** ἀναζωπυρησάτω ἡ πίστις αὐτοῦ *let faith in God be rekindled* 1 Cl 27:3.

❷ intr. (Dionys. Hal. 7, 54; Plut., Timol. 247 [24, 1], Pomp. 640 [41, 2]; Gen 45:27; 1 Macc 13:7; JosAs 19:3 cod B ἀναζωοπύρησαν; Jos., Ant. 11, 240) **to take on new life, *kindle into flame*** ἀναζωπυρήσαντες ἐν αἵματι θεοῦ *inflamed with new life through God's blood* IEph 1:1.—See Anz 284f.—M-M.

ἀναθάλλω (θάλλω 'sprout, grow') 1 aor. pl. ἀνεθήλαμεν Just., D. 119, 3; 2 aor. ἀνέθαλον (W-S. §13, 10; B-D-F §101 s.v. θάλλειν; Rob. 348).

❶ intr. **to be in a state identical with a previous state, *grow up again, bloom again*** (lit. of plants, e.g. schol. to Nicander, Ther. 677. Also Oenomaus in Eus., PE 5, 34, 14 end γῆ ἀνέθαλεν=the earth bloomed again; PGM 4, 1611) also fig. (Aelian, VH 5, 4; Ps 27:7; Wsd 4:4; Sir 46:12; 49:10; Just., D. 119, 3 λαὸς ἕτερος ἀνεθήλαμεν) ἡ ἐσκοτωμένη διάνοια ἡμῶν ἀναθάλλει εἰς τὸ φῶς *our darkened mind grows up again into the light* (like a plant) 1 Cl 36:2. For **Phil 4:10** s. 2.

❷ factitive **to cause to be in a state, identical with a previous state, *cause to grow/bloom again*** (lit. Sir 50:10; Ezk 17:24 and fig. Sir 1:18; 11:22)—**Phil 4:10** both 1 and 2 are prob. ἀνεθάλετε τὸ ὑπὲρ ἐμοῦ φρονεῖν either: *you have revived, as far as your care for me is concerned* or: *you have revived your care for me.*—M-M.

ἀνάθεμα, ατος, τό =ἀνατεθειμένον (ἀνατίθημι) 'something placed' or 'set up', H. Gk. form for the older (Hom. et al.) ἀνάθημα (Moeris 188; Phryn. 249 Lob.; s. SIG index).

❶ **that which is dedicated as a votive offering, *a votive offering*** set up in a temple (Plut., Pelop. 291 [25, 7]; 2 Macc 2:13; Philo, Mos. 1, 253) **Lk 21:5 v.l.**

❷ **that which has been cursed, *cursed, accursed*** (LXX as a rule=חֵרֶם: what is 'devoted to the divinity' can be either consecrated or accursed. The mng. of the word in the other NT passages moves definitely in the direction of the latter [like Num 21:3; Dt 7:26; Josh 6:17; 7:12; Judg 1:17; Zech 14:11, but also the curse-tablets from Megara, as IDefixWünsch 1, 17]) οὐδεὶς ἐν πνεύματι θεοῦ λαλῶν λέγει· ἀνάθεμα Ἰησοῦς *no one who speaks by God's Spirit says 'Jesus be cursed'* **1 Cor 12:3** (on this subject Laud. Therap. 22 ὅταν ὁ δαίμων ἀλλοιώσας τὸν ἐνεργούμενον, ἐκεῖνος ὅλος λαλεῖ, τὸ στόμα τοῦ πάσχοντος ἴδιον τεχναζόμενος ὄργανον=when the divinity has altered the one it has influenced, then it is altogether the divinity that speaks, for it has skillfully made the victim's mouth its own instrument; NBrox, BZ n.s. 12, '68, 103–11). As a formula ἀνάθεμα ἔστω **Gal 1:8f.** For this ἤτω ἀ. **1 Cor 16:22.** Likew. ηὐχόμην ἀνάθεμα εἶναι αὐτὸς ἐγὼ ἀπὸ τοῦ Χριστοῦ *I could wish that I myself would be accursed (and therefore separated) from Christ* **Ro 9:3** (CSchneider, D. Volks- u. Heimatgefühl b. Pls: Christentum u. Wissensch. 8, '32, 1–14; PBratsiotis, Eine Notiz zu Rö 9:3 u. 10:1: NovT 5, '62, 299f).

❸ **the content that is expressed in a curse, *a curse.*** The expr. ἀναθέματι ἀνεθεματίσαμεν ἑαυτοὺς μηδενὸς γεύσασθαι **Ac 23:14** means that the conspirators bound themselves to the plot with a dreadful oath, so that if they failed the curse would fall upon them (ἀ. ἀναθεματίζειν as Dt 13:15; 20:17). S. Dssm., LO 74 (LAE 92f); Nägeli 49; Schürer II 432f; Billerb. IV 293–333: D. Synagogenbann.—S. also ἀνάθημα, a spelling that oft. alternates w. ἀνάθεμα in the texts, in so far as the fine distinction betw. ἀνάθημα='votive offering' and ἀνάθεμα='a thing accursed' is not observed.—GBornkamm, Das Ende des Gesetzes[4] '63, 123–32; KHofmann, RAC I 427–30.—EDNT I 80f. M-M. TW. Sv.

ἀναθεματίζω (s. ἀνάθεμα and DELG s.v. τίθημι p. 1117) fut. ἀναθεματιῶ LXX; 1 aor. ἀνεθεμάτισα. Pass. fut. 3 sg. ἀναθεματισθήσεται 2 Esdr 10:8; pf. ptc. ἀναθεματισμένον Num. 18:14 (LXX mostly=carry out a curse: Num 21:2f; Dt 13:16; 20:17; Josh 6:21 al.) **to invoke consequences if what one says is not true**

ⓐ trans. ***put under a curse*** τινά *someone* (cp. curse-tablets from Megara [IDefixWünsch 1, 5, 8, s. ἀνάθεμα 2]) pleonastically ἀναθέματι ἀ. ἑαυτόν **Ac 23:14** s. ἀνάθεμα 3; ἀ. ἑαυτόν vss. **12, 21, 13 v.l.** (cp. En 6:4 ἀναθεματίσωμεν πάντες ἀλλήλους μὴ … μέχρις οὗ …; ἀνεθεμάτισαν ἀλλήλους vs. 5).

ⓑ intr. ***curse*** ἤρξατο ἀναθεματίζειν καὶ ὀμνύναι means that Peter put himself under curses and took oaths in the course of his denial **Mk 14:71** (OSeitz, TU 73, '59, 516–19; HMerkel, CFDMoule Festschr., '70, 66–71).—M-M. TW.

ἀναθεωρέω look at again and again = 'examine, observe carefully' (so both lit. and fig. Theophr., HP 8, 6, 2; Diod. S. 12, 15, 1 ἐξ ἐπιπολῆς θεωρούμενος 'examining superficially' in contrast to ἀναθεωρούμενος καὶ μετ' ἀκριβείας ἐξεταζόμενος; 2, 5, 5; 14, 109, 2; Lucian, Vit. Auct. 2, Necyom. 15; Plut., Cato Min. 765 [14, 3], Mor. 1119b).

❶ lit. **to examine someth. carefully, *look carefully at*** ἀναθεωρῶν τὰ σεβάσματα ὑμῶν *I looked carefully at the objects of your devotion* **Ac 17:23.**

❷ fig. **to give careful thought to, *consider,*** of spiritual things τὶ (Philostrat., Vi. Apollon. 2, 39 p. 81, 17) ὧν ἀναθεωροῦντες τὴν ἔκβασιν τῆς ἀναστροφῆς *considering the outcome of their lives* **Hb 13:7.**

ἀνάθημα, ατος, τό (ἀνατίθημι 'to set up'; on the forms ἀνάθημα and ἀνάθεμα s. DELG s.v. τίθημι) (Hom.+) **a dedication to a deity, *votive offering*** (since Soph., Ant. 286; Hdt. 1, 14; 92; ins, pap; 3 Macc 3:17; Jdth 16:19; TestSol 2:1 D; EpArist 40; Philo; Jos., Bell. 6, 335, Ant. 17, 156 al.) **Lk 21:5** (the expr. used here, ἀναθήμασι κοσμεῖν: Hdt. 1, 183, 3; Ps.-Pla., Alcib. 2, 12, 148c; Epict. in Stob. 59 Sch.; 2 Macc 9:16). S. ἀνάθεμα.—M-M. TW.

ἀναίδεια, ας, ἡ also -εία, -ία (αἰδώς 'respect, self-respect'; Hom. et al.; PCairZen 534, 21 [III BC]; Sir 25:22; Jos., Bell. 1, 224, Ant. 17, 119; SibOr 4, 36; on the spelling s. Kühner-Bl. II 276, 1; B-D-F §23) **lack of sensitivity to what is proper, carelessness about the good opinion of others, *shamelessness, impertinence, impudence, ignoring of convention*** (a fundamental cultural consideration in the Gr-Rom. world, here with focus on tradition of hospitality) **Lk 11:8,** either of the one who is doing the calling out (simply εἶπον vs. 5) to his friend within, in which case the 'shamelessness' consists in disturbing the peace at an inappropriate hour *shameless disturbance* (ἀ. itself does not mean 'persistence', of which the text make no explicit mention; but many translations draw semantic support from the explanation—cp. vs. 6, where 'knocking' is introduced—and render 'persistence') or of the sleepy neighbor, who does not wish to lose face by shameless disregard of conventions concerning hospitality (s. NLevison, Exp. 9th ser. 3, 1925, 456–60 and AFridrichsen, SymbOsl 13, '34, 40–43; AJohnson, JETS 22, '79, 123–31; DCatchpole, JTS 34, '83, 407–24 [lit.]). On shame culture in Lk s. DDaube, in: Paul and Paulinism (Festschr. CK-Barrett), ed. MHooker, SWilson '82, 355–72. In gener. s. entire issue of Semeia 68, '96 ('Honor and Shame in the World of the Bible').—M-M. TW. Spicq.

ἀναιδεύομαι 1 aor. ptc. ἀναιδευσάμενος (s. prec. and DELG s.v. αἴδομαι; Aristoph., Eq. 397; Philod., Rhet. I 251 Sudh.; Phryn. 66f Lob.; PRyl 141, 19 [37 AD]; Pr 7:13 Theod.) lit. 'be shameless', **to be unconcerned about convention,** ***be unabashed, bold*** ἀ. αὐτὴν ἐπηρώτησα *unabashed, I asked her* Hv 3, 7, 5.

ἀναιδής, ές (s. ἀναίδεια; Hom. et al.; OGI 665, 16 [adv.]; PLond II, 342, 14 [185 AD] p. 174; LXX; Test12Patr) ***shameless, bold*** (Jos., Bell. 6, 337; Just., D. 105, 3; Mel., HE 4, 26, 5) ἀ. εἶ *you are shameless* Hv 3, 3, 2; w. ἰταμός (as Menand., Epitr. 527 S. [351 Kö.) and πολύλαλος m 11:12.

ἀναίρεσις, εως, ἡ (αἱρέω 'grasp, seize', s. also next entry; var. aspects of 'removal': Eur., Thu. et al.; TestSol 13:4; TestJud 23:3; TestGad 2:4; Philo, Aet. M. 5 al.) ***murder, killing*** (X., Hell. 6, 3, 5; Plut., Mor. 1051d; Herodian 2, 13, 1; Num 11:15; Jdth 15:4; 2 Macc 5:13; Jos., Ant. 5, 165, Vi. 21; TestJud 23:3; GrBar 4:9; Tat. 10, 3) ἦν συνευδοκῶν τῇ ἀναιρέσει αὐτοῦ (Saul) *consented to his murder* **Ac 8:1** (**22:20 v.l.** infl. by 8:1); **13:28** D.—M-M.

ἀναιρέω (s. prec.) fut. ἀναιρήσω and ἀνελῶ (B-D-F §74, 3), the latter (Dionys. Hal. 11, 18, 2; Jdth 7:13; Just., D. 112, 2 [ἀνεῖλε A]) formed after 2 aor. ἀνεῖλον, which appears also in the forms (B-D-F §81, 3) ἀνεῖλα (ἀνείλατε **Ac 2:23,** ἀνεῖλαν **10:39**); subj. ἀνέλω; mid. ἀνειλόμην (v.l.) and ἀνειλάμην (ἀνείλατο **7:21** [-ετο v.l.]; cp. CIG 4137, 3; Ex 2:5, 10; B-D-F §81, 3; s. W-S. §13, 13; Mlt-H. 226 s.v. αἱρέω); fut. pass. ἀναιρεθήσομαι LXX; 1 aor. pass ἀνῃρέθην; pf. act. inf. ἀνῃρηκέναι (Just., D. 73, 6); pf. pass. ἀνῄρημαι LXX (also Just., Tat., Mel.) (Hom.+).

❶ **to remove or take away,** ***take away*** of things πνοήν 1 Cl 21:9. *Do away with, abolish* (Aeschin. 3, 39 νόμον; Isaeus 1, 14; Polyb. 31, 20, 3; TestGad 5:3 τὸ ζῆλος; Dio Chrys. 59 [76], 2) **Hb 10:9** (opp. στῆσαι). *Take up* a martyr's bones MPol 18:1.

❷ **to get rid of by execution,** ***do away with, destroy,*** of pers. τινά *someone,* mostly of killing by violence, in battle, by execution, murder, or assassination (trag., Hdt.+; SIG 226, 20; 709, 35; UPZ 8, 15 [161 BC]; PAmh 142, 8; LXX; EpArist 166; Jos., Bell. 1, 389, Ant. 17, 44; Just., Tat., Ath.; Mel., P. 96, 736; Iren. 4, 33, 7 [Harv. II 261, 6]; Orig., C. Cels. 1, 61, 8) ἀ. πάντας τοὺς παῖδας **Mt 2:16** (PSaintyves, Le massacre des Innocents: Congr. d'Hist. du Christ. I 229–72); ἀνελεῖν πάντα τὰ βρέφη GJs 22:1 (follows ἀνελεῖται corr. to ἀναιρεῖται; cp. ἀνελεῖν τὰ βρέφη ApcEsdr 4, 11 p. 28: 13 Tdf.). ἐζήτουν τὸ πῶς ἀνέλωσιν αὐτόν *they sought a way to dispose of him* **Lk 22:2.** τοῦτον **Ac 2:23**; cp. **5:33, 36; 7:28** (Ex 2:14); **9:23f, 29; 22:20; 23:15, 21; 25:3;** 1 Cl 4:10 (Ex 2:14). ἀ. ἑαυτόν *commit suicide* (Parthenius 17, 7; Jos., Ant. 20, 80) **Ac 16:27.** Of execution (Chariton 4, 3, 5) **Lk 23:32; Ac 10:39; 12:2; 13:28.** ἀκρίτως AcPl Ha 9, 19 (restored). Synon. w. θανατοῦν 1 Cl 39:7 (Job 5:2). Of the destruction of the Lawless One ὃν ὁ Κύριος Ἰησοῦς ἀνελεῖ (vv.ll. ἀνελοῖ, ἀναλοῖ, ἀναλώσει, s. ἀναλίσκω) τῷ πνεύματι τοῦ στόματος αὐτοῦ *whom the Lord Jesus will slay with the breath of his mouth* **2 Th 2:8** (after Is 11:4). Pregnant constr., of martyrs ἀναιρούμενοι εἰς θεόν *those who come to God by a violent death* IEph 12:2. Of the tree of knowledge: *kill* οὐ τὸ τῆς γνώσεως (sc. ξύλον) ἀναιρεῖ ἀλλ' ἡ παρακοὴ ἀναιρεῖ Dg 12:2.—Pass. ἀναιρεῖσθαι **Ac 23:27; 26:10;** AcPl Ha 9, 20 (restored); ἀναιρεθῆναι **Lk 23:32; Ac 5:36; 13:28;** *be condemned to death* **26:10;** Papias (11:2; 12:2); AcPl Ha 4, 21f; 5, 5f; 8, 19.

❸ mid. **to take up for oneself,** ***take up, claim (for oneself)*** (Jos., Ant. 5, 20) of the baby Moses, whom Pharaoh's daughter rescued from the river after his exposure (Ex 2:5, 10; Philo, Mos. 1, 17) **Ac 7:21,** with focus on the act of rescue (sim. Dio Chrys. 65 [15], 9 ἀλλότρια εὑρόντες ἐν τῇ ὁδῷ παιδία ἀνελόμενοι [opp. ἐκτίθημι] ἔτρεφον ὡς αὐτῶν; cp. Aristocritus [III BC]: 493 fgm. 3 Jac. p. 465, 3; Aristoph., Nub. 531; Men., Sam. 159; Epict. 1, 23, 7 [opp. ῥιπτῶ 'expose']; Plut., Anton. 932 [36, 3], 'own, acknowledge', Mor. 320e al.; BGU 1110; PSI 203, 3; POxy 37, 6 [act.] and 38, 6 [mid.], both 49 AD; s. Preis.). The pap exx. involve exposed children taken up and reared as slaves, and the junction of ἀναιρέομαι and ἀνατρέφω in our pass. suggests Hell. nursing contracts (reflected in the LXX choice of diction Ex 2:9–10; s. New Docs 2, 7 and ins cited there). The rendering 'adopt' lacks philological precision and can be used only in a loose sense (as NRSV), esp. when Gr-Rom. terminology relating to adoption procedures is taken into account.—M-M. TW.

ἀναισθητέω (αἰσθάνομαι 'perceive by the senses'; Demosth. 18, 221; Plut., Mor. 1103d; 1105a; TestLevi 3:10; Philo, Ebr. 6; 154; Ath. 15, 3, R. 78, 2) **to be without feeling,** ***be unfeeling, insensible*** τινός *toward something* (Plut., Mor. 1062c; Jos., Bell. 4, 165, Ant. 11, 176; Ath. 15, 3) τῆς χρηστότητος αὐτοῦ *having no feeling for his goodness* IMg 10:1. Abs. (Epicurus, Ep. 1 p. 59, 6 [p. 21 Us.]) *lack perception* Dg 2:8f.

ἀναίσθητος, ον (Thu. et al., Philo; Jos., Ant. 11, 41) ***without feeling/perception*** (Hippocr., VM 15; Thrasymachus [IV BC]: 85 fgm. B 1; Pla., Tim. 75e; Philostrat., Imag. 1, 23 p. 326, 20; Herm. Wr. 9, 9 ὁ θεὸς οὐκ ἀ.; Diogenes p. 116, 21 Malherbe) of cultic images of deities Dg 2:4; 3:3 (Ar. 13, 1).—DELG s.v. 1 ἀΐω.

ἀναίτιος, ον ***innocent*** (s. αἴτιος; Hom. et al.; PTebt 43, 32 [II BC]; Philo; Jos., Bell. 4, 543, Ant. 17, 174; LXX only in the expr. ἀ. αἷμα, which occurs also in the prayers for vengeance from Rheneia [Dssm., LO 352–54 (LAE 423ff)=SIG 1181, 12f]) **Ac 16:37** D. ψυχή 2 Cl 10:5; ἀ. εἶναι **Mt 12:5, 7.**—M-M. TW.

ἀνακαθίζω 1 aor. ἀνεκάθισα **to sit up from a reclining position,** ***sit up, sit upright*** (s. καθίζω; Ps.-Xenophon, Cyn. 5, 7; 19; Plut., Alex. 671 [14, 4]; POxy 939, 25 [IV AD]; in medical writers [Hobart 11f], also Hippiatr. I 177, 24; Gen 48:2 v.l. [ed. ARahlfs 1926]); ἀνεκάθισεν ὁ νεκρός *the dead man sat up* **Lk 7:15** (v.l. ἐκάθισεν); cp. **Ac 9:40.**—DELG s.v. ἕζομαι A. M-M.

ἀνακαινίζω fut. 2 sg. ἀνακαινιεῖς Ps 103:30; 1 aor. ἀνεκαίνισα. Pass. fut. 3 sg. ἀνακαινισθήσεται Ps 102:5; aor. ἀνεκαινίσθην LXX (s. καινίζω and DELG s.v. καινός; Isocr. et al.; Plut., Marcell. 300 [6, 3]; Appian, Mithridates 37 §144; Ps.-Lucian, Philopatris 12 δι' ὕδατος ἡμᾶς ἀνεκαίνισεν [prob. against the Christians]; Philo, Leg. ad Gai. 85 v.l.; Jos., Ant. 9, 161; 13, 57; Ps 38:3; 102:5; 103:30; La 5:21; 1 Macc 6:9; En 106:13; JosAs; GrBar 8:4f) ***renew, restore*** ἀ. εἰς μετάνοιαν *restore to repentance* **Hb 6:6.** ἀνακαινίσας ἡμᾶς ἐν τῇ ἀφέσει τῶν ἁμαρτιῶν *since he made us new by forgiveness of sins* (in baptism) B 6:11; ἀ. τὸ πνεῦμα *renew our spirit* Hs 9, 14, 3; cp. 8, 6, 3.—DELG s.v. καινός. TW.

ἀνακαινόω (καινόω 'make new'; act. Orig., C. Cels. 4, 20; mid. Heliod. Philos., In EN 221, 13) ***renew*** only in Paul, in pass., and fig. of the spiritual rebirth of the Christian (opp. διαφθείρειν) ὁ ἔσω ἡμῶν (ἄνθρωπος) ἀνακαινοῦται *our inner* (spiritual) *person is being renewed* **2 Cor 4:16.** ἀ. εἰς ἐπίγνωσιν *renew for full knowledge* **Col 3:10.**—DELG s.v. καινός. M-M. TW.

ἀνακαίνωσις, εως, ἡ (ἀνακαινόω s. also ἀνακαινίζω; not found outside Christian lit.; Nägeli 52.—καίνωσις Jos.,

Ant. 18, 230) ***renewal;*** of a person's spiritual rebirth μεταμορφοῦσθαι τῇ ἀ. τοῦ νοός *be changed by the renewal of your minds* **Ro 12:2.** λουτρὸν ἀ. πνεύματος ἁγίου *washing of renewal through the Holy Spirit* (w. παλιγγενεσία) **Tit 3:5.** ἀ. τῶν πνευμάτων ὑμῶν *the renewal of your spirit* of the imparting of a new spirit Hv 3, 8, 9.—TW.

ἀνακαλύπτω fut. ἀνακαλύψω, 1 aor. ἀνεκάλυψα. Pass.: aor. ἀνεκαλύφθην LXX; pf. ἀνακεκάλυμμαι (s. καλύπτω; Eur., X. et al.; Polyb., Plut.; SIG 1169, 62; POxy 1297, 9 [IV AD]; LXX; En 16:3; 98:6; TestSol 6:3; TestJud 14:5; ParJer; Philo, Congr. Erud. Grat. 124 ἀ. πρόσωπον=unveil) ***uncover, unveil*** ἀνακεκαλυμμένῳ προσώπῳ *w. unveiled face* (w. ref. to Ex 34:34, of the relation betw. Christians and their Lord) **2 Cor 3:18** (ἀνακεκαλυμμένῳ πρ. as in Pel.-Leg. 4, 14). κάλυμμα μένει μὴ ἀνακαλυπτόμενον *a veil remains unlifted* vs. **14** (cp. TestJud 14:5; Dt 23:1 v.l. ἀνακαλύψει συγκάλυμμα; PGM 57, 17 ἀνακάλυψον τὸν ἱερὸν πέπλον; Maximus Tyr. 26, 2c ἀποκαλύψαντες τὰ προκαλύμματα). S. WvanUnnik, NovT 6, '63, 153–69.—DELG s.v. καλύπτω. M-M. TW. Spicq.

ἀνακάμπτω fut. ἀνακάμψω; 1 aor. ἀνέκαμψα (s. κάμπτω; Hdt. 2, 8+; LXX; s. Anz 314; New Docs 4, 141f ins [c. 290 BC]; TestJob 4:7 σὲ ἐπὶ τὰ ὑπάρχοντα 'restore you to' i.e. 'get you back' to your possessions; Just., D. 56, 6 [on Gen 18:14] for ἀναστρέψω) intr.

❶ **to go back to a point or area from which an entity has departed, *return***—ⓐ lit. (Diod. S. 16, 3, 6; 16, 8, 1 al.; PMagd 8, 10; PEdgar 34 [=Sb 6740], 5 [255/254 BC]; Ex 32:27; Philo, Aet. M. 58; cp. 31 [w. πρός and acc.]; Jos., Bell. 2, 116; SibOr 5, 33) μὴ ἀ. πρὸς Ἡρῴδην **Mt 2:12.** πρὸς ὑμᾶς **Ac 18:21.** Abs. **Hb 11:15.**

ⓑ fig. (cp. BGU 896, 6 πάντα τὰ ἐμὰ ἀνακάμψει εἰς τὴν θυγατέρα) of a religious greeting ἐφ' ὑμᾶς ἀνακάμψει *it will return to you* **Lk 10:6** (ἀ. ἐπί w. acc. as Pla., Phd. 72b; Περὶ ὕψους 36, 4; M. Ant. 4, 16).

❷ **to return to a former way of thinking, *turn back again*** ἀπὸ τ. παραδοθείσης ἐντολῆς **2 Pt 2:21 v.l.**—DELG s.v. κάμπτω. M-M.

ἀνάκειμαι impf. ἀνεκείμην (s. κεῖμαι; Pind., Hdt.+; ins, pap, LXX; TestJob 15:4 [for ἐνέκειντο]; ParJer 9:9 [of deceased Jer.]; Jos., Ant. 3, 38 al.; Ath. 37, 1 ἀνακείσθω ... ὁ λόγος of Ath.'s apologetic statement 'suffice, be concluded'), functions as pass. of ἀνατίθημι.

❶ gener. (opp. ἑστηκέναι, of one who appears to be dead ParJer 9:9) ***lie, recline*** **Mk 5:40 v.l.;** Hv 3, 12, 2. (Most ancient writers prefer κεῖμαι in this sense, s. Phryn. in 2.)

❷ otherw. always of reclining at table, equals ***dine*** (Aristot. and Diphilus [300 BC] in Athen. 1, 23c; Polyb. 13, 6, 8; 1 Esdr 4:11; for discussion on proper usage s. Phryn. 216f Lob. A character in a drama cited Ath. 1, 23c sarcastically asks in ref. to a banquet scene whether statues were being entertained on the couch.) αὐτοῦ ἀνακειμένου ἐν τῇ οἰκίᾳ *as he was dining in the house* **Mt 9:10.—26:7; Mk 14:18; 16:14; Lk 7:37 v.l.** ἀ. μετά τινος **Mt 26:20.** σύν τινι **J 12:2;** ἀ. ἐν τῷ κόλπῳ τινός *lean on someone's chest*=take the place of honor, if it was the chest of the head of the house **13:23** (cp. Lk 16:23, where sc. ἀνακείμενον [some mss. supply ἀναπαυόμενον]; Pliny, Epist. 4, 22, 4 cenabat Nerva cum paucis; Veiento proximus atque etiam in sinu recumbebat). ἐργάτας ἀνακειμένους GJs 18:2 (not pap) *laborers reclining for dinner*—ὁ ἀνακείμενος *the one who is reclining, the guest* **Mt 22:10f; Mk 6:26** (v.l. συνανάκειμαι q.v.); **Lk 22:27** (opp. ὁ διακονῶν); **J 6:11; 13:28.**—On the v.l. κατάκειμαι s. GKilpatrick, JTS n.s. 17, '66, 67–69; For pictures on ancient reliefs and vases s. e.g. JJung, Leben u. Sitten d. Römer I 1883, 24; ABaumeister, Denkmäler d. klass. Altert. I 1885, 365f.—DELG s.v. κεῖμαι. M-M. TW.

ἀνακεφαλαιόω 1 aor. mid. ἀνεκεφαλαιωσάμην, pass. 3 sg. ἀνεκεφαλαιώθη (to be read for ἐνεκ-) GJs 13:1 (κεφάλαιον 'sum, sum total', s. DELG s.v. κεφαλή; Aristot. et al.; in OT only Theod. and the Quinta at Ps 71:20).

❶ used of literary or rhetorical summation ***sum up, recapitulate*** (Aristot., fgm. 133, 1499a, 33; Dionys. Hal. 1, 90; Quintil. 6,1 rerum repetitio et congregatio, quae graece ἀνακεφαλαίωσις dicitur). Of individual commandments ἐν τῷ λόγῳ τούτῳ ἀνακεφαλαιοῦται everything is *summed up in this word/statement* (the command. of love; s. λόγος) **Ro 13:9** (s. 2 below). ἀνακεφαλαιώσασθαι τὰ πάντα ἐν τῷ Χριστῷ *to bring everything together in Christ* **Eph 1:10** (Ps.-Aristot., De Mundo 4,1 τὰ ἀναγκαῖα ἀνακεφαλαιούμενοι=sum up the necessary points). ἀ. τὸ τέλειον τῶν ἁμαρτιῶν *complete the total of the sins* B 5:11 (κεφαλαιώσει cod. V; s. 2 below). μήτι ἐν ἐμοὶ ἀνεκεφαλαιώθη ἡ ἱστορία (τοῦ Ἀδάμ); *is (Adam's) history to be repeated in me?* GJs 13:1.—CClassen, WienerStud 107f, 1994f, 322f (rhetorical term)

❷ of a mathematical total ***sum up,*** *complete the total of the sins* B 5:11 (s.1 above; κεφαλαιώσει cod. V). The interpretive var. κεφαλαιόω (q.v.) suggests that ἀ. was also used in a commercial sense, or that it could be readily so understood, but that κεφαλαιόω is the more normal term for such a sense. In **Ro 13:9** (s. 1 above) the immediate context suggests a commercial frame of ref. for the understanding of ἀ. as 'ledger entry', with retention of the full force of the prefix: ἐν τῷ λόγῳ τούτῳ ἀνακεφαλαιοῦται=*is summed up completely under this (ledger) entry* (cp. the use of πληρόω Gal 5:14 and s. s.v. λόγος 2a).—SHanson, Unity of the Church in the NT '46, 123–26. WStaerck, RAC I 411–14.—M-M. (no reff.). TW.

ἀνακλίνω fut. ἀνακλινῶ; 1 aor. ἀνέκλινα. Pass.: 1 fut. ἀνακλιθήσομαι; 1 aor. pass. ἀνεκλίθην (Hom. et al.; 3 Macc 5:16; TestSol 2:11 D; SibOr, fgm. 3, 37).

❶ **to cause someone to lie down, *to lay down, lay,*** *put to bed* of a child ἀ. αὐτὸν ἐν φάτνῃ **Lk 2:7;** αὐτήν GJs 5:2; 22:2 v.l. (for ἔβαλεν, s. deStrycker). ἐμὲ ἀνέκλιναν εἰς τὸ μέσον αὐτῶν *they caused me to lie down in their midst* Hs 9, 11, 7. The context that precedes (κοιμάω vs. 6) suggests slumber, but the succeeding context (vs. 8) suggests mng. 2.

❷ **to cause to recline at a meal, *place as guest*** (Polyb. 30, 26, 5; TestGad 1:5) ἀνακλινεῖ αὐτούς *he will have them recline* **Lk 12:37** (normally it is vice versa: Lucian, Ep. Sat. 1, 22; 3, 32); cp. **9:15 v.l.—Mk 6:39** (B-D-F §392, 4). Pass. *lie down, recline* at a meal, abs. **Lk 7:36 v.l.** ἐπὶ τ. χόρτου on *the grass* **Mt 14:19.** ἐπὶ τ. χλωρῷ χόρτῳ *on the green grass* **Mk 6:39 v.l.** ἀνακλίνεσθαι εἰς τοὺς ἐξέχοντας τόπους *recline in the preferred places* (viz. the seats of honor) **Mt 20:28** D=Agr 22. In transf. sense, of the Messianic banquet w. the idea *dine in style* (or some similar rendering, not simply 'eat' as NRSV) **Mt 8:11; Lk 13:29** (DZeller, BZ 15, '71, 222–37).—DELG s.v. κλίνω. M-M.

ἀνακοινόω 1 aor. mid. ptc. ἀνακοινωσαμένου 2 Macc 14:20 (X. et al.; pap, usu. in mid., as Diod. S. 4, 40, 2; PCairZen 520, 6 [III BC]; 2 Macc 14:20; Jos., Ant. 19, 19) **to make another privy to what one knows, *communicate*** τινί (τι) ***(something) to someone*** Dg 8:9 (ἀνακοινοῦν τινί τι Syntipas p. 9, 17; 47, 8).—DELG s.v. κοινός.

ἀνακόπτω 1 aor. ἀνέκοψα (Hom. et al.; Jos., Ant. 2, 338) ***hinder, restrain*** (so Plut.; Lucian; Philo, Spec. Leg. 1, 67; Jos., Bell. 1, 180; PFlor 36, 3; Wsd 18:23; 4 Macc 13:6) οἵτινες τὴν θεοῦ πρόνοιαν ἀνακόπτουσιν *who obstruct God's* (*beneficent*) *concern* AcPlCor 2:19; **Gal 5:7 v.l.** (s. Tdf. and s.v. ἐγκόπτω). Of desires *restrain* (Procop. Gaz., Ep. 117 σωφροσύνη νεότητος ἀλόγους ὁρμὰς ἀνακόπτουσα = moderation, which restrains the irrational impulses of youth) mid. *abstain* ἀνακόπτεσθαι ἀπὸ τῶν ἐπιθυμιῶν Pol 5:3.—DELG s.v. κόπτω. M-M.

ἀνακράζω 1 aor. ἀνέκραξα (BGU 1201, 11 [II AD]; Judg 7:20; **Mk 1:23**); 2 aor. ἀνέκραγον (**Lk 23:18;** -ξαν v.l.); fut. mid. 3 sg. ἀνακεκράξεται **J 4:16** (Hom. et al.; Polyb., Plut., pap, LXX. TestSol, TestJob; Just., D. 122, 4) ***cry out*** (Jos., Ant. 2, 235; Just., D. 122, 4) of the cry of the possessed (of the departing evil spirit itself: Neo-plat. Damascius [VI AD], Vi. Isidori 56 Westerm.) **Mk 1:23,** w. φωνῇ μεγάλῃ (בְּקוֹל גָּדוֹל; 1 Km 4:5; 1 Macc 2:27—but also Phlegon: 257 fgm. 36, 3, 9 Jac. p. 1176, 19: ἀνεκεκράγει μεγάλῃ τῇ φωνῇ λέγων) added, *with a loud voice* **Lk 4:33,** cp. **8:28; Mk 1:26 v.l.** Of the cries of frightened men **Mk 6:49;** of an aroused multitude **Lk 23:18.**—Of the loud speech of an angry person ἀ. φωνῇ μεγάλῃ Hv 3, 8, 9.—DELG s.v. κράζω. M-M. TW.

ἀνακραυγάζω (TestSol 6:9 P ἀνεκραύγασαν; Epict. 2, 19, 15; Vi. Aesopi G 16) ***cry out*** **Lk 4:35** D.—Frisk s.v. κράζω.

ἀνακρίνω (κρίνω 'separate, decide') fut. ἀνακρινῶ LXX, 1 aor. ἀνέκρινα, pass. ἀνεκρίθην (Thu. et al.; ins, pap, LXX; TestSol 1:3 A; TestAbr A 13 p. 92, 13f [Stone p. 32]).

❶ **to engage in careful study of a question, *question, examine,*** of general questions (s. ἀνάκρισις; Epict. 1, 1, 20; 2, 20, 27 τὴν Πυθίαν; 1 Km 20:12; Sus 13; Jos., Ant. 5, 329) ἀ. τὰς γραφάς *examine the Scriptures* **Ac 17:11** (ἀ. εἰ as Jos., Ant. 8, 267; 12, 197). ἀ. τοὺς λόγους *inquire about the words* (of the elders) Papias (2:4) (expiscabar Rufin.). μηδὲν ἀνακρίνοντες *without asking questions* **1 Cor 10:25, 27; Ac 11:12 v.l.** (for διακρίνω).

❷ **to conduct a judicial hearing, *hear a case, question,*** administrative term w. acc. of pers. examined (SIG 953, 46 [II BC] ἀνακρινάντω δὲ καὶ τ. μάρτυρας; Sus 51 Theod.; Jos., Ant. 17, 131) ἀ. τοὺς φύλακας *examine the guards* **Ac 12:19.—28:18; 1 Cor 4:3f; 9:3;** GJs 21:2 (not pap); pass. **1 Cor 4:3.** Abs. *conduct an examination* (Sus 48) **Lk 23:14.** W. indication of the matter investigated ἀ. περὶ πάντων τούτων *about all these matters* **Ac 24:8.**—W. the reasons for the hearing given ἐπὶ εὐεργεσίᾳ *because of a benefaction* **4:9** (an incongruous situation, w. Peter in effect challenging his audience to avoid shame, for ordinarily in the Gr-Rom. world a civic award was in order for an act of rescue, s. στέφανος and σῴζω). Judicial diction may be implied **1 Cor 2:15,** but s. 3.

❸ **to examine with a view to finding fault, *judge, call to account, discern*** (Demosth. 57, 66; 70; POxy 1209, 19; 1706, 20) πάντα **1 Cor 2:15;** pass. vs. **14f; 14:24** (w. ἐλέγχειν). But s. 2 above.—M-M. TW.

ἀνάκρισις, εως, ἡ a judicial hearing, *investigation, hearing,* esp. ***preliminary hearing*** (s. ἀνακρίνω; X., Symp. 5, 2; Pla., Leg. 766d; Isaeus 6, 13; SIG 780, 28, OGI 374, 6; PSI 392, 2 [III BC]; PTebt 86, 1ff; PLips 4, 15; PLond II, 251, 7 [337–50 AD] p. 317; 3 Macc 7:5; Jos., Ant. 17, 121; Tat. 42, 1 ἀνάκρισιν τῶν δογμάτων *examination of the teachings;* Iren. 1, 11, 1 [Harv. I 101, 10]) τῆς ἀ. γενομένης **Ac 25:26.**—DELG s.v. κρίνω. M-M. TW.

ἀνακτάομαι fut. ἀνακτήσομαι TestJob 40:4; 1 aor. ἀνεκτησάμην (trag., Hdt. et al.; ins, pap; Sym. 1 Km 30:12 al.; TestJob 44:4) w. ἑαυτόν ***regain one's strength, renew one's energy*** (Epict. 3, 25, 4; PFay 106, 18 ὅπως δυνηθῶ ἐμαυτὸν ἀνακτήσασθαι; Jos., Ant. 9, 123; 15, 365; OdeSol 11:11). ἀνακτήσασθε (ἑαυτοὺς ἐν πίστει) ITr 8:1 is J-BCotelier's conjecture for the ἀνακτίσασθε of the mss.—DELG s.v. κτάομαι.

ἀνακτίζω (κτίζω 'create'; Strabo 9, 2, 5; Ps 50:12 Aq.; TestSol 1:1 L; Jos., Bell. 1, 165, Ant. 11, 12) ***create anew*** mid. *have oneself created anew* ITr 8:1; s. ἀνακτάομαι.

ἀνακυλίω pf. pass. ἀνακεκύλισμαι (κυλίω 'roll along'; Alexis Com. 116, 7 [in Athen. 6, 237c]; Lucian, Luct. 8 al.) ***roll away*** of the stone at the grave **Mk 16:4 v.l.**—DELG s.v. κυλίνδω.

ἀνακύπτω 1 aor. ἀνέκυψα, impv. ἀνάκυψον, inf. ἀνακύψαι (also -ῦψαι; s. PKatz-Walters, The Text of the Septuagint, '73, 97)

❶ **to raise oneself up to an erect position, *stand erect, straighten oneself,*** lit. (opp. κύπτω 'bend forward, stoop'; X., De Re Equ. 7, 10 et al.; Sus 35; Jos., Ant. 19, 346) **J 8:7, 10.** Of a body bent by disease μὴ δυναμένη ἀνακύψαι **Lk 13:11** (medical t.t., acc. to Hobart 20ff, but s. Cadbury, Style 44f).

❷ **to take heart in expectation of deliverance, *stand tall,*** fig. (as Hdt. 5, 91; X., Oec. 11, 5; Diod. S. 14, 9, 3 ἀ. ταῖς ἐλπίσιν; UPZ 70, 23 [152/151 BC] ἀ. ὑπὸ τῆς αἰσχύνης; Job 10:15; Philo, In Flacc. 160; Jos., Bell. 6, 401) **Lk 21:28** (w. ἐπαίρειν τὴν κεφαλήν).—DELG s.v. κύπτω. M-M.

ἀναλαλάζω 1 aor. ἀνηλάλαξα (ἀλαλάζω 'cry aloud'; since Eur., Xen. of outcry for various reasons) ***cry out*** fr. pain GJs 20:1.—DELG s.v. λαλέω.

ἀναλαμβάνω (λαμβάνω 'take'; Hdt.+) 2 aor. ἀνέλαβον; pf. ἀνείληφα. Mid.: fut. ἀναλήψομαι; 2 aor. 3 sg. ἀνελάβετο TestJos 16:5. Pass.: 1 fut. ἀναληφθήσομαι LXX; 1 aor. ἀνελή(μ)φθην (B-D-F §101 λαμβ.; Mlt-H. 246f).

❶ **to lift up and carry away, *take up*** εἰς τὸν οὐρανόν (4 Km 2:10f; 1 Macc 2:58; Philo, Mos. 2, 291; TestAbr A 7 p. 84, 16 [Stone p. 16], B 4 p. 108, 16 [Stone p. 64] al.; Just., D. 80, 4; cp. Did., Gen. 148, 2; cp. ἀνάλημψις AssMos p. 64 Denis [=p. 272 Tromp] and PtK fgm. 4 p. 15, 36) pass. of Christ **Mk 16:19; Ac 1:11** (Just., D. 32, 3; Mel., P. 70, 510; of dead pers. εἰς οὐρανούς TestJob 39:12). Of Paul εἰς τὸν ἅγιον τόπον ἀνελήμφθη *he was taken up into the realm of the blessed* 1 Cl 5:7. In same sense without εἰς τ. οὐ. (cp. Sir 48:9; 49:14; TestAbr A 15 p. 95, 15 [Stone p. 38] ἀφ' ὑμῶν; ParJer 9:3) **Ac 1:2** (PvanStempvoort, NTS 5, '58/59, 30–42 takes **Ac 1:2** to refer to the death of Christ; JDupont, NTS, '61/62, 154–57, to his ascension. Cp. also BMetzger, The Mng. of Christ's Ascension, RTStamm memorial vol., '69, 118–28), **22; 1 Ti 3:16;** GPt 5:19. Perh. of a deceased woman (Christian ins ἀνελήμφθη='has died', like our 'is in heaven': Byzantion 2, 1926, 330; Ramsay, CB I /2, 561, no. 454) Hv 1, 1, 5 (see handbooks ad loc.). Of a sheet **Ac 10:16.**

❷ **to take up in order to carry, *take up*** ἀ. τὴν σκηνὴν τοῦ Μολόχ *you took along the tent of Moloch* **Ac 7:43** (Am 5:26).—Of weapons *take* (Hdt. 3, 78, 2; 9, 53, 16 et al.; SIG 742, 45; 49; 2 Macc 10:27; Jdth 6:12; 7:5; 14:3 ἀναλαβόντες τὰς πανοπλίας; Jos., Ant. 20, 110 πανοπλ. ἀναλ.; 121) τὴν πανοπλίαν τοῦ θεοῦ **Eph 6:13.** τὸν θυρεὸν τῆς πίστεως vs. **16.**

❸ **to make someth. one's own by taking, w. focus on moral or transcendent aspects, *take to one's self, adopt*** (TestJob 21:4 λογισμόν; ParJer 9:22 [Christ.] ὁμοιότητα; Ar. 15, 1 σάρκα [of Christ]; Tat. 10, 1 ἀετοῦ μορφήν; Orig., C. Cels.

3, 28, 49 Βίον, ὃν Ἰησοῦς ἐδίδαξεν) τὴν πραϋπάθειαν ITr 8:1. ζῆλον ἄδικον καὶ ἀσεβῆ 1 Cl 3:4; μιαρὸν καὶ ἄδικον ζῆλον 45:4.—*Accept* παιδείαν 56:2 (s. παιδεία 1).—ἀ. τὴν διαθήκην ἐπὶ στόματός σου *take the covenant in your mouth* 35:7 (Ps 49:16).—τὴν δύναμίν τινος *take back someone's power* Hs 9, 14, 2. τὴν ζωήν *receive life* s 9, 16, 3.

❹ **take someone along on a journey,** ***take along*** of a travel companion (Thu., X.; 2 Macc 12:38; Jos., Bell. 2, 551, Ant. 4, 85; TestJos 16:5) **2 Ti 4:11;** of Paul's escort **Ac 23:31.**—*Take on board* (Thu. 7, 25, 4) **20:13f.**

❺ **take up someth. for scrutiny,** ***take in hand*** (βύβλοι 'divisions of a book or treatise' Polyb. 3, 9, 3; βιβλίον 1 Esdr 9:45) τὴν ἐπιστολὴν τ. μακαρίου Παύλου 1 Cl 47:1.—DELG s.v. λαμβάνω. M-M. TW.

ἀναλημφθείς s. ἀναλαμβάνω.

ἀνάλημψις, εως, ἡ also ἀνάληψις (s. λαμβάνω; Hippocr. et al. in var. mngs.; ins, pap, Philo, AssMos fgm. c; Eus., HE 2, 13, 3f cites Just., A I, 26, 1 but reads ἀνάληψιν for Justin's ἀνέλευσιν; ἀνάλημψις ἀρετῆς Did., Gen. 50, 17; on spelling cp. B-D-F §101 λαμβ.; Mlt-H. 246f) in the Gk. Bible only **Lk 9:51** αἱ ἡμέραι τῆς ἀ. αὐτοῦ. Here it is usu. interpr. to mean ***ascension*** (into heaven); this is its mng. in PtK 4 p. 15, 35; TestLevi 18:3 v.l.; AssMos fgm. c Denis p. 64 (s. the Latin text TestMos 10:12) (cp. ἔνσαρκον εἰς τοὺς οὐρανοὺς ἀνάλημψιν τοῦ ἠγαπημένου Χριστοῦ Ἰησοῦ Iren. 1, 10, 1 [Harv. I 91, 3] and s. ἀναλαμβάνω 1); also in the subscriptions at the end of Mk, e.g. in the Ferrar family (Min. 13 et al.; see on Ῥωμαϊστί) ἐγράφη ιβ´ ἔτη τῆς ἀναλήψεως τ. κυρίου.—But ἀ. can also mean *death, decease* (cp. PsSol 4:18 τὸ γῆρας αὐτοῦ εἰς ἀνάλημψιν; Christian ins from Aphrodisias: Byzantion 2, 1926, 331; Ps.-Clem., Hom. 3, 47).—DELG s.v. λαμβάνω. M-M. TW.

ἀναλίσκω (Pr 24:22d; Ezk 15:4; Jos., Ant. 3, 236; 19, 352; TestSol 14:5; TestAbr A 4 p. 81, 23 [Stone p. 10]; TestJob; ApcEsdr 6:24 p. 32:4 Tdf.; Tat.) or **ἀναλόω** (Bel 12 Theod., cp. EpJer 9; Jos., Bell. 7, 321) fut. ἀναλώσω LXX, TestNapht 4:2; 1 aor. ἀνήλωσα. Pass.: fut. ἀναλωθήσομαι; aor. ἀνηλώθην; pf. ἀνήλωμαι LXX, En 103:9 (Pind., Thu.+) **to do away with someth. completely by using up,** ***destroy, consume*** τινά of fire **Lk 9:54** (as in Alex. Aphr., An. Mant. 111, 20, Quaest. 2, 23 p. 73, 17, Mixt. 9, p. 223, 5 Bruns; Jo 1:19; 2:3; Ezk 19:12; 2 Macc 2:10; Jos., Bell. 7, 321; Ar. 10, 9). Fig., of annihilation (cp. Gen 41:30; Pr 23:28; En 103:9; SibOr 3, 646; Jos., Ant. 2, 287) **2 Th 2:8 v.l.** (ἀναιρέω 2. Ael. Dion. α, 121 ἀναλοῦντες· ἀντὶ τοῦ ἀναιροῦντες) **Mk 9:49 v.l.** Semantically more complex is βλέπετε μὴ ὑπ᾽ ἀλλήλων ἀναλωθῆτε (w. κατεσθίειν as Pr 30:14) **Gal 5:15.** For a prob. commercial metaphor: *see to it that you are not squandered by one another,* s. s.v. λόγος and πληρόω.—DELG s.v. ἁλίσκομαι. Frisk s.v. ἀναλίσκω. M-M.

ἀνάλλομαι (ἄλλομαι, 'spring, leap'; Aristoph., X.+; PGM 36, 138) ***jump up*** ἀνήλατο **Ac 14:10** D.

ἀναλογία, ας, ἡ (s. λόγος; Pre-Socr. et al.; Philo; Jos., Ant. 15, 396; Just., A I, 17, 4; Ath., R. 75, 28; Iren. 1, 14, 5 [Harv. I 139, 3]) **a state of right relationship involving proportion,** ***proportion*** κατὰ (τὴν) ἀναλογίαν *in right relationship to, in agreement w.*, or *in proportion to* (Pla., Polit. 257b; PFlor 50, 91 [III AD]; Lev 27:18 acc. to Field, Hexapla κατὰ ἀναλογίαν τῶν ἐτῶν. Cp. Philo, Virtut. 95) κατὰ τὴν ἀ. τῆς πίστεως *in agreement w.* (or *in proportion to*) *the share of commitment one has* (REB: *in proportion to our faith;* i.e. each gift is accompanied by a distribution of commitment or fidelity adequate for implementing the gift [s. Ro 12:3 ὡς ὁ θεὸς ἐμέρισεν μέτρον πίστεως]) **Ro 12:6.** For the understanding of πίστις here in the sense of 'the Christian faith' s. πίστις 3.—DELG s.v. λέγω. M-M. TW. Sv.

ἀναλογίζομαι 1 aor. ἀνελογισάμην (s. λογίζομαι; Thu. 8, 83, 3 et al.; Stoic. III p. 246, 15; Polyb. 10, 37, 10; Diod. S. 20, 8, 1; Plut., Anton. 951 [75, 6]; Lucian, Tox. 17; PTebt 183 commercial term; 3 Macc 7:7; Wsd 17:12 v.l.; PsSol 8:7; Jos., Ant. 4, 312) **to reason with careful deliberation,** ***consider*** τινά (Diod. S. 4, 83, 2) **Hb 12:3.** Abs. ἀναλογισώμεθα *let us consider* 1 Cl 38:3.—M-M.

ἄναλος, ον (Aristot., Probl. 21, 5, 1; Plut., Mor. 684f; Aq. Ezk 13:10; 22:28) ***without salt,*** *deprived of its salt content* **Mk 9:50.** Salt produced by natural evaporation on the shores of the Dead Sea is never pure; when dampness decomposes it, the residue is useless.—FPerles, La parab. du Sel sourd: REJ 82, 1926, 119–23; JdeZwaan, Het smakelooze zout bij Mc 9:50: NThSt 11, 1928, 176–78; s. ἅλας.

ἀναλόω s. ἀναλίσκω.

ἀνάλυσις, εως, ἡ (s. ἀναλύω; Soph. et al.) lit. 'loosing up'; then, like our 'breaking up', ***departure*** (Philo, In Flacc. 115; Jos., Ant. 19, 239); euphem., of departure from life, *death* (Philo, In Flacc. 187 τ. ἐκ τοῦ βίου τελευταίαν ἀνάλυσιν. ἀνάλυσις alone='death' in contrast to γένεσις in Joannes Sard., Comm. in Aphth. p. 87, 4; Iren. 5, 2, 3 [Harv II 324, 2 end of the world]) καιρὸς τῆς ἀ. μου **2 Ti 4:6.** ἔγκαρπον καὶ τελείαν ἔχειν τ. ἀνάλυσιν *a fruitful and perfect departure* (i.e. after a fruitful and perfect life) 1 Cl 44:5; s. ἀναλύω 2.—TW. Sv.

ἀναλύω 1 aor. ἀνέλυσα, pf. ptc. ἀναλελυκώς 2 Macc 9:1; aor. pass. ἀνελύθην LXX, Tat. 12, 4 (Hom.+)

❶ trans. ***loose, untie*** (Callim., Del. 237 ζώνην; IAndrosIsis 144f δεσμῶν ἀνάγκαν) pass. τὰ δεσμὰ ἀνελύθη **Ac 16:26 v.l.** (Just., A I, 20, 2 acc. to the Stoics θεὸν εἰς πῦρ ἀναλύεσθαι=God turns into fire).

❷ intr. ***depart, return*** (Polyb.; pap in APF 1, 1901, p. 59 ln. 10; Tob 2:9; 2 Macc 8:25; 12:7; Jos., Ant. 6, 52; 11, 34 [after a dinner]) ἔκ τινος *from something* (Aelian, VH 4, 23 v.l. ἐκ συμποσίου; Wsd 2:1; 2 Macc 9:1) ἐκ τῶν γάμων **Lk 12:36.**—Fig., *depart* (sc. ἐκ τοῦ ζῆν) euphemistic for *die* (Lucian, Philops. 14 ὀκτωκαιδεκαέτης ὢν ἀνέλυεν; Socrat., Ep. 27, 5; IG XIV, 1794, 2; Diog. Oen. 58 I, 11 [BCH 21, 1897, 401]=fgm. 2 II, 11 Ch. ἀ. [ἐκ τ]οῦ ζῆν) ἐπιθυμίαν ἔχων εἰς τὸ ἀναλῦσαι **Phil 1:23** (GOsnes, TTK 11, '40, 148–59).—M-M. TW.

ἀναμάρτητος, ον (s. ἁμαρτάνω; Hdt. [5, 39, 2]+; Musonius 6, 16 H.; Epict. 4, 8, 6; 4, 12, 19; Plut., Mor. 419a; Appian, Liby. 51 §224 πρὸς τ. θεούς; ins [Muratori, Nov. Thes. vet. ins IV, p. 2062, 6 Ναρκίσσῳ τέκνῳ ἀναμαρτήτῳ]; pap; Dt 29:19; 2 Macc 8:4; 12:42; En 99:2; TestBenj 3:8; ApcSed 14:8 p. 136, 11 Ja; EpArist 252; Philo, Mut. Nom. 51; Jos., Bell. 7, 329 πρὸς τ. θεὸν Ar. 15:11 [Milne 76, 41]; Just., D. 47, 5 al.; ἀναμαρτήτως 44, 4) ***without sin,*** i.e. not having sinned (Teles p. 55, 13=ἐκτὸς ἁμαρτίας) ὁ ἀ. ὑμῶν **J 8:7.**—M-M.

ἀναμαρυκάομαι (μηρυκάομαι 'chew the cud'; Lucian, Gall. 8; Lev 11:26 v.l.; Dt 14:8 v.l.) ***ruminate*** fig., w. ref. to Lev 11:3; Dt 14:6 τὸν λόγον κυρίου *ruminate on the word of the Lord,* i.e. think on it again and again B 10:11.—S. μαρυκάομαι.

ἀναμένω fut. 2 pl. ἀναμενεῖτε Jer. 13:16; 1 aor. ἀνέμεινα, impv. ἀνάμεινον (Hom. et al.; pap, LXX; pseudepigr., Philo, Joseph.; Just., D. 11, 4 al.—Abs.: Ps.-Callisth. 2, 19, 5; POxy 1773, 32; Just. D., 115, 3) ***wait for, expect*** someone or something (Attic wr.; Epict. 4, 8, 42; Jdth 8:17; Sir 2:7; Is 59:11; JosAs 24:9; Jos., Bell. 3, 72; ApcSed 14:8; Just., D. 32, 1), esp. the Messiah ἀ. τ. υἱὸν αὐτοῦ ἐκ τῶν οὐρανῶν *wait for God's Son (coming) from heaven* **1 Th 1:10.** ὃν δικαίως ἀνέμενον IMg 9:3. W. εἰς αὐτὸν ἐλπίζειν IPhld 5:2. ἀνάμεινον τὸ τρίτον (ἔτος) *wait until the third year!* GJs 7:1.—Fig., of time μακάριος αὐτὸν ἀναμένει χρόνος *a blessed time awaits (the devout)* 2 Cl 19:4 (cp. TestAsh 5:2). P-ÉLangevin, Jésus Seigneur '67, 67–73. GFriedrich, TZ 21, '65, 504f (on 1 Th 1:10).—M-M.

ἀναμέσον s. ἀνά 1.

ἀναμιμνῄσκω pres. by-form ἀναμνήσκω TestJob 41:4 P; fut. ἀναμνήσω; 1 aor. ἀνέμνησα LXX. Pass.: fut. ἀναμνησθήσομαι LXX; aor. ἀνεμνήσθην (s. μιμνήσκομαι; Hom.+; ins, pap, LXX; En 103:15; 104:1; TestJob 14:3 al.; Philo, Joseph., Just.) ***remind*** τινά τι ***someone of something*** (X., An. 3, 2, 11; Diod. S. 17, 10, 6) ὃς ὑμᾶς ἀναμνήσει τὰς ὁδούς μου *who will remind you of my directives* i.e. instructions, teachings **1 Cor 4:17** (ὁδός 3c). τινά w. inf. ἀ. σε ἀναζωπυρεῖν *I remind you to rekindle* **2 Ti 1:6.**—Pass. *be reminded, remember* (SIG 557, 26; PGrenf I, 1 col. 1, 2; 22; Just., D. 34, 1; 64, 7) w. acc. of thing (X., An. 7, 1, 26; Pla., Phd. 72e; Jos., Bell. 3, 396; B-D-F §175; Rob. 509) ἀνεμνήσθη ὁ Πέτρος τὸ ῥῆμα *Peter remembered the word* **Mk 14:72.** ἀ. τὴν ὑπακοήν **2 Cor 7:15.** ἀ. τὰς πρότερον ἡμέρας **Hb 10:32.** Cp. **Ac 16:35** D.—W. gen. (Thu. 2, 54, 2; 2 Esdr 19:17; TestJob 51:4; Jos., Bell. 4, 174, Ant. 2, 137; PCairMasp 2 III, 6; Just., D. 34, 1; 64, 7) τῆς περυσινῆς ὁράσεως *the vision of the previous year* Hv 2, 1, 1.—Abs. (Hdt. 3, 51, 1 ὁ δὲ ἀναμνησθεὶς εἶπε) ἀναμνησθεὶς ὁ Πέτρος λέγει **Mk 11:21.**—M-M. TW.

ἀνάμνησις, εως, ἡ (s. ἀναμιμνῄσκω; Pla. et al.; ins, LXX, Philo; Jos., Ant. 4, 189; Just.) ***reminder, remembrance*** τινός ***of something*** (Diod. S. 20, 93, 7 τῆς φιλίας ἀν.; Wsd 16:6; Jos., Bell. 3, 394; Just., D. 27, 4; 117, 3) ἀ. ἁμαρτιῶν *a reminder of sins,* of the sacrifices repeated every year **Hb 10:3.** In the account of the Eucharist εἰς τὴν ἐμὴν ἀνάμνησιν *in remembrance (memory) of me* **1 Cor 11:24f; Lk 22:19** (εἰς ἀ. Appian, Hann. 1 §2; Hierocles 11, 440 εἰς ἀ. τοῦ νόμου, 441 εἰς ἀ. τοῦ ὀρθοῦ λόγου='to remind them of'; Lev 24:7; Ps 37:1; 69:1; Jos., Ant. 19, 318. Cp. μνήμη 2. In Diod. S. 3, 57, 8 Basileia is honored as a deity by the people from whose midst she has disappeared. And when they offer sacrifices or show other honors to her, they beat kettledrums and cymbals, as Basileia did, and put on a representation [ἀπομιμουμένους] of her experiences; POxy 494, 22ff; Ltzm., Messe u. Herrenmahl[4] 1926; ELohmeyer, JBL 56, '37, 244f; JJeremias, D. Abendmahlsworte Jesu '67; DJones, JTS 6, '55, 183–91; HKosmala, NovT 4, '60, 81–94.—For the mng. *memorial sacrifice,* cp. Num 10:10 and s. L-S-J-M, but s. GCaird, JTS 19, '68, 458; cp. EPeters, CBQ 10, '48, 248f).—πρὸς ἀ. γράφειν *to remind (you)* 1 Cl 53:1.—M-M. TW. Sv.

ἀναναπαύστως (hapax leg.) adv. ***without cessation*** ἀ. ἕξουσιν τὴν κόλασιν *they will have no relief from their punishment* ApcPt Bodl. 9f (Bouriant, verso 33=Dieterich, lines 107f μηδέποτε παυόμενοι τῆς τοιαύτης κολάσεως).

ἀνανεόω fut. 3 sg. ἀνανεώσει Job 33:24; 1 aor. ἀνενέωσα, mid. ἀνενεωσάμην LXX; aor. pass. ptc. gen. pl. ἀνανεωθέντων Ath., R. 58, 20 (ἀνα-, νέος, s. ἀνανέωσις; trag. et al.; ins [e.g. OGI 90, 35 (II BC); ÖJh 64, 1995, p. 72 (III AD)]; pap, LXX; TestBenj 9:1; Apc4Esdr fgm. d [mid.]; Jos., Ant. 12, 321; Ath., R. 58, 20).

❶ trans. ***renew.*** The act. is not found very oft. w. this mng. (in a dedication to Aristonous of Corinth [III BC] fgm. 2b Diehl[2] [AnthLG II, 6 p. 139] Δελφοὶ ἀνενέωσαν τὰν πάτριον προξενίαν; M. Ant. 4, 3, 3 σεαυτόν; 6, 15, 1; Herm. Wr. 9, 6; ins; pap; Job 33:24; 1 Macc 12:1; Iren., 3, 3, 3 [Harv. II 11, 1]) ἀ. τὴν ζωήν (of the angel of repentance) *restore life* Hs 9, 14, 3. Much more freq. (since Thu. 7, 33, 4) is the mid. (Diod. S. 33, 28a, 3 Dind.; 37, 15, 2; Chion, Ep. 16, 8; Appian, Maced. 11 §6; SIG 721, 13; 475, 10; 554, 6; 591, 53, cp. index; OGI 90, 35; Esth 3:13b; 1 Macc 12:3, 10, 16 al.; Jos., Bell. 1, 283, Ant. 1, 290), which seems not to have the reflexive sense 'renew oneself'. Hence ἀνανεοῦσθαι τῷ πνεύματι τοῦ νοός is better taken as a pass. *be renewed=(let yourselves) be renewed in the spirit of your minds* **Eph 4:23** (on the figure Cornutus 33 p. 70, 10 ἀνανεάζειν ἐκ τῶν νόσων καὶ ἐκδύεσθαι τὸ γῆρας). ἀνανεοῦται τὸ πνεῦμα *his spirit is renewed* Hv 3, 12, 2; 3, 13, 2, cp. 3, 12, 3.

❷ intr. ***become young again*** μηκέτι ἔχοντες ἐλπίδα τοῦ ἀνανεῶσαι Hv 3, 11, 3.—New Docs 3, 61f. DELG s.v. νέος. M-M. TW. Sv.

ἀνανέωσις, εως, ἡ (s. ἀνανεόω; Thu. et al; Herm. Wr. 3, 4; SIG 1059 II, 9; IEgChr [IGA V] 561, 16; POxy 274, 20; PStras 52, 7; 1 Macc 12:17; Jos., Ant. 9, 161; 12, 324) ***renewal*** of the Christian ἀ. λαμβάνειν τῶν πνευμάτων *renewal of the spirit* (pl., since several pers. are involved) Hv 3, 13, 2. ἐλπὶς ἀνανεώσεώς τινος *hope of some renewal* s 6, 2, 4.—New Docs 3, 62. TW.

ἀνανήφω 1 aor. ἀνένηψα (Aristot. et al.) 'become sober' (rather oft. transferred to the spiritual, esp. ethical realm in later Gk.: Cebes 9, 3; Dio Chrys. 4, 77; Ps.-Lucian, Salt. 84; M. Ant. 6, 31; Philo, Leg. All. 2, 60 ἀνανήφει, τοῦτο δ' ἐστὶ μετανοεῖ; Jos., Ant. 6, 241; s. Nägeli 30; s. νήφω) ***come to one's senses again*** ἀ. ἐκ τῆς τοῦ διαβόλου παγίδος *come to one's s. and escape from the snare of the devil* **2 Ti 2:26.** Abs. ἀνανῆψαι *become sober again* ISm.

Ἁνανίας, ου, ὁ (also Ἀν-; חֲנַנְיָה) (AscIs 2:9; EpArist 48; Joseph.—Diod. S. 20, 97, 7 Ἀνανίας is the name of a Rhodian general. See also Athen. 12, 3, 511c Ἀνάνιος or Ἄνανις) ***Ananias.***

❶ one of the three youths in the fiery furnace 1 Cl 45:7 (cp. Da 3:24 LXX; Just., A I, 46, 3).

❷ a member of the Christian community in Jerusalem, husband of Sapphira **Ac 5:1, 3, 5** (cp. the scene in Jos., Ant. 8, 266–73).—WBornemann, A. u. S.: Christl. Welt 13, 1899, 987–91; RSchumacher, A. u. S.: ThGl 5, 1913, 824–30. P-HMenoud, Goguel Festschr., '50, 146–54; Haenchen, ad loc.

❸ a Christian in Damascus, who instructed Paul and baptized him **Ac 9:10, 12f, 17; 22:12** (EFascher, Z. Taufe des Paulus: TLZ 80, '55, 643–48).

❹ a Jewish high priest, son of Nedebaeus, in office c. 47–59 (Jos., Ant. 20, 103; 131; 205; 208–10; 213, Bell. 2, 243; 426; 429; 441f) **Ac 22:5 v.l.; 23:2; 24:1.** See Schürer II 231.

ἀναντίρρητος, ον (also ἀναντίρητος; W-S. §5, 266b) pass. (ῥητός 'spoken'; Polyb. 6, 7, 7; Diod. S. 31, 27, 7; Plut., Them. 124a [24, 4], Mor. 339b; Job 11:2 Sym.) ***not to be***

contradicted, undeniable (Herm. Wr. 2, 11 ἀ. ὁ λόγος; Jos., C. Ap. 1, 160) ἀ. ὄντων τούτων *since this is undeniable* **Ac 19:36.** βραβεῖον ἀ. ἀποφέρεσθαι *carry off an incontestable prize* MPol 17:1.—DELG s.v. εἴρω.

ἀναντιρρήτως (also ἀναντιρήτως w. one ρ as in OGI 335, 138 [II/I BC]) adv. of ἀναντίρρητος, in NT only in act. mng. (Polyb. 22, 8, 11; pap; Job 33:13 Sym.) ***without raising any objection*** ἔρχεσθαι **Ac 10:29.**

ἀναντλέω (ἀντλέω 'bail out bilge-water, draw water') 1 aor. ἀνήντλησα; pf. ptc. ἀνηντληκώς lit. 'draw up' of water, ***drain out, empty*** fig., of dealing incessantly with toil or hardships ***bear patiently*** (Dionys. Hal. 8, 51 πόνους; Phalaris, Ep. 19 πόνους; Dio Chrys. 11 [12], 51; UPZ 60, 14 [168 BC] τοιούτους καιροὺς ἀνηντληκυῖα) ταῦτα πάντα 1 Cl 26:3 (Job 19:26). ἀνηντληκὼς κόπους Hs 5, 6, 2 (Bonner 58).—DELG s.v. ἄντλος.

ἀνάξιος, ον (s. ἄξιος; Soph., Hdt. et al.; Epict. 2, 8, 18; PStras 5, 8 [262 AD]; Sir 25:8; TestAbr A 9 p. 86, 22 [Stone p. 20]; Philo, Aet. M. 85; Jos., Ant. 6, 17; Just., A II, 2, 14; D. 4, 6; 76, 5; Ath., R. 58, 11 al.) ***unworthy*** τινός: ἀνάξιοί ἐστε κριτηρίων ἐλαχίστων; *are you not good enough* or *not competent to settle trivial cases?* **1 Cor 6:2** (Simplicius in Epict. p. 60, 33 τοὺς μηδὲ ἀξίους ὄντας τῶν τοιούτων κριτάς). πράσσειν ἀ. (Hippocr., Ep. 9, 1; Herm. Wr. fgm. XXIII 41 [478, 33 Sc.]; EpArist 205; 217; cp. Aeschin., Ep. p. 254, 33 Malherbe w. ποιεῖν) θεοῦ IEph 7:1. ἀ. ζωῆς *unworthy of* (eternal) *life* Dg 9:1. τῆς ἐν Χριστῷ ἀγωγῆς 1 Cl 47:6. ἀνάξιοι *unworthy people* Hs 6, 3, 4.—M-M. TW.

ἀναξίως (Soph., Hdt. et al.; Teles p. 56, 9; Sb 1267, 5; 2 Macc 14:42) adv. of ἀνάξιος *in an unworthy/careless manner* ἐσθίειν, πίνειν of the Eucharist **1 Cor 11:27 (29 v.l.).** For partaking of the Eucharist in an improper manner, and the results thereof, s. ConNeot 15, '55, p. 27f.

ἀναπάρτιστος, ον (cp. ἀπαρτίζω 'to complete'; Diog. L. 7, 63) ***imperfect*** ὡς ἔτι ὢν ἀ. *as one who is not yet perfected* IPhld 5:1 (v.l. ἀνάρπαστος; s. the text-crit. notes in Zahn, Lghtf., Bihlmeyer).—DELG and Frisk s.v. ἄρτι.

ἀνάπαυσις, εως, ἡ (s. ἀναπαύω; Mimnermus, Pind. et al.; ins; PFlor 57, 56; BGU 180, 5; LXX; En 23:3; TestSol, TestAbr B; TestZeb 10:4; JosAs 15:7 cod. A [s. 61, 18 Bat.]; ParJer 5:32; ApcSed 16:5 p. 197, 11 Ja; Just.)

❶ **cessation from an activity in which one is engaged, *stopping, ceasing*** (Just. D. 87, 3 ἀ.... ποιεῖσθαι, τοῦτ' ἔστιν ... πέρας ποιεῖσθαι) ἀνάπαυσιν οὐκ ἔχουσιν λέγοντες *they say without ceasing* **Rv 4:8;** cp. **14:11.**

❷ **cessation from wearisome activity for the sake of rest, *rest, relief*** (Diocles, fgm. 142 p. 186, 13; LXX; TestSol, TestAbr B 7 p. 111, 20 [Stone p. 70]; 9 p. 114, 2 [Stone p. 76]; EpArist 94; Philo, Fuga 174 ἡ ἐν θεῷ ἀ.; Jos., Ant. 3, 281 al.; Just., D. 8, 2) εὑρίσκειν ἀ. (Sir 6:28; 11:19; 22:13; Is 34:14; La 1:3) εὑρίσκειν ἀ. ταῖς ψυχαῖς **Mt 11:29** (ParJer 5:32 τῶν ψυχῶν; Heraclid. Crit. fgm. 1, 1 ψυχῆς ἀνάπαυσις; cp. Sir 51:27); cp. 2 Cl 6:7; perh. also GMary 463, 2 (s. note on line 1 Roberts p. 22). ἀ. διδόναι τινί (Ps 131:4; Aristobul. in Eus., PE 13, 12, 9 [Holladay p. 176, 7]; Jos., Bell. 4, 88) *give someone rest* Hs 6, 2, 7.—ἀ. τῆς μελλούσης βασιλείας καὶ ζωῆς αἰωνίου *rest in the coming kingdom and in eternal life* 2 Cl 5:5.

❸ **a location for resting, *resting-place*** (Heraclid. Crit., fgm. 1, 6; Gen 8:9; Num 10:33; Ps 131:8; Just., D. 138, 3) ζητεῖν ἀ. (Ruth 3:1; Sir 24:7) *look for a resting-place* **Mt 12:43; Lk 11:24.** PVielhauer, ἀνάπαυσις in Apophoreta (EHaenchen Festschr.), '64, 281–99.—M-M. TW. Sv.

ἀναπαύω fut. ἀναπαύσω; 1 aor. ἀνέπαυσα, impv. ἀνάπαυσον. Mid.: fut. ἀναπαύσομαι; aor. ἀνεπαυσάμην ParJer; ApcMos 9; pf. mid. and pass. ἀναπέπαυμαι; 1 aor. pass. ἀνεπαύθην, 1 pl. ἀνεπαύθημεν La 5:5; aor. pass. inf. (Schwyzer I 808) ἀναπαῆναι Hs 9, 5, 1f (v.l. ἀναπαυθῆναι); 2 fut. pass. ἀναπαήσομαι **Rv 14:13** (-παύσωνται v.l.; s. W-S. §13, 9; B-D-F §78) (s. παύω; Hom. et al., ins, pap, LXX; En 23:2; TestSol, TestAbr; Test12Patr; JosAs 10:8 cod. A [p. 51, 17 Bat.]; Philo).

❶ **to cause someone to gain relief from toil,** trans. (mid.: ApcEsdr 1:12 p. 25, 5) ***cause to rest, give*** (someone) ***rest, refresh, revive*** w. acc. (X., Cyr. 7, 1, 4; Appian, Mithrid. 45 §176; Arrian, Anab. 3, 7, 6 τὸν στρατόν; 1 Ch 22:18; Pr 29:17; Sir 3:6; Jos., Ant. 3, 61) κἀγὼ ἀναπαύσω ὑμᾶς *and I will give you rest* **Mt 11:28.** ἀνέπαυσεν αὐτήν (Anna) *let her* (Mary) *rest* GJs 6:3 (ἀπέπαυσεν pap). ἀ. τὸ πνεῦμα **1 Cor 16:18.** τὴν ψυχήν *set at rest* Hs 9, 5, 4. ἀνάπαυσόν μου τὰ σπλάγχνα *refresh, cheer my heart* **Phlm 20** (s. Nägeli 64f). κατὰ πάντα *in every way* IEph 2:1; Mg 15; Tr 12:1; Sm 9:2; 10:1; 12:1. Abs. IRo 10:2. ἀναπαύσασα τὴν κάλπιν *when she had set the pitcher down* GJs 11:1.—Pass. (TestAbr A 5 p. 82, 2 [Stone p. 12]) ἀναπέπαυται τὸ πνεῦμα αὐτοῦ *his spirit has been set at rest* **2 Cor 7:13.** τὰ σπλάγχνα ἀναπέπαυται (their) *hearts have been refreshed* **Phlm 7.**—μετὰ το ἀναπαῆναι GJs 2:4.

❷ **to bring someth. to a conclusion, *end, conclude, finish,*** trans. ἀναπαύσαντος τὴν προσευχήν *when* (Paul) *finished his prayer* AcPl Ha 4, 31.

❸ **to take one's rest, *rest*** mid. (also act. TestAbr B) (Cornutus 32 p. 69, 17; Artem. 1, 8 p. 14, 7; Plotinus, Enn. 6, 9, 9 ἀναπαύεται ψυχή; Julian, Letters 97, 382d; Herm. Wr. V 5 [408, 27 Sc.]; Ex 23:12; Is 14:30; 57:20; Esth 9:17f; TestSol; TestAbr A 5 p. 81, 34 [Stone p. 10]; B 5, p. 109, 18 [Stone p. 66] al.; TestJob; JosAs cod. A [p. 51, 17 Bat.]; Philo; Jos., Vi. 249).

ⓐ of persons who are drowsy ἀναπαύεσθε **Mt 26:45; Mk 14:41** (s. λοιπός 3αα); who have just eaten B 10:11; who are tired **Mk 6:31;** Hs 9, 5, 1f; GJs 4:4. ἀ. ἐκ τῶν κόπων *rest from their labors* **Rv 14:13** (cp. Pla., Critias 106a ἐκ μακρᾶς ἀναπεπαυμένος ὁδοῦ; Arrian, Anab. 3, 9, 1 ἐκ τῆς ὁδοῦ; Jos., Ant. 3, 91 ἀ. ἀπὸ παντὸς ἔργου). *Take life easy* **Lk 12:19; 16:23** D al.—ἀ. χρόνον μικρόν *remain quiet* (i.e. wait) *for a short time* (Da 12:13) **Rv 6:11.** τὴν μίαν ἡμέραν GJs 15:1.—Of sheep Hs 9, 1, 9.

ⓑ fig., abs. as goal of gnosticism Ox 654 (=ASyn 187, 20//GTh 2), 8f: [ἀναπα]ήσεται; cp. GHb 187, 17 (cp. Wsd 4:7; TestAbr B 7, p. 111, 20 [Stone p. 70] and 9 p. 114, 2 [Stone p. 76]).

❹ **to settle on an object,** mid. w. prep. ***rest upon*** in imagery (Is 11:2 ἀναπαύσεται ἐπ' αὐτὸν πνεῦμα τ. θεοῦ) τὸ τ. θεοῦ πνεῦμα ἐφ' ὑμᾶς ἀναπαύεται **1 Pt 4:14;** cp. Hs 2:5 Joly (s. ἐπαναπαύομαι).—Of God ἅγιος ἐν ἁγίοις ἀναπαυόμενος *holy, abiding among the holy* 1 Cl 59:3 (Is 57:15). Lit. s. ἀνάπαυσις.—M-M. TW. Sv.

ἀναπαφλάζω (Eutecnius 1 p. 13, 9; Hesych.; Ps.-Caesarius of Naz., Dial. 3, 146 [MPG XXXVIII 1096] of the Tigris. The simplex form παφλάζω Hom. et al.) ***boil, bubble up*** ApcPt 9, 24.—DELG s.v. παφλάζω.

ἀναπείθω 1 aor. pass. ἀνεπείσθην (s. πείθω; Hdt. et al.; ins, pap, LXX) **to move someone to do something by persuasion,**

induce. With an improper objective in mind (so Hdt. 3, 148; 5, 66, 1; X., Cyr. 1, 5, 3; PMagd 14, 3f [221 BC]; POxy 1295, 10; Jer 36:8; 1 Macc 1:11; Mel., HE 4, 26, 9) τινά w. inf. foll. (cp. Philo, Leg. All. 3, 212; Jos., Bell. 7, 438, Ant. 14, 285; 15, 72; PEnteux 49, 4) ἀ. τοὺς ἀνθρώπους *incites people* **Ac 18:13.** Pass. Hs 9, 13, 8.—DELG s.v. πείθομαι. M-M.

ἀνάπειρος, ον (s. πηρός; Tob 14:2 S) ***crippled* Lk 14:13, 21** (v.l. ἀνάπηρος; LXX mss. [2 Macc 8:24] also have both forms [Thackeray 83]; Phrynichus, Praep. Soph. p. 13, 4f Borries [1911] διὰ τοῦ η τὴν τρίτην, οὐ διὰ τῆς ει διφθόγγου ὡς οἱ ἀμαθεῖς 'w. η on the third-last syllable, not w. the dipthong ει as the unsophisticated do'.) See W-S. §5, 15; B-D-F §24; Mlt-H. 72.—DELG s.v. πηρός.

ἀναπέμπω fut. ἀναπέμψω; 1 aor. ἀνέπεμψα (s. πέμπω; Pind., Aeschyl.+; ins, pap; TestJob 48:3; Philo, Joseph., Just.; Mel., P. 91, 687).

❶ **to send up from a lower position to a higher, *send up*** (Ps.-Aristot., Mirabilia 114 φλόγα πυρός) toward heaven (Bias in Diog. L. 1, 88 εἰς θεοὺς ἀνάπεμπε) τὸ ἀμήν MPol 15:1 (cp. Just., A I, 65, 3 δόξαν; 67, 5 εὐχαριστίας).

❷ **to send on to someone in authority, *send*** (up), i.e. to one in a higher position (Plut., Marius 415 [17, 3]; Jos., Bell. 2, 571; OGI 329, 51; PHib 1, 57 [III BC]; PTebt 7, 7; hence t.t. for sending to the proper pers. or gov. agency [Jos., Ant. 4, 218; Nägeli 34]) τινὰ πρός τινα **Lk 23:7** (HHoehner, CFDMoule Festschr., '70, 84–90 [Antipas]); **Ac 25:21;** for this τινά τινι **27:1 v.l.**

❸ **to send back to a previous location, *send back*** (Plut., Sol. 80 [4, 6]; PParis 13, 22 [157 BC]; POxy 1032, 50 [162 AD]; Mel., P. 91, 687) τινά τινι **Lk 23:11** (v.l. πέμπω P[75] et al.); **Phlm 12;** τινὰ πρός τινα **Lk 23:15;** 1 Cl 65:1.—M-M. Spicq.

ἀνάπεσε, εἶν s. ἀναπίπτω.

ἀναπετάννυμι 1 aor. ptc. ἀναπετάσας Job 39:26; 1 aor. pass. ἀνεπετάσθην (πετάννυμι 'spread out'; Hom. et al.; PMich 425, 16 [198 AD]; Job 39:26 ['spread wings']; Joseph.) in our lit. pass. w. act. sense ***fly open, spring open, open*** of guarded doors [οἱ κεκλισμένοι πυ]λῶνες ἐν [ὀνό]ματι θεοῦ ἀνεπετ[άσθησαν] *then the gates [that had been closed] opened in the name of God* AcPl Ha 3, 24.—DELG s.v. πετάννυμι.

ἀναπηδάω 1 aor. ἀνεπήδησα (s. πηδάω; Hom. et al.; PHib, LXX; En 89:48; TestSol 9:3; Jos., Vi. 265) 'jump up' also w. weakened force ***stand up*** (Epict. 3, 4, 4; Tob 2:4; 7:6; PGM 1, 93; Jos., Ant. 8, 360) **Mk 10:50.**

ἀνάπηρος, ον (s. ἀνάπειρος, πηρός; the Attic form, as Soph. et al.; TestAbr A 1 p. 77, 7 [Stone p. 2]; Jos., Ant. 7, 61) subst. ***a cripple*** w. πτωχός, χωλός, τυφλός (Pla., Cri. 53a χωλοὶ καὶ τυφλοὶ καὶ ἄλλοι ἀνάπηροι; Aelian, VH 11, 9 p. 115, 23; Diog. L. 6, 33) **Lk 14:13 v.l., 21 v.l.**

ἀναπίπτω fut. 3 sg. ἀναπεσεῖται Sir 25:18; 2 aor. ἀνέπεσον and the later ἀνέπεσα (W-S. §13, 13; B-D-F §81, 3; Mlt-H. 208) (s. πίπτω; trag. et al.; UPZ 78, 4 [II BC], LXX; TestAbr A; Jos., Ant. 8, 256).

❶ **to recline on a couch to eat, *lie down, recline*** (Diod. S. 4, 59, 5, in a story about Procrustes ἐπί τινος κλίνης; Syntipas 48, 29 ἀ. ἐπὶ τ. κλίνης), esp. at a meal (Alexis Com. 293 [in Athen. 1, 23e]; Ps.-Lucian, Asin. 23; PGM 1, 24; Tob 2:1; 7:9 S; Jdth 12:16; s. Anz 301f) **Lk 11:37; 17:7; 22:14; J 13:12.** ἀ. εἰς τὸν ἔσχατον τόπον *occupy the humblest place* **Lk 14:10; Mt 20:28** D=Agr 22=ASyn. no. 263, p. 353. ἀνέπεσαν πρασιαὶ *they took their places in groups* to eat **Mk 6:40;** cp. **J 6:10.** ἀ. ἐπὶ τῆς γῆς *take their places on the ground* **Mk 8:6;** ἀ. ἐπὶ τὴν γῆν **Mt 15:35.**

❷ **to lean while reclining at a meal, *lean, lean back*** (Pla., Phdr. 254b and e; Polyb. 1, 21, 2) *leaned back from where he lay* (Goodsp.) **J 13:25** (ἐπιπίπτω v.l.); **21:20.**—M-M. TW.

ἀναπλάσσω 1 aor. mid. ἀνεπλασάμην; fut. pass. 2 sg. ἀναπλασθήσῃ JosAs 15:4 (s. πλάσσω; Hdt. et al.; PHal 1, 183 [III BC]; Jos., C. Ap. 2, 248; Just., D. 8, 4 Χριστόν τινα; Ath. 27, 1 εἴδωλα 'fashion cult images', R. 13 p. 63, 15 'make up, devise'; Mel., P. 47, 333; 83, 621 ἄνθρωπον 'create') **to form anew, *form, remold.***

ⓐ lit. of a potter, who reshapes a vessel he has spoiled πάλιν αὐτὸ ἀ. 2 Cl 8:2 (cp. Wsd 15:7).

ⓑ fig., of a person's spiritual transformation B 6:11, 14.—Sv.

ἀναπληρόω fut. ἀναπληρώσω; 1 aor. ἀνεπλήρωσα. Pass.: fut. 3 pl. ἀναπληρωθήσονται Is 60:20; aor. ἀνεπληρώθην LXX; pf. 3 pl. ἀναπεπλήρωνται Gen 15:16 (s. πληρόω; Eur.+).

❶ **to complete the quantity of someth., *make complete*** fig. (Appian, Bell. Civ. 3, 47 §191 a body of troops, 4, 89 §374 of outstanding obligations; schol. on Nicander, Ther. 447 τὴν ἡλικίαν=period of childhood; EpArist 75; Just., D. 81, 3 χίλια ἔτη) ἀ. αὐτῶν τὰς ἁμαρτίας (cp. Gen 15:16) *fill up the measure of their sins* **1 Th 2:16** (unless this belongs in 2 as a commercial metaphor).

❷ **to carry out an agreement or obligation, *fulfill*** (a contract: UPZ 112 V, 3 [203/202 BC]; O. Wilck. I 532–34. A duty: POxy 1121, 11. An order for work: Jos., Ant. 8, 58) of prophecies (1 Esdr 1:54 εἰς ἀναπλήρωσιν τ. ῥήματος τ. κυρίου) ἀναπληροῦται αὐτοῖς ἡ προφητεία *with them the prophecy is being fulfilled* **Mt 13:14.** Of claims upon one: ἀ. τὸν νόμον τ. Χριστοῦ **Gal 6:2.** ἀ. πᾶσαν ἐντολήν B 21:8.

❸ **to supply what is lacking, *fill a gap, replace*** (Pla., Symp. 188e; SIG 364, 62; OGI 56, 46; PLille I, 8, 14 [III BC]; Jos., Bell. 4, 198, Ant. 5, 214) τὸ ὑστέρημα (Herm. Wr. 13, 1 τὰ ὑστερήματα ἀναπλήρωσον; TestBenj 11:5) w. gen. of pers. *make up for someone's absence* or *lack, represent one who is absent* (PMonac 14, 17f [VI AD] τῷ βικαρίῳ Ἑρμώνθεως ἀναπληροῦντι τὸν τόπον τοῦ τοποτηρητοῦ) **1 Cor 16:17; Phil 2:30;** 1 Cl 38:2. τὸν τ. ὑπακοῆς τόπον ἀναπληρῶσαι *take the attitude of obedience* 1 Cl 63:1. τοὺς τύπους τῶν λίθων ἀ. *fill up the impressions left by the stones* (cp. EpArist 75) Hs 9, 10, 1.

❹ **to occupy a place, *occupy, fill*** ὁ ἀναπληρῶν τ. τόπον τ. ἰδιώτου **1 Cor 14:16,** because of the ἰδ. of vss. 23f, cannot mean 'the one who occupies the position' (for this mng. of τόπος see s.v. 1e; ἀναπληρ. in such a connection: Ps.-Clem., Hom. 3, 60; cp. the use of ἀποπληρόω Epict. 2, 4, 5; Jos., Bell. 5, 88) of an 'outsider', i.e., in contrast to those speaking in tongues, one who is not so gifted (PBachmann, w. ref. to Talmudic usage; Ltzm., w. ref. to Whitaker, s. below; JSickenberger; H-DWendland). Rather ἀ. τὸν τόπον τινός means *take* or *fill someone's place* (cp. Diod. S. 19, 22, 2 τὸν τόπον ἀ.; Hero Alex. I p. 8, 20 τὸν κενωθέντα τόπον ἀ.; Pla., Tim. 79b ἀ. τὴν ἕδραν), and τόπος here means a place actually occupied by an ἰδιώτης in the meeting (a view not shared by most Eng. translators), but it is not necessary to assume that a section was reserved for catechumens (so GHeinrici; JWeiss). On the other hand, Ltzm. asks whether baptized Christians would be better informed. S. ἰδιώτης 2 and GWhitaker, JTS 22, 1921, 268.—M-M. TW.

ἀναπνέω 1 aor. ἀνέπνευσα (s. πνέω; Hom. et al.; also Job 9:18; Philo, Joseph.) ***draw breath, revive*** ἀνέπνευσεν ἡ ματρῶνα *the* (married) *woman* (Artemilla) *revived* (from a swoon) AcPl Ha 4, 2.

ἀναπολόγητος, ον (s. ἀπολογέομαι; Polyb. 29, 10, 5; Dionys. Hal. 7, 46; Plut., Brut. 1006 [46, 2]; Cicero, Ad Att. 16, 7 et al.; Jos., C. Ap. 2, 137; Just., A I, 3, 5; cp. 28, 3) ***without excuse, inexcusable*** (Polyb. 12, 21, 10; Dio Chrys. 2, 39) εἰς τὸ εἶναι αὐτοὺς ἀναπολογήτους *so that they are without excuse* **Ro 1:20;** ἀ. εἶ **2:1.**

ἀναπράσσω (s. πράσσω; Thu. et al., ins, pap) as a commercial term ***demand, exact*** of a payment **Lk 19:23 v.l.**

ἀναπτύσσω fut. 3 pl. ἀναπτύξουσι (Dt 22:17), 1 aor. ἀνέπτυξα ***unroll*** of a book in scroll form (s. πτύσσω; so Hdt. et al.; Epict. 1, 17, 21; Aesop, Fab. 332 H.=264 P.; 4 Km 19:14; TestSol 22:6 P; TestAbr B 10 p. 115, 1 [Stone p. 78]; Jos., Vi. 223; Iren. 1, 10, 3 [Harv. I 96, 9]) **Lk 4:17;** PtK 4, p. 15, 30.—Renehan '82, 24f.

ἀνάπτω fut. ἀνάψω LXX; 1 aor. ἀνῆψα LXX. Pass.: fut. ἀναφθήσομαι LXX; aor. pass. ἀνήφθην ***kindle*** (s. ἅπτω; so Eur., Hdt. et al.; PGiss 3, 8; PGM 13, 681; 2 Ch 13:11; Just.) ὕλην (cp. Polyaenus 4, 7, 9 πῦρ … ἀνῆψε τὴν ὕλην; Philo, Aet. M. 127; PsSol 12:2 πῦρ ἀνάπτον καλλονήν; Ath. 19, 1 ἀνάψας πυράν; Tat. 5, 2) *a forest* **Js 3:5.** Cp. **Ac 28:2 v.l.** Of fire (Eur., Or. 1137; TestAbr A 4 p. 80, 24 [Stone p. 8]=TestSol 6:10 L λύχνους; Jos., Ant. 3, 207) ἀνήφθη *has been kindled*=is now burning **Lk 12:49** (Diod. S. 13, 84, 2 ὅταν ἀναφθῇ πῦρ=when a fire would be kindled, or would burn). Just., D. 8, 1 πῦρ ἐν τῇ ψυχῇ ἀνήφθη.—M-M.

ἀναρίθμητος, ον (s. ἀριθμέω; Pind., Hdt. et al.; LXX; JosAs 16:13 cod. A [p. 65, 1 Bat.]; Jos., Ant. 17, 214; Just., Iren.) ***innumerable*** of the grains of sand on the seashore **Hb 11:12;** cp. Just., D. 120, 2 ἡ ἄμμος … ἀ.—DELG s.v. ἀριθμός.

ἀναρπάζω 1 aor. ἀνήρπασα (Hom. et al. in var. mngs.; Judg 9:25 A; EpArist 146; Joseph.; Mel., P. 50, 358; 91, 683)

❶ ***lift up*** GJs 6:1.—❷ ***carry up*** ἐν τῷ ἁγιάσματι τοῦ κοιτῶνος *in the consecrated area of the bedroom* 6:3.

ἀνασείω (Hes. et al.; PTebt 28, 20 [II BC]; Jos., Bell. 5, 120) (lit. 'shake', 'brandish', e.g. a shield Hes., Sc. 344; syn. σείω q.v.) **to cause to be disturbed, *stir up, disturb, upset, incite*** (cp. our colloq. 'shake up') (Diod. S. 13, 91, 4; 14, 10, 3; 17, 62, 5; 18, 10, 1; Is 36:18 Aq., Sym.) w. acc. τ. ὄχλον **Mk 15:11.** τ. λαόν **Lk 23:5** (cp. Dionys. Hal. 8, 81 τὸ πλῆθος; Philod., Rhet. II 290 Sudh.) τὴν Ἰκονείων πόλιν ἀνασείει, ἔτι δὲ καὶ τὴν σὴν Θέκλαν AcPl Ox 6, 20 (=Aa I 242, 1).—M-M. TW.

ἀνασκάπτω pf. pass. ptc. n. pl. ἀνεσκαμμένα (Aristot., Theophr. et al.; Ps. 7:16; 79:17; Joseph.) ***dig up, raze, destroy*** **Ac 15:16 v.l.** (s. κατασκάπτω).

ἀνασκευάζω (σκευάζω 'prepare, make ready'; Thu. et al. in var. mngs.; POxy 745, 5 [I AD]; Jos., Bell. 6, 282, Ant. 14, 406; 418; Iren.; Theoph. Ant. 3, 4 [p. 212, 1]) lit. 'tear down, dismantle' (a process of packing up instead of making ready) then fig. **to cause inward distress, *upset, unsettle,*** w. ταράσσειν (cp. Vett. Val. 212, 20 ἀνασκευασθήσεται καὶ ἐπιτάραχον γενήσεται) ἀνασκευάζειν τὰς ψυχάς **Ac 15:24.**—M-M. TW.

ἀνασπάω fut. ἀνασπάσω; 1 aor. ἀνέσπασα; 1 aor. pass. ἀνεσπάσθην (s. σπάομαι; Hom. et al.; PTebt 420, 25; BGU 1041, 8; PGM 4, 2498; 2973; Hab 1:15; Da 6:18; Bel 42 Theod.; TestSol 6:13 D; TestAbr A 11 p. 90, 4 [Stone p. 28]; ParJer 3:13; Jos., Ant. 2, 259 al.) ***draw/pull up*** **Lk 14:5.** Of the sheet, which Peter saw in his vision ἀνεσπάσθη εἰς τ. οὐρανόν **Ac 11:10** (Pherecrates Com., fgm. 180 K. κάδους ἀνασπῶν).—M-M.

ἀνάστα s. ἀνίστημι.

ἀνάστασις, εως, ἡ (s. ἀνίστημι; Aeschyl., Hdt.+ in var. mngs.).

❶ **a change for the better in status, *rising up, rise*** (La 3:63; Zech 3:8; Jos., Ant. 17, 212; 18, 301 [here of the 'erection' of a statue]) κεῖται εἰς πτῶσιν καὶ ἀ. πολλῶν *he is destined for the fall and rise of many* of Jesus **Lk 2:34,** i.e. because of him many will fall and others will rise, viz. in relation to God (for contrast w. πτῶσις cp. Evagrius Pont., Sent. 5, 19 p. 327 Frankenberg: ἡ μικρὰ τ. σώματος ἀνάστασίς ἐστιν ἡ μετάθεσις αὐτοῦ ἐκ πτώσεως τ. ἀσελγείας εἰς τὴν τ. ἁγιασμοῦ ἀνάστασιν).—Esp.

❷ **resurrection from the dead, *resurrection*** (Aeschyl., Eum. 648 ἅπαξ θανόντος οὔτις ἐστ' ἀ. [cp. Job 7:9f; 16:22]; Ps.-Lucian, De Salt. 45; Ael. Aristid. 32, 25 K.=12 p. 142 D.; 46 p. 300 D.; IGR IV 743, 25 [o]ἱ δὴ δ[είλ]αιοι πάντ[ες] εἰς ἀ[νά]στασιν|[----][the stone breaks off after ἀ. and some think that βλέποντες or the like is to be supplied]; 2 Macc 7:14; 12:43), and so

ⓐ in the past: of Jesus' res. (Orig., C. Cels. 5, 57, 25) **Ac 1:22; 2:31; 4:33; Ro 6:5; Phil 3:10** (JFitzmyer, BRigaux Festschr., '70, 411–25); **1 Pt 3:21;** 1 Cl 42:3; ISm 3:1, 3; in more detail ἀ. ἐκ νεκρῶν **1 Pt 1:3;** ἀ. νεκρῶν *res. from the dead* **Ro 1:4;** w. the passion of Jesus IEph 20:1; Mg 11; Tr ins; Phld ins; 8:2; 9:2; Sm 7:2; 12:2; cp. 1:2. τὸν Ἰησοῦν καὶ τὴν ἀ. εὐαγγελίζεσθαι *proclaim Jesus and the res.* i.e. his res., and in consequence, the possibility of a general res. **Ac 17:18** (but s. 3 below. τὸν Ἰησοῦν καὶ τὴν ἀνάστασιν could also mean 'the res. of Jesus', as perh. Nicol Dam.: 90 fgm. 130, 18 p. 400, 17 Jac. μνήμη τἀνδρὸς καὶ φιλοστοργίας='... the love of the man'); cp. vs. **32** and **4:2.** Of the raisings from the dead by Elijah and Elisha ἔλαβον γυναῖκες ἐξ ἀ. τοὺς νεκροὺς αὐτῶν *women* (i.e. the widow of Zarephath and the Shunammite woman 3 Km 17:23; 4 Km 4:36) *received their dead by res.* **Hb 11:35.**

ⓑ of the future res. (Theoph. Ant. 1, 13 [p. 86, 25]), linked with Judgment Day: described as ἀ. νεκρῶν (Did., Gen. 96, 13) **Mt 22:31; Ac 23:6; 24:15, 21; 26:23; 1 Cor 15:12f; 21; 42; Hb 6:2;** D 16:6; or ἀ. ἐκ νεκρῶν **Lk 20:35;** B 5:6; AcPlCor 2:35 (cp. Ar. 15, 3; Just., D. 45, 2); cp. IPol 7:1; Pol 7:1; MPol 14:2. ἀ. σαρκός (not found in the NT) AcPlCor 1:12; 2:24 (Just., D. 80, 5; σωμάτων Tat. 6, 1; Ath., R. 11 p. 59, 14). Of Jesus: τὴν ἀ. ποιεῖν *bring about the res. (of the dead)* B 5:7. Jesus' Passion as our *res.* ISm 5:3. ἀθάνατος τῆς ἀ. καρπός 2 Cl 19:3. Described as ἀ. κρείττων **Hb 11:35** in contrast w. the res. of the past, because the latter was, after all, followed by death. ἡ μέλλουσα ἀ. (Theoph. Ant. 2, 15 [p. 138, 17]) *the future res.* 1 Cl 24:1. ἡ κατὰ καιρὸν γινομένη ἀ. *the res. that comes at regular intervals* (i.e. seasons, day and night), as a type of the future res. 24:2.—More details in J, who mentions an ἀ. ἐν τῇ ἐσχάτῃ ἡμέρᾳ *on the Last Day* **J 11:24** and differentiates betw. the ἀ. κρίσεως *res. for judgment* for the wicked and the ἀ. ζωῆς *res. to life* for those who do good **5:29.** Christ calls himself ἡ ἀ. and ἡ ζωή **11:25,** since he mediates both to humans.—Paul seeks to demonstrate the validity of belief in Jesus' res. in terms of the res. of the dead in general **1 Cor 15:12ff** (s. MDahl, The Res. of the Body. A Study of 1 Cor 15, '62 and s. τάγμα 1b). γνῶναι … τὴν δύναμιν τῆς ἀ. αὐτου **Phil 3:10.—Lk 14:14** mentions only a res. of the just, as in some intertestamental belief; likew. B 21:1.

Hebraistically υἱοὶ τῆς ἀ. (w. υἱοὶ θεοῦ) *children of the res.*=sharers in the resurrection **Lk 20:36.** A second res. is presupposed by the ἀ. ἡ πρώτη of **Rv 20:5f**. Denial of res. by the Sadducees **Mt 22:23, 28, 30f; Mk 12:18, 23; Lk 20:27, 33, 35f** (on this see Schürer II 391; 411); by the Epicureans **Ac 17:18** (ERohde, Psyche[3] 1903 II 331–35; cp. the ins 2 above, beg.); and by Christians **1 Cor 15:12** (prob. in the sense of Just., D. 80, 4 λέγουσι μὴ εἶναι νεκρῶν ἀνάστασιν, ἀλλ' ἅμα τῷ ἀποθνήσκειν τὰς ψυχὰς αὐτῶν ἀναλαμβάνεσθαι εἰς τ. οὐρανόν 'they say there is no resurrection of the dead, but that at the time of death their souls are taken up into heaven'; s. JWilson, ZNW 59, '68, 90–107); **2 Ti 2:18** (cp. Menander in Iren. 1, 23, 5 [Harv. I 195] resurrectionem enim per id quod est in eum baptisma, accipere eius discipulos, et ultra non posse mori, sed perseverare non senescentes et immortales [Menander teaches that] 'his followers receive resurrection by being baptized into him, and that they face death no more, but live on without growing old, exempt from death'; cp. Just., A I, 26, 4; Valentinus in Clem. of Alex., Str. 4, 13, 91; Tertull., Carn. Resurr. 25 agnitio sacramenti [=ἡ τοῦ μυστηρίου γνῶσις] resurrectio).—FNötscher, Altoriental. u. atl. Auferstehungsglaube 1926; JLeipoldt, Sterbende u. auferstehende Götter 1923; Cumont[3] '31; ANikolainen, D. Auferstehungsglauben in d. Bibel u. in ihrer Umwelt. I Relgesch. Teil '44. II NT '46.—WBousset, Rel.[3], 1926, 269–74 al.; Billerb. IV 1928, 1166–98.—AMeyer, D. Auferstehung Christi 1905; KLake, The Historical Evidence of Res. of Jesus Christ 1907; LBrun, D. Auferst. Christi in d. urchr. Überl. 1925; PGardner-Smith, The Narratives of the Resurrection 1926; SMcCasland, The Res. of Jesus '32; MGoguel, La foi à la résurr. de Jésus dans le Christianisme primitif '33; EFascher, ZNW 26, 1927, 1–26; EFuchs, ZKG 51, '32, 1–20; AThomson, Did Jesus Rise from the Dead? '40; EHirsch, D. Auferstehungsgeschichten u. d. chr. Glaube '40; PAlthaus, D. Wahrheit des kirchl. Osterglaubens[2] '41; WMichaelis, D. Erscheinungen des Auferstandenen '44; ARamsey, The Res. of Christ '45; JLeipoldt, Zu den Auferstehungsgeschichten: TLZ 73, '48, 737–42 (rel.-hist.); KRengstorf, Die Auferstehung Jesu[2] '54; GKoch, Die Auferstehung J. Christi '59; HGrass, Ostergeschehen u. Osterberichte '56; ELohse, Die Auferstehung J. Chr. im Zeugnis des Lk '61; HvCampenhausen, Tradition and Life in the Early Church, '68, 42–89; WCraig, Assessing the NT Evidence for the Historicity of the Resurrection of Jesus '89; GLüdemann, Die Auferstehung Jesu '94. S. also τάφος 1.—KDeissner, Auferstehungshoffnung u. Pneumagedanke b. Pls 1912; GVos, The Pauline Doctrine of the Res.: PTR 27, 1929, 1–35; 193–226; FGuntermann, D. Eschatologie d. hl. Pls '32; HMolitor, Die Auferstehung d. Christen und Nichtchristen nach d. Ap. Pls '33; LSimeone, Resurrectionis iustorum doctr. in ep. S. Pauli '38; DStanley, Christ's Resurrection in Pauline Soteriology '61; CMoule, NTS 12, '65/66, 106–23; MdeBoer, The Defeat of Death '88; JHolleman, A Traditio-Historical Study of Paul's Eschatology in 1 Cor 15 (NovT Suppl. 84), '96.—RGrant, Miracle and Nat. Law '52, 221–63. JBuitkamp, Auferstehungsglaube in den Qumrantexten, diss. Groningen '64; GWild, Auferstehungsglaube des späten Israel, diss. Bonn. '67; W. Pannenberg, Grundzüge der Christologie[6] '82, 74ff.

❸ **a deity within a polytheistic system,** ***Resurrection*** **Ac 17:18.** This interpr., first set forth by Chrysostom (Hom. in Act. 38, 1), has found modern supporters (s. Haenchen ad loc.). The semantic issue arises from the fact that the narrative presents the auditors as theologically ignorant. Their assumption is that Paul seemed to be a proclaimer of 'new divinities' (vs. 18a). From their perspective the term ἀ. suggests a divinity named Resurrection (abstractions identified as divinities were not uncommon in the Gr-Rom. world, s. EA 19 '92, 71–73). But the omniscient author informs the reader that bodily resurrection (as in 2 above) is meant.—DELG s.v. ἵστημι. M-M. TW. Sv.

ἀναστατόω fut. 3 sg. ἀναστατώσει Da 7:23, 1 aor. ἀνεστάτωσα (late Gk.: pap, e.g. BGU 1858, 12 [I BC]; POxy 119, 10; PGM 4, 2244; LXX, Aq., Sym. [Nägeli 47f]) **to upset the stability of a pers. or group,** ***disturb, trouble, upset*** τὴν οἰκουμένην **Ac 17:6.** Of the leaders of a party disturbing the church **Gal 5:12** (cp. BGU 1079, 20 [41 AD] μὴ ἵνα ἀναστατώσῃς ἡμᾶς). Abs. ὁ ἀναστατώσας *the man who raised a revolt* **Ac 21:38.**—DELG s.v. ἵστημι. M-M.

ἀνασταυρόω (s. σταυρόω; Hdt. et al.) always simply ***crucify*** (ἀνά=up; cp. Pla., Gorg. 473c; Hellen. Oxy. XV, 5; Polyb. 1, 11, 5; 1, 24, 6; Diod. S. 2, 1, 10; 2, 44, 2; 13, 111, 5; 14, 53, 5; Plut., Fab. 177 [6, 5], Cleom. 823 [39, 2]; Chariton 4, 2, 6; Aesop., Fab. 152 P. [=σταυρόω 264 H.]; POxy 842, col. 18, 22; Jos., Bell. 2, 306; 5, 449, Ant. 2, 73; 11, 246, Vi. 420); hence **Hb 6:6** ἀνασταυροῦντας ἑαυτοῖς τὸν υἱὸν τ. θεοῦ may mean *since, to their own hurt, they crucify the Son of God,* of apostate Christians; but the context seems to require the fig. mng. *crucify again* (ἀνά=again), and the ancient translators and Gk. fathers understood it so; cp. L-S-J-M s.v., and Lampe s.v. 2.—AVitti, Verb. Dom. 22, '42, 174–82.—TW.

ἀναστενάζω 1 aor. ἀνεστέναξα (s. στενάζω; Aeschyl., Choëph. 335; Hdt. 1, 863; PGM 4, 2492f; Sir 25:18; La 1:4; Sus 22 Theod.; JosAs; ApcMos 9) ***sigh deeply*** ἀναστενάξας τῷ πνεύματι αὐτοῦ λέγει *he sighed deeply in his spirit* (=to himself; cp. Mk 2:8) *and said* **Mk 8:12** (cp. 2 Macc 6:30; JGibson, BT 38, '87, 122–25). ἀνεστενάζων ὅτι ἐθριαμβεύετο ὑπὸ τῆς πόλεως *distressed over being subject to ridicule by the city, as though he were being exhibited in a triumphal procession* AcPl Ha 4, 12f (for distress in an apparently hopeless situation cp. Il. 10, 9 al.).—Error for ἀτενίζω or ἐνατενίζω GJs 3:1; 12:2 (s. deStrycker p. 298; s. also the sequence ἀνεστέναξε καὶ ἦν ἀτενίζουσα JosAs 8:8).—CBonner, HTR 20, 1927, 171–81.—DELG s.v. στένω.

ἀνάστηθι s. ἀνίστημι.

ἀναστρέφω fut. ἀναστρέψω LXX; 1 aor. ἀνέστρεψα. Pass. fut. 3 sg. ἀναστραφήσεται Sir 39:3; 50:28; 2 aor. ἀνεστράφην, ptc. ἀναστραφείς; pf. 3 sg. ἀνέστραπται Josh 5:6 (s. στρέφω; Hom.+ in var. mngs.; ins, pap, LXX, TestSol 18:12; TestAsh 6:3; Philo, Joseph.; Just., A I, 53, 3).

❶ **to overturn completely,** ***upset, overturn,*** trans. (Polyb. 5, 9, 3; Ps.-Apollod. 3, 8, 1; Dionys. Hal. 9, 6, 2, all acc. to the mss.) τὶ ***something*** τὰς τραπέζας *overturn the tables* **J 2:15 v.l.** for ἀνατρέπω (s. Hdb. ad loc.).

❷ **to spend time in a locality,** ***stay, live*** pass. in act. sense ἐν (Pla., Rep. 8, 558a μένειν καὶ ἀ. ἐν; X., Hell. 6, 4, 16; Polyb. 3, 33, 18; Epict. 1, 2, 26; Plut., Fab. 179 [9, 5]; Josh 5:6; Ezk 19:6. Cp. PKatz, JTS 47, '46, 31) **Mt 17:22 v.l.**

❸ **to conduct oneself in terms of certain principles,** ***act, behave, conduct oneself, live,*** pass. in act. but nonliteral sense, ext. of 2 ('to turn back and forth') (X. et al.; Polyb. 1, 9, 7; 1, 74, 13 al.; Chion, Ep. 7, 1; Crates, Ep. 35, 2 p. 216 H.; Vett. Val. index; ins, pap; Dssm. B 83, NB 22 [BS 88; 194], LO 264f [LAE 315]; Nägeli 38; Thieme 14; Hatch 136; Pr 20:7; Ezk 22:30; Jos., Ant. 15, 190; Just., A I, 53, 3); always with the kind of behavior more exactly described

ⓐ by an adv. (Ael. Dion. σ, 41 ἀμαθῶς ἀναστρέφεσθαι; SIG and OGI indices; Jos., Ant. 19, 72 εὐπρεπῶς) ἁγνῶς

(Hatch, op. cit. III 73 Cilic. ins) Hs 9, 27, 2. ἰσχυρῶς καὶ ἀνδρείως ἀ. *conduct oneself w. strength and courage* 5, 6, 6. καλῶς ἀ. (SIG 717, 95, OGI 322, 8) **Hb 13:18.** ἀμέμπτως (OGI 323, 5) 1 Cl 63:3; ἀ.... ὁσίως καὶ δικαίως (SIG 800, 20f) 2 Cl 5:6.

ⓑ by prep. phrases (X., Ages. 9, 4 ἀ. ἐν μέσαις εὐφροσύναις; EpArist 252; Just., A I, 53, 3 τὰ παλαιά, ἐν οἷς ... ἀνεστράφησαν) ἐν ταῖς ἐπιθυμίαις τῆς σαρκός *live in the passions of the flesh*=be a slave to physical passion **Eph 2:3.** ἐν παλαιοῖς πράγμασιν *according to ancient* (i.e. Israelite) *customs* IMg 9:1. ἐν τρυφαῖς πολλαῖς Hm 11:12. ἐν πλάνῃ **2 Pt 2:18.** ἀ. ἐν οἴκῳ θεοῦ *conduct oneself in the household of God* **1 Ti 3:15.** ἐν φόβῳ ἀ. *live in fear* **1 Pt 1:17.**

ⓒ w. adv. and prep. phrase (Simplicius in Epict. p. 24, 16 ἀλύτως ἐν τούτοις ἀναστρεφώμεθα; Jos., Vi. 273) ὁσίως ἀ. ἐν καθαρᾷ διανοίᾳ *live in holiness w. a pure mind* 1 Cl 21:8.

ⓓ w. more than one ἐν in var. mngs. ἐν ἁπλότητι ... τοῦ θεοῦ, καὶ οὐκ ἐν σοφίᾳ σαρκικῇ ἀλλ' ἐν χάριτι θεοῦ ἀνεστράφημεν ἐν τῷ κόσμῳ *we have conducted ourselves in the world in sincerity before God, not w. earthly wisdom, but in the grace of God* **2 Cor 1:12.**—Somewhat as the phrase ἀ. ἐν τῷ κόσμῳ above—i.e. not in the active sense of practicing something—οὕτως ἀ. **Hb 10:33** *to live in such a way* (i.e. amid reproach and affliction) means *to be treated in such a way.*

❹ **to be involved with someone in close proximity, *associate,*** intr., μετά τινος ***w. someone*** (Jos., Ant. 1, 55 μετά; difft. πρός τινος Epict. 4, 1, 116, where the emphasis is placed on personal face-to-face encounter and dealings with another) B 19:6; D 3:9.

❺ **to go back to a locality, *return, come back,*** intr. (Appian, Bell. Civ. 5, 51 §215; Polyaenus 1, 48, 1; 8, 12; Crates, Ep. 28, 8 [Malherbe p. 78]; Sus 49 Theod.; Jdth 15:7; 1 Macc 5:8; 10:52, 55 v.l.; Jos., Ant. 7, 226) **Ac 5:22; 15:16.**—M-M. TW.

ἀναστροφή, ῆς, ἡ (in var. mgs. since Aeschyl., Pre-Socr. et al.; ins, pap, LXX; Jos., Ant. 18, 359 al.; Just., A I, 10, 2) **conduct expressed according to certain principles *way of life, conduct, behavior*** (Polyb. 4, 82, 1 [FKälker, Quaest. de elocut. Polyb.=Leipz. Stud. III/2, 1880, 301]; Teles p. 41, 2; Diog. L.; Epict. 1, 9, 24; 1, 22, 13; ins: SIG index; IG XII/1, 1032, 6 [II BC]; IMagnMai 91b, 6; IPergamon 86; PTebt 703, 270 [IIIBC] Tob 4:14; 2 Macc 6:23; EpArist 130; 216) ἠκούσατε τ. ἐμὴν ἀ. ποτε ἐν τῷ Ἰουδαϊσμῷ *you have heard of my conduct when I was still in Judaism* **Gal 1:13.** κατὰ τὴν προτέραν ἀ. *according to your former* (i.e. pre-Christian) *way of life* **Eph 4:22** (GDI 4320, 5f κατὰ τὰν ἄλλαν ἀναστροφάν [Rhodes]). ἡ ἐν φόβῳ ἁγνὴ ἀ. **1 Pt 3:2;** cp. vs. **1.** ἡ ἀγαθὴ ἐν Χριστῷ ἀ. vs. **16.** ἡ καλὴ ἀ. **Js 3:13; 1 Pt 2:12.** ἡ ματαία ἀ. πατροπαράδοτος *the futile* (i.e. directed toward futile ends) *way of life handed down by your fathers* **1:18.** ἡ ἐν ἀσελγείᾳ ἀ. **2 Pt 2:7.** ἡ ἔκβασις τῆς ἀ. **Hb 13:7.** ἅγιον ἐν πάσῃ ἀ. γίνεσθαι *be holy in all your conduct* **1 Pt 1:15.** W. λόγος, ἀγάπη κτλ. **1 Ti 4:12.** Pl. ἅγιαι ἀ. καὶ εὐσέβειαι *holy conduct and piety* (pl. to include all varieties; cp. EpArist 130) **2 Pt 3:11.**—DDaube, Alexandrian Methods of Interpretation and the Rabbis: Festschr. HLewald '53, 27–44.—DELG s.v. στρέφω. M-M. TW. Spicq.

ἀνασῴζω pass. fut. 3 pl. ἀνασωθήσονται Ezk 7:16; aor. ptc. ἀνασωθείς LXX; pf. ptc. ἀνασεσῳσμένος LXX (s. σῴζω; Soph., Hdt. et al.; Hippocr., Ep. 11, 3 H. ἀνασῴζω τι; OGI 493, 21; UPZ 19, 12; PTebt 920, 24 [both II BC]; Jer 27:29; Zech 2:11; Jos., Ant. 5, 214; 6, 364; 365) ***rescue, save*** pass. τοὺς ἀνασῳζομένους **Hb 10:14** P^{46} (for τ. ἁγιαζομένους).—New Docs 4, 142, no. 41. DELG s.v. σῶς. TW.

ἀνατάσσομαι 1 aor. ἀνεταξάμην lit. 'arrange in proper order'; fig., ***to organize in a series*** (s. τάσσω; Plut., Mor. 968c; Iren. 3, 21, 2 [Harv. II 114, 12]) διήγησιν ἀ. *draw up, compose/compile a narrative* **Lk 1:1,** implying use of traditional material and, as the context indicates, with emphasis on orderly sequence (synon. συντάσσεσθαι 'compile'; cp. Syr., Copt., Goth. versions; Athanasius' 39th Festival Letter: EPreuschen, Analecta[2] II 1910, p. 43, 9; so Hippiatr. 1, 1 in a prologue reminiscent of **Lk 1:1;** EpArist 144). Cp. PCorssen, GGA 1899, 317f; Zahn on **Lk 1:1;** PScheller, De hellenist. conscribendae historiae arte, diss. Leipz. 1911, 23; JMansion, Serta Leodiensia 1930, 261–67; HCadbury, JBL 52, '33, 56–58; LAlexander, The Preface to Luke's Gospel '93, 110f. S. also on παρακολουθέω 4.—M-M. TW.

ἀνατεθραμμένος s. ἀνατρέφω.

ἀνατέλλω (s. ἀνατολή) fut. ἀνατελῶ; 1 aor. ἀνέτειλα; pf. ἀνατέταλκα.

❶ trans. (Hom. +; Philo, Conf. Ling. 63; Gen 3:18; ApcMos 24; ApcZeph; cp. Anz 265f) **cause to spring/rise up** (Jos., Ant. 1, 31; Just., D. 107, 3) ξύλον *a tree* Dg 12:1 (PsSol 11:5; cp. Aeschyl., fgm. 193, 7f [300 N.] Αἴγυπτος Δήμητρος ἀνατέλλει στάχυν). τροφὴν τοῖς ζῴοις *cause food to grow for the living creatures* 1 Cl 20:4. ἥλιον *cause the sun to rise* **Mt 5:45;** GNaass 59, 23 (cp. Nicephorus: Rhet. Gr. I p. 500, 2 μετὰ τόκον ἀστέρα καινὸν ἀνέτελλε).

❷ intr. (Soph., Hdt. et al.; LXX, TestJob 37:8; TestSim 18:3 al.; JosAs; ApcEsdr 4:29 p. 29, 4 Tdf.; Ar., Just.; Mel., fgm. 8b 34, 45; Joseph.) **to move upward above the horizon, *rise, spring up, dawn.***

ⓐ of heavenly bodies and atmospheric phenomena (Neugebauer-Hoesen no. 137c II, 9). Of the sun (oft. in Gk. lit.; also Michel 466, 10 ἅμα τῷ ἡλίῳ ἀνατέλλοντι; PHib 27, 52; Gen 32:31; Ex 22:3; Sir 26:16; Philo; Ar. 6, 1. Of stars En 2:1; TestLevi 18:3; JosAs, ApcEsdr; Ar. 4, 2; Just., D. 106, 4 al.) **Mt 13:6; Mk 4:6; 16:2; Js 1:11.** Of Christ ἕως οὗ φωσφόρος ἀνατείλῃ ἐν ταῖς καρδίαις ὑμῶν *until the morning star rises in your hearts* **2 Pt 1:19** (for usage of ἀ. in Hellenistic ruler cult, cp. Sb 8420; PFouad 8, 13; Sb 4284, 7 as συνα.; PGiss 3, 2). Of a cloud *come up* **Lk 12:54.** Fig. ἡ ζωὴ ἡμῶν ἀνέτειλεν *our life has arisen* IMg 9:1. Death is likened to the setting, resurr. to the rising, of a heavenly body IRo 2:2.

ⓑ in imagery φῶς ἀνέτειλεν αὐτοῖς *light has dawned for them* **Mt 4:16** (cp. Is 58:10; Esth 1:1k); ὑμῖν AcPl Ha 8, 33.

❸ intr. **to be a descendant, w. implication of distinction, *be a descendant*** **Hb 7:14** (cp. TestSim 7:1; Jer 23:5 ἀναστήσω τῷ Δαυὶδ ἀνατολὴν δικαίαν; Apollon. Rhod. 1, 810).

❹ Other expressions, all fig. and intr.: of the robes of the righteous ***shine brightly*** B 3:4 (cp. Is 58:8; on the text, s. Hdb. ad loc.; cp. also **Mk 9:3**). Of someth. that is said to *spring forth* (Jos., Bell. 1, 406 πηγαί): of horns B 4:5.—M-M. TW.

ἀνατίθημι fut. 2 sg. ἀναθήσεις Mi 4:13; 2 aor. ἀνέθηκα LXX; pf. ptc. ἀνατεθηκώς Just., A I, 14, 2; 2 aor. mid. ἀνεθέμην; aor. pass. ἀνετέθην LXX.—ἀνάκειμαι, q.v., functions as the pass. of this vb. (s. τίθημι; Hom. et al. w. var. mngs.; ins, pap, LXX, TestIss 2:5; Philo, Joseph., Just.; Ath., R. 70, 8) lit. 'place upon'.

❶ act. **to attribute someth. to someone, *ascribe, attribute*** τινί τι (schol. on Eur., Hippol. 264 τὸ μηδὲν ἄγαν τῷ Χίλωνι) τῷ θεῷ τὴν κατὰ πάντων ἐξουσίαν *ascr. to God power over all things* MPol 2:1 (cp. Alex. Aphr., Fat. 30, CAG suppl. II/2 p.

201, 26 πρόγνωσιν ἀνατιθέναι τοῖς θεοῖς; Jos., Ant. 1, 15, C. Apion. 2, 165).

❷ otherw. only mid. **to lay someth. before someone for consideration, *communicate, refer, declare*** w. connotation of request for a person's opinion (Polyb. 21, 46, 11; Diog. L. 2, 141; Alciphron 3, 23, 2; PParis 69d, 23; 2 Macc 3:9) τινί τι (Plut., Mor. 772d τὴν πρᾶξιν ἀνέθετο τ. ἑταίρων τισί; Artem. 2, 59 v.l. ἀ. τινι τὸ ὄναρ; Mi 7:5) ὁ Φῆστος τῷ βασιλεῖ ἀνέθετο τὰ κατὰ τὸν Παῦλον **Ac 25:14.** ἀνεθέμην αὐτοῖς τὸ εὐαγγέλιον *I laid my gospel before them* **Gal 2:2.** Cp. Nägeli 45; on the use of ἀ. as an administrative term s. Betz, Gal, 86, 268.—M-M. TW.

ἀνατολή, ῆς, ἡ (s. ἀνατέλλω; poetic form ἀντ-, some mss. Pre-Socratics, Hdt.; ins, pap, LXX, En, TestSol 9:7 P; TestAbr A 11 p. 88, 28 [Stone p. 24]; TestJob, Test12Patr, JosAs; ApcEsdr 5:12 p. 30, 22 Tdf.; ApcMos, Philo, Joseph.; Mel., HE 4, 26, 14 [fgm. 8b 43 = Goodsp., Apol. p. 309]).

❶ **upward movement of celestial bodies, *rising,*** of stars (Aeschyl. et al.; PHib 27, 45 πρὸς τ. δύσεις καὶ ἀνατολὰς τ. ἄστρων; PTebt 276, 38; Neugebauer-Hoesen index; PGM 13, 1027; 1037; Philo, Spec. Leg. 3, 187) ἐν τῇ ἀνατολῇ *at its rising, when it rose* **Mt 2:2,** because of the sg. and the article in contrast to ἀπὸ ἀνατολῶν, vs. **1,** prob. not a geograph. expr. like the latter, but rather astronomical (B-D-R §235, 5; cp. B-D-F); likew. vs. **9;** GJs 21:1, 3 (cp. Petosiris, fgm. 6, ln. 31 of the moon ἅμα τῇ ἀνατολῇ=simultaneously with its rising; 12, ln. 133 ἐν τῇ τοῦ ἄστρου ἀνατολῇ; FBoll, ZNW 18, 1918, 44f; a distinction is also made by PGM 36, 239 ἐξ ἀνατολῆς τ. χωρίου πλησίον ἀνατολῶν ἡλίου. Cp. EHodous, CBQ 6, '44, 81f ['near the horizon'], and L-S-J-M s.v. 2).

❷ **the position of the rising sun, *east, orient*** (Hdt. et al.; LXX).—ⓐ sg. ἀπὸ ἀ. ἡλίου (cp. Aeschyl., Pr. 707 ἐνθένδ' ἡλίου πρὸς ἀντολάς) *from the east* **Rv 7:2; 16:12** (Just., D. 28, 5 [Mal 1:11 ἀνατολῶν]); simply ἀπὸ ἀ. (SIG 1112, 25) **21:13;** (opp. δύσις; cp. Appian, Mithrid. 68 §288 ἀπό τε δύσεως καὶ ἐξ ἀνατολῆς; OGI 199, 32; Jos., Bell. 6, 301) **short ending of Mk;** πρὸς τὴν ἀ. *toward the east* (Jos., Ant. 1, 37, C. Ap. 1, 77) Hv 1, 4, 1; 3 (cp. Mel., HE 4, 26, 14). Gener. of the orient (opp. δύσις) 1 Cl 5:6; IRo 2:2.

ⓑ pl. (Hdt. et al.; Diod. S. 5, 42, 3; Jos., C. Ap. 1, 65; B-D-F §141, 2; Rob. 408) 1 Cl 10:4 (Gen 13:14). ἀπὸ ἀνατολῶν *from the east* (pap, s. Preis.; Gk. Parchments fr. Avroman IIa, 8: JHS 35, 1915, p. 30 ἀπὸ τ. ἀνατολῶν; Num 23:7) μάγοι ἀπὸ ἀ. **Mt 2:1.** ἐξέρχεσθαι ἀπὸ ἀ. *come* from the east (of lightning) **Mt 24:27.** ἀπὸ ἀ. καὶ δυσμῶν (this contrast Apollon. Rhod. 1, 85; Epict. 3, 13, 9; Sb 385, 2; Mal 1:11; Zech 8:7; Is 59:19; Philo, In Flacc. 45) *from east and west*=fr. the whole world **Mt 8:11.** The four points of the compass (Ps 106:3) **Lk 13:29** (cp. En 18:6f εἰς ἀ. . . . πρὸς ἀ. Mel., P. 47, 335 [B] κατὰ ἀνατολὰς ἐν Ἐδέμ to the east, in Eden [on Gen. 2:8]).

❸ **a change from darkness to light in the early morning, *the dawn,*** fig., of the coming of the Messiah (cp. Damasc., Vi. Isidori 244 φέρειν τ. θείαν ἀνατολήν [s. ἀνατέλλω 2]; of Augustus: Kaibel 978, 4 ὃς (σ)ωτ[ὴ]ρ Ζεὺ[ς ἀ]ν[έ]τ[ειλε] μέγας; [s. ἀνατέλλω 2]; Mel. fgm. 8b, 45 περὶ λουτροῦ 4, Perler p. 232 = Goodsp., Apol. p. 311: ἥλιος ἀνατολῆς) ἀ. ἐξ ὕψους *the dawn from heaven* **Lk 1:78,** interpr. by AJacoby, ZNW 20, 1921, 205ff as *sprout* or *scion* of God, and sim. by Billerb. II, 1924, 113 as *Messiah of Yahweh.*—FDölger, Sol Salutis[2], 1925, 149ff.—B. 871. DDD s.v. 'Helel' (הילל). DELG s.v. τέλλω. M-M. TW. Sv.

ἀνατολικός, ή, όν (s. ἀνατολή; Epicurus, fgm. 346b; Strabo 2, 3, 2; Plut., Mor. 888a; Herodian 3, 2, 2; 3, 4, 3; TestSol 10:15 C; Philo, Leg. ad Gai. 289; Jos., Ant. 20, 220; PFlor 278 V, 1; Job 1:3 Sym. al.) ***eastern*** **Ac 19:1 v.l.** ἐν τοῖς ἀ. τόποις *in the eastern lands* 1 Cl 25:1.

ἀνατομή, ῆς, ἡ (s. τέμνω; Aristot., Plut., Philo) ***cutting up, mutilation*** of the human body; pl. of tortures IRo 5:3 (text uncertain; s. the text-crit. notes of Lghtf., Hilgenfeld, Bihlmeyer ad loc.).—DELG s.v. τέμνω 1103.

ἀνατρέπω fut. 3 sg. ἀνατρέψει; 1 aor. ἀνέτρεψα. Pass.: aor. ἀνετράπην LXX; pf. ptc. ἀνατετραμμένος Just., A I, 27, 5; 2 (s. τρέπω; Aeschyl.+; ins, pap, LXX; TestAsh 1:7; Philo, Mut. Nom. 239; Jos., Bell. 4, 318, Vi. 250; Just.)

❶ **to cause someth. to be overturned, *cause to fall, overturn, destroy,*** lit. τὰς τραπέζας (Teles p. 18, 9 H.; Plut., Galba 1055 [5, 3]; Ps.-Lucian, Asin. 40; Ps.-Apollod. 3, 7, 7, 6) *overturn* **J 2:15** (v.l. ἀνέστρεψεν; cp. ἀναστρέφω 1 and Hdb. ad loc.).

❷ **to jeopardize someone's inner well-being, *upset, ruin*** fig. ext. of 1 (Pla., Ep. 7, 336b; Appian, Bell. Civ. 4, 131 §550 ἐλπίδα; TestAsh 1:7; Just., D. 87, 1 λεγόμενα) ἀνατρέπουσιν τήν τινων πίστιν *they are upsetting the faith of some* **2 Ti 2:18** (AcPlCor 1:2; ἀ. πίστιν also Diod. S. 1, 77, 2). ὅλους οἴκους ἀ. *they ruin whole families,* i.e. by false teachings **Tit 1:11** (cp. Plut., Mor. 490b; UPZ 144 IX, 37 [II BC] τῆς πατρικῆς οἰκίας ἀνατετραμμένης).—M-M.

ἀνατρέφω 1 aor. ἀνέθρεψα, mid. ἀνεθρεψάμην. Pass.: 2 aor. ἀνετράφην; pf. ἀνατέθραμμαι (s. τρέφω; Aeschyl. et al.; LXX, Joseph.). **to provide nurture**

ⓐ of physical nurture ***bring up, care for*** (X., Mem. 4, 3, 10 et al.; PLips 28, 12 et al. since III BC; Wsd 7:4) of the infant Moses **Ac 7:20** (cp. Jos., Ant. 9, 142; Eutecnius 4 p. 41, 18 Διόνυσον ἐκ τοῦ κιβωτίου δεξάμενος ἀνεθρέψατο). Of Jesus **Lk 4:16 v.l.,** where it may also have sense b. Pass. *be nourished,* of the worm generated within the body of the phoenix 1 Cl 25:3.

ⓑ of mental and spiritual nurture ***bring up, rear, train*** (Epict. 2, 22, 26; 3, 1, 35; Herodian 1, 2, 1; 4 Macc 10:2) ἀνεθρέψατο αὐτὸν ἑαυτῇ εἰς υἱόν *she brought him up as her own son* **Ac 7:21** (Jos., Ant. 2, 232). ἀνατεθραμμένος ἐν τ. πόλει ταύτῃ **22:3** (WvanUnnik, Tarsus or Jerusalem '62). Of Mary ἡ ἀνατραφεῖσα εἰς τὰ ἅγια τῶν ἁγίων *brought up in the holy of holies* GJs 13:2; 15:3. ἐν ναῷ κυρίου *in the Lord's temple* 19:1.—Spicq.

ἀνατρέχω 2 aor. ἀνέδραμον (s. τρέχω; Hom. et al.; PTebt 711, 10; ApcSed 11:13 p. 134, 30 Ja.; Philo, Ebr. 8, Aet. M. 33) (lit. 'run back'; cp. Tat. 20, 3 'return') ***make up for, make amends for*** (Plut., Mor. 2c; Lucian, Adv. Ind. 4) w. acc. of thing ἵν' ὃ οὐκ εἰργάσαντο, νῦν ἀναδράμωσιν *that they may now make up for what they neglected to do* Hs 9, 20, 4.

ἀνατυλίσσω (τυλίσσω 'twist'; cp. ἐντυλίσσω) 1 aor. ἀνετύλιξα (lit. 'unroll', βίβλια Lucian, Ind. 16) fig., ***think over*** or ***call to mind again*** τί (Lucian, Nig. 7 τ. λόγους, οὓς τότε ἤκουσα συναγείρων καὶ πρὸς ἐμαυτὸν ἀνατυλίττων) τὰ ἀπ' ἀρχῆς γενόμενα 1 Cl 31:1.—DELG s.v. τύλη.

ἀναφαίνω 1 aor. ἀνέφανα (Doric; B-D-F §72; Mlt-H. 214f); fut. mid. ἀναφανοῦμαι LXX; 2 aor. pass. ἀνεφάνην LXX; impv. ἀναφανήτω En 10:16 (s. φαίνω; Hom. et al.; LXX; TestSol 10:3 C; TestBenj 5:5; GrBar 7:3; Tat. 13, 3).

❶ act. ***light up, cause to appear*** ἀναφάναντες (v.l. ἀναφανέντες, cp. Theophanes, Chronograph. I p. 721 Classen

[CSHB] οἱ Ἄραβες περιεφέροντο ἐν τῷ πελάγει. ἀναφανέντων δὲ αὐτῶν τὴν γῆν, εἶδον αὐτοὺς οἱ στρατηγοί) τὴν Κύπρον *we came within sight of Cyprus,* i.e. we *sighted* it **Ac 21:3** (B-D-F §309,1; Rob. 817), prob. a nautical t.t. (cp. Lucian, D. Mar. 10, 1; Philostrat., Her. 19, 6 p. 212, 10 τὴν νῆσον; s. Theophanes above).

❷ Exc. for the v.l. cited above, the pass. is used in the sense ***appear*** (Job 13:18; 40:8; En 10:16; TestSol 10:3 C; TestJob 42:1; TestBenj 5:5; GrBar 7:3; Philo; Jos., Ant. 2, 339; 7, 333; PGM 36, 107) **Lk 19:11.**—M-M.

ἀναφέρω fut. ἀνοίσω LXX (also Just., D. 112 al.), 2 aor. ἀνήνεγκα (late form) and ἀνήνεγκον (B-D-F §80; 81; W-S. §13, 13; Mlt-H. 263); pf. ἀνενήνοχα LXX. Pass.: fut. ἀνενεχθήσομαι LXX; aor. ἀνηνέχθην (s. φέρω; Hom.+ in var. mngs.; ins, pap, LXX; TestSol 10:9 L; TestAbr, TestJob, Test12Patr; JosAs 10:4; ParJer; GrBar 8:4; ApcSed [-φέρυσται 10:3; -φέρνεται p. 133, 36 Ja.]; ApcMos 32; ApcZeph; Philo, Aet. M. 64; Jos., Bell. 1, 234, C. Ap. 1, 232)

❶ **to cause to move from a lower position to a higher, *take, lead, bring up,*** of pers. ἀ. αὐτοὺς εἰς ὄρος ὑψηλόν *he led them up a high mountain* **Mt 17:1; Mk 9:2.** Pass. ἀνεφέρετο εἰς τ. οὐρανόν *he was taken up into heaven* (of Romulus: Plut., Numa 60 [2, 4]; of Endymion: Hes., fgm. 148 Rz. τὸν Ἐνδυμίωνα ἀνενεχθῆναι ὑπὸ τοῦ Διὸς εἰς οὐρανόν; schol. on Apollon. Rhod. 4, 57 and 58 p. 264, 17) **Lk 24:51** (MParsons, The Departure of Jesus in Luke-Acts '87). ἀναφερόμενοι εἰς τὰ ὕψη IEph 9:1.

❷ **to carry and hand over someth. to someone, *deliver*** ἀνήνεγκεν τῷ ἱερεῖ (Mary) *delivered to the priest* her purple and scarlet embroidery work GJs 12:1 (pap; mss. v.l. ἀπ-). Of food, syn. w. αἴρω GJs 18:2 (s. αἴρω 2b).

❸ **to offer as a sacrifice, *offer up,*** specif. a cultic t.t. (SIG 56, 68; Lev 17:5; 1 Esdr 5:49; Is 57:6; 2 Macc 1:18; 2:9 al.; ParJer 9:1f; Did., Gen. 219, 15) ἀ. θυσίας ὑπέρ τινος *offer sacrifices for someth.* **Hb 7:27.** ἀ. τινὰ ἐπὶ τὸ θυσιαστήριον (Gen 8:20; Lev 14:20; Bar 1:10; 1 Macc 4:53; Just., D. 118, 2 θυσίας) *offer up someone on the altar* **Js 2:21.** Of Jesus' sacrifice: ἑαυτὸν ἀνενέγκας *when he offered up himself* **Hb 7:27.** τὰς ἁμαρτίας ἡμῶν αὐτὸς ἀνήνεγκεν ἐν τῷ σώματι αὐτοῦ ἐπὶ τὸ ξύλον *he himself brought our sins in his body to the cross* **1 Pt 2:24** (cp. Dssm., B 83ff [BS 88f]). Pol 8:1 (Is 53:12).—Fig. (schol. on Apollon. Rhod. 2, 214b χάριν=render thanks to the divinity) ἀ. θυσίαν αἰνέσεως *offer up a sacr. of praise* **Hb 13:15** (cp. 2 Ch 29:31). ἀ. πνευματικὰς θυσίας **1 Pt 2:5.** ἀ. προσευχάς *offer prayers* 2 Cl 2:2. ἀ. δέησιν περί τινος *offer up a petition for someth.* B 12:7.

❹ **take up as a burden, *take up.*** In Is 53:11 ἀ. is used to translate סָבַל, in vs. 12 for נָשָׂא, and in the corresponding passages in our lit. ἀ. is often rendered 'bear' or 'take away'. But ἀ. seems not to have these meanings. Very often, on the contrary, it has a sense that gives ἀνα its full force: *lay* or *impose a burden on* someone, *give* something to someone *to bear,* as a rule, in fact, to someone who is not obligated to bear it (Aeschyl., Choeph. 841 ἄχθος; Polyb. 1, 36, 3; 4, 45, 9; Diod. S. 15, 48, 4; 32, 26, 1; Appian, Liby. 93; Syr. 41, where the other defendants were τὴν αἰτίαν ἐς τὸν Ἐπαμεινώνδαν ἀναφέροντες, i.e. putting the blame on Epaminondas. The Lex. Vind. p. 12, 3 sees in Eur., Or. 76 ἐς Φοῖβον ἀναφέρουσα τ. ἁμαρτίαν and in Procop. Soph., Ep. 7 p. 535 H. proof that ἀναφέρειν is used ἀντὶ τοῦ τὴν αἰτίαν εἰς ἕτερον τιθέναι.) In a case in which a man takes upon himself the burden that another should have borne, then ἀ.=*take upon oneself* (Thu. 3, 38, 3 ἡ πόλις τὰ μὲν ἆθλα ἑτέροις δίδωσιν, αὐτὴ δὲ τοὺς κινδύνους ἀναφέρει=the city gives the prizes to others, but she takes the dangers upon herself). *Christ was once for all offered up in this respect* (εἰς 5) *that he assumed the sins of many* **Hb 9:28.** Cp. 1 Cl 16:12, 14.—M-M. TW. Spicq.

ἀναφωνέω 1 aor. ἀνεφώνησα (s. φωνέω; Epicurus 63, 28 [p. 24, 16 Us.]; Polyb. 3, 33, 4; Ps.-Aristot., De Mundo 6 p. 400a, 18; Artem. I, 58; UPZ 162 V, 26; PFay 14, 2 [both IIBC]; 1 Ch 15:28 al.; 2 Ch 5:13; TestJob 31:7) ***cry out,*** ἀ. κραυγῇ μεγάλῃ *cry out loudly* **Lk 1:42** (s. ἀναβοάω)—DELG s.v. φωνή. M-M.

ἀναχθείς s. ἀνάγω.

ἀνάχυσις, εως, ἡ (ἀναχέω 'pour out'; Strabo 3, 1, 9; Plut., Mar. 419 [25, 5]; Philo, Decal. 41, Aet. M. 102, Spec. Leg. 1, 34; Somn. 2, 278) lit. 'pouring out', then ***wide stream*** (Ocellus Luc. c. 41 of the sea; Maximus Tyr. 26, 1a; 38, 3e ἀ. θαλάττης) only fig. ἡ τῆς ἀσωτίας ἀ. *flood of dissipation* **1 Pt 4:4.**—DELG s.v. χέω III. M-M.

ἀναχωρέω 1 aor. ἀνεχώρησα; pf. ἀνακεχώρηκα (s. χωρέω; Hom.+; ins, pap, LXX; pseudepigr., Philo, Joseph.; Just. D. 76, 5 [for ἀπο- **Mt 7:23**]).

❶ **to depart from a location—ⓐ** gener. ***go away*** (Epict. 2, 1, 8; 2, 12, 6; 4, 1, 96; Herodian 1, 12, 2; 2 Macc 10:13; Jos., Vi. 151) **Mt 2:13; 9:24; 27:5;** Hv 3, 1, 8; s 9, 5, 1f. μικρόν *a little way* s 9, 5, 1 v.l. ἀπό τινος s 9, 11, 2. Fig. τόπος ἀνακεχωρηκώς *a secluded place* v 3, 1, 3 (cp. the metaph. expressions L-S-J-M III).

ⓑ ***withdraw, retire, take refuge*** (common in pap of obligations to the state, e.g. POxy 251, 10 εἰς τὴν ξένην; 252, 9 [19/20]; PLille 3, 76 [241 BC]; cp. Wilcken, APF 5, 1908, 222; HBraunert, JJP 9/10, '55/56, 59ff; HHenne, MPER n.s. V, '56, 59ff; also s. Ex 2:15; 2 Macc 5:27 εἰς) εἰς Αἴγυπτον **Mt 2:14.** εἰς τὰ μέρη τῆς Γαλιλαίας **2:22;** cp. **15:21.** εἰς τὴν Γαλιλαίαν **4:12.** εἴς τινα τόπον *to a certain place* Hv 2, 1, 4. πρὸς (v.l. εἰς, read by Tdf.) τὴν θάλασσαν *to the sea = westward* like יָמָּה **Mk 3:7** (ἀ. πρός w. acc. as Jos., Ant. 1, 85). εἰς τὸ ὄρος **J 6:15.** ἀπὸ τ. Ἀθηνῶν **Ac 18:1** D. ἐκεῖθεν **Mt 12:15.** ἐκεῖθεν εἰς ἔρημον τόπον *from there to a lonely place* **14:13;** κατ' ἰδίαν ibid. **Ac 23:19.** Abs. **26:31;** AcPl Ha 3, 3; 15.

❷ **to go back to an area from which one has departed, *return*** (εἰς Polyb. 1, 11, 15; SIG 1168, 117; OGI 335, 121; Jos., Bell. 2, 407, Ant. 17, 58) εἰς τ. χώραν αὐτῶν *to their own country* **Mt 2:12;** GJs 21:4.—DELG s.v. χώρα. M-M.

ἀνάψας s. ἀνάπτω.

ἀνάψυξις, εως, ἡ (ψύξις 'a cooling'; s. ἀναψύχω; Diocles, fgm. 15; Strabo 10, 2, 19; Heraclit. Sto. 10 p. 17, 17; Herm. Wr. fgm. XXV, 10 [512, 4 Sc.]; Philo, De Abrah. 152 w. ἄνεσις; Ex 8:11; ApcSed 16:5 [p. 137, 11 Ja.]; late pap [cp. ἀναψυχή in PLond I, 42, 19 p. 30 [172 BC] and note in Witkowski no. 35 p. 63; s. also New Docs 4, 262]) **experience of relief from obligation or trouble, *breathing space, relaxation, relief*** fig., of the Messianic age καιροὶ ἀναψύξεως *times of rest* **Ac 3:20.** Cp. ADieterich, Nekyia 1893, 95f.—DELG s.v. ψυχρός C1 ψύχω 1295. TW. Sv.

ἀναψύχω (s. ἀνάψυξις) fut. ἀναψύξω (JosAs 3:3); 1 aor. ἀνέψυξα; pf. ptc. acc. sg. ἀνεψυκότα 2 Macc 13:11; 1 aor. pass. ptc. ἀναψυχθείς (TestSol 4:11 D).

❶ trans. (Hom.+; Plut.; TestSol 4:11 D; Jos., Ant. 15, 54. [Nägeli 16; Anz 303]) **to provide relief from obligation or trouble, *give*** someone ***a breathing space, revive, refresh*** τινά IEph

2:1; Tr 12:2. πολλάκις με ἀνέψυξεν *he often refreshed me* **2 Ti 1:16.**

❷ intr. (Diphilus [c. 300 BC] 81; POslo 153, 10 [early II AD]; POxy 1296, 7; Sb 3939, 28, in a letter on a wood tablet fr. a mummy requesting someth. for 'repose'; cp. JSvennung, Aretos, Acta Philol. Fenn., n.s. II, '58, 183; also 1 Km 16:23; Ps 38:14; En 103:13; JosAs 3:3; ParJer 6:7; Babrius 95, 57) **to experience relief from obligation or trouble,** ***be refreshed*** μετά τινος *together with someone* **Ro 15:32** D.—DELG s.v. ψυχρός C1 ψύχω 1295. M-M. TW. Spicq.

ἀνδρ- Some words with this prefix show erosion of emphasis on maleness.

ἀνδραποδιστής, οῦ, ὁ (ἀνδράποδον 'one taken in war and sold as a slave'; Aristoph., Pla., X.+; Demosth. 4, 47; Polyb. 13, 6, 4; Dio Chrys. 52 [69], 9; Chariton 5, 7, 4; Philo, Spec. Leg. 4, 13) **one who acquires pers. for use by others,** ***slave-dealer, kidnapper*** **1 Ti 1:10** (here perh. w. the mng. 'procurer.' Vulg. plagiarius; s. New Docs 1, 50).—DELG s.v. ἀνήρ A end. M-M.

Ἀνδρέας, ου, ὁ a Gk. name (Diod. S. 8, 24; SIG 649, 5; EpArist; Joseph.; a Jew Ἀ. also in Cass. Dio 68, 32, 2) ***Andrew,*** brother of Simon Peter; acc. to **J 1:44** he was from Bethsaida on the Sea of Galilee, and according to vss. **35, 40** was orig. a disciple of John the Baptist. **Mt 4:18; 10:2; Mk 1:16, 29; 3:18; 13:3; Lk 6:14; J 6:8; 12:22; Ac 1:13;** GPt 14:60=ASyn. 361, 36; GEb 34, 60f; Papias (2:4).—PPeterson, Andrew, Brother of Simon Peter: NovT Suppl. 1, '58.—M-M.

ἀνδρεῖος, εία, εῖον (s. ἀνήρ; trag., Hdt. et al.; ins; PLips 119 II, 3; LXX; Jos., C. Ap. 2, 292; Test12Patr) **pert. to being manly,** ***manly, courageous*** subst. τὰ ἀνδρεῖα *heroic deeds* worthy of a brave person (Philo, Mut. Nom. 146) ἐπιτελεῖσθαι πολλὰ ἀ. *do many heroic deeds,* of famous women (sim. Aristot., Pol. 1277b, 22) 1 Cl 55:3.—DELG s.v. ἀνήρ B. TW.

ἀνδρείως (Aristoph., Pax 498; 1 Macc 9:10 v.l.; 2 Macc 6:27; Philo, Mos. 2, 184; Jos., Ant. 12, 302) adv. fr. ἀνδρεῖος in a ***manly*** i.e. ***brave*** *way* ἀ. ἀναστρέφεσθαι *conduct oneself bravely* (w. ἰσχυρῶς) Hs 5, 6, 6. ἀ. ἑστηκέναι *stand firm,* of young women s 9, 2, 5. (On courage of women s. Plut., Mor. 242e–63c.)

ἀνδρίζομαι fut. ἀνδριοῦμαι LXX; 1 aor. mid. impv. ἄνδρισαι Na 2:2 (s. ἀνδρεῖος, ἀνήρ; Pla., X. et al.; Lucian, Anach. 15 et al.; PSI 402, 3; 512, 29; PPetr II, 40a, 12 [c. 233 BC] μὴ οὖν ὀλιγοψυχήσητε, ἀλλ' ἀνδρίζεσθε; LXX; JosAs 24:7; Jos., Bell. 6, 50) ***conduct oneself in a courageous way*** w. κραταιοῦσθαι (like חֲזַק וֶאֱמָץ; cp. 2 Km 10:12; Ps 26:14; 30:25) **1 Cor 16:13;** w. ἰσχύειν (Dt 31:6, 7, 23; Josh 1:6, 7 al.) MPol 9:1. ἀνδρίζου *act like a man!* Hv 1, 4, 3. Of an old man, whose hope in life has been renewed v 3, 12, 2. Also of a woman who is girded and of manly appearance v 3, 8, 4.—DELG s.v. ἀνήρ B. M-M. TW.

Ἀνδρόνικος, ου, ὁ a common name (Diod. S. 19, 59, 2; Appian, Maced. 16; SIG[2] and OGI indices; IPriene 313 [I BC]; Preisigke, Namenbuch; 2 Macc 4:31, 32, 34, 38; 5:23; Jos., Ant. 13, 75; 78) ***Andronicus,*** greeted in **Ro 16:7;** w. Junia or Junias described by Paul as συγγενεῖς μου καὶ συναιχμάλωτοι and called ἐπίσημοι ἐν τ. ἀποστόλοις.—BBacon, ET 42, '31, 300–304. GBarton, ibid. 43, '32, 359–61.—M-M.

ἀνδροφόνος, ου, ὁ (s. ἀνήρ, φόνος; Hom. et al.; OGI 218, 99 [III BC]; Kaibel 184, 6 [III BC]; POslo 18, 4 [162 AD]; 2 Macc 9:28; Philo, Just.; Ath. 35, 1; Iren. 1, 6, 3 [Harv. I 55, 14] adj.) ***murderer*** (lit. 'man-slayer'; Lex. Vind. p. 192, 13: a murderer of women and children as well as of men) **1 Ti 1:9.**—DELG s.v. ἀνήρ A, θείνω. M-M.

ἀνέβην s. ἀναβαίνω.

ἀνεγκλησία, ας, ἡ (ἀ- + ἐγκαλέω; s. ἀνέγκλητος; pap oft.=indemnity) ***blamelessness*** (Bardesanes in Eus., PE 6, 10, 10 p. 274d) ἀ. τοῦ θεοῦ *bl. before God* **Phil 3:14 v.l.**—DELG s.v. καλέω (κλη-).

ἀνέγκλητος, ον (s. ἀνεγκλησία; Pla., X. et al.; Epict. 1, 28, 10; SIG 911, 25 [III/II BC]; 556d, 5 [207/6 BC]; Socratics 31, 26 p. 298 Malherbe; pap; 3 Macc 5:31; Jos., Ant. 10, 281; 17, 289; Just., D. 35, 8) ***blameless, irreproachable*** of Christians gener. ὃς βεβαιώσει ὑμᾶς ἀ. ἐν τ. ἡμέρᾳ τ. κυρίου *who will establish you as blameless in the day of the Lord*=so that you will be bl. when it comes **1 Cor 1:8;** w. ἅγιος and ἄμωμος **Col 1:22.** Of Christian leaders **1 Ti 3:10; Tit 1:6f.**—M-M. TW.

ἀνέγνων s. ἀναγινώσκω.

ἀνεθέμην s. ἀνατίθημι.

ἀνέθην, ἀνείς s. ἀνίημι.

ἀνεθρεψάμην s. ἀνατρέφω.

ἀνεῖλα, ἀνεῖλον s. ἀναιρέω.

ἀνεκδιήγητος, ον (ἀ- + ἐκδιηγέομαι q.v.; Rhet. Gr. III 747, 8; Hesych.; EpArist 99 v.l.; Just., D. 43, 3; 76, 2; A I, 51, 1 [each on Is 53:8]; Ath. 10, 1; Mel., P. 31, 210; 105, 814 [B]) ***indescribable*** in good sense ἐπὶ τῇ ἀ. αὐτοῦ δωρεᾷ **2 Cor 9:15.** Of God's power ἀ. κράτος 1 Cl 61:1 (cp. δυνάμει ἀ. Ath. 10, 1). τὸ ὕψος, εἰς ὃ ἀνάγει ἡ ἀγάπη, ἀ. ἐστι 49:4. νερτέρων ἀ. κρίματα (so the mss.; κλίματα is an unnecessary emendation) *the indescribable judgments of the underworld* 20:5 (s. Knopf, Hdb. ad loc.).—DELG s.v. ἡγέομαι. M-M.

ἀνεκλάλητος, ον (ἀ- + ἐκλαλέω q.v.; Diosc., Eup. preface Wellm.; Heliod. 6, 15, 4; Ps.-Callisth. 1, 40, 5; Herm Wr. 1, 4, 31; Eunap. 486 [Vi. Soph.. 10, 2, 1]; Iren. 1, 14, 5 [Harv. I 137, 11) ***inexpressible*** χαρᾷ ἀ. καὶ δεδοξασμένῃ **1 Pt 1:8;** Pol 1:3. φῶς ἀ. (JosAs 14:3) of the radiance of the star at Jesus' birth IEph 19:2.—DELG s.v. λαλέω B.

ἀνέκλειπτος, ον (ἀ- + ἐκλείπω q.v.; Hyperid. et al.; Diod. S. 1, 36, 1; 4, 84, 2; Plut., Mor. 438d; OGI 383, 70 [I BC]; PLond III 1166, 7 p. 105 [42 AD]; EpArist 89; 185) ***unfailing, inexhaustible*** of the treasure of good works θησαυρὸς ἀ. (cp. Wsd 7:14; 8:18) **Lk 12:33.**—S. DELG s.v. λείπω (*λειπτος). M-M.

ἀνεκτός, όν (s. ἀνέχομαι; Hom. et al.; SIG[2] 793, 3; IGR IV, 293 II, 4 [II BC, Pergam.]; Jos., Bell. 7, 68, Ant. 18, 348) ***bearable, endurable*** ἀνεκτὸν ἦν, εἰ *it could be endured, if* 2 Cl 10:5.—Comp. (Memnon [I BC/I AD]: 434, fgm. 1, 2, 1 p. 338, 15; 1, 6, 3 p. 343, 22 Jac. ἀνεκτότερον; Cicero, Att. 12, 45, 2; Christian letter POxy 939, 25 ἀνεκτότερον ἐσχηκέναι) Τύρῳ καὶ Σιδῶνι ἀνεκτότερον ἔσται *it will be more tolerable for Tyre and Sidon* **Mt 11:22; Lk 10:14.** ἀ. ἔ. γῇ Σοδόμων **Mt 10:15; 11:24;** cp. **Mk 6:11 v.l.; Lk 10:12.**—DELG s.v. ἔχω 393. M-M. TW.

ἀνελεήμων, ον (ἀ- + ἐλεήμων q.v.; Aristot. Rhet. ad Alex. 1442a, 13; Cat. Cod. Astr. II 173; Pr 5:9; Job 30:21 al.; PLond VI, 1915, 7f; 27 w. ἄθεος) (adv. ἀνελεημόνως ApcMos 2) ***unmerciful*** **Ro 1:31; Tit 1:9 v.l.** (in a catalogue of vices in Ptolem., Apotel. 3, 14, 28).—DELG s.v. ἔλεος. TW.

ἀνελεῖν, ἀνέλω s. ἀναιρέω.

ἀνέλεος, ον (s. ἔλεος; Att. ἀνηλεής [also TestAbr A 12 p. 90, 15=Stone p. 28]; cp. Phryn. 710 Lob.; B-D-F §120, 2. TestAbr A 16 p. 96, 18 [Stone p. 4] βλέμμα; contrast A 17 p. 99, 4f [Stone p. 46] βλέμματι . . . ἀνίλεῳ) ***merciless*** κρίσις ἀ. *judgment is merciless* **Js 2:13** (v.l. ἀνίλεως).—M-M. TW.

ἀνελήμφθην s. ἀναλαμβάνω.

ἀνεμίζω (Att. ἀνεμόω) pass. ***be moved by the wind*** (schol. on Od. 12, 336) κλύδων ἀνεμιζόμενος καὶ ῥιπιζόμενος *surf moved and tossed by the wind* **Js 1:6.**—DELG s.v. ἄνεμος. M-M.

ἄνεμος, ου, ὁ (Hom.+)—❶ **a blowing atmospheric phenomenon,** ***wind*** **Rv 7:1;** playing among the reeds **Mt 11:7; Lk 7:24;** scattering chaff B 11:7 (Ps 1:4); desired by the sailor IPol 2:3, or not ἐναντίος ἄ. *a contrary wind* **Mt 14:24; Mk 6:48.** ὁ ἄ. ἰσχυρός *the storm* **Mt 14:30;** cp. **32; Mk 4:39, 41; 6:51.** ἄ. μέγας *a strong wind* **J 6:18; Rv 6:13.** ἄ. τυφωνικός *a violent, hurricane-like wind* **Ac 27:14,** cp. **15.** For this, λαῖλαψ ἀνέμου *a storm-wind* **Mk 4:37; Lk 8:23,** cp. **Mk 4:41; Lk 8:24** (on the stilling of the storm POxy 1383, 1 [III AD] κελεύειν ἀνέμοις.—WFiedler, Antik. Wetterzauber '31, esp. 17–23).—Pl. without the art. (Jos., Bell. 4, 286) **Js 3:4.** οἱ ἄ. (Jos., Bell. 4, 299; also thought of as personified, cp. IDefixWünsch 4, 6 τὸν θεὸν τῶν ἀνέμων καὶ πνευμάτων Λαιλαμ) **Mt 7:25, 27; 8:26f** (the par. **Mk 4:39** has the sg.); **Lk 8:25; Jd 12.** ἄ. ἐναντίοι *contrary winds* **Ac 27:4.** οἱ τέσσαρες ἄ. τῆς γῆς **Rv 7:1** (cp. Zech 6:5; Jer 25:16; Da 7:2; En 18:2 τοὺς τέσσαρας ἀ. τὴν γῆν βαστάζοντας; on the angels of the winds cp. PGM 15, 14; 16, and on control of the winds Diod. S. 20, 101, 3 Aeolus as κύριος τῶν ἀνέμων; Ps.-Apollod., Epit. 7, 10 Zeus has appointed Aeolus as ἐπιμελητὴς τῶν ἀνέμων, καὶ παύειν καὶ προΐεσθαι; Ael. Aristid. 45, 29 K.; IAndrosIsis, Kyme 39; POxy 1383, 9 ἀπέκλειε τὰ πνεύματα).

❷ οἱ τέσσαρες ἄνεμοι can also be ***the four directions,*** or ***cardinal points*** (Sb 6152, 20 [93 BC]; CPR 115, 6; PFlor 50, 104 ἐκ τῶν τεσσ. ἀ.; Ezk 37:9 v.l.; Zech 2:10; 1 Ch 9:24; Jos., Bell. 6, 301, Ant. 8, 80; PGM 3, 496; 4, 1606f) **Mt 24:31; Mk 13:27;** D 10:5. ἀνέμων σταθμοί *stations* or *quarters* of the wind 1 Cl 20:10 (Job 28:25; s. Lghtf. and Knopf ad loc.).

❸ **a tendency or trend that causes one to move from a view or belief,** ***wind*** fig. ext. of 1 (cp. 4 Macc 15:32), περιφερόμενοι παντὶ ἀ. τ. διδασκαλίας *driven about by any and every didactic breeze* **Eph 4:14.**—B. 64.—DELG. M-M. TW.

ἀνεμπόδιστος, ον (s. ἐμποδίζω; Aristot., EN 7, 12 [1153a, 15]; 13 [1153b, 10f] et al.; Epict. 3, 22, 41; 4, 4, 5; Vett. Val. 246, 5; SIG[2] 517, 32 [SIG 955, 32 restores this passage difft.]; OGI 383, 129; pap since II BC], e.g. UPZ 191, 13; 192, 23; 193, 23; PAmh 38, 12; Wsd 17:19; 19:7; Just., D. 3, 2) ***unhindered*** only adv. in our lit **ἀνεμποδίστως** (Diod. S. 1, 36, 10; PTebt 6, 48; 43, 40 [118 BC] al. in pap; Jos., Ant. 16, 172) κλῆρον ἀ. ἀπολαβεῖν *receive my lot unhindered* IRo 1:2.—DELG s.v. πούς.

ἀνένδεκτος, ον (s. ἐνδέχομαι; Artem. 2, 70; Diog. L. 7, 50; PLond IV, 1404, 8) ***impossible*** ἀ. ἐστιν *it is imp.* **Lk 17:1** (s. B-D-F §400, 4; Mlt-H. 305; Rob. 1171).—DELG s.v. δέχομαι.

ἀνενέγκαι s. ἀναφέρω.

ἀνεξεραύνητος, ον ***unfathomable,*** lit. 'unsearchable', of God's judgments τὰ κρίματα αὐτοῦ **Ro 11:33** (s. ἐξεραυνάω; Hell. by-form of ἀνεξερεύνητος—so Heraclitus fgm. B 18 [in Clem. Al., Strom. 2, 17, 4 Stählin]; Cass. Dio 69, 14; Sym. Pr 25:3; Jer 17:9. Cp. W-S. §5, 21a; B-D-F §30, 4; Nägeli 16; 23; Mlt. 46).—DELG s.v. 1. ἐρέω. Frisk s.v. ἐρευνάω. M-M.

ἀνεξίκακος, ον (s. ἀνέχομαι, κακός; Lucian, Jud. Voc. 9; Vett. Val. 38, 21; Cat. Cod. Astr. VIII/2 p. 156, 15; Pollux 5, 138; PTebt 272, 19 [II AD]; Just., A. I, 16, 1; Ath. 34, 2.—ἀνεξικακία Epict., Ench. 10; Wsd 2:19; Jos., Bell. 1, 624; perh. also Acta Alex. X, 40f: [ἔγνω]|σται μὲν ἡ ἐμ[ὴ ἄνεξι]|κακία) **pert. to bearing evil without resentment,** ***patient, tolerant*** of Christians **2 Ti 2:24** (w. ἤπιος, διδακτικός).—TW.

ἀνεξιχνίαστος, ον (ἀ-, ἐξιχνιάζω 'track out'; Cat. Cod. Astr. VIII/2 p. 156, 16; Etym. Mag. p. 709, 50; Job 5:9; 9:10; 34:24; Prayer of Manasseh [=Odes 12] 6) lit. 'not to be tracked out', ***inscrutable, incomprehensible,*** of God's ways **Ro 11:33.** Of the riches in Christ *fathomless* **Eph 3:8** (RThomas, ET 39, 1928, 283). ἀ. δημιουργία *inscrutable creation* Dg 9:5.—1 Cl 20:5. Cp. FPfister, SBHeidAk 1914, no. 11, p. 8.—DELG s.v. ἴχνος. TW. Sv.

ἀνεπαίσχυντος, ον (s. ἐπαισχύνομαι; Jos., Ant. 18, 243; Agapetus, De Offic. Boni Princ. 57 p. 174 Groebel) **pert. to having no need to be ashamed,** ***unashamed*** of a Christian leader: ἐργάτης ἀ. **2 Ti 2:15.**—DELG s.v. αἶσχος. M-M.

ἀνέπεσα s. ἀναπίπτω.

ἀνεπιδεής, ές (ἐπιδεής 'in need of'; Pla., Leg. 12 p. 947e; Lucian, Dial. Mort. 26, 2) **pert. to not lacking anything,** ***lacking nothing*** of God (Philo, Plant. 35; Ath. 29, 2 τὸ θεῖον) PtK 2 p. 13, 25.—DELG s.v. 2 δέω.

ἀνεπίλη(μ)πτος, ον (s. ἐπιλαμβάνω; Eur., Thu. et al.; Lucian, Pisc. 8; Ps.-Lucian, Salt. 81; Dio Chrys. 11 [12], 66; Ath. 31, 2 ἄνθρωπος; PTebt 5, 48; 61b, 237f; 72, 176; IPontEux II 52, 9) ***irreproachable*** **1 Ti 3:2; 5:7;** w. ἄσπιλος **6:14.** ἀ. πολιτεία *irrepr. conduct* (Philo, Spec. Leg. 3, 24; cp. PGiss 55, 10 ἀ. βίον ἔχειν; on the moral requirement cp. PTebt 27, 27: ἀξιολόγος) MPol 17:1.—DELG s.v. λαμβάνω. M-M. TW.

ἀνέρχομαι pres. 2 sg. ἀνέρχεσαι (ApcSed 11:16 p. 134, 35 Ja.); fut. ἀνελεύσεται (Just., A I, 54, 7f); 2 aor. ἀνῆλθον; pf. ἀνελήλυθα (Just., Tat.) (s. ἔρχομαι; Hom.+) **to move from a lower to a higher place,** ***go up, come up*** (X., Hell. 2, 4, 39 εἰς τ. ἀκρόπολιν; 3 Km 13:12; Jos., Ant. 6, 314; Just., A I, 21, 3) εἰς τὸ ὄρος **J 6:3** (on the journey to Jerusalem s. ἀναβαίνω 1aα) ἀ. εἰς Ἱεροσόλυμα **Gal 1:17f** (of journey to the capital Epict. 1, 11, 32 νῦν ἐν Ῥώμῃ ἀνέρχῃ; PTebt 412, 3 ἄνελθε εἰς μητρόπολιν; 411, 5; Jos., Ant. 16, 91 εἰς τ. Ῥώμην). Of coming up out of a river ἀ. ἀπὸ ὕδατος GEb 18, 36.—M-M.

ἀνερωτάω 1 aor. inf. ἀνερωτῆσαι and mid. ἀνερωτήσασθαι (Just.); pass. ἀνερωτηθῆναι (Just., D. 124, 1); pf. ptc. ἀνηρωτημένος (Just., D. 68, 3) (s. ἐρωτάω; Hom. et al.) ***ask*** τινά (Just., D. 67, 8 al.; Dio Chrys. 13 [7], 5; Ael. Aristid. 36, 48 K.=48 p. 457 D.) MPol 9:2.

ἄνεσις, εως, ἡ (s. ἀνίημι; Hdt. 5, 28 et al.; SIG 880, 53; 884, 16; pap [e.g. PGiss 59, 7 of relief fr. liturgy]; LXX; TestSol 6:10 P; TestBenj 2:5c; ApcEsdr 5, 10 p. 30, 4 Tdf.; EpArist 284) 'relaxing, loosening'.

❶ lit. **relaxation of custodial control,** ***some liberty,*** ἀ. ἔχειν *have some freedom* **Ac 24:23** (cp. Jos., Ant. 18, 235 φυλακὴ μὲν γὰρ καὶ τήρησις ἦν, μετὰ μέντοι ἀνέσεως).

❷ **relief from someth. onerous or troublesome,** ***rest, relaxation, relief*** (Pla., Leg. 4, 724a; Strabo 10, 3, 9; M. Ant. 1, 16, 6; Philo, Rer. Div. Her. 156) ἵνα ἄλλοις ἄ. (sc. ᾖ), ὑμῖν θλῖψις *that* *others should have relief, and you be burdened* **2 Cor 8:13.** ἀ. ἔχειν (Jos., Bell. 3, 319) **2:13; 7:5.** ε̣ἰ̣ς̣ [ἄ]ν̣ε̣σ̣ι̣[ν]|τὸ λοιπὸν τὰ δάκρυα αὐτοῦ γενέ[σ]θαι *so that his tears finally brought relief* AcPl Ha 6, 5f. ἄνεσιν διδόναι τινί (Diod. S. 19, 26, 10 αὐτῷ δοὺς ἄνεσιν; 2 Ch 23:15; 1 Esdr 4:62; Jos., Ant. 3, 254; 281) B 4:2. ἀνταποδοῦναι τ. θλιβομένοις ἄνεσιν *grant, in turn, rest to those who are oppressed* **2 Th 1:7.**—DELG s.v. ἵημι. M-M. TW.

ἀνέστην s. ἀνίστημι.

ἀνετάζω 1 aor. ἀνήτασε Esth 2:23 v.l. (s. ἐξετάζω, the usual term; PSI 380, 9 [249/48 BC]; POxy 34 I, 13 [127 AD]; Judg 6:29A; Sus 14 Theod.) ***give someone*** (τινά) ***a hearing*** judicial t.t. (Anaphora Pilati A 6 [Ea p. 439 Tdf.; Just., A I, 11, 1]) **Ac 22:29.** μάστιξιν ἀ. *give a hearing, and use torture* (in the form of a lashing) *in connection w. it,* vs. **24.**—DELG s.v. ἑτάζω 'examine'. M-M.

ἄνευ prep. w. gen., never used in compos. (Hom.+; and s. lit. s.v. ἀνά) ***without*** (cp. ἄτερ, χωρίς, fr. which it can scarcely be distinguished in usage).

ⓐ of pers. *without the knowledge and consent of* (Od. 2, 372; Appian, Bell. Civ. 5, 100 §416; Ael. Aristid. 28, 105 K.=49 p. 525 D.: ἄνευ θεοῦ; UPZ 69, 4 [152 BC] ἄνευ τ. θεῶν οὐθὲν γίνεται; PPetr II, Append. p. 3; O. Wilck I 559f). ἀ. τοῦ πατρὸς ὑμῶν **Mt 10:29** (cp. Am 3:5); ἀ. θεοῦ B 19:6; IPol 4:1 (cp. Just., D. 102, 7). IMg 7:1; ITr 2:2.

ⓑ of things (Jos., Bell. 2, 1, Ant. 7, 72, Vi. 167) ἀ. λόγου *without a word* (opp. διὰ τῆς ἀναστροφῆς contrast Just., A I, 46, 4 [opp. μετὰ λόγου] of non-Christians) **1 Pt 3:1.** ἀ. γογγυσμοῦ *without complaining* **4:9.** ἀ. χειρῶν (Da 2:34) built *without hands* **Mk 13:2** D. ἀ. ζυγοῦ ἀνάγκης *without the yoke of constraint* (=free from the yoke of compulsion) B 2:6; ἀ. γνώμης σου *without your consent* IPol 4:1; ἀ. γνώσεως *without understanding* Dg 12:4, 6; ἀ. ζωῆς ἀληθοῦς *without real life* 12:4; ἀ. ἀλήθεια *without truth* 12:5. W. χωρίς: οὐ δύναται κεφαλὴ χ̣ωρὶς γεννηθῆναι ἀ. μελῶν *the head cannot be born separately, without limbs* ITr 11:2.—DELG. M-M.

ἀνεύθετος, ον (s. εὔθετος. Hesychius; Suda; beginning of the lexicon of Photius ed. RReitzenstein 1907; Anecd. Gr. p. 399, 11) **pert. to being unfavorably situated and therefore unusable, *unsuitable, poor,*** of a harbor λιμὴν ἀ. πρὸς παραχειμασίαν *not suitable for wintering in* **Ac 27:12** (of the harbor Καλοὶ Λιμένες on Crete).—DELG s.v. τίθημι. M-M.

ἀνευρίσκω 2 aor. ἀνεῦρα **Lk 2:16** (vv.ll. ἀνεῦρον, εὗρον, εὗραν; s. W-S. §13, 13) ptc. ἀνευρών; mid. ἀνευράμενος 4 Macc 3:14 (s. εὑρίσκω; Aeschyl., Hdt.+) ***look/search for*** (w. finding presupposed) τινά: τὴν Μαριὰμ καὶ τὸν Ἰωσὴφ καὶ τὸ βρέφος **Lk 2:16.** τοὺς μαθητάς **Ac 21:4.**—M-M.

ἀνευφημέω impf. ἀνευφήμουν (Soph., Pla. et al.; Jos., Bell. 2, 608; 4, 113) ***praise loudly*** τ. κύριον θεόν ApcPt 5:19 (cp. Ps 62:8 Sym.; Achilles Tat. 3, 5, 6 τ. θεοὺς ἀ.).—DELG s.v. φημί.

ἀνέχω in our lit. only mid.: impf. ἀνειχόμην (ἠνειχόμην) 3 Macc 1:22, Just.; fut. ἀνέξομαι; 2 aor. ἀνεσχόμην **Ac 18:14;** v.l. ἠνεσχόμην on the augm. s. W-S. §12, 7; B-D-F §69, 2; Rob. 368 (s. ἀνοχή, ἔχω; Hom.+).

❶ **to regard w. tolerance, *endure, bear with, put up with;*** on its constr. s. B-D-F §176, 1; Rob. 508.**—**ⓐ τινός *someone* (Pla., Polit. 8, 564e; Teles p. 18, 6 H.; Gen 45:1; Is 63:15; 3 Macc 1:22; Just., D. 2, 3; 68, 1 μου; 109, 1 λέγοντός μου al.) Hm 4, 4, 1. ὑμῶν **Mt 17:17; Mk 9:19; Lk 9:41.** μου **2 Cor 11:1b** (Appian, Samn. 4 §10 τίς ἀνέξεταί μου).πάντων IPol 1:2. ἀλλήλων ἐν ἀγάπῃ *bear w. one another in love* **Eph 4:2;** cp. **Col 3:13.** τῶν ἀφρόνων *foolish people* **2 Cor 11:19.**

ⓑ *something*—**α.** w. gen. (Synes., Prov. 2, 6 p. 226c ἀνέχεσθαι φαύλων εἰκόνων = put up with second-rate pictures; Philo, Omn. Prob. Lib. 36; Jos., C. Ap. 2, 126) τ. λόγου τ. παρακλήσεως *listen patiently to the word of exhortation* **Hb 13:22.** τῆς ὑγιαινούσης διδασκαλίας **2 Ti 4:3.**

β. w. acc. (Procop. Soph., Ep. 161 p. 597 κακά; Is 1:13; Job 6:26) or w. gen. (Od. 22, 423; Polyaenus 8, 10, 1; Job 6:26 v.l.; 2 Macc 9:12) of thing πάντα 1 Cl 49:5. τὰ σάββατα *Sabbath-observances* B 2:5; 15:8 (Is 1:13). ταῦτα ἀ. (w. ὑπομένειν) Dg 2:9. ἀ. μου μικρόν τι ἀφροσύνης *put up w. a little foolishness from me* **2 Cor 11:1a** (Ltzm. ad loc.; the rhetorical topos as Demosth. 18, 160.—Appian, Bell. Civ. 1, 103 §480 ἀνέχεσθαι=be pleased with something, consent). ὀλίγα μου ῥήματα ἔτι ἀνάσχου *put up w. a few more words from me* Hm 4, 2, 1. Cp. Appian, Bell. Civ. 2, 63 §264 Καῖσαρ οὐδὲ τοῦτ' ἀνασχόμενος; Job 6:26; Jos., Ant. 19:12.

γ. w. adv. καλῶς ἀνέχεσθε *you put up with it quite easily* **2 Cor 11:4** (cp. εὖ ἀ. PAmh. 3a II, 14 and s. καλῶς 6 [lit.]).

δ. w. εἰ foll. **2 Cor 11:20**

ⓒ abs.; but the obj. is easily supplied fr. the context (Vi. Aesopi G 3 [I 36 P.]; Is 42:14; Job 6:11; Just., D. 2, 5 οὐκ ἠνειχόμην εἰς μακρὰν ἀποτιθέμενος 'I could no longer endure the prospect of spending so much time [on many branches of learning]': *forbear, put up with* Dg 9:1f.

❷ **to undergo someth. onerous or troublesome without giving in, *endure,*** ἐν ταῖς θλίψεσιν αἷς ἀνέχεσθε *in the trials that you endure* (αἷς can be attraction for ἅς as well as for ὧν, s. W-S §24, 4e; Rob. 716) **2 Th 1:4.** διωκόμενοι ἀνεχόμεθα *when we are persecuted we endure it* **1 Cor 4:12** (use w. ptc. is quite common Thu. et al.; s. e.g. Epict. index Schenkl).

❸ ***accept a complaint*** legal t.t. κατὰ λόγον ἂν ἀνεσχόμην ὑμῶν *I would have been justified in accepting your complaint* **Ac 18:14.**—DELG s.v. 1 ἔχω 392. M-M. TW.

ἀνεψιός, οῦ, ὁ (Hom. et al.) ***cousin*** (IG IV^2/1, 693, 4 [III AD]; ISyriaW 2053c; PLond III, 1164k, 20, p. 167 [212 AD]; PTebt 323, 13; Sb 176 ἀ. πρὸς πατρός and πρὸς μητρός; Num 36:11; Tob 7:2; Philo, Leg. ad Gai. 67; Jos., Bell. 1, 662, Ant. 1, 290; 15, 250 al.) Μᾶρκος ὁ ἀ. Βαρναβᾶ **Col 4:10.** JKalitsunakis, Mittel-u. neugriech. Erklärungen bei Eustathius 1919, 42ff. —B. 116; 118. DELG. M-M.

ἀνέῳγα, ἀνέῳξα s. ἀνοίγω.

ἀνήγαγον s. ἀνάγω.

ἀνήγγειλα, ἀνηγγέλην s. ἀναγγέλλω.

ἄνηθον, ου, τό (not to be confused w. ἄννησον, 'anise' [L-S-J-M]; since Alc. and Sappho [ἄνητον]; Aristoph., Nub. 982; Theocr. 15, 119; SIG 1170, 26; pap) ***dill,*** a plant used for seasoning, w. ἡδύοσμον and κύμινον (s. Hippiatr. II 164, 13 πήγανον, κύμινον, ἄνηθον), acc. to rabb. tradition (Maaseroth 4, 5) subject to the tithe **Mt 23:23; Lk 11:42 v.l.** Goodsp., Probs. 37f.—DELG. M-M. TW.

ἀνῆκα s. ἀνίημι.

ἀνήκω (Soph., Hdt.+; ins, pap, LXX).**—**❶ **to have come to a point so as to have some connection, *refer, relate, belong*** εἴς τι *to someth.* (Demosth. 60, 6 [prob. spurious work]; SIG 589, 63 ἃ ἀνήκει εἰς τ. τροφήν; 742, 15; BGU 1120, 32 [I BC]; Sir Prol. ln. 12; Jos., Ant. 4, 198) διακονία εἰς τὸ κοινὸν ἀνήκουσα *a* *service related to the association (of Christians), a service to the church* IPhld 1:1. τὰ ἀνήκοντα εἰς τ. ἐκκλησίαν *what concerns the church* ISm 8:1. τὰ ἀ. εἰς σωτηρίαν *what relates to salvation* 1 Cl 45:1; B 17:1. οἰκοδομὴ εἰς τ. κύριον ἡμῶν ἀνήκουσα *edification that pertains to our Lord* Pol 13:2. Instead of the prep., τινί to *someth.* (BGU 300, 7; 638, 14 al.) τὰ ἀ. τῇ θρησκείᾳ ἡμῶν *what pertains to our religion* 1 Cl 62:1. τὰ ἀ. τῇ βουλήσει θεοῦ *what is in harmony w. God's will* 35:5. εὐποιΐα θεῷ ἀνήκουσα *a good deed that concerns God* IPol 7:3. τὰ ἀ. ταῖς ψυχαῖς *what your souls need* D 16:2. παραβολὴ ἀνήκουσα τῇ νηστείᾳ *a parable that has to do w. fasting* Hs 5, 2,1.

❷ **to reach a point of connection, w. focus on what is appropriate,** impers. (Nägeli 48; Thieme 15) ἀνήκει ***it is proper, fitting*** (Ael. Dion. α, 138 ἀνήκει: ʼΑντιφῶν [fgm. 103 Blass] ἀντὶ τοῦ καθήκει; BGU 417, 17 ὅτι καὶ σοὶ τοῦτο ἀνήκει καὶ συμφέρει; 1 Macc 10:42) ὡς ἀνῆκεν *as is fitting* **Col 3:18** (on the use of the impf. B-D-F §358, 2; Rob. 920; Mlt-Turner 90f, but s. Lohmeyer ad loc.). ἃ οὐκ ἀνῆκεν **Eph 5:4** (τὰ οὐκ ἀνήκοντα v.l.). τὸ ἀνῆκον *what is proper, one's duty* (IMagnMai 53, 65 [III BC] τὰ ἀνήκοντα τῇ πόλει what one owes the city; PFay 94, 9, 24; PTebt 6, 41; 1 Macc 11:35; 2 Macc 14:8) ἐπιτάσσειν σοι τὸ ἀνῆκον *order you to do the right thing* (an appeal for reciprocity) **Phlm 8.** τὰ ἀν[ή]κοντα τῇ ἀρχῇ *what belongs to the authorities* PEg[2] 49.—DELG s.v. ἥκω. M-M. TW.

ἀνήμερος, ον (since Anacr. 1, 7 [348, 7 Page]; Epict. 1, 3, 7; Dio Chrys. 11 [12], 51; Aelian, NA 15, 25; Socratics p. 292, 16 Malherbe; JosAs 12:9 cod. A [p. 56, 1 Bat.]; EpArist 289; Philo et al. [Nägeli 16; 25]) lit. 'untamed', ***savage, brutal,*** w. other undesirable qualities **2 Ti 3:3.**—DELG s.v. ἥμερος. M-M.

ἀνήνεγκον s. ἀναφέρω.

ἀνήρ, ἀνδρός, ὁ (Hom.+, common in all the mngs. known to our lit.) a male person

❶ **an adult human male, *man, husband*—ⓐ** in contrast to woman *man* (Pla., Gorg. 514e; X., Hell. 4, 5, 5 et al.) **Mt 14:21; 15:38; Mk 6:44; Lk 9:14; J 1:13; Ac 4:4; 8:3, 12; 1 Cor 11:3, 7ff;** Hm 5, 2, 2; 6, 2, 7; 12, 2, 1 al. Hence ἄνδρα γινώσκειν (יָדְעָה אִישׁ Gen 19:8; Judg 11:39) of a woman *have sexual intercourse w. a man* **Lk 1:34** (cp. Just., D. 78, 3 ἀπὸ συνουσίας ἀνδρός). Esp. *husband* (Hom. et al.; Diod. S. 2, 8, 6; Sir 4:10; Jos., Ant. 18, 149; Ar. 12, 2; fgm. Milne p. 74 ln. 3; Just., A II, 2, 5ff; for this shift from the general to the specific cp. our 'that's her man', 'my man') **Mt 1:16, 19; Mk 10:2, 12; Lk 2:36; J 4:16ff; Ac 5:9f; Ro 7:2f** (Sb 8010, 21 [pap I AD] μέχρι οὗ ἐὰν συνέρχωμαι ἑτέρῳ ἀνδρί; PLond V, 1731, 16 [VI AD] κολλᾶσθαι ἑτέρῳ ἀνδρί); **1 Cor 7:2ff, 10ff; 14:35; Gal 4:27; Eph 5:22ff; Col 3:18f; 1 Ti 3:2, 12; 5:9; Tit 1:6** (on the four last ref. εἷς 2b, the comm. and JFischer, Weidenauer Studien 1, 1906, 177–226; comparison w. non-Christian sources in J-BFrey, Signification des termes μονάνδρα et Univira: RSR 20, 1930, 48–60; GDelling, Pls' Stellung z. Frau u. Ehe '31, 136ff; BEaston, Past. Epistles, '47, 216ff; WSchulze, Kerygma und Dogma [Göttingen] 4, '58, 287–300) **2:5; 1 Pt 3:1, 5, 7;** Hm 4, 1, 4ff; 1 Cl 6:3; Pol 4:2; AcPl Ha 4, 5.—**1 Ti 2:12** (cp. Ocellus Luc. c. 49: the wife wishes ἄρχειν τοῦ ἀνδρὸς παρὰ τὸν τῆς φύσεως νόμον). Even *a bridegroom* can be so called (cp. אִישׁ Dt 22:23) ὡς νύμφην κεκοσμημένην τῷ ἀνδρὶ αὐτῆς **Rv 21:2.** Freq. in address, esp. in formal assemblies: ἄνδρες *men, gentlemen* (X., An. 1, 4, 14; 1 Esdr 3:18; 4:14, 34) **Ac 14:15; 19:25; 27:10, 21, 25.** ἄνδρες ἀδελφοί *(my esteemed) brothers* (4 Macc 8:19; cp. X., An. 1, 6, 6 ἄ. φίλοι) **Ac 15:7, 13; 23:1, 6; 28:17;** 1 Cl 14:1; 37:1; 43:4; 62:1. AcPl Ha 6, 18; 7, 13; 8:9. ἀ. ἀδελφοὶ καὶ πατέρες **Ac 7:2.** Of soldiers (1 Macc 5:17; 16:15) οἱ ἄ. οἱ συνέχοντες αὐτόν *the men who were holding him* **Lk 22:63.**—In **Ac 17:34** ἀνήρ appears to = ἄνθρωπος, but the term was probably chosen in anticipation of the contrasting γυνή (is Damaris the wife of one of the men?).

ⓑ in contrast to boy (Tob 1:9; but ἀ. of a child IK VII/2, 14) ὅτε γέγονα ἀ. *when I became a man* **1 Cor 13:11.** ἀ. τέλειος *a full-grown man* (X., Cyr. 1, 2, 4) **Eph 4:13;** in sense of maturity w. ethical component *perfect* **Js 3:2** (s. 1dα).

ⓒ used w. a word indicating national or local origin, calling attention to a single individual, or even individualizing the pl.; hence in address (X., An. 1, 7, 3 ὦ ἄ. Ἕλληνες; Jdth 4:9; 15:13; 1 Macc 2:23); the sg. is omitted in transl., the pl. rendered *men, gentlemen* (in direct address = esteemed people) of a certain place: ἀνὴρ Αἰθίοψ **Ac 8:27** (X., An. 1, 8, 1 ἀ. Πέρσης; Palaeph. 5; Maximus Tyr. 5, 1a ἀ. **Φρύξ;** Tat. 6, 1 Βηρωσσὸς ἀ. Βαβυλώνιος); ἄ. ʼΑθηναῖοι (Lysias 6, 8) **17:22;** ἄ. Γαλιλαῖοι **1:11;** ἄ. ʼΕφέσιοι **19:35;** AcPl Ha 1, 24; ἀ. ʼΙουδαῖος **Ac 10:28;** ἄ. ʼΙουδαῖοι (Jos., Ant. 11, 169) **2:14;** ἄ. ʼΙσραηλῖται (Jos., Ant. 3, 189) **2:22** (cp. vs. **22b** of Jesus, in an adroit rhetorical ploy); **5:35; 13:16; 21:28;** ἄ. Κορίνθιοι AcPlCor 2:26; ἄ. Κύπριοι καὶ Κυρηναῖοι **Ac 11:20;** ἀ. Μακεδών **16:9.** (Cp. B-D-F §242.)

ⓓ with focus on personal characteristics, either pos. or neg.

α. used w. adj.: ἀ. ἀγαθός **Ac 11:24;** ἀ. ἀγαθὸς καὶ δίκαιος **Lk 23:50** (cp. ἀνδραγαθία Aeschin., C. Ctesiph. 42 al.; δεδοκιμασμένοι ἄ. 1 Cl 44:2; cp. Tat. 38, 1 ἄ. δοκιμώτατος; δίκαιος Hm 4, 1, 3; 11, 9, 13f; δίκαιος καὶ ἅγιος **Mk 6:20;** ἀ. δίψυχος, ἀκατάστατος **Js 1:8;** ἀ. ἐλλόγιμος 1 Cl 44:3; ἀ. ἔνδοξος Hv 5:1; ἀ. εὐλαβής **Ac 8:2; 22:12;** ἀ. λόγιος **18:24;** ἀ. μεμαρτυρημένος IPhld 11:1; ἀ. πιστὸς καὶ ἐλλογιμώτατος 1 Cl 62:3; ξένος AcPl Ox 6, 11 (= Aa I 241, 14); ἀ. πονηρός **Ac 17:5** (PsSol 12:1f); ἀ. πραΰς D 15:1; ἀ. συνετός **Ac 13:7** (Just., D. 2, 6); ἀ. φρόνιμος **Mt 7:24;** ἀ. μωρός vs. **26.** ἀ. χρυσοδακτύλιος *someone with gold rings on the fingers* (satirical='Mr. Gold Rings') **Js 2:2.** τέλειος ἀ. **3:2** (s. 1b).— Oft. in circumlocutions for nouns, somet. pleonastic (like Heb. אִישׁ) οἱ ἄ. τοῦ τόπου (Gen 26:7) *the local residents* **Mt 14:35.** ἀ. πλήρης λέπρας=*a leper* (in serious condition) **Lk 5:12;** ἀ. πλήρης πίστεως **Ac 6:5, 11:24.** ἀ. ἁμαρτωλός (Sir 12:14; 27:30 al.) *a sinner* **Lk 5:8; 19:7.**—In noun combinations (Ps.-Pla., Axioch. 12 p. 371a ἀ. μάγος; Chion, Ep. 14, 4 ἀ. δεσπότης; Maximus Tyr. 19, 2a ποιμὴν ἀ.) ἀ. προφήτης (Judg 6:8) *a prophet* **24:19.** ἀ. πρεσβύτης (s. πρεσβύτης) MPol 7:2.

β. w. special emphasis on courage or endurance, an aspect w. strong Homeric color (Hom. et al.; Philostrat., Vi. Apoll. 1, 16 p. 17, 2 [opp. ἄνθρωποι real 'men' in contrast to mere 'people']) of the apostles 1 Cl 6:1.—AcPl Ha 1, 25; 28.

❷ equiv. to τὶς ***someone, a person*** (Theognis 1, 199 Diehl[2]; X., Cyr. 2, 2, 22; Sir 27:7) **Lk 9:38; 19:2; J 1:30; Ro 4:8** (Ps 32:2). Pl. *some* people (1 Macc 12:1; 13:34; Just., D. 108, 2 al.) **Lk 5:18; Ac 6:11.** ἀνήρ τις **Lk 8:27; Ac 10:1.** ἀνὴρ ὅς Lat. is qui (like אִישׁ אֲשֶׁר; cp. 1 Macc 7:7; PsSol 6:1; 10:1 and as early as Pind., P. 9, 87 ἀνήρ τις, ὅς . . .); **Js 1:12.** οἱ κατ' ἄνδρα (Dio Chrys. 15 [32], 6; cp. κατ' ἄνδρα καὶ οἶκον PsSol 9:5) *man for man, individually* IEph 4:2 (of presbyters, but s. JKleist, note ad loc., *rank and file*); 20:2; ITr 13:2; ISm 5:1; 12:2; IPol 1:3.

❸ **a transcendent figure—ⓐ *a figure of a man*** of heavenly beings who resemble men (SibOr 3, 137 the Titans are so called; Just., D.56, 5 [s. Gen. 18:2], 10 ἐν ἰδέᾳ ἀνδρός) GPt 9:36; 10:39.

ⓑ of Jesus as the judge of the world, appointed by God: ὁ θεὸς . . . μέλλει κρίνειν τὴν οἰκουμένην ἐν ἀνδρὶ ᾧ ὥρισεν **Ac 17:31** (cp. Oenomaus in Eus., PE 5, 19, 3 Minos is the ἀνήρ, ὃν ἀποδεικνύναι ἐμέλλετε κοινὸν ἀνθρώπων δικαστήν=whom you [Gods] intended to make the common judge of humanity).—On Jesus as θεῖος ἀνήρ figure, s. EKoskenniemi, Apollonius von Tyana in der neutestamentlichen Exegese '94 (lit.).—MVock, Bedeutung u. Verwendung von ΑΝΗΡ u. ΑΝΘΡΩΠΟΣ etc., diss. Freiburg 1928; HSeiler, Glotta 32, '53, 225–36.—B. 81; 96. DELG. M-M. TW. Sv.

ἀνηρέθην s. ἀναιρέω.

ἀνήφθην s. ἀνάπτω.

ἀνήχθην s. ἀνάγω.

ἀνθέξομαι s. ἀντέχω.

ἀνθέω fut. ἀνθήσω; 1 aor. ἤνθησα; pf. ἤνθηκα LXX (Hom. et al.; also Just., A II, 11, 4 ἀνθοῦντι … προσώπῳ) ***bloom*** τὴν γῆν ἀνθοῦσαν ἀμαράντοις ἄνθεσι *blooming w. unfading flowers* ApcPt 5:15 (w. the dat. ἄνθος as Hom. Hymn Ap. 139).—DELG s.v. ἄνθος.

ἀνθηρός, ά, όν (s. ἀνθέω. Soph. et al.; Cornutus 30 p. 59, 16; Longus 1, 15, 3) of hair ***splendid, brilliant*** ApcPt 3:10.—DELG s.v. ἄνθος.

ἀνθίστημι fut. ἀντιστήσομαι LXX; 2 aor. ἀντέστην; pf. ἀνθέστηκα; 1 aor. pass. ἀντεστάθην Hm 12, 2, 3 (ἀντί, ἵστημι; Hom. et al.) 'set against'; the forms occurring in our lit. have the mid. sense

❶ **be in opposition to, *set oneself against, oppose*—ⓐ** pers. τινί *someone* (PGiss 65, 9) **Mt 5:39; Ac 13:8;** κατὰ πρόσωπον αὐτῷ ἀντέστην (Dt 7:24; 9:2; 11:25) *I opposed him to his face* **Gal 2:11;** ἀ. Μωϋσεῖ **2 Ti 3:8;** ἀ. τῷ διαβόλῳ **Js 4:7;** cp. **1 Pt 5:9;** Hm 12, 5, 2 and 4; ἀντιστήτω μοι *let him oppose me* B 6:1 (Mel., P. 101, 774 [both Is 50:8]).

ⓑ impers. τινί τῇ σοφίᾳ **Lk 21:15; Ac 6:10.** τ. βουλήματι αὐτοῦ **Ro 9:19** (cp. Demosth. 18, 49 τοὺς ἀνθισταμένους τ. ὑμετέροις βουλήμασι).θεοῦ διαταγῇ **13:2.** τῷ κράτει τῆς ἰσχύος αὐτοῦ 1 Cl 27:5 (cp. Wsd 11:21). τῇ ἀληθείᾳ **2 Ti 3:8.** τοῖς ἡμετέροις λόγοις **4:15** (cp. Jdth 8:28). ἐπιθυμίαις Hm 12, 2, 3f. ἀ. τῇ ὀξυχολίᾳ *resist ill temper* m 5, 2, 8.

❷ **to be resistant to power, *resist,*** abs. (BGU 747 II, 10; Esth 9:2; 3 Macc 6:19) ἵνα δυνηθῆτε ἀντιστῆναι *that you might be able to stand your ground* **Eph 6:13** (cp. PPetr II, 37, 2a, 14 [III BC] οὐ δύναμαι ἀνθιστάνειν). ἀντιστῶμεν *let us take a firm stand* B 4:9. οἱ ἀνθεστηκότες *those who resist* **Ro 13:2b** (sc. τ. διαταγῇ).—DELG s.v. ἵστημι. M-M.

ἀνθομολογέομαι impf. ἀνθωμολογούμην (ἀντί, ὁμολογέομαι; w. many mngs. Demosth. et al.; pap [incl. PYadin 17, 16], LXX; TestJud 1:3; Jos., Ant. 8, 257; 362) ***praise, thank*** (publicly express: thanks Plut., Aemil. Paul. 11, 1; recognition: Diod. S. 1, 70, 6) τῷ θεῷ (Ps 78:13; Da 4:37 [here alternating w. ἐξομολογοῦμαι; cp. Sir 17:27, 28]; 3 Macc 6:33) **Lk 2:38.**—DELG s.v. λέγω, ὁμός. M-M. TW.

ἄνθος, ους, τό (Hom.+).—❶ ***blossom, flower*** specif., of a grape blossom 1 Cl 23:4. Type of that which does not last (Quint. Smyrn. 14, 207 ἀνδρῶν γὰρ γένος ἐστὶν ὁμοίιον ἄνθεσι ποίης=like the flowers of the grass (Zohary, Plants 172f); Aristaen., Ep. 2, 1 πέπαυται τὰ ἄνθη) ἀ. χόρτου *wild flower* **Js 1:10,** cp. vs. **11. 1 Pt 1:24ab** (both Is 40:6f). Colorful splendor ApcPt 3:10 (descr. of κόμη as in Anacr., fgm. 46 Diehl.[2] [414 Page]). ἄ. ἀμάραντα *unfading flowers* 15.

❷ ***fragrance of flowers*** ApcPt 5:16.—B. 527. DELG. M-M.

ἀνθρακιά, ᾶς, ἡ (s. ἄνθραξ; Hom. et al.; Sir 11:32; 4 Macc 9:20) ***a charcoal fire*** ἀ. ποιεῖν (PGM 4, 2468) **J 18:18.** ἀ. κειμένη *a charcoal fire on the ground* **21:9** (the Latin vers.: incensos= ἀ. καιομένη would mean: a pile of burning charcoal). For ἀνθ. used in preparing fish, and the connection with **J 21:9,** cp. Creophylus of Ephesus [400 BC]: 417 fgm. 1 Jac. p. 314, 23f ἁλιέας ἀριστοποιεῖσθαι … τῶν ἰχθύων … σὺν ἀνθρακιᾷ.

ἄνθραξ, ακος, ὁ (Thu., Aristoph. et al.) ***charcoal*** only in the proverb ἄνθρακας πυρὸς σωρεύειν ἐπὶ τὴν κεφαλήν τινος *heap burning embers on someone's head* **Ro 12:20,** i.e., prob., cause the pers. to blush w. shame and remorse (Pr 25:22). Cp. AWright, Interpreter 16, 1920, 159; ERoberts and FJarrat, ibid. 239; AFryer, ET 36, 1925, 478; SBartstra NThT 23, '34, 61–68; SMorenz, TLZ 78, '53, 187–92; KStendahl, HTR 55, '62, 343–55, esp. 346–48 (Qumran); WKlassen, NTS 9, '63, 337–50; LRamarosan, Biblica 51, '70, 230–34.—DELG. M-M.

ἀνθρωπαρεσκέω (s. ἄνθρωπος, ἀρέσκω; hapax leg., but s. next entry) **be a people-pleaser, *court/curry the favor of people*** (connoting sacrifice of principle; cp. our colloq. 'play up to' or 'be an apple-polisher') οὐ θέλω ὑμᾶς ἀνθρωπαρεσκῆσαι IRo 2:1 (cp. Gal 1:10).—DELG s.v. ἀρέσκω.

ἀνθρωπάρεσκος, ον (s. prec.; Ps 52:6; PsSol 4:7, 8, 19; cp. Nägeli 61; ADebrunner, Griech. Wortbildungslehre, 1917, 51) as subst., **one who tries to make an impression on others, *fawner, timeserver*** of slaves who practice obsequious obedience when their owner is watching **Eph 6:6; Col 3:22.**—In wordplay w. ἑαυτῷ ἀρέσκειν (people-pleaser–self-pleaser) 2 Cl 13:1 (WvanUnnik, ZNW Beiheft 26, '60, 221–34).—M-M. TW.

ἀνθρώπινος, η, ον (s. ἄνθρωπος; Pre-Socr., Hdt.+. Just. has fem. -ος A I, 11, 1f, otherw. -η) **pert. to being a person, *human.***

ⓐ gener. (ἀνθρώπινόν τι πάσχειν=die: PPetr I, 11, 9ff; PGen 21, 15; BGU 1149, 34; SIG 1042, 13) ἀ. ἔργα *human deeds* 1 Cl 59:3 (Just., D. 76, 1 [sg.]); φόβοι ἀ. *human fears* i.e. such as humans are heir to 2 Cl 10:3; συνήθεια ἀ. IEph 5:1; φόβῳ (sc.) ἀ. AcPl Ha 11, 17; σάρξ ἀ. (Wsd 12:5; Philo, Spec. Leg. 4, 103) IPhld 7:2; πειρασμὸς ἀ. *a temptation common to humanity* (cp. Epict. 1, 9, 30, Ench. 26; Num 5:6), i.e. bearable (Pollux 3, 27, 131 also mentions τὸ ἀνθρώπινον among the concepts which form a contrast to ὃ οὐκ ἄν τις ὑπομένειεν) **1 Cor 10:13.** ἀνθρώπινον λέγειν *speak in human terms* i.e. as people do in daily life **Ro 6:19** (cp. Plut., Mor. 13c; Philo, Somn. 2, 288); ἀ. ὁ λόγος *the saying is commonly accepted* **1 Ti 3:1** D*, cp. **1:15 v.l.** (favored by Zahn, Einl. I 487; GWohlenberg ad loc.; EKühl, Erläuterung d. paul. Briefe II 1909, 179; WLock, ICC ad loc. and Intr. xxxvi, 'true to human needs').

ⓑ in contrast to animal (Diod. S. 3, 35, 5; Ezk 4:15; Da 7:4, 8) δεδάμασται τῇ φύσει τῇ ἀ. *has been tamed by human nature* or *humankind* **Js 3:7;** ὁ λέων … εἶπεν τῷ Παύλῳ ἀ. γλώσσῃ (cp. TestAbr A 3 p. 79, 18f [Stone p. 6] ἀ. φωνῇ of a tree. ParJer 7, 2 of an eagle).

ⓒ in contrast to the divine (Maximus Tyr. 38, 5e; SIG 526, 29f [III BC]; 721, 33; 798, 10 [c. 37 AD]; Job 10:5; 4 Macc 1:16f; 4:13; Jos., Bell. 6, 429) ἀ. μυστήρια (merely) *human secrets* Dg 7:1. ὑπὸ χειρῶν ἀ. θεραπεύεται **Ac 17:25** (χ. ἀ. Jos., Bell. 5, 387; 400; Just., A I, 20, 5). ἀ. σοφία *human wisdom* (Philo, Rer. Div. Her. 126.—Jos., Ant. 3, 223 σύνεσις ἀ; Just., D. 80, 3 διδάγματα ἀ.) **1 Cor 2:4 v.l., 13.** ἀ. ἡμέρα *a human court* **4:3.** πρόσκλισις ἀ. *human partiality* 1 Cl 50:2. δόγμα ἀ. *human opinion* Dg 5:3. ἀ. κτίσις *human institution* of the authorities **1 Pt 2:13.**—DELG s.v. ἄνθρωπος. M-M. TW.

ἀνθρωπίνως adv. (s. ἀνθρώπινος; Thu.; Andoc. 1, 57; 2, 6 et al.; PSI XII, 1248, 17 [III AD]; TestSol 10:3 C; Jos., Ant. 19, 4;

Tat. 4:1) ***as a human being*** θεοῦ ἀ. φανερουμένου *when God appeared in human form* IEph 19:3.—M-M.

ἀνθρωποκτόνος, ου, ὁ (κτείνω 'kill'; rare: Eur., Cycl. 127, Iph. T. 389; Tat. 8, 3; Mel. all as adj.; Ps.-Plut., De Fluv. 1165a; Nicetas Eugen. 8, 225H) ***murderer,*** of one who hates his brother **1J 3:15** (cp. **Mt 5:21f**). Of the devil ἀ. ἦν ἀπ' ἀρχῆς *he was a murderer from the beginning,* not w. ref. to the murder of Abel, but to designate the devil as the one who brought death into the world by misleading Adam (Wsd 2:24) **J 8:44.**—DELG s.v. κτείνω. M-M.

ἀνθρωπόμορφος, ον (s. μορφή; Epicur., fgm. 353 Us. θεός; [acc. to Diod. S. 40, 3, 4 Moses refused to believe in a θ. ἀνθρωπόμορφος]; Diod. S. 3, 62, 2 [Dionysus]; 22, 9, 4 θεοὶ ἀ.; Strabo 16, 2, 35 τὸ θεῖον; Cornutus 27 p. 49, 7; Diog. L.; Plut., Mor. 149cd; 167d; TestSol 18:1; Philo, Op. M. 69) ***in human form*** θηρία ἀ. *wild beasts in human form* (Philo, Abr. 33) of dissidents ISm 4:1.—DELG s.v. μορφή.

ἀνθρωποποίητος, ον lit. 'something made by a human being' προσφορὰ ἀ. ***an offering of human origin*** B 2:6.—DELG s.v. ποιέω.

ἄνθρωπος, ου, ὁ (Hom.+; loanw. in rabb.; ἡ ἄνθρωπος [Hdt. 1, 60, 5] does not appear in our lit.) 'human being, man, person'.

❶ **a person of either sex, w. focus on participation in the human race, *a human being*—ⓐ** ἐγεννήθη ἀ. **J 16:21;** εἰς χεῖρας ἀ. **Mk 9:31;** ψυχὴ ἀνθρώπου **Ro 2:9;** συνείδησις ἀ. **2 Cor 4:2;** μέτρον ἀ. **Rv 21:17.**

ⓑ in contrast to animals, plants, etc. **Mt 4:19; 12:12; Mk 1:17; Lk 5:10; 1 Cor 15:39; 2 Pt 2:16; Rv 9:4, 7; 13:18** al. To angels (cp. Aristaen. 1, 24, end σάτυροι οὐκ ἄνθρωποι) **1 Cor 4:9; 13:1.** To God (Aeschyl., Ag. 663 θεός τις οὐκ ἄνθ.; Aeschines 3, 137 θεοὶ κ. δαίμονες; Ael. Aristid. 30 p. 578 D.; Herm. Wr. 14, 8 θεοὺς κ. ἀνθρ.; οὐκ ἐλογίσατο ὅτι ἀ. ἐστιν PsSol 2:28) **Hb 13:6** (Ps 117:6); **Mt 10:32f; 19:6; Mk 10:9; J 10:33** (ἄνθ. ὤν='as a mortal human', a favorite formula: X., An. 7, 6, 11; Menand., Epitr. 592 Kö.; fgm.: 46; 395, 2 Kö; Comp. I 282; Alexis Com., fgm. 150; Polyb. 3, 31, 3; Chariton 4, 4, 8 [WBlake '38]; Heliod. 6, 9, 3; As early as Eur., Hipp. 472ff ἄνθρωπος οὖσα … κρείσσω δαιμόνων εἶναι θέλειν); **Ac 10:26; 12:22; 14:11, 15; 1 Th 2:13; Phil 2:7.** ἐντάλματα ἀνθρώπων *human precepts* **Mt 15:9; Mk 7:7** (Is 29:13); w. οὐρανός (=God) **Mt 21:25; Mk 11:30.** ἀδύνατα παρὰ ἀνθρώποις **Lk 18:27,** cp. **Mt 19:26.** δοῦλοι ἀνθρώπων *people's slaves* **1 Cor 7:23.** πείθειν and ἀρέσκειν ἀ. **Gal 1:10.** μεσίτης θεοῦ καὶ ἀ. **1 Ti 2:5** al. θεὸς πάντας ἀνθρώπους θέλει σωθῆναι **1 Ti 2:4** (cp. Epict. 3, 24, 2 ὁ θεὸς πάντας ἀνθρώπους ἐπὶ τὸ εὐδαιμονεῖν ἐποίησεν).

ⓒ in pl. w. gener. mng. (cp. Hom., Il. 21, 569; Od. 1, 351) οἱ ἀ. *people,* also one's *associates* (Jos., Ant. 9, 28) **Mt 5:13, 16; 6:1f, 5, 14, 18; 7:12; 8:27; 23:5; Mk 8:27** and often. οἱ τότε ἀ. *the people of that time* Pol 3:2.—οἱ υἱοὶ τῶν ἀνθρώπων *the offspring of human beings* or simply *human beings, people* (Gen 11:5; 1 Esdr 4:37; Ps 10:4; En10:7 al.; PsSol 9:4) **Mk 3:28; Eph 3:5.** Sim. ὁ υἱὸς τοῦ ἀ. as a self-designation of Jesus but s. next, also 2a and υἱός 2dγ.

ⓓ Jesus Christ is called ἀ. as one who identifies with humanity (cp. ὁ Σωτὴρ ἀ. γενόμενος Did., Gen. 41, 28) **1 Ti 2:5; Hb 2:6a** (Ps 8:5a; cp. Just., A II, 6, 4). He is in contrast to Adam **Ro 5:15; 1 Cor 15:21,** the πρῶτος ἀ. **1 Cor 15:45, 47** (cp. Philo, Abr. 56; s. DDD 112) as δεύτερος ἀ. vs. **47.** On the nature and origin of this concept cp. Ltzm. and JWeiss on **1 Cor 15:45ff;** WBousset, Kyrios Christos[2] 1921, 120 ff, Jesus der Herr 1916, 67ff; Rtzst., Mysterienrel.[3] 343ff, Erlösungsmyst. 107ff; ARawlinson, The NT Doctrine of the Christ 1926, 124ff; BStegmann, Christ, the 'Man from Heaven', a Study of 1 Cor 15:45–47: The Cath. Univ., Washington 1927; CKraeling, Anthropos and Son of Man 1927. S. on Ἀδάμ and on οὐρανός 2b.—On ὁ υἱὸς τοῦ ἀ. as a self-designation of Jesus s.c end, above, and υἱός 2dγ.

❷ **a member of the human race, w. focus on limitations and weaknesses, *a human being*—ⓐ** of physical aspect **Js 5:17;** subject to death **Hb 9:27; Rv 8:11; Ro 5:12;** sunken in sin (cp. fr. a different perspective Menand., fgm. 432 Kö [499 K.] ἄνθρωπος ὢν ἥμαρτον; Herodas 5, 27 ἄνθρωπός εἰμι, ἥμαρτον; schol. on Apollon. Rhod. 4, 1015–17a σὺ ἄνθρωπος εἶ, οἷς τὸ ἁμαρτάνειν γίνεται ῥᾳδίως; cp. Orig. C. Cels. 3, 62, 17) **5:18f** al., hence judged to be inferior **Gal 1:1, 11f; Col 2:8, 22** (Is 29:13) or even carefully to be avoided προσέχειν ἀπὸ τ. ἀ. *beware of* (evil) *men* **Mt 10:17;** cp. **Lk 6:22, 26.**

ⓑ of status κατὰ ἄνθρωπον (Aeschyl., Sept. 425; Pla., Phileb. 370f; Diod. S. 16, 11, 2; Athen. 10, 444b; Plut., Mor. 1042a; Witkowski 8, 5 [252 BC]) *in a human way, from a human standpoint* emphasizes the inferiority of human beings in comparison w. God; λαλεῖν **1 Cor 9:8;** λέγειν **Ro 3:5; Gal 3:15;** περιπατεῖν **1 Cor 3:3.** κ. ἀ. ἐθηριομάχησα perh. *like an ordinary man* (opp. as a Christian sure of the resurrection) **15:32.** Of the gospel οὐκ ἔστιν κ. ἀ. **Gal 1:11.** Pl. κ. ἀνθρώπους (opp. κ. θεόν) **1 Pt 4:6.**

❸ **a male person, *man*—ⓐ** adult male, *man* (Pla., Prot. 6, 314e, Phd. 66, 117e; Gen. 24:26ff; PsSol 17:17; TestAbr A 3 p. 79, 25 [Stone p. 6]; ParJer 5:20) **Mt 11:8; Lk 7:25.** σκληρὸς εἶ ἀ. **Mt 25:24;** cp. **Lk 19:21f.** In contrast to woman (Achilles Tat. 5, 22, 2; PGM 36, 225f; 1 Esdr 9:40; Tob 6:8) **Mt 19:5;** prob. **Lk 13:19** (cp. vs. 21); **Eph 5:31** (both Gen 2:24); **1 Cor 7:1;** Ox 840, 39.

ⓑ married person *husband* **Mt 19:10.**

ⓒ an immediate descendant *son,* opp. father (Sir 3:11) **Mt 10:35.**

ⓓ a person owned and therefore under the control of another *slave* (X., Mem. 2, 1, 15, Vect. 4, 14; Herodas 5, 78; BGU 830, 4; POxy. 1067, 30; 1159, 16) **Lk 12:36.** οἱ τοῦ πυρὸς ἀ. *the persons in charge of the fire* MPol 15:1; ἀ. τοῦ μεγάλου βασιλέως AcPl Ha 9, 1 (Aa I 111, 10). Perh. **J 6:7.**

❹ practically equiv. to the indef. pron., w. the basic mng. of ἀ. greatly weakened (cp. 1c.) ***someone, one, a person.*—ⓐ** without the art.—**α.** used w. τίς: ἐὰν γένηταί τινι ἀνθρώπῳ **Mt 18:12.** ἄνθρωπός τις κατέβαινεν *a man was going down* **Lk 10:30.** ἀνθρώπου τινὸς πλουσίου **12:16.** ἀ. τις ἦν ὑδρωπικός **14:2,** cp. vs. **16; 15:11; 16:1, 19; 19:12.** ἦν τις ἀ. ἐκεῖ **J 5:5.** τινῶν ἀ. αἱ ἁμαρτίαι **1 Ti 5:24.**

β. without τίς, and somet. nearly equiv. to it (Paus. 5, 7, 3 ἐξ ἀνθρώπου=from someone) εἷς ἀ.=εἷς τις *an individual* **J 11:50,** cp. **18:14.** εἶδεν ἄνθρωπον καθήμενον *he saw someone sitting* **Mt 9:9.** ἰδοὺ ἀ. χεῖρα ἔχων ξηράν *there was someone with a shriveled hand* **12:10.** λαβὼν ἀ. *a person took* **13:31;** cp. **Mk 1:23; 3:1; 4:26; 5:2; 7:11; 10:7** (Gen 2:24); **Lk 2:25; 4:33; 5:18; 6:48f; 13:19; J 3:4, 27** al. Used w. negatives ἀ. οὐκ ἔχω *I have nobody* **J 5:7.** οὐδέποτε ἐλάλησεν οὕτως ἀ. *nobody has ever spoken like that* **7:46.**

γ. in indef. and at the same time general sense, oft.=*one* (Ger. man, Fr. on) οὕτως ἡμᾶς λογιζέσθω ἀ. lit. *this is how one* or *a person* (i.e. *you*) *should regard us* **1 Cor 4:1;** cp. **Mt 16:26; Ro 3:28; 1 Cor 7:26; 11:28; Gal 2:16; 6:7; Js 2:24.**

δ. w. relative foll. δεῦτε ἴδετε ἀ. ὃς εἶπέν μοι *come and see someone who* (contrast w. ἀνήρ vss. 16–18) *told me* **J 4:29.** ἀ. ὃς τὴν ἀλήθειαν ὑμῖν λελάληκα **8:40.** For **Ac 19:16** s. 6 below.

ε. used pleonastically w. a noun (cp. usage s.v. ἀνήρ 1dα) (Il. 16, 263; Lev 21:9; Sir 8:1; 1 Macc 7:14) ἄ. φάγος *a glutton* **Mt 11:19; Lk 7:34;** ἄ. ἔμπορος *a merchant* **Mt 13:45;** ἄ. οἰκοδεσπότης vs. **52; 21:33;** ἄ. βασιλεύς (Horapollo 2, 85; Jos., Ant. 6, 142) **18:23; 22:2;** ἄ. θηριομάχος AcPl Ha 5, 30.—Likew. w. names indicating local or national origin (X., An. 6, 4, 23; Ex 2:11 ἄ. Αἰγύπτιος) ἄ. Κυρηναῖος *a Cyrenaean* **Mt 27:32;** ἄ. Ἰουδαῖος **Ac 21:39;** ἄ. Ῥωμαῖος **16:37; 22:25.** W. adj., giving them the character of nouns (Menand., fgm. 518 Kö ἄ. φίλος; PFlor 61, 60; PAmh 78, 13 ἄ. αὐθάδης; PStras 41, 40 πρεσβύτης ἄ. εἰμι; Sir 8:2 al.) ἄ. τυφλός (EpJer 36) *a blind person* **J 9:1;** ἄ. ἁμαρτωλός (Sir 11:32; 32:17) vs. **16;** ἄ. αἱρετικός **Tit 3:10.** Likew. w. ptc. ἄ. σπείρων *a sower* **Mt 13:24.**

ζ. pleonastic are also the combinations τίς ἄ.; *who?* **Mt 7:9; Lk 15:4;** πᾶς ἄ. (PsSol 2:9; 17:27 [both times after οὐ]; ParJer 8:7; cp. Just., D. 3) *everyone* **J 2:10; Js 1:19;** πάντες ἄ. *all people* **Ac 22:15,** *everyone* **1 Cor 7:7;** εἷς ἄ. **J 11:50;** δύο ἄ. **Lk 18:10.** Likew. the partitive gen. ἀνθρώπων w. οὐδείς (cp. Mimnermus 1, 15f Diehl[2] οὐ δέ τίς ἐστιν ἀνθρώπων) **Mk 11:2; Lk 19:30,** μηδείς **Ac 4:17,** τίς **19:35; 1 Cor 2:11.**—MBlack, An Aramaic Approach[3], '67, 106f.

ⓑ w. the generic art. (Wsd 2:23; 4 Macc 2:21; PsSol 5:16; Just., D. 20, 2) ὁ ἀγαθὸς ἄ. *the good person,* opp. ὁ πονηρὸς ἄ. *the evil person* **Mt 12:35.** οὐκ ἐπ' ἄρτῳ ζήσεται ὁ ἄ. *no one can live on bread* (Dt 8:3) **4:4.** κοινοῖ τὸν ἄ. *defiles a person* **15:11, 18;** cp. **Mk 7:15, 20;** τὸ σάββατον διὰ τὸν ἄ. ἐγένετο **2:27;** τί ἦν ἐν τῷ ἀ. **J 2:25;** κρίνειν τὸν ἄ. **7:51;** ὁ νόμος κυριεύει τοῦ ἀ. **Ro 7:1;** ὁ ποιήσας ἄ. *everyone who does it* **10:5** (Lev 18:5; 2 Esdr 19:29); κακὸν τῷ ἀ. τῷ διὰ προσκόμματος ἐσθίοντι *wrong for anyone who eats w. misgivings* **Ro 14:20** al.

ⓒ w. qualifying gen. ἄνθρωποι εὐδοκίας **Lk 2:14** (εὐδοκία 1). ὁ ἄ. τῆς ἀνομίας (v.l. ἁμαρτίας) **2 Th 2:3.** ἄ. (τοῦ) θεοῦ *man of God* **1 Ti 6:11; 2 Ti 3:17; 2 Pt 1:21 v.l.** (3 Km 12:22; 13:1; 17:24; 4 Km 1:9ff; 2 Ch 8:14 al.; TestJob 53:4; EpArist 140; Philo, Gig. 61, Deus Imm. 138f. But also Sextus 2; 3; Herm. Wr. 1, 32; 13, 20; PGM 4, 1177, where no comma is needed betw. ἄ. and θ. Cp. Callim. 193, 37 [Pf.]).

❺ **a being in conflict at a transcendent level**—ⓐ the two sides of human nature as ὁ ἔξω ἄ. ***the outer being,*** i.e. human beings in their material, transitory, and sinful aspects **2 Cor 4:16,** and, on the other hand, ὁ ἔσω ἄ. ***the inner being,*** i.e. humans in their transcendent significance, striving toward God **Ro 7:22; 2 Cor 4:16; Eph 3:16** (cp. Pla., Rep. 9, 589a ὁ ἐντὸς ἄνθρωπος; Plotinus, Enn. 5, 1, 10 ὁ εἴσω ἄ.; Philo, Plant. 42 ὁ ἐν ἡμῖν πρὸς ἀλήθειαν ἄ., τουτέστιν ὁ νοῦς, Congr. Erud. Grat. 97, Det. Pot. Insid. 23; Zosimus in Rtzst., Poim. 104 ἔσω αὐτοῦ ἄνθρωπος πνευματικός. Cp. Rtzst., Mysterienrel.[3] 354f; WGutbrod, D. paulin. Anthropologie '34; KSchäfer, FTillmann Festschr. '34, 25–35; RJewett, Paul's Anthropological Terms, '71, 391–401). Similar in mng. is ὁ κρυπτὸς τῆς καρδίας ἄ. *the hidden person of the heart*=ὁ ἔσω ἄ. **1 Pt 3:4.**

ⓑ from another viewpoint, w. contrast of παλαιὸς and καινὸς (νέος) ἄ. **Ro 6:6; Eph 4:22, 24; Col 3:9** (cp. Dg 2:1; Jesus as καινὸς ἄ. IEph 20:1 is the ***new being,*** who is really God), or of ὁ ψυχικὸς ἄ. and ὁ πνευματικὸς ἄ. **1 Cor 2:14f** (s. πνευματικός 2aγ). τὸν τέλειον ἄ. GMary 463, 27.

❻ **a person who has just been mentioned in a narrative,** w. the art. ***the person*** (Diod. S. 37, 18 ὁ ἄ. εἶπε; Just., A II, 2, 12) **Mt 12:13; Mk 3:5; 5:8; J 4:50; Ac 19:16** al.

❼ **a pers. perceived to be contemptible,** ***a certain person*** w. a connotation of contempt (Diogenianus Epicureus [II AD] in Eus., PE 6, 8, 30 calls Chrysippus, his opponent, contemptuously ὁ ἄ.; Artem. 5, 67 ἡ ἄνθρωπος of a prostitute; UPZ 72, 6 [152 BC]; BGU 1208 I, 25; Plut., Mor 870c.—ASvensson [ὁ, ἡ, τό beg.]; AWilhelm, Anzeiger der Ak. d. W. in Wien, phil.- hist. Kl. '37 [XXIII–XXVI 83–86]) οὐκ οἶδα τὸν ἄ. *I don't know the fellow* (of Jesus, as oft. in these exx.) **Mt 26:72, 74; Mk 14:71.** προσηνέγκατέ μοι τὸν ἄ. τοῦτον **Lk 23:14;** ὁ ἄ. οὗτος AcPl Ox 6, 18 (= Aa I 242, 1). εἰ ὁ ἄ. Γαλιλαῖός ἐστιν **Lk 23:6.** τίς ἐστιν ὁ ἄ. **J 5:12.** ἰδοὺ ὁ ἄ. *here's the fellow!* **19:5** (on the attempt to arouse pity, cp. Nicol. Dam.: 90 fgm. 68, 4 Jac., Cyrus in connection w. the downfall of Croesus; Diog. L. 2:13 Pericles in the interest of Anaxagoras, his teacher; Jos., Ant. 19, 35f). μὴ οἰέσθω ὁ ἄ. ἐκεῖνος *such a person must not expect* **Js 1:7.**

❽ in address, varying from a familiar tone to one that is more formal ἄνθρωπε *friend* (X., Cyr. 2, 2, 7; Plut., Mor. 553e) indicating a close relationship between the speaker and the one addressed **Lk 5:20;** *sir* Ἄνθρωπε, ποῦ πορεύῃ; 'Sir, where are you going?' GJs 19:1 (not pap), the woman is a stranger to Joseph. W. a reproachful connotation, *man!* (Diogenes the Cynic in Diog. L. 6, 56; Diod. S. 33, 7, 4; Chariton 6, 7, 9; Ps.-Callisth. 1, 31, 1) **Lk 12:14; 22:58, 60;** Hm 10, 1, 2 (ἄνθρωπος Joly). Also in rhetorical address, in a letter **Ro 2:1, 3; 9:20** (Pla., Gorg. 452b σὺ δὲ . . . τίς εἶ, ὦ ἄνθρωπε); **Js 2:20.** (Cp. Pla., Apol. 16 p. 28b; Epict. index Schenkl; Mi 6:8; Ps 54:14.—JWackernagel, Über einige antike Anredeformen: Progr. Gött. 1912.)

❾ **a heavenly being that looked like a person,** ***a human figure*** of GPt 11:44 (cp. Just., D. 58, 10 ἐν ἰδέᾳ ἀνθρώπου [on Gen 32:25]; Tat. 21, 1 θεὸν ἐν ἀνθρώπου μορφῇ γεγονέναι).—JNielen, D. Mensch in der Verkünd. der Ev.: FTillmann Festschr. '34, 14–24; Gutbrod op. cit. 2cα; WKümmel, Man in the NT, tr. JVincent, '63; also Vock and Seiler ἀνήρ end.—B. 80. EDNT (lit.). DELG. M-M. TW. Sv.

ἀνθυπατεύω (s. ἀνθύπατος; Plut., Cic. 887 [52, 7]; Herodian 7, 5, 2; OGI 517, 10) ***be proconsul*** **Ac 18:12 v.l.** ἀνθυπατεύοντος Στατίου Κοδράτου *when Statius Quadratus was proconsul* MPol 21. DELG s.v. ὕπατος.

ἀνθύπατος, ου, ὁ (ἀντί, ὕπατος; orig. 'highest' then 'consul'; Polyb. et al.; freq. in lit.; Jos., Ant. 14, 236; 244 al.; Mel.; ins [s. e.g. PHermann, Inschriften von Sardeis: Chiron 23, '93, 233–48: of an honorand, 211 AD, pp. 238f]; pap [incl. Ox 850 verso 15: AcJ]) **head of the govt. in a senatorial province,** ***proconsul*** (s. Hahn 39f; 115; 259, w. lit.). Those mentioned are the proconsul of Cyprus, Sergius Paulus **Ac 13:7,** cp. vss. **8** and **12;** of Achaia, Gallio **18:12;** cp. **19:38;** of Asia MPol 3:1; 4; 9: 2, 3; 10:2; 11:1; 12:1.—DELG s.v. ὕπατος. M-M.

ἀνίατος, ον (α- priv., ἰάομαι 'to heal'; Hippocr., Pla. et al.; IG III add. 171a, 23 p. 474 of an 'incurable' sore healed by Asclepius; pap, LXX; TestSol 18:20, 23; Jos., Ant. 19, 325 [adv.]; Just., D. 132, 2) ***incurable*** only fig. (Aeschines 3, 156 κακά; TestReub 6:3) ἁμαρτία μεγάλη καὶ ἀ. *a great and unforgivable sin* Hm 5, 2, 4 (cp. Philo, Somn. 1, 87 τὰ ἀνίατα τ. ἁμαρτημάτων; Pla., Gorg. 525c διὰ τοιαῦτα ἀδικήματα ἀνίατοι).—DELG s.v. ἰάομαι.

ἀνίημι fut. ἀνήσω LXX; 1 aor. ἀνῆκα; 2 aor. subj. ἀνῶ, ptc. ἀνείς. Pass.: 1 aor. ἀνέθην (no augm., B-D-F §67, 2); pf. ptc. ἀνειμένος LXX (s. ἵημι; Hom. et al.; ins, pap, LXX, Joseph.; s. Nägeli 16; 20).

❶ ***loosen, unfasten*** of chains (Od. 8, 359; Callim., fgm. 260, 29 [Hecale] Pf. δεσμά; Plut., Alex. 705 [73, 9] τοὺς δεσμούς; Just., D. 9, 2 [a person]) πάντων τὰ δεσμὰ ἀνέθη **Ac 16:26** (s. ἀναλύω). Of ropes ἀ. τὰς ζευκτηρίας **27:40.**

❷ ***abandon, desert*** τινά *someone* οὐ μή σε ἀνῶ (word for word as in Philo, Conf. Lingu. 166; s. PKatz, Biblica 33, '52, 523–25) *I will never desert you* **Hb 13:5.**

❸ ***give up, cease from*** τὶ *someth.* (Thu. 3, 10, 4; Plut., Alex. M. 704 [70, 6] τὴν ὀργήν; Jos., Ant. 14, 286) ἀ. τὴν ἀπειλήν *give up threatening* **Eph 6:9.**—DELG s.v. ἵημι. M-M. TW.

ἀνίλεως gen. ω ***merciless*** (Herodian [?], Epim. [=Partitiones] 257 JBoissonade; TestGad 5:11; TestAbr A 12 p. 91, 7 [Stone p. 30] al.; ApcEsdr 4:9 p. 28, 9 Tdf. [κρίσις]) κρίσις **Js 2:13 v.l.** (for ἀνέλεος, q.v.).—DELG s.v. ἱλάσκομαι.

ἀνίπταμαι (ἀνά, πέτομαι; Maximus Tyr. 20, 6d; Cass. Dio 56, 42, 3; Themist. 27 p. 406, 11 D.; Cyranides 3 p. 100, 11; on the form [for ἀναπέτομαι] Kühner-Bl. II 450) ***fly up, flutter about*** νοσσοὶ ἀνιπτάμενοι B 11:3 (Is 16:2).—Lampe. Frisk s.v. πέτομαι.

ἄνιπτος, ον (α- priv., νίπτω; Hom. et al.) ***unwashed*** χεῖρες (Il. 6, 266; Philo, Spec. Leg. 2, 6) **Mt 15:20.** κοιναῖς χερσίν, τουτέστιν ἀνίπτοις **Mk 7:2, 5 v.l.** Acc. to a rabb. rule, going beyond the Torah, it was necessary to wash one's hands before a meal; see Schürer II 477.—DELG s.v. νίπτω. TW.

ἀνίστημι (α- priv., ἵστημι; Hom. +) fut. ἀναστήσω; 1 aor. ἀνέστησα; pf. 3 sg. ἀνέστακεν 1 Km 15:12; 2 aor. ἀνέστην, impv. ἀνάστηθι and ἀνάστα: **Eph 5:14, Ac 9:11 v.l.; 11:7 v.l.; 12:7** (cp. TestAbr B 2 p. 106, 2 [Stone p. 60] al.; ParJer 1:1 opp. vs. 10). Ptc. ἀναστάς, W-S. §14, 15, B-D-F §95, 3; fut. mid. ἀναστήσομαι; aor. pass. subj. 3 sg. ἀνασταθῇ 1 Esdr 2:18, n. ptc. ἀνασταθέντα 2 Macc 5:16. Trans. (1–5 below): fut. and 1 aor. act.; intr. (6–11 below): 2 aor. and all mid. forms.

❶ **to cause to stand or be erect, *raise, erect, raise up*** trans.,—ⓐ of images of deities (oft. of statues SIG 867, 68; 1073, 45; BGU 362 VI, 4 et al.). PtK 2 p. 14, 16 (Ath. 26, 2 [pass.])

ⓑ of one lying down, esp. one sick (Artem. 2, 37 p. 139, 23 τοὺς νοσοῦντας ἀνίστησιν; Jos., Ant. 7, 193) δοὺς αὐτῇ χεῖρα ἀνέστησεν αὐτήν *he gave her his hand and raised her up* **Ac 9:41.**

❷ **to raise up by bringing back to life, *raise, raise up,*** trans.—esp. of the dead *raise up, bring to life* (Ps.- X., Cyn. 1, 6; Paus. 2, 26, 5 [Asclepius] ἀνίστησι τεθνεῶτας; Ael. Aristid. 45, 29 K. = 8 p. 95 D.: [Sarapis] κειμένους ἀνέστησεν; Palaeph. p. 35, 8; Himerius, Or. [Ecl.] 5, 32; 2 Macc 7:9; Just., D. 46, 7 al.; Orig., C. Cels. 2, 48, 20) **J 6:39f, 44, 54;** in full ἀ. ἐκ νεκρῶν **Ac 13:34** (Herodas 1, 43 ἐκ νερτέρων ἀνίστημί τινα). Esp. of Jesus' resurrection **Ac 2:24, 30 v.l., 32; 3:26** (in wordplay w. ἀ. vs. 22); **13:33f; 17:31.** Ign. says of Jesus ἀνέστησεν ἑαυτόν ISm 2 (cp. Theodore Prodr. 5, 88 H. ἂν . . . ἑαυτὸν αὐτὸς ἐξαναστήσῃ πάλιν).

❸ **to cause to be born, *raise up,*** trans., in the idiom ἀνιστάναι σπέρμα *raise up seed=to beget, to procreate* σπέρμα τῷ ἀδελφῷ *children for his brother* **Mt 22:24** (Gen 38:8) w. ref. to levirate marriage. Of procreation in gener. σπέρμα ἐν τῷ 'Ισραὴλ ἀνέστησαν the upright *have left descendants in Is.* GJs 1:3 (s. ἐξανίστημι 2).

❹ **to cause to appear for a role or function, *raise up,*** trans. (Plut., Marcell. 314 [27, 2]; Synes., Ep. 67 p. 210c; EpJer 52; PsSol 17:21; cp. Did., Gen. 139, 7) προφήτην ὑμῖν **Ac 3:22** (after Dt 18:15 and in wordplay w. ἀ. Ac. 3:26, s. 2 above). Through election τίνα ἀναστήσουσιν εἰς τὸν τόπον τοῦ Ζαχαρίου GJs 24:4.

❺ **to erect a structure,** trans. (Jos., Ant. 19, 329 ναούς) **Mk 14:58** D.

❻ **to stand up from a recumbent or sitting position, *stand up, rise*** to speak, intr. (X., An. 3, 2, 34 ἀναστὰς εἶπε) ἀναστὰς ὁ ἀρχιερεὺς εἶπεν **Mt 26:62;** cp. **Mk 14:57, 60; Lk 17:12 v.l.;** out of bed (2 Km 11:2; cp. of God Just., D. 127, 2 οὔτε καθεύδει οὔτε ἀνίσταται) **11:7, 8.** *Rise* and come together for consultation (Mitt-Wilck. II/2, 83, 15f: ἀναστὰς εἰς συμβούλιον καὶ σκεψάμενος μετὰ τῶν . . .) **Ac 26:30.** Of one recovered from illness **Mk 9:27** or come back to life (Proverbia Aesopi 101 P.) ἀνέστη τὸ κοράσιον **Mk 5:42;** cp. **Lk 8:55.** W. inf. foll. to show purpose ἀ. ἀναγνῶναι *stand up to read* (scripture) **Lk 4:16;** ἀ. παίζειν **1 Cor 10:7** (Ex 32:6); ἀ. ἄρχειν **Ro 15:12;** Is 11:10). Short for *stand up and go* (Sus 34) ἀναστὰς ὁ ἀρχιερεὺς εἰς μέσον *he stood up and went before them* **Mk 14:60;** ἀ. ἀπὸ τῆς συναγωγῆς **Lk 4:38;** ἀ. ἀπὸ τῆς προσευχῆς **22:45.** ἀπὸ τοῦ σάκκου GJs 13:2; ἀπο τοῦ ὕπνου 14:2. Of a tree that is bent over and rises again B 12:1.

❼ **to come back to life from the dead, *rise up, come back from the dead,*** intr. (Il. 21, 56; Hdt. 3, 62, 4) **J 11:23f; 1 Cor 15:51** D (PBrandhuber, D. sekund. LAA b. 1 Cor 15:51: Biblica 18, '37, 303–33; 418–38); **1 Th 4:16;** IRo 4:3; ISm 7:1; B 11:7 (Ps 1:5); 2 Cl 9:1; AcPl BMM verso 38; in full ἐκ νεκρῶν ἀ. (Phlegon: 257 fgm. 36, 3, 3 Jac. ἀνέστη ὁ Βούπλαγος ἐκ τῶν νεκρῶν) **Mk 9:10; 12:25;** Qua (apolog.). **Lk 16:30 v.l.** w. ἀπό. Partic. of Jesus' resurrection (cp. Hos 6:2 ἐν τῇ ἡμέρᾳ τῇ τρίτῃ ἀναστησόμεθα; cp. 1 Cor 15:4); **Mt 17:9 v.l.; 20:19 v.l.; Mk 8:31; 9:9f, 31; 10:34; 16:9; Lk 18:33; 24:7, 46; J 20:9; Ac 17:3; Ro 14:9 v.l.; 1 Th 4:14;** IRo 6:1; B 15:9. Intr. used for the pass. ὑπὸ τ. θεοῦ ἀναστάντα *raised by God* (from the dead) Pol 9:2; περὶ τῶν ὑπὸ τοῦ χριστοῦ ἐκ νεκρῶν ἀναστάντων Papias (11:2). Fig., of a spiritual reawakening ἀνάστα ἐκ τ. νεκρῶν *arise from the dead* **Eph 5:14** (cp. Cleopatra ln. 127f and Rtzst., Erlösungsmyst. 6; 135ff).—For lit. s. ἀνάστασις, end.

❽ **to show oneself eager to help, *arise,*** intr., to help the poor, of God 1 Cl 15:6 (Ps 11:6).

❾ **to come/appear to carry out a function or role, *rise up, arise,*** intr. (1 Macc 2:1; 14:41; Jdth 8:18; 1 Esdr 5:40) of a king **Ac 7:18** (Ex 1:8). Of a priest **Hb 7:11, 15.** Of accusers in court **Mt 12:41; Lk 11:32** (s. ἐγείρω 12); **Mk 14:57** (cp. the use of קוּם 'stand up' in 11Q Temple 61, 7). Of a questioner who appears in a group of disciples **Lk 10:25,** cp. **Ac 6:9** (s. 2 Ch 20:5). Of an enemy ἀ. ἐπί τινα (Gen 4:8; 2 Ch 20:23; Sus 61 Theod.; ApcEsdr 3:12 p. 27, 23 Tdf. [for ἐπαναστήσονται Mt 10:21; Mk 13:12]) *rise up* or *rebel against someone* **Mk 3:26.**

❿ **to initiate an action,** intr., gener., w. weakened basic mng., to indicate the beginning of an action (usu. motion) expr. by another verb: ***rise, set out, get ready*** (X., Cyr. 5, 2, 14; Gen 13:17; 19:14; 1 Macc 16:5; Tob 8:10; 10:10; Sus 19 Theod.; Jos., Ant. 14, 452; Just., D. 9, 2) ἀναστὰς ἠκολούθησεν αὐτῷ *he got ready and followed him* **Mt 9:9; Lk 5:28; Mk 2:14.** ἀ. ἐξῆλθεν **1:35;** ἀ. ἀπῆλθεν **7:24;** ἀ. ἔρχεται **10:1;** ἀ. ἔδραμεν **Lk 24:12;** ἀναστᾶσα ἐπορεύθη (cp. Gen 43:8) **Lk 1:39,** cp. **15:18.** ἀναστάντες ἐξέβαλον **4:29;** ἀναστᾶσα διηκόνει vs. **39;** ἀ. ἔστη **6:8;** ἀ. ἦλθεν **15:20;** ἀνάστηθι καὶ πορεύου *get up and go!* **Ac 8:26,** cp. **27.** For this ἀναστὰς πορεύθητι (but v.l. ἀνάστα πορ.) **9:11.** ἀνάστηθι καὶ εἴσελθε vs. **6.** ἀνάστηθι καὶ στρῶσον vs. **34.** ἀναστὰς κατάβηθι **10:20** al.

⓫ **to become a standing structure, *rise, go up,*** intr. (Mel., P. 36 ἔργον) **Mk 13:2 v.l.**—Dalman, Worte 18f. B. 668. DELG s.v. ἵστημι. M-M. TW. Sv.

'Αννα, ας, ἡ ('Αν- var. edd.; חַנָּה) (1 Km 1:2ff; Philo, Deus Imm. 5ff, Ebr. 145ff, Mut. Nom. 143f, Somn. 1, 254; Jos., Ant. 5, 342; 344–47; BCH 3, 1879, p. 344, 23; ISyriaW 1965; oft. pap s. Preis., Namenbuch) ***Hannah,*** or ***Anna*** w. the Vulgate and numerous other translations (s. B-D-F §39, 3; 40; 53, 3).

❶ Prophet, daughter of Phanuel **Lk 2:36.**—❷ Mother of Mary, the mother of Jesus GJs 2:1, 3, 4; 3:1; 4:1, 2, 4; 5:2; 6:3; 7:1.

Ἄννας, α, ὁ (Ἄν- other edd.; Herodas 8, 14; 43; 66 [as a man's name, accented Ἀννᾶς by the editions]; PGen 42, 8; Cyprian ins from an Egyptian temple: Κυπρ. I p. 293 no. 21)

❶ ***Hannas*** or ***Annas*** (s. B-D-F §40; 53, 2; Rob. 225; short for Ἄνανος, חנניה Yahweh is gracious), high priest 6–15 AD, **Lk 3:2; J 18:24; Ac 4:6.** Father-in-law of Caiaphas **J 18:13.** Cp. Jos., Ant. 18, 26; 20, 197. Schürer II 216; 230; 232–34; PGaechter, Petrus u. seine Zeit, '58, 67–104.

❷ ***Annas,*** name of a Scripture scholar or scribe GJs 15:1.

ἀνοδία, ας, ἡ (Polyb. 5, 13, 6 al.; Diod. S. 19, 5, 3; Plut., Mar. 427 [37, 9], Mor. 508d; Job 12:24 Sym.; En 89:44) **a place with no roads, *wayless area*** Hv 1, 1, 3. Opp. ὁδός (Philo, Somn. 2, 161, Mos. 2, 138) 3, 2, 9. Pl. (Jos., Bell. 4, 109) 3, 7, 1; m 6, 1, 3.—DELG s.v. ὁδός. TW.

ἀνόητος, ον (s. νόημα; predom., and in our lit., always in active sense, as in Pre-Socr., Soph.; Pla., Gorg. 464d et al.; LXX; EpArist 136; Philo; Jos., Ant. 9, 225, C. Ap. 2, 255; Just., D. 64, 5; Tat. 16:1; Ath.) ***unintelligent, foolish, dull-witted.***

ⓐ of pers., opp. σοφός (cp. Pr 17:28) **Ro 1:14;** w. ἄφρων (Plut., Mor. 22c τοῖς ἄφροσι καὶ ἀνοήτοις; Epict. 2, 21, 1) 1 Cl 21:5; w. βραδὺς τ. καρδίᾳ **Lk 24:25.** In address (Diog. L. 2, 117 ἀνόητε=you fool! 4 Macc 8:17) 1 Cl 23:4; 2 Cl 11:3; Hm 10, 2, 1.—**Gal 3:1** (Chariton 6, 7, 9; Alciphron 4, 7, 4; Philostrat., Vi. Apoll. 8, 7 p. 307, 13 ὦ ἀνόητοι; Philo, Somn. 2, 181 ὦ ἀνόητε); vs. **3** (Chariton 5, 7, 3 οὕτως ἀ.; Maximus Tyr. 36, 4 τίς οὕτως ἀ.; Jos., Ant. 9, 255). Of the intellectual and spiritual condition of people before becoming Christians ἦμεν γάρ ποτε καὶ ἡμεῖς ἀ. **Tit 3:3** (cp. Herm. Wr. 1, 23 τοῖς ἀνοήτοις πόρρωθέν εἰμι).

ⓑ w. a noun denoting a thing (Soph., Ajax 162 γνῶμαι; Just., D. 68, 8 γνώμην; Pla., Phileb. 12d δόξαι; Herm. Wr. 6, 3b; γελοῖα καὶ ἀ. Just., D. 23, 1 and 68, 9; ἄθεα καὶ ἀ. 80, 3) ἐπιθυμίας ἀ. *foolish desires* **1 Ti 6:9** (v.l. ἀνονήτους).—B. 1215. DELG s.v. νόος. M-M. TW.

ἄνοια, ας, ἡ ('the characteristic of one who is ἄνοος' i.e. without understanding [s. νοῦς]; Theognis 453 et al.; Pla., Tim. 86b δύο ἀνοίας γένη, τὸ μὲν μανία, τὸ δ' ἀμαθία; Herm. Wr. 14, 8; LXX; Philo; Jos., Bell. 2, 110, C. Ap. 210; Ar. 9, 5 ὢ τῆς ἀ.) ***folly*** of exploitative and dissident teachers **2 Ti 3:9** (AcPlCor 1:16). Gener. of human ignorance w. πονηρία (Jos., Ant. 8, 318) 2 Cl 13:1. Of angry pers. ἐπλήσθησαν ἀνοίας *they were filled w. fury* **Lk 6:11**; cp. PEg² 51 (the ms. rdg.; for the restoration [δι]|άνοια s. the entry).—DELG s.v. νόος. TW.

ἀνοίγω (ἀνά, οἴγω 'open'; Hom. +) on this by-form of ἀνοίγνυμι see Kühner-Bl. II 496f; W-S. §12, 7 and §15 (p. 130); B-D-F §101; Rob. 1212f; Mayser 404. Fut. ἀνοίξω; 1 aor. ἀνέῳξα **J 9:14** (vv.ll. ἠνέῳξα, ἤνοιξα), ἠνέῳξα vs. **17** (vv.ll. ἤνοιξα, ἀνέῳξα), mostly ἤνοιξα **Ac 5:19; 9:40** al.; 2 pf. (intr.) ἀνέῳγα; pf. pass. ἀνέῳγμαι **2 Cor 2:12** (v.l. ἠνέῳγμαι), ptc. ἀνεῳγμένος (ἠνεῳγμένος 3 Km 8:52; ἠνοιγμένος Is 42:20), inf. ἀνεῴχθαι (Just., D. 123, 2). Pass.: 1 aor. ἠνεῴχθην **Mt 3:16; v.l. 9:30; Jn 9:10; Ac 16:26** (vv.ll. ἀνεῴχθην, ἠνοίχθην); inf. ἀνεῳχθῆναι **Lk 3:21** (ἀνοιχθῆναι D); 1 fut. ἀνοιχθήσομαι **Lk 11:9f v.l.;** 2 aor. ἠνοίγην **Mk 7:35** (vv.ll. ἠνοίχθησαν, διηνοίγησαν, διηνοίχθησαν); **Ac 12:10** (v.l. ἠνοίχθη); Hv 1, 1, 4 (Dssm. NB 17 [BS 189]); 2 fut. ἀνοιγήσομαι **Mt 7:7; Lk 11:9f** (v.l. ἀνοίγεται). The same circumstance prevails in LXX: Helbing 78f; 83ff; 95f; 102f. Thackeray 202ff.

❶ **to move someth. from a shut or closed position,** trans. *a door* (Menand., Epitr. 643 Kö.; Polyb. 16, 25, 7; OGI 222, 36; 332, 28, SIG 798, 19; 1 Km 3:15; PsSol 8:17; GrBar 11:5f; Jos., Ant. 13, 92 ἀ. τ. πύλας, Vi. 246; Just., D. 36, 5 τὰς πύλας τῶν οὐρανῶν) τὰς θύρας (really the wings of a double door) **Ac 5:19; 12:10** (w. act. force, see 6 below); **16:26f** (s. OWeinreich, Türöffnung im Wunder-, Prodigien- u. Zauberglauben d. Antike, d. Judentums u. Christentums: WSchmid Festschr. 1929, 200–452). ἀ. τὸν πυλῶνα *open the outer door* of the house **Ac 12:14.** τ. θύραν τ. ναοῦ fig., of the mouth of the believer, who is the temple of God B 16:9 (with this figure cp. Philosoph. Max. 488, 6 τοῦ σοφοῦ στόματος ἀνοιχθέντος, καθάπερ ἱεροῦ, τὰ τῆς ψυχῆς καλὰ βλέπεται ὥσπερ ἀγάλματα=when the mouth of the wise man opens like the door of a temple, the beauties of his soul are as visible as statues [of deities]). Without *door* as obj. acc., or as subject of a verb in the pass., easily supplied from the context (Achilles Tat. 2, 26, 1) **Mt 7:7f; Lk 11:9f; Mt 25:11; Lk 13:25;** GJs 12:2.—Used fig. in var. ways (PTebt 383, 29 [46 AD]; Epict. Schenkl index θύρα: ἡ θύρα ἤνοικται=I am free to go anywhere) **Rv 3:20,** cp. **3:7f** (s. Is 22:22; Job 12:14). πύλη δικαιοσύνης 1 Cl 48:2, cp. 4. Of preaching that wins attention ἤνοιξεν τοῖς ἔθνεσιν θύραν πίστεως *God gave the gentiles an opportunity to become believers* **Ac 14:27.** Cp. θύρας μοι ἀνεῳγμένης *since a door was opened for me,* i.e. I was given an opportunity to work **2 Cor 2:12** (for **1 Cor 16:9** s. 6 below). Likew. ἀ. θύραν τοῦ λόγου **Col 4:3.**

❷ **to render someth. readily accessible, *open,*** trans., closed places, whose interior is thereby made accessible: a sanctuary 1 Cl 43:5; pass. **Rv 11:19; 15:5** heaven (Kaibel 882 [III AD] οὐρανὸν ἀνθρώποις εἶδον ἀνοιγόμενον; PGM 4, 1180; 36, 298; Is 64:1; Ezk 1:1; cp. 3 Macc 6:18) **Mt 3:16; Lk 3:21; Ac 10:11; Rv 19:11;** GEb 18, 36; Hv 1, 1, 4; the nether world **Rv 9:2;** graves (SIG 1237, 3 ἀνοῖξαι τόδε τὸ μνῆμα; Ezk 37:12, 13) **Mt 27:52.** Fig., of the throat of the impious τάφος ἀνεῳγμένος ὁ λάρυγξ αὐτῶν *their gullet is an open grave* (breathing out putrefaction?) **Ro 3:13** (Ps 5:10; 13:3).

❸ **to disclose contents by opening, *open,*** trans., τ. θησαυρούς (SIG² 587, 302 τῷ τ. θησαυροὺς ἀνοίξαντι; 601, 32; 653, 93; Eur., Ion 923; Arrian, Cyneg. 34, 2 ἀνοίγνυται ὁ θησαυρός; Is 45:3; Sir 43:14; Philo, Leg. All. 3, 105; Ath. 1, 1) *treasure chests* **Mt 2:11.** κεράμιον οἴνου ἢ ἐλαίου *open a jar of wine or oil* D 13:6. ἀ. βιβλίον *open a book* in scroll form (Diod. S. 14, 55, 1 βιβλίον ἐπεσφραγισμένον … ἀνοίγειν; 2 Esdr 18:5; Da 7:10) **Lk 4:17 v.l.; Rv 5:2ff; 10:2, 8** (cp. 2 Esdr 16:5; TestAbr A 12 p. 91, 22 [Stone p. 30]); 20:12.

❹ **to remove an obstruction, *open,*** trans., a seal (X., De Rep. Lac. 6, 4; SIG 1157, 47 [I AD] τὰς σφραγῖδας ἀνοιξάτω) **Rv 5:9; 6:1–12; 8:1.**

❺ **to cause to function, *open,*** trans., of bodily parts

ⓐ mouth ἀ. τὸ στόμα *open the mouth* of another person 1 Cl 18:15 (cp. Ps 50:17); of a fish, to take something out **Mt 17:27;** of a mute (Wsd 10:21) **Lk 1:64.**—*Open* one's own *mouth* to speak (oft. in OT; SibOr 3, 497, but e.g. also Aristoph., Av. 1719) **Mt 5:2; 6:8** D; **Ac 8:35; 10:34; 18:14;** GEb 34, 60. More specif. ἐν παραβολαῖς=he spoke *in parables* **Mt 13:35** (Ps 77:2; cp. Lucian, Philops. 33 ὁ Μέμνων αὐτὸς ἀνοίξας τὸ στόμα ἐν ἔπεσιν ἑπτά). εἰς βλασφημίας (opened its mouth) *to blaspheme* **Rv 13:6.**—*Not to open* one's *mouth,* remain silent **Ac 8:32;** 1 Cl 16:7 (both Is 53:7, as also Mel., P. 64, 462).—Fig., of the earth when it opens to swallow something ἤνοιξεν ἡ γῆ τὸ στόμα αὐτῆς **Rv 12:16** (cp. Num 16:30; 26:10; Dt 11:6).

ⓑ eyes ἀ. τοὺς ὀφθαλμούς of a blind person (Is 35:5; 42:7; Tob 11:7; Mel., P. 78, 565) **Mt 9:30; 20:33; J 9:10, 14, 17, 21, 26, 30, 32; 10:21;** B 14:7 (Is 42:7).—One's own eyes, to see (Epict. 2, 23, 9 and 12; PGM 4, 624) **Ac 9:8, 40.**—Fig., of spiritual sight **Lk 24:31 v.l.; Ac 26:18.** τοὺς ὀφθαλμοὺς τ. καρδίας

1 Cl 36:2; 59:3 (cp. Just., D. 123, 2 προσηλύτων ... ἀνεῷχθαι τὰ ὄμματα).

ⓒ ears (Epict. 2, 23, 10; PGM 7, 329) of a deaf man **Mk 7:35.**

ⓓ heart, fig. ἀ. τ. καρδίαν πρὸς τ. κύριον *open one's heart to the Lord* Hv 4, 2, 4.

❻ **to be in a state of openness, *be open,*** intr. (only 2 pf., except that the 2 aor. pass. ἠνοίγη **Ac 12:10** [s. 1 above] is the practical equivalent of an intr. Other exx. of 2 pf.: Hippocr., Morb. 4, 39 ed. Littré VII 558; Plut., Mor. 693d, Coriol. 231 [37, 2]; Lucian, Nav. 4; Polyaenus 2, 28, 1) in our lit. in contexts connoting opportunity θύρα μοι ἀνέῳγεν **1 Cor 16:9** (s. 1 above; Lucian, Soloec. 8 ἡ θύρα ἀνέῳγέ σοι τῆς γνωρίσεως αὐτῶν. Cp. Just., D. 7, 3 φωτὸς ἀνοιχθῆναι πύλας).—Cp. τ. οὐρανὸν ἀνεῳγότα **J 1:51.**

❼ **to be candid, *be open,*** intr. (s. 6 beg. for grammatical ref.; s. also 5a) τὸ στόμα ἡμῶν ἀνέῳγεν πρὸς ὑμᾶς *our mouth is open toward you,* i.e. I have spoken freely and openly **2 Cor 6:11** (cp. Ezk 16:63; 29:21 and ἄνοιξις).—B. 847. DELG s.v. οἴγνυμι. M-M.

ἀνοικοδομέω (ἀνά, οἰκοδομέω) fut. ἀνοικοδομήσω; 1 aor. ἀνῳκοδόμησα LXX. Pass.: fut. ἀνοικοδομηθήσομαι LXX; aor. ἀνῳκοδομήθη (Just., D. 34, 7) (Hdt., Aristoph.+; ins, pap, LXX; TestSol; EpArist 100; Jos., Ant. 2, 203 al.; Just., D. 34, 7; 80, 1 in mngs. 'build' and 'build again') ***build up again*** (so Ephoros [IV BC]: 70 fgm. 132 Jac.; PPetr II, 12, 1, 15 [p. 28]; Mitt-Wilck. I/2, 96 VIII, 4; SIG 454, 11f τῶν τειχῶν τ. πεπτωκότων συνεπεμελήθη ὅπως ἀνοικοδομηθεῖ) τ. σκηνὴν Δαυίδ *the tabernacle of David* **Ac 15:16a** (Am 9:11); τὰ κατεστραμμένα αὐτῆς *its ruins* vs. **16b;** the temple B 16:4.—ἀγαπητοὶ ἀνοικοδομεῖσθε, mid. *dear people, build yourselves up* **Jd 20** P[72].—DELG s.v. δέμω. M-M.

ἄνοιξις, εως, ἡ (s. ἀνοίγω; since Thu. 4, 68, 5; Plut., Mor. 738c χειλῶν; PGM 5, 285; 36, 312; Jos., Ant. 18, 30) the act of ***opening*** ἵνα μοι δοθῇ λόγος ἐν ἀνοίξει τ. στόματός μου *that I may be given a message when I open my mouth* **Eph 6:19** (cp. ἀνοίγω 7).—DELG s.v. οἴγνυμι. M-M.

ἀνοίσω s. ἀναφέρω.

ἀνοιχθήσομαι s. ἀνοίγω.

ἀνομέω 1 aor. ἠνόμησα, ptc. ἀνομήσας; pass. inf. ἀνομηθῆναι 3 Km 8:32 (s. ἀνομία; Hdt. 1, 144; pap since III BC; LXX; JosAs 12:5; TestLevi 10:3; TestGad 4:1 v.l.; s. Helbing 12; syn. παρανομέω Suda) ***be lawless, sin*** εἴς τινα (Num 32:15; Ps 118:78) *against someone* Hv 1, 3, 1. Abs. 1 Cl 53:2; B 4:8; 14:3 (all three Ex 32:7). (Ἰωσήφ) ἠνόμησεν σφόδρα *sinned exceedingly* or *flagrantly* GJs 15:2.—DELG s.v. 1. νέμω.

ἀνόμημα, ατος, τό (s. ἀνομέω; Stoic. III 136; Diod. S. 1, 77, 2; 17, 5, 4; PGM 4, 3099; LXX; En 9:10; TestDan 1:9; TestGad 2:5 [v.l. ἀνομία]; Jos., Ant. 8, 251; CSchmidt and WSchubart, Altchr. Texte 1910, p. 111) ***lawless action, iniquity*** w. ἁμαρτία Hv 1, 3, 1; w. ἀνομία and ἁμαρτία 1 Cl 18:2f (Ps 50:3f).

ἀνομία, ας, ἡ (Eur., Hdt., Pre-Socr. et al.; pap, LXX, pseudepigr., Philo; Jos., Bell. 1, 493, Ant. 15, 348; Ar. 11, 7; Just., D. 14, 1; 18, 2; 24, 3; Ath., R. 71, 6; Mel., P. 68, 486; Orig., C. Cels. 6, 44, 31; Did., Gen. 44, 17)

❶ **state or condition of being disposed to what is lawless, *lawlessness,*** opp. δικαιοσύνη (Hdt. 1, 96; X., Mem. 1, 2, 24 ἀνομίᾳ μᾶλλον ἢ δικαιοσύνῃ χρώμενοι) **Ro 6:19a; 2 Cor 6:14;** Dg 9:5; Hm 4, 1, 3; w. ὑπόκρισις **Mt 23:28;** oft. (as Ps 58:3) w. ἁμαρτία, w. which it is identified **1J 3:4:** cp. 1 Cl 8:3; 18:3 (Ps 50:4; 30:19; 102:10); Hs 7:2. ἔργα τῆς ἀ. *lawless deeds,* which originate in a lawless frame of mind B 4:1; Hs 8, 10, 3. υἱοὶ τῆς ἀ. *lawless pers.,* those who despise the law (cp. Ps 88:23) Hv 3, 6, 1; ApcPt 1:3; διὰ τὴν τῶν ἀνθρώπων ἀ. AcPl Ha 2, 27. ἀ. characterizes this aeon as Satan's domain, ending of Mk in the Freer ms. 2. ὁ ἄνθρωπος τῆς ἀ. (v.l. ἁμαρτίας) of the Lawless One **2 Th 2:3** (regarded as transl. of Beliar by Bousset, D. Antichr. 1895, 86; s. also Ps 93:20 θρόνος ἀνομίας and cp. 1QH 5:36; but see BRigaux, Les Épîtres aux Thess. '56, 656–67). μυστήριον τῆς ἀ. *the secret of lawlessness,* secret because (and as long as) the Antichrist has not made his appearance vs. **7** (cp. Genesis Apocryphon col. I, 2; JFitzmyer, Essays on the Semitic Background of the NT '71, 103f, n. 9); on the ἀ. in the last days **Mt 24:12;** D 16:4. μέθυσμα ἀνομίας *wanton drunkenness* Hm 8:3. ἡ τῆς πλάνης ἀ. *lawless deceit* B 14:5. ὁ καιρὸς ὁ νῦν τῆς ἀ. *the present time, when lawlessness reigns* 18:2; cp. 15:7 (cp. TestDan 6:6). Of God μισεῖν ἀ. (Ps 44:8) **Hb 1:9** (v.l. ἀδικίαν).

❷ **the product of a lawless disposition, *a lawless deed*** **Ro 6:19b.** λυτρώσασθαι ἀπὸ πάσης ἀ. (Ps 129:8) *redeem fr. all lawlessness,* i.e. l. deeds **Tit 2:14.** ἐργάζεσθαι ἀ. (oft. LXX) **Mt 7:23;** Hm 10, 3, 2; ἐργάτης ἀ. 2 Cl 4:5; ἀ. ποιεῖν (Hos 6:9; Is 5:7 al.; TestDan 3:2; TestGad 2:5 v.l.; cp. πράττειν ἀ. Ar. 11, 7) **Mt 13:41; 1J 3:4;** 1 Cl 16:10 (Is 53:9); more specif. ἐν στόματι *commit sin with the mouth* B 10:8; λαλεῖν ἀ. κατά τινός 1 Cl 15:5 (Ps 34:19); ἁρπάζειν ἐν ἀ. *seize lawlessly* 10:4. Of Salome *woe is me for my sin and unbelief!* GJs 20:1 (not pap). Pl. *lawless deeds, trangressions* (POxy 1121, 20; Herm. Wr. 1, 23; oft. LXX; Just., D. 18, 2) **Ro 4:7** (Ps 31:1); **Hb 8:12 v.l.; 10:17;** 1 Cl 16:5, 9 (Is 53:8); 18:5, 9 (Ps 50:7, 11); 50:6 (Ps 31:1); 60:1; B 5:2 (Is 53:5); Hv 2, 2, 2; 3, 6, 4; s 5, 5, 3. (In ms. tradition ἀ. is oft. interchanged w. synonyms; so **Hb 1:9** [ἀδικία]; **2 Th 2:3** [ἁμαρτία]; 1 Cl 35:5 as v.l. for πονηρία.)—AcPl BMM recto 26 restored fr. POxy 1602, 27 [ἀν]ομίας (for this ἐπιθυμίας AcPl Ha 8, 20), cp. AcPlCor 2:11.—Dodd 76–81. DELG s.v. νέμω. M-M. TW.

ἀνόμοιος, ον (s. ὅμοιος; Pind., Pla. et al.; POxy 237 VI, 29; Wsd 2:15; Philo; Tat. 12:3; Ath. 8:1) ***unlike*** w. dat. (Pla., Gorg. 513b; Wsd) of a star πόθεν ἡ καινότης ἡ ἀ. αὐτοῖς *whence the new thing, unlike them* (the other stars), *might come* IEph 19:2.—DELG s.v. ὁμός.

ἄνομος, ον (Soph., Hdt., Thu.+; IDefixAudollent 188; POxy 237 VII, 11 [II AD]; PGM 58, 9; 11f; LXX, En, Test12Patr; ParJer 7:24; AscIs; Ar. 15, 6; Just.; Ath. R. 73, 14; Orig., C. Cels. 7, 63, 3 [superl.]) 'lawless'.

❶ **pert. to behaving contrary to law, *lawless,*** w. ref. to any law ἄ. κριτής *an unjust judge,* who cares nothing for the law B 20:2; D 5:2.

❷ **pert. to being without adherence to a moral code *outside law, without law.*—**ⓐ of obligation to God, without ref. to a moral code μὴ ὢν ἄ. θεοῦ *though I am not free fr. obedience to God* **1 Cor 9:21c** (opp. ἔννομος; on the constr. of ἄ. θεοῦ s. Mlt. 236).

ⓑ w. ref. to the Mosaic law, used of gentiles as persons who do not know it (s. 3b), w. no criticism implied (Pla., Pol. 302e [Nägeli 14]; Esth 4:17u) τοῖς ἀ. ὡς ἄ. *to those without (Mosaic) law* (= 'gentiles') **1 Cor 9:21a.** W. the phrase ὡς ἄνομος vs. **21b** Paul indicates empathy for those outside Mosaic tradition.

❸ **pert. to violating moral standards, *lawless.*—**ⓐ w. ref. to God's moral law. Hence *wicked* in gener. (oft. LXX) in personal address ἄνομε *You wicked one!* 1 Cl 35:9 (Ps. 49:21); w. ἀνυπότακτος **1 Ti 1:9;** w. ἀσεβής (1 Macc 7:5; PGM 58, 11; IDefixAudollent 188) 1 Cl 18:13 (Ps 50:15); Dg 9:4; w. ἄδικος

(Just., D. 35, 5 ἀθέους καὶ ἀσεβεῖς καὶ ἀδίκους καὶ ἀνόμους; PLond II, 358, 13 [150 AD] p. 172 ἄνομα καὶ ἄδικα) 1 Cl 56:11 (Job 5:22). Opp. δίκαιος (Pr 21:18) 45:4; cp. Dg 9:5; ἅγιος Dg 9:2. μετὰ ἀνόμων λογισθῆναι *be classed among the criminals* **Mk 15:28; Lk 22:37** (SHall, Studia Evangelica '59, 499–501); cp. 1 Cl 16:13 (all three Is 53:12). ὑπὲρ πᾶσαν ἁμαρτίαν ἀνομώτερος *wicked beyond measure* B 5:9. τὸ γένος ἄ. *the wicked kind* Hs 9, 19, 1.—Of things ἄ. βίος w. ἄδικος MPol 3; ἄ. ἔργα **2 Pt 2:8** (Nicol. Dam.: 90 fgm. 58, 2 Jac. ἔργον ἄνομον ἐργάσασθαι). ὁ ἄ. καιρός *wicked time* B 4:9 (cp. 18:2).

ⓑ w. reference to those who are outside Israelite legal tradition (s. 2b) and act contrary to its moral standards (Wsd 17:2; Just., D. 123, 3 υἱοὶ ἄ.). διὰ χειρὸς ἀνόμων *by lawless hands* **Ac 2:23.** ἐκ χειρὸς ἀνόμου AcPl Ha 8, 10 (ἀνόμων Ox 1602, 2//BMM recto 10); AcPlCor 1:8. Φαραὼ . . . ὄντος ἄ. AcPl Ha 8, 12. οἱ ἄνομοι MPol 16:1. τὰ ἄ. ἔθνη (3 Macc 6:9) *the lawless people* 9:2.

❹ ὁ ἄ. **the epitome of lawlessness, *the lawless one*** (Ezk 18:24; 33:8; PsSol 17:11) of the Lawless One or Antichrist (s. Iren., 3, 7, 2 [Harv. II 26f]) **2 Th 2:8** (cp. vs. **3**). This prob. explains ὁ καιρὸς τοῦ ἄ. *the time of iniquity* B 15:5 (cp. 18:2; TestDan 6:6 ἐν καιρῷ τῆς ἀνομίας).—DELG s.v. νέμω. M-M. TW.

ἀνόμως adv. fr. ἄνομος (Eur., Thu. et al.; PMagd 6, 11; BGU 1200, 20; 2 Macc 8:17; Philo, Leg. All. 1, 35 v.l.; Jos., C. Ap. 1, 147, Ant. 15, 59) **without participation in an organized legal system, *lawlessly,*** ὅσοι ἀ. ἥμαρτον ἀ. καὶ ἀπολοῦνται *those who sin without law will also be lost without law,* i.e. those who sin without awareness of the Mosaic law (expressed from the vantage point of Israel's chosen status) will also perish without reference to it: **Ro 2:12** (=χωρὶς νόμου **7:9;** cp. Isocr. 4, 39 ἀ. ζῆν= live without the advantage of organized law, i.e. without polity, uncivilized: expressed from the vantage point of Athenian achievement. For the term ἀ. and the theme of relative advantage s. also Jos., C. Ap. 2, 151). Synon. ἀτάκτως, q.v.

ἀνονειδίστως adv. fr. ἀνονείδιστος (Nicol. Dam.: 90 fgm. 130, 62 p. 403, 14 Jac. ἀνονείδιστα) ***without reproaching*** w. ἀδιστάκτως: χορηγεῖν τινι Hs 9, 24, 2.—DELG s.v. ὄνειδος.

ἀνόνητος, ον (αν- priv., ὀνητός 'profitable', s. ὀνίναμαι; Soph., Pla. et al.; Mitt-Wilck. II/2, 88 IV, 9; PPrinc 119, 56 [IV AD]; Wsd 3:11; 4 Macc 16:7, 9; Jos., Bell. 1, 464, Vi. 422 al.) ***useless*** ἐπιθυμίαι ἀ. w. βλαβεραί **1 Ti 6:9 v.l.** (for ἀνοήτους).—DELG s.v. ὀνίνημι.

ἀνορθόω fut. ἀνορθώσω; 1 aor. ἀνώρθωσα LXX. Pass.: aor. ἀνωρθώθη **Lk 13:13** (ἀνορθώθη v.l.; s. B-D-F §67, 2; Helbing 72f); pf. ptc. ἀνωρθωμένος LXX (ὀρθόω 'set straight'; Eur., Hdt.+; LXX; ApcEsdr p. 26, 15 Tdf.)

❶ **to build someth. up again after it has fallen, *rebuild, restore*** (Hdt. 1, 19 τὸν νηόν; OGI 710, 3f [II AD] τὸ π[ρ]οπύλα[ιον]| χρόνῳ [διαφθαρὲ]ν [ἀ]νώρθωσεν; 2 Km 7:26 v.l.; 1 Ch 17:24) **Ac 15:16.**

❷ **to become erect from a bent position, *straighten up*** of a crippled woman, who was healed, pass., act. sense ἀνωρθώθη *she became erect once more* **Lk 13:13** (JosAs 11 end [p. 54, 18 Bat.] cod. A; ἐπὶ τὰ γόνατα [cp. Hobart 22]). τὰ παραλελυμένα γόνατα ἀ. *strengthen your weakened knees* **Hb 12:12.**—DELG s.v. ὀρθός. M-M.

ἀνόσιος, ον (s. ὅσιος; Aeschyl., Hdt.+) **pert. to being in opposition to God or what is sacred, *unholy.*** The view that certain actions make holy beings or places off limits to their agents invites the connotation of moral turpitude: *wicked,* i.e. revolting to God or to a well-minded person. (For various perspectives s. ἁγνεία and lit. cited s.v.; on the subject s. esp. Plato, Laws 4, 716d, cited SIG 983 n. 3.)

ⓐ of pers. (PBrem 1, 4 [116 AD]=CPJ 438, 4; PGiss 41 II, 4 [117 AD]=CPJ 443 II, 4 [all ἀνόσιοι Ἰουδαῖοι]; PGM 4, 2476; 2 Macc 7:34; 8:32; 4 Macc 12:11; EpArist 289; Just., A I, 5, 4 δαίμονας; Ath. 32, 1 Δία) **1 Ti 1:9;** cp. **2 Ti 3:2;** w. ἄνομος 1 Cl 45:4; AcPl Ha 8, 12.

ⓑ of things (Diod. S. 34+35, fgm. 14 πρᾶξις; PThead 21, 15 πρᾶγμα; Wsd 12:4; 3 Macc 5:8; Just., D. 108, 2; Ath. 1, 2) ἀ. στάσις *unholy discord* 1 Cl 1:1. αἰκίσματα δεινὰ καὶ ἀ. *terrible and wicked tortures* 6:2.—DELG s.v. ὅσιος. M-M. TW.

ἀνοχή, ῆς, ἡ (s. ἀνέχω; X. et al.) lit. 'a holding back'.

❶ **a state of respite from someth. onerous or disagreeable, *relief*** (1 Macc. 12:25; Jos., Bell. 1, 173, Ant. 6, 72; w. ἔχειν Diod. S. 11, 36, 4 ἀνοχὴν ἔχειν; POxy 1068, 15 ἡμερῶν ἀνοχὴν ἔχω) ἀνοχὴν οὐκ ἔχειν *have no relief* Hs 6, 3, 1.

❷ **a temporary cessation, *pause*** (Jos., Ant. 6, 72) ἀ. τῆς οἰκοδομῆς *a pause in the building* Hs 9, 5, 1; 9, 14, 2.

❸ **the act of being forbearing, *forbearance, clemency, tolerance*** (Epict. 1, 29, 62 ἀ. ἔχω I enjoy clemency; En 13:2; PSI 632, 13 [III BC]; cp. Nägeli 45) ἐν τῇ ἀ. τοῦ θεοῦ *in God's forbearance* **Ro 3:26** (for a neg. expression of this idea s. SIG 985, 34f [I AD]: καὶ τοὺς παραβαίνοντας τὰ παραγ[γέλματα οὐκ ἀνέ]ξονται said of the great gods, FDanker in Gingrich Festschr., '72, 102f). W. μακροθυμία **2:4.**—DELG s.v. 1. ἔχω. M-M. TW.

ἀνταγωνίζομαι (ἀντί, ἀγωνίζομαι; Thu. et al.; 4 Macc 17:14; Jos., C. Ap. 1, 56; w. πρός τινα IPriene 17, 15 [III BC]) ***to struggle*** ἀ. πρὸς τ. ἁμαρτίαν *in your bout/struggle against sin* **Hb 12:4.**—DELG s.v. ἄγω. M-M. TW.

ἀντακούω fut. ἀντακούσομαι (s. ἀκούω; trag. et al.; X., An. 2, 5, 16; Philostrat., Imag. 1, 28 p. 333, 24; PLond 1708, 57) ***hear in turn*** ὁ τὰ πολλὰ λέγων καὶ ἀντακούσεται *one who speaks much hears much in return* 1 Cl 30:4 (Job 11:2).

ἀνταλλαγή, ῆς, ἡ (Maximus Tyr. 39, 1c v.l.; PCol IV, 100, 12 [III BC]; Hesych.; Simplicius, in Aristot., Phys. 1350, 32: in a definition of ἀντιπερίστασις [interchange], Simplicius explains it as 'exchange [ἀνταλλαγή] of places made when one body is thrust out by another'; Theophilus Antecessor [VI AD] 2, 6 p. 281 [ed. OReitz 1751]; other reff. DGE) ***exchange*** ὢ τῆς γλυκείας ἀ. *what a sweet exchange* (from being sinners to righteous people) Dg 9:5.—DELG s.v. ἄλλος.

ἀντάλλαγμα, ατος, τό (Eur. et al.; Ruth 4:7; Job 28:15; Jer 15:13; Sir 6:15; Philo, fgm. 110 Harris; Jos., Bell. 1, 355, Ant. 14, 484) ***someth. given in exchange*** τί δώσει ἄνθρωπος ἀ. τ. ψυχῆς αὐτοῦ; *what will one give in exchange for his soul?* there is nothing that would compensate for such a loss **Mt 16:26; Mk 8:37.**—DELG s.v. ἄλλος. TW.

ἀνταναιρέω fut. 2 sg. ἀντανελεῖς Ps 103:29; 2 aor. ἀντανεῖλον. Pass.: fut. ἀνταναιρεθήσομαι LXX: 1 aor. ἀντανῃρέθην (s. ἀναιρέω; Demosth. et al.; pap, LXX) ***take away*** as a punishment τὶ ἀπό τινος 1 Cl 18:11 (Ps 50:13).—DELG s.v. αἱρέω.

ἀνταναπληρόω (Demosth. 14, 16 and 17; Cass. Dio 44, 48, 2; Apollon. Dysc., Synt. p. 14, 1; 114, 7f al. [p. 21, 5; 158,

1 al.]) **take one's turn in filling up someth.** (for the reciprocal force of ἀντί cp. Xen., Hell. 2, 4, 11 and 12 ἐμπίπλημι … ἀντεμπίπλημι one group of soldiers fills a road, and a second group forms another line) ***fill up on one's part, supplement*** τὰ ὑστερήματα τῶν θλίψεων τοῦ Χριστοῦ *I supplement what is lacking in Christ's tribulations* **Col 1:24** (on the inevitability of sufferings incurred because of witness to Christ, resulting in a variety of benefits cp. 2 Cor 1:5; 4:10; 1 Th 3:3). Paul rejoices in supplying what his Master has left him to suffer (s. Photius, Ep. 253 p. 190–93, esp. p. 193, 77–82). After receiving his apostolic assignment, Paul assumes the burden of sufferings that would befall Christ were the latter to undertake the apostolic mission in person. See Lightfoot, comm. ad loc. for detailed discussion of this view.—For other interpretations, including ref. to 'Messianic woes', s. PO'Brien, WBC: Colossians, Philemon, '82, ad loc. S. also WMoir, Col 1:24: ET 42, '31, 479f; EPercy, Die Probleme der Kolosser- und Epheserbriefe '46, 128–34; ELohse, Märtyrer u. Gottesknecht '55, 202ff; JKremer, Was an den Leiden Christi noch mangelt: Bonner Biblische Beiträge 12, '56; HGustafson, Biblical Research 8, '63, 28–42 and lit. on πάθημα 1. S. θλῖψις.—DELG s.v. πίμπλημι. M-M.

ἀνταποδίδωμι fut. ἀνταποδώσω; 2 aor. ἀνταπέδωκα (2 pl. -εδώκατε Gen 44:4; 3 pl. -έδωκαν Mel., P. 72, 531); 2 aor. inf. ἀνταποδοῦναι; 1 fut. pass. ἀνταποδοθήσομαι (s. ἀποδίδωμι; Hdt.+) lit. 'give back, tender in repayment'.

❶ **to practice reciprocity with respect to an obligation, *repay, pay back, requite*** τινί τι (PLond II, 413, 8 [IV AD] ἵν' ἀνταποδώσω σοι τὴν ἀγάπην; Sb 7600, 8f ἀ. τὰς χαρίτας; cp. SEG VIII, 549, 33; Pr 25:22; Sir 30:6; 1 Macc 10:27) εὐχαριστίαν τῷ θεῷ ἀ. *requite God with thanks* **1 Th 3:9;** without obj. οὐκ ἔχουσιν ἀ. σοι *they have no way to repay you* **Lk 14:14** (cp. EpJer 33; the thought strikes both a neg. and a positive note for one rooted in Gr-Rom. tradition: on the one hand, the virtuous pers. should be more interested in giving than in taking, but one ought to give to the right kind of pers.; s. e.g. Aristot., EN 1120a). Pass. (Jos., Ant. 14, 212) ἀνταποδοθήσεται αὐτῷ *it will be paid back to him* **Ro 11:35** (Is 40:14 v.l.).

❷ **to exact retribution, *repay, pay back*** τινί τι (PGM 3, 7; 115; Lev 18:25; Ps 7:5; 34:12 al.) ἀ. τοῖς θλίβουσιν ὑμᾶς θλῖψιν **2 Th 1:6.** Abs. ἐγὼ ἀνταποδώσω *I will repay* **Ro 12:19; Hb 10:30** (both Dt 32:35).—DELG s.v. δίδωμι. M-M. TW.

ἀνταπόδομα, ατος, τό (s. prec.; LXX)—❶ **that which is given in requital for a benefit, *repayment, reward*** (Is 1:23; Sir 20:10) B 20:2; D 5:2. μὴ γένηται ἀ. σοι *that no repayment may come to you* **Lk 14:12** (cp. M. Ant. 5, 6, 2).

❷ **that which is given in return for behavior, *recompense.***—As punishment, as mostly in LXX (w. σκάνδαλον) εἰς ἀ. αὐτοῖς *as retribution for them* **Ro 11:9.**—Neutrally, of the last judgment, *recompense,* which dispenses both reward and punishment (w. ἀνάστασις) B 21:1.—TW.

ἀνταπόδοσις, εως, ἡ (s. ἀνταποδίδωμι; Thu. et al. [s. Nägeli 36]: ins, pap, LXX; En 22:11; TestAbr A; TestJob 14:4, mostly sensu malo; Mel., P. 46, 324 'antitype' [opp. τύπος]) **that which is given to someone in exchange for what has been done, *repaying, reward*** ἀπολαμβάνειν τὴν ἀ. τῆς κληρονομίας *receive the inheritance as a reward* **Col 3:24** (cp. Judg 9:16 B; Ps 18:12). ἡμέρα τῆς ἀ. (Is 63:4; cp. ὁ καιρὸς τῆς ἀ. Did., Gen. 232, 14) *day of recompense* of divine judgment B 14:9 (Is 61:2); cp. **Ro 2:5** A.—M-M. TW.

ἀνταποδότης, ου, ὁ (s. ἀνταποδίδωμι; Jer 28:56 Sym.) **one who gives in return for services rendered, *recompenser, paymaster*** ὁ τοῦ μισθοῦ καλὸς ἀ. *the good paymaster* D 4:7; B 19:11.

ἀνταποκρίνομαι 1 aor. mid. 3 sg. ἀνταπεκρίνατο (Just.); pass. ἀνταπεκρίθην (s. ἀποκρίνομαι; mathematical t.t.=correspond to [Nicomachus Gerasenus, Arithmet. 1, 8, 10f]; LXX; TestJob 5:1; 41:1; Just. A I, 17, 2 [Mt 22:21 par.]) ***answer in turn*** (Aesop 301a, 6 [Ch.]; schol. on Pind., P. 9, 65; Syntipas p. 80, 12; Leontios 35 p. 68, 23 τινί; Judg 5:29 A; Job; TestJob 5:1 al.) οὐκ ἴσχυσαν ἀ. πρὸς ταῦτα *they could make no reply to this* **Lk 14:6** (cp. Job 32:12). ὁ ἀνταποκρινόμενος τῷ θεῷ *one who answers back to God* **Ro 9:20** (cp. Job 16:8; Pind., P. 2, 88 χρὴ δὲ πρὸς θεὸν οὐκ ἐρίζειν=one must not contend against God).—DELG s.v. κρίνω. TW.

ἀντασπάζομαι 1 aor. ἀντησπασάμην (s. ἀσπάζομαι; X.; Plut., Tim. 254 [38, 6]; s. ZPE 7, '71, 164a) ***greet in return*** τινά *someone* Hv 4, 2, 2; 5:1.

ἀντεῖπον 2 aor. (used in place of the missing aor. of ἀντιλέγω, q.v.; but ἀντιείπατε Just., D. 71, 3, cp. ἀντεῖπας **Rv 2:13 v.l.** [if the unaccented form in Tdf. app. is to be read as a verb] and s. Borger, TRu 52, '87, 45–47); fut. ἀντερῶ LXX (Aeschyl., Thu. et al.; LXX; Jos., Ant. 1, 11; 19, 208; SibOr 2, 276) **to say someth. in reply, *say in return*** ἀ. τινί (PMich 219, 9) *contradict someone* **Lk 21:15;** Hm 3:3. οὐδὲν εἶχον ἀντειπεῖν *they had nothing to say in reply* **Ac 4:14** (cp. Aeschyl., Prom. 51 οὐδὲν ἀντειπεῖν ἔχω; POxy 237 V, 13 [186 AD] ἐσιώπησεν οὐδὲν ἀντειπεῖν δυνάμενος). ἀντιεῖπεν ὁ Ἰωσὴφ λέγων GJs 9:2.—DELG s.v. ἔπος.

ἀντέχω fut. ἀνθέξομαι; 2 aor. 3 sg. ἀντέσχε 4 Macc. 7:4 (ἀντί, ἔχω; in our lit. only in the mid., which is quotable fr. Pindar's time, and common in the Hellenistic era [Nägeli 54]).

❶ **to have a strong attachment to someone or someth., *cling to, hold fast to, be devoted to*** τινός (PTebt 40, 9; POxy 1230, 30; PStras 74, 18; also s. Preis.; Is 56:2, 4, 6; Jer 2:8; 1 Macc 15:34 [hold fast to]; Pr 4:6; Jer 8:2 [be devoted to]; Jos., Bell. 4, 323; Ar. [Milne 74, 7]; Tat. 27, 1) ἑνὸς ἀνθέξεται *will be devoted to the one* **Mt 6:24; Lk 16:13** (cp. Pind., N. 1, 33 ἀντ. Ἡρακλέος). τῶν ἀγαθῶν τ. μελλόντων *hold fast to the good things to come* Hv 1, 1, 8. τοῦ πιστοῦ λόγου *cling to the trustworthy message* **Tit 1:9** (cp. Ael. Aristid. 36, 112 K.=48 p. 484 D.: ἀληθείας ἀντέχεσθαι; POxy 1203, 30 al.: τῶν δικαίων ἄ.). Since the last passage concerns an eccl. superintendent, who could be expected to do more than hold fast to correct instruction, perh. mng. 2 is to be preferred.

❷ **to have strong interest in,** hence ***help*** τινός *someone* or *someth.* (Diod. S. 2, 33, 3; 3, 71, 4; 14, 4, 5 al.; TestNapht 8:4; UPZ 170 [127/26 BC] A, 24=B, 23 οὐθενὸς δικαίου ἀντεχόμενοι [also s. Preis.]; Dt 32:41; Pr 3:18; Zeph 1:6; Jos., Ant. 20, 120) ἀ. τῶν ἀσθενῶν **1 Th 5:14.**—M-M s.v. ἀντέχομαι. TW.

ἀντί prep. w. gen. (Hom.+; for lit. s. on ἀνά, beg.); orig. mng. local, 'opposite', then of various types of correspondence ranging from replacement to equivalence. A marker

❶ **indicating that one person or thing is, or is to be, replaced by another, *instead of, in place of*** ἀντὶ τοῦ πατρὸς αὐτοῦ Ἡρῴδου *in place of his father Herod* **Mt 2:22** (cp. Hdt. 1, 108; X., An. 1, 1, 4; Appian, Mithrid, 7 §23 Νικομήδης ἀντὶ Προυσίου ἐβασίλευε, Syr. 69 §364; 3 Km 11:43; Tob 1:15, 21; 1 Macc 3:1; 9:31 al.; Jos., Ant. 15, 9). ἀ. ἰχθύος ὄφιν *instead of a fish, a snake* **Lk 11:11** (Paroem. Gr.: Zenobius [Hadr.] 1, 88 ἀντὶ πέρκης σκορπίον, prob. from Attic comedy: Kock III 678 [Adesp.]; Paus. 9, 41, 3 Cronos receives ἀντὶ Διὸς πέτρον to swallow). ἀ. τῆς προκειμένης αὐτῷ χαρᾶς ὑπέμεινεν σταυρόν **Hb 12:2** (cp. PHib 170 [247 BC] ἀντὶ φιλίας ἔχθραν; 3 Macc 4:6, 8); sense 3 is also prob., depending on the mng. of πρόκειμαι (q.v. 2 and 3). Cp. Hs 1:8; 9, 29, 4.

❷ **indicating that one thing is equiv. to another,** ***for, as, in place of*** (Diod. S. 3, 30, 3) κόμη ἀ. περιβολαίου *hair as a covering* **1 Cor 11:15.** ὀφθαλμὸν ἀ. ὀφθαλμοῦ καὶ ὀδόντα ἀ. ὀδόντος **Mt 5:38** (Ex 21:24). κακὸν ἀ. κακοῦ ἀποδίδωμι (cp. Ael. Aristid. 38 p. 711 D.: ἴσα ἀντ' ἴσων ἀποδ.; Pr 17:13; Mel., P. 72, 531 κακὰ ἀντὶ ἀγαθῶν [cp. Ps 34:12].—SIG 145, 9 τὰ κακὰ ἀντὶ τ. ἀγαθῶν) **Ro 12:17; 1 Th 5:15; 1 Pt 3:9.** λοιδορίαν ἀ. λοιδορίας ibid. (Dionys. Soph., Ep. 40 χάριν ἀντὶ χάριτος= gift in return for gift). Differently to be understood is χάριν ἀ. χάριτος *grace after* or *upon grace* (i.e. God's favor comes in ever new streams; cp. Philo, Poster. Cain. 145 διὰ τὰς πρώτας χάριτας . . . ἑτέρας ἀντ' ἐκείνων καὶ τρίτας ἀντὶ τ. δευτέρων καὶ ἀεὶ νέας ἀντὶ παλαιοτέρων . . . ἐπιδίδωσι. Theognis 344 ἀντ' ἀνιῶν ἀνίας) **J 1:16** (JBover, Biblica 6, 1925, 454–60; PJoüon, RSR 22, '32, 206; WNewton, CBQ 1, '39, 160–63).

❸ **indicating a process of intervention.** Gen 44:33 shows how the sense 'in place of' can develop into ***in behalf of, for*** someone, so that ἀ. becomes =ὑπέρ (s. Rossberg [s.v. ἀνά] 18.—Diod. S. 20, 33, 7 αὐτὸν ἀντ' ἐκείνου τὴν τιμωρίαν ὑπέχειν=he would have to take the punishment for him [i.e., his son]; Ael. Aristid. 51, 24 K.=27 p. 540 D.: Φιλουμένη ψυχὴν ἀντὶ ψυχῆς κ. σῶμα ἀντὶ σώματος ἀντέδωκεν, τὰ αὑτῆς ἀντὶ τῶν ἐμῶν) δοῦναι ἀ. ἐμοῦ καὶ σοῦ *pay (it) for me and for yourself* **Mt 17:27.** λύτρον ἀ. πολλῶν *a ransom for many* **20:28; Mk 10:45** (Appian, Syr. 60 §314 διδόναι τι ἀντὶ τῆς σωτηρίας, Bell. Civ. 5, 39 §166 ἐμοὶ ἀντὶ πάντων ὑμῶν καταχρήσασθαι=inflict punishment on me in place of all of you; Jos., Ant. 14, 107 τὴν δοκὸν αὐτῷ τὴν χρυσῆν λύτρον ἀ. πάντων ἔδωκεν; cp. Eur., Alc. 524). S. the lit. on λύτρον.—W. articular inf. (Ael. Aristid. 34 p. 654 D.; Jos., Ant. 16, 107) ἀ. τοῦ λέγειν ὑμᾶς *instead of (your) saying* **Js 4:15** (B-D-F §403; Rob. 574; Mlt-Turner 258).—Replacing the gen. of price (even in Hdt. et al., s. Kühner-G. I 454; cp. Hdt. 3, 59 νῆσον ἀντὶ χρημάτων παρέλαβον; Pla., Rep. 371d; Jos., Ant. 4, 118) ἀ. βρώσεως μιᾶς ἀπέδοτο *(in exchange) for a single meal* **Hb 12:16.** So perh. also vs. **2** (s. 1 above).

❹ **indicating the reason for someth.,** ***because of, for the purpose of,*** ἀ. τούτου *for this reason* **Eph 5:31.** W. attraction of the rel. ἀνθ' ὧν *in return for which=because* (Soph., Ant. 1068; X., An. 1, 3, 4; OGI 90, 35 [196 BC]; PLeid D I, 21; LXX; AscIs 2:14; Jos., Ant. 17, 201; SibOr 5, 68; B-D-F §294, 4) **Lk 1:20; 19:44; Ac 12:23; 2 Th 2:10.**

❺ **indicating result, w. implication of being a replacement for someth.,** ***wherefore, therefore, so then*** (Aeschyl., Prom. 31; Thu. 6, 83, 1; 4 Macc 18:3; Jdth 9:3; Jos., Ant. 4, 318) **Lk 12:3.**—DELG s.v. ἄντα. M-M. EDNT. TW.

ἀντιβάλλω (s. βάλλω; Thu. et al.; SEG XXVI, 1295 [II AD]; pap, LXX) lit. 'put/place against', **to be engaged in an exchange,** ***exchange*** metaph. ***discuss*** τὶ πρός τινα (2 Macc 11:13 ἀ. πρὸς ἑαυτόν) τίνες οἱ λόγοι οὓς ἀντιβάλλετε πρὸς ἀλλήλους; *what are the words you are exchanging with each other?* i.e. *what is the subject of your discussion?* **Lk 24:17** (Vi. Pol. [IV AD] 11, 3 πρὸς ἀλλήλους κατ' ἰδίαν ἀντέβαλλον; Theophanes Conf., Chron. 461, 18 ἀντιβάλλειν πρὸς ἀλλήλους=dispute).—M-M. TW. Spicq.

ἀντιβλέπω (s. βλέπω; Pherecr. fgm. 20D [V AD]; X. et al.; Mitt-Wilck. I/2, 38, 27 Stud. Pal. V, 52 I, 27 [III AD]; PGM 5, 323; Jos., Ant. 6, 10, C. Ap. 2, 235) ***look (straight) at*** πρός τινα (cp. Plut., Pomp. 656 [69, 5]; Aelian, NA 3, 33) *someone* ApcPt 3:6.

ἀντίγραφον, ου, τό (s. next; Lysias, Demosth. et al.; Strabo 8, 6, 15; ins, pap, LXX, EpArist; Jos., Ant. 13, 126; 17, 145; Test12Patr; Just., A I, 68, 4f, D. 72, 3) ***a copy*** of a book MPol 22:2; Epil Mosq 5.

ἀντιγράφω 1 aor. ἀντέγραψα (s. γράφω; since Isaeus, Lysias, Isoc, Demosth., also pap; 1 Esdr 2:10; 1 Macc 8:22; 12:23; EpArist 41; Joseph.; En 104:10 ['falsify']) ***write back*** ἀντίγραψον ἡμῖν *give us an answer in writing* AcPlCor 1:8.

ἀντιδιατίθημι (s. διατίθημι; Diod. Sic. 34, 12; Philo 30, 85; 31, 103 [Nägeli 30] word of the higher Koine) mid. ***oppose oneself, be opposed*** (Περὶ ὕψους 17, 1 πρὸς τὴν πειθὼ τ. λόγων πάντως ἀντιδιατίθεται) παιδεύειν τοὺς ἀντιδιατιθεμένους *correct his opponents* **2 Ti 2:25.**— B. 1432. DELG s.v. τίθημι. Spicq.

ἀντίδικος, ου, ὁ (s. δίκη; Aeschyl. et al.)—❶ **one who brings a charge in a lawsuit,** ***accuser, plaintiff*** (so X. et al.; SIG 656, 24; 953, 5 and 15; very oft. pap, e.g. POxy 37 I, 8; 237 VII, 24 and 32; VIII, 12; BGU 592, 7; Pr 18:17; Jer 27:34; Philo, Aet. M. 142; Jos., Ant. 8, 30; loanw. in rabb.) **Mt 5:25; Lk 12:58; 18:3.** Of the devil, since he appears in court as an accuser **1 Pt 5:8** (cp. **Rv 12:10;** Job 1:6ff; Zech 3:1); but here and in **Lk 18:3** it could mean

❷ **one who is continuously antagonistic to another,** ***enemy, opponent*** in gener. (so Aeschyl., Ag. 41; Philod., Ira p. 65 W.; PGM 3, 6; 1 Km 2:10; Is 41:11; Sir 36:6; Jos., Ant. 13, 413). This would corresp. to the designation of the devil as ἐχθρός TestDan 6:3f.—B. 1432. DELG s.v. δίκη. M-M. TW.

ἀντίδοτος, ου, ἡ (s. ἀντιδίδωμι; Plut., Mor. 42d and 54e Straton Epigramm. [II AD]: Anth. Pal. 12, 13; Diosc. 2, 110, 1 W.; Galen: CMG V 4, 2 p. 147, 15; 191, 21; Philumen. p. 21, 1 al.) ***antidote*** (w. φάρμακον) ἀ. τοῦ μὴ ἀποθανεῖν *against death* IEph 20:2.—DELG s.v. δίδωμι. Sv.

ἀντίζηλος, ου, ὁ (s. ζῆλος; as adj., Vett. Val. 198, 11; Lev 18:18; Sir 26:6; 37:11) ***jealous one, adversary*** (TestJos 7:5 ἡ ἀντίζηλός σου) w. βάσκανος and πονηρός of the devil MPol 17:1.

ἀντίθεσις, εως, ἡ (s. τίθημι; Pre-Socr.+; Plut., Mor. 953b; Lucian, Dial. Mort. 10, 10; Herm. Wr. 10, 10; Philo, Ebr. 187) **a statement that involves contradiction or inconsistency,** ***contradiction*** ἀ. τῆς ψευδωνύμου γνώσεως **1 Ti 6:20** (γνῶσις 3; and for rhet. usage L-S-S-M s.v. 3).—DELG s.v. τίθημι. M-M.

ἀντικαθίστημι (s. καθίστημι) 2 aor. (intr.) ἀντικατέστην; fut. mid. 3 sg. ἀντικαταστήσεται Dt 13:21 'place against'; intr. ***oppose, resist*** (so Thu. 1, 62, 5; 1, 71, 1 et al.; freq. in pap as legal t.t. POxy 97, 9 [II AD]; BGU 168, 11; Mi 2:8 A) μέχρις αἵματος ἀ. *resist unto death* **Hb 12:4.**—DELG s.v. ἵστημι. M-M. Spicq.

ἀντικαλέω (s. καλέω) 1 aor. ἀντεκάλεσα ***invite in return*** τινά *someone* of an invitation to a meal in return for a previous invitation (so X., Symp. 1, 15) **Lk 14:12.**—TW.

ἀντίκειμαι fut. ἀντικείσομαι LXX (s. κεῖμαι; Hdt. et al. in the mng. 'be opposite, form a contrast to'; s. Nägeli 39. So also Jos., Bell. 4, 454; Ath. 3, 1 πρὸς τὴν ἀρετὴν τῆς κακίας ἀντικειμένης, cp. R. 75, 13) **be opposed to someone,** ***be in opposition to*** τινί (ViEzk 20 [p. 76, 10 Sch.]; Cass. Dio

39, 8 ἀλλ' ἐκείνῳ τε ὁ Μίλων ἀντέκειτο): ταῦτα ἀλλήλοις ἀντίκειται *these things are in opposition to each other* **Gal 5:17.** ἀ. τῇ ὑγιαιούσῃ διδασκαλίᾳ **1 Ti 1:10.** ὡς ἀντικείμενος αὐτῇ GMary463, 21.—ὁ ἀντικείμενος *opponent, enemy* (UPZ 69, 6 [152 BC] Μενέδημον ἀντικείμενον ἡμῖν. Ex 23:22; Esth 9:2; 2 Macc 10:26 al. LXX; ApcEsdr 3:15 p. 27, 28 Tdf. [for ἐπι-]; EpArist 266) w. dat. of pers. **Lk 13:17; 21:15.** Abs. **1 Cor 16:9; Phil 1:28.** Of God's endtime *adversary* **2 Th 2:4** ('anteciminus', Ps.-Philo, Liber Antiq. Bibl. 45, 6). Of the devil (Berl. Kopt. Urk. I/6, 25) 1 Cl 51:1; MPol 17:1; perh. also **1 Ti 5:14.**—Lampe. M-M. TW. Spicq.

ἀντικνήμιον, ου, τό (ἀντί, κνήμη ['leg'] + suffix -ιον; Hipponax [VI BC] 49; Aristoph., Hippocr., X. et al.; oft. pap) ***shin*** MPol 8:3.—DELG s.v. κνήμη.

ἄντικρυς adv. (s. ἀντί; Hom. et al.; oft. Joseph.; ἀντικρύ t.r.; on the form s. Kühner-Bl. I p. 298f; W-S. §5, 28b; B-D-F §21; Mlt-H. 328; Thackeray p. 136) ***opposite*** (Ath. 4, 1 'frankly' declaring that there is no god) functions as prep. w. gen. (Themistocl., Ep. 20 ἄ. τοῦ θρόνου. POxy 43 verso III, 20 ἄ. οἰκίας Ἐπιμάχου. PTebt 395, 4; 3 Macc 5:16; Philo, Op. M. 79; Jos., Ant. 15, 410) ἄ. Χίου **Ac 20:15;** ἄ. αὐτῶν ApcPt 11:26 (cp. POxy 471, 81f ἄ. τοῦ δεῖνα).—DELG s.v. ἀντικρύ. M-M.

ἀντιλαμβάνω (s. λαμβάνω) in our lit. only mid. (which is common Thu. et al.; LXX, En; Philo, Joseph.; Just., D. 4, 7; 103, 8) fut. ἀντιλήψομαι LXX; 2 aor. ἀντελαβόμην.

❶ **to take someone's part by assisting, *take part, come to the aid of,*** w. gen. (Diod. S. 11, 13, 1 [of divine help]; Cass. Dio 40, 27; 46, 45; Plut., Pyrrh. 399 [25, 2]; OGI 51, 9f; 697, 1; PPetr II, 3b, 7; UPZ 47, 23 [II BC]; LXX; En 1:8; 100:8; 103:15; PsSol 16:3, 5) ἀντελάβετο Ἰσραὴλ *God has helped Israel* **Lk 1:54** (cp. Is 41:8f). ἀ. τῶν ἀσθενούντων *help the weak* **Ac 20:35** (cp. 2 Ch 28:15). ἀ. ἀλλήλων Hv 3, 9, 2.

❷ **to commit oneself wholeheartedly to someth., *take part in, devote oneself to, practice,*** w. gen. (X., Cyr. 2, 3, 6 τ. πραγμάτων. PRein 47, 4 τῆς γεωργίας. PLond II, 301, 6f p. 256 τῆς χρείας=the assignment; likew. POxy 1196, 12ff. Is 26:3; Bar 3:21; Jos., Ant. 5, 194; 19, 238) οἱ τῆς εὐεργεσίας ἀντιλαμβανόμενοι *who devote themselves to kindness* **1 Ti 6:2** (the assoc. w. εὐεργεσία suggests pers. of exceptional merit, cp. OGI 339, 32 τῆς εὐσχημοσύνης; s. also 51, 9f). Others make the masters the beneficiaries of the slaves' service (s. 4).

❸ **to be involved w. someth. through close contact, *perceive, notice*** τινός *someth.* (Ps.-Pla., Ax. 370a; s. MMeister, Axioch. Dial., diss. Breslau 1915, 43) εὐωδίας ἀ. *notice a fragrance* MPol 15:2 (Philo, Leg. All. 3, 56, Det. Pot. Ins. 101: tones; Just., D. 4, 7 κολάσεως 103, 8). Some expand this mng. into

❹ **derive benefit fr. someth., *enjoy, benefit by*** **1 Ti 6:2,** w. 'masters' as subject, on the basis that it fits well into the context (so REB, NRSV; s. Field, Notes 210; WLock, ICC ad loc.; but s. 2).—M-M. TW.

ἀντιλέγω for the aor. used in place of ἀντέλεξα, s. 2 aor. ἀντεῖπον (**Lk 21:15** et al.) as separate entry (trag., Hdt. et al.; ins, pap, LXX; Just.; Ath. 231; R. 58, 4; Mel., P. 102, 778).

❶ ***speak against, contradict*** τινί ***someone*** or ***someth.*** (s. ἀντιλογία 1; Thu. et al.; Sir 4:25; Jos., Ant. 3, 217 μηδὲν ἀ. δύνασθαι τούτοις=be able to say nothing against them) τοῖς ὑπὸ Παύλου λαλουμένοις **Ac 13:45.** Abs. (Thu. 8, 53, 2b οἱ ἀντιλέγοντες. EpArist 266; Jos., Ant. 1, 338) τοὺς ἀντιλέγοντας ἐλέγχειν *refute those who contradict* **Tit 1:9;** οἱ μὴ ἀντιλέγοντες **2:9** (cp. 3 Macc 2:28).— **Ac 28:19, 22.**—Foll. by μή w. inf. *deny* (Dio Chrys. 21 [38], 14; this constr. is found in the sense 'speak out against a thing' Thu. 3, 41) ἀ. ἀνάστασιν μὴ εἶναι *they deny that there is a resurrection* **Lk 20:27** (B-D-F §429, 2). On ἀντεῖπας **Rv 2:13 v.l.** s. ἀντεῖπον and Ἀντιπᾶς.

❷ ***oppose, refuse*** (Appian, Liby. 94, §442; Lucian, Abdic. 24, Dial. Mort. 30, 3; Achilles Tat. 5, 27; POxy 1148, 5ff; pap letter in Dssm., LO 160, 23 [LAE 194, 23]; Is 22:22; 4 Macc 8:2) ἀ. τῷ Καίσαρι **J 19:12.** λαὸν ἀντιλέγοντα ὁδῷ δικαίᾳ μου *that opposes my righteous way* B 12:4 (cp. Is 65:2). τῇ δωρεᾷ τοῦ θεοῦ *refuse the gift of God* ISm 7:1. Abs. (Diod. S. 18, 2, 3 οἱ ἀντιλέγοντες=the opponents) λαὸν ἀπειθοῦντα καὶ ἀντιλέγοντα *a disobedient and obstinate people* **Ro 10:21** (Is 65:2).—σημεῖον ἀντιλεγόμενον *a sign that is opposed* **Lk 2:34.**—*reject* a writing as spurious: Plut., Mor. 839c Aphareus composed 37 tragedies, ὧν ἀντιλέγονται δύο; alternatively, in Plut., Mor. 839f, of the 64 λόγοι of Isaeus 50 are γνήσιοι=genuine.—Schlageter, Wortschatz 11. M-M. TW.

ἀντίλημψις, εως, ἡ (s. ἀντιλαμβάνω, λῆμψις; Thu. et al. in var. mngs.; Just., D. 125, 5 ἐν ἀντιλήψει τοῦ πάθους 'through acceptance of suffering'; on the spelling w. or without μ cp. W-S. §5, 30; Mayser 194f; WSchulze, Orthographica 1894 I p. xivff) ***help*** (so UPZ 42, 40 [162 BC]; PAmh 35, 58; BGU 1187, 27; LXX; TestSol 20:17; Jos., Ant. 18, 4; s. Dssm B 87 [BS p. 92]; Nägeli 39) ἀντιλήμψεις *helpful deeds* **1 Cor 12:28** (for the pl. cp. 2 Macc 8:19; 3 Macc 5:50).—DELG s.v. λαμβάνω. M-M.

ἀντιλήπτωρ, ορος, ὁ (s. prec.; BGU 1138, 19 of a Rom. official: τὸν πάντων σωτῆρα κ. ἀντιλ(ήμπτορα). UPZ 14, 17f [158 BC] the royal couple: ὑμᾶς τ. θεοὺς μεγίστους καὶ ἀντιλήμπτορας; LXX of God; En 103:9) ***helper, protector*** ὁ βοηθὸς καὶ ἀ. ἡμῶν *our helper and protector* 1 Cl 59:4 (ἀ. and βοηθός Ps 118:114; 17:3; 58:17).—DELG s.v. λαμβάνω. Sv.

ἀντίληψις s. ἀντίλημψις.

ἀντιλογία, ας, ἡ (Hdt.et al.; ins, pap, LXX; Tat. 35, 2).

❶ ***contradiction, dispute*** χωρὶς πάσης ἀντιλογίας (s. ἀντιλέγω 1; BGU 1133, 15; PStras 75, 10; PLond II, 310, 16 p. 208) *beyond all doubt* **Hb 7:7.** πάσης ἀ. πέρας **6:16.**

❷ ***hostility, rebellion*** (s. ἀντιλέγω 2; PPetr II, 17 [3], 7 p. 56 [III BC]; Pr 17:11; Jos., Ant. 2, 43; 17, 313) ἡ εἰς ἑαυτὸν ἀ. *hostility toward himself* **Hb 12:3.** τῇ ἀντιλογίᾳ τοῦ Κόρε *in the rebellion of Korah* **Jd 11.** διὰ τὴν ἀ. αὐτῶν *because of their* (Korah's faction) *rebellion* GJs 9:2.—DELG s.v. λέγω. M-M. TW.

ἀντιλοιδορέω (s. λοιδορία; Plut., Anton. 935 [42, 5], Mor. 88e; Lucian, Conviv. 40; PEnteux 79, 5; PPetr III, 21g, 20 [III BC] ἐμοῦ δέ σε ἀντιλοιδοροῦντος foll. by ἐλοιδόρησας φαμένη) ***revile in return,*** of Christ λοιδορούμενος οὐκ ἀντελοιδόρει **1 Pt 2:23.**—DELG s.v. λοιδορέω. M-M. TW.

ἀντίλυτρον, ου, τό (Polyaenus, Exc. 52, 7 Melber; Orphica: Lithica 593 Abel πάντων ἀ; schol. on Nicander, Alexiph. 560 ἀντ. . . . ὑπὲρ τῶν βοῶν; Origen, Hexapla II 170 Field on Ps 48:9; Hesych.; Cosmas and Damian 40, 30; a late pap PLond IV, 1343, 31 [VIII AD]) ***ransom*** ἀ. ὑπὲρ πάντων **1 Ti 2:6** (s. Mlt. 105; Jos., Ant. 14, 107 λύτρον ἀντὶ πάντων=ransom for the return of all).—TW. Spicq. DELG s.v. λύω.

ἀντιμετρέω fut. pass. ἀντιμετρηθήσομαι (s. μετρέω; perh. as early as Caecilius Calactinus p. 147 Ofenloch; then Ps.-Lucian, Amor. 19; Rhet. Gr. I 523, 12 [mid.]) ***measure in return*** τινί *to someone* (Psellus p. 169, 1) **Mt 7:2 v.l.; Lk 6:38;** Pol 2:3.—DELG s.v. μέτρον. M-M.

ἀντιμιμέομαι (s. μιμέομαι; Appian, Bell. Civ. 5, 41 §174; 5, 94 §393) ***follow the example*** τινά ***of someone*** IEph 10:2.—DELG s.v. μῖμος.

ἀντιμισθία, ας, ἡ (so far found only in Christian writers; Theoph., Ad Autol. 2, 9; Clem. Al.) expresses the reciprocal (ἀντί) nature of a transaction as **requital based upon what one deserves,** ***recompense, exchange,*** either in the positive sense of *reward* or the negative sense *penalty,* depending on the context. τὴν αὐτὴν ἀ. πλατύνθητε καὶ ὑμεῖς *widen your hearts* (cp. 2 Cor 6:11) *in the same way in exchange* **2 Cor 6:13** (on the acc. s. B-D-F §154; Rob. 486f).—ἀπολαμβάνειν τὴν ἀ. *receive the penalty* **Ro 1:27** (FDanker, in Gingrich Festschr. 95). ἀ. διδόναι τινί *make a return* 2 Cl 1:3; 9:7. ἀντιμισθίας ἀποδιδόναι τινί 11:6; 15:2. μισθὸν ἀντιμισθίας διδόναι *give a recompense in return* 1:5.—DELG s.v. μισθός. M-M. TW.

Ἀντιόχεια, ας, ἡ (lit., ins, Joseph., SibOr) ***Antioch.***

❶ *A.* on the Orontes, the largest city in Syria (Jos., Ant. 16, 148), capital of the Seleucid Empire, later seat of the Rom. legate. Many Jews lived there (Jos., Bell. 7, 43; Just., A I, 26, 4). Of the origin of the Christian community in A. we know only what is reported in **Ac 11:19–26.** Paul labored there **Ac 13:1; 14:26; 15:22ff; 18:22,** and had a difference of opinion w. Peter **Gal 2:11.** Ignatius, superintendent (bishop) of the church there, mentions the city IPhld 10:1; ISm 11:1; IPol 7:1.—OMüller, Antiquitates Antiochenae 1839; TMommsen, Röm. Gesch. V 456ff; RFörster, A. am Orontes: Jahrb. d. K. D. Arch. Inst. 12, 1897, 103–49; HLeclerq, Antioche: DAC I 2359–427; KBauer, A. in der ältesten Kirchengesch. 1919; HDieckmann, Antiochien 1920; KPieper, A. am Orontes im ap. Zeitalter: ThGl 22, 1930, 710–28; VSchultze, Antiocheia 1930; LEnfrey, Antioche 1930; CKraeling, The Jewish Commun. at Antioch: JBL 51, '32, 130–60; MTenney, BiblSacra 107, '50, 298–310; JKollwitz, RAC I '50, 461–69; GDowney, A History of Antioch in Syria from Seleucus to the Arab Conquest, '61; WMeeks/RWilcken, Jews and Christians in Antioch in the First Four Centuries of the Common Era '78; RBrown/JMeier, Antioch and Rome '83; Schürer index.

❷ Pisidian A. (Strabo 12, 8, 14; Pliny the Elder, NH 5, 94; OGI 536, 2), belonging to the province of Galatia, seat of the civil and military administration in S. Galatia. Visited several times by Paul **Ac 13:14; 14:19, 21; 2 Ti 3:11.**—Ramsay, Bearing 282ff; WCalder, JRS 2, 1912, 79–109; PGaechter, Petrus u. seine Zeit, '58, 155–212; Schürer III 32.

Ἀντιοχεύς, έως, ὁ (lit., ins, pap, Joseph.) *an* ***Antiochene*** (Syrian A.), of the proselyte Nicolaus **Ac 6:5.**

ἀντιπαλαίω 1 aor. ἀντεπάλαισα, inf. ἀντιπαλαῖσαι (παλαίω 'wrestle'; POxy1099; schol. on Aristoph, Ach. 570; schol. on Thu. 2, 89; TestSol 25:4) ***wrestle*** (w. καταπαλαίω), abs. of the devil Hm 12, 5, 2.

ἀντιπαρέλκω (παρέλκω 'draw aside') only pass. ***let oneself be dragged over to the opposite side*** 2 Cl 17:3.—DELG s.v. ἕλκω.

ἀντιπαρέρχομαι 2 aor. ἀντιπαρῆλθον (s. παρέρχομαι; Diog. Oenoand., fgm. 28 VI, 13; Straton Epigramm.: Anth. Pal. 12, 8 [7], 1 codd. Jacobs; Wsd 16:10) ***pass by on the opposite side*** (cp. Heliodor. 7, 27, 6 ἀντιπαρήει) **Lk 10:31f.**—DELG s.v. ἔρχομαι. M-M. TW.

Ἀντιπᾶς, ᾶ, ὁ (Ἀντεί- Tdf., Ἀντί- other edd.; declinable like Σατανᾶς, cp. gen. σατανᾶ Ac 26:18 and Rv 2:13, and for the form Ἀντίπα s. W-H., Introd: 'Notes on Select Readings' 137f [on **Rv 2:13**].—Sb 4206, 65; 255 [I BC]; RCharles, ICC Rv I 62 declared it like Κλέοπας for Κλεόπατρος short for Ἀντίπατρος [cp. Jos., Ant. 14, 10; on hypocoristic names in -ᾶς in Attic ins s. Threatte II, 71–75], found IPergamon 524, 2 et al.; but the textual problem is far more complex than indicated in N. app.: s. ἀντιλέγω, ἀντεῖπον, and Borger below) ***Antipas*** martyr (s. μάρτυς 3) in Pergamum **Rv 2:13** (unless Ἀντιπᾶς is understood as indeclinable [s. GMussies, The Morphology of Koine Greek '71, 94; idem, Antipas: NovT 7, '64, 242ff; but s. above], the syntax in N. must be considered barbarous).—WSchulze, Kl. Schr.[2] '66, 67; 275 n. 1; RBorger, TRu 52, '87, 45–47.—M-M.

Ἀντιπατρίς, ίδος, ἡ *Antipatris* city in Judea founded by Herod the Great and named after his father (Jos., Ant. 16, 143, Bell. 1, 417), on the road fr. Lydda to Caesarea **Mt 13:54** ℵ*. Paul went through the city while being taken as captive to Caesarea **Ac 23:31.**—Schürer II 167f.

ἀντιπέρα adv. (πέρα 'beyond, further'; B-D-F §26; Rob. 638f; Jos. only Ant. 2, 341 τὴν ἀντιπέραν γῆν) ***opposite,*** functions as prep. w. gen (Polyb. 4, 43, 4; Diod. S. 2, 47, 1; POslo 26, 8 [5/4 BC]; as ἀντιπέρας as early as Thu. 2, 66, 1) Gerasa ἀ. τῆς Γαλιλαίας *opposite Galilee,* i.e. on the east shore of Lake Gennesaret **Lk 8:26.**—M-M.

ἀντιπίπτω (s. πίπτω; Aristot. et al.) ***resist, oppose*** (so since Polyb. 24, 11, 5; oft. in Plut., also pap, e.g. UPZ 36, 21 [162/61 BC]; Num 27:14; Demetr.: 722 fgm. 2, 3 Jac. [w. acc. and inf.]; s. Anz 343) w. dat. (Polyb., loc. cit.; BGU 1300, 22 [III/II BC]; UPZ 81 III, 6 the divine command) τῷ πνεύματι τ. ἁγίῳ **Ac 7:51.**—M-M.

ἀντιστῆναι s. ἀνθίστημι.

ἀντιστρατεύομαι (s. στρατεύομαι; X., Cyr. 8, 8, 26; Diod. S. 22, 13, 2 Dind.; this is also the act., as Jos., Ant. 2, 240.—Nägeli 18; 23; cp. the noun ἀντιστράτηγος IXanthus VII p. 79, no. 37, 2 [I AD]) ***be at war with*** τινί, only fig. (cp. Aristaen. 2, 1 Ἔρωτες ἀ. τοῖς ὑπερηφανοῦσι) ἀ. τῷ νόμῳ τοῦ νοός μου *at war w. the law of my mind* **Ro 7:23.**—DELG s.v. στρατός.

ἀντιτάσσω fut. ἀντιτάξομαι LXX (s. τάσσω; Aeschyl., Hdt. et al.; in our lit., as in OGI 654, 4; pap, LXX; TestJob 47:10; TestDan 5:4; Jos., Bell. 2, 194; 3, 15, Vi. 202, only mid.) ***oppose, resist*** w. dat. of pers. or thing opposed. Of pers. (3 Km 11:34; Hos 1:6) ὑπερηφάνοις **Js 4:6; 1 Pt 5:5;** 1 Cl 30:2; IEph 5:3 (all Pr 3:34). οὐκ ἀ. ὑμῖν *he offers you no resistance* **Js 5:6.** τῇ ἐξουσίᾳ **Ro 13:2.** μηδενί (w. ἡσύχιον εἶναι) Hm 8:10.—Of things (Esth 3:4; 4 Macc 16:23 S) τῷ θελήματι θεοῦ *oppose the will of God* 1 Cl 36:6. τῷ νόμῳ Hs 1:6. ταῖς ἡδοναῖς *oppose their pleasures* (Procop. Soph., Ep. 117 ἀντιτάξει τ. ἡδοναῖς) Dg 6:5. Abs. **Ac 18:6.**—M-M.

ἀντίτυπος, ον (since Anaximander pre-Socr.; Theognis 2, 1244; Aeschyl., Septem 521, also IG XIV, 1320; Esth 3:13d v.l.; Philo) of someth. that corresponds to another; esp. used metaph.

❶ **pert. to that which corresponds to someth. else,** adj. ***corresponding to*** (Polyb. 6, 31, 8 ἀντίτυπος τίθεμαί τινι I am placed opposite) someth. that has gone before (τύπος, cp. the oracular saying in Diod. S. 9, 36, 3 τύπος ἀντίτυπος and Ex 25:40). In a compressed statement, with rescue through water as the dominant theme ὃ (i.e. ὕδωρ) καὶ ὑμᾶς ἀ. νῦν σῴζει βάπτισμα *baptism correspondingly now saves you,* i.e. the salvation of Noah and family via water (δι' ὕδατος), which supported the ark, is the τύπος for the salutary function of the water of baptism **1 Pt 3:21.** A Platonic perspective (s. 2, below) is not implied in the passage.—PLundberg, La Typologie Baptismale dans l'ancienne Église, '42, 110ff; ESelwyn, The First Epistle of St Peter, '46, 298f; BReicke, The Disobedient Spirits and Christian Baptism, '46, 144f. LHurst, JTS 34, '83, 165–68, argues for the same mng. **Hb 9:24** (s. 2 below).

❷ subst. τὸ ἀ. ***copy, antitype, representation*** (ISyriaW 1855; pap, e.g. POxy 1470, 6; PYadin 23, 24 al.; Plotin. 2, 9, 6 [ὁ ἀ.]; Proclus on Pla., Cratyl. p. 76, 28 Pasquali; in different sense Just., D. 5, 2 ἀντιτυπίαν resistance), acc. to Platonic doctrine, w. ref. to the world of things about us, as opposed to the true heavenly originals, or ideas (the αὐθεντικόν). So χειροποίητα ἅγια, ἀ. τῶν ἀληθινῶν *a sanctuary made w. hands, a (mere) copy of the true (sanctuary)* **Hb 9:24** (s. 1 above). The flesh is ἀντίτυπος τοῦ πνεύματος 2 Cl 14:3a; the spirit, on the other hand, is τὸ αὐθεντικόν vs. 3b.—RHanson, Allegory and Event, '59, 67–69; CFritsch, TCVriezen Festschr. '66, 100–107.—DELG s.v. τύπτω. M-M. TW.

ἀντίχριστος, ου, ὁ (s. χριστός; cp. ἀντίθεος: Heliod. 4, 7, 13; Iambl., Myst. 3, 31; PGM 7, 635 πέμψον μοι τὸν ἀληθινὸν Ἀσκληπιὸν δίχα τινὸς ἀντιθέου πλανοδαίμονος; Philo, Somn. 2, 183) ***antichrist,*** adversary of the Messiah, to appear in the last days (ApcEsdr 4:31 p. 29, 8 Tdf.; ApcSed 15:5 p. 136, 33 Ja.; Iren. 3, 7, 2 Lat. [Harv. II, 26]) **1J 2:18, 22; 4:3; 2J 7;** Pol 7:1. Pl. ἀ. πολλοί **1J 2:18.** The word is not found outside Christian circles, but the concept is. For the general idea in the NT without the word s. 2 Th 2:1–12 and Rv 12–14. Cp. WBousset, Der Antichrist 1895, Rel.[3] 254–56 al.; KErbes, Der A. in d. Schriften d. NTs 1897; JGeffcken, D. Sage v. Antichrist: PJ 102, 1900, 385ff; MFriedländer, Der Antichrist in d. vorchr. jüd. Quellen 1901; AJeremias, D. Antichrist in Gesch. u. Gegenwart 1930; PRigaux, L'Antéchrist '32; HSchlier, KBarth Festschr. '36, 110–23; OPiper, JBL 66, '47, 444f; MDibelius, Hdb.[3] 11, '37, 47–51; RCharles, ICC Rv II, 76–87; ELohmeyer, RAC I, '50, 450–57; RSchütz, RGG[3] I, 431f (lit.); BMcGinn, Antichrist: Two Thousand Years of the Human Fascination w. Evil '94.—DELG s.v. χρίω. EDNT. M-M. TW.

ἀντίψυχον, ου, τό (s. ψυχή) ***ransom*** (cp. 4 Macc 6:29; 17:21. The adj. ἀντίψυχος, ον=someth. given in return for sparing one's life: Lucian, Lex. 10 χρήματα ἀντίψυχα διδόναι; Cass. Dio 59, 8, 3 ἀντίψυχοι.) IEph 21:1; ISm 10:2; IPol 2:3; 6:1.—TW. Sv.

ἀντλέω (ἄντλος, in Hom. 'hold of a ship', then 'bilgewater') fut. ἀντλήσω LXX; 1 aor. ἤντλησα (s. ἄντλημα; Theognis, Hdt. et al.).

❶ **to draw a liquid from a source, *draw,*** water understood (so Hdt. et al.; POxy 985; PLond III, 1177, 66 p. 183; LXX; TestAbr A; ParJer 2:5; Jos., Bell. 4, 472) w. acc. (Biogr. p. 428; Gen 24:13; Is 12:3) **J 2:9; 4:7.** Abs. (Hdt.6, 119; Diog. L. 7, 168 and 169) **2:8; 4:15.**

❷ fig. ***endure*** (trag. and later; Lucian, De Merc. Cond. 17 δουλείαν) πολλοὺς κόπους ἀ. Hs 5, 6, 2 (cod. A, s. ἀναντλέω). The fig. develops out of the idea of constantly drawing from a source, in this case troubles.—M-M. Spicq.

ἄντλημα, ατος, τό ***a bucket*** for drawing water (Plut., Mor. 974e; schol. on Aristoph., Ran. 1297; PFlor 384, 17 [V AD]) **J 4:11.**—DELG s.v. ἄντλος. Spicq.

ἀντοφθαλμέω 1 aor. inf. ἀντοφθαλμῆσαι Wsd 12:14 (s. ὀφθαλμός; oft. in Polyb., w. whom it is a characteristic word, in var. mngs.; also UPZ 110, 43 [II BC]) the term suggests an eye that is focused directly on someth. ***look directly at,*** of the sun εἰς τὰς ἀκτῖνας αὐτοῦ B 5:10 (cp. Antig. Car. 46; GrBar 7:4). τινί *look someone in the face:* τῷ ἐργοπαρέκτῃ *his employer* 1 Cl 34:1. ἀ. τῇ ἀληθείᾳ *look the truth in the face* honestly or defiantly (Περὶ ὕψους 34, 4 α. τοῖς ἐκείνου πάθεσιν=the passions of that person; Wsd 12:14) **Ac 6:10** D. Metaph. of a ship τοῦ πλοίου μὴ δυναμένοι ἀ. τῷ ἀνέμῳ *since the ship was not able to face the wind,* i.e. with its bow headed against the force of the waves **Ac 27:15** (s. Breusing 167f; CVoigt, Hansa 53, 1916, 728).—DELG s.v. ὄπωπα. M-M.

ἀνυβρίστως adv. fr. ἀνύβριστος (s. ὕβρις; Ath. 32, 3).

❶ ***without being insulted/injured*** (Ps.-Phoc. 157 H. Jos., Ant. 17, 308; adj. Plut., Pel. 282 [9]; PRyl 117, 26 [III AD]), but perh. in an act. sense

❷ ***without insolence, decorously*** (Democr. 73; adj. Plut., Sert. 582 [26]) ἀ. ἀγαλλιᾶσθαι Hs 1:6. The context suggests that the Christian need have no fear of acting insolently when behaving in a correct manner that is misconstrued by worldlings.—DELG s.v. ὕβρις.

ἄνυδρος, ον (s. ὕδωρ; since Hes., fgm. 24 Rz.; Eur., Hdt.; OGI 199, 21; POxy 918 II, 10; LXX; Jos., C. Ap. 1, 277) ***waterless, dry,*** τόποι ἄ. *waterless places* (Plut., Lucull. 516 [36, 3]; Ps.-Callisth. 2, 9, 1; cp. Pr 9:12c; Is 44:3; Jos., C. Ap. 2, 25) as the abode of hostile spirits (cp. Is 13:21; Bar 4:35; Rv 18:2) **Mt 12:43; Lk 11:24.** Fig. πηγαὶ ἄ. *springs without water* of sinners **2 Pt 2:17.** νεφέλαι ἄ. (cp. Pr 25:14 Hebr.; Vergil, Georg. 3, 197 arida nubila) *clouds that yield no rain* **Jd 12.**—Subst. ἐν τῇ ἐρήμῳ καὶ τῇ ἀνύδρῳ *in the waterless desert* AcPl Ha 8, 16.—M-M.

ἀνυπέρβλητος, ον (αν- priv., ὑπερβάλλω 'shoot beyond the mark'; X., Pla. et al.; Polyb. 8, 12, 12; Diod. S. 1, 55, 10; 13, 56, 5; Dio Chrys. 58 [75], 8; Ael. Aristid. 25, 18K.=43 p. 803 D.; Herm. Wr. 6, 3; 11, 5; SIG 839, 9; 893, 16f; PFlor 382, 48; POxy 1070, 21; 1121, 7; PGM 2, 150; 4, 1201; 1873; 3172; Jdth 16:13; EpArist 92; Philo, Mos. 2, 207; Jos., Bell. 2, 198, Ant. 11, 44) ***unsurpassable, unexcelled*** τελειότης *perfection* 1 Cl 53:5. εὔνοια MPol 17:3. ὡς ἀ. εἶναι τὸ τῆς χαρᾶς μέγεθος *so that the full measure of his joy could not be surpassed* AcPl Ha 6, 9.—DELG s.v. βάλλω.

ἀνυπόκριτος, ον (s. ὑποκρίτης; schol. on Aristoph., Av. 798; Iambl., Vi. Pyth. §69, 188 αἰδώς; Ps.-Demetr., De Eloc. 194; Wsd 5:18; 18:15) **pert. to being without pretense, *genuine, sincere,*** lit. 'without play-acting' ἀγάπη (ApcSed 1:4) **Ro 12:9; 2 Cor 6:6.** φιλαδελφία **1 Pt 1:22.** πίστις **1 Ti 1:5; 2 Ti 1:5.** σοφία **Js 3:17.**—DELG s.v. κρίνω. M-M. TW. Spicq.

ἀνυποκρίτως adv. fr. ἀνυπόκριτος (M. Ant. 8, 5, 2) ***with no insincerity/hypocrisy*** 2 Cl 12:3.—DELG s.v. κρίνω.

ἀνυπότακτος, ον (s. ὑποτάσσω; since Polyb. 3, 36, 4).

❶ **not made subject, *independent*** (Epict. 2, 10, 1; 4, 1, 161; Artem. 2, 30; Vett. Val. 9, 18; 41, 3 al.; Philo, Rer. Div. Her. 4; Jos., Ant. 11, 217) οὐδὲν ἀφῆκεν αὐτῷ ἀ. *he has left nothing that was not made subject to him* i.e. he has withheld nothing from his sovereignty **Hb 2:8.**

❷ **pert. to refusing submission to authority, *undisciplined, disobedient, rebellious*** (Ptolem., Apotel. 2, 3, 13; 18; 45; 4, 5, 3; 5; Sym. 1 Km 2:12 and 10:27; Moeris p. 31 groups ἀ. with ἀφηνιαστής 'rebel' and ὑπερήφανος; PGM 4, 1367; PCair-Masp 97 II, 49) w. ἄνομος **1 Ti 1:9.** Of flagrant law-breakers **Tit 1:10.** Of spoiled children **1:6.**—DELG s.v. τάσσω. M-M. TW.

ἀνυστέρητος, ον (s. ὑστερέω) ***not lacking*** w. gen. ***in anything*** ἐκκλησίᾳ ἀ. οὔσῃ παντὸς χαρίσματος *not lacking in any spiritual gift* ISm ins; ἀπὸ πάντων τῶν αἰτημάτων σου ἀ. ἔσῃ *all your requests will be granted* Hm 9:4.—DELG s.v. ὕστερος.

ἄνω adv. of place (the usual adv. form of ἀνά; Hom.+).—❶ **at a position above another position, *above*** (opp. κάτω as Aristot. p. 6a, 13; Aeneas Tact. 1674; Philo, Conf. Ling. 139, Deus Imm. 175 al.; Jos., C. Ap. 1, 77; Tat.; Ath. 22, 6; Mel., P. 44, 314f) ἐν τ. οὐρανῷ ἀ. *in the heaven above* **Ac 2:19** (Jo 3:3 v.l.; cp. Ex 20:4; Dt 4:39; 5:8 al.; Herm. Wr., fgm. XXIV 1 [in Stobaeus I 407, 23 W.=Sc. 494, 28]), where ἄ. is seemingly pleonastic. The pious person ἄνω μετὰ τῶν πατέρων ἀναβιώσας εὐφρανθήσεται *on high the pious will live in (eternal) joy with the ancestors* 2 Cl 19:4. ἡ χεὶρ αὐτοῦ ἔστη ἄ. *the hand* (of the shepherd, who intended to strike) *was arrested mid-air* GJs18:3 (not pap). ἕως ἄ. (2 Ch 26:8) γεμίζειν *fill to the brim* **J 2:7.**—As adj. (Diod. S. 4, 55, 7 οἱ ἄνω τόποι; Appian, Syr. 12 §47 ἡ Ἀσία ἡ ἄνω; Arrian, Ind. 5, 13; UPZ 162 V, 28 [117 BC]; Jos. Ant. 12, 135 οἱ ἄνω τόποι, 147; 13, 223 ἡ ἄ. Συρία, Vi. 67; Mel., P. 44, 314f) ἡ ἄ. Ἰερουσαλήμ (opp. ἡ νῦν Ἰ.) *the Jerus. above, the heavenly* (or future) *Jerus.* **Gal 4:26** (Mel., P. 45, 316; ParJer 5:35 πόλις; s. Ἱεροσόλυμα 3 and cp. Jos., Bell. 5, 400 ὁ ἄ. δικαστής; TestAbr A 7 p. 84, 16 [Stone p. 16] ὁ ἄ. βασιλεύς, both of God).—As subst. τὰ ἄ. *what is above*=heaven (cp. Herm. Wr. 4, 11 τὴν πρὸς τὰ ἄνω ὁδόν; Theoph. Ant. 2, 17 [p. 142, 18] τὰ ἄνω φρονοῦντες) ἐγὼ ἐκ τῶν ἄ. εἰμί *I am from the world above* **J 8:23.** τὰ ἄ. ζητεῖν *seek what is above* (heavenly) **Col 3:1.** τὰ ἄ. φρονεῖν vs. **2.**

❷ **extension toward a goal which is up, *upward(s), up*** (Alex. Aphr., Fat. 27, II 2 p. 198, 28 ἄνω φέρεσθαι=raise oneself upward; POxy 744, 8 [I BC]; I Esdr 9:47; En 14:8; Philo, Spec. Leg. 1, 207 ἀπὸ γῆς ἄνω πρὸς οὐρανόν) ἄ. ὁρᾶν *look upward* Dg 10:2 (in prayer as ἄνω βλέπω in Moschus, fgm. 4 p. 139 v. Wilam. [1906]; cp. Herm. Wr. fgm. IV 1 [406, 19 Sc.] ἄ. βλέπειν; Celsus 3, 62). Also ἦρεν τοὺς ὀφθαλμοὺς ἄνω, where ἄ. is superfluous **J 11:41.** πάντων ἦν τὰ πρόσωπα ἄ. βλέποντα *all looked up* GJs 18:2 (not pap). ῥίζα ἄ. φύουσα *a root growing up* **Hb 12:15** (Dt 29:17). ἡ ἄνω κλῆσις *the upward call* **Phil 3:14** (cp. GrBar 4:15 ἐν αὐτῷ μέλλουσιν τ. ἀνάκλησιν [ἄνω κλῆσιν James, p. 87, 33] προσλαβεῖν, καὶ τ. εἰς παράδεισον εἴσοδον).—DELG s.v. ἀνά. M-M. TW.

ἀνῶ s. ἀνίημι.

ἀνώγαιον, ἀνώγεον s. ἀνάγαιον.

ἄνωθεν adv. of place (trag., Hdt.+; ins, pap, LXX, En; TestSol 12:6 C; JosAs 21:4 [cod. A and Pal. 364]; ApcrEzk [Epiph 70, 10]; Just., Ath.).

❶ **in extension fr. a source that is above, *from above*** (SIG 969, 63; PHib 110, 66; 107; 109; Gen 49:25; Josh 3:16; EpJer 61; En 28:2; TestSol 12:6 C; Philo, Rer. Div. Her. 64; 184, Fug. 138, Somn., 2, 142; Jos., Ant. 3, 158) σχισθῆναι ἀπ᾽ ἄ. ἕως κάτω *be torn fr. top to bottom* **Mk 15:38.** For this ἄ. ἕως κάτω **Mt 27:51** (where ἀπ᾽ is added by many witnesses, foll. Mk). ἐκ τῶν ἄ. ὑφαντὸς δι᾽ ὅλου *woven from the top in one piece* (i.e. altogether without seam) **J 19:23.** Esp. *from heaven* (cp. ἄνω 1 and schol. on Pla. 856e of the seer: ἄνωθεν λαμβάνειν τὸ πνεῦμα; Philo, Mos. 2, 69) ἄ. ἐκ τ. οὐρανοῦ **J 3:27 v.l.** ὁ ἄ. ἐρχόμενος *he who comes from heaven* (explained in the same vs. by ὁ ἐκ τοῦ οὐρανοῦ ἐρχόμενος) **3:31.** Of the Holy Spirit πνεῦμα ἄ. ἐρχόμενον Hm 11:21; also simply τὸ πνεῦμα τὸ ἄ. 11:8. ἡ δύναμις ἡ ἄ. ἐρχομένη 11:20. ἡ σοφία ἄ. κατερχομένη **Js 3:15.** Also ἡ ἄ. σοφία vs. **17.** ἄ. εἶναι *come from above* Hm 9:11; 11:5; **Js 1:17.** Some would place 2 Cl 14:2 here, but the temporal sense seems more prob., s. 2. ἄ. δεδομένον *bestowed from above* (i.e. by God; cp. Procop. Soph., Ep. 109 θεοῦ ἄ. ἐπινεύοντος) **J 19:11.** ἄ. γεννᾶσθαι *be born from above* **J 3:3, 7** (Epict. 1, 13, 3: all humans are begotten of their ancestor Zeus ἐκ τῶν αὐτῶν σπερμάτων καὶ τῆς αὐτῆς ἄ. καταβολῆς; Just., D. 63, 3), but. s. 4 on the wordplay in these verses (Nicodemus thinks of physical rebirth [vs. 4], but the narrator shows Jesus with another dimension in mind).

❷ **from a point of time marking the beginning of someth., *from the beginning*** (Hippocr., VM 3; Pla.; Demosth. 44, 69; SIG 1104, 11; POxy 237 VIII, 31; En 98:5; JosAs 21:4 cod. A [p. 71, 19 Bat.]; Philo, Mos. 2, 48; Ath., R. 68, 19) παρακολουθεῖν ἄ. *follow from the beginning* **Lk 1:3** (w. suggestion of thoroughness rather than temporal precision: LAlexander, The Preface to Luke's Gospel, '93, 130); cp. **Ac 26:5** and s. 3. Opp. νῦν 2 Cl 14:2 (Lghtf.).

❸ **for a relatively long period in the past, *for a long time*** (SIG 685, 81 and 91; 748, 2; PTebt 59, 7 and 10; Jos., Ant. 15, 250; Just. [throughout]; Ath.) προγινώσκειν ἄ. *know for a long time* **Ac 26:5** (Ael. Aristid. 50, 78 K.=26 p. 525 D. ἄ. Ἀριστείδην γιγνώσκω) beside ἀπ᾽ ἀρχῆς vs. 4 (cp. Aelian NA 17, 40 οὐκ ἄνωθεν, οὐδὲ ἐξ ἀρχῆς=not for a long time nor from of old). For **Lk 1:3** s. 2.

❹ **at a subsequent point of time involving repetition, *again, anew*** (Pla., Ep. 2 p. 310e ἄ. ἀρξάμενος; Epict. 2, 17, 27; Jos., Ant. 1, 263; IG VII, 2712, 59; BGU 595, 5ff) ἄ. ἐπιδεικνύναι MPol 1:1. Oft. strengthened by πάλιν (CIG 1625, 60; Wsd 19:6) **Gal 4:9.**—ἄ. γεννηθῆναι *be born again* **J 3:3, 7** (ἄ. γεννᾶσθαι in the physical sense Artem. 1, 13) is designedly ambiguous and suggests also a transcendent experience *born from above* (s. 1 above on these pass. fr. J). JLouw, NThSt 23, '40, 53–56; ESjöberg, Wiedergeburt u. Neuschöpfung im paläst. Judentum: Studia Theologica 4, '51, 44–85.—DELG s.v. ἀνά. M-M.

ἀνωτερικός, ή, όν (s. ἀνώτερος; Hippocr.; Galen [Hobart 148]; Hippiatr. I 69, 22) ***upper*** τὰ ἀ. μέρη *the upper* (i.e. *inland*) *country, the interior* **Ac 19:1** (like ἄνω for the interior, Jdth 1:8; 2:21 al. LXX).

ἀνώτερος, έρα, ον (comp. of ἄνω=ἀνώτερον εἶναί τινος 'to be higher than someth. else'; Tatian; Vi. Da. [p. 77, 1 Sch. 'Upper Beth-Horon']); in our lit. only neut. as adv. (Aristot. et al.; SIG 674, 55; Lev 11:21; 2 Esdr 13:28; En 14:17 τὸ ἀ.; 15:9 [prob. corruption for ἀνθρώπων]; TestLevi 3:4; cp. B-D-F §62; Rob. 298).

❶ **pert. to a position that enhances status, *higher*** προσαναβαίνω ἀ. *go up higher,* i.e. to a more prestigious place **Lk 14:10.**

❷ **pert. to being precedent in a series, *preceding, above, earlier*** (as we say 'above' in ref. to someth. expressed previously; PCairZen 631, 10 [III BC] ἀνώτερον γεγράφαμεν; Polyb. 3, 1, 1 τρίτῃ ἀνώτερον βίβλῳ; Jos., Ant. 19, 212 καθάπερ ἀν. ἔφην; cp. AHeisenberg and LWenger, Byz. Pap. in d. Staatsbibl. zu München 1914, no. 7, 47) ἀ. λέγειν **Hb 10:8.**—DELG s.v. ἀνά. M-M.

ἀνωφελής, ές (s. ὄφελος) adj. (Aeschyl., Thu. et al.; LXX; PsSol 16:8; EpArist 253; Philo 253; Ar. 3, 2; Just., D. 2, 3; 19, 2).

❶ **pert. to not being of any advantage, *useless*** (PLond III, 908, 31, cp. 28f [adv.] p. 133; Wsd 1:11; Is 44:10; Jer 2:8; Jos.,

Ant. 4, 191) νηστεία Hs 5, 1, 3. τὸ ἀνωφελές *uselessness* (Lucian, Dial. Mort. 15, 4) διὰ τὸ ἀσθενὲς καὶ ἀ. *because of its weakness and usel.* **Hb 7:18.** Of fantastic stories IMg 8:1; controversies **Tit 3:9** (cp. Is 44:9: οὐκ ὠφελέω w. μάταιος), but s. 2.

❷ **pert. to being damaging, *harmful*** (Pla., Protag. 21, 334a; Pr 28:3; PsSol 16:8 ἁμαρτία ἀ.). This interpretation has been proposed for **Tit 3:9** (cp. Is 44:9), but 1 appears more prob., esp. since the reff. cited above (Pla. etc.) include specific contextual indications of harmfulness that are not present in the NT passages.—DELG s.v. ὀφέλλω. M-M.

ἀξιαγάπητος, ον ***worthy of love,*** of pers. (w. ἀξιοθαύμαστος) IPhld 5:2.—Of things ὄνομα 1 Cl 1:1; ἦθος 21:7.—DELG s.v. ἄξιος and ἀγαπάω.

ἀξίαγνος s. ἀξιόαγνος.

ἀξιέπαινος, ον (s. ἄξιος, ἔπαινος; X. et al.; Appian, Ital. 6, Liby. 51 §224; Aelian, NA 2, 57) ***worthy of praise*** of Christians in Rome IRo ins.

ἀξίνη, ης, ἡ (since Hom.; Alcmaeonis (Ep.), fgm. 1, 3 Kinkel p. 76 and Bernabé p. 33; et al. BGU 1529, 4 [III BC]; PCairZen 783, 4; LXX; Just., D. 86, 6) ***ax*** used for cutting wood (X., An. 1, 5, 12; Jer 26:22) **Mt 3:10; Lk 3:9; 13:7** D.—B. 561. M-M.

ἀξιόαγνος, ον (s. ἄξιος, ἅγνος) ***worthy of sanctification*** IRo ins (Lghtf. ἀξίαγνος).

ἀξιοεπίτευκτος, ον (s. ἄξιος, ἐπιτυγχάνω [cp. ἐπιτευκτικος 'able to achieve']) ***worthy of success*** IRo ins (s. Lghtf. ad loc.).—DELG s.v. τυγχάνω.

ἀξιοθαύμαστος, ον (s. ἄξιος, θαῦμα, θαυμαστός; X., Mem. 1, 4, 4; Appian, Bell. Civ. 1, 6 §24; Herm. Wr., fgm. XXIII, 5 [458, 16 Sc.]; EpArist 282) ***worthy of admiration*** (w. ἀξιαγάπητος) IPhld 5:2.—DELG s.v. θαῦμα.

ἀξιόθεος, ον ***worthy of God*** (Oenomaus [II AD] in Eus., PE 5, 34, 4; Studia Pontica III no. 173 τῇ ἀξιοθέᾳ μητρί) of the church at Tralles ITr ins; at Rome IRo ins. Of pers. Mg 2:1; Sm 12:2; τὰ ἀ. πρόσωπα IRo 1:1.

ἀξιόλογος, ον adj. (s. ἄξιος, λόγος; ISmyrnaMcCabe .0004, 10; SEG XLII, 1212, 6f [superl.]; since Hdt.; pap; EpArist 322 [adv. -ως 72; 184]; TestSol D 5; Joseph.; Ath. 17, 1 [comp. adv.]) of pers. ***important,*** comp. (ἀξιολογώτερος; cp. the superl. in the same sense Thu. 2, 10 et al.) *more important* [μὴ ἀ]ξιολογοτέραν ἡ[μ]ῶν [αὐτὴν]| [ἀποδείξαι ἤθ]ε[λε]; *did he (the Savior) wish to show that she (Mary Magadelene) is more important than we?* (namely, by communicating secretly to Mary) GMary463, 15f, as reconstructed by Otero, I no. 9, p. 101.

ἀξιομακάριστος, ον (s. ἄξιος, μακάριος; X., Apol. 34; Cyrillus of Scyth. p. 235, 27) ***worthy of blessing*** IEph ins; IRo ins and 10:1; of Paul IEph 12:2.—DELG s.v. μάκαρ.

ἀξιονόμαστος, ον (s. ἄξιος, ὄνομα) ***worthy of the name*** πρεσβυτέριον IEph 4:1.

ἀξιόπιστος, ον adj. (s. ἄξιος, πιστός)—❶ **pert. to being deemed worthy of credence, *trustworthy*** (X., Pla., et al.; pap; Pr 28:20; 2 Macc 15:11; Jos., C. Ap. 1, 4; Just., D. 72. Suda: ἀξιόπιστος οὐχὶ ὁ κατάπλαστος λέγεται ὑπὸ τῶν παλαιῶν καὶ τεραταίᾳ χρώνενος, ἀλλ' ὁ πιστὸς καὶ δόκιμος καὶ ἀξιόχρεως=one who is ἀξιόπιστος is defined by the ancients as one who does not make things up nor tell tall tales, but is trustworthy, reliable, and credible) in our lit. used at two levels of sense: a characteristic as perceived or traditionally projected and the reality as established contextually οἱ δοκοῦντες ἀ. εἶναι καὶ ἑτεροδιδασκαλοῦντες *who seem to be worthy of confidence and yet teach error* IPol 3:1.

❷ **pert. to having the appearance of being trustworthy, *betraying confidence, pretentious, specious*** (Lucian, Alex. 4; Chariton 6, 9, 7; so the adv. Jos., Bell. 1, 508) φιλόσοφοι Dg 8:2. In a sharp oxymoron λύκοι ἀ. IPhld 2:2.—DELG s.v. πείθομαι. Spicq.

ἀξιόπλοκος, ον (s. ἄξιος, πλέκω) ***worthily woven*** στέφανος, fig., of a group of worthy pers. IMg 13:1.

ἀξιοπρεπής, ές (s. ἄξιος, πρέπω; X., Symp. 8, 40; Sym. Ps 89:16) ***worthy of honor*** of Roman Christians IRo ins; ἀξιοπρεπέστατος ἐπίσκοπος *most esteemed superintendent (bishop)* IMg 13:1.

ἄξιος, ία, ον (Hom.+; loanw. in rabb.) adj. for *ἄγ-τιος, cp. ἄγω in the sense 'draw down' in the scale, 'weigh', hence ἄξιος of someone or someth. that is evaluated. Whether the evaluation results in an advantage or a penalty depends on the context or use of a negative particle.

❶ **pert. to having a relatively high degree of comparable worth or value, *corresponding, comparable, worthy,*** of things, in relation to other things,

ⓐ of price *equal in value* (Eur., Alc. 300; Ps.-Demosth. 13, 10; Herodian 2, 3 [of the value of a thing]; Pr 3:15; 8:11; Sir 26:15; s. Nägeli 62) οὐκ ἄξια τὰ παθήματα πρὸς τ. μέλλουσαν δόξαν *the sufferings are not to be compared w. the glory to come* **Ro 8:18** (Arrian, Anab. 6, 24, 1 οὐδὲ τὰ ξύμπαντα … ξυμβληθῆναι ἄξια εἶναι τοῖς … πόνοις=all [the trials] are not worthy to be compared with the miseries). οὐδενὸς ἀ. λόγου *worthy of no consideration* Dg 4:1 (λόγου ἀ. Hdt. 4, 28; Pla., Ep. 7, 334e; Diod. S. 13, 65, 3 οὐδὲν ἄξιον λόγου πράξας; Dionys. Hal. 1, 22, 5; Dio Chrys. 22 [39], 1; Vit. Hom. et Hes. 4); cp. vs. 4.

ⓑ gener., of any other relation (Diod. S. 4, 11, 1 ἄξιον τῆς ἀρετῆς=worthy of his valor; Jos., Vi. 250 βοὴ εὐνοίας ἀξία; Just., A I, 4, 8 οὐδὲν ἀ. τῆς ὑποσχέσεως) καρποὶ ἀ. τῆς μετανοίας *fruits in keeping with your repentance* i.e. such as show that you have turned from your sinful ways **Lk 3:8; Mt 3:8.** For this ἀ. τῆς μετανοίας ἔργα **Ac 26:20.** καρπὸς ἀ. οὗ ἔδωκεν *fruit that corresponds to what he gave us* 2 Cl 1:3. ἀ. πρᾶγμα ISm 11:3 (cp. Just., A I, 19, 5 ἀ. θεοῦ δύναμιν). ἄκκεπτα IPol 6:2. ἔργα ἀ. τῶν ῥημάτων *deeds corresponding to the words* 2 Cl 13:3. πάσης ἀποδοχῆς ἀ. *worthy of full acceptance* **1 Ti 1:15; 4:9** (Heraclid. Crit. [III BC] fgm. I 17 πάσης ἄξιος φιλίας; Just., D. 3, 3 ἀποδοχῆς ἄξια). οὐδὲν ἀ. θανάτου *nothing deserving death* (cp. ἄξιον … τι θανάτου Plut., Marcus Cato 349a [21]) **Lk 23:15; Ac 25:11, 25.** θανάτου ἢ δεσμῶν ἀ. *nothing deserving death or imprisonment* **23:29; 26:31** (cp. Hyperid. 3, 14; Appian, Iber. 31 §124 ἄξια θανάτου; Jos., Ant. 11, 144; Herm. Wr. 1, 20 ἀ. τοῦ θανάτου). Foll. by rel. clause ἀ. ὧν ἐπράξαμεν **Lk 23:41.**

ⓒ impers. ἄξιόν ἐστι *it is worthwhile, fitting, proper* (Hyperid. 2, 3; 6, 3; 4 Macc 17:8; EpArist 4; 282; Just., A II, 3, 2) w. articular inf. foll. (B-D-F §400, 3; Rob. 1059) τοῦ πορεύεσθαι **1 Cor 16:4.** καθὼς ἀ. ἐστιν **2 Th 1:3.**

❷ **pert. to being correspondingly fitting or appropriate, *worthy, fit, deserving*** of pers.—ⓐ in a good sense, but one which is sometimes negated. The negative particle in such cases generates the equivalent of ἀνάξιος 'unworthy'. W. gen. of the thing of which one is worthy τῆς τροφῆς *entitled to his food* **Mt 10:10;** D 13:1f. τῆς αἰωνίου ζωῆς **Ac 13:46.** τοῦ μισθοῦ

Lk 10:7; 1 Ti 5:18. πάσης τιμῆς 6:1 (Dio Chrys. 14 [31], 93; Lucian, Tox. 3 τιμῆς ἄ. παρὰ πάντων).ἄ. μετανοίας Hs 8, 6, 1.—W. gen. of the pers. οὐκ ἔστιν μου ἄ. *he is not worthy of me*=does not deserve to belong to me (perh. 'is not suited to me', s. 1 above) **Mt 10:37**f; cp. PtK 3 p. 15, 17; D 15:1; ἄ. θεοῦ (Wsd 3:5; Just., D. 5, 3) IEph 2:1; 4:1; cp. 15:1; IRo 10:2; ὧν οὐκ ἦν ἄ. ὁ κόσμος *of whom the world was not worthy*='they were too good for this world' (New Life version) **Hb 11:38.**—W. inf. foll. (M. Ant. 8, 42 οὐκ εἰμι ἄξιος with inf.; BGU 1141, 15 [13 BC]; Jos., Ant. 4, 179; Just., A I, 22, 1) οὐκέτι εἰμὶ ἄ. κληθῆναι υἱός σου *I am no longer fit to be called your son* **Lk 15:19, 21;** cp. **Ac 13:25; Rv 4:11; 5:2, 4, 9, 12** (WvUnnik, BRigaux Festschr. '70, 445–61); B 14:1; IEph 1:3; Mg 14; Tr 13:1; Sm 11:1; Hs 8, 2, 5.—W. gen. of the inf. (ParJer 4:5) MPol 10:2. Foll. by ἵνα (B-D-F §393, 4; Rob. 658) ἄ. ἵνα λύσω τὸν ἱμάντα *good enough to untie the thong* **J 1:27** (ἱκανός P[66, 75]; s. ἱκανός end). Foll. by a rel. clause ἄ. ἐστιν ᾧ παρέξῃ τοῦτο **Lk 7:4** (B-D-F §5, 3b; 379; Rob. 724). Abs. (PPetr II, 15 [3], 8 ἄ. γάρ ἐστιν ὁ ἄνθρωπος; 2 Macc 15:21; Just., D. 39, 2 ὡς ἄξιοί εἰσι) ἄ. εἰσιν *they deserve to* **Rv 3:4; 16:6.** Cp. **Mt 10:11, 13; 22:8;** IEph 2:2; Mg 12; Tr 4:2; IRo 9:2; ISm 9:2; IPol 8:1; B 9:9; 21:8; with a negative or negative implication in the context Hs 8, 11, 1; B 9:9; 14:4. ἄ. τινα ἡγεῖσθαι (Job 30:1) Hv 2, 1, 2; 3, 3, 4; 4, 1, 3; m 4, 2, 1; s 7:5; s 9, 28, 5 (w. ἵνα foll. in some of these pass. fr. Hermas). ὁ σωτὴρ ἀξίαν αὐτὴν ἡγήσατο *the Savior considered her worthy* GMary 463, 22. As an epithet of persons IMg 2. Subst. ἀκούει τῶν ἀξίων (God) *heeds the deserving* AcPt Ox 849, 28 (cp. Just., A I, 52, 3).—Comp. ἀξιώτερος (SIG 218, 25) Hv 3, 4, 3.—Ins: Larfeld I, 493f.

ⓑ in a context in which the evaluation is qualified by unpleasant consequences to the one evaluated (Ael. Aristid. 34 p. 650 D. ἄ. ὀργῆς) ἄ. πληγῶν (Dt 25:2; cp. Jos., Ant. 13, 294) *deserving blows* **Lk 12:48.** ἄ. θανάτου (Nicol. Dam.: 90 fgm. 4 p. 335, 12f Jac.; Appian, Bell. Civ. 2, 108 §452; Mel., HE 4, 26, 6) **Ro 1:32.** καθὼς τις ἄξιός ἐστιν *as each deserves* Hs 6, 3, 3 of punishments.—JKleist, 'Axios' in the Gospels: CBQ 6, '44, 342–46; KStendahl, Nuntius 7, '52, 53f.—EDNT. M-M. TW.

ἀξιόω impf. ἠξίουν (s. B-D-F §328); fut. ἀξιώσω; 1 aor. ἠξίωσα. Pass. pres. impv. ἀξιούσθω; 1 fut. ἀξιωθήσομαι; 1 aor. ἠξιώθην Gen. 31:28; pf. ἠξίωμαι (trag., Hdt.+).

❶ **to consider suitable for requital or for receipt of someth. *consider worthy, deserving*** τινά τινος (Diod. S. 17, 76, 3 τιμῆς ἠξίωσαν αὐτόν; schol. on Nicander, Alex. 8; 2 Macc 9:15; Jos., Vi. 231; Tat.; Mel., P. 97, 940) *someone of someth.* σὲ λόγου (Eur., Med. 962 ἡμᾶς ἀξιοῖ λόγου) *you of a discussion* MPol 10:2; cp. 14:2. ἵνα ὑμᾶς ἀξιώσῃ τ. κλήσεως ὁ θεός *that God may count you worthy of the call* (so KJV, 20th Century, Goodsp., REB et al.; 'make worthy' NRSV et al. lacks lexical support) that you are already heeding **2 Th 1:11;** pass. Dg 9:1 (opp. 'be adjudged unworthy' of eternal life); also pass. (Diod. S. 16, 59, 2 τ. στρατηγίας ἠξιωμένος; schol. on Apollon. Rhod. 4, 1212–14a; Jos., Ant. 2, 258 τιμῆς) διπλῆς τιμῆς ἀξιούσθαι **1 Ti 5:17** (cp. Tat. 10, 2 τιμῆς καὶ δωρεᾶς). δόξης **Hb 3:3.** In connection with an undesirable consequence (Hdt. 3, 145; Diod. S. 16, 64, 1 ὑπὸ τοῦ δαιμονίου τιμωρίας ἠξιώθησαν) χείρονος τιμωρίας **Hb 10:29** (Diod. S. 34+35, fgm. 3 τῆς αὐτῆς τιμωρίας ἀξιῶσαί τινα). W. inf. foll. οὐδὲ ἐμαυτὸν ἠξίωσα πρὸς σὲ ἐλθεῖν *I did not consider myself worthy to come to you* **Lk 7:7;** MPol 20:1. Pass. w. inf. foll. *be considered worthy* (Simplicius in Epict. p. 110, 37 ἀξιοῦσθαι μανθάνειν; Gen 31:28; Just., D. 123, 1 λαὸς κεκλῆσθαι ἠξιωμένοι) IEph 9:2; 21:2; IMg 2:14; IRo 1:1.

❷ **to make an evaluation concerning the suitability of someth., esp. an activity** (Appian, Bell. Civ. 1, 34 §154; Philo, Spec. Leg. 1, 319; Jos., Ant. 1, 307; Just., A I, 68, 3 al.; Ath. 2, 3 al.)

ⓐ ***deem, hold an opinion,*** w. inf. foll. (EpJer 40; Just., A I, 16, 14 [acc. w. inf.]; 23:1 al.; Ath.) ἠξίου, μὴ συνπαραλαμβάνειν τοῦτον *he insisted* (impf.) *that they should not take him along* **Ac 15:38.** ἀξιοῦμεν παρὰ σοῦ ἀκοῦσαι *we would like to hear from you* **Ac 28:22.** Cp. Dg 3:2; 7:1.

ⓑ ***request, ask*** (a sense characteristic of later Gk.), w. implication of evaluation of need and ability of the potential giver to meet it (X., Mem. 3, 11, 12; Herodas 6, 79; so mostly LXX; Just., D. 106, 1) w. inf. foll. (Demet.: 722 fgm. 1, 6 Jac.; Jos., ant. 1. 338; Alex. Aphr., An. Mant. II, 1 p. 184, 2 ἀξ. παρὰ θεῶν μαθεῖν=ask to learn from the gods; Just., A I, 3, 12 al.; Mel., HE 4, 26, 13) **Ac 13:42** and **43** both v.l.; 1 Cl 51:1; 53:5; 59:4. W. acc. of pers. and ἵνα foll. Hv 4, 1, 3. Only w. acc. of pers. 1 Cl 55:6. In the passages from 1 Cl and H the request is directed to God (so UPZ 78, 22 [159 BC]. Prayers for vengeance from Rheneia in Dssm., LO 352, 354 [LAE 423ff]=SIG 1181, 1f [II/I BC] ἐπικαλοῦμαι καὶ ἀξιῶ τ. θεὸν τὸν ὕψιστον. Jer 7:16; 11:14; EpArist 245).—DELG s.v. ἄξιος. M-M. TW.

ἀξίως adv. fr. ἄξιος (Soph., Hdt.+; ins, pap, LXX; ApcEsdr 2:20 p. 26, 12 Tdf.; EpArist 32:39; Just.; Tat. 7, 2) ***worthily, in a manner worthy of, suitably*** w. gen. in ref. to a deity or person τοῦ θεοῦ (Hyperid. 3:25 τῆς θεοῦ; Just., A I, 15, 5, D. 58, 2) **1 Th 2:12; 3J 6;** cp. Pol 5:2; 1 Cl 21:1. τοῦ κυρίου **Col 1:10** (on these formulas, which have many counterparts in ins relating to public-spirited pers., s. Dssm. NB 75f [BS 248f]; Nägeli 54; Thieme 21; their use in connection with ordinary Christians suggests an extraordinary status in the new order). τῶν ἁγίων **Ro 16:2.** ὑπηρετῶν Dg 11:1. W. gen. of thing (Diod. S. 1, 51, 7 τῆς ἀληθείας ἀ.; Appian, Bell. Civ. 5, 36 §146 ἀ. τῆς ἀνάγκης=in a manner corresponding to the necessity; Wsd 7:15) τοῦ εὐαγγελίου **Phil 1:27.** τῆς κλήσεως **Eph 4:1.** τῆς ἐντολῆς Pol 5:1. Without such a gen. ἀγαπᾶν τινα ἀ. *love someone in a suitable manner* (='as the pers. deserves'; cp. Thu. 3, 40, 8 κολάσατε ἀξίως τούτους. Wsd 16:1; Sir 14:11;Tat. 7, 2) MPol 17:3.—M-M. s.v. ἄξιος.

ἀοίκητος, ον (Hes., Hdt. et al.; pap [imperial per.]; LXX; TestNapht 3:5 [Charles brackets ἀ.]) ***uninhabited, uninhabitable*** τὸ χωρίον . . . γενέσθαι the property of Judas had become uninhabitable Papias (3:3) (v.l. ἄοικον s. next entry).

ἄοικος, ον (s. οἶκος; Hes., trag., et al.; BGU 372, 13; Philo; Just., D. 117, 5) lit. 'without a house', then ***deserted,*** so Papias (3:3 v.l.) in the sense of ἀοίκητος (s. prec. entry).

ἄοκνος, ον (s. ὀκνέω; Hes., et al.; pap; Pr 6:11a) ***untiring*** ἀγάπη IPol 7:2. ὃν ἀγαπητὸν λίαν ἔχετε καὶ ἄοκνον *whom you hold esp. dear to you, and who is resolute* (lit.'without hesitation') ibid. S. next.—DELG s.v. 1 ὄκνος.

ἀόκνως adv. fr. ἄοκνος (Hippocr. et al.; SIG 762, 30; PSI 621, 6 [III BC]; UPZ 145, 46 [164 BC]; Jos., Ant. 5, 238; Ath. 3, 2) in the Gr-Rom. world of pers. distinguished for eagerness to engage in public service (in add. to some of the reff. cited above, s. e.g. IPriene 17, 45; SEG XLI, 1556, 10) ***without hesitation*** προσέρχεσθαί τινι 1 Cl 33:8.

ἀόρατος, ον (s. ὁράω; Isocr., et al.; LXX, pseudepigr.; Philo, Joseph.; apolog. exc. Mel.) **pert. to not being subject to being**

seen, ***unseen, invisible,*** of God (Diod. S. 2, 21, 7; Cornutus 5 p. 5, 3; Maximus Tyr. 2, 10a; 11, 9d; PGM 5, 123; 12, 265; 13, 71; Herm. Wr. 11, 22; 14, 3; Philo, Op. Mundi 69, Mos. 2, 65, Spec. Leg. 1, 18; 20; 46 al.; Jos., Bell. 7, 346; SibOr fgm. 1, 8; Ar.; Tat. 4, 1; Ath. HDaxer, Ro 1:18–2:20 im Verh. z. spätjüd. Lehrauffassung, diss. Rostock 1914, 11. Cp. Ltzm., Hdb. on Ro 1:20 [lit.]; FBoll, Studien über Claud. Ptolem. 1894, 68; RBultmann, ZNW 29, 1930, 169–92; EFascher, Deus invisibilis: Marb. Theol. Studien '31, 41–77) **Col 1:15; 1 Ti 1:17; Hb 11:27;** 2 Cl 20:5; PtK 2 p. 13, 24; Dg 7:2. Of divine attributes δύναμις (cp. Philo, Somn. 2, 291) Hv 1, 3, 4; 3, 3, 5. τὰ ἀ. τοῦ θεοῦ *God's invisible attributes* **Ro 1:20.** Of Christ, who is described as ἀ. ἐπίσκοπος IMg 3:2 or as ὁ ἀ., ὁ δι' ἡμᾶς ὁρατός IPol 3:2. τὰ ἀ. *the invisible world* (opp. τὰ ὁρατά the visible world, as in Philo, Congr. Erud. Gr. 25; Tat. 5, 1) **Col 1:16;** ITr 5:2; IRo 5:3; IPol 2:2. ἄρχοντες ὁρατοί καὶ ἀ. *rulers visible and invisible* ISm 6:1. θησαυροὶ ἀ. B 11:4 (Is 45:3). ψυχή (Philo, Virt. 57, 172) Dg 6:4. θεοσέβεια ibid.—M-M. TW.

ἀόργητος, ον (s. ὀργή; Aristot., et al.; Stoic t.t. in sense 'without passions'; cp. Philo, Praem. 77 [Moses]) ***free from anger*** of God (w. χρηστός, ἀγαθός, and ἀληθής) Dg 8:8. ἀ. ὑπάρχει πρὸς πᾶσαν τ. κτίσιν αὐτοῦ *(God) is free from wrath toward all the creation* 1 Cl 19:3. τὸ ἀόργητον αὐτοῦ *his* (the supervisor's) *freedom from passion* IPhld 1:2 (τὸ ἀ. Epict. 3, 20, 9; M. Ant. 1, 1).—Sv.

ἀπαγγέλλω impf. ἀπήγγελλον; fut. ἀπαγγελῶ; 1 aor. ἀπήγγειλα; pf. ἀπήγγελκα Jdg 14:16 cod. B, ptc. ἀπηγγελκότες Sir 44:3. Pass. 1 aor. 3 sg. ἀπηγγέλθη (Just., A II, 2, 6); 2 aor. ἀπηγγέλην B-D-F §76, 1; Mlt-H. 226 (s. ἀγγέλλω; Hom.+).

❶ **to give an account of someth., *report (back), announce, tell*** (Jos., Vi. 62 al.; Just., A II, 2, 6 [nominative and inf.]; Tat. 24, 1) w. dat. of the pers. **Mt 2:8; 14:12; 28:8; Mk 16:10, 13; Ac 22:26; 23:16.** W. dat. of pers. and acc. of thing (Gen 37:5; 42:29; 44:24 al.) **Mt 28:11; Mk 6:30** al.; 1 Cl 65:1; Hs 5, 2, 11. Only w. acc. of thing: πάντα **Mt 8:33.** περί τινος **1 Th 1:9.** τὶ περί τινος **Ac 28:21.** τινὶ περί τινος (X., An. 1, 7, 2; Gen 26:32; Esth 6:2; 1 Macc 14:21) **Lk 7:18; 13:1** (ἐν τούτῳ παρῆσαν οἱ τὴν συμφορὰν ἀπαγγέλοντες Plut., Mor. 509c); **J 16:25.** τὶ πρός τινα (Hyperid. 3, 14; Epict. 3, 4, 1; 2 Km 15:13) **Ac 16:36, 38** D. ἀ. εἰς τὴν πόλιν *bring a report into the city* (X., Hell. 2, 2, 14) **Mk 5:14; Lk 8:34** (cp. Jos., Ant. 5, 357 ἀπαγγελθείσης τῆς ἥττης εἰς τὴν Σιλω; Am 4:13; 1 Macc 6:5). Used w. λέγων **J 4:51 v.l.; Ac 5:22.** W. dat. of pers. foll. by acc. and inf. IPhld 10:1. Foll. by a relative clause **Mt 11:4; Lk 7:22; Ac 4:23; 23:19.** W. πῶς foll. **Lk 8:36; Ac 11:13.** W. ὅτι foll. **Lk 18:37; J 5:15 v.l.; 20:18 v.l.;** GJs 24:3 (Bodmer for ἀν-). W. acc. and inf. **Ac 12:14.** W. ὡς foll. (1 Esdr 5:37) **Lk 8:47** (B-D-F §396; Rob. 726).

❷ **to make someth. known publicly, *proclaim*** (of someth. in the present or fut.) κρίσιν τοῖς ἔθνεσιν **Mt 12:18;** (w. μαρτυρεῖν) τὴν ζωήν **1J 1:2;** cp. vs. **3;** τὸ ὄνομά σου τοῖς ἀδελφοῖς **Hb 2:12;** ἀ. ἐνώπιόν τινος (Ps 141:3) in the sense *tell openly* or *frankly* (Gen 12:18; 1 Km 9:19) ἀπήγγειλεν ἐνώπιον παντὸς τοῦ λαοῦ *she confessed before all the people* **Lk 8:47;** cp. **1 Cor 14:25.** W. dat. and inf. foll. τ. ἔθνεσιν ἀ. μετανοεῖν καὶ ἐπιστρέφειν *they declared to the gentiles that they should repent* ... **Ac 26:20;** cp. **17:30 v.l.** Foll. by ἵνα to introduce a command that is to be transmitted to another **Mt 28:10** (cp. Polyaenus 7, 15, 2 Xerxes' command: ἄπιτε κ. τοῖς Ἕλλησιν ἀπαγγείλατε, ὅσα ἑωράκατε).—Anz 283f. M-M. TW.

ἀπάγχω (ἄγχω 'to squeeze, strangle') 1 aor. mid. ἀπηγξάμην (Hom.+; Jos., Ant. 12, 256; 15, 176) mid. ***hang oneself*** (so since Aeschyl., Hdt.; Epict.; PSI 177, 10; PGM 4, 1911; 2 Km 17:23; Tob 3:10.—Mlt. 155) of Judas **Mt 27:5** (ἀπελθὼν ἀπήγξατο like Epict. 1, 2, 3). S. Ἰούδας 6.

ἀπάγω fut. ἀπάξω LXX; 2 aor. ἀπήγαγον. Pass.: fut. ἀπαχθήσομαι LXX; 1 aor. ἀπήχθην **Ac 12:19;** pf. ptc. ἀπηγμένος; plupf. 3 sg. ἀπῆκτο Gen 40:3 (Hom.+).

❶ **to lead or move someone or someth. from a place, *lead off, take away,*** to water **Lk 13:15.** W. acc. of pers. and indication of goal (Ps 59:11; 3 Km 1:38) με εἰς τὴν Ἀρκαδίαν Hs 9, 1, 4 (Diod. S. 5, 51, 4 Διόνυσος ἀπήγαγε τὴν Ἀριάδνην εἰς τὸ ὄρος). σὲ ἀ. ἐν τῷ ναῷ Κυρίου GJs 6:1. ποῦ σε ἀπάξω καὶ σκεπάσω σου τὴν ἀσχημοσύνην; *where shall I take you to hide your shame?* 17:3. Abs. **Ac 24:6(7) v.l.** (cp. next).

❷ **to conduct a pers. from one point to another in a legal process,** legal t.t.—ⓐ ***bring before*** πρὸς Καϊάφαν **Mt 26:57;** πρὸς τὸν ἀρχιερέα **Mk 14:53.** ἐπὶ βασιλεῖς **Lk 21:12.** εἰς τὸ συνέδριον **Lk 22:66.** εἰς τὸ ἱερόν GJs 15:2.—**Mt 27:2.** Of a witness **Ac 23:17.**

ⓑ ***lead away*** a prisoner or condemned man (cp. Andoc. 4, 181; Demosth. 23, 80; PPetr II, 10 [2], 7; PLille 7, 12f οὗτος ἀπήγαγέν με εἰς τὸ δεσμοτήριον; OGI 90, 14; Gen 39:22; Philo, De Jos. 154) **Mk 14:44; 15:16;** AcPl Ha 4, 13. Cp. intr. **Rv 13:10 v.l.**

ⓒ ***lead away*** to execution (Diod. S. 13, 102, 3; POxy 33, I 8, al.; Sus 45 Theod.; EpJer 17; En 10:13 εἰς τὸ χάος τοῦ πυρός; Jos., Bell. 6, 155, Ant. 19, 269; Just., A I, 31, 6 al.) ἀ. εἰς τὸ σταυρῶσαι *to crucify (him)* **Mt 27:31.** With no addition (Aesop., Fab. 56 P. [for this Halm 112 and H-H. 56 ὑπάγω]; Esth 1:1o) **Lk 23:26; J 19:16 v.l.,** but s. also P[66] Supplement v.l., '58, 38. Pass. ἐκέλευσεν ἀπαχθῆναι *he ordered that they be led away* (Polyaenus 5, 2, 16 ἀπαχθῆναι προσέταξεν) to execution **Ac 12:19.** εἰς Ῥώμην IEph 21:2.

❸ intr. **to mark an extension along a route.** Of a road ***lead, run*** (like Lat. ducere) εἴς τι (Vita Aesopi W 4 ἀπάγουσα ὁδὸς εἰς τὴν πόλιν; Stephanus Byzantius [VI AD], Ethnica ed. Meineke I p. 287 Εὔτρησις, κώμη ... κεῖται παρὰ τ. ὁδὸν τὴν ἐκ Θεσπιῶν εἰς Πλαταιὰς ἀπάγουσαν): εἰς τ. ἀπώλειαν *to destruction* **Mt 7:13** (TestAbr A 11 p. 90, 7 [Stone p. 28]; B 8 p. 113, 2 [Stone p. 74]). εἰς τ. ζωήν vs. **14.** Of pers. *leave* (s. ἄγω 5) ἀπάγει ἀπὸ τῶν ἀδελφῶν AcPl Ha 7, 18.

❹ **to cause to depart from correct behavior,** pass. ***be misled, carried away*** (Lucian, Catapl. 26 πρὸς ὕβριν) πρὸς τὰ εἴδωλα *led astray to idols* **1 Cor 12:2.** ἡδοναῖς καὶ ἐπιθυμίαις ἀπαγόμενοι *carried away by pleasures and desires* Dg 9:1 ἀπαγομένους κα[ὶ κα]τανδραποδιζομένους *led off and enslaved* AcPl Ha 1, 10.—M-M.

ἀπαθής, ές (s. πάσχω; Theognis I, 1177 et al.).—❶ **pert. to not being subject to suffering, *free of suffering*** (so Plato et al.; Stoic term: Stoic. II p. 99, 23; Teles p. 56, 14; Porphyr., Abst. 2, 61; Herm. Wr. 2, 12; Philo; Jos., Bell. 5, 417; POxy 526, 3f; Just., Ath. Cp. Theognis 1177; X., An., 7, 7, 33 al.) of Christ (opp. παθητός as in Proclus, Theol. 80 p. 74, 33) IEph 7:2; IPol 3:2.

❷ **pert. to emergence from suffering or injury without mishap, *without suffering, uninjured*** (Hdt. 1, 32; 2, 119; Dio Chrys. 19 [36], 40 Zoroaster emerges from fire unharmed; Appian, Liby. 111 §522; Jos., Ant. 1, 284; also med. term, e.g. Galen 5, 122) Βαρσαβᾶς ... ἰὸν ἐχίδνης πιὼν ... ἀ. διεφυλάχθη *despite his having drunk snake-venom, he suffered no ill effects* Papias (11:2).—TW.

ἀπαίδευτος, ον (s. παιδεύω; Eur., Pla. et al.; PSI 1282, 59 Hymn to Demeter; POxy 2339, 18; BGU 1578, 14; LXX; Philo; Jos., Ant. 2, 285, C. Ap. 2, 37; SibOr 3, 670, mostly of pers.; adv. Tat. 2, 1) ***uninstructed, uneducated*** (w. ἄφρων, ἀσύνετος, μωρός) 1 Cl 39:1. ζητήσεις *uninformed speculations* **2 Ti 2:23** (cp. Xenophon, Ep. 2 Ad Crit. p. 789 γνώμη ἀ.; Pla., Phdr. 269b ῥῆμα ἀ.).—M-M. TW.

ἀπαίρω fut. ἀπαρῶ; 1 aor. ἀπῆρα LXX; pf. ἀπῆρκα; 1 aor. pass. ἀπήρθην (s. αἴρω; Eur., Hdt. et al.; TestSol 26:6; TestLevi 7:4; ParJer 3:8; LXX; Jos., Bell. 4, 87, Vi. 422).

❶ trans. ***take away*** τινὰ ἀπό τινος, in our lit. only pass. ὅταν ἀπαρθῇ ἀπ᾽ αὐτῶν ὁ νυμφίος *when the bridegroom is taken away from them* **Mt 9:15; Mk 2:20** (GBraumann, NovT 6, ’63, 264–67); **Lk 5:35.** Yet there is no need to assume the necessity of force **Ac 1:9** D.

❷ intr. ***go on a journey, depart, leave*** (cp. our ‘take off’, as for a vacation) PPetr II, 13 [5], 5 [III BC] ἀπηρμένος=gone on a journey. Cp. PLips 47, 12 [IV AD]; POxy 1873, 13 [V AD]) Παῦλος . . . ἀπῆρεν εἰς Μακεδονίαν *Paul . . . has left for Macedonia* AcPl Ha 5, 26; ἀπάραντος τοῦ πλοίου *after the boat had left* 7, 22; uncert. ἀπέ[ρομ]ε εἰς Ῥώμην (ἀπέρομε=ἀπαίρομαι Schubart) 7, 14.—M-M.

ἀπαιτέω 1 aor. pass. ptc. ἀπαιτηθείς Wsd 15:8; fut. 2 sg. pass. ἀπαιτηθήσῃ Is 30:33; inf. ἀπαιτηθήσεσθαι (Just., A I, 17, 4) and ἀπαιτήσεσθαι (Ath. 36, 1) (s. αἰτέω; trag., Hdt.+)

❶ **to demand someth. back or as due, *ask for, demand*** of a loan (as in ‘payment on demand’=*dun*) or stolen property (Theophr., Char. 10, 2; Phalaris, Ep. 83, 1; 2; SIG 955, 18; pap, e.g., BGU 183, 8; PYadin 17, 9 al.; Poxy 3058, 13 [II AD]; Sir 20:15; Philo, De Jos. 227; Just., D. 125, 2 τὰ ἴδια παρὰ πάντων) τὶ ἀπό τινος **Lk 6:30.** W. obj. supplied from the context ἀπό τινος Hs 8, 1, 5; cp. D 1:4. Abs. 1:5. Using the image of life as a loan (Cicero, De Rep. 1, 3, 4; cp. Epict. 4, 1, 172; Wsd 15:8; other reff. Horst, Ps.-Phocyl., p. 190) τὴν ψυχὴν ἀπαιτοῦσιν ἀπὸ σοῦ *they are demanding your soul fr. you,* i.e. *your soul will be demanded of you* **Lk 12:20** (v.l. αἰτοῦσιν).

❷ gener. **to ask for with a note of urgency, *demand, desire*** (Diod. S. 16, 56, 3; Dio Chrys. 31, 3; Jos., Ant. 12, 181; PBerl 11662, 26 [I AD]=Olsson 34, p. 100: ὁ τόπος ἀπαιτεῖ=the place demands) ὁ καιρὸς ἀπαιτεῖ σε *the time demands you,* i.e. a person like you IPol 2:3 (Procop. Soph., Ep. 54 καιρὸς γράμματα ἀπαιτῶν=time that demands a letter). **1 Pt 3:15 v.l.**—DELG s.v. αἰτέω. M-M. TW.

ἀπαλγέω pf. ἀπήλγηκα (ἀλγέω ‘suffer’; Thu. 2, 61, 4 et al.; Philo, Exs. 135).

❶ **to be so inured that one is not bothered by the implications of what one is doing, *become callous, dead to feeling,*** without a sense of right and wrong (Polyb. 16, 12, 7; cp. Nägeli 34) ἀπηλγηκότες *dead to all feeling* (REB; so, with variations, most translations) **Eph 4:19.** For a diff t. perspective s. 2.

❷ **to be filled with a heavy sense of loss or deprivation, *be despondent*** (Polyb. 1, 35, 5 ἀπηλγηκυίας ψυχάς; Cass. Dio 48, 37) **Eph 4:19** (cp. the v.l. ἀπηλπικότες ‘despairing’, and cp. 2:12 ἐλπίδα μὴ ἔχοντες; their hopelessness leads them into vice: ἑαυτοὺς παρέδωκαν τῇ ἀσελγείᾳ). S. 1 above.

ἀπαλλάσσω fut. ἀπαλλάξω LXX; 1 aor. ἀπήλλαξα; pf. 3 sg. ἀπήλλαγεν 1 Km 14:29. Mid.: fut. ἀπαλλάξομαι Just., D. 68, 1. Pass.: fut. ἀπαλλαγήσομαι TestJob 25:10; 2 aor. ἀπηλλάγην; pf. ἀπήλλαγμαι (s. ἀλλάσσω; Aeschyl., Hdt.+).

❶ **to set free from a controlling state or entity, *free, release***

ⓐ act. trans. τούτους **Hb 2:15** (cp. Jos., Ant. 11, 270; 13, 363; Just., A I, 57, 3; A II, 4, 4; ἵν᾽ [ὁ Ἰησοῦς] αὐτοὺς ἀπαλλάξῃ τῆς ἁμαρτίας Orig., C. Cels. 4, 19, 30). αὐτόν from an evil spirit **Lk 9:40** D.

ⓑ pass. (PTebt 104, 31 and POxy 104, 26 of separation from a spouse; PGen 21, 12; Philo, Spec. Leg. 3, 107 of a death penalty) sick people *are released = are cured* ἀπὸ πάσης ἀσθενείας **Ac 5:15** D (Jos., Ant. 2, 33).

❷ **to go away, *leave, depart*** intr. (Philo, Spec. Leg. 2, 85; Jos., Ant. 5, 143; Just., A II, 2, 7; D. 56, 5 al.; Mel., P. 24, 175) ἀπό τινος (X., An. 7, 1, 4; Phlegon: 257 fgm. 36, 1, 2 Jac.; Mitt-Wilck. II/2, 284, 12; PRyl 154, 26 ἀπαλλασσομένης ἀπ᾽ αὐτοῦ; Just., D. 126, 4 ἀπαλλάσσονται ἀπὸ Ἀβραάμ [Gen. 18:16]) of diseases **Ac 19:12** (cp. Ps.-Pla., Eryx. 401c εἰ αἱ νόσοι ἀπαλλαγείησαν ἐκ τ. σωμάτων; PGM 13, 245). τοῦ κόσμου *depart from the world* euphem. for *die* 1 Cl 5:7. For this τοῦ βίου (Eur., Hel. 102; PFay 19, 19 ἀπαλλάσσομαι τοῦ βίου; TestAbr A 18 p. 100, 22 [Stone p. 48; act.]; Ath. 31, 3) MPol 3:1. Abs. Qua (opp. ἐπιδημεῖν). εἰς οἶκον *go home* GPt 14:59=ASyn. 361, 35; 2 Cl 17:3.

❸ **to settle a matter with an adversary, *come to a settlement, be quit of*** pass. w. act. sense (X., Mem. 2, 9, 6: a defendant ‘does everything’ to be rid of his accuser) δὸς ἐργασίαν ἀπηλλάχθαι ἀπ᾽ αὐτοῦ *do your best to come to a settlement w. (your adversary)* lit., get rid of . . . **Lk 12:58.**—DELG s.v. ἄλλος. M-M. TW.

ἀπαλλοτριόω fut. ἀπαλλοτριώσω LXX; 1 aor. ἀπηλλοτρίωσα. Pass.: aor. ἀπηλλοτριώθην; pf. ptc. ἀπηλλοτριωμένος LXX (Hippocr., Pla. et al.; ins [e.g. IMagnSip 19, 5f: AD 154/55; ISmyrnaMcCabe .0421, 5]; pap, LXX, TestJob; TestBenj 10:10; ApcMos) ***estrange, alienate*** τινά τινος (s. ἀλλότριος; SIG 495, 164 [III BC]; Sir 11:34; Jos., Ant. 4, 3) γαμετὰς ἀνδρῶν *wives from their husbands* 1 Cl 6:3. ἡμᾶς τοῦ καλῶς ἔχοντος *us from what is right* 14:2.—Pass. (Polyb. 1, 79, 6; Ezk 14:5, 7; 3 Macc 1:3; TestBenj 10:10; Herm. Wr. 13, 1 τ. κόσμου) ἀπηλλοτριωμένοι τῆς ζωῆς τοῦ θεοῦ *estranged from the life of God* **Eph 4:18.** τῆς πολιτείας τοῦ Ἰσραήλ *excluded from the corporate life of Israel* **2:12.** W. ἐχθρός **Col 1:21.** New Docs 3, 62.—DELG s.v. ἄλλος. M-M. TW.

ἁπαλός, ή, όν (Hom.+; PEdg 22, 9=Sb 6728 [257/56 BC] text restored, superl.: of barley; LXX; TestNapht 1:7; Jos., Bell. 2, 120; Ath. 27, 1 ψυξή) ***tender*** (not hard or tough) of the young shoots of the fig tree ὅταν ὁ κλάδος αὐτῆς ἁ. γένηται *when its branch becomes tender,* i.e. sprouts **Mt 24:32; Mk 13:28** (a favorite expression relative to plants in Theocr. 5, 55; 8, 67; 11, 57; 15, 113). Of calves (Gen 18:7) δώδεκα μόσχους ἁ. GJs 4:3 (w. var. in the mss.; not pap).

ἀπαναίνομαι 1 aor. 3 sg. ἀπηνήνατο Ps 76:3 (ἀναίνομαι ‘reject, spurn’; Hom. et al.; PGrenf I, 1 [1], 5; LXX; Just., D. 117, 1) ***reject, disown*** w. acc. (Hippocr., Mul. 2, 179 the wife τὸν ἄνδρα ἀπαναίνεται) νουθέτημα παντοκράτορος 1 Cl 56:6 (Job 5:17).

ἀπάνθρωπος, ον (s. ἄνθρωπος; trag., et al.; Jos., Ant. 8, 117; 16, 42; Tat.; pap [e.g. PFlor 367, 4: III AD]) ***inhuman*** βασανισταί MPol 2:3.

ἀπαντάω fut. ἀπαντήσω (Polyaenus 2, 1, 17 for the older and customary mid.); 1 aor. ἀπήντησα (ἠπήντησα GJs 19:3; 24:1); pf. ἀπήντηκα Gen 33:8; fut. mid. ἀπαντήσομαι LXX; aor. 3 sg. pass. ἀπηντήθη En 102:5 (ἀντάω ‘meet face to face’; Eur., Hdt.+. Ath. 4, 1; 31, 2: ‘respond, counter’, ‘meet charges’; s. Anz 351) ***meet*** τινί ***someone*** (Appian, Liby. 109 §515, Bell. Civ.

4, 36 §152; 1 Km 25:20; Jos., Ant. 1, 179; 6, 189) **Mk 14:13; Ac 16:16 v.l.;** GJs 19:3; 24:1 (both ὑπ- Tdf.). Without obj. (Hyperid., fgm. 205) ἀπήντησαν δέκα λεπροὶ ἄνδρες *ten lepers came toward him* **Lk 17:12** (v.l. ὑπήντησαν; gener. in mss. ὑπαντάω is interchanged w. ἀ.: **Mt 28:9; Mk 5:2; Lk 14:31; J 4:51; Ac 16:16**).—οὐδέν σοι ἀπήντησεν; *did nothing meet you?* Hv 4, 2, 3 (fr. the context = come toward, not = happen to. ἀπ. has the latter mng. in Polyb. 4, 38, 10; Diod. S. 15, 58, 4; Gen 49:1; Jer 13:22; Sir 31:22; 33:1; En 98:9; 102:5).—B. 1366. DELG s.v. ἄντα 1. M-M.

ἀπάντησις, εως, ἡ (s. ἀπαντάω; Soph.+; Polyb. 5, 26, 8; Diod. S. 18, 59, 3 et al.; ins, pap, LXX; TestJob 9:7; EpArist 91; Jos., Ant. 7, 276; Philo, Quod Deus 10, 166; s. Nägeli 30; Mlt. 14, n. 4; 242; loanw. in rabb.) ***meeting*** only in the formula εἰς ἀπάντησιν (LXX freq. in friendly and hostile mng.) *to meet.* Abs. (PTebt 43 I, 7 [118 BC] παρεγενήθημεν εἰς ἀ.; 1 Km 13:15) ἐξέρχεσθαι εἰς ἀ. [αὐτοῦ] **Mt 25:6** (many mss. variously read a gen. or dat. pronoun, and some omit it [s. also the variants for **J 12:13**]). W. dat. (1 Km 4:1; 13:10; 1 Ch 14:8; Jos., Ant. 13, 101) ἔρχεσθαι εἰς ἀ. τινι (Jdth 5:4) **Ac 28:15.** W. gen. (Pel.-Leg. p. 19; 1 Km 30:21; 2 Km 19:26) **Mt 27:32** D. ἁρπάζεσθαι εἰς ἀ. τοῦ κυρίου εἰς ἀέρα *be snatched up to meet the Lord in the air* **1 Th 4:17** (s. EPeterson, D. Einholung des Kyrios: ZST 7, 1930, 682–702.—Diod. S. 34+35, fgm. 33, 2 of bringing in the Great Mother of the gods by the Romans).—DELG s.v. ἄντα 1. M-M. TW.

ἅπαξ adv. (Hom.+; Tat. 6, 1 [Hb 9:26?]) 'once'.—**❶** as a numer. term **pert. to a single occurrence, *once,*** ἅ. ἐλιθάσθην *I was stoned once* **2 Cor 11:25.** ἅ. πεφανέρωται **Hb 9:26.** ἅ. ἀποθανεῖν vs. **27** (Proverbia Aesopi 141 P.: ‹πλέον ἢ› ἅπαξ οὐδεὶς ἄνθρωπος θνήσκει); cp. **1 Pt 3:18.** ἅ. προσενεχθείς **Hb 9:28.** W. gen. foll. ἅ. τοῦ ἐνιαυτοῦ (Hdt. 2, 59; Ex 30:10; Lev 16:34) *once a year* **Hb 9:7.** ἔτι ἅ. (2 Macc 3:37; Judg 16:18, 28; TestAbr A 85, 15 [Stone p. 18] al.) *once more*=for the last time (Aeschyl., Ag. 1322; Judg 6:39) 12:26f (Hg 2:6). ἅ. καὶ δίς (Dionys. Hal. 8, 56, 1 οὐχ ἅ. ἀλλὰ καὶ δίς; Ael. Aristid. 36, 91 K.=48 p. 474 D.: ἅ. ἢ δίς; Anna Comn., Alexias 3, 3 ed. Reiff. I 102, 17 καὶ ἅ. καὶ δίς; 1 Km 17:39; 2 Esdr 23:20; 1 Macc 3:30) *again and again, more than once* (LMorris, NovT 1, '56, 205–8) **Phil 4:16; 1 Th 2:18;** 1 Cl 53:3 (Dt 9:13). W. weakening of the numer. idea ἐπεὶ ἅ. (Thu. 7, 44, 7; X., An. 1, 9, 10; Menand., PDidot 36 S. p. 329; Menand., Dyscolos 392; Chion, Ep. 14, 1; POxy 1102, 8 ἐπεὶ ἅ. προσῆλθε τῇ κληρονομίᾳ) *since for once* Hv 3, 3, 4; m 4, 4, 1.

❷ pert. to a single occurrence and decisively unique, *once and for all* (Hippocr., Ep. 27, 41; Aelian, VH 2, 30; Philostrat., Ep. 7, 2; PLips 34, 20; 35, 19; Ps 88:36; PsSol 12:6; TestAbr 20 p. 103, 1 [Stone p. 54]; Philo, Ebr. 198; Jos., Bell. 2, 158, Ant. 4, 140; Just., A I, 61, 5) **Hb 10:2; Jd 3, 5.**—Sim. *once* (Alciphron 1, 8, 4; 1, 10, 2) **Hb 6:4.**—DELG s.v. πάξ and πήγνυμι. EDNT. M-M. TW. Spicq.

ἁπαξαπλῶς adv. (intensive of ἁπλῶς) (since II AD; also TestJob 25:9; 29:3; Tat. 21, 3; 32, 1) ***in general*** ἅπαξα[πλῶς] at the end of a recital of Jesus' deeds AcPl BMM verso 12.—DELG s.v. ἁπλόος.

ἀπαράβατος, ον (s. παραβαίνω; belonging to later Gk. [Phryn. 313 Lob.]; not LXX) **Hb 7:24** usu. interpr. 'without a successor'. But this mng. is found nowhere else. ἀ. rather has the sense ***permanent, unchangeable*** (Stoic. II 266, 1; 293, 31 [Chrysipp.]; Plut., Mor. 410f; 745d; Epict. 2, 15, 1, Ench. 51, 2; Herm. Wr. fgm. XXIII, 48 [494, 26 Sc.], fgm. XXIV, 1; Philo, Aet. M. 112; Jos., Ant. 18, 266, C. Ap. 2, 293; Just., A I, 43, 7; as legal t.t. over a long period of time in pap: PRyl 65, 18 [I BC]; PLond III, 1015, 12 p. 257 [VI AD] ἄτρωτα καὶ ἀσάλευτα καὶ ἀπαράβατα; Mitt-Wilck. II /2, 372 V, 19; PEllingworth, JSNT 23 '85, 125f).—M-M. TW. Spicq.—DELG s.v. βαίνω.

ἀπαρασκεύαστος, ον (s. παρασκευάζω; X. et al.; Jos., Ant. 4, 293; s. Nägeli 16) ***not ready, unprepared*** (actually a military t.t.) εὑρεῖν τινα ἀ. *find someone not in readiness* **2 Cor 9:4.**—DELG s.v. σκεῦος.

ἀπαρθῇ, -ῶ s. ἀπαίρω.

ἀπαρνέομαι fut. ἀπαρνήσομαι; 1 aor. ἀπηρνησάμην. Pass.: 1 fut. ἀπαρνηθήσομαι; pf. ἀπήρνημαι ISm 5:2; (W-S. §13, 9; B-D-F §78; 311); variant act. aor. ἀπαρνῆσαι Hs 1:5 (Soph., Hdt. et al.; Is 31:7; JosAs 12:11 cod. A for ἠρνήσαντο; Mel., P. 26, 181; 73, 537) 'deny'.

❶ to refuse to recognize/acknowledge, *deny* τινά (Is 31:7) Christ (of Peter's denial; MGoguel, Did Peter Deny his Lord? HTR 25, '32, 1–27; ELinnemann, Die Verleugnung des Petrus: ZTK 63, '66, 21) **Mt 26:34f, 75; Mk 14:30f, 72; Lk 22:61.** In full ἕως τρίς με ἀπαρνήσῃ εἰδέναι *until you have three times denied that you know me* vs. **34** (on the v.l. μὴ εἰδέναι cp. Soph., Ant. 442 καταρνῇ μὴ δεδρακέναι τάδε;). τὸν κύριον Hv 3, 6, 5; cp. 8, 8, 2; ISm 5:2 (Lucian, M. Peregr. 13 p. 337 θεούς). W. acc. of thing (Diod. S. 20, 63, 4 ἀ. τὴν ἐπιστήμην=deny, refuse to acknowledge his [former] trade [as a potter]—opp. καυχάομαι=be proud of it; SibOr 4, 27f νηοὺς κ. βωμούς) τ. νόμον s 1:5. Pass. (Soph., Philoct. 527; Pla., 7th Letter 338e; Herodas 4, 74) ἀπαρνηθήσεται ἐνώπιον τῶν ἀγγέλων *the person will be denied* (i.e. not recognized) *before the angels* **Lk 12:9** (Ps.-Callisth. 2, 8, 10 ἀπαρνέομαι=reject, wish to know nothing of).

❷ to act in a wholly selfless manner, *deny oneself* (opp. Mel., P. 26, 181 'to avoid being killed') **Mt 16:24; Mk 8:34; Lk 9:23 v.l.** AFridrichsen, 'S. selbst verleugnen': ConNeot 2, '36, 1–8; 6, '42, 94–96. SEÅ 5, '40, 158–62; JLebreton, La doctrine du renoncement dans le NT: NouvRT 65, '38, 385–412.—DELG s.v. ἀρνέομαι. M-M. TW.

ἀπαρτί adv. (Hdt., Hippocr. et al.; Teleclides [V BC]; Schwyzer I 632f) ***exactly, certainly, expressly*** (ἀ. = ἀπηρτισμένως, τελείως, ἀκριβῶς Phryn. 20f Lob.; s. Suda s.v. and Bekker, Anecd. Gr. 418, 15; this mng. is also prob. for Aristoph., Pl. 388) considered by some to be the correct rdg. for ἀπ' ἄρτι **Rv 14:13** (so N.[24, 25]; ἀπάρτι Tdf.), if ναί is rejected as a gloss; also **Mt 26:29, 64** (B-D-F §12 ; ADebrunner, after AFridrichsen [w. inclusion of J 13:19 and 1:51 (52)], ConNeot 11, '47, 45–49). In all the pass. cited above, exc. J 1:51 (here as v.l.), N. reads ἀπ' ἄρτι, s. ἄρτι.—Cp. DELG s.v. ἄρτι. M-M.

ἀπάρτι ***just now, even now*** (not an Attic use) **J 13:19; 14:7; Rv 13:13** (all Tdf.), s. ἀπ' ἄρτι s.v. ἄρτι 3.

ἀπαρτίζω 1 aor. ἀπήρτισα; pf. pass. ἀπήρτισμαι, ptc. ἀπηρτισμένος (Aeschyl. [Septem 374, but the rdg. is in question as a late expression: Moeris 75f (82); Phryn. 447 Lob.], Hippocr. et al.; pap; 3 Km 9:25 A; TestLevi 9:11; Just.; Mel.; πράγματα ἀπηρτισμένα Theoph. Ant. 3, 17 [p. 238, 14]) **to make or do something in a precise or conclusive manner, *finish, complete*** (ἀρτίζω 'prepare'; Polyb. 31, 12, 10; 31, 13, 1; Diod. S. 1, 11, 6 et al.; POxy 908, 23; 936, 22; PLips 105, 11; and see Preis.; 3 Km 9:25 A; Jos., Ant. 3, 146; 8, 130) τι someth. ἔργον τελείως ἀ. *complete a task perfectly* IEph 1:1

(Mel., P. 38, 265; cp. πρᾶξιν Just., D. 134, 3). τὸν ἴδιον κλῆρον *fulfill his destiny* MPol 6:2. ὅταν αὐτὸ ἀπαρτίσητε *when you complete it* IPol 7:3. Of God ὁ ἀπαρτίσας αὐτά *who perfected them* Hs 5, 5, 2. Also τινά (POxy 724, 11 [II AD] ἐὰν αὐτὸν ἀπαρτίσῃς) *make someone complete* με ἀπαρτίσει IPhld 5:1. Pass. παρὰ θεῷ ἀπηρτισμένος IEph 19:3. ἀπήρτισμαι ἐν Ἰ. Χριστῷ 3:1. Cp. ἀποτελέω.—DELG s.v. ἀραρίσκω, ἄρτι. M-M. s.v. ἀπαρτισμός.

ἀπάρτισμα, ατος, τό s. ἀπαρτίζω (3 Km 7:9 Sym.) ***completion*** ἀ. ἀφθαρσίας *consummation of immortality* IPhld 9:2. Cp. DELG s.v. ἀραρίσκω.

ἀπαρτισμός, οῦ, ὁ (s. ἀπάρτισμα; Chrysippus: Stoic. II 164; Dionys. Hal., De Comp. Verb. 24; Apollon. Dysc., De Adv. p. 532, 8; pap, in Mitt-Wilck. II/2, 88 IV, 26; PGiss 67, 8ff; Sb 7173, 30 [all II AD]) ***completion*** ἀ. (sc. πύργου) **Lk 14:28.**—M-M.

ἀπαρχή, ῆς, ἡ (cp. ἀπάρχομαι 'make a beginning' in sacrifice; orig. of hair cut from the forehead and cast into the fire Il. 19, 254; Od. 14, 422 al., hence ἀπαρχή='beginning of a sacrifice' Eur., Or. 96; such sacrifices would begin with 'firstlings' or 'first fruits', freq. distinguished also for quality) (Soph., Hdt. et al.; ins, pap, LXX; PsSol 15:3; Test12Patr, Philo, Joseph.; Celsus 8, 33)

❶ cultic t.t. ***first fruits, first portion*** of any kind (incl. animals, both domesticated and wild [for the latter Arrian, Cyneg. 33, 1]), which were holy to the divinity and were consecrated before the rest could be put to secular use (cp. Theopomp. [IV BC]:115 fgm. 344 Jac. p. 608, 5; Cornutus 28 p. 55, 9; Ael. Aristid. 45 p. 136 D.; Theophyl. Sym., Ep. 29 Πανὶ τοῦ ποιμνίου τὰς ἀπαρχάς; OGI 179, 12 [I BC]; PSI 690, 14; Porphyr., Abst. 2, 61 θεοῖς ἀρίστη μὲν ἀπαρχὴ νοῦς καθαρός; SEG XLII, 17 lit.).

ⓐ lit. εἰ ἡ ἀ. ἁγία, καὶ τὸ φύραμα *if the first fruits (of dough) are holy, so is the whole lump* **Ro 11:16** (on first fruits of bread dough, Num 15:18–21, cp. The Mishnah, tr. HDanby '58 ['33] 83–88 [Hallah]). In full ἀ. γεννημάτων ληνοῦ καὶ ἅλωνος, βοῶν τε καὶ προβάτων *the first fruits of the produce of wine-press and threshing floor, of cattle and sheep* D 13:3, cp. 5f (s. Ex 22:28); ἀ. τῆς ἅλω 1 Cl 29:3. Assigned to a prophet, as to the priests and seers among the gentiles (Artem. 3, 3) and in the OT to the priest D 13:3, 6f.

ⓑ fig., w. the components of a above strongly felt—α. of persons *first fruits* of Christians ἀ. τῆς Ἀσίας, i.e. the first convert in Asia **Ro 16:5.** ἀ. τῆς Ἀχαΐας **1 Cor 16:15.** Also **2 Th 2:13** (v.l. ἀπ' ἀρχῆς) the first converts of Thessalonica (so Harnack, SBBerlAk 1910, 575ff); pl. 1 Cl 42:4. Gener. ἀ. τις τῶν αὐτοῦ κτισμάτων *a kind of first fruits of his creatures* **Js 1:18** (cp. Philo, Spec. Leg. 4, 180 of the Jews: τοῦ σύμπαντος ἀνθρώπων γένους ἀπενεμήθη οἷά τις ἀπαρχὴ τῷ ποιητῇ καὶ πατρί; Alex. Aphr., Fat. 1, II 2 p. 164, 10 τινὰ ἀπαρχὴν τῶν ἡμετέρων καρπῶν=a sort of first fruit of our [spiritual] harvest. LElliott-Binns, NTS 3, '56/57, 148–61). Here as **Rv 14:4** the emphasis is less on chronological sequence than on quality (schol. on Eur., Or. 96 ἀπαρχὴ ἐλέγετο οὐ μόνον τ. πρῶτον τῇ τάξει, ἀλλὰ καὶ τ. πρῶτον τ. τιμῇ). The orig. mng. is greatly weakened, so that ἀ. becomes almost = πρῶτος; of Christ ἀ. τῶν κεκοιμημένων *the first of those who have fallen asleep* **1 Cor 15:20;** cp. vs. **23** (HMontefiore, When Did Jesus Die? ET 62, '60, 53f; s. also BSpörlein, Die Leugnung der Auferstehung, '71 [1 Cor 15]); 1 Cl 24:1.

β. of things (Dio Chrys. 54 [71], 2 ἀπαρχαὶ τῆς σοφίας) τὴν ἀ. τοῦ πνεύματος ἔχοντες *since we possess the first fruits of the Spirit,* i.e. as much of the Spirit as has been poured out so far and a foretaste of things to come **Ro 8:23** (cp. Thieme 25f), but s. 2 below. διδόναι ἀπαρχὰς γεύσεώς τινος *give a foretaste of someth.* B 1:7.—ESanders, Jewish Law fr. Jesus to the Mishnah '90, 283–308.

❷ ***birth-certificate*** also suits the context of **Ro 8:23;** cp. Mitt-Wilck. II/2, 372, 4, 7; PFlor 57, 81; 86; 89; PTebt 316, 10; 49; 82; HJones, JTS 23, 1922, 282f; RTaubenschlag, Opera Minora 2, '59, 220–21 (identification card); L-S-J-M s.v. 7.—HBeer, Ἀπαρχή, diss., Würzb. 1914; EMoutsonlas: Sacris erudiri XV 5–14 (Steenbrugge, '64); COke, Int 11, '57, 455–60.—DELG s.v. ἄρχω A. O. Wilck I 345f §140. EDNT. M-M. TW. Sv.

ἅπας, ασα, αν intensive form of πᾶς 'all, the whole', pl. 'all together' (Hom.+. Beside πᾶς in Attic after consonants; for πᾶς after vowels, s. HDiels, GGA 1894, 298ff; but the distinction is not maintained in the NT: B-D-F §275; Rob. 771; s. also Mayser 161f. On its use w. the art. W-S. §20, 11.)

❶ used w. a subst and the art. **the totality of a mass or object, *whole, all*** ἅ. τὸν λαόν (cp. Jos., Ant. 7, 63; 211; Just., D. 77, 4 al.) *the whole people* (opp. an individual) **Lk 3:21;** cp. GPt 8:28=ASyn. 351, 7. ἅ. τὸ πλῆθος **Lk 8:37; 19:37; 23:1; Ac 25:24.** ἅ. τὸν βίον **Lk 21:4 v.l.** (for πάντα).ἅ. τὰ γενόμενα *all that had happened* **Mt 28:11.** τὴν ἐξουσίαν ταύτην ἅπασαν *this whole domain* **Lk 4:6.** ὁ λαὸς ἅ. (Jos., Ant. 6, 199; 8, 101) **19:48.** ἐν ἁπάσῃ τῇ πράξει αὐτοῦ *in all that he did* Hs 7:4.

❷ without a subst. (Just., A I, 15, 9; Ath. 1, 2), masc. ἅπαντες ***all, everybody, everything*** **Mt 24:39; Lk 5:26; 7:16 v.l.; 9:15; 21:4 v.l.; Ac 2:7; 4:31; 5:12,16; 16:3,28; 27:33; Gal 3:28 v.l.; Js 3:2.**—Neut. ἅπαντα *everything* (TestAbr A 12 p. 92, 18 [Stone p. 32]; Ar. 15, 3; Just., D. 60, 2 al.) **Mk 8:25; Lk 2:39 v.l.; 11:41 v.l.; 15:13 v.l.** ἔχειν ἅ. κοινά *have everything in common* **Ac 2:44; 4:32.** χρῄζειν τούτων ἅ. *need all this* **Mt 6:32.** Cp. D 3:2–6.—DELG s.v. πᾶς. M-M. TW.

ἀπασπάζομαι 1 aor. ἀπησπασάμην (Tob 10:12 S; Himerius, Eclog. in Phot. 11, 1 p. 194) ***take leave of, say farewell to*** τινά *someone* (Chariton 3, 5, 8) ἀπησπασάμεθα ἀλλήλους *we said farewell to one another* **Ac 21:6.** Abs. 20:1 D (s. FBlass, Acta apost. 1895 ad loc.).—TW.

ἀπατάω fut. ἀπαντήσω LXX; 1 aor. ἠπάτησα LXX; TestJud 12:3; Tat. 8, 3. Pass.: fut. ἀπατηθήσομι; aor. ἠπατήθην (s. ἀπάτη; Hom. et al.; not in ins; rare in pap [e.g. PSI 152, 24 (II AD) in a fragmentary context, perh. ἠπάτ[ων]; PLond IV, 1345, 13: sp. ηπαιτησας (VII AD)]; Epicurus p. 298, 29 Us.; Plut.; Epict. 4, 5, 32; Herodian 2, 1, 10; LXX; PsSol 16:8; TestSol, TestJob, Test12Patr; GrBar 4:8; ApcEsdr 2:15 p. 26, 18 Tdf.; ApcSed, ApcMos; Philo, Aet. M. 117; Joseph., Just., Tat., Ath.).

❶ ***deceive, mislead*** τινά τινι (Is 36:14) *someone with someth.* μηδεὶς ὑμᾶς ἀπατάτω κενοῖς λόγοις *let nobody deceive you w. empty words* **Eph 5:6** (cp. TestNapht 3:1; Jos., Vi. 302 λόγοις ἀ. τινὰ). ἀπατῶν αὐτοὺς τ. ἐπιθυμίαις τ. πονηραῖς Hs 6, 2, 1. ἀ. καρδίαν ἑαυτοῦ *deceive oneself* **Js 1:26** (cp. Job 31:27; Just., D. 141, 2 al.; Ath. 36, 2); Hs 6, 4, 1 and 4. W. acc. of pers. Dg 2:1; Hm 11:13. Pass. (Jos., Ant. 12, 20; w. the mng. 'be led astray' C. Ap. 2, 245) Ἀδὰμ οὐκ ἠπατήθη **1 Ti 2:14** (v.l. has the simplex also in ref. to Eve). ἀπατηθεὶς τῷ κάλλει τῶν γυναικῶν τούτων *led astray by the beauty of these women* Hs 9, 13, 9 (TestJud 12:3 ἠπάτησέ με τὸ κάλλος αὐτῆς. PsSol 16:8 μὴ ἀπατησάτω με κάλλος γυναικὸς παρανομούσης.—ἀ.='seduce sexually' as early as Eratosth. p. 22, 10).

❷ mid. ***enjoy oneself, live pleasurably*** (w. τρυφᾶν cp. Sir 14:16 and s. ἀπάτη 2) Hs 6, 4, 1; 6, 5, 3f.—DELG s.v. ἀπάτη. M-M. TW.

ἀπάτη, ης, ἡ (s. ἀπατάω; Hom.+).—❶ ***deception, deceitfulness*** (Jdth 9:10, 13; 4 Macc 18:8; Jos., Ant. 2, 300; SibOr 5, 405 ἀ. ψυχῶν) ἡ ἀ. τοῦ πλούτου *the seduction which comes from wealth* **Mt 13:22; Mk 4:19;** ἀ. τῆς ἁμαρτίας *deceitfulness of sin* **Hb 3:13** (note that sense 2 is also probable for the synoptic passages and Hb 3:13; cp. PRein inv. 2069 V, 73 LRobert, Hellenica XI/XII, '60, 5ff). ἀ. τοῦ κόσμου Dg 10:7 (cp. Herm. Wr. 13, 1 ἡ τοῦ κόσμου ἀπάτη). [τ]ὰς ἐπὶ τὴν ἀπάτην ἀγούσας *(paths?) that lead to deceit* AcPl Ha 9, 13 (the text is fragmentary, s. ed.'s note and also s. ἄγω 3 end); w. φιλοσοφία (cp. Heraclid. Crit., Descriptio Graeciae 1, 1 [p. 72, 15 Pfister]) *empty deceit* **Col 2:8.** ἐν πάσῃ ἀ. ἀδικίας *w. every kind of wicked deception* **2 Th 2:10** (of deceptive trickery, like Jos., Ant. 2, 284). ἐπιθυμία τ. ἀπάτης *deceptive desire* **Eph 4:22.** W. φιλαργυρία 2 Cl 6:4; w. εἰκαιότης Dg 4:6; listed w. other sins Hm 8:5. Personified (Hes., Theog. 224; Lucian, De Merc. Cond. 42) Hs 9, 15, 3.

❷ esp. (since Polyb. 2, 56, 12; 4, 20, 5; IPriene 113, 64 [84 BC; cp. Rouffiac 38f]; Moeris p. 65 ἀπάτη· ἡ πλάνη παρ' Ἀττικοῖς . . . ἡ τέρψις παρ' Ἕλλησιν; Philo, Dec. 55) ***pleasure, pleasantness*** that involves one in sin, w. τρυφή Hs 6, 2, 1; 6, 4, 4; 6, 5, 1 and 3f. Pl. (Ps.-Dicaearch. p. 104f. ψυχῆς ἀπάται) Hm 11:12; s 6, 2, 2 and 4; 6, 5, 6; (w. ἐπιθυμίαι) ἀπάται τοῦ αἰῶνος τούτου Hs 6, 3, 3 v.l. Hence ἐντρυφῶντες ἐν ταῖς ἀ. (v.l. ἀγάπαις; the same variant **Mk 4:19;** Eccl 9:6 v.l.; see AvHarnack, Z. Revision d. Prinzipien d. ntl. Textkritik 1916, 109f and ἀγάπη 2) *reveling in their lusts* **2 Pt 2:13.**—M-M. TW. Spicq.

ἀπατηλός, ή, όν (s. ἀπάτη; Hom. et al.; also 4 Macc 18:8 v.l.; Philo; Just., A II, 2, 11; Ath. 27, 2) ***deceptive*** ἀνδρὶ ξένῳ ἀπα[τηλοὺς] καὶ ποικίλους καὶ κενοὺς λόγους διδάσκοντι *a foreigner who makes deceptive, specious, and nonsensical statements* AcPl Ox 6, 11f (=Aa I 241, 14).

ἀπατρικός, όν ***without a father*** (otherwise unknown and mistakenly restored in Ox 1081, 34 α.[. . .ι]κου $\overline{\pi\rho\varsigma}$ as ἀπατρικοῦ πατρός; the ed. cites Dr. Bartlet's suggestion: ἀγγελικοῦ). Instead read ἀγεννήτου (s. SJCh 90, 12; s. also ἀγέννητος).—DELG s.v. πατήρ.

ἀπάτωρ, ορος (Soph. et al.; oft. in pap) ***fatherless, without a father*** of children who are orphaned, abandoned, estranged, or born out of wedlock; in our lit. only of Melchizedek (Gen 14:18ff) w. ἀμήτωρ, ἀγενεαλόγητος **Hb 7:3.** The context suggests that he is to be understood as a kind of transcendent being (as Pollux, Onom. 3, 25f ὁ οὐκ ἔχων μητέρα ἀμήτωρ, καθάπερ ἡ Ἀθηνᾶ, καὶ ὁ οὐκ ἔχων πατέρα ἀπάτωρ ὡς ὁ Ἥφαιστος; Anth. Pal. 15, 26; schol. on Theocr. 1, 3/4d Wendel [1914] of Pan; PGM 5, 282 of the god Horus; Ἀπάτωρα καὶ Δημιουργὸν αὐτὸν . . . καλοῦσιν Iren., 1, 51 [Harv. I 42, 12]; s. also ἀμήτωρ).—DELG s.v. πατήρ. M-M. TW. Sv.

ἀπαύγασμα, ατος, τό (s. αὐγάζω; Heliod. 5, 27, 4 φωτὸς ἀ.; TestAbr A 16 p. 97, 17 [Stone p. 42]; Philo; Wsd 7:26; Tat. 15, 3 τῆς . . . ὕλης καὶ πονηρίας [of hostile spirits]; Plut. has ἀπαυγασμός Mor. 83d and 934d; PGM 4, 1130 καταύγασμα) act. ***radiance, effulgence,*** in the sense of brightness from a source; pass., ***reflection,*** i.e. brightness shining back. The mng. cannot always be determined w. certainty. The pass. is prob. to be preferred in Plut. The act. seems preferable for Wsd and Philo (Op. Mundi 146, Spec. Leg. 4, 123, Plant. 50), corresp. to Hesychius: ἀ.=ἡλίου φέγγος. Philo uses the word of the relation of the Logos to God. Christ is described as ἀ. τῆς δόξης *radiance of his glory* **Hb 1:3** (the act. mng. in the Gk. fathers Orig.; Gregory of Nyssa; Theodoret; Chrysostom: φῶς ἐκ φωτός. Likew. Theodore of Mopsu.; Severian of Gabala; Gennadius of Constantinople: KStaab, Pauluskommentare '33, 201; 346; 421). For this ἀ. τῆς μεγαλωσύνης 1 Cl 36:2.—FDölger, AC I 1929, 269ff. DELG s.v. αὐγή.

ἀπαφρίζω (ἀφρίζω 'to foam'; Galen, CMG V 4, 2 p. 120, 3; 125, 21; Oribas. 5, 33, 4; Geopon. 8, 29; 32) ***cast off like foam*** τὶ **Jd 13 v.l.**—DELG s.v. ἀφρός.

ἀπαχθῆναι s. ἀπάγω.

ἀπέβαλον s. ἀποβάλλω.

ἀπέβην s. ἀποβαίνω.

ἀπέδειξα s. ἀποδείκνυμι.

ἀπέδετο Later Gk. for ἀπέδοτο; s. ἀποδίδωμι.

ἀπεδίδουν s. ἀποδίδωμι.

ἀπέθανον s. ἀποθνῄσκω.

ἀπεθέμην s. ἀποτίθημι.

ἀπεῖδον s. ἀφοράω.

ἀπείθεια, ας, ἡ (s. ἀπειθής; X., Mem. 3, 5, 5 et al.; ins; pap; 4 Macc 8:9, 18: 12:4; PsSol 17:20) ***disobedience,*** in our lit. always of disob. toward God (cp. Jos., Ant. 3, 316); somet. w. the connotation of ***disbelief*** in the Christian gospel (see ἀπειθέω). Those who oppose God are called υἱοὶ τῆς ἀ. **Eph 2:2; 5:6; Col 3:6** (some mss. om.; s. KKuhn, NTS 7, '61, 339 for Qumran parallels). Of disob. of Israelites **Ro 11:30; Hb 4:6, 11;** of all humanity **Ro 11:32.** Personified Hs 9, 15, 3.—DELG s.v. πείθομαι. M-M. TW.

ἀπειθέω (opp. πείθομαι; s. ἀπείθεια) impf. ἠπείθουν; 1 aor. ἠπείθησα (for ἀπιθέω [Hom.] since Aeschyl., Pla.+) ***disobey, be disobedient*** (cp. PYadin 24a, 10 [restored] of refusal); in our lit. disobedience is always toward God, God's ordinances, or revelation (like Eur., Or. 31; Pla., Leg. 741d; Lucian, Dial. Deor. 8, 1; SIG 736, 40 [92 BC] τὸν δὲ ἀπειθοῦντα ἢ ἀπρεπῶς ἀναστρεφόμενον εἰς τὸ θεῖον μαστιγούντω οἱ ἱεροί; Dt 1:26; 9:23; Josh 5:6; Is 36:5; 63:10; Bar 1:18f). W. dat. of pers. (Num 14:43 κυρίω) τῷ θεῷ (Diod. S. 5, 74, 4 ἀ. τοῖς θεοῖς; Hierocles 24, 473 τῷ θεῷ; Jos., Ant. 9, 249) **Ro 11:30,** cp. Pol 2:1. τῷ υἱῷ **J 3:36.**—W. dat. of thing (Diod. S. 5, 71, 5 τοῖς νόμοις) τῇ ἀληθείᾳ **Ro 2:8** (Theoph. Ant. 1, 14 p. 92, 5). τῷ εὐαγγελίῳ **1 Pt 4:17.** τῷ λόγῳ **2:8; 3:1.** τοῖς εἰρημένοις 1 Cl 59:1. τοῖς ἐμοῖς ἐλέγχοις 57:4 (Pr 1:25).—Abs. (Dicaearchus fgm. 23 [Athen. 13 p. 603b] ἀπειθήσας=disobedient) of members of a synagogue at Corinth **Ac 19:9.** Of a part of Israel **Ro 11:31.** Of people of Judea **15:31.** οἱ ἀπειθήσαντες Ἰουδαῖοι *the disobedient* (but see below, end) *Judeans* **Ac 14:2.** λαὸς ἀπειθῶν **Ro 10:21;** B 12:4 (both Is 65:2). οἱ ἀπειθοῦντες IMg 8:2; 1 Cl 58:1. Of gentiles οἱ ἀπειθήσαντες **Hb 11:31.**—Gener. **3:18; 1 Pt 3:20.** In a number of pass. NRSV and REB, among others, with less probability render ἀ. 'disbelieve' or an equivalent.—DELG s.v. πείθομαι. M-M. TW.

ἀπειθής, ές (s. ἀπειθέω) ***disobedient*** (so Thu. et al.; LXX; TestDan 5:11; Jos., Ant. 17, 186; Just., D. 120, 5; 140, 2).—ⓐ w. dat. of pers. γονεῦσιν (Theoph. Ant. I, 2 [p. 60, 30]) *to parents* **Ro 1:30; 2 Ti 3:2** (cp. Dt 21:18).—W. dat. of thing τῇ οὐρανίῳ ὀπτασίᾳ *to the heavenly vision* **Ac 26:19.**

ⓑ abs. (Num 20:10; Just., D. 120, 5) opp. δίκαιος **Lk 1:17;** w. βδελυκτός **Tit 1:16;** w. ἀνόητος, πλανώμενος **3:3.** Of the people of Israel λαὸς ἀ. B 12:4 (cod. Sin. [cp. Is 30:9; SibOr 3, 668] for ἀπειθοῦντα [Is. 65:2]).—DELG s.v. πείθομαι. M-M. TW.

ἀπειλέω (s. ἀπειλή) impf. ἠπείλουν; fut. 3 sg. ἀπειλήσει Is 66:14; 1 aor. mid. ἠπειλησάμην (on the mid. cp. B-D-F §316, 1); pass. inf. ἀπειληθῆναι LXX (Hom. et al.; pap, LXX; Jos., Ant. 5, 144; Test12Patr, Just.) ***threaten, warn*** τινί someone, foll. by μή and inf. *warn (them) no longer to* **Ac 4:17** (v.l. adds ἀπειλῇ). τὶ (4 Macc 9:5; Jos., Ant. 13, 143 πόλεμον) *with someth.* πῦρ MPol 11:2; cp. Just., A I, 2, 1 θάνατος. Abs., of Christ πάσχων οὐκ ἠπείλει *although he suffered he did not threaten* **1 Pt 2:23.**—B. 1279. M-M.

ἀπειλή, ῆς, ἡ (s. ἀπειλέω; Hom. et al.; pap, LXX; PsSol 17:25; TestJob 17:3; JosAs 7:5; 4 Esdr 8:23 fgm. c; ApcEsdr; Jos., Bell. 6, 257, Ant. 8, 362; Ath., R. 72, 9) ***threat*** ἐμπνέων ἀπειλῆς κ. φόνου *breathing murderous threats* **Ac 9:1** (CBurchard, ZNW 61, '70, 163–65). ἀνιέναι τὴν ἀ. *stop threatening* **Eph 6:9.** ἡ ἀ. τοῦ διαβόλου Hm 12, 6, 2. ἀπειλῇ ἀπειλεῖσθαι μή w. inf. *warn sharply* **Ac 4:17 v.l.** (s. ἀπειλέω). Pl. (SibOr 3, 71; 97) φυγεῖν τὰς ἀ. *escape the threats* 1 Cl 58:1. ἐφορᾶν ἐπὶ τὰς ἀ. **Ac 4:29.**—DELG s.v. ἀπειλέω. M-M.

I. ἄπειμι (s. εἰμί) ptc. ἀπών; fut. sg. ἀπέσται Pr 25:10 (Hom.+; ins, pap, LXX; Test12Patr; Jos., C. Ap. 2, 212; Just., A I, 21, 5) ***be absent/away*** πόρρω ἀ. ἀπό τινος *be far away fr. someone* 1 Cl 3:4 (v.l. ἀπέστη); 15:2 (v.l. ἀπέχει); 2 Cl 3:5 (v.l. ἀπέστην). Opp. παρών (Socrat., Ep. 7, 1; Ael. Aristid. 13, p. 222 D.; SIG 1044, 43; PTebt 317, 32; BGU 1080, 6ff; Wsd 11:11; 14:17) **2 Cor 10:11; 13:2;** ISm 9:2; cp. Pol 3:2. ἀπὼν θαρρῶ **2 Cor 10:1;** ἀ. γράφω **13:10;** ἀ. ἀκούω **Phil 1:27.** More specif. ἀ. τῷ σώματι *be absent in body* **1 Cor 5:3;** for this τῇ σαρκὶ ἄ. **Col 2:5**—M-M.

II. ἄπειμι (s. εἶμι) impf. ἀπῄειν (Hom.+) **to move from a position, *go away, go, come,*** *go away* ἀπό τινος *fr. someth.* (SIG 1218, 19). εἰς τὰ ὄρη AcPl Ha 5, 8. Simply *go, come* (Demetr.: 722 fgm. 1, Jac. εἰς Χανάαν; Jos., Ant. 14, 289) εἰς τ. συναγωγήν (cp. 4 Macc 4:8) **Ac 17:10.** εἰς τὴν δωδεκάφυλον GJs 1:3 (some mss., not pap). ἐν τῷ οἴκῳ 10:2; 16:3. πρὸς τὴν συγγενίδα 12:2; πρὸς τὸν ἱερέαν 15:2. ἄ. οὗ ἐὰν βούλησθε *wherever you wish* 1 Cl 54:2. ἀπῄει μετ' αὐτοῦ (the midwife) *went with him* (Joseph) GJs 19:1. Of the day *depart* (cp. Ins. 10, 1: Eranos 13, 1913, p. 87) 1 Cl 24:3.—DELG s.v. εἶμι.

ἀπεῖπον (s. εἶπον) 2 aor. (no present in use; LXX; Just.; Ath. 1:4), to which (since Hdt.; O. Wilck II, 1156, 3f; LXX; Nägeli 23) the mid. ἀπειπάμην belongs (on the form s. W-S. §13, 13 note); perf. pass. ptc. ἀπειρημένος 'forbidden' (4 Macc 1:33); inf. ἀπειρῆσθαι (Just., A I, 29, 2).

❶ ***forbid,*** act. Ox 1224 fgm. 2 verso I, 2.—❷ ***disown, renounce*** τὶ, mid. (cp. Hdt. 4, 120 συμμαχίην; Polyb. 33, 12, 5 φιλίαν; Job 6:14) ἀπειπάμεθα τὰ κρυπτὰ τ. αἰσχύνης *we have renounced the things that one hides out of a sense of shame* **2 Cor 4:2.**—DELG s.v. ἔπος. M-M.

ἀπείραστος, ον (s. πειράζω; Philod., Rhet. I p. 45, 3 Sudh.; Empirikerschule p. 91, 18 KDeichgräber [1930]; Galen: CMG V 4, 1, 1 p. 62, 30; Alciphron 2, 35, 3 Sch. after Cobet; Jos., Bell. 5, 364 and 7, 262 codd.) for the older ἀπείρατος (Pind. et al.) ***without temptation,*** either active = who does not tempt, or passive = who cannot be tempted. Of God ὁ θεὸς ἀ. ἐστιν κακῶν **Js 1:13,** certainly pass. because δέ in the next clause introduces a new thought, *God cannot be tempted to do evil* (Leontios 8 p. 17, 3 of God as One who cannot and dare not be tempted [cp. Eur., Bellerophon TGF 292, 7 εἰ θεοί τι δρῶσιν αἰσχρόν, οὐκ εἰσὶν θεοί=if gods do someth. shameful, they can't be gods]; for the gen. κακῶν cp. X., Cyr. 3, 3, 55 ἀπαίδευτος ἀρετῆς, and s. B-D-F §182, 3; Rob. 516). Of humans ἀνὴρ ἀδόκιμος ἀπείραστος (παρὰ θεῷ is added by Const. Apost. 2, 8, 2) *an untempted man is untried* Agr 21.—DELG s.v. πεῖρα. M-M. TW.

I. ἄπειρος, ον pert. to lack of knowledge or capacity to do someth., *unacquainted with, unaccustomed to* ('lacking the ability to make trial [s. πεῖρα] of'; Pind., Hdt., et al.; Epict. 2, 24, 3; OGI 669, 11; pap e.g. PSI 522, 4 [also s. Preis.]; LXX; Philo, Agr. 160 [a beginner is ἄ.], Op. M. 171; Jos., Bell. 6, 291; Iren. 1, 8, 1 [Harv. I 68, 5]), of an immature Christian ἄ. λόγου δικαιοσύνης *unacquainted w. the teaching about uprightness* **Hb 5:13** (the gen. as freq., e.g. PGiss 68, 17 ἄ. τῶν τόπων; Jos., Ant. 7, 336; Ath. 27, 1).—DELG s.v. πεῖρα. M-M. TW.

II. ἄπειρος, ον (cogn. πέρας; cp. ἀπέραντος) ***boundless*** (Pind., Hdt.+; OGI 383, 43 and 113 [I BC]; magical pap: PWarr 21:31; Herm. Wr. 3, 1; Philo; Jos., Ant. 4, 163; TestJud 13:4; TestLevi 2:8; JosAs 2:7 cod. A [Bat.] ἱματισμός . . . ἄ.; SibOr 3, 236; Just., Tat.) θάλασσα 1 Cl 20:6.—DELG πεῖραρ. Sv.

ἀπεκαλύφθην s. ἀποκαλύπτω.

ἀπεκατεστάθην, ἀπεκατέστην s. ἀποκαθίστημι.

ἀπεκδέχομαι (s. δέχομαι) impf. ἀπεξεδεχόμην ***await eagerly*** (so Alciphron 3, 4, 6; Heliod. 2, 35, 3; 7, 23, 5; Sext. Emp., Math. 2, 73; TestAbr A 16 p. 96, 23 [Stone p. 40]) τινά or τί : Onesiphorus went out to meet Paul on the road that leads to Lystra and *waited to welcome him* καὶ εἱστήκει ἀ[πεκδεχόμενος αὐτόν] AcPl Ant 13, 22 (restoration after AcPlTh 3 [Aa I 237, 5]); in our lit. always of Christian hope w. its var. objects: σωτῆρα **Phil 3:20;** Christ **Hb 9:28.**—τὴν ἀποκάλυψιν τῶν υἱῶν τοῦ θεοῦ *the revelation of the sons of God* **Ro 8:19;** cp. **1 Cor 1:7.** υἱοθεσίαν **Ro 8:23** (for this and other passages JSwetnam suggests *infer, understand in a certain sense:* Biblica 48, '67, 102–8). ἐλπίδα δικαιοσύνης **Gal 5:5.**—Abs. *wait* δι' ὑπομονῆς *wait patiently* **Ro 8:25.** Of God's forbearance **1 Pt 3:20.**—M-M. TW.

ἀπεκδύομαι 1 aor. ptc. ἀπεκδυσάμενος (s. ἐκδύω; Proclus on Pla., Rep. I p. 16, 10 WKroll; Jos., Ant. 6, 330 Cod. Marc.; Eustath, ad Il., p. 664, 23).

❶ ***take off, strip off*** of clothes (opp. ἐπενδύομαι) only fig. (of σῶμα Dox. Gr. 573, 22) τὸν παλαιὸν ἄνθρωπον *the old (sinful) self* **Col 3:9** (cp. Philo, Mut. Nom. 233 ἐκδύεσθαι τὰ ἁμαρτήματα). Perh. fig. **Col 2:15,** but s. 2.

❷ ***disarm*** τινά (on the mid. for the act. s. B-D-F §316, 1; Rob. 805) τὰς ἀρχὰς καὶ τ. ἐξουσίας *the principalities and powers* **Col 2:15.**—S. 1 and on θριαμβεύω.—DELG s.v. δύω. TW.

ἀπέκδυσις, εως, ἡ (s. ἀπεκδύομαι; found nowhere independently of Paul; does not reappear until Eustath. ad Il. p. 91, 28; s. Nägeli 50) ***removal, stripping off*** of clothes; only fig. ἐν τῇ ἀ. τοῦ σώματος τ. σαρκός *in stripping off your fleshly* (i.e. sinful) *body,* because Christians have, as it were, a new body (*with no material circumcision that cuts flesh from the body* Moffatt) **Col 2:11.**—DELG s.v. δύω. M-M. TW.

ἀπεκριθείς, ἀπεκρίθην s. ἀποκρίνομαι.

ἀπεκτάνθην, ἀπέκτεινα s. ἀποκτείνω.

ἀπέλαβον s. ἀπολαμβάνω.

ἀπελαύνω fut. ἀπελάσω Ezk. 34:12; 1 aor. ἀπήλασα; pf. pass. 3 sg. ἀπελήλαται (s. ἐλαύνω; trag., Hdt.+; Cyranides p. 101, 2 δαίμονας; pap; LXX; TestBenj 8:3; Joseph.; Ath., R. 67, 5) ***drive away*** τινὰ ἀπό τινος (X., Cyr. 3, 2, 16; Ezk 34:12) αὐτοὺς ἀπὸ τοῦ βήματος *them away from the tribunal* **Ac 18:16** (D ἀπέλυσεν.—Cp. Jos., Bell. 1, 245 τ. λοιποὺς ἀπήλασεν).—πάντα θήξει ὑπὸ τοῦ δρόμου αὐτῶν ἀπηλαύνετο *then all at once everything took its course again* GJs 18:3 (not pap; textual trad. uncertain: variants include διελαύνω, ἐλαύνω, συνελαύνω, ἡσυχάζω).—M-M.

ἀπελεγμός, οῦ, ὁ (ἀπελέγχω 'expose, refute', s. ἐλέγχω; found only in Christian writings) **criticism relating to questionable conduct,** ***refutation, exposure, discredit*** εἰς ἀ. ἐλθεῖν (Vulg. in redargutionem venire) *come into disrepute* **Ac 19:27** (GKilpatrick, JTS 10, '59, 327 [reproof, public criticism]).—M-M.

ἀπελεύθερος, ου, ὁ (s. ἐλεύθερος; since Ps.-X., De Rep. Athen. 1, 10; X.; Pla.; oft. in pap and ins; Jos., Ant. 7, 263; 14, 75; s. Hahn 241, 10; 244, 4; 246, 3; Thalheim in Pauly-W. VII 95ff; JBaunack, Philol 69, 1910, 473ff) ***freedperson*** Διόφαντος AcPl Ha 2, 9; τῇ ἀ. Εὐβούλᾳ 3, 3; fig., of Christians ἀ. κυρίου *a freedperson of the Lord,* because he has freed us fr. the powers of darkness, the slaveholders of this age **1 Cor 7:22.** Likew. ἀ. Ἰησοῦ Χριστοῦ IRo 4:3 (Epict. 1, 19, 9 ἐμὲ ὁ Ζεὺς ἐλεύθερον ἀφῆκεν.—Dssm., LO 277; 323 [LAE 332f]; Magie 70; JWeiss on 1 Cor 7:22). WElert, TLZ 72, '47, 265ff.—M-M. TW.

ἀπελεύσομαι, ἀπεληλύθειν, ἀπελθών s. ἀπέρχομαι.

ἀπέλιπον s. ἀπολείπω.

Ἀπελλῆς, οῦ, ὁ (OGI 265, 12; 444, 7; IPriene 248; Philo, Leg. ad Gai. 203ff; Jos., Ant. 12, 270) ***Apelles,*** greeted in **Ro 16:10.** The name was common among Jews (cp. credat Judaeus Apella: Hor., Sat. 1, 5, 100). **Ac 18:24** and **19:1 v.l.** for Ἀπολλῶς; s. B-D-F §29, 4; 125, 1.—M-M.

ἀπελπίζω 1 aor. ἀπήλπισα LXX; pf. ptc. ἀπηλπικώς **Eph 4:19 v.l.,** ἀφηλπικώς Hv 3, 12, 2 (as BGU 1844, 13 [I BC]; ἀ. τῆς ζωῆς τοῦ θεοῦ Iren. 1, 13, 7 [Harv. I 126, 5]; s. Reinhold 36) (s. ἐλπίζω; Hyperid. 5, 35; Epicurus p. 111, 13 [62, 6 Us.]; Polyb. 1, 19, 12; Diod. S. 17, 106, 7 et al.; SIG 1173, 7; PCairZen 642, 4 [III BC]; LXX; En 103:10; Jos., Bell. 4, 397; 5, 354).

❶ ***despair*** abs. **Eph 4:19 v.l.** ἀ. ἑαυτόν *despair of oneself* Hv 3, 12, 2. Pass.: in act. sense (LXX; En 103:10) ἀπηλπισμένος (Is 29:19) *despairing* 1 Cl 59:3.

❷ ***expect back*** **Lk 6:35** δανείζετε μηδὲν ἀπελπίζοντες, because of the contrast w. παρ' ὧν ἐλπίζετε λαβεῖν vs. 34 (in a play on words, 'hoping nothing back'), demands the meaning *lend, expecting nothing in return* (whether in kind or in other goods or services) which, although it is contrary to contemporary usage, is quotable fr. Gk. lit. at least since Chrysostom, and then introduced widely through the Vulg. W. the v.l. μηδένα *without disappointing anyone* (=without causing anyone to despair).—M-M. TW. Spicq.

ἀπέναντι (s. ἔναντι; Polyb. 1, 86, 3+; pap since III BC [PPetr II, 17 (3), 3; s. Mayser 242; 457]; ins since II BC [Priene]; LXX; TestJob 34:5; JosAs 24:19; ApcMos 29; JWackernagel, Hellenistica 1907, 3ff).

❶ **in a position that faces against an object or other position,** ***opposite***—ⓐ as adv. σταθεὶς … ἀπέν[αντι πρὸς ἀνατολὰς προσηύ]ξατο *Paul stood facing east and prayed* AcPl Ha 10, 21 (κατέναντι Aa I 115, 13); [καὶ ἀπέ]ναντι ἱστήκει = εἱστήκει (the light-bearer) *stood opposite* 3, 30.

ⓑ used as prep. w. gen. *opposite* someone or someth.—**α.** strictly of place (Diod. S. 18, 34, 6 ἀ. τῆς Μέμφεως) καθήμεναι ἀ. τοῦ τάφου *opposite the tomb* **Mt 27:61;** cp. **Mk 12:41 v.l.** and **Mt 21:2 v.l.** (SIG 756, 17f ἀ. τῆς εἰσόδου; PGrenf I, 21, 14; Jdth 3:9; 7:3, 18); *before, in the presence of* someone (cp. 1 Macc 6:32) ἀ. τοῦ ὄχλου *before the crowd* **Mt 27:24 v.l.** (for κατέναντι); ἀ. πάντων ὑμῶν **Ac 3:16.** ἀ. Ἀρτεμύλλας AcPl Ha 3, 11. βλέπω ἀ. μου *I see before me* Hv 2, 1, 3.

β. fig. ἀ. τῶν ὀφθαλμῶν αὐτῶν *before their eyes* (לְנֶגֶד עֵינָיו)=with them **Ro 3:18** (Ps 13:3; 35:2). ἀ. τ. ὀ. μου (cp. Sir 27:23)=so that I see it 1 Cl 8:4 (Is 1:16); cp. Pol 6:2.

❷ **marker of hostility or strong opposition,** ***against, contrary to*** (Sir 37:4) ἀ. τῶν δογμάτων Καίσαρος πράσσειν *act contrary to the decrees of Caesar* **Ac 17:7.**—DELG s.v. ἄντα 2. M-M.

ἀπενεγκεῖν, ἀπενεχθῆναι s. ἀποφέρω.

ἀπέπεσα s. ἀποπίπτω.

ἀπέπλευσα s. ἀποπλέω.

ἀπεπνίγην s. ἀποπνίγω.

ἀπέραντος, ον (cp. περαίνω 'to complete, finish'; Pind., Thu.+; Herm. Wr. 1, 11; 4, 8 p. 43, 20; Job 36:26; 3 Macc 2:9; Philo, Congr. Erud. Gr. 53; Jos., Ant. 17, 131; Just., A I, 28, 1=D. 119, 5 αἰῶνα; τὸ ἀπέραντον Iren. 1, 17, 2 [Harv. I 168, 6]) ***endless, limitless*** ὠκεανὸς ἀ. ἀνθρώποις *the ocean, whose limits can never be reached by humans* 1 Cl 20:8 (cp. 3 Macc 2:9); γενεαλογίαι **1 Ti 1:4** (Polyb. 1, 57, 3 of tiresome detailed enumeration). Ox 1081, 6f is prob. to be read τ[ῶν ἀ]περάντων [ἀ]κο[ύει]ν (=SJCh 89, 5f): (one who has ears) *to hear the things that are without limits/that never end.*—DELG s.v. πεῖραρ. Spicq.

ἀπερινόητος, ον (περινοέω 'consider a matter thoroughly'; Epicurus p. 10, 5 Us.; Sext. Emp., Pyrrh. 2, 70 ed. Mutschm. v.l.; Damascius, De Princ. 4; TestSol 1:2 C; ParJer 9:6 [of God]; Philo, Mut. Nom. 15 [of God]; PGM 4, 1138) ***incomprehensible*** of the divine λόγος Dg 7:2.—DELG s.v. νόος.

ἀπερίσπαστος, ον (s. περισπάω; Polyb. 2, 20, 10; 4:18, 6; Diod. S. 17, 9, 4; pap e.g. BGU 1057, 22 [I BC]; POxy 898, 15; PLond 932, 9 [also s. Preis.; Wsd 16:11; Sir 41:1; s. Nägeli 30) ***not distracted*** ἀ. διανοίᾳ *with undisturbed mind* IEph 20:2 (cp. Epict. 3, 22, 69; Diod. S. 40, 3, 7).—DELG s.v. σπάω.

ἀπερισπάστως adv. of ἀπερίσπαστος (Polyb. 2, 20, 10; 4, 18, 6; Epict. 1, 29, 59) ***without distraction*** πρὸς τὸ εὐπάρεδρον τ. κυρίῳ ἀ. *that you might adhere faithfully to the Lord without distraction* **1 Cor 7:35** (on the theme, s. Epict. 3, 22, 69 ἀπερίσπαστον εἶναι δεῖ τὸν Κυνικὸν ὅλον πρὸς τῇ διακονίᾳ τοῦ θεοῦ; for this reason he should keep himself free from marriage and all other earthly obligations, cp. 2 [4] Esdr 16:40–45. Diod. S. 40, 3, 7 Moses places the priests on a higher economic level than nonpriests, ἵνα ἀπερίσπαστοι προσεδρεύωσι ταῖς τοῦ θεοῦ τιμαῖς). DBalch, 1 Cor 7:32–35 and Stoic Debates about Marriage, Anxiety, and Distraction: JBL 102, '83, 429–39. S. ἀμέριμνος.—M-M. Spicq.

ἀπερίτμητος, ον (s. περιτέμνω; oft. LXX; Philo; Jos., Bell. 1, 34, Ant. 20, 45; in Plut., Mor. 495c=unmutilated).

❶ lit. ***uncircumcised*** (so also PEdgar 84, 14=Sb 6790, 14 [257 BC]; Just.) ἔθνη ἀπερίτμητα ἀκροβυστίᾳ (v.l. ἀκροβυστίαν) *gentiles w. uncircumcised foreskin* B 9:5a (Jer 9:25).

❷ fig. ***obdurate,*** ἀ. καρδίαις καὶ τοῖς ὠσίν *uncir. in heart and ears* **Ac 7:51** (after Lev 26:41; Jer 6:10; Ezk 44:7, 9); ἀ. καρδίας B 9:5b (Jer 9:25b). Cp. Dssm., B 151 (BS 153).—DELG s.v. τέμνω. M-M. TW.

ἀπέρχομαι fut. ἀπελεύσομαι; aor. ἀπῆλθον; 3 pl. ἀπῆλθαν **J 11:46** P[66]; GJs 9:1 [s. B-D-F §81, 3]; ἀπήλθασιν GJs 10:1; 24:1; -οσαν Jdth 13:4; cp. -ωσαν GJs 23:2; pf. ἀπελήλυθα **Js 1:24,** ptc. ἀπεληλυθώς Hs 9, 5, 4; plpf. ἀπεληλύθειν **J 4:8;** s. B-D-F §101 ἔρχεσθαι; sim. W-S. §15 (Hom.+).

❶ **to move from a ref. point,** of pers. or things—ⓐ ***go away, depart,*** w. no indication of place (1 Macc 9:36; 2 Macc 14:34; 1 Esdr 4:11) **Mt 8:21; 13:25; 16:4; Mk 5:20; Ac 10:7; 28:29 v.l.; Js 1:24.**—Ptc. ἀπελθών w. ind., subj., or impv. of another verb=*go away and* (Epict. index Sch.; Gen 21:14, 16 al.) **Mt 13:28, 46; 18:30; 25:18, 25; Mk 6:27, 37; Lk 5:14.**—W. indication of place or person ἀπό τινος (Thu. 8, 92, 2; UPZ 61, 6f [161 BC] ἀφ᾽ ὑμῶν ἀπελήλυθα; Epict. 3, 15, 11; 3 Km 21:36; Tob 14:8): ἀπὸ τ. ὁρίων αὐτῶν **Mk 5:17.** ἀπ᾽ αὐτῆς **Lk 1:38.** ἀπ᾽ αὐτῶν **2:15; 8:37.**—ἔξω τοῦ συνεδρίου **Ac 4:15** (cp. Jdth 6:12). In a ship **J 6:22.**

ⓑ ***go*** (opp. ἐξέρχεται GrBar 9:2; πόθεν ἔρχει καὶ ποῦ ἀπέρχει TestAbr B 2, p. 106, 4ff [Stone p. 60] cod. C) w. indication of place εἰς (Simplicius in Epict. p. 134, 51 ἀ. εἰς τὸ ἱερόν): (on **Mt 4:24** s. 3); εἰς ἔρημον τόπον **Mk 1:35;** cp. **6:36, 46; 7:24; Mt 8:33; 14:15;** but ἐπὶ τὸν τόπον **Lk 23:33 v.l.** εἰς τὸν οἶκον **Mt 9:7; Mk 7:30; Lk 1:23;** Hs 9, 11, 2; εἰς τὴν Γαλιλαίαν **Mt 28:10; J 4:3, 43 v.l.** εἰς Σπανίαν **Ro 15:28;** cp. **2 Cor 1:16 v.l.** (for διελθεῖν). **Gal 1:17. J 6:66** s. b end. ἐπί τι (Jos., Vi. 151): ἐπὶ τὸ μνημεῖον **Lk 24:24** (cp. 3 Km 19:19 v.l.; Epict. 4, 7, 30). ἐν: Hs 1:6 (cp. Diod. S. 23, 18, 5 ἀπῆλθεν ἐν Μεσσήνῃ; Pel.-Leg. p. 7, 3; Epict. 2, 20, 33 ἀπελθεῖν ἐν βαλανείῳ). W. the simple dat. (PFay 113, 12 [100 AD] τῇ πόλει πέμψας) ποίῳ τόπῳ ἀπῆλθεν Hv 4, 3, 7.—Of a possessive spirit/demon (Thrasyllus [I AD]: 622 fgm. 1, 2, 3 Jac. [in Ps- Plut., Fluv. 16, 2]; PGM 13, 244) ἀ. εἰς τοὺς χοίρους **Mt 8:32.**—ἀ. πρός τινα (PFay 123, 19 [100 AD]; BGU 884 II, 13f; 1 Km 25:5; 1 Macc 7:20) *come* or *go to someone* **Mt 14:25 v.l.; Mk 3:13; Rv 10:9.** Perh. also πρὸς αὐτούς **J 20:10** (v.l. ἑαυτούς s. ἑαυτοῦ), which may be a colloquial expression = rejoined their party or group, i.e. the disciples (so Twentieth Century NT). The rendering of NSRV et al., 'returned to their homes', seems improbable (cp. CBarrett, Comm. ad loc.) in view of the description of the huddled disciples vs. 19. What appears to be 'loose' writing (taking a reader's knowledge of the story line for granted) is characteristic of numerous displays of colloquial syntax in John's gospel.—The v.l. (πρὸς) ἑαυτούς **20:10** gives the mng. *go home,* as πρὸς ἑαυτὸν **Lk 24:12** (v.l. αὐτόν). On these two pass. s. FNeirynck, ETL 54, '78, 104–18; RBorger, GGA 130f; idem, TU 52, '87, 34; for the rdg. αὐτούς N[25] in **J 20:10** cp. Jos., Ant. 8, 124; but s. also Metzger 254, 615f.—**J 16:7** πρὸς τὸν πατέρα is to be supplied from the context (PPetr II, 13 [19], 7 [252 BC] εἰς θεοὺς ἀπελθεῖν).—Also of a journey in a boat εἰς τὸ πέραν *go over to the opposite side* **Mt 8:18; Mk 8:13.** εἰς ἔρημον τόπον **Mk 6:32.** W. no place indicated (the context supplies the goal as POxf 16, 16: to a festival) **Lk 17:23.**—W. purpose inf. (s. ἔρχομαι 1aε) GJs 9:3.—Of stones, w. connotation of being appropriate *go* εἰς τ. οἰκοδομήν *into the building* Hs 9, 5, 3 and 4; 9, 14, 2.—Abs. ἀ. εἰς τὰ ὀπίσω *draw back* a short distance **J 18:6.** For **6:66** s. 5.

❷ **to discontinue as a condition or state,** of diseases, etc. (Cebes 14, 3 οὐ μὴ ἀπέλθῃ ἀπ᾽ αὐτῶν ἡ κακία; Ex 8:25) ἀπῆλθεν ἀπ᾽ αὐτοῦ ἡ λέπρα *the leprosy left him* **Mk 1:42; Lk 5:13;** ἡ ὀπώρα ἀ. ἀπὸ σοῦ *your fruit is gone* **Rv 18:14.**—Gener. *pass away* (SSol 2:11) **Rv 9:12; 11:14; 21:1, 4.**

❸ **to go from a source and spread out,** ***go out,*** of a message *go out and spread* εἰς ὅλην τ. Συρίαν **Mt 4:24.**

❹ **to endeavor to attain someth.,** ***go after,*** of the Sodomites ἀ. ὀπίσω σαρκὸς ἑτέρας *go after flesh other than their own,* i.e., as humans soliciting sexual relations with transcendent figures **Jd 7.**

❺ **to abandon an association w. someone,** ***go off, go away, leave*** ἀπῆλθον εἰς ὀπίσω **J 6:66.**

❻ idiom, ἀ. ὀπίσω τινός (Job 21:33) **to leave a place to become an adherent of someone,** ***go after, follow someone*** of the disciples **Mk 1:20;** of the world **J 12:19.**—DELG s.v. ἐλεύσομαι. M-M. TW.

ἀπεστάλην, ἀπέσταλκα, ἀπέστειλα s. ἀποστέλλω.

ἀπέστην, ἀπέστησα s. ἀφίστημι.

ἀπεστράφην s. ἀποστρέφω.

ἀπέχω 2 aor. ἀπέσχον; pf. 3 sg. ἀπέσχηκεν LXX; fut. mid. ἀφέξομαι; aor. ἀπεσχόμην LXX; inf. ἀποσχέσθαι; pf. 1 pl. ἀπεσχήμεθα 1 Km 21:6 al. (Hom.+; ins, pap, LXX, En, TestAbr A, Test12Patr; ParJer 7:37; Philo, Joseph., Just., Ath.).

❶ **to receive in full what is due,** ***to be paid in full, receive in full,*** act., commercial t.t. = 'provide a receipt for a sum paid in full', used both lit. and fig. (Callim., Epigr. 50, 4 [Pf.] of a nurse who receives thanks in the form of a memorial; SIG[2] 845, 7 [200 BC] τὰν τιμὰν ἀπέχει; M. Ant. 9, 42 ἀπέχει τὸ ἴδιον. Oft. pap and ostraca; s. Dssm., NB 56 [BS 229]; LO 88ff [LAE 110f]; Erman, APF 1, 1901, 77ff; Mayser 487; O. Wilck I 86; Nägeli 54f; Anz 318f; Gen 43:23; Num 32:19; Jos., Bell. 1, 596 ἀ. τῆς ἀσεβείας τὸ ἐπιτίμιον) τὸν μισθόν (Plut., Sol. 90 [22, 4], Mor. 334a) **Mt 6:2, 5, 16;** τὴν παράκλησιν **Lk 6:24;** πάντα **Phil 4:18;** τὸ τέλειον τῆς γνώσεως *perfect knowledge* B 13:7; ἀ. τὴν ἀποκάλυψιν *to have received the revelation* Hv 3, 13, 4.—Sim. **Phlm 15** ἵνα αἰώνιον αὐτὸν ἀπέχῃς *that you might have him back forever* (opp. χωρίζεσθαι πρὸς ὥραν). Some would here put the difficult impers. ἀπέχει in the sense *the account is closed* **Mk 14:41;** s. JdeZwaan, Exp. 6th ser., 12, 1905, 459–72, who takes the informant of vs. 42 as the subj. *he has received the money.* S. 2 and 3.

❷ **to meet the need of the moment,** ***to suffice, be enough,*** Vulg. has for ἀπέχει **Mk 14:41** 'sufficit' *it is enough,* which is supported by some comparatively late evidence (Anacreontea Carmina 16, 33 [Preis., West, Campbell]; PStras 4, 19 note [550 AD]; PLond 1343, 38 [709 AD] dub. l.) and is followed in numerous translations, incl. REV, NRSV ('Enough!'); that the expression is not found in this sense in other lit. is not surprising, for it is a colloquialism that emerges, as in the case of the Anacreontea, in dramatic statement. In this instance, as w. ἀπελπίζω (Lk 6:35) q.v., context is a strong semantic determinant.

❸ The rather freq. expr. οὐδὲν ἀπέχει='nothing hinders' (Pla., Cra. 23 p. 407b; Plut., Mor. 433a; 680e) would suggest for ἀπέχει in **Mk 14:41** *that is a hindrance* (referring to the extreme drowsiness of the disciples at the decisive moment). But s. 1 and 2.—Ms. D has ἀ. τὸ τέλος *this is the end* (B-D-F §129; JWackernagel, Syntax. I[2] [1926] 119. Cp. Kaibel 259, 4 [II AD] ἀπέσχε τέλος [=death]. MBlack, An Aramaic Approach, '46, 16f, suggests an Aram. background).—GBoobyer, NTS 2, '55, 44–48 'he (Judas) is taking possession of' me.

❹ **to be at some distance from a position,** ***be distant,*** intr. (Hdt. et al.; PStras 57, 6; PLille 1, 5; 2, 2; Jos., Ant. 5, 161; Just., A I, 34, 2; Ath. 32, 1) αὐτοῦ μακρὰν ἀπέχοντος *when he was* *still far away* **Lk 15:20** (Diod. S. 12, 33, 4 μακρὰν ἀπ.; Gen 44:4; Jo 4:8; En 32:2). W. indication of the place from which (as 1 Macc 8:4; 2 Macc 11:5) οὐ μακρὰν ἀπέχων ἀπὸ τ. οἰκίας *being not far fr. the house* **Lk 7:6;** cp. MPol 5:1; of a ship at some distance from the land **Mt 14:24** (as Michel 466, 9 ἀπέχον ἀπὸ τῆς γῆς). W. the exact distance given (so since Thu. 2, 5, 2) κώμη ἀπέχουσα σταδίους ἑξήκοντα ἀπὸ Ἰερουσαλήμ *sixty stades fr. Jerusalem* **Lk 24:13** (Demetr. of Kallatis [200 BC]: 85 fgm. 2 Jac. ἀπεχούσης τῆς νήσου ἀπὸ τῆς ἠπείρου σταδίους υ΄. Cp. the comic poet Euphro [III BC] 11, 3 Kock; Appian, Ital. 5 §1; 2 Macc 12:29; Jos., Bell. 2, 516; Just., A I, 34, 2).—Fig. πόρρω ἀ. ἀπό τινος (=רחק מן) *be far from someone* **Mt 15:8; Mk 7:6** (both Is 29:13); so also PEg[2] 57f.

❺ **to avoid contact w. or use of someth.,** ***keep away, abstain, refrain from*** mid. w. gen. of thing (Hom. et al.; SIG 768, 16 [31 BC]; PHerm 52, 21; StudPal V, 52, 21; 1 Esdr 6:26; Wsd 2:16; σου PsSol 8:32; τούτου TestAbr A 2 p. 79, 8 [Stone p. 6]; Jos., Bell. 2, 581, Ant. 11, 101; Just., A II, 7, 7 al.; Ath.) εἰδωλοθύτων καὶ αἵματος καὶ πνικτῶν καὶ πορνείας *abstain fr. things offered to idols, blood, things strangled, and irregular sexual union* **Ac 15:29** (s. Lev 18:6–30), cp. vs. **20** (s. αἷμα 1b). πάσης ἀδικίας (Hyperid., fgm. 210 τ. ἀδικημάτων; SIG 1268 I, 18 [III BC] κακίας ἀπέχου; Ath. 1, 2 τοῦ ἀδικεῖν) Pol 2:2; cp. 6:1, 3; Hv 1, 2, 4; 2, 2, 3; 3, 8, 4; m 3:5; Dg 4:6. τῶν κακῶν βοτανῶν IPhld 3:1; cp. ITr 6:1. βρωμάτων **1 Ti 4:3.** εὐχαριστίας κ. προσευχῆς *keep away fr. the Lord's Supper and prayer* ISm 7:1; the response to those who absent themselves from the Lord's meal is to discontinue social relations with them, vs. 2 (Schol. Pl. Euthyphr. 2 A ἀπέχεσθαι μυστηρίων=remain aloof from the Mysteries). τῶν σαρκικῶν ἐπιθυμιῶν **1 Pt 2:11;** D 1:4. τῆς γλώσσης=*control the tongue* Hv 2, 2, 3. λατρείας Dg 3:2.—W. ἀπό τινος (oft. LXX; En 104:6; TestAbr A 4 p. 81, 4 [Stone p. 10]; EpArist 143; w. ἐκ ParJer 7:37 [7, 32 Harris]): ἀπὸ τῆς πορνείας **1 Th 4:3;** cp. **Ac 15:20** (v.l. ἀπό); ἀπὸ παντὸς εἴδους πονηροῦ *fr. every kind of evil* **1 Th 5:22.** ἀπὸ παντὸς κακοῦ 1 Cl 17:3 (Job 1:1, 8; 2:3). ἀπέχεσθε ἀπὸ τ. ἀνθρώπων *keep hands off the men* **Ac 5:39** D.—Pol 5:3; Hm 2:3; 4, 1, 3 and 9; 5, 1, 7; 5, 2, 8; 7:3; 9:12; 11:4, 8, 21; 12, 1, 3; 12, 2, 2; s 4:5.—DELG s.v. ἔχω. M-M. TW. Spicq.

ἀπήγαγον s. ἀπάγω.

ἀπηγξάμην s. ἀπάγχω.

ἀπῆεσαν s. ἄπειμι II.

ἀπήλασα s. ἀπελαύνω.

ἀπῆλθα, ἀπῆλθον s. ἀπέρχομαι.

ἀπηλλάχθαι s. ἀπαλλάσσω.

ἀπήρθη s. ἀπαίρω.

ἀπίδω s. ἀφοράω.

ἀπιστέω impf. ἠπίστουν; 1 aor. ἠπίστησα; pass. ἠπιστήθην (Just., A I, 33, 2; Ath. 32:2) (s. ἄπιστος; Hom. et al.; LXX, TestSol; TestAbr A 6 p. 83, 24 [Stone p. 14]; TestLevi 4:1; Philo; Just.; Ath.).

❶ ***disbelieve, refuse to believe,*** intr.—ⓐ gener. (POxy 471, 4 [II AD]; Jos., Ant. 2, 58); **Mk 16:11; Lk 24:41.** ἠπίστουν *refused to believe* **Ac 28:24.** ἀ. τινι *someone* (Jos., Ant. 2, 330) **Lk 24:11.**—SIG 1168, 24 (w. verb for 'sneer'); 30; 31; Philo, Mos. 1, 212; 2, 261 show the transition to usage

ⓑ in description of response to a deity or divine activity or to reports about divine activity (Iambl., Vi. Pyth. 28, 148 περὶ θεῶν μηδὲν θαυμαστὸν ἀπιστεῖν. Herm. Wr. 9, 10; Wsd 1:2; 10:7; 18:13; 2 Macc 8:13; Jos., Ant. 2, 270) ὁ ἀπιστήσας *one who gives no credence (to the message)* **Mk 16:16;** οἱ ἀπιστοῦντες *the unbelievers* (Iambl., Vi. Pyth. 28, 139) **1 Pt 2:7;** IEph 18:1.

❷ ***not believe in someone,*** trans. οἵτινες τὸν οὕτως ἀναστάντα ἀπιστοῦσι *who do not believe in the one who thus rose* AcPlCor 2:25 (cp. Just., A I, 33, 2 [J 14:29]; Ath. 12, 3 ἀπιστούμεθα θεοσεβεῖν). In reciprocity-shame-oriented Mediterranean societies negative attitudes and responses in the face of divine beneficence merit strong rebuke.

❸ ***be unfaithful*** of one lacking a sense of obligation (X., An. 2, 6, 19 of disloyal soldiers) of relation of humans to God or Jesus **Ro 3:3; 2 Ti 2:13.**—DELG s.v. πείθομαι. M-M. TW.

ἀπιστία, ας, ἡ (s. ἀπιστέω; Hes., Hdt. et al.; LXX, Philo, Joseph.; Just.; Tat. 32, 2; Ath. R. 60, 15 al.; s. Mayser 11f, 130)

❶ **unwillingness to commit oneself to another or respond positively to the other's words or actions,** ***lack of belief, unbelief*** (Mitt-Wilck. I/2, 155, 11; Jos., Ant. 2, 327; 19, 127) in our lit. always with God or divine action as referent (cp. Cercidas Iamb. [III BC], fgm. 18 II, 8 Coll. Alex. p. 217 [=Anon. in turpilucrum 74: AnthLG, Diehl[3] fasc.3=Knox 1929 p. 234]; Plut., Coriol. 232 [38, 4], Alex. 706 [75, 2] ἀ. πρὸς τὰ θεῖα καὶ καταφρόνησις αὐτῶν, De Superstit. 2 p. 165b; Ael. Aristid. 47, 66 K.=23 p. 462 D.; Philo, Leg. ad Gai. 118 ἀ. πρὸς τὸν τοῦ κόσμου παντὸς εὐεργέτην [w. ἀχαριστία], Mut. Nom. 201 al.; Jos., Ant. 10, 142). As response to Jesus by inhabitants of Nazareth **Mt 13:58; Mk 6:6;** a parent of a possessed pers. **9:24;** disciples **Mt 17:20 v.l.** (for ὀλιγοπιστίαν); of some Judeans [ἀ]πιστεί[α] PEg[2] 19; of Israelites toward God **Ro 11:20** (τῇ ἀπιστίᾳ=because of their unbelief; ACharue, L'Incrédulité des Juifs dans le NT 1929; on the dat. of cause Schmid III 57; IV 59; M. Ant. 3, 1; ins in ENachmanson, Eranos 11, 1911, 220–25), **23; Hb 3:19.** διακρίνεσθαι τῇ ἀπιστίᾳ *waver in disbelief* **Ro 4:20.** ἐποίησα ἐν ἀ. *while I was still an unbeliever* **1 Ti 1:13.** καρδία πονηρὰ ἀπιστίας *an evil, unbelieving heart* **Hb 3:12** (on the gen. s. Mlt. 74).—Among Christians w. διψυχία 2 Cl 19:2; w. ἀνομία GJs 20:1 (not pap). Personif. as one of the chief sins Hs 9, 15, 3. (Opp. πίστις) IEph 8:2.—As a characteristic of this age (w. ἀνομία) ending of Mark (**16:14**) in the Freer Ms. ln. 2.

❷ **lack of commitment to a relationship or pledge,** ***unfaithfulness*** (X., An. 3, 2, 4 et al.; UPZ 18, 5 [163 BC]; Wsd 14:25; Philo, Spec. Leg. 2, 8, Decal. 172; Jos., Ant. 14, 349) **Ro 3:3** (JGriffiths, ET 53, '41, 118).—M-M. TW.

ἄπιστος, ον (s. πιστός; Hom. et al.; LXX, Philo, Joseph., Just., Ath.; Mel., P. 16, 111).

❶ ***unbelievable, incredible*** (Bacchylides 17, 117; X., Cyr. 3, 1, 26; Pla., Theag. 130; Herm. Wr. 9, 10; EpArist 296; Philo, Op. M. 114 al.; Jos., Ant. 6, 198; Just., D. 73, 5f et al; Ath. 30, 3) τί ἄπιστον κρίνεται παρ' ὑμῖν; *why does it seem incredible to you?* **Ac 26:8** (Jos., Ant. 18, 76 ἄπιστα αὐτὰ κρίνειν).

❷ ***without faith, disbelieving, unbelieving*** (in relation to a divine activity as early as SIG 1168, 32 [c. 320 BC], a patient sneers in disbelief at healings recorded in a shrine of Asclepius and subsequently receives the sobriquet Ἄπιστος; Hymn to Demeter: PSI 1282, 42; Is 17:10; Pr 28:25 v.l.; Philo, Leg. All. 3, 164, Leg. ad Gai. 3; Just., D. 91, 3 al.; Ath. 24, 4; Mel, P. 16, 111) γενεά **Mt 17:17; Mk 9:19; Lk 9:41;** of Thomas **J 20:27.**—Esp. of gentiles οἱ ἄ. **1 Cor 6:6; 7:15; 10:27; 14:22;** 2 Cl 17:5; Dg 11:2; MPol 16:1; IMg 5:2; Papias (11:2); condemned at the Last

Judgment **Lk 12:46** (cp. Paroem. Gr.: Zenob. [II AD] 2, 6 p. 33, 4f: αἱ ἀμυήτων ψυχαί are tormented in Hades); w. ἰδιώτης **1 Cor 14:23f;** ἄ. γυνή **7:12, 14;** ἀνήρ vs. **13f** (s. JKöhne, Die Ehen zw. Christen u. Heiden in d. ersten christl. Jahrhunderten '31). W. the connotation of evil-doing **2 Cor 6:14f; 1 Ti 5:8;** w. μεμιαμμένοι **Tit 1:15;** cp. **Rv 21:8.**—Of teachers of error ITr 10; ISm 2; 5:3.—ἐν οἷς ὁ θεὸς τ. αἰῶνος τούτου ἐτύφλωσεν τὰ νοήματα τῶν ἀ. *in their case, the god of this age has blinded their unbelieving minds* **2 Cor 4:4.**—DELG s.v. πείθομαι. M-M. TW.

ἀπλανής, ές, gen. **οῦς** adj. (πλάνης 'wanderer'; since Pla., Aristot., also EpArist 2; Philo; Jos., Ant. 20, 261; Tat. 9, 2; Ath. 6, 3) **pert. to not straying from an established or recognized course,** ***unerring, undeviating, correct*** τὴν ἀπλανῆ θεοσέβειαν *faultless worship of God* AcPlCor 2:10.—DELG s.v. πλανάομαι.

ἁπλότης, ητος, ἡ (s. ἁπλοῦς 'single', opp. of διπλοῦς 'twofold'; X., Pla., et al.; OGI 764, 1; Kaibel 716, 5; LXX; Test12Patr; TestJob 26:6; Philo; Joseph.; s. Nägeli 52) 'singleness'.

❶ In our lit. esp. of personal integrity expressed in word or action (cp. our colloq. 'what you see is what you get') ***simplicity, sincerity, uprightness, frankness*** ἐν ἁ. τῆς καρδίας ὑπακούειν *obey w. a sincere heart* (as vs. 6 indicates, not with an outward show that conceals improper motivation) **Eph 6:5;** cp. **Col 3:22** (Diod. S. 5, 66, 4, ἁπλότης τῆς ψυχῆς =inmost sincerity; 1 Ch 29:17; Wsd 1:1; TestReub 4:1; TestSim 4:5; TestLevi 13:1); w. εἰλικρίνεια **2 Cor 1:12;** cp. the Syr. rendering of 1 Cl 60:2 (text: ὁσιότης). ἐν ἁ. λέγειν *speak simply, plainly,* i.e., without ambiguity B 8:2 (cp. Dionys. Hal., Ars Rhet. 9, 14). ἐν ἁ. δηλῶσαι 17:1. ἐν ἁ. εὑρίσκεσθαι *be found sincere* Hm 2:7. ἡ ἁ. ἡ εἰς Χριστόν *sincere devotion to Christ* **2 Cor 11:3** (WWood, Exp. 9th ser., 2, 1925, 450–53).—Of simple goodness, which gives itself without reserve, 'without strings attached', 'without hidden agendas' (Jos., Bell. 5, 319, Ant. 7, 332; TestIss 3:8) *ingenuousness* **Ro 12:8; 2 Cor 8:2; 9:11, 13.** Hermas is esp. fond of this mng.: w. ἀκακία (Philo, Op. M. 170) Hv 1, 2, 4; 3, 9, 1; w. ἐγκράτεια Hv 2, 3, 2; w. νηπιότης s 9, 24, 3; ἐμμένειν τῇ ἁ. *continue in your sincerity* Hv 3, 1, 9. For this ἁ. ἔχειν m 2:1. Personif. w. other Christian virtues Hv 3, 8, 5 and 7; s 9, 15, 2.

❷ The interpretation ***generosity, liberality*** has frequently been proposed for **Ro 12:8; 2 Cor 8:2; 9:11, 13** (w. support sought in TestIss 3:8 [s. RCharles, Test12Patr, 1908, on TestIss 3:1, 2, 8]; Kaibel 716, 5=IG XIV, 1517 [s. L-S-J-M s.v. II, 3]), but this sense (adopted by NRSV et al.) is in dispute, and it is prob. that mng. 1 in the sense of *sincere concern, simple goodness* is sufficient for all these pass. Aristot., EN 4, 1, 13f, 1120a documents the Gr-Rom. cultural perspective: giving should be done with enthusiasm and without grudging.—JAmstutz, ΑΠΛΟΤΗΣ '68 (no pap or ins).—DELG s.v. ἁπλόος. EDNT. New Docs 5, 77. M-M. TW. Spicq.

ἁπλοῦς, ῆ, οῦν (Att. contr.; Aeschyl., Thu.+) **pert. to being motivated by singleness of purpose so as to be open and aboveboard,** ***single, without guile, sincere, straightforward*** i.e. without a hidden agenda (Plut., Mor. 63f: the gods take delight in beneficence for its own sake, but a flatterer's performance is with mixed motives) εἶναι ἁ. τῇ καρδίᾳ *be guileless* B 19:2 (cp. SIG 1042, 12 ἁ. τῇ ψυχῇ; Pr 11:25; Ps.-Phocyl. 50). ἁ. διάνοια *a sincere mind* 1 Cl 23:1. W. ἄκακος (Diod. S. 13, 76; Nicol. Dam.: 90 fgm. 61, 2 Jac.; Appian, Bell. Civ. 5, 136 §566) Hs 9, 24, 2. Of the eye (Damasc., Vi. Isid. 16 [p. 16, 9–11 Z.], with ref. to frank expression) *single = unjaundiced, sincere* (s. ἁπλότης 1; opp. πονηρός, whose mng. is apparent fr. Mt 20:15; Mk 7:22. Cp. Sir 14:10; 31:13; TestIss 3:2 πορευόμενος ἐν ἁπλότητι ὀφθαλμῶν; also IArsameia, Antiochus I, lines 210–20 [tr. Danker, Benefactor 251]: of attempt to conceal jealousy over another's good fortune and 'melting one's eye' in the process) **Mt 6:22** (the Kommagene ins helps explain the intercalation of vss. 22f between two logia on approach to riches); **Lk 11:34** (s. Jülicher, Gleichn. 98ff esp. 100f; WBrandt, ZNW 14, 1913, 189ff; CEdlund, D. Auge der Einfalt: ASNU 19, '52, 51–122; HCadbury, The Single Eye: HTR 47, '54, 69–74 holds out for *generous;* opposed by TThienemann, Gordon Review 1, '55, 10–22. Plut., Mor. 63f distinguishes ἁ. 'unreserved' fr. ἐλευθέριος 'liberal.' See also λύχνος b, ὀφθαλμός 1, πονηρός 1b and 3a. Zahn, Mt p. 291 and Betz, SM 451 adopt a physiological sense for ἁ.: 'healthy.').—As of animals gener. (Aristot., HA 9, 1), so the superl. ἁπλούστατος (the form in X., Mem. 4, 2, 16; Polyb. 9, 10, 5; Strabo 7, 3, 7; Philo, Vi. Cont. 82) *quite simple, guileless,* of doves **Mt 10:16** D.—The comp. ἁπλούστερον *very simply* B 6:5 (s. ἁπλῶς).—CSpicq, La vertu de Simplicité dans l'A. et le N. Test.: RSPT 22, '33, 1–26; ESjöberg, StTh 5, '51, 89–105; HBacht, Geist u. Leben 29, '56, 416–26; JAmstutz, ΑΠΛΟΤΗΣ '68; Betz, SM 437–53, esp. 449–53.—DELG s.v. ἁπλόος. M-M. TW. Spicq. Sv.

ἁπλόω (s. ἁπλοῦς; Hero Alex. III p. 130, 7; Cornutus 32 p. 66, 7; Soranus p. 76, 16; Aelian, NA 12, 27; Ps.-Callisth. p. 36, 10; Herm. Wr. fgm. XXIII 52 [488, 6 Sc.]; Anth. Pal. 11, 107, 4; also ἁπλώσῃς τὴν ὁδόν σου [ἀπώσῃς BS*] Job 22:3; νεκρὰν ἡπλωμένην TestJob 40:8; ἥπλωσε τὰς πτέρυγας αὐτοῦ GrBar 6:7; ἁπλώσας τὰς χεῖρας of hands outstretched in a receptive gesture ApcMos 37) ***make single, unfold*** pass. in act. sense (TestJob 40:8; Aelian, NA 14, 26) χάρις ἁπλουμένη *unfolding grace,* i.e. generosity that is constantly reaching out Dg 11:5.

ἄπλυτος, ον (ἀ-, πλυτός 'washed'; Semonides 7, 5; Dio Chrys. 11[12], 43; Galen XIII 664 K.) ***unwashed*** τὸ ἔντερον ἄ. φαγεῖν *eat the entrails unwashed* B 7:4.—DELG s.v. πλύνω.

ἁπλῶς adv. fr. ἁπλοῦς (Aeschyl.+).—❶ **pert. to being straightforward,** ***simply, above board, sincerely, openly*** of guileless response to someth. that arrests one's attention (Demosth. 23, 178; M. Ant. 3, 6, 3 al.; Epict. 2, 2, 13; Philo, Ebr. 76; Just., D. 65, 2; Ath., R. 60, 32 al.; Iren. 5, 30, 1 [Harv. II 407, 6; w. ἀκακῶς]) w. διδόναι *without reservation* **Js 1:5** (s. MDibelius ad loc.; HRiesenfeld, ConNeot 9, '44, 33–41); Hm 2:4 *without having second thoughts about the donation* (s. ἁπλότης 1) ἁ. τι τελέσαι *fulfill someth. without reservation* Hm 2:6a, cp. b. *Pray wholeheartedly, with confidence* προσευχὰς ἀναφέρειν 2 Cl 2:2. Comp. ἁπλούστερον (Isaeus 4, 2) γράφειν *write very plainly* B 6:5 (cp. Iren. 1, prol. 3 [Harv. I 6, 5]).

❷ **pert. to simplicity in verbal expression**—ⓐ ***in short, in a word*** (Epict. 3, 15, 3; 3, 22, 96; Just., A I, 67, 6 ἁ. πᾶσι τοῖς ἐν χρείᾳ οὖσι 'in brief, all who are in need', D. 5, 4 al.; Iren., 1, 18, 3 [Harv. I 172, 17]) ἁ. εἰπεῖν (TestAbr 10 p. 87, 27 [Stone p. 22]; 17 p. 99, 28 [St. p. 46]) *to put it succinctly* Dg 6:1 (the mng. *frankly* or *bluntly* i.e. not obliquely or deviously [M. Ant. 5, 7, 2; schol. on Apollon. Rhod. 2, 844–47a ἁπλῶς κ. κατὰ ἀλήθειαν ἐξειπεῖν=to state it simply and as it really is] is less prob. here, for the preceding context consists of explicit details).

ⓑ ***simply, at all*** w. neg. expr. (reff. in Riesenf., op. cit. 37f, and Theopomp. [IV BC]: 115 fgm. 224 Jac. p. 582, 18 ἁ. οὐδείς; Diod. S. 3, 8, 5 ἁ. οὐ; Just., A II, 2, 16, D. 6, 1; Eur., Rhesus 851) ἁ. οὐ δύναμαι ἐξηγήσασθαι *I simply cannot describe* ApcPt 3:9.—M-M. Spicq.

ἀπό (Hom.+) prep. w. gen. (see the lit. on ἀνά, beg., also for ἀπό: KDieterich, IndogF 24, 1909, 93–158; LfgrE s.v.). Basic sense 'separation from' someone or someth., fr. which the other uses have developed. In the NT it has encroached on the domain of Att. ἐκ, ὑπό, παρά, and the gen. of separation; s. Mlt. 102; 246; Mlt-Turner 258f.

➊ **a marker to indicate separation from a place, whether person or thing, *from, away from*—ⓐ** w. all verbs denoting motion, esp. those compounded w. ἀπό: ἀπάγεσθαι, ἀπαλλάσσεσθαι, ἀπελαύνειν, ἀπέρχεσθαι, ἀπολύεσθαι, ἀποπλανᾶσθαι, ἀποστέλλειν, ἀποφεύγειν, ἀποχωρεῖν, ἀποχωρίζεσθαι; but also w. ἀνίστασθαι, διαστῆναι, διέρχεσθαι, ἐκδημεῖν, ἐκκινεῖν, ἐκπλεῖν, ἐκπορεύεσθαι, ἐξέρχεσθαι, ἐξωθεῖν, ἐπιδιδόναι, μεταβαίνειν, μετατίθεσθαι, νοσφίζειν, παραγίνεσθαι, πλανᾶσθαι, πορεύεσθαι, ὑπάγειν, ὑποστρέφειν, φεύγειν; s. the entries in question.

ⓑ w. all verbs expressing the idea of separation ἐκβάλλειν τὸ κάρφος ἀ. τοῦ ὀφθαλμοῦ *remove the splinter fr. the eye* **Mt 7:4 v.l.** (for ἐκ). ἐξέβαλον ἀπὸ τῆς πήρας αὐτῶν δῶρα *they set forth gifts out of their travel bags* GJs 21:3. ἀπολύεσθαι ἀ. ἀνδρός *be divorced fr. her husband* **Lk 16:18,** cp. **Ac 15:33.** ἀποκυλίειν, ἀπολαμβάνεσθαι, ἀποστρέφειν, ἐπιστρέφεσθαι, ἐπανάγειν, αἴρειν, ἀφαιρεῖν, ἀπολέσθαι, μερίζειν et al., s. the pertinent entries. So also κενὸς ἀ. τινος Hs 9, 19, 2. ἔρημος ἀ. τινος (Jer 51:2) 2 Cl 2:3. W. verbs which express the concept of separation in the wider sense, like loose, free, acquit et al. ἀπορφανίζειν, ἀποσπᾶν, διεγείρεσθαι, δικαιοῦν, ἐκδικοῦν, ἐλευθεροῦν, λούειν, λύειν, λυτροῦν, ῥαντίζειν, σαλεύειν, στέλλειν, σῴζειν, φθείρειν, s. the entries; hence also ἀθῷος (Sus 46 Theod. v.l.) **Mt 27:24.** καθαρὸς ἀ. τινος (Tob 3:14; but s. Dssm. NB 24 [BS 196; 216]) **Ac 20:26;** cp. Kuhring 54.

ⓒ verbs meaning *be on guard, be ashamed,* etc., take ἀπό to express the occasion or object of their caution, shame, or fear; so αἰσχύνεσθαι, βλέπειν, μετανοεῖν, προσέχειν, φοβεῖσθαι, φυλάσσειν, φυλάσσεσθαι; s. 5 below.

ⓓ w. verbs of *concealing, hiding, hindering,* the pers. *from* whom someth. is concealed is found w. ἀπό; so κρύπτειν τι ἀπό τινος, παρακαλύπτειν τι ἀπό τινος, κωλύειν τι ἀπό τινος; s. the entries.

ⓔ in pregnant constr. like ἀνάθεμα εἶναι ἀ. τοῦ Χριστοῦ *be separated fr. Christ by a curse* **Ro 9:3.** μετανοεῖν ἀ. τ. κακίας (Jer 8:6) **Ac 8:22.** ἀποθνῄσκειν ἀ. τινος *through death become free from* **Col 2:20.** φθείρεσθαι ἀ. τ. ἁπλότητος *be ruinously diverted from wholehearted commitment* **2 Cor 11:3.** Cp. Hs 6, 2, 4.

ⓕ as a substitute for the partitive gen. (Hdt. 6, 27, 2; Thu. 7, 87, 6; PPetr III, 11, 20; PIand 8, 6; Kuhring 20; Rossberg 22; Johannessohn, Präp. 17) τίνα ἀ. τῶν δύο; **Mt 27:21,** cp. **Lk 9:38; 19:39** (like PTebt 299, 13; 1 Macc 1:13; 3:24; Sir 6:6; 46:8). τὰ ἀ. τοῦ πλοίου *pieces of the ship* **Ac 27:44.** ἐκχεῶ ἀ. τοῦ πνεύματός μου **Ac 2:17f** (Jo 3:1f). λαμβάνειν ἀ. τ. καρπῶν *get a share of the vintage* **Mk 12:2** (cp. Just., A I, 65, 5 μεταλαβεῖν ἀπὸ τοῦ … ἄρτου).—Of foods (as in Da 1:13, 4:33a; 2 Macc 7:1) ἐσθίειν ἀ. τ. ψιχίων *eat some of the crumbs* **Mt 15:27; Mk 7:28.** χορτάζεσθαι ἀ. τινος *eat one's fill of someth.* **Lk 16:21.** αἴρειν ἀ. τῶν ἰχθύων *pick up the remnants of the fish* **Mk 6:43.** ἐνέγκατε ἀ. τ. ὀψαρίων *bring some of the fish* **J 21:10** (the only instance of this usage in J; s. M-EBoismard, Le chapitre 21 de Saint Jean: RB 54 ['47] 492).—Of drink (cp. Sir 26:12) πίνειν ἀπὸ τ. γενήματος τῆς ἀμπέλου *drink the product of the vine* **Lk 22:18.**

➋ **to indicate the point from which someth. begins, whether lit. or fig.—ⓐ** of place *from, out from* (Just., D. 86, 1 ἀπὸ τῆς πέτρας ὕδωρ ἀναβλύσαν 'gushing out of the rock') σημεῖον ἀ. τ. οὐρανοῦ *a sign fr. heaven* **Mk 8:11.** ἀ. πόλεως εἰς πόλιν *from one city to another* **Mt 23:34.** ἀπ᾿ ἄκρων οὐρανῶν ἕως ἄκρων αὐτῶν (Dt 30:4; Ps 18:7) *from one end of heaven to the other* **24:31,** cp. **Mk 13:27.** ἀπ᾿ ἄνωθεν ἕως κάτω *from top to bottom* **Mt 27:51.** ἀρξάμενοι ἀ. Ἰερουσαλήμ *beginning in Jerusalem* **Lk 24:47** (s. also **Lk 23:5; Ac 1:22; 10:37**). ἀφ᾿ ὑμῶν ἐξήχηται ὁ λόγος τ. κυρίου *the word of the Lord has gone out from you and sounded forth* **1 Th 1:8.** ἀπὸ βορρᾶ, ἀπὸ νότου *in the north, in the south* (PCairGoodsp 6, 5 [129 BC] ἐν τῷ ἀπὸ νότου πεδίῳ; Mitt-Wilck. I/2, 11A col. 1, 12f [123 BC] τὸ ἀπὸ νότου τῆς πόλεως χῶμα; ln. 7 ἀπὸ βορρᾶ τῆς πόλεως; 70, 16 al.; Josh 18:5; 19:34; 1 Km 14:5) **Rv 21:13.**

ⓑ of time *from … (on), since* (POxy 523, 4; Mel., HE 4, 26, 8; s. Kuhring 54ff).—**α.** ἀ. τῶν ἡμερῶν Ἰωάννου *from the days of John* **Mt 11:12.** ἀ. τῆς ὥρας ἐκείνης **9:22.** ἀπ᾿ ἐκείνης τ. ἡμέρας (Jos., Bell. 4, 318, Ant. 7, 382) **Mt 22:46; J 11:53.** ἔτη ἑπτὰ ἀ. τῆς παρθενίας αὐτῆς *for seven years fr. the time she was a virgin* **Lk 2:36.** ἀ. ἐτῶν δώδεκα *for 12 years* **8:43.** ἀ. τρίτης ὥρας τῆς νυκτός **Ac 23:23.** ἀ. κτίσεως κόσμου **Ro 1:20.** ἀ. πέρυσι *since last year, a year ago* **2 Cor 8:10; 9:2.**—ἀπ᾿ αἰῶνος, ἀπ᾿ ἀρχῆς, ἀπ᾿ ἄρτι (also ἀπαρτί and ἄρτι), ἀπὸ καταβολῆς κόσμου, ἀπὸ τότε, ἀπὸ τοῦ νῦν; s. the pertinent entries.

β. w. the limits defined, forward and backward: ἀπὸ … ἕως (Jos., Ant. 6, 364) **Mt 27:45.** ἀπὸ … ἄχρι **Phil 1:5.** ἀπὸ … μέχρι **Ac 10:30; Ro 5:14; 15:19.**

γ. ἀφ᾿ ἧς (sc. ὥρας or ἡμέρας, which is found **Col 1:6, 9;** but ἀφ᾿ ἧς became a fixed formula: ParJer 7:28; Plut., Pelop. [285] 15, 5; s. B-D-F §241, 2) *since* **Lk 7:45** (Renehan '75, 36f); **Ac 24:11;2 Pt 3:4** (cp. X., Hell. 4, 6, 6; 1 Macc 1:11). ἀφ᾿ οὗ (sc.—as in X., Cyr. 1, 2, 13—χρόνου; Att. ins in Meisterhans.[3]-Schw. and s. Witkowski, index 163; ἀφ᾿ οὗ is also a formula) *since, when once* (X., Symp. 4, 62; Demetr.: 722 fgm. 1, 16 Jac.; Lucian, Dial. Mar. 15, 1; Ex 5:23 GrBar 3:6) **Lk 13:25; 24:21; Rv 16:18** (cp. Da 12:1; 1 Macc 9:29; 16:24; 2 Macc 1:7; TestAbr B 13 p. 117, 23; GrBar; Jos., Ant. 4, 78). τρία ἔτη ἀφ᾿ οὗ (cp. Tob 5:35 S) **Lk 13:7.** ἀφότε s. ὅτε 1aγ end.

ⓒ the beg. of a series *from … (on).*—**α.** ἀρξάμενος ἀ. Μωϋσέως καὶ ἀ. πάντων τ. προφητῶν *beginning w. Moses and all the prophets* **Lk 24:27.** ἕβδομος ἀ. Ἀδάμ **Jd 14** (Diod. S. 1, 50, 3 ὄγδοος ὁ ἀπὸ τοῦ πατρός [ancestor]; Appian, Mithrid. 9 §29 τὸν ἕκτον ἀπὸ τοῦ πρώτου Μιθριδάτην; Arrian, Anab. 7, 12, 4; Diog. L. 3, 1: Plato in the line of descent was ἕκτος ἀπὸ Σόλωνος; Biogr. p. 31: Homer δέκατος ἀπὸ Μουσαίου). ἀ. διετοῦς καὶ κατωτέρω **Mt 2:16** (cp. Num 1:20; 2 Esdr 3:8).

β. w. both beg. and end given ἀπὸ … ἕως (Sir 18:26; 1 Macc 9:13) **Mt 1:17; 23:35; Ac 8:10.** Sim., ἀ. δόξης εἰς δόξαν *fr. glory to glory* **2 Cor 3:18.**

➌ **to indicate origin or source, *from*—ⓐ** lit., with verbs of motion—**α.** *down from* πίπτειν ἀ. τραπέζης **Mt 15:27.** καθεῖλεν δυνάστας ἀ. θρόνων *God has dethroned rulers* **Lk 1:52.**

β. *from* ἔρχεσθαι ἀ. θεοῦ **J 3:2;** cp. **13:3; 16:30.** παραγίνεται ἀ. τῆς Γαλιλαίας **Mt 3:13;** ἀ. ἀνατολῶν ἥξουσιν **8:11** (Is 49:12; 59:19); ἀ. τοῦ ἱεροῦ ἐπορεύετο **24:1;** ἀ. Παμφυλίας **Ac 15:38.** ἐγείρεσθαι ἀ. τ. νεκρῶν *be raised from the dead* **Mt 14:2.**

ⓑ lit., to indicate someone's local origin *from* (Hom. et al.; Soph., El. 701; Hdt. 8, 114; ins [RevArch 4 sér. IV 1904 p. 9 ἀπὸ

Θεσσαλονίκης]; pap [HBraunert, Binnenwanderung '64, 384, s.v.; PFlor 14, 2; 15, 5; 17, 4; 22, 13 al.]; Judg 12:8; 13:2; 17:1 [all three acc. to B]; 2 Km 23:20 al.; Jos., Bell. 3, 422, Vi. 217; Just., A I, 1 τῶν ἀπὸ Φλαουΐας Νέας πόλεως; s. B-D-F §209, 3; Rob. 578) ἦν ἀ. Βηθσαϊδά *he was from B.* **J 1:44;** cp. **12:21.** ὄχλοι ἀ. τῆς Γαλιλαίας *crowds fr. Galilee* **Mt 4:25.** ἄνδρες ἀ. παντὸς ἔθνους **Ac 2:5.** ἀνὴρ ἀ. τοῦ ὄχλου *a man fr. the crowd* **Lk 9:38.** ὁ προφήτης ὁ ἀ. Ναζαρέθ **Mt 21:11.** οἱ ἀ. Κιλικίας *the Cilicians* **Ac 6:9.** οἱ ἀδελφοὶ οἱ ἀ. Ἰόππης **10:23** (Musaeus 153 παρθένος ἀπ' Ἀρκαδίας; Just., A I, 58, 1 Μαρκίωνα . . . τὸν ἀπὸ Πόντου). οἱ ἀ. Θεσσαλονίκης Ἰουδαῖοι **17:13.** οἱ ἀ. τῆς Ἰταλίας *the Italians* **Hb 13:24,** who could be inside as well as outside Italy (cp. Dssm., Her. 33, 1898, 344, LO 167, 1 [LAE 200, 3]; Mlt. 237; B-D-F §437).—Rather denoting close association οἱ ἀ. τῆς ἐκκλησίας *members of the church* **Ac 12:1;** likew. **15:5** (cp. Plut., Cato Min. 4, 2 οἱ ἀπὸ τ. στοᾶς φιλόσοφοι; Ps.-Demetr. c. 68 οἱ ἀπ' αὐτοῦ=his [Isocrates'] pupils; Synes., Ep. 4 p. 162b; 66 p. 206c; PTebt 33, 3 [112 BC], Ῥωμαῖος τῶν ἀπὸ συγκλήτου; Ar. 15, 1 Χριστιανοὶ γενεαλογοῦνται ἀπὸ . . . Ἰησοῦ Χριστοῦ; Ath.).—To indicate origin in the sense of material fr. which someth. is made (Hdt. 7, 65; Theocr. 15, 117; IPriene 117, 72 ἀπὸ χρυσοῦ; 1 Esdr 8:56; Sir 43:20 v.l.) ἔνδυμα ἀ. τριχῶν καμήλου *clothing made of camel's hair* **Mt 3:4.**

ⓒ fig., w. verbs of asking, desiring, to denote the pers. *of* or *from* whom a thing is asked (Ar. 11, 3): δανίσασθαι ἀπό τινος *borrow fr. someone* **Mt 5:42.** ἐκζητεῖν ἀ. τῆς γενεᾶς ταύτης **Lk 11:51.** ἀπαιτεῖν τι ἀπό τινος **Lk 12:20.** ζητεῖν τι ἀπό τινος **1 Th 2:6.** λαμβάνειν τι ἀπό τινος **Mt 17:25f; 3J 7.**

ⓓ fig., w. verbs of perceiving, to indicate source of the perception (Lysias, Andoc. 6; Ps.-Aristot., De Mundo 6, 399b ἀπ' αὐτῶν τῶν ἔργων θεωρεῖται ὁ θεός; Appian, Liby. 104 §493 ἀπὸ τῆς σφραγῖδος=[recognize a corpse] by the seal-ring; Demetr.: 722 fgm. 2, 1 στοχάζεσθαι ἀπὸ τῶν ὀνομάτων; Just., D. 60, 1 τοῦτο νοοῦμεν ἀπὸ τῶν λόγων τῶν προλελεγμένων; 100, 2 ἀπὸ τῶν γραφῶν): ἀ. τῶν καρπῶν αὐτῶν ἐπιγνώσεσθε αὐτούς *by their fruits you will know them* **Mt 7:16, 20.** μανθάνειν παραβολὴν ἀ. τῆς συκῆς *learn a lesson from the fig tree* **24:32; Mk 13:28.** ἀπὸ τῶν σπερμάτων μὴ ποιεῖσθαι τὴν παραβολήν *if we are not to derive our parable solely from reference to seeds* (cp. **1 Cor 15:37**) AcPlCor 2:28.—Also μανθάνειν τι ἀπό τινος *learn someth. fr. someone* **Gal 3:2; Col 1:7.**

ⓔ γράψαι ἀφ' ὧν ἠδυνήθην, lit., *write from what I was able,* i.e. *as well as I could* B 21:9 (cp. Tat. 12, 5 οὐκ ἀπὸ γλώττης οὐδὲ ἀπὸ τῶν εἰκότων οὐδὲ ἀπ' ἐννοιῶν etc.).

❹ **to indicate distance fr. a point,** ***away from,*** for μακρὰν ἀ. τινος *far fr. someone,* ἀπὸ μακρόθεν *fr. a great distance* s. μακράν, μακρόθεν. ἀπέχειν ἀπό τινος s. ἀπέχω 4. W. detailed measurements (corresp. to Lat. 'a', s. B-D-F §161, 1; Rob. 575; WSchulze, Graeca Latina 1901, 15ff; Hdb. on J 11:18; Appian, Bell. Civ. 3, 12 §42; Ramsay, CB I/2, 390 no. 248) ἦν Βηθανία ἐγγὺς τῶν Ἱεροσολύμων ὡς ἀπὸ σταδίων δεκαπέντε *Bethany was near Jerusalem, about 15 stades* (less than 3 km.) *away* **J 11:18.** ὡς ἀπὸ πηχῶν διακοσίων *about 200 cubits* (c. 90 meters) **21:8.** ἀπὸ σταδίων χιλίων ἑξακοσίων *about 1600 stades* (c. 320 km.) **Rv 14:20;** cp. Hv 4, 1, 5 (for other examples of this usage, s. Rydbeck 68).—Hebraistically ἀπὸ προσώπου τινός (Gen 16:6; Jer 4:26; Jdth 2:14; Sir 21:2; 1 Macc 5:34; En 103:4; Just., A I, 37, 1 ἀπὸ προσώπου τοῦ πατρὸς ἐλέχθησαν διὰ Ἠσαίου . . . οἶδε οἱ λόγοι 'in the name of the father . . . through Isaiah'; 38, 1 al.)=מִפְּנֵי פ׳ *(away) from the presence of someone* **2 Th 1:9** (Is 2:10, 19, 21); **Rv 12:14** (B-D-F §140; 217, 1; Mlt-H. 466).

❺ **to indicate cause, means, or outcome—ⓐ** gener., to show the reason for someth. *because of, as a result of, for* (numerous ref. in FBleek on Hb 5:7; PFay 111, 4; POxy 3314, 7 [from falling off a horse]; Jdth 2:20; 4 [6] Esdr [POxy 1010]; AscIs 3:13; Jos., Ant. 9, 56) οὐκ ἠδύνατο ἀ. τοῦ ὄχλου *he could not because of the crowd* **Lk 19:3;** cp. **Mk 2:4** D. οὐκ ἐνέβλεπον ἀπὸ τῆς δόξης τοῦ φωτός *I could not see because of the brilliance of the light* **Ac 22:11.** ἀ. τοῦ πλήθους τ. ἰχθύων **J 21:6** (M-EBoismard, ad loc.: s. 1f end). ἀ. τοῦ ὕδατος *for the water* Hs 8, 2, 8. ἀ. τῆς θλίψεως *because of the persecution* **Ac 11:19.** οὐαὶ τῷ κόσμῳ ἀ. τ. σκανδάλων **Mt 18:7** (s. B-D-F §176, 1; Mlt. 246). εἰσακουσθεὶς ἀ. τῆς εὐλαβείας *heard because of his piety* **Hb 5:7** (but the text may be corrupt; at any rate it is obscure and variously interpr.; besides the comm. s. KRomaniuk, Die Gottesfürchtigen im NT: Aegyptus 44, '64, 84; B-D-F §211; Rob. 580; s. on εὐλάβεια).

ⓑ to indicate means *with the help of, with* (Hdt. et al.; Ael. Aristid. 37, 23 K.=2 p. 25 D.; PGM 4, 2128f σφράγιζε ἀπὸ ῥύπου=seal with dirt; En 97:8) γεμίσαι τὴν κοιλίαν ἀ. τ. κερατίων *fill one's stomach w. the husks* **Lk 15:16 v.l.** (s. ἐκ 4aζ; cp. Pr 18:20). οἱ πλουτήσαντες ἀπ' αὐτῆς **Rv 18:15** (cp. Sir 11:18).

ⓒ to indicate motive or reason *for, from, with* (Appian, Bell. Civ. 5, 13 §52 ἀπ' εὐνοίας=with goodwill; 1 Macc 6:10; pap exx. in Kuhring 35) κοιμᾶσθαι ἀ. τῆς λύπης *sleep from sorrow* **Lk 22:45.** ἀ. τῆς χαρᾶς αὐτοῦ **Mt 13:44;** cp. **Lk 24:41; Ac 12:14.** ἀ. τοῦ φόβου κράζειν **Mt 14:26,** ἀ. φόβου καὶ προσδοκίας *with fear and expectation* **Lk 21:26.** Hence verbs of fearing, etc., take ἀ. to show the cause of the fear (s. above 1c) μὴ φοβεῖσθαι ἀ. τ. ἀποκτεννόντων τὸ σῶμα *not be afraid of those who kill only the body* **Mt 10:28; Lk 12:4** (cp. Jdth 5:23; 1 Macc 2:62; 3:22; 8:12; En 106:4).

ⓓ to indicate the originator of the action denoted by the verb *from* (trag., Hdt. et al.) ἀ. σοῦ σημεῖον ἰδεῖν **Mt 12:38.** γινώσκειν ἀπό τινος *learn fr. someone* **Mk 15:45.** ἀκούειν ἀ. τοῦ στόματός τινος *hear fr. someone's mouth,* i.e. fr. him personally **Lk 22:71** (Dionys. Hal. 3, 8 ἀ. στόματος ἤκουσεν); cp. **Ac 9:13; 1J 1:5.** τὴν ἀ. σοῦ ἐπαγγελίαν *a promise given by you* **Ac 23:21** (cp. Ath. 2, 3 ταῖς ἀπὸ τῶν κατηγόρων αἰτίαις 'the charges made by the accusers'). ἀφ' ἑνὸς ἐγενήθησαν **Hb 11:12.** Prob. παραλαμβάνειν ἀ. τοῦ κυρίου **1 Cor 11:23** is to be understood in the same way: Paul is convinced that he is taught by the Lord himself (for direct teaching s. EBröse, Die Präp. ἀπό 1 Cor 11:23: StKr 71, 1898, 351–60; Dssm.; BWeiss; Ltzm.; H-DWendland. But for indirect communication: Zahn et al.). παραλαβὼν ἀπὸ τῶν θυγατέρων Φιλίππου, ὅτι Papias (11:2); opp. παρειληφέναι ὑπὸ τῶν θ. Φ. (2:9).—Of the more remote cause ἀπ' ἀνθρώπων *from human beings* (as opposed to transcendent revelation; w. δι' ἀνθρώπου; cp. Artem. 1, 73 p. 66, 11 ἀπὸ γυναικῶν ἢ διὰ γυναικῶν; 2, 36 p. 135, 26) **Gal 1:1.** ἀ. κυρίου πνεύματος *fr. the Lord, who is the Spirit* **2 Cor 3:18.** ἔχειν τι ἀπό τινος *have (received) someth. fr. someone* **1 Cor 6:19; 1 Ti 3:7; 1J 2:20; 4:21.**—In salutation formulas εἰρήνη ἀ. θεοῦ πατρός ἡμῶν *peace that comes from God, our father* **Ro 1:7; 1 Cor 1:3; 2 Cor 1:2; Gal 1:3; Eph 1:2;** cp. **6:23; Phil 1:2; Col 1:2; 1 Th 1:1 v.l.; 2 Th 1:2; 1 Ti 1:2; 2 Ti 1:2; Tit 1:4; Phlm 3.** σοφία ἀ. θεοῦ *wisdom that comes fr. God* **1 Cor 1:30.** ἔπαινος ἀ. θεοῦ *praise fr. God* **4:5.** καὶ τοῦτο ἀ. θεοῦ *and that brought about by God* **Phil 1:28.** The expr. εἰρήνη ἀπὸ 'ὁ ὢν καὶ ὁ ἦν καὶ ὁ ἐρχόμενος' **Rv 1:4** is quite extraordinary. It may be an interpretation of the name Yahweh already current, or an attempt to show reverence for the divine name by preserving it unchanged, or simply one more of the grammatical peculiarities so frequent in Rv (Meyer[6]-

Bousset 1906, 159ff; Mlt. 9, note 1; cp. PParis 51, 33 ἀπὸ ἀπηλιότης; Mussies 93f, 328).

ⓔ to indicate responsible agents for someth., *from, of*—**α.** the self, st. Gk. usage (Thu. 5, 60, 1; X., Mem. 2, 10, 3; Andoc., Orat. 2, 4 οὗτοι οὐκ ἀφ' αὑτῶν ταῦτα πράττουσιν; Diod. S. 17, 56; Num 16:28; 4 Macc 11:3; En 98:4; TestAbr A 15 p. 95, 26 [Stone p. 38]; 18 p. 101, 6 [Stone p. 50]; Just., A I, 43, 8) the expr. ἀφ' ἑαυτοῦ (pl. ἀφ' ἑαυτῶν) *of himself* and ἀπ' ἐμαυτοῦ *of myself* are common **Lk 12:57; 21:30; 2 Cor 3:5,** esp. so in J: **5:19, 30; 8:28; 10:18; 15:4.—7:17f; 11:51; 14:10; 16:13; 18:34.** So also ἀπ' ἐμαυτοῦ οὐκ ἐλήλυθα *I did not come of myself* (opp. the Father sent me) **7:28; 8:42.**

β. fr. others. W. verbs in the pass. voice or pass. mng. ὑπό is somet. replaced by ἀπό (in isolated cases in older Gk. e.g. Thu. 1, 17 et al. [Kühner-G. II/1 p. 457f]; freq. in later Gk.: Polyb. 1, 79, 14; Hero I 152, 6; 388, 11; Nicol. Dam.: 90 fgm. 130, 130 Jac.; IG XII/5, 29, 1; SIG 820, 9; PLond III, 1173, 12 p. 208; BGU 1185, 26; PFlor 150, 6 ἀ. τῶν μυῶν κατεσθιόμενα; PGM 4, 256; Kuhring 36f; 1 Macc 15:17; Sir 16:4; ParJer 1:1 ᾐχμαλωτεύθησαν … ἀπὸ τοῦ βασιλέως; Philo, Leg. All. 3, 62; Just., A I, 68, 6 ἐπιστολὴν … γραφεῖσάν μοι ἀπὸ Σερήνου, D. 121, 3 ἀπὸ παντὸς [γένους] μετάνοιαν πεποιῆσθαι. See B-D-F §210; Rob. 820; GHatzidakis, Einl. in d. neugriech. Gramm. 1892, 211; AJannaris, An Histor. Gk. Grammar 1897, §1507). Yet just at this point the textual tradition varies considerably, and the choice of prep. is prob. at times influenced by the wish to express special nuances of mng. **Lk 8:29b v.l.** (ὑπό text); **43b** (ὑπό v.l.); **10:22** D; ἀποδεδειγμένος ἀ. τ. θεοῦ *attested by God* **Ac 2:22.** ἐπικληθεὶς Βαρναβᾶς ἀ. (ὑπό v.l.) τ. ἀποστόλων *named B. by the apostles* **4:36.** κατενεχθεὶς ἀ. τοῦ ὕπνου *overcome by sleep* **20:9.** ἀθετούμενος ἀπὸ τῶν παραχαρασσόντων τὰ λόγια αὐτοῦ *inasmuch as (Jesus) is being rejected by those who falsify his words* AcPlCor 2:3. νεκροῦ βληθέντος ἀπὸ τῶν υἱῶν Ἰσραὴλ ἐπ' αὐτά *when a corpse was cast upon them* (the bones of Elisha) 2:32. In such cases ἀπό freq. denotes the one who indirectly originates an action, and can be transl. *at the hands of, by command of:* πολλὰ παθεῖν ἀ. τ. πρεσβυτέρων *suffer much at the hands of the elders* **Mt 16:21;** cp. **Lk 9:22; 17:25,** where the emphasis is to be placed on παθεῖν, not on ἀποδοκιμασθῆναι. In ἀ. θεοῦ πειράζομαι the thought is that the temptation is caused by God, though not actually carried out by God **Js 1:13.** ἡτοιμασμένος ἀ. τοῦ θεοῦ *prepared by God's command,* not by God in person **Rv 12:6.**

❻ In a few expr. ἀπό helps to take the place of an adverb. ἀπὸ μέρους, s. μέρος 1c.—ἡμέρα ἀφ' ἡμέρας *day by day* GJs 12:3.—ἀπὸ μιᾶς (acc. to Wlh., Einl.[2] 26, an Aramaism, min hădā=at once [s. MBlack, An Aramaic Approach[3], '67, 113]; but this does not explain the fem. gender, found also in the formulaic ἐπὶ μιᾶς Maxim. Tyr. 6, 3f En 99:9 [s. SAalen, NTS 13, '67, 3] and in Mod. Gk. μὲ μιᾶς *at once* [Thumb §162 note 2]. PSI 286, 22 uses ἀπὸ μιᾶς of a payment made 'at once'; on the phrase s. New Docs 2, 189. Orig. γνώμης might have been a part of the expr. [Philo, Spec. Leg. 3, 73], or ὁρμῆς [Thu. 7, 71, 6], or γλώσσης [Cass. Dio 44, 36, 2], or φωνῆς [Herodian 1, 4, 8]; cp. ἀπὸ μιᾶς φωνῆς Plut., Mor. 502d of an echo; s. B-D-F §241, 6) *unanimously, alike, in concert* **Lk 14:18.** Sim. ἀπὸ τ. καρδιῶν *fr. (your) hearts, sincerely* **Mt 18:35.**—Himerius, Or. 39 [=Or. 5], 6 has as a formula διὰ μιᾶς, probably = continuously, uninterruptedly, Or. 44 [=Or. 8], 2 fuller διὰ μιᾶς τῆς σπουδῆς=with one and the same, or with quite similar zeal.—M-M.

ἀποβαίνω fut. ἀποβήσομαι; 2 aor. ἀπέβην (s. βαίνω; Hom.+; ins, pap, LXX; TestJob 43:6).

❶ lit. **to get off or depart,** ***go away, get out*** e.g. from a ship to the land (X., An. 5, 7, 9 ἀ. εἰς τ. χώραν; Diogenes, Ep. 37, 1) ἀ. εἰς τὴν γῆν **J 21:9.** Abs. (Thu. 1, 116, 2; Jos., Bell. 4, 660) ἀποβάντες *when they had gotten out* **Lk 5:2.**

❷ fig. **to result in a state or condition,** ***turn out, lead*** (to) (Hdt.+; Artem. 3, 66; SIG 851, 9f εἰ καὶ ἑτέρως τοῦτο ἀπέβη; PPetr III, 42H (8) f, 5f=Witkowski p. 15; Job 30:31 εἰς πάθος; TestJob 43:6 εἰς κρίμα; Jos., Ant. 1, 20 ἀ. εἰς; Just., Tat., Theoph. Antioch 2, 11 [p. 226, 19]) ἀ. εἰς μαρτύριον *lead to testifying* **Lk 21:13.** ἀ. εἰς σωτηρίαν *turn out to salvation* **Phil 1:19** (Job 13:16).—M-M.

ἀποβάλλω fut. ἀποβαλῶ; 2 aor. ἀπέβαλον; pf. ἀποβέβληκα. Mid.: fut. 3 sg. ἀποβαλεῖται Tob 11:8 B. Pass.: 1 aor. ἀπεβλήθην; pf. ptc. ἀποβεβλημένος (s. βάλλω; Hom.+).

❶ **to remove someth. that is affixed or an established part,** ***take off, shed***—ⓐ lit., a garment **Mk 10:50.** Of a tree ἀ. τὰ φύλλα (Is 1:30) *shed (its) leaves* Hs 3:3 (ἀποβ.=drop, let fall [unintentionally]: Ps.-Demetr. 65).

ⓑ fig. *take off, doff* (schol. on Nicander, Alexiph. 450 τὸν ὕπνον ἀποβ.=shake off) of characteristics, which can be put on and taken off like a garment (w. ἐνδύσασθαι) Hm 10, 3, 4; ἀ. τὰς πονηρίας s 6, 1, 4; ἀ. πᾶσαν λύπην v 4, 3, 4; ἀ. πονηρίαν ἀπὸ σεαυτοῦ *doff wickedness* m 1:2; ἀ. τὰς ἐπιθυμίας s 9, 14, 1; τὰ ἔργα τούτων τ. γυναικῶν s 9, 14, 2.—Mid. **Ro 13:12 v.l.**

❷ **to get rid of as undesirable or substandard,** ***throw away, reject***—ⓐ lit. ἀ. λίθους *reject* or *throw away* stones Hv 3, 2, 7; 3, 5, 5. Pass.: 3, 7, 5; s 9, 8, 4ff; 9, 9, 4; 9, 13, 3, and 6, and 9; 9, 30, 1. ἀποβάλλεσθαι ἀπὸ τοῦ πύργου s 9, 8, 3; ἀπὸ τοῦ οἴκου s 9, 13, 9; ἐκ τῆς οἰκοδομῆς s 9, 7, 1; 9, 9, 5. W. indication of the goal ἀποβάλλεσθαι εἰς τὸν ἴδιον τόπον *be put back in their place* s 9, 12, 4. ἀποβάλλεσθαι πρὸς τ. λοιπούς *be thrown away w. the rest* s 9, 8, 7.

ⓑ fig. *reject* τινά (Theocr. 11, 19; Hippocr., Ep. 10, 4) 2 Cl 4:5. Pass.: 1 Cl 45:3; Hs 9, 18, 3f; 9, 22, 3. ἐσκανδαλισμένους ἀπὸ τ. πίστεως ἀ. (not to) *reject those who have been led astray from the faith* Hm 8:10 (cp. schol. on Nicander, Ther. 270 ἀποβαλλομένη τῆς εὐθείας ὁδοῦ=led astray fr. the correct path).

❸ **to come to be without someth.,** ***lose*** τὶ *someth.* (Hdt. et al.; Epict. 2, 10, 15 ἀ. αἰδῶ; Dio Chrys. 17 [34], 39 ἀ. τὴν παρρησίαν; Dt 26:5; Philo, Abr. 235; 236, Spec. Leg. 3, 202; Jos., Bell. 1, 90, Ant. 8, 225; 14, 77; Ar. 13, 5) τ. παρρησίαν **Hb 10:35** (but *throw away* [Lucian, Dial. Mort. 10, 1; Aelian, VH 10, 13 et al.] is also prob.). Of gold ἀποβάλλει τὴν σκωρίαν *puts away, loses its dross* Hv 4, 3, 4. ἐὰν μὴ … ἀποβάλῃ ἐξ αὐτοῦ τι *unless it loses some part of it* v 3, 6, 6.

❹ **to remove from an official position,** ***remove, depose*** τινά τινος: ἀ. τῆς ἐπισκοπῆς *depose from the supervisory office* (s. Ltzm. ZWT 55, 1913, 135) 1 Cl 44:4. Pass. ἀ. τῆς λειτουργίας *be removed fr. his office* 44:3.—M-M.

ἀποβλέπω impf. ἀπέβλεπον; 1 aor. ἀπέβλεψα (trag., Hdt.+) ***look, pay attention*** εἴς τι *at* or *to someth.* (Epict. 1, 6, 37; SIG 867, 10; PSI 414, 9; Ps 9:29; 10:4; Philo, Spec. Leg. 1, 293; Just., D. 112, 1; Mel.; πρός Just., A I, 18, 1; Tat., 21, 2; Ath., R. 67, 23) fig., of Moses ἀ. εἰς τ. μισθαποδοσίαν *intent on the reward* **Hb 11:26** (cp. Jos., Bell. 2, 311, Ant. 20, 61).—M-M. Spicq.

ἀπόβλητος, ον verbal adj. of ἀποβάλλω (Hom. et al.; pap, Aq., Sym.; Philo, Spec. Leg. 2, 169 [cp. Nägeli 25]) ***rejected*** (Herm. Wr. 6, 1)=unclean (opp. κάλος) **1 Ti 4:4.**—DELG s.v. βάλλω.

ἀποβολή, ῆς, ἡ (s. ἀποβάλλω; Pla. et al.; PLond 1659, 10) corresp. to the var. mngs. of ἀποβάλλω.

❶ *rejection,* of the (temporary) rejection of Israelites by God (Jos., Ant. 4, 314 not of people as such, but repeated loss of their cities and temple through divine providence) **Ro 11:15** (opp. πρόσλημψις).

❷ *loss* (PCairZen 569, 25 and 106 [III BC]; 55th letter of Apollonius of Tyana [Philostrat. I 358, 19] by death; Philo, Praem. 33 of a ship; Jos., Ant. 2, 147; Tat. 15, 4; Sextus 257) ἀ. ψυχῆς οὐδεμία ἔσται ἐξ ὑμῶν *not a single one of you will be lost* **Ac 27:22** (Straton of Lamps., fgm. 124 ἀ. ζωῆς).—DELG s.v. βάλλω.

ἀπογίνομαι 2 aor. ἀπεγενόμην (in our lit. opp. ζῆν) ***die*** (Hdt., Thu. [cp. 1, 39, 3 τῶν ἁμαρτημάτων ἀπογενόμενοι, in the sense 'have no part in'], Teles 59, 11f; Dionys. Hal. 4, 15; SIG 1099, 15; SIG[2] 850, 12; pap, e.g. PMagd 29, 3; PRyl 65, 9; PGrenf II, 69, 10; PLips 29, 9; 10; 13; also s. Preis.; PGM 4, 719; cp. Jos., Ant. 5, 1) **1 Pt 2:24;** Ox 1081, 12; 16 (=SJCh 89, 14) [οὐκ ἀπο]γείν[εται].—New Docs 3, 62. DELG s.v. γίγνομαι. M-M. TW.

ἀπογινώσκω 2 aor. 3 sg. ἀπέγνω Dt 33:9; pf. ἀπεγνωκα; pass. pf. ptc. ἀπεγνωσμένος (Jdth 9:11) **to give up as hopeless, *despair*** (so Lysias et al.; SIG 326, 30; PCairZen 298, 4; 2 Macc 9:22; Jdth 9:11; Ath., R. 68, 2 al.) τὶ *of someth.* (Aristot., EN 1115b, 2 et al.; UPZ 144, 10 [II BC]; PGiss 72, 12f τοῦτο ἀπέγνων; Jos., Ant. 2, 140 τ. σωτηρίαν; 336 al.): ἀ. ἑαυτόν (Polyb. 22, 9, 14; Plut., Tib. Gracch. 830 [13]; Philo, Somn. 1, 60; Jos., Bell. 5, 537) *despair of oneself* Hv 1, 1, 9; s 9, 26, 4. τὴν ζωήν *of life* m 12, 6, 2 (cp. Philo, Leg. ad Gai. 352 τὸ ζῆν ἀ.). ὁ τὰ ἀπεγνω[σμένα .....] ἐπιστρ[έφ]ων εἰς σέ *(you) who turn despairing [hearts] to yourself (Jesus)* Ox 850 (AcJ), 6f.

ἀπογνωρίζω ***dispossess, reject*** pass. ἀπογνωρίζεσθαι ἀπὸ τ. ζωῆς *be dispossessed of one's life* Hv 2, 2, 8; in wordplay w. ἀρνέομαι: deny-disaffirm.—DELG s.v. γιγνώσκω.

ἀπογραφή, ῆς, ἡ (s. ἀπογράφω; Lysias, Pla. et al.; SIG 1023, 45 and 71; 1109, 34; 1157, 33, OGI 338, 11 and 34; very freq. pap; LXX, EpArist, Joseph.; Just., A I, 34, 2, D. 78, 4) administrative term 'list, inventory' of the statistical reports and declarations of citizens for the purpose of completing the tax lists and family registers (s. Mitt-Wilck. I/1 175f; 178; 202ff; 225ff, I/2 198ff, esp. 202, the census edict of C. Vibius Maximus, 104 AD [=PLond III, 904, 25f, restored]; on this Dssm., LO 231f [LAE 268f]). **Lk 2:2** the word means ***census, registration,*** of the census taken by Quirinius. Joseph. puts a census taken by Q. in 6/7 AD (cp. Jos., Bell. 7, 253, Ant. 18, 3). Presumably **Ac 5:37** ἐν τ. ἡμέραις τ. ἀπογραφῆς also refers to this census. The chronology is full of problems, on which see the handbooks. See Schürer I 399–427 (lit.); Ramsay, Bearing 238ff; Zahn, Lk 129–35 and Exk. IV; EKlostermann, Hdb. on Lk 2:1–3; M-JLagrange, RB n.s. 8, 1911, 60–84; EGroag, Prosopogr. Beitr. VII (JÖAI 21/22, 1924 Beiblatt, cols. 445–78); HWindisch, NThT 16, 1927, 106–24; AvPremerstein, Ztschr. d. Savigny-Stiftg. f. Rechtsgeschichte 48, 1928, Rom. Abt. 449ff; LRTaylor, AJP 54, '33, 120–33; RSyme, The Roman Revolution '39, 397–401; ESeraphin, CBQ 7, '45, 91–96; FHauck, Theol. Hndkomm., Lk p. 37; Goodsp., Probs. 71f; MHombert-CPréaux, Recherches sur le recensement dans l'Egypte romaine, '52; EStauffer, Jesus, Gestalt u. Geschichte, '57, Die Dauer des Census Augusti: Studien zum NT u. zur Patristik, '61, 9–34; HInstinsky, D. Jahr der Geburt Christi, '57; HBraunert, Historia 6, '57, 192–214, Cives Romani und ΚΑΤ' ΟΙΚΙΑΝ ΑΠΟΓΡΑΦΑΙ: Antidoron MDavid in Papyrologica Lugd.-Bat. vol. 17, '68, 11–21 (lit.; EStauffer, Festschr. Klostermann '61, 9ff; JThorley, The Nativity Census: What Does Luke Actually Say?: Greece and Rome, ser. 2, 26, '79, 81–84; Haenchen ad loc.; BPalme, ProBib 2, '93, 1–24). S. also on ἡγεμονεύω and Κυρήνιος.—Boffo, Iscrizioni 182f (lit.). New Docs 6, 115–19. DELG s.v. γράφω. M-M.

ἀπογράφω mid.: fut. ἀπογράψομαι; 1 aor. ἀπεγραψάμην. Pass.: 2 aor. ἀπεγράφην LXX; pf. ptc. ἀπογεγραμμένος (Hdt. et al.; ins, pap, LXX, En; TestSol 28:8 B; TestAbr) to 'write-off' i.e. to copy, a common term for the making of copies of official documents. Hence **to enter into a list, *register***

ⓐ of official registration in tax lists (Philol 71, 1912, 24; POxy 249, 5; 250, 1; PLond III, 904, 32 [I AD] p. 126 et al.; cp. ἀπογραφή) mid. as t.t. *register (oneself)* (Arrian, Anab. 3, 19, 6) **Lk 2:3, 5;** pass. vs. **1;** w. obj. of Joseph ἀπογραψομαι τοὺς υἱούς μου *I shall have my sons registered* GJs 17:1, foll. by πῶς αὐτὴν (Μαρίαν) ἀπογράψομαι; in the same sense prob. ἀπογράψασθαι ὅσοι εἰσὶν ἐν Βηθλεέμ loc. cit. (For the sense 'declare' [property] s. PTaur LVII, 11 [II BC]; cp. POxy 246, 10 [I AD]; add. reff. DGE s.v.)

ⓑ of records kept by God, fig. ext. of a (the Book of Life; cp. En 98:7 and 8; TestAbr A 12 p. 91, 11 [Stone p. 30] al.; ApcPl 10 p. 39f Tdf. πάντα τὰ πραττόμενα παρ' ὑμῶν καθ' ἡμέραν ἄγγελοι ἀπογράφονται [='write down'] ἐν οὐρανοῖς=daily the angels write down in heaven the things that we do) πρωτότοκοι ἀπογεγραμμένοι ἐν οὐρανοῖς *firstborn registered in heaven* **Hb 12:23.** S. ἀπογραφή.—EDNT. M-M s.v. ἀπογράφομαι. New Docs 1, 79f, w. examples of a typical return (BGU 2223) and an extract from a register (BGU 2228), both II AD.

ἀποδείκνυμι 1 aor. ἀπέδειξα. Pass.: 1 aor. ἀπεδείχθην LXX; pf. 3 sg. ἀποδέδεικται (Ar. 13, 8; Just.); ptc. ἀποδεδειγμένος (Pind., Hdt.+) gener. to 'point away' and 'direct attention' to a specific object.

❶ **to show forth for public recognition as so and so, *make, render, proclaim, appoint,*** esp. as administrative term w. double acc. (in var. senses: X., Cyr. 1, 2, 5 παῖδας βελτίστους ἀ.; Socrat., Ep. 28, 11 [=Malherbe 292, 10]; Diod. S. 2, 26, 6; Arrian, Anab. 6, 2, 1; Da 2:48; 2 Macc 14:26 [Swete]; Jos., Ant. 8, 162; Just., D. 86, 4 ῥάβδος . . . ἀρχιερέα αὐτὸν ἀπέδειξε '[Aaron's] rod . . . declared him highpriest') of God (Jos., Ant. 11, 3; TestJos 2:7) ἡμᾶς τοὺς ἀποστόλους ἐσχάτους ἀπέδειξεν *he has made/exhibited us (as) the last ones* perh. in a triumphal procession **1 Cor 4:9;** Paul's use of irony suggests a double sense. W. ὅτι foll. instead of the second acc. ἀποδεικνύντα ἑαυτὸν ὅτι ἔστιν θεός *proclaiming that he himself is God* **2 Th 2:4.** Pass. (Diod. S. 3, 59, 2) διάκονοι, ἀποδεδειγμένοι ἐν γνώμῃ Ἰησοῦ *assistants, appointed w. the approval of Jesus* IPhld ins (cp. PPetr III, 36a verso, 17 ἀποδεδειγμένοι ἐπίσκοποι: PGen 36, 2; Jos., Ant. 7, 356).

❷ **to show forth the quality of an entity, *show forth, display*** (PLond III, 904, 34 [104 AD] p. 126; BGU 388 II, 19) τὸ ἀκέραιον τῆς πραΰτητος αὐτῶν βούλημα ἀποδειξάτωσαν *let them display a sincere and gentle disposition* 1 Cl 21:7. Pass. ἄνδρα ἀποδεδειγμένον ἀπὸ τοῦ θεοῦ *attested by God* **Ac 2:22** (cp. Esth 3:13c; also Diod. S. 20, 40, 6 ἀποδεδειγμένος εἰς τ. πόλιν=well-liked in the city).

❸ **to demonstrate that someth. is true, *prove*** τὶ *someth.* (4 Macc 1:8; TestAbr B 115:17f [Stone p. 78]; Just., A I, 52, 1 [acc. w. inf.]; D. 100, 1; 68, 1 ὅτι; 59, 1 πῶς al.) **Ac 25:7.**—EPeterson, Deissmann Festschr. 1926, 320ff.

❹ like δείκνυμι **to draw attention to a specific object,** ***show*** (Hdt. 3, 122, 4; Thu. 1, 129, 1) προῆγεν αὐτ[οὺς . . .] |.[.φ]ωσ[τὴ]ρ ἀπεδίκνυεν *(Christ) went ahead of them [and like] a star showed them the way* AcPl Ha 7, 34f; **Lk 10:1** D.—M-M.

ἀπόδειξις, εως, ἡ (s. ἀποδείκνυμι; Pre-Socr., Hdt.+) **a pointing away to someth. for the purpose of demonstration,** ***proof*** (esp. of or for an intervention by a divinity, as Diod. S. 15, 49, 4; Theoph. Ant. 1, 13 [p. 86, 26]) ἀ. πνεύματος καὶ δυνάμεως lit. *proof of spirit and power,* i.e. proof consisting in possession of the Holy Spirit and miracle-working power (opp. πειθοὶ λόγοι) **1 Cor 2:4** (Philo, Mos. 1, 95 ἀ. διὰ σημείων κ. τεράτων in contrast to διὰ τ. λόγων; on assoc. w. ancient rhetoric s. GDautzenberg, EDNT I 127; HHommel/KZiegler, Pauly-W. IV 1396–1414).—M-M. TW. Sv.

ἀποδεκατεύω (Ion.-Att.; SEG IX, 72, 56 τῷ θεῷ; cp. δεκατεύω Hdt. et al.; Alexis Com. 200, 4 K. [in Athen. 6, 226a]) **to give one tenth of someth.,** ***tithe*** πάντα **Lk 18:12 v.l.**—DELG s.v. δέκα.

ἀποδεκατόω inf. ἀποδεκατοῦν (ἀποδεκατοῖν **Hb 7:5 v.l.,** s. B-D-F §91; 343; Mlt. 53) fut. ἀποδεκατώσω; 1 aor. ἀπεδεκάτωσα (LXX; TestLevi 9:4; Mich. Glycas 263, 6 IBekker [1836]).

❶ **to give one tenth,** ***tithe*** τὶ *(of) someth.* (Gen 28:22) **Mt 23:23; Lk 11:42; 18:12** (v.l. ἀποδεκατεύω; cp. ἀποδεκατοῦτε Just., D. 17, 4 and ἀποδεκατοῦντες 112, 4).

❷ **to collect one tenth,** ***collect a tithe*** (1 Km 8:15, 16, 17) τινά *fr. someone* τὸν λαόν **Hb 7:5.**—DELG s.v. δέκα.

ἀπόδεκτος, ον (s. ἀποδέχομαι) is accented thus almost exclusively in the NT tradition (but s. CGregory, Prolegomena to Tdf. NT[8] 1894, 100f), but ἀποδεκτός elsewhere (Plut., Mor. 1061a; Sext. Emp., Math. 11, 83; so also OGI 441, 100 ἀποδεκ[τὰ ὑπάρχει]ν δεῖν). Strictly speaking, ἀποδεκτός means ***acceptable, welcome*** and ἀπόδεκτος ***pleasing*** (W-S. §6, 4; Mlt-H. 58). The former is given Dg 8:3 (cp. Just., A I, 43, 2 οὔθ' οὗτος ἀπόδεκτος οὐδὲ ἐκεῖνος μεμπτέος); the latter has been given preference in **1 Ti 2:3; 5:4,** but the accentuation ἀποδεκτός for these pass. in the sense ***be approved, find approval*** deserves review, esp. when the administrative aspect of the next entry is considered in relation to the official-sounding tone of the Pauline pass.—M-M. TW.

ἀποδέχομαι 1 aor. ἀπεδεξάμην; pass. ἀπεδέχθην (Hom.+) gener. to 'receive' or 'accept' someone or someth. from a source. Hence

❶ **receive someone favorably,** ***welcome*** (Polyb. 21, 35, 5; Diod. S. 1, 18, 5; SIG 601, 9; POxy 939, 11; 2 Macc 3:9; 13:24) **Lk 8:40; 9:11; Ac 18:27; 21:17; 28:30;** IEph 1:1; ITr 1:2; AcPl Ha 7, 37.

❷ **to show approval by accepting,** ***accept*** someth. (En 103:14; Philo, Abr. 90; Jos., Ant. 9, 176; Just., D. 8, 3; Tat. 11, 1; Mel., P. 66, 469 πάθη) τ. λόγον (this expr. in Pla. et al.) **Ac 2:41;** cp. Dg 8:2.

❸ **to approve or commend as praiseworthy,** ***recognize, acknowledge, praise*** someone or someth. (Diod. S. 4, 31, 8 τὴν ἀνδρείαν; Appian, Bell. Civ. 2, 82 §347; Aesop, Fab. 308 H.//173 P.=183a H-H.; Himerius, Or. 65 [=Or. 19], 2; IG II, 481, 60; 4 Macc 3:20; EpArist 194; 274 al.; Philo, Gig, 37; Jos., Ant. 9, 176; 20, 264) **Ac 24:3** (sc. ταῦτα; typical administrative prose, s. Welles index VII s.v. ἀποδέχομαι and p. 316); τὴν ἐν θεῷ γνώμην *godly frame of mind* IPol 1:1. τινά τινος *someone for someth.* (POxy 705, 59 ἀποδεχόμεθά σε ταύτης τ. ἐπιδόσεως; Jos., Ant. 6, 340; 7, 160) τῆς προθυμίας σε ταύτης *I praise you for this eagerness* Dg 1.—**Ac 15:4 v.l.** (for παραδέχομαι).—DELG s.v. δέχομαι. M-M. TW.

ἀποδημέω 1 aor. ἀπεδήμησα (s. ἀπόδημος; Pind., Hdt. et al.; ins, pap; Ezk 19:3 A; TestJos 3:5) lit. 'be away from one's deme' (a district in a city-state); opp. ἐνδημέω (cp. [ἐνδημῶν καὶ] ἀπ[οδημῶν] Mitt-Wilck. II/2, 284, 3 [II BC]).

❶ **to travel away from one's domicile,** ***go on a journey*** εἰς (PSI 436, 2 [248 BC]; 413, 24f) χώραν μακράν *to a distant country* **Lk 15:13.** Abs. (PSI 416, 3 [III BC]; Jos., Ant. 6, 227, C. Ap. 2, 259) **Mt 21:33; 25:15; Mk 12:1; Lk 20:9.** ἄνθρωπος ἀποδημῶν *a man who was about to go on a journey* **Mt 25:14** (related imagery Epict. 4, 1, 58 of a slave's master who ἀποδημεῖ but ἥξει); sim. Hs 5, 2, 2.—Fig., euphem. ἀ. τῆς σαρκός *be absent fr. the flesh*=die (cp. ἤδη ἄγγελοι ἦσαν vs. 3), or perh.=be in a trance MPol 2:2 (=die: Epict. 3, 24, 88; Ar. [Milne 76, 38f] προπέμπουσιν ὡς ἀποδημοῦντα cp. MMeister, Axioch. Dial., diss. Breslau 1915, 87, 1).

❷ **to be distant from,** ***be away, absent*** (Pind. et al.) ἀπὸ τ. κυρίου *fr. the Lord* **2 Cor 5:6 v.l.; Mk 13:34 v.l.** (cp. PTebt 104, 17 ἐνδημῶν [q.v.] κ. ἀποδημῶν).—DELG s.v. δῆμος. M-M. TW.

ἀποδημία, ας, ἡ (s. ἀποδημέω; Hdt. et al.; SIG 1109, 50; pap, e.g. POxy 471, 134; PTebt 330, 3; SB V/2, 7835, 12; Jos., Ant. 17, 69) **being away from a place,** ***absence, journey*** Hs 5, 5, 3. εἰς ἀ. ἐξέρχεσθαι *go on a journey* 5, 2, 2.

ἀπόδημος, ον (s. ἀποδημέω; Pind. et al.; Plut., Mor. 799e; SIG 279, 24; 524, 30; POxy 1446, 84; 89; 1547, 23; Jos., Ant. 2, 165; Just., D. 3, 2) ***away on a journey*** ἄνθρωπος ἀ. *a man who is away on a journey* **Mk 13:34** (JDupont, BRigaux Festschr. '70, 89–116).—M-M.

ἀποδιδράσκω 2 aor. ἀπέδραν, 3 sg. ἀπέδρα; in late Gk. the subj. ἀποδράσῃ and fem. ptc. ἀποδράσασα (the latter TestJob 39:2) are found; cp. inf. ἀποδρᾶσαι (Vita Jon 5 [p. 84, 2 Sch.]) (Hom. et al.; pap, LXX; En 102:1; TestJob 39:2; TestBenj 5:3; SibOr 4, 124; Philo, Post. Cai. 43; Jos., Ant. 12, 378; Just., D. 60, 3 ἀπεδίδρασκες [Gen 35:1]) ***run away, escape*** ἀπό τινος (Jdth 11:3; TestBenj 5:3; Cleopatra ln. 126) *fr. someone* 1 Cl 28:4. ἀπὸ προσώπου τινός (Gen 16:6; Jdth 10:12; 11:16) 4:8.—DELG s.v. διδράσκω, 1 δράω. New Docs 4, 96f.

ἀποδίδωμι ptc. ἀποδιδοῦν (for -δόν) **Rv 22:2** (B-D-F §94, 1; Rob. 312); impf. ἀπεδίδουν **Ac 4:33,** H 67:5; fut. ἀποδώσω; 1 aor. ἀπέδωκα; 2 aor. subj. 2 sg. ἀποδῷς, 3 sg. ἀποδῷ, ἀποδοῖ Hv 1, 3, 4, impv. ἀπόδος, ἀπόδοτε; 2 aor. mid. ἀπεδόμην, 3 sg. ἀπέδετο **Hb 12:16** (-δοτο v.l.). Pass.: fut. ἀποδοθήσομαι; 1 aor. ἀπεδόθην, inf. ἀποδοθῆναι (the ms. tradition varies in the aor. subj. act., s. B-D-F §95, 2); pf. ptc. ἀποδεδομένος Num 8:16 (s. δίδωμι; Hom.+) gener. 'give out' something.

❶ **to give out,** ***give, give up, yield,*** τὸ σῶμα **Mt 27:58** (for the syntax cp. Diod. S. 14, 84, 2 τοὺς νεκροὺς ἀπέδωκαν). Of divine generosity τινί τι 1 Cl 23:1 (τὰς χάριτας). Of plants καρπόν *yield fruit* (POxy 53, 11 καρποὺς ἀ.; Lev 26:4) **Rv 22:2;** Hs 2:8; fig., **Hb 12:11.** στέφανον ἀ. *award a crown* **2 Ti 4:8.**

❷ **to meet a contractual or other obligation,** ***pay, pay out, fulfill***—ⓐ of wages or produce τὸν μισθόν (X., An. 1, 2, 12; Dio Chrys. 13 [7], 12; SIG 127, 27; Sb 3924, 20 [19 AD]; Tob 2:12; Jer 22:13; Philo, Virt. 88) *pay out wages* **Mt 20:8;** 2 Cl 20:4;

B 11:8. τὴν ἀντιμισθίαν τινὶ ἀ. 2 Cl 11:6; 15:2. Of proceeds, *give* **Mt 21:41.** μαρτύριον ἀ. (4 Macc 6:32) *give testimony* **Ac 4:33.**

ⓑ of taxes, *pay* (Philo, Op. M. 85) **Mt 22:21; Mk 12:17; Lk 20:25** (cp. Sextus 20).

ⓒ of fulfilling various responsibilities ἀ. τῷ ὑψίστῳ τὰς εὐχάς *pay vows to the Highest* 1 Cl 52:3 (Ps 49:14; cp. Dt 23:22; Jos., Ant. 11, 9 τ. εὐχὰς ἀπεδίδοσαν τ. θεῷ; X., Mem. 2, 2, 10 τ. θεοῖς εὐχὰς ἀ.; Diod. S. 4, 48, 7; 4, 49, 2; 8 τὰς εὐχὰς ἀποδοῦναι τοῖς θεοῖς; 14, 13, 5 Ἄμμωνι; PGiss 27, 9f [II AD] ἵνα τ. θεοῖς τ. ὀφειλομένας σπονδὰς ἀποδῶ). τὴν ὀφειλήν τινι ἀ. *fulfill one's duty to someone* **1 Cor 7:3;** pl. **Ro 13:7.** τὴν ἐπαγγελίαν *keep the promise*=give that which we promised GJs 7:1; sim. of God B 5:7; Hv 1, 3, 4. τοὺς ὅρκους ἀ. *keep oaths* **Mt 5:33** (cp. POxy 1026, 6). λόγον ἀ. *give account* (s. λόγος 2a) **Mt 12:36; Lk 16:2; Ac 19:40; Ro 14:12 v.l.; Hb 13:17; 1 Pt 4:5;** Hv 3, 9, 10; m 2:5.

❸ **to restore to an original possessor, *give back, return***

ⓐ of things τὶ (Philo, Spec. Leg. 4, 67; Jos., Vi. 335; Just., D. 105, 5 τὸ πνεῦμα) Hm 3:2; s 8, 6, 3. τινί τι (X., Hell. 2, 2, 9 et al.) **Lk 9:42;** Hs 2:7. τινί v 2, 1, 3. τῷ ὑπηρέτῃ **Lk 4:20.** *Pay back a debt* **Mt 5:26; 18:25ff, 34; Lk 7:42; 12:59;** D 1:5; *repay* an advance **Lk 10:35;** *give back* taxes unjustly collected **19:8** (cp. Num 5:7f). Mid. τὰς ῥάβδους Hs 8, 1, 5.

ⓑ of persons τὴν παρθένον GJs 16:1; Salome prays ἀπόδος με τοῖς πένησιν *return me to the poor* 20:2 (not pap). ἵνα αὐτὸν ἐγείρας ἀποδῷ σοι *so that* (Peter) *might raise him* (your son) *and return him to you* AcPt Ox 849.

❹ **to recompense, whether in a good or bad sense, *render, reward, recompense,*** cp. ἀνταποδίδωμι, of God **Mt 6:4, 6, 18.** ἑκάστῳ κατὰ τὰ ἔργα αὐτοῦ **Ro 2:6** (Ps 61:13; Pr 24:12; PsSol 2:16); cp. **2 Ti 4:14; Rv 22:12;** 1 Cl 34:3. ἑκάστῳ κατὰ τ. πρᾶξιν αὐτοῦ **Mt 16:27** (Sir 35:22). τινί τι 1 Cl 18:12 (Ps 50:14; Just. D. 121, 3). κακὸν ἀντὶ κακοῦ (cp. Pr 17:13; ApcSed 7:7) *evil with evil* **Ro 12:17** (cp. 1QS 10:17); **1 Th 5:15; 1 Pt 3:9;** Pol 2:2. ἀμοιβὰς ἀ. (Dionys. Hal. 6, 73; POxy 705, 61 ἀποδιδοὺς ἀμοιβήν; Ps 27:4 Aq.; Just. A I, 43, 2) *make a return* **1 Ti 5:4.** Abs. ἀπόδοτε αὐτῇ ὡς καὶ αὐτὴ ἀπέδωκεν *render to her as she herself has rendered to others* **Rv 18:6** (cp. Ps 136:8).—IBroer, Das Ius Talionis im NT: NTS 40, '94, 1–21.

❺ mid. **to make an exchange—ⓐ *sell, trade*** (Hdt. 1, 70 et al.; ins, pap) τὸν Ἰωσήφ **Ac 7:9** (Gen 37:28; 45:4; Philo, De Jos. 15; 238). τί τινος *someth. for someth.* (Pla., Phd. 98b; X., Hell. 2, 3, 48) τοσούτου τὸ χωρίον *sell the piece of ground for so much* **Ac 5:8** (ἀ. τὸ χ. as Jos., Ant. 3, 283). τὶ ἀντί τινος (as TestIss 2:2) *trade* **Hb 12:16.**

ⓑ τὸν ἴδιον υἱὸν λύτρον *(God's) own son as a ransom* Dg 9:2.—EDNT. M-M. TW.

ἀποδιορίζω (διορίζω 'draw a boundary through'; s. ὅρος; Aristot., Pol. 4, 4, 13 p. 1290b, 25; Herm. Wr. 3, 2a codd.) 'mark off by dividing or separating', hence the metaph. sense ***divide, separate*** in ref. to pers. (opp. ἐποικοδομεῖν) abs. οὗτοι εἰσιν οἱ ἀποδιορίζοντες *these are the ones who cause a division* **Jd 19.**—DELG s.v. ὅρος. M-M. TW.

ἀποδιϋλίζω ***to strain/filter*** (s. διϋλίζω; Lghtf. ad loc.) of purification through a filtering process in which the undesirable portion is left behind; ἀπὸ παντὸς ἀλλοτρίου χρώματος *cleared of every foreign color* metaph., of true teaching IRo ins.—DELG s.v. ὕλη.

ἀποδιϋλισμός, οῦ, ὁ (s. ἀποδιϋλίζω) ***filtering*** fig., *purification* fr. evil elements (opp. μερισμός) IPhld 3:1.

ἀποδοκιμάζω fut. ἀποδοκιμῶ Jer 38:35; 1 aor. ἀπεδοκίμασα. Pass.: fut. 3 sg. ἀποδοκιμασθήσεται Sir 20:20; 1 aor. ἀπεδοκιμάσθην; pf. ptc. ἀποδεδοκιμασμένος (Solon and Hdt. 6, 130, 1+; Vett. Val. 278, 18; 313, 26; LXX; TestSol) 'reject' (after scrutiny), 'declare useless', **to regard as unworthy/unfit and therefore to be rejected, *reject***

ⓐ of things (Epicurus in Diog. L. 10, 31; Appian, Bell. Civ. 5, 32 §126; Ps.-Demetr. c. 200; SIG 306, 52; PTebt 860, 13 PGiss 47, 14ff; PCairIsid 44, 9; 72, 38; Jer 6:30; Jos., Ant. 15, 321) of stones **Mt 21:42; Mk 12:10; Lk 20:17; 1 Pt 2:4, 7;** B 6:4 (all these after Ps 117:22); Hs 9, 7, 4; 9, 23, 3. λίθους ἀ. ἐκ τ. οἰκοδομῆς *reject stones fr. the building* 9, 12, 7. Of coins *reject as counterfeit* Agr 11 (of a τραπεζίτης Epict 3, 3, 3; cp. Theophr., Char. 4, 11 ἀργύριον; Jer 6:30).

ⓑ of pers. (Pla., Tht. 181b; X., Mem. 2, 2, 13) pass., *be rejected* (Aristoxenus, fgm. 18) of Jesus **Mk 8:31; Lk 9:22; 17:25** (Just., D. 76, 7; 100, 3). Gener., *be rejected* by God (Jer 6:30; 7:29; 14:19 al.) **Hb 12:17.** IRo 8:3 (in latter pass.=not to become a martyr, opp. παθεῖν).—DELG s.v. δοκάω III. M-M. TW.

ἀποδοχή, ῆς, ἡ (s. ἀποδέχομαι; Thu. et al.) ***acceptance, approval*** (so since Polyb. [1, 5, 5 ὁ λόγος ἀποδοχῆς τυγχάνει]; Diod. S. 1, 47, 4; Letter 2 of Apollonius of Tyana [Philostrat. I 345, 12] ἀποδοχῆς ἄξιον; Diog. L. 5, 64; Hierocles in Stob., Ecl. 4, 27, 20 p. 662, 1f ἔργον πολλῆς ἄξιον ἀποδοχῆς; IPriene 108, 312; SIG 867, 20f ἀνδρὸς … πάσης τειμῆς καὶ ἀποδοχῆς ἀξίου; EpArist 257; 308; Jos., Ant. 6, 347; Just., D. 3, 3. S. also Nägeli 34f) of a saying πάσης ἀ. ἄξιος **1 Ti 1:15; 4:9.**—DELG s.v. δέχομαι B. M-M. TW. Spicq.

ἀποδύομαι 1 aor. ἀπεδυσάμην (δύω 'put on' e.g. armor; Hom. et al.; TestAbr A 17 p. 99, 12 [Stone p. 46]; Jos., Bell. 1, 452 codd.) ***take off*** τὸ ἔνδυμα καὶ τὴν δύναμιν Hs 9, 13, 8 (cp. Athen. 11, 507e as a saying of Plato: τὸν τῆς δόξης χιτῶνα ἀποδυόμεθα; PLips 40 III, 22 τὸ ἱμάτιον).—DELG s.v. δύω.

ἀποδῴη, ἀποδῷς s. ἀποδίδωμι.

ἀποθανοῦμαι s. ἀποθνῄσκω.

ἀποθαυμάζω 1 aor. ἀπεθαύμασμα LXX (s. θαυμάζω; since Od. 6, 49; Hdt. et al., seldom in good Attic prose; LXX, TestJob 28:5; Joseph.) ***be astounded*** τὰ μεγέθη τ[ῶν θηρίων]|| ἀποθα[υ]μ‹ά›ζειν *the hugeness of the beasts* AcPl Ha 1, 34f.—DELG s.v. θαῦμα.

ἀπόθεσις, εως, ἡ (s. ἀποτίθημι; Hippocr., Pla.+ in var. senses; ins, pap; TestSim 2:9) ***removal, getting rid of,*** only fig. ἀ. ῥύπου *of dirt* in baptism **1 Pt 3:21.** ἡ ἀ. τ. σκηνώματός μου *of my tent* euphem. for death **2 Pt 1:14.**—DELG s.v. τίθημι. M-M.

ἀποθήκη, ης, ἡ (s. ἀποτίθημι; Thu. 6, 97, 5+; SIG 1106, 84; PRyl 97, 11; PTebt 347, 1; 5; BGU 32, 3; 816, 5; 931, 2; LXX; ApcEsdr 5:23 p. 30, 26 Tdf.; Jos., Ant. 9, 274; loanw. in rabb.) of a place where one puts someth. ***storehouse, barn*** συνάγειν εἰς τὴν ἀ. *gather into the barn* **Mt 3:12; 6:26; 13:30; Lk 3:17** (Just., D.49, 3). S. on ἀλοάω.—**Lk 12:18;** w. ταμιεῖον (Jos., loc. cit.) **12:24;** *cellar* for oil and wine Hm 11:15.—B. 492. M-M.

ἀποθησαυρίζω (s. θησαυρίζω; Diod. S. 3, 31, 3; 5, 75, 4; Epict 3, 22, 50; Lucian, Alex. 23; Aelian, NA 14, 18; Artem. 1, 73 p. 66, 22; Vett. Val. 16, 21; 18:12; Jos., Bell. 7, 299 et al. [Nägeli 30]; Sir 3:4) ***store up, lay up*** fig. ἀ. θεμέλιον καλόν *lay up a good foundation* **1 Ti 6:19** (cp. θεμέλιος γὰρ τῷ φαύλῳ κακία καὶ πάθος=baseness and passion are a bad man's support Philo, Sacr. Ab/C 81). The metaphor is "telescoped" (cp. Pind.,

P. 10, 51–54; s. BGildersleeve, Pindar 1885, 355).—DELG s.v. θησαυρός.

ἀποθλίβω 1 aor. 3 sg. ἀπέθλιψεν Num 22:25 (s. θλίβω; Eur. et al. in var. senses, but esp. of someth., such as a grape, which loses its contents when squeezed; pap [Mayser 381]; Num 22:25; Jos., Ant. 2, 64; 6, 118) **to apply squeezing pressure,** ***press upon, crowd*** (UPZ 162 II, 13 [117 BC]) τινά *someone,* of a throng (w. συνέχειν) **Lk 8:45.**—DELG s.v. θλίβω. M-M.

ἀποθνῄσκω impf. ἀπέθνῃσκον; fut. ἀποθανοῦμαι; 2 aor. ἀπέθανον; pf. 3 sg. ἀποτέθνηκεν (Tat. 2, 1) (s. θνῄσκω, θάνατος; Hom.+; on the ῃ s. B-D-F §2; Rob. 194) intensive of θνῄσκω 'die'.

➊ **to cease to have vital functions, whether at an earthly or transcendent level,** ***die***—ⓐ of death on an earthly level—**α.** of pers. **Mt 9:24; 22:24** (Dt 25:5), **27; Mk 5:35, 39; 9:26; Lk 8:42** (ἀπέθνῃσκεν *was about to die,* as in Jos., Ant. 5, 4), **52; Ro 6:10; 7:2f** (Artem. 4, 71 p. 246, 2 πάντων ὁ θάνατός ἐστι λυτικός); **Phil 1:21; Hb 9:27** (Archinus: Orat. Att. II p. 167 πᾶσι ἀνθρώποις ὀφείλεται ἀποθανεῖν; Just., A I, 18, 1 τὸν κοινὸν πᾶσι θάνατον ἀπέθανον); GEg 252, 48 al. Of violent death (also as pass. of ἀποκτείνω=be killed: Hdt. 1, 137, 2; 7, 154, 1; Lycurgus 93; Pla., Ap. 29d; 32d; Nicol. Dam.: 90 fgm. 30 Jac.; Lucian, Dial. Mort. 4, 4 ὑπὸ τοῦ παιδὸς ἀποθανών; Iambl., Vi. Pyth. 28, 143 ἱεροσυλῶν ἐλήφθη κ. ἀπέθανε; Josh 20:3) **Mt 26:35** (for κἂν δέῃ ἀποθανεῖν cp. Lucian, Timon 43; Jos., Ant. 6, 108); **J 19:7; Ac 25:11.** θανάτῳ ἀ. (Od. 11, 412; Gen 2:17; 3:4) **J 12:33; 18:32;** cp. Hs 8, 7, 3. W. ἐπί τινι *on the basis of* (Dio Chrys. 47 [64], 3) ἐπὶ δυσὶν ἢ τρισὶν μάρτυσιν ἀ. *suffer death on the basis of (the testimony of) two or three witnesses* lit., **Hb 10:28** (Dt 17:6). W. ὑπέρ τινος *for (the benefit of)* (Epict 2, 7, 3 ὑπὲρ αὐτοῦ; Lucian, Peregr. 23; 33: Per. dies ὑπὲρ τ. ἀνθρώπων, cp. Tox. 43; 2 Macc 7:9; 8:21; 4 Macc 1:8, 10; Jos., Ant. 13, 5; 6) **J 11:50f; Ac 21:13; Ro 5:6ff.** διά (4 Macc 6:27; 16:25) Ἰησοῦν Χριστὸν ἀ. IRo 6:1 v.l. (the rdg. varies betw. διά, εἰς, ἐν). Esp. of Christ's death **Ro 5:8; 14:15; 1 Cor 15:3; 2 Cor 5:14f; 1 Th 5:10; 1 Pt 3:18 v.l.;** ITr 2:1; IRo 6:1; Pol 9:2. ἀ. ἐν κυρίῳ *die in the Lord* of martyrs **Rv 14:13.** For this ὑπὲρ θεοῦ ἀ. IRo 4:1. Not specif. of a martyr's death τῷ κυρίῳ ἀ. *die for the Lord* **Ro 14:8** (cp. Alciphron 4, 10, 5 δεῖ γὰρ αὐτὸν ἢ ἐμοὶ ζῆν ἢ τεθνάναι Θεττάλῃ). W. the reason given ἀ. ἔκ τινος *die because of someth.* (Hdt. 2, 63 ἐκ τ. τρωμάτων) **Rv 8:11;** ὑπὸ τοῦ πλήθους τῆς χαλάζης AcPl Ha 5, 10. The extraordinary expr. ἀ. εἰς τὸ αὐτοῦ (i.e. Jesus') πάθος may be transl. *die in order to share his experience (=his death;* s. JKleist, note ad loc.) IMg 5:2.

β. of animals and plants ἀ. ἐν τοῖς ὕδασιν *drown* **Mt 8:32.** Of grains of wheat placed in the ground *decay* **J 12:24; 1 Cor 15:36;** w. regard to what is being illustrated, this is called *dying.* Of trees *die* **Jd 12.** fig.

ⓑ of death on a transcendent level—**α.** of losing the ultimate, eternal life **Ro 8:13; Rv 3:2.** So almost always in J: **6:50, 58; 8:21, 24; 11:26** al. ἡ ἁμαρτία ἀνέζησεν, ἐγὼ δὲ ἀπέθανον *sin came back to life, and I died* **Ro 7:9, 10.** Of worldly Christians: τὸ ἥμισυ ἀπέθανεν Hs 8, 1. ζῆν ἡμᾶς ἐν θεῷ . . . [καὶ μὴ ἀπο]|θανεῖν ἐν ἁμαρτίαις AcPl Ha 1, 15f (cp. Tat. 11:2 πολλάκις ἀποθνήσκεις). Cp. μὴ εἰδό[τες τὴν δια]φ[ο]ρὰν τα[ύτην ἀπέ]θανον *not recognizing this distinction* (between the transitory and the intransitory), *they died* Ox 1081, 22–24 (=SJCh 89, 19f) as read by Till p. 218 app.

β. of mystical death with Christ ἀπεθάνομεν σὺν Χριστῷ **Ro 6:8** (EKlaar, ZNW 59, '68, 131–34). Cp. **2 Cor 5:14; Col 3:3.**

γ. w. dat. of pers. or thing fr. which one is separated by death, however death may be understood: τ. θεῷ Hs 8, 6, 4; 9, 28, 5; νόμῳ **Gal 2:19;** τ. ἁμαρτίᾳ **Ro 6:2;** ἀ. (τούτῳ) ἐν ᾧ κατειχόμεθα *dead to that which held us captive* **7:6** (for the dative constr. cp. Plut., Agis et Cleom. 819f; see s.v. ζάω 3b and CFDMoule, BRigaux Festschr., '70, 367–75).—W. ἀπό τινος instead of the dat. **Col 2:20** (cp. Porphyr., Abst. 1, 41 ἀπὸ τ. παθῶν).

➋ **the prospect of death or realization of mortality** ***be about to die, face death, be mortal*** (Phalaris, Ep. 52 ἀποθνήσκοντες=be in danger of death; Philosoph. Max 495, 125 ὁ τῶν ἀσώτων βίος ὥσπερ καθ' ἡμέραν ἀποθνήσκων ἐκφέρεται; Athen. 12, 552b καθ' ἑκάστην ἡμέραν ἀποθνήσκειν; Seneca, Ep. 24, 20 (cotidie morimur); Philo, In Flacc. 175; PGiss 17, 9 ἀποθνήσκομεν ὅτι οὐ βλέπομέν σε καθ' ἡμέραν) καθ' ἡμέραν ἀ. *I face death every day* **1 Cor 15:31** (cp. Ps 43:23). ὡς ἀποθνήσκοντες καὶ ἰδοὺ ζῶμεν **2 Cor 6:9.** ἀποθνήσκοντες ἄνθρωποι *mortal people* **Hb 7:8.**—B. 287. DELG s.v. θάνατος. M-M.

ἀποίητος, ον (ποιητός 'made', s. ποιέω; in var. senses, e.g. Pind., O. 2, 16 'undone'=ἄπρακτον; StudPal XX, 144, 9 of wine inadequately fermented; Pind. et al.) ***not made, uncreated*** in wordplay of God ἀποίητος ὃς πάντα ἐποίησεν PtK 2 p. 13, 26.—DELG s.v. ποιέω.

ἀποκαθιστάνω s. next.

ἀποκαθίστημι/ἀποκαθιστάνω (the latter form: SIG 588, 56 [196 BC]; Polyb. 3, 98, 9; Diod. S. 18, 57; Jos., Ant. 16, 170; **Mk 9:12; Ac 1:6;** B-D-F §93; W-S. §14, 14; Rob. 1216).—The form ἀποκαθίστημι: pres. also as by-form -ιστάω (Duris of Samos [IV/III BC]: 76 fgm. 7 Jac.; Diod. S. 1, 78, 2; Arist., Met. 1074a, 3 v.l.) as v.l. **Mk 9:12** (3 sg. ἀποκαθιστᾷ); also as by-form 3 sg. ἀποκαταστάνει (**Mk 9:12 v.l.**). Impf. 3 pl. ἀπεκαθίστων Gen 29:3; fut. ἀποκαταστήσω; 1 aor. ἀπεκατέστησα LXX, GrBar 17:2 (ἀπο- Gen 40:21 cod. R); 2 aor. ἀπεκατέστην. Pass.: 1 fut. ἀποκατασταθήσομαι; 1 aor. ἀπεκατεστάθην (for the double augm., see, e.g., PTebt 413, 4; s. B-D-F §69, 3; Rob. 368; KBrugmann[4]-AThumb, Griech. Gramm. 1913, p. 311; Schwyzer I 656; DELG s.v. ἵστημι); pf. ptc. ἀποκαθεσταμένη Mel., P. 78, 563 Ch. (X.+; s. Anz 330f.)

➊ **to change to an earlier good state or condition,** ***restore, reestablish*** (OGI 90, 18; Demosth. 18, 90; Dionys. Hal. 3, 23; Herodian 2, 6, 11; IPriene 361, 2 [IV BC]; PGM 4, 629f; Gen 29:3; Ezk 16:55; 1 Macc 15:3; Tat. 18, 3 εἰς τὸ ἀρχαῖον) of Elijah (Mal 3:23) πάντα **Mt 17:11; Mk 9:12** (s. Schürer II 515f; Bousset, Rel.[3] 232f; Billerb. IV 764–98). τινί τι (Diod. S. 16, 45, 9; 20, 32, 2 τ. πολίταις τ. δημοκρατίαν ἀποκατέστησε) ἀ. τὴν βασιλείαν τῷ Ἰσραήλ **Ac 1:6** (s. the discussion s.v. ἀποκατάστασις). Abs. 1 Cl 56:6 (Job 5:18).—Medical t.t. *cure* (Diosc., Mat. Med. I 64, 4; Vi. Aesopi G 7 ἀ. τὴν φωνήν=restore the voice of a mute; Ex 4:7; Lev 13:16) intr. ἀπεκατέστη *he was cured* (EpArist 316) **Mk 8:25.** Pass. ἀπεκατεστάθη ὑγιής *it was restored* **Mt 12:13; Mk 3:5; Lk 6:10** (TestSim 2:13; cp. Mel., P. 78, 563; 89, 669); ἀπεκατεστάθη τὸ οὖς **22:51** D. Fig., of the tortured body of a persecuted church ISm 11:2. ἐπί τι (Diod. S.2, 9, 3) ἐπὶ τὴν σεμνὴν τ. φιλαδελφίας ἀγωγήν *to the venerable practice of brotherly love* 1 Cl 48:1.

➋ **to return someone to a former place or relationship,** ***bring back, give back, restore*** (Polyb. 3, 98, 7; Diod. S. 18, 65, 1; POxy 38, 12f ὑφ' οὗ καὶ ἀποκατεστάθη μοι ὁ υἱός et al. in pap; 2 Km 9:7; Job 8:6; 2 Macc 11:25; Jos., Ant. 15, 195; Tat. 18, 3 τοῖς οἰκείοις) ἵνα ἀποκατασταθῶ ὑμῖν *that I might be* *restored to you* **Hb 13:19.** τινὰ εἴς τι (Polyb. 8, 29, 6; 1 Esdr 6:25; Jer 16:15; 23:8; GrBar 17:2; Jos., Ant. 11, 2, Vi. 183) εἰς τ. τόπον Hs 7:6 (v.l. οἶκον).—B. 751. EDNT. M-M. TW. Sv.

ἀποκαλύπτω fut. ἀποκαλύψω; 1 aor. ἀπεκάλυψα. Pass.: 1 fut. ἀποκαλυφθήσομαι; aor. ἀπεκαλύφθην; pf. ptc. ἀποκεκαλυμμένοι Pr 27:5; plupf. 3 sg. ἀποκεκαλύπτο (Just., D. 78, 7) (s. ἀποκάλυψις, καλύπτω; Hdt. et al.; pap, LXX; TestSol, Test12Patr; ParJer 5:24; JosAs, GrBar, ApcEsdr; ApcSed 2:1; ApcMos; Jos., Bell. 5, 350, Ant. 14, 406; Just.) the lit. sense 'uncover' as of head (Hdt. 1, 119, 6) does not appear in our lit. (but s. ἀκατακάλυπτος). **to cause someth. to be fully known, *reveal, disclose, bring to light, make fully known***

ⓐ in a gener. sense (Appian, Syr. 5 §18) pass. *be revealed* (opp. καλύπτω) **Mt 10:26; Lk 12:2; J 12:38** (in act. sense) and 1 Cl 16:3 (Is 53:1); **Ro 1:17** (cp. Ps 97:2), **18; Lk 2:35** (cp. Josh 2:20; Sir 27:16f; Ezk 16:57; 1 Macc 7:31; AcPlCor 1:8).

ⓑ esp. of divine revelation of certain transcendent secrets (Ps 97:2; Da 2:19, 22 [both Theod.], 28; 1 Km 2:27; 3:21; Is 56:1) ἀ. τινί τι *reveal someth. to someone* (TestJos 6:6; Just., D. 100, 2) **Mt 11:25; 16:17; Lk 10:21; Phil 3:15;** IEph 20:1; w. ὅτι foll. (TestLevi 1:2) **1 Pt 1:12.** The revealers are Christ **Mt 11:27; Lk 10:22,** and the Holy Spirit **1 Cor 2:10; 14:30; Eph 3:5.** For **Gal 1:16** s. ἐν 9 and s. ADenis, RB 64, '57, 335–62; 481–515. Abs. (w. φανεροῦν) ἀ. διά τινος Dg 8:11. τὰ ἀποκαλυφθέντα ἡμῖν *the revelations that have come to us* 11:8.

ⓒ of the interpr. of prophetic visions ἀ. τινί Hv 2, 2, 4; 2, 4, 1; 3, 3, 2ff; 3, 4, 3; 3, 8, 10; 3, 13, 4. ἀ. τινὶ ἀποκάλυψιν *impart a revelation to someone* 3, 12, 2. ἀ. τινὶ περί τινος *give someone a revelation about someth.* (TestReub 3:15) 3, 10, 2. ἀπεκαλύφθη μοι ἡ γνῶσις τῆς γραφῆς *a knowledge of the scripture was disclosed to me* 2, 2, 1.

ⓓ of the revelation of certain pers. and circumstances in the endtime (Da 10:1 Theod.): of the Human One (Son of Man) **Lk 17:30.** Of the Lawless One **2 Th 2:3, 6, 8.** Of the final judgment **1 Cor 3:13.** ἡ μέλλουσα δόξα ἀποκαλυφθῆναι *the glory that is about to be revealed* **Ro 8:18;** cp. **1 Pt 5:1.** σωτηρία **1:5.** πίστις **Gal 3:23.** The disciples say to the risen Lord ἀποκάλυψον σοῦ τὴν δικαιοσύνην ἤδη *reveal, now, your righteousness* **ending of Mk** in the Freer ms.—RBultmann, D. Begriff d. Offenbarung im NT 1929. EFScott, The NT Idea of Rev. '35. ESelwyn, I Peter, '46, 250–52; HSchulte, D. Begriff d. Offenbarung im NT, diss. Heidelberg '47; WBulst, Offenbarung: Bibl. u. Theolog. Begriff '60; BVawter, CBQ 22, '60, 33–46.—M-M. TW. Spicq.

ἀποκάλυψις, εως, ἡ (s. ἀποκαλύπτω; Philod., Vit. [περὶ κακιῶν] p. 38 Jensen) (Plut., Cato Mai. 34 8 [20, 8], Aemil. 262 [14, 3], Mor. 70f ἀ. τῆς ἁμαρτίας; Sir 11:27; 22:22; 41:26 v.l.; TestAbr A 6 p. 83, 27 [Stone p. 14]; GrBar, ApcEsdr ins, Just.) the lit. sense 'uncovering' as of head (s. Philod. above) does not appear in our lit., which uses the term in transcendent associations.

❶ **making fully known, *revelation, disclosure*—ⓐ** of the revelation of truth gener., w. obj. gen., **Ro 16:25.** πνεῦμα σοφίας κ. ἀ. **Eph 1:17.** φῶς εἰς ἀ. ἐθνῶν *a light of revelation for gentiles* **Lk 2:32.**

ⓑ of revelations of a particular kind, through visions, etc.: w. gen. of the author ἀ. Ἰησοῦ Χριστοῦ **Gal 1:12; Rv 1:1** (w. ὀπτασία) ἀ. κυρίου **2 Cor 12:1.** κατὰ ἀποκάλυψιν *because of a rev.* **Gal 2:2;** MPol 22:3, Epil Mosq 5. κατὰ ἀ. ἐγνωρίσθη μοι τὸ μυστήριον *the secret was made known to me by revelation* **Eph 3:3.** Cp. **1 Cor 2:4** D; **14:6, 26; 2 Cor 12:7.**—In the visions of Hermas the ἀ. are not only transcendent rev. for eye and ear, but also the interpretations given to such rev. The ἀ. is ὁλοτελής *complete* only when it is explained and understood v 3, 10, 9; 3, 13, 4a. W. ὁράματα 4, 1, 3. Cp. 3, 1, 2; 3, 3, 2; 3, 10, 6–9; 3, 12, 2; 3, 13, 4b; 5 ins.—MBuber, Ekstatische Konfessionen 1909.

ⓒ of the disclosure of secrets belonging to the last days ἀ. τῆς δόξης τοῦ Χριστοῦ **1 Pt 4:13.** Of the parousia ἐν ἀποκαλύψει, Ἰ. Χ. **1 Pt 1:7, 13;** cp. **1 Cor 1:7; 2 Th 1:7.** τὴν ἀ. τ. υἱῶν τ. θεοῦ ἀπεκδέχεσθαι *wait for the revealing of the children of God,* i.e. for the time when they will be revealed in their glorified status **Ro 8:19.** ἀ. δικαιοκρισίας τ. θεοῦ **2:5.**

❷ as part of a book title ***Revelation*** (Porphyr., Vi. Plot. 16 συγγράμματα …, ἀποκαλύψεις Ζωροάστρου κ. Ζωστριανοῦ κτλ.) ἀ. Ἰωάννου Rv ins ἀ. Ἰακώβ GJs ins and subscr.—EDNT. TRE XXV 109–46. DELG s.v. καλύπτω. M-M. TW. Spicq.

ἀποκαραδοκία, ας, ἡ (ἀποκαραδοκέω, from κάρα 'head' and δοκέω 'think, imagine') (only in Christian writers—cp. Hesychius; Suda; Anecd. Gr. p. 428, 14; Etym. Gud. 171, 14—but ἀποκαραδοκέω in Polyb. 16, 2, 8; 18, 48, 4 ἀ. τὴν Ἀντιόχου παρουσίαν; 22, 19, 3; Sostratus [I BC]: 23 fgm. 4, p. 187 Jac. [in Stob. 4, 20, 70]; Aesop, Fab. 177 P. and 194 P.=H-H. 187 and 208; Jos., Bell. 3, 264; Ps 36:7 Aq.) ***eager expectation*** ἡ ἀ. τῆς κτίσεως = ἡ ἀποκαραδοκοῦσα κτίσις *the eagerly awaiting creation* **Ro 8:19** (GSchläger, D. ängstl. Harren d. Kreatur: NorTT 19, 1930, 353–60; GBertram, ZNW 49, '58, 264–70; DDenton, ibid. 73, '82, 138–40). κατὰ τὴν ἀ. μου (w. ἐλπίς) *according to my eager expectation* **Phil 1:20.**—DELG s.v. (1) κάρα. EDNT. M-M. TW. Sv.

ἀποκαταλλάσσω 1 aor. ἀποκατήλλαξα; 2 aor. pass. ἀποκατηλλάγην (s. καταλλάσσω; found only in Christian writers; s. Nägeli 52) ***reconcile*** (Anecd. Gr. p. 428, 15=φιλοποιῆσαι) ἀ. τὰ πάντα εἰς αὐτόν *reconcile everything in his own person,* i.e. the universe is to form a unity, which has its goal in Christ **Col 1:20** (cp. MDibelius, Hdb. ad loc.; s. also CBreytenbach, Versöhnung '89, esp. 190f); some prefer to transl. *reconcile everything to himself* (i.e. God). ἀ. τοὺς ἀμφοτέρους τῷ θεῷ **Eph 2:16.** Abs. ἀποκατήλλαξεν **Col 1:22** (v.l. ἀποκατηλλάγητε and ἀποκαταλλαγέντες).—EDNT. DELG s.v. ἄλλος. TW.

ἀποκαταστάνω by-form of ἀποκαθίστημι, q.v. ***restore, reestablish*** **Mk 9:12 v.l.**—DELG s.v. ἵστημι.

ἀποκατάστασις, εως, ἡ (s. ἀποκαθίστημι; Aristot. EM 2, 7, 1204b, 36; Epicurus p. 41, 26 [8, 9 Us.]; Polyb.; Diod. S. 20, 34, 5 al.; ins [e.g. SEG XLI, 1003 II, 42], pap; Herm. Wr. 8, 4; 11, 2; τέλειος λόγος in Lact., Inst. 7, 18, 3; Iambl., Myst. 1, 10; EpArist 123; Philo, Rer. Div. Her. 293; Jos., Ant. 11, 63; 98; Just., D. 134, 4; Iren. 1, 17, 1 [Harv. I 167, 1] of the sun's cycle) ***restoration,*** which can be var. understood ἄχρι χρόνων ἀποκαταστάσεως πάντων *until the time for restoring everything* to perfection or, as of stars in their orbits, to their starting points (Diod. S. 12, 36, 2; in diplomatic documents: e.g. OGI 90, 18; SIG 814, 42, in which the cognate vb. ἀποκαθίστημι is used of states restored by benefactors to normal conditions and stability) **Ac 3:21** (cp. the cognate vb. ἀποκαθίστημι Ac 1:6).—AMéhat, Apocatastase (Origen, Clem. Al., Ac 3:21) VigChr 10, '56, 196–214; CRabinowitz, Personal and Cosmic Salvation in Origen, ibid. 39, '84, 319–29; CLenz, RAC I 510–16; Danker, Benefactor 423.—DELG s.v. ἵστημι. M-M. TW. Sv.

ἀπόκειμαι (s. κεῖμαι; Pind.+) used as pass. of ἀποτίθημι 'be put away, stored up' (so X.+; pap, LXX, TestSol; JosAs 15:10; Just.; Tat. 6, 2; Ath., R. 68, 26)

➊ **to put away for safekeeping** lit. (POxy 69, 5 ἀπὸ τῶν ἐν τ. οἰκίᾳ ἀποκειμένων; BGU 275, 9; PTebt 340, 13; Job 38:23; Philo, Det. Pot. Ins. 128; Jos., Vi. 119; Tat. 6, 2) ἡ μνᾶ, ἣν εἶχον ἀποκειμένην ἐν σουδαρίῳ *the mina, which I kept laid away in a piece of cloth* **Lk 19:20.**

➋ **to reserve as award or recompense,** ***reserve,*** a common term in honorary documents expressing appreciation for sense of civic or other communal responsibility, fig. ext. of 1: ἀπόκειταί μοι . . . στέφανος *a crown is reserved for me* **2 Ti 4:8** (cp. Iambl., Myst. 8, 7 p. 270 P. τὰ ἀπὸ τ. εἱμαρμένης ἀποκείμενα κακά; Demophilus, Similitud. 22 p. 6 Orelli; OGI 383, 189–91 οἷς ἀποκείσεται παρὰ θεῶν χάρις εὐσεβείας; UPZ 144, 47 [II BC] ἀπόκειται παρὰ θεοῦ μῆνις τοῖς . . . ; 2 Macc 12:45; Jos., Ant. 6, 368; Just., A I, 18, 2 κόλασις αἰωνία). FPfister, ZNW 15, 1914, 94–96. διὰ τὴν ἐλπίδα τ. ἀποκειμένην ὑμῖν ἐν τ. οὐρανοῖς *because of the hope that is reserved for you in heaven* **Col 1:5** (the 'hope' is the totality of blessing that awaits the Christian in the life to come).

➌ Impers. ἀπόκειταί τινι **it is unavoidable in view of inevitable circumstance,** ***it is certain, one is destined*** (Ael. Aristid. 39 p. 764 D.) w. inf. foll. ἅπαξ ἀποθανεῖν **Hb 9:27** (cp. Kaibel 416, 6 ὡς εἰδώς, ὅτι πᾶσι βροτοῖς τὸ θανεῖν ἀπόκειται; 4 Macc 8:11).—M-M. TW.

ἀπόκενος, ον (s. κενός; Diosc. 5, 36 W. et al.; GrBar 15:3f) ***quite empty*** (Hero, [Spiritalia] Pneumatica 2, 24; PCairZen 680, 3 [III BC]) w. δίψυχος Hm 5, 2, 1; 12, 5, 2ff.

ἀποκεφαλίζω 1 aor. ἀπεκεφάλισα (s. κεφαλή; Philod., περὶ σημ. 13, 29 G.; Epict 1, 1, 19; 24 al.; Artem. 1, 35; Cass. Dio 71, 28, 1; PHamb 57, 25 [160 BC]; Acta Alex. III col. IV, 24 (restored); IX rec. B, 8f (restored); Ps 151:7; Phryn. p. 341 L.) ***behead*** Ἰωάννην **Mt 14:10; Mk 6:16, 27; Lk 9:9.**

ἀποκλείω fut. ἀποκλείσω LXX; 1 aor. ἀπέκλεισα. Pass.: fut. 3 sg. ἀποκλεισθήσεται; 1 aor. inf. ἀποκλεισθῆναι Ps 67:38; perf. 3 sg. ἀποκέκλεισται 1 Kgm 23:7, ptc. ἀποκεκλεισμέναι Judg 3:24 cod. A (s. κλείω; trag., Hdt. et al.; pap, LXX; En 101:2; Ath. 8, 2 'be limited to') ***close, shut*** τὴν θύραν (Iambl., Myst. 2, 8; Achilles Tat. 6, 10, 6; POxy 1272, 5; Gen 19:10; 2 Km 13:17f al.; En 101:2; Jos., Vi. 246) **Lk 13:25.** τὴν μήτραν (1 Kgm 1:6 συνέκλεισεν τὰ περὶ τῆς μ. αὐτῆς) GJs 2:3.—DELG s.v. κλείς. M-M.

ἀποκνέω fut. ἀποκνήσω; 1 aor. inf. ἀποκνῆσαι (Ath. R. 65, 20) (s. ὀκνέω; Thu. et al.; Ael. Aristid. 34 p. 664, 9 D. al.; PCairZen 416, 3; PColZen 64, 6; 10 [both III BC]; PBad 51, 6) ***hesitate, have misgivings*** Ox 654, 22 (ASyn. 256, 54).—DELG s.v. 1 ὄκνος.

ἀποκομίζω fut. ptc. acc. ἀποκομιοῦντας 2 Macc. 2:15; 1 aor. subj. ἀποκομίσω (s. κομίζω; Hdt. et al.; ins, pap, LXX; GrBar 11:9; Joseph.; apolog.; Theoph. Ant. 3, 25 [p. 258, 9]) ***take along*** (Polyb. 28, 10, 7) γράμματα *a letter* Pol 13:1.—DELG s.v. κομέω 2. κομίζω.

ἀποκόπτω fut. ἀποκόψω; 1 aor. ἀπέκοψα LXX; 2 aor. 3 pl. pass. ἀπεκόπησαν Judg 5:22 cod. A; inf. ἀποκοπῆναι (s. κόπτω; Hom. et al.; pap, LXX, Philo, Joseph.) **to cut so as to make a separation,** ***cut off, cut away***

ⓐ of body parts (Hom. et al.; Hdt. 6, 91 χεῖρας; Diod. S. 17, 20, 7 ἀπέκοψε τὴν χεῖρα; Dt 25:12; Judg 1:6f; Jos., Bell. 6, 164, Vi. 177) **Mk 9:43, 45** (Epict 2, 5, 24 of ἀποκόπτειν the foot ὑπὲρ τοῦ ὅλου; cp. Ael. Aristid. 48, 27 K.=24 p. 472 D.: παρατέμνειν one limb ὑπὲρ σωτηρίας of the whole body); ear **J 18:10, 26** (on the implications of mutilation cp. Lev 21:16–23; BViviano, RB 96, '89, 71–80). Private parts implied *make a eunuch of, castrate* (Lucian, Eunuch. 8; Cass. Dio 79, 11; Dt 23:2; Philo, Leg. All. 3, 8, Spec. Leg. 1, 325; Theoph. Ant. 3, 8 [p. 222, 3]) mid. (Epict. 2, 20, 19; §317; Rob. 809) ὄφελον καὶ ἀποκόψονται *would that they might make eunuchs of themselves* **Gal 5:12.** So interpr. by many since Chrysostom and Ambrosiaster, also PDebouxhtay, RevÉtGr 39, 1926, 323–26 (against ChBruston, ibid. 36, 1923, 193f); GDuncan, Gal '34, 154; 161.

ⓑ of noncorporal things τὰ σχοινία *cut the ropes* (cp. Od. 10, 127; X., Hell. 1, 6, 21; Polyaenus 5, 8, 2; 6, 8) **Ac 27:32;** branches κλάδους in pruning procedure Hs 8, 1, 2 Joly (ἔκοπτε W.); building-stones πολὺ δεῖ ἀπ᾿ αὐτῶν ἀποκοπῆναι *a great deal must be cut away from them* Hs 9, 9, 2.—M-M. TW.

ἀπόκριμα, ατος, τό (s. ἀποκρίνομαι; quotable since Polyb., 12, 26b, 1 as a t.t., esp. freq. in ins [Dssm., NB 85=BS 257; Nägeli 30]; PTebt 286, 1; Jos., Ant. 14, 210. Cp. UWilcken, Her 55, 1920, p. 32, 1, and s. PCol 123) ***official report, decision*** ἀ. τ. θανάτου **2 Cor 1:9** (Theodoret III 291 N. ἀ. δὲ θανάτου τὴν τοῦ θανάτου ψῆφον ἐκάλεσε).—M-M. TW.

ἀποκρίνομαι 1 aor. mid. ἀπεκρινάμην (occas. NT, but the usual form in Joseph.). Pass.: 1 fut. ἀποκριθήσομαι; aor. ἀπεκρίθην (freq. in NT; in Jos. only Ant. 9, 35 and in Just. only D. 3, 6) (Ammonios, De Adfin. Voc. Diff. 67 [KNikkau '66] states the purist's position: ἀποκριθῆναι . . . ἐστι τὸ ἀποχωρισθῆναι, ἀποκρίνασθαι δὲ τὸ ἐρωτηθέντα λόγον δοῦναι = ἀποκριθῆναι has to do w. making distinctions, ἀποκρίνασθαι with making a reply; cp. Phryn. 108 Lob; on developments in the Koine s. M-M; also B-D-F §78; W-S. §13, 9; Rob. 334; Mayser I 2^2, 158; Thackeray 239; DELG s.v. κρίνω).

➊ ***answer, reply*** (so occas. in Hdt. and fr. Thu. on; ins, pap, LXX; En 106:9; TestSol, TestAbr, TestJob; JosAs 4:16; ParJer, ApcMos, ApcrEsdr [Epiph. 70, 14], EpArist; Philo, e.g. Aet. M. 4 [ἀπεκρίνατο]; Just.; diff. and more precisely Ath. ['separate oneself']) τινί and in Lk πρός τινα *to someone* (Thu. 5, 42, 2; Iambl., Myst. 7, 5 at end) **Lk 4:4; 6:3; Ac 3:12; 25:16.** To a question **Mt 11:4; 13:11; 19:4; Mk 12:28, 34; Lk 3:11; 7:22; J 1:21, 26, 48; 3:5** al.; MPol 8:2. To requests, exhortations, commands, etc., the answer being quoted directly **Mt 4:4; 12:39; 13:37;** 1 Cl 12:4; MPol 10, 1 al. Freq. in Hermas: v 1, 1, 5 and 7; 3, 3, 1; 3, 4, 1 and 3; 3, 6, 5f al. Not preceded by a question expressed or implied, when the sentence is related in content to what precedes and forms a contrast to it, *reply* (as a reaction) **Mt 3:15; 8:8; 12:48; 14:28; 15:24, 28; Mk 7:28; J 2:18; 3:9; Ac 25:4** al. τινί τι **Mt 15:23; 22:46; Mk 14:40; Lk 23:9** (cp. Epict. 2, 24, 1 πολλάκις ἐπιθυμῶν σου ἀκοῦσαι ἦλθον πρός σε καὶ οὐδέποτέ μοι ἀπεκρίνω). οὐ γὰρ ᾔδει τί ἀποκριθῇ **Mk 9:6;** οὐδεν **Mt 26:62; 27:12; Mk 14:61;** πρός τι *to someth.* (Pla., Protag. 338d) οὐκ ἀπεκρίθη αὐτῷ πρὸς οὐδὲ ἓν ῥῆμα *he made no reply to him, not even to a single word* or *charge* **Mt 27:14** (cp. Jesus, son of Ananias, before the procurator Albinus: πρὸς ταῦτα οὐδ᾿ ὁτιοῦν ἀπεκρίνατο Jos., Bell. 6, 305; TestAbr A 16 p. 98, 11 [Stone p. 44] ὁ θάνατος . . . οὐκ ἀπεκρίθη αὐτῷ [Abraham] λόγον; Eupolis Com. [V BC] K. ὡς ὑμῖν ἐγὼ πάντως ἀποκρινοῦμαι πρὸς τὰ κατηγορούμενα.—Artem. 3, 20 ὁ μηδὲν ἀποκρινόμενος μάντις . . . καὶ ἡ σιγὴ ἀπόκρισις ἀλλ᾿ ἀπαγορευτική= . . . a negative answer, to be sure. Just., A II, 9, 1 πρὸς τοῦτο; D. 50, 1 πρὸς πάντα). W. inf. foll. **Lk 20:7** (on the rhetorical exchange 20:2–8 cp. Pla., Meno 76a and b); w. acc. and inf. foll. (X., Hell. 2, 2, 18) **Ac 25:4** (cp. Just., D. 67, 9); foll. by ὅτι and direct discourse **Mk 8:4; Ac 25:16;** IPhld 8:2; foll. by dir. disc. without ὅτι **Mk 9:17; J 1:21** (cp. Just., D. 35, 2 al.).

❷ Of the continuation of discourse like עָנָה (וַיַּעַן וַיֹּאמֶר, cp. the Homeric ἀμειβόμενος προσέειπε Il. 3; 437, s. DGE s.v. ἀμείβω; ἀπαμειβόμενος προσέφη Il. 1, 84 al.; for related pleonasm s. L-S-J-M λέγω III 7) ***continue*** **Mt 11:25; 12:38; 15:15; 22:1; 26:25; Mk 10:24;** *begin, speak up* **Mt 26:63 v.l.; Mk 9:5; 10:51; 11:14; 12:35; Lk 1:19; 13:14; 14:3; J 5:19; Ac 5:8** (cp. Dt 21:7; 26:5; Is 14:10; Zech 1:10; 3:4; 1 Macc 2:17; 8:19; 2 Macc 15:14). Used formulaically w. εἰπεῖν or λέγειν, and oft. left untransl.: 2 Cl 5:3; ἀπεκρίθη καὶ εἶπεν **J 2:19;** ἀποκριθεὶς εἶπεν **Mt 16:16** al. (TestAbr B 4, p. 108, 21 [Stone p. 64]; TestJob; ParJer 7:2); ἀποκριθεὶς ἔφη **Lk 23:3;** GPt 11:46; ἀπεκρίθη καὶ λέγει **Mk 7:28; J 1:49 v.l.; 4:17;** ἀποκριθήσονται λέγοντες **Mt 25:37;** ἀπεκρίθη λέγων Hs 5, 4, 3 Joly (cp. Hdt. 5, 67, 2 χρᾷ φᾶσα=[the Pythia] declared and said; TestLevi 19:2; B-D-F §420, 1; Mlt. 131; Schwyzer II 301; Dalman, Worte 19f [Eng. 24f]; PJoüon, 'Respondit et dixit': Biblica 13, '32, 309–14).—B. 1266. M-M. TW.

ἀπόκρισις, εως, ἡ (ἀποκρίνομαι; Theognis, Hdt.+; SIG 344, 62; 591, 28; pap, LXX; TestSol 1:4 H; TestLevi 3:7; EpArist; Jos.; Ant. 7, 119; Just.) ***answer*** **Lk 2:47; 20:26.** ἀ. διδόναι τινί (SIG 683, 15; Job 32:4; 33:5; 35:4 al.; without dat. Diod. S. 16, 25, 2; 18, 48, 3; Jos., Ant. 20, 89) **J 1:22; 19:9.**—M-M. TW.

ἀποκρύπτω fut. ἀποκρύψω; 1 aor. ἀπέκρυψα. Pass.: 1 fut. ἀποκρυβήσομαι (JosAs 6:2); 2 aor. ἀπεκρύβην LXX; pf. ptc. ἀποκεκρυμμένος (s. κρύπτω; Hom.+) gener. 'put something out of sight'.

❶ **to provide a hiding-place for someth. or someone, *hide, conceal*** by digging **Mt 25:18 v.l.** A son from persecutors, GJs 22:3; 23:1.

❷ **to keep from being known, *keep secret*** τὶ ἀπό τινος (Is 40:27; Jer 39:17; Just., D. 55, 3) **Lk 10:21;** Hs 9, 11, 9. ἀποκεκρυμμένος *hidden, kept secret* (Pla., Phdr. 273c ἀποκεκρυμμένη τέχνη; Ps.-Demetr. c. 155 κατηγορίαι ἀποκεκρυμμέναι; Just., D. 115, 1 Ζαχαρίᾳ … ἀποκεκρυμμένως κηρύσσοντι) **1 Cor 2:7; Eph 3:9; Col 1:26.**—M-M. TW.

ἀπόκρυφος, ον (Pre-Socr., Eur.+; Vita Philonidis [Crönert, SBBerlAk 1900, 942ff], fgm. 3; Vett. Val. Index; Kaibel 1028, 10; PGM 4, 1115; 12, 321; 13, 343f; 730f; LXX, En; TestSol 10:53 C; Jos., Bell. 3, 340) ***hidden*** οὐκ ἔνι τόπος ἀ. *there was no hiding place* GJs 22:3. Of treasures (Da 11:43 Theod.; 1 Macc 1:23=Jos., Ant. 12, 250), fig., of secret wisdom (IAndrosIsis [I BC] 15, 10 ἀπόκρυφα σύνβολα; Philo, Sacr. Abel. 62 ἐν ἀποκρύφοις αὐτὸν ἐθησαυρίσαντο) θησαυροὶ ἀ. **Col 2:3;** B 11:4 (Is 45:3; cp. Tat. 30, 1). Opp. φανερός (Philo, Abr. 147) **Mk 4:22; Lk 8:17.**—DELG s.v. κρύπτω. M-M. TW. Sv.

ἀποκτείνω, ἀποκτέννω (the latter form **Mt 10:28; Mk 12:5; Lk 12:4 v.l.,** Tdf. in text; s. Borger, GGA 131; **2 Cor 3:6; Rv 6:11;** 2 Cl 5:4; s. B-D-F §73; Rob. 1213; W-S. §15 s.v. κτείνω; mss. rdgs. vary greatly betw. ἀποκτέννω, ἀποκτένω, ἀποκτεννύω, ἀποκτιννύω) fut. ἀποκτενῶ; 1 aor. ἀπέκτεινα. Pass.: 1 aor. ἀπεκτάνθην (s. B-D-F §76, 2; 315; W-S.§15, 5); pf. ptc. ἀπεκταμμένων 1 Macc 5:51; pf. inf. ἀπεκτάνθαι 2 Macc. 4: 36 cod. L for ἀπεκτονῆσθαι (Hom.+).

❶ lit., **to deprive of life, *kill***—ⓐ of bodily life **Mt 14:5; 16:21; 17:23; 21:35, 38, 39; Mk 6:19; 9:31ab; Lk 11:47; J 16:2** (killing of an unbeliever considered a service to God: Synes., Ep. 4 p. 160a.—Lycophron 1172 δῆμος τὸν κτανόντ᾽ ἐπαινέσει by public decree every Trojan who kills one of the accursed Locrians is publicly praised; thereupon blood-lust breaks out against these unfortunates); **18:31** (Ltzm., SBBerlAk '31 XIV; ZNW 30, '31, 211–15; ibid. 31, '32, 78–84; FBüchsel, ibid. 30, '31, 202–10; 33, '34, 84–87; MGoguel, ibid. 31, '32, 289–301; PFiebig, StKr 104, '32, 213–28; UHolzmeister, Biblica 19, '38, 43–59; 151–74; HvanHille, Mnemosyne 10, '42, 241–50; JBlinzler, D. Prozess Jesu '51; JJeremias ZNW 43, '51, 145–50 [lit.]); **Rv 6:8; 9:5** al. Of God ὁ ἀποκτείνων κ. ζῆν ποιῶν 1 Cl 59:3. ἀ. ἑαυτόν *commit suicide* (Dio Chrys. 47 [64], 3; Artem. 2, 49 p. 151, 13; Jos., Ant. 9, 39) **J 8:22.** Also of things as causing death: of a falling tower **Lk 13:4;** of plagues **Rv 9:18.—Mk 3:4; Lk 6:9 v.l.** ἀποκτεῖναι is either abs. or to be taken w. ψυχήν (like Eur., Tro. 1214).

ⓑ of life in a transcendent sense **Ro 7:11.** τὸ γράμμα ἀ. *the letter* (of the law) *kills,* in so far as the legal letter causes humans to die **2 Cor 3:6.** ἀ. τὴν ψυχήν **Mt 10:28** (s. ψυχή 1b; cp. Epict. 3, 23, 21 [after Pla., Apol. 30c] ἐμὲ ἀποκτεῖναι μὲν δύνανται, βλάψαι δ᾽ οὔ. On this topic s. LAlfonsi, VigChr 16, '62, 77f). τὴν δὲ ψυχὴν μὴ ἀπ[οκτενεῖς] *but my soul* (opp. σῶμα) *you cannot kill* AcPl Ha 1, 4.

❷ fig. of abstract things **to do away w., *put to death, eliminate*** (Eur., Hipp. 1064 τὸ σεμνόν; Philippus [=Demosth. 12] 9 φιλίαν; Mel., P. 66, 472 πνεύματι ἀπέκτεινεν τὸν … θάνατον) *the enmity* τὴν ἔχθραν **Eph 2:16.**—B. 288. DELG s.v. κτείνω. M-M.

ἀποκυέω 1 aor. ἀπεκύησα (because the aor. is found in this form [not ἀπέκυσα] **Js 1:18,** W-H. Vog. M. in 1:15 accent ἀποκυεῖ; s. W-S. §15 p. 129); aor. pass. ἀπεκυήθη (Just., A I, 32, 14; 46, 5). (κυέω or κύω 'to be pregnant'; Aristot., fgm. 76 Rose; Dionys. Hal. 1, 70 [interpol.]; Plut., Sull. 475 [37, 7]; Lucian, D. Mar. 10, 1; Aelian, VH 5, 4 et al.; Herm. Wr. 1, 16; BGU 665 II, 19 [I AD]; APF 3, 1906, 370 II, 4; Sb 6611, 15; PFamTebt 20, 15; 20; 22; 4 Macc 15:17; Philo, Ebr. 30 al.) ***give birth to***

ⓐ of delivery of that with which one has been pregnant, w. ἀπό retaining its force *give birth to,* ὃς ἐ[κ]υοφορήθη|[. . . . . .]. ὑπ᾽ αὐτῆς ὡς ἀποκυῆσε (=ἕως ἀποκυῆσαι) αὐτήν, καὶ γεννῆσαι ['Ιησοῦν] τὸν Χριστόν *who was carried (in the womb) by her (Mary) until she gave birth and bore [Jesus] the Messiah* AcPl Ha 8, 27f.

ⓑ otherwise in our lit. only fig., ἡ ἁμαρτία ἀ. θάνατον *sin gives birth to* (i.e. *brings forth*) *death* **Js 1:15.** But the term is not confined to the human female faculty (cp. Herm. Wr. 1, 9); of God (s. γεννάω) ἀπεκύησεν ἡμᾶς λόγῳ ἀληθείας *gave birth to us (brought us into being) through the word of truth* **Js 1:18.**—C-MEdsman, Schöpferwille u. Geburt Jk 1:18: ZNW 38, '39, 11–44.—DELG s.v. κυέω I. M-M. TW. Spicq.

ἀποκυλίω fut. ἀποκυλίσω; 1 aor. 3 sg. ἀπεκύλισε LXX; pf. pass. ἀποκεκύλισμαι (s. B-D-F §101 p. 46) (s. κυλίω; Diod. S. 14, 116, 6; Ps.-Apollod. 3, 15, 7; Lucian, Rhet. Praec. 3; Jos., Ant. 4, 284; 5, 359; LXX) ***roll away*** τὶ (Ἀρχαιολογικὴ Ἐφημερίς 1923, 39 λίθους [IV BC]) ἀ. τὸν λίθον (Gen 29:3, 8, 10) **Mt 28:2;** GPt 12:53; ἀ. τ. λίθον ἐκ τ. θύρας *roll the stone away from the entrance* **Mk 16:3;** cp. vs. **4.** λίθος ἀποκεκυλισμένος ἀπὸ τ. μνημείου **Lk 24:2** (so also the ptc. **Mk 16:4 v.l.;** the passive also has the same mng. as the intr. *roll away:* Diod. S. 20, 14, 6). S. ἀνακυλίω.—DELG s.v. κυλίνδω.

ἀποκύω s. ἀποκυέω.

ἀπολακτίζω 1 aor. ἀπελάκτισα (s. λακτίζω; Theognis et al.) intr. **to engage in a kicking motion,** ***kick away, kick off, kick up, kick*** (M. Ant. 10, 28, 1 [of a kicking and screaming pig]; Ps.- Lucian, Asin. 18 [the ass kicks out with its hind legs as it runs off]). So in the use of Dt 32:15 in 1 Cl 3:1 (cp. Just., D. 20, 1), where the mng. in the light of the context prob. = 'kick up (the heels)', in a demonstration of proud independence *spurn* (cp. Aeschyl. Prom. 651; Plut., Ant. 36, 2 τὰ καλά; as a saying of Plato in Diog. L. 5, 2 [Aristotle 'kicks up' at Plato, i.e. leaves him behind in the Academy]).—DELG s.v. λάξ (adv. 'with the foot').

ἀπολαλέω impf. 3 sg. ἀπελάλει (s. λαλέω; Lucian, Nigrin. 22 blurt out) ***speak out (freely)*** (Jos., Ant. 6, 9, 2 [178]) **Ac 18:25** D.

ἀπολαμβάνω fut. ἀπολή(μ)ψομαι; 2 aor. ἀπέλαβον; pf. ptc. ἀπειληφότες 4 Macc 18:23. Mid.: 2 aor. ptc. ἀπολαβόμενος; pf. ptc. ἀπειλημμένων Is. 5:17 (s. λαμβάνω; Eur., Hdt.+).

❶ **to obtain someth. from a source,** ***receive*** τί: τ. υἱοθεσίαν *adoption* **Gal 4:5.** τὴν ἐπαγγελίαν B 15:7; pl. Hv 2, 2, 6, cp. 5:7. πάντα Hm 9:4. τ. ἐκκλησίαν 2 Cl 14:3. τ. αἰώνιον ζωήν 8:6.—As commercial t.t. (s. ἀπέχω) *receive* (UPZ 162 VIII, 28 [117 BC] τ. τιμὴν ἀπολαβεῖν) τὰ ἀγαθά σου *you have already received your good things* **Lk 16:25** (difft. KBornhäuser, NKZ 39, 1928, 838f); cp. 2 Cl 11:4. Esp. of wages (since Hdt. 8, 137 μισθόν; Sb 7438, 13 [VI AD]; GrBar 15:3 μισθόν) ἀ. πολλαπλασίονα *receive many times more* **Lk 18:30;** ἄξια ἀ. **23:41;** τ. μισθόν 2 Cl 9:5; Hs 5, 6, 7; μισθὸν πλήρη **2J 8;** ἀντιμισθίαν ἀ. **Ro 1:27;** ἀπὸ κυρίου ἀ. τ. ἀνταπόδοσιν **Col 3:24;** τ. κλῆρον ἀ. *obtain one's lot* IRo 1:2; τ. μέλλοντα αἰῶνα *the future age* (w. its glory) Pol 5:2; τ. τῆς ἀφθαρσίας στέφανον MPol 19:2 (cp. τὴν δόξαν TestJob 43:15). It appears to be used abs. οὐ γὰρ | ἐν τοῖς ζωοῖς μόνοις ἀπολαμβάνουσιν οἱ κακοῦργοι τῶν ἀν(θρώπ)ων ἀλλὰ [κ]αὶ| κόλασιν ὑπομένουσιν καὶ πολ[λ]ὴν| βάσανον Ox 840, 4–7, but the primary obj. is probably κόλασις which does duty for the two clauses, w. β. being an additional feature in the endtime: *not only among the living do human evildoers receive punishment, but they also await it and much torment as well.*—EPreuschen, ZNW 9, 1908, 4.

❷ **to receive back someth. that one previously possessed,** ***recover, get back*** (Jos., Ant. 5, 19; Just., A I, 18, 6 τὰ . . . ἑαυτῶν σώματα) τὰ ἴσα *the same amount* **Lk 6:34** (a commercial term as Sb 7516, 24 [II AD] τὰ ὀφειλόμενα). ὑγιαίνοντα αὐτὸν ἀπέλαβεν *he has gotten him back safe and sound* **15:27.** Fig. τ. λαὸν καθαρόν *take his people back pure* Hs 9, 18, 4. τὸ ἴδιον μέγεθος ISm 11:2.

❸ **to lead or take away from a particular point,** ***take away*** of persons (so since Hdt. 1, 209; Aristoph., Ran. 78 αὐτὸν μόνον; PLond I, 42, 13 p. 30; Witkowski 32, 13 p. 62; sim. 36, 10f p. 65 for confinement; Jos., Bell. 2, 109 ἀπολαβόμενος αὐτὸν κατ' ἰδίαν; 2 Macc 6:21) mid. ἀπολαβόμενος αὐτὸν ἀπὸ τ. ὄχλου κατ' ἰδίαν *he took him aside, away fr. the crowd, by himself* **Mk 7:33.**

❹ **to accept someone's presence with friendliness,** ***welcome*** (PLips 110, 6; PIand 13, 17f ἵνα μετὰ χαρᾶς σε ἀπολάβωμεν) **3J 8 v.l.;** τὴν πολυπληθίαν ὑμῶν *your entire congregation* IEph 1:3. ὃν ἐξεμπλάριον τ. ἀφ' ὑμῶν ἀγάπης ἀπέλαβον *whom I have welcomed as a living example of your love* 2:1.—M-M. TW.

ἀπόλαυσις, εως, ἡ (ἀπολαύω 'have enjoyment of'; Eur., Thu.+; OGI 383, 12 and 150; 404, 10; pap; 3 Macc 7:16 v.l.; TestJos 5:4; Philo, Mos. 2, 70; Jos., Ant. 2, 52 and 174 εἰς ἀ. ἀγαθῶν; Tat. 14, 2; Ath. R. 78, 3) **having the benefit of something, and so enjoying it,** ***enjoyment*** πρόσκαιρον ἔχειν ἁμαρτίας ἀπόλαυσιν *enjoy the short-lived pleasures of sin* **Hb 11:25.** (Opp. ἐπαγγελία) ἡ ἐνθάδε ἀ. 2 Cl 10:3f. πρὸς ἀπόλαυσιν (Clearchus, fgm. 44; Palaeph. p. 84, 13; OGI 669, 8; IG XII/3, 326, 12; BGU 1563, 18) *for enjoyment* 1 Cl 20:10, a H. Gk. expression, like εἰς ἀ. (Diod. S. 14, 80, 2; Nägeli 30): εἰς ἀ. διδόναι τί τινι D 10:3; for this εἰς ἀ. παρέχειν τί τινι **1 Ti 6:17.** Of food delicacies in the endtime τὰς διὰ βρωμάτων εἶπεν (Παπίας) ἐν τῇ ἀναστάσει ἀπολαύσεις *the enjoyment of foods in the (endtime) resurrection* Papias (9). αἰσθητῶν τινων βρωμάτων ἀπόλαυσιν εἶναι τὴν τῶν οὐρανῶν βασιλείαν *the kingdom of heaven means enjoyment of certain real foods* Papias (10).—DELG s.v. ἀπολαύω. M-M. Spicq.

ἀπολείπω impf. ἀπέλειπον; fut. ἀπολείψω; 1 aor. ἀπέλειψα LXX; 2 aor. ἀπέλιπον, mid. ἀπελιπόμην, 3 sg. pass. ἀπελείφθη LXX (Hom.+).

❶ **to cause or permit to remain in a place upon going away,** ***leave behind*** (s. Nägeli 23) τινά or τὶ ἔν τινι (1 Macc 9:65) **2 Ti 4:13, 20; Tit 1:5.**

❷ **to be reserved for future appearance or enactment,** pass. ***remain*** ἀ. σαββατισμός *a Sabbath rest remains* **Hb 4:9** (Polyb. 6, 58, 9 ἐλπὶς ἀπολείπεται σωτηρίας).ἀ. θυσία *a sacrifice remains*=can be made **10:26** (cp. Polyb. 3, 39, 12; Diog. L. 7, 85 ἀ. λέγειν). Abs. ἀ. w. inf. and acc. foll. (B-D-F §393, 6) *it is reserved* or *certain* **4:6.**

❸ **to depart from a place, with a suggestion of finality,** ***desert*** (Apollon. Rhod. 4, 752 δώματα=[leave] a house; Appian, Bell. Civ. 3, 92 §377, 380; UPZ 19, 6 [163 BC]; Job 11:20; Jos., Ant. 1, 20; Just., D. 39, 2 τὴν ὁδὸν τῆς πλάνης) τὸ ἴδιον οἰκητήριον *their own abode* **Jd 6;** [ἀπολείπ]εται (read ἀπολείπετε, Schubart) τὸ σκότος AcPl Ha 8, 32.

❹ **to cease to have an interest in someth.,** ***put aside, give up*** (Polycrates: 588 fgm. 1 Jac.; Dio Chrys. 45 [62], 2; Socrat., Ep. 6, 2 οὐδέν; Sir 17:25; Pr 9:6), also *leave behind, overcome* (Isocr., 4 [Panegyr.] 50; 12 [Panathen.] 159; Harpocration p. 47, 6 Dind.: ἀπολελοιπότες· ἀντὶ τοῦ νενικηκότες; Lex. Vind. p. 7, 33) τὸν φόβον τοῦ θεοῦ *abandon the fear of God* 1 Cl 3:4. τὰς κενὰς φροντίδας *empty cares* 7:2. τὴν ματαιοπονίαν 9:1. μιαρὰς ἐπιθυμίας 28:1. τ. κενὴν ματαιολογίαν Pol 2:1; cp. 7:2.—M-M. Spicq.

ἀπολεῖται, -ολέσαι, -ολέσῃ s. ἀπόλλυμι.

ἀπολείχω impf. ἀπέλειχον (s. λείχω; Apollon. Rhod. 4, 478; Athen. 6, 13, 250a) ***lick, lick off*** **Lk 16:21 v.l.**

ἀπολιμπάνω by-form of ἀπολείπω (Sappho et al.; POxy 1426, 12; Jos., Ant. 19, 99) **1 Pt 2:21** P[72] v.l. for ὑπολιμπάνω, q.v.—DELG s.v. λείπω.

ἀπόλλυμι for its conjug. s. B-D-F §101 (s.v. ὄλλυμι); W-S. §14, 18; Rob. 317; fut. ἀπολέσω Hs 8, 7, 5; Att. ἀπολῶ **1 Cor 1:19** (Is 29:14; ParJer 1:1, 8); 1 aor. ἀπώλεσα; 1 pf. ἀπολώλεκα. Mid.: fut. ἀπολοῦμαι **Lk 13:3;** 2 aor. ἀπωλόμην; the 2 pf. ἀπόλωλα functions as a pf. mid.; ptc. ἀπολωλώς (Hom.+).

❶ **to cause or experience destruction—ⓐ** act. ***ruin, destroy*—α.** of pers. (Sir 10:3) **Mk 1:24; Lk 4:34.** W. ref. to eternal destruction μὴ ἐκεῖνον ἀπόλλυε do not bring *about his ruin* **Ro 14:15.** Esp. *kill, put to death* (Gen 20:4; Esth 9:6 v.l.; 1 Macc 2:37; Jos., C. Ap. 1, 122; Mel., P. 84, 635 [Ch.] τὸν ἐχθρόν σου) Hs 9, 26, 7. παιδίον **Mt 2:13;** Jesus **12:14; 27:20; Mk 3:6; 11:18; Lk 19:47;** B 12:5; the wicked tenants κακοὺς κακῶς ἀ.

(s. κακός 1a) *he will put the evildoers to a miserable death* **Mt 21:41.** τοὺς γεωργούς **Mk 12:9; Lk 20:16;** τ. φονεῖς **Mt 22:7;** τ. μὴ πιστεύσαντας *those who did not believe* **Jd 5;** πάντας **Lk 17:27, 29.** W. σῶσαι (like Chariton 2, 8, 1) **Js 4:12;** Hs 9, 23, 4. Of eternal death (Herm. Wr. 4, 7; Tat. 11:2 ἀπώλεσεν ἡμᾶς τὸ αὐτέξουσιον) ψυχὴν κ. σῶμα ἀ. ἐν γεέννῃ **Mt 10:28;** ψυχήν B 20:1; τ. ψυχάς Hs 9, 26, 3 (cp. Sir 20:22).

β. w. impers. obj. ἀ. τ. σοφίαν τ. σοφῶν *destroy the wisdom of the wise* **1 Cor 1:19** (Is 29:14). ἀ. τ. διάνοιαν *destroy the understanding* Hm 11:1 (cp. Just., D. 93, 1 τὰς φυσικὰς ἐννοίας).

γ. without obj. **J 10:10.**

ⓑ mid. ***perish, be ruined*—α.** of pers. *perish, die* (schol. on Nicander, Ther. 188 ἀπόλλυται ὁ ἀνήρ=the man dies; Tat. 21, 2 τοὺς ἀνθρώπους … ἀπόλλυσθαι) 1 Cl 51:5; 55:6; B 5:4, 12; D 16:5; Hs 6, 2, 1f. As a cry of anguish ἀπολλύμεθα *we are perishing!* (Epict. 2, 19, 16 [in a storm-tossed vessel]; PPetr II, 4 [1], 4f νυνὶ δὲ ἀπολλύμεθα) **Mt 8:25; Mk 4:38; Lk 8:24** (Arrian, Peripl. 3, 3 of disaster that the stormy sea brings to the seafarer). ἐν μαχαίρῃ ἀ. *die by the sword* **Mt 26:52.** λιμῷ *of hunger* (Ezk 34:29) **Lk 15:17.** τῇ ἀντιλογίᾳ τοῦ Κόρε **Jd 11c** (because of 11a and b it should perh. = *be corrupted;* cp. Polyb. 32, 23, 6). ὑπό τινος (Hdt. 5. 126; Dio Chrys. 13 [7], 12) ὑπὸ τ. ὄφεων *killed by the snakes* **1 Cor 10:9;** cp. vs. **10.** Abs. of a people *perish* **J 11:50.** Of individuals (Lev 23:30) **Ac 5:37; 2 Pt 3:9;** 1 Cl 12:6; 39:5 (Job 4:20).—Esp. of eternal death (cp. Ps 9:6f; 36:20; 67:3; 72:27; 82:18; 91:10; Is 41:11) **J 3:16; 17:12.** ἀπολέσθαι εἰς τὸν αἰῶνα *perish forever* **10:28** (Bar 3:3 ἡμεῖς ἀπολλύμενοι τὸν αἰῶνα). ἀνόμως ἀ. **Ro 2:12;** μωρῶς ἀ. IEph 17:2 (cp. ἀσκόπως Just., D. 8, 4); ἐν καυχήσει *because of boasting* ITr 4:1; cp. IPol 5:2. Abs. **1 Cor 8:11; 15:18;** 2 Cl 17:1.—οἱ ἀπολλύμενοι (opp. οἱ σῳζόμενοι, as in Plut., Mor. 469d) *those who are lost* **1 Cor 1:18; 2 Cor 2:15; 4:3; 2 Th 2:10;** 2 Cl 1:4; 2:5. For this τὸ ἀπολωλός **Lk 19:10 (Mt 18:10 v.l.**—Ezk 34:4, 16). τὰ ἀπολλύμενα 2 Cl 2:7 (cp. SIG 417, 9 τά τε ἀπολωλότα ἐκ τ. ἱεροῦ ἀνέσωσαν). S. also 3b end.

β. of things *be lost, pass away, be ruined* (Jos., Bell. 2, 650 of Jerusalem; Tat. 17, 2 πάθος … ἀπολλύμενον) of bursting wineskins **Mt 9:17; Mk 2:22; Lk 5:37;** fading beauty **Js 1:11;** transitory beauty of gold **1 Pt 1:7.** AcPl Ha 2, 24; [χρυσὸς]| γὰρ ἀπόλλυται 9:8f; passing splendor **Rv 18:14** (w. ἀπό as Jer 10:11; Da 7:17). Of earthly food **J 6:27;** spoiled honey Hm 5, 1, 5; σαρκὸς ἀπολλυμένης AcPlCor 2:15. Of the heavens which, like the earth, will pass away **Hb 1:11** (Ps 101:27). Of the end of the world Hv 4, 3, 3, Of the way of the godless, which is lost in darkness B 11:7 (Ps 1:6). μὴ … τὸ μνημόσυνον [ὑμῶν]| ἀπόλιτε (read ἀπόληται) AcPl Ha 1, 22f.

❷ to fail to obtain what one expects or anticipates, *lose out on, lose* (X., Pla.+; PPetr III, 51, 5; POxy 743, 23; PFay 111, 3ff; Sir 6:3; 9:6; 27:16 al.; Tob 7:6 BA; 4 Macc 2:14; Tat. 8, τὸν ἐρώμενον; 15, 1) τ. μισθόν *lose the reward* **Mt 10:42; Mk 9:41;** Hs 5, 6, 7. δραχμήν (Dio Chrys. 70 [20], 25) **Lk 15:8f;** ἀ. ἃ ἠργασάμεθα *lose what we have worked for* **2J 8.** διαθήκην B 4:7, 8. τὴν ζωὴν τ. ἀνθρώπων Hm 2:1; cp. s 8, 6, 6; 8, 7, 5; 8, 8, 2f and 5. τὴν ἐλπίδα m 5, 1, 7.

❸ to lose someth. that one already has or be separated from a normal connection, *lose, be lost*—ⓐ act. w. colloq. flavor ἵνα πᾶν ὃ δέδωκέν μοι μὴ ἀπολέσω ἐξ αὐτοῦ *that I should lose nothing of all that he has given me* **J 6:39** (B-D-F §466, 3 on Semitic assoc.; Rob. 437; 753).—ἀ. τὴν ψυχήν (cp. Sir 20:22) *lose one's life* **Mt 10:39; 16:25; Mk 8:35; Lk 9:24; 17:33;** cp. **J 12:25.** For this ἀ. ἑαυτόν *lose oneself* **Lk 9:25** (similar in form is Tyrtaeus [VII BC], fgm. 8 Diehl[2] lines 11–14: 'One who risks his life in battle has the best chance of saving it; one who flees to save it is most likely to lose it').

ⓑ mid. (Antiphon: Diels, Vorsokrat. 87, fgm. 54 ἀπολόμενον ἀργύριον; X., Symp. 1, 5; 1 Km 9:3; Tat. 9, 2) ISm 10:1. Of falling hair **Lk 21:18; Ac 27:34;** a member or organ of the body **Mt 5:29f;** remnants of food **J 6:12.** Of wine that has lost its flavor Hm 12, 5, 3.—Of sheep gone astray **Mt 10:6; 15:24; Lk 15:4, 6;** B 5:12 (cp. Jer 27:6; Ezk 34:4; Ps 118:176). Of a lost son **Lk 15:24** (Artem. 4, 33 ἡ γυνὴ … τ. υἱὸν ἀπώλεσε καὶ … εὗρεν αὐτόν); of humanity in general ἀπολλύμενος ἐζητήθη ἵνα ζωοποιηθῇ διὰ τῆς υἱοθεσίας *when lost, humanity was sought, so that it might regain life through acceptance into sonship* AcPlCor 2:8 (cp. 1bα.—JSchniewind, D. Gleichn. vom verl. Sohn '40). ἀ. θεῷ *be lost to God* Hs 8, 6, 4 (cod. A for ἀπέθανον).—B. 758. DELG s.v. ὄλλυμι. M-M. TW.

Ἀπολλύων, ονος, ὁ (pres. ptc. of ἀπολλύω, 'destroy') ***Apollyon, the Destroyer,*** tr. of Ἀβαδδών (q.v., which itself is a tr. of אֲבַדּוֹן) **Rv 9:11.** (Whether the writer of Rv implied a connection with the deity Apollo cannot be determined. Indeed, it is questionable, for Apollo was the god of purity and recognized for his civilizing influence. For ancient association of Apollo with the theme of retribution, s. Archilochus Lyr. [VII BC], fgm. 30 Ἄπολλον … ὄλλυ' ὥσπερ ὀλλύεις=Apollo …, destroy them [the guilty ones] even as you do destroy! For an etymological connection of Apollo w. the verb ἀπόλλυμι Aeschyl., Ag. 1080–82; s. EFraënkel, Aeschylus: Agammemnon '50, III 492.)—JSolomon, ed., Apollo '94. DDD 138–43, 456–63. TW.

Ἀπολλωνία, ας, ἡ *Apollonia,* a city in Macedonia ca. 56 km. east of Thessalonica, on the Egnatian Way (X., Hell. 5, 2, 11; Athen. 8, 334e, ins), which Paul passed through **Ac 17:1** (Ἀπολλωνίδα D).—Pauly-W. II/1, 14.

Ἀπολλώνιος, ου, ὁ *Apollonius,* a name freq. found (SIG, OGI, IMagnMai indices; Papias; Joseph.); of a πρεσβύτερος in Magnesia IMg 2:1.—**Ac 18:24** D s. Ἀπολλῶς.

Ἀπολλῶς, ῶ, ὁ (-ώς other edd.; cp. B-D-F §55, 1; O. Wilck II, 1319; 1577; very oft. in pap, e.g. PLond III, 929, 44 and 66 [pp. 42 and 43 resp.]; III, 1233, 8 p. 58) ***Apollos*** a Christian born and educated at Alexandria, who worked in Ephesus and Corinth **Ac 18:24; 19:1; 1 Cor 1:12** (cp. Epict. 1, 9, 1–4: not Ἀθηναῖος ἢ Κορίνθιος, ἀλλὰ κόσμιος); **3:4–6, 22; 4:6; 16:12; Tit 3:13;** 1 Cl 47:3. On the form of the name, which is short for Ἀπολλώνιος (as this man is called **Ac 18:24** D), and prob. also for Ἀπολλόδωρος and Ἀπολλωνίδης, s. W-S. §16, 9 end; Rob. 172; 189; 260; B-D-F §125, 1; Ltzm., Hdb., exc. on **1 Cor 16:18** and s. on Ἀπελλῆς.—RSchumacher, D. Alexandriner Apollos 1916; GBarton, Some Influences of Apollos in the NT: JBL 43, 1924, 207–23; EBuonaiuti, Paolo ed Apollo: Ricerche Religiose 1, 1925, 14–34; HPreisker, Ap. u. d. Johannesjünger in Ac 18:24–19:6: ZNW 30, '31, 301–4; SBugge, NorTT 44, '43, 83–97.—LGPN I. M-M. TW.

ἀπολογέομαι impf. ἀπελογούμην; fut. ἀπολογήσομαι Jer 12:1; 1 aor. ἀπελογησάμην; pf. inf. ἀπολελογῆσθαι; 1 aor. pass. inf. ἀπολογηθῆναι (**Lk 21:14;** TestSol 5:6) (s. ἀπολογία; Eur., Hdt.+; OGI 609, 39; PStras 5, 15 et al.; LXX, pseudepigr., Joseph., Just., Ath.) **to speak in one's own defense against charges presumed to be false, *defend oneself*** (Jos., Ant. 4, 169; 15, 35; Ath. 31, 2 ἐμαυτόν). Abs. (opp. κατηγορέω) **Ro 2:15** (cp. assoc. of charge and defense Dionys., Hal. 7, 58, 1); **Lk 21:14.** ὁ Παῦλος ἀπελογεῖτο **Ac 26:1. Ending of Mark** in the Freer ms. 1. W. acc. ταῦτα αὐτοῦ ἀπολογουμένου *as he spoke thus in his defense* **Ac 26:24.** πῶς ἢ τί ἀπολογήσησθε *how or what you should answer* **Lk 12:11.** τὰ περὶ ἐμαυτοῦ ἀ. *I make my defense* **Ac 24:10.** ἀ. περί τινος *defend oneself against someth.* (Demosth. 19, 214; Diod. S. 4, 53, 1; Just., A II, 2, 8) **26:2** (ἐπί τινος *before someone;* sim. Ath. 11, 2).—W. dat. of pers. (Pla., Prot. 359a; esp. later writers [Nägeli 43]; Epict. 2, 16, 42 σοὶ [God] ἀπολογήσομαι [ὑπέρ τινος πρός τινα=in a matter before someone]; Maximus Tyr. 3, 7a; Vett. Val. 209, 13 βασιλεῖ ἀπολογήσεται) ἀ. τῷ δήμῳ *make a defense before the people* **Ac 19:33;** ὑμῖν ἀ. **2 Cor 12:19;** αὐτοῖς MPol 10:2.—W. ὅτι foll. τοῦ Παύλου ἀπολογουμένου, ὅτι *when Paul said in his defense* (direct quot. foll.) **Ac 25:8.**—DELG s.v. λέγω B. M-M.

ἀπολογία, ας, ἡ (s. ἀπολογέομαι; Pre-Socr., Thu. et al.; pap, e.g. BGU 531, 21 [I AD]; PLips 58, 18; Wsd 6:10; TestSol; Jos. C. Ap. 2, 147; Ar., Just.) freq. as legal term.

❶ **a speech of defense,** ***defense, reply*** ἀκούσατέ μου τῆς πρὸς ὑμᾶς νυνὶ ἀπολογίας *hear the defense which I now make to you* **Ac 22:1** (ἀ. πρός τινα as X., Mem. 4, 8, 5). ἡ ἐμὴ ἀ. τοῖς ἐμὲ ἀνακρίνουσιν *my reply to those who sit in judgment over me* **1 Cor 9:3.** *Written defense, apology* Qua (1).

❷ **the act of making a defense,** ***defense***—ⓐ in court (Jos., Bell. 1, 621) ἐν τ. πρώτῃ μου ἀ. *at my first* defense **2 Ti 4:16** (s. πρῶτος 1aαℵ). τόπον ἀπολογίας λαμβάνειν περί τινος *receive an opportunity to defend himself concerning someth.* **Ac 25:16.**

ⓑ gener. of eagerness to defend oneself **2 Cor 7:11.** Of defending the gospel **Phil 1:7, 16.** ἕτοιμοι πρὸς ἀπολογίαν παντί *ready to make a defense to anyone* **1 Pt 3:15.**

❸ **claim of extenuating circumstance,** ***excuse,*** οὐκ ἔχειν ἀπολογίαν εἰπεῖν *be unable to say in defense* PtK 3 p. 15, 23 (cp. Just., A I, 42, 2 ἀ. παρέχειν).—DELG s.v. λέγω B. M-M.

ἀπολούω 1 aor. mid. ἀπελουσάμην (s. λούω; Hom. et al.; Job 9:30) in our lit. only mid., **wash someth. away from oneself,** ***wash oneself,*** used in imagery of purification (as Philo, Mut. Nom. 49; Just., D. 13, 1 τὸν φόνον καὶ τὰς ἄλλας ἁμαρτίας; Lucian, Cataplus 24 ἁπάσας τ. κηλῖδας τῆς ψυχῆς ἀπελουσάμην) τὰς ἁμαρτίας *wash away one's sins* **Ac 22:16.** Abs. (w. ἁγιάζεσθαι) **1 Cor 6:11.**—TW.

ἀπόλυσις, εως, ἡ (λύω; Hdt. et al.; pap, 3 Macc; TestSol 1:4 A; EpArist; Jos., Ant. 17, 204 as 'release', 'deliverance'; in Polyb. oft. as 'departure') euphem. for death (Theophr., Hist. Pl. 9, 16, 8; Dio Chrys. 60+61 [77+78], 45; Diog. L. 5, 71) **a state of deterioration,** ***dissolution*** γίνεσθαι πρὸς ἀ. τοῦ ἀποθανεῖν *come to the dissolution of death,* 1 Cl 25:2.

ἀπολύτρωσις, εως, ἡ orig. 'buying back' a slave or captive, i.e. 'making free' by payment of a ransom (λύτρον, q.v.; prisoners of war could ordinarily face slavery). The word is comp. rare (Diod. S., fgm. 37, 5, 3 p. 149, 6 Dind.; Plut., Pomp. 631 [24, 5]; EpArist 12; 33; Philo, Omn. Prob. Lib. 114; Jos., Ant. 12, 27; Da 4:34; Just., D. 86, 1. An ins fr. Cos (IKosPH 29, 7) so designates sacral manumission of slaves: RHerzog, Koische Forschungen u. Funde 1899, 39f. Dssm., LO 278 [LAE 327]; KLatte, Heiliges Recht 1920), and usage may diverge freely fr. the orig. mng.

❶ **release from a painful interrogation,** ***release,*** offered in return for apostasy (Philo, loc. cit.; for the story 2 Macc 7:24; 4 Macc 8:4–14) **Hb 11:35** from torture.

❷ **release from a captive condition,** ***release, redemption, deliverance*** fig. ext. of the orig. use in connection with manumission of captives or slaves: the release fr. sin and finiteness that comes through Christ.

ⓐ *redemption, acquittal,* also the *state of being redeemed* διὰ τῆς ἀ. τῆς ἐν Χριστῷ Ἰησοῦ **Ro 3:24.** εἰς ἀ. τῶν παραβάσεων *for redemption fr. the transgressions* **Hb 9:15.** ἐγγίζει ἡ ἀ. ὑμῶν **Lk 21:28.** ἡ ἀ. τοῦ σώματος ἡμῶν *the freeing of our body* fr. earthly limitations or *redemption of our body* (σῶμα=σάρξ as 2 Cor 5:8) **Ro 8:23.** ἔχομεν τὴν ἀ. διὰ τ. αἵματος αὐτοῦ **Eph 1:7;** cp. **Col 1:14 v.l.** ἐσφραγίσθητε εἰς ἡμέραν ἀπολυτρώσεως *you were sealed for the day of redemption* **Eph 4:30.** εἰς ἀ. τῆς περιποιήσεως *for a redemption, through which you become God's property* **1:14.**

ⓑ abstr. for concr. *redeemer* Christ ἐγενήθη ἡμῖν ἀ. **1 Cor 1:30.**—JWirtz, D. Lehre von d. Apolytrosis1906; JStamm, Erlösen u. Vergeben im AT '40; BWarfield, The NT Terminol. of 'Redemption': PTR 15, 1917, 201–49; ELohmeyer, D. Begriff d. Erlösung im Urchristentum 1928; EvDobschütz, ThBl 8, 1929, 34–36; 99f; JBohatec, TZ 4, '48, 268–70; DaConchas, Verbum Domini 30, '52, 14–29; 81–91; 154–69; ELohse, Märtyrer u. Gottesknecht, '55; DWhitely, JTS 8, '57, 240–55; DHill, Gk. Words and Hebr. Mngs. '67, 49–81; SLyonnet, Sin, Redemption, and Sacrifice '70, 79–103. FBüchsel, RAC I 543–45. JHarril, The Manumission of Slaves in Early Christianity '95.—DELG s.v. λύω. TW. Spicq. Sv.

ἀπολύω impf. ἀπέλυον; fut. ἀπολύσω; 1 aor. ἀπέλυσα, inf. ἀπολῦσαι; pf. 1 pl. ἀπολελύκαμεν 3 Macc 7:7. Pass.: 1 fut. ἀπολυθήσομαι; 1 aor. ἀπελύθην; pf. ἀπολέλυμαι (Hom. et al.; ins, pap, LXX, EpArist, Joseph.).

❶ As legal term, **to grant acquittal,** ***set free, release, pardon*** τινά a prisoner (PGiss 65a, 4; 66, 11; POxy1271, 5; 2 Macc 4:47; 12:25; 4 Macc 8:2; Jos., Bell. 2, 4; Just., D. 4, 5 [ψυχὴ] ἀπολυθεῖσα τοῦ σώματος al.) ἀ. ἕνα τῷ ὄχλῳ δέσμιον *release a prisoner for the crowd* (JMerkel, D. Begnadigung am Passahfeste: ZNW 6, 1905, 293–316; RMerritt, JBL 104, '85, 57–68;—ἀπολύω=pardon: Diod. S. 3, 71, 5; Appian, Bell. Civ. 5, 4 §15; OGI 90, 14 [196 BC]; UPZ 111, 2 [163 BC]; Just., A I, 7, 4 ἀπολύηται ὡς Χριστιανός; Mel., P. 101, 775 τὸν κατάδικον) **Mt 27:15–26;** cp. **Mk 15:6–15; Lk 23:16–25; J 18:39; 19:10, 12; Ac 3:13; 5:40; 16:35f; 26:32; 28:18;** AcPl Ha 10, 4; on GJs 16:3 cp. 3 below, on Lk 22:68 see JDuplacy in: Neutest. Aufsätze, Festchr. JSchmid, '63, 42–52 (for genuineness); *release* from threat of being sold **Mt 18:27.**—Abs. ἀπολύετε καὶ ἀπολυθήσεσθε *pardon* (your debtors) *and you will be pardoned* **Lk 6:37.**

❷ **to release from a painful condition,** ***free,*** pass. *be freed* (Tob 3:6; 2 Macc 12:45; Jos., Ant. 2, 65 τ. δεσμῶν) of diseases (Diog. L. 3, 6; Jos., Ant. 3, 264 τ. νόσου) ἀπολέλυσαι (v.l.+ ἀπὸ) τῆς ἀσθενείας σου **Lk 13:12.**

❸ **to permit or cause someone to leave a particular location** ***let go, send away, dismiss*** (X., Hell. 6, 5, 21; UPZ 62, 18 [161 BC]; Tob 10:12 S; 1 Macc 11:38; 2 Macc 14:23; Jos., Ant. 5, 97) of a crowd (Jos., Ant. 11, 337 ἀ. τὸ πλῆθος) **Mt 14:15, 22; 15:32, 39; Mk 6:36, 45; 8:9** al.; ἀ. τὴν ἐκκλησίαν *dismiss the assembly* **Ac 19:40.** Also of individuals (Ps 33 ins; ParJer 3:22) **Mt 15:23; Lk 8:38; 14:4;** GJs 21:2 (not pap); **Lk 22:68 v.l.** Perh. GJs 16:3 (s. 1 above). W. the goal indicated (Jos., Vi. 271 εἰς) εἰς οἶκον (send them away) *to their homes* **Mk 8:3.** εἰς τὰ τείχη *let (them) go into the building* Hs 8, 2, 5; cp. 8, 2, 1. πρὸς ... τὸν ἄνδρα αὐτῆς AcPl Ha 4, 5. Pass. *be dismissed, take leave, depart* (Philo, In Flacc. 96; Jos., Ant. 5, 99) **Ac 4:23; 15:30, 33,** also **Hb 13:23,** unless the ref. is to a release fr. imprisonment (s. 1 above) or simply mng. 6 (s. WWrede, D. Literar. Rätsel d. Hb. 1906, 57ff).—Euphem. for *let die* (Ps.-Plut., Consol. ad Apoll. 13 p. 108c ἕως ἂν ὁ θεὸς ἀπολύσῃ ἡμᾶς; M. Ant. 12, 36, 2 and 5; a veteran's gravestone [Sb 2477]

Ἡλιόδωρε ἐντείμως ἀπολελυμένε, εὐψύχει; Gen 15:2; Num 20:29; Tob 3:6; 2 Macc 7:9) νῦν ἀπολύεις τὸν δοῦλόν σου **Lk 2:29** (some interpret this as modal *now mayest thou* … JKleist, Mk. '36, 147–50 and AFridrichsen, ConNeot 7, '42, 5f; s. also Goodsp., Probs. 77–79). Perh. *discharge* fr. Simeon's long vigil (vs. 26); cp. POxy 2760, 2f (179/80 AD), of a cavalryman's discharge (on the desire for departure cp. TestAbr A 9 p. 87, 5f [Stone p. 22]). **Mt 15:23** is semantically dense: as the context indicates, the riddance is to be expedited by granting the woman's request (s. 4).

❹ **to grant a request and so be rid of a pers.,** ***satisfy*** **Mt 15:23** (cp. 3).

❺ **to dissolve a marriage relationship,** ***to divorce*** τὴν γυναῖκα *one's wife,* or *betrothed* (1 Esdr 9:36; cp. Dt 24:1ff; the expr. ἀ. τ. γυν. Dionys. Hal. 2, 25, 7) **Mt 1:19; 5:31f** (Just., A I, 15, 3); **19:3, 7–9** (BWitherington, Matthew 5:32 and 19:9—Exception or Exceptional Situation?: NTS 31, '85, 571–76); **Mk 10:2, 4, 11** (GDelling, NovT 1, '56, 263–74); **Lk 16:18;** Hm 4, 1, 6; ἀπ' ἐμοῦ GJs 14:1. Of the woman ἀ. τὸν ἄνδρα *divorce her husband* (Diod. S. 12, 18, 1) **Mk 10:12.** This is in accord not w. Jewish (Jos., Ant. 15, 259), but w. Gr-Rom. custom (D has simply ἐξελθεῖν ἀπὸ τοῦ ἀνδρός; on Roman custom relating to women s. MMcDonnell, American Journal of Ancient History 8, '83, 54–80). See on divorce TEngert, Ehe- u. Familienrecht d. Hebräer 1905; AOtt, D. Auslegung d. ntl. Texte über d. Ehescheidung 1910; HNordin, D. ehel. Ethik d. Juden z. Zt. Jesu 1911; AEberharter, D. Ehe- u. Familienrecht d. Hebräer 1914; LBlau, D. jüd. Ehescheidung u. d. jüd. Scheidebrief 1911/12; RCharles, The Teaching of the NT on Divorce 1921; Billerb. I 303–21 al.; SJohnson, Jesus' Teaching on Divorce '45; FCirlot, Christ and Divorce '45; JDerrett, Law in the NT, '70; HCronzel, 363–88, L'Église primitive face au divorce, '71; JFitzmyer, The Matthean Divorce Texts and Some New Palestinian Evidence: TS 37, '76, 197–226; BVawter, CBQ 39, '77, 528–42.

❻ mid. **to make a departure from a locality,** ***go away*** (Thu., Polyb.; PHal 1, 174 [III BC]; Ex 33:11; EpArist 304; Anz 285. ἀπολυόμενος τὰς διαβολάς 'refuting the calumnies' Ath. 2, 3) **Ac 28:25;** perh. **Hb 13:23.**—B. 768. EDNT. DELG s.v. λύω. M-M. TW.

ἀπολῶ, ἀπολωλός s. ἀπόλλυμι.

ἀπομάσσω (μάσσω of hand motions used, e.g., in kneading or molding; Aristoph. et al.; POxy 1381, 133; Tob 7:16 S) ***wipe off,*** mid. *oneself* (Galen, Protr. 1, p. 26 [10 p. 34, 5 John]; Ps.-Callisth. 1, 18, 10) τὸν κονιορτὸν ἀπομασσόμεθα ὑμῖν *we wipe off the dust (in protest) against you* **Lk 10:11.** S. on ἐκτινάσσω.—DELG s.v. μάσσω.

ἀπομένω (s. μένω; PFamTebt 42, 11 [180 AD], w. doubtful mng., as PFlor 378, 6 [V AD]) ***remain behind*** (so TestJob 12:4; JosAs 19:1 cod. A [p. 69, 3 Bat.]; Alciphron 3, 24, 2) **Lk 2:43 v.l.**

ἀπομνημονεύω 1 aor. ἀπεμνημόνευσα (s. μνημονεύω; Hdt., Pla. et al.; APF 5, 13 p. 416, 10; Joseph., Just.) ***remember*** Papias (2:15).—DELG s.v. μιμνήσκω. M-M. s.v. ἀπομνημόνευμα.

ἀπονέμω 1 aor. ἀπένειμα LXX; aor. pass. ptc. acc. sg. fem. ἀπονεμηθεῖσαν (Just., D. 103, 4) (νέμω 'distribute'; Simonides, Pind.+; OGI 90, 18; 116, 19; BGU 168, 4; POxy 71 II, 3; 1185, 6; LXX; JosAs 28 [p. 84, 9 Bat.] cod. A; EpArist 24; Philo, Spec. Leg. 1, 148; Just., D. 88, 2; 103, 4; 130, 4; Ath. 32, 3; R. 75, 28) **to grant that which is appropriate in a relationship,** ***assign, show, pay, accord*** τινὶ τιμήν (Pla., Laws 8, 837c; Isocr., [Paneg.] 178; Alex. Ep. XV 11 τὰς ἰσοθέους τιμὰς ἀ. Herodian 1, 8, 1; Jos., Ant. 1, 156; Ath. 32, 3) *show honor to someone* **1 Pt 3:7;** 1 Cl 1:3; MPol 10:2. τινὶ πᾶσαν ἐντροπήν *show all respect to someone* IMg 3:1.—Frisk s.v. νέμω C. M-M.

ἀπονεύω (s. νεύω 'to incline' in some direction; Pla., Theophr., et al.) w. ἀπό τινος ***withdraw, turn away from*** (Epict. 4, 10, 2; 4, 12, 18). Of Jesus: ἀπένευσεν ἀπ' [αὐτῶν] *he withdrew from* [them] PEg[2], 31. The imprisoned Paul οὐκ ἀπένευεν AcPl Ha 2, 2 (cp. Thecla in AcPlTh 7 [Aa I 240, 10]; Just., D. 125, 4 ἀπένευσε τότε ὁ διάβολος [end of the story of Jesus' temptation]).

ἀπονίπτω (Od. 18, 179 v.l.; Diod. S. 4, 59, 4; LXX; JosAs 29:5. An earlier form is ἀπονίζω Hom. et al.) 1 aor. mid. ἀπενιψάμην (this formation Hom. et al. [s. νίπτω, beg.], also SIG 1168, 63 [III BC]) ***wash off*** mid. ***(for) oneself*** (Plut., Phoc. 749 [18, 3]; Philostrat., Vi. Apoll. 8, 13 p. 330, 26; Achilles Tat. 8, 3, 2 μὲ ἀ. τὸ πρόσωπον) τ. χεῖρας (Theophr., Char. 16, 2) as a sign of innocence (Jewish, not Roman custom acc. to Origen, Comm. on Mt., Ser. Lat. 124 [ed. EKlostermann '33, 259]; s. Dt 21:6f=Jos., Ant.4, 222; Ps 25:6; 72:13; EpArist 305f=Jos., Ant. 12, 106; Sota 9, 6.—Anticlides Hist. [III BC]: 140 fgm. 6 Jac. in Suppl. III B p. 743, 21–23 says of the Greeks that acc. to an old custom still practiced ὅταν ἢ φόνον ἀνθρώπων ἢ καὶ ἄλλας σφαγὰς ἐποίουν, ὕδατι ἀεννάῳ τὰς χεῖρας ἀπονίπτειν εἰς τοῦ μιάσματος κάθαρσιν=whenever they killed a pers. or engaged in other kinds of slaughter, they would wash their hands with running water to purify themselves from the pollution) **Mt 27:24.**—DELG s.v. νίζω. M-M.

ἀπόνοια, ας, ἡ (s. νοῦς; Thu. et al.) ***madness, frenzy*** εἰς τοσοῦτον ἀπονοίας *to such a degree of madness* 1 Cl 1:1 (w. στάσις, as Cat. Cod. Astr. II 18). εἰς τοσαύτην ἀ. ἔρχεσθαι 46:7 (cp. SIG 643, 19 [171 BC] εἰς τοῦτο ἦλθεν ἀπονοίας; Philo, Somn. 2, 277 ἐπὶ τοσοῦτον ἀπονοίας).—W. ὥστε foll., as Hyperid. 2, 5.

ἀποπαύω 1 aor. ἀπέπαυσα (s. παύω; Hom., Hdt. et al.; Ps 88:45 Sym.; ApcMos 6; Jos., Ant. 7, 308 [Naber], also s. Jos. Lex. s.v. on 6, 117; ApcMos 6; Tat. 17, 1) **to make to cease from an activity,** ***put to rest.*** After nursing Mary, Anna ἀπέπαυσεν αὐτὴν ἐν τῷ κοιτῶνι *put her to rest in the bedroom* GJs 6:3 Bodm. (ἀνέπαυσεν Strycker, who suggests that the copyist of Bodmer mistook ν for π (s. ἀναπαύω); v.l. ἀνεκλινεν.

ἀποπέμπω 1 aor. ἀπέπεμψα (s. πέμπω; Hom. et al.; pap; Judg 3:19 Sym.; Joseph.; Just., D. 2, 5) ***send out*** **J 17:3 v.l.**

ἀποπίπτω fut. ἀποπεσοῦμαι LXX; aor. ἀπέπεσα (ἀπέπεσον LXX) (Hom.+; UPZ 70, 27 [II BC]; LXX). In our lit. ἀ. is used w. ἀπό and gen. (Hdt. 3, 130; Job 24:24) or w. gen. (Hdt. 3, 64; Jdth 11:6); but not simply without a gen. (as Il. 14, 351).

❶ lit. **to fall from a point or location,** ***fall*** (Jos., Ant. 6, 2) ἀ. αὐτοῦ ἀπὸ τ. ὀφθαλμῶν *there fell fr. his eyes* **Ac 9:18.** ἡ χείρ μου πυρὶ ἀποπίπτει ἀπ' ἐμοῦ *my hand, burned by fire, falls off* GJs 20:1.

❷ fig. **to depart from a norm,** ***to deviate*** (Polyb.; Diod. S.; Jdth 11:6; Jos., Bell. 1, 527) ἀ. τῆς ὁδοῦ τ. δικαίας *fall from the right way* 2 Cl 5:7 (cp. Proclus, Inst. 13 ἀ. τἀγαθοῦ).—Schlageter 11. M-M.

ἀποπλανάω fut. ἀποπλανήσω Sir 13:6; 1 aor. ἀπεπλάνησα LXX, pass. ἀπεπλανήθην (s. πλανάω; Hippocr. et al.; Ps.-Pla., Ax. 369d; Polyb. 3, 57, 4; Dionys. Hal.; Plut.; Epict. 4, 6, 38; Sb 7464, 6; LXX; En; TestSol 8:9; TestReub 4:1 [some mss. omit]; Just., D. 124, 3) *mislead* τινά (2 Ch 21:11; Pr 7:21; Sir 13:6; En 98:15) only fig. of false teachers ἀ. τ. ἐκλεκτούς *mislead the elect* **Mk 13:22;** cp. Hm 5, 2, 1; Pol 6:3. Pass. (Sir 4:19; 13:8; 2 Macc 2:2) ἀποπλανᾶσθαι ἀπό τινος *wander away fr. someone* or *someth.* ἀ. ἀπὸ τ. πίστεως *they have gone astray fr. the faith* **1 Ti 6:10** (Dionys. Hal., Comp. Verb. 4 ἀπὸ τ. ἀληθείας). ἀποπλανώμενος ἀπὸ τ. θεοῦ *wandered away fr. God* Hs 6, 3, 3; ἀ. ἀπὸ τ. διανοίας αὐτῶν *wander away fr. their understanding* Hm 10, 1, 5. Abs. *be led into error* (En 8:2) s 9, 20, 2. τὰ ἀποπεπλανημένα = τοὺς ἀ. *those who have gone astray* Pol 6:1.—DELG s.v. πλανάομαι. TW.

ἀποπλέω 1 aor. ἀπέπλευσα (s. πλέω; Hom. et al.; PLille 3, 5 [III BC]; Jos., Ant. 16, 16 al.) nautical t.t. ***sail away*** ἐκεῖθεν **Ac 20:15.** W. εἰς to indicate destination (Thu. 6, 61, 6; PEdgar 6, 3=Sb 6712 [258/7 BC]) **13:4; 14:26; 27:1.**

ἀπόπληκτος, ον (s. πλήσσω; Hdt., Hippocr. et al.) **pert. to experiencing physical change because of profound emotional disturbance, *in shock, in a swoon*** ὥστε . . . [τὴν Ἀρτεμύλλαν] μικροῦ δεῖν ἀ. γενέσθαι *so that . . . [Artemilla] was almost in a swoon* AcPl Ha 3, 34f.

ἀποπληρόω (s. πληρόω; since Hippocr., Pla.; also Joseph., Tat.) ***fulfill*** **Gal 6:2 v.l.** (for ἀναπλη.).

ἀποπλύνω impf. ἀπέπλυνον; 1 aor. ἀπέπλυνα (s. πλύνω; Hom. et al.; Epict.; Philostrat., Vi. Apoll. 8, 22 p. 337, 14; LXX; JosAs after 18:7 cod. A [p. 68, 15 Bat.] and Pal. 364; Jos., Ant. 3, 114; 8, 417; Just., D. 54, 1) ***wash off/out*** **Lk 5:2 v.l.** (for ἔπλυνον).

ἀποπνίγω 1 aor. ἀπέπνιξα; 2 aor. pass. ἀπεπνίγην (s. πνίγω; Hdt., Aristoph. et al.; POxy 2111, 29 and 36; LXX) **to check normal breathing or growth through pressure or other restricting measure**

ⓐ ***choke*** trans. (BCH 16, 1892, p. 384 no. 81; Na 2:13; Tob 3:8 BA; TestSol 2:2; TestAbr A 19 p. 102, 2 [Stone p. 52]; Jos., Bell. 1, 551) of rank weeds (Theophr.) ἄκανθαι ἀ. αὐτά **Mt 13:7 v.l.; Lk 8:7.** Pass. intr. sense, of Judas (Ἰούδας) ἐπεβίω καθαιρεθεὶς πρὸ τοῦ ἀποπνιγῆναι *Judas (did not die by hanging but) lived on, for he was taken down before he choked to death* Papias (3:1, but not in the renderings of mss. egh).

ⓑ ***drown*** (Diod. S. 3, 57, 5; Syntipas p. 19, 4) pass. w. intr. sense ἡ ἀγέλη ἀπεπνίγη *the drove drowned* **Lk 8:33** (cp. Demosth. 32, 6; Epict. 2, 5, 12; Diog. L. 9, 12; TestAbr A 19 p. 102, 2).—M-M. TW.

ἀπορέω impf. ἠπόρουν; fut. 3 sg. ἀπορήσει Pr 31:11 (πόρος 'way', 'means' of achieving someth.; Pre-Socr., Hdt.+) orig. 'be without resources' (so also esp. ins, pap) **to be in a confused state of mind, *be at a loss, be in doubt, be uncertain*** act. (Thu. 5, 40, 3; X., Hell. 6, 1, 4; Alex. Ep. XIII 1; POxy 472, 8; 939, 23f; Wsd 11:17; Philo, Leg. All. 1, 70; Jos., Ant. 2, 271 and 304, Vi. 161) πολλὰ ἠπόρει *he was at a loss* **Mk 6:20** (so Goodsp., Probs. 58f: 'he was very much disturbed'; but s. FZorell, Lex. s.v. and CBonner, HTR 37, '44, 41–44, 336 'he was wont to raise many questions'; s. also L-S-J-M s.v. I 2; but the καί foll. is prob. adversative: 'he was much perplexed when he listened to John, yet readily continued to give him an audience'. On the textual problem s. KRomaniuk, ἠπόρει ου ἐποίει en Mc 6:20?: ETL 69, '93, 140f).—Elsewh., in our lit. mid. (X., An. 6, 1, 21; 7, 3, 29 et al.; SIG 226, 35; 1 Macc 3:31; Jos., Bell. 4, 226; Just., D. 72, 3; s. Renehan '82, 34) τί ἐν σεαυτῷ διαλογίζῃ καὶ ἀπορῇ; *why this inward debate and perplexity?* Hs 9, 2, 6. περί τινος *about someth.* **Lk 24:4** (v.l. διαπορέω q.v.); Hs 8, 3, 1. W. indir. question foll. ἀπορούμενοι περί τίνος λέγει *uncertain as to which one he meant* **J 13:22.** πρός τι PEg[2], 63. W. acc. foll. ἀπορούμενος τὴν (v.l. εἰς τὴν) περὶ τούτων ζήτησιν *since I was at a loss how to investigate these matters* **Ac 25:20** (B-D-F §148, 2; Rob. 472). ἔν τινι *because of someone* **Gal 4:20.** Abs. ἀπορούμενοι ἀλλ' οὐκ ἐξαπορούμενοι *(sometimes) at a loss, but not losers* (an attempt to reproduce the wordplay; REB: *bewildered, but never at our wits' end*) **2 Cor 4:8.** ἠπορούμην ἐπὶ ταῖς παρθέναις Hs 9, 2, 5.—M-M.

ἀπο(ρ)ρήγνυμι fut. ἀπορρήξω LXX; 1 aor. 3 sg. ἀπέρρηξε 4 Macc 9:25; pf. ἀπέρρηγα, ptc. ἀπερρηγώς; fut. pass. 3 sg. ἀπορραγήσεται Eccl 4:12 (s. ῥήγνυμι 'break, shatter'; Hom. et al.; PMichZen 87, 3 [III BC]; Philo, Aet. M. 118; Jos., Ant. 17, 320; on the spelling s. B-D-F §11, 1) ***break up*** τόπος κρημνώδης καὶ ἀ. ἀπὸ τ. ὑδάτων *steep place broken up by the waters* Hv 1, 1, 3.—DELG s.v. ῥήγνυμι.

ἀπορία, ας, ἡ (s. ἀπορέω; Pind., Hdt. et al.; ins, pap, LXX; TestJob; Jos., Bell. 1, 198, Ant., 8, 328; Ath., R. 74, 32 'lack' of money or possessions) orig. 'lack of means/resources' (so esp. ins, pap) ***perplexity, anxiety*** ἀ. ἤχους θαλάσσης *anxiety because of the roaring of the sea* **Lk 21:25** (cp. Herodian 4, 14, 1 ἀ. τοῦ πρακτέου).—DELG s.v. πόρος, w. ref. to πείρω. Frisk s.v. πείρω. M-M. Sv.

ἀπο(ρ)ρίπτω fut. ἀπορρίψω LXX; 1 aor. ἀπέριψα (v.l. ἀπέρριψα **Ac 27:43;** W-S §5, 26b, B-D-F §11, 1). Pass.: 2 aor. ἀπερίφην Hv 3, 5, 5; 3, 6, 1; fut. ἀπορριφήσομαι LXX; pf. ἀπέρριμμαι LXX (s. ῥίπτω; Hom. et al.; pap, LXX; OdeSol 11:10; Test12Patr; JosAs; Philo, Ebr. 7; Joseph.; Just.; Tat. 20, 1).

❶ **cause quick downward movement or separation away from a point or location, *throw away*** in rejection (Jon 2:4) pass. ἀπὸ τοῦ πύργου Hs 9, 23, 3; cp. v 3, 5, 5; 3, 6, 1.

❷ **to cause a sudden or forcible separation, *drive/scare away,*** fig. ext. of 1 (Aeschyl. et al.; Himerius, Or. [Ecl.] 36, 1 τινὰ εἴς τι) μὴ ἀπορίψῃς με ἀπὸ τοῦ προσώπου σου *do not drive me away fr. your presence* 1 Cl 18:11 (Ps 50:13; gener. freq. in LXX; Jos., Bell. 1, 624 ἀ. ἀπό=drive away from.—ἀ.=reject, of God, in Celsus 3, 71.—Procop. Soph., Ep. 77 ἀπερριμμένοι=rejected ones; 94). μέριμναν ἀπορίψαντες *casting care* **1 Pt 5:7** P[72]. ἀ. ἀφ' ἑαυτῶν πᾶσαν ἀδικίαν *casting away fr. ourselves all unrighteousness* 1 Cl 35:5 (cp. Ezk 18:31; 20:7f; SibOr 1, 338 ἀ. ἐκ κραδίης κακίας; of the *casting off* of a garment Jos., Bell. 1, 197, Ant. 6, 113; OdeSol 11:10; 1 Tat. 20:1).

❸ **propel oneself downward** intr. (Lucian, Ver. Hist. 1, 30; Chariton 3, 5, 6; s. Moulton, ClR 20, 1906, 216) *throw oneself down, jump* **Ac 27:43** (s. B-D-F §308; Rob. 797).—M-M. TW.

ἀπορρέω pass.: fut. ἀπορυήσομαι and 2 aor. 3 sg. ἀπερρύη (s. ῥέω; trag., Hdt. et al.; Eudoxos-Papyrus [=PParis 1] 14, 328 [II BC]; LXX, Just., Ath.) lit. 'flow down'; fig., of leaves (Demosth. 22, 70; cp. Sb 7350 of hair falling out) ***fall down*** B 11:6, 8 (Ps 1:3).

ἀπόρροια, ας, ἡ (ἀπορρέω; since Xen., Hell. 5, 2, 5, also Wsd 7:25; Philo, Ath.) lit. 'a flowing off, a stream'; esp. ***emanation*** αὐτὴ ἡ ἀ. τῆς ἐννοίας *she, the emanation itself of the (divine) mind* Ox 1081 30f (SJCh 90, 7f)=Otero I no. 3 p. 83 (cp. Herm. fgm. 23, 3 al. and Rtzst., Poim., p. 16, n. 4).—DELG s.v. ῥέω C.

ἀπορφανίζω 1 aor. pass. ptc. ἀπορφανισθείς (ὀρφανίζω 'make orphan'; Aeschyl.; BCH 46, 1922, 345; Philo [Nägeli 25]) ***make an orphan of*** someone, fig., of the apostle separated fr. his church ἀπορφανισθέντες ἀφ' ὑμῶν *made orphans by separation fr. you* **1 Th 2:17.**—Cp. Straub 23. DELG s.v. ὀρφανός.

ἀποσκευάζω fut. 3 sg. ἀποσκευάσει (Ath. 2, 1); 1 aor. inf. ἀποσκευάσαι Lev 14:36; mid. ἀπεσκευασάμην (s. σκευάζω; mostly mid.; Polyb. et al.; cp. SIG 588, 54 [196 BC]; 633, 68; Lev 14:36; Philo, Deus Imm. 135; Ath. 2, 1; 9, 2) ***lay aside, get rid of*** τὶ (Jos., Bell. 1, 260; 618) τ. συνήθειαν *lay aside the habit* Dg 2:1. **Ac 21:15 v.l.,** ἀ. prob. means *pack up and leave.*—DELG s.v. σκεῦος. M-M.

ἀποσκίασμα, ατος, τό (ἀποσκιάζω 'cast a shadow'; Aëtius [100 AD] 2, 30, 3: Dox. Gr. 361b, 21. ἀποσκιασμοί Plut., Pericl. 155 [6, 5]) ***shadow*** τροπῆς ἀ. *a shadow cast by variation* (in position of heavenly bodies) **Js 1:17** (Theopomp. [?]: 115 fgm. 400 Jac. τὸ ἀποσκίασμα τῆς τοῦ ἡλίου ἀνταυγείας). JRopes, ICC ad loc. and Goodsp., Probs. 189f prefer the rdg. of B et al. (παρ.) ἡ τροπῆς ἀποσκιάσματος '(no variation) of changing shadow'. MDibelius, Meyer[7] 1921 ad loc. would emend to put both nouns in the genitive and transl. the clause 'who is without change and knows neither turning nor darkness.'—DELG s.v. σκιά. M-M. TW.

ἀποσμήχω 1 aor. mid. ἀπεσμηξάμην (σμήχω 'wipe off'; since Pherecydes of Athens [V BC]: 3 fgm. 33 p. 70, 32 Jac.; Jos., Bell. 2, 123 [Herwerden]) ***wipe, wipe off*** in our lit. only mid.: with acc. *purify* τὴν κεφαλήν GJs 2:4; w. gen. *purify oneself* τῆς ἀφέδρου of giving birth 5:2.—DELG s.v. σμήω.

ἀποσπάω fut. ἀποσπάσω LXX, ἀποσπῶ Jer 12:14; 1 aor. ἀπέσπασα. Pass.: aor. ἀπεσπάσθην; pf. ptc. ἀπεσπασμένοι Is 28:9 (σπάω 'draw, pull'; Pind., Hdt. et al.; SEG XLII, 613, 5; pap, LXX; ApcSed 10:4; Just., Tat.).

❶ lit. **to pull/draw out,** ***draw out*** ἀ. τ. μάχαιραν *draw a sword* **Mt 26:51.** ἀ. τοὺς ἥλους ἀπὸ τ. χειρῶν *draw out the nails fr. the hands* GPt 6:21=ASyn. 347, 62.

❷ fig. **to draw away from a place or point of view—ⓐ** act. ***draw away, attract, proselyte*** (cp. Artem. 5, 43 τινά τινος someone from someone; Josh 8:6; Jer 12:14; Jos., Vi. 321, Ant. 8, 277 ἀπὸ τ. θεου) ἀπὸ τ. εἰδώλων *fr. cult images* 2 Cl 17:1 (cp. Sb 1161, 40; 6156, 32 [both I BC]; Polyaenus 8, 51 of the bringing out of one who has fled to a temple for refuge); ἀ. τοὺς μαθητὰς ὀπίσω ἑαυτῶν *draw away the disciples after them* (and thereby alienate them) **Ac 20:30** (cp. Aelian, VH 13:32; Diog. L. 2, 113 ἀ. τινὰ ἀπό τινος alienate pupils from someone, proselyte; PPetr III, 43 [3], 12; PCairZen 60, 3 [III BC]; BGU 1125, 9 [13 BC] οὐκ ἀποσπάσω αὐτὸν ἀπὸ σοῦ; POxy 275, 22 [66 AD]). εἰς τὸ ἀπὸ τ. ἁμαρτιῶν ἀποσπασθῆναι *so that they might be wrested from their sins* AcPlCor 2:9.

ⓑ pass. in mid. sense ἀ. ἀπό τινος ***tear oneself away*** **Ac 21:1;** Hs 6, 2, 3.—***Withdraw*** (Diod. S. 20, 39; Job 41:9; POxy 275, 22 [66 AD]; Jos., Bell. 2, 498; 6, 379) ἀπό τινος **Lk 22:41.**—DELG s.v. σπάω. M-M.

ἀποσταλῶ, ἀποσταλείς s. ἀποστέλλω.

ἀποστασία, ας, ἡ (s. ἀφίστημι; a form quotable since Diod. S. outside the Bible [Nägeli 31] for the older ἀπόστασις [Phryn. 528 Lob.]) **defiance of established system or authority,** ***rebellion, abandonment, breach of faith*** (Josh 22:22; 2 Ch 29:19; 1 Macc 2:15; Just., D. 110, 2; Tat. 8:1) ἀπό τινος (Plu., Galb. 1053 [1, 9] Z. v.l. ἀπὸ Νέρωνος ἀ.; Jos., Vi. 43) ἀποστασίαν διδάσκεις ἀπὸ Μωϋσέως *you teach (Judeans) to abandon Moses* **Ac 21:21.** Of the rebellion caused by the Lawless One in the last days **2 Th 2:3** (cp. Just., D. 110, 2).—DELG s.v. ἵστημι. M-M. TW. Sv.

ἀποστάσιον, ου, τό (a legal t.t. found as early as Lysias, Hyperid. [fgm. Or. 17] and Demosth. [cp. Renehan '75, 38], and freq. in pap [cp. Wilcken, APF 2, 1903, 143 and 388f; 4, 1908, 183 and 456f; Preisigke, Fachwörter 1915; Taubenschlag, Law[2] 274] since PHib 96, 3 [258 BC]; PSI 551, 9 [III BC] in the sense of relinquishment of property after sale, abandonment, etc. The consequent giving up of one's claim explains the meaning that the word acquires in Jewish circles:) δοῦναι βιβλίον ἀποστασίου (Jer 3:8; Just., D. 114, 5) ***notice of divorce*** *give (one's wife) a certificate of divorce* **Mt 19:7.** διδόναι ἀποστάσιον, w. the same mng. **5:31.** For this γράφειν β. ἀ. (Dt 24:1, 3) **Mk 10:4.**—S. lit. on ἀπολύω 5; also Mishnah Gitten (Certificates of Divorce).—DELG s.v. ἵστημι. EDNT. M-M.

ἀπόστασις, ἡ (s. ἀφίστημι; Hdt. et al.; PParis 36, 13 'revolt'; Epict. 4, 4, 39 'giving up') ***cessation, renunciation, desisting from*** πραγμάτων α. *giving up of things (hoped for)* **Hb 11:1** P[13] (cp. Epict. 4, 4, 39 ἀ. τῶν ἀπροαιρέτων=giving up interest in things that are outside one's control).

ἀποστάτης, ου, ὁ (s. ἀφίστημι; Polyb. et al.; SIG 705, 50 [112 BC]; PAmh 30, 33ff; Mitt-Wilck. I/2, 10, 12 [=Witkowski 52, 12]; PTebt 781, 7; 888, 11; 1043, 45 and 54 [all II BC]; LXX; TestSol 13:1 C; Berosus 680: fgm. 8, 135 p. 389, 3 Jac. in Jos., Ant. 10, 221=C. Ap. 1, 136; Just.) ***deserter, rebel*** w. ἔθνη Hv 1, 4, 2; w. προδότης s 8, 6, 4; w. βλάσφημος and προδότης s 9, 19, 1. W. obj. gen. (Polyb. 5, 57, 4 and Diod. S. 15, 18, 1 τ. βασιλέως) τ. νόμου *from the law* (2 Macc 5:8 τ. νόμων ἀ.) **Js 2:11 v.l.** —DELG s.v. ἵστημι.

ἀποστεγάζω (s. στέγη) 1 aor. ἀπεστέγασα (in the sense 'uncover': Strabo; IG XII/3, 325, 30 [Thera, II AD]; Jer 49:10 Sym.; in the sense 'cover': Theoph., De Causis Plantarum 5, 6, 5; Aristot., Problemata 924a, 37) ***unroof*** τ. στέγην *remove the roof* **Mk 2:4** (so Strabo 4, 4, 6 pass. of a custom of unroofing and roofing a temple on the same day; 8, 3, 30 of a statue of Zeus: if Z. stood up he would unroof the temple; Artem. 2, 36 p. 137, 26; SIG 852, 29f στοὰ . . . ἀπεστέγασται μὲν ὅλη).—S. lit. on στέγη.—DELG s.v. στέγω.

ἀποστέλλω fut. ἀποστελῶ; 1 aor. ἀπέστειλα; ἀποστείλω **Ac 7:34** (Ex 3:10) is perh. not hortat. subj. but pres. ind. as in the Pontic dial. (Thumb 18; s. M-M s.v.) or fut. (see v.l.); pf. ἀπέσταλκα, pass. ἀπέσταλμαι; 2 aor. pass. ἀπεστάλην (Soph., Hdt.+).

❶ **to dispatch someone for the achievement of some objective,** ***send away/out*** (Diod. S. 34 + 35, 14)—ⓐ w. only the obj. given **Mt 13:41; Mk 11:1; 12:5** al.

ⓑ more exactly defined—**α.** w. indication of the pers. to whom someone is sent: by the dat. (UPZ 61, 20) **Mt 22:16;** εἴς τινα **Mt 15:24; Lk 11:49; Ac 26:17.** πρός τινα (Epict. 3, 22, 74; Jos., Ant. 7, 334) **Mt 21:34, 37; 23:34, 37; 27:19; Mk 3:31; 12:4, 6; J 1:19** al.

β. w. indication of the place to which someone is sent, w. εἰς (PCairZen 578, 3): **Mt 14:35; 20:2; Mk 8:26; Lk 1:26; 10:1; J 3:17** al. W. ἐν (4 Km 17:25; 2 Ch 7:13) ἐν μέσῳ λύκων **Mt 10:16; Lk 10:3** (cp. Jer 32:27). ἔξω τ. χώρας *outside the country* **Mk 5:10.** W. ὧδε *here* **Mk 11:3.** ἀ. πρεσβείαν ὀπίσω τινός *send an embassy after someone* **Lk 19:14** (cp. 4 Km 14:19). ἀ. ἔμπροσθέν τινος (cp. Gen 45:5, 7; 46:28) *send before someone* **J 3:28;** cp. ἀ. ἄγγελον πρὸ προσώπου σου **Mt 11:10; Mk 1:2** (Ex 23:20; cp. Mal 3:1); cp. **Lk 9:52; 10:1.**

γ. w. the purpose of the sending indicated by ἵνα (Gen 30:25) **Mk 12:2, 13; Lk 20:10; J 1:19; 3:17; 7:32;** Hv 5:2 al. By ὅπως

(1 Macc 16:18) **Ac 9:17.** By the inf. (Num 16:12; 31:4) **Mt 22:3; Mk 3:14; Lk 1:19; 4:18a** (Is 61:1); **9:2; 14:17; J 4:38; Ac 5:21; 1 Cor 1:17; Rv 22:6;** B 14:9 (Is 61:1); Hm 12, 6, 1; cp. AcPlCor 2:9 in c below. By ἐπί (or εἰς) w. acc. (Apollon. Paradox. 1; PFlor 126, 8; Sb 174, 5f [III BC] ἀ. ἐπὶ τ. θήραν τ. ἐλεφάντων; UPZ 15, 24) ἐπὶ τοῦτο *for this purpose* **Lk 4:43.** εἰς διακονίαν *to render service* **Hb 1:14** (cp. Jdth 11:7; Gen 45:5). By the simple acc. τοῦτον ἄρχοντα καὶ λυτρωτὴν ἀπέσταλκεν *this man he sent as leader and deliverer* **Ac 7:35.** ἀ. τὸν υἱὸν αὐτοῦ ἱλασμόν **1J 4:10.** ἀ. τ. υἱόν σωτῆρα vs. **14** (cp. ἐκεῖνον . . . κατάσκοπον . . . ἀποσταλέντα Just., D. 113, 1).

δ. in pass. ἀποστέλλεσθαι παρὰ θεοῦ (Vi. Aesopi I c. 31 p. 295, 1 ed. Eberh. ἀπεστάλην παρὰ τ. θεοῦ μου; cp. Sir 15:9; 34:6) **J 1:6.** πνεύματος ἁγίου ἀπὸ οὐρανοῦ παρὰ τοῦ πατρὸς ἀποσταλέντος εἰς αὐτὴν (Μαρίαν) AcPlCor 2:5; ἀπὸ τ. θεοῦ (Epict. 3, 22, 23 ἀπὸ τοῦ Διός; Vi. Aesopi G 119 P.: the prophets of Heliopolis say ἡμεῖς ἀπεστάλημεν ἀπὸ τοῦ θεοῦ) **Lk 1:26** (v.l. ὑπό); cp. 1 Cl 65:1. ἀπὸ Κορνηλίου πρὸς αὐτόν **Ac 10:21 v.l.** ἀπὸ Καισαρείας **11:11** (cp. 1 Macc 15:1). ἀπ' οὐρανοῦ **1 Pt 1:12;** ἀπὸ τοῦ ἀγγέλου Hv 5:2.

ⓒ esp. of the sending out of the disciples by Jesus **Mt 10:5; Mk 3:14; 6:7; Lk 9:2; J 4:38; 17:18,** as well as God's sending forth of Jesus (of the divine mission, esp. of prophets, very oft. in LXX; on the Heb. שָׁלִיחַ see LKopf, VetusT 7, '58, 207–9 and ἀπόστολος 2c.—Philo, Migr. Abr. 22; Just., A I, 63, 5; D. 75, 3. The Cynic ἀπὸ τ. Διὸς ἀπέσταλται Epict. 3, 22, 23; cp. 46.—Cornutus 16 p. 30, 19 ὁ Ἑρμῆς ὁ λόγος ὤν, ὃν ἀπέστειλαν πρὸς ἡμᾶς ἐξ οὐρανοῦ οἱ θεοί) **Mt 15:24; Mk 9:37; Lk 9:48; J 3:17, 34; 5:36, 38; 6:29, 57; 7:29; 8:42; 11:42; 17:3** (ἀποπέμπω v.l.), **8, 21, 23, 25; 20:21; Ac 3:20.** Σιλωάμ tr. ἀπεσταλμένος **J 9:7** (for a prob. mystic sense cp. Philo, Poster. Cai. 73; difft. VIs 2 [p. 69, 5 Sch.].—The abs. ὁ ἀπεσταλμένος [Diod. S. 16, 50, 2]=the emissary). John the Baptist ἀπεσταλμένος παρὰ θεοῦ **1:6.**— ἀπέστειλε πρώτοις Ἰουδαίοις προφήτας εἰς τὸ ἀπὸ τῶν ἁμαρτιῶν ἀποσπασθῆναι *sent prophets first to Judaeans so that they might be rescued from their sins* AcPlCor 2:9.—Also of the Holy Spirit **1 Pt 1:12** (cp. w. ref. to the breath or wind of God, Jdth 16:14; Ex 15:10).—Of angels Hv 4, 2, 4 (cp. Da 4:13, 23; 2 Macc 11:6; 15:22f; Tob 3:17).

❷ to dispatch a message, *send, have someth. done*—ⓐ w. ref. to content of the message τοῖς ἔθνεσιν ἀπεστάλη τοῦτο τὸ σωτήριον *this salvation has been dispatched to the gentiles* **Ac 28:28** (cp. the passages fr. Lk and Ac in c end).

ⓑ When used w. other verbs, ἀ. often functions like our verbal auxiliary 'have' and means simply that the action in question has been performed by someone else (Gen 31:4; 41:8, 14; Ex 9:27; 2 Km 11:5 al.; X., Cyr. 3, 1, 6; Plut., Mor. 11c μεταπέμψας ἀνεῖλε τ. Θεόκριτον) ἀποστείλας ἀνεῖλεν *he had (them) killed* **Mt 2:16.** ἀ. ἐκράτησεν τ. Ἰωάννην *he had John arrested* **Mk 6:17.** ἀ. μετεκαλέσατο *he had (him) summoned* **Ac 7:14.** ἐσήμανεν ἀ. διὰ τ. ἀγγέλου αὐτοῦ *he had it made known by his angel* **Rv 1:1.** Sim. ἀπέστειλαν αἱ ἀδελφαὶ πρὸς αὐτὸν λέγουσαι *the sisters had word brought to him* **J 11:3.** ἀ. ἐν ἀφέσει *set free* **Lk 4:18b** (Is 58:6).

ⓒ in related vein w. impers. obj. (Demetr.: 722 fgm. 1, 15 Jac.; cp. En 101:3; PsSol 7:4): ἀ. τὸ δρέπανον *(one) sends for the sickle*='sends for the reapers'; a species of synecdoche **Mk 4:29** (Field, Notes 26, argues for 'put forth'='put in' on the basis principally of Jo 3:13, ἐξαποστείλατε δρέπανα, ὅτι παρέστηκεν τρύγητος, a clause formally sim. to the phrase in Mk. The sense linguistically remains the same: reapers must perform the task with a sickle. In the impv. construction of Jo the subject is specified and the action defined as a directive; in Mk the subj. is to be inferred and the directive implied). ἀ. αὐτούς, the owner arranges for dispatch of donkeys **Mt 21:3.** ἀ. τὸν λόγον *send out a message* (Ps 106:20; 147:7; cp. PLips 64, 42 τὸ περὶ τούτου ἀποσταλὲν πρόσταγμα) **Ac 10:36; 13:26 v.l.;** cp. **Lk 24:49.** Pass. **Ac 28:28** (s. a above).

ⓓ abs. μήπως ἀποστείλῃ ὁ δεσπότης ἐφ' ἡμᾶς *lest the Lord dispatch* (his wrath) *upon us* GJs 7:1 (Ezk 7:7).—See lit. s.v. ἀπόστολος.—B. 710. DELG s.v. στέλλω A. M-M. TW.

ἀποστερέω fut. ἀποστερήσω LXX; 1 aor. ἀπεστέρησα; perf. pass. ptc. ἀπεστερημένος (στερέω 'rob'; Aeschyl., Hdt., et al.; ins, pap, LXX; Ath., Just.)

❶ to cause another to suffer loss by taking away through illicit means, *rob, steal, despoil, defraud* τινά *someone* (UPZ 32, 33 [162/161 BC] ἀποστεροῦντες ἡμᾶς; Jos., Vi. 128) ἀποστερεῖτε, καὶ τοῦτο ἀδελφούς *you engage in fraud, yes, even against your own fellow-members* **1 Cor 6:8.** W. gen. of thing (PRyl 116, 16 βουλόμενοι ἀποστερέσαι τῶν ἐμῶν; Sir 29:6; Jos., Ant. 2, 303 τῆς ἐπιμελείας) τῆς ἀληθείας **1 Ti 6:5.** W. acc. of thing (Heraclit., Ep. 7 p. 202, 9 Malherbe; UPZ 16, 7; Herm. Wr. 5, 8; Sir 4:1; 34:21) ἀ. τὴν ζωὴν ὑμῶν *rob you of (eternal) life* Hv 3, 9, 9. Abs. (UPZ 42, 35 [163/162 BC]) μὴ ἀποστερήσῃς *do not steal* **Mk 10:19** (perh. w. ref. to property held on deposit: CCoulter, ClPh 35, '40, 60–63; Pliny, Ep. to Trajan 96, 7; Lev 5:20–25 [=6:2–5 MT]).—Pass. ὁ μισθὸς ὁ ἀπεστερημένος (Sir 34:22; Mal 3:5; cp. Philo, Mos. 1, 142; Jos., Ant. 4, 288—SIG 1199, 5: ἀ.=acquire illegally, embezzle) *wages stolen* or *held back* fr. the workers **Js 5:4.** τίς πλέον ἀποστερηθῇ; *who has suffered greater loss?* IEph 10:3. *Let oneself be robbed* **1 Cor 6:7** (permissive pass.: Gildersleeve, Syntax I §167). W. gen. *lose someth.* (Jos., Vi. 205) **Ac 16:19** D.

❷ to prevent someone from having the benefit of someth., *deprive,* fig. ext. of 1: μὴ ἀποστερεῖτε ἀλλήλους *do not deprive each other* of marital rights **1 Cor 7:5** (cp. PLond VI, 1917, 19; cp. Ex 21:10 and s. Nägeli 20).—DELG s.v. στέρομαι. M-M.

ἀποστέρησις, εως, ἡ (s. ἀποστερέω; since Thu. 7, 70, 6; POxy 71, 10; Jos., Ant. 18, 7) **withholding what is due,** ***fraud*** (Diod. S. 4, 33, 1 ἀποστέρησις τοῦ μισθοῦ) in a catalogue of vices Hm 8:5.—DELG s.v. στέρομαι.

ἀποστερητής, οῦ, ὁ (s. ἀποστερέω; Pla., Rep. 5, 344b et al.; POxy 745, 7 [I AD]) ***defrauder, cheat,*** classed w. other sinners Hs 6, 5, 5. οἱ ψευδόμενοι γίνονται ἀποστερηταὶ τοῦ κυρίου *liars become defrauders of the Lord* m 3:2.—DELG s.v. στέρομαι.

ἀποστῇ, ἀποστῆναι, ἀποστήσομαι, ἀπόστητε s. ἀφίστημι.

ἀποστιβάζω (s. στιβάζω) apparently occurs only here, ***to make empty,*** ἀ. τ. ἀποθήκην *empty the storeroom* Hm 11:15.

ἀποστολή, ῆς, ἡ (s. ἀποστέλλω; Eur., Thu., et al. in var. mngs.; Diod. S. 36, 1 [ἀ. στρατιωτῶν='sending out' of troops]; ins, pap, LXX; TestNapht 2:1; EpArist 15; Jos., Ant. 20, 50, Vi. 268) in our lit. only of God's elite emissaries for the Christian message **office of a special emissary, *apostleship, office of an apostle, assignment*** w. διακονία **Ac 1:25.** Used esp. by Paul to designate his position: ἡ σφραγίς μου τ. ἀποστολῆς *the seal* (official confirmation) *of my apostleship* **1 Cor 9:2.** ἐνεργεῖν τινι εἰς ἀ. *make someone capable of being an apostle* **Gal 2:8.** λαμβάνειν ἀποστολὴν εἰς ὑπακοὴν πίστεως *receive apostleship, to bring about obedience that is consonant with faith* **Ro 1:5.**—DELG s.v. στέλλω A. M-M. TW.

ἀποστολικός, ή, όν (s. ἀποστέλλω; schol. on Pind., P. 2, 6b, I. 2 ins a; Proclus in Phot., Bibl. p. 322b; Athen. 14, 631d [of a dance style: relating to a diplomatic mission?]) *apostolic* ἐν ἀ. χαρακτῆρι in *apostolic fashion*=as the apostles did in their letters ITr ins διδάσκαλος ἀ. καὶ προφητικός an *apost. and prophetic teacher* of Polycarp MPol 16:2. τὰς ἀ. διηγήσεις *the apostolic accounts* Pa (2:12).—Sv.

ἀπόστολος, ου, ὁ (s. ἀποστέλλω). In older Gk. (Lysias, Demosth.) and later (e.g. Posidon.: 87 fgm. 53 p. 257, 21 Jac. [Strabo 3, 5, 5]) ὁ ἀ. is a naval expedition, prob. also its commander (Anecd. Gr. 217, 26). τὸ ἀπόστολον with (Pla., Ep. 7, 346a) or without (Vi. Hom. 19) πλοῖον means a ship ready for departure. In its single occurrence in Jos. (Ant. 17, 300; it is not found elsewh. in Jewish-Gk. lit.) it prob. means 'sending out'; in pap mostly 'bill of lading' (s. Preisigke, Fachwörter 1915), less freq. 'certificate of clearance (at a port)' (BGU V §64 [II AD]=Gnomon des Idios Logos). It can also be 'letter of authorization (relating to shipping)': Mitt-Wilck. I/2, 443, 10 (15 AD); PHerm 6, 11f (cp. Dig. 49, 6, 1 litteras dimissorias sive apostolos). In contrast, in isolated cases it refers to persons who are dispatched for a specific purpose, and the context determines the status or function expressed in such Eng. terms as 'ambassador, delegate, messenger' (Hdt. 1, 21; 5, 38; Synesius, Providence 2, 3 p. 122a ἀπόστολοι of ordinary messengers; Sb 7241, 48; BGU 1741, 6 [64 BC]; 3 Km 14:6A; Is 18:2 Sym.). Cp. KLake, The Word Ἀ.: Beginn. I 5, '33, 46–52. It is this isolated usage that is preferred in the NT w. nuances peculiar to its lit. But the extensive use of ἀποστέλλω in documents relating to pers. of merit engaged in administrative service prob. encouraged NT use of the noun, thus in effect disavowing assoc. w. the type of itinerant philosophers that evoked the kind of pejorative term applied by Paul's audience Ac 17:18.

❶ of messengers without extraordinary status ***delegate, envoy, messenger*** (opp. ὁ πέμψας) **J 13:16.** Of Epaphroditus, messenger of the Philippians **Phil 2:25.—2 Cor 8:23.**

❷ of messengers with extraordinary status, esp. of God's ***messenger, envoy*** (cp. Epict. 3, 22, 23 of Cynic wise men: ἄγγελος ἀπὸ τ. Διὸς ἀπέσταλται).

ⓐ of prophets **Lk 11:49; Rv 18:20;** cp. **2:2; Eph 3:5.**

ⓑ of Christ (w. ἀρχιερεύς) **Hb 3:1** (cp. ApcEsdr 2:1 p. 25, 29 T.; Just., A I, 12, 9; the extra-Christian firman Sb 7240, 4f οὐκ ἔστιν θεὸς εἰ μὴ ὁ θεὸς μόνος. Μααμετ ἀπόστολος θεοῦ). GWetter, 'D. Sohn Gottes' 1916, 26ff.

ⓒ but predominately in the NT (of the apologists, only Just.) of a group of highly honored believers w. a special function as God's envoys. Also Judaism had a figure known as apostle (שָׁלִיחַ; Schürer III 124f w. sources and lit.; Billerb. III 1926, 2–4; JTruron, Theology 51, '48, 166–70; 341–43; GDix, ibid. 249–56; 385f; JBühner, art. ἀ. in EDNT I 142–46). In Christian circles, at first ἀ. denoted one who proclaimed the gospel, and was not strictly limited: Paul freq. calls himself an ἀ.: **Ro 1:1; 11:13; 1 Cor 1:1; 9:1f; 15:9; 2 Cor 1:1; Gal 1:1; Eph 1:1; Col 1:1; 1 Ti 1:1; 2:7; 2 Ti 1:1; Tit 1:1.**—1 Cl 47:1. Of Barnabas **Ac 14:14; 15:2.** Of Andronicus and Junia (less prob. Junias, s. Ἰουνία) **Ro 16:7.** Of James, the Lord's brother **Gal 1:19.** Of Peter **1 Pt 1:1; 2 Pt 1:1.** Then esp. of the 12 apostles οἱ δώδεκα ἀ. (cp. ParJer 9:20; AscIs 3:21; 4:3) **Mt 10:2; Mk 3:14; Lk 22:14** (v.l. οἱ δώδεκα); cp. **6:13; 9:10; 17:5; Ac 1:26** (P-HMenoud, RHPR 37 '57, 71–80); **Rv 21:14;** PtK 3 p. 15, 18. Peter and the apostles **Ac 2:37; 5:29.** Paul and apostles Pol 9:1 (cp. AcPlTh Aa I, 235 app. of Thecla). Gener. the apostles **Mk 6:30; Lk 24:10; 1 Cor 4:9; 9:5; 15:7; 2 Cor 11:13; 1 Th 2:7; Ac 1:2; 2:42f; 4:33, 35, 37; 5:2, 12, 18, 34 v.l., 40; 6:6; 8:1, 14, 18; 9:27; 11:1; 14:4; 2 Pt 3:2; Jd 17;** IEph 11:2; IMg 7:1; 13:2; ITr 2:2; 3:1; 7:1; IPhld 5:1; ISm 8:1; D ins; 11:3, 6. As a governing board, w. the elders **Ac 15:2, 4, 6, 22f; 16:4.** As possessors of the most important spiritual gift **1 Cor 12:28f.** Proclaimers of the gospel 1 Cl 42:1f; B 5:9; Hs 9, 17, 1. Prophesying strife 1 Cl 44:1. Working miracles **2 Cor 12:12.** W. overseers, teachers and attendants Hv 3, 5, 1; s 9, 15, 4; w. teachers s 9, 25, 2; w. teachers, preaching to those who had fallen asleep s 9, 16, 5; w. var. Christian officials IMg 6:1; w. prophets **Eph 2:20;** D 11:3; Pol 6:3. Christ and the apostles as the foundation of the church IMg 13:1; ITr 12; 2; cp. **Eph 2:20.** οἱ ἀ. and ἡ ἐκκλησία w. the three patriarchs and the prophets IPhld 9:1. The Holy Scriptures named w. the ap. 2 Cl 14:2 (sim. ApcSed 14:10 p. 136, 17 Ja.). Paul ironically refers to his opponents (or the original apostles; s. s.v. ὑπερλίαν) as οἱ ὑπερλίαν ἀ. *the super-apostles* **2 Cor 11:5; 12:11.** The orig. apostles he calls οἱ πρὸ ἐμοῦ ἀ. **Gal 1:17;** AcPlCor 2:4.—Harnack, Mission[4] I 1923, 332ff (Eng. tr. I 319–31). WSeufert, D. Urspr. u. d. Bed. d. Apostolates 1887; EHaupt, Z. Verständnis d. Apostolates im NT 1896; EMonnier, La notion de l'Apostolat des origines à Irénée 1903; PBatiffol, RB n.s. 3, 1906, 520–32; Wlh., Einleitung[2], 1911, 138–47; EBurton, AJT 16, 1912, 561–88, Gal comm. 1921, 363–84; RSchütz, Apostel u. Jünger 1921; EMeyer I 265ff; III 255ff. HVogelstein, Development of the Apostolate in Judaism, etc.: HUCA 2, 1925, 99–123; JWagenmann, D. Stellg. d. Ap. Pls neben den Zwölf 1926; WMundle, D. Apostelbild der AG: ZNW 27, 1928, 36–54; KRengstorf, TW I 406–46 (s. critique by HConzelmann, The Theol. of St. Luke '60, 216, n. 1), Apost. u. Predigtamt '34; J-LLeuba, Rech. exégét. rel. à l'apostolat dans le NT, diss. Neuchâtel '36; PSaintyves, Deux mythes évangéliques, Les 12 apôtres et les 72 disciples '38; GSass, Apostelamt u. Kirche . . . paulin. Apostelbegr. '39; EKäsemann, ZNW 40, '41, 33–71; RLiechtenhan, D. urchr. Mission '46; ESchweizer, D. Leben d. Herrn in d. Gemeinde u. ihren Diensten '46; AFridrichsen, The Apostle and His Message '47; HvCampenhausen, D. urchristl. Apostelbegr.: StTh 1, '47, 96–130; HMosbech, ibid. 2, '48, 166–200; ELohse, Ursprung u. Prägung des christl. Apostolates: TZ 9, '53, 259–75; GKlein, Die 12 Apostel, '60; FHahn, Mission in the NT, tr. FClarke, '65; WSchmithals, The Office of the Apostle, tr. J-Steely, '69; KKertelge, Das Apostelamt des Paulus, BZ 14, '70, 161–81. S. also ἐκκλησία end, esp. Holl and Kattenbusch; also HBetz, Hermeneia: Gal '79, 74f (w. additional lit.); FAgnew, On the Origin of the Term ἀπόστολος: CBQ 38, '76, 49–53 (survey of debate); KHaacker, NovT 30, '88, 9–38 (Acts). Ins evidence (s. e.g. SIG index) relating to the verb ἀποστέλλω is almost gener. ignored in debate about the meaning of the noun.—DELG s.v. στέλλω A. EDNT. M-M. TW. Spicq.

ἀποστοματίζω (s. στόμα) is found since Pla. (Euthyd. 276c; 277a) w. the mngs. 'dictate for recitation' or 'repeat from memory' (ἀπὸ στόματος), which do not fit the context of **Lk 11:53** (note that the passage is not text-critically certain; see Tdf.), but a transf. sense such as ***question closely, interrogate, quiz*** τινά περί τινος (so L-S-J-M s.v. I 2; cp. Pla. in Pollux 2, 102 [pass.]) is prob.; but s. Wlh. ad loc. Ancient commentators interpreted it as *catch* (him) *in someth. he says*=vs. 54; then approx. *watch his utterances closely,* but such exposition imposes excessive semantic burden on the context. On the analogy of ἐπιστοματίζω 'to silence' someone, Luke's usage may be rendered *have him talk* (about many things); the opposition expects Jesus to say someth. that would be incriminating, vs. 54.—DELG s.v. στομα. M-M.

ἀποστρέφω fut. ἀποστρέψω; 1 aor. ἀπέστρεψα. Pass.: fut. ἀποστραφήσομαι LXX; 2 aor. ἀπεστράφην; pf. ἀπέστραμμαι (Hom.+).

❶ gener. **to turn someth. away from someth.,** ***turn away,*** freq. τὶ ἀπό τινος (BGU 955, 1; Ex 23:25; Job 33:17; Pr 4:27;

Sir 4:5 al.) lit. of bodily gestures ἀπὸ τ. ἀληθείας τ. ἀκοὴν ἀ. *turn away one's ear fr. the truth*=be unwilling to listen to the truth **2 Ti 4:4.** ἀ. τὸ πρόσωπον (oft. LXX) *turn away one's face* 1 Cl 18:9 (Ps 50:11). ἀπέστραπται τὸ πρόσωπον αὐτοῦ *his face is turned away* 16:3 (Is 53:3). ἀπεστραμμένοι ἦσαν *they* (i.e. their faces) *were turned away* Hv 3, 10, 1.

❷ **to cause change in belief or behavior,** fig. ext. of 1.

ⓐ positive ***turn, turn away,*** ἀ. ψυχὴν εἰς τὸ σωθῆναι *turn a soul to salvation* 2 Cl 15:1 (cp. PsSol 18:4). τ. ὀργὴν ἀπό τινος (cp. 1 Macc 3:8) *turn away wrath fr. someone* Hv 4, 2, 6. ἀποστρέψει ἀσεβείας ἀπὸ Ἰακώβ *will remove ungodliness fr. Jacob* **Ro 11:26** (Is 59:20). Prob. also **Ac 3:26** (w. numerous translators; cp. Job 33:17), but some interpret intr. (cp. Ezk 3:18, 19, 20; Sir 8:5; 17:26: B-D-F §308; Rob. 800).

ⓑ neg. ***mislead*** ἀ. τὸν λαόν *mislead the people, cause them to revolt* **Lk 23:14** (cp. 2 Ch 18:31; Jer 48:10); **Ac 20:30** D (foll. by ὀπίσω ἑαυτῶν). τ. γυναῖκας κ. τὰ τέκνα *mislead, alienate* **Lk 23:2 v.l.** (Marcion).

❸ **turn away from by rejecting, *reject, repudiate*** mid. (also 2d aor. pass. in act. sense) ἀ. τινά or τὶ (so w. acc. since Aristoph., Pax 683; X., Cyr. 5, 5, 36; PSI 392, 11 [III BC] ὁ δεῖνα οὐκ ἀπεστραμμένος αὐτόν; PGM 13, 620 Σάραπι, … μὴ ἀποστραφῇς με; Hos 8:3; Jer 15:6; 3 Macc 3:23; 4 Macc 1:33; 5:9; τὴν δέησιν ἡμῶν PsSol 5:5; EpArist 236; Philo, Det. Pot. Ins. 93 al.; Jos., Ant. 4, 135; 6, 340; 20, 166) ἀ. με πάντες *everybody has turned away fr. me* **2 Ti 1:15.** ἀ. τὸν ἐνδεόμενον *turn away fr. the needy* D 4:8; 5:2; B 20:2. ἀ. τὸν θέλοντα ἀπὸ σοῦ δανείσασθαι *turn away fr. him who wants to borrow fr. you* **Mt 5:42.** ἀ. τὸν ἀπ᾽ οὐρανῶν *reject the one fr. heaven* **Hb 12:25.** τὴν ἀλήθειαν **Tit 1:14** (Appian, Bell. Civ. 5, 25 §99 τὴν πολιτείαν=reject the form of government; Jos., Ant. 2, 48 τὴν ἀξίωσιν; 4, 135). ὅτι οὐκ ἀπεστράφη ἐπ᾽ αὐτούς *because (God) did not turn away (in wrath) against them* GJs 8:1; but the unusual phrase has undergone other interpretation, s. 5. For **Ac 3:26** s. 2a.

❹ **to return someth. to its customary place, *return, put back*** τὶ **Mt 27:3 v.l.;** ἀ. τ. μάχαιραν εἰς τ. τόπον αὐτῆς **Mt 26:52** (cp. Jer 35:3).

❺ ***turn back*** w. 2 aor. pass. in act. sense (Heraclides Pont., fgm. 49 Wehrli: the statue of Hera ἀπεστράφη=turned around; Noah's raven οὐκ ἀπεστράφη πρὸς αὐτὸν εἰς τὴν κιβωτόν, cp. ApcMos 42) fig. ἀπεστράφησαν ἐν τ. καρδίαις εἰς Αἴγυπτον **Ac 7:39** D. Various forms of GJs 8:1 (s. 3 end; the text of Tdf. and the vv.ll. in de Strycker) point to the rendering *because (Mary) did not turn back to go with them.*—DELG s.v. στρέφω. M-M. TW.

ἀποστροφή, ῆς, ἡ (s. ἀποστρέφω; Aeschyl. and Hdt. et al.; PLond IV, 1344, 4 of return of fugitives; LXX; Philo; Jos., Bell. 2, 212, Ant. 19, 131; Just., A II, 13, 1) ***turning, return*** πρὸς σὲ ἡ ἀ. αὐτοῦ *he shall turn to you* 1 Cl 4:5 (Gen 4:7).—DELG s.v. στρέφω.

ἀποστυγέω 1 aor. subj. 2 pl. ἀποστυγήσητε (Tat.) (στυγέω 'hate, abhor'; trag.; Hdt. 2, 47; 6, 129; Parthenius 20, 2; 36, 2; Tat. 19, 4) **to have a vehement dislike for someth., *hate strongly, abhor*** τὸ πονηρόν *the evil* (opp. κολλᾶσθαι τ. ἀγαθῷ) **Ro 12:9.**—DELG s.v. στυγέω II.

ἀποσυνάγωγος, ον (unknown in nonbibl. lit. and LXX) **expelled from the synagogue, *excluded, put under a curse/ban*** (חֵרֶם) ἀ. ποιεῖν *exclude fr. the synagogue* **J 16:2;** ἀ. γενέσθαι *be excommunicated* **9:22; 12:42.**—Schürer II 431–33; 462f; Billerb. IV 293–333; JDöller, ZKT 37, 1913, 1–24; KCarroll, BJRL 40, '57, 19–32.—M-M. TW.

ἀποσυνέχω (s. συνέχω; found only in our passage) apparently **confine to an isolated position, *hold, keep*** w. ἀπό emphasizing isolation ἑαυτὸν εἰς ὁδὸν σκότους *hold to the way of darkness* B 5:4 (in view of the ref. to fowlers' nets *ensnare,* tr. RKraft, Didache and Barnabas, '65, 93).—DELG s.v. ἔχω.

ἀποσύρω 1 aor. 3 pl. ἀπέσυραν 4 Macc. 9:28 cod. A; inf. ἀποσῦραι (Thu. et al.; 4 Macc 9:28; Jos., Bell. 3, 243, C. Ap. 2, 114) **to tear away someth. and so lay bare, *tear/scrape off*** τὶ *someth.* of skin (Alciphron 3, 32, 2 τὸ δέρμα τ. κεφαλῆς) MPol 8:3.—DELG s.v. σύρω.

ἀποτάσσω 1 aor. 3 sg. ἀπέταξεν LXX; in our lit. only mid., as in later usage gener. (cp. Eccl 2:20; Just., D. 119, 5; A I, 49, 5; Tat. 1:3) 1 aor. ἀπεταξάμην; pf. pass. ptc. ἀποτεταγμένος LXX (Pla., Polyb. et al.)

❶ **to express a formal farewell, *say farewell (to), take leave (of)*** τινί (Vi. Aesopi G 124 P.; POxy 298, 31 [I AD]; BGU 884 II, 12 [II/III AD]; Jos., Ant. 8, 354; s. Nageli 39; in pap most freq. in sense of bidding farewell, s. Wilcken on PBrem 16, 12; so also Jos., Ant. 11, 345; opp. POxy 1669, 4) τοῖς ἀδελφοῖς **Ac 18:18.** αὐτοῖς **2 Cor 2:13.** τοῖς εἰς τ. οἶκόν μου *to my people at home* **Lk 9:61;** cp. **Mk 6:46.** (Opp. ἀκολουθεῖν τινι.) τ. ἀγγέλῳ τ. πονηρίας *say farewell to the angel of wickedness* Hm 6, 2, 9. τῷ βίῳ to life IPhld 11:1 (cp. Cat. Cod. Astr. VIII/3 p. 136, 17). Abs. **Ac 18:21; 21:15** D.

❷ **to renounce interest in someth., *renounce, give up*** fig., w. impers. obj. (POxy 904, 8; Philo, Leg. All. 3, 142 al.; Just., Tat.; s. Rtzst., Hist. Mon. 104; Jos., Ant. 11, 232) 2 Cl 6:4f (opp. χρᾶσθαι). ταῖς ἡδυπαθείαις 16:2. πᾶσιν τοῖς ἑαυτοῦ ὑπάρχουσιν **Lk 14:33.**—DELG s.v. τάσσω. M-M. TW.

ἀποτελέω fut. ἀποτελοῦμαι **Lk 13:32** D; 1 aor. ἀπετέλεσα, pass. ἀπετελέσθην (s. τελέω; Hdt., X. et al.; ins, pap, LXX, En, TestSol; Philo, Aet. M. 41 al., De Prov. in Eus., PE 7, 21, 2; Ar. 4, 2; Just., Ath.).

❶ **to bring an activity to an end, *bring to completion, finish*** (1 Esdr 5:70 v.l.; Jos., C. Ap. 1, 154) of the constr. of a tower Hs 9, 5, 1f; 9, 26, 6. τὰ ῥήματα πάντα *finish all the words* v 2, 4, 2. Fig., pass. in act. sense *come to completion, be fully formed* (Aristot., De Cael. 26, 268b τὸ σῶμα ἀπετελέσθη; Luc., Herm. 8 ὃς ἂν ἀποτελέσθῃ πρὸς ἀρετήν; Synesius, Dio 1 p. 36 Petau Δίων φιλόσοφος ἀπετελέσθη) ἡ ἁμαρτία ἀποτελεσθεῖσα *sin, when it has run its course* **Js 1:15** (in the sense of being completed in action, cp. Pla., Leg. 823d ἀ. τὰ προσταχθέντα, 7th Letter 336c ἀ. βουλήσεις).

❷ **to accomplish someth., but without special reference to a beginning, *perform*** (Pla., Gorg. 503d; Isocr. 10, 63; X., Cyr. 5, 1, 14; PTebt 276, 14; 2 Macc 15:39; En 5:2; Jos., C. Ap. 2, 179; Ar. 4, 2; Just., D. 134, 2) ἰάσεις *cures* **Lk 13:32** (v.l. ἐπιτελῶ; for D s. beg. of this entry; s. ἐπιτελέω).—DELG s.v. τέλος. M-M.

ἀποτίθημι fut. ἀποθήσω; aor. ἀπέθηκα LXX (the act. does not occur in our lit.); 2 aor. mid. ἀπεθέμην, 3 pl. ἀπέθοντο Hs 8, 5, 1; 1 aor. pass. ἀπετέθην (s. τίθημι; Hom. et al.; ins, pap, LXX, TestSol, JosAs; ParJer 5:14; ApcSed 9:1) gener. 'put off'.

❶ ***take off***—ⓐ lit. of clothes (Teles p. 16, 7 ἱμάτιον; Alciphron 3, 6, 2; 2 Macc 8:35; JosAs 13:2 al.; Jos., Ant. 8, 266) τὰ ἱμάτια ἀ. MPol 13:2; *take off and lay down* **Ac 7:58.**

ⓑ fig. *lay aside, rid oneself of* τὰ ἔργα τ. σκότους **Ro 13:12.** ἀλαζονείαν 1 Cl 13:1. αὐθάδειαν 57:2. τὰς μαλακίας Hv 3, 12, 3. τὴν νέκρωσιν τ. ζωῆς s 9, 16, 2f. τὰ πάντα, ὀργὴν κτλ. **Col 3:8** (Plut., Cor. 223 [19, 4] ὀργήν). τὸ τῆς λύπης AcPl Ha 8, 8//BMM recto 7. τὸ νέφος 2 Cl 1:6. τὸν παλαιὸν ἄνθρωπον

Eph 4:22 (w. acc. of pers. in Callim., Epigr. 21, 6 [Pf.]; Maximus Tyr. 1 4e in the theater ἀποθέμενος τὸν θεατὴν ἀγωνιστὴς γενέσθαι=stop being a spectator and become a contestant). τὸ ψεῦδος vs. **25.** πᾶσαν ῥυπαρίαν **Js 1:21.** πᾶσαν κακίαν **1 Pt 2:1.** ὄγκον πάντα καὶ τὴν ἁμαρτίαν **Hb 12:1** (of vices since Demosth. 8, 46; Lucian, Dial. Mort. 10, 8f; EpArist 122 et al. [Nägeli 20]).—νηστίαν . . . ἀποθέ[ντος] *(Paul) having ended a fast* AcPl Ha 6, 37.—αἵρεσιν *give up a way of thinking* Hs 9, 23, 5; *lose* cracks s 8, 5, 1.

❷ **to put aside for a special purpose,** ***lay aside*** (as alms) Hs 5, 3, 7 (some mss. omit; cp. Just., A I, 67, 6).

❸ **to remove from a locality and place elsewhere,** ***put away, lay down*** (Hom. et al.; PFlor 125, 2; PRyl 125, 14; Jos., Ant. 11, 11) a martyr's bones MPol 18:1 (Appian, Syr. 63 §336 ἀπέθετο of the 'laying away' or 'depositing' of the remains [τὰ λείψαντα] of a cremated body; ApcSed 9:1 transfer of [Sedrach's] soul to Paradise); *put* (rods) *away* 1 Cl 43:2; *put back* (opp. αἴρω) stones Hs 9, 5, 4; 9, 9, 4 (cp. 1 Macc 4:46).—ἀ. τινὰ ἐν φυλακῇ *put someone in prison* **Mt 14:3** (cp. Polyb. 24, 8, 8; Diod. S. 4, 49, 3; PEleph 12, 2 [223/222 BC] ἀποθέσθαι αὐτοὺς εἰς τ. φυλακήν; PTebt 769, 51 al. [III BC]. Lev 24:12; Num 15:34; 2 Ch 18:26).—DELG s.v. τίθημι. M-M.

ἀποτίκτω 1 aor. pass. ptc. ἀποτεχθέντες 4 Macc 13:21 (s. τίκτω; Pla., Plut.; Artem. 1, 16; 4 Macc 13:21; 14:16; Philo, Virt. 139, Aet. M. 60; Ath. 22, 4; 27, 1) ***bring to birth*** τὰ ἀποτικτόμενα *children* born after a full-term pregnancy (in contrast to premature births or abortions) ApcPt fgm. 3 p. 12, 31.—DELG s.v. τίκτω.

ἀποτινάσσω 1 aor. ἀπετίναξα; fut. mid. ἀποτινάξομαι Judg 16:20 cod. A; pf. 3 sg. ἀποτετίνακται 1 Kgm 10:2 (τινάσσω 'shake, brandish'; Eur., Bacch. 253; Galen: CMG V 4, 2 p. 458, 8=VI 821 K.; LXX) ***shake off*** τὶ, of a snake which has bitten a hand τὸ θηρίον εἰς τὸ πῦρ **Ac 28:5.** τὸν κονιορτὸν (Amulet of Parisinus 2316 leaf 318 verso ff: Rtzst., Poim. 297f κονιορτὸν ἀποτινάξαι) ἀπὸ τ. ποδῶν ἀ. *shake the dust fr. one's feet* **Lk 9:5** (s. on ἐκτινάσσω 1).—Of St. Paul's beheading καὶ ἀπετ[ίναξεν . . . ὡς δὲ ὁ σπεκουλάτωρ ἀπ]ε̣τ̣ί̣ν̣α̣|ξεν αὐτοῦ τὴν κ̣[εφαλήν] AcPl Ha 10, 26f *[the executioner] beheaded him [. . . But after the executioner] had beheaded him.* —DELG s.v. τινάσσω.

ἀποτίνω fut. ἀποτίσω; 1 aor. 3 sg. opt. ἀποτείσαι LXX, 2 sg. subj. ἀποτείσῃς Pr 22:27, 3 sg. impv. ἀποτεισάτω Lev 24:18 (s. τίνω; Hom. et al.; ins [SIG index]; pap [POxy 275, 27 et al.; OGradenwitz, Einführg. in die Papyruskunde 1900, 85]; LXX; Jos., Ant. 4, 282, Vi. 298; SibOr 5, 191) legal t.t. **to make compensation,** ***pay damages*** abs. ἐγὼ ἀποτίσω (better ἀποτείσω, B-D-F §23) *I will pay the damages* (PTebt 821, 11 [III BC]; PPetr III, 26, 8 [III BC]; BGU 759, 23 [II AD] et al.) **Phlm 19.**—B. 796f. DELG s.v. τίνω. M-M.

ἀποτολμάω (s. τολμάω; Thu. et al.; Polyb.; Diod. S.; Plut.; SIG 1169, 94; BGU 1574, 22; PLond IV, 1343, 42; Philo, Post. Cai. 42; Jos., C. Ap. 2, 180) ***be bold*** abs. Ἠσαΐας ἀποτολμᾷ καὶ λέγει *Isaiah is so bold as to say* **Ro 10:20** (cp. Demosth. 19, 199 τολμήσει . . . καὶ ἐρεῖ).—DELG s.v. τόλμη. TW.

ἀποτομία, ας, ἡ (ἀποτέμνω 'cut off'; Diod. S. 12, 16, 3; Dionys. Hal. 8, 61; Plut., Mor. 13d τὴν ἀ. τῇ πραότητι μιγνύναι; Ps.-Demetrius, Eloc. 292 Roberts; POxy 237 VII, 40; PSI 1052, 9; BGU 1024 V, 13; Na 3:1 Sym.; Philo, Spec. Leg. 2, 94, In Flacc. 95) ***severity*** (opp. χρηστότης) ἀ. θεοῦ **Ro 11:22** (twice).—DELG s.v. τέμνω. M-M. TW.

ἀπότομος, ον (s. ἀποτομία; Soph., Hdt. et al.; LXX; TestAbr A) ***relentless*** ἐν κρίσει *in judgment* Pol 6:1 (cp. in this fig. mng. [lit. 'steep'] Wsd 6:5 al.; Diod. S. 1, 76, 1; 2, 57, 5; Περὶ ὕψους 27, 1 ἀπειλή; Jos., Ant. 19, 329 τιμωρία).—DELG s.v. τέμνω. TW.

ἀποτόμως adv. fr. ἀπότομος (Isocr. et al.; Polyb. 18, 11, 2; Plut., Mor. 131c; Cic., Att. 10, 11, 5; Wsd 5:22) ***severely, rigorously*** ἔλεγχε αὐτοὺς ἀ. *correct them rigorously* **Tit 1:13.** ἵνα μὴ ἀ. χρήσωμαι = ἀποτομίᾳ χρ. *that I may not have to deal sharply* **2 Cor 13:10.**—DELG s.v. τέμνω. M-M.

ἀποτρέπω 1 aor. subj. 3 pl. ἀποτρέψωσι (Just.); pres. mid. impv. 2 sg. ἀποτρέπου; 2 aor. pass. ptc. ἀποτραπέντες 3 Macc 1:23 (s. τρέπω; Hom. et al.; Jos., Bell. 3, 500, Ant. 18, 283; Just., A I, 14, 1) mid. **purposely to avoid associating w. someone,** ***turn away from, avoid*** w. acc. (so trag., Polyb., Plut. [Nägeli 25]; 4 Macc 1:33 A) **2 Ti 3:5;** AcPlCor 2:21, 39.—DELG s.v. τρέπω. M-M.

ἀποτρέχω aor. 3 sg. ἀπέδραμεν LXX (Hdt. et al.; ins, pap, LXX; En 107:2; Test12Patr; Just., D. 39, 8) ***hurry away*** (lit. *run away*) Hv 3, 3, 1.—DELG s.v. τρέχω.

ἀποτυγχάνω 2 aor. 3 pl. ἀπέτυχον Job 31:16, 3 sg. subj. ἀποτύχῃ (s. τυγχάνω; Hippocr., X., Pla. et al.; pap; Job 31:16; Test12Patr; EpArist 191; 192; Just., D. 2, 5) **to have no success,** ***fail*** w. gen. (Diod. S. 1, 75, 3 τῆς προαιρέσεως=in the intention; Appian, Hann. 43, §183 τ. πείρας=in the attempt; BGU 1816, 12 [I BC] τ. ἐπιβολῆς; PSI 96, 5 [V AD] τ. παρακλήσεως; Jos., Ant. 19, 289) ἡ διψυχία πάντων ἀ. τῶν ἔργων αὐτῆς *double-mindedness fails in all its works* Hm 9:10; cp. 10, 2, 2. W. inf. foll. τοῦ πεῖσαι αὐτόν *they failed to persuade him* MPol 8:3.—DELG s.v. τυγχάνω.

ἀποτυφλόω (s. τυφλόω; Aristot.; Diod. S. 3, 37, 9; Plut., Arat. 1031 [10, 4], Mor. 1107c; LXX lit. and fig.) ***to blind*** aor. pass. inf. ἀποτυφλωθῆναι (Tob 2:10 Sin.) fig. (Epict. 1, 16, 19) ἀ. ἀπὸ τ. διανοίας τ. ἀγαθῆς *be blinded and cease to have good intentions* Hm 5, 2, 7.—DELG s.v. τύφομαι B (τυφλός).

ἀπουσία, ας, ἡ (s. ἄπειμι; Aeschyl., Thu., Plut. [Nägeli 16]; Philo, Leg. All. 3, 113; Jos., Ant. 2, 56; PCairZen 631, 12 [III BC]; PAmh 135, 5 [II AD]; BGU 195, 39; 242, 8; IG II/2, 839, 84 [III BC]) ***absence*** ἐν τῇ ἀ. μου *while I am absent* **Phil 2:12** (opp. παρουσία as Aristoxenus, fgm. 37; Ps.-Demetr., Form. Ep. p. 12, 15f).—DELG s.v. εἰμί. M-M.

ἀποφαίνομαι fut. ἀποφανοῦμαι (Just., Tat.); 1 aor. ἀπεφηνάμην 2 Macc 6:23; 15:4, act. ἀπέφηνα LXX (Pind., Hdt.+) ***show, declare, pronounce*** (some creature) θεόν Dg 8:3.—DELG s.v. φαίνω.

ἀποφέρω fut. ἀποίσω LXX; aor. ἀπήνεγκα, inf. ἀπενεγκεῖν. Mid.: fut. ἀποίσομαι LXX; aor. ἀπηνεγκάμην LXX. Pass.: fut. 3 pl. ἀπενεχθήσονται; 1 aor. ἀπηνέχθην (Hom.+).

❶ **to carry off from a point,** ***carry/take away*** someone or someth. to a place **Lk 16:22;** Hv 3, 10, 1ab; s 9, 4, 7; 9, 8, 3; 9, 9, 5f. Of being transported in or by the spirit **Rv 17:3;** cp. **21:10;** Hv 1, 1, 3; 2, 1, 1; GHb 20, 61 by the hair.

❷ **to bring from one point to another,** ***take, bring*** ἀ. τὴν χάριν ὑμῶν εἰς Ἰερουσαλήμ *take your gift to Jer.* **1 Cor 16:3.** τὶ ἐπί τινα **Ac 19:12;** or τινί **Lk 19:24** D. ἐκεῖ AcPt Ox 849, 9.

❸ **to conduct w. constraint away fr. a point,** ***lead off, lead away*** (POxy 37 I, 18; BGU 22, 29ff; Da 11:8) of a prisoner **Mk 15:1; J 21:18 v.l.**

❹ **to deprive someone of someth.,** ***take away*** by force τὴν ζωήν Hs 9, 21, 4.

❺ **to gain someth. for oneself,** ***carry off, win*** mid. (Diod. S. 4, 76, 5 δόξαν; Jos., Ant. 4, 234; Ath. 36, 2) athletic imagery βραβεῖον *a prize* MPol 17:1 (Thu. et al. in sim. connections; Diod. S. 17, 6, 1 τὸ πρωτεῖον ἀπηνέγκατο; Lev 20:19; EpArist 39; Jos., Vi. 360).—DELG s.v. φέρω. M-M.

ἀποφεύγω 3 sg. fut. ἀποφεύξεται Sir. 22:22; 2 aor. ἀπέφυγον (since Theognis 1159; Pind., Hdt.; also PRyl 77, 39 [192 AD]; JosAs 13:1 cod. A).

❶ ***escape, escape from*** w. acc. of pers. or thing fr. which one escapes (Alex. Aphr. Fat. 8 II 2 p. 173, 9) **2 Pt 2:18, 20.** W. gen. of thing (cp. Aesop 80d, 8 Ch. v.l. τούτων ἐκφεύγειν) τῆς ἐν τ. κόσμῳ ἐν ἐπιθυμίᾳ φθορᾶς *from the destruction in the world caused by desire* **1:4.**

❷ ***avoid, shun*** τινά *someone* Hm 11:13 (opp. ἐγγίζειν). ἀπό τινος from someth. ἀπὸ τῆς διδασκαλίας αὐτῶν ἀποφεύγετε *flee from their teaching* AcPlCor 2:21.—DELG s.v. φεύγω I. M-M.

ἀποφθέγγομαι (s. φθόγγος; fut. 3 pl. ἀποφθέγξονται Ps 58:8; 1 aor. 3 sg. ἀπεφθέγξατο TestJob 48:3) **to express oneself orally, w. focus on sound rather than content,** ***speak out, declare*** boldly or loudly (of the speech of a wise man Diog. L. 1, 63; 73; 79; but also of an oracle-giver, diviner, prophet, exorcist, and other inspired persons Diod. S. 16, 27, 1; Plut., Mor. 405e; Vett. Val. 73, 24; 112, 15; 113, 1; Philostrat., Vi. Apollon. 1, 19 p. 20, 7; Diogenes 21, 8 p. 114 Malherbe; Mi 5:11; Zech 10:2; Ezk 13:9, 19; TestJob; Philo, Mos. 2, 33) τὶ: σωφροσύνης ῥήματα **Ac 26:25;** ἀ. τινι *declare to someone w. urgency* **2:14,** also abs. vs. **4.**—DELG s.v. φθέγγομαι. M-M. TW.

ἀπόφθεγμα, τό (X. et al., gener. 'a sententious saying'; cp. the title of some of Plutarch's works: Mor. 172b; 208a) ***saying, utterance*** τὰ ἀποφθέγματα τοῦ σωτῆρος *the Savior's utterances* GMary Ox 3525, 14. Prob. here in sense of a revelatory/oracular statement (as Cass. Dio 62, 13, 3 τὸ ἀ. τῆς Πυθιάδος).

ἀποφορτίζομαι nautical t.t. (fig. Jos., Bell. 1, 172; 266), mostly of 'jettisoning' cargo in a storm (Philo Mech. 2, 143; Athen. 2, 5, 37cf; Philo, Praem. 33; Pollux 1, 99), but also of regular unloading (Dionys. Hal. 3, 44 αἱ μείζους νῆες ἀπογεμίζονται καὶ ἀποφορτίζονται σκάφαις) ***unload*** τ. γόμον *the cargo* **Ac 21:3** (Mod. Gk. ἀποφορτώνω).—DELG s.v. φόρτος.

ἀπόχρησις, εως, ἡ (s. χράομαι) ***consuming, using up*** (so Dionys. Hal. 1, 58; Plut., Mor. 267f.—ἀποχράομαι Polyb. 1, 45, 2; PHib 52, 7 [c. 245 BC]) ἐστὶν εἰς φθορὰν τῇ ἀποχρήσει *are meant for destruction by being consumed* (εἰς κόπρον γὰρ ἅπαντα μεταβάλλεται Theodoret III p. 491 N.) **Col 2:22.**—DELG s.v. χρή deriv. χράομαι 1274. M-M, but without a ref. to the use of the noun: PStras 35, 6 (IV–V AD) in sense of 'need, necessity'.

ἀποχωρέω 1 aor. ἀπεχώρησα; pf. ptc. ἀποκεχωρηκώς 2 Macc. 4:33 (s. χωρέω; Eur., Thu. et al.; pap, LXX; En 14:23 [of angels]; TestSol 13:3 P; Jos., Bell. 1, 24, Ant. 1, 261; Ath. R. 57, 10) **to move away from a point,** ***go away*** ἀπό τινος Hv 3, 6, 3. Also more strongly in the sense ***leave, desert*** (Sb. 7835, 14 [I BC] ἀ. ἐκ . . . εἰς=desert from . . . to; 3 Macc 2:33) **Ac 13:13** or *depart* (Jer 26:5; 2 Macc 4:33) ἀποχωρεῖτε ἀπ' ἐμοῦ *depart from me!* **Mt 7:23** (Vi. Aesopi I, 6 p. 239, 19 Eberh. ἀποχώρει=away w. you!), also of defeated opponents (Jos., Ant. 15, 149) **Lk 20:20 v.l.** Of spirits *withdraw fr. someone* **Lk 9:39.** Hm 5, 2, 6; of the devil m 12, 5, 4; of personified virtues [ἀποχ]ωρήσουσιν *they will leave* Hs 10, 3, 2 (Ox 404, 5).—ὁ δὲ λίθος . . . ἀπεχώρησε παρὰ μέρος *the stone went off to the side* GPt 9:37=ASyn. 352, 82 (ἀ. emendation [not noted as such in ASyn.] by Gebhardt and Blass for επεχωρεσε [ἐπιχώρησε] cod. C; s. ἐπιχωρέω, ὑποχωρέω).—DELG χώρα. M-M.

ἀποχωρίζω (s. χωρίζω; Pla. et al.; pap; Ezk 43:21 [pf. pass. ptc. ἀποκεχωρισμένος]; TestSol; AcThom 99 [Aa II/2, 211, 20]) *separate* **Mt 19:6** D.—Pass. *be separated* ἀπό τινος (PLond V, 1731, 11 [585 AD]; PAnt 93, 9f ἀ. ἀλλήλων [IV AD]) **Ac 15:39.** ὁ οὐρανὸς ἀπεχωρίσθη *the sky was split* **Rv 6:14** (cp. Boll 17, 9, 1).—DELG s.v. χώρα.

ἀποψύχω lit. 'breathe out, stop breathing', hence either ***faint*** (Od. 24, 348) or ***breathe one's last, die*** (Soph., Thu., et al.; 4 Macc 15:18; Philo, Aet. M. 128; Jos., Ant. 19, 114) ἀπὸ φόβου *of* or *from fear* **Lk 21:26.**—DELG s.v. ψυχρός C1 ψύχω.

Ἀππίου φόρον=Lat. Appii Forum, ***the Forum of Appius,*** a market town on the Appian Way, 43 Rom. miles (c. 62 km.) fr. Rome (CIL X 6825; acc. to Horace, Sat. 1, 5, 1ff, full of sailors and rascals; cp. Cicero, Ad Att. 2, 10). Paul was met there on his journey to Rome by some fellow Christians **Ac 28:15.**

ἀπρεπής, ές (s. πρέπει) lit. 'not fitting' **pert. to not meeting a standard and therefore subject to rejection,** ***unsuitable*** (fig. Thu.; Pla., Laws 788b; Epicrates Com. 11, 33 Edmonds; Lucian, Dial. Deor. 13, 1; Aelian, VH 14, 19; PTebt 765, 4; 802, 15; PAmh 142, 8; 4 Macc 6:17; Philo, Cher. 92; Jos., Ant. 18, 314, Vi. 146) lit. (Artem. 2, 3 p. 88, 6 ἀ. ἐσθῆτες) λίθοι ἀ. ἐν τ. οἰκοδομῇ *stones that are not suitable for the building* Hs 9, 4, 6f.—DELG s.v. πρέπω.

ἀπροσδεής, ές (H. Gk.; προσδεής 'lacking' someth.) ***needing nothing, self-sufficient*** of God (Philod., περὶ θεῶν [ed. H Diels, ABA 1916f] 3, 13; Plut., Aristid. et Cat. 354 [4, 2]; 2 Macc 14:35; 3 Macc 2:9; EpArist 211; Philo, Deus Imm. 56; Jos., Ant. 8, 111) 1 Cl 52:1 (Albinus 10; Ath.: 13:1; R. 61, 23; s. Norden, Agn. Th. 13f).—DELG s.v. δέω.

ἀπρόσδεκτος, ον (προσδεκτέος 'one must admit/accept'; Polyb. 36, 12, 4 et al.; ins; BGU 1113, 21 [I BC]; POxy 268, 18 in var. mngs.) ***unacceptable,*** fr. God's perspective (IG III, 73, 14; 75, 8: θυσία; Porphyr., Ad Marc 24 εὐχή) μήπως . . . ἀ. ἔσται τὸ δῶρον ἡμῶν *lest perchance . . . our gift prove unacceptable* GJs 7:1.—DELG s.v. δέχομαι.

ἀπροσδόκητος, ον (προσδεκτέος 'one must admit/expect'; Aeschyl., Hdt. et al.; SIG 742, 9; 814, 9; PFay 19, 3; Wsd 17:14; 3 Macc 3:8 al.; Philo, De Prov. in Eus., PE 8, 14, 60; Jos., Ant. 12, 308) ***unexpected*** ἀ. εὐεργεσίαι Dg 9:5.—DELG s.v. δέχομαι.

ἀπρόσιτος, ον (προσιτός 'approachable'; since Ctesias 688 fgm. 14 p. 467, 23 Jac.=Pers. 41; Polyb. 3, 49, 7; Diod. S. 1, 32, 1; Dio Chrys. 13 [7], 51; Lucian; Philo, Mos. 2, 70; Jos., Bell. 7, 280, Ant. 3, 76; PSI 1103, 15) ***unapproachable*** of God φῶς οἰκεῖν ἀπρόσιτον *dwell in unapproachable light* **1 Ti 6:16** (Ath. 16, 2; φέγγος . . . ἀ Tat. 20:2) cp. DDD 688.—DELG s.v. εἶμι. TW.

ἀπρόσκοπος, ον (s. προσκόπτω) gener. 'without offense'

❶ **pert. to being without fault because of not giving offense,** ***undamaged, blameless*** (PGiss 17, 7; 22, 9; PBad 39 III, 14; Sb 6297, 3 [all II AD]; EpArist 210) ἀ. συνείδησις *a clear conscience* **Ac 24:16;** w. εἰλικρινής: ἀ. εἰς ἡμέραν Χριστοῦ *blameless for the day of Christ* **Phil 1:10.**

❷ **pert. to not causing offense,** ***giving no offense*** (Sext. Emp., Math. 1, 195; Sir 32:21) ἀ. τινι γίνεσθαι **1 Cor 10:32.** See Nägeli 43.—DELG s.v. κόπτω. M-M. TW.

ἀπροσκόπως adv. fr. ἀπρόσκοπος (PGiss 79 IV, 8 ἀπροσκόπως ἐξέλθωμεν ἀπ᾽ αὐτῶν) ***without stumbling*** (w. ὁμαλῶς) περιπατεῖν Hm 6, 1, 4; *without disturbance* λειτουργίαν ἐπιτελεῖν 1 Cl 20:10; *blamelessly* διέπειν τ. ἡγεμονίαν 61:1.

ἀπροσωπολήμπτως (on the form -λημπ- s. W-S. §5, 30; Reinhold §7) adv. fr. ἀπροσωπόλημπτος (ἀπροσωπόλημπτος TestJob 4:8; Cos. and Dam. 1, 17; Psellus p. 163, 8 ἀ. δικαστής) ***impartially,*** i.e. without ref. to rank or status κρίνειν **1 Pt 1:17;** B 4:12; ἀ. πάντα ποιεῖν 1 Cl 1:3. Cp. προσωπολημπτέω, -λήμπτης, -λημψία, πρόσωπον λαμβάνειν.—DELG s.v. λαμβάνω. M-M. TW.

ἄπταιστος, ον (s. πταίω; X., Equ. 1, 6+ [of a horse]; fig., Epict. [Stob., Flor. 9, 44] no. 52 p. 475 Sch.; M. Ant. 5, 9, 5; Vett. Val. ind.; 3 Macc 6:39; EpArist 187; Philo, Agr. 177, Ebr. 199; SibOr 3, 289) ***without stumbling*** φυλάξαι ὑμᾶς ἀ. *keep you from stumbling* **Jd 24.**—M-M. TW.

ἅπτω 1 aor. ἧψα, ptc. ἅψας. Mid.: fut. ἅψομαι LXX; 1 aor. ἡψάμην; pf. 3 sg. ἧπται; ptc. ἡμμένος LXX. Pass.: fut. 3 sg. ἀφθήσεται Jer 31:9 B S (Hom.+).

❶ **to cause illumination or burning to take place,** ***light, kindle*** (Aeschyl., Hdt.; PGM 7, 543; POxy 1297, 4; 7; 13; LXX, Joseph.) λύχνον ἅ. (Herodas 8, 6; PAthen 60, 6; Epict. 1, 20, 19; Diog. L. 4, 66; 6, 41; TestSol 6:10 λύχνους; Philo, Gig. 33 [mid.]; Jos., Ant. 3, 199) **Lk 8:16; 11:33; 15:8.** ἅ. πῦρ *kindle a fire* (Eur., Hel. 503; Phalaris, Ep. 122, 2; Jdth 13:13; TestSol 7:5; Jos., Ant. 4, 55) **Lk 22:55 v.l.; Ac 28:2.** Pass. **Mk 4:21 v.l.** (cp. PGM 13, 683 λύχνους ἡμμένους).

❷ **to make close contact,** mid. w. gen. (Hom. et al.; En, PsSol, GrBar; Jos., Ant. 6, 308 al; Just., Ath.; Mel., P. 52, 383).

ⓐ gener. ***touch, take hold of, hold*** τινός *someone* or *someth.* **Lk 7:39;** IRo 5:2. Dg 12:8. MPol 13:2. Hs 1:11; the sky by throwing a stone m 11:18.—*Touch* someone's chest, spontaneously, of one who is speaking Hv 1, 4, 2; cp. 3, 1, 6. Cp. GHb 356, 39=ISm 3:2. ἅψαι τοῦ παιδίου *take hold of the child* GJs 20:3. Fig., *take hold of* τ. βασιλείας *the Kingdom* B 7:11.—JBauer, Agraphon 90 Resch: ZNW 62, '71, 301–3.

ⓑ ***cling to*** μή μου ἅπτου *stop clinging to me!* (s. BHaensler, BZ 11, 1913, 172–77; KKastner, ibid. 13, 1915, 344–53; KRösch, ibid. 14, 1917, 333–37; BViolet, ZNW 24, 1925, 78–80; FPerles, ibid. 25, 1926, 287; WCotter, ET 43, '32, 45f; TNicklin, ibid. 51, '39/40, 478; JMaiworm, ThGl '38, 540–46) **J 20:17** (Arrian, Anab. 6, 13, 3: Alexander is severely wounded in the chest by an arrow and his soldiers cannot believe that he is still alive. When he appears among them, recovered from his wound, they take hold [ἁπτόμενοι] of his hands, knees, and clothing in astonishment and delight).

ⓒ freq. of touching as a means of conveying a blessing (divine working by a touch of the hand: Anton. Lib. 4, 7 Ἀπόλλων ἁψάμενος αὐτοῦ τῇ χειρὶ πέτρον ἐποίησεν; Ps.-Apollod. 2, 1, 3, 1 Zeus transforms by touching [ἅπτεσθαι]) **Mk 10:13; Lk 18:15** (here perh. *hold*), esp. to bring about a healing (SIG 1169, 62). Gener. of touching persons who are ill **Mt 8:3; 17:7; Mk 1:41; 8:22; Lk 5:13.** ἅψαι αὐτῆς ἐκ τ. χειρῶν σου **Mk 5:23** D. Esp. of touching parts of the body (SIG 1170, 23 ἥψατό μου τῆς δεξιᾶς χιρός) τ. γλώσσης (cp. Philo, De Prov. in Eus., PE 8, 14, 18) **Mk 7:33.** τ. ὀφθαλμῶν **Mt 9:29;** cp. **20:34; 8:15; Lk 22:51.** Likew. τῆς σοροῦ *touch the coffin,* if the purpose was to raise the dead man, not simply to halt the bearers (cp. Aphrodite touching a chariot Pind., P. 9, 11) **Lk 7:14.** Of those who are ill, touching the healer **Mk 3:10; 6:56; Lk 6:19; 8:45ff.** Also of touching the clothes of the healer (cp. Athen. 5, 212f ἑκάστου σπεύδοντος κἂν προσάψασθαι τῆς ἐσθῆτος) ἅ. τ. ἱματίου *touch his cloak* **Mt 9:21; Mk 5:27; 6:56.** τ. ἱματίων **5:28, 30f.** τ. κρασπέδου *the hem* or *tassel* **Mt 9:20; 14:36; Lk 8:44.**

❸ **to partake of someth., w. cultic implications,** ***have contact with, touch.*** Of contact w. unclean things **2 Cor 6:17** (Num 16:26; Is 52:11). The abs. μὴ ἅψῃ *you must not touch* or *handle* **Col 2:21** can be interpreted in this sense. On the other hand, ἅπτεσθαι can mean *eat,* like our 'touch food' (Od. 4, 60; Plut., Anton. 923 [17]; Chariton 6, 2, 8 οὐχ ἥπτετο τροφῆς; Arrian, Anab. 4, 9, 5 σίτου ἅπτεσθαι; Aelian, VH 12, 37 ἐπ᾽ ἀπορίᾳ τροφῶν ἥψατο τῶν καμήλων=he seized [and ate] the camels; Diog. L. 6, 73 κρεῶν; Philostrat., Vi. Apoll. 3, 27 p. 105, 9; Philo, Exs. 134; Jos., Ant. 4, 234; 8, 362; 13, 276; En 25:4f [tree of life, as in GrBar 4:8]). We would, then, have in this passage the anticlimax *eat, taste, touch.* Finally, θιγγάνω, like ἅπτ. and γεύομαι (q.v. 1) can mean *eat* (cp. Iambl., Vi. Pyth. 31, 191 κυάμων μὴ θιγγάνειν; 13, 61 γεύεσθαι=Porphyr., Vi. Pyth. 24 θιγγάνειν; POxy 1185, 10f [c. 200 AD], where three difft. expr. for 'eat' are grouped together: τὸν παῖδα δεῖ ἄρτον ἐσθίειν, ἅλας ἐπιτρώγειν, ὀψαρίου μὴ θιγγάνειν [eat, eat [with], not eat at all]). The combination ἐσθ., τρωγ., θιγγ. might corresp. to **Col 2:21** ἅπτ., γεύ., θιγγ., taken to mean *eat, enjoy, consume* (ἅ. and γεύ. together, both='eat' in Teles p. 34, 5). The verbs, perh. used in association w. var. foods (s. POxy 1185) by the false spirits, are effectively combined by Paul, in order to picture the feeling of dread which he castigates.

❹ **to touch intimately,** ***have sexual contact,*** of intercourse w. a woman (Pla., Leg. 8, 840a; Aristot., Pol. 7, 14, 12 [1335b]; Plut., Alex. 676 [21, 9]; M. Ant. 1, 17, 13; Jos., Ant. 1, 163; Gen 20:6; Pr 6:29) γυναικὸς μὴ ἅ. **1 Cor 7:1** (ἅπτεσθαι w. gen. of 'touching' a woman in general: Vi. Aesopi G103).

❺ **to make contact with a view to causing harm,** ***touch*** for the purpose of harming, *injure* (Diod. S. 1, 84, 1; Arrian, Alex. Anab. 4, 4, 2; Ps 104:15; 1 Ch 16:22; Zech 2:12; Demetr.: 722 fgm. 1, 7 Jac.) ὁ πονηρὸς οὐχ ἅπτεται αὐτοῦ *the evil one cannot harm him* (or *cannot even touch him;* cp. 1 Esdr 4:28; PsSol 13:6; TestAbr A 15 p. 96, 11 [Stone p. 40]) **1J 5:18.**—Fig. οὐχ ἅψηταί σου κακόν *no evil shall touch you* 1 Cl 56:8 (Job 5:19; cp. PsSol 13:6; 15:4).—OHeick, Hapto in the NT: Luth. Church Quart. 12, '39, 90–95.—B. 76; 1061. DELG. M-M s.v. ἅπτομαι. TW. Sv.

Ἀπφία, ας, ἡ (a name freq. found in western Asia Minor [KBuresch, Aus Lydien 1898, 44; Lghtf., Col. and Phlm. 304f; Thieme 9; 39], also in Colossae, CIG III p. 1168 no. 4380k, 3, 1) ***Apphia,*** the name of a Christian, prob. wife of Philemon, at Colossae, **Phlm 2; ins v.l.; subscr. v.l.**—LGPN I. M-M.

ἀπωθέω (ὠθέω 'push') fut. ἀπ(ε)ώσομαι; 1 aor. ἀπ(ε)ωσάμην; pf. ἀπῶσμαι; aor. pass. ἀπεώθην all LXX (Hom. et al.; pap, e.g. PFay 124, 19; LXX; TestAsh 1:8; TestJos 2:5; Philo, Aet. M. 74; Joseph.) in our lit. only mid. 'push' someth. 'away' or 'aside.'

❶ ***push aside*** lit., w. acc. (4 Km 4:27; Jos., Ant. 17, 91) ἀπώσατο αὐτόν **Ac 7:27** (like POxy 1206, 10).

❷ ***reject, repudiate,*** fig. ext. of 1 (sc. Moses) **Ac 7:39.** τὶ *something* (Appian, Syr. 5 §21; Quint. Smyrn. 9, 96) the word of God (Jer 23:17) **13:46;** a good conscience **1 Ti 1:19** (cp. Jos., Ant. 4, 123; perh. maritime imagery Straub 27). Esp. of God: *repudiate* the people Israel **Ro 11:1f** (Ps 93:14; cp. 94:4 v.l.

and oft. in LXX); of humans gener. Dg 9:2. τινὰ ἀπό τινος (Ps 118:10) *force someone out of someth.* B 4:13.—DELG s.v. ὠθέω. M-M.

ἀπώλεια, ας, ἡ (s. ἀπόλλυμι; Demades [IV BC]: Or. Att. II 52 p. 313 in the sense 'loss'; later writers; ins, pap, oft. LXX, pseudepigr., Philo, Jos., Ar., Just.; Mel., P.).

❶ **the destruction that one causes, *destruction, waste*** trans. (Aristot., EN 4, 1, 1120a 2; Polyb. 6, 11a, 10 opp. τήρησις; PTebt 276, 34) εἰς τί ἡ ἀ. αὕτη τ. μύρου; *why this waste of ointment?* **Mk 14:4;** cp. **Mt 26:8.**

❷ **the destruction that one experiences, *annihilation*** both complete and in process, ***ruin*** intr. (so usu. LXX; EpArist 167; Philo, Aet. M. 20; 74; Jos., Ant. 15, 62, Vi. 272; TestDan 4:5; Ar. 13, 8; Just., D. 56, 5; Mel.; but also in Aristot., Prob. 29, 14, 952b 26; Polyb., Plut., Epict. et al. [Nägeli 35]; Diod. S. 15, 48, 1 with φθορά; Herm. Wr. 12, 16; PGM 4, 1247f παραδίδωμι σε εἰς τὸ μέλαν χάος ἐν τ. ἀπωλείαις) **Ac 25:16 v.l.;** AcPl Ha 4, 16. (w. ὄλεθρον) βυθίζειν εἰς ὄ. καὶ ἀ. *plunge into utter destruction* **1 Ti 6:9;** πρὸς τ. ἰδίαν αὐτῶν ἀ. *to their own ruin* **2 Pt 3:16;** (w. πλάνη) 2 Cl 1:7 (Ar. 13:8). Esp. of eternal destruction as punishment for the wicked: **Mt 7:13;** εἰς ἀ. ὑπάγειν *go to destr.* **Rv 17:8, 11.** (Opp. περιποίησις ψυχῆς) **Hb 10:39.** (Opp. σωτηρία) **Phil 1:28.** ἡμέρα κρίσεως καὶ ἀπωλείας (Job 21:30) τ. ἀσεβῶν ἀνθρώπων *day of judgment and* (consequent) *destruction of wicked men* **2 Pt 3:7.** Hence the end of the wicked is described as ἀ.: τὸ ἀργύριόν σου σὺν σοὶ εἴη εἰς ἀπώλειαν *to hell with you and your money* (Phillips) **Ac 8:20** (for the phrasing cp. Da 2:5 and 3:96 Theod.); ὧν τὸ τέλος ἀ. **Phil 3:19.** σκεύη ὀργῆς, κατηρτισμένα εἰς ἀ. *objects of (God's) anger, ready for destruction* **Ro 9:22** (Is 54:16). It will come quickly **2 Pt 2:1;** is not sleeping vs. **3** (on the topic cp. Od. 2, 281–84). Appears as a consequence of death (cp. Job 28, 22): ὁ θάνατος ἀ. ἔχει αἰώνιον Hs 6, 2, 4; God laughs at it 1 Cl 57:4 (Pr 1:26). Those destined to destruction are υἱοὶ τῆς ἀ. **J 17:12;** ApcPt 1:2. The Lawless One is also υἱὸς τῆς ἀ. **2 Th 2:3.** αἱρέσεις ἀπωλείας *heresies that lead to destr.* **2 Pt 2:1;** δόγματα τῆς ἀ. ApcPt 1:1.—DELG s.v. ὄλλυμι. M-M. TW.

ἀπώλεσε, ἀπώλετο, ἀπωλόμην s. ἀπόλλυμι.

ἀπών s. ἄπειμι.

ἀπωσάμην s. ἀπωθέω.

Ἅρ s. Ἁρμαγεδ(δ)ών.

ἀρά, ᾶς, ἡ (Hom. et al.; OGI 383, 236; IMagnMai 105, 53; LXX; PsSol 4:14; Philo; Jos., Ant. 17, 3 and 88, Vi. 101; 'prayer, vow', but mostly pl., as in our lit., in the sense of 'malediction') ***curse*** (w. πικρία) τὸ στόμα ἀρᾶς γέμει **Ro 3:14** (Ps 9:28; 13:3).—M-M. TW.

ἄρα (Hom.+ [s. Kühner-G. II p. 317ff]) transitional/inferential (illative) particle; in older Gk. (Hom., Hdt., Pla., X. et al. [Aristot., Mech. 851a 22 is corrupt]) never at the beginning of its clause (Denniston 41). Strengthened to ἄρα γε Gen 26:9; **Mt 7:20; 17:26; Ac 17:27.**—LfgrE s.v.; Rob. 1189f and index; s. also Denniston 32–43.

❶ **marker of an inference made on the basis of what precedes**—ⓐ in declarative statement, and w. colloqu. flavor ***so, then, consequently, you see*** (B-D-F §451, 2) **Ac 11:18.** εὑρίσκω ἀ. τὸν νόμον *so I find the law* **Ro 7:21.** οὐδὲν ἄρα νῦν κατάκριμα *so there is no condemnation now* **8:1.** γινώσκετε ἄρα *you may be sure, then* **Gal 3:7.** After ἐπεί: *for otherwise* (B-D-F §456, 3) **1 Cor 5:10; 7:14.** After εἰ: *if then, if on the other hand* (SIG 834, 12; Gen 18:3; s. B-D-F §454, 2) **15:15** (εἴπερ ἄρα—*really* is also prob. here); Hv 3, 4, 3; 3, 7, 5; s. 6, 4, 1; 8, 3, 3; 9, 5, 7; s. εἰ 6a.

ⓑ freq. in questions which draw an inference fr. what precedes; but oft. simply to enliven the question (Jos., Ant. 6, 200; B-D-F §440, 2) τίς ἄρα *who then* **Mt 18:1; 19:25; 24:45; Mk 4:41; Lk 8:25; 12:42; 22:23.** τί ἀ. *what then* **Mt 19:27; Lk 1:66; Ac 12:18;** Hm 11:2; GJs 13:1; AcPl Ha 5, 20; 7, 2 and 3 (cp. GrBar 4:12). εἰ ἄρα *then* (X., An. 3, 2, 22) **Ac 7:1 v.l.;** οὐκ ἄ. are you *not, then* **Ac 21:38;** μήτι ἄ. **2 Cor 1:17.** After οὖν 1 Cl 35:3; B 15:7. S. also 3 below.

❷ **to express result**—ⓐ ***then, as a result*** w. suggestion of emphasis (Herm. Wr. 11, 13 ed. Nock; B-D-F §451, 2d) **Mt 12:28; Lk 11:20; 1 Cor 15:14; 2 Cor 5:14; Gal 2:21; 3:29; 5:11; Hb 12:8;** 2 Cl 14:4; B 6:19; IEph 8:1. Also **1 Cor 15:18** ἄ. is used to emphasize a further result, and continues the apodosis of vs. 17.

ⓑ at the beg. of a sentence: *so, **as a result, consequently*** **Lk 11:48; Ro 10:17; 2 Cor 7:12; Hb 4:9.** Strengthened to ἄρα γε (Gen 26:9) **Mt 7:20; 17:26;** to ἄρα οὖν (never elided) *so then;* here ἄ. expresses the inference and οὖν the transition **Ro 5:18; 7:3, 25** (s. ἆρα); **8:12; 9:16, 18; 14:12, 19; Gal 6:10; Eph 2:19; 1 Th 5:6; 2 Th 2:15;** 2 Cl 8:6; 14:3; B 9:6; 10:2; ITr 10.

❸ **to express someth. tentative, *perhaps, conceivably.***—KClark, Gingrich Festschr. '72, 70–84 (w. survey fr. LXX to Mod. Gk.): in addition to its inferential mng., ἄρα is employed in the context of the tentative, the uncertain, the unresolved, the contingent, e.g. *possibly* **Ac 12:18;** *conceivably* **Mk 4:41,** or it may be rendered by a phrase: *would you say?* **Mt 24:45** (on these three last pass. s. 1b).—Also in indirect questions εἰ ἄ. *whether (perhaps)* (PPetr II, 13 [19] 9; Num 22:11) **Mk 11:13; Ac 5:8** D; **8:22; 17:27** (εἰ ἄρα γε); s. εἰ 6a.—JGrimm, Die Partikel ἄρα im frühen griech. Epos, Glotta 40, '62, 3–41; Denniston 32–43; JBlomqvist, Gk. Particles in Hell. Prose, diss. Lund, '69.—EDNT. M-M.

ἆρα (Pind.+ [Kühner-G. II p. 527f]; ἆρα POxy 33 IV, 7; μὴ ἆρα 120 recto 14 and verso 9; in Sym. more oft. than in the other transl. of the OT; TestJob; JosAs 14:2; 16:4 cod A; GrBar 4:13; apolog. exc. Mel.) interrog. particle (Aeschyl. et al.) introducing direct questions (B-D-F §440, 2; Rob. 1176); usu. incapable of concordant transl., but in gener. **marker of a tone of suspense or impatience in interrogation, *then*** w. the onus for a correct answer put on the addressee ἆ. εὑρήσει τ. πίστιν; *will he find* (the necessary) *faith?* **Lk 18:8;** ἆ. Χριστὸς ἁμαρτίας διάκονος; *is Christ, then, a servant of sin?* **Gal 2:17** (s. B-D-F, loc. cit.). In a question which forms the apodosis of a conditional sentence Hm 4, 1, 4. Strengthened and enlivened ἆρά γε (Aristoph., X. et al.; Gen 37:10; Jer 4:10 Swete; Jos., Bell. 6, 330; Just., D. 56, 17 [Gen 18:13]; Tat. 23, 1; Ath. R. 71, 28) **Ac 8:30;** Dg 7:3. Zahn, Ro 370f, also takes **Ro 7:25** (s. ἄρα 2b) as a question: ἆρα οὖν; (Περὶ ὕψους 33, 4; Ael. Aristid. 32 p. 607 D. twice; 34 p. 660; 39 p. 745; Maximus Tyr. 8, 6c; Jos., C. Ap. 2, 232).—Denniston 44–51.—DELG s.v. ἆρα and ἦ. M-M. Sv.

Ἀραβία, ας, ἡ (Hdt. 3, 107 et al.; TestSol; EpArist 119; Philo; Joseph. Ἀρρ-; Just. On Ἀ. w. and without the art. s. B-D-F §261, 6; PFlor 278 στρατηγῷ Ἀραβίας) ***Arabia*** as a geogr. concept includes the territory west of Mesopotamia, east and south of Syria and Palestine, to the isthmus of Suez. In Roman times independent kingdoms arose like that of the Nabataeans south of Damascus, which could be called simply Arabia (Diod. S. 19, 94, 1 χώρα τῶν Ἀράβων τῶν καλουμένων Ναβαταίων; Stephan. Byz. s.v. Γοαρήνη: χώρα Ἀραβίας πλησίον Δαμασκοῦ;

Appian, Bell. Civ. 2, 71 §294 describes Ἄραβες and Ἑβραῖοι as neighbors), and is regularly so called by Joseph. This seems to have been the country visited by Paul after his conversion **Gal 1:17** (CBriggs, The Ap. Paul in Arabia: Biblical World 41, 1913, 255–59). Of Arabia in the narrower sense, w. special ref. to the Sinai peninsula **Gal 4:25.** As the home of the phoenix 1 Cl 25:1.—BMoritz, Arabien 1923; HPhilby, Arabia 1930; JMontgomery, A. and the Bible '34; FAbel, Géographie de la Palestine '33/38, I 288–94; II 164–68. ANegev, ANRW II/8, '77, 520–686.—EDNT. M-M.

Ἀραβικός, ή, όν (Diod. S. 19, 94, 4; Diosc. 1, 17; Plut., Anton. 69, 4; PGen 29, 8 [II AD]; Jos., Bell. 1, 267, Ant. 16, 288; Ἀρρ- Just., A I, 62, 3, D. 78, 10) ***Arabian*** ἡ Ἀ. χώρα *Arabia* 1 Cl 25:3.

Ἄραβοι ***Arabs*** **Ac 2:11** D (for Ἄραβες) could have been wrongly formed fr. the gen. pl. Ἀράβων (Appian, Syr. 51 §257 ἐξ Ἀράβων; Ps 71:10; EpArist 114; Jos., Ant. 2, 213; Ἀρράβων Just., D. 34, 4; 119, 4), perh. as ἄλα fr. ἅλατος (s. ἅλας beg.).

ἀραβών s. ἀρραβών.

ἄραγε s. ἄρα.

ἆραι s. αἴρω.

Ἀράμ, ὁ (רָם) indecl. ***Aram*** in genealogy of Jesus **Mt 1:3f; Lk 3:33 v.l.** (cp. 1 Ch 2:9f; Ruth 4:19 v.l.; TestJud 10:1; TestIss 1:5).

ἀράομαι 1 aor. ἠρασάμην (s. ἀρά; Hom. et al.; LXX, Philo Vi. Mos. 278) lit. 'pray', then (since trag.) w. neg. content **to invoke evil on someone, *wish evil, imprecate*** τί ἀράσωμαι σε (for σοι) *what evil, then, shall I invoke upon you?* GJs 2:3.—Schmidt, Syn. I 181–83. DELG s.v. ἀρά. TW.

ἄραφος, ον (ἄρραφος t.r. Bov., N[25]—ῥάπτω 'sew'; s. ῥαφίς; Galen, De Usu Part. II 177, 18; 179, 14 H. of bones= without sutures) ***seamless*** **J 19:23** (cp. Jos., Ant. 3, 161 the high priest's χιτών is not ῥαπτός).—PRieger, Versuch e. Technologie u. Terminol. d. Handwerke in d. Mischna, diss. Bresl. 1894, 36ff; FConybeare, Exp. 6th ser. 9, 1904, 458–60; JRepond, Le costume du Christ: Biblica 3, 1922, 3–14; Bultmann, comm. ad loc.—DELG s.v. ῥάπτω.

Ἄραψ, βος, ὁ an ***Arab*** (Strabo 1, 2, 34; Appian, Syr. 51 §256; UPZ 72, 2 [152 BC]; TestSol; EpArist 114; Philo; SibOr; oft. Joseph.) **Ac 2:11** (s. Κρής); B 9:6.—EGüting, ZNW 66, '75, 149–69.

ἀργέω 1 aor. ἤργησα (s. ἀργός; Soph., Hippocr. et al.; pap fr. PPetr II, 4 [9], 4 [225/224 BC] on; LXX; OdeSol 11:23; ApcrEzk, Denis p. 122 [Epiph 64, 70, 14]; Jos., C. Ap. 2, 282) **to stop doing someth., *slack off, become idle*** (w. ἐγκαταλείπειν) ἀπὸ τῆς ἀγαθοποιΐας 1 Cl 33:1. Abs. (Agatharchides: 86 fgm. 20, 209 Jac. [in Jos., C. Ap. 1, 209]) τὸ κρίμα ἔκπαλαι οὐκ ἀργεῖ *from ancient times (their) condemnation has not been idle* i.e. it is being prepared **2 Pt 2:3** (cp. 1 Esdr 2:26 ἤργει ἡ οἰκοδομή=the construction was delayed).—M-M. TW.

ἀργός, ή, όν (contr. fr. ἄεργος 'without performance', s. ἔργον; Aeschyl., Hdt. et al.; Herm. Wr. 11, 5; ins, pap, LXX; Philo; Joseph.; on the number of endings s. Nägeli 31; B-D-F §69, 1).

❶ **pert. to being without anything to do, *unemployed, idle*** (BGU 1078, 6ff [39 AD] οὐ γὰρ ἀργὸν δεῖ με καθῆσθαι). Of unemployed in the marketplace **Mt 20:3, 6** (Aesop, Fab. 81 H.=291 P.=Babr. 20, 3 ἀργὸς εἱστήκει=stood idle). Of unoccupied widows **1 Ti 5:13** (twice). μὴ ἀ. μεθ' ὑμῶν ζήσεται Χριστιανός D 12:4.

❷ **pert. to being unwilling to work, *idle, lazy*** (Sir 37:11) ἀ. πρὸς τ. ἔντευξιν *neglectful of, careless in prayer* Hs 5, 4, 3f (ἀ. πρός τι as Vi. Aesopi I c. 15 p. 268, 2 Eberh.; Wsd 15:15). ἐπὶ πᾶν ἔργον ἀγαθόν *for every good work* 1 Cl 34:4 (w. παρειμένος). ὄρνεα ἀ. καθήμενα B 10:4. Of Cretans γαστέρες ἀργαί *lazy gluttons* **Tit 1:12** (fr. Epimenides? cp. Vorsokr.[5] 3 fgm. B 1. f [=4th ed. II 188]; Plut., Mor. 1108c. See MDibelius, Hdb. ad loc.—With this unfavorable description of persons cp. Diod. S. 19, 41, 1 ὦ κακαὶ κεφαλαί).

❸ **pert. to being unproductive, *useless, worthless*** (SIG 884, 23f; PAmh 97, 9f; Wsd 14:5; 15:15; Philo, Spec. Leg. 2, 86; 88; Jos., Ant. 12, 378) ἡ πίστις χωρὶς τ. ἔργων ἀ. ἐστιν *faith without deeds is useless* **Js 2:20** (νεκρά v.l. and κενή P[74]); ἀ. εἰς τ. Χριστοῦ ἐπίγνωσιν (w. ἄκαρπος) **2 Pt 1:8** (cp. OdeSol 11:23); ῥῆμα ἀ. *a careless utterance* which, because of its worthlessness, had better been left unspoken (Pythagoras in Stob., Flor. III 34, 11 p. 684 W. αἱρετώτερόν σοι ἔστω λίθον εἰκῇ βαλεῖν ἢ λόγον ἀργόν; cp. Jos., Ant. 15, 224) **Mt 12:36** (EbNestle, Philologica Sacra, 1896, 58f; Jülicher, Gleichn. 126; JViteau, La Vie spirituelle '31, 16–28: abuse, slander; EStauffer, Von jedem unnützen Wort: EFascher Festschr., '58, 94–102).—B. 315. DELG s.v. ἔργον. M-M. TW. Spicq.

ἀργύρεος s. ἀργυροῦς.

ἀργύριον, ου, τό (s. ἄργυρος; Hdt., Aristoph.+; 'silver, money')

❶ **the precious metal known as silver, *silver*** **1 Cor 3:12 v.l.** (s. ἄργυρος). χρυσῷ τελε[ίῳ καὶ ἀργυ]ρίῳ AcPl Ha 1, 11.

❷ **silver used as money, *silver money*—ⓐ** silver money beside gold (Gen 24:35; Num 31:22 al.; En 97:8; 98:2; Jos., Ant. 15, 5) **Ac 3:6; 20:33;** cp. **1 Pt 1:18.** ᾧ ὠνήσατο Ἀβραὰμ τιμῆς ἀργυρίου *which Abraham had bought for a sum of silver* **Ac 7:16** (cp. Gen 23:16).

ⓑ money gener. (Aristoph., Plut. 131; Appian, Artem. 1, 2 p. 4, 16 al.; Diog. L. 6, 95; Alex. Aphr., Fat. 8 II 2 p. 172, 30; Synes., Ep. 6 p. 169a. Gen 42:25, 35) **Lk 9:3; Ac 8:20.** τοῦ ἀ. τὴν ἀπαρχήν D 13:7 (s. ἀπαρχή 1a); ἀποκρύπτειν τὸ ἀ. **Mt 25:18;** ἀ. αἰτεῖν *ask for money* D 11:6; ἀ. δοῦναί τινι *give* or *pay money to someone* **Mk 14:11; Lk 22:5;** cp. D 11:12. Otherw. διδόναι τὸ ἀ. *give the money*=entrust **Lk 19:15.** διδόναι τὸ ἀ. ἐπὶ τράπεζαν *put money into a bank* vs. **23.** For this τὰ ἀ. (cp. Aristoph., Av. 600; Demosth. 25, 41 v.l.; cp. Pollux 3, 86) **Mt 25:27.** διδόναι ἀ. ἱκανά *offer an ample bribe* **Mt 28:12;** λαμβάνειν ἀ. (Appian, Iber. 34 §138 ἀργ. λαμβάνειν; Gen 23:13) vs. **15** (=allow oneself to be bribed, as Artem. 4, 82).

ⓒ of particular silver coins (so as loanw. in rabb. ἀργύρια=silver coins: Pla., Leg. 5, 742d; Pollux 3, 86; 9, 89f; PGM 4, 2439) τριάκοντα ἀργύρια *30 silver shekels* (each worth about 4 drachmas; s. below) **Mt 26:15; 27:3, 9;** cp. vs. **5f** (=שֶׁקֶל כֶּסֶף or simply כֶּסֶף, cp. Zech 11:12f). ἀργυρίου μυριάδας πέντε *50,000* (Attic silver) *drachmas* **Ac 19:19** (=a worker's wage for 137 years with no days off; cp. Jos., Ant. 17, 189).—FPrat, Le cours des Monnaies en Palest. au temps de J.-Chr.: RSR 15, 1925, 441–48; ORoller, Münzen, Geld u. Vermögensverhältnisse in den Evv. 1929; Billerb. I 290–94; CSeltmann, Greek Coins '33; AReifenberg, Ancient Jewish Coins[2], '47.—B. 773. DELG s.v. ἄργυρος. New Docs 4, 7–10. M-M.

ἀργυροκόπος, ου, ὁ (s. ἄργυρος, κόπτω; Plut., Mor. 830e; IK Eph VI, 2212, 6 [I AD]; SIG 1263, 1 [fr. Smyrna];

BGU 781 IV, 5; PGiss 47, 22; POxy 1146, 12; PLond III, 983, 1 p. 229; Jer 6:29) ***silversmith*** (Judg 17:4 B) **Ac 19:24** (for ins at Ephesus s. Hemer, Acts 235); Dg 2:3.—M-M.

ἄργυρος, ου, ὁ (ἀργός 'shining', not to be confused with the homograph ἀργός 'idle') (Hom.+; ins, pap, LXX, pseudepigr.; Mel. fgm. 8b 3; Ath. 5, 1; R. 76, 29, but much less freq. than ἀργύριον).

❶ **silver as a commodity,** ***silver*** (Diod. S. 2, 16, 4; 2, 36, 2; Appian, Bell. Civ. 4, 75 §320) w. gold (Jos., Ant. 9, 85; TestLevi 13:7) **Ac 17:29; Rv 18:12;** MPol 15:2; **1 Cor 3:12** (s. ἀργύριον 1). W. still other materials (Diod. S. 4, 46, 4; 5, 74, 2) 2 Cl 1:6; PtK 2 p. 14, 14; Dg 2:2. It rusts acc. to **Js 5:3.**

❷ **money made of silver,** ***silver money, silver*** (w. χρυσός: Herodian 2, 6, 8; Jos., Ant. 6, 201, C. Ap. 2, 217) **Mt 10:9** (s. ἀργύριον 2).—B. 610. DELG. M-M.

ἀργυροῦς, ᾶ, οῦν made of silver, ***silver.*** The contracted form of this word (common Hom.+; freq. in LXX [s. Helbing, Grammatik, 34f]) predominates in our lit. and the pap (also found En 99:7; TestSol 21:3; TestJob 32:9; Jos., Ant. 3, 221). σκεύη χρυσᾶ καὶ ἀ. (Gen 24:53 al.) **2 Ti 2:20;** ναοὶ ἀ. **Ac 19:24** (Artem. 4, 31 ἀργυροῦς νεώς); τὰ εἴδωλα τὰ ἀ. **Rv 9:20** (cp. Da 5:4, 23 LXX + Theod.).—ἀργύρεος (SIG 579, 3; 1168, 39; Sb 6949, 30; PLond III, 1007, 3; 9 p. 262f; TestJob 25:8): θεοὶ ἀ. *gods made of silver* Dg 2:7 (cp. Ex 20:23; EpJer 3; 10 and 29).—DELG s.v. ἄργυρος. M-M s.v. ἀργύρεος.

Ἄρειος πάγος, ὁ (Ἄριος π. Tdf.—Hdt. 8, 52 et al.; Diod. S. 11, 77, 6; Paus., Attic. 1, 28, 5; Meisterhans[3]-Schw. 43, 3; 47, 21; SIG index IV) ***the Areopagus*** or ***Hill of Ares*** (Ares, the Gk. god of war = Rom. Mars, hence the older 'Mars' Hill'), northwest of the Acropolis in Athens **Ac 17:19, 22.** But the A. is to be understood here less as a place (where speakers were permitted to hold forth freely, and listeners were always at hand) than as the council, which met on the hill (ἐπὶ τὸν Ἀ.=*before the A.*; cp. 16:19, 17:6). For the opp. view s. MDibelius below. In Rom. times it was the most important governmental body in Athens; whether its functions included that of supervising education, particularly of controlling the many visiting lecturers (Thalheim [s. below] 632; Gärtner [s. below] 56ff), cannot be determined w. certainty.—Thalheim in Pauly-W. II 1896, 627ff; ECurtius, Pls. in Athen: SBBerlAk 1893, 925ff; WFerguson, Klio 9, 1909, 325–30; Ramsay, Bearing 101ff; AWikenhauser, Die AG 1921, 351ff; Beginn. IV '33, 212f; JAdams, Paul at Athens: Rev. and Exp. 32, '35, 50–56; MDibelius, Pls. auf d. Areopag. '39; WSchmid, Philol 95, '42, 79–120; MPohlenz, Pls. u. d. Stoa: ZNW 42, '49, 69–104; NStonehouse, The Areopagus Address '49; HHommel, Neue Forschungen zur Areopagrede: ZNW 46, '55, 145–78; BGärtner, The Areopagus Speech and Natural Revelation '55; EHaenchen, AG '56, 457–74; WNauck, ZTK 53, '56, 11–52; BAFCS II 447f.—DELG s.v. Ἄρης.

Ἀρεοπαγίτης, ου, ὁ (also -είτης Tdf. On -ίτης s. Lobeck on Phryn. 599; 697f; B-D-F §30, 2; Mlt-H. 277; 366; Aeschin. 1, 81; Menand., Fab. Inc. 11 J.; Alciphron 1, 16, 1; SIG 334, 35; 856, 8.—Ἀρευπαγίτης Michel 687, 52 [III BC]; 823, 7 [220 BC]) ***Areopagite,*** member of the council or court of the Areopagus (s. prec.); of Dionysius **Ac 17:34.** (Tdf. Ἀρεοπαγείτης as SIG 856, 8).—Hemer, Acts 119. DELG s.v. Ἄρης. EDNT.

ἀρεσκεία, ας, ἡ (better ἀρέσκεια w. L-S-J-M, DGE et al., but for ἀρεσκεία s. Mlt-H. 339; Rbt. 153, 231—cp. ἀρεσκεύομαι 'be obsequious', s. ἀρέσκω; Aristot., Theophr. et al.; TestReub 3:4; mostly in pejorative sense: obsequiousness. In favorable sense: that by which one gains favor, Pr 31:30; also, esp. in public documents, of exceptional public service or expression of devotion IPontEux II, 5 χάριν τῆς εἰς τ. πόλιν ἀρεσκείας; IPriene 113, 73; POxy 729, 24 πρὸς ἀ. τοῦ Σαραπίωνος. Of one's relation w. God Philo, Op. M. 144, Fuga 88 ἕνεκα ἀ. θεοῦ, Spec. Leg. 1, 176) **desire to do someth. that produces satisfaction,** ***desire to please*** εἰς πᾶσαν ἀ. *to please* (the Lord) *in all respects* **Col 1:10.**—DELG s.v. ἀρέσκω. M-M.

ἀρέσκω impf. ἤρεσκον; fut. ἀρέσω; 1 aor. ἤρεσα. Mid. impf. ἠρέσκετο (Tat. 2, 1) (s. ἀρεσκεία; Hom.+). In Gk. lit. ἀ. is used in a variety of senses ranging from conciliatory action (s. Od. 22, 55, of satisfaction pledged to Odysseus) to undertaking of civic responsibility that meets with public approval (s. 2 below). Most oft. w. dat. of pers.

❶ **to act in a fawning manner,** ***win favor, please, flatter,*** w. focus on the winning of approval (Aristot., EN 2, 7, 13; 4, 6, 1; Theophr., Char. 5 [e.g. in a dispute the flatterer endeavors to please friend and foe alike; and he will tell foreigners that they speak with greater sense of justice than do his fellow citizens]. That the original sense of basic civility in human relations [s. 2a below] suffered debasement is affirmed by Anaxandrides Com., cited Athen. 6, 255b: τὸ γαρ κολακεύειν νῦν ἀρέσκειν ὄνομ' ἔχει 'flattery' is now called 'being accommodating'; s. ἀνθρωπαρεσκέω, ἀνθρωπάρεσκος) ἀνθρώποις (Pla., Ep. 4, 321b; Simplicius in Epict. p. 118, 30 ἀρέσκειν ἀνθρώποις βουλόμενος) **Gal 1:10ab** (conative impf.); **1 Th 2:4** here in both a neg. and a positive sense: 'flattering' humans, but 'pleasing' God (in the sense of 2 below), who tests (δοκιμάζω) for motivation.

❷ **to give pleasure/satisfaction,** ***please, accommodate.***

ⓐ a favored term in the reciprocity-conscious Mediterranean world, and frequently used in honorary documents to express interest in accommodating others by meeting their needs or carrying out important obligations. Oft. almost *serve* Nägeli 40. The use of the term in a good sense in our lit. contributes a tone of special worth and diginity to some of the relationships that are depicted. τινί *someone* τῷ πλησίον **Ro 15:2** (w. τὸ ἀγαθόν and οἰκοδομή as decisive semantic components); cp. Hs 5, 2, 7 a servant doing good work. Lord/God ἀ. τ. κυρίῳ **1 Cor 7:32; 1 Th 4:1;** inability to do so **Ro 8:8;** cp. **1 Th 2:15;** rather than humans **1 Th 2:4** (s. 1 above); IRo 2:1 (note the semantic problem cited 1 above). God/Lord as commander (military imagery) IPol 6:2; cp. **2 Ti 2:4.**—Concern for a broad public is a common theme in honorary documents (e.g. OGI 339, 29f; s. Danker, Benefactor 336f) and other lit. (cp. Demosth., Ep. 3, 27 πᾶσιν ἀ.; Ath. 26:1 τοῖς πολλοῖς ἀρέσκοντες θεοί) πάντα πᾶσιν ἀ. *in everything I endeavor to please all,* i.e. without deference to one at the expense of another, **1 Cor 10:33** (w. σύμφορον, q.v., along w. συμφέρω, for cultural significance); sim. κατὰ πάντα τρόπον πᾶσιν ἀ. ITr 2:3. (Cp. the negative appraisal **1 Th 2:15.**)—Sacrifice of self-interest is a major component of the foregoing theme, hence the caution μὴ ἑαυτῷ ἀ. **Ro 15:1,** and the exhibition of Jesus as role model vs. **3;** cp. 2 Cl 13:1 (w. ἀνθρωπάρεσκος s. 1 above); Hs 9, 22, 1; in a marriage relationship, wife or husband ἀ. τ. γυναικί **1 Cor 7:33;** ἀ. τ. ἀνδρι vs. **34.**

ⓑ of pleasure (without any suggestion of mere amusement) as a condition generated by an action (cp. POxy 1153, 25 ἐὰν αὐτῷ ἀρέσκῃ; PGiss 20, 15). A fine line cannot always be drawn between a focus on endeavor to please and focus on the impact of pleasure produced by the activity. Some of the pass. cited in 2a may equally belong here and some of those included here could be cited above. But the gener. sense in those that follow is satisfaction produced by the behavior of another *please God* ἀ. θεῷ

(Theopomp. [IV BC]: 115 fgm. 344 Jac. τ. θεοῖς ἀ. here the concern is to meet divine expectations; Num 23:27; Ps 68:32; Mal 3:4; Jos., Ant. 6, 164; 13, 289) **Ro 8:8; 1 Th 2:15;** cp. Hs 5, 2, 7; ἀ. τ. κυρίῳ **1 Cor 7:32** (on these four last pass. s. also a above); 1 Cl 52, 2 (Ps 68, 32); wife/husband 1 Cor 7:33f (s. a above); **2 Ti 2:4;** Herod **Mt 14:6; Mk 6:22.** W. focus on someth. that provides pleasure (Ael. Aristid. 46, 380 D.: θεοῖς ἀρέσκοντα) Hv 1, 4, 2; s 5, 6, 6. ἤρεσεν ὁ λόγος ἐνώπιον (for לִפְנֵי or בְּעֵינֵי) τοῦ πλήθους (= τῷ πλήθει) *the saying pleased the whole group* (cp. 2 Ch 30:4; 1 Macc 6:60; 8:21; Jos., Vi. 238) **Ac 6:5** (B-D-F §4, p. 4, 5; 187, 2; 214, 6).—Salome, daughter of Herodias, pleases Herod and his company, and in keeping w. Mediterranean reciprocity system receives her award, in this instance a grisly one **Mt 14:6; Mk 6:22.**—Implied, i.e. impers. (Philo, Aet. M. 87; Jos., Ant. 14, 205; 207) ἀρέσκει μοι *it pleases me* (=mihi placet) w. inf. foll. (Hdt. 8, 19; Josh 24:15; 1 Macc 14:23; 15:19; Jos., Ant. 14, 352) Hm 6, 1, 5.—B. 1099. DELG. M-M. TW. Sv.

ἀρεστός, ή, όν (Semonides, Hdt.+) **pert. to being satisfying, *pleasing*** τὰ ἀ. τ. θεῷ ποιεῖν (the Pythagorean Ecphantus in Stob. 4, 7, 65 H.; Porphyr., Abst. 1, 25; Sir 48:22) *do what is pleasing to God* **J 8:29.** Also ἐνώπιον τοῦ θεοῦ (Is 38:3; Tob 4:21; Da 4:37a) **1J 3:22** (s. ἀρέσκω 2b). ἔστιν ἀ. τῷ θεῷ B 19:2 (cp. Just., A I, 10, 3); τ. κυρίῳ D 4:12.—Of pers. (Aristoxenus, fgm. 70 πλήθει [=the masses] ἀρεστὸν εἶναι; SEG I, 572, 6; Sb 6649, 5; Tob 4:3; 2 Esdr 19 [Neh 9]: 37; Jos., Ant. 16, 135) τ. Ἰουδαίοις **Ac 12:3;** οὐκ ἀ. ἐστιν w. acc. and inf. foll. *it is not desirable* **6:2** (B-D-F §408). S. εὐάρεστος.—DELG s.v. ἀρέσκω. M-M. TW.

Ἁρέτας, α, ὁ (on the spelling s. Dssm. NB 11 [BS 183f]) a name which, in the form Ḥâritat, is often found in Nabataean inscriptions and among the Arabs, and was borne by Nabataean kings (Joseph. index). The one named **2 Cor 11:32** was Aretas IV (ruled c. 9 BC to 40 AD). Cp. Schürer I 581–83; ASteinmann, Aretas IV: BZ 7, 1909, 174–84, 312–41; also separately 1909; Ltzm., Hdb. Exk. on 2 Cor 11:32f; HWindisch, KEK[9] 1924 ad loc. (lit.); JStarcky, Dict. de la Bible, Suppl. VII '66, 913–16.—M-M.

ἀρετή, ῆς, ἡ (Hom.+, a term denoting consummate 'excellence' or 'merit' within a social context, hence freq. w. δικαιοσύνη; cp. the tripartite appraisal Pla., Protag. 329c: δικαιοσύνη, σωφροσύνη, ὁσιότης). Exhibition of ἀρετή invites recognition, resulting in renown or glory. In Homer primarily of military valor or exploits, but also of distinction for other personal qualities and associated performance that enhance the common interest. The term is a favorite subject in Stoic thought relating to morality. Theognis 147f summarizes Gk. thinking: ἐν δὲ δικαιοσύνῃ συλλήβδην πᾶσ' ἀρετή 'στι,| πᾶς δέ τ' ἀνὴρ ἀγαθός, Κύρνε, δίκαιος ἐών=in a word, Cyrnus, all excellence lies in uprightness, and a good person is one who is upright.

❶ **uncommon character worthy of praise, *excellence of character, exceptional civic virtue*** (Theognis 147; Aristot., EN a detailed discussion of ἀ.; s. indexes in OGI, SIG, IPriene, et al.; Herm. Wr. 9, 4; 10, 9; Wsd; 2, 3, 4 Macc; EpArist; Philo; Jos., Ant. 1, 113 al.; διὰ τὴν ἀ. Orig. C. Cels. 5, 2, 26 [as distinguished merit]; τέσσαράς φησιν εἶναι ἀρετάς Hippol., Ref. 1, 19, 16 [in a list of virtues]; Did., Gen. 102, 15; 17 [accompanied by 'trouble']) **Phil 4:8** (w. ἔπαινος, in ref. to recognition of distinguished merit that was customary in Gr-Rom. society; cp. AcJ 5 [Aa II/1, 153, 29]). W. πίστις (as OGI 438, 6ff ἄνδρα διενένκαντα πίστει καὶ ἀρετῇ καὶ δικαιοσύνῃ καὶ εὐσεβείαι=a gentleman distinguished for fidelity, admirable character, uprightness [concern for people], and devotion [to deities]; cp. Dssm. LO 270 [LAE 322]; Danker, Benefactor 460–61) ἐπιχορηγήσατε ἐν τῇ πίστει ὑμῶν τὴν ἀρετήν *bring the finest character to your commitment* **2 Pt 1:5a;** ἐν δὲ τῇ ἀρετῇ τὴν γνῶσιν *and to the finest character knowledge* **5b.** ἐνδύσασθαι πᾶσαν ἀ. δικαιοσύνης *put on every virtue of uprightness* (='aspire to the highest standards of uprightness'; opp. πονηρία, which is low-grade behavior; on the rhetorical form s. HFischel, HUCA 44, '73, 119–51) Hm 1:2; s 6, 1, 4. ἐργάζεσθαι πᾶσαν ἀ. καὶ δικαιοσύνην s 8, 10, 39 (=be a model member of the human community); cp. m 12, 3, 1; διώκειν τὴν ἀ. 2 Cl 10:1. ἀ. ἔνδοξος Hm 6, 2, 3.

❷ **manifestation of divine power, *miracle*** (a usage in keeping w. the primary mng.; Oenom. in Eus., PE 5, 22, 4; SIG 1151, 2; 1172, 10 πλείονας ἀρετὰς τ. θεοῦ, see on this Dittenberger's note 8 w. further exx. and lit.; 1173, 5; MAI 21, 1896, 77; POxy 1382 [II AD]; Sb 8026, 1; 8266, 17 [261/260 BC] of the miracles of the deity Amenothis; PGM 5, 419; Philo, Somn. 1, 256; Jos., Ant. 17, 130; s. Dssm., B 90–93 [BS 95f]; Nägeli 69; OWeinreich, Neue Urkunden zur Sarapisrel. 1919, index; SReiter, Ἐπιτύμβιον, Swoboda Festschr. 1927, 228–37), also that which causes such things: *the power of God* (IG IV[2], 128, 79 [280 BC]; PGM 4, 3205; Herm. Wr. 10, 17; Jos., Ant. 17, 130 ἀ. τοῦ θείου; cp. 1, 100) **2 Pt 1:3** (Dssm., B 277ff [BS 360ff]).—In accordance w. a usage that treats ἀ. and δόξα as correlatives (ἀ.=excellence that results in approbation and therefore δόξα=renown), which finds expression outside the OT (Is 42:8, 12) in the juxtaposition of the two terms (Herodian; Pausanias, Arcadia 52, 6 ins on a statue in honor of Philopoemen at Tegea; Dionys. Hal.; Diod. Sic. 2, 45, 2 of a woman, self-styled 'Daughter of Ares', reputed for her valor; s. Wetstein on 2 Pt 1:3), the LXX transl. הוֹד majesty, high rank (Hab 3:3; Zech 6:13; cp. Il. 9, 498 ἀ. w. τιμή and βίη; 23, 578 w. βίη) and also תְּהִלָּה praise sg. (Is; cp. Od. 14, 402 ἀ. w. ἐϋκλείη 'good repute') with ἀ. pl. The latter sense 'praise' (pl.=laudes) has been maintained for **1 Pt 2:9,** which is probably influenced by Is 42:12; 43:21. It is poss. that Semitically oriented auditors of 1 Pt interpreted the expression along such lines, but Gr-Rom. publics would in the main be conditioned to hear a stress on performance, which of course would elicit praise (cp. Plut., Mor. 535d).—AKiefer, Aretalogische Studien, diss. Freib. 1929; VLongo, Aretalogie nel mondo Greco: I, Epigrafi e Papiri '69; MSmith, JBL 90, '71, 174–99; JKube, TEXNH und APETH '69; Danker, Benefactor '82, passim.—DELG. M-M. TW. Sv.

ἄρη s. αἴρω.

ἀρήν, ἀρνός, ὁ nom. found only in early ins (VII–VI BC, HSearles, A Lexicograph. Study of the Gk. Ins. 1898, 21; Meisterhans[3]-Schw. §58, 1; Kühner-Bl. I 429, 14; s. L-S-J-M s.v.), but the oblique cases Hom.+. Gen. pl. ἀρνῶν; acc. ἄρνας ***lamb*** as an animal for slaughter B 2:5 (Is 1:11). As a type of weakness ὡς ἄρνας ἐν μέσῳ λύκων **Lk 10:3** (cp. Kaibel 1038, 38 ὡς ἄρνας κατέχουσι λύκοι; Is 65:25; Just., A I, 58, 2.—The contrast is as old as Hom. [Il. 22, 263]).—DELG. M-M. TW.

ἀριθμέω fut. 2 pl. ἀριθμήσετε Lev 23:15; 1 aor. ἠρίθμησα, impv. ἀρίθμησον. Pass. fut. ἀριθμηθήσομαι LXX; aor. ἠριθμήθην; pf. ἠρίθμημαι (Hom. et al.; ins, pap, LXX; TestNapht 7:2 v.l.; ApcEsdr p. 27, 4 Tdf.; Jos., Ant. 10, 243; 14, 194) ***count*** ὄχλον **Rv 7:9;** ἀστέρας 1 Cl 10:6 (Gen 15:5); pass. **Mt 10:30; Lk 12:7.**—DELG s.v. ἀριθμός. M-M. TW.

ἀριθμός, οῦ, ὁ (s. ἀριθμέω; Hom.+)—❶ **a cardinal number, *number*** ὄντα ἐκ τοῦ ἀριθμοῦ τῶν δώδεκα (like Lat. e numero esse) *belonging to the number of the twelve,* i.e. being one of the twelve **Lk 22:3;** cp. εὑρεθῆναι ἐν τῷ ἀ. τινος *be found among the number* 1 Cl 35:4; sim. 58:2; MPol 14:2; Hs 5, 3, 2;

9, 24, 4. W. specif. numbers ἀ. τῶν ἀνδρῶν **Ac 4:4; 5:36.** τὸν ἀριθμὸν ὡς πεντακισχίλιοι *about 5,000 in number* (Hdt., X. et al.; SIG 495, 115 [III BC]; POxy 1117, 15; PFlor 53, 7; 16; PGen 16, 22f ἀδελφοὶ ὄντες τ. ἀριθμὸν πέντε; 2 Macc 8:16; 3 Macc 5:2; Jos., Vi. 15) **J 6:10;** cp. **Rv 5:11; 7:4; 9:16.** W. non-specif. numbers **Ro 9:27; Rv 20:8** (both Is 10:22). ὡς μὴ εἶναι ἀριθμόν *so that one could not count* (them) AcPl Ha 7, 6.—**Rv 13:17f, 15:2** refer to numerology, which was quite familiar to people of ancient times; acc. to it, since each Gk. letter has a numerical value, a name could be replaced by a number representing the total of the numerical values of the letters making up the name (cp. PGM 13, 155=466 σὺ εἶ ὁ ἀριθμὸς τ. ἐνιαυτοῦ Ἀβρασάξ [α=1 + β=2 + ρ=100 + α=1 + σ=200 + α=1 + ξ=60 makes 365, the number of days in a year]; IGR IV 743, 7f ἰσόψηφος δυσὶ τούτοις Γάϊος ὡς ἅγιος, ὡς ἀγαθὸς, προλέγω [the name and both adjs. each have a num. value of 284]; PGM 1, 325 κλῄζω δ' οὔνομα σὸν Μοίραις αὐταῖς ἰσάριθμον; 2, 128; 8, 44ff; SibOr 1, 141–45; Artem. 3, 28; 3, 34; 4, 24; Dssm., LO 237f [LAE 276f]; FBücheler, RhM n.s. 61, 1906, 307f); on the interpr. of the number 666 s. χξς'.

❷ **a numerical total,** ***number, total*** (Dt 26:5; 28:62) ἀ. τῶν ἐκλεκτῶν *the number of the elect* 1 Cl 2:4; cp. 59:2. ἐπληθύνετο ὁ ἀ. *the total continued to grow* **Ac 6:7;** περισσεύειν τῷ ἀ. **16:5;** πολὺς ἀ. (Diod. S. 13, 2, 5; 14, 43, 3; Sir 51:28) **11:21.** κατὰ ἀριθμὸν ἀγγέλων *acc. to the number of angels* 1 Cl 29:2 (Dt 32:8).—B. 917. DELG. M-M. TW. Sv.

Ἁριμαθαία, ας, ἡ (Ἀ. other edd.) ***Arimathea,*** a city in Judea (acc. to Dalman, Orte[3] 139 [Eng. tr. 225 n. 12, 226] and PThomsen, Philol. Wochenschr. 49, 1929, 246=Rentis); home of Joseph (s. Ἰωσήφ 6) **Mt 27:57; Mk 15:43; Lk 23:51; J 19:38.**

Ἄριος πάγος s. Ἄρειος πάγος.

Ἀρίσταρχος, ου, ὁ (common name: SIG and OGI, index; Preisigke, Namenbuch) ***Aristarchus*** of Thessalonica, **Ac 20:4,** cp. **19:29,** accompanied Paul on his collection-journey and when he left for Rome **27:2; Phlm 24,** named as Paul's συνεργός; **Col 4:10** as his συναιχμάλωτος.

ἀριστάω 1 aor. ἠρίστησα (s. ἄριστον).—❶ ***eat breakfast*** (oft. so since Hippoc., Vict. 6, p. 594; X., Cyr.6, 4, 1) **J 21:12, 15** (cp. vs. 4)

❷ of the main meal (Aelian, VH 9, 19; Gen 43:25), then of a meal without ref. to a particular time of day or type of food ***eat a meal, dine*** (3 Km 13:7; Jos., Ant. 6, 362; 8, 240) **Lk 11:37; 15:29** D.—DELG s.v. ἄριστον.

ἀριστερός, α, όν (Hom.+) ***left*** (opp. to right) ὅπλα δεξιὰ καὶ ἀ. weapons used w. the right hand, and those used w. the left=*weapons for offense and defense* (cp. Scipio cited in Plut, Mor. 201d and Polyaenus 8, 16, 4 ἀριστερά and δεξιά of weapons for defense and offense) **2 Cor 6:7.** ἡ ἀριστερὰ (sc. χείρ B-D-F §241, 6; Rob. 652) *the left hand* **Mt 6:3** (cp. Damasc., Vi. Isid. 283 the proverb: give not w. one hand, but w. both). τὰ ἀ. μέρη *the left side* (on the pl. B-D-F §141, 2) Hv 3, 1, 9; 3, 2, 1; hence ἐξ ἀριστερῶν (sc. μερῶν) *on the left* (Diogenes the Cynic in Diog. L. 6, 48; UPZ 121, 7 [156 BC]; Sb 8952, 21 [76 AD]; BGU 86, 27; LXX; TestAbr A 12 p. 91, 2 [Stone p. 30] al.) **Mk 10:37; Lk 23:33;** Hs 9, 6, 2. περιέβλεπεν τὰ δεξιὰ καὶ τὰ ἀ. *she looked to the right and the left* GJs 11:1 (cp. ParJer 7:11 μὴ ἐκκλίνῃς εἰς τὰ δεξιὰ μήτε εἰς τὰ ἀ.). σύνεσιν γὰρ ἕξετε δεξιὰν καὶ ἀριστεράν *you will have right and left understanding*=you will be able to distinguish between what is true and what is false (apparently with ref. to true and false prophets) D 12:1 (the text can also be read: γνώσεσθε—σύνεσιν γὰρ ἕξετε—δ. κ. ἀ. *you will know—for you will have understanding—(the distinction between) right and left* i.e., true/good and false/evil; cp. Jon 4:11).—B. 866. DELG s.v. ἀρείων (comparative of ἀγαθός). M-M.

Ἀριστίων, ωνος, ὁ (name in use since VI BC [adherent of Peisistratos], also pap) ***Aristion,*** an early Christian, called 'a disciple of the Lord' Papias (2:4).

Ἀριστόβουλος, ου, ὁ (common name: SIG and OGI, index; Preisigke, Namenbuch; s. Denis 18d, p. 217ff; Joseph.) ***Aristobulus;*** οἱ ἐκ τῶν Ἀριστοβούλου *those who belong to (the household of) A.* **Ro 16:10.**—PFeine, Die Abfassung d. Phil. in Ephesus 1916, 128–30.—M-M.

ἄριστον, ου, τό (s. ἀριστάω) in early Gk. meal eaten early in the day (later called ἀκράτισμα, from the custom of dipping bread in wine), then the noon meal.

❶ ***breakfast*** (so Hom. et al.; GDI 5495, 45 [Ionic]; POxy 519, 17; 736, 28; PTebt 116, 36; Sus 13 Theod., cp. 12 LXX) **Lk 14:12** differentiated fr. δεῖπνον (as Polyaenus 4, 3, 32 ἄριστον κ. δεῖπνον; Jos., Ant. 8, 356).

❷ ***noon meal*** (Thu. 4, 90, 3; 7, 81, 1; Athen. 1, 9, 10, 11b δεῖπνον μεσημβρινόν, cp. 2 Km 24:15; Tob 2:1; JosAs 3:3; Demetr.: 722 fgm. 1, 14 Jac.; Jos., Ant. 5, 190) **Mt 22:4** and *meal* gener. (PTebt 120, 82 [I BC]; Tob 12:13; Bel 34; 37; ViHab 7 [p. 86, 10 Sch.]; Jos., Ant. 2, 2) **Lk 11:38; 14:15 v.l.**—In both mngs. loanw. in rabb.—B. 354. DELG. M-M.

Ἀρκαδία, ας, ἡ (Hom. et al.; ins) ***Arcadia,*** a province in the interior of the Peloponnesus in Greece, to which Hermas was taken in a vision Hs 9, 1, 4 (on the text s. Joly 289–91, n. 6).—Rtzst., Poim. 33; MDibelius, Harnack-Ehrung 1921, 116; Hdb. ad loc.

ἀρκετός, ή, όν (B-D-F §187, 8; 405, 2; Rob. 80) ***enough, sufficient, adequate*** (s. ἀρκέω; Chrysippus Tyanensis [I AD] in Athen. 3, 79, 113b; Vett. Val. 304, 25; Herm. Wr.: fgm. 23, 14, in Stob. I 49, 44=p. 464, 18 Sc.; Anth. Pal. 4, 18, 10 ἀρκετὸν οἴνῳ αἴθεσθαι κραδίην; BGU 33, 5; 531 II, 24 [I AD]; 33, 5; Kaibel, p. xii: praefatio, 288c, 10; Dt 25:2 Aq.; TestJob 24:6; Jos., Bell. 3, 130) τίς ἀ. ἐξειπεῖν; *who is in a position to declare?* 1 Cl 49:3. τινί *for someone* or *someth.* w. inf. foll. ἀ. (v.l. ἡμῖν or ὑμῖν) ὁ παρεληλυθὼς χρόνος . . . κατειργάσθαι **1 Pt 4:3.** ἀρκετὴ σοι ἡ ὑπόμνησις αὕτη *this reminder is enough for you* Hv 3, 8, 9. τὴν αὐτάρκειαν τὴν ἀ. σοι *an adequate competence* Hs 1:6. ἀρκετὸν (B-D-F §131) τῇ ἡμέρᾳ ἡ κακία αὐτῆς **Mt 6:34** (s. κακία 3). W. ἵνα foll. (s. B-D-F §393, 2) ἀ. τῷ μαθητῇ *it is* (=must be) *enough for the disciple* **Mt 10:25.**—As a substantive τὸ ἀ. τ. τροφῆς *an adequate amount of food* Hv 3, 9, 3.—B. 927. DELG s.v. ἀρκέω. M-M.

ἀρκέω (s. ἀρκετός) fut. 3 sg. ἀρκέσει LXX; 1 aor. ἤρκεσα. Pass.: 1 fut. pl. ἀρκεσθησόμεθα **1 Ti 6:8.;** aor. 3 sg. ἠρκέσθη and ptc. ἀρκεσθείς LXX.

❶ act. ***be enough, sufficient, adequate*** (trag., Thu.+; pap; Num 11:22; 3 Km 8:27; Wsd 14:22; PsSol 16:12; TestSol 14:5; TestJos 7:6; Jos., Ant. 9, 266; Ath., R 65, 17 al.) ἀρκεῖ τινί τι *someth. is enough for someone* (Epict. 2, 19, 19; Jos., Ant. 13, 291) ἀ. σοι ἡ χάρις μου *my grace is sufficient for you* (=you need nothing more than my grace) **2 Cor 12:9.** ἀρκοῦσίν σοι αἱ ἀποκαλύψεις αὗται *these revelations are enough for you* Hv 3, 10, 8. μή ποτε οὐ μὴ ἀρκέσῃ (sc. τὸ ἔλαιον) ἡμῖν καὶ ὑμῖν *there may not be enough for us and you* **Mt 25:9.** διακοσίων δηναρίων ἄρτοι οὐκ ἀ. αὐτοῖς, ἵνα *loaves of bread worth 200* *denarii would not be enough* (for each one to have a bite) **J 6:7.** τὰ ἀρκοῦντα αὐτῷ *what was enough for him* Hs 5, 2, 9 (cp. PLond V, 1833, 4 τὸ ἀρκοῦν=a sufficient quantity).—Impers. (Ael. Aristid. 47, 23 K.=23 p. 451 D. and Vi. Aesopi W 64: ἀρκεῖ P.) ἀρκεῖ ἡμῖν *it is enough for us* **J 14:8** (cp. PLond III, 964, 13f p. 212, ἵνα ἀρκέσῃ ἡμῖν).

❷ pass. ἀρκέομαί τινι ***be satisfied/content w. someth.*** (Hdt., X. et al.; Epict., pap [Nägeli 55]; Pr 30:15; 2 Macc 5:15; 4 Macc 6:28; Jos., Ant. 12, 294; Ar., Just.) **1 Ti 6:8.** ἀρκεῖσθε τοῖς ὀψωνίοις ὑμῶν *be content w. your wages* **Lk 3:14.** ἀ. τοῖς παροῦσιν (this expr. in Democrit., fgm. 191 Diels; Teles 11, 5; 38, 10; 41, 12; Dio Cassius 38, 8 and 38; 56, 33; s. GGerhard, Phoinix v. Kolophon 1909, 56f) *be content w. what one has* **Hb 13:5;** τοῖς ἐφοδίοις τ. θεοῦ (or τ. Χριστοῦ) ἀ. *be satisfied w. the travel-allowance that God* (or Christ) *has given us* 1 Cl 2:1; τοῖς συμβίοις ἀ. *be content w. their husbands* IPol 5:1.—W. ἐπί τινι (PLond I, 45, 13 p. 36; UPZ 162 II, 18 [117 BC] οὐκ ἀρκεσθέντες δὲ ἐπὶ τῷ ἐνοικεῖν ἐν τ. ἐμῇ οἰκίᾳ; B-D-F §235, 2): μὴ ἀρκούμενος ἐπὶ τούτοις (i.e. λόγοις) *not being satisfied w. words* (opp. deeds; an ironical personality sketch in view of Gr-Rom. expectations of pers. of merit) **3J 10** (UPZ 19, 20 [165 BC] οὐκ ἀρκεσθεῖσα ἐπὶ τούτοις).—DELG. M-M. TW.

ἄρκος, ου, ὁ, ἡ (on this form, found also Heraclides, Pol. 38; Aelian, NA 1, 31; IG XIV, 1302, 1; 2325, 4; 2328, 5; 2334, 6; IDefixAudollent 249 [I AD]; Anth. Pal. 11, 231; LXX; Jos., Ant. 6, 183; TestSol 12:6 C; TestAbr A 19 p. 102, 13 [Stone p. 52]; TestJud 2:4; TestGad 1:3; Just., D. 22, 4 instead of ἄρκτος [Hom. et al.; Herm. Wr. 5, 4; Philo; SibOr 3, 26; Ath. 16, 1; Tat.] s. W-S. §5, 31; B-D-F §34, 4) ***a bear*** **Rv 13:2** (Da 7:5).—B. 186. DELG s.v. ἄρκτος. M-M s.v. ἄρκτος. TW.

ἀρκούντως adv. fr. pres. ptc. of ἀρκέω (Aeschyl., Thu. et al.; Jos., Ant. 13, 73) ***sufficiently*** ἀ. μανθάνειν Dg 4:6.

ἄρκτος s. ἄρκος.

ἅρμα, ατος, τό (Hom.+) **carriage—ⓐ** ***traveling-chariot*** (Dio Chrys. 64 [14], 20 and Ps.-Apollod. 3, 5, 7, 5 ἐφ' ἅρματος; Gen 41:43; 46:29; Jos., Ant. 8, 386 ἐφ' ἅρματος καθεζομένῳ) **Ac 8:28f, 38.**

ⓑ esp. ***war-chariot*** (X., Cyr. 6, 3, 8; Jos., Ant. 2, 324) **Rv 9:9** (cp. Jo 2:5); 1 Cl 51:5 (cp. Ex 14:23, 26, 28; 15:19).—DELG. M-M.

Ἁρμαγεδ(δ)ών (W-H. Ἅρ Μαγεδών; t.r. Ἀρμαγεδδών) indecl. ***Armageddon*** a mythical place-name, said to be Hebrew **Rv 16:16;** it has been identified w. Megiddo and Jerusalem, but its interpr. is beset w. difficulties that have not yet been surmounted. See comm., and JJeremias, ZNW 31, '32, 73–77; BViolet, ibid. 205f; CTorrey, HTR 31, '38, 237–50; JMichael, JTS 38, '37, 168–72; HKraft, TRu 38, '73, 81–98; MOberweis, Biblica 76, '95, 305–24.

ἁρμογή, ῆς, ἡ (s. ἁρμόζω; Polyb. et al.; POslo 13 II, 14f grammatical t.t.; Mel., P. 55, 405) ***joint*** in masonry, where one stone touches the others (Jos., Ant. 15, 399) Hv 3, 2, 6; 3, 5, 1f; s 9, 9, 7.—DELG s.v. ἅρμα.

ἁρμόζω fut. 3 sg. ἁρμόσει Eccl 17:7; 1 aor. ἥρμοσα, mid. ἡρμοσάμην. Pass.: 1 aor. ἡρμόσθην; pf. ἥρμοσμαι (s. ἁρμογή; Hom.+; on the spelling s. Crönert 135; 245).

❶ **to be appropriate as part of a whole, *fit, fit in*** intr. τινί *with someth.* (Diod. S. 23, 12, 1; PSI 442, 12 [III BC]; Jos., Bell. 3, 516; cp. C. Ap. 2, 188; Just., D. 67, 10) of stones in a building ἁ. τοῖς λοιποῖς *fit in w. the others* Hs 9, 7, 2; cp. v 3, 7, 6. For this ἁ. μετὰ τῶν λοιπῶν λίθων s 9, 7, 4; ἁ. εἴς τι *fit into someth.* v 3, 2, 8; 3, 6, 5; 3, 7, 5; s 9, 9, 3.

❷ **to bring into close association, *join*** trans. (Maximus Tyr. 15, 3a λίθους; Jos., Ant. 6, 189 a stone into a sling; φθόγγους Ath. 16, 2) τὶ εἴς τι Hs 9, 8, 4. Pass. Hv 3, 2, 6; s 9, 4, 2f; 9, 8, 5ff; 9, 9, 4; 9, 15, 4.—*Harmonize,* pass. *be harmonized* μετακόσμια ἁρμόζεται *are harmonized* Dg 12:9 (text uncertain, s. μετακόσμιος). τὰ πρὸς τ. πυρὰν ἡρμοσμένα ὄργανα *the material* (wood) or *instruments of wood prepared for the pyre* MPol 13:3 (cp. Just., D. 19, 6 ἁρμοσάμενος πρὸς τὸν λαόν; s. ὄργανον).—Of betrothal and marriage *join* or *give in marriage, betroth* (t.t. Pind., Hdt.+ [Nägeli 25]; Pr 19:14; Jos., Ant. 20, 140), mid. ἁρμόζεσθαι τ. θυγατέρα τινός *become engaged to someone's daughter* (cp. POxy 906, 7). The mid. is used for the act. in one isolated case (B-D-F §316, 1) ἡρμοσάμην ὑμᾶς ἑνὶ ἀνδρί *I betrothed you to one man* **2 Cor 11:2** (cp. Parthenius 6, 3; Philo, Leg. All. 2, 67 τὸν πιστόν, ᾧ τὴν Αἰθιόπισσαν αὐτὸς ὁ θεὸς ἡρμόσατο, Abr. 100; s. Mlt. 160).—Batey, NT Nuptial Imagery, '71.—DELG s.v. ἅρμα. M-M. Sv.

ἁρμός, οῦ, ὁ (s. ἁρμόζω; Soph., X. et al.; SIG 970, 9; 972, 106; Sir 27:2; ApcSed 11:8 p. 134, 21 Ja; EpArist 71; Jos., Ant. 1, 78 v.l.) ***joint*** (schol. on Nicander, Ther. 781; 4 Macc 10:5; TestZeb 2:5) **Hb 4:12.**—M-M.

ἄρνας s. ἀρήν.

ἀρνέομαι fut. ἀρνήσομαι; 1 aor. ἠρνησάμην (B-D-F §78; BGU 195, 22); pf. ἤρνημαι; mid.-pass. aor. inf. ἀρνηθῆναι (Just., D. 69, 4) (Hom.+).

❶ **to refuse consent to someth., *refuse, disdain*** (Hes., Works 408; Appian, Syr. 5 §19; Artem. 1, 78 p. 72, 26; 5, 9; Diog. L. 2, 115; 6, 36; Jos., Ant. 4, 86; 5, 236, Vi. 222) w. inf. foll. (Hdt. 6, 13, 2; Wsd 12:27; 17:9) ἠρνήσατο λέγεσθαι υἱός *he refused to be known as the son* **Hb 11:24** (JFeather, ET 43, '32, 423–25).

❷ **to state that someth. is not true, *deny*** (Hippol., Ref. 6, 42, 1; opp. ὁμολογεῖν=admit, say 'yes', as Diog. L. 6, 40; Jos., Ant. 6, 151; Did., Gen. 176, 14) w. ὅτι foll.: ἀ. ὅτι Ἰησ. οὐκ ἔστιν ὁ Χριστός **1J 2:22** (the neg. is redundant as Demosth. 9, 54 ἀ. ὡς οὐκ εἰσὶ τοιοῦτοι; Alciphron 4, 17, 4 v.l.). W. acc. τὶ *someth.* (Jos., Ant. 6, 151 τ. ἁμαρτίαν, Vi. 255) IMg 9:1. W. acc. and inf. foll. PtK 2 p. 14, 22. W. inf. foll. (Epict. 3, 24, 81; Wsd 16:16) ἠρνησάμην δεδωκέναι *I said that I had not given* (it) Hv 2, 4, 2. Abs. (SIG 780, 25; Gen 18:15) **Lk 8:45; J 1:20; Ac 4:16.**

❸ **to disclaim association with a pers. or event, *deny, repudiate, disown*** (verbally or nonverbally) w. acc. *someone* (Appian, Bell. Civ. 2, 39 §154 ἀρνούμενοι τὸν Δύρραχον) or *someth.,* or abs., with obj. supplied fr. the context; usu. of backsliders.

ⓐ of repudiating Moses **Ac 7:35**

ⓑ of repudiating Christ ἀ. με ἔμπροσθεν τ. ἀνθρώπων **Mt 10:33a; Lk 12:9;** ἀ. (αὐτὸν) κατὰ πρόσωπον Πιλάτου **Ac 3:13;** cp. vs. **14;** ἀ. τὸν κύριον Hv 2, 2, 8; s 9, 26, 6; 9, 28, 8; Dg 7:7. τὸν Ἰησοῦν 2 Cl 17:7; cp. 3:1. Ἰησοῦν Χριστόν **Jd 4.** τὸν υἱόν **1J 2:23.** τὸν δεσπότην (s. below c) **2 Pt 2:1;** cp. ISm 5:1. Of Peter's denial (MGoguel, Did Peter Deny His Lord? HTR 25, '32, 1–27) **Mt 26:70, 72; Mk 14:68, 70; Lk 22:57; J 13:38; 18:25, 27.** ἀ. τὴν ζωήν = τὸν Χριστόν Hv 2, 2, 7. Without obj. **2 Ti 2:12a;** Hv 2, 3, 4; s 9, 26, 5; 9, 28, 4 and 7; MPol 9:2.

ⓒ of repudiating God (Aesop, Fab. 323 P.=Babrius 152 Crus. τὸν πρότερόν σου δεσπότην [Apollo] ἠρνήσω) ἀ. θεὸν τοῖς ἔργοις *disown God by deeds* **Tit 1:16.** ἀ. τὸν πατέρα καὶ τ. υἱόν **1J 2:22.** μὴ θέλειν ἀ. θεόν Dg 10:7.

ⓓ of Christ's repudiation of pers. (cp. the Egypt. ins HTR 33, '40, 318 τοῦτον ἀπηρνήσαντο θεοί) **Mt 10:33b; 2 Ti 2:12b.**

ⓔ w. impers. obj. *refuse, reject, decline* someth. (Lycophron v. 348 γάμους=marriage; Himerius, Or. 18 [Ecl. 19], 2 the χάρις of a god, the gracious gift offered by the deity; 4 Macc 8:7; 10:15; Nägeli 23) ἀ. τὴν πίστιν *repudiate the* (Christian) *faith* **1 Ti 5:8; Rv 2:13.** τὸ ὄνομά μου **3:8.** τὸν νόμον Hs 8, 3, 7.

ⓕ of behavior that in effect repudiates one's standards for self-identity ἀ. ἑαυτόν *be untrue to oneself* **2 Ti 2:13.**

ⓖ gener. ἀ. ποικίλαις ἀρνήσεσι *deny in many different ways* Hs 8, 8, 4.

❹ **to refuse to pay any attention to, *disregard, renounce*** ἀ. ἑαυτόν *deny, disregard oneself*=act in a wholly selfless way **Lk 9:23** (s. ἀπαρνέομαι). ἀ. τὴν δύναμιν εὐσεβείας *deny the function of piety* (by contradictory conduct) **3:5.** τὴν ἀσέβειαν ἀ. *renounce impiety* **Tit 2:12.**—HRiesenfeld, The Mng. of the Verb ἀρνεῖσθαι: ConNeot 11, '47, 207–19; CMasson, Le reniement de Pierre: RHPR 37, '57, 24–35; MWilcox, NTS 17, '70/71, 426–36; s. lit. s.v. ἀπαρνέομαι.—B. 1269; 1273. DELG. EDNT. M-M. TW. Spicq. Sv.

ἄρνησις, εως, ἡ (s. ἀρνέομαι; Aeschyl.+; PCairZen 228, 8; Job 16:8 Aq.; Jos., Ant. 16, 216, C. Ap. 2, 276) ***repudiation, rejection*** (opp. ὁμολόγησις) Hs 9, 28, 7; 8, 8, 4 (s. ἀρνέομαι 3g). εἰς ἄ. τινα τρέπειν *bring someone to a denial* (of the person's faith) MPol 2:4.—EDNT. TW.

Ἀρνί, ὁ indecl. name (Ἀρνεί v.l.) ***Arni,*** in the genealogy of Jesus **Lk 3:33** (Ἀράμ t.r.).

ἀρνίον, ου, τό dim. of ἀρήν, but no longer felt to be such in NT times. (Lysias et al.; pap since III BC, e.g. BGU 377, 2; 7; PStras 24, 7f; PGen 68, 7; LXX [rare]; Philo, Leg. ad Gai. 362; Jos., Ant. 3, 221; 226; Just., D. 72, 2f; Mel., P. 63, 454 [both Jer 11:19]) **a sheep of any age, *sheep, lamb,*** in our lit. only in imagery: in Rv a designation of Christ **5:6, 8, 12f; 6:1, 16; 7:9f, 14, 17; 12:11; 13:8; 14:1, 4, 10; 15:3; 17:14; 19:7, 9; 21:9, 14, 22f, 27; 22:1, 3;** cp. the parody figure **13:11.** τὰ ἀ. (as πρόβατα elsewh.) of the Christian community **J 21:15.** As a type of weakness 2 Cl 5:2ff. Cp. Boll 45, 6; FSpitta, Streitfragen d. Gesch. Jesu 1907, 174; HWindisch, D. messian. Krieg 1909, 70; ELohmeyer, Hdb., exc. on Rv 5:6; THoltz, D. Christologie der Apokalypse, diss. Halle '59.—B. 159. DELG s.v. ἀρήν. M-M. TW.

ἀρνῶν s. ἀρήν.

ἆρον s. αἴρω.

ἀροτριάω fut. ἀροτριάσω LXX; 1 aor. 2 pl. ἠροτριάσατε Judg 14:18 [cod. B]; fut. pass. 3 sg. ἀροτριαθήσεται LXX (s. ἄροτρον; Theophr., HP 8, 6, 3 et al. [Nägeli 31]; PCairZen 729, 5; PPetr III, 31, 7 et al.; LXX; TestAbr A 10 p. 87, 21f [Stone p. 22]; Jos., Bell. 2, 113) ***to plow*** (w. ποιμαίνειν) **Lk 17:7.** ὀφείλει ἐπ᾽ ἐλπίδι ὁ ἀροτριῶν ἀροτριᾶν *the plowman should plow in hope* (of reaping a crop) **1 Cor 9:10**—DELG s.v. ἀρόω. M-M.

ἄροτρον, ου, τό (s. ἀροτριάω; Hom. et al.; PRein 17, 20; PFlor 134, 1; PStras 32, 3; LXX; Jos., Ant. 2, 84 al.) ***a plow*** ἐπιβάλλειν τ. χεῖρα ἐπ᾽ ἄ. *put one's hand to the plow* **Lk 9:62** (cp. Hes., Works 467 ἀρχόμενος ἀρότρου ἄκρον ἐχέτλης χειρὶ λαβών=when you begin the plowing take hold of the plowhandle).—B. 495. DELG s.v. ἀρόω. M-M.

ἁρπαγή, ῆς, ἡ (s. ἁρπάζω; since Solon 3, 13 AnthLG Diehl[3] [ἀφαρπαγῇ West]; Aeschyl.; ins, pap, LXX; TestAbr A 19 p. 102, 10 [Stone p. 52]; Test12Patr; GrBar 8:5; Jos., C. Ap. 2, 200; Tat. 37, 1; 39, 3; Ath., R. 76, 12)

❶ **the act of seizure, *robbery, plunder*** (Aeschyl.; Thu. 4, 104, 2; SIG 679, 85; BGU 871, 5; PLips 64, 53; 4 Macc 4:10; Jos., Ant. 5, 25; TestJud 23:3) of forcible confiscation of property in a persecution **Hb 10:34.** καθῆσθαι εἰς ἁρπαγήν *sit (waiting) for prey* B 10:10. Pl. *robberies* (Appian, Liby. 115 § 545; 1 Macc 13:34; GrBar 8:5) D 5:1; B 20:1.

❷ **the product of seizure, *what has been stolen, plunder*** (so trag.; Thu. 8, 62, 2; mostly LXX; Jos., Vi. 380) of cup and dish ἔσωθεν γέμουσιν ἐξ ἁρπαγῆς **Mt 23:25.** The Luke parallel refers not to the cup, but to the Pharisees themselves, so that ἁ. takes on mng. 3.

❸ **the inner state of mind that leads to seizure, *greediness, rapacity*** (w. πονηρία) **Lk 11:39** (X., Cyr. 5. 2, 17).—DELG s.v. ἁρπάζω. M-M. TW.

ἁρπαγμός, οῦ, ὁ (rare in nonbibl. Gk.; not found at all in the Gk. transl. of the OT; in our lit. only in **Phil 2:6**).

❶ **a violent seizure of property, *robbery*** (s. ἁρπάζω; Plut., Mor. 12a; Vett. Val. 122, 1; Phryn., Appar. Soph.: Anecd. Gr. I 36. Also Plut., Mor. 644a ἁρπασμός), which is next to impossible in **Phil 2:6** (W-S. §28, 3: the state of being equal w. God cannot be equated w. the act of robbery).

❷ As equal to ἅρπαγμα, **someth. to which one can claim or assert title by gripping or grasping, *someth. claimed*** w. change fr. abstr. to concr. (as θερισμός Rv 14:15, cp. J 4:35; ἱματισμός J 19:24). This mng. cannot be quoted fr. non-Christian lit., but is grammatically justifiable (Kühner-Bl. II p. 272; RLipsius, Hand-Comment. ad loc.). Christian exx. are Eus., In Luc. 6 (AMai, Nova Patrum Bibliotheca IV 165), where Peter regards death on the cross as ἁρπαγμός 'a prize to be grasped eagerly', and Cyrill. Alex., De Ador. 1, 25 (MPG, LXVIII 172c), Lot does not regard the angels' demand (Gen 19:15ff) as a ἁρπαγμός 'prize'.—Acc. to FVokes, on Phil 2:5–11 in Studia Evangelica 2, '64, 670–75, forms in -μα may approach -μος forms in mng., but not vice versa, cp. πορισμός 1 Ti 6:5 (for rejoinder s. RMartin, Carmen Christi '67, 137).

ⓐ If ἁρπαγμός approaches ἅρπαγμα in mng., it can be taken 'sensu malo' to mean ***booty, (a) grab*** (so for ἅρπαγμα LXX), and only the context and an understanding of Paul's thought in general can decide whether it means holding fast to someth. already obtained (ἁ.='res rapta'; so the Gk fathers, s. Lampe, s.v. B 1) or the appropriation to oneself of someth. that is sought after (ἁ.='res rapienda').

ⓑ But a good sense is also poss., ***a piece of good fortune, windfall, prize, gain*** (Heliod., 7, 11, 7; 7, 20, 2 [=ἕρμαιον]; 8, 7, 1; Plut., Mor. 330d; Nägeli 43f)=ἕρμαιον (Isid. Pelus., Ep. 4, 22); again it remains an open question whether the windfall has already been seized and is waiting to be used, or whether it has not yet been appropriated. In favor of the former is the contrast between Adam (implied as a dramatic foil) and his anxiety about death and equality w. God and Jesus' majestic freedom from such anxiety, with culmination in the ultimate vindication of Jesus, whose destiny contrasts with Adam's implied fate: οὐχ ἁρπαγμὸν ἡγήσατο τὸ εἶναι ἴσα θεῷ *did not consider equality w. God a prize to be tenaciously grasped.* (Cp. the fortunes of Zeus: Diod. S. 3, 61, 4–6.)

❸ Another, and less probable, mng. is (mystical) ***rapture,*** s. ἁρπάζω 2b and LHammerich, An Ancient Misunderstanding (Phil. 2:6 'robbery'), '66, who would translate the phrase 'considered that to be like God was no rapture'; a similar view was expressed by PFlorensky (1915), quoted in Dictionnaire de la Bible, Suppl. V, '57, col. 24 s.v. kénose.—LSaint-Paul, RB n.s. 8, 1911, 550ff (pretext, opportunity); WJaeger, Her. 50, 1915, 537–53 (w. further support, RHoover, HTR 64, '71, 95–119);

AJülicher, ZNW 17, 1916, 1–17; PSchmidt, PM 20, 1916, 171–86; HSchumacher, Christus in s. Präexistenz u. Kenose nach Phil 2:5–8, I 1914, II 1921; FLoofs, StKr 100, 1927/28, 1–102; ELohmeyer, Kyrios Jesus: SBHeidAk 1927/28, 4 Abh.; WFoerster, ZNW 29, 1930, 115–28; FKattenbusch, StKr 104, '32, 373–420; EBarnikol, Mensch u. Messias '32, Philipper 2, '32; KBornhäuser, NKZ 44, '33, 428–34; 453–62; SMowinckel, NorTT 40, '39, 208–11; AStephenson, CBQ 1, '39, 301–8; AFeuillet, Vivre et Penser, Sér. 2, '42, 61f; AFridrichsen: AKaritz Festschr. '46, 197ff; HAlmqvist, Plut. u. d. NT, '46, 117f; JHering, D. bibl. Grundlagen des Christl. Humanismus '46, 31f; AEhrhardt, JTS 46, '45, 49–51 (cp. Plut., Mor. 330d; Diod. S. 3, 61, 6); EKäsemann, ZTK 47, '50, 313–60; HKruse, Verbum Domini 27, '49, 355–60; 29, '51, 206–14; LBouyer, RSR 39, '51, 281–88; DGriffiths, ET 69, '57/58, 237–39; RMartin, Carmen Christi (Phil 2:5–11) '67, esp. 134–64; 320–39 (lit.). NWright, JTS 37, '86, 321–52; SVollenweider, NTS 45, '99, 413–33 (surveys of debate).—S. also s.v. κενόω 1b.—EDNT. DELG s.v. ἁρπάζω. M-M. TW. Sv.

ἁρπάζω fut. ἁρπάσω **J 10:28;** 1 aor. ἥρπασα; pf. 3 sg. ἥρπακεν Hos 6:1. Mid.: fut. ἁρπῶμαι LXX. Pass.: 2 fut. ἁρπαγήσομαι **1 Th 4:17;** 1 aor. ἡρπάσθην **Rv 12:5** (cp. Jos., Bell. 2, 69); 2 aor. ἡρπάγην **2 Cor 12:2, 4;** Wsd 4:11 (Jos., Ant. 6, 14; 12, 144; B-D-F § 71, 2) (s. ἁρπαγή; Hom.+) 'snatch, seize', i.e. take suddenly and vehemently, or take away in the sense of

❶ **to make off w. someone's property by attacking or seizing, *steal, carry off, drag away*** (so mostly LXX; En 102:9) τὶ *someth.* of wild animals (Gen 37:33; Ps 7:3; JosAs 12:10) **J 10:12** (X., Mem. 2, 7, 14); 1 Cl 35:11 (Ps 49:22). Of thieving people (SIG 1168, 111 [IV BC]; TestJob 18:1; Jos., Ant. 20, 214) τὰ σκεύη *his property* **Mt 12:29.** τὰ ἀλλότρια *other people's property* B 10:4.

❷ **to grab or seize suddenly so as to remove or gain control, *snatch/take away*—ⓐ** forcefully τινά *someone* (Appian, Bell. Civ. 4, 113 §474; Polyaenus 8, 34; Ps.-Apollod. 1, 5, 1, 1 of Persephone; Ps.-Callisth. 1, 24, 3; Judg 21:21; TestJob 39:1) ἁ. αὐτόν *take him away* **J 6:15** (cp. Jos., Bell. 4, 259, Ant. 19, 162; Philogonius, who ἐκ μέσης τ. ἀγορᾶς ἁρπασθείς was made a bishop [Chrysost. I p. 495d Montf.]; AcThom 165 [Aa II/2, 278, 5]); **Ac 23:25 v.l.** Of an arrest ἁ. τινὰ ἐκ μέσου αὐτῶν *take someone away fr. among them* **Ac 23:10.** Of seed already sown *tear out* **Mt 13:19.** ἁ. ἐκ τ. χειρός *snatch fr. the hand* (cp. 2 Km 23:21) **J 10:28f;** Hv 2, 1, 4. Of rescue from threatening danger (JosAs 12:8): ἐκ τοῦ πυρὸς ἁ. *snatch fr. the fire* **Jd 23.**

ⓑ in such a way that no resistance is offered (Herodian 1, 11, 5; Quint. Smyrn. 11, 291 [Aphrodite 'snatches away' Aeneas, who is in danger]; Wsd 4:11; ApcEsdr 5:7; ApcMos 37 εἰς τὴν Ἀχερουσίαν λίμνην; cp. ViEzk 15 [p. 75, 14 Sch.]; cp. Jos., Ant. 7, 113), esp. of the πνεῦμα κυρίου, which carries someone away **Ac 8:39** (v.l. has ἄγγελος κυρίου.—On the word πνεῦμα, which can signify either 'spirit' or 'wind', cp. Apollon. Rhod. 3, 1114, where ἀναρπάζειν is used of winds which transport a person from one place to another far away). Pass. ἁρπαγῆναι ἕως τρίτου οὐρανοῦ *be caught up to the third heaven* **2 Cor 12:2** (Hesych. Miles. [VI AD], Vir. Ill. c. 66 JFlach [1880]: Tribonian, a polytheist, says of Emperor Justinian ὅτι οὐκ ἀποθανεῖται, ἀλλὰ μετὰ σαρκὸς εἰς οὐρανοὺς ἁρπαγήσεται); ἁ. εἰς τ. παράδεισον vs. **4;** ἁ. ἐν νεφέλαις εἰς ἀέρα **1 Th 4:17;** ἁ. πρὸς τ. θεόν **Rv 12:5.**—The mng. of ἁ. τὴν βασιλείαν τ. οὐρανῶν **Mt 11:12** is difficult to determine; ἁ. beside βιάζειν (as Plut., Mor. 203c et al.; s. HAlmqvist, Plut. u. d. NT, '46, 38; 117f; s. βιάζω 1a) prob. means someth. like *seize* or *claim for oneself* (cp. X., An. 6, 5, 18; 6, 6, 6; Epict. 4, 7, 22; Plut., Mor. 81c; Iren. 1, 16, 2 [Harv. I 161, 9]; s. WKnox, HTR 41, '48, 237). Another possibility is *plunder* (Libanius, Or. 1 p. 147, 4 F. κώμας ἁ.; Polyaenus 8, 11 τ. πόλεως ἁρπαγή=plundering of the city).—Finally ἁ. τι *grasp something quickly, eagerly, with desire* (Musonius in Stob. 3, 7, 23 [III 315, 4 H.] ἅρπαζε τὸ καλῶς ἀποθνήσκειν; Aelian, NA 2, 50; Libanius, Declam. 4, 81 vol. V 281, 16 F. ἁ. τὴν δωρεάν).—B. 744. DELG. EDNT. M-M. TW. Sv.

ἅρπαξ, αγος (ἁρπάζω) adj. (Hes.+; X., LXX; TestBenj 11:1; Ar. 8:2; Just., A. II, 2, 16; Theoph. Ant. 1, 2 [p. 60, 27]; in a vice list).

❶ ***rapacious, ravenous*** of wolves (Gen 49:27) **Mt 7:15.**

❷ subst., ὁ ἅ. ***robber*** (Jos., Bell. 6, 203; PRossGeorg V, 22, 16); to differentiate it fr. λῃστής perh. better *swindler* or *rogue* (Dssm., LO 269, 4 [LAE 321, 1]; ἅρπαξ and λῃστής in juxtaposition: Artem. 4, 56) w. ἄδικοι, μοιχοί **Lk 18:11;** cp. **1 Cor 5:10f; 6:10; Tit 1:9 v.l.;** D 2:6.—DELG s.v. ἁρπάζω. M-M.

ἀρραβών, ῶνος, ὁ (Python, fgm. 1, 18 TGF et al.; Semit. loanw.; Hebr. עֵרָבוֹן Gen 38:17–20=ἀρραβών LXX; Lat. arra or arrabo [TLL II 633]. For the spelling ἀραβών s. W-S. § 5, 26 c; B-D-F §40; Thackeray 119; Dssm. NB 11 [BS 183–84]) legal and commercial t.t. (since Isaeus 8, 23 and Aristot., freq. ins, pap, ostraca [Nägeli 55; Preisigke, Fachw.]) **payment of part of a purchase price in advance, *first installment, deposit, down payment, pledge*** (s. Taubenschlag, Law², 408ff), which secures a legal claim to the article in question, or makes a contract valid (s. e.g. UPZ 67, 13 [153 BC]; PLond II, 143, 13 p. 204; PFay 91, 14; POxy 299, 2f; BGU 446, 5); in any case, ἀ. is a payment that obligates the contracting party to make further payments. It is also used fig. (Antiphanes Com. 123, 6 K.; Aristot., Pol. 1, 11 [1259a, 12]; Stob. IV 418, 13 H. ἔχειν ἀρραβῶνα τ. τέχνην τοῦ ζῆν) δοὺς τὸν ἀ. τοῦ πνεύματος ἐν ταῖς καρδίαις ἡμῶν *has deposited the first installment of the Spirit in our hearts* **2 Cor 1:22** (on association w. baptism: EDinkler, OCullmann Festschr. '62, 188f); cp. **5:5.** The Spirit is the *first installment* τῆς κληρονομίας **Eph 1:14.** Jesus Christ is ἀ. τῆς δικαιοσύνης ἡμῶν *pledge of our righteousness* Pol 8:1.—S. BAhern, CBQ 9, '47, 179–89.—DELG. New Docs 1, 83. M-M. TW.

ἄρραφος s. ἄραφος.

ἄρρην s. ἄρσην.

ἄρρητος, ον (cp. ῥῆμα; Hom.+; Sb 7600, 7; TestSol 8:7 D; JosAs 12:5 cod. A 27:2; GrBar ins 1; ApcZeph; Philo; Jos., Bell. 7, 262; Just., D. 127, 2 al.; Ath. 6, 1; Tat. 34, 3; for spelling B-D-F §11, 1)

❶ of someth. **that cannot be expressed, since it is beyond human powers, *inexpressible*** (Pla., Symp. 189b; Plut., Mor. 564f; Herm. Wr. 1, 31; PGM 13, 763 explains it: ἐν ἀνθρώπου στόματι λαληθῆναι οὐ δύναται).

❷ of someth. **that must not be expressed, since it is holy, *not to be spoken*** (since Eur., Bacch. 472; Hdt. 5, 83, 3; Thessalus [I AD] adjures Asclepius δι' ἀρρήτων ὀνομάτων: Cat. Cod. Astr. VIII/3, 137. Not infreq. on sacral ins [Nägeli 55]. PGM 3, 205; 12, 237; Vett. Val. 19, 1; Plut., Mor. 360f; Mesomedes in: Alex. Coll. p. 198, no. 36, 14=IAndrosIsis, Mesomedes p. 145 ln. 14; Philo, Det. Pot. Ins. 175) ἄ. ῥήματα *words too sacred to tell* **2 Cor 12:4** (cp. Lucian, Epigr. 11).—DELG s.v. 2 εἴρω. M-M. TW.

ἀρρωστέω (s. ῥώννυμι; since Heraclit. 58; ins, pap; Sir 18:21; Jos., Ant. 10, 221, C. Ap. 1, 136; Test12Patr) ***be ill, sick***

Mt 14:14 D (οἱ ἀρρωστοῦντες as Diod. S. 14, 71, 4).—DELG s.v. ῥώννυμι. M-M. s.v. ἄρρωστος.

ἄρρωστος, ον (s. ἀρρωστέω; for spelling B-D-F §11, 1) ***sick, ill,*** lit. powerless (so Hippocr.+; SIG[2] 858, 17; restored in PEdgar 4, 5=PCairZen 18, 5=Sb 6710 [259/258 BC]; Sir 7:35; Mal 1:8; Jos., Bell. 5, 526) **1 Cor 11:30** (w. ἀσθενής).—**Mt 14:14; Mk 6:5, 13; 16:18.**—B. 298; 302. DELG s.v. ῥώννυμι. M-M.

ἀρσενικός, ή, όν (s. ἄρσην; Callim., Epigr. 25; PLille 1, 10 [III BC]; POxy 38, 7; PGM 4, 2519; oft. LXX; TestSol 1:7; TestJob 53:1 [ἀρρ-]; ApcMos 15) ***male*** φρονεῖν τι ἀ. περί τινος *think anything male about someone*='think of someone as a male' (with emphasis on sexuality) w. a female as subj. 2 Cl 12:5.—DELG s.v. ἄρσην.

ἀρσενόθηλυς, ὁ (ἄρσην + θῆλυς; Orphic Fragments 56 Kern; Porphyr. in Eus., PE 3, 11; Manetho 5, 140; cp. Diod. S. 8 fgm. 23; also ἀρρενόθηλυς) **a pers. of both sexes, *hermaphrodite*** ἀπεκόπη γάρ, φησίν, ὁ Ἄττις, τοῦτ' ἔστιν ἀπὸ τῶν χοϊκῶν τῆς κτίσεως κάτωθεν μερῶν, καὶ ἐπὶ τὴν αἰωνίαν ἄνω μετελήλυθεν οὐσίαν, ὅπου, φησίν, 'οὐκ ἔστιν οὔτε θῆλυ οὔτε ἄρσεν', ἀλλὰ καινὴ κτίσις, 'καινὸς ἄνθρωπος', ὅ ἐστιν ἀρσενόθηλυς=for, says the Naassene, Attis has been emasculated, that is, has moved from the earthly elements of the world below to the eternal substance above, where, the N. says, 'there is neither male nor female', but a new creation, 'a new human being', that is, a hermaphrodite GNaass 252, 59f.—DELG s.v. ἄρσην.

ἀρσενοκοίτης, ου, ὁ (ἄρσην 'male' + κοίτη 'bed'; Bardesanes 719 fgm. 3b 10, 25 p. 653 Jac. [in Eus., PE 6, 10, 25]; Anth. Pal. 9, 686, 5 and Cat. Cod. Astr. VIII/4 p. 196, 6 and 8 have the sp. ἀρρενοκοίτης; Theoph. Ant. 1, 2 [p. 60, 27]; in a vice list—ἀρσενοκοιτεῖν SibOr 2, 73; AcJ 36 [Aa II/1, 169]; cp. the association of ἄρσην and κοίτη Lev 20:13, s. Soph. Lex.: ἀ.= ὁ μετὰ ἄρσενος κοιμώμενος κοίτην γυναικείαν='one who has intercourse w. a man as w. a woman'; cp. the formation of μητροκοίτης [μήτηρ + κοίτη] 'one who has intercourse w. his mother' Hipponax 15, 2 Diehl[3] [=Degani 20, 2]) **a male who engages in sexual activity w. a pers. of his own sex, *pederast* 1 Cor 6:9** (on the impropriety of RSV's 'homosexuals' [altered to 'sodomites' NRSV] s. WPetersen, VigChr 40, '86, 187–91; cp. DWright, ibid. 41, '87, 396–98; REB's rendering of μαλακοὶ οὔτε ἀρσενοκοῖται w. the single term 'sexual pervert' is lexically unacceptable), of one who assumes the dominant role in same-sex activity, opp. μαλακός (difft. DMartin, in Biblical Ethics and Homosexuality, ed. RBrawley, '96, 117–36); **1 Ti 1:10;** Pol 5:3. Cp. Ro 1:27. Romans forbade pederasty w. free boys in the Lex Scantinia, pre-Cicero (JBremmer, Arethusa 13, '80, 288 and notes); Paul's strictures against same-sex activity cannot be satisfactorily explained on the basis of alleged temple prostitution (on its rarity, but w. some evidence concerning women used for sacred prostitution at Corinth s. LWoodbury, TAPA 108, '78, 290f, esp. note 18 [lit.]), or limited to contract w. boys for homoerotic service (s. Wright, VigChr 38, '84, 125–53). For condemnation of the practice in the Euphrates region s. the ref. to Bardesanes above.—RBurton, The Book of the Thousand Nights and a Night, 1934, vol. 6, 3748–82, lit. reff. and anthropological data relating to a variety of Mediterranean cultures; DBailey, Homosexuality and the Western Christian Tradition, '55; KDover, Greek Homosexuality '78; RScroggs, The NT and Homosexuality '83; JBoswell, Christianity, Social Tolerance, and Homosexuality '80; JBremmer, Greek Pederasty, in JBremmer, ed. From Sappho to de Sade[2] '91, 1–14; ECantarella, Bisexuality in the Ancient World '92.—Pauly-W. 8, 1333f; 1459–68. DELG s.v. ἄρσην. M-M.

ἄρσην, εν, gen. **ενος** (Hom.+; SIG 1033; 1044, 3; 13; PSI 569, 6; 7 [III BC]; PGM 15, 18; LXX; TestSol 1:7 B; TestJob [ἀρρ-]; TestJos 3:7; JosAs 2:11; ParJer 8:3; EpArist 152; SibOr 3, 133; Ath. 20, 2; 22, 5; 34, 1; Just., D. 88, 1. The Attic form ἄρρην appears in **Ac 7:19 v.l.; Ro 1:27a v.l.; 1:27ab** Tdf., S. [but the last reads ἄρσεσιν for the third occurrence]; **Rv 12:5 v.l., 13 v.l.,** S., Vog.; oft. pap, also Philo, Joseph., TestJob, TestJos; JosAs 2:11; Ar. 8:2; Just.; Ath. 22:4, R. 76, 20; Mel., P. 53, 392; GEg 252, 57; B 10:7. See W-S. §5, 27b; B-D-F §34, 2; Mlt-H. 103f) ***male*** (opp. θῆλυς, as Pla., Leg. 2, 9 p. 665c; PGM 15, 18) subst. τὸ ἄ. W. strong emphasis on the sex (syn. ἀνήρ 'man', s. ἀρσενοκοίτης) *males* **Ro 1:27abc** (cp. Demetr.: 722 fgm. 1, 9 Jac.; Jos., C. Ap. 2, 199). ἄρσεν καὶ θῆλυ ἐποίησεν αὐτούς *God created them male and female* (Gen 1:27; cp. PGM 5, 105) **Mt 19:4; Mk 10:6;** 1 Cl 33:5; 2 Cl 14:2. οὐκ ἔνι ἄρσεν καὶ θῆλυ **Gal 3:28;** cp. GEg 252, 57; 2 Cl 12:2, 5; GNaass 252, 60 (s. ἀρσενόθηλυς); πᾶν ἄρσεν **Lk 2:23.** The masc. as subst. εἴτε ἄρσενα εἴτε θήλειαν *a son or a daughter* GJs 4:1. The neut. ἄρσεν **Rv 12:5,** difft. vs. **13,** comes fr. Is 66:7 and is in apposition to υἱόν. On the juxtaposition s. FBoll, ZNW 15, 1914, 253; BOlsson, Glotta 23, '34, 112.—Cp. ἄνθρωπος. Schmidt, Syn. II 385–95. B. 84. DELG. M-M.

Ἀρτεμᾶς, ᾶ, ὁ (CLobeck, Pathologiae Sermonis Graeci Prolegomena 1843, 505f; SIG 851, 16; IMagnMai 122d, 13; BGU 1205, 25 [28 BC]; POxy 745, 2 [1 AD]) ***Artemas,*** a friend of Paul (short for Ἀρτεμίδωρος W-S. §16, 9; B-D-F §125, 1) **Tit 3:12.**

Ἄρτεμις, ιδος, ἡ (Hom. et al.) *Artemis,* a deity whose worship was widespread (Diana is her Roman name; on the association, s. esp. Catullus 34). The center of her worship in Asia Minor was at Ephesus (DHogarth, Excav. at Eph. The Archaic Artemisia, 1908; CPicard, Ephèse et Claros 1922.—Jos., Ant. 15, 89; SibOr 5, 293; Ath. 17:3; Tat. 3:1) **Ac 19:24, 27f, 34f.** As here, A. is called 'The Great' in the lit. (X. Eph. 1, 11, 5) and in ins fr. Ephesus (CIG 2963c, 10; τῇ μεγίστῃ θεᾷ Ἐφεσίᾳ Ἀρτέμιδι IBM III, 481, 324f; JWood, Discoveries at Ephesus 1877 app., Ins. fr. the Theater no. 1 col. 1, 9; 4, 48) and elsewh. (IG XII/2, 270 and 514; cp. PGM 4, 2720–22). S. BMüller, ΜΕΓΑΣ ΘΕΟΣ 1913, 331–33.—Jessen, Ephesia: Pauly-W. V 1905, 2753–71; AWikenhauser, comm. Ac 1921, 363–67; JdeJongh, Jr., De tempel te Ephese en het beeld van Diana: GereformTT 26, 1926, 461–75; LTaylor, Beginn. V, '33, 251–56; HThiersch, Artemis Ephesia I: AGG III 12, '35; Haenchen, ad loc.; Kl. Pauly I 6118–25; ROster, The Ephesian Artemis as an Opponent of Early Christianity: JAC 19, '76, 24–44; PScherrer, JÖAI 60, '90, 87–101; RStrelan, Paul, Artemis, and the Jews in Ephesus: BZNW 80, '96; s. also HEngelmann, ZPE 97, '93 279–89 on the imperial cult; EDNT I 158. DDD 168–80. S. on Ἔφεσος.—DELG.

Ἀρτεμύλλα, ας ***Artemilla,*** wife of the governor in Ephesus AcPl Ha 2, 12 al. (mentioned 12 times).

ἀρτέμων, ωνος, ὁ (etym. uncertain) prob. ***foresail*** (Fr. 'voile d'artimon') ἐπαίρειν τὸν ἀ. *hoist the foresail* (cp. Plut., Mor. 870b ἐπαιρόμενος τὰ ἱστία) **Ac 27:40.** S. Breusing 79f; HBalmer, D. Romfahrt d. Ap. Pls. 1905; LCasson, Ships and Seamanship, '71, 240, n. 70; Hemer, Acts 151 n. 145; Haenchen, ad loc.—DELG. M-M.

Ἀρτέμων, ωνος name since VI BC (Anacr. fgm. 14, 1 [Diehl = 27, 2 Page]; also name of a dissident Eus., HE 5, 28, 1) ***Artemon,*** captain of the ship carrying Paul to Italy AcPl Ha 7, 19;

22;37; 8, 4 restored. The choice of this name may have been influenced by the term ἀρτέμων **Ac 27:40.**

ἀρτηρία, ας, ἡ (Soph., Hippocr. et al.; Philo) *artery* MPol 2:2.—DELG s.v. 2 ἀείρω.

ἄρτι temp. adv. (Pind.+) of the immediate moment—❶ as class. (Phryn. p. 18 Lob.; 2 Macc 3:28), **ref. to the immediate past,** ***just (now)*** (Dio Chrys. 4, 61; Ael. Aristid. 48, 35 K.=24 p. 474 D.; Appian, Hann. 51 §219) ἄ. ἐτελεύτησεν *she has just died* **Mt 9:18.** ἄ. ἐγένετο ἡ σωτηρία *salvation has just now come* **Rv 12:10.**—GHb 20, 60; GMary 463, 20.

❷ also as class., **ref. to the immediate present,** ***at once, immediately, now*** (cp. Hippocr., Ep. 9, 2; Lucian, Soloec. 1, 553; Jdth 9:1; 2 Macc 10:28) παραστήσει μοι ἄ. *at once he will put at my disposal* **Mt 26:53;** ἀκολουθεῖν ἄ. *follow immediately* **J 13:37;** ἄφες ἄ. *let it be so now* (on the position of ἄ. s. B-D-F §474, 3) **Mt 3:15.**

❸ later Gk. uses ἄ. as **ref. to the present in general,** ***now, at the present time*** (Jos., Ant. 1, 125 alternating w. νῦν; 15, 18; Epict. 2, 17, 15; PMich 203, 10; BGU 294, 5; PLond III, 937b, 9f p. 213 οὐ δύναμαι ἄρτι ἐλθεῖν πρὸς σέ) ἄ. βλέπει *now he can see* **J 9:19, 25;** cp. **13:7, 33** (πλὴν ἄρτι P^{66}); **16:12, 31; 1 Cor 13:12; 16:7; Gal 1:9f; 4:20; 1 Th 3:6; 2 Th 2:7; 1 Pt 1:6, 8;** 2 Cl 17:3. After an aor. Hs 5, 5, 1.—Used w. prep. ἀπ᾽ ἄρτι *fr. now on* (Plato Com., fgm. 143 K. ἀπαρτί for ἄρτι ἀπὸ νῦν [but s. L-S-J-M s.v. ἀπαρτί end]) ἀπ᾽ ἄ. λέγω **J 13:19;** ἀπ᾽ ἄ. γινώσκετε **14:7;** ἀποθνήσκοντες ἀπ᾽ ἄ. **Rv 14:13** (see s.v. ἀπαρτί and B-D-F §12); w. fut. (Aristoph., Plut. 388 ἀπαρτὶ πλουτῆσαι ποιήσω) ἀπ᾽ ἄ. ὄψεσθε **Mt 26:64; J 1:51 v.l.;** ἀπ᾽ ἄ. ἕως . . . **Mt 23:39; 26:29;** ἕως ἄ. *up to the present time, until now* (POxy 936, 23; Sb 4630, 3; 7036, 4; ApcSed 11:14) **Mt 11:12; J 2:10; 5:17** (SBacchiocci, Andrews U. Seminary Studies 19, '81, 3–19 ['culmination' of God's activity]); **16:24; 1 Cor 4:13; 8:7; 15:6; 1J 2:9.**—In attributive position ἄ. has adj. mng. as in older Gk. (Pla., Tht. 153e; Jos., Ant. 9, 264 ὁ ἄ. βίος) ἄχρι τῆς ἄ. ὥρας *up to the present moment* **1 Cor 4:11** (cp. PGM 4, 1469 ἐν τῇ ἄ. ὥρᾳ; 1581; 1935; 5, 195; 7, 373; 546). μέχρι τῆς ἄρτι ὥρας **Ac 10:30** D. Nägeli 36, 1.—DELG. M-M. TW.

ἀρτιγέννητος, ον (s. ἄρτι, γεννητός; Lucian, Alex. 13; Longus 1, 9, 1; 2, 4, 3) ***newborn*** βρέφη infants **1 Pt 2:2** (Lucian, Dial. Marit. 12, 1 βρέφος ἀρτιγέννητον; cp. Sallustius 4 p. 8, 24 N.=FPhGr III, 33, col. 2, 6 γάλακτος τροφή, ὥσπερ ἀναγεννωμένων).—RPerdelwitz, D. Mysterienrel. u. d. Problem d. 1 Pt 1911, 16ff; WBornemann, 1 Pt e. Taufrede d. Silvanus: ZNW 19, 1920, 143–65.—M-M. TW.

ἄρτιος, ία, ον (Hom.+; Epict. 1, 28, 3; IG XIV, 889, 7 ἄ. εἴς τι; TestAbr A 8 p. 85, 12 [Stone p. 18]; Ath., R. 77, 4 ἀρτίως; Philo) **pert. to being well fitted for some function,** ***complete, capable, proficient***=able to meet all demands **2 Ti 3:17.**—DELG s.v. ἄρτι. M-M. TW.

ἄρτος, ου, ὁ (Hom.+)—❶ **a baked product produced fr. a cereal grain,** ***bread*** also ***loaf of bread***—ⓐ gener. (Did., Gen. 190, 25) **Mt 4:4** (Dt 8:3); **14:17, 19; 15:26, 33f; 16:8ff; Mk 6:38, 44, 52** (QQuesnell, The Mind of Mark, '69); **7:27; 8:4ff, 14** (JManek, NovT 7, '64, 10–14), **16f; Lk 4:4** (Dt 8:3); **9:13; 11:5; J 6:5, 23, 26; 21:9; 2 Cor 9:10** (Is 55:10). Opp. λίθος **Mt 4:3** and **Lk 4:3** (Ps.-Clem., Hom. 2, 32 Simon Mag. ἐκ λίθων ἄρτους ποιεῖ); **Mt 7:9; Lk 11:11 v.l.** W. water (Dt 9:9, 18; Sir 29:21; Hos 2:7) Hs 5, 3, 7. The father of the household opened a meal (s. Billerb. IV 620ff) by taking a loaf of bread, giving thanks, breaking it, and distributing it: λαμβάνειν τὸν ἄ., (κατα)κλάσαι τὸν ἄ. (Jer 16:7) **Mt 14:19; 15:36; Mk 6:41; 8:19; Lk 9:16; 24:30; J 6:11; 21:13; Ac 20:11; 27:35.** Cp. **Lk 24:35; Ac 2:42, 46; 20:7.** Usu. taken along on journeys **Mk 6:8; Lk 9:3;** cp. **Mt 16:5, 7; Mk 8:14.** W. gen. of price διακοσίων δηναρίων ἄρτοι **J 6:7; Mk 6:37.** ἄρτοι κρίθινοι (Judg 7:13; 4 Km 4:42) *loaves of barley bread* **J 6:9, 13.** The martyr's body in the fire is compared to baking bread MPol 15:2.—Dalman, Arbeit IV: Brot, Öl u. Wein '35.

ⓑ of a bread-offering ἄρτοι τῆς προθέσεως (Ex 40:23; 1 Km 21:7; 1 Ch 9:32; 23:29; 2 Ch 4:19; cp. 2 Ch 13:11; 2 Macc 10:3; Dssm. B 155f [BS 157]. Cp. OGI 56, 73; UPZ 149, 21 [III BC] πρόθεσις τ. ἄρτων in a temple ln. 31) *consecrated bread* (Billerb. III 719–33) **Mt 12:4; Mk 2:26; Lk 6:4; Hb 9:2.**—S. πρόθεσις.

ⓒ of the bread of the eucharist, which likew. was broken after giving thanks, and then eaten (Orig., C. Cels. 8, 33, 25) **Mt 26:26; Mk 14:22; Lk 22:19;** perh. **Ac 2:42, 46; 20:7; 1 Cor 10:16f** (the acc. τὸν ἄρτον vs. **16** is by attraction to the rel. ὅν; cp. Gen 31:16); **11:23, 26ff;** D 14:1; IEph 20:2; AcPl Ha 4, 4 (s. κλάω, κατακλάω, εὐχαριστέω 2, εὐχαριστία 3 and Aberciusins. 16.—Diog. L. 8, 35: acc. to Pythagoras the εἷς ἄρτος [1 Cor 10:17] has served as a symbol of the union of the φίλοι from time immemorial to the present. Partaking of the same bread and wine [τ. αὐτὸν ἄρτον, οἶνον] as proof of the most intimate communion: Theodor. Prodr. 8, 400ff H.; Herodas 4, 93f: in the temple of Asclepius those who offer a sacrifice—in this case women—receive consecrated bread called ὑγιή [ὑγίεια] to eat; Athen. 3, 115a ὑγίεια καλεῖται ἡ διδομένη ἐν ταῖς θυσίαις μᾶζα ἵνα ἀπογεύσωνται=the barley-cake that is given everyone to taste at the sacrifices is called Health; Anecd. Gr. 313, 13).—PdeBoer, Divine Bread, Studies in the Rel. of Anc. Israel, '72, 27–36. S. καλάσις 2.

❷ **any kind of food or nourishment,** ***food*** gener. (since bread is the most important food; cp. לֶחֶם e.g. Is 65:25; Am 8:11; 4 [6] Esdr [POxy 1010]) περισσεύεσθαι ἄρτων *have more than enough bread,* i.e. *plenty to eat* **Lk 15:17** (cp. Pr 20:13). διαθρύπτειν πεινῶσι τὸν ἄ. *break bread for the hungry,* i.e. give them someth. to eat B 3:3, cp. 5 (Is 58:7, 10). Hence ἄ. ἐσθίειν *eat, dine, eat a meal* (Gen 37:25; 2 Km 12:20; Eccl 9:7; Orig., C. Cels 7, 28, 43; cp. Did., Gen. 190, 12) **Mt 15:2; Mk 3:20; 7:2, 5; Lk 14:1.** δωρεὰν ἄ. φαγεῖν παρά τινος *eat someone's bread without paying* **2 Th 3:8.** Opp. τὸν ἑαυτοῦ ἄρτον ἐσθίειν vs. **12.** Of an ascetic way of life μὴ ἐσθίων ἄρτον μήτε πίνων οἶνον *neither eating bread nor drinking wine,* i.e. fasting **Lk 7:33** (cp. 1 Esdr 9:2). On ἄ. ἐπιούσιος **Mt 6:11; Lk 11:3;** D 8:2 s. ἐπιούσιος.—τρώγειν τινὸς τὸν ἄ. *be the guest of someone* **J 13:18** (cp. Ps 40:10). Since according to a concept widespread among Israelites and gentiles, eternal bliss was to be enjoyed in the form of a banquet, φαγεῖν ἄ. ἐν τῇ βασιλείᾳ τοῦ θεοῦ=share eternal bliss, or salvation **Lk 14:15.**—In J ἄ. ἐκ τ. οὐρανοῦ (after Ps 77:24; cp. Ex 16:4; 2 Esdr 19:15; Ps 104:40; Wsd 16:20; SibOr fgm. 3, 49) is Christ and his body in the Eucharist **J 6:31ff, 41, 50, 58** or simply Christ himself. For this ἄ. τῆς ζωῆς (JosAs 8:5; 15:4) vs. **35, 48;** ὁ ἄ. ὁ ζῶν vs. **51.** Sim. ἄ. τ. θεοῦ IEph 5:2; IRo 7:3; ἄ. τ. Χριστοῦ 4:1.—BGärtner, J 6 and the Jewish Passover: ConNeot 17, '59; GVermes, MBlack Festschr., '69, 256–63.

❸ **means of support,** ***support, livelihood*** τὸν ἄ. λαμβάνειν *take his bread* (i.e. support) D 11:6 (difft. Orig., C. Cels. 2, 68, 20: 'take bread [from someone's hand]').

❹ **reward for labor,** ***reward, proceeds*** λαμβάνειν τὸν ἄ. τοῦ ἔργου *receive the reward of (one's) labor* 1 Cl 34:1.—EBattaglia, 'Artos', il lessico della panificazione nei paperi greci '89.—B. 357. DELG. EDNT. M-M. TW.

ἀρτύω fut. ἀρτύσω. Pass.: fut. ἀρτυθήσομαι; pf. ἤρτυμαι (Hom.+; Polyb 15, 25, 2; Jos., Bell. 2, 614) gener. 'prepare' w. connotation of skillful use of material. Of food preparation **to add condiments to someth.,** ***season*** (Hippocr.; Aristot., EN 3, 13 p. 1118a, 29 τὰ ὄψα; Theophr., De Odor. 51 [fgm. 4, 11] ἠρτυμένος οἶνος, cp. SSol 8:2 Sym.; Athen. 3, 79, 113b; PTebt 375, 27; POxy 1454, 4) lit. *season, salt* **Mk 9:50; Lk 14:34** (JWackernagel, TLZ 33, 1908, 36). Fig., λόγος ἅλατι ἠρτυμένος *speech seasoned w. salt* to make it interesting and fruitful **Col 4:6** (s. MDibelius, Hdb. ad loc.).—DELG s.v. ἀραρίσκω. M-M.

Ἀρφαξάδ, ὁ indecl. (אַרְפַּכְשַׁד), in Jos., Ant. 1, 146 Ἀρφαξάδης, ου, ***Arphaxad,*** son of Shem (Gen 10:22, 24), in genealogy of Jesus **Lk 3:36.**

ἀρχ- On ἀρχ- formations s. New Docs 2, 18f; also M-M. s.v. ἀρχι-.

ἀρχάγγελος, ου, ὁ (s. ἀρχή, ἄγγελος; En 20:8; TestSol; TestAbr A B; TestLevi 3:5 v.l.; ParJer 9:5; GrBar; ApcEsdr 1:3 p. 24, 7 Tdf.; ApcSed 14:1 p. 135, 33 Ja.; ApcMos; AssMos fgm. k; Philo, Confus. Lingu. 146, Rer. Div. Her. 205, Somn. 1, 157; Porphyr., Ep. ad Anebonem [GParthey, Iambl. De Myst. Lib. 1857 p. xxix–xlv] c. 10; cp. Iambl., Myst. 2, 3 p. 70, 10; Theologumena Arithmetica ed. VdeFalco 1922, p. 57, 7; Agathias: Anth. Pal. 1, 36, 1; ins in Ramsay, CB I/2 557 no. 434 ὁ θεὸς τῶν ἀρχαγγέλων; Gnost. ins, CIG 2895; PGM 1, 208; 3, 339; 4, 1203; 2357; 3052; 7, 257 τῷ κυρίῳ μου τῷ ἀρχαγγέλῳ Μιχαήλ; 13, 257; 328; 744) **a member of the higher ranks in the celestial hierarchy,** ***chief angel, archangel*** PtK 2 p. 14, 27. Michael (En 20:5; 8; ParJer 9:5) is one of them **Jd 9.** He is also prob. the archangel who will appear at the last judgment **1 Th 4:16** (the anonymous sing. as PGM 4, 483, where the archangel appears as a helper of Helios Mithras).—See WLueken, D. Erzengel Michael 1898; Rtzst., Mysterienrel.[3] 171, 2; UHolzmeister, Verb. Dom. 23, '43, 176–86; s. on ἄγγελος.—DDD 149–53. M-M. TW.

ἀρχαῖος, αία, αῖον (s. ἀρχή; Pind., Hdt.+) adj.—**❶ pert. to what has existed from the beginning or for a long time, w. connotation of present existence,** ***old*** (Sir 9:10; 2 Macc 6:22) ὁ ὄφις ὁ ἀ. *the old/ancient serpent* **Rv 12:9; 20:2.** Of a Christian assembly βεβαιοτάτη καὶ ἀ. *old, established* 1 Cl 47:6; ἀ. μαθητής *a disciple of long standing* (perh. *original disc.*) **Ac 21:16** (cp. IMagnMai 215b, 3 [I AD] ἀρχαῖος μύστης; Thieme 26; Sir 9:10 φίλος ἀ.).

❷ pert. to what was in former times, long ago, ***ancient*** (Ps 78:8; 88:50; Sir 16:7; ViJer 14 [p. 73, 16 Sch.]; Jos., Ant. 9, 264) ἀ. ὑποδείγματα *examples from ancient times* 1 Cl 5:1; ἀ. κόσμος the world before the deluge **2 Pt 2:5.** Of ages past (Diod. S. 1, 6, 2) ἀφ' ἡμερῶν ἀ. (Is 37:26; La 1:7; 2:17) **Ac 15:7;** ἐκ γενεῶν ἀ. (Sir 2:10 εἰς ἀ. γενεάς; PsSol 18:12 ἀπὸ γενεῶν ἀ.) **15:21;** ἐξ ἀ. χρόνων (Sb 7172, 12 [217 BC]) Pol 1:2.—οἱ ἀρχαῖοι *the ancients, people of ancient times, of old* (Thu. 2, 16, 1; Cornutus p. 2, 18; 4, 9; Ps.-Demetr. c. 175 [here ἀρχαῖοι is used to intensify παλαιοί: very, very old = obs. Eng. 'primoprimitive']; Sir 39:1; 3 Km 5:10; Philo, Rer. Div. Her. 181 [w. ref. to Plato]; Jos., Ant. 7, 171) **Mt 5:21, 27 v.l.; 33** (grammatically, τοῖς ἀρχαίοις can mean *by the ancients* as well as *to the ancients;* since Hdt. 6, 123; Thu. 1, 51; 118 the dat. w. the passive often replaces ὑπό w. gen., esp. in later writers such as Polyb. and Arrian. Cp. Lk 23:15 πράσσω 1a). Of the ancient prophets (cp. Jos., Ant. 12, 413) **Lk 9:8, 19;** D 11:11 (cp. ἀ. ἀνήρ [=one of the earliest Christians] of Papias in Papias [1:4=Eus., HE 3, 39, 1]). τὰ ἀρχαῖα (Ps 138:5; Wsd 8:8; Is 43:18) *what is old* **2 Cor 5:17** (cp. τὸ ἀρχαῖον=the old, or earlier, state of things OGI 672, 9; Sb 5233, 17; Is 23:17).—B. 959. DELG s.v. ἄρχω E, 1 p. 121. M-M. TW.

ἀρχέγονος, ον 'primal, original' (Diod. S. 1, 4; Cornutus, ND 17; Philo, De Vita Cont. 2; PGM IV, 1459), in our lit. only as subst. (paroxytone 1Cl 59:3, s. Lghtf. ad loc.; Rob. 232f) ***original author, originator, source*** τινός *of someth.* (s. ἀρχή, γεννάω; Heraclit. Sto. 22 p. 32, 20 ἀ. ἁπάντων; Damoxenus 2:8 [in Athen. 3, 102a] ἡ φύσις ἀρχέγονον πάσης τέχνης; Cornutus 8 p. 8, 11 ἀ. πάντων; Proclus, Theol. 152 p. 134, 21 τῶν ὅλων ἀ.; PGM 4, 1459) of God's name τὸ ἀρχεγόνον πάσης κτίσεως 1 Cl 59:3.—DELG s.v. ἄρχω B, 2a p. 120.

ἀρχεῖον, ου, τό (s. ἀρχή; X. et al.; ins, pap; Jos., Vi. 38, C. Ap. 1, 143; IHierapJ 212, 6 ἐν τῷ ἀρχίῳ τ. Ἰουδαίων; loanw. in rabb.) orig. the government building, in which the official records were kept, hence also 'archives', and in a transf. sense the documents that were stored ***official records, original documents*** (so Dionys. Hal., Ant. 2, 26; Jul. Africanus to Aristides: TU 34 p. 61, 9 WReichardt [in Eus., HE 1, 7, 13; 1, 13, 5]) ἐὰν μὴ ἐν τοῖς ἀρχείοις εὕρω *if I do not find it in the original documents* (prob.=the OT) IPhld 8:2. ἐμοὶ δὲ ἀρχεῖά ἐστιν Ἰ. Χρ., τὰ ἄθικτα ἀρχεῖα ὁ σταυρὸς αὐτοῦ *for me the original documents are Jesus Christ, the taboo* (=holy, cp. Aeschyl., Ag. 371) *original documents are his cross* ibid.—DELG s.v. ἄρχω E, 2 p. 121.

Ἀρχέλαος, ου, ὁ ***Archelaus,*** a common (Diod. S. 18, 37, 4; SIG and OGI index; Preisigke, Namenbuch) name, deriv. fr. the adj. ἀρχέλαος 'leading the people' (Aeschyl., Pers. 297); in NT, the son of Herod I, ethnarch of Judaea, Idumaea and Samaria fr. his father's death in 4 BC to AD 6, when he was deposed by Emperor Augustus; noted for his cruelty (Jos., Ant. 17, 342ff, Bell. 1, 668ff; Just., D. 103, 3f) **Mt 2:22.**—Schürer I 353–57 (sources and lit.).—EDNT.

ἀρχή, ῆς, ἡ (Hom.+)—**❶ the commencement of someth. as an action, process, or state of being,** ***beginning,*** i.e. a point of time at the beginning of a duration.

ⓐ gener. (opp. τέλος; cp. Diod. S. 16, 1, 1 ἀπ' ἀρχῆς μέχρι τοῦ τέλους; Ael. Aristid. 30, 24 K.=10 p. 123 D.: ἐξ ἀ. εἰς τέλος; Appian, Bell. Civ. 5, 9, §36; Wsd 7:18) B 1:6; IEph 14:1; IMg 13:1; IRo 1:2, cp. vs. 1. W. gen. foll. (OGI 458, 10 life) ἡμέρας ὀγδόης B 15:8; ἡμερῶν (2 Km 14:26) **Hb 7:3;** τῶν σημείων *first of the signs* **J 2:11** (ἀ. τοῦ ἡμετέρου δόγματος Orig., C. Cels. 2, 4, 20; cp. Isocr., Paneg. 10:38 Blass ἀλλ' ἀρχὴν μὲν ταύτην ἐποιήσατο τ. εὐεργεσιῶν, τροφὴν τοῖς δεομένοις εὑρεῖν=but [Athens] made this the starting point of her benefactions: to provide basic needs for livelihood; Pr 8:22; Jos., Ant. 8, 229 ἀ. κακῶν); ὠδίνων **Mt 24:8; Mk 13:8;** κακῶν ISm 7:2. As the beginning, i.e. initial account, in a book (Ion of Chios [V BC] 392 fgm. 24 Jac. [=Leurini no. 114] ἀρχὴ τοῦ λόγου; Polystrat. p. 28; Diod. S. 17, 1, 1 ἡ βύβλος τὴν ἀ. ἔσχε ἀπὸ …; Ael. Aristid. 23, 2 K.=42 p. 768 D.: ἐπ' ἀρχῇ τοῦ συγγράμματος; Diog. L. 3, 37 ἡ ἀρχὴ τῆς Πολιτείας; cp. Sb 7696, 53; 58 [250 AD]) ἀ. τοῦ εὐαγγελίου Ἰ. Χ. *Beginning of the gospel of J. C.* **Mk 1:1** (cp. Hos 1:2 ἀ. λόγου κυρίου πρὸς Ὡσηέ; s. RHarris, Exp. 8th ser., 1919, 113–19; 1920, 142–50; 334–50; FDaubanton, NThSt 2, 1919, 168–70; AvanVeldhuizen, ibid., 171–75; EEidem, Ingressen til Mkevangeliet: FBuhl Festschr. 1925, 35–49; NFreese, StKr 104, '32, 429–38; AWikgren, JBL 61, '42, 11–20 [ἀρχή=*summary*]; LKeck, NTS 12, '65/66, 352–70). ἀ. τῆς ὑποστάσεως *original commitment* **Hb 3:14.** ἀρχὴν ἔχειν w.

gen. of the inf. *begin to be someth.* IEph 3:1. ἀρχὴν λαμβάνειν *begin* (Polyb.; Aelian, VH 2, 28; 12, 53; Diog. L., Prooem. 3, 4; Sext. Emp., Phys. 1, 366; Philo, Mos. 1, 81) λαλεῖσθαι *to be proclaimed at first* **Hb 2:3;** cp. IEph 19:3.—W. prep. ἀπ᾽ ἀρχῆς *from the beginning* (Paus. 3, 18, 2; SIG 741, 20; UPZ 160, 15 [119 BC]; BGU 1141, 44; JosAs 23:4; Jos., Ant. 8, 350; 9, 30) **J 6:64 v.l.; 15:27; 1J 2:7, 24; 3:11; 2J 5f; Ac 26:4;** MPol 17:1; Hs 9, 11, 9; Dg 12:3. οἱ ἀπ᾽ ἀ. αὐτόπται *those who fr. the beginning were eyewitnesses* **Lk 1:2.** Also ἐξ ἀρχῆς (Diod. Sic. 18, 41, 7; Appian, Bell. Civ. 5, 45 [189]; SIG 547, 9; 634, 4; UPZ 185 II 5; PGen 7, 8; BGU 1118, 21; Jos., Bell. 7, 358) **J 6:64; 16:4;** 1 Cl 19:2; Pol 7:2; Dg 2:1. πάλιν ἐξ ἀ. (Ael. Aristid. 21, 10 K.=22 p. 443 D.; SIG 972, 174) *again fr. the beginning* (=*afresh, anew;* a common expr., Renehan '75, 42) B 16:8. ἐν ἀρχῇ (Diod. S. 19, 110, 5; Palaeph. p. 2, 3; OGI 56, 57; PPetr II, 37, 2b verso, 4; PTebt 762, 9; POxy 1151, 15; BGU 954, 26; ViHab 14 [p. 87, 4 Sch.]) *at the beginning, at first* **Ac 11:15;** AcPlCor 2:4. ἐν ἀ. τοῦ εὐαγγελίου *when the gospel was first preached* **Phil 4:15;** sim., word for word, w. ref. to beg. of 1 Cor: 1 Cl 47:2.—τὴν ἀ. **J 8:25,** as nearly all the Gk. fathers understood it, is emphatically used adverbially=ὅλως *at all* (Plut., Mor. 115b; Dio Chrys. 10 [11], 12; 14 [31], 5; 133; Lucian, Eunuch. 6 al.; Ps.-Lucian, Salt. 3; POxy 472, 17 [c. 130 AD]; Philo, Spec. Leg. 3, 121; Jos., Ant. 1, 100; 15, 235 al.; as a rule in neg. clauses, but the negation can inhere in the sense: 48th letter of Apollonius of Tyana [Philostrat. I 356, 17]; Philo, Abrah. 116, Decal. 89; Ps.-Clem., Hom. 6, 11; without art. ApcSed 10:3; cp. Hs 2:5 cj. by W., endorsed by Joly; s. Field, Notes, 93f) τὴν ἀ. ὅτι καὶ λαλῶ ὑμῖν *(how is it) that I even speak to you at all?* But s. B-D-F §300, 2. More prob. the mng. is somewhat as follows: *What I said to you from the first* (so NT in Basic English; sim. REB et al.; cp. τὴν ἀρχήν 'at the beginning' Thu 2, 74, 2; s. also RFunk, HTR 51, '58, 95–100; B-D-F §300, 2, but appeal to P[66] is specious, s. EMiller, TZ 36, '80, 261).

ⓑ *beginning, origin* in the abs. sense (ἀ. τῆς τῶν πάντων ὑποστάσεως Orig. C. Cels. 6, 65, 4) ἀ. πάντων χαλεπῶν Pol 4:1; ἀ. κακῶν ISm 7:2 (cp. 1 Ti 6:10, which has ῥίζα for ἀ., and s. e.g. Ps 110:10; Sir 10:13); ἀ. κόσμου B 15:8; ἀ. πάντων PtK 2, p. 13, 21. ἀπ᾽ ἀρχῆς *fr. the very beginning* (Is 43:13; Wsd 9:8; 12:11; Sir 24:9 al.; PsSol 8:31; GrBar 17:2) **Mt 19:4, 8; J 8:44; 1J 1:1** (of the hist. beg. of Christianity: HWendt, D. Johannesbriefe u. d. joh. Christent. 1925, 31f; HWindisch, Hdb. ad loc.; difft. HConzelmann, RBultmann Festschr., '54, 194–201); **3:8; 2 Th 2:13;** ὁ ἀπ᾽ ἀ. **1J 2:13f;** Dg 11:4; οἱ ἀπ᾽ ἀ. *those at the very beginning, the first people* 12:3; τὰ ἀπ᾽ ἀ. γενόμενα 1 Cl 31:1; ἀπ᾽ ἀ. κτίσεως **Mk 10:6; 13:19; 2 Pt 3:4** (on ἀ. κτίσεως cp. En 15:9); ἀπ᾽ ἀ. κόσμου **Mt 24:21.** Also ἐξ ἀ. (X., Mem. 1, 4, 5; Ael. Aristid. 43, 9 K.=1 p. 3 D. [of the existence of Zeus]; TestAbr A 15 p. 96, 11 [Stone p. 40]; B 4 p. 109, 7 [St. p. 66]; Ath., R. 16, p. 67, 18; Philo, Aet. M. 42, Spec. Leg. 1, 300; Did., Gen. 50, 1) Dg 8:11; ἐν ἀ. *in the beginning* (Simplicius in Epict. p. 104, 2; Did., Gen. 29, 25 al.) **J 1:1f;** ἐν ἀ. τῆς κτίσεως B 15:3. κατ᾽ ἀρχάς *in the beg.* **Hb 1:10** (Ps 101:26; cp. Hdt. 3, 153 et al.; Diod. S.; Plut.; Philo, Leg. All. 3, 92, Det. Pot. Insid. 118; Ps 118:152; Just., D. 2, 3).

❷ **one with whom a process begins,** ***beginning*** fig., of pers. (Gen 49:3 Ῥουβὴν σὺ ἀρχὴ τέκνων μου; Dt 21:17): of Christ **Col 1:18.** W. τέλος of God or Christ **Rv 1:8 v.l.; 21:6; 22:13** (Hymn to Selene 35 ἀ. καὶ τέλος εἶ: Orphica p. 294, likew. PGM 4, 2836; 13, 362; 687; Philo, Plant. 93; Jos., Ant. 8, 280; others in Rtzst., Poim. 270ff and cp. SIG 1125, 7–11 Αἰών, … ἀρχὴν μεσότητα τέλος οὐκ ἔχων, expressed from the perspective of historical beginning).

❸ **the first cause,** ***the beginning*** (philos. t.t. ODittrich, D. Systeme d. Moral I 1923, 360a, 369a;—Ael. Aristid. 43, 9 K.=1 p. 3 D.: ἀρχὴ ἁπάντων Ζεύς τε καὶ ἐκ Διὸς πάντα; Jos., C. Ap. 2, 190 God as ἀρχὴ κ. μέσα κ. τέλος τῶν πάντων [contrast SIG 1125, 10f]) of Christ ἡ ἀ. τῆς κτίσεως **Rv 3:14;** but the mng. *beginning*='first created' is linguistically probable (s. above 1b and Job 40:19; also CBurney, Christ as the Ἀρχή of Creation: JTS 27, 1926, 160–77). [ὁ γὰ]ρ π̅ρ̅ (=πατὴρ) [ἀρ]|χὴ ἐ[σ]τ[ιν τῶν μ]ελλόν|των *for the Father is the source of all who are to come into being* in contrast to the προπάτωρ, who is without a beginning Ox 1081, 38f (SJCh 91, 1 ἀρχή; on the context, s. WTill, TU 60/5, '55 p. 57).

❹ **a point at which two surfaces or lines meet,** ***corner*** (from the perspective of an observer the object appears to begin at that point), pl. *corners* of a sheet **Ac 10:11; 11:5** (cp. Hdt. 4, 60; Diod. S. 1, 35, 10).

❺ **a basis for further understanding,** ***beginning*** τὰ στοιχεῖα τῆς ἀ. *elementary principles* **Hb 5:12** (perh. w. an element of gentle satire: 'the discrete items or ABC's that compose the very beginning [of divine instructions]'; cp. MKiley, SBLSP 25, '86, 236–45, esp. 239f). ὁ τῆς ἀ. τοῦ X. λόγος *elementary Christian teaching* **6:1.**

❻ **an authority figure who initiates activity or process,** ***ruler, authority*** (Aeschyl., Thu. et al.; ins; pap, e.g. PHal 1, 226 μαρτυρείτω ἐπὶ τῇ ἀρχῇ καὶ ἐπὶ τῷ δικαστηρίῳ; Gen 40:13, 21; 41:13; 2 Macc 4:10, 50 al., s. Magie 26; so as a loanw. in rabb. ἀ. = νόμιμος ἐπιστασία Did., Gen. 60, 9) w. ἐξουσία **Lk 20:20;** pl. (Oenomaus in Eus., PE 6, 7, 26 ἀρχαὶ κ. ἐξουσίαι; 4 Macc 8:7; Jos., Ant. 4, 220) **Lk 12:11; Tit 3:1;** MPol 10:2 (αἱ ἀρχαί can also be *the officials* as persons, as those who took part in the funeral procession of Sulla: Appian, Bell. Civ. 1, 106 §497.—The same mng. 2, 106 §442; 2, 118 §498 al. Likewise Diod. S. 34+35 fgm. 2, 31).—Also of angelic or transcendent powers, since they were thought of as having a political organization (Damascius, Princ. 96 R.) **Ro 8:38; 1 Cor 15:24; Eph 1:21; 3:10; 6:12; Col 1:16; 2:10, 15;** AcPl Ha 1, 7. Cp. TestJob 49, 2; Just., D. 120, 6 end.

❼ **the sphere of one's official activity,** ***rule, office*** (Diod. S. 3, 53, 1; Appian, Bell. Civ. 1, 13 §57; Jos., C. Ap. 2, 177, Ant. 19, 273), or better ***domain, sphere of influence*** (Diod. S. 17, 24, 2; Appian, Syr. 23 §111; Arrian, Anab. 6, 29, 1; Polyaen. 8:55; Procop. Soph., Ep. 139) of angels **Jd 6.** Papias (4 v.l. for ἄρχω).—S. the lit. on ἄγγελος and HSchlier, Mächte u. Gewalten im NT: ThBl 9, 1930, 289–97.—DDD 144–50 ('Archai'). EDNT. DELG s.v. ἄρχω D. M-M. TW. Sv.

ἀρχηγός, οῦ, ὁ (s. entries beg. ἀρχ-; on the predilection for such forms in the Koine s. New Docs 2, 18f)

❶ **one who has a preeminent position,** ***leader, ruler, prince*** (Aeschyl.+; POxy 41, 5; 6 and mostly LXX; Ar. 2, 1; Tat. 31, 1) ἀ. καὶ σωτήρ **Ac 5:31** (this combin. also 2 Cl 20:5; cp. AcPh 143 [Aa II/2, 83, 10]).—τ. ζωῆς **3:15,** where mng. 3 is also poss.

❷ **one who begins someth. that is first in a series,** thereby providing impetus for further developments (Aristot., Metaph. 1, 3, 983b 20 of Thales ὁ τῆς τοιαύτης ἀρχηγὸς φιλοσοφίας; Aristoxenus, fgm. 83 Ὄλυμπος ἀ. γενέσθαι τ. Ἑλληνικῆς μουσικῆς; Polyb. 5, 10, 1; Plut., Mor. 958d; 1135b; OGI 219, 26 ἀ. τοῦ γένους; Sb 8232, 12; 1 Macc 9:61; 10:47; Mi 1:13; Jos., C. Ap. 1, 130 [of Moses]) in bad sense ***instigator*** 1 Cl 14:1 ἀ. ζήλους; 51:1 ἀ. στάσεως (cp. Herodian 7, 1, 11 ἀ. τ. ἀποστάσεως).

❸ **one who begins or originates,** hence the recipient of special esteem in the Gr-Rom. world, ***originator, founder*** (Diod. S. 15, 81, 2 ἀ. τῆς νίκης=originator; 16, 3, 5 τῆς βασιλείας ἀ.=founder; Jos., Ant. 7, 207. Oft. of God: Pla., Tim. 21e al.; Isocr. 4, 61 τῶν ἀγαθῶν; Diod. S. 5, 64, 5; OGI 90, 47; SIG 711 L, 13 Apollo ἀ. τ. εὐσεβείας) ἀ. τῆς ἀφθαρσίας 2 Cl 20:5; ἀ. τῆς σωτηρίας **Hb 2:10;** τῆς πίστεως ἀ. **12:2.**—PGMüller, ΧΡΙΣΤΟΣ ΑΡΧΗΓΟΣ '73.—EDNT. DELG s.v. ἄγω and ἄρχω B1. M-M. TW. Sv.

ἀρχιερατικός, όν (s. ἀρχιερεύς; CIG 4363; OGI 470, 21; JÖAI 15, 51; Jos., Bell. 4, 164, Ant. 4, 83; 6, 115) ***highpriestly*** γένος ἀ. (Jos., Ant. 15, 40; Just., D. 116, 3) *the high priest's family* **Ac 4:6** (on this Schürer II 232–36).—M-M. TW.

ἀρχιερεύς, έως, ὁ (*ἀρχ- + ἱερεύς; Hdt.+; on the freq. use of the title in polytheistic cults s. Brandis in Pauly-W. II 471–83; Magie 64).

❶ one who serves as head priest, *high priest*—ⓐ gentile MPol 21=Ἀσιάρχης (q.v.) 12:2.

ⓑ Israelite—**α.** president of the Sanhedrin (Schürer II 215–18): in Jesus' trial **Mt 26:57, 62f, 65; Mk 14:60f, 63; J 18:19, 22, 24.** Those named are Ἀβιαθάρ, Ἀνανίας, Ἅννας, Καϊάφας, Σκευᾶς; see these entries.

β. by fig. extension, of Christ, who serves as high priest by atoning for the sins of humans **Hb 2:17; 3:1** (w. ἀπόστολος); **5:10; 6:20; 7:26; 8:1; 9:11;** 1 Cl 61:3; 64; IPhld 9:1; MPol 14:3. ἀ. μέγας (1 Macc 13:42; Philo, Somn. 1, 219; Michel 1231, 1; cp. also the ἀ. μέγιστος=pontifex maximus of imperial ins) **Hb 4:14** (GFriedrich, TZ 18, '62, 95–115); ἀ. τῶν προσφορῶν 1 Cl 36:1. Cp. ANairne, The Epistle of Priesthood 1913, 135ff; HWindisch, Hdb., exc. on Hb 9:14; JUbbink, NThSt 22, '39, 172–84 (on Hb); MDibelius, D. himml. Kultus nach Hb: ThBl 21, '42, 1–11; HWenschkewitz, D. Spiritualisierung d. Kultusbegriffe Tempel, Priester u. Opfer im NT '32; OMoe, D. Priestert. Christi im NT ausserhalb des Hb: TLZ 72, '47, 335–38; GSchille, Erwägungen zur Hohepriesterlehre des Hb: ZNW 56, '55, 81–109; AJansen, Schwäche u. Vollkommenheit des H-priesters Christus, diss. Rome, '57.

❷ a priest of high rank, *chief priest*—ⓐ in Israel's cultic life. The pl. is used in the NT and in Joseph. (Schürer II 233, 25; 235, 34) to denote members of the Sanhedrin who belonged to highpriestly families: ruling high priests, those who had been deposed, and adult male members of the most prominent priestly families (s. Schürer II 232–36 w. ref. [235, 36] to the view of a jurisdictional body proposed by JJeremias, Jerusalem in the Time of Jesus '69, 175–81, s. also GSchrenk, TW III 271, 37). ἀρχιερεῖς w. ἄρχοντες **Lk 23:13; 24:20;** w. γραμματεῖς and πρεσβύτεροι **Mt 16:21; 27:41; Mk 8:31; 11:27; 14:43, 53; 15:1; Lk 9:22; 20:1;** w. γραμματεῖς (IMagnMai 197, 11f; 193, 10; Thieme 21f) **Mt 2:4; 20:18; 21:15; Mk 10:33; 11:18; 14:1; 15:31; Lk 20:19; 22:2, 66; 23:10;** GJs 6:2; w. πρεσβύτεροι **Mt 21:23** (cp. Lk 20:1); **26:3, 47; 27:1, 3, 12, 20; Ac 4:23; 23:14; 25:15;** w. Σαδδουκαῖοι **Ac 4:1 v.l.;** ἀ. καὶ τὸ συνέδριον ὅλον **Mt 26:59; Mk 14:55; Ac 22:30** (πᾶν τὸ συν.). οἱ ἀρχιερεῖς alone=*the Sanhedrin* **Ac 9:14.** Cp. **Hb 10:11 v.l.;** 1 Cl 40:5; 41:2; GJs 6:2.—On ἀ. τ. ἐνιαυτοῦ ἐκ. **J 11:49, 51; 18:13** s. ἐνιαυτός 1.

ⓑ by fig. ext., of Christian prophets D 13:3 and ApcPt 20 (Harnack's text, Wilamowitz ἀδελφῶν, Schubert ἀρχηγῶν).—Pauly-W. II 471–83. EDNT. M-M. TW. Sv.

ἀρχιληστής, οῦ, ὁ (Herodian Gr. I 82, 26; Ps.-Callisth. 1, 36; PCairMasp I, 2 III, 22 [Byz.]; Jos., Bell. 1, 204, V 105; loanw. in rabb.) ***robber chieftain*** s. Tdf. on the Syriac trad. of **J 18:40** (cp. the use of ἀ. passim in the Byzantine story, ed. JWortley, De Latrone Converso, The Tale of the Converted Robber: Byzantion 66, '96, 219–43 [text 235–37; first published AnalBoll 100, '82, 351–63]).—DELG s.v. λεία (on ληστής).

ἀρχιποίμην, ενος, ὁ (s. ποιμήν; Herodian Gr. I 16, 19; wooden tablet of imperial times in Dssm., LO 77f [LAE 97ff]=Sb 3507, 2; 8087, 7; PLips 97 XI, 4 Καμήτι ἀρχιποιμένι; PSI 286, 6; 4 Km 3:4 Sym.; TestJud 8:1: cited in WJost, ΠΟΙΜΗΝ, diss. Giessen, '39, 47–50) *chief shepherd* of Christ **1 Pt 5:4** (cp. the ποιμὴν μέγας **Hb 13:20** and the ἀρχιβουκόλος of the Dionysus mysteries; RPerdelwitz, D. Mysterienrel. u. d. Problem d. 1 Pt 1911, 100f).—M-M. TW. Spicq.

Ἄρχιππος, ου, ὁ ***Archippus*** a common name (Diod. S. 18, 58, 1; SIG index; PHib 124–26; 130; Tat. 31, 3), found also in west. Asia Minor (CIG 3143 I, 22; 3224 Smyrna). Of a Christian in Colossae **Col 4:17,** called συστρατιώτης (perh. w. a play on the name Ἀ., in popular etymology suggestive of military association) of Paul and Titus, **Phlm 2.** Cp. also inscription v.l. and subscr. v.l.—LGPN I.

ἀρχιστράτηγος, ου (LXX; Jos., Ant. 6, 235 al. of such commanders as Abner and Joab [w. constant v.l. ἀντιστράτηγος, s. Jos., Lex, s.v. ἀρχισ-]; Philo, De Cong. 125 allegorically of a learner) of a transcendent being (Just., D. 34, 2; 61, 1; 62, 5 of Christ) ἀρχιστρά[τηγον] ***commander,*** of a heavenly messenger (so Josh 5:13, 15; Da 8:11) PCairCat 10735 verso, 8f (=ASyn. 3, 24 and Otero I 86, no. 6; s. προβαδίζω).

ἀρχισυνάγωγος, ου, ὁ (s. συναγωγή; Just., D. 137, 2 exx. fr. ins and lit. in Schürer II 434–36 and III 100f; Sb 5959, 3 [time of Augustus]; SEG VIII, 170, 2ff; on this ZNW 20, 1921, 171; Dssm., LO 378–80 [LAE 439–41] w. lit.) ***leader/president of a synagogue,*** a term found also in polytheistic cult (Poland, Gesch. 355–57) and given simply as a title (Schürer II 435; for ins evidence relating to Jewish women s. BBrooten, Women Leaders in the Ancient Synagogue, '82; men and women: New Docs 4, 214–20), in our lit. only w. ref. to the Jewish synagogue, of an official whose duty it was esp. to take care of the physical arrangements for the worship services (Hebr. רֹאשׁ הַכְּנֶסֶת) **Mk 5:22, 35f, 38; Lk 8:49; 13:14; Ac 13:15; 14:2** D; **18:8, 17.** Those named are Ἰάϊρος, Κρίσπος and Σωσθένης; s. these entries.—WThieling, Der Hellenismus in Kleinafrika 1911, 76; TRajak/DNoy, JRS 83, '93, 75–93.—M-M. TW.

ἀρχιτέκτων, ονος, ὁ (s. τέκτων; Hdt. et al.; ins, pap, LXX, Philo; Jos., V 156; loanw. in rabb.) ***master builder*** σοφὸς ἀ. (Is 3:3; cp. Philo, Somn. 2, 8) **1 Cor 3:10** (Pla., Amat. 135b τέκτονα μὲν ἂν πρίαιο πέντε ἢ ἓξ μνῶν, ἄκρον ἀρχιτέκτονα δ' οὐδ' ἂν μυρίων δραχμῶν. 10,000 drachmas [i.e. 100 minas]=you might be able to buy a carpenter for 6 minas, but you'd need more than 10,000 drachmas for a master builder).—M-M. TW. Sv.

ἀρχιτελώνης, ου, ὁ (*ἀρχ- + τελώνης) (not found elsewh.) *chief tax collector* **Lk 19:2.**—DELG s.v. τέλος (on τελώνης). TW.

ἀρχιτρίκλινος, ου, ὁ (τρίκλινος a banquet room 'with three couches') (the slave who was responsible for managing a banquet: in Lat architriclinus, tricliniarcha; Heliod. 7, 27, 7 ἀρχιτρίκλινοι καὶ οἰνοχόοι) ***head waiter, butler*** **J 2:8f.** For the view that the context suggests equivalence of ἀ. with συμποσίαρχος *toastmaster, master of the feast* (cp. ἡγούμενος Sir 32:1f) s. comm.—DELG s.v. κλίνω (on τρίκλινος).

ἀρχοντικός, ή, όν (s. ἄρχων; Herm. Wr. 1, 25; Anth. Pal. 9, 763; Vett. Val. 14, 24f; 70, 8; 355, 33; pap) **pert. to primary leadership obligations at various administrative levels, *commanding*** (s. ἄρχων 2; used of angels ἀρχοντικός Celsus 6, 27; 35; Kephal. I, 53, 7) in ref. to angels συστάσεις ἀ. *assemblages of the (celestial) commanders* ITr 5:2.—DELG s.v. ἄρχω C p. 120.

ἄρχω fut. ἄρξω; 1 aor. ἦρξα LXX. Mid.: fut. ἄρξομαι; 1 aor. ἠρξάμην; pf. ἦργμαι (Hom.+) lit. *be first.*

❶ **to rule or govern, w. implication of special status, *rule*** act. w. gen. *over someth.* or *someone* (Hom., Hdt. et al.; UPZ 81 col. 2, 18 [II BC] as an epithet of Isis: τῶν ἐν τῷ κόσμῳ ἄρχουσα; En 9:7; EpArist 190; Demetr.: 722 fgm. 1, 12 Jac.; Philo, Congr. Erud. Gr. 6; Just., D. 90, 4; 111, 1) τῶν ἐθνῶν **Mk 10:42; Ro 15:12** (Is 11:10). εἰς πόλιν ἄρχουσαν δύσεως *into the city that rules over the West* ApcPt Rainer 15f. τῶν θηρίων τ. γῆς B 6:12 (cp. Gen 1:26, 28). τῆς περὶ τὴν γῆν διακοσμήσεως ἔδωκεν ἄ. (angels) *authority to govern the earth* Papias (4).

❷ **to initiate an action, process, or state of being, *begin*** mid., except for GMary s. 2αα.—ⓐ w. pres. inf. (DHesseling, Z. Syntax v. ἄρχομαι: ByzZ 20, 1911, 147–64; JKleist, Mk '36, 154–61 Marcan ἤρξατο; GReichenkron, Die Umschreibung m. occipere, incipere u. coepisse: Syntactica u. Stilistica, Festschr. EGamillscheg '57, 473–75; MReiser, Syntax u. Stil (Mk), '84, 43–45).

α. lit., to denote what one begins to do, in pres. inf. (Polyaenus 3, 9, 40 σφαγιάζειν) λέγειν (Jos., Ant. 8, 276; 18, 289) **Mt 11:7;** ὀνειδίζειν vs. **20;** τύπτειν **24:49;** κηρύσσειν **4:17; Mk 5:20;** cp. the use of the act. GMar 463 ἀπ[ελθὼ]ν ἦρχεν κη[ρύσ]|[σειν τὸ εὐαγγέλι]ο̣ν̣ [κατὰ Μάριαμ] *(Levi) went off and began to proclaim [the gospel according to Mary];* παίζειν Hs 9, 11, 5 al.; εἶναι IRo 5:3. Emphasis can be laid on the beginning **Lk 15:14; 21:28, Ac 2:4; 11:15,** or a contrast can be implied, as w. continuation **Mk 6:7; 8:31;** IEph 20:1; w. completion **Mt 14:30; Lk 14:30; J 13:5;** w. an interruption **Mt 12:1; 26:22; Ac 27:35.**—μὴ ἄρξησθε λέγειν ἐν ἑαυτοῖς *don't even begin to think*=do not cherish the unfortunate thought **Lk 3:8.**

β. Oft. ἄ. only means that the pers. in question has been doing something else and that the activity now takes a new turn (GrBar 4:11 ὅταν ... ἐξῆλθε Νῶε τῆς κιβωτοῦ, ἤρξατο φυτεύειν 'after Noah left the Ark, he began to beget') **Mt 26:37, 74; Lk 4:21; 5:21; 7:15, 24, 38, 49** al. In such cases it is freq. almost superfluous as an auxiliary, in accordance w. late Semitic usage (Jos., Ant. 11, 131; 200; Dalman, Worte 21f; s. JHunkin, 'Pleonastic' ἄρχομαι in the NT: JTS 25, 1924, 390–402). So ὧν ἤρξατο ὁ Ἰησ. ποιεῖν **Ac 1:1**=simply *what Jesus did* (sim. Lat. coepio).

ⓑ abs. (sc. the inf. fr. the context) ἦν Ἰησοῦς ἀρχόμενος ὡσεὶ ἐτῶν τριάκοντα **Lk 3:23** prob. *Jesus was about 30 years old when he began his work.* In ἀρξάμενος Πέτρος ἐξετίθετο (Aesop, Fab. 100 P.=H-H. 102 [Halm 155 ἀχθόμενος] Μῶμος ἀρξάμενος ἔλεγε; X. Eph. 5, 7, 9 ἀρξαμένη κατέχομαι) ἀ. receives its content fr. the foll. καθεξῆς: *P. began and explained in order* **Ac 11:4.**

ⓒ w. indication of the starting point ἄ. ἀπὸ τότε *begin fr. that time* **Mt 4:17; 16:21;** ἄ. ἀπό τινος (Pla. et al., also Arrian, Cyneg. 36, 4; PMeyer 24, 3; Ezk 9:6; Jos., Ant. 7, 255 ἀπὸ σοῦ; in local sense SIG 969, 5; PTebt 526; Jos., Ant. 13, 390) ἀρξάμενος ἀπὸ Μωϋσέως *beginning w. Moses* **Lk 24:27;** ἀ. ἀπὸ τῆς γραφῆς ταύτης *beginning with this passage of Scripture* **Ac 8:35; J 8:9; 1 Pt 4:17.** Locally **Lk 24:47; Ac 10:37.** With both starting point and end point given (Lucian, Somn. 15 ἀπὸ τῆς ἕω ἀρξάμενος ἄχρι πρὸς ἑσπέραν; Gen 44:12) ἀπό τινος ἕως τινός: ἀπὸ τ. ἐσχάτων ἕως τῶν πρώτων **Mt 20:8; Ac 1:22;** local **Lk 23:5.**—B. 976; 1319. EDNT. DELG. M-M s.v. ἄρχομαι. TW.

ἄρχων, οντος, ὁ (Aeschyl., Hdt.+) actually ptc. of ἄρχω, used as subst.: one who is in a position of leadership, esp. in a civic capacity.

❶ **one who has eminence in a ruling capacity, *ruler, lord, prince***—ⓐ of earthly figures, οἱ ἄ. τῶν ἐθνῶν **Mt 20:25;** cp. B 9:3 (Is 1:10); οἱ ἄ. *the rulers* **Ac 4:26** (Ps 2:2). W. δικαστής of Moses (in quot. of Ex 2:14): **7:27, 35** and 1 Cl 4:10.

ⓑ of Christ ὁ ἄ. τ. βασιλέων τ. γῆς *the ruler of the kings of the earth* **Rv 1:5;**

ⓒ of transcendent figures. Evil spirits (Kephal. I p. 50, 22; 24; 51, 25 al.), whose hierarchies resembled human polit. institutions. The devil is ἄ. τ. δαιμονίων **Mt 9:34; 12:24; Mk 3:22; Lk 11:15** (s. Βεελζεβούλ.—Porphyr. [in Eus., PE 4, 22, 15] names Sarapis and Hecate as τοὺς ἄρχοντας τ. πονηρῶν δαιμόνων) or ἄ. τοῦ κόσμου τούτου **J 12:31; 14:30; 16:11;** ἄ. καιροῦ τοῦ νῦν τῆς ἀνομίας B 18:2; ὁ ἄ. τοῦ αἰῶνος τούτου (Orig., C. Cels. 8, 13, 13) IEph 17:1; 19:1; IMg 1:2; ITr 4:2; IRo 7:1; IPhld 6:2. (Cp. AscIs 1, 3; 10, 29.) At AcPlCor 2, 11 the ed. of PBodmer X suggests on the basis of a Latin version (s. ZNW 44, 1952–53, 66–76) that the following words be supplied between πολλοῖς and θέλων εἶναι: [ὁ γὰρ ἄρχων ἄδικος ὢν| (καὶ) θεὸς] (lat.: nam quia injustus princeps deus volens esse) *[the prince (of this world) being unjust] and desiring to be [god]* (s. ASchlatter, D. Evglst. Joh. 1930, 271f). Many would also class the ἄρχοντες τοῦ αἰῶνος τούτου **1 Cor 2:6–8** in this category (so from Origen to H-DWendland ad loc., but for possible classification under mng. 2 s. TLing, ET 68, '56/57, 26; WBoyd, ibid. 68, '57/58, 158). ὁ πονηρὸς ἄ. B 4:13; ὁ ἄδικος ἄ. MPol 19:2 (cp. ὁ ἄρχων τ. πλάνης TestSim 2:7, TestJud 19:4). ὁ ἄ. τῆς ἐξουσίας τοῦ ἀέρος **Eph 2:2** (s. ἀήρ, end). W. ἄγγελος as a messenger of God and representative of the spirit world (Porphyr., Ep. ad Aneb. [s. ἀρχάγγελος] c. 10) Dg 7:2; οἱ ἄ. ὁρατοί τε καὶ ἀόρατοι *the visible and invisible rulers* ISm 6:1.

❷ gener. **one who has administrative authority, *leader, official*** (so loanw. in rabb.) **Ro 13:3; Tit 1:9 v.l.** (cp. PsSol 17:36). For **1 Cor 2:6–8** s. 1b above.

ⓐ of Jewish leaders (Schürer, index; PLond III, 1177, 57 p. 183 [113 AD] ἀρχόντων Ἰουδαίων προσευχῆς Θηβαίων; IGR I, 1024, 21; Jos., Ant. 20, 11) of the high priest **Ac 23:5** (Ex 22:27). Of those in charge of a synagogue (IG XIV, 949, 2) **Mt 9:18, 23;** cp. ἄ. τῆς συναγωγῆς **Lk 8:41; Ac 14:2** D. Of members of the Sanhedrin **Lk 18:18; 23:13, 35; 24:20;** ἄ. τ. Ἰουδαίων (cp. Epict. 3, 7, 30 κριτὴς τῶν Ἑλλήνων) **J 3:1;** cp. **7:26, 48; 12:42; Ac 3:17; 4:5, 8** (ἄρχοντες καὶ πρεσβύτεροι as 1 Macc 1:26); **13:27; 14:5.** τὶς τῶν ἀρχόντων τ. Φαρισαίων *a member of the Sanhedrin who was a Pharisee* **Lk 14:1.** Of a judge **12:58.**

ⓑ of gentile officials (Diod. S. 18, 65, 6; s. the indexes to SIG and OGI) **Ac 16:19** (OGI 441, 59 and note); 1 Cl 60:2; MPol 17:2. W. ἡγούμενοι 1 Cl 60:4. W. βασιλεῖς and ἡγούμενοι 1 Cl 32:2.—B. 1324. DDD 153–59 ('Archon'). EDNT. DELG s.v. ἄρχω. M-M. TW.

ἄρωμα, ατος, τό (Hippocr.+) nearly always pl. (X., An. 1, 5, 1; SIG 999, 17; OGI 383, 143; pap, e.g. POxy 1211, 10; BGU 149, 1; LXX; TestAbr A 20, p. 103, 22 [Stone p. 54]; ApcMos 29; EpArist; Philo, Leg. All. 1, 42; Jos., Ant. 14, 72; En), **any kind of fragrant substance, *fragrant spice/salve/oil/perfume,*** esp. used in embalming the dead (Diod. S. 18, 26, 3 [the ἀρώματα in Alexander's coffin were put there to preserve the corpse]; Chariton 1, 8, 2; Plut., Sulla 475 [38, 3]; for details 2 Ch 16:14) **Mk**

16:1; Lk 23:56; 24:1; J 19:40; 1 Cl 25:2. τίμια ἀ. *precious perfumes* MPol 15:2. The earth ἀρωμάτων πλήρη *full of fragrant things* ApcPt 5:15.—DELG. M-M.

ἀσάλευτος, ον (s. σαλεύω; Eur., Pla., et al; ins; pap; TestSol 13:5 C; ApcEsdr 4:29, p. 29, 5 Tdf.; ApcMos 32; Philo; Jos., Bell. 1, 405; LXX in special sense)

❶ lit., **not being subject to movement,** of part of a ship that has run aground ἡ πρῷρα ἔμεινεν ἀ. the *bow remained immovable* **Ac 27:41.**

❷ **not subject to alteration of essential nature or being,** ***unshakable, enduring,*** fig. ext.of 1 (so Polystrat. p. 10 [πίστις]; Diod. S. 2, 48, 4 [ἐλευθερία]; 3, 47, 8; 5, 15, 3 al.; Plut., Mor. 83e; TestSol 13:5 C; Philo, Mos. 2, 14; IMagnMai 116, 26 [διάταξις]; Kaibel 855, 3; 1028, 4; BGU 1826, 16 [52/51 BC]; PFamTebt 19, 24 [118 AD] and see pap since IV AD e.g. PLips 34, 18; 35, 20) βασιλεία ἀ. *a kingdom that cannot be shaken* **Hb 12:28.**—DELG s.v. σάλος. M-M.

Ἀσάφ, ὁ (אָסָא 1 Ch 3:10) indecl. (cp. Jos., Ant. 11, 80 οἱ Ἀσάφου παῖδες) ***Asa(ph),*** in genealogy of Jesus **Mt 1:7f** (v.l. Ἀσά both times); **Lk 3:23ff** D.

ἄσβεστος, ον (σβεστός + α- priv., s. σβέννυμι; Hom. et al.; PHolm index; TestSol 11:7; ParJer 9:14 [Christ.] λύχνος; ApcEsdr 1:24 p. 25, 20 Tdf. φλόξ; Jos., Bell. 2. 425; Just., D. 120, 5) of something whose state of being cannot be nullified or stopped; hence

❶ of fire ***inextinguishable*** (syn. αἰώνιος Mt 18:8; 25:41) πῦρ ἄ. (this combin. also Dionys. Hal. 1, 76; Strabo 15, 3, 15; Plut., Num 9, 15, Mor. 410b; 411c; Ael. Aristid. 26, 99 K.=14 p. 365 D.; Aelian, NA 5, 3; Philo, Spec. Leg. 1, 285, Ebr. 134; Job 20, 26 v.l.; Just.; PGM 4, 3070; PWarr 21, 2, 21) **Mt 3:12; Mk 9:43, 45 v.l.; Lk 3:17;** 2 Cl 17:7; IEph 16:2; AcPl Ha 1, 22.

❷ ἡ ἄ. (sc. τίτανος, 'white earth' hence 'chalk') of lime that has not been disintegrated by addition of water ***unslaked lime*** (Diosc. 5, 115 W.; Plut., Sert. 576 [17, 3]) Hs 9, 10, 1.—DELG s.v. σβέννυμι. TW.

ἀσβόλη, ης, ἡ (Semonides 7, 61 Diehl; Diosc. 5, 161 W.; La 4:8 for ἡ ἄσβολος; Galen XVI 623, 8 ὑπὸ τ. πολλῶν ἀσβόλην, ἣν ἄσβολον οἱ Ἕλληνες. Cp. Lob., Phryn. p. 113) ***soot,*** typical of blackness Hs 9, 1, 5; 9, 6, 4.—DELG s.v. ἄσβολος.

ἀσέβεια, ας, ἡ (s. ἀσεβής; Eur., X., Pla.+; Antiphon 5:88 [=6:6] and Diod. S. 1, 44, 3 εἰς τοὺς θεοὺς ἀσέβεια; Epict., ins; PEleph 23, 1; 9f; PCairZen 11 verso I, 3; Sb 5680, 20; PSI 515, 18 [all III BC]; BGU 1578, 8; 1823, 23; PGrad 4, 20; LXX, En; EpArist 166; Philo; Jos., Ant. 9, 266, C. Ap. 2, 291; Test12Patr; Ar. 11, 7; Just.) in general ἀσέβεια is understood vertically as a lack of reverence for deity and hallowed institutions as displayed in sacrilegious words and deeds: ***impiety;*** its corollary ἀδικία refers horizontally to violation of human rights: ἐπὶ πλεῖον προκόπτειν ἀσεβείας *progress further in impiety* **2 Ti 2:16;** ἀρνεῖσθαι τὴν ἀ. **Tit 2:12;** φυγεῖν τὴν ἀ. 2 Cl 10:1; ἔργα ἀσεβείας='impious deeds', i.e. deeds that are the product of distorted views of God **Jd 15** (En 1:9). Of polytheists, who are indicted for dishonoring God **Ro 1:18** (cp. Dt 9:5). ἀσεβείας ὑπόδειγμα Papias (3:2). In imagery τῆς ἀ. πλησθήσονται *they will be sated w. their impiety* 1 Cl 57:6 (Pr 1:31).—Pl. (Pla., Leg. 890a; LXX; ViMi 1 [p. 81, 7 Sch.]; Jos., Bell. 7, 260) ἀποστρέψει ἀσεβείας ἀπὸ Ἰακώβ **Ro 11:26** (Is 59:20). ἐπιθυμίαι τ. ἀσεβειῶν *profane desires* **Jd 18** (cp. En 13:2 ἔργα τ. ἀσεβειῶν).—Dodd 76–81; BGärtner, The Areopagus Speech and Natural Revelation '55, 73ff.—M-M. TW. Sv.

ἀσεβέω fut. 3 sg. ἀσεβήσει (Dt 17:13); 1 aor. ἠσέβησα; pf. ἠσέβηκα LXX (s. next entry; Aeschyl., Hdt.; ins; Sb 6152, 11; 6153, 13; LXX; En 1:9; JosAs 12:5f; Philo; Jos., Ant. 9, 262; 11, 91, C. Ap. 2, 194; Test12Patr; Just., Ath.; Mel., P. 86, 645; Orig.) **to violate the norms of a proper or professed relation to deity,** ***act impiously*** **2 Pt 2:6 v.l.;** 2 Cl 17:6. ἔργα ἀσεβείας ἀσεβεῖν *commit impious deeds* **Jd 15** (En 1:9).—DELG s.v. σέβομαι. M-M. TW.

ἀσεβής, ές acc. sing. ἀσεβῆν **Ro 4:5 v.l.,** B-D-F §46, 1 (s. prec. entry; Aeschyl., Thu.+) **pert. to violating norms for a proper relation to deity,** ***irreverent, impious, ungodly.***

ⓐ of pers., ἁμαρτωλὸς ἀ. **Jd 15** (En 1:9). οἱ ἀ. ἄνθρωποι (UPZ 162 III, 8 [117 BC] ὑπὸ ἀσεβῶν ἀνθρώπων) **2 Pt 3:7.** Mostly subst. ὁ ἀ. *impious (person)* (Diod. S. 1, 96, 5; 3, 61, 5; 5, 71, 2 and 6; OGI 90, 23; 26; LXX; TestZeb 10:3) **Ro 5:6; 2 Pt 2:5; 2:6; Jd 4, 15;** 1 Cl 14:5 (Ps 36:35); 18:13 (Ps 50:15); 57:7 (Pr 1:32); B 10:10 (Ps 1:1); 11:7 (Ps 1:4ff); (w. ἁμαρτωλός) **1 Ti 1:9;** (w. ἄνομος) B 15:5; Dg 9:4; (w. κεκριμένοι τῷ θανάτῳ) B 10:5; in contrast to those who serve God and in the fear of God are eager to live uprightly οἱ κρινόμενοι ἀ. *the ungodly who are* (already) *condemned* 2 Cl 18:1. Punished w. eternal fire MPol 11:2 (Diod. S. 4, 74, 2 the ἀσεβεῖς in everlasting torment in a subterranean place of punishment).—The collective sg. (as Lucian, Bacch. 7 ὁ γέρων = οἱ γέροντες; Ps.-Dicaearch. p. 146 F. πολὺς ὁ καταπλέων ἐστίν; EpArist 13) **Ro 4:5; 1 Pt 4:18** (Pr 11:31).—ÅStröm, Vetekornet, Studier över individ och kollektivi NT '44.

ⓑ of human characteristics (w. ἄδικος, as Philo, Rer. Div. Her. 90; Jos., Ant. 8, 251; cp. ἀσεβέσιν ὁδοῖς ApcSed 15:5) ζῆλος ἀ. 1 Cl 3:4. Impers. (Epict. 4, 7, 11; SIG 204, 52 ὅπως ἂν μηδὲν ἀσεβὲς γίγνηται) πῶς οὐκ ἀσεβές; *how is it not impious?* Dg 4:3. V.l. for ἀσθενής 1 Cl 59:4 (vide).—M-M. TW.

ἀσέλγεια, ας, ἡ (ἀσελγής; Pla., Isaeus et al.; Polyb. 1, 6, 5; 5, 28, 9 al.; Plut., Alcib. 8, 2 [195]; Lucian, Gall. 32; BGU 1578, 15 [II/III AD]; PMagd 24, 2; PLond V, 1711, 34; Wsd 14:26; 3 Macc 2:26; Jos., Ant. 4, 151; 8, 252; 318; 20, 112; TestJud 23:1; Ar.; Just., A II, 2, 3; Tat.; Mel., P. 50, 364) **lack of self-constraint which involves one in conduct that violates all bounds of what is socially acceptable,** ***self-abandonment.*** In sg. and pl. ἑαυτὸν παραδιδόναι τῇ ἀ. *give oneself over to licentiousness* **Eph 4:19;** πορεύεσθαι ἐν ἀσελγείαις *live licentiously* **1 Pt 4:3;** cp. Hm 12, 4, 6. τὴν χάριτα μετατιθέναι εἰς ἀ. *pervert favor into licentiousness* (i.e. they interpret divine goodness as an opportunity to ignore God and do what they please) **Jd 4** (cp. Diod. S. 16, 87, 1, where ἀ. is used of the insolence of a scoffer); πολλοὶ ἐξακολουθήσουσιν ταῖς ἀ. *many will follow in their licentious tracks* **2 Pt 2:2.** Cp. Hv 2, 2, 2. Esp. of sexual excesses (Philo, Mos. 1, 305; Hippol., Ref. 9, 13, 4) w. κοῖται **Ro 13:13;** w. ἀκαθαρσία (cp. **Eph 4:19**) and πορνεία **2 Cor 12:21; Gal 5:19,** in a long catalogue of vices, like **Mk 7:22;** Hs 9, 15, 3. ἡ ἐν ἀ. ἀναστροφή *indecent conduct* **2 Pt 2:7;** cp. vs. **18.** αἱ ἐπιθυμίαι τῆς ἀ. *licentious desires* Hv 3, 7, 2 (cp. Polyb. 36, 15, 4 ἀ. περὶ τ. σωματικὰς ἐπιθυμίας).—DELG s.v. ἀσελγής. M-M. TW.

ἀσελγής, ές gen. οῦς (s. prec. entry; Pherecr., Com. fgm. 176; Aristoph., Eupolis et al.; TestLevi 17:11; EpArist 205; Philo, Post Caini 156; Joseph., Just.; Mel., P. 53, 388 [cp. ἀσελγέστερος]; cp. adv. -ῶς Hos 7:14 Aq., Sym.; Philo, Det.

Pot. Ins. 95) ***licentious, lewd*** ταῖς ἐντολαῖς . . . τοῦ διαβόλου ταῖς . . . ἀσελγέσι *the lewd ordinances of the devil* Hm 12, 4, 6.—DELG.

ἄσημος, ον (σῆμα; trag. Hdt.+; ins, pap, LXX) 'without (distinguishing) mark' (cp. the numismatic metaphor Philo, Migr. Abr. 79).

❶ **pert. to being unmarked, *insignificant, unimportant*** (Gen 30:42; 3 Macc 1:3; Philo, Virt. 222; Jos., Bell. 6, 81, Ant. 16, 243 οὐκ ἄ., Vi. 1 οὐκ ἄ.) in litotes οὐκ ἄ. πόλις *no unimportant city* **Ac 21:39** (Eur., Ion 8 οὐκ ἄ. πόλις, likewise Strabo 8, 6, 15; a favorite expr., s. Wetstein ad loc. opp. διάσημος of Alexandria: Acta Alex. fgm. 4 col. 3, 10, p. 13; Renehan '82, 38).

❷ **of words or statements whose meaning or intent is not readily grasped, *obscure, unclear*** (Aeschyl., Prom. 662 χρησμοί; Hdt. 1, 86, 4) τὰ γεγραμμένα Dg 12:3.—DELG s.v. σῆμα. M-M. TW.

ἄσηπτος, ον (Hippocr. et al.; LXX; TestSol 19:2 P; TestSim 8:2; almost always w. ξύλον) ***not rotted*** of sticks Hs 8, 6, 5, fr. the context in the sense *not worm-eaten*.—DELG s.v. σήπομαι.

Ἀσήρ, ὁ (אָשֵׁר), indecl. (LXX, Philo, Test12Patr; JosAs 20:5.—In Joseph. Ἄσηρος, ου [Ant. 7, 59]) ***Asher*** son of Jacob (Gen 30:13; 49:20; 2 Ch 30:11), ancestor of the tribe to which the prophet Anna belonged **Lk 2:36.** In the list of the 12 tribes **Rv 7:6** (cp. Demetr.: 722 fgm. 1, 8 Jac.).

ἀσθένεια, ας, ἡ (σθένος 'strength', s. next entry; Hdt., Thu.+)

❶ **a state of debilitating illness, *sickness, disease*** (X., Mem. 4, 2, 32; Appian, Bell. Civ. 5, 16 §65; Herodian 1, 4, 7; pap; 2 Macc 9:21f; Jos., Bell. 1, 76, Ant. 15, 359) **Ac 5:15** D; w. νόσος **Mt 8:17;** ἔχειν ἀ. *be ill* **Ac 28:9;** ἀσθένειαν τῇ σαρκὶ αὐτῶν ἐπισπῶνται Hv 3, 9, 3; θεραπεύεσθαι ἀπὸ τῶν ἀ. **Lk 5:15.** For this ἀπολύεσθαι τῆς ἀ. **13:12;** ἔτη ἔχειν ἐν ἀ. (s. ἔτος end) **J 5:5,** cp. **11:4;** Hs 6, 3, 4. δι' ἀσθένειαν τῆς σαρκός *because of a bodily ailment* (Persaeus [III BC]: 584 fgm. 3a Jac. διὰ τὴν τοῦ σώματος ἀσθένειαν; Dio Chrys. 28 [45], 1 σώματος ἀσθ., likew. Ael. Aristid. 27, 2 K.=16 p. 382 D.—PLond III, 971, 4 p. 128 [III/IV AD] ἀδύνατος γάρ ἐστιν ἡ γυνὴ διὰ ἀσθένιαν τῆς φύσεως, cp. also PFlor 51, 5 σωματικῆς ἀσθενείας) **Gal 4:13.** ἀσθένειαι (pl., as **2 Cor 12:5, 9f**) *times of weakness, weaknesses* **1 Ti 5:23.** Caused by hostile spirits, the πνεύματα ἀσθενείας **Lk 8:2; 13:11.**

❷ **incapacity for someth. or experience of limitation, *weakness***—ⓐ gener., Hv 3, 11, 4; 3, 12, 2. Opp. δύναμις (Diod. S. 4, 8, 3: many do not believe the writers of history when they relate the marvelous deeds of one like Heracles, because they judge the δύναμις of the divine hero in comparison with the ἀσθένεια of contemporary pers.) of inability to function as effectively as one might wish **1 Cor 15:43.** δυναμοῦσθαι ἀπὸ ἀ. *come out of weakness to strength* **Hb 11:34.** In Paul's ἀ., which appears in τὰ τῆς ἀ. μου **2 Cor 11:30** or αἱ ἀσθένειαι (s. 1 above) **12:5, 9f,** all of which suggest ineffectualness, God's δύναμις manifests itself **12:9** (s. τελέω 1 end), thus in effect converting displays of weakness into heroic performance.

ⓑ gener., of the frailty to which all human flesh is heir (Pla., Leg. 854a ἀ. τ. ἀνθρωπίνης φύσεως; Diod. S. 1, 2, 3 ἡ τῆς φύσεως ἀ.; 13, 24, 4 and 6; Orig., C. Cels. 3, 42, 11; Did., Gen. 55, 19) of Christ (Orig., C. Cels. 3, 42, 11) ἐσταυρώθη ἐξ ἀ. (opp. ἐκ δυνάμεως θεοῦ) *he was crucified as a result of his weakness* (his vulnerability as a human being) **2 Cor 13:4.** περίκειται ἀσθένειαν **Hb 5:2.** For this ἀ. ἔχειν **7:28.**

❸ **lack of confidence or feeling of inadequacy, *weakness.*** Of Paul's *self-effacement, timidity* (w. φόβος and τρόμος) **1 Cor 2:3.** Of a sense of *helplessness* (Paul's friends wish that Paul would remain with them 'because of their weakness', i.e. they cannot get along without him) AcPl Ha 6, 36. Of weakness in judgment (cp. Orig., C. Cels. 1, 9, 22) τῆς σαρκός **Ro 6:19.** Of lack of spiritual insight **8:26.** Of moral deficiency 1 Cl 36:1; Hm 4, 3, 4. συμπαθῆσαι ταῖς ἀ. *sympathize w. weaknesses* **Hb 4:15.**—MBarré, CBQ 42, '80, 216–27 (background of persecution in Qumran).—DELG s.v. σθένος. M-M. TW.

ἀσθενέω fut. ἀσθενήσω; 1 aor. ἠσθένησα; pf. ptc. τὸ ἠσθενηκός Ezk 34:4 (s. prec. entry; Eur., Thu. et al.; ins, pap, LXX, TestSol 1:2 codd. VW; Test12Patr, Philo, Joseph.)

❶ **to suffer a debilitating illness, *be sick*** (SIG 596, 16 ἰατρὸν τὸν θεραπεύσοντα τοὺς ἀσθενοῦντας; 620, 43; POxy 725, 40; BGU 844, 12; PLond II, 144, 8 p. 253 [I AD?] et al.; for others s. Preis. index) **Mt 25:39; Lk 7:10 v.l.; J 4:46; 11:1, 2, 3, 6; Phil 2:26f; 2 Ti 4:20; Js 5:14;** ἀ. νόσοις ποικίλαις *suffer from various diseases* **Lk 4:40.**—Pres. ptc. oft. as subst. *sick person* **J 5:7, 13 v.l.;** mostly pl., **Mt 10:8; Mk 6:56; Lk 9:2 v.l.; J 5:3; 6:2; Ac 19:12;** 1 Cl 59:4.—The aor. means *I was sick* **Mt 25:36** or *I have become sick* **Ac 9:37** (Palaeph. p. 44, 2 ἡ Ἕλλη ἀσθενήσασα ἀπέθανεν).

❷ **to experience some personal incapacity or limitation, *be weak*** of weakness in general **2 Cor 12:10;** ἀ. εἴς τινα (opp. δυνατεῖν ἔν τινι) *be weak toward someone* **2 Cor 13:3;** cp. vss. **4, 9.**—Of weakness caused by fear or caution **2 Cor 11:21** (for the satire cp. Demosth. 18, 320). Of weakness in determining correct courses of action **Ro 14:2; 1 Cor 8:11f;** 2 Cl 17:2; ἀ. τῇ πίστει *be weak in faith* **4:19; 14:1** (i.e. over-scrupulous). W. σκανδαλίζεσθαι **Ro 14:21 v.l.** Gener. of faint-heartedness and timidity **2 Cor 11:29.**—*Be weakened, disabled* (Oenomaus in Eus., PE 5, 24, 3; Jos., Bell. 2, 329, Ant. 6, 370; Sb 5113, 19) of the law's weakness: ἐν ᾧ ἠσθένει *because it was weakened* **Ro 8:3.**

❸ **to experience lack of material necessities, *be in need*** (Eur.; Aristoph., Pax 636; PHib 113, 17; UPZ 110, 22; ἠσθενηκότες PTebt 188 [II/I BC]) **Ac 20:35** (s. ἀσθενής 2c).—DELG s.v. σθένος. M-M. TW.

ἀσθένημα, ατος, τό (s. ἀσθενής; Aristot. HA 10, 7, 638a, 37; Gen. An. 1, 18, 726a, 15; uncertain rdg. in BGU 903, 15 [II AD]) ***weakness;*** pl., of conscientious scruples caused by weakness of faith (s. ἀσθενέω 2) **Ro 15:1.**—M-M. TW.

ἀσθενής, ές (Pind., Hdt.+; loanw. in rabb.) adj., of that which lacks strength: 'weak, powerless'.

❶ **pert. to suffering from a debilitating illness, *sick, ill*** ἄνθρωπος ἀ. **Ac 4:9.** Subst. ὁ ἀ. *the sick person* (Diod. S. 1, 34, 4) **Mt 25:43f; Lk 9:2; 10:9; Ac 5:15f;** 1 Cl 59:4 (ἀσεβεῖς cod. H); Pol 6:1. W. ἄρρωστος **1 Cor 11:30** (on the connection betw. wrongdoing and disease cp. PMich Inv. 3690, 7–11 [ZPE 4, '69, 123]).

❷ **pert. to experiencing some incapacity or limitation, *weak***—ⓐ of physical weakness. Opp. ἰσχυρός (cp. Ael. Aristid. 36 p. 690 D.; Philo, Aet. M. 58) 1 Cl 38:2; cp. Hv 3, 11, 4; ἡ σὰρξ ἀ. *the flesh is weak,* gives up too easily **Mt 26:41; Mk 14:38;** Pol 7:2. ἀ. τῇ σαρκί Hs 9, 1, 2. Of woman (PAmh 141, 16 [restored]; PFlor 58, 14 γυνὴ ἀσθενής; cp. POxy 2713, 8f; EpArist 250) ἀσθενέστερον σκεῦος *weaker vessel,* i.e. sex **1 Pt 3:7;** ἀ. τῷ σώματι *physically weak* (cp. PFlor 382, 41; abs. Tat. 32, 3) 1 Cl 6:2. ἡ παρουσία τοῦ σώματος ἀ. *his personal presence is weak* i.e. unimpressive **2 Cor 10:10** (cp. Demosth. 18, 152, s. FDanker, in: Persuasive Artistry [GAKennedy Festschr.]

'91, 276). Acc. to many modern scholars, of spirit beings that can do nothing (w. πτωχός) τὰ ἀ. στοιχεῖα *the weak elementary spirits* **Gal 4:9** (s. στοιχεῖον 2). In imagery of the Christian community: comp., of inferior stones *too weak,* i.e. incapable of standing great strain Hs 9, 8, 4; 6.

ⓑ of relative ineffectiveness, whether external or inward *weak, feeble, ineffectual* ἡμεῖς ἀ. **1 Cor 4:10;** τὰ μέλη ἀσθενέστερα *the weaker, less important members* **12:22.** W. φθαρτός the heart viewed as a shrine B 16:7.—τὸ ἀσθενές = ἡ ἀσθένεια (Thu. 2, 61, 2; POxy 71 II, 4 τὸ τῆς φύσεως ἀ.; Jos., Ant. 13, 430) w. τὸ ἀνωφελές **Hb 7:18;** τὸ ἀ. τοῦ θεοῦ *the weakness of God:* even *what is weak* acc. to human standards becomes effective as soon as it comes *fr. God* **1 Cor 1:25.**—τὰ ἀ. τοῦ κόσμου *what is weak in* (the eyes of) *the world* **1:27.**

ⓒ of the inner life. ὄντων ἡμῶν ἀ. (=ἁμαρτωλῶν vs. 8) *helpless* in a moral sense **Ro 5:6.** Of a weakness in faith, which, through lack of advanced knowledge, considers externals of the greatest importance (cp. Epict. 1, 8, 8 ἀπαιδεύτοις κ. ἀσθενέσι) **1 Cor 8:7, 9f** (WMcGarry, Eccl. Rev. 94, '37, 609–17). ἐγενόμην τοῖς ἀ. ἀ. *to those who are weak in faith I became as they are* **1 Cor 9:22;** ἀντέχεσθαι τῶν ἀ. *take care of the weak* **1 Th 5:14.**—*Weak, without influence* συγγένεια 1 Cl 10:2. οἱ ἀσθενέστεροι Dg 10:5 (but here ἀ. could have the mng. *economically weak, poor,* as pap, e.g. UPZ 17, 23; BGU 1815, 6; 1843, 14; 1863, 10; PHib 113, 17; PThéad 20, 15 τὰς ἀσθενεστέρας κώμας; s. ἀσθενέω 3).—ERiggenbach, StKr 66, 1893, 649–78; MRauer, D. 'Schwachen' in Korinth u. Rom nach den Pls-briefen 1923.—B. 298. New Docs 4, 132–34. DELG s.v. σθένος. M-M.

Ἀσία, ας, ἡ (Pind., Hdt. et al.; ins, LXX, Philo, Joseph., Mel.; on the use of the art. s. B-D-F §261, 5) ***Asia,*** a Rom. province (Asia proprie dicta) in western Asia Minor, formed in 133–130 BC, from the time of Augustus ruled by proconsuls. **Ac 2:9; 16:6; 19:1** D, **10, 22, 26f; 20:4 v.l., 16, 18; 21:27; 24:19; 27:2; 6:9** (καὶ Ἀσίας is lacking in AD*).—**Ro 16:5; 1 Cor 16:19; 2 Cor 1:8; 2 Ti 1:15; 1 Pt 1:1; Rv 1:4;** IEph ins; ITr ins; IPhld ins; ISm ins; MPol 12:2.—See JMarquardt, Röm. Staatsverwaltung I² 1881, 339–49; Mommsen, Röm. Geschichte V 299ff; VChapot, La province romaine procons. d'Asie 1904; DMagie, Roman Rule in Asia Minor '66; AHMJones, The Cities of the Eastern Roman Provinces², '71; KRigsby, TAPA 118, '88, 123–53; Pauly-W. II 1538ff; Kl.-Pauly I 636f.

Ἀσιανός, οῦ, ὁ (Thu. 1, 6, 5; et al.; Philo) **a person from the Roman province of Asia,** ***Asian*** of Tychicus and Trophimus **Ac 20:4.**

Ἀσιάρχης, ου, ὁ (Strabo 14, 1, 42; ins) ***Asiarch,*** plainly equiv. to the ἀρχιερεὺς Ἀσίας (cp. Ramsay, CB I/2, 465 no. 299, where ἀρχιερεῖς is used in the sense 'Asiarchs') MPol 12:2 (cp. 21). Many would understand it so also in **Ac 19:31** (s. e.g. JMarquardt, Röm. Staatsverwaltung I² 1881, 513ff; Lghtf., Ign. and Pol. III² 1889, 404ff; Ramsay, Bearing 88). But the titles are sometimes differentiated (SIG 900, 5), and the pl. in Ac rather favors a ref. to deputies of the κοινὸν Ἀσίας, the assembly of Asia, which met in Ephesus (so finally Beyer; Bauernfeind). Cp. Brandis, Pauly-W. II 1564ff (lit.); JWeiss RE X 538f; Thieme 17; LTaylor: Beginn. I 5, '33, 256–62; DMagie, Roman Rule in Asia Minor, '50, 449f, 1298–1301, 1526; Haenchen, ad loc.—RKearsley, in: BAFCS II, '94, 363–76; idem, New Docs 4, 46–55. DDD 1350. EDNT. M-M.

ἀσιτία, ας, ἡ (s. next entry; Eur., Hdt. et al.; JosAs 11 [p. 12 n. 12, line 4 Istrin] Vatican cod. 364; Jos., Ant. 12, 290; PRyl 10, 6 and 12 [theol. text] in the sense 'a fast, hunger'; so ἀσιτέω Esth 4:16; 1 Macc 3:17) ***lack of appetite*** (Hippocr., Aphor. 7, 6; Hippiatr. I 54, 10; ἄσιτος='without appetite' in Ostracon 2, 35 in Preisendanz, PGM II p. 234 H.) πολλῆς ἀ. ὑπαρχούσης *since almost nobody wanted to eat* because of anxiety or seasickness (seasickness: Ael. Aristid. 48, 68 K.=24 p. 483 D. ἀσιτίαι οὐκ ὀλίγαι in a storm.—JMadan, JTS 6, 1905, 116–21.—Hippiatr. I 3, 7 ἀσιτίας μενούσης) **Ac 27:21.**—DELG s.v. σῖτος ('grain'). M-M.

ἄσιτος, ον (s. prec. entry; Hom.+; Arrian, Anab. 4, 9, 4; TestZeb 4:4) ***without eating, fasting*** **Ac 27:33** (Galen XI 242 K. ἄ. διετέλεσε; cp. Jos., Ant. 10, 258).—M-M.

ἀσκανδάλιστος, ον (since Clem. Al., in act. and pass. senses [s. Lampe s.v.]; Hesych. 6848 gloss on ἀπρόσκοπος; 6852 on ἀπρόσπταιστος [=ἀπρόσκοπος]) ***without being misled*** ὅπως ἀ. μείνῃ ἡ Κορινθίων ἐκκλησία *so that the Corinthian congregation might be free of stumbling* (through erroneous teaching) AcPlCor 1:16. S. σκανδαλίζω.

ἀσκέω impf. ἤσκουν; 1 aor. ἤσκησα Ath. 22, 6; pf. pass. ptc. ἠσκημένος Ath. (s. next entry; Hom.+) **to apply oneself w. commitment to some activity,** ***practice, engage in*** τὶ someth. (so trag., Hdt. et al.; cp. 2 Macc 15:4) ἐμπορίαν ἀ. *engage in business* w. θεοσέβειαν *practice piety* 2 Cl 20:4 (UPZ 144, 24 [164 BC] εὐσέβειαν ἀσκήσαντα; cp. SibOr 4, 170.—Eur., Bacch. 476 ἀσέβειαν; Philo, Cher. 42 εὐσ., Virt. 94 ὁσ.); ἀ. πᾶσαν ὑπομονήν *practice patience to the limit* Pol 9:1 (in Eus., HE 3, 36, 13; ὑπομένειν cod. Vat.) δικαιοσύνην ἀ. (Hdt. 1, 96; Pla., Gorg. 527e; Nicol. Dam.: 90 fgm. 103m, 2 Jac. ἀσκοῦσι εὐσέβειαν κ. δικαιοσύνην; 103w, 2; EpArist 168) Hm 8:10; ἀκακίαν ἀ. Papias (8); βίον παράσημον ἀ. *lead a peculiar kind of life* Dg 5:2 (cp. Sb 5100, 4 epitaph for Abbot David: τὸν μοναδικὸν ἀσκήσας βίον). ἡ εἰς ζωὴν ἀσκουμένη γνῶσις *knowledge which is applied to life* 12:5 (Eur., Electra 1073 γυνὴ . . . , ἥτις ἐκ δόμων ἐς κάλλος ἀσκεῖ=who, outside of her home, pays too much attention to beautifying herself). Abs. ἐν τούτῳ ἀσκῶ w. inf. foll. *therefore I do my best* **Ac 24:16** (cp. X., Cyr. 5, 5, 12, Mem. 2, 1, 6; Epict. 3, 12, 10).—HDressler, Ἀσκέω and its cognates in Gk. Documents to 100 AD, diss. Cath. Univ. of America '47.—New Docs 3, 153. DELG. M-M. TW. Sv.

ἄσκησις, εως, ἡ (s. prec. entry; Thu., et al.; 4 Macc 13:22; Philo, Migr. Abr. 31, Vi. Cont. 28; Jos., C. Ap. 2, 171; Tat. 19, 1; Ath., R. 67, 2 ἀρετῆς ἄ.; PSI I, 422, 29) ***practice*** lit., of athletes, transferred to martyrs, w. ἑτοιμασία MPol 18:3.—FPfister, Deissmann Festschr. 1927, 76–81.—TW. Sv.

ἀσκός, οῦ, ὁ (Hom.+; ins, pap, LXX, TestSol) ***a leather bag,*** esp. ***wine-skin*** (Dio Chrys. 13 [7], 46; Ps.-Apollod., Epit. 7, 4; Jos., Ant. 6, 55 ἀ. οἴνου) **Mt 9:17; Mk 2:22; Lk 5:37f.**—DELG. M-M.

ἄσκυλτος, ον ('not pulled about' Heliodorus Med. [I–II AD] in Oribasius 50, 47, 5; Philumenus Med. [II AD] in Aëtius 9, 23; 'undisturbed' Sextus Emp. P. 1, 71. In pap freq. 'undisturbed' e.g. BGU 638, 13 [II AD]; 650, 20; PFlor 39, 11; POxy 125, 15, s. Preis. index; so also AcThom 12 [Aa II/2, 118, 6] 'lead an untroubled/undisturbed life'). In our lit. only in one passage, where the transf. sense is ***unmoved, without moving:*** Polycarp asks not to be nailed in place, promising that he will not move ἄσκυλτον ἐπιμεῖναι MPol 13:3.—DELG s.v. σκύλλω.

ᾆσμα, ατος, τό (Pl. +; LXX; TestSol 8:2 D; Philo; Jos., C. Ap. 1, 12) *song* ἐποιήσεν ᾆσμα κυρίῳ τῷ θεῷ *Anna sang a song for the Lord God* GJs 6:3.—DELG s.v. ἀείδω.

ἀσμένως adv. fr. ἄσμενος (Aeschyl.+; SIG 742, 52; PGrenf II, 14, 17f; UPZ 110, 160; 145, 31; 2 and 3 Macc; EpArist 5; Jos., Bell. 1, 309 al.; Just., D. 1, 2 al.) ***gladly*** ἀ. ἀποδέχεσθαι *receive* someone *gladly* (Cebes 26, 1 ἀσμ. ὑποδέχεσθαί τινα; Philo, Rer. Div. Her. 295 v.l.; Jos., Ant. 4, 131 ἀ. δέχ. τ. λόγους) **Ac 2:41 v.l.; 21:17.**—DELG s.v. ἄσμενος. M-M.

ἄσοφος, ον (s. σοφός; Theognis, Pind. et al.; PRyl 62, 12; Pr 9:8 v.l.; Just., D. 103, 9) **of one who lacks the power of proper discernment, *unwise, foolish,*** subst. ὁ ἄ. (Philostrat., Vi. Apoll. 6, 39 p. 250, 10) 2 Cl 19:2. Opp. σοφός (Philostrat., op. cit. 3, 43 p. 117, 26f) **Eph 5:15.**—M-M. TW.

ἀσπάζομαι fut. ptc. ἀσπασομένους 3 Macc. 1:8; 1 aor. ἠσπασάμην (s. next entry; Hom.+) 'greet'.

❶ **to engage in hospitable recognition of another** (w. varying degrees of intimacy), ***greet, welcome*** τινά *someone* Just., A I, 65, 2

ⓐ through word or gesture or both: of those entering a house **Mt 10:12; Lk 1:40; Ac 21:19;** Hv 5:1. Of those meeting others (Jos., Ant. 8, 321) **Lk 10:4;** *welcome, greet someone* (Philostrat., Vi. Apoll. 1, 12) **Mk 9:15;** Hv 1, 1, 4; 1, 2, 2; 4, 2, 2; AcPl Ha 7:38; 8:3. Of those departing *take leave of* (X., An. 7, 1, 8; Nicol. Dam.: 90 fgm. 68, 7 Jac.; Plut., Aemil. P. 270 [29, 1] ἀσπασάμενος ἀνέζευξεν) **Ac 20:1, 12** D; **21:6 v.l.;** AcPl Ha 5, 13.—**Mt 5:47** ἀ. here denotes more than a perfunctory salutation and requires some such rendering as *spend time in warm exchange* (cp. X., Cyr. 1, 4, 1; Ael. Aristid. 31, 6 K.=11 p. 128 D.; Aelian, VH 9, 4; Appian, Bell. Civ. 3, 79 §322 τ. ἐναντίους); w. ἀγαπάω (vs. 46), of which it is almost a synonym (as Plut., Mor. 143b; s. HAlmqvist, Plut. u. das NT, '46, 34; Ptolem., Apotel. 1, 3, 17.—W. φιλέω: Hierocles 19, 460; opp. μισέω: Simplicius in Epict. p. 31, 6). See FPorporato, Verb. Domini 11, '31, 15–22.—Freq. in written greetings (cp. the exx. in Ltzm., Griech. Papyri [Kleine Texte 14][2] 1910, nos. 7, 8, 9, 10, 11, 13.—FZiemann, De Epistularum Graec. Formulis Soll., diss. Halle 1911, 325ff; FXJExler, The Form of the Ancient Gk. Letter 1923; ORoller, D. Formular d. paul. Briefe '33, 67ff; HKoskenniemi, Studien z. Idee u. Phraseologie d. griech. Briefes '56, 148ff); the impv. may be transl. *greetings to* (*someone*) or *remember me to* (*someone*); other moods than impv. may be rendered *wish to be remembered, greet, send greetings* **Ro 16:3, 5ff; 1 Cor 16:19f; 2 Cor 13:12; Phil 4:21f; Col 4:10, 12, 14f; 2 Ti 4:19, 21; Tit 3:15; Phlm 23; Hb 13:24; 1 Pt 5:13f; 2J 13; 3J 15;** IMg ins; 15; ITr ins; 12:1; 13:1; IRo ins; 9:3; IPhld ins; 11:2; ISm 11:1; 12:1f; 13:1f; IPol 8:2f. Another person than the writer of the letter sometimes adds greetings of his own **Ro 16:22** (sim. POxy 1067, 25 κἀγὼ Ἀλέξανδρος ἀσπάζομαι ὑμᾶς πολλά). ἀ. πολλά (besides the pap just mentioned also PParis 18, 3 [Dssm., B 215]; POxy 930, 22; 935, 22; PGrenf II, 73, 4 [=Ltzm. Pap. nos. 13, 14, 15]) *greet warmly* **1 Cor 16:19;** ἀ. κατ' ὄνομα (PParis 18, 15 [Dssm., B 216]; POxy 930, 26 [=Ltzm. Pap. no. 13]) *greet by name* **3J 15;** ISm 13:2 (πάντας κατ' ὄνομα as PMich 206, 20ff [II AD]); ἄσπασαι τοὺς φιλοῦντας ἡμᾶς ἐν πίστει (PFay 119, 25ff ἀσπάζου τοὺς φιλοῦντες [sic] ἡμᾶς πρὸς ἀλήθιαν. Sim. BGU 814, 38) **Tit 3:15.** Among friends the greeting is accompanied by a kiss (Ps.-Lucian, De Asin. 17 φιλήμασιν ἠσπάζοντο ἀλλήλους; Heliod. 10, 6; φιλήματι Just., A I, 65, 2; cp. the apocryphal preface Ath. 32, 3 [Resch, Agrapha 137]), hence: ἀ. ἐν φιλήματι **Ro 16:16; 1 Cor 16:20; 2 Cor 13:12; 1 Th 5:26; 1 Pt 5:14.** Of homage to a king *hail, acclaim* (Dionys. Hal. 4, 39; Plut., Pomp. 624 [12, 4]; 13, 7; cp. Jos., Ant. 10, 211) **Mk 15:18** (cp. Philo, In Flacc. 38).

ⓑ of short friendly visits, 'look in on' **Ac 18:22; 21:7;** IRo 1:1. Of official visits *pay one's respects to* (Sb 8247, 13; 15 [II AD]; BGU 248, 12; 347 I, 3 and II, 2; 376 I, 3; Jos., Ant. 1, 290; 6, 207) **Ac 25:13** (OGI 219, 43 [III BC]) s. Schwyzer II 301, also 297. Of the greeting given to a priest in a liturgical service τοῦ ἀσπάσασθαι αὐτὸν ἐν εὐχῇ *to greet him with prayer* GJs 24:1.

❷ **to express happiness about the arrival of someth., *welcome, greet,*** fig. ext. of 1 in ref. to someth. intangible (Eur., Ion 587; Chariton 6, 7, 12; Alciphron 1, 3, 3; Diog. L. σοφίαν ἀσπαζόμενος; POxy 41, 17 τὴν παρ' ὑμῶν τιμήν; CPR 30 II, 39; Philo, Det. Pot. Ins. 21; Jos., Ant. 6, 82; 7, 187; TestGad 3:3; Just.) τὰς ἐπαγγελίας *the promises* **Hb 11:13.**—DELG. M-M. TW.

ἀσπασμός, οῦ, ὁ (s. ἀσπάζομαι; Theognis et al.; Epict. 4, 4, 3; 37; POxy 471, 67; TestSol 18:21 H; EpArist 246; 304; Jos., Ant. 15, 210) ***greeting.***

ⓐ of personal salutations **Lk 1:29, 41, 44;** φιλεῖν etc. **Mt 23:7; Mk 12:38; Lk 11:43; 20:46.** ὥρα τοῦ ἀ. GJs 24:1 (s. ἀσπάζομαι 1b end).

ⓑ of written greetings ὁ ἀ. τῇ ἐμῇ χειρὶ Παύλου **1 Cor 16:21; Col 4:18; 2 Th 3:17.**—DELG s.v. ἀσπάζομαι. M-M. TW.

ἄσπιλος, ον (s. σπίλος; since IG II/5, 1054c, 4 [c. 300 BC, Eleusis] of stones; Nägeli 38; Just., D. 110, 6; Mel., P. 12, 78)

❶ **pert. to being of highest quality and without defect, *spotless,*** of an outward condition (ἵππος Herodian 5, 6, 7; μῆλον Antiphilus [I AD]: Anth. Pal. 6, 252, 3; ἀλέκτωρ PGM 2, 25; 3, 693; 13, 370; Cyranides p. 25, 26 λίθος; 36, 27) ἀμνὸς ἄμωμος καὶ ἄ. *a lamb unblemished and spotless* **1 Pt 1:19.** ἀμνάδας ἀ. GJs 4:3.

❷ **pert. to being of untainted character, *pure, without fault*** of inward condition, as of character (Job 15:15 Sym.) of Christians (w. ἀμώμητος) **2 Pt 3:14,** cp. **Jd 25** P[72] et al. W. καθαρός Hv 4, 3, 5.—Of flesh (=person) w. ἀμίαντος Hs 5, 6, 7. ἄσπιλον ἑαυτὸν τηρεῖν ἀπὸ τ. κόσμου *keep oneself unspotted by the world* **Js 1:27** (on the constr. w. ἀπό s. PGM 12, 260); τηρεῖν τὴν ἐντολὴν ἄ. **1 Ti 6:14;** τηρεῖν τὴν σφραγῖδα ἄ. 2 Cl 8:6.—DELG s.v. 2 σπίλος. M-M. TW.

ἀσπίς, ίδος, ἡ (Hdt., et al.; Antig. Car. 16; Aelian, NA 2, 24; 6, 38; Plut., 380f; Ps.-Oppian, Cyn. 3, 433; OGI 90, 43; Sb 8232, 11; PGM 4, 2116; LXX; Test12Patr; TestAbr AB; TestJob 43:12; JosAs 26:7 [shield]; Philo; Jos., C. Ap. 2, 86; SibOr 3, 794) 'asp, Egyptian cobra', gener. of venomous snakes ἰὸς ἀσπίδων *venom of asps* **Ro 3:13** (Ps 13:3; 139:4).—DELG. M-M. TW.

ἄσπλαγχνος, ον (s. σπλάγχνον, fig. as seat of the emotions; Soph., et al.) since the ancients freq. associated emotion with the inward parts, a lack of compassion could be indicated by metaphorical use of the term σπλάγχνον + α- priv., ***merciless*** (so Chrysipp. II 249; Dt 32:33 Aq.; Ezk 31:12 Sym.; Pr 17:11) *ruthless* w. πικρός Hs 6, 3, 2.—DELG s.v. σπλήν. TW.

ἄσπονδος, ον (σπονδή 'treaty') **of one who is unwilling to negotiate a solution to a problem involving a second party, *irreconcilable*** (so Aeschyl., et al.; Demosth. 18, 262; Polyb. 1, 65, 6; Cicero, Ad Att. 9, 10, 5; Philo, Virt. 131, Mos. 1, 242; Jos., Ant. 4, 264) in a list of vices **Ro 1:31 v.l.; 2 Ti 3:3** (in both passages w. ἄστοργος, as schol. on Nicander, Ther. 367).—DELG s.v. σπένδω. M-M.

ἀσσάριον, ου, τό (Lat. loanw.: assarius [nummus]; s. Hahn index; Schürer II 66; OGI 484, 13 w. n. 14; Kubitschek in Pauly-W. II 1742ff.—s. ἀργύριον end) **a Roman copper coin, worth**

about one-sixteenth of a denarius, *as, assarion* (s. δηνάριον), or a similar native coin ἀσσαρίου πωλεῖσθαι *be sold for a paltry sum* **Mt 10:29** (a cliché, s. e.g. Cato in Seneca, Ep. 94, 27 quod non opus est, asse carum est=even an 'as' is too high a price for something you don't need); **Lk 12:6** (two assaria = [only] an hour's work; 'two pennies' NRSV does not reflect economic reality; DMacDonald, Historia 38, '89, 120–23; TMartin, Biblical Research 38, '93, 69–73). Dssm., LO 196 (LAE 272–75).—M-M.

Ἀσσάρων, ωνος Ac 9:35 v.l.; s. Σαρ(ρ)ων.

ἆσσον adv. (comp. of ἄγχι) ***nearer*** (Hom., et al.; Jos., Ant. 1, 328; 19, 198) ἆσσον παρελέγοντο τὴν Κρήτην *they sailed along closer* (or *close;* B-D-B §244, 2) *to Crete* **Ac 27:13.** (The Vulg. understands Ἄσσον, s. next entry)—DELG s.v. ἄγχι.

Ἄσσος, ου, ἡ *Assos,* a city on the coast of Mysia, in the Rom. province of Asia (Stephan. Byz. s.v. Ἄσσος after Alexander Cornelius Polyhistor) **Ac 20:13f.**

ἀστατέω (s. ἄστατος, ἵστημι, ἵσταμαι; Plut., Crass. 533 [17, 1]; Vett. Val. 116, 30; Anth. Pal. App. 3, 146, 4 [App. Nova Epigrammatum ed. ECougny 1890]; mostly = 'be unsteady'; Nägeli 44) **to be without a permanent residence, *be unsettled, be homeless*** (Is 58:7 Aq.) of Paul's way of life **1 Cor 4:11** (Field, Notes 170, 'vagabond').—DELG s.v. ἵστημι. M-M. TW.

ἄστατος, ον (s. ἀστατέω, ἵστημι; Aristot. et al. in various senses) lit. of someth. that does not remain fixed: 'unsteady, unstable' (Polyb. et al.); in our lit., and only once, it appears to be used in the sense ***unweighed*** (Nicander, Ther. 602; IG I, 32b, 25 al.; PSI 368, 49): in PEg[2] 62, in a fragmentary context (the first half of the line is missing entirely), the second half of the line is restored thus: τ̣ὸ̣ βάρος̣ α̣ὐτοῦ ἄστ̣α̣τ̣ο(ν). The editors translate it (p. 28): 'its weight unweighed(?)' (s. L-S-J-M s.v. ἵστημι A, IV). Perh. in the sense 'undetermined', if the the ref. is to a seed so fertile that its produce defies accurate weighing.—DELG s.v. ἵστημι.

ἄστεγος, ον (s. στέγος; Manetho 1, 173; Appian, Iber. 78 §336; Philo, Fuga 189; Ps.-Phoc. 24) of one who may be said to have no roof (over the head) ***homeless*** B 3:3 (Is 58:7).—DELG s.v. στέγος.

ἀστεῖος, α, ον (Aristoph. et al.; X., Pla.; LXX, Philo; Jos., Ant. 7, 147; Just., D. 1, 6) adj., fr. ἄστυ. In Greece 'the city' (ἄστυ) was Athens and in Egypt it was Alexandria. The splendid edifices and culture of such sites would offer a striking contrast to conditions in the countryside (ἀγρός), hence ἀστεῖος 'befitting a city' (Lat. urbanus) denotes good breeding, refinement (our colloq. 'class'; as applied to conduct s. Philo, Mos. 1, 18; Spec. Leg. 1, 284 ἄξιον αὑτὸν παρεχέτω τῶν εὐπραγιῶν ἀστεῖος ὤν 'let him show himself worthy of such benefits by appropriate behavior'; Num 22:32; of personal grace and charm, PHib 54, 16; PCairZen 562, 21; Judg 3:17; Jdth 11:23; Sus 7) ***handsome*** of Moses (s. Ex 2:2), who bears the marks of good breeding **Hb 11:23** (the narrative structure suggests that Moses would be a match for Pharaoh, cp. vs. 24). Sim. ***well-bred*** ἀ. τῷ θεῷ **Ac 7:20** of Moses, whose shepherd background would be a mark of ill-breeding to Egyptians, but God considers him a person of refined status, a perspective developed in the narrative that follows (s. vss. 22, 35f). For the probability that τ. θεῷ functions as a superl. 'very well-bred pers.' (cp. Jon 3:3 of Nineveh μεγάλη τῷ θεῷ 'a very great city') s. θεός 3gβ.—DELG s.v. ἄστυ. Schmidt, Syn. II 505. M-M. Spicq.

ἀστήρ, έρος, ὁ (Hom.+; ins, a few times in astron. and magic. pap [e.g. PGM 4, 574; 580; 2891; 2894; 2939], LXX, pseudepigr., Philo [e.g. Plant. 12 ἀστέρες as living beings endowed w. reason], apolog., loanw. in rabb.) **a luminous body (other than the sun) visible in the sky, *star, single star, planet*** (Achilles, Comm. in Arat. p. 41 ἀστήρ ἐστιν εἷς ἀριθμῷ; schol. on Pind., O. 1, 9d) IEph 19:2. Of the star of the Magi **Mt 2:2, 7, 9f;** GJs 21:1; περὶ τοῦ ἀ. vs. 2; εἶδον ἀστέρας . . . καὶ προῆγαν αὐτούς vs. 3 (pap). (FBoll, ZNW 18, 1918, 40–48. Diod. S. 16, 66, 3: a marvelous, divinely sent heavenly body leads the fleet of Timoleon toward Italy. When he and his companions noticed this heavenly manifestation, περιχαρεῖς ἦσαν [16, 66, 5].—On the star s. μάγος 1.) Falling fr. heaven in the last tribulation **Mt 24:29; Mk 13:25; Rv 6:13** (all three Is 13:10; cp. Artem. 2, 36 p. 137, 15 καταπίπτοντες εἰς γῆν οἱ ἀστέρες). Single stars **8:10; 9:1** (cp. Artem. 5, 23 τ. οὐρανοῦ ἀστέρα ἐκπεσεῖν; Ps.-Callisth. 3, 33, 26: at the death of Alexander μέγας ἀστὴρ πεσὼν ἐκ τ. οὐρανοῦ ἐπὶ τὴν θάλασσαν.—Boll, Offb. 135). Changed at Christ's parousia B 15:5. W. sun and moon (Dt 4:19; TestNapht 3:2) **1 Cor 15:41; Rv 8:12; 12:1** (Eratosth. 33 ἔχει ἀστέρας ἐπὶ τ. κεφαλῆς); 1 Cl 20:3; B 15:5. Of the stars as numberless (Gen 22:17; 1 Ch 27:23 al.) 1 Cl 10:6 (Gen 15:5); 32:2 (Gen 22:17).—As to the seven stars that the Son of Man holds in his right hand **Rv 1:16; 2:1; 3:1,** it has been conjectured that the imagery is based on a constellation, prob. that of the Great Bear (Strabo 1, 1, 21 τοὺς ἑπτὰ τῆς μεγάλης ἄρκτου ἀστέρας; almost the same thing in Diod. S. 3, 48, 1.—Philo, Op. M. 114, Leg. All. 1, 8; PGM 4, 700; ADieterich, Mithraslit. 1903, 14; 16f; 72f; Boll, Offb. 21f). In **1:20** they are interpr. to mean the ἄγγελοι (PGM 1, 74f star=angel; cp. 154; Chrysipp., Stoic. II 1076 and Diod. S. 2, 30, 6 stars=gods; En 18:14=heavenly beings) of the seven churches, by which are meant the guardian angels (so fr. Origen, Hom. 12 and 13 In Luc., De Orat. 11, to Bousset, Charles, Lohmeyer; JSickenberger, Röm. Quartalschr. 35, 1927, 135–49), not overseers/bishops (Primasius and Bede to Zahn, JWeiss, Billerb., Allo.—ἀ. to designate a prominent pers.: Plut., Marcell. 316 [30, 8] ὁ μέγας πατρίδος ἀ.). ἀ. ὁ πρωϊνός *the morning star* (Venus) likened to Christ **22:16;** δώσω αὐτῷ τὸν ἀ. τὸν πρωϊνόν **2:28** (on both passages s. Boll, Offb. 47–50). Other pass. that associate pers. w. celestial bodies—a practice going back largely, as some hold, to Babyl. apocalyptic—are **8:11, 12; 12:1, 4,** which also contain the word ἀ.—ἀστέρες πλανῆται *wandering stars* (Cicero, De Nat. Deor. of stars 'quae falso vocantur errantes'), perh. meteors, typical of dissident teachers **Jd 13** (cp. En 18:14; also chap. 21).—FBoll, Sternglaube u. Sterndeutung[4] '31 (lit.); EZimer, Sternglaube u. Sternforschung '53.—B. 56. DDD 1530–40. DELG. EDNT. M-M. TW.

ἀστήρικτος, ον (s. στηρίζω; Περὶ ὕψους 2, 2; Anth. Pal. 6, 203, 11; Vett. Val., Ind.; Galen, De Usu Part. II 1, 30, 9 [II 459 Helmr., index]; Dionys. Byz. §20; Schol. on Pl.144a) ***unstable, weak*** ψυχαὶ ἀ. *unst. persons* **2 Pt 2:14.** Subst. οἱ ἀ. (w. ἀμαθεῖς) **3:16.**—DELG s.v. στηρίζω. M-M. TW.

ἀστομάχητος, ον (στομαχικός 'of the stomach', 'with stomach disorder'; Alciphron 4, 17, 2; CIG 6647; PBad II, 35, 17 [87 AD]) lit. of one who does not have a disorder in the stomach; metaph. ***not easily angered*** (w. μακρόθυμος) Hv 1, 2, 3 (on the association of emotive aspect with inner bodily parts, s. ἄσπλαγχνος).—DELG s.v. στόμα.

ἄστοργος, ον (s. στέργω; Aeschin. et al.; Hellen. poets; Plut.; M. Ant. [Nägeli 17]; Athen. 14 p. 655c; IAndrosIsis 44;

Kaibel 146, 6; 1028, 44; cp. adv. ἀστοργῶς IKyme 41, 21f) of one who is **lacking in good feelings for others,** thereby jeopardizing the maintenance of relationships (e.g. political and familial) that are essential to a well-ordered society; ***hardhearted, unfeeling, without regard for others*** in a catalogue of vices **Ro 1:31; 2 Ti 3:3.**—DELG s.v. στέργω. M-M.

ἀστοχέω (στοχάζομαι 'aim at' someth., s. ἀστόχημα; fr. III BC, Polyb. et al.; ins, pap, LXX; TestSol 18:28; Jos., Bell. 4, 116; s. Nägeli 31) orig. 'miss the mark', then of the inner life **to go astray by departing from moral or spiritual standards, *miss, fail, deviate, depart*** w. gen. *fr. someth.* (Plut., Mor. 414f; SIG 543, 28 [214 BC]; POxy 219, 21; UPZ 6, 26 [163 BC] ἀστοχήσαντες τοῦ καλῶς ἔχοντος; Sir 7:19; 8:9) **1 Ti 1:6;** ἀ. περί τι (Plut., Mor. p. 46a; 705c) περὶ τὴν πίστιν *miss the mark w. regard to the faith* **6:21;** ἀ. περὶ τὴν ἀλήθειαν **2 Ti 2:18.** κατά τινος *wrong someone* D 15:3. Abs. (BGU 531 II, 19 [I AD]) οἱ ἀστοχήσαντες *those who have gone astray* (in word and deed) w. ἀρνησάμενοι 2 Cl 17:7.—DELG s.v. στόχος. M-M.

ἀστόχημα, ατος, τό (s. ἀστοχέω; Plut. Curios. 520b) ***mistake, error*** ἐν πολλοῖς ὧν ἀστοχήμασι *since I must deal w. numerous errors* (in teaching) AcPlCor 2:2.

ἀστραπή, ῆς, ἡ (s. ἀστράπτω; Aeschyl., Hdt.+; PGM 7, 785; LXX, TestSol, TestAbr A, JosAs; GrBar 16:3; Jos., Ant. 2, 343; 5, 201; Just., D. 67, 10; Mel., fgm. 8b, 25; 30)

❶ ***lightning*** (Hdt. et al.) illuminating the whole sky **Mt 24:27.** Proceeding fr. God's throne **Rv 4:5** (cp. Ezk 1:13; PGM 4, 703). Accompanying cosmic phenomena (En 14:8) **8:5; 11:19; 16:18** (cp. PGM 4, 681f; 694ff. The combin. w. βρονταί also Diod. S. 4, 2, 3; Epict. 2, 18, 30; hymn to Isis POxy 1380, 238; Jos., Ant. 3, 184). Type of the greatest speed **Lk 10:18** (cp. TestSol 20:17; FSpitta, ZNW 9, 1908, 160–63) and brilliance **17:24; Mt 28:3** (cp. Na 2:5). ἀ. πυρός *fiery lightning* ApcPt fgm. 1.

❷ Of a lamp ***light*** (Aeschyl., fgm. 386) **Lk 11:36.**—B. 56. DDD 970–73. DELG s.v. ἀστεροπή (cp. ἀστήρ). M-M. TW.

ἀστράπτω (s. ἀστραπή; Hom. et al.; Epict. 1, 29, 61; PGM 5, 150; 7, 234; 8, 92; LXX; TestAbr A 7 p. 84, 5 [Stone p. 16] al.; JosAs 23:14 cod. A; Philo, Aet. M. 86) ***flash, gleam*** ἀστραπὴ ἀστράπτουσα (cp. Ps 143:6) *lightning flashing* **Lk 17:24.** Of clothing *gleam* like lightning **24:4** (suggesting the opposite of a scene of mourning such as one might normally expect, cp. Aeschin. 3, 77).—EDNT. M-M.

ἄστρον, ου, τό (Hom.+ [the sg. is non-Hom. and rarely used in older Gk.]; ins, pap, LXX; En 18:14; PsSol 1:5; TestSol; Test12Patr; JosAs 2:11; 18:7 cod. A; ApcEsdr 5:4 p. 29, 28 Tdf.; Philo; Jos., Ant. 1, 31, C. Ap. 2, 117; Ar. 4, 2; Just.; Tat.; Mel., fgm. 8b, 18; 37; 41; Ath. 13:2) ***star, constellation,*** also ***single star*** (=ἀστήρ: Posidon. in Stob., Flor. 1, 24 p. 518 [HDiels, Doxogr. Graec. 1879 p. 466, 20] διαφέρειν ἀστέρα ἄστρου. εἰ μὲν γάρ τίς ἐστιν ἀστήρ, καὶ ἄστρον ὀνομασθήσεται δεόντως, οὐ μὴν ἀνάπαλιν; PGM 1, 75; Galen CMG V 10, 1 [XVIIa p. 16, 6ff K.]; s. Boll, ZNW 18, 1918, 4ff) w. sun and moon (Pla., Leg. 10 p. 898d; Dio Chrys. 80 [30], 28; Epict. 2, 16, 32; 3, 13, 16 al.; Jo 2:10; Ezk 32:7) **Lk 21:25;** Dg 4:5; 7:2; (w. ἀστήρ) IEph 19:2. Normally showing sailors the way at night **Ac 27:20.** Typical of a large number **Hb 11:12** (Ex 32:13; Dt 1:10; 10:22 al.; Philo, Rer. Div. Her. 86; Jos., Ant. 1, 183). τὸ ἀ. τοῦ θεοῦ Ῥαιφάν *the constellation of the god R.* **Ac 7:43** (Am 5:26) s. Ῥαιφάν. In contrast to the star over Bethlehem ἀστέρα … λάμψαντα ἐν τοῖς ἄ. τούτοις GJs 21:2 (not pap).—Of the harmonious stellar movements created by God ἄστρων ἐναρμόνιος κίνησις Hm, 12, 4, 1 v.l.—DELG s.v. ἀστήρ. M-M. TW.

ἀσυγκρασία, ας, ἡ (α- priv. + σύγκρασις 'commixture'; not found elsewh.) ***lack of sharing/community spirit*** Hv 3, 9, 4.—DELG s.v. κεράννυμι.

ἀσύγκριτος, ον (α- priv. + σύγκριτος 'comparable'; Theophr. et al.; Epicurus [in Diog. L. 10, 83]; Plut., Marcell. 307 [17, 7]; Herm. Wr. 6, 5; GDI 4481, 8 [Laconia]; IGal 110, 8f; BGU 613, 20; PGen 55, 4ff; POxy 1298, 1; Philo; TestLevi 2:9; Jewish ins: RGarrucci, Dissert. Archeol. II 1865, p. 179, no 8; 182 no. 21; Tat. 15, 2) ***incomparable*** ISm 13:2 (here w. εὔτεκνος, scarcely a proper name; s. the foll. entry) πρᾶξις ἀ. *conduct beyond compare* Hm 7:1.—DELG s.v. κρίνω.

Ἀσύγκριτος, ου, ὁ (CIL VI, 12565 [Rome]; IX, 114; 224; XII, 3192; PLips 98 I, 2; POxy 1413, 21f; perh. also IG III, 1093h, 5) ***Asyncritus*** **Ro 16:14.** S. the preceding entry.—New Docs 2, 108. M-M.

ἀσύμφορος, ον (s. σύμφορος; Hes., Thu. et al.; Dio Chrys. 3, 91; 10 [11], 13; Pr 25:20; Philo) adj. 'pert. to unsuitability', then ***disadvantageous, harmful*** ἀ. ἐστί τινι *it is harmful for someone* 2 Cl 6:1; Hm 4, 3, 6; 5, 1, 4; 5, 2, 2; 6, 2, 6; s 1:10; w. inf. foll. 1:5.—Frisk s.v. φέρω.

ἀσύμφωνος, ον (s. σύμφωνος; Pla. et al.; Bel 17; Philo) 'pert. to harmony of voiced sounds', 'discordant' (Wsd 18:10), then of personal relationships, ***in disagreement w.*** (Pla., Gorg. 482c; Plut., Agis 800 [10, 8]; Jos., C. Ap. 1, 38; cp. Vett. Val., Ind. II; Tat. 25, 2) *being in disagreement with* ἀ. ὄντες πρὸς ἀλλήλους (Diod. S. 4, 1) *they disagreed w. each other* **Ac 28:25.**—DELG s.v. φωνή. M-M.

ἀσύνετος, ον (s. συνετός; Hdt. et al.; POxy 471, 89; LXX; TestSol 16:5; TestLevi 7:2; GrBar 16:2; Jos., Bell. 6, 170, Ant. 1, 117; Ar. 12:6; Just.) the noun σύνεσις (fr. συνίημι) refers to bringing together of things or persons (juncture of two rivers Hom., Od. 10, 515), then to inward organization ('understanding'); one who lacks σύνεσις is **void of understanding, *senseless, foolish,*** implying also a lack of high moral quality (Kaibel 225, 3; Sir 15:7; TestLevi 7:2).

ⓐ of pers. (as Job 13:2) **Mt 15:16; Mk 7:18;** B 2:9; Hv 3, 10, 9; m 10, 1, 2f; ἀ. ἄνθρωπος Hv 3, 8, 9; ἔθνος ἀ. **Ro 10:19** (Dt 32:21); ἀσύνετόν τινα ποιεῖν Hv 3, 10, 9. In a play on words σύνιε ἀσύνετε *understand, you fool* s 9, 12, 1 and ἀσυνέτους ἀσυνθέτους *senseless, faithless* **Ro 1:31;** in the latter pass. ἀσύνετος prob. refers to gross lack of understanding respecting one's obligations in society (ἀ. in a list of vices also Dio Chrys. 2, 75. W. ἀσύνθετος [and ἄφρων] PCairMasp 97 verso D, 84). W. ἄφρων Hs 9, 14, 4 (cp. Ps 91:7). ἀ. εἰς τὰ μέλλοντα *without understanding of the future* B 5:3. W. μωρός Hv 3, 6, 5; s 9, 22, 4. W. ἄφρων, μωρός and other characteristics 1 Cl 39:1. W. ἄφρων, δίψυχος Hm 12, 4, 2.

ⓑ used w. an impers. noun (Aristoph., Av. 456 φρὴν ἀ.) καρδία **Ro 1:21;** 1 Cl 51:5 (cp. Ps 75:6); ἡ ἀ. καὶ ἐσκοτωμένη διάνοια *the foolish and darkened mind* 1 Cl 36:2; (w. πονηρός) διψυχία Hm 9:9.—DELG s.v. ἵημι. M-M. TW.

ἀσύνθετος, ον (s. συντίθημι; Pla.+; PFamTebt 15, 69 and 90; Eth. Epicur. col. 19, 19; Herm. Wr. 14, 6) **pert. to such as renege on their word, *faithless.*** The noun συνθήκη refers to a formal agreement or compact; an ἀσύνθετος pers. does not keep an agreement (Hesychius and Sudas explain ἀ.: μὴ ἐμμένων ταῖς συνθήκαις; cp. Demosth. 19, 136; Jer 3:7–11) **Ro 1:31.** In favor of the sense *undutiful* in this pass. is the ref. to disobedience that precedes (γονεῦσιν ἀπειθεῖς; cp. PCairMasp 97 verso D, 84 ἀ. παῖς). The term appears in a list of vices (as Ptolem., Apotel. 3, 14, 35 Boll-B.); s. also ἀσύνετος a.—AFridrichsen, ConNeot. 9, '44, 47f: 'self-willed.'—DELG s.v. τίθημι. M-M.

ἀσύνκ., s. ἀσύγκ.

ἀσφάλεια, ας, ἡ (s. ἀσφαλής; Aeschyl.+; loanw. in Aramaic and in rabb. Heb. [s. LAlexander, The Preface to Luke's Gospel '93, 141, n. 44]) the verb σφάλλω freq. refers to the act of making someone fall or trip; ἀ. marks 'security against stumbling/falling'; hence, in var. transf. senses

❶ **a stable and salutary circumstance,** ***safety, security*** (Jos., Ant. 2, 245) w. εἰρήνη **1 Th 5:3** (X., Mem. 3, 12, 7; Epict. 1, 9, 7; in ins w. ἀσυλία and ἀτέλεια, s. index SIG and OGI; LXX). ὡς . . . ἐν ἀ. ἤδη ἦσαν AcPl Ha 3, 21.

❷ **stability of idea or statement,** ***certainty, truth*** τ. λόγων **Lk 1:4** (=be clear about the accounts; difft. X., Mem. 4, 6, 15 ἀ. λόγου of rhetorical procedure; ἀ. is also a legal t.t. for a written guarantee ='security' [Epict. 2, 13, 7; PAmh 78, 16 ἀσφάλιαν γραπτήν; PTebt 293, 19]).—J Ropes, St Luke's Preface; ἀσφάλεια and παρακολουθεῖν: JTS 25, 1924, 67–71; FVogel, NKZ 44, '33, 203ff; CMoule, memorial volume for TWManson '59, 165–79; LAlexander, s. above, 140f.

❸ **detention that restricts movement,** ***security*** κεκλεισμένος ἐν πάσῃ ἀ. *securely locked* **Ac 5:23** (Jos., Bell. 3, 398 φρουρεῖν μετὰ πάσης ἀσφαλείας; SIG 547, 30; 2 Macc 3:22). χωρὶς τῆς ὑμετέρας ἐκ τῶν ἥλων ἀσφαλείας *without being fastened w. nails by you* MPol 13:3.—DELG s.v. σφάλλω. M-M. TW. Spicq.

ἀσφαλής, ές (s. ἀσφάλεια; Hom. et al.; Epict., ins, pap, LXX, TestSol, Philo, Joseph., Just.; Ath., R.)

❶ **pert. to being stable,** ***firm*** ἄγκυρα **Hb 6:19** (w. βέβαιος, as Cebes 18, 3; 31, 1; Sext. Emp., Adv. Math. 8, 374; BGU 419, 18; Wsd 7:23; Dio Chrys. 34, 17 and 37; cp. 33, 17). τὸν ἀ. θεμέλιον *the sure foundation* 1 Cl 33:3 (cp. Wsd 4:3).

❷ fig. (Philo, Exs. 153; Jos., Bell. 2, 524) **pert. to expression that ensures certainty about someth.,** ***certain,*** ἀσφαλές τι γράφειν *write someth. definite* **Ac 25:26;** τὸ ἀ. *the certainty = the truth* (in ref. to ferreting out the facts; cp. Mitt-Wilck, I/2, 17, 8 [Traj.] ἵνα τὸ ἀ. ἐπιγνῶ) γνῶναι **21:34; 22:30;** ἡ ἀ. γνῶσις 1 Cl 1:2; Dg 12:4.

❸ **pert. to being in someone's best interest,** ***safe, secure*** (Demosth. 10, 70 βίος ἀ.; Jos., Ant. 3, 41 ἀ. καὶ σῶφρον=the safest and wisest) ὑμῖν (ἐστιν) ἀσφαλές *it is* (a) *safe* (course) *for you* **Phil 3:1.** ἀσφαλὲς εἶναι ISm 8:2.—B. 756; 1237. DELG s.v. σφάλλω. M-M. TW. Spicq.

ἀσφαλίζω (ἀσφαλής) 1 aor. pass. ἠσφαλίσθην; in our lit. the mid. ἠσφαλισάμην is used for the act. (so since Epicurus 215 p. 164, 22; Polyb. 6, 22, 4; 9, 3, 3; and often, e.g. Diod. S. 18, 52, 4; OGI 613, 4; PTebt 53, 29; POxy 1033, 13; LXX; TestSol 6:5 D; TestAbr A 13 p. 92, 23 [Stone p. 32]; TestJob 5:3; 39:8 al.; EpArist 104; Jos., Ant. 13, 22; 183).

❶ **to ensure security by preventive measures—**ⓐ ***guard*** τινά *someone* against escape (PTebt 283, 18–20 [I BC] τὸν προγεγραμμένον Π. ἀσφαλίσασθαι [actively]; cp. 800, 35 [I BC]; PRyl 68, 19) **Ac 16:30** D.

ⓑ ***fasten, secure*** τοὺς πόδας εἰς τὸ ξύλον *fasten (their) feet in the stocks* **16:24.**

ⓒ ***make secure,*** against tampering τ. τάφον (BGU 1036, 11 κέλλα ἠσφαλισμένη 'storage room secured'; PHamb 29, 12f) **Mt 27:64ff.**

❷ fig. **to cause to be safe,** ***safeguard, watch over*** ἀ. τινα (Epicurus [see above]; Is 41:10) IPhld 5:1.—DELG s.v. σφάλλω. M-M. s.v. ἀσφαλίζομαι. TW. Spicq.

ἀσφαλῶς adv. fr. ἀσφαλής (Hom. et al.; Epict. 2, 13, 21; 2, 17, 33; ins [e.g. SIG, ind.]; PGiss 19, 14; PHib 53, 3; JosAs 7:6 cod. A (for ἰσχυρῶς); 10:5; EpArist 46; 312; Joseph., Ar.)

❶ **in a manner that ensures continuing detention,** ***securely,*** ἀ. τηρεῖν τινα *guard someone securely* **Ac 16:23;** ἀπάγειν ἀ. *lead away under guard* **Mk 14:44.**

❷ **pert. to being certain,** ***assuredly, certainly,*** of intellectual and emotive aspects (Appian, Bell. Civ. 2, 125 §521; EpArist 312; Jos., Ant. 1, 106) ἀ. γινώσκειν *know beyond a doubt* **Ac 2:36** (cp. Wsd 18:6). πάν|τως γὰρ ἐκεῖνος εἰδὼς αὐτὴν ἀσ|φ[αλ]ῶ[ς] ἠγάπησεν *he* (the Savior), *knowing her* (Mary Magdalene) *well* (πάντως), *was certainly fond of her* GMary 463, 23f. The Coptic version appears to link ἀ. w. εἰδώς, in which case the Gk. could be rendered *for he certainly knew her.*—DELG s.v. σφάλλω. TW. Spicq.

ἀσχημονέω fut. 3 sg. ἀσχημονήσει (s. ἀσχήμων; Eur.; X., Pla., pap, oft. = incur disgrace by virtue of circumstances; so LXX; Just. D. 9, 2; Tat. 33, 1) the noun σχῆμα refers to someth. that has a pattern or form, freq. of a type that the public considers standard or laudable; to act contary to the standard=***behave disgracefully, dishonorably, indecently*** (X. et al.; Dionys. Hal. 4, 65; Plut., Cat. Min. 770 [24, 6]; Vett. Val. 64, 10; 67, 7; 81, 25; SB 6222, 20; PTebt 44, 17 [114 BC]; Philo, Cher. 94) **1 Cor 13:5** (v.l. εὐσχημονεῖ, q.v.). εἴ τις ἀσχημονεῖν ἐπὶ τὴν παρθένον αὐτοῦ νομίζει *if anyone thinks he is behaving dishonorably toward his fianceé* **7:36** (s. γαμίζω).—DELG s.v. ἔχω. M-M.

ἀσχημοσύνη, ης, ἡ (ἀσχήμων)—❶ **behavior that elicits disgrace,** ***shameless deed*** (Anacharsis [600 BC] in Diog. L. 1, 103 in pl.; Pla.; PLond 1915, 23; Epict. 2, 5, 23; Vett. Val. 61, 31; Sir 26:8; 30:13; TestLevi 10:3; Philo, Leg. All. 2, 66; 3, 158; Jos., Ant. 16, 223; SibOr 5, 389) **Ro 1:27** in a vice list.

❷ **appearance that deviates from a standard,** ***unbecoming appearance,*** *abnormality,* of Judas's genitals Papias (3:2); *embarrassing condition,* of Mary's pregnant condition GJs 17:3.

❸ **a state of disgrace,** ***disgracefulness,*** associated w. nakedness **Rv 3:18 v.l.** (s. αἰσχύνη 2).

❹ **someth. considered too private for public exposure,** ***nakedness*** euphem.= *genitals* (Ex 20:26; Dt 23:14; Lev 18:6ff Hb. עֶרְוָה) βλέπειν τὴν ἀ. **Rv 16:15.**—DELG s.v. ἔχω. M-M.

ἀσχήμων, ον (s. ἀσχημονέω, ἀσχημοσύνη; Eur., Hdt. et al.; Epict. 2, 16, 18; 4, 9, 5; Vett. Val. 62, 16; SIG 736, 4; BGU 1247, 10; PTebt 44, 10; PRyl 144, 18; 150, 11; LXX; EpArist 211; Jos., Ant. 16, 363; freq. of someth. that is not openly done, displayed, or discussed in reserved society because it is considered 'shameful, unpresentable, indecent', or 'unmentionable', opp. εὐσχήμων). The word is applied esp. to sexual matters in Dio Chrys. 2 (40), 29; LXX Gen 34:7, Dt 24:1; Theod. Sus 63 (s. ἀσχημοσύνη 1). Hence τὰ ἀ. (it is prob. unnecessary to supply μέλη) *the unpresentable parts* i.e. those that elicit special modesty, *genitalia* **1 Cor 12:23** (on the topic cp. περὶ ὕψους 43, 5)—DELG s.v. ἔχω. M-M.

ἀσώματος, ον (σῶμα; Pla. et al.; Philostrat., Vi. Apoll. 8, 18 p. 333, 26; Plotinus 1, 6, 6 al.; Herm. Wr. 2, 4b θεῖον ἢ θεός; Celsus 3, 32; PGM 4, 1777; ὁ ἀ. [Michael] TestAbr A 3 p. 79, 29 [Stone p. 6] al.; πνεύματα ἀ. TestSol 2:5 L; Philo; Just.; Tat. 25, 2; Ath.) ***bodiless*** δαιμόνιον (q.v. 2) ISm 3:2; w. δαιμονικός ISm 2.—TW. Sv.

ἀσωτία, ας, ἡ (s. σῴζω; Pla. et al.; Polyb. 32, 11, 10; 39, 7, 7; PFay 12, 24 [103 BC]; Pr 28:7; 2 Macc 6:4; TestJud 16:1; TestAsh 5:1 v.l.) the verb σῴζω refers to preservation, hence ἀσωτία gener. denotes 'wastefulness' (for a detailed discussion of the topic Aristot., EN 4, 1–45), then **reckless abandon, *debauchery, dissipation, profligacy,*** esp. exhibited in convivial gatherings (Athen. 11, 485a ἀπὸ τῶν εἰς τ. μέθας κ. τ. ἀσωτίας πολλὰ ἀναλισκόντων) *debauchery* **Eph 5:18;** *wild living* **Tit 1:6;** *flood of dissipation* τῆς ἀ. ἀνάχυσις **1 Pt 4:4.**—DELG s.v. σῶς. M-M. TW. Spicq.

ἀσώτως (s. ἀσωτία; Theopomp. [IV BC]: 115 fgm. 224; Demosth. 40, 58) adv. of ἄσωτος 'profligate' (Soph. et al.; Pr 7:11; Test12Patr; Just., A I, 61, 11 of madness that knows no bounds; Tat. 12:3; loanw. in rabb.) ***wastefully, prodigally*** ζῆν of a spendthrift lifestyle (Aesop, Fab. 304 H.=169 P.; Lucian, Catapl. 17; ζῆν ἀσώτως, opp. κοσμίως Theopomp. [IV BC]: 115 fgm. 224 p. 582, 34 Jac. [in Athen. 4, 62, 167c]; cp. Diogenes of Babylon, in Stoic. III 221 [in Athen. 4, 62, 168e πάντα γὰρ ἀνήλωσε τὰ πατρῷα εἰς ἀσωτίαν; in the same context 168f Athen. cites as an example of ἀσωτία provision for the washing of feet with spiced wine]; Jos., Ant. 12, 203) of a wasteful son **Lk 15:13** (PFlor 99, 6ff ἐπεὶ ὁ υἱὸς ἡμῶν Κάστωρ μεθ' ἑτέρων [Zahn ἑταιρῶν, cp. Lk 15:30] ἀσωτευόμενος ἐσπάνισε τὰ αὑτοῦ πάντα καὶ ἐπὶ τὰ ἡμῶν μεταβὰς βούλεται ἀπολέσαι κτλ.; Philo, De Prov., in Eus., PE 8, 14, 4 τῶν ἀσώτων υἱέων οὐ περιορῶσιν οἱ τοκέες); GHb 297, 20.—DELG s.v. σῶς. Spicq.

ἀτακτέω (s. ἄτακτος) 1 aor. ἠτάκτησα. Of such as are not at their appointed posts or do not conform to established law or custom, hence acting with self-interest and not for the common good (s. X., Cyr. 8, 1, 22; Demosth. 3, 11; Plut., Mor. 184f; IG IV^2/1, 68, 83 [IV BC]; PEleph 2, 13 [III BC]; PCairZen 596, 18; BGU 1125, 8 [13 BC]; POxy 275, 24f [66 AD]; 725, 39f) **to violate prescribed or recognized order, *behave inappropriately*** in our lit. only **2 Th 3:7** οὐκ ἠτακτήσαμεν ἐν ὑμῖν *we did not treat you in a free-wheeling manner* (cp. our colloq. 'be out of line'; opp. observance of ἡσυχία vs. 12: cp. Ps.-Sotades 7:8f [Coll. Alex. p. 241] ἀτακτεῖν w. ἡσυχία). As the subsequent clause οὐδὲ δωρεὰν ἄρτον ἐφάγομεν παρά τινος indicates, Paul conforms to societal proprieties and did not act as though he were entitled to free sustenance; to support his claim, he states that he 'worked night and day so as not to be a burden to them'. Cp. 1 Cor 10:31–11:1 (for the Gr-Rom. perspective, s. Aristot. EN 4, 15–18). The trans. *be idle, lazy* does not take adequate account of Gr-Rom. social history, but s. comm.; Milligan, Thess. 152ff; CSpicq, Studia Theologica 10, '56, 1–13.—New Docs 2, 104 no. 82. DELG s.v. τάσσω. M-M. Spicq.

ἄτακτος, ον (s. ἀτακτέω) gener. 'not in the proper order' (3 Macc 1:19; TestNapht 2:9; Philo; Jos., Bell. 2, 517; 649, Ant. 15, 152; Ath. 25:3 [ἀταξία ibid. 3:2]; loanw. in rabb.)

❶ of volitional state, **pert. to being out of step and going one's own way, *disorderly, insubordinate*** (Hdt., Thu. et al.; Sb 6152, 13; 6153, 16; PFlor 332, 4; Philo, Sacr. Abel. 32) **1 Th 5:14** (cp. SEG XXVII, 261 B, 99; s. CSpicq, Studia Theologica 10, '56, 1–13); but some prefer the sense *idle, indolent* (s. ἀτακτέω and ἀτάκτως; also the orator Lycurgus 39 ἄτακτος='not at one's post').—GHolland, SBLSP 24, '85, 327–41.

❷ of affective state **pert. to being without socially recognized constraint, *undisciplined*** φορά *impulse* Dg 9:1 (cp. Pla., Leg. 2 p. 660b ἄτακτοι ἡδοναί; Plut., Mor. 5a likew.).—M-M. TW. Spicq.

ἀτάκτως (since Thu. 3, 108, 3; PFay 337, 16 [II AD]; POxy 842; PGM 4, 2628; Philo, Sacr. Abel. 45; Jos., C. Ap. 2, 151) adv. of ἄτακτος **in defiance of good order, *disorderly,*** holding religious services without regard to established times *arbitrarily* 1 Cl 40:2 (w. εἰκῇ 'at random'). ἀτάκτως περιπατεῖν *behave irresponsibly* **2 Th 3:6** (Isocr. 2m 31 ἀ. ζῆν) apparently without respect for established custom or received instruction, as the qualifying clause καὶ . . . ἡμῶν indicates (cp. Mk 7:5), **11;** the specific manner in which the irresponsible behavior manifests itself is described in the context: freeloading, sponging.—On contractual obligations in the Rom. world s. PCsillag, The Problems of Labour Relations in Roman Law: Oikumene 2, '78, 239–63. DELG s.v. τάσσω. TW. Spicq.

ἀταράχως (Epicurus, Ep. 1 p. 14 Us.; PSI 798, 15; Diod. S. 17, 54, 1; Jos., Ant. 14, 157) adv. of ἀτάραχος (Aristot. et al.; LXX; EpArist 213; ἀτάραχοι Just. A I, 46, 4) ***without confusion, undisturbed*** 1 Cl 48:4.—DELG s.v. ταράσσω.

ἀτεκνία, ας, ἡ (Aristot..; Plut., Thes. 12; LXX; En 98:5; PsSol 4:18; Philo, Det. Pot. Ins. 51; Mel.; PSI 1289 B II, 11 [II AD]; PRyl 659, 8 [322 AD]) ***childlessness*** GJs 2:1.

ἄτεκνος, ον (s. τέκνον; Hes.+; Polyb. 20, 6, 5; Plut.; Lucian; ins [SIG^2 838, 6: II BC; 858, 13; epitaphs 11 and 22, 7: ZNW 22, 1923, 281; 283]; pap [PLond I, 23, 13 p. 38; s. also Preis.]; LXX; En 98:5; TestJud 8:3; 19:2; Philo in Eus., PE 8, 11, 13; Jos., Bell. 1, 563, Ant. 4, 254) ***childless*** **Lk 20:28f.** Subst. ἡ ἄτεκνος GJs 4:4 (cp. Is 49:21).—DELG s.v. τίκτω. M-M.

ἀτενίζω 1 aor. ἠτένισα (Hippocr. et al.) ***look intently at, stare at someth.*** or *someone* εἴς τι (Polyb. 6, 11, 5; BGU 1816, 25; Lucian, Charon 16; 3 Macc 2:26; TestSol 24:5; TestAbr B 8 p. 112, 19f [Stone p. 72]; TestReub 4:2; JosAs 8:8; 16:7 cod. A; ApcMos 33; Jos., Bell. 5, 517) **Ac 1:10; 7:55; 2 Cor 3:7, 13;** 1 Cl 7:4; 17:2; 36:2; GJs 3:1; 12:2 (varying w. ἀναστενάζω, cp. de Strycker 298). εἴς τινα (Diog. L. 6, 6, 61; Sext. Emp., Math. 1, 306 Pyrr. 1, 75) **Ac 3:4; 6:15; 11:6; 13:9;** 1 Cl 9:2; 19:2. πρὸς κυρίου GJs 13:1. W. dat. of pers. (PGM 4, 556; 711; JosAs 8:8) **Lk 4:20; 22:56; Ac 3:5** D, **12; 10:4; 14:9; 23:1.** Abs. (Herm. Wr. 13, 3) **3:3** D. AcPt Ox 849, 13. Without personal referent, in this instance Paul, AcPl Ox 6, 8f (=Aa I, 241, 13).—FSolmsen, Beiträge z. griech. Wortforschung I 1909, 22.—DELG s.v. τανυ- E. τείνω. M-M. TW. Spicq.

ἄτερ prep. w. gen. ***without*** (Hom.+, but in prose first IPriene 109, 106 [c. 120 BC], then in imperial times [B-D-F §216, 2]: Dionys. Hal. 3, 10; Plut., Num. 14, 7, Cato Min. 5, 6; Vett. Val. 136, 9; 271, 9; 341, 3; perh. PLond III, 1171 verso c, 3 p. 107 [42 AD], ed.: ἄνευ[?]; POxy 936, 18; PHolm η 4; PGM 13, 56; 2 Macc 12:15; Ath. 1:3) ἀ. ὄχλου *apart fr. the crowd,* perh. *without a disturbance* **Lk 22:6;** ἄ. βαλλαντίου *without a purse* vs. **35;** ἄ. γραφῆς PtK 4 p. 16, 6; ἄ. θεοῦ *without God, apart fr. God's will* D 3:10 (Polyaenus 6, 53 θεῶν ἄτερ); ἀ. ἀλλήλων Hs 5, 7, 4; cp. 5, 4, 5; 5, 6, 2; 9, 12, 8; 9, 27, 2; ἄ. ζυγοῦ ἀνάγκης B 2:6 v.l.—DELG. M-M.

ἀτιμάζω 1 aor. ἠτίμασα. Pass.: fut. ἀτιμασθήσομαι LXX; 1 aor. ἠτιμάσθην; pf. ptc. ἠτιμασμένοι 2 Km 10:5 (s. τιμή; Hom.+) **deprive someone of honor or respect, *to dishonor/shame,*** an especially grievous offense in the strongly honor-shame oriented Semitic and Gr-Rom. societies (Ael. Aristid. 53 p. 620 D.: τὰ τῶν θεῶν ἀ.) τινά *someone* **Mk 12:4** (exposure of the head to public ridicule is perh. implied; s. ἀτιμάω and ἀτιμόω); **Lk 20:11; J 8:49; Ro 2:23; Js 2:6** (cp. Pr 14:21); IPhld 11:1.—Pass. **Ac 5:41;** Dg 11:3. τοῦ ἀτιμάζεσθαι τὰ σώματα αὐτῶν *that their bodies might be degraded* **Ro 1:24.** ἠτιμάσθη καὶ οὐκ ἐλογίσθη *he was dishonored and despised* 1 Cl 16:3 (Is 53:3).—DELG s.v. τιμή. M-M.

ἀτιμάω 1 aor. ἠτίμησα (Hom.+; Philostrat., Ep. 28 p. 240, 10; Mel., P. 73, 335). Mng. same as ἀτιμάζω (q.v.); ἠτίμησαν **Mk 12:4** D (s. also ἀτιμόω).

ἀτιμία, ας, ἡ (s. ἄτιμος; Hom. et al.; Epict. 4, 1, 60; PSI 330, 7; PGiss 40 II, 5; LXX; En 98:3; Test12Patr, Philo; Jos., Ant. 4, 229; 15, 24; Mel., P. 49; Ath. R. 76, 13; Did., Gen. 238, 26) **a state of dishonor or disrespect, *dishonor,*** of pers.: a disaster in Gr-Rom. society, in which civic-minded pers. placed a high premium on honor (τιμή) and enjoyment of repute (δόξα) **2 Cor 6:8** (opp. δόξα); ἐν ταῖς ἀτιμίαις δοξάζονται *in dishonor* (or *by shameful treatment*) *they are held in esteem* Dg 5:14 (pl. as Pla., Pol. 309a; Demosth. 18, 205).—Of things, a vessel to which no special value is attached εἰς ἀ. *for ordinary (use)* **Ro 9:21; 2 Ti 2:20.**—Of affective state πάθη ἀτιμίας *shameful passions* (=passions that disgrace a pers.) **Ro 1:26;** ἀ. αὐτῷ ἐστιν *it is a disgrace for him* **1 Cor 11:14.** ἐν ἀ. *in humiliation* (opp. δόξα) **15:43** (PsSol 2:27). κατὰ ἀ. λέγω *to my shame I must confess* **2 Cor 11:21** in self-deprecating irony (sim. Demosth. 18, 320; s. FDanker, in: Persuasive Artistry [GKennedy Festschr.], ed. DWatson, '91, 274).—DELG s.v. τιμή. M-M. TW.

ἄτιμος, ον (s. ἀτιμία; Hom.+; Epict. 4, 6, 3; OGI 218, 103; 140; 338, 29; 527, 8; pap; LXX; TestJob 18:3; ἀτίμως 24:10; Philo; Jos., Ant. 4, 136, C. Ap. 2, 191; Just., Mel., P. 37, 256 al.)

❶ pert. to being without honor or respect, *dishonored, despised,* of pers. *in disrepute* **1 Cor 4:10** (opp. ἔνδοξος 'held highly'); 1 Cl 3:3 (opp. ἔντιμος as Synes., Ep. 79, 226d [comp.]; cp. Is 3:5); *despised* εἶδος 16:3 (Is 53:3); οὐκ ἄ. εἰ μή *honored everywhere, except* **Mt 13:57; Mk 6:4.**

❷ pert. to being considered relatively unimportant, *insignificant* of things that do not elicit special admiration or attention, comp. *held in less esteem* μέλη **1 Cor 12:23** (of parts of the body also Aristot., Part. An. 3, 672b, 21 τὸ τιμιώτερον κ. ἀτιμότερον, 'more esteemed . . . less esteemed', a distinction made in terms of dependency, lower members being at the service of upper ones; Artem. 4, 25. On the subject-matter s. Heraclit. Sto. 19 p. 29, 3 ἡ κεφαλὴ ἐν τῷ σώματι τὴν κυριωτάτην εἰληχυῖα τάξιν=the head has the most distinguished position in the body; line 9 κυριώτατον μέρος. S. also εὐσχήμων 1). ἀτιμοτάτη ὑπηρεσία *the lowliest service* Dg 2:2.—DELG s.v. τιμή. M-M.

ἀτιμόω 1 aor. ἠτίμωσα LXX. Pass.: fut. ἀτιμωθήσομαι LXX; 1 aor. ἠτιμώθην; pf. ptc. ἠτιμωμένος (s. ἄτιμος; Aeschyl., Hdt. et al.; SIG 64, 6; 112, 10; LXX; PsSol 2:5; Just.; Ath. 34, 1). Mng. same as ἀτιμάζω (q.v.). Pass. *be disgraced* ἀπέστειλαν ἠτιμωμένον **Mk 12:4 v.l.** (s. ἀτιμάω); Dg 5:14.—M-M.

ἀτμίς, ίδος, ἡ (since Hdt. 4, 75, 1; Pla., Tim., p. 86e; perh. PCairZen 534 I, 7 [III BC]; PGM 7, 639; 743; LXX; ApcMos 33) ***vapor*** ἀ. καπνοῦ *smoky vapor* (like that of a volcanic eruption) **Ac 2:19** (Jo 3:3). Typical of what passes away **Js 4:14** (cp. Eccl 1:2 and 12:8 Aq.). ἀ. ἀπὸ κύθρας *steam that rises from a pot,* typical of nothingness 1 Cl 17:6 (quot. of unknown orig.; s. RHarris, JBL 29, 1910, 190–95).—DELG s.v. ἀτμός. M-M.

ἄτομος, ον (Pre-Socr. et al.; Philo) 'uncut' (s. τέμνω) then of someth. that is viewed as such a unit that it cannot be cut, esp. because of smallness (e.g. particle of matter, uncompounded word) ***indivisible*** (Is 54:8 Sym. ἐν ἀτόμῳ ὀργῆς in a short outburst of wrath=LXX ἐν θυμῷ μικρῳ), used of time by Aristot. (Phys. 236a, 6 ἐν ἀτόμῳ) ἐν ἀ. *in a moment* **1 Cor 15:52** (Nägeli 31).—DELG s.v. τέμνω. Sv.

ἄτονος, ον (ἀτονέω 'be relaxed, not stretched or in torsion'; Theophr., HP 3, 18, 11; Plut.; Epict. 3, 16, 7; Vett. Val. 233, 12 and15; 337, 19; PStras 95, 11; PLond VI, 1929, 14; Job 5:16 Aq.; Ps 81:3 Sym.; Jos., Bell. 1, 203; 3, 114; Tat. 32, 2) ***slack, powerless*** of the devil's threats ἄ. ὥσπερ νεκροῦ νεῦρα *as powerless as the sinews of a corpse* Hm 12, 6, 2 (ἄ. w. νεκρός as Epict., loc. cit.).—DELG s.v. τανυ- E. τείνω.

ἄτοπος, ον (s. τόπος; Eur., Pre-Socr. et al.; pap, LXX [Job; Pr 30:20; 2 Macc 14:23], Philo, Joseph., Just., Tat., Ath.; Ath. R. 73, 15 al.) from the perception of someth. 'not in its proper place', 'out of place', it is but a short step to the metaph. sense of someth. that is 'unusual', i.e. does not correspond to normal expectation (τόπος; cp. the wordplay τρία σώματα ἔσται ἐν τῷ αὐτῷ τόπῳ ἀτοπωτάτου τούτου ὑπάρχοντος Albinus 11).

❶ pert. to being out of the ordinary, *unusual, surprising* (Thu. 3, 38, 5; Pla., Leg. 1 p. 646b; PTebt 800, 37), 'abnormal', or 'hazardous' (Thu. 2, 49, 2; Herodian 4, 11, 4; Jos., Ant. 8, 378 the enemies of Samuel are not able to sustain any charges of 'unusual' conduct; 11, 134 of hazards that might befall travelers) μηδὲν ἄ. εἰς αὐτὸν γινόμενον *nothing unusual happened to him* **Ac 28:6** (the normal expectation in the case of a pers. bitten by a poisonous snake would be extraordinary divine retribution, s. vs 4). Cp. the self-vindication of the Roman poet Horace after a wolf fled from him (Odes 1, 22, 9–12).

❷ pert. to being behaviorally out of place, *evil, wrong, improper* (Plut., Mor. 27f; SEG XLI, 328, 41; PPetr II, 19 (1a), 5f; UPZ 5, 12 [163 BC]; Philo, Leg. All. 3, 53; Jos., Ant. 6, 88; Job 11:11; 35:13) (w. πονηρός) ἄνθρωποι **2 Th 3:2;** ποιεῖν τὰ ἄ. (Polyb. 5, 11, 1; Job 34:12) *do what is improper* Pol 5:3; οὐδὲν ἄ. ἔπραξεν (ἄ. πράσσειν: Dio Chrys. 10 [11], 65; Aristipp. in Diog. L. 2, 93; PPetr III, 43 (3), 17f [III BC]; UPZ 5, 12; BGU 757, 21 [12 AD]; PBrem 2:12 [II AD]; Job 27:6; Pr 30:20; 2 Macc 14:23) **Lk 23:41;** cp. **Ac 25:5.** ἄτοπόν ἐστιν *it is wrong, absurd* (Philo, Mos. 1, 308) IMg 10:3.—DELG s.v. τόπος. M-M.

ἄτρεπτος, ον (s. τρέπω; Chrysipp.+ [Stoic. II 158]; Plut.; Aelian; Herm. Wr.; IG IX/2, 317, 2; Job 15:15 Sym.; Philo, Leg. All. 1, 51 al.; Jos., Ant. 11, 57; τὸν ἄ. . . . θεόν Just., A I, 13, 4) ***unchangeable*** δόξα IEph ins.—DELG s.v. τρέπω.

Ἀττάλεια, ας, ἡ (Ἀτταλία v.l., oth. edd.) *Attalia,* a seaport in Pamphylia **Ac 14:25.**—Ramsay, Hist. Geogr. 420.

Ἄτταλος, ου, ὁ *Attalus,* a Christian in Smyrna IPol 8:2. The name was common in Asia Minor; specif. in Smyrna: CIG 3141; 3142, 2; 3239; 3288, 1 al.

αὐγάζω 1 aor. inf. αὐγάσαι (s. αὐγή) relates to brightness or clarity in various senses

❶ *see* (so in poets Soph. et al.; Lycophron v. 941 αὐγάζων φάος=seeing the light; Philod.: Anth. Pal. 5, 123, 3 and Philo, Mos. 2, 139; cp. Nägeli 25f) τὶ *someth.* Metaph., of the gospel's light **2 Cor 4:4** (s. φωτισμός 1). This is the most likely interpr. (see e.g. Ltzm., Windisch, H-DWendland, NRSV).

❷ intr. ***shine forth*** (PGM 3, 143; 4, 1636; 2558; Lev 13:24ff; 14:56; GrBar 9:8) suggested by some (for example, Sickenberger) for **2 Cor 4:4** (s. 1) can hardly do without αὐτοῖς, which is actually added in many mss.—DELG s.v. αὐγή. M-M. TW.

αὐγή, ῆς, ἡ (Hom.+; orig. 'light' esp. 'daylight') since the sun is perceived as the ultimate expression of brightness, the term αὐ. readily refers to ***dawn*** (Polyaenus 4, 6, 18 κατὰ τὴν πρώτην αὐγὴν τ. ἡμέρας; Is 59:9) ἄχρι αὐ. *until daybreak* **Ac 20:11.**—B. 993. DELG. M-M.

Αὔγουστος, ου, ὁ (so accented L-S-J-M, DGE; on the sp. Ἄγουσ- s. M-M) ***Augustus,*** title (usu. transl. Σεβαστός, q.v.) given Octavian, first Rom. emperor (31 BC–14 AD) in 27 BC; **Lk 2:1.** Ἀόστου GJs 17:1.—HDieckmann, Kaisernamen u. Kaiserbezeichnungen b. Lk: ZKT 33, 1919, 213–34; EPeterson, Kaiser A. im Urteil d. antiken Christent.: Hochland 30, '33, 289ff; RAC I 933–1004.—M-M.

αὐθάδεια, ας, ἡ (s. αὐθάδης; Pla. et al.; Aristot., EE 1221a, 8; Is 24:8; TestSol 18:14 A; Philo, Rer. Div. Her. 21; Jos., Bell. 4, 94, Ant. 12, 29; 15, 101; lit. 'self-satisfaction'; the poet. form αὐθαδία [Aeschyl. et al.] becomes prominent in later colloq. Gk. [Crönert 32], and is predom. in ins and pap) **preoccupation w. one's own interests,** the polar end of ἀρεσκεία, ***arrogance, willfulness, stubbornness*** 1 Cl 30:8 (w. θράσος, cp. Pr 21:24); ὑπερήφανος αὐ. *proud willfulness* 57:2; Hs 9, 22, 2f. In a list of vices D 5:1; B 20:1.—DELG s.v. αὐθάδης.

αὐθάδης, ες (s. αὐθάδεια; Aeschyl., Hdt.+; Polyb. 4, 21; Plut., Lycurg. 11, 6, Lucull. 7, 2; PAmh 78, 13f; Sb 4284, 9; Gen 49:3, 7; Pr 21:24; Jos., Ant. 1, 189; 4, 263; TKellis 22, 27) ***self-willed, stubborn, arrogant*** **Tit 1:7; 2 Pt 2:10;** 1 Cl 1:1 (w. προπετής); Hs 5, 4, 2; 5, 5, 1; 9, 22, 1; D 3:6. Field, Notes, 219; to the Gk. mind=hybris, s. Reader, Polemo 296.—DELG and Frisk. M-M. TW. Spicq.

αὐθαίρετος, ον (s. αὐτός and αἱρέω; trag., Thu. et al.; OGI 583, 8; pap; Sym. Ex 35:5, 22; Philo, Mos. 1, 50 v.l.; Jos., Bell. 6, 310; Ath. 24, 4) **pert. to being self-chosen,** ***of one's own accord*** **2 Cor 8:3, 17.**—DELG s.v. αὐτός 2. M-M.

αὐθαιρέτως adv. of αὐθαίρετος (Plut., Pel. 290 [24, 8]; Philostrat., Vi. Apoll. 8, 7 p. 306, 22; IMagnMai 163, 15ff; PLond II, 280, 8 p. 193 [55 AD], restored; BGU 581, 6 et al.; 2 Macc 6:19; 3 Macc 6:6; 7:10) ***voluntarily*** ἀποθανεῖν IMg 5:2.

αὐθεντέω (s. αὐθέντης; Philod., Rhet. II p. 133, 14 Sudh.; Jo. Lydus, Mag. 3, 42; Moeris p. 54; cp. Phryn. 120 Lob.; Hesychius; Thom. Mag. p. 18, 8; schol. in Aeschyl., Eum. 42; BGU 1208, 38 [27 BC]; s. Lampe s.v.) **to assume a stance of independent authority,** ***give orders to, dictate to*** w. gen. of pers. (Ptolem., Apotel. 3, 14, 10 Boll-B.; Cat. Cod. Astr. VIII/1 p. 177, 7; B-D-F §177) ἀνδρός, w. διδάσκειν, **1 Ti 2:12** (practically = 'tell a man what to do' [Jerusalem Bible]; Mich. Glykas [XII AD] 270, 10 αἱ γυναῖκες αὐθεντοῦσι τ. ἀνδρῶν. According to Diod. S. 1, 27, 2 there was a well-documented law in Egypt: κυριεύειν τὴν γυναῖκα τἀνδρός, cp. Soph., OC 337–41; GKnight III, NTS 30, '84, 143–57; LWilshire, ibid. 34, '88, 120–34).—DELG s.v. αὐθέντης. M-M.

αὐθέντης, ου, ὁ (s. αὐθεντέω; Hdt. et al.; on the mng. s. PKretschmer, Glotta 3, 1912, 289–93; FZucker, SBLeipzAk 107, 4, '62; the adj. is a loanw. in rabb., and the noun is the source of Turk. 'effendi'; cp. Jos., Bell. 2, 240) ***master*** (Eur., Suppl. 442; epitaph PCairZen 532, 15; Sb 6754, 15; PGM 13, 258) τοῦ πύργου Hs 9, 5, 6.—DELG. Sv.

αὐθεντικός, ή, όν (POxy 260, 20; 719, 30; 33 al. in pap) ***original*** τὸ αὐ. (opp. ἀντίτυπον) 2 Cl 14:3 (so PGiss 34, 4 τὰ αὐ.; the adj. in the pap passages above, not used as subst., has the same mng.).—DELG s.v. αὐθέντης.

αὐθεντικῶς adv. of αὐθεντικός (Cicero, Att. 9, 14, 2; 10, 9, 1) ***w. perfect clarity*** PtK 4 p. 15, 31.

αὐλέω 1 aor. ηὔλησα (Alcman, Hdt. et al.; SIG 1084–88 al.; StudPal XXII, 47, 5; Sb 7557, 5) ***play the flute*** τινί (X., Symp. 2, 8) *for someone* (to dance) **Mt 11:17; Lk 7:32** (Aesop 27 H.=11 P., H-H. ὅτε ηὔλουν, οὐκ ὠρχεῖσθε; similarly 134 H.; Proverbia Aesopi 115 P.). τὸ αὐλούμενον *what is played on the flute* **1 Cor 14:7.**—DELG s.v. αὐλός.

αὐλή, ῆς, ἡ (Hom.+)—**❶ an area open to the sky, freq. surrounded by buildings, and in some cases partially by walls,** ***enclosed open space, courtyard*** (Dio Chrys. 60 and 61 [77 + 78], 35 περὶ τὰς αὐλὰς κ. πρόθυρα; pap, e.g. PLond I, 45, 15 p. 36 [II BC]; BGU 275, 6f; POxy 104; 105 al.; PFay 31; 32 al.; Tob 2:9; TestSol 2:1 P εἰς τὰ πρόθυρα τῆς αὐλῆς; Jos., Ant. 1, 196) **Mt 26:58, 69; Mk 14:54, 66; Lk 22:55; J 18:15.** Used also as *a fold* for sheep (Il. 4, 433; PHib 36, 4; POxy 75, 20) **J 10:1, 16.**—*(outer) court* of the temple (αὐ. τοῦ ἱεροῦ SIG 485, 28; 547, 46 al.; Ex 27:9 al.) **Rv 11:2;** B 2:5 (Is 1:12).

❷ a dwelling complex (the social and business uses of the αὐ., as well as the juxtaposition of the courtyard and other quarters, encouraged extension of the term αὐ. to the entire complex)

ⓐ of ordinary property ***farm, house*** (Dionys. Hal. 6, 50; PGiss 32, 7; 19; PFlor 81, 8; s. FLuckhard, D. Privathaus, diss. Giess. 1914, 79) **Lk 11:21,** where *palace* is also prob. (see b).

ⓑ of royal property, the 'court' of a prince (lit., ins, pap), then ***palace*** (Suda αὐλή· ἡ τοῦ βασιλέως οἰκία. So Polyb.; Diod. S. 16, 93, 7; Epict. 1, 10, 3; 4; 1 Macc 11:46; 3 Macc 2:27; 5:46; Jos., Bell. 2, 328, Vi. 66; 295; Just., D. 22, 11) **Mt 26:3; Mk 15:16** (=πραιτώριον).—B. 463. DELG. M-M.

αὐλητής, οῦ, ὁ (s. αὐλέω; Theognis, Hdt. et al.; ins, pap) ***flutist*** for festive occasions **Rv 18:22,** and for mourning (Jos., Bell. 3, 437; s. EReiner, Die rituelle Totenklage der Griechen '38, 67–70; for influence of Asia Minor on use of flute-players in funereal rites, ibid. p. 61, n. 1) **Mt 9:23.**—DELG s.v. αὐλός. M-M.

αὐλητρίς, ίδος, ἡ (s. αὐλέω; Simonides et al.; X., Pla., ins, pap; freq. as entertainer at a symposium, Pla., Prot. 347cd, cited Athen. 3, 97ab) ***flutist*** in pl. w. πόρναι Ox 840, 36; cp. GHb 297, 21 (Euhem.: 63 fgm. 1 Jac. [in Athen. 14, 77 p. 658f], of a flutist who apparently served her king in a special capacity; Phylarch. [III BC]: 81 fgm. 42 Jac. and Dio Chrys. 53 [70], 9 pl. w. ἑταῖραι; Theophyl. Sim., Ep. 12 αὐ. as πορνίδιον).—DELG s.v. αὐλός.

αὐλίζομαι impf. ηὐλιζόμην. Pass.: fut. αὐλισθήσομαι LXX; JosAs 9:5; 1 aor. ηὐλίσθην (s. αὐλή; Hom.+; OGI 730, 7 [III BC]; pap; LXX; JosAs 9:4f; Joseph.) orig. of spending the night in the αὐλή, viz. in the open air, then also of temporary lodging, w. context indicating whether outdoors ('bivouac') or indoors.

❶ gener. **to have a temporary sleeping arrangement,** ***spend the night*** (Eupolis [V BC] 322; Nicol. Dam.: 90 fgm. 4 p. 332, 17 Jac. [indoors]; Arrian, Anab. 6, 25, 5 [army bivouacking]; Ctesias: 688 fgm. 24 Jac. [=Ps.-Demetr., Eloc. §216] 'where noble men must spend the night'—in euphem. ref. to the death of Cyrus as sleep; Judg 19:6f, 10f; 20:4B; Ruth 3:13 αὐλίσθητι τὴν νύκτα al. LXX; Jos., Ant. 1, 279) ἐκεῖ (Judg 19:7; Tob 6:1BA) **Mt 21:17;** εἴς τι **Lk 21:37** (cp. Tob 14:9BA μηκέτι αὐλισθῆτε εἰς Νινευή, but the sense here is 'stay', s. 2 below; *spend some time* is also poss. for the Lk pass., but *bivouac* is certainly prob. in view of the chosen locale, s. 22:39). ἕως οὗ αὐλισθῇ *until he finds lodging* (again) D 11:6 (indoors).

❷ **to have housing, without special ref. to nighttime, *live, stay*** (Epict., Gnomolog., fgm. 47; Himerius, Or. 54 [15], 1 αὐλίζ. ἡμέραν μίαν, accordingly not at night; of stabling animals BASP 24/1–2, '87, p. 10, lines 17f [PCol inv. 316] αὐ[λι]ζέσθω; Sir 51:23; Jos., Bell. 1, 334; 2, 301) 1 Cl 4:11.—DELG s.v. αὐλή. M-M.

αὐλός, οῦ, ὁ (Hom. et al.; PHib 54, 6 [c. 245 BC]; PFuad I Univ no. XII, 37; LXX; Ath. 9, 1) ***flute*** **1 Cor 14:7** (w. κιθάρα, as Dio Chrys. 16 [33], 35; Ps.-Lucian, Salt. 16; Himerius, Or. 8 [23], 11; Is 30:32).—CSachs, Real-Lexikon d. Musikinstrumente '62, 23; KSchlesinger, Greek Aulos[2] '39. S. also lit. on κύμβαλον.—DELG. M-M.

αὐξάνω/αὔξω (both forms as early as Pindar with the shorter predominating, as usu. in the earlier lit.; later the longer form becomes more freq. [e.g., Just., D. 88, 2] and the shorter one [Epict.; Heraclit. Stoic. p. 2, 7; 78, 12; Hierocles the Stoic—II AD—in BKT IV pap 9780 col. 6, 16 p. 28f; SIG index; OGI 51, 12; 56, 9 and 22; POxy 1450, 3; 21; 4 Macc 13:22; OdeSol 11:19; TestZeb 1:3; TestJos 19:4, based on the Armenian version, as rendered by Charles; GrBar; ParJer 9:16; EpArist 208; Philo, Aet. M. 71; Jos., Ant. 1, 61; 4, 59; Ar. 6, 3; Mel., fgm. 8b, 8] becomes rare; both in the same sentence Aëtius 132, 13 αὐξανομένου τ. πάθους αὔξει κ. τὰ συμπτώματα) B-D-F §101; W-S. §15; Meisterhans[3]-Schw. 176; Mayser 465. Impf. ηὔξανον; fut. αὐξήσω and αὐξανῶ Gen 48:4; Lev 26:9; 1 aor. ηὔξησα. Pass.: fut. αὐξηθήσομαι LXX, En 5:9; aor. ηὐξήθην.

❶ **to cause to become greater in extent, size, state, or quality, *grow*** someth., ***cause to grow, increase*** trans. (Pind., Hdt., Pla. et al.; ins, pap, LXX; Jos., Ant. 2, 205 [Nägeli 35]) the fruits of righteousness **2 Cor 9:10.** Abs. **1 Cor 3:6f**=God made it grow; Hv 1, 1, 6; 3, 4, 1.

❷ **to become greater, *grow, increase*** intr.—ⓐ pass. used actively (Hes., Hdt.+; LXX; En oft.; on GrBar s. under b; Jos., Ant. 18, 129, Vi. 193; Ar. 6:3; Mel., HE 4, 26, 7; Did., Gen. 190, 25). Of humans and plants: the human race 1 Cl 33:6; B 6:12, 18 (Gen 1:28); children (Hdt. 5, 92, 5; Gen 21:8; 25; 27) **1 Pt 2:2;** plants (Ps.-Phocyl. 38) **Mt 13:32; Mk 4:8;** καρπὸς αὐξανόμενος ibid. v.l. (Diosc., Mat. Med. 2, 199 add. πρὸ τοῦ τὸν καρπὸν αὐξηθῆναι).—Of nonphysical entities (Pind., N. 8, 40 αὔξεται δ' ἀρετά = ἀρετή grows; Did., Gen. 119, 8 [of the soul]) the gospel **Col 1:6;** faith **2 Cor 10:15;** knowledge **Col 1:10;** unrighteousness D 16:4. Cp. **Lk 22:28** D.

ⓑ The use of the act. in the same intr. sense belongs to later Gk. (Aristot.; Polyb.; Diod. S.; Maximus Tyr. 6, 4f; Olympiodor., Comm. in Alcib. Plat. 18 ed. Creuzer 1821: αὐξούσης τ. σελήνης; PGM 4, 2553; 13, 65; EpArist 208; GrBar; Jos., Ant. 2, 189; 4, 59; Ar. 12, 2; POxy 1778, 13; Just., D. 88, 2; not LXX) lit. of plants **Mt 6:28; Lk 12:27;** Ox 655, 9f (ASyn. 67, 33; on the last 3 passages s. ξαίνω); **Lk 13:19.** ἐκ τοῦ ἑνὸς πλείονα *fr. one (grain) many grow* 1 Cl 24:5. Of children **Lk 1:80; 2:40.** Of a people **Ac 7:17.** Of a house εἰς ναόν **Eph 2:21.** Of the word of God **Ac 6:7; 12:24; 19:20** (on the theme of growth s. DBalch, SBLSP '89, 354; cp. Polyb. 6, 43, 2). αὐ. τὴν αὔξησιν **Col 2:19;** ἔν τινι **2 Pt 3:18;** αὐ. εἰς Χριστόν *grow up into* (union w.) *Christ* **Eph 4:15.** Abs. **Mt 20:28 v.l.** = Agr 22; ὡς . . . αὔξιν [=αὔξειν] . . . τὴν ψυχὴν τοῦ Παύλου *so that . . . Paul's spirits rose* AcPl Ha 6, 10. Of Jesus *increase* **J 3:30.** This is usu. considered a direct ref. to success in attracting followers, but αὐ. can also be used of the increase of sunlight (Calendarium of Antiochus [c. 200 AD] on Dec. 25 Ἡλίου γενέθλιον· αὔξει φῶς [FBoll, SBHeidAk 1910, 16; Abh. p. 40ff]; Cosmas of Jerusalem [FCumont, Natalis Invicti: Extr. des compt. rend. de l'Ac. des Inscr. et Bell. Lett. 1911, 292f]). Cp. 3:19–21, where φῶς occurs five times, and marks the leading concept. May this not also be true of 3:30? At any rate the Gk. and Lat. fathers understood 3:30 in the solar sense. S. also on ἐλαττοῦσθαι and s. ENorden, D. Geburt des Kindes 1924, 99–112.—DELG s.v. αὔξω. M-M. TW.

αὔξησις, εως, ἡ (s. αὐξάνω; Pre-Socr., Hdt.+; Epict. 1, 14, 14; ins [57/56 BC] in Mitt-Wilck. I/2, 70, 12; Sb 1161, 18; 4224, 23; PMich XIII, 659, 227 [VI AD] of taxes; 2 Macc 5:16; ParJer 5:30; Philo; Jos., Ant. 1, 60; 4, 261; Just., A II, 5, 2; D. 88, 2; Ath., R. 69, 9) ***growth, increase*** αὐ. ποιεῖσθαι *cause growth* (for this phrase s. Aristot., HA 6, 12, 566b, 18 growth of a dolphin) εἴς τι **Eph 4:16** mystical sense of the Christian community growing as a body in its sense of unity and understanding of God's purpose in Christ; sim. αὔξειν τὴν αὐ. τοῦ θεοῦ; *grows w. divine growth* **Col 2:19** (cp. Herm. Wr. 3, 3 εἰς τὸ αὐξάνεσθαι ἐν αὐξήσει; OdeSol 11:19).—DELG s.v. αὔξω. M-M.

αὔξω s. αὐξάνω.

αὔρα, ας, ἡ (Hom. et al.; TestSol; Philo; Tat. 8, 5) ***breeze*** 1 Cl 39:3 (Job 4:16).—DELG.

αὔριον adv. (Hom. et al.; ins, pap, LXX; PsSol 5:13; ParJer 6:15; Joseph.; Ath. 12, 2) orig. in ref. to the day following today, then of a brief period of time.

❶ ***next day*** **Ac 23:15 v.l., 20; 25:22;** σήμερον ἢ αὐ. **Js 4:13.** W. art., w. ἡμέρα to be supplied (as Soph., Trach. 945; Diod. S. 19, 32, 2 ἡ αὐ.; PFlor 118, 5 μετὰ τὴν αὐ.; PTebt 417, 7 al.; Ex 8:19; 32:30; 1 Km 11:11 al.; Jos., Ant. 17, 91) ἡ αὐ. **Mt 6:34b; Js 4:14** (Simonides, fgm. 6 Diehl[2] [521, 1 Page] as ἄνθρωπος you do not know what the αὔριον will be; εἰς τὴν αὐ. Ariston of Ceos [III BC], fgm. 24 [ed. Wehrli '52]; BGU 511 I, 18; Esth 5:12; 3 Macc 5:38; Jos., Ant. 3, 231) **Mt 6:34a** (Epict. 1, 9, 19 discourages care περὶ τῆς αὐ., πόθεν φάγητε; Artem. 4, 84 περὶ τῆς αὐ. φοβεῖσθαι ἢ ἐλπίζειν.—The opposite of **Mt 6:34** among the Pythagoreans: Philosoph. Max. 504, 1: διδάσκει ἀεί τι τοῦ παρόντος εἰς τὸ μέλλον καταλιπεῖν, καὶ τῆς αὐ. ἐν τῇ σήμερον μνημονεύειν = [the saying ἐπὶ χοίνικος μὴ καθίζειν, not to sit on a food container] 'instructs us always to leave someth. for the future, and to be mindful of the morrow in the present'; a line of thought related to the Delphic maxim γνῶθι σαυτόν); **Ac 4:3;** Hs 6, 5, 3; εἰς αὐ. ἦν τὰ θηριομαχία AcPl Ha 2, 36; μέχρι τῆς αὐ. Hs 9, 11, 7; ἐπὶ τὴν αὐ. *on the next day* **Lk 10:35; Ac 4:5** (B-D-F § 233, 3); ἐπὶ τὴν αὐ. ἡμέραν **4:5 v.l.** (ἡ αὐ. ἡμέρα as PCairZen 78, 8). In metaph. σήμ. . . . αὐ. *now . . . soon* **Mt 6:30; Lk 12:28.** Cp. **13:32f** (on σήμ. καὶ αὐ. καὶ τῇ τρίτῃ vs. **32** cp. Ex 19:10f and τρίτος 1a). These three last pass. may also be classed in 2.

❷ **a brief time lapse without ref. to a nocturnal period, *soon, in a short time*** **1 Cor 15:32** (Is 22:13; Ath. 12, 2). Perh. also **Mt 6:30; Lk 12:28.** Cp. **13:32f** (s. 1 end).—B. 999. DELG. M-M.

αὐστηρός, ά, όν (αὖος [αὗος Att.] 'dry, stale'; αὔω 'be' or 'become dry'; Hippocr., Pla. et al.; ins, pap, TestAbr A 19 p. 101, 4 [Stone p. 50]; Philo) adj. **pert. to being strict in requirement, *punctilious, strict,*** used esp. of pers. who practice rigid personal discipline or are strict in the supervision of others (Polyb. 4, 20, 7 of pers. who maintain a very severe life-style; sim. Plut., Mor. 300d; Vett. Val. 75, 11; Diog. L. 7, 26 opp. of the condition expressed by the verb διαχέω 'be relaxed'; 117 applied to pers. who are like wine that is used medicinally; PTebt 315, 19 [II AD] of a 'punctilious' govt. finance inspector ὁ γὰρ ἄνθρωπος λείαν ἐστὶν αὐστηρός; grave ins ZNW 22, 1923, 280 αὐ. παράκοιτις;

2 Macc 14:30) **Lk 19:21f** (imagery of a tough, uncompromising, punctilious financier).—DELG s.v. αὖος. M-M.

αὐτάρκεια, ας, ἡ (s. αὐτάρκης) 'self-sufficiency' in the sense of 'independence', then gener. 'sufficiency'

❶ external, **state of having what is adequate,** ***sufficiency, a competence*** (Pla. et al. αὐ. means the state of one who supports himself without aid fr. others, cp. Theoph. Ant. I 6 [p. 72, 2], but in POxy 729, 10 [137 AD] it is 'sufficient supply'; of God's allocation ἐν συμμετρίᾳ αὐταρκείας PsSol 5:16; sufficient citation of Biblical references Just., D. 73, 6) Hs 1:6; πᾶσαν αὐ. ἔχειν (PFlor 242, 8 ἵνα δυνηθῇς ἔχειν τ. αὐτάρκιαν) *have enough of everything* **2 Cor 9:8.**

❷ internal, **state of being content w. one's circumstances,** ***contentment, self-sufficiency,*** a favorite virtue of the Cynics and Stoics (Epicurus in Diog. L. 10, 130; Stoic. III p. 67, 3; 68, 5; Stob. III p. 101, 16 [Epict.]; 265, 13 H.; Teles p. 5, 1; cp. 11, 5; 38, 10f H.; Sextus 98. Cp. GGerhard, Phoinix v. Kolophon 1909, 57ff; Tat.) **1 Ti 6:6;** Hm 6, 2, 3.—DELG s.v. ἀρκέω. M-M. TW. Sv.

αὐτάρκης, ες (s. αὐτός, ἀρκέω; Aeschyl., Hdt. et al.; ins, pap, LXX; Philo, Op. M. 146; Jos., C. Ap. 2, 190 [of God]; Albinus 12 p. 167, ln. 2; Just., A I, 53, 1) of pers. ***content, self-sufficient*** (Pla., Rep. 369b; Polyb. 6, 48, 7; Diog. L. 2, 24 of Socrates αὐτάρκης καὶ σεμνός; Sir 40:18; Philo; Jos., C. Ap. 2, 291) εἶναι *be content,* perh. *self-sufficient* **Phil 4:11.**—DELG s.v. ἀρκέω. M-M. TW. Sv.

αὐτεπαίνετος, ον (αὐτός, ἐπαινετός 'laudable') adj. (not yet found elsewhere) ***praising oneself*** subst. 1 Cl 30:6.—DELG s.v. αἶνος.

αὐτοκατάκριτος, ον adj. (s. αὐτός, κατακρίνω; in Philo in the fgm. fr. the Sacra Parallela ed. Mangey II 652; s. RHarris, Fragments of Philo 1886. Otherw. only in Christian writers) ***self-condemned*** **Tit 3:11.**—DELG s.v. κρίνω. TW.

αὐτολεξεί (αὐτή, λέξις) adv. (Philo, Leg. ad Gai. 353; Just.) ***expressly, in the very words*** PtK 4 p. 15, 32.—DELG s.v. λέγω A1.

αὐτόματος, η, ον (fr. αὐτός + -ματος [cp. μένος 'strength']) also w. two endings (Crönert 183) **pert. to someth. that happens without visible cause,** ***by itself*** (Hom. et al.; Josh 6:5; Job 24:24; Wsd 17:6; Philo; Jos., Ant. 1, 54; loanw. in rabb.) of doors opening by themselves (Il. 5, 749; X., Hell. 6, 4, 7; Apollon. Rhod. 4, 41; Plut., Timol. 241 [12, 9]; Cass. Dio 44, 17; cp. Artapanus de Judaeis: 726 fgm. 3, 23 Jac. [in Eus., PE 9, 27, 23] νυκτὸς . . . τὰς θύρας πάσας αὐτομάτως ἀνοιχθῆναι τοῦ δεσμωτηρίου. S. ἀνοίγω 1) **Ac 12:10.** Of plants growing without help (Hes., Works 118 and Hdt. et al.; Theophr., HP 4, 8, 8; Diod. S. 1, 8, 1; Lev 25:5, 11; Philo, Op. M. 167; Jos., Ant. 12, 317, Vi. 11) **Mk 4:28** (on this parable s. KWeiss, Voll Zuversicht 1922; BZ 18, 1929, 45–67; JFreundorfer, BZ 17, 1926, 51–62; 68; TManson, JTS 38, '37, 399f; KClark, ClW 36, '42, 27–29; GHarder, Theologia Viatorum 1, '48/49, 51–70). The connection is uncertain AcPl Ha 7, 1 [. . . 11 . . . α]ὐτόμ̣α̣τ̣ο̣ς̣ εἰς μέρη α̣ν̣ [. . . 18 . . .] (something seems of itself to break into pieces).—DELG s.v. αὐτός 1. M-M. Spicq. Sv.

αὐτομολέω (αὐτός, cp. 2 aor. μολεῖν 'go') fut. 3 sg. αὐτομολήσει Pr 6:11a (A); 1 aor. ηὐτομόλησα LXX (Hdt., Aristoph. et al.; PGissUniv 46 IV 30; Philo, Aet. M. 76; Jos., Bell. 4, 380, Vi. 107; 239) ***desert*** ἀπό τινος (*fr.*) *someone* 1 Cl 28:2.—DELG s.v. αὐτός 1 and βλώσκω (aor. ἔμολον).

αὐτόπτης, ου, ὁ (αὐτός, ὀπτεύω = ὁράω 'seeing with one's own eyes'; Hdt. et al.; Polyb. 3, 4, 13; Vett. Val. 260, 30; PSI 1314, 10; POxy 1154, 8 [both I AD]; Jos., Bell. 3, 432) ***eyewitness*** αὐ. γενόμενος (Dionys. Hal., Pomp. 6, 3; Maximus Tyr. 16, 3h; Jos., Ant. 18, 342; 19, 125, C. Ap. 1, 55) **Lk 1:2;** Papias (2:2; 12:2).—DELG s.v. αὐτός and ὁράω. M-M. TW. Spicq.

αὐτός, ή, ό (Hom.+; W-S. §22; B-D-F index) reflexive pron. 'self'—❶ **intensive marker, setting an item off fr. everything else through emphasis and contrast,** ***self,*** used in all pers., genders, and numbers.

ⓐ used w. a subject (noun or pron.)—**α.** specif. named (X., Cyr. 1, 4, 6; Plut., Caes. 710 [7, 9] αὐ. Κικέρων; 2 Macc 11:12) αὐ. Δαυίδ *David himself* **Mk 12:36f; Lk 20:42;** αὐ. Ἰησοῦς **Lk 24:15; J 2:24; 4:44;** αὐ. ὁ Ἰησοῦς **short ending of Mk.**

β. or otherw. exactly designated αὐ. ὁ θεός (Jos., Bell. 7, 346) **Rv 21:3;** αὐ. τ. ἐπουράνια **Hb 9:23** (cp. 4 Macc 17:17; Sir 46:3b; GrBar); αὐ. ἐγώ *I myself* **Ro 15:14** (cp. 3 Macc 3:13; POxy 294, 13f [22 AD]); αὐ. ἐγὼ Παῦλος **2 Cor 10:1;** αὐτοὶ ὑμεῖς **J 3:28** (cp. 4 Macc 6:19; En 103:7); αὐτοὶ οὗτοι (Thu. 6, 33, 6) **Ac 24:15;** ἐν ὑμῖν αὐτοῖς *among yourselves* **1 Cor 11:13.**

ⓑ to emphasize a subject already known: of Jesus **Mt 8:24; Mk 8:29; Lk 5:16f; 9:51; 10:38; 24:36** (cp. the Pythagorean αὐτὸς ἔφα Schwyzer II 211). Of God **Hb 13:5** (cp. Wsd 6:7; 7:17; Sir 15:12; 1 Macc 3:22 and oft. LXX).

ⓒ differentiating fr. other subjects or pointing out a contrast w. them αὐτὸς καὶ οἱ μετ' αὐτοῦ **Mk 2:25; J 2:12; 4:53; 18:1; Lk 24:15; 1 Cor 3:15.** αὐ. οὐκ εἰσήλθατε καὶ τοὺς εἰσερχομένους ἐκωλύσατε *you yourselves did not come in* etc. **Lk 11:52;** cp. vs. **46.**—**J 7:9; 9:21; Mt 23:4; Lk 6:11; Ac 18:15; 1 Th 1:9; 1 Cor 2:15.** αὐτὸς ἐγώ *I alone* **2 Cor 12:13. Ro 7:25** s. e below.—εἰ μὴ αὐ. *except himself* **Rv 19:12.** αὐ. ὄγδοός ἐστιν *he is the eighth* **17:11;** s. also 2a. In anticipation of an incorrect inference Ἰησοῦς αὐ. οὐκ ἐβάπτιζεν *Jesus did not personally baptize* **J 4:2** opp. 'his disciples.' Of bodily presence, αὐ. παραγενοῦ *come in person* (as opp. to letter-writing) AcPlCor 1:7; with component of surprise that the subject specified is actually present *in person* (Philo, De Jos. 238: Jos. to his brothers αὐ. εἰμι ἐγώ) **Lk 24:36, 39.**

ⓓ of one whose action is independent or significant without ref. to someth. else (Hyperid. 1, 19, 11; 3, 2) without help **J 2:25; 4:42; 6:6; Ac 20:34;** αὐ. ᾠκοδόμησεν *he built at his own expense* **Lk 7:5;** αὐ. ὁ πατὴρ φιλεῖ ὑμᾶς *the Father personally loves you* **J 16:27** (i.e. they require no intermediary).

ⓔ of one viewed as a solitary figure '(be) by oneself, alone' w. μόνος (cp. μόνος 1aβ) **Mk 6:47; J 6:15.** W. κατ' ἰδίαν **Mk 6:31.**—*thrown on one's own resources* αὐ. ἐγὼ τῷ νοΐ δουλεύω νόμῳ θεοῦ *thrown on my own resources I am enslaved in mind to God's interests but in my flesh to the interests of sin* **Ro 7:25** (JWeiss, Beitr. zur Paulin. Rhetorik, in BWeiss Festschr., 1897, 233f; JKürzinger, BZ 7, '63, 270–74).

ⓕ with climactic force in connection with one or more lexical units καὶ αὐτός *even* (Sir prol. line 24 καὶ αὐ. ὁ νόμος *even the law;* 4 Macc 17:1; GrBar 4:13; 9:4 al.) καὶ αὐ. ἡ κτίσις *even the created world* **Ro 8:21.** καὶ αὐ. Σάρρα *even Sara* **Hb 11:11** (on the rdg. here s. Windisch ad loc. and B-D-F §194, 1; Rob. 686; Mlt-Turner 220; cp. Ps.-Callisth. 1, 10, 3 καὶ αὐτὸν τὸν Φίλιππον = and even Philip; but the text of the Hb passage is prob. corrupt; s. καταβολή). οὐδὲ ἡ φύσις αὐ. διδάσκει; *does not even nature teach?* **1 Cor 11:14.**—Without ascensive particle, **Ro 9:3** Paul expresses extraordinary devotion to his people *(imagine!) I myself.*

ⓖ w. attention directed to a certain pers. or thing to the exclusion of other lexical units, so that αὐ. can almost take on demonstrative sense (s. 2a, also Aeschyl., 7 against Thebes 528; Hes., Works 350): αὐ. τὰ ἔργα *the very deeds* **J 5:36;** αὐ. ὁ Ἰωάννης (POxy 745, 3 [I AD] αὐ. τὸν Ἀντᾶν) *this very* (or *same*) *John* **Mt 3:4** (s. Mlt. 91); αὐτῆς τῆς Ἡρωδίαδος **Mk 6:22 v.l.** (s. 2bα for the rdg. αὐτοῦ W-H., N. and s. on this RBorger, TRu 52, '87, 25f); ἐν αὐ. τ. καιρῷ (cp. Tob 3:17 BA; 2:9; SIG 1173, 1 αὐταῖς τ. ἡμέραις) *just at that time* **Lk 13:1.—23:12; 24:13.—2:38; 10:21; 12:12.—10:7.** αὐτὸ τοῦτο *just this, the very same thing* (Oenomaus in Eus., PE 5, 22, 3; PRyl 77, 39; POxy 1119, 11; cp. Phoenix Coloph. 6, 8 Coll. Alex. p. 235) **2 Cor 7:11; Gal 2:10; Phil 1:6;** εἰς αὐ. τοῦτο **Ro 9:17; 13:6; 2 Cor 5:5; Eph 6:22; Col 4:8.** The phrases τοῦτο αὐ. **2 Cor 2:3** and αὐ. τοῦτο **2 Pt 1:5** are adverbial accusatives *for this very reason* (Pla., Prot. 310e [pl.]; X., An. 1, 9, 21; PGrenf I, 1, 14).

❷ **a ref. to a definite person or thing, *he, him, she, her, it, they, them*—ⓐ** αὐτός refers w. more or less emphasis, esp. in the nom., to a subject, oft. resuming one already mentioned: αὐ. παρακληθήσονται *they* (not others) *shall be comforted* **Mt 5:4;** cp. vs. **5ff.** οὐκ αὐ. βλασφημοῦσιν; **Js 2:7.** αὐ. σώσει **Mt 1:21** (cp. Ps 129:8). αὐ. ἀποδώσει **6:4 v.l.—Mk 1:8; 14:15** al. Freq. the emphasis is scarcely felt: **Mt 14:2; Lk 4:15; 22:23; J 6:24; Ac 22:19** (cp. Gen 12:12; Tob 6:11 BA; Sir 49:7; Vett. Val. 113, 16.—JWackernagel, Syntax II^2 1928, 86).—Perh. the development of αὐ. in the direction of οὗτος (which it practically replaces in Mod. Gk.) is beginning to have some influence in the NT (Pla., Phdr. 229e αὐτά=this; X., An. 4, 7, 7 αὐτό; Dio Chrys. 3, 37; 15 [32], 10 αὐτοί; Aelian, NA 6, 10; Mél. de la fac. orient ... Beyrouth 1, 1906, 149 no. 18 εἰς αὐτὸ ἐγεννήθης=for this [purpose] you were born; Schmid IV 69; 616 αὐτός = οὗτος; Synes., Ep. 3, 159a; 4, 165a; Agathias [VI AD], Hist. 1, 3 p. 144, 17 D.) καὶ αὐ. ἦν Σαμαρίτης **Lk 17:16** (cp. **3:23; 19:2** and 1g above; on **5:1** s. Mussies 169). Yet here αὐ. could mean *alone* (examples of this from Hom. on in many writers in WSchulze, Quaestiones epicae 1892, p. 250, 3) *he alone was a Samaritan*; but Luke's thematic interest in unexpected candidates for the Kingdom (cp. 5:30–32; 15:2; 19:2 [καὶ αὐτός]; 23:43) militates against the view.

ⓑ The oblique cases of αὐ. very oft. (in a fashion customary since Hom.) take the place of the 3rd pers. personal pron.; in partic. the gen. case replaces the missing possessive pron.

α. w. ref. to a preceding noun διαφέρετε αὐτῶν **Mt 6:26;** καταβάντος αὐτοῦ **8:1;** ἀπεκάλυψας αὐτά **11:25.—26:43f; Mk 1:10; 4:33ff; 12:19; Lk 1:22; 4:41.** The gen. is sometimes put first for no special reason (Esth 1:1e) αὐτοῦ τὰ σημεῖα **J 2:23,** cp. **3:19, 21, 33; 4:47; 12:40.** αὐτῶν τὴν συνείδησιν **1 Cor 8:12.** Sim. **Lk 1:36** αὐτῇ τῇ καλουμένῃ στείρᾳ *w. her who was called barren.* Forms of αὐ. are sometimes used without qualifiers in a series, referring to difft. pers.: φέρουσιν αὐτῷ (Jesus) τυφλόν, καὶ παρακαλοῦσιν αὐτὸν (Jesus) ἵνα αὐτοῦ (i.e. τοῦ τυφλοῦ) ἅψηται **Mk 8:22.** On problems related to the rdg. τῆς θυγατρὸς αὐτοῦ Ἡρωδιάδος εἰσελθούσης *when his* (Herod's) *daughter Herodias came in* (?) **Mk 6:22,** s. Borger in 1g, and entry Ἡρῳδιάς.

β. w. ref. to a noun to be supplied fr. the context, and without suggestion of contrast or disparagement: ἐν ταῖς συναγωγαῖς αὐτῶν (i.e. τ. Γαλιλαίων) **Mt 4:23.** ἐν ταῖς πόλεσιν αὐτῶν **11:1.** ἐκήρυσσεν αὐτοῖς (i.e. the inhabitants) **Ac 8:5.** παρακαλέσας αὐτούς **20:2.** ἀποταξάμενος αὐτοῖς **2 Cor 2:13.** τὰ γινόμενα ὑπ' αὐτῶν **Eph 5:12.** ἐδημηγόρει πρὸς αὐτούς **Ac 12:21.** τὸν φόβον αὐτῶν **1 Pt 3:14** (cp. **13** and s. Is 8:12). **Mt 12:9** (cp. vs. **2**); **Lk 2:22; 18:15; 19:9; 23:51; J 8:44; 20:15; Ac 4:5; Ro 2:26; Hb 8:9.**

γ. freq. used w. a verb, even though a noun in the case belonging to the verb has already preceded it (cp. Dio Chrys. 6, 23; 78 [29], 20; Epict. 3, 1, 22; POxy 299 [I AD] Λάμπωνι ἔδωκα αὐτῷ δραχμὰς η'; FKälker, Quaest. de Eloc. Polyb. 1880, 274) τοῖς καθημένοις ἐν σκιᾷ θανάτου φῶς ἀνέτειλεν αὐτοῖς **Mt 4:16.—5:40; 9:28; 26:71; J 15:2; 18:11; Js 4:17; Rv 2:7, 17; 6:4** al.

δ. used pleonastically after a relative, as somet. in older Gk., e.g. Soph., X., Hyperid. (B-D-F §297; Rob. 683), freq. in the LXX fr. Gen 1:11 (οὗ τὸ σπέρμα αὐτοῦ ἐν αὐτῷ; GrBar 2:11 ὃν οὐδεὶς δύναται πειρᾶσαι αὐτόν al.) on (Helbing, Grammatik p. iv; Thackeray 46), and quotable elsewh. in the Koine (Callim., Epigr. 43 [42], 3 ὧν ... αὐτῶν; Peripl. Eryth. c. 35; POxy 117, 15f ἐξ ὧν δώσεις τοῖς παιδίοις σου ἓν ἐξ αὐτῶν): οὗ τὸ πτύον ἐν τῇ χειρὶ αὐτοῦ **Mt 3:12; Lk 3:17.** οὗ οὐκ εἰμὶ ἱκανὸς ... τῶν ὑποδημάτων αὐτοῦ **Mk 1:7; Lk 3:16.** ἧς εἶχεν τὸ θυγάτριον αὐτῆς **Mk 7:25.** πᾶν ὃ δέδωκεν ... ἀναστήσω αὐτό **J 6:39; Ac 15:17.** ἣν οὐδεὶς δύναται κλεῖσαι αὐτήν **Rv 3:8.** οἷς ἐδόθη αὐτοῖς **7:2,** cp. **13:12.** οὗ ἡ πνοὴ αὐτοῦ 1 Cl 21:9.—Cp. in ref. to an anticipatory noun τὰ Ἐλισαίου ὀστᾶ ... νεκροῦ βληθέντος ... ἐπ' αὐτά *when a corpse was cast on the bones of Elisha* AcPlCor 2:32.

ε. continuing a relative clause (an older Gk. constr.; B-D-F §297; Rob. 724): ἐξ οὗ τὰ πάντα καὶ ἡμεῖς εἰς αὐτόν **1 Cor 8:6;** οἷς τὸ κρίμα ... καὶ ἡ ἀπώλεια αὐτῶν (for καὶ ὧν ἡ ἀπώλεια) **2 Pt 2:3.**

ζ. w. a change of pers. **Lk 1:45; Rv 18:24.**

η. w. a change of number and gender ἔθνη ... αὐτούς **Mt 28:19.** τοῦ παιδίου ... αὐτῇ **Mk 5:41.** φῶς ... αὐτόν **J 1:10.** λαόν ... αὐτῶν **Mt 1:21.—14:14; Mk 6:45f; 2 Cor 5:19.**

❸ **pert. to someth. that is identical with, or closely related to, someth.,** w. art. ὁ αὐτός, ἡ αὐτή, τὸ αὐτό ***the same*** (Hom. et al.; Ps 101:28, s. Mussies 171).

ⓐ w. a noun τὸν αὐ. λόγον **Mt 26:44; Mk 14:39;** τὸ αὐ. φύραμα **Ro 9:21;** cp. **Lk 23:40; 1 Cor 1:10; 10:3f; 12:4ff; 15:39; Phil 1:30.**

ⓑ without a noun τὸ (τὰ) αὐ. ποιεῖν (Jos., Ant. 5, 129; 9, 271) **Mt 5:46; Lk 6:33; Eph 6:9.** τὰ αὐτὰ πράσσειν **Ro 2:1.** τὸ αὐ. λέγειν *agree* (not only in words; s. on λέγω 1aα) **1 Cor 1:10.** ἀπαγγέλλειν τὰ αὐτά **Ac 15:27.** τὸ αὐ. as adv. *in the same way* (X., Mem. 3, 8, 5) **Mt 27:44; 18:9** D.—ἐπὶ τὸ αὐ. (Hesychius: ὁμοῦ, ἐπὶ τὸν αὐ. τόπον; Iambl., Vi. Pyth. 30, 167; SIG 736, 66 [92 BC]; BGU 762, 9 [II AD] ἀπὸ τῶν ἐπὶ τὸ αὐ. καμήλων ε' of the five camels taken together; PTebt 14, 20; 319, 9 al.; 2 Km 2:13; Ps 2:2 al.; 3 Macc 3:1; Sus 14 Theod.) of place *at the same place, together* (En 100:2; Jos., Bell. 2, 346; s. συνέρχομαι 1a) **Mt 22:34; 1 Cor 11:20; 14:23;** B 4:10; IEph 5:3; εἶναι ἐπὶ τὸ αὐ. (TestNapht 6:6) **Lk 17:35; Ac 1:15; 2:1.** προστιθέναι ἐπὶ τὸ αὐ. *add to the total* **Ac 2:47** (see M-M.). κατὰ τὸ αυ. of pers. being together as a body *in each other's company, together* (PEleph 1, 5 εἶναι δὲ ἡμᾶς κατὰ ταὐτό) and also with ref. to simultaneous presence *at the same time* (Aelian, VH 14, 8 δύο εἰκόνας εἰργάσατο Πολύκλειτος κατὰ τ. αὐ.; 3 Km 3:18) **Ac 14:1;** the mng. *in the same way* may also apply (ENestle, Acts 14:1: ET 24, 1913, 187f) as in Hs 8, 7, 1 (cod. A; s. καθά; but s. Bonner 105, n. 17, who restores κατ' αὐ[τοὺς αἱ ῥάβ]δοι; so also Joly).—In combinations ἓν καὶ τὸ αὐ. (also Pla., Leg. 721c; Aristot., Metaph. 1039a, 28; other exx. in GKypke, Observ. II 1755, 220; Diod. S. 3, 63, 2 εἷς καὶ ὁ αὐτός) *one and the same thing* **1 Cor 11:5;** cp. **12:11** (Diod. S. 22, 6, 3 μίαν καὶ τὴν αὐτὴν ἀπόκρισιν; Epict. 1, 19, 15 μία καὶ ἡ αὐ. ἀρχή). W. gen. foll. τὰ αὐ. τῶν παθημάτων *the same sufferings as* **1 Pt 5:9.** Without comparison: ὁ αὐ. (Thu. 2, 61, 2; Plut., Caesar 729 [45, 7], Brutus 989 [13, 1]) εἶ *thou art the same* **Hb 1:12** (Ps 101:28);

cp. **13:8.** On the variation betw. αὐτοῦ and αὑτοῦ, αὐτῶν and αὑτῶν in the mss., s. ἑαυτοῦ, beg.—WMichaelis, D. unbetonte καὶ αὐτός bei Lukas: StTh 4, '51, 86–93; MBlack, An Aramaic Approach[3], '67, 96–100; MWilcox, The Semitisms of Ac, '65, 93–100 (Qumran).—Mussies 168–73. DELG. M-M. Sv.

αὐτοσώρας (αὐτός, ὥρα) adv. ***at the same time*** (like αὔθωρον ParJer 3:19 cod. C; s. HUsener, NGG 1892, 45; HDiels, Parmenides' Lehrgedicht 1897, 95) GPt 5:20.

αὐτοῦ neut. gen. of αὐτός functioning as deictic adv. designating a position relatively near or far (Hom.+; Epict. 4, 4, 14; Vett. Val. 264, 12; SIG 167, 37; 273, 20; 1024, 26; pap [Mayser 457; PSI 374, 14]; LXX; TestAbr A; Jos., Ant. 8, 14, Vi. 116) ***here*** καθίσατε αὐ. (Gen 22:5) **Mt 26:36; Mk 6:33 v.l.; Lk 9:27;** ***there*** **Ac 15:34 v.l.; 18:19; 21:4.**

αὐτόφωρος, ον (αὐτός, φώρ 'thief'; Soph. et al.; Sym. Job 34:11) ***(caught) in the act*** in the expr. ἐπ' αὐτοφώρῳ (since Hdt. 6, 72; PColZen 74, 25 [248 BC]; POslo 21, 9 [71 AD]; BGU 372 II, 11 [II AD]; Philo, Spec. Leg. 3, 52; Jos., Ant. 15, 48; 16, 213) first of a thief (φώρ=Lat. fur), then also of other wrongdoers (Plut., Eumen. 583 [2, 2] al.), esp. adulterers (X., Symp. 3, 13; Aelian, NA 11, 15: μοιχευομένην γυναῖκα ἐπ' αὐ. καταλαβών; Achilles Tat. 5, 19, 6) **J 8:4.**—DELG s.v. φώρ. M-M.

αὐτόχειρ, ρος (s. αὐτός, χείρ; trag. et al.; Isocr.; Pla., Leg. p. 824a; Epict. 4, 9, 12; Herodian 7, 2, 8; Vett. Val., Ind.; SIG 709, 42; epitaph Sb 6754, 22; perh. PGissUniv 46 II, 10; Jos., Bell. 7, 393, Ant. 13, 363) ***w. one's own hand*** ῥίπτειν **Ac 27:19.**—DELG s.v. χείρ III. M-M.

αὐχέω (αὔχη 'boasting, pride'; Aeschyl., Hdt. et al.; Vett. Val. 241, 9; ins; Is 10:15; Tat. 34, 1; Ath. 34, 1) ***boast*** w. acc. (Ael. Aristid. 13 p. 164 D.; Kaibel 567, 3; 822, 5; Jos., C. Ap. 1, 22, Vi. 340) μεγάλα αὐχεῖ *boasts of great things* **Js 3:5** (v.l. μεγαλαυχέω q.v.; cp. Kaibel 489, 1 in a grave inscription [ὃν μεγάλ' αὐ]χήσασα πατρὶς Θή[β]η=in whom his homeland Thebes took great pride).—M-M. TW.

αὐχμηρός, ά, όν (αὐχμός 'drought'; Soph., Hippocr. et al.; Just., A II, 11, 5) gen. in the sense 'dry' but the rendering ***dark*** or ***gloomy*** (Aristot., De Color. 3, 793a 10ff τὸ λαμπρὸν ἢ στίλβον … ἢ τοὐναντίον αὐχμηρὸν καί ἀλαμπές; Hesych. αὐ. σκοτῶδες; Suda αὐ. στυγνὸν ἢ σκοτεινόν; Kaibel 431, 3) of a place (Pla., Leg. 761b 'very dry' τόποι) is required for **2 Pt 1:19.** τόπος αὐχμηρότατος *very dreary* ApcPt 6:21.—DELG s.v. αὖος. M-M.

ἀφαιρέω 2 fut. ἀφελῶ (B-D-F §74, 3; cp. Schwyzer I 746 n. 5; 785 n. 1); 2 aor. ἀφεῖλον, inf. ἀφελεῖν. Mid. 2 aor. ἀφειλόμην, -άμην LXX. Pass. 1 fut. ἀφαιρεθήσομαι; 1 aor. ἀφῃρέθην; pf. ἀφῄρημαι (Hom.+; Ath. 1, 4 [cp. Mt 5:39f; Lk 6:29]; 12, 1).

❶ **to detach someth. by force, *take away, remove, cut off,*** act. τὶ *someth.* τὸ ἔριον B 7:8; *cut off* (Parthenius 8, 9 τ. κεφαλήν) τὸ ὠτίον *the ear* (cp. Ezk 23:25) **Mt 26:51; Mk 14:47; Lk 22:50;** AcPl Ha 5:11.

❷ **to cause a state or condition to cease, *take away, do away with, remove*—ⓐ** act. ὄνειδος **Lk 1:25;** ὀνειδισμόν GJs 6:3 (for both cp. Gen 30:23). ἁμαρτίας **Hb 10:4** (cp. Sir 47:11). τὶ ἀπό τινος (Theophr., Char. 2, 3; Num 21:7; Josh 5:9; 1 Esdr 4:30; Jer 11:15) *take away someth. fr. someone or someth.* τὰς πονηρίας ἀπὸ τ. ψυχῶν 1 Cl 8:4 (Is 1:16). ἐὰν ἀφέλῃς ἀπὸ σοῦ σύνδεσμον καὶ χειροτονίαν καὶ ῥῆμα γογγυσμοῦ *if you put away fr. you bonds and scorn and the complaining word* B 3:5 (Is 58:9). τὸ μέρος αὐτοῦ ἀπὸ τοῦ ξύλου τῆς ζωῆς *take away* or *cut off the person's share in the tree of life* **Rv 22:19b** (on the ἐκ τῆς πόλεως foll. cp. Is 22:19). W. omission of the obj., to be supplied fr. context (cp. Num 11:17) ἀπὸ τ. λόγων *take away anything fr. the words* **22:19a** (cp. Diod. S. 12, 75, 4 ἀφ. ἀπὸ τῶν συνθηκῶν = take someth. away from the agreements; Artem. 2, 70 p. 167, 25 a request to the readers of the βιβλία: μήτε προσθεῖναι μήτε τι τῶν ὄντων ἀφελεῖν; Ael. Aristid. 30, 20 K.=10 p. 121 D.; En 104:11; Jos., C. Ap. 1, 42); ἀ. ἀπὸ τοῦ πόνου τῆς ψυχῆς *take away some of the torment of his soul* 1 Cl 16:12 (Is 53:10). Abs. (opp. προστιθέναι as Socrat., Ep. 28, 13) B 19:11; D 4:13.

ⓑ mid. and pass.—**α.** *take away* mid. as act. τὶ ἀπό τινος (Aristoph., Vesp. 883; Ezk 26:16) *someth. fr. someone* τ. οἰκονομίαν **Lk 16:3.**

β. *do away with, remove,* of sins, mid. as act. w. acc. of thing (EpArist 244; Jos., Ant. 15, 39) τὰς ἁμαρτίας **Ro 11:27** (Is 27:9); pass. *be taken away* Hs 9, 28, 3.

❸ **to deprive by taking, *take away,*** pass. νοσσιᾶς ἀφῃρημένοι (-μένης v.l.) *when they are taken from the nest* B 11:3 (cp. Is 16:2). W. gen. of the pers. deprived of someth. ἥτις οὐκ ἀφαιρεθήσεται αὐτῆς *which shall not be taken away fr. her* **Lk 10:42.**—DELG s.v. αἱρέω. M-M.

ἀφάνεια, ας, ἡ (s. ἀφανής; Pind., Aeschyl., Thu.; also Ezk 23:33 Theod.; Philo, Div. Rer. Hered. 157) 'invisibility', then ***annihilation, destruction*** ἵνα ἀρχὴν λάβῃ αὐτοῦ ἡ ἀφ. *so that his annihilation* (cp. 2 Th 2:8) *might begin* ApcPt Rainer 4:9 (at ApcPt 14).

ἀφανής, ές (Aeschyl., Hdt.+) ***invisible, hidden*** **Hb 4:13;** Ox 1081, 28 (opp. ἐμφανής ln. 2; cp. SJCh 90, 5). On the probability of the use of this word in the corrupt text AcPl Ha 3, 27, s. Schubart's note.—DELG s.v. φαίνω B. M-M. TW.

ἀφανίζω fut. ἀφανιῶ LXX and ἀφανίσω LXX, Da 2:44; 1 aor. ἠφάνισα LXX. Pass.: fut. ἀφανισθήσομαι LXX; aor. ἠφανίσθην; pf. 3 sg. ἠφάνισται Job 2:9 (s. ἀφανής; Soph.; Hdt.+)

❶ **to cause someth. to disappear—ⓐ** act. ***destroy, ruin,*** of treasures (X., An. 3, 2, 11; Kaibel 531, 2; PRyl 152, 14; POxy 1220, 20; PLond II, 413, 14f p. 300 [the 3 last passages of destruction by animals]; LXX; mislead people PsSol 17:11) **Mt 6:19f.**

ⓑ pass. freq. in act. sense ***be destroyed, perish, disappear*** (Diod. S. 15, 48, 3 [people and cities because of an earthquake]; Philostrat., Vi. Apoll. 1, 36 p. 38, 20 τὸ γένος αὐτῶν; Jos., Ant. 1, 76; Ath.) of the earth in a holocaust **2 Pt 3:10 v.l.;** of scoffers **Ac 13:41** (Hab 1:5). In imagery of the bond of wickedness IEph 19:3. Of honey *be spoiled* Hm 5, 1, 5. Of someth. that is seen and forthwith disappears (Antig. Car. 12; Artem. 2, 36 p. 134, 26; Eunap.Vi. Soph. 7, 6, 9 p. 63; Philo, Deus Imm. 123, Virt. 164; Jos., Ant. 9, 28) of mist *evanesce* **Js 4:14.**

❷ **to cause to become unrecognizable through change in appearance, *render invisible/unrecognizable,*** of one's face (opp. φαίνομαι in a play on words as Js 4:14; Aristot., HA 6, 7, 11 [583b 19]; Ps.-Aristot., De Mundo 6, 22) by covering the head (cp. Jer 14:4; 2 Km 15:30; Esth 6:12) or neglect of cleanliness (cp. POxy 294, 15 [22 AD]) **Mt 6:16** in theatrical imagery (s. ὑποκριτής) of Pharisees who seem to don masks during their fasting (for the poss. rendering *disfigure* [s. M'Neile comm. ad loc.] cp. PAmh 2, 3, but the passage is too corrupt to determine the mng. with any precision; on the topic of a highly zealous piety s. Plut., Mor. 168d).—DELG s.v. φαίνω B. M-M. TW.

ἀφανισμός, οῦ, ὁ the condition of being no longer visible, freq. in the transferred sense ***destruction*** (s. ἀφανίζω; Polyb. et al.; Diod. S. 15, 48, 1; Herm. Wr. p. 364 Sc.; LXX; En 12:4; ParJer 3:13; 4:10; Jos., Ant. 1, 70) ἐγγὺς ἀφανισμοῦ *is near destruction* **Hb 8:13.**—DELG s.v. φαίνω. M-M.

ἄφαντος, ον (Hom. et al., chiefly in poets, then also in prose; ApcMos 20) ***invisible*** ἄ. γίνεσθαι (Diod. S. 3, 60, 3 of Hesperus; 4, 65, 9 ἐμπεσὼν εἰς τὸ χάσμα . . . ἄφ. ἐγένετο; 5, 22, 4; Plut., Mor. 409f; AcTh 77 [Aa II/2, 192, 12f] ἄφαντοι γεγόνασιν οἱ δαίμονες; 13 p. 119, 2 v.l.) *vanish* **Lk 24:31** (on ἀπό τινος *fr. someone* [as Pel.-Leg. 6, 24; 11, 24] s. JPsichari, Essai sur le Grec de la LXX: REJ 55, 1908, 161–208, esp. 204ff).—DELG s.v. φαίνω. M-M.

ἄφεδρος, ου, ἡ (cp. next entry; LXX) of ***childbirth*** (Lev 12:2, 5) GJs 5:2.

ἀφεδρών, ῶνος, ὁ (ἀπό, cp. ἕδρα 'seat'; the older Gk. term is ἄφοδος) ***toilet, latrine*** (OGI 483, 220f [prechristian] τ. δημοσίων ἀφεδρώνων καὶ τ. ἐξ αὐτῶν ὑπονόμων; Geopon. 6, 2, 8; Anecd. Gr. p. 469, 23; Etym. Gud. 240, 14) εἰς ἀ. ἐκβάλλεται *passes into the latrine* **Mt 15:17; Mk 7:19** (cp. ὅταν . . . καταβῇ τὰ δύο[τροφή, ὕδωρ] εἰς τὸν ἀ. TestJob 38:3).—DELG s.v. ἕζομαι B2. M-M.

ἀφέθην, ἀφεθήσομαι s. ἀφίημι.

ἀφειδία, ας, ἡ (ἀφειδής 'unsparing'; Ps.-Pla., Def. 412d; Plut., Mor. 762d; Nägeli 52) from the sense 'spare nothing', i.e. lavish on someth., there is a tranference to ***sparing very little for*** someth. as in *severe treatment* σώματος *of the body* (=asceticism) **Col 2:23** (ἀφειδεῖν τοῦ σώματος also in sense 'harden' [Lucian, Anach. 24]).—DELG s.v. φείδομαι. M-M.

ἀφεῖδον s. ἀφοράω.

ἀφεῖλον s. ἀφαιρέω.

ἀφεῖναι s. ἀφίημι.

ἀφείς, ἀφεῖς s. ἀφίημι.

ἀφελεῖν s. ἀφαιρέω.

ἀφελότης, ητος, ἡ (older Gk. ἀφέλεια; Mel., P. subscr. [B]; Dio Chrys.; Vett. Val. 240, 15; 153, 30) *simplicity* of heart **Ac 2:46.**—DELG s.v. ἀφελής. M-M.

ἀφελπίζω s. ἀπελπίζω.

ἀφελῶ, ἀφέλωμαι s. ἀφαιρέω.

ἄφεσις, έσεως, ἡ (s. ἀφίημι; Pla.+)—**❶ the act of freeing and liberating from someth. that confines, *release*** fr. captivity (Polyb. 1, 79, 12; SIG 374, 21; PGrenf I, 64, 5; 1 Esdr 4, 62; Philo, Mut. Nom. 228 [after Lev 25:10]; Jos., Ant. 12, 40; 17, 185) **Lk 4:18ab** (Is 61:1; 58:6); B 3:3 (Is 58:6); 14:9 (Is 61:1).

❷ the act of freeing from an obligation, guilt, or punishment, *pardon, cancellation* (Pla., Leg. 9, 869d φόνου; Diod. S. 20, 44, 6 ἐγκλημάτων; 32, 2, 6 τῆς τιμωρίας; Dionys. Hal. 8, 50 al.; En 13:4 and 6; Philo, Mos. 2, 147 ἀ. ἁμαρτημάτων, Spec. Leg. 1, 215; 237; Jos., Bell. 1, 481; exx. fr. ins and pap in Nägeli 56. Cp. also Dt 15:3; Jdth 11:14; 1 Macc 10:34; 13:34. For history of the word Dssm., B 94–97 [BS 98–101]) ἁμαρτιῶν *forgiveness of sins* i.e. cancellation of the guilt of sin (Iren. 1, 21, 2 [Harv. I 182, 4]; Theoph. Ant. 2, 16 [p. 140, 9]) **Mt 26:28; Mk 1:4; Lk 1:77; 3:3; 24:47; Ac 2:38; 5:31** (δοῦναι ἄφεσιν as Diod. S. 20, 54, 2); **10:43** (λαβεῖν; likew. TestSol 6:10 A; Just., D. 141, 2 al.); **13:38; 26:18; Col 1:14;** B 5:1; 6:11; 8:3; 11:1; 16:8; Hm 4, 3, 1ff; AcPl Ha 2, 30. For this ἄ. τ. παραπτωμάτων **Eph 1:7;** τοῖς παραπτώμασιν ἄ. Hm 4, 4, 4 (cp. ἄφεσις ἁμαρτημάτων Orig., C. Cels. 1, 47, 4); ἄ. abs. in same sense (Hippol., Ref. 6, 41, 2) **Mk 3:29; Hb 9:22; 10:18.** τὸ τῆς ἀφέσεως *what is offered for forgiveness of sins* GJs 1:1; αἰτεῖσθαι ἄφεσίν τινι *ask forgiveness for someone* 1 Cl 53:5 (εὔχεσθαί τε καὶ αἰτεῖν . . . παρὰ τοῦ θεοῦ Just., A I, 61, 2).—ERedlich, The Forgiveness of Sins '37; VTaylor, Forgiveness and Reconciliation (in the NT) '41; HThyen, Studien z. Sündenvergebung im NT '70.—DELG s.v. ἵημι. EDNT. M-M. TW. Spicq.

ἄφετε, ἀφέωνται s. ἀφίημι.

ἁφή, ῆς, ἡ (s. ἅπτω; Hdt. et al.; SIG 1170, 11; LXX; TestSol 12:5 C; EpArist; Philo; s. Nägeli 18; on its use as medic. t.t. s. Lghtf. on Col 2:19 and JRobinson on Eph 4:16) ***ligament,*** lit. 'joint, connection', **Eph 4:16, Col 2:19.** CBruston, Rev. des Ét. grecques 24, 1911, 77ff.—DELG s.v. ἅπτω. M-M.

ἀφῆκα s. ἀφίημι.

ἀφήκω fut. ἀφήξω (Pla., Rep. 7 p. 530e; Antiphon: Anecd. Gr. p. 470 s.v. ἀφήκοντος) ***go away*** (Cass. Dio 41, 8; PMich 218, 5; Sb 7250, 5) ποῦ ἀφήξω; *where shall I go?* 1 Cl 28:3.—DELG s.v. ἥκω.

ἀφήσω s. ἀφίημι.

ἀφθαρσία, ας, ἡ (ἄφθαρτος, α- priv. + φθείρω) **the state of not being subject to decay/dissolution/interruption, *incorruptibility, immortality*** ('higher Koine' [Nägeli 41, 1; 31]: Epicurus 60, 3 [PLinde, Epicuri Vocab. 1906, 43]; Chrysipp.; Strabo; Plut., Aristid. 322 [6, 3], Mor. 881b al.; Herm. Wr. 12, 14; Wsd 2:23; 6:19; 4 Macc 9:22; 17:12; Philo, Aet. M. 27 ἀ. τ. κόσμου; OdeSol 11:12; JosAs 8:5; 15:4; Just., Tat.; Mel., P. 49, 351; Ath., R. 63, 14 al.) **1 Cor 15:42, 50, 53f;** IPol 2:3. As a quality of the future life (w. ζωή) **2 Ti 1:10;** 2 Cl 14:5; (w. δόξα, τιμή) ἀ. ζητεῖν **Ro 2:7;** ἀ. προσδέχεσθαι Dg 6:8 (cp. ἐνδύεσθαι τὴν ἀ. Theoph. Ant. 1, 7 [p. 74, 1] al.; κληρονομεῖν τὴν ἀ. 2, 27 [p. 166, 4]); πνεῖν ἀφθαρσίαν IEph 17:1; μεταλαμβάνειν ἀ. 2 Cl 14:5; ἀρχηγὸς τῆς ἀ. (of Christ) 20:5; ἀγὼν τῆς ἀ. 7:5; ἀπάρτισμα ἀ. *the imperishable completed work* (of the gosp.) IPhld 9:2; διδαχὴ ἀ. *teaching that assures immort.* IMg 6:2; ὁ τῆς ἀ. στέφανος *the crown that is immortality* MPol 17:1; 19:2; ἐν ἀ. πνεύματος ἁγίου 14:2.—ἀγαπᾶν . . . ἐν ἀφθαρσίᾳ have an undying love **Eph 6:24** (NRSV), but some prefer as ref. either to those who love the Lord, and as such are now partakers of the future life, or to the Lord himself, who reigns in immortal glory. The presence of ἀ. in **Tit 2:7 v.l.** is prob. due to a misunderstanding of the rare word ἀφθορία. [τὸ] δὲ γε[ι]νό|μεν[ον ἀπὸ] ἀφ[θ]αρ|σίας [οὐκ ἀπο]γείν[εται]| ἀλλ[ὰ μ]έν[ει] ἀφ[θαρ]|τον ὡς ἀπὸ ἀ[φ]θ[αρσί|α]ς γεγονός *what is born of incorruption remains incorruptible inasmuch as it is born of incorruption* Ox 1081, 14–19, s. 15f and 18f (=SJCh 89, 10–17 Coptic).—DELG s.v. φθείρω. M-M. TW.

ἄφθαρτος, ον (s. φθείρω) **pert. to imperviousness to corruption and death, *imperishable, incorruptible, immortal*** ('higher Koine' [Nägeli 41, 1; 31]: Philochorus [IV/III BC]: 328 fgm. 188b Jac.; Aristot., Epicurus, Diod. S., Dionys. Hal.; Cornutus 1 p. 2, 8; Lucian; Philostrat., Dial. p. 259, 7 K.; Sallust. p. 12, 24; 30, 7; CIG 4240d, 5; OGI 569, 24; PGM 4, 497; 519; 13, 912; Ox 1081, 5; 17f [s. below]; Wsd 12:1; 18:4; JosAs 12:12; ApcEsdr 4:36 p. 29, 14 Tdf.; Ar. 4, 1; Just.; Mel., P. 2, 10 al.;

Ath., R. 10 p. 58, 23 al.) of God (Diod. S. 6, 2, 2 of gods: ἀΐδιοι and ἄφθαρτοι; Zoroaster in Philo of Bybl.: 790 fgm. 4 Jac. [in Eus., PE 1, 10, 52]; Antipater of Tarsus [150 BC]: 3 p. 249, 13 [in Plut., Stoicor. Repugn. 38, p. 1105f]; Herm. Wr. 11, 3; PGM 4, 559 θεοῦ ζῶντος ἀφθάρτου; SibOr, fgm. 3, 17; Philo, Sacr. Abel. 95, Mos. 2, 171; Jos., Ant. 3, 88; 10, 278; Ar. 4, 1; Just., D. 5, 4.—Cp. Orig., C. Cels. 4, 14, 29) **Ro 1:23; 1 Ti 1:17;** PtK 2, p. 13, 26; of Christ Dg 9:2 (ὁ ἄφθαρτος καὶ μόνος θεός Theoph. Ant. 3, 30 [p. 268, 27]). Of the resurrected body **1 Cor 15:52.** ναός B 16:9; στέφανος **1 Cor 9:25;** κληρονομία **1 Pt 1:4;** σπορά vs. **23; short ending of Mk;** ἀγάπη ἄ. *an imperishable love-feast* IRo 7:3; ἀγὼν ἄ. 2 Cl 7:3; ἀγαθὰ ἄ. (Philo, Deus Imm. 151) 6:6; καρπὸς ἄ. ITr 11:2; φυτά (Philo, Sacr. Abel. 97) ApcPt 5, 15.—Subst. τὸ ἄ. (SIG 798, 10 [37 AD]) B 19:8; ἐν τῷ ἄ. τοῦ πραέως πνεύματος *w. the imperishable quality of a gentle spirit* (s. πνεῦμα 3c) **1 Pt 3:4.** On the basis of the Coptic SJCh 89, 1–3, the text of Ox 1081, 3–5 can be restored as follows: [διαφο]||ρά τε πολλὴ [μεταξὺ]|| τῶν ἀφθάρ[τ]ω[ν] (there exists) *a great difference between the incorruptible things.* For ἄ. Ox 1081, 17f [SJCh 90, 15 Coptic] s. prec. entry, end.—DELG s.v. φθείρω. M-M. TW.

ἀφθονία, ας, ἡ (s. φθονέω; Pind.+; POslo 78, 16 [136 AD='abundance']; OdeSol 11:6; TestAbr A 4 p. 80, 20 [Stone p. 8] al.; Philo, Mos. 1, 6; Jos., Bell. 3, 505, Ant. 12, 133; Just., A II, 7, 3) 'freedom fr. envy', hence ***willingness*** (so Pla., Prot. 327b) **Tit 2:7 v.l.**—Sv.—DELG s.v. φθόνος.

ἀφθορία, ας, ἡ (s. φθείρω) ***soundness,*** lit. incorruption (corresp. to ἄφθορος Diod. S. 4, 7, 3; Artem. 5, 95; Phalaris, Ep. 70; BGU 1106, 11; 1107, 7; PGM 5, 376; 7, 544; Esth 2:2) of pure doctrine **Tit 2:7.**—M-M. TW.

ἀφίδω s. ἀφοράω.

ἀφιερόω (ἱερόω 'consecrate') 1 aor. ἀφιέρωσα (pass. in Aeschyl., Eumen. 451; Jos., Ant. 11, 148) in H. Gk. cultic t.t. ***consecrate*** (Diod. S. 1, 90, 4; Plut.; Philo Bybl. [c.100 AD]: 790 fgm. 1, 29 Jac. [in Eus., PE 1, 9, 29]; OGI, index, and oft. in ins; Sb 7687, 7; 4 Macc 13:13; Philo Alex.; Jos., Ant. 15, 364) ἀφιέρωσαν αὐτὸν (sc. τὸν θεόν) ἐν τῷ ναῷ *they have consecrated God through the temple* instead of conversely basing the consecration of the temple on God B 16:2.—DELG s.v. ἱερός.

ἀφίημι (Hom.+) pres. act. ind. 2 sg. ἀφεῖς (Rob. 315; W-S. §14, 16; M-M.) and ἀφίεις (ApcSed 12:4 p. 135, 14 Ja.), 3 sg. ἀφίησιν (TestSim 3:2) and ἀφίει (TestJud 18:3); 1 pl. ἀφίομεν (ἀφίεμεν v.l.; B-D-F §94, 3) **Lk 11:4;** 3 pl. ἀφίουσιν **Rv 11:9.** Impf. 2 sg. ἠφίεις Sus 53 LXX, 3 sg. ἤφιε (B-D-F §69, 1); ptc. ἀφίοντες Hs 8, 6, 5. Fut. ἀφήσω. 1 aor. ἀφῆκα, 2 sg. ἀφῆκες **Rv 2:4** (W-H.; B-D-F §83, 2); impv. ἄφησον ApcEsdr 1:3 p. 24, 8 Tdf.; 2 aor. impv. ἄφες (as אֲפֵס in rabb.), ἄφετε; subj. ἀφῶ, 2 pl. ἀφῆτε; inf. ἀφεῖναι **Mt 23:23 v.l.; Lk 5:21;** ptc. ἀφείς. Mid. aor. impv. 2 sg. ἄφησαι (TestAbr A 20 p. 102, 29 [Stone p. 52]). Pass.: pres. ἀφίεμαι, 3 pl. ἀφίονται **Mt 9:2** D; fut. ἀφεθήσομαι; 1 aor. ἀφέθην, 3 sg. ἀφείθη Just. D. 141, 3; pf. 3 pl. ἀφέωνται **Mt 9:2 v.l.; Mk 2:5 v.l.; Lk 5:20, 23; 7:48; J 20:23; 1J 2:12** (B-D-F §97, 3); impv. 3 sg. ἀφείσθω Ath. 2:4. Gener., to cause someone or someth. to undergo separation.

❶ to dismiss or release someone or someth. from a place or one's presence—ⓐ w. personal obj. ***let go, send away*** (X., Cyr. 1, 2, 8; Polyb. 33, 1, 6; Tob 10:5; Sir 27:19; Jos., Ant. 16, 135 τ. ἐκκλησίαν) crowds **Mt 13:36; Mk 4:36; 8:13** (mng. 3a is also prob.).

ⓑ w. impers. obj. ***give up, emit*** obj. τὸ πνεῦμα *give up one's spirit* **Mt 27:50** (cp. ἀ. τ. ψυχήν Hdt. 4, 190 and oft. in Gk. lit.; Gen 35:18; 1 Esdr 4:21; Jos., Ant. 1, 218; 14, 369 al.). φωνὴν μεγάλην *utter a loud cry* **Mk 15:37** (φων. ἀ. Hdt. et al.; Appian, Bell. Civ. 3, 68 §279; Epict. 2, 22, 12 al.; Gen 45:2; Philo, Sacr. Abel. 34; Jos., Bell. 4, 170, Ant. 8, 325, Vi. 158).

ⓒ in a legal sense ***divorce*** γυναῖκα (Hdt. 5, 39) **1 Cor 7:11ff.**—Lit.—LEpstein, Marriage Law in the Bible and the Talmud '42; MHumbert, Le remariage à Rome '72; CPréaux, in La Femme I, '79, 161–65 [Hellen. period]; JMurphy-O'Connor, JBL 100, '81, '601–6; JMoiser, JSNT 18, '83, 103–22.

❷ to release from legal or moral obligation or consequence, *cancel, remit, pardon* τὸ δάνειον *the loan* **Mt 18:27** (OGI 90, 12; PGrenf I, 26, 9; Dt 15:2). ὀφειλήν *a debt* vs. **32** (cp. 1 Macc 15:8 πᾶν ὀφείλημα βασιλικὸν ἀ.). Also of remission of the guilt (debt) of sin (Hdt. 6, 30 ἀπῆκέ τ' ἂν αὐτῷ τὴν αἰτίην; 8, 140, 2; Lysias 20, 34 ἀφιέντας τ. τῶν πατέρων ἁμαρτίας; Herodas 5, 26 ἄφες μοι τὴν ἁμαρτίην ταύτην; 38, 72f; 1 Macc 13:39.—In another construction Diod. S. 9, 31, 4 Κῦρος αὐτὸν ἀφίησι τῶν ἁμαρτημάτων = absolves him of his misdeeds), in OT and NT predom. in sense of divine forgiveness. W. dat. of pers. and acc. of thing: ὀφειλήματα *remit, forgive debts* (Appian, Ital. 9 §1 ἠφίει τοῖς ἑαυτοῦ χρήσταις τὰ ὀφλήματα) **Mt 6:12a;** cp. **b** (s. Sir 28:2 and ὡς 3αβ; FFensham, The Legal Background of Mt 6:12: NovT 4, '60, 1f [Deut 15:2 LXX]; on the text FBurkitt, 'As we have forgiven' Mt 6:12: JTS 33, '32, 253–55); *forgive* ἁμαρτίας (Ex 32:32; Num 14:19; Job 42:10 al.; Jos., Ant. 6, 92) **Lk 11:4; 1J 1:9.** παραπτώματα **Mt 6:14f; Mk 11:25;** vs. **26 v.l.** Pass. (Lev 4:20; 19:22; Is 22:14; 33:24 al.) ἁμαρτίαι **Lk 5:20, 23; 7:47b; 1J 2:12;** 1 Cl 50:5; Hv 2, 2, 4; s 7:4; PtK 3 p. 15, 12; ἁμαρτήματα **Mk 3:28** (s. GDalman, Jesus-Jeshua [Eng. tr. PLevertoff 1929], 195–97; JWilliams, NTS 12, '65, 75–77); PtK 3 p. 15, 27; cp. **Mt 12:31f.** W. dat. of pers. only **Mt 18:21, 35; Lk 17:3f; 23:34** (ELohse, Märtyrer u. Gottesknecht, Exkurs: Lk 23:34, '55). Pass. (Lev 4:26, 31, 35; Num 15:25f al.) **Lk 12:10; Js 5:15.—J 20:23b** (s. JMantey, JBL 58, '39, 243–49 and HCadbury ibid. 251–54). W. impers. obj. only **Mt 9:6; Mk 2:7, 10; Lk 5:21, 24; 7:49; J 20:23.** Pass. **Mt 9:2, 5; Mk 2:5, 9** (s. HBranscomb, JBL 53, '34, 53–60; B-D-F §320); **Lk 7:47f.** ἀνομίαι **Ro 4:7;** 1 Cl 50:6 (both Ps 31:1). Abs. ἀφίετε 1 Cl 13:2.

❸ to move away, w. implication of causing a separation, *leave, depart from*—ⓐ lit. of pers. or physical things as obj. (PGrenf I, 1, 16; BGU 814, 16; 18) **Mt 4:11; 8:15; 26:44; Mk 1:20, 31; 12:12; Lk 4:39.** The spirit *left* the possessed man **9:42** D; *abandon* (Soph., Phil. 486; Hyperid. 5, 32; X., Hell. 6, 4, 5) **Mt 26:56; Mk 14:50.**—W. impers. obj. (PFay 112, 13; Jer 12:7; Eccl 10:4; 1 Esdr 4:50): **J 10:12;** *house* **Mk 13:34;** cp. **Mt 23:38; Lk 13:35** (Diod. S. 17, 41, 7: Apollo appears and explains that he would leave Tyre, which is doomed to destruction); *Judaea* **J 4:3** (Jos., Ant. 2, 335 τ. Αἴγυπτον); *the way* Hv 3, 7, 1; *everything* **Mt 19:27, 29; 10:28f; Lk 5:11; 18:28f.**

ⓑ fig. of impers. obj. *give up, abandon* (Aeschyl., Prom. 317 ὀργάς; Arrian, Anab. 1, 10, 6; Jos., Ant. 9, 264 ἀ. τ. ἄρτι βίον) τὴν πρώτην ἀγάπην **Rv 2:4;** τ. φυσικὴν χρῆσιν **Ro 1:27;** *leave (behind)* to go on to someth. else (in orators; Plut., Mor. 793a; Epict. 4, 1, 15 al.) τὸν τῆς ἀρχῆς τοῦ Χρ. λόγον **Hb 6:1;** *neglect* (Diod. S. 1, 39, 11; POxy 1067, 5) also *omit* (Diod. S. 8, 12, 11) τὰ βαρύτερα τοῦ νόμου *what is more important in the law* **Mt 23:23;** τὴν ἐντολήν **Mk 7:8** (Hyperid. 5, 22 νόμον).

❹ to have someth. continue or remain in a place. ***Leave standing/lying*** (without concerning oneself further about it as, in a way, Diod. S. 5, 35, 3 a fire without putting it out) αὐτόν **Mt 22:22;** τὰ δίκτυα **4:20; Mk 1:18;** ἐκεῖ τὸ δῶρον **Mt 5:24;** cp. **18:12;**

J 4:28; ἡμιθανῆ *half dead* **Lk 10:30** (cp. Jdth 6:13).—*Leave (behind)* w. pers. obj. (2 Km 15:16; 3 Km 19:3; Tob 11:2) as orphans **J 14:18** (Epict. 3, 24, 14; Jos., Ant. 12, 387). τινὰ μόνον **8:29; 16:32.**—τινί τι ἀ. *let someone have someth.* (cp. Jos., Ant. 7, 274 τ. υἱὸν ἄφες μοι) **Mt 5:40.** W. acc. only τέκνον, σπέρμα **Mk 12:19ff;** vs. **21 v.l.** τινί τι *leave, give* (Eccl 2:18; Ps 16:14); **Mt 22:25;** εἰρήνην ἀφίημι ὑμῖν *I leave you peace* (cp. Diod. S. 25, 16 τὸν πόλεμον ἀφίημι=I leave [you] war) **J 14:27;** *leave (over, remaining)* (Da 4:15) **Hb 2:8.**—Pass. *be left, remain* (Da 4:26) οὐ μὴ ἀφεθῇ λίθος ἐπὶ λίθον *not a stone will be left on another* **Mt 24:2; Mk 13:2;** cp. **Lk 21:6** (on the hyperbole cp. Reader, Polemo p. 338).

❺ to convey a sense of distancing through an allowable margin of freedom, **leave it to someone to do something, *let, let go, allow, tolerate***

ⓐ w. acc. (Arrian, Anab. 1, 25, 2; Himerius, Or. [Ecl.] 4, 1; 4 Km 4:27; PsSol 17:9) **Mt 15:14; Mk 5:19; 11:6; 14:6; Lk 13:8; Ac 5:38.** ἀφεῖς τ. γυναῖκα Ἰεζάβελ *you tolerate the woman Jezebel* **Rv 2:20.** ἐὰν ἀφῶμεν αὐτὸν οὕτως *if we let him go on like this* (i.e. doing miracles) **J 11:48.**—Related types of usage *allow, let, permit, leave* w. double acc. οὐκ ἀμάρτυρον αὐτὸν ἀφῆκεν *God has not left himself without a witness* **Ac 14:17** (cp. Soph., Oed. Col. 1279 ἀ. τινὰ ἄτιμον; PFay 112, 13; POxy 494, 5f ἐλεύθερα ἀφίημι δοῦλά μου σώματα; 1 Macc 1:48). W. acc. and inf. (BGU 23, 7; POxy 121, 15; Ex 12:23; Num 22:13; PsSol 17:27) **Mt 8:22; 13:30; 19:14; 23:13; Mk 1:34; 7:12, 27; 10:14; Lk 8:51; 9:60; 12:39; 18:16; J 11:44; 18:8; Rv 11:9;** Hv 1, 3, 1; 3, 1, 8; s 9, 11, 6. W. ἵνα foll. **Mk 11:16.**

ⓑ The imperatives ἄφες, ἄφετε are used w. the subjunctive esp. in the first pers. (this is the source of Mod. Gk. ἄς; B-D-F §364, 1 and 2; Rob. 931f) ἄφες ἐκβάλω τὸ κάρφος *let me take out the speck* **Mt 7:4; Lk 6:42** (cp. Epict. 4, 1, 132 ἄφες σκέψωμαι; POxy 413, 184 [II 1d] ἄφες ἐγὼ αὐτὸν θρηνήσω). ἄφες (ἄφετε) ἴδωμεν *let us see* **Mt 27:49; Mk 15:36** (cp. Epict. 3, 12, 15 ἄφες ἴδω). It is also used w. the third pers. (Epict. 1, 15, 7 ἄφες ἀνθήσῃ). And w. ἵνα in a colloquially expressed sentence ἄφες αὐτήν, ἵνα τηρήσῃ αὐτό *let her be, so that she can keep it for the day of my burial* **J 12:7.** (The usage Epict. 4, 13, 19 ἄφες οὖν, ἵνα κἀγὼ ταὐτὰ ὑπολάβω is not strictly parallel, for the impv. is not followed by a pronoun. The rendering *let her keep it* [s. Mlt. 175f] treats ἄφες as an auxiliary. NRSV's addition, 'She bought it', is unnecessary.) The second pers. is rare ἄφες ἴδῃς Hs 8, 1, 4 acc. to PMich. Abs. *let it be so, let it go* (Chariton 4, 3, 6) **Mt 3:15;** GEb 18, 40 (w. ὅτι foll.='for').—B. 768; 839; 1174. DELG s.v. ἵημι. M-M. TW. Sv.

ἀφικνέομαι fut. 3 sg. ἀφίξεται Judg 8:32; 2 aor. ἀφικόμην; pf. 3 sg. ἀφῖκται Just., D. 127, 2 (ἱκνέομαι 'come'; Hom.+) **to arrive at a certain point, *reach*** (the central mng. 'come to' in ref. to physical space is not used in the NT) of a report εἴς τινα *someone* ἡ ὑπακοὴ εἰς πάντας ἀφίκετο *the report of your obedience has reached* (become known to) *everyone* **Ro 16:19** (cp. Aristot., EN 1, 5, 1097a, 24 ὁ λόγος εἰς ταὐτὸν ἀφ.; Sir 47:16; Jos., Ant. 17, 155; 19, 127 εἰς τὸ θέατρον ἀφίκετο ὁ λόγος). ὡς ἂν ἀφίκηται ὑμῖν ἄφνω θόρυβος *when sudden confusion comes upon you* 1 Cl 57:4 (Prov 1:27). With ref. to passage of time ὥστε καὶ εἰς τοὺς ἡμετέρους χρόνους τινὲς αὐτῶν ἀφίκοντο *so that some of them* (the healed) *remained alive to our own time* Qua.—B. 703. DELG s.v. ἵκω. M-M.

ἀφιλάγαθος, ον (s. φιλέω, ἀγαθός) **pert. to lack of generous interest in the public good, *without interest in the (public) good*** (cp. cognate φιλαγαθία=generosity OGI 146, 4 and oft.; φιλαγάθως 339, 27 [II BC] et al. in connection with expenditures for choral production. Cp. also POxy 33 II, 13 [II AD] ἀφιλοκαγαθία [s. ed.'s note] prob. a shortened form for *ἀφιλοκαλοκαγαθία [opp. φιλοκαγαθία CIG 4078, 12, s. note SEG VI, 68; PLond 1927, 40]; POxy 33 II, 11 φιλάγαθος and s. Nägeli 52). In a list of vices **2 Ti 3:3** (so far the word is found only here, but this is prob. due to the fact that the affirmative φιλάγαθος is freq. in honorary ins and the unfavorable term ἀ. would not suggest itself in such a medium, whereas **2 Ti 3:3** projects a [satirical?] sketch of pers. who are the opp. of public expectation).—M-M. TW.

ἀφιλάργυρος, ον (s. φιλέω, ἄργυρος; Diod S. 9, 11, 2; Diog. L. 4, 38; IPriene 137, 5 [II BC]; SIG 708, 17 [II BC]; 1104, 25 [36/35 BC]; POxy 33 II, 11 [II AD] s. below; other ref. in Nägeli 31) ***not loving money, not greedy*** (in instructions for midwives in Soranus p. 5, 27 and for generals in Onosander [I AD] 1, 1; 2; 4; 8 w. σώφρων and νήπτης [=νηφάλιος]). The noun ἀφιλαργυρία appears beside ἀρετή (q.v.) and φιλαγαθία (s. φιλάγαθος as a mark of an exceptionally fine pers. Sb 8267, 44; cp. POxy 33 II, 11=Acta Alex. fgm. 11 B II, 11 ἀφιλάργυρος w. φιλόσοφος and φιλάγαθος, in a portrait of an ideal pers.) **1 Ti 3:3; Hb 13:5;** D 15:1; Pol 5:2.—M-M. TW. Spicq.

ἀφιλοξενία, ας, ἡ (s. φιλέω, ξένος) ***inhospitality*** (SibOr 8, 304) 1 Cl 35:5.—DELG s.v. ξένος.

ἄφιξις, εως, ἡ (s. ἀφικνέομαι, hence usu. of 'arrival': Hdt. et al.; so also Lysimachus [200 BC]: 382 fgm. 6 Jac.; Diod. S. 8, 19, 2; pap; 3 Macc 7:18; EpArist 173; Jos., Ant. 20, 51, Vi. 104; Tat.) in our lit. the point from which one moves is emphasized ***departure*** (cp. Demosth., Ep. 1, 2; 3, 39 ἀ. οἴκαδε; Ael. Aristid. 48, 7 K.=24 p. 467 D.; Jos., Ant. 2, 18; 4, 315; 7, 247; PMich 497, 12; other pass. in Gk. lit. may appear to be ambiguous to the modern reader, but not be, because the ancient writer views the departure in terms of movement toward a destination) **Ac 20:29.**—JWackernagel, Glotta 14, 1925, 59.—DELG s.v. ἵκω. M-M.

ἀφίστημι pres. 3 sg. ἀφιστᾷ TestJud 18:3; 3 pl. ἀφιστῶσι TestJud 14:2; ptc. fem. ἀφιστῶσα TestAsh 2:1 v.l.; fut. ἀποστήσω LXX; 1 aor. ἀπέστησα, 2 aor. ἀπέστην, impv. ἀπόστα Hm 6, 2, 6; pf. ἀφέστηκα LXX, PsSol, ptc. ἀφεστηκώς LXX, pl. ἀφεστῶτες Tat. 26, 3, w. act. mng. ἀφέστακα Jer 16:5. Mid. ἀφίσταμαι, impv. ἀφίστασο; fut. ἀποστήσομαι (Hom.+; ins, pap, LXX, En, TestSol; TestAbr B 13 p. 117, 23 [Stone p. 82]; TestJob, Test12Patr, JosAs; ApcMos 12; EpArist 173; Joseph., Just., Tat.) of action that results in the distancing of pers. or thing from pers., thing, place, or condition.

❶ **to cause someone to move from a reference point,** trans., in our lit. in ref. to altering allegiance ***cause to revolt, mislead*** (Hdt. 1, 76 et al.; Dt 7:4; Jos., Ant. 8, 198; 20, 102 τ. λαόν) λαὸν ὀπίσω αὐτοῦ *the people, so that they followed him* **Ac 5:37.**

❷ **to distance oneself from some pers. or thing** (mid. forms, and 2 aor., pf., and plupf. act.) intrans.—ⓐ ***go away, withdraw*** τινός (Hdt. 3, 15; Epict. 2, 13, 26; 4, 5, 28; BGU 159, 4; Sir 38:12; En 14:23; Jos., Ant. 1, 14; Just., D. 106, 1) **Lk 2:37.** ἀπό τινος (PGM 4, 1244; Sir 23:11f; Jdth 13:19; 1 Macc 6:10, 36; Just., D. 6, 2) **Lk 1:38** D; **13:27** (Ps 6:9); **24:51** D; **Ac 12:10; 19:9;** Hs 9, 15, 6. ἐκ τοῦ τόπου Hm 5, 1, 3. Abs. (Aesop, Fab. 194 H.=86 P.=H-H. 88; cp. Ch. 158; Just., A I, 50, 12) s 8, 8, 2. *Desert* ἀπό τινος *someone* (as Appian, Iber. 34 §137; cp. Jer 6:8) **Ac 15:38;** GJs 2:3.—*Fall away* (Hdt. et al.), *become a backslider* abs. (Appian, Iber. 38 §156 ἀφίστατο=he revolted; Jer 3:14; Da 9:9 Theod.; 1 Macc 11:43; En 5:4) **Lk 8:13.** ἀπό τινος (X., Cyr. 5, 4, 1; Polyb. 1, 16, 3; oft. LXX, mostly of falling away fr. God)

Hb 3:12; Hv 2, 3, 2; s 6, 2, 3; 8, 8, 5; 8, 9, 1 and 3; 8, 10, 3; τινός (Polyb. 14, 12, 3; Herodian 6, 2, 7; Wsd 3:10; Jos., Vi. 158; Just., A I, 14, 1, D. 78, 9; τοῦ θεοῦ 79, 1) Hv 3, 7, 2; **1 Ti 4:1;** AcPl Ha 8, 20. Of transcendent figures, the Holy Spirit Hm 10, 2, 5; an evil spirit m 5, 2, 7; 6, 2, 6f.—Fig. of conditions and moral qualities *depart, withdraw* affliction Hs 7:7; life s 8, 6, 4; understanding s 9, 22, 2; righteousness and peace 1 Cl 3:4 cod. H; wickedness Hv 3, 6, 1.

ⓑ *keep away* (Diod. S. 11, 50, 7; PsSol 4:10; Jos., Vi. 261) ἀπό τινος (UPZ 196 I, 15 [119 BC]) **Lk 4:13; Ac 5:38; 2 Cor 12:8;** AcPl Ha 8, 11; cp. **Ac 22:29;** Hs 7:2. Fig. of moral conduct (Sir 7:2; 35:3 ἀποστῆναι ἀπὸ πονηρίας; Tob 4:21 BA) *abstain* **2 Ti 2:19;** Hs 6, 1, 4.—DELG s.v. ἵστημι. M-M.

ἄφνω adv. (Aeschyl., Thu. et al.; pap, LXX; TestSol H; TestAbr B 14 p. 118, 21 [Stone p. 84]; JosAs 27:6; Jos., Vi. 126; Mel., P. 30, 203) **pert. to a very brief interval between a state or event that precedes and one that follows,** ***of a sudden,*** ἐγένετο ἄφνω . . . ἦχος *suddenly there was a sound* **Ac 2:2; 16:26;** 1 Cl 57:4; ApcPt 4:11.—*Immediately, at once* (Diod. S. 14, 104, 2) **Ac 28:6.**—DDaube, The Sudden in the Scriptures '64, 29f. DELG.

ἀφοβία, ας, ἡ lit., being without fear about what may happen, 'fearlessness' (s. ἀφόβως, φόβος; Pla. et al.; Epict.; EpArist 243). In ref. to relationship to God, failure to recognize one's dependence is misplaced fearlessness or ***lack of reverence*** (Pr 15:16; Ps.-Clem., Hom. 1, 18) D 5:1 (Const. Apost.; cp. Lat. tr.: deum [sc. by a second hand] non timentes). ἀ. θεοῦ B 20:1.—DELG s.v. φέβομαι. TW.

ἀφόβως adv. of ἄφοβος 'without fear' (s. ἀφοβία; X. et al.; SEG XLI 1619, 22 [III/IV AD]; PTebt 24, 74 [II BC]; PHarr 55, 21; Sb 7517, 7; Pr 1:33; Wsd 17:4 v.l.; Philo, Migr. Abr. 169; Jos., Ant. 7, 322; Just.) **pert. to being without fear of what might happen,** ***fearlessly*** **Lk 1:74; Phil 1:14;** 1 Cl 57:7; *without cause to be afraid* (Horapollo 2, 72) **1 Cor 16:10.** In **Jd 12** ἀ. can be rendered either *boldly* or *without reverence, shamelessly,* the point being arrogant disregard of responsibility for one's manner of life.—DELG s.v. φέβομαι. M-M.

ἀφόδευσις, εως, ἡ (ἀφοδεύω 'excrete') (Erotian [I AD] s.v. ἀπόπατοι ed. ENachmanson 1918; cp. also schol. on Nicander, Ther. 933) ***anus*** of hares: πλεονεκτεῖν τὴν ἀ. *grows a new anus* B 10:6 (cp. Pliny, NH 8, 81, 218 Archelaus auctor est, quot sint corporis cavernae ad excrementa lepori, totidem annos esse aetatis=according to Archelaus the number of apertures for a hare's excrements equals the years of its lifespan.; Aelian, NA 2, 12; Varro, De Re Rust. 3, 12).—DELG s.v. ὁδός.

ἀφομοιόω aor. 3 sg. ἀφωμοίωσεν Wsd 13:14 S (s. ὁμοιόω, Xen., Pla. et al.) ***make like/similar*** pass. *become like* (Herm. Wr. 454, 17 Sc.), in past tenses *be like, resemble* (Diod. S. 1, 86, 3; Aesop, Fab. 137 H.=88 P.=90 H-H.: Ἑρμῆς ἀφομοιωθεὶς ἀνθρώπῳ; ἀφομοιωθῆτε EpJer 4; ἀφωμοιωμένα 62; ἀφωμοίωνται 70) pf. pass. ptc. ἀφωμοιωμένος τῷ υἱῷ τοῦ θεοῦ **Hb 7:3.**—DELG s.v. ὁμός. TW.

ἀφοράω (ὁράω; Hdt., Pla. et al.; pap; Philo, Omn. Prob. Lib. 28, Aet. M. 4) 2 aor. for this vb. ἀπεῖδον, subj. ἀφίδω, also ἀπίδω v.l. **Phil 2:23** (B-D-F §14)

❶ **to direct one's attention without distraction,** ***fix one's eyes*** trustingly εἴς τινα *on someone* (Epict. 2, 19, 29 εἰς τὸν θεόν; 3, 26, 11 al.; Herm. Wr. 7, 2a; 4 Macc 17:10; Jos., Bell. 2, 410) εἰς τὸν τῆς πίστεως ἀρχηγόν **Hb 12:2.**

❷ **to develop more precise knowledge about someth. in the offing,** ***determine, see*** (Jon 4:5) ὡς ἂν ἀφίδω τὰ περὶ ἐμέ *as soon as I see how things go w. me* **Phil 2:23.**—DELG s.v. ὁράω. M-M. Spicq.

ἀφορίζω impf. ἀφώριζον; fut. ἀφορίσω **Mt 25:32**—Attic (also LXX) ἀφοριῶ **13:49;** 1 aor. ἀφώρισα. Pass.: 1 aor. ἀφωρίσθην LXX; impv. 2 pl. ἀφορίσθητε; pf. ptc. ἀφωρισμένος (s. ὁρίζω, ὅρος; Soph., Pla.+; ins, pap, LXX; TestJob 9:3 al.; ParJer, Philo; Jos., Bell. 2, 488; Just.; Hippol., Ref. 1, 8, 10 'undertake to do someth.') lit. to mark off or set apart as if by a line or boundary.

❶ **to remove one party from other parties so as to discourage or eliminate contact,** ***separate, take away*** **Ac 19:9.** τινὰ ἀπό τινος (Is 56:3; Sir 47:2) **Mt 25:32** (cp. Diod. S. 5, 79, 2 Rhadamanthys was appointed judge in Hades to διακρίνειν τοὺς εὐσεβεῖς καὶ τοὺς πονηρούς). τινὰ ἐκ μέσου τινῶν *take out* **13:49.** ἑαυτόν (Is 45:24) *separate oneself, hold aloof* **Gal 2:12.** *Exclude, excommunicate* **Lk 6:22.** Pass., w. middle mng. *be separate* **2 Cor 6:17** (Is 52:11).

❷ **to select one pers. out of a group for a purpose,** ***set apart, appoint*** (Nägeli 35) τινά **Gal 1:15** (no purpose mentioned; JDoeve, Paulus d. Pharisäer u. Gal 1:13–15, NovT 6, '63, 170–81). W. the purpose given εἴς τι (POxy 37, 9; 4 Macc 3:20) εἰς εὐαγγέλιον *to proclaim the gospel* **Ro 1:1.** ἀ. εἰς τὸ ἔργον **Ac 13:2.**—GDelling, Jüd. Lehre u. Frömmigkeit in den ParJer '67, 44.—DELG s.v. ὅρος. M-M. TW.

ἀφορμάω (s. ἀφορμή, ὁρμάω, ὁρμή: terms relating to motion; Hom. et al.; in act. trag., X.+; TestSol 11:21 L for ἐφ-; Demetr.: 722 fgm. 1, 2 Jac.) **to initiate movement from one point to another,** ***start, set out*** εἰς τοὐπίσω *start back again, return* 1 Cl 25:4.—DELG s.v. ὄρνυμαι I; Frisk s.v. ὁρμή.

ἀφορμή, ῆς, ἡ (s. ἀφορμάω) lit. a base or circumstance from which other action becomes possible, such as the starting-point or base of operations for an expedition, then gener. the resources needed to carry through an undertaking (e.g. even commercial capital), in our lit. (also Ar. 2, 7; Just.; Tat.; Mel., HE 4, 26, 5; Ath., R. 49, 235 al.) a set of convenient circumstances for carrying out some purpose ***occasion, opportunity*** for someth., a meaning found in Attic Gk. and also quite common in the Koine (Nägeli 15) ἐκκόπτειν τὴν ἀ. τῶν θελόντων ἀ. *cut off the opportunity of those who wish an opportunity* **2 Cor 11:12** (numerous transl. var. render: 'cut the ground out from under those who look for opportunity'); ἀ. διδόναι τινί (Polyb. 28, 6, 7 μὴ διδόναι τ. ἐχθροῖς ἀφορμὴν εἰς διαβολήν; Pr 9:9; Philo, Leg. ad Gai. 200; cp. Diod. S. 1, 83; 13, 22, 5; 3 Macc 3:2) *give someone an occasion*: τῷ ἀντικειμένῳ λοιδορίας χάριν *to the opponent for reviling* **1 Ti 5:14;** *excuse* (to future believers for moral laxity) Hm 4, 3, 3; τινός *for someth.* **2 Cor 5:12** (for the gen. cp. Epict. 1, 8, 6; 1, 9, 20; Dio Chrys. 16 [33], 38; Jos., Bell. 7, 441, Ant. 5, 57); ἀ. διδόναι τινί, ἵνα Hm 4, 1, 11. Pl. (Polyb., Epict., Vett. Val.; IPriene 105, 13 and 16; Joseph.) ἀφορμὰς διδόναι τινί, ἵνα ITr 8:2; ἀ. λαμβάνειν (a favorite expr.; e.g. in Polyb.; Dionys. Hal.; Philo, In Flacc. 47; Ar. 11, 7 ἀφορμήν; cp. Just., A I, 44, 9 ἀφορμάς) *grasp an opportunity* **Ro 7:8, 11;** w. gen. of the one who gives the opportunity **Lk 11:53/54 v.l.** (the expr. ἀ. ζητεῖν is used difft. POxy 34 III, 13 ἀ. ζητοῦντες ἁμαρτημάτων=looking for opportunity to commit illegal acts). W. εἴς τι *for someth.* (Appian, Bell. Civ. 5, 53 §222 ἔχειν ἀφορμὴν ἔς τι; Philo) 2 Cl 16:1; εἰς ἀ. τῇ σαρκί *to give the flesh an opportunity* (to become active) **Gal 5:13.**—M-M. TW. Sv.

ἀφότε s. ὅτε 1aγ end.

ἄφραστος, ον (s. φράζω; Hom. Hymns et al.; Aeschyl.) ***too wonderful for words*** (Soph., Trach. 694; so also in later prose; Eunap. 45; TestLevi 8:15; PGM 3, 592 ἄ. ὄνομα) ἔννοια *plan* Dg 8:9 (perh. there is an implied parallel here to the code of silence accorded Gr-Rom. mystery rites).—DELG s.v. φράζω.

ἀφρίζω (ἀφρός; Soph., El. 719 horses; Diod. S. 3, 10, 5 elephants; Athen. 11, 43 p. 472a; TestSol 12:2) **to produce a foam, *foam (at the mouth)*** of a sick person, prob. in an epileptic seizure **Mk 9:18, 20.**—DELG s.v. ἀφρός.

ἀφροντιστέω (s. φροντίζω; X., Pla. et al.; Diod. S. 5, 32, 7; Philostrat., Vi. Apoll. 1, 38 p. 41, 1; PRein 57, 11; Just., A I, 17, 4 ἀφροντισθήσετε) **to make no use of one's mental faculties in certain circumstances, esp. with ref. to lack of attention to practical matters, *be careless, unconcerned*** Dg 8:10.—DELG s.v. φρήν.

ἀφρόνως adv. of ἄφρων (Soph., Aj. 766; Diod. S. 16, 70, 2; Artem. 1, 50 p. 46, 21; Gen 31:28; Just., D. 112, 2) **pert. to lack of judgment or prudence, *foolishly*** ἀποκρίνεσθαι Hv 5:4.—DELG s.v. φρήν.

ἀφρός, οῦ, ὁ (Hom. et al.; POxy 1088, 33; PSI 1180, 34; PGM 4, 942 and 3204; medical use in Hobart 17f) **a frothy mass, *foam*** in our lit. only of froth appearing at the mouth in epileptic seizures (Jos., Ant. 6, 245) μετὰ ἀφροῦ *so that he foams* **Lk 9:39.**—DELG. M-M.

ἀφροσύνη, ης, ἡ (s. ἄφρων; Hom. et al.; Artem. 2, 37 p. 141, 15; LXX, En; OdeSol 11:10; Test12Patr; Philo; Jos., Ant. 17, 277, Vi. 323; SibOr 4, 38; Just., D. 5, 5; Hippol., Ref. 4, 46, 1) **the state of lack of prudence or good judgment, *foolishness, lack of sense,*** moral and intellectual **Mk 7:22; 2 Cor 11:1, 17, 21;** 1 Cl 13:1; 47:7; Hm 5, 2, 4; s 6, 5, 2f; 9, 15, 3; 9, 22, 2f; Dg 3:3; 4:5.—DELG s.v. φρήν. TW.

ἄφρων, ον, gen. ονος (s. φρήν; Hom.+; PFay 124, 12; LXX; En; TestJob 26:6; JosAs 6:6f; GrBar 13:3; Philo; Jos., Bell. 1, 630; 2, 303; Ar. 12, 1) **pert. to lack of prudence or good judgment, *foolish, ignorant*** (opp. φρόνιμος as Dio Chrys. 73 [23], 3; Pr 11:29; En 98:1, 9; PsSol 16:7; Philo, Poster. Cai. 32) **2 Cor 11:19;** 1 Cl 3:3; (w. ἀνόητος) 21:5; (w. ἀσύνετος as Ps 91:7) 39:1; voc. Hm 12, 4, 2—**Lk 11:40; 12:20; Ro 2:20; 1 Cor 15:36; 2 Cor 11:16; 12:6, 11; Eph 5:17; 1 Pt 2:15;** 1 Cl 39:7f (Job 5:2, 3); ITr 8:2; Hm 4, 2, 1; 5, 2, 2; 4; 6, 2, 4; 11:4; s 1:3; 6, 4, 3; 6, 5, 2; 9, 14, 4; 9, 22, 2.—DELG s.v. φρήν. EDNT. M-M. TW.

ἀφύλακτος, ον (s. φυλακή, φυλάσσω; Aeschyl., Hdt. et al.; Sb 6002, 15 [II BC]; Jos., Ant. 14, 169; cp. Ezk 7:22; 23:39 A) **pert. to absence of security, *without guarding*** (them) of cult images made of ordinary substance as opp. to those kept in temples open to the public Dg 2:7 (v.l. ἀφυλάκτως).—DELG s.v. φύλαξ.

ἀφυπνόω (s. ὕπνος, ὑπνόω) 1 aor. ἀφύπνωσα ***fall asleep, drop off to sleep*** (the opp. of the more freq. ref. to being 'awake' in the use of the cognate terms in older Gk.; but for the sense 'fall asleep' s. Heliod. 9, 12; schol. on Pind., P. 1, 10b, I. 4, 33c; Achmes 174, 16; AcAndr/Mt 16 [Aa II/1, 84, 7f]; Paulus Aegineta [VII AD] 1, 98; cp. Lob., Phryn. p. 224) **Lk 8:23;** Hv 1, 1, 3; AcPl Ha 7, 27.—DELG s.v. ὕπνος. M-M. TW.

ἀφυστερέω 1 aor. ἀφυστέρησα LXX; pf. pass. ptc. ἀφυστερημένος (s. ὑστερέω; Polyb. et al.; pap, LXX) gener. to be behind with respect to an anticipated objective or expectation (Polyb. 1, 52, 8; 21, 22, 2; Dionys. Hal. 10, 26) in our lit. only trans. (cp. 2 Esdr 19:2) **to be remiss in paying what is due, *withhold*** μισθός **Js 5:4 v.l.** for ἀπεστερημένος.—DELG s.v. ὕστερος. M-M. TW.

ἀφῶ, ἀφῶμεν s. ἀφίημι.

ἄφωνος, ον (s. φωνέω, φωνή; since Theognis 669 [of one whom poverty makes mute]; Aeschyl., Pind., Hdt. et al.; SIG 1168, 41; Kaibel 402, 1; PGM 1, 117; Wsd 4:19; 2 Macc 3:29; Philo; Jos., Ant. 6, 337; 12, 413; Mel., P. 44, 311 [B] after Is 53:7).

❶ **pert. to making no sound with vocal chords, *silent, mute*** of animals that can otherwise make sounds (Timaeus Hist. [IV–III BC]: 566 fgm. 43a, 20 Jac.; Strabo 6, 1, 9 p. 260 [certain grasshoppers]) sheep **Ac 8:32;** 1 Cl 16:7; B 5:2 (all 3 Is 53:7).

❷ **incapable of vocal utterance, *mute*** of inanimate obj. (Kaibel 402, 1 a memorial monument that was silent when unmined); of deified images **1 Cor 12:2.**

❸ **incapable of human speech, *speechless*** of Balaam's ass, which lacked the facility of human speech (ὑποζύγιον ἄφωνον), yet spoke with a human voice (ἐν ἀνθρώπου φώνῃ) **2 Pt 2:16.**

❹ **incapable of conveying meaning as a language normally does, *without conveying meaning*** τοσαῦτα … γένη φωνῶν εἰσιν ἐν κόσμῳ καὶ οὐδὲν ἄφωνον *there are numerous languages spoken in the world, with none devoid of meaning* **1 Cor 14:10.**—B. 321. DELG s.v. φωνή. M-M. TW.

Ἀχάζ, ὁ (Ἄχας W-H.; אָחָז) indecl. (in Jos. Ant. 9, 247 Ἄχαζος, ου) ***Ahaz,*** a king of Judah (1 Ch 3:13; cp. 4 Km 16:1ff; 2 Ch 28:16ff; Is 1:1; 7:1ff); in genealogy of Jesus **Mt 1:9; Lk 3:23ff** D (here Ἀχας, as also the v.l. in Mt).

Ἀχαΐα, ας, ἡ (Hdt. et al.; Joseph.) ***Achaia*** in NT the Rom. province created 146 BC, including the most important parts of Greece, i.e. Attica, Boeotia (perh. Epirus) and the Peloponnese (Mommsen, Röm. Gesch. V 233ff) **Ac 18:2** D, **12, 27; 19:21; 2 Cor 1:1; 11:10; 1 Th 1:7f.** The country for its inhabitants, esp. the Christians living in it **Ro 15:26; 16:5 v.l.; 1 Cor 16:15; 2 Cor 9:2.**—JMarquardt, Röm. Staatsverw. I[2] 1881, 321ff; Pauly-W. I 1894, 190–98; RE VII 160ff; Kl. Pauly I, 32–38; Ramsay, Bearing 404f; Hahn, index.

Ἀχαϊκός, οῦ, ὁ (CIG 1296; 3376, 5; IG III, 1030, 34; 1138, 15 al.) ***Achaicus*** a Christian at Corinth **1 Cor 16:17; 16:15 v.l.; subscr.**

ἀχαριστέω (s. ἀχάριστος, χαρίζομαι; in lit. and ins; SyrBar 13:12 [?]; Jos., Bell. 2, 400; PGM XXII a 1, 5) ***be ungrateful,*** a cardinal sociocultural crime in the Gr-Rom. world (Antiphon Soph. 54; Demosth. 18, 119; X., Mem. 2, 2, 2 et al.) τινί *toward someone* (Plut., Phocyl. 758 [36, 5]; Vi. Philonidis p. 13 Crönert) τῷ θεῷ PtK 2 p. 14, 21.—DELG s.v. χάρις.

ἀχάριστος, ον (s. ἀχαριστέω; Hom. et al.; ApcMos 26; Just.; Tat. 4, 1; Mel., P. 87, 651) ***ungrateful*** (so since Hdt. 1, 90; Epict. 2, 23, 5; IG XIV, 2012, 14; UPZ 199, 22 [131 BC]; POxy-Hels 47a, 14 [II AD]; Wsd 16:29; Sir 29:16; 4 Macc 9:10; Philo, De Jos. 99; Jos., Ant. 13, 388, Vi. 172) **Lk 6:35** (w. πονηρός as Demosth. 131; Lucian, Timon 48, 2; Celsus 6, 53; Jos., Ant. 6, 305); **2 Ti 3:2.**—M-M. TW.

Ἀχάς s. Ἀχάζ.

ἀχειροποίητος, ον (Ps.-Callisth. 1, 34, 6 [p. 38, 18]—χειροποίητος freq. since Hdt.; ins reff. SEG XLII, 1226; s. Nägeli 52) ***not made by*** (human) ***hand.*** Of circumcision **Col**

2:11. Of a transcendent temple **Mk 14:58.** Of the heavenly body **2 Cor 5:1.**—DELG s.v. χείρ II. M-M. TW.

Ἀχελδαμάχ s. Ἀκελδαμάχ.

Ἀχερούσιος, α, ον (Aeschyl., Thu. et al.) **pert. to Acheron (Ἀχέρων), a body of water in the netherworld,** ***Acherusian*** (Acherontic) βάπτισμα ἐν σωτηρίᾳ Ἀχερουσίας λίμνης *b. in the saving waters of the Acherusian lake,* i.e., the Acherusian waters are instrumental in effecting salvation, ApcPt Rainer 4 and 5 (s. ApcPt 14 Ethiopic text; cp. SibOr 2, 338 λίμνης . . . ἀχερουσιάδος; ApcMos 37 εἰς τὴν ἀχέρουσαν λίμνην a seraph washes Adam 'before God' in Lake Acheron; for the mythological background and location in the Elysian field, s. Od. 4, 561–69; Hes., Works 167–73).

ἀχθῆναι, ἀχθήσεσθαι s. ἄγω.

ἄχθομαι, ὁ (Hom. et al.; pap, Joseph.; Just., D. 29, 3) **to be afflicted with mental agitation,** ***be vexed*** ἐπί τινι *over someth.* (Xen., Hell. 7, 1, 32 al.) ὡς πάντας ἄχθεσθαι ἐπὶ τῇ σεμνότητι Παύλου *so that all were vexed by Paul's composure* (i.e. they were annoyed by his self-possessed demeanor, for he ought to have been cowed by the imminent attack of a wild beast; s. σεμνότης) AcPl Ha 4, 14.—DELG.

Ἀχίμ, ὁ (Ἀχείμ v.l. Tdf. W-H. S.) indecl. *Achim* in genealogy of Jesus **Mt 1:14.**

ἀχλύς, ύος, ἡ (Hom. et al.; in prose Hippocr. et al.; Polyb. 34, 11, 15; Ezk 12:7 Aq.; Job 3:5 Sym.; Philo, Cher. 61; Jos., Ant. 9, 56)

❶ lit. **someth. that comes upon one like a fog and obscures vision,** ***mist*** (w. σκότος as Dio Chrys. 11 [12], 36; Philo, Deus Imm. 130) of darkening of the eyes in a man who is being blinded **Ac 13:11** (cp. Il. 16, 344; Od. 20, 357; κατ' ὀφθαλμῶν δ' ἔχυτ' ἀχλύς 'a mist came over his eyes' 22, 88; schol. on Apollon. Rhod. 2, 259b; also medic. t.t.: Galen, Medicus 16 [XIV 774 K.]; further exx. in Hobart 44f).

❷ fig. **someth. that beclouds one's understanding,** ***mistiness,*** in the eyes of the mind (Heraclit. Sto. 33 p. 48, 14; Plut., Mor. 42c διάνοια ἀχλύος γέμουσα; Himerius, Or. 35 [=Or. 34, 3] p. 146, 20 Colonna ἡ ἀχλὺς τῆς ψυχῆς) 2 Cl 1:6.—DELG.

ἀχρεῖος, ον (χρεῖος 'useful'; Hom. et al.; pap, LXX; Jos., Vi. 50; 117; Ath., R. 70, 16 al.)—❶ **pert. to being of no use or profit, esp. economic,** ***useless, worthless*** of slaves (Ps.-Pla., Alcib. 1, 17 p. 122b τῶν οἰκετῶν τὸν ἀχρειότατον; Achilles Tat. 5, 17, 8; PParis 68, 54 ἀ. δούλους) in wordplay of one who fails to make a good investment *profitless* **Mt 25:30.**

❷ **pert. to being unworthy of any praise,** ***unworthy.***—As suggested by the the words that immediately follow it, the clause λέγετε ὅτι δοῦλοι ἀχρεῖοί ἐσμεν **Lk 17:10** may play on commercial associations of the cognate noun χρεῖος 'debt' *Say, 'We are slaves who are now debt-free'* (as respects the obligations cited in vs. 9), but the statement may simply be typical of servile self-abasement. ἀ. can mean more gener. *unworthy, miserable* (2 Km 6:22; Is 33:9 Sym., Theod.; Ezk 17:6), or simply *worthless* without moral connotation (Arrian, Anab. 1, 24, 3; 2, 7, 3). Therefore it is not nec. to omit the adj., as some commentators, following the Sin. Syr., have done (e.g. FBlass; AMerx; Wlh.; JWeiss; APott, D. Text des NTs.[2] 1919, 103; Moffatt, NT).—CdeVillapadierna, in ACacciari Festschr. '94, 327–35 renders 'simple slaves':—DELG s.v. χρή. M-M.

ἀχρειόω (s. ἀχρεῖος) (t.r., S., Vog.; by-form ἀχρεόω Tdf., W-H., M., Bov., N[25]; SIG 569, 31; s. B-D-F §30, 2) 1 aor. inf. ἀχρειῶσαι LXX; 3 pl. pf. ἠχρείωκαν Da 6:21. Pass. 1 aor. ἠχρεώθην; pf. ptc. ἠχρειωμένος (Philo Mech. 60, 16; Polyb. 3, 64, 8 al.; Vett. Val. 290, 1; OGI 573, 16: LXX; ἠχρειώθησαν Just., D. 27, 3; Theoph. Ant. 2, 35 [p. 188, 29]) in our lit. only pass.

❶ ***make useless,*** outwardly, in symbolism, of damaged sticks Hs 8, 3, 4.—❷ of becoming a liability to society because of moral depravity ***become depraved, worthless*** of pers. **Ro 3:12** (Ps 13:3; 52:4).—M-M.

ἄχρηστος, ον (s. χρηστός, χράομαι; Theognis+) **pert. to not serving any beneficial purpose** (in Gr-Rom. society gener. pert. to lack of responsibility within the larger social structure, s. antonyms εὔχρηστος, χρηστός) ***useless, worthless,*** perh. in wordplay on the name Onesimus and certainly w. the term εὔχρηστος (as Hv 3, 6, 7; cp. s 9, 26, 4; Jos., Ant. 12, 61) **Phlm 11** τόν ποτέ σοι ἄ. *who was once useless to you* (ἄ. τινι as EpArist 164); ἄ. of a slave Epict. 1, 19, 19 and 22 (cp. wordplay χρήσιμον ἐξ ἀχηρήστου Pla, Rep. 411a). W. περισσός Dg 4:2.—Hv 3, 6, 2; s 9, 26, 4; ὀξυχολία ἄ. ἐστιν *ill temper leads to no good* m 5, 1, 6.—DELG s.v. χρή. M-M. TW.

ἄχρι (Hom.+) this form, which is Attic (Phryn. 14; Moeris 32; Meisterhans[3]-Schw. 219, 39) is found in NT almost exclusively (Just., only D. 64, 6; Tat. 38, 2); the H. Gk. ἄχρις (SIG 958, 37; s. Schwyzer I 405 on Hom. usage) occurs only **Gal 3:19** (throughout the ms. tradition) and **Hb 3:13** (predom.), each case before vowels. For the adoption of ἄχρις, in accordance w. t.r., in other edd. s. S. and Vog. on **Ac 7:18; 1 Cor 11:26; 15:25; Phil. 1:6;** S., Vog., Bov. on **Ac 11:5;** S., Vog., M. on **Rom 11:25;** S., Vog., M., Bov. on Rv 2:25 (Just. has ἄχρις ἂν three times; once [A I, 35, 1] ἄχρις before verb with initial vowel. On the Apostol. Fathers s. Reinhold 37. On the whole, B-D-F §21; W-S. §5, 28b; Mayser 243f; Crönert 144, 3). A function word used to indicate an interval between two points

❶ **marker of continuous extent of time up to a point,** ***until***

ⓐ used as prep. w. gen. (Hom., less oft. in Att., but s. Demosth.; B-D-F §216, 3)

α. of time *until* (2 Macc 14:15; Tat. 38, 2) ἄ. ἧς ἡμέρας *until the day when* **Mt 24:38; Lk 1:20; 17:27; Ac 1:2, 22 v.l.;** ἄ. τῆς ἡμέρας ταύτης (BChilds, JBL 82, '63, 279–92: OT background) **2:29; 23:1; 26:22;** ἄ. καιροῦ *for a while* **Lk 4:13** (ἄ. χρόνου D); *until the time determined by God* **Ac 13:11.** ἄ. χρόνων ἀποκαταστάσεως **3:21.** ἄ. αὐγῆς *until sunrise* **Ac 20:11** (cp. Jos., Ant. 6, 215 ἄχρι τῆς ἕω); ἄ. τοῦ δεῦρο (Plut., Anton. 34, 9 [without art.]; Jos., Ant. 10, 265) *until now* **Ro 1:13;** ἄ. τοῦ νῦν (Timostratus [II BC] 1; cp. Lucian, Tim. 39; Plut., Rom. 15, 3; Philo, Abr. 182) **8:22; Phil 1:5.—1 Cor 4:11; 2 Cor 3:14; Gal 4:2; Phil 1:6;** ἄ. τέλους (Plut., Demosth. 851 [13, 2], Fab. Max. 183 [16, 8]) *to the end* **Hb 6:11; Rv 2:26;** ἄ. ἡμερῶν πέντε *within five days* **Ac 20:6.** ἄ. νόμου *until the time when* (or better, *before*) *the law was given* **Ro 5:13** (cp. Jos., Ant. 4, 248 ἄ. νομίμων γάμων=until the time of the lawful marriage). Cp. **Mt 13:30 v.l.**

β. in ref. to acts or conditions that prevail up to a certain point (SIG 1109, 84 ἄ. πληγῶν ἔρχεσθαι; Simplicius in Epict. p. 29, 7 ἄ. θανάτου σχεδόν of the lashings by the Spartans) διώκειν ἄ. θανάτου *persecute to the death* **Ac 22:4;** πιστὸς ἄ. θανάτου *faithful unto death* **Rv 2:10;** cp. **12:11** (s. SibOr 2, 47). ἄ. τῆς ἀγνοίας *so long as he does not know* Hm 4, 1, 5.

ⓑ used as conj. (B-D-F §383; 455, 3; Rob. 974)—**α.** w. rel. ἄχρι οὗ (=ἄχρι χρόνου ᾧ) *until the time when* w. past indic. (X., Hell. 6, 4, 37 ἄχρι οὗ ὅδε ὁ λόγος ἐγράφετο; Jos., Ant. 11, 111) ἄ. οὗ ἀνέστη **Ac 7:18;** ἄ. οὗ ἡμέρα ἤμελλεν γίνεσθαι *until the day began to dawn* **27:33.** W. aor. subj. (Hdt. 1, 117; SIG 799, 26; POxy 104, 18; 507, 30; BGU 19 I, 5; Job 32:11) **Lk 21:24;**

Ro 11:25; 1 Cor 11:26; 15:25; Gal 3:19; w. ἄν: ἄχρι οὗ ἄν (Hippocr., περὶ συρίγγων 3 [6, 450]) **Gal 3:19 v.l.; Rv 2:25.**—*as long as* (X., Cyr. 5, 4, 16; Plut., Mor. 601e; cp. 2 Macc 14:10) ἄ. οὗ τὸ σήμερον καλεῖται *as long as it is still called 'today'* **Hb 3:13.**

β. without rel., used w. aor. subj. *until* (POxy 491, 8; 1215, 3; Just., A I, 35, 1) **Rv 7:3; 15:8; 17:17 v.l.; 20:3, 5.** W. ἄν and aor. subj. (X., An. 2, 3, 2; SIG 972, 26f; BGU 419, 11; 830, 13 ἄ. ἄν σοι ἔλθω; PGM 5, 58; Jos., Ant. 12, 152; ParJer 7:24; Just., D. 103, 3) **Gal 3:19 v.l.** W. fut. ind. (SibOr 1, 273) **Rv 17:17.**—LRydbeck, Fachprosa, '67, 144–53.

❷ **marker of extension up to a certain point,** ***as far as*** (SIG 937; Judg 11:33 B; Just., D. 64, 6) **short ending of Mk;** ἦλθεν ἄ. ἐμοῦ *it came to where I was* **Ac 11:5;** cp. **13:6; 20:4 v.l.; 28:15;** ἄ. τούτου τοῦ λόγου *as far as this word* **22:22;** ἄ. καὶ ὑμῶν **2 Cor 10:13f;** ἄ. μερισμοῦ *as far as the separation* **Hb 4:12;** cp. **Rv 14:20; 18:5.**—DELG. M-M.

ἄχρονος, ον **pert. to not being affected or limited by the passage of time,** ***timeless***=eternal (s. χρόνος; Plut., Mor. 393a; Philo, Sacr. Abel. 76) of God (Proclus, Theol. 124 p. 110, 26; Lampe s.v.) IPol 3:2 (Martyr. Carpi 16 HMusurillo, Acts of the Christian Martyrs p. 24 ὁ θεὸς ἡμῶν ἄ. ὤν).

ἄχυρον, ου, τό (Hdt. et al. in pl. and sg.; ins, pap, LXX; Jos., Bell. 3, 223, Ant. 2, 289; SibOr 3, 791) **the husks of grain,** ***chaff*** **Mt 3:12; Lk 3:17.** On the burning of ἄ. cp. O. Wilck II, 1168 ἄ. εἰς τὰς καμείνους. For heating bath water BGU 760, 9 (II AD).—DELG s.v. ἄχυρα. M-M.

ἀχώρητος, ον (s. χῶρος; Just., Ath., Hesychius ὁ μὴ χωρούμενος) **pert. to not being confined to a space,** ***uncontained*** of God, in wordplay Hm 1:1 God 'contains' (χωρέω) all things but remains 'uncontained'; PtK 2 p. 13, 24; of the name of God's Son *illimitable, incomprehensible* Hs 9, 14, 5.—DELG s.v. χώρα.

ἀχώριστος, ον (s. χωρίζω; X., Pla. et al.; ApcMos 42; Just., D. 128, 3) ***inseparable*** w. gen. foll. (Cornutus 14 p. 15, 14; Philo, Gig. 48) ἀ. θεοῦ (Lghtf. suggests omission of θεοῦ w. the Armenian vers.) Ἰ. Χ. *inseparable fr. our God Jesus Christ* ITr 7:1 (cp. Herm. Wr. 2, 16 τὸ ἀγαθὸν ἀ. τοῦ θεοῦ; Sextus 423; Jos., Ant. 9, 273).—DELG s.v. χώρα.

ἀψευδής, ές (s. ψεῦδος; Hes., Hdt. et al.; BGU 432 II, 2; PSI 1102, 21; Wsd 7:17; Philo; Ar. [Milne 74, 13]) **free fr. all deceit,** ***truthful, trustworthy*** in our lit. only of God (cp. Archilochus [VII BC] 84 Diehl[2]; Eur., Or. 364 ἀψευδὴς θεός; Pla., Rep. 2, 382e; Orphica 168 Kern [of Zeus]; PGM 7, 571; Philo, Ebr. 139) **Tit 1:2;** MPol 14:2 w. ἀληθινός; and of Christ, who is called IRo 8:2 τὸ ἀ. στόμα ἐν ᾧ ὁ πατὴρ ἐλάλησεν ἀληθῶς (cp. Aeschyl. in Pla., Rep. 2, 383b τὸ Φοίβου θεῖον ἀ. στόμα=Ath. 21, 5).—DELG s.v. ψεύδομαι B. M-M.

ἄψευστος, ον (later form of ἀψευδής; Crinagoras no. 21, 5; Plut., Artox. 1025 [28, 2]; Sb 1070; PGM 13, 788; Philo, fgm. 51 Harris 1886) ***free fr. lies, truthful*** of πνεῦμα (SibOr 3, 701) Hm 3:2.—DELG s.v. A. TW.

ἀψηλάφητος, ον (s. ψηλαφάω; Polyb. 8, 19, 5; schol. on Pind., O. 6, 87; Cat. Cod. Astr. VIII/1 p. 188, 24; ὁ ἀ. θάνατος Mel., P. 23, 156; Hesych. gloss on ἄψαυστος 'untouched') **pert. to not being in a state or condition to be physically touchable despite groping efforts of the searcher,** ***impalpable*** of God IPol 3:2.—DELG s.v. ψηλαφάω.

ἀψίνθιον, ου, τό (Hippocr. et al.; X., An. 1, 5, 1; PSI 1180, 55; StudPal XX, 27, 9; PRyl IV ind.; Pr 5:4 Aq.; Jer 9:15; 23:15; so in rabb.) and **ἄψινθος, ου, ἡ** (Aretaeus [II AD], χρονίων νούσων θερ. 1, 13 Hude; on the art. s. Mussies 197) a plant of the genus 'Artemisia', proverbially bitter to the taste, yielding a dark green oil (the rendering ***wormwood*** derives from its association with medicinal use to kill intestinal worms) τὸ ἐλάχιστον ἀ. *a very little bit of wormwood* Hm 5, 1, 5. In imagery, water changed to wormw., i.e. the water became bitter as wormw. **Rv 8:11b.** As name of a star, and (prob. because of ὁ ἀστήρ) masc. ὁ Ἄψινθος ibid. **a** (s. Boll 41f).—DELG s.v. ἄψινθος.

ἄψυχος, ον (s. ψυχή; since Archilochus [VII BC] 104 Diehl[2]; Simonides 116 D.; PGM 7, 441; LXX, Philo; Just., A I, 9, 1; Ath.) ***inanimate, lifeless*** of musical instruments (Eur., Ion 881; Plut., Mor. 9c) **1 Cor 14:7.**—Of cult images (Wsd 13:17; 14:29; Just. A I, 9, 1.—Of statues of deities: Heraclitus in Celsus 1, 5; Timaeus Hist.: 566 fgm. 32 p. 610, 9 Jac. [Athen. 6, 250a]; Philo, Congr. Erud. Grat. 48; Ath. 23, 1) Dg 2:4.—M-M. TW.

ἄωρος, ον (s. ὥρα; Aeschyl., Hdt.+; PSI 1057, 11 and 17; PBon 19, 10 and 15; PGM 4, 2877; 5, 332; LXX; TestAbr A 18 p. 100, 25 [Stone p. 48] ἀώρως; 19 p. 102, 22f v.l. -ος; Jos., Bell. 4, 502) ***untimely***=*too early* (a term found esp. in grave ins RLattimore, Themes in Gk. and Lat. Epitaphs '62, 185f; ZNW 22, 1923, 281 nos. 5, 3; 6, 5; 7, 2 al.; JKazazis, Hellenika 40, '89, 21–33; s. also Preis. ind.) of children οἵτινες ἄ. ἐτίκτοντο *who were born prematurely* ApcPt 11, 26.

B

β′ numerical sign = *2* (δύο: Jos., C. Ap. 1, 157; Ar. [Milne 76, 28]) Hs 8, 9, 1 (cod. A for δύο) **Lk 10:35** P[75] (β); or *2d* (δευτέρα), i.e. ἐπιστολή (in the superscriptions of 2 Cor, 2 Th, 2 Ti, 2 Pt, 2J, 2 Cl, and in the subscriptions of 2 Th, 2 Ti, 2J), or ὅρασις (in the superscr. of Hv 2), or ἐντολή (in the superscr. of Hm 2).

Βάαλ, ὁ indecl. (בַּעַל lord; Jos., Ant. 9, 135f; 138 ὁ Βάαλ) ***Baal,*** a deity worshipped by the Semites gener., bitterly opposed by Elijah and later Hebr. prophets, κάμπτειν γόνυ τῇ B. *bow the knee before B.* **Ro 11:4** (3 Km 19:18 τῷ B.). The fem. art. (4 Km 21:3; Jer 2:8; 12:16 al.; AscIs 2:12; Just., D. 136, 3) may be due to the Hebr. custom of substituting αἰσχύνη (בֹּשֶׁת) for the names of foreign deities; s. ADillmann, Mon.-Ber. d. Berl. Akad. 1881, 601–20; RAC I 1063–1113; W-S. §10, 6; B-D-F§ 53, 4; Mlt-H. 152; Rob. 254.—M-M.

Βαβυλών, ῶνος, ἡ (Alcaeus Lyr. [VII/VI BC] 82, 10 D. [48, 10 L-P.]; Aeschyl., Pers. 52 et al.; LXX, ParJer, Philo, Joseph.,

SibOr; TestSol 26:6 B; Just.—בָּבֶל Gen 11:9; Babyl. *Bâb-îlu* or *Bâbili,* which the Babylonians interpreted by folk etymology to mean 'gate of the gods') ***Babylon,*** capital of Babylonia (Diod. S. 19, 100, 7 Βαβυλῶνα τὴν πόλιν); used also for the country (Bar 1:1, 4, 9, 11 al.; 1 Esdr 1:53; 2:11; 4:44 al.), so μετοικεσία Βαβυλῶνος *deportation to Babylonia* (B-D-F §166) **Mt 1:11f, 17;** cp. **Ac 7:43** (cp. Ps.-Callisth. 3, 33, 15 ἐπάνω τῆς Βαβυλωνίας).—Among Israelites Rome began to take on the name and many of the characteristics of Babylon as a world-power hostile to God, denounced by the prophets (SyrBar 67, 7; SibOr 5, 143; 159; Billerb. III 816). So also **1 Pt 5:13** (s. the v.l. Ῥώμη and also CHunzinger, HHertzberg Festschr., '65, 67–77 [Bab., Ro and 1 Pt].—Others, incl. GManley, EvQ 16, '44, 138–46 and RAltheim-Stiehl, Christentum am Roten Meer II, '73, 298, argue with less probability for the Bab. in Egypt [Diod. S. 1, 56, 3; Strabo 17, 1, 30; Jos., Ant. 2, 315]. The Bab. in Mesopotamia is also suggested by some, but at the time of Diod. S. [2, 9, 9], i.e. I BC, it was almost entirely uninhabited). The association w. Rome is preferred by most for Rv (otherwise GAvan den Bergh van Eysinga, NThT 16, 1927, 33ff; JOman, Book of Rv 1923, 29 al.; JSickenberger, BZ 17, 1926, 270–82; Lohmeyer), where B. is always called *the Great* (cp. Da 4:30; Jos., Ant. 8, 153; Alcaeus, loc. cit., spoke of Βαβύλωνος ἱρας=holy Babylon) **Rv 16:19; 17:5; 18:10, 21;** ἔπεσεν, ἔπεσεν Β. **14:8; 18:2** (cp. Is 21:9; Jer 28:8).—RAC I 1118–34. M-M. TW.

βαδίζω fut. βαδιοῦμαι; 1 aor. ἐβάδισα LXX (Stesichorus, perh. POxy 2360 I, 4, s. ed. note on the fragmentary text; et al., but rare in poetry) ***walk*** (in this sense since Hippocr. Int. 7 p. 274; Aristoph., Thesm 617; X+). Fig. (Galen: CMG V 4, 1, 1 p. 23, 12 β. ἐπὶ σωφροσύνην δι' ἐγκρατείας; Proverb. Aesopi 121 P.: β. τῶν νόμων ἐνώπιον; SibOr fgm. 1, 23; Psellus p. 213, 26) of human conduct, as (w. περιπατεῖν, πορεύεσθαι, πολιτεύεσθαι) β. κατὰ τὰς ἐπιθυμίας 1 Cl 3:4.—DELG s.v. βαίνω p. 157. M-M.

βάδος, ὁ Lk 16:6 v.l.; s. βάτος, ὁ.

βαθέως s. βαθύς end.

βαθμός, οῦ, ὁ (s. βαίνω; in various senses Strabo, Luc., et al.; LXX, ins, pap, 4 Esdr, Ps.-Soph. Philo, Joseph.)

❶ **a structured rest for the foot marking a stage in ascending or descending, *step*** (cp. βαίνω 'take a step, walk'; Soph.; Hellen. writers [Nägeli 26], LXX; ApcEsdr 4:8 p. 28, 7 Tdf. al.; Jos., Bell. 5, 206, Ant. 8, 140 in physical sense) ἐπὶ τρίτου βαθμοῦ τοῦ θυσιαστηρίου *on the third step of the altar* GJs 7:3; cp. **Ac 12:10** D.

❷ **a stage in intellectual or spiritual progress** (Dio Chrys. 24 [41], 6; Philo, Aet. M. 58) ***grade*** (Jos., Bell. 4, 171 οἱ τῶν τολμημάτων βαθμοί), *rank* (cp. IG XII/2, 243, 16 τοῖς τᾶς ἀξίας βασμοῖς ἀνελόγησε=he kept up to the degrees of his rank): β. ἑαυτῷ καλὸν περιποιεῖσθαι *win a good standing* (or *rank*) *for oneself* **1 Ti 3:13.** Perh. a t.t. of the mysteries underlies the last ref. (a 'step' in the soul's journey heavenward); cp. Herm. Wr. 13, 9 ὁ βαθμὸς οὗτος, ὦ τέκνον, δικαιοσύνης ἐστὶν ἕδρασμα. Furthermore, philosophy seems also to have used β. to denote the gradual attainment of wisdom (s. OImmisch, Philol. n.s. 17, 1904, 33, 1).—On the form of the word s. RSchöll, SBBayAk 1893 II 500.—DELG s.v. βαίνω p. 157. M-M.

βάθος, ους, τό (s. βαθύς; Aeschyl., Hdt.+) gener., distance beneath someth.

❶ **the space or distance beneath a surface, *depth*** (w. ὕψος Is 7:11; Herm. Wr. 11, 20b) Dg 7:2; (w. other dimensions; s. Aristot., Phys. 4, 1, 209a, 5; Dio Chrys. 76 [26], 6; Plut., Mor. 937f; SIG 973, 6ff μῆκος, πλάτος, β. [of a ditch]; Philo, Decal. 25; Jos., Ant. 1, 77) **Eph 3:18** (cp. the magic formula γενέσθω φῶς πλάτος βάθος μῆκος ὕψος αὐγή PGM 4, 970f and 978f; 12, 157; s. Straub 56). Of soil **Mt 13:5; Mk 4:5** (Jos., Ant. 8, 63 τῆς γῆς β.; Theophr., HP 6, 5, 4 χώρας βάθος; BGU 1122, 16 of plants ἔχον τὸ καθῆκον β.). Of the depths of the sea B 10:10 (cp. schol. on Apollon. Rhod. 1, 461; 4, 865f; Ps 68:3; Am 9:3; Mi 7:19 al. LXX). Of deep water **Lk 5:4.** Of eyes sunken because of swelling Papias (3:2). ὕψωμα οὔτε βάθος **Ro 8:39,** since they are said to be creatures and the context speaks apparently only of transcendent forces, are prob. astral spirits; they are both astronomical t.t., and β. means the celestial space below the horizon fr. which the stars arise (PGM 4, 575 ἀστὴρ ἐκ τ. βάθους ἀναλάμπων).

❷ **someth. nonphysical perceived to be so remote that it is difficult to assess, *depth*** fig. (Aeschyl. et al.) ἡ κατὰ βάθους πτωχεία αὐτῶν *their poverty reaching down into the depths* (Strabo 9, 3, 5 ἄντρον κοῖλον κατὰ βάθους)=*extreme poverty* **2 Cor 8:2;** β. πλούτου (Soph., Aj. 130; cp. Jos., Ant. 1, 271 τὸ τῆς τριχὸς βάθος; Pr 18:3; Aelian, VH 3, 18 πλοῦτος βαθύς; Norden, Agn. Th. 243, 3) *depth* (i.e. inexhaustibility) *of the wealth* **Ro 11:33;** τὰ β. τῆς θείας γνώσεως *depths of divine knowledge* 1 Cl 40:1 (Philo, Poster. Cai. 130 β. τῆς ἐπιστήμης); τὰ β. τοῦ θεοῦ *the depths of God* **1 Cor 2:10** (TestJob 37:6 τοῦ κυρίου); τὰ βάθη τοῦ σατανᾶ **Rv 2:24 v.l.** (cp. Jdth 8:14 βάθος καρδίας ἀνθρώπου; τὰ βάθη τῆς καρδίας καὶ τοῦ νοῦ Just., D. 121, 2; Eunap., Vi. Soph. 23, 3, 8 p. 113 β. τῆς ψυχῆς; w. κακῶν Aeschyl., Pers. 465).—DELG s.v. βαθύς. M-M. TW. Spicq.

βαθύνω 1 aor. ἐβάθυνα LXX; pass. 3 pl. ἐβαθύνθησαν Ps 91:6 (Hom. et al.; LXX; Jos., Bell. 1, 405) ***make deep*** (Jos., Bell. 5, 130) and intr. ***go down deep*** (Proclus, In Rem Publ. II p. 347, 2 Kroll; Philo, Post. Cai. 118 ὁ τῆς διανοίας ὀφθαλμὸς εἴσω προελθὼν καὶ βαθύνας τὰ ἐν αὐτοῖς σπλάγχνοις ἐγκεκρυμμένα κατεῖδε) ἔσκαψεν καὶ ἐβάθυνεν *dug and went deep, dug deep* **Lk 6:48.**—DELG s.v. βαθύς. M-M.

βαθύς, εῖα, ύ (s. βάθος; Hom. et al.; ins, pap, LXX; TestJud 7:3; Ath.)

❶ **pert. to distance beneath a surface, *deep*** (En 24:2; EpArist 118; Jos., Ant. 10, 170) of a well (Pythag., Ep. 3, 3 and Chariton 8, 1, 10 φρέαρ β.) **J 4:11.**

❷ **pert. to someth. nonphysical perceived to be so remote that it is difficult to assess, *deep*** τὰ βαθέα τοῦ σατανᾶ *the* (hidden) *depths of Satan* **Rv 2:24** (cp. Da 2:22 and s. βαθός 2).

❸ **pert. to an extreme point on a scale of extent**

ⓐ ***profound,*** of sleep (Theocr. 8, 65; Lucian et al.; Jos., Ant. 5, 148; Sir 22:9; 3 Macc 5:12; Ath. 12, 2) **Ac 20:9;** AcPl Ha 3, 25f οἱ δὲ φύλακε[ς βα]θεῖ ὕπνῳ. Of peace (Lucian, Tox. 36; Herodian 4, 10, 1; 7, 9, 5; 4 Macc 3:20; Philo, Somn. 2, 229; SibOr 12, 87; Ath. 1:3) 1 Cl 2:2.

ⓑ ***at the extreme of, very, exceedingly,*** ὄρθρου βαθέως (Aristoph., Vesp. 216; Pla., Crito 43a, Prot. 310a ἔτι βαθέος ὄρθρου; Phlegon: 257 fgm. 36, 1, 9 p. 1171, 4 Jac.; Philo, Mut. Nom. 162, Mos. 1, 179, Spec. Leg. 1, 276; PLips 40 II, 10) *early in the morning* **Lk 24:1** (β. [v.l. βαθέος] is to be taken, not as an adv., but as gen. of βαθύς, like πραέως [πραέος] **1 Pt 3:4.** Cp. W-S. §9, 5; Rob. 495; B-D-F §46, 3).—DELG. M-M.

βαΐον, ου, τό (Egypt. word, Coptic 'bai'.—The accents βάϊον and βάϊς are preferred by PKatz, TLZ 82, '57, 112; 83, '58, 316 and B-D-F §6) ***palm branch*** (1 Macc 13:51; SSol 7:8

Sym.; PFlor 37, 3; CWessely, Stud. z. Paläogr. u. Pap.-kunde 22, 1922, no. 157 [II AD]; cp. PTebt II p. 69. The pap prefer the form βαΐς [as N., but s. B-D-F §6], found also in Chaeremon Alex. in Porphyr., Abst. 4, 7.—Loanw. in rabb.) τὰ β. τῶν φοινίκων *the palm branches* **J 12:13** (where τῶν φ. is not really needed; but TestNapht 5:4 βαΐα φοινίκων and PLeid 13, 6, 7 [I AD] βαΐα φοινί[κων]). WFarmer, JTS 3, '52, 62–66.—DELG s.v. βαΐς. M-M.

Βαλαάμ, ὁ indecl. (בִּלְעָם) ***Balaam,*** a seer (Num 22–24; 31:16; Dt 23:5f; Josh 13:22; 24:9; Mi 6:5; Philo, Mos. 1, 264ff, Migr. Abr. 113–15; Jos., Ant. [Βάλαμος, ου] 4, 104; 107–9; 111; 126; 157; Pirqe Aboth 5, 19). Viewed as a typical deceiver and false prophet **Rv 2:14; Jd 11** (βαλαακ P[72]); **2 Pt 2:15.**—RAC II 362–73.

Βαλάκ, ὁ indecl. (בָּלָק) (LXX; Philo, Conf. Ling. 65.—In Joseph. βάλακος, ου [Ant. 4, 107]) ***Balak,*** a Moabite king (Num 22:2ff; 23:7; 24:10; Josh 24:9; Mi 6:5), involved w. Balaam (s. above) **Rv 2:14.**—Βαλαάκ **Jd 11** P[72] for Βαλαάμ, q.v.

βαλανεῖον, ου, τό (Aristoph. et al.; ins, pap, TestSol; Just., D. 13; loanw. in rabb.) **a structure designed for bathing and sociability, *bathhouse*** MPol 13:1.—FYegül, Baths and Bathing in Classical Antiquity '92.—DELG s.v. βαλανεύς.

βαλλάντιον, ου, τό (also βαλάντιον; s. B-D-F §11, 2; Rob. 213; W-S. §5, 26a n. 51; Helbing 15f. Found since Ps.-Simonides 157 Diehl[2]; Epicharmus [V BC] fgm. 10 p. 95: Com. Gr. Fgm. I/1, 1899 Kaibel; O. Bodl 348 recto, 10 [I BC]; PSI 1128, 26 [III AD]; Athen. 3, 98 in a pun w. βάλλω; Philo, De Jos. 180 and 207; LXX) ***money-bag, purse*** (Plut., Mor. 62b; 802d; Herodian 5, 4, 3 βαλλάντια χρημάτων μεστά) **Lk 10:4; 12:33; 22:35f.**—B. 776. DELG. TW.

βάλλω fut. βαλῶ; 2 aor. ἔβαλον, 3 pl. ἔβαλον **Lk 23:34** (Ps 21:19); **Ac 16:23** and ἔβαλαν **Ac 16:37** (B-D-F §81, 3; Mlt-H. 208); pf. βέβληκα (on this form s. lit. in LfgrE s.v. βάλλω col. 25). Pass.: 1 fut. βληθήσομαι; 1 aor. ἐβλήθην; pf. βέβλημαι; plpf. ἐβεβλήμην (Hom.+) gener. to put someth. into motion by throwing, used from the time of Hom. either with a suggestion of force or in a gentler sense; opp. of ἁμαρτάνω 'miss the mark'.

❶ to cause to move from one location to another through use of forceful motion, *throw*—ⓐ w. simple obj. *scatter seed on the ground* (Diod. S. 1, 36, 4; Ps 125:6 v.l. [ARahlfs, Psalmi cum Odis '31]) **Mk 4:26;** 1 Cl 24:5; AcPlCor 2:26; in a simile, of the body τὸ σῶμα . . . βληθέν vs. 27; εἰς κῆπον **Lk 13:19;** *cast lots* (Ps 21:19; 1 Ch 25:8 al.; Jos., Ant. 6, 61) **Mt 27:35; Mk 15:24; Lk 23:34; J 19:24;** B 6:6.

ⓑ *throw* τινί τι **Mt 15:26; Mk 7:27.** τὶ ἔμπροσθέν τινος **Mt 7:6** (β.=*throw* something before animals: Aesop, Fab. 275b H.//158 P.//163 H.). τὶ ἀπό τινος *throw someth. away* (fr. someone) **Mt 5:29f; 18:8f** (Teles p. 60, 2 ἀποβάλλω of the eye). τὶ ἔκ τινος: ὕδωρ ἐκ τοῦ στόματος ὀπίσω τινός *spew water out of the mouth after someone* **Rv 12:15f;** β. ἔξω = ἐκβάλλειν *throw out* **J 12:31 v.l.;** 2 Cl 7:4; s. ἐκβάλλω 1. Of worthless salt **Mt 5:13; Lk 14:35;** of bad fish *throw away* **Mt 13:48** (cp. Κυπρ. I p. 44 no. 43 κόπρια βάλλειν probably = throw refuse away); τὶ ἐπί τινα: *throw stones at somebody* **J 8:7, 59** (cp. Sir 22:20; 27:25; Jos., Vi. 303); in a vision of the future *dust* on one's *head* **Rv 18:19;** as an expression of protest τὶ εἴς τι *dust into the air* **Ac 22:23** (D εἰς τ. οὐρανόν *toward the sky*); *cast, throw* nets into the lake **Mt 4:18; J 21:6;** cp. vs. **7;** *a fishhook* **Mt 17:27** (cp. Is 19:8). Pass., into the sea, lake **Mt 13:47; Mk 9:42;** βλήθητι εἰς τὴν θάλασσαν *throw yourself into the sea* **Mt 21:21; Mk 11:23.**—*Throw* into the fire (Jos., Ant. 10, 95 and 215) **Mt 3:10; Mk 9:22; Lk 3:9; J 15:6;** into Gehenna **Mt 5:29; 18:9b;** 2 Cl 5:4; into the stove **Mt 6:30; 13:42, 50** (cp. Da 3:21); **Lk 12:28;** 2 Cl 8:2. β. ἑαυτὸν κάτω *throw oneself down* **Mt 4:6; Lk 4:9** (cp. schol. on Apollon. Rhod. 4, 1212–14a εἰς τὸν κρημνὸν ἑαυτὸν ἔβαλε; Jos., Bell. 4, 28).—**Rv 8:7f; 12:4, 9** (schol. on Apollon. Rhod. 4, 57; 28 p. 264, 18 of throwing out of heaven ἐκβληθέντα κατελθεῖν εἰς Ἅιδου), **13; 14:19; 18:21; 19:20; 20:3, 10, 14f;** *thrown* into a grave AcPlCor 2:32 (cp. τὰ νεκρούμενα καὶ εἰς γῆν βαλλόμενα Just., A I, 18, 6).—Of physical disability βεβλημένος *lying* (Jos., Bell. 1, 629) ἐπὶ κλίνης β. **Mt 9:2;** cp. **Mk 7:30.** *Throw on a sickbed* **Rv 2:22.** Pass. abs. (Conon [I BC/I AD] 26 fgm. 1, 17 Jac. βαλλομένη θνήσκει) *lie* on a sickbed (cp. Babrius 103, 4 κάμνων ἐβέβλητο [ἔκειτο L-P.]) **Mt 8:6, 14.** ἐβέβλητο πρὸς τὸν πυλῶνα *he lay before the door* **Lk 16:20** (ἐβέβλητο as Aesop, Fab. 284 H.; Jos., Ant. 9, 209; Field, Notes 70).—Fig. εἰς ἀθυμίαν β. τινά *plunge someone into despondency* 1 Cl 46:9.

ⓒ to cause or to let fall down, *let fall* of a tree dropping its fruit **Rv 6:13;** *throw down* **18:21a,** to destruction ibid. **b.**

❷ to force out of or into a place, *throw (away), drive out, expel* ἐβλήθη ἔξω *he is* (the aor. emphasizes the certainty of the result, and is gnomic [B-D-F §333; Rob. 836f; s. Hdb. ad loc.]) *thrown away/out,* i.e. expelled fr. the fellowship **J 15:6.** *drive out* into the desert B 7:8; *throw* into prison **Mt 18:30; Rv 2:10** (Epict. 1, 1, 24; 1, 12, 23; 1, 29, 6 al.; PTebt 567 [53/54 AD]). Pass. *be thrown* into the lions' den 1 Cl 45:6 (cp. Da 6:25 Theod. v.l.; Bel 31 Theod. v.l.); εἰς τὸ στάδιον AcPl Ha 4, 13. Fig. *love drives out fear* **1J 4:18.**

❸ to put or place someth. in a location, *put, place, apply, lay, bring*—ⓐ w. simple obj. κόπρια β. *put manure on, apply m.* **Lk 13:8** (POxy 934, 9 μὴ οὖν ἀμελήσῃς τοῦ βαλεῖν τὴν κόπρον).

ⓑ w. indication of the place to which τὶ εἴς τι: *put* money into the temple treasury **Mk 12:41–44; Lk 21:1–4** (in the context **Mk 12:43f; Lk 21:3f** suggest sacrifical offering by the widow); τὰ βαλλόμενα *contributions* (s. γλωσσόκομον and cp. 2 Ch 24:10) **J 12:6;** put a finger into an ear when healing **Mk 7:33;** difft. **J 20:25, 27** (exx. from medical lit. in Rydbeck 158f); to determine virginal purity by digital exploration GJs 19:3; *put* a sword into the scabbard **J 18:11;** *place bits into mouths* **Js 3:3;** εἰς τὴν κολυμβήθραν *take into the pool* **J 5:7;** cp. Ox 840, 33f; πολλὰ θηρία εἰς τὸν Παῦλον *many animals let loose against Paul* AcPl Ha 5, 4f (here β. suggests the rush of the animals); β. εἰς τὴν καρδίαν *put into the heart* **J 13:2** (cp. Od. 1, 201; 14, 269; Pind., O. 13, 16 [21] πολλὰ δ' ἐν καρδίαις ἔβαλον; schol. on Pind., P. 4, 133; Plut., Timol. 237 [3, 2]; Herm. Wr. 6, 4 θεῷ τῷ εἰς νοῦν μοι βαλόντι). Of liquids: *pour* (Epict. 4, 13, 12; PLond III, 1177, 46 p. 182 [113 AD]; Judg 6:19 B) wine into skins **Mt 9:17; Lk 5:37f;** water into a basin (TestAbr B 3 p. 107, 18 [Stone p. 62] βάλε ὕδωρ ἐπὶ τῆς λεκάνης ἵνα νίψωμεν τοὺς πόδας τοῦ ξένου [cp. TestAbr A 3 p. 80, 1 [Stone p. 8] ἔνεγκέ μοι ἐπὶ τῆς λ.]; Vi. Aesopi W 61 p. 92, 29f P. βάλε ὕδωρ εἰς τ. λεκάνην καὶ νίψον μου τοὺς πόδας; PGM 4, 224; 7, 319 βαλὼν εἰς αὐτὸ [the basin] ὕδωρ) **J 13:5;** wormwood in honey Hm 5, 1, 5; ointment on the body **Mt 26:12.**—βάρος ἐπί τινα *put a burden on some one* **Rv 2:24.** δρέπανον ἐπὶ τὴν γῆν *swing the sickle on the earth* as on a harvest field **Rv 14:19.** Cp. ἐπ' αὐτὸν τὰς χεῖρας **J 7:44 v.l.** (s. ἐπιβάλλω 1b). *Lay down* crowns (wreaths) before the throne **Rv 4:10.**

ⓒ other usage ῥίζας β. *send forth roots, take root* like a tree, fig. (Polemon, Decl. 2, 54 ὦ ῥίζας ἐξ ἀρετῆς βαλλόμενος) 1 Cl 39:8 (Job 5:3).

❹ to bring about a change in state or condition, εἰρήνην, μάχαιραν ἐπὶ τὴν γῆν *bring peace, the sword on earth* **Mt**

10:34 (Jos., Ant. 1, 98 ὀργὴν ἐπὶ τὴν γῆν βαλεῖν); χάριν ἐπ' αὐτήν *God showed her* (Mary) *favor* GJs 7:3. τὶ ἐνώπιόν τινος: σκάνδαλον *place a stumbling-block* **Rv 2:14.**

❺ to entrust money to a banker for interest, *deposit money* (τί τινι as Quint. Smyrn. 12, 250 in a diff t. context) *w. the bankers* (to earn interest; cp. Aristoxenus, fgm. 59 τὸ βαλλόμενον κέρμα; so also Diog. L. 2, 20) **Mt 25:27.**

❻ to move down suddenly and rapidly, *rush down,* intr. (Hom.; Epict. 2, 20, 10; 4, 10, 29; POslo 45, 2; En 18:6 ὄρη . . . εἰς νότον βάλλοντα 'in a southern direction'. Cp. Rdm.[2] 23; 28f; Rob. 799; JStahl, RhM 66, 1911, 626ff) ἔβαλεν ἄνεμος *a storm rushed down* **Ac 27:14.** (s. Warnecke 36 n. 9).—B. 673. Schmidt, Syn. III 150–66. DELG. M-M. TW.

βάναυσος, ον (deriv. fr. βαῦνος or βαυνός 'furnace, forge' may be folk etym. Frisk; Soph., Pla. et al.) **pert. to the artisan class, being socially inferior or crude in manner** (the artisan class was considered necessary to a city's existence [s. Aristot., Pol. 1291a, 1], but at a low rung socially, hence the transf. sense 'vulgar' Aristot., EN 1123a, 19 of the nouveau riche) ***base, vulgar*** (as in mod. Gk.) οὐδὲν βάναυσον ἐν ἀγάπῃ *there is nothing shabby in love* 1 Cl 49:5 (φορτικὰ καὶ βάναυσα Just., D. 3, 3).—DELG and Frisk.

βαπτίζω fut. βαπτίσω; 1 aor. ἐβάπτισα. Mid.: ἐβαπτισάμην. Pass.: impf. ἐβαπτιζόμην; fut. βαπτισθήσομαι; 1 aor. ἐβαπτίσθην; pf. ptc. βεβαπτισμένος (Hippocr., Pla., esp. Polyb.+; UPZ 70, 13 [152/151 BC]; PGM 5, 69; LXX; ApcSed 14:7 [p. 136, 8f Ja.]; Philo; Joseph.; SibOr 5, 478; Just.; Mel., fgm. 8, 1 and 2 Goodsp.=8b, 4 and 14 P.—In Gk. lit. gener. to put or go under water in a variety of senses, also fig., e.g. 'soak' Pla., Symp. 176b in wine) in our lit. only in ritual or ceremonial sense (as Plut.; Herm. Wr. [s. 2a below]; PGM 4, 44; 7, 441 λουσάμενος κ. βαπτισάμενος; 4 Km 5:14; Sir 34:25; Jdth 12:7; cp. Iren. 1, 21, 3 [Harv. I 183, 83]).

❶ wash ceremonially for purpose of purification, *wash, purify,* of a broad range of repeated ritual washing rooted in Israelite tradition (cp. Just., D. 46, 2) **Mk 7:4; Lk 11:38;** Ox 840, 15.—WBrandt, Jüd. Reinheitslehre u. ihre Beschreibg. in den Ev. 1910; ABüchler, The Law of Purification in Mk 7:1–23: ET 21, 1910, 34–40; JDöller, D. Reinheits- u. Speisegesetze d. ATs 1917; JJeremias, TZ 5, '49, 418–28. See 1QS 5:8–23; 2:25–3:12; 4:20–22.

❷ to use water in a rite for purpose of renewing or establishing a relationship w. God, *plunge, dip, wash, baptize.* The transliteration 'baptize' signifies the ceremonial character that NT narratives accord such cleansing, but the need of qualifying statements or contextual coloring in the documents indicates that the term β. was not nearly so technical as the transliteration suggests.

ⓐ of dedicatory cleansing associated w. the ministry of John the Baptist (Orig., C. Cels. 1, 47, 4), abs. **J 1:25, 28; 3:23a; 10:40;** hence John is called ὁ βαπτίζων **Mk 1:4; 6:14, 24** (Goodsp., Probs. 50–52).—Pass. **Mt 3:16;** ISm 1:1; oft. *have oneself baptized, get baptized* **Mt 3:13f; Lk 3:7, 12, 21; 7:30; J 3:23b;** GEb 18, 35f; IEph 18:2 al. (B-D-F §314; s. §317).—(ἐν) ὕδατι *w. water* **Mk 1:8a; Lk 3:16a; Ac 1:5a; 11:16a;** ἐν (τῷ) ὕδατι **J 1:26, 31, 33;** ἐν τῷ Ἰορδ. (4 Km 5:14) **Mt 3:6; Mk 1:5;** εἰς τὸν Ἰορδ. (cp. Plut., Mor. 166a βάπτισον σεαυτὸν εἰς θάλασσαν; Herm. Wr. 4, 4 βάπτισον σεαυτὸν εἰς τὸν κρατῆρα) **Mk 1:9.**—W. the external element and purpose given ἐν ὕδατι εἰς μετάνοιαν **Mt 3:11a** (AOliver, Is β. used w. ἐν and the Instrumental?: RevExp 35, '38, 190–97).—βαπτίζεσθαι τὸ βάπτισμα Ἰωάννου *undergo John's baptism* **Lk 7:29.** εἰς τί ἐβαπτίσθητε; **Ac 19:3** means, as the answer shows, *in reference to what (baptism) were you baptized?* i.e. what kind of baptism did you receive (as the context indicates, John's baptism was designed to implement repentance as a necessary stage for the reception of Jesus; with the arrival of Jesus the next stage was the receipt of the Holy Spirit in connection with apostolic baptism in the name of Jesus, who was no longer the 'coming one', but the arrived 'Lord')? β. βάπτισμα μετανοίας *administer a repentance baptism* vs. **4;** GEb 13, 74.—S. the lit. on Ἰωάν(ν)ης 1, and on the baptism of Jesus by John: JBornemann, D. Taufe Christi durch Joh. 1896; HUsener, D. Weihnachtsfest[2] 1911; DVölter, D. Taufe Jesu durch Joh.: NThT 6, 1917, 53–76; WBundy, The Meaning of Jesus' Baptism: JR 7, 1927, 56–75; MJacobus, Zur Taufe Jesu bei Mt 3:14, 15: NKZ 40, 1929, 44–53; SHirsch, Taufe, Versuchung u. Verklärung Jesu '32; DPlooij, The Baptism of Jesus: RHarris Festschr. (Amicitiae Corolla), ed. HWood '33, 239–52; JKosnetter, D. Taufe Jesu '36; HRowley, TManson memorial vol., ed. Higgins '59, 218–29 (Qumran); JSchneider, Der historische Jesus u. d. kerygmatische Christus '61, 530–42; HKraft, TZ 17, '61, 399–412 (Joel); FLentzen-Dies, D. Taufe Jesu nach den Synoptikern, '70. More reff. s.v. περιστερά.

ⓑ of cleansing performed by Jesus **J 3:22, 26; 4:1;** difft. **4:2** with disclaimer of baptismal activity by Jesus personally.

ⓒ of the Christian sacrament of initiation after Jesus' death (freq. pass.; s. above 2a; Iren. 3, 12, 9 [Harv. II 63, 3]) **Mk 16:16; Ac 2:41; 8:12f, 36, 38; 9:18; 10:47; 16:15, 33; 18:8; 22:16; 1 Cor 1:14–17;** D 7 (where baptism by pouring is allowed in cases of necessity); ISm 8:2.—β. τινὰ εἰς (τὸ) ὄνομά τινος (s. ὄνομα 1dγב) *baptize in* or *w. respect to the name of someone:* (τοῦ) κυρίου **Ac 8:16; 19:5;** D 9:5; Hv 3, 7, 3. Cp. **1 Cor 1:13, 15.** εἰς τ. ὄν. τ. πατρὸς καὶ τ. υἱοῦ καὶ τ. ἁγίου πνεύματος **Mt 28:19** (on the original form of the baptismal formula see FConybeare, ZNW 2, 1901, 275–88; ERiggenbach, BFCT VII/1, 1903; VIII/4, 1904; HHoltzmann, Ntl. Theologie[2] I 1911, 449f; OMoe: RSeeberg Festschr. 1929, I 179–96; GOngaro, Biblica 19, '38, 267–79; GBraumann, Vorpaulinische christl. Taufverkündigung bei Paulus '62); D 7:1, 4. Likew. ἐν τῷ ὀν. Ἰ. Χριστοῦ **Ac 2:38 v.l.; 10:48;** ἐπὶ τῷ ὀν. Ἰ. Χρ. **Ac 2:38** text; more briefly εἰς Χριστόν **Gal 3:27; Ro 6:3a.** To be baptized εἰς Χρ. is for Paul an involvement in Christ's death and its implications for the believer εἰς τὸν θάνατον αὐτοῦ ἐβαπτίσθημεν vs. **3b** (s. Ltzm. ad loc.; HSchlier, EvTh '38, 335–47; GWagner, D. relgeschichtliche Problem von Rö 6:1–11, '62, tr. Pauline Bapt. and the Pagan Mysteries, by JSmith, '67; RSchnackenburg, Baptism in the Thought of St. Paul '64, tr. of D. Heilsgeschehen b. d. Taufe nach dem Ap. Paulus '50). The effect of baptism is to bring all those baptized εἰς ἓν σῶμα **1 Cor 12:13** (perh. wordplay: 'plunged into one body').—W. the purpose given εἰς ἄφεσιν τ. ἁμαρτιῶν **Ac 2:38** (IScheftelowitz, D. Sündentilgung durch Wasser: ARW 17, 1914, 353–412).—Diod. S. 5, 49, 6: many believe that by being received into the mysteries by the rites (τελεταί) they become more devout, more just, and better in every way.—ὑπὲρ τ. νεκρῶν **1 Cor 15:29a,** s. also vs. **29b,** is obscure because of our limited knowledge of a practice that was evidently obvious to the recipients of Paul's letter; it has been interpr. (1) *in place of the dead,* i.e. vicariously; (2) *for the benefit of the dead,* in var. senses; (3) locally, *over* (the graves of) *the dead;* (4) *on account of the dead,* infl. by their good ex.; of these the last two are the least probable. See comm. and HPreisker, ZNW 23, 1924, 298–304; JZingerle, Heiliges Recht: JÖAI 23, 1926; Rtzst., Taufe 43f; AMarmorstein, ZNW 30, '31, 277–85;

AOliver, RevExp 34, '37, 48–53; three articles: Kirchenblatt 98, '42 and six: ET 54, '43; 55, '44; MRaeder, ZNW 46, '56, 258–60; BFoschini, 5 articles: CBQ 12, '50 and 13, '51.—On the substitution of a ceremony by another person cp. Diod. S. 4, 24, 5: the boys who do not perform the customary sacrifices lose their voices and become as dead persons in the sacred precinct. When someone takes a vow to make the sacrifice for them, their trouble disappears at once.

❸ **to cause someone to have an extraordinary experience akin to an initiatory water-rite, *to plunge, baptize.*** Cp. 'take the plunge' and s. OED 'Plunge' II 5 esp. for the rendering of usage 3c, below.

ⓐ typologically of Israel's passage through the Red Sea εἰς τὸν Μωϋσῆν ἐβαπτίσαντο *they got themselves plunged/baptized for Moses,* thereby affirming his leadership **1 Cor 10:2 v.l.** (if the pass. ἐβαπτίσθησαν is to be read with N. the point remains the same; but the mid. form puts the onus, as indicated by the context, on the Israelites).

ⓑ of the Holy Spirit (fire) β. τινὰ (ἐν) πνεύματι ἁγίῳ **Mk 1:8** (v.l. + ἐν); **J 1:33; Ac 1:5b; 11:16b;** cp. **1 Cor 12:13** (cp. Just., D. 29, 1). ἐν πν. ἁγ. καὶ πυρί **Mt 3:11b; Lk 3:16b** (JDunn, NovT 14, '72, 81–92). On the oxymoron of baptism w. fire: REisler, Orphisch-dionysische Mysteriengед. in d. christl. Antike: Vortr. d. Bibl. Warburg II/2, 1925, 139ff; CEdsman, Le baptême de feu (ASNU 9) '40. JATRobinson, The Baptism of John and Qumran, HTR 50, '57, 175–91; cp. 1QS 4:20f.

ⓒ of martyrdom (s. the fig. uses in UPZ 70, 13 [152/151 BC]; Diod. S. 1, 73, 6; Plut., Galba 1062 [21, 3] ὀφλήμασι βεβ. 'overwhelmed by debts'; Chariton 2, 4, 4, βαπτιζόμενος ὑπὸ τ. ἐπιθυμίας; Vi. Aesopi I c. 21 p. 278, 4 λύπῃ βαπτιζόμενος; Achilles Tat. 3, 10, 1 πλήθει βαπτισθῆναι κακῶν; Herm. Wr. 4, 4 ἐβαπτίσαντο τοῦ νοός; Is 21:4; Jos., Bell. 4, 137 ἐβάπτισεν τ. πόλιν 'he drowned the city in misery') δύνασθε τὸ βάπτισμα ὃ ἐγὼ βαπτίζομαι βαπτισθῆναι; **Mk 10:38** (perh. the stark metaph. of impending personal disaster is to be rendered, 'are you prepared to be drowned the way I'm going to be drowned?'); cp. vs. **39; Mt 20:22 v.l.;** in striking contrast to fire **Lk 12:50** (GDelling, Novum Testamentum 2, '57, 92–115).—PAlthaus, Senior, D. Heilsbedeutung d. Taufe im NT 1897; WHeitmüller, Im Namen Jesu 1903, Taufe u. Abendmahl b. Paulus 1903, Taufe u. Abendmahl im Urchristentum 1911; FRendtorff, D. Taufe im Urchristentum 1905; HWindisch, Taufe u. Sünde im ältesten Christentum 1908; ASeeberg, D. Taufe im NT² 1913; AvStromberg, Studien zu Theorie u. Praxis der Taufe 1913; GottfrKittel, D. Wirkungen d. chr. Wassertaufe nach d. NT: StKr 87, 1914, 25ff; WKoch, D. Taufe im NT³ 1921; JLeipoldt, D. urchr. Taufe im Lichte der Relgesch. 1928; RReitzenstein, D. Vorgesch. d. christl. Taufe 1929 (against him HSchaeder, Gnomon 5, 1929, 353–70, answered by Rtzst., ARW 27, 1929, 241–77); FDölger, AC I 1929, II 1930; HvSoden, Sakrament u. Ethik bei Pls: ROtto Festschr., Marburger Theologische Studien '31, no. 1, 1–40; MEnslin, Crozer Quarterly 8, '31, 47–67; BBacon, ATR 13, '31, 155–74; CBowen: RHutcheon, Studies in NT, '36, 30–48; GBornkamm, ThBl 17, '38, 42–52; 18, '39, 233–42; HSchlier, EvTh '38, 335–47 (Ro 6); EBruston, La notion bibl. du baptême: ÉTLR '38, 67–93; 135–50; HMarsh, The Origin and Signif. of the NT Baptism '41; KBarth, D. kirchl. Lehre v. d. Taufe² '43 (Eng. tr., The Teaching of the Church Regarding Baptism, EPayne '48); FGrant, ATR 27, '45, 253–63; HSchlier, D. kirchl. Lehre v. d. Taufe: TLZ 72, '47, 321–26; OCullmann, Baptism in the NT (tr. JReid) '50; MBarth, D. Taufe ein Sakrament? '51; RBultmann, Theology of the NT, tr. KGrobel '51, I 133–44; JSchneider, D. Taufe im NT '52; DStanley, TS 18, '57, 169–215; EFascher, Taufe: Pauly-W. 2. Reihe IV 2501–18 ('32); AOepke, TW I '33, 527–44; GBeasley-Murray, Baptism in the NT '62; MQuesnel, Baptisés dans l'Esprit '85 (Acts); DDaube, The NT and Rabbinic Judaism '56, 106–40; NMcEleney, Conversion, Circumstance and the Law: NTS 20, '74, 319–41; HBraun, Qumran u. d. NT II '66, 1–29; OBetz, D. Proselytentaufe der Qumransekte u. d. NT: RevQ 1, '58, 213–34; JYsebaert, Gk. Baptismal Terminology, '62. S. τέκνον 1aα.—B. 1482. DELG s.v. βάπτω. M-M. EDNT. TW. Sv.

βάπτισμα, ατος, τό (s. βαπτίζω; found only in Christian writers; ApcSed 14:6 [p. 136, 7 and 9 Ja.]; Just., D.; Mel., fgm. 6 al.)

❶ **the ceremonious use of water for purpose of renewing or establishing a relationship w. God, *plunging, dipping, washing, water-rite, baptism***

ⓐ of John's rite (Orig., C. Cels. 1, 44, 13 al. [T. Jesus]) **Mt 3:7; 21:25; Mk 11:30; Lk 7:29; 20:4; Ac 1:22; 10:37; 18:25; 19:3;** β. μετανοίας **Mk 1:4; Lk 3:3** (in these two passages with εἰς ἄφεσιν ἁμαρτιῶν *[proclaiming] a baptism-with-repentance to receive forgiveness of sins*) **Ac 13:24; 19:4;** GEb 13, 74.

ⓑ of Christian rite β. φέρον ἄφεσιν ἁμαρτιῶν B 11:1; β. εἰς τὸν θάνατον **Ro 6:4** (s. βαπτίζω 2b). ἓν β. **Eph 4:5.** The person baptized is at the same time buried w. Christ **Col 2:12 v.l.; 1 Pt 3:21** (s. ἀντίτυπος). Compared to a soldier's weapons IPol 6:2. τηρεῖν τὸ β. ἁγνὸν καὶ ἀμίαντον 2 Cl 6:9. Ritual directions D 7:1, 4.

❷ **an extraordinary experience akin to an initiatory purification rite, *a plunge, a baptism.***—ⓐ metaph. of martyrdom **Mk 10:38f; Lk 12:50; Mt 20:22f v.l.** (s. GDelling, NovT 2, '58, 92–115, and βαπτίζω 3c).

ⓑ metaph. of salvation β. ἐν σωτηρίᾳ Ἀχερουσίας λίμνης *b. in the saving waters of the Acherusian lake* ApcPt Rainer 1, 4f (s. Ἀχερούσιος; EPeterson, Frühkirche, Judentum u. Gnosis '59, 310ff).—M-M. TW.

βαπτισμός, οῦ, ὁ (s. βαπτίζω; Antyllus the physician [II AD] in Oribasius 10, 3, 9, 'act of immersion or dipping')

❶ **water-rite for purpose of purification, *washing, cleansing,*** of dishes **Mk 7:4, 8 v.l.** Of other ritual *washings* (Jos., Ant. 18, 117 of John's baptism) **Hb 9:10.**—ESanders, Jewish Law fr. Jesus to the Mishnah '90, 258–71 (purification).

❷ **water-rite for purpose of renewing or establishing a relationship w. God, *plunging experience, baptism*** burial with Christ in *baptism* **Col 2:12.** βαπτισμῶν διδαχή **Hb 6:2** (a ref. to various water-rites, including prob. John's baptism and Christian baptism).—M-M. TW.

βαπτιστής, οῦ, ὁ ***Baptist, Baptizer,*** surname of John **Mt 3:1; 11:11f; 14:2, 8; 16:14; 17:13; Mk 6:25** (in vs. 24 ὁ βαπτίζων); **8:28; Lk 7:20, 33; 9:19** (found only in Christian writers [Just., D. 50, 2; 84, 4; name of a Hebraic sect Just., D. 80, 4, but, argues J., not to be identified w. Ἰουδαῖοι], except for Jos., Ant. 18, 116, where it refers to J. Bapt. But cp. Epict. 2, 9, 21 ἡμεῖς παραβαπτισταί).

βάπτω fut. βάψω; 1 aor. ἔβαψα; pf. pass. ptc. βεβαμμένος (this form Epict. 2, 9, 20 of the experience [τὸ πάθος] that causes a Ἕλλην to become a Ἰουδαῖος); aor. ἐβάφην (Hom.+, pap, LXX) **to dip someth. in a liquid, *dip, dip in* J 13:26,** ἐμβάπτω P⁶⁶ et al. (cp. Ruth 2:14); ἄκρον τοῦ δακτύλου ὕδατος *the tip of the finger in water* (on the gen. ὕδατος cp. B-D-F §172; Arat., Phaenomena 651 βάπτων ὠκεανοῖο; 858 Maass) **Lk 16:24.**

The dat. also occurs (ἔβαψεν τῷ ὕδατι 4 Km 8:15 v.l.) ibid. v.l.; ἱμάτιον βεβαμμένον αἵματι **Rv 19:13** (the text is uncertain; v.l. ῥεραντισμένον, περιρεραμμένον, ἐρραμμένον s. ῥαντίζω, περιρραίνω, ῥαίνω) *a garment dipped in blood* = *dyed in blood* (s. JScott, ClJ 16, 1920, 53f for exx. of β.='stain' w. blood fr. Batrachom. 220 and Lucian, Ver. Hist. 1, 17. For the act of dipping into dye s. GThGk A 8 [Ea p. 148 note, a portion of text from the fragmentary ms.Paris Bibl. nat. gr. 239]; s. also Hdt. 7, 67 εἵματα βεβαμμένα; PCairZen 630, 1 [III BC]; POxy 736, 6 [I AD]; Jos., Bell. 4, 563, Ant. 3, 102); the imagery vss. **11–13** is that of a regal figure, who would be caparisoned in a garment with hue of indigo, the standard color for a head of state (s. πορφύρα); the blood of Jesus suggests such royal purple dye in a climactic contrast to the woman described 17:4 and the 'great city' 18:16.—B. 415. DELG. M-M. TW.

Βαρ s. Βαριωνᾶ.

Βαραββᾶς, ᾶ, ὁ (בַּר אַבָּא) a common (e.g. SEG VII, 489, 1) name, ***Barabbas*** = 'son of Abba' (Billerb, I 1031).

❶ the prisoner released by Pilate **Mt 27:16f, 20f, 26; Mk 15:7, 11, 15; Lk 23:18; J 18:40.** In GHb (339, 50f), acc. to Jerome, the name was rendered in Lat. filius magistri eorum (=בַּר רַבָּן). Origen, In Mt Comm. Ser. 121 (ed. EKlosterenann '33, 255–57) found the name written in full in old mss. as Ἰησοῦς ὁ Β., and this v.l. occurs **Mt 27:16f.**—WBrandt, Ev. Geschichte 1893, 94ff; JMerkel, ZNW 6, 1905, 293ff; LCouchoud and RStahl, Jesus B.: Hibbert Journ. 25, 1927, 26–42; ADeissmann, Mysterium Christi '31, 32–36; HRigg, Jr., Barabbas: JBL 64, '45, 417–56 (many reff.; against him MHengel, D. Zeloten '61, 348); JBlinzler, D. Prozess Jesu[3] '60, 220–35; MMarco, EstBîbl 30, '71, 137–60; Schürer I 385; 439.

❷ associate of Paul and Barnabas **Ac 15:22** D (B. for Βαρσαββᾶς, q.v. 2).—TW.

Βαράκ, ὁ indecl. (בָּרָק; in Jos. βάρακος, ου [Ant. 5, 203]) ***Barak,*** an Israelite general (Judg 4f), mentioned w. other heroes **Hb 11:32.**

Βαραχίας, ου, ὁ (בֶּרֶכְיָה; also Jos., Ant. 9, 250) ***Barachiah,*** name of the father of a certain Zechariah (Gk. Zacharias), who was killed in the temple (s. Ζαχαρίας 2) **Mt 23:35; Lk 11:51 v.l.** Acc. to GHb 284, 150f (as ViZech [p. 96, 25 Sch.]) this Zechariah was the son of Jehoiada, not of B., and so identified w. the Zech. who was stoned to death in the temple court, 2 Ch 24:20ff. Zech., the son of Berechiah, is the well-known prophet (Zech 1:1), who seems elsewh. to have been confused w. the murdered Z. (Pesikta R. Kahana 15). If the ref. in the gospels is to a biblical pers., the Zech. of 2 Ch (the last book in the Hebrew canon; Billerb. I 943; IV 422) must be meant, in which case Mt. has classified him with the prophets (for other views, incl. the possibility of a gloss, s. comm., esp. Allen and Zahn) Since this Z. was not the last prophet or just person to be killed, some scholars hold that the allusion is to Zacharias, son of Baruch, whom the Zealots killed 67/68 AD (Jos., Bell. 4, 334ff). See EbNestle, ZNW 6, 1905, 198–200; Wlh., Einl. 118–23; JChapman, JTS 13, 1912, 398–410; Rtzst., Herr der Grösse 34ff; JKennard, Jr., ATR 29, '47, 173–79.

βάρβαρος, ον (onomatopoetic formation; Aeschyl., Hdt.+; loanw. in rabb. [Dalman, Gram.[2] 183, 185]) gener. pert. to what is foreign (esp. from the perspective of one who knows Greek and is familiar w. Hellenic culture; the components 'foreign in language' and 'foreign in culture' are ordinarily linked) 'non-Hellenic'

❶ w. focus on strangeness of language: **pert. to using a language that is unintelligible to outsiders,** ***foreign-speaking, of foreign tongue*** adj. or noun **1 Cor 14:11** (cp. Hdt. 2, 158; Aristoph., Av. 199 and its scholia [Ltzm. on 1 Cor 14:11]; Ovid, Tristia 5, 10, 37 barbarus hic ego sum, quia non intellegor ulli 'I'm a *barbarus* here, because no one understands me'; Ps 113:1).

❷ w. focus on non-Hellenic association: **pert. to not speaking Greek or participating in Gk. culture—ⓐ** adj. ***not Hellenic*** πόλεις Ἑλληνίδας κ. βαρβάρους Dg 5:4.

ⓑ subst. ***a non-Hellene, foreigner*** (the Engl. loanw. 'barbarian' is freq. used in a derogatory sense and is therefore inappropriate for rendering [as NRSV, REB et al.] the Gk. term when it appears without the negative contexts of some texts composed after the Persian wars, e.g. Demosth. 26, 17) contrasted w. Hellenes (the Neo-Platonist Amelius [III AD] calls the writer of John's gospel a β.: Eus., PE 11, 19, 1) Ἕλληνες κ. βάρβαροι **Ro 1:14** (cp. Ps.-Eur., Rhes. 404; Pla., Theaet. 175a; Chariton 6, 3, 7; SIG 360, 12 and 27; 867, 32; OGI 765, 16ff; IAndrosIsis p. 124, 31 ἐγὼ διαλέκτους Ἕλλησι καὶ βαρβάροις ἔταξα=125, 27 [but διετάξάμην]; Philo, Abr. 267; Jos., Ant. 4, 12; 8, 284 al.—The Romans refused to be classified as β.: Jüthner [s. Ἕλλην 1] p. 62; MPohlenz, Stoa II '49, 139); cp. **Col 3:11** (44th Ep. of Apollonius of Tyana [Philostrat. I 354, 25]: there is no difference betw. people εἴτε βάρβαρος εἴτε καὶ Ἕλλην.—THermann, ThBl 9, 1930, 106f). Of the inhabitants of Malta, who apparently spoke in their native language **Ac 28:2, 4** (here β. certainly without derogatory tone; indeed, Luke transforms the 'foreigners' into 'Hellenes' by noting their extraordinary hospitality παρεῖχον οὐ τὴν τυχοῦσαν φιλανθρωπίαν; cp. Warnecke, Romfahrt 111–18).—AEichhorn, βάρβαρος quid significaverit, diss. Leipz. 1904; HWerner, Barbarus: NJklA 41, 1918, 389–408; RAC I 1173–76; JAC 10, '67, 251–96. S. Ἕλλην 1.—DELG. M-M. TW. Sv.

βαρέω 1 aor. ἐβάρησα. Pass.: pres. ptc. βαρούμενος, impv. βαρείσθω; 1 aor. ἐβαρήθην; pf. 3 sg. βεβάρηται Ex 7:14; ptc. βεβαρημένος (s. βάρος; Hom. et al.; ins, pap; seldom LXX; pseudepigr.; Jos., Ant. 15, 55; SibOr fgm. 3, 39; Tat. 23, 1 βεβαρημένους; s. Anz 266–68; Nägeli 26) **to press down as if with a weight,** ***weigh down, burden***

ⓐ of physical weariness. Of eyelids that have dropped ὀφθαλμοὶ βεβαρημένοι=*they could not keep awake* (Philo, Ebr. 131 βεβαρημένος τ. ὀφθαλμούς) **Mt 26:43; Mk 14:40 v.l.** W. ὕπνῳ (Anth. Pal. 3, 22, 17; 4, 8, 12; 7, 290) *heavy w. sleep* **Lk 9:32;** cp. διὰ τὰς νηστείας καὶ τὰς διανυκτερεύσεις . . . βαρηθεὶς ὁ Παῦλος ἀφύπνωσεν (some restoration) *weary from fastings and wakefulness at night, Paul fell off to sleep* AcPl Ha 7, 26.

ⓑ of a mental or psychological condition. Of minds that lose their alertness (cp. Ex 7:14) in drunkenness (β. οἴνῳ is a common expr. Hom. et al.) **Lk 21:34.** Of misfortune or injustice (cp. POxy 525, 3 [II AD] καθ' ἑκάστην ἡμέραν βαροῦμαι δι' αὐτόν; SIG 888, 85; 904, 3–4) καθ' ὑπερβολὴν ὑπὲρ δύναμιν ἐβαρήθημεν *we were burdened altogether beyond our strength* (='the load was so heavy we did not have the strength to keep going' New Life) **2 Cor 1:8** (cp. PTebt 23, 5 [II BC] καθ' ὑπερβολὴν βεβαρυμμένοι). Abs. βαρούμενοι *oppressed* **5:4** (Epict. 1, 25, 17; s. βαρύνω end). Of financial burdens (Cass. Dio 46, 32; OGI 595, 15 [174 AD] ἵνα μὴ τὴν πόλιν βαρῶμεν; so also IG XIV, 830, 15; of Opramoas, Lycian philanthropist, who bore costs for the erection of statues in his honor so that the 'province might not be burdened' IGR III, 9 [30], 56–57) μὴ βαρείσθω ἡ ἐκκλησία *the congregation is not to be burdened* **1 Ti 5:16.**—DELG s.v. βαρύς. M-M. TW.

βαρέως adv. of βαρύς (Hdt. et al.; PTebt 747, 12 [III BC]; UPZ 59, 28 [168 BC]; Sb 6263, 26 [II AD]; LXX; Jos., Ant. 20, 60; 94) ***with difficulty*** ἀκούειν *be hard of hearing* (X., An. 2, 1, 9 β. ἀκούειν means 'hear with anger') **Mt 13:15; Ac 28:27** (both Is 6:10).

Βαρθολομαῖος, ου, ὁ (בַּר תַּלְמַי; cp. 2 Km 3:3; 13:37; Joseph. index Niese Θολεμαῖος and Θολομαῖος; Preisigke, Namenbuch) ***Bartholomew,*** name of one of the 12 apostles **Mt 10:3; Mk 3:18; Lk 6:14; Ac 1:13.** Efforts have been made to identify him under other names, including Ναθαναήλ q.v.; s. UHolzmeister, Biblica 21, '40, 28–39.

Βαριησοῦ, ὁ (so Tdf., whose app. s. for variants, then supplement w. N. app.; בַּר יֵשׁוּעַ) indecl. ***Bar-Jesus,*** name of a false prophet (cp. Ἐλύμας, and ref. there) **Ac 13:6.** MWilcox, The Semitisms of Ac, '65, 89.

Βαριωνᾶ/Βαριωνᾶς, ᾶ, ὁ (Βάρ Ἰωνᾶ t.r.; Βαριωνά N[25]; בַּר יוֹנָה) ***Bar-Jona*** (=son of Jonah; cp. Jon 1:1; 4 Km 14:25) surname of the apostle Simon (Peter) **Mt 16:17.** Judaicon 158, 74 υἱὲ Ἰωάννου=בַּר יוֹחָנָן, which agrees w. J 1:42 (cp. 21:15–17). S. Dalman, Gramm.[2] 179, 5; HHirschberg, JBL 61, '42, 171–91, opposed by RMarcus ibid. 281; MHengel, Die Zeloten '61, 55–57.

Βαρναβᾶς, ᾶ, ὁ (Βαρνάβας edd.; ברנבו? SEG VII, 381, 5.—See Dssm., B 175ff, NB 16 [BS 187ff, 307ff], ZNW 7, 1906, 91f; Dalman, Worte 32, Gram.[2] 178, 4; HCadbury, Semitic Personal Names in Luke-Acts: RHarris Festschr. [Amicitiae Corolla], ed. HWood '33, 47f, JBL 52, '33, 59) ***Barnabas,*** a Levite fr. Cyprus, whose first name was Joseph (**Ac 4:36**), uncle of John Mark **Col 4:10** (cp. **Ac 15:37**) and freq. cited in association w. Paul **Ac 9:27; 11:22, 30; 12:25; chs. 13–15** (18 times); **1 Cor 9:6; Gal 2:1, 9, 13; Col 4:10; 2 Cor subscr.;** B subscr. In **Ac 4:36** his name is translated υἱὸς παρακλήσεως *son of consolation,* but it is not quite clear how this rendering, prob. a popular etymology, is derived.—RTaylor, CQR 136, '43, 59–79; Bruce, Acts 160.—M-M.

βάρος, ους, τό (trag., Hdt.+; ins, pap, LXX [rare]; TestAbr B 11 p. 115, 22 [Stone p. 78]; EpArist 93; Philo, Joseph.) gener. 'weight, burden'; in our lit. only fig.

❶ **experience of someth. that is particularly oppressive,** ***burden*** (Diod. S. 13, 81, 3 τοῦ πολέμου; Jos., Bell. 1, 461; 4, 616) of a day's work that proves exhausting βαστάζειν τὸ β. τῆς ἡμέρας **Mt 20:12** (cp. Babrius 111, 20 βάρος διπλοῦν βαστάσας). Of temptations ἀλλήλων τὰ β. βαστάζετε **Gal 6:2.** ἀναδέχεσθαι τὸ β. τοῦ πλησίον Dg 10:6. Of the burden of a law (Polyb. 1, 31, 5 τὸ β. τῶν ἐπιταγμάτων) βάλλειν β. ἐπί τινα *impose a burden on someone* **Rv 2:24.** For this ἐπιτιθέναι τινὶ β. (X., Oec. 17, 9; Dionys. Hal. 4, 10 ἅπαν ἐπιθεὶς τ. β. τοῖς πλουσίοις; PGiss 19, 18) **Ac 15:28;** β. ἄστατον *an unweighed burden* PEg[2], 62 (s. ἄστατος).

❷ **influence that someone enjoys or claims,** ***claim of importance*** (cp. our colloq. 'throw one's weight around'. Polyb. 4, 32, 7 πρὸς τὸ β. τὸ Λακεδαιμονίων; Diod. S. 4, 61, 9; Plut., Per. 172 [37, 1]) ἐν β. εἶναι *wield authority, insist on one's importance* **1 Th 2:7.**

❸ **a high point in a scale of evaluation,** ***fullness*** (β. πλούτου Eur., El. 1287, Iph. Taur. 416; Plut., Alex. M. 692 [48, 3]; cp. 3 Macc 5:47) αἰώνιον β. δόξης *an everlasting fullness of glory* 2 Cor 4:17 (the thing being evaluated is viewed as an accumulated mass that promotes pleasure instead of discomfort [in wordplay, cp. βαρούμενοι 2 Cor 5:4]; s. Rtzst., Mysterienrel.[3] 355).—DELG s.v. βαρύς. M-M. TW.

Βαρσα(β)βᾶς, ᾶ, ὁ (Βαρσαβᾶς t.r. [so Aa I 108, 13]; Βαρζάβας AcPl Ha 11, 10–11; בַּר סָאבָא or בַּר שְׁבָא) ***Barsabbas*** (Diod. S. 32, 15, 7 as the name of a king of the Thracians, but with only one β.; PBenoit et al., Discoveries in the Judean Desert, II, '61, 25, 5 [133 AD]).

❶ patronymic of a certain Joseph, surnamed Justus, a member of the earliest Christian community **Ac 1:23;** Pa. (2:9; 11:2); name used for a servant of Nero AcPl Ha 11, 10; s. index of names Aa I 298.

❷ patronymic of a certain Judas who, with Silas, was appointed by the Jerusalem apostles as a companion of Paul and Barnabas when they returned to Antioch fr. the meeting described **Ac 15:22.** (On the name and spelling s. Dalman, Gramm.[2] 180; Cadbury, Harris Festschr. [s. Βαρναβᾶς] 48–50.)—M-M.

Βαρτιμαῖος, ου, ὁ (בַּר טִמַּי, s. Billerb. II 25; Βαρτειμίας D it) ***Bartimaeus,*** name of a blind man **Mk 10:46,** where ὁ υἱὸς Τιμαίου explains Βαρτιμαῖος. *Timai* (cp. LXX; Jos., C. Ap. 1, 16; 221) may be an abbreviation, perh. of Timotheus (Wlh. ad loc.).—EbNestle, Marginalien u. Materialien 1893, 83–92: D. blinde Bettler B., Mk 10:46.

βαρύνω 1 aor. ἐβάρυνα. Pass.: fut. βαρυνθήσομαι LXX; aor. ἐβαρύνθην LXX; pf. 3 sg. βεβάρυνται Na 2:10 (s. βαρύς; Hom.+; OGI 669, 5 and 18; PTebt 23, 5 [c. 115 BC]; POxy 298, 26; BGU 1563, 7 [both I AD]; PHamb 87, 10; PSI 1406, 9f [both II AD]; LXX; En 103:11; PsSol 2:22; 5:6; Philo, Exs. 154; Jos., Bell. 4, 171, Ant. 6, 32; SibOr 3, 462) **to cause pressure through someth. weighty,** ***burden, weigh down*** τ. δίκαιον **Ac 3:14** D. β. δεσμοῖς *weigh down w. chains* 2 Cl 20:4.—**Ac 28:27 v.l.; 2 Cor 5:4 v.l.; Lk 21:34 v.l.**—DELG s.v. βαρύς. M-M. TW.

βαρύς, εῖα, ύ (s. βαρύνω; Hom.+; LXX, TestSol; TestJud 7:1; JosAs; ParJer 5:9; Philo; Joseph.; Just., D. 86, 6; Mel., P. 95, 728 [B]; Ath., R. 72, 23) gener. 'heavy', in our lit. in imagery and metaphors pert. esp. to things or pers. that are burdensome because of demands or threats.

❶ **pert. to being relatively weighty,** ***heavy,*** regulations, rules, and legal matters φορτία βαρέα (Ps 37:5 the psalmist's sins likened to a heavy burden) *heavy burdens* metaph. (Procop. Soph., Ep. 141 β. φορτίον; cp. Jos., Ant. 19, 362) of the law **Mt 23:4;** *in a deep sleep* **Ac 20:9** D. In these pass. the component of heaviness resident in the object depicted dominates, but the statements as a whole are metaphorical.

❷ **pert. to being a source of difficulty or trouble because of demands made.**—ⓐ in criticism of Paul's letters ἐπιστολαί ***severe*** **2 Cor 10:10** (w. ἰσχυρός, q.v. 2).—In a negation of unbearableness or difficulty in compliance (for an evaluation of demands s. Polyb. 1, 31, 7; Philo, Mos. 1, 37) *not difficult to carry out* ἐντολαὶ αὐτοῦ β. οὐκ εἰσίν **1J 5:3** (cp. Philo, Spec. Leg. 1, 299 αἰτεῖται ὁ θεὸς οὐδὲν βαρύ).

ⓑ ***burdensome, troublesome*** (Dio Chrys. 26 [43], 7 οὐδὲν οὐδενὶ βαρύς εἰμι; Appian, Samn. 5β. εἶναί τινι; Wsd 2:14; 17:20) β. γίνεσθαί τινι *become a burden to someone* IRo 4:2 (if Ignatius becomes a meal for lions he will not be a burden to his survivors).

❸ **pert. to being important because of unusual significance.** In positive affirmation of certain legal directives ***weighty, important*** (Herodian 2, 14, 3; Jos., Ant. 19, 362 of administrative responsibilities) τὰ βαρύτερα τοῦ νόμου *the more important provisions of the law* **Mt 23:23.**—Of serious *charges* αἰτιώματα **Ac 25:7** (cp. Synes., Ep. 69 p. 217d ἁμαρτίαι β.).

❹ **pert. to being of unbearable temperament,** ***fierce, cruel, savage*** (Il. 1, 89; X., Ages. 11, 12 ἀνταγωνιστὴς β.; 3 Macc 6:5;

Philo, Agr. 120 β. ἐχθροί; Jos., Ant. 15, 354) of arrogant leaders likened to wolves who prey on sheep λύκοι β. **Ac 20:29.**—B. 1072. DELG. M-M. TW. Spicq.

βαρύτιμος, ον (βαρύς, τιμή) **pert. to being of great value,** ***very expensive, very precious*** (in this sense Strabo 17, 1, 13; Cyranides p. 12, 9) of ointments (Peripl. Eryth. 49 μύρον οὐ β.) **Mt 26:7** (s. πολύτιμος).

βασανίζω impf. ἐβασάνιζον; fut. 3 sg. βασανίσει Sir 4:19 and βασανιεῖ 2 Macc 7:17; 1 aor. ἐβασάνισα. Pass.: 1 fut. βασανισθήσομαι; 1 aor. pass. ἐβασανίσθην (s. βάσανος; PreSocr.+) prim. 'put to a test, prove'.

❶ **to subject to punitive judicial procedure,** ***torture*** (Thu. 8, 92, 2; Chariton 4, 3, 2; BGU 1847, 16; PAnt 87, 13; 2 Macc 7:13; 4 Macc 6:5 al.; Jos., Ant. 2, 105; 16, 232) MPol 2:2; used on slaves (Antiphon 2, 4, 8; POxy 903, 10) 6:1.

❷ **to subject to severe distress,** ***torment, harass***—ⓐ ***harass*** (Maximus Tyr. 11, 2a βασανίζειν τὸν χρυσὸν ἐν πυρί =torture the gold with fire [in the smelting process]) πλοῖον βασανιζόμενον ὑπὸ τῶν κυμάτων *a boat harassed by the waves* **Mt 14:24;** cp. **Mk 6:48** *they had rough going in the waves* or *they were straining (at the oars?) to make headway.* Synon. τυμπανίζω. In these pass. the lit. component dominates, in b and c the metaphorical.

ⓑ mostly physical: in diseases (Lucian, Soloec. 6 censures this use; Jos., Ant. 9, 101; 12, 413; POxyHels 46, 19 [I/II AD]) **Mt 8:6.** Of birth-pangs (Anth. Pal. 9, 311 βάσανος has this mng.) **Rv 12:2.** Of Jesus as threat to evil spirits ἦλθες βασανίσαι ἡμᾶς; **Mt 8:29;** cp. **Mk 5:7; Lk 8:28.** Of prophetic testimony as source of annoyance **Rv 11:10.—9:5; 14:10; 20:10;** GPt 4:14; Hv 3, 7, 6; s 6, 4, 1f; 4; 6, 5, 3f; 6.

ⓒ essentially affective IEph 8:1; ἑαυτόν *torment oneself* Hs 9, 9, 3 (Epict. 2, 22, 35; Philo, Deus Imm. 102). For this τὴν ἑαυτοῦ ψυχήν (TestAsh 6:5 ἡ ψυχὴ βασανίζεται) m 4, 2, 2 (w. ταπεινοῦν); ψυχὴν δικαίαν ἀνόμοις ἔργοις ἐβασάνιζεν (Lot) *felt his upright soul tormented by the lawless deeds* (of the Sodomites) **2 Pt 2:8** (s. Harnack, Beitr. VII 1916, 105f).—M-M. DELG s.v. βάσανος. TW.

βασανισμός, οῦ, ὁ (s. βασανίζω; Alexis Com. 290 [in Athen. 1, 56 p. 30f]; 4 Macc 9:6; 11:2)

❶ **infliction of severe suffering or pain associated with torture or torment,** ***tormenting, torture*** **Rv 9:5b.—**❷ **the severe pain experienced through torture,** ***torment*** **vs. 5a; 14:11; 18:10, 15;** (w. πένθος) **vs. 7.** Synon. βάσανος.—TW.

βασανιστής, οῦ, ὁ (since Antiphon and Demosth. 37, 40, also Plut., Mor. 498d; TestAbr AB; Philo, Spec. Leg. 4, 82, Omn. Prob. Lib. 108, In Flacc. 96) **guard in a prison, freq. under orders to torture prisoners,** ***oppressive jailer,*** **Mt 18:34** someth. like *merciless jailer* seems to be required. In the background may be the image of a wealthy estate owner who would have a detention center for recalcitrant slaves (SEG VIII, 246, 8 [II AD] uses βασανίζω of the treatment of a debtor fr. whom everything possible is to be exacted); MPol 2:3; ἄγγελοι β. *avenging angels* ApcPt 8, 23.—DELG s.v. βάσανος. TW.

βάσανος, ου, ἡ (Theognis, Pind.+, orig. 'touchstone, test', then of procedures or 'torment' used to extract a confession; ins, pap, LXX, En; TestSol 1:3; Philo; Jos., Ant. 12, 255; 13, 241; Just.)

❶ **severe pain occasioned by punitive torture,** ***torture, torment*** (Herodas 2, 88 and Diod. S, 15, 58, 2 of torture ordered by a court to extort a confession; SIG 780, 12; PLille 29 I, 22; LXX, esp. oft. 4 Macc; Philo, De Jos. 86; Jos., Bell. 1, 635; Ant. 16, 245) MPol 2:3, 4; Ox 840, 7. Of the tortures in the nether world (cp. Wsd 3:1; 4 Macc 13:15) and as synon. of 'unquenchable fire' 2 Cl 17:7b; ὑπάρχειν ἐν β. *be in torment* **Lk 16:23.** Descriptive of place in the nether world τόπος τῆς β. *place of torment* vs. **28.** Cp. 2 Cl 10:4.—Of persecutions of Christians 1 Cl 6:1; 2 Cl 17:7a.—Cp. Hv 3, 7, 6; s 6, 3, 4; 6, 4, 3f; 6, 5, 1; 3; 7.

❷ gener. **severe pain caused by someth. oppressive,** ***severe pain, torment*** (w. νόσοι; cp. Sext. Emp., Eth. 153 [Adv. Math. 11, 153]; 1 Macc 9:56; Philo, Abr. 96) **Mt 4:24.**—Papias (3:3).—PduBois, Torture and Truth 1991. B. 1115. DELG. M-M. TW.

βασιλεία, ας, ἡ (Heraclit. fgm. 52; Hdt.+) a term relating to royal administration

❶ **the act of ruling—**ⓐ gener. ***kingship, royal power, royal rule*** (1 Km 15:28; 20:31; Sir 10:8; Jdth 1:1; Esth 3:6; 1 Macc 1:16 al. LXX; En 98:2; TestJob 33:9; Just., Tat., Ath.; οὐ βασιλείαν ἀλλὰ τυράνιδα Mel., P. 49, 354; Orig.) λαβεῖν ἑαυτῷ βασιλείαν *obtain royal power (for oneself)* **Lk 19:12, 15;** without dat. **Rv 17:12** (cp. Jos., Ant. 13, 220); δοῦναί τινι τὴν β. vs. **17;** ἔχειν β. ἐπί τινων vs. **18;** ἐποίησεν ἡμᾶς βασιλείαν *he gave us royal jurisdiction* **1:6;** cp. **5:10;** *royal rule* **Lk 1:33; 22:29; 23:42 v.l.** (ἐν τῇ β. σου *in your royal power*); **Ac 1:6; Hb 1:8** (Ps 44:7); **1 Cor 15:24** (παραδιδόναι as Diod. S. 1, 43, 6); B 4:4 (Da 7:24). Ps 95:10 (Justin, A I, 41, 4, D. 73: ὁ κύριος ἐβασίλευσεν ἀπὸ τ. ξύλου) is the basis for β. Ἰησοῦ ἐπὶ ξύλου *the rule of Jesus on the cross* B 8:5 (s. Windisch, Hdb. ad loc.).—**Hb 11:33;** 1 Cl 61:1.

ⓑ esp. of God's rule ***the royal reign*** of God (usually rendered 'kingdom of God', and oft. understood as royal realm but with dilution of the primary component of reigning activity), a chiefly eschatological concept, beginning to appear in the prophets, elaborated in apocalyptic passages (Mi 4:7f; Ps 102:19; 144:11–13; Wsd 6:4; 10:10; Da 3:54; 4:3; cp. SibOr 3:47f.—Diod. S. 5, 71, 1 Zeus takes over the βασιλεία from Cronus; Sextus 311 κοινωνεῖ βασιλείας θεοῦ σοφὸς ἀνήρ) and taught by Jesus. The expressions vary; β. τοῦ θεοῦ and τῶν οὐρανῶν have essentially the same mng., since Israelites used οὐρανός (-οί) as well as other circumlocutions for θεός (cp. **Mt 19:23f;** s. Bousset, Rel.[3] 314f); the latter term may also emphasize the heavenly origin and nature of the reign.—Dalman, Worte 75–119; JWeiss, D. Predigt Jesu v. Reiche Gottes[2] 1900, 1–35; ESellin, D. isr.-jüd. Heilandserwartung 1909, D. alt. Prophetismus 1912, 136ff; BDuhm, D. kommende RG 1910; SMowinckel, Psalmenstudien II 1922, 146ff; LDürr, Ursprung u. Ausbau d. isr. Heilandserwartung 1925; Bousset, Rel[3] 1926, 213ff; AvGall, βασιλεία τ. θεοῦ 1926; JWissing, Het begrip van het Koningrijk Gods, diss., Leiden 1927; HGressmann, Der Messias 1929; MBuber, Königtum Gottes '32; PVolz, D. Eschatologie der jüd. Gemeinde im ntl. Zeitalter '34; Ltzm., D. Weltheiland 1909; TManson, The Teaching of Jesus '55, 116–284; SAalen, NTS 8, '61/62, 215–40 ('house' or 'community' of God); GLadd, JBL 81, '62, 230–38 ('realm'); FNötscher, Vom A. zum NT '62, 226–30 (ethical).

α. β. τῶν οὐρανῶν mostly in **Mt: 3:2; 4:17; 5:3, 10, 19f** al.; otherw. (Did., Gen. 52, 11; 60, 28) **J 3:5 v.l.;** AcPl Ha 8, 31.

β. β. τοῦ θεοῦ (cp. Orig., C. Cels. 3, 40, 21) **Mt 6:33; 12:28; 21:31, 43; Mk 1:15; 4:11, 26, 30** al.; **Lk 4:43; 6:20; 7:28; 8:1** al.; **Ac 1:3; 8:12; 14:22; 19:8; 28:23, 31; J 3:3, 5; Ro 14:17** (defined as δικαιοσύνη, εἰρήνη, χαρά); **1 Cor 4:20** al.; Ox 1 verso, 7f; Dg 9:1; B 21:1; Pol 2:3; β. θεοῦ **1 Cor 6:10,** cp. **9; 15:50; Gal 5:21;** Pol 5:3; β. τοῦ Χριστοῦ καὶ θεοῦ **Eph 5:5;** τοῦ Χριστοῦ 1 Cl 50:3.

γ. β. τοῦ πατρός **Mt 13:43; 26:29.—δ.** β. αὐτοῦ (=τοῦ υἱοῦ τοῦ ἀνθρώπου) **Mt 13:41; Lk 24:26 v.l.;** cp. **Col 1:13.**

ε. β. τοῦ πατρὸς ἡμῶν Δαυίδ **Mk 11:10,** since the Davidic kgdm. is to be reestablished under the Son of David, the Messiah (cp. Is 9:5f; Jer 23:5f).

ζ. ἡ β. τοῦ κυρίου B 4:13; ἡ β. αὐτοῦ (=κυρίου) ἡ ἐπουράνιος **2 Ti 4:18;** EpilMosq 5; ἡ οὐράνιος β. MPol 22:3; ἡ ἐν οὐρανῷ β. Dg 10:2.

η. αἰώνιος β. τοῦ κυρίου (cp. Da 4:3; Just.; CIG II, 2715a, 3 ἐπὶ τῆς τῶν κυρίων Ῥωμαίων αἰωνίου ἀρχῆς, Dssm., B 277f) **2 Pt 1:11;** cp. MPol 20:2.—The greatest blessings conceivable are found in the β. **Mt 13:44f.** The foll. expr. refer to obtaining it = participate in its benefits: ἅψασθαι τῆς β. B 7:11; δέχεσθαι **Mk 10:15;** διδόναι **Lk 12:32;** εἰσέρχεσθαι εἰς τὴν β. **Mt 5:20; 7:21; 18:3; 19:23; Mk 10:23ff; Lk 24:26** P[75] (first hand); **J 3:5; Ac 14:22;** Hs 9, 12, 3f (HWindisch, D. Sprüche v. Eingehen in d. Reich Gs: ZNW 27, 1928, 163–92); εἰσήκειν εἰς τὴν β. 2 Cl 11:7; ἔρχεσθαι εἰς τὴν β. 9:6; ἑτοιμάζειν **Mt 25:34;** εὔθετον εἶναι τῇ β. **Lk 9:62;** εὑρεθῆναι εἰς τὴν β. Hs 9, 13, 2; ζητεῖν **Mt 6:33; Lk 12:31;** καταξιοῦσθαι τῆς β. **2 Th 1:5;** κατοικεῖν ἐν τῇ β. Hs 9, 29, 2; κληρονομεῖν **Mt 25:34; 1 Cor 6:9f; 15:50;** IPhld 3:3; cp. κληρονόμος τῆς β. **Js 2:5;** μαθητεύεσθαι τῇ β. **Mt 13:52;** μεθιστάναι εἰς τὴν β. **Col 1:13;** φθάνει ἡ β. ἐπί τινα **Lk 11:20.** The phrase ὁρᾶν τὴν β. *see the kgdm.*='realize the fulfillment of God's promises to Israel' occurs **Mk 9:1; Lk 9:27; J 3:3;** Hs 9, 15, 3. The mysteries of the kgdm. can be revealed to those for whom they are intended **Mt 13:11; Mk 4:11;** διαγγέλλειν **Lk 9:60;** διαμαρτυρεῖσθαι **Ac 28:23;** κηρύσσειν καὶ εὐαγγελίζεσθαι **Lk 8:1;** sim. **16:16;** cp. κηρύσσειν τὸ εὐαγγέλιον τῆς β. **Mt 4:23; 9:35; 24:14;** κηρύσσειν τὴν β. **Lk 9:2; Ac 28:31;** λαλεῖν περὶ τῆς β. **Lk 9:11.** Keep fr. entering: κλείειν **Mt 23:13;** cp. κλεῖδες τῆς β. **16:19** (s. κλεῖς 1); αἴρειν ἀπό τινος **21:43.**—Spoken of as present **Mt 12:28; Lk 11:20,** perh. also **17:20f** (see s.v. ἐντός). Viewed as future, but close at hand ἤγγικεν ἡ β. **Mt 3:2; 10:7; Mk 1:15; Lk 10:9, 11;** perh. **Mk 1:15;** ἐγγύς ἐστιν **Lk 21:31;** ἔρχεται **Mt 6:10; Mk 11:10; Lk 11:2; 17:20;** μέλλει ἀναφαίνεσθαι **19:11;** προσδέχεσθαι τὴν β. **Mk 15:43;** ἐκδέχεσθαι τὴν β. 2 Cl 12:1; μέλλει ἔρχεσθαι 1 Cl 42:3; ἡ μέλλουσα β. 2 Cl 5:5; ἥξει ἡ β. 12:2. Conceived of as a banquet (Billerb. IV 1154ff): ἀνακλιθῆναι ἐν τῇ β. **Mt 8:11;** sim. **26:29; Mk 14:25; Lk 13:28f; 22:16, 18, 30;** cp. the parables **14:15ff; Mt 22:2ff.** Participants in it are called υἱοὶ τῆς β. **Mt 8:12** (of mere external connection); **13:38.** Prerequisite for participation is μετάνοια **Mt 4:17; Mk 1:15;** the willingness to become like children **Mt 18:3f; 19:14; Mk 10:14f; Lk 18:16f.** Only uprightness will inherit the β. **Mt 5:20.** Degrees and grades **5:19; 18:1, 4.** The prosperous have difficulty entering **19:23f; Mk 10:23–25; Lk 18:24f** (cp. vs. 29), those who persist in sin have no prospects at all **Mt 13:24ff, 36ff, 47ff.**—Paul thinks of the β. as someth. that effects changes in pers. resulting in righteousness, peace (w. God) and joy **Ro 14:17.** It manifests itself in deeds, not in words **1 Cor 4:20.** Those committed to sin will not inherit it **6:9f; Gal 5:21; Eph 5:5** (cp. 2 Cl 9:6); the latter passages show that for Paul the kgdm. is essentially future, since Christians await the complete victory of the spirit over the flesh. Cp. also **2 Ti 4:1.** Flesh and blood will not inherit it, i.e. bodies under the direction of the spirit of Christ are required for entrance **1 Cor 15:50** (JJeremias, NTS 2, '56, 151–59). None other than God calls people into it **1 Th 2:12.**—HJWesterink, Het Koninkrijk Gods bij Pls '37.—The most important lit. to 1931 in PFeine, Theol. d. NTs[7] '36, 73. Additional lit.: GGloege, Reich Gs u. Kirche im NT 1929; RFrick, D. Gesch. des R.-Gs-Gedankens in d. alten Kirche 1929; EScott, The Kgdm. of God in the NT '31; H-DWendland, Reichsidee u. Gottesreich '34; ROtto, Reich Gottes u. Menschensohn '34 (Eng. tr., The Kgdm. of God and the Son of Man, tr. Filson and Woolf, '43 and '51); TW I 562–95; WKümmel, D. Eschatologie der Evangelien '36, Verheissg. u. Erfüllg. '45 and '53; JHéring, Le Royaume de Dieu et sa Venue (Jesus, Paul) '38 and '59; JTheissing, D. Lehre Jesu v. d. ew. Seligkeit '40; FGrant, The Gospel of the Kgdm. '40; JWellhagen, Anden och Riket '41 (Lk); WMichaelis, D. Herr verzieht nicht d. Verheissung '42; RLiechtenhan, D. Kommen des RGs nach dem NT '44; GKnight, From Moses to Paul, '49, 173–87; WArndt, CTM 21, '50, 8–29; JBright, The Kgdm. of God: The Biblical Concept and Its Mng. for the Church '53; RSchnackenburg, Gottes Herrschaft u. Reich,[4] '65, tr. JMurray,[2] '68; ELadd, Jesus and the Kgdm., '64; NPerrin, The Kgdm. of God in the Teaching of Jesus, '66; MWolter, NTS 41, '95, 541–63 [Lk].—OT background: WSchmidt, Königtum Gottes in Ugarit u. Israel, '61; KBernhardt, D. Problem der altorientalischen Königs-Ideologie im AT, VetusT suppl. 8, '61.—Patristics: GLampe, JTS 49, '48, 58–73.

❷ **territory ruled by a king,** ***kingdom*** (Diod. S. 4, 68, 4; Appian, Mithrid. 105 §496 ἡ βασ. ὅλη=the whole kingdom; OGI 383, 25 [I BC]; Ps 67:33; 134:11; Bar 2:4; Tob 1:21; 1 Macc 1:6; 3:27; 2 Macc 9:25; 3 Macc 6:24 al. LXX) **Mt 12:25f; 24:7; Mk 3:24; 6:23** (Socrat., Ep. 1, 10 τ. βασιλείας μέρος διδόναι); **13:8; Lk 11:17f; 21:10;** αἱ β. τοῦ αἰῶνος τούτου IRo 6:1. In the account of the temptation **Mt 4:8; Lk 4:5** (in a manner very different from Jesus, Alexander [Diod. S. 17, 51, 2] asks his father, Zeus Ammon, for τὴν ἁπάσης τῆς γῆς ἀρχήν and finds a hearing).—EDNT. DELG s.v. βασιλεύς. M-M. TW. Spicq. Sv.

βασίλειος, ον (Hom. et al.; LXX; PsSol 17:4, 6; TestSol 5:5; TestJud) **pert. to a king,** ***royal*** (oracular saying in Diod. S. 7, 17 κράτος βασίλειον) β. ἱεράτευμα **1 Pt 2:9** (Ex 19:6; 23:22; but s. JElliott, The Elect and the Holy, '66, 149–54). Used as a noun the pl. τὰ β. (since Hdt. 1, 30, 1; also SIG 495, 45; PSI 488, 11; PColZen 39, 8; PCairZen 664, 1; 758, 7 [all III BC]; PGM 2, 181; 4, 1061–62; Esth 1:9; Philo, In Flacc. 92; Jos., Ant. 13, 138) and more rarely the sg. τὸ β. (X., Cyr. 2, 4, 3; Pr 18:19; PsSol ['royal majesty', sim. TestSol, TestJud]; Philo, Sobr. 66; Jos., Ant. 6, 251) means *the (royal) palace* **Lk 7:25.**—In 2 Cl τὸ β. = ἡ βασιλεία (B-D-F 50; cp. TestJud 17:6, 22f; SibOr 3, 159; Just., A I, 32, 2; D. 31, 5 [Da 7:22]; Gaius in Eus., HE 3, 28, 2.—Polyaenus 8, 55 uses the pl. τὰ βασίλεια = ἡ βασιλεία): εἰσέρχεσθαι εἰς τὸ β. τοῦ θεοῦ 6:9; ὁρᾶν τὸ β. τοῦ κόσμου 17:5.—DELG s.v. βασιλεύς. M-M. TW. Spicq.

βασιλεύς, έως, ὁ (Hom. +; loanw. in rabb.)—❶ **one who rules as possessor of the highest office in a political realm,** ***king,*** gener. of a male ruler who has unquestioned authority (exceptions are client rulers who owe their power to the grace of Rome) in a specific area ποιεῖν τινα β. *make someone king* **J 6:15.** βασιλεῖς τῆς γῆς *earthly kings* **Mt 17:25; Rv. 1:5; 6:15** (Ps 2:2; 88:28) al.; **Ac 4:26** (Ps 2:2); β. τῶν ἐθνῶν **Lk 22:25;** (w. ἡγεμόνες; cp. ἡγούμενοι ἐθνῶν καὶ β. Orig., C. Cels. 2, 32, 22) **Mt 10:18; Mk 13:9; Lk 21:12.** Of kings gener. (w. προφῆται; 2 Macc 2:13; Boll 139) **Lk 10:24.** Of Pharaoh **Ac 7:10** (Tat. 38, 1); David **Mt 1:6; Ac 13:22** (Just., A I, 35, 6); Herod I (Jos., Ant. 14, 382; 385; OGI 414, 2; 415, 1; 416, 2; 417, 3; Just., A I, 40, 6; D. 78, 1]) **Mt 2:1, 3; Lk 1:5;** Herod Antipas (not really a king [Jos., Ant. 17, 188; OGI 414, 2; 415, 1; 416, 2; 417, 3], but occasionally given that title: Cicero, Verr. 4, 27) **Mt 14:9; Mk 6:14;** GPt 1:2 (ASyn. 341, 20); Herod Agrippa I (Jos., Ant. 18, 237; 19, 274; OGI 418, 1; 419, 1; 428, 4) **Ac 12:1;** Agrippa II (Jos., Bell. 2, 223; OGI 419, 2; 423, 1; 425, 3; 426, 2) **25:13, 24, 26;** Aretas, king of the Nabataeans **2 Cor 11:32;** Melchizedek, king of Salem **Hb 7:1f** (Gen 14:18). Of the Rom. emperor (Appian, Iber. 102 §444, Bell. Civ. 2, 86 §362 Ῥωμαίων β. Ἁδριανός al.; Herodian 2, 4, 4; IG III, 12, 18; CIG II, 2721, 11; POxy 33 II, 6; 35 verso, 1; BGU 588, 10; PGM 4, 2448 Ἁδριανὸς β.; 2452; Jos., Bell. 3, 351; 4, 596; 5, 563, Vi. 34; Magie 62; βασιλεῦ Ar. 1, 1 al. Tat. 4, 1; 19, 1; Mel., HE 4, 26, 6) **1 Ti 2:2** (the pl. is generic as Appian, Prooem. 15 §62; Jos., Ant. 2, 71; PEg[2] 48; on the topic s. LBiehl, D. liturg. Gebet für Kaiser u. Reich '37); **1 Pt 2:13, 17** (s. Pr 24:21 and esp. Vi. Aesopi I c. 26 p. 288, 17 Eberh.: τέκνον, πρὸ πάντων σέβου τὸ θεῖον, τὸν βασιλέα δὲ τίμα); **Rv 17:9;** 1 Cl 37:3.

❷ **one who possesses unusual or transcendent power,** ext. of mng. 1 (Ael. Aristid. 46 p. 285 D.: β. Θεμιστοκλῆς) esp.

ⓐ of the Messianic king β. τῶν Ἰουδαίων (so Alex. Jannaeus: Jos., Ant. 14, 36; Herod 16, 311; Aristobolus: Diod. S. 40, 2) **Mt 2:2; 27:11, 29, 37; Mk 15:2, 9, 12, 18, 26; Lk 23:3, 37f; J 18:33** al.; β. (τοῦ) Ἰσραήλ **Mt 27:42; Mk 15:32; J 1:49; 12:13;** GPt 3:7 (ASyn. 341, 20); 4:11 (ASyn. 344, 74). Hence of Jesus as king of the Christians (Orig., C. Cels. 1, 61, 27; Did., Gen. 215, 10) MPol 9:3; 17:3; AcPl BMM verso 37 (difft. AcPl Ha 8, 29). He is also the κύριος referred to D 14:3, which quotes β. μέγας fr. Mal 1:14; for the latter phrase s. also AcPl Ha 9:1f (cp. 9:7). Cp. **Mt 21:5** (Zech 9:9); **25:34, 40; J 18:37** (for the judge's question: βασιλεὺς εἶ σύ; cp. Μαρτύριον Κάρπου 24, in: Musurillo, Ac. Chr. M. p. 24: βουλευτὴς εἶ;). β. βασιλέων (as 2 Macc 13:4; Philo, Spec. Leg. 1:18, Decal. 41; cp. PGM 13, 605.—Of Zeus: Dio Chrys. 2, 75) **Rv 17:14; 19:16** (GBeale, NTS 31, '85, 618–20, w. ref. to Da 4:37; in support TSlater, ibid. 39, '93, 159f); this title is still current for kings in the early Christian era (Dssm., LO 310f [LAE 367f]; Diod. S. 1, 47, 4 an ancient royal inscr. β. βασιλέων; 1, 55, 7 β. βασιλέων καὶ δεσπότης δεσποτῶν Σεσόωσις; Memnon [I BC/I AD] 434 fgm. 1, 31, 3 Jac. βασ. βασ. of Tigranes; Appian, Bell. Civ. 2, 67 §278; Ezk 26:7; Da 2:37; 2 Esdr 7:12; Mussies 96f; WHuss, Der 'König der Könige' und der 'Herr der Könige': ZDPV 93, '77, 131–40) and purposely reserved by the Christians for their Lord, in strong contrast to earthly kings (cp. Pass. Scilit. 6 p. 24 vGebh.).—B 11:5 (Is 33:17). ὁ β. τῶν οὐρανῶν AcPl Ha 7, 29.

ⓑ of God (Pla., Ep. 2, 312e ὁ πάντων βασιλεύς; Plut., Mor. 383a: ἡγεμών ἐστι κ. βασιλεὺς ὁ θεός of human souls who have entered eternal bliss) μέγας β. (SEG VIII, 32, 3 [III AD] of Zeus; Tob 13:16; Philo, Migr. Abr. 146 al.; SibOr 3, 499 and 616; of human kings since Hdt. 1, 188, 1; Jdth 2:5; 3:2; EpArist; Philo) **Mt 5:35** (cp. Ps 47:3); Hv 3, 9, 8; β. τῶν ἐθνῶν (Jer 10:7; s. ed. HSwete v.l.) **Rv 15:3;** β. τῶν αἰώνων (Tob 13:7, 11; En 9:4; cp. Ps 144:13; Ex 15:18; Jos., Ant. 1, 272 δέσποτα παντὸς αἰῶνος, also 14:24 β. τῶν ὅλων [β. τῶν ὅλων is also a designation of the god Uranus in Diod. S. 3, 56, 5]; PGM 12, 247 αἰώνων βασιλεῦ καὶ κύριε) **1 Ti 1:17; Rv 15:3 v.l.;** ἐπουράνιος β. τῶν αἰ. 1 Cl 61:2; β. τῶν βασιλευόντων **1 Ti 6:15** (as 3 Macc 5:35 v.l.; Pel.-Leg. 21, 8; 24, 21). β. τῆς δόξης AcPl BMM verso 24; 26. WGrafBaudissin, Kyrios III 1929, 70–76.

ⓒ of a king of spirits in the nether world, Abaddon **Rv 9:11.**—WSchubart, Das hell. Königsideal nach Inschr. u. Pap., APF 12, '37, 1–26; PCarlier, La royauté en Grèce avant Alexandre '84 (for summary and ins reff. s. SEG XXXIX, 1792).—B. 1321; 1324. M-M. TW. Sv.

βασιλεύω fut. βασιλεύσω; 1 aor. ἐβασίλευσα; pf. 3 sg. βεβασίλευκεν 2 Km 5:10 (Hom.+)

❶ **to exercise authority at a royal level, *be king, rule*** (B-D-F §177; 233, 2; 234, 5; Rob.: 801, 833, 902).—ⓐ of temporal princes τινός *over (of) someth.* (1 Esdr 1:37; 6:16; 1 Macc 1:16; 11:9 al.) τῆς Ἰουδαίας **Mt 2:22** of Archelaus, who was called king without having the official title (Jos., Vi. 5 βασιλεύοντος Ἀρχελάου, Ant. 17, 188ff; 317ff; 18, 93 βασιλεὺς Ἀ.); τοῦ Ἰσραήλ GJs 23:2; τῶν περάτων τῆς γῆς IRo 6:1; ἐπί τινα (Gen 37:8; 1 Km 8:9; 12:1 al.) **Lk 19:14, 27.**—βασιλεῖαι βασιλεύσουσιν ἐπὶ τ. γῆς *royal powers will reign on (the) earth* (s. ἐπί 1a) B 4:4. On βασιλεὺς τ. βασιλευόντων **1 Ti 6:15** s. βασιλεύς 2b.

ⓑ of God and those closely united w. him—**α.** God (Ps.-Phoc. 111) **Rv 11:17; 19:6** (s. 2 below for a difft. interpr. of both pass.).

β. Christ **Lk 1:33; 1 Cor 15:25;** εἰς τ. αἰῶνας MPol 21.

γ. God and Christ together: their βασιλεία ... βασιλεύσει (s. 1a above: B 4:4) εἰς τ. αἰῶνας τ. αἰώνων (cp. Ps 9:37) **Rv 11:15.**

δ. faithful Christians, who have been called to rule w. God **Ro 5:17b; Rv 5:10** (ἐπὶ τ. γῆς, as 1a above); **20:4, 6; 22:5** (cp. Da 7:27).

ⓒ fig. death **Ro 5:14** (ἐπί τινα), **17a;** sin **21a;** grace **21b;** sinful desire **6:12.**

❷ **to obtain royal power, *become king,*** so esp. in aor. (Hdt. 1, 130, 1; Thu. 2, 99, 3; Polyb. 5, 40, 6; 4 Km 14:29; 15:1, 7, 10; 1 Macc 1:10 al.) **Rv 11:17; 19:6** (for both s. 1bα above); GHb 70, 16–18; Ox 654, 8 (GTh 2). χωρὶς ἡμῶν ἐβασιλεύσατε *without us you have become kings* **1 Cor 4:8** (Appian, Basil. 1a §5 β. has the sense 'seize the rule').—DELG. M-M. TW. Spicq.

βασιλικός, ή, όν (Aeschyl., Hdt.+) ***royal*** of a king's official robe (ChronLind C 89 τὰν βασιλικὰν στολάν; Esth 8:15) ἐσθὴς β. *royal robe* (cp. Diod. S. 17, 47, 4; 17, 116, 2 and 3) **Ac 12:21** (described Jos., Ant. 19, 344). νόμος β. *royal law,* so called either because of its transcending significance (somewhat in the sense of Ps.-Pla., Minos 317c τὸ μὲν ὀρθὸν νόμος ἐστὶ βασιλικός; Epict. 4, 6, 20; Philo, Post. Cai. 101; 102; 4 Macc 14:2), or more prob. because it is given by the king (of the kingdom of God) **Js 2:8** (cp. OGI 483, 1 ὁ βασ. νόμος; BGU 820, 2; 1074, 15; 1 Esdr 8:24; 2 Macc 3:13). χώρα β. (OGI 221, 41; 68) *the king's country* **Ac 12:20.** κατὰ τὴν βασιλικὴν *on the royal road* AcPl Ant 13:20 (cp. Aa I 237, 4). τὸ κεφαλοδέσμιον ... χαρακτῆρα ἔχει βασιλικόν *the headband bears a royal mark* GJs 2:2.—The β. **J 4:46, 49** could be a relative of the royal (Herodian) family (Lucian, Dial. Deor. 20, 1; Ps.-Lucian, De Salt. 8; Plut., Mor. 546e), but more prob. the ref. is to a royal official (not necessarily a Jew: AMead, JSNT 23, '85, 69–72; perh. an 'adviser' GSchwartz, ZNW 75, 138 [Aramaic trad.]); reff. in Hdb. ad loc. Appian, Mithrid. 80 §358 οἱ βασιλικοί are soldiers of King Mithridates.—DELG s.v. βασιλεύς. M-M. TW. Spicq. Sv.

βασιλίσκος, ου, ὁ (Polyb. 3, 44, 5; Plut., Mor. 1d v.l.; Athen. 13, 20 p. 566b; OGI 200, 18; POxy 1566, 9; Sb 6949, 18 and 28; TestAbr A) dim. of βασιλεύς ***petty king,*** v.l. in **J 4:46** and **49.**—DELG s.v. βασιλεύς.

βασίλισσα, ης, ἡ (for Attic βασιλίς [τῇ βασιλίδι Ῥώμῃ Just., A I, 26, 2; 56, 2] and βασίλεια [Phryn. p. 225 Lob.; Moeris 192], first in Alcaeus Comicus [V/IV BC] 6 and X., Oec. 9, 15, later freq., incl. ins [SIG and OGI index; Meisterhans-Schw. 101, 5; Schweizer, 140; Nachmanson 121]; pap [Mayser 214; 222; 255]; APF 2, 1903, 541; 6, 1920, 453; LXX, TestSol, JosAs; EpArist 41; Philo, Congr. Erud. Gr. 45; Jos., Bell. 1, 76, Ant. 11, 190 al.; Tat. 33, 3) **a female ruler within a specific area and with authority to pass her ruling power on to a successor, *queen*** **Mt 12:42; Lk 11:31** (TestSol 19:3; 21:1); **Ac 8:27; Rv 18:7.**—DELG s.v. βασιλεύς. M-M. TW.

βάσις, εως, ἡ (s. βαίνω; Aeschyl. et al.; ins; pap [PGM 7, 518]; LXX, TestSol, EpArist, Philo, Joseph.; SibOr 5, 54; loanw. in rabb.) in various senses relating to 'step' but in our lit. **that with which one steps, usually of the area below the ankle, *foot*** (so since Pla., Tim. 92a; Diod. S. 3, 28, 2; medical use in Hobart 34f; Philo, Op. M. 118 διτταὶ χεῖρες διτταὶ βάσεις, Post. Cai. 3; Jos., Ant. 7, 113; 303 [w. χεῖρες]; Wsd 13:18) αἱ β. **Ac 3:7.**—Synon. πούς.—DELG s.v. βαίνω p. 156. M-M.

βασκαίνω fut. 3 sg. βασκανεῖ Dt 28:56; 1 aor. ἐβάσκανα, s. B-D-F §72 (s. two next entries; IG XII/7, 106 [VI BC]; Euphorion [?] fgm. 175, 2 Coll. Alex. p. 58; Aristot. et al.; LXX; TestSol 18:39 [cp. PVindobBosw 18, 39 [β]ασκένω]).

➊ **to exert an evil influence through the eye, *bewitch,*** as with the 'evil eye' τινά *someone* (Aristot., Probl. 34, 20 [926b, 24] με; Diod. S. 4, 6, 4; Alex. Aphr., Probl. 2, 53 παῖδας; Dt 28:56; TestSol 18:39) prob. metaph. Gal 3:1 (one can ward off βασκανία by spitting 3 times ὡς μὴ βασκανθῶ τρὶς ἔπτυσα: Theocr. 6, 39; s. ἐκπτύω Gal 4:14; πτύω Mk 8:23). Cp. the adj. ἀβάσκαντος POxy 3312, 3.—For lit. on the 'evil eye' s. JHElliott, Biblical Interpretation 2/1, '94, 80–84; add SEitrem, SymbOsl 7, 1928, 73 n. 5 (lit.); MDickie, Heliodorus and Plutarch on the Evil Eye: ClPh 86, '91, 17–29; idem, Glotta 71, '93, 174–77.

➋ **to be resentful of someth. enjoyed by another, *envy*** (Demosth. 20, 24; Theocr. 5, 13; Jos., Vi. 425, C. Ap. 1, 2) τινί (Demosth. 20, 24) or τινά *somebody* (Demosth. 8, 19; Dt 28:54, 56; Sir 14:6, 8) οὐδέποτε ἐβασκάνατε οὐδένι *you have never grudged anyone* (the opportunity of witnessing to the death) IRo 3:1.—On assoc. of envy and the evil eye s. Elliott (1 above), The Fear of the Leer, the Evil Eye from the Bible to Li'l Abner: Forum 4/4, '88, 42–71. B. 1495. M-M. (Lat. fascinum). TW. Spicq.

βασκανία, ας, ἡ (s. βασκαίνω Pla., Demosth. et al.) ***envy*** (Dio Chrys. 28 [45], 5; Vi. Aesopi W 16 P.; 4 Macc 1:26; 2:15; TestIss 4:5; Philo; Jos., Ant. 3, 268) IRo 7:2.—Welles p. 321. M-M s.v. βασκαίνω.

βάσκανος, ου, ὁ (s. two preceding entries; both noun and adj. Demosth. et al.; ins reff. SEG XLI, 1526. Philo, In Flacc. 29; Jos., Ant. 6, 59; TestIss 3:3; 4:5 v.l.; Mel., HE 4, 26, 9) ***envious one*** (as noun e.g. Demosth. 18, 132; Menand., Per. 529 S.=279 Kö.; on a clay figure Sb 6295; Vett. Val. 2, 2; 358, 5; Sir 18:18; 37:11; Jos., Bell. 1, 208) w. ἀντίζηλος, πονηρός MPol 17:1.—S. φθόνος. DELG. Sv.

Βάσσος, ου, ὁ ***Bassus,*** a congregation leader in Magnesia IMg 2. The name is not rare in W. Asia Minor (CIG II, 3112b, 1; 3148, 4; 3151, 13; 3493, 23; IPergamon 361; 362, 2 and oft.) and found specif. in Magnesia (IMagnMai122g, 5; coins ibid. p. xxiv).

βαστάζω fut. βαστάσω; 1 aor. ἐβάστασα (-ξα Sir 6:25, AcPl Ha 8, 4; cp. Sir 6:25; B-D-F §71) (Hom.+) in all senses with suggestion of a burden involved.

➊ **to cause to come to a higher position, *pick up, take up*** (Jos., Ant. 7, 284 β. τ. μάχαιραν ἀπὸ τ. γῆς) stones **J 10:31** (cp. 8:59).

➋ **to sustain a burden, *carry, bear*—ⓐ** a physical object Hs 9, 2, 4; AcPl Ha 8, 4; a jar of water **Mk 14:13; Lk 22:10;** a bier **7:14,** cp. 1 Cl 25:3; stones Hs 9, 3, 4f; 9, 4, 1 (abs.); 3; 9, 6, 7; *support:* heaven 9, 2, 5; πύργον 9, 4, 2; κόσμον 9, 14, 5.—A cross **J 19:17** (Chariton 4, 2, 7; 4, 3, 10 σταυρὸν ἐβάστασα; Artem. 2, 56 σταυρὸν β.); of drugs used for magical purposes φάρμακα εἰς τὰς πυξίδας β. *carry drugs in boxes* Hv 3, 9, 7; of animals used for riding **Rv 17:7** (cp. Epict. 2, 8, 7). Pass. Hv 3, 8, 2; s 9, 4, 3; 9, 6, 7; 9, 14, 5 (see 9, 24, 6 for interpretation: those who joyfully bear the name of the Son of God are *borne* by him). Of pers. who are carried **Ac 3:2; 21:35;** GJs 20:3 (not pap).—Esp. of pregnant women: ἡ κοιλία ἡ βαστάσασά σε **Lk 11:27.—10:4; Ro 11:18;** B 7:8.—The meaning AcPl Ha 2, 4 is unclear because of the fragmentary context.

ⓑ fig. ext. of 2a—α. of bearing anything burdensome (4 Km 18:14; Sir 6:25): a cross (following Jesus in his suffering) **Lk 14:27;** legal requirements **Ac 15:10** (JNolland, NTS 27, '80, 113–15); ζυγὸν τοῦ κυρίου Christian conduct D 6:2.—ἀλλήλων τὰ βάρη βαστάζετε, **Gal 6:2;** cp. vs. **5.**

β. be able to bear up under especially trying or oppressive circumstances *bear, endure* (Epict. 1, 3, 2, Ench. 29, 5; Aesop, Fab. 391 P. misfortune and trouble; PBrem 36, 8f [Mitt-Wilck. I/2, 352] οὐ βαστάζουσι τοσοῦτο τέλεσμα; Job 21:3 v.l.) the burden and heat of the day **Mt 20:12;** κακούς **Rv 2:2.** δύνασθαι β. *be able to bear* words, of divine mysteries **J 16:12;** Hv 1, 3, 3; *bear patiently, put up with:* weaknesses of the weak **Ro 15:1;** cp. IPol 1:2; evil **Rv 2:3;** κρίμα *bear one's judgment* = must pay the penalty **Gal 5:10.** ὃ δύνασαι βάστασον *tolerate* or *accept* what you can D 6:3 (counsel respecting restrictions about food, followed by caution against eating food offered in a polytheistic setting).

ⓒ without the idea of outward or inward stress *carry, bear,* marks **Gal 6:17** (s. Dssm. B 265ff [BS 352ff]); the name (message) of Jesus β. τὸ ὄνομά μου ἐνώπιον ἐθνῶν **Ac 9:15** (cp. POxy 1242 I, 17, where Alexandrian Gentiles and Jews appear before Trajan ἕκαστοι βαστάζοντες τ. ἰδίους θεούς); Hs 8, 10, 3; 9, 28, 5.

➌ **to carry someth. (freq. burdensome) from a place, *carry away, remove*** (PFay 122, 6 [c. 100 AD]; Bel 36 Theod.).

ⓐ without moral implication, a corpse (Jos., Ant. 3, 210; 7, 287; POxy 2341, 8) **J 20:15.** Of sandals *remove* **Mt 3:11** (cp. PGM 4, 1058 βαστάξας τὸ στεφάνιον ἀπὸ τ. κεφαλῆς; NKrieger, Barfuss Busse Tun, NovT 1, '56, 227f). Of disease *remove* (Galen, De Compos. Medic. Per. Gen. 2, 14, citing a 1st cent. physician Asklepiades ψώρας τε θεραπεύει καὶ ὑπώπια βαστάζει; s. also Rydbeck, Fachprosa, '67, 155f) **Mt 8:17;** IPol 1:3 (unless this pass. is to be understood in the sense of 2bα).

ⓑ with moral implication *take surreptitiously, pilfer, steal* (Polyb. 32, 15, 4; Diog. L. 4, 59; Jos., Ant. 1, 316; 7, 393; PTebt 330, 7; BGU 46, 10; 157, 8; PFay 108, 16; POxy 69, 4) **J 12:6.**—B. 707. DELG. M-M. TW.

I. βάτος, ου, ἡ, ὁ (acc. to Moeris 99 the fem. is Hellenistic [Just., D. 60, 3; 127, 4; 128, 1], and ὁ βάτος, as in **Mk 12:26,** Ex 3:2–4 [Just., D. 60, 4] and Philo, Mos. 1, 67 is Attic, but Thackeray, and PKatz in ZNW 46, '55, 136 with n. 8a [s. B-D-F §49, 1] show that the reverse is true.—Hom. et al.; Kaibel 546, 6; 548, 2; LXX; Just.) a spiny or thorny shrub of the genus 'Rubus' ***thorn-bush,*** of the bush in which Moses saw a vision of God (Ex 3:2–4; cp. Dt 33:16; Jos., Ant. 2, 266) **Mk 12:26** (ὁ); ἐπὶ τ. βάτου *in the passage about the thorn-bush* **Lk 20:37** (ἡ); **Ac 7:30, 35** (ἡ), s. Zohary 140f; 1 Cl 17:5 (ἡ). Symbol of unfruitfulness **Lk 6:44** (cp. Job 31:40). Zohary 140f identifies the bush of Moses as 'Cassia senna', a shrub that grows up to 1 m. high w. a thick foliage of pinnate leaves—DELG. M-M. TW.

II. βάτος, ου, ὁ a Hebr. liquid measure 'bath', *jug* (Hb. loanw. בַּת; cp. 2 Esdr 7:22; En 10:19) acc. to Jos., Ant. 8, 57 β.=72 sextarii, or c. 34 liters (FHultsch, Griech. u. röm. Metrologie^2 1882, 488:36, 371; OViedebannt, Forschungen z. Metrologie d. Altertums 1917, 127ff: 32, 61) **Lk 16:6** (vv.ll.: βάδος, κάδος κάβος).—DELG. M-M.

βάτραχος, ου, ὁ (Batr., Hdt. et al.; PGM 36, 324; 326; LXX; Philo; Jos., Ant. 2, 296) ***frog.*** As the form in which unclean spirits appeared **Rv 16:13** (Artem. 2, 15 βάτραχοι ἄνδρας γόητας προσαγορεύουσι).—FSteinmetzer, D. Froschsymbol in Offb. 16: BZ 10, 1912, 252–60.—DELG. M-M.

βατταλογέω (βαττολογέω v.l.; s. Rdm. 44; Mlt-H. 272) 1 aor. subj. βατταλογήσω onomatopoetic word; **to speak in a way that images the kind of speech pattern of one who stammers, *use the same words again and again,*** *speak without thinking* (explained by πολυλογία) **Mt 6:7; Lk 11:2** D. Except for writers dependent on the NT the word has been found only in Vi. Aesopi W 109, where Perry notes the v.l. βατολογέω for βαττολογέω (it is missing in the corresp. place ed. Eberhard I c. 26 p. 289, 9. But Vi. Aesopi G 50 P. has the noun βαττολογία=foolish talk, but in a different context), and in Simplicius (c. 530 AD), Comm. in Epict. p. 91, 23 in the spelling βαττολογέω='prate'. It is perh. a hybrid form, rendering Aram. אמר בטלהא='talk idly' (B-D-F §40). Differently FBussby, ET 76, '64, 26.—S. DELG s.v. βατταρίζω for discussion of this type of word. M-M.

βδέλυγμα, ατος, τό (βδελυρός 'disgusting'; Aesop, Fab. 452 P. τοσοῦτον βδέλυγμα, τοσοῦτον μίασμα; oft. LXX; TestReub 3:12; JosAs; Suda—βδελυγμία as early as Cratinus: Phryn., Praep. Soph. p. 54, 4 Borries [1911]; X., Mem. 3, 11, 13) gener. someth. that causes revulsion or extreme disgust, a 'loathsome, detestable thing', in our lit. in ref. to what is detested by God.

❶ **someth. disgusting that arouses wrath, *loathsome thing*** B 2:5 (Is 1:13) ='I loathe incense'. β. ἐνώπιον τοῦ θεοῦ *detestable in the sight of God* (cp. Pr 11:1) **Lk 16:15.**—As in the OT (e.g. Dt 29:16; 3 Km 11:6, 33; 4 Km 23:13; 2 Ch 28:3) of everything connected w. polytheistic cult: (w. ἀκάθαρτα; cp. Pr 17:15) **Rv 17:4f.** ποιεῖν β. καὶ ψεῦδος *practice someth. foul or false* **21:27** (cp. REB).

❷ **someth. that is totally defiling, *abomination, pollutant*** the phrase τὸ β. τῆς ἐρημώσεως appears to refer to someth. that is abhorred because it defiles a sacred place and causes it to be left desolate **Mt 24:15; Mk 13:14** (τὸ β. ἑστηκότα is a 'constructio ad sensum', as Appian, Bell. Civ. 4, 48 §205 τὸ γύναιον . . . φέρουσα) is taken fr. Da (9:27; 11:31; 12:11), whence 1 Macc (1:54) had also taken it; β. τ. ἐρ. (cp. the similar gen. β. ἀνομίας Sir 49:2) is prob. *the desolating sacrilege* (NRSV) of the holy place; some interpret it as denoting the Antichrist.—GHölscher, ThBl 12, '33, 193ff; ELohmeyer, Mk 275ff; Dodd 23 and JRS 37, '47, 47ff; FBusch, Z. Verständnis d. synopt. Eschatologie: Mk 13 neu untersucht '38; WKümmel, Verheissung[2] '53; RPesch, Naherwartungen: Tradition u. Redaktion in Mk 13 (diss. Freiburg im Br.) '68; GBeasley-Murray, A Commentary on Mk 13, '57, 59–72. For Mk 13 see also s.v. σημεῖον.—DDD 4f. DELG s.v. βδελυρός. M-M. TW.

βδελυκτός, ή, όν (s. βδέλυγμα; Aretaeus p. 84, 21; schol. on Lucian p. 81, 25 Rabe; Syntipas p. 126, 8; Hesych.; 2 Macc 1:27; TestGad 3:2 v.l. [s. βδελύσσομαι]; Philo, Spec. Leg. 1, 323) **pert. to a pers. or thing that stirs up feelings of repugnance, *abhorrent, detestable.***

ⓐ of pers. (w. ἀπειθής) **Tit 1:16** (cp. Pr 17:15; Sir 41:5 v.l.).—ⓑ impers. (TestGad 3:2 v.l.) of divisions 1 Cl 2:6; of inordinate desires and pride 30:1.—TW.

βδελύσσομαι fut. βδελύξομαι; 1 aor. ἐβδελυξάμην; pf. mid. 3 sg. ἐβδέλυκται (Pr 28:9); aor. pass. ἐβδελύχθην (all LXX) (s. two preced. entries; Hippocr.; Achaeus, TGF fgm. 12, p. 749; Aristoph. et al. [Nägeli 15; Anz 305]; PLond VI, 1927 [IV AD], 34; PCairMasp 353, 16; LXX; PsSol 2:9; TestLevi 16:2; TestGad 3:2; JosAs 11 cod. A [p. 53, 18 Bat.]; ApcrEzk P 1 recto 15; Tat.; Theoph., Ant.; Pel.-Leg. p. 9, 9) **to detest someth. because it is utterly offensive or loathsome, *abhor, detest*** τὶ *someth.* (cp. Phalaris, Ep. 141, 2; Eratosth. p. 17, 10; Polyb. 33, 18, 10; Jos., Bell. 6, 172, Ant. 14, 45; Gen 26:29; Lev 11:11, 13 al.; CPJ I, 141, 9 of hatred for Jews): cult images **Ro 2:22.** The perf. pass. ptc. ἐβδελυγμένος (cp. Lev 18:30; Pr 8:7; Job 15:16; 3 Macc 6:9) = βδελυκτός (w. δειλός, ἄπιστος) *detestable* (because of polytheistic worship) **Rv 21:8.**—DELG s.v. βδελυρός. M-M. TW.

βέβαιος, α, ον (s. the next βεβαι- entries; Aeschyl., Hdt. et al.; ins, pap, rare in LXX, freq. in Philo; Jos., Ant. 13, 187; 14, 398; Just.) gener. relating to stability: 'firm, permanent'.

❶ **of something that can be relied on not to cause disappointment, *reliable,*** in metaph. of an anchor (w. ἀσφαλής) *unshifting* **Hb 6:19** of hope (cp. Dionys. Hal. 6, 51; Plut., Ant. 917 [3, 7]; 4 Macc 17:4) whose realization can be counted on because it does not move, being set down in the 'holy of holies'. Sim. ἡ ἐλπὶς ἡμῶν βεβαία ὑπὲρ ὑμῶν *our hope for you is firm* **2 Cor 1:7** (=our expectation [of things to be fulfilled] for you is not misplaced). ἔχομεν βεβαιότερον (for superl.; cp. Stob., Flor. IV 625, 2 βεβαιοτέραν ἔχε τ. φιλίαν πρὸς τ. γονεῖς) τὸν προφητικὸν λόγον *we possess the prophetic word as something that is (now) all the more reliable* **2 Pt 1:19** (on β. ἔχειν cp. Thu. 1, 32; Appian, Bell. Civ. 5, 19 §78 ἔχειν τι βέβαιον=have a firm hold on something; UPZ 162 II, 10 [117 BC]; s. also Diod. S. in 2); for other interpretations see comm. Of things revealed *reliable* (w. ἰσχυρός, τεθεμελιωμένος) Hv 3, 4, 3.

❷ **pert. to having continuity or being unwavering and persistent, *abiding*** (ψυχή Did., Gen. 197, 4; of a just pers. TKellis 22, 103 [w. ἁγνός]): of boldness and hope that remain *constant, steadfast* **Hb 3:6 v.l.;** of πίστις *unwavering* (Appian, Liby. 64 §284 πίστις ἐστὶ βέβαιος; Diod. S. 2, 29, 4 πιστεύοντες βεβαιότερον=accept all the more confidently; Simplicius in Epict. p. 110, 37 πίστις βεβαία=firm faith in the immortality of the soul on the basis of a declaration by a μάντις; Esth 3:13c; 3 Macc 5:31) 1 Cl 1:2. Of love *steadfast* MPol 1:2. ἀρχὴν τῆς ὑποστάσεως βεβαίαν κατέχειν *hold firm the original commitment* **Hb 3:14.** (W. ἀσφαλής) ISm 8:2. ἐπὶ τὸν τῆς πίστεως βέβαιον δρόμον καταντῆσαι *steadfastly finish the course of faith* 1 Cl 6:2. Of the Corinthian congregation *well-established, dependable* (Appian, Iber. 37 §150 ἀνὴρ β., Bell. Civ. 2, 13 §47 a servant) 47:6.—ἡ βεβαία τῆς πίστεως ὑμῶν ῥίζα *dependable root of your faith* Pol 1:2 in ref. to constancy in a productive Christian life.

❸ **pert. to having validity over a period of time, *in force, valid*** of a promise that applies to all pers. **Ro 4:16;** of the eucharist ISm 8:1. ὁ λόγος ἐγένετο βέβαιος (on λόγος β. cp. Pla., Phd. 90c λόγος β. καὶ ἀληθής) *the word was in force* **Hb 2:2** (β. of the Mosaic law as Philo, Mos. 2, 14); a last will and testament *valid* (opp. οὐκ ἰσχύει 'lack force'; legal t.t., s. JBehm, Διαθήκη 1912, 87, 4) **Hb 9:17.** βεβαίαν τὴν κλῆσιν ποιεῖσθαι *keep the call in force* i.e. confirm it so that it does not lapse (cp. Ael. Aristid. 13 p. 250 D.: βεβ. ἐλευθερία) **2 Pt 1:10;** β. εἶναι *be in force* IRo 3:1 (Ignatius fears that the instructions given by the Romans to others about dying for the faith will not apply to him; he wants them to be consistent).—B. 1237. DELG. M-M. TW. Spicq.

βεβαιόω fut. βεβαιώσω; 1 aor. ἐβεβαίωσα, pass. ἐβεβαιώθην (s. βέβαιος; Thu.+; ins, pap, rare in LXX; Philo, Op. M. 99; Jos., Ant. 1, 273; 17, 42; 20, 28; Tat. 32, 2; Ath. 22, 7) w. acc.

❶ **to put someth. beyond doubt,** ***confirm, establish,*** τὸν λόγον *confirm the preaching* **Mk 16:20** (Ael. Aristid. 25, 64 K.=43 p. 821 D., τὸν λόγον; Sextus 177 τ. λόγους. Cp. Epict. 2, 18, 32 τότε βεβαιώσεις τὸ τοῦ Ἡσιόδου ὅτι ἀληθές ἐστιν Iren. 4, 18, 5 [Harv. II 205, 3] τὴν γνώμην). τὰς ἐπαγγελίας *prove the promises reliable, fulfill (them)* **Ro 15:8** (cp. Polyb. 3, 111, 10 βεβαιώσειν ἡμῖν πέπεισμαι τὰς ἐπαγγελίας; Diod. S. 1, 5, 3; IPriene 123, 9 ἐβεβαίωσεν τὴν ἐπαγγελίαν). Of faith ταῦτα πάντα βεβαιοῖ 1 Cl 22:1.—Pass. τὸ μαρτύριον τοῦ Χριστοῦ ἐβεβαιώθη ἐν ὑμῖν *our attestation of Christ was ratified in you* **1 Cor 1:6** (i.e. Paul's proclamation concerning God's beneficence displayed in Christ was validated by the gifts evident in the Corinthian congregation, vs. 7). (ἡ σωτηρία) εἰς ἡμᾶς ἐβεβαιώθη *the saving message was guaranteed to us* **Hb 2:3** (as of someth. legally validated; cp. Ael. Aristid. 46 p. 288 D.: σωτηρίαν β. τινι; POxy 1119, 17; β. is also legal t.t. to designate properly guaranteed security: PFay 92, 19; POxy 899; 1036; s. Dssm., B 100ff [BS 104ff] and s. βεβαίωσις). For **Hb 13:9** s. below.

❷ **to make a pers. firm in commitment,** ***establish, strengthen*** (cp. Ps 40:13; 118:28) ὁ βεβαιῶν ἡμᾶς εἰς Χριστόν *the one who strengthens us in Christ*=makes us faithful disciples **2 Cor 1:21** (EDinkler, OCullmann Festschr., '62, 177–80: baptismal terminology). ὃς καὶ βεβαιώσει ὑμᾶς ἀνεγκλήτους *who will strengthen you, so that you are blameless* **1 Cor 1:8.** Pass. *be confirmed* in faith **Col 2:7;** in instruction IMg 13:1. **Hb 13:9** *make firm, strengthen* belongs here, since the imagery of a heart made firm is semantically equivalent in ancient culture to inward strengthening of the pers.—M-M. TW. Spicq.

βεβαίως adv. of βέβαιος (Aeschyl., Thu. et al.; PYadin 19, 23; Lev 25:30; 3 Macc 5:42; Philo; Jos., C. Ap. 2, 221; Just., D. 58, 3; Ath., R. 63, 13).

❶ **pert. to being high on a scale of reliability,** ***certainly, truly, reliably*** (w. ἀληθῶς) πράττεσθαι *certainly done* IMg 11; (w. ἀκριβῶς; cp. Jos., C. Ap. 1, 15) *reliably, dependably* (PGM 7, 710; 836) διδάσκειν Pol 3:2.

❷ **pert. to being valid because in keeping w. established procedure,** ***valid, proper,*** συναθροίζεσθαι *meet in valid manner = hold valid meetings* i.e. as authorized by the ecclesiastical overseer IMg 4 (cp. ISm 8).

βεβαίωσις, εως, ἡ (s. βέβαιος; Thu. et al.; pap, LXX, Philo) **process of establishing or confirming something,** ***confirmation, validation*** τοῦ εὐαγγελίου *confirmation, establishment of the gospel* **Phil 1:7;** εἰς β. ὁ ὅρκος *an oath serves as confirmation* (Philo, Abr. 273 ἡ δι' ὅρκου β.) **Hb 6:16.** The last passage esp. is a reminder that β. is a legal t.t. for *guaranteeing, furnishing security* (PParis 62 II, 8 [II BC] εἰς τ. βεβαίωσιν; cp. Lev 25:23; Wsd 6:18). Dssm., B 100ff (BS 104ff); NB 56 (BS 230); Mitt-Wilck. II/1, 188ff; Preisigke, Fachwörter; Taubenschlag, Law index.—M-M. TW. Spicq.

βεβαιωσύνη, ης, ἡ **the act of putting into an unwavering condition,** ***confirming, establishing*** στηρίζειν ἐν β. *set them firmly so that they do not waver* IPhld ins.

βεβαμμένος s. βάπτω.

βέβηλος, ον (s. βεβηλόω; Aeschyl., Thu. et al.; SIG 22, 25; Theosphien p. 180 §56, 1=Holladay p. 104 ln. 6; LXX; GrBar 4:3; Philo; Joseph.) pert. to being gener. public, in NT not in a ritualistic sense (Polyaenus 5, 2, 19 ['profane' in contrast to the temple vessels]; LXX; Philo, Mos. 2, 158, Leg. All. 1, 62; Jos., Bell. 6, 271, Ant. 15, 90)

❶ **pert. to being accessible to everyone and therefore devoid of real significance,** ***pointless, worthless*** οἱ β. καὶ γραώδεις μῦθοι *foolish tales, such as are told by elderly women* **1 Ti 4:7** (satirical indictment of cosmic speculations, opp. edifying discourse). κενοφωνίαι *pointless and empty talk, frivolous talk* (cp. 3 Macc 4:16) **6:20; 2 Ti 2:16.**

❷ of pers. (Ael. Aristid. 17, 18 K.=15 p. 380 D.; 3 Macc 2:14 al.; cp. Orig., C. Cels. 1, 7, 17) **pert. to being worldly as opp. to having an interest in transcendent matters,** ***totally worldly*** (w. ἀνόσιος, as 3 Macc 2:2) **1 Ti 1:9;** of Esau, devoid of interest in divine blessing (w. πόρνος; cp. Philo, Spec. Leg. 1, 102) **Hb 12:16.**—DELG. M-M. TW. Spicq.

βεβηλόω fut. βεβηλώσω LXX; 1 aor. ἐβεβήλωσα. Pass.: aor. ἐβεβηλώθην LXX; pf. 3 pl. βεβήλωνται 1 Macc 3:51; ptc. βεβηλωμένος LXX. (s. βέβηλος; Heliod. 2, 25; 10, 36; oft. LXX; Test12Patr, Just., Hesychius, Suda) **to cause someth. highly revered to become identified with the commonplace,** ***violate sanctity, desecrate, profane*** the Sabbath (2 Esdr 23:17; Ezk 20:13; 1 Macc 1:43, 45 al. Opp. φυλάσσειν τ. σαββ. Is 56:2) **Mt 12:5;** the sanctuary (Ezk 28:18; 2 Macc 8:2) **Ac 24:6;** God's name (Lev 18:21; 21:6 al.) Hs 8, 6, 2 (cod. A for βλασφημήσωσιν τὸν νόμον).—DELG s.v. βέβηλος. TW. Spicq.

βέβληκα, βέβλημαι s. βάλλω.

βέβρωκα s. βιβρώσκω.

Βεελζεβούλ, ὁ indecl. (v.l. Βεελζεβούβ and Βεεζεβούλ W-S. §5, 31, cp. 27 n. 56) ***Beelzebul,*** orig. a Philistine deity; the name בַּעַל זְבוּב means *Baal* (lord) *of flies* (4 Km 1:2, 6; Sym. transcribes βεελζεβούβ; Vulgate Beelzebub; TestSol freq. Βεελζεβούλ, -βουέλ). Whether בַּעַל זְבוּל (=lord of filth?) represents an intentional change or merely careless pronunciation cannot be determined w. certainty. For various derivations from Ugaritic and various periods of Hebrew, including the Dead Sea Scrolls, see IDB s.v. 'Beelzebul'. In NT B. is prince of hostile spirits: ἄρχων τῶν δαιμονίων **Mt 12:24; Lk 11:15.** B. ἔχειν *be possessed by the devil himself* **Mk 3:22.** Jesus is called B. by his enemies **Mt 10:25;** his exorcisms are ascribed to the help of B. (practically a charge of witchcraft) **Mt 12:24ff; Lk 11:15, 18f.**—WGrafBaudissin, RE II 514ff; EKautzsch, Gramm. d. bibl. Aram. 1884, 9; PJensen, D. Gilgameschepos I 1906, 644; WAitken, Beelzebul: JBL 31, 1912, 34–53; HBauer, D. Gottheiten von Ras Schamra: ZAW 51, '33, 89; LGaston, Beelzebul: TZ 18, '62, 247–55.—TW.

Βελζεθά s. Βηθζαθά.

Βελιάρ, ὁ indecl. ***Beliar*** (βελίαρ some edd.; also βελιάλ [Belial, the sp. used by most translators]=בְּלִיַּעַל 'worthlessness'; on the interchange of λ and ρ s. W-S. §5, 27a; other variants Βελιάβ, Βελιάν; s. B-D-F §39, 6) name for the devil (e.g. TestReub 2; 4; 6; TestSol 1:2, 5 D; AscIs; Jubil. 15, 33; CD 4:13 al. and oft. in 1QM and 1QH). The Antichrist, too, is given this name (TestDan 5; SibOr 2, 167; 3, 63; 73; perh. also AscIs 4:2 [not pap]). Both mngs. are prob. **2 Cor 6:15** (cp. 'either-or' TestNapht 2).—WBousset, D. Antichrist 1895, 86f; 99ff, Rel.[3] 528a (index); WGrafBaudissin, RE II 548f; MFriedlaender, D. Antichrist 1901, 118ff; RCharles, Rev. of St. John 1920 II 76ff. On B. in the OT: PJoüon, Biblica 5, 1924, 178–83; JHogg, JSL 44, 1928, 56–61.—HHuppenbauer, TZ 15, '59, 81–89 (Qumran texts); DThomas in RCasey memorial vol. '63, 11–19; Pvon der Osten-Sacken, Gott u. Belial, '69.—TW.

βελόνη, ης, ἡ (s. βέλος; Aristoph. et al.; Batr. 130; Memnon [I BC/I AD]: 434 fgm. 1, 4, 7 p. 341, 2 Jac.; Maximus Tyr. 29, 4a; PGM 7, 442; 36, 237; s. HCadbury, JBL 52, '33, 59f) ***needle*** τρῆμα β. *eye of a needle* **Lk 18:25.** There is no sound evidence that this is imagery for a narrow gate; s. HDB s.v. 'needle's eye', and Exp., 1st ser. 3, 1876, 373–79.—B. 412. DELG s.v. βάλλω p. 162. M-M.

βέλος, ους, τό (Hom.+; loanw. in rabb.) someth. w. a sharp point, a term used for projectiles of various kinds, in our lit. ***arrow*** βέλη πεπυρωμένα *flaming arrows* **Eph 6:16** (cp. Ps.-Apollod. 2, 5, 2, 2 De Hercule βάλλων βέλεσι πεπυρωμένοις; Jos., Ant. 1, 203; Ps.-Scylax, Peripl. 95 p. 40 Fabr.=112 GGM I p. 94: Αἰθίοπες χρῶνται βέλεσι πεπυρακτωμένοις).—B. 1389. DELG s.v. βάλλω p. 162. M-M. TW.

βελτιόω (s. βελτίων; Plut., Mor. 85c; SIG 888, 5; StudPal XX, 86, 19; pap, e.g. PCairMasp 97 recto, 36; PLond III, 1044, 22 p. 255; Philo, Det. Pot. Ins. 56, Sacr. Abel. 42) **to enhance in value or quality, *improve,*** pass. ***become better*** of the soul (cp. Philo, Dec. 17) Dg 6:9.—DELG s.v. βέλτερος.

βελτίων, ον (Soph., Thu. et al.; ins, pap, LXX, Philo [Leiseg. on ἀγαθός p. 50]; Just., D. 85, 5; 134, 1; Ath. 10, 1) **pert. to being relatively superior,** comp. of ἀγαθός ***better:*** ὁδός Hv 3, 7, 1; βελτίω ποιεῖν *make better* (Jer 33:13; 42:15) 1 Cl 19:1. βελτίω γενέσθαι (Cebes 33, 4; 5) Dg 1. W. gen. foll. β. τινός *better than someone* (Is 17:3; Sir 30:16; Jos., Ant. 18, 268) Hv 3, 4, 3.—Neut. βέλτιόν ἐστιν w. inf. foll. (pap, e.g. PColZen 9, 3; POxy 1148, 2; Num 14:3; Just., D. 134, 1) 2 Cl 6:6; Hs 1:9. As adv. βέλτιον γινώσκειν *know very well* (B-D-F §244; Rob. 665) **2 Ti 1:18;** cp. **Ac 10:28** D.—DELG s.v. βέλτερος. M-M.

Βενιαμ(ε)ίν, ὁ indecl. (בִּנְיָמִין.—LXX; JosAs [Βενιαμήν]; AscIs, Philo, Test12Patr. On spelling B-D-F §38.—In Joseph. βενιαμ(ε)ίς, gen. εῖ [Ant. 2, 122]) ***Benjamin,*** Israelite tribe (K-DSchunck, Benjamin. Untersuchungen zur Entstehung u. Gesch. eines israel. Stammes '63) **Ac 13:21; Ro 11:1; Phil 3:5; Rv 7:8.**

Βερνίκη, ης, ἡ (colloq. abbreviation IG III, 2618, 1; PPetr III, 1 II, 7; PTebt 407, 14 for Βερενίκη [s. Gignac I 306]; Tat. 10, 1; Polyaenus 8, 50; OGI 263, 2; 717, 6; Sb 307, 1; 438, 2; s. also Preisigke, Namenbuch; Acta Pilati 7=ASyn. 95, 90) ***Bernice,*** daughter of Agrippa I and sister of Agrippa II and Drusilla, b. 28, d. after 79 AD. She lived in marital relations w. various men, incl. her brother Agrippa. Both visited Festus in Caesarea **Ac 25:13, 23; 26:30.** Chief sources: Joseph., index Niese; Tacit., Hist. 2, 2 and 81; Sueton., Tit. 7; Juvenal, Sat. 6, 156–60; OGI 428, 3.—Schürer I 450f; 474–76; 479; 485; 571f; Wilcken, Pauly-W. III 287ff; MWahl, De Regina Berenice 1893; EMireaux, La reine Bérénice '51; Boffo, Iscrizioni p. 338 (lit.); Hemer, Acts 173; 238.—M-M.

Βέροια, ας, ἡ (Thu. 1, 61, 4; Ptolem. 3, 12, 36; Strabo 7, fgm. 26 p. 330; Ps.-Lucian, Asin. 34; ins) ***Beroia,*** very old city in Macedonia on the river Astraeus in the province of Emathia at the foot of Mt. Bermion, where Paul preached on his journey fr. Thessalonica to Achaia **Ac 17:10, 13.**—HKiepert, Lehrb. d. alten Geogr. 1878, §278; Pauly-W. III 304–8; Kl. Pauly I, 869; other lit. PECS 150f.

Βεροιαῖος, α, ον *of or from Beroia,* subst. *the Beroian* (SIG 636, 6f; SIG[2] 848, 2) of Sopater, a companion of Paul **Ac 20:4.**

Βεώρ, ὁ indecl. (בְּעוֹר) ***Beor,*** father of Balaam (Num 22:5; 31:8; Dt 23:5) **2 Pt 2:15 v.l.** for Βοσόρ (s. BWeiss, TU VIII/3, 1892, 74).

Βηθαβαρά, ἡ (Origen declines it) ***Bethabara;*** Orig. (Comm. in Io. VI 40, 204 Pr.) prefers this reading in **J 1:28,** though attested by fewer witnesses, to Βηθανία, found in Heracleon and most contemporary mss.; he could find no place called Bethany along the Jordan. S. Βηθανία 2.

Βηθανία, ας, ἡ also indecl. Βηθανιά as v.l. **Mt 21:17; Mk 11:1; Lk 19:29** (acc. to the Onomastica בֵּית עֲנִיָּה) ***Bethany.***

❶ village on the Mt. of Olives, 15 stades = 2.775 km. fr. Jerusalem (AscIs 2:12). Acc. to **J 11:1, 18** (with art., but v.l. without art.); **12:1** home of Mary, Martha, and Lazarus; acc. to **Mt 26:6; Mk 14:3** home of Simon the leper. Last station on the pilgrim road fr. Jericho to Jerusalem **Mk 11:1; Lk 19:29,** used by Jesus for lodging **Mt 21:17; Mk 11:11f.** Cp. **8:22 v.l.** Place of the ascension **Lk 24:50.**—HVincent, RB n.s. 11, 1914, 438ff; BHHW I 230f; CKopp, Holy Places of the Gospels, '63, 278–81.

❷ place on the east side of the Jordan where John baptized **J 1:28** (v.l. Βηθαβαρά).—FFenner, D. Ortslage v. Bethanien 1906; TZahn, NKZ 18, 1907, 265–94; ESchwartz, NGG 1908, 520f; Dalman, Orte[3] index; KErbes, D. Tauforte des Joh. nebst d. Salem des Melchisedek: Theol. Arb. aus d. Rhein. wiss. Predigerverein, n.s. 24, 1928, 71–106; DBuzy, RSR 21, '31, 444–62; PParker, JBL 74, '55, 257–61; WWiefel, Bethabara jenseits des Jordans: ZDPV 83, '67, 72–81; Kopp (s. 1 above), 113–29. On the rdg. Βηθαβαρά s. that word.

Βηθαραβά error for Βηθαβαρά, q.v.

Βηθεσδά, ἡ indecl. (בֵּית חֶסְדָּא house of mercy?), name of a pool in Jerusalem **J 5:2 v.l.** The editions of Tdf., W-H., S., N[25] have Βηθζαθά (q.v.) in the text; another v.l. is Βηθσαϊδά. Cp. W-S. §5, 27g; Hdb. ad loc.—See HVincent: Vincent-Abel, Jérusalem II, 1926, Sect. XXVIII Sainte Anne et ses sanctuaires; JJeremias, ZNW 31, '32, 308–12, Die Wiederentdeckung von Bethesda '49 (the double pool of St. Anna), Eng. tr., The Rediscovery of Bethesda '66; CPronobis, Bethesda z. Zt. Jesu: TQ 114, '33, 181–207; BHHW I, 232f. Perh. בֵּית אֶשְׁדָּה 'place of outpouring', cp. the dual form in 3Q 15, 11, 12, JMilik, Discoveries in the Judaean Desert of Jordan III, '62. 271f, 297; EVardaman, BT 14, '63, 27–29; DWieand, NTS 12, '66, 392–404.

Βηθζαθά, ἡ indecl. ***Bethzatha*** **J 5:2** (Eus., Onom. 58, 2; also D Βελζεθα); s. Βηθεσδά. Acc. to 1 Macc 7:19 and Jos., Bell. 2, 328; 530; 5, 149; 151; 246 Bethz. is the name of the northern extension of the city, which may give a hint as to the location of the pool.—HVincent and FAbel, Jérusalem I 1912, 685ff; GDalman, Jerus. u. s. Gelände 1930. On the name s. FBurkitt, The Syriac Forms of NT Proper Names 1912, 20f; BHHW I 232f.

Βηθλέεμ, ἡ (other edd. -λεέμ; s. B-D-F §56, 3) indecl. (בֵּית לֶחֶם house of bread; LXX; TestReub 3:13; AscIs; Just. In Joseph. Βήθλεμα, Βηθλέεμα [Ant. 5, 323], -ων [5, 136] and Βηθλ[ε]έμη, ης [7, 312]) ***Bethlehem,*** a town in Judaea, 7 km. south of Jerusalem, birthplace of Benjamin (Gen. 1:16; Demetr.: 722 fgm. 1, 10 Jac. εἰς Ἐφραθά, ἣν εἶναι B.) and home of David (1 Km 17:12; 20:6=Jos., Ant. 6, 227), hence the birthplace of the Messiah: **Mt 2:1, 5f** (Mi 5:1), **8, 16; Lk 2:4, 15; J 7:42;** GJs 17:1; 18:1; 21:1, 2 (v.l.). Cp. Baedeker[7] 1910, 94ff; TZahn, D. Geburtsstätte in Gesch., Sage u. bildender Kunst: NKZ 32, 1921, 669ff; Dalman, Orte[3] 18–60 [Eng. tr. 17–55]; WFoerster, ZDPV 57, '34, 1–7; CKopp, Holy Places of the Gospels, '63, 1–47; BHHW I 233; OEANE I 302.

Βηθσαϊδά(ν), ἡ indecl. (בֵּית צַיְדָה) ***Bethsaida.***—**❶** place north of Lake Gennesaret (Jos., Ant. 18, 28), east of the Jordan, near where it empties into the lake. Acc. to **J 1:44; 12:21** home of Philip, Andrew, and Peter. **Mt 11:21; Mk 6:45; 8:22; Lk 9:10; 10:13** (Βηδ'σαϊδα P[75]). Its distinction from another B. located farther west, B. τῆς Γαλιλαίας (**J 12:21**), awaits solution.—Schürer II 171f (sources and lit.); Dalman, Orte[3] 173ff (Eng. tr. 161–83); CMcCown, The Problem of the Site of Beths.: JPOS 10, 1930, 32–58; LVaganay, Mk 6:45: RB 49, '40, 5–32; PVannutelli, Synoptica '40 III–VIII; CKopp, Dominican Studies 3, '50, 11–40. BHHW I 234; OEANE I 302–5. S. Καφαρναούμ.

❷ J 5:2 P[75] et al. (s. Βηθεσδά, Βηθζαθά).

Βηθφαγή, ἡ indecl. (בֵּית פַּגֵּא house of unripe figs; in Talmud a place בית פאגי near Jerusalem: Dalman, Gramm.[2] 191) ***Bethphage,*** place on Mt of Olives **Mt 21:1; Mk 11:1; Lk 19:29** (Just., D. 53, 2; Eus., Onomast. 58 Kl.).—Billerb. I 839f; Dalman Orte[3] 268ff [Eng. tr. 250–58]; ILöw, Bethphagé: REJ 62, 1911, 232–35; CKopp, Holy Places of the Gospels, '63, 267–77; BHHW I 233f.

βῆμα, ατος, τό (s. βαίνω; Hom. Hymns, Pind.+; ins, pap, LXX, TestSol; TestAbr A 13 p. 92, 21 [Stone p. 32]; Joseph., Just.) orig. movement by raising a step, 'step'; then

❶ a step forward made by a foot, *step* (Hero Alex., Deff. [spurious] 131 = a little less than a meter) ἑπτὰ βήματα περιπατήσασα *when she had taken seven steps* GJs 6:1.

❷ a very limited space, *step* οὐδὲ β. ποδός *not even a square meter of ground* less than the space covered by one taking a stride **Ac 7:5** ('foothold', REB; cp. Dt 2:5).

❸ a dais or platform that required steps to ascend, *tribunal* (Thu. 2, 34, 8; Epict. 4, 10, 21; Jos., Bell. 2, 172; 2 Esdr 18:4; 2 Macc 13:26). A magistrate would address an assembly from a chair placed on the structure. Esp. *judicial bench* (Isocr., Ep. 8, 7; Ps.-Demosth. 48, 31; POxy 237 V, 13; PTebt 316, 11; PAmh 80, 7 al. S. καθίζω 3 and s. Reisch in Pauly-W. III 264; Preisigke, Fachwörter) **Mt 27:19; J 19:13; Ac 18:12, 16f; 25:6, 10, 17;** also God's judgment seat (SibOr 2, 218; 8, 222 and 242) **Ro 14:10** and Christ **14:10 v.l.; 2 Cor 5:10;** Pol 6:2.—**Ac 12:21, 23** D of the throne-like *speaker's platform* (Appian, Liby. 115 §546; Arrian, Anab. 7, 8, 3; 7, 11, 1; Jos., Ant. 4, 209; 7, 370) of Herod Agrippa I. In mng. 2 בִּימָה is a loanw. in rabb.—DELG s.v. βαίνω p. 157. M-M. TW.

βήρυλλος, ου, ὁ, ἡ (of Dravidian origin; Strabo 16, 4, 20; Dionys. Periegeta [II AD] 1012; PHolm η 8, 10; Tob 13:17 BA; Jos., Bell. 5, 234, Ant. 3, 168.—βηρύλλιαν Ex 28:20 al.; Ezk 28:13) semiprecious stone usually of sea-green color, *beryl* (Cyranides p. 12, 9 λευκὸς λίθος; Michel Psellus, in Lapidaires p. 202 lines 11–15 [various hues]) **Rv 21:20** (cp. Plin., HN 37, 20; 38, 5).—DELG. Lit. s.v. ἀμέθυστος.

βία, ας, ἡ (s. βιάζομαι; Hom.+; loanw. in rabb.) **strength or energy brought to bear in varying degrees on things or pers., *force***

ⓐ of violent natural forces (Dio Chrys. 17 [34], 33 β. τῆς θαλάττης; PPetr II, 37 IIa, 6 ἡ βία τοῦ ὕδατος; Wsd 4:4 ὑπὸ βίας ἀνέμων) ὑπὸ τῆς β. τῶν κυμάτων **Ac 27:41.**

ⓑ of pers. (Jos., Vi. 303) μετὰ βίας (Isocr. 10, 59; Plut., Mor. 96d; SIG 705, 41; 780, 33; PTebt 5, 57; Ex 1:14; TestJos 8:2; PsSol 17:5) **Ac 5:26;** cp. **24:7 v.l.;** *compulsion:* β. οὐ πρόσεστι τῷ θεῷ (s. I πρόσειμι) Dg 7:4.—A mob pressing forward διὰ τὴν β. τοῦ ὄχλου **Ac 21:35.**—DELG. M-M. TW. Sv.

βιάζω (Hom.+) nearly always as a mid. dep. βιάζομαι; aor. mid. ἐβιασάμην, pass. 2 sg. ἐβιάσθης Sir 31:21. Apart fr. Dg. 7:4; 10:15 most of this entry concerns probabilities relating to β. in **Mt 11:12** and par. **Lk 16:16.** The principal semantic problem is whether β. is used negatively ('in malam partem') or positively ('in bonam partem'), a problem compounded by the question of the function of these vss. in their literary context. In Gk. lit. β. is most often used in the unfavorable sense of attack or forcible constraint (s. L-S-J-M).

❶ to inflict violence on, *dominate, constrain* w. acc. (Herodas 2, 71; Menand., Dyscolus 253 [opp. πείθειν use of persuasion]; 371; Appian, Bell. Civ. 5, 35 §139; PAmh 35, 17 [213 BC] βιασάμενος αὐτούς; PGiss 19, 13; LGötzeler, Quaestiones in Appiani et Polybii dicendi genus 1890, 63; Esth 7:8 [rape]; En 103:14; 104:3) *mistreat the poor people* β. τοὺς ὑποδεεστέρους Dg 10:5.—With β. taken as pass., **Mt 11:12** ἡ βασιλεία τ. οὐρανῶν βιάζεται is frequently understood in the unfavorable sense *the reign/kingdom of heaven is violently treated, is oppressed* (so the pass. e.g. Thu. 1, 77, 4; POxy 294, 16 [22 AD]; Sir 31:21. On the topic of violence to the divine, cp. Paus. 2, 1, 5 τὰ θεῖα βιάσασθαι=(it is difficult for a mere human) to coerce things in the realm of the divine.—GSchrenk, TW I 608ff; NRSV 'has suffered violence'; its mng., w. β. understood as mid.: 'has been coming violently', s. 2 end); var. ways by which the violence is suffered have been suggested—(a) through hindrances raised against it (βιάζομαι=be hindered, be obstructed: cp. the use of the mid. in this sense: Synes., Provid. 1, 1, 89c of the evil man's power, which strives εἴ πῃ τὸν θεῖον νόμον βιάσαιτο=[to see] whether it could perhaps 'hinder' the divine law; Jos., Ant. 1, 261). For the pass. in this sense, s. the versions: It., Vulg., Syr. Sin. and Cur. S. also Dalman, Worte 113–16; MDibelius, Joh. d. T. 1911, 26ff: hostile spirits.—(b) through the efforts of unauthorized pers. to compel its coming (s. HScholander, ZNW 13, 1912, 172–75)—(c) through attempts to *occupy* (an area) *by force* (a territory, Appian, Bell. Civ. 3, 24 §91).

❷ to gain an objective by force, *use force,* intr. (X., Mem. 3, 9, 10; Diod. S. 4, 12, 5 οἱ βιαζόμενοι=the ones who use force, the intruders; Plut., Mor. 203c; Epict. 4, 8, 40; Lucian, Necyom. 20, Hermot. 22; SIG 1042, 8 [Dssm., NB 85f (BS 258)]; 888, 24; 1243, 4f; PTebt 6, 31; PFlor 382, 54; Dt 22:25, 28; Philo, Mos. 1, 215; Jos., Bell. 3, 493; 518) of compulsion οὐ βιαζόμενος *without using force* (opp. πείθειν) Dg 7:4.—Of forcing one's way (Demosth. 55, 17; Appian, Hann. 24 §106) w. εἴς τι *enter forcibly into someth.* (Thu. 1, 63, 1; 7, 69, 4; Polyb. 1, 74, 5; Plut., Otho 1072 [12, 10]; Philo, Mos. 1, 108 of a gnat forcing its way into bodily orifices εἰς τἀντὸς βιάζεται; Jos., Bell. 3, 423) ἡ βασιλεία τοῦ θεοῦ εὐαγγελίζεται καὶ πᾶς εἰς αὐτὴν βιάζεται *the reign of God is being proclaimed and everyone takes* (or *tries to take* [cp. Polemo Soph. B 11 Reader, s. p. 266f]) *it by force* **Lk 16:16** (hyperbolic usage; on the question whether this is a perspective attributed to Jesus or to his opposition concerning moral miscalculation, s. FDanker, JBL 77, '58, 234–36).—*Makes its way w. triumphant force* is preferred for **Mt 11:12** by FBaur; TZahn; AHarnack, SBBerlAk 1907, 947–57; WBrandt, ZNW 11, 1910, 247f; ROtto, Reich Gottes u. Menschensohn '34, 84–88; cp. NRSV mg. 'has been coming violently'.—EGraesser, D. Problem der Parusieverzögerung, ZNW Beih. 22, '57, 180ff; OBetz, Jesu heiliger Krieg, NovT 2, '57, 116–37.

❸ go after someth. w. enthusiasm, *seek fervently, try hard,* the sense *is sought w. burning zeal* is preferred by HHoltzmann; FDibelius, StKr 86, 1913, 285–88; et al. for **Mt 11:12.** A variation of this interpretation is the sense *try hard,* but the support sought in Epict. 4, 7, 20f is questionable, for this latter pass. rather refers to attempts at forced entry when one is not welcome.

❹ *constrain (warmly)* if βιάζεται **Lk 16:16** is to be understood as a passive, as POxy 294, 16 (22 AD), or in the same sense as the mid. in Gen 33:11; Judg 13:15, the sense would be *invite urgently* of the 'genteel constraint imposed on a reluctant guest' (so vHoffmann et al.; s. FDibelius [s. 3 above]; cp. the sense of Lk 14:23 ἀνάγκασον εἰσελθεῖν 'compel them to come in').—On usage at Qumran s. BThiering, NovT 21, '79, 293–97.—DELG s.v. βία. M-M. TW. Spicq. Sv.

βίαιος, α, ον (Hom. et al.; ins, pap, LXX, Philo; Jos., Ant. 14, 43; Just., A I, 16, 4 κατά τινα βιαιοτέραν ὁλκήν; Ath., R. 74, 5; βιαίως Ar. 11, 4) **pert. to being violent or strong in use of force, *violent, forcible.***

ⓐ of human force συναλλάγματα *forcibly exacted agreements* B 3:3 (Is 58:6).—ⓑ of natural force *violent, strong* of a wind **Ac 2:2** (Aristot., Meteor. 3, 1, 370b, 9; Polyb. 21, 31, 6 ἄνεμος; Diod. S. 17, 106, 6 βιαίου πνεύματος φερομένου; Paus. 10, 17, 11 νότος; Ex 14:21; Ps 47:8 πνεῦμα; Philo, Somn. 2, 166 πν.; Jos., Bell. 3, 422 πν.).—DELG s.v. βία. M-M.

βιαστής, οῦ, ὁ (Aretaeus 4, 12, 12; Eustathius Macrembolita [c. 900 AD] 5, 3, 5 IHilberg [1876]; Philo, Agric. 89 v.l., all three in a pejorative sense) *violent, impetuous pers.* transf. sense **Mt 11:12** (s. βιάζω). S. Thiering s.v. βιάζομαι end.—DELG s.v. βία. TW.

βιβλαρίδιον, ου, τό dim. of βίβλος (Galen XVI p. 5 K. has βιβλιαρίδιον) **a small document with writing, *little scroll/roll*** containing a message **Rv 10:2,** vs. **8 v.l., 9f** (s. Mussies 116 on the textual trad.; cp. Artem. 2, 45 p. 149, 6: ἐσθίειν βιβλία in a dream . . . θάνατον σύντομον προαγορεύει); Hv 2, 1, 3. Of a letter 2, 4, 3. The form βιβλιδάριον (Aristoph. acc. to Pollux 7, 210; Arrian [II AD] βιβλιδάριον περὶ κομητῶν, ascribed to Agatharchides [II BC] 111 [GGM I 194]; Cat. Cod. Astr. VIII/3, p. 92, 9) appears as v.l. for βιβλαρίδιον in Rv and Hermas; s. AWikenhauser, BZ 6, 1908, 171.—DELG s.v. βύβλος. TW.

βιβλάριον, ου, τό (PLille 1, 7, 7 [III BC]; Anth. Pal 11, 78, 2); dim. of βίβλος *little scroll* **Rv 10:8 v.l.** (for βιβλίον); **10:2 v.l., 9 v.l.** (for βιβλαρίδιον).—DELG s.v. βύβλος.

βιβλιδάριον s. βιβλαρίδιον.—DELG s.v. βύβλος.

βιβλίδιον, ου, τό (Demosth. et al., ins, pap) dim. of βιβλίον ***brief document*** (Plut., Cim. 486 [12, 4], Caesar 938 [65, 1]; BGU 432 II, 3f; POxy 1032, 4; esp. of petitions PTebt 293, 8, cp. Mitt-Wilck. I/1, XXXI, 2; Preisigke, Fachwörter 40) Hv 2, 1, 3f; 2, 4, 1. Of a letter (Polyaenus 7, 33, 1) IEph 20:1.—DELG s.v. βύβλος. M-M. s.v. βιβλίον.

βιβλίον, ου, τό (Hdt., Aristoph.+; s. Preisigke, Fachwörter) der. from βύβλος, Egyptian papyrus, from whose strips writing material was manufactured.

❶ **brief written message, *document*** (Demosth., Ep. 1, 3; Appian, Iber. 41 §167 β. ἐσφραγισμένα; Polyaenus 7, 19 [of an ἐπιστολή]; Jos., C. Ap. 1, 101; later pap: APF 5, 263; Mitt-Wilck. I/2, 42, 8 [314 AD]; s. Preis.) β. ἀποστασίου *certificate of divorce* (Dt 24:1, 3) which, acc. to law, an Israelite had to give his wife when he dismissed her **Mt 19:7; Mk 10:4.**—S. ἀπολύω 5.

❷ **long written composition** (either of a total work or of parts of a work), ***scroll, book,*** **Rv 6:14** (Is 34:4); **20:12;** of the scroll of the Law (Synes., Ep. 4 p. 162b and prob. as early as Diod. S. 34+35 fgm. 1, 3 [Hecataeus of Abdera—III BC?] of a stone figure of Moses μετὰ χεῖρας ἔχον βιβλίον) **Gal 3:10** (Vi. Aesopi G 81 P. τὸ βιβλίον τοῦ τῆς πόλεως νόμου); **Hb 9:19** (Ex 24:7); of the scroll of a prophet **Lk 4:17, 20;** B 12:9 (Ex 17:14), cp. **Hb 10:7** (Ps 39:8); of John's gospel **J 20:30** (Plut., Mor. 189d ταῦτα ἐν τοῖς βιβλίοις γέγραπται); cp. **21:25.** W. μεμβράναι **2 Ti 4:13.** Esp. of apocal. books **Rv 1:11; 5:1ff** (ERussell, BiblSacra 115, '58, 258–64 [mancipatio]—s. σφραγίς; Diod. S. 14, 55, 1 βιβλίον ἐπεσφραγισμένον . . . ἀνοίγειν καὶ ποιεῖν τὰ γεγραμμένα); **10:8; 22:7, 9f, 18f;** Hv 1, 2, 2; 2, 4, 2. Of holy writings gener. τὰ β. (w. ἀπόστολοι) 2 Cl 14:2 (s. AvHarnack, Zentralbl. f. Bibliothekswesen 45, 1928, 337–42). Cp. Papias (2:4, in contrast to τὰ παρὰ ζώσης φωνῆς). β. τῆς ζωῆς *book of life* **Rv 13:8; 17:8; 20:12; 21:27** (s. βίβλος 2). Of the works of Papias (1:4, 8, 9).—CMcCown, Codex and Roll in the NT: HTR 34, '41, 219–50.—DELG s.v. βύβλος. M-M. TW. Sv.

βίβλος, ου, ἡ (Aeschyl., Hdt.+; also s. Preisigke, Fachwörter) 'book', later esp. 'sacred, venerable book' (Pla., Rep. 364e; Lucian, Philops. 12, M. Peregr. 11; Ps.-Lucian, Amor. 44; Celsus 1, 16; PParis 19, 1; POxy 470, 24; PGM 3, 424 ἱερὰ βίβλος, 13, 15 Ἑρμῆς ἐν ἑαυτοῦ ἱερᾷ βύβλῳ [=βίβλῳ], lines 231, 232f; EpArist 316; L'Ànnée Épigraphique 1977, '81, no. 840, 12 [III AD]; SibOr 3, 425).

❶ **a specific composition or class of composition, *book*** (β. τῆς διαθήκης Did., Gen. 121, 23) β. Μωϋσέως (1 Esdr 5:48; 7:6, 9) **Mk 12:26;** β. λόγων (cp. Tob 1:1) Ἠσαΐου **Lk 3:4;** β. ψαλμῶν (subscription of Psalter in Sahidic version: ARahlfs, Psalmi cum Odis '31, 340; β. τῶν ψ. Orig., C. Cels. 4, 49, 39) **20:42; Ac 1:20.** Gener. β. τῶν προφητῶν **7:42.**—Pl. PtK 4 p. 15, 30; β. ἱεραί (Diod. S. 1, 70, 9; 34+35 fgm. 1, 4 [in the latter passage of the sacred scriptures of the Jews]; Ael. Aristid. 45, 29 K.=8 p. 95 D.; OGI 56, 70; 2 Macc 8:23; Philo; Jos., Ant. 2, 347; 3, 81; 105; Orig., C. Cels. 4, 17, 14—sg. in PGM s. above) 1 Cl 43:1. Of books of magic (Ps.-Phoc. 149; PGM 13, 739; s. Field, Notes 129; so βιβλία Celsus 6, 40) **Ac 19:19** (cp. Dssm., Baudissin Festschr. 1917, 121–24).—RAC II 664–731; BHHW I 276–79.—β. γενέσεως Ἰησοῦ X. **Mt 1:1** s. γένεσις 3 and Goodsp., Probs. 9f; EKrentz, The Extent of Matthew's Prologue, JBL 83, '64, 409–14.

❷ **a book of accounts, *record-book,*** esp. β. τῆς ζωῆς *book of life* **Phil 4:3; Rv 3:5** (cp. Ex 32:32f; JosAs 15:3); **13:8 v.l.; 20:15.** Pl. Hv 1, 3, 2. More exactly β. ζώντων 1 Cl 53:4; Hs 2:9; judgment will be rendered on the basis of books. See Bousset, Rel.[3] 258; BMeissner, Babylonien u. Assyrien II 1925, 124ff; LRuhl, De Mortuorum Judicio 1903, 68, 101ff; WSattler, ZNW 21, 1922, 43–53; LKoep, D. himmlische Buch in Antike u. Christentum, '52.—Straub 34. DELG s.v. βύβλος. M-M. New Docs 2, 84. TW. Sv.

βιβρώσκω pf. βέβρωκα; plpf. 3 sg. βεβρώκει 1 Km 30:12. Pass.: fut. 3 sg. βρωθήσεται LXX; 1 aor. ἐβρώθην; pf. ptc. βεβρωμένος (s. βρῶμα, βρώσιμος, βρῶσις; Hom.+; pap, LXX; Jos., Bell. 6, 210, Ant. 17, 345) **to take food in through the mouth, *eat, consume,*** οἱ βεβρωκότες *those who had eaten* **J 6:13** (thus Aristot. HA 629b, 9; Polyb. 3, 72, 6). Of sticks *be eaten, gnawed* (Diosc. 3, 9 W. ῥίζα βεβρ.) Hs 8, 1, 6f; 8, 4, 6; 8, 5, 2ff; 8, 6, 4.—ἐβρώθη ἡ δίαιτα (*their*) *abode was consumed* 1 Cl 39:8 (Job 5:3).—B. 327. DELG. M-M.

Βιθυνία, ας, ἡ (X. et al.; ins; Philo, Leg. ad Gai. 281; Joseph.) ***Bithynia,*** province in northern Asia Minor **Ac 16:7; 1 Pt 1:1;** JWeiss, RE X 553f (lit.).—RAC II 416–22; Kl. Pauly I 908–11.

βίος, ου, ὁ (s. βιόω; Hom.+; Hermas prefers ζωή) 'life' in its appearance and manifestations freq. distinguished from ζωή, the condition of being alive, cp. Plotin. 3, 7, 11, 4; Schmidt, Syn.

327–30. Although there is freq. overlapping in usage, βίος may be said to denote the manner in which one's ζωή finds expression (cp. Plut., Mor. 114d τῆς ζωῆς βίος), and the latter term may be used to connote quality of existence as such (cp. IPriene 105, 10 the birth of Augustus marked the 'beginning of life (βίος) and living (ζωή)'; s. also line 49; cp. Od. 15, 491; X. Mem. 3, 3, 11 and Cass. Dio 69, 19 'Here lies Similis, alive [βιόω] for a number of years, but really living [ζάω] for seven'.). Hence, as the semantic history shows, the loss of βίος need not terminate ζωή (q.v.).

❶ **life and activity associated w. it,** ***life*** (Hdt. 6, 109, 3; cp. Aeschyl., Prom. 537 al.; pap, LXX) 2 Cl 1:6. χρόνος τοῦ βίου *time of life* **1 Pt 4:3 v.l.** εἰσέρχεσθαι εἰς τὸν β. *come to life* Dg 1 of a new way of living. ἀποτάσσεσθαι τῷ βίῳ *bid farewell to life* (as the world knows it) IPhld 11:1; ὁ νῦν β. *the present life* (Ael. Aristid. 30, 20 K.=10 p. 121 D.) 2 Cl 20:2 and its ἡδοναί *pleasures* (cp. Jos., Ant. 4, 143) **Lk 8:14;** IRo 7:3. Contrasted w. it is life beyond the grave μέλλων β. (Diod. S. 8, 15, 1; Maximus Tyr. 41, 5f) 2 Cl 20:2 or ἄλλος β. (Sallust. 18 p. 34, 10 ἕτερος β., which involves punishment; Jos., C. Ap. 2, 218 β. ἀμείνων) IEph 9:2 (ὅλον cj.). αἱ τ. βίου πραγματεῖαι *the affairs of everyday life* **2 Ti 2:4.** W. qualifying terms denoting personal conduct (Himerius, Or. 41 [=Or. 7], 1 ἥμερος β.; BGU 372 II, 2 ἀνδράσι πονηρὸν καὶ λῃστρικὸν βίον ποιουμένοις; Wsd 4:9; 5:4; 4 Macc 1:15; 7:7; 8:8 Ἑλληνικὸς β.) ἄνομος β. MPol 3. Opp. ἐνάρετος β. 1 Cl 62:1; β. παράσημον ἀσκεῖν *lead a strange/outlandish life* Dg 5:2. Pl. of the way of life of several pers. (Diod. S. 3, 34, 8; 3, 35, 1; Strabo 3, 3, 7; Jos., Vi. 256b) 5:10. Prob. **1 Ti 2:2** has a sim. thrust *lead an orderly life* (=one that does not disturb the peace) ἡσύχιον β. διάγειν (Ath. 37, 1; cp. PSI 541 ἵνα εὐσχημονῶν κ. ἀνέγκλητος ... τὸν βίον ἔχω).

❷ (Hes. et al.; Hdt., X.) **resources needed to maintain life,** ***means of subsistence*** (UPZ 14, 32 [158 BC]; Pr 31:14) Dg 5:4. Specif. *property* (Eur., Suppl. 861 in Diog. L. 7, 22; Diod. S. 12, 40, 3; Vett. Val. index; SIG 708, 33; 762, 40; PCairPreis 2, 13; PGM 13, 636f αὔξησόν μου τὸν βίον ἐν πολλοῖς ἀγαθοῖς; SSol 8:7; 2 Esdr 7:26; Jos., Ant. 1, 326) **Mk 12:44; Lk 8:43; 15:12, 30; 21:4** (Julian, Anth. Pal. 6, 25, 5f: the insignificant gift of poor Cinyres to the nymphs was his ὅλος βίος); β. τοῦ κόσμου *worldly goods* **1J 3:17.** ἀλαζονεία τοῦ β. **2:16.**—B. 285; 769. Schmidt, Syn. IV 40–53. DELG. M-M. TW. Sv.

βιόω fut. βιώσω Job 29:18; 1 aor. ptc. acc. pl. βιώσαντας Wsd. 12:23, inf. βιῶσαι (B-D-F §75; the form βιῶσαι as early as Aristot., EN 9, 8, 9, also Dionys. Hal. 3, 37, 1; Ps.-Lucian, Macrob. 8; Herm. Wr. 3, 4; Jos., Ant. 1, 152 v.l.); pf. ptc. neut. pl. βεβιωκότα Wsd 4:4 cod. Sin.; pass. βεβιωμένων (Ath., R. 79, 5) (s. βίος; Hom. et al.; ins, pap, LXX; EpArist 32; 39; Jos., C. Ap. 2, 151) **to spend one's life,** ***live*** τὸν ἐπίλοιπον ἐν σαρκὶ χρόνον *the remaining time in the flesh* **1 Pt 4:2** (s. Job 29:18; P^{72} reads σῶσαι **1 Pt 4:2**).—DELG s.v. βίος. M-M. TW.

Βίτων, ωνος, ὁ (Diod. S. 14, 53, 6) ***Bito,*** a Roman whose praenomen was Valerius, w. others the bearer of 1 Cl; s. 65:1.

βίωσις, εως, ἡ (Sir Prol. ln. 14; Jew. ins in Ramsay, Phrygia I/2, 650 ἐνάρετος β.) ***manner of life*** **Ac 26:4.**—M-M.

βιωτικός, ή, όν (since Aristot., HA 9, 17 [Lob. on Phryn. 355]; pap) **pert. to daily life and living,** ***belonging to (daily) life*** (so Polyb. et al.; cp. χρεῖαι β. 'necessities of daily life' Polyb. 4, 73, 8; Diod. S. 2. 29, 5; Philo Bybl. [100 AD]: 790 fgm. 1, 29 Jac. [in Eus., PE 1, 9, 29]; Artem. 1, 31; Philo Alex., Mos. 2, 158) μέριμναι β. **Lk 21:34;** β. πράξεις Hv 1, 3, 1; β. πράγματα 3, 11, 3; m 5, 2, 2; βάσανοι β. *tortures that befall one during his earthly life* s 6, 3, 4; β. κριτήρια **1 Cor 6:4** (s. κριτήριον); cp. vs. **3** βιωτικά *ordinary (everyday) matters* (τὰ β. in a somewhat different sense Epict. 1, 26, 3; 7; Vett. Val. 286, 14; PRyl 125, 11; Philo, Omn. Prob. Liber 49; Field, Notes 171). In connection with 1 Cor 6:1–6, s. ERohde, Z. griech. Roman (Kleine Schriften II) 1901, 38f; also Philostrat., Vi. Soph. 1, 25, 3, concerning quarrels in daily life which, in contrast to grave offenses, are not to be brought to court, but settled at home.—DELG s.v. βίος. M-M.

βλαβερός, ά, όν (s. βλάβη; Hom. Hymns, Hes. et al.; Epict.; SIG 454, 14; PTebt 725, 5 [II BC]; Pr 10:26; TestSol; EpArist 192; Ath., R. 75, 4) ***harmful*** (w. ἀνόητος) ἐπιθυμίαι **1 Ti 6:9** (X., Mem. 1, 3, 11 β. ἡδοναί); ἀσυγκρασία β. *harmful lack of community spirit* Hv 3, 9, 4. τρυφαί Hs 6, 5, 5ff. W. dat. of pers. (X., Mem. 1, 5, 3) Hm 6, 1, 3. Anton. τὸ συμφέρων, -ουσα, -ον, ὠφέλιμος.—DELG s.v. βλάβη. M-M. TW. Spicq.

βλάβη, ης, ἡ (s. βλαβερός, βλάπτω; trag., Thu. et al.) ***harm*** βλάβην οὐ τὴν τυχοῦσαν ... ὑποίσομεν *we shall suffer no insignificant harm* 1 Cl 14:2. βλάβην παρατιθέναι τινί *cause harm to someone* ITr 5:1.—DELG s.v. βλάβη. Sv.

βλάπτω 1 aor. ἔβλαψα, subj. βλάψω. Pass.: fut. 1 pl. βλαβησόμεθα Just., A 1, 17, 4;1 aor. inf. βλαφθῆναι 1 Cl 1:1; 2 aor. 3 pl. ἐβλάβησαν Wsd 10:8; (s. two prec. entries; Hom.+) ***to harm, injure*** τινά *someone* (PHib 55, 5f [250 BC] σαυτὸν βλάψεις; 4 Macc 9:7; EpArist 232; Jos., Ant. 14, 355) MPol 10:2. οὐ μὴ αὐτοὺς βλάψῃ *it will not hurt them* **Mk 16:18.** τὶ *someth.* (SIG 360, 28; 839, 15; Pr 25:20a) τὸ πνεῦμα 2 Cl 20:4; τὴν σάρκα Hv 3, 10, 7 (preparation for visions imposes strain on the flesh, Joly p. 127, n. 3).—W. double acc. (Appian, Hann. 28 §119, Mithrid. 15 §51, Bell. Civ. 2, 131 §550; Jos., Ant. 8, 241) μηδὲν βλάψαν αὐτόν *without doing him any harm* **Lk 4:35.**—Pass. *be harmed* (Jos., Ant. 3, 193) underlies the Lat. and Syr. versions of 1 Cl 1:1, but the Gk trad. has the word βλασφημέω (q.v. bη).—B. 760. DELG s.v. βλάβη. M-M. TW.

βλαστάνω (also βλαστάω schol. on Pind., P. 4, 113a; **Mk 4:27** [for vv.ll. s. Tdf. app.] Hs 4:1f; TestJud 24:6; s. B-D-F §101; Rob. 1213. Both forms in LXX) fut. βλαστήσω LXX; 1 aor. ἐβλάστησα (Aelian, NA 9, 37; LXX; Just., D. 119, 3); pf. βεβλάστηκε Jo 2:22. Esp. in ref. to plants: to cause growth or to spring up as new growth.

❶ **to cause someth. to grow,** ***produce*** (Hippocr. et al.: CMG I, 1 p. 84, 21; Apollon. Rhod. 1, 1131; Gen 1:11; Sir 24:17; EpArist 230) ἡ γῆ ἐβλάστησεν τὸν καρπὸν αὐτῆς **Js 5:18** (Philo, Op. M. 47 ἐβλάστησε ἡ γῆ).

❷ **to emerge as new growth,** ***bud, sprout*** intr. (s. βλαστός; Pind. et al.; Jos., Ant. 3, 176; 17, 215; Jo 2:22; Sir 39:13; ParJer; Just., D. 119, 3) of wheat **Mt 13:26;** of seed (Philo, Leg. All. 3, 170 σπαρὲν βλαστάνειν) **Mk 4:27** (βλαστᾷ). Of Aaron's sprouting rod **Hb 9:4;** cp. 1 Cl 43:4f (s. Num 17:23). Of budding trees (opp. ξηρά) Hs 4:1f.—DELG. M-M.

βλαστός, οῦ, ὁ (s. βλαστάνω 2; Hdt. et al.; pap, LXX; TestJud 24:4; Philo, Op. M. 41; Ar.; Just., D. 86, 4) ***bud, sprout*** of a vine (Strabo 7, 5, 8) βλαστὸς γίνεται *it begins to bud* 1 Cl 23:4=2 Cl 11:3. Of the edible shoots (or fruits) of a shrub B 7:8.

Βλάστος, ου, ὁ ***Blastus*** (common name: IG XII, 4, 274; 5, 1016; IG III, 3052, 1; 3053, 1; CIL VIII, 5549f; IX 4547; 5880 al.; BGU 37, 3 [51 AD]), chamberlain of Herod Agrippa I **Ac 12:20.**—M-M.

βλασφημέω impf. ἐβλασφήμουν; 1 aor. ἐβλασφήμησα. Pass.: 1 fut. βλασφημηθήσομαι; 1 aor. ἐβλασφημήθην (s. next two entries; Pla. et al.; PSI 298, 14; LXX; Alex., Ep. XVI 2f; TestJob 16:7; AssMos fgm. j p. 67 Denis; Philo, Joseph., Just.) prim. 'to demean through speech', an esp. sensitive matter in an honor-shame oriented society. **to speak in a disrespectful way that demeans, denigrates, maligns**

ⓐ in relation to humans ***slander, revile, defame*** (Isocr. 10, 45 w. λοιδορεῖν) τινά *someone* (Socrat., Ep. 22, 2; Chion, Ep. 7, 1 ἡμᾶς) μηδένα (Philo, Spec. Leg. 4, 197; Jos., Vi. 232; Hippol., Ref. 7, 32, 6) *speak evil of* **Tit 3:2.** Pass. **Ro 3:8; 1 Cor 4:13 v.l.; 10:30** (ὑπὲρ οὗ = ὑπ. τούτου ὑπ. οὗ); Dg 5:14. Abs. **Ac 13:45; 18:6.**

ⓑ in relation to transcendent or associated entities ***slander, revile, defame, speak irreverently/impiously/disrespectfully of or about***

α. a Gr-Rom. deity (for Gr-Rom. attitudes respecting deities Ps.-Pla., Alc. II 149c; Diod. S. 2, 21, 7; Philo, Spec. Leg. 1, 53; Jos., Ant. 4, 207, C. Apion 2, 237 [s. βλασφημία bγ]; Orig., C. Cels. 8, 43, 27; s. bε below and at the very end of the entry) τὴν θεὸν ἡμῶν **Ac 19:37.**

β. God in Israelite/Christian tradition (4 Km 19:4) τὸν θεόν (cp. Philo, Fuga 84b; Jos., Ant. 4, 202; 6, 183; Hippol., Ref. 7, 11) **Rv 16:11, 21.** Abs. (2 Macc 10:34; 12:14; Orig., C. Cels. 8, 43, 31; Hippol., Ref. 1, Pr. 2) **Mt 9:3; 26:65** (JKennard, Jr., ZNW 53, '62, 25–51); **Mk 2:7; J 10:36; Ac 26:11; 1 Ti 1:20; 1 Pt 4:4** (the last 3 passages may be interpr. as not referring exclusively to God). βλασφημίαι, ὅσα ἐὰν βλασφημήσωσιν *whatever impious slanders they utter* **Mk 3:28** (cp. Pla., Leg. 7, 800c βλ. βλασφημίαν; Tob 1:18 S).

γ. God's name **Ro 2:24** (contrast the approval expressed OGI 339, 30); 2 Cl 13:2a; ITr 8:2b (all three Is 52:5); **1 Ti 6:1; Rv 13:6; 16:9;** 2 Cl 13:1, 2b (quot. of unknown orig.), 4; Hs 6, 2, 3 v.l.

δ. God's Spirit εἰς τὸ πνεῦμα τὸ ἅγιον **Mk 3:29; Lk 12:10.** On impious slander of the Holy Spirit s. WWeber, ZWT 52, 1910, 320–41; HWindisch, in Porter-Bacon Festschr. 1928, 218–21; EBuonaiuti, Ricerche Religiose 6, 1930, 481–91; OEvans, ET 68, '57, 240–44; GFitzer, TZ 13, '57, 161–82; JWilliams, NTS 12, '65, 75–77; CColpe, JJeremias Festschr., '70, 63–79.

ε. Christ **Mt 27:39; Mk 15:29; Lk 23:39;** ἕτερα πολλὰ β. **22:65** (cp. Vett. Val. 67, 20 πολλὰ βλασφημήσει θεούς). τὸν κύριον Hs 8, 6, 4; 8, 8, 2; 9, 19, 3; ISm 5:2; εἰς τ. κύριον Hv 2, 2, 2; s 6, 2, 4; τὸν βασιλέα μου MPol 9:3.—The name of Christ **Js 2:7.**

ζ. angels δόξας β. **2 Pt 2:10; Jd 8.** Angels are also meant in ὅσα οὐκ οἴδασιν β. **Jd 10** and ἐν οἷς ἀγνοοῦσιν β. *defaming where they have no knowledge* **2 Pt 2:12** (B-D-F §152, 1; Rob. 473). S. δόξα 4.

η. things that constitute the significant possessions of Christians τὴν ὁδὸν τ. δικαιοσύνης ApcPt 7:22; cp. **2 Pt 2:2.** Here and elsewh. pass. ὁ λόγος τ. θεοῦ **Tit 2:5;** ὑμῶν τὸ ἀγαθόν **Ro 14:16;** τὸ ἐν θεῷ πλῆθος ITr 8:2a; τὸ ὄνομα ὑμῶν μεγάλως β. 1 Cl 1:1; τὸν νόμον τοῦ κυρίου Hs 8, 6, 2.—In our lit. β. is used w. the acc. of the pers. or thing (Plut.; Appian [Nägeli 44]; Vett. Val. [s. bε above]; Philo [s. bα and bβ above]; Joseph. [s. bα and bβ above]; 4 Km 19:22) or w. εἰς and acc. (Demosth. 51, 3; Philo, Mos. 2, 206; Jos., Bell. 2, 406. Specif. εἰς θεούς and the like, Pla., Rep. 2 p. 381e; Vett. Val. 44, 4; 58, 12; Philo, Fuga 84a; Jos., Ant. 8, 392; Da 3:96; Bel 8 Theod.).—S. βλασφημία end. DELG. M-M. s.v. -ος. TW.

βλασφημία, ας, ἡ (s. βλασφημέω; Eur., Democr., Pla.+; LXX, Philo, Joseph.; Just., A I, 26, 5; Ath. 31, 2, R.72, 27; AssMos fgm. j p. 67 Denis; loanw. in rabb.) **speech that denigrates or defames, *reviling, denigration, disrespect, slander***

ⓐ gener., of any kind of speech that is defamatory or abusive, w. other vices **Mk 7:22; Eph 4:31; Col 3:8.** πᾶσα β. *all abusive speech* Hm 8:3; cp. **Mt 12:31a.** Pl. (Jos., Vi. 245) **Mt 15:19; 1 Ti 6:4.**

ⓑ specif., against humans and transcendent entities—**α.** humans (Cleanthes [IV–III BC] 1 p. 135, 21 [in Diog. L. 7, 17, 3]; Polyb. 11, 5, 8; Jos., Ant. 3, 307, Vi. 260) β. ἔκ τινος *slander of* (i.e. emanating from) *someone* **Rv 2:9;** cp. IEph 10:2.

β. the devil κρίσιν βλασφημίας *a reviling judgment* **Jd 9** (but s. Field [Notes 244], who favors 'accusation of [the devil for] blasphemy').

γ. God and what is God's (Comp. II 153f [Menand., fgm. 715 Kock] ἡ εἰς τὸ θεῖον β.; Ezk 35:12; 1 Macc 2:6; 2 Macc 8:4; 10:35; 15:24; Philo, Leg. ad Gai. 368) **Mt 26:65** (OLinton, NTS 7, '61, 258–62); **Mk 2:7 v.l.; 14:64; Lk 5:21** (pl.); **J 10:33; Rv 13:5** (pl.); 2 Cl 13:3; D 3:6; β. πρὸς τὸν θεόν (Iambl., Vi. Pyth. 32, 216; cp. εἰς τὸν πατέρα Hippol., Ref. 9, 12, 19) **Rv 13:6.** βλασφημίας ἐπιφέρεσθαι τῷ ὀνόματι κυρίου 1 Cl 47:7; προσέθηκαν κατὰ ὄνομα τοῦ κυρίου βλασφημίαν Hs 6, 2, 3; β., ὅσα ἐὰν βλασφημήσωσιν **Mk 3:28,** s. βλασφημέω bβ; ἡ τοῦ πνεύματος (obj. gen.) β. **Mt 12:31b,** s. βλασφημέω bδ. ὀνόματα βλασφημίας (gen. of qual.) **Rv 13:1; 17:3.** ῥήματα βλασφημίας **Ac 6:11 v.l.**—The passages in β and γ generate an emotive aspect associated with denigration of a prestigious entity (cp. Origen's rejoinder to Celsus: C. Celsum 8, 38 with reff. to Ex 22:27; Ro 12:14; 1 Cor 6:10). Hence the caution about denigrating the devil. Impious denigration of deity is esp. heinous and many translations reflect this emotive value in the loanword 'blasphemy'. But Greco-Roman and Semitic minds would first of all, as Ac 19:37 and Rom 2:24 indicate, think in terms of disrespect shown or harm done to a deity's reputation, a fact obscured by the rendering 'blasphemy', which has to some extent in Eng. gone its own emotive way semantically and has in effect become a religious technical term, which is not the case with βλασφημέω. On the range of expressions for denigration of God s. ESanders, Jewish Law fr. Jesus to the Mishnah '90, 57–67.—DELG s.v. βλασφημέω. M-M. TW.

βλάσφημος, ον (s. two prec. entries; Demosth. et al.; Plut., Herodian; LXX; JosAs 13:9; Just.) ***defaming, denigrating, demeaning*** ῥήματα β. *demeaning words* **Ac 6:11, 13 v.l.;** cp. **Rv 13:5 v.l.** (Dio Chrys. 3, 53 τὶ βλάσφημον περὶ τῶν θεῶν; Herodian 7, 8, 9 βλάσφημα πολλὰ εἰπὼν εἰς τὴν Ῥώμην καὶ τὴν σύγκλητον; Philo, De Ios. 247; Jos., Vi. 158; 320). β. κρίσιν φέρειν *pronounce a demeaning judgment* **2 Pt 2:11.** Of pers.: *slanderer* (Wsd 1:6; Sir 3:16; 2 Macc 9:28; 10:36) **1 Ti 1:13; 2 Ti 3:2;** Hs 9, 18, 3; w. προδόται 9, 19, 3; β. εἰς τὸν κύριον 9, 19, 1.—DELG s.v. βλασφημέω. M-M. TW.

βλέμμα, ατος, τό—❶ the aspect one projects through facial gesture, *look, mien, expression of countenance* (s. βλέπω; Eur. et al.; Demosth.; Epict. 4, 1, 145; 4, 8, 17; Lucian, Dial. Mar. 15:2; POxy 471, 60; Philo, Conf. Lingu. 11; Jos. Ant. 16, 223; 19, 39; TestReub 5:3; TestSol 5:2, 3; TestAbr A; 4 Esdr 8:23 fgm. c) περίπικρον β. *a very bitter look* Hs 6, 2, 5 (Maximus Tyr. 14, 1c β. ἰταμόν).

❷ the act of seeing, *seeing* (Lot was profoundly disturbed) *by what he saw* w. ἀκοή **2 Pt 2:8.**—DELG s.v. βλέπω. M-M.

βλέπω fut. βλέψω; 3 pl. fut. βλέψονται Is 29:18; 1 aor. ἔβλεψα (s. βλέμμα; Pind.+ 'see': on the use of βλέπω and ὁράω s. Reinhold 97ff. Esp. oft. in Hermas [70 times]).

❶ **to perceive w. the eye,** *see*—ⓐ w. acc. of what is seen: beam, splinter **Mt 7:3; Lk 6:41f—Mt 11:4; 13:17; 24:2; Mk 8:23f; Lk 10:23f; Ac 2:33; 9:8f; Rv 1:11f; 5:3f; 22:8.** Large buildings **Mk 13:2** (cp. Choliamb. in Ps.-Callisth. 1, 46a, 8 lines 4, 8, 19: ὁρᾷς τὰ τείχη ταῦθ'; . . . τὰ θεμέλια ταῦτα . . . ὁρᾷς ἐκείνους τοὺς οἴκους;); a woman **Lk 7:44;** light (Artem. 5, 20 τὸ φῶς ἔβλεπεν; 5, 77) **8:16,** cp. **11:33;** Jesus **J 1:29;** B 5:10; signs **Ac 8:6;** B 4:14; a vision **Ac 12:9;** nakedness **Rv 16:15;** the beast **17:8;** smoke **18:9, 18.**—*Seeing* contrasted w. hoping **Ro 8:24f.** Of angels βλέπουσι τὸ πρόσωπον τοῦ πατρός (expr. fr. oriental court life = have access constantly, 2 Km 14:24; cp. 4 Km 25:19) **Mt 18:10** (s. πρόσωπον 1bα). Pass. πάντων βλεπομένων *since everything is seen* 1 Cl 28:1. W. acc. and ptc. instead of a dependent clause (SIG1104, 42; UPZ 68, 6 [152 BC] βλέπω Μενέδημον κατατρέχοντά με=that M. runs after me; 1 Macc 12:29; Jos., Ant. 20, 219); τὸν ὄχλον συνθλίβοντά σε *that the crowd is pressing around you* **Mk 5:31.** τὸν λίθον ἠρμένον *that the stone was taken away* **J 20:1;** cp. **Mt 15:31; Lk 24:12; J 20:5; 21:9.** τὸν πατέρα ποιοῦντα **5:19;** sim. **21:20; Ac 4:14; Hb 2:9.** ὑπὲρ ὃ βλέπει με *beyond what he sees in me* **2 Cor 12:6.**

ⓑ abs.: **Mt 13:16; Ro 11:10** (Ps 68:24); **Rv 9:20.** τὰ βλεπόμενα (Ael. Aristid. 46 p. 406 D.; Wsd 13:7; 17:6) *what can be seen* **2 Cor 4:18.** *Look on, watch* (Jos., Bell. 1, 596. Ant. 3, 95 βλεπόντων αὐτῶν while they looked on, before their eyes) **Ac 1:9;** 1 Cl 25:4.

ⓒ w. prep. phrase: ἐν τῷ κρυπτῷ *who sees in secret* **Mt 6:4, 6;** cp. vs. **18** (s. 4 Macc 15:18). In imagery δι' ἐσόπτρου ἐν αἰνίγματι **1 Cor 13:12.**

ⓓ βλέπων βλέπω *see w. open eyes* **Mt 13:14** (Is 6:9). βλέπων οὐ βλέπει *though he looks he does not see* **13:13; Lk 8:10** (the theme is transcultural, cp. Aeschyl., Prom. 447f; Soph. O.T. 413; Ps.-Demosth. 25, 89; Polyb. 12, 24, 6; Lucian, D. Mar. 4, 3; Lucretius 2:14 o pectora caeca! qualibus in tenebris vitae 'O blind hearts! In what darkness of life . . . '; s. ἀκούω).

❷ **to have the faculty of sight,** *be able to see,* in contrast to being blind (trag.; Antiphon 4, 4, 2; X., Mem. 1, 3, 4; Aelian, VH 6, 12; SIG 1168, 78 blind man βλέπων ἀμφοῖν ἐξῆλθε; POxy 39, 9 [52 AD] ὀλίγον βλέπων=of weak sight; Ex 4:11; 23:8; 1 Km 3:2; Ps. 113:14; al.) **Mt 12:22; 15:31; Lk 7:21; J 9:7, 15, 25; Ac 9:9; Rv 3:18.** ὀφθαλμοὶ τοῦ μὴ β. (Ps 68:24, cp. 9:32; Sus 9; B-D-F §400, 2) *eyes unable to see* **Ro 11:8** (Dt 29:3); Hs 6, 2, 1. θεοὶ . . . δυνάμενοι μήτε βλέψαι μήτε ἀκοῦσαι AcPl Ha 1, 20 (cp. Ps 113:14).—Fig. of grasp of transcendent matters (cp. Diog. L. 6, 53 with reference to Pla.: β. with the eyes of the νοῦς) **J 9:39.**

❸ **to take in the sight of someth.,** *look at, observe* εἰς w. acc. (Anaxandrides Com. [IV BC] 34, 9 K. εἰς τοὺς καλούς; Ael. Aristid. 28, 126 K.=49 p. 531f D.; Aelian, VH 14, 42; Herodian 3, 11, 3; Jdth 9:9; Pr 16:25; Sir 40:29; 4 Macc 15:18) **Lk 9:62; J 13:22** (εἰς ἀλλήλους as Proverb. Aesopi 49 P.) **Ac 1:11 v.l.** (Ps.-Apollod., Epit. 5, 22 and PGM 13, 833 εἰς τ. οὐρανὸν β.); **3:4.** W. dat. [ὁ δὲ λέων . . . .ἔβλ]επεν τῷ Παύλῳ| καὶ ὁ Παῦλο[ς τῷ λέοντι] *the lion looked at Paul and Paul [at the lion]* AcPl Ha 4, 36. W. acc. *look at a woman* (cp. Synes., Calvitii encomium 23, 86b ὅστις ἀδίκοις ὀφθαλμοῖς ὁρᾷ τὴν τοῦ γείτονος) **Mt 5:28** (ὅστις ἂν ἐμβλέψῃ γυναικί Just., A I, 15, 1). *See* magic rites D 3:4. βιβλίον *look into a book* **Rv 5:3f.**

❹ **to pay esp. close attention to someth.,** *notice, mark* someth.: w. acc. **2 Cor 10:7** (impv.). W. εἴς τι (Polyb. 3, 64, 10 εἰς τ. παρουσίαν) εἰς πρόσωπον β. *look at someone's face* = *regard someone's opinion* in the sense of being afraid of what someone might think **Mt 22:16; Mk 12:14.**

❺ **be ready to learn about someth. that is needed or is hazardous,** *watch, look to, beware of,* **Mk 13:9; Phil 3:2** (GKilpatrick, PKahle memorial vol. '68, 146–48: *look at, consider*); **2J 8.** Followed by μή, μήποτε, μήπως and aor. subj. (Pythag., Ep. 4; Epict. 2, 11, 22; 3, 20, 16; PLond III, 964, 9 p. 212 [II/III AD] βλέπε μὴ ἐπιλάθῃ οὐδέν; PLips 106, 17 [I BC]) *beware, look out* **Mt 24:4; Mk 13:5; Lk 21:8; Ac 13:40; 1 Cor 8:9; 10:12; Gal 5:15; Hb 12:25,** or fut. indic. **Col 2:8.** W. ἀπό τινος (BGU 1079, 2426 [41 AD]=CPJ 152, 24ff βλέπε σατὸν [=σαυτὸν] ἀπὸ τῶν Ἰουδαίων; APF 4, 1908, 568) *beware of* the leaven of the Pharisees **Mk 8:15;** of the scribes **12:38.**

❻ **to process information by giving thought,** ***direct one's attention to someth., consider, note*** (Jos., Bell. 7, 351, Ant. 20, 57).

ⓐ abs. βλέπετε *keep your eyes open* **Mk 13:33.**—ⓑ w. acc. (2 Ch 10:16) **1 Cor 1:26; 10:18;** on **Phil 3:2** s. 5; **Col 2:5; 4:17.** βλέπων τ. ἐντολήν *w. regard to the commandment* B 10:11a.

ⓒ w. indir. question foll. **Mk 4:24; Lk 8:18; 1 Cor 3:10; Eph 5:15;** 1 Cl 56:16; B 10:11b.—W. ἵνα foll. **1 Cor 16:10.**

❼ **to develop awareness of someth.,** ***perceive, feel***—ⓐ by the senses: a strong wind **Mt 14:30.**

ⓑ of inner awareness *discover, find* a law **Ro 7:23** (cp. PFay 111, 16 ἐὰν βλέπῃς τὴν τιμὴν [price] παντὸς ἀγόρασον). W. acc. and ptc. 2 Cl 20:1; B 1:3. W. ὅτι foll. (BGU 815, 4; EpArist 113) **2 Cor 7:8; Hb 3:19; Js 2:22.**

❽ **to be oriented in a particular direction,** ***looking to, in the direction of, facing*** (rather freq. and w. var. preps.; w. κατά and acc. Ezk 11:1; 40:6 al.; JosAs 5:2 θυρίδα . . . βλέπουσαν κατὰ ἀνατολάς 'a window looking out toward the east') **Ac 27:12** (s. λίψ and s. Field, Notes 144).—FHahn, Sehen u. Glauben im J: OCullmann Festschr., '72, 125–41; FThordarson, SymbOsl 46, '71, 108–30.—B. 1042. DELG. M-M. TW. Sv.

βλέφαρον, ου, τό (Hom. et al.; pap, LXX; ApcEsdr 4:22 p. 28, 25 Tdf.; SibOr 2, 178; 181) ***eyelid*** τὰ β. τῶν ὀφθαλμῶν Papias (3:2); but prob. *eyelash* in οὔτε θρὶξ οὔτε β. AcPlCor 2:30.—S. DELG and Frisk on etym.

βληθήσομαι s. βάλλω.

βλητέος, α, ον the only verbal adj. in -τέος in NT (B-D-F §65, 3; Rob. 157), fr. βάλλω ***must be put*** (s. βάλλω 3b) **Lk 5:38;** cp. **Mk 2:22 v.l.**—JViteau, Revue de Philol. n.s. 18, 1894, 38.

βληχρός, ά, όν (Pind.+; Diod. S., Plut.) **pert. to lack of strength,** ***feeble*** of prayer (w. μικρός) Hs 2:5. Of pers. (w. ἀργός) πρός τι *too weak for someth.* 5, 4, 3.—DELG.

Βοανηργές (var. other spellings are found in the mss., e.g. Βοανεργές, which is also used by Just.) of Aram. composition ***Boanerges***=Hebr. בְּנֵי רֶגֶשׁ **Mk 3:17,** transl. υἱοὶ βροντῆς *Sons of thunder* (cp. Diod. S. 8, 11, 2 of a house that had been struck by lightning: ὀνομάζεται Ἐμβρονταῖον=House of Thunder); surname given by Jesus to the sons of Zebedee (s. Lk 9:54). See EKautzsch, Gramm. d. Bibl. Aram. 1884, 9; Dalman, Gramm.[2] 144, Worte 33; 39, 4, Jesus 11; RHarris, Exp. 7th ser. III 1907, 146–52, ET 36, 1925, 139; JBoehmer, StKr 85, 1912, 458–64; EPreuschen, ZNW 18, 1918, 141–44 (s. Fischer, ibid. 23, 1924, 310f); FSchulthess, D. Problem d. Sprache Jesu 1917, 52f, ZNW 21, 1922, 243–47; GBardy, RSR 15, 1925, 167f; 18, 1928, 344; PJoüon, ibid. 438ff; AFridrichsen, SymbOsl 13, '34, 40: 'thunderstrokes'; JMontgomery, JBL 56, '37, 51f; B-D-F §162, 6. (The difficulty pert. to the vowels of Boa is not yet solved; s. ThNöldeke, GGA 1884, 1022f. Nor is it certain that rges=רְגַשׁ; Kautzsch points to רֹגֶז *wrath,* which would make the word mean *the hot-tempered.* Wlh.[2] ad loc. draws attention to the name Ragasbal. Schulthess first cj. benē reḥēm=fratres uterini, *full brothers,* then benē regeš=partisans, adherents. JRook, JBL 100, '81, 94f attributes the problem to a transliteration technique involving an ayin/gamma change.—Pairs of brothers or sisters known by a special name: AKrappe: Amicitiae Corolla 133–46.)

βοάω impf. ἐβόων **Ac 21:34 v.l.;** fut. βοήσω and βοήσομαι LXX; 1 aor. ἐβόησα, impv. βόησον (s. βοή; Hom.+)

❶ **to use one's voice at high volume,** ***call, shout, cry out,*** oft. w. φωνῇ μεγάλῃ (Phlegon: 257 fgm. 36, 1, 1 Jac.; Plut., Coriol. 225 [25, 3]; Gen 39:14; 1 Macc 3:54; 13:45 al. LXX; Sus 46 and Bel 18 Theod.).

ⓐ of emotionally charged cries: of joy abs. ῥῆξον κ. βόησον *break forth and shout* **Gal 4:27;** 2 Cl 2:1f (both Is 54:1; interpreted as prayer to God 2 Cl 2:2). —Of the shouts of excited crowds (Jos., Ant. 13, 376; cp. X., An. 4, 3, 22) **Ac 17:6; 25:24;** AcPl Ha 4, 35; 5, 11; 9, 21; 10, 30; MPol 12:2 v.l.

ⓑ of pleading petitions or anguished outcries (Ael. Aristid. 48, 54 K.=24 p. 479 D.; β. τὸν θεόν) abs. B 3:5 (Is 58:9). W. dat. foll. (Sus 60 Theod. v.l. ἐβόησαν τ. θεῷ) **Lk 18:7.** W. πρός and acc. (Num 12:13; PsSol 1:1) ἐξ ἑνὸς στόματος β. πρὸς αὐτόν 1 Cl 34:7; πρὸς τὸν θεόν AcPl Ha 3, 8.—Of cry of anguish or for help: Jesus on the cross **Mt 27:46 v.l.; Mk 15:34;** evil spirits when leaving a person **Ac 8:7** (in these three pass. β. φωνῇ μεγάλῃ; s. above); sick people **Lk 9:38; 18:38** (s. ἀναβοάω; ἐβόησεν λέγων as Diog. L. 6, 44 ἐβόα λέγων; Ps.-Callisth. 1, 25, 1; 1 Km 5:10; Jdth 6:18; for pap relating to requests for healing s. New Docs 4, 245–50).

ⓒ of solemn proclamation (Menand. Com. fgm. 215, 5 Kö., in Diog. L. 6, 83 τὰ βοώμενα; Aelian, VH 3, 42 ἡ τραγῳδία βοᾷ; SibOr 3, 212) φωνὴ βοῶντος (φωνή 2e) **Mt 3:3; Mk 1:3; Lk 3:4; J 1:23;** B 9:3 (all Is 40:3).

❷ ***to roar,*** of a lion ἐβόησεν μεγάλως AcPl Ha 2, 6.—B. 1250. Schmidt, Syn. I 125–35. DELG s.v. βοή. M-M. TW.

Βόες, ὁ (Βοές Tdf., W-H.; v.l. Βόος, Βόοζ; B-D-F §39, 4; s. Βόος; ARahlfs, Studie über d. griech. Text d. Buches Ruth 1922, 73) indecl. (in Jos., Ant. 5, 323ff Βοώζης [Ant. 5, 323] or Βόαζος, ου [Ant. 5, 326]) ***Boaz*** (בֹּעַז), in the genealogy of Jesus **Mt 1:5.** Cp. 1 Ch 2:11f; Ruth 4:21.

βοή, ῆς, ἡ (s. βοάω; Hom. et al.; pap, LXX; pl. 2 Macc 4:22; Jos., Bell. 4, 306; 310; Just., A I, 68, 8 [Hadrian]) ***cry (out), shout*** AcPl Ha 5, 34; pl. **Js 5:4** (cp. Jos., Ant. 8, 339 μεγάλῃ βοῇ καλεῖν τ. θεούς).—DELG. M-M.

βοήθεια, ας, ἡ (s. βοηθέω; Thu.+)—❶ **assistance offered to meet a need,** ***help*** εὔκαιρος β. *timely help* **Hb 4:16** (cp. OGI 762, 3f ὁ δῆμος ὁ τῶν Κιβυρατῶν τῷ δήμῳ τῷ Ῥωμαίων βοηθείτω κατὰ τὸ εὔκαιρον; SIG 693, 12.—Of divine help: Diod. S. 3, 40, 7 τῶν θεῶν β.; Ael. Aristid. 31 p. 600 D.: παρὰ τ. θεῶν; Ps 19:3; 34:2; PsSol; JosAs 23:4; Jos., Ant. 13, 65, Vi. 290).

❷ **material things that help,** ***an aid, a help,*** pl. *(makeshift) aids, helps* (Diod. S. 3, 8, 5) βοηθείαις ἐχρῶντο prob. a nautical t.t. (cp. Philo, De Ios. 33 κυβερνήτης ταῖς τῶν πνευμάτων μεταβολαῖς συμμεταβάλλει τὰς πρὸς εὔπλοιαν βοηθείας; cp. Diod. S., 3, 40, 5 βοηθέω of the bringing of aid for a ship in danger) *they used supports* (perh. cables) **Ac 27:17.** See lit. s.v. ὑποζώννυμι and comm.—DELG s.v. βοή. M-M. TW.

βοηθέω fut. βοηθήσω, 1 aor. ἐβοήθησα, impv. βοήθησον. Pass. fut. βοηθηθήσομαι (cp. Is 44:2; Da 11:34 Theod.); 1 aor. ἐβοηθήθην LXX (s. βοήθεια; Aeschyl., Hdt.+) **to render assistance to someone in need,** ***furnish aid.*** βοηθεῖτε *help!* (Aristoph., Vesp. 433 ὦ Μίδα καὶ Φρὺξ βοηθεῖτε δεῦρο) **Ac 21:28.**—Render assistance *help, come to the aid of* τινί *someone* **Mt 15:25; Mk 9:22; Ac 16:9** (cp. Epict. 2, 15, 15 νοσῶ, κύριε· βοήθησόν μοι; Josh 10:6; Jos., Bell. 1, 56); **Hb 2:18; Rv 12:16;** 1 Cl 39:5 (Job 4:20); 2 Cl 8:2; IRo 7:1; D 12:2; AcPl Ha 6, 34; 10, 3 (cp. MartPl 4 [=Aa I 114, 12]). βοήθει μου τῇ ἀπιστίᾳ *help my lack of faith,* or = μοι ἀπιστοῦντι **Mk 9:24.**—God as helper (Sb 158 ὁ θεὸς αὐτῷ ἐβοήθησε; PGM 13, 289 βοήθησον ἐν ἀνάγκαις; EPeterson, Εἷς θεός 1926, 3f; 309 al.) **2 Cor 6:2** (Is 49:8).—B. 1353. Schmidt, Syn. IV 148–61. DELG s.v. βοή. M-M. TW.

βοηθός, όν (s. βοήθεια, βοηθέω; Hdt. et al.; LXX; JosAs; ParJer 9:32; Just., Tat.) ***helpful,*** subst. *helper* (Hdt. et al., ins, pap, ostraca, LXX; Jos., Bell. 1, 317, Ant. 13, 276; 358) of Christ β. τῆς ἀσθενείας ἡμῶν *who helps us in our weakness* 1 Cl 36:1. Of God (Herodian 3, 6, 7; UPZ 52, 8 [162 BC] Sarap.; PLond II, 410, 7f p. 298 [c. 346 AD] μετὰ τὸν θεὸν οὐδένα ἔχομεν βοηθόν; POxy 1381, 83; LXX, Philo; Jos., Ant. 2, 274; Jew. ins: ISyriaW 2451) **Hb 13:6** (Ps 117:7). τῶν κινδυνευόντων *helper of those in danger* 1 Cl 59:3; cp. vs. 4.—βοηθοί *auxiliaries* B 2:2.—DELG s.v. βοή. M-M. TW.

βόησον s. βοάω.

βόθρος, ου, ὁ (s. next; Hom. et al.; Paus. 9, 39, 6; Philostrat., Her 18, 3 p. 195, 16; perh. PRossGeorg V, 55, 1; LXX; Jos., Ant. 9, 35; TestReub 2:9; Just., A I, 18, 5; Moeris 105 βόθρος ἀττικόν· βόθυνος κοινόν 'β. is Attic, βόθυνος common/vulgar'; X. has both forms [Schmid IV 282]) **a hollowed out area in the ground,** ***hole,*** prob. *pit* or *hole* **Mt 15:14** D; *cistern* B 11:2. Sv.—TMavrojannis, Rivista di Antichità 3/2, '94, 298 n. 39 (lit.).

βόθυνος, ου, ὁ (s. prec.; since Cratinus 210; X., Oec. 19, 3; Clidemus [350 BC]: 323 fgm. 14 Jac.; PHal 1, 97 [III BC]; BGU 1122, 17 [14 BC]; PMert 27, 12; LXX; cp. Is 24:18; 47:11) =βόθρος q.v.; *pit* **Mt 12:11; 15:14; Lk 6:39** (εἰς βόθ. ἐμπ. as Jer 31:44; on this topic cp. Philo, Virt. 7).—M-M.

βολή, ῆς, ἡ (Hom. et al.; LXX) 'act of propelling through the air by a forward motion'; in our lit. in the transf. sense **distance travelled by something propelled,** ***a throw*** ὡσεὶ λίθου βολήν *as far as one can throw a stone, about a stone's throw* (TestGad 1:3) **Lk 22:41** (Thu. 5, 65, 2 μέχρι λίθου βολῆς ἐχώρησαν; Herodian 2, 6, 13; 7, 12, 5; cp. Gen 21:16; Jos., Ant. 20, 213).—DELG s.v. βάλλω p. 162.

βολίζω (via βόλος 'a throw w. a net', and βολή [s. prec.]) 1 aor. ἐβόλισα **to use a weighted line to determine depth,** ***take soundings, heave the lead*** (the sounding would be taken with a βολίς, an implement shaped like a missile [s. βολίς next entry] and prob. made of lead, μόλυβδος, hence Sch. Il. 24, 80 renders βολίς 'sounding-lead') **Ac 27:28** twice (elsewh. only in Geoponica 6, 17 [pass.='sink'] and Eustathius on Homer 563, 30; 731, 46). LCasson, Ships and Seamanship in the Anc. World, '71, 246, n. 85; further details Hemer, Acts 147 n. 131.—DELG s.v. βάλλω. M-M.

βολίς, ίδος, ἡ (s. βολίζω) ***missile, arrow, javelin*** (Zech 9:14; Plut., Demetr. 890 [3, 2]; Hesych.; Suda) **Hb 12:20 v.l.** (Ex 19:13).—DELG s.v. βάλλω p. 162.

Βόος, ὁ indecl. (v.l. Βόοζ) ***Boaz,*** in the genealogy of Jesus **Lk 3:32;** s. Βόες.

βορά, ᾶς, ἡ (Aeschyl., Hdt.+; LXX; cp. Job 38:39; 3 Macc 6:7; En 25:5; 6:7; TestJob 43:8; JosAs 10:14; Just.; Tat. 25, 5; PCairMasp 141, 14 κυνὸς β.) **food, esp. for carnivorous animals,** *food* ἄφετέ με θηρίων εἶναι βοράν IRo 4:1 (Eur., Phoen. 1603 θηρσὶν ἄθλιον βορ.; Jos., Bell. 4, 324 β. θηρίων).—DELG s.v. βιβρώσκω.

βόρβορος, ου, ὁ (Aeschyl., Pla., al.; Jer 45:6; Jos., Ant. 10, 121; ParJer 3:13; Tat. 21, 4)

❶ **boiling mire in the netherworld,** *mire* ApcPt 8:23; 9:24; 16:31 (cp. Diogenes the Cynic [IV BC] in Diog. L. 6, 39: the wicked are tormented in the next world ἐν τῷ βορβόρῳ; AcThom 56; MartMt 3 [Aa II/2, 172, 9; II/1, 220, 1]).

❷ **sullied mud,** *slime, mud* (cp. TestBenj 8:3 κόπρον και β.) in which swine wallow ὗς λουσαμένη εἰς κυλισμὸν βορβόρου **2 Pt 2:22.** This is usu. taken to mean *a sow, after she has washed herself, (turns) to wallowing in the mud* (the ptc. is mid., Mlt. 155f; 238f; s. JHarris, The Story of Aḥikar 1898, lxvii, also in Charles, APOT II, 772; RSmend, Alter u. Herkunft d. Achikar-Romans 1908, 75). But the idea was also current that swine preferred to bathe in mud or slime (Sext. Emp., Pyrrhon. Hypot. I 56 σύες τε ἥδιον βορβόρῳ λούονται … ἢ ὕδατι … καθαρῷ; cp. Clem. Al., Protr. 92, 4; Aristot., HA 8, 6 p. 595a, 31; Galen, Protr. 13, p. 42, 22 John); the tr. might then be *a sow, having (once) bathed herself (in mud), (returns) to wallowing in the mire* (CBigg, ICC, 1901 ad loc.), or *a sow that washes herself by wallowing in the mire* (M-M. s.v. λούω); cp. PWendland, Ein Wort des Heraklit im NT: SBBerlAk 1898, 788–96. On swine wallowing in mud, lit. and fig., see Semonides 7, 2ff; Heraclitus, fgm. 37; Epict. 4, 11, 29 (cp. 31) χοίρῳ διαλέγου, ἵν' ἐν βορβόρῳ μὴ κυλίηται; Plut., Mor. 129a; Ael. Aristid. 33, 31 K.=51 p. 582 D.; Philo, Spec. Leg. 1, 148, Agr. 144; Clem. Al., Protr. 92, 4. In the light of Israelite and Gr-Rom. emphasis on purification before participation in religious rites, the imagery is esp. forceful in its devastating satire. S. BHHW I 20.—Schmidt, Syn. II 193f, and s. πηλός. DELG. M-M. Sv.

βορρᾶς, ᾶ, ὁ (this colloq. form, interchangeable even in class. writers w. βορέας [Kühner-Bl. I 386f; Schwyzer I 274], is predom. in pap [Mayser 252; cp. 221] and LXX; it is found En 32:4; PsSol 11:3; JosAs; GrBar 11:8; ApcEsdr 4:25 p. 28, 29 Tdf.; Jos., Bell. 5, 144; Just., D. 52, 10 [on Zech 2:10], and in ins [OGI 176, 8; 178, 10], and is the only form used by Koine writers like Vett. Val.; cp. B-D-F §34, 3; 45; Rdm. 59; Rob. 254) ***the north*** ἀπὸ βορρᾶ *on the north* **Rv 21:13** (ἀπό 2a); ἀπὸ β. καὶ νότου *from north and south* **Lk 13:29** (on the absence of the art. s. B-D-F §253, 5; Rob. 793ff). W. the three other points of the compass 1 Cl 10:4 (Gen 13:14).—B. 872. DELG s.v. βορέας. M-M.

Βόρρος s. Βοῦρρος.

βόσκω fut. βοσκήσω; 1 aor. ἐβόσκησα; fut. pass. βοσκηθήσομαι, all LXX (Hom. et al.; ins, pap, LXX; ApcrEzk P 1 verso 13; Philo distinguishes betw. β. and ποιμαίνω, Det. Pot. Ins. 25).

❶ **to tend to the needs of animals,** ***herd, tend,*** of herders (Jos., Ant. 6, 254) lambs **J 21:15** (on the fig. use cp. 3 Km 12:16 νῦν βόσκε τὸν οἶκόν σου, Δαυίδ; Aberciusins 4 β. πρόβ.). Sheep vs. 17; Hs 6, 1, 6. Swine **Lk 15:15.** ὁ βόσκων *herdsman* (cp. Aristot. HA 5, 2, 540a, 18; Jer 38:10) **Mt 8:33; Mk 5:14; Lk 8:34.**

❷ **to feed on herbage,** ***graze, feed,*** pass. of livestock (Is 5:17; 11:7; Jos., Bell. 6, 153; SibOr 3, 789) ἀγέλη βοσκομένη **Mt 8:30; Mk 5:11; Lk 8:32.** πρόβατα βοσκόμενα (PTebt 298, 53) Hs 6, 2, 4, cp. 7; sim. 9, 1, 8.—B. 146. DELG. M-M.

Βοσόρ, ὁ indecl. (ApcSed 11:2 p. 134, 12 Ja.) ***Bosor*** **2 Pt 2:15** (v.l.: Βεώρ, q.v.).

βοτάνη, ης, ἡ (fr. βόσκω q.v.; Hom.+; pap, LXX; En 7:1; TestSol; TestAbr A 4 p. 80, 23 [Stone p. 8]; AscIs 2:11; Philo) a generic term for smaller green plants, freq. serving as pasturage for animals, s. βόσκω.

❶ **vegetation in general,** ***herb, plant,*** lit. Hs 9, 1, 5ff; 9, 21, 1; 3; 9, 22, 1; 9, 23, 1; 9, 24, 1; β. εὔθετος *useful vegetation* **Hb 6:7;** πᾶσαν φάγε β. *eat every plant* GEg 252, 53; s. also under 2, ITr 6:1; semina et herbam Pa (1, 3).—Esp. of *weeds* (for pap s. Preis.) Hm 10, 1, 5; s 5, 2, 3ff; 5, 4, 1; 5, 5, 3; 9, 26, 4.

❷ **someth. likened to a plant,** ***plant,*** of evil persons (foll. **Mt 13:24ff**) β. τοῦ διαβόλου *a plant of the devil* IEph 10:3; ἀπέχεσθαι κακῶν βοτανῶν IPhld 3:1. Of false teachings ἀλλοτρίας βοτάνης ἀπέχεσθαι ITr 6:1.—B. 521. DELG s.v. βόσκω. M-M.

βότρυς, υος, ὁ (Hom. et al; Epict. 1, 15, 7; BGU 1118, 14 [22 BC]; PLips 30, 4; LXX; En 32:4; EpArist 63; 70; 75; Jos., Ant. 12, 68; 75) ***bunch of grapes*** **Rv 14:18** (Ps.-Callisth. 3, 21, 2 βότρυες σταφυλῆς). The word is also found in the Phrygian Papias of Hierapolis, in a passage in which he speaks of the enormous size of the grapes in the new aeon (in the Lat. transl. in Irenaeus 5, 33, 2f): dena millia botruum Papias (1:2). On this see Stephan. Byz. s.v. Εὐκαρπία: Metrophanes says that in the district of Εὐκαρπία in Phrygia Minor the grapes were said to be so large that one bunch of them caused a wagon to break down in the middle; cp. Lucian, Ver. Hist. 2, 13 on an extraterrestrial viticultural phenomenon.—B. 378. DELG. M-M.

βουλευτής, οῦ, ὁ (s. βουλεύω; Hom. et al.; IGR I, 25, 3; Job 3:14; 12:17; 'councillor, senator') **a member of an advisory or legislative body,** ***councillor*** (ins, pap, loanw. in rabb.); of Joseph of Arimathaea: member of the Sanhedrin (Jos., Bell. 2, 405 οἱ ἄρχοντες καὶ βουλευταί) **Mk 15:43; Lk 23:50.**—DELG s.v. βούλομαι. M-M. TW.

βουλεύω in our lit. only mid. βουλεύομαι; impf. ἐβουλευόμην; fut. βουλεύσομαι **Lk 14:31;** 1 aor. ἐβουλευσάμην; pf. βεβούλευμαι LXX; B 6:7.

❶ **to think about a course of action,** ***deliberate*** (w. oneself) w. indir. question foll. (Jos., Ant. 1, 339) εἰ **Lk 14:31** (cp. X., Mem. 3, 6, 8 Diog. L. 1, 64); ἐβουλεύσαντο οἱ ἱερεῖς τίνα ἀναστήσουσιν GJs 24:4; *consider* τὶ *someth.* (Appian, Hann. 54 §227 β. ἀπόστασιν=consider a revolt) Hv 1, 1, 2 and 8; s 9, 28, 5.

❷ **to reach a decision about a course of action,** ***resolve, decide*** w. acc. ἅ (Jdth 9:6; 12:4) **2 Cor 1:17;** βουλὴν πονηράν B 6:7 (Is 3:9). W. inf. foll. (PTebt 58, 28; PFay 116, 9; 2 Ch 30:23; Wsd 18:5; 1 Macc 8:9; Jos., C. Ap. 2, 296 v.l.; Just., D. 72, 3) **Ac 5:33 v.l.; 15:37 v.l.; 27:39.** W. ἵνα foll. (B-D-F §392, 1a) **J 11:53** (EBammel, CMoule Festschr., '70, 11–40); **12:10.**—DELG s.v. βούλομαι. M-M.

βουλή, ῆς, ἡ (s. βουλεύω)—❶ **that which one thinks about as possibility for action,** ***plan, purpose, intention*** (Hom.+; s. also Iren. 5, 5, 2 [Harv. II 332, 10]: β. τοῦ θεοῦ) *purpose, counsel* 1 Cl 61:2; Hv 1, 2, 4; s 9, 28, 4f; pl. 9, 28, 8; βουλαὶ τῆς καρδίας *motives of the heart* **1 Cor 4:5;** μεστοὶ ὁσίας βουλῆς *full of holy plans* 1 Cl 2:3; perh. B 10:10 (Ps 1:1), but s. 3 below.

❷ **that which one decides,** ***resolution, decision***—ⓐ of humans (Jos., Ant. 2, 23) **Lk 23:51** (w. πρᾶξις as Philo, Poster. Cai. 86).—**Ac 5:38.** β. τίθεσθαι (Judg 19:30; Ps 12:3) *decide*

27:12 (w. inf. foll.). στρατιωτῶν β. ἐγένετο (w. ἵνα foll.) vs. **42.** βουλὴν βουλεύεσθαι of evil designs (Vi. Aesopi I, 33 p. 298, 6 Eberh.): βουλεύεσθαι βουλὴν πονηράν *form an evil plot* B 6:7 (Is 3:9); λαμβάνειν β. πονηρὰν κατά τινος *plot evil against someone* (but in Leontius 11 p. 21, 11 λαμβάνει βουλήν τινος=he receives [bad] advice from someone) 19:3; D 2:6. Cp. Hs 6, 3, 5.

ⓑ of the divine will (Herm. Wr. 1, 8; 18; 31; Quint. Smyrn. 6, 141 βουλῇ Διός; oft. LXX; Jos., Ant. 4, 42; SibOr 3, 574.—Dodd 126–32) 1 Cl 57:4f (Pr 1:25, 30); **Ac 2:23; 4:28; 13:36; 20:27;** Dg 8:10; ἡ ἔνδοξος β. Hv 1, 3, 4; τὸ ἀμετάθετον τῆς β. αὐτοῦ *the unchangeable nature of his resolve* **Hb 6:17;** κατὰ τὴν β. τοῦ θελήματος αὐτοῦ *acc. to the purpose of his will* **Eph 1:11;** cp. **Ac 19:1** D; τὴν β. τοῦ θεοῦ ἠθέτησαν εἰς ἑαυτούς *they frustrated the purpose of God for themselves* **Lk 7:30.** οὐδὲν λέληθεν τὴν β. αὐτοῦ *nothing is hidden from God's directing counsel* 1 Cl 27:6.

❸ **an assembly that takes up proposals or deliberates,** ***council meeting*** (Hom. et al.; Diod. S. 14, 4, 5; Philo; PsSol 8:20; Jos., Bell. 2, 641 al.; loanw. in rabb.) B 11:7 (Ps 1:5); B 10:10 (Ps 1:1, but see 1 above).—DELG s.v. βούλομαι. M-M. TW.

βούλημα, ατος, τό (Aristoph., Pla. et al.; Epict.; SIG 799, 12; pap, LXX, EpArist, Philo; Jos., Ant. 1, 278; Just.; Tat. 7, 2) ***intention*** τὸ ἀκέραιον αὐτῶν β. *their pure purpose* 1 Cl 21:7; τὸ β. τῶν ἐθνῶν *what the gentiles desire to do* **1 Pt 4:3** (v.l. θέλημα); κωλύειν τινὰ τοῦ β. *hinder someone in an intention* **Ac 27:43.** Of God's *will* (Cornutus 16 p. 22, 2 β. τῶν θεῶν; Philo, Mos. 1, 287 τοῦ θεοῦ β.; Jos., Ant. 2, 304; Just., D. 103, 3; Tat. 7, 2) **Ro 9:19;** 1 Cl 23:5; 33:3. τὸ παντοκρατορικὸν β. αὐτοῦ 8:5; τὸ μακρόθυμον αὐτοῦ β. 19:3.—DELG s.v. βούλομαι. M-M. TW.

βούλησις, εως, ἡ (Eur., Thu.+; Epict., ins; PTebt 43, 35; PHamb 73, 10; POxy 2267, 11; TestSol 1:3 D; Jos., C. Ap. 1, 45) **the act of willing,** ***will,*** of God's will (Plato, Tim. 41b; Ephorus [IV BC]: 70 fgm. 31b Jac.; Diod. S. 17, 66, 7; Phlegon: 257 fgm. 36, 1, 1; 36, 1, 4; 36, 1, 7 Jac.; Parthenius 4, 5; 15, 4 β. θεῶν; OGI 458, 15; 669, 17; PAmh 144, 11; POxy 130, 11; expressed in a dream, UPZ 81 IV, 19 [II BC]; EpArist 234; Philo, Rer. Div. Her. 246; Jos., Ant. 2, 232; Just., D. 5, 4; 63, 1; Eupolemus: 723 fgm. 2b, 2 [in Eus., PE 9, 30, 2]) ἡ ἔνδοξος β. αὐτοῦ 1 Cl 9:1; ἡ ἄμωμος β. αὐτοῦ 35:5; ἡ ὑπέρτατος αὐτοῦ β. 40:3; παρὰ τὸ καθῆκον τῆς βουλήσεως αὐτοῦ *contrary to what conforms to his will* 41:3.—The history of tradition of the Lat. text (voluntas) of 42:4 is uncertain.—DELG s.v. βούλομαι. TW.

βούλομαι 2 sg. βούλει (B-D-F §27; Mayser 328) beside Att. βούλῃ (**Lk 22:42 v.l.;** Hs 9, 11, 9 v.l.); impf. ἐβουλόμην (on the augment s. B-D-F §66, 3; Rob. 368; W-S. §12, 3), also ἠβούλετο (Hs 5, 6, 5); fut. βουλήσεται Job 39:9; 1 aor. ἐβουλήθην; ἠβουλήθην **2J 12 v.l.** (MPol 7:1; AcPt Ox 849); pf. inf. βεβουλῆσθαι Just., D. 23, 1. (Hom.+) 'wish, be willing' (no longer difft. in mng. fr. θέλω: B-D-F §101 s.v. θέλειν, but cp. Epict. 1, 12, 13; s. RRödiger, Glotta 8, 1917, 1ff; WFox, PhilolWoch 37, 1917, 597ff; 633ff; FZucker, Gnomon 9, '33, 191–201; GSchrenk, TW I 628–31; AWifstrand, D. griech. Verba für wollen: Eranos 40, '42, 16–36).

❶ **to desire to have or experience someth., with implication of planning accordingly,** ***wish, want, desire*** w. inf. foll. (Jos., Ant. 5, 280) ἐβουλόμην ἀκοῦσαι *I should like to hear* **Ac 25:22** (B-D-F §359, 2; Rob. 1055f; cp. Dionys. Hal., De Dem. 42 p. 1087 ἐβουλόμην ἔτι πλείω παρασχέσθαι παραδείγματα). ὃν ἐβουλόμην πρὸς ἐμαυτὸν κατέχειν (on the analogy of θέλω w. inf.=opt. w. ἄν) *whom I would have been glad to keep with me* **Phlm 13.** οἱ βουλόμενοι πλουτεῖν *those who desire to be rich* **1 Ti 6:9;** πλέον ἔχειν βούλεσθαι *desire to have more* Dg 10:5.—**Js 4:4.** W. a thing as obj. in the acc. Hm 12, 5, 4; s 5, 6, 5; 6, 5, 3; β. τὸν θάνατον τοῦ ἁμαρτωλοῦ *desire the death of the sinner* 1 Cl 8:2 (Ezk 33:11); β. εἰρήνην *wish for peace* 15:1; αἷμα ταύρων … οὐ βούλομαι *I do not desire* B 2:5 (Is 1:11); νηστείαν β. Hs 5, 1, 4; ὅσον ἂν βούλωνται *as much as they wished* of food and drink MPol 7:2. φέρε, ὃ βούλει *Come, do what (ever) you wish* MPol 11:2; λέγει, φησίν, ὃ βούλει Hm 12, 5, 1.

❷ **to plan on a course of action,** ***intend, plan, will***—ⓐ of human beings—**α.** w. acc. τοῦτο β. **2 Cor 1:17.**

β. w. aor. inf. foll. **Mt 1:19; Mk 15:15; Ac 5:28, 33; 12:4; 15:37; 17:20; 18:27; 19:30; 22:30; 23:28; 27:43; 28:18; 2 Cor 1:15;** 1 Cl 7:5; IRo 7:1; GPt 1:1 (ASyn. 341, 20); MPol 3:1 end.

γ. w. pres. inf. foll. **Ac 18:15;** εἰ βούλοιτο πορεύεσθαι *whether he was willing to go* **25:20;** β. φιλοπονεῖν 2 Cl 19:1; β. πιστεύειν Dg 9:6; β. πείθειν MPol 3:1; β. μένειν 5:1.

δ. foll. by acc. and inf. (Jos., Ant. 14, 233 βούλομαι ὑμᾶς εἰδέναι; 246) γινώσκειν ὑμᾶς βούλομαι *I want you to know* **Phil 1:12.—1 Ti 2:8; 5:14; Tit 3:8; Jd 5;** 1 Cl 39:1; AcPl Ha 1, 14 (restored).

ε. w. aor. subj. foll., in which case β. introduces a deliberative question βούλεσθε ἀπολύσω ὑμῖν; *shall I release to you?* **J 18:39** (B-D-F §366, 3; Rob. 935).

ζ. w. omission of the inf. which is to be supplied fr. the context ὅπου ἡ ὁρμὴ … βούλεται (sc. μετάγειν) **Js 3:4.** τοὺς βουλομένους (sc. ἐπιδέχεσθαι) κωλύει **3J 10.** οὐκ ἐβουλήθην (sc. γράφειν) **2J 12.**—1 Cl 54:2; 2 Cl 13:2; MPol 7:1; Dg 11:7. καθὼς βούλεται *as he (it) wills* Hm 5, 1, 3; cp. 11:2, 9; 12, 1, 1; 12, 2, 5; s 6, 5, 2; 9, 11, 9; cp. ὡς ἐβουλόμεθα Dg 9:1. εἴ τι βούλει (sc. εἰπεῖν) Hs 5, 5, 5. εἰ ἄρα βούλει *if you so desire* AcPt Ox 849, 6f.

ⓑ of transcendent beings. Of God (though θέλω is more common in ref. to deity, s. BGildersleeve, Pindar, 1885, p. 245 and also θέλω 2; βούλομαι is the more common administrative term, s. Welles, index) (Dio Chrys. 28 [45], 15 βουλομένων θεῶν; Ael. Aristid. 50, 1 K.=26 p. 502 D.; BGU 248, 11 [I AD] θεῶν δὲ βουλομένων; 249, 13; Herm. Wr. 13, 21; LXX; Jos., Ant. 9, 189) abs. **Lk 22:42.** ἃ βούλομαι 2 Cl 13:2. βουληθεὶς ἀπεκύησεν ἡμᾶς λόγῳ ἀληθείας *acc. to his will he brought us into being through the word of truth* **Js 1:18.** W. aor. inf. foll. **Hb 6:17;** 1 Cl 16:10, 12 (Is 53:10); AcPlCor 2:10, 12. Foll. by acc. w. inf. **2 Pt 3:9;** 1 Cl 8:5.—Of Jesus **Mt 11:27; Lk 10:22.**—Of the Holy Spirit **1 Cor 12:11.**—Of the day of the Lord GJs 17:1.—B. 1160. Schmidt, Syn. III 602–20. DELG. M-M. TW.

βουνός, οῦ, ὁ (found first in Aeschyl., Suppl. 109, prob. of Doric origin [Mayser p. 8; B-D-F §126, 1bα; Rob. 111], occurring more freq. since Polyb. [3, 83, 1 and 3 and 4; 5, 22, 1f] in lit., ins, pap, LXX; En 1:6; PsSol 11:4; TestSol D 6:1; AscIs 2:11; Philo, Poster. Cai. 57; Jos., Bell. 2, 619, Ant. 6, 156; SibOr 3, 680; Just., D. 111, 1) ***hill*** **Lk 3:5** (Is 40:4); **23:30** (w. ὄρη, Hos 10:8; in sg. Strabo 3, 2, 9): Hv 1, 3, 4.—B. 24. DELG. M-M.

Βοῦρρος, ου, ὁ *Burrus* (both Gk. and Lat. forms of the name are well attested; cp. Hdb. on IEph 2:1), a ministrant (διάκονος) in Ephesus, termed σύνδουλος by Ign., IEph 2:1.—διὰ βούρου IPhld 11:2; likew. ISm 12:1 (v.l. Βόρρου).

βοῦς, βοός acc. pl. βόας **J 2:14** (as Il. 5, 556; Arrian, Ind. 7, 7; Polyaenus 6, 52; Aelian, VH 12, 44; POxy 729, 16; Gen 18:7 al.; B-D-F §46, 2) ***head of cattle*** (Hom.+; ins, pap, LXX; TestSol 13:1 A; TestAbr A 2 p. 78, 14 [Stone p. 4] and B 2 p. 105, 8 [St.

p. 58]; TestJob; TestJud 2:7; TestJos 19:5–7 [Armenian Vers., s. Charles]; GrBar; Philo, Aet. M. 23; Joseph.; Just., A I, 27, 1; Ath., R. 61, 11) ὁ *ox,* ἡ *cow* **Lk 13:15; 14:5.** ἐν πάθνῃ βοῶν *in a cattle stall* GJs 22:2. W. πρόβατα (Gen 13:5; 33:13 al.) **J 2:14f;** D 13:3; ζεῦγος β. (TestAbr A 2 [s. above]; TestJob 10:5; Jos., Ant. 12, 192) **Lk 14:19.** Used in threshing **1 Cor 9:9; 1 Ti 5:18** (both Dt 25:4; cp. Philo, Virt. 145; Jos., Ant. 4, 233. Cp. Pherecrates Com. [V BC] 65 ὑποζυγίοις ἀλοᾶν).—B. 152. DELG. M-M. TW.

βραβεῖον, ου, τό (s. βραβεύω; Menand., Monost. 124 J.=653 Meineke [IV p. 359]; Ps.-Oppian, Cyn. 4, 197; Vett. Val. 174, 21; 288, 8; ins: Étude Delphiques [BCH Suppl. IV] '77, 103–21, line 40 [III BC]; IPriene 118, 3 [I BC]; CIG 3674, 15 al. [Nägeli 37, 3]; horoscope in PPrinc 75, 13; PGM 4, 664) 'prize', but ἆθλον and νικητήριον are more common in Gk. lit. **an award for exceptional performance,** ***prize, award***

ⓐ of competition in the games, the prim. sense **1 Cor 9:24**

ⓑ of moral/spiritual performance, fig. ext. of a (cp. Herm. Wr. 18, 10; GrBar 12:6; Philo, Praem. 6; SibOr 2, 149) of the award of victory of Christians β. τῆς ἄνω κλήσεως *the prize that is the object of* (and can only be attained in connection with) *the upward call* **Phil 3:14;** (w. στέφανος) β. ἀναντίρρητον *incontestable prize* MPol 17:1. Gener. *reward* ὑπομονῆς β. *reward for endurance* 1 Cl 5:5 (cp. Menand., loc. cit. β. ἀρετῆς).—AEhrhardt, An Unknown Orphic-Writing . . . and St. Paul, ZNW 48, '57, 101–10.—DELG s.v. βραβεύς. M-M (add. reff. APapathomas, NTS 43, '97, 234 n. 48). New Docs 2, 78f. TW.

βραβεύω (s. βραβεῖον) prim. 'award prizes in contests', then gener. **be in control of someone's activity by making a decision,** ***be judge, decide, control, rule*** (Eur.+; Polyb. 2, 35, 3; Diod. S. 14, 65, 3; Plut., Lycurg. 58 [30, 2], Pomp. 649 [55, 6], Brut. 1002 [40, 8] al.; Herm. Wr. 18, 16; Michel 163, 11; SIG 685, 32 [139 BC]; UPZ 20, 22 [163 BC]; 110, 70; 161 [164 BC]; Wsd 10:12; Philo, Mos. 1, 163 al.; Jos., Bell. 5, 503; 6, 143 al.; Theoph. Ant. 3, 15 [p. 234, 19]) abs. ἡ εἰρήνη τοῦ Χ. βραβευέτω ἐν ταῖς καρδίαις ὑμῶν *let the peace of Christ rule in your hearts* (=be the decisive factor) **Col 3:15.**—DELG s.v. βραβεύς. M-M.

βραδέως adv. of βραδύς (Thu. et al.; Epict. 1, 18, 19; pap, e.g. PFay 97, 37; POxy 1088, 50; 2 Macc 14:17; Jos., Bell. 3, 274; Tat. 32, 2) ***slowly*** β. ἐγένετο *it took a long time* Hs 9, 6, 8.—DELG s.v. βραδύς.

βραδύγλωσσος, ον (Vi. Aesopi W 1 and 2 P.; in 3 this is explained: λαλεῖν μὴ δυνάμενος διὰ τὸ τῆς γλώσσης βραδύ; Leontius 40 p. 79, 2; Cat. Cod. Astr. II 167.—Ps.-Lucian, Philopatris 13 the word refers to Moses as the author of the creation story. This is plainly influenced by the Bible.) ***slow of tongue*** of Moses 1 Cl 17:5 (Ex 4:10).

βραδύνω fut. βραδυνῶ LXX; 1 aor. 1 pl. ἐβραδύναμεν Gen 43:10. Intr. (s. βραδύς; Aeschyl.+; OGI 515, 53: PFlor 278 II, 11; POxy 118, 37; 2228, 20; magical pap in PWarren 21, 28 and 32; Gen 43:10; Dt 7:10; Jos., Bell. 5, 566, Vi. 89; ParJer; ApcMos 31) ***hesitate, delay*** **1 Ti 3:15;** Hs 9, 19, 2. τί βραδύνεις; *why do you delay?* MPol 11:2; *hold back* τινός *from someth.* (B-D-F §180, 5; Rob. 518) *in hesitation:* τῆς ἐπαγγελίας *from* (fulfillment of) *the promise* (poss.: *the Lord of the promise does not delay*) **2 Pt 3:9.**—DELG s.v. βραδύς. M-M.

βραδυπλοέω (Artem. 4, 30; Anecd. Gr. p. 225, 15; cp. βραδυπλοία in POxy 2191, 8 [II AD]) ***sail slowly*** **Ac 27:7.**—M-M.

βραδύς, εῖα, ύ (s. βραδέως; Hom. et al.; SIG 502, 12; TestAbr A 6 p. 83, 19 [Stone p. 14] τῇ ὀψὲ βραδείᾳ) ***slow,*** opp. ταχύς (Ps.-Isocr., ad Demon. 34; Aristot., EN 6, 10, 1142b; Philo, Conf. Lingu. 48) εἰς τὸ λαλῆσαι *slow to speak* **Js 1:19** (B-D-F §402, 2; Rob. 658; βραδὺ φθέγγεσθαι is praised Dio Chrys. 15 [32], 2); β. εἰς ὀργήν ibid. (cp. Dionys. Soph., Ep. 9 β. εἰς ἐπιστολήν; Jos., Ant. 15, 107 βραδὺς εἰς τ. ἀποδόσεις.—Menand., Monost. 99 J. [60 Meineke] πρὸς ὀργὴν β.). Fig., of mental and spiritual slowness (Aristoph., Nub. 129; Polyb. 4, 8, 7; Dion. Hal., Orat. Vet. 2 p. 448; Sext. Emp., Math. 7, 325 w. ἀσύνετος; cp. Il. 10, 226, with a difft. adj.) β. τῇ καρδίᾳ *slow of heart*='dull', w. inf. foll. (as Thu. 3, 38, 6 προνοῆσαι β.) τοῦ πιστεύειν *too dull to believe* (B-D-F §400, 8) **Lk 24:25.** Comp. βραδύτερος (Thu. 4, 8, 1; Theocr. 29, 30; Chion, Ep. 3, 2; Mayser 297): αἴτημα β. λαμβάνειν *receive* (the answer to) *a petition rather slowly* Hm 9:7; β. μετανοεῖν *be slower in repentance* s 8, 7, 3; 8, 8, 3. βράδιον (Hes., Op. 528; OGI 502, 17) *rather tardy* 1 Cl 1:1.—DELG. M-M.

βραδύτης, ητος (on accent -ής, -ῆτος [t.r. Tdf. W-H. S. Vog. Bov.] cp. JWackernagel, NGG 1909, 58ff; Schwyzer I 382), ἡ (s. βραδύς; Hom. et al.; Plut., Mor. 549; Appian, Bell. Civ. 4 p. 1052, 16 Mendelssohn; Vett. Val. 289, 24; Sb 7741, 12 [II AD]; Philo, Op. M. 156; Jos., Ant. 7, 74; 13, 47) ***slowness*** ὥς τινες βραδύτητα ἡγοῦνται *as some count slowness* **2 Pt 3:9.**—M-M.

βραχίων, ονος, ὁ (Hom.+) ***arm,*** anthropomorphic symbol of God's power (Ex 15:16; Is 51:5; 52:10; Ps 70:18; 76:16;—Eur., Suppl. 738 'youthful strength'; Philo, Spec. Leg. 1, 145 β. ἰσχύος κ. ἀνδρείας σύμβολον): ἐν β. αὐτοῦ *with his arm* **Lk 1:51** (Ps 88:11); β. κυρίου (PsSol 13:2) **J 12:38;** 1 Cl 16:3 (both Is 53:1f). μετὰ βραχίονος ὑψηλοῦ *with uplifted arm* (Ex 6:1; 32:11; Dt 3:24 al.) **Ac 13:17;** cp. 1 Cl 60:3.—B. 237. DELG. M-M. TW.

βραχύς, εῖα, ύ (Pind., Hdt. +) prim. 'short'.—❶ **pert. to having little length,** ***short,*** of space: βραχύ (so Thu. 1, 63, 2; 2 Km 16:1) διαστήσαντες *a little farther on* **Ac 27:28.**

❷ **pert. to being brief in duration,** ***brief, short,*** of time: β. (τι) *for a short time* (Ael. Aristid. 13 p. 276 D.) **Ac 5:34; Hb 2:7** (quotes Ps 8:6, which refers to rank; in Is 57:17 β. τι denotes time), **9;** μετὰ β. *a little later* **Lk 22:58.**

❸ **pert. to being low in quantity,** ***little, small*** (1 Km 14:29, 43; Jos., Bell. 1, 597, Ant. 9, 48 ἔλαιον βραχύ): *a small amount* β. τι *a little* **J 6:7** (cp. Thu. 2, 99, 5). διὰ βραχέων *in a few words, briefly* **Hb 13:22** (besides the exx. in FBleek ad loc., s. also Just., A I, 8, 3; Tat. 41, 3; Ocellus Luc. 35; Ptolem., Apotel. 1, 1, 3; Lucian, Toxaris 56; Ps.-Lucian, Charid. 22; Ael. Aristid. 13 p. 183 D.; Achilles Tat. 7, 9, 3; PStras 41, 8 διὰ βραχέων σε διδάξω; EpArist 128; Jos., Bell. 4, 338). LTrudinger, JTS 23, '72, 128–30.—**1 Pt 5:12** P[72].—B. 883. DELG. M-M.

βρέφος, ους, τό—❶ **a child that is still unborn,** ***fetus, child*** (Il. 23, 266; Plut., Mor. 1052f; Diosc. 5, 74; SIG 1267, 23; IAndrosIsis, Kyme 18; PGM 8, 1 ἐλθέ μοι κύριε Ἑρμῆ ὡς τὰ βρέφη εἰς τ. κοιλίας τ. γυναικῶν; PFlor 93, 21 τὸ ἐν γαστρὶ βρέφος; Sir 19:11; Ps.-Phocyl. 184; Jos., Ant. 20, 18; s. ἐξαμβλόω) **Lk 1:41, 44.**

❷ **a very small child,** ***baby, infant*** (Pind.+; PFamTebt 20, 15; PMich 423/24, 13; 17; 20; BGU 1104, 24; POxy 1069, 22 al.; 1 Macc 1:61; 2 Macc 6:10; 4 Macc 4:25; TestSol 13:3, 4; ApcSed 9; ApcEsdr p. 28, 13 Tdf.; Philo; ViJer 7; Jos., Bell. 6, 205; Tat. 30, 1) **Lk 2:12, 16;** GJs 9:2; 22:2 (Diod. S. 2, 4, 5 herdsmen find a divine child, Semiramis [εὑρεῖν τὸ βρέφος]; of Plato as infant s. παρίστημι 1bα); **Lk 18:15; Ac 7:19;** νήπια β. (Dio Chrys.

10 [11], 29; En 99:5 [restored]) Hs 9, 29, 1; cp. 3; ἀπὸ βρέφους *from childhood* **2 Ti 3:15** (Ptolem., Apotel. 2, 3, 40; Philo, Spec. Leg. 2, 33; more freq. ἐκ β.: Philo, Somn. 1, 192; Anth. Pal, 9, 567). In imagery **1 Pt 2:2.**—On caution respecting usage in grave ins s. New Docs 4, 40f.—B. 92. DELG. M-M. TW.

βρέχω 1 aor. ἔβρεξα. Pass.: fut. 3 sg. βραχήσεται Is 43:3; 2 aor. ἐβράχην (Pind., Hdt. et al.; pap, LXX; TestSol 10:7 C; GrBar; ApcSed 8:10 p. 133, 16 Ja.; Ar. 4, 3).

❶ to cause someth. to become wet, ***to wet*** (B-D-F §309, 2) τινί *with something* (schol. on Apollon. Rhod. 2, 819) τοῖς δάκρυσιν τοὺς πόδας *feet with tears* **Lk 7:38, 44** (cp. Ps 6:7; IG XIV, 1422, 5 δακρύοισιν ἔβρεξαν ὅλον τάφον). Without obj. ἵνα μὴ ὑετὸς βρέχῃ *that no rain may fall* **Rv 11:6** (τ. ἡμ. is acc. of duration of time; B-D-F §161, 2; Rob. 469ff).

❷ to cause rain to fall, ***send rain*** (Phryn. 291 Lob.; Polyb. 16, 12, 3; ἐὰν ἐπὶ πλέον βραχῇ, φθείρεται ἡ γῆ Ar. 4, 3) pers. (B-D-F §129) of God (Gen 2:5 ἐπὶ τὴν γῆν; s. Philo, Leg. All. 1, 25; 26; 29; POxy 1482, 6 [II AD] ὁ Ζεὺς ἔβρεχε.—Proverbially of Zeus, who sometimes lets the sun shine and sometimes sends rain: Theognis 25; Theocritus 4, 43; Liban., Declam. 1, 78 vol. V p. 57, 1 F.) βρέχει *causes it to rain* **Mt 5:45;** GNaass 59, 24. ἔβρεξεν πῦρ καὶ θεῖον **Lk 17:29** (s. Gen 19:24, but w. κύριος as the subj.; cp. Ezk 38:22; PGM 36, 301; SibOr 5, 508), but cp. vs. 28, a formulaic parallel, w. meteorological phenomenon as subj.

❸ to fall in drops, ***rain,*** impers. βρέχει *it rains* (so since the comic poet Teleclides [V BC]; Epict. 1, 6, 26; SibOr 5, 377) **Js 5:17;** perh. **Lk 17:29** (s. 2 end).—DELG. M-M.

βριμάομαι (Aristoph. et al.) ***be indignant*** **J 11:33** P[75] for ἐμβρ., q.v.—DELG s.v. βρίμη.

βροντή, ῆς, ἡ (βρέμω 'roar'; Hom.+; PGM 36, 356; LXX; En 17:3; TestAbr A, GrBar; ApcSed 11:2 p. 134, 12; Jos., Ant. 2, 343; SibOr 5, 303) ***thunder*** βροντὴν γεγονέναι **J 12:29** (speech that is loud and energetic [Philostrat., Vi. Ap. 7, 28, 3 Polyphemus; Diog. L. 2, 36 Xanthippe] or that makes extravagant demands [Herodas 7, 66] is compared to thunder). φωνὴ βροντῆς *crash of thunder* **Rv 6:1; 14:2; 19:6** (cp. Ps 76:19; 103:7; Sir 43:17; CBezold-FBoll, Reflexe astral. Keilinschriften bei griech. Schriftstellern [SBHeidAk 1911, 7. Abt.] 21, 1). φωναὶ καὶ βρονταί (s. φωνή 1) **4:5; 8:5; 11:19; 16:18.** The 7 thunders which speak **10:3f** may be the thunders of the 7 planetary spheres (Boll, Offb. 22). On υἱοὶ βροντῆς **Mk 3:17** cp. Βοανηργές and Appian, Syr. 62 §330 Πτολεμαίῳ Κεραυνὸς ἐπίκλησις.—B. 58. DELG s.v. βρέμω. M-M. TW.

βροτός, ή, όν ***mortal*** (opp. ἀθάνατος, θεός) subst. ὁ β. *mortal pers.* (Hom. et al.; Job freq.; TestSol 5:7 P; Mel., fgm. 8b, 44) 1 Cl 39:4 (Job 4:17).—DELG.

βροχή, ῆς, ἡ (Phryn. 291 Lob.; pap since III BC 'irrigation' [Mayser 421; POxy 280, 5; 593]) ***rain*** (Democrit. fgm. 14, 8; Ps 67:10; 104:32; Philo, Leg. All. 1, 26; SibOr fgm. 1, 32 and in Mod. Gk. [HKennedy, Sources of NT Gk. 1895, 153; Thumb 226]) of a torrential rain **Mt 7:25, 27.**—B. 68. DELG s.v. Βρέχω. M-M.

βρόχος, ου, ὁ (Hom. et al.; POxy 51, 16; LXX; Mel., P. 79, 573; 93, 701 [Bodm.]) ***noose*** βρόχον ἐπιβάλλειν τινί *put or throw a noose on someone* to catch or restrain him (an expr. fr. war or hunting [β. περιβάλλειν τινί: Arrian, Cyneg. 23, 4; 24, 3; Philo, Mos. 2, 252; Jos., Bell. 7, 250]); only fig. **1 Cor 7:35**=to impose restrictions.—DELG. M-M.

βρυγμός, οῦ, ὁ (Eupolis [V BC] 347; Hippocr., περὶ διαίτης 6 p. 634 [3, 84]) ***gnashing*** of teeth striking together (Galen, Glossar. Hippocr. XIX p. 90 K. βρυγμός· ὁ ἀπὸ τ. ὀδόντων συγκρουομένων ψόφος; s. also Erotian [I AD], Vocum Hippocraticarum Coll. ed. ENachmanson 1918 p. 28, 9; 29, 4; Anecd. Gr. 30, 28; Hesych.; Suda.—Pr 19:12; Sir 51:3), ὁ β. τῶν ὀδόντων *chattering* or *gnashing of the teeth* **Mt 8:12; 13:42, 50; 22:13; 24:51; 25:30; Lk 13:28** (always w. κλαυθμός).—Chattering of teeth because of cold: Sallust. 19 p. 34, 22 souls are being punished in τόποι ψυχροί. Cp. Plut., Mor. 567c; ApcPl 42.—Grinding of teeth because of pain: Quint. Smyrn. 11, 206.—DELG s.v. βρύκω. M-M. TW.

βρύχω impf. ἔβρυχον; fut. 3 sg. βρύξει; 1 aor. 3 sg. ἔβρυξεν LXX **to grind one's teeth,** ***gnash,*** a sign of violent rage (Theodor. Prodr. 5, 49 H.) τοὺς ὀδόντας ἐπ' αὐτόν *they gnashed their teeth against him* **Ac 7:54** (cp. Lex. Vind. p. 34, 5 βρύχει τ. ὀδόντας ἄνθρωπος, βρυχᾶται δὲ λέων=humans gnash their teeth, lions roar; Job 16:9; Ps 34:16; 36:12; SibOr 2, 203; Hippocr., 8 p. 16 [Mul. 1, 2], Epid. 5, 86 and other medical wr. [Hobart 208] of chattering of the teeth in chills and fevers). The expression may also be intended as metaph. *become enraged* (so NRSV with others, unless the translators are thinking in terms of functional equivalence).—Frisk.

βρύω (Hom. et al.; usu. intr. as Jos., Ant. 13, 66; SibOr 6, 8) trans. (as Aelian, fgm. 25 p. 197, 20 Herch.; Himerius, Or. 1, 19; Anacreont. 44, 2 Χάριτες ῥόδα βρύουσιν; JosAs 16 cod. A [p. 64, 15 Bat.] αἱ σάρκες σου βρύουσιν ἄνθη ζωῆς; JosAs 10:14 cod. A [p. 52, 15 Bat.]; Just., D. 114, 4; Ps.-Clemens, Hom. 2, 45) of someth. that is teeming w. a substance ***pour forth*** **Js 3:11.**—DELG. M-M.

βρῶμα, ατος, τό (s. βιβρώσκω; Thu., X. et al.; pap, LXX; En; TestSol 1:1 C; Test12Patr; Jos., Ant. 3, 29 and 30; 17, 62; Ar.; Just., D. 20, 1; 12:6; cp. TestReub 2:7 βρῶσις βρωμάτων)

❶ that which is eaten, ***food*** lit. **Ro 14:15ab, 20; 1 Cor 8:8, 13;** GEb 13, 79. Pl. (Hippocr. et al.; oft. LXX; En 98:2; Hippol., Ref. 1, 24, 1) **Lk 3:11; 9:13; 1 Cor 6:13ab; 1 Ti 4:3; Hb 13:9;** B 10:9; PtK 2 p. 14, 20.—Esp. *solid food* (opp. γάλα) **1 Cor 3:2** (in imagery, but w. lit. components dominant). Pl. (w. ποτά, as 2 Esdr 3:7) ITr 2:3; (w. πόματα, as Plato, Leg. 11 p. 932a; Epict., Ench. 33, 2; TestReub 2:7) **Hb 9:10.**—The mng. 'filth', 'stench', as in Mod. Gk. (Rdm. 12) is most unlikely for **Mt 14:15, Mk 7:19** (B-D-F §126, 3).—Of manna: τὸ πνευματικὸν β. **1 Cor 10:3.**—In the endtime Papias (9:10); s. ἀπόλαυσις.

❷ nourishment of a transcendent nature, ***means of sustenance, food*** (πνεῦμα ἅγιον, ὅ ἐστι βρῶμα ζωῆς Iren. Haer. 4, 2 [Harv. II 294, 11]; ὁ περὶ β. ἀληθῶν καὶ πνευματικῶν λόγος Orig., C. Cels. 2, 2, 49) doing the will of God is Jesus' food **J 4:34;** ἔσται μου ἡ εὐχὴ βρώματα καὶ πώματα *prayer will be my food and drink* GJs 1:4 (cp. Aeschyl., Cho. 26; Soph., El. 363f). Cp. **1 Cor 3:2** above.—B. 329. DELG s.v. βιβρώσκω. M-M. TW.

βρώσιμος, ον (Aeschyl., Prom. 479; 'Anti-Atticist' [Anecd. Gr. 84, 25]; SIG 624, 38; PSI 306, 7; StudPal XXII 75, 58; PGM 10, 1; Lev 19:23; Ezk 47:12; 2 Esdr 19:25) ***eatable*** τὶ β. *anything to eat* **Lk 24:41.**—DELG s.v. βιβρώσκω. M-M.

βρῶσις, εως, ἡ (Hom. et al.; pap, LXX; TestAbr B 13 p. 117, 22 [Stone p. 82]; EpArist 129; Philo; Joseph.; Just., D. 57, 3; Mel., P. 47, 337).

❶ the act of partaking of food, ***eating*** (w. πόσις [this combin. since Od. 1, 191; also Diod. S. 1, 45, 2; Plut., Mor. 114c; Da 1:10; Philo, Mos. 1, 184]) **Ro 14:17; Col 2:16.** W. obj. gen.

(as Pla., Rep. 10, 619c; Jos., Ant. 1, 334; TestReub 2:7 βρῶσις βρωμάτων) β. τῶν εἰδωλοθύτων *eating of meat sacrificed to idols* **1 Cor 8:4;** ἄρτος εἰς β. (as Is 55:10) *bread to eat* **2 Cor 9:10;** ὡς περὶ β. *as if they referred to eating* B 10:9; ἔχετε τελείως περὶ τῆς β. *you are fully instructed on eating,* i.e. on dietary laws 10:10 (cp. ὁ περὶ βρώσεων καὶ πόσεων . . . νόμος Orig., C. Cels. 2, 2, 17); εἰς β. *to eat* PtK 2 p. 14, 17.

❷ **the process of causing deterioration by consuming,** ***consuming*** w. σής **Mt 6:19f,** where β. is used as a general term for *consuming,* which could be done by a variety of insects (in Mal 3:11 LXX A, e.g., β. is used to render אוכל='grasshopper'; מַאֲכוֹלֶת=*wood worm* has been suggested [HGressmann, Hdb. ad loc.]). Cp. EpJer 10, where a few mss. have βρῶσις instead of βρώματα w. ἰός. This combin. argues against the identification of βρῶσις w. ἰός in Mt, and it is not likely that a hendiadys is present. The interpretation *corrosion, rust* finds no support outside this passage. In the medical passages that have been adduced (cp. Galen 6, 422 [pl.]; 12, 879 ed. Kühn 1823) β.='decay' of teeth. The balanced structure of the passage implies garments as victims of 'moth and eating', and other possessions as plunder of thieves.

❸ **that which one eats,** ***food*** (Soph. fgm. 182, 2 TGF; Philostrat., Vi. Apoll. 8, 7 p. 307, 27; PLond III, 1223, 9 p. 139 [121 AD] χόρτον εἰς βρῶσιν προβάτων; PLips 118, 15; POxy 1686, 10; Gen 25:28; Jer 41:20; 2 Km 19:43 v.l. βρῶσιν ἐφάγαμεν; Philo, Op. M. 38).

ⓐ lit. of a meal **Hb 12:16;** D 6:3; Dg 4:1; GJs 1:4 v.l. for βρωτόν and βρώματα.—ⓑ fig. **J 4:32; 6:27, 55.**—DELG s.v. βιβρώσκω. M-M. TW.

βρωτός, ή, όν (Aeneas Tact. 8, 4; Archestr [IV BC], fgm. 28; Porphyr., Abst. 1, 27 PSI 64, 21 [I BC]) verbal adj. of βιβρώσκω ***given for food*** PtK 2 p. 14, 20 (the ref. is to animals given to humanity for food and honored by it through use in sacrifice, unless β. refers to animals worshipped as gods and means *eatable*).—οὐ καταβήσομαι οὔτε ἐπὶ βρωτὸν οὔτε ἐπὶ ποτόν *I will come down neither for food nor drink* GJs 1:4.

βυθίζω 1 aor. ἐβύθισαν 2 Macc. 12:4, pass. ἐβυθίσθην; fut. 3 pl. pass. βυθισθήσονται JosAs 12:3 (s. βυθός; Soph. et al.; mag. pap in PWarren 21, 43; 2 Macc 12:4)

❶ **to cause to go down in water,** ***to sink,*** only pass. in act. sense (Jos., C. Ap. 1, 308) of ships (Polyb. 2, 10, 5; 16, 3, 2; Diod. S. 13, 40, 5; Dio Chrys. 46 [63], 3; Epict. 3, 2, 18 βυθιζομένου τοῦ πλοίου) ὥστε βυθίζεσθαι αὐτά (i.e. τὰ πλοῖα) *so that they began to sink* **Lk 5:7.** W. εἰς (AcJ 112 [Aa II/1 p. 211, 8f]) of the Egyptian military forces ἐβυθίσθησαν εἰς θάλασσαν *sank into the sea* 1 Cl 51:5.

❷ **to cause someone to experience disastrous consequences,** ***plunge, expose to*** fig. (cp. Philod., De Morte 33 [DBassi, Pap. Ercolanesi 1914]; Alciphron 1, 16, 1 τὸ νῆφον ἐν ἐμοὶ συνεχῶς ὑπὸ τοῦ πάθους βυθίζεται; Philostrat., Vi. Apoll. 4, 32 p. 151, 17 of the utter ruin of Sparta; SIG 730, 7 [I BC] καταβυθ.) *plunge* τινά *someone* εἰς ὄλεθρον καὶ ἀπώλειαν *into ruin and destruction* **1 Ti 6:9.**—B. 679. DELG s.v. βυθός. M-M.

βυθός, οῦ, ὁ (s. βυθίζω; Aeschyl., Hippocr. et al.; Alex. Ep. II, 10; Herm. Wr. 16, 5; mag. pap: POxy 886, 10; PGM 13, 1072; LXX, TestSol; JosAs 12:10 cod. A βυθὸν τῆς θαλάσσης; Philo; SibOr 3, 481; Mel., fgm. 8b, 17 and 35 P.) **depth of the sea,** ***sea, deep water*** ἐν τῷ β. *adrift at sea* **2 Cor 11:25.** Of deep sea fish ἐν τῷ β. νήχεται *they swim* (only) *in deep water* B 10:5 (cp. Aelian, NA 2, 15; 9, 57). Of water gener.: ἐκ (τοῦ) β. (SibOr 4, 60) Hv 3, 2, 5f; 3, 5, 2; s 9, 3, 3 and 5; 9, 4, 3f; 9, 5, 3; 9, 15, 4; 9, 16, 1 and 5; 9, 17, 3.—DELG. M-M.

βυρσεύς, έως, ὁ (Dio Chrys. 38 [55], 22; Artem. 4, 56; IGR IV, 1216, 8; PTebt 801, 2 [II BC]; PCorn 26, 6; PFay 121, 15; PWarren 15, 25 [all II AD]; loanw. in rabb.) ***tanner,*** surname of Simon, a Christian in Joppa **Ac 9:43; 10:6, 32.**—DELG s.v. βύρσα. M-M.

βύσσινος, η, ον (s. βύσσος; Aeschyl., Hdt.+; Plut.; Diod. S. 1, 85, 5; OGI 90, 17; 29; pap [PRev 103, 1; PEleph 26, 4; 27a, 11ff et al.]; LXX; JosAs 3:19; 13:2 cod. A; ApcMos 40; EpArist 87; 320; Jos., Ant. 3, 153; Test12Patr) ***made of fine linen,*** subst. τὸ β. *fine linen, linen garment* (PHolm 15, 26; PGM 1, 332; 4, 663; Esth 1:6; Is 3:23; Da 10:5; 12:6f) **Rv 18:12** (s. βύσσος end), **16; 19:8, 14.**—DELG s.v. βύσσος. M-M.

βύσσος, ου, ἡ (Semit. loanw.=בּוּץ [HLewy, D. sem. Fremdwörter im Griech. 1895, 125]; Empedocles [V BC] fgm. 93; Theocr. 2, 73; Paus. 5, 5, 2; 7, 21, 7; Pollux 7, 17, 75; PGen 36, 19 and 26; PSI 1152, 7; PLund IV, 9, 24; PTebt 313, 20; 598; LXX; TestAbr A; TestJob 25:7; JosAs; Philo, Congr. Erud. Grat. 117; Jos., Ant. 3, 103 al.) ***fine linen*** (Pliny, HN 19, 1, [9], 26); for prominent people (Philostrat., Vi. Apoll. 2, 20) πορφύρα καὶ β. (Pr 31:22; Jos., Ant. 3, 154; cp. Esth 1:6; JosAs 5:6 β. χρυσοϋφής) **Lk 16:19; Rv 18:12 v.l.;** GJs 10:2.—PBatiffol, RB n.s. 9, 1912, 541–43.—DELG. M-M.

βύω 1 aor. ἔβυσα (Hom. et al., 'to plug') **to plug an obj. w. someth.,** ***stop, plug*** the ears (as Lucian, Catapl. 5 β. τὰ ὦτα, Charon 21; Ps 57:5) in imagery, against dissident teaching IEph 9:1.—DELG s.v. βυνέω.

βωμός, οῦ, ὁ (Hom. et al.; ins, pap, LXX, Philo; Jos., Bell. 1, 39, Ant. 1, 157; Orig., C. Cels. 8, 20, 27 al.; loanw. in rabb.; cp. EMaass, ARW 23, 1925, 226f) ***altar*** **Ac 17:23;** ὁ τοῦ Ἡλίου β. 1 Cl 25:4.—B. 1466f. DELG. M-M. TW.

Γ

γ' numerical sign = *3* (τρεῖς: pap; Jos., C. Ap. 1, 157; cp. SibOr 5:24; Ar. [JTS 25, '24, 76, ln. 28; Mel., P. 90 B]) or *3d* (τρίτη) in the superscr. of **3J** (sc. ἐπιστολή), of Hv 3 (ὅρασις); Hm 3 (ἐντολή); Hs 3 (παραβολή). S. also TestSol; PVindobBosw 18, 37 superscr. (δεκατός).

Γαββαθᾶ indecl. (an Aram. word whose mng. is still uncertain. Acc. to Jos., Bell. 5, 51 Γαβὰθ Σαοὺλ is to be rendered λόφος Σαούλου) ***Gabbatha,*** a locality in Jerusalem which also had the Gk. name Λιθόστρωτον (q.v.) **J 19:13.** CTorrey ZAW 65, '53, 232f thinks the word is Latin, viz. gabata='platter' and was adapted to Aramaic; the stone pavement resembled such a dish.

Γαβριήλ, ὁ indecl. (גַּבְרִיאֵל, God's valiant one) ***Gabriel,*** name of an archangel (Da 8:16; 9:21; En 9:1 al.; TestSol 18:6; ApcEsdr; ApcMos 4; ISyrW 2068; PGM 1, 302; 3, 149 and 535; 4, 1815; 7, 1013 and 1017; 36, 310; Bousset, Rel.[3] 325–28; Billerb. II 126ff; RAC V 239–45) **Lk 1:19, 26;** GJs 12:2 (Just., D. 100, 5; for an angel announcing a birth, cp. Judg 13:2ff, which is peculiarly embellished Jos., Ant. 5, 276–84).

γάγγραινα, ης, ἡ a disease involving severe inflammation, which if left unchecked can become a destructive ulcerous condition, ***gangrene, cancer,*** of spreading ulcers, etc. (medical term since Hippocr.). Fig. (as Plut., Mor. 65d of slanders) **2 Ti 2:17.**—DELG.

Γάδ, ὁ indecl. (גָּד) ***Gad*** (Gen 30:11; 49:19; Test12Patr, JosAs; Philo, Somn. 2, 34.—In Joseph. Γάδας [Ant. 1, 306] or Γάδης [Ant. 2, 182], ου [Ant. 6, 99]) φυλὴ Γ. **Rv 7:5** (s. Δάν).

Γαδαρηνός, ή, όν pert. to Gadara, a city in Transjordania: ***from Gadara;*** ὁ Γ. *the Gadarene* (Jos., Vi. 42; 44) **Mt 8:28; Mk 5:1 v.l.; Lk 8:26 v.l., 37 v.l.** Origen held Gadara could not be the name intended in these passages and adopted the rdg. Γεργεσηνῶν (q.v.); s. his comments In Joannem 6, 6, 41, 208ff Pr. (cp. 10, 19, 113). The rdg. Γερασηνῶν (q.v.) was also known in his time.—Difficulties caused by similar-sounding names in the tradition are old. A scholion on Od. 1, 85 (in Hes., fgm. 70 Rz.) says w. reference to the Homeric νῆσον ἐς Ὠγυγίην that Antimachus (IV BC) calls the island Ὠγυλίη. The scholion goes on to say: διαφέρουσι δὲ οἱ τόποι.—TZahn, D. Land der Gadarener, Gerasener, Gergesener: NKZ 13, 1902, 923–45; GDalman, Pj 7, 1911, 20ff, Orte[3] 1924 (tr., Sacred Sites, index); OProcksch, Pj 14, 1918, 20; DVölter, D. Heilg. d. Besessenen im Lande der Gerasener od. Gadarener od. Gergesener: NThT 9, 1920, 285–97; Pauly-W. VII 1242–45; BHHW I 508–33. SEG XLII, 1431 (ins).

Γάζα, ης, ἡ (עַזָּה) *Gaza* (Diod. S. 19, 59, 2; Strabo 16, 2, 21; Arrian, Anab. 2, 26 and elsewhere in the story of Alexander; ins; Gen 10:19 al.; EpArist; Joseph.; SibOr 3, 345), one of the 5 chief cities of the Philistines, in southwest Palestine; it was touched by the caravan route leading to Egypt **Ac 8:26** (where the added phrase αὕτη ἐστὶν ἔρημος refers to ὁδός.—WPhythian-Adams, The Problem of 'Deserted' Gaza: PEF 1923, 30–36). Schürer II 98–103; MMeyer, History of the City of Gaza 1907; IBenzinger, Pauly-W. VII 1910, 880ff; PThomsen, Reallex. der Vorgesch. IV 1926, 178ff; BHHW I 516; RAC IX 1123–34; PECS 345–46.—M-M.

γάζα, ης, ἡ (cp. Persian ganj; treasure; found as a loanw. in Gk. since Theophr., HP 8, 11, 5; Polyb., Diod. S., Plut.; Appian, Mithrid. 23 §93; OGI 54, 22; LXX, cp. Hebr. גִּזְבָּר treasurer) ***the*** (royal) ***treasury*** ὃς ἦν ἐπὶ πάσης τῆς γάζης αὐτῆς *who was her chief treasurer* **Ac 8:27.**—HSchaeder, Iran. Beiträge I 1930, 47.—DELG. M-M.

γαζοφυλάκιον, ου, τό (v.l. γαζοφυλακεῖον N[25] but -φυλάκιον preferred by B-D-F §13; s. DELG s.v. φύλαξ)

❶ **a place for the storing of valuables,** ***treasure room, treasury*** (Diod. S. 9, 12, 2; Strabo 7, 6, 1; OGI 225, 16; Esth 3:9; 1 Macc 3:28). In this sense our sources of information on the Jerusalem temple speak of γαζοφ. in the pl. (2 Esdr 22: 44; Jos., Bell. 5, 200; 6, 282) and sg. (1 Macc 14:49; 2 Macc 3:6, 24, 28, 40; 4:42; 5:18; 2 Esdr 23: 5, 7; Jos., Ant. 19, 294). It can be taken in this sense **J 8:20** (sing.) *in* (or *at*) *the treasury* (for the use of ἐν in the sense of 'near' [the public would of course not be permitted in the treasure room(s)] see s.v. ἐν 1c. But it is quite prob. that J may be using the term γ. loosely of the area generally known as the 'treasury', which would have the equivalent of a vault; the prep. would then be used in its customary locative sense).

❷ For **Mk 12:41, 43; Lk 21:1** the mng. ***contribution box*** or ***receptacle*** is attractive. Acc. to Mishnah, Shekalim 6, 5 there were in the temple 13 such receptacles in the form of trumpets. But even in these passages the general sense of 'treasury' is prob., for the contributions would go the treasury via the receptacles.—Billerb. II 37–46. GKaminski, JDAI 106, '91, 63–181.—M-M.

Γάϊος, ου, ὁ (Γαῖος W-H.; found frequently, e.g. Diod. S. 11, 60, 1; 13, 104, 1; 19, 73, 1) ***Gaius*** name of several Christians about whom little is known.

❶ fr. Derbe **Ac 20:4.**—❷ fr. Macedonia, companion of Paul in Ephesus **19:29.**—❸ fr. Corinth, baptized by Paul **1 Cor 1:14.** Paul lived w. him when he wrote **Ro 16:23.** See Goodsp. s.v. Τίτιος.—❹ the man to whom **3J** was addressed (vs. **1**).

❺ name of the copyist of the Martyrdom of Polycarp, MPol 22:2; Epil Mosq 1:5.—JChapman, JTS 5, 1904, 366 identifies 1 and 4, perh. 3.—M-M.

γάλα, γάλακτος, τό (Hom.+) ***milk***—ⓐ as material fluid **1 Cor 9:7;** B 6:17. W. honey as sign of fertility 6:8, 10, 13 (cp. Ex 3:8, 17; 13:5 al.; Lucian, Saturn. 7, Ep. Sat. 1, 20; Himerius, Or. 13, 7 W. ῥεῖν μέλι καὶ γάλα; Dio Chrys. 18 [35], 18 Indian rivers, in which milk, wine, honey and oil flow). As product of human mammary gland γάλα τ. γυναικῶν (Hippocr., Mul. 8: VII, p. 206 L.) ApcPt, fgm. 2 p. 12, 24 (s. πήγνυμι 3). Of extraordinary circumstance [ὅτι τραχηλοκοπη]θείσης τῆς κεφαλῆς αὐτοῦ γάλα ἐξῆλθεν *when (Paul) was beheaded, milk came out from him* (evidently in contrast to blood) AcPl Ha 11, 1.

ⓑ fig. (cp. Philo, Agr. 9 ἐπεὶ δὲ νηπίοις μέν ἐστι γάλα τροφή, τελείοις δὲ τὰ ἐκ πυρῶν πέμματα, καὶ ψυχῆς γαλακτώδεις μὲν ἂν εἶεν τροφαὶ κτλ., Omn. Prob. Lib. 160, Migr. Abr. 29 al.; Epict. 2, 16, 39; 3, 24, 9. For Hebraic associations s. FDanker, ZNW 58, '67, 94f) of elementary Christian instruction **1 Cor 3:2; Hb 5:12f.** τὸ λογικὸν ἄδολον γ. *the unadulterated spiritual milk* **1 Pt 2:2** (Sallust. 4, 10 p. 8, 24 of the mysteries: γάλακτος τροφὴ ὥσπερ ἀναγεννωμένων). S. HUsener, Milch u. Honig: RhM 57, 1902, 177–95=Kleine Schriften IV 1914, 398ff; ADieterich, Mithraslit. 1903, 171; RPerdelwitz, D. Mys. 1911, 56ff; KWyss, D. Milch im Kultus d. Griech. u. Römer 1914; FLehmann, D. Entstehung der sakralen Bedeutung der Milch: ZMR 22, 1917, 1–12; 33–45; ESelwyn, 1 Pt. '46, ad loc. and 308f; BHHW II 1215f; Kl. Pauly III 1293f.—DELG. M-M. TW.

Γαλάτης, ου, ὁ (since Demetrius of Byz. [c. 275 BC] who described in 13 books τὴν Γαλατῶν διάβασιν ἐξ Εὐρώπης εἰς Ἀσίαν [no. 162 Jac.; s. Diog. L. 5, 83]; ins; 1 Macc 8:2; 2 Macc 8:20; Joseph.; SibOr index) **an inhabitant of Galatia,** ***a Galatian*** (so Demetr. of Byz.; Strabo 12, 5, 2 et al.; s. the foll. entry) **Gal 3:1** (cp. Callim., Hymn. 4, Delos, 184 Γαλάτῃσι ἄφρονι φύλῳ. In a Hamburg pap [III BC] Coll. Alex. p. 131, 9 the Galatians are called ἄφρονες); superscr. of Gal.

Γαλατία, ας, ἡ (Diocles 125; Appian, Mithr. 17 §60; 65 §272 al.; Cass. Dio 53, 26; ins) ***Galatia,*** a district in Asia Minor, abode of the Celtic Galatians, and a Roman province to which, in addition to the orig. Galatia, Isauria, Cilicia, and northern Lycaonia belonged. The exact mng. of G. in the NT, esp. in Paul, is a much disputed question. **Gal 1:2; 1 Cor 16:1; 2 Ti 4:10** (in this pass. some mss. have Γαλλίαν, and even the better attested rdg. Γαλατίαν can be understood as referring to Gaul: Diod. S. 5, 22, 4 al.; Appian, Celts 1, 5 al.; Polyaenus 8, 23, 2; Jos., Ant. 17, 344; other ref. in Zahn, Einl. I 418.—To avoid confusion, it was possible to say something like Γαλατία τῆς ἑῴας=eastern [Appian, Bell. Civ. 2, 49 §202] or Γαλάται οἱ ἐν Ἀσίᾳ [Appian, Bell. Civ. 4, 88 §373]); **1 Pt 1:1.** For the NT there are only two possibilities, both of which involve the Galatia in Asia Minor. The view that G. means the district orig. inhabited by the Galatians (North Gal. theory) found favor with Mommsen (ZNW 2, 1901, 86), ASteinmann (esp. detailed, D. Leserkreis des Gal. 1908), vDobschütz, Jülicher, MDibelius, Feine, Ltzm., JMoffatt, Goguel, Sickenberger, Lagrange, Meinertz, Oepke, EHaenchen (comm. on Ac 16:6), et al. Impressive support is given this point of view by Memnon of Asia Minor, a younger contemporary of Paul. For him the Galatians, of whom he speaks again and again (no. 434 fgm. 1, 11ff Jac.), are the people with a well-defined individuality, who came to Asia Minor from Europe. Paul would never have addressed the Lycaonians as Γαλάται.—The opp. view, that G. means the Rom. province (South Gal. theory), is adopted by Zahn, Ramsay, EMeyer, EBurton (Gal 1921), GDuncan (Gal '34), esp. VWeber (Des Pls Reiserouten 1920). S. also FStähelin, Gesch. d. kleinasiat. Galater[2] 1907; RSyme, Galatia and Pamphylia under Aug.: Klio 27, '34, 122–48; CWatkins, D. Kampf des Pls um Galatien 1913; JRopes, The Singular Prob. of the Ep. to the Gal. 1929; LWeisgerber, Galat. Sprachreste: JGeffcken Festschr. '31, 151–75; Hemer, Acts 277–307 (North-Gal. hypothesis 'unnecessary and improbable' p. 306) Pauly-W. VII 519–55; Kl. Pauly II, 666–70.—New Docs 4, 138f. M-M.

Γαλατικός, ή, όν (Diod. S. 5, 39, 7; Arrian, Anab. 2, 4, 1; Polyaenus 4, 6, 17; ins) **pert. to Galatia, *Galatian*** χώρα *the Galatian country* **Ac 16:6; 18:23.** Here prob. the district, not the Rom. province, is meant; but s. WRamsay, St. P. the Traveler and Rom. Citizen, 1896, 104; 194 (s. Γαλατία).

γαλεάγρα, ας, ἡ (Hyperid., fgm. 34; Theophr., HP 5, 7, 6; Ezk 19:9; TestJob 27:1; AscIs 3:6) prim.: device for catching a weasel 'weasel-trap' or 'weasel-cage' then gener. ***animal-cage*** AcPl Ha 4, 22.—DELG s.v. γαλέη.

γαλῆ, ῆς, ἡ (contr. fr. γαλέη; Hdt. and Batr. et al.—The form γαλὴ in Lycophron 843) a name given to various members of the 'weasel' family: ***weasel*** PtK 2 p. 14, 19; acc. to Moses (Lev 11:29) its flesh was not to be eaten B 10:8 (on the odd view expressed by B cp. Aristot., GA 3, 6, 756b; Aelian, NA 2, 55; 9, 65; Plut., Mor. 380f; Anton. Lib. 29, 3; EpArist 144; 163; 165; Physiologus 21 p. 253f L.; s. MCurley, Physiologus '79, 86).—DELG s.v. γαλέη.

γαλήνη, ης, ἡ (Hom. et al.; Epict. 2, 18, 30; Sym. Ps 106:29; loanw. in rabb.) **an unruffled surface on a body of water, *a calm,*** on a lake (Diod. S. 3, 21, 1; Appian, Bell. Civ. 4, 115 §480; Lucian, Dial. Mar. 1, 3; 15, 3; in imagery, Philo; Jos., Bell. 3, 195) **Mt 8:26; Mk 4:39; Lk 8:24.**—DELG. M-M. TW.

γαληνιάω (s. γαλήνη; Anth. Pal. 5, 35, 7 [Rufinus c. 130 AD]; Orphica) ***be clear, be calm*** τὰ ὕδατα ταῦτα γαληνιῶντα καὶ σκιρτῶντα *these waters calm and then dancing* GJs 3:3 in imagery of a period of sterility followed by the joy of conception.

Γαλιλαία, ας, ἡ *Galilee* (fr. גָּלִיל circle, district, really גְּלִיל הַגּוֹיִם district of the gentiles, Is 8:23 [9:1]; **Mt 4:15,** Aram. גְּלִילָא; Strabo 16, 2, 34 and 40; LXX; Philo, Leg. ad Gai. 326; Joseph.; B-D-F. §56, 2), after the Exile, the northern part of Palestine, bounded by Syria, Sidon, Tyre, Ptolemais, Carmel, the plain of Jezreel, and the Jordan (Jos., Bell. 3, 35–40). It was divided into Northern (Upper) and Southern (Lower) Gal. (Jos., Bell. 3, 35; 2, 568; 573, Vi. 187f; Jdth 1:8; Mishnah, Shebiith 9, 2), and fr. the death of Herod the Great in 4 BC until 39 AD it belonged to the tetrarchy of Herod Antipas. Mentioned w. Samaria **Lk 17:11; Ac 9:31;** w. the Decapolis **Mt 4:25;** w. Judea **Lk 5:17; Ac 9:31; J 4:47, 54.** Used to specify names of places, well-known or otherwise: Ναζαρὲτ τῆς Γ. **Mt 21:11; Mk 1:9;** Κανὰ τῆς Γ. **J 2:1, 11; 4:46; 21:2;** Βηθσαϊδὰ τῆς Γ. **12:21;** θάλασσα τῆς Γ. the Lake of Tiberias, or Gennesaret **Mt 4:18; 15:29; Mk 1:16; 7:31; J 6:1;** τὰ μέρη τῆς Γ. *the district of Gal.* (s. μέρος 1bγ) **Mt 2:22;** ἡ περίχωρος τῆς Γ. *the surrounding country of G.* **Mk 1:28; Lk 4:41 v.l.; 23:6 v.l.**—Outside the gospels only **Ac 9:31; 10:37; 13:31.**—HGuthe, RE VI 336ff, XXIII 496f; VSchwöbel, D. Landesnatur Palästinas I and II 1914; CWatzinger, Denkmäler Palästinas II '35; GBertram, ARW 32, '35, 265–81; GSchrenk, Gal. z. Zt. Jesu '41; WMeeks, Galilee and Judea in the 4th Gosp., JBL 85, '66, 159–69; BHHW I 510–12; RAC VIII 796–821. RHorsley, Galilee: History, Politics, People '95; OEANE II 369–76.

Γαλιλαῖος, α, ον (Joseph.; Just., D 108, 2 Ἰησοῦ τινος Γ.; 80, 4 name of a Jewish sect) ***Galilean,*** ὁ Γ. *the Galilean,* inhabitant of Galilee **Mt 26:69; Ac 2:7;** cp. **J 7:52;** recognizable by his dialect **Mk 14:70; Lk 22:59.—Lk 13:1f; 23:6; J 4:45; Ac 1:11** (Epict. 4, 7, 6 οἱ Γαλιλαῖοι=Christians). τὴν Μαρίαν τὴν Γ. AcPl Ha 8, 26f; AcPlCor 2:14. Surname of the insurrectionist Judas **Ac 5:37.**—TW.

Γαλλία 2 Ti 4:10 v.l., s. Γαλατία.

Γαλλίων, ωνος, ὁ *Gallio* (Prosopogr. Imp. Rom. II p. 237; Tacit., Annal. 15, 73 Junius Gallio, Senecae frater) proconsul of Achaia 51/52, **Ac 18:12, 14, 17.** For the ins relating to him SIG 801D; MPlassart, Fouilles de Delphes III/4, 286; JOliver, Hesperia 40, '71, 239–40.—ADeissmann, Paulus[2] 1925, 203–25 (lit., esp. p. 210f; Eng. tr. Paul[2] 1926, 261–86); LHennequin, Dict. de la Bible, Suppl. II '34, 355–73; MGoguel, RHPR 12, '32, 321–33; Haenchen, index; DSlingerland, JBL 110, '91, 439–49, and rejoinder by JMurphy-O'Connor, Paul and Gallio: JBL 112, '93, 315–17 (lit.); Boffo, Iscrizioni no. 29 (lit.); Hemer, Acts 251–53; SEG XLII, 474 (lit.); Kl. Pauly II 686; BHHW I 512f.—M-M.

Γαμαλιήλ, ὁ indecl. (גַּמְלִיאֵל, Num 1:10; 2:20 al., in Joseph. Γαμαλίηλος, ου [Ant. 20, 213]) ***Gamaliel.*** The NT knows only Rabban G. the Elder, a Pharisee and renowned teacher of the law in Jerusalem **Ac 5:34.** Acc. to **22:3** Paul's teacher.—Schürer II 372f; WBacher, Jewish Encycl. V 1903, 558ff; Billerb. II 636–39; HBöhlig, Der Rat des G. in Ac 5:38f: StKr 86, 1913, 112–20; HSteege, Beth-El 27, '35, 298–304 (on Ac 5:34); MEnslin, Paul and G.: JR 7, 1927, 360–75; JSwain, G's Speech and Caligula's Statue: HTR 37, '44, 341–49; BHHW I 513; Haenchen, index.

γαμετή, ῆς, ἡ (s. γαμέω; Hes. et al.; PTebt 104, 17 [I BC]; POxy 795, 4; SIG 921, 110; OGI 206, 9; Jos., Bell. 1, 475, Ant. 1, 209; 4 Macc 2:11) a woman with married status (opp. concubine) ***wife*** 1 Cl 6:3.—DELG s.v. γαμέω.

γαμέω impf. ἐγάμουν **Lk 17:27;** 1 aor. ἔγημα **Lk 14:20,** inf. γῆμαι 2 Macc 14:25, subj. γήμω **1 Cor 7:28,** ptc. γήμας **Mt 22:25;** the form ἐγάμησα also occurs **Mt 5:32; Mk 6:17; 10:11** (subj.); perf. act. γεγάμηκα **1 Cor 7:10;** plpf. ἐγεγαμήκει Just., D. 140, 1; aor. mid. inf. γήμασθαι Just., A I, 29, 1; 1 aor. pass. ἐγαμήθην **1 Cor 7:39.** See W-S. §15; B-D-F §101; Rob. 1213; Mlt-H. 231 (Hom.+; ins, pap; Phryn. 742 Lob.; LXX; En 106:14; TestJud 12:2; JosAs 4:15; ParJer 8:4; Just.; Tat. 8:1). In our lit., **to take another person as spouse, *marry.***

ⓐ said of a man (Hom.+ gener.)—**α.** w. acc. *marry, take someone as wife* (Hom. et al.; OGI 391, 8; 392, 11; IDefixAudollent 78; Demetr.: 722 fgm. 1, 3 Jac.; Esth 10:3c; Jos., Ant. 6, 309; 7, 70; Just., D. 134, 3; Orig., C. Cels. 5, 27, 13) **Lk 14:20** (the aor. form ἔγημα is exceptional in the NT, and the more usual expr. is λαβεῖν [γυναῖκα] as in ms. D of 14:20; cp. 20:28, 29, 31; 1 Cor 7:28 v.l.; GKilpatrick, JTS 18, '67, 139f); a divorced woman **Mt 5:32; Mk 6:17; Lk 16:18b;** another woman **Mt 19:9; Mk 10:11; Lk 16:18a;** Hm 4, 1, 6.

β. abs. *marry, enter matrimony* (POxy 1213, 4; PFlor 332, 24; 2 Macc 14:25; 4 Macc 16:9; Jos., C. Ap. 2, 201; Just., A I, 29, 1; Tat. 8, 1) **Mt 19:10; 22:25, 30; 24:38; Mk 12:25; Lk 17:27; 20:34f; 1 Cor 7:28, 33;** Hm 4, 1, 8; IPol 5:2; Agr 18.

ⓑ of a woman—**α.** act.—**א.** w. acc. (Eur., Med. 606 ironically; Menander, Hero 3 S.; s. also Nauck, TGF, Adespota 194 and note on the disputed pass.) **Mk 10:12** (v.l. γαμηθῇ ἄλλῳ is adapted to more common usage; s. bγ).

ב. abs. (Chariton 3, 2, 17 Ἀφροδίτη γαμεῖ) **1 Cor 7:28b, 34; 1 Ti 5:11, 14.**

β. mid. (Hom. et al.), esp. ptc. ἡ γαμουμένη (as POxy 496, 5; 905, 10; Just., A I, 29, 1 τὸ γήμασθαι) IPol 5:2.

γ. pass. *get married, be married* (X., An. 4, 5, 24; Plut., Romul. 18 [2, 1]; Anton. Lib. 16, 2; 20, 7; Ps.-Apollod. 1, 147 Μήδεια γαμηθεῖσα, Αἰγεῖ παῖδα γεννᾷ; POxy 361, 1 [I AD]; 257, 25; 30; PGrenf II, 76, 10f ἀλλ' ἐξεῖναι αὐτῇ γαμηθῆναι ὡς ἂν βουληθῇ; JosAs 4:15 ABH γαμηθήσομαι [γαμήσομαι DEF] τῷ υἱῷ τοῦ βασιλέως; Philo, Spec. Leg. 1, 110; Jos., Ant. 6, 308) **Mk 10:12 v.l.** (s. bαא); **1 Cor 7:39.**—For lit. s. γαμίζω 2 and s. also HPreisker, Christent. u. Ehe in d. ersten drei Jahrh. 1927, Ehe u. Charisma b. Pls: ZST 6, 1929, 91–95; WMichaelis, Ehe u. Charisma b. Pls: ibid. 5, 1928, 426–52; HSchumacher, D. Eheideal d. Ap. Pls '32; FBüchsel, D. Ehe im Urchristent.: ThBl 21, '42, 113–28; AOepke, RAC IV, '59, 650–731; AIsaksson, Marriage and Ministry in the New Temple, '65; RSchnackenburg, Schriften zum NT, '71, 414–34; KNiederwimmer, Askese u. Mysterium '75; STreggiari, Roman Marriage '91. S. also γυνή 1.

ⓒ of both sexes *marry* (M. Ant. 4, 32; PEleph 2, 8 [285/284 BC]; BGU 717, 16 οἱ γαμοῦντες) **1 Cor 7:9f, 36; 1 Ti 4:3;** Hm 4, 4, 1f; Dg 5:6.—EDNT I 235–38. B. 98. DELG. M-M. TW

γαμίζω impf. pass. ἐγαμιζόμην (Apollon. Dysc., Synt. p. 280, 11 H. [3, 153 p. 400 Uhlig] ἔστι γὰρ τὸ μὲν πρότερον [i.e. γαμῶ] γάμου μεταλαμβάνω, τὸ δὲ γαμίζω γάμου τινὶ μεταδίδωμι=the former [γαμῶ] means 'I receive in marriage', whereas γαμίζω means 'I give in marriage'.—Otherw. the word is found only in Christian writings.)

❶ **to cause (a woman) to become married, *give (a woman) in marriage*** abs. **Mt 24:38; Mk 12:25** D. Pass. *be given in marriage, be married* **Mt 22:30; Mk 12:25; Lk 17:27; 20:35.**—In **1 Cor 7:38,** γ. abs. and w. acc. may be understood in this sense of a father who gives his daughter (or a guardian who gives his ward) in marriage (v.l. ἐκγαμίζων). But mng. 2 appears more probable.

❷ Because of the context in 1 Cor 7:36–38, where the relation of virgins to Christ is featured, it is best to take γ. vs. **38**=γαμέω **to take as spouse,** ***marry*** (on this s. Ltzm., Hdb. ad loc.; B-D-F §101 p. 44 agrees; s. also Mlt-H. 409f. It is hard to say how far the rule of Apollon., quoted above, applies, since there are so few exx. of γ. In any case, his observation indicates that mistakes could be made in the use of either term. On the increasing frequency of formations in -ίζω s. Psaltes p. 325–31. γαμίζω='marry' is also found in Methodius, Sympos. 3, 14 p. 44, 21 Bonwetsch). In the context of vss. 36–38 παρθένος would then mean either a Christian's fiancée (s. ref. to Goodsp. below and NRSV), or perh. even his 'spiritual bride', who lived with him as a virgin. S. παρθένος a.—EGrafe, Theol. Arbeiten aus d. Rhein. wiss. Predigerverein n.F. 3, 1899, 57–69; HAchelis, Virgines subintroductae 1902; AJülicher, ARW 7, 1904, 373–86, PM 22, 1918, 97–119; JSickenberger, BZ 3, 1905, 44–69; HKoch, ibid. 3, 1905, 401–7; FFahnenbruch, ibid. 12, 1914, 391–401; AvanVeldhuizen, TSt 23, 1905, 185–202, NThSt 2, 1919, 297–309; RSteck, SchTZ 34, 1917, 177–89; StSchiwietz, ThGl 19, 1927, 1–15; KHolzhey, ibid. 307f; AJuncker, D. Ethik d. Ap. Pls II 1919, 191ff; KMüller, D. Forderung d. Ehelosigkeit für d. Getauften in d. alten Kirche 1927; HKoch, Quellen z. Gesch. d. Askese '33; Goodsp., Probs. 158f; RKugelman, CBQ 10, '48, 63–71; LRichard: Mémorial JChaine '50, 309–20; AOepke, TLZ 77, '52, 449–52; WKümmel: Bultmann Festschr. '54, 275–95; JO'Rourke, CBQ 20, '58, 292–98; RSebolt, CTM 30, '59, 103–10; 176–89; HBaltensweiler, Die Ehe im NT, '67; HGreeven, NTS 15, '69, 365–88.—DELG s.v. γαμέω. M-M.

γαμίσκω (Aristot., Pol. 7, 14, 4; Stob. et al.)=γαμίζω act. ***give in marriage*** **Mt 22:30 v.l.; Mt 24:38 v.l.;** pass., *be given in marriage* of a woman (Aristot., loc. cit.; Heraclides Hist. 64 [Aristot., Fgm. ed. VRose 1886, 383]; PLond V, 1708, 98; 168; 177 ἐγαμίσκετο ἀνδρί) **Mk 12:25 v.l.; Lk 20:34, 35 v.l.**

γάμος, ου, ὁ (Hom.+; sg. and pl. are oft. used interchangeably w. no difference in mng.; cp. SIG 1106, 101-3 διδότω ὁ ἱερεὺς εἰς τοὺς γάμους τὰ γέρη τῷ τὸν γάμον ποιοῦντι; AcThom 4 [Aa II/2 p. 105, 3]. Joseph. distinguishes in Ant. 14, 467f betw. γάμος=wedding and γάμοι=wedding celebration. But for 'marriage' he somet. uses the sg. [s. 1a below], somet. the pl. [Ant. 20, 141]; Field, Notes, 16).

❶ **public ceremony associated with entry into a marriage relationship, *wedding celebration***—ⓐ gener., pl. (the pl. is used in this sense as early as Hom.; s. also Isaeus 8, 18; 20; BGU 892, 10; 13; 909, 3; Sb 7745, 2; PGiss 31, 16; POxy 111, 2; 927, 2.—Joseph., s. above) γάμους ποιεῖν *give a wedding celebration* **Mt 22:2** (on γ. ποιεῖν cp. Demosth. 30, 21; Menand., fgm. 450 K. [=454 Edm. III/2 p. 732]; Achilles Tat. 1, 3, 3; Xenophon Eph. 2, 7, 1; Michel 1001 II, 19; Tob 6:13; 8:19; 1 Macc 9:37; 10:58). καλεῖσθαι εἰς τοὺς γ. *be invited to the wedding* (POxy 1486) **22:3, 9** (cp. Tob 9:5 S).—**22:4** (on the parable Mt 22:1–14 s. JSickenberger, ByzZ 30, 1930, 253–61; VHasler, TZ 18, '62, 25–35). Sg. (LXX) **Mt 22:8; J 2:1f;** ἔνδυμα γάμου *a wedding garment* **Mt 22:11, 12** (cp. Aristoph., Av. 1692 γαμικὴν χλανίδα; Achilles Tat. 2, 11, 2f).—εἰσέρχεσθαι εἰς τοὺς γ. **Mt 25:10** (for the pl. cp. Diog. L. 3, 2 s. b). Colloq. usage may be embedded **Mt 22:10,** but s. 3 below.

ⓑ Banqueting was integral to marriage celebration (cp. Diog. L. 3, 2; Esth 2:18) **Mt 22:4; Rv 19:9** δεῖπνον τοῦ γάμου (cp. Diog. L. 3, 2 ἐν γάμοις δειπνῶν; for the theme of an apocalyptic feast [sometimes referred to as 'Messianic Banquet' s. ABD IV 788] s. Is 25:6; 4 Esdr 2:38), but the term itself does not mean 'wedding banquet'; nor do Herodas 7, 86; Diod. S. 4, 81, 4 support such interpretation.—Whether **Lk 12:36; 14:8** refer to wedding celebrations or simply *feasts* (cp. Esth 9:22) cannot be determined w. certainty (s. IMarshall, Comm. on Luke '78, 536).

❷ **the state of being married**—ⓐ of socially recognized nuptials *marriage* (Diod. S. 2, 5, 1; Maximus Tyr. 26, 6a; 26, 9d; Chion, Ep. 10; Herodian 3, 10, 5; POxy 905, 4 [170 AD] al.; pap; Wsd 14:24, 26; Jos., Ant. 6, 210, Vi.; Just., Tat., Ath.; πρὸς γάμον διδόναι Theoph. Ant. 3, 27 [p. 260, 23]) **Hb 13:4;** IPol 5:2.—Fig. of the Lamb's apocalyptic nuptials **Rv 19:7, 9.**

ⓑ of socially unrecognized nuptials (Dem. 18, 129, prostitution; Eur. Tro. 932) ἔκλεψεν τοὺς γ. αὐτῆς of Joseph: 'he has stolen her nuptials' *has eloped with her* (unacceptable in a society in which all aspects of entry into a marriage were governed by protocol) GJs 15:2; cp. vs. 4.

❸ **a relatively large room that could serve as a place for celebration of a wedding, *wedding hall*** ἐπλήσθη ὁ γάμος (v.l. νυμφών q.v.) ἀνακειμένων *the hall was filled w. guests* **Mt 22:10** (cp. Twentieth Century NT et al.). But the absence of any confirmatory usage suggests that this pass. might better be considered under 1a (Mft.: 'The marriage-banquet was supplied w. guests').—B. 98. DELG s.v. γαμέω. M-M. TW. Sv.

γάρ (Hom.+) conj. used to express cause, clarification, or inference. Never comes first in its clause; usu. second, but also third (**Hb 11:32**), or even fourth (**2 Cor 1:19,** as e.g. Menand., Epitr. 883 S. [=563 Kö.]; Lucian, Pisc. 10, Philops. 15; s. B-D-F §452; 475, 2; Denniston 56–114; Schwyzer II 560).

❶ **marker of cause or reason, *for*—ⓐ** abs. **Mk 1:22; 9:49; Lk 1:15; 21:4; J 2:25; Ac 2:25; Ro 1:9; 1 Cor 11:5** and oft.—It should be noted that γάρ w. a verb (and nothing else) can form a sentence (Demosth. 21, 28 δίδωσι γάρ.; Epicurus in Diog. L. 10, 32 κινεῖ γάρ.; Menand., Sam. 666 S. [=321 Kö.] δεῖ γάρ.; Alexis Com. 286 Kock παύσει γάρ.; Axionicus Com. [IV BC] 6, 6 K.: Ael. Aristid. 13 p. 273 D.; Maximus Tyr. 10, 8g δύναται γάρ.; Lucian, Dial. Mort. 3, 3; Synes., Ep. 4 p. 163d ἠνεχυρίαστο γάρ.=for it had been seized as security; Aristaen., Ep. 2, 7; Anna Comn., Alexias 5, 1 vol. I p. 156, 8 R. προπέποτο γάρ.; et al.— Ps.-Demetrius, Form. Ep. p. 12, 2 as conclusion of a letter ὀφείλω γάρ.; Vi. Aesopi G 67 P. as the ending of a story: οὐκ ἔχεις γάρ.=you don't have any [understanding, common sense]; Polyaenus 3 the introduction ends with the words: πρόδηλον γάρ.—See also CKraeling, JBL 44, 1925, 357f; RRottley, JTS 27, 1926, 407–9; RLightfoot, Locality and Doctrine in the Gosp. '38, 10ff; CMoule, NTS 2, '55/56, 58f) ἐφοβοῦντο γάρ. **Mk 16:8** (s. φοβέω 1a). Conclusions of this kind at the end of Mk are also found in other lit. (Horapollo 2, 80 οὗτος γάρ; Plotin. V 5, 13, 36f κρεῖττον γὰρ τὸ ποιοῦν τοῦ ποιούμενου· τελειότερον γάρ. [Pvan der Horst, JTS n.s. 23, '72, 121–24]).

ⓑ used w. other particles and conjunctions ἰδοὺ γάρ (Jdth 5:23; 9:7; 12:12; 1 Macc 9:45) **Lk 1:44, 48; 2:10; 6:23; 17:21; Ac 9:11; 2 Cor 7:11** al.; s. ἰδού 1c. καὶ γάρ (B-D-F §452, 3; B-D-R §452, 3) *for* (=Lat. etenim, Kühner-G. II 338; s. Chariton 3, 3, 16; 2 Macc 1:19; 4 Macc 1:2; 5:8) **Mk 10:45; Lk 22:37; J 4:23; Ac 19:40; 1 Cor 5:7; Hb 5:12; 12:29;** Hs 9, 8, 2; *for also, for even* (B-D-F §452, 3; ZNW 19, 1920, 175f) **Mt 8:9; Lk 6:32f; 7:8; 11:4; J 4:45; Ro 11:1; 15:3; 16:2; 2 Cor 2:10.** S. FGrosheide, καὶ γάρ in het NT: TSt 33, 1915, 108–10. γὰρ καί *for also, for precisely* **2 Cor 2:9** (ParJer 7:6 εἰς τοῦτο γὰρ καὶ ἀπεστάλην). τε γάρ *for indeed* (X., Mem. 1, 1, 3) **Ro 1:26; 7:7; Hb 2:11** (s. τέ 2b). μὲν γάρ (3 Macc 2:15f) often followed by δέ, ἀλλά **Ac 13:36; 23:8; 28:22; 2 Cor 9:1; 11:4; Hb 7:20; 12:10** (s. μέν 1aα, β); ὅτι μὲν γὰρ … ἀλλά **Ac 4:16.** καὶ γὰρ οὐ **1 Cor 11:9;** οὐ γάρ **Mt 10:20; Mk 4:22; 6:52; J 3:17; Ac 2:34; Ro 1:16; 2:11, 13, 28; 4:13; 1 Cor 1:17; 2 Cor 1:8; Gal 4:30** and oft. μὴ γάρ **Js 1:7** (TestAbr A 2, 79, 9 [Stone p. 6]; GrBar 6:6; 8:7). οὐδὲ γάρ **Lk 20:36; J 5:22; 7:5; 8:42; Ro 8:7; Gal 1:12** (s. οὐδέ 2). οὔτε γὰρ … οὔτε (Wsd 12:13; Sir 30:19) *for neither … nor* **1 Th 2:5.**

ⓒ γάρ is somet. repeated. It occurs twice either to introduce several arguments for the same assertion, as (Sir 37:13f; 38:1f; Wsd 7:16f) **J 8:42; 1 Cor 16:7; 2 Cor 11:19f;** or to have one clause confirm the other, as (Jdth 5:23; 7:27; 1 Macc 11:10) **Mt 10:19f; Lk 8:29; J 5:21f, 46; Ac 2:15; Ro 6:14; 8:2f;** Hv 5:3; or to have various assertions of one and the same sentence confirmed one after the other **Mt 3:2f; J 3:19f** (cp. Wsd 1:5f; EpJer 6; 7). γάρ also occurs three times (Wsd 9:13–15; 14:27–29) **Mt 16:25–27; Lk 9:24–26; Ro 4:13–15; 2 Cor 3:9–11;** four times **Mk 8:35–38; Ro 1:16–18;** even five times **1 Cor 9:15–17.**

ⓓ the general is confirmed by the specific **Mk 7:10; Lk 12:52; Ro 7:2; 1 Cor 12:8;**—the specific by the general **Mt 7:8; 13:12; 22:14; Mk 4:22, 25; Ro 2:2 v.l.**

ⓔ oft. the thought to be supported is not expressed, but must be supplied fr. the context: (He has truly been born) *for we have seen his star* **Mt 2:2.** (Let no one refuse) ὃς γὰρ ἐὰν θέλῃ **Mk 8:35; Lk 9:24.** (Let no disciple fail to testify) ὃς γὰρ ἐὰν ἐπαισχυνθῇ με **Mk 8:38.** This is common; cp. **Ac 13:36; 21:13; 22:26; Ro 8:18; 14:10; 1 Cor 1:18; 5:3; 9:9, 17; 14:9.** Sim. w. other particles καὶ γάρ **Mt 15:27; 2 Cor 5:2; 13:4; Phil 2:27; 1 Th 3:4; 4:10.** καὶ γὰρ οὐ **2 Cor 3:10.** μὲν γάρ **Ro 2:25; 1 Cor 5:3; 11:7; 2 Cor 9:1; Hb 7:18.** οὐ γάρ **Mt 9:13; Mk 9:6; Lk 6:43f; Ac 4:20; Ro 8:15; 2 Cor 1:13** (also s. καί 2iα, and μέν 1aα).

ⓕ oft. in questions, where the English idiom leaves the word untransl., adds *then, pray,* or prefixes *what!* or *why!* to the question (Hyperid., fgm. 219; Ael. Aristid. 47, 27 K.=23 p. 452 D.; TestJob 23:8 τὶ γὰρ μοι ἡ θρίξ …; Jos., Bell. 1, 589, Ant. 9, 92) ἱνατί γὰρ … κρίνεται *for what reason … should be judged* **1 Cor 10:29.** ποῖον γὰρ κλέος; *what credit is there?* **1 Pt 2:20.** μὴ γὰρ … ἔρχεται; *what! Is the Messiah to hail fr. Galilee?* **J 7:41.** μὴ γὰρ οἰκίας οὐκ ἔχετε; *what! Have you no houses?* **1 Cor 11:22.** S. μή 3a.—ποία γὰρ ἡ ζωὴ ὑμῶν; *what, pray, is your life?* **Js 4:14 v.l.** πῶς γὰρ ἂν δυναίμην; *how in the world can I?* **Ac 8:31.**—Esp. τίς γάρ; τί γάρ; in direct questions: **Mt 9:5; 16:26; 23:17, 19** al. τί γὰρ κακὸν ἐποίησεν; *why, what crime has he committed?* **27:23;** sim. **Mk 15:14; Lk 23:22.** τί γάρ; transitional, *well, then* **Ro 3:3;** *what does it matter?* **Phil 1:18.**

❷ **marker of clarification, *for, you see*** (Dionys. Hal., De Isocr. p. 542 Raderm.; Lucian, Dial. Mort. 10, 9 p. 373 κοῦφα γὰρ ὄντα; BGU 830, 20 ἐπεὶ γὰρ καὶ γείτων αὐτοῦ εἰμί=since I am also, as you see, his neighbor; Ps.-Demetr. 153 p. 35, 16 R.; Ps.-Callisth. 3, 2, 2 ἐγὼ γάρ=for I) **Mt 12:40, 50; 23:3; 24:38; Mk 7:3; Lk 8:40; 9:14; J 3:16; 4:8f; Ro 7:2; Hb 2:8; 3:4; 2 Pt 2:8;** AcPlCor 2, 4; 35.—Brief, explanatory parenthetical clauses (En 107:3 μυστηριακῶς γὰρ ἐδήλωσεν αὐτῷ; Diod. S. 13, 66, 6 ἦν γὰρ ὁ Κλέαρχος χαλεπός) **Mt 4:18; Mk 1:16; 2:15; 5:42; 16:4; Ro 7:1; 1 Cor 16:5; Gal. 4:25 v.l.** (cp. γὰρ δή 1 Cl 42:5). Akin to explanatory function is the use of γάρ as a narrative marker to express continuation or connection (in later Gk. writers, where more recent users of the texts, not finding the causal force they expect, would often prefer to see it replaced by δέ; unnecessarily, since the grammarian Trypho Alex. [I BC], fgm. 54 ed. AvVelsen 1853 shows clearly that γάρ under certain circumstances εἷς οὖν ἐστὶν ἀντὶ τοῦ δέ=is one and the same thing as δέ). Indeed, in many instances γάρ appears to be used adverbially like our 'now' (in which the temporal sense gives way to signal an important point or transition), 'well, then', 'you see' (e.g. Diod. S. 20, 35, 1 'now'; Iambl., Vi. Pyth. §1; 120; 158; 197 [LDeubner, Bemerkungen z. Text der Vi. Pyth. des Jambl.'35, 30f]; Arrian, Ind. 33, 1 ἀλλὰ ἔπλωον γὰρ … =well, then, they sailed …; schol. on Od. 4, 22 p. 174, 10 Dind.; 'moreover' SIG 1109, 28 [II AD]; 'in the first place' Jos., Bell. 7, 43, 'now' Ant. 1, 68): **Ro 1:18; 2:25** ('indeed', 'to be sure' as Jos., Ant. 11, 8); **4:3, 9; 5:7** ('but'); **12:3; 14:5; 1 Cor 10:1** (v.l. δέ); **2 Cor 1:12; 10:12; 11:5** (B δέ); **Gal 1:11** (v.l. δέ); **5:13; 1 Ti 2:5.** Cp. ἡμεῖς γὰρ **J 9:28 v.l.**—Confirming (Arrian, Ind. 22, 6 ἀλλὰ ἐκπεριπλῶσαι γὰρ … μέγα ἔργον ἐφαίνετο=but to sail seaward seemed indeed a dangerous undertaking; Philo, Leg. All. 3, 192 ἅπασαι μὲν γὰρ . . . =What has just been stated is apparent from the fact that all . . .). Especially in replies γάρ confirms what has been asked about (B-D-F §452, 2) *yes, indeed; certainly* **1 Th 2:20; 1 Cor 9:10.**

❸ **marker of inference, *certainly, by all means, so, then.*** In self-evident conclusions, esp. in exclamations, strong affirmations, etc. (Diogenes the Cynic in Diog. L. 6, 47 παῦσαι γάρ=stop, then) μὴ γὰρ οἰέσθω ὁ ἄνθρωπος ἐκεῖνος *not for a moment let such a person think* **Js 1:7;** μὴ γάρ τις ὑμῶν πασχέτω *by no means let any of you suffer* **1 Pt 4:15;** ἀναλογίσασθε γὰρ τὸν . . . ὑπομεμενηκότα *yes indeed, consider him who endured* **Hb 12:3;** οὐ γάρ *no, indeed!* **Ac 16:37** (Aristoph., Nub. 232, Ran. 58; Pla., Rep. 492e; Lucian, Jupp. Conf. 16). In weakened sense it is somet. resumptive, esp. in long periodic sentences: ηὐδόκησαν γάρ *they decided, then* **Ro 15:27.** ἐλεύθερος γὰρ ὤν *though I am free, then* **1 Cor 9:19** (cp. vs. 1). Sim. **2 Cor 5:4.** Many questions w. γάρ have both inferential and causal force.—S. τοιγαροῦν.—CBird, Some γάρ Clauses in St Mark's Gospel: JTS n.s. 4, '53, 171–87.—DELG. M-M.

γαστήρ, τρός, ἡ (Hom.+) gener. inner regions of the body, with its various parts, such as stomach and womb

❶ ***belly*—ⓐ** of the body's inner regions, but w. ref. to moral obligation τὰ ταμιεῖα τῆς γαστρός *innermost chambers of the being* (so rendered in OT, An American Translation: Pr 20:27) 1 Cl 21:2 (Pr 20:27).

ⓑ metaph., of pers. defined by primary interest *glutton* (Hes., Theog. 26 et al.) γαστέρες ἀργαί (ἀργός 2) **Tit 1:12.**

❷ ***womb*** ἡ γαστὴρ αὐτῆς ὀγκοῦτο GJs 12:3; συλλαμβάνειν ἐν γαστρί (Gen 25:21 LXX Sixtina; Demetr.: 722 fgm 1, 4 Jac.) **Lk 1:31;** ἐν γαστρὶ λαμβάνειν GJs 4:2, 4 (LXX; En 7:2; ApcMos 1). ἐν γαστρὶ ἔχειν *be pregnant* (Hdt. 3, 32 et al.; med. wr. since Hippocr. [Hobart 92]; Paus. 4, 33, 3; Artem. 2, 18; 3, 32, 4 et al.; PCairZen 328, 20 and PEnteux 71, 6; PMagd 4, 6 [the three III BC]; PFlor 130, 3; LXX; En 99:5) **Mt 1:18, 23** (cp. Is 7:14); **24:19; Mk 13:17; Lk 21:23; 1 Th 5:3; Rv 12:2.** ἐν τῇ γαστρὶ (εἶναι) B 13:2 (Gen 25:23); GJs 13:3.—B. 253. DELG. M-M. Spicq.

γαυριάω (X. et al.; Demosth.; Jdth 9:7 [aor. ἐγαυρίασαν]) **to bear oneself proudly, *be proud, exult*** (cp. X., Eq. 10, 16 a prancing horse) *to glory* ἐν τῷ πλούτῳ *in riches* Hv 1, 1, 8; 17:6 v.l.

γαυρόω (act. in Plut., et al.) mostly pass. γαυροῦμαι; fut. 3 sg. γαυρωθήσεται; aor. ptc. acc. γαυρωθέντα; pf. ptc. γεγαυρωμένος (all LXX) =γαυριάω 'to be proud, exult': ***pride oneself*** (Eur., Or. 1532; X., Hiero 2, 15; Wsd 6:2; 3 Macc 3:11; 6:5; Philo, Mos. 1, 284) ἐν τῷ πλούτῳ Hv 3, 9, 6 (Ps.-Phoc. 53 γ. ἐνὶ πλούτῳ. PFlor 367, 11 πλούτῳ γαυρωθείς).—DELG s.v. γαῦρος.

γέ (Hom.+; apolog. exc. Ar.) enclit. particle, appended to the word or words it refers to; as in Hom.+ it serves to "focus the attention upon a single idea, and place it, as it were, in the limelight: differing thus from δή, which emphasizes the reality of a concept (though in certain respects the usages of the two particles are similar)" (Denniston 114). In oral utterance it would be accompanied by a change in pitch of voice at certain points in the context, and a translator may use an adverb or indicate the point through word order, choice of typeface, or punctuation ***at least, even, indeed,*** etc.

ⓐ without other particles**—α.** limiting *at least, at any rate* (cp. Just., A I, 4, 4 ὅσον γε ἐκ τοῦ ὀνόματος 'at least so far as [one can derive a reason for punishment] from the name Christian'): *at least* διά γε τὴν ἀναίδειαν *at least because of (his) shamelessness, persistence* (?) **Lk 11:8.** διά γε τὸ παρέχειν μοι κόπον *yet because she bothers me* **18:5.**

β. intensive (Mel., HE 4, 26, 11 πολύ γε φιλανθρωποτέραν [γνώμην]; cp. Just., D. 127, 2 [of God] ὅς γε ἦν καὶ πρὶν τὸν κόσμον γενέσθαι): *even* ὅς γε τοῦ ἰδίου υἱοῦ οὐκ ἐφείσατο *who did not spare even his own son* **Ro 8:32.** ἁμαρτία γέ ἐστιν *indeed, it is a sin* Hv 1, 1, 8.

ⓑ added to other particles (for ἄρα γε s. ἄρα, ἆρα; for ἀλλά γε s. ἀλλά):**—α.** εἴ γε *if indeed, inasmuch as* (Kühner-G. II 177c) **Eph 3:2; 4:21; Col 1:23.** τοσαῦτα ἐπάθετε εἰκῇ; εἴ γε καὶ εἰκῇ *have you experienced so many things in vain? If it really was in vain* **Gal 3:4.** εἴ γε καὶ ἐκδυσάμενοι οὐ γυμνοὶ εὑρεθησόμεθα *assuming, of course, that we shall not be found naked after having put off (our earthly habitation)* (sim. NRSV; difft. REB) **2 Cor 5:3.** S. also AcPl Ha 8, 24f s.v. εἰ 6b.

β. εἰ δὲ μή γε *otherwise* (Pla. et al.; Epict. 3, 22, 27; Jos., Bell. 6, 120, Ant. 17, 113; IRG IV, 833; POxy 1159, 6; Mitt-Wilck I/2, 167, 25; PGM 4, 2629; Da 3:15; Bel 8).

א. after affirmative clauses: εἰ δὲ μή γε (sc. προσέχετε), μισθὸν οὐκ ἔχετε *otherwise you have no reward* **Mt 6:1;** cp. **Lk 10:6.** Elliptically: κἂν μὲν ποιήσῃ καρπὸν εἰς τὸ μέλλον· εἰ δὲ μή γε, ἐκκόψεις αὐτήν *if in the future it bears fruit* (very well); *otherwise have it cut down* **13:9.**

ב. after a negative statement: οὐδὲ βάλλουσιν οἶνον νέον εἰς ἀσκοὺς παλαιούς. εἰ δὲ μή γε, ῥήγνυνται *new wine is not poured into old skins; otherwise they burst* **Mt 9:17;** cp. **Lk 5:36.** *No one is to consider me foolish; but if you do, treat me as you would a fool* (i.e. let me enjoy some of the prerogatives) **2 Cor 11:16.**

γ. καί γε (without a word between [older Gk. sometimes inserts a word between καί and γε: e.g., Pla., Phd. 58d, Pol. 7, 531a]: Hippocr., Septim. 9 vol. VII 450; Cornutus 9 p. 40, 12; Περὶ ὕψους 13, 2; Apsines Rhetor [III AD] p. 332, 17 Hammer; LXX; TestReub 4:4 al.) limiting: *at least* **Lk 19:42 v.l.** Intensive: *even* (Jos., Ant. 20, 19) **Ac 2:18** (Jo 3:2 v.l.). καί γε οὐ μακρὰν *though he is really not far* **17:27.** Cp. Hm 8:5; 9:9.—Kühner-G. II 176b; B-D-F §439, 2; Rdm. 35f, 37; Rob. 1129. S. also καί 2iβ.

δ. καίτοι γε *and yet; though, of course* (Epict. 3, 24, 90) **J 4:2;** Dg 8:3.—Kühner-G. II 151–52; B-D-F §439, 1; 450, 3; Rob. 1129. S. also καί 2iδ.

ε. μενοῦνγε in NT somet. at the beginning of its clause, contrary to older usage (Phryn. 342 Lob.), stating a correction *rather* **Lk 11:28 v.l.;** Ro 9:20; **10:18; Phil 3:8.**—B-D-F §450, 4; Hdb. on Ro 9:20. S. also μενοῦν.

ζ. μήτι γε *not to mention, let alone* **1 Cor 6:3** (also Pla., Ep. 4, 321a; Demosth. 21, 148; Strabo 1, 1, 13; other exx. in Wettstein; PLond I, 42, 23 p. 30 [II BC]; B-D-F §427, 3). S. also μήτι.

η. γέ τοι *indeed,* only in the stereotyped transition formula πέρας γέ τοι *and furthermore* B 5:8; 10:2; 12:6; 15:6, 8; 16:3 (s. πέρας 3 and τοί).

θ. ὄφελόν γε *would that indeed* **1 Cor 4:8.**—S. also γοῦν.—DELG. M-M.

γέγονα s. γίνομαι.

Γεδεών, ὁ indecl. (גִּדְעוֹן) ***Gideon,*** an Israelite hero (Judg 6–8; Philo; Jos., Ant. 5, 213ff [in the form Γεδεών, ῶνος]). Named w. other heroes of faith **Hb 11:32.**—BHHW I 570f.

γέεννα, ης, ἡ ***Gehenna,*** Grecized fr. גֵּי(א) הִנֹּם (B-D-F §39, 8; Josh 15:8b; 18:16b; Neh 11:30) cp. Targum גֵּיהִנָּם (s.

Dalman, Gramm.[2] 183), really גֵּי(א) בֶן־הִנֹּם (Josh 15:8a; 18:16a; 2 Ch 28:3; Jer 7:32; cp. 2 Kings 23:10, where the kethibh has the pl.: sons of Hinnom) *Valley of the Sons of Hinnom,* a ravine south of Jerusalem. There, acc. to later Jewish popular belief, God's final judgment was to take place (cp. Just., A I, 19, 8). In the gospels it is the place of punishment in the next life, *hell:* κρίσις τῆς γ. *condemnation to G.* **Mt 23:33.** βάλλεσθαι (εἰς) (τὴν) γ. (cp. SibOr 2, 291) **5:29; 18:9; Mk 9:45, 47;** ἐμβαλεῖν εἰς τὴν γ. **Lk 12:5;** ἀπελθεῖν εἰς (τὴν) γ. **Mt 5:30; Mk 9:43;** ἀπολέσαι ἐν γ. **Mt 10:28;** υἱὸς γ. *a son of hell* **23:15** (dominantly a Semitism, s. υἱός 2 cβ; Bab. Rosh ha-Shana 17b בני גיהנם. Cp. the oracle Hdt. 6, 86, γ: the perjurer is Ὅρκου πάϊς; Menand. Dyskolos 88 υἱὸς ὀδύνης). ἔνοχον εἶναι εἰς τὴν γ. (sc. βληθῆναι) **5:22.** As a place of fire γ. (τοῦ) πυρός (PGM 4, 3072 γέννα πυρός; ApcEsdr 1:9 p. 25, 1 Tdf.; SibOr 1, 103) *hell of fire* **5:22; 18:9;** 2 Cl 5:4. Of the tongue φλογιζομένη ὑπὸ τῆς γ. *set on fire by hell* **Js 3:6.**—GDalman, RE VI 418ff; PVolz, Eschatol. d. jüd. Gem.'34, 327ff; GBeer, D. bibl. Hades: HHoltzmann Festschr, 1902, 1–29; Billerb. IV 1928, 1029–1118.—B. 1485. M-M.

Γεθσημανί (-νῆ v.l.; גַּת שְׁמָנֵי oil-press; גֵּיא שׁ׳ oil valley [Jerome]), indecl. ***Gethsemane,*** name of an olive orchard on the Mt. of Olives, called a χωρίον **Mt 26:36; Mk 14:32.** On form and mng. s. EKautzsch in W-S. §5, 13, a; Dalman, Gramm.[2] 191, Orte[3] 340ff (Eng. tr. 321–23), Jesus 27; GReymann, Pj 5, 1909, 87–96; HTrusen, Geschichte v. G.: ZDPV 33, 1910, 50–97; BMeistermann, Gethsémani 1920; MDibelius, Gethsemane: Crozer Quart. 12, '35, 254–65; GKuhn, EvTh 12, '52/53, 260–85 (Mk 14:32–41); CKopp, Holy Places of the Gospels, '63, 335–50; TLescow, ZNW 58, '67, 215–39; RBarbour, NTS 16, '69/70, 231–51 JTaylor, The Garden of Gethsemane Not the Place of Jesus' Arrest: BAR 21, '95, 26–35, 62.—EDNT.

γείτων, ονος, ὁ and **ἡ** (Hom.+; ins, pap, LXX; TestAbr A 1 p. 77, 7 [Stone p. 2]; Philo, Aet. M. 144; 148; Joseph.; Just., A I, 16, 4; II, 1, 2) ***neighbor*** (w. φίλοι, φίλαι as 3 Macc 3:10; Jos., Ant. 18, 376; cp. Epict. 1, 12, 20 with ἀδελφός and others in a related series) **Lk 15:6, 9; 14:12.—J 9:8.**—B. 1349. DELG. M-M. TW.

γελάω fut. γελάσω and γελάσομαι; 1 aor. ἐγέλασα (Hom. [s. LfgrE II 124] +; ins, pap, LXX, TestSol, TestAbr B, Philo; Jos., Bell. 4, 386 al.; Tat.) ***laugh*** **Lk 6:21, 25** (opp. κλαίω as Theognis 1041 παρὰ κλαίοντι γελῶντες=laughing in the presence of one who is weeping; 1217; Porphyr., Vi. Pyth. 35); Hv 1, 1, 8; 1, 2, 3; εἶδεν αὐτὴν γελοῦσαν *he saw her laughing* GJs 17:2, followed by πρόσωπόν σου βλέπω … γελοῦντα (form of the ptc. as in OdeSol 11:12; s. B-D-F §90 and deStrycker 246).—B. 1106f. DELG. M-M (w. ref. to PGM 13 IV, 162: the exclamation χά=ha!). TW.

γέλως, ωτος, ὁ (Hom.+) ***laughter,*** turned to weeping **Js 4:9.**—SHalliwell, The Uses of Laughter in Gk Culture: ClQ 41, '91, 279–96. DELG s.v. γελάω. M-M. TW.

γεμίζω fut. γεμίσω (ApcSed); 1 aor. ἐγέμισα; pass. ἐγεμίσθην (Aeschyl.+) **to put someth. into an object to the extent of its capacity** (the procedure of filling, in contrast to the result expressed by γέμω, next entry) ***fill***

ⓐ τί τινος (Aeschyl., Ag. 443; Demosth. 34, 36; Ar. 4, 3 [γῆ] γεμίζεται νεκρῶν; OGI 383, 146; PSI 429, 12 [III BC] τὸ πλοῖον γεμίσαι ξύλων) *an object w. someth.* a sponge w. vinegar **Mk 15:36;** jars w. water **J 2:7;** jars w. wine Hm 12, 5, 3; baskets w. fragments **J 6:13.** Pass. ἐγεμίσθη ὁ ναὸς καπνοῦ *the temple was filled w. smoke* **Rv 15:8.**

ⓑ τὶ ἔκ τινος **Lk 15:16** (v.l. ἀπὸ τῶν κερατίων) of filling a censer with fire from an altar **Rv 8:5** (PEnteux 27, 14=PMagd 11, 14 [221 BC] γεμίσαι τὸ πλοῖον ἐκ τῶν τόπων; 4 Macc 3:14 v.l. πηγήν, ἐξ αὐτῆς ἐγέμισαν τ. βασιλεῖ τὸ ποτόν).

ⓒ abs. in pass. (PEnteux 27 verso περὶ τοῦ γεμισθῆναι τὸ πλοῖον [restored]; PSI 429, 12; BGU 1303, 31) (begin to) *be filled* (with water) **Mk 4:37.** Of a house *be filled* (with guests) **Lk 14:23.** Cp. **Rv 10:10 v.l.** (with a little scroll).

ⓓ w. acc. of content: *fill* a vessel ἔλαβεν τὴν κάλπιν καὶ ἐξῆλθεν γεμίσαι ὕδωρ GJs 11:1 (sim. Paus. 3, 13, 3; s. deStrycker 268). S. ὕδωρ.—DELG s.v. γέμω. M-M. TW.

γέμω impf. ἔγεμον (Aeschyl., Hdt.+) **to be full of someth.** (of state rather than procedure), ***be full.***

ⓐ w. simple gen. τινός (Thu. 7, 25, 1 et al.; LXX; GrBar 12:1; PGM 8, 94 πυρὸς γ.) *of someth.*: of bones of the dead **Mt 23:27** (cp. Just., D. 17, 4; 112, 4); GNaass 284, 153; of sins B 11:11 (cp. Isocr., Panath. 10, 29 πολλῶν ἁμαρτημάτων γέμοντες); of rapacity and wickedness **Lk 11:39** (cp. Isocr., Areop. 17, 43 πλείστων γ. ἐπιθυμιῶν; Plut., Pomp. 657 [72, 4], Aemil. 271 [31, 4]); of cursing and bitterness (cp. Philod., Ira p. 56 W. πικρίας) **Ro 3:14** (Ps 9:28; 13:3); of incense **Rv 5:8** (cp. GrBar 12:1–5); of pollutions **17:4;** of the seven plagues **21:9;** of God's wrath **15:7.** ζῷα γέμοντα ὀφθαλμῶν *living creatures full of eyes* (of heavily loaded animals, Posidon.: 87 fgm. 2 Jac. ὄνους γέμοντας οἴνου; Aesop, Fab. 322a H.//180 P.//266 Ch.//191 H-H. S. also Appian, Bell. Civ. 2, 15 §55 γέμων ῥύπου, covered with filth) **4:6, 8.** ὄρος σχισμῶν ὅλον ἔγεμεν *the mountain was all full of cracks* Hs 9, 1, 7; *be full* of mistiness 2 Cl 1:6 (contrast Diod. Sic. 13, 84, 3 ἡ πόλις ἔγεμε φωτός). Pregnant constr. θεοῦ γ. *be full of God* IMg 14 (cp. Vergil in Seneca Rhet., Suasoria 3, 5 HMüller: plena deo, of the Sibyl; Lucan 9, 564; Pollux 1, 15 πλήρης θεοῦ; schol. on Pla. 856e of μάντις· ἄνωθεν λαμβάνειν τὸ πνεῦμα καὶ πληροῦσθαι τοῦ θεοῦ).

ⓑ w. prep. and gen. ἔκ τινος of extortion **Mt 23:25.**

ⓒ w. acc. of thing: θηρίον γέμοντα (constr. ad sensum) ὀνόματα βλασφημίας full of sacrilegious names **Rv 17:3** (s. AThumb, Hdb. d. neugriech. Volkssprache[2] 1910 §50c; B-D-F §159, 1; KWolf, Studien z. Sprache d. Malalas II, diss. Munich 1912, 33).—DELG. M-M. TW.

γενεά, ᾶς, ἡ (Hom.+; ins, pap, LXX, En; TestSol C 13:7; TestJob, Test12Patr; GrBar 10:3; Philo, Joseph., SibOr, Just., Tat.) a term relating to the product of the act of generating and with special ref. to kinship, frequently used of familial connections and ancestry. Gener. those descended fr. a common ancestor, a 'clan' (Pind., P. 10, 42 the Hyperboreans are a ἱερὰ γενεά; Diod. S. 18, 56, 7; Jos., Ant. 17, 220), then

❶ **those exhibiting common characteristics or interests,** ***race, kind*** gener. as in **Lk 16:8** εἰς τὴν γ. τὴν ἑαυτῶν the people of the world are more prudent *in relation to their own kind* than are those who lay claim to the light (difft. GBeasley-Murray, A Commentary on Mk 13, '57, 99–102).

❷ **the sum total of those born at the same time, expanded to include all those living at a given time and freq. defined in terms of specific characteristics,** ***generation, contemporaries*** (Hom. et al.; BGU 1211, 12 [II BC] ἕως γενεῶν τριῶν); Jesus looks upon the whole contemp. generation of Israel as a uniform mass confronting him ἡ γ. αὕτη (cp. Gen 7:1; Ps 11:8) **Mt 11:16; 12:41f; 23:36; 24:34; Mk 13:30; Lk 7:31; 11:29–32, 50f; 17:25; 21:32** (EGraesser, ZNW Beih. 22,[2] '60). S. also 1 above. This generation is characterized as γ. ἄπιστος καὶ διεστραμμένη **Mt 17:17; Mk 9:19** D; **Lk 9:41;** ἄπιστος **Mk 9:19;** πονηρά **Mt 12:45; 16:4** D; **Lk 11:29;** πονηρὰ κ.

μοιχαλίς **Mt 12:39; 16:4;** μοιχαλὶς καὶ ἁμαρτωλός **Mk 8:38** (JGuillet, RSR 35, '48, 275–81). Their contemporaries appeared to Christians as γ. σκολιὰ καὶ διεστραμμένη (the latter term as **Mt 17:17; Mk 9:19 v.l.; Lk 9:41,** the former **Ac 2:40;** cp. Ps 77:8) **Phil 2:15** (Dt 32:5).—Cp. Wsd 3:19. A more favorable kind of γ. is mentioned in Ps 23:6; 111:2; 1QS 3:14.—The desert generation **Hb 3:10** (Ps 94:10). ἰδίᾳ γ. ὑπηρετήσας *after he had served his own generation* **Ac 13:36;** γ. ἡμῶν 1 Cl 5:1; αἱ πρὸ ἡμῶν γ. 19:1; πρώτη γ. *the first generation* (of Christians) Hs 9, 15, 4 (Paus. 7, 4, 9 τετάρτη γενεᾷ=in the fourth generation).

❸ **the time of a generation,** ***age*** (as a rule of thumb, the time between birth of parents and the birth of their children; since Hdt. 2, 142, 2; Dionys. Hal. 3, 15; Gen 50:23; Ex 13:18; 20:5; EpJer 2; Philo, Mos. 1, 7; Jos., Ant. 5, 336; SibOr 3, 108). Here the original sense gradually disappears, and the mng. 'a period of time' remains.

ⓐ of periods of time defined in terms of a generation: *age, generation* **Mt 1:17** (a similar list of numbers in Hellanicus [400 BC]: 323a, fgm. 22a Jac. ἐννέα γενεαῖς ὕστερον . . . ἓξ γενεαῖς ὕστερον ... τρισὶ γενεαῖς ὕστερον; Just., D. 92, 5 γενεαὶ ἀνθρώπων; Tat. 41, 1 μιᾷ τῶν Τρωϊκῶν προγενέστερος ... γενεᾷ [of Heracles]); **Lk 1:48;** 1 Cl 50:3; ἐν γενεᾷ καὶ γ. (Ps 44:18; 89:1) *in one generation after the other* 7:5.

ⓑ of an undefined time period *period of time* gener. εἰς γενεὰς καὶ γενεάς (Ps 48:12; 88:2 al.; Just., D. 92, 2 μετὰ τοσαύτας γ.) *to all ages* **Lk 1:50** (v.l. εἰς γενεὰς γενεῶν and εἰς γενεὰν καὶ γενεάν); cp. 1 Cl 61:3; εἰς πάσας τὰς γ. (Ex 12:14) *to all generations* **Eph 3:21;** ἀπὸ τῶν γ. *from earliest times* **Col 1:26** (for the combination αἰῶνες and γενεαί cp. Tob 1:4; 8:5 S; 13:12; Esth 10:3k). ἐκ γενεῶν ἀρχαίων *fr. ancient times* **Ac 15:21** (cp. Sir 2:10); ἀπὸ γενεᾶς εἰς γ. (Ex 17:16; Ps 9:27) *fr. generation to g.* **Lk 1:50 v.l.;** MPol 21; ἐν πάσαις ταῖς γ. *in all generations* 1 Cl 60:1; GJs 6:2; 7:2; cp. 1 Cl 11:2; ἐν πάσαις ταῖς γενεαῖς τῆς γῆς GJs 12:1 (TestJob 4:6); ἑτέραις γ. *at other times* **Eph 3:5** (cp. Jo 1:3; Ps 47:14); ἐν ταῖς παρῳχημέναις γ. *in past ages* **Ac 14:16.**

❹ in the quot. fr. Is 53:8 τὴν γ. αὐτοῦ τίς διηγήσεται; **Ac 8:33;** 1 Cl 16:8 γ. is prob. to be taken in the sense of ***family history.***—MMeinertz, 'Dieses Geschlecht' im NT, BZ n.F. 1, '57, 283–89.—DELG s.v. γίγνομαι p. 222. M-M. TW. Sv.

γενεαλογέω 1 aor. 3 sg. ἐγενεαλογήθη 1 Ch 5:1 (Hdt. et al.; Sb 7835, 15 [I BC]; Demetr.: 722 fgm. 2, 2 Jac. [in Eus., PE 9, 29, 2]; 1 Ch 5:1; Ar. 15:1 ἀπὸ τοῦ κυρίου [Christians]; Ath., R. 68, 9) ***trace descent*** γενεαλογούμενος ἐξ αὐτῶν *having his descent from them* **Hb 7:6**—S. DELG s.v. γίγνομαι p. 222, λεγω p. 626. M-M.

γενεαλογία, ας, ἡ (s. prec.; Pla., Crat. 396c; Polyb. 9, 2, 1; Dionys. Hal. 1, 11; TestSol D 1:12; Philo, Congr. Erud. Gr. 44; Jos., Ant. 11, 71, C. Ap. 1, 16) an account of ancestry: ***genealogy* 1 Ti 1:4** (for the combination w. μῦθοι cp. FGrH I 47f, in reference to myths cast in genealogical form, as in Hesiod; Polyb., loc. cit. περὶ τὰς γενεαλογίας καὶ μύθους; Julian, Or. 7, 205c); **Tit 3:9,** since Irenaeus 1 praef.; Tertullian, Praescr. Haer. 33, it has oft. been interpr. as referring to Gnostic teachings, esp. groups of Aeons; s. MDibelius, comm. Hermeneia ser. ad loc.—The interpr. which holds that the errors in question have a Jewish background and involve rabbinical speculation begins w. Ambrosiaster and Jerome, and is more or less favored by GKittel, D. γενεαλογίαι d. Past.: ZNW 20, 1921, 49–69; JJeremias[4] '47 ad loc.; RAC IX 1145–1268.—M-M. TW.

γενέθλιος, ον (Aeschyl. et al.; ins, pap) in gener. 'pert. to one's birth'

❶ γ. ἡμέρα ***birthday*** (Epicurus, fgm. 217 Us.; Plut., Pomp. 661 [79, 5]; Lucian, Enc. Dem. 26; OGI ind. VIII, s. esp. no. 458, 4f; Sb 1626; 2 Macc 6:7; Philo, Mos. 1, 207; Jos., Bell. 7, 37; 39) in imagery of Polycarp's date of martyrdom MPol 18:3.—τὰ γενέθλια (Diod. S. 34+35, fgm. 14; Lucian, Gall. 9; Porphyr., Vi. Plotini 2, 39ff, p. 103, 26; 27 Westerm.) **Mk 6:21** D prob. belongs here, for otherwise δεῖπνον would be pleonastic.

❷ τὰ γενέθλια ***birthday celebration*** (OGI 56, 5; 90, 46 τὰ γ. τοῦ βασιλέως; pap, s. Preis.; B-D-F §141, 3; s. also γενέσια) is poss. **Mk 6:21** D, but s. 1 above. On variation in the title of GJs, s. deStrycker 211.—DELG s.v. γίγνομαι p. 223.

γενέσθαι s. γίνομαι.

γενέσια, ίων, τά (fr. adj. γενέσιος, ον, cp. Jos., Ant. 12, 196 ἡ γενέσιος ἡμέρα; 215; OGI 583, 14) ***birthday celebration*** (=Att. γενέθλια, whereas γενέσια earlier [Hdt. 4, 262 al.] meant a commemorative celebration on the birthday of a deceased pers.; s. Phryn. 103f Lob.; ERohde, Psyche[3] I 235) **Mt 14:6; Mk 6:21** (so Alciphron 2, 15, 1; 3, 19, 1; PFay 114, 20; POxy 736, 56; loanw. in rabb.—On the locative [dat.] of time Mk 6:21 cp. PCairZen 332, 1 [284 BC] τοῖς γενεθλίοις; BHHW I 529; BGU 1, 9 γενεσίοις; 149, 15 γενεθλίοις). S. B-D-F §200, 3; Schürer I 346–48 n. 26; ZNW 2, 1901, 48ff; WSchmidt, Geburtstag im Altertum 1908; POslo III p. 49. On GJs s. deStrycker 211. S. γενέθλιον.—RAC IX, 217–43. DELG s.v. γίγνομαι p. 223. M-M.

γένεσις, εως, ἡ (Hom.+)—❶ the term is used in Gk. lit. of ancestry as point of origin (e.g. Diod. S. 17, 51, 3; 17, 108, 3 of Alexander ἡ ἐξ Ἄμμωνος γ.; Orig., C. Cels. 8, 57, 27; Did., Gen. 24, 1), but also of one's **coming into being at a specific moment,** ***birth*** (Diod. S. 2, 5, 1; 4, 39, 2; IPriene 105, 48; OGI 56, 25; O. Wilck II, 1601, 1; Gen 40:20; Hos 2:5; Eccl 7:1 v.l.; PsSol 3:9; Jos., Ant. 2, 215; 234; Orig., C. Cels. 1, 57, 19; Did., Gen. 118, 11) **Mt 1:18,** with special ref. to circumstances under which the birth took place (s. γέννησις.—The superscription here has a counterpart in the subscription of the infancy narrative of Pythagoras in Iambl., Vi. Pyth. 2, 8: περὶ τῆς γενέσεως τοσαῦτο.—Arrian, Anab. answers the question [7, 29, 3] whether Alex. rightly ἐς θεὸν τὴν γένεσιν τὴν αὑτοῦ ἀνέφερεν with the reflection [7, 30, 2] οὐδὲ ἐμοὶ ἔξω τοῦ θείου φῦναι ἂν δοκεῖ ἀνὴρ οὐδενὶ ἄλλῳ ἀνθρώπων ἐοικώς=it seems to me that a man who is different from all other men could not have come into being apart from divinity); **Lk 1:14** (γεννήσει v.l.). As book title (in LXX; Mel., HE 4, 26, 4; Just.) Γένεσις Μαρίας GJs, so also in the subscr.

❷ **state of being**—ⓐ ***existence*** (Pla., Phdr. 252d τ. πρώτην γένεσιν βιοτεύειν; Ps.-Aristid., Ἀπελλᾷ γενεθλιακός 30, 27 Keil; POxy 120, 8; PGM 13, 612; Jdth 12:18; Wsd 7:5) πρόσωπον τῆς γ. αὐτοῦ *his natural face* (i.e. the way he has turned out to be, the way he really looks; s. γίνομαι) **Js 1:23.**

ⓑ ***life, human experience*** ὁ τροχὸς τῆς γενέσεως **Js 3:6** was used in the Orphic mysteries w. the mng. 'wheel of human origin' (Simplicius on Aristot., De Caelo 2 p. 377 Heiberg ἐν τῷ τῆς εἱμαρμένης τε καὶ γενέσεως τροχῷ οὗπερ ἀδύνατον ἀπαλλαγῆναι κατὰ τὸν Ὀρφέα, s. ERohde, Psyche[3] II 130f). In Js it seems to have lost its orig. mng. and to signify *course of life, whole of life* (cp. Anacreontea 32, 7f Preis.: τροχὸς ἅρματος γὰρ οἷα βίοτος τρέχει κυλισθείς).—For lit. s. τροχός.

❸ **an account of someone's life,** ***history, life.*** The expr. βίβλος γενέσεως **Mt 1:1** is fr. the OT: Gen 2:4; 5:1; in the former of these two pass. it = *history of the origin* (cp. Diod. S. 1, 10, 3 ἡ γ. τῶν ἀνθρώπων; schol. on Apollon. Rhod. 3, 1–5a . . . δύο ἱστοροῦνται γενέσεις Μουσῶν=there are two accounts given of the origin of the Muses), which some consider a fitting heading for Mt 1; Zahn ad loc. regards the expr. as constituting the superscription of the whole gospel: *Book of the History.* But if the phrase applies to vv. 1–17, the term γ. refers to

❹ **persons of successive generations forming an ancestral line,** ***lineage, family line,*** which describes the contents of **Mt 1:1–17.**—JLindblom: Teologiska Studier for EStave 1922, 102–9; OEissfeldt, 'Toledot', in Studien zum NT u. zur Patristik '61, 1–8.—DELG s.v. γίγνομαι p. 223. M-M. TW. Sv.

γενετή, ῆς, ἡ coming into being through birth, ***birth,*** ἐκ γενετῆς *fr. birth* (Hom. et al.; Lev 25:47; Esth 4:17m; Jos., Ant. 8, 157; Just., A I, 22, 6, D. 69, 6 [cp. J 9:1]) of blind pers. **J 9:1** (so also Heraclides, Pol. 30 τυφλὸς ἐκ γ.; Paus. 4, 12, 7; Sext. Emp., Math. 11, 238; Philostrat., Ep. 12 p. 230, 31 μακαρίων τῶν ἐκ γενετῆς τυφλῶν; Mel., P. 90, 670).—KBornhäuser, NKZ 38, 1927, 433–37.—DELG s.v. γίγνομαι p. 223. M-M.

γένημα, ατος, τό (on the sp. s. B-D-F §11, 2; 34, 3; Rob. 213) **that which comes into being through production,** ***product, fruit, yield*** of vegetable produce **Lk 12:18 v.l.** (other rdgs. are γεννήματα and τὸν σῖτον; s. GKilpatrick in: Essays in Memory of GMacgregor, '65, 190; 202); of wine as the *product of the vine* (cp. Is 32:12 ἀμπέλου γένημα; pap refer to οἴνου γένημα [BGU 774, 3 al.; so also O. Fay 7] or οἰνικὸν γένημα [BGU 1123, 9; POxy 729, 36 al.]; γ. τοῦ Δίωνος ἀμπελῶνος PTebt 772, 8; Just., D. 91, 1 γεννημάτων for γεν- [Dt 33:14]) **Mt 26:29; Mk 14:25; Lk 22:18** (in all these passages t.r. γεννήματος). In imagery τὰ γ. τῆς δικαιοσύνης ὑμῶν (Hos 10:12) *the harvest of your righteousness* **2 Cor 9:10** (v.l. γεννήματα). The word is a new formation in H. Gk. from γίνεσθαι and has no affinity w. the older γέννημα. It is found since III BC in pap (Dssm. B 105f; NB 12 [BS 110, 184]; Mayser 214; Nägeli 32), ins (CIG 4757, 62; OGI 262, 9), LXX (Thackeray 118); TestLevi 9:14 v.l. (d, e, g; in text: πρωτογεννήματος), and in writers like Polyb. (1, 71, 1; 1, 79, 6; 3, 87, 1 acc. to the best mss.).—New Docs 2, 79. DELG s.v. γίγνομαι p. 222. M-M. TW.

γενναῖος, α, ον (Hom. et al.; OGI 589, 1; PMerton 12, 18; StudPal XXII, 33, 15; BGU 801, 5; LXX, Philo; Jos., C. Ap. 1, 319; 2, 24 al.; Tat. 32, 2) gener. pert. to meeting standards of ancestral prestige, then **of characteristics associated with high-born pers.,** ***noble, illustrious*** epithet of martyrs or their witness (as 4 Macc) οἱ γενναιότατοι μάρτυρες τους Χριστοῦ *the most noble witnesses of Christ* MPol 2:2; ὁ γενναιότατος . . . Γερμανικός 3:1; γενναῖα τὰ μαρτύρια 2:1; τὰ γ. ὑποδείγματα *noble examples* 1 Cl 5:1; τὸ γενναῖον τῆς πίστεως αὐτοῦ κλέος he won *glorious renown for his faith* 5:6. γέρας γενναῖον λαμβάνειν *receive a noble reward* 6:2 (cp. Aeschyl. fgm. 281, 5 TGF μέλος; of inanimate things: Περὶ ὕψους 8, 1; 9, 1 al.). As epithet for Christians gener. *brave, able* 54:1 (cp. 4 Macc 6:10; PLond IV, 1353, 13 [VII AD] ναύτας γενναίους). Sim. of the phoenix *strong, powerful* (Menand., fgm. 223, 12 Kock=1, 12 S. ἀλεκτρυών) 25:3.—τὸ γενναῖον as substantive (=γενναιότης, as Soph., Oed. Col. 569; Xenophon; Nicol. Dam: 90 fgm. 9; 47, 4 Jac.) τὸ γενναῖον αὐτῶν *their nobility* MPol 2:2.—DELG s.v. γίγνομαι p. 222.

γενναιότης, ητος, ἡ (s. prec.; Eur., Thu. et al.; 2 Macc 6:31; 4 Macc 17:2; Philo; Jos., Ant. 17, 333; 19, 212; lit. PHamb 138, 6f) **the quality associated with one who is γενναῖος,** ***nobility, bravery*** εἰς τοσοῦτον γενναιότητος ἐλθεῖν *reach such a degree of noble courage* MPol 2:2; cp. 3.

γεννάω fut. γεννήσω; 1 aor. ἐγέννησα; pf. γεγέννηκα. Pass.: fut. pl. γεννηθήσεσθε Sir 41:9; 1 aor. ἐγεννήθην; pf. γεγέννημαι (Pind., Hdt.+).—See ARahlfs, Genesis 1926, 39. Gener., to cause someth. to come into existence, primarily through procreation or parturition.

❶ **become the parent of,** ***beget***—ⓐ by procreation (oft. LXX, fr. Gen 4:18 on) **Mt 1:2–20** (cp. Diod. S. 4, 67, 2–68, 6, the genealogy of the Aeolians: 67, 4 Ἄρνη ἐγέννησεν Αἰόλον κ. Βοιωτόν; 67, 7 Ἱππάλκιμος ἐγέννησε Πηνέλεων; 68:1 Σαλμωνεὺς ἐγέννησε θυγατέρα . . . Τυρώ; 68, 3 Ποσειδῶν ἐγέννησε Πελίαν κ. Νηλέα; 68, 6 Νηλεὺς παῖδας ἐγέννησε δώδεκα. Interchanged with ἐγέννησε are ἐτέκνωσε, ἦν υἱός, παῖδες ἐγένοντο, etc.; cp. PMich 155, 7. The continuity is not formalized to the degree in Mt, but in Diod. S. 4, 69, 1–3 ἐγέννησε is repeated six times in a short space, and 4, 75, 4f ἐγέννησε occurs four times with the names of fathers and sons; Did., Gen. 144, 27); **Ac 7:8, 29.** ἐκ w. gen. of the mother (Hdt. 1, 108, 2; Diod. S. 4, 2, 1; 4, 62, 1; Palaeph. 44; PLond V, 1730, 10 οἱ ἐξ αὐτῆς γεννηθέντες υἱοί; Tob 1:9; 2 Esdr 10:44; Demetr.: 722 fgm. 2, 2 Jac.; TestJob 1:6; Jos, Ant. 12, 189) **Mt 1:3, 5f.**—Pass. *be fathered* (Orig., C. Cels. 8, 66, 23) ἐκ τῆς παιδίσκης κατὰ σάρκα *w. the slave-woman, according to the flesh* (i.e. in line with human devising; opp. δι' ἐπαγγελίας) **Gal 4:23.** ὁ κατὰ σάρκα γεννηθείς *he that was fathered by human design*, opp. ὁ κατὰ πνεῦμα *he that was fathered by the Spirit's design*, i.e. in keeping with the divine promise, vs. 23) vs. **29.** τὸ ἐν αὐτῇ γεννηθὲν ἐκ πνεύματός ἐστιν *that which is conceived in her is of the Spirit* **Mt 1:20** (τὸ γεννηθέν of that which is yet unborn: Diod. S. 17, 77, 3). Here the male principle is introduced by ἐκ (Lucian, Dial. Deor. 20, 14 ἐκ κύκνου γεγεννημένη; Phlegon: 257 fgm. 36, 2, 4 Jac.; Ps- Callisth. 1, 30, 3 ἐξ Ἄμμωνος ἐγεννήθη; TestSim 2:2) as **J 1:13** (ἐγενήθ. P^{75}et al.); but in **3:6** the imagery is complex, involving a maternal aspect in vs. **4.** W. ἀπό (En 15:8 οἱ γίγαντες οἱ γεννηθέντες ἀπὸ τ. πνευμάτων κ. σαρκός) ἀφ' ἑνὸς ἐγεννήθησαν *they were fathered by one man* **Hb 11:12** (numerous edd. ἐγενήθησαν). ἐκ πορνείας οὐ γεγεννήμεθα (v.l. ἐγεννήθημεν) **J 8:41** (cp. StudPal XX, 4, 30 ἐξ ἀγράφων γάμων γεγεννῆσθαι). ἐν ἁμαρτίαις σὺ ἐγεννήθης ὅλος *you're a born sinner, totally!* **9:34.**—**Lk 1:35** (where mng. 2 is also prob. [as in τὸ γεννώμενον Philo, Plant. 15]. S. AFridrichsen, SymbOsl 6, 1928, 33–36; HAlmqvist, Plut. u. d. NT '46, 60f).

ⓑ by exercising the role of a parental figure, ext. of 1a (Philo, Leg. ad Gai. 58 μᾶλλον αὐτὸν τῶν γονέων γεγέννηκα), of a teacher on pupils ἐν Χ. Ἰ. διὰ τοῦ εὐαγγελίου ὑμᾶς ἐγέννησα *I became your father as Christians through the gospel* **1 Cor 4:15; Phlm 10** (s. Ltzm. and JWeiss on 1 Cor 4:15; ADieterich, Mithraslit. 1903, 146ff).—Pass. ἐκ (τοῦ) θεοῦ γεννᾶσθαι **J 1:13** (on the rdg. of the Lat. ms. b, s. JPryor, NovT 27, '85, 296–318); **1J 2:29; 3:9; 4:7; 5:1, 4, 18.** On γεννᾶσθαι ἐξ ὕδατος κ. πνεύματος **J 3:5** cp. 1QS 4:20–22 and s. YYadin, JBL 74, '55, 40–43. Also ἄνωθεν γ. **J 3:3, 7.** πᾶς ὁ ἀγαπῶν τὸν γεννήσαντα ἀγαπᾷ τὸν γεγεννημένον ἐξ αὐτοῦ *everyone who loves the father* (=God) *loves the child* (=Christ or one's fellow Christian) **1J 5:1** (on γεννᾶσθαι ἐκ θεοῦ s. Hdb. on J 3:3 and 1J 3:9 and the sources and lit. listed there; s. also παλιγγενεσία). Cp. σήμερον γεγέννηκά σε (Ps 2:7) 1 Cl 36:4; GEb 18, 37; **Ac 13:33** (held by some to have been the orig. rdg. **Lk 3:22 v.l.;** s. JHillmann, Die Kindheitsgesch. Jesu nach Lucas: Jahrbücher f. Protestantische Theologie 17/2, 1891, 192–261; HUsener, D. Weihnachtsfest[2] 1911, 38ff); **Hb 1:5; 5:5.**

❷ **to give birth to, *bear*** (Aeschyl., Suppl. 48; X., De Rep. Lac. 1, 3; Lucian, Sacrif. 6; Plut., Mor., 3c; Ps.-Callisth. 1, 9, 2 ἐκ θεοῦ γεννήσασα παῖδα=a woman who has borne a child to a god; BGU 132 II, 5; Judg 11:1 B; Is 66:9; 4 Macc 10:2) **Lk 1:13, 57; 23:29; J 16:21** w. τίκτειν; AcPl Ha 8, 28 εἰς δουλείαν γεννῶσα *who bears children for slavery* **Gal 4:24.** Pass. *be born* (ἐκ παρθένου Did., Gen. 96, 13) ἐγεννήθη Μωϋσῆς **Ac 7:20;** cp. **Hb 11:23.** γεγεννημένος ἐν Ταρσῷ **Ac 22:3;** μήπω . . . γεννηθέντων **Ro 9:11;** πρὶν ἡμᾶς γεννηθῆναι *before we were born* 1 Cl 38:3. εἰς τὸν κόσμον *come into the world* **J 16:21; Mt 2:1, 4; 19:12; 26:24** (=1 Cl 46:8); **Mk 14:21** (cp. En 38:2); **Lk 1:35** (1a is also prob.; a v.l. adds ἐκ σοῦ, which can be rendered 'the child to whom you give birth'). ἐκ Μαρίας ἐγεννήθη AcPlCor 1:14; 2:5 (cp. **Mt 1:16**); **J 3:4; 9:2, 19f, 32;** IEph 18:2; ITr 11:2; ἀληθῶς γ. *be in fact born* (in opp. to Docetism) 9:1. γεγεννημένα (v.l. γεγενημένα) εἰς ἅλωσιν **2 Pt 2:12.** εἰς τοῦτο *for this purpose* **J 18:37.** διάλεκτος ἐν ᾗ ἐγεννήθημεν *the language in which we were born* i.e., which we have spoken fr. infancy **Ac 2:8.** ἐγὼ δὲ καὶ γεγέννημαι *but I was actually born* a Roman citizen **22:28.** οὗτος ἐγεννήθη βασιλεύς *born a king* GJs 20:4 codd. γεννῶνται και γεννῶσιν **Lk 20:34 v.l.**

❸ **to cause someth. to happen, *bring forth, produce, cause,*** fig. of various kinds of production (Pla. et al.; Polyb. 1, 67, 2 στάσις ἐγεννᾶτο; Philo, De Jos. 254; Jos., Ant. 6, 144) **2 Ti 2:23.**—γ. καρπόν *produce fruit* (Philo, Op. M. 113) ITr 11:1. Forged writing γεγεννημένον for γεγενημένον GJs 24:3.—B. 280. DELG s.v. γίγνομαι p. 222. M-M. TW.

γέννημα, ατος, τό product of the activity expressed by γεννάω **that which is produced or born** (of living creatures; s. B-D-F §11, 2; 24, 3), ***child, offspring*** (Soph., OT 1167; Pla., Tim. 24d; 69c; Sir 10:18 γεννήματα γυναικῶν; TestIss 3:6 πρῶτον γ. v.l. [for πρωτογένημα]; Philo, Just., Ath.; Orig., C. Cels 1, 35, 14) γεννήματα ἐχιδνῶν *brood of vipers* (cp. the Syntipas collection of Aesop's Fables 57 p. 549 P. ὄφεως γεννήματα=brood of snakes; of snakes also schol. on Nicander, Ther. 8) **Mt 3:7; 12:34; 23:33; Lk 3:7;** cp. AcPlCor 2:38 (τεκνήματα pap; sensu malo Dio Chrys. 41 [58], 5 ὦ κακὸν γ.). γεννήματα ληνοῦ καὶ ἅλωνος, βοῶν τε καὶ προβάτων D 13:3 is justifiable because the last two nouns refer to animals. The variant γέννημα, which is found everywhere for γένημα (q.v.), does not merit serious consideration.—DELG s.v. γιγνομαι p. 222. TW. Sv.

Γεννησαρέτ indecl., **ἡ** (more correctly Γεννησάρ as 1 Macc 11:67; Joseph., Talmud; so also the foll. witnesses in Mt and Mk: D, It., Syr. Sin. and Cur., Pesh.; s. RHarris, ET 40, 1929, 189f) ***Gennesaret,*** prob. name of the fertile and (in I AD) thickly populated plain south of Capernaum, now El-Ghuweir (Jos., Bell. 3, 516ff) **Mt 14:34; Mk 6:53.** This was also the name of the large lake adjacent to the plain, λίμνη Γ. (Jos., Bell. 3, 506 λίμνη Γεννησάρ; 1 Macc 11:67 τὸ ὕδωρ τοῦ Γεννησάρ; Stephan. Byz. s.v. Τιβεριάς: this is a city πρὸς τῇ Γεννεσιρίτιδι λίμνῃ) **Lk 5:1,** less precisely termed θάλασσα τῆς Γαλιλαίας (Mt 4:18; Mk 1:16), and θάλ. τῆς Τιβεριάδος (J 21:1).—Dalman, Orte[3] 118 (Eng. tr. 121–22); Westm. Hist. Atlas 17 etc.; CKopp, Holy Places of the Gospels, '63, 167–203; BHHW I 546f.

γέννησις, εως, ἡ (s. γένεσις; Eur., Pla.; SIG 1109, 130; PLond V, 1731, 10 [VI AD]; PGM 13, 981; Eccl 7:1 v.l. ἡμέρα γεννήσεως; TestSol C 10:4; Just., D. 100, 3; ἐκ παρθένου γ. τοῦ θεοῦ Orig., C. Cels. 6, 73, 2) ***birth*** **Mt 1:18 v.l.; Lk 1:14 v.l.; 1J 5:18 v.l.;** IMg 11. Variant in book title of GJs, s. deStrycker 211.—M-M. DELG s.v. γίγνομαι p. 222.

γεννητός, ή, όν (oft. in Pla.; Diod. S. 1, 6, 3; Dionys. Hal. 5, 29; Lucian, Icarom. 2; Just.) **pert. to having been born, *born*** γεννητὸς γυναικός *person that is born of woman*=human being (Job 11:2, 12; 14:1; 15:14; 25:4; cp. 1QH 18, 13) 1 Cl 30:5 (Job 11:2f). Pl. **Mt 11:11; Lk 7:28.** Of Christ γ. καὶ ἀγέννητος *begotten and unbegotten* IEph 7:2. (Just., D. 66, 1 ἐκ παρθένου γ.)—DELG s.v. γίγνομαι p. 222. TW. Sv.

γένος, ους, τό (Hom.+; loanw. in rabb.) a noun expressive of relationship of various degrees and kinds.

❶ **ancestral stock, *descendant*** ἐκ γένους ἀρχιερατικοῦ *of high-priestly descent* (s. Jos., Ant. 15, 40) **Ac 4:6** (PTebt 291, 36 ἀπέδειξας σεαυτὸν γένους ὄντα ἱερατικοῦ, cp. 293, 14; 18; BGU 82, 7 al. pap). υἱοὶ γένους Ἀβραάμ **13:26** (s. Demetr.: 722 fgm. 2, 1 Jac.; Jos., Ant. 5, 113; Just., D. 23, 3 ἀπὸ γένους τοῦ Ἀ.); γ. Δαυίδ **Rv 22:16;** IEph 20:2; ITr 9:1; ISm 1:1. τοῦ γὰρ καὶ γένος ἐσμέν *we, too, are descended from him* **Ac 17:28** (quoted fr. Arat., Phaenom. 5; perh. as early as Epimenides [RHarris, Exp. 8th ser. IV, 1912, 348–53; CBruston, RTQR 21, 1913, 533–35; DFrøvig, SymbOsl 15/16, '36, 44ff; MZerwick, VD 20, '40, 307–21; EPlaces, Ac 17:28: Biblica 43, '62, 388–95]. Cp. also IG XIV, 641; 638 in Norden, Agn. Th. 194 n.; Cleanthes, Hymn to Zeus 4 [Stoic. I 537] ἐκ σοῦ γὰρ γένος . . .; Dio Chrys. 80 [30], 26 ἀπὸ τ. θεῶν τὸ τῶν ἀνθρώπων γένος; Ep. 44 of Apollonius of Tyana [Philostrat. I 354, 22] γένος ὄντες θεοῦ; Hierocles 25, 474, vs. 63 of the Carmen Aur.: θεῖον γένος ἐστὶ βροτοῖσιν), cp. **Ac 17:29.**—Also of an individual *descendant, scion* (Hom.; Soph., Ant. 1117 Bacchus is Διὸς γ.). Jesus is τὸ γένος Δαυίδ **Rv 22:16** (cp. Epimenides [VI BC]: 457 fgm. 3 Jac., the saying of Musaeus: ἐγὼ γένος εἰμὶ Σελήνης; Quint. Smyrn. 1, 191 σεῖο θεοῦ γένος ἐστί).

❷ **a relatively small group with common ancestry, *family, relatives*** (Appian, Bell. Civ. 5, 54 §228; Reg. 1a§1; BGU 1185, 18; Jos., Ant. 17, 22; 18, 127; Ath. 32, 3) τὸ γ. Ἰωσήφ **Ac 7:13.**

❸ **a relatively large people group, *nation, people*** (Appian, Bell. Civ. 2, 71 §294 Ἑβραίων γένος; 2, 90 §380 Ἰουδαίων γ., the latter also Diod. S. 34+35 fgm. 1, 1; 40, 3, 8; Maximus Tyr. 23, 7b; Ael. Aristid. 45 p. 108 D.: τῶν Ἑλλήνων γ.; Achilles Tat. 1, 3, 1; 3, 19, 1; Synes., Ep. 121 p. 258b τὸ Ἐβραίων γ.; TestLevi 5:6 and PsSol 7:8 τὸ γένος Ἰσραήλ; Jos., Bell. 7, 43, Ant. 10, 183 τὸ Ἑβραίων γ.; Just., D. 49, 3 ἐν τῷ γ. ὑμῶν; Demetr.: 722 fgm. 3 τὸ Ἰουδαίων γ.) **Ac 7:19; Gal 1:14; Phil 3:5;** B 14:7 (Is 42:6). Of Christians: γένος ἐκλεκτόν *a chosen nation* **1 Pt 2:9** (Is 43:20; TestJob 1:5; cp. Esth 8:12t; s. JFenton, CBQ 9, '47, 141f); καινὸν γ. Dg 1; τρίτῳ γένει *as a third people* (beside gentiles and Jews) PtK 2 p. 15, 8 (s. Harnack, Mission[4] I 1924, 259–89); γ. τῶν δικαίων MPol 14:1; 17:1; Hs 9, 17, 5; cp. 9, 19, 1 ἄνομον; 9, 30, 3 ἄκακον. θεοφιλὲς καὶ θεοσεβὲς γ. τῶν Χριστιανῶν *godly and pious race of the Christians* MPol 3:2 (Plut., Mor. 567f: the Greeks acc. to the divine verdict are τὸ βέλτιστον κ. θεοφιλέστατον γένος; Mel., HE 4, 26, 5 τὸ τῶν θεοσεβῶν γ.). ἄνομον Hs 9, 19, 1. τῷ γένει w. name of a people to denote nationality (Menand., Peric. 9 Kö. [129 S.]; Plut., Dem. 859 [28, 3]; Jos., Ant. 20, 81; BGU 887, 3 and 15; 937, 9 δοῦλος γένει Ποντικός; cp. 2 Macc 5:22; 3 Macc 1:3; B-D-F §197) **Mk 7:26; Ac 4:36; 18:2, 24.** Pregnant constr. κίνδυνοι ἐκ γένους *perils from the people*=my compatriots, fellow-Israelites **2 Cor 11:26.**

❹ **entities united by common traits, *class, kind*** (Ps.-Xenophon, Cyneg. 3, 1 τὰ γένη τῶν κυνῶν; Apollon. Rhod. 4, 1517 and Just., D. 60, 2 snakes; PTebt 703, 133 [III BC] καθ' ἕκαστον γένος; PGiss 40, 9 παντὸς γένους πολιτευμάτων and oft. pap; Wsd 19:21; Philo; Just., A II, 7, 5 ἀγγέλων ... ἀνθρώπων; D. 23:5 τὸ θῆλυ γ.) of plants (BGU 1119, 27 [I BC] ταὐτὰ γένη 'the same species of plants'; 1120, 34; 1122, 23) Hs 8, 2, 7; of fish (Heniochus Com. 3; Jos., Bell. 3, 508) **Mt 13:47;** of draught animals Hs 9, 1, 8; of cattle in gener. 9, 24, 1; of hostile spirits **Mt 17:21; Mk 9:29** (Herm. Wr. 13, 2 τοῦτο τὸ γένος οὐ διδάσκεται). γένη γλωσσῶν (s. γλῶσσα 3) **1 Cor 12:10, 28;** γ. φωνῶν **14:10;** all humanity B 14:7 (Is 42:6; cp. Ar. 2, 1 τὸ ἀνθρώπινον γ.; Just., A I, 43, 3 al. τὸ ἀνθρώπειον γ.; 46, 2 al. πᾶν γ' ἀνθρώπων).—B. 85; 1317. DELG s.v. γίγνομαι p. 222. M-M.

γεραίρω (s. next; Hom. et al.; 3 Macc 5:17) **to offer material exhibition of esteem, *honor*** τινά τινι *someone w. someth.* Dg 3:5 (Aelian, NA 7, 44 τῇ θυσίᾳ γεραίρων τὸ θεῖον; cp. Ps.-Phoc. 222; SibOr 5, 407).—DELG s.v. γέρας.

γέρας, ως, τό (s. prec.; Hom. et al.; ins, pap, LXX; Just., D. 3, 4; Mel, HE 4, 26, 6) **material exhibition of esteem, *prize, reward*** in our lit. given by God (Philo, Spec. Leg. 2, 183; Jos., Ant. 1, 14) 1 Cl 6:2. λαμβάνειν (SIG 624, 45 [τὰ γέρ]η; 1037:1, 4, 5, 7) ApcPt fgm. 2 p. 12, 24.—DELG.

Γερασηνός, ή, όν *from Gerasa,* a city in Perea, east of the Jordan, about 53 km. SE of Lake Genessaret; ὁ Γ. *the Gerasene* (s. Joseph. index Niese; Schürer II 149–55; Dalman, Pj 1907–12; HGuthe, Gerasa [D. Land der Bibel III 1, 2] 1919; JStarr, A New Jewish Source for Gerasa: JBL 53, '34, 167–69; CKraeling, Gerasa '38.—The word is found Stephan. Byz. s.v. Βάργασα and Γέρασα; IGR IV, 374, 11). Readings antedating Origen **Mt 8:28 v.l.; Mk 5:1** (HSahlin, Studia Theolog. 18, '64, 159–72: Gentile emphasis in the pericope); **Lk 8:26, 37** (s. the foll. entry and Γαδαρηνός).—EDNT. PECS 348–49. M-M.

Γεργεσηνός, ή, όν *from Gergesa,* a town on the eastern shore of Lake Genessaret; ὁ Γ. *the Gergesene.* Origen (Comm. on J. 6, 41) suggests this rdg. in place of Γερασηνός, Γαδαρηνός, q.v., though in the form Γεργεσαῖος, for **Mt 8:28; Mk 5:1; Lk 8:26, 37.** He does not say whether his suggestion is supported by mss., but it is now a v.l. in all the above pass.; s. Γαδαρηνός.—Dalman, Orte[3] 190–93 (Eng. tr. 177–79); RClapp, JBL 26, 1907, 62–83; FBurkitt, 27, 1908, 128–33.

Γερμανικός, οῦ, ὁ ***Germanicus*** name of a martyr in Smyrna MPol 3:1.

γερουσία, ας, ἡ (s. next; Eur., X.+; s. OGI index VIII; Thieme 16; SEG XXXIX, 1318, 2; XL, 1121, 5 [both II AD]; APF 3, 1906, 138 no. 21, 5; PRyl 599, 12; LXX; Philo, In Flacc. 76; 80, Leg. ad Gai. 229; Joseph. Of various boards or councils [e.g. the Roman Senate: Diod. S. 14, 113, 7 and 8], some having a sacred character [SIG 1112, 1f ἔδοξεν τῇ ἱερᾷ γερουσίᾳ τοῦ Σωτῆρος Ἀσκληπιοῦ; the ἱερὰ γερουσία of Eleusis IG III, 702, 2; 10]) ***council of elders,*** esp. the Sanhedrin in Jerusalem (Jdth 4:8; 1 Macc 12:6; 2 Macc 1:10 al.; Jos., Ant. 13, 166) **Ac 5:21** (on the juxtaposition of συνέδριον and γερουσία cp. IGR IV, 836, 8 τῷ σεμνοτάτῳ συνεδρίῳ γερουσίας). GJs 4:3; 6:2.—Schürer II 199–209. DELG s.v. γέρων. M-M. TW.

γέρων, οντος, ὁ (Hom. et al.; ins, pap, LXX, TestSol; TestReub 4:7; ParJer 5:27; AscIs 2:9; ApcEsdr; ViJer 5 [p. 71, 13 Sch.]; Jos., Bell. 6, 271) ***elderly/old man*** (Diog. L. 8, 10: acc. to Pythagoras a γ. is between 60 and 80 yrs. old; age played an important role in selection of pers. for special social and political functions) **J 3:4.**—B. 959. DELG. M-M. TW.

γεύομαι fut. γεύσομαι, 1 aor. ἐγευσάμην (Hom. et al.; pap, LXX; TestReub 1:10 [v.l. ἔφαγον]; TestZeb 4:2; TestJos 6:3; JosAs 10:20; ApcEsdr 7:1 p. 32, 8 Tdf.; ApcMos, Philo, Joseph.) to have perception of someth. either by mouth or by experience, esp. in ref. to relatively small quantity.

➊ **to partake of someth. by mouth, *taste, partake of*** w. acc. (rarely in Gk. lit. with this verb [for acc. w. verbs of consumption, but not γεύομαι, s. Kühner-G. I 356, 2]: Anth. Pal. 6, 120 ἔρσης ἰκμάδα γευόμενος 'tasting the juicy dew'; also Sb 1106 οἱ συμπόσιον γευόμενοι; 1 Km 14:43; Job 12:11; 34:3; Tob 7:12 BA) *water* **J 2:9.** μηδὲν εἰ μὴ ἄρτον καὶ ὕδωρ Hs 5, 3, 7. W. gen. of thing (Crates, Ep. 14 ἰχθύος κ. οἴνου; Dio Chrys. 2, 47; POxy 658, 12; 1576, 4 τοῦ οἴνου; 1 Km 14:24; 2 Km 3:35 al.): *a meal*=take part in it **Lk 14:24.** μηδενός (Jos., Ant. 7, 42) **Ac 23:14;** poisonous plants ITr 11:1. The obj. of the verb is indicated by the context **Mt 27:34; Ac 20:11.** μὴ ἅψῃ μηδὲ γεύσῃ μηδὲ θίγῃς **Col 2:21** (s. ἅπτω 3).—Abs. with apparent ref. to the initial phase of dining γεύομαι=*eat* (ins Sb 1944; Tob 2:4 BA 'left his meal untouched'; Jos., Ant. 6, 119 'taste' in contrast to 'eat' [ἐσθίω]; 338 the witch of Endor urges Saul to 'take some food' [in contrast to his fasting]; cp. Appian, Bell. Civ. 2, 98 §407 'dine') **Ac 10:10.**

➋ **to experience someth. cognitively or emotionally, *come to know someth.*** fig. ext. of 1 (Hom. et al.; Pr 31:18; Pfuhl-Möbius II, 1310, 8 'taste of words', or lit.). W. gen. of thing (Pind., N. 6, 24 πόνων; Hdt. 6, 5 ἐλευθερίης; Lycophron vs. 1431 φυγῆς [of Xerxes]; Dio Chrys. 15 [32], 72 πολέμου; Ael. Aristid. 28, 60 K.=49 p. 510 D.: ἀλαζονείας; Maximus Tyr. 33, 4c ἡδονῶν): θανάτου (analogous to rabb. טְעַם מִיתָה [Billerb. I 751f; 4 Esdr 6:26]; Leonidas in Anth. Pal. 7, 662 ἀδελφὸν ἀστόργου γευσάμενον θανάτου; cp. γ. ζωῆς IGUR III, 1216, 1; s. HRüger, ZNW 59, '68, 113f) **Mt 16:28; Mk 9:1; Lk 9:27; J 8:52; Hb 2:9;** Ox 654, 5 (where θανάτου is supplied)=ASyn. 247, 20; *partake of* knowledge 1 Cl 36:2 (cp. Herm. Wr. 10, 8 γ. ἀθανασίας; Philo, Virt. 188 σοφίας al.; Jos., Bell. 2, 158); *obtain* a gift **Hb 6:4.** W. acc. of thing (B-D-F §169): a word of God vs. **5.** W. ὅτι foll.: γεύσασθαι ὅτι χρηστὸς ὁ κύριος *experience the Lord's kindness* **1 Pt 2:3** (Ps 33:9); RPerdelwitz, D. Mysterienrel. u. d. Problem des 1 Pt 1911, 65ff.—B. 1030. DELG. M-M. New Docs 4, 41. TW.

γεῦσις, εως, ἡ (s. prec.; Democr. 11d; Aristot. et al.; Paradoxogr. Flor. 20; LXX; TestReub 2:5, 7; JosAs 4:4 cod. A; Philo; Mel., P. 49) **a small amount that is tasted, *taste*** δοὺς ἀπαρχὰς ἡμῖν γεύσεως *gave us a foretaste* B 1:7. μέλι ἄγριον, οὗ ἡ γεῦσις ἦν τοῦ μάννα *wild honey which tasted like manna* GEb 13, 79.

γεωργέω 1 aor. 2 sg. ἐγεώργησας (Mel., P. 93, 707) (s. two next entries; Hyperid. 5, 26, X., Pla.+) ***cultivate*** βοτάνας ἅστινας οὐ γεωργεῖ Ἰ. Χρ. *plants that Jesus Christ does not cultivate* IPhld 3:1. Pass. (Jos., Bell. 7, 145 γῆ) δι' οὓς γεωργεῖται (ἡ γῆ) *on whose account the land is tilled* **Hb 6:7.**—M-M.

γεώργιον, ου, τό (s. next; Philo Mech. 96, 49; Strabo 14, 5, 6; Dionys. Hal.; Theagenes in schol. on Pind., N. 3, 21; SIG 311, 9 [323 BC]; pap since III BC, incl. e.g. UPZ 110, 48 [164 BC]; PTebt 72, 370 [114/113 BC]; and s. Preis.; Gen 26:14; Pr 6:7 al.; Philo, Plant. 2) **an area of land used for cultivation** (opp. pasture land), ***cultivated land, field*** fig. of a Christian congregation as God's field **1 Cor 3:9.**—AFridrichsen, Ackerbau u. Hausbau: StKr Sonderheft 1922, 185f; 102; 1930, 297ff, Serta Rudbergiana '31, 25f; Straub 72f.— M-M.

γεωργός, οῦ, ὁ gener. one who is occupied in agriculture or gardening

❶ **one who owns a farm,** ***farmer*** (Hdt., Aristoph.+) **2 Ti 2:6** (on association of γ. w. the teacher s. AHenrichs, ZPE 1, '67, 50–53); **Js 5:7.**

❷ **one who does agricultural work on a contractual basis,** ***vine-dresser, tenant farmer*** (Pla., Theaet. p. 178d; Aelian, NA 7, 28; Gen 9:20) **Mt 21:33ff, 38, 40f; Mk 12:1f, 7, 9; Lk 20:9f, 14, 16** (ELohmeyer, ZST 18, '41, 243–59: wicked tenants; BIersel, 'D. Sohn' in den synoptischen Jesusworten[2] '64, 124–45); **J 15:1** (God as γ. Herm. Wr. 9, 6; 14, 10; PGM 1:26 ἧκέ μοι ἀγαθὲ γεωργέ, Ἀγαθὸς Δαίμων). Goodsp., Probs. 111f 'cultivator'.—B. 487. S. DELG s.v. γῆ and ἔργον. M-M.

γῆ, γῆς, ἡ (Hom.+)—❶ **surface of the earth as the habitation of humanity,** ***earth*** (as heavenly body: Tat. 27, 2 τῷ λέγοντι . . . τὴν σελήνην γῆν 'one who says . . . the moon is an earth')

ⓐ in contrast to heaven (Heracl. Sto. 34, p. 50, 4 ἀπὸ γῆς εἰς οὐρ.; Ael. Aristid. 24, 44 K.=44 p. 838 D.: ἐκ θεῶν ἥκειν ἐπὶ γῆν; Maximus Tyr. 16, 6d ἐκ γῆς ἐπ' οὐρανόν; Ar. 3, 1 τοῦ οὐρανοῦ καὶ τῆς γῆς) **Mt 5:18, 35; 6:10, 19; 16:19; Lk 2:14; 21:25; Col 1:16; Hb 1:10** (Ps 101:26); **11:13; 2 Pt 3:5, 7, 10;** AcPl Ha 1, 7; AcPlCor 2:9, 19. τὰ ἐπὶ τῆς γῆς *earthly things* (TestJob 48:1 τὰ τῆς γῆς φρονεῖν; Ocellus Luc. 36 γῆ κ. πάντα τὰ ἐπὶ γῆς; Ps.-Aristot., De Mundo 6, 5; Lucian, Vit. Auct. 18) **Col 3:2, 5** (Maximus Tyr. 25, 6b: in contrast to the ἄνω the γῆ is the seat of all earthly weakness and inferiority). αἷμα δίκαιον ἐξ[έχεας ἐπὶ] τῆς γῆς *on earth* AcPl Ha 11, 8; s. also b below. Established on the waters Hv 1, 3, 4. Vanishing w. heaven at the end of time 2 Cl 16:3 and replaced by a new earth **2 Pt 3:13; Rv 21:1** (Is 65:17; 66:22).

ⓑ as the inhabited planet (Ar. 12, 1 τῶν ἐθνῶν τῶν ἐπὶ τῆς γῆς; Just., A I, 54, 9 τὴν πᾶσαν γῆν; Appian, Mithrid. 57 §234 γῆς ἄρξειν ἁπάσης) **Lk 21:35; Ac 10:12; 11:6; 17:26** et al. ἕως ἐσχάτου τῆς γῆς *to the remotest parts of the earth* **1:8** (PsSol 1:4) difft. OSchwartz, JBL 105, '86, 669–76 (limited to Palestine). Hence

❷ **the inhabitants of the earth,** ***people, humanity,*** associative sense **Mt 5:13; 10:34; Lk 12:49, 51;** cp. **Rv 13:3.** ἐπὶ τῆς γῆς *on earth*=among people **Lk 18:8; J 17:4; Ro 9:28; Eph 6:3** (Ex 20:12; Dt 5:16; En 102:5; PsSol 17:2); **Js 5:5;** Hs 5, 6, 6; s. also 1b. ἀπὸ τῆς γῆς *from the earth*=from the midst of humanity **Ac 8:33** (Is 53:8; cp. PsSol 2:17; 4:22; 17:7); 22:22; **Rv 14:3.**

❸ **portions or regions of the earth,** ***region, country*** **Ac 7:3f** (Gen 12:1); vs. **6** (Gen 15:13). In a territorial sense (X., An. 1, 3, 4) Israel **Mt 2:20f;** Gennesaret **14:34;** Midian **Ac 7:29;** Judah **Mt 2:6** (where ENestle in his critical apparatus [s. e.g. N[25]] listed the conjecture of JDrusius van den Driessche [†1616], γῆς, accepted by PSchmiedel, as indicated in Zürcher Bibel '31, appendix to NT, p. 5); Zebulon and Naphtali **4:15** (Is 9:1); Judea **J 3:22;** AcPl Ha 8, 14; Canaan **Ac 13:19;** AcPl Ha 8, 14; Egypt **Ac 7:36, 40; 13:17; Hb 8:9** (Jer 38:32); of the Chaldaeans **Ac 7:4;** *native land* vs. **3.** The inhabitants included **Mt 10:15; 11:24.** ἡ γῆ abs.=Palestine **Mt 27:45; Mk 15:33; Lk 4:25.** On κληρονομεῖν τ. γῆν **Mt 5:5;** D 3:7 s. κληρονομέω 2.

❹ **dry land as opposed to sea,** ***land*** (X., An. 1, 1, 7; Dio Chrys. 63 [80], 12; Sb 5103, 6 ἐν γῇ κ' ἐν θαλάσσῃ; BGU 27, 5; PsSol 2:26, 29; Jos., Ant. 4, 125; 11, 53) **Mk 4:1; 6:47; Lk 5:3, 11; J 6:21; 21:8f, 11; Ac 27:39, 43f.**

❺ **earth-like surface that forms the bottom of a body of water,** ***ground, bottom*** of the sea B 10:5.

❻ **earth w. ref. to limited areas and the material that forms its surface**

ⓐ of earth-surface: ***ground*** **Mt 10:29** (πίπτειν ἐπὶ τ. γῆν as Jos., Ant. 7, 381); **15:35; 25:18, 25** (Artem. 2, 59 οὐ γὰρ ἄνευ τοῦ τὴν γῆν ἀνασκαφῆναι θησαυρὸς εὑρίσκεται); **Mk 8:6; 9:20; 14:35; Lk 22:44; 24:5; J 8:6, 8** (writing on it as Ael. Aristid. 50, 21 K.=26 p. 508 D.); **Ac 9:4, 8;** GPt 6:21a. οἰκοδομεῖν οἰκίαν ἐπὶ τὴν γῆν χωρὶς θεμελίου *build a house on the ground without any foundation* **Lk 6:49.** The earth opens in the service of a divinity in order to swallow something (Quint. Smyrn. 13, 548f, a person; cp. En 99:2 ἐν τῇ γῇ καταποθήσονται; ParJer 3:19) **Rv 12:16.**

ⓑ of ground for agricultural use ***soil, earth,*** receiving seed (Just., A I, 55, 3 γῆ . . . ἀροῦται) **Mt 13:5, 8, 23; Mk 4:5, 8, 20, 26, 28, 31; J 12:24;** AcPlCor 2:26; watered by rain **Hb 6:7;** yielding fruit (Jos., Ant. 18, 22) **Js 5:7:** 1 Cl 20:4. καταργεῖν τ. γῆν *waste, use up the ground* **Lk 13:7.**—Dalman, Arbeit II.—B. 17. Schmidt, Syn. III 55–69. DELG. TW. Sv.

γηγενής, ές (Soph., Hdt. et al.; Diod. S. 1, 86, 3; Herm. Wr. 1, 27; Proclus, Hymn. 1, 15; 3, 5; LXX; TestSol 5:3; TestJos 2:5) ***earth-born*** (par. θνητός; cp. Philo, Spec. Leg. 2, 124) 1 Cl 39:2.—DELG s.v. γῆ p. 218. TW.

γῆρας (Hom.+), **ως** (Jos., Bell. 5, 461; Ant. 6, 32; Ath. R. 69, 11) or **ους** (TestJud 15, 4), **τό,** dat. γήρᾳ or γήρει (1 Ch 29:28; Ps 91:15; Da 6:1 al.; s. Helbing 42) as in Ionic (W-S. §9, 2; B-D-F §47, 1; Mlt-H. 140) **advancement in years or age w. ref. to passage of a relatively long period of time** (in our lit. of pers.), ***old age*** ἐν γήρει **Lk 1:36** (TestAbr A 8 p. 85, 19 [Stone p. 18]); but ἐν γήρᾳ (as **Lk 1:36 v.l.;** Sir 3:12; 25:3) 1 Cl 10:7. ἕως γήρους (Ps 70:18) *to old age* 63:3 (s. Reinhold 51).—DELG. M-M.

γηράσκω (s. prec.; Hom. et al.; PSI 685, 13; POxy 904, 2; LXX; TestZeb 6:5; ApcSed 16:2 p. 137, 4 Ja.; Philo, Aet. M. 61; Jos., Ant. 19, 170 al.; Ar. 7, 1; Tat. 21, 2) 1 aor. ἐγήρασα; pf. γεγήρακα (Diod. S. 16, 20, 3; 18, 24, 2; Ath., R. 69, 2) ***grow old*** **J 21:18;** 1 Cl 23:3. παλαιούμενον καὶ γηράσκον *becoming obsolete and growing old* **Hb 8:13.** κάλλος γηρᾷ AcPl Ha 2, 25.—M-M.

γίνομαι (in the form γίγνομαι [s. below] Hom.+; as γίν. since Aristot.+; and s. Kühner-Bl. II p. 391; Schwyzer I 215; KBrugmann[4]-AThumb, Griech. Gramm. 1913, 126; Mayser p. 165 and lit. there). Impf. ἐγινόμην; fut. γενήσομαι; 2 aor. ἐγενόμην, 3 sg. opt. γένοιτο; very rare v.l. (B-D-F §81, 3) γενάμενος (GJs 6:1; 16;1; 25:1 [s. deStrycker 249]; also found in Ps.-Callisth. 1, 20, 1; 1, 41, 11; ApcEsdr 1:3 p. 24, 7 Tdf.; Mel., P. 49, 346 [Bodm.]). Pass.: fut. ptc. τῶν γενηθησομένων (Eccl 1:11 v.l.); 1 aor. ἐγενήθην (Doric, H. Gk.; Phryn. 108 Lob.; pap fr. III BC, Mayser I/2[2] '38, 157f [w. lit.]; ins [Schweizer 181; Nachmanson 168; Thieme 13]; LXX), impv. γενηθήτω; pf. γεγένημαι (Meisterhans[3]-Schw.: Att. ins since 376 BC; Mayser 391) uncontested use in NT only **J 2:9;** GJs 24:3 (γεγένν- pap); apolog. On pf. γέγονα s. Meisterhans[3]-Schw.: since 464 BC; Mayser 372; on the aoristic use of γέγονα s. Mlt. 145f; 238; 239; PChantraine, Histoire du parfait grec 1927, 233–45; 3 pl. γέγοναν **Ro 16:7** (v.l. γεγόνασιν) and **Rv 21:6;** s. KBuresch, Γέγοναν: RhM 46, 1891, 193ff; Mlt. 52 n.; ptc. γεγονώς; plpf. 3 sg. ἐγεγόνει (1 Macc. 4:27; 2 Macc. 13:17; **J 6:17;** Just.), without augment γεγόνει (**Ac 4:22;** v.l. ἐγεγόνει), s. B-D-F §78; Mlt-H. 190. On the variation γίνομαι and γίγνομαι s. W-S. §5, 31; B-D-F §34, 4; Mlt-H. 108. A verb with numerous nuances relating to being and manner of being. Its contrast to the more static term εἰμί can be seen in Kaibel 595, 5 οὐκ ἤμην καὶ ἐγενόμην=I was not and then I came to be (cp. Ath. 4, 2 in 3 below).

❶ **to come into being through process of birth or natural production, *be born, be produced*** (SIG 1168, 6; Epict. 2, 17, 8; Wsd 7:3; Sir 44:9; Just., A I, 13, 3; Tat. 26, 2) **J 8:58;** w. ἔκ τινος foll. (Diod. S. 3, 64, 1; Appian, Basil. 5 §1; Parthenius 1, 4; Athen. 13, 37 p. 576c ἐξ ἑταίρας; PPetr III, 2, 20; PFlor 382, 38 ὁ ἐξ ἐμοῦ γενόμενος υἱός; 1 Esdr 4:16; Tob 8:6; Jos., Ant. 2, 216) **Ro 1:3; Gal 4:4** (cp. 1QS 11:21). Also of plants **1 Cor 15:37.** Of fruits ἔκ τινος *be produced by a tree* **Mt 21:19** (cp. X., Mem. 3, 6, 13 ὁ ἐκ τ. χώρας γιγνόμενος σῖτος). W. ἀπό τινος foll. Ox 1081 (SJCh), 11 γε[ινόμε]νον, 14 γέγ[ονος], 14f γε[ι]νομεν[ον], 19 γέγονος.

❷ **to come into existence, *be made, be created, be manufactured, be performed*—ⓐ** gener. ὃ γέγονεν **J 1:3c** (s. ref. to Vawter, below); w. διά τινος vs. **3a** (MTeschendorf, D. Schöpfungsged. im NT: StKr 104, '32, 337–72). W. χωρίς τινος vs. **3b** (IAndrosIsis, Cyrene 15 [103 AD] Ἐμοῦ δὲ χωρὶς γείνετ' οὐδὲν πώποτε; Cleanthes, Hymn to Zeus 15 [Stoic. I 537=Coll. Alex. no. 1 p. 227] οὐδέ τι γίγνεται ἔργον σοῦ δίχα; note the related style 1QH 1:20; on the syntax of J 1:3f see BVawter, CBQ 25, '63, 401–6, who favors a full stop after οὐδὲ ἕν, s. εἷς 2b and lit. cited there on J 1:3). W. ἔκ τινος **Hb 11:3.** Of cult images διὰ χειρῶν γινόμενοι *made w. hands* **Ac 19:26** (cp. PRyl 231, 3 [40 AD] τοὺς ἄρτους γενέσθαι). Of miracles: *be done, take place* (Tob 11:15; Wsd 19:13 v.l. Swete) **Mt 11:20f, 23; Lk 10:13; Ac 8:13.** ἐφ' ὃν γεγόνει τὸ σημεῖον τοῦτο *on whom this miracle had been performed* **4:22.** W. mention of the author διά τινος (cp. 4 Macc 17:11) **2:43; 4:16, 30; 12:9; 24:2.** διὰ τῶν χειρῶν τινος **Mk 6:2; Ac 14:3.** ὑπό τινος (Herodian 8, 4, 2; OGI 168, 46 [115 BC] τὰ γεγονότα ὑπὸ τοῦ πατρὸς φιλάνθρωπα; UPZ III, 3, 7 [116 BC]; PTebt 786, 14 [II BC]; Wsd 9:2; Jos., Ant. 8, 111; 347; Just., D. 35, 8 τῶν ἀπὸ τοῦ ὀνόματος αὐτοῦ [Jesus] καὶ νῦν γινομένων δυνάμεων) **Lk 9:7 v.l.; 13:17; 23:8; Eph 5:12.** Of commands, instructions *be fulfilled, performed* γενηθήτω τὸ θέλημά σου *thy will be done* (Appian, Liby. 90 §423 τὸ πρόσταγμα δεῖ γενέσθαι; Syntipas p. 25, 3 γενέσθω τὸ αἴτημα) **Mt 6:10; 26:42; Lk 11:2;** cp. **22:42.** γέγονεν ὃ ἐπέταξας *your order has been carried out* **14:22.** γενέσθαι τὸ αἴτημα αὐτῶν *that their demand should be granted* **23:24.** Of institutions: *be established,* the Sabbath for the sake of humans **Mk 2:27** (Crates, Ep. 24 οὐ γεγόνασιν οἱ ἄνθρωποι τ. ἵππων χάριν, ἀλλ' οἱ ἵπποι τ. ἀνθρώπων).

ⓑ w. mention of the special nature of an undertaking: ἵνα οὕτως γένηται ἐν ἐμοί *in order to have such action taken in my case* **1 Cor 9:15.** ἐν τῷ ξηρῷ τί γένηται; *what will be done when it* (the wood) *is dry?* **Lk 23:31.**

❸ **come into being as an event or phenomenon from a point of origin, *arise, come about, develop*** (Alcaeus 23 Diehl[2] [320 L-P.] καί κ' οὐδὲν ἐκ δένος γένοιτο=nothing could originate from nothing; Ath. 4:2 τὸ ὂν οὐ γίνεται ἀλλὰ τὸ μὴ ὄν)

ⓐ of events or phenomena in nature (Sir 40:10; Ex 10:22; Job 40:23; Jos., Ant. 9, 36): lightning, thunder (X., An. 3, 1, 11) **J 12:29; Rv 8:5; 11:19;** calm (on the sea) **Mt 8:26; Mk 4:39; Lk 8:24;** storm **Mk 4:37;** a cloud (cp. Jos., Ant. 9, 36) **9:7; Lk 9:34;** Hv 4, 3, 7; flood **Lk 6:48;** earthquake (Parian Marbles [III BC]=FGrH: 239B, 24) **Mt 8:24; 28:2; Ac 16:26; Rv 6:12; 11:13; 16:18;** darkness **Mt 27:45; Mk 15:33; Lk 23:44; J 6:17;** hail, fire **Rv 8:7.** Of a dawning day ὅτε δὲ ἡμέρα ἐγένετο (cp. περὶ ἀρχομένην ἡμέραν 'about dawn' Jos., Vi 15: in a related story of shipwreck) **Ac 27:39.**

ⓑ of other occurrences (Arrian, Anab. 4, 4, 3 τὰ ἱερὰ οὐκ ἐγίγνετο=the sacrifice did not turn out [favorably]; 1 Macc 1:25; 4:58; 9:27; 13:44; Jdth 7:29; 14:19 al.): complaining **Ac 6:1;** persecution, oppression **Mt 13:21; 24:21; Mk 4:17; 13:19; Ac 11:19;** discussion **J 3:25; Ac 15:7;** tumult **Mt 26:5; 27:24;** GJs 21:1 and 25:1; a sound **Ac 2:2, 6;** weeping **20:37;** clamor **23:9; Mt 25:6;** AcPl Ha 4, 6; famine **Lk 4:25; 15:14; Ac 11:28;** ὁρμή (q.v.) **14:5;** war **Rv 12:7;** sharp contention **Ac 15:39;** tear (in a garment) **Mt 9:16; Mk 2:21; Lk 6:49;** silence (s. σιγή) **Ac 21:40; Rv 8:1;** στάσις (q.v. 2) **Lk 23:19; Ac 15:2; 23:7, 10;** concourse **21:30;** confusion **19:23;** shout, loud voice **2:6; 19:34; Rv 11:15;** dispute **Lk 22:24;** envy, strife **1 Ti 6:4;** astonishment AcPl Ha 4, 25; joy 6, 3; prayer 6, 7; offering 6, 37.

ⓒ of the various divisions of a day (Jdth 13:1; 1 Macc 5:30; 4 Macc 3:8 al.) γενομένης ἡμέρας *when day came* (Jos., Ant. 10, 202, Vi. 405) **Lk 4:42; Ac 12:18; 16:35; 23:12;** cp. **Lk 6:13; 22:66; Ac 27:29, 33, 39.** Difft. **Mk 6:21** γενομένης ἡμέρας εὐκαίρου *when a convenient/opportune day arrived.* ὀψέ (cp. Gen 29:25; 1 Km 25:37) **11:19.** ὀψίας γενομένης **Mt 8:16; 14:15, 23; 16:2; 26:20; 27:57; Mk 1:32; 6:47; 14:17; 15:42;** cp. **J 6:16.** πρωΐας **Mt 27:1; J 21:4.** νύξ **Ac 27:27.** ὥρας πολλῆς γενομένης *when it had grown late* **Mk 6:35;** cp. **15:33; Lk 22:14; Ac 26:4.**

❹ **to occur as process or result, *happen, turn out, take place*** (Dicaearch., fgm. 102 W.: a campaign 'takes place'; Diod. S. 32 fgm. 9c τὰς εἰς τ. πατέρα γεγενημένας ἁμαρτίας=the misdeeds 'perpetrated' against his father; 2 Macc 1:32; 13:17; 3 Macc 1:11; 4:12; 5:17 al.)

ⓐ gener. τοῦτο ὅλον γέγονεν *all this took place* w. ἵνα foll. **Mt 1:22; 26:56.** ἕως ἂν πάντα γένηται *until all has taken place* (=is past) **5:18.** πάντα τὰ γενόμενα *everything that had happened* (cp. Appian, Bell. Civ. 2, 121 §508 τὰ γενόμενα; 1 Esdr 1:10; Jdth 15:1; 1 Macc 4:20; 2 Macc 10:21; 3 Macc 1:17) **18:31;** cp. **21:21; 24:6, 20, 34; 26:54; 27:54; 28:11; Mk 5:14.** ἴδωμεν τὸ ῥῆμα τοῦτο τὸ γεγονός *let us see this thing that has taken place* **Lk 2:15** (TestAbr A 15 p. 96, 15 [Stone p. 40]) θανάτου γενομένου *since a death has occurred,* i.e. *since he has died* **Hb 9:15.** τούτου γενομένου *after this had happened* (Jos., Ant. 9, 56; 129) **Ac 28:9.** τὸ γεγονός *what had happened* (Diod. S. 12, 49, 4; Appian, Bell. Civ. 2, 18 §496; Jos., Ant. 14, 292) **Lk 8:34; 24:12.** τὰ γεγονότα AcPl Ha 11, 1.—μὴ γένοιτο strong negation, in Paul only after rhet. questions (cp. TestJob 38:1; JosAs 25:8; Epict., index p. 540e; Lucian, Dial. Deor. 1, 2, Dial. Meretr. 13, 4; Achilles Tat. 5, 18, 4; Aristaen., Ep. 1, 27) *by no means, far from it, God forbid* (Goodsp., Probs., 88; AMalherbe, HTR 73, '80, 231–41) **Lk 20:16; Ro 3:4, 6, 31; 6:2, 15; 7:7, 13; 9:14; 11:1, 11; 1 Cor 6:15; Gal 2:17; 3:21.** In more extensive phrasing (the LXX has exx. only of this usage: Gen 44:17; 3 Km 20:3 al.; cp. Josh 22:29; Demosth. 10, 27; Alciphron 2, 5, 3 al.; Ael. Aristid. 23, 80 K.=42 p. 795 D.; 30 p. 578 D.; 54 p. 679 ὃ μὴ γένοιτο) **Gal 6:14;** w. ἵνα foll. AcPl Ha 7, 40. τί γέγονεν ὅτι (cp. Eccl 7:10) *why is it that* **J 14:22.**—Of festivals: *be held, take place, come* (X., Hell. 7, 4, 28 τὰ Ὀλύμπια; 4, 5, 1; 4 Km 23:22f; 2 Macc 6:7) feast of dedication **J 10:22;** passover **Mt 26:2;** sabbath **Mk 6:2;** wedding **J 2:1.**—Abs. impv. (put twice for emphasis as Lucian, Pisc. 1 βάλλε, βάλλε; Philostrat., Ep. 35, 1 λάβε λάβε; Procop. Soph., Ep. 45) γενηθήτω γενηθήτω *so let it be* as a closing formula **1 Cor 16:24 v.l.** (cp. Herodas 4, 85, where the sacristan closes his prayer to Asclepius with the words: ὧδε ταῦτ' εἴη=so may it be).—On γένοιτο ἀμήν GJs 6:2 s. ἀμήν 1a.

ⓑ w. dat. of pers. affected—**α.** w. inf. foll. (UPZ 24, 29 al.; 1 Macc 13:5; Jos., Ant. 6, 232) ὅπως μὴ γένηται αὐτῷ χρονοτριβῆσαι *so that he would not have to lose time* **Ac 20:16.**

β. w. adv. or adv. phrase added (1 Esdr 6:33) κατὰ τὴν πίστιν ὑμῶν γενηθήτω ὑμῖν *according to your faith let it be done to you,* i.e. *you believe, and you won't be disappointed* **Mt 9:29;** cp. **8:13.** γένοιτό μοι κατὰ τὸ ῥῆμά σου *may that happen to me as you have said* **Lk 1:38.** πῶς ἐγένετο τῷ δαιμονιζομένῳ *what had happened to the possessed man* **Mk 5:16.** ἵνα εὖ σοι γένηται *that it may be well w. you* **Eph 6:3** (Dt 5:16; cp. Epict. 2, 5, 29 εὖ σοι γένοιτο; Aelian, VH 9, 36). γενηθήτω σοι ὡς θέλεις *let it be done for you as you desire,* i.e. *your wish is granted* **Mt 15:28.**

γ. w. nom. of thing (1 Macc 4:25; Sir 51:17; Ar. 15:5) γίνεταί τινί τι *someth. happens to* or *befalls a person* **Mk 9:21.** ἵνα μὴ χεῖρόν σοί τι γένηται *lest someth. worse come upon you* **J 5:14.** τί ἐγένετο αὐτῷ *what has happened to him* **Ac 7:40** (Ex 32:1, 23; AcPl Ha 5, 20). τὸ γεγενημένον αὐτῷ **Ac 3:10** D. ἐγίνετο πάσῃ ψυχῇ φόβος *fear came upon everyone* (cp. Tob 11:18) **2:43.** λύπη AcPl Ha 6, 16. Freq. γέγονε ἐμοί τι *someth. has come to me=I have someth.*: πώρωσις τῷ Ἰσραὴλ γέγονεν *a hardening (of heart) has befallen Israel* **Ro 11:25;** σωτηρία τῷ Ἰσραὴλ γεγένηται GJs 19:2; cp. **Lk 19:9;** διὰ τὴν ὀπτασίαν τὴν γενομένην Παύλῳ AcPl Ha 3, 15; ἐὰν γένηταί τινι ἀνθρώπῳ ἑκατὸν πρόβατα *if a man has a hundred sheep* **Mt 18:12.** τοῖς ἔξω ἐν παραβολαῖς τὰ πάντα γίνεται *those outside receive everything in parables* **Mk 4:11.** μήποτε γένηται ἀνταπόδομά σοι *that you may receive no repayment* **Lk 14:12;** cp. **19:9; J 15:7; 1 Cor 4:5.**

ⓒ w. gen. of pers. (Diod. S. 16, 64, 2 τὸν τῆς Ἑλένης γεγενημένον ὅρμον=the necklace that had belonged to Helen): ἐγένετο ἡ βασιλεία τοῦ κόσμου τοῦ κυρίου ἡμῶν *the kingdom of the world has come into the possession of our Lord* **Rv 11:15.**

ⓓ γίνεταί τι ἐπί τινι *someth. happens in the case of* or *to a person* **Mk 5:33 v.l.;** ἐν v.l. This can also be expressed w. εἴς τινα **Ac 28:6** or the double nom. τί ἄρα ὁ Πέτρος ἐγένετο *what had become of Peter* **12:18** (cp. Jos., Vi. 296 οἱ εἴκοσι χρυσοῖ τί γεγόνασιν).

ⓔ w. inf. foll., to emphasize the actual occurrence of the action denoted by the verb: ἐὰν γένηται εὑρεῖν αὐτό *if it comes about that he finds it=if he actually finds it* **Mt 18:13** (s. PCatt V, 19f [=Mitt-Wilck. II/2, 372 V] ἐὰν γένηταί με ἀποδημεῖν; PAmh 135, 10; BGU 970, 5). ἐγένετο αὐτὸν παραπορεύεσθαι *he happened to be passing* **Mk 2:23;** cp. **Lk 6:1, 6.** ἐγένετο ἀνεῳχθῆναι τὸν οὐρανόν *just then the heaven opened* **Lk 3:21;** cp. **16:22** (ἐν τῷ ἀποθανεῖν P[75]); **Ac 4:5; 9:3, 32, 37, 43; 11:26; 14:1; 16:16; 19:1; 21:1, 5; 22:6, 17; 27:44; 28:8** (UPZ 62, 29 [161 BC] γίνεται γὰρ ἐντραπῆναι).

ⓕ καὶ ἐγένετο (ἐγένετο δέ) periphrastic like וַיְהִי with וְ foll. to indicate the progress of the narrative; it is followed either by a conjunction like ὅτε, ὡς etc., or a gen. abs., or a prepositional constr., and joined to it is a finite verb w. καί (Jdth 5:22; 10:1; Sus 19 Theod.; 1 Macc 1:1; 5:1; Gen 39:7, 13, 19; 42:35; JosAs 11:1; 22:1; AscIs 3:2) **Mt 9:10; Mk 2:15 v.l.; Lk 2:15; 5:1, 12, 17; 8:1, 22; 14:1.**—Without the second καί (Jdth 2:4; 12:10; 13:12; 1 Macc 6:8; 7:2 v.l.; 9:23; Sus 28 Theod.; Bel 18 Theod.; TestAbr B 1 p. 105, 1 [Stone p. 58] and 6 p. 109, 27 [Stone p. 66]; TestJob 31:1; JosAs 1:1; 3:1) **Mt 7:28; 11:1; 13:53; 19:1; 26:1; Mk 1:9; 4:4; Lk 1:8, 23, 41, 59; 2:1, 6, 46; 6:12** al. At times it is followed by an inf. The phrase is usually omitted in translation; older versions transl. *it came to pass.*—Mlt. 16f; MJohannessohn, Das bibl. καὶ ἐγένετο u. s. Geschichte: ZVS 53, 1926, 161–212 (LXX); s. MDibelius, Gnomon 3, 1927, 446–50; HPernot, Études sur la langue des Évangiles 1927, 189–99; KBeyer, Semitische Syntax im NT, '62, 29–62; JReiling, BT 16, '65, 153–63; EDelebecque, Études grecques sur l'Évangile de Luc '76, 123–65.

❺ **to experience a change in nature and so indicate entry into a new condition, *become someth.***—ⓐ w. nouns (Lamellae Aur. Orphicae ed. AOlivieri 1915, p. 16, 5 θεὸς ἐγένου ἐξ ἀνθρώπου [IV/III]; Arrian, Anab. 5, 26, 5; Sir 51:2; 1 Esdr 4:26; Wsd 8:2; 4 Macc 16:6; En 103:11; Tat. 19, 2 τοῦ θανάτου καταφρονηταὶ γίνεσθε): ὅπως γένησθε υἱοὶ τοῦ πατρὸς ὑμῶν *that you may become sons of your father* **Mt 5:45;** ποιήσω ὑμᾶς γενέσθαι ἁλιεῖς ἀνθρώπων *I will turn you into fishers of people* **Mk 1:17;** a traitor **Lk 6:16;** friends **23:12** (cp. Jos., Ant. 11, 121); children of God **J 1:12;** children of light **12:36;** a Christian **Ac 26:29;** apostle AcPlCor 2:4; a father **Ro 4:18;** a fool **1 Cor 3:18;** a spectacle **4:9;** a man, an adult **13:11** (Tob 1:9); a curse **Gal 3:13.** οὐχ ἑαυτὸν ἐδόξασεν γενηθῆναι ἀρχιερέα *he did not exalt himself to be made high priest* **Hb 5:5;** ἐγένετο ἀντὶ αὐτοῦ Σαμουήλ *Samuel became (high priest) in his place* GJs 10:2. W. double nom. (Ps.-Apollod., Epit. 3, 15 δράκων λίθος ἐγένετο; Quint. Smyrn. 12, 507; Bel 28; 4 Macc 18:7) οἱ λίθοι ἄρτοι γίνονται *the stones turn into loaves* **Mt 4:3.** τὸ αἷμα αὐτοῦ λίθον γεγενημένον GJs 24:3. ὁ λόγος σὰρξ ἐγένετο **J 1:14** (the reverse PBerl 13044, col. III, 28ff [UWilcken, SBBerlAk 1923, 161f] τί ποιῶν ἄν τις γένοιτο θεός;). τὸ ὕδωρ γενήσεται πηγή **4:14.** ἡ περιτομὴ ἀκροβυστία γέγονεν **Ro 2:25.** ἐγενόμην ἐγὼ διάκονος *I became a courier* **Col 1:23** (cp. Herodian 2, 6, 8 ἀνὴρ ἔπαρχος γενόμενος).—Also γ. εἴς τι (Menand., Peric. 49f Kö. [169f S.] τὸ κακὸν εἰς ἀγαθὸν ῥέπει γινόμενον; 1 Km 4:9; Jdth 5:18; 1 Macc 2:11, 43; 3:58; En 19:2 al.; B-D-F §145, 1): ἐγένετο εἰς δένδρον *it became a tree* **Lk 13:19;** εἰς κεφαλὴν γωνίας **Mt 21:42; Mk 12:10; Lk 20:17; Ac 4:11; 1 Pt 2:7** (all in ref. to Ps 117:22); εἰς χαρὰν γ. *change* (or, *turn*) *into joy* **J 16:20.** εἰς οὐδέν *come to nothing* **Ac 5:36.** εἰς παγίδα **Ro 11:9** (Ps 68:23); εἰς κενὸν γ. *be done in vain* **1 Th 3:5.** εἰς ἄψινθον **Rv 8:11.** Cp. AcPl Ha 6, 6. Also w. γίνεσθαι omitted: εἰς κατάκριμα (sc. ἐγένετο τὸ κρίμα) **Ro 5:18.**

ⓑ used w. an adj. to paraphrase the passive (Jdth 11:11; 1 Esdr 7:3; 2 Macc 3:34; Sus 64 Theod.; En 103:9; Ath. 37, 1 πάντων ὑποχειρίων γιγνομένων): ἁπαλὸν γ. *become tender* **Mt 24:32; Mk 13:28;** ἀπειθὴ γ. **Ac 26:19;** ἀποσυνάγωγον γ. *be expelled fr. the synagogue* **J 12:42;** ἄφαντον γ. *disappear* **Lk 24:31;** σκωληκόβρωτον γ. *be eaten by worms* **Ac 12:23;** γνωστόν, φανερὸν γ. *become known* (Just., A I, 63, 6) **Mk 6:14; Ac 1:19; 9:42; 19:17; 1 Cor 3:13; 14:25; Phil 1:13;** δόκιμον γ. *pass the test* **Js 1:12;** ἑδραῖον γ. **1 Cor 15:58;** ἔκδηλον γ. **2 Ti 3:9;** AcPlCor 1:16; ἔξυπνον γ. **Ac 16:27** (1 Esdr 3:3=Jos., Ant. 11:34); s. ἀπόπληκτος, ἐλεύθερος, ἐμφανής, ἔμφοβος, ἐνεργής, ἔντρομος, καθαρός, μέγας, περιδάκρυτος, περικρατής, πλήρης, πρηνής, τυφλός, ὑγιής, ὑπήκοος, ὑπόδικος, φανερός 1.

ⓒ w. ἐν of a state of being (Stoic. III 221, 16; Diod. S. 20, 62, 4 ἐν ἀνέσει γ.; Plut., Tit. Flam. 378 [16, 1] ἐν ὀργῇ γ.; Lucian, Tim. 28; PPetr II, 20; III, 12 [252 BC] ἐν ἐπισχέσει γ.; BGU 5 II, 19 ἐν νόσῳ; POxy 471 IV, 77f; 4 Km 9:20; 1 Macc 1:27 v.l.; Sus 8 Theod.; Jos., Bell. 1, 320, Ant. 16, 372; Mel., P. 18 ἐν πόνοις . . . ἐν πληγαῖς etc.) ἐν ἀγωνίᾳ **Lk 22:44.** ἐν ἐκστάσει **Ac 22:17.** ἐν πνεύματι *under the Spirit's influence* **Rv 1:10; 4:2;** AcPl Ha 6, 28. ἐν ὁμοιώματι ἀνθρώπων *be like human beings* **Phil 2:7.** ἐν ἀσθενείᾳ, φόβῳ, τρόμῳ **1 Cor 2:3.** ἐν δόξῃ **2 Cor 3:7.** ἐν ἑαυτῷ γ. *come to one's senses* (Soph., Phil. 950; X., An. 1, 5, 17; Polyb. 1, 49, 8; Chariton 3, 9, 11) **Ac 12:11;** γ. ἐν Χριστῷ *be a Christian* **Ro 16:7.** Cp. 7 below.

❻ **to make a change of location in space, *move***—ⓐ εἴς τι (Hdt. 5, 87 al.; Philo, Op. M. 86; 2 Macc 1:13; also ἐν: Just., A II, 9, 3 ἐγενόμεθα ἐν ἐκείνῳ τῷ τόπῳ): εἰς Ἱεροσόλυμα γ. (Jos., Ant. 10, 42) **Ac 20:16; 21:17; 25:15.** εἰς τὸν ἀγρόν Hv 3, 1, 4. Of a voice: ἐγένετο εἰς τὰ ὦτά μου *reached my ear* **Lk 1:44.** Fig. (cp. Bar 4:28) of Abraham's blessing εἰς τὰ ἔθνη *come to the Gentiles* **Gal 3:14;** cp. **2 Cor 8:14** (s. περίσσευμα 1, ὑστέρημα 1).

ⓑ ἔκ τινος (Job 28:2): γ. ἐκ μέσου *be removed,* Lat. e medio tolli (cp. Ps.-Aeschin., Ep. 12, 6 ἐκ μέσου γενομένων ἐκείνων; Plut., Timol. 238 [5, 3]; Achilles Tat. 2, 27, 2) **2 Th 2:7** (HFulford, ET 23, 1912, 40f: 'leave the scene'). Of a voice fr. heaven: ἐκ τ. οὐρανῶν γ. *sound forth fr. heaven* (2 Macc 2:21; cp. Da 4:31 Theod.) **Mk 1:11; Lk 3:22; 9:35;** cp. vs. **36.**

ⓒ ἐπί τι: ἐπὶ τὸ μνημεῖον *go to the tomb* **Lk 24:22;** ἐπὶ τοὺς ἀναβαθμούς *when he was at the steps* **Ac 21:35.** Of fear that befalls someone (2 Macc 12:22) **Lk 1:65; 4:36; Ac 5:5.** Of ulcers: *break out on someone* **Rv 16:2** (Ex 9:10f). Of divine commands: *go out to someone* **Lk 3:2.** ἐπί is somet. used w. the gen. (Appian, Liby. 93 §440; Alex. Aphr., Mixt. II 2 p. 213, 21) instead of the acc.: γενόμενος ἐπὶ τοῦ τόπου *when he had arrived at the place* **22:40** (Mitt-Wilck. I/2, 327, 18 ἐπὶ τ. τόπων γινόμενος).—**J 6:21.**

ⓓ w. κατά and gen. of place: τὸ γενόμενον ῥῆμα καθ' ὅλης τῆς Ἰουδαίας *the message that has spread throughout all Judea* **Ac 10:37.** W. acc. of place (X., Cyr. 7, 1, 15; Apollon. Paradox. 3 κατὰ τόπους γ.; Jos., Ant. I, 174; cp. 2 Macc 9:8): γενόμενος κατὰ τὸν τόπον **Lk 10:32;** γενόμενοι κατὰ τὴν Κνίδον **Ac 27:7.**

ⓔ w. πρός and acc. of the direction and goal (PLond III, 962, 1 p. 210 [III AD] γενοῦ πρὸς Ἄταϊν τὸν ποιμένα; PFlor 180, 45) **1 Cor 2:3; 2J 12.** Of divine instructions *be given to someone* (Gen 15:1, 4; Jer 1:2, 11; 13:8; Ezk 6:1; Hos 1:1; cp. ἐπί w. acc.) **J 10:35; Ac 7:31 v.l.; 10:13; 13:32.**

ⓕ w. σύν and the dat. *join someone* (X., Cyr. 5, 3, 8; 2 Macc 13:13) **Lk 2:13.**

ⓖ w. ἐγγύς (X., An. 1, 8, 8, Cyr. 7, 1, 7; cp. γίν. πλησίον Philo, Mos. 1, 228; Jos., Ant. 4, 40): ἐγγὺς τοῦ πλοίου γίνεσθαι *come close to the boat* **J 6:19.** Fig. of the relation of believers to Christ: *come near* **Eph 2:13.**

ⓗ w. ὧδε *come here* **J 6:25;**

ⓘ ἔμπροσθέν τινος γ. **J 1:15, 30** s. on ἔμπροσθεν 1bζ and ὀπίσω 2b.

❼ **to come into a certain state or possess certain characteristics,** ***to be, prove to be, turn out to be*** (on relation to the forms of εἰμί [here and in 8–10] s. ALink, StKr 69, 1896, 420ff). Used w. the nom. (Wsd 16:3; Jdth 16:21; Sir 31:22; 1 Macc 3:58) γίνεσθε φρόνιμοι *be prudent* **Mt 10:16.** ἄκαρπος γίνεται **13:22; Mk 4:19.**—W. other words: vs. **22; 9:50; Lk 1:2; 2:2; 6:36** and very oft. Freq. the dat. of advantage (dat. commodi) is added (1 Macc 10:47; 2 Macc 7:37; 4 Macc 6:28; 12:17): ἀγαπητόν τινι γ. *be dear to someone* **1 Th 2:8.** ἀπρόσκοπον γ. τινι *be inoffensive to someone* **1 Cor 10:32;** γ. τινι μαθητήν **J 15:8;** μισθαποδότην γ. τινι *be a rewarder of someone* **Hb 11:6;** γ. ὁδηγόν τινι **Ac 1:16.** Cp. παρηγορία, σημεῖον, τύπος.—γ. ὁμοθυμαδόν *come together in unanimity* or *reach unanimity* **Ac 15:25.**—τὶ γίνεταί τινί τι *a thing results in someth. for someone* τὸ ἀγαθὸν ἐμοὶ ἐγ. θάνατος; **Ro 7:13.** ἡ ἐξουσία πρόσκομμα τοῖς ἀσθενέσιν **1 Cor 8:9.**—γίνομαι ὡς, ὥσπερ, ὡσεί τις (Ps 21:15; 31:9; 37:15; 82:11; 87:5 al.) *be, become, show oneself like* **Mt 6:16; 10:25; 18:3; 28:4; Lk 22:26, 44; 1 Cor 4:13; 9:20f; Gal 4:12.** καθὼς ἐγένετο … οὕτως ἔσται *as it was … so it will be* **Lk 17:26, 28.** οὐ χρὴ ταῦτα οὕτως γίνεσθαι *this should not be so* **Js 3:10.** ὁσίως καὶ δικαίως καὶ ἀμέμπτως ὑμῖν ἐγενήθημεν *we proved/showed ourselves … toward you* **1 Th 2:10.**—In statements pert. to age (Aristoxenus, fgm. 16 γεγονότα [sc. τὸν Πυθαγόραν] ἐτῶν τεσσαράκοντα; Demetr. of Phaleron [IV–III BC], fgm. 153 Wehrli ['49]; Demetr: 722 fgm. 1, 1 Jac.; Jos., Ant. 10, 50) ἐτῶν δώδεκα **Lk 2:42;** cp. **1 Ti 5:9.**—Here prob. also belongs ἐγένετο γνώμης *he decided* **Ac 20:3** (cp. Plut., Phoc. 752 [23, 4] ἐλπίδος μεγάλης γ.; Cass. Dio 61, 14 τ. ἐπιθυμίας γ.; Jos., Bell. 6, 287).

❽ **to be present at a given time,** ***be there*** ([Ps.-]Jos., Ant. 18, 63) **Mk 1:4; J 1:6,** hence *exist* (Diod. S. 3, 52, 4 γέγονε γένη γυναικῶν=there have been nations of women; Appian, Maced. 18 §3 τὸ χρυσίον τὸ γιγνόμενον=the gold that was at hand; Bar 3:26; 2 Macc 10:24) **Ro 11:5; 1J 2:18.** ἐγένετο *there lived* **Lk 1:5.** ἔν τινι **2 Pt 2:1.** ἐπὶ τῆς γῆς **Rv 16:18** (Da 12:1 Theod.).

❾ **to be closely related to someone or someth.,** ***belong to*** ⓐ gen. of the possessor (Appian, Bell. Civ. 5, 79 §336 a slave γεγένητο Πομπηίου=had belonged to Pompey: B-D-F §162, 7) *belong to someone* **Lk 20:14, 33** (Appian, Bell. Civ. 2, 83 §350 γυνὴ Κράσσου γεγενημένη=who had been the wife of [the younger] Crassus).

ⓑ w. dat. of pers. *belong to someone* (PPetr II, 40b, 7 [277 BC]; O. Wilck II, 1530, 2f [120 BC] τὸ γινόμενόν μοι=what belongs to me) of a woman ἀνδρὶ ἑτέρῳ **Ro 7:3f** (cp. Ruth 1:12f; Dt 24:2).

ⓒ w. prep. μετά τινος (Josh 2:19) **Ac 9:19; 20:18.** οἱ μετ' αὐτοῦ γενόμενοι *his intimate friends* **Mk 16:10.** πρός τινα *be w. someone* **1 Cor 16:10** (*make him* [Timothy] *feel quite at home with you* Mft.) ὑπό τινα *be under the authority of someone* or *someth.* (1 Macc 10:38) **Gal 4:4.**

ⓓ Here perh. belongs ἰδίας ἐπιλύσεως οὐ γίνεται *it is not a matter of private interpretation* **2 Pt 1:20.**

❿ **to be in or at a place,** ***be in, be there***—ⓐ ἔν τινι to designate one's present or future place of residence (X., An. 4, 3, 29; Appian, Bell. Civ. 5, 4 §15 Ἀντώνιος ἐν Ἐφέσῳ γενόμενος; Aelian, VH 4, 15; Herodian 2, 2, 5; POxy 283, 11; 709, 6 ἐν Μένφει γενόμενος; PTebt 416, 3; BGU 731 II, 6 ἐν οἰκίᾳ μου; Num 11:35; Judg 17:4; 1 Ch 14:17; Jdth 5:7 al. Demetr.: 722 fgm. 1, 18 Jac.) **Mt 26:6; Mk 9:33; Ac 7:38; 13:5; 2 Ti 1:17; Rv 1:9;** AcPl Ha 7, 23.

ⓑ w. adv.: ἐκεῖ (X., An. 6, 5, 20; 3 Km 8:8 v.l.; Jos., Ant. 10, 180) **Ac 19:21.** κατὰ μόνας **Mk 4:10.**—B. 637. DELG s.v. γίγνομαι. M-M. TW.

γινώσκω (in the form γιγνώσκω [s. below] since Homer; γιν. in Attic ins in Meisterhans[3]-Schw. index, from 325 BC; in pap fr. 277 BC [Mayser 165]; likew. LXX, pseudepigr., Philo, Joseph., apolog.) impf. ἐγίνωσκον; fut. γνώσομαι; 2 aor. ἔγνων, impv. γνῶθι, γνώτω, subj. 1 sg. γνῶ and 3 sg. γνῷ (γνοῖ **Mk 5:43; 9:30; Lk 19:15;** Hm 4, 1, 5; B-D-F §95, 2; W-S. §13, 22; Mlt-H. 83; Rob. 1214); 2 sg. γνώσῃς (TestAbr A 8 p. 86, 5 [Stone p. 20]); opt. 1 sg. γνῴην; 3 sg. γνοίη Job 23:3, 5; inf. γνῶναι, ptc. γνούς; pf. ἔγνωκα, 3 pl. ἔγνωκαν **J 17:7** (W-S. §13, 15 n. 15); plpf. ἐγνώκειν. Pass.: 1 fut. γνωσθήσομαι; 1 aor. ἐγνώσθην; pf. ἔγνωσμαι. (On the spellings γινώσκειν and γιγνώσκειν s. W-S. §5, 31; B-D-F §34, 4; Mlt-H. 108.) This verb is variously nuanced in contexts relating to familiarity acquired through experience or association with pers. or thing.

❶ **to arrive at a knowledge of someone or someth.,** ***know, know about, make acquaintance of***—ⓐ w. acc. of thing: mysteries (Wsd 2:22; En 104:12) **Mt 13:11; Mk 4:11 v.l.; Lk 8:10;** will of the Master (Just., D. 123, 4) **12:47f;** that which brings peace **19:42;** truth (Jos., Ant. 13, 291) **J 8:32;** times **Ac 1:7;** sin **Ro 7:7;** affection **2 Cor 2:4;** spirit of truth **J 14:17;** way of righteousness **2 Pt 2:21** P[72]; God's glory 1 Cl 61:1.—Abs. γνόντες (Is 26:11) *when they had ascertained it* **Mk 6:38;** ἐκ μέρους γ. *know fragmentarily, only in part* **1 Cor 13:9, 12.**—W. prep. γ. τι ἔκ τινος (X., Cyr. 1, 6, 45; Jos., Vi. 364) *know a thing by someth.* (Diod. S. 17, 101, 6): a tree by its fruit **Mt 12:33; Lk 6:44; 1J 4:6;** γ. τι ἔν τινι (Sir 4:24; 26:9) **1J 4:2.** Also γ. τι κατά τι (Gen 15:8): κατὰ τί γνώσομαι τοῦτο; *by what (=how) shall I know this?* **Lk 1:18.**

ⓑ w. personal obj. (Plut., Mor. 69c ἄνδρα τοιοῦτον οὐκ ἔγνωμεν; Did., Gen. 45, 24 evil powers): God (Ael. Aristid. 52, 2 K.=28 p. 551 D.: γ. τὸν θεόν; Herm. Wr. 1, 3; 10, 19a; Sallust. 18, 3 p. 34, 9 θεούς; 1 Km 2:10; 3:7; 1 Ch 28:9; 3 Macc 7:6; PsSol 2:31; Da 11:32 Theod.; Philo, Ebr. 45; Ar. 15, 3; Just., D. 14, 12; Orig., C. Cels. 6, 66, 26f) **J 14:7ab; 17:3, 25; Ro 1:21; Gal 4:9; 1J 2:3, 13; 3:1, 6; 4:6ff; 5:20** (for 1J s. M-EBoismard, RB 56, '49, 365–91); PtK 2. Jesus Christ **J 14:7; 17:3; 2 Cor 5:16** (*even though we have known Christ* [irrealis, 'contrary to fact', is also prob.=*even if we had known;* cp. Gal 5:11], *we now no longer know him;* on this pass. s. κατά B7a; σάρξ 5); **1J 2:3f** (Just., D. 28, 3). τινὰ ἔν τινι *someone by someth.* (Ps 47:4; Sir 11:28; TestNapht 3:4) **Lk 24:35.**

ⓒ w. ὅτι foll. (BGU 824, 8; Philo, Det. Pot. Ins. 22) **Mt 25:24; J 6:69; 7:26; 8:52; 14:20, 31; 17:7f, 25; 19:4.** W. ὅθεν preceding *by this* one knows (EpJer 22) **1J 2:18.** ἐν τούτῳ (Gen 42:33; Ex 7:17; Josh 3:10 al.) **J 13:35; 1J 2:3, 5; 4:13; 5:2.** W. combination of two constr. ἐν τούτῳ γινώσκομεν ὅτι μένει ἐν ἡμῖν, ἐκ τοῦ πνεύματος *by this we know that (Jesus Christ) remains in us, namely by the spirit* **3:24;** cp. **4:13.** W. an indir. question foll. (1 Km 14:38: 25:17; 2 Km 18:29; Ps 38:5) **Mt 12:7; J 7:51.** W. combination of two questions (double interrogative) ἵνα γνοῖ τίς τί διεπραγματεύσατο *that he might know what each one had gained in his dealings* **Lk 19:15.**

❷ **to acquire information through some means,** ***learn (of), ascertain, find out*****—ⓐ** w. acc. as obj. (1 Km 21:3; 1 Ch 21:2; 4 Macc 4:4) τοῦτο (1 Km 20:3) **Mk 5:43.** τὰ γενόμενα *what has happened* **Lk 24:18.** τὸ ἀσφαλές **Ac 21:34; 22:30.** τὰ περὶ ἡμῶν *our situation* **Col 4:8;** *your faith* **1 Th 3:5.** Pass. *become known to someone* w. or without dat. of the pers. who is informed: of secret things **Mt 10:26; Lk 8:17; 12:2.** Of plots **Ac 9:24** (cp. 1 Macc 6:3; 7:3, 30 al.).

ⓑ w. ὅτι foll. (PGiss 11, 4 [118 AD] γεινώσκειν σε θέλω ὅτι; 1 Esdr 2:17; Ruth 3:14) **J 4:1; 5:6; 12:9; Ac 24:11 v.l.**

ⓒ abs. (1 Km 14:29; 3 Km 1:11; Tob 8:12 al.) μηδεὶς γινωσκέτω *nobody is to know of this* **Mt 9:30.** ἵνα τις γνοῖ *that anyone should obtain knowledge of it* **Mk 9:30.**

ⓓ γ. ἀπό τινος *ascertain fr. someone* **15:45.**

❸ **to grasp the significance or meaning of someth.,** ***understand, comprehend*****—ⓐ** w. acc. foll. (Sir 1:6; 18:28; Wsd 5:7 v.l.; 9:13; Bar 3:9 al.; Just., A I, 63, 5; D. 68, 1 σκληροκάρδιοι πρὸς τὸ γνῶναι νοῦν … τοῦ θεοῦ): parables **Mk 4:13;** what was said **Lk 18:34;** (w. ἀναγινώσκειν in wordplay) **Ac 8:30.** ταῦτα **J 3:10; 12:16;** what one says **J 8:43;** God's wisdom **1 Cor 2:8;** the nature of God vs. **11;** the nature of the divine spirit vs. **14;** the love of Christ **Eph 3:19** (s. γνῶσις 1); God's ways **Hb 3:10** (Ps 94:10); τὸν νόμον *know the law* **J 7:49; Ro 7:1** (here perh.=*have the law at one's fingertips,* cp. Menand., Sicyonius 138f, τῶν τοὺς νόμους εἰδότων; Just., D. 123, 2). πῶς οὖν [ταῦτα γιγν]ώσκομεν; *how then shall we know these things?* Ox 1081, 25f (=SJCh 90, 1f), as read by Till p. 220 app.

ⓑ abs. **Mt 24:39.**

ⓒ w. ὅτι foll. (Wsd 10:12; EpJer 64; 1 Macc 6:13; 7:42; 2 Macc 7:28 al.) **Mt 21:45; 24:32; Mk 12:12; 13:28f; Lk 21:30f; J 4:53; 8:27f; 2 Cor 13:6; Js 2:20.**

ⓓ w. indir. question foll. (Job 19:29) **J 10:6; 13:12, 28.**

❹ **to be aware of someth.,** ***perceive, notice, realize*****—ⓐ** w. acc.: their wickedness **Mt 22:18;** γ. δύναμιν ἐξεληλυθυῖαν *that power had gone out* **Lk 8:46** (on the constr. w. the ptc. cp. PHamb 27, 13 [III BC]; BGU 1078 [I AD] γίνωσκε ἡγεμόνα εἰσεληλυθότα; POxy 1118, 7; Jos., Ant. 17, 342; Just., D. 39, 2 al.).

ⓑ abs. (Ex 22:9; 1 Km 26:12) **Mt 16:8; 26:10; Mk 7:24; 8:17.**

ⓒ w. ὅτι foll. (Gen 3:7; 8:11; 1 Macc 1:5 al.): ἔγνω τῷ σώματι ὅτι ἴαται *she felt in her body that she was healed* **Mk 5:29;** cp. **15:10; J 6:15; 16:19; Ac 23:6.**

❺ **to have sexual intercourse with,** ***have sex/marital relations with,*** euphemistic ext. of 1 (Menand., fgm. 558, 5 Kock; Heraclid. Lembus, Pol. 64 [Aristot., Fgm. ed. VRose 1886, 383]; oft. in Plut. and other later authors, and LXX [Anz 306]) w. acc., said of a man as agent (Gen 4:1, 17; 1 Km 1:19; Jdth 16:22; ApcMos 4; Did., Gen. 143, 9) **Mt 1:25** (in connection w. the topic of 1:25f see Plut., Mor. 717e; Olympiodorus, Vi. Plat. 1 [Westermann, 1850]: φάσμα Ἀπολλωνιακὸν συνεγένετο τῇ μητρὶ αὐτοῦ τῇ Περικτιόνῃ καὶ ἐν νυκτὶ φανὲν τῷ Ἀρίστωνι ἐκέλευσεν αὐτῷ μὴ μιγνύναι τῇ Περικτιόνῃ μέχρι τ. χρόνου τῆς ἀποτέξεως. Ὁ δ' οὕτω πεποίηκεν: 'an apparition of Apollo had relations with [Plato's] mother Perictione, and in a nocturnal appearance to Ariston [Plato's father] ordered him not to have intercourse w. P. until the time of her parturition. So he acted accordingly.'—The legend of Plato's birth is traceable to Plato's nephew Speusippus [Diog. L. 3:2; Jerome, Adv. Iovin. 1, 42]); of a woman (Judg 11:39; 21:12; Theodor. Prodr. 9, 486 H.) **Lk 1:34** (DHaugg, D. erste bibl. Marienwort '38; FGrant, JBL 59, '40, 19f; HSahlin, D. Messias u. d. Gottesvolk, '45, 117–20).

❻ **to have come to the knowledge of,** ***have come to know, know*** (Nägeli 40 w. exx.)**—ⓐ** w. acc.**—α.** of thing (Bar 3:20, 23; Jdth 8:29; Bel 35; Just., D. 110, 1 καὶ τοῦτο γ.): τὴν ποσότητα 1 Cl 35:3; hearts (Ps 43:22) **Lk 16:15;** will **Ro 2:18;** truth (Just., D. 139, 5; Tat. 13, 1) **2J 1; 2 Cor 5:21;** grace **8:9;** πάντα (2 Km 14:20; Just., D. 127, 2) **1J 3:20.** τὶ **1 Cor 8:2a.** W. object clause preceding: ὃ κατεργάζομαι οὐ γ. *what I am accomplishing I really do not know* **Ro 7:15** (here γ. almost=*desire, want, decide* [Polyb. 5, 82, 1; Plut., Lycurg. 41[3, 9] ἔγνω φυγεῖν; Appian, Syr. 5 §18; Arrian, Anab. 2, 21, 8; 2, 25, 8; Paradox. Vat. 46 Keller ὅ τι ἂν γνῶσιν αἱ γυναῖκες; Jos., Ant. 1, 195; 14, 352; 16, 331]; mngs. 3 *understand* and 7 *recognize* are also prob.). W. attraction of the relative ἐν ὥρᾳ ᾗ οὐ γ. *at an hour unknown to him* **Mt 24:50; Lk 12:46.** W. acc. and ptc. (on the constr. s. 4a above) τὴν πόλιν νεωκόρον οὖσαν *that the city is guardian of the temple* **Ac 19:35.**

β. of pers. *know someone* (Tob 5:2; 7:4; Is 1:3) **J 1:48; 2:24; 10:14f, 27; Ac 19:15; 2 Ti 2:19** (Num 16:5); Ox 1 recto, 14 (GTh 31). W. acc. and ptc. (s. α above, end and e.g. Just., A I, 19, 6) **Hb 13:23.**

ⓑ w. acc. and inf. (Da 4:17; Just., D. 130, 2 al.) **Hb 10:34.**

ⓒ w. ὅτι foll. (Sir 23:19; Bar 2:30; Tob 3:14) **J 21:17; Ac 20:34; Phil 1:12; Js 1:3; 2 Pt 1:20; 3:3;** γ. τοὺς διαλογισμοὺς ὅτι εἰσὶν μάταιοι *he knows that the thoughts are vain* **1 Cor 3:20** (Ps 93:11).—Oft. γινώσκετε, ὅτι *you may be quite sure that* **Mt 24:33, 43; Mk 13:28f; Lk 10:11; 12:39; 21:31; J 15:18; 1J 2:29** (cp. UPZ 62, 32 [161 BC] γίνωσκε σαφῶς ὅτι πρός σε οὐ μὴ ἐπέλθω; 70, 14; 3 Macc 7:9; Judg 4:9; Job 36:5; Pr 24:12). In τοῦτο ἴστε γινώσκοντες, ὅτι **Eph 5:5** the question is whether the two verbs are to be separated or not. In the latter case, one could point to Sym. Jer 49:22 ἴστε γινώσκοντες and 1 Km 20:3.

ⓓ w. indir. question (Gen 21:26; 1 Km 22:3; Eccl 11:5; 2 Macc 14:32; Just., A I, 63, 3 τί πατὴρ καὶ τί υἱός) **Lk 7:39; 10:22; J 2:25; 11:57.**

ⓔ w. adv. modifier γ. Ἑλληνιστί *understand Greek* **Ac 21:37** (cp. X., Cyr. 7, 5; 31 ἐπίστασθαι Συριστί).

ⓕ abs. (Gen 4:9; 18:21; 4 Km 2:3; Sir 32:8) **Lk 2:43.** τί ἐγὼ γινώσκω; *how should I know?* Hs 9, 9, 1.

❼ **to indicate that one does know,** ***acknowledge, recognize*** as that which one is or claims to be τινά (Plut., Ages. 597 [3, 1]; Jos., Ant. 5, 112) οὐδέποτε ἔγνων ὑμᾶς *I have never recognized you* **Mt 7:23;** cp. **J 1:10.** ἐὰν γνωσθῇ πλέον τ.

ἐπισκόπου *if he receives more recognition than the supervisor (bishop)* IPol 5:2. Of God as subject *recognize someone as belonging to God, choose,* almost=*elect* (Am 3:2; Hos 12:1; SibOr 5, 330) **1 Cor 8:3; Gal 4:9.** In these pass. the γ. of God directed toward human beings is conceived of as the basis of and condition for their coming to know God; cp. the language of the Pythagoreans in HSchenkl, Wiener Studien 8, 1886 p. 265, no. 9 βούλει γνωσθῆναι θεοῖς· ἀγνοήθητι μάλιστα ἀνθρώποις; p. 277 no. 92 σοφὸς ἄνθρωπος κ. θεὸν σεβόμενος γινώσκεται ὑπὸ τ. θεοῦ; Porphyr., ad Marcellam 13 σοφὸς ἄνθρωπος γινώσκεται ὑπὸ θεοῦ; Herm. Wr. 1, 31 θεός, ὃς γνωσθῆναι βούλεται καὶ γινώσκεται τοῖς ἰδίοις; 10, 15 οὐ γὰρ ἀγνοεῖ τὸν ἄνθρωπον ὁ θεός, ἀλλὰ καὶ πάνυ γνωρίζει καὶ θέλει γνωρίζεσθαι. S. Rtzst., Mysterienrel.[3] 299f; Ltzm. on 1 Cor 8:3; RAC XI 446–659.—On the whole word: BSnell, D. Ausdrücke für die Begriffe des Wissens in d. vorplatonischen Philosophie 1924; EBaumann, ידע u. seine Derivate: ZAW 28, 1908, 22ff; 110ff; WBousset, Gnosis: Pauly-W. VII 1912, 1503ff; Rtzst., Mysterienrel.[3] 66–70; 284–308; PThomson, 'Know' in the NT: Exp. 9th ser. III, 1925, 379–82; AFridrichsen, Gnosis (Paul): ELehmann Festschr. 1927, 85–109; RPope, Faith and Knowledge in Pauline and Johannine Thought: ET 41, 1930, 421–27; RBultmann, TW I '33, 688–715; HJonas, Gnosis u. spätantiker Geist I '34; [2]'55; EPrucker, Gnosis Theou '37; JDupont, La Connaissance religieuse dans les Épîtres de Saint Paul, '49; LBouyer, Gnosis: Le Sens orthodoxe de l'expression jusqu'aux pères Alexandrins: JTS n.s. 4, '53, 188–203; WDavies, Knowledge in the Dead Sea Scrolls and Mt 11:25–30: HTR 46, '53, 113–39; WSchmithals, D. Gnosis in Kor. '55, [3]'69; MMagnusson, Der Begriff 'Verstehen' (esp. in Paul), '55; RCasey, Gnosis, Gnosticism and the NT: CDodd Festschr., '56, 52–80; IdelaPotterie, οἶδα et γινώσκω (4th Gosp.), Biblica 40, '59, 709–25; HJSchoeps, Urgemeinde, Judenchristentum, Gnosis '56; EKäsemann, Das Wandernde Gottesvolk (Hb)[2], '57; HJonas, The Gnostic Religion, '58; JDupont, Gnosis, '60; UWilckens, Weisheit u. Torheit (1 Cor 1 and 2) '59; DGeorgi, Die Gegner des Pls im 2 Cor, '64; DScholer, Nag Hammadi Bibliography, 1948–69, '71.—B. 1209f. DELG s.v. γιγνώσκω. EDNT. M-M. TW. Sv.

γλεῦκος, ους, τό (Aristot. et al.; Plut.; Lucian, Philops. 39; Galen XII p. 88, 6 K., XIII p. 45, 18 al.; Athen. 1, 31e; GDI 4993; PPetr II, 40[b], 8 [277 BC]; PSI 544, 2; PGrenf II, 24, 12 al.; s. Preis.; Job 32:19; Jos., Ant. 2, 64) ***sweet new wine*** (schol. on Nicander, Alexiph. 493 γλεῦκος, ὃ λέγεται ἐν συνηθείᾳ μοῦστος= 'γλεῦκος, commonly referred to as must'; cp. PStras 1, 7 [V AD]) **Ac 2:13.**—DELG s.v. γλυκύς. M-M.

γλυκύς, εῖα, ύ (Hom.+; ins, pap, LXX; TestGad 5:1; JosAs 12 p. 56, 19f Bat.; GrBar 4:15 [Christian]; Just.) ***sweet*** of water (Diod. S. 5, 43, 2; Arrian, Anab. 6, 26, 5; Jos., Bell. 3, 50, Ant. 3, 38) **Js 3:11f** (opp. πικρός as Hdt. 4, 52; Plut., Mor. 13d; Demetr.: 722 fgm. 4 Jac.; Philo, Rer. Div. Her. 208, Aet. M. 104; Just., D. 20, 3; 86, 1); of honey Hm 5, 1, 5f. In imagery, of a book *be sweet as honey,* i.e. pleasant to read **Rv 10:9f;** of blackberries(?) B 7:8. (Gen. of food Just., D. 20, 3.) Fig. of commandments Hm 12, 4, 5; of patience m 5, 1, 6; of an exchange Dg 9:5.—The superl. freq. of persons to express affection (Menand., Epitr. 143 S.=17 Kö.; OGI 382, 7f; 526, 4; SIG 889, 20; IMakedD I, 414, 2 children; SEG XLI, 867, 4f daughter; POxy 907, 3; 935, 22f τ. γλυκύτατον ἀδελφόν) IMg 6:1.—B. 1032. DELG. M-M.

γλυκύτης, ητος, ἡ (s. γλυκύς; Hdt. et al.; Judg 9:11; Philo; ApcMos 24) ***sweetness*** of honey (Jos., Ant. 3, 28) Hm 5, 1, 5. Since sweet viands or liquids afforded pleasing sensations, metaph. use of γ. became common (s. L-S-J-M, s.v. I, 2): *sweetness, tenderness,* of God 1 Cl 14:3 (cp. Sappho 90 γλυκεῖα μᾶτηρ; Wsd 16:21; Cat. Cod. Astr. VIII/2 p. 156, 21 of Aphrodite).—JZiegler, Dulcedo Dei '37.

γλυπτός, ή, όν ***carved*** (γλύφω 'carve'; Theophr., Lap. 5 et al.; LXX) τὸ γ. *carved image* (Judg 18:18 al. and freq. pl. in LXX; ViElisha 3 [p. 95, 5 Sch.]; loanw. in rabb.) B 12:6 (Dt 27:15).—TW.

γλῶσσα, ης, ἡ (Hom.+; ins, pap, LXX, En; TestJob 43:12; Test12Patr; JosAs 13:8; GrBar 3:6; ApcSed; AscIs 3:18; Philo, Joseph., Just., Tat.)

❶ **organ of speech, *tongue***—ⓐ lit. (Did., Gen. 88, 26) **Lk 16:24;** as an organ of speech (Iambl., Vi. Pyth. 31, 195 χαλεπώτατόν ἐστιν τὸ γλώττης κρατεῖν; Did., Gen. 46, 26 ὄργανον λόγου ἐστὶν ἡ γ.) **Mk 7:33, 35;** (Vi. Aesopi I G 7 P.: Isis heals the mute Aesop τὸ τραχὺ τῆς γλώττης ἀποτεμοῦσα, τὸ κωλῦον αὐτὸν λαλεῖν 'cutting off the rough part of his tongue that prevented him from speaking') **Lk 1:64; Ro 3:13** (Ps 5:10; 13:3; cp. Hes., Op. 322–26); **14:11** (Is 45:23); **Js 1:26; 3:5f, 8** (Apion in the schol. on Od. 3, 341 κράτιστον τῶν μελῶν ἡ γλῶσσα.—JGeffcken, Kynika usw. 1909, 45–53; GAvdBergh vEysinga, NThT 20, '31, 303–20). **1J 3:18;** διὰ τῆς γ. *w. the tongue,* i.e., in *speaking* **1 Cor 14:9** (Just., A I, 16, 8 διὰ γλώττης). παύειν τὴν γ. ἀπὸ κακοῦ *keep the tongue from (saying) evil things* **1 Pt 3:10;** 1 Cl 22:3 (both Ps 33:14). Synon. στόμα 35:8 (Ps 49:19); **Rv 16:10;** 1 Cl 15:4f (Ps 77:36; 11:4f). τὸ ἐπιεικὲς τῆς γ. *moderation of the tongue* 21:7. μάστιξ γλώσσης *words of reproof* 56:10 (Job 5:21). Conceited speech 57:2 (cp. 3 Macc 2:17). Of *evil tongues* Hv 2, 2, 3. ἠγαλλιάσατο ἡ γλῶσσά μου *my tongue exulted* (the organ for the pers., cp. πούς 1b) **Ac 2:26;** 1 Cl 18:15 (both Ps 15:9). τὴν γ. προβάλλειν *put out the tongue, hiss* of a dragon Hv 4, 1, 9.

ⓑ fig., of forked flames **Ac 2:3** (=לְשׁוֹן אֵשׁ Is 5:24; cp. En 14:9f).

❷ **a body of words and systems that makes up a distinctive language, *language, tongue***—ⓐ of the language itself (Hom. et al.; PGiss 99, 9; Philo, Mos. 2, 40; Jos., Ant. 10, 8; 158; Just., D. 102, 4) **Ac 2:6 v.l., 11;** *language* λαλεῖν ἑτέραις γλώσσαις **Ac 2:4.** On this s. ἕτερος 2 end.; B-D-F §480, 3.

ⓑ of language viewed in terms of pers. using it, *language, tongue:* πᾶσα γ. *every language*=every person, regardless of the language that pers. speaks **Ro 14:11; Phil 2:11** (Is 45:23; cp. POxy 1381, 198: Ἑλληνὶς δὲ πᾶσα γλῶσσα τὴν σὴν λαλήσει ἱστορίαν καὶ πᾶς Ἕλλην ἀνὴρ τὸν τοῦ Φθᾶ σεβήσεται Ἰμούθην; PGM 12, 188) IMg 10:3. As a distinctive feature of nations γ. can be used as a synonym of φυλή, λαός, ἔθνος (Is 66:18; Da 3:4, 7 al.; Jdth 3:8; AscIs 3:18) **Rv 5:9; 7:9; 10:11; 11:9; 13:7; 14:6; 17:15;** 2 Cl 17:4 (Is 66:18).

❸ **an utterance outside the normal patterns of intelligible speech and therefore requiring special interpretation, *ecstatic language, ecstatic speech, tongue,*** γλῶσσαι, γένη γλωσσῶν, (ἐν) γλώσσῃ/-αις λαλεῖν (λαλούντων διὰ τοῦ πνεύματος γλώσσαις Iren. 5, 6, 1 [Harv. II 334, 3]) **1 Cor 14:1–27, 39; 12:10, 28, 30; 13:1, 8; Ac 10:46; 19:6.** Always without the article (in **1 Cor 14:22** αἱ is anaphoric; vs. 9 belongs under mng. 1a). There is no doubt about the thing referred to, namely the strange speech of persons in religious ecstasy. The phenomenon, as found in Hellenistic religion, is described esp. by ERohde (Psyche[3] 1903, Eng. tr. 1925, 289–93) and Reitzenstein; cp. Celsus 7, 8; 9. The origin of the term is less clear. Two explanations are prominent today. The one (Bleek, Heinrici et al.) holds that γλῶσσα here means antiquated, foreign, unintelligible, mysterious utterances (Diod. S. 4, 66, 7 κατὰ γλῶτταν=according to an old expression). The other (Rtzst., Bousset et al.) sees in glossolalia a speaking in marvelous, celestial languages. On ἑρμηνεία γλωσσῶν **1 Cor 12:10** (cp. **14:26**) s. ἑρμηνεία.—γλώσσαις καιναῖς λαλεῖν **Mk 16:17**.—On 'speaking in tongues' s. HGunkel, Die Wirkungen d. hl. Geistes[2] 1899; HWeinel, D. Wirkungen d. Geistes u. d. Geister im nachap. Zeitalter 1899; ELombard, De la Glossolalie chez les premiers chrétiens 1910; EMosiman, Das Zungenreden geschichtl. u. psychol. unters. 1911. WReinhard, D. Wirken d. hl. Geistes 1918, 120ff; KLSchmidt, Die Pfingsterzählung u. d. Pfingstereignis 1919 (against him PSchmiedel, PM 24, 1920, 73–86); HGüntert, Von der Sprache der Götter u. Geister 1921, 23ff; AMackie, The Gift of Tongues 1922; HRust, D. Zungenreden 1924; FBüchsel, D. Geist Gottes im NT 1926, 242ff; 321ff; GCutten, Speaking with Tongues 1927; IMartin, 3rd, Glossolalia in the Apostolic Church: JBL 63, '44, 123–30; JDavies, Pentecost and Glossolalia: JTS n.s. 3, '52, 228–31; FBeare, JBL 83, '64, 229–46; SCurrie, Int 19, '65, 274–94; RHarrisville, CBQ 38, '76, 35–48; RAC XI 225–46; EDNT I 251–55.—B. 230; 1260. Frisk. DELG s.v. γλῶχες. M-M. TW. Sv.

γλωσσόκομον, ου, τό (κομέω 'tend, care for'; H. Gk. for γλωττοκομεῖον, Phryn. 98 Lob.; s. B-D-F §119, 5; Mlt-H. 272; loanw. in rabb.) orig. a 'case' for the mouthpiece or reed of a flute, then gener. 'case, container' for anything at all (Michel 1001 VIII, 25; 31 [c. 200 BC]; pap, e.g., PGrenf I, 14, 3 [II BC]; PTebt 414, 21; POxy 521, 12; PGM 13, 1009; and s. Preis.; LXX; Jos., Ant. 6, 11) in NT of a container for money, ***money-box, purse*** (Plut., Galba 1060 [16, 2]; PRyl 127, 25 [29 AD]; 2 Ch 24:8, 10) **J 12:6;** τὸ γλωσσόκομον εἶχεν Ἰούδας *Judas was in charge of the (common) purse* **13:29** (in ref. to Judas' function as treasurer of the band of disciples).—M-M.

γλωσσώδης, ες (s. γλῶσσα, -ώδης; Aesop 248b H.//141 v.l. P.//146 H-H.//202 Ch.; Sextus 13 γυνὴ γ. ὥσπερ σάλπιγξ πολεμίων; Ps 139:12; Sir 8:3; 9:18; 25:20) ***talkative, garrulous,*** perh. *glib of tongue* B 19:7 v.l. (for δίγλωσσος).

γναφεύς, έως, ὁ (Hdt. et al.; the older spelling was κναφεύς [s. Kühner-Bl. I 147f; Meisterhans[3]-Schw. 74, 1; Schwyzer I 343]; the form w. γν. as early as an Att. ins of IV BC, and gener. in the Ptolemaic pap [Mayser 170, further ref. there], also Mitt-Wilck., I/2, 315, 8 [88 AD]; LXX. But κν. reappears, as e.g. Dio Chrys. 55 [72], 4; Artem. 4, 33 p. 224, 4; Diog. L. 5, 36; Celsus 3, 55) gener. a specialist in one or more of the processes in the treatment of cloth, incl. fulling, carding, cleaning, bleaching. Since the Eng. term 'fuller' refers to one who shrinks and thickens cloth, a more general rendering such as ***cloth refiner*** is required to cover the various components. In our lit. (only **Mk 9:3**) ref. is to the bleaching aspect, without suggesting that the term applies only to one engaged in that particular feature. Hence such glosses as 'bleacher' or 'fuller' would overly limit the professional niche.—DELG s.v. κνάπτω. M-M.

γνήσιος, α, ον (Hom. et al.; ins, pap, LXX, TestAbr A, EpArist, Philo, Joseph.)

➊ one who is considered a valid member of a family, *legitimate, true.* In the Hellenic world ancestral connections were highly prized; hence this term referred orig. to having connection with the γένος by birth: 'belonging to the race.' Hence lit. of children *born in wedlock, legitimate* (X., Cyr. 8, 5, 19; OGI 194, 12; Mitt-Wilck. I/2, 145, 21 legitimacy of a son affirmed on basis of birth from a freewoman; PFlor 79, 21; 294, 12 γνησίων τέκνων; POxy 1267, 15 γ. υἱός; PLips 28, 17f; cp. PEleph 1, 3 γ. γυνή; Sir 7:18; Philo, Mos. 1, 15 γ. παῖς, Spec. Leg. 4, 203 τέκνα; Jos., Ant. 17, 45 τέκνα); fig., of affective relationship, esp. as developed through sharing of values or experiences (Herm. Wr. 13, 3 γνήσιος υἱός εἰμι; Eunap. Vi. Soph. 7, 1, 13 p. 49: pupils as παῖδες γ.) γ. τέκνον ἐν πίστει *true child in the faith* **1 Ti 1:2;** cp. **Tit 1:4;** γ. σύζυγε **Phil 4:3** (cp. BGU 86, 19 γ. φίλος; PLond III, 1244, 5 p. 244 [III AD]; EpArist 41; TestAbr A 16 p. 97, 7 [Stone p. 42] al.).

➋ pert. to possession of apparent or reputed good character or quality, *genuine* of things (of 'genuine' writings: Harpocration s.v. Ἀλκιβιάδης; Galen XV 748 K.; Athen. 4, 25, 144e; 14, 63, 650d) γνησιώτερος λόγος *more reliable teaching* B 9:9 (Harpocration s.v. ναυτοδίκαι: Lysias says εἰ γνήσιος ὁ λόγος; Philo, Poster. Cai. 102 γ. φιλοσοφία). ἀγάπη 1 Cl 62:2 (Michel 394, 48f γ. φιλοστοργία). τὸ γ. *genuineness, sincerity* of love **2 Cor 8:8** (OGI 339, 7 [c. 120 BC] τὸ πρὸς τὴν πατρίδα γνήσιον).—DELG s.v. γίγνομαι p. 223. TW. Spicq.

γνησίως adv. of γνήσιος (Eur. et al.; ins, pap, LXX) ***sincerely, genuinely*** (so the horoscope in PLond I, 130, 3 p. 133 [I/II AD]; PTebt 326, 11; 2 Macc 14:8; 3 Macc 3:23) μεριμνᾶν **Phil 2:20** (cp. IMagnMai 188, 8ff).—M-M s.v. γνήσιος.

γνούς, γνόντος s. γινώσκω.

γνόφος, ου, ὁ (later form for the earlier and poetic δνόφος; e.g. ChronLind D, 28; Heraclid. Miles., fgm. 28 [LCohn 1884]; Ps.-Aristot., De Mundo 2 p. 392b; Lucian, Peregr. 43; Vett. Val. 145, 16; Cleopatra 15, 44 of Hades; ins Guarducci IV 276–78, line 8; Sb 5620, 8; LXX; SibOr 5, 378) ***darkness*** **Hb 12:18** (Dt 4:11).—New Docs 4, 143. DELG s.v. δνόφος. TW. Sv.

γνώμη, ης, ἡ (s. γινώσκω; w. var. mngs. since Pind., Pre-Socr.; BSnell, Die Ausdrücke f. den Begriff des Wissens in der vorplatonischen Philosophie 1924, 20–30; Hdt.+)

➊ that which is purposed or intended, *purpose, intention, mind, mind-set* ἐν αὐτῇ γνώμῃ *in unity of mind* **1 Cor 1:10;** sim. **Rv 17:13** (μία γνώμη as Demosth. 10, 59; Plut., Cam. 150 [40, 2]; Ael. Aristid. 23, 31 K.=42 p. 778 D.; SIG 135, 21; Pollux 8, 151 μίαν γ. ἔχειν; Philo, Mos. 1, 235; Jos., Ant. 7, 60; 276; s. WvanUnnik in: Studies in John Presented to Prof. Dr. JSevenster, '70, 209–20). ἐν Ἰησοῦ Χριστοῦ γνώμῃ *under the control of the mind of J. C.* IEph 3:2; IPhld ins; ἡ εἰς θεὸν γ. *mind directed toward God* IRo 7:1; IPhld 1:2; ἡ ἐν θεῷ γ. *mind fixed in God* IPol 1:1. γ. τοῦ θεοῦ *purpose/will of God* IEph 3:2 (here also Christ as τοῦ πατρὸς ἡ γ., i.e., the personification of what God has in mind for appropriate conduct.—Jos., Ant. 2, 309; 3, 16; 17 τοῦ θεοῦ γ. is clearly *God's will.* Likew. Appian, Bell. Civ. 4, 100 §421 κατὰ γνώμην θεῶν; IAndrosIsis, Kyme 40 p. 124 Peek; OGI 383, 110 [I BC]; Just., D. 95, 2; 125, 4; Tat. 32, 2); IRo 8:3; ISm 6:2; IPol 8:1; ἡ τ. ἐπισκόπου γ. IEph 4:1; of the devil θλιβέντες τῇ γνώμῃ αὐτοῦ *oppressed by his design* IPhld 6:2 (γνώμῃ as instrumental dat. in Pind., N. 10, 89). γ. ἀγαθή *good will* or *motive* B 21:2 (cp. SIG 75, 28).—γ. ὀρθή IEph 1:1 v.l. (Lghtf.); γ. ἀλλοτρία=(behaves) in a contrary state of mind IPhld 3:3 (cp. 2 below).—As used in diplomatic parlance (s. OGI 315, 82f al.) B 2:9 of divine *attitude* or *disposition = mind-set.*

➋ a viewpoint or way of thinking about a matter, *opinion, judgment, way of thinking* (earliest use Hdt. 1, 120 [Parm. 8, 61 is questionable]; Dio Chrys. 55 [72], 12 ἑπτὰ σοφῶν τ. γνώμας; Vi. Aesopi G 20 ἡ τοῦ φίλου γνώμη; Sir 6:23; 2 Macc 14:20; 4 Macc 9:27; Jos., Ant. 13, 416) **Ac 4:18** D; κατὰ τὴν ἐμὴν γ. *in my judgment* **1 Cor 7:40** (κατὰ τ. γ. as PPetr II, 11; I, 1; Wsd 7:15); γ. διδόναι *express an opinion, appraise a matter, offer counsel* or *direction* (for the phrase cp. Diod. S. 20, 16, 1 τ. ἐναντίαν δοὺς γνώμην; for the sense 'direction, guidance'

s. also Iren. 4, 37, 2 [Harv. II 287, 8]) **1 Cor 7:25; 2 Cor 8:10;** ἀλλοτρία γ. *alien view* IPhld 3:3 (cp. Just., D. 35, 6 of heresies). This mng. is poss. **Phlm 14,** and the phrase χωρὶς τῆς σῆς γ. can be understood in the sense *without your input,* but s. 3 below.

❸ the act of expressing agreement with a body of data, *approval* (Polyb. 2, 21, 3 Appian, Bell. Civ. 4, 96 §403 γ. δημοκρατικῆς διανοίας=showing preference for republican government; Jos., Ant. 18, 336) χωρὶς τῆς σῆς γ. **Phlm 14:** numerous versions (incl. NRSV, REB) and comm. favor *approval, consent* (s. 2 above); also ἄνευ γνώμης σου IPol 4:1 (exx. fr. Hellenistic times for both in Nägeli 33; also Diod. S. 16, 50, 8 ἄνευ τῆς ἐκείνου γνώμης; IAndrosIsis [δοξάζω 2]; UPZ 112, III 3 [III BC] al.). μετὰ γνώμης τινός *w. someone's approval* (Isaeus 2, 8; Demosth. 25, 10; Diod. S. 16, 91, 2 μετὰ τῆς τῶν θεῶν γνώμης; UPZ 27, 1 [II BC al.) IPol 5:2. S. Renehan '82, 49.

❹ a declaration that expresses formal consideration of a matter, *declaration, decision, resolution* (freq. used as a t.t. for official proposals and proclamations: s. Herodas 2, 86 γνώμη δικαίη of judges; IPriene 105, 31 [9 BC] γνώμη τοῦ ἀρχιερέως; POxy 54, 12; PFay 20, 4; PBrem 15, 8 al.) of God **Rv 17:17;** w. impv. foll. γ. ἀγαθή *gracious pronouncement* i.e. a declaration that displays God's gracious disposition 1 Cl 8:2. Sim. *resolve, decision* (Thu. 1, 53, 2; 2, 86, 5 γ. ἔχοντες μὴ ἐκπλεῖν; POxy 1280, 5 ἑκουσίᾳ καὶ αὐθαιρέτῳ γνώμῃ; En 6:4; Philo, In Flacc. 145, Spec. Leg. 2, 88 al.; Jos., Ant. 10, 253; Tat. 7:2 αὐτεξουσίῳ γ.; Ath. 34, 1 ὑπὸ χειρὸς καὶ γνώμης) **Ac 20:3** (γίνομαι 7); of a proposal Hs 5, 2, 8.—SMouraviev, Glotta 51, '73, 69–78. B. 1240. DELG s.v. γιγνώσκω. M-M. TW. Sv.

γνωρίζω fut. γνωρίσω (γνωριῶ [POxy 1024, 18; LXX; Just., D. 14, 8] **Col 4:9 v.l.** [Tdf. S. Vog.]); 1 aor. ἐγνώρισα. Mid.: ἐγνωρισάμην. Pass.: 1 fut. γνωρισθήσομαι; 1 aor. ἐγνωρίσθην; pf. 3 sg. ἐγνώρισται 2 Esdr 7:24 (Aeschyl. et al.; pap, LXX, pseudepigr., Philo, Joseph.; Ar. 12, 6; Just., Ath. 3, 1)

❶ to cause information to become known: *make known, reveal* (Aeschyl., Prom. 487; Diod. S. 1, 6, 2; 1, 9, 2; 10, 3, 1; Plut., Fab. Max. 186 [21, 3]; Cato Maj. 336 [1, 2] al.; LXX; TestJob 41:5; Jos., Ant. 8, 102) γ. τι **Ro 9:22f; Eph 6:19;** τί τινι **Lk 2:15;** Hs 9, 5, 4; ways of life **Ac 2:28** (Ps 15:11); sins Hv 2, 1, 2; words 2, 2, 3f; the past and the future B 1:7; cp. 5:3. πάντα **Eph 6:21; Col 4:7, 9; J 15:15;** cp. Hs 9, 5, 4; name **17:26.—2 Cor 8:1; 2 Pt 1:16.** Pass. **Eph 3:5, 10;** Hv 2, 4, 2. τινὶ τὸ μυστήριον **Eph 1:9;** pass. **3:3.** περί τινος **Lk 2:17.** W. ὅτι foll. **1 Cor 12:3;** τινί τι, ὅτι **Gal 1:11.** W. indir. quest. foll. **Col 1:27;** Hv 4, 3, 1; m 8:2; s 2:5; 8, 3, 1. W. attraction of the relat. D 9:2f; 10:2. Abs. Hm 12, 1, 3. Pass. γνωριζέσθω πρὸς τ. θεόν *let* (your requests) *be made known to God* **Phil 4:6.** γνωρίζεσθαι εἰς πάντα τὰ ἔθνη *be made* known *among all the nations* **Ro 16:26.** Reflexive ἐγνωρίσθη Ἰωσὴφ τοῖς ἀδελφοῖς *J. made himself known to his brothers* **Ac 7:13 v.l.** (ἀνεγν. N., as in Gen 45:1; cp. Ruth 3:3).—In **1 Cor 15:1,** where apparently the discussion deals with someth. already known, γ. is nevertheless correctly used because of the instruction, which evidently introduces someth. new.

❷ to have information or be knowledgeable about someth., *know* (Dio Chrys. 4, 33; Plut., Coriol. 224 [23, 4]; Herodian 2, 1, 10; Achilles Tat. 7, 14, 1 and 3; Herm. Wr. 10, 15; POxy 705, 39; 1024, 18; 1643, 8. Λόγος τέλειος: PGM 3, 602ff; Pr 3:6; 15:10; Job 4:16 Sym. ἐγνώρισα=LXX ἐπέγνων; TestAbr A 6 p. 83, 4 [Stone p. 14]; 8 p. 86, 9 [Stone p. 20]; Philo, De Jos. 165, Conf. Ling. 183; Jos., Ant. 2, 97, Vi. 420; Just., D. 3, 2 γνωρίζεις με al.; 80, 2 'share a point of view'; Ath. 3:1 'note, recognize' of animals) w. indir. question foll.: τί αἱρήσομαι οὐ γ. *which I shall choose I do not know* **Phil 1:22.** Abs. (w. ἰδεῖν) Dg 8:5.—DELG s.v. γιγνώσκω p. 225. M-M. TW.

γνώριμος, ον (Pla.+; OGI 90, 53 [196 BC]; PCairZen 225, 4 [253 BC] al.; LXX; Just.; ParJer 5:7) ***acquainted with*** w. dat. of pers. (Pla., 7th Epistle, 324d γνώριμοι ἐμοί; PTebt 286, 6; 703, 55; Ruth 2:1; 4 Macc 5:4) **J 18:16 v.l.** παρὰ τῶν ἐκείνοις γνωρίμων *of those who were acquainted with them* (the apostles) Papias (2:2).—DELG s.v. γιγνώσκω p. 225.

γνῶσις, εως, ἡ (Pre-Socr. [s. Snell s.v. γνώμη], Thu.+; Herm. Wr., ins, pap, LXX; PsSol 9:3; TestSol C 10:42; Test12-Patr; ParJer 6:13; ApcSed 7:1; Philo; Jos., Ant. 8, 171, Vi. 239 al.; Just., Tat., Ath.; τὸ μὲν ξύλον τὸ τῆς γνώσεως Theoph. Ant. 2, 25 [p. 160, 1, of the 'tree of knowledge'])

❶ comprehension or intellectual grasp of someth., *knowledge* as possessed by God **Ro 11:33** and humans (Orig., C. Cels. 3, 59, 18; 6, 13, 26; Did., Gen. 113, 3) **1 Cor 8:1, 7, 10f** (Just., D. 1, 4 al.); κλεὶς τῆς γ. *key to knowledge* **Lk 11:52;** *grasp* of a piece of writing Hv 2, 2, 1 (cp. Just., D. 69, 1 τὴν ἐν ταῖς γραφαῖς γ.); ἀναγγέλλειν γ. *impart knowledge* 1 Cl 27:7 (Ps 18:2f). In B γ., besides ref. to content, refers specif. to understanding of the Scriptures: 6:9; 9:8. Mentioned w. other significant concepts **2 Cor 6:6; 2 Pt 1:5ff** (w. εὐσέβεια also Herm. Wr. 1, 27; 9, 4a); D 10:2; B 2:3; κατὰ γ. *knowledgeably* (as the context indicates, in awareness of female vulnerability and common Christian hope) **1 Pt 3:7** (BReicke, Bultmann Festschr., '54, 296–304: *with understanding*); γ. ἐξειπεῖν *utter profound Christian knowl.* 1 Cl 48:5; φωτισμὸς τῆς γ. *enlightening of the knowl.* **2 Cor 4:6.** τελεία καὶ ἀσφαλής 1 Cl 1:2. ἀθάνατος 36:2. θεία 40:1; τὸ τέλειον τῆς γ. *perfection of knowledge* B 13:7; cp. 1:5. W. λόγος (on this combination cp. the Λόγος τέλειος in PGM 3, 591–609) **1 Cor 1:5** (on πᾶσα γ. cp. Sir 21:14; **Ro 15:14; 1 Cor 13:2**); **2 Cor 8:7; 11:6;** w. σοφία **Col 2:3** (cp. Eccl 1:17; 2:26 al.). Although here γ. and σοφία are almost synonymous, Paul distinguishes betw. them **1 Cor 12:8;** he places γ. betw. ἀποκάλυψις and προφητεία **14:6,** and beside μυστήρια **13:2,** and thus invests the term w. the significance of extraordinary mystical knowledge, a mng. which the word has in H. Gk., esp. in the mystery cults (s. 2 below). Despite the fact that the text has the sg. **1 Cor 13:8,** the pl. γνώσεις (Lucian, Apol. 12) is fairly well attested as a v.l.—In an oxymoron: **Eph 3:19** γνῶναι … τὴν ὑπερβάλλουσαν τῆς γνώσεως ἀγάπην τοῦ Χριστοῦ *to comprehend the love of Christ, which transcends comprehension* (s. γινώσκω 3a).—Because of the frequent blend of abstract and concrete in the use of γ. in our lit. some of the passages cited above will fall under 2 and some in 2 may also apply here.

❷ the content of what is known, *knowledge, what is known* μόρφωσις τῆςγ. *embodiment of knowledge* in the law **Ro 2:20** (some would place this under 1; on γνῶσις among the Hellenistic Jews s. WBousset, NGG 1915, 466ff). Of Christians: γ. τοῦ θεοῦ (a formulation foreign to Gr-Rom. polytheism; obj. gen. as Wsd 2:13; 14:22; Philo, Deus Imm. 143; Just., D. 14, 1; Tat. 12, 4) **2 Cor 10:5;** IEph 17:2. πρὸς αὐτόν 2 Cl 3:1; γ. σωτηρίας **Lk 1:77;** ὁδοῦ δικαιοσύνης γ. B 5:4; γ. δογμάτων 10:10. τῶν δικαιωμάτων θεοῦ 21:5 (cp. Musonius p. 34, 9 γνῶσις δικαιοσύνης; 92, 10). Given by God B 19:1, and hence sharing in the heavenly fragrance (s. ὀσμή 2) **2 Cor 2:14.** W. διδαχή B 18:1. Paul had seen Christ the God-man, and the γ. Χριστοῦ Ἰησοῦ *personal acquaintance w. Christ Jesus* (IPontEux I, 47, 6f ἡ τ. Σεβαστῶν γ.=personal acquaintance w. the Augusti [Augustus and Tiberius]; Dssm., LO 324, 7 [LAE 383, 8]) was a matter of inestimable value for him **Phil 3:8.** Cp. the experience of the devotees in the mystery religions, in which mystical knowledge was intensified and issued in what was called a divine vision (Λόγος τέλ.=PGM 3, 591–609 [a slightly different restoration of the text is given in Rtzt., Mysterienrel.[3] 285–87 and Herm. Wr. 374–77

Scott] χάριν σοι οἴδαμεν, . . . ἄφραστον ὄνομα τετιμημένον τῇ τ. θεοῦ προσηγορίᾳ . . . , χαρισάμενος ἡμῖν νοῦν, λόγον, γνῶσιν . . . χαίρομεν, ὅτι σεαυτὸν ἡμῖν ἔδειξας, χαίρομεν ὅτι ἐν πλάσμασιν ἡμᾶς ὄντας ἀπεθέωσας τῇ σεαυτοῦ γνώσει 'we acknowledge our gratitude to you, . . . ineffable name, honored in address as God . . . ; having endowed us w. mind, reason, knowledge . . . we rejoice, for you have revealed yourself to us; we rejoice, for when we were in common clay you deified us through knowledge of yourself'; Plut., Mor. 352a ὧν τέλος ἐστὶν ἡ τοῦ πρώτου καὶ κυρίου καὶ νοητοῦ γνῶσις); on the expression cp. ἐν χάριτι καὶ γ. τοῦ κυρίου ἡμῶν καὶ σωτῆρος Ἰησοῦ Χριστοῦ **2 Pt 3:18.**—For lit. s. γινώσκω 7.

❸ **a dissident variety of knowledge, *knowledge*** ἀντιθέσεις τῆς ψευδωνύμου γνώσεως *the oppositions of so-called knowledge* **1 Ti 6:20** (cp. the title of Irenaeus' chief work, and Marcion's 'Antitheses'; on the latter s. WBauer, Rechtgläubigkeit u. Ketzerei '34, 229; MRist, JR 22, '42, 39ff; JKnox, Marcion and the NT '42, 73–76. The lack of knowledge about any clearly definable 'Gnostic' system as object of attack in 1 Ti suggests that the definition of γ. be left sufficiently general for this passage; s. MDibelius-HConzelmann, The Pastoral Epistles, Eng. tr. '72, 92). ἀλλοτρία γ. *strange* (=dissident) *knowledge* IPhld 3:3.—DELG s.v. γιγνώσκω p. 224. M-M. TW. Sv.

γνώστης, ου, ὁ (Plut., Flam. 370 [4, 3]; PLips 106, 10; 1 Km 28:3; SibOr fgm. 1, 4) **one who is knowledgeable about someth.,** *one acquainted with, expert in* (cp. the pap [III AD] in the Berlin Library in Dssm. LO 313, 1–2 [LAE 367] = Sb 421, if rightly restored by Dssm: ἐπεὶ γν[ω]στ[ὴς ἐγενόμην τοῦ]| εὐανγελ[ίο]υ; LXX) τῶν ἐθῶν **Ac 26:3.**—DELG s.v. γιγνώσκω p. 224. M-M.

γνωστός, ή, όν (Aeschyl. et al.; Pla., X.; SIG 800, 34; LXX; En 98:12; PsSol 14:8; ApcSed).

❶ **pert. to being familiar or known: *known*** (the usual mng. in LXX)—ⓐ of things: a *remarkable* miracle **Ac 4:16.** γνωστόν ἐστί τινι *it is known to someone* **2:14;** εἰς τὸ γ. εἶναι πᾶσιν *that it might be known to all* 1 Cl 11:2. W. ὅτι foll. (En 98:12) **Ac 4:10; 13:38; 28:28** (MWilcox, The Semitisms of Ac, '65, 90f). περὶ τῆς αἱρέσεως ταύτης γ. ἡμῖν ἐστιν *concerning this sect it is known to us* **28:22.** γνωστόν τινι ποιεῖν τι *make someth. known to someone* Hs 5, 5, 1. γνωστὸν γίνεσθαί τινι *become known to someone* **Ac 1:19; 19:17.** Abs. **9:42.**—κύριος (ὁ) ποιῶν ταῦτα γ. ἀπ' αἰῶνος *the Lord who makes this known from of old* **15:17f.**

ⓑ of pers.: γ. w. gen. or dat., subst. *acquaintance, friend, intimate* (4 Km 10:11; 2 Esdr 15:10; Ps 30:12; 54:14; 87:9, 19) **J 18:15f;** pl. (SibOr 1, 76) **Lk 23:49.** Abs. in **2:44.**

❷ **pert. to being able to be known, *capable of being known, intelligible*** (Pla.; Epict. 2, 20, 4; Gen 2:9; also prob. Sir 21:7; PLaur III, 60, 17 [restored]; Hippol., Ref. 6, 24, 4) γνωστὰ αὐτῷ γίνονται τὰ ῥήματα *the words become intelligible to him* Hs 5, 4, 3; τὸ γ. (PAmh 145, 9): τὸ γνωστὸν τοῦ θεοῦ *what can be known about God* or *God, to the extent that he can be known* (cp. Philo, Leg. All. 1, 60f) **Ro 1:19** (s. PSchjött, ZNW 4, 1903, 75–78; AKlöpper, ZWT 47, 1904, 169–80; HDaxer, Ro 1:18–2:10, diss. Rostock 1914, 4ff; AFridrichsen, ZNW 17, 1916, 159–68).—DELG s.v. γιγνώσκω p. 224. M-M. New Docs 4, 143. TW.

γογγύζω impf. ἐγόγγυζον; fut. γογγύσω Sir 10:25; D 4:7; 1 aor. ἐγόγγυσα (for Att. τονθορύζω/-ίζω 'mumble'; acc. to Phryn. 358 Lob. γ. and γογγυσμός are Ionic [denied by WSchmid, GGA 1895, 33f; defended by Thumb 215; PMelcher, De Sermone Epict., diss. Halle 1905, 61], in the pap since 241/239 BC [Nägeli 27], in lit. M. Ant. 2, 3, 3 al.; Lucian, Ocyp. 45; Epict., LXX; TestSol 8:12 P; 9:3; gener. to express oneself in low tones that are not readily distinguishable).

❶ **to express oneself in low tones of disapprobation, *grumble, murmur*** (M. Ant. 2, 3, 3; PPetr II, 9 [3], 9; III, 43 [3], 20) κατά τινος (Ex 16:7 A) *against someone* **Mt 20:11.** περί τινος *speak complainingly about someone* (Num 14:27) **J 6:41;** but περὶ αὐτοῦ can also be construed as a neuter =*about it,* as περὶ τούτου vs. **61.** πρός τινα (Ex 17:3) *against someone* **Lk 5:30.** μετ' ἀλλήλων *among yourselves* **J 6:43.** Abs. (Jdth 5:22; Sir 10:25) **1 Cor 10:10** (Num 14:2, 36); GPt 8:28; D 4:7; B 19:11.

❷ **to express oneself in low tones of affirmation, *speak secretly, whisper*** τὶ περί τινος **J 7:32.**—DELG. M-M. TW.

γογγυσμός, οῦ, ὁ (s. γογγύζω; γογγυσμός since Anaxandrides Com. [IV BC] fgm. 31; M. Ant. 9, 37, 1; Cat. Cod. Astr. VII 139, 11; PRossGeorg III, 2, 11 [III AD]; PCairMasp 159, 27 [VI AD]; LXX; TestJob 14:5; GrBar) **utterance made in a low tone of voice** (the context indicates whether the utterance is one of discontent or satisfaction), ***behind-the-scenes talk.***—Negative aspect: *complaint, displeasure,* expressed in murmuring: ἐγένετο γ. τινος πρός τινα *complaints arose fr. someone against someone* **Ac 6:1** (cp. PRossGeorg above: μή τις γονγυσμὸς καθ' ἡμῶν γένηται). χωρὶς γογγυσμῶν (ἄνευ γ. PsSol 5:13) *without complaining* **Phil 2:14;** cp. **1 Pt 4:9** (on the topic of ungrudging hospitality s. Athen. 8, 364). ῥῆμα γογγυσμοῦ *grumbling speech* B 3:5 (Is 58:9).—In ref. to both discontent and satisfaction: *secret talk, whispering* γ. περὶ αὐτοῦ ἦν πολύς *there was much secret discussion about him* **J 7:12** (some say Jesus is ἀγαθός; others, πλανᾷ τὸν ὄχλον).—Field, Notes 92. M-M. New Docs 4, 143f. TW.

γόγγυσος, ον (s. γογγύζω and γογγυσμός; Pr 16:28 Theod.; Herodian Gr. 1, 213, 19) ***complaining:*** subst. *grumbler* D 3:6.

γογγυστής, οῦ, ὁ (s. γογγύζω and γογγυσμός; Sym. Pr 26:22; Theod. Pr 26:20) **grumbler** γογγυσταὶ μεμψίμοιροι *fate-blaming grumblers* **Jd 16.**—TW.

γόης, ητος, ὁ orig. 'sorcerer, conjurer' (so Eur., Hdt.+; Diod. S. 5, 55, 3; 5, 64, 4; Plut., Mor. 407c; Lucian, Piscat. 25; Jos., C. Ap. 2, 145; 161; POxy 1011, 64; TestSol 19:3 B; Tat. 17:1.—Nägeli 14); in our lit. more in the sense ***swindler, cheat*** (s. esp. Lucian, Alex.; Dio Chrys. 15 [32], 11; Ael. Aristid. 28, 11 K.=49 p. 494 D.; Philo, Spec. Leg. 1, 315, Rer. Div. Her. 302; Jos., Bell. 4, 85, Ant. 20, 97; Apollonaretal., Berl. Gr. Pap. 11517 [II AD], ed. WSchubart, Her 55, 1920, 191, ln. 45 in the eyes of his opponent Apollo's prophet is a 'hungry γόης') of pers. who veer from correct instruction and lead others into error *impostors* **2 Ti 3:13.** πλάνη τῶν γοήτων Dg 8:4.—H-DBetz, Der Apostel Paulus u. die Sokratische Tradition '72, 19–39; THopfner in Pauly-W. XIV 1928, 373ff; FPfister, ibid. Suppl. IV 1924, 324ff.—B. 1495. DELG s.v. γοάω ('cry out in lamentation'). M-M. TW.

Γολγοθᾶ, ἡ always with acute accent in W-H. and t.r. for **Mt 27:33,** and for **Mk 15:22** N[25] Γολγοθάν.—(גָּלְגָּתָא? unusual formation fr. Aram. גֻּלְגַּלְתָּא=Hebr. גֻּלְגֹּלֶת 'skull' s. Wlh. on Mk 15:22; Dalman, Gramm.[2] 166; B-D-F §39, 6) ***Golgotha*** translated Κρανίου Τόπος ***Skull Place*** (name of an eminence near Jerusalem, used as a place of execution) **Mt 27:33; J 19:17** (unaccented in text). Acc. Γολγοθᾶν **Mk 15:22** (-ᾶ v.l.).—Dalman, Pj 9, 1913, 98ff; 16, 1920, 11ff, Orte[3] 364ff (Eng. tr. 346–81); JBoehmer, ZAW 34, 1914, 300ff, Studierstube 11, 1919, Suppl. 1ff; 21, 1929, 128–35; JHerrmann, StKr 88, 1916, 381ff; CSachsse, ZNW 19, 1920, 29–34; FBower, CQR 91, 1920,

106–38 (lit.); Wandel, StKr 94, 1922, 132–61; JJeremias, Golgotha 1926; Vincent-Abel, Jérusalem II 1926, 92ff; AParrot, D. Tempel v. Jerus., Golg. u. d. hl. Grab '56, 95ff; CKopp, Holy Places of the Gospels, '63, 374–88; BHHW I 584.

Γόμορρα, ων, τά (Heb. עֲמֹרָה; double ρ also AscIs 2:16; Just., D. 56, 23 Γομόρροις) and **ας, ἡ** (s. B-D-F §57; Mlt-H. 109; W-S. §6, 8b; Thackeray 168, 3) ***Gomorrah,*** name of a ruined city that lay in a depression now occupied by the Dead Sea; example of awesome divine punishment (Gen 19:24–29; TestLevi 14:6; ApcEsdr) **Mt 10:15; Mk 6:11 v.l.; Ro 9:29** (Is 1:9); **2 Pt 2:6; Jd 7** (Γόμορα P^{72} in the 2 last passages).—M-M.

γόμος, ου, ὁ (s. γέμω) **that which is carried by a conveyance, *load, freight*** (Aeschyl., Hdt. et al.; Ex 23:5; 4 Km 5:17) *cargo* of a ship (OGI 209 note 3; POxy 63, 6; 708, 3 and16) **Ac 21:3.** W. gen. of owner **Rv 18:11.** W. gen. of content (B-D-F §167; Rob. 499; O. Wilck II, 1010, 5; 1258, 3 γόμος ἀχύρου) γ. χρυσοῦ *a cargo of gold* vs. **12.**—DELG s.v. γέμω. M-M.

[γονεύς, έως, ὁ] in our lit. only pl. **οἱ γονεῖς, έων** acc. τοὺς γονεῖς (as Hyperid. 3, 6; Anton. Lib. 30, 3; OGI 731, 2 [c. 200 BC]; SIG 796b, 13 [c. 40 AD]; pap [Mayser I/2², '38, p. 30]; Pr 29:15; 4 Macc 2:10; TestSol 2:2; TestAbr B 2, p. 106, 12 [Stone p. 60]; TestLevi 13:4; TestZeb 1:3; JosAs; GrBar 4:17; ApcEsdr; Jos., Ant. 3, 92) ***parents*** (since Hom. Hymns and Hes.; ins, pap, LXX, EpArist; Demetr.: 722 fgm. 1, 1 Jac.; Philo, Joseph., Just.) **Mt 10:21; Mk 13:12** (Petosiris, fgm. 8, 8: when the sun presents a certain appearance, there will be στάσεις πατράσι πρὸς παῖδας καὶ τὸ ἀνάπαλιν as well as many other calamities [πόλεμοι, θόρυβοι etc.]); **Lk 2:27, 41, 43; 8:56; 18:29; 21:16; J 9:2f, 18, 20, 22f; Ro 1:30; 2 Cor 12:14; Eph 6:1; Col 3:20; 2 Ti 3:2; Tit 1:11 v.l.;** Hv 1, 3, 1; 2, 2, 2; GJs 8:1.—B. 104. DELG s.v. γίγνομαι p. 223. M-M.

γόνιμος, ον (also fem. -η) (Aristoph., Eur., Hippocr., pap, Philo, Joseph.) **pert. to being productive** (cp. γονή 'offspring') ***fruitful*** of birds and esp. of animals GJs 3:2 (3 times).—DELG s.v. γίγνομαι p. 223.

γόνυ, ατος, τό (Hom.+; Tat. 10, 2 Ἐν γόνασιν [astral figure]) ***knee*** τὰ παραλελυμένα γ. *the weakened knees* **Hb 12:12** (Is 35:3; PsSol 8:5.—Laud. Therap. 20 παραλύσεις γονάτων). τιθέναι τὰ γ. (Latinism: ponere genua, but s. Eur., Tr. 1307; B-D-F §5, 3b) *bend the knee* as a sign of respect for superiors (w. προσκυνεῖν) **Mk 15:19.** Sim. προσπίπτειν τοῖς γ. τινος (s. προσπίπτω 1) **Lk 5:8.** τιθέναι τὰ γ. as a posture in prayer (w. προσεύχεσθαι) **Lk 22:41; Ac 9:40; 20:36; 21:5;** Hv 1, 1, 3; 2, 1, 2; 3, 1, 5; cp. **Ac 7:60.** Also κάμπτειν τὰ γ. (1 Ch 29:20; 1 Esdr 8:70 al.) w. πρός τινα *before someone* **Eph 3:14.** W. dat. τῇ βάαλ *bow the knee before Baal* **Ro 11:4** (cp. 3 Km 19:18). ἔκλινεν τὰ γόνατα πρὸς τὸν δεσπότην GJs 20:2 (not pap). οὐκ ἔκλαυσαν οὐδὲ γό[νατα ἔκλι]ναν AcPl Ha 1, 31f.—Intr. (like Is 45:23) ἐμοὶ κάμψει πᾶν γόνυ *every knee shall bow to me* **Ro 14:11.** Sim. **Phil 2:10.**—Fig. κάμπτειν τὰ γ. τῆς καρδίας *bow the knees of the heart* (cp. Prayer of Manasseh [=Odes 12] 11) 1 Cl 57:1.—B. 243. M-M. TW.

γονυπετέω 1 aor. ptc. γονυπετήσας (Polyb. 15, 29, 9; 32, 25, 7; Heliod. 9, 11; PCairMasp 2 III, 20 [VI AD]; Hesychius= παρακαλεῖ) ***kneel down*** τινά *before someone in petition* (cp. Tacitus, Annals 11, 30; 12, 18) **Mt 17:14; Mk 10:17.** Abs. (Cornutus 12 p. 12, 7) **Mk 1:40;** *fall on one's knees* ἔμπροσθέν τινος **Mt 27:29.**

γοργός, ή, όν (trag. et al.; ins, pap, Lucian) ***vigorous, strenuous*** 1 Cl 48:5 (Lghtf.) as quoted (for ἁγνός) in Clem. Al., Strom. 1, 38, 8; 6, 65, 3. S. app. Bihlmeyer.

γοῦν (γε + οὖν) **marker of result, esp. from a cognitive process, *hence, then*** in later usage (Hyperid. 5, 2; Aeneas Tact. 154, 2 and numerous others in many places, e.g. 2 Macc 5:21 [οὖν codex A]; 4 Macc 2:2 al; TestSol; Jos., e.g. Ant. 15, 153; 16, 22; Just., Tat., Mel.—Ath. [2, 1; 6, 4 'in any event'] follows earlier usage, e.g. Demosth. 20, 16)=οὖν MPol 16:1; 17:2. Cp. Hs 8, 8, 2 v.l. B 16:3.

γραῖς, ιδος, ἡ (since Chariton 6, 1; Athanasius; PLond I, 125, 21 p. 124 [mag.; V AD]; prob. w. suggestion of wrinkled appearance, cp. γέρων) ***elderly/old woman*** AcPt (25f) Ox 849, 6 (Lat. text Aa I 73, 17 matrem ipsius).—On views in antiquity about aged women s. JLong, IJCT 2, '96, 327 n. 23 (lit.).—DELG s.v. γραῦς.

γράμμα, ατος, τό (s. γράφω; Aeschyl., Hdt.+).—**❶ a unit of an alphabet,** in our lit. only of a Greek character: ***letter*** (Ps.-Aristot., Mirabilia 133 ἐπιγραφὴ ἀρχαίοις γράμμασιν an inscription in old-fashioned letters; Diod. S. 2, 13, 2 a rock-cut inscription Συρίοις γράμμασιν; Procop. Soph., Ep. 28; Lev 19:28; Jos., Bell. 5, 235, Ant. 3, 178; Tat. 9, 3 al.) **Lk 23:38 v.l.** (UPZ 108, 30 [99 BC] official placard in Gk. and Egypt. script. Naturally script and language coincide, as plainly in Diod. S. 19, 23, 3 ἡ ἐπιστολὴ Συρίοις γεγραμμένη γράμμασιν=the letter was written in the Syrian language); **2 Cor 3:7** (CHickling, NTS 21, '74/75, 380–95); **Gal 6:11** (cp. Plut., Cato Maj. 348 [20, 7] συγγράψαι ἰδίᾳ χειρὶ κ. μεγάλοις γράμμασιν; PHib 29, 9 [265 BC]). Letter as a numeral B 9:7f. μεταγράφεσθαι πρὸς γ. *copy letter for letter* Hv 2, 1, 4. δι' ὀλίγων γραμμάτων *in a few lines,* IRo 8:2; IPol 7:3.

❷ a set of written characters forming a document or piece of writing, *a document, piece of writing,* mostly in pl., even of single copies (Appian, Hann. 52 §221 al.; Polyaenus 7, 7; 7, 19; Alciphr. 4, 15; 4, 16, 1; pap; 1 Esdr 3:9, 13f; Esth 8:5, 10 al.; Jos., Ant. 7, 137; 8, 50 al.).

ⓐ a piece of correspondence *letter, epistle* (since Hdt. 5, 14; PGrenf I, 30, 5 [103 BC]; PAmh 143, 10; 1 Macc 5:10; EpArist 43.—γράμματα of a single letter: Diod. S. 13, 93, 1; GDI 4566, 10 [Laconia]; Sb 7995, 17; 7997, 3) **Ac 28:21;** Pol 13:1.

ⓑ a promissory *note* (Jos., Ant. 18, 156; PTebt 397, 17; cp. βιβλίον in **Rv 5:1** and see ORoller, ZNW 36, '37, 98–113) **Lk 16:6f.**

ⓒ a relatively long written publication *writing, book* (Ael. Aristid. 46, 41 K.=3 p. 46 D.: ἀσεβῆ γράμματα; Arrian, Peripl. 19, 4 ἐν πολλοῖς γράμμασιν; Biogr. p. 29 δύο γράμματα; Esth 6:1; Just., A I, 2, 3) of the books of Moses **J 5:47.** Of the OT gener. ἱερὰ γράμματα (in the same sense τὰ ἱερ. γ.: Philo, Mos. 2, 290; 292, Praem. 79, Leg. ad Gai. 195; Jos., Ant. 1, 13; 10, 210, C. Ap. 1, 54. Cp. OGI 56, 36 [339 BC] τῇ ἡμέρᾳ, ἐν ᾗ ἐπιτέλλει τὸ ἄστρον τὸ τῆς Ἴσιος, ἣ νομίζεται διὰ τῶν ἱερῶν γραμμάτων νέον ἔτος εἶναι, and the description of imperial letters as ἱερὰ or θεῖα γράμματα in Dssm., LO 321f [LAE 380]) **2 Ti 3:15** (because of the technical character of the expression no article is needed; cp. Philo, Rer. Div. Her. 106 ἐν ἱεραῖς γραφαῖς; 159, Poster. Cai. 158; Ro 1:2;16:26; 2 Pt 1:20).—Of the literally correct form of the law **Ro 2:27** (BSchneider, CBQ 15, '53, 163–207, 'Book of the Law' in contrast to the more general referents for γράμματα and γραφή, s. esp. 188–91). Opp. spirit (cp. Pla., Gorg. 484a.—Heraclitus, Ep. 9, 2 opp. γ. . . . θεός. Ps.-Archytas [IV BC] in Stob., Ecl. 4, 135 ed. Hense, IV p. 82, 21: νόμος ὁ μὲν ἔμψυχος βασιλεύς, ὁ δὲ ἄψυχος γράμμα=the law, if it is alive, is indeed king; but if it is lifeless, it is nothing but a letter.—Romualdus, Stud. Cath. 17, '41, 18–32) **Ro 2:29; 7:6; 2 Cor 3:6.**

❸ pl. ***learning, knowledge.*** The mng. of γράμματα **J 7:15** is connected w. 1 above; γ. without the article used w. a verb like ἐπίστασθαι, εἰδέναι means *elementary knowledge* esp. reading and writing (X., Mem. 4, 2, 20; Dio Chrys. 9 [10], 28; SIG[2] 844, 6. Very oft. in pap: POxy 264, 19; 275, 43; 485, 48; PFay 24, 21; 91, 45; PGen 8, 31; 9, 27; Is 29:12; Da 1:4; Jos., Ant. 12, 209; s. ἀγράμματος; J 7:15 therefore implies an evaluation of social status). On the other hand, τὰ γ. can also mean *higher learning* (X., Cyr. 1, 2, 6; Pla., Apol. 26d; Aristoxenus, fgm. 31 p. 16, 29: Pythagoras γράμματα ἐν Κορίνθῳ ἐδίδασκε; Sext. Emp., Gramm. 1, 2, 48 γραμμάτων ἔμπειρον . . . , τουτέστιν οὐ τ. στοιχείων, ἀλλὰ τ. συγγραμμάτων; PLond I, 43, 3 [II BC]; Da 1:4; EpArist 121; TestReub 4:1, TestLevi 13:2) **Ac 26:24.**—Field, Notes 92f; Goodsp., Probs. 102–4.—B. 1285; 1286. DELG s.v. γράφω. M-M. EDNT. TW.

γραμματεύς, έως, ὁ (Thu., X.+) gener., one who has special functions in connection with documents.

❶ **chief executive officer of a governmental entity, *secretary (of state), clerk,*** title of a high official in Ephesus (32nd letter of Apollonius of Tyana [Philostrat. I 352, 7] Ἐφεσίων γ.; γραμματεὺς τοῦ δήμου IBM III/2, 482 B, 5; 500, 11; 528, 4; OGI 493, 11; FImhoof-Blumer, Kleinas. Münzen 1901, p. 55 nos. 46; 47 al. Cp. Schulthess in Pauly-W. VII/2, 1747ff) **Ac 19:35.**

❷ **an expert in matters relating to divine revelation,**

ⓐ specialists in the law of Moses: ***experts in the law, scholars versed in the law, scribes;*** mentioned together w. high priests (s. ἀρχιερεύς), w. whom and the elders (oft. referred to in the same context) their representatives formed the Sanhedrin (Just., D. 76, 7 ὑπο τῶν γ. καὶ φαρισαίων; 100, 3 ὑπὸ τῶν φ. καὶ γ.) **Mt 2:4; 16:21; 20:18; 21:15; 27:41; Mk 8:31; 10:33; 11:18, 27; 14:1, 43, 53; 15:1, 31;** GPt 8:31 al. W. the Pharisees **Mt 5:20** (Just., D. 105, 6); **12:38; 15:1; 23:2, 13ff; Mk 2:16; 7:1, 5; Ac 23:9.** Ἄννας ὁ γρ. GJs 15:1 (cp. 15:2). W. σοφός: ποῦ γρ.; *where is the expert in the law?* **1 Cor 1:20.**—Schürer II 322–80; Billerb. I 79–82; 691–95; II 647–61; JJeremias, Jerusalem z. Zt. Jesu II A, 1924, 27–32 and B/1, 1929, 101–14; 122–27; GKilpatrick, JTS 1, '50, 56–60.

ⓑ interpreter of teaching connected with the ministry of Jesus, ext. of 2a ***scribe, instructor*** (cp. Lucian, M. Peregr. 11: Χριστιανῶν γραμματεῖς in Palestine) **Mt 13:52** (Jülicher, Gleichn. 128–33) and most prob. 23:34 (JHoh, D. christl. γρ.: BZ 17, 1926, 256–69).—BHHW III, 1736f. DELG s.v. γράφω. M-M. EDNT. TW.

Γραπτή, ῆς, ἡ (pref. accent Γράπτη, cp. Schwyzer I 420; PKatz, TLZ 83, '58, 316, n. 13.—Jos., Bell. 4, 567; Mélanges de la Faculté Orientale de l'Université de Beyrouth VII [1914–21] p. 4 no. 3 Μειδύλος Γραπτῇ; Kaibel 517d; MAMA III '31, no. 794) ***Grapte,*** name of a Christian Hv 2, 4, 3.

γραπτός, ή, όν (Eur. et al.; ins, pap) **pert. to being set down in writing, *written*** (so Gorgias, fgm. B 11a [Palamedes] 30 [V BC]; PPetr III, 21g, 38; PAmh 78, 17; cp. EpArist 56; LXX; Just., A I, 19, 2) τὸ ἔργον τ. νόμου γραπτὸν ἐν τ. καρδίαις **Ro 2:15** (cp. 1QH 18:27f 'write on the heart'. Similarly Plut., Mor. 780c; TestJud 20:3 v.l.).—DELG s.v. γράφω. M-M.

γραφεῖον, ου, τό (Aristot. et al.; ins, pap) prim. a pencil or other writing instrument, then also ***the thing written, writing.*** In eccl. usage the pl. somet. designated the third part of the Hebr. canon, also called ἁγιόγραφα. 1 Cl 28:2 may be an early example of this usage (s. Knopf, Hdb. ad loc.).—DELG s.v. γράφω.

γραφή, ῆς, ἡ (s. γράφω; trag., Hdt.+) gener. that which is written: 'writing'.

❶ **a brief piece of writing, *writing*** (γ.=piece of writing: Diod. S. 1, 91, 3 price-list; Maximus Tyr. 16, 1b indictment; GDI 4689, 49 and 58 [Messenia]; PHib 78, 18; 1 Ch 28:19; 1 Macc 14:27; Tat. 38, 1) Hv 2, 2, 1.

❷ **sacred scripture,** in the NT exclusively so—ⓐ ἡ γ. individual ***scripture passage*** (4 Macc 18:14; Philo, Rer. Div. Her. 266; Just., D. 65, 2 al.; Mel., P. 1, 3.—S. also TestNapht 5:8 γραφὴ ἁγία of a written word of a divine sort outside the Bible) **Mk 12:10; 15:28 v.l.; Lk 4:21; J 13:18; 19:24, 36f; Ac 1:16; 8:35; Ro 11:2; 2 Ti 3:16; Js 2:8, 23;** 1 Cl 23:3.

ⓑ ***scripture in its entirety*—α.** the pl. αἱ γραφαί designates collectively all the parts of Scripture: *the scriptures* (Philo, Fug. 4, Spec. Leg. 1, 214 αἱ ἱεραὶ γ.; Rer. Div. Her. 106; 159; Jos., C. Ap. 2, 45 τ. τῶν ἱερῶν γραφῶν βίβλοις; Just., D. 68, 8; 137, 3 al.; Did., Gen. 70, 13: θεῖαι γ.) **Mt 21:42; 22:29; 26:54; Mk 12:24; 14:49; Lk 24:27, 32, 45; J 5:39; Ac 17:2, 11; 18:24, 28; Ro 15:4; 2 Pt 3:16;** PtK 2 p. 15, 4; αἱ γ. τῶν προφητῶν *the writings of the prophets* **Mt 26:56** (cp. αἱ τῶν προφητῶν τοῦ θεοῦ καὶ τῶν ἀποστόλων τοῦ Ἰησοῦ γ. Orig. C. Cels. 5, 5, 10). αἱ ἱεραὶ γ. 1 Cl 45:2; 53:1 (s. Philo and Joseph. above); γ. ἅγιαι **Ro 1:2** (Just., D. 55, 3); προφητικαί **16:26** (Just., D. 85, 5 γ. προφητικῶν; on the absence of the art. in both Ro passages and 2 Pt 1:20 [β next] s. γράμμα 2c).

β. the sg. as designation of Scripture as a whole (Philo, Mos. 2, 84; EpArist 155; 168; cp. 1 Ch 15:15; 2 Ch 30:5, 18; Just., Mel; ἡ θεία γ. Theoph. Ant. 2, 10 [p. 122, 33]; Did., Gen. 71, 15) **Ac 8:32; J 20:9; 2 Pt 1:20** (s. bα above); εἶπεν ἡ γ. **J 7:38, 42;** λέγει **Ro 4:3; 9:17; 10:11; Gal 4:30; 1 Ti 5:18; Js 4:5;** 1 Cl 23:5; 34:6; 35:7; 42:5; 2 Cl 2:4; 6:8; 14:1f; B 4:7, 11; 5:4; 6:12; 13:2, also 16:5 in a quot. fr. En 89:56ff (Just., D. 123, 1 al.); περιέχει ἐν γ. **1 Pt 2:6;** πεπλήρωται, ἐπληρώθη ἡ γ. **J 17:12;** cp. **19:28 v.l.;** πιστεύειν τῇ γ. **J 2:22;** οὐ δύναται λυθῆναι ἡ γ. *scripture cannot be set aside* **10:35.** W. Scripture personified: προϊδοῦσα ἡ γ. *scripture foresaw* **Gal 3:8.** συνέκλεισεν ὑπὸ ἁμαρτίαν vs. **22.**—κατὰ τὴν γ. (w. ref. to a contract CPR I, 224, 6 [Dssm., NB 78=BS 112f]; PAmh 43, 13; 2 Ch 30:5; 35:4; 1 Esdr 1:4) **Js 2:8;** κατὰ τὰς γ. (BGU 136, 10 κατὰ γ. w. ref. to the laws) *according to* (the prophecy of) *the holy scriptures* **1 Cor 15:3f** (Just., D. 82, 4) ἄτερ γραφῆς *without scriptural proof* PtK 4 p. 16, 6.—JHänel, D. Schriftbegriff Jesu 1919, 13ff; Harnack, D. AT in d. paul. Briefen u. in d. paul. Gemeinden: SBBerlAk 1928, 124–41; OMichel, Pls u. s. Bibel 1929; HvanCampenhausen, D. Entstehung d. christl. Bibel '68. S. νόμος, end.—'Scripture' in the early Christian period always means the OT, and only after some passage of time was this term used in ref. to the writings of the NT. Quotation of the Gospels as such begins to make its appearance in Justin, but concern for literal accuracy is first to be found in Irenaeus. In general, the authors of our lit. quote the Gospels with as little care for precision as that exhibited e.g. by Maximus Tyr. in his citation of 'the ancients' (KDürr, Philol. Suppl. VIII 1900, 150f). The close acquaintance of Christians with Scripture has its parallels in the familiarity of the Greeks with Homer. Heraclit. Sto. I p. 2 ln. 3ff: ἐκ πρώτης ἡλικίας a child is trained on Homer and is to be occupied to the end of life with his epics.—DELG s.v. γράφω. M-M. EDNT. TW. Sv.

γράφω impf. ἔγραφον; fut. γράψω; 1 aor. ἔγραψα; pf. γέγραφα; 1 pl. γεγραφήκαμεν 2 Macc 1:7 v.l. Pass.: 2 aor.

ἐγράφην; pf. γέγραμμαι; 3 sg. plpf. ἐγέγραπτο LXX (Hom.+) 'write'.

❶ **to inscribe characters on a surface, *write*** (X., Mem. 4, 2, 20; Demosth. 9, 41; Just., D. 46, 5 γεγραμμένων χαρακτήρων) πηλίκοις γράμμασιν ἔγραψα **Gal 6:11** (ἔγραψα as epistolary aorist, as Ps.-Callisth. 2, 19, 2, at the beginning of a letter ἔγραψα σοι=I am writing to you). οὕτως γράφω *this is my handwriting* of one's own signature **2 Th 3:17;** cp. **Phlm 19** (on the conclusion of a letter in one's own hand ORoller, D. Formular d. paul. Briefe '33).—**J 8:6 v.l., 8** (s. καταγράφω).

❷ **to express thought in writing—ⓐ** of brief statements ***write*** w. λέγων foll. (4 Km 10:6; Da 6:26; 1 Macc 8:31; 11:57.—EKieckers, IndogF 35, 1915, 34ff) ἔγραψεν λέγων· Ἰωάννης ἐστὶν ὄνομα αὐτοῦ *he wrote, 'His name is John'* **Lk 1:63.** μὴ γράφε· ὁ βασιλεύς **J 19:21.** γράψον· μακάριοι **Rv 14:13.** ἐπιγραφὴν ἐπί τινι **Lk 23:38 v.l.** τὶ ἐπί τι (Dt 4:13; 6:9; 10:2; Pr 3:3 v.l.) **Rv 2:17; 19:16.** τὶ ἐπί τινα **3:12.** ἐπί τινος (Ex 34:1; 36:37; Da 5:5) **14:1.**

ⓑ of pronouncements and solemn proceedings ***write down, record:*** a vision **Rv 1:19;** commandments, parables Hv 5:5f. ταῦτα πάντα 5:7. εἰς βιβλίον (Tob 12:20) **Rv 1:11.** Pass. ἐν τ. βιβλίῳ **J 20:30;** of the book of life ἐν τῷ β. (τῇ β.), ἐπὶ τὸ β. **Rv 13:8; 17:8; 20:15; 21:27;** cp. **20:12; 22:18f** (s. EpArist 311). Esp. freq. is the perf. γέγραπται (abundantly attested as a legal expr.: Dssm., B 109f, NB 77f [BS 112ff, 249f]; Thieme 22. Cp. also 2 Esdr 20:35, 37; Job 42:17a; Jos., Vi. 342) as a formula introducing quotations fr. the OT (cp. Jos., C. Ap. 1, 154) **Mt 4:4, 6f, 10; 21:13; Mk 11:17; 14:27; Lk 4:8; 19:46.** ὡς γέγραπται (SIG 45, 44; Inschr. d. Asklepieion von Kos A, 14 ed. RHerzog, ARW 10, 1907, 401; Just., D. 56, 8; 86, 5 al.) **Mk 7:6.** καθὼς γέγραπται (SIG 736, 44 [92 BC]; CPR I,154, 11; cp. 1 Esdr 3:9; Da 9:13 Theod.; 2 Ch 23:18) **Mk 1:2; Ac 15:15; Ro 1:17; 2:24; 3:4, 10; 4:17; 8:36; 9:13, 33; 10:15; 11:8;** 1 Cl 48:2 al. οὕτως γέγραπται 1 Cl 17:3. καθάπερ γέγραπται (PCauer, Delectus Inscr.[2] 1883, 457, 50f [III BC]; IPergamon 251, 35 [II BC]; oft. in pap, e.g. PRev 29, 9 [258 BC] καθάπερ ἐν τ. νόμῳ γέγρ.); as v.l. in **Ro 3:4; 9:13; 10:15;** and **11:8.** γέγραπται γάρ **12:19; 14:11; 1 Cor 1:19;** 1 Cl 36:3; 39:3; 46:2; 50:4, 6. γεγραμμένον ἐστίν **J 2:17; 6:31, 45; 10:34** (γεγραμμένον ἐν τῷ νόμῳ as 2 Esdr 18:14. Cp. Inschr. d. Asklepieion [s. above] ln. 9 τὰ γεγραμμένα ἐν τοῖς ἱεροῖς νόμοις; Just., D. 8, 4 τὰ ἐν τῷ νόμῳ γ.; 57, 3 γ. ἐστίν, so also w. acc. and inf. 79, 2); **12:14.** ὁ λόγος ὁ γεγραμμένος (cp. 4 Km 23:24; 1 Ch 29:29; 2 Ch 16:11) **1 Cor 15:54.** κατὰ τὸ γ. (SIG[2] 438, 13 and 84; SIG 955, 22f; 1016, 6 al.; PEleph 2, 13 [285 BC]; 2 Esdr 3:4; 18:15; cp. 1 Esdr 1:12; Bar 2:2) **2 Cor 4:13.** ἐγράφη **Ro 4:23; 1 Cor 9:10; 10:11.** W. a specif. ref. (4 Km 14:6; 2 Ch 23:18; 1 Esdr 1:12; Da 9:13; Just., D. 34, 6 and 8; 79, 4. Cp. Diod. S. 9, 30 ὡς γέγραπται ἐν τῷ περὶ διαδοχῆς βασιλέων=in the book of the succession of kings; Philod., Περὶ εὐσεβ. p. 61 Gomp. ἐν τοῖς ἀναφερομένοις εἰς Μουσαῖον γέγραπται; Ael. Aristid. 33 p. 618 D.: γέγραπται γὰρ ἐν αὐτῇ [a peace treaty]; 34 p. 654): in the book of Psalms **Ac 1:20;** in the second Psalm **13:33;** in the book of the prophets **7:42;** in Isaiah **Mk 1:2** (cp. 2 Ch 32:32); in the Decalogue B 15:1. Also of noncanonical apocalypses: (Diod. S. 34+35, fgm. 33, 2 ἐν τοῖς τῆς Σιβύλλης χρησμοῖς εὑρέθη γεγραμμένον ὅτι κτλ.): Eldad and Modat Hv 2, 3, 4; Enoch B 4:3, cp. 16:6. Of dominical words 4:14; 14:6 (JFitzmyer, NTS 7, '60/61, 297–333). Pilate's official pronouncement bears the mark of administrative parlance: ὃ γέγραφα, γέγραφα *what I have written I have written,* i.e., it will not be changed (on the pf. cp. the expr. taken over fr. the Romans κέκρικα=I have decided once for all Epict. 2, 15, 5. Pilate's action means that Caesar has spoken, Dig. Just. 1, 19, 1. For the repetition of the same form of the pf. s. Gen 43:14; for the repetition of the word γ. see Aeschrion Iamb. [IV BC] 6, 9 [Diehl[3], '52, fasc. 3, p. 122] ἔγραψεν ὅσσ' ἔγραψ'.) **J 19:22.** Cp. the solemn tone **Rv 5:1** (s. Ezk 2:10) βιβλίον γεγραμμένον ἔσωθεν καὶ ὄπισθεν *a scroll covered w. writing inside and on the back.*—W. acc. of pers. or thing (Bar 1:1; Tob 7:13 S; 1 Esdr 2:25 al.): *write about someone* or *someth.* ὃν ἔγραψεν Μωϋσῆς *about whom Moses wrote* **J 1:45;** of righteousness **Ro 10:5.** Also περί τινος (Diod. S. 2, 36, 3; 14, 96, 3; 1 Esdr 2:17; Esth 1:1p; 1 Macc 11:31) **Mt 26:24; Mk 14:21; J 5:46; Ac 13:29** (on ἐτέλεσαν τὰ γεγραμμένα cp. Diod. S. 14, 55, 1 and Just., D. 8, 4 ποιεῖν τὰ γεγρ.). ἐπί τινα *w. reference to someone* **Mk 9:12f;** ἐπί τινι **J 12:16.** τὰ γεγραμμένα διὰ τ. προφητῶν τῷ υἱῷ τ. ἀνθρώπου **Lk 18:31** (on διὰ τ. π. cp. Esth 8:10 [= ὑπό 9:1]; the dat. designating the pers. written *about* is made easier to understand by ref. to 3 Macc 6:41; 1 Esdr 4:47). W. ὅτι foll. (cp. X., An. 2, 3, 1; Just., D. 49, 5 al.) **Mk 12:19; Ro 4:23; 1 Cor 9:10.**—In a traditional formulation: μὴ ὑπὲρ ἃ γέγραπται *not beyond what has been written* **1 Cor 4:6** (s. ὑπέρ B).

ⓒ of correspondence *write (to) someone* τινί (Plut., Pomp. 634 [29, 3]; pap; 1 Macc 12:22; 2 Macc 2:16; Da 6:26; ParJer; Jos., Ant. 12, 16; Mel., HE 4, 26, 10) **Ro 15:15; 2 Cor 2:4, 9 v.l.; 7:12; Phlm 21; 2 Pt 3:15; 1J 2:12ff.** δι' ὀλίγων *briefly, a few lines* **1 Pt 5:12.** διὰ μέλανος καὶ καλάμου *w. pen and ink* **3J 13** (cp. ParJer 6:19). The content of the writing is quoted: **Rv 2:1, 8, 12, 18; 3:1, 7, 14;** *write someth. to someone* τινί τι (Plut., Cic. 879 [37, 1]; pap; 1 Macc: 10:24; 11:29; 13:35) **1 Cor 14:37; 2 Cor 1:13; Gal 1:20; 3J 9.** τινί τι περί τινος (1 Macc 11:31) **Ac 25:26; 1J 2:26.** τινὶ περί τινος (1 Macc 12:22; Jos., Vi. 62; Mel., HE 4, 26, 10) **2 Cor 9:1; 1 Th 4:9; 5:1; Jd 3.** περὶ δὲ ὧν ἐγράψατε (μοι v.l.) *as to the matters about which you wrote (me)* **1 Cor 7:1** (Pla., Ep. 13 p. 361a περὶ δὲ ὧν ἐπέστελλές μοι; Socrat., Ep. 7, 1 ὑπὲρ ὧν γράφεις); γ. τινί *give someone directions in writing* w. inf. foll. **Ac 18:27;** also w. ὅπως **ibid.** D.—γ. διά τινος signifies either that the person referred to in the διά-phrase participated in writing the document (Dionys. of Cor. in Eus., HE 4, 23, 11; cp. IG XIV, 956B, 10f ὑπογράψαντες διὰ τοῦ ἀδελφοῦ ἡμῶν) **1 Pt 5:12,** as some comm. hold, or that this person is its bearer IRo 10:1; IPhld 11:2; ISm 12:1; Pol 14. The latter mng. obtains in διὰ χειρός τινος **Ac 15:23.**

ⓓ of literary composition *compose, write* βιβλίον (Jer 39:25, 44; Mal 3:16; 2 Ch 32:17; Tat. 36, 2 Ἰόβας Περὶ Ἀσσυρίων γράφων) **Mk 10:4** (Dt 24:1, 3); **J 21:25b;** δύο βιβλαρίδια Hv 2, 4, 3. τίτλον **J 19:19.** ἐπιστολήν (SIG 679, 19f; 1 Macc 13:35; 2 Macc 9:18; 3 Macc 3:11; 6:41; ParJer 7:24; Just., A I, 68, 6 [Hadrian]) **Ac 23:25** (cp. 3 Macc 3:30); **2 Pt 3:1.** In a wider sense: ἐντολήν (4 Km 17:37) *give a written commandment, fix a comm. in writing* **Mk 10:5; 1J 2:7f; 2J 5.**—FHitchcock, The Use of γράφειν: JTS 31, 1930, 271–75.—B. 1283. DELG. M-M. TW. Sv.

γραώδης, ες (γραῦς 'elderly/old woman' + -ώδης s. γραΐς; Chrysipp.: Stoic. II 255; Strabo 1, 2, 3 γ. μυθολογία; Cleom. 2, 1 p. 162, 14. μυθαρίῳ γραώδει πιστεύσας; Galen; Heliod.; on the Lat. anicula, s. APease, Ciceronis De Natura Deorum, '55, I 341 n.) ***characteristic of an elderly woman*** of speculative or legendary accounts that lack Christian pedagogical value **1 Ti 4:7** (cp. γραῶν ὕθλος 'gossip of elderly women' Pla., Theat. 176b; γραολογία Tat. 3, 2 of Pherecydes' cosmology; cp. Tibullus 1, 3, 83–85 story-teller; 'anilis superstitio' Cicero, De Domo 105. VRosivach, Classical World 88, '94, 113; JLong, IJCT 2, '96, 327 n. 23 [lit. on views of older women]). DELG s.v. γραῦς.

γρηγορέω (on this new formation in H. Gk. fr. ἐγρήγορα, the pf. of ἐγείρω [Herm. Wr.; Achilles Tat. 4, 17, 3; Cyril of Scyth. p.

80, 19; Phryn. 118 Lob.], found also PSI 1413, 9; LXX; PsSol 3:2; JosAs 10:2; Jos., Ant. 11, 47; TestBenj 10:1 [Thackeray 263; Helbing 82; 84] s. B-D-F §73; Nägeli 44; Mlt-H. 386; PKatz, Philo's Bible 160) fut. γρηγορήσω Jer 38:28; 1 aor. ἐγρηγόρησα.

❶ **to stay awake,** ***be watchful*** (Herm. Wr. 11, 21b; 1 Macc 12:27; 2 Esdr 17:3) **Mt 24:43; 26:38, 40; Mk 13:34; 14:34, 37; Lk 12:37, 39 v.l.**

❷ **to be in constant readiness** ***be on the alert*** (fig. ext. of 1; cp. Bar 2:9 al.; cp. our 'keep one's eyes open') **Mt 24:42; 25:13; 26:41; Mk 13:35, 37; 14:38; Ac 20:31; 1 Cor 16:13; 1 Th 5:6; 1 Pt 5:8; Rv 3:2f; 16:15;** IPol 1:3. ὑπὲρ τῆς ζωῆς *be vigilant for your life* D 16:1. Of alertness in prayer γρηγοροῦντες ἐν αὐτῇ (=προσευχῇ) *be wide awake about it* **Col 4:2**

❸ **to remain fully alive,** ***be alive*** (opp. to be dead, fig. ext. of 1) γ. and καθεύδω, *be alive* and *be dead* **1 Th 5:10** (this opposition develops in association w. the popular consolatory motif of death as a sleep, s. καθεύδω 3). S. ἐγρηγορέω.—DELG s.v. ἐγείρω. M-M.

γρόνθος, ου, ὁ =πυγμή 'clenched hand' (Moeris p. 323 πύξ Ἀττικῶς, γ. Ἑλληνικῶς; schol. on Il. 219; PAmh 141, 10 [IV AD]; Aq. Ex 21:18, Judg 3:16, Is 58:4) ***fist*** γ. ἀντὶ γρόνθου *blow for blow* Pol 2:2.—DELG.

γρύζω 1 aor ἔγρυξα, inf. γρύξαι (Aristoph.; Herodas 3, 37; 85; Dio Chrys. 13 [7], 26; Ael. Aristid. 35 p. 676 D. al.; Ex 11:7; Josh 10:21; Jdth 11:19) to say γρῦ: ***mutter, complain*** (w. στενάζειν, as Eus., HE 5, 1, 51) MPol 2:2.—DELG s.v. γρῦ.

γυμνάζω pf. pass. ptc. γεγυμνασμένος (s. γυμνός; Aeschyl. et al.; ins, pap; 2 Macc 10:15; Philo; Joseph.; SibOr 3, 230; Ath., R. 56, 14; Hippol., Ref. 4, 15, 1) commonly in literature of gymnastic exercises in the nude: 'exercise naked, train'; but also fig. of mental and spiritual powers: ***to train, undergo discipline*** (Isocr., Ad Nicocl. 10; Ps.-Isocr., 1. 21 Ad Demonicum γύμναζε σεαυτὸν πόνοις ἑκουσίοις; Epict.; SIG 578, 28; Did., Gen. 237, 9) τινί *in* or *by someth.* (Ps.-Isocr. [s. above]; Philo, De Jos. 26; Jos., Ant. 3, 15) τῷ νῦν βίῳ *train oneself by the present life* (w. ἀθλέω) 2 Cl 20:2. Also διά τινος (Philo, Sacrif. Abel. 78) **Hb 12:11;** γ. (τινὰ) πρός τι (Epict. 2, 18, 27; 3, 12, 7 al.; Philo, Mos. 1, 48) **5:14.** γύμναζε σεαυτὸν πρὸς εὐσέβειαν **1 Ti 4:7.** καρδία γεγυμνασμένη πλεονεξίας *a heart trained in greed* **2 Pt 2:14** (cp. Philostrat., Her. 2:15 θαλάττης οὔπω γεγ.).—DELG s.v. γυμνός. M-M. TW.

γυμνασία, ας, ἡ (since Pla., Leg. 648c; SIG 1073, 19; 4 Macc 11:20) ***training*** ἡ σωματικὴ γ. *of the body* **1 Ti 4:8.**—M-M. TW.—DELG s.v. γυμνός.

γυμνητεύω s. γυμνιτεύω.—Dio Chrys. 75 (25), 3; Cass. Dio 47, 34, 2; Tat. 20, 3; Plut., Aem. 263 [16, 8] Z. w. v.l. γυμνιτεύω; PRossGeorg III, 28, 8 (here γυμνιεύοντα for γυμνιτεύοντα). The same sentence that contains γυμνητεύω in HSchenkl, Pythagoreerspr. 17 (WienerStud 8, 1886 p. 266) and Porphyr., Ad Marcellam 33 N., has the spelling γυμνιτεύω in Demophilus, Sent. 8 (JOrelli, Opuscula Gr. Vet. Sententiosa I 1819 p. 38). B-D-F §24; Mlt-H. 72; 399. DELG s.v. γυμνός.

γυμνιτεύω (γυμνητεύω v.l.) ***be poorly clothed*** (so Dio Chrys. 75 [25], 3) **1 Cor 4:11.**

γυμνός, ή, όν (Hom.+; also s. Just. A I, 37, 8 γυμνὸν σκέπε [ref. Is 58:7]; Mel.)

❶ **pert. to being without covering—ⓐ** lit. ***naked, stripped, bare*** (PFay 12, 20; Gen 2:25, 3: 7, 10f al.; Job 1:21; Mel., P. 97, 739 γύμνῳ τῷ σώματι) **Mk 14:52** (Appian, Bell. Civ. 5, 140 §582 γυμνοὶ ... ἔφευγον; TestJos 8:3 ἔφυγον γυμνός); **Ac 19:16** (cp. Philo, In Flaccum 36); **Rv 3:17; 16:15; 17:16.** περιβεβλημένος σινδόνα ἐπὶ γυμνοῦ *who wore a linen garment over his naked body* (Tyndale: 'cloothed in lynnen apon the bare') **Mk 14:51** (for the subst. τὸ γυμνόν=the naked body cp. Lucian, Nav. 33 τὰ γυμνά). πόδες (Euphorion [III BC] 53, 1 Coll. Alex. p. 40; Jos., Ant. 8, 362) Hs 9, 20, 3.

ⓑ fig. ***uncovered, bare*** (cp. Diod. S. 1, 76, 2; Themistocl., Ep. 16 p. 756 H. γ. ἀλήθεια; Lucian, Tox. 42, Anachars. 19 ὡς γυμνὰ τὰ γεγενημένα οἱ Ἀρεοπαγῖται βλέποιεν; Heliod., Aeth. 10, 29 w. ἀπαρακάλυπτος; Job 26:6; Philo, Migr. Abr. 192; Jos., Ant. 6, 286; Ar. 13, 5 αἰσχύνην; Mel., fgm. 9, 19 P. a bared sword) **Hb 4:13.** Of the soul, whose covering is the body: *naked* **2 Cor 5:3** (cp. Pla., Cratyl. 20, 403b ἡ ψυχὴ γυμνὴ τοῦ σώματος, also Gorg. 523ce; 524f; Aelian, HA 11, 39. Artem. 4, 30 p. 221, 10f the σῶμα is the ἱμάτιον of the ψυχή; 5, 40; M. Ant. 12, 2 of the divine element in man, 'which God sees without any covering'.—Of the νοῦς: Herm. Wr. 10, 17). S. on this EKühl, Über 2 Cor 5:1–10, 1904; JUbbink, Het eeuwige leven bij Pls, Groningen diss. 1917, 14ff; WMundle, D. Problem d. Zwischenzustandes ... 2 Cor 5:1–10: Jülicher Festschr. 1927, 93–109; LBrun, ZNW 28, 1929, 207–29; Guntermann (ἀνάστασις 2b); RBultmann, Exeg. Probl. des 2 Kor: SymbBUps 9, '47, 1–12; JSevenster, Studia Paulina (JdeZwaan Festschr.) '53, 202–14; EEllis, NTS 6, '60, 211–24. γ. κόκκος *a naked kernel* **1 Cor 15:37,** where an adj. is applied to a grain of wheat, when it properly belongs to the bodiless soul which is compared to it; s. σπέρματα γ. 1 Cl 24:5 and AcPlCor 2:26.

❷ **pert. to being inadequately clothed,** ***poorly dressed*** (Demosth. 21, 216; BGU 846, 9; PBrem 63, 30; Job 31:19; Tob 1:17; 4:16) **Mt 25:36, 38, 43f; Js 2:15;** B 3:3 (Is 58:7).

❸ **pert. to being lightly clad,** ***without an outer garment,*** without which a decent person did not appear in public (so Hes., Op. 391, oft. in Attic wr.; PMagd 6, 7 [III BC]; 1 Km 19:24; Is 20:2) **J 21:7** (Dio Chrys. 55 [72], 1 the ναύτης wears only an undergarment while at work).—Pauly-W. XVI 2, 1541–49; BHHW II 962–65; RAC X 1–52.—B. 324f. M-M. TW.

γυμνότης, ητος, ἡ (M. Ant. 11, 27; TestZeb 7:1; Philo, Leg. All. 2, 59; Dt 28:48).

❶ **being without clothing,** ***nakedness*** (Cornutus 30 p. 59, 18) αἰσχύνη τῆς γ. *disgraceful nakedness* **Rv 3:18.—❷ being without adequate clothing, with connotation of destitution,** ***lack of sufficient clothing, destitution*** (Ps.-Dionys. Hal., De Arte Rhet. 10, 6; Dt 28:48: ἐν λιμῷ κ. ἐν δίψει κ. ἐν γ.; TestZeb 7:1) **Ro 8:35; 2 Cor 11:27.**—DELG.

γυμνόω 1 aor. ἐγύμνωσεν Jdth 9:1. Pass. aor. ἐγυμνώθη Gen 9:21; pf. γεγύμνωμαι (Hom. et al. [Hom. only mid. and pass.]; Herm. Wr. 1, 26a; POxy 903, 7; PLips 37, 18; Sb 4317, 25; LXX; Jos., Ant. 12, 212; Mel., P. 97) **to make naked,** ***strip, lay bare;*** pass. *be made naked* Dg 12:3.—DELG s.v. γυμνός.

γυναικάριον, ου τό (Diocles Com. [V BC] 11; M. Ant. 5, 11; Epict. index Sch.; on the suffix s. Phryn. p. 180 Lob.) dim. of γυνή, lit. 'little woman' (with derogatory connotation, Mussies 86f) ***idle/foolish/weak woman*** pl. **2 Ti 3:6.**—DELG s.v. γυνή. M-M (w. suggestion of higher societal status).

γυναικεῖος, α, ον (Hom. et al.; ins, pap, LXX; TestReub 3:10, 12; Philo; Jos., Ant. 13, 108) ***feminine*** σκεῦος γ. periphrasis for *woman, wife* (σκεῦος 3), ἀσθενεστέρῳ σκ. τῷ γυν. **1 Pt 3:7** (POxy 261, 12 διὰ γυναικείαν ἀσθένειαν).—DELG s.v. γυνή. M-M.

γυνή, αικός, ἡ (Hom.+; loanw. in rabb.)—❶ **an adult female person,** ***woman*** (virgins are included, e.g., Eur., Or. 309 of Electra) **Mt 9:20** (=AcPl BMM verso 16); **13:33; 27:55; Lk**

1:42 (cp. Semonides of Amorgos, fgm. 7, 88f [Diehl[3] fasc. 3, 56] ἀριπρεπὴς μὲν ἐν γυναιξὶ γίγνεται πάσῃσι); **8:2f** (cp. Appian, Bell. Civ. 1, 63 §282 γύναια πολλὰ πολυχρήματα assist Marius); **13:11; 1 Cor 14:34f; 1 Ti 2:11f** (Democr., fgm. 110 γυνὴ μὴ ἀσκείτω λόγον· δεινὸν γάρ=no woman should practice using her tongue; it just means trouble; Ael. Aristid. 45 p. 41 D.: ὁ ἀνὴρ λεγέτω, γυνὴ δὲ οἷς ἂν ἀκούσῃ χαιρέτω=it is appropriate for a man to speak, but let a woman be content with what she hears.—NGeurts, Het Huwelijk bij de Griekse en Romeinse Moralisten 1928; PTischleder, Wesen u. Stellg. d. Frau nach d. Lehre des hl. Pls 1923; HWindisch, Christl. Welt 44, 1930, 411–25; 837–40; GDelling, Pls' Stellg. z. Frau u. Ehe '31, s. OMichel, StKr 105, '33, 215–25; PKetter, Christ and Womankind, tr. IMcHugh, '52; KRengstorf, Mann u. Frau im Urchristentum, '54; JLeipoldt, D. Frau i. d. antiken Welt u. im Urchristentum '62; EKähler, Die Frau in d. paulinischen Briefen, '60; JBalsdon, Roman Women '62; SPomeroy, Goddesses, Whores, Wives, and Slaves '75; MLefkowitz/MFant, Women in Greece and Rome '77 [sources]; GClark, Roman Women: Greece and Rome ser. 2, 28, '81; JWhite, The Improved Status of Women in the Hellenistic Period: Biblical Research 39, '94, 62–79; JNeyrey, BTB 24, '94, 77—91 [on cultural stereotyping 89–91]; KTorjesen, When Women Were Priests: Women's Leadership in the Early Church and the Scandal of Their Subordination in the Rise of Early Christianity '93. Cp. the lit. on γαμέω end, and on σιγάω also s. προστάτις); **3:11** (JStiefel, NTS 41, '95, 442–57); Hv 1, 1, 4; 3, 8, 2. Opp. ἀνήρ (Diog. L. 1, 33; 1 Esdr 9:41) **Ac 5:14; 8:3; 1 Cor 11:3, 5ff** (on vs. **11** cp. Philosoph. Max. FGrPh I 491, 73 οὔτε γυνὴ χωρὶς ἀνδρὸς οὔτε …; on vs. **12b** cp. 1 Esdr 4:15f); 1 Cl 6:2; 55:3; γ. πρεσβῦτις *an elderly woman* Hv 1, 2, 2.—The voc. (ὦ) γύναι is by no means a disrespectful form of address (Il. 3, 204; Od. 19, 221; Soph., Oed. R. 655; Chariton 3, 2, 1; 5, 9, 3; Cass. Dio 51, 12, 5: Augustus to Cleopatra; Jdth 11:1; Jos., Ant. 1, 252; 17, 74. Cp. Alexander's reassuring ὦ μῆτηρ Diod. S. 17, 37, 6.—Only rarely is there a tone of disrespect in ὦ γύναι, as, e.g., Quint. Smyrn. 1, 575) **Mt 15:28; Lk 22:57; J 2:4** (Goodsp., Probs. 98–101); **19:26** (s. GDalman, Jesus-Jeshua [Eng. tr. PLevertoff] 1929, 201–3); **20:13, 15;** Hv 1, 1, 7; AcPl Ha 2, 18. S. JWackernagel, Über einige antike Anredeformen 1912, 25f.—σὺν γυναιξὶ κ. τέκνοις (Dio Chrys. 20 [37], 33; SIG 695, 20; 1 Macc 5:23; Jos., Vi. 99) **Ac 21:5.** σὺν γυναιξίν **1:14** (Diog. L. 3, 46: after the death of Plato, his μαθηταί are listed by name, and the list closes: σὺν οἷς καὶ γυναῖκες δύο, who are also named).—On the woman in heaven **Rv 12:1–17** cp. 1QH 3:7–12, also Boll 98–124 and against him JFreundorfer, D. Apk. des Ap. Joh. 1929. Cp. also PPrigent, Apocalypse 12: Histoire de l'exégèse, '59.

❷ **a married woman,** ***wife*** (Hom.+) **Mt 5:28, 31f; 14:3; 18:25; 19:5=Mk 10:7; 19:29 v.l.; Lk 1:5, 13, 18, 24; 8:3; 1 Cor 7:2ff; 9:5; Eph 5:22ff; Col 3:18f;** 1 Cl 1:3; 11:2; 21:6; ISm 13:1; Pol 4:2; Hv 1, 1, 2; m 4, 1, 1; 4ff; AcPl Ha 2, 9; AcPl Ant 13, 6 (=Aa 1 236, 7); et al. Those who understand **1 Ti 3:2, 12; Tit 1:16** as inclining toward celibacy may compare Ramsay, CB I/1, 151 no. 46: Apellas a priest makes himself liable to punishment by his god because he wishes to remain μετὰ γυναικός.—Of *widows* γ. χήρα **Lk 4:26** (3 Km 17:9=Jos., Ant. 8, 320). γυνὴ τοῦ πατρός *father's wife* (Lev 18:8, 11. Of a stepmother UPZ 189, 6 [112/111 BC]), who need not necessarily have been officially married to the man in question **1 Cor 5:1** (for the idea s. Ps.-Phoc. 179–81).

❸ **a newly married woman,** ***bride,*** to be considered in some contexts (Gen 29:21; Dt 22:24) δείξω σοι τὴν νύμφην τὴν γυναῖκα τ. ἀρνίου **Rv 21:9;** cp. **19:7; Mt 1:20, 24; Lk 2:5 v.l.** Perh. also **J 8:3f.**—B. 82; 96. DELG. M-M. TW. Sv.

Γώγ, ὁ, indecl. (גּוֹג) ***Gog*** symbol. name beside Magog (Ezk 38 and 39; cp. SibOr 3, 319; 512), to designate the enemy to be conquered by the Messiah **Rv 20:8.**—WBousset, ZKG 20, 1900, 113–31, Rel.[3] 219f; JKlausner, D. Mess. Vorstellungen des jüd. Volkes im Zeitalter d. Tannaiten 1904, 99ff; JBoehmer, Wer ist G. von Magog? ZWT 40, 1897, 321–55; Billerb. III 831–40; BHHW I 581; FBruce, Bulletin JOSCS 12, '79, 17ff. Variant rdg. for Ωγ AcPl Ha 8:12 (in the same context Ωγ AcPl Ox 1602, 8).

γωνία, ας, ἡ (on alleged connection w. γόνυ s. Frisk s.v. γωνία; Hdt.+; loanw. in rabb.) ***corner*** τῶν πλατειῶν *street corners* **Mt 6:5.** κεφαλὴ γωνίας (Ps 117:22) *corner-stone* or *keystone* (s. κεφαλή 2b) **Mt 21:42; Mk 12:10; Lk 20:17; Ac 4:11; 1 Pt 2:7;** B 6:4. αἱ τέσσαρες γωνίαι τῆς γῆς *the four corners of the earth* **Rv 7:1; 20:8** (X., De Rep. Lac. 12, 1; TestAsh 7:2; PGM 8, 8 ἐν ταῖς δ' γωνίαις τ. οὐρανοῦ). Of the corners of a stone Hs 9, 4, 1; of a structure (BGU 1002, 11 [55 BC] μέχρι γωνίας τῆς οἰκίας; Jos., Bell. 3, 243) s 9, 2, 3; 9, 15, 1.—Of a hidden place (Pla., Gorg. 485d βίον βιῶναι ἐν γωνίᾳ; Epict. 2, 12, 17; Orig., C. Cels 6, 78; Sus 38 Theod.) **Ac 26:26** (AMalherbe, Paul and the Popular Philosophers '89, 147–63: Christians not a socially undesirable group). Of false prophets: κατὰ γωνίαν προφητεύειν *prophesy in a corner* Hm 11:13.—B. 900. DELG. M-M.

δ' numerical sign = *4* (τέσσαρες: Jos., C. Ap. 1, 158; Mel., P. 90, 673 [B]; cp. SibOr 5, 40) Hs 9, 10, 7; or *4th* (τετάρτη) in the titles Hv 4; m 4; s 4 (uncertain, s. the app.). ἐν τῷ δ' τῆς ἐξηγήσεως τῶν κυριακῶν λόγων Papias (3:1).

Δαβίδ s. Δαυίδ.

Δαθάν, ὁ indecl. (דָּתָן) (LXX.—In Joseph. Δαθάμης, ου [Ant. 4, 19]) ***Dathan*** 1 Cl 4:12; GJs 9:2; s. Ἀβ(ε)ιρών. BHHW I 323.

δαιμονιάζομαι by-form of δαιμονίζομαι.

δαιμονίζομαι 1 aor. pass. ptc. δαιμονισθείς **Mk 5:18; Lk 8:36** ***be possessed by a hostile spirit*** (s. δαιμόνιον and δαίμων; the word is known since Soph., but found in this sense in the comic wr. Philemon 191; Plut., Mor. 706d; Cat. Cod. Astr. XI/2 p. 119, 20; Ps 90:6 Aq.; TestSol 17:3). Of a girl κακῶς δαιμονίζεται *is cruelly tormented by a spirit* **Mt 15:22.** Elsewh. only as a ptc. ὁ δαιμονιζομένους *the one possessed* (Thrasyllus [I AD] in Ps.-Plut., Fluv. 16; Cyranides p. 69, 17; Jos., Ant. 8, 47;

PGM 13, 242; 4, 3009 acc. to ADieterich, Abraxas 1891, 138; Preisendanz has δαιμονιαζομένους) **Mt 4:24; 8:16, 28, 33; 9:32; 12:22; Mk 1:32; 5:15f; Lk 8:35** D; **J 10:21; Ac 19:14** D. δαιμονιαζομένους καθα[ρίζων] AcPl BMM verso 12. Also δαιμονισθείς s. above.—JWeiss, RE IV 410–19.—M-M. TW.

δαιμονικός, ή, όν (Plut.; Physiogn. I 345, 8; 12; Cat. Cod. Astr. X 112, 10; Proclus on Pla., Cratyl. p. 93, 9 Pasqu.; Ath. 25, 3; Clem. Al., Strom. 6, 12, 98; TestSol 1:2 PQ) **pert. to being like a spirit or phantom,** ***like spirits/phantoms, ghost-like*** w. ἀσώματος of 'unbelieving' teachers ISm 2; both adjectives are chosen because of the saying in 3:2.—DELG s.v. δαίμων.

δαιμόνιον, ου, τό (substant. neut. of the adj. δαιμόνιος [s. 2 below δαιμόνιον πνεῦμα], quotable since Homer; OGI 383, 175; Herm. Wr. 10, 19; Ps.-Phoc. 101; En 19:1; TestSol; GrBar 16:3; Philo; Jos., Bell. 1, 373; 6, 429) in Gk. lit. the δαιμον-family refers in general to powerful entities that transcend ordinary experience. After Homer's time, the adj. δαιμόνιος means anything 'sent from heaven' or 'that which is divine' and the subst. τὸ δ. comes to mean 'divine manifestation' or 'heaven', as in our expression 'what heaven decrees' (Hdt. 5, 87, 2; cp. SIG 601, 15; Jos., Bell. 1, 69); or simply 'the divine' (Eur., Bacch. 894); cp. SIG 545, 14 (of religious piety). In our lit. the subst. gener. denotes a malevolent force.

➊ **transcendent incorporeal being w. status between humans and deities,** ***daemon*** (as distinguished from demon, which in Eng. gener. connotes inimical aspect), ***semi-divine being, a divinity, spirit, (higher) power,*** without neg. connotation. The subst. was freq. used by Hellenes in a gener. sense esp. of independent numinous beings or divinities, as distinguished from a more personalized θεός, e.g. nymphs, Panes, and Sileni (Pla., Symp. 23 p. 202e πᾶν τὸ δαιμόνιον μεταξύ ἐστι θεοῦ τε καὶ θνητοῦ='every δ. is between a god and a mortal'; cp. Philo, Mos. 1, 276; UPZ 144, 43; 50 [164 BC]; Vett. Val. 355, 15; Ps.-Lucian, Asinus 24 p. 592 οὐδὲ τὰ δ. δέδοικας; 'aren't you afraid of the spirits [powers]?' The term is common in adjurations, e.g., δαιμόνιον πνεῦμα, w. ref. to the spirit of the departed as possessing extraordinary powers: lead tablet fr. Hadrumetum [Dssm., B 26, 35 (BS 271ff)]; PGM 4, 3038; 3065; 3075). ξένων δ. καταγγελεύς *a preacher of strange divinities* **Ac 17:18** (cp. Pla., Apol. 26b; X., Mem. 1, 1, 1 καινὰ δαιμόνια εἰσφέρειν).

➋ **a hostile transcendent being w. status between humans and deities,** ***spirit, power, hostile divinity, evil spirit,*** the neg. component may be either specific or contextual, and w. the sense commonly associated w. the loanword 'demon' (δ. φαῦλα: Chrysipp. [Stoic. II 338, 32, no. 1178]; Plut., Mor. 1051c. φαῦλ. δ.: Plut., Mor. 277a, Dio 2, 5. Vett. Val. 67, 5; 99, 7. Herm. Wr. 9, 3; PGM 4, 3081; 5, 120; 165; 170; LXX; En 19:1). Beings of this type are said to enter into persons and cause illness, esp. of the mental variety (GrBar 16:3 ἐν μαχαίρᾳ . . . ἐν δαιμονίοις as punishment; Jos., Bell. 7, 185 [of the spirits of deceased wicked people], Ant. 6, 166ff; 211; 214; 8, 45ff): δ. εἰσέρχεται εἴς τινα **Lk 8:30;** δ. ἔχειν **Mt 11:18; Lk 7:33; 8:27; J 7:20; 8:48f, 52; 10:20.** ἔχων πνεῦμα δαιμονίου ἀκαθάρτου *who was under the control of an unclean power* **Lk 4:33.** ῥίψαν αὐτὸν τὸ δ. vs. **35;** cp. ἔρρηξεν **9:42.** Hence the healing of a sick person is described as the driving out of malignant forces ἐκβάλλειν (τ.) δ. (Jos., Ant. 6, 211) **Mt 7:22; 9:34; 10:8; 12:24, 27f; Mk 1:34, 39; 3:15, 22; 6:13; 7:26; 9:38; 16:9, 17; Lk 9:49; 11:14f, 18ff; 13:32.** Pass. **Mt 9:33.** ἐξουσίαν ἐπὶ πάντα τὰ δ. **Lk 9:1.** τὰ δ' ὑποτάσσεται ἡμῖν **10:17.** ἐξέρχεται τὸ δ. (s. ἐξέρχομαι 1aβב.—Thrasyllus [I AD] in Ps.-Plut., Fluv. 16, 2 ἀπέρχεται τὸ δαιμόνιον) **Mt 17:18; Mk 7:29f; Lk 4:41; 8:2, 33, 35, 38.** Some live in deserted places **8:29,** hence a ruined city is a *habitation of (malevolent) powers* **Rv 18:2** (cp. Is 13:21; 34:11, 14; Bar 4:35). Their ruler is βεελζεβούλ (q.v.) **Mt 12:24, 27; Lk 11:15, 18f.** Erroneous instruction is διδασκαλίαι δαιμονίων (subj. gen.) **1 Ti 4:1.** The ability of such beings to work miracles is variously described **J 10:21** and **Rv 16:14.** They are objects of polytheistic worship **9:20** (Dt 32:17; Bar 4:7; cp. Ps 95:5; 105:37; En 19:1; 99:7; Just., Tat.; SibOr fgm. 1, 22. Likew. among Persians and Babylonians: Cumont[3] 305, 97) **1 Cor 10:20f** (w. satirical reference to the secondary status of these members of the spirit-world relative to deity); B 16:7. On **Js 2:19** s. φρίσσω.—Of the evil spirit of slander Hm 2:3; of vengeance s 9, 23, 5; of arrogance s 9, 22, 3.—The δ. can appear without a tangible body, and then acts as a *phantom* or *ghost* ISm 3:2.—JGeffcken, Zwei griech. Apologeten 1907, 216ff; JTambornino, De Antiquorum Daemonismo 1909; RWünsch, D. Geisterbannung im Altertum: Festschr. Univ. Breslau 1911, 9–32; WBousset, Z. Dämonologie d. späteren Antike: ARW 18, 1915, 134–72; FAndres, Daimon: Pauly-W. Suppl. III 1918, 267–322; MPohlenz, Stoa '49 (index).—HDuhm, D. bösen Geister im AT 1904; GBarton, EncRelEth IV 1911, 594–601; AJirku, Die Dämonen u. ihre Abwehr im AT 1912; ALods, Marti Festschr. 1925, 181–93; HKaupel, D. Dämonen im AT 1930; Bousset, Rel.[3] 1926, 331ff; Billerb. IV 1928, 501–35; TCanaan, M.D., Dämonenglaube im Lande der Bibel 1929 1–20.—WAlexander, Demonic Possession in the NT 1902; JSmit, De Daemonicis in Hist. Evang. 1913; RBultmann, Gesch. d. syn. Tradition[2] '31, 223ff; HEberlein, NKZ 42, '31, 499–509; 562–72; FFenner, D. Krankheit im NT 1930; ATitius, NBonwetsch Festschr. 1918, 25–47; GSulzer, D. Besessenheitsheilungen Jesu 1921; HSeng, D. Heilungen Jesu in med. Beleuchtung[2] 1926; WWrede, Z. Messiaserkenntnis d. Dämonen bei Mk: ZNW 5, 1904, 169–77; OBauernfeind, D. Worte d. Dämonen im Mk-Ev. 1928; AFridrichsen, Theology 21, '31, 122–35; SMcCasland, By the Finger of God '51; SEitrem, Some Notes on the Demonology in the NT: SymbOsl, suppl. 12, '50, 1–60; JKallas, The Satanward View (Paul), '66; GTillesse, Le Secret Messianique dans Mk, '68, 75–111; RAC IX 546–797; RMacMullen, VigChr 37, '83, 174–92; G. Francois, Le polythéisme et l'emploi au singulier des mots ΘΕΟΣ ΔΑΙΜΩΝ '57 (lit.); GRiley, Demon: DDD 445–55. S. also the lit. s.v. ἄγγελος.—B. 1488. DELG s.v. δαίμων. M-M. TW.

δαιμονιώδης, ες (astrolog. text PMich 149 [II AD] VI, 33; VII, 11; VIII, 8 and 13; Proclus on Pla., Tim. I p. 113, 21 Diehl; Syntipas p. 13, 22; schol. on Aristoph., Ran. 295; Leontius 8 p. 16, 13; Etym. Mag. p. 336, 38 φάντασμα δαιμονιῶδες ὑπὸ τῆς Ἑκάτης πεμπόμενον; Ps 90:6 Sym.) **originating from the lower spirit-world,** ***infernal, demonic*** (as opp. to that which is ἄνωθεν) **Js 3:15.**—TW.

δαίμων, ονος, ὁ (Hom.+ in the sense 'a divinity' [between θεός and ἥρως Pla., Rep. 392a; cp. Menand., Epitr. 1083 S.=725 Kö., specific or unspecified, sometimes 'destiny', s. JRexine, Daimon in Classical Gk. Lit. 30, '85, 335–61; Herm. Wr., ins, pap, Philo, Joseph., SibOr]) means ***(evil) spirit/demon*** in the only place, apart from v.l., in the NT text (so Chariton 6, 2, 9 δ. κακός; Epict. 1, 22, 16; Appian, Bell. Civ. 4, 86 §366; Alex. Aphr., Probl. 2, 46; Iambl., Myst. 3, 31, 15 πονηρ.; Himerius, Or. 8 [23], 13 [here the πονηρὸς δ. of the disease strangles his victim with the βρόχος]; Sextus 604; Synes., Ep. 79 p. 227d; Eutecnius 2 p. 30, 13 [of a harpy]; PGM 4, 1227 [ἐκβάλλειν];

2516 [πονηρός]; 3081; 5, 131; POxy 1380, 164; BGU 954, 9; Is 65:11; Philo, Gig. 16b; Jos., Bell. 1, 628, Ant. 8, 45, Vi. 402; TestJud 23:1; Theoph. Ant. 2, 8 [p. 118, 7]. Cp. δαιμόνιον 2; for a positive view of daemons as beneficent beings s. Hes., Op. 123–26) **Mt 8:31** in wordplay to emphasize the source of the plight of the two possessed men δύο δαιμονιζόμενοι: the 'possessors' of the two 'possessed'. As v.l. also **Mk 5:12; Lk 8:29; Rv 16:14; 18:2.**—EOwen, Δαίμων and Cognate Words: JTS 32, '31, 133–53; HSchibli, Xenocrates' Daemons and the Irrational Soul: ClQ 43, '93, 143–67 (p. 147 n. 21 lit.; n. 23 on 'bad' daemons that can suffer pain).—EDNT. LexThK^3 III 1–6. TRE VIII 275–86 (lit.). DDD 445–55. DELG. M-M. TW. Sv.

δαίρω if this word has an independent existence and is not, as PKatz thinks, to be rejected as an itacistic spelling of δέρω, it means ***beat (severely)*** Hs 6, 2, 7 v.l. (δαιρόμενα for δερόμενα; s. also variously Tdf. and S. for v.l. δαιρ- in place of δερ- in **Mk 12:5; Lk 22:63; J 18:23; Ac 22:19; 1 Cor 9:26; 2 Cor 11:20;** the same edd. also variously include as v.l. δηρ-/ἐδηρ- for δειρ-/ἐδειρ- in **Mt 21:35; Mk 12:3; Lk 20:10f; Ac 5:40; 16:37;** s. δέρω).

δάκνω fut. δήξομαι LXX; 2 aor. ἔδακον (LXX, Just., D. 91, 4; 131, 4). Pass. 1 aor. ἐδήχθην, subj. δηχθῶ ; pf. ptc. δεδηγμένος (Just., D. 112, 1) (Hom. et al.; LXX, Just.)

❶ **to cause harm by biting, *bite*** of snakes B 12:5. Pass. (Diog. L. 5, 78 ὑπ᾽ ἀσπίδος δηχθείς) vs. 7 (cp. Num 21:6ff).

❷ **to cause discomfort to, *harm,*** fig. ext. of 1 (Hdt. 7, 16, 1; X., Cyr. 4, 3, 3; Epict. 2, 22, 28 δάκνειν ἀλλήλους καὶ λοιδορεῖσθαι; Appian, Syr. 10 §40=offend, nettle; PBrem 56, app. 11; Hab 2:7; Philo, Leg. All. 2, 8) w. κατεσθίειν (q.v.) **Gal 5:15.**—B. 266f. DELG. M-M.

δάκρυον, ου, τό (Hom.+) dat. pl. δάκρυσιν (**Lk 7:38, 44;** LXX; JosAs 13:5 cod. A [p. 57, 12 Bat.]; ApcSed 14:3 p. 136, 1 Ja.; ApcEsdr 6:23 p. 32, 1f Tdf.; Just., D. 90, 5; Jos., Ant. 1, 275, Vi. 138; Mel., P. 18, 121. Remnant of the poet. δάκρυ? B-D-F §52; δακρύοις Empedocles, fgm. 6, 3 D in Ath. 22, 1) **fluid that drops from the eye, *tear*** **Rv 7:17; 21:4** (both Is 25:8). Elsewh. pl. (Polyb. 2, 56, 6; 7; Philo) **Lk 7:38, 44** (Theodor. Prodr. 9, 275 H.: bathing feet w. tears). The pl.=*weeping* **2 Ti 1:4;** AcPl Ha 6, 6. μετὰ δακρύων (Nicol. Dam.: 90 fgm. 68, 3; fgm. 130, 17 p. 399, 14 Jac.; Diod. S. 34+35, 11 and 34+35 fgm. 26; Lucian, Ver. Hist. 1, 21; PPetr II, 1, 4 [260 BC]; Jos., Bell. 5, 420, Vi. 420; TestZeb 1:7; 2:1) **Mk 9:24 v.l.; Ac 20:19, 31; Hb 5:7; 12:17;** διὰ πολλῶν δ. **2 Cor 2:4** (διά A3c. On the 'letter written w. many tears' cp. Synes., Ep. 140 p. 276c τί ταῖς ἐπιστολαῖς τῶν δακρύων ἐγχεῖς; why do you moisten your letters with tears?).—B. 1130. DELG s.v. δάκρυ. M-M.

δακρύω fut. 3 sg. δακρύσει Sir 12:16; 1 aor. ἐδάκρυσα (Hom. et al.; grave ins Sb 373, 2; 4; 6178, 2; LXX; TestAbr AB; TestNapht 7:4; TestJos 8:1; Jos., Ant. 9, 9, Vi. 210) **to shed tears, *weep*** ἐδάκρυσεν ὁ Ἰησοῦς *Jesus burst into tears* **J 11:35** (as Diod. S. 17, 66, 4; 27, 6, 1; Appian, Samn. 4 §13 ὁ πρεσβύτης ἐδάκρυσε).—M-M.

δακτύλιος, ου, ὁ (Sappho, Hdt. et al.; ins, pap, LXX, TestSol; TestJob 46:5 τὸ δακτύλιον; Philo, Joseph.) **a ring for the finger, *ring*** **Lk 15:22;** used to make a seal (in wax, etc.) for someth. (Diod. S. 16, 52, 6; Appian, Hann. c. 50 and 51; Diog. L. 4, 59; 7, 45; Esth 8:8, 10; Da 6:18 al.; Jos., Bell. 1, 667; 2, 24) 1 Cl 43:2.—B. 443. M-M. TW.

δάκτυλος, ου, ὁ (Hdt.+) ***finger*** βαλεῖν τὸν (τοὺς) δ. **J 20:25; Mk 7:33;** GJs 19:3; φέρε τὸν δ. σου ὧδε **J 20:27;** *move w. the finger* of the slightest movement (Simplicius in Epict. p. 53, 25 ἄκρῳ δακτύλῳ=very lightly indeed 'acc. to the proverb') **Mt 23:4; Lk 11:46;** ἄκρον τοῦ δ. (cp. 4 Macc 10:7; Jos., Ant. 11, 234 ἄκροις τ. δακτύλοις) *tip of the finger* **Lk 16:24;** write w. the finger (cp. Ex 31:18; Dt 9:10) **J 8:6, 8 v.l.**—*The finger of God*=God's power (Ex 8:15 [BCouroyer, Le 'Doigt de Dieu', RB 63, '56, 481–95]; Philo, Mos. 1, 112; PGM II p. 209 no. 1, 6ff κατὰ τοῦ δ. τοῦ θεοῦ) **Lk 11:20;** in another sense γεγραμμένας τῷ δ. τῆς χειρὸς τοῦ κυρίου *written w. the Lord's own hand* B 4:7; 14:2 (Ex 31:18).—ILöw, D. Finger in Lit. u. Folklore der Juden: Gedenkbuch z. Erinnerung an D. Kauffmann 1900, 61–85; RAC IX 909–46;—B. 239f. DELG p. 249f. M-M. TW.

Δαλμανουθά, ἡ indecl. ***Dalmanutha,*** a place of uncertain location near Lake Gennesaret, perh. another name for Magdala, which also has many variants in the tradition (Dalman, Gramm.[1] 133; on this MRossi, Rivista storico-critica delle Scienze Teolog. 5, 1909, 345–50) **Mk 8:10.** The derivation of the name is as uncertain as the location.—EbNestle, Philologica sacra 1896, 17; Dalman, Worte 52f; OProcksch, Pj 14, 1918, 16f; JSickenberger, ZDPV 57, '34, 281–85; BHjerl-Hansen, Dalmanoutha: RB 53, '46, 372–84.

Δαλματία, ας, ἡ ***Dalmatia,*** southern Illyricum, across the Adriatic fr. S. Italy (Mommsen, Röm. Gesch. V 19f; 183ff; Stephan. Byz. s.v. Ἴσσα: κατὰ Δαλματίαν καὶ Ἰλλυρίαν; Phlegon: 257 fgm. 36, 12 Jac.; Jos., Bell. 2, 369; CIL III 1 p. 271; 279ff; Pauly-W. IV, 2448–59, IX, 1085–88, Suppl. VIII, 21–59; Kl. Pauly I 1364–68; HKrahe, D. alten balkanillyr. geogr. Namen, diss. Heidelb. 1925) **2 Ti 4:10.** On the v.l. Δελματίαν s. B-D-F. §41, 1 and M-M.

δαμάζω (Hom. et al.; Da 2:40; Schwyzer I 734) fut. 3 sg. δαμάσει (Da 2:40 Theod. [-ζει Cod. A†]); 1 aor. ἐδάμασα (cp. Mel., P. 17, 115); 3 sg. ἐδάμασσεν (Ath. 21, 4 [Hom., Il. 14, 316]); pf. pass. 3 sg. δεδάμασται; aor. inf δαμῆναι (Ath. 21, 2 [Hom., Il. 16, 434]) **to reduce from an uncontrolled to a controlled state, *subdue, tame, control***

ⓐ of persons and animals: a possessed person **Mk 5:4** (cp. Dionys. Hal. 6, 27, 3 on uncontrollable debtors); animals (TestAbr A 2 p. 79, 6 [Stone p. 6] ἵππους … δεδαδασμένους) *subdue, tame* **Js 3:7** (Field, Notes, 237f).

ⓑ of a part of the body *control* (Jos., Ant. 3, 86 τὸ φρόνημα; Mel., P. 17, 115 ὁ ἄγγελος … τὸν … Φαραὼ διὰ πένθους ἐδάμασεν) the tongue **Js 3:8.**—DELG s.v. δάμνημι. M-M.

δάμαλις, εως, ἡ (Aeschyl.+; also SIG 1026, 5 and 22; PAbinn 80, 7; 8; 21) **young female of cattle, *heifer, young cow.*** The red heifer (Num 19; Jos., Ant. 4, 80 [here the gen. is δαμάλιδος]) **Hb 9:13;** B 8:1 (Just., D. 13, 1).—DELG s.v. δάμνημι. M-M. TW.

Δάμαρις, ιδος, ἡ ***Damaris*** name of an Athenian converted by Paul **Ac 17:34.** The fragmentary state of SEG XI, 669 (IV–III BC) does not permit a reliable restoration in that inscription; cp. the restoration in IG V/1, 972 (II AD). On the view that this name is a variant of Damalis (the rdg. of Lat. vers. h [s. Merk app.]) s. Hemer, Acts 232, esp. n. 34 (to the lit. add Bechtel 589 w. ref. to IG XII, 7, which reads: [Δ]άμαλις); s. also Hdb. ad loc.; Beginn, IV 220. LGPN I 113.

Δαμᾶς, ᾶ, ὁ ***Damas,*** overseer of Magnesian Christians IMagnMai 2. The name appears in inscriptions, and is esp. well attested for western Asia Minor (CIG 2562; 2869; 2880; 2507), specif. for Magnesia by InsMagnMai 321; s. also 287. Cp. Δημᾶς.

Δαμασκηνός, ή, όν ***from Damascus*** ὁ Δ. *the Damascene* (Strabo, Athen., Geopon., Joseph.) **2 Cor 11:32.**

Δαμασκός, οῦ, ἡ (דַּמֶּשֶׂק Gen 14:15 al.; Just., D. 78, 10 al.) ***Damascus*** (Diod. S. 19, 100, 5 Δ. τῆς Συρίας; Nicol. Dam. in Jos., Ant. 7, 101; Strabo, Joseph.), capital of Coelesyria w. a large Jewish population (Jos., Bell. 2, 561; 7, 368). The city belonged to the Seleucids, the Nabataeans, and finally to the Romans (Schürer II 127–29). **Ac 9:2ff; 22:5f, 10f; 26:12, 20; 2 Cor 11:32; Gal 1:17.**—HvKiesling, Damaskus, Altes u. Neues aus Syrien 1919; CWatzinger u. KWulzinger, Damaskus 1921; IBenzinger, Pauly-W. IV 1901, 2042–48; LJalabert, Dict. d'Arch. IV 119ff; JSauvaget, Esquisse d'une histoire de la ville de Damas '35. On the political situation reflected in 2 Cor 11:32 s. ESchwartz, NGG 1906, 367f; 1907, 275; Schürer I 581f; II 97; 129f; Zahn, NKZ 15, 1904, 34; UKahrstedt, Syr. Territorien in hellenist. Zeit 1926; Kl-Pauly I 1371–73; BHHW I 313–15.—S. Ἁρέτας.

Δάν, ὁ indecl. (דָּן; LXX; En 13:7; Test12Patr; TestSol 18:20 A; JosAs, Philo, Joseph. The last has both Δάν [Ant. 1, 305] and Δάνος, ου [2, 181]) ***Dan,*** name of an Israelite tribe (Gen 30:6; 49:16) **Rv 7:5 v.l.** for Γάδ (cp. ViEzk 17 [p. 76, 4 Sch.] τὴν φυλὴν Δὰν καὶ τοῦ Γάδ). BHHW I 317f.

Δαναΐδες, ων, αἱ ***the Danaids,*** daughters of Danaus (all of whom, except Hypermestra, at the behest of their father killed their husbands on their wedding night) 1 Cl 6:2 (the D. linked with Tantalus, Tityus, and Sisyphus in [Plato] Axiochus 371e, and are said to suffer punishment by filling leaky jars with water, but the traditions vary; s. RKnopf, Hdb. ad loc. The rdg. Δαναΐδες κ. Δίρκαι, found in all mss., is also defended by APlummer, ET 26, 1915, 560–62. For satirical use of the myths s. Tat. 26, 1).—Kl. Pauly I 1379f; II 99.

δαν(ε)ίζω (s. two next entries) fut. δανιῶ LXX; 1 aor. ἐδάνισα, mid. ἐδανισάμην (on the spelling s. B-D-F §23; cp. B-D-R 23, 3; Mlt-H. 77)

❶ **to lend money, *lend,*** act. (Aristoph. et al.; X., Pla., ins, pap, LXX; Jos., Ant. 4, 266) **Lk 6:34ab, 35** (cp. Just., A I, 15, 10; Ath. 12, 3); at excessive interest ApcPt 16:31.

❷ **to borrow money, *borrow,*** mid. (Aristoph., X. et al.; ins, pap; 2 Esdr 15:4; Ps 36:21; Jos., Ant. 16, 296) ἀπό τινος (Pla., Tim. 42e; Philo, Rer. Div. Her. 282) **Mt 5:42** (cp. Just., A I, 15, 10).—B. 792f. DELG s.v. δάνος. M-M.

δάν(ε)ιον, ου, τό (s. prec. and next; since Demosth. 34, 12, Aristot.; ins, pap, Dt 15:8, 10; 24:11; 4 Macc 2:8; Philo; Jos., Ant. 3, 282; 14, 370) ***loan*** ἀφιέναι τὸ δ. *cancel the loan* **Mt 18:27.**—DELG s.v. δάνος. M-M.

δαν(ε)ιστής, οῦ, ὁ (since Demosth.; Plut., Sol. 85 [13, 5], Mor. 830d; ins, pap; 4 Km 4:1; Ps 108:11; Sir 29:28; Philo; Jos., Ant. 18, 147 al.; loanw. in rabb.) ***money-lender, creditor*** **Lk 7:41** (opp. χρεοφειλέτης as Pr 29:13).—DELG s.v. δάνος. M-M.

Δανιήλ, ὁ indecl. (דָּנִיֵּאל; LXX; En 6:7; SibOr 2, 247; Just.; Mel., HE 4, 26, 14.—EpArist 49 and Joseph. have Δανίηλος, ου [Ant. 10, 193], likew. **Mt 24:15** D) ***Daniel,*** the prophet **Mt 24:15; Mk 13:14 v.l.;** 1 Cl 45:6; 2 Cl 6:8; B 4:5.—BHHW I 318; RAC III 575–85.

δαπανάω (fr. δάπτω 'devour' [of wild beasts Il. 16, 159 al.] via δαπάνη) fut. δαπανήσω; 1 aor. ἐδαπάνησα, impv. δαπάνησον. Pass.: aor. 3 sg. ἐδαπανήθη 2 Macc 1:32; pf. ptc. δεδαπανηνένος LXX (Hdt., Thu.+; ins, pap, LXX; TestAbr A 6 p. 83, 12 [Stone p.14]; EpArist, Philo, Joseph.; Just., A I, 13, 1)

❶ **to use up or pay out material or physical resources, *spend, spend freely*** w. acc. as obj. *property* **Mk 5:26** (cp. 1 Macc 14:32; Jos., Ant. 15, 303; SEG XLI, 311, 3 [II AD]). τὶ εἴς τι (Diod. S. 11, 72, 2; Appian, Bell. Civ. 3, 32 §126; Artem. 1, 31 p. 33, 11f; Sb 8331, 17f [98 AD] πολλὰ δαπανήσας ἰς τὸ ἱερόν; OGI 59, 15; Bel 6 LXX, 3 Theod.; Jos., Ant. 4, 277) *spend someth. for* or *on someth.* Hs 1:8; also ἔν τινι (BGU 149, 5 ἐν πυρῷ κατ' ἔτος δαπανᾶται τὰ ὑπογεγραμμένα) ἐν ταῖς ἡδοναῖς ὑμῶν *on your pleasures* **Js 4:3.** ἐπί τινι *spend (money) on someone*=pay someone's expenses **Ac 21:24;** cp. ὑπέρ τινος **2 Cor 12:15** (s. BBetzinger, ZNW 18, 1918, 201; Seneca, Providentia 5, 4 boni viri . . . impendunt, impenduntur, et volentes quidem=good men expend, are expended, and, in fact, voluntarily).—W. the connotation of wastefulness (Hesychius; Suda δαπ.: οὐ τὸ ἁπλῶς ἀναλίσκειν, ἀλλὰ τὸ λαμπρῶς ζῆν καὶ σπαθᾶν καὶ δαπανᾶν τὴν οὐσίαν=not a matter of mere spending, but of living luxuriously, and squandering and wasting one's estate): πάντα *spend* or *waste everything* **Lk 15:14** (though the neutral sense *use everything up* is also prob.). Cp. also **Js 4:3** above.—In a bold fig. αἱ δεδαπανημέναι καρδίαι τ. θανάτῳ *hearts indentured to death,* i.e., they were extravagantly handed over to death (the phrase is amplified by the succeeding phrase: 'given over to lawless wandering') B 14:5; the bridge to mng. 2 is apparent.

❷ **to cause destruction by external means, *wear out, destroy*** fig. ext. of 1 (Jos., Bell. 3, 74) τοὺς ἀνθρώπους Hm 12, 1, 2; pass. (Appian, Bell. Civ. 4, 41 §171; 4, 108 §456; cp. Cat. Cod. Astr. VIII/3 p. 135, 19 ὑπὸ τ. λύπης ἐδαπανώμην) ibid. of base desire.—Of fire (Dio Chrys. 4, 32; 2 Macc 1:23; 2:10; Philo, Exsecr. 153; Jos., Ant. 4, 192; SibOr 2, 197; Just., A I, 13, 1 τὰ . . . εἰς διατροφὴν γενόμενα . . . πυρὶ δαπανᾶν) πυρί σε ποιῶ δαπανηθῆναι *I will cause you to be consumed by fire* MPol 11:2; cp. 16:1.—DELG s.v. δάπτω. M-M.

δαπάνη, ης, ἡ (s. prec. entry; Hes., Pind., Hdt. et al.; ins, pap, LXX, EpArist; Jos., Bell. 1, 605, Ant. 12, 200) ***cost, expense*** ψηφίζειν τὴν δ. *calculate the cost* **Lk 14:28.** συνοψίζειν τὴν ποσότητα τῆς δ. *estimate the amount of the expense* Hs 5, 3, 7.—The rdg. AcPl BMM verso 27 is uncertain: δ[απ]άνης.—B. 805. DELG s.v. δάπτω. M-M.

δασύπους, οδος, ὁ (Cratinus 400; Aristot., HA 511a, 31; Eutecnius 2 p. 22, 22; TestAsh 2:9) an animal of the family Leporidae, genus Lepus (Hb. אַרְנֶבֶת), termed 'shaggy-of-foot' (δασύς + πούς foot) in Gk. because of the dense growth of hair on the animal's soles: ***hare,*** whose flesh was forbidden to the Jews B 10:6 (Dt 14:7; cp. Lev 11:5; TestAsh 2:9).

Δαυίδ, ὁ indecl. (Δαυείδ is another spelling, in late mss. also Δαβίδ, s. B-D-F §38; 39, 1; Mlt-H. 110; on the abbrev. Δ̅α̅δ s. LTraube, Nomina Sacra 1907) ***David*** (דָּוִד) (LXX; SibOr index; Eupolemus the Jew [II BC]: 723 fgm. 2b, 3ff Jac., in Eus., PE 30, 5 and 7f [Δαβίδ]; Philo, Conf. Lingu. 149 [Δαβίδ]; Just.; Mel. [Δαυίδ B, Δαυείδ Ch].—In Joseph. Ant. 6, 199; also 7, 101 in a quot. fr. Nicol. Dam. Δαυίδης, ου or Δαβίδης), king of Israel, in genealogy of Jesus **Mt 1:6, 17; Lk 3:31.** Acc to **Mt 1:20; Lk 1:27; 2:4** Joseph was of Davidic descent. Jesus is called υἱὸς Δ. **Mt 1:1; 9:27; 12:23; 15:22; 20:30f; 21:9, 15; Mk 10:47f; 12:35; Lk 18:38f;** ἐκ σπέρματος Δ. **Ro 1:3; 2 Ti 2:8;** IEph

18:2; IRo 7:3; AcPlCor 2:5; ἐκ γένους Δ. IEph 20:2; ITr 9:1; ISm 1:1; cp. **Rv 22:16.**—ἕως τῶν ἡμερῶν Δ. **Ac 7:45.** David called to be king **13:22** (conflation of Ps 88:21, 1 Km 13:14 and Is 44:28); beneficiary of divine promises **13:34** (Is 55:3). David eating showbread (1 Km 21:1–6) **Mt 12:3; Mk 2:25; Lk 6:3.** His fidelity to Saul and clemency to Nabal AcPl Ha 6, 21ff (1 Km 25). His wars 1 Cl 4:13. His death **Ac 13:36** (3 Km 2:10). His grave **Ac 2:29** (cp. Jos., Bell. 1, 61; Ant. 16, 179). As singer of psalms **Mk 12:36f; Lk 20:42, 44; Ac 2:25; Ro 4:6; 11:9; Hb 4:7;** B 10:10; AcPl Ha 7, 11; also inspired **Mt 22:43, 45; Ac 1:16; 2:34; 4:25;** prophesying B 12:10. Ancestor of the Messiah **Mt 22:42; Mk 12:35; Lk 20:41;** B 12:10. The messianic reign described as kgdm. of David **Mk 11:10;** the restoration of the 'fallen tent of David' **Ac 15:16** (Am 9:11). David's throne **Lk 1:32** (Is 9:6). The Messiah has the key, i.e. sovereignty, of David **Rv 3:7** (Is 22:22 v.l.). Bethlehem is the city of David **Lk 2:4, 11; J 7:42.** On ἡ ῥίζα Δ. **Rv 5:5; 22:16** s. ῥίζα 2. On λίμνη τοῦ Δ. Ox 840, 25 s. λίμνη 1b.—D. is exemplar of faith **Hb 11:32;** described as μεμαρτυρημένος 1 Cl 18:1; ἐκλεκτός 52:2.—The mng. of ἄμπελος Δ. in the eucharistic prayer D 9:2 is debated (s. ἄμπελος b).—EDNT. RAC III 594–603. TW.

δαφνιδέα, ας, ἡ (δαφνηδαία v.l.; hapax leg.) ***laurel tree*** GJs 2:4; 3:1; s. de Strycker 299.

Δάφνος, ου, ὁ ***Daphnus,*** a Christian in Smyrna ISm 13:2; in Corinth AcPlCor 1:1. On the name s. Hdb. ad loc.

δέ (Hom.+) one of the most common Gk. particles, used to connect one clause to another, either to express contrast or simple continuation. When it is felt that there is some contrast betw. clauses—though the contrast is oft. scarcely discernible—the most common translation is 'but'. When a simple connective is desired, without contrast being clearly implied, 'and' will suffice, and in certain occurrences the marker may be left untranslated (Denniston 162–89; Schwyzer 2, 562; B-D-F §447).—Usually δέ comes second in its clause, somet. third (Menand., Epitr. 355 S. [=179 Kö.]; Lucian, Tim. 48, Dial. Mar. 4, 2; Alex. Aphr., Fat. 36, II 2 p. 208, 20; 209, 6) **Mt 10:11; 18:25; Mk 4:34; Lk 10:31; Ac 17:6; 28:6** al., occasionally fourth (Menand., Epitr. 281 S. [105 Kö.]; Archimed. II 150, 10 Heib.; Lucian, Adv. Ind. 19 p. 114; PHib 54, 20 [245 BC]; Wsd 16:8; 1 Macc 8:27; 4 Macc 2:15) **Mt 10:18; J 6:51; 8:16; 1 Cor 4:18; 1J 1:3,** or even fifth (Lucian, Apol. 12 p. 722; Alex. Aphr., An. II, 1 p. 34, 8; 57, 15; 1 Esdr 1:22; 4 Macc 2:9) **J 8:17; 1J 2:2;** IEph 4:2.

❶ a marker connecting a series of closely related data or lines of narrative, *and, as for.* Freq. used in lists of similar things, with a slight call of attention to the singularity of each item (cp. Hom., Il. 3, 144–48).—In tightly knit lists **Mt 1:2–16; 2 Pt 1:5–8;** relating one teaching to another (in this respect δέ is similar to the use in 2) **Mt 5:31; 6:16; Ro 14:1; 1 Cor 7:1; 8:1; 12:1; 15:1; 16:1.** Freq. w. the art. in narrative to mark change in the dramatis personae, e.g. **Mt 14:17f, Mk 14:31.**

❷ a marker linking narrative segments, *now, then, and, so, that is* Mt 1:18, 24; 2:19; 3:1; 8:30; Mk 5:11; 7:24; 16:9; Lk 3:21; 12:2, 11, 13, 15f, 50; 13:1, 6, 10; 15:1, 11 al.; **Ac 4:5; 6:1, 8; 9:10; 12:10, 17, 20; 23:10; 24:17; Ro 8:28; 14:1** (s. 1 above); **16:1; 1 Cor 16:12, 17; 2 Cor 4:7; 8:1; Gal 3:23.** Esp. to insert an explanation *that is* (Aeschyl., Choeph. 190) **Ro 3:22; 9:30; 1 Cor 10:11; 15:56; Eph 5:32; Phil 2:8.** So in parentheses (Thu. 1, 26, 5 ἔστι δὲ ἰσθμὸς τὸ χωρίον al.) ἦσαν δὲ ἡμέραι τῶν ἀζύμων **Ac 12:3.** Freq. to indicate change of speaker, e.g. **Mk 15:12–14; Lk 18:19–23; 20:3–5; 22:33–34.**—Resuming a discourse that has been interrupted (Thu. 2, 36, 1; Theocr. 5, 104 after the parenthetical 100–103) **Mt 3:4; Lk 4:1; Ro 5:8; 2 Cor 10:2.**

❸ a marker with an additive relation, with possible suggestion of contrast, *at the same time* Παῦλος δοῦλος θεοῦ ἀπόστολος δὲ Ἰησοῦ Χριστοῦ *Paul, God's slave, and at the same time apostle of Jesus Christ* **Tit 1:1.**

❹ marker of contrast, *but, on the other hand,*—ⓐ adversative function gener. **Mt 6:1, 6, 15, 16, 17; 8:20; 9:17; 23:25; Mk 2:21f; Lk 5:36f; 10:6; 12:9f; 13:9; 1 Cor 2:15** and oft.

ⓑ for correlative use μέν . . . δέ s. μέν.

ⓒ after a negative *rather* (Wsd 2:11; 4:9; 7:6 al.; 2 Macc 4:5; 5:6 al.; 3 Macc 2:24; 3:15) **Mt 6:33; Lk 10:20; Ac 12:9, 14; Ro 3:4; Eph 4:15; Hb 4:13, 15; 6:12; 9:12;** intensified δὲ μᾶλλον **12:13; Mt 10:6, 28.**

ⓓ introducing an apodosis after a hypothetical or temporal protasis, and contrasting it with the protasis (Kühner-G. II 275f; Epict. 1, 4, 32; 1 Macc 14:29; 2 Macc 1:34; AcThom 98 [Aa II/2, p. 210, 25]) **Ac 11:17 v.l.; 2 Pt 1:5** (for the protasis vs. 3f); **Col 1:22** (where the participial constr. vs. 21 represents the protasis; EpArist 175; 315).

❺ marker of heightened emphasis, in combination w. καί ***but also*—ⓐ** δὲ καί *but also, but even* (2 Macc 12:13; 15:19; EpArist 40 al.; TestJob 15:8 al.) **Mt 3:10 v.l.; 10:30; 18:17;** *so also, similarly, likewise, too* **Lk 11:18;** ἀπέθανεν δὲ καὶ ὁ πλούσιος=*the rich man died too* **16:22; 22:68 v.l.; J 2:2; 3:23; 18:2, 5; Ac 22:28; 1 Cor 15:15;** Papias (4).—ἔτι δὲ καί *and (even)* (EpJer 40; 2 Macc 10:7; EpArist 35; 151) **Lk 14:26 v.l.; Ac 2:26** (Ps 15:9)

ⓑ καί . . . δέ *and also, but also* (Kühner-G. II 253; Wsd 7:3; 11:20; 1 Esdr 1:47; 1 Macc 12:23; 2 Macc 11:12; 4 Macc 2:9; EpArist index) **Mt 10:18; 16:18; J 6:51; 8:16f; 15:27; Ac 3:24; 22:29; 1 Ti 3:10; 2 Ti 3:12; 1J 1:3.** Cp. Hatch 141f.—Epict. index p. 542 Sch.; s. the grammars and Aland, Vollst. Konk.; HMeecham, The Letter of Aristeas '35, 136; 154f.—EDNT.

δεδώκει s. δίδωμι.

δέησις, εως, ἡ (Lysias, Pla.+; Diod. S. 14, 106, 1; Plut., ins, pap, LXX, pseudepigr.; Mel., HE 26, 6; Nägeli 40) 'entreaty', in our lit., as almost always LXX (but not 1 Macc 11:49) **urgent request to meet a need, exclusively addressed to God, *prayer*** (so Plut., Coriol. 227 [30, 2]; Ps.-Lucian, Amor. 19; pap; Jos., C. Ap. 2, 197) **Lk 1:13; 2:37; Phil 1:19; 2 Ti 1:3; 1 Pt 3:12;** 1 Cl 22:6 (last two both Ps 33:16); Pol 7:2; GJs 2:4; 4;1, 2; 20:3. W. ἱκεσία (OGI 569, 11; PPetr II, 19 [1a], 2 μετὰ δεήσεως καὶ ἱκετείας οὕνεκα τοῦ θεοῦ) 1 Cl 59:2. W. προσευχή, the more general term, to denote a more specif. supplication (3 Km 8:45; 2 Ch 6:29; cp. Alex. Aphr., An. Mant. II, 1 p. 186, 3 εὐχαὶ καὶ δεήσεις; Orig., C. Cels. 5, 4, 19 πᾶσαν . . . δέησιν καὶ προσευχὴν καὶ ἔντευξιν καὶ εὐχαριστίαν ἀναπεμτέον) **Ac 1:14 v.l.; Eph 6:18; Phil 4:6; 1 Ti 2:1; 5:5;** IMg 7:1. W. προσκαρτέρησις **Eph 6:18;** w. ἱκετηρία **Hb 5:7;** ἐν δεήσει Hv 3, 10, 7; δ. ποιεῖσθαι *pray* (PParis 69 II, 11 ἔνθα σπονδάς τε καὶ δεήσεις ποιησάμενος; BGU 180, 17; StudPal V, 6, 1; 3 Macc 2:1; cp. Jos., Bell. 7, 107) **Lk 5:33; Phil 1:4; 1 Ti 2:1.** ἀναφέρειν δέησιν *offer prayer* (to God) B 12:7. ἐν δεήσει *in* or *with* (your) *prayer* Hv 3, 10, 7. W. addition of the object ὑπέρ τινος **Ro 10:1; 2 Cor 1:11; 9:14; Phil 1:4; 1 Ti 2:1f.** περί τινος (En 13:6) **Eph 6:18;** πολὺ ἰσχύει δ. **Js 5:16.** RAC VIII 1134–1258; IX 1–36.—DELG s.v. δέω 2 p. 270. M-M.

δεῖ inf. (τὸ) δεῖν **Lk 18:1, Ac 25:24;** AcPlCor 1:9, subj. δέῃ, impf. ἔδει (B-D-F §358, 1; Rob. 885f), fut. δεήσει Josh 18:4; impers. verb from δέω; for Attic ins forms s. Threatte II 634f

(Hom.+) Strict classification of usage is not possible because of the multifunctional adaptability of this verb, esp. in colloquial discourse.

❶ **to be under necessity of happening, *it is necessary, one must, one has to,*** denoting compulsion of any kind.—ⓐ of that which takes place because of circumstances or inner necessity, with the context determining the cause (Hdt. [8, 53 ἔδεε κατὰ τὸ θεοπρόπιον]; Appian, Liby. 122 §578 ἁλῶναι ἔδει Καρχηδόνα=it was necessary that Carthage be captured, i.e. it could not escape being captured [Appian's theological perspective surfaces, s. e.g. 7, 53; 8, 51; 57; 61; 62; 92]; Da 2:28f, 45 Theod; Wsd 16:4; Just., D. 6, 2; 32, 4) **Mt 17:10; 24:6** (δεῖ γενέσθαι as Jos., Ant. 10, 142); **26:54; Mk 9:11; 13:7, 10; Lk 4:43; 21:9; 24:46 v.l.; J 3:14, 30; 9:4; 10:16; 20:9; Ac 1:16; 3:21; 4:12; Ro 1:27; 1 Cor 15:53; 2 Cor 5:10; Rv 1:1; 4:1; 22:6;** 2 Cl 2:5.

ⓑ of the compulsion of law or custom ᾗ ἔδει θύεσθαι τὸ πάσχα *when the paschal lamb had to be sacrificed* **Lk 22:7.**—**Mt 23:23; Lk 11:42; 13:14; J 4:20, 24; Ac 15:5; 18:21 v.l.** Of the compulsion of Roman law **25:10.**

ⓒ of an inner necessity growing out of a given situation, **Mt 26:35** (Jos., Ant. 6, 108 κἂν ἀποθανεῖν δέῃ; PFay 109, 5 ἐάν σε δῇ [=δέῃ] τὸ εἱμάτιόν σου θεῖναι ἐνέχυρον; Ath. 24, 1 τί δὲ δεῖ πρὸς ὑμᾶς . . . μνημονεύειν;), **Mk 14:31; J 4:4; Ac 14:22; 21:22 v.l.; 27:21; 2 Cor 11:30.**—ὥστε . . . [τὴν Ἀρτεμύλλαν] μικροῦ δεῖν ἀπόπληκτον γενέσθαι *so that Artemilla was on the point of fainting* AcPl Ha 3, 33–35 (Demosth. 27, 29; Jos., C. Ap. 2, 119 al.).

ⓓ of compulsion caused by the necessity of attaining a certain result **Lk 12:12; 19:5; Ac 9:6; 1 Cor 11:19;** 2 Cl 1:1; B 4:1; IEph 7:1.—τὰ δέοντα (PPetr II, 11 [1], 6; BGU 251, 5 al.; pap; Pr 30:8; 2 Macc 13:20) *the needs* Hs 2, 5 and 8.

❷ **to be someth. that should happen because of being fitting,**—ⓐ gener. (Epict. 2, 22, 20 φίλος ἔσομαι οἷος δεῖ; 3, 23, 21 ὡς δεῖ, as Just., D. 114, 1; 2 Macc 6:20; 4 Macc 7:8) **2 Ti 2:6, 24.** καθὸ δεῖ *as is proper* **Ro 8:26.**—δέον ἐστίν *it is necessary, one must* (Polyb.; POxy 727, 19f; 1061, 13; BGU 981 II, 6; Sir. Prol. ln. 3; 1 Macc 12:11; EpArist) **Ac 19:36;** 1 Cl 34:2; without ἐστίν (POxy 899, 40; EpArist 227; 242; Philo, Aet. M. 107; Jos., Bell. 2, 296; Just., A I, 4, 6; A II, 2, 7; D. 11, 2) ITr 2:3; Pol 5:3. εἰ δέον ἐστίν *if it must be* **1 Pt 1:6** (s. εἰμί 11d); οὐ δέον v.l. for οὐδέν Papias (4).—On the constr. of δεῖ, note that as a rule the acc. and inf. follow it (Jos., C. Ap. 2, 254; Lucian, Charon 13, Pisc. 17; Just., D. 11, 2 al.; B-D-F §408), occasionally the inf. alone **Mt 23:23** (Jos., C. Ap. 1, 53a; Just., A I, 4, 6 al.—B-D-F §407); **26:54; Ac 5:29.**—To convey the idea that someth. should *not* happen, δεῖ is used w. the negative οὐ **Lk 13:16; 2 Tim 2:24;** 2 Cl 1:1; AcPlCor 1:10 or μή. **Tit 1:11** (ἃ μὴ δεῖ *what is not proper* [also Ael. Aristid. 54 p. 687 D.] is prob. a mixture of τὰ μὴ δέοντα **1 Ti 5:13** and ἃ οὐ δεῖ [Job 19:4]; s. B-D-F §428, 4; Rob. 1169); **Ac 15:24.** εἰ δὲ δεῖ ἡμᾶς . . . μὴ ποιεῖσθαι τὴν παραβολήν AcPlCor 2:28.

ⓑ of that which one should do (Wsd 12:19; 16:28; EpJer 5; Tob 12:1): *one ought* or *should* οὐκ ἔδει σε ἐλεῆσαι; *should you not have had mercy?* **Mt 18:33.**—**Lk 2:49; 15:32; 18:1; Ac 5:29; 1 Th 4:1; Tit 1:11;** 1 Cl 62:2.—In τί με δεῖ ποιεῖν; *what shall I do?* **Ac 16:30,** δ. stands for the deliberative subj. (B-D-F §366, 4).

ⓒ to indicate that something that happened should by all means have happened, expressed w. the impf. ἔδει (Jos., Bell. 4, 232; Just., D. 88, 6; 141, 1 al.) *had to* **Lk 15:32; 22:7; 24:26; J 4:4; Ac 1:16; 17:3.**

ⓓ to indicate that someth. that did not take place really should have happened, also expressed w. the impf. ἔδει *should have, ought to have* **Mt 18:33; 23:23; Ac 24:19** (Ath. 21, 1; ὃν ἔδει w. inf. TestJos 14:3; οὓς ἔδει w. inf.: Isocr. 3, 40, 35a; Lysias 14, 29; Lucian, Philops. 21); **27:21; 2 Cor 2:3.** Cp. B-D-F. §358.—EFascher, Theol. Beobachtungen zu δεῖ im AT: ZNW 45, '54, 244–52, Theol. Beobachtungen zu δεῖ: RBultmann Festschr., '54, 228–54; CCosgrove, NovT 26, '84, 168–90 (Luke-Acts).—JKube, ΤΕΧΝΗ und ΑΡΕΤΗ '69, 46. Cp. χρή. B. 640f. Schmidt, Syn. III 702–5. DELG s.v. δέω 2. EDNT. M-M. TW. Sv.

δεῖγμα, ατος, τό (s. two next entries; Eur., X., Pla. et al.; ins, pap, Philo, Joseph., loanw. in rabb.).

❶ ***indicator, proof*** τινός *of someth.* (Eur., Supp. 354; Menand., Georg. fgm. 3, 4 J.; Cass. Dio 55, 7, 4; Jos., Ant. 8, 34; pap) Dg 4:5; 7:9.

❷ ***example*** (δεῖγμα καὶ τύπον Theoph. Ant. II 15 [p. 138, 7]) παρέχειν (Dionys. Hal., Rhet. 6, 5 p. 282, 19 R. τ. ἀρετῆς; Philostrat., Vi. Apoll. 6, 12 p. 224, 23) *give an example* Dg 3:3; προκεῖσθαι δ. *stand as an ex.* **Jd 7** (*sample* ELee, NTS 8, '61/62, 167). Cp. εἰς τὸ δεῖγμα **2 Pt 2:6** P^{72}.—Schmidt, Syn. III 416f. DELG s.v. δείκνυμι. M-M.

δειγματίζω 1 aor. ἐδειγμάτισα (s. prec. and next entries; PCairZen 484, 18; PColZen 82, 10 [both III BC]; PTebt 576 [I BC]; PSI 442, 18; MartIs 3:13 [in PAmh 1 VIII, 21]; AcPtPl 33 [Aa I 194, 3]. Exx. of the noun δειγματισμός in Mayser 436; also BGU 246, 5, where δ.=public disgrace) ***expose, make an example of, disgrace*** τινά *someone* (schol. on Eur., Hippol. 426) a woman **Mt 1:19** (on the public disgrace of an adulteress cp. Heraclides [IV BC], Polit. 14; Nicol. Dam.: 90 fgm. 103, l [Pisidians] Plut., Mor. 291ef; Dio Chrys. 47 [64] 3 mentions a Cyprian law, according to which an adulteress had to cut her hair and was subjected to contempt by the community; Aelian, VH 11, 6; Hermogenes Rhet. p. 90, 2; among interpreters of Mosaic law such a woman was threatened w. more serious perils: cp. **J 8:3ff** [Hdb. ad loc.]; GJs14:1); *mock, expose* **Col 2:15.**—DELG s.v. δείκνυμι. M-M. TW.

δείκνυμι (s. prec. two entries) fut. δείξω; 1 aor. ἔδειξα, impv. δεῖξον; pf. δέδειχα LXX; B 13:3. Pass.: fut. 3 sg. δειχθήσεται (Just., Tat., Ath.); 1 aor. 2 pl. ἐδείχθητε (Just., D. 93, 1), inf. δειχθῆναι LXX (Just., A I, 12, 10); ptc. δειχθείς **Hb 8:5;** Dg 11:2; pf. 3 sg. δέδεικται (Ath. 10:1), ptc. δεδειγμένον Ex 25:29; 26:30 (Hom.+. The alternate form δεικνύω, as old as Hdt., also Ps.-Aeschin., Ep. 12, 6; B-D-F §92; Rob. 311) gener. to exhibit or make someth. known, *show.*

❶ **to exhibit someth. that can be apprehended by one or more of the senses, *point out, show, make known*** (τύπον . . . τοῦ σταυροῦ Just., D. 111, 1) τινί τι or τινα *someth.* or *someone to someone:* kingdoms **Mt 4:8; Lk 4:5.** δεῖξον σεαυτὸν τῷ ἱερεῖ (cp. Lev 13:49) **Mt 8:4; Mk 1:44; Lk 5:14;** mountains 1 Cl 10:7; trees Hs 3:1; an upper room **Mk 14:15; Lk 22:12;** denarius **Lk 20:24;** hands and feet **Lk 24:40;** hands **J 20:20;** good works **10:32;** land **Ac 7:3** (Gen 12:1); a pattern **Hb 8:5** (Ex 25:40). σημεῖον (EpJer 66; Jos., Bell. 2, 259, Ant. 18, 211; Just., A I, 55, 6; cp. TestAbr A 6 p. 83, 26 [Stone p. 14] θαυμάσια) **J 2:18.** ἃ δεῖ σε ἰδεῖν Hv 3, 1, 2.—Of apocalyptic visions (Zech 3:1) **Rv 1:1; 4:1; 17:1; 21:9f; 22:1, 6, 8.** The Father **J 14:8f** (Nicol. Dam.: 90 fgm. 3 p. 331, 13 Jac. ὁ Ἀρβάκης ἐδεήθη αὐτοῦ δεῖξαι οἱ τὸν βασιλέα. σφόδρα γὰρ ἐπιθυμεῖν τὸν δεσπότην ὅστις εἴη θεάσασθαι=A. asked him (the eunuch) to show him the king, for he was eager to see what the ruler was like). Of divine revelation (Hermes fgm. XXIII, 5 [Stob. I 386, 22 W.=458, 20 Sc.; PGM 3, 599]) **J 5:20.** Of the future manifestation of Jesus Christ **1 Ti 6:15.**—1 Cl 5:5; B 5:9.—By fig. ext., of direction to transcendent matters (1 Km

12:23; Mi 4:2) **1 Cor 12:31;** the salvation of God 1 Cl 35:12 (Ps 49:23).

❷ **to prove or make clear by evidence or reasoning,** ***explain, prove*** (Ps.-Callisth. 3, 22, 10 ἄρτι δέ σοι δείξω=I will soon prove [it] to you; cp. Just., A I, 57, 1 ὡς δείκνυται al.; Did., Gen. 71, 6) τὶ (cp. Just., A I, 68, 10) *someth.* **Js 2:18a;** B 5:6. τινί τι 1 Cl 26:1. W. ὅτι foll. B 7:5 (cp. Just., D. 23, 5); τινί w. ὅτι foll. (3 Macc 6:15) **Mt 16:21;** τινί w. inf. foll. **Ac 10:28.** τὶ ἔκ τινος (Alex. Aphr., Quaest. 3, 3 II 2 p. 83, 10) **Js 2:18b; 3:13.** W. double acc. τὸν σωτῆρα δείξας δυνατόν *he has revealed the Savior as powerful* Dg 9:6; ἑαυτὸν τύπον ἔδειξε (Christ) *displayed himself as exemplar* (of the resurrection) AcPlCor 2:6 (cp. TestJob 26:6; Just., A I, 57, 3 ἑαυτοὺς . . . φαύλους δεικνύουσιν).—JGonda, Δείκνυμι 1929. B. 1045. Schmidt, Syn. III 401–15. DELG. M-M. TW.

δειλαίνω aor. pass. 3 sg. subj. δειλανθῇ 1 Macc 5:41 ('act the coward' Aristot. et al.) mid. ***be cowardly, fearful*** (Ps.-Lucian, Ocy. 153; PTebt 58, 27 [III BC]; PLond VI, 1914, 24; 1 Macc 5:41) IRo 5:2. μηδὲν δειλαινόμενος *without fearing* Hs 9, 1, 3.—DELG s.v. δείδω p. 256.

δειλία, ας, ἡ (s. next entry; Soph., Hdt. et al.; BGU 372 I, 26; PGiss 40 II, 11; Herm. Wr. fgm. XVII 2, p. 444, 3 Sc.; LXX; TestAbr A 16 p. 96, 21 [Stone p. 40]; TestJos 2:5; Philo; Jos., Vi. 172, C. Ap. 2, 148) **lack of mental or moral strength,** ***cowardice*** πνεῦμα δειλίας *spirit of cowardice* **2 Ti 1:7;** διὰ τὴν δ. *through cowardice* Hs 9, 21, 3; *timidity* GJs 22:3; cp. MPol 3; μετὰ φόβου καὶ δειλίας *in fear and terror* AcPl Ha 11, 12.—On Gr-Rom. views of cowardice, s. Reader, Polemo pp. 345–47. DELG s.v. δείδω p. 256. M-M. Spicq.

δειλιάω fr. δειλία; 1 aor. ἐδειλίασα (Ezk. Trag. 267; Diod. S. 20, 78, 1 Fischer v.l.; PParis 68c, 4; LXX; TestSol 1:9 P; TestSim 2:3; ViEliae 3 [p. 93, 13 Sch.]; Pel.-Leg. 12, 12) **to lack courage,** ***be cowardly/fearful*** (w. ταράσσεσθαι as Is 13:7f) *be afraid* **J 14:27;** *be fearful* (Cyril Scyth. p. 95, 22; 78, 28; 208, 16) before wild beasts MPol 4.—DELG s.v. δείδω. M-M. Spicq.

δειλινός, ή, όν (Diocles 141 p. 180, 12; Strabo, Plut., Lucian, pap, LXX) ***in the afternoon*** τὸ δειλινόν as adv. *toward evening* (Menand., Kon. 7; Lucian, Lex. 2; Gen 3:8) **Ac 3:1** D (d: ad vesperum).—DELG s.v. δείελος.

δειλόομαι 1 aor. ptc. δειλωθείς (Soph., Ichneutai fgm. 314, 150 v.l., s. APearson p. 246; Diod. S. 20, 78; 1 Macc. 16:6) ***be afraid, be frightened*** [ὥστε καὶ Παῦλο]ν ἐκπεσεῖν της προσευχῆς διλωθέντα *[so that Paul] in fright stopped praying* AcPl Ha 2, 8.—DELG s.v. δείδω p. 256.

δειλός, ή, όν (Hom. et al.; LXX; Philo; Jos., Bell. 3, 365, Ant. 6, 215; Just., D. 5, 5) ***cowardly, timid*** (w. ἄπιστος et al.) **Rv 21:8;** of a pers. lacking confidence (Dio Chrys. 47 [64], 11 τί δέδοικας, ὦ δειλέ;) **Mt 8:26** w. ὀλιγόπιστος; **Mk 4:40** w. πίστις; Hs 9, 28, 4.—DELG s.v. δείδω p. 256. M-M. Spicq.

δεῖνα, ὁ, ἡ, τό (Thu., Aristoph. et al.; pap, Aq., Sym.) **a pers. or thing one cannot or does not wish to name,** ***so-and-so, somebody,*** in our lit. only masc. *a certain man* **Mt 26:18.**—DELG. M-M.

δεινός, ή, όν (Hom.+; s. Nägele 56) **pert. to causing or being likely to cause fear,** ***fearful, terrible*** of punishments 2 Cl 17:7; MPol 2:4; Hs 6, 3, 3 (Just., A I, 31, 6); of tortures (Ael. Aristid. 49, 16 K.=25 p. 492 D.) 1 Cl 6:2; δ. ῥήματα *threatening words* MPol 8:3. Superl. δεινότατος (Philo; Just., D. 9:1) of grief δεινοτάτη τοῖς δούλοις τοῦ θεοῦ *very bad* Hm 10, 1, 2. Subst. τὸ δεινόν=danger (of death) (Diod. S. 19, 83, 5; Appian, Bell. Civ. 5, 90 §378; Philo; Jos., Ant. 1, 164) ἄλλα δεινά *other afflictions* **ending of Mk** in the Freer ms. 8.— [[τὰ]] μὲν ὧδε δυνά (=δεινά) *what is powerful here* (on earth) AcPl Ha 2, 23 (opp. τὰ δὲ ἐκεῖ θαυμάσια).—LVoit, Δεινότης '34; ESchlesinger, Δεινότης: Philol 91, '37, 59–66. DELG s.v. δείδω p. 256.

δεινῶς adv. of δεινός (Hdt.+; Aelian [oft.]; ins, pap, LXX, TestSol, Jos., Ant. 2, 304; 3, 1) **an extreme negative point on a scale relating to values,** ***terribly*** βασανιζόμενος *tortured* **Mt 8:6** (BGU 595, 14 ὁ υἱός μου ἀσθενεῖ δεινῶς; SIG 1168, 114); καταφθαρῆναι δ. *become disgustingly corrupt* Hv 1, 3, 1 Joly; δ. ἐνέχειν *act in a very hostile manner* **Lk 11:53.** δαπανᾶσθαι *be dreadfully ruined* Hm 12, 1, 2.—M-M.

δειπνέω fut. δειπνήσω; 1 aor. ἐδείπνησα (s. δεῖπνον; Hom. et al.; ins, pap, LXX; TestJob15:2; EpArist 180; Jos., Ant. 1, 252) **to eat a meal (without ref. to time of day or type of food),** ***eat, dine*** **Lk 17:8; 22:20; 1 Cor 11:25** (of the Passover Jos., Ant. 2, 312; of a polytheistic cult meal POxy 110; 523.—μετὰ τὸ δειπνῆσαι as Plut., Mor. 645d); **Rv 3:20;** AcPl Ha 3, 3; **Mt 20:28 v.l.** (addition in D); Hs 9, 11, 8a; the continuation in ibid. b uses it fig. δ. ῥήματα κυρίου.—DELG s.v. δεῖπνον. M-M. TW. Spicq.

δειπνοκλήτωρ, ορος, ὁ (Artem. in Athen. 4, 70, 171b= ἐδέατρος [ἐλέατρος] steward; Hesych.; Glykas 337, 5) one who καλεῖ to the δεῖπνον: ***host*** **Mt 20:28 v.l.** (addition in D). S. EbNestle, ZNW 7, 1906, 362ff; HVogels, BZ 12, 1914, 384f.

δεῖπνον, ου, τό (s. δειπνέω; Hom.+) **the main meal of the day** (distinguished fr. ἄριστον, a meal taken earlier in the day, cp. **Lk 14:12;** Polyaenus, Exc. 3, 8).

ⓐ of an everyday meal, ***dinner, supper*** περὶ δείπνου ὥραν *about dinner time* (cp. POxy 110 δειπνῆσαι . . . ἀπὸ ὥρας θ´) MPol 7:1; cp. Lk 14:17.

ⓑ of a formal meal w. guests ***feast, dinner*—α.** gener. in our lit. of an elaborate dinner celebration (Iren., 1, 13, 4 [Harv. I 120, 9]) **Mt 23:6; Mk 12:39; Lk 11:43 v.l.; 14:12, 17, 24; 20:46; 1 Cor 10:27 v.l.; Rv 19:9;** Hs 5, 5, 3.—δεῖπνον μέγα (Vi. Aesopi W 77 P. p. 99, 43 ἐπὶ μέγα δεῖπνον ἐκάλει τινά) **Lk 14:16; Rv 19:17.** ποιεῖν δ. *give a dinner* (PMeyer 20, 34 δεῖπνον ἐπόει μοι; PGM 1, 106; Da 5:1 Theod.) **Mk 6:21; Lk 14:12, 16; J 12:2;** Hs 5, 2, 9=the feast of 5, 5, 3. δείπνου γινομένου *when a dinner was being held* **J 13:2** (Athen. 4, 8, 132c πότερον ἐν ἄστει γίνεται βελτίω δεῖπνα ἢ ἐν Χαλκίδι;). τελεσθέντος τοῦ δ. *at the end of the meal* GJs 6:3. W. temporal ref. τῇ ὥρᾳ τοῦ δ. (cp. POxy 110 cited in a above) **Lk 14:17.**

β. a cultic meal, such as the Passover **J 13:4; 21:20** (exx. of δ.=a cult meal in JBehm, TW II 34f; Biogr. p. 92 at the sacrifice a priest calls out: Πίνδαρος ἴτω ἐπὶ τὸ δεῖπνον τοῦ θεοῦ). κυριακὸν δ. *the Lord's Feast (Supper)* **1 Cor 11:20.** On τὸ ἴδιον δεῖπνον προλαμβάνει vs. **21** s. ἴδιος 1b and προλαμβάνω 1c. Cp. ESchweizer, D. Herrenmahl im NT. Ein Forschungsbericht: TLZ 79, '54, 577–92; TRE I 43–278.—Billerb. IV 611–39; Pauly-W. XIV 524–27; RAC III 658–66; VI 612–35; B. 352 and 354. DELG. M-M. TW.

δεῖπνος, ου, ὁ (a late form of the prec. entry; Diod. S. 4, 3 v.l.; schol. on Aristoph., Pax 564; Ursing 23; TestAbr B 5 p. 109, 16 [Stone p. 66] al.; JosAs 3:6 δ. μέγαν 10:14 [DG]; 13:7 [DH]) for δεῖπνον only as v.l. **Lk 14:16; Rv 19:9, 17.**—B-D-F §49, 2; Mlt-H. 123.

δεισιδαιμονία, ας, ἡ In the ancient Mediterranean world δ. refers to concern about one's relations to the transcendent realm (e.g. Polyb. 6, 56, 7; Dio Chrys. 44 [61], 9) exhibited especially in time of war; also viewed as a motivating force (Diod. S. 1, 70, 8; 11, 89, 6; 8; Jos. Ant. 10, 42). Because such concern is ordinarily expressed in observance of specific religious rites or customs, δ. can denote 'rite' or 'ceremony' (OGI 455, 11).

❶ When fear of offending divinity expresses itself in extraordinary ways, δ. denotes ***religious scruple, religiosity*** (e.g., Jos., Ant. 14, 228; 15, 277; Jos., Bell. 2, 174). To Romans, for whom public order was of primary interest, and to Hellenes, who valued moderation, excessive anxiety could be prejudicial to the interests of the State, and was described through qualified use of the term δ. (Polyb. 12, 24, 5; Plut., Sol. 12, 4 [84], Alex. 75, 1 [706], Mor. 66c, s. his work Περί τῆς δεισιδαιμονίας; Agatharchides in Jos., Ant. 12, 5f 'ill-timed religious scruples or piety'; idem C. Ap. 1, 208; Herm. Wr. 9, 9; extreme forms of δ. are satirized as 'superstition' Theophr., Char. 16, and distinguished from εὐσέβεια Philo, Spec. Leg. 4, 147; s. also Tatian's contemptuous description: 22, 1). Such negative viewpoint (gener. expressed in the Lat. 'superstitio'; in ref. to Christians cp. Pliny, Ep. Traj. 10, 96 [97], 9; Suetonius, Nero 16, 2) is reflected Dg 1:1; 4:1 (cp. M. Ant. 6, 30 θεοσεβὴς χωρὶς δεισιδαιμονίας 'god-fearing without fussy piety').

❷ **system of cultic belief or practice,** ***religion*** (OGI 455, 11; Jos., Ant. 14, 228; 19, 290 on Rom. religious tolerance; reciprocity is expected from others: Jews are forbidden by Claudius τὰς τ. ἄλλων ἐθνῶν δεισιδαιμονίας ἐξουθενίζειν='to ridicule the religious practices of other nationalities'; cp. Ac 19:37; Ro 9:22) ζητήματα περὶ τῆς ἰδίας δεισιδαιμονίας εἶχον *they had some points of dispute about their religion* **Ac 25:19** (because of the author's apparent appreciation of Rom. religious tolerance it is not prob. that satire is to be inferred here).—HBolkestein, Theophrastos' Charakter der Δεισιδαιμονία als religionsgesch. Urkunde 1929; PKoets, Δεισιδαιμονία, diss. Utrecht 1929; SEitrem, SymbOsl 31, '55, 155–69; HMoellering, Plutarch on Superstition '63; MSmith, Superstitio: SBLSP 20, '81, 349–55.—B. 1492f. EDNT. M-M. DELG. s.v. δαίμων. TW. Spicq. Sv. S. next entry.

δεισιδαίμων, ον, gen. **ονος** can, like δεισιδαιμονία, be used in a denigrating sense 'superstitious' (cp. Maximus Tyr. 14, 6f in critique of the δ. as a κόλαξ 'flatterer' of the gods μακάριος εὐσεβὴς φίλος θεοῦ, δυστηχὴς δὲ ὁ δεισιδαίμων [s. H. app. and T.'s rdg.]; Philo, Cher. 42; s. Field, Notes 125–27), but in the laudatory introduction of Paul's speech before the Areopagus **Ac 17:22** it must mean ***devout, religious*** (so X., Cyr. 3, 3, 58, Ages. 11, 8; Aristot., Pol. 5, 11 p. 1315a, 1; Kaibel 607, 3 πᾶσι φίλος θνητοῖς εἴς τ' ἀθανάτους δεισιδαίμων) comp. for superl. (as Diog. L. 2, 132): δεισιδαιμονεστέρους ὑμᾶς θεωρῶ *I perceive that you are very devout people* **Ac 17:22** (the Athenians as the εὐσεβέστατοι τ. Ἑλλήνων: Jos., C. Ap. 2, 130. Cp. Paus. Attic. 24, 3 Ἀθηναίοις περισσότερόν τι ἢ τοῖς ἄλλοις ἐς τὰ θεῖά ἐστι σπουδῆς).—DELG s.v. δαίμων. TW. Spicq.

δέκα indecl. *ten* (Hom.+; loanw. in rabb.; Jos., Bell. 2, 146 as a round number; Ath. 6, 1 μέγιστος ἀριθμὸς … ὁ δέκα πυθαγορικούς) **Mt 20:24; 25:1, 28; Mk 10:41; Lk 15:8; 17:12, 17; 19:15, 16f, 24f.** ἐν δ. χιλιάσεν **14:31;** δ. ἀπόστολοι **Ac 2:14** D; ἡμέρας … ὀκτὼ ἢ δ. **25:6;** θλῖψιν ἡμερῶν δ. **Rv 2:10** (ten days as a relatively short period of time as Gen 24:55; Da 1:12, 14); horns **12:3; 13:1; 17:3, 7, 12, 16** (Da 7:7, 20, 24); soldiers IRo 5:1; kingdoms B 4:4f (Da 7:24, 7); cp. **Rv 17:12;** δ. λόγοι *the Ten Commandments* (Ex 34:28; Dt 10:4) B 15:1.—**δεκαδύο** (ins in Meisterhans[3]-Schw. p. 159; Schweizer 164; Nachmanson 147; pap in Mayser 316; Polyb., Plut., EpArist, Joseph., LXX; TestJob 15:4) ***twelve*** **Ac 19:7; 24:11** both v.l.; B 8:3; GEb 34, 62 (cp. Just., A I, 39, 3 ἄνδρες δ.).—**δεκαέξ,** expressed var. (ins, pap, LXX, Strabo 2, 5, 42): ἦν ἐτῶν ιϛ' (δέκα ἕξ most codd., δέκα ἑπτά H; cp. TestJob 26:1) *was* ***sixteen*** *years of age* GJs 12:3. For ἑξακόσιαι δεκαέξ or ἑξακόσιαι δέκα ἕξ *six hundred and sixteen* **Rv 13:18 v.l.** see Dssm., LO 237 (=LAE 276–78; s. M-M s.v. δεκαέξ) and L-S-J-M s.v. δέκα.—**δεκαοκτώ** (ins in Meisterhans[3]-Schw. 161 and Schweizer 165; Cleonides [II AD], Introductio Harmonica 2; pap, LXX; Jos., C. Ap. 1, 230; TestJud 9:2; ApcMos 1) ***eighteen*** **Lk 13:4, 11 (16** δ. καὶ ὀκτώ as JosAs 27:2; s. Thackeray 188); B 9:8 (Jos., Ant. 1, 178).—**δεκαπέντε** (ins in Meisterhans[3] -Schw. 160, 12; pap in Mayser 316; Polyb., Diod. S., Plut., Joseph., LXX; ParJer 7:7; GrBar 4:10; πέντε καὶ δέκα ἐτῶν TestAbr B 9 p. 113, 19 [Stone p. 74]) ***fifteen*** **J 11:18; Ac 27:5 v.l., 28; Gal 1:18** (ἡμ. δεκ. means our *two weeks* as Appian, Liby. 108 §507 [πεντεκαίδεκα ἡμ.]; Jos., Ant. 13, 427; Beros[s]us 680: fgm. 8 [140] p. 390, 15 Jac. [in Jos., C. Ap. 1, 140]; OGI 210, 7 [247/48]).—**δεκατέσσαρες** (ins in Schweizer 165; OGI 672, 13; pap in Mayser 316; Polyb., Diod. S., Strabo, Plut., Joseph., LXX; TestAbr A 17 p. 99, 18 [Stone p. 46]; TestJob 25:1; TestIss 1:10) ***fourteen*** **Mt 1:17** (on the numerical difficulties here s. HSchöllig, ZNW 59, '68, 261–68); **2 Cor 12:2; Gal 2:1** (LDieu, Quatorze ans ou quatre ans?: ETL 14, '37, 308–17; PFriesenhahn, Hellenistische Wortzahlenmystik, '35).—DELG s.v. δέκα. DELG s.v. δέκα. M-M. TW.

δεκαδύο, δεκαέξ, δεκαοκτώ, δεκαπέντε s. δέκα. —M-M.

Δεκάπολις, εως, ἡ (Jos., Bell. 3, 446; IGR III, 1057, 5) ***Decapolis*** name of a league orig. consisting of ten cities (αἱ δέκα πόλεις: Jos., Vi. 341f), whose region (except for Scythopolis) lay east of the Jordan. Damascus marked the boundary to the north, Philadelphia to the south. **Mt 4:25; Mk 5:20; 7:31.**—Schürer II 125–58; on the gentile cults II 36–39; HGuthe, D. griech.-röm. Städte d. Ostjordanlandes 1918; Kl.-Pauly I 1436f; BHHW 1, 332f. HBietenhard, Die Syrischen Dekapolis von Pompeius bis Traian: ANRW II/8, '77, 220–61; SEG XLII, 1484 (sources and lit.). OEANE II 127–30.—M-M.

δεκατέσσαρες s. δέκα.

δέκατος, η, ον (s. δέκα and next entry; Hom.+)—❶ **pert. to being tenth in a series,** ***tenth*** (ordinal number) a precious gem **Rv 21:20;** ὅρος Hs 9, 1, 9; 9, 27, 1; hour (prob.=4 p.m.; 3 Macc 5:14) **J 1:39; Ac 19:9** D.

❷ **pert. to being a tenth part of someth.,** ***part,*** as subst. (sc. μέρις)—ⓐ gener. τὸ δ. ***a tenth (part)*** (Appian, Ital. 8 §2; Lucian, Sat. 14; Ex 16:36; Lev 5:11 al.; Philo, Congr. Erud. Gr. 102) **Rv 11:13.**

ⓑ specific **ἡ δεκάτη** a tenth of someth. offered for a specific purpose ***tenth part, tithe*** (Simonides 106b Diehl[2]; Hdt. 2, 135; 4, 152) of booty (Maximus Tyr. 24, 5b [for the gods from the spoils of war]) **Hb 7:2, 4** (Gen 14:20). Of the gift of a tithe prescribed by the Jewish law (LXX; Ps.-Hecataeus: 264 fgm. 21 [188] Jac. [in Jos., C. Ap. 1, 188]; Philo, Congr. Erud. Gr. 98 al.; Joseph.; cp. on sim. sacred gifts Diod. S. 20, 14, 2; IDelosChoix 5, 2 [Artemis]; SEG XXVIII, 1541 [III/II BC]; IG XI, 1243 [III/II BC]; PHib 115, 1 [c. 250 BC]; μόσχων δεκάτης; PTebt 307, 8; O. Wilck I 348f; s. SWallace, Taxation in Egypt, '38, index) pl. (as Lysias 20, 24; 2 Esdr 22:44; 1 Macc 3:49; 10:31; 11:35; Jos., Ant. 14, 203) **Hb 7:8f** (δεκ. λαμβάνειν as Diod. S. 5, 42, 1; Ps.-Lucian, Salt. 21).—JBaumgarten, JBL 103, '84, 245–51 (Hb. background for nonliteral use).—Kl. Pauly I 1438. DELG s.v. δέκα. M-M. New Docs 3, 65.

δεκατόω pf. δεδεκάτωκα, pass. δεδεκάτωμαι (s. prec. entry; 2 Esdr 20:38; Dositheus 77, 7; Suda in conjunction w. Hb 7:9) ***collect, receive tithes*** τινά *fr. someone* **Hb 7:6.** Pass. in act. sense *pay tithes* vs. **9.**—DELG s.v. δέκα; M-M.

δεκτός, ή, όν (Alciphron 3, 34, 4; Iambl., Protr. 21, 19 p. 117, 27 Pistelli; LXX; verbal adj. of δέχομαι).

❶ **pert. to being met with approval in someone's company, *acceptable, welcome,*** of pers. (Hesych.: δεκτόν· εὐπρόσδεκτον): prophets **Lk 4:24** (cp. the experience of Aesop οἱ δὲ ὄχλοι ἡδέως μὲν αὐτοῦ ἠκροοῦντο, οὐδὲν δὲ αὐτὸν ἐτίμησαν Vi. Aesopi W 124 P.); Ox 1 recto, 10 (ASyn. 33, 85; cp. GTh 31), only here of human recognition; in all other references in this entry always of acceptance by God. W. dat. **Ac 10:35.**

❷ **pert. to being pleasing because of being approved, *pleasing, acceptable,*** of things: sabbaths B 15:8; sacrifices (w. εὐάρεστος) **Phil 4:18;** MPol 14:1; Hs 5, 3, 8 (cp. Sir 35:6; Herm. Wr. 13, 21; SIG 1042, 8f ἀπρόσδεκτος ἡ θυσία παρὰ τ. θεοῦ); fasting B 3:2 (Is 58:5); Hs 5, 1, 3; 5 (both w. dat.); generosity s 2:7, w. παρά τινι (Pr 12:22; 15:8, 28).

❸ **pert. to being appropriate to circumstances, *favorable,*** of time **2 Cor 6:2** (Is 49:8); year **Lk 4:19;** B 14:9 (both Is 61:2). In these passages the concrete temporal element points to the abstract feature of God's favorable attitude finding climactic expression.—The rdg. in ApcPt Rainer 19f is uncertain: δεκτὸς τῆς ἐπαγγελίας (Ethiopic indicates ἐκλεκτός *beneficiary of the promise*)—DELG s.v. δέχομαι p. 268. M-M. TW.

δελεάζω 'to lure by the use of bait' (δέλεαρ 'bait', Pla., Tim. 69d ἡδονὴν μέγιστον κακοῦ δέλεαρ) then **to arouse someone's interest in someth. by adroit measures, *lure, entice*** (in fig. sense since Isocr. and X.; Jos., Bell. 5, 120; ApcMos 19 and 26) to sin, w. ἐξέλκεσθαι **Js 1:14** (cp. M. Ant. 2, 12 τὰ ἡδονῇ δελεάζοντα; Philo, Omn. Prob. Lib. 159 πρὸς ἐπιθυμίας ἐλαύνεται ἢ ὑφ' ἡδονῆς δελεάζεται, Agr. 103.—Cp. schol. on Nicander, Ther. 793 δελεάζοντες τοὺς ἰχθῦς. Since ἐξέλκω is likewise a t.t. of a fisher's speech [e.g. Od. 5, 432], a fishing metaphor is probable: 'drawn out and enticed by his own desire'). Of false teachers who entice unstable Christians to veer from the true path **2 Pt 2:14, 18.**—DELG s.v. δέλεαρ.

Δελματία s. Δαλματία.

δένδρον, ου, τό (Hdt.+ [in Hom. δένδρεον]) **a relatively large woody plant, *tree* Mt 21:8; Lk 21:29; Rv 7:1, 3; 8:7; 9:4.** Freq. of fruit-bearing varieties, and in contexts pointing to fig. use: **Mt 3:10; Lk 3:9** (ELohmeyer, V. Baum u. Frucht: ZST 9, '32, 377–79); the sound tree and the rotten tree, of good and bad people (Paroem. Gr.: Diogenian. 5, 15 ἐκ τ. καρποῦ τὸ δένδρον) **Mt 7:17ff; 12:33** (s. IEph 14:2); **Lk 6:43f.** Lacking fruit δ. φθινοπωρινὰ ἄκαρπα **Jd 12.** In a good sense δ. ὡραῖον B 11:10; (εἰς) δ. γίνεσθαι *become a tree* **Lk 13:19; Mt 13:32.** ὡς δένδρα ὁρῶ *like trees* **Mk 8:24** (cp. SIG 1168, 121).—Used by Hermas in various figures Hs 2:2; 3:1, 3; 4:1–4; 8, 1, 3f; 8, 2, 7 and 9; 8, 3, 1f; 8, 6, 1; 9, 1, 9f; 9, 27, 1; 9, 28, 1 and 3.—B. 49. DELG s.v. δένδρεον. M-M.

δεξιοβόλος (not found elsewh.; but ἀδεξιοβόλος is found in Ps.-Callisth. 1, 24, 10 in ms. A) **Ac 23:23 v.l.** (s. δεξιολάβος).

δεξιολάβος, ου, ὁ **Ac 23:23** (ms. A has δεξιοβόλος), a word of uncertain mng., military t.t., acc. to Joannes Lydus (in Constantinus Porphyrog., De Themat. 1, 5) and Theophyl. Sim., Hist. 4, 1 a light-armed soldier, perh. ***bowman, slinger;*** acc. to a scholion in CMatthaei p. 342 *body-guard.* Acc. to EEgli, ZWT 17, 1884, 20ff δεξιόλαβος *left-handed* (?). *Spearman* Goodsp., NRSV; 'security officer', GKilpatrick, JTS 14, '63, 393f. W-S. §6, 4; Mlt-H. 272f.—Bruce, Acts 470. M-M.

δεξιός, ά, όν (Hom.+; Ath. 15, 2 κατὰ τὴν τέχνην 'artistically appropriate')

❶ **right as opposed to left in a frame of reference, *right.***

ⓐ Used w. a noun χείρ (Hippocr.; Epid. 5, p. 88 [2, 8]) **Mt 5:30; Lk 6:6; Ac 3:7; Rv 1:16f; 10:5** (Dt 32:40); **13:16;** eye (Hippocr., Epid. 3, 1, 3 [44] ed. Kühlewein I 218, 19) **Mt 5:29** (the right eye is esp. valuable because its loss is a handicap to the warrior: Jos., Ant. 6, 69–71; here in 71 also the thought: it is better to suffer the loss of the right eye than to ἀπολωλέναι in possession of all the other members); cheek vs. **39** (s. D 1:4); ear (s. on οὖς 1) **Lk 22:50; J 18:10;** shoulder Hs 9, 2, 4; foot (Artem. 2, 51; 5, 70) **Rv 10:2.** τὰ δ. μέρη *the right side* **J 21:6;** Hv 3, 1, 9; 3, 2, 1 (as the lucky side as Il. 12, 239; 13, 821; Artem. 5, 92; Quint. Smyrn. 12, 58).—Abs. ἡ δ. (sc. χείρ) *the right hand* (Hom.+; LXX; ApcEsdr 3:7 p. 27, 15 Tdf.; Jos., Ant. 17, 184) **Mt 6:3** in a warning against 'strategic' giving; **27:29; Rv 1:17, 20; 2:1; 5:1, 7**—τὰ δ. (sc. μέρη; s. above) *the right side* (X., An. 1, 8, 4); περιέβλεπεν τὰ δ. καὶ τὰ ἀριστερά GJs 11:1 (s. ἀριστερός). ἐκ δεξιῶν *on the right* (X., Cyr. 8, 5, 15 al.; oft. pap [Mayser 226]; LXX; En 13:7; Jos., Ant. 4, 305) w. gen. (Tob 1:2; Zech 4:3; Sir 12:12 al.; TestAbr A 12 p. 91, 2 [Stone p. 30] al.; TestJob 33:3) **Mt 25:33f** (cp. Plut., Mor. 192f ἐκέλευε τοὺς μὲν ἐπὶ δεξιᾷ τοῦ βήματος θεῖναι, τοὺς δ' ἐπ' ἀριστερᾷ … τ. βελτίονας … τοὺς χείρονας); **Mk 15:27; Lk 1:11;** Pol 2:1; abs. (1 Esdr 9:43; Ex 14:22, 29; 3 Km 7:25, 35 al.) **Mt 27:38; Lk 23:33;** B 11:10; Hv 3, 2, 1f; 4; s 9, 6, 2. Also ἐν τοῖς δ. **Mk 16:5** or δεξιά (s. εὐώνυμος, end) Hs 9, 12, 8. Pl. ἐκ δεξιῶν τινος εἶναι *stand at someone's side* **Ac 2:25** (Ps 15:8; of geographical location En 13:7 Ἑρμωνοεὶμ δύσεως 'to the right of Hermon').—In imagery of spiritual equipment ὅπλα δ. καὶ ἀριστερά *weapons for the right side and the left side* **2 Cor 6:7** (sword and shield, offense and defense).

ⓑ freq. in symbolism (on symbolic use s. SFlory, Medea's Right Hand: Promise and Revenge: TAPA 108, '78, 69–74; cp. δεξιτερή [sc. χείρ] Il. 22, 320 Achilles is about to avenge the death of Patroclus; s. also Soph., Phil. 813. The pl. δεξιαί is used in Hom. of pledges given in good faith with the right hand Il. 2, 341=4, 159; for use of the term in contracts s. Preis. s.v., esp. PFay 124, 13 [II AD]) and imagery relating to prestige or power. Abs. (sc. χεῖρ): of position at the *right hand* of an eminent pers., esp. a royal figure (for a king's right hand as emblematic of prestige s. 1 Cl 28:3 [Ps 138:10]); B 12:11 (Is 45:1). δ. διδόναι *give the right hand* (on this abs. use cp. the Eng. expression 'give me five') as a sign of friendship and trust (X., An. 1, 6, 6; 2, 5, 3; Alex. Ep. XIV, 31; Diod. S. 13, 43, 4; Appian, Liby. 64, 284; 1 and 2 Macc; Jos., Ant. 18, 326; 328.—Dssm., NB 78f [BS 251]; Nägeli 24) **Gal 2:9** (KGrayston, BRigaux Festschr., '70, 485: 'came to terms'; JSampley, Pauline Partnership in Christ '80, 26–35). ἐπιτιθέναι τὴν δ. ἐπὶ τ. κεφαλήν τινος *lay one's right hand on someone's head* B 13:5a (Gen. 48:18a ἐπιβάλλειν); also μετατιθέναι … τινος *transfer one's right hand on someone's head* vs. 5b (Gen 48:18b ἐπιτιθέναι). ἐν δεξιᾷ *at the right* (Arrian, Anab. 6, 2, 2): ἐν δ. τινος *at someone's right:* God's (Ael. Aristid. 37, 6 K.=2 p. 15 D., w. allusion to Pind., calls Athena δεξιὰν κατὰ χεῖρα τοῦ πατρὸς [Zeus] καθεζομένη.—Pind., N. 11, 2 names Hera as the ὁμόθρονος of Zeus) **Ro 8:34; Eph**

1:20; Col 3:1; Hb 10:12; 1 Pt 3:22.** τῆς μεγαλωσύνης **Hb 1:3;** τοῦ θρόνου **8:1; 12:2.**—The right hand in imagery of power (of God: PsSol 13, 1; Jos., Bell. 1, 378) τῇ δεξιᾷ of God (as Is 63:12) *by* or *with his right hand* (cp. Maximus Tyr. 4, 8a) **Ac 2:33; 5:31** (BWeiss; Zahn; HHoltzmann; Felten; Beyer; Steinmann; Moffatt Ac 2:33); it may also be dat. of place (B-D-F §199; Rob. 526; 543) *at* or *to his right hand* (Weizsäcker; Wendt; Knopf; Belser; Hoennicke; OHoltzmann; Moffatt Ac 5:31). Pl. καθίσαι ἐκ δ. τινος *sit at someone's right,* i.e. at the place of honor (3 Km 2:19; Jos., Ant. 8, 7) of the Messiah **Mt 20:21, 23; Mk 10:37, 40;** of God **Mt 22:44** (Ps 109:1); **26:64; Mk 12:36** (Ps 109:1); **14:62; 16:19; Lk 20:42** (Ps 109:1); **22:69; Ac 2:34; Hb 1:13;** 1 Cl 36:5; B 12:10 (the last 4 Ps 109:1); *stand on the right* as the place of honor (Ps 44:10) **Ac 7:55f;** Hs 9, 6, 2 (s. Bihlmeyer app.).—AGornatowski, Rechts u. Links im ant. Abergl., diss. Breslau '36; JDaniélou, TU 73, '59, 689–98; BLiow-Gille, 'Dexter' et 'sinister' et leur équivalents: Glotta 69, '91, 194–201.

❷ **pert. to being morally or spiritually correct,** ***true*** σύνεσις δ., ἀριστερά *understanding of what is true and what is false* D 12:1 (for other interpretations s. ἀριστερός and σύνεσις).—B. 865. DELG. M-M. TW.

δέομαι (s. δέησις) pass. dep. impf. 3 sg. ἐδεῖτο **Lk 8:38** (Tdf. and other edd. have the Ion. form ἐδέετο, so also TestJob 39:8; s. B-D-F §89; Helbing 110; Thackeray 243); fut. δεηθήσομαι LXX; 1 aor. ἐδεήθην, impv. δεήθητι, pl. δεήθητε; pf. δεδέημαι 3Km 8:59 (in var. mngs. Hdt.+). In our lit. only w. the mng. **to ask for something pleadingly,** ***ask, request,*** which predominates also in LXX and En (Jos., Vi. 310 al.), w. gen. of pers.

ⓐ gener. of address to humans *ask, request*—**α.** w. inf. foll. (X., Cyr. 1, 5, 4; Herodian 2, 11, 9; Jdth 12:8; 3 Macc 1:16; 5:25; pap esp. in petitions since III BC; e.g. PCairZen 236, 4; BGU 1297, 6; UPZ 50, 24) **Lk 8:38; 9:38; Ac 26:3** (σου) v.l.

β. w. acc. of thing (X., Cyr. 1, 4, 2; Pla., Apol. 17c; 1 Esdr 8:53 v.l.) δεόμενοι ἡμῶν τὴν χάριν *begging us for the favor* **2 Cor 8:4.** Without gen. of pers. δέομαι τὸ μὴ παρὼν θαρρῆσαι *I ask that when I am present I need not show boldness* **10:2.**

γ. w. direct discourse foll., *(I) beg (of you),* or *please* (Gen 19:18; 44:18; PCairZen 639, 15 δέομαί σου, μή με περιίδῃς; Vi. Aesopi W 100, 6f P. δέομαί σου, δέσποτα, διαλλάγηθι Σαμίοις) δέομαί σου, ἐπίτρεψόν μοι *please allow me* **Ac 21:39;** sim. **8:34; Lk 8:28; Gal 4:12.** W. λέγων added **Lk 5:12.** Without gen. of the pers., but w. ὑπὲρ Χριστοῦ (s. ὑπέρ A1c) added **2 Cor 5:20.**

δ. w. ἵνα foll. (Sir 37:15; 38:14; 1 Esdr 4:46; Jos., Ant. 12, 121) **Lk 9:40; 11:37** D; B 12:7; Hs 5, 4, 1.

ⓑ of petition to God (w. αἰτεῖσθαι) δεώμεθα … ἀπὸ τοῦ ἐλέους αὐτοῦ, ἵνα 1 Cl 50:2. W. gen. (cp. Epict. 2, 7, 12 in a simile about petitioning a bird-augur as one would a deity; PsSol 2:22 of one petitioning τοῦ προσώπου κυρίου) τοῦ θεοῦ *praying to God* **Ac 10:2;** τοῦ κυρίου ἵνα Hv 3, 1, 2; Pol. 6:2. Other constructions in address to God: w. εἰ ἄρα foll. **Ac 8:22,** ὅπως (cp. Ael. Aristid. 35, 28 K.=9 p. 108 D.; Aesop, Fab. 63 P.=117 H.: ἐδεήθη αὐτῶν ὅπως; Jos., Ant. 9, 9) **Mt 9:38; Lk 10:2;** δ. πρὸς τὸν κύριον (Ps 29:9; 141, 1; Is 37:4) w. ὑπὲρ τινος and ὅπως foll. **Ac 8:24** (ParJer 7:24).—Without ref. to the one petitioned: περί τινος (Jdth 8:31; Sir 21:1; 28:4; Da 4:27; Jos., Ant. 10, 203) B 13:2 (Gen 25:21); w. ἵνα foll. **Lk 21:36; 22:32;** w. εἰς and inf. foll. **1 Th 3:10;** δ. ἐπὶ τῶν προσευχῶν *ask in prayer* w. εἴ πως foll. **Ro 1:10.** Abs. (Tob 3:11; 3 Macc 1:24; 2:10; En 12:6) δεηθέντων αὐτῶν **Ac 4:31;** αὐτὸς δὲ ἐδεήθη AcPl Ha 4, 6; οἱ δεόμενοι *those who pray* (Lucian, Tim. 5; 8; Wsd 16:25) 1 Cl 59:4.—DCrump, Jesus the Intercessor '92.—DELG s.v. δέω 2. M-M. TW.

δέον s. δεῖ 2a.—M-M.

δέος, ους, τό (Hom. et al.; Epicharmus Com. fgm. 221 K.; Polemo Soph. 1, 41 p. 14, 21 H.=p. 124, 1 R.; Epict. 2, 23, 38; Lucian, Necyom. 10, Dial. Deor. 2, 1; 2 Macc; Jos., Ant. 12, 246; 16, 235; Just.; Ath. 1, 2) **emotion of profound respect and reverence for deity,** ***awe*** (w. εὐλάβεια) **Hb 12:28.**—1 Cl 2:4 v.l. (Lghtf.) for ἔλεος.—B. 1153. DELG s.v. δείδω. M-M. TW.

δεπόσιτα, ων, τά ***deposits (of money)*** Lat. loanw. 'deposita'; military t.t. When gifts of money were given the army on special occasions, the individual soldier received only half of what was due him; the rest was deposited to his credit in the regimental treasury (Lat. depositum apud signa), and he received it (as ἄκκεπτα, q.v.) if and when he was honorably discharged (Sueton., Domit. 7; Vegetius, De Re Milit. 2, 20; PFay 105 II, 1; III, 13ff [c. 180 AD]; Geneva Lat. pap in JNicole and ChMorel, Archives militaires du 1er siècle 1900, and the lit. on it, e.g. Mommsen, Her 35, 1900, 443ff; HBlümner NJklA 5, 1900, 432–43; AvPremerstein, Klio 3, 1903, 1ff, here a ref. to an unedited Berlin pap no. 6866 of c. 180 AD and further lit.) IPol 6:2.—Kl. Pauly I 1492f; RAC III 778–84.

Δερβαῖος, α, ον ***from Derbe*** ὁ Δ. (Stephan. Byz. s.v. Ἄβαι) of Gaius **Ac 20:4.** The difficulty caused by the fact that a certain Gaius is called a Macedonian 19:29 is prob. the reason for the v.l. Δουβ[ή]ριος in D (of a Maced. city); K and SLake, JBL 53, '34, 44f; s. Haenchen (Ger. 65f; Eng. tr. 52f).

Δέρβη, ης, ἡ ***Derbe,*** a city in Lycaonia, in the Roman province of Galatia (Strabo 12, 6, 3; Ptolemaeus 5, 6, 71) **Ac 14:6, 20; 16:1.**—JWeiss, RE X 560, 43ff; WRamsay, The Cities of St. Paul 1907. See Haenchen, end of preceding entry. Definitely located at Kerti Hüyük: see Bible dictionaries s.v. Derbe; GOgg, NTS 9, '63, 367–70; BHHW I 336; Kl. Pauly I 1493.

δέρμα, ατος, τό (δέρω 'to skin, flay'; Hom. et al.; ins, pap, LXX, TestSol, Philo; Jos., Ant. 1, 270) **skin of an animal separated from the body and usually with attached hair and sometimes tanned,** ***skin, hide*** αἴγειον *goatskin* (PEdgar 11, 8=PCairZen 60, 8=Sb 6717 [257 BC]; PFay 107, 2 δέρματα αἴγεια) **Hb 11:37;** 1 Cl 17:1; δ. αἴ. λευκόν Hv 5:1; s 6, 2, 5.—B. 200. DELG s.v. δέρω. M-M.

δερμάτινος, η, ον (Hom. et al.; SIG 736, 23; PTebt 112; BGU 814, 10; LXX; Philo) ***(made of) leather,*** ζώνη *belt* (4 Km 1:8; Jos., Ant. 9, 22) **Mt 3:4; Mk 1:6;** GEb 13, 79.—B. 407. DELG s.v. δέρω. New Docs 4, 66. M-M.

δέρρις, εως, ἡ (Thu. 2, 75, 5 et al. [in forms of δέρσις]; SIG 736, 55 [92 BC]; Sb 6801, 26 [246/245 BC]; LXX, esp. Zech 13:4; JosAs 10:4) ***skin.*** John the Baptist described as ἐνδεδυμένος δέρριν καμήλου (δ. as clothing: Eupolis Com. [V BC] 328) **Mk 1:6 v.l.** (cp. ms. a: pellem). EbNestle[4]-EvDobschütz, Einführung in d. Griech. NT 1923, 7 and comm. on the passage.—DELG s.v. δέρω. M-M.

δέρω 1 aor. ἔδειρα. Pass.: 2 fut. δαρήσομαι; 2 aor. ἐδάρην (Hom. et al.; LXX) orig. 'skin, flay' (Il. 23, 167 et al.; PCairZen III 354, 4 [240 BC]); in our lit. only in imagery ***beat, whip*** (so, in colloq. speech, since Aristoph., Ran. 618; Epict. 3, 19, 5; 3, 22, 54f al.; SIG 1109, 91; POxy 653 [b]; Sb 7523, 3, 12; PMich 204, 9; Ath. 1, 4; not LXX) τινά **Mt 21:35; Mk 12:3, 5; Lk 20:10f; 22:63; J 18:23; Ac 5:40; 16:37; 22:19.** Pass. **Mk**

13:9 (FDanker, NovT 10, '68, 162f); Hs 6, 2, 7 (s. also δαίρω). τινὰ εἰς πρόσωπον *strike someone in the face* **2 Cor 11:20.** δαρήσεται πολλάς, ὀλίγας (Aristoph., Nub. 968 τυπτόμενος πολλάς, to which a scholiast adds πληγὰς δηλονότι. X., An. 5, 8, 12 ὀλίγας παίειν; s. πληγή 1) *he will receive many, few blows* **Lk 12:47f;** ἀέρα δ. *beat the air* of unskillful boxers, who miss their mark **1 Cor 9:26** (not a t.t., but s. schol. on Lucian, p. 93, 16 Rabe πύκται … μὴ … πρὸς ἀέρα δέρειν).—Abs. δέρεσθαι καὶ νικᾶν *endure punishment and yet win* IPol 3:1.—B. 553; 567. DELG. M-M (add for the metaph. sense the reff. by APapathomas, NTS 43, '97, 238f, n. 70).

δεσέρτωρ, ορος, ὁ (Lat., loanw. desertor, also in Basilius Magn., Ep. 258: MPG XXXII 997c) ***deserter,*** military term (on the Roman perspective s. Reader, Polemo p. 345f) IPol 6:2.

δεσμεύω 1 aor. 3 sg. ἐδέσμευσε (TestSol); subj. 2 sg. (Sir 12:12 B[corr]). Pass.: impf. ἐδεσμευόμην; aor. inf. δεσμευθῆναι (TestSol 13:7)

❶ ***bind*** (Eur.; X.; Pla., Leg. 7, 808d; Epict. 4, 1, 127; PGM 4, 1246:5, 320; Judg 16:11 B; cp. 3 Macc 5:5; TestSol; ParJer 7:26 [ABH]; Jos., Ant. 14, 348) τινά **Lk 8:29; Ac 22:4;** τὴν πᾶσαν σάρκα ἀνθρώπων πρὸς ἡδονὴν ἐδέσμευεν (the devil) *bound all flesh of humans to pleasure* AcPlCor 2:11.

❷ ***tie up (in a bundle)*** (Hes., Op. 481 grain in a sheaf; Polyb.; PHib 214, 1 [c. 250 BC]; Sb 9386, 4; 9409 [1], 76 and 77; PLond I, 131 recto, 426 and 437 p. 182f; PFlor 322, 31; Gen 37:7; Jdth 8:3; Am 2:8) in imagery φορτίον *tie up a burden, load* which is then put on a person's shoulder **Mt 23:4** (cp. Cicero, Tusc. Disp. II, 4, 11).—DELG s.v. δέω 1. M-M.

δεσμέω (Aristot., De Plant. 1, 2 p. 817b, 21; Heliod. 8, 9; Jos., Bell. 1, 71 al.) **Lk 8:29 v.l.** for δεσμεύω, q.v.

δέσμη (Lobeck, Paralipomena Gramm. Graec. 1837, 396, or δεσμή as the gramm. Herodian I 324, 10; II 426, 6 [Lentz] would accent it) **ης, ἡ** ***bundle*** (since Demosth. and Theophr., HP 9, 17, 1; Diod. S. 19, 99, 2 δέσμη καλάμων; Dionys. Hal. 3, 61, 2; pap [Mayser 285; 435]; Ex 12:22) δῆσαι εἰς δέσμας *tie up in bundles* **Mt 13:30.**—DELG s.v. δέω 1. M-M. TW.

δέσμιος, ου, ὁ ***prisoner*** (so trag. +; δ. τῆς ἁμαρτίας, Hippol., Ref. 1, prol. 3.—Nägeli 26) **Mt 27:15f; Mk 15:6.** Of Christians and others in prison **Ac 16:25, 27; 23:18; 25:14, 27; 28:16 v.l., 17; Hb 10:34; 13:3;** 1 Cl 59:4; AcPl Ha 4, 1; 11, 9. Paul calls himself δ. (τοῦ) Χριστοῦ Ἰησοῦ **Phlm 1, 9; Eph 3:1;** AcPlCor 2:1; cp. **2 Ti 1:8.** Also δ. ἐν κυρίῳ **Eph 4:1.** S. on this Rtzst., Mysterienrel.[3] 196ff; 214; UWilcken, UPZ I 52–77; LDelekat, Katoche, Hierodoulie u. Adoptionsfreilassg. '64.—Straub 39. DELG s.v. δέω 1. M-M. TW.

δεσμός, οῦ, ὁ pl. δεσμά (Diod. S. 14, 103, 3; Nicander, Ther. 317 and 728; JosAs 20:1 [cod. A and Pal 364]; Jos., Bell. 4, 143, Ant. 2, 60; Just., Ath.; Sb 7569, 21 [II BC], s. also Mayser 285; PGM 36, 143 and 57, 5) **Lk 8:29; Ac 16:26; 20:23;** 1 Cl 5:6; 55:2; IEph 11:2; ITr 12:2; ISm 10:2; IPol 2:3; AcPlCor 2:35; δεσμοί (Hom., Od. 8, 296b; Nicander, Ther. 479; Polyaenus 2, 31, 3; SIG[2] 588, 6; PTebt 886, 69; POxy 2424, 16; Sb 9379 IV 2, 4 al.; Ath. 21:3) **Phil 1:13.** Both forms also in Attic ins (Meisterhans[3]-Schw. 143, 3) and LXX (Thackeray 154); Philo (Somn. 1, 181 -ά, Sacr. Abel. 81 -οί); δέσμοις En 14:5; TestSol; TestJos.—B-D-F §49, 3; W-S. §8, 12; Crönert 175, 3; Reinhold 54; Mlt-H. 121f.

❶ **that which serves as a means of restraint by tying or fastening, *bond, fetter*** (Hom.+)—ⓐ lit. of the bond or hindrance that prevents mutes **Mk 7:35** or crippled persons **Lk 13:16** from using their members (s. Dssm., LO 258ff [LAE 306ff], and cp. SIG 1169, 43). Pl. *bonds, fetters* (δ. λύειν Orig., C. Cels. 2, 34, 15) **Lk 8:29; Ac 16:26; 20:23; 22:30 v.l.; 23:29; 26:29, 31; Jd 6** (on the mythological aspect s. LfgrE s.v. for ancient reff.); δ. φορεῖν *be in* bonds (=δεσμοφορέω) 1 Cl 5:6; sim. ἔχω AcPlCor 2:35; παραδιδόναι εἰς δ. *give over to bondage* 55:2; τὰ δ. περιφέρειν IEph 11:2; cp. IMagnMai 1, 2. πεῖραν λαμβάνειν δεσμῶν (cp. Vett. Val. 68, 17 δεσμῶν πεῖραν λαμβάνοντες) *become acquainted w. bonds* **Hb 11:36.** On B 14:7 (Is 42:7) cp. πεδάω. ῥαγῆναι τὰ δεσμὰ ἀπὸ τῶν χερῶν μου *so that the fetters broke away from my hands* AcPl Ha 3, 12; ἔλυσεν τὰ δεσμά *released the bonds* 3, 14; ἐπὶ τῶν δ. *about the bonds* 3, 16 (cp. Mel., fgm. 10 ἵνα δεσμῶν Ἰσαὰκ λυθῇ).—Oft. simply in ref. to the locale where bonds or fetters are worn *imprisonment, prison* (Diod. S. 14, 103, 3; Lucian, Tox. 29; Jos., Ant. 13, 294; 302, Vi. 241; Just., A I, 67, 6 al.) **Phil 1:7, 13f, 17; Col 4:18; Phlm 10.** μέχρι δεσμῶν **2 Ti 2:9.** ἐν τοῖς δ. τοῦ εὐαγγελίου *in imprisonment for the gospel* **Phlm 13;** cp. ISm 11:1; Pol 1:1.

ⓑ fig. (Herm. Wr. 7, 2b φθορᾶς δ.) δ. κακίας IEph 19:3 (cp. τῆς ἁμαρτιάς Did., Gen. 47, 17). Without qualification (Orig., C. Cels. 8, 57, 2) IPhld 8:1; πεπίστευκα θεῷ, ὃς ἐκ δ. ἐρύσατο τὸν κόσμον ὅλον *I believe that God has released the entire world from its fetters* AcPl Ha 3, 7. Of divine punishment 2 Cl 20:4 (s. Bihlmeyer app.).

❷ **someth. that holds pers. together in a common interest, *bond*** fig. ext. of the lit. sense in 1 (Timagenes [I BC]: 88 fgm. 5 Jac. [in Jos., Ant. 13, 319] 'bond of circumcision'; EpArist 265 εὐνοίας δ.; Tat. 15, 2 δ. τῆς σαρκὸς ψυχή; sim. Iren. 1, 21, 5 [Harv. I 188, 8]; δ. τοῦ σώματος Hippol., Ref. 7, 38, 5) δ. τῆς ἀγάπης τοῦ θεοῦ *bond of God's love* 1 Cl 49:2 (cp. Theodor. Prodr. 5, 245 H. τὰ δεσμὰ τῆς ἀγάπης).—EDNT. DELG s.v. δέω 1 p. 270. M-M. TW.

δεσμοφύλαξ, ακος, ὁ (s. δέσμος and φύλαξ; Lucian, Tox. 30; Artem. 3, 60; Vett. Val. 68, 26; Cass. Dio 76, 10, 3; pap since III BC [Mayser 467], also BGU 1138, 12ff; TestJos 2:3; Jos., Ant. 2, 61; AcThom 118 [Aa II/2, 228, 15] al. ἀρχιδεσμοφύλαξ Gen 39:21–23; 41:10 v.l.) ***jailer, keeper of a prison* Ac 16:23, 27, 36.**—M-M.

δεσμωτήριον, ου, τό (Hdt., Thu. et al., also pap since III BC, LXX, En, Philo; Jos., Bell. 4, 385, C. Ap. 2, 247; Just., A II, 2, 11; Mel., P. 48) place for detention (prisons in the Rom. world were ordinarily used for temporary custody to prevent escape pending sentencing, not for rehabilitation; Rom. law did not permit the chaining of free citizens) ***prison, jail* Mt 11:2** (a longer detention for political reasons); **Ac 5:21, 23; 16:26;** παραδοθῆναι εἰς δ. *be thrown into prison* Hs 9, 28, 7.—S. οἴκημα 2. BAFCS III passim; on honor-shame implications, s. 283–312. Kl. Pauly I 1496–97. DELG s.v. δέω 1 p. 270. M-M. TW.

δεσμώτης, ου, ὁ (Aeschyl., Hdt. et al.; PPetr II, 5 c, 2; 13 [3], 9; PSI 423, 3, 39; PColZen 58, 12; PCairZen 707, 4 [all III BC]; LXX; Jos., Ant. 2, 61; 18, 193; SibOr 11, 29) ***prisoner* Ac 27:1, 42.**—DELG s.v. δέω 1 p. 269. M-M. TW.

δεσπόζω fut. 2 sg. δεσπόσεις (4 Macc 5:38) (s. next; Hom. Hymns, Hdt.+, Polyb., Lucian, Philostrat.; pap, s. Mayser 33; Herm. Wr., fgm. XXIII 38 [p. 476, 33 Sc.]; LXX, TestSol, TestJob; Philo, Op. M. 148; Jos., Bell. 4, 575, Ant. 2, 52 al.; Just., A I, 14, 3; 44, 13) **to have complete power over another, *be lord/master*** τινός *of someth.* (Lucian, Catapl. 2; Ps.-Callisth. 3, 33, 19 τῷ πάντων δεσπόζοντι μεγάλῳ Σεράπιδι; Philostrat., Vi. Apoll. 1, 13 p. 13, 14; TestJob 45:4; Theoph. Ant. 1, 7 [p. 72,

8]) τῆς κτίσεως πάσης *of all creation* Hv 3, 4, 1.—DELG s.v. δεσπότης. TW. Sv.

δεσπότης, ου, ὁ (s. prec. entry; Sappho 97, 8 D. [95, 8 EVoigt '71], Pind., Hdt.+) voc. δέσποτα

❶ **one who has legal control and authority over persons, such as subjects or slaves, *lord, master*—ⓐ** of slaves (Pla., Parm. 133d, Leg. 757a al.; Paroem. Gr.: Zenob. [Hadrian] 2, 81 τ. ἰδίους δεσπότας et al.; Tat. 4, 1) **1 Ti 6:1f; Tit 2:9;** Phlm subscr.; **1 Pt 2:18;** Hs 5, 2, 2. A slave metaphor is present in some of the pass. in 1b, AChang, BiblSacra 142, '85, 52–63.

ⓑ of subjects. Ruler of a city Hs 1:6.—Esp. of God (Eur., Hipp. 88; X., An. 3, 2, 13; Pla., Euthyd. 302d and oft. in Gk. writings incl. Herm. Wr. 16:3 [p. 264, 14 Sc.]; OGI 619, 3; UPZ 1, 1 [IV BC]; PGM 36, 227 δέσποτα; LXX; TestAbr A I p. 77, 12 [Stone p. 2]; Artapanus: 726 fgm. 3, 22 Jac. [in Eus., PE 9, 27, 22]; Ezk. Trag. 124; 188 [in Eus., PE 9, 29, 11]; Philo, Rer. Div. Her. 22ff [PKatz, Philo's Bible, '50, 59f]; Jos., Bell. 7, 323, Ant. 8, 111; 18, 23; Just., A II, 6, 2 al.) **Lk 2:29; Ac 4:24; Rv 6:10;** 1 Cl 7:5; 9:4; 11:1; 24:1, 5; 36:2, 4; 40:1 al.; B 1:7; 4:3; Dg 8:7; Hv 2, 2, 4f; s 1:9; δ. ἁπάντων (cp. Job 5:8; Wsd. 6:7; 8:3; Sir 36:1; TestJos 1:5; Herm. Wr. 5, 4; PGM 3, 589; 4, 1164; 12, 250; δ. τῶν ὅλων Jos., Ant. 1, 72 and Just., D. 140, 4 [sim. Tat. 12, 4]; τοῦ παντὸς δ. Did., Gen. 99, 22) 1 Cl 8:2; 20:11; 33:2; 52:1; [ὁ τῶν ὅλ]ων δεσπότης Ox 1081, 36f (Coptic SJCh 90, 15); δ. καὶ δημιουργὸς τῶν ὅλων θεός Dg 8:7; τοῦ πάντων δ. GJs 11:2; ὁ δ. μου 23:3 (but s. deStrycker ad loc.). Of Christ **Lk 13:25** P[75]; **2 Pt 2:1; Jd 4** (δεσπ. and κύριος as Jos., Ant. 20, 90).

❷ **one who controls a thing, *owner*** of a vessel **2 Ti 2:21;** of honey Hm 5, 1, 5.—B. 1330. Schmidt, Syn. 116–24. DELG. M-M. TW. Sv.

δεσπότις, ιδος, ἡ (Soph., Eur., Pla. et al.; SEG VIII, 548, 25 [Isisaretal. I AD] term used by a slave in address to an owner POxy 48, 7; Sb 5616, 6) ***mistress*** [ἡ τ]οῦ χρυσοῦ πολλοῦ δ. mistress of much gold AcPl Ha 2, 19.—DELG s.v. δεσπότης.

δεῦρο adv. (Hom.+)—❶ of place, funct. as interjection *over here, (come) here, come!* w. impv. foll. (Hom. et al.; Menand., Epitr. 541 Kö. [861 S.]; Lucian, Catapl. 24 δεῦρο προσίτω; Gen 24:31; 2 Km 13:11; 3 Km 1:13 al.) δ. ἀκολούθει μοι *come! follow me* **Mt 19:21; Mk 10:21** ("almost a verb" Rob 302); **Lk 18:22.** Cp. δεῦρο καὶ ἴδε GJs 19:1 (not pap). Foll. by 1 pers. aor. subj., hortatory (Eur., Bacch. 341; Gen 31:44; 37:13; 4 Km 14:8 al. Cp. B-D-F §364, 1; Rob. 931f): **Ac 7:34** (Ex 3:10); **Rv 17:1; 21:9.**—Abs. (Pla., Tht. 144d: Θεαίτητε, δεῦρο παρὰ Σωκράτη) δεῦρο εἰς τ. γῆν *away into the country* [=*come away/go into the country*] **Ac 7:3** (Gen 12:1 v.l., influenced by **Ac 7:3** [ARahlfs, Genesis 1926], s. MWilcox, The Semitisms of Ac, '65, 26f; DTabachovitz, Die Septuaginta u. das NT, '56, 101; also 3 Km 1:53; 1 Macc 12:45). As in other lit., where δ. functions like a word for *come!* (s. the variant δεῦρο B for ἐλθέ A in Judg 18:19 and cp. Num 10:29; 1 Km 17:44; 4 Km 10:16; Od. 8, 292; Theognis 1, 1041; Hipponax [VI BC] 4, 4 Diehl[3] [=2, 2 Degani]; Pla., Rep. 5, 477d; Chariton 3, 7, 4 Χαιρέα, δεῦρο; Aristaen., Ep. 2, 7 p. 163 H.; PGM 12, 238 δεῦρό μοι; 13, 268) δεῦρο is used with related force in δεῦρο ἔξω *come out* (Menand., Epitr. 904 S. [Kö. 584]) **J 11:43;** δ. πρὸς τὸν πατέρα IRo 7:2.

❷ of time ***until now*** (μέχρι τοῦ δεῦρο: Thu. 3, 64, 3; SIG 821e, 2; 3; PLond II, 358, 16 p. 172; PStras 56, 12; 73, 16; Jos., Ant. 11, 93; Just., A I, 31, 5, D. 56, 10) ἄχρι τοῦ δ. *thus far* **Ro 1:13** (Sext. Emp., Math. 8, 401 ἄχρι δ.; PLond II, 409, 25f ἄχρεις δεῦρο).—DELG. M-M.

δεῦτε adv. (serves as pl. of δεῦρο) s. on δεῦρο, ***come here! come on!*** mostly as hortatory particle w. pl. (Hom.+). W. impv. or aor. subj. foll. (impv.: Josh 10:4; 4 Km 6:13; Ps 65:16 and oft.; Jos., Ant. 6, 111; aor. subj.: Gen 11:3f; 37:27; Ps 94:6 al.; En 6:2) δ. ἴδετε **Mt 28:6; J 4:29;** δ. ἀριστήσατε *come! eat* (=*come, it's time for breakfast*) **21:12;** δ. συνάχθητε *come! gather* **Rv 19:17;** δ. ἀκούσατε 1 Cl 22:1 (Ps 33:12); δ. ἀποκτείνωμεν αὐτόν *come on, let's kill him* **Mt 21:38; Mk 12:7; Lk 20:14 v.l.;** δ. καὶ διελεγχθῶμεν *come and let us reason together* 1 Cl 8:4 (Is 1:18).—Abs. (Aesop, Fab. 353a H.//319d Ch. p. 514//226 IIIδγ H-H.; LXX; Mel., P. 103, 787; JosAs 23:5; Just., D. 24, 3 σὺν ἐμοί) w. ὀπίσω τινός: δ. ὀπίσω μου *follow me* (4 Km 6:19) **Mt 4:19; Mk 1:17.** W. εἴς τι: *come on to the wedding* **Mt 22:4;** *come to an unfrequented place* **Mk 6:31.** W. πρός τινα: δ. πρός με *come here to me* **Mt 11:28** (on the theme, s. AFridrichsen, E. Unbeachtete Parallele [Epict. 4, 8, 28] in Wikenhauser Festschr., '53, 83–85); δ. οἱ εὐλογημένοι τοῦ πατρός μου *come, you whom my Father has blessed* **25:34.**—DELG, and also M-M s.v. δεῦρο.

δευτεραῖος, αία, ον (Hdt.; X., Cyr. 5, 2, 2; Diod. S. 13, 39, 1; Jos., Ant. 1, 178; SIG 982, 6f; PCairZen 736, 39 [III BC]) ***on the second day*** δευτεραῖοι ἤλθομεν *we came on the second day* **Ac 28:13** (B-D-F §243; Rob. 298).—DELG s.v. δεύτερος.

Δευτερονόμιον, ου, τό ***Deuteronomy*** title in the LXX for the last book of the Pentateuch B 10:2 (Mel., HE 4, 26, 14).—WRamsay, ET 26, 1915, 170, where the word is quoted from a Phrygian gravestone 248/49 AD. M-M.

δευτερόπρωτος, ον a word of doubtful mng., only in the phrase ἐν σαββάτῳ δ. **Lk 6:1 v.l.;** many editions (but not Tdf.), following most mss., omit the word or put it in brackets. Even many ancient interpreters, understandably, could make nothing of it (Jerome, Epistle 52, 8, 2), and it may owe its origin solely to a scribal error. It might correspond (but s. M-M.) to δευτερέσχατος (=next to the last) and mean ***first but one (?)*** (cp. Epiphan., Haer. 30, 32; 51, 31 δευτερόπρωτον = δεύτερον σάββατον μετὰ τὸ πρῶτον; Eustratius, Life of Eutychius [MPG LXXXVI 2381] ἡ δευτεροπρώτη κυριακή=the first Sunday after Easter Sunday), reckoned from Passover.—CTrossen, ThGl 6, 1914, 466–75, esp. 470f; HMeulenbelt, Lk 6:1: NThSt 5, 1922, 140–42; ASchlatter, D. Ev. des Lk '31, 67f; Goodsp., Probs. 83–85; JBover, Estudios Ecclesiasticos 7, 1928, 97–106; J-P Audet, Jésus et le 'Calendrier sacerdotal ancien', Sciences Ecclésiastiques (Montreal) 10, '58, 361–83; GBuchanan-CWolfe, JBL 97, '78, 259–62.—M-M.

δεύτερος, α, ον (Hom.+) 'second'—❶ **next to the first in a sequence or series, *second.*** In a numerical sequence: **Mt 22:26** of the second of seven brothers; **J 4:54** second sign (a similar close in Appian, Bell. Civ. 1, 33 §150 τρίτον τόδε ἔργον ἦν); D 2:1. In a series (cp. Just., A I, 13, 3 χριστὸν . . . ἐν δευτέρᾳ χώρᾳ ἔχοντες =holding Christ in second position [in the Trinity] 60, 7; Ath. 35, 1 τὸ πρότερον . . . τὸ δεύτερον of two charges made against Christians): **Mt 22:39; Mk 12:31; Lk 19:18; 1 Cor 15:47; 2 Pt 3:1; Rv 4:7; 6:3; 16:3; 21:19.** δευτέρα (sc. ἐπιστολή) in the subscr. of 2 Th and 2 Ti. Of position: the second sentinel's post **Ac 12:10;** the second curtain **Hb 9:3;** cp. vs. **7.** Of that which comes later in time (cp. Just., D. 110, 2 δ. παρουσία) as the second item in a class: **Hb 8:7; 10:9; Rv 2:11; 11:14; 20:14; 21:8; 2 Cor 1:15; Tit 3:10;** ὥρα δ. Hs 9, 11, 7 (cp. Jos., Vi. 220); φυλακὴ δ. *second watch* in the night (Arrian, Anab. 6, 25, 5; Jos., Bell. 5, 510) **Lk 12:38.** δευτέρᾳ (sc. ἡμέρᾳ) *on the second* (day of the month) MPol 21.

❷ neut. δεύτερον, τὸ δεύτερον used as adv. ***for the second time*** (Sappho [POxy 1231 fgm. 1 col. 1, 11=Campbell p. 64]; Hdt. et al.; Appian to Fronto [I p. 537f Viereck-R.] §6; OGI 82, 7 [III BC]; Gen 22:15; Jer 40:1; Jos., Bell. 1, 25, Vi. 389; s. MBoismard, Le chapitre 21 de StJean: RB 54, '47, 480) δ. εἰσελθεῖν **J 3:4;** παρὼν τὸ δ. **2 Cor 13:2;** δ. εἴρηκαν *they said for the second time* **Rv 19:3.** Also ἐκ δευτέρου (Diosc. 5, 41; Galen, CMG VII 159, 15 al.; PTebt 297, 19; PHolm 1, 32; Jon 3:1; Jer 1:13; 1 Macc 9:1; JosAs 14:6; 4 [6] Esdr [POxy 1010]; Jos., Ant. 6, 94; TestAbr A 7 p. 84, 9f [Stone p. 16]; Ath. 32, 3 [Resch, Agrapha 137] on caution with respect to kissing) **Mk 14:72; J 9:24; Ac 11:9; Hb 9:28; 2 Ti** subscr.; making πάλιν more definite (Heraclit. Sto. 32 p. 48, 8 ἐκ δευτέρου πάλιν; reversed 4 [6] Esdr [POxy 1010]) **Mt 26:42; Ac 10:15;** also πάλιν δεύτερον (cp. Herodas 5, 47) **J 21:16;** ἐν τῷ δ. *the second time* **Ac 7:13** (TestJob 36:6). In enumerations *secondly* (PTebt 56, 9–11 [II BC] εὐχαριστῆσαι πρῶτον μὲν τοῖς θεοῖς, δεύτερον δὲ σῶσαι ψυχάς; Sir 23:23; 2 Macc 14:8; Tat. 40, 1; 42, 1) **1 Cor 12:28;** D 1:2; Hm 10, 3, 2. τὸ δ. ἀπώλεσεν *the second time he destroyed* **Jd 5** (NRSV renders 'afterward', but this is not to be construed as a difft. mng. for Jude's use of δ.: in Jude's pregnant statement the point lies in a contrast between two special moments of display of divine power, one in salvation, and the second in destruction).—DELG. M-M. Sv.

δευτερόω fut. δευτερώσω LXX; 1 aor. ἐδευτέρωσα (LXX) (PsSol 5:131) ***do someth. a second time*** ὁ δὲ Παῦλος ἐδευτέρου καὶ εἶπεν αὐτῷ *Paul spoke to it* (the lion) *a second time* AcPl Ha 5, 3.—DELG s.v. δεύτερος.

δέχομαι fut. δέξομαι (LXX; Just., D. 22, 8). Pass.: fut. 3 sg. δεχθήσεται LXX; 1 aor. ἐδεξάμην, ἐδέχθην; pf. δέδεγμαι (Hom.+)

❶ **to receive someth. offered or transmitted by another, *take, receive*** τινά εἰς τὰς ἀγκάλας *take someone up in one's arms* **Lk 2:28;** one's spirit **Ac 7:59;** GJs 23:3. Of letters (Procop. Soph., Ep. 20; PFlor 154, 2) **Ac 22:5;** cp. **28:21** (Jos., Ant. 13, 259; Just., A I, 68, 6 [Hadrian]). τὰ παρ' ὑμῶν *the things,* i.e. *gifts, from you* **Phil 4:18.** τὰς ῥάβδους αὐτῶν *the staffs* of assembled widowers GJs 9:1. λόγια **Ac 7:38.** εὐαγγέλιον **2 Cor 11:4.**

❷ **to take someth. in hand, *grasp*** lit. τί *someth.* (2 Ch 29:22; TestJob τὸ γραμματεῖον) τὰ γράμματα *the (promissory) note* **Lk 16:6f;** a cup **22:17;** a helmet **Eph 6:17.**

❸ **to be receptive of someone, *receive, welcome,*** gener. 1 Cl 28:2; 54:3; IEph 6:1; IPhld 11:1. Esp. of hospitality τινὰ εἰς τ. οἶκον *welcome someone into one's house* **Lk 16:4,** cp. vs. **9** (Epict. 3, 26, 25; X., An. 5, 5, 20). *Receive* as a guest, *welcome* **Mt 10:14, 40f; Lk 9:5, 11 v.l., 53; 10:8, 10; J 4:45; Col 4:10; Hb 11:31;** D 11:1f, 4; 12:1. Of welcoming children **Mt 18:5; Mk 9:37; Lk 9:48;** a child dedicated in the temple GJs 7:2. W. adv. ἀσμένως *welcome heartily* (Aelian, VH 12, 18; Herodian 7, 5, 2; Jos., Ant. 12, 382; cp. 18, 101) **Ac 21:17 v.l.** μετὰ φόβου καὶ τρόμου *with fear and trembling* **2 Cor 7:15;** *as an angel of God* **Gal 4:14.** τινὰ εἰς ὄνομά τινος IRo 9:3 (s. ὄνομα 1dγב). Of places receptive to pers. ὃν δεῖ οὐρανὸν (subj.) δέξασθαι *whom the heaven must receive* **Ac 3:21** (cp. Pla., Tht. 177a τελευτήσαντας αὐτοὺς ὁ τῶν κακῶν καθαρὸς τόπος οὐ δέξεται). W. τόπος as subj. **Mk 6:11** and 1 Cl 54:3; w. κόσμος 28:2. Elizabeth petitions: ὄρος θεοῦ, δέξαι με μητέρα μετὰ τέκνου *mountain of God, receive me, the mother, with my child* GJs 22:3; ἐδέξατο αὐτήν ibid.

❹ **to overcome obstacles in being receptive, *put up with, tolerate*** *someone* or *someth.* (Gen 50:17; Jdth 11:5; Sir 2:4; Mel., P. 48, 341 λίχνον σύμβουλον) ὡς ἄφρονα **2 Cor 11:16.**

❺ **to indicate approval or conviction by accepting, *be receptive of, be open to, approve, accept,*** *of things* (Appian, Bell. Civ. 5, 66 §277; Ath. 2:3 ψῆφον) **Mt 11:14.** τὰ τοῦ πνεύματος *what comes fr. the Spirit* **1 Cor 2:14** (Herm. Wr. 4, 4 [N-F.] τ. νοῦν); τὴν παράκλησιν *request, appeal* **2 Cor 8:17** (of a request also Chion, Ep. 8); love for the truth **2 Th 2:10;** τὸν λόγον (since Eur. and Thu. 4, 16, 1; also Polyb. 1, 43, 4; Diod. S. 4, 52, 1; Pr 4:10; Zech 1:6; Jos., Ant. 18, 101; Just., A I, 9, 1) *teaching* **Lk 8:13; Ac 8:14; 11:1; 13:48** D; **17:11; 1 Th 1:6; 2:13; Js 1:21;** the reign of God **Mk 10:15; Lk 18:17;** grace, favor (Plut., Themist. 125 [28, 3] δέξασθαι χάριν) **2 Cor 6:1;** δ. συμβουλήν *accept advice* 1 Cl 58:2. τὰ μιμήματα τῆς ἀληθοῦς ἀγάπης Pol 1:1.— S. also λαμβάνω. Schmidt, Syn. III 203–33. DELG. M-M. TW. Sv.

δέω 3 sg. pres. δεῖται (Ath. 21, 3); fut. δήσω LXX; 1 aor. ἔδησα, subj. δήσω; pf. ptc. δεδεκώς **Ac 22:29.** Pass.: 1 aor. inf. δεθῆναι **21:33;** pf. δέδεμαι (Hom.+)

❶ **to confine a pers. or thing by various kinds of restraints, *bind, tie***—ⓐ of things τὶ *someth.* 1 Cl 43:2; τὶ εἴς τι (Ezk 37:17): tie weeds in bundles **Mt 13:30.** τί τινι (cp. Ezk 27:24): τοὺς πόδας κειρίαις **J 11:44.** ἔδησαν (τὸ σῶμα) ὀθονίοις μετὰ τῶν ἀρωμάτων *they bound (the corpse) in linen cloths with spices* **19:40.**

ⓑ of binding and imprisoning pers. δ. τινὰ ἁλύσεσι (cp. Lucian, Necyom. 11; Wsd. 17:16) *bind someone w. chains,* of a possessed person **Mk 5:3f;** of prisoners (PLips 64, 58) **Ac 12:6; 21:33;** Taubenschlag, Op. Min. II 722f. Also simply δ. τινά (Judg 16:5, 7f) **Mt 12:29** (cp. TestLevi 18:12); **14:3; 27:2; Mk 3:27; 15:1; J 18:12; Ac 9:14; 21:11, 13; 22:29;** B 6:7 (Is 3:10). (τοὺς) πόδας καὶ (τὰς) χεῖρας *bind hand and foot* (the acc. as Jos., Ant. 19, 294) **Mt 22:13; Ac 21:11;** δ. τινὰ ἐν φυλακῇ *bind someone (and put him) in prison* (4 Km 17:4) **Mk 6:17.** Pass. (Biogr. p. 238) δέδεμαι *be bound,* i.e., *a prisoner* **15:7.** κατέλιπε δεδεμένον *leave behind as a prisoner* **Ac 24:27** (δεδεμένος=in prison, as Diog. L. 2, 24 of Socrates); ἀπέστειλεν δ. **J 18:24.** Cp. **Col 4:3;** IEph 1:2 al. in Ignatius. Παύλου δεδεμένου AcPl Ha 2, 1. δέδεμαι ἐν τῷ ὀνόματι *be a prisoner because of the name* (=being a Christian) IEph 3:1. Also δ. ἐν Ἰησοῦ Χριστῷ ITr 1:1; IRo 1:1. δεδεμένον ἄγειν τινά *bring someone as prisoner* (Jos., Bell. 7, 449) **Ac 9:2, 21; 22:5;** cp. IRo 4:3. Pass. δ. ἀπάγεσθαι IEph 21:2; δ. θεοπρεπεστάτοις δεσμοῖς *bound w. chains that befit God's majesty* (i.e. through his bondage Ignatius displays his total devotion to God, s. IEph 3:1 above) ISm 11:1; δ. ἢ λελυμένος *a prisoner or one (recently) freed* 6:2.—Fig. ὁ λόγος τ. θεοῦ οὐ δέδεται *God's message cannot be imprisoned* (though the speaker can) **2 Ti 2:9.**—Mid. (s. L-S-J-M s.v. δέω A, II) οὐκ ἔξεστί μοι δήσασθαι αὐτό (viz. τὸ κεφαλοδέσμιον) *I am not allowed to put on the headscarf* GJs 2:2 (vv.ll. ἀναδήσασθαι and περιδήσασθαι).—A metaphorical use derived from ancient perceptions of illness explains the expr. ἣν ἔδησεν ὁ σατανᾶς *whom Satan had bound* of a deformed woman **Lk 13:16** (cp. SIG 1175, 14ff; 32–35 Ἀριστὼ ἐγὼ ἔλαβον καὶ ἔδησα τὰς χεῖρας καὶ τοὺς πόδας καὶ τὴν γλῶσσαν καὶ τὴν ψυχήν). For another transcendent binding cp. δεδεμένος τῷ πνεύματι *bound by the Spirit* **Ac 20:22** (similar imagery, perh., in Apollon. Rhod. 4, 880 ἀμηχανίῃ δῆσεν φρένας 'perplexity bound his mind').—On the binding of the dragon **Rv 20:2** s. JKroll, Gott u. Hölle '32, esp. 316ff; Tob 8:3; TestLevi 18:12.

❷ **to tie someth. to someth., *tie to*** an animal (4 Km 7:10) **Mt 21:2; Mk 11:2, 4** (πρὸς θύραν); **Lk 19:30;** angels **Rv 9:14.** δ. δέκα λεοπάρδοις *tied to ten leopards* (on the language: Soph., Aj. 240 κίονι δήσας = πρὸς κίονα 108; cp. Jos., Ant. 18, 196) IRo 5:1 v.l.—*Fasten* someth. (ParJer 7:35 τὴν ἐπιστολὴν εἰς τὸν τράχηλον τοῦ ἀέτου) a linen cloth at its four corners **Ac 10:11 v.l.**

❸ **to constrain by law and duty,** ***bind*** w. dat. of pers. *to someone:* of a wife to her husband **Ro 7:2;** of a husband to his wife **1 Cor 7:27** (for the form cp. Posidippus [III BC]: Anth. Pal. 9, 359, 5f ἔχεις γάμον; οὐκ ἀμέριμνος ἔσσεαι· οὐ γαμέεις; ζῇς ἔτ᾽ ἐρημότερος=You are married? You won't be without cares. You remain unmarried? You'll live still lonelier.). Abs. vs. **39** (cp. Achilles Tat. 1, 11, 2 v.l. ἄλλῃ δέδεμαι παρθένῳ; Iambl., Vi. Pyth. 11, 56 τὴν μὲν ἄγαμον . . . τὴν δὲ πρὸς ἄνδρα δεδεμένην); τοῖς λαϊκοῖς προστάγμασιν *be bound by the rules for the people* (those without official duties) 1 Cl 40:5.

❹ The combination δ. καὶ λύειν ***bind and loose*** (Ael. Aristid. 40, 7 K.=5 p. 55 D. of Prometheus: ὅσα δήσειεν ὁ Ζεύς, ταῦτ᾽ ἐξὸν Ἡρακλεῖ λῦσαι; 41, 7 K.; Teleclides Com. [V BC] fgm. 42 K. δέω—ἀναλύω) is found **Mt 16:19; 18:18.** On the meaning δέω has here cp. J 20:22f (cp. 1QH 13:10). Another interpretation starts fr. the rabbinic viewpoint. Aram. אֲסַר and שְׁרָא are academic language for the decision of the rabbis as to what was to be regarded as 'bound' (אָסִיר), i.e. forbidden, or 'loosed' (שְׁרֵי), i.e. permitted; s. Dalman, Worte 175ff; Billerb. I 738–47. Binding and loosing in magical practice are emphasized by WKöhler, ARW 8, 1905, 236ff; ADell, ZNW 15, 1914, 38ff. S. also VBrander, Der Katholik 94, 1914, 116ff; KAdam, Gesammelte Aufsätze '36, 17–52; JMantey, JBL 58, '39, 243–49; HCadbury, ibid. 251–54 (both on J 20:23; Mt 16:19;18:18).—B. EDNT. DELG s.v. δέω 1. M-M. TW.

δή (Hom. et al.; pap, LXX, En, TestSol, TestJob, JosAs, apologists, exc. Ar.) a marker that invites attention to what is being stated.

❶ **a marker denoting that a statement is definitely established,** ***indeed*** (cp. Eur., Alc. 233 for the deictic force; freq. = our colloq. 'you see') B 6:11. ὃς δὴ καρποφορεῖ *who indeed bears fruit* **Mt 13:23** (relat. w. δή as EpArist 4; 125; Jos., Ant. 17, 19; Just., D. 7, 1).—W. expr. denoting time ἐκ γὰρ δὴ πολλῶν χρόνων *for* (already; or, the fact is that) *many years ago* 1 Cl 42:5 (cp. Just., D. 71, 3 καὶ δὴ τὴν ἀπόδειξιν ποιήσομαι 'and you can be sure I will prove it'.—οὐ γὰρ δή γε 'for of course . . . not' Just., D. 13, 1.)—In indirect qu. τί δή ποτε Dg 1. S. δήποτε, δήπου.

❷ ***now, then, therefore,*** w. exhortations or commands, to give them greater urgency (B-D-F §451, 4; somewhat like our colloq. 'well', 'well, now'; cp. En 104:2; JosAs [s. Philonenko, p. 30]; Jos., Vi. 209; Just., D. 137, 1 μὴ δὴ . . . εἴπητε) διέλθωμεν δή *well, let's go* **Lk 2:15.** δοξάσατε δὴ τὸν θεόν *therefore glorify God* **1 Cor 6:20.** σύνετε δή *understand then* 1 Cl 35:11. ἄγε δή *come then* (Lucian, Pisc. 21) Dg 2:1. ἐπιστρέψαντες δὴ ἐπισκεψώμεθα **Ac 15:36; 6:3 v.l.; 13:2.** On D 1:6 s. Bihlmeyer app.—Denniston 203–62. DELG. M-M.

δηλαδή (Epicharm., fgm. 149, 1 Kaibel; Hdt. et al.; pap, TestSol 10:25 C; Just., D. 5, 1; Tat. 21, 3) adv. **pert. to being readily perceived by the mind,** ***obviously, plainly*** Papias (4).—DELG s.v. δή.

δηλαυγῶς (s. αὐγή) adv. lit. 'shining clearly', then **being relatively clear to the mind,** ***quite clearly*** (Hesych.: δηλαυγῶς· ἄγαν φανερῶς; Democr. [JFabricius, Biblioth. Gr. IV p. 333] δηλαυγέσι τεκμηρίοις; PGM 4, 775; 1033; s. on this WCrönert, Stud. z. Paläogr. u. Papyruskunde 4, 1905, 101) **Mk 8:25 v.l.** (s. τηλαυγῶς). The adv. of the comp. δηλαυγέστερον Hs 6, 5, 1 (Joly [τηλαυγέστερον B.]; s. PMich 129, Bonner p. 73f, n. on ln. 18; s. τηλαυγής).—M-M.

δηλονότι = δῆλον ὅτι IEph 6:1 v.l.

δῆλος, η, ον (Hom. et al.; pap, LXX; TestJob 36:6; ParJer 7:3; Philo, Joseph.; apologists, exc. Ar.) pert. to someth. being clearly visible (Hom., Il. 10, 466), then **clear to the understanding,** ***clear, plain, evident*** (Pla., Rep. 550d καὶ τυφλῷ γε δῆλον; X., Cyr. 8, 5, 7) δ. τινα ποιεῖν *reveal someone* **Mt 26:73** (v.l. ὁμοιάζει); δ. εἶναι ἔν τινι *reveal itself in someth.* 2 Cl 12:4.—δῆλον (sc. ἐστίν) w. ὅτι foll. *it is clear that* (Herm. Wr. 11, 11; TestJob 36:6; Philo, Aet. M. 75; 129 [w. ἐστί 93]; Just., D. 83, 2; Ath. 20, 4) **1 Cor 15:27; Gal 3:11; 1 Ti 6:7 v.l.;** IEph 6:1 (cp. Thu. 3, 38, 2; X., An. 1, 3, 9; Hero Alex. III p. 314, 11; POxy 1101, 12; PFlor 36, 28; 4 Macc 2:7; Philo, Op. M. 25; Jos., C. Ap. 1, 277; 2, 13). Cp. 2 Cl 14:2 Lghtf.—B. 1233. Cp. φανερός, ἐναργής; s. Schmidt, Syn. III 418–34. DELG. M-M. TW.

δηλόω fut. δηλώσω; 1 aor. ἐδήλωσα, impv. δήλωσον pf. δεδήλωκα (Just.) Pass.: 1 aor. ἐδηλώθην; pf. δεδήλωμαι (Hom.+)

❶ **to make some matter known that was unknown or not communicated previously,** ***reveal, make clear, show*** τὶ *someth.* Secrets 1 Cl 18:6 (Ps 50:8); future things (Polyaenus 5, 12, 1 νίκην οἱ θεοὶ δηλοῦσιν ἡμῖν; SibOr 3, 819) **1 Cor 3:13;** PtK 3 p. 15, 21. ApcPt Rainer, 14; cp. Hv 3, 12, 3; s 9, 1, 2 (PGM 13, 614f δήλου μοι πάντα, addressed to an angel). *Report* (Diod. S. 15, 25, 3) τινί *to someone* ITr 1:1; IPol 7:1; *set forth* MPol 22:3. Preceded by a ὅτι- clause (as Demetr.: 722 fgm. 1, 13 Jac.) and w. ὡς λέγει foll. **Lk 20:37** D. *Give information* τινὶ περί τινος w. ὅτι foll. **1 Cor 1:11** (cp. PGrenf II, 73, 18); τινί τι *to someone about someth.* (Jos., C. Ap. 1, 101) the Colossians' affection **Col 1:8.** *Notify* w. acc. and ptc. foll. (Lucian, Dial. Deor. 7, 1; Just., D. 76, 1; 103, 3) οἷς δηλώσατε ἐγγύς με ὄντα *notify them that I am nearby* IRo 10:2.

❷ **to make someth. clear to the understanding,** ***explain, clarify*** τινί **2 Pt 1:14.** τινί τι: *explain a parable* Hs 5, 4, 1; pass. 5, 4, 2; 5. σοι δηλώσω *I will explain to you* m 4, 3, 3; *indicate, refer to* τινά *someone* B 9:8; τὶ *someth.* τὸ ἔτι ἅπαξ δηλοῖ τὴν μετάθεσιν *the phrase 'once again' indicates the removal* **Hb 12:27.** ἡμέρα καὶ νὺξ ἀνάστασιν ἡμῖν δηλοῦσιν *day and night point out a resurrection to us* 1 Cl 24:3. Also εἴς τι **1 Pt 1:11.** *Give information* τινί B 17:1; Hs 6, 4, 1; 3. W. acc. and inf. foll. **Hb 9:8** (Just., D. 33, 2; 86, 2).—DELG s.v. δῆλος. M-M. TW. Sv.

Δημᾶς, ᾶ, ὁ *Demas* (short form of Δημήτριος? B-D-F §125, 1 or Δημάρατος? Cp. Δαμᾶς above and s. Vi. Aesopi I, 33 p. 299, 6 Eberh.; SIG 585, 202 Δημᾶς Καλλικράτεος; Sb. 8066, 95 [ins 78 BC]; grave-inscription 1, 2: ZNW 22, 1923, 280; PLond III, 929, 38 [II/III AD] p. 42; BGU 10, 12; 715 II, 13) a companion of Paul **Phlm 24; Col 4:14; 2 Ti 4:10.**—LGPN I. M-M.

δημηγορέω impf. ἐδημηγόρουν (s. δῆμος, ἀγορεύω 'speak in the assembly'; Aristoph., Lysias et al.; Pr 30:31; 4 Macc 5:15; Jos., Bell. 2, 619, Vi. 92) ***deliver a public address*** πρός τινα **Ac 12:21**—DELG s.v. δῆμος.

Δημήτριος, ου, ὁ (occurs freq.: SIG, OGI ind.; LXX; Demetr.: 722 Jac.; Joseph.) ***Demetrius*—❶** an otherwise unknown Christian **3J 12.**

❷ a silversmith in Ephesus, leader of a demonstration against Paul **Ac 19:24, 38.** JChapman, JTS 5, 1904, 364ff identifies 1 w. Δημᾶς; VBartlet, ibid. 6, 1905, 208f, 215 identifies the two Demtr. of the NT. See ABludau, D. Aufstand d. Silberschmieds

Dem. Ac 19:23–40: Der Katholik 86, 1906, 81–92; 201–13; 258–72; Haenchen ad loc.; also reff. in SEG XXXVI, 1028; XLII, 1029.—LGPN I. M-M.

δημιουργέω 1 aor. ἐδημιούργησα; pf. 3 pl. δεδημιουργήκασι (Tat. 17, 2). Pass.: aor. ἐδημιουργήθην; pf. pass. 3 sg. δεδημιούργηται (Ath. 6, 3); ptc. δεδημιουργημένος 2 Macc 10:2 (s. δῆμος, ἔργον, 'to work for the public'; Pla. et al.; Herm. Wr. 1, 13; 4, 1; 5, 11; LXX; Philo; Jos., Ant. 8, 88; apolog., exc. Mel.) **to engage in construction of someth.,** orig. of any craft activity, then also of divine construction ***create*** (Dio Chrys. 11 [12], 83; Ael. Aristid. 45 p. 126 D.; Chariton 3, 3, 16; Herm. Wr. 4, 1a; Philo, Op. M. 16) 1 Cl 20:10; 38:3. καιρὸν δ. *create an era* or *epoch* Dg 9:1.—S. next entry. TW.

δημιουργία, ας, ἡ (s. δημιουργέω Pla. et al.; Herm. Wr. 10, 18; ins; Philo, Ebr. 85; Jos., Ant. 12, 42; Tat. 4, 2; Ath., R. 62, 9 al.) orig. handicraft production and other creative construction, then of cosmic construction (Damascius [V–VI AD], De Princ. 283; s. Plato's use of δημιουργός in the sense of divine creator, next entry) ***creative act*** ὢ τῆς ἀνεξιχνιάστου δημιουργίας *O, the unfathomable act of creativity* (that is revealed in redemption) Dg 9:5. κατὰ τὴν δ. αὐτοῦ *in accordance w. his creative activity* 1 Cl 20:6.

δημιουργός, οῦ, ὁ (s. δημιουργέω; Hom.+; ins; 2 Macc 4:1; Philo, Joseph.; apolog., exc. Mel.) **one who designs someth. and constructs it, *craftsworker, builder, maker, creator,*** also of divine activity (so e.g. Pla., Tim. 28a and c; 29a; 31a al., Rep. 7, 530a; X., Mem. 1, 4, 7; 9; Epict. 2, 8, 21; Maximus Tyr. 41, 4d ὕλην ὑποβεβλημένην δημιουργῷ ἀγαθῷ; Philostrat., Vi. Apoll. 8, 7, 312, 26; Herm. Wr. 1, 9–11; Damascius, De Principiis §270, II 137 Ruelle; Philo, Op. M. 10, Mut. Nom. 29; Jos., Ant. 1, 155 and 272; 7, 380. On gnostic views s. AHilgenfeld, Ketzergeschichte 1884 index under Demiurg; for later lit. KRudolph, ABD II 1039f), as in our lit. (also TestJob 39:12; ApcEsdr 32:16 Tdf.) throughout: (w. τεχνίτης; cp. Lucian, Icar. 8; Philo, Mut. Nom. 29–31; Orig., C. Cels. 1, 37, 12 al.; w. ποιητής Theoph. Ant. 2, 34 [p. 186, 1]; w. ἄρχων and βασιλεύς Did., Gen. 57, 10) **Hb 11:10;** Dg 7:2; (w. δεσπότης) ὁ μέγας δ. 1 Cl 20:11; cp. 33:2; Dg 8:7; ὁ δ. τῶν ἁπάντων (Ael. Aristid. 37, 2 K.=2 p. 13 D.; Herm. Wr. 9, 5 θεός, πάντων δημιουργὸς ὤν; Philostrat., Vi. Soph. 2, 5, 11) 1 Cl 26:1; 59:2; (w. πατήρ; cp. Hierocles 1, 417; Herm. Wr. 5, 11; Did., Gen. 22, 4) 35:3.—Harnack, SBBerlAk 1909, 60, 1; TSchermann, TU 34, 2b, 1909, 23; FPfister, SBHeidAk 1914 no. 11, 9; Dodd 136–44 al.; AvdOudenrijn, Demiourgos: diss. Utr. '51; WTheiler, RAC III '56, 694–711 (lit.); HWeiss, Untersuchungen z. Kosmologie: TU 97, '66, 44–52; Kl. Pauly I 1472f.—EDNT. DELG s.v. ἔργον. M-M. TW. Sv.

δῆμος, ου, ὁ (Hom. et al.; ins, pap, LXX; Jos., Ant. 12, 120; 123; 14, 24; SibOr 5, 419; apolog.; loanw. in rabb.)

➊ **a gathering of people for any purpose, *people, populace, crowd*** **Ac 12:22;** πεῖσον τὸν δ. *try to convince the crowd* (so that it will intercede for you) MPol 10:2.

➋ **in a Hellenistic city, a convocation of citizens called together for the purpose of transacting official business, *popular assembly*** προάγειν εἰς τὸν δ. **Ac 17:5;** εἰσελθεῖν εἰς τὸν δ. *go into the assembly* **19:30;** ἀπολογεῖσθαι τῷ δ. *make a defense before the assembly* vs. **33** (cp. in the ins the common expr. δεδόχθαι or ἔδοξεν τῷ δήμῳ). Ferguson 38–41; Kl. Pauly I 1482.—LfgrE II 275 (lit.). M-M. TW. Sv.

δημόσιος, ία, ιον (Hdt., Aristoph.+; ins, pap; EpArist 81; Jos., Bell. 5, 518 al.; TestJud 23:2; Just., Tat., Ath.)

➊ **pert. to belonging to the state, *public,*** ἐν τηρήσει δ. *in the public prison* (loanw. in rabb. דִּימוֹסִין, public jail) **Ac 5:18** (but s. 2). ὁδός *a public road* (oft. pap) Hv 4, 1, 2.

➋ **pert. to being able to be known by the general public, *in the open, public,*** δημοσίᾳ as adv. *publicly* (Epict. 3, 4, 1; 3, 22, 2; Vett. Val. 71, 22; SIG 1173, 9; 13; 18; often in pap, e.g. BGU 1086 II, 3; 2 Macc 6:10; 3 Macc 2:27; 4:7; Jos., Bell. 2, 455; Just., A II, 3, 2; 12, 5; Tat. 18, 3; 25, 1; 26, 3) **Ac 16:37** (cp. SIG² 680, 3 μαστιγοῦσθαι δημοσίᾳ); **18:28** (as opposed to κατ' οἰκόν 'house by house', s. cod. E); **20:20** (w. κατ' οἰκούς). This adv. use is preferred Beg. IV 57 et al. for **Ac 5:18:** 'publicly put them in custody', but it is to be noted that the other passages in Ac explictly refer to someth. taking place within public view, whereas **Ac 5:19** clearly indicates that the guarding cited vs. 18 is done in special quarters.—DELG. M-M.

δηνάριον, ου, τό (Lat. denarius as δηνάριον first in two ins fr. Acraephiae of the time of Sulla [IG IX/2, 415 b, 89]. Exx. fr. later times in Hahn 271 word-index; OGI ind. VIII; cp. Preis. III 346; loanw. in rabb.) ***denarius,*** a Roman silver coin orig. c. 4.55 g; the debasement of coinage under Nero reduced it in value; it was a worker's average daily wage (cp. Tob 5:15; Talmud Babli: Aboda Zara 62a; SBastomsky, Greece and Rome, ser. 2, 37, '90, 37) **Mt 18:28; 20:2, 9f, 13; 22:19; Mk 6:37; 12:15; 14:5; Lk 7:41; 10:35; 20:24; J 6:7; 12:5; Rv 6:6.** τὸ ἀνὰ δηνάριον *a denarius each,* like the others before them **Mt 20:10** (B-D-F §266, 2).—Hultsch, Pauly-W. V 202ff; KRegling, Wörterbuch der Münzkunde, ed. FSchrötter, 1930, 126ff; Kl. Pauly I, 1488–90; IDB III 428, illustr. 29 p. 433; Schürer II 65.—Other reff. s. ἀργύριον end.—M-M.

δήποτε adv. (Hom. et al.; pap, e.g., PLond III, 904, 22 [104 AD] p. 125; PFamTebt 15, 41; PTebt 381, 14; LXX) ***at any time;*** w. relative *whatever* **J 5:4 v.l.;** τί δ. *just why* (Maximus Tyr. 1, 5a; Lucian, Jupp. Conf. 16; Jos., Ant. 11, 89) Dg 1 (earlier style).—M-M.

δήπου adv. (Hom. et al.; PCairZen 454, 4; Jos., C. Ap. 1, 127; Tat. 5, 2; Ath., R. 70, 23 al.) like μέν, γέ, δή a marker of emphasis, but the suffix που is rhetorically significant, for it softens the process of inference, while yet strongly asserting the conclusion, by graciously taking the auditor into the logical process, somewhat in the sense 'one would agree, I'm sure' ***of course, surely*** **Hb 2:16** (so also Hom., trag. et al., s. Denniston 267–68; B-D-F §441, 3).

Δία, Διός see Ζεύς.

διά prep. w. gen. and acc. (Hom.+) (for lit. s. ἀνά, beg.); the fundamental idea that finds expression in this prep. is separation, esp. in the gen., with the gener. sense 'through'; in the acc. the gener. sense also is 'through' (cp. the semantic range in Eng.), but primarily with a causal focus 'owing to'.

A. w. gen.—➊ **marker of extension through an area or object, *via, through***—ⓐ w. verbs of going διέρχεσθαι διὰ πάντων (sc. τόπων, EpArist 132) *go through all the places* **Ac 9:32;** cp. **Mt 12:43; Lk 11:24.** ἀπελεύσομαι δι' ὑμῶν εἰς *I will go through your city on the way to* **Ro 15:28;** cp. **2 Cor. 1:16.** διαβαίνειν **Hb 11:29.** διαπορεύεσθαι διὰ σπορίμων **Lk 6:1.** εἰσέρχεσθαι διὰ τῆς πύλης (Jos., Ant. 13, 229) **Mt 7:13a;** τ. θύρας **J 10:1f;** cp. vs. **9.** παρέρχεσθαι διὰ τ. ὁδοῦ *pass by along the road* **Mt 8:28;** cp. **7:13b.** παραπορεύεσθαι **Mk 2:23; 9:30.** περιπατεῖν διὰ τοῦ φωτός *walk about through* or *in the light* **Rv 21:24.** ὑποστρέφειν διὰ Μακεδονίας *return through M.* **Ac 20:3.**—Ἰησ. ὁ ἐλθὼν δι' ὕδατος καὶ αἵματος **1J 5:6**

first of all refers quite literally to Jesus' passing *through* water at the hand of John and *through* blood at his death (on the expression 'come through blood' in this sense cp. Eur., Phoen. 20 in Alex. Aphr., Fat. 31 II 2 p. 202, 10, of the oracle to Laius the father of Oedipus, concerning the bloody downfall of his house: πᾶς σὸς οἶκος βήσεται δι' αἵματος). But mng. 3c may also apply: Jesus comes *with* the water of baptism and *with* the blood of redemption for his own.—AKlöpper, 1J 5:6–12: ZWT 43, 1900, 378–400.—The ῥῆμα ἐκπορευόμενον διὰ στόματος θεοῦ **Mt 4:4** (Dt 8:3) is simply the *word that proceeds out of the mouth of God* (cp. Theognis 1, 18 Diehl[3] τοῦτ' ἔπος ἀθανάτων ἦλθε διὰ στομάτων; Pittacus in Diog. L. 1, 78 διὰ στόματος λαλεῖ; Chrysippus argues in Diog. L. 7, 187: εἴ τι λαλεῖς, τοῦτο διὰ τοῦ στόματός σου διέρχεται, i.e. if one e.g. says the word ἅμαξα, a wagon passes through the person's lips; TestIss 7:4 ψεῦδος οὐκ ἀνῆλθε διὰ τ. χειλέων μου. Cp. also δέχεσθαι διὰ τῶν χειρῶν τινος Gen 33:10 beside δέχ. ἐκ τ. χειρ. τινος Ex 32:4).

ⓑ w. other verbs that include motion: οὗ ὁ ἔπαινος διὰ πασῶν τ. ἐκκλησιῶν (sc. ἀγγέλλεται) *throughout all the congregations* **2 Cor 8:18.** διαφέρεσθαι δι' (v.l. καθ') ὅλης τῆς χώρας *be spread through the whole region* **Ac 13:49.** διὰ τ. κεράμων καθῆκαν αὐτόν *they let him down through the tile roof* **Lk 5:19.** διὰ τοῦ τείχους καθῆκαν *through an opening in the wall* (Jos., Ant. 5, 15) **Ac 9:25;** cp. **2 Cor 11:33.** (σωθήσεται) ὡς διὰ πυρός *as if he had come through fire* **1 Cor 3:15.** διασῴζεσθαι δι' ὕδατος *be brought safely through the water* **1 Pt 3:20.**—δι' ὅλου **J 19:23** s. ὅλος 2.

❷ **marker of extension in time—**ⓐ of a whole period of time, to its very end ***throughout, through, during*** διὰ παντός (sc. χρόνου. Edd. gener. write διὰ παντός, but Tdf. writes διαπαντός exc. **Mt 18:10**) *always, continually, constantly* (Hdt. 1, 122, 3; Thu. 1, 38, 1; Vett. Val. 220, 1; 16; PLond I, 42, 6 [172 BC] p. 30; BGU 1078, 2; PGM 7, 235; LXX; GrBar 10:7; EpArist index; Jos., Ant. 3, 281; SibOr fgm. 1, 17; Just., D. 6, 2; 12, 3 al.) **Mt 18:10; Mk 5:5; Lk 24:53; Ac 2:25** (Ps 15:8); **10:2; 24:16; Ro 11:10** (Ps 68:24); **2 Th 3:16; Hb 9:6; 13:15;** Hm 5, 2, 3; s 9, 27, 3. διὰ νυκτός *during the night, overnight* (νύξ 1b) **Ac 23:31.** δι' ὅλης νυκτός *the whole night through* **Lk 5:5; J 21:6 v.l.** (X., An. 4, 2, 4; Diod. S. 3, 12, 3 δι' ὅλης τῆς νυκτός; PGM 4, 3151; Jos., Ant. 6, 37; cp. δι' ἡμέρας *all through the day:* IPriene 112, 61 and 99; 1 Macc 12:27; 4 Macc 3:7). δι' ἡμερῶν τεσσεράκοντα **Ac 1:3** means either *for forty days* (Philo, Vi. Cont. 35 δι' ἓξ ἡμερῶν. So AFridrichsen, ThBl 6, 1927, 337–41; MEnslin, JBL 47, 1928, 60–73) or (s. b below) *now and then in the course of 40 days* (B-D-F §223, 1; Rob. 581; WMichaelis, ThBl 4, 1925, 102f; Bruce, Acts). διὰ παντὸς τοῦ ζῆν *throughout the lifetime* **Hb 2:15** (cp. διὰ παντὸς τοῦ βίου: X., Mem. 1, 2, 61; Pla., Phileb. 39e; Dionys. Hal. 2, 21; δι' ὅλου τοῦ ζῆν EpArist 130; 141; 168).

ⓑ of a period of time within which someth. occurs ***during, at*** (PTebt 48, 10) διὰ (τῆς) νυκτός *at night, during the night* (Palaeph. 1, 10; PRyl 138, 15 κατέλαβα τοῦτον διὰ νυκτός; Jos., Bell. 1, 229. S. νύξ 1b end) **Ac 5:19; 16:9; 17:10.** διὰ τῆς ἡμέρας *during the day* **Lk 9:37** D (Antig. Car. 128 διὰ πέμπτης ἡμέρας=on the fifth day). διὰ τριῶν ἡμερῶν *within three days* **Mt 26:61; Mk 14:58.**

ⓒ of an interval of time, ***after*** (Hdt. 6, 118, 3 δι' ἐτέων εἴκοσι; Thu. 2, 94, 3; X., Mem. 2, 8, 1; Diod. S. 5, 28, 6 of transmigration of souls: δι' ἐτῶν ὡρισμένων [=after the passing of a certain number of years] πάλιν βιοῦν; OGI 56, 38; 4 Macc 13:21; Jos., Ant. 4, 209): δι' ἐτῶν πλειόνων *after several years* **Ac 24:17.** διὰ δεκατεσσάρων (s. under δέκα) ἐτῶν *after 14 years* **Gal 2:1.** δι' ἡμερῶν *several days afterward* **Mk 2:1.** διὰ ἱκανοῦ χρόνου *after (quite) some time* **Ac 11:2** D (X., Cyr. 1, 4, 28 διὰ χρόνου).

❸ **marker of instrumentality or circumstance whereby someth. is accomplished or effected, *by, via, through***

ⓐ of means or instrument γράφειν διὰ χάρτου καὶ μέλανος *write w. paper and ink* **2J 12;** cp. **3J 13** (Plut., Sol. 87 [17, 3]). διὰ πυρὸς δοκιμάζειν *test by fire* **1 Pt 1:7.** διὰ χρημάτων κτᾶσθαι **Ac 8:20.** Hebraistically in expr. denoting activity διὰ χειρῶν τινος (LXX) **Mk 6:2; Ac 5:12; 14:3; 19:11, 26.** Differently γράφειν διὰ χειρός τινος *write through the agency of someone* **15:23;** cp. **11:30.** εἰπεῖν διὰ στόματός τινος *by the mouth of someone* (where the usage discussed in A1a is influential) **1:16; 3:18, 21; 4:25.** εὔσημον λόγον διδόναι διὰ τῆς γλώσσης *utter intelligible speech with the tongue* **1 Cor 14:9.** διὰ τοῦ νοὸς λαλεῖν *speak, using one's reason* (=consciously; opp., ecstatic speech) vs. **19 v.l.** Of the work of Christ: περιποιεῖσθαι διὰ τοῦ αἵματος *obtain through his blood* **Ac 20:28;** cp. **Eph 1:7; Col 1:20.** Also διὰ τοῦ θανάτου **Ro 5:10; Col 1:22; Hb 2:14;** διὰ τοῦ σώματος **Ro 7:4;** διὰ τῆς ἰδίας σαρκός AcPlCor 2:6; cp. 2:15; διὰ τοῦ σταυροῦ **Eph 2:16;** διὰ τῆς θυσίας **Hb 9:26;** διὰ τῆς προσφορᾶς τοῦ σώματος Ἰησοῦ *through the offering of the body of Jesus* **10:10;** διὰ παθημάτων **2:10.**

ⓑ of manner, esp. w. verbs of saying: ἀπαγγέλλειν διὰ λόγου *by word of mouth* **Ac 15:27;** cp. **2 Th 2:15.** δι' ἐπιστολῶν *by letter* (POxy 1066, 9; 1070, 14f πολλάκις σοι γράψας διὰ ἐπιστολῶν πολλῶν; Tat. 12:3 δια γραφῆς in writing) **1 Cor 16:3; 2 Cor 10:11;** cp. **2 Th 2:2, 15.** διὰ λόγου πολλοῦ *w. many words* **Ac 15:32.** δι' ὁράματος εἰπεῖν *in a vision* **18:9.** διὰ παραβολῆς *in an illustrative way, in a parable* **Lk 8:4.** διὰ προσευχῆς καὶ δεήσεως προσεύχεσθαι *call on (God) w. prayer and supplication* **Eph 6:18.** διὰ βραχέων ἐπιστέλλειν *write briefly* **Hb 13:22** (cp. **1 Pt 5:12** P^{72}; Isocr. 14, 3; Lucian, Tox. 56; EpArist 128; Ath. 17:1 σκέψασθε . . . διὰ βρ.). Also δι' ὀλίγων γράφειν **1 Pt 5:12** (Pla., Phileb. 31d; UPZ 42, 9 [162 BC]; 2 Macc 6:17).

ⓒ of attendant or prevailing circumstance (Kühner-G. I 482f; X., Cyr. 4, 6, 6 διὰ πένθους τὸ γῆρας διάγων; Just., D. 105, 2 δι' οὗ πάθους ἔμελλενἀποθνήσκειν; PTebt 35, 9 [111 BC] διὰ τῆς γνώμης τινός=with someone's consent; Jos., Bell. 4, 105) σὲ τὸν διὰ γράμματος καὶ περιτομῆς παραβάτην νόμου *you who,* (though provided) *with the written code and circumcision, are a transgressor/violator of the law* **Ro 2:27.** δι' ὑπομονῆς **8:25.** διὰ προσκόμματος *eat with offense* (to the scruples of another) **14:20.** δι' ἀκροβυστίας *in a state of being uncircumcised* **4:11.** διὰ πολλῶν δακρύων *with many tears* **2 Cor 2:4.** Cp. **6:7.** διὰ τῆς ἐπιγνώσεως **2 Pt 1:3** (*through recognition* [of God as source of the gifts], s. Danker, Benefactor 457). διὰ πυρός *in fiery form* AcPlCor 2:13.—Here prob. belongs σωθήσεται διὰ τῆς τεκνογονίας **1 Ti 2:15** (opp. of the negative theme in Gen. 3:16), but s. d next. On **1J 5:6** s. A1a above.

ⓓ of efficient cause *via, through* διὰ νόμου ἐπίγνωσις ἁμαρτίας (*only*) *recognition of sin comes via the law* **Ro 3:20;** cp. **4:13.** τὰ παθήματα τὰ διὰ τοῦ νόμου *passions aroused via the law* **7:5.** διὰ νόμου πίστεως *by the law of faith* **3:27; Gal 2:19.** ἀφορμὴν λαμβάνειν διὰ τῆς ἐντολῆς **Ro 7:8, 11;** cp. **13.** διὰ τ. εὐαγγελίου ὑμᾶς ἐγέννησα (spiritual parenthood) **1 Cor 4:15.** Perh. **1 Ti 2:15** but s. c, above. διὰ τῆς σοφίας *with its wisdom* **1 Cor 1:21;** opp. διὰ τῆς μωρίας τοῦ κηρύγματος *through the folly of proclamation = foolish proclamation* ibid. διὰ τῆς Λευιτικῆς ἱερωσύνης **Hb 7:11.** Freq. διὰ (τῆς) πίστεως **Ro 1:12; 3:22, 25, 30f; Gal 2:16; 3:14, 26; Eph 2:8; 3:12, 17** al. Cp. AcPl Cor 2:8. πίστις δι' ἀγάπης ἐνεργουμένη *faith which works through* (=expresses itself in) *deeds of love* **Gal 5:6.** διὰ θελήματος θεοῦ *if God is willing* **Ro 15:32;** *by the will of God* **1 Cor 1:1; 2 Cor 1:1; 8:5; Eph 1:1; Col 1:1; 2 Ti 1:1.**

ⓔ of occasion διὰ τῆς χάριτος *by virtue of the grace* **Ro 12:3; Gal 1:15** (Just., D. 100, 2).—**3:18; 4:23; Phlm 22.** διὰ δόξης καὶ ἀρετῆς *in consequence of his glory and excellence* **2 Pt 1:3 v.l.**

ⓕ in wording of urgent requests διὰ τῶν οἰκτιρμῶν τοῦ θεοῦ *by the mercy of God* **Ro 12:1;** cp. **15:30; 1 Cor 1:10; 2 Cor 10:1.**

❹ **marker of pers. agency,** ***through, by***—ⓐ with focus on agency *through* (*the agency of*), *by* (X., An. 2, 3, 17 δι' ἑρμηνέως λέγειν; Menand., fgm. 210, 1 οὐθεὶς δι' ἀνθρώπου θεὸς σῴζει . . . ἑτέρου τόν ἕτερον; Achilles Tat. 7, 1, 3 δι' ἐκείνου μαθεῖν; Just., D. 75, 4 διὰ παρθένου γεννηθῆναι; PMert 5, 8 γεομετρηθῆναι δι' αὐτοῦ) ῥηθὲν διὰ τοῦ προφήτου **Mt 1:22; 2:15, 23; 4:14** al. (cp. Just., A I, 47, 5 διὰ Ἠσαίου τοῦ πρ.). γεγραμμένα διὰ τῶν προφητῶν **Lk 18:31;** cp. **Ac 2:22; 10:36; 15:12** al. δι' ἀνθρώπου *by human agency* **Gal 1:1.** διὰ Μωϋσέως *through Moses* (Jos., Ant. 7, 338; Mel., P. 11, 77 διὰ χειρὸς Μωυσέως) **J 1:17;** *under Moses' leadership* **Hb 3:16.** δι' ἀγγέλων *by means of divine messengers* (TestJob 18:5 διὰ τοῦ ἀγγέλου; cp. Jos., Ant. 15, 136, but s. n. by RMarcus, Loeb ed., ad loc.) **Gal 3:19; Hb 2:2.** πέμψας διὰ τ. μαθητῶν εἶπεν *sent and said through his disciples* **Mt 11:2f.** Cp. the **short ending of Mk.** γράφειν διά τινος of the bearer IRo 10:1; IPhld 11:2; ISm 12:1, but also of pers. who had a greater or smaller part in drawing up some document (Dionys. of Cor. in Eus., HE 4, 23, 11) **1 Pt 5:12** (on the practice s. ERichards, The Secretary in the Letters of Paul '91). In this case διά comes close to the mng. *represented by* (LWenger, D. Stellvertretung im Rechte d. Pap. 1906, 9ff; Dssm., LO 98 [LAE 123f]). So also κρίνει ὁ θεὸς διὰ Χρ. Ἰ. *God judges, represented by Christ Jesus* **Ro 2:16.** Christ as intermediary in the creation of the world **J 1:3, 10; 1 Cor 8:6; Col 1:16.**—εὐχαριστεῖν τ. θεῷ διὰ Ἰ. Χρ. *thank God through Jesus Christ* **Ro 1:8; 7:25; Col 3:17.**—Occasionally the mediation becomes actual presence (references for this usage in BKeil, Anonymus Argentinensis 1902, p. 192, 1; 306 note) διὰ πολλῶν μαρτύρων *in the presence of many witnesses* **2 Ti 2:2** (Simplicius in Epict. p. 114, 31 διὰ θεοῦ μέσου=in the presence of God as mediator; Philo, Leg. ad Gai. 187 τὸ διὰ μαρτύρων κλαίειν=weeping in the presence of witnesses).

ⓑ with focus on the originator of an action (Hom. et al.; pap, LXX, EpArist)—**α.** of human activity (PSI 354, 6 [254 BC] τὸν χόρτον τὸν συνηγμένον δι' ἡμῶν=by us; 500, 5; 527, 12; 1 Esdr 6:13; 2 Macc 6:21; 4 Macc 1:11) **2 Cor 1:11** (where διὰ πολλῶν resumes ἐκ πολλῶν προσώπων). ᾧ παρέλαβε κανόνι διὰ τῶν μακαρίων προφήτων καὶ τοῦ ἁγίου εὐαγγελίου AcPlCor 2:36.

β. of divine activity:—of God (Aeschyl., Ag. 1485; Pla., Symp. 186e ἡ ἰατρικὴ πᾶσα διὰ τ. θεοῦ τούτου [Asclepius] κυβερνᾶται; Ael. Aristid., Sarap. [Or. 8 Dind.=45 Keil] 14 K. πάντα γὰρ πανταχοῦ διὰ σοῦ τε καὶ διὰ σὲ ἡμῖν γίγνεται; Zosimus in CALG p. 143 and a magic ring in introd. 133; EpArist 313) **1 Cor 1:9** δι' οὗ ἐκλήθητε (v.l. ὑπό s. καλέω 4); **Ro 11:36** (s. Norden, Agn. Th. 240–50; 347f); **Hb 2:10b** (s. B 2a, below; cp. Ar. 1:5 δι' αὐτοῦ . . . τὰ πάντα συνέστηκεν).—Of Christ **Ro 1:5; 5:9, 17f, 21; 8:37; 2 Cor 1:20** al. (ASchettler, D. paulin. Formel 'durch Christus' 1907; GJonker, De paulin. formule 'door Christus': ThSt 27, 1909, 173–208).—Of the Holy Spirit **Ac 11:28; 21:4; Ro 5:5.**

❺ At times διά w. gen. seems to have causal mng. (Rdm. 142; POxy 299, 2 [I AD] ἔδωκα αὐτῷ διὰ σοῦ=because of you; Achilles Tat. 3, 4, 5 διὰ τούτων=for this reason; in Eng. cp. Coleridge, Anc. Mariner 135–36: Every tongue thro' utter drouth Was wither'd at the root, s. OED s.v. 'through' I B 8) διὰ τῆς σαρκός *because of the resistance of the flesh* **Ro 8:3.**—**2 Cor 9:13.**—On the use of διά w. gen. in Ro s. Schlaeger, La critique radicale de l'épître aux Rom.: Congr. d' Hist. du Christ. II 111f.

B. w. acc.—❶ **marker of extension through an area,** ***through*** (Hom. and other early Gk. only in poetry, e.g. Pind. P. 9, 123 δι' ὅμιλον 'through the throng'; Hellenistic prose since Dionys. Hal. [JKäser, D. Präpositionen b. Dionys. Hal., diss. Erlangen 1915, 54]; ISyriaW 1866b τὸν πάτρωνα διὰ πάντα of the governor of a whole province) διήρχετο διὰ μέσον Σαμαρείας καὶ Γαλιλαίας **Lk 17:11** (cp. SibOr 3, 316 ῥομφαία διελεύσεται διὰ μέσον σεῖο).

❷ **marker of someth. constituting cause**—ⓐ the reason why someth. happens, results, exists: ***because of, for the sake of*** (do something for the sake of a divinity: UPZ 62, 2 [161 BC] διὰ τὸν Σάραπιν; JosAs 1:10 δι' αὐτήν; ApcSed 3:3 διὰ τὸν ἄνθρωπον; Tat. 8:2 διὰ τὸν . . . Ἄττιν; Ath. 30, 1 διὰ τὴν Δερκετώ) hated because of the name **Mt 10:22;** persecution arises because of teaching **13:21;** because of unbelief vs. **58;** because of a tradition **15:3;** διὰ τὸν ἄνθρωπον (the sabbath was designed) *for people* **Mk 2:27;** because of Herodias **Mk 6:17** (cp. Just. D. 34, 8 διὰ γυναῖκα); because of a crowd **Lk 5:19; 8:19** al; because of Judeans **Ac 16:3.** διὰ τὸν θόρυβον **21:34;** because of rain **28:2.** Juristically to indicate guilt: imprisoned *for insurrection and murder* **Lk 23:25.** δι' ὑμᾶς *on your account*=through your fault **Ro 2:24** (Is 52:5). διὰ τὴν πάρεσιν *because of the passing over* **3:25** (but s. WKümmel, ZTK 49, '52, 164). διὰ τὰ παραπτώματα *on account of transgressions* **4:25a** (cp. Is 53:5; PsSol 13:5); but διὰ τὴν δικαίωσιν *in the interest of justification* vs. **25b;** s. **8:10** for a sim. paired use of διά. διὰ τὴν χάριν *on the basis of the grace* **15:15.** δι' ἀσθένειαν τῆς σαρκός *because of a physical ailment* (cp. POxy 726, 10f [II AD] οὐ δυνάμενος δι' ἀσθένειαν πλεῦσαι. Cp. ἀσθένεια 1) **Gal 4:13.** διὰ τὸ θέλημα σου *by your will* **Rv 4:11.** διὰ τὸν χρόνον *according to the time = by this time* **Hb 5:12** (Aelian, VH 3, 37 δ. τὸν χρ.=because of the particular time-situation).—W. words denoting emotions *out of* (Diod. S. 5, 59, 8 διὰ τὴν λύπην; 18, 25, 1 διὰ τὴν προπέτειαν=out of rashness; Appian, Celt. 1 §9 δι' ἐλπίδα; 2 Macc 5:21; 7:20; 9:8; 3 Macc 5:32, 41; Tob 8:7): διὰ φθόνον *out of envy* **Mt 27:18; Phil 1:15.** διὰ σπλάγχνα ἐλέους *out of tender mercy* **Lk 1:78.** διὰ τ. φόβον τινός *out of fear of someone* **J 7:13.** διὰ τὴν πολλὴν ἀγάπην *out of the great love* **Eph 2:4.** διὰ τ. πλεονεξίαν *in their greediness* B 10:4.—Of God as the ultimate goal or purpose of life, whereas διά w. gen. (s. A4bβ above) represents God as Creator, **Hb 2:10a** (s. Norden, op. cit.; PGM 13, 76 διὰ σὲ συνέστηκεν . . . ἡ γῆ). Cp. J 6:57 (s. Bultmann ad loc.) PtK 2.

ⓑ in direct questions διὰ τί; ***why?*** (Hyperid. 3, 17; Dio Chrys. 20 [37], 28; Ael. Aristid. 31 p. 597 D.; oft. LXX; TestJob 37:8; TestLevi 2:9; GrBar, Tat; Mel., fgm. 8b, 42) mostly in an interrogative clause **Mt 9:11, 14; 13:10; 15:2f; 17:19; 21:25; Mk 2:18; 11:31; Lk 5:30; 19:23, 31; 20:5; 24:38; J 7:45; 8:43, 46; 12:5; 13:37; Ac 5:3; 1 Cor 6:7; Rv 17:7.** Simply διὰ τί; (Hyperid. 3, 23) **Ro 9:32; 2 Cor 11:11.** Also διατί (always in t.r. and often by Tdf.; TestJob 46:2) B 8:4, 6; Hm 2:5; s 5, 5, 5. Kvan Leeuwen Boomkamp, Τι et Διατι dans les évangiles: RevÉtGr 39, 1926, 327–31.—In real and supposed answers and inferences διὰ τοῦτο *therefore* (X., An. 1, 7, 3; 7, 19; oft. LXX; JosAs 7:7; Ar. 12, 2; Just., A I, 44, 5 al.; Demetr.: 722 fgm. 2, 3 Jac.) **Mt 6:25; 12:27, 31; 13:13, 52; 14:2; 18:23; 21:43; 23:13 v.l.; 24:44; Mk 11:24; 12:24; Lk 11:19** al. Also διὰ ταῦτα (Epict.) **Eph 5:6.** διὰ τοῦτο ὅτι *for this reason, (namely) that* **J 5:16, 18; 8:47; 10:17; 12:18, 39; 15:19; 1J 3:1.** διὰ τοῦτο ἵνα *for this reason,* *(in order) that* (Lucian, Abdic. 1) **J 1:31; 2 Cor 13:10; 1 Ti 1:16; Phlm 15.** Also διὰ τοῦτο ὅπως **Hb 9:15.**

ⓒ διά foll. by inf. or acc. w. inf., representing a causal clause, ***because*** (Gen 39:9; Dt 1:36; 1 Macc 6:53; GrBar 8:4; Demetr.: 722 fgm 1:1 al.) διὰ τὸ μὴ ἔχειν βάθος *because it had no depth* **Mt 13:5f; Mk 4:5f** (διὰ τὸ μή w. inf.: X., Mem. 1, 3, 5; Hero Alex. I 348, 7; III 274, 19; Lucian, Hermot. 31); *because lawlessness increases* **Mt 24:12;** διὰ τὸ εἶναι αὐτὸν ἐξ οἴκου Δ. **Lk 2:4;** *because it was built well* **6:48** al. διὰ τὸ λέγεσθαι ὑπό τινων *because it was said by some* **Lk 9:7** (for the constr. cp. Herodian 7, 12, 7 διὰ τὸ τὰς ἐξόδους ὑπὸ τ. πυρὸς προκατειλῆφθαι=because the exit-routes were blocked by the fire).

ⓓ instead of διά w. gen. to denote the efficient cause we may have διά, ***by*—α.** w. acc. of thing (schol. on Pind., N. 4, 79a; 2 Macc 12:11; EpArist 77) διὰ τὸ αἷμα *by the blood* **Rv 12:11.** διὰ τὰ σημεῖα *by the miracles* **13:14.**

β. w. acc. of pers. and freq. as expr. of favorable divine action (Aristoph., Plut. 468; Dionys. Hal. 8, 33, 3, 1579 μέγας διὰ τ. θεοὺς ἐγενόμην; Ael. Aristid. 24, 1 K.=44 p. 824 D.: δι' οὓς [= θεούς] ἐσώθην; SIG 1122; OGI 458, 40; PGM 13, 579 διῳκονομήθη τ. πάντα διὰ σέ; EpArist 292; Sir 15:11; 3 Macc 6:36: other exx. in SEitrem and AFridrichsen, E. christl. Amulett auf Pap. 1921, 24). ζῶ διὰ τὸν πατέρα **J 6:57** (cp. PKöln VI, 245, 16 of Isis σὺ κυρεῖς τὰ πάντα, διὰ σὲ δ' εἰσορῶ φαός 'you are responsible for everything and thanks to you I can see light'). διὰ τὸν ὑποτάξαντα *by the one who subjected it* **Ro 8:20.**—DELG. M-M. TW.

διαβαίνω fut. διαβήσομαι LXX; 2 aor. διέβην, ptc. διαβάς (Hom. et al.; ins, pap, LXX; En 32:2; ApcrEzk P 1 verso 18 [Denis 126]; Joseph.; Just., D. 86, 5) **to proceed from one side to another over a geographical area, *go through, cross*** w. acc. τὴν ἐρυθρὰν θάλασσαν *the Red Sea* **Hb 11:29** (Anonym. Alex. Hist. [II BC]: 151 fgm. 1, 2 Jac.: Alex. the Great experiences a similar miracle at the Pamphylian Sea. Before him ἐσπάσθη τὸ πέλαγος which leaves τὸν χερσωθέντα τόπον free. ἄνεμοι ἀντέσχον τῷ πελάγει, until Alex. and his men διέβησαν.—Ps.-Apollod. 1, 4, 3, 1 διαβ. τὴν θάλασσαν by Poseidon's favor); *cross* a river, w. acc. (Hdt. 1, 75 al.; Gen 31:21 al.; Jos., Ant. 7, 128; SibOr 4, 139) Hv 1, 1, 3; *come over* εἰς Μακεδονίαν **Ac 16:9** (Memnon [I BC/I AD]: 434 fgm. 1, 8, 1 Jac. εἰς τὴν Μακεδονίαν διαβαίνειν; PLille 6, 3; PFay 110, 15f διάβα εἰς Διονυσιάδα; Num 32:7 al.; Jos., Bell. 7, 21); over a chasm πρός τινα **Lk 16:26** (cp. 1 Macc 5:40; Jos., Ant. 12, 103).—M-M.

διαβάλλω 1 aor. pass. διεβλήθην; pf. pass. 3 sg. διαβέβληται (Just., D. 10, 1) (s. βάλλω, διάβολος; trag., Hdt. et al.; pap, LXX, Joseph.) **to make a complaint about a pers. to a third party, *bring charges, inform*** either justly or falsely. The former (Hdt. 8, 22, 3 of incriminating information provided indirectly; Thu. 3, 4, 4; Aristoph., Thesm. 1169; Philostratus, Ep. 37; PTebt 23, 4; Da 3:8; 2 Macc 3:11; Jos., Ant. 12, 176): διεβλήθη αὐτῷ ὡς διασκορπίζων *he was informed that (the manager) was squandering* **Lk 16:1** (dat. as Hdt. 5, 35, 1; Pla., Rep. 8, 566b al.; ὡς w. ptc. as X., Hell. 2, 3, 23; Pla., Epist. 7, 334a). Of malicious accusation (BGU 1040, 22; POxy 900, 13; 4 Macc 4:1; Jos., Ant. 7, 267): Papias (2:17) includes a story περὶ γυναικὸς ἐπὶ πολλαῖς ἁμαρτίαις διαβληθείσης ἐπὶ τοῦ κυρίου *of a woman accused before the Lord of many sins.*—M-M. TW. Sv.

διαβεβαιόομαι (since Demosth. 17, 30; oft. in H. Gk. writers; pap, e.g. CPR I, 18, 29; PFamTebt 19, 14; PWarr 13, 14; BGU 19, 7; PLond I, 113; I, 21 [VI AD] p. 201; EpArist 99; Just., A I, 19, 2) mid. dep. ***speak confidently, insist*** περί τινος (Polyb. 12, 12, 6; Plut., Fab. 182 [14, 4]; Sext. Emp., Pyrrh. 1, 191; Jos., C. Ap. 2, 14) *concerning* or *on someth.* **1 Ti 1:7; Tit 3:8;** *confirm* Papias (2:3).—S. DELG s.v. βέβαιος. M-M.

διάβημα, ατος, τό (Damascius, De Princ. 423; LXX; PsSol 16, 9; Hesych.) **a foot movement, *step*** κατευθύνειν τὰ δ. τινος *guide someone's* steps 1 Cl 60:2 (cp. Ps 36:23; 39:3; 118, 133).—DELG s.v. βαίνω p. 157.

διαβλέπω fut. διαβλέψω; 1 aor. διέβλεψα (Pla. et al.; PAbinn 7, 19; PCairZen 639, 5; PLond II 418, 19 [346 AD] p. 302)

❶ **to stare w. eyes wide open, *look intently,*** or ***open one's eyes (wide)*** (Plut., Mor. 973f; s. HAlmqvist, Plut. u. d. NT '46, 55f) **Mk 8:25** (ERoos, Eranos 51, '53, 155–57).

❷ **to be able to see clearly, *see clearly*** w. inf. foll. in imagery **Mt 7:5; Lk 6:42;** Ox 1 verso, 1 (ASyn. 68, 44; cp. GTh 26).—M-M.

διαβόητος, ον (Plut.; Dio Chrys.; Lucian, Alex. 4; X. Eph. 1, 7, 3 al.; SIG 888, 28) **pert. to having word spread about a pers. or thing, *talked about, renowned*** of the church at Ephesus IEph 8:1 (for the dat. τ. αἰῶσιν cp. X. Eph. 1, 2, 7 δ. τοῖς θεωμένοις ἅπασιν; for the content s. the entry αἰών)—DELG s.v. βοή.

διαβολή, ῆς, ἡ (s. διάβολος; Epicharmus, Hdt. et al.; PSI 441, 19 [III BC]; Sb 9558, 7; LXX; TestJos 1:7; EpArist; Jos., Ant. 6, 285 and 286, Vi. 80; Mel., HE 4, 26, 9; Ath.) ***slander*** (w. καταλαλιά) Pol 4:3. (For usage in magical pap, PUps 8, p. 115.)—DELG s.v. βάλλω p. 162. TW.

διάβολος, ον (s. διαβολή)—❶ **pert. to engagement in slander, *slanderous*** (since Aristoph.; Thuc. 6, 15, 2 as adv.; Herm. Wr. 13, 13b; 22b; Philo, Sacr. Abel. 32 p. 215, 6) Pol 5:2. γυναῖκες **1 Ti 3:11.** πρεσβύτιδες **Tit 2:3.—2 Ti 3:3.**

❷ subst. ὁ δ. **one who engages in slander** (since X., Ages. 11, 5; Athen. 11, 508e; Esth 7:4; 8:1; pap first Christian; cp. PLond VI, 1923, 9 [IV AD] 'the devil'; Tat. 22, 1), in our lit. as title of the principal transcendent evil being ***the adversary/devil,*** already current in the LXX as transl. of הַשָּׂטָן (Job 2:1, but here not 'as an entity opposed to the divine will', JGammie, HUCA 56, '85, 1–19 [s. p. 13]; Zech 3:1f; 1 Ch 21:1; cp. Wsd 2:24; TestNapht 8:4, 6; TestSol, TestJob; JosAs 12:9; GrBar 4:8; ApcSed, ApcMos, AssMos; Just., Mel., P. 67, 477 al.; δ. ὁ ἄρχων τοῦ κόσμου τούτου Hippol., Ref. 6, 33) **Mt 4:1, 5, 8, 11; 13:39; 25:41; Lk 4:2f, 6, 13; 8:12; J 13:2; Ac 10:38; Eph 4:27; 6:11; Hb 2:14; Js 4:7.** κρίμα … τοῦ διαβόλου *the judgment that befalls the devil* **1 Ti 3:6;** παγὶς τοῦ διαβόλου *devil's trap* **3:7; 2 Ti 2:26** (s. IScheftelowitz, Das Schlingen- u. Netzmotiv 1912, 11). ὁ ἀντίδικος ὑμῶν διάβολος *your adversary, the devil* **1 Pt 5:8;** Μιχαὴλ … τῷ δ. διακρινόμενος **Jd 9.** In **Rv 12:9; 20:2** w. ὄφις and σατανᾶς; s. also **2:10; 12:12; 20:10.** τοῦ δ. βοτάνη *weed of the devil* IEph 10:3; ἐνέδραι τοῦ δ. *the devil's ambuscades* ITr 8:1; cp. MPol 3:1. Of tortures inflicted by the devil IRo 5:3. τῷ δ. λατρεύειν *serve the devil* ISm 9:1; ὄργανα τοῦ δ. *tools of the devil* (of non-Christians) 2 Cl 18:2; πολυπλοκία τοῦ δ. *the devil's cunning* Hm 4, 3, 4; tempting to sin (cp. πειράζων τὸν σωτῆρα δ. Orig., C. Cels. 6, 43, 29) m 4, 3, 6; dwells in anger m 5, 1, 3; ἔργα τοῦ δ. m 7:3; doubt described as the devil's daughter m 9:9; likew. evil desire m 12, 2, 2. The πνεῦμα or basic character of the devil is mentioned m 11:3; it is a πνεῦμα ἐπίγειον m 11:17 (Just., D. 82, 3 ἀκάθαρτον); ἐντολαὶ τοῦ δ. m 12, 4, 6; παλαίειν μετὰ τοῦ δ. s 8, 3, 6.—In imagery, those who oppose divine interests or purpose (s. πατήρ 3b) are υἱοὶ δ. **Ac 13:10;** τέκνα τοῦ δ. **1J 3:10;** they are descended ἐκ τοῦ δ. vs. **8;** the devil is their father **J 8:44.** (Cp. οἱ μὲν τοῦ θεοῦ, οἱ δὲ τοῦ διαβόλου Orig., C. Cels. 8, 25, 16.) On the designation of Judas as δ. **6:70** (sim. Peter as σατανᾶς Mk 8:33), cp. **13:2** (cp. εἰσῆλθεν εἰς ἐκεῖνον ὁ σατανᾶς 13:27).—Lit. under δαιμόνιον end, and ἄγγελος end. BNoack, Satanas u. Soteria '48, 55f.—B. 1487. EDNT. TW.

διαγγέλλω fut. 2 pl. διαγγελεῖτε Lev 25:9; 2 aor. 3 sg. subj. διαγγείλῃ Jos 6:10, 2 aor. pass. διηγγέλην, subj. διαγγελῶ (s. ἀγγέλλω; Pind., Thu. et al.; PSI 329, 4; 559, 5; PPetr II, 1, 12 [all III BC]; LXX, Philo, Joseph.)

❶ **to make someth. known far and wide, *proclaim, spread the news concerning/about*** (Pind., N. 5, 3 in imagery of the poet's sweet song speeding in every available vessel to announce a certain boy's victory in the pancratium; Demosth. 12, 16; Jos., Vi. 98; Just., D. 60, 3) the reign of God **Lk 9:60.** τὸ ὄνομα τοῦ θεοῦ **Ro 9:17** (Ex 9:16). Cp. **Mk 5:19 v.l.**

❷ **to make a report, *announce, report*** (X., An. 1, 6, 2; Jos., Ant. 7, 201) completion of the days of purification **Ac 21:26.** Of the church δ. καιροὺς *announce* seasons (fulfillment of prophecies) Dg 11:5. TW.

διάγε s. γέ aα.

διαγίνομαι (s. γίνομαι) 2 aor. διεγενόμην ***to pass/elapse*** of time (Lysias, Or. 1, 15 χρόνου μεταξὺ διαγενομένου; X., Isaeus et al.; Joseph., s. below; PStras 41, 42 πολὺς χρόνος διαγέγονεν [250 AD]; POxy 68, 18; PLond V, 1676, 40; PFamTebt 15, 139; Mitt-Wilck. I/2, 41, col. III, 25; cp. διά A2a; LXX has the word only 2 Macc 11:26 in another mng.) διαγενομένου τοῦ σαββάτου *when the Sabbath was over* **Mk 16:1.** ἡμερῶν διαγενομένων τινῶν *several days afterward* **Ac 25:13** (cp. Jos., Ant. 7, 394). ἱκανοῦ χρόνου διαγενομένου *since* or *when considerable time had passed* **27:9.**—M-M.

διαγινώσκω fut. διαγνώσομαι; 2 aor. 3 pl. διέγνωσαν; plupf. 1 sg. διεγνώκειν LXX; pf. pass. 1 pl. διεγνώσμεθα (Just., A I, 2, 4), ptc. διεγνωσμένον 2 Macc. 3:23 (s. γινώσκω; Hom. et al.; ins, pap [e.g. PTebt 55, 2 of a decision to travel], LXX, Philo; Jos., Ant. 4, 121; 6, 205). In our lit. as a legal term (cp. Aeschyl., Antiphon et al.; Dionys. Hal. 2, 14; PRev 14, 1; POxy 1032, 53; 1117, 3 al.; Philo, Agr. 116; Just. A I, 2, 4; 68, 9 [Hadrian?]).

❶ **to give careful attention (to facts or a subject) as a basis for forming a judgment, *determine*** w. specific ref. to factors entering into a decision ἀκριβέστερον τὰ περὶ αὐτοῦ *to make a more thorough examination of his case* **Ac 23:15** (NRSV).

❷ **to make a judicial decision, *decide/hear (a case)*** [μέχρις ἂν αὐτὸς] διαγνοῖ τὰ περ[ὶ αὐτῶν] *until (Nero) himself should decide their* (the Christians') *case* AcPl Ha 9:23. τὰ καθ' ὑμᾶς *decide your case* **Ac 24:22** prob. refers to the total judicial process.—M-M.

διαγνωρίζω 1 aor. διεγνώρισα (s. διάγνωσις; Philo, Det. Pot. Insid. 97) ***give an exact report*** περί τινος **Lk 2:17 v.l.** (for ἐγνώρισαν).—DELG s.v. γιγνώσκω.

διάγνωσις, εως, ἡ (s. διαγνωρίζω; as legal term e.g. Pla., Leg. 9, 865c; Wsd 3:18; Jos., Ant. 8, 133; 15, 358; loanw. in rabb.) **a judicial inquiry or investigation that culminates in a decision, *decision*** (pap, e.g., PHib 93, 10 [c. 250 BC] ἡ δ. περὶ αὐτοῦ ἔστω πρὸς βασιλικά; PLond II, 358, 17 p. 172 [c. 150 AD]; PCollYoutie I, 30, 17 [198/99 AD]) τηρεῖσθαι εἰς τὴν τοῦ Σεβαστοῦ δ. *to be kept in custody for the Emperor's decision* (cognitio) **Ac 25:21** (IG XIV, 1072, 4f ἐπὶ διαγνώσεων τοῦ Σεβαστοῦ; Jos., Bell. 2, 17).—M-M.

διαγογγύζω impf. διεγόγγυζον; fut. 3 sg. διαγογγύσει Sir 31:24; 1 aor. 3 pl. διεγόγγυσαν LXX (s. γογγύζω; Heliod. 7, 27, 4; LXX; TestJob 14:4) ***complain, grumble*** (aloud) w. λέγων foll. **Lk 15:2; 19:7.**—TW.

διαγρηγορέω (s. γρηγορέω) aor. διεγρηγόρησα

❶ ***keep awake*** (Herodian 3, 4, 4; Niceph. Gregoras, Hist. Byz. p. 205f; 571a); for διαγρηγορήσαντες εἶδον **Lk 9:32** this would give the mng. *since they had kept awake, they saw.* But δ. can also mean

❷ ***awake fully*** (Niceph., op. cit. 205f, δόξαν ἀπεβαλόμην ὥσπερ οἱ διαγρηγορήσαντες τὰ ἐν τοῖς ὕπνοις ὀνείρατα); in this case: *when they were fully awake, they saw.* The latter rendering appears more probable in view of the subsequent ref. to the disciples' ignorance (vs. 45) of the destiny of Jesus at Jerusalem (vs. 31).—S. DELG s.v. ἐγείρω.

διάγω fut. διάξω Sir 31:24; 1 aor. διήγαγον LXX (s. ἄγω; Hom., Od. 20, 187; Thu. 4, 78; LXX; Just., D. 138, 2; Mel., P. 84, 634) with or without the acc. βίον very common in Gk. writers (cp. also 2 Macc 12:38; 3 Macc 4:8; TestSol, TestAbr A, Test12Patr; Jos., C. Ap. 2, 229; Just.) in the sense ***spend one's life, live.*** ἐν τρυφῇ **Lk 7:25 v.l.** (cp. TestJos 3:4); ἐν κακίᾳ **Tit 3:3.** ἐν Χριστῷ ITr 2:2 (cp. Pla., Phdr., 259d ἐν φιλοσοφίᾳ; Plut., Timol. 3, 1 ἐν εἰρήνῃ διάγοντες; TestJos 9:3 ἐν σωφροσύνῃ; TestAbr A 10 p. 88, 19 [Stone p. 24] ἐν ἁμαρτίᾳ; gravestone: Sb 6648, 4 ἐν σκοτίᾳ; Just., A I, 20, 4 εἰς). ἤρεμον καὶ ἡσύχιον βίον *lead a peaceful and quiet life* **1 Ti 2:2.**—M-M.

διαδέχομαι fut. ptc. τὸν διαδεξόμενον (2 Macc. 9:23 v.l.); 1 aor. διεδεξάμην; fut. pass. 3 sg. διαδεχθήσεται (Sir 14:20 cod. A) (Hdt. et al.; Just., Ath.) **to receive in turn from a former possessor, *receive in turn, succeed to*** freq. as t.t. in reference to one who succeeds another either in manifestation of character exhibited by the predecessor: 'inherit' in the sense of reception by genetic transmission (SIG 495, 6 [Protogenes manifests the goodwill of his father]) or in public office (Polyb. 9, 28, 8 [Alexander succeeds Philip] et al.; SIG 700, 32; OGI 335, 132; 210, 2f τὴν ἀρχιερωσύνην; PTebt 489; PHamb 27, 14; POxy 495, 11; 13; 4 Macc 4:15; TestSol D 4:6; Philo, Mos. 1, 207; Jos., Ant. 7, 337; Just., D. 139, 4; Ath. 37, 1) the sense used 1 Cl 44:2: τὴν λειτουργίαν *ministry*—Abs. (as Hdt. 8, 142; s. Field, Notes 116) of the Israelites' tabernacle *in turn* **Ac 7:45.**—M-M.

διάδημα, ατος, τό (since X., Cyr. 8, 3, 13; Alex. Ep. XIII, 27; XIV, 4; Epict. 1, 24, 17; 4, 8, 30; OGI 248, 17; 383, 103; O. Bodl 262, 1 BC; pap; LXX; TestSol D 7:4; Test12Patr; JosAs; ApcSol) fr. διαδεῖν to bind around: 'band, fillet', Eng. loanw. 'diadem': properly the sign of royalty among the Persians, a blue band trimmed with white, on the tiara, hence a symbol of royalty gener.: ***royal headband, crown*** (Diod. S. 4, 4, 4; Lucian, Pisc. 35 βασιλείας γνώρισμα; Ezk. Trag. 71 [in Eus., PE 9, 29, 5]; Philo, Fuga 111; Jos., Bell. 1, 70, Ant. 12, 389; TestJud 12:4) **Rv 12:3; 13:1; 19:12** (divinities w. diadems: PGM 4:521, 675, 2840). Pol 1:1. Kl. Pauly I 1504f.—DELG s.v. δέω 1. TW.

διαδίδωμι fut. διαδώσω LXX; 1 aor. διέδωκα, 2 aor. impv. διάδος. Pass.: impf. 3 sg. διεδίδετο; aor. 3 sg. διεδόθη (PsSol 1:4); ptc. διαδοθείς LXX; (s. on this form B-D-F §94, 1; W-S. §14, 11; Mlt-H. 206) **to apportion among various parties, *distribute, give*** (so Thu. et al.; X., Cyr. 1, 3, 7; SIG 374, 12; POxy 1115, 6; 1194, 17; PLips 35, 10; LXX; TestJob; TestBenj 11:1) τὰ σκῦλα *the spoils* **Lk 11:22.** τί τινι (Thu. 4, 38, 4; Jos., Ant. 7, 86) **18:22; Rv 17:13** t.r. (Erasmian rdg. s. Tdf. app.; RBorger, TRu 52, '87, 57); τὰ λοιπὰ τοῖς συνδούλοις *the rest to his fellow* *slaves* Hs 5, 2, 9. In **Lk 12:42 v.l.** the recipient of τὸ σιτομέτριον is implied. τινί *to someone* **J 6:11** (v.l. ἔδωκεν N[25] app., Tdf. in text; s. RBorger, op. cit, 34f). Pass. **Ac 4:35.**—M-M.

διαδοχή, ῆς, ἡ (s. διάδοχος; Aeschyl., Thu. et al.; ins, pap, in var. mgs., esp. of persons; TestLevi 18:8; TestAbr A, 2 p. 78, 31 [Stone p. 4; of Abraham's transfer from this life to the next]; Philo, Joseph., Just., Tat.; Ath. 28, 3) **the quality or state of being later, *succession*** ἐσχάτην εὐλογίαν, ἥτις διαδοχὴν οὐκ ἔχει *the ultimate blessing that has no successor*=the unsurpassable blessing GJs 6:2.—DELG s.v. δέχομαι p. 268. M-M. s.v. διάδοχος.

διάδοχος, ου, ὁ one who comes next in a series, esp. of a political figure, *successor* (Aeschyl. et al.; Hdt. 5, 26; ins, pap; Sir 46:1; 48:8; Philo; Jos., Ant. 1, 228 al.; Just., D. 103, 3; 113, 3; Mel., HE 4, 26, 7) λαμβάνειν δ. *receive as successor* **Ac 24:27** (cp. Jos., Ant. 20, 182).—M-M. Sv.

διαζώννυμι 1 aor. διέζωσα, mid. διεζωσάμην; pf. pass. ptc. διεζωσμένος (s. ζώννυμι; Thu. et al.; IG II, 763b, 16 et al. in ins; Ezk 23:15 A; TestSol 23:3 B; Philo, Op. M. 112) ***tie around.*** δ. ἑαυτόν *tie* (a towel) *around oneself* **J 13:4.** ἦν διεζωσμένος *he had tied around himself* vs. **5.** Mid. τὸν ἐπενδύτην *tie around* oneself (i.e. *put on*) *an outer garment* **21:7** (Lucian, Somn. 6 ἐσθῆτα, Anach. 6 al.; Jos., Ant. 7, 283 διεζωσμένος μάχαιραν). MSoards, JBL 102, '83, 283f ('belted his smock').—DELG s.v. ζώννυμι. M-M. TW.

διαθήκη, ης, ἡ (Democr., Aristoph.+; ins, pap, LXX, En, TestSol, TestAbr, Test12Patr; ParJer 6:21; ApcEsdr, ApcMos; AssMos fgm. a; Philo, Joseph., Just.; Mel., HE 4, 26, 14) apart from the simplex θήκη 'case, chest', for the mng. of this word one must begin with the mid. form of the verb διατίθεμαι, which is freq. used in legal and commercial discourse of disposition of things (s. L-S-J-M s.v. διατιθημι B), w. implication of promissory obligation. Disposition of one's personal effects would naturally come under testamentary law, hence

❶ ***last will and testament*** (so exclusively in Hellenistic times, Eger [s. 3 below] 99 note; exx. e.g. in Riggenbach 292ff; Behm 10, 1; 2; Philo, Joseph., Test12Patr; loanw. in rabb.) **Hb 9:16f;** δ. κεκυρωμένη *a will that has been ratified* **Gal 3:15;** cp. **17,** where δ. shades into mng. 2 (s. κυρόω 1, προκυρόω); s. also EBammel, below, and JSwetnam, CBQ 27, '65, 373–90. On Jewish perspective s. RKatzoff, An Interpretation of PYadin 19— A Jewish Gift after Death: ProcXXCongPap 562–65.

❷ As a transl. of בְּרִית in LXX δ. retains the component of legal disposition of personal goods while omitting that of the anticipated death of a testator. A Hellenistic reader would experience no confusion, for it was a foregone conclusion that gods were immortal. Hence a δ. decreed by God cannot require the death of the testator to make it operative. Nevertheless, another essential characteristic of a testament is retained, namely that it is the declaration of one person's initiative, not the result of an agreement betw. two parties, like a compact or a contract. This is beyond doubt one of the main reasons why the LXX rendered בְּרִית by δ. In the 'covenants' of God, it was God alone who set the conditions; hence ***covenant*** (s. OED s.v. 'covenant' sb. 7) can be used to trans. δ. only when this is kept in mind. So δ. acquires a mng. in LXX which cannot be paralleled w. certainty in extra-Biblical sources, namely 'decree', 'declaration of purpose', 'set of regulations', etc. Our lit., which is very strongly influenced by LXX in this area, seems as a rule to have understood the word in these senses (JHughes, NovT 21, '79, 27–96 [also Hb 9:16–20; Gal 3:15–17]). God has issued *a declaration of his purpose* **Ro 11:27** (Is 59:21); 1 Cl 15:4 (Ps 77:37); 35:7 (Ps 49:16), which God bears in mind (cp. Ps 104:8f; 105:45 al.) **Lk 1:72;** it goes back to ancestral days **Ac 3:25** (PsSol 9:10; ParJer 6:21). God also issued an *ordinance* (of circumcision) **7:8** (cp. Gen 17:10ff). Since God's holy will was set forth on more than one occasion (Gen 6:18; 9:9ff; 15:18; 17:2ff; Ex 19:5 and oft.), one may speak of διαθῆκαι *decrees, assurances* (cp. διαθῆκαι πατέρων Wsd 18:22; 2 Macc 8:15.—But the pl. is also used for a single testament: Diog. L. 4, 44; 5, 16. In quoting or referring to Theophr. sometimes the sing. [Diog. L. 5, 52; 56] is used, sometimes the pl. [5, 51; 57]) **Ro 9:4; Eph 2:12.** Much emphasis is laid on the δ. καινή, mentioned as early as Jer 38:31, which God planned for future disposition (**Hb 8:8–10; 10:16**). God's *decree* or *covenant* directed toward the Christians is a καινὴ δ. (δ. δευτέρα Orig., C. Cels. 2, 75) **Lk 22:20; 1 Cor 11:25; 2 Cor 3:6; Hb 8:8; 9:15a;** PtK 2 p. 15, 5, or δ. νέα **Hb 12:24;** PtK 2 p. 15, 6 which, as a δ. αἰώνιος (cp. Jer 39:40; En 99:2) **Hb 13:20,** far excels **7:22; 8:6** the παλαιὰ δ. **2 Cor 3:14,** or πρώτη δ. **Hb 9:15b,** with which it is contrasted. Both are mentioned (Did., Gen. 46, 4; 235, 26) **Gal 4:24;** B 4:6ff (Ex 34:28; 31:18; Just., D. 67, 9). Blood was shed when the old covenant was proclaimed at Sinai **Hb 9:20** (Ex 24:8); the same is true of the new covenant **Hb 10:29.** τὸ αἷμά μου τ. διαθήκης **Mt 26:28; Mk 14:24** (ELohse, Märtyrer u. Gottesknecht[2], '63, 122–29) is prob. to be understood in connection w. this blood (s. WWrede, ZNW 1, 1900, 69–74; TRobinson, My Blood of the Covenant: KMarti Festschr. 1925, 232–37; for a critique of this view s. GWalther, Jesus, D. Passalamm des Neuen Bundes, '50, 22–27 and JJeremias TLZ, '51, 547. For Syriac background JEmerton, JTS 13, '62, 111–17; s. also ÉDelebrecque, Études grecques sur l'évangile de Luc '76, 109–21).—The v.l. **Lk 22:29** may be derived from Jer 39:40 or Is 55:3 LXX (for the cognate acc. s. Aristoph., Aves 440).—δ. may also be transl. *decree* in the Ep. of Barnabas (4:6ff; 6:19; 9:6; 13:1, 6; 14:1ff δ. δοῦναί τινι); but the freq. occurrence of the idea of inheritance (6:19; 13:1, 6; 14:4f), makes it likely that the 'decree' is to be thought of as part of a will.

❸ The mng. ***compact, contract*** seems firmly established for Gr-Rom. times (FNorton, A Lexicographical and Historical Study of Διαθήκη, Chicago 1908, 31ff; EBruck, D. Schenkung auf d. Todesfall im griech. u. röm. Recht I 1909, 115ff; JWackernagel, D. Kultur d. Gegenw. I 8[2] 1907, 309). It remains doubtful whether this mng. has influenced our lit. here and there (exc. quite prob. **Lk 22:29 v.l.** with its administrative tenor; the phrase διατίθεμαι δ. as Aristoph., Av. 440 of a treaty agreement), but the usage of the term δ. in such sense would again serve as a bridge to LXX usage.—The expr. ἡ κιβωτὸς τ. διαθήκης *covenant chest* i.e. the sacred box (Eng. 'ark' as loanw. from Lat. arca) that symbolized God's pledge of presence w. Israel (Ex 31:7; 39:14 al.) **Hb 9:4; Rv 11:19** or αἱ πλάκες τ. διαθ. (Ex 34:28; Dt 9:9, 11) **Hb 9:4** would have required some acquaintance with Israelite tradition on the part of ancient readers.—ERiggenbach, D. Begriff d. Διαθήκη im Hb: Theol. Stud. f. TZahn 1908, 289ff, Hb[2] 1922, 205ff al.; ACarr, Covenant or Testament?: Exp. 7th ser., 7, 1909, 347ff; JBehm, D. Begriff D. im NT 1912; ELohmeyer, Diatheke 1913; WFerguson, Legal Terms Common to the Macedonian Inscr. and the NT, 1913, 42–46 (testamentary exhibits); HKennedy, Exp. 8th ser., 10, 1915, 385ff; GVos, Hebrews, the Epistle of the Diatheke: PTR 13, 1915, 587–632; 14, 1916, 1–61; OEger, ZNW 18, 1918, 84–108; EBurton, ICC Gal 1921, 496–505; LdaFonseca, Διαθήκη foedus an testamentum?: Biblica 8, 1927; 9, 1928; EBammel, Gottes διαθήκη (Gal 3:15–17) u. d. jüd. Rechtsdenken, NTS 6, '60, 313–19; NDow, A Select Bibliography on the Concept of Covenant, Austin Seminary Bulletin 78, 6, '63; CRoetzel, Biblica 51, '70, 377–90 (Ro 9:4);

DMcCarthy, Berit and Covenant (Deut.), '72, 65–85; EChristiansen, The Covenant in Judaism and Paul '95.—DELG s.v. θήκη. M-M. TW. Sv.

διαθρύπτω fut. διαθήσομαι; 2 aor. pass. διεθρύβην LXX τινί τι (s. θρύπτω; Hom. et al.) **to break someth. in pieces,** ***break*** τινί τι bread for the hungry B 3:3 (Is 58:7).—DELG s.v. θρύπτω.

διαίρεσις,εως,ἡ (s. διαιρέω) gener. a state or circumstance of being divided up

❶ **division or distribution of someth. to pers.,** ***apportionment, division*** (Hdt. et al.; ins, pap; Jdth 9:4; Sir14:15; Philo) διαιρέσεις χαρισμάτων *allotments of spiritual gifts* **1 Cor 12:4;** cp. vss. **5, 6** (this interpr. is supported by vs. 11 διαιροῦν ἑκάστῳ καθὼς βούλεται). Another tenable interpr. for this passage is

❷ **a state of difference in the nature of objects or events,** ***difference, variety*** (Pla., Soph. 267b τίνα μείζω διαίρεσιν ἀγνωσίας τε καὶ γνώσεως θήσομεν; Lucian, Hermot. 52; Epict. 2, 6, 24; Tat. 12, 1; Ath. 10, 3; 12, 2, R. 71, 16).

❸ **division through violent action,** ***tearing apart*** (of political conflicts TestJud 22:1 διαιρέσεις κατ' ἀλλήλων) of the body in certain kinds of torture and execution IRo 5:3 (text uncertain; s. ἀνατομή; cp. Artem. 1, 67 p. 62, 7 διαιρέσεις ὑπὸ σιδήρου; Philo, Agr. 129 ἄνευ τομῆς κ. διαιρέσεως).—DELG s.v. αἱρέω. M-M. TW. Sv.

διαιρέω s. διαίρεσις; fut. διελῶ LXX; 2 aor. διεῖλον, subj. διέλω. Pass.: fut. 3 sg. διαιρεθήσεται LXX; aor. διῃρέθην LXX; pf. διῄρημαι LXX (Hom. et al.; ins, pap, LXX) ***distribute, divide*** (Jos., Ant. 5, 88 τί) τινί τι *someth. to someone* (X., Cyr. 4, 5, 51, Hell. 3, 2, 10; often pap, e.g. PLond III, 880, 11 [113 BC] p. 9 διειρῆσθαι τὰ ὑπάρχοντα αὐτῷ ἔγγαια τοῖς ἑαυτοῦ υἱοῖς; Josh 18:5; Jdth 16:24; 1 Macc 1:6) διεῖλεν αὐτοῖς τὸν βίον *he divided his property between them* **Lk 15:12;** *apportion someth. to someone* (Michel 1001 VI, 18 ὁ ἀρτυτὴρ ['officiant'] διελεῖ τὰ ἱερὰ τοῖς παροῦσι) **1 Cor 12:11.** Abs. ἐὰν ὀρθῶς μὴ διέλῃς *if you did not divide* (the sacrifice) *rightly* 1 Cl 4:4 (Gen 4:7).—DELG s.v. αἱρέω. M-M.—TW.

δίαιτα, ης, ἡ (cp. διαιτάομαι 'lead one's life, live'; Pind., Hdt. et al.; LXX; TestSol 11:2 P; TestJos 3:5 [v.l. τροφήν]; Jos., Bell. 2, 151, C. Ap. 2, 240) orig. 'way of life'.

❶ ***food, diet*** Dg 5:4.—❷ ***habitation, dwelling-place*** (Diod. S. 3, 30, 2; Ps.-Aristot., De Mundo 6, 398b, 32; Plut., Mor. 515e; OGI 383, 27 [I BC]; Jos., Ant. 15, 331; Tat. 9, 1 τῆς ἐν οὐρανῷ διαίτης *life in heaven.* So as loanw. in rabb.) 1 Cl 39:8 (Job 5:3). δ. τῆς σκηνῆς σου οὐ μὴ ἁμάρτῃ *the dwelling-place of your tent shall not suffer want* 56:13 (Job 5:24).—DELG.

διακαθαίρω 1 aor. inf. διακαθᾶραι (s. καθαρίζω; Aristoph., Pla. et al.; BCH 27, 1903, 73 ln. 79) **to make free of someth. unwanted,** ***thoroughly purge, clean out*** τί a threshing-floor **Lk 3:17** (Alciphron 2, 23, 1 ἄρτι μοι τὴν ἅλω διακαθήραντι).—M-M.

διακαθαρίζω fut. διακαθαριῶ (not found elsewh.; s. preceding entry) ***clean out*** τί someth. **Mt 3:12; Lk 3:17 v.l.**—DELG s.v. καθαρός.

διακατελέγχομαι impf. διακατηλεγχόμην (s. ἐλέγχω; not found elsewh.) ***confute, overwhelm in argument*** τινί: τοῖς Ἰουδαίοις **Ac 18:28.**—TW.

διακελεύω (s. κελεύω; the mid. since Hdt., the act. only in Philostrat., Vi. Apollon. 1, 31 v.l.; POxy 2340, 11 [192 AD]; and Suda) ***command, order*** τινί w. inf. foll. **J 8:5 v.l.**

διακονέω (s. two next entries) impf. διηκόνουν; fut. διακονήσω; 1 aor. διηκόνησα; pf. inf. δεδιηκονηκέναι (AssMos fgm. k, Denis p. 67); aor. pass. διηκονήθην, for augm. s. B-D-F §69, 4; W-S. §12, 6; Mlt-H. 192 (Soph., Hdt. et al.; rare in ins, pap; never in LXX, but in Philo, Joseph.) gener. to render service in a variety of ways either at someone's behest or voluntarily and freq. with suggestion of movement.

❶ **to function as an intermediary,** ***act as go-between/agent, be at one's service*** w. intermediary function either expressed or implied (lead tablet Sb 4947, 2 διακόνησόν μοι; in lover's petition 'serve as intermediary [medium] for me' PWarr 21, 4; 8; Lucian, Cont. 1 of Hermes as messenger for Zeus; Theophr. Char. 2, 9 fetch things; Just., D. 79, 2; cp. the role of Repentance JosAs 15:7) w. dat. of pers. and acc. of thing οὐχ ἑαυτοῖς ὑμῖν δὲ διηκόνουν αὐτά *they were not acting as agents in their own behalf but for yours in the things* **1 Pt 1:12** (for a service consisting in the delivery of a message cp. Jos., Ant. 6, 298). For a similar contrast, and with suggestion of an intermediary's mission: οὐκ ἦλθεν διακονηθῆναι ἀλλὰ διακονῆσαι *came not to be served, but to serve* **Mt 20:28; Mk 10:45** (i.e. the Human One [Son of Man] came to carry out an assignment not to benefit himself but others [by giving his life in ransom]; cp. **Mt 4:11;** par. **Mk 1:13** [service rendered by divine messengers]). Of Jesus carrying out his mission [ἀ]νῆλθε[ν δια]κονῶν AcPl BMM verso 13f.—**Phlm 13** suggests that Onesimus can be used by Paul on assignment in behalf of the gospel. πορεύομαι … διακονῶν τοῖς ἁγίοις *on an errand to God's people* (REB) **Ro 15:25** (s. 3).—Of delivery of an object: χάρις διακονουμένη ὑφ' ἡμῶν *gift that we are transmitting* (a ref. to the collection for whose delivery they have accepted responsibility) **2 Cor 8:19;** cp. vs. **20.** In imagery, ἐπιστολὴ Χριστοῦ διακονηθεῖσα ὑφ' ἡμῶν *a letter of Christ, delivered by us* **2 Cor 3:3** (WBaird, Letters of Recommendation: JBL 80, '61, 190).

❷ **to perform obligations,** without focus on intermediary function—ⓐ of unspecified services ***perform duties, render assistance, serve*** τινί *someone* (Demosth. 9, 43; UPZ 18, 23 [163 BC]; δαίμοσι δ. Orig., C. Cels. 2, 51, 38) **Mt 8:15; Mk 1:31; Lk 4:39;** GJs 6:3; διακονοῦσαι αὐτῷ *being at his service* **Mt 27:55;** cp. **Mk 15:41.** διακόνει μοι *serve me* Hs 8, 4, 1, cp. 2; **J 12:26; Ac 19:22.** Also εἰς ἑαυτοὺς αὐτὸ δ. *serve one another w. it* **1 Pt 4:10.** W. acc. of thing ὅσα διηκόνησεν *what services he rendered* **2 Ti 1:18;** cp. Hs 2:10. Abs. (POxy 275, 10 [I AD]) **1 Pt 4:11.** Pass. (Jos., Ant. 10, 242); ἁπλῶς δ. *complete a service in simplicity of heart* Hm 2:6.

ⓑ of attention at meals ***wait on someone*** (τινί) ***at table*** (Menand., fgm. 272; Pyrgion [Hellenistic times]: 467 fgm. 1 Jac. [a communal meal in Crete]; Diod. S. 4, 36, 2; 5, 28, 4; Philo, Vi. Cont. 70; TestJob 12:1 al.; Jos., Ant. 11, 163; 166) **Lk 12:37; 17:8.** Abs. **10:40; J 12:2;** GJs 6:3. In imagery ὡς ὁ διακονῶν *waiter* **Lk 22:26f.**

❸ **to meet an immediate need,** ***help*** w. dat. (Iren. 1, pr. 3 [Harv. I 7, 1]) πότε οὐ διηκονήσαμέν σοι; *when did we not help you?* **Mt 25:44** (but s. 4, Collins). ἐκ τῶν ὑπαρχόντων *helped to support them w. their means* **Lk 8:3** (KTorjesen, When Women Were Priests '93, 53ff); the saints **Ro 15:25** (JO'Rourke, CBQ 29, '67, 116–18; but s. 1); **Hb 6:10.**

❹ **to carry out official duties,** ***minister,*** in cultic context (of holy service at the altar Jos., Ant. 3, 155; cp. PGM 36, 304 and 335 παρὰ θεοῖς δ.) of διάκονοι **1 Ti 3:10;** καλῶς δ. vs. **13.** ἁγνῶς καὶ σεμνῶς Hv 3, 5, 1. Opp. κακῶς s 9, 26, 2. Collins

(s. below) p. 65 argues for placement of **Mt 25:44** in this classification: those consigned to perdition plead their total dedication to the Lord's interests.

❺ **Ac 6:2** poses a special problem: ***care for, take care of*** w. dat. of thing τραπέζαις *look after tables* can be understood of serving food at tables (cp. βούλομαι … διακονῆσαι τοῖς πτωχοῖς σήμερον ἐν τῇ σῇ τραπέζῃ TestJob 12:1), but it is improbable that some widows would be deprived of food at a communal meal. The term διακονία vs. 1 more probably refers to administrative responsibility (s. διακονία 5), one of whose aspects is concern for widows without specifying the kind of assistance that is allotted. Vs. **2** may contain wordplay involving the phrase τὸν λόγον τοῦ θεοῦ, w. λόγος designating a ledger entry, in which case τράπεζα, which is also a banker's term (s. L-S-J-M s.v. II), may here denote *accounts* (s. τράπεζα 1c).—WBrandt, Dienst u. Dienen im NT '31; ESchweizer, D. Leben des Herrn in d. Gemeinde u. ihren Diensten '46; PBoulton, Διακονέω and Its Cognates in the 4 Gospels: TU 73, '59, 415–22. JCollins, Diakonia '90.—DELG s.v. διάκονος. M-M. TW.

διακονία, ας, ἡ (s. διακονέω, διάκονος; Thu. et al.; IG XII/5, 600, 14 [III BC]; PFouad 25 verso I, 1 [II AD]; 1 Macc 11:58; Esth 6:3, 5 [both v.l.]; TestJob 11:1ff, 15:1; Joseph.)

❶ **service rendered in an intermediary capacity, *mediation, assignment,*** δ. τῆς λειτουργίας *mediation of this public obligation* **2 Cor 9:12;** cp. **13.** ἡ δ. ἡ εἰς Ἰερουσαλήμ *my embassy in behalf of J.* (=my role as delivery agent [for the gift] for J. The v.l. δωροφορία indicates that δ. denotes intermediary function; the context informs the reader that the mission involves the bringing of a gift) **Ro 15:31;** cp. **2 Cor 8:4; 9:1.**—On the 'collection': ELombard, RTP 35, 1902, 113–39; 262–81; MGoguel, RHPR 4, 1925, 301–18; KNickle, The Collection '66.—πνεύματα εἰς δ. ἀποστελλόμενα *spirits sent out on assignment* **Hb 1:14.**

❷ **performance of a service**—ⓐ gener. ***service*** πρὸς τὸν καταρτισμὸν τ. ἁγίων εἰς ἔργον διακονίας *to prepare God's people for productive service* **Eph 4:12** (the rendering [as later edd. of RSV, also NRSV, REB] assumes that no comma, as in KJV, RV, RSV[1], JB et al., is to be placed before εἰς [difft. 3 below]); δ. τοῦ λόγου **Ac 6:4;** ἡ ὑμῶν δ. service *to you* **2 Cor 11:8.**—**1 Cor 16:15; 2 Ti 4:11; Rv 2:19.**

ⓑ specif. ***engagement in preparations for a social event,*** such as a meal (s. Plut., Philopoem. 357 [2, 3]: a Megarian hostess mistakes the statesman P. for one of his aides and sets him to chop wood as part of the διάκονια or preparations for a meal; Jos., Ant. 2, 65; 11, 163 διακονεῖν τινι τὴν ἐπὶ τοῦ πότου διακονίαν) περιεσπᾶτο περὶ πολλὴν δ. *(Martha) was distracted w. many preparations* **Lk 10:40.**

❸ **functioning in the interest of a larger public, *service, office*** of the prophets and apostles **1 Ti 1:12;** κλῆρος τῆς δ. **Ac 1:17;** τόπος τῆς δ. vs. **25.** Of the service of the Levites 1 Cl 40:5; the *office* of an ecclesiastical overseer IPhld 1:1; 10:2; ISm 12:1; Hs 9, 27, 2; δ. λαμβάνειν *receive a ministry* **Ac 20:24.** διαιρέσεις διακονιῶν **1 Cor 12:5;** δ. τοῦ θανάτου *ministry of death:* of the OT law **2 Cor 3:7.** Also δ. τῆς κατακρίσεως *min. of condemnation* vs. **9.** Opp. δ. τῆς δικαιοσύνης *min. of righteousness* ibid.; δ. τοῦ πνεύματος *min. of the Spirit* vs. **8** of service in behalf of the Gospel; cp. **Ac 21:19; Ro 11:13; 2 Cor 4:1; 6:3; Col 4:17; 2 Ti 4:5;** δ. τῆς καταλλαγῆς *ministry of reconciliation* **2 Cor 5:18;** τὴν δ. τελέσαι *carry out this assignment* Hm 2:6; concerning obedience and exhortation 12, 3, 3; s 1:9; 2:7. τελειῶσαι … τὴν δ' *discharge … my responsibility* **Ac 20:34.**—**Eph 4:12** belongs here if, with KJV, RV, RSV[1] et al. and contrary to N. and other edd., a comma is placed before εἰς (s. Collins [at 5, end, below] 233f).

❹ **rendering of specific assistance, *aid, support*** (Arrian, Peripl. 3, 1 εἰς διακονίαν=for support), esp. of alms and charitable giving (AcThom 59 [Aa II/2, 176, 2] χρήματα πολλὰ εἰς διακονίαν τῶν χηρῶν=much money to take care of the widows) **Ac 6:1.** εἰς δ. πέμψαι τί τινι *send someone someth. for support* **11:29;** cp. **12:25.**

❺ **an administrative function, *service*** as attendant, aide, or assistant (Eng. loanw. 'deacon'; Hippol., Ref. 7, 36, 3) **Ro 12:7** (Ltzm., ZWT 55, 1913, 110); IMg 6:1; IPhld 10:2; Hs 9, 26, 2.—PAbbing, Diakonia, diss. Utrecht '50; BReicke, Diakonie, Festfreude u. Zelos usw. '51, 19–164; RAC III 909–17; WBrandt, Dienst u. Duienen im NT '31 (diss. Münster: Diakonie u. das NT, 1923); JCollins, Diakonia '90.—DELG s.v. διάκονος. M-M. TW. Sv.

διάκονος, ου, ὁ, ἡ (s. διακονέω, διακονία; trag., Hdt. et al.; ins, pap, LXX; TestSol 6:10 L, for δράκοντας; TestJud 14:2; Philo, Joseph., Just., Tat., Iren., Hippol.) gener. one who is busy with someth. in a manner that is of assistance to someone

❶ **one who serves as an intermediary in a transaction, *agent, intermediary, courier*** (cp. Jos., Ant. 1, 298 of Rachel who brought Jacob to Laban; s. also Ant. 7, 201; 224 al.; Jos., Ant. 8, 354 Elisha is Ἠλίου καὶ μαθητὴς καὶ δ.; Epigonos is δ. καὶ μαθητής of Noetus in Hippol., Ref. 9, 7, 1). Of a deity's intermediaries: gener. θεοῦ δ. (Epict. 3, 24, 65 Diogenes as τοῦ Διὸς διάκονος; Achilles Tat. 3, 18, 5 δ. θεῶν; cp. Philo, De Jos. 241; Jos., Bell. 3, 354) **2 Cor 6:4; 1 Th 3:2** (cp. **1 Cor 3:5**) s. below; **Tit 1:9b v.l.;** Hs 9, 15, 4; δ. Χριστοῦ **2 Cor 11:23; Col 1:7; 1 Ti 4:6** (cp. Tat. 13, 3 δ. τοῦ πεπονθότος θεοῦ); of officials understood collectively as a political system *agent* ἡ ἐξουσία *the* (governmental) *authorities* as θεοῦ δ. **Ro 13:4,** here understood as a fem. noun (Heraclit. Sto. 28 p. 43, 15; of abstractions Epict. 2, 23, 8; 3, 7, 28). W. specific ref. to an aspect of the divine message: of apostles and other prominent Christians charged with its transmission (δ. τῆς διδασκαλίας Orig., C. Cels. 1, 62, 30) **Col 1:23; Eph 3:7;** δ. καινῆς διαθήκης **2 Cor 3:6;** δ. δικαιοσύνης (opp. δ. τοῦ σατανᾶ) **2 Cor 11:15.** δ. τοῦ θεοῦ ἐν τ. εὐαγγελίῳ *God's agent in the interest of the gospel* **1 Th 3:2 v.l.** (for συνεργός); cp. δ. χριστοῦ Ἰησοῦ (if Timothy provides proper instruction he will be considered an admirable transmitter of the gospel tradition) **1 Ti 4:6;** δ. ἐν κυρίῳ **Eph 6:21; Col 1:25** indirectly as δ. ἐκκλησίας; of Christ as God's agent δ. περιτομῆς *for the circumcision*=for descendants of Abraham, **Ro 15:8.** Cp. Phoebe **Ro 16:1** and **subscr. v.l.;** of Tychicus as faithful *courier* **Col 4:7** (Pla., Rep. 370e 'intermediary, courier'; of Hermes, s. G Elderkin, Two Curse Inscriptions: Hesperia 6, '37. 389, table 3, ln. 8; Jos., Ant. 7, 201; 224 al.).

❷ **one who gets someth. done, at the behest of a superior, *assistant*** to someone (the context determines whether the term, with or without the article ὁ, οἱ is used inclusively of women or exclusively) **Mt 20:26; 23:11; Mk 10:43;** of all **9:35;** Pol 5:2. Of table attendants (X., Mem. 1, 5, 2; Polyb. 31, 4, 5; Lucian, Merc. Cond. 26; Athen. 7, 291a; 10, 420e; Jos., Ant. 6, 52) **J 2:5, 9.** Of a king's retinue **Mt 22:13.**—Of Jesus' adherents gener.: those in the service of Jesus **J 12:26.** Satirically, ἁμαρτίας δ. *agent for sin* **Gal 2:17** (cp. the genitival constructions in 1 above; cp. Tat. 19, 2 of divination as instrument or medium for immoderate cravings πλεονεξιῶν … δ.). One who serves as assistant in a cultic context (Hdt. 4, 71, 4 'aide, retainer'; Pausanias 9, 82, 2 'attendants') *attendant, assistant, aide* (the Eng. derivatives 'deacon' and 'deaconess' are technical terms, whose mng. varies in ecclesiastical history and are therefore inadequate for rendering NT usage of δ.) as one identified for special ministerial service in a Christian community (s. Just., A I, 65, 5; 67, 5; Iren. 1, 13, 5 [Harv. I 121, 6]; Hippol., Ref. 9, 12, 22) esp. of males (the δ. as holder of a religious office outside Christianity: IMagnMai 109 [c. 100 BC]; IG IV, 474, 12; 824, 6; IX, 486, 18; CIG II, 1800, 1; 3037, 4; II addenda 1793b, 18 p. 982; Thieme 17f; MAI 27, 1902, p. 333f no. 8, 22) **Phil 1:1** (EBest, Bishops and Deacons, TU 102, '68, 371–76); **1 Ti 3:8, 12; 4:6; Tit 1:9a v.l.; Phlm subscr. v.l.;** 1 Cl 42:4f (Is 60:17); Hv 3, 5, 1; s 9, 26, 2; IEph 2:1; IMg 2; 6:1; 13:1; ITr 2:3; 3:1; 7:2; IPhld: ins; 4; 7:1; 10:1f; 11:1; ISm 8:1; 10:1; 12:2; IPol 6:1; Pol 5:3; D 15:1.—Harnack, D. Lehre d. Zwölf Apostel: TU II 1; 2, 1884, 140ff, Entstehung u. Entwicklung d. Kirchenverfassung 1910, 40ff; FHort, The Christian Ecclesia 1898, 202–8; Ltzm., ZWT 55, 1913, 106–13=Kleine Schriften I, '58, 148–53; HLauerer, D. 'Diakonie' im NT: NKZ 42, '31, 315–26; WBrandt, Dienst u. Duienen im NT '31 (diss. Münster: Diakonie u. das NT, 1923); RAC III, 888–99; JCollins, Diakonia '90 (p. 254: 'Care, concern, and love—those elements of meaning introduced into the interpretation of this word and its cognates by Wilhelm Brandt—are just not part of their field of meaning'.) Further lit. s.v. ἐπίσκοπος and πρεσβύτερος.—Since the responsibilities of Phoebe as διάκονος **Ro 16:1** and **subscr. v.l.** seem to go beyond those of cultic attendants, male or female (for females in cultic settings: ministra, s. Pliny, Ep. 10, 96, 8; cp. CIG II 3037 διάκονος Τύχη; ἡ δ. Marcus Diaconus, Vi. Porphyr. p. 81, 6; MAI [s. above] 14, 1889, p. 210; Pel.-Leg. 11, 18; many documentary reff. in New Docs 4, 239f), the reff. in Ro are better classified 1, above (but s. DArchea, Bible Translator 39, '88, 401–9). For the idea of woman's service cp. Hv 2, 4, 3; hence Hs 9, 26, 2 may include women. Further lit. s.v. χήρα b.—Thieme 17f. B. 1334. DELG. M-M. TW. Sv.

διακόσιοι, αι, α (Hom.+; pap, LXX; TestSol, Test12Patr; Jos., Vi. 90; 115; Tat. 31, 3) ***two hundred*** **Mk 6:37; J 6:7; 21:8; Ac 23:23; 27:37** (on the number of pers. s. Hemer, Acts 149; cp. a related experience involving c. 600 Jos., Vi. 15); **Rv 11:3; 12:6.**—Mussies 220f. DELG.

διακοσμέω aor. pass. διεκοσμήθην LXX; pf. pass. 3 sg. διακεκόσμηται (Ath. 10:1); ptc. διακεκοσμημένος 2 Macc 3:25 (s. διακόσμησις, κοσμέω; Hom. et al.) to make an orderly arrangement ***set in order, regulate*** τί (Jos., Ant. 6, 31) the heavens (Philo, Op. M. 53) 1 Cl 33:3 (as a cosmolog. expr. as early as the Ionic nature philosophers, later esp. in Stoic wr.; s. Knopf, Hdb. ad loc.).—DELG s.v. κόσμος.

διακόσμησις, εως, ἡ (s. διακοσμέω, Pla.+; Stoic term; Sb 8858, 46 [III BC]; 2 Macc. 2:29; Ps 32:6 Sym.; SSol 7:5 Sym.; Philo; Jos. Ant. 1, 69; Ar. 1:1; Tat.) ***regulation, orderly arrangement*** Papias (4).—DELG s.v. κόσμος.

διακούω (X. et al.) fut. διακούσομαι as legal t.t. **give someone an opportunity to be heard in court,** ***give someone*** (τινός) ***a hearing*** **Ac 23:35** (so Polyb., Plut.; Cass. Dio 36, 53 [36]; IMagnMai 93a, 10; 105, 1 et al. in ins; BGU 168, 28; PFay 119, 12 et al. in pap; Dt 1:16; Job 9:33; Jos., Bell. 2, 242).—M-M.

διακρίνω fut. διακρινῶ; 1 aor. διέκρινα LXX; impf. mid. διεκρινόμην. Pass.: fut. διακριθήσομαι LXX; 1 aor. διεκρίθην (s. κρίνω, διάκρισις; Hom.+).

❶ **to differentiate by separating,** ***separate, arrange*** (Jos., Ant. 11, 56; Ath. 13, 2; 22, 1; Mel. P. 82, 611) of created things πάντα κατὰ τάξιν δ. *effect an orderly arrangement for everything* Dg 8:7. ἑαυτὸν δ. *separate oneself* IEph 5:3 (but the ominous tone of the context favors 3b below).

❷ **to conclude that there is a difference,** ***make a distinction, differentiate*** (PGM 5, 103f σὺ διέκρινας τὸ δίκαιον καὶ τὸ ἄδικον; 4 Macc 1:14; Jos., Bell. 1, 27; Just., D. 20, 3; Ath. 15, 1) μεταξὺ ἡμῶν τε καὶ αὐτῶν *betw. us and them* **Ac 15:9.** τίς σε διακρίνει; *who concedes you any superiority?* **1 Cor 4:7** (Appian, Bell. Civ. 5, 54 §228 δ. τινά=concede superiority to someone, beside ἐπιλέγεσθαί τινα=select someone; cp. Philo, Op. M. 137 διακρίνας ἐξ ἁπάσης τὸ βέλτιστον). μηθὲν διακρίνων τίνι δῷ *without distinguishing to whom he should give* Hm 2:6; cp. **Ac 11:12.**—Pass. διακρίνεσθαί τινος *be differentiated fr. someone* Dg 5:1.

❸ **to evaluate by paying careful attention to,** ***evaluate, judge***—ⓐ *judge correctly* (Job 12:11; 23:10) the appearance of the sky **Mt 16:3;** *evaluate* oneself **1 Cor 11:31;** *recognize* τὸ σῶμα vs. **29.**

ⓑ *pass judgment on* w. acc. ἑαυτόν *on oneself* IEph 5:3 (mng. 1 is also prob.); προφήτην D 11:7; abs. **1 Cor 14:29.**

❹ **to render a legal decision,** ***judge, decide,*** legal t.t. (X., Hell. 5, 2, 10; Appian, Bell. Civ. 5, 76 §324 δίκαι διεκρίνοντο; SIG 545, 18; OGI 43, 4 and11; pap; EpArist 110; Just. A II, 7, 2) ἀνὰ μέσον τινός *decide* betw. pers. (as Ezk 34:17, 20) **1 Cor 6:5;** s. EvDobschütz, StKr 91, 1918, 410–21 and ἀνά 1b, μέσος 1b.

❺ **to be at variance w. someone,** mid., w. pass. aor. (B-D-F. §78)—ⓐ because of differing judgments ***dispute*** τινί *w. someone* (Polyb. 2, 22, 11) **Jd 9.**

ⓑ by maintaining a firm opposing position or adverse judgment ***take issue*** πρός τινα *w. someone* (Hdt. 9, 58, 2; Ezk 20:35f; Jo 4:2) **Ac 11:2** (=*criticize*).

❻ **to be uncertain,** ***be at odds w. oneself, doubt, waver*** (this mng. appears first in NT; with no dependence on the NT, e.g., Cyril of Scyth. p. 52, 17; 80, 10; 174, 7) **Mt 21:21; Mk 11:23; Ro 14:23; Jd 22.** ἐν ἑαυτῷ *in one's own mind* **Lk 11:38** D; **Js 2:4;** GJs 11:2. W. εἰς **Ro 4:20** μηδὲν διακρινόμενος *without any doubting* **Js 1:6;** *hesitate* **Ac 10:20.**—DELG s.v. κρίνω. M-M. TW.

διάκρισις, εως, ἡ (s. διακρίνω; Pre-Socr., X. et al.; pap; LXX only Job 37:16; TestNapht 2:8; EpArist; Philo; Tat. 12, 1; Ath. 15, 2 'separation' [of the elements]).

❶ **the ability to distinguish and evaluate,** ***distinguishing, differentiation*** of good and evil **Hb 5:14** (Sext. Emp., Hyp. Pyrrh. 3, 168 διάκρισις τῶν τε καλῶν καὶ κακῶν; Ath., R. 66, 21 πρὸς δ. νοητῶν). πνευμάτων *ability to distinguish betw. spirits* **1 Cor 12:10** (cp. Pla., Leg. 11, 937b ψευδομαρτυριῶν; Diod. S. 17, 10, 5 ἡ τῶν σημείων διάκρισις=critical examination of miraculous signs. ELerle, Diakrisis Pneumaton, diss. Hdlbg. '46). σοφὸς ἐν διακρίσει λόγων *skillful in the interpretation of discourse* 1 Cl 48:5.

❷ **engagement in verbal conflict because of differing viewpoints,** ***quarrel*** (Polyb. 18, 28, 3; Dio Chrys. 21 [38], 21) **Ac 4:32** D. προσλαμβάνεσθαι μὴ εἰς δ. διαλογισμῶν *welcome, but not for the purpose of getting into quarrels about opinions* **Ro 14:1.**—M-M. TW. Sv.

διακυβερνάω (κυβερνάω 'to pilot a vessel'; Pla. et al.; UPZ 59, 15 [168 BC]; LXX) ***direct, govern*** of Michael, the guardian angel of Christians Hs 8, 3, 3.—DELG s.v. κυβερνάω.

διακωλύω impf. διεκώλυον; 1 aor. inf. διακωλῦσαι (s. κωλύω; Soph., Hdt.+; SIG 685, 81; PTebt 72, 363; BGU 1187,

11; 1844, 10 and 14; pap, e.g. PRyl 579, 16; JosAs 25:1; Jos., Bell. 2, 287, Ant. 11, 29) **to keep someth. from happening,** ***prevent*** διεκώλυεν αὐτόν *he tried to prevent him* (cp. Jdth 12:7; the impf. tense with conative force as Hierocles 11 p. 442 τῷ κωλύοντι τὴν πονηρίαν θεῷ=to the god who is endeavoring to prevent the injustice [the present participle takes over the function of the imperfect]) **Mt 3:14.**—M-M.

διαλαλέω (s. λαλέω; Eur. et al.; POxy 1417, 24; Sym. Ps 50:16 al.; Just., D. 9:3) ***discuss*** (Appian, Bell. Civ. 2, 20 §72; Jos., Bell. 4, 601) to exchange opinions or viewpoints διελάλουν πρὸς ἀλλήλους (πρός as Polyb. 22, 9, 6; Diod. S. 36, 3, 3) *they discussed w. each other* **Lk 6:11.** Pass. διελαλεῖτο πάντα τὰ ῥήματα ταῦτα *all these things were talked about* **1:65** (cp. Polyb. 1, 85, 2; Sb 7033, 18 [V AD]=TAPA 53, 1922, p. 116 'he talked of arresting Cyrus' [a bishop]).—M-M.

διαλέγομαι impf. διελεγόμην **Ac 18:19 v.l.;** 1 aor. διελεξάμην (s. λέγω; Hom.; Polyaenus 3, 9, 40; 7, 27, 2) **Ac 17:2; 18:19;** pf. 3 sg. διείλεκται (Tat. 21, 3). Pass.: fut. 3 sg. διαλεχθήσεται (Sir 14:20); aor. διελέχθην ([Att.] LXX; Just., D. 2, 4) **Mk 9:34; Ac 18:19 v.l.** (Hom.+).

❶ **to engage in speech interchange,** ***converse, discuss, argue*** (freq. in Attic wr., also PPetr III, 43 [3], 15 [240 BC]; BGU 1080, 11; Epict. 1, 17, 4; 2, 8, 12; TestAbr A 5 p. 82, 3 [Stone p. 12] τὰ διαλεγόμενα ὑμῶν; Tat. 21, 3), esp. of instructional discourse that frequently includes exchange of opinions **Ac 18:4; 19:8f; 20:9.** περί τινος (Ps.-Callisth. 3, 32, 2; Just., D. 100, 3; Ath. 9:1) **24:25.** πρός τινα (X., Mem. 1, 6, 1; 2, 10, 1; Ex 6:27; Ps.-Callisth., loc. cit.; Jos., Ant. 7, 278; AssMos fgm. a Denis p. 63=Tromp p. 272) **Ac 24:12.** τινί *w. someone* (for the syntax, s. 1 Esdr 8:45 'inform, tell'; 2 Macc 11:20; EpArist 40; Just., D. 2, 4: the three last 'discuss, confer') **17:2, 17; 18:19; 20:7;** sim. *converse* MPol 7:2.—Of controversies πρός τινα *with someone* (Judg 8:1 B) **Mk 9:34.** περί τινος *about someth.* (cp. Pla., Ap., 19d; Plut., Pomp. 620 [4, 4]; PSI 330, 8 [258 BC] περὶ διαφόρου οὐ διαλ.; PFlor 132, 3; Just., A II, 3, 3) **Jd 9.**

❷ **to instruct about someth.,** ***inform, instruct*** (Isocr. 5 [Phil.] 109; Epict.; PSI 401, 4 [III BC]; 1 Esdr 8:45; Philo; Joseph.; EHicks, ClR 1, 1887, 45) δ. may have this mng. in many of the above pass. (e.g. **Ac 18:4**), clearly so **Hb 12:5** (δ. of a Scripture pass. also Philo, Leg. All. 3, 118).—GKilpatrick, JTS 11, '60, 338–40.—Frisk s.v. λέγω. M-M. TW. Sv.

διαλείπω fut. διαλείψω LXX; 2 aor. διέλιπον (s. λείπω; Hom. et al.) **to desist from an action or activity,** ***stop, cease*** w. neg. and w. ptc. foll. οὐ διέλιπεν (v.l. διέλειπεν) καταφιλοῦσα *she has not stopped kissing* (X., Apol. 16 οὐ πώποτε διέλειπον ζητῶν, sim. Isocr. et al.; UPZ 47, 22 [II BC]; POxy 281, 16; BGU 747 I, 7 οὐ διέλιπον παραινῶν; PGiss 14, 4f al.; Jer 17:8; EpArist 274; Jos., Ant. 8, 302; 11, 119) **Lk 7:45.** Also *constantly:* μὴ διαλίπῃς νουθετῶν *admonish constantly* Hv 1, 3, 2. μὴ διαλίπῃς λαλῶν (cp. Περὶ ὕψους 38, 5 οὐ διαλ. λέγων) 4, 3, 6. μὴ δ. αἰτούμενος m 9:8.—B. 981. M-M.

διάλεκτος, ου, ἡ (s. διαλέγομαι; Aristoph., Hippocr. et al.; LXX, TestJob 48ff; Just., A I, 33, 7; Tat.) ***language*** of a nation or a region (so Aristot., Probl. 10, 38 p. 895a, 6 τοῦ ἀνθρώπου μία φωνή, ἀλλὰ διάλεκτοι πολλαί; Polyb. 1, 80, 6; 3, 22, 3; 39, 1, 3; Diod. S. 1, 37, 9; Plut., Mor. [Apophth.] 185f Περσικὴ δ.; SIG 1267, 30; IAndrosIsis, Kyme 31 pl.; IMaronIsis 27 sg.; PGM 13, 139; 444; 699; Esth 9:26; Da 1:4; Philo, Mos. 2, 38, Jos., C. Ap. 1, 180 al.—AThumb, Hdb. d. griech. Dialekte 1909, 22f; RMunz, Über γλῶττα u. διάλεκτος: Glotta 11, 1921, 85–94) **Ac 1:19; 2:6, 8** (unless in these two last verses a regional variety of a language is meant); **21:40; 22:2; 26:14;** Papias (2:16). δ. τινὶ παρηλλαγμένῳ Dg 5:2.—B. 1261. Frisk, and DELG s.v. λέγω. M-M. TW. Sv.

διαλιμπάνω (διά + λιμπάνω, by-form of λείπω) impf. διελίμπανον (Galen CMG V/10, 1 p. 111, 16 codd. [XVII 1 p. 220 K.]; AcPh 45 [Aa II/2 p. 20, 22]) ***stop, cease*** w. ptc. (Tob 10:7 οὐ διελίμπανεν θρηνοῦσα) ὃς πολλὰ κλαίων οὐ διελίμπανεν *who could not cease shedding many tears* **Ac 8:24** D. cp. **17:13** D.—DELG s.v. λείπω. M-M.

διαλλάσσομαι pass.: 3 sg. fut. διαλλαγήσεται 1 Km 29:4; 2 aor. διηλλάγην, impv. διαλλάγηθι; pf. ptc. διηλλαγμένος LXX **to be restored to normal relations or harmony w. someone,** ***become reconciled*** τινί *to someone* (s. ἀλλάσσω, διαλλαγή, καταλλάσσω, καταλλαγή; Aeschyl.; Pla., Symp. 193c; Thu. 8, 70, 2; Plut., Them. 114 [6, 3]; BGU 846, 10; PGiss 17, 13f; 1 Km 29:4; 1 Esdr 4:31; Jos., Ant. 16, 125; 335) **Mt 5:24** (impv. as Vi. Aesopi W 100 P.). Abs. D 14:2.—Cp. act. 'alter, change' (Just., D. 10, 3; Ath. 24, 5; Wsd 19:18) or 'be different' ἑπτὰ ὄρη τοῦ ἑκατέρου διαλλάσσοντα En 24:2 (cp. Wsd 15:4 χρώμασι διηλλαγμένοις).—DELG s.v. ἄλλος. M-M. TW. Spicq.

διαλογίζομαι mid. dep.; impf. διελογιζόμην; fut. διαλογιοῦμαι LXX; 1 aor. διελογισάμην LXX (s. λογίζομαι; Democr., X., Pla. et al.; ins, pap, LXX; TestSol, TestJob; Just., D. 8, 1).

❶ **to think or reason carefully, esp. about the implications of someth.,** ***consider, ponder, reason*** (EpArist 256) τὶ ἐν ἑαυτῷ *someth. in one's own mind* (TestJob 2:3; Philo, Spec. Leg. 1, 213) Hs 9, 2, 6; GJs 4:1 (cod. D. not Bodm pap). ἐν ἑαυτοῖς **Mt 16:7f; 21:25; Mk 2:8; Lk 12:17.** Also ἐν τῇ καρδίᾳ Hv 1, 1, 2. ἐν ταῖς καρδίαις **Mk 2:6, 8; Lk 5:22;** Hv 3, 4, 3. ἐν τ. καρδίαις περί τινος **Lk 3:15.** παρ' ἑαυτοῖς **Mt 21:25 v.l.** πρὸς ἑαυτούς (Pla., Soph. 231c πρὸς ἡμᾶς αὐτοὺς διαλογισώμεθα; Diod. S. 20, 12, 5 διελογίζετο πρὸς αὑτόν; Just., D. 8:1) **Mk 11:31.** W. indirect quest. foll. Hv 3, 4, 3; **Lk 1:29;** GJs 14:1. Abs. **Lk 5:21;** Hv 3, 1, 9; 4, 1, 4. δ. ταῦτα *harbor these thoughts* m 9:2 (cp. Ps 76:6).

❷ **to discuss a matter in some detail,** ***consider and discuss, argue*** (X., Mem. 3, 5, 1; Ps 139:9) πρός τινα *w. someone* **Mk 8:16;** perh. **11:31** (s. 1); **Lk 20:14.** W. ὅτι foll. **Mk 8:17.** Abs. **9:33.**—DELG s.v. λέγω p. 626. M-M. TW.

διαλογισμός, οῦ, ὁ (s. διαλογίζομαι; since Demosth. 36, 23; Polyb., Epict., Plut., ins, pap [incl. POxy 3313, 7 (II AD)], LXX; TestJob 22:6; TestJud 14:3).

❶ **the process of reasoning,** ***reasoning*** of polytheists ἐματαιώθησαν ἐν τοῖς δ. αὐτῶν **Ro 1:21.**

❷ **content of reasoning or conclusion reached through use of reason,** ***thought, opinion, reasoning, design*** (Ps.-Pla., Axioch. 367a φροντίδες καὶ διαλογισμοί; mostly LXX; EpArist 216; Jos., Bell. 1, 320; TestJud 14:3) **Lk 2:35; 5:22; 6:8; 9:47** (for the nuance in vs. **46** s. 3) **Ro 14:1** (διάκρισις 2). διαλογισμοὺς ποιεῖσθαι *devise plans* (PEdg 60 verso, 2; 7=PCairZen 362 verso, 2; 7 [243/242 BC]) 1 Cl 21:3. The thoughts of the wise of this world are known to God **1 Cor 3:20** (Ps 93:11); *evil machinations* **Mt 15:19; Mk 7:21.** κριταὶ δ. πονηρῶν *judges w. evil thoughts* **Js 2:4** (but here δ. can also be the legal t.t. *decision* [BGU 19 I, 13; 226, 22; PTebt 27:35 (113 BC)]: *judges who give corrupt decisions*).

❸ **verbal exchange that takes place when conflicting ideas are expressed,** ***dispute, argument*** εἰσῆλθεν δ. *an argument* *arose* **Lk 9:46** (cp. the nuance in vs. **47** s. 2); χωρὶς δ. *without dispute* **Phil 2:14; 1 Ti 2:8.**

❹ **reasoning that gives rise to uncertainty,** ***doubt*** δ. ἀναβαίνουσιν *doubts arise* **Lk 24:38**—M-M. TW.

διάλυσις, εως, ἡ (s. διαλύω; Eur., Thu. et al.; POxy 104, 20; 1034; 2 Esdr 11:7; Philo; Jos., C. Ap. 2, 276) ***dissolution, decay*** (cp. Philod., Περὶ θεῶν 3, 6 [ed. HDiels, ABA 1916 and 1917] the antithesis διάλ. and γένεσις; Diod. S. 3, 29, 7 διάλυσις τ. σώματος; Herm. Wr. 8, 1a δ. σώματος; 4; Philo, Aet. M. 28; Ath. 36, 3 δ. τῶν σωμάτων, cp. R. 67, 23) of a seed 1 Cl 24:5.—DELG s.v. λύω. M-M s.v. διαλύω.

διαλύω fut. διαλύσω LXX; 1 aor. διέλυσε 4 Macc 14:10. Mid.: pf. ptc. διαλελυμένος (Ath. 37, 1). Pass.: fut. 3 sg. διαλυθήσεται Sir 22:16; 1 aor. διελύθην; pf. 3 sg. διαλέλυται Job 13:17 (s. διάλυσις; Eur., Hdt. et al.; ins, pap, LXX; PsSol 4:9; TestJos 15:3; JosAs 27:8; Philo, Joseph., Just., Ath.)

❶ **to break up into elements,** ***break up, dissolve,*** pass. with act. force.—ⓐ of a seed *break down, decay* 1 Cl 24:5.—ⓑ of a ship's stern *break up* **Ac 27:41 v.l.**

❷ **to put an end to someth.,** ***destroy*** fig. ext. of 1 (Philo, Aet. M. 36 δεσμόν; Just., A I, 43, 1 [resolve an intellectual problem by offering appropriate explanation]; Ath. 11:2 τὰς ἀμφιβολίας) δ. στραγγαλιάς *loose the entanglements* B 3:3 (Is 58:6; w. λύω); *destroy, put an end to* (UPZ 19, 21 [163 BC] τῷ λιμῷ διαλυθῆναι; 11, 27 [160 BC]; PsSol 4:9; ApcrEzk P 1 recto 7f [Denis p. 125]; Jos., Ant. 14, 284) τὶ *someth.* (SIG 1268 II, 22 [III BC] ἔχθραν) λογισμοὺς ἐθνῶν 1 Cl 59:3.

❸ **to cause a group to be broken up,** ***disperse, scatter,*** fig. ext. of 1, of a crowd (Hdt. 8, 11 al. 'disperse'): pass. in act. sense (Appian, Iber. 42 §172 διελύθησαν [people] *scattered;* BGU 1012, 12 [II BC] διαλυθῆναι αὐτά sc. τὰ πρόβατα; Jos., Ant. 20, 124) **Ac 5:36** (Appian, Mithrid. 19 §75 διελύθησαν of military forces; likewise 90 §412; Ath. R. 59, 14 τῶν διαλυθέντων σωμάτων).—M-M. TW.

διαμαρτάνω (strengthened form of ἁμαρτάνω) 2 aor. διήμαρτον (Thu. et al.; Diod. S. 5, 76, 4 διαμ. τῆς ἀληθείας=transgress against the truth; PSI 383, 11; 441, 5; PCairZen 147, 11; 481, 2 [all III BC]; POxy 473, 6; Num 15:22; Philo; Jos., Bell. 1, 214, Ant. 13, 331 al.) **to be completely unsuccessful or seriously in error,** ***miss the mark badly, be quite wrong,*** in mode of worship Dg 3:2; of failure to meet divine expectations *sin* 1 Cl 40:4; Hm 4, 1, 2; οὐδέν *in no respect* Hs 4:5. οὐδέποτε m 4, 1, 1 (Manetho in Jos., C. Ap. 1, 287 οὐ πολὺ τῆς ἀληθείας διημάρτανεν).

διαμαρτύρομαι fut. διαμαρτυροῦμαι (Just., D. 22, 8 [Ps. 49:7]); 1 aor. διεμαρτυράμην (since X., Pla. et al.; pap, LXX; TestZeb 7:1) gener. to state something in such a way that the auditor is to be impressed with its seriousness.

❶ **to make a solemn declaration about the truth of someth.** ***testify of, bear witness to*** (orig. under oath) (X., Hell. 3, 2, 13) τινί τι (Ezk 16:2 διαμάρτυραι τῇ Ἰερουσαλὴμ τὰς ἀνομίας αὐτῆς.—En 104:11 διαμαρτυρέομαί τινί τι; cp. Jos., Ant. 9, 167) of repentance to Judeans and Hellenes **Ac 20:21.** τὶ *the gospel* vs. **24;** *God's kingdom* **28:23;** *my cause in Jerusalem* **23:11.** Abs. **8:25; 1 Th 4:6.** W. λέγων foll. **Ac 20:23; Hb 2:6.** W. ὅτι foll. (PSI 422, 7 [III BC]) **Ac 10:42.** W. acc. and inf. foll. **Ac 18:5.**

❷ **to exhort with authority in matters of extraordinary importance, freq. w. ref. to higher powers and/or suggestion of peril,** ***solemnly urge, exhort, warn*** (X., Cyr. 7, 1, 17; Polyb. 3, 110, 4; Diod. S. 18, 62, 2; Plut., Cim. 489 [16, 9]; Jos., Ant. 6, 39 al.; Ex 19:10, 21; 1 Km 8:9; 2 Ch 24:19 al.) w. dat. of pers. addressed *warn* δ. αὐτοῖς **Lk 16:28** (w. ἵνα μή foll.). W. ἐνώπιον τ. θεοῦ *charge* **1 Ti 5:21** (ἵνα); **2 Ti 2:14** (μή w. inf. as Polyb. 1, 33, 5; Plut., Crass. 533 [16, 6]). Abs. **Ac 2:40.** W. two constr. mixed: δ. ἐνώπιον θεοῦ καὶ Ἰ. Χ. καὶ τὴν ἐπιφάνειαν αὐτοῦ *I charge you before God and J. Chr., and by his appearing* **2 Ti 4:1.** διαμαρτυρομένου ταῦτα Παύλου *while Paul was earnestly entreating (God) for this* (release from his bonds) AcPl Ha 3, 12 (cp. X., Cyr. 7, 1, 9).—DMacDowell, The Law in Classical Athens, '78, 212–19.—DELG s.v. μάρτυς. M-M. TW.

διαμάχομαι impf. διεμαχόμην; fut. 3 sg. διαμαχήσεται Sir 38:28; pf. 3 sg. διαμεμάχηται Sir 51:19 v.l. (s. μάχομαι; Eur., Hdt., Thu. et al.; Sir; Jos., Bell. 2, 55, Ant. 14, 475; Tat. 25, 2; 27, 1) ***contend sharply*** **Ac 23:9.**—DELG s.v. μάχομαι.

διαμένω impf. διέμενον; fut. 3 sg. διαμενεῖ LXX; 1 aor. διέμεινα; pf. διαμεμένηκα (s. μένω; Pre-Socr., X., Pla. et al.; ins, pap, LXX; En 23:2; TestJud 21:1; JosAs 21:3 cod. A and Pal. 364 [p. 71, 14 Bat.]; EpArist; Philo; Jos., Ant. 14, 266; 20, 225; Just.; Tat. 20, 2; Ath., R. 61, 17 al.) gener. 'remain'.

❶ **to continue in an activity, state, or condition,** ***remain*** πάντα οὕτως δ. *everything remains as it was* **2 Pt 3:4.** μετὰ νηπιότητος δ. ἔν τινι *remain with innocence in someth.* Hs 9, 29, 2. τὸ δένδρον τοῦτο ὑγιὲς διέμεινεν *remained healthy* Hs 8, 1, 4. διαμείνατε τοιοῦτοι *remain as you are* (Epict. 2, 16, 4) Hs 9, 24, 4; cp. 9, 29, 3. διέμενεν κωφός *he remained mute* **Lk 1:22** (cp. SIG 385, 8; EpArist 204 πλούσιος δ.). ἔν τινι (PTebt 27, 40) *remain somewhere permanently* Hs 9, 28, 5; *continue in someth.* (Pla., Prot. 344b; 3 Macc 3:11) ITr 12:2; IPol 8:3; Hs 9, 29, 1; διαμένουσι λαμπροί *they will stay bright* Hs 9, 30, 2. Abs. *remain, continue* (Dio Chrys. 57 [74], 21; LXX; EpArist 226; 258; 259) Pol 1:2.

❷ **continue to exist,** ***live on*** opp. ἀπολέσθαι **Hb 1:11** (Ps 101:27).

❸ **to continue in association with someone,** ***remain continually w. someone*** δ. πρός τινα **Gal 2:5;** cp. **Ac 10:48** D; δ. μετά τινος *stand by someone* (Sir 12:15) **Lk 22:28.**—DELG s.v. μένω. M-M.

διαμερίζω impf. διεμέριζον; fut. διαμεριῶ (LXX, Just.); 1 aor. διεμέρισα. Mid.: 3 pl. διαμερίσονται (TestAbr B 12 p. 116, 26f [Stone p. 80]); 1 aor. διεμερισάμην. Pass.: fut. 3 pl. διαμερισθήσονται Zech 14:1; 1 aor. διεμερίσθην; pf. ptc. διαμεμερισμένος (s. μερίζω, διαμερισμός; Pla. et al.; pap, LXX; TestAbr A 14 p. 94, 18 [Stone p. 36]; B 12 p. 116, 26f [Stone p. 80]; TestJob; EpArist 183; Joseph.; Just., D. 113, 3).

❶ **to divide into separate parts,** ***divide, separate*** (Pla., Leg. 8, 849d; Gen 10:25) the nations 1 Cl 29:2 (Dt 32:8).—Mid. διαμεριζόμεναι γλῶσσαι ὡσεὶ πυρός *divided tongues, just like fire* (cp. NRSV) **Ac 2:3** prob. in imagery of the jagged effect produced by a flame; but s. 2.

❷ **to distribute objects to a series of pers.,** ***distribute*** (Pla., Polit. 289c; LXX) εἴς τινα *share with someone* **Lk 22:17** (Appian, Bell. Civ. 1, 96 §448 ἐς τούσδε διεμέριζεν; PLond III, 982, 4 [IV AD] p. 242 διεμερίσαμεν εἰς ἑαυτούς. Cp. the treatment of a defeated enemy Diod. S. 17, 70, 5). τί τινι (2 Km 6:19; Ezk 47:21) **Ac 2:45** (cp. Just., D. 113, 3 γῆν ἑκάστῳ).—Mid. *divide among themselves* (Jos., Bell. 5, 440) clothes (cp. Artem. 2, 53 γυμνοὶ σταυροῦνται) **Mt 27:35; Mk 15:24; Lk 23:34; J 19:24** (B-D-F §310, 2); GP 4:12 (all after Ps 21:19). Some would interpret **Ac 2:3** in this sense: *like tongues of fire distributed among them* (REB).

❸ **to be divided into opposing units,** ***be divided,*** fig. ext. of 1, and only pass. (Lucian, Gall. 22 πρὸς τοσαύτας φροντίδας διαμεριζόμενος) ἐπί τινα *against someone* **Lk 11:17f; 12:53;** also ἐπί τινι **12:52f.** For this sense s. also διαμερισμός.—DELG s.v. μείρομαι. M-M.

διαμερισμός, οῦ, ὁ (=division Pla. et al.; POxy 12 VI, 17; LXX; Jos., Ant. 10, 274) **division into partisan and contentious units,** ***dissension, disunity*** (like διαμερίζομαι 3; opp. εἰρήνη) **Lk 12:51.**—DELG s.v. μείρομαι p. 679.

διανέμω 1 aor. 3 sg. διένειμεν Dt 29:25; fut. mid. 3 sg. διανεμεῖται TestLevi; aor. mid. 3 pl. διενείμαντο (Tat.); 1 aor. pass. διενεμήθην (s. μένω; Pind. +; ins; Stud. Pal. V, 8 II, 9; TestLevi 8:16; Philo, Aet. M. 147; Joseph.; Just., D. 113, 3; Tat.; Ath. 10, 4) ***distribute*** (so Aristoph., X. et al.; OGI 493, 29; SIG 604, 9; POslo 78, 18; Dt 29:25; Jos., Bell. 1, 308, Ant. 20, 101) εἰς τὸν λαόν *spread* (a report) *among the people* **Ac 4:17.**—DELG s.v. νέμω. M-M.

διανεύω to express an idea through motion of a part of the body, such as head ('nod'), eye, or hand ('gesture'), ***give a sign*** (s. νεύω, ἐννεύω, κατανεύω; Diod. S. 3, 18, 6 'with head'; 17, 37, 5; Lucian, Icar. 15, Ver. Hist. 2, 25 both of flirtatious manner, implying use of eye; Ps 34:19 and Sir 27:22 with eyes) τινὶ *to someone* (Alexis Com. [IV BC] fgm. 261, 12 [II 392 Kock]; Lucian, Ver. Hist. 2, 25) ἦν διανεύων αὐτοῖς *he kept making signs to them* the manner not specified, but prob. hand gestures **Lk 1:22.**—DELG s.v. νεύω.

διανοέομαι (s. νοέω, διανόημα, νόημα; Hdt. et al.; Nicol. Dam.: 90 fgm. 13 p. 339, 24 Jac.; PCairZen 573, 6; Mitt-Wilck. I/2, 1 col. II, 5 [restored]; Herm. Wr. 1, 7; LXX; En 1:2; 2:2; 5:1; Philo; Jos., Vi. 245; Just., D. 72, 1 [in a citation from Esdr., perh. after 2 Esdr 6:21, according to Swete, Introd. 424]) **to have in mind,** ***consider*** GPt 11:44—ὁ Παῦλο[ς τῷ λέοντι καὶ διενοή]θη Παῦλος *Paul (was looking) [at the lion and] Paul [noted] (that this was the lion who had come to him and was baptized)* AcPl Ha 4, 37.—DELG s.v. νόος.

διανόημα, ατος, τό (s. διανοέομαι; X., Pla. et al.; pap [late]; LXX) **product of a thought process,** ***thought*** εἰδὼς τὰ δ. *he knew their thoughts* **Lk 11:17;** cp. ἐπιγνοὺς τὰ δ. **3:16** D.—DELG s.v. νόος. TW.

διάνοια, ας, ἡ (s. διανοέομαι; Aeschyl., Hdt+.; in LXX nearly always for לֵב, לֵבָב).

❶ the faculty of thinking, comprehending, and reasoning, ***understanding, intelligence, mind*** as the organ of νοεῖν (SibOr 3, 421; Iren. 1, 14, 3 [Harv. I 135, 3]. Of God Hippol., Ref. 1, 19, 2) Hm 10, 1, 5. κατὰ διάνοιαν 1 Cl 19:3. Described as the seat of the λογισμοί Dg 2:1; as the organ of ζωή, πίστις, ἐγκράτεια 1 Cl 35:2. Darkened **Eph 4:18;** 1 Cl 36:2; 2 Cl 19:2; hence πηρὸς τῇ δ. *maimed* or *blind in understanding* 2 Cl 1:6 (cp. Ex 36:1 σοφὸς τῇ δ.; Job 9:4). In contrast, fixed on God (cp. Philochorus, cited 2, below) 1 Cl 35:5. *Insight* **1J 5:20** (Just., D. 5, 6 ἐπ᾽ ἄπειρον ἀεὶ τὴν δ. πέμπων). Of moral understanding **Hb 8:10; 10:16** (both Jer 38:33); Hm 5, 2, 7; 11:1. W. heart and soul and *mind* (s. IDefixWünsch 1, 10) **Mt 22:37; Mk 12:30** (ἐξ ὅλης τ. διανοίας Epict. 2, 2, 13); **Lk 10:27** (Dt 6:5 v.l.); cp. 2 Cl 3:4. On τετρωμένοι κατὰ διάνοιαν GPt 7:26 s. τιτρώσκω.

❷ mind as a mode of thinking, ***disposition, thought, mind*** (Jos., Ant. 2, 19; Ath. 32, 3) εἰλικρινὴς δ. **2 Pt 3:1;** καθαρὰ δ. 1 Cl 21:8; ἁπλῆ δ. 23:1; ἄμωμος δ. ITr 1:1; ὑπερήφανος διανοίᾳ καρδίας αὐτοῦ (1 Ch 29:18; Bar 1:22) *proud in the thoughts of his heart* **Lk 1:51;** ἐχθρὸς τῇ δ. *hostile in attitude* **Col 1:21;** ἀπερισπάστῳ δ. *w. undisturbed mind* IEph 20:2. The mind becomes discouraged Hv 3, 11, 3; disturbed 2 Cl 20:1; corrupted away fr. the Lord Hs 4:7 (contrast Philochorus [IV/III BC]: 328 fgm. 188b Jac. in a hymn to a goddess concerning the devotee's 'pure mind'). In imagery *gird up the loins of the mind* **1 Pt 1:13.**

❸ mind focused on objective, ***purpose, plan*** (Jos., Vi. 158) εἰδὼς [τὴν δι]άνοιαν (as restored by edd., but w. proviso PEg[2] p. 22 [s. ἄνοια]) PEg[2] 50f =ASyn. 280, 45. So prob. in 1 Cl 33:4, if κατὰ διάνοιαν (lacking in Lat., Syr., and Coptic transl.) is orig.: *in accordance with plan.*

❹ mind as fantasizing power, ***imagination,*** in an unfavorable sense 1 Cl 39:1.

❺ mind in sensory aspect, ***sense, impulse,*** in a bad sense (Num 15:39) pl. **Eph 2:3.**—B. 1240. EDNT. M-M. TW. Sv.

διανοίγω fut. διανοίξω LXX; 1 aor. διήνοιξα. Pass.: 3 sg. fut. διανοιχθήσεται; aor. διηνοίχθην, 3 pl. also διηνοίγησαν **Mk 7:35 v.l.;** pf. 3 sg. διήνοικται Job 28:19 (s. ἀνοίγω; since Pla., Lys. 210a; LXX; TestSol 1:4 C; TestAbr A 8 p. 85, 18 [Stone p. 18]; Mel., fgm. 8b, 21 p. 230 P. [s. note]).

❶ ***open***—ⓐ a womb πᾶν ἄρσεν διανοῖγον μήτραν *every male that opens the womb=every first-born male* **Lk 2:23** (Ex 13:2 al.); the heavens **Ac 7:56.**

ⓑ fig., ears (Lucian, Charon 21) **Mk 7:34, 35 v.l.** eyes (=make understanding possible, as Gen 3:5, 7; 4 Km 6:17) **Lk 24:31;** heart (=enable someone to perceive, as 2 Macc 1:4; Themist., Orat. 2 De Constantio Imp. p. 29 Harduin διανοίγεταί μου ἡ καρδία κ. διαυγεστέρα γίνεται ἡ ψυχή) **Ac 16:14;** mind **Lk 24:45** (cp. Hos 2:17).

❷ ***explain, interpret*** (Aeneas Gaz. [V/VI AD], Theophr. p. 5b Boiss. δ. τὰ τῶν παλαιῶν ἀπόρρητα) the Scriptures **Lk 24:32; Ac 17:3** (τὰς γραφάς is to be supplied fr. what precedes).—DELG s.v. οἴγνυμι. TW.

διανυκτέρευσις, εως, ἡ (s. διανυκτερεύω; τοῦ πάσχα δ. Eus., HE 6, 9, 2) ***night-watch*** διὰ [τ]ὰς [νησ]τίας κα[ὶ τὰς]| δι[α]νυκτερεύσις τὰς πρὸς τοὺς ἀδελφούς *through fasting and night-watches with his fellow Christians* AcPl Ha 7, 25f.—DELG s.v. νύξ.

διανυκτερεύω (νυκτερεύω 'pass the night'; s. νύξ and prec. entry; Xen., HG 5, 4, 3 et al.; PTebt, Dictys, fgm. 268, 73) ***spend the whole night*** (intr. Diod. S. 13, 62, 1; 13, 84, 5; Plut., Mor. 950b; M. Ant, 7, 66; Herodian 1, 16, 4 al.; Job 2:9c [=TestJob 24:3]; Philo, Aet. M. 4, In Flacc. 36; Jos., Bell. 3, 418, Ant. 6, 311) ἐν τῇ προσευχῇ **Lk 6:12** (Appian, Bell. Civ. 3, 71 §294 διενυκτέρευσεν ἐν τοῖς ὅπλοις). ἐν θελήματι τοῦ θεοῦ AcPl Ha 7, 12.—M-M.

διανύω 1 aor. διήνυσα (ἀνύω 'effect, accomplish'; Hom. et al.)—**❶ to carry out an activity,** ***complete*** w. acc. (Hom. Hymns et al.; Vett. Val. 81, 27; 109, 4; 330, 9; POxy 1469, 4; 2407, 7; Jos., Bell. 5, 51, Ant. 10, 36) τὸν πλοῦν *the voyage* (Achilles Tat. 5, 17, 1) **Ac 21:7;** but *continue* is also probable here (as Xenophon Eph. 3, 2, 12 διενύετο εὐτυχῶς ὁ πλοῦς [Erotici, ed. RHercher, I 361, 29f]; 1, 11, 2 τ. πλοῦν; 5, 1, 1; 5, 10, 3; 5, 11, 1. S. Field, Notes 134f w. emphasis on Xenophon Eph.; Beginn. IV ad loc.; s. also Eur., Or. 1663). Either aspect is poss. for δρόμον δ. 1 Cl 20:2 (cp. Mel., fgm. 8 b, 3 Goodsp. w. cod. Ambr. [διανοίσας cod. Vat.; in Perler's text p. 230 ln. 21 διανοίξας]).

❷ ***arrive (at),*** intr., *travel (to)* (Polyb. 3, 53, 9; Diod. S. 17, 39, 1 εἰς Βαβυλῶνα; 2 Macc 12:17, also w. εἰς) 1 Cl 25:3.—DELG s.v. ἄνυμι. M-M.

διαπαντός s. διά A2a.

διαπαρατριβή, ῆς, ἡ (heightened form of παρατριβή 'irritation, friction' Polyb. 2, 36, 5 et al.; B-D-F §116, 4) **that which is characterized by constant argumentativeness and therefore irritating, *wrangling*** pl. *frictional wranglings* (AMalherbe, Paul and the Popular Philosophers '89, 125, n. 9) **1 Ti 6:5** (v.l. παραδιατριβαί).—DELG s.v. τρίβω.

διαπειράζω (s. πειράζω) (3 Macc 5:40; Jos., Ant. 2, 97; 15, 97) and **διαπειράω** (act. Plut., Pomp. 646 [51, 2]; POxy 1101, 21 [IV AD]; mostly mid. since Hdt.; Antiphon, Or. 5:34) 1 aor. inf. διαπειράσαι (Tdf.) or διαπειρᾶσαι (deStrycker) **to find out by investigation, *determine*** δ. εἰ ἵσταται *whether (the child) could stand up* GJs 6:1.

διαπειράω s. διαπειράζω.

διαπέμπω 1 aor. διεπεμψάμην, pass. inf. διαπεμφθῆναι (2 Macc 3:37) (s. πέμπω; Hdt. et al.; ins, pap; EpArist 6; Philo, De Jos. 14; Joseph.; Just., A I, 31, 2f) ***send on*** τινί τι (Thu. 1, 129 ἐπιστολήν; freq. pap) MPol 20:1.

διαπεράω fut. διαπεράσω; 1 aor. διεπέρασα (περάω 'traverse'; Eur., X.+; PFlor 247, 8; PBrem 18, 9; TestSol 25:7; ParJer 8:3; Joseph.; Ar. [Milne 76, 47] τὸν κόσμον τοῦτον) in our lit. **movement across the area between two sides of a geographical object, *cross (over)*** abs. (Jos., Bell. 1, 613) **Mt 9:1; 14:34.** W. the destination given (Jos., Vi. 153) **Mk 5:21** (cp. Dt 30:13 δ. εἰς τὸ πέραν; PGM 13, 287); **6:53;** εἰς Φοινίκην *to Ph.* **Ac 21:2** (Aristot., fgm. 485 Rose εἰς Ἰταλίαν). W. point of departure and goal ἐκεῖθεν πρὸς ἡμᾶς δ. **Lk 16:26.**—DELG s.v. πέρα. M-M.

διαπλανάω (s. πλανάω; ordinarily in a negative sense: PGissUniv 1, 11f [II BC]; PBrem 12, 13 [II AD]; Arrian; Plut., Mor. 917e; Epict. 1, 20, 10 'mislead'; in pap e.g. Sb 5242, 8 [I AD]; BGU 36, 7; 436, 7; PRyl 125, 20 'prevaricate, deceive') perh. **to cause a diversion** (without neg. sense, as Photius, MPG CIII 536C) ***amuse, entertain*** GJs 6:1 (on the variants s. Tdf., and deStrycker p. 303).

διαπλέω 1 aor. διέπλευσα (s. πλέω; Thu., Aristoph.+; SIG 633, 100; PCairZen 34, 5=PSI 435, 5 [III BC]; Jos., Bell. 2, 103, Ant. 15, 46) **to cross an area by ship, *sail through*** τὸ πέλαγος *the sea* (Plut., Mor. 206cd; Kaibel 642, 13 πέλαγος διέπλευσε) **Ac 27:5.**—DELG s.v. πλέω. M-M.

διαπονέομαι pres. ptc. διαπονούσης (Ath., R. 63, 2); impf. διεπονούμην. Pass.: fut. 3 sg. διαπονηθήσεται Eccl 10:9; 1 aor. ptc. διαπονηθείς (πονέομαι, s. πόνος; Aeschyl. et al.; Sb 5678, 12; Eccl 10:9; Philo; Jos., Ant. 8, 165) **to feel burdened as the result of someone's provocative activity, *be (greatly) disturbed, annoyed*** (POxy 743, 22 [2 BC] ἐγὼ ὅλος διαπονοῦμαι; Aq. Gen 6:6 and 1 Km 20:30) **Mk 14:4** D; **Ac 4:2; 16:18.**—DELG s.v. πένομαι. M-M s.v. διαπονέω.

διαπορεύομαι impf. διεπορευόμην; fut. 3 sg. διαπορεύσεται (En 100:3); aor. ptc. διαπορευθείς Job 2:2 (s. πορεύομαι; Hdt. et al.; pap, LXX; PsSol 13:2; TestZeb 6:3; EpArist 322).

❶ **of movement by way of someth., *go, walk through*** *someth.* διά τινος (En 100:3) a gate Hs 9, 3, 4; field of grain διὰ (τῶν) σπορίμων (prob. via a path running through it) **Mk 2:23 v.l.; Lk 6:1.**

❷ **of movement from one part or locality to another within a geographical area, *pass through*** (w. acc. of place X., An. 2, 5, 18; schol. on Apollon. Rhod. 2, 168a; Job 2:2; Jos., Ant. 5, 67) τὰς πόλεις **Ac 16:4.** κατὰ πόλεις **Lk 13:22.** διαπορευόμενος *on the way, in passing* (X., An. 2, 2, 11) **Ro 15:24;** *go by* **Lk 18:36.**—DELG s.v. πόρος. M-M.

διαπορέω impf. διηπόρουν (s. ἀπορέω; Pla.+; Hellenistic wr., e.g., Alex. Ep. XII, 34f; PEdfou 5, 13; Ps 76:5 and Da 2:1 Sym.; TestSol 4:4 D; JosAs 16:1 cod. A; Demetr.: 722 fgm. 1, 14 Jac.; Philo, Leg. All. 1, 85; Jos., Ant. 1, 18; Ath. 5:1) ***be greatly perplexed, be at a loss*** **Lk 9:7.** θαυμάζοντος καὶ διαποροῦντος AcPl Ha 11, 2f. ἐν ἑαυτῷ *in one's own mind* **Ac 10:17.** περί τινος *about someth.* (Polyb. 4, 20, 2; PCairZen 78, 5 [257 BC]) **5:24** (the constr. δ. περί τινος τί . . . as Jos., Ant. 11, 289). ἐπί τινι (Polyb. 4, 71, 5; ἐπί τινος Ath. 5, 1) *about someth.* Hs 9, 2, 5.—Mid. abs. in the same sense **Lk 24:4 v.l.; Ac 2:12;** Hs 9, 2, 6 v.l.—DELG s.v. πόρος.

διαπραγματεύομαι mid. dep., 1 aor. διεπραγματευσάμην (s. πραγματεύομαι Pla., Phd. 77d; 95e=examine thoroughly) ***gain by trading, earn*** (Dionys. Hal. 3, 72; POxy 1982, 16) τί διεπραγματεύσαντο *what they had gained by trading* **Lk 19:15** (v.l. τίς τί -σατο).—DELG s.v. πράσσω. M-M. TW.

διαπρίω impf. pass. διεπριόμην lit., like πρίω 'saw through, saw asunder' (so Aristoph., Hippocr. et al.; Diod. S. 4, 76, 5; SIG[2] 587, 160; 304; 1 Ch 20:3). Pass., fig. ***be cut to the quick, be infuriated*** **Ac 5:33.** ταῖς καρδίαις inwardly **7:54.**—DELG s.v. πρίω. M-M.

διαρθρόω (ἀρθρόω 'fasten by a joint'; Hippocr. et al.; Ath., R. 69, 7 σπερμάτων . . . διαρθρωθέντων) ***render capable of articulate speech*** (Lucian, Enc. Dem. 14 τ. γλῶτταν; Plut., Demosth. 850 [11:1]) pass. (Alex. Aphr., An. Mant. II/1 p. 153, 2 διηρθρωμένως λέγει) **Lk 1:64 v.l.**—DELG s.v. ἀραρίσκω.

διαρπάζω impf. 3 pl. διηρπάζοσαν PsSol; 1 aor. διήρπασα; fut. mid. 3 pl. διαρπῶνται Zech 2:9. Pass. 2 fut. διαρπαγήσομαι LXX; 1 aor. inf. διαρπασθῆναι 3 Macc. 5:41; 2 aor. διηρπάγην LXX; pf. ptc. διηρπασμένος LXX (s. ἁρπάζω; Hom. et al.; pap, e.g. PLond I, 35, 21 [161 BC] p. 25; LXX; PsSol 8:11; JosAs ch. 13 cod. A [p. 57, 24 Bat.]) ***plunder thoroughly*** τὶ *someth.* (Hdt. 1, 88 πόλιν; Diod. S. 12, 76, 5; Appian, Iber. 52 §220; Gen 34:27; Jos., Ant. 7, 77) a house (Zech 14:2; Da 2:5 Theod.; Jos., Bell. 4, 314) **Mt 12:29 v.l.; Mk 3:27b;** *rob* τὶ *someth.* (Hdt. et al.) **Mk 3:27a** (cp. IGR IV, 1029, 18f, restored thus: διαρπασάν[των]| δὲ καὶ τὰ [σκεύη τῶν σ]ωμάτ[ων]=slaves); *steal* ζωήν τινος *someone's livelihood* Hs 9, 26, 2. Of pers. *snatch away, abduct* or *take captive* τινά someone (Diod. S. 13, 19, 2; 'despoil' Dt. 28:29; Ps 88:42; Mel., HE 4, 26, 5) IRo 7:1.—**Mt 12:30 v.l.**—M-M.

δια(ρ)ρήγνυμι/διαρήσσω (Ion.; B-D-F §101 s.v. ῥήγνυμι; W-S. §15 and Rob. 1219 s.v. ῥήσσω.—Hom. et al.; LXX, TestSol; TestJob 19:2; TestJos 5:2; ParJer) fut. διαρρήξω LXX; 1 aor. διε(ρ)ρηξα; pf. ptc. trans. διερρηχώς LXX, intr. διερρωγώς (s. ParJer 2:1, 10). Pass.: fut. διαρραγήσομαι (s. TestSol 5:5; 15:8); 2 aor. 3 sg. διε(ρ)ράγη GPt 5:20; pf. ptc. διερρηγμένος LXX.

❶ **to cause something to come apart through violent action or pressure.—ⓐ** Of fabric ***tear*** τὶ *someth.*: garments (as a sign of grief Gen 37:29; Jdth 14:19; Esth 4:1 al.; Philippides Com. [IV/III BC] 25, 5, vol. III p. 308 K.; Phlegon of Tralles [Hadr.]: 257 fgm. 36, I, 5, Jac.; PHib 200, 10 [III BC] χιτῶνα λινοῦν διέρρηξεν; PCairIsid 63, 25 τὴν ἐσθῆταν διαρήξαντες; PLips 37, 19 τὴν ἐπικειμένην αὐτοῦ ἐσθῆτα διαρήξαντες; Philo, De Jos. 217; Jos., Bell. 2, 322; TestJos 5:2.—S. ἀλαλάζω 1)

Mt 26:65; Mk 14:63; Ac 14:14.—Pass. intr. *tear, burst* (Hero Alex. I p. 18, 21 διαρραγήσεται τὸ τεῖχος; 264, 20; Aesop, Fab. 135 P.=218 H.; 139 P.=239 H.; Lucian, Hist. Conscrib. 20; PGM 36, 263 πέτραι; Bel 27) of nets **Lk 5:6** (διερρήγνυτο v.l. for -ήσσετο); of the temple curtain GPt 5:20.

ⓑ Of chains and fetters ***break*** τὶ *someth.*(Chariton 4, 3, 3; Ps.-Apollod. 2, 5, 11, 117; PGM 12, 279; 57, 4; Ps 2:3; 106:14; Na 1:13; Jer 5:5; Jos., Ant. 5, 300) **Lk 8:29** (spelled [s. above] διαρήσσων as PGM 4, 1022).

❷ ***shatter, destroy*** τι *someth.*, fig. ext. of 1 ἰσχὺν βασιλέων B 12:11 (Is 45:1).—DELG s.v. ῥήγνυμι. M-M.

διασαφέω fut. 1 pl. διασαφήσομεν (Just.); 1 aor. διεσάφησα; pf. 3 sg. διασεσάφηκε (Aristobul., PE 13, 12, 12 [= Denis p. 225; Holladay p. 184 lines 79f]), pf. pass. 3 sg. διασεσάφηται (Mel., P. 1, 4) gener. to cause someth. to be clear to the understanding.

❶ **to clarify someth. that is obscure, *explain,*** lit. 'make clear' (Eur., Phoen. 398; Pla., Leg. 6, 754a; Polyb. 2, 1, 1; 3, 52, 5; Lucian, M. Peregr. 11; Da 2:6; EpArist 171; Jos., Ant. 2, 12; PYale 41, 9; Just., A I, 33, 3 al.) τινί τι: *a parable to someone* **Mt 13:36** (cp. Jos., Ant. 5, 293).

❷ **to inform by relating someth. in detail, *tell plainly, tell in detail, report*** (Polyb. 1, 46, 4; 2, 27, 3; Vett. Val. index; ins; PEleph 18, 3; UPZ 59, 7; 64, 10 al.; 1 Macc 12:8; 2 Macc 1:18; 2:9; 11:18; TestSol C prol. 2; EpArist 51; 297; Aristobul., PE VIII 10, 5 [Denis p. 218; Holladay p. 136 ln. 34]; Jos., Ant. 18, 199, Vi. 374; Mel., P. 1, 4) what had happened **Mt 18:31.**—W. acc. and inf. **Ac 10:25** D. τινὶ περί τινος GJs 21:2.—On allegorical assoc. s. NWalter, Der Thoraausleger Aristobulos, TU 86, '64, 136.—DELG s.v. σάφα. M-M. Sv.

διασείω 1 aor. διέσεισα, aor. pass. ptc. διασεισθέντες 3 Macc 7:21 (s. σείω; Hdt. et al.; Philo, Leg. All. 2, 99; Jos., Bell. 3, 221 al.) **extort money by force or threat of violence, *extort*** (lit. 'shake violently'; cp. our colloq. 'shake down') legal t.t. (UPZ 162 VIII, 13 [117 BC]; 192, 7; 193, 8; POxy 240, 5 [37 AD] διασεσεισμένῳ ὑπὸ στρατιώτου; 284, 5 [50 AD]; PTebt 43, 26 [118 BC] συκοφαντηθῶμεν διασεσεισμένοι; 3 Macc 7:21) w. acc. (UPZ 161, 37 [119 BC]; PAmh 81, 6) μηδένα *from no one* **Lk 3:14.**—M-M.

διασκορπίζω fut. διασκορπιῶ LXX; 1 aor. διεσκόρπισα. Pass.: 1 fut. διασκορπισθήσομαι; 1 aor. διεσκορπίσθην; pf. ptc. διεσκορπισμένον Zech 11:1 (s. σκορπίζω; Polyb. 1, 47, 4; 27, 2, 10; Aelian, VH 13, 46; BGU 1049, 7; PIand 142 II, 22; oft. LXX; Test12Patr, Joseph. [s. below]; Just., D. 130, 3 prob. OT citation)

❶ ***scatter, disperse*** of a flock **Mt 26:31; Mk 14:27** (both Zech 13:7 v.l.); God's children **J 11:52;** the proud (as Num 10:34; Ps 67:2; 88:11) **Lk 1:51;** on the field of battle (Jos., Ant. 8, 404) **Ac 5:37;** of the components of the bread of the Lord's Supper D 9:4. Of seed *scatter,* unless it could be taken to mean *winnow* (cp. Ezk 5:2 δ. τῷ πνεύματι; s. L-S-J-M) **Mt 25:24, 26.**

❷ ***waste, squander*** a fig. extension of mng. 1: **Lk 15:13; 16:1.**—M-M. TW.

διασπαράσσω 1 aor. διεσπάραξα; pass. ptc. n. διασπαραχθείς (Just.) (s. σπαράσσω; Aeschyl. et al.; Parthenius 10, 3 [of dogs]; TestSol 4:1 D; JosAs 12:10 cod. A; Just., A I, 21, 2 al. Διόνυσον) ***tear in pieces*** of wolves (Aesop, Fab. 165 H.= Syntipas 6, 2f [H-H.]: the wolf tears the sheep) τὰ ἀρνία 2 Cl 5:3.

διασπάω fut. 3 sg. διασπάσει Hos 13:8; 1 aor. διέσπασα LXX. Pass. 1 aor. διεσπάσθην; pf. inf. διεσπάσθαι (s. σπάω; Eur., Hdt.+; SIG 364, 10 [III BC]; pap, e.g. PCairZen 443, 4; LXX; TestJud 2:4; Jos., Ant. 6, 186; Just., A I, 37, 8, D. 15, 4 διάσπα [both Is 58:6 διάλυε]; Tat. 6:2; Ath., R. 64, 20) ***tear apart, tear up*** of a possessed person breaking chains (cp. Jer 2:20) **Mk 5:4;** a document B 3:3 (Is 58:6); of an angry mob μὴ διασπασθῇ ὁ Παῦλος ὑπ' αὐτῶν *that Paul would be torn in pieces by them* **Ac 23:10** (Dio Chrys. 26 [43], 6 ὑπὸ τῶν συγγενῶν διασπασθῆναι; Appian, Bell. Civ. 2, 147 §613; Biogr. p. 444 Ὑπατία διεσπάσθη ὑπὸ τῶν Ἀλεξανδρέων=Hypatia [the philosopher] torn limb from limb by Alexandrian [monks]; cp. Hdt. 3, 13; Lucian, Phal. 1, 4). Fig. (w. διέλκειν) *tear apart* the members of Christ, i.e. the churches 1 Cl 46:7 (cp. Dio Chrys. 28 [45], 8 εἰς μέρη δ. τὴν πόλιν; Ael. Aristid. 24, 39 K.=44 p. 836 D.: τὸ σῶμα τ. πόλεως; Iambl., Vi. Pyth. 33, 240 τὸν ἐν ἑαυτοῖς θεόν).—DELG s.v. σπάω. M-M.

διασπείρω fut. διασπερῶ LXX; 1 aor. διέσπειρα LXX. Pass.: fut. 2 pl. διασπαρήσεσθε Jer 30:21; 2 aor. διεσπάρην; pf. ptc. διεσπαρμένος LXX (s. σπείρω; Soph., Hdt. et al.; PLond II, 259, 73 p. 38; also Test12Patr) ***scatter*** τινά *someone* υἱοὺς Ἀδάμ 1 Cl 29:2 (Dt 32:8). Pass. of scattered communities (cp. Lucian, Tox. 33; Iambl., Vi. Pyth. 35, 253; Jos., Ant. 7, 244; 12, 278) of Christians **Ac 8:1, 4; 11:19.**—DELG s.v. σπείρω. M-M. TW.

διασπορά, ᾶς, ἡ (s. διασπείρω; Philo, Praem. 115; Plut., Mor. 1105a; Just.) LXX of dispersion of Israel among the gentiles (Dt 28:25; 30:4; Jer 41:17; s. also PsSol; TestAsh 7:2).

❶ **state or condition of being scattered, *dispersion*** of those who are dispersed (Is 49:6; Ps 146:2; 2 Macc 1:27; PsSol 8:28) ἡ δ. τῶν Ἑλλήνων *those who are dispersed among the Greeks* **J 7:35.**—Schürer III 1–176; JJuster, Les Juifs dans l'Empire romain 1914; ACausse, Les Dispersés d'Israël 1929; GRosen, Juden u. Phönizier 1929; KKuhn, D. inneren Gründe d. jüd. Ausbreitung: Deutsche Theologie 2, '35, 9–17; HPreisker, Ntl. Zeitgesch. '37, 290–93 (lit.); JRobinson, NTS 6, '60, 117–31 (4th Gosp.).

❷ **the place in which the dispersed are found, *dispersion, diaspora*** (Jdth 5:19; TestAsh 7:2). Fig., of Christians who live in dispersion in the world, far fr. their heavenly home αἱ δώδεκα φυλαὶ αἱ ἐν τῇ δ. **Js 1:1.** παρεπίδημοι διασπορᾶς **1 Pt 1:1.**—Hengel, Judaism II index. DELG s.v. σπείρω. TW.

διάσταλμα, ατος, τό (BGU 913, 9 [III AD]) **state or condition of being distinctive or carefully defined, *distinguishing*** δ. ῥήματος *special point* or *meaning* of the teaching (prob. a ref. to specific allegorical equations) B 10:11.—PHaeuser, D. Barnabasbr. 1912, 64f.

διαστέλλω (s. διαστολή; Hippocr., Pla. et al.; PLond I, 45, 29 [160/159 BC] p. 36; LXX; PsSol 2:34; TestReub 6:8; Philo, Mos. 2, 237; Jos., Bell. 5, 62; Just.; Ath. 23, 6) fut. διαστελῶ LXX; 1 aor. διέστειλα LXX. Mid.: impf. διεστελλόμην; 1 aor. διεστειλάμην. Pass.: 2 fut. διασταλήσομαι LXX; 2 aor. διεστάλην LXX; pf. 3 sg. διέσταλται (Just., D. 10:3), ptc. διεσταλμένος LXX; 'divide, distinguish' (Gen 30:35; Just., D. 20, 2; Ath. 23, 6); in our lit. only mid. **to define or express in no uncertain terms what one must do, *order, give orders*** (cp. our colloq. 'spell something out to someone') (Pla., Rep. 7, 535b; Polyb. 3, 23, 5; Ezk 3:18f; Jdth 11:12 al.; EpArist 131) w. dat. of pers. (UPZ 42, 23 [162 BC]; 110, 211 [164 BC]; Sb 5675, 3; POxy 86, 10) **Mk 7:36b; 8:15; Ac 15:24.** W. dat. of pers. and ἵνα foll. **Mt 16:20; Mk 7:36a; 9:9.** διεστείλατο αὐτοῖς πολλά *he gave them strict orders* **5:43.** Pass. τὸ διαστελλόμενον *the* *command* **Hb 12:20** (cp. 2 Macc 14:28 τὰ διεσταλμένα).—Anz 326f. DELG s.v. στέλλω. M-M. TW.

διάστημα, ατος, τό (Pla. et al.; pap, LXX; GrBar 2:4; EpArist, Philo, Joseph.; Ar. 4:2; Ath., R. 68, 5.—D in **Ac 5:7** spells it διάστεμα [B-D-F §109, 3 app.]) **a space of time between events, *interval*** ἐγένετο ὡς ὡρῶν τριῶν δ. *after an interval of about three hours* **Ac 5:7** (cp. Aristot., Aud. 800b, 5; Polyb. 9, 1, 1 τετραετὲς δ.; Philo; PParis 1, 381; PGiss 40 II, 15 μετὰ τὸ πληρωθῆναι τὸ τοῦ χρόνου διάστημα); δ. ποιεῖν (Gen 32:17) *leave an interval* B 9:8.—DELG s.v. ἵστημι. M-M. Sv.

διαστολή, ῆς, ἡ (s. διαστέλλω; in var. senses since Anaximander 23 [? s. Aetius 3, 3, 1]; Eupolis, fgm. 11, 15 Demiańczuk; ins, pap, LXX; PsSol 4:4; EpArist, Philo; Just., D. 20, 2) ***difference, distinction*** (so Chrysipp.: Stoic. II 158; Philod., De Pietate 123G; Ex 8:19 δώσω δ.; Philo, Mos. 2, 158—New Docs 2, 80 notes lack of evidence for this sense in ins and pap) **Ro 3:22;** δ. Ἰουδαίου τε καὶ Ἕλληνος *distinction betw. a Jew and a Gentile* **10:12.** ἐὰν διαστολὴν τοῖς φθόγγοις μὴ δῷ *if they* (musical instruments) *make no clear distinction in their tones* **1 Cor 14:7** (s. Straub 83f).—DELG s.v. στέλλω. M-M. TW.

διαστρέφω fut. διαστρέψω LXX; 1 aor. διέστρεψα. Pass.: 2 fut. διαστραφήσομαι LXX; 2 aor. διεστράφην; pf. pass. ptc. διεστραμμένος (Aeschyl., Hippocr. et al.; LXX, En; PsSol 10:3; TestSol 18:12 HP; TestAbr A 15 p. 95, 9 [Stone p. 38]; Test12Patr; SibOr 3, 106).

❶ **to cause to be distorted, *deform*** (Philosoph. Max. 489, 37 δ. of objects that turn out as failures in the hands of a clumsy workman, and whose shape is therefore distorted) of a vessel on the potter's wheel: *become misshapen* 2 Cl 8:2 (cp. PGissUniv 26, 12f).

❷ **to cause to depart from an accepted standard of oral or spiritual values, *make crooked, pervert*** (Demosth. 18, 140 τἀληθές; Dio Chrys. 59 [76], 4; En 99:2; τὴν ζωτικὴν δύναμιν τῆς ψυχῆς δ. Did., Gen. 130, 4): τὰς ὁδοὺς τοῦ κυρίου τ. εὐθείας *make crooked the Lord's straight ways* **Ac 13:10** (cp. Pr 10:9; 11:20); μετὰ στρεβλοῦ δ. *w. a perverse pers. you will deal perversely* 1 Cl 46:3 (Ps 17:27). διεστραμμένος *perverted* in the moral sense, *depraved* (Sent. Aesopi 33 p. 255 P. ψυχῆς διεστραμμένης; Did., Gen. 103, 4 δ. συμβιώσεις for the pf. ptc. s. Dio Chrys. 67 [17], 22) γενεά w. ἄπιστος **Mt 17:17; Lk 9:41; Phil 2:15** (Dt 32:5; cp. Pr 6:14; Epict. 3, 6, 8 οἱ μὴ παντάπασιν διεστραμμένοι τῶν ἀνθρώπων; 1, 29, 3). λαλεῖν διεστραμμένα *teach perversions* (of the truth) **Ac 20:30** (cp. Alciphron 4, 17, 2 διεστραμμένοι κανόνες).

❸ **to cause to be uncertain about a belief or to believe something different, *mislead*** τινά *someone* 1 Cl 46:8; 47:5. τὸ ἔθνος **Lk 23:2** (cp. Polyb. 5, 41, 1; 8, 24, 3; 3 Km 18:17f). πολλούς 1 Cl 46:9; *turn away* τινὰ ἀπό τινος (Ex 5:4) **Ac 13:8.**—M-M. TW.

διασῴζω (on the orthography s. B-D-F §26; Mlt-H. 84; W-S. §5:11a; Mayser 134) 1 aor. διέσωσα. Pass. 1 fut. διασωθήσομαι LXX; 1 aor. διεσώθην; pf. διασέσω(σ)μαι 2 Km 1:3 (s. σῴζω; Eur., Hdt.+) **to rescue or deliver from a hazard or danger, *bring safely through,*** also ***save, rescue*** without special feeling for the mng. of διά (X., Mem. 2, 10, 2; PGM 4, 1936; 8, 32; En 100:6; Philo, Aet. M. 35) act. and pass. δι' ὕδατος (s. διά A1b) **1 Pt 3:20;** cp. 1 Cl 9:4 (Jos., C. Ap. 1, 130 περὶ τῆς λάρνακος, ἐν ᾗ Νῶχος διεσώθη, Ant. 1, 78; Did., Gen. 139, 8). **1 Pt 3:20** has a phrase w. εἰς in connection w. δ. (like Lucian, Ver. Hist. 2, 35). ἐκ τῆς θαλάσσης *fr. the shipwreck* **Ac 28:4** (Witkowski 36, 6f=White, LAC 35, 6f=UPZ 60, 6f: διασεσῶισθαι ἐγ μεγάλων κινδύνων; SIG 528, 10; Philo, Vi. 3); cp. vs. **1.** ἐπὶ τὴν γῆν *bring safely to land* **27:44** (δ. ἐπί τι as Polyaenus 7:12; cp. εἰς τὰ ὑψηλὰ ὄρη Did., Gen. 192, 13). ἵνα τὸν Παῦλον διασώσωσι πρὸς Φήλικα *that they might bring Paul safely to Felix* **23:24** (δ. πρός τινα as Jos., Ant. 5, 15); *save* fr. danger (Jon 1:6) **27:43;** 1 Cl 12:5f.—Pass. *escape death* (EpJer 54; Jos., Ant. 9, 141) MPol 8:2. Of sick persons *be cured* **Mt 14:36;** also act. **Lk 7:3.**—M-M. TW.

διαταγή, ῆς, ἡ that which has been ordered or commanded, *ordinance, direction* (s. διατάσσω, τάσσω; Vett. Val. 342, 7; 355, 18; Ps.-Callisthenes 1, 33; ins; pap [s. Nägeli 38; Dssm., LO 70f=LAE 86ff; IGR IV, 661, 17; 734, 12; PFay 133, 4]; 2 Esdr 4:11; Just., D. 67, 7) of God **Ro 13:2;** 1 Cl 20:3. ἐλάβετε τὸν νόμον εἰς διαταγὰς ἀγγέλων *you received the law by* (εἰς 9) *directions of angels* (i.e. by angels under God's direction [to transmit it]) **Ac 7:53** (cp. Gal 3:19; Hb 2:2; LXX Dt 33:2; Philo, Somn. 1, 141ff; Jos., Ant. 15, 136 and s. Ltzm., Hdb. on Gal 3:19).—New Docs 1, 83; DELG s.v. τάσσω. M-M. TW.

διάταγμα, ατος, τό an official ordinance, *edict, command* t.t. (s. διατάσσω; Philod., Rhet. II 289 Sudh.; Diod. S. 18, 64, 5; Plut., Marcell. 312 [24, 13]; Epict. 1, 25, 4; ins, pap, LXX; Philo, Sacr. Abel. 88 al.; Joseph.; loanw. in rabb.; Mel.) of the king (so SEG VIII, 13, 1 [concerning Nazareth I AD=Ehrenberg-Jones no. 322; on this imperial edict s. Boffo, Iscrizione no. 39 (lit.); s. also Benner (below) 63–66 on its authenticity] of Augustus; PGiss 40 II, 8 of Caracalla; 2 Esdr 7:11; Esth 3:13d; Jos., Ant. 11, 215; 19, 292; Preisigke, Fachwörter) **Hb 11:23** (v.l. δόγμα). διατάγματα τ. ἀποστόλων ITr 7:1.—JStroux-LWenger, Die Augustus-Inschrift auf dem Marktplatz von Kyrene: ABayAW 34, 2 (1928) 25. On δ. and related terms and lit. s. MBenner, The Emperor Says (Studia Graeca et Latina Gothoburgensia 33) '75, 25–30.—DELG s.v. τάσσω. M-M.

διάταξις, εως, ἡ (διατάσσω; since Hdt. 9, 26, 1) a formal arrangement of things or matters, then in official parlance ***command*** (Polyb., Plut., ins, pap, LXX; TestAbr A 4 p. 81, 27 [Stone p. 10] al.; Philo; Ath., R. 67, 2; loanw. in rabb.) of God (PParis 69C, 18 αἱ θεῖαι διατάξεις; BGU 473, 15; cp. CPR I, 20, 15; SIG 876, 5; EpArist 192) of sea animals whose existence is arranged by God 1 Cl 33:3.—DELG s.v. τάσσω. TW.

διαταράσσω 1 aor. pass. διεταράχθην (X., Pla. et al.; Polyb. 11, 1, 9; Diod. S. 18, 7, 6 [pass.]; TestSim 4:9; Jos., Ant. 2, 120, Vi. 281 [pass.]; 3 Km 21:43 Sym.) ***confuse, perplex*** (greatly) ἐπὶ τῷ λόγῳ διεταράχθη *she was greatly perplexed at the saying* **Lk 1:29.**

διατάσσω fut. 2 sg. διατάξεις Ezk 21:25; 1 aor. διέταξα. Mid.: fut. διατάξομαι; 1 aor. διεταξάμην. Pass.: 1 fut. inf. διαταχθήσεσθαι; 1 aor. διετάχθην, ptc. διαταχθείς (Just.); 2 aor. διετάγην (Just.), ptc. διαταγείς; pf. 3 sg. διατέτακται (Da 7:2; AcPl Ha 9, 6), ptc. διατεταγμένος; plpf. 3 sg. διετέτακτο (Just., D. 44, 2) (s. διάταγμα, τάσσω; Hes., Hdt.+) gener. to make orderly arrangements or to cause someone to do someth. that advances one's objective, freq. of an official nature.

❶ **to put into a proper order or relationship, *make arrangements*** (X., Cyr. 8, 5, 16) οὕτως διατεταγμένος ἦν *he had arranged it so* **Ac 20:13.**—To make provisions for someone *arrange* (accommodations) Hv 3, 1, 4 (syntax as Ac 24:23 below).

❷ **to give (detailed) instructions as to what must be done, *order*** (Jos., Ant. 4, 308; 15, 113) w. dat. of pers. (Hippol., Ref. 10, 15, 5) **Mt 11:1; 1 Cor 9:14; 16:1;** 1 Cl 20:6. W. inf. foll.

(Jos., Ant. 4, 205) **Lk 8:55; Ac 18:2.** Pass. Dg 7:2. τοῦτο γὰρ διατέτακται μηδένα ἀποκλεισθῆναι *for it is ordained* (by God) *that no one be excluded* AcPl Ha 9, 6. Military terminology τὰ διατασσόμενα *orders* 1 Cl 37:2. Also τὸ διατεταγμένον *order* (EpArist 92; POxy 105, 7 τὰ ὑπ᾽ ἐμοῦ διατεταγμένα) **Lk 3:13.** κατὰ τὸ δ. αὐτοῖς *in accordance w. their orders* (POxy 718, 25 κατὰ τὰ διατεταγμένα) **Ac 23:31;** cp. 1 Cl 43:1. τὰ διαταχθέντα *what was ordered* **Lk 17:9,** cp. **10;** (ὁ νόμος; so Hes., Op. 274; Just., D. 45, 2) διαταγεὶς δι᾽ ἀγγέλων *ordered (by God) through angels* **Gal 3:19** (s. διαταγή, end).—Mid. (in same sense Pla. et al.; SIG 709, 26; OGI 331, 53; Philo) *order, command* w. dat. of pers. **Tit 1:5;** IEph 3:1; ITr 3:3; IRo 4:3. W. dat. of pers. and inf. foll. **Ac 24:23.** Abs. οὕτως ἐν τ. ἐκκλησίαις πάσαις δ. *I make this rule in all the churches* **1 Cor 7:17.** καθὼς διετάξατο *just as he directed* **Ac 7:44.** W. acc. of thing (Just., A II, 9, 4 νόμους) τὰ λοιπά *the rest I will take care of when I come* **1 Cor 11:34.**—M-M. TW.

διατελέω 1 aor. διετέλεσα Jer 20:7; trans. 'complete' (TestJob 41:4 κλαυθμόν [but κλαίων δ. cod. V]; Mel., P. 15, 95 διατελέσας τὸ μυστήριον) intr. ***continue, remain*** w. ptc. or adj. to denote the state in which one remains (Hdt.+; Thu. 1, 34, 3 ἀσφαλέστατος διατελεῖ; Diod. S. 11, 49, 4 καλῶς πολιτευόμενοι διετέλεσαν; ins [freq. of generous public service, s. SIG index] and pap, e.g., PHib 35, 5; UPZ 59, 4 [168 BC]; BGU 287, 6–8 ἀεὶ θύων τοῖς θεοῖς διετέλεσα; 2 Macc 5:27; Dt 9:7; EpArist 187; Philo, Aet. M. 19; 93; Jos., Ant. 15, 263, Vi. 423; Ath. 11, 2, R. 79, 2) ἄσιτοι διατελεῖτε *you have been continually without food* **Ac 27:33** (Aristotle in Apollon. Paradox. 25 ἄποτος διετέλεσεν; B-D-F §414, 1).—DELG s.v. τελέω. M-M.

διατηρέω impf. διετήρουν; fut. διατηρήσω; 1 aor. διετήρησα. Pass. 1 aor. διετηρήθην ; pf. ptc. διατετηρημένος (all LXX) (Pla. et al.; ins [e.g. OGI 229, 16 al.; SEG XXVIII, 1540, 18: 62/61 BC]; pap, LXX; TestDan 6:8; TestAsh 6:3; JosAs 13:12; EpArist; Philo, Aet. M. 35; Jos., Ant. 6, 101; 10, 42) gener. of careful watching.

❶ **to keep someth. mentally with implication of duration, *keep*** τὰ ῥήματα ἐν τῇ καρδίᾳ *treasure the words in the heart* **Lk 2:51** (=συνετήρει 2:19; cp. Gen 37:11; Da 7:28 Theod. v.l.); βουλήν *keep counsel* Dg 8:10 (cp. Diod. S. 4, 16, 3 ὅρκον διετήρησε; EpArist 206 τ. ἀλήθειαν; Jos., C. Ap. 1, 210).

❷ **to keep oneself from doing something, *keep free of*** δ. ἑαυτὸν ἔκ τινος *keep oneself free fr. someth.* **Ac 15:29** (cp. Pr 21:23; TestDan 6:8 ἑαυτοὺς ἀπό).—DELG s.v. τηρέω. M-M. New Docs 3, 65. TW.

διατί s. διά B2b.

διατίθημι (Hdt.+) aor. 3 sg. διέθηκεν 2 Macc 9:28, impv. διάθες (TestAbr B 7, p. 112, 4 [Stone 72, 4]); pf. 3 pl. διατεθείκασιν (Ath. 20, 1). Pass.: διάκειμαι functions as the pf. pass. (LXX, Just., Ath.); pf. pass. inf. διατεθεῖσθαι (Just., D, 142, 1); διεκείμην functions as the plpf. pass. (LXX, Just., Ath.); lit. 'put in order' then 'arrange, prepare' (2 Macc 9:28; Just., A I, 9, 2 al.; Ath. 20, 1 'analyze, describe'); in our lit. only mid. διατίθεμαι (X. et al.): fut. διαθήσομαι; 2 aor. διεθέμην, ptc. διαθέμενος.

❶ **to make formal arrangements for someth. to be done or brought about, *decree, ordain*** (Ps 104:9; 2 Ch 7:18) τὶ *someth.* (Appian, Bell. Civ. 4, 95 §401 τοιαῦτα=this sort of thing) τὰ δικαιώματά μου *my ordinances* B 10:2 (cp. Pla., Leg. 834a δ. νόμους).—διαθήκην (q.v. 2) δ. *issue a decree* (LXX; PsSol 9:10; TestNapht 1:1; the same expr.='conclude an agreement' in Aristoph., Av. 440) τινί *to* or *for someone* **Hb 8:10;** PtK 2 p. 15, 5; 6; 7 (both Jer 38: 31–33). ἐν ἡμῖν *among us* B 14:5. πρός τινα *to someone* (Ex 24:8; Dt 4:23; Josh 9:15) **Ac 3:25; Hb 10:16.**

❷ **to make a disposition of someth., *arrange*** τὶ *someth.* (X., Cyr. 5, 2, 7 τ. θυγατέρα; Andoc. 4, 30) *confer* w. dat. of the pers. favored κἀγὼ διατίθεμαι ὑμῖν καθὼς διέθετό μοι ὁ πατήρ βασιλείαν *I confer on you as the Father has conferred on me the right to rule* **Lk 22:29** (cp. 2 Km 5:3; albeit in sense 3, Jos., Ant. 13, 407 τ. βασιλείαν διέθετο; for the formulation δ. διαθήκην w. dat. vs. **29 v.l.,** s. Aristoph., Av. 440) w. a play on the word διαθήκη vs. **20.**

❸ **to arrange for disposition of property after one's death, *dispose of property by a will, make a will*** (Pla., Isaeus et al.; PEleph 2, 2; POxy 104, 4; 105, 2; 489, 3; PLips 29, 8 al.; Jos., Ant. 13, 407; Test12Patr) ὁ διαθέμενος *the testator* (Isaeus+; BGU 448, 24; POxy 99, 9; 15; OGI 509, 6 and 16; s. JBehm, Διαθήκη im NT 1912, 8; 87, 6) **Hb 9:16f.**—M-M. TW.

διατρίβω impf. διέτριβον; fut. διατρίψω LXX; 1 aor. διέτριψα, ptc. διατρίψας (Hom.+) lit.'rub through, wear away'; in our lit. fig. **to remain or stay in a place, *spend time,*** usually rendered *stay* in sense of duration, esp. when associated with place or pers. (Il. 19, 150, abs. 'waste time'; Hdt. et al.) w. acc. τὸν χρόνον (Lysias 3, 12; BGU 1140, 4 [5 BC] διατρείψας ἐνταῦθα τὸν πάντα χρόνον; cp. Demetr.: 722 fgm. 1, 3 Jac. of Jacob indentured by Laban ἑπτὰ ἔτη; Jos., Ant. 6, 297; Just., D. 2, 3 δ. ἱκανὸν μετ᾽ αὐτοῦ χρόνον) ἱκανὸν μὲν οὖν χρόνον διέτριψαν=*they stayed quite a while* (in Iconium) **Ac 14:3;** sim. vs. **28.** ἡμέρας τινάς (X., Hell. 6, 5, 49; cp. Lev 14:8) **16:12;** cp. **20:6; 25:6, 14.** Abs. *stay, remain, stay* μετά τινος *with someone* (Pla., Apol. 33b, Phd. 59d al.) **J 3:22; 11:54 v.l.;** MPol 5:1.—**Ac 12:19; 14:19 v.l.** W. the place given ἐν Ἀντιοχείᾳ **15:35;** cp. **14:7** D (PHal 1, 182f ἐν Ἀπόλλωνος πόλει δ.; Sb 1002, 9; 2 Macc 14:23; Jdth 10:2; Jos., Bell. 1, 387; Tat. 9, 1 ἐν οὐρανῷ). ἐπὶ γῆς *on earth* Dg 5:9 (Alciphron 2, 22, 2 ἐπὶ Κεραμεικοῦ; POxy 2756 [78/79 AD], 8f ἐπὶ Ἀλλεξανδρίας). ἐκεῖ (Jos., Ant. 8, 267) **Ac 25:14.**—B. 569. DELG s.v. τρίβω. M-M.

διατροφή, ῆς, ἡ that which sustains or nourishes the body, *support, sustenance* (X., Vect. 4, 49; Diod. S. 19, 32, 2; Plut.; PTebt 52, 16 [114 BC]; POxy 275, 19; 494, 16 al.; 1 Macc 6:49; Jos., Ant. 2, 88; 4, 231; ApcMos 29; Just., A I, 13, 1; Mel., P. 87, 656) pl. in same sense ***means of subsistence, food*** (with ἔχειν as Epict., Ench. 12, 1) **1 Ti 6:8.**—DELG s.v. τρέφω. M-M.

διαυγάζω 1 aor. διηύγασα (Philo Bybl.:790 fgm. 4, 49 Jac. [in Eus., PE 1, 10, 50]; Plut., Mor. 893e; Dionys. Periegetes [II AD] 1120 ed. GBernhardy [1828]; horoscope in PLond I, 130, 70 [I/II AD] p. 135; PGM 4, 991; 13, 165; Job 25:5 Aq.; Jos., Ant. 5, 349 [pass.=a light dawned on him]) gener. to emit light through someth.

❶ ***shine through*** (Philo Mech. 57, 27) **2 Cor 4:4 v.l.**

❷ ***dawn, break*** ἕως οὗ ἡμέρα διαυγάσῃ *until the day dawns* **2 Pt 1:19** (cp. Polyb. 3, 104, 5 ἅμα τῷ διαυγάζειν; Passio Andreae 8 [Aa I I/1 p. 18, 30]). JBoehmer, ZNW 22, 1923, 228–33.—DELG s.v. αὐγή. M-M.

διαυγής, ές (Pre-Socr. et al.; PGM 4, 497; Pr 16:2 Aq.; Philo; Jos., Ant. 3, 37 ὕδωρ; 17, 169) **possessing the property of being able to be seen through, *transparent, pure*** ὕαλος **Rv 21:21** (s. διαφανής).—DELG s.v. αὐγή.

διαφαίνω (pass. since Hom., also Wsd 17:6; act. since Aristot, also Philo, Joseph.) ***allow light to shine through*** ἦν τὸ ὄρος ἐκεῖνο διαφαῖνον αὐτῇ φῶς *that mountain allowed light to* *pass through it for (Elizabeth)* GJs 22:3 (for other translations s. deStrycker 177, n. 6).—DELG s.v. φαίνω.

διαφανής, ές (Soph., Hdt.+) ***transparent*** (so Aristoph., Hippocr. et al.; Achilles Tat. 4, 18, 4 ὕαλος διαφανής; SIG 736, 16 and 21; Ex 30:34; Philo, Leg. ad Gai. 364; Tat. 39, 2 αἱ διαφανέστεραι πράξεις) **Rv 21:21** t.r. (Erasmian rendering?, s. Tdf. app.; s. διαυγής).—DELG s.v. φαίνω. M-M.

διάφαυμα, ατος, τό (fr. IV AD in patr., s. Lampe; fr. VI AD in pap) ***daybreak*** GJs 23:3.

διαφέρω fut. 3 sg. διοίσει LXX; 1 aor. διήνεγκα; pf. 3 pl. διενηνόχασιν (Ath. 20. 4); impf. mid. διεφερόμην; pf. pass. ptc. διενηνεγμένων 2 Macc 4:39 (Hom. Hymns, Pind.+).

❶ **to carry someth. through a place or structure, *carry through*** (cp. 1 Esdr 5:53) σκεῦος διὰ τοῦ ἱεροῦ *a vessel (through) the temple* **Mk 11:16** (perh. in ref. to taking a shortcut; cp. Mishnah, Berakoth 9, 5). Stones through a gate Hs 9, 4, 1; 9, 4, 5; 9, 4, 8; 9, 15, 5.—Of a teaching (Lucian, D. Deor. 24, 1 ἀγγελίας δ.; Plut., Mor. 163c φήμη διηνέχθαι) διεφέρετο δὲ ὁ λόγος τοῦ κυρίου δι' ὅλης τῆς χώρης *the word of the Lord was borne (=spread) throughout the region* **Ac 13:49.**

❷ **to cause to move from one locality to another, *carry hither and yon*** (Pompey's bier PsSol 2:27); *drive* or *carry about, drift* of a ship (Philo, Migr. Abr. 148 σκάφος ὑπ' ἐναντίων πνευμάτων διαφερόμενον; Strabo 3, 2, 7; Lucian, Hermot. 28; Plut., Mor. 552c, Galba 1065 [26, 5] al.) **Ac 27:27.**

❸ **to be unlike, *differ, be different*** τινός *from someone or someth.* οὐδέν *in no respect, not at all* (Pla., Apol. 35b οὗτοι γυναικῶν οὐδὲν διαφέρουσι; Epict. 1, 5, 6; 2, 19, 6 al.; cp. TestAbr B 6 p. 110, 10 [Stone p. 68] τ. ἀνθρώπων; Jos., Ant. 2, 153; Just., D. 10, 3 al.; Ath. 20, 4; 24, 5) οὐδὲν δ. δούλου **Gal 4:1.**—Dg 3:5.—δ. τινὸς ἔν τινι (Pla., Pol. 568a; Demosth. 18, 189) *differ fr. someth. w. respect to someth.* **1 Cor 15:41.**—Impers. οὐδέν μοι διαφέρει *it makes no difference to me* (Pla., Prot. 316b al.; Demosth. 9, 50; Polyb. 3, 21, 9; Dionys. Hal., De Lys. 25; Aelian, VH 1, 25 al.; POxy 1348) **Gal 2:6** (JJaquette, Paul, Epictetus, and Others on Indifference to Status: CBQ 56, '94, 68–80).

❹ **differ to one's advantage fr. someone or someth., *be worth more than, be superior to*** τινός (Pla. et al.; Dio Chrys. 27 [44], 10; POxy 1061, 12 [22 BC] διαφέρετε τοῦ Πτολεμαίου ἐμπειρίᾳ; 3 Macc 6:26; Jos., Ant. 4, 97; 8, 42; 20, 189) **Mt 6:26; 10:31; 12:12; Lk 12:7, 24.** Some mss. read πολλῷ instead of πολλῶν **Mt 10:31** and **Lk 12:7** (s. app. N[25], Merk, Tdf.) giving the mng. 'You differ by far from sparrows', a qualitative sense rather than the quantitative; s. RBorger, TRu 52, 87, 21f on probability for the v.l. Abs. τὰ διαφέροντα *the things that really matter* (Ps.-Pla., Eryx. 6, 394e.—Opp. τὰ ἀδιάφορα) **Ro 2:18; Phil 1:10** (cp. Plut., Mor. 43e; 73a ὑπὲρ μεγάλων . . . καὶ σφόδρα διαφερόντων al. [PWendland, Philol. 57, 1897, 115]; Ptolemaeus, Ep. ad Floram 5, 2, 8 [GQuispel, Sources chrétiennes 24 p. 60, 52 w. πνευματικά]; LBW 410, 3 τὰ δ. αὐτ[οῖς]=what is important for them).—DELG s.v. φέρω. M-M. TW.

διαφεύγω fut. διαφεύξομαι LXX; aor. διέφυγον; pf. διαπέφευγα LXX ***escape*** (Hdt.+) **Ac 27:42;** IMg 1:2.—DELG s.v. φεύγω. M-M.

διαφημίζω 1 aor. διεφήμισα, pass. διεφημίσθην **to make extensively known by word of mouth, *make generally known, spread abroad*** (φημίζω, 'spread a report'; Arat., Phaen. 221; Dionys. Hal. 11, 46; Palaeph. p. 21, 12; Vett. Val. index; TestSol D 8:1; Jos., Bell. 2, 594; 6, 116) τινά **Mt 9:31.** τὸν λόγον (cp. Jos., Bell. 1, 651) *spread widely, disseminate, advertise* **Mk 1:45;** pass. **Mt 28:15.**—DELG s.v. φημί. M-M.

διαφθείρω fut. διαφθερῶ; 1 aor. διέφθειρα LXX. Pass.: fut. 3 sg. διαφθαρήσεται Da Theod.; 2 aor. διεφθάρην; pf. 3 sg. διέφθαρται Zeph 3:7, ptc. διεφθαρμένος (s. φθείρω; Hom.+)

❶ **to cause the destruction of someth., *spoil, destroy*** of rust eating into iron Dg 2:2; of moths (Philo, Abr. 11), that eat clothes **Lk 12:33.**—IMg 10:2 (imagery of food spoilage); *destroy* persons and nations (Aristot., Pol. 1323a, 31; Diod. S. 5, 54, 3; 12, 68, 2; Plut., Demosth. 859 [28, 4]; LXX; Jos., Ant. 2, 26; 11, 211) **Rv 11:18a** (in wordplay, s. 11:18b in 2 below; cp. Jer 28:25); Hv 4, 2, 3; s 9, 1, 9; 9, 26, 1; 7. Pass. *be destroyed* of a person's physical being **2 Cor 4:16** (cp. Ps.-Pla., Alcib. 1, 135a διαφθαρῆναι τ. σῶμα; Lucian, Dial. Deor. 13, 2; Philo, Decal. 124). οὐδὲν αὐτοῦ διεφθάρη *no part of him was impaired* AcPlCor 2:30—Hv 2, 3, 3. Of ships (Diod. S. 11, 19, 3; 13, 13, 4; schol. on Apollon. Rhod. 2, 1111–12b διαφθαρείσης τῆς νεώς) **Rv 8:9;** a kingdom IEph 19:3. Of the bodies of starving persons *waste away* (Appian, Bell. Civ. 2, 66 §274 λιμῷ διαφθαρῆναι; POxy 938, 4; Philo, Leg. ad Gai. 124) Hv 3, 9, 3.

❷ **to cause to become morally corrupt, *deprave, ruin*** (Diod. S. 16, 54, 4 τὰ ἤθη τ. ἀνθρώπων; Dio Chrys. 26 [43], 10 τοὺς νέους; Jos., C. Ap. 2, 264; Just.): the earth (i.e. its people) **Rv 11:18b** (s. on 11:18a in 1 above); **19:2 v.l.;** δ. τὴν εἰς θεὸν γνώμην IRo 7:1. διεφθαρμένοι ἄνθρωποι τὸν νοῦν **1 Ti 6:5.** Of the mind pass. *be corrupted* Hs 4:7 (cp. Pla., Leg. 10, 888a and Jos., Ant. 9, 222 δ. τὴν διάνοιαν; Aeschyl., Ag. 932 and Dionys. Hal. 5, 21 τ. γνώμην; Dio Chrys. 60 + 61 [77 + 78], 45 ψυχὴ διεφθαρμένη).—B. 762. DELG s.v. φθείρω. M-M. TW.

διαφθορά, ᾶς, ἡ (s. διαφθείρω; Aeschyl., Hdt. et al.; LXX, TestGad 8:2; JosAs 7:6; Philo; Jos., C. Ap. 2, 259; Just., D. 134, 2 and Tat. 1:4 in moral sense) **the condition or state of rotting or decaying, *destruction, corruption*** of the body ἰδεῖν δ. (εἶδον 4) **Ac 2:27, 31; 13:35ff** (all Ps 15:10; s. JRegula, PM 15, 1911, 230–33; RMurphy, Šaḥat in the Qumran Lit., Biblica 39, '58, 61–66); ὑποστρέφειν εἰς δ. *return to decay* (i.e. prob. the realm of the dead) vs. **34** (cp. ἐλθεῖν εἰς δ. Job 33:28; καταβαίνειν εἰς δ. Ps 29:10).—DELG s.v. φθείρω. TW.

διαφορά, ᾶς, ἡ the state or relation of being different, freq. in ref. to worth, *difference* (s. διαφέρω 3; Thu. et al.; UPZ 110, 96 [164 BC]; pap; Sir Prol., ln. 26; 1 Macc 3:18; Wsd 7:20; TestAbr A 5 p. 82, 4 [Stone p. 12] τὴν δ. τῆς ὁμιλίας 'worthwhile conversation' [cp. Just., A I, 21, 4] εἰς δ. καὶ προτροπὴν τῶν ἐκπαιδευομένων 'for the improvement and encouragement of the young'; Tat.; Ath., R. 76, 20) δ. πολλή *a great difference* (Jos., Vi. 2; cp. Philo, Op. M. 134) B 18:1; D 1:1. [διαφο]||ρά τε πολλὴ [μεταξὺ]|| τῶν ἀφθάρ[τ]ω[ν] (there exists) *a great difference [between] the incorruptible things* Ox 1081, 3–5 (restored after Coptic SJCh 89, 1f). μεταξύ τινος καὶ ἄλλου *betw. someone and another* MPol 16:1. μὴ εἰδότ[ες τὴν διά]||φ[ο]ραν τα[ύτην ἀπέ]||θανον (restoration of Ox 1081, 22–24 by Till based on Coptic SJCh 89, 19–20) *inasmuch as* (erring human beings) *did not recognize this distinction* (between the transitory and the intransitory), *they died.*—DELG, and Frisk s.v. φέρω. M-M s.v. διάφορος.

διάφορος, ον (s. διαφέρω 3; Hdt., Pla.+)—❶ **pert. to being different, w. focus on distinctiveness, *different*** (so Hdt. et al.; pap, e.g. POxy 1033, 88; PGrenf II, 92, 8; Da 7:7 Theod.; Jos., Ant. 1, 166; TestSol, Test12Patr, Just., Tat.) χαρίσματα *spiritual gifts* **Ro 12:6.** βαπτισμοί *washings* **Hb 9:10.**

❷ **pert. to being different, w. focus on value,** ***outstanding, excellent*** (since Antiphanes Com. 175, 3; Diod. S. 1, 15, 9; 2, 57, 2; Sb 1005; EpArist 97; Jos., Bell. 5, 161; the rare comparative διαφορώτερος also Sext. Emp., Phys. 1, 218 [Adv. Math. 9:218]) διαφορώτερον ὄνομα *a more excellent name* **Hb 1:4** (=1 Cl 36:2). διαφορώτεραι λειτουργίαι **8:6.**—DELG, and Frisk s.v. φέρω. M-M. TW.

διαφυλάσσω fut. 3 sg. διαφυλάξει LXX; 1 aor. διεφύλαξα. Pass.: fut. 3 sg. διαφυλαχθήσεται Jer 3:5; 1 aor. 3 sg. διεφυλάχθη Hos 12:13. (s. φυλάσσω; Hdt.+; ins, pap; a special favorite of the magical lit. [SEitrem and AFridrichsen, E. chr. Amulett 1921, 6 and 25]; TestZeb 5:4; TestJos 18:4, EpArist 272; Philo, Aet. M. 36; 74; Jos., Ant. 11, 155 al.—In LXX, as well as PsSol 16:9; TestJos 18:4; JosAs 25:5 [-ττει] 26, 2; GrBar ins 2 and Mel., P. 84, 629 esp. of God's care, as Diod. Sic. 3, 40, 7 θεὸς διεφύλαξεν; PGiss 17, 7 (Hadrian); BGU 1081, 3f εὔχομαι τοῖς θεοῖς ὑπέρ σου, ἵνα σε διαφυλάξουσι; 984, 27 al.; PGM 4, 2516; 13, 633) ***guard, protect*** τινά *someone* of God 1 Cl 59:2; GJs 9:3; of angels **Lk 4:10** (Ps 90:11); GJs 22:3.—Βαρσαβᾶς . . . ἀπαθὴς διεφυλάχθη *(after drinking a snake's poison) Barsabas was preserved from harm* Papias (11:2) (s. ἀπαθής 2).—DELG s.v. φύλαξ. M-M.

διαχειρίζω 1 aor. mid. διεχειρισάμην (χειρίζω, 'handle, manage'; Andoc., Lysias et al.; PTebt 112 introd. extract 3); in our lit. only mid. **take hold of someone forcibly with malicious intent and frequently ending in the taking of life,** ***lay violent hands on, murder, kill*** (Polyb. 8, 23, 8; Diod. S. 18, 46; Plut., Mor. 220b; Herodian 3, 12, 1; Jos., Bell. 1, 113, Ant. 15, 173 al.) τινά *someone* **Ac 5:30;** AcPlCor 2:11. Cp. **Ac 26:21.**—DELG s.v. Χείρ. M-M.

διαχλευάζω (s. χλευάζω; Demosth. 50, 49; Polyb. 18, 4, 4; Ps.-Pla., Axioch. 364b; Jos., Bell. 2, 281, Ant. 15, 220) **to laugh at someone in scorn,** abs. ***jeer*** **Ac 2:13.** S. PvanderHorst, JSNT 25, '85, 49–60 (Hellen. parallels).—DELG s.v. Χλεύη.

διαχωρίζω 1 aor. διεχώρισα LXX; aor. pass. διεχωρίσθην LXX; pf. pass. ptc. διακεχωρισμένος LXX (s. χωρίζω; Aristoph. et al., X., Pla.; PTebt 802, 14; POxy 1673, 5; LXX; TestJob 38:3; Test12Patr; GrBar 16:13; Philo, Joseph.; Mel., P. 55, 407) **to cause a distance to be put between objects or persons,** ***separate*** τὶ ἀπό τινος *someth. fr. someth.* 1 Cl 33:3 (cp. Gen 1:4, 6f; Jos., Bell. 1, 535; TestJos 13:6). Mid. and pass. *be separated, part, go away* (mid. Diod. S. 4, 53, 4; pass. of a divorced woman Jos., Ant. 15, 259) ἀπό τινος (in a love charm PGM 12, 458f ποίησον τὸν δεῖνα διαχωρισθῆναι ἀπὸ τοῦ δεῖνος get so-and-so separated from so-and-so; Herm. Wr. 1, 11b; Gen 13:9, 11; Sus 13 Theod.) mid. **Lk 9:33;** pass. 1 Cl 10:4 (Gen 13:14).—DELG s.v. Χώρα. M-M.

διγαμία, ας, ἡ ***second marriage*** (Cat. Cod. Astr. XII 174, 10; Just., A I, 15, 5) **Tit 1:9 v.l.** (s. δίγαμος).

δίγαμος, ον—❶ ***married to two people at the same time*** (Manetho, Apotel. 5, 291). See 2 for **Tit 1:9 v.l.**

❷ ***married for the second time*** (Stesichorus [VII/VI BC] fgm. 17, 4 Diehl [223, 4 Page; on this schol., Eur., Or. 249] δ. w. τρίγαμος of women who leave their husbands and marry a second or third time [s. DELG s.v. γαμέω]. Eccl. writers [Hippol., Elench. 9, 12, 22 Wendl. al.] use it of a normal second marriage; δίγ. in this sense Leontius 13 p. 26, 10; τρίγαμος γυνή=married for the third time Theocr. 12, 5. Normal marriage is also kept in mind in Ptolem., Apotel. 4, 5, 1; 2: ἄγαμος=unmarried, μονόγαμος=married once, πολύγαμος [also 4, 5, 4] married several times) **Tit 1:9 v.l.** in a prohibition against laying hands on persons who have entered a second marriage, the ideal being to be married only once, s. on **1 Ti 3:2, 12; Tit 1:6,** s.v. εἷς 2b.—DELG s.v. γαμέω.

διγλωσσία, ας, ἡ **doubleness of speech that conceals true intentions by deceitful words,** ***duplicity, insincerity*** (=our colloq. 'speaking with forked tongue') D 2:4; B 19:7 v.l. s. γλῶσσα.

δίγλωσσος, ον (in the sense of 'bilingual' since Thu. 8, 85, 2; also Diod. S. 17, 68, 5; schol. on Pla., Rep. 600a) **pert. to being insincere in one's speech,** ***insincere, deceitful*** (of snakes schol. on Nicander, Ther. 371 οἵτινες δύο γλώσσας ἔχουσιν. Also of humans: Pr 11:13; Sir 5:9, 14f; 28:13; Philo, Sacr. Abel. 32 p, 215, 12; SibOr 3, 37.—Theognis 1, 91 likew. speaks of one ὃς μιῇ γλώσσῃ δίχ' ἔχει νόον 'whose mind is twofold and his tongue but one') D 2:4; B 19:7 (s. διγλωσσία, γλωσσώδης).

διγνώμων, ον (schol. on Eur., Or. 633; Simplicius in Epict. p. 134, 53) ***double-minded, fickle*** D 2:4; B 19:7.—DELG s.v. γιγνώσκω.

διδακτικός, ή, όν ***skillful in teaching*** (s. διδάσκω; Philod., Rhet II p. 22, 10 Sudh.; Philo, Praem. 27, Congr. 35) **1 Ti 3:2; 2 Ti 2:24.**—DELG s.v. διδάσκω. M-M. TW.

διδακτός, ή, όν (s. διδάσκω; Pind., X., Pla. et al.=teachable; so also PsSol 17:32; EpArist 236; Philo).

❶ **pert. to being taught,** ***taught, instructed*** of pers. as recipients of instruction (1 Macc 4:7) διδακτοὶ θεοῦ *taught by God* **J 6:45** (Is 54:13; cp. PsSol 17:32 βασιλεὺς δίκαιος διδακτὸς ὑπὸ θεοῦ; Socrat., Ep. 1, 10 προηγόρευσα . . . διδάσκοντος τ. θεοῦ).

❷ **pert. to being communicated as instruction,** ***imparted, taught*** (Jos., Bell. 6, 38) w. gen. (Soph., El. 344 νουθετήματα κείνης διδακτά taught by her) ἐν διδακτοῖς ἀνθρωπίνης σοφίας λόγοις *in words imparted by human wisdom,* opp. ἐν δ. πνεύματος *in that which is imparted by the Spirit to someone* **1 Cor 2:13.**—M-M.

διδασκαλία, ας, ἡ (s. διδάσκω; Pind.+).—❶ **the act of teaching,** ***teaching, instruction*** (X., Oec. 19, 15 ἆρα ἡ ἐρώτησις δ. ἐστίν; Epict. 2, 14, 1; SIG 672, 4 [II BC] ὑπὲρ τᾶς τῶν παίδων διδασκαλίας al.; POxy 1101, 4; Sir 39:8; Philo; Jos., Ant. 3, 5; 13, 311; Just., A II, 10, 1; Ath. 33, 2) **Ro 12:7.** Of Timothy in role as superintendent or overseer **1 Ti 4:13, 16;** εἰς δ. ἐγράφη *was written for instruction* **Ro 15:4;** ὠφέλιμος πρὸς δ. *useful for instr.* **2 Ti 3:16** (perh. a rabbinic-type expr., לְלַמֵּד, cp. Sanh. 73a, underlies the usage of δ. with a prep. in these two passages). πρὸς τ. χρείας *as the needs required* Papias (2:15).

❷ **that which is taught,** ***teaching, instruction*** (cp. X., Cyr. 8, 7, 24 παρὰ τῶν προγεγενημένων μανθάνετε. αὕτη γὰρ ἀρίστη δ.; Sir 24:33; Pr 2:17; ancient Christian prayer [CSchmidt: Heinrici Festschr. 1914 p. 71, 26] δ. τῶν εὐαγγελίων; Just., D. 35, 2 καθαρᾶς δ. al.) w. ἐντάλματα ἀνθρώπων (after Is 29:13) **Mt 15:9; Mk 7:7; Col 2:22;** δ. δαιμονίων **1 Ti 4:1** (cp. αἱ δ. τῆς πλάνης Theoph. Ant. 2, 14 [p. 136, 21]); κακὴ δ. IEph 16:2; δυσωδία τῆς δ. 17:1.—**Eph 4:14.** Freq. of the teachings of eccl. Christianity (αἱ δ. τῆς ἀληθείας Theoph. Ant. 2, 14 [p. 136, 14]): δ. τοῦ σωτῆρος ἡμῶν θεοῦ **Tit 2:10** (on the gen. cp. En 10:8 ἡ δ. Ἀζαήλ); δ. ὑγιαίνουσα **1 Ti 1:10; 2 Ti 4:3; Tit 1:9; 2:1;** καλὴ δ. **1 Ti 4:6;** ἡ κατ' εὐσέβειαν δ. *godly teaching* **6:3.** Of dissident teaching: ἀπὸ τῆς δ. αὐτῶν ἀποφεύγετε AcPlCor 2:21.W. no modifiers w. λόγος **5:17; 6:1; 2 Ti 3:10; Tit 2:7.** παραβολὰς και διδασκαλίας Papias (2:11).—M-M. TW. Sv.

διδάσκαλος, ου, ὁ (s. διδάσκω; Hom. Hymns, Aeschyl.+) ***teacher*** δ. ἐθνῶν Dg 11:1; πέποιθας σεαυτὸν εἶναι δ. νηπίων *you are sure that you are* (i.e. can be) *a teacher of the young* **Ro 2:19f.** ὀφείλοντες εἶναι διδάσκαλοι *although you ought to be teachers* **Hb 5:12.** W. μαθητής (Epict. 4, 6, 11; Jos., Ant. 17, 334; Did., Gen. 66, 25) **Mt 10:24f; Lk 6:40;** IMg 9:2. Used in addressing Jesus (corresp. to the title רַב,רַבִּי rabbi) **Mt 8:19; 12:38; 19:16; 22:16, 24, 36; Mk 4:38; 9:17, 38; 10:17, 20, 35; 12:14, 19, 32; 13:1; Lk 3:12; 7:40; 9:38; 10:25; 11:45; 12:13; 18:18; 19:39; 20:21, 28, 39; 21:7; J8:4;** IEph 15:1; IMg 9:2f. Also as designation for Jesus (ὁ δ. ἡμῶν Orig., C. Cels. 6, 36, 32; θεῖος δ. 1, 37, 19), w. other titles Dg 9:6. He is called βασιλεὺς καὶ δ. MPol 17:3. Ῥαββί w. translation **J 1:38** (cp. **3:2**), also Ῥαββουνί **20:16.** W. the art. (=רַבָּא) **Mt 9:11; 17:24; 23:8; 26:18; Mk 5:35; 14:14; Lk 6:40b; 8:49; 22:11; J 11:28** (Philo, Leg. ad Gai. 53 πάρεστιν ὁ δ.). ὁ δ. καὶ ὁ κύριος (=מָרִי) as a title of respect **13:13f.** Used of John the Baptist **Lk 3:12.** Of Scripture scholars in Jerusalem **Lk 2:46; J 3:10** (Petosiris, fgm. 36b, 13 ὁ διδάσκαλος λέγει=the [well-known] teacher says; sim. **Mk 14:14** and par.).—As an official of a Christian assembly **Ac 13:1; 1 Cor 12:28f; Eph 4:11; 2 Ti 1:11; Js 3:1** (TOrbiso, VD 21, '41, 169–82); D 15:1f; paid 13:2. Cp. Hv 3, 5, 1; m 4, 3, 1; s 9, 15, 4; 9, 16, 5; 9, 25, 2; B 1:8; 4:9. HGreeven, ZNW 44, '52/53, 16–31. Of Paul δ. ἐθνῶν **1 Ti 2:7.** Of Polycarp δ. ἀποστολικὸς καὶ προφητικός MPol 16:2; δ. ἐπίσημος 19:1; ὁ τῆς Ἀσίας δ. 12:2. Of dissident teachers δ. πονηρίας Hs 9, 19, 2. υἱὸς διδασκάλου as transl. of Barabbas (q.v.) underlies the Lat. text 'filius magistri' of GHb 339, 51 (s. Peter of Laodicea in Kl. T. 8^3 p. 10, ln. 9ff app.).—EReisch in Pauly-W. V, 1905, 401ff; Dalman, Worte 272ff; Schürer II 322–36, 417–22; GMoore, Judaism I 1927, 37–47, 308–22.—AHarnack, Lehre d. Zwölf Ap.: TU II/1/2 1884, 93ff, Mission I^4 1923, 345ff; CDodd, Jesus as Teacher and Prophet: Mysterium Christi 1930, 53–66; FFilson, JBL 60, '41, 317–28; EFascher, TLZ 79, '54, 325–42; HBraun, Qumran u. d. NT II, '66, 54–74 (Jesus and the Teacher of Righteousness).—DELG s.v. διδάσκω. M-M. TW. Sv.

διδάσκω impf. ἐδίδασκον; fut. διδάξω; 1 aor. ἐδίδαξα; pf. 3 sg. δεδίδαχεν Pr 30:3. Pass.: aor. ἐδιδάχθην; pf. 1 pl. δεδιδάγμεθα (Just.), ptc. δεδιδαγμένος LXX (Hom.+)

❶ **to tell someone what to do, *tell, instruct*** ἐποίησαν ὡς ἐδιδάχθησαν *they did as they were told* **Mt 28:15.**

❷ **to provide instruction in a formal or informal setting, *teach*—ⓐ** abs. **Mt 4:23; Mk 1:21; J 7:14; 1 Cor 4:17; 1 Ti 4:11; 6:2;** IEph 15:1; Pol 2:3. Of the activity of the Christian διδάσκαλοι Hv 3, 5, 1. W. κηρύσσειν **Mt 11:1.**

ⓑ w. acc. of pers. (SIG 593, 15; PLond I, 43, 6 [II BC] p. 48 παιδάρια) **Hb 8:11** (Jer 38:34); **Mt 5:2; Mk 9:31; Lk 4:31; J 7:35** al.; **Col 3:16** w. νουθετεῖν; Israel B 5:8.

ⓒ w. acc. of thing (X., Cyr. 1, 6, 20; SIG 578, 34 τὰ μουσικά; Jos., Ant. 9, 4; Did., Gen. 58, 4 al.) **Mt 15:9** (Is 29:13); **22:16; Ac 18:11, 25;** φόβον θεοῦ B 19:5 (cp. Ps 33:12); τὸν περὶ ἀληθείας λόγον Pol 3:2; cp. Papias (2:3); AcPl Ha 8, 8 τὸν λόγον τοῦ θεοῦ; **Ac 15:35** (w. εὐαγγελίζεσθαι).—AcPl Ox 6, 14; AcPl Ha 6, 12 (Herm. Wr. 1, 29 τ. λόγους διδάσκων, πῶς σωθήσονται); τ. εὐαγγέλιον MPol 4; ταῦτα **1 Ti 4:11** (w. παραγγέλλειν); so also **6:2** (w. παρακαλεῖν). Cp. AcPl Cor 1:9.

ⓓ w. acc. of pers. and thing *teach someone someth.* (X., Mem. 1, 2, 10, Cyr. 1, 6, 28; Sallust. 3 p. 12; SIG 450, 5f δ. τοὺς παῖδας . . . τὸν ὕμνον; Philo, Rer. Div. Her. 39; Jos., Ant. 8, 395) ὑμᾶς διδάξει πάντα *he will instruct you in everything* **J 14:26.—Mk 4:2; Ac 21:21; Hb 5:12.** Pass. διδάσκομαί τι (Solon 22, 7 Diehl^3; OGI 383, 165 διδασκόμενοι τὰς τέχνας; Philo, Mut. Nom. 5) **Gal 1:12.** παραδόσεις ἃς ἐδιδάχθητε *traditions in which you have been instructed* **2 Th 2:15.**—Also τινὰ περί τινος (OGI 484, 5; PStras 41, 8; Jos., Ant. 2, 254) **1J 2:27.**

ⓔ w. dat. of pers. (Plut., Marcell. 304 [12, 4]; Aesop, Fab. 210c, 8f v.l. Ch.) and inf. foll. ἐδίδασκεν τῷ Βαλὰκ βαλεῖν **Rv 2:14.**

ⓕ w. acc. of pers. and inf. foll. (SIG 662, 12 δ. τοὺς παῖδας ᾄδειν; Philo, Omn. Prob. Lib. 144; Aesop 260 H.=149, 6 P.=H-H. 154, III, 8) **Mt 28:20; Lk 11:1;** Pol 4:1. W. ὅτι instead of inf. (Diod. S. 11, 12, 5; 18, 10, 3; Aelian, VH 3, 16; Philo, Mut. Nom. 18, Fuga 55) **1 Cor 11:14;** also recitative ὅτι **Mk 8:31** and **Ac 15:1.**—GBjörck, HN ΔΙΔΑΣΚΩΝ, D. periphrastischen Konstruktionen im Griechischen '40.—B. 1222f.—DELG. M-M. TW. Sv.

διδαχή, ῆς, ἡ (s. διδάσκω; Hdt. et al.; BGU 140, 16 [II AD]; once in LXX; EpArist, Philo, Joseph., Just.).

❶ **the activity of teaching, *teaching, instruction*** (Hdt. 3, 134, 2; Pla., Phdr. 275a; Ps 59:1; Jerus. ins: SEG VIII, 170, 5 [before 70 AD] δ. ἐντολῶν; Philo, Spec. Leg. 2, 3; Jos., Ant. 17, 159; Just., A II, 5, 4 διὰ διδαχῆς θυμάτων) λαλεῖν (ἐν) δ. *speak in the form of teaching* **1 Cor 14:6;** ἐν πάσῃ δ. *in every kind of instruction* **2 Ti 4:2.** Of Jesus' teaching activity **Mk 4:2; 12:38.**

❷ **the content of teaching, *teaching*** (EpArist 207; 294; Just., A I, 40, 1) by Pharisees and Sadducees **Mt 16:12;** by Jesus **J 7:16f; 18:19;** apostles **Ac 2:42** (Iren. 4, 33, 8 [Harv. II 262, 6]; Just., A I, 53, 3 παρὰ τῶν ἀποστολῶν).—**Ac 5:28; 13:12; Ro 16:17; 1 Cor 14:26; 2J 9f; Rv 2:24;** D ins; 1:3; 2:1; 6:1; 11:2; B 9:9; 16:9; 18:1. κατὰ τ. διδαχήν *in accordance w. the teaching* **Tit 1:9;** βαπτισμῶν δ. *teaching about baptisms* **Hb 6:2.** τύπος διδαχῆς *pattern of teaching* (of Christian belief and practice) **Ro 6:17** (GRoss, Exp. 7th ser., 5, 1908, 469–75; CLattey, JTS 29, 1928, 381–84; 30, 1929, 397–99; JMoffatt, JBL 48, 1929, 233–38; FBurkitt, JTS 30, 1929, 190f.—S. also παραδίδωμι 1b end, and τύπος 4); δ. καινή **Mk 1:27** (cp. the apocryphal gospel Ox 1224 fgm. 2 verso, I, 2–5 [Kl. Texte 8^3, p. 26, 19ff] π[ο]ίαν σέ| [φασιν διδα]χὴν καιν[ὴν] δι|[δάσκειν, ἢ τί β]ά[πτισμ]α καινὸν| [κηρύσσειν;] *what's this new teaching all about that they say you're promoting, or what's this new baptism you're proclaiming?*); **Ac 17:19;** δ. ἀφθαρσίας *teaching that assures immortality* IMg 6:2. Of offensive teachings **Rv 2:14f; Hb 13:9;** κακὴ δ. IEph 9:1; δ. ξέναι, μωραί Hs 8, 6, 5. The teaching of the wicked angel m 6, 2, 7.

❸ Either mng. can be defended **Mt 7:28; 22:33; Mk 1:22; 11:18; Lk 4:32.**—CDodd, TManson memorial vol., '59, 106–18 ('catechetical' instr. in the early church).—DELG s.v. διδάσκω. M-M. TW. Sv.

δίδραχμον, ου, τό (τὸ δίδραχμα cod. W; s. MBlack, BRigaux Festschr. '70, 61f; the adj. δίδραχμος since Thu.; the noun τὸ δ. in Aristot., Ἀθην. πολ. 10, 7; Pollux; Lucian, Dial. Meretr. 7, 2 ἐὰν ὁ σκυτοτόμος αἰτῇ τὸ δίδραχμον; Galen; Cass. Dio 66, 7; IG^2 I, 792; PTebt 404, 12; LXX; Philo, Rer. Div. Her. 186f; Jos., Ant. 18, 312) ***a double drachma, two-drachma piece*** (two δ.=1 stater) monetary unit of the Aegean, Corinthian, Persian, and Ital.-Sic. coinage system; a coin worth two Attic drachmas, but no longer in circulation in NT times; it was about equal to a half shekel (two days' wage) among the Jews, and was the sum required of each person annually as the temple tax; even though this tax was paid with other coins, the amount was termed a δ. **Mt 17:24** (also Mel., P. 86, 649; a διδραχμία as a gift for the temple of the god Suchos: Mitt-Wilck. I/2, 289, 9 [125 BC]; BGU 748 [I AD].—Schürer II 62–65, 271–72; Mitt-Wilck. I/2, p. 85f; Dssm., LO 229 [LAE 269]). On the pl. in **Mt 17:24,**

s. MBlack, BRigaux Festschr. '70, 60–62. S. also on ἀργύριον end.—S. SEG XLII, 1822 on economics of cult in the ancient world. IDB III 428. M-M.

Δίδυμος, ου, ὁ ***Didymus*** (as a name e.g. OGI 519, 8; 736, 27; SEG XLI, 1648; IKourion 139, 12; 29; POxy 243, 4 and 46; 251, 1; 255, 2; 263, 8 al.; PFay 16), lit. *twin,* Greek name of the apostle Thomas (תאמ=twin) **J 11:16; 20:24; 21:2.**—M-M.

δίδωμι (Hom.+) by-form διδῶ (B-D-F §94, 1; Rob. 311f) **Rv 3:9** (δίδω Tregelles, δίδωμι v.l.), 3 sg. διδοῖ (GrBar 7:2), 3 pl. διδόασι; impf. 3 sg. ἐδίδου, ἐδίδει (Hs 6, 2, 7; cp. **Mk 4:8** cod. W), 3 pl. ἐδίδουν, ἐδίδοσαν **J 19:3;** ptc. διδῶν (Hs 8, 3, 3); fut. δώσω; 1 aor. ἔδωκα, subj. 3 sg. δώσῃ **J 17:2; Rv 8:3 v.l.** (on this W-S.§14, 9; B-D-F §95, 1; Rob. 308f), 1 pl. δώσωμεν **Mk 6:37 v.l.,** 3 pl. δώσωσιν **Rv 4:9 v.l.;** pf. δέδωκα; plpf. ἐδεδώκειν (and without augm. δεδώκειν **Mk 14:44; Lk 19:15; J 11:57**); 2 aor. subj. 3 sg. δῷ **J 15:16** (δώῃ v.l.); also in the form δώῃ **Eph 1:17; 2 Ti 2:25** (in both δῷ as v.l.): in all these cases read δώῃ subj., not δῴη opt., s. below; δοῖ **Mk 8:37** (B-D-F §95, 2; Mlt. 55; Rdm.[2] 97f and Glotta 7, 1916, 21ff; GKilpatrick in Festschrift JSchmid '63, 135), pl. δῶμεν, δῶτε, δῶσιν; 2 aor. opt. 3 sg. Hellenist. (also LXX) δῴη for δοίη **Ro 15:5; 2 Th 3:16; 2 Ti 1:16, 18** (on **Eph 1:17; 2 Ti 2:25** s. above); 2 aor. impv. δός, δότε, inf. δοῦναι, ptc. δούς; pf. δέδωκα LXX. Pass.: 1 fut. δοθήσομαι (W-S. §14, 8ff); 1 aor. ἐδόθην; pf. δέδομαι.

❶ **to give as an expression of generosity,** ***give, donate*** as a gen. principle: μακάριόν ἐστιν μᾶλλον διδόναι ἢ λαμβάνειν *it is more blessed to give than to receive* **Ac 20:35** (Theophyl. Sim., Ep. 42 τὸ διδόναι ἢ τὸ λαβεῖν οἰκειότερον); cp. 1 Cl 2:1; Hm 2:4ff (the contrast δίδωμι . . . λαμβάνω is frequently found: Epicharmus, fgm. 273 Kaibel; Com. Fgm. Adesp. 108, 4 K.; Maximus Tyr. 32, 10c ὀλίγα δούς, μεγάλα ἔλαβες; Sir 14:16; Tat. 29, 2).—On the logion **Ac 20:35** s. Unknown Sayings 77–81: *giving is blessed, not receiving* (cp. EHaenchen on Ac 20:35; Aristot., EN 4, 3, 26; Plut., Mor. 173d). S. μᾶλλον 3c. δὸς τοῖς πτωχοῖς *give to the poor* **Mt 19:21** (HvonCampenhausen, Tradition u. Leben '60, 114–56). τινὶ ἔκ τινος *give someone some* (of a substance: Tob 4:16; Ezk 48:12) **Mt 25:8.** S. also **7:11; 14:7.**

❷ **to give someth. out,** ***give, bestow, grant*** δ. δακτύλιον εἰς τὴν χεῖρα *put a ring on the finger* **Lk 15:22** (cp. Esth 3:10—δίδωμί τι εἰς τ. χεῖρα also Aristoph., Nub. 506; Herodas 3, 70). *give* τινί τι *someth. to someone* τὸ ἅγιον τοῖς κυσίν **Mt 7:6** (Ps.-Lucian, Asin. 33 τὰ ἔγκατα τοῖς κυσὶ δότε).—A certificate of divorce to one's wife **5:31** (Dt 24:1; conversely of the wife Just., A II, 2, 6 ῥεπούδιον δοῦσα); without dat. **19:7.** Of bread (w. dat. or acc. somet. to be supplied fr. the context) **26:26f; Mk 2:26; 14:22; Lk 6:4; 11:7f; 22:19; J 21:13** (difft. **Mt 14:19; 15:36; Mk 6:41; 8:6** the disciples transfer to others what they have received). W. inf. foll. δ. τινὶ φαγεῖν *give someone someth. to eat* **Mt 14:16; 25:35, 42; Mk 5:43; 6:37; J 6:31** al. (cp. Gen 28:20; Ex 16:8, 15; Lev 10:17); *someth. to drink* **Mt 27:34; Mk 15:23; J 4:7; Rv 16:6** (Hdt. 4, 172, 4; Aristoph., Pax 49; Jos., Ant. 2, 64; schol. on Nicander, Alexiph. 146 δὸς πιεῖν τί τινι, without dat. 198; PGM 13, 320 δὸς πεῖν[=πιεῖν]; Jos., Ant. 2, 64).—τὰς ῥάβδους GJs 9:1.—**Lk 15:29** (Hipponax 43 Deg.).

❸ **to express devotion,** ***give*** δόξαν δ. θεῷ *give God the glory,* i.e. *praise, honor, thanks* (Josh 7:19; Ps 67:35; 1 Esdr 9:8; 2 Ch 30:8 and oft.) **Lk 17:18; J 9:24** (practically=promise under oath to tell the truth); **Ac 12:23** al. δόξαν καὶ τιμήν (2 Ch 32:33) *give glory and honor* **Rv 4:9.** Through a sacrificial offering θυσίαν δ. *bring an offering* **Lk 2:24** (cp. Jos., Ant. 7, 196 θυσίαν ἀποδοῦναι τ. θεῷ).

❹ **to cause to happen, esp. in ref. to physical phenomena,** ***produce, make, cause, give*** fig. extension of mng. 1 ὑετὸν δ. (3 Km 17:14; Job 5:10; Zech 10:1; PsSol 5:9) *yield rain* **Js 5:18;** *send rain* **Ac 14:17.** τέρατα *cause wonders to appear* **Ac 2:19** (Jo 3:3). Of heavenly bodies φέγγος δ. *give light, shine* **Mt 24:29; Mk 13:24** (cp. Is 13:10). Of a musical instrument φωνὴν δ. (cp. Ps 17:14; 103:12; Jdth 14:9; Pind., N. 5, 50b [93]) *produce a sound* **1 Cor 14:7f.**

❺ **to put someth. in care of another,** ***entrust***—ⓐ of things *entrust* τινί τι *someth. to someone* money **Mt 25:15; Lk 19:13, 15;** the keys of the kgdm. **Mt 16:19;** perh. **Lk 12:48.** W. εἰς τὰς χεῖρας added **J 13:3** (cp. Gen 39:8; Is 22:21; 29:12 al.) or ἐν τῇ χειρί τινος **3:35** (cp. Jdth 9:9; Da 1:2; 7:25 Theod.; 1 Macc 2:7). Of spiritual things **J 17:8, 14; Ac 7:38.**

ⓑ of pers. τινά τινι *entrust someone to another's care* **J 6:37, 39; 17:6, 9, 12, 24; Hb 2:13** (Is 8:18).

❻ **to engage in a financial transaction**—ⓐ of payment ***pay, give*** τινί τι **Mt 20:4; 26:15; 28:12; Mk 14:11; Lk 22:5; Rv 11:18.** Fig. *repay* someone (Mélanges Nicole, var. contributors, JNicole Festschr. 1905, p. 246 [HvanHerwerden=PLips 40 III, 3 p. 129] λίθῳ δέδωκεν τῷ υἱῷ μου; Ps 27:4) **Rv 2:23.** Of taxes, tribute, rent, etc. τινὶ ἀπό τινος *pay rent of someth.* **Lk 20:10** (cp. 1 Esdr 6:28). τὶ *pay (up), give someth.* **Mt 16:26; 27:10; Mk 8:37;** δ. κῆνσον, φόρον καίσαρι *pay tax to the emperor* (Jos., Bell. 2, 403) **Mt 22:17; Mk 12:14; Lk 20:22.** Of inheritance *pay out* a portion of property **Lk 15:12.**

ⓑ as commercial t.t. for bookkeeping λόγον δ. ***render account*** (POxy 1281, 9 [21 AD]; PStras 32, 9 δότω λόγον; cp. Phil 4:15) **Ro 14:12.**

ⓒ of a bank deposit, equivalent to τιθέναι ***put, place, deposit*** ἀργύριον ἐπὶ τράπεζαν *put money in the bank* **Lk 19:23.**

❼ **appoint to special responsibility,** ***appoint*** (Num 14:4) κριτάς *judges* **Ac 13:20;** w. double acc. *appoint someone someth.* (PLille 28, II [III BC] αὐτοῖς ἐδώκαμεν μεσίτην Δωρίωνα) τοὺς μὲν ἀποστόλους *some* (to be) *apostles* **Eph 4:11.** τινὰ κεφαλήν *make someone head* **1:22.** Also δ. τινὰ εἴς τι B 14:7 (Is 42:6).

❽ **to cause someth. to happen,** ***give*** (Philo, Leg. All. 3, 106 δ. χρόνον εἰς μετάνοιαν) δ. γνῶσιν σωτηρίας=*to give (his people) knowledge of salvation = to tell (his people) how to be saved* **Lk 1:77.**

❾ **to bear as a natural product,** ***yield, produce*** of a field and its crops καρπὸν δ. *yield fruit* (Ps 1:3) **Mt 13:8; Mk 4:7f;** fig. ἔδωκεν μοὶ Κύριος καρπὸν δικαιοσύνης αὐτοῦ GJs 6:3 (Pr 11:30).

❿ **to dedicate oneself for some purpose or cause,** ***give up, sacrifice*** τὸ σῶμά μου τὸ ὑπὲρ ὑμῶν διδόμενον *my body, given up for you* **Lk 22:19** (cp. Thu. 2, 43, 2; Libanius, Declam. 24, 23 Förster οἱ ἐν Πύλαις ὑπὲρ ἐλευθερίας τ. Ἑλλήνων δεδωκότες τὰ σώματα; of Menas δ. ἀπροφασίστως ἑαυτόν 'gave of himself unstintingly' OGI 339, 19f; Danker, Benefactor 321–23; for use of δ. in a testamentary context cp. Diog. L. 5, 72); ἑαυτὸν (τὴν ψυχὴν) δ. *give oneself up, sacrifice oneself* (ref. in Nägeli 56; 1 Macc 6:44; 2:50) w. dat. **2 Cor 8:5.** λύτρον ἀντι πολλῶν *give oneself up as a ransom for many* **Mt 20:28; Mk 10:45** (ἀντί 3). Also ἀντίλυτρον ὑπέρ τινος **1 Ti 2:6.** ὑπέρ τινος *for* or *because of a person* or *thing* **J 10:15 v.l.; Gal 1:4; Tit 2:14;** AcPl Ha 8, 24 (on the form of these passages s. KRomaniuk, NovT 5, '62, 55–76). ἑαυτὸν δ. τῷ θανάτῳ ISm 4:2 (cp. Just., A I, 21, 2 πυρί); δ. ἑαυτὸν εἰς τὸ θηρίον *face the beast* Hv 4, 1, 8.

⓫ **to cause (oneself) to go,** ***go, venture somewhere*** (cp. our older 'betake oneself') (Polyb. 5, 14, 9; Diod. S. 5, 59, 4; 14, 81,

2; Jos., Ant. 7, 225; 15, 244) εἰς τὸ θέατρον **Ac 19:31;** εἰς τὴν ἔρημον GJs 1:4.

⑫ **to use an oracular device, *draw/cast lots* Ac 1:26.**

⑬ **to grant by formal action, *grant, allow,*** freq. of God (cp. 7 above) ἐξουσίαν δ. (Hippol., Ref. 5, 26, 21 *grant someone the power* or *authority, give someone the right,* etc. (cp. TestJob 20:3; Jos., Ant. 2, 90, Vi. 71) **Mt 9:8; 28:18; 2 Cor 13:10; Rv 9:3;** 1 Cl 61:1; τοῦ πατεῖν ἐπάνω τινός *tread* on *someth.* **Lk 10:19.** τὴν σοφίαν τοῦ γράψαι τὴν ἱστορίαν ταύτην *the ability to write this account* GJs 25:1. ἔδωκεν αὐτοῖς δύναμιν καὶ ἐξουσίαν ἐπί **Lk 9:1** (cp. Just., D. 30, 3 ἔδωκεν αὐτῷ δύναμιν). ταῦτά σοι πάντα δώσω i.e. put them under your control **Mt 4:9** of the devil. Simple δ. w. inf. (Appian, Liby. 19 §78 ἢν [=ἐὰν] ὁ θεὸς δῷ ἐπικρατῆσαι 106 §499) δέδοται *it is given, granted* to someone γνῶναι τὰ μυστήρια *to know the secrets* **Mt 13:11;** cp. ἡ δοθεῖσα αὐτῷ γνῶσις B 9:8 (Just., D. 7, 3 εἰ μή τῳ θεός δῷ συνιέναι) ἔδωκεν ζωὴν ἔχειν *he has granted (the privilege) of having life* **J 5:26.** μετὰ παρρησίας λαλεῖν *to speak courageously* **Ac 4:29** and oft. Rather freq. the inf. is to be supplied fr. the context (Himerius, Or. 38 [4], 8 εἰ θεὸς διδοίη=if God permits) οἷς δέδοται sc. χωρεῖν **Mt 19:11.** ἦν δεδομένον σοι sc. ἐξουσίαν ἔχειν **J 19:11.** W. acc. and inf. foll. (Appian, Mithrid. 11, §37; Heliodorus 5, 12, 2 δώσεις με πιστεύειν) οὐδὲ δώσεις τὸν ὅσιόν σου ἰδεῖν διαφθοράν *you will not permit your holy one to see corruption* **Ac 2:27; 13:35** (both Ps 15:10). ἔδωκεν αὐτὸν ἐμφανῆ γενέσθαι *granted that he should be plainly seen* **10:40.** δὸς … ῥαγῆναι τὰ δέσμα *grant that our chains be broken* AcPl Ha 3,11f. Pregnant constr.: *grant, order* (Diod. S. 9, 12, 2 διδ. λαβεῖν=permit to; 19, 85, 3 τὶ=someth.; Appian, Bell. Civ. 4, 125 §524 ὁ καιρὸς ἐδίδου=the opportunity permitted; Biogr. p. 130 ἐδίδου θάπτειν τ. ἄνδρα) ἐδόθη αὐτοῖς ἵνα μὴ ἀποκτείνωσιν *orders were given them not to kill* **Rv 9:5;** cp. **19:8.**—Of an oath w. double inf. **Lk 1:73f.** S. also 17 below.

⑭ **to cause to come into being, *institute*** περιτομὴν δ. *institute circumcision* B 9:7.

⑮ **give up, someth. that has been under one's control for a relatively long time, *give up, give back*** ἡ θάλασσα τ. νεκρούς *the sea gave up its dead* **Rv 20:13.**

⑯ **to proffer someth., *extend, offer*** χεῖρα *hold out one's hand (to someone)* **Ac 9:41** (cp. 1 Macc 6:58; 2 Macc 12:11; Jos., Bell. 6, 318). (τὸν) μαστὸν τῇ παιδὶ GJs 5:2; 6:3.

⑰ In many phrases this word relates to an activity or an abstract object, and with tr. freq. determined by the noun object; cp. 13 above.

ⓐ of humans: of a plan conceived in a meeting ***give*** counsel or advice: δ. for ποιεῖν (cp. κατά A2b β and s. s.v. συμβούλιον), which is read by some mss., in συμβούλιον δ. *conspired (against Jesus)* **Mk 3:6.** ἀφορμὴν δ. *give an occasion* (for someth.) **2 Cor 5:12;** Hm 4, 1, 11; μαρτυρίαν δ. *give testimony* 1 Cl 30:7; δ. τὸ μαρτύριον *bear witness* AcPl Ha 4, 28; γνώμην δ. *give an* opinion **1 Cor 7:25; 2 Cor 8:10;** ἐγκοπὴν δ. *cause a hindrance* **1 Cor 9:12;** ἐντολὴν δ. *command, order* **J 11:57; 12:49; 1J 3:23;** ἐντολὴν καινὴν δ. *give a new commandment* **J 13:34;** εὔσημον λόγον δ. *speak plainly* or *intelligibly* **1 Cor 14:9;** παραγγελίαν δ. *give an instruction* **1 Th 4:2;** δ. τὴν ἐν [κυρίῳ σφραγίδα] *seal in the Lord* AcPl Ha 11, 23 (restored after the Coptic); προσκοπὴν δ. *put an obstacle in (someone's) way* **2 Cor 6:3;** δ. ἐκδίκησιν *take vengeance* **2 Th 1:8;** ῥάπισμα δ. τινί *slap someone* **J 18:22; 19:3;** σημεῖον δ. *give a sign* **Mt 26:48;** τόπον δ. τινί *make room for someone* (Plut., Gai. Gracch. 840 [13, 3]) **Lk 14:9;** fig. *leave room for* **Ro 12:19** (cp. τόπος 4); **Eph 4:27.** ὑπόδειγμα δ. *give an example* **J 13:15;** φίλημα δ. τινί *give someone a kiss* **Lk 7:45.**—δὸς ἐργασίαν **Lk 12:58** is prob. a Latinism=da operam *take pains, make an effort* (B-D-F §5, 3b note 9; Rob. 109), which nevertheless penetrated the popular speech (OGI 441, 109 [senatorial decree 81 BC]; POxy 742, 11 [colloq. letter 2 BC] δὸς ἐργασίαν; PMich 203, 7; 466, 33f [Trajan]; PGiss 11, 16 [118 AD]; PBrem 5, 8 [117/119 AD]).

ⓑ esp. oft. of God (Hom. et al.) and Christ: *give, grant, impose* (of punishments etc.), *send,* of gifts, peace τινί τι **Eph 4:8;** 1 Cl 60:4; τινί τινος *give someone some of a thing* **Rv 2:17.** Also τινὶ ἔκ τινος **1J 4:13.** τὶ εἴς τινα **1 Th 4:8** (Ezk 37:14); εἰς τὰς καρδίας *put into the hearts* **Rv 17:17** (cp. X., Cyr. 8, 2, 20 δ. τινί τι εἰς ψυχήν). Also ἐν τ. καρδίαις δ. (cp. ἐν 3) **2 Cor 1:22; 8:16** (cp. Ezk 36:27). εἰς τὴν διάνοιαν **Hb 8:10** (Jer 38: 33); ἐπὶ καρδίας **Hb 10:16** (δ. ἐπί w. acc. as Jer 6:21, and s. Jer 38:33 ἐπὶ καρδίας αὐτῶν γράψω). W. ἵνα foll. *grant that* **Mk 10:37.**—The pass. occurs very oft. in this sense (Plut., Mor. 265d; 277e) **Lk 8:10; Rv 6:4; 7:2; 13:7, 14f** and oft. ἐκδίκησιν διδόναι τινί *inflict punishment on someone* **2 Th 1:8;** βασανισμὸν καὶ πένθος δ. τινί *send torment and grief upon someone* **Rv 18:7;** ὄνομα δ. GJs 6:2, χάριν δ. (Jos., Bell. 7, 325) **Js 4:6; 1 Pt 5:5** (both Pr 3:34); GJs 14:2; υἱοθεσίαν AcPl Ha 2, 28; 9,12; ἄφεσιν ἁμαρτιῶν 2, 30f; μεγαλεῖα 6,13. W. gen. foll. *over someone* **Mt 10:1; Mk 6:7; J 17:2.**—B. 749. Schmidt, Syn. 193–203. DELG. M-M. TW.

διέβην s. διαβαίνω.

διεγείρω 1 aor. διήγειρα; pass. impf. διηγειρόμην or διεγειρόμην (B-D-F §67, 2); 1 aor. διηγέρθην (s. ἐγείρω; Hippocr. et al.; UPZ 81, 3, 12 [II BC]; PTebt 804, 15; PGM 13, 279; LXX; TestSol; TestJob 14:2; Test12Patr) ***wake up, arouse*** someone who is asleep (Teles p. 18, 3; Polyb. 12, 26, 1; 3 Macc 5:15; Jos., Ant. 8, 349) **Mk 4:38 v.l.; Lk 8:24.** Pass. *awaken* (Esth 1:11; Philo, Vi. Cont. 89; Jos., Ant. 2, 82 ἐκ τ. ὕπνου) **Mt 1:24 v.l.; Mk 4:39; Ac 16:10** D. Fig. (the pass. of the rekindling of a battle: Quint. Smyrn. 3, 20) of a calm sea: διηγείρετο *was becoming aroused* **J 6:18.** Act. fig. *arouse, stir up* w. acc. (2 Macc 7:21; 15:10; Jos., Bell. 2, 181 τὰς ἐπιθυμίας; TestDan 4:2 τ. ψυχήν) ἐν ὑπομνήσει *by way of a reminder* **2 Pt 1:13; 3:1.** DELG s.v. ἐγείρω.—M-M.

διεγρηγορέω (not found elsewhere; s. γρηγορέω) ***be awake*** P[45] the ptc. διεγρηγορήσαντες **Lk 9:32.**—JBirdsall, JTS 14, '63, 390f.

διεῖλον s. διαιρέω.

διελαύνω (s. ἐλαύνω; trans. Hom. et al.; Judg 4:21 A; 5:26 A [both aor. 3 sg. διήλασεν]; intr. X et al.; Jos., Bell. 1, 100 ['march across']) ***proceed*** mid. in a suspect passage *completed its course* or *began to proceed again, pushed on,* πάντα … διηλαύνετο GJs 18:3 v.l. (for ἀπηλαύνετο).—DELG s.v. ἐλαύνω.

διελέγχω 1 aor. pass. διηλέγχθην; 1 fut. διελεγχθήσεται Mi 6:2 (Pla. et al.; Appian, Bell. Civ. 3, 54 §224; pap; Philo, Spec. Leg. 1, 64; Jos., C. Ap. 2, 149; var. 'prove wrong, convict') in our lit., only pass. ***engage in dispute,*** *let us debate, argue* διελεγχθῶμεν 1 Cl 8:4 (Is 1:18).—DELG s.v. ἐλέγχω.

διελέχθην s. διαλέγομαι.

διέλκω (Pla. et al.; pap, e.g. UPZ 145, 7; PTebt 711, 8 [both II BC]; BGU 1116, 21; 1120, 35 [I BC]; 'to tear asunder, open wide') **to divide (into factions), *rend, tear apart*** (w. διασπάω) the members of Christ 1 Cl 46:7.—DELG s.v. ἕλκω.

διενέγκω s. διαφέρω.

διενθυμέομαι (only in Christian wr.; s. ἐνθυμέομαι) **to give serious thought to someth.,** ***ponder*** περὶ τοῦ ὁράματος *on the vision* **Ac 10:19.** S. θυμός.

διεξέρχομαι fut. 2 sg. διεξελεύσῃ Ezk 12:5; 2 aor. διεξῆλθον (Soph., Hdt.+; SIG ind.; pap, e.g. PStras 92, 12; 15 [III BC]; PLond III, 977, 15 [330 AD] p. 232) ***come out*** **Ac 28:3 v.l.**—M-M.

διέξοδος, ου, ἡ (s. ἔξοδος; Hdt. et al.; Vett. Val. 334, 16; LXX; TestJud 6:2; EpArist 105; Philo, Joseph.) δ. τῶν ὁδῶν **Mt 22:9** is somet. taken to mean 'street-crossing', but is prob. **the place where a main street cuts (through) the city boundary and goes (out) into the open country,** ***outlet, way out of town*** (Diod. S. 17, 12, 5 ἐν ταῖς διεξόδοις καὶ τάφροις=among the street-ends and the trenches; Eutecnius 3 p. 35, 33 outlet fr. a fox-hole; Num 34:4f; Josh 15:4, 7 al.; Jos., Ant. 12, 346. In pap of the 'conclusion' of legal proceedings PEnteux 54, 11f; 65, 6; PTebt 762, 8 [all III BC].—On the beggars at street-crossings cp. Lucian, Necyom. 17). Corresp. δ. τῶν ὑδάτων, the point where a stream of water flowing underground suddenly breaks *through* and flows *out* freely, *a spring* (Hesychius Miles.: 390 fgm. 1, 3 Jac [=FGrH IV p. 147 Müller: διέξοδοι of two rivers]; 4 Km 2:21) B 11:6 (Ps 1:3).—DELG s.v. ὁδός. M-M. TW.

διέπω (Hom. et al.; ins, pap; Wsd 9:3; 12:15; Jos., C. Ap. 2, 294; SibOr 3, 360) **to be in charge of or direct someth.,** ***conduct, administer*** τὴν ἡγεμονίαν (as OGI 614, 4; cp. 519, 24) 1 Cl 61:1f; τὴν ἐπαρχικὴν ἐξουσίαν δ. (s. ἐπαρχικός) Phlm subscr.; τὰ ἐπίγεια *manage earthly things* Dg 7:2.—DELG s.v. ἕπω.

διερμηνεία, ας, ἡ (not found elsewh.; s. ἑρμηνεία) ***explanation, interpretation, translation*** **1 Cor 12:10 v.l.** (s. next two entries).—DELG s.v. ἑρμηνεύς. TW.

διερμηνευτής, οῦ, ὁ (s. prec. entry; does not occur again until the Byz. gramm. Eustath., Ad Il. p. 106, 14; Nägeli 50) ***interpreter, translator*** of ecstatic speech **1 Cor 14:28** (s. ἑρμηνευτής).—M-M. TW. Spicq.

διερμηνεύω 1 aor. διερμήνευσα (B-D-F §67, 2)—❶ **to translate from one language to another,** ***translate*** (Polyb. 3, 22, 3; UPZ 162 V, 4 [117 BC]; 2 Macc 1:36; EpArist 15, 308; 310; Philo, Poster. Cai. 1, Deus Imm. 144, Migr. Abr. 12; 73) Ταβιθά, ἣ διερμηνευομένη λέγεται Δορκάς *T. which, translated, means Dorcas* [=gazelle] **Ac 9:36.**

❷ **to clarify someth. so as to make it understandable,** ***explain, interpret*** (Philod., Rhet. I 84 S. as διερμηνεῖσθαι; Philo, Op. M. 31; GrBar 11:7) τὶ *someth.* ecstatic speech **1 Cor 12:30; 14:5, 13, 27** (mng. 1 is also prob. here); the mng. of prophecies **Lk 24:27.** Pass., of the holy scriptures **Ac 18:6** D.—DELG s.v. ἑρμηνεύς. M-M. TW. Spicq.

διέρχομαι impf. διηρχόμην; fut. διελεύσομαι; 2 aor. διῆλθον; pf. διελήλυθα, διεληλυθώς, inf. διεληλυθέναι (Just., D. 86, 2 [on διέβην Gen. 32:11]), ptc. διεληλυθώς **Hb 4:14** (Hom. et al.; ins, pap, LXX, TestSol; TestAbr A 10 p. 87, 28 [Stone p. 22]; TestJud 7:7; ParJer 7:13; GrBar.; ApcEsdr 2:18 p. 26, 10 Tdf.; EpArist 131; Philo, Joseph.).

❶ **to move within or through an area,** ***go (through)***—ⓐ to travel or move about *go about fr. place to place, spread* δ. κατὰ τὰς κώμας *go about among the villages* **Lk 9:6; Ac 10:38.** W. ἐν (Sir 39:4; 1 Macc 3:8): ἐν οἷς διῆλθον κηρύσσων *among whom I went about proclaiming* **Ac 20:25.** Abs. διασπαρέντες διῆλθον *they were scattered and went about fr. place to place* **8:4;** Paul at Athens **17:23.** Fig. of a report διήρχετο μᾶλλον ὁ λόγος *spread even farther* **Lk 5:15** (cp. Thu. 6, 46, 5; X., An. 1, 4, 7 διῆλθε λόγος; Jos., Vi. 182).—W. acc. of place (EpArist 301; Jos., Bell. 2, 67) an island **Ac 13:6.** τὰ ἀνωτερικὰ μέρη *the interior* **19:1;** regions **20:2.**

ⓑ of movement through someth. *go through*—**α.** w. the force of διά retained: *go* or *travel through* w. acc. of place names (Diod. S. 16, 44, 4 τὴν Συρίαν; Jos., Ant. 14, 40) Jericho **Lk 19:1;** Pisidia **Ac 14:24;** cp. **15:3, 41; 16:6; 18:23; 19:21; 1 Cor 16:5.**—τοὺς οὐρανούς *go through the heavens* **Hb 4:14.** W. prep. δ. διά τινος *go through someth.* (Hdt. 6:31, 2 al.; Philo; SibOr 2, 253) through deserts (cp. Jos., Ant. 15, 200 τὴν ἄνυδρον δ.) **Mt 12:43; Lk 11:24;** through a gate Hs 9, 13, 6; διὰ μέσον Σαμαρίας καὶ Γαλιλαίας prob. *through the region between Samaria and Galilee* **Lk 17:11** (s. διά B1) cp. **J 4:4;** through all the places **Ac 9:32;** through the sea **1 Cor 10:1;** δι' ὑμῶν εἰς Μακεδονίαν *through your city to M.* **2 Cor 1:16;** through a person GJs 6:1 κοινὸν καὶ ἀκάθαρτον οὐκ εἴα διέρχεσθαι δι' αὐτῆς (Anna) *did not permit anything common or unclean to pass through (Mary)* (of food, perh. also fig. of thoughts, cp. Mt 15:17f; Mk 7:19ff).

β. of movement toward a destination *come, go:* εἴς τινα of death: to all people **Ro 5:12.** εἴς τι (Jos., Ant. 14, 414) of journeys: *go over, cross over* εἰς τὸ πέραν *to the other side* **Mk 4:35; Lk 8:22;** cp. **Ac 18:27.** εἰς τὸ πεδίον *go off into the country* 1 Cl 4:6 (Gen 4:8). διέλθε[τε διὰ τῶν] ἀφανῶν κα[ὶ εἰ]ς τ̣ὸ̣ [τέλο]ς (or: τ̣ε̣[λο]ς) τῶν φαινο[μέ]νων *come out of the realm of the latent and to the end of the things that are apparent:* rev. of Ox 1081, 27–30 based on the Coptic of SJCh 90, 4–7 (Till). Also ἕως τινός (1 Macc 1:3): ἕως Βηθλέεμ *to B.* **Lk 2:15;** ἕως Φοινίκης **Ac 11:19, 22 v.l.;** ἕως ἡμῶν **9:38.** ἐνθάδε *come here* **J 4:15.**—δ. ἀπὸ τῆς Πέργης *they went on fr. Perga* **Ac 13:14.** Abs. ἐκείνης (sc. ὁδοῦ) ἤμελλεν διέρχεσθαι *he was to come through that way* **Lk 19:4;** διερχόμενος *as he went through* **Ac 8:40**

❷ **go through someth. in one's mind,** ***review*** (Hom. Hymn Ven. 276 δ. τι μετὰ φρεσί al.) τὰς γενεάς 1 Cl 7:5 (εἰς τ. γ. is read by some mss.).—διερχ[. . .] AcPl BMM verso 21.

❸ **to pass into or through an obstacle,** ***penetrate.*** Of a sword (cp. Il. 20, 263; 23, 876; Jdth 6:6; 16:9) δ. τὴν ψυχήν *pierces the soul* **Lk 2:35** (cp. SibOr 3, 316); *pass* a guard **Ac 12:10;** through a closed room διὰ τοῦ . . . κοιτῶνος AcPl Ha 5, 31 (restored); διὰ μέσου αὐτῶν *through the midst of them* **Lk 4:30; J 8:59 v.l.;** through a needle's eye **Mt 19:24; Mk 10:25; Lk 18:25 v.l.**—Papias (3:2) ὥστε μηδὲ ὁπόθεν ἅμαξα ῥαδίως διέρχεται ἐκεῖνον δύνασθαι διέλθειν *so that he (Judas) was not able to pass through where a wagon would have no difficulty*—DELG s.v. ἔρχομαι. M-M. TW. Sv.

διερωτάω 1 aor. διηρώτησα (X., Pla. et al.; Cass. Dio 43, 10; 48, 8; Jos., Bell. 1, 234; 653) ***ask about, find by inquiry*** οἰκίαν **Ac 10:17.**—DELG s.v. ἐρέω 1.

διεσπάρην s. διασπείρω.

διεστειλάμην, διεστραμμένος s. διαστέλλω.

διέστη s. διΐστημι.

διέστραμμαι, διεστραμμένος s. διαστρέφω.

διεταράχθην s. διαταράσσω.

διετής, ές (s. next entry; Hdt. et al.; ins, pap; 2 Macc 10:3; ApcEsdr 4:11 p. 28, 12 Tdf.; Jos., Ant. 2, 74) ***two years old*** ἀπὸ διετοῦς καὶ κατωτέρω *two years old and under* **Mt 2:16**

(masc., not neut.; cp. Num 1:3, 20; 1 Ch 27:23; 2 Ch 31:16); GJs 7:1.—For διετία GJs 7:1 v.l.—DELG s.v. ἔτος. M-M.

διετία, ας, ἡ (s. prec. entry; Cleomedes [II AD] I, 3; IMagnMai 164, 12; SIG and OGI ind.; oft. pap, e.g. POxy 707, 24; BGU 180, 7; also see Preis.; Graec. Venet. Gen 41:1 and 45:5; Philo, In Flacc. 128.—Joseph. does not have δ., but ἑπταετία [Ant. 1, 302])

❶ **a span of two years,** ***two years*** διετίας πληρωθείσης *when two years had elapsed* **Ac 24:27** (on this s. Beginn. V 465f; 471 n. 1: it is difficult to establish whether δ. refers to Paul or Felix); δ. ὅλην he stayed *two full years* 28:30. For another view on these Ac pass. s. 2 below.—**Mt 2:16 D;** GJs 22:1 pap πάντα τὰ βρέφη ἀπὸ διετίας καὶ κάτω *all infants two years old and under.*

❷ **a two-year period of limitation,** ***biennium,*** legal and administrative t.t. (=Lat. biennium). It has been argued (s. Beginn. V, 326–36 [citing esp. KLake, TT 47, 1913, 356ff, on the juridical aspects of a period of limitation on capital cases; for earlier lit. on Luke's alleged legal interests s. ibid. 298, n. 4]; s. also HTajra, The Trial of St. Paul '89, 132; 193–96) that after a two-year period of limitation had run out (διετίας πληρωθείσης) Paul's case would have been dismissed. But s. above and BAFCS III 322f.—DELG s.v. ἔτος. M-M.

διευθύνω 1 aor. impv. διεύθυνον (Manetho 4, 90; Lucian, Prom. 19 'straighten me out' on the matter; pap; EpArist 188; Philo, Agr. 177; Ath. 24, 3) **to regulate the activities or course of someth.,** ***guide, direct, govern*** of various created things maintaining their assigned functions under divine control *direct* 1 Cl 20:8. τὴν βουλὴν κατὰ τὸ καλόν *direct their minds according to what is good* 61:2; εὐσεβῶς καὶ δικαίως δ. (sc. τὸν βίον) *conduct one's life in piety and righteousness=remain undeviatingly in p. and r.* 62:1.—DELG s.v. εὐθύς.

διεφθάρην, διέφθαρμαι s. διαφθείρω.

διήγειρα s. διεγείρω.

διηγέομαι fut. διηγήσομαι; 1 aor. διηγησάμην (s. two next entries; Heraclitus, Thu. et al.) **to give a detailed account of someth. in words,** ***tell, relate, describe*** τὶ *someth.* **Lk 8:39** (cp. Jos., Vi. 60). τὴν γενεὰν αὐτοῦ (γενεά 4) **Ac 8:33;** 1 Cl 16:8 (both Is 53:8). δόξαν θεοῦ 27:7 (Ps 18:2). τὰ δικαιώματα θεοῦ *recount God's ordinances* 35:7 (Ps 49:16). τινί τι (Lucian, Nigrin. 3; πάντα σοι διήγηται BGU 846, 14f [=Hunt-Edgar 120, 14f] *someth. to someone* **Mk 9:9; Lk 9:10; Ac 16:10** D; τινί **Mk 5:16;** Dg 11:2 (of explanation to an inner circle). W. indir. quest. foll. **Mk 5:16; Ac 9:27; 12:17; 16:40** D; AcPl Ant 13, 11f (=Aa I 237, 1). περί τινος *about someone* (Lucian, D. Mar. 15, 1) **Hb 11:32.**—M-M.

διήγημα, τό (Phoenicides com.; Polyb. et al.; pap, LXX, Philo, Joseph.; Tat. 21, 1; Mel., P. 40, 279; 46, 327) ***narrative, account*** AcPlTh 8 [Aa I 241, 11], used for θεώρημα (q.v.) in Ox 6, 2.—DELG s.v. ἡγέομαι.

διήγησις, εως, ἡ (s. two prec. entries; Pla.+; PSI I 85, 8; POxy 1468, 11; LXX; TestSol ins H; GrBar ins 1; EpArist 1; 8; 322; Philo; Jos., Ant. 11, 68; Tat. 30, 2; 36, 1; Thom. Mag. p. 96, 8 R. διήγησις ὅλον τὸ σύγγραμμα, διήγημα δὲ μέρος τι; Iren. 5, 28, 3 [Harv. II 402, 6]) **an orderly description of facts, events, actions, or words** ***narrative, account.*** Of Luke's Gospel **Lk 1:1** (of a historical report also Diod. S. 11, 20, 1 ἡ διήγησις ἐπὶ τὰς πράξεις; Luc., Hist. Conscrib. 55 ἅπαν γὰρ ἀτεχνῶς τὸ λοιπὸν σῶμα τῆς ἱστορίας δ. μακρά ἐστιν 'all the rest of the history is simply a lengthy narration'. Polyb. [3, 36, 1; 38, 4; 39, 1, s. Mausberger s.v.; s. also 2 Macc 2:32; 6:17; Jos., Vi. 336; EpArist 8] distinguishes the δ. from a preface or excursus. In forensic rhetoric=Lat. narratio). Of other accounts composed by apostles and their disciples: διήγησιν παρειλειφέναι θαυμασίαν ὑπὸ τῶν τοῦ Φιλίππου θυγατέρων *that (Papias) had been the recipient of a marvelous recital attributed to Philip's daughters* Papias (2:9). Ἀριστίωνας . . . τῶν τους κυρίου λόγων διηγήσεις (opp. Ἰωάννου παραδόσεις) *Aristion's recitals of the dominical words* Pa (2:14).—ἀποστολικὰς . . . δ. *apostolic treatments* (for δ. in the sense of 'discussion, presentation' see Orig., C. Cels. 1, 9, 18; Hippol., Ref. Pr. 5) of eschatology Pa (2:12).—LAlexander '93, 111. DELG s.v. ἡγέομαι. M-M. TW.

διηνεκής, ές (s. next entry; Hom. et al.; ins, pap, Philo; Jos., Ant. 16, 149) **pert. to being continuous,** ***without interruption, always*** of time εἰς τὸ δ. *for all time, without interruption* (Appian, Bell. Civ. 1, 4, §15; IG XII/1, 786, 16; pap, e.g. PRyl 427, fgm. 24; in a decree [II AD] calling for a national celebration in honor of Emperor Pertinax ὑπέρ τε τοῦ διηνεκοῦς αὐτοκρατοῦς 'for an unbroken reign' Mitt-Wilck. I/2, 490, 22=BGU 646, 22; Ps 47:15 Sym.) μένει ἱερεὺς εἰς τὸ διηνεκές *remains a priest for all time* (i.e. Melchizedek's priesthood goes on without lapse) **Hb 7:3;** an offering *good for all time* vs. **12;** pers. made perfect *for all time* vs. **14.** *constantly* (Hippocr., Ep. 17, 44; IX p. 372) **10:1** (TestJob 33:7).—DELG. M-M.

διηνεκῶς adv. (s. prec. entry; Aeschyl., Ag. 319 [Hom., Hes. διηνεκέως; Mayser 13, n. 4]; OGI 194, 12; 544, 19; PGM 4, 1219; LXX; Philo, Sacr. Abel. 94) adv. fr. διηνεκής ***continually, without lapse*** 1 Cl 24:1.—M-M. s.v. διηνεκής.

διθάλασσος, ον (s. θάλασσα; Strabo 1, 1, 8; 2, 5, 22; Dio Chrys. 5, 9 [in the Syrtis]; Dionys. Perieget. 156; SibOr 5, 334) 'with the sea on both sides'. τόπος δ. **Ac 27:41** is a semantic unit signifying **a point** (of land jutting out with water on both sides); s. Warnecke, Romfahrt 86–90; for other explanations s. Breusing 202 'a reef', based on Strabo 1, 1, 8; 'sandbank' AWeiser, Die Apostelgesch. '85, 658 and 665, so also JRoloff, Die Apostelgesch. '81, 357; 'canal' JSmith, The Voyage and Shipwreck of St. Paul[4] 1880, 143; sim. HBalmer, D. Romfahrt des Ap. Pls 1905, 413ff; 'a small strait' FBrannigan, ThGl 25, '33, 186. L-S-J-M 'headland'; REB 'cross-currents'. S. Haenchen ad loc.; for critique of H. and others s. Warnecke, loc. cit.

διϊκνέομαι intr. (Thu. et al.; Ex 26:28) **to move through a three-dimensional space,** ***pierce, penetrate*** **Hb 4:12** (Jos., Ant. 13, 96 of missiles; sim. Cornutus 31 p. 63, 22f).—DELG s.v. ἵκω.

διΐστημι fut. διαστήσεις Ezk 5:1; 1 aor. (διέστησα), ptc. διαστήσας; 2 aor. διέστην, ptc. διαστάς; pf. 3 pl. διεστᾶσι (Ath. 15, 1); ptc. διεστηκώς Esth. 8:13 'separate, divide'.

❶ **to move from, separate from, or take leave of,** ***go away, part*** intr. (2 aor.) (Hom. et al.; pap; 3 Macc 2:32; Philo, Aet. M. 75; Jos., Ant. 18, 136) ἀπό τινος (Herm. Wr. 14, 5) *fr. someone* **Lk 24:51.**

❷ **to cause separation through movement,** ***go on*** trans. (1 aor.—Appian, Iber. 36 §144 διαστῆσαι τὸ πλῆθος=divide the crowd; Sir 28:14 of pers. driven from place to place by malicious gossip; PGM 13, 476 διέστησεν τὰ πάντα; 4, 1150; Jos., Ant. 13, 305) βραχὺ διαστήσαντες (cp. Hippiatr. I 388, 5) *after they had sailed a short distance farther* **Ac 27:28** (FBlass, Acta Apost.

1895, 279 equates: βραχὺ διάστημα ποιήσαντες *after a short distance*).

❸ **to mark the passage of time,** ***pass*** intr. (2 aor.) διαστάσης ὡσεὶ ὥρας μιᾶς *after about an hour had passed* **Lk 22:59.**—DELG s.v. ἵστημι. M-M.

διϊστορέω (Philod., Rhet. II 150 fgm. 6 S.) ***examine carefully*** **Ac 17:23** D (first hand) for ἀναθεωρῶν.—DELG s.v. οἶδα

διϊσχυρίζομαι impf. διϊσχυριζόμην **to be emphatic or resolute about someth.,** ***insist, maintain firmly*** (so since Lysias, Isaeus, Pla.; Aelian, HA 7, 18; Cass. Dio 57, 23; PMich XIII, 659, 14 [VI AD]; Jos., Ant. 17, 336; Just., A I, 68, 8 [Hadrian]) **Lk 22:59; Ac 15:2** D. W. inf. foll. (Jos., Ant. 2, 106) **Ac 12:15.**—New Docs 2, 81.—DELG s.v. ἰσχύς.

δικάζω fut. δικάσω; 1 aor. 2 sg. ἐδίκασας La 3:58, mid. impv. 3 sg. δικασάσθω Judg 6:32; 1 fut. pass. δικασθήσομαι (Hom.+; Maximus Tyr. 3, 81 δ. θεός; pap; SEG XLIII, 850, 11, 986, 8 [both II BC]; LXX; TestAbr A 10 p. 87, 25 [Stone p. 22]; ApcEsdr [mid. 'press a suit, go to law with']; Ps.-Phocyl. 11; Philo; Jos., C. Ap. 2, 207; SibOr 4, 183; Tat. 6:1; Ath.) ***judge, condemn*** w. neg. (opp. δίκην τίνειν) Hm 2:5; **Lk 6:37 v.l.** (for κατα-, q.v.)—Schmidt, Syn. I 348–60. M-M. DELG s.v. δίκη.

δικαιοκρισία, ας, ἡ (POxy 71, I, 4; 904, 2; PMich 426, 5f; PVindBosw 4, 6; PFlor 88, 26; Sb 7205, 3; TestLevi 3:2; 15:2; Quinta in Origen's Hexapla Hos 6:5.—δικαιοκρίτης of God: SibOr 3, 704) ***just/fair verdict*** **Ro 2:5** ('fair' because of the criterion: 'according to each one's performance'); **2 Th 1:5 v.l.**—DELG s.v. δίκη. M-M. TW.

δικαιοπραγία, ας, ἡ (Aristot. et al.; schol. on Pla. 107e; PCairMasp 2, 1; 3, 6 [both VI AD]; TestDan 1:3; -ξία Just.) ***righteous action*** 1 Cl 32:3.—DELG s.v. πράσσω.

δίκαιος, αία, ον (s. δικαιοσύνη; Hom.+; loanw. in rabb.)

❶ **pert. to being in accordance with high standards of rectitude,** ***upright, just, fair***—ⓐ of humans—α. In Gr-Rom. tradition a δ. pers. is one who upholds the customs and norms of behavior, including esp. public service, that make for a well-ordered, civilized society (Hom, Od. 6, 120f hospitality and fear of God mark an upright pers.; Dem. 3, 21 a δίκαιος πολίτης gives priority to the interest of the state). Such perspective opened a bridge to Greco-Romans for understanding of Jewish/Christian perspectives: e.g. the description of an eccl. overseer (w. σώφρων, ὅσιος) **Tit 1:8.** Both polytheistic and monotheistic societies closely associated uprightness, with special reference to behavior toward humans (cp. Pla., Rep. 4, 443; Aristot. EN 5, 1, 1129a-1130a), and piety in reference esp. to familial obligations and deity (Augustus enshrined the perspective, taking pride in being awarded a crown for his δικαιοσύνη and εὐσέβεια Res Gestae 34). In keeping with OT tradition, NT writers emphasize a connection between upright conduct and sense of responsibility to God; δ. like צַדִּיק=conforming to the laws of God and people. General definition ὁ ποιῶν τὴν δικαιοσύνην δ. ἐστιν *one who does what is right, is righteous* **1J 3:7;** cp. **Rv 22:11.**—**Ro 5:7.** δικαίῳ νόμος οὐ κεῖται *law does not apply to an upright person* **1 Ti 1:9.** οὐκ ἔστιν δίκαιος **Ro 3:10** (cp. Eccl 7:20); δ. παρὰ τῷ θεῷ *righteous in the sight of God* **Ro 2:13;** δ. ἐναντίον τοῦ θεοῦ (Gen 7:1; Job 32:2) **Lk 1:6.** W. φοβούμενος τὸν θεόν of Cornelius **Ac 10:22.** W. εὐλαβής (Pla., Pol. 311ab ἤθη εὐλαβῆ κ. δίκαια, τὸ δικαιον κ. εὐλαβές) **Lk 2:25.** W. ἀγαθός (Kaibel 648, 10; Jos., Ant. 8, 248; 9, 132 ἀνὴρ ἀγ. κ. δίκ.; s. ἀγαθός 2aα) **23:50;** ἀθῷος (Sus 53) 1 Cl 46:4; ὅσιος (En 103:9) 2 Cl 15:3; ταπεινός B 19:6. (ὡς δίκαιον καὶ ἀναμάρτητον Just., D. 47, 5). Serving God w. a pure heart makes one δ. 2 Cl 11:1. Hence the δίκαιοι=*the just, the upright* in a specif. Israelite-Christian sense **Mt 13:43** (cp. Da 12:3 Theod.) **Lk 1:17; 1 Pt 3:12** (Ps 33:16); 1 Cl 22:6 (Ps 33:16); 33:7; 45:3f; 48:3 (Ps 117:20); 2 Cl 6:9; 17:7; 20:3f; B 11:7 (Ps 1:5f); MPol 14:1; 17:1; also of those who only appear upright (cp. Pr 21:2) **Mt 23:28; Lk 18:9; 20:20;** specifically of Christians **Mt 10:41; Ac 14:2** D; **1 Pt 4:18** (Pr 11:31); Hv 1, 4, 2. W. apostles MPol 19:2; cp. 1 Cl 5:2. Esp. of the *righteous* of the OT: πατέρες δ. 1 Cl 30:7. W. prophets **Mt 13:17; 23:29** (perh. *teachers:* DHill, NTS 11, '64/65, 296–302). Of Abel (Did., Gen. 181, 10) **Mt 23:35** (construction with τοῦ αἵματος deserves consideration: GKilpatrick, BT 16, '65, 119); **Hb 11:4;** Enoch 1 Cl 9:3; Lot **2 Pt 2:7f** (Noah: Just., D. 20, 1; 138, 1; δίκαιοι καὶ πατριάρχαι ibid. 67, 7); John the Baptist (w. ἅγιος) **Mk 6:20;** δ. τετελειωμένοι *just persons made perfect* (i.e., who have died) **Hb 12:23.** Opp. ἄδικοι (Pr 17:15; 29:27; En 99:3; 100:7) **Mt 5:45; Ac 24:15; 1 Pt 3:18;** ἁμαρτωλοί (Ps 1:5; En 104:6 and 12; PsSol 2:34) **Mt 9:13; Mk 2:17; Lk 5:32; 15:7;** ἁμαρτωλοί and ἀσεβεῖς (Ps 1:5f) **1 Ti 1:9; 1 Pt 4:18** (Pr 11:31); πονηροί (Pr 11:15) **Mt 13:49** (μοχθηροί Tat. 3, 2). W. regard to the Last Judgment, the one who stands the test is δ. *righteous* **Mt 25:37, 46.**—**Ro 1:17** (s. ζάω 2bβ); **Gal 3:11; Hb 10:38** (all three Hab 2:4; cp. Larfeld I 494); **Ro 5:19.** Resurrection of the just **Lk 14:14;** prayer **Js 5:16;** cp. **5:6** (1bβ below). Joseph, who is interested in doing the right thing *honorable, just, good* (Jos., Ant. 15, 106; Diod. S. 33, 5, 6 ἀνδρὸς εὐσεβοῦς κ. δικαίου; Conon [I BC–I AD]: 26 fgm. 1, 17 Jac.; Galen CMG V/10, 3 p. 33, 13f [XVIII/1 p. 247 K.] ἄνδρες δ.) **Mt 1:19** (w. connotation of 'merciful' DHill, ET 76, '65, 133f; s. δικαιοσύνη 3b).

β. of things relating to human beings ἔργα **1J 3:12;** αἷμα δ. (Jo 4:19; La 4:13=αἷμα δικαίου Pr 6:17, where αἷ. δίκαιον is a v.l.) *blood of an upright,* or better, *an innocent man* **Mt 23:35** (s. 1bβ below), and esp. **27:4,** where δ. is v.l. for ἀθῷον; AcPl Ha 11, 8; ψυχὴ δ. *upright soul* (cp. Pr 10:3; s. also GrBar 10:5) **2 Pt 2:8;** πνεῦμα δ. *upright spirit* Hm 5, 2, 7; ἐντολή (w. ἁγία and ἀγαθή) **Ro 7:12.** κρίσις (Dt 16:18; Is 58:2; 2 Macc 9:18; 3 Macc 2:22; Jos., Ant. 9, 4) **J 5:30; 7:24; 8:16 v.l.; 2 Th 1:5;** B 20:2. Pl. **Rv 16:7; 19:2.** φύσει δικαίᾳ *by an upright nature* IEph 1:1 (Hdb. ad loc.; Orig., C. Cels. 5, 24, 8); ὁδὸς δ. (Vi. Aesopi I G 85 P. of the 'right way') 2 Cl 5:7; B 12:4; pl. **Rv 15:3.**

ⓑ of transcendent beings. Because of their privileged status as authority figures, the idea of fairness or equity is associated w. such entities (for δ. in the sense of 'equitable' in a very explicit form s. Strabo 4, 18, 7).

α. God (NRhizos, Καππαδοκικά 1856, p. 113: it is gener. assumed that deities are *just* or *fair,* but the attribute is esp. affirmed in an ins fr. Tyana Θεῷ δικαίῳ Μίθρᾳ.—JMordtmann, MAI 10, 1885, 11–14 has several exx. of ὅσιος κ. δίκαιος as adj. applied to gods in west Asia Minor.—δικ. of Isis: PRoussel, Les cultes égypt. à Delos 1916, p. 276.—Oft. in OT; Jos., Bell. 7, 323, Ant. 11, 55 [w. ἀληθινός]; Just., A II, 12, 6, D. 23, 2) *just, righteous* w. ref. to God's judgment of people and nations κριτὴς δ. *a righteous judge* (Ps 7:12; 2 Macc 12:6; PsSol 9:2; cp. the description of Rhadamanthys, Pind., O. 2, 69) **2 Ti 4:8;** δ. ἐν τοῖς κρίμασιν 1 Cl 27:1; 60:1; cp. 56:5 (Ps 140:5); πατὴρ δ. **J 17:25;** cp. **Ro 3:26; 1J 2:29;** cp. **3:7;** ὁ θεὸς ὁ παντοκράτωρ δ. AcPlCor 2:12. W. ὅσιος (Ps 144:17; Dt 32:4) **Rv 16:5.** W. πιστός **1J 1:9.**

β. of Jesus who, as the ideal of an upright pers. is called simply ὁ δ. *the upright one* (HDechent, D. 'Gerechte', Eine Bezeichnung für d. Messias: StKr 100, 1928, 439–43) **Ac 7:52; 22:14; Mt 27:19,** cp. **24 v.l.; 1J 2:1; 3:7b ; Lk 23:47** (for Gr-Rom.

associations in favor of *upright,* esp. in **Lk 23:47** s. Danker, Benefactor '82, 345f. GKilpatrick, JTS 42, '41, 34–36, prefers *innocent,* so also Goodsp., Probs. 90f, but against this interp. s. RHanson, Hermathena 60, '42, 74–78; RKarris, JBL 105, '86, 65–74). W. ἅγιος **Ac 3:14.** On the qu. whether **Js 5:6** applies to Jesus, s. K-Aland, TLZ '44, 103 and MDibelius, Commentary (Hermeneia), ad loc. (but s. Greeven's note in this comm. p. 240, 58: 'perhaps a veiled, melancholy allusion to the death of James').—Also of angels Hs 6, 3, 2.

❷ The neuter denotes that which is **obligatory in view of certain requirements of justice,** ***right, fair, equitable*** (Dio Chrys. 67 [17], 12; Jos., Ant. 15, 376; cp. Strabo 4, 18, 7; s. Larfeld I 494) δ. παρὰ θεῷ *it is right in the sight of God* **2 Th 1:6.** Also δ. ἐνώπιον τοῦ θεοῦ **Ac 4:19;** δ. καὶ ὅσιον *it is right and holy* 1 Cl 14:1, pl. **Phil 4:8;** δ. ἐστιν *it is right* **Eph 6:1;** w. inf. foll. **Phil 1:7;** 1 Cl 21:4 (cp. Hyperid. 6, 14; PSI 442, 14 [III BC] οὐ δίκαιόν ἐστι οὕτως εἶναι; Sir 10:23; 2 Macc 9:12; 4 Macc 6:34); δ. ἡγοῦμαι *I consider it right* (Diod. S. 12, 45, 1 δ. ἡγοῦντο) **2 Pt 1:13;** τὸ δ. (Appian, Bell. Civ. 4, 97 §409 τὸ δ.=the just cause; Arrian, Anab. 3, 27, 5; Polyb.; IMagnMai; SEG XLI, 625, 5; pap; 2 Macc 4:34; 10:12; 3 Macc 2:25; EpArist; Jos., Bell. 4, 340 Ant. 16, 158; το νῦν δ. Tat. 1, 3) *what is right* **Lk 12:57.** τὸ δ. παρέχεσθαι *give what is right* **Col 4:1.** ὃ ἐὰν ᾖ δ. δώσω ὑμῖν *whatever is right I will give you* **Mt 20:4** (Diod. S. 5, 71, 1 τὸ δίκαιον ἀλλήλοις διδόναι; 8, 25, 4). Abstract for concrete (Philipp. [=Demosth. 12] 23 μετὰ τοῦ δ.; Dio Chrys. 52 [69], 6 ἄνευ νόμου κ. δικαίου; Ael. Aristid, 46 p. 302 D.) τὸ δίκαιον ὀρθὴν ὁδὸν ἔχει *uprightness goes the straight way* Hm 6, 1, 2. Pl. (Diod. S. 15, 11, 1; 19, 85, 3; Appian, Samn. 11 §4 al.; Lucian, Dial. Mort. 30, 1; Jos., Ant. 19, 288; SibOr 3, 257; Just., A I, 68, 3 δ. ἀξιοῦν; D. 28, 4 φυλάσσει τὰ αἰώνια δ.) δίκαια βουλεύεσθαι *have upright thoughts* Hv 1, 1, 8 (cp. λαλεῖν Is 59:4; ἐκζητήσεται 1 Macc 7:12; κρίνειν Ar. 15, 4; Just., A II, 15, 5).—B. 1180. DELG s.v. δίκη. M-M. TW. Spicq. Sv.

δικαιοσύνη, ης, ἡ (s. δίκαιος; Theognis, Hdt.+) gener. the quality of being upright. Theognis 1, 147 defines δ. as the sum of all ἀρετή; acc. to Demosth. (20, 165) it is the opp. of κακία. A strict classification of δ. in the NT is complicated by freq. interplay of abstract and concrete aspects drawn from OT and Gr-Rom. cultures, in which a sense of equitableness combines with awareness of responsibility within a social context.

❶ **the quality, state, or practice of judicial responsibility w. focus on fairness,** ***justice, equitableness, fairness***—ⓐ of human beings (a common theme in honorary ins, e.g. IPriene 71, 14f; 22f of a judge named Alexis; Danker, Benefactor 346–48; cp. Aristot., EN 5, 1, 8, 1129a τὸ μὲν δίκαιον ἄρα τὸ νόμιμον καὶ τὸ ἴσον 'uprightness consists of that which is lawful and fair'; Ath. 34:2 ἔστι δὲ δ. ἴσα ἴσοις ἀμείβειν 'uprightness means to answer like with like'; for association of δ. with judgment s. also Diog. L. 3, 79; in contexts of praise δ. suggests authority involving juridical responsibility FX 7, '81, 255 n. 229) δ. κρίσεως ἀρχὴ καὶ τέλος *uprightness is the beginning and end of judgment* B 1:6. Melchizedek as βασιλεὺς δικαιοσύνης **Hb 7:2.** ἐργάζεσθαι δικαιοσύνην *administer justice* **Hb 11:33;** κρίνειν ἐν δ. (Ps 71:2f; 95:13; Sir 45:26; PsSol 8:24) *judge justly* **Ac 17:31,** cp. **Mk 16:14 v.l.** (Freer ms. line 5 in N. app.); **Ro 9:28 v.l.** (Is 10:22). ποιεῖν κρίμα καὶ δ. *practice justice and uprightness* 1 Cl 13:1 (Jer 9:23). καθιστάναι τοὺς ἐπισκοποὺς ἐν δ. *appoint overseers in uprightness=who will serve justly* 1 Cl 42:5 (Is 60:17). David rejoices in God's δ. 1 Cl 18:15 (Ps 50:16; s. ἀγαλλιάω, end).

ⓑ of transcendent figures (Pla. τὴν δ. θεοῦ νόμον ὑπελάμβανεν 'considered divine justice [i.e. apportionment of reward or retribution in accordance with behavior] a principle' or 'system' that served as a deterrent of crime Diog. L. 3, 79). Of an apocalyptic horseman ἐν δικαιοσύνῃ κρινεῖ **Rv 19:11.**

❷ **quality or state of juridical correctness with focus on redemptive action,** ***righteousness.*** Equitableness is esp. associated w. God (cp. Paradoxogr. Vat. 43 Keller αἰτεῖται παρὰ τ. θεῶν οὐδὲν ἄλλο πλὴν δικαιοσύνης), and in our lit. freq. in connection w. exercise of executive privilege in conferring a benefit. Hence God's δ. can be the opposite of condemnation **2 Cor 3:9** (s. below); in it God is revealed as judge **Rom 3:5**—in contrast to human wrath, which beclouds judgment—displaying judicial integrity **3:25** (on this pass. s. also below). Cp. ἐκάλεσά σε ἐν δ. B 14:7 (Is 42:6). Also of equitable privilege allotted by God **2 Pt 1:1.**—In Pauline thought the intimate association of God's interest in retaining a reputation for justice that rewards goodness and requites evil, while at the same time working out a plan of salvation for all humanity, complicates classification of his use of δικαιοσύνη. On the one hand, God's δ. is pardoning action, and on the other a way of sharing God's character with believers, who then exhibit righteousness in the moral sense. God achieves this objective through exercise of executive privilege in dispensing justice equitably without reference to νόμος by making salvation available to all humanity (which shares a common problem of liability to wrath by being unanimously in revolt against God Ro 3:9–18, 23) through faith in God's action in Jesus Christ. The genitival constr. δ. θεοῦ accents the uniqueness of this δ.: **Ro 1:17; 3:21f, 25, 26** (s. these pass. also below; Reumann, 3c end); **10:3,** and δ. alone **5:21; 9:30** (3 times); **2 Cor 3:9** (opp. κατάκρισις; cp. Dg 9:3; 5). **2 Cor 5:21** may belong here if δ. is viewed as abstract for concrete=δικαιωθέντες (but s. below). All these refer to *righteousness bestowed by God* cp. ἡ δωρεὰ τῆς δ. **Ro 5:17,** also **1 Cor 1:30** (sim. 1QS 11, 9–15; 1QH 4, 30–37). In this area it closely approximates *salvation* (cp. Is 46:13; 51:5 and s. NSnaith, Distinctive Ideas of the OT '46, 207–22, esp. 218–22; EKäsemann, ZTK 58, '61, 367–78 [against him RBultmann, JBL 83, '64, 12–16]). According to some interpreters *hunger and thirst for uprightness* **Mt 5:6** perh. offers (but s. 3a below) a related eschatological sense ('Kingdom of God', FNötscher, Biblica 31, '50, 237–41=Vom A zum NT, '62, 226–30).—Keeping the law cannot bring about *uprightness* **Ro 3:21; Gal 2:21; 3:21,** because δ. ἐκ τοῦ νόμου *uprightness based on the law* **Ro 10:5** (cp. **9:30f**), as ἰδία δ. *one's own* (self-made) *upr.* **10:3,** is impossible. God's δ. without ref. to νόμος is to be apprehended by faith **Ro 1:17; 3:22, 26; 4:3ff, 13; 9:30; 10:4, 6, 10** (cp. **Hb 11:7** ἡ κατὰ πίστιν δ. *righteousness based on faith;* s. B-D-F §224, 1), for which reason faith is 'calculated as righteousness' (Gen 15:6; Ps 105:31; 1 Macc 2:52) **Ro 4:3, 5f, 9, 11, 13, 22; Gal 3:6** (cp. **Hb 11:7; Js 2:23;** AMeyer, D. Rätsel des Jk 1930, 86ff; 1 Cl 10:6; B 13:7). Of Jesus as *our righteousness* **1 Cor 1:30.**—As gift and power **Ro 5:17, 21,** and because it is intimately associated with the δύναμις of Christ's resurrection **Phil 3:9f** (s. below), this righteousness enables the redeemed to respond and serve God faithfully **Ro 6:13** (in wordplay opp. of ἀδικία), **16, 18ff;** cp. **1 Cor 1:30** of Christ as instrument of God's gift of δ.; **2 Cor 3:9.** Thus God's δ. functions as δύναμις **6:7** within Christians **5:21** (i.e. the way God acts in justifying or restoring people to a relationship with God's self serves as a model for Christian interaction; for a difft. view, s. above) through the Spirit (Ro 8:9) and assures them they will have life that will be fully realized at the end of the age **Ro 8:10f;** for the time being it is a matter of hope ἐλπὶς δικαιοσύνης **Gal 5:5** (cp.Is 51:5); cp. ἡ ἐκ θεοῦ δ. **Phil 3:9.** Pol 8:1 shares Paul's view: Christ as ἀρραβὼν τῆς δ.—God's uprightness as gift τοῦ κυρίου τοῦ ἐφ' ὑμᾶς στάξαντος τὴν δ.

who distills uprightness on you Hv 3, 9, 1.—Such perspectives offer a transition to specific ways in which the redeemed express uprightness.

❸ **the quality or characteristic of upright behavior, *uprightness, righteousness*—ⓐ** of uprightness in general: **Mt 5:6** (cp. **6:33;** some interpret **5:6** in an eschatological sense, s. 2 above; on desire for δ. cp. ἐπιθυμία τῆς δ. Hm 12, 2, 4); **Mt 5:10, 20** (s. b, below); Hm 10, 1, 5; Dg 10:8; λόγος δικαιοσύνης **Hb 5:13;** Pol 9:1 (s. also Epict., fgm. Stob. 26; when a man is excited by the λόγος in meetings, he should give expression to τὰ τῆς δικαιοσύνης λόγια). πάσχειν διὰ δ. **1 Pt 3:14.** ἄγγελος τῆς δ. Hm 6, 2, 1; 3; 8; 10. ῥήματα δ. 8:9. 10, 1, 5; Dg 10:8; Pol 2:3; 3:1; ἐντολὴ δ. *commandment of upr.* Pol 3:3; 9:1.—**Mt 6:33** of the kind of δ. God expects (on δ. as characteristic required by God acc. to Jewish perspective s. Bousset, Rel.[3] 387ff; 379ff; 423; cp. KFahlgren, Ṣedāḳā, nahestehende u. entgegengesetzte Begriffe im Alten Testament, diss. Uppsala '32.—S. Diog. L. 3, 83 on Plato's view of δικαιοσύνη περὶ θεούς or δ. πρὸς τοὺς θεούς=performance of prescribed duties toward gods; s. also ref. to 3, 79 at 1b above). Christ's δ. Dg 9:3, 5. διαλέγεσθαι περὶ δ. **Ac 24:25.** Opp. ἀδικία (Hippol., Ref. 4, 43, 12; Did., Gen. 20, 27) 2 Cl 19:2; Dg 9:1. As ἀρετή Hm 1:2; s 6, 1, 4; 8, 10, 3. Opp. ἀνομία **2 Cor 6:14;** cp. **2 Cor. 11:15** (ironical); **Hb 1:9** (Ps 44:8); ἁμαρτία, which is the dominating power before δ. θεοῦ comes into play **Ro 6:16, 18–20;** cp. **1 Pt 2:24.** ἐργάζεσθαι δ. (Ps 14:2) *do what is right* **Ac 10:35;** *accomplish righteousness* **Js 1:20** (W-S. §30, 7g); Hv 2, 2, 7; 2, 3, 3; m 5, 1, 1; 12, 3, 1; 12, 6, 2; s 9, 13, 7. Also ἔργον δικαιοσύνης ἐργάζεσθαι 1 Cl 33:8. Opp. οὐδὲν ἐργάζεσθαι τῇ δ. Hs 5, 1, 4; ποιεῖν (τὴν) δ. (2 Km 8:15; Ps 105:3; Is 56:1; 58:2; 1 Macc 14:35 al.) *do what is right* **1J 2:29; 3:7, 10; Rv 22:11;** 2 Cl 4:2; 11:7. Also πράσσειν τὴν δ. 2 Cl 19:3; διώκειν τὴν δ. (cp. Sir 27:8 διώκ. τὸ δίκαιον) *seek to attain/achieve upr.* **Ro 9:30; 1 Ti 6:11; 2 Ti 2:22;** 2 Cl 18:2; δ. ἀσκεῖν Hm 8:10. ὁδὸς (τῆς) δ. (ὁδός 3ab) **Mt 21:32; 2 Pt 2:21;** B 1:4; 5:4. προπορεύσεται ἔμπροσθέν σου ἡ δ. 3:4 (Is 58:8); cp. 4:12. κατορθοῦσθαι τὰς ὁδοὺς ἐν δ. *walk uprightly* Hv 2, 2, 6; τῇ δ. ζήσωμεν *live uprightly* **1 Pt 2:24.** πύλη δ. *gate of upr.* 1 Cl 48:2 (Ps 117:19), cp. vs. 4. ἐν οἷς δ. κατοικεῖ (cp. Is 32:16) *in which righteousness dwells* **2 Pt 3:13.** Of Christ's body δικαιοσύνης ναός AcPlCor 2:17. παιδεία ἡ ἐν δ. *training in uprightness* **2 Ti 3:16.** ἔργα τὰ ἐν δ. *righteous deeds* **Tit 3:5.** λαμπρότης ἐν δ. *rejoicing in uprightness* 1 Cl 35:2; ἐχθρὸς πάσης δ. *enemy of every kind of upr.* **Ac 13:10.** W. ὁσιότης (Wsd 9:3): *holiness and upr.* (as the relig. and moral side of conduct; cp. 1QS 1:5; 8:2; 11:9–15; 1QH 4:30f) **Lk 1:75** (λατρεύειν ἐν δ. as Josh 24:14); **Eph 4:24;** 1 Cl 48:4. W. πίστις (OGI 438, 8; 1 Macc 14:35; Just., D. 110, 3) Pol 9:2; cp. **2 Pt 1:1.** With εἰρήνη (Is 39:8; 48:18) and χαρά **Ro 14:17;** cp. 1 Cl 3:4; **Hb 7:2** (but s. 1a, above). W. ἀλήθεια (Is 45:19; 48:1) **Eph 5:9;** 1 Cl 31:2; 62:2; Hs 9, 25, 2. W. ἀγάπη 2 Cl 12:1. W. ἀγαθωσύνη **Eph 5:9.** W. ἁγνεία Hs 9,16, 7. W. γνῶσις κυρίου (cp. Pr 16:8) D 11:2. ὅπλα (τῆς) δ. *tools* or *weapons of uprightness* **Ro 6:13; 2 Cor 6:7;** Pol 4:1; θώραξ τῆς δ. (Is 59:17; Wsd 5:18) *breastplate of upr.* **Eph 6:14.** τέκνα δικαιοσύνης (opp. ὀργῆς) AcPlCor 2:19. διάκονοι δικαιοσύνης *servants of upr.* **2 Cor 11:15;** Pol 5:2; μισθὸς δ. D 5:2; B 20:2; μέρος δ. *portion in* (eternal salvation) which is meant for righteousness ApPt Rainer 6; καρπὸς δικαιοσύνης (Pr 3:9; 11:30; 13:2) *produce of uprightness* (ApcSed 12:5) **Phil 1:11; Hb 12:11; Js 3:18;** Hs 9, 19, 2; GJs 6:3. ὁ τῆς δ. στέφανος *the crown of upr.* (w. which the upright are adorned; cp. TestLevi 8:2; Rtzst., Mysterienrel.[3] 258; a common theme in honorary ins recognizing distinguished public service, s. indexes SIG, OGI and other ins corpora; Danker, Benefactor 345–47; s. also the boast of Augustus, s.v. δίκαιος 1aα) **2 Ti 4:8;** cp. ἡ τ. δικαιοσύνης δόξα *the glory of upr.* **ending of Mk** in the Freer ms. ln. 11f. Described as a characteristic to be taught and learned, because it depends on a knowledge of God's will: κῆρυξ δ. *preacher of upr.* **2 Pt 2:5** (cp. Ar. 15:2 τῇ δ. τοῦ κηρύγματος). διδάσκειν δ. *teach upr.* (of Paul) 1 Cl 5:7. μέρος τι ἐκ τῆς δ. *a portion of uprightness* Hv 3, 1, 6; cp. 3, 6, 4; δ. μεγάλην ἐργάζεσθαι m 8:2.—ἐλέγχειν περὶ δικαιοσύνης *convict w. regard to uprightness* (of Jesus) **J 16:8, 10** (s. WHatch, HTR 14, 1921, 103–5; HWindisch: Jülicher Festschr. 1927, 119f; HTribble, Rev. and Expos. 32, '37, 269–80; BLindars, BRigaux Festschr., '70, 275–85).

ⓑ of specific action *righteousness* in the sense of fulfilling divine expectation not specifically expressed in ordinances (Orig., C. Cels. 7, 18, 39; Did., Gen. 188, 27: οἱ κατὰ δ. ζῶντες) **Mt 3:15**=ISm 1:1; of a superior type **Mt 5:20** (s. JMoffatt, ET 13, 1902, 201–6, OOlevieri, Biblica 5, 1924, 201ff; Betz, SM 190f); not to win plaudits **6:1.** To please outsiders as well as oneself 2 Cl 13:1. W. characteristic restriction of mng. *mercy, charitableness* (cp. Tob 12:9) of God, whose concern for the poor **2 Cor 9:9** (Ps 111:9) is exemplary for the recipients of the letter vs. **10;** participation in such activity belongs, according to **Mt 6:1f** (cp. δίκαιος 1:19: Joseph combines justice and mercy), to the practice of piety (on the development of the word's mng. in this direction s. Bousset, Rel.[3] 380). Pl. (B-D-F §142; W-S. §27, 4d; Rob. 408 δικαιοσύναι *righteous deeds* (Ezk 3:20; 33:13; Da 9:18) 2 Cl 6:9. δικαιοσύναι *righteous deeds* (Ezk 3:20; 33:13; Da 9:18; TestAbr A 12 p. 91, 12 [Stone p. 30]) 2 Cl 6:9. ἀρετὴ δικαιοσύνης Hm 1:2; s 6, 1, 4; cp. 8, 10, 3.

ⓒ uprightness as determined by divine/legal standards δ. θεοῦ *upr. that meets God's standard* **Js 1:20** (W-S. 30, §7g).—**Ro 10:5; Gal 2:21; 3:21; Phil 3:6; 3:9.**—ASchmitt, Δικαιοσύνη θεοῦ: JGeffcken Festschr. '31, 111–31; FHellegers, D. Gerechtigkeit Gottes im Rö., diss. Tüb. '39; AOepke, TLZ 78, '53, 257–64.—Dodd 42–59; ADescamps, Studia Hellenistica, '48, 69–92.—S. also JRopes, Righteousness in the OT and in St. Paul: JBL 22, 1903, 211ff; JGerretsen, Rechtvaardigmaking bij Pls 1905; GottfrKittel, StKr 80, 1907, 217–33; ETobac, Le problème de la Justification dans S. Paul 1908; EDobschütz, Über d. paul. Rechtfertigungslehre: StKr 85, 1912, 38–87; GWetter, D. Vergeltungsged. b. Pls 1912, 161ff; BWestcott, St. Paul and Justification 1913; WMacholz, StKr 88, 1915, 29ff; EBurton ICC, Gal. 1921, 460–74; WMichaelis, Rechtf. aus Glauben b. Pls: Deissmann Festschr. 1927, 116–38; ELohmeyer, Grundlagen d. paul. Theologie 1929, 52ff; HBraun, Gerichtsged. u. Rechtfertigungslehre b. Pls. 1930; OZänker, Δικαιοσύνη θεοῦ b. Pls: ZST 9, '32, 398–420; FFilson, St. P.'s Conception of Recompense '31; WGrundmann, ZNW 32, '33, 52–65; H-DWendland, D. Mitte der paul. Botschaft '35; RGyllenberg, D. paul. Rechtfertigungslehre u. das AT: Studia Theologica (Riga) I '35, 35–52; HJager, Rechtvaardiging en zekerheid des geloofs (Ro 1:16f; 3:21–5:11) '39; HHofer, D. Rechtfertigungsverk. des Pls nach neuerer Forschg. '40; VTaylor, Forgiveness and Reconciliation '41; RBultmann, Theologie des NT '48, 266–80, Eng. tr. KGrobel '51, I 270–85; SSchulz, ZTK 56, '59, 155–85 (Qumran and Paul); CMüller, FRL 86, '64 (Ro 9–11); JBecker, Das Heil Gottes, '64; PStuhlmacher, Gerechtigkeit Gottes b. Paulus, '65; JReumann, Int 20, '66, 432–52 (Ro 3:21–31); HBraun, Qumran II, '66, 165–80; JZiesler, The Mng. of Righteousness in Paul, '72; ESanders, Paul and Palestinian Judaism, '77 (s. index 625; appendix by MBrauch 523–42 rev. of discussions in Germany); SWilliams, JBL 99, '80, 241–90.—CPerella, De justificatione sec. Hb: Biblica 14, '33, 1–21; 150–69. S. also the lit. on πίστις and ἁμαρτία.—On the whole word s. RAC X 233–360; AKöberle, Rechtfertigung u.

Heiligung 1930; EDNT I 325–30.—DELG s.v. δίκη. M-M. EDNT.TW. Sv.

δικαιόω fut. δικαιώσω; 1 aor. ἐδικαίωσα. Pass.: 1 fut. δικαιωθήσομαι; 1 aor. ἐδικαιώθην, subj. δικαιωθῶ, ptc. δικαιωθείς; pf. δεδικαίωμαι **Ro 6:7; 1 Cor 4:4;** ptc. δεδικαιωμένος **Lk 18:14** (Soph., Hdt.; Aristot., EN 1136a; et al.; pap, LXX; En 102:10; TestAbr A 13 p. 93, 14 [Stone p. 34]; Test12Patr; ApcSed, 14:8 p. 136, 15 Ja.; Jos., Ant. 17, 206; Just.; Ath., R. 53, 1; 65, 14) to practice δικαιοσύνη.

❶ **to take up a legal cause, *show justice, do justice, take up a cause*** τινά (Polyb. 3, 31, 9 ὑμᾶς δὲ αὐτοὺς . . . δικαιώσεσθε 'you will (find it necessary to) take up your own cause' = you will sit in judgment on yourselves; Cass. Dio 48, 46 'Antony was not taking Caesar's side' in the matter; 2 Km 15:4; Ps 81:3) δικαιῶσαι δίκαιον *take up the cause of an upright pers.* 1 Cl 16:12 (Is 53:11); τινί χήρᾳ (χήραν v.l.) 8:4 (Is 1:17 'take up the cause of the widow').

❷ **to render a favorable verdict, *vindicate.***—ⓐ as activity of humans *justify, vindicate, treat as just* (Appian, Liby. 17 §70; Gen 44:16; Sir 10:29; 13:22; 23:11 al.) θέλων δ. ἑαυτόν *wishing to justify himself* **Lk 10:29;** δ. ἑαυτὸν ἐνώπιόν τινος *j. oneself before someone*='you try to make out a good case for yourselves before the public' **16:15** (δ. ἑαυτόν as En 102:10; but s. JJeremias, ZNW 38, '39, 117f [against him SAalen, NTS 13, '67, 1ff]). ὁ δικαιούμενός μοι *the one who vindicates himself before* (or *against*) *me* B 6:1 (cp. Is 50:8). τελῶναι ἐδικαίωσαν τὸν θεόν βαπτισθέντες *tax-collectors affirmed God's uprightness and got baptized* i.e. by ruling in God's favor they admitted that they were in the wrong and took a new direction (opp. τὴν βουλὴν τ. θεοῦ ἀθετεῖν) **Lk 7:29** (cp. PsSol 2:15; 3:5; 8:7, 23; 9:2).

ⓑ of experience or activity of transcendent figures, esp. in relation to humans

α. of wisdom ἐδικαιώθη ἀπὸ τῶν τέκνων αὐτῆς *is vindicated by her children* (on δικ. ἀπό cp. Is 45:25. S. also Appian, Basil. 8: δικαιόω=consider someth. just or correct) **Lk 7:35;** also ἀπὸ τῶν ἔργων αὐτῆς **Mt 11:19** (v.l. τέκνων). On this saying s. DVölter, NThT 8, 1919, 22–42; JBover, Biblica 6, 1925, 323–25; 463–65; M-JLagrange, ibid. 461–63. Of an angel Hm 5, 1, 7.

β. of God *be found in the right, be free of charges* (cp. TestAbr A 13 p. 93, 14 [Stone p. 34] 'be vindicated' in a trial by fire) **Mt 12:37** (opp. καταδικάζειν). δεδικαιωμένος **Lk 18:14;** GJs 5:1; δεδικαιωμένη (Salome) 20:4 (not pap). **Ac 13:39** (but s. 3 below); **Rv 22:11 v.l;** Dg 5:14.—Paul, who has influenced later wr. (cp. Iren. 3, 18, 7 [Harv. II 102, 2f]), uses the word almost exclusively of God's judgment. As affirmative verdict **Ro 2:13.** Esp. of pers. δικαιοῦσθαι *be acquitted, be pronounced and treated as righteous* and thereby become δίκαιος, receive the divine gift of δικαιοσύνη through faith in Christ Jesus and apart from νόμος as a basis for evaluation (MSeifrid, Justification by Faith—The Origin and Development of a Central Pauline Theme '92) **3:20** (Ps 142:2), **24, 28; 4:2; 5:1, 9; 1 Cor 4:4; Gal 2:16f** (Ps 142:2); **3:11, 24; 5:4; Tit 3:7; Phil 3:12 v.l.;** B 4:10; 15:7; IPhld 8:2; Dg 9:4; (w. ἁγιάζεσθαι) Hv 3, 9, 1. οὐ παρὰ τοῦτο δεδικαίωμαι *I am not justified by this* (after **1 Cor 4:4**) IRo 5:1. ἵνα δικαιωθῇ σου ἡ σάρξ *that your flesh* (as the sinful part) *may be acquitted* Hs 5, 7, 1; δ. ἔργοις *by* (on the basis of) *works, by what one does* 1 Cl 30:3; cp. **Js 2:21, 24f** (ἔργον 1a and πίστις 2dδ); δι' ἑαυτῶν δ. *by oneself*=as a result of one's own accomplishments 1 Cl 32:4. (cp. κατὰ νόμον Hippol., Ref. 7, 34, 1).—Since Paul views God's justifying action in close connection with the power of Christ's resurrection, there is sometimes no clear distinction between the justifying action of acquittal and the gift of new life through the Holy Spirit as God's activity in promoting uprightness in believers. Passages of this nature include **Ro 3:26, 30; 4:5** (on δικαιοῦν τὸν ἀσεβῆ cp. the warning against accepting δῶρα to arrange acquittal Ex 23:7 and Is 5:23; δικαιούμενοι δωρεάν **Ro 3:24** is therefore all the more pointed); **8:30, 33** (Is 50:8); **Gal 3:8;** Dg 9:5. For the view (held since Chrysostom) that δ. in these and other pass. means 'make upright' s. Goodsp., Probs. 143–46, JBL 73, '54, 86–91.

❸ **to cause someone to be released from personal or institutional claims that are no longer to be considered pertinent or valid, *make free/pure*** (the act. Ps 72:13) in our lit. pass. δικαιοῦμαι *be set free, made pure* ἀπό *from* (Sir 26:29; Test-Sim 6:1, both δικ. ἀπὸ [τῆς] ἁμαρτίας) ἀπὸ πάντων ὧν οὐκ ἠδυνήθητε ἐν νόμῳ Μωϋσέως δικαιωθῆναι *from everything fr. which you could not be freed by the law of Moses* **Ac 13:38;** cp. vs. **39.** ὁ ἀποθανὼν δεδικαίωται ἀπὸ τ. ἁμαρτίας *the one who died is freed fr. sin* **Ro 6:7** (s. KKuhn, ZNW 30, '31, 305–10; EKlaar, ibid. 59, '68, 131–34). In the context of **1 Cor 6:11** ἐδικαιώθητε means *you have become pure.*—In the language of the mystery religions (Rtzst., Mysterienrel.[3] 258ff) δικαιοῦσθαι refers to a radical inner change which the initiate experiences (Herm. Wr. 13, 9 χωρὶς γὰρ κρίσεως ἰδὲ πῶς τὴν ἀδικίαν ἐξήλασεν. ἐδικαιώθημεν, ὦ τέκνον, ἀδικίας ἀπούσης) and approaches the sense 'become deified'. Some are inclined to find in **1 Ti 3:16** a similar use; but see under 4.

❹ **to demonstrate to be morally right, *prove to be right,*** pass. of God *is proved to be right* **Ro 3:4;** 1 Cl 18:4 (both Ps 50:6). Of Christ **1 Ti 3:16.**—Lit. s. on δικαιοσύνη 3c.—HRosman, Iustificare (δικαιοῦν) est verbum causativum: Verbum Domini 21, '41, 144–47; NWatson, Δικ. in the LXX, JBL 79, '60, 255–66; CCosgrove, JBL 106, '87, 653—70.—DELG s.v. δίκη. M-M. EDNT. TW. Spicq.

δικαίωμα, ατος, τό (Thu.+; ins, pap, LXX; En 104:9; Par-Jer 6:23; Just., D. 46, 2)

❶ **a regulation relating to just or right action, *regulation, requirement, commandment*** (so mostly LXX; Philo, Det. Pot. Ins. 68; Jos., Bell. 7, 110, Ant. 17, 108; Cass. Dio 36, 23 of the laws; POxy 1119, 15 τῶν ἐξαιρέτων τῆς ἡμετέρας πατρίδος δικαιωμάτων) w. ἐντολαί and κρίματα (as Num 36:13; Dt 4:40; cp. 6:1; 7:11 al. cp. Theoph. Ant. 3, 11 [p. 226, 29]) **Lk 1:6;** (w. προστάγματα, as Gen 26:5) 1 Cl 2:8; 35:7 (Ps 49:16); τὰ δεδομένα δ. *the commandments which were given* 58:2 (δικ. διδόναι: Jos., C. Ap. 2, 37); δ. τοῦ νόμου *the requirements of the law* **Ro 2:26; 8:4.** Esp. of God's requirements: δ. τοῦ θεοῦ **Ro 1:32;** B 4:11; 10:2 (cp. Dt 4:1). κυρίου Hm 12, 6, 4. ἐκζητεῖν τὰ δ. κυρίου *seek out the Lord's requirements* B 2:1. μανθάνειν 21:1; γνῶσις τῶν δ. 21:5. λαλεῖν δ. κυρίου *speak of the law of the Lord* 10:11; σοφία τῶν δ. *the wisdom revealed in his ordinances* 16:9; δ. λατρείας *regulations for worship* **Hb 9:1;** δ. σαρκός *regulations for the body* vs. **10.**

❷ **an action that meets expectations as to what is right or just, *righteous deed*** (Aristot. EN 1135a, 12f, Rhet. 1359a, 25; 1373b, 1; 3 Km 3:28; Bar 2:19) δι' ἑνὸς δικαιώματος (opp. παράπτωμα) **Ro 5:18.**—B 1:2 (cp. Wengst, Barnabasbrief 196, n. 4); **Rv 15:4** (here perh.='sentence of condemnation' [cp. Pla., Leg. 9, 864e; ins fr. Asia Minor: LBW 41, 2 [κατὰ] τὸ δι[καί]ωμα τὸ κυρω[θέν]='acc. to the sentence which has become valid']; difft. Wengst, s. above); **19:8.**

❸ to clear someone of a violation **Ro 5:16** (opp. κατάκριμα) it is prob. chosen because of the other words in -μα, and is equiv. in mng. to δικαίωσις (on the linguistic possibility s. Kühner-Bl. II 272 and Schwyzer I 491: forms in -μα, which express the result of an action.—En 104:9 δικαίωμα may stand for δικαιοσύνη [cp. Ezk 18:21 and v.l.], but the text appears to be corrupt).—DELG s.v. δίκη. M-M. TW. Spicq.

δικαίως adv. of δίκαιος (Hom.+).—**❶ pert. to being just or right in a juridical sense, *justly, in an upright manner***

ⓐ of a judge's hearing of a case *(judge) uprightly, fairly* (IPriene 63, 20 and oft. in ins; Diod. S. 15, 11, 2 δ. κρίνειν; Sir 35:18 v.l.) **1 Pt 2:23;** B 19:11; D 4:3. Sarcastically GPt 3:7.

ⓑ of treatment in a deserving manner for one's way of life *uprightly, justly, in (all) justice* (X., Symp. 4, 60; Lucian, Dial. Mort. 30, 1 δ. κολασθήσομαι; Just., A I, 43, 8 δ. κολάσεως ἐτύγχανεν; Tat. 7:1) πάσχειν (Wsd 19:13; TestSim 4:3; Just., D. 110, 6) Hs 6, 3, 6. λέγειν 1:4. ἀπολέσθαι B 5:4; καὶ ἡμεῖς μὲν δ. *and we have been justly condemned* **Lk 23:41.** Opp. οὐ δ. *quite unjustly* 1 Cl 44:3 (Just., D. 107, 3).

❷ pert. to quality of character, thought, or behavior, *correctly, justly, uprightly* (w. ὁσίως, ἀμέμπτως) **1 Th 2:10;** (w. ὁσίως) PtK 2 p. 15, 2 (Pla., Rep. 1, 331a ὁσίως κ. δικαίως; IPriene 46, 12 [I BC]; 60, 8f [II BC]; UPZ 144, 13 [164 BC] τοῖς θεοῖς, πρὸς οὓς ὁσίως . . . καὶ δικαίως πολιτευσάμενος; En 106:18 δ. κ. ὁσίως; Jos., Ant. 6, 87; cp. Ar. 15, 10); ἀναστρέφεσθαι 2 Cl 5:6; (w. σωφρόνως, εὐσεβῶς) ζῆν **Tit 2:12** (Heraclides, Pol. 39 δ. κ. σωφρόνως βιοῦσι); cp. 1 Cl 51:2; 62:1. ἀγαπᾶν *love rightly* IEph 15:3. νοεῖν *understand rightly* B 10:12. ἐκνήφειν *be sober, as you ought* **1 Cor 15:34;** δ. ἀναμένειν τινά *wait for someone in uprightness* IMagnMai 9, 3; δ. νοεῖν *understand correctly* B 10:12.—M-M. s.v. δίκαιος.

δικαίωσις, εως, ἡ *justification, vindication, acquittal* (so Thu. et al.; Lev 24:22 and Sym. Ps 34:23; PsSol 3:3) as a process as well as its result διὰ τὴν δ. **Ro 4:25** (s. DSharp, ET 39, 1928, 87–90). εἰς δ. ζωῆς *acquittal that brings life* **5:18.**—DELG s.v. δίκη. TW. Spicq.

δικαστής, οῦ, ὁ (Aeschyl., Hdt. et al.; ins, pap, LXX, Philo; Jos., Bell. 1, 630 [God], Ant. 7, 229 al., C. Ap. 1, 157 [δ. as chief administrator in Tyre]) **one who presides over and decides cases in court, *judge*** (w. ἄρχων) **Ac 7:27, 35;** 1 Cl 4:10 (all three Ex 2:14); **Lk 12:14 v.l.** (Diod. S. 4, 33, 4 δ.=arbitrator).—DELG s.v. δίκη. M-M. TW. Spicq.

δίκη, ης, ἡ (Hom.+; ins, pap, LXX; TestAbr A 2 p. 78, 18 [Stone p. 4] δίκην 'like'; TestSol 1:9 and ApcSed 3:1 'complaint' or 'charge'; Philo, Joseph., Just., Ath. [the last also δίκην 'like']; loanw. in rabb. Originally='direction, way', hence adverbial acc. δίκην 'in manner of, like' w. gen.; Hom.=what is right, esp. in terms of custom or usage.)

❶ punishment meted out as legal penalty, *punishment, penalty* (Pre-Socr., trag.+; pap, e.g. UPZ 1, 13 [IV BC]; PFay 21, 24 [II AD]; LXX) δίκην τίνειν (trag.; Pla.; Epict. 3, 24, 4; 3, 26, 20; Plut., Mor. 553f; 559d; 561b; 592e; Aelian, VH 9, 8; Philo, Spec. Leg. 3, 175, Mos. 1, 245; Just., A I, 17, 4; Ath., R. 74, 2) *pay a penalty, suffer punishment, be punished* τὶ *of* or *with someth.* **2 Th 1:9;** Hm 2:5; s 9, 19, 3. Also δ. διδόναι (freq. trag.+; Jos., C. Ap. 2, 143, Vi. 343; Just., D. 1:5) D 1:5 (δ. διδόναι of divine punishment also Diod. S. 16, 31, 4. But s. RKraft, The Didache and Barnabas '65, p. 141 *will be called to account*) and δ. ὑπέχειν (not infreq. since Soph., Oed. Rex 552; also Diog. L. 3, 79; Jos., Ant. 14, 45; 168) **Jd 7;** δ. αἰτεῖσθαι κατά τινος **Ac 25:15 v.l.**

❷ *Justice* personified as a deity **Ac 28:4** (Soph., Ant. 538 ἀλλ' οὐκ ἐάσαι τοῦτο γ' ἡ Δίκη σ', ἐπεὶ κτλ.; Ael. Aristid. 52 p. 606 D.; Arrian, Anab. 4, 9, 7 Δίκη as πάρεδρος of Zeus; Pind., O. 7, 17 al.; Pla., Leg. 716a; Plotin. V 8, 4, 40ff; Damasc., Vi. Isid. 138; Procop. Soph., Ep. 17; 149; Herm. Wr. p. 420, 1 Sc.; 4 Macc; Philo; Joseph.; Warnecke, Romfahrt 118f).—RHirzel, Themis, Dike u. Verwandtes 1907; WJaeger, Paideia '34, 144ff (s. Eng. tr. '39, vol. 1, 68); DLoenen, Dike '48; Kl. Pauly II 24–26.—B. 1358. DELG. LfgrE s.v. (lit.). DDD 476–80. M-M. TW. Spicq. Sv. S. δικάζω.

δίκτυον, ου, τό (Hom. et al.; PTebt 701, 88; Ps.-X., Cyn. 2, 5; Epict. 2, 1, 8; LXX; TestAbr A 8 p. 86, 3 [Stone p. 20]; TestDan 2:4; Jos., Ant. 9, 92) a generic term 'net', but in NT only of ***fishnet*** (since Od. 22, 386; also Diod. S. 5, 76, 4; Paus. 2, 30, 3; Lucian, Herm. 65; Alciphron 1, 14 al.; s. on ἀμφιβάλλω) **Mt 4:20f; Mk 1:18f; Lk 5:2, 4ff; J 21:6, 8, 11** (ἕλκειν τὸ δίκτ.: Theocr., Idyll 1, 40; Vi. Aesopi G 26); for catching birds (old Eng. *fowler's net*) (Pr 1:17).—B 5:4. DELG. M-M.

δίλογος, ον (Pollux 2, 118, but='repeating'. Likew. Diod. S. 20, 37, 1 διλογεῖν τι=say someth. twice; cp. Nägeli 52) ***insincere*** (cp. our 'double-talking' [in the U.S.A. 'double-tongued' may convey a different mng.]) **1 Ti 3:8.**—Pol 5:2.—B 5:4. M-M.

διό inferential conjunction (δι' ὅ; s. B-D-F §451, 5) (Heraclitus, Thu.+) ***therefore, for this reason*** **Mt 27:8; Mk 5:33 v.l.; Lk 7:7; Ac 15:19; 20:31; 25:26; 26:3; 27:25, 34; Ro 1:24; 2:1; 13:5** (RBultmann, TLZ 72, '47, 200 would omit the two last verses as glosses); **Hb 3:7, 10;** B 4:9; 1 Cl 7:2; 9:1; AcPlCor 1:16 al. διὸ καί (B-D-F §442, 12; 451, 5) *therefore . . . also,* denoting that the inference is self-evident (Jos., Ant. 19, 294) **Lk 1:35; Ac 10:29; 24:26; Ro 4:22; 15:22; 2 Cor 1:20; 5:9; Phil 2:9;** AcPlCor 2:8 al. P[72] reads δι' οὗ, w. ref. to Christ **2 Pt 1:12.**—EMolland, Διο: Serta Rudbergiana '31, 43–52. See διότι 2.—M-M.

Διόγνητος, ου, ὁ (found freq.; Demosth.; Polyb.; M. Ant. 1, 6; ins, pap) ***Diognetus,*** addressee of Epistle to Diognetus, Dg 1.

διοδεύω impf. διώδευον; 1 aor. διώδευσα, pass. 3 sg. διωδεύθη Wsd 5:11 (Aristot. et al.; ins, pap, LXX; TestZeb 4:6 v.l.; JosAs 11:1 cod. A and Pal. 364; ApcMos. 19; Joseph., SibOr).

❶ *go, travel through* (Lucian, Dial. Mort. 27, 2; OGI 613, 3; 665, 22; SEG XXVI, 1392, 40f; pap, e.g. PAmh 36, 131 PTebt 736, 12) τόπον τινά (cp. Wsd 5:7; 11:2) **Ac 17:1.**

❷ *go about,* intr. (IKNikaia I, 1, 7; PAmh II, 36, 13 [II BC]; Jos., Bell. 2, 340; Jer 2:6; 1 Macc 12:32 διώδ. ἐν πάσῃ τῇ χώρᾳ; SibOr 3, 250) κατὰ πόλιν και κώμην *fr. one city and village to another* **Lk 8:1.**—Anz 344. New Docs 4, no. 48. DELG s.v. ὁδός. M-M.

διοίκησις, εως, ἡ *administration, management* (X.+; OGI 11, 24; 458, 65; pap; Tob 1:21; Jos., Bell. 1, 669, Ant. 15, 68; 355 δ. Καίσαρος; Just., A II, 8) of a political body: of God's rule of the world (Epict. 3, 5, 8; 10; 4, 1, 100 al.; Philo, Spec. Leg. 4, 187; cp. Herm. Wr. 10, 23; Ar. [Milne 76, 50]; Just., Ath.) τῇ δ. αὐτοῦ *at his direction* 1 Cl 20:1.—Dg 7:2.—DELG s.v. οἶκος p. 782. Sv.

Διονύσιος, ου, ὁ (very freq.) ***Dionysius,*** name of an Athenian (s. Jos., Ant. 14, 149–52), member of the Areopagus, converted by Paul, **Ac 17:34.**—DELG s.v. Διόνυσος. M-M.

διόπερ inferential conj. (δι' ὅπερ) (Epicharm. 85a, 5 [CGFP]; Democr., Thu. et al.; Diod. S, 4, 33, 6; ins, pap, LXX; Jos., Ant. 16, 118; Tat., Ath.) ***therefore, for this very reason*** **1 Cor 8:13; 10:14; 14:13 v.l.**—M-M.

διοπετής, ές lit. 'fallen from Zeus' or 'the sky'. Orig. of meteorites viewed as heaven-sent cult objects ***fallen from heaven*** (of images of deities Eur., Iph. T. 86–88; 977; 1384f Artemis; Dionys. Hal. 2, 66 Athena; Appian, Mithrid. 53 §213 Athena; Herodian 5, 3, 5 of a very large stone representative of the sun god Elagabalus; cp. Livy, Hist. 29, 11, 14, image of 'Magna Mater' brought from Pessinus to Rome in 204 BC) in our lit. only as neut. subst. τὸ διοπετές *the image* (of Artemis) fallen *fr. heaven* at Ephesus **Ac 19:35** (B-D-F §241, 7).—EvDobschütz, Christusbilder: TU 18, 1899, 11ff; 41; on the cult of meteorites: ACook, Zeus III, '40, xii, 881–942. CHemer, The Letters to the Seven Churches of Asia in Their Local Setting '86, 227 n. 39.—DELG s.v. πέτομαι. M-M.

διόπτρα, ας, ἡ (formed like ἀντόπτρα, see HSchoene, Hermes 38, 1903, 281) ***optical instrument*** (Euclid, Polyb. et al.); Papias (3:2) states that the eyes of Judas were so swollen that a physician could not even examine them with the aid of a δ., perh. designed to aid in prying eyelids apart (cp. Aëtius 16, 89; Paulus Aegineta med. CMG 6, 73).—DELG s.v. ὄπωπα.

διορθόω 1 aor. διώρθωσα LXX, mid. διωρθωσάμην. Pass. 1 fut. διορθωθήσομαι LXX; aor. διωρθώθην (s. two next entries; Pind. et al.; ISardGauthier 1, 2, et al.; PPetr III, 53k, 4, et al.; LXX; Jos., Ant. 2, 46 al.) ***set on the right path*** ἐπὶ τὸ ἀγαθὸν δ. *lead to what is good* 1 Cl 21:6.—DELG s.v. ὀρθός.

διόρθωμα, ατος, τό (s. prec. and next entry; Hippocr., Aristot.+; Michel 469, 17; PRev 57, 1; PParis 62 1, 7 al.) **that which results from correcting a wrong or undesirable situation, *improvement, reform,*** of improvements in internal administration **Ac 24:2** (cp. κατόρθωμα v.l.).—SLösch, TQ 112, '31, 307–12.—Frisk s.v. ὀρθός. M-M.

διόρθωσις, εως, ἡ (s. prec. two entries; Hippocr. et al.; pap; TestSol 1:7 D; Philo, Sacr. Abel. 27; Jos., Bell. 1, 389; 2, 449, Ant. 2, 51) **a process leading to a new order viewed as something yet to be realized, *improvement, reformation, new order*** (Pla., Leg. 1, 642a; Polyb. 1, 1, 1; PGM 13, 707f πρὸς διόρθωσιν βίου) καιρὸς δ. *the time of the new order=until the time comes to set things right* NRSV (in contrast to that of the law w. its stipulations relating to things merely affecting the body) **Hb 9:10.**—Frisk s.v. ὀρθός. M-M. TW.

διορίζω (Aeschyl., Hdt.+; also T. Kellis 22, 46f) fut. 3 sg. διοριεῖ Ex 26:33; 1 aor. mid. inf. διορίσασθαι (TestSol D 4:8); pf. pass. ptc. διωρισμένου (En 22:4) ***set limits to*** someth., pass. Dg 7:2.—DELG s.v. ὅρος.

διορύσσω 1 aor. διώρυξα LXX; 1 aor. pass. inf. διορυχθῆναι (-ορυγῆναι **Mt 24:43 v.l.; Lk 12:39 v.l.**) (Hom. et al.; pap, LXX; TestAbr A 10 p. 88, 11 [Stone p. 24]; Philo, In Flacc. 73; Ar. 4, 3; Ath., R. 64, 19) to break through a wall or barrier. In our lit. of a thief who *digs through* the (sun-dried brick) wall of a house and gains entrance, ***break through, break in*** (Aristoph., Plut. 565 κλέπτειν καὶ τοὺς τοίχους διορύττειν; X., Symp. 4, 30; Lucian, Gall. 22; OGI 483, 118; Job 24:16.—Joseph. does not have the verb, but Ant. 16, 1 τοιχωρύχος=house-breaker, house-invader) abs. **Mt 6:19f.** W. acc. (Mitt-Wilck. II/2, 45, 2=PPetr III, 28 verso b, 2 [260 BC] ὅτι διώρυξεν οἰκίαν; PMich 421, 6) pass. **24:43; Lk 12:39** *he would not have permitted his house to be broken into = he would not have let anyone break in.*—DELG s.v. ὀρύσσω. M-M.

Διός s. Ζεύς.

Διόσκουροι, ων, οἱ fr. Δίος κοῦροι 'Sons of Zeus' (Hom., Pind. et al.; ins; pap, e.g. BGU 248, 13 [I AD]; Mayser 10f; B-D-F §30, 3; Rob. 199—Ionic form) ***the Dioscuri*** title (first used in IG 359 and then Hom. Hymns 33, 1) of Castor and Pollux (Πολυδεύκης), twin sons of Zeus and Leda, serving as insignia and also tutelary deities (οἱ σωτῆρες 'the Savior Gods' IG XII/3, 422 et al.; on their temple and epiphanies at Rome s. Dionys. Hal. 6, 13) of an Alexandrian ship **Ac 28:11** (cp. Lucian, Navig. 9; Epict. 2, 18, 29; Ael. Aristid. 43, 26 K.=1 p. 10 D.: Δ. σῴζουσι τοὺς πλέοντας et al.).—AFurtwängler, art. 'Dioskuren', in Roscher, I 1154–77; RHarris, The Cult of the Heavenly Twins, 1906; KJaisle, D. Dioskuren als Retter z. See, diss. Tüb. 1907; ACook, Zeus, 1914, I 760–75; LFarnell, Greek Hero Cults, 1921, pp. 175–233; Kl. Pauly II 92–94; RAC III 1122–38—DDD. DELG s.v. Ζεύς. M-M.

διότι conj. (Hdt.+) (B-D-F §294, 4; 456, 1; Rob. ind.; Meisterhans^3-Schw. 252f; Mayser 161; Thackeray 138f; FKälker, Quaest. de Eloc. Polyb. 1880, 243f; 300) a marker used to establish an intimate connection between two statements.

❶ **marker of a causal connection between two statements,** ***because*** (=διὰ τοῦτο ὅτι 'for the reason that, in view of the fact that') in causal clauses **Lk 2:7; 21:28; Ac 17:31 v.l.; Ro 8:21 v.l.** (but s. 4); **1 Cor 15:9; Phil 2:26; 1 Th 2:8; 4:6; Hb 11:5** (Gen 5:24), 23; **Js 4:3;** Dg 6:5; Hv 3, 5, 4; m 12, 3, 4; s 9, 14, 4.

❷ **marker used to introduce an inference, *therefore*** (=διὰ τοῦτο) **Ac 13:35; 20:26.**

❸ **marker used to indicate why someth. just stated can reasonably be considered valid,** used in place of ὅτι (TestAbr A 11 p. 90, 6 [Stone p. 28]; TestJob 49:3): ***for*** **Lk 1:13; Ac 10:20 v.l.; 18:10; 22:18; Ro 1:19–21; 3:20; 8:7; Gal 2:16 v.l.; 1 Th 2:18; 1 Pt 1:16ab** (v.l.), **24** (ὅτι P[72]); **2:6.**

❹ **marker of discourse content, *that*** (Teles p. 46, 4; 47, 12; 48, 11; Antig. Car. 149; 152; Diod. S. 4, 10, 7; 4, 23, 2 al.; Epict. 4, 7, 8; Dio Chrys. 21 [38], 14; Celsus 2, 49; SIG 1169, 24f; Sb 7638, 8 [257 BC]; UPZ 15, 24 [156 BC] ἐπίγνωσιν διότι=ὅτι; UPZ 16, 15 in a parallel concept of the same petition]; EpArist 151; Jos., Bell. 3, 475, Ant. 15, 142) **Ro 8:21 v.l.** (s. 1 above).—M-M.

Διοτρέφης, ους, ὁ (also -ής, -οῦς; for the adj. διοτρεφής s. LfgrE s.v.) ***Diotrephes*** (Thu. 8, 64, 2; Diod. S. 15, 14, 1; SIG^2 868, 8; OGI 219, 1), a Christian, influential in his congregation **3J 9** (LCountryman, The Rich Christian in the Church of the Early Empire '80, 179 n. 27).—BHHW I 345. DELG s.v. τρέφω p. 1135. LGPN I. M-M.

Διόφαντος, ου, ὁ (the name since IV BC, also SIG index p. 20; ISyriaW 710; 757) ***Diophantos,*** freedperson of the proconsul in Ephesus AcPl Ha 2, 9; 11; 13; 3, 1; 4, 10.

διπλοκαρδία, ας, ἡ ***duplicity,*** lit. 'double-heartedness', in a list of vices D 5:1; B 20:1.

διπλοῦς, ῆ, οῦν contracted form of διπλόος (Hom.+; loanw. in rabb.) ***double, two-fold*** τιμή (POslo 43, 8 [140/41 AD] ἐκτείσω σοι τὴν τιμὴν διπλῆν) **1 Ti 5:17** (s. τιμή 3 and PGM 4, 2454, where the emperor διπλᾶ ὀψώνια ἐκέλευσεν δίδοσθαι to the prophet for his services.—Diod. S. 5, 45, 5 τ. ἱερεῦσι μόνοις δίδοται διπλάσιον; 13, 93, 2 διπλοῦς ποιήσειν τοὺς μισθούς). τὰ κτίσματα τοῦ θεοῦ δ. ἐστί *are of two kinds* Hm 8:1; δ. εἰσιν αἱ ἐνέργειαι 6, 1, 1; cp. ἡ ἐγκράτεια δ. ἐστιν 8:1. διπλοῦν τὸν καρπὸν ἀποδιδόναι *yield fruit twofold* s 2:8; δῶρα . . . διπλᾶ GJs 1:1; τὰ διπλᾶ *double,* διπλοῦν τὰ δ. *pay back double* **Rv 18:6a** (cp. PYadin 5a II, a). Neuter διπλοῦν *double* (SIG 962, 70; PSI 1120, 4) κεράσαι **Rv 18:6b.**—Comp., strikingly derived fr. the poetic form διπλός, displays pattern of late Koine: διπλότερος (Appian, Prooem. 10 §40 διπλότερα τούτων; B-D-F §61, 2; W-S. §11, 5; Mlt-H. 166). Neut. as adv. *twice as much* υἱὸς γεέννης δ. ὑμῶν *twice as bad as you* **Mt 23:15** (B-D-F §102, 4; Rob. 299; Just., D. 122, 2 says on Mt 23:15 [cp. διπλότερον υἱοὶ γεέννης Just., D. 122, 1]: διπλότερον ὑμῶν βλασφημοῦσιν).—DELG s.v. διπλόος. M-M.

διπλόω 1 aor. ἐδίπλωσα (since X., Hell. 6, 5, 19) ***to double*** τὰ διπλᾶ *pay back double* **Rv 18:6** (Cp. the adj. διπλοῦς PYadin 5a ii, 9 and n. p. 40.)—DELG s.v. διπλόος.

Δίρκη, ης, ἡ ***Dirce,*** wife of the Theban king Lycus; she was dragged to death by a wild bull. Pl. (with Δίρκαι=people like Dirce cp. Themist., Or. 285c . . . Τιμάιους, Δικαιάρχους=men like Timaeus, Dicaearchus; Himerius, Or. [Ecl.] 5, 24 Θησεῖς κ. Κόδροι; schol. on Plato, Tht. 169b; Synesius, Calvit. 21 p. 85b) of Christian women who were martyred 1 Cl 6:2; s. Δαναΐδες (cp. Diod. S. 14, 112, 1 τραγικήν τινα τιμωρίαν λαμβάνειν=receive a punishment of the kind found in tragedy). Kl. Pauly II 99.

δίς adv. (Hom.+; ins, pap, LXX; JosAs 28:13; ApcEsdr 1:5 p. 24, 10 Tdf.; Jos., Vi. 355; Just., D. 85, 5 τὰ δὶς δύο πόσα ἐστί 'how much is two times two') ***twice*** **Mk 14:30, 72.** (On Rv 9:16 s. δισμυρίας). ἅπαξ καὶ δ. (ἅπαξ 1) *once and again=several times* **Phil 4:16; 1 Th 2:18;** 1 Cl 53:3 (Dt 9:13). W. gen. foll. (Diod. S. 5, 41, 6 δὶς τοῦ ἐνιαυτοῦ; Jos., Ant. 3, 199) δ. τοῦ σαββάτου *twice in a week* **Lk 18:12;** δ. ἀποθνήσκειν *die twice* **Jd 12** (cp. Paroem. Gr.: Apostol. 14, 27 δὶς ἀποθανουμένη ψυχή; the same Plut., Mor. 236d).—DELG. M-M.

δισμυριάς, άδος, ἡ (so Tdf. S. Vog. M. Bov.) ***a double myriad*** (i.e. 20,000) **Rv 9:16** (also written separately δὶς μυριάς H.; δύο μυριάδες v.l., but precision would require δισμυριὰς μ., since only one double-myriad of tens of thousands appears to be in view); the undefined pl. suggests several units of twenty-thousand multiplied by 10,000. An indefinite number of incalculable immensity is indicated (as indefinite as the ἀναρίθμητοι μυριάδες of Theopompus in Περὶ ὕψους 43, 2). If the Hb. רִבֹּתַיִם רִבּוֹת, in which the first part expresses multiplication through the fem. dual form, underlies the Gk. phrase, δισμ. might well be the equivalent of this dual and with similar mng. *ten thousand times ten thousand,* i.e. 'a very great number'. S. GMussies, Δύο in Rv 9:12 and 16: NovT 9, '67, 151–54; s. also his Morphology pp. 223–25.—DELG s.v. δίς.

δισσός, ή, όν (s. next entry; trag., Pla., X. et al.; PTebt 27, 53 et al. pap; LXX; ParJer 7:30; AssMos fgm. f [διττ-] p. 65 Denis; Philo, Aet. M. 20; SibOr 1, 327; Ath. 19, 2) **pert. to being twice in quantity, whether similar or different in kind, *double*** δ. ἕξουσιν τὴν κρίσιν *they will incur double punishment* 2 Cl 10:5; δ. φόβοι *two kinds of fear* Hm 7:4.—Frisk s.v. δίς.

δισσῶς adv. (s. prec. entry; trag. et al.; PMich 465, 31; Sir 23:11; Test12Patr) ***doubly*** κολάζεσθαι *be punished doubly* Hs 9, 18, 2.

δισταγμός, οῦ, ὁ (Agatharchides [II BC] 21 [GGM I 120, 8]; Plut., Mor. 214f; schol. on Apollon. Rhod. 3, 539a) **pert. to being uncertain as to what side or position one should take in a disputed matter, *doubt*** εἰς δ. βάλλειν *plunge into doubt* 1 Cl 46:9. ἐν δ. γενέσθαι *become uncertain* Hs 9, 28, 4.—B. 1244. DELG s.v. δίς.

διστάζω (δίς + ?) fut. διστάσω; 1 aor. ἐδίστασα (Pla.+; OGI 315, 66; UPZ 110, 57; PSI 1315, 6 [both II BC]; PGiss 18, 9; BGU 388, 17; Sb 6663, 35 al. pap; EpArist 53; Jos., Bell. 2, 182) gener. 'to be uncertain, to have second thoughts about a matter'.

❶ **to have doubts concerning something, *doubt, waver*** abs. (Diod. S. 20, 15, 3) **Mt 14:31;** 28:17 (IEllis, NTS 14, '67/68, 574–80; KMcKay, JSNT 24, '85, 71f the subject is a subgroup of the apostles; for another interpr. of Mt 28:17 s. 2 below); GMary Ox 3525, 10. τῇ ψυχῇ *within oneself* 1 Cl 23:3. Also τῇ καρδίᾳ 2 Cl 11:2. ἐν τῇ καρδίᾳ Hm 9:5. περί τινος *have doubts concerning someth.* (Diod. S. 4, 62, 3; 19, 36, 5; Plut., Mor. 62a) 1 Cl 11:2; Hs 9, 28, 7. W. indirect quest. foll. (Pla., Aristot.; Polyb. 12, 26c, 2) τίνι δῷς *consider to whom you should give* Hm 2:4.

❷ **to be uncertain about taking a particular course of action, *hesitate*** in doubt (Diod. S. 10, 4, 4; Dositheus 71, 5; Just., D. 28, 2; 39, 6) perh. **Mt 28:17** abs.; w. inf. foll. δοῦναι D 4:7 and B 19:11; αἰτεῖσθαι *to make a request* Hs 5, 4, 3.—DELG s.v. δίς. M-M. TW.

δίστομος, ον (Soph.+; PMichZen 48, 4 [251 BC]; LXX) **pert. to having two edges, *double-edged*** of a sword (so Eur., Hel. 983; LXX) μάχαιρα (Judg 3:16; Pr 5:4; cp. PGM 13, 92 ἔχε . . . μαχαῖριν ὁλοσίδηρον δίστομον. But τὰ δίστομα 'gifted with two languages' GrBar 6:16) **Hb 4:12.** ῥομφαία (Ps 149:6; Sir 21:3) **Rv 1:16; 2:12; 19:15 v.l.** (w. ὀξεῖα).—DELG s.v. δίς. M-M. Spicq.

δισχίλιοι, αι, α (Hdt.+; Aberciusins. 21; pap; LXX; JosAs 27:6; Jos., Bell. 1, 172, Ant. 11, 15; 18 al.; Just. A I, 31, 8) ***two thousand*** **Mk 5:13.**—DELG s.v. δίς.

διϋλίζω (in fig. sense in Pseudo-Archytas [c. 360 BC; Stob. III/1, p. 58, 7 H.]. In lit. mng., of wine Plut., Mor. 692d; Diosc. 2, 86; 5, 72; Artem. 4, 48; POxy 413, 154; Am 6:6) ***filter out, strain out*** fr. a liquid (the KJV 'strain at' is widely considered a misprint [so Goodsp., Relig. in Life 12, '42/43, 205–10 and Probs. '45, 38f], but for the view that it is an archaic usage s. OED s.v. 'strain', verb, 14e and esp. 21, and CHopf, Rev. of Engl. Studies 20, '44, 155f; 'strain at'='strain [the liquid] at [seeing]' a gnat) τὸν κώνωπα *a gnat* fr. a drink **Mt 23:24.**—DELG s.v. ὕλη.

δίχα adv. (Hom. et al.; POxy 237 VIII, 37; PGiss 66, 3; BGU 908, 22; Sir 47:21); functions in our lit. as a prep. w. gen. ***apart from, without*** (trag., X. et al.; Philo, Aet. M. 52; 74; Jos., Bell. 1, 346; 6, 95, Ant. 3, 76; 18, 336; Mel., P. 35, 237 [B]; Ath. 22, 8) δ. πάσης παρεκβάσεως *without any divergence at all* 1 Cl 20:3; δ. ἐλλείψεως *without interruption* vs. 10; cp. 37:4f; 49:5; 50:2; 63:1.—DELG s.v. δίς.

διχάζω 1 aor. ἐδίχασα, pass. 3 sg. ἐδιχάσθη (TestAbr A 10 p. 88, 9f [Stone p. 24]) (=divide in two, separate Pla., Pol. 264d; Galen, De Usu Part. II 313, 24 Helmr.; mystery pap [I AD]: APF 13, '39, 212=PSI 1290, 10; Aq. Lev 1:17 and Dt 14:6) ***to divide in two,*** pass. πῶς ἐδιχάσθη ἡ γῆ *how the earth was split* GJs 9:2; ἐδιχάσθη τὸ ὄρος 22:3.—In imagery *cause a separation, separate* (so PCairMasp 155, 16 [VI AD] φθόνος πονηρὸς ἐδίχασε ἡμᾶς; Eustath. ad Od. 7, 325 p. 1582, 12) τινὰ κατά τινος *turn someone against someone* **Mt 10:35.**—DELG s.v. δίς. M-M.

διχηλέω (Aristot., Part. Anim. 695a, 18 v.l.; LXX; EpArist 153; Philo, Spec. Leg. 4, 106) ***to have a divided hoof*** πᾶν διχηλοῦν *every animal w. a divided hoof* B 10:11 (Lev 11:3).—DELG s.v. χηλή.

διχοστασία, ας, ἡ (s. two next entries; Solon 3, 37 Diehl[2]; Bacchylides 11, 67 BSnell ['34]; Hdt. 5, 75; Dionys. Hal. 8, 72, 1; Plut., Mor. 479a; Michel 448, 19; 1 Macc 3:29; TestSol 18:16; Ps.-Phocyl. 151; SibOr 4, 68) **the state of being in factious opposition, *dissension*** (w. ἐριθεῖαι, αἱρέσεις) **Gal 5:20;** cp. 1 Cl

46:5; 51:1. διχοστασίας ποιεῖν *cause dissensions* **Ro 16:17;** cp. Hs 8, 7, 5; 8, 10, 2; **1 Cor 3:3 v.l.;** Hv 3, 9, 9; m 2:3.—DELG s.v. δίς and ἵστημι. M-M.

διχοστατέω 1 aor. ἐδιχοστάτησα (s. prec. and next entry; trag.+).

❶ **to adopt a factious position (opp. of being in harmony),** ***disagree*** γῆ μὴ διχοστατοῦσα *without dissent, in harmony* 1 Cl 20:4. Context suggests that this is the place also for Hs 8, 7, 2; 8, 8, 5.

❷ **to be divided within oneself,** ***feel doubts, be insecure*** (Alex. Aphr., Probl., Praef.) Hs 8, 7, 2; 8, 8, 5. But both of these passages may belong in 1 above.

διχοστάτης, ου, ὁ (s. prec. two entries) ***one who causes dissensions*** (w. παράνομοι) Hs 8, 7, 6. S. DELG s.v. δίς and ἵστημι.

διχοτομέω fut. διχοτομήσω; 1 aor. impv. 2 pl. διχοτομήσατε (GrBar 16:3) (Pre-Socr., Pla. et al.; Polyb. 6, 28, 2; 10, 15, 5; Plut., Pyrrh. 399 [24, 5]; ins fr. Lycaonia [JHS 22, 1902, p. 369 nr. 143 A, 9f]; Ex 29:17; Jos., Ant. 8, 31) ***cut in two*** of the dismemberment of a condemned person **Mt 24:51; Lk 12:46** (GrBar 16:3 διχοτομήσατε αὐτοὺς ἐν μαχαίρᾳ. For this idea cp. Od. 18, 339; Hdt. 2, 139; Epict. 3, 22, 3; Sus 55 σχίσει σε μέσον; 59 τὴν ῥομφαίαν ἔχων πρίσαι σε μέσον both Theod.; Hb 11:37). In the light of the context of these two passages the figurative extension of mng. *punish w. utmost severity* has been suggested (L-S-J-M, but no exact linguistic parallels have been found to support either this rendering or the NRSV marginal rdg. 'cut him off').—M-M. S. DELG s.v. δίς and τέμνω. TW.

διψάω 3 sg. διψᾷ (Ps.-Pla., Ax. 366a) **J 7:37; Ro 12:20** (Pr 25:21); fut. διψήσω; 1 aor. ἐδίψησα (Hom. et al.; IG XIV, 1890, 10 [12]; PGM 36, 112; 148; LXX; Philo; Jos., Bell. 6, 318 al.) gener. 'to be thirsty'.

❶ **to have a desire for liquid,** ***be thirsty,*** *suffer fr. thirst* **Mt 25:35, 37, 42, 44; J 4:13, 15; 19:28** (s. GDalman, Jesus-Jeshua [tr. PLevertoff], 1929, 207–9); **Ro 12:20** (Pr 25:21). W. πεινάω to denote the severest privations (Ps 106:5) **1 Cor 4:11; Rv 7:16** (Is 49:10; on liberation fr. hunger and thirst cp. Eur., Bacch. 142f, s. VLeinieks, The City of Dionysos '96); ISm 6:2. In imagery γῆ διψῶσα *thirsty (=dry) ground* 1 Cl 16:3 (Is 53:2). For **J 4:14; 6:35; 7:37** s. 2, below.

❷ **to have a strong desire to attain some goal,** ***thirst,*** i.e. *long for someth.,* fig. ext. of 1 (Pla., Rep. 8, 562c; Plut., Cato Mai. 342 [11, 5]; Philo, Fug. 139 τοὺς διψῶντας κ. πεινῶντας καλοκἀγαθίας; Ps 41:3; Sir 51:24) of thirst for the water of life **J 4:14; 6:35; 7:37; Rv 21:6; 22:17** (cp. Is 55:1). τ. δικαιοσύνην **Mt 5:6** (for the acc. cp. Philipp. Epigr. [I AD] in Anth. Plan. bk. 4=Anth. Pal. 16, 137 Düb. φόνον; Jos., Bell. 1, 628 αἷμα; Cos. and Dam. 10, 64 τ. σωτηρίαν. W. acc. of pers. Ps 62:2 v.l. [Psalmi cum Odis ed. ARahlfs '31]).—For the idea JBover, Estudios Eclesiásticos 16, '42, 9–26; FBraun, Avoir Soif (J 4 and 7), BRigaux Festschr., '70, 247–58.—Abs., opp. drunkenness Ox 1 verso, 16f (ASyn. 240, 41; cp. GTh 28; s. LWright, JBL 65, '46, 180f).—DELG s.v. δίψα. M-M. TW. Spicq.

δίψος, ους, τό (s. διψάω; X., al.; Epict.; PTebt 272, 17 [med. pap]; LXX; s. Thackeray 157; Philo; Jos., Ant. 3, 37; 38; 18, 192. S. also Nägeli 14) ***thirst*** (w. λιμός, as Dio Chrys. 7 [8], 16; 13 [7], 55; Pythag., Ep. 4, 4; Socrat., Ep. 12; Is 5:13) **2 Cor 11:27.**—B. 333. DELG s.v. δίψα. M-M. TW.

διψυχέω (s. two next entries) 1 aor. ἐδιψύχησα (not in nonbibl. wr., LXX, or NT) **to be uncertain about the truth of someth.,** ***be undecided, be changeable, doubt*** (of indecision about becoming a Christian or believing in specif. Christian teachings or hopes, etc.). Abs. 1 Cl 23:2; 2 Cl 11:5; Hv 2, 2, 7; 4, 1, 4; 7; 4, 2, 4; m 9:8; s 8, 8, 3; 5; 8, 9, 4; 8, 10, 2; οἱ διψυχοῦντες *those who waver* Hv 3, 2, 2; m 9:6. ἔχω τι διψυχῆσαι *I am doubtful about someth.* Hv 4, 1, 4; cp. 3, 3, 4.—w. περί τινος *be in doubt about someth.* Hs 6, 1, 2. Also ἐπί τινι s 8, 11, 3. μηδὲν ὅλως δ. w. inf. foll. *not hesitate at all to* ... m 9:1. W. indir. quest. foll. *doubt whether* B 19:5; D 4:4. W. ὅτι foll. Hm 9:7.—S. DELG s.v. δίς and ψυχή.

διψυχία, ας, ἡ (s. prec. and foll. entries; neither LXX nor NT.—Hesych. διψυχία· ἀπορία) the state or condition of being uncertain about someth. *indecision, doubt* (in our lit. in sacred matters) Hv 3, 10, 9; m 9:7, 9ff; w. ἀπιστία 2 Cl 19:2; w. μαλακίαι Hv 3, 11, 2; w. ὀξυχολία m 10, 1, 1f; 10, 2, 4. αἴρειν τὴν δ. *remove the doubt* m 9:1; also αἴρειν τὰς δ. v 2, 2, 4; διὰ τὴν δ. m 10, 2, 2; ἀπὸ τῆς δ. *because of doubt* v 3, 7, 1. Called the daughter of the devil m 9:9.—ABaumeister, Die Ethik des Pastor Hermae, 1912, 107–10.—Sv.

δίψυχος, ον (s. prec. two entries; not in non-bibl. wr. or LXX; the title in Philo, fgm. II 663 Mangey is not fr. Philo's hand.—But Parmenides 6, 5 speaks of δίκρανοι=double-headed people, who stagger helplessly here and there in their thinking) **pert. to being uncertain about the truth of someth.,** ***doubting, hesitating,*** lit. *double-minded* **Js 4:8** (cp. Pind., N. 10, 89 οὐ γνώμᾳ διπλόαν θέτο βουλάν='he entertained no double purpose in his mind'); ἀνὴρ δ. *a doubter* **1:8;** Hm 9:6; ὁ δ. m 10, 2, 2; οἱ δ. (w. διστάζοντες) 1 Cl 11:2; 23:3; 2 Cl 11:2.—Hv 3, 4, 3; 4, 2, 6; m 9:5; 11:1f, 4; s 8, 7, 1; 9, 21, 1ff. W. ἀπόκενος m 5, 2, 1. κενός m 11:13. ἀσύνετος m 12, 4, 2. ἄφρων, ταλαίπωρος s 1:3. βλάσφημος s 9, 18, 3. κατάλαλος s 8, 7, 2.—OSeitz, JBL 63, '44, 131–40; 66, '47, 211–19, NTS 4, '57/58, 327–34 (Hermas and the Thanksgiving Scroll); WWolverton, ATR 38, '56, 166–75 (Essene Psychology).—M-M. TW. Sv.

διωγμίτης, ου, ὁ (s. three next entries; OGI 511, 10, also editor's note 3 w. further exx.) **one who engages in pursuit,** ***detective,*** *(mounted) security officer* (cp. Old Eng. 'manhunter') MPol 7:1 (JMarquardt, Röm. Staatsverw. I[2] 1881, 213).—DELG s.v. διώκω.

διωγμός, οῦ, ὁ (s. two next entries; Aeschyl. et al.; Polyb. 3, 74, 2; Plut.; LXX, AscIs) **a program or process designed to harass and oppress someone,** ***persecution*** (in our lit. only for reasons of belief) δ. μέγας *a severe persecution* **Ac 8:1.** μετὰ διωγμῶν (D -οῦ; other v.l. -όν) *not without persecutions* **Mk 10:30** (s. MGoguel, RHPR 8, 1928, 264–77). ἐπεγείρειν δ. ἐπί τινα *stir up a persecution against someone* **Ac 13:50;** δ. ὑποφέρειν *suffer persecution* **2 Ti 3:11.** καταπαύειν τ. διωγμόν *bring the persecution to an end* MPol 1:1. W. θλῖψις **Mt 13:21; Mk 4:17; 2 Th 1:4;** στενοχωρία **2 Cor 12:10.** W. both **Ro 8:35.** W. παθήματα **2 Ti 3:11.** W. ἀκαταστασία 1 Cl 3:2. DELG s.v. διώκω. TW.

διώκτης, ου, ὁ (s. prec. and next entry; not outside Jewish/Christian wr., but cp. ἐργοδιώκτης 'taskmaster'=our colloq. 'slave-driver' PPetr II, 4/1, 2 [III BC; s. JMahaffy's comm. in the same vol. p. 6]; Hos 6:8 Sym.) ***persecutor*** (w. βλάσφημος, ὑβριστής) **1 Ti 1:13;** δ. ἀγαθῶν *persecutor of the good* D 5:2; B 20:2.—DELG s.v. διώκω. M-M.

διώκω impf. ἐδίωκον; fut. διώξω (B-D-F §77); 1 aor. ἐδίωξα, pass. ἐδιώχθην; pf. pass. ptc. δεδιωγμένος (Hom.+)

❶ **to move rapidly and decisively toward an objective, *hasten, run, press on*** (Il. 23, 344; Aeschyl., Sept. 91; X., An. 6, 5, 25; Hg 1:9; Is 13:14; Philo, Virt. 30 διώκουσι καὶ ἐπιτρέχουσιν) κατὰ σκοπόν *toward the goal* **Phil 3:14;** cp. vs. **12** (on the combination w. καταλαμβάνω cp. Hdt. 9, 58, 4; Lucian, Herm. 77; Sir 11:10; La 1:3 v.l.).

❷ **to harass someone, esp. because of beliefs, *persecute*** (OGI 532, 25) τινά *someone* (1 Macc 5:22; En 99:14; Jos., Ant. 12, 272; apolog.) **Mt 5:11f, 44; 10:23; Lk 11:49; 21:12; J 5:16; 15:20; Ac 7:52; 9:4f; 22:4, 7f; 26:11, 14f; Ro 12:14; 1 Cor 4:12; 15:9; Gal 1:13, 23; 4:29; Phil 3:6; Rv 12:13;** AcPl Ha 11:17f; D 1:3; 16:4; B 20:2; Dg 7:5; ἐν θανάτῳ δ. *persecute to death* B 5:11. Pass. (Lucian, D. Mar. 9, 1) **Mt 5:10** (=Pol. 2:3); **2 Cor 4:9; Gal 5:11; 6:12; 2 Ti 3:12;** IMg 8:2; ITr 9:1; 1 Cl 4:13; 5:2; 6:2; 45:4; Dg 5:11, 17. Of plots against Joseph 1 Cl 4:9.

❸ **to cause to run or set in motion, *drive away, drive out*** (Od. 18, 409; Hdt. 9, 77, 2a μέχρι Θεσσαλίης, 2b ἐκ τ. γῆς, 3; POxy 943, 5; BGU 954, 7–9 ὅπως διώξῃς ἀπ᾽ ἐμοῦ τ. δαίμονα [VI AD?, Christ.]; Cat. Cod. Astr. VIII/2 p. 174, 20); w. ἐκ **Mt 10:23 v.l.** (cp. our 'run someone out of town'); w. ἀπό **23:34** (δ. εἴς τι as Appian, Bell. Civ. 2, 14 §52).

❹ **to follow in haste in order to find someth., *run after, pursue*—ⓐ** lit. μηδὲ διώξητε *do not run after (them)* **Lk 17:23** (cp. X., Mem. 2, 8, 6; SIG 1168, 112).

ⓑ fig. *pursue, strive for, seek after, aspire to* someth. (Thu. 2, 63, 1 τιμάς; Pla., Gorg. 482e ἀλήθειαν; Dio Chrys. 60 + 61 [77 + 78], 26 πλούτους; Ael. Aristid. 29, 1 K.=40 p. 751 D.; Is 5:11; Hos 6:3; Sir 31:5; Philo, Somn. 1, 199 ἡδονὴν δ.; Jos., Ant. 6, 263 τὸ δίκαιον) δικαιοσύνην (Pr 15:9) *uprightness* **Ro 9:30; 1 Ti 6:11; 2 Ti 2:22;** 2 Cl 18:2. νόμον δικαιοσύνης **Ro 9:31** (cp. 2 Esdr 9:4); hospitality **12:13.** Pursue what makes for peace **14:19;** cp. **Hb 12:14.**—OT citation: **1 Pt 3:11** (Ps 33:15); 1 Cl 22:5; cp. 2 Cl 10:2.—Love **1 Cor 14:1;** virtue (Maximus Tyr. 15, 7c) 2 Cl 10:1; what is good (Alex. Aphr., An. Mant. II/1 p. 155, 31 δ. τὸ καλόν) **1 Th 5:15.**—διώκοντες ἀνταπόδομα *in pursuit of recompense* D 5:2 = B 20:2 (Is 1:23); cp. 2 Cl 20:4.—B. 700. DELG. M-M. TW. Sv.

δόγμα, ατος, τό (s. δογματίζω, δοκέω; X., Pla.+; loanw. in rabb.).

❶ **a formal statement concerning rules or regulations that are to be observed—ⓐ** of formalized sets of rules ***ordinance, decision, command*** (Pla., Rep. 3, 414b; Demosth. 25, 16; Plut., Mor. 742d; Da 3:10; 4:6; 6:13 Theod. al.; Mel., HE 4, 26, 5; Did., Gen. 221, 20) **Hb 11:23 v.l.** Of the *rules* or *commandments* of Jesus B 1:6; IMg 13:1; of the gospel D 11:3; of the apostles **Ac 16:4** (cp. the Christian prayer in CSchmidt, GHeinrici Festschr. 1914, p. 71, 24). τριῶν γραμμάτων δόγματα λαμβάνειν *receive instructions from three letters* (of the alphabet) B 9:7; cp. 10:1, 9f. Of the Mosaic law (3 Macc 1:3; Philo, Gig. 52, Leg. All. 1, 54; 55 διατήρησις τ. ἁγίων δογμάτων; Jos., C. Ap. 1, 42) νόμος τῶν ἐντολῶν ἐν δ. *law of commandments consisting in* (single) *ordinances* **Eph 2:15.** τὸ καθ᾽ ἡμῶν χειρόγραφον τοῖς δ. *the bond that stood against us, w. its requirements* **Col 2:14.**

ⓑ of an imperial declaration (SEG IX, 8) ***decree*** (Jos., Bell. 1, 393; PFay 20, 22 a δ. of Alex. Severus) ἐξῆλθεν δ. (cp. Da 2:13 Theod.) παρὰ Καίσαρος **Lk 2:1.** ἀπέναντι τῶν δογμάτων Καίσαρος πράττειν *act contrary to the decrees of Caesar* **Ac 17:7** (EJudge, The Decrees of Caesar at Thessalonica: Reformed Theological Review 30, '71, 1–7).

❷ **something that is taught as an established tenet or statement of belief, *doctrine, dogma*** (Pla. et al.; Plut., Mor. 14e; 779b; 1000d; Epict. 4, 11, 8; Herodian 1, 2, 4; Philo, Spec. Leg. 1, 269; Jos., Bell. 2, 142; apolog.; Theoph. Ant. 3, 3 [p. 210, 4]; ἡμέτερον δόγμα [=the Gospel] Orig., C. Cels. 2, 4, 20) of philosophical position δ. ἀνθρώπινον Dg 5:3. Of false prophets δ. ποικίλα τῆς ἀπωλείας διδάσκειν *teach various doctrines that lead to perdition* ApcPt 1 (Diod. S. 1, 86, 2 of relig. teaching [about the sacred animals of the Egyptians]). τὰ τοῦ πονηροῦ . . . δόγματα AcPlCor 2:2.—RAC III 1257–60; IV 1–24; Ferguson, Legal Terms, 47–49; Mason 39; Sherk, lit. on senatorial decrees p. 2f.—M-M. DELG s.v. δοκάω etc. New Docs 4, 146. S. διάταγμα. TW. Sv.

δογματίζω (s. δόγμα) 1 aor. ἐδογμάτισα LXX; pf. δεδογμάτικα 1 Esdr 6:33; pf. pass. ptc. δεδογματισμένον 3 Macc 4:11; 1 aor. pass. ἐδογματίσθη (=decree, ordain, since II BC; s. Nägeli 32; Da 2:13 and elsewhere LXX, Just., Tat.; Ath.: 'state position' or 'viewpoint') **to put under obligation by rules or ordinances, *obligate:*** pass. *submit to rules and regulations* **Col 2:20** here permissive pass. (s. Gildersleeve, Syntax I 73)=*permit yourselves to be put under* etc. τὰ δεδογματισμένα ὑπό τινος *things decreed by someone* 1 Cl 20:4; 27:5 (cp. 3 Macc 4:11).—M-M. DELG s.v. δοκάω etc. TW.

δοθείς s. δίδωμι.

δοῖ s. δίδωμι.

δοκέω impf. ἐδόκουν, 3 pl. ἐδοκοῦσαν Hs 9, 9, 5 (s. B-D-F §84, 3); fut. δόξω; 1 aor. ἔδοξα; pf. pass. 3 sg. δέδοκται 1 Esdr 8:11; ptc. δεδογμένον LXX (s. δόγμα; Hom.+).

❶ **to consider as probable, *think, believe, suppose, consider,*** trans., of subjective opinion (Hom.+; pap; rare LXX).

ⓐ w. inf. foll., when its subj. is identical w. that of the inf. (X., An. 2, 2, 14; Diod. S. 17, 27, 2 τοὺς δοκοῦντας νενικηκέναι; Pr 28:24; 4 Macc 13:14; Just., D. 2, 4 δοκεῖς κατόψεσθαι): μὴ δόξητε λέγειν *do not suppose that you are to say* **Mt 3:9.** ἐδόκουν πνεῦμα θεωρεῖν *they thought they saw a ghost* **Lk 24:37.** ὃ δοκεῖ ἔχειν *what he thinks he has* **8:18** (cp. Jos., Bell. 3, 319). ὁ δοκῶν πνεῦμα ἔχειν *the one who thinks he has the Spirit* Hm 11:12; cp. **J 5:39; 16:2; Ac 27:13; 1 Cor 7:40; Phil 3:4; Js 1:26;** 2 Cl 17:3; Dg 3:5; 8:10; Hm 10, 2, 4.

ⓑ foll. by the inf. w. a nom. ὅσῳ δοκεῖ μᾶλλον μείζων εἶναι *the greater he thinks he is* (or *seems to be,* s. 2 below) 1 Cl 48:6. εἴ τις δοκεῖ σοφὸς εἶναι *if anyone thinks that he is wise* **1 Cor 3:18.** εἴ τις δοκεῖ προφήτης εἶναι **14:37.** εἴ τις δοκεῖ φιλόνεικος εἶναι *if anyone is disposed to be contentious* **11:16.—Gal 6:3.**

ⓒ foll. by acc. and inf. w. subj. not identical (X., An. 1, 7, 1; PTebt 413, 6 μὴ δόξῃς με, κυρία, ἠμεληκέναι σου τῶν ἐντολῶν; Gen 38:15; 2 Macc 7:16; 3 Macc 5:5; Demetr.: 722 fgm. 1, 1 Jac.; Jos., Ant. 2, 340; Just. A I, 3, 1; D. 118, 2) μή τίς με δόξῃ ἄφρονα εἶναι *no one is to consider me foolish* **2 Cor 11:16.** ἃ δοκοῦμεν ἀτιμότερα εἶναι (the bodily members) *which we consider less worthy of special attention* **1 Cor 12:23.**

ⓓ w. ὅτι foll. (Arrian, Alex. An. 4, 28, 2) **Mt 6:7; 26:53; Mk 6:49; Lk 12:51; 13:2, 4; J 5:45; 11:13, 31; 1 Cor 4:9 v.l.; 2 Cor 12:19; Js 4:5;** Hv 4, 3, 7; 5:3.

ⓔ used parenthetically (B-D-F §465, 2; Rob. 434; cp. Anacreontea 35, 15 Preis. πόσον δοκεῖς πονοῦσιν; Aristoph., Acharn. 12; Epict. 2, 19, 7; POxy 1218, 6f ἡ μήτηρ μου Θαῆσις εἰς 'Αντινόου, δοκῶ, ἐπὶ κηδίαν ἀπῆλθεν) πόσῳ δοκεῖτε χείρονος ἀξιωθήσεται τιμωρίας; *how much more severely, do you think, will he be punished?* **Hb 10:29.** τί δοκεῖτε ποιήσει; *what, do you think, will he do?* Hs 9, 28, 8; cp. **1 Cor 4:9.** οὔ, δοκῶ *I suppose not* **Lk 17:9 v.l.**

ⓕ elliptically (2 Macc 2:29) ᾗ οὐ δοκεῖτε ὥρᾳ ὁ υἱὸς τ. ἀνθρώπου ἔρχεται *the Human One / Son of Man is coming at an hour when you do not think (he will come)* **Mt 24:44;** cp. **Lk 12:40.** τί δοκεῖτε; *what do you think?* 1 Cl 43:6; 2 Cl 7:5. τί δοκεῖς τοὺς κεκλημένους; *what do you think about those who have been called?* Hs 9, 14, 5 (cp. X., An. 5, 7, 26 τούτους τί δοκεῖτε;).

❷ to appear to one's understanding, *seem, be recognized as*—ⓐ intr. (Hom. et al.; so mostly LXX)—**α.** *have the appearance* w. dat. of pers. τίς τούτων … πλησίον δοκεῖ σοι γεγονέναι; *who of these, do you think, proved to be a neighbor?* **Lk 10:36** (on τίνα … δοκεῖς … γεγονέναι; v.l. cp. 1c). δ. καταγγελεὺς εἶναι *he seems to be a preacher* **Ac 17:18;** cp. **1 Cor 12:22; 2 Cor 10:9; Hb 12:11;** Dg 8:10 (παρὰ πᾶσι σπέρματα ἀληθείας δοκεῖ εἶναι Just., A I, 44, 10). εἴ τινι μὴ δοκοίη κἂν ταῦτα ἱκανά *if that should seem to anybody to be insufficient* Dg 2:10 (cp. Just., D. 42, 4). οὐδέν μοι δοκοῦσι διαφέρειν *they seem to me to differ in no way* 3:5 (παράδοξον λέγειν μοι δοκεῖς Just., D. 49, 6). ἔδοξα ἐμαυτῷ δεῖν πρᾶξαι=Lat. mihi videbar *I was convinced that it was necessary to do* **Ac 26:9** (cp. Aristoph., Vesp. 177, 1265; Aeschin. 3, 53 [Schwyzer II 193]). GMary 463, 9. τὸ δοκεῖν *in appearance* (only) (Sextus 64; Sb 7696, 55 [250 AD]; Jos., Vi. 75, Ant. 14, 291 v.l. for τῷ δοκεῖν; s. Hdb. on ITr 10) ITr 10; ISm 2; 4:2. ὁ δοκῶν ἐνθάδε θάνατος *what seems to be death in this world* Dg 10:7 (τὰ δοκούντα καλά Just., A II, 1, 6; τῶν ἐν βαρβάροις … δοξάντων σοφῶν A I, 7, 3). As an expression serving to moderate a statement **Hb 4:1.**

β. *be influential, be recognized as being someth., have a reputation* (cp. Sus 5; 2 Macc 1:13). οἱ δοκοῦντες (Eur., Hec. 295; Petosiris, fgm. 6 ln. 58 οἱ δ.=the prominent dignitaries; Herodian 6, 1, 2; Jos., C. Ap. 1, 67) *the influential men* **Gal 2:2, 6b.** A fuller expr. w. the same mng., w. inf. added (X., Cyr. 7, 1, 41; Pla., Gorg. 472a, Euthd. 303c οἱ δοκοῦντες εἶναί τι; Plut. Mor. 212b δοκοῦντας εἶναί τινας; Epict., Ench. 33, 12; Herodian 4, 2, 5; Philo, Mos. 2, 241) vss. **6a, 9** (Pla., Apol. 6, 21b οἱ δοκοῦντες σοφοὶ εἶναι). WFoerster, D. δοκοῦντες in Gal 2: ZNW 36, '38, 286–92 (against him, HGreeven, ZNW 44, '52, 41 n. 100).— οἱ δοκοῦντες ἄρχειν *those who are reputed to be rulers* **Mk 10:42** (cp. Plut., Arat. 1047 [43, 2] ᾧ δουλεύουσιν οἱ δοκοῦντες ἄρχειν).

ⓑ impers. δοκεῖ μοι ***it seems to me*** (Ael. Aristid. 47 p. 427 D.: ἔμοιγε δοκεῖ; Jos., Ant. 6, 227 δοκεῖ σοι; Just., D. 5, 2 οὕτως δοκεῖ ὀρθῶς ἔχειν).

α. *I think, believe* (cp. 1 above): τί σοι δοκεῖ; *what do you think?* **Mt 17:25; 22:17.** τί ὑμῖν δοκεῖ; **18:12; 21:28; 26:66; J 11:56.** W. περί τινος foll. (Lucian, Dial. Deor. 6, 4) **Mt 22:42;** GMary 463, 6 (PRyl 3, 463). W. acc. and inf. foll. (Ael. Aristid. 46 p. 344 D.) οὐ δοκεῖ σοι τὸ μετανοῆσαι σύνεσιν εἶναι; *do you not think that repentance is understanding?* Hm 4, 2, 2; cp. m 8:6; 11; 10, 1, 2. τὸ δοκοῦν τινι *someone's discretion* (Diod. S. 19, 91, 1 αὐτῷ τὸ δοκοῦν=his discretion; Just., A II, 14, 1 τὸ ὑμῖν δοκοῦν) κατὰ τὸ δ. αὐτοῖς *at their discretion* (Lucian, Tim. 25; cp. Thu. 1, 84, 2 παρὰ τὸ δοκοῦν ἡμῖν) **Hb 12:10.**

β. *it seems best to me, I decide, I resolve* w. inf. foll. (X., An. 1, 10, 17; Diod. S. 18, 55, 2; Appian, Iber. 63 §265; SIG 1169, 77 [IV BC]; Jos., Ant. 6, 321) **Lk 1:3** (decretal style; cp. the foll. pass.); as administrative t.t. (freq. ins, e.g. IPriene 105, 20 [9 BC]) **Ac 15:22, 25, 28** (cp. Jos., Ant. 16, 163 ἔδοξέ μοι κ. τῷ ἐμῷ συμβουλίῳ … χρῆσθαι; Dio Chrys. 80 [30], 8 ἔδοξε τῷ θεῷ; s. Ferguson, Legal Terms 50–53 on the socio-cultural implications of these Ac pass.; Danker, Benefactor 310–13; s. also MSimon, BJRL 52, '69/70, 437–60; CPerrot, RSR 69, '81, 195–208); ἄλογον γάρ μοι δοκεῖ *I decided that is was unreasonable* 25:27. Cp. MPol 12:3. ὡς ἂν σοι δόξῃ *as it may seem best to you* D 13:7 (Arrian, Cyneg. 3. 4 ὥς μοι δοκεῖ).—Cp. the contrast of the two mngs.: τὰ ἀεὶ δοκοῦντα … τῷ δοκοῦντι εἶναι ἀληθῆ='that which *seems* true is true to one who *thinks* it' Pla., Tht. 158e (s. L-S-J-M δ. end).—EHamp, ClPh 63, '68, 285–87.—B. 1121. DELG. Schmidt, Syn. I 321–28 s. δόξα. M-M. EDNT. TW. Sv.

δοκιμάζω (s. four next entries) fut. δοκιμάσω, δοκιμῶ LXX; 1 aor. ἐδοκίμασα; pf. 2 sg. δεδοκίμακας Jer 12:3, pass. δεδοκίμασμαι (Hdt., Thu.+)

❶ to make a critical examination of someth. to determine genuineness, *put to the test, examine* (so mostly LXX.—EpArist 276; Jos., Ant. 1, 233; 3, 15; TestAsh 5:4; Tat., Ath.; Iren. 1, prol. 2 [Harv. I 3, 9]) w. acc., *test* oxen for their usefulness **Lk 14:19** (Hdt. 2, 38 of the Apis bulls). ἑαυτόν *examine oneself* **1 Cor 11:28; 2 Cor 13:5;** one's own work **Gal 6:4;** the works of God **Hb 3:9 v.l.** (Ps 94:9); of God's self (w. πειράζω); ApcPt (Ox 849, 25); τὰ διαφέροντα **Ro 2:18; Ph 1:10;** φθοριμαίοις (cod. φθοριμειοις) λόγοις, οὓς σὺ (cod. σοι) δοκίμασον *destructive statements, which you must evaluate* AcPlCor 1:3; everything **1 Th 5:21;** spirits (of bogus prophets) **1J 4:1;** cp. D 12:1; Hm 11, 7, 16; 1 Cl 42:4; believers in general Hs 8, 2, 5; fig. οἰκοδομήν 9, 5, 2; heaven and earth **Lk 12:56a;** τὸν καιρόν **56b;** *be convinced* of someone's faithfulness 1 Cl 1:2; *try to learn* τί ἐστιν εὐάρεστον τῷ κυρίῳ *what is pleasing to the Lord* **Eph 5:10.**—Of the examination of prospects for special service in the Christian community (acc. to Attic usage: Lysias 16, 3; Pla., Leg. 6, 765c; Attic ins) **1 Ti 3:10.** Of God **1 Th 2:4b** (Jer 11:20; 17:10; 20:12; Ps 7:10; 26:2; Jos., Ant. 1, 233).—Of opponents Βαρσαββᾶς … δοκιμαζόμενος ὑπὸ τῶν ἀπίστων *Barsabbas … was put to the test by the unbelievers* Papias (11:2).—For **Ro 2:18,** and **12:2** s. 2b below.

❷ to draw a conclusion about worth on the basis of testing, *prove, approve,* here the focus is on the result of a procedure or examination.

ⓐ *prove by testing,* of gold (Isocr., Panathen. 14, 39; SIG 334, 45 [on monetary assoc. s. other reff. in SEG XLII, 1851]; Pr 8:10; Sir 2:5; Wsd 3:6) **1 Pt 1:7** (on testing of character cp. Pind., P. 10, 67f); Hv 4, 3, 4; cp. **1 Cor 3:13** (JGnilka, Ist 1 Cor 3:10–15 ein Schriftzeugnis für d. Fegefeuer? '55). τὰς ψυχάς ApcPt 3.

ⓑ *accept as proved, approve* (PEleph 1, 10; POxy 928, 7 ἵνα ἐὰν δοκιμάσῃς ποιήσῃς; PTebt 326, 10) w. acc. τὶ ISm 8:2. οὓς ἐὰν δοκιμάσητε *whom you consider qualified* **1 Cor 16:3.** ἐδοκιμάσαμεν σπουδαῖον ὄντα *we have tested and found him zealous* **2 Cor 8:22.** ἐδοκίμασε γὰρ ὑμᾶς ὁ κύριος καὶ ἐνέγραψεν ὑμᾶς εἰς τὸν ἀριθμὸν τὸν ἡμέτερον Hs 9, 24, 4; cp. λίθους v 3, 5, 3. δ. τὸ ἀγάπης γνήσιον *prove the genuineness of love* **2 Cor 8:8.** ἐν ᾧ δοκιμάζει *for what he approves* **Ro 14:22.** δ. τὰ διαφέροντα *approve* (or *discover* s. under 1) *what is essential* **Ro 2:18; Phil 1:10.** W. inf. (Appian, Iber. 90 §392, Bell. Civ. 2, 114 §475; Jos., Ant. 2, 176, Vi. 161 simply = intend, wish) οὐκ ἐδοκίμασαν τὸν θεὸν ἔχειν ἐν ἐπιγνώσει *they did not see fit to have a true knowledge of God* **Ro 1:28** (anticipating the opposite in **12:2.**—WReiss, 'Gott nicht kennen' im AT, ZAW 58, '40/41, 70–98). W. indir. quest. foll. δ., τί τὸ θέλημα τ. θεοῦ *approve* (or *discover* s. under 1) *what God's will is* 12:2. Pass. (Prov. Aesopi 171 P. φίλος καὶ ἵππος ἐν ἀνάγκῃ δοκιμάζονται=stand the test; Jos., Ant. 3, 71) δεδοκιμάσμεθα *we have been found worthy* w. inf. foll. **1 Th 2:4a.** δεδοκιμασμένος *tested, approved* of genuine prophets D 11:11 (Diod. S. 4, 7, 1 δεδοκιμασμένος of the story writer who has a good reputation; cp. SIG 807, 9; PFay 106, 23; 2 Macc 4:3); cp. Hm 11, 7, 16 (s. 1 above); πνεῦμα δεδοκιμασμένον v 2, 4; of Jesus **Ac 2:22** D.—B. 652. DELG s.v. δοκάω etc. EDNT. M-M. TW. Spicq.

δοκιμασία, ας, ἡ (s. δοκιμάζω, δοκιμή, δοκίμιον, δόκιμος; Lysias et al.; Polyb., Plut., Epict.; SIG 972, 29; PSI 1105, 18 [II AD]; PMert 26, 11 [III AD]; PLeid X vii, 12; 20; ix, 12; Sir 6:21; PsSol 16:14; TestSol 19:3 P.; Jos., Ant. 4, 54) **an examination for genuineness,** ***testing, examination*** πειράζειν ἐν δ. *put to the test* **Hb 3:9.** πύρωσις τῆς δ. *trial by fire* D 16:5.—M-M. TW. Spicq. Sv.

δοκιμή, ῆς, ἡ (s. δοκιμάζω, δοκίμιον, δόκιμος; several mss. of Diosc., Mater. Med. 4, 184 Wellm. II p. 333, 9 n.; Achmes 24, 9; Cat. Cod. Astr. X 67, 7; Ps 67:31 Sym.—B-D-F §110, 2; Mlt-H. 352).

❶ **a testing process,** ***test, ordeal*** (Sextus 7a δ. πίστεως) ἐν πολλῇ δοκιμῇ θλίψεως *in a great ordeal of affliction* **2 Cor 8:2.**

❷ **the experience of going through a test with special ref. to the result,** ***standing a test, character*** **Ro 5:4** (a pregnant constr.: ὑπομονή as a process of enduring something amounts to a test that promotes and validates the character of the one undergoing it. This success in turn promotes ἐλπίς). γινώσκειν τὴν δ. τινος *make determination of someone's attitude* **2 Cor 2:9;** *make proof of someone's character* or *value* **Phil 2:22.** δ. τῆς διακονίας *the approved character of your service* **2 Cor 9:13.**— δ. ζητεῖν *desire proof* or *evidence* **13:3.**—M-M. TW. Spicq.

δοκίμιον, ου, τό (s. three prec. entries and δόκιμος; on the spelling s. Mlt-H. 78; B-D-F §23; B-D-R §13, 3; 263, 5; δοκιμεῖον preferred by PKatz, TLZ 83, '58, 314f; WGrundmann, TW II 259).

❶ **the process or means of determining the genuineness of someth.,** ***testing, means of testing*** (Dionys. Hal., Rhet. 11, 1; Herodian 2, 10, 6; Plut., Mor. 230b; Περὶ ὕψους 32, 5 γλῶσσα γεύσεως δοκίμιον; Pr 27:21) τὸ δ. ὑμῶν τῆς πίστεως κατεργάζεται ὑπομονήν *the testing of your faith* (temptation) *produces endurance* **Js 1:3.**

❷ **genuineness as result of a test,** ***genuine, without alloy,*** neut. sg. of the adj. δοκίμιος (esp. of metals: BGU 1045 II, 12; 1065, 8; PTebt 392, 22; s. Dssm., NB 86ff [BS 259ff]) τὸ δ. ὑμῶν τῆς πίστεως *the genuineness of your faith* (on the usage B-D-F §263, 2) **1 Pt 1:7** (δόκιμον P[72] et al.; cp. **Js 1:3 v.l.;** s. δόκιμος 1).—DELG s.v. δοκάω etc. III p. 291. M-M. TW. Spicq.

δόκιμος, ον (s. four prec. entries; Pre-Socr., Hdt.+; superlative: Tat. 1, 1; 38, 1) CArbenz, Die Adj. auf -ιμος, diss. Zürich '33, 38ff; Schwyzer I 494f.

❶ **pert. to being genuine on the basis of testing,** ***approved (by test), tried and true, genuine*** (Alcaeus 6, 12 L-P [119 + 120 + 122 Diehl] of a man: νῦν τις ἀνὴρ δόκιμος γενέσθω; TestJos 2:7) **Js 1:12; 2 Cor 10:18; 13:7; 2 Ti 2:15.** δ. τραπεζῖται *approved money changers* (who put genuine money or legal tender [cp. Epict. 1, 7, 6 δραχμὰς δοκίμους κ. ἀδοκίμους; Socrat., Ep. 6, 12] in circulation) Agr 11. ὁ δ. ἐν Χριστῷ the approved one in Christ=*the tried and true Christian* **Ro 16:10;** οἱ δ. **1 Cor 11:19.**

❷ **pert. to being considered worthy of high regard,** ***respected, esteemed*** (Hdt., al.; Philo, Op. M. 128, De Jos. 201; Jos., C. Ap. 1, 18) δ. τοῖς ἀνθρώποις *among people* (in contrast to God) **Ro 14:18.**

❸ **pert. to being valuable,** ***precious*** comp. of Polycarp's bones *more precious than gold* (cp. **1 Pt 1:7 v.l.**) MPol 18:2.—DELG s.v. δοκάω etc. III p. 291. M-M. TW. Spicq. Sv.

δοκός, οῦ, ἡ (s. δέχομαι) (Hom. et al.; ins, pap, LXX; Jos., Bell. 3, 214f, Ant. 14, 106; loanw. in rabb.) **a piece of heavy timber such as a beam used in roof construction or to bar a door,** ***beam of wood*** **Mt 7:3ff; Lk 6:41f** (cp. Ox 1 verso, 1–4).—GKing, HTR 17, 1924, 393–404; 26, '33, 73–76; CWebster, ET 39, 1928, 91f; PHedley, ibid. 427f; SKaatz, Jeschurun 16, 1929, 482–84.—B. 599. DELG s.v. δέχομαι. M-M.

δόλιος, ία, ον (s. four next entries; Hom. et al.; LXX; TestSol 26:5 B; Jos., Bell. 4, 208, Ant. 1, 335) **pert. to violation of trust in effort to deceive,** ***deceitful, treacherous;*** ἐργάται δ. *dishonest workmen* **2 Cor 11:13;** χείλη δ. *deceitful lips* 1 Cl 15:5 (Ps 30:19; 11:4). W. κατάλαλος: οἱ δ. *treacherous persons* (cp. Sir 11:29) Hs 9, 26, 7.—DELG s.v. δόλος. M-M.

δολιότης, ητος, ἡ (Vett. Val. 2, 3; LXX; Test12Patr) ***deceit, treachery*** περιπλέκειν δολιότητα *weave deceit* 1 Cl 35:8 (Ps 49:19). W. πονηρία Hs 8, 6, 2.—DELG s.v. δόλος.

δολιόω impf. 3 pl. ἐδολιοῦσαν B-D-F §84, 3; Mlt-H. 195; Rdm.[2] 92, 95 (schol. on Soph., Trach. 412 p. 303 P.; LXX) ***deceive*** **Ro 3:13** (Ps 5:10; 13:3).—DELG s.v. δόλος.

δόλος, ου, ὁ (s. three prec. entries and δολόω; Hom.+; ins, pap, LXX; PsSol 4:8; Test12Patr; ApcEl [PSI 7 verso, 3]; SibOr 3, 191; EpArist 246; Philo; Jos., C. Ap. 2, 200 al.; Just., D. 14, 2; Iren. 5, 29, 2 [Harv. II 404, 2]; loanw. in rabb.) **taking advantage through craft and underhanded methods,** ***deceit, cunning, treachery.*** In the following lists of vices (cp. Herm. Wr. 13, 7b) δ. may be rendered by *deceit* **Mk 7:22; Ro 1:29;** D 5:1; B 20:1; pl. 1 Cl 35:5. ἐν ᾧ δ. οὐκ ἔστιν *in whom there is nothing false* (Theogn. 416 πιστὸν ἑταῖρον, ὅτῳ μή τις ἔνεστι δόλος; LXX) **J 1:47;** cp. **1 Pt 2:22;** 1 Cl 16:10 (both Is 53:9); 50:6; **Rv 14:5 v.l.** (both Ps 31:2); Pol 8:1 (after 1 Pt 2:22); πλήρης παντὸς δ. *monster of underhandedness* (Goodsp.) **Ac 13:10** (Just., D. 14, 2 μεμεστωμένοι . . . δόλου). W. κακία **1 Pt 2:1** (FDanker, ZNW 58, '67, 93–95); λαλεῖν δ. *speak deceitfully* **3:10;** 1 Cl 22:3 (both Ps 33:14).—δόλῳ *by cunning* or *stealth* (Hom. et al.; Ex 21:14; Dt 27:24 al.; ViAhiae [Ahijah] 3 [p. 92, 2 Sch.]; Philo, Spec. Leg. 4, 183; Jos., Ant. 10, 164; prayers for vengeance fr. Rheneia: SIG 1181, 3 and in Dssm., LO 352; 354ff [LAE 423ff]; cp. μετὰ δόλου Did., Gen. 126, 20) **Mt 26:4; 2 Cor 12:16.** δόλῳ πονηρῷ *w. base cunning* (SIG 693, 2; 5, cp. 9; OGI 629, 112; BGU 326 II, 3 [Hunt-Edgar 85 II, 3]) IEph 7:1. Also ἐν δ. (Soph., Phil. 102; Wsd 14:30; 1 Macc 1:30) **Mk 12:14 v.l.; 14:1; 1 Th 2:3.**—B. 1171. DELG. M-M. TW.

δολόω (s. four prec. entries) 1 aor. ἐδόλωσεν Ps 14:3; 35:2 (Hes., Hdt. et al.; Vett. Val. 248, 2; SIG 1168, 102) gener. to beguile by craft, then: **to make false through deception or distortion,** ***falsify, adulterate*** (so Diosc. 1, 67; 68 W.; Lucian, Hermot. 59 τὸν οἶνον; PLeid X, v, 37; xii, 2 [chem. pap]) **1 Cor 5:6** D; δ. τὸν λόγον τοῦ θεοῦ **2 Cor 4:2.**—DELG s.v. δόλος. M-M.

δόμα, δόματος, τό (Ps.-Pla., Defin. 415b; Plut.; pap [Mayser 435]; LXX; EpArist 224; Philo, Cher. 84; Just., D. 39, 2 al. Cp. the entry δῶμα) ***gift*** δ. ἀγαθά *good gifts* (cp. Sir 18:17) **Mt 7:11; Lk 11:13.** διδόναι δόματά τινι **Eph 4:8** (cp. Ps 67:19; Just., D. 39, 4); οὐχ ὅτι ἐπιζητῶ τὸ δ. *not that I desire the gift* **Phil 4:17.**—DELG s.v. δίδωμι A. M-M.

δόξα, ης, ἡ (s. δοξάζω; in var. mngs. Hom.+; in Ath. 'meaning'). In many of the passages in our lit. the OT and Gr-Rom. perceptions of dependence of fame and honor on extraordinary performance deserve further exploration. SIG 456, 15 is typical:

concern for others leads to enhancement of one's δόξα or reputation. The Common Gk. usage of δ. in sense of 'notion, opinion' is not found in the NT.

❶ **the condition of being bright or shining, *brightness, splendor, radiance*** (a distinctive aspect of Hb. כָּבוֹד).—ⓐ of physical phenomena (PGM 13, 189 τὴν δόξαν τοῦ φωτός, cp. 298ff. On this Rtzst., Mysterienrel.[3] 357ff, also 314 δόξα ἐκ τ. πυρός [cp. Just., D. 128]; 315 φῶς κ. δόξαν θεῖαν [=Cleopatra 150]; LXX; TestJob 43:6 τῆς λαμπάδας αὐτοῦ) οὐκ ἐνέβλεπον ἀπὸ τῆς δ. τοῦ φωτός *I could not see because of the brightness of the light* **Ac 22:11;** ὁρᾶν τὴν δ. *see the radiance* **Lk 9:32;** cp. vs. **31.** Everything in heaven has this radiance: the radiant bodies in the sky **1 Cor 15:40f** (cp. PGM 13, 64 σὺ ἔδωκας ἡλίῳ τὴν δόξαν κ. δύναμιν; 448; Sir 43:9, 12; 50:7).

ⓑ of humans involved in transcendent circumstances, and also transcendent beings: cherubim (Sir 49:8; Ezk 10:4) **Hb 9:5;** angels **Lk 2:9; Rv 18:1.** Esp. of God's self (Ex 24:17; 40:34; Num 14:10; Bar 5:9 τὸ φῶς τῆς δόξης αὐτου; Tob 12:15; 13:16 BA; 2 Macc 2:8; SibOr 5, 427) ὁ θεὸς τῆς δ. (En 25:7) **Ac 7:2** (Ps 28:3); cp. **J 12:41** (Is 6:1); **Ac 7:55; 2 Th 1:9; 2 Pt 1:17b; Rv 15:8; 19:1; 21:11, 23.** ὁ πατὴρ τῆς δ. **Eph 1:17;** βασιλεὺς τῆς δ. AcPl BMM verso 24 and 26. But also of those who appear before God: Moses **2 Cor 3:7–11, 18** (Just., D. 127, 3; cp. Ἀδὰμ τῆς δ. θεοῦ ἐγυμνώθη GrBar 4:16); Christians in the next life **1 Cor 15:43; Col 3:4.** The δόξα τοῦ θεοῦ as it relates to the final judgment **Ro 3:23; 5:2** (but s. 3); Jesus himself has a σῶμα τῆς δ. *radiant, glorious body* **Phil 3:21;** cp. 2 Cl 17:5. Christ is the κύριος τ. δόξης **1 Cor 2:8** (cp. En 22:14; 27:3, 5; 36:4; 40:3 of God; PGM 7, 713 κύριοι δόξης of deities).—The concept has been widened to denote the *glory, majesty, sublimity* of God in general (PGM 4, 1202 ἐφώνησά σου τ. ἀνυπέρβλητον δόξαν; Orig., C. Cels. 4, 1, 24 οἰκοδομεῖν . . . ναὸν δόξης θεοῦ) ἀλλάσσειν τὴν δ. τοῦ θεοῦ *exchange the majesty of God* **Ro 1:23;** κατενώπιον τῆς δόξης αὐτοῦ **Jd 24** (cp. En 104:1)=before himself. Christ was raised fr. the dead διὰ τῆς δ. τοῦ πατρός *by the majesty* (here, as in **J 2:11,** the thought of *power, might* is also present; cp. Rtzst., Mysterienrel.[3] 344, 359 and PGM 4, 1650 δὸς δόξαν καὶ χάριν τῷ φυλακτηρίῳ τούτῳ; Wsd 9:11 φυλάξει με ἐν τ. δόξῃ; Philo, Spec. Leg. 1, 45.—JVogel, Het sanscrit woord tejas [=gloedvuur] in de beteekenis van magische Kracht 1930) *of the Father* **Ro 6:4;** cp. **Mt 16:27; Mk 8:38;** AcPl Ha 10, 9; ὄψῃ τὴν δ. τοῦ θεοῦ **J 11:40;** κράτος τῆς δ. *majestic power* **Col 1:11;** πλοῦτος τῆς δ. *the wealth of his glory* **Ro 9:23; Eph 1:18;** cp. **Eph 3:16; Phil 4:19; Col 1:27;** δ. τῆς χάριτος (PGM 4, 1650, s. above) **Eph 1:6;** w. ἀρετή **2 Pt 1:3** (τῆς ἐπ᾽ ἀρετῇ καὶ δόξῃ διαλήψεως, ins at Aphrodisias II, 14: ZPE 8, '71, 186); ἀπαύγασμα τῆς δ. **Hb 1:3;** τὴν ἐπιφάνειαν τῆς δ. τοῦ μεγάλου θεοῦ **Tit 2:13.** Some would classify **Ro 2:7, 10** here, but these and related pass. w. the formulation δόξα καὶ τιμή prob. are better placed in 3 below because of their focus on honor and prestige. Doxol. σοῦ ἐστιν ἡ δ. εἰς τ. αἰῶνας, ἀμήν (Odes 12:15 [Prayer of Manasseh]) **Mt 6:13 v.l.;** AcPl Ha 2, 33; εἰς ἔπαινον τῆς δ. αὐτοῦ **Eph 1:12, 14;** cp. **1:6.—1 Th 2:12; 1 Pt 5:10.** Pl. Hv 1, 3, 3. κατὰ τὸ εὐαγγέλιον τῆς δ. τοῦ μακαρίου θεοῦ **1 Ti 1:11.** Transferred to Christ: **Mt 19:28; 24:30; 25:31; Mk 10:37; 13:26; Lk 9:26; 21:27; J 1:14; 2:11; Js 2:1** (AMeyer, D. Rätsel d. Js 1930, 118ff); B 12:7; AcPl Ha 7:7. τὸν φωτισμὸν τοῦ εὐαγγελίου τῆς δ. τοῦ χριστοῦ *the news that shines with the greatness of Christ* **2 Cor 4:4;** cp. **4:6** (cp. Just., A I, 51, 8 παραγίνεσθαι μετὰ δόξης μέλλει). Of Christ's prestige promoted by Paul's associates **2 Cor 8:23** (but s. d and 3 below).

ⓒ The state of being in the next life is thus described as participation in the radiance or glory

α. w. ref. to Christ: εἰσελθεῖν εἰς τὴν δ. αὐτοῦ *enter into his glory* **Lk 24:26** (βασιλείαν P[75] first hand); ἀνελήμφθη ἐν δ. **1 Ti 3:16;** cp. τὰς μετὰ ταῦτα δ. **1 Pt 1:11** (but s. β below; pl. because of the παθήματα; cp. also Wsd 18:24; Isocr. 4, 51; POslo 85, 13 [III AD]), **21.** ἐν τῇ ἀποκαλύψει τῆς δ. αὐτοῦ **4:13.** Also of Christ's preëxistence: **J 17:5, 22, 24.**

β. w. ref. to his followers (cp. Da 12:13; Herm. Wr. 10, 7): **Ro 8:18, 21; 1 Cor 2:7; 2 Cor 4:17; 1 Th 2:12; 2 Th 2:14; 2 Ti 2:10; Hb 2:10; 1 Pt 5:1, 4** (στέφανος τ. δόξης; on this expr. cp. Jer 13:18; TestBenj 4:1); εἰς . . . δ. καὶ τιμὴν ἐν ἀποκαλύψει Ἰησοῦ Χριστοῦ **1 Pt 1:7** (perh. **1:11** belongs here, in ref. to sufferings that are endured in behalf of Christ). πνεῦμα τῆς δ. w. πν. τοῦ θεοῦ **4:14.** ἵνα πνευματικὴν καὶ ἄφθαρτον τῆς δικαιοσύνης δόξαν κληρονομήσωσιν **ending of Mk 16:14 v.l.** (Freer ms. ln. 11f) (Cleopatra 146f ἐνέδυσεν αὐτοὺς θείαν δόξαν πνευματικήν); ἥτις ἐστὶν δ. ὑμῶν (my troubles) *promote your glory* **Eph 3:13** (s. MDibelius, comm. on Col 1:24ff) τόπος τῆς δ.=the hereafter 1 Cl 5:4.

ⓓ of reflected radiance *reflection* ἀνὴρ . . . εἰκὼν καὶ δόξα θεοῦ *man* (as distinguished from woman) *is the image and reflection of God* **1 Cor 11:7** (perh. this thought finds expression **Ro 3:23; 5:2,** but s. 3, below); also γυνὴ δόξα ἀνδρός **ibid.** (cp. the formal similarity but difft. mng. in the Jewish ins in Lietzmann comm. ad loc.: ἡ δόξα Σωφρονίου Λούκιλλα εὐλογημένη; s. also AFeuillet, RB 81, '74, 161–82). Some interpret δ. Χριστοῦ **2 Cor 8:23** in ref. to Paul's associates (but s. 1b).

❷ **a state of being magnificent, *greatness, splendor,*** anything that catches the eye (1 Esdr 6:9; 1 Macc 10:60, 86; 2 Macc 5:20): fine clothing (Sir 6:31; 27:8; 45:7; 50:11) of a king **Mt 6:29; Lk 12:27;** of royal *splendor* gener. (Bar 5:6; 1 Macc 10:58; Jos., Ant. 8, 166) **Mt 4:8; Lk 4:6; Rv 21:24, 26.** Gener. of human splendor of any sort **1 Pt 1:24** (Is 40:6).

❸ **honor as enhancement or recognition of status or performance, *fame, recognition, renown, honor, prestige*** (s. s.v. ἀγαθός and δικαιο- entries; Diod. S. 15, 61, 5 abs. δόξα= good reputation; Appian, Bell. Civ. 2, 89 §376 δ. ἀγαθή good reputation, esteem; Polyaenus 8 Prooem. δόξα ἀθάνατος=eternal renown; Herm. Wr. 14, 7; PsSol 1:4; 17:6; Jos., Ant. 4, 14, Vi. 274; Just., A II, 10, 8 δόξης . . . καταφρονήσαντος) of public approbation (cp. Orig., C. Cels. 7, 24, 1; Did., Gen. 238, 25) ἐνώπιον πάντων τῶν συνανακειμένων σοι **Lk 14:10;** δ. λαμβάνειν (En 99:1; Diog. L. 9, 37 of Democr. οὐκ ἐκ τόπου δόξαν λαβεῖν βουλόμενος) **J 5:41, 44a** al.; sim. of God **Rv 4:11** and the Lamb **5:12** receiving honor. **J 8:54** (=make high claims for myself); **12:43a** (cp. **8:50**); **Ro 9:4; 2 Cor 6:8** (opp. ἀτιμία); **1 Th 2:6;** 1 Cl 3:1; B 19:3; Hv 1, 1, 8. Gener. γυνὴ . . . ἐὰν κομᾷ, δόξα αὐτῇ ἐστιν, i.e. she enjoys a favorable reputation **1 Cor 11:15** (opp. ἀτιμία). Oxymoron ὧν . . . ἡ δόξα ἐν τῇ αἰσχύνῃ αὐτῶν *whose prestige is in their disgrace* **Phil 3:19.** Of enhancement of divine prestige as an objective **J 7:18;** Lazarus' illness redounds to *God's honor* **11:4; Ro 15:7.** Of divine approbation of pers. δ. τοῦ θεοῦ **J 5:44b; 12:43b** (cp. 1QH 17:15; 1QS 4:23); **Ro 3:23; 5:2.** Here also belong pass. w. the form δὸξα καὶ τιμή / τιμὴ καὶ δόξα (LXX; ins, e.g. OGI 223, 12; 244, 19f; 763, 37; Welles 42, 6; also PGM 4, 1616f δὸς δ. καὶ τιμὴν κ. χάριν; Just., D. 42, 1) **Ro 2:7, 10; 1 Ti 1:17; Hb 2:7, 9** (Ps 8:6); cp. **3:3; 1 Pt 1:7; 2 Pt 1:17; Rv 4:9, 11; 5:12, 13; 21:26.** Of pers. who bestow renown through their excellence: of Jesus **Lk 2:32** (cp. **Ro 9:4**); of Paul's epistolary recipients ὑμεῖς ἡ δ. ἡμῶν *you bring us renown* **1 Th 2:20** (cp. the Jewish ins in Lietzmann, 1d above: Loucilla brings renown to Sophronius).—Israel's liturgy furnishes the pattern for the liturg. formula δ. θεῷ *praise is* (BWeiss; HHoltzmann; Harnack; Zahn; EKlostermann; ASchlatter; Rengstorf) or *be* (Weizsäcker; JWeiss; OHoltzmann) *to God* **Lk 2:14.** Cp. **19:38; Ro 11:36; 16:27; Gal 1:5; Eph 3:21; Phil 4:20; 2 Ti 4:18** (perh. Christ as referent); **Hb 13:21; 1 Pt 4:11;** 1 Cl 20:12; 50:7 al.; τιμὴ καὶ δ. **1 Ti 1:17** (s. also above as extra-biblical formulation, esp. OGI 223, 12; 244, 19f; 763, 37); cp. **Jd 25 v.l.; Rv 5:13; 7:12.** Doxologies to Christ **2 Pt 3:18; Rv 1:6;** εἰς (τὴν) δ. (τοῦ) θεοῦ *to the praise of God* **Ro 15:7; 1 Cor 10:31; 2 Cor 4:15; Phil 1:11; 2:11;** cp. **Ro 3:7.** Also πρὸς δ. **2 Cor 1:20;** πρὸς τὴν αὐτοῦ τοῦ κυρίου (Christ) δ. **8:19.** Hence the expr. δ. διδόναι τῷ θεῷ *praise God* (Bar 2:17f; 1 Esdr 9:8; 4 Macc 1:12): in thanksgiving **Lk 17:18; Rv 19:7;** as a form of relig. devotion: **Ac 12:23; Ro 4:20; Rv 4:9; 11:13; 14:7; 16:9;** as an adjuration δὸς δ. τῷ θεῷ *give God the praise* by telling the truth **J 9:24.**—GBoobyer, 'Thanksgiving' and the 'Glory of God' in Paul, diss. Leipzig 1929; LChampion, Benedictions and Doxologies in the Epistles of Paul '35; MPamment, The Meaning of δόξα in the Fourth Gospel: ZNW 74, '83, 12–16, God's glory is manifested through the gift of Jesus' voluntary self-surrender on the cross.

❹ **a transcendent being deserving of honor, *majestic being,*** by metonymy (cp. Diod. S. 15, 58, 1 of citizens who stood out from among all others in ἐξουσίαι καὶ δόξαι=offices and honors) of angelic beings (s. Philo, Spec. Leg. 1, 45; PGM 1, 199) δόξαι *majestic (heavenly) beings* **Jd 8; 2 Pt 2:10** (s. also Ex 15:11 LXX; TestJud 25:2 αἱ δυνάμεις τ. δόξης. Also the magical text in Rtzst., Poim. p. 28 [VI 17] χαιρέτωσάν σου αἱ δόξαι (practically = δυνάμεις) εἰς αἰῶνα, κύριε). Cp. JSickenberger, Engels- oder Teufelslästerer? Festschrift zur Jahrhundertfeier d. Univers. Breslau 1911, 621ff. The mng. *majesties* and by metonymy *illustrious persons* is also prob.—On the whole word Rtzst., Mysterienrel.[3] 289; 314f; 344; 355ff; AvGall, D. Herrlichkeit Gottes 1900; IAbrahams, The Glory of God 1925.—AForster, The Mng. of Δόξα in the Greek Bible: ATR 12, 1929/1930, 311ff; EOwen, Δόξα and Cognate Words: JTS 33, '32, 139–50; 265–79; CMohrmann, Note sur doxa: ADebrunner Festschr. '54, 321–28; LBrockington, LXX Background to the NT Use of δ., Studies in the Gospels in memory of RLightfoot '55, 1–8.—HBöhlig, D. Geisteskultur v. Tarsos 1913, 97ff; GWetter, D. Verherrlichung im Joh.-ev.: Beitr. z. Rel.-wiss. II 1915, 32–113, Phos 1915; RLloyd, The Word 'Glory' in the Fourth Gospel: ET 43, '32, 546–48; BBotte, La gloire du Christ dans l'Evangile de S. Jean: Quest. liturgiques 12, 1927, 65ff; HPass, The Glory of the Father; a Study in St John 13–17, '35; WThüsing, Die Erhöhung u. Verherrlichung Jesu im J, '60.—GKittel, D. Rel. gesch. u. d. Urchristentum '32, 82ff; JSchneider, Doxa '32; HKittel, D. Herrlichkeit Gottes '34; MGreindl, Κλεος, Κυδος, Ευχος, Τιμη, Φατις, Δοξα, diss. Munich '38; AVermeulen, Semantic Development of Gloria in Early-Christian Latin '56.—RAC IV 210–16; XI 196–225.—B. 1144f. DELG s.v. δοκάω etc. II p. 291. Schmidt, Syn. I 321–28, s. δοκέω. M-M. EDNT. TW. Spicq. Sv.

δοξάζω (s. δόξα) impf. ἐδόξαζον; fut. δοξάσω; 1 aor. ἐδόξασα, impv. δόξασον; pf. 1 pl. δεδοξάκαμεν (Just., D. 1:4). Pass.: 1 aor. pass. ἐδοξάσθην; pf. pass. δεδόξασμαι **J 17:10** (Xenophanes and trag.+; LXX; pseudepigr., Philo, Joseph., Mel., P. 92, 692; Just and Ath. oft. 'express an opinion').

❶ **to influence one's opinion about another so as to enhance the latter's reputation, *praise, honor, extol*** (Thu. 3, 45, 4; Polyb. 6, 53, 10 δεδοξασμένοι ἐπ' ἀρετῇ; OGI 168, 56 [115 BC]; cp. ViJer 2 [Sch. 71, 5]; LXX; EpArist; Jos., Ant. 4, 183) τινά *someone* **Mt 6:2;** oneself **Rv 18:7** (cp. 2 below); the Father **Mt 5:16;** God (SibOr fgm. 1, 21) **9:8; 15:31; Mk 2:12; Lk 5:25f; 7:16; 13:13; 17:15; 18:43; 23:47; Ac 11:18; 21:20; Ro 15:6, 9; 1 Pt 2:12;** MPol 14:3; 19:2; AcPl Ha 6, 13; τ. κύριον 20:1; Hv 3, 4, 2; AcPl Ha 7, 24 (δόξαι pap, perh. = δοξάσαι). ἔν τινι *in the person of someone* **Gal 1:24** (FNeugebauer, In Christus, etc. '61, 43); cp. **1 Cor 6:20;** ἐν τῷ ὀνόματι (μέρει v.l.) τούτῳ *in this name* (that of a Christian) **1 Pt 4:16.** κατὰ δὲ ὑμᾶς δοξάζεται *among you God's spirit is honored* **4:14 v.l.** ἐπί τινι *for, because of someth.* (w. αἰνεῖν) **Lk 2:20** (s. Polyb. above); **Ac 4:21;** διά τινος and ἐπί τινι **2 Cor 9:13;** διὰ Ἰησοῦ Χριστοῦ **1 Pt 4:11.** W. εὐχαριστεῖν **Ro 1:21** (the cardinal sin is not to be grateful for benefactions; reciprocity requires glorification of the benefactor, hence the freq. ref. in ins to the effect that one knows how to acknowledge benefits, e.g. IPriene 3, 26f; 6, 24–27); the name (Nicol. Dam.: 90 fgm. 19 Jac. [in Jos., Ant. 1, 160] τοῦ Ἀβράμου ἔτι κ. νῦν τὸ ὄνομα δοξάζεται=revered) of God **Rv 15:4** (Ps 85:9); Hv 2, 1, 2; 3, 4, 3 (Just., D. 41, 3). τὸ ὄνομα *the name,* i.e. God's, IPhld 10:1 (cp. POxy 924, 13 ἵνα τὸ ὄνομά σου ᾖ διὰ παντὸς δεδοξασμένον; PGM 36, 165). Of Christ **Lk 4:15;** IEph 2:2; ISm 1:1; Pol 8:2. τόν σε λυτρωσάμενον ἐκ θανάτου *him who redeemed you fr. death* B 19:2; *someone's love* IPol 7:2. Abs.=*praise God* ITr 1:2. τὴν διακονίαν μου δοξάζω *I take pride in my ministry* or *I take my assignment seriously* **Ro 11:13.**—δοξάζεται μέλος *a member is honored* **1 Cor 12:26.** δοξασθεὶς μεγάλως *given high honors* 1 Cl 17:5.

❷ **to cause to have splendid greatness, *clothe in splendor, glorify,*** of the glory that comes in the next life (s. δόξα 1c) **Ac 3:13** (cp. Is 52:13); **Ro 8:30;** B 21:1; **J 7:39; 12:16, 23, 28; 13:31, 32; 17:1, 5, 10.** It is a favorite term in J (s. Thüsing et al. s.v. δόξα, end), in which the whole life of Jesus is depicted as a glorifying of the Son by the Father: **J 8:54; 12:28; 13:31; 17:1, 4** (cp. GCaird, NTS 15, '68/69, 265–77) and, at the same time, of the Father by the Son: **13:31f; 14:13; 17:1.** The glorifying of the Son is brought about by the miracles which the Father has him perform **11:4** (cp. PGM 7, 501ff κυρία Ἶσις, δόξασόν με, ὡς ἐδόξασα τὸ ὄνομα τοῦ υἱοῦ σου Ὧρος; IAndrosIsis, Kyme 40 [s. also Peek's comm. p. 63] spoken by the deity: οὐδεὶς δοξάζεται ἄνευ τ. ἐμῆς γνώμης), through the working of the Paraclete **16:14** and through 'his own' **17:10,** who also glorify the Father **15:8,** esp. in martyrdom **21:19** (on δοξάζεσθαι ἐν **13:31f; 14:13; 15:8; 17:10** cp. Diod. S. 12, 36, 2; 16, 82, 7 ἐν συνέσει δεδοξασμένος; Sir 48:4; 1 Macc 2:64).—**2 Cor 3:10;** τὸν λόγον τοῦ κυρίου **Ac 13:48;** cp. **2 Th 3:1;** B 6:16 (Is 49:5); IPol 8:1. χαρὰ δεδοξασμένη *joy filled w. glory* **1 Pt 1:8;** Pol 1:3. οὐχ ἑαυτὸν ἐδόξασεν γενηθῆναι ἀρχιερέα *he did not presume for himself the prestige of the high priesthood* **Hb 5:5.**—On **Rv 18:7** s. 1, above. δοξάζοντες **J 11:31 v.l.** Lit., s. δόξα, end, also ESelwyn, First Ep. of Peter '46, 253–58.—DELG s.v. δοκάω etc. II p. 291. M-M. TW. Spicq. Sv.

δοξολογία, ας, ἡ (on the prefix δοξο- s. DELG s.v. δοκάω etc. II p. 291; Orig., De Or. 14, 2 p. 331, 6 al. in patristic lit.; Iambl., Myst 2, 10; TestAbr A 20 p.103, 29 [Stone p. 54]) ***paean, prayer*** ἐν τῇ ὥρα τῆς δ. αὐτους *at the time of his prayer* GJs 13:1.

Δορκάς, άδος, ἡ (Eur., Hdt. et al.; pap, LXX; Test12Patr) ***Dorcas,*** meaning *gazelle,* as tr. of a name (s. Ταβιθά) **Ac 9:36, 39** (Δορκάς as a name e.g. in Jos., Bell. 4, 145; Lucian, Dial. Meretr. 9; SIG[2] 854, 11; 12; 23; IG VII, 942; XIV, 646). Goodsp., Probs. 130.—DELG. M-M.

δόρυ, ρατος, τό (Hom. et al.; ins, LXX; JosAs 26:7; SibOr 4, 63; Jos., Bell. 5, 313, Ant. 6, 187; Tat.2, 2; loanw. in rabb.) orig. of a tree or portion of a tree used for planks, masts, or shafts of spears, then of the ***spear;*** in description of armor of an upright person IPol 6:2.—B. 48; 1390. DELG.

δόσις, εως, ἡ (s. δότης)—**❶** ***gift*** (so since Hom.; Theogn. 444 ἀθανάτων δ.; Sir 18:15, 16, 18; 20:14; 26:14 al.; EpArist 229 θεοῦ δ.; Philo, Cher. 84; Jos., Ant. 1, 181) **Js 1:17** (TestZeb 1:3 δ. ἀγαθή of a gift fr. God; HGreeven, TZ 14, '58, 1–13).

❷ ***giving*** (Antiphon, Hdt.; LXX; EpArist 22; Jos., Ant. 17, 327) **Mt 6:1 v.l.** δ. καὶ λῆμψις (Epict. 2, 9, 12; Artem. 1, 42 p. 39, 24; Vett. Val. [ind. III]; PTebt 277, 16; Sir 41:21; 42:7) *giving and receiving, debit and credit* **Phil 4:15** (on the implied reciprocity system cp. the ground-breaking anthropological perspective of MMaus, Essai sur le don, forme archaïque de l'échange: L'Année Sociologique, n.s. 1, 1923/1924, 30–126); cp. Hm 5, 2, 2. Kl.Pauly II 151–53.—DELG s.v. δίδωμι. M-M.

δότης, ου, ὁ (s. δόσις; Herodian. Gramm. I 60, 26; II 678, 22; Cass. Dio fgm. 66, 2; Etym. Mag. p. 177, 25; 435, 49) ***giver*** ἱλαρὸς δ. *one who gives cheerfully* **2 Cor 9:7** (Pr 22:8a).—DELG s.v. δίδωμι B. M-M. TW.

Δουβέριος Ac 20:4. For this v.l. of D see s.v. Δερβαῖος; s. also Haenchen ad loc.; AClark, Acts[2] '33, xlixf; 374–76.

δουλαγωγέω (Diod. S. 17, 70, 6; Epict. 3, 24, 76; 4, 7, 17; Just., A II, 11, 7, D. 110, 4; Ath., R. 72, 6) ***enslave, subjugate*** fig. (Chariton 2, 7, 1; Περὶ ὕψους 44, 6; Theophyl. Sim., Ep. 36; Herm. Wr. fgm. XXIII, 48 p. 484, 13 Sc.; Procop., Hist., Aed. 1, 9, 4) the body (w. ὑπωπιάζω) Paul makes a slave out of his body, i.e. he directs it for useful service: *I make it obey me* (New Life) **1 Cor 9:27.**—S. DELG s.v. ἄγω p. 18 and δοῦλος. M-M. TW.

δουλεία, ας, ἡ (δουλία Tdf.; Pind.+)—**❶ the state or condition of being held as chattel by another, *slavery*** (the basic perspective of the ancient world that one can be owned by only one master is expressed Mt 6:24; Lk 16:13) μέχρι δουλείας ἐλθεῖν *come into slavery* of Joseph (TestJos 1:5; 10:3) 1 Cl 4:9; ἑαυτὸν παραδιδόναι εἰς δ. *give oneself up to slavery* 55:2.

❷ state or condition of being subservient, *servility,* fig. ext. of mng. 1 (Herm. Wr. fgm. II B p. 392, 10 Sc.; Mel., P. 49, 353 and 67, 477) πνεῦμα δ. *a spirit of servility* **Ro 8:15.** Fear of death leads to slavery **Hb 2:15.** Of serving the Mosaic law (cp. Lucian, Abdic. 23 ὑπὸ δουλείαν γενέσθαι νόμου) ζυγῷ δουλείας ἐνέχεσθαι *be held fast in a yoke of slavery* **Gal 5:1;** cp. **4:24;** δ. τῆς φθορᾶς **Ro 8:21.** Of Christ's life on earth Hs 5, 6, 7.—DELG s.v. δοῦλος. M-M. EDNT. TW. Sv.

δουλεύω fut. δουλεύσω; 1 aor. ἐδούλευσα; pf. δεδούλευκα **J 8:33,** ptc. δεδουλευκώς 2 Cl 17:7 (Aeschyl., Hdt.+; the basic diff. between master and slave is stated Aeschyl., Pr. 927).

❶ to be owned by another, *be a slave, be subjected*—ⓐ lit., of Hagar and Jerusalem **Gal 4:25.** τινί *to someone* (Jos., Ant. 4, 115.—C. Ap. 2, 128 the Egyptians claim τὸ μηδενὶ δουλεῦσαι. Likew. in Appian, Bell. Civ. 4, 67 §286 the Rhodians are proud ἕνεκα τύχης ἐς τὸ νῦν ἀδουλώτου; Diod. S. 5, 15, 3 the Iolaës of Sardinia have maintained their freedom ἅπαντα τὸν αἰῶνα … μέχρι τοῦ νῦν; in 5, 15, 4 even the Carthaginians οὐκ ἠδυνήθησαν [αὐτοὺς] … καταδουλώσασθαι) **J 8:33; Ac 7:7** (Gen 15:14); **Ro 9:12;** B 13:2 (both Gen 25:23; cp. Jos., Ant. 1, 275); 13:5 (Gen 48:19 altered after 25:23); 1 Cl 31:4 (Jacob by Laban [Gen 29:15, 20]; cp. Just., D. 134, 3).

ⓑ in imagery: of a change in masters **Ro 7:6.**

❷ to act or conduct oneself as one in total service to another, *perform the duties of a slave, serve, obey.*—ⓐ be in service to personal beings—**α.** to humans, w. dat. of pers. (PHal 1, 219 [III BC] ὁ Ἀλεξανδρεὺς τῷ Ἀλεξανδρεῖ μὴ δουλευέτω) **Mt 6:24; Lk 16:13;** 2 Cl 6:1 (on being a slave to more than one master s. Billerb. on Mt 6:24; Mitt-Wilck. I/2, 203 II, 13f; 206, 16ff). τοσαῦτα ἔτη δ. σοι *I have slaved for you so many years* **Lk 15:29,** a statement about toil rather than actual status (cp. Gen 31:41). Abs. ἐν καθαρᾷ καρδίᾳ 2 Cl 11:1; μᾶλλον δ. *let them be all the better slaves* **1 Ti 6:2;** πλέον δ. IPol 4:3. On Eph 6:7, see β. Fig., of loving service ἀλλήλοις **Gal 5:13.** δίκαιον εὖ δουλεύοντα πόλλοις 1 Cl 16:12 (Is 53:11).

β. to transcendent beings, esp. in expressions relating to God or Jesus Christ as recipients of undivided allegiance, for, as indicated in α, a slave can take orders from only one master δ. τῷ θεῷ *serve God,* where God is thought of as κύριος, and a human as δοῦλος (Eur., Or. 418; Ex 23:33; Philo, Cher. 107, Somn. 2, 100; Jos., Ant. 7, 367; 8, 257; SibOr 3, 740; Orig., C. Cels. 8, 8, 17; cp. τοῖς κτισθεῖσιν ἀντὶ θεοῦ 3, 15, 17): **Mt 6:24; Lk 16:13** (on both cp. Sextus 574 οὐκ ἔστιν ἅμα δουλεύειν ἡδονῇ κ. θεῷ); **1 Th 1:9;** 2 Cl 11:1; 17:7; Pol 2:1 (Ps 2:11); 6:3; MPol 9:3; Hm 8:6; 12, 6, 2; s 4:2; Dg 2:5 τῷ δημιουργῷ; 1 Cl 26:1. τῷ Χριστῷ **Ro 14:18;** cp. **16:18; Col 3:24;** abs. μετ' εὐνοίας δ. *render service* (to your masters) *w. good will* **Eph 6:7** (through wordplay Jesus Christ, as κύριος, is here viewed as the ultimate recipient of the slave's service); τῷ κυρίῳ (Judg 2:7; 1 Km 7:4; 12:20) **Ac 20:19; Ro 12:11** (v.l. τῷ καιρῷ.—δ. τῷ καιρῷ means 'accommodate oneself to the occasion' [Plut., Arat. 1047 [43, 2]; Pallad.: Anth. Pal. 9, 441; Procop. Soph., Ep. 113 H. δουλεύειν τῇ χρείᾳ καὶ πείθεσθαι τῷ καιρῷ. The contrast is with πράττειν ὅσα τις βούλεται, or Herodas 2, 9f: ζῶμεν οὐχ ὡς βουλόμεσθ', ἀλλ' ὡς ἡμέας ὁ καιρὸς ἕλκει], and can have the unfavorable connotation 'be an opportunist'; for this reason it is expressly rejected for this pass. by Athanas., Origen-Rufinus, and Jerome, but they may be interested in sanitizing the text. S. Ltzm. ad loc.); Hv 4, 2, 5; s 1:7; 4:5ff; 6, 3, 6; 8, 6, 2; the Holy Spirit 5, 6, 5; 7; elements or elemental spirits **Gal 4:9,** cp. vs. **8** (in a relig. sense also PGM 13, 72 κύριε, δουλεύω ὑπὸ τὸν σὸν κόσμον τῷ σῷ ἀγγέλῳ; lesser divinities [δαίμονες] Just., D. 83, 4; Tat. 17, 3).

ⓑ to things, by fig. ext. of mng. in a: Be a slave to sin **Ro 6:6;** the law (Orig., C. Cels. 5, 6, 28) **7:25;** desire Hm 12, 2, 5; **Tit 3:3** (X., Mem. 1, 5, 5, Apol. 16; Pla., Phdr. 238e ἡδονῇ; Polyb. 18, 15, 16; Herodian 1, 17, 9; Philo, Cher. 71; Jos., Ant. 15, 91 δ. ταῖς ἐπιθυμίαις; Iren., 1, 6, 3 [Harv. I 56, 2]); the virtues Hv 3, 8, 8; m 12, 3, 1; faith m 9:12; τῇ κοιλίᾳ *the belly,* i.e. *appetite* (γαστρί X., Mem. 1, 6, 8; Anth. 11, 410, 4; cp. Ath. 31, 2) **Ro 16:18.** εἰς τὸ εὐαγγέλιον *serve in the gospel* **Phil 2:22.** For **Ro 12:11 v.l.** καιρῷ s. 2aβ.—M-M. TW.

δούλη, ης, ἡ (Hom. et al.; pap, LXX, En 98:5; TestSol 12, 1 C; TestAbr A 20 p. 103, 13; TestJob 7:7f; JosAs; ApcMos 42; Philo; Jos., Ant. 1, 215 al.; Just., D. 140, 1) ***female slave, bondwoman*** of women claimed by God w. δοῦλοι **Ac 2:18** (cp. Jo 3:2); IPol 4:3. As an oriental expr., used by one of humble station in addressing one of a higher rank or a deity **Lk 1:38, 48** (1 Km 1:11); GJs 11:3.—DELG s.v. δοῦλος. TW.

δοῦλος, η, ον (s. next entry; Soph. et al.; PGiss 3, 5 ᾧ πάντα δοῦλα; Ps 118:91; Wsd 15:7; Philo; Jos., Ant. 16, 156; Ar. [Milne, 76, 49]; SibOr 3, 567) **pert. to being under someone's total control, *slavish, servile, subject*** τὰ μέλη δ. τῇ ἀκαθαρσίᾳ *the members enslaved to impurity* **Ro 6:19;** τῇ δικαιοσύνῃ **ibid.**—Subst. τὰ δοῦλα *things subservient* PtK 2 (s. ὕπαρξις 1).—DELG. TW.

δοῦλος, ου, ὁ (trag., Hdt.et al.; ins, pap, LXX, Philo, Joseph., Test12Patr)

❶ **male slave as an entity in a socioeconomic context,** ***slave*** ('servant' for 'slave' is largely confined to Biblical transl. and early American times [s. OED s.v. servant, 3a and b]; in normal usage at the present time the two words are carefully distinguished [Goodsp., Probs., 77–79]). Opp. ἐλεύθερος **1 Cor 7:21.** Lit., in contrast

ⓐ to a master (Did., Gen. 66, 25): **Mt 8:9; 10:24f;** cp. **J 13:16; 15:20.—Mt 13:27f; 21:34ff; 24:45f, 48, 50; 25:14, 19, 21, 23, 26, 30;** cp. **Lk 19:13, 15, 17, 22.—Mt 26:51;** cp. **Mk 14:47; Lk 22:50; J 18:10, 26** (on δοῦλος of the ἀρχιερεύς s. Jos., Ant. 20, 181).—**Mk 12:2, 4; 13:34; Lk 7:2f, 8, 10; 12:37, 43, 45ff; 17:7, 9f; J 4:51; Col 4:1** (Billerb. IV 698–744: D. altjüd. Sklavenwesen; SZucrow, Women, Slaves, etc. in Rabb. Lit. '32; JJeremias, Jerusalem IIb '37, 184–88; 217–24).—οἱ δ. και οἱ ὑπηρέται **J 18:18.**—Of slaves sent out with invitations **Mt 22:3f, 6, 8, 10;** par. **Lk 14:17, 21ff;** of one who could not pay his debt **Mt 18:23, 26ff** (but s. 2bα on these pass. fr. Mt). Opp. δεσπότης (as Diod. S. 15, 8, 2f ὡς δοῦλος δεσπότῃ; Ps.-Lucian, Asin. 5) **1 Ti 6:1; Tit 2:9;** οἱ δ. in direct address **Eph 6:5; Col 3:22.**—For lit. on Christianity and slavery (Ath. 35, 1 δ. εἰσιν ἡμῖν 'we have slaves' [who can attest our innocence of the charges]) s. on χράομαι 1a.—Christ, the heavenly κύριος, appears on earth in μορφὴ δούλου *the form of a slave* (anticipating vs. 8 w. its ref. to crucifixion, a fate reserved for condemned slaves; for the contrast cp. Lucian, Catapl. 13 δοῦλος ἀντὶ τοῦ πάλαι βασιλέως) **Phil 2:7** (lit. on κενόω 1b); cp. Hs 5, 2ff (on this MDibelius, Hdb. 564f).—On **Ac 2:18** s. under 2bβ.

ⓑ to a free pers. (opp. ἐλεύθερος: Pla., Gorg. 57 p. 502d; Dio Chrys. 9 [10], 4; SIG 521, 7 [III BC]; Jos., Ant. 16, 126; Just., D. 139, 5) **1 Cor 7:21f** (cp. the trimeter: Trag. Fgm. Adesp. 304 N., quot. fr. M. Ant. 11, 30 and Philo, Omn. Prob. Lib. 48, δοῦλος πέφυκας, οὐ μέτεστί σοι λόγου=you are a slave, with no share in discussions); **12:13; Gal 3:28; 4:1; Eph 6:8; Col 3:11; Rv 6:15; 13:16; 19:18;** IRo 4:3. W. παιδίσκη D 4:10.—House slave in contrast to a son **J 8:35; Gal 4:7.**

ⓒ in contrast to being a fellow Christian οὐκέτι ὡς δοῦλον, ἀλλὰ ὑπὲρ δοῦλον, ἀδελφὸν ἀγαπητόν **Phlm 16.**

❷ **one who is solely committed to another,** ***slave, subject;*** ext. of mng. 1. Mt 6:24; Lk 16:13 express the ancient perspective out of which such extended usage develops: slaves are duty-bound only to their owners or masters, or those to whom total allegiance is pledged.

ⓐ in a pejorative sense δ. ἀνθρώπων *slaves to humans* **1 Cor 7:23.** παριστάναι ἑαυτόν τινι δοῦλον **Ro 6:16.** δ. τῆς ἁμαρτίας *slave of sin* **J 8:34; Ro 6:17, 20.** τῆς φθορᾶς *of destruction* **2 Pt 2:19** (cp. Eur., Hec. 865 and Plut., Pelop. 279 [3, 1] χρημάτων; Thu. 3, 38, 5; Dio Chrys. 4, 60 τ. δόξης; Athen. 12, 531c τῶν ἡδονῶν; 542d; Aelian, VH 2, 41 τοῦ πίνειν; Achilles Tat. 6, 19, 4 τ. ἐπιθυμίας).

ⓑ in a positive sense—α. in relation to a superior human being (here the perspective is Oriental and not Hellenic). Of humble service (opp. πρῶτος) **Mt 20:27; Mk 10:44.** According to oriental usage, of a king's officials (cp. SIG 22, 4; IMagnMai 115, 4; I Km 29:3; 4 Km 5:6; Jos., Ant. 2, 70) *ministers* **Mt 18:23, 26ff** (s. Spicq, I 383, n. 14 [Lexique 394, n. 4]); cp. the slaves sent out with invitations **22:3f, 6, 8, 10; Lk 14:17, 21ff** (but s. 1a above).

β. esp. of the relationship of humans to God (with roots in both OT and Hellenic thought; s. δουλεύω 2aβ) δ. τοῦ θεοῦ *slave of God=subject to God,* owned body and soul (Eur., Ion 309 τοῦ θεοῦ καλοῦμαι δοῦλος εἰμί τε; Cass. Dio 63, 5, 2; CFossey, Inscr. de Syrie: BCH 21, 1897, p. 60 [Lucius calls himself the δοῦλος of the θεὰ Συρία]; PGM 12, 71 δ. τοῦ ὑψ. θεοῦ; 13, 637ff δοῦλός εἰμι σὸς . . . Σάραπι; 59, 2; 4; LXX; ParJer 6:17 [Baruch]; ApcSed 16:7 p. 137, 15; Philo, Rer. Div. Her. 7 al.; Jos., Ant. 11, 90; 101): of Moses (4 Km 18:12; 2 Esdr 19:14; Ps 104:26; Jos., Ant. 5, 39) **Rv 15:3.** Of recipients of gifts from God's spirit **Ac 2:18** (Jo 3:2). Of Christian prophets **Rv 10:7; 11:18** (prophets are also called slaves of God in the OT Jer 25:4; Am 3:7; Da 9:6, 10 Theod.). Of the apostles **Ac 4:29; 16:17** (δ. τοῦ θεοῦ τ. ὑψίστου as Da 3:93 Theod.); **Tit 1:1;** AcPl Ha 6, 35; Christ as master (cp. oriental usage, of a king's official *minister,* and the interpretation of δ. in such sense [s. 2bα]) puts his slaves, the apostles, at the disposal of the Corinthians **2 Cor 4:5.** Of God-fearing people gener. (Ps 33:23; 68:37 al.) **Rv 1:1; Lk 2:29; 1 Pt 2:16; Rv 2:20; 7:3; 19:2, 5; 22:3, 6;** 1 Cl 60:2; 2 Cl 20:1; Hv 1, 2, 4; 4, 1, 3; m 3:4 al. The one who is praying refers to himself as *your* (God's) *slave* (cp. Ps 26:9; Ch 6:23; Da 3:33, 44) **Lk 2:29; Ac 4:29** (FDölger, ΙΧΘΥΣ I 1910, 195ff).—In the same vein, of one's relation to Christ δ. Χριστοῦ, self-designation of Paul (on the imagery s. Straub 37; DMartin, Slavery as Salvation: The Metaphor of Slavery in Pauline Christianity '90) **Ro 1:1; Gal 1:10; Phil 1:1;** cp. **Col 4:12; 2 Ti 2:24; Js 1:1; 2 Pt 1:1; Jd 1; Rv 1:1; 22:3; 1 Cor 7:22; Eph 6:6.**—On δοῦλοι and φίλοι of Christ (for this contrast s. Philo, Migr. Abr. 45, Sobr. 55; PKatz, Philo's Bible '50, 85ff) **J 15:15,** s. φίλος 2aα.—Dssm., LO 271ff [LAE 323ff]; GSass, δ. bei Pls: ZNW 40, '41, 24–32; LReilly, Slaves in Ancient Greece (manumission ins) '78; COsiek, Slavery in the Second Testament World: BTB 22, '92, 174–79; JHarril, The Manumission of Slaves in Early Christianity '95, s. 11–67 on ancient slavery; KBradley, Slavery and Society at Rome '94; also lit. on χράομαι 1a.—JVogt/HBellen, eds., Bibliographie zur antiken Sklaverei, rev. ed. EHermann/NBrockmeyer '83 (lists over 5000 books and articles); JCMiller, Slavery and Slaving in World History, A Bibliography 1990–91 '93 (lit. p. 196–225).—B. 1332. Schmidt, Syn. IV 124–29 s. δεσπότης. New Docs 2, 52–54. DELG. SEG XLII, 1837 (ins reff.). M-M. TW. Spicq. Sv.

δουλόω fut. δουλώσω; 1 aor. ἐδούλωσα. Pass.: 1 aor. ἐδουλώθην; pf. δεδούλωμαι, ptc. δεδουλωμένος (Aeschyl., Hdt. et al.; LXX; TestSol 13:3 C; Philo; Jos., Ant. 11, 300; Test12Patr; Just., A II, 5, 4)

❶ **to make someone a slave** (δοῦλος), ***enslave*** a people **Ac 7:6** (Gen 15:13). Pass δεδούλωμαί τινι *become a slave to someone,* of one who is defeated in battle **2 Pt 2:19.**

❷ **to make one subservient to one's interests,** ***cause to be like a slave,*** fig. ext. of mng. 1 (Thu. et al.; Hippol., Ref., proem. 2) πᾶσιν ἐμαυτὸν ἐδούλωσα *I have made myself a slave to everyone* **1 Cor 9:19.** Pass. *to be bound (as a slave)* (Menand., Sam. 280 J. [625 S.]; Dio Chrys. 68 [18], 12 δεδουλωμένοι τὴν γνώμην; Did., Gen. 212, 27) ἐν τοῖς τοιούτοις *in such cases* **1 Cor 7:15.** ὑπὸ τὰ στοιχεῖα τοῦ κόσμου *be enslaved by the elemental spirits* (or: *be subject to rudimentary knowledge*) **Gal 4:3;** cp. Dg 2:10; B 16:9; *be* God's *slave* **Ro 6:22;** to righteousness vs. **18** (cp. Heraclit. Sto. 69 p. 90, 3 δεδουλωμένοι ἡδονῇ; Porphyr., Abst. 1, 42 ἐδουλώθημεν τῷ τοῦ φόβου φρονήματι; Just., A II, 5, 4 πάθεσιν ἐπιθυμιῶν); to wine **Tit 2:3** (Philostrat., Vi. Apoll. 2, 36 p. 78, 25 δεδουλωμένος ὑπὸ τοῦ οἴνου; Libanius, Epist. 316, 3 Förster δουλεύειν οἴνῳ).—S. lit. s.v. δούλος. DELG s.v. δοῦλος. M-M. TW.

δοῦναι, δούς s. δίδωμι.

δοχή, ῆς, ἡ (Eur., Pla. al.=receptacle) ***reception, banquet*** (so Machon [280 BC] V 106 [in Athen. 8, 348f]; Plut., Mor. 1102b; pap, LXX; TestSol 16:7) ποιεῖν δ. *give a banquet* (Gen 21:8; 26:30; 1 Esdr 3:1; Esth 1:3; Da 5:1) **Lk 5:29; 14:13;** GJs 6:2.—DELG s.v. δέχομαι p. 268 col. 2. M-M. TW.

δράκων, οντος, ὁ (Hom.+; loanw. in rabb.; oft. synon. w. ὄφις [PGM 36, 183; 196], which strictly defined its species and δράκων genus, but s. LfgrE II, col. 345f on Homer; Boll 42, 5; 103) ***dragon, serpent,*** a sobriquet for the devil (cp. PGM 4, 994 θεὲ θεῶν . . . κατέχων δράκοντα; 190; PsSol 2, 25) **Rv 12:3** (Damasc., Vi. Isid. 67 δράκοντας ἐξαισίους κατὰ μέγεθος ἑπτακεφάλους. Cp. Apollon. Rhod. 4, 127ff the description of the frightful δράκων that guards the golden fleece. Also the Hydra: acc. to Alcaeus ἐννεακέφαλος, acc. to Simonides, πεντηκοντακέφαλος [schol. on Hesiod, Theogony 313]; Pisander Epic. [VI BC] in Paus. 2, 37, 4 al.), **4, 7, 9** (ὁ δ. ὁ μέγας as PGM 4, 2770), **13, 16f; 13:2, 4, 11** (Arrian, Anab. 3, 3, 5 acc. to Ptolemaeus, son of Lagus: δράκοντας δύο . . . φωνὴν ἱέντας show Alexander the way through the desert; cp. Lucian, Ver. Hist. 1, 30 w. whale over 300 km. in length); **16:13; 20:2.**—Lit. on ὄφις 3; also PJoüon, Le Grand Dragon: RSR 17, 1927, 444–46; BRenz, D. oriental. Schlangendrache 1930; JKroll, Gott u. Hölle '32; WFoerster, D. Bilder in Offb. 12f und 17f: StKr 104, '32, 279–310 (on this RSchütz, ibid. 105, '33, 456–66); RLehmann-Nitzsche, D. apokal. Drache Rv 12: Ztschr. f. Ethnologie 65, '33, 193–230; PPrigent, Apoc. 12: Histoire de l'exégèse, in Beitr. zur Gesch. d. bibl. Exegese no. 2, '59; JGammie, The Angelology and Demonology in the Septuagint of the Book of Job: HUCA 56, '85, 1–19 (esp. 13–19). RAC IV 226–50.—DELG s.v. δέρκομαι. M-M. EDNT. TW.

δραμεῖν, -ών s. τρέχω.

δράξ, δρακός, ἡ (s. δράσσομαι; Batr. et al.; Aberciusins.; Herm. Wr. XXIII, 52, 486, 4 Sc.; LXX; ApcEsdr 7:5 p. 32, 17 [acc. δρακήν for δρακί Is 40:12]; Philo, Somn. 2, 74; Jos., Ant. 3, 251; 8, 322) **the hand spread out, *hand*** B 16:2 (Is 40:12).—DELG s.v. δράσσομαι.

δράσσομαι fut. δράξομαι; 1 aor. ἐδραξάμην (cp. δράξ, δραχμή; Hom. et al.; Aberciusins. 14; BGU 1816, 17 [60/59 AD]; POxy 1298, 10; LXX; Jos., Bell. 3, 385, Ant. 14, 425) lit. to take by the handful, grasp by the hand, hence ***catch, seize*** (w. acc.: Dionys. Hal. 9, 21, 4; Lev 2:2; 5:12; Num 5:26) τινά *someone* **1 Cor 3:19.**—DELG. M-M.

δραχμή, ῆς ἡ (s. δρασσομαι; Hdt.+; loanw. in rabb.; lit. 'as much as one can hold in one's hand') ***drachma,*** a Greek silver coin, combining weight and value; varying in weight and value in all Gk. currencies, depending on currency standards, times, and social circumstances **Lk 15:8f** (Dio Chrys. 70 [20], 5 concern over the loss of just one drachma). Its purchasing power was by no means insignificant; acc. to Demetr. of Phal. (300 BC): 228 fgm. 22 Jac. it was the price of a sheep, or one-fifth the price of an ox. Under specially favorable circumstances it was even possible to buy a whole ox for one drachma, or a slave for four: Appian, Mithrid. 78 §344. Conversely, the soldiers of Mark Antony look upon a gift of 100 dr. per man as proof of stinginess, acc. to Appian, Bell. Civ. 3, 43 §177. On wages and living costs see AJohnson, Roman Egypt to Diocletian, in TFrank, An Economic Survey of Ancient Rome II, '59, 301–21.—Lit. s.v. ἀργύριον 2c.—KChrist, Antike Numismatik '67 (lit.); Pauly-W V 2, 1613–33; Kl. Pauly II 155f.—DELG s.v. δράσσομαι. M-M.

δράω 1 aor. ἔδρασα (Hom.+; Aristot., Poetics 1448b; OGI 765, 34; PPetr II, 9 [1], 2 [III BC]; POxy 259, 35; LXX; TestDan 3:4; GrBar 4:16; EpArist 194; Philo; Jos., Ant. 16, 99, Vi. 357; Just., D. 1, 5; 3, 3) ***do, accomplish,*** οἱ ταῦτα δράσαντες *the men who have done these things* (cp. Wsd 14:10; 4 Macc 11:4; Jos., Ant. 1, 102) 1 Cl 45:7.—B. 537. DELG s.v. δράω 1. Sv.

δρέπανον, ου, τό (δρέπω 'pluck'; Hom. et al.; pap, LXX; TestAbr A; ApcEsdr 4:31 p. 29, 6; Jos., Bell. 3, 225) **an agricultural implement consisting of a curved blade and a handle, used for a variety of purposes,*sickle:*** for cutting branches of a willow Hs 8, 1, 2; 3 (cp. Polyaenus 1, 18); in imagery **Rv 14:14–19** of harvests including grapes, s. below (cp. here the two Phryg. ins in Ramsay, CB I/2 565 no. 466 ἐὰν δέ τις αὐτῶν μὴ φοβηθῇ τούτων τ. καταρῶν τὸ ἀρᾶς δρέπανον εἰσέλθοιτο εἰς τὰς οἰκήσις αὐτῶν=if any one of them does not fear these curses, let the sickle of the curse enter into their houses). OT ἀποστέλλειν τὸ δ. (cp. Jo 4:13) *put in the sickle* for harvesting grain **Mk 4:29;** cp. **Rv 14:15** (w. θερίζω as Mesomedes 7, 9; s. ἀποστέλλω 2c), **18f** (vinedresser's tool as Geopon. 5, 22, 1; Cornutus 27 p. 51, 6).—B. 507. DELG s.v. δρέπω. M-M.

δρομαῖος, α, ον (δραμεῖν 'run'; Soph. et al.; TestAbr A 5 p. 82, 24; Jos., Ant. 13, 228.—Adv. -ως TestAbr A 5 p. 82, 13 [Stone p. 12]; TestSol 1:9, 11) ***running at full speed, swift*** ἀπῄει δρομαῖος πρὸς τὸν ἱερέαν (Annas) *went on the run to the priest* GJs 15:2.–DELG s.v. δραμεῖν.

δρόμος, ου, ὁ (Hom.+; loanw. in rabb.)—**❶ movement on a path from one point to another, *course*** of heavenly bodies (Ps.-Pla., Axioch. 370b; Dio Chrys. 19 [36], 42; Sext. Emp., Math. 9, 27; M. Ant. 7, 47; Herm. Wr. 4, 8 al.; PGM 12, 251; 13, 575; Jos., Ant. 1, 32; Mel., Tat.) Dg 7:2. τὸν δ. διανύειν *complete* or *continue their course* 1 Cl 20:2.—πάντα . . . τῷ δρόμῳ αὐτῶν ἀπηλαύνοντο *everything returned to its course* GJs 18:3 (Tdf., Ea p. 35, 4f after codd., not pap; ὑπὸ τοῦ δρόμου αὐτῶν ἀπηλαύνετο deStrycker). Of a race, in a fig. context (Philo, Leg. All. 3, 48) **2 Ti 4:7** (s. τελέω 1 beg.); of martyrs ἐπὶ τὸν τῆς πίστεως βέβαιον δ. κατήντησαν *they securely reached the goal in the race of faith* 1 Cl 6:2. GMary 463, 1.

❷ carrying out of an obligation or task, *course of life, mission,* fig. ext. of 1 πληροῦν τὸν δ. *complete one's course* **Ac 13:25;** τελεῖν *finish* **Ac 20:24.** προστιθέναι τῷ δ. *hasten on in your course* IPol 1:2 (s. JKleist, transl., '46, note ad loc.).—DELG s.v. δραμεῖν. M-M. TW.

δροσίζω 1 aor. ptc. δροσίσας 3 Macc 6:6, aor. pass. ἐδροσίσθην (since Aristoph. [mid.]; LXX) **to wet with dew, *bedew*** fig. in a spiritual sense *refresh with dew* IMg 14 (on the fig. use of dew cp. Dt 32:2; Pr 19:12; OdeSol 11:14).—DELG s.v. δρόσος.

Δρούσιλλα, ης, ἡ ***Drusilla*** (also the name of the Emperor Gaius's sister), youngest daughter of Herod Agrippa I, sister of Agrippa II; betrothed as a child to Antiochus Epiphanes of Commagene (Jos., Ant. 19, 355), but never married to him (Ant. 20, 139); married 53 AD to Azizus of Emesa, but left her husband and married Felix the procurator (Ant. 20, 141ff), to whom she bore a son, Agrippa (20, 143) **Ac 24:24, 27 v.l.** HTajra, The Trial of St. Paul '89, 130–32.—Schürer I 446, 449, 453, 461f (lit. here, notes 24 to 26), 577. RSullivan, ANRW II/8, '77, 296–354.

δύναμαι (Hom.+) dep.; pres. 2 sg. δύνῃ and δύνασαι; impf. ἠδυνάμην (also TestJob; TestZeb 2:5; ParJer; Ath. 8, 1; Just. [after οὐκ]) and ἐδυνάμην (also Just.); fut. δυνήσομαι; pass. 1 aor. ἠδυνήθην (LXX; En 21:7; TestJud 9:4; GrBar 7:4; Jos., Ant. 12, 278; Ar. 10, 6 and 8), ἐδυνήθητε (Just., D. 16, 4), ἐδυνήθησαν (2 Macc 2:6), ἠδυνάσθην (LXX; En 14:19) and ἐδυνάσθην (Da 2:47 LXX.—B-D-F §66, 3; 79; 93; 101; Mlt-H. 188; 206; 234); pf. δεδύνημαι (Just.) **to possess capability (whether because of personal or**

external factors) for experiencing or doing someth., *can, am able, be capable.*

ⓐ w. inf. foll.—α. pres. inf. (Poyaenus 8, 10, 3 φέρειν δύν.) οὐδεὶς δύναται δυσὶ κυρίοις δουλεύειν **Mt 6:24; Lk 16:13.**—**Mt 9:15; 19:12; Mk 2:7, 19** al. καθὼς ἠδύναντο ἀκούειν **Mk 4:33** (w. ref. to level of understanding; cp. Epict. 2, 24, 11). Expressed with strong emotion in rejection of what is heard τίς δύναται αὐτοῦ ἀκούειν *Who can listen to such talk!* (REB) **J 6:60.** οὐ δ. ἀναστὰς δοῦναί σοι *I'm in no position to get up and grant your request* **Lk 11:7.** οὐ δυνάμεθα … μὴ λαλεῖν *we cannot remain silent* τὶ *about someth.* **Ac 4:20.** In questions πῶς δύνασθε ἀγαθὰ λαλεῖν; *how can you say good things?* **Mt 12:34.** πῶς δύναται σατανᾶς σατανᾶν ἐκβάλλειν; *how can Satan drive out Satan?* **Mk 3:23;** cp. **J 6:52; Lk 6:42.**

β. aor. inf. (IAndrosIsis, Kyme 4; Just. A I, 2, 4 ἀποκτεῖναι μὲν δύνασθε, βλάψαι δ' οὔ; Ath. 15, 1 διακρῖναι οὐ δυνάμενοι) δύνασθαι … εἰσελθεῖν **Mk 1:45.—2:4; 5:3; Lk 8:19; 13:11; 14:20** and oft. The impf. ἐδύνατο τοῦτο πραθῆναι *this could have been sold* **Mt 26:9** (B-D-F §358, 1; cp. Wsd 11:19f).

γ. likew. the impf. w. pf. inf. ἀπολελύσθαι ἐδύνατο *he could have been set free* **Ac 26:32.**

ⓑ abs., whereby the inf. can easily be supplied (cp. Eur., Or. 889; Thu. 4, 105, 1; X., An. 4, 5, 11 al.; Sir 43:30; Bar 1:6; 1 Macc 6:3; 9:9, 60; 4 Macc 14:17b; ParJer 4:6 cod. C ἠδυνήθητε ἐπ' αὐτῇ [s. ἰσχύω]; Just., A II, 15, 2 ἵνα εἰ δύναιντο μεταθῶνται 'in the hope that they might possibly be converted') **Mt 16:3** (sc. διακρίνειν); **20:22b; Mk 10:39** (sc. πιεῖν); **6:19** (sc. ἀποκτεῖναι); cp. **Lk 9:40; 16:26; 19:3; Ac 27:39; Ro 8:7.** καίπερ δυνάμενος *although he was able to do so* 1 Cl 16:2. οὔπω γὰρ ἐδύνασθε (sc. χρῆσθαι τῷ βρώματι) *you were not yet strong enough* (='you were not yet up to it') **1 Cor 3:2.** ὑπὲρ ὃ δύνασθε (sc. ἐνεγκεῖν) *beyond your capability* **10:13.**

ⓒ w. acc. foll., w. ποιεῖν to be supplied *be capable of, have capacity for someth.* (Maximus Tyr. 1, 2h τοῦτο δύναται λόγος; PRyl 77, 38 οὐ γὰρ δύναμαι κοσμητείαν; POxy 115, 10; 472 II, 22; Ath. 26, 3 τί δὲ χαλκὸς δύναται καθ' αὐτόν; Just., A I, 12, 6 πράττετε ὃ δύνασθε; 19, 5 μηδὲν ἄλλο δύνασθαι μηδὲ τὸν θεόν) οὐ δυνάμεθά τι κατὰ τ. ἀληθείας *we can do nothing against the truth* **2 Cor 13:8** (cp. PsSol 17:39 τίς δύναται πρὸς αὐτόν; 'who is effectual against [the Lord]?') οὐδὲ ἐλάχιστον δ. *not capable of even the smallest thing* **Lk 12:26.** εἴ τι δύνῃ *if you can do anything* (Vi. Aesopi I, 21 p. 279, 11 Eberh.: Αἴσωπε, εἴ τι δύνασαι, λέγε τῇ πόλει) **Mk 9:22** (also perh.: *if you possibly can,* as X., Hell., 7, 5, 15; Heliod. 1, 19, 2; Ael. Aristid. 48, 1 K.=24 p. 465 D.); πλείονα δ. *accomplish more* IPhld 1:1 (Ammonius, Vi. Aristot. p. 11, 15 πολλὰ δ.; Just., A I, 45, 6 οὐ πλέον τι δύνασθε … τοῦ φονεύειν). Of God ὁ πάντα δυνάμενος *the one who has all power* (Lucian, Nav. 28 δύνανται πάντα οἱ θεοί; Iambl., Vi. Pyth. 28, 148; Philo, Abr. 268) Hm 12, 6, 3; cp. v 4, 2, 6.—DELG. M-M. TW.

δύναμις, εως, ἡ (Hom.+; loanw. in rabb.) gener. 'capability', with emphasis on function.

➊ **potential for functioning in some way, *power, might, strength, force, capability*—ⓐ** general, λαμβάνειν δ. *receive power* **Ac 1:8** (cp. Epict. 1, 6, 28; 4, 1, 109; Tat. 16, 1 δραστικωτέρας δ.); ἰδίᾳ δ. *by one's own capability* **3:12.** Of kings τὴν δύναμιν καὶ ἐξουσίαν αὐτῶν τῷ θηρίῳ διδόασιν **Rv 17:13** (cp. Just., A I, 17, 3 βασιλικῆς δ.).—Of God's power (Nicol. Dam.: 90 fgm. 66, 33 Jac. θεῶν δ., Diod. S. 1, 20, 6 τοῦ θεοῦ τὴν δύναμιν of Osiris' function as benefactor to humanity; 5, 71, 6; 27, 12, 1; 34 + 35 fgm. 28, 3; Dio Chrys. 11 [12], 70, 75; 84; 23 [40], 36; Herm. Wr. 14, 9 ὁ θεὸς …, ἡ [ᾧ v.l.] πᾶσα δύναμις τοῦ ποιεῖν πάντα; PGM 4, 641; 7, 582; 12, 250; LXX; Aristobulus in Eus., PE 13, 12, 4; 7 [fgm. 4, ln. 22 p. 164; ln. 84 p. 172]; EpArist; Jos., Ant. 8, 109; 9, 15; SibOr 3, 72; Just., A I, 32, 11 al.) **Mt 22:29; Mk 12:24; Lk 22:69; Ro 1:16, 20** (Jos., C. Ap. 2, 167 God is known through his δ.); **9:17** (Ex 9:16); **1 Cor 1:18, 24; 2:5; 6:14; 2 Cor 4:7; 6:7; 13:4; Eph 3:7; 2 Ti 1:8; 1 Pt 1:5; Rv 1:16; 11:17; 12:10; 15:8;** cp. **2 Cor 12:9a; Rv 5:12;** 1 Cl 11:2; 33:3; Dg 7:9; 9:1f; δ. ὑψίστου **Lk 1:35.** In doxology (1 Ch 29:11f; on the doxol. in the Lord's Prayer HSchumaker, Cath. World 160, '45, 342–49) **Mt 6:13 v.l.;** D 8:2; 9:4; 10:5. Cp. **Rv 4:11; 7:12; 19:1.**—IMg 3:1; ISm 1:1; Hv 3, 3, 5; m 5, 2, 1; PtK 2. Hence God is actually called δ. (Philo, Mos. 1, 111, Mut. Nom. 29; Ath. 16, 2) **Mt 26:64; Mk 14:62** (cp. Wsd 1:3; 5:23 and Dalman, Worte 164f). Christ possesses a θεία δ. (this expr. in Aristot., Pol. 4 [7], 4, 1326a 32; PGM 12, 302 al.; s. Orig., C. Cels. 3, 40, 20 al.; Did., Gen. 60, 8; s. θεῖος 1a) **2 Pt 1:3;** cp. **1:16** and **1 Cor 5:4;** of Christ's potential to achieve someth. through Paul **2 Cor 12:9b** (cp. SEG XXXIV, 1308, 5f [50 BC–50 AD]). In Hs 9, 26, 8, the potential associated with the women in black leads to destruction. δ. leaves Christ at his death GPt 5:19 (s. LVaganay, L'Évangile de Pierre 1930, 108; 254ff). ἐν τῇ τοῦ κυρίου δ. AcPlCor 2:39.—*Power* of the Holy Spirit (Jos., Ant. 8, 408; Just., D. 87, 4f al.) **Lk 4:14; Ac 1:8; Ro 15:13, 19** (ἐν δ. πν. [θεοῦ]); Hm 11:2, 5. ἐν ἀποδείξει πνεύματος καὶ δυνάμεως **1 Cor 2:4;** cp. ἐγείρεται ἐν δ. **15:43,** foll. by σῶμα πνευμάτικον. δυνάμει κραταιωθῆναι *be strengthened in power* (i.e. with ability to function) by the Spirit **Eph 3:16.** Hence the Spirit given the Christian can be called πνεῦμα δυνάμεως, i.e. in contrast to an unenterprising spirit, πνεῦμα δειλίας, God offers one that functions aggressively, **2 Ti 1:7;** cp. **1 Pt 4:14 v.l.;** AcPl Ha 8, 25//BMM 32f//Ox 1602, 39. The believers are ἐν πάσῃ δ. δυναμούμενοι *equipped w. all power* **Col 1:11;** cp. **Eph 1:19; 3:20** (for Eph 1:19 cp. 1QH 14:23; 11:29 al.; for Eph 3:16, 6:10 cp. 1QH 7:17, 19; 12:35; 1QM 10:5; see KKuhn, NTS 7, '61, 336); esp. the apostles and other people of God **Lk 24:49; Ac 4:33; 6:8;** cp. AcPl Ha 6, 21. ἐν πνεύματι καὶ δ. Ἠλίου **Lk 1:17.**—Of the devil's destructive capability **Lk 10:19;** cp. **Rv 13:2.** ἡ δύναμις τῆς ἁμαρτίας ὁ νόμος *what gives sin its power to function is the law* **1 Cor 15:56.**

ⓑ specif., the *power* that works wonders (SEG VIII, 551, 39 [I BC]; POxy 1381, 206ff; PGM 4, 2449; 12, 260ff; Just., D. 49, 8 κρυφία δ.; s. JZingerle, Heiliges Recht 1926, 10f; JRöhr, D. okkulte Kraftbegriff im Altertum 1923, 14f) **Mt 14:2; Mk 6:14;** Hv 1, 3, 4. ἔχρισεν αὐτὸν ὁ θεός δυνάμει (God endowed him to perform miracles) **Ac 10:38** (Dio Chrys. 66 [16], 10 of Jason: χρισάμενος δυνάμει τινί, λαβὼν παρὰ τῆς Μηδείας; Diod. S. 4, 51, 1 τ. τρίχας δυνάμεσί τισι χρίσασα=she anointed her hair with certain potions; 4, 51, 4; 17, 103, 4 ὁ σίδηρος κεχριμένος ἦν φαρμάκου δυνάμει=with a poisonous potion. Diod. S. 1, 97, 7 a powerful medium=φάρμακον; s. ἐξουσία 7; also RAC II 415–58). τὴν ἐξ αὐτοῦ δ. ἐξελθοῦσαν *potency emanated from him* **Mk 5:30;** cp. **Lk 8:46;** δ. παρ' αὐτοῦ ἐξήρχετο **6:19;** cp. **5:17;** perh. also (but s. 3 below) **Gal 3:5; 1 Cor 12:28f** (on the pl. δυνάμεις s. X., Cyr. 8, 8, 14; Herm. Wr. 13, 8 al.; on this ADieterich, E. Mithraslit. 1903, 46f; cp. PKöhn VI, 245, 18 Athena; for parallels and lit. s. Ptocheia [=ASP 31] '91, 55). ἐν δ. *with power, powerful(ly)* (TestJob 47:9; Synes., Ep. 90 p. 230d τοὺς ἐν δ.) **Mk 9:1; Ro 1:4; Col 1:29; 2 Th 1:11;** μετὰ δυνάμεως **Mt 24:30; Mk 13:26; Lk 21:27.**—κατὰ δύναμιν w. gen. (Lucian, Imag. 3) *by the power of* **Hb 7:16.** Hebraist.=δυνατός (but readily understood in the Greek world as a defining gen., e.g. λόγου ἄνοια=vocal frenzy Soph. Antig. 603; s. Judg 3:29; 20:46 [ἄνδρες δυνάμεως B =ἄνδρες δυνατοί A]; Wsd 5:23): τῷ ῥήματι τῆς δ. αὐτοῦ *by his* *powerful word* **1:3;** μετ' ἀγγέλων δυνάμεως αὐτοῦ *w. messengers of his power* i.e. angels who exercise Jesus' power **2 Th 1:7** (unless this is to be rendered with KJV et al. *his mighty angels*) (cp. En 20:1; GrBar 1:8; 2:6); μὴ ἔχων δ. *powerless* Hv 3, 11, 2; m 9:12. ἰσχυρὰν δ. ἔχειν *be very powerful* m 5, 2, 3; cp. 9:11; ἐν ποίᾳ δ.; *by what power?* (s. under 5) **Ac 4:7.** ὕψος δυνάμεως *pride in (one's) power* B 20:1.—Effectiveness in contrast to mere word or appearance **1 Cor 4:19f; 1 Th 1:5.** ἔχοντες μόρφωσιν εὐσεβείας, τὴν δὲ δύναμιν αὐτῆς ἠρνημένοι *they have the outward appearance of piety, but deny its function* **2 Ti 3:5** (cp. Jos., Ant. 13, 409 τὸ ὄνομα τ. βασιλείας εἶχεν, τ. δὲ δύναμιν οἱ Φαρισαῖοι=[Alexandra] bore the title queen, but the Pharisees were in control). δ. πίστεως *the power of faith* in contrast to verbal profession IEph 14:2. Sim. δ. w. ἐξουσία (Dio Chrys. 11 [12], 65) *potent authority* i.e. the word of Jesus is not only authoritative but functions effectively ἐν ἐξουσίᾳ, for the unclean spirits depart **Lk 4:36; 9:1.**—W. ἰσχύς **2 Pt 2:11** (Ath. 24, 2); w. ἐνέργεια Hm 6, 1, 1 (cp. Galen X, 635); τὴν δ. τῆς ἀναστάσεως *the effectiveness of his (Christ's) resurrection,* which brings about the resurrection of the believers **Phil 3:10.**—Of the peculiar power inherent in a thing (of the healing power of medicines since Hippocr.; cp. Diod. S. 1, 20, 4; 1, 97, 7; 17, 103, 4; Plut., Mor. 157d al.; Dio Chrys. 25 [42], 3; Galen, Comp. Med. XIII 707 K.). δ. πυρός **Hb 11:34** (Diod. S. 15, 50, 3 δ. τοῦ φωτός=the intensity of the light).

❷ **ability to carry out someth.,** ***ability, capability*** (cp. Democrit, fgm. B 234; Pla., Philb. 58d; cp. Aristot., Metaph. 4, 12, 1019a 26; Epict. 2, 23, 34; 4 Km 18:20; Ruth 3:11; Jos., Ant. 10, 54; Just., D. 4, 1) δύναμιν εἰς καταβολὴν σπέρματος **Hb 11:11** (s. entry καταβολή). κατὰ δύναμιν *according to ability* (Diod. S. 14, 81,6 v.l.; SIG 695, 9; 44 [129 BC]; PGM 4, 650; POxy 1273, 24; BGU 1050, 14; Sir 29:20; Jos., Ant. 3, 102; Just., A II, 13, 6; also ὅση δ. A I, 13, 1; 55, 8 al.; ὡς δ. μου D. 80, 5) **2 Cor 8:3a;** ἑκάστῳ κατὰ τὴν ἰδίαν δ. *to each according to his special capability* (cp. SIG 695, 55) **Mt 25:15;** AcPl Ha 7, 17. Opp. *beyond one's ability* ὑπὲρ δύναμιν (Demosth. 18, 193; Appian, Bell. Civ. 2, 1 §3; 2, 13 §49; POxy 282, 8; Sir 8:13) **2 Cor 1:8** or παρὰ δ. (Thu. 3, 54, 4; PPetr II, 3b, 2 [III BC]; POxy 1418, 3; Jos., Ant. 14, 378) **8:3b.**

❸ **a deed that exhibits ability to function powerfully,** ***deed of power, miracle, wonder*** (Ael. Aristid. 40, 12 K.=5 p. 59 D.: δυνάμεις ἐμφανεῖς; 42, 4 K.=6 p. 64 D. al.; Eutecnius 4 p. 41, 13; POxy 1381, 42; 90f τ. δυνάμεις ἀπαγγέλλειν; Steinleitner, nos. 3, 7f and 17; 8, 10 [restored] al.; Ps 117:15; Just., A I, 26, 22 al.) w. σημεῖα **2 Th 2:9;** also in pl. **Ac 2:22; 2 Cor 12:12; Hb 2:4;** in this sense δ. stands mostly in pl. δυνάμεις **Mt 7:22; 11:20f, 23; 13:54, 58; Mk 6:2; 9:39; Lk 10:13; 19:37; Ac 8:13; 19:11; 1 Cor 12:10, 28f; Gal 3:5** (on the two last pass. s. 1b above); **Hb 6:5.** Sg. **Mk 6:5.**

❹ **someth. that serves as an adjunct of power,** ***resource*** μικρὰν ἔχειν δ. *have few resources* **Rv 3:8.** Also *wealth* (X., An. 7, 7, 36, Cyr. 8, 4, 34; Dt 8:17f) ἐκ τῆς δ. τοῦ στρήνους *fr. the excessive wealth* **Rv 18:3.** Esp. of military *forces* (Hdt. et al. very oft.; cp. OGI ind. VIII; LXX; Jos., Ant. 18, 262; Just., D 131, 3), even of the heavenly bodies thought of as armies δ. τῶν οὐρανῶν *the armies of heaven* (Is 34:4 v.l.; 4 Km 17:16; Da 8:10 Theod.; En 18:14) **Mt 24:29; Lk 21:26;** cp. **Mk 13:25.**

❺ **an entity or being, whether human or transcendent, that functions in a remarkable manner,** ***power*** as a personal transcendent spirit or heavenly agent/angel ([cp. Pla., Crat. 438c] Aristot., Met. 4, 12, 1019a, 26 divinities δυνάμεις [likewise TestAbr A 14 p. 94, 21=Stone p. 36] λέγονται; Eth. Epic. col. 9, 16, w. θεοι; Porphyr., Abst. 2, 2 p. 133 Nauck δαίμοσιν ἢ θεοῖς ἤ τισι δυνάμεσιν θῦσαι; Sallust. 15 p. 28, 15 αἱ ἄνω δυνάμεις; Herm. Wr. 1, 26; 13, 15; Synes., Ep. 57 p. 191b; PGM 4, 3051; 4 Macc 5:13; Philo, Conf. Lingu. 171, Mut. Nom. 59) **Ro 8:38; 1 Cor 15:24; Eph 1:21; 1 Pt 3:22;** αἱ δ. τοῦ σατανᾶ IEph 13:1. (Cp. αἱ πονηραὶ δ., διάβολος καὶ οἱ ἄγγελοι αὐτοῦ Did., Gen. 45, 4.) θεὸς ἀγγέλων καὶ δ. MPol 14:1 (cp. the ins in FCumont, Étud. syr. 1917, p. 321, 5 ὁ θεὸς τ. δυνάμεων=BCH 26, 1902, 176; Just., D. 85, 6 ἄγγελοι . . . καὶ δ.)—Desig. of a personal divine being as a power (i.e. an effective intermediary or expression; s. DDD 509–16) of the most high God (Ael. Aristid. 37, 28 K.=2 p. 27 D.: Athena as δ. τοῦ Διός; Just., A I, 14, 5 δ. θεοῦ ὁ λόγος αὐτοῦ ἦν; cp. 23, 2; Tat. 5, 1) οὗτός ἐστιν ἡ δύναμις τοῦ θεοῦ ἡ καλουμένη μεγάλη *this man is what is called the Great Power of God* **Ac 8:10** (cp. ins of Saïttaï in Lydia εἷς θεὸς ἐν οὐρανοῖς μέγας Μὴν οὐράνιος, μεγάλη δύναμις τοῦ ἀθανάτου θεοῦ: ILydiaKP 110; PGM 4, 1275ff ἐπικαλοῦμαί σε τὴν μεγίστην δύναμιν τὴν ἐν τῷ οὐρανῷ ὑπὸ κυρίου θεοῦ τεταγμένην. S. New Docs 1, 107. Cp. HKippenberg, Garizim u. Synagoge: RVV '71, 122–24.—GWetter, 'D. Sohn Gottes' 1916, 8f; WSpiegelberg, Die ägypt. Gottheit der 'Gotteskraft': Ztschr. f. äg. Sprache 57, 1922, 145ff; FPreisigke, D. Gotteskraft der frühchristl. Zeit 1922).

❻ **the capacity to convey thought,** ***meaning*** (Pla., Crat. 394b; Polyb. 20, 9, 11; Dionys. Hal. 1, 68; Dio Chrys. 19 [36], 19; Cass. Dio 55, 3; Philo, Congr. Erud. Gr. 125; Just., D. 125, 1 ἡ δ. τοῦ 'Ισραὴλ ὀνόματος; 138, 1 ὀγδόης ἡμέρας . . . δυνάμει . . . πρώτης) of language **1 Cor 14:11;** of stones Hv 3, 4, 3; cp. 3, 8, 6f.—OSchmitz, D. Begriff δ. bei Pls: ADeissmann Festschr. 1927, 139–67; WGrundmann, D. Begriff d. Kraft in d. ntl. Gedankenwelt '32; Dodd 16–20; EFascher, Dynamis Theou: ZTK n. s. 19, '38, 82–108; LBieler, Δύναμις u. ἐξουσία: Wiener Studien 55, '38, 182–90; AForster, The Mng. of Power for St. Paul, ATR 32, '50, 177–85; MBarré, CBQ 42, '80, 216–27 (contrast w. 'weakness' in Qumran lit.)—DELG. Lampe s.v. δύναμις VI B and VII. RAC IV 441–51. EDNT. M-M. TW.

δυναμόω 1 aor. impv. δυνάμωσον (Ps 67:28), pass. ἐδυναμώθην (Polemo Soph. 2, 30 p. 26, 11; Porphyr., Sent. 35 p. 29, 6 Mommert, πρὸς Γαῦρον [ABA 1895] 16, 5 p. 57, 8; Herm. Wr. 1, 27 ὑπ' αὐτου [=θεοῦ] δυναμωθείς; Sallust. 16 p. 28, 25; PGM 4, 197; 216; 12, 266; 13, 279; LXX; TestGad 4:2) **to cause someone to be able to do someth.,** ***enable*** ἐν πάσῃ δυνάμει δυναμούμενοι *endowed w. all capability* **Col 1:11;** δ. ἀπὸ ἀσθενείας *pass fr. weakness to strength* **Hb 11:34; Eph 6:10 v.l.** δυναμοῦσθε for ἐνδυν. (s. ἐνδυναμόω 2b). ὁ κτίσας τὰ πάντα καὶ δυναμώσας Hs 5, 5, 2; cp. 7:4. ἐγώ σε δυναμώσω ἐν αὐταῖς (viz. ταῖς ἐντολαῖς) *I will enable you to keep (the instructions I give you)* s 5, 5, 2. Also Hv 3, 12, 3 v.l.—DELG s.v. δύναμαι. M-M. TW.

δυνάστης, ου, ὁ (trag., Hdt.+; ins, pap, LXX; TestJud 6:3 v.l.; 9:5; Ath., R. 72, 25) gener. one who is in a position to command others.

❶ **one who is in relatively high position,** ***ruler, sovereign***

ⓐ of God (Soph., Antig. 608 of Zeus; Herm. Wr. fgm. XXIII 27, p. 472, 10 Sc.; ZPWess 665 τ. δυνάστας μεγάλους θεούς; PGM 4, 180, 265; 988; Sir 46:5; 2 Macc 12:15; 15:3ff al.; 3 Macc 2:3; SibOr 3, 719) ὁ μακάριος κ. μόνος δ. *the blessed and only Sovereign* **1 Ti 6:15.**

ⓑ of humans (Ctesias: 688 fgm. 11 Jac. [in Apollon. Paradox. 20]; Diod. S. 5, 21, 6 βασιλεῖς καὶ δυνάστας; Appian, Mithr. 102 §472; 108 §516; Lucian, Phal. 2, 1 ἀνὴρ δ.; Appian, Iber. 29 §115; ViDa 7 [Sch. p. 77, 13]; Philo, Spec. Leg. 1, 142; Jos., Bell. 6, 438, Ant. 14, 36; TestJud 9:5; SibOr 3, 636) καθαιρεῖν δ. ἀπὸ θρόνων *dethrone rulers* **Lk 1:52** (cp. Job 12:19).

❷ **one who is in a relatively minor position,** ***court official*** (Gen 50:4) fr. the court of the queen of Ethiopia **Ac 8:27.** S. Κανδάκη.—DELG s.v. δύναμαι. M-M.

δυνατέω (cp. ἀδυνατέω; Philod., Περὶ σημ. 11, 8 Gomperz; s. B-D-F §108, 2; Mlt-H. 390) **to display capability,** ***be effective, be able,*** **2 Cor 13:3;** w. aor. inf. foll. **Ro 14:4; 2 Cor 9:8.** Analogous formation: ἀδυνατέω, q.v.—DELG s.v. δύναμαι. TW.

δυνατός, ή, όν (Pind., Hdt.+; loanw. in rabb.).—❶ **pert. to being capable or competent**—ⓐ in general sense, ***able, capable, powerful*** of beings and their attributes, esp. political power or influence

α. of transcendent beings: God (Plut., Numa 65 [9, 2]; IG XII, 8, 74; ILydiaKP [s. δύναμις 5] no. 224 p. 117; Ps 23:8; 44:4, 6; Ps.-Phocyl. 54; EpArist 139; Just., D. 129, 1) D 10:4. God as ὁ δ. (Ps 119:4; Zeph 3:17) **Lk 1:49.** Of angelic beings Hs 9, 4, 1.

β. of humans: prominent people (Thu. 1, 89, 3; X., Cyr. 5, 4, 1; Polyb. 9, 23, 4; oft. LXX; Philo, Mos. 1, 49; Jos., Bell. 1, 242 Ἰουδαίων οἱ δυνατοί; Just., A I, 14, 4 δ. βασιλέων) **Ac 25:5; 1 Cor 1:26; Rv 6:15** t.r. (Erasmian rdg.; s. RBorger, TRu 52, '87, 57). Of pers. gener. (PsSol 5:3) δ. εἰμι *I am empowered* **2 Cor 12:10; 13:9;** ἄνδρες λίαν καλοὶ καὶ δ. *very handsome and powerful men* Hs 9, 3, 1. Of women, fig. for virtues 9, 15, 3. Of faith w. ἰσχυρά Hm 9:10. Of the spirit 11:21.

ⓑ specificially, w. ref. to an area of competence or skill—**α.** of pers. *competent* δυνατός (εἰμι)=δύναμαι *I am able* or *in a position, skilled, adept* Hs 1:8. W. pres. inf. foll. (X., An. 7, 4, 24; Pla., Ep. 7, 340e; Jos., C. Ap. 1, 187 λέγειν δ.) **Tit 1:9** *be expert in* exhortation; **Hb 11:19** *be capable of* raising the dead. W. aor. inf. foll. (PEleph 8, 18; PHib 78, 15; Num 22:38; EpJer 40; 63; Da 3:17) **Lk 14:31; Ac 11:17, Ro 4:21; 11:23; 14:4 v.l.; 2 Cor 9:8 v.l.; 2 Ti 1:12; Js 3:2;** 1 Cl 48:5; 61:3; Dg 9:1. W. ἔν τινι *be strong, capable in someth.=distinguish oneself* in it (Ps 23:8; Sir 21:7; 47:5; Jdth 11:8): in word and deed **Lk 24:19** (cp. Thu. 1, 139, 4 Pericles λέγειν τε καὶ πράσσειν δυνατώτατος 'very effective in speech and action'); cp. **Ac 7:22** (in both passages the phrase connotes pers. worthy of exceptional honor, s. ἔργον 1a); in the Scriptures=*well-versed* **18:24;** in everything one does Hm 7:1; οἱ δ. *those who are strong (in faith)* **Ro 15:1.** W. ἑρμηνεύειν *able to translate* Papias (2:16).

β. of things (Polyb. 10, 31, 8 προτείχισμα; Zeph 1:14; Wsd 10:12; Jos., Ant. 14, 364): ὅπλα δ. πρός τι *weapons powerful enough for someth.* **2 Cor 10:4.** Of commandments Hs 6, 1, 1. Of God's created works v 1, 1, 3.

❷ **pert. to being possible** (neut.).—ⓐ *it is possible* δυνατόν ἐστι (Pind., Hdt. et al.; pap; 2 Macc 3:6) w. acc. and inf. (EpArist 230; Just., A I, 39, 4) **Ac 2:24;** Dg 9:4. W. inf. foll. (Horapollo 1, 21 p. 31 μαθεῖν; Just., A I, 63, 9 ἀναγράψαι πάντα al.) 9:6. εἰ δ. *if (it is) possible* (EpArist 9; Jos., Ant. 4, 310; 13, 31; B-D-F §127, 2) **Mt 24:24; Mk 13:22; Ro 12:18; Gal 4:15;** ISm 4:1; more completely εἰ δ. ἐστιν (PPetr II, 11 [1], 3; Menand., Epitr. 587 Kö. [907 S.] in a prayer εἴπερ ἐστὶ δυνατόν) **Mt 26:39; Mk 14:35.** ὡς δ. ἡμῖν … παρέξει ὁ κύριος ἐπιτελεῖν *as soon as possible* MPol 18:3.—W. dat. of pers. (w. or without copula) for someone (Lucian, Icar. 21 μὴ δυνατόν ἐστί μοι … μένειν; Just., D. 120, 4; Tat. 16, 2) **9:23; 14:36** (Iambl., Vi. Pyth. 28, 139 τ. θεοῖς πάντα δυνατά; Philo, Virt. 26 πάντα θεῷ δ.); **Ac 20:16;** Hs 5, 7, 3 (PGiss 79 II, 4; Jos., Ant. 3, 189). W. παρά τινι *with someone = for someone* **Mt 19:26; Mk 10:27; Lk 18:27.**

ⓑ τὸ δ. = ἡ δύναμις (Polyb. 1, 55, 4; Appian, Bell. Civ. 5, 45 §191; EpArist 229; cp. τὸ ὁμοιωθῆναι τῷ θεῷ κατὰ τὸ δ.; Did., Gen 145, 6) *God's power* (EpArist 133) **Ro 9:22.** ἐν δυνατῷ εἶναι *be in the realm of possibility* (OGI 771, 49; PCairZen 42, 4 [257 BC]; 209, 1 [254 BC]) B 17:1.—B. 295f. DELG s.v. δύναμαι. M-M. TW.

δυνατῶς adv. of δύνατος (Hdt. 7, 11; Michel 1001 VII, 27 [c. 200 BC]; ISardGauthier 4, 8; Plut.; 1 Ch 26:8; Wsd 6:6) ***strongly*** δ. ὁρᾶν *see as keenly as possible* Hs 9, 1, 3 (cp. Philo, Det. Pot. Ins. 130. Hermas' use of the δυν- family is quite imagistic).—M-M. s.v. δυνατός.

δύνω 1 aor. ἔδυσα and ἔδυνα (2 Ch 18:34 δύναντος B; Just., D. 132, 1); 2 aor. ἔδυν (B-D-F §75; 101; W-S. §15 under δύειν; Mlt-H. 208; 234) (s. δυσμή; Hom. et al.; pap, LXX, En; TestAbr B 4 p. 108, 18 [Stone p. 64]; TestJob, JosAs; GrBar 8:1; Ar, Just., D. 132, 1) ***go down, set*** of the sun (Hom. et al.; Gen 28:11 al.; En 100:2; TestJob 37:8; GrBar 8:1; Bell. 4, 317, Ant. 8, 415) **Mk 1:32; Lk 4:40;** GPt 2:5. In imagery (cp. Pr 11:8 v.l.) δῦναι ἀπὸ κόσμου=*die* IRo 2:2.—B. 679. M-M. TW.

δύο gen. and acc. δύο, dat. δυσί (as early as Thu. 8, 101, 1 codd., then Aristot.+; Polyaenus 2, 3, 8; 3, 9, 47; TestJob 38:8; pap in Mayser I²/2, 73; ins e.g. IPriene s. index; B-D-F §63, 1; Mlt-H. 170), dual gen. δυοῖν (Demetr.: 722 fgm. 1, 8 Jac.) (Hom.+; loanw. in rabb.) 'two'.

ⓐ as simple adj. or subst. ***two***—**α.** nom.—**א.** used w. subst.: δ. δαιμονιζόμενοι *two possessed pers.* **Mt 8:28;** δ. τυφλοί **9:27; 20:30;** cp. **26:60; 27:38** and oft.

ב. w. ἐκ foll.: δ. ἐξ ὑμῶν *two of you* **18:19;** δ. ἐξ αὐτῶν *two of them* **Lk 24:13;** cp. **J 1:35; 21:2.**

ג. δ. ἢ τρεῖς *two or three* used approximately for a small number (Ananius Lyr. [VI BC] fgm. 2 [AnthLG³] in Athen. 3, 78f δύ' ἢ τρεῖς ἀνθρώπους; X., An. 4, 7, 5; Jos., C. Ap. 2, 232) **Mt 18:20; J 2:6; 1 Cor 14:29.** In the same sense δ. καὶ τρεῖς (Ael. Aristid. 45 p. 4 D.; 11 D.; Polyaenus 6, 1, 2) **2 Cor 13:1.**

ד. w. the art. (PGiss 2 II, 5; 14; TestJob 35:3; 39:4) **Mt 19:5; Mk 10:8; 1 Cor 6:16; Eph 5:31** (Gen 2:24).

β. gen. **Mt 18:16** (Dt 19:15); **Lk 12:6; J 8:17; Ac 12:6** al.

γ. dat. **Mt 6:24; Mk 16:12; Lk 16:13; Ac 12:6; 21:33; Hb 10:28** (Dt 17:6).

δ. acc. **Mt 4:18, 21; 10:10, 29; 14:17; 18:8** and oft.

ⓑ in idiomatic phrases: w. prep. εἰς δ. *in two* (Lucian, Tox. 54; PGM 13, 262; TestJud 2:6) **Mt 27:51a; Mk 15:38;** ἀνὰ δ. *two apiece* **Lk 9:3;** ἀνὰ δύο δύο *two by two* **Lk 10:1;** cp. **J 2:6;** κατὰ δ. *two at a time* **1 Cor 14:27.** Also δύο δύο *two by two* **Mk 6:7** (this way of expressing a distributive number is found also in LXX, Gen 7:3, 9, 15 and is widely regarded as a Semitism [Wlh., Einl.² 1911, 24; JWackernagel, TLZ 34, 1909, 227]. Nevertheless it occurs as early as Aeschyl., Pers. 981 [but s. Mussies 218: perh. not distributive but w. emotional value]; Soph., fgm. 191 Nauck²; POxy 121, 9 [III AD] τρία τρία; cp. the mixed expr. κατὰ δύο δύο in the magical pap POxy 886, 19 [III AD], in Medieval Gk. [KDieterich, Unters. z. Gesch. d. griech. Sprache 1898, 188], and in Mod. Gk. [JPsichari, Essai sur le Grec de la Septante: Rev. des Ét. juives 55, 1908, 161–208, esp. 183ff]. Cp. Dssm., LO 98f [LAE 122f]; Mlt. 21 n. 3; 97; Mlt-H. 270; 439f; Thumb 128; B-D-F §248, 1; Rdm.² 72; s. also HThesleff, Studies on Intensification in Early and Classical Greek '54). On **Mk 6:7** see JJeremias, NT Essays: Studies in Memory of TWManson '59, 136–43.—In **Rv 9:12** it can be understood as a translation of the Heb. dual *double, twofold* (cp. TestJob 53:2 διπλῶς τὸ οὐαί).—JGonda, Reflections on the Numerals 'One' and 'Two' in Ancient IE Languages '53. S. also entry δισμυριάς. DELG.—M-M.

δυσ- inseparable prefix, opp. εὖ-, ***un-, mis-.*** It negates the good sense of a word, w. notion of *hard, bad, difficult,* as in next entry.—DELG.

δυσβάστακτος, ον (s. βαστάζω; Plut., Mor. 915f; schol. on Pind., N. 10, 37b; Philo, Omnis Prob. Lib. 28; Pr 27:3; SibOr 8, 327) **pert. to being burdensome or difficult to endure,** ***hard to bear*** φορτία *burdens* **Mt 23:4** (ἀδυσβάστακτα D first hand); **Lk 11:46.**—M-M. TW.

δύσβατος, ον (s. βαίνω; Pind., Pla. et al.; Philo, Ebr. 150; Jos., Ant. 14, 432; SibOr 7, 103) ***impassable, hard to walk in*** fig. (cp. Pind., N. 7, 97 ἀμηχανίαι δύσβατοι) of commandments Hm 12, 4, 4.—DELG s.v. βαίνω 157.

δυσεντέριον, ου, τό (ἔντερον, piece of the intestine; H. Gk. form for δυσεντερία [Hdt. et al.; Jos., Ant. 6, 3]; cp. Phryn. 518 Lob.; Moeris 129; Etym. Mag. p. 494, 33. S. also Hobart 52f) ***dysentery,*** w. fever **Ac 28:8** (v.l. δυσεντερίᾳ; pl. forms of both genders as v.l.).—M-M.

δυσερμήνευτος, ον (s. ἑρμηνεύω; Diod. S. 2, 52, 5=difficult to describe; Artem. 3, 66; Cat. Cod. Astr. I 114, 26; Philo, Somn. 1, 188) **pert. to being difficult to tell the meaning of someth.,** ***hard to explain*** πολὺς ὁ λόγος καὶ δ. *there is much to be said, and it is hard to explain* (as the context indicates, not because of the subject matter but because of a problem with the hearers) **Hb 5:11.**

δυσθεράπευτος, ον (s. θεραπεύω; since Soph., Aj. 609; Hippocr., περὶ ἰητροῦ 10 [CMG I/1, p. 23, 26]; Philo, Plant. 32) **pert. to being difficult to restore to a sound and healthful condition,** ***hard to cure*** (like θεραπεύω, which is used of care and concern for physical [s. Hippocr., above] as well as inner well-being [Pl., Crat. 440c, R. 403d; Philo Mech. 1, 334 naïveté]) of false Christians IEph 7:1 (cp. Philo, Deus Imm. 182 δ. . . . τὰ τῆς ψυχῆς ἀρρωστήματα).

δύσις, εως, ἡ (Aeschyl. et al.; Heraclitus fgm.120; ins, pap; Ps 103:19; En; TestSol 10:14 C; TestJob 37:8; GrBar 7:6; ApcMos 15) 'setting' (of the sun: Ael. Aristid. 49, 17 K. = 25 p. 492 D.; En 17:4), in our lit. ***west*** as the direction of the setting sun (Jos., Ant. 14, 401; opp. ἀνατολή, as Philo, Cher. 22; cp. SibOr 3, 26) **short ending of Mk;** IRo 2:2; 1 Cl 5:6 (s. ὄπυσις); τὸ τέρμα τῆς δ. *the extreme west* 5:7 (s. τέρμα).—B. 871. DELG s.v. δύω. M-M.

δύσκολος, ον (Thales, Eur. et al.; Athen. 262a; ins, pap; Jer 30:2; Jos., Bell. 6, 36; orig. only of persons, in our lit. always objectively) **pert. to that which is difficult to fulfill or do,** ***hard, difficult*** (X., Oec. 15, 10 ἡ γεωργία δύσκολός ἐστι μαθεῖν; OGI 339, 54; SIG 409, 33) of commandments Hm 12, 4, 6. δύσκολόν ἐστιν *it is hard* w. inf. foll. (OGI 458, 16; Jos., Ant. 6, 43; Philo, Praem. 49 [without copula]) **Mk 10:24;** Hs 9, 20, 3. W. dat. of pers. and inf. foll. *it is difficult for someone* IRo 1:2. Abs. ὅπερ δύσκολον (sc. ἐστίν) ISm 4:1.—B. 651. DELG s.v. κόλον. M-M. Spicq.

δυσκόλως adv. of δύσκολος (s. δύσκολος; Isocr., Pla.+; Vett. Val. 123, 2; POxy 1294, 10; PPrinc 102, 9; Jos., Ant. 4, 87) ***hardly, w. difficulty*** εἰσέρχεσθαι εἰς τὴν βασιλείαν **Mt 19:23; Mk 10:23;** Hs 9, 20, 2. εἰσπορεύεσθαι **Lk 18:24.** ζῆν *attain (eternal) life* Hm 4, 3, 6; s 9, 23, 3. σῴζεσθαι m 9:6. ἀποθανεῖσθαι s 8, 10, 2; ἡμεροῦσθαι m 12, 1, 2. κολλᾶσθαί τινι s 9, 20, 2.—M-M. s.v. δύσκολος. Spicq.

δυσμαθής, ές 'pert. to being hard to learn' (δυς- + -μαθής; in this sense Aeschyl. et al.), then act. **pert. to lacking sharpness or quickness in understanding,** ***obtuse, slow to learn, hard to teach*** (so Pla. et al.; Cebes 35, 2; Philo, Mos. 2, 261) of complacent Christians Hs 9, 22, 1.—DELG s.v. μανθάνω.

δυσμή, ῆς, ἡ the action of appearing to sink and so disappear from view, ***going down, setting*** (of the sun) (s. δύνω; Aeschyl., Hdt. et al.; ins, pap, LXX), also as direction of the setting sun, *west* (Aeschyl. et al.) in our lit. (also LXX, En, TestSol 1:2 and 4 VW; TestJud 5:2; GrBar 8:1; Philo; Jos., e.g. Ant. 3, 199; 7, 16; SibOr, e.g. 4, 102; 5, 371 and 374; Just., D. 137, 4) exclusively pl., elsewh., nearly so (opp. ἀνατολαί) of east and west (BGU 1049, 8; Ps 106:3; TestJud 5:2) **Mt 8:11; Lk 13:29;** ἀπὸ δ. *in the west* **Rv 21:13** (s. ἀπό 2a). ἐπὶ δυσμῶν *in the west* (cp. Num 22:1; 33:48; Dt 11:24, 30) **Lk 12:54.** Of lightning that flashes across the whole sky ἐξέρχεται ἀπὸ ἀνατολῶν καὶ φαίνεται ἕως δ. *it comes fr. the east and shines to the west* **Mt 24:27** (cp. 1 Ch 12:16; Bar 4:37).—B. 871. DELG s.v. δύω. M-M.

δυσνόητος, ον (s. νοέω, νόημα; Aristot., Plant. 1, 1, 816a, 3; Lucian, Alex. 54; Diog. L. 9, 13 δυσνόητόν τε καὶ δυσεξήγητον) ***hard to understand*** **2 Pt 3:16;** δ. τινι *for someone* Hs 9, 14, 4.—TW.

δυσφημέω 1 aor. 3 pl. ἐδυσφήμησαν 1 Macc. 7:41 (s. φημί; Hipponax: POxy 2174 fgm. 9, 8 [=78, 8 Degani] trag.; PLond V, 1708, 51 [VI AD]; Just., A I, 49, 6) ***to slander, defame*** **1 Cor 4:13.**

δυσφημία, ας, ἡ (s. δυσφημέω; Soph. et al.; Dionys. Hal. 6, 48; Plut., Mor. 587f; SIG 799, 15; PLond V, 1660, 25; 1677, 16 [both VI AD]; 1 Macc 7:38; 3 Macc 2:26; Jos., Ant. 16, 90) **the act of detracting from or damaging another's reputation,** ***defamation, slander, calumny*** (opp. εὐφημία 'affirmation'; cp. Ael. Aristid., Τέχναι ῥητορικαί 1, 12 Dindorf II p. 763 τὸ ἐναντίον τῇ εὐφημίᾳ δυσφημία) **2 Cor 6:8.**—M-M.

δύσχρηστος, ον (s. χρηστός; Hippocr.; Philo, Sacr. Abel. 32 p. 214, 17) **pert. to being hard to be involved with,** ***inconvenient, annoying*** δ. ἡμῖν ἐστιν *he irritates us* B 6:7 (Just., D. 17, 2 al.; Mel., P. 72, 533, all Is 3:10).

δυσωδία, ας, ἡ (ὄζω 'to emit an odor'; Aristot. et al.; Diod. S. 14, 71, 2; Longus 4, 17, 2; schol. on Nicander, Ther. 308; SEG 8, 621; Is 34:3 Sym.; Philo, Mos. 1, 100; 2, 262; TestBenj 8:3; TestJob [pl. 34:4] AcThom 55 [Aa II/2, 171, 17]) 'a strong offensive odor, stench', then also that which causes the stench, ***filth*** (Anna Comn., Alex. 13, 10 ed. Reiff. II 205, 10) ApcPt 11, 26. Fig. *filth of erroneous teaching* IEph 17:1.—DELG s.v. ὄζω.

δύω s. δύνω.

δῷ, δώσῃ, etc., s. δίδωμι.

δώδεκα indecl. (Hom.+; ins [Meisterhans³-Schw. 159]; pap [Mayser 316]; et al.) ***twelve*** **Mt 9:20; Mk 5:25, 42; Lk 2:42** (Plut., Mor. 839a γίνεσθαι ἐτῶν δώδεκα; on Jesus at 12 yrs. of age s. RBultmann, Gesch. d. syn. Tradition³ '57, 327f.—At the beginning of the story an external parallel in Ps.-Callisth. 1, 14, 1 ὁ δὲ Ἀλέξανδρος ηὔξανε τῇ ἡλικίᾳ, καὶ γενόμενος δωδεκαέτης μετὰ τοῦ πατρός . . .) al.; οἱ δ. the twelve (sc. μαθηταί; AscIs 3:13 ἡ τῶν δ. μαθητεία; Orig., C. Cels. 1, 64, 12.—οἱ δ. is to be expanded differently, e.g. Lucian, Jupp. Trag. 26 [12 Olympian deities]; Jos., Vi. 56; Ps.-Clem., Hom. 6, 14) **1 Cor 15:5** (the separation of Judas the informer, for which the v.l. ἕνδεκα would make allowance, does not make it impossible to use the fixed expression 'the 12': X., Hell. 2, 4, 23 still speaks of οἱ τριάκοντα, despite the fact that acc. to 2, 4, 19 Critias and Hippomachus have already been put to death; but s. Orig., C. Cels. 2, 65, 6: οἱ δ., τοῦ Ματθίου ἀντὶ τοῦ Ἰούδα καταταχθέντος; of Jacob's sons 7, 7, 30); cp. **Mt 10:1f, 5; 11:1; 20:17; 26:14** et al.—1 Clem 43:2; Hm 12, 3, 2; s 8, 17, 1f al. Cp. δεκαδύο under δέκα.—RMeye, Jesus and the Twelve '68, the term 'the Twelve' goes back to Jesus; difft. GSchille, Die urchristliche Kollegialmission '67, of later origin as honorary recognition of the earliest associates of Jesus. S. also the lit. s. on ἀπόστολος and ἐκκλησία, end. EDNT. TW.

δωδεκαετής, ες **pert. to a period of time lasting twelve years, *twelve years*** (1 Esdr 5:41; Jos., Ant. 15, 9, 6 [341] 'within twelve years'; Plut.) *twelve years old* γενομένης δὲ δωδεκαετοῦς (for ιβ' ἐτοῦς pap)*when she* (Mary) *was twelve years old* GJs 8:2 (As read by Tdf., s. his and deStrycker's app.)—DELG s.v. δώδεκα.

δωδεκακώδων, ωνος, ὁ (δώδεκα + κώδων 'bell'; hapax leg.) ***ornamentation with twelve small bells*** on the highpriest's official robe GJs 8:3 (s. Ex 28:33f; deStrycker p. 103 n. 7).

δωδεκάσκηπτρον, ου, τό (δώδεκα + σκῆπτρον) ***scepter of the twelve tribes*** (of Israel) 1 Cl 31:4 (Knopf, Hdb. ad loc.).

δωδέκατος, η, ον (Hom. et al.; ins, pap [Mayser 318]; LXX; ParJer 5:34 [AB]; EpArist 50) **twelfth in a series, *twelfth*** **Rv 21:20;** MPol 19:1; Hs 9, 1, 10; 9, 29, 1.—DELG s.v. δώδεκα. M-M. TW.

δωδεκάφυλος, ον (δωδεκα + φῦλον 'race, tribe' SibOr 3, 249; cp. δεκάφυλος, τετράφυλος Hdt. 5, 66, 2; SibOr 2, 171) **consisting of or pert. to twelve tribes**

ⓐ ***of twelve tribes*** as adj. ἡ δ. (βίβλος) *the twelve-tribe (record)=the record of the twelve tribes* GJs 1:3.

ⓑ subst. as a collective (B-D-F §263, 3) τὸ δ. ***the twelve tribes***=our twelve-tribe entity **Ac 26:7;** δ. τοῦ Ἰσραήλ 1 Cl 55:6.—M-M. TW.

δῴη, δώῃ s. δίδωμι.

δῶμα, ατος, τό (='house' and 'room' since Hom.) in our lit. **the level surface of a flat roof, *roof, housetop*** (also Babrius 5, 5; pap since III BC, e.g. POxy 475, 22 [II AD]; 1641, 5; PTebt 241 verso; PGM 1, 56 and 75; 4, 2469 and 2712; LXX; JosAs 12:12 [prob. for δόματα]; Just., D. 21, 4 [for δόμασιν Ezk 20:26]). Proverbially κηρύσσειν ἐπὶ τῶν δ. *proclaim on the housetops*=quite publicly **Mt 10:27; Lk 12:3** (cp. 2 Km 16:22 ἐπὶ τὸ δῶμα . . . κατ' ὀφθαλμοὺς παντὸς Ἰσραήλ); ἀναβαίνειν ἐπὶ τὸ δ. *go up to the roof* **Lk 5:19; Ac 10:9.** ὁ ἐπὶ τοῦ δώματος *the one who happens to be on the housetop* **Mt 24:17; Mk 13:15; Lk 17:31** (ἐπὶ τοῦ δ. as Jos., Ant. 6, 49). Cp. RMeister, SBBerlAk 1911, 7, 633; Ltzm., ZNW 20, 1921, 172; RAC III 517–57; BHHW 1, 311.—DELG. M-M.

δωμάτιον, ου, τό (Aristoph., Pla. et al.; PGM 1, 70; Jos., Bell. 2, 610, C. Ap. 2, 246, Ant. 5, 191) dim. of δῶμα 'room' δ. ὑπερῷον ***a little room upstairs*** MPol 7:1.—B. 464.

δωρεά, ᾶς, ἡ (Aeschyl., Hdt. et al.; ins [e.g. Res Gestae of Caesar Augustus ch. 15 'grant'], pap, LXX, Philo, Joseph.; Ath., R. 67, 6; loanw. in rabb.) **that which is given or transferred freely by one pers. to another, *gift, bounty,*** of God (Pla., Leg. 2, 672a; Diod. S. 3, 47, 3; Athen. 15, 48, 693d τὴν τοῦ θεοῦ δωρεάν; Herm. Wr. 4, 5; Philo, Poster. Cai. 81 δωρεαὶ . . . τ. θεοῦ καλαὶ πᾶσαι; Jos., Ant. 3, 223) **J 4:10; Ac 8:20.** Pl. 1 Cl 19:2; 23:2; 32:1; 35:4; δ. διδόναι (Aeschyl., Hdt. et al.; SIG 1118, 3; Tat.; Mel., P. 88, 665; 90, 674) **Ac 11:17.** ἀντιλέγειν τῇ δ. τοῦ θεοῦ *oppose the gift of God* ISm 7:1. W. χάρις (Demosth. 21, 172; Polyb. 1, 31, 6; Diod. S. 3, 73, 6; Philo, Rer. Div. Her. 26; Jos., Ant. 5, 54 θεοῦ χ. καὶ δ.) **Ro 5:17;** MPol 20:2; τῆς δ. πνευματικῆς χάριν λαμβάνειν *receive the favor of the spiritual gift* B 1:2; ἡ δ. ἐν χάριτι *the gift given in generosity* **Ro 5:15;** ἐπὶ τῇ ἀνεκδιηγήτῳ δ. *for the indescribable gift* **2 Cor 9:15;** δ. ἐπουράνιος *the heavenly gift* **Hb 6:4.** W. gen. δ. τοῦ πνεύματος *receive the Spirit as a gift* **Ac 2:38;** cp. **10:45.** ἡ ἔμφυτος δ. τῆς διδαχῆς B 9:9; δ. δικαιοσύνης *the gift of uprightness* **Ro 5:17;** δ. τῆς χάριτος *the gift of grace* **Eph 3:7.** κατὰ τὸ μέτρον τῆς δ. τοῦ Χριστοῦ *acc. to the measure that Christ has given* **4:7.**—For the acc. δωρεάν used as adv., s. next entry.—DDunn, ET 81, '69/70, 349–51; RAC X 685–703.—DELG s.v. δίδωμι B. M-M. TW.

δωρεάν acc. of δωρεά used as adv. (since Hdt. 5, 23 [δωρεήν]; ins, pap, LXX; PsSol 7:1; TestSol; Joseph.).

❶ **pert. to being freely given, *as a gift, without payment, gratis*** (so, in addition to the ref. in Nägeli 35f and Poland 496 note **, GDI 2569, 4 [Delphi]; PSI 400, 16; 543, 19 al. [both III BC]; 1401, 8; PTebt 5, 187; 250 [both II BC]; Gen 29:15; Ex 21:11 δωρεὰν ἄνευ ἀργυρίου al.; Tat. 19, 1) δ. λαμβάνειν (Jos., Vi. 425), διδόναι (Bell. 1, 274, Vi. 38) *receive or give without payment* **Mt 10:8** (cp. Sextus 242; of an emissary who paid his own traveling expenses IPriene 108, 165); cp. **Rv 21:6; 22:17;** δ. εὐαγγελίσασθαι **2 Cor 11:7.** δικαιούμενοι δ. *justified, made upright, as a gift* **Ro 3:24.** οὐδὲ δ. ἄρτον ἐφάγομεν παρά τινος *we have not eaten bread with* (or *from*) *anyone without paying for it* **2 Th 3:8.**

❷ **pert. to being without contributory fault, *undeservedly, without reason/cause*** ἐμίσησάν με δ. *they hated me without reason* **J 15:25** (Ps 34:19; 68:5; PsSol 7:1; cp. Ps 118:161; 1 Km 19:5).

❸ **pert. to being without purpose, *in vain, to no purpose*** (Job 1:9; Ps 34:7) δ. ἀποθνήσκειν **Gal 2:21;** ITr 10.—DELG s.v. δίδωμι. M-M. s.v. δωρεά. TW.

δωρέομαι 1 aor. ἐδωρησάμην; pf. δεδώρημαι, ptc. δεδωρημένος; aor. pass. ptc. neut. δωρηθέν (the act. is scarce in post-Homeric times; the mid. is found Hom.+) **to present someth. as a gift or confer a benefit, prob. with some suggestion of formality** (cp. Philostrat., Vi. Soph. 2, 10, 7 [589] s.v. δῶρον) ***present, bestow*** τινί τι *someth. to (on) someone* (Aeschyl., Hdt. et al.; OGI 90, 31; 517, 7; POxy 1153, 15 [I AD]; IDefixWünsch 4, 30; of God Iren. 3, 18, 7 [Harv. II 100, 4]; Hippol., Ref. 9, 30, 4; Did., Gen. 66, 5; of Jesus 81, 25) τὸ πτῶμα τῷ Ἰωσήφ *the body to Joseph* **Mk 15:45.** τ. θείας δυνάμεως δεδωρημένης *since the divine power has bestowed* **2 Pt 1:3.** Hence in vs. **4** prob. mid., not pass. (of a divine gift Ael. Aristid. 13 p. 297 D.).—Dg 11:5.—DELG s.v. δίδωμι B. M-M. TW.

δώρημα, ατος, τό (Aeschyl., Hdt. et al.; IG IV^2, 128, 53 [c. 280 BC] δ. of Asclepius; Kaibel 1039, 13; Sir 34:18; Ezk. Trag. 35 [in Eus., PE 9, 28] θεοῦ δ.; Philo, Somn. 1, 103 δ. παρὰ θεοῦ) ***gift, present*** δ. τέλειον *a perfect gift* **Js 1:17** (Philo, Abr. 54 δ. τέλ.; EpArist 276 θεοῦ δ. καλόν; Jos., Ant. 4, 318 δ. κάλλιστον; PSI 29, 33 τἀγαθὰ δορήματα). οὐχ ὡς δι' ἑνὸς ἁμαρτήσαντος τὸ δ. *the gift* (of grace) *is not like the effects of one man's sin* **Ro 5:16;** ἐκ τῶν ἰδίων δ. *from the gifts that oneself has received* Hm 2:4. δ. τοῦ κυρίου s 2:7.—DELG s.v. δίδωμι B. M-M. TW.

δῶρον, ου, τό (Hom.+; ins, pap, LXX; En 100:12; Test12 Patr; JosAs 7:4; EpArist, Philo; Jos., C. Ap. 2, 207; Just., D. 28, 4.—Philostrat., Vi. Soph. 2, 10, 7 [589] distinguishes betw. δωρεά [special grant or privilege] and δῶρον [material gift]) ***gift, present.*** Of gifts in general: προσφέρειν δ. *bring gifts* (cp. Gen 43:26; Did., Gen. 228, 1 10: αὐτὴν ὡς δῶρον) **Mt 2:11;** cp. ἐξέβαλον ἀπὸ τῆς πήρας αὐτῶν δῶρα χρυσόν … *they took a gift of gold out of their traveling bag* GJs 21:3; δῶρα πέμπειν ἀλλήλοις *send gifts to each other* **Rv 11:10.** Of God's gifts (Hom. et al.; Sotades Lyr. [III BC] 9, 7 p. 242 Coll.; oracular saying Diod. S. 8, 18, 1; Strabo 16, 2, 35; Herm. Wr. 10, 9; EpArist 231; 272; Philo, Congr. Erud. Gr. 38; Did., Gen. 161, 2) 1 Cl 35:1; w. ἐπαγγελίαι Hv 3, 2, 1; καὶ τοῦτο οὐκ ἐξ ὑμῶν, θεοῦ τὸ δ. *and you have not done this of your own strength; it is a gift of God* **Eph 2:8.** Of sacrificial *gifts* and *offerings* (Pla., Euthphr. 15a; SIG 1141; 1154 Διὶ δ.; OGI 407, 4; Just., D. 28, 4) **Hb 11:4;** 1 Cl 4:2 (Gen 4:4); GJs 7:1. εἰς τὰ δ. βάλλειν *cast into the gifts* (i.e. those already in the offering receptacle) **Lk 21:4;** cp. vs. **1.** προσφέρειν τὸ δ. *bring one's offering* (Lev. 1:2, 14; 2:1, 4 and oft.; TestIss 5:3) **Mt 5:23f; 8:4; Hb 5:1; 8:3f; 9:9** (w. θυσίαι as Lev 21:6; cp. EpArist 234); GJs 1:1f; 5:1; cp. 1 Cl 44:4. ἀφιέναι τὸ δ. *leave one's offering* **Mt 5:24;** δ. as transl. of קָרְבָּן (Jos., Ant. 4, 73, C. Ap. 1, 167) **Mk 7:11;** cp. **Mt 15:5;** ἁγιάζειν τὸ δ. *sanctify the offering* **23:19;** cp. vs. **18.** Of a child consecrated for temple service προσάξω (αὐτὸ) δῶρον Κυρίῳ τῷ θεῷ μου GJs 4:1 (cp. 1 Km 1:11).—V.l. for λόγον Qua (1).—DELG s.v. δίδωμι B. M-M. TW.

δωροφορία, ας, ἡ (δῶρον + φέρω via -φορος) bringing of presents (Alciphron 1, 6; Pollux 4, 47; B-D-F §119, 1) *bringing of a gift* of a collection **Ro 15:31 v.l.** for διακονία.—S. DELG s.v. φέρω. M-M.

E

E

ε′ numerical sign = ***5*** (πέντε) or ***5th*** (πέμπτη); **Ac 19:9** D. In titles: Hv 5; m 5; s 5 (Apollon. Paradox. 46 Θεόφραστος ἐν τῇ ε′ τῶν φυτικῶν αἰτιῶν φησίν; freq. pap, e.g. PWisc II, 80, 15 al.).

ἔα (Aeschyl. et al. in Attic poets; rare in prose: Pla., Prot. 314d; Epict. 2, 24, 22; 3, 20, 5; Job 15:16; 25:6) **an exclamatory particle expressing surprise or displeasure, *ah!, ha!* Mk 1:24 v.l.; Lk 4:34.** Some connection w. ἔα, impv. of ἐάω, *let alone!* seems likely in 1 Cl, and poss. in Mk and Lk (cp. Vulg. and NRSV mng., **Lk 4:34**). S. ἐάω 2.

ἐάν (Hom.+) fundamentally introduces a situation in which given X, Y will follow (B-D-F §31, 1; 107; 371, 4; 372, 1a; 373; Mlt. and Rob., indices)

❶ as conj., **marker of condition, with probability of activity expressed in the verb left open and thereby suited esp. for generalized statements, *if*** (only rarely [**1 Cor 6:4; 11:14,** as e.g. Lucian, Vit. Auct. 11 καὶ ἰδιώτης γὰρ ἐὰν ᾖς] anywhere else than at the beg. of the subordinate clause).

ⓐ used w. subjunctive to denote what is expected to occur, under certain circumstances, from a given standpoint in the present, either general or specific (B-D-F. §371, 4; Mlt-Turner 114f)

α. w. pres. subj., and pres. in apodosis: ἐὰν θέλῃς δύνασαί με καθαρίσαι **Mt 8:2; Mk 1:40; Lk 5:12.** ἐὰν ἀγαθοποιῆτε, ποία ὑμῖν χάρις ἐστίν; **6:33.** ἐὰν μαρτυρῶ, ἡ μαρτυρία μου οὐκ ἔστιν ἀληθής **J 5:31** (but s. bβ below) cp. **8:16; 15:14.** περιτομὴ ὠφελεῖ ἐὰν νόμον πράσσῃς **Ro 2:25;** cp. **13:4; 14:8; 1 Cor 13:1ff** al. W. pres. subj., and aorist in apodosis: ἐὰν ὁ πούς σου σκανδαλίζῃ σε, ἀπόκοψον **Mk 9:45;** cp. vs. **47;** w. fut. in apod.: ἐὰν ᾖ …, ἐπαναπαήσεται **Lk 10:6;** ἐὰν ὁδηγῇ, πεσοῦνται **Mt 15:14.**

β. mostly w. aor. subj., and pres. in apodosis: ἐὰν ἀγαπήσητε, τίνα μισθὸν ἔχετε; **Mt 5:46,** cp. **47; 18:15ff.** ἐὰν μερισθῇ, οὐ δύναται σταθῆναι **Mk 3:24.** ἐὰν γαμήσῃ, μοιχᾶται **10:12.** ἐὰν ἀπολέσῃ, οὐχὶ ἅπτει; **Lk 15:8.** ἐὰν μείνητε, μαθηταί μού ἐστε **J 8:31;** cp. **19:12.** ἐὰν χωρισθῇ, μενέτω **1 Cor 7:11;** cp. vs. **39.** ἐὰν φάγωμεν, περισσεύομεν **8:8.** W. aor. subj., and aor. in apodosis ἐὰν εἴπωσιν, μὴ ἐξέλθητε **Mt 24:26.** ἐὰν ἁμάρτῃ, ἐπιτίμησον … ἐὰν μετανοήσῃ, ἄφες **Lk 17:3;** ἐὰν εἴπω, οὐ μὴ πιστεύσητε **22:67;** cp. vs. **68.** W. aor. subj., and fut. in apod. (cp. Aesop, Fab. 408b H.//250 I, H-H.): ἐὰν ἀφῆτε, ἀφήσει καὶ ὑμῖν **Mt 6:14.** ἐὰν ἅψωμαι, σωθήσομαι **9:21.** ἐὰν ἐμπέσῃ, οὐχὶ κρατήσει; **12:11;** cp. **24:48, 50; 28:14; Mk 8:3; Lk 4:7; 14:34; J 15:10** al. (w. aor. opt. in apodosis Just., A II, 15, 2).

γ. w. pres. and aor. subj. at the same time: ἐὰν δὲ καὶ ἀθλῇ τις (*is an athlete* by profession), οὐ στεφανοῦται, ἐὰν μὴ νομίμως ἀθλήσῃ (*competes acc. to the rules* single or repeated action) **2 Ti 2:5.—1 Cor 14:23:** ἐὰν συνέλθῃ (antecedent action) καὶ λαλῶσιν (repeated and lasting), εἰσέλθωσιν δέ (once); cp. vs. 24. ἐὰν ἔχητε πίστιν καὶ μὴ διακριθῆτε **Mt 21:21.**

ⓑ used w. the indic. (exx. in Dssm., NB 29f [BS 201f]; B-D-F §372, 1a; Mlt. 168; Mlt-Turner 115f; Rdm.[2] 200; Rob. 1009f).

α. w. fut. ind., in the same mng. (CIG II, 2485 ἐὰν θελήσει; pap; TestReub 4:11; TestJob 4:4 ἐὰν ἐπιχειρήσεις; B-D-F §373, 2): ἐὰν οὗτοι σιωπήσουσιν, οἱ λίθοι κράξουσιν **Lk 19:40** (vv.ll. σιγήσουσιν, σιωπήσωσιν). ἐὰν μή τις ὁδηγήσει με **Ac 8:31** (v.l. ὁδηγήσῃ). ἐὰν ἡμᾶς μιμήσεται …, οὐκ ἔτι ἐσμέν IMg 10:1; ἐὰν μετανοήσουσιν Hv 1, 3, 2; ἐὰν προσθήσω m 4, 3, 7; ἐὰν ἔσῃ m 5, 1, 2.

β. w. pres. ind. (Ocellus [II BC] 5; Cyril of Scyth. p. 145, 5 ἐὰν ἔστιν; CIG II, 2485 ἐὰν βούλονται; TestJud 15:2 v.l.; Just., D. 47, 1 and 3; 67, 2) ἐὰν στήκετε ἐν κυρίῳ **1 Th 3:8** (v.l. στήκητε); IMg 5:2; Hv 3, 12, 3; ἐὰν οἴδαμεν **1J 5:15** (on this and **J 5:31** [s. aα above] s. B-D-F §372, 1=B-D-R §373, 3n. 12) ἐὰν πάσχομεν Pol. 8:2.

γ. w. aor. ind. In **Mt 15:5=Mk 7:11,** N[24] accents ὠφελήθης instead of ὠφεληθῇς (N.), giving us an example of ἐάν w. aor. ind., strongly supported by B-D-F §360, 1. This constr. is rare but occasionally found in the late κοινή (Rob. 1009).

ⓒ w. other particles—**α.** ἐὰν καί *even if* **Gal 6:1;** likew. ἐὰν δὲ καί (POxy 472 II, 7) *but if* **1 Cor 7:11, 28; 2 Ti 2:5.** ἐὰν δὲ καὶ παρακούσῃ *but if the pers. refuses to listen* **Mt 18:17.**

β. ἐὰν μή *if not, unless* w. pres. subj. ἐὰν δὲ μὴ ᾖ ἀξία **Mt 10:13;** cp. **Lk 13:3; J 3:2f, 5, 27.** Mostly w. aor. subj. ἐὰν μὴ περισσεύσῃ **Mt 5:20; 6:15; 12:29; 18:3; 21:21; Mk 3:27; 4:22** (s. KBeyer, Semitische Syntax im NT, ’62, 131); **J 4:48; 6:44; 7:51; Ro 10:15; 1 Cor 9:16; 14:6;** *unless, without* ἐὰν μὴ αὐτὸ πίω **Mt 26:42.** W. fut. ἐὰν μὴ μετανοήσουσιν **Rv 2:22.**

γ. ἐάνπερ *if indeed, if only, supposing that* ‘referring to still another condition (fact)’ (B-D-F §454, 2) w. pres. subj. (Pla., Ap. 12, 25b; X., Cyr. 4, 6, 8; PFay 124, 9) **Hb 6:3;** IRo 1:1 and aor. (Plut., Lyc. 40 [3, 2]; BGU 1141, 30) 1:2; IPol 7:1; **Hb 3:6, 14** (v.l. ἐάν).

δ. ἐάν τε ... ἐάν τε *whether ... or whether* (X., Cyr. 3, 3, 17, Mem. 2, 4, 6; Ael. Aristid. 53 p. 622 D.; Maximus Tyr. 1, 9a) **Ro 14:8.** (On the single occurrence ἐάν τε **2 Cor 10:8** s. Rad[2] 5.)

ε. ἐὰν οὖν s. οὖν 2d. Also s. κἄν.

❷ as conj., **marker of the prospect of an action in a point of time coordinated with another point of time.** Thus at times the mng. of ἐάν approaches closely that of ὅταν ***whenever, when*** (Is 24:13; Am 7:2; Tob 6:17 BA ἐὰν εἰσέλθῃς, cp. S ὅταν εἰσ.; 4:3 BA, cp. vs. 4) **1J 2:28** (v.l. ὅταν); **J 12:32** (v.l. ὅταν) **14:3; Hb 3:7** (Ps 94:7).

❸ marker of the possibility of any number of occurrences of the same event, *ever* freq. in place of ἄν (q.v.) after relatives (so Lysias 24, 18 Thalh. v.l. acc. to mss.; pap since 246 BC [Mayser 152f]; LXX [Thackeray 67]; Mel., P. 35, 236 [B] πάντα ὅσα ἐὰν γείνηται.—Dssm., NB 29f [BS 201f]; Mlt. 42f; B-D-F §107; Rdm.[2] 203f; Crönert 130f; Rob. 190f; acc. to Rydbeck most freq. in I–II AD, esp. in vernacular texts) ὃς ἐάν = ὃς ἄν (PTebt107, 8 [II BC]; Gen 15:14) **Mt 5:19, 32;** 1 Cl 32:1. ὅπου ἐάν = ὅπου ἄν **Mt 8:19.** ὁσάκις ἐάν = ὁσάκις ἄν **Rv 11:6.** οὗ ἐάν = οὗ ἄν **1 Cor 16:6.**—Rydbeck 119–44. DELG. M-M.

ἐάνπερ s. ἐάν 1 cγ.—M-M.

ἐαρινός, ή, όν (Hom. [εἰαρ-] et al.; Diod. S. 5, 41, 6; ins, pap; Philo, Mos. 2, 186 al.) **pert. to the season between winter and summer, *of spring*** καιροὶ ἐ. *seasons of spring* (as Philo, Op. M. 153 ἐαριναὶ ὧραι) 1 Cl 20:9.—DELG s.v. ἔαρ 2.

ἑαυτοῦ, ῆς, οῦ, pl. ἑαυτῶν, reflexive pron. (Hom.+; JosAs 7:6 [oft. cod. A; 3:2 αὑτοῦ]). Editors variously replace contract forms αὑτοῦ and αὑτῶν of later mss. w. uncontracted forms or w. αὐτοῦ, αὐτῶν; cp., e.g., the texts of **Mk 9:16; Lk 23:12; J 2:24; 20:10; Ac 14:17; Ro 1:24; Eph 2:15; Hb 5:3; 1J 5:10; Rv 8:6; 18:7** in GNT[1-3] w. GNT[4]; s. also Merk’s treatment of these same pass. Cp. the ms. evidence for **Phil 3:21** in GNT[1-3] w. its absence in GNT[4]. (W-S. §223 16; B-D-F §64, 1; Mayser 305; I[2]/2, 65; Rob. 226; Mlt-Turner 190; M-M. s.v. αὑτοῦ; RBorger, TRu 52, ’88, 17–19).

❶ indicator of identity w. the pers. speaking or acting, *self*—ⓐ of the third pers. sing. and pl. ταπεινοῦν ἑαυτόν *humble oneself* **Mt 18:4; 23:12.** Opp. ὑψοῦν ἑ. *exalt oneself* **23:12;** δοξάζειν ἑ. *glorify oneself* **Rv 18:7 v.l.** ἀπαρνεῖσθαι ἑ. *deny oneself* **16:24; Mk 8:34** (Mel, P. 26, 181). ἀμάρτυρον ἑ. ἀφεῖναι *leave oneself without witness* **Ac 14:17 v.l.;** ἑτοιμάζειν ἑ. *prepare oneself* **Rv 8:6 v.l.** εὐνουχίζειν ἑ. *make a eunuch of oneself* **Mt 19:12;** σῴζειν ἑ. (Jos., Ant. 10, 137) **27:42;** κατακόπτειν ἑ. *beat oneself* **Mk 5:5;** πιστεύειν ἑαυτόν τινι **J 2:24 v.l.** et al.; ἀγοράζειν τι ἑαυτῷ *buy someth. for oneself* **Mt 14:15; Mk 6:36;** θησαυρίζων ἑαυτῷ *lay up assets for oneself* **Lk 12:21.** ὑποτάσσειν ἑ. **Phil 3:21 v.l.** W. the middle (cp. X., Mem. 1, 6, 13 ποιεῖσθαι ἑαυτῷ φίλον; Sir 37:8): διεμερίσαντο ἑαυτοῖς *they divided among them* **J 19:24** (Ps 21:19).—The simple dat. may also be used to emphasize the subject as agent (Hdt. 1, 32; Strabo 2, 1, 35; POxy 2351, 49; Ps 26:12; SSol 1:8) βαστάζων ἑαυτῷ τὸν σταυρόν *bearing the cross without help* **J 19:17;** ἑαυτοῖς κρίμα λήμψονται *they themselves will be responsible for the judgment they are to receive* **Ro 13:2;** οὐκ ἐπαινοῦμεν τοὺς προσιόντας ἑαυτοῖς *we do not commend those who take the initiative in advancing themselves* MPol 4; cp. στρῶσον σεαυτῷ *make your own bed* **Ac 9:34.**—Rydbeck 51–61.—Used esp. w. prep.

α. ἀφ’ ἑαυτοῦ (ἀπό 5ea; TestAbr A 19 p. 101, 6 [Stone p. 50]; Just., A I, 43, 8 ἀφ’ ἑαυτοῦ ἑλόμενος τὸ ἀγαθόν; Tat. 17, 4 ἐχθρὸν ἀμυνεῖται): ποιεῖν τι *do someth. of one’s own accord* **J 5:19.** λαλεῖν *speak on one’s own authority* (Diod. S. 12, 66, 2 ἐκήρυξέ τις ἀφ’ ἑαυτοῦ; i.e. without orders from a higher authority) **7:18; 16:13;** λέγειν **11:51; 18:34 v.l.** (M. Ant. 11, 19 τοῦτο οὐκ ἀπὸ σαυτοῦ μέλλεις λέγειν). καρπὸν φέρειν *bear fruit by itself* **15:4.** ἱκανὸν εἶναι *be competent by oneself* **2 Cor 3:5** (ἀφ’ ἑαυτῶν interchanging w. ἐξ ἑαυτῶν; s. also 1aδ). γινώσκειν *know by oneself* **Lk 21:30.** κρίνειν *judge for oneself* **12:57** (ἐξετάζειν Ath. 18, 1).

β. δι’ ἑαυτοῦ (POxy 273, 21; PTebt 72, 197; TestJob 16:4): κοινὸς δι’ ἑαυτοῦ *unclean in itself* **Ro 14:14** (EpJer 26; Just., A I, 54, 8; A II, 10, 8; D. 56, 1).

γ. ἐν ἑαυτῷ *to* or *in oneself,* εὐπαρεπέστατον ἦν ἐν αὐτῷ τὸ ὄρος Hs 9, 1, 10. **J 13:32 v.l.; Ro 1:24 v.l.; Eph 2:15 v.l.** Otherw. mostly w. verbs of speaking, in contrast to audible utterance; s. διαλογίζομαι 1, εἶπον 6, λέγω 1bζ; otherw. ἔχειν τι ἐν ἑαυτῷ *have someth. in oneself* (cp. Jdth 10:19; Jos., Ant. 8, 171; Just., D. 8, 2; Ath. 10, 2) **J 5:26, 42; 6:53; 17:13; 2 Cor 1:9.** Gener., of what takes place in the inner consciousness διαπορεῖν **Ac 10:17.** Esp. γίνεσθαι ἐν ἑαυτῷ *come to one’s senses* **12:11** (X., An. 1, 5, 17 ὁ Κλέαρχος ἐν ἑαυτῷ ἐγένετο; Polyb. 1, 49, 8; Chariton 3, 9, 11 ἐν ἑαυτῷ γενόμενος). Also:

δ. ἐξ ἑαυτῶν (Soph., El. 343 ἐκ σαυτῆς; Theophr. fgm. 96 [in Ps.-Demetr. 222] ἐξ αὑτοῦ) *of (our) own strength* **2 Cor 3:5.**

ε. εἰς ἑαυτὸν ἔρχεσθαι *come to one’s senses* **Lk 15:17** (Diod. S. 13, 95, 2; Epict. 3, 1, 15; GrBar 17:3).

ζ. καθ’ ἑαυτόν *by oneself* (X., Mem. 3, 5, 4; Plut., Anton. 940 [54, 1 and 2]; 2 Macc 13:13; Just., D. 4, 5; 74:2; Ath. 15, 2 al.) μένειν *live by oneself* (in a private house) **Ac 28:16.** πίστις νεκρά ἐστιν καθ’ ἑαυτήν *faith* (when it remains) *by itself is dead* **Js 2:17** (Diog. L. 1, 64 from a letter of Solon: religion and lawgivers can do nothing καθ’ ἑαυτά=if they are dependent on themselves alone).—βασιλεία μερισθεῖσα καθ’ ἑαυτῆς *a kingdom that is divided against itself* **Mt 12:25.**—μεθ’ ἑαυτοῦ, μεθ’ ἑαυτῶν *with oneself, themselves* (cp. 1 Km 9:3; 24:3 ἔλαβεν μεθ’ ἑ.) **Mt 12:45; 25:3.**

η. παρ’ ἑαυτῷ τιθέναι τι *put someth. aside* **1 Cor 16:2** (X., Mem. 3, 13, 3; cp. Jos., Ant. 9, 68 οἴκαδε παρ’ αὑτῷ; Tat. 7, 2 λόγου δύναμις ἔχουσα παρ’ ἑαυτῇ τὸ προγνωστικόν ‘has in itself’).

θ. περὶ ἑ. προσφέρειν *make offering for himself* **Hb 5:3.** τὰ περι ἑαυτοῦ *the passages about himself* **Lk 24:27.**

ι. πρὸς ἑαυτὸν προσεύχεσθαι *pray to oneself* (=in silence) **18:11** (cp. Aristaen., Ep. 1, 6; 2 Macc 11:13; Jos., Ant. 11, 210; Vi. Aesopi G 9 P. πρὸς ἑαυτὸν εἶπεν; 38; Just., D. 62, 2 πρὸς ἑαυτὸν ἔλεγεν ὁ θεός ... πρὸς ἑαυτοὺς λέγομεν). ἀπῆλθεν πρὸς ἑαυτόν, θαυμάζων τὸ γέγονος *(Peter) went home, (all the while) marveling at what had taken place* **Lk 24:12** (FNeirynck, ETL 54, ’78, 104–18). ἀπέρχεσθαι πρὸς ἑαυτούς *go home* **J 20:10 v.l.** (for αὐτούς, cp. Polyb. 5, 93, 1; Num 24:25; Jos., Ant. 8, 124; s. MBlack, An Aramaic Approach[3], ’67, 102f). **Lk 23:12 v.l.**

ⓑ for the first and second pers. pl. (gener. H. Gk.; s. FKälker, Quaest. de elocut. Polyb. 1880, 277; Mlt. 87; B-D-F §64, 1;

Mayser 303, w. further lit. in note 3; Rob. 689f) ἑαυτούς = ἡμᾶς αὐτούς (Themistocl., Ep. 15; Jos., Bell. 5, 536; Just., A I, 53, 3; D. 32, 5; 34, 1 al.; Tat. 30, 1; Ath. 12, 1) **1 Cor 11:31.** ἐν ἑαυτοῖς = ἐν ἡμῖν αὐτοῖς **Ro 8:23; 2 Cor 1:9;**=ἐν ὑμῖν αὐτοῖς **Ro 11:25 v.l.** (En 6:2 ἐκλεξώμεθα ἑαυτοῖς γυναῖκας). δι' ἑαυτῶν = δι' ἡμῶν αὐ. 1 Cl 32:4; παρ' ἑαυτοῖς = παρ' ὑμῖν αὐτοῖς **Ro 11:25** (cp. Just., D. 141, 1 and Tat. 11:2 δι' ἑαυτούς). ἑαυτοῖς = ὑμῖν αὐτοῖς (cp. En 15:3; TestJob 45:3; TestDan 6:1; Jos., Ant. 4, 190; 8, 277) **Mt 23:31; Ro 11:25 v.l.;** 1 Cl 47:7.—This replacement of the first and second pers. by the third is very much less common in the sg. (Ps.-Pla., Alc. 2, 143c; Dio Chrys. 30 [47], 6 σὺ ... αὐτόν; Aelian, VH 1, 21; Galen, Protr. 10 p. 30, 10 John; Syntipas p. 115, 10 μεθ' ἑαυτοῦ=with me; TestJob 2:3 διελογιζόμην ἐν ἑαυτῷ; GrBar 17:3 εἰς ἑαυτὸν ἐλθὼν δόξαν ἔφερον τῷ θεῷ. Transjordanian ins: NGG Phil.-hist. Kl. Fachgr. V n.s. I/1 '36, p. 3, 1; other exx. in Mlt. 87, n. 2; Mayser 304; Hauser 100), and can hardly be established w. certainty for the NT gener.: s. **J 18:34 v.l.; Ro 13:9 v.l.;** cp. ISm 4:2 (v.l. ἐμαυτόν); Hv 4, 1, 5 Joly (ἐμαυτῷ B.); s 2:1.

❷ **marker of reciprocal relationship,** for the reciprocal pron. ἀλλήλων, ἀλλήλοις, ἀλλήλους (also in earlier auth., Kühner-G. I 573; pap in Mayser 304; LXX; 4 [6] Esdr [POxy 1010] ἔδονται τά(ς) σάρκας αὐτῶν καὶ τὸ αἷμα αὐτῶν πίονται; Tat. 3, 3.—W-S. §22, 13; B-D-F §287; Rob. 690) ***each other, one another*** συζητεῖν πρὸς ἑαυτούς **Mk 9:16 v.l.** (s. VTaylor, Comm. ad. loc.; ASyn. app., w. correction of Tdf. app.); λέγοντες πρὸς ἑαυτούς *as they said to each other* **Mk 10:26;** cp. **J 12:19** (πρὸς ἑ. as Antig. Car. 39 μάχεσθαι πρὸς αὑτούς; Lucian, Philops. 29, Ver. Hist. 1, 35; Tat. 26, 3 πολεμοῦντες ... ἑαυτοῖς ἀλλήλους καθαιρεῖτε). χαρίζεσθαι ἑαυτοῖς *forgive one another* **Eph 4:32; Col 3:13.** νουθετεῖν ἑαυτούς *admonish one another* vs. **16.** εἰρηνεύειν ἐν ἑαυτοῖς *live in peace w. one another* **1 Th 5:13;** τὴν εἰς ἑαυτοὺς ἀγάπην **1 Pt 4:9.**

❸ **marker of possession by the pers. spoken of or acting,** in place of the possessive pron. ***his, her*** (Mayser 304f; Mlt. 87f) **Mt 8:22; 21:8; 25:1; Lk 2:39; 9:60; 11:21; 12:36** al. ESchwartz, Index lectionum 1905, 8f; DTabachovitz, Eranos 93, '55, 76ff; ADihle, Noch einmal ἑαυτῷ: Glotta 39, '60, 83–92; s. Rydbeck (1a beg.).—DELG. M-M.

ἐάω impf. εἴων; fut. ἐάσω; 1 aor. εἴασα, impv. ἔασον, opt. 3 sg. ἐάσαι 1 Cl 33:1; 1 aor. pass. 3 pl. εἰάθησαν (3 Macc 5:18); inf. ἐαθῆναι (Hom.+)

❶ **to allow someone to do someth.,** ***let, permit*** w. acc. and inf. (Lucian, Dial. Mort. 13, 5; Tat. 12, 4) εἴασεν πάντα τὰ ἔθνη πορεύεσθαι *(God) let all the nations go* **Ac 14:16.—23:32; 27:32; 28:4;** 1 Cl 38:2; 53:3 (Ex 32:10); 55:4; Dg 9:1. W. neg. οὐκ ἐᾶν *not permit, prevent* (Appian, Bell. Civ. 5, 92 §384; PSI 380, 5 [249 BC]; 402, 11; 602, 10; Job 9:18; 1 Macc 12:40; 15:14; 2 Macc 12:2) **Mt 24:43; Lk 4:41** (w. pres. inf. as Polyaenus 7, 21, 5 and 6); **1 Cor 10:13; Mk 16:14 v.l.** (Freer ms. 3); 1 Cl 33:1; IEph 3:2; 9:1; Hv 3, 1, 9; GJs 6:3. W. ἵνα instead of the inf. Hv 2, 3, 1. W. omission of the inf. (Soph., Ant. 538; POxy 1293, 21) οὐκ εἴασεν αὐτοὺς τὸ πνεῦμα Ἰησοῦ (sc. πορευθῆναι) *the Spirit of Jesus prevented them* (fr. going) **Ac 16:7.** οὐκ εἴων αὐτὸν (sc. εἰσελθεῖν) οἱ μαθηταί **19:30.**

❷ **to refrain from bothering, detaining, or using,** ***let go, leave alone*** (Demosth. 9, 26, Ael. Aristid. 34, 42 K.=50 p. 562 D.: ἐῶ τὰ ἄλλα; PFay 122, 6; PTebt 319, 24; Jos., C. Ap. 2, 118; GrBar 16:1; Just., D. 85, 5; Ath. 6:1) τὶ *someth.* τὴν στρεβλήν (sc. ὁδόν) *avoid the crooked way* Hm 6, 1, 2. W. relative as obj. s 9, 2, 7; =ἀφιέναι τινά *let someone go* (Maximus Tyr. 8, 5g; 6h) **Ac 5:38 v.l.; Rv 2:20** t.r. (Erasmian rdg.? s. Tdf.); *leave someone to oneself* Hv 2, 3, 1. Abs. ἐᾶτε ἕως τούτου *Stop! No more of this!* **Lk 22:51** (cp. Il. 21, 221 ἔασον). ἔα δέ *let alone, not to speak of, much more* or *less* 1 Cl 39:5, but s. also ἔα (Job 4:19 v.l., 15, 16. Cp. PKatz, JTS 47, '46, 168f).

❸ perh. nautical t.t. ἐᾶν τὰς ἀγκύρας εἰς τὴν θάλασσαν *leave the anchors in the sea* **Ac 27:40.**—DELG. M-M.

ἑβδομάς, άδος, ἡ ***week*** (Hippocr., Aphorism. 2, 24; Lydus, Mens. 2, 4 p. 21 W et al.; PPrinc III, 179, 16 [V–VI AD]; LXX; ApcEsdr, Philo; TestLevi 16:1; 17:10.—In Jos.=sabbath: Bell. 2, 147 and 4, 99, C. Ap. 2, 175) B 16:6 (quot. of uncertain origin; s. Windisch, Hdb. ad loc.).—B. 1005. DELG s.v. ἑπτά. TW.

ἑβδομήκοντα indecl. (Hdt.+) ***seventy*** **Lk 10:1 v.l.; 17 v.l.** (οἱ ἑβδ. w. someth. to be supplied as Plut., Mor. 345d; Jos., Vi. 56b; 58); **Ac 23:23.** ἑ. δύο *seventy-two* (TestAbr A 20, 3 p. 102, 24 [Stone p. 52] ἑβδομήκοντα δύο εἰσὶν θάνατοι; EpArist 50: the 72 translators [other exx. from the pseudepigr. in MPhilonenko, JosAs, p. 74]; Antig. Car. 111, the 72 children of Heracles; Plut., Mor. 356b: the 72 fellow-conspirators of Typhon) **Lk 10:1, 17** (B Metzger, NTS 5, '59, 299–306; SJellicoe, ibid. 6, '60, 319–21). ἑ. πέντε *seventy-five* **Ac 7:14** (Demetr.: 722 fgm. 1, 1f Jac.). ἑ. ἕξ *seventy-six* **27:37** (ἑ. ἑπτά 'seventy-seven' ParJer 9:15; on the number of persons s. Hemer, Acts 149).—DELG s.v. ἑπτά. M-M. TW.

ἑβδομηκοντάκις ***seventy times*** ἑ. ἑπτά may be short for ἑ. ἑπτάκις *seventy times seven times* (cp. PGM 1, 143 ἑπτάκις ἑπτά seven times seven), but is more likely *seventy-seven times* (as Gen 4:24; cp. TestBenj 7:4) **Mt 18:22** (Mlt. 98, but s. Mlt-H. 175; B-D-F §248, 2; Goodsp., Probs., 29–31. In Polyaenus 8, 33; Plut., Mor. 245d the number 7777 is found, denoting an incalculable throng).—DELG s.v. ἑπτά. M-M. TW.

ἕβδομος, η, ον (Hom.+) ***seventh*** **Jd 14; Rv 8:1; 10:7; 11:15; 16:17; 21:20;** Hs 9, 1, 8; 9, 24, 1; hour (Polyaenus 8, 16, 1 ὥρα ἑβ.) **J 4:52;** day **Ac 21:27** D; **Hb 4:4b;** B 15:3 and 5 (3 times Gen 2:2); month GJs 5:2 (deStrycker for ἑπτά; s. p. 206 of his text). ἡ ἑβδόμη (sc. ἡμέρα; cp. Antig. Car. 140; GDI 4705, 8 [Thera] ἐπάγεσθαι τὰν ἑβδόμαν of the celebration 'of the seventh'; Bar 1:2; Ezk 30:20; Philo, Vit. Cont. 30; 32; Just., D 24, 1) **Hb 4:4a.** ἐν τῷ ἑβδόμῳ *the seventh time* 1 Cl 56:8 (Job 5:19).—DELG s.v. ἑπτά. M-M. TW.

ἐβεβλήκει, ἐβέβλητο s. βάλλω.

Ἔβερ, ὁ (Ἕβερ v.l.) indecl. ***Eber,*** son of Shelah (Gen 10:24f.—In Joseph. Ἔβερος, ου [Ant. 1, 147]), in the genealogy of Jesus **Lk 3:35.**

ἐβλήθην s. βάλλω.

Ἑβραϊκός, ή, όν (Philo; Jos., Ant. 1, 5; PGM 4, 3085; cp. IDefixWünsch 1, 12; 15; Mel., P. 1, 1; 94, 174) **pert. to the Hebrew people,** ***Hebrew*** γράμμασιν Ἑ. *with Hebrew letters* (EpArist 3; 30), which takes for granted that the language was also Hebrew (Jos., Ant. 1, 5; 12, 48) **Lk 23:38 v.l.;** cp. Kleine Texte 8³, p. 9, 27=Asyn. 297, 19.—TW. Sv.

Ἑβραῖος, ου, ὁ (W-H. Ἐβ.; s. their Introd.[2] §408; B-D-F §39, 3) 'a Hebrew' (Paus. 1, 5, 5; Appian, Bell. Civ. 2, 71; Plut.; Porphyr., Vi. Pyth. 11; Sallust. 9 p. 18, 17; Damasc., Vi. Isidori 56 ὁ Ἑβραίων θεός; 141; PGM 4, 3019, corresp. to what Jews oft. called themselves; LXX; TestSol 6:8; JosAs 1:7; ch. 11 cod. A and Pal. 364 [p. 54, 6 Bat.]; Ezk. Trag., Philo, Joseph., SibOr; TestJos 12:2; 3; ins [exx. in Schürer III 97, 29]; συναγωγὴ

Ἑβραίων s. on συναγωγή 2a; MDibelius, Hdb.[2] on Phil 3:5 exc.; Just., D. 1, 3)

❶ **ethnic name for an Israelite,** ***Hebrew*** in contrast to other nations (in this sense Eus. applies the term Ἑβρ. to such Jews as Philo [Eus., HE 2, 4, 2] and Aristobulus [PE 8, 8, 56//Holladay T 11 (10) p. 123] who spoke Gk. and were Gk. scholars; s. the Jew. grave-ins in Rome and Lydia: Ltzm., Hdb.[3] on 2 Cor 11:22 exc.; MAMA III, 32; Just., D. 1, 3) **2 Cor 11:22; Phil 3:5** (on these pass. s. 2). The word prob. has this mng. in the **title** πρὸς Ἑβρ. of **Hb,** as well as in the name of the GHb in the old orig. Gk. in Clem. Al. and Origen (Kl. T. 8[3], p. 7, 2; 12; note on ln. 8; cp. p. 5, 9f; 18; 22; 11, 25f) τὸ καθ' Ἑβραίους εὐαγγέλιον. Papias (2:17). The author of GJs 6:1; 7:2; 18:1 compares Palestinian and Egyptian conditions (deStrycker 147, n. 2).

❷ **Hebrew-/Aramaic-speaking Israelite in contrast to a Gk.-speaking Israelite,** ***Hebrew-speaking Israelite*** (s. Ἑλληνισταί; GWetter, ARW 21, 1922, 410ff; Haenchen) **Ac 6:1** in contrast to Gk.-speaking Israelites (Philo, Conf. Ling. 129, makes a difference betw. Ἑβρ. and ἡμεῖς, who speak Gk. [Congr. Erud. Grat. 43f]). Windisch proposes that Paul emphasizes his fluency in his ancestral language **2 Cor 11:22; Phil 3:5** (s. 1).—S. on Ἰσραήλ, end. HKosmala, Hebräer-Essener-Christen '59; MHengel, ZTK 72, '75. 151–206.—M-M. EDNT. TW.

Ἑβραΐς, ΐδος, ἡ (ἑβρ- S., M.; Ἐβρ- W-H.—Fem. of Ἑβραῖος, Jos., Ant. 2, 225f and of Ἑβραϊκός, Kühner-Bl. II 274, 1) ἡ Ἑ. διάλεκτος (cp. Ἑ. φωνή 4 Macc 12:7; 16:15; Just., A I, 31, 1 and 3 al.) ***the Hebr. language*** **Ac 21:40; 22:2; 26:14;** Papias (2:16). These pass. refer to the Aramaic spoken at that time in Palestine.—Zahn. Einl.[3] I 18f; Dalman, Jesus 6ff (Eng. 7ff). But PNepper-Christensen, Das Matthäusevangelium '58, 101–35 and JGrintz, JBL 79, '60, 32–47 hold that some form of Hebrew was commonly spoken.—TW.

Ἑβραϊστί Ἐβ- W-H. adv. (Sir., Praef., ln. 22; Jos., Ant. 10, 8; Sb VIII/2, 9843, 14 [Bar-Kokhba revolt]; PGM 5, 475; 13, 81; 150 ἁβραιστί) *in Hebrew/Aramaic* (s. on Ἑβραΐς) **J 5:2; 19:13, 17, 20; 20:16; Rv 9:11; 16:16;** AcPl Ha 10, 24.—New Docs 5, 22f. M-M. TW.

ἐγγεννάω (ἐν + γεννάω; Polyb. 6, 55, 4; Cornutus 20 p. 37, 12; Plut., Mor. 132e; Herm. Wr. 10, 15b; Sir 22:4 v.l.) **to cause someth. to come into being in someth.,** ***generate in someth.;*** pass. *be generated,* of a worm in the flesh of the dead phoenix 1 Cl 25:3 v.l. (for γεννᾶται).—S. DELG s.v. γίγνομαι A 2.

ἐγγίζω (fr. ἐγγύς) Att. fut. ἐγγιῶ; 1 aor. ἤγγισα; Att. reduplication ἐνήγγισα and ἠνήγγισα GJs (deStrycker 242 and 299f); pf. 3 pl. ἠγγίκασιν Dt 31:14. In our lit. only intr. *approach, come near* (so in Aristot., Polyb., Diod. S., Epict. et al., pap, LXX, En; OdeSol 11:6; TestSol, TestAbr B, TestJob, Test12Patr, JosAs 3:2; GrBar 12:6; MartIs, ApcMos, Philo, Joseph.; Tat. 37, 1; s. Nägeli 36; Anz 344f; KClark, JBL 59, '40, 367–74)

❶ **to move in space and so draw closer to a reference point,** ***draw near, come near, approach*** of humans and transcendent beings.

ⓐ abs. of someone approaching (Gen 18:23; 27:27) **Ac 23:15;** ἤγγικεν ὁ παραδιδούς με *my betrayer is near* **Mt 26:46; Mk 14:42;** thief **Lk 12:33;** the tribune **Ac 21:33;** blind man **Lk 18:40;** Jesus **19:41; 24:15.**

ⓑ modified—**α.** without prep.: W. gen. of thing (Gen. 33:3; Jdth 13:7; En 14:9) ἐγγίσαντες αὐτοῦ *when they came near it* (the grave) AcPl Ha 11, 19. W. dat. of pers. (Gen 27:21; TestAbr B 2, p. 106, 4 [Stone p. 60]) or thing (Polyb. 18, 4, 1; Ex 32:19; Jos., Bell. 5, 408 τ. πόλει) τῷ παιδί B 6:1 (Is 50:8); τῇ πύλῃ τῆς πόλεως *the city gate* **Lk 7:12;** the house **15:25;** Damascus **Ac 9:3; 22:6;** cp. **10:9;** the grave GPt 9:36.—Jesus **Lk 15:1; 22:47.** τῷ θεῷ *draw near to God* (Philo, Leg. All. 2, 57, Deus Imm. 161; Theodor. Prodr. 7, 475 H. θεοῖς ἐγγ.) of priestly service (Ex 19:22; 34:30; Lev 10:3 al.), fig. of the spiritual service of Christians **Hb 7:19; Js 4:8; Mt 15:8 v.l.** (cp. Jdth 8:27; Ps 148:14; Is 29:13 al.).

β. w. prep.: W. εἰς, only with indications of place (Tob 11:1; En 14:10): Jerusalem **Mt 21:1; Mk 11:1.—Lk 18:35; 19:29.** εἰς τὴν κώμην *to the village* **24:28;** εἰς συναγωγήν Hm 11:13.—W. πρός and dat. to show place (Pr 5:8; OdeSol 11:6 πρὸς τὰ χείλη μου) **Lk 19:37.** W. ἐπί, τινα **Lk 10:9** (cp. Ps 26:2; 68:4 v.l.; ἐπὶ τὴν θάλασσαν AcPl Ha 3, 30; ἐπὶ μίλιον τρίτον *for three miles* GJs 17:2).

❷ **to draw near in a temporal sense,** ***draw near, come near, approach*** (POxy 1202, 8; w. dat., Epict. 3, 10, 14; Tat. 37:1). W. indications of time (KClark, JBL 59, '40, 367–83) the hour **Mt 26:45;** the day (Ezk 7:4; 12:23) **Ro 13:12; Hb 10:25;** the (feast) day GJs 1:2; 2:2; ὁ καιρός (La 4:18; 1 Macc 9:10) **Lk 21:8;** cp. **Mt 21:34;** ὁ χρόνος **Ac 7:17;** the Passover **Lk 22:1;** the end **1 Pt 4:7;** the final stumbling-block B 4:3; cp. **ending of Mk** in the Freer ms. 8; the judgment GPt 7:25; destruction of the temple **Lk 21:20;** redemption vs. **28.** μέχρι θανάτου ἐ. *come close to dying* **Phil 2:30** (cp. Job 33:22; Sir 51:6 ἤγγισεν ἕως θανάτου). PKatz, TZ 5, '49, 7; ADebrunner, Mus. Helv. 11, '54, 58f.—Esp. of the approaching Reign of God: ἤγγικεν ἡ βασιλεία τῶν οὐρανῶν (or τοῦ θεοῦ) **Mt 3:2; 4:17; 10:7; Mk 1:15; Lk 10:9, 11** (WHutton, ET 64, '52/53, 89–91: *has come* for the Lk passages); AcPl Ha 8, 31=BMM verso 2f. Of the Lord's return **Js 5:8.**—On 'realized eschatology' s. CDodd, Parables of the Kgdm.[3] '36, 44–51, ET 48, '36/37, 138–42; JCampbell, ET 48, '36/37, 91–94; RFuller, The Mission and Achievement of Jesus '54, 20–25; RBerkey, JBL 82, '63, 177–87; MBlack, An Aramaic Approach[3], '67, 208–11.—DELG s.v. ἐγγύς. M-M. TW. Sv.

ἔγγιστα superl. of the adv. ἐγγύς, q.v., beg., 1a, 2b, 3.—DELG s.v. ἐγγύς. M-M.

ἔγγραφος, ον (ἐν + -γραφος, s. ἐγγράφω; Polyb.; Dio Chrys. 59 [76], 2 ἔ. νόμος; Plut.; Lucian; TestSol 1:3 C; TestJob 11:7; Just., D. 120, 6; Mel., HE 4, 26, 10; ins; POxy 70, 4, al. in pap; adv. -ως Demetr.: 722 fgm. 3 Jac.; freq. used as an administrative term) **pert. to being officially recorded,** ***recorded, enrolled*** ἔ. γίνεσθαι 1 Cl 45:8; *recorded* Hs 5, 3, 8.—DELG s.v. γράφω.

ἐγγράφω (s. preceding entry; ἐνγρ. Tdf., W-H.) fut. ἐγγράψω (Just., D. 72, 3; 80, 3; Ath., R. 69, 12); 1 aor. ἐνέγραψα; pass. 2 fut. ἐγγραφήσομαι; pf. pass. ἐγγέγραμμαι (Aeschyl., Hdt. et al.; ins, pap, LXX, En, Philo, Joseph.) mostly a tech. term for recording of information.

❶ **to record information,** esp. names in official documents (inscribed on pillars Hdt. 2, 102 and SIG 966, 38) ***write in, record*** ἐγγράφειν εἰς τ. ἀριθμόν *enroll among the number* Hs 9, 24, 4; 5, 3, 2 (Ps.-Pla., Axioch. 5 p. 336e εἰς τ. ἐφήβους; Appian, Maced. 4 §2; SIG 736, 163f ἐ. εἰς τοὺς πολεμάρχους; 858, 10). τὰ ὀνόματα ἐγγέγραπται ἐν τοῖς οὐρανοῖς *the names are recorded in heaven* **Lk 10:20;** cp. ISm 5:3 (s. SAalen, NTS 13, '67, 7 on En 104:1), ἐγγραφήσονται εἰς τὰς βίβλους τῆς ζωῆς *they will be recorded in the books of life* Hv 1, 3, 2; cp. m 8:6 (Lucian, Philops. 38; SIG 921, 97 ἐ. εἰς τὸ γραμματεῖον).

❷ **to communicate a message in writing,** ***write down, inscribe*** (cp. schol. on Pla. 504d ἐ. ἐν τῷ πίνακι; in a letter Jos., Vi. 261) in imagery ἐπιστολὴ ἐγγεγραμμένη ἐν ταῖς καρδίαις ἡμῶν *a letter, inscribed on our hearts* **2 Cor 3:2** (cp. Pind., O. 10, 2f; Plut., Mor. 779b; En 103:3; Jos., Ant. 4, 210 νόμους . . . ταῖς ψυχαῖς ἐγγραφέντας). In the continuation vs. **3** the imagery of a handwritten document ἐγγεγραμμένη οὐ μέλανι, ἀλλὰ πνεύματι θεοῦ, *written not w. ink. but w. God's Spirit* points to ἐγγρ. as equivalent to γράφω (as PLond II 358, 15 p. 172 [c. 150 AD]; Herm. Wr. 13, 15; Nägeli 48), but the related clause οὐκ ἐν πλαξὶν λιθίναις ἀλλ' ἐν πλαξὶν καρδίαις σαρκίναις suggests engraved letters. Like the Gk. term ἐγγρ., which can be used of handwriting as well as engraving, the Eng. rendering 'inscribe' does double duty for Paul's imagery and is in harmony with the official flavor (numerous official letters were inscribed on stone) of his prose in 2 Cor.—DELG s.v. γράφω. M-M. TW.

ἔγγυος, ον pert. to assurance for the fulfillment of someth., ***under good security,*** as noun ὁ ἔ. *guarantee* (X. et al.; ins, pap; Sir 29:15f; 2 Macc. 10:28 [adj.]. Linguistic exx. and discussion of the subj. in JPartsch, Griech. Bürgschaftsrecht I 1909, 105ff; 228ff; 281ff; Mitt-Wilck. II/1, 264ff; JBehm, D. Begriff διαθήκη 1912, 77; ELohmeyer, Diatheke 1913, p. 145) κρείττονος διαθήκης ἔ. *guar. of a better covenant* **Hb 7:22.**—Frisk s.v. ἐγγύη, cp. DELG s.v. *γύη etc. M-M. TW. Spicq.

ἐγγύς adv. freq. funct. as prep.(Hom.+) comp. ἐγγύτερον (X. et al.; Jos., Ant. 19, 217 [cp. C. Ap. 2, 224 ἐγγίω]); superl. ἔγγιστα (Antiphon, Hippocr. et al.; ins [BCH 18, 1894, p. 324 no. 2, 26; OGI index]; BGU 69, 8; 759, 9; LXX; TestAbr A 2, p. 78, 14 [Stone p. 4], B 13 p. 117, 24 [Stone p. 82]; TestJob 2:2; Joseph. [always; e.g., Bell. 1, 289, Ant. 4, 254]).

❶ **pert. to being in close proximity spatially,** ***near, close to***

ⓐ abs. ἐ. εἶναι *be close by* **J 19:42;** IRo 10:2; Hs 9, 6, 6; αἱ ἐγγὺς κῶμαι *the neighboring villages* **Mk 1:38** D (Appian, Iber. 42 §174 οἱ ἐγγὺς βάρβαροι; likew. Appian, Syr. 42 §220). αἱ ἔγγιστα ἐκκλησίαι *the closest assemblies* IPhld 10:2; cp. **Mk 6:36** D οἱ ἔγγιστα ἀγροί (Dionys. Hal. 1, 22, 1 ἡ ἔγγιστα νῆσος; Ps.-Callisth. 2, 11, 6).

ⓑ w. gen. (Hom. et al.; also Joseph. as a rule [Schmidt 379f]; TestDan 6:11; TestJob 2:2) ἐ. τοῦ Σαλίμ **J 3:23;** ἐ. Ἰερουσαλήμ **Lk 19:11; J 11:18; Ac 1:12;** ἐ. τῆς πόλεως **J 19:20;** ἐ. τοῦ τόπου **6:23;** ἐ. τῆς ἐρήμου **11:54;** ἐ. ὑδάτων Hv 3, 2, 9; 3, 7, 3. W. gen. of pers. Hs 8, 6, 5; 9, 6, 2; ApcPt 20:34.

ⓒ w. dat. (Il. 22, 453; X., Cyr. 2, 3, 2; al. in later writers as Polyb. 21, 28, 8; Dionys. Hal. 6, 52. Cp. Kühner-G. I 408; JObrecht, D. echte u. soziative Dativ bei Pausanias, Zürich diss. 1919, 14; Ps 33:19; 144:18; Jos., Ant. 1, 335; 7, 218) **Ac 9:38; 27:8.**

ⓓ ἐ. γίνεσθαι *come near* (opp. μακρὰν εἶναι) **Eph 2:13.** W. gen. (Vett. Val. 196, 28f) 2 Cl 7:3; 18:2; ἐ. τοῦ πλοίου γίνεσθαι **J 6:19;** ἐ. τινος ἔρχεσθαι (Theophanes, Chron. 389, 12f de Boor ἐγγύς σου ἐλθεῖν=come to you; BGU 814, 30f [III AD]) Hv 4, 1, 9 (Unknown Sayings 85f quotes Ox 1224, fgm. 2 recto I, 5 [ἐγγὺς ὑμῶν γ]ενήσεται).

❷ **pert. to being close in point of time,** ***near***—ⓐ of the future: καιρός **Mt 26:18; Rv 1:3; 22:10.** Of summer (Herodas 3, 45 ὁ χειμὼν [winter] ἐγγύς) **Mt 24:32; Mk 13:28; Lk 21:30.** Of a festival **J 2:13; 6:4; 7:2; 11:55.** Of God's reign **Lk 21:31.** Of the parousia **Phil 4:5;** 1 Cl 21:3; B 21:3. Of death Hs 8, 9, 4. ἐγγύτερον ἡμῶν ἡ σωτηρία, ἤ . . . *our salvation is nearer than* . . . **Ro 13:11.** Abs. soon ἐ. τὸ ἔργον τελεσθήσεται *will soon be completed* Hs 9, 10, 2.

ⓑ of the past ἔγγιστα *a very short time ago* 1 Cl 5:1.

❸ **pert. to being close as experience or event,** ***close,*** extension of mng 1 (Vi. Aesopi I 6 p. 241, 7 Eberh. ἐγγὺς ἡ γνώμη=his purpose is obvious) ἐ. σου τὸ ῥῆμά ἐστιν *the word is close to you,* explained by what follows: in your mouth and your heart **Ro 10:8** (Dt 30:14); κατάρας ἐ. *close to being cursed*=under a curse **Hb 6:8** (cp. Ael. Aristid. 26, 53 K.=14 p. 343 D.: ἀμήχανον καὶ κατάρας ἐγγύς); ἐ. ἀφανισμοῦ *ready to disappear altogether* **8:13;** οἱ ἐ. (opp. οἱ μακράν as Is 57:19; Esth 9:20; Da 9:7 Theod.; TestNapht 4:5) *those who are near* **Eph 2:17;** ἐ. (εἶναι) *be near* of God Hv 2, 3, 4 (cp. Dio Chrys. 14 [31], 87 τινὲς σφόδρα ἐγγὺς παρεστῶτες τοῖς θεοῖς); πάντα ἐ. αὐτῷ ἐστιν *everything is near (God)* 1 Cl 27:3; cp. IEph 15:3 (Just., A I, 21, 6); ἐ. μαχαίρας ἐ. θεοῦ *close to the sword* (martyrdom) *is close to God* ISm 4:2 (cp. Paroem. Gr. II p. 228, Aesop 7 ὁ ἐγγὺς Διός, ἐγγὺς κεραυνοῦ; Pla., Philebus 16c ἐγγυτέρω θεῶν; X., Mem. 1, 6, 10; Pythag., Ep. 2; Crates, Ep. 11 ἐγγυτάτω θεοῦ; Lucian, Cyn. 12 οἱ ἔγγιστα θεοῖς; Wsd 6:19). Agr 3 s.v. πῦρ c. ἐ. ἐπὶ θύραις *at* (your) *very door* **Mt 24:33; Mk 13:29.**—B. 867. DELG. M-M. TW.

ἐγεγόνει s. γίνομαι.

ἐγείρω fut. ἐγερῶ; 1 aor. ἤγειρα. Pass.: pres. ἐγείρομαι, impv. 2 sg. ἐγείρου, pl. ἐγείρεσθε; 1 fut. ἐγερθήσομαι; 1 aor. ἠγέρθην; pf. ἐγήγερμαι (B-D-F §101 and 78; Rob. 1215) (Hom.+).

❶ **to cause someone to wake from sleep,** ***wake, rouse*** **Mt 8:25; Mk 4:38; Ac 12:7.**

❷ **to cease sleeping,** ***wake up, awaken*** fr. sleep, pass. intr. (PStras 100, 15 [II BC] ἐγερθεὶς ἐκάλουν βοηθούς) ἀπὸ τοῦ ὕπνου **Mt 1:24** (cp. διεγείρω). Abs. **25:7; Mk 4:27; J 11:12** P[75]. Fig., ἐξ ὕπνου ἐγερθῆναι *awaken fr. sleep* (i.e. thoughtless indolence) **Ro 13:11** (cp. Epict. 2, 20, 15 ἐ. ἐκ τῶν ὕπνων, fr. the sleep of carelessness); cp. AcPl Ha 4, 32.

❸ **to cause to stand up from a position lower than that of the pers. rendering assistance,** ***raise, help to rise,*** pers. sitting down **Ac 3:7** (ἵνα σταθῶ). Lying down **Mk 1:31; 9:27.** Stretched out **Ac 10:26** (En 14:25). Fallen **Mt 12:11;** 1 Cl 59:4; Hv 3, 2, 4.

❹ **to move to a standing position,** ***rise, get up,*** pass. intr. of those who have awakened **Mt 2:13f, 20f; 8:26; Lk 11:8;** who were sitting down (EpArist 94) **Mt 9:19; Lk 13:25; J 11:29;** Hv 1, 4, 1; AcPl Ox 6; kneeling Hv 2, 1, 3; of the sick **Mt 8:15; 9:6f; Mk 2:12;** of those called back to life (cp. 4 Km 4:31) **Mt 9:25; Lk 7:14.** ἐκ τοῦ δείπνου *rise from the table* **J 13:4;** of one who has fallen **Mt 17:7; Ac 9:8** (on ἀπὸ τ. γῆς cp. 2 Km 12:17; Ps 112:7).

❺ **to cause to come into existence,** ***raise up, bring into being*** (Judg 2:16, 18 ἤγειρε αὐτοῖς κύριος κριτάς; 3:9, 15 σωτῆρα; Pr 10:12; TestLevi 18:2 ἱερέα; Jos., Ant. 8, 199) κέρας σωτηρίας *a horn of salvation* **Lk 1:69;** τέκνα τινί **Mt 3:9; Lk 3:8.** ἤγειρεν τὸν Δαυὶδ αὐτοῖς εἰς βασιλέα *he gave them David as (their) king* **Ac 13:22** (cp. Jos., Ant. 19, 295). W. double acc. and dat. of advantage vs. **23 v.l.;** τὶ *someth.* (Theognis 549 πόλεμον ἐ.; Appian, Hann. 41 §177 θόρυβον; Nicol. Dam.: 90 fgm. 50 Jac. μάχην; Tat. 19, 3 στάσεις καὶ μάχας) *cause* θλῖψιν **Phil 1:17** (Lucian, Syr. Dea 18 πένθος τινι).

❻ **to cause to return to life,** ***raise up*** (the ancients closely associated death with sleep; s., e.g., Kaibel 559, 7f; RLattimore, Themes in Greek and Latin Epitaphs '62, 164f al.) (Apollodor. [II BC]: 244 fgm. 138a Jac., of Asclepius. Similarly schol. on Lucian p. 55, 23 Rabe; Sir 48:5 ὁ ἐγείρας νεκρὸν ἐκ θανάτου; PGM 4, 195) **Mt 10:8; J 5:21; Ac 26:8; 2 Cor 1:9;** AcPt Ox 849 verso, 10; AcPl Ha 8, 35=BMM verso 9. Of the raising of Jesus **Ac 5:30; 10:40; 13:37; 1 Cor 6:14; 15:15ff; 2 Cor 4:14.** More fully ἐ. τινὰ ἐκ νεκρῶν (mostly of Jesus' resurr.) **J 12:1, 9, 17; Ac 3:15; 4:10; 13:30; Ro 4:24; 8:11; 10:9; Gal 1:1; Eph 1:20;**

Col 2:12; 1 Th 1:10; Hb 11:19; 1 Pt 1:21; IMg 9:3; Pol 2:1f; AcPlCor 2:6. ἀπὸ νεκρῶν ITr 9:2. Of the raising of Christ's flesh ISm 7:1.

❼ to enter into or to be in a state of life as a result of being raised, ***be raised, rise,*** pass. intr., of one who has died (Is 26:19; TestJob 4:9; cp. 4 Km 4:31) approaches ἀναστῆναι in mng. (cp. mss. and synopt. parallels; s. ἀνίστημι 7) gen. νεκροὶ ἐγείρονται **Mk 12:26; Lk 7:22; 20:37; 1 Cor 15:15f, 29, 32, 35, 52.** Of Lazarus ἐγερθήσεται **J 11:12 v.l.** σώματα . . . ἠγέρθησαν **Mt 27:52;** ἐγείρεται σῶμα πνευμάτικον **1 Cor 15:44;** cp. **15:42f;** τὸ σῶμα ἐγείρεται AcPlCor 2:27; cp. 2:26 (in imagery after 1 Cor 15:37). ἐάν τις ἀπὸ νεκρῶν ἐγερθῇ **Lk 16:30 v.l.;** ἐάν τις ἐκ νεκρῶν ἐγερθῇ **16:31** P^{75}.—Of John the Baptist ἀπὸ τῶν νεκρῶν **Mt 14:2;** cp. ἐκ νεκρῶν **Mk 6:14; Lk 9:7.**—Of Christ: ἐκ νεκρῶν **Mt 17:9; J 2:22; 21:14; Ro 6:4, 9; 7:4; 1 Cor 15:12, 20** (cp. Just., D. 108, 2 ἐγηγέρθαι); **2 Ti 2:8.** Also ἀπὸ τῶν νεκρῶν **Mt 27:64; 28:7;** ἀπὸ νεκρῶν ITr 9:2. Without this qualification τῇ τρίτῃ ἡμέρᾳ ἐγερθῆναι **Mt 16:21; 17:23.** καθὼς εἶπεν **28:6;** ὄντως εἶπεν **26:34.** διὰ τὴν δικαίωσιν ἡμῶν **Ro 4:25;** ὑπὲρ αὐτῶν (τῶν ζώντων) **2 Cor 5:15.** Abs. **Mt 26:32; Mk 14:28; 16:6; Lk 24:6, 14** (v.l. ἐκ νεκρῶν); **Ro 8:34** (v.l. ἐκ ν.); **1 Cor 15:13f, 16f;** AcPlCor 2:31.—For lit. s. on ἀνάστασις 2 end.

❽ to raise up from sickness, ***raise up=restore to health*** (the sick pers. is ordinarily recumbent) **Js 5:15;** AcPl BMM verso 11 (Did., Gen. 168, 17).

❾ to change to a previous good state or condition, ***restore, erect*** of buildings (Dio Chrys. 11 [12], 18; Aelian, NA 11, 10; Herodian 3, 15, 3; 8, 2, 5; Lucian, Alex. 19; Anth. Pal. 9, 696; OGI 677, 3; 1 Esdr 5:43; Sir 49:13; ἐ. τρόπαιον Hippol., Ref. 1, 24, 6; θυσιαστήριον Did., Gen. 223, 19) temple (ναόν: Appian, Bell. Civ. 1, 26 §120; Lucian, Sacr. 11; Jos., Ant. 15, 391; 20, 228) **J 2:19f.**

❿ to move someth. from its position by exerting effort in overcoming resistance, ***lift up*** ἔγειρον τ. λίθον *lift up the stone, push the stone aside* (Seleucus of Alex. [I AD]: 341 fgm. 4 Jac. in buffoonery at a symposium, of a stone pushed out from under a participant who has put his head in a noose and has been given a small scimitar to cut the rope before it strangles him) (Ox 1 recto, 6 [=GTh 77]); LWright, JBL 65, '46, 182; Unknown Sayings 95–98; AWalls, VigChr 16, '62, 71–76.—*Raise* κονιορτόν (Polyaenus 4, 19; 7, 44, 1) Hv 4, 1, 5 (Jos. Bell. 5, 471 speaks in the pass. of the dust that 'is raised'). Cp. **Mt 12:11.**

⓫ to move against in hostility, ***rise up,*** pass. intr., of nations rising in arms (Jer 6:22 v.l.) ἐ. ἐπί τινα *against someone* one nation against another **Mt 24:7; Mk 13:8; Lk 21:10** (for ἐπί τινα cp. Appian, Liby. 68 §307; Jer 27:9; Jos., Ant. 8, 199).

⓬ to make an appearance, ***appear,*** pass. intr. of prophets **Mt 11:11; Lk 7:16; J 7:52;** of false prophets **Mt 24:11, 24; Mk 13:22.** Of accusers in court (w. ἐν τῇ κρίσει; s. ἀνίστημι 9) **Mt 12:42; Lk 11:31** (on omission of ἐν τῇ κρίσει in ms. D, see MBlack, An Aramaic Approach[3], '67, 134).

⓭ in a command to evoke movement from a fixed position ἔγειρε, ἐγείρου ***get up!, come!*** impv.—ⓐ act. intr. only in impv. (Eur., Iph. A. 624; Aristoph., Ran. 340; Aesop-mss. [Ursing 80]) **Mt 9:5f; Mk 2:9** (v.l. ἐγείρου), **11; 3:3; 5:41; 10:49; Lk 5:23f; 6:8; 8:54** (v.l. ἐγείρου); **J 5:8; Ac 3:6** ἔγειρε καὶ περιπάτει; **Rv 11:1;** AcPl Ha 7, 28. Awakening of the 'dead' (with καθεύδειν and ἐγείρειν associated in figurative use, as in Plut., Mor. 462) in **Mk 5:41; Lk 8:54** (v.l. ἐγείρου); **Eph 5:14** (MDibelius, Hdb. ad loc., but without Gnostic motif acc. to KKuhn, NTS 7, '60/61, 341–46; cp. PsSol 16:1–4) parallels the aspect of motion in passages cited in 1, 3–10, and others here in a above.

ⓑ pass. intr. ἐγείρου *get up!* **Mk 2:9 v.l.; Lk 8:54 v.l.;** ἐγείρεσθε, ἄγωμεν *get up! let us be going* **Mt 26:46; Mk 14:42; J 14:31.**—B. 271; 670. DELG. M-M. EDNT. TW.

ἔγερσις, εως, ἡ (Pre-Socr. et al.; LXX; ParJer 8 cod. C; EpArist 160) **a coming back to life,** ***resurrection,*** lit. 'awakening' of a dead person (so Menander of Ephesus: 783 fgm. 1, 118 Jac. [in Jos., Ant. 8, 146=C. Ap. 1, 119]; PGM 13, 277 ἔγερσις σώματος νεκροῦ; AcThom 80 [Aa II/2, 196, 5]) of Jesus **Mt 27:53;** PtK 4 p. 15, 35.—DELG s.v. ἐγείρω. M-M. TW.

ἐγκάθετος, ον (ἐν + κατά + ἵημι; ἔνκ- Tdf., W-H.—Hyperid., fgm. 56; Demosth., Ep. 3, 34; Polyb. 3, 15, 1; Ps.-Pla., Axioch. 368e; Jos., Bell. 2, 27; 6, 286; Job 19:12; 31:9) **pert. to having the task of obtaining information secretly,** ***hired to lie in wait,*** subst. ἐγκάθετοι *spies* **Lk 20:20.**—S. DELG s.v. ἵημι.

ἐγκάθημαι (ἐν + κατά + ἕζομαι; Aristoph., X.+; Herm. Wr. 16, 14; LXX) gener. 'to sit in', **to take a position in,** ***reside, dwell*** εἴς τι (Judg 2:2) fig., of grief in the heart Hm 10, 3, 3 (Polyb. 2, 23, 7 ἐγκαθημένου τ. ψυχαῖς τοῦ φόβου).—S. DELG s.v. ἕζομαι.

ἐγκαίνια, ίων, τά (s. ἐγκανίζω; B-D-F §141, 3; 2 Esdr 6:16f; 22:27; Da 3:2 Theod.; Philo, Congr. Erud. Gr. 114; lit. 'renewal') ***festival of rededication*** **J 10:22,** known also as Hanukkah and the Feast of Lights, beg. the 25th of Chislev (roughly=November-December) to commemorate the purification and rededication of the temple by Judas Maccabaeus on that date in 165 BC. Cp. 1 Macc 4:36–39 (vs. 56 ὁ ἐγκαινισμὸς τ. θυσιαστηρίου; vss. 36, 54; 5:1 ἐγκαινίζειν). 2 Macc 10:1–8; Jos., Ant. 12, 316ff; Schürer I 163; w. lit.; TSchärf, D. gottesdienstl. Jahr d. Juden 1902, 92–96; Billerb. II 539–41; BHHW III 1951.—DELG s.v. καινός. TW.

ἐγκαινίζω fut. 3 sg. ἐγκαινιεῖ Dt. 20:5; 1 aor. ἐνεκαίνισα. Pass. 1 aor. ἐνεκαινίσθην LXX; pf. ἐγκεκαίνισμαι (cp. ἐγκαίνια; Pollux 1, 11; LXX; OdeSol 11:11; perh. UPZ 185 II, 6 [II BC], where it is restored).

❶ to give newness to someth., ***renew*** (1 Km 11:14) πνεῦμα ἐ. a spirit 1 Cl 18:10 (Ps 50:12).—**❷ to bring about the beginning of someth., with implication that it is newly established,** ***ratify, inaugurate, dedicate*** (w. solemn rites IG XII/5, 712, 58; Dt 20:5; 3 Km 8:63; 2 Ch 7:5) **Hb 9:18** the Sinai covenant ('ratified' Twentieth Century; cp. Chrysostom, MPG XII, 159a); *inaugurate, open* a 'new and living way' **10:20.**—DELG s.v. καινός. M-M. s.v. ἐν-. M-M. TW. Spicq.

ἐγκακέω 1 aor. ἐνεκάκησα (ἐν + κακός; Polyb. 4, 19, 10; BGU 1043, 3; Sym., Gen 27:46; Num 21:5; Is 7:16; Pr 3:11 Theod.)

❶ to lose one's motivation in continuing a desirable pattern of conduct or activity, ***lose enthusiasm, be discouraged*** w. ptc. foll. (B-D-F §414, 2) **2 Th 3:13** (ἐκκ- v.l.); w. ptc. preceding **Gal 6:9** (ἐκκ- v. l.—both of these passages play on the opposition of τὸ καλόν and τὸ κακόν in Gr.-Rom. thought respecting civic responsibility); οὐκ ἐγκακοῦμεν *we do not lose our enthusiasm, lose heart* for 'this service' **2 Cor 4:1** (in contrast to falling into deceptive behavior patterns, vs. 2); **16.** αἰτοῦμαι μὴ ἐγκακεῖν ἐν ταῖς θλίψεσιν *I ask you not to be disappointed in connection with my tribulations* **Eph 3:13.** On these three last s. 2. Abs. *give up* **Lk 18:1.**

❷ to be afraid in the face of a great difficulty, ***be afraid,*** of women in childbirth 2 Cl 2:2. (In all NT pass. t.r. has ἐκκακέω, q.v.) Some would put **2 Cor 4:1, 16; Eph. 3:13** here.—M-M. s.v. ἐν-. TW. Spicq.

ἐγκαλέω (ἐν + καλέω; s. ἔγκλημα) impv. 3 pl. ἐγκαλείτωσαν; impf. ἐνεκάλουν; fut. ἐγκαλέσω; 1 aor. ἐνεκάλεσα LXX. Pass. fut. ptc. gen. pl. ἐγκληθησομένων (Ath., R. 77, 17); 1 aor. 3 sg. ἐνεκλήθη (Just., A II, 10, 5) (Soph., X., Pla.+). Legal t.t. **bring charges against, *accuse*** τινί (Soph., Pla. et al.; PEleph 1, 7; Sir 46:19; Wsd 12:12; Jos., C. Ap. 2, 138; w. the cause as obj. τῇ αὐτῶν κακίᾳ ἐγκαλεῖτε Just., D. 30, 1) *someone* **Ac 19:38** (ἐ. ἀλλήλοις as PHib 96 [s. below]; Jos., Ant. 3, 213); **23:28;** also ἐ. κατά τινος **Ro 8:33.** Pass. (Just., A II, 10, 5 [here w. acc.] Σωκράτης τὰ αὐτὰ ἡμῖν ἐνεκλήθη Socrates experienced the same kind of charges that are levelled against us): περί τινος *because of someth.* (the act. Diod. S. 11, 83, 3; UPZ 63, 9 [158 BC]; PHamb 25, 3; Jos., Ant. 12, 172) περὶ ζητημάτων τοῦ νόμου αὐτῶν *because of questions concerning their law* **Ac 23:29;** because of a hope **26:7.** τινός *because of someth.* (not earlier than IV BC [Demades 61 Blass] and rare; Plut., Aristid. 324 [10, 7]; Cass. Dio 58, 4 ἀσεβείας ἐς τὸν Τιβέριον ἐγκληθείς; Jos., Ant. 5, 56; B-D-F §178) ἐ. στάσεως **19:40;** περὶ πάντων ὧν ἐγκαλοῦμαι *on all the charges made against me* **26:2** (PHib 96, 6; 22 [259 BC] περὶ ὧν ἐνεκάλεσαν ἀλλήλοις; cp. OGI 229, 42).—B. 1439. Renehan '75, 75. M-M. TW.

ἐγκάρδια, ίων, τά from the adj. ἐγκάρδιος, ον 'found in the heart' (Democr.+; Philo, Spec. Leg. 1, 6) ***what is in the heart*** 2 Cl 9:9 (cod. H; cp. Philod., παρρ. fgm. 28, 6 p. 14 Ol. τἀγκ. τις ἐρεῖ; Syntipas p. 10, 1). But the correct rdg. is perh. τὰ ἐν καρδίᾳ (2 Ch 32:31; Dt 8:2; 1 Km 9:19 al.).—S. DELG s.v. καρδία.

ἔγκαρπος, ον (ἐν + καρπός; Soph., Pla. et al.; PTebt 815, 6; 55 [III BC]; PFlor 369, 13; Jer 38:12) **pert. to being conducive to a bountiful yield, *fruitful,*** fig. (Ael. Aristid. 46 p. 404 D.: λόγος ἔ.; Maximus Tyr. 34, 4b βίος) ἀνάλυσις *a fruitful departure* 1 Cl 44:5; μνεία *fruitful remembrance* 56:1.—DELG s.v. καρπός.

ἔγκατα, άτων, τά (Hom.+; Theocr. 22, 202; Pollux 6, 51; schol. on Nicander, Ther. 694; TestSol 18:13 A) ***inmost parts*** 1 Cl 18:10 (Ps 50:12). Addition to Papias 3:2 (s. Preuschen, Antilegomena p. 98).—DELG (etym. uncertain).

ἐγκατάλειμμα, ατος, τό (ἐν + κατά + λείπω, s. next entry; Aristot., fgm. 13 Rose; PPetr II, 4 [11], 2 [255/254 BC]; LXX; TestSim 6:3) **something that is left (over), *remnant, posterity*** 1 Cl 14:5 (Ps 36:37).—DELG s.v. λείπω.

ἐγκαταλείπω impf. ἐγκατέλειπον; fut. ἐγκαταλείψω; 1 aor. 3 pl. ἐγκατέλειψαν (TestJob 43:10); 2 aor. ἐγκατέλιπον, subj. ἐγκαταλίπω; perf. ἐγκαταλέλοιπα LXX. Pass.: 1 fut. ἐγκαταλειφθήσομαι; 1 aor. ἐγκατελείφθην; perf. 3 sg. ἐγκαταλέλειπται Ps 9:35, ptc. ἐγκαταλελειμμένος LXX, inf. ἐγκαταλελεῖφθαι (s. prec. entry; Hes., Hdt.+)

❶ **to cause someth. to remain or to exist after a point in time, *leave*** of posterity **Ro 9:29** (Is 1:9.—Cp. Lucian, Dial. Deor. 25, 1 εἰ μὴ ἐγὼ . . . , οὐδὲ λείψανον ἀνθρώπων ἐπέμεινεν ἄν).

❷ **to separate connection with someone or someth., *forsake, abandon, desert*** (Socrat., Ep. 14, 10 [Malherbe p. 258] of soul and body; SIG 364, 88; 97; 495, 135 [III BC]; UPZ 71, 8 [152 BC]; POxy 281, 21; PTebt 27, 16; LXX; TestJos 2:4) τινά someone (X., Cyr. 8, 8, 4; Polyb. 3, 40, 7; Diod. S. 11, 68, 3; 18, 7, 6; Appian, Mithrid. 105 §493 desert one who is in danger; Jos, Vi. 205) **2 Ti 4:10, 16.** Of feeling or being forsaken by God (TestJos 2:4) **Mt 27:46; Mk 15:34** (both Ps 21:2; cp. Billerb. II 574–80; Dalman, Jesus [tr. 204–7]; WHasenzahl, D. Gottverlassenh. des Christus . . . u. d. christolog. Verständnis des griech. Psalters '37; FDanker, ZNW 61, '70, 48–69 [lit.]); **2 Cor 4:9; Hb 13:5** (Josh 1:5; Dt 31:6, 8; 1 Ch 28:20); B 4:14; Hm 9:2 (as Dt 31:6, 8); s 2:9; 1 Cl 11:1; *abandon* the fountain of life B 11:2 (Jer 2:13); God's commandments D 4:13; B 19:2; ἐ. τὴν ἀγάπην *forsake love* 1 Cl 33:1 (Dio Chrys. 57 [74], 8 τ. φιλίαν; Jos., Ant. 2, 40 τ. ἀρετήν).—*Cease* assembling **Hb 10:25** (*do* or *carry on someth. in a negligent manner, be remiss* is also prob.: Diod. S. 15, 9, 1 τὴν πολιορκίαν; Mitt-Wilck. I/2, 72, 8ff μηδένα δὲ τῶν ἱερέων ἢ ἱερωμένων ἐνκαταλελοιπέναι τὰς θρησκείας).—*Leave* (Menand., Epitr. 550 τούτοις μή μ' ἐγκαταλίπῃς), *allow to remain* (cp. Demosth. 57, 58) τὴν ψυχὴν εἰς ᾅδην *the soul in Hades* **Ac 2:27** (Ps 15:10), **31** (for ἐ. τινὰ εἰς cp. PsSol 2:7).—DELG s.v. λείπω. M-M. Spicq.

ἐγκαταστηρίζω 1 aor. ἐγκατεστήριξα (Cornutus 6 p. 7, 14) **to fix firmly in, *establish*** τί τινι the Logos in the hearts Dg 7:2.—DELG s.v. στηρίζω.

ἐγκατασφραγίζω 1 aor. pass. ἐγκατεσφραγίσθην **to mark within with an authenticating seal, *seal*** τὶ εἴς τι the covenant in the hearts B 4:8 (s. FDölger, Sphragis 1911, 108f; AvStromberg, Taufe [s. βαπτίζω end] 1913, 87).—DELG s.v. σφραγίζω.

ἐγκατοικέω (Eur.; Hdt. 4, 204; Lycophron 1204; Polyb. 18, 26, 13; Jos., C. Ap. 1, 296) **to live as a resident, *live, reside*** ἐν αὐτοῖς *among them* **2 Pt 2:8.** Fig. of love ἐν ὑμῖν B 1:4.—DELG s.v. οἶκος IIC.

ἐγκαυχάομαι (Aesop, Fab. 230 H.=H-H. 340 [Synt. 38]; schol. on Lucian p. 166, 18; Ps 51:3; 73:4; 96:7; 105:47; TestJud 13:3) **to be proud of someone or someth. and express oneself accordingly, *boast*** ἔν τινι (so in all the Ps-passages above) *of someone* **2 Th 1:4.** ἐν ἀλαζονείᾳ *in arrogance* 1 Cl 21:5.—DELG s.v. καυχάομαι. M-M. s.v. ἐν-. TW.

ἔγκειμαι (Hom. et al.; ins, pap, LXX, Test12Patr, Joseph.) **to be emphatic about someth., *insist, warn urgently*** (so Hdt. 7, 158, 1; Thu. 2, 59, 2; Herodas 5, 3; Plut., Fab. Max. 179 [9, 2]; Lucian, Demon. 12; Jos., Vi. 19, Ant. 15, 31) MPol 9:3.—ITr 12:3 cj. (for περίκειμαι).—DELG s.v. κεῖμαι.

ἐγκεντρίζω (ἐν + κεντέω 'prick, pierce') 1 aor. ἐνεκέντρισα, pass. ἐνεκεντρίσθην; 1 fut. pass. ἐγκεντρισθήσομαι **to cause** (a shoot or bud: scion) **to unite with the stock of a growing plant, *graft*** of trees (so Aristot., De Plant. 6 p. 820b, 34 al.; Theophr., HP 2, 2, 5; M. Ant. 11, 8, 6. W. the mng. 'sting' Wsd 16:11; En 103:12 'goad') εἴς τι *on someth.* **Ro 11:24;** also τινί vs. **24.** Abs. vss. **19, 23.** ἐ. ἐν αὐτοῖς *graft in among them* vs. **17.** ABaxter/JZiesler, JSNT 24, '85, 25–32.—DELG s.v. κεντέω. M-M. s.v. ἐν-. TW.

ἐγκεράννυμι pf. pass. ptc. ἐγκεκραμένος (Hom. et al.; Ps.-Lucian, Amor. 32) **to combine w. another, *mix,*** pass. *be united* τινί *w. someone* IEph 5:1.—DELG s.v. κεράννυμι.

ἐγκλείω aor. pass. impv. ἐγκλείσθητι Ezk 3:24, ptc. ἐγκλεισθείς 2 Macc 5:8; pf. pass. ἐγκέκλεισμαι (Soph., Hdt. et al.; pap, LXX, TestSol; Just., A II, 8, 3) **to hold within a location, *lock up, shut up, enclose*** τινά τινι Dg 2:7; 6:7; 7:2. Also τινὰ ἔν τινι (Jos., Ant. 8, 255; 13, 221) **Lk 3:20** D; *keep within bounds* 1 Cl 33:3.—DELG s.v. κλείς.

ἔγκλημα, τος, τό (s. ἐγκαλέω; Soph., Thu.+; ins, pap, Joseph., Ath., AssMos fgm. k) gener. 'the act or action of finding fault with someone'

❶ **an indictment or charge brought against someone through judicial proceedings, *charge, accusation,*** legal t.t. (OGI 229, 41; 43; Appian, Bell. Civ. 1. 96 §446; Jos., Bell. 7, 450) ἀπολογία περὶ τοῦ ἐ. *defense against the accusation* **Ac**

25:16; ἔ. ἄξιον θανάτου ἢ δεσμῶν *a charge deserving death or imprisonment* **23:29.**

❷ **the act or action of expressing disapproval,** ***reproach*** (Diod. S. 20, 33, 7; Heraclit. Sto. 21 p. 31, 13; 25 p. 39, 15; Ael. Aristid. 47, 67 K.=23 p. 462 D.; Jos., Ant. 2, 120, C. Ap. 2, 182; Ath. 3:1 al.) φυλάσσεσθαι τὰ ἐ. *guard against reproaches* ITr 2:3.—**Ac 23:25 v.l.**—New Docs 3, 66. DELG s.v. καλέω. M-M. TW.

ἐγκομβόομαι (ἐν + κόμβος 'band') 1 aor. ἐνεκομβωσάμην **to put or tie someth. on oneself,** ***put on*** (ἐ. τὴν ἐπωμίδα [tunic] Apollod. of Carystus Com.: fgm. 4 Kock III 281; cp. ἐγκόμβωμα=any garment which is tied on) ἀλλήλοις τ. ταπεινοφροσύνην ἐγκομβώσασθε *in your relations w. each other clothe yourselves w. humility* **1 Pt 5:5** (Selwyn, ad loc.).—DELG s.v. κόμβος M-M. TW. Spicq.

ἐγκοπή, ῆς, ἡ (ἐν + κόπτω) **that which holds back the progress of someth.,** ***hindrance*** (so Heraclitus fgm.131; Diod. S. 1, 32, 8; Dionys. Hal., Comp. Verb. 22; Περὶ ὕψους 41, 3 [but not a rhetorical t.t., CClassen, in: ΣΦΑΙΡΟΣ, WienerStud 107/8, '94/95: HSchwabl Festschr. I, 333]; Vett. Val. Index) ἐγκοπὴν (v.l. ἐκκοπὴν) διδόναι τινί *cause a hindrance to someth.* **1 Cor 9:12.**—DELG s.v. κόπτω A2. M-M. s.v. ἐκκοπή. TW.

ἐγκόπτω (ἐν +κόπτω) 1 aor. ἐνέκοψα; impf. pass. ἐνεκοπτόμην (Hippocr. et al., ins, pap; Jos., Bell. 1, 629; 6, 111; Just., D. 45, 1 τοῖς λόγοις 'interrupt' and thus hinder the progress of a discussion; Ath. 26, 1 [cause wounds]) **to make progress slow or difficult,** ***hinder, thwart*** (so Hesych.: ἐμποδίζω, διακωλύω; Polyb. 23, 1, 12; M. Ant. 11, 1, 2; PAlex, 4, 3 [=Witkowski 33, 1, III BC; and Sb 4305]; PMichZen 56, 6 [III BC]) in NT w. the acc. (B-D-F §152, 4) τίς ὑμᾶς ἐνέκοψεν; foll. by inf. w. μή as neg. (B-D-F §429; Rob. 1094) *who hindered you?* **Gal 5:7;** cp. **1 Th 2:18.** εἰς τὸ μὴ ἐγκόπτεσθαι τὰς προσευχὰς ὑμῶν *in order that your prayers may not be hindered* **1 Pt 3:7.** ἐνεκοπτόμην τὰ πολλά w. gen. of the inf. foll. (B-D-F §400, 4) *I have so often been prevented* **Ro 15:22.**—ἵνα μὴ ἐπὶ πλεῖόν σε ἐγκόπτω **Ac 24:4** is understood by Syr. and Armen. versions to mean *in order not to weary you any further;* cp. ἔγκοπος *weary* Diog. L. 4, 50; LXX; and ἔγκοπον ποιεῖν *to weary* Job 19:2; Is 43:23. But *impose on* is also prob.; *detain* NRSV—B. 1355. DELG s.v. κόπτω. M-M s.v. ἐκκόπτω. TW.

ἐγκράτεια, είας, ἡ (ἐν + -κράτεια, s. next entry; X., Pla. et al.; Diod. S. 10, 5, 2; Epict. 2, 20, 13; Vett. Val. index; Herm. Wr. 13, 9; PFay 20, 21; Sir 18:29 [v.l. in a superscr.]; 4 Macc 5:34; Test12Patr; EpArist 278; Philo; of Essenes in Jos., Bell. 2, 120; 138, and a prophet Ant. 8, 235; Just., D. 2, 2; 8:3 w. καρτερία; Ath., R. 75, 19 w. σωφροσύνη; Theoph. Ant. III 15 [p. 234, 14]) **restraint of one's emotions, impulses, or desires,** ***self-control*** (for detailed discussion s. Aristot., EN 7, 1145a–1154b; esp. w. ref. to matters of sex; cp. Simplicius in Epict. p. 117, 18; 123, 14; TestNapht 8:8; Hippol., Ref. 7, 28, 7) 2 Cl 15:1. In a list of virtues **Gal 5:23.** W. other virtues (Lucian, Demosth. Enc. 40; PFay s. above; cp. Christian ins: Sb 8705 πίστις, ἐλπίς, ἀγάπη, δικαιοσύνη, εἰρήνη, ἀλήθεια, μακροθυμία, ἐγκράτεια) 1 Cl 35:2; 62:2; 64; w. δικαιοσύνη **Ac 24:25;** w. γνῶσις and ὑπομονή **2 Pt 1:6;** w. μακροθυμία B 2:2; w. ἁπλότης Hv 2, 3, 2; w. πίστις and φόβος m 6, 1, 1. (W. ἀγαθὴ πρᾶξις Iren., 1, 6, 4 [Harv. I 58, 2].) ἀγαπᾶν ἐν πάσῃ ἐ. *in all chastity* Pol 4:2; ἐ. διπλῆ Hm 8:1. Personified as a virtue v 3, 8, 4; 7; s 9, 15, 2. Bestowed by God 1 Cl 38:2.—DELG s.v. κράτος. M-M. TW. Spicq. Sv.

ἐγκρατεύομαι mid. dep. aor. ἐνεκρατευσάμην LXX (Pythag.; Aristot., Eth. Eud. 2, 7 p. 1223b, 13 and later writers; Gen 43:31; Ar. 15, 6; Just., Tat. 9, 1) **to keep one's emotions, impulses, or desires under control,** ***control oneself, abstain,*** ἀπὸ παντὸς πονηροῦ πράγματος *abstain fr. every evil deed* Hs 5, 1, 5; cp. m 8:1ff, where ἐ. takes the acc., gen. (Sir 19:6 v.l.), ἀπό, ἐπί, and the inf. after it (B-D-F §154). Esp. of sexual continence **1 Cor 7:9;** 1 Cl 30:3 (Ar. 15, 6; also Milne 74 recto, 4 and 6; Just.). As a consequence of the fear of God Hm 1:2. W. acc. of content (Abel §43f, 4) πάντα ἐ. *exercise self-control in all respects* of athletes **1 Cor 9:25.**—LBouvet, L'ascèse dans S. Paul, diss. Lyon '36; MHansen, Het ascetisme en Pl's verkondiging van het nieuwe leven '38.—DELG s.v. κράτος. M-M. TW.

ἐγκρατής, ές (Pre-Socr. et al.; trag., Hdt., ins, pap, LXX; Jos., Vi. 396) **pert. to having one's emotions, impulses, or desires under control,** ***self-controlled, disciplined*** abs. (as Ps.-Pla., Def. 415d; Aristot., EN 7, 4 p. 1146b, 10ff; 8:21; Sir 26:15; Philo, De Jos., 54) w. δίκαιος and ὅσιος **Tit 1:8;** cp. 2 Cl 4:3; Pol 5:2. As an epithet: Ἑρμᾶς ὁ ἐ. Hv 1, 2, 4.—DELG s.v. κράτος. M-M. TW.

ἐγκρίνω (ἐν + κρίνω) 1 aor. ἐνέκρινα, inf. ἐγκρῖναι (Eur.+; Pla., X.; CIG II, 2715a, 11 ἐ. εἰς τοὺς ἐφήβους; IG 7, 29, 6; Sb 9559, 10 [III BC]; EpArist 228; Jos., Bell. 2, 138) **to make a judgment about someth. and classify it in a specific group,** ***to class*** τινά τινι *someone w. someone* (Synes., Ep. 105 p. 250c) **2 Cor 10:12** (in a play on words w. συγκρῖναι *compare*).—M-M. s.v. ἐνκρίνω. TW.

ἐγκρίς, ίδος, ἡ (etym. uncertain; Stesichorus [VII/VI BC] 2; Pherecrates [V BC] 83; LXX) ***pancake, fritter*** ἐ. ἐν ἐλαίῳ (cp. Athen. 14, 645e defines as πεμμάτιον ἑψόμενον ἐν ἐλαίῳ κ. μετὰ τοῦτο μελιτούμενον 'a small cake cooked in olive oil and sweetened with honey'; Num 11:8; Ex 16:31; Philo, Det. Pot. Insid. 118) *a pancake baked in oil* of the food of John the Baptist (for ἀκρίδες) GEb 13, 79.

ἐγκρύπτω (ἐν + κρύπτω) fut. 2 sg. ἐγκρύψεις Ezk 4:12; 1 aor. ἐνέκρυψα; pf. pass. 3 sg. ἐγκέκρυπται Jos 7:21; aor. subj. 3 pl. ἐγκρυβῶσιν Am 9:3 (Hom. et al.; LXX; Jos., Ant. 9, 142) **to put into, and so out of sight,** ***hide*** τὶ εἴς τι (Ps.-Apollod., Bibl. 1, 5, 1, 4 εἰς πῦρ) *put someth. into someth.* (Ps.-Lucian, Asin. 31; PMich 154 I 23) **Mt 13:33; Lk 13:21.**—DELG s.v. κρύπτω.

ἔγκυος, ον (ἐν + κυέω [s. κύω]; Hdt. et al.; SIG 1168, 12; 14; 17; BGU 1104, 21; POxy 267, 20; 1273, 33; Sir 42:10; Philo, Spec. Leg. 3, 108; Jos., Ant. 4, 278, C. Ap. 2, 245) ***pregnant*** **Lk 2:5;** GJs 13:1 v.l. (for ὠγκωμένην).—B. 283. DELG s.v. κυέω. M-M. s.v. ἔνκυος.

ἐγκύπτω perf. ἐγκέκυφα (ἐν + κύπτω; Hdt., Pla. et al.; LXX) **to give someth. close attention,** ***examine*** *look closely* εἴς τι *into someth.* (Hdt. 7, 152; Bel 40; EpArist 140) εἰς ἐπιστολάς Pol 3:2 (of looking at a piece of lit. PLond IV, 1356, 35; 1359, 4 [both 710 AD]). Fig. *gain an insight into, study* someth.: divine knowledge 1 Cl 40:1; holy scriptures 45:2; oracles of God 53:1; cp. 62:3.—CEvans, VigChr 38, '84, 200f.—DELG s.v. κύπτω.

ἔγνωκα, ἔγνων, ἔγνωσμαι s. γινώσκω.

ἐγρηγορέω (cp. the pf. of ἐγείρω: ἐγρήγορα; transmitted only as f.l. or v.l.: X., Cyn. 5, 11; Ps.-Aristot., Probl. 877a 9; 2 Esdr 17:3 [cod. B]; cp. Hom., Od. 20, 6 ἐγρηγορόων [s. Schwyzer, I 540, n. 4] fr. pf. ἐγρήγορα. S. γρηγορέω) ***be awake*** **Mt 26:38,**

40 (both v.l.); also **Rv 3:2** Sin. first hand. τοῖς ἐγρηγοροῦσιν (ἀγρηγ- pap) ἐγὼ λαλῶ *I speak to the alert* Ox 1081, 8f (SJCh 89, 7f).—JBirdsall, JTS 14, '63, 390f.—DELG s.v. ἐγείρω.

ἐγχρίω (ἐν + χρίω) 1 aor. ἐνέχρισα, inf. ἐγχρῖσαι (or ἔγχρισαι aor. mid. impv.) **to smear/rub on a substance such as salve or oil, *smear on, anoint*** (so Duris [IV/III BC] et al.; LXX) τὶ *someth.* (on) the eyes (PGM 7, 336 ἔνχριε [anoint] τοὺς ὀφθαλμούς σου; 5, 64; Jer 4:30; cp. Tob 6:9; 11:8) **Rv 3:18.**—DELG s.v. χρίω. M-M. TW.

ἐγχώριος, ον (ἐν + χῶρα; Pind. Hdt. et al.; pap, LXX; Jos., C. Ap. 1, 314) **pert. to that which relates to or belongs to a particular locale, *local*** ἔθη *local customs* Dg 5:4.—DELG s.v. χώρα.

ἐγώ (Hom.+) pers. pron. of the first pers. ἐμοῦ (μου), ἐμοί (μοι), ἐμέ (με); pl. ἡμεῖς, ἡμῶν, ἡμῖν, ἡμᾶς: ***I,*** used w. a verb to emphasize the pers.: ἐγὼ ἀποστέλλω **Mt 10:16;** ἐγὼ λέγω **21:27;** ἐγὼ ἐπιτάσσω σοι **Mk 9:25;** ἐγὼ καταλύσω **14:58.** Esp. in the antitheses of the Sermon on the Mount **Mt 5:22–44** (s. ELohse, JJeremias Festschr. '70, 189–203 [rabb.]). ἐγώ εἰμι *it is I* (in contrast to others) **Mt 14:27; Lk 24:39; J 6:20;** *I am the man* **9:9;** w. strong emphasis: *I am the one* (i.e. the Messiah) **Mk 13:6; Lk 21:8; J 8:24, 28;** cp. vs. **58.**—For the solemn I-style in J, esp. **10:7–14,** cp. the Isis ins in Diod. S. 1, 27, 4; IG XII/5, 14 (SIG 1267) passim; PGM 5, 145ff (all three in Dssm., LO 109–12 [LAE 134ff]; further material there 109, 3 and in Hdb., excur. on **J 8:12.** See IAndrosIsis; GWetter, 'Ich bin es': StKr 88, 1915, 224–38; KZickendraht, ibid. 94, 1922, 162–68; ESchweizer, Ego Eimi '39; WManson, JTS 48, '47, 137–45; HSahlin, Zur Typologie des Joh-evangeliums '50, 63–71; Bultmann 167, 2; GMacRae, CMoule Festschr., '70, 122–34 [Gnostics]; JBergman, Ich bin Isis, 1968; RMerkelbach, Isis Regina—Zeus Sarapis '95).—On **J 8:58** s. EFreed, JSNT 17, '83, 52–59 (esp. p. 57f, n. 3, lit.).—ἰδοὺ ἐγώ (oft. LXX; s. PKatz, Philo's Bible '50, 75ff) **Mt 23:34; 28:20; Mk 1:2 v.l.** (Mal 3:1); **Lk 24:49.** ἰδοὺ ἐγώ, κύριε *here I am, Lord* **Ac 9:10** (cp. Gen 22:1; 27:1 al.).—ἐγώ *I (will),* or *yes* (Judg 13:11; cp. Epict. 2, 12, 18 ἔγωγε) **Mt 21:30.**—In gospel mss. ἐ. is also found without special emphasis, either as a Hebraism, **Mk 12:26** (Ex 3:6); **J 10:34** (Ps 81:6), or as a copyist's addition (B-D-F §277, 2).—On the interchange of pl. and sg. (cp. Apollon. Rhod. 3, 784 ἄμμι [=ἡμῖν], on which the scholion reads: ἀντὶ ἑνικοῦ [=singular] τοῦ ἐμοὶ κεῖται τὸ ἄμμι. 3, 1111; Appian, Bell. Civ. 3, 18 §67 ἡμῖν=to me. Likew. 3, 48 §196 ἡμῖν in the words of Octavian; 3, 38 §152 μετεβάλομεν=I; Jos., Ant. 2, 68; Just., D. 1, 4) s. Mlt. 86f, esp. in Paul s. B-D-F §280; Rob. 406f; KDick, D. schriftstellerische Pl. b. Pls. 1900; EAskwith, Exp. 8th Ser., 1, 1911, 149–59; EvDobschütz, Wir u. Ich b. Pls: ZST 10, '33, 251–77; WLofthouse, ET 64, '52/53, 241–45; ARogers, ibid. 77, '66, 339f. For J, s. AvHarnack, Das 'Wir' in den joh. Schriften: SBBerlAk 1923, 96–113.—FSlotty, Der sog. Pl. modestiae: IndogF 44, 1927, 155–90; on the pl. in Ac 27f s. Hemer, Acts 312–34 (lit.); UHolzmeister, De 'plurali categoriae' in NT a Patribus adhibito: Biblica 14, '33, 68–95.—In the oblique cases the longer forms ἐμοῦ, ἐμοί, ἐμέ are used as a rule where the main emphasis lies on the pron. ὁ ἀκούων ὑμῶν, ἐμοῦ ἀκούει **Lk 10:16;** τῆς πίστεως ὑμῶν τε καὶ ἐμοῦ **Ro 1:12** al., where the emphasis is suggested by the position of the pron.—The enclit. forms occur where the main emphasis lies on the noun or verb οὐκ ἔστιν μου ἄξιος **Mt 10:37;** τίς μου ἥψατο; **Mk 5:31;** ἀπαγγείλατέ μοι **Mt 2:8** al. With prep. (Mayser 302f) the enclit. forms are used only in the case of ἔμπροσθεν and ὀπίσω, somet. ἐνώπιον (**Ac 10:30;** but cp. **Lk 4:7** ἐ. ἐμοῦ), as well as w. πρός w. acc. after verbs of motion (δεῦτε πρός με **Mt 11:28;** cp. **3:14; J 6:37 v.l.;** ἐρχέσθω πρός με **7:37;** ἀπεσταλμένοι πρός με **Ac 11:11** al.). Only the enclit. forms are used as substitutes for the possessive adj. ὁ λαός μου *my people* **Mt 2:6;** μενεῖτε ἐν τῇ ἀγάπῃ μου *you will remain in my love,* i.e. make it possible for me to continue to love you **J 15:10.** μου stands as objective gen. μιμηταί μου γίνεσθε *become imitators of me* **1 Cor 4:16.**—The expr. τί ἐμοὶ καὶ σοί; is Hebraistic (=מַה־לִּי וָלָךְ), but it also made its way into vernac. Gk. (cp. Epict. 1, 22, 15; 1, 27, 13; 2, 19, 19; 1, 1, 16; ESchwartz, GGN 1908, p. 511, 3; DHesseling: Donum natalicium Schrijnen 1929, 665–68; FBurkitt, JTS 13, 1912, 594f; CLattey, ibid. 20, 1919, 335f); it may be rendered *what have I to do w. you? what have we in common? leave me alone! never mind!* It serves to refuse a request or invitation (2 Km 16:10; 19:23; 4 Km 3:13) **J 2:4** (s. PGächter, ZKT 55, '31, 351–402. Difft. JDerrett, Law in the NT, '70, 238–42.—Apparent indifference toward close relatives compared with the things of God, as Epict. 3, 3, 5 οὐδὲν ἐμοὶ καὶ τῷ πατρί, ἀλλὰ τῷ ἀγαθῷ) and as a protest against hostile measures (Judg 11:12; 3 Km 17:18; 2 Ch 35:21; 1 Esdr 1:24) **Mk 5:7; Lk 8:28;** likew. τί ἡμῖν κ. σοί; (s. τίς 1 aβב) **Mt 8:29; Mk 1:24; Lk 4:34** (cp. OBauernfeind, D. Worte d. Dämonen im Mk 1927).—On the 'I' **Ro 7:7ff** s. WKümmel, Rö 7 u. d. Bekehrung des Pls 1929; RBultmann: Imago Dei '32, 53–62; BMartin, SJT 34, '81, 39–47 (in support of Kümmel for pre-Christian identity). Also s. οἴμοι.—DELG. M-M. TW.

ἐδαφίζω Att. fut. ἐδαφιῶ Ps 136:9; Na 3:10; 1 aor. ἠδάφισα Hos 10:14; Ezk 31:12, pass. ἠδαφίσθην (Mel., P. 26 and 99); fut. pass. ἐδαφισθήσομαι Hos 14:1; Is 3:26 (s. ἔδαφος; Aristot. et al.; ins, LXX; Mel. P. 26; 99 [B]) ἔδαφος refers to ground level, hence the verb means **to destroy or tear down by causing someth. to be brought to ground level, *dash to the ground*** (Ps 136:9; Hos 10:14; 14:1 al.) and of a city ***raze to the ground*** (Is 3:26) both mngs. at once **Lk 19:44.**—DELG s.v. ἔδαφος. M-M.

ἔδαφος, ους, τό (s. ἐδαφίζω Hom.+) **the surface of the earth, *ground*** πίπτειν εἰς τὸ ἔ. (4 Macc 6:7; cp. Jos., Ant. 8, 119; BGU 1253, 5 ἐπὶ τὸ ἔ. ῥίψαντες) *fall to the ground* **Ac 22:7.** κάθισον εἰς τὸ ἐ. *sit on the ground* AcPl Ha 2, 20.—B. 17f; 471. DELG. M-M.

ἔδεσμα, ατος, τό (on the old epic pres. ἔδω s. LfgrE s.v.; Pla. et al.; ViHab 5 [Sch. 86, 7]; Jos., Ant. 1, 43) ***food*** in our lit. only pl. (as Batr. 31; X., Hiero 1, 23; OGI 665, 59; LXX; TestJob 13:4; Test12Patr) Hv 3, 9, 3a; m 5, 2, 2; 6, 2, 5; 8:3; 12, 2, 1; s 5, 2, 9ff; 5, 3, 7; 5, 5, 3. μὴ ἔχειν ἐδέσματα *have nothing to eat* v 3, 9, 3b.—DELG s.v. ἔδω.

ἔδομαι s. ἐσθίω.

ἑδράζω fut. 3 sg. ἑδράσει Wsd 4:3; 1 aor. ἥδρασα. Pass. aor. ptc. ἑδρασθείσης 3 Km 3:1, inf. ἑδρασθῆναι LXX; perf. ptc. ἡδρασμένος (ἕδρα 'seat'; Simias Rhod., fgm 8, 1 Diehl[2]=24, 1 p. 72 HFränkel=Anth. Pal. 15, 24, 1; Dionys. Hal., Comp. Verb. 6; Heliod. 9, 25; Herm. Wr. 5, 4; LXX; Ath. 13, 1) **to firmly establish in a certain place, *establish, fix, settle;*** fig. ἑ. ἐπὶ τὸν τοῦ βουλήματος θεμέλιον *fix* (someth.) *upon the foundation of his will* 1 Cl 33:3; τὰ γενόμενα ἑ. *establish what exists* 60:1. Pass. (Callixenus [III BC] : 627 fgm. 1, 37 Jac. [in Athen. 5, 204d]; Dio Chrys. 1, 78 ἡδρασμένος) ἐν ὁμονοίᾳ θεοῦ *established in godly harmony* IPhil. ins; ἐν ἀγάπῃ ISm 1:1; πίστει *in faith* 13:2; γνώμη ἡ. ὡς ἐπὶ πέτραν *attitude founded as if upon a rock* IPol 1:1 (cp. Sir 22:17).—DELG s.v. ἕζομαι B2.

ἑδραῖος, (αία,) αῖον (s. ἕδράζω) **pert. to being firmly or solidly in place,** ***firm, steadfast*** (so Eur., Pla.; Vett. Val. 9, 15; PStras 40, 24; Sym.; ParJer 1:2 ὡς στῦλος ἑ.) ἑ. γίνεσθαι *be firm* **1 Cor 15:58;** ἑστηκέναι ἑ. *stand firm* (Herm. Wr. 2, 7) **7:37;** cp. IPol 3:1. W. τεθεμελιωμένος **Col 1:23;** ἑ. τῇ πίστει *steadfast in the faith* **1 Pt 5:9** P[72]; IEph 10:2.—DELG s.v. ἕζομαι B2. M-M. TW.

ἑδραίωμα, ατος, τό (s. ἑδράζω; only in Christian wr.) **that which provides a firm base for someth.,** perh. ***mainstay,*** fig. ἑ. τῆς ἀληθείας **1 Ti 3:15.**—DELG s.v. ἕζομαι. M-M. TW.

ἔδραμον s. τρέχω.

Ἑζεκίας, ου, ὁ (freq. 'E-) ***Hezekiah,*** in the genealogy of Jesus **Mt 1:9f** (1 Ch 3:13; 4 Km 18:1ff; 20:1ff; Is 1:1; 38:1ff; TestSol, AscIs, Joseph.; Just., D. 33, 1 al.); **Lk 3:23ff** D (here the gen. is Ἑζεκία).

ἔζην s. ζάω.

ἐθελο- Compounds with ἐθελο- can mean—❶ **to be or do someth. designedly or on purpose** (ἐθελοδουλεία, -έω, -ος; ἐθελοκακέω; ἐθελουργία, -έω etc.).

❷ **to wish to be or do someth. that a person is not or cannot do, so that it remains a wish and nothing more** (ἐθελοπρόξενος Thu. 3, 70, 3=represent oneself as a πρόξ. and wish to regulate other people's affairs without the proper authority.—ἐθελοφιλόσοφος Etym. Magn. p. 722, 17=one who wants to be a philosopher but is not.—ἐθελοκωφέω Strabo 1, 2, 30=be unwilling to hear, pretend to be deaf). The second mng. is of value for our lit.; s. the following two entries.—DELG s.v. ἐθέλω.

ἐθελοδιδάσκαλος, ου, ὁ (s. entry ἐθελο-) ***self-made/self-proclaimed teacher*** in contrast to one authorized by God's people (the church) Hs 9, 22, 2.

ἐθελοθρησκία, ας, ἡ (s. θρησκεύω; Hesych.; Suda ἐθελοθρησκεῖ: ἰδίῳ θελήματι σέβει τὸ δοκοῦν=by his own volition he worships what seems best; Schleusner, s.v.—A Christian formation; Nägeli 51) ***self-made religion, do-it-yourself religion, idiosyncratic religion,*** perh. *would-be religion* **Col 2:23.** (B-D-F §118, 2; Mlt-H. 290; BReicke, Studia Theologica 6, '52, 45f).—DELG s.v. θρησκεύω. M-M. TW.

ἐθέλω Dg 10:6 (Just. D. 12, 3; Tat. 30, 2; Ath., R. 70, 10 al.; Mel., HE 4, 26, 9) s. θέλω.

ἐθέμην, ἔθηκα s. τίθημι.

ἐθίζω (s. ἔθος) aor. subj. 2 sg. ἐθίσῃς Sir 23:9; perf. pass. ptc. εἰθισμένος (Eur., Thu. et al.; ins, pap, LXX; TestSol; Philo, e.g. Mos. 2, 205; Jos., Ant. 11, 16, C. Ap. 1, 225) **to conform to custom or tradition,** ***accustom*** κατὰ τὸ εἰθισμένον τοῦ νόμου *acc. to the custom of* (i.e., required by) *the law* **Lk 2:27** (Mitt-Wilck. II/2, 12=BGU 1073, 12 κατὰ τὰ εἰθισμένα).—DELG s.v. εἴωθα etc.; Frisk s.v. ἔθος and εἴωθα. M-M. Spicq.

ἐθνάρχης, ου, ὁ a title used w. var. mngs., but in gener. a pers. appointed to rule over a particular area or constituency on behalf of a king (Strabo 17, 1, 13; Ps.-Lucian, Macrob. 17; SEG XXVI, 1623, 25; OGI 616, 2f=στρατηγὸς νομάδων; epitaph in Dschize: ZDPV 20, 1897, 135; coins [Ztschr. f. Numismatik 35, 1903, 197ff]; 1 Macc 14:47; 15:1, 2; Jos., Bell. 2, 93, Ant. 14, 117; 19, 283. Cp. Philo, Rer. Div. Her. 279) **head of an ethnic community/minority,** ***ethnic head/leader*** **2 Cor 11:32.**—ESchürer, StKr 72, 1899, 95ff, History I 333f, 12; TZahn, NKZ 15, 1904, 34ff; ESchwartz, GGN 1906, 367f; JStarcky, Dict. de la Bible, Suppl. VII '66, 915f; EKnauf, ZNW 74, '83, 145–47 (someth. like a consul). S. also Ἀρέτας.—M-M.

ἐθνικός, ή, όν (since Polyb. 30, 13, 6; BGU 1764, 13 [I BC] and Philo, Mos. 1, 69; 188=national; so also Jos., Ant. 12, 36) in our lit. **pert. to nationhood foreign to a specific national group, w. focus on morality or belief,** ***unbelieving, worldly, polytheistic*** (a Christian source in Kaibel 430, 6 [III/IV AD] ἐθνικῇ ἐν σοφίᾳ=in gentile learning) φιλίαι ἐθνικαί *friendships w. unbelievers* Hm 10, 1, 4. In the NT only as subst. ὁ ἐθνικός *the non-Israelite/gentile* in contrast to descendants of Abraham **Mt 5:47; 6:7.** W. τελώνης **Mt 18:17.**—**3J** 7 evangelists look for support only fr. Christians.—M-M. TW.

ἐθνικῶς adv. of ἐθνικός (Apollon. Dysc., Synt. p. 190, 5 Bekker; Diog. L. 7, 56 ἐθνικῶς τε καὶ ἑλληνικῶς=in the manner of other peoples as distinguished fr. the Hellenic mode) ***in the manner of the nations,*** ἐθνικῶς καὶ οὐχὶ Ἰουδαικῶς ζῆν *live* (w. focus on distinctive dietary practice) *like the rest of the world and not like a Judean* **Gal 2:14.**—TW.

ἔθνος, ους, τό (Hom.+).—❶ **a body of persons united by kinship, culture, and common traditions,** ***nation, people,*** τὸ ἔθνος τῆς Σαμαρείας *the Samaritan people* **Ac 8:9** (cp. Jos., Ant. 18, 85). τῶν Ἰουδαίων **10:22** (Polyb. in Jos., Ant. 12, 135; Agatharchides: 86 fgm. 20b Jac. [in Jos., Ant. 12, 6]; Diod. S. 34 + 35 fgm. 1, 2 τὸ τῶν Ἰουδαίων ἔθνος; Philo, Decal. 96 al.; Just., D. 56, 10 ὑμῶν al.) ἔ. the (specific) people, contextually the people of Israel (cp. Orig., C. Cels. 5, 15, 24; Did., Gen. 209, 14) **J 11:48, 50ff; 18:35.** δώδεκα ἔ. Hs 9, 17, 2.—B 13:2 (Gen 25:23); ἔθνη ἑπτὰ ἐν γῇ Χανάαν *seven nations in Canaan* **Ac 13:19** (Dt 7:1). The people in contrast to heads of state **9:15.** ἔθνος ἐπὶ ἔθνος *one nation against another* **Mt 24:7; Mk 13:8; Lk 21:10** (cp. 2 Ch 15:6); πάντα τὰ ἔ. (Ar. 12, 1; Ath. 14, 2; cp. Appian, Bell. Civ. 2, 106 §440 ἐν ἔθνεσιν ἅπασι; Jos., Ant. 11, 215 ἅπαντα τὰ ἔ.) **Mt 24:14; 28:19** (SKio, BT 41, '90, 230–38, prefers 2 below); **Mk 11:17** (Is 56:7); **13:10.** More specif. πάντα τὰ ἔ. τοῦ κόσμου **Lk 12:30;** cp. ἅπαντα τὰ ἔ. 1 Cl 59:4; ἐν πᾶσιν τοῖς ἔ. 2 Cl 13:2. πᾶν ἔθνος ἀνθρώπων *every nation of humankind* **Ac 17:26.** ἄρχοντες ἐθνῶν **Mt 20:25;** also οἱ δοκοῦντες ἄρχειν τῶν ἐ. **Mk 10:42;** οἱ βασιλεῖς τῶν ἐ. **Lk 22:25** (cp. Ath. 34, 2 ἡγεμόνας τῶν ἐ.).—In **Mt 21:43** ἔ. (not gentiles) in contrast to the leaders described vv. 23; 45.

❷ (τὰ) ἔθνη **people groups foreign to a specific people group** (corresp. to Heb. גּוֹיִם in LXX; a nationalistic expression, also usu. in Gk. for foreigners: Aristot., Pol. 1324b, 10 [opp. Ἕλληνες]; Ael. Aristid. 45, p. 3 D.; Cass. Dio 36, 41; Ps.-Callisth. 2, 7, 4 [opp. ἡ Ἑλλάς]; IG II/1, 445 fgm. ab, 8; fgm. c, 5; 448, 15 and 17 [c. 150 BC]; SIG 760; PStras 22, 19; PFay 20, 11; this is an expression favored by Appian in Rome for foreign peoples in contrast to the Italians: Bell. Civ. 2, 26 §99; 2, 28 §107; 3, 35 §140; 4, 57 §246 and oft.; s. Nägeli 46; B-D-F §254, 3) in our lit.

ⓐ those who do not belong to groups professing faith in the God of Israel, ***the nations, gentiles, unbelievers*** (in effect='polytheists') w. ἡγεμόνες κ. βασιλεῖς **Mt 10:18.** Named w. Israelites (Jos., Ant. 13, 196; cp. SibOr 3, 663; Just., A I, 53, 3ff and D. 123, 2 al.) **Ac 14:5; 21:21; 26:17; Ro 3:29; 9:24; 15:10** (Dt 32:43); ISm 1:2. They, too, are to share in salvation (Did., Gen. 182, 19); cp. **Ac 11:1, 18; 14:27; 15:3, 7;** cp. 2 Cl 13:3 (Just., D. 26, 1 al.) (MKiddle, The Admission of the Gentiles in Lk and Ac: JTS 36, '35, 160–73; JJeremias, Jesu Verheissung für die Völker '56 [lit.], Eng. tr. Jesus' Promise to the Nations

'58). But s. **Mt 10:5f** (MHooker, ET 82, '71, 361–65). Their sacrificial rites **1 Cor 10:20 v.l.** Paul as διδάσκαλος ἐθνῶν **1 Ti 2:7; 2 Ti 1:11 v.l.** Contrasted w. Christians Hs 1:10. Offended by Christian behavior ITr 8:2.

ⓑ ***non-Israelite Christians, gentiles*** of Christian congregations composed of more than one nationality and not limited to people of Israel (οἱ ἀπὸ τῶν ἐθνῶν πιστεύοντες Orig., C. Cels. 2, 1, 9; 8, 29, 24): πᾶσαι αἱ ἐκκλησίαι τῶν ἐθνῶν **Ro 16:4,** and their members: μετὰ τῶν ἐθνῶν συνήσθιεν *it was his custom to eat w. gentile (non-Israelite) Christians* **Gal 2:12;** cp. vs. **14.** ὑπὲρ ὑμῶν τῶν ἐθνῶν *for you gentile Christians* **Eph 3:1.** Somet. the word connotes Israelite allegations of religious and moral inferiority of gentiles **Mt 6:32** (s. Goodsp., Probs., 26f); **Lk 12:30;** Hm 4, 1, 9; ἔ. καὶ ἁμαρτωλοί s 4:4 al. ἄνομα ἔ. *lawless gentiles (=polytheists)* MPol 9:2. Contrasted w. the δίκαιοι (w. ἀποστάται) Hv 1, 4, 2; cp. 2, 2, 5.—RFeldmeier/UHeckel, edd., Die Heiden '94 (essays by a number of scholars); JLaGrand, Proliferation of the 'Gentile' in the NRSV: BR 41, '96, 77–87 (against use of 'Gentiles' as a rendering of ἔθνη).—B. 1315; 1489. M-M. TW. Sv.

ἔθος, ους, τό (trag.+).—**❶ a usual or customary manner of behavior,** ***habit, usage*** καθὼς ἔ. τισίν (EpArist 311; Jos., Ant. 20, 28; Iren. 1, 20, 1 [Harv. I 177, 9]) *as the habit of some people is* **Hb 10:25;** cp. **J 19:40; Ac 25:16.** ἔθος ἔχειν *be accustomed* w. inf. foll. (Philo, Deus Imm. 167) **19:14** D. ἐπορεύθη κατὰ τὸ ἔ. *he went, as usual, as was his wont* **Lk 22:39** (cp. Lucian, Alex. 54; POxy 370; PLond II, 171b, 19 p. 176 [III AD]; Bel 15 Theod.). ὡς ἔθος αὐτοῖς λέγειν (cp. 1 Macc 10:89; 2 Macc 13:4; PFay 125, 5 ὡς ἔθος ἐστί σοι) *as they are accustomed to say* MPol 9:2. cp. 13:1. 18:1; cp. 9:2 ἕτερα, ὧν ἔ. αὐτοῖς λέγειν.

❷ long-established usage or practice common to a group, ***custom*** τὰ ἔ. τὰ πατρῷα *the customs of the fathers* **Ac 28:17** (Just., D. 63, 5; SIG 1073, 20f κατὰ τὸ πάτριον ἔθος; Jos., Bell. 7, 424; 4 Macc 18:5 v.l.; Just., D. 87, 3 κατὰ τὸ παλαιὸν ἔ.). τὰ ἔ. ἃ παρέδωκεν ἡμῖν Μωϋσῆς *the customs that Moses handed down* **6:14;** cp. **15:1** (on the dat. τῷ ἔθει cp. PHolm 2, 18 τῇδε τάξει=acc. to this recipe); **16:21** (ἤθη v.l.); τοῖς ἔ. περιπατεῖν *live acc. to our customs (way of life)* **21:21** (DBalch, '. . . you teach all the Jews' etc.: SBLSP '93, 369–83); τὰ κατὰ Ἰουδαίους ἔ. *customs of the Judeans* (cp. Jos., Ant. 15, 286) **26:3** (ἠθῶν v.l.); κατὰ τὸ ἔ. τῆς ἱερατείας *as the custom is in the priestly office* **Lk 1:9;** cp. GJs 24:1; κατὰ τὸ ἔ. τῆς ἑορτῆς *acc. to the custom (prevailing) at the festival* **2:42** (on κατὰ τὸ ἔ. cp. pap in Dssm., NB 79 [BS 251f]; ins in SIG, index). τὰ ἐγχώρια ἔθη *the customs of the country* Dg 5:4; w. country and language 5:1.—B. 1358. Schmidt, Syn. IV 570–75, s. λαός. DELG s.v. εἴωθα; Frisk s.v. ἔθος and ἔθων (also s. LfgrE s.v. ἔθων). M-M. TW. Spicq. Sv.

ἔθρεψα s. τρέφω.

ἔθω s. εἴωθα.

εἰ (Hom.+)—**❶ marker of a condition, existing in fact or hypothetical,** ***if*** (B-D-F §371f, neg. §428, 1; 2; Rob., indexes; JBoyer, Grace Theological Journal 2, '81, 75–141, marker of a 'simple, logical connection between protasis and apodosis').

ⓐ w. the indic.—**α.** in all tenses, to express a condition thought of as real or to denote assumptions relating to what has already happened εἰ υἱὸς εἶ τοῦ θεοῦ *if you really are the Son of God* **Mt 4:3;** sim. **5:29f; 6:23; 8:31; Ac 5:39.** εἰ σὺ Ἰουδαῖος ἐπονομάζῃ *if you call yourself a Judean* **Ro 2:17.** εἰ κατακαυχᾶσαι, οὐ σὺ βαστάζεις *if you do boast, (remember) you do not support* **11:18** al. In Paul the verb is freq. missing, and is to be supplied fr. the context: εἰ Χριστὸς ἐν ὑμῖν (sc. ἐστιν), τὸ μὲν σῶμα νεκρόν (sc. ἐστιν) **8:10.** εἰ τέκνα (sc. ἐστέ) *if you are children, then* . . . vs. **17,** εἰ χάριτι (γέγονεν), οὐκέτι ἐξ ἔργων **11:6** al. The negative in clauses where the reality of the condition is taken for granted is οὐ (earlier Gk. μή [for exception s. Goodwin p. 138f]; s. B-D-F §428, 1): εἰ οὐ δύναται τοῦτο παρελθεῖν **Mt 26:42.** εἰ δὲ ὑμεῖς οὐκ ἀφίετε **Mk 11:25 [26] v.l.** εἰ πιστοὶ οὐκ ἐγένεσθε **Lk 16:11f;** εἰ οὐκ ἀκούουσιν vs. **31.** εἰ οὐ φοβοῦμαι **Lk 18:4;** cp. **J 5:47; 10:37; Ro 8:9; 11:21; 1 Cor 7:9; 9:2; 11:6; 15:13ff, 29, 32; 16:22** al. εἰ is rarely found w. the future εἰ πάντες σκανδαλισθήσονται **Mt 26:33; Mk 14:29;** εἰ ἀρνησόμεθα **2 Ti 2:12** (cp. Just., A I, 31, 6 εἰ μὴ ἀρνοῖντο Ἰησοῦν); εἰ ὑπομενεῖτε **1 Pt 2:20;** εἰ καὶ οὐ δώσει (class. ἐὰν καὶ μὴ δῷ B-D-F §372, 3; Rob. 1012) **Lk 11:8.** W. aor., when events are regarded as having taken place **Mt 24:22; Mk 3:26; 13:20.**

β. w. the pres., impf., aor., or plpf. indic. to express an unreal (contrary to fact) condition (B-D-F §360; 372; Rob. 1012ff). ἄν is usu. found in the apodosis (regularly in class.) εἰ ἐν Τύρῳ καὶ Σίδωνι ἐγένοντο αἱ δυνάμεις, πάλαι ἂν μετενόησαν *if the wonders had been done in T. and S., they would have repented long ago* **Mt 11:21.** εἰ ἤμεθα ἐν ταῖς ἡμέραις τῶν πατέρων ἡμῶν *if we had lived in the days of our fathers* **23:30.** εἰ ᾔδει ὁ οἰκοδεσπότης *if the master of the house had known* **24:43** (cp. Just., A I, 12, 2 εἰ . . . ταῦτα ἐγίνωσκον; 18, 1 al.) εἰ ἦν προφήτης, ἐγίνωσκεν ἄν *if he were a prophet, he would know* **Lk 7:39** al. The pres. indic. εἰ ἔχετε (v.l. εἴχετε) πίστιν . . . ἐλέγετε ἄν *if you had faith . . . you would say* **Lk 17:6.** Somet. ἄν is lacking in the apodosis (Polyaenus 2, 3, 5 εἰ ἐπεποιήκειμεν . . . νῦν ἐχρῆν=if we had done . . . it would have been necessary; Mitt-Wilck. II/2, 16, 18 [II BC]; PRein I, 7 [II BC]; POxy 526, 10; 530, 8 and 17; Just., A I, 10, 6; 11:2 al.—PMelcher, De sermone Epict., diss. Halle 1905, 75; Mlt. 200f) εἰ μὴ ἦν οὗτος παρὰ θεοῦ, οὐκ ἠδύνατο *if this man were not from God, he would not have been able to* . . . **J 9:33.** εἰ μὴ ἦλθον, ἁμαρτίαν οὐκ εἴχοσαν *if I had not come, they would not have sin* **15:22;** cp. vs. **24.** W. the apodosis placed first **Mk 9:42** (v.l. περιέκειτο), **Lk 17:2; J 19:11.**

ⓑ εἰ w. subj., as καὶ εἴ τις θελήσῃ **Rv 11:5** (s. 7 below), is unusual, perh. a textual error; B-D-F §372, 3 conjectures κἄν for καὶ εἰ. But εἰ w. subj. is found in the older poets and Hdt. (Kühner-G. II 474), in Aristoph., Equ. 698 et al., in var. dialects (EHermann, Griech. Forschungen I 1912, 277f) and in later times (e.g. Epict., Vett. Val., Lucian [ed. CJacobitz, Index graec. 473a]; Philostrat., Vi. Apoll. p. 84, 28; 197, 9; ins [Rdm.[2] 199]; PRyl 234, 12; POxy 496, 11; Dt 8:5); B-D-F §372, 3; Mlt. 187; Reinhold 107; OSchulthess, AKaegi Festschr. 1919, 161f.

ⓒ εἰ w. the optative is rare: εἰ καὶ πάσχοιτε . . . μακάριοι *even if you should suffer, . . . you would be blessed* **1 Pt 3:14.** εἰ θέλοι (v.l. θέλει) τὸ θέλημα τοῦ θεοῦ *if it should be God's will* vs. **17.** εἴ τι ἔχοιεν (sc. κατηγορεῖν; cp. Just., A I, 3, 1 εἰ . . . μηδὲν ἔχοι τις ἐλέγχειν) πρὸς ἐμέ *if they should have any charges to bring against me* **Ac 24:19.** εἰ δυνατὸν εἴη (Jos., Ant. 12, 12) *if it should be possible* **20:16** (but s. B-D-F §385, 2; Just., A II, 15, 2 εἰ δύναιντο). εἰ τύχοι is used as a formula (oft. in later wr., incl. Philo; s. KReik, D. Opt. bei Polyb. u. Philo 1907, 154; Just., A I, 27, 3) *it may be, for example, perhaps* **1 Cor 15:37;** used to tone down an assertion which may be too bold **14:10** (Lucian, Icar. 6 καὶ πολλάκις, εἰ τύχοι, μηδὲ ὁπόσοι στάδιοι Μεγαρόθεν Ἀθήναζέ εἰσιν, ἀκριβῶς ἐπιστάμενοι 'and many times, so it appears, not even knowing how many stades it is from Megara to Athens').

❷ marker of an indirect question as content, ***that*** (Kühner-G. II 369, 8; Rob. 965. Cp. Appian, Bell. Civ. 5, 67 §283 ἀγανακτέω εἰ=be exasperated that; Sir 23:14 θελήσεις εἰ μὴ ἐγεννήθης; 2 Macc 14:28; 4 Macc 2:1; 4:7. S. on θαυμάζω 1aγ) ἐθαύμασεν εἰ ἤδη τέθνηκεν *he was surprised that he was already dead* **Mk 15:44a.** μὴ θαυμάζετε εἰ μισεῖ ὑμᾶς ὁ κόσμος *do not wonder that the world hates you* **1J 3:13;** θαυμαζόντων . . . , εἰ τοσαύτη σπουδὴ ἦν τοῦ συλληφθῆναι *that there was such interest in arresting* MPol 7:2; AcPlCor 2:2 (cp. Just., A II, 8, 3 οὐδὲν . . . θαυμαστόν, εἰ). Sim. also (Procop. Soph., Ep. 123 χάριν ἔχειν εἰ=that) μαρτυρόμενος . . . εἰ παθητὸς ὁ Χριστός *testifying . . . that the Christ was to suffer* (s. πάσχω 3aα) **Ac 26:23.**—οὐ μέγα εἰ *it is not surprising that* **2 Cor 11:15** (cp. Aeschin., In Ctes. 94 ἐστὶ δεινὸν εἰ; Diod. S. 23, 15, 5, παράδοξον . . . εἰ=incredible . . . that; ibid. θαυμαστὸν εἰ; Gen 45:28 μέγα μοί ἐστιν εἰ).—*That* is also poss. after verbs of knowing or not knowing, e.g. **J 9:25; Ac 19:2b; 1 Cor 1:16; 7:16;** so CBurchard, ZNW 52, '61, 73–82 but s. 5bα.

❸ marker in causal clauses, when an actual case is taken as a supposition, where we also can use *if* instead of *since:* εἰ τὸν χόρτον . . . ὁ θεὸς οὕτως ἀμφιέννυσιν *if God so clothes the grass* **Mt 6:30; Lk 12:28;** cp. **Mt 7:11; Lk 11:13; J 7:23; 10:35; 13:14, 17, 32; Ac 4:9; 11:17; Ro 6:8; 15:27; Col 2:20; Hb 7:15; 1 Pt 1:17; 1J 4:11.**

❹ marker of strong or solemn assertion, without apodosis (=in aposiopesis; B-D-F §482; Rob. 1203) εἰ ἔγνως *if you only knew* **Lk 19:42.** εἰ βούλει παρενέγκαι *if you would only let (this) pass* **22:42 v.l.** (cp. the letter fr. IV BC in Dssm., LO 120, note 5 [LAE 149]).—Hebraistic in oaths, like אִם: *may this or that happen to me, if . . .* (cp. 2 Km 3:25; GBuchanan, HTR 58, '65, 319–24); this amounts to a strong negation *certainly not* (cp. Ps 7:4f; Gen 14:23) ἀμὴν λέγω ὑμῖν εἰ δοθήσεται *truly, I tell you, it will not be given* **Mk 8:12** (NColeman, JTS 28, 1927, 159–67 interprets this as strongly positive; against him FBurkitt, ibid. 274–76). εἰ εἰσελεύσονται *they shall certainly not enter* **Hb 3:11; 4:3, 5** (all 3 Ps 94:11); B-D-F §372, 4; 454, 5; Mlt-H. 468f; Rob. 94; 1024.

❺ marker of direct and indirect questions (without particle following)**—ⓐ** (not in earlier Gk., B-D-F §440, 3; Rob. 916) w. direct questions (Gen 17:17; 44:19; Am 3:3–6; 6:12; TestAbr A 15 p.96, 8 [Stone p. 40]; 18 p. 100, 13 [St. p. 48]): εἰ ἔξεστιν; *is it permitted, may one?* **Mt 12:10; 19:3** (cp. **Mk 10:2**); **Lk 14:3 v.l.; Ac 21:37; 22:25.** εἰ ὀλίγοι οἱ σωζόμενοι; *are there only a few who will be saved?* **Lk 13:23;** cp. **Mk 8:23; Lk 22:49; Ac 1:6; 7:1; 19:2a.** Cp. 6aβ.

ⓑ freq. in indir. questions *whether* (Hom. et al.)**—α.** w. pres. indic. (Gen 27:21; 42:16; TestJob 31:1; Jos., Ant. 10, 259; 16, 225; Ar 8, 1; Just., A I, 2, 2; A II, 2, 10) εἴπῃς εἰ σὺ εἶ ὁ Χριστός *whether you are the Christ* **Mt 26:63.** εἰ ἁμαρτωλός ἐστιν *whether he is a sinner* **J 9:25;** εἰ πνεῦμα ἅγιον ἔστιν *whether there is a holy spirit* **Ac 19:2b** (s. 2 above). ἴδωμεν εἰ ἔρχεται **Mt 27:49; Mk 15:36** (Lucian, Dial. Mort. 20, 3 φέρ' ἴδω εἰ=let me see whether, Merc. Cond. 6); cp. **Mk 10:2; Lk 14:31; 1 Cor 3:12; 2 Cor 13:5; 1J 4:1.**—W. the fut. indic. (4 Km 1:2; Job 5:1) εἰ θεραπεύσει αὐτόν *whether he would heal him* **Mk 3:2** (v.l. θεραπεύει); **Lk 6:7 v.l.;** εἰ σώσεις *whether you will save* **1 Cor 7:16.**—W. the aor. indic. (Esth 4:14; w. plpf. Just., D. 56, 2) εἰ πάλαι ἀπέθανεν *whether he had already died* **Mk 15:44b;** εἰ ἐβάπτισα **1 Cor 1:16.**

β. w. subj. διώκω εἰ καταλάβω *I press on (to see) whether I can capture* **Phil 3:12** (B-D-F §368; 375; Rob. 1017).

γ. w. opt. (X., An. 1, 8, 15; 2, 1, 15; 4 Macc 9:27; 11:13) ἀνακρίνοντες . . . εἰ ἔχοι ταῦτα *examining . . . to see whether this was really* so **Ac 17:11.** εἰ βούλοιτο πορεύεσθαι **25:20;** cp. **17:27.**

❻ In combination w. other particles, w. the other particles foll.**—ⓐ** εἰ ἄρα**—α.** expressing possibility *if, indeed; if, in fact; whether (perhaps)* (X., An. 3, 2, 22; SIG 834, 12; Gen 18:3; s. B-D-F §454, 2) **1 Cor 15:15** (εἴπερ ἄρα); Hv 3, 4, 3; 3, 7, 5; s 6, 4, 1; 8, 3, 3; 9, 5, 7; AcPt Ox 849, 6.

β. introducing a direct question εἰ ἄρα ταῦτα οὕτως ἔχει; *is it (really) so?* **Ac 7:1 v.l.;** indirect qu. *on the chance that* (PPetr II, 13 [19] 9 'should you find it impossible'; Num 22:11) **Mk 11:13; Ac 5:8** D; **8:22;** *in the hope that* **17:27** (εἰ ἄρα γε); AcPt Ox 849, 2; 22. Cp. εἰ δέ . . . ; *What if . . . ?* **Ac 23:9.**

ⓑ εἴ γε *if indeed, inasmuch as* (Kühner-G. II 177c) **Eph 3:2; 4:21; Col 1:23.** τοσαῦτα ἐπάθετε εἰκῇ; εἴ γε καὶ εἰκῇ *have you experienced so many things in vain? If it really was in vain* **Gal 3:4.** εἴ γε καὶ ἐκδυσάμενοι οὐ γυμνοὶ εὑρεθησόμεθα *assuming, of course, that having put it off we shall not be found naked* **2 Cor 5:3.** [εἴ γ]ε οὕτως ὡς [ἔστιν καὶ παρελάβετε τὸν λόγον] AcPl BMM recto, 31f (restoration based on duplicate Ox 1602 verso, 37f and AcPl Ha 8, 24f, which has a slightly difft. text after εἴ γε [s. also the text of Ghent 62, 17 in HSanders, HTR 31, '38, 79, n. 2]). S. γέ bα.

ⓒ εἰ δὲ καί (Just., D. 110, 1) *but if, and if* **Lk 11:18; 1 Cor 4:7;** *and even if* **2 Cor 4:3** (but s. Lietzmann, Hdb.); **11:6.** *If, on the other hand, . . . then* AcPlCor 2:28 (εἰ . . . δέ . . . καί . . . μή).

ⓓ εἰ δὲ μή (γε) *if not, otherwise***—α.** after affirmat. clauses, w. the aor. ind, and ἄν in the apodosis **J 14:2;** or pres. ind. (Demosth., Prooem. 29, 3) and fut. (Gen 30:1; Bel 29 Theod.; PLond 1912, 98) **Rv 2:5, 16;** or pres. impv. **J 14:11.**—εἰ δὲ μή γε (μήγε some edd.) *otherwise* (Pla. et al.; Epict. 3, 22, 27; Jos., Bell. 6, 120, Ant. 17, 113; Just., D. 105, 6; IGR IV, 833; POxy 1159, 6; Mitt-Wilck. I/2, 167, 25; PGM 4, 2629; Da 3:15; Bel 8; TestSol 13:3 P): εἰ δὲ μή γε (sc. προσέχετε), μισθὸν οὐκ ἔχετε *otherwise you have no reward* **Mt 6:1;** cp. **Lk 10:6.** Elliptically: κἂν μὲν ποιήσῃ καρπὸν εἰς τὸ μέλλον· εἰ δὲ μή γε, ἐκκόψεις αὐτήν *who knows, it may bear fruit next year; if not, fine, then cut it down (=have it cut down)* **13:9.**

β. after negat. clauses, *otherwise* (X., An. 7, 1, 8; Diod. S. 3, 47, 4; Dio Chrys. 10 [11], 100; LBW 1651 μὴ ἀδικεῖν. . . , εἰ δὲ μή; UPZ 196 I, 33 [119 BC]; Job 32:22) **Mk 2:21f.**—After a negative statement: οὐδὲ βάλλουσιν οἶνον νέον εἰς ἀσκοὺς παλαιούς. εἰ δὲ μή γε, ῥήγνυνται *people do not pour new wine into old skins; otherwise they burst* **Mt 9:17;** cp. **Lk 5:36.** μή τίς με δόξῃ ἄφρονα εἶναι· εἰ δὲ μή γε, κἂν ὡς ἄφρονα δέξασθέ με *no one is to consider me foolish; otherwise at least accept me as a fool* **2 Cor 11:16.**

ⓔ εἰ καί *even if, even though, although* **Lk 11:8; 18:4; 1 Cor 7:21; 2 Cor 4:16; 7:8; 12:11; Phil 2:17; Col 2:5; Hb 6:9;** AcPlCor 2:32.

ⓕ εἰ μὲν γάρ *for if* **Ac 25:11 v.l.** (for εἰ μὲν οὖν); **2 Cor 11:4; Hb 8:4 v.l.** (for εἰ μὲν οὖν).

ⓖ εἰ μὲν οὖν *if, then* **Hb 7:11.** W. εἰ δέ foll. (X., Cyr. 8, 7, 22; Ael. Aristid. 28, 156 K.=49 p. 542 D.) **Ac 19:38.**

ⓗ εἰ μέντοι *if, on the other hand* **Js 2:8.**

ⓘ εἰ μή (=πλήν) *but* **1 Cor 7:17** (= *in general*) (B-D-F §376).—After negatives

α. *except, if not,* mostly without a verb depending on εἰ μή (X., An. 2, 1, 12; JosAs 12:11; Just., A I, 29, 1) **Mt 11:27; 12:24; 16:4; J 3:13; Ro 7:7; Gal 1:19** (HKoch, Z. Jakobusfrage Gal 1:19: ZNW 33, '34, 204–9); but also with a verb (Jos., Ant. 8, 316) **Mt 5:13; Mk 6:5; Ac 21:25 v.l.**

β. *but* (OGI 201, 20f οὐκ ἀφῶ αὐτοὺς καθεσθῆναι εἰς τὴν σκιάν, εἰ μὴ ὑπὸ ἡλίου ἔξω; in note 33 the ed. gives exx. fr. Aristoph. for this use) without a verb **Mt 12:4;** w. a verb (Theod. Prodr. 7, 426 H.) **Gal 1:7,** s. ἄλλος 2b. For ἐκτὸς εἰ μή s. ἐκτός 3a.

ⓙ εἰ μήτι *unless indeed, unless perhaps* (Ael. Aristid. 46 p. 198 D.; Jos., Ant. 4, 280; Tat. 10, 2) **Lk 9:13; 2 Cor 13:5;** w. ἄν (Ps.-Clem., Hom. 16, 4) **1 Cor 7:5** (s. Dssm., NB 32, 1 [BS 204 n.]; B-D-F §376; Mlt. 169; 239; Reinhold 35; JTrunk, De Basilio Magno sermonis Attic. imitatore 1911, 56; JWackernagel, Antike Anredeformen 1912, 27f).

ⓚ εἰ οὖν *if, therefore* **Mt 6:23; Lk 11:36; 12:26; J 13:14; 18:8; Col 3:1; Phlm 17.**

ⓛ εἴπερ *if indeed, if after all, since* (X., An. 1, 7, 9; Menand., Epitr. 907 S. [587 Kö.]; PHal 7, 6; UPZ 59, 29 [168 BC]; Jdth 6:9; TestJob 3:6; Just., Tat., Ath.) **Ro 3:30** (ἐπείπερ v.l.); **8:9, 17; 2 Th 1:6.**—*if indeed, provided that* εἴπερ ἄρα (ἄρα 1a) **1 Cor 15:15.** καὶ γὰρ εἴπερ *for even if* (cp. Od. 1, 167; B-D-F §454, 2) **1 Cor 8:5;** on 2 Cor 5:3 s. εἴ γε καί 6b above. Doubtful IEph 6:2; s. ἤ 2aβ.

ⓜ *if perchance, if haply* εἰ δέ που . . . τις ἔλθοι *if perchance . . . anyone came* Papias (2:4).

ⓝ εἴ πως (the spelling εἴπως is also correct; B-D-F §12) *if perhaps, if somehow*—**α.** w. opt. (X., An. 2, 5, 2; 4, 1, 21; POxy 939, 15) εἴ πως δύναιντο παραχειμάσαι *in the hope that they could spend the winter* **Ac 27:12.**

β. w. fut. indic. (3 Km 21:31; 4 Km 19:4; Jer 28:8; TestJos 6:6) εἴ πως εὐοδωθήσομαι *whether, perhaps, I shall succeed* **Ro 1:10;** cp. **11:14; Phil 3:11.**

ⓞ εἴτε . . . εἴτε (Soph. et al.; ins since 416 BC [Meisterhans³-Schw.]; pap [Mayser II/3, 159]; LXX; JosAs 5:9; ApcrEzk [Epiph 70, 11]; Jos., Ant. 16, 33 and 37; Just., Ath. B-D-F §446; 454, 3; Rob. ind.) *if . . . (or) if, whether . . . or*

α. w. a verb in pres. indic. (Herm. Wr. 12, 22 thrice) **1 Cor 12:26; 2 Cor 1:6;** or pres. subj. **1 Th 5:10.**—**β.** w. no verb (Just., D. 86, 3 al.) **Ro 12:6–8; 1 Cor 3:22; 8:5; 2 Cor 5:10** al. εἴτε only once **1 Cor 14:27.** εἴτε ἄρσενα εἴτε θήλειαν (ἤτε . . . ἤτε pap) GJs 4:1.

❼ Used w. the indef. pron.: εἴ τις, εἴ τι *everyone who* or *whoever; everything that* or *whatever* **Mt 16:24; 18:28; Mk 4:23; 9:35; Lk 9:23; 14:26; 1 Ti 3:1, 5; 5:4, 8, 16** al. Cp. **1 Cor 12:31 v.l.** (ADebrunner, ConNeot XI, '47, 37). W. subj. εἴ τις θελήσῃ **Rv 11:5** s. 1b, above.—DELG. M-M.

εἰ μήν, more correctly **εἶ μήν** (B-D-F §24; Rob. 1150) for the older ἦ μήν (Hom. et al. [s. Denniston 350f], but found also Jos., Ant. 13, 76; 17, 42), in Hellenistic-Roman times (SIG 993, 20 [III BC]; 736, 27 [92 BC]; IG IV, 840, 15 [EHermann, Gr. Forschungen I 1912, 312]; pap since 112 BC [Mayser 78]; LXX e.g. Ezk 33:27; 34:8 al.; Num 14:28; Jdth 1:12; Bar 2:29 [Thackeray 83]) formula used in oaths ***surely, certainly*** **Hb 6:14** (Gen 22:17).—Dssm., NB 33ff (BS 205ff).—M-M.

εἴα, ἔιασα s. ἐάω.

εἶδα s. ὁράω.

εἰδέα, ας, ἡ (this sp. is found, e.g., in Artem. 2, 44 φαίνονται οἱ θεοὶ ἐν ἀνθρώπων ἰδέᾳ [v.l. εἰδέᾳ] τε καὶ μορφῇ; PGen 16, 17=Mitt-Wilck. I/2, 354 I, 17; StudPal XVII, lines 272 and 335; TestJob 46:7; TestBenj 10:1 v.l.; GrBar 4:3; PAmh I, col. IX, 3 and 5 [AscIs 3:13]; Philo, Spec. Leg. 4, 113 with v.l.) **Mt 28:3** (incorrect spelling, s. B-D-R §23; N.[25] notes that ἰδέα is preferable); cp. AcPl Ant 13, 14 (= Aa I 237, 2). For the mng. in these pass. s. ἰδέα 1.—M-M. TW.

εἰδέναι, εἰδήσω s. οἶδα.

-ειδής suffix to adjectives indicating that something is 'like, similar to'; Schwyzer I 418; cp. -ώδης (related to ὄζω).

εἶδον (Hom.+) used as the 2 aor. of ὁράω; mixed forms fr. 1 and 2 aor. somet. occur, and freq. as vv.ll. (B-D-F §81, 3; W-S. §13, 13; Rob. 337–39): εἶδα **Rv 17:3 v.l.;** εἴδαμεν **Mk 2:12 v.l.; Ac 4:20,** εἴδατε as v.l. **Lk 7:22** and **J 6:26,** εἶδαν **Mt 13:17; Mk 6:33 v.l.; Lk 10:24** al.; **Ac 9:35.** In gener., wherever εἶδον is read, the mixed form is found as v.l. Numerous mss. have both this and the phonetic spelling (B-D-F §23) ἴδον **Rv 4:1; 6:1ff;** ἴδες **1:19;** ἴδεν **Lk 5:2; Rv 1:2;** ἴδομεν **Lk 5:26;** ἴδατε **7:22;** ἴδετε **Phil 1:30** (all as v.l.); subj. ἴδω; opt. ἴδοιμι; impv. ἴδε (Moeris p. 193 ἰδέ ἀττικῶς· ἴδε ἑλληνικῶς. W-S. §6, 7d; B-D-F §13; 101 p. 47 [ὁρᾶν]; Rob. 1215 [εἰδέω]; cp. PRyl 239, 21; LXX); inf. ἰδεῖν; ptc. ἰδών; mid. inf. ἰδέσθαι *see.* Since εἶδον functions as the aor. form of ὁράω, most of the mngs. found here will be duplicated s.v. ὁράω.

❶ **to perceive by sight of the eye, *see, perceive.***—ⓐ w. acc. τινά, τὶ *someone, someth.* a star **Mt 2:2;** cp. vs. **9f;** a child vs. **11;** the Spirit of God as a dove **3:16;** a light **4:16** (Is 9:2); two brothers vss. **18, 21** al. W. ἀκούειν (Lucian, Hist. Conscrib. 29) **Lk 7:22; Ac 22:14; 1 Cor 2:9; Phil 1:27, 30; 4:9; Js 5:11.** Contrasted w. πιστεύειν **J 20:29** (cp. 2 Cor 5:7); *look at* someone **Mk 8:33; J 21:21;** at someth. critically **Lk 14:18.**—Also of visions that one sees (Sir 49:8): εἶδον κ. ἰδοὺ θύρα ἠνεῳγμένη ἐν τ. οὐρανῷ . . . κ. θρόνος . . . κ. ἐπὶ τὸν θρόνον καθήμενος . . . **Rv 4:1f** (TestLevi 5:1 ἤνοιξέ μοι ὁ ἄγγελος τ. πύλας τοῦ οὐρανοῦ. κ. εἶδον τὸν ὕψιστον ἐπὶ θρόνον καθήμενον). ἰδεῖν ὅραμα **Ac 10:17; 11:5; 16:10.** ἐν ὁράματι *in a vision* **9:12; 10:3;** also ἐν τῇ ὁράσει **Rv 9:17.** ὑπ' (πάρ' Joly) ἐμοῦ πάντα ἰδεῖν Hs 9, 1, 3 B. ἰδεῖν τοῖς ὀφθαλμοῖς *see w. one's own eyes* **Mt 13:15; J 12:40; Ac 28:27** (all three Is 6:10; cp. Just., A I, 32, 4 ὄψει . . . ἰδεῖν). The combination ἰδὼν εἶδον *I have surely seen* **7:34** (Ex 3:7) is Hebraistic (but cp. Lucian, D. Mar. 4, 3 Jacobitz). The ptc. with and without acc. freq. serves to continue a narrative **Mt 2:10; 5:1; 8:34; Mk 5:22; 9:20; Lk 2:48** al. The acc. is to be supplied **Mt 9:8, 11; 21:20; Mk 10:14; Lk 1:12; 2:17; Ac 3:12** al.

ⓑ w. acc. and a ptc. (LXX; En 104:6; Lucian, Philops. 13 εἶδον πετόμενον τὸν ξένον; Tat. 23, 1 εἶδον ἀνθρώπους . . . βεβαρημένους) ἰδὼν πολλοὺς ἐρχομένους *when he saw many coming* **Mt 3:7.** εἶδεν τὴν πενθερὰν αὐτοῦ βεβλημένην *he saw his mother-in-law lying in bed (with fever)* **8:14;** cp. **9:9; 16:28; Ac 28:4** (cp. Jos., Ant. 7, 241); B 7:10; Hm 5, 2, 2 al.

ⓒ w. indir. question foll.: ἰδεῖν τὸν Ἰησοῦν τίς ἐστιν *to see just who Jesus was* **Lk 19:3;** ἰ. τί ἐστιν τὸ γεγονός *what had happened* **Mk 5:14.** ἴδωμεν εἰ ἔρχεται Ἠλίας *let us see whether Elijah will come* **15:36** (s. εἰ 5bα). ἴδωμεν τί καλόν 1 Cl 7:3. ἴδετε πηλίκοις ὑμῖν γράμμασιν ἔγραψα *notice with what large letters I write to you* **Gal 6:11.**

ⓓ w. ὅτι foll. **Mk 2:16; 9:25; J 6:24; 11:31; Rv 12:13.**

ⓔ the formulas (s. also ἴδε) ἔρχου καὶ ἴδε *come and see* **J 1:46; 11:34;** cp. **1:39** and ὑπάγετε ἴδετε **Mk 6:38,** borrowed fr. Semitic usage (cp. δεῦρο καὶ ἴδε, δεῦτε ἴδετε 4 Km 6:13; 7:14; 10:16; Ps 45:9; 65:5; ἐξέλθατε καὶ ἴδετε SSol 3:11), direct attention to a particular object.

❷ **to become aware of someth. through sensitivity, *feel*** (Alexis Com. 222, 4 ὀσμήν; Diod. S. 1, 39, 6 the blowing of the wind; Oenomaus in Eus., PE 5, 28, 2 τὴν θείαν φωνήν; Aristaen., Ep. 2, 7 ὄψει τὸ πήδημα [the beating of the heart]; Ezk 3:13 εἶδον φωνήν) σεισμόν **Mt 27:54.**

❸ **to take special note of someth., *see, notice, note*** (Philo, Abr. 191; Just., D. 120, 1 ἴδοις ἂν ὃ λέγω) *faith* **Mt 9:2;** *thoughts* vs. **4; Lk 9:47 v.l.;** *God's kindness* **Ro 11:22.** W. ὅτι foll. **Mt 27:3, 24; Ac 12:3; Gal 2:7, 14.** W. indir. question foll. (X., Symp. 2, 15; Ar. 2, 1 al.) *consider, ponder* someth. ἴδετε ποταπὴν ἀγάπην δέδωκεν *consider the outstanding love the Father has shown* **1J**

3:1. W. περί τινος (Epict. 1, 17, 10; 4, 8, 24, 'see about' someth.): περὶ τ. λόγου τούτου *deliberate concerning this matter* **Ac 15:6** (cp. 18:15, a Latinism [?] videre de, 'look into, see to, deal with', JNorth, NTS 29, '83, 264–66).

❹ **to experience someth.,** *see someth.=experience someth.* (Ps 26:13); prosperous days **1 Pt 3:10** (Ps 33:13); τ. βασιλείαν **J 3:3.** θάνατον *see death=die* **Lk 2:26,** echoed in GJs 24:4; cp. **Hb 11:5** (cp. Ps 88:49; Anth. Pal. 6, 230 ἰδεῖν Ἀΐδην). πένθος *grief* **Rv 18:7** (cp. 1 Macc 13:3 τὰς στενοχωρίας; Eccl 6:6 ἀγαθωσύνην).τὴν διαφθοράν *experience decay* =decay **Ac 2:27, 31; 13:35–37** (all Ps 15:10); τ. ἡμέραν (Soph., Oed. R. 831; Aristoph., Pax 345; Polyb. 10, 4, 7; 32, 10, 9; Ael. Aristid. 32 p. 601 D.; Lam 2:16; En 103:5; Jos., Ant. 6, 305): τὴν ἡμέραν τ. ἐμήν **J 8:56;** μίαν τῶν ἡμερῶν **Lk 17:22.**

❺ **to show an interest in,** ***look after, visit*** (X., An. 2, 4, 15; Appian, Bell. Civ. 4, 19 §73e visit a country place; 5, 62 §266 visit or look after a sick woman) **Lk 8:20; Ac 16:40; 1 Cor 16:7.** τὸ πρόσωπόν τινος (Lucian, Dial. Deor. 24, 2) *visit someone* **1 Th 2:17; 3:10;** *come* or *learn to know* someone (Epict. 3, 9, 14 Ἐπίκτητον ἰδεῖν) **Lk 9:9; 23:8; J 12:21; Ro 1:11; Phil 2:26 v.l.;** w. προσλαλῆσαι **Ac 28:20.** See ἴδε, ἰδού, and ὁράω.—B. 1041. DELG s.v. ἰδεῖν. M-M. TW.

εἰδός s. εἰδώς and ὁράω.

εἶδος, ους, τό (Hom.+.—CRitter, Neue Unters. über Plato 1910, 228–320)

❶ **the shape and structure of someth. as it appears to someone,** ***form, outward appearance*** (X., Cyr. 1, 2, 1; Pla., Symp. 210b; Philostrat., Ep. 51; Gen 41:2–4; Ezk 1:26; Philo; Jos., Ant. 6, 296; TestSim 5:1; Mel., P. 47, 334 [Perler]) σωματικῷ εἴδει *in bodily form* **Lk 3:22;** cp. GEb 18, 36 (Just., D. 88, 4 ἐν εἴδει περιστερᾶς and oft.). τὸ εἶδος τοῦ προσώπου αὐτοῦ *the appearance of his face* **Lk 9:29** (ApcEsdr 4:29 p. 29, 3 Tdf.). Of God (cp. Ex 24:17; Theoph. Ant. 1, 3 [p. 62, 8]) εἶδος αὐτοῦ (w. φωνή) **J 5:37.** Of the form of polytheists' gods Dg 2:1. οὐκ ἔχειν εἶδος *have no comeliness* 1 Cl 16:3 (Is 53:2). τὸ πῦρ καμάρας εἶδος ποιῆσαν *formed the shape of a vaulted room* MPol 15:2.

❷ **a variety of someth.,** ***kind*** (X., Pla. et al.; PTebt 58, 20f [111 BC]; PFay 34, 6; POxy 905, 6; Sir 23:16; 25:2; Philo; Jos., Ant. 10, 37 πᾶν εἶδος πονηρίας; Just., Tat., Ath. [here the 'form' of matter]) ἀπὸ παντὸς εἴδους πονηροῦ *fr. every kind of evil* **1 Th 5:22** (Unknown Sayings, p. 92 [money-changing?])

❸ **the act of looking/seeing,** ***seeing, sight*** (Num 12:8; Ps.-Clem., Hom. 17, 18 στόμα κατὰ στόμα, ἐν εἴδει καὶ οὐ δι' ὁραμάτων καὶ ἐνυπνίων. So also the interpr. of 2 Cor 5:7 in Severian of Gabala [Pauluskomm. aus d. griech. Kirche ed. KStaab '33, 291] and in Theodoret III 314 Noesselt) διὰ πίστεως, οὐ διὰ εἴδους *by faith, not by sight* **2 Cor 5:7** (the same contrast betw. πιστεύειν and ἰδεῖν [s. εἶδον 1a] also **J 20:29**).—PBrommer, ΕΙΔΟΣ et ΙΔΕΑ '40. DELG and Frisk. B. 874. EDNT. M-M. TW.

εἰδυῖα, εἰδῶ s. οἶδα.

εἰδωλεῖον, ου, τό (on the spelling εἰδώλιον s. B-D-F §13; 111, 5; PKatz, TLZ '36, 283; Rob. 154) **place of worship with a cult image,** ***idol's temple*** **1 Cor 8:10** (cp. 1 Esdr 2:7; Bel 10; 1 Macc 10:83; TestJob 5:2 εἰς τόν ναὸν τοῦ εἰδωλίου in the temple with a cult image).—DELG s.v. εἶδος. M-M. TW.

εἰδωλόθυτος, ον (s. εἴδωλον and θύω; 4 Macc 5:2), only subst. τὸ εἰδωλόθυτον, ***someth. offered to a cultic image/idol,*** *food sacrificed to idols* an expr. which (s. εἴδωλον 2) was possible only within Israelite tradition (cp. Ps.-Phoc. 31 [an interpolation prob. based on Ac 15:29]; Just., D. 34, 8; 35, 1), where it was used in a derogatory sense. Polytheists said ἱερόθυτον (s. ἱερόθυτος). It refers to sacrificial meat, part of which was burned on the altar as the deities' portion (cp. Orig., C. Cels. 8, 30, 1: τό εἰδωλόθυτον θύεται δαιμονίοις), part was eaten at a solemn meal in the temple, and part was sold in the market (so Artem. 5, 2) for home use. Within the Mosaic tradition it was unclean and therefore forbidden. **Ac 15:29** (for lit. s. πνικτός); **21:25; 1 Cor 8:1, 4, 7, 10; 10:19, 28 v.l.; Rv 2:14, 20;** D 6:3. (Iren. 6, 3 [Harv. I 55, 10]).—MRauer, D. 'Schwachen' in Korinth u. Rom 1923, 40–52; HvSoden, Sakrament u. Ethik b. Pls: Marburger Theol. Stud. 1, '31, 1ff; GFee, Biblica 61, '80, 172–97; WWillis, Idol Meat in Corinth: SBLDS 68, '85; PTomson, Paul and the Jewish Law: CRINT III/1, '90, 187–220; BWitherington III, Why Not Idol Meat?: BRev 10/3, '94, 38–43; 54f.—EDNT. TW.

εἰδωλολατρέω (s. εἴδωλον, λατρεύω and the two following entries; TestLevi 17:11; Just., D. 19, 6 al.) w. derogatory connotation ***be/become an image-worshiper/idolater*** (=commit idolatry) of Christians who consult oracles Hm 11:4, or become apostate under persecution s 9, 21, 3.

εἰδωλολάτρης, ου, ὁ (s. εἰδωλολατρέω and next entry; SibOr 3, 38) like the two preceding terms derogatory ***image-worshiper/idolater*** (=idolater) **1 Cor 5:10; Rv 21:8; 22:15.** Of those who are covetous, etc. (s. εἰδωλολατρία) Eph 5:5; cp. **1 Cor 5:11.** W. πόρνοι, μοιχοί **6:9;** εἰ. γίνεσθαι *take part in image-worship/idolatry* **10:7.** Of Christians who consult false prophets Hm 11:4.—DELG s.v. λάτρον. M-M. TW.

εἰδωλολατρία, ας, ἡ (on the sp. -εία s. B-D-F §23; 119, 2; TestJud 19:1; GrBar 8:5; Just., Orig.) derogatory term ***image-worship, idolatry*** D 3:4. In a catalogue of vices **Gal 5:20;** B 20:1; D 5:1. Of greed **Col 3:5** (cp. Eph 5:5; Pol 11:2 and s. HWeinel, D. Wirkungen des Geistes u. der Geister 1899, 14f). The unregenerate heart is πλήρης εἰδωλολατρίας *full of idolatry* B 16:7; φεύγειν ἀπὸ τῆς εἰ. **1 Cor 10:14** (cp. κινεῖσθαι ἀπὸ τῆς εἰ. Did., Gen. 210, 12). Pl. πορεύεσθαι ἐν ἀθεμίτοις εἰ. *walk in unlawful idolatry,* i.e. commit unlawful deeds connected w. polytheistic worship **1 Pt 4:3.**—M-M. TW.

εἰδωλομανής, -ές (s. εἴδωλον, μανία; only in Christian wr.; Ath. 27, 1 et al. [Lampe]) **pert. to insane interest in idols,** ***idol-mad*** καιόμενοι τῇ καύσει τῶν εἰδωλομανῶν *aflame with the burning of the idol-crazed* ApcPt Bodl. 5–8. For this rdg., which requires the restoration κ[αιόμ]ενοι τῇ [κ]αύσει τῶ[ν ε]ἰδωλομ[αν]ῶν, s. JTS 12, 1910–11, 368f.

εἴδωλον, ου, τό (Hom. et al. ordinarily in the sense: form, image, shadow, phantom; cp. Ath. 27, 1; Hippol., Ref. 4, 50, 2; AcJ 28 [Aa II/1] 166, 13 used by a Christian of his bodily appearance as opposed to his real Christian self; LexGrMin 53, 20–24). In the LXX εἴδωλον bridges two views: the deities of the nations have no reality, and so are truly the products of fantasy; and they are manufactured by human hands (cp. the satire expressed, e.g., 3 Km 18:27; Jer 2:27f; Is 44:12–17).

❶ **cultic image/representation of an alleged transcendent being,** ***image, representation*** (cp. Chaeremon fgm. 25 Db p. 38 H.: the falcon as εἰ. of the sun signifies a deity; Is 30:22; 2 Ch 23:17; Tob 14:6; EpJer 72; Just., A I, 64, 1 τὸ εἰ. τῆς λεγομένης Κόρης; Ath. 15, 1; Orig., C. Cels. 3, 15, 15 [w. ἀγάλματα]; cp. Polyb. 30, 25, 13 θεῶν ἢ δαιμόνων εἴδωλα 'images of gods or demi-gods'; Vett. Val. 67:5; 113, 17; Cat. Cod. Astr. VII p. 176, 22; OGI 201, 8; PStras 91, 10; PSI 901, 13 and 22). Sacrifices were made to it (Nicol. Dam.: 90 fgm. 13, 23 p. 407, 31 Jac.

πρὸς τῷ εἰδώλῳ ἀποσφάττεσθαι; Num 25:2; 1 Macc 1:43; cp. Orig., C. Cels. 1, 36, 32 ἀπὸ τῶν εἰ. μαντείαν λαβεῖν; since Mosaic law forbade material representation of God, all references in our lit. to a divine image, usu. transliterated 'idol', relate to polytheistic Gr-Rom. depiction) **Ac 7:41;** gold and silver (Ps 113:12) **Rv 9:20.** εἴδωλα ἄφωνα *images that cannot speak* **1 Cor 12:2** (but s. 2 below; cp. Hab 2:18; 3 Macc 4:16; JosAs 3:10 πρόσωπα τῶν εἰ.; 8:5 εἴ. νεκρὰ καὶ κωφά al.; Ar. 13, 1 θεοποιούμενοι τὰ κωφὰ καὶ ἀναίσθητα εἴ. 'making gods out of mute and insensible images'.—Polytheists also know that the images of the gods are lifeless: e.g. Artem. 4, 36 ταῦτα οὐ ζῇ; for Ancient Near East s. MGruber, DDD 240. τούτων εἰδώλων τῶν πλάνων 'these deceptive [deified] images' ApcPt Bodl. ἵνα μηκέτι εἰδώλοις λατρεύῃς καὶ κνίσαις 'so that you might no longer devote yourselves to images and sacrificial smoke' AcPl Ha 2, 32. Cp. εἴδωλα, ἔργα χειρῶν ἀνθρώπων Theoph. Ant. 2, 34 [p.184, 25]).

❷ through metonymy the image and the deity or divinity alleged to be represented are freq. associated in such manner that the image factor is less significant than the component of unreality or spuriousness of what is represented (cp. Is 44:6–20; 46;1–7; Wsd 13–14) **fabricated/imaged deity,** ***idol*** (oft. LXX, also Philo; Jos., Ant. 9, 273; 10, 50; TestReub 4:6; TestSol; TestJos 4:5; 6:5; JosAs; Just., A I, 49, 5 al.; Iren. 1, 15, 4 [Harv. I 153, 7] al.; Orig., C. Cels. 5, 43, 11 [w. δαίμονες]) βδελύσσεσθαι τὰ εἴ. *abhor idols* **Ro 2:22;** cp. B 4:8. . . . ὅτι εἴ. τί ἐστιν; (do I mean to say) *that an imaged deity is anything?* **1 Cor 10:19** (i.e. the cult object as alleged image is evident, but its subject has no real existence as a god; Paul means that if any transcendent reality is at all to be assigned to an εἴδωλον, its status is not that of a god but of the lesser beings known as δαίμονες 1 Cor 10:20). Cp. **1 Cor 12:2** (s. 1 above). Contrasted w. the temple of God, i.e. God's people **2 Cor 6:16.** Contrasted w. God (cp. θεοὶ δὲ οὐ τὰ εἴδωλα ἢ δαίμονες Did., Gen. 248, 6) **1 Th 1:9.** ἀπὸ τῶν εἰ. ἀποσπᾶν *tear away fr. imaged deities* 2 Cl 17:1; οὐδὲν εἴ. ἐν κόσμῳ (in wordplay w. οὐδεὶς θεός) *no idol has any real existence in the universe* (Twentieth Century NT) **1 Cor 8:4** (cp. the contrast between humanity as being οὐδέν and heaven that abides for the immortals Pind., N. 6, 3). τῇ συνηθείᾳ (v.l. συνειδήσει) *because of their consciousness, up to now, that this is an imaged deity* vs. **7; Ac 15:20;** ἱερεῖς τῶν εἰ. *priests of the imaged deities* B 9:6. φυλάσσειν ἑαυτὸν ἀπὸ τῶν εἰ. *keep oneself fr. deified illusions* or *ghosts* (i.e. views of God that are divorced from the truth of God's self-revelation in Jesus Christ; in contrast to this ἀλήθεια, the εἴδωλα are but phantoms in the Gr-Rom. sense of the term) **1J 5:21.** JSuggit, JTS 36, '85, 386–90. TPodella, Das Lichtkleid '96, esp. 164–85.—B. 1491. DELG s.v. εἶδος. DDD s.v. 'AZZABIM and GILLULIM'. M-M. TW. Sv.

εἰδώς, υῖα, ός s. οἶδα.

εἴθισμαι s. εἰθίζω.

εἰκάζω 1 aor. inf. εἰκάσαι (Wsd 19:18), opt. εἰκάσαιμι, pass. subj. εἰκασθῇ (Jer 26:23) **to form a mental image of someth.,** ***suppose, imagine*** (so Aeschyl., Hdt. et al.; PBerlSchubart 4, 32 [III AD, lit.]; Wsd; En 21:7; EpArist 105; Philo, Fuga 179; Jos., Ant. 17, 136, Vi. 148) Dg 2:3 cj. Lachmann; 7:2. Cp. 'appraise, value (at)' in pap fr. III BC, also PMichael 18 Acol. 1, 6 (III AD).—DELG s.v. ἔοικα. Sv.

εἰκαιότης, ητος, ἡ (s. εἰκῇ; Philod.; Diog. L. 7, 48; Philo, Det. Pot. Ins. 10 et al.; Pr 30:8 Aq.) **the state or condition of lacking seriousness by engaging in triviality,** ***silliness*** w. ἀπάτη Dg 4:6.—DELG s.v. εἰκῇ.

εἰκῇ adv. (Xenophanes et al.; ins, pap; Pr 28:25; TestJob 39:11; Just; for the spelling εἰκῆ s. B-D-F §26; W-S. §5, 11 n. 22; Rob. 295f).

❶ **pert. to there being no cause or reason,** ***without cause*** (Xenophanes, fgm. B 2, 13 Diels; Artem. 2, 60; UPZ 106, 15; 107, 17; 108, 14 and 24 [all I BC]) **Mt 5:22 v.l.** (PWernberg-Møller, NTS 3, '56/57, 71–73); εἰ. φυσιούμενος *puffed up without cause* **Col 2:18.**

❷ **pert. to being without success or result,** ***to no avail*** (TestJob 39:11; Lucian, Anach. 19) πάσχειν *experience* **Gal 3:4.** κοπιάζειν *work* **4:11.**

❸ **pert. to being without purpose,** ***to no purpose*** (Lucian, Jupp. Tr. 36; EpArist 161; 168; Just., A II, 4, 2 and D. 97, 1) of the government τὴν μάχαιραν φορεῖν *carry the sword to no purpose* **Ro 13:4.**

❹ **pert. to being without careful thought,** ***without due consideration, in a haphazard manner*** (Heraclitus fgm. 47 Diels; Epict. 1, 6, 7; 1, 28, 28; Arrian, Anab. 6, 3, 2; Apollon. Dysc.: Gramm. Gr. II/2 p. 215, 1 U.; Sb 5675, 12 [II BC]; PLips 104, 29 [I BC]; POslo 159, 9 [III AD]; Pr 28:25; EpArist 51; 162; Jos., C. Ap. 2, 234) w. ἀτάκτως *thoughtlessly* (perh. *at random*) *and in disorder* 1 Cl 40:2. πιστεῦσαι **1 Cor 15:2** (here mng. 3 is also prob.).—DELG s.v. εἰκῇ. New Docs 2, 81. M-M. TW.

εἰκός neut. of the ptc. of ἔοικα (trag., Hdt. et al.; pap; EpArist 223; Philo; Jos., Bell. 6, 52 al.; Ath., R. 62, 23; Hesych. εἰκός: τάχα, ἴσως, s. Blakeney, The Ep. to Diognetus '43, 41) ***probable, reasonable*** Dg 3:3.—Sv.

εἴκοσι indecl. (Hom.+) ***twenty*** **Lk 14:31; Ac 1:15; 27:28;** Hv 4, 1, 1; μόγις εἴ. ἐκύλιον **Lk 23:53** D (cp. Jos., Bell. 6, 293 μόλις ὑπ' ἀνθρώπων εἴ.); εἴ. τρεῖς (s. B-D-F §63, 2) *twenty-three* **1 Cor 10:8;** εἴ. τέσσαρες (Hippocr.; TestJos 15:1; Joseph.) **ibid. v.l.; Rv 4:4, 10; 5:8; 11:16; 19:4;** εἰκοσιτέσσαρες **5:14 v.l.** (Erasmian rdg.); εἴ. πέντε (Demosth. 35, 10 [document]; Joseph.) **J 6:19.** As numeric symbol κ' (κζ' = εἴ. ἑπτά TestJob 41:2) Hs 9, 4, 3; 9, 5, 4; 9, 15, 4.—DELG. M-M. TW.

εἰκοσιπέντε, εἰκοσιτέσσαρες, εἰκοσιτρεῖς better written as two words (cp. Athen. 13, 585b), s. εἴκοσι.

εἰκτικῶς adv. of εἰκτικός (fr. εἴκω) 'readily yielding' (Philod., Περὶ σημ. 18, 2 Gomp.; Maximus Tyr. 7, 3b) ***readily yielding*** 1 Cl 37:2 (s. Bihlmeyer's note; s. Lightf. app. on the reading of cod. Alexandrinus).—DELG s.v. εἴκω.

εἴκω 1 aor. εἶξα, inf. εἶξαι (Hom. et al.; Epict., pap; Wsd 18:25; 4 Macc 1:6; Jos., Ant. 1, 115 τ. θεῷ; 2, 304; 4, 143 τ. ἐπιθυμίαις; Ath. 21, 2 ὀργῇ καὶ λύπῃ) ***yield*** (Pind., I. 1, 6; Diog. L. 2, 143) τινί *to someone* (Appian, Hann. 19 §84, Bell. Civ. 1, 1 §1 ἀλλήλοις) to give way before expression of force or argument οἷς οὐδὲ πρὸς ὥραν εἴξαμεν *to whom we did not yield even for a moment* **Gal 2:5** (ὥρα 2b). ἡμῖν 1 Cl 56:1.—DELG.

εἰκών, όνος, ἡ (Aeschyl., Hdt.+; loanw. in rabb.)—❶ **an object shaped to resemble the form or appearance of someth.,** ***likeness, portrait*** (cp. Did., Gen. 82, 6) of the emperor's head on a coin (so Artem. 4, 31; of an emperor's image Jos., Bell. 2, 169; 194, Ant. 19, 185; cp. AcThom 112 [Aa II/2, 223, 19]; s. DShotter, Gods, Emperors, and Coins: Greece and Rome, 2d ser. 26, '79, 48–57) **Mt 22:20; Mk 12:16; Lk 20:24.** Of an image of a god (Diod. S. 2, 8, 7 [Zeus]; Appian, Mithrid. 117 §575 θεῶν εἰκόνες; Lucian, Sacr. 11; 2 Ch 33:7; Is 40:19; Just., A I, 55, 7; Ath. 18, 1; s. TPodella, Das Lichtkleid '96, esp. 83–88) **Rv 13:14f; 14:9, 11; 15:2; 16:2; 19:20; 20:4.**

❷ **that which has the same form as someth. else** (not a crafted object as in 1 above), ***living image,*** fig. ext. of 1 εἰκὼν τοῦ θεοῦ (ἄνθρωπος πλάσμα καὶ εἰκὼν αὐτοῦ [God] Theoph. Ant. 1, 4 [p. 64, 17]; w. ὁμοίωσις Did., Gen. 56, 28) of a man (cp. Mitt-Wilck. I/2, 109, 11 [III BC] Philopator as εἰκὼν τοῦ Διός; Rosetta Stone=OGI 90, 3 [196 BC] Ptolemy V as εἰκὼν ζῶσα τοῦ Διός, cp. APF 1, 1901, 483, 11; Plut., Themist. 125 [27, 4]; Lucian, Pro Imag. 28 εἰκόνα θεοῦ τ. ἄνθρωπον εἶναι; Diog. L. 6, 51 τ. ἀγαθοὺς ἄνδρας θεῶν εἰκόνας εἶναι; Sextus 190; Herm. Wr. 1, 12 al.; Apuleius as image of God, Rtzst., Mysterienrel.[3] 43; JHehn, Zum Terminus 'Bild Gottes': ESachau Festschr. 1915, 36–52) **1 Cor 11:7** (on the gradation here cp. Herm. Wr. 11, 15a); of Christ (Helios as εἰκών of deity: Pla., Rep. 509; Proclus, Hymni 1, 33f [Orphica p. 277 Abel]; Herm. Wr. 11, 15; Stob. I 293, 21=454, 1ff Sc.; Hierocles 1, 418: the rest of the gods are εἰκόνες of the primeval god.—The Logos: Philo, Conf. Ling. 97; 147. Wisdom: Wsd 7:26) **2 Cor 4:4; Col 1:15** (εἰ. τοῦ θεοῦ ἐστιν ὁ υἱὸς αὐτοῦ ὁ μονογενής Did., Gen. 58, 3; cp. εἰκὼν γὰρ τοῦ . . . θεοῦ ὁ λόγος ἐστὶ αὐτοῦ Orig., C. Cels. 4, 85, 24.—EPreuschen, ZNW 18, 1918, 243).—εἰ. τοῦ χοϊκοῦ, τοῦ ἐπουρανίου *image of the earthly, heavenly* (human being) **1 Cor 15:49.** (See SMcCasland, The Image of God Acc. to Paul: JBL 69, '50, 85–100). The image corresponds to its original (cp. ὁμοίωμα 2ab; Doxopatres [XI AD]: Rhet. Gr. II 160, 1 εἰ. καὶ ὁμοίωμα διαφέρει; Mel., P. 36, 245 διὰ τῆς τυπικῆς εἰκόνος; 38, 262 τοῦ μέλλοντος ἐν αὐτῷ τὴν εἰκόνα βλέπεις and oft. in typological exegesis of the OT).

❸ **that which represents someth. else in terms of basic form and features,** ***form, appearance*** (Istros [III BC]: no. 334 fgm. 53 Jac. ἀνθρωποειδὴς εἰκών=a human figure; Artem. 1, 35 p. 36, 5 τὸ πρόσωπον κ. τὴν εἰκόνα=the face and the form; Ps.-Callisth. 2, 27; Hierocles 20, 465: to his followers Pythagoras has θείαν εἰκόνα=the appearance of a god; Cleopatra ln. 154 ἐτελειώθη ἡ εἰκὼν σώματι κ. ψυχῇ κ. πνεύματι; Herm. Wr. 1, 12 of the first human being, the son of the πατὴρ πάντων: τὴν τοῦ πατρὸς εἰκόνα ἔχων; 5, 6; En 106:10) ὁμοίωμα εἰκόνος φθαρτοῦ ἀνθρώπου *the likeness of mortal human form* **Ro 1:23** (MHooker, NTS 6, '60, 297–306). συμμόρφους τῆς εἰ. τοῦ υἱοῦ *conformed to the appearance of his Son* **8:29;** cp. **2 Cor 3:18;** εἰ. τ. πραγμάτων *form of things* in contrast to their σκιά **Hb 10:1.**—The infl. of Gen 1:26f is very strong (κατ' εἰκόνα θεοῦ; TestNapht 2:5; Tat. 12, 1 al.; Just., A I, 63, 16 εἰκόνος ἀσωμάτου. See AStruker, D. Gottesebenbildlichkeit d. Menschen in d. christl. Lit d. zwei erst. Jahrh. 1913). Humans made by God ἐκ τῆς ἰδίας εἰ. *in God's own form* Dg 10:2; cp. τῆς ἑαυτοῦ εἰ. χαρακτήρ 1 Cl 33:4; cp. vs. 5; B 5:5; 6:12. Gen 1:27 also infl. **Col 3:10:** the new human is made new κατ' εἰκόνα τοῦ κτίσαντος αὐτόν. (Philo, Leg. All. 3, 96, in Platonic fashion, expresses the thought that first of all an image proceeded fr. God, which, in turn, served as a model for humans; against this view s. FEltester, Eikon im NT, '58, 157).—EKäsemann, Leib u. Leib Christi: Beiträge zur hist. Theol. 9, '33, 81–88, 147–50; J Bover, 'Imaginis' notio apud B. Paulum: Biblica 4, 1923, 174–79; HWillms, Εἰκών I '35; ESelwyn, Image, Fact and Faith: NTS 1, '55, 235–47; GLadner, RAC IV, '59, 771–86 (lit.); JJervell, Imago Dei (Genesis, late Judaism, Gnosis, NT) FRLANT no. 58, '60; KPrümm, Verbum Domini 40, '62, 232–57 (Paul); ELarsson, Christus als Vorbild, '62.—DELG s.v. ἔοικα. M-M. EDNT. TW. Spicq. Sv.

εἰλάμην s. αἱρέομαι.

εἰλευθέρωσεν s. ἐλευθερόω.

εἰλέω fut. 2 sg. εἰλήσεις (Job 40:26 A Vat); 1 aor. εἴλησα (4 Km 2:8); pf. pass ptc. εἰλημένος (LXX) (Hippocr.: CMG I/1 p. 97, 14; Lycophron vs. 1202 ἐν σπαργάνοις εἰλημένον et al.; Hesych.; TestSol) ***wrap*** τινί *in someth.* (cp. Is 11:5) GPt 6:24 acc. to the mss. (s. ἐνειλέω; the same variation in Herodian 2, 1, 1 with v.l.).—DELG s.v. εἰλέω 1.

εἴλημμαι, εἴληπται, εἴληφα s. λαμβάνω.

εἰλικρίνεια, ας, ἡ (also εἰλικρινία s. W-S. §5, 13c; Mlt-H. 100; 348. Since Aristot. et al.; POxy 1252 verso II, 38; PAberd 52, 8; Wsd 7:25 v.l.; fr. εἰλικρινής) **the quality or state of being free of dissimulation,** ***sincerity, purity of motive*** w. ἀλήθεια **1 Cor 5:8.** ἐξ εἰλικρινείας *out of pure motives* **2 Cor 2:17;** (w. ἁπλότης; v.l. ἁγιότης) ἐν εἰ. τοῦ θεοῦ *in godly sincerity* **1:12.**—M-M. TW. Spicq.

εἰλικρινής, ές, gen. **οῦς** (s. εἰλικρίνεια; the etym. 'judge in the light of the sun' is dubious, s. Boisacq 223, n. 1 and Chantraine, DELG 320; Hippocr., X., Pla. et al.; Sb 7684, 3f; Wsd 7:25; Philo; Jos., Ant. 19, 321) gener. 'unmixed, without alloy', then in moral sense **pert. to being sincere, without hidden motives or pretense,** ***pure*** (so Pla., Phd. 66a εἰλικρινεῖ τῇ διανοίᾳ χρώμενος [cp. Just. D. 4, 1]; 81c ψυχὴ εἰ.; Ael. Aristid. 13 p. 158 D.; OGI 227, 12; 763, 40; TestBenj 6:5), *sincere* w. ἀπρόσκοπος **Phil 1:10.** W. ἀκέραιος 1 Cl 2:5; εἰ. διάνοια *pure mind* (s. Plato above) **2 Pt 3:1;** καρδία 2 Cl 9:8.—Frisk. M-M. TW. Spicq.

εἰλικρινῶς adv. of εἰλικρινής (Pla.; Epict. 4, 2, 6; OGI 441, 5; Michel 394, 48; Philo; Albinos, Didasc. 11; Ath., R. 54, 28) ***sincerely, candidly*** κατανοεῖν *consider* 1 Cl 32:1.

εἰλίσσω s. ἑλίσσω.

εἷλκον, εἵλκυσα s. ἕλκω.

εἵλκωμαι s. ἑλκόομαι.

εἱλόμην s. αἱρέω.

εἰμί (Hom.+) impv. ἴσθι, ἔσο IPol 4:1, ἔστω—also colloq. ἤτω (BGU 276, 24; 419, 13; POxy 533, 9; Ps 103:31; 1 Macc 10:31) **1 Cor 16:22; Js 5:12;** 1 Cl 48:5; Hv 3, 3, 4;—3 pers. pl. ἔστωσαν (ins since 200 BC Meisterhans[3]-Schw. 191; PPetr III, 2, 22 [237 BC]) **Lk 12:35; 1 Ti 3:12;** GJs 7:2. Inf. εἶναι. Impf. 1 pers. only mid. ἤμην (Jos., Bell. 1, 389; 631; s. further below); ἦν only **Ac 20:18** D, 2 pers. ἦσθα (Jos., Ant. 6, 104) **Mt 26:69; Mk 14:67** and ἦς (Lobeck, Phryn. 149 'say ἦσθα'; Jos., Ant. 17, 110 al.; Sb 6262, 16 [III AD]) **Mt 25:21, 23** al., 3 sg. ἦν, 1 pl. ἦμεν. Beside this the mid. form ἤμην (pap since III BC; Job 29:16; Tob 12:13 BA), s. above, gives the pl. ἤμεθα (pap since III BC; Bar 1:19) **Mt 23:30; Ac 27:37; Eph 2:3.** Both forms in succession **Gal. 4:3.** Fut. ἔσομαι, ptc. ἐσόμενος. The mss. vary in choice of act. or mid., but like the edd. lean toward the mid. (W-S. §14, 1; Mlt-H. 201–3; Rob. index; B-D-F §98; Rdm.[2] 99; 101f; Helbing 108f; Reinhold 86f). Also s. ἔνι.

❶ ***be, exist, be on hand*** a pred. use (for other pred. use s. 3a, 4, 5, 6, 7): of God (Epicurus in Diog. L. 10, 123 θεοί εἰσιν; Zaleucus in Diod. S. 12, 20, 2 θεοὺς εἶναι; Wsd 12:13; Just., D. 128, 4 angels) ἔστιν ὁ θεός *God exists* **Hb 11:6;** cp. **1 Cor 8:5.** ὁ ὢν καὶ ὁ ἦν *the one who is and who was* (cp. SibOr 3, 16; as amulet PMich 155, 3 [II AD] ὁ ὢν θεὸς ὁ Ἰάω κύριος παντοκράτωρ=the god . . . who exists.) **Rv 11:17; 16:5.** ὁ ὢν καὶ ὁ ἦν καὶ ὁ ἐρχόμενος, in this and the two preceding passages ἦν is treated as a ptc. (for the unusual use of ἦν cp. Simonides 74 D.: ἦν ἑκατὸν φιάλαι) **1:4; 4:8** (cp. Ex 3:14;

Wsd 13:1; Paus. 10, 12, 10 Ζεὺς ἦν, Ζ. ἔστι, Ζ. ἔσσεται; cp. Theosophien 18. S. OWeinreich, ARW 19, 1919, 178f). οὐδ᾽ εἶναι θεὸν παντοκράτορα AcPlCor 1:11. ἐγώ εἰμι (ins in the Athena-Isis temple of Saïs in Plut., Is. et Os. 9, 354c: ἐγώ εἰμι πᾶν τὸ γεγονὸς κ. ὂν κ. ἐσόμενον. On the role of Isis in Gk. rel. s. IBergman, Ich bin Isis '68; RMerkelbach, Isis Regina—Zeus Sarapis '95; for further lit. s. MGustafson in: Prayer fr. Alexander to Constantine, ed. MKiley et al. '97, 158.) **Rv 1:8** (s. ἐγώ beg.). ὁ ὤν, . . . θεός **Ro 9:5** is classed here and taken to mean Christ by JWordsworth ad loc. and HWarner, JTS 48, '47, 203f. Of the λόγος: ἐν ἀρχῇ ἦν ὁ λ. **J 1:1** (for ἦν cp. Herm. Wr. 1, 4; 3, 1b ἦν σκότος, fgm. IX 1 p. 422, 23 Sc. γέγονεν ἡ ὕλη καὶ ἦν).—Of Christ πρὶν Ἀβραὰμ γενέσθαι, ἐγὼ εἰμί *before Abraham was born, I am* **8:58** (on the pres. εἰμί cp. Parmenides 8, 5: of the Eternal we cannot say ἦν οὐδ᾽ ἔσται, only ἔστιν; Ammonius Hermiae [Comm. in Aristotl. IV 5 ed. ABusse 1897] 6 p. 172: in Timaeus we read that we must not say of the gods τὸ ἦν ἢ τὸ ἔσται μεταβολῆς τινος ὄντα σημαντικά, μόνον δὲ τὸ ἔστι='was' or 'will be', suggesting change, but only 'is'; Ps 89:2; DBall, 'I Am' in John's Gospel [JSNT Suppl. 124] '96).—Of the world πρὸ τοῦ τὸν κόσμον εἶναι *before the world existed* **17:5.** Satirically, of the beast, who parodies the Lamb, ἦν καὶ οὐκ ἔστιν **Rv 17:8.** Of God's temple: ἔστιν B 16:6f *it exists.* τὸ μὴ ὄν *that which does not exist, the unreal* (Sallust. 17 p. 32, 7 and 9; Philo, Aet. M. 5; 82) Hm 1:1. τὰ ὄντα *that which exists* contrasted w. τὰ μὴ ὄντα **Ro 4:17;** cp. **1 Cor 1:28;** 2 Cl 1:8. Of God κτίσας ἐκ τοῦ μὴ ὄντος τὰ ὄντα *what is out of what is not* Hv 1, 1, 6 (on the contrast τὰ ὄντα and τὰ μὴ ὄντα cp. Ps.-Arist. on Xenophanes: fgm. 21, 28; Artem. 1, 51 p. 49, 19 τὰ μὴ ὄντα ὡς ὄντα; Ocellus Luc. 12; Sallust. 17, 5 p. 30, 28–32, 12; Philo, Op. M. 81; PGM 4, 3077f ποιήσαντα τὰ πάντα ἐξ ὧν οὐκ ὄντων εἰς τὸ εἶναι; 13, 272f τὸν ἐκ μὴ ὄντων εἶναι ποιήσαντα καὶ ἐξ ὄντων μὴ εἶναι; Theoph. Ant. 1, 4 [p. 64, 21] τὰ πάντα ὁ θεὸς ἐποίησεν ἐξ οὐκ ὄντων εἰς τὸ εἶναι).—Of existing in the sense *be present, available, provided* πολλοῦ ὄχλου ὄντος *since a large crowd was present* **Mk 8:1.** ὄντων τῶν προσφερόντων *those are provided who offer* **Hb 8:4.** οὔπω ἦν πνεῦμα *the Spirit had not yet come* **J 7:39.** ἀκούσας ὄντα σιτία *when he heard that grain was available* **Ac 7:12.**—Freq. used to introduce parables and stories *(once) there was:* ἄνθρωπός τις ἦν πλούσιος *there was (once) a rich man* **Lk 16:1, 19.** ἦν ἄνθρωπος ἐκ τ. Φαρισαίων *there was a man among the Pharisees* **J 3:1.**—*There is, there are* ὥσπερ εἰσὶν θεοὶ πολλοί *as there are many gods* **1 Cor 8:5.** διαιρέσεις χαρισμάτων εἰσίν *there are various kinds of spiritual gifts* **12:4ff; 1J 5:16** al. Neg. οὐκ ἔστι *there is (are) not, no* (Ps 52:2; Simplicius in Epict. p. 95, 42 as a quot. from 'tragedy' οὐκ εἰσὶν θεοί) δίκαιος *there is no righteous man* **Ro 3:10** (Eccl 7:20). ἀνάστασις νεκρῶν οὐκ ἔστιν *there is no resurr. of the dead* **1 Cor 15:12;** οὐδ᾽ εἶναι ἀνάστασιν AcPlCor 1:12; 2:24; cp. **Mt 22:23; Ac 23:8** (cp. 2 Macc 7:14). εἰσὶν οἵ, or οἵτινες *there are people who* (Hom. et al.; LXX; Just., D. 47, 2 εἰ μήτι εἰσὶν οἱ λέγοντες ὅτι etc.—W. sing. and pl. combined: Arrian, Ind. 24, 9 ἔστι δὲ οἳ διέφυγον=but there are some who escaped) **Mt 16:28; 19:12; Mk 9:1; Lk 9:27; J 6:64; Ac 11:20.** Neg. οὐδείς ἐστιν ὅς *there is no one who* **Mk 9:39; 10:29; Lk 1:61; 18:29.** As a question τίς ἐστιν ὅς; *who is there that?* **Mt 12:11**—In an unusual (perh. bureaucratic terminology) participial construction **Ac 13:1** ἡ οὖσα ἐκκλησία *the congregation there* (cp. Ps.-Pla., Eryx. 6, 394c οἱ ὄντες ἄνθρωποι=the people with whom he has to deal; PLond III 1168, 5 p. 136 [18 AD] ἐπὶ ταῖς οὔσαις γειτνίαις=on the adjoining areas there; PGen 49; PSI 229, 11 τοῦ ὄντος μηνός of the current month); cp. **14:13.**—αἱ οὖσαι (sc. ἐξουσίαι) *those that exist* **Ro 13:1** (cp. UPZ 180a I, 4 [113 BC] ἐφ᾽ ἱερέων καὶ ἱερειῶν τῶν ὄντων καὶ οὐσῶν).

❷ to be in close connection (with), *is,* freq. in statements of identity or equation, as a copula, the equative function, uniting subject and predicate. On absence of the copula, Mlt-Turner 294–310.

ⓐ gener. πραΰς εἰμι *I am gentle* **Mt 11:29.** ἐγώ εἰμι Γαβριήλ **Lk 1:19.** σὺ εἶ ὁ υἱὸς τοῦ θεοῦ **Mk 3:11; J 1:49** and very oft. ἵνα . . . ὁ πονηρὸς . . . ἐλεγχθῇ [το? s. app. in Bodm.] μὴ ὢν θεός AcPlCor 2:15 (Just., D. 3, 3 φιλολόγος οὖν τις εἶ σύ).—The pred. can be supplied fr. the context: καὶ ἐσμέν *and we are* (really God's children) **1J 3:1** (Eur., Ion 309 τ. θεοῦ καλοῦμαι δοῦλος εἰμί τε. Dio Chrys. 14 [31], 58 θεοφιλεῖς οἱ χρηστοὶ λέγονται καὶ εἰσίν; Epict. 2, 16, 44 Ἡρακλῆς ἐπιστεύθη Διὸς υἱὸς εἶναι καὶ ἦν.—The ptc. ὤν, οὖσα, ὄν used w. a noun or adj.and serving as an if-, since-, or although-clause sim. functions as a copula πονηροὶ ὄντες **Mt 7:11; 12:34.—Lk 20:36; J 3:4; 4:9; Ac 16:21; Ro 5:10; 1 Cor 8:7; Gal 2:3** al.).—W. adv. of quality: οὕτως εἶναι *be so* preceded by ὥσπερ, καθώς or followed by ὡς, ὥσπερ **Mt 13:40; 24:27, 37, 39; Mk 4:26; Lk 17:26.** W. dat. of pers. οὕτως ἔσται ὁ υἱὸς τ. ἀ. τῇ γενεᾷ ταύτῃ *so the Human One (Son of Man) will be for this generation* **11:30.** εἰμὶ ὡς/ὥσπερ *I am like* **Mt 6:5; Lk 18:11.** W. dat. ἔστω σοι ὥσπερ τελώνης *he shall be to you as a tax-collector* **Mt 18:17.** εἰμὶ ὥς τις *I am like someone* of outward and inward similarity **28:3; Lk 6:40; 11:44; 22:27** al. καθώς εἰμι *as I am* **Ac 22:3; 1J 3:2, 7; 4:17.**—W. demonstr. pron. (Just., A I, 16, 1 ἃ ἔφη, ταῦτά ἐστι: foll. by a quotation; sim. 48, 5 ἔστι δὲ ταῦτα; and oft.) τὰ ὀνόματά ἐστιν ταῦτα **Mt 10:2.** αὕτη ἐστὶν ἡ μαρτυρία **J 1:19.** W. inf. foll. θρησκεία αὕτη ἐστίν, ἐπισκέπτεσθαι **Js 1:27.** W. ὅτι foll. αὕτη ἐστὶν ἡ κρίσις, ὅτι τὸ φῶς ἐλήλυθεν **J 3:19;** cp. **21:24; 1J 1:5; 3:11; 5:11.** W. ἵνα foll. τοῦτό ἐστιν τὸ ἔργον, ἵνα πιστεύητε **J 6:29;** cp. vs. **39f; 15:12; 17:3; 1J 3:11, 23; 5:3.** W. τηλικοῦτος: τὰ πλοῖα, τηλικαῦτα ὄντα *though they are so large* **Js 3:4.** W. τοσοῦτος: τοσούτων ὄντων *although there were so many* **J 21:11.** W. τοιοῦτος: τοιοῦτος ὢν **Phlm 9** (cp. Just., A I, 18, 4 ὅσα ἄλλα τοιαῦτά ἐστι).—W. interrog. pron. ὑμεῖς τίνα με λέγετε εἶναι; *who do you say I am?* **Mt 16:15;** cp. **21:10; Mk 1:24; 4:41; 8:27, 29; Lk 4:34** al.; σὺ τίς εἶ; **J 1:19; 8:25; 21:12** al. (cp. JosAs 14:6 τίς εἶ συ tell me 'who you are'). σὺ τίς εἶ ὁ κρίνων; (Pla., Gorg. 452b; Strabo 6, 2, 4 σὺ τίς εἶ ὁ τὸν Ὅμηρον ψέγων ὡς μυθογράφον;) **Ro 14:4;** ἐγὼ τίς ἤμην; (cp. Ex 3:11) **Ac 11:17;** τίς εἰμι ἐγὼ ὅτι *who am I, that* GJs 12:2 (Ex 3:11). W. πόσος: πόσος χρόνος ἐστίν; *how long a time?* **Mk 9:21.** W. ποταπός *of what sort* **Lk 1:29.**—W. relative pron. οἷος **2 Cor 10:11;** ὁποῖος **Ac 26:29; 1 Cor 3:13; Gal 2:6;** ὅς **Rv 1:19;** ὅστις **Gal 5:10, 19.**—W. numerals ἦσαν οἱ φαγόντες πεντακισχίλιοι ἄνδρες **6:44** (cp. Polyaenus 7, 25 ἦσαν οἱ πεσόντες ἀνδρῶν μυριάδες δέκα); cp. **Ac 19:7; 23:13.** Λάζαρος εἷς ἦν ἐκ τῶν ἀνακειμένων *L. was one of those at the table* **J 12:2;** cp. **Gal 3:20; Js 2:19.** τῶν πιστευσάντων ἦν καρδία καὶ ψυχὴ μία **Ac 4:32.** εἷς εἶναι *be one and the same* **Gal 3:28.** ἓν εἶναι *be one* **J 10:30; 17:11, 21ff; 1 Cor 3:8.**—οὐδ᾽ εἶναι τὴν πλάσιν τὴν τῶν ἀνθρώπων τοῦ θεοῦ *(that) the creation of humankind is not God's doing* AcPlCor 1:13.—To establish identity the formula ἐγώ εἰμι is oft. used in the gospels (corresp. to Hebr. אֲנִי הוּא Dt 32:39; Is 43:10), in such a way that the predicate must be understood fr. the context: **Mt 14:27; Mk 6:50; 13:6; 14:62; Lk 22:70; J 4:26; 6:20; 8:24, 28; 13:19; 18:5f** and oft.; s. on ἐγώ.—In a question μήτι ἐγώ εἰμι; *surely it is not I?* **Mt 26:22, 25.**

ⓑ to describe a special connection betw. the subject and a predicate noun ἡμεῖς ναὸς θεοῦ ἐσμεν ζῶντος *we are a temple of the living God* **2 Cor 6:16.** ἡ ἐπιστολὴ ὑμεῖς ἐστε *you are our letter (of recommendation)* **3:2.** σφραγίς μου τῆς ἀποστολῆς ὑμεῖς ἐστε *you are the seal of my apostleship* **1 Cor 9:2** and oft.

ⓒ in explanations:—**α.** to show how someth. is to be understood *is a representation of, is the equivalent of;* εἰμί here, too, serves as copula; we usually translate *mean,* so in the formula τοῦτ᾽ ἔστιν *this* or *that means, that is to say* (Epict., Ench. 33, 10; Arrian, Tact. 29, 3; SIG 880, 50; PFlor 157, 4; PSI 298, 9; PMert 91, 9; Jos., C. Ap. 2, 16; ApcMos 19; Just., D. 56, 23; 78, 3 al.) **Mk 7:2; Ac 19:4; Ro 7:18; 9:8; 10:6, 8; Phlm 12; Hb 7:5** al.; in the sense *that is (when translated)* (Polyaenus 8, 14, 1 Μάξιμος ἀνηγορεύθη· τοῦτο δ᾽ ἂν εἴη Μέγιστον) **Mt 27:46; Ac 1:19.** So also w. relative pron.: ὅ ἐστιν **Mk 3:17; 7:11, 34; Hb 7:2.** After verbs of asking, recognizing, knowing and not knowing (Antiphanes Com. 231, 1f τὸ ζῆν τί ἐστι;) μάθετε τί ἐστιν *learn what (this) means* **Mt 9:13.** εἰ ἐγνώκειτε τί ἐστιν **12:7;** cp. **Mk 1:27; 9:10; Lk 20:17; J 16:17f; Eph 4:9.** W. an indir. question (Stephan. Byz. s.v. Ἀγύλλα: τὶς ἠρώτα τί ἂν εἴη τὸ ὄνομα) τί ἂν εἴη ταῦτα **Lk 15:26;** τί εἴη τοῦτο **18:36.** τίνα θέλει ταῦτα εἶναι *what this means* **Ac 17:20;** cp. **2:12,** where the question is not about the mng. of terms but the significance of what is happening.—Esp. in interpr. of the parables (Artem. 1, 51 p. 48, 26 ἄρουρα οὐδὲν ἄλλο ἐστὶν ἢ γυνή=field means nothing else than woman) ὁ ἀγρός ἐστιν ὁ κόσμος *the field means the world* **Mt 13:38;** cp. vss. **19f, 22f; Mk 4:15f, 18, 20; Lk 8:11ff** (cp. Gen 41:26f; Ezk 37:11; Ath. 22, 4 [Stoic interpr. of myths]). On τοῦτό ἐστιν τὸ σῶμά μου **Mt 26:26; Mk 14:22; Lk 22:19** and its various interpretations, see lit. s.v. εὐχαριστία. Cp. Hipponax (VI BC) 45 Diehl αὕτη γάρ ἐστι συμφορή=this means misfortune.

β. to be of relative significance, be of moment or importance, amount to someth. w. indef. pron. εἰδωλόθυτόν τί ἐστιν *meat offered to idols means anything* **1 Cor 10:19.** Esp. εἰμί τι *I mean someth.* of pers. **1 Cor 3:7; Gal 2:6; 6:3;** and of things vs. **15.** εἰμί τις **Ac 5:36.**—Of no account ἐμοὶ εἰς ἐλάχιστόν ἐστιν (telescoped fr. ἐλάχ. ἐστιν and εἰς ἐλάχ. γίνεται, of which there are many exx. in Schmid, I 398; II 161, 237; III 281; IV 455) *it is of little or no importance to me* **1 Cor 4:3.**

❸ **be in reference to location, persons, condition, or time, *be*—ⓐ** of various relations or positions involving a place or thing: w. ἀπό: εἶναι ἀπό τινος *be* or *come from a certain place* (X., An. 2, 4, 13) **J 1:44.**—W. ἐν: ἐν τοῖς τ. πατρός μου *in my father's house* **Lk 2:49** (cp. Jos., Ant. 16, 302 καταγωγὴ ἐν τοῖς Ἀντιπάτρου). ἐν τῇ ὁδῷ *on the way* **Mk 10:32.** ἐν τῇ ἐρήμῳ **Mt 24:26.** ἐν ἀγρῷ **Lk 15:25.** ἐν δεξιᾷ τ. θεοῦ *at God's right hand* **Ro 8:34;** in heaven **Eph 6:9.**—W. εἰς: τὴν κοίτην **Lk 11:7;** τὸν κόλπον **J1:18.**—W. ἐπί w. gen. *be on someth.* of place, roof **Lk 17:31;** head **J 20:7** (cp. 1 Macc 1:59); also fig., of one who *is over someone* (1 Macc 10:69; Jdth 14:13 ὁ ὢν ἐπὶ πάντων τῶν αὐτοῦ) **Ro 9:5** (of the angel of death Mel., P. 20, 142 ἐπὶ τῶν πρωτοτόκων); also ἐπάνω τινός **J 3:31.**—W. dat. *be at someth.* the door **Mt 24:33; Mk 13:29.**—W. acc. *be on someone:* grace **Lk 2:40; Ac 4:33;** spirit (Is 61:1) **Lk 2:25;** εἶναι ἐπὶ τὸ αὐτό *be in the same place, together* (Gen 29:2 v.l.) **Ac 1:15; 2:1, 44; 1 Cor 7:5.**—W. κατά w. acc. εἶναι κατὰ τὴν Ἰουδαίαν *be in Judea* **Ac 11:1;** εἶναι ἐν Ἀντιοχείᾳ κατὰ τὴν οὖσαν ἐκκλησίαν *were at Antioch in the congregation there* **13:1.**—W. ὑπό w. acc. τι or τινα of place *be under someth.* **J 1:48; 1 Cor 10:1.**—W. παρά w. acc. παρὰ τὴν θάλασσαν *by the sea-* (i.e. *lake-*) *shore* **Mk 5:21; Ac 10:6.**—W. πρός τι *be close to, facing someth.* **Mk 4:1.**—W. adv. of place ἐγγύς τινι *near someth.* **Ac 9:38; 27:8.** μακρὰν (ἀπό) **Mk 12:34; J 21:8; Eph 2:13;** also πόρρω **Lk 14:32.** χωρίς τινος *without someth.* **Hb 12:8.** ἐνθάδε **Ac 16:28.** ἔσω **J 20:26.** ἀπέναντί τινος **Ro 3:18** (Ps 35:2). ἐκτός τινος **1 Cor 6:18;** ἀντίπερά τινος **Lk 8:26;** ὁμοῦ **J 21:2;** οὗ **Mt 2:9;** ὅπου **Mk 2:4; 5:40.** ὧδε **Mt 17:4; Mk 9:5; Lk 9:33.** Also w. fut. mng. (ESchwartz, GGN 1908, 161 n.; on the fut. use of the pres. cp. POxy 531, 22 [II AD] ἔστι δὲ τοῦ Τῦβι μηνὸς σοὶ ὃ θέλεις) ὅπου εἰμί **J 7:34, 36; 12:26; 14:3; 17:24.** As pred., to denote a relatively long stay at a place, *stay, reside* ἴσθι ἐκεῖ *stay there* **Mt 2:13,** cp. vs. **15;** ἐπ᾽ ἐρήμοις τόποις in *lonely places* **Mk 1:45;** ἦν παρὰ τὴν θάλασσαν *he stayed by the lakeside* **5:21.**

ⓑ involving humans or transcendent beings: w. adv. ἔμπροσθέν τινος **Lk 14:2.** ἔναντί τινος **Ac 8:21;** ἐνώπιόν τινος **Lk 14:10; Ac 4:19; 1 Pt 3:4; Rv 7:15;** ἐντός τινος **Lk 17:21;** ἐγγύς τινος **J 11:18; 19:20; Ro 10:8** (Dt 30:14).—W. prep. ἐν τινί equiv. to ἔκ τινος εἶναι *be among* **Mt 27:56;** cp. **Mk 15:40; Ro 1:6.** Of God, who is among his people **1 Cor 14:25** (Is 45:14; Jer 14:9); of the Spirit **J 14:17.** Of persons under Christ's direction: ἐν θεῷ **1J 2:5; 5:20** (s. Norden, Agn. Th. 23, 1). ἔν τινι *rest upon, arise from someth.* (Aristot., Pol. 7, 1, 3 [1323b, 1] ἐν ἀρετῇ; Sir 9:16) **Ac 4:12; 1 Cor 2:5; Eph 5:18.**—εἴς τινα *be directed, inclined toward* **Ac 23:30; 2 Cor 7:15; 1 Pt 1:21.**—κατά w. gen. *be against someone* (Sir 6:12) **Mt 12:30; Mk 9:40** and **Lk 9:50** (both opp. ὑπέρ); **Gal 5:23.**—σύν τινι *be with someone* (Jos., Ant. 7, 181) **Lk 22:56; 24:44; Ac 13:7;** *accompany, associate w. someone* **Lk 8:38; Ac 4:13; 22:9;** *take sides with someone* (X., Cyr. 5, 4, 37; 7, 5, 77; Jos., Ant. 11, 259 [of God]) **Ac 14:4.**—πρός τινα *be with someone* **Mt 13:56; Mk 6:3; J 1:1f.** *I am to be compared w.* IMg 12.—μετά and gen. *be with someone* (Judg 14:11) **Mt 17:17; Mk 3:14; 5:18; J 3:26; 12:17;** ἔστω μεθ᾽ ὑμῶν εἰρήνη AcPlCor 2:40; of God, who *is with someone* (Gen 21:20; Judg 6:13 al.; Philo, Det. Pot. Ins. 4; Jos., Ant. 6, 181; 15, 138) **Lk 1:66; J 3:2; 8:29; Ac 10:38** al.; also *be with* in the sense *be favorable to, in league with* (Ex 23:2) **Mt 12:30; Lk 11:23;** of punishment attending a pers. τὸ πῦρ ἐστι μετ᾽ αὐτοῦ AcPlCor 2:37.—παρά and gen. *come from someone* (X., An. 2, 4, 15; Just., D. 8, 4 ἔλεος παρὰ θεοῦ) fr. God **J 6:46; 7:29;** w. dat. *be with, among* persons **Mt 22:25; Ac 10:6.** W. neg. *be strange to someone, there is no . . . in someone* **Ro 2:11; 9:14; Eph 6:9.**—ὑπέρ w. gen. *be on one's side* **Mk 9:4** and **Lk 9:50** (both opp. κατά); w. acc. *be superior to* (Sir 25:10; 30:16) **Lk 6:40.**

ⓒ of condition or circumstance: κατά w. acc. *live in accordance with* (Sir 28:10; 43:8; 2 Macc 9:20) κατὰ σάκρα, πνεῦμα **Ro 8:5.** οὐκ ἔστιν κατὰ ἄνθρωπον *not human* (in origin) **Gal 1:11.**—Fig. ὑπό w. acc. *be under* (the power of) someth. **Ro 3:9; 6:14f; Gal 3:10, 25.**—W. ἐν of existing ἐν τῷ θεῷ εἶναι of humankind: have its basis of existence in God **Ac 17:28.** Of states of being: ἐν δόξῃ **2 Cor 3:8;** ἐν εἰρήνῃ **Lk 11:21;** ἐν ἔχθρᾳ *at enmity* **23:12;** ἐν κρίματι *under condemnation* vs. **40.** ἐν ῥύσει αἵματος *suffer from hemorrhages* **Mk 5:25; Lk 8:43** (cp. Soph., Aj. 271 ἦν ἐν τῇ νόσῳ; cp. TestJob 35:1 ἐν πληγαῖς πολλαῖς). Periphrastically for an adj. ἐν ἐξουσίᾳ *authoritative* **Lk 4:32.** ἐν βάρει *important* **1 Th 2:7.** ἐν τῇ πίστει *true believers, believing* **2 Cor 13:5.** Be involved in someth. ἐν ἑορτῇ *be at the festival*=take part in it **J 2:23.** ἐν τούτοις ἴσθι *devote yourself to these things* **1 Ti 4:15** (cp. X., Hell. 4, 8, 7 ἐν τοιούτοις ὄντες=occupied w. such things; Jos., Ant. 2, 346 ἐν ὕμνοις ἦσαν=they occupied themselves w. the singing of hymns).—Fig., *live* in the light **1J 2:9;** cp. vs. **11; 1 Th 5:4;** in the flesh **Ro 7:5; 8:8;** AcPlCor 1:6. ἐν οἷς εἰμι *in the situation in which I find myself* **Phil 4:11** (X., Hell. 4, 2, 1; Diod. S. 12, 63, 5; 12, 66, 4; Appian, Hann. 55 §228 ἐν τούτοις ἦν=he was in this situation; Jos., Ant. 7, 232 ἐν τούτοις ἦσαν=found themselves in this sit.; TestJob 35:6 ἐν τίνι ἐστίν; s. ZPE VIII 170). ἐν πολλοῖς ὢν ἀστοχήμασι AcPlCor 2:1. Of characteristics, emotions, etc. ἔν τινί ἐστιν, e.g. ἀδικία **J 7:18;** ἄγνοια **Eph 4:18;** ἀλήθεια **J 8:44; 2 Cor 11:10** (cp. 1 Macc 7:18); ἁμαρτία **1J 3:5.**

ⓓ of time ἐγγύς of καιρός *be near* **Mt 26:18; Mk 13:28.** πρὸς ἑσπέραν ἐστίν *it is toward evening* **Lk 24:29** (Just., D. 137, 4 πρὸς δυσμὰς . . . ὁ ἥλιός ἐστι).

❹ **to be alive in a period of time,** ***live,*** denoting temporal existence (Hom., trag., Thu. et al.; Sir 42:21; En 102:5 Philo, De Jos. 17; Jos., Ant. 7, 254) εἰ ἤμεθα ἐν ταῖς ἡμέραις τῶν πατέρων ἡμῶν *if we had lived in the days of our fathers* **Mt 23:30.** ὅτι οὐκ εἰσὶν *because they were no more* **2:18** (Jer 38:15). ἦσαν ἐπὶ χρόνον ἱκανόν (those who were healed and raised by Christ) *remained alive for quite some time* Qua.

❺ **to be the time at which someth. takes place** w. indications of specific moments or occasions, ***be*** (X., Hell. 4, 5, 1, An. 4, 3, 8; Sus 13 Theod.; 1 Macc 6:49; 2 Macc 8:26; Jos., Ant. 6, 235 νουμηνία δ' ἦν; 11, 251): ἦν ὥρα ἕκτη *it was the sixth hour* (=noon acc. to Jewish reckoning) **Lk 23:44; J 4:6; 19:14.—Mk 15:25; J 1:39.** ἦν ἑσπέρα ἤδη *it was already evening* **Ac 4:3.** πρωΐ **J 18:28.** ἦν παρασκευή **Mk 15:42.** ἦν ἑορτὴ τῶν Ἰουδαίων **J 5:1.** σάββατόν ἐστιν vs. **10** et al. Short clauses (as Polyaenus 4, 9, 2 νὺξ ἦν; 7, 44, 2 πόλεμος ἦν; exc. 36, 8 ἦν ἀρίστου ὥρα; Jos., Ant. 19, 248 ἔτι δὲ νὺξ ἦν) χειμὼν ἦν **J 10:22;** ἦν δὲ νύξ (sim. Jos., Bell. 4, 64) **13:30;** ψύχος *it was cold* **18:18;** καύσων ἔσται *it will be hot* **Lk 12:55.**

❻ **to take place as a phenomenon or event,** ***take place, occur, become, be, be in*** (Hom., Thu. et al.; LXX; En 104:5; 106:6.—Cp. Just., D. 82, 2 of Christ's predictions ὅπερ καὶ ἔστι 'which is in fact the case'.) ἔσται θόρυβος τοῦ λαοῦ *a popular uprising* **Mk 14:2.** γογγυσμὸς ἦν *there was* (much) *muttering* **J 7:12.** σχίσμα *there was a division* **9:16; 1 Cor 1:10; 12:25.** ἔριδες . . . εἰσίν *quarrels are going on* **1:11.** δεῖ αἱρέσεις εἶναι **11:19.** θάνατος, πένθος, κραυγή, πόνος ἔσται **Rv 21:4.** ἔσονται λιμοὶ κ. σεισμοί **Mt 24:7.** Hence τὸ ἐσόμενον *what was going to happen* (Sir 48:25) **Lk 22:49.** πότε ταῦτα ἔσται; *when will this happen?* **Mt 24:3.** πῶς ἔσται τοῦτο; *how can this be?* **Lk 1:34.** Hebraistically (הָיָה; s. KBeyer, Semitische Syntax im NT, '62, 63–65) καὶ ἔσται w. fut. of another verb foll. *and it will come about that* **Ac 2:17** (Jo 3:1); **3:23** (w. δέ); **Ro 9:26** (Hos 2:1).—W. dat. ἐστί τινι *happen, be granted, come, to someone* (X., An. 2, 1, 10; Jos., Ant. 11, 255; Just., D. 8, 4 σοὶ . . . ἔλεος ἔσται παρὰ θεοῦ) **Mt 16:22; Mk 11:24; Lk 2:10;** GJs 1:1; 4:3; 8:3; τί ἐστίν σοι τοῦτο, ὅτι *what is the matter with you, that* GJs 17:2.—Of becoming or turning into someth. *become someth.* εἰς χολὴν πικρίας εἶναι *become bitter gall* **Ac 8:23.** εἰς σάρκα μίαν **Mt 19:5; Mk 10:8; 1 Cor 6:16; Eph 5:31** (all Gen 2:24. Cp. Syntipas p. 42, 24 οὐκ ἔτι ἔσομαι μετὰ σοῦ εἰς γυναῖκα); τὰ σκολιὰ εἰς εὐθείας **Lk 3:5** (Is 40:4); εἰς πατέρα **2 Cor 6:18; Hb 1:5** (2 Km 7:14; 1 Ch 22:10; 28:6); εἰς τὸ ἕν **1J 5:8.**—*Serve as someth.* (IPriene 50, 39 [c. II BC] εἶναι εἰς φυλακὴν τ. πόλεως; Aesop., Fab. 28 H.=18 P.; 26 Ch.; 18 H-H. εἰς ὠφέλειαν; Gen 9:13; s. also εἰς 4d) **1 Cor 14:22; Col 2:22; Js 5:3.**—Of something being ἀνεκτότερον ἔσται *it will be more tolerable* τινί *for someone* **Lk 10:12, 14.**

❼ **to exist as possibility** ἔστιν w. inf. foll. ***it is possible, one can*** (Περὶ ὕψους 6; Diog. L. 1, 110 ἔστιν εὑρεῖν=one can find; Just., A I, 59, 10 ἔστι ταῦτα ἀκοῦσαι καὶ μαθεῖν; D. 42, 3 ἰδεῖν al.; Mel., P. 19, 127); neg. οὐκ ἔστιν νῦν λέγειν *it is not possible to speak at this time* **Hb 9:5.** οὐκ ἔστιν φαγεῖν *it is impossible to eat* **1 Cor 11:20** (so Hom. et al.; UPZ 70, 23 [152/151 BC] οὐκ ἔστι ἀνακύψαι με πώποτε . . . ὑπὸ τῆς αἰσχύνης; 4 Macc 13:5; Wsd 5:10; Sir 14:16; 18:6; EpJer 49 al.; EpArist 163; Jos., Ant. 2, 335; Ath. 22, 3 ἔστιν εἰπεῖν).

❽ **to have a point of derivation or origin,** ***be,/come from somewhere*** ἐκ τῆς ἐξουσίας Ἡρῴδου *from Herod's jurisdiction* **Lk 23:7;** ἐκ Ναζαρέτ (as an insignificant place) **J 1:46;** ἐκ τῆς γῆς **3:31;** ἐκ γυναικός **1 Cor 11:8** al. ἐξ οὐρανοῦ, ἐξ ἀνθρώπων *be of heavenly (divine), human descent* **Mt 21:25; Mk 11:30; Lk 20:4.** *Be generated by* (cp. Sb 8141, 21f [ins I BC] οὐδ' ἐκ βροτοῦ ἦεν ἄνακτος, ἀλλὰ θεοῦ μεγάλου ἔκγονος; En 106:6) **Mt 1:20.** Esp. in Johannine usage ἐκ τοῦ διαβόλου εἶναι *originate from the devil* **J 8:44; 1J 3:8.** ἐκ τοῦ πονηροῦ **3:12;** ἐκ τοῦ κόσμου **J 15:19; 17:14, 16; 1J 4:5.** ἐκ τῆς ἀληθείας εἶναι **2:21; J 18:37** etc. Cp. 9 end.

❾ **to belong to someone or someth. through association or genetic affiliation,** ***be, belong*** w. simple gen. (X., Hell. 2, 4, 36; Iambl., Vi. Pyth. 33, 230 τῶν Πυθαγορείων) οἱ τῆς ὁδοῦ ὄντες *those who belong to the Way* **Ac 9:2.** εἰμὶ Παύλου *I belong to Paul* **1 Cor 1:12; 3:4;** cp. **Ro 8:9; 2 Cor 10:7; 1 Ti 1:20; Ac 23:6.** ἡμέρας εἶναι *belong to the day* **1 Th 5:8,** cp. vs. **5.** W. ἔκ τινος **1 Cor 12:15f; Mt 26:73; Mk 14:69f; Lk 22:58** al. (cp. X., Mem. 3, 6, 17; oft LXX). ἐκ τοῦ ἀριθμοῦ τῶν δώδεκα *belong to the twelve* **22:3.** ὅς ἐστιν ἐξ ὑμῶν *who is a fellow-countryman of yours* **Col 4:9.**—To belong through origin **2 Cor 4:7.** Of Mary: ἦν τῆς φυλῆς τοῦ Δαυίδ was of David's line GJs 10:1. Cp. 8 above.

❿ **to have someth. to do with someth. or someone,** ***be.*** To denote a close relationship ἐξ ἔργων νόμου εἶναι *rely on legal performance* **Gal 3:10.** ὁ νόμος οὐκ ἔστιν ἐκ πίστεως *the law has nothing to do with faith* vs. **12.**—To denote a possessor **Mt 5:3, 10;** 19:14; **Mk 12:7; Lk 18:16; 1 Cor 6:19.** Esp. of God who owns the Christian **Ac 27:23; 1 Cor 3:23; 2 Ti 2:19** (Num 16:5). οὐδ' εἶναι τὸν κόσμον θεοῦ, ἀλλὰ ἀγγέλων AcPlCor 1:15 (cp. Just., A II, 13, 4 ὅσα . . . καλῶς εἴρηται, ἡμῶν τῶν χριστιανῶν ἐστι).—W. possess. pron. ὑμετέρα ἐστὶν ἡ βασιλεία **Lk 6:20.** οὐκ ἔστιν ἐμὸν δοῦναι **Mk 10:40** (cp. Just., A I, 4, 2 ὑμέτερον ἀγωνιᾶσαί ἐστι 'it is a matter for your concern').—To denote function (X., An. 2, 1, 4) οὐχ ὑμῶν ἐστιν *it is no concern of yours* **Ac 1:7**—Of quality παιδεία οὐ δοκεῖ χαρᾶς εἶναι *discipline does not seem to be* (partake of) *joy* **Hb 12:11.—10:39.**

⓫ as an auxiliary: very commonly the simple tense forms are replaced by the periphrasis εἶναι and the ptc. (B-D-F §352–55; Mlt. 225–27, 249; Mlt-H. 451f; Rdm.[2] 102, 105, 205; Kühner-G. I 38ff; Rob. 374–76, 1119f; CTurner, Marcan Usage: JTS 28, 1927 349–51; GKilpatrick, BT 7, '56, 7f; very oft. LXX).

ⓐ (as in Hom et al.) w. the pf. ptc. to express the pf., plpf. and fut. pf. act. and pass. (s. Mayser 329; 377) ἦσαν ἐληλυθότες *they had come* **Lk 5:17.** ἦν αὐτῶν ἡ καρδία πεπωρωμένη *their hearts were hardened* **Mk 6:52.** ἠλπικότες ἐσμέν *we have set our hope* **1 Cor 15:19.** ὁ καιρὸς συνεσταλμένος ἐστίν *the time has become short* **7:29.** ἦν ἑστώς (En 12:3) *he was standing* (more exactly *he took his stand*) **Lk 5:1.**

ⓑ w. pres. ptc. (B-D-F §353).—**α.** to express the pres. ἐστὶν προσαναπληροῦσα τὰ ὑστερήματα *supplies the wants* **2 Cor 9:12** (Just., A I, 26, 5 Μαρκίων . . . καὶ νῦν ἔτι ἐστὶ διδάσκων; Mel., P. 61, 441 ἐστὶν . . . κηρυσσόμενον).

β. impf. or aor. ἦν καθεύδων *he was sleeping* **Mk 4:38.** ἦσαν ἀναβαίνοντες . . . ἦν προάγων **10:32;** cp. **Lk 1:22; 5:17; 11:14** al. (JosAs 1:3 ἦν συνάγων τὸν σίτον; Mel., P. 80, 580 ἦσθα εὐφραινόμενος). ἦν τὸ φῶς τὸ ἀλήθινόν . . . ἐρχόμενον εἰς τὸν κόσμον *the true light entered the world* **J 1:9,** w. ἦν introducing a statement in dramatic contrast to the initial phrase of vs. **8.**—To denote age (Demetr.: 722 fgm. 1, 2 al. Jac.; POxy 275, 9 [66 AD] οὐδέπω ὄντα τῶν ἐτῶν; Tob 14:11) **Mk 5:42; Lk 3:23; Ac 4:22;** GJs 12:3.—Mussies 304–6.

γ. fut. ἔσῃ σιωπῶν *you will be silent* **Lk 1:20;** cp. **5:10; Mt 24:9; Mk 13:13; Lk 21:17, 24** al.; 2 Cl 17:7 Bihlm. (the child) *shall serve him* (God).

ⓒ w. aor. ptc. as plpf. (Aelian, NA 7, 11; Hippiatr. 34, 14, vol. I p. 185, 3 ἦν σκευάσας; ISyriaW 2070b ἦν κτίσας; AcThom 16; 27 [Aa II/2 p. 123, 2f; p. 142, 10]; B-D-F § 355 m.—JVogeser, Z. Sprache d. griech. Heiligenlegenden, diss. Munich 1907, 14; JWittmann, Sprachl. Untersuchungen zu Cosmas Indicopleustes, diss. Munich 1913, 20; SPsaltes, Gramm. d. byzant. Chroniken 1913, 230; Björck [διδάσκω end] 75; B-D-F §355). ἦν βληθείς *had been thrown* **Lk 23:19; J 18:30 v.l.**—GPt 6:23; 12:51. (Cp. Just., A II, 10, 2 δι' εὑρέσεως . . . ἐστὶ πονηθέντα αὐτοῖς 'they achieved through investigation').

ⓓ Notice esp. the impersonals δέον ἐστίν *it is necessary* (Pla. et al.; POxy 727, 19; Sir praef. ln. 3; 1 Macc 12:11 δέον ἐστὶν καὶ πρέπον) **Ac 19:36;** εἰ δέον ἐστίν *if it must be* **1 Pt 1:6** (s. δεῖ 2a); 1 Cl 34:2; πρέπον ἐστίν *it is appropriate* (Pla. et al.; POxy 120, 24; 3 Macc 7:13) **Mt 3:15; 1 Cor 11:13.**

ⓔ In many cases the usage w. the ptc. serves to emphasize the duration of an action or condition (BGU 183, 25 ἐφ' ὃν χρόνον ζῶσα ἦ Σαταβούς); JosAs 2:1 ἦν . . . ἐξουθενοῦσα καὶ καταπτύουσα πάντα ἄνδρα). ἦν διδάσκων *he customarily taught* **Mk 1:22; Lk 4:31; 19:47.** ἦν θέλων *he cherished the wish* **23:8.** ἦσαν νηστεύοντες *they were keeping the fast* **Mk 2:18.** ἦσαν συλλαλοῦντες *they were conversing for a while* **9:4.** ἦν προσδεχόμενος *he was waiting for* (the kgdm.) **15:43.** ἦν συγκύπτουσα *she was bent over* **Lk 13:11.**

ⓕ to emphasize the adjectival idea inherent in the ptc. rather than the concept of action expressed by the finite verb ζῶν εἰμι *I am alive* **Rv 1:18.** ἦν ὑποτασσόμενος *he was obedient* **Lk 2:51.** ἦν ἔχων κτήματα πολλά *he was very rich* **Mt 19:22; Mk 10:22.** ἴσθι ἐξουσίαν ἔχων *you shall have authority* **Lk 19:17** (Lucian, Tim. 35 ἴσθι εὐδαιμονῶν). ἦν καταλλάσσων (God) *was reconciling* **2 Cor 5:19** (cp. Mel., P. 83, 622 οὗτος ἦν ὁ ἐκλεξάμενός σε; Ath. 15, 2 οὗτός ἐστιν ὁ . . . καρπούμενος).—LMcGaughy, Toward a Descriptive Analysis of EINAI as a Linking Verb in the Gk. NT, diss. Vanderbilt, '70 (s. esp. critique of treatment of εἰμί in previous edd. of this lexicon pp. 12–15).—Mlt. 228. B. 635. DELG. M-M. EDNT. TW. Sv.

εἶμι (Hom.+ in pres. w. pres. mng. 'I go') in Att. used as fut. of ἔρχομαι=***I shall go*** (rare in H. Gk.) **J 7:34 v.l.,** cp. **36; 12:26; 14:3; 17:24** where εἰμί may also be read as εἶμι (B-D-F §99, 1).—DELG.

εἵνεκεν prep. w. gen. (Pind.+; IAsMinLyk 109; Sb 1568, 7; PGiss 40 II, 21; PGM 5, 385; LXX) ***on account of*** **Lk 4:18** (Is 61:1); **Ac 28:20 v.l.; 2 Cor 3:10;** s. ἕνεκα.

εἶξα s. εἴκω.

εἶπα, εἰπεῖν s. εἶπον and related forms s. v. εἶδον.

εἴπερ s. εἰ 6l.

εἶπον (Hom.+) used as 2 aor. of λέγω 'say' (B-D-F §101, p. 46); subj. εἴπω, impv. εἶπον; inf. εἰπεῖν, ptc. εἰπών. Somet. takes 1 aor. endings (Meisterhans[3]-Schw. 184, 6; Schweizer 182; Mayser 331; EpArist index) εἶπα, εἶπας, εἶπαν; impv. εἰπόν **Mk 13:4; Lk 22:67; Ac 28:26** (on the accent s. W-S. §6, 7d; Mlt-H. 58. On the other hand, εἶπον acc. to PKatz, TLZ 61, '36, 284 and B-D-F §81, 1), εἰπάτω, εἴπατε (GrBar 13:2), εἰπάτωσαν; ptc. εἴπας **Ac 7:37,** fem. εἴπασα **J 11:28 v.l.;** Hv 3, 2, 3; 4, 3, 7. Fut. ἐρῶ; pf. εἴρηκα, 3 pl. εἰρήκασιν and εἴρηκαν (**Rv 19:3**), inf. εἰρηκέναι; plpf. εἰρήκειν. Pass. 1 aor. ἐρρέθην (ἐρρήθην **v.l. Ro 9:12, 26; Gal 3:16**), ptc. ῥηθείς; pf. εἴρηται, ptc. εἰρημένος (B-D-F §70, 1; 81, 1; 101 p. 46; W-S. §13, 13; Rob. index) 'say, speak'.

❶ **to express a thought, opinion, or idea,** ***say, tell***—ⓐ w. direct or indirect obj. or equivalent τὸν λόγον **Mt 26:44.** ὅσα **Lk 12:3.** τί vs. **11;** a parable *tell* (Artem. 4, 80 Μενεκράτης εἶπεν ὄνειρον) **19:11;** the truth **2 Cor 12:6** and oft. τοῦτο ἀληθές this as someth. true=*this truly* **J 4:18.** τί εἴπω; *what shall I say?* **J 12:27.** As a rhetor. transition formula (s. also 3 below) τί ἐροῦμεν; *what shall we say* or *conclude? what then?* **Ro 3:5; 6:1; 7:7; 9:14, 30.** λόγον εἴς τινα *say someth. against someone* **Lk 12:10;** also κατά τινος **Mt 5:11; 12:32.** τί τινι *say someth. to someone* **Gal 3:16.** ἔχω σοί τι εἰπεῖν *I have someth. to say to you* (cp. Lucian, Tim. 20) **Lk 7:40.** τί εἴπω ὑμῖν; *what shall I say to you?* **1 Cor 11:22.** τὶ πρός τινα *say someth. to someone* (Pla., Prot. 345c; Herodas 2, 84; Philostrat., Vi. Apoll. 6, 20, 6; Ex 23:13; Jos., Vi. 205) a parable **Lk 12:16;** *speak w. reference to someone* **Mk 12:12; Lk 20:19.** Also πρὸς ταῦτα *to this* **Ro 8:31.** τὶ περί τινος *say someth. about someone or someth.* (X., Vect. 4, 13) **J 7:39; 10:41.** εἰρήκει περὶ τοῦ θανάτου *he had referred to death* **11:13.** ὑπὲρ (περὶ v.l.) οὗ ἐγὼ εἶπον *of whom I spoke* **J 1:30** (introducing dir. speech). W. acc. of pers. ὃν εἶπον *of whom I said* vs. **15;** cp. ὁ ῥηθείς *the one who was mentioned* **Mt 3:3.** εἰπεῖν τινα καλῶς *speak well of someone* **Lk 6:26.** κακῶς *speak ill of someone* **Ac 23:5** (Ex 22:27). W. omission of the nearer obj., which is supplied fr. the context **Lk 22:67; J 9:27** al. As an answer σὺ εἶπας sc. αὐτό *you have said it* is evasive or even a denial (as schol. on Pla. 112e Socrates says: σὺ ταῦτα εἶπες, οὐκ ἐγώ. S. also the refusal to give a clearly affirmative answer in Const. Apost. 15, 14, 4 οὐκ εἶπεν ὁ κύριος 'ναί', ἀλλ' ὅτι 'σὺ εἶπας'.—λέγω 2e end) **Mt 26:25, 64.**—W. indication of the pers., to whom someth. is said: in the dat. **Mt 5:22; 8:10, 13, 19, 21** and oft. τινὶ περί τινος *tell someone about someth.* **17:13; J 18:34.** Also πρός τινα for the dat. (Lucian, Dial. Mort. 1; Jos., Ant. 11, 210) **Mk 12:7; Lk 1:13, 34, 61** and very oft. (w. acc. εἶπον τὸν ἄγγελον GrBar 6:3; 10:7).

ⓑ w. direct discourse foll.: **Mt 2:8; 9:22; 12:24, 49; 14:29; 15:16, 32; 17:17** and very oft. οὐδὲ ἐροῦσιν=*nor will they be able to say* **Lk 17:21** (cp. Herodas 4, 73 οὐδ' ἐρεῖς, with direct discourse foll. as in Lk); of someth. said in the past **J 14:28.**—As a formula introducing an objection (Diod. S. 13, 21, 5 ἐροῦσί τινες ἴσως; Dio Chrys. 14 [31], 47 ἴσως οὖν ἐρεῖ τις) ἀλλὰ ἐρεῖ τις (X., Cyr. 4, 3, 10; Appian, Bell. Civ. 3, 16 §59 ἀλλὰ . . . ἐρεῖ τις; Ps.-Clem., Hom. 9, 16 p. 98, 1; 5 Lag.) **1 Cor 15:35; Js 2:18** (on various views, DVerseput, NTS 43, '97, 108 n. 22). ἐρεῖς οὖν **Ro 11:19;** w. μοι added **9:19.** πρὸς ἡμᾶς **Ac 21:13** D. Inserted τίς οὖν αὐτῶν, εἰπέ, πλεῖον ἀγαπήσει αὐτόν; *which one, tell me, will love him more?* **Lk 7:42 v.l.**

ⓒ w. ὅτι foll. (Diod. S. 12, 16, 5; 12, 74, 3; Jos., Vi. 205) **Mt 28:7, 13; J 7:42; 8:55; 16:15; 1J 1:6, 8, 10; 1 Cor 1:15; 14:23** al.

ⓓ w. acc. and inf. foll. **Ro 4:1** (text uncertain).

ⓔ regularly used w. quotations: **Tit 1:12;** usually fr. the OT ἐρρέθη **Ro 9:12;** καθὼς εἴρηκεν **Hb 4:3.** τὸ ῥηθὲν ὑπὸ κυρίου διὰ τοῦ προφήτου **Mt 1:22.** ὑπὸ τ. θεοῦ **22:31.** διὰ τοῦ προφήτου **Ac 2:16;** cp. **Mt 2:17, 23; 4:14; 8:17; 12:17; 13:35; 24:15** (Just., D. 27, 1 διὰ . . . Ἠσαίου οὕτως εἴρηται) al. τὸ εἰρημένον *what is written* **Lk 2:24; Ac 13:40; Ro 4:18.**—EHowind, De ratione citandi in Ciceronis Plutarchi Senecae Novi Testamenti scriptis obvia, diss. Marburg 1921.

ⓕ with questions w. direct discourse foll. (Epict. 3, 23, 18a=ask; Zech 1:9a) **Mt 9:4; 17:19, 24; 18:21; 20:32; 26:15** al. W. dat. of pers. **Mt 13:10, 27.**

ⓖ w. adv. modifier ὁμοίως **Mt 26:35.** ὡσαύτως **21:30;** or an adv. expr. ἐν παραβολαῖς *in parables=parabolically* **22:1.** διὰ παραβολῆς *using a parable* **Lk 8:4.** W. καθὼς of someth. said in the past (Jos., Ant. 8, 273 καθὼς εἶπεν ὁ προφήτης; cp. Dt

to (Jos., Vi. 115 εἰς τ. κώμην) εἰς (τὴν) θάλασσαν **Mk 7:31; 3:7 v.l.; Mt 17:27.** εἰς πόλιν (Hdt. 2, 169; 4, 200, 1; Diod. S. 15, 32, 2 παραγενόμενος εἰς πόλιν) **J 4:5;** cp. vs. **28.** εἰς τό μνημεῖον **11:31, 38; 20:1, 3f** (cp. vs. **6**). ἐγγίζειν εἰς (Tob 11:1) **Mt 21:1; Mk 11:1; Lk 18:35; 19:29.** εἰς τοὺς φραγμούς *to the hedges* **14:23.** κλίνειν τὸ πρόσωπον εἰς τ. γῆν *toward the ground* **24:5.**

β. with focus on the area within the point reached. After verbs of sending, moving, etc., which result in movement or include a movement of the body *to, into, among* εἰς τὴν πόλιν *into the city* **Mt 26:18** al.; boat **Mt 8:23; J 6:17;** world **J 1:9;** εἰς τ. ναόν **2 Th 2:4;** εἰς (τὸ) μέσον (Sir 27:12; cp. 48:17): ἔστη εἰς τὸ μέσον (X., Cyr. 4, 1, 1), *he (came and) stood among them* **J 20:19, 26;** cp. **Mk 14:60; Lk 6:8,** also ἔγειρε εἰς τὸ μ. *get up and come here* **Mk 3:3.**—δέχεσθαι εἰς τὰς ἀγκάλας *take in* (into) *one's arms* **Lk 2:28** (cp. Jos., Ant. 8, 28).

γ. of movement directed at a surface of an area *on, in:* of striking (PRyl 145, 13f [38 AD] ἔδωκεν πληγὰς πλείους εἰς πᾶν μέρος τοῦ σώματος=gave many blows all over his body; cp. PTebt 39, 32) τύπτειν εἰς τ. κεφαλήν *on the head* **Mt 27:30** (cp. Arrian, Anab. 2, 26, 4 ἐμβάλλειν εἰς τ. κεφαλήν). ῥαπίζειν εἰς τὴν σιαγόνα *on the cheek* **5:39.**—εἰς τ. ὄμματα **Mk 8:23;** εἰς τ. ὁδόν **11:8;** ἀναπίπτειν εἰς τ. ἔσχατον τόπον *sit in the lowest place* **Lk 14:10;** cp. vs. **8.** εἰς τὴν χεῖρα, τοὺς πόδας *on his hand, his feet* **Lk 15:22.**

δ. of a position within a certain area *be at, be in, be on* εἰς is freq. used where ἐν would be expected (s. 1bβ below; for Mark usage s. JO'Rourke, JBL 85, '66, 349–51)—(Hdt. 7, 239, 1; Diod. S. 13, 101, 3; 20, 30, 2; Vett. Val. index III p. 394b; PTebt 38, 14 [113 BC] εἰς ὃν ἐνοικεῖ . . . οἶκον; POxy 294, 6 [22 AD]; 929, 12; BGU 385, 5; 423, 7; Kaibel 134; LXX. Cp. GHatzidakis, Einl. in die neugr. Gramm. 1892, 210f; Mlt. 62f, 234f; Rob. 592f; Rdm.[2] 14; 140; B-D-F §205; EOldenburger, De Or. Sib. Elocutione, diss. Rostock 1903, 26ff) εἰς τ. κοίτην εἶναι **Lk 11:7.** εἰς τὴν οἰκίαν **Mk 10:10.** οἱ εἰς τ. οἶκόν μου (ὄντες) **Lk 9:61.** οἱ εἰς μακρὰν (ὄντες) **Ac 2:39.** καθημένου εἰς τὸ ὄρος **Mk 13:3** (cp. Musonius 43, 18 H. καθῆσθαι εἰς Σινώπην). ὁ εἰς τὸν ἀγρὸν (ὤν) *he who is in the field* **13:16.** γίνεσθαι εἰς τὴν Καφαρναούμ *happen in Capernaum* **Lk 4:23.** εἰς συναγωγὰς δαρήσεσθε *you will be beaten in the synagogues* **Mk 13:9.** εὑρέθη εἰς Ἄζωτον *he found himself in A.* **Ac 8:40** (cp. Esth 1:5 τοῖς ἔθνεσιν τοῖς εὑρεθεῖσιν εἰς τ. πόλιν; Gen 37:17). ἀποθανεῖν εἰς Ἰερ. **Ac 21:13** (cp. Aelian, VH 7, 8 Ἡφαιστίων εἰς Ἐκβάτανα ἀπέθανε). κατοικεῖν εἰς Ἰερ. **Ac 2:5;** cp. **Mt 2:23; 4:13; Ac 7:4; Hb 11:9** (cp. Thu. 2, 102, 6; X., An. 1, 2, 24; Num 35:33; 2 Ch 19:4). χάριν, εἰς ἣν στῆτε *the favor in which you stand* **1 Pt 5:12.** ἔχειν βιβλίον εἰς τὰς χεῖρας *have a book in one's hands* Hv 1, 2, 2. πηλὸς γάρ ἐσμεν εἰς την χεῖρα τοῦ τεχνίτου *for we are clay in the hand of the artisan.* εἰς ταύτην τὴν πόλιν *in this city* 2, 4, 3 al.—εἰς=*at* or *on* (BGU 845, 20f; τραπέζας . . . εἰς ἃς ἤσθιον οἱ πτωχοί TestJob 25:5) ὁ ὢν εἰς τ. κόλπον τ. πατρός *who leans on the breast* (or *reclines in the lap*) *of the Father* (=who is on intimate terms w. the Father, s. κόλπος) **J 1:18.** In AcPlCor 2:35 the prepositions εἰς and ἐν appear to be carefully distinguished: τὰ δεσμὰ εἰς τὰς χεῖρας ἔχω . . . καὶ τὰ στίγματα ἐν τῷ σώματί μου.

ε. of presence in an area determined by other objects, esp. after verbs of sending, moving, etc. including ἀπολύω, ἀποστέλλω, βάλλω, βαπτίζω, δέχομαι, δίδωμι, ἐγκεντρίζω, ἐκβάλλω, ἐκπέμπω, ἐκχέω, ἐμβάπτω, ἐξαποστέλλω, καθίημι, μεταπέμπομαι, παρακύπτω, πέμπω, χαλάω; s. these entries. ἐμπίπτειν εἰς τοὺς λῃστάς *fall among robbers* **Lk 10:36.** εἰς τὰς ἀκάνθας *among the thorns* **Mk 4:7;** εἰς τ. λαόν **Ac 4:17** et al., where the transl. depends on the verb in question. πνεύματος ἁγίου . . . ἀποσταλέντος εἰς αὐτήν (Μαρίαν) *sent into her* AcPlCor 2:5; cp. 2:10 ἔπεμψεν εἰς τοὺς προφήτας *into the prophets;* 2:14 κατέπεμψε . . . εἰς Μαρίαν.—ἔστη εἰς τὸ κριτήριον *she stood before the tribunal* GJs 15:2 (difft. **J 20:19, 26,** s. 1aβ).

ⓑ of direction toward something without ref. to bodily motion.—**α.** w. verbs of looking (fr. Od. 10, 37; Il. 3, 364; LXX) ἀναβλέπειν εἴς τι *look up toward someth.* (2 Macc 7:28; Sus 35 Theod.) **Mk 6:41; Lk 9:16; Ac 22:13;** cp. ἀτενίζω, βλέπω, ἐμβλέπω, ὁράω (Just., D. 112, 1).—ἐπαίρειν τοὺς ὀφθαλμοὺς εἴς τινα *raise one's eyes toward someone* **Lk 6:20.**

β. after verbs of saying, teaching, proclaiming, preaching, etc. (trag.; Hdt. 8:26, 3; Thu. 1, 72, 2; 5, 45, 1 and many later wr., incl. LXX) λαλεῖν εἰς τ. κόσμον *say to the world* **J 8:26.** τὸ εὐαγγέλιον εἰς ὅλον τ. κόσμον *the gospel in the whole world* **Mk 14:9.** εἰς πάντα τὰ ἔθνη **13:10; Lk 24:47.** εἰς ὑμᾶς **1 Th 2:9.** εὐαγγελίζεσθαι εἴς τινα **2 Cor 10:16; 1 Pt 1:25;** γνωρίζειν **Ro 16:26.** ἀπαγγέλλειν τι εἴς τινα **Mk 5:14; Lk 8:34.** διαμαρτύρεσθαι εἰς Ἰερουσαλήμ, μαρτυρεῖν εἰς Ῥώμην *bear witness in Jerusalem, Rome* **Ac 23:11.** ἵνα εἰς Νινευὴ μὴ κηρύξῃ AcPlCor 2:29. In these and similar cases εἰς approaches ἐν in mng.; s. 1aδ.

γ. The same is true of βαπτίζεσθαι εἰς τὸν Ἰορδάνην **Mk 1:9** and νίπτεσθαι εἰς τὴν κολυμβήθραν **J 9:7;** these expr. look like exx. of the interchange of εἰς and ἐν, but were orig. formed on the analogy of X., Cyr. 1, 3, 5 ἀποκαθαίρει τὴν χεῖρα εἰς τὰ χειρόμακτρα= lit. 'into the towels'; cp. Epict. 3, 22, 71 ἵν' αὐτὸ (sc. τὸ παιδίον) λούσῃ εἰς σκάφην; Alciphron, Ep. 3, 7, 1; Athen. 10, 438e.

❷ **extension in time, *to, until, on*—ⓐ** w. indication of specific time—**α.** up to which someth. continues εἰς τέλος *to the end* (Epict. 1, 7, 17) **Mt 10:22; 24:13; Mk 13:13.** εἰς ἐκείνην τὴν ἡμέραν *until that day* **2 Ti 1:12** (Ath. 2, 1 εἰς . . . τὴν σήμερον ἡμέραν). εἰς ἡμέραν Χριστοῦ **Phil 1:10.** εἰς Χριστόν *until the coming of the Messiah* **Gal 3:24.**

β. *for* or *on* which someth. happens μεριμνᾶν εἰς τὴν αὔριον *be anxious for tomorrow* **Mt 6:34;** cp. Hs 6, 5, 3; εἰς τὸ μέλλον *for the future* **1 Ti 6:19.** εἰς τὸ μεταξὺ σάββατον *on the next Sabbath* **Ac 13:42.** εἰς ἡμέραν (UPZ 66, 5 [153 BC]) *for the day* **Phil 2:16;** cp. **Eph 4:30; Rv 9:15.**

γ. at which someth. takes place (Appian, Mithrid. 74 §321 ἐς ἑσπέραν=in the evening; Epict. 4, 10, 31 αὔριον ἢ εἰς τὴν τρίτην; En 1:1 οἵτινες ἔσονται εἰς ἡμέραν ἀνάγκης) εἰς τὸν καιρὸν αὐτῶν *in their time* **Lk 1:20;** εἰς τὸ μέλλον *in the future* **13:9.** εἰς τέλος *in the end, finally* (Hdt. 3, 403; Gen 46:4; Ps.-Clem., Hom. 18, 2) **18:5** (B-D-F §207, 3 prefers mng. 3 below and ὑπωπιάζω 3; s. also Mlt-Turner 266). εἰς τὸ πάλιν=πάλιν **2 Cor 13:2;** s. Schmid I 167; II 129; III 282; IV 455; 625. εἰς ταχεῖαν *soon* AcPlCor 2:3.

ⓑ to indicate duration of time ***for, throughout*** (Nicol. Dam.: 90 fgm. 4 p. 332, 16 Jac. εἰς νύκτα; Arrian, Anab. 4, 30, 1 ἐς τρεῖς ἡμέρας; Just., D. 2, 5 εἰς μακρὰν *for a long time*) εἰς ἔτη πολλά *for many years* **Lk 12:19.** εἰς τὸν αἰῶνα, εἰς τοὺς αἰῶνας (αἰών 1b) *forever* **Mt 21:19; Mk 3:29; 11:14; Lk 1:33; J 8:35** and oft. εἰς ἡμέραν αἰῶνος *to the day of eternity* **2 Pt 3:18.** εἰς γενεὰς καὶ γενεάς *for generation after generation* **Lk 1:50.** εἰς τὸ διηνεκές *forever* **Hb 7:3; 10:1, 12, 14** (cp. Thu. 2, 64, 3 ἐς ἀΐδιον).

❸ **marker of degree, *up to:*** εἰς τέλος *completely, fully, absolutely* (s. Just, A I, 44, 12 and on τέλος 2bγ) **1 Th 2:16;** B 4:7; 19:11; Hv 3, 7, 2; m 12, 2, 3; s 8, 6, 4; 8, 8, 5; 8, 9, 3.—**J 13:1** combines in εἰς τέλος the mngs. *to the end* (s. 2aα above) and *to* *the uttermost* (cp. Appian, Mithrid. 58 §239 ἡμῶν ἀμυναμένων ἤδη καὶ ἀμυνουμένων ἐς τέλος=we have defended ourselves up to now and will defend ourselves ἐς τέλος). εἰς τὰ ἄμετρα **2 Cor 10:13, 15** (cp. PVat A 12=Witkowski 36, 12 [168 BC] εἰς τὰ ἔσχατα). εἰς περισσείαν **10:15.** εἰς ὑπερβολήν (Eur., Hipp. 939; Aeschin., F. Leg. 4) **4:17.** εἰς τὸ παντελές (q.v. 2) **Lk 13:11; Hb 7:25** (Tat. 6, 1).

❹ marker of goals involving affective/abstract/suitability aspects, *into, to*—ⓐ of entry into a state of being w. verbs of going, coming, leading, etc., used in a fig. sense: ἀπέρχεσθαι εἰς κόλασιν αἰώνιον **Mt 25:46** (cp. Sir 41:10). εἰσφέρειν εἰς πειρασμόν **6:13.** πορεύεσθαι εἰς θάνατον **Lk 22:33.** ὑπάγειν εἰς ἀπώλειαν **Rv 17:8, 11.** βάλλειν εἰς θλῖψιν **2:22.** παραδιδόναι εἰς θλῖψιν **Mt 24:9;** cp. **2 Cor 4:11; Lk 24:20.** συγκλείειν εἰς ἀπείθειαν **Ro 11:32.** ἐμπίπτειν εἰς κρίμα **1 Ti 3:6f;** cp. **6:9** (and Ath. 24, 5 εἰς ἐπιθυμίαν πεσόντες παρθένων). ἄγειν εἰς μετάνοιαν **Ro 2:4;** cp. **Hb 2:10** εἰς δόξαν. (Just., A I, 10, 4 εἰς πίστιν; 42, 11 εἰς ἐπίστασιν καὶ ἀνάμνησιν.) αἰχμαλωτίζειν εἰς ὑπακοήν **2 Cor 10:5.** ἀνακαινίζειν εἰς μετάνοιαν **Hb 6:6;** cp. **2:10.** Sim. ἀπάγω, ἀποβαίνω, εἰσέρχομαι, εἰσφέρω, ἐκβάλλω, ἐλευθερόω, ἐπιστρέφω, κατευθύνω, μεταβαίνω, ὁδηγέω et al.; s. these entries.

ⓑ of change from one state to another w. verbs of changing: στρέφειν (Esth 4:17h; 1 Macc 1:39), μεταστρέφειν (Sir 11:31; 1 Macc 9:41; 3 Macc 6:22) τι εἴς τι **Rv 11:6; Ac 2:20** (Jo 3:4); **Js 4:9.** μεταλλάσσειν **Ro 1:26.** μετασχηματίζεσθαι (q.v. 2) **2 Cor 11:13f;** μετατίθεσθαι εἰς *turn away to* **Gal 1:6.**

ⓒ of actions or feelings directed in someone's direction in hostile or friendly sense (Thu. 1, 38; 66; 130; X., Cyr. 1, 3, 5; Paus. 7, 9, 3; 7, 10, 2; Aelian, VH 11, 10).

α. in a hostile sense (Arrian, Anab. 1, 1, 4; PEleph 1, 9 [311/310 BC] κακοτεχνεῖν εἰς Δημητρίαν; UPZ 170b, 47 [127 BC]): ἁμαρτάνειν εἴς τινα (Herodian 7, 9, 11; EpJer 12; Jdth 5:20; 11:10) *sin against someone* **Lk 15:18, 21.** βλασφημεῖν εἴς τινα (Bel 8 Theod.; Just., D. 122, 2) *defame someone* **Mk 3:29; Lk 12:10; 22:65;** θαρρεῖν εἴς τινα **2 Cor 10:1.** ψεύδεσθαι εἴς τινα (Sus 55; 59 Theod.) **Col 3:9.** Also w. nouns and adj. (Paus. 7, 8, 4; PFay 12, 7 [c. 103 BC] ἀδικήματα εἴς με; En 97:7 μνημόσυνον εἰς ὑμᾶς κακόν) **Ac 6:11; 23:30; Ro 8:7.**

β. in a friendly sense: μακροθυμεῖν **2 Pt 3:9.** τὸ αὐτὸ φρονεῖν **Ro 12:16.** So also πιστεύειν εἴς τινα *trust* or *believe in someone* **Mt 18:6; Mk 9:42** and oft. (s. πιστεύω 1aε). Also w. nouns (OGI 49, 10 [III BC] φιλοτιμία εἰς; 51, 4; UPZ 22, 18 [162 BC]; 39, 5 εἰς τὸ θεῖον εὐσέβεια; 2 Macc 9:26 εὔνοια; Tat. 16:2 τῆς εἰς αὐτοὺς [δαίμονας] θρησκείας) ἀγάπη **Ro 5:8; 2 Cor 2:4, 8; Col 1:4; 1 Th 3:12.** ἐλπίς (2 Macc 9:20; Synes., Ep. 104 p. 264a εἰς τὸν κομήτην ἐ.) **Ac 24:15.** κοινωνία **Phil 1:5** (Tat. 18, 2); πεποίθησις **2 Cor 8:22.** δύναμις **Eph 1:19.** πίστις (Jos., Ant. 16, 48; 18, 334) **Ac 20:21; 24:24; 26:18; Col 2:5;** and adj. φιλόξενος **1 Pt 4:9;** χρηστός **Eph 4:32.** διακονία **Ro 15:31** (cp. the v.l. Ac 12:25 and s. JDupont, NovT 1, '56, 275–303); **2 Cor 8:4.** The context of **1 Pt 1:11** suggests consolation of Christians for the sufferings they endure in a hostile environment, hence REB: *sufferings in Christ's cause;* for εἰς Χρ. construed genitivally (UPZ 180a II, 2 [113 BC] χωρὶς τοῦ εἰς αὐτὴν οἴκου; PTebt 16:9f contains a restoration of εἰς) s. NRSV 'sufferings destined for Christ' (for a parallel expr. in a hostile sense cp. Polyb. 1, 7, 12 τῆς εἰς ἐκείνους τιμωρίας; 1, 69, 7; 38, 1 [4], 13; s. [s.v. ἀνά beg.] Kuhring 13; Rudberg 201).

ⓓ w. the vocation, use, or end indicated *for, as:* αἱρέομαι εἴς τι **2 Th 2:13.** ἀφορίζω **Ro 1:1; Ac 13:2.** προγράφω **Ro 15:4; Jd 4.** ἀποστέλλω **Hb 1:14.** πέμπω **Phil 4:16; 1 Th 3:2, 5.** ποιῶ τι εἰς **1 Cor 10:31; 11:24.** S. also under κεῖμαι, προορίζω, τάσσω, τίθημι.—εἰμὶ εἴς τι *serve as someth.* (s. εἰμί 6; also ins 134, 33ff fr. the Delphinion at Miletus [I AD] 1914; s. Dssm., LO 97, 1 [LAE 123]; Ar. 5, 1 ὕδωρ . . . εἰς χρῆσιν τῶν ἀνθρώπων γέγονε) **1 Cor 14:22;** for destruction **Col 2:22;** as a testimony **Js 5:3.** Used w. a noun σκεῦος εἰς τιμήν, ἀτιμίαν *a vessel meant for honorable, dishonorable use* **Ro 9:21;** cp. vs. **22f; 2 Ti 2:20f;** φύλλα τοῦ ξύλου εἰς θεραπείαν **Rv 22:2.** φῶς εἰς ἀποκάλυψιν *a light serving* as *a revelation* **Lk 2:32.** θεράπων εἰς μαρτύριον τῶν λαληθησομένων *a servant to bear witness to what would be said* **Hb 3:5.** (Cp. Just., A I, 66, 1 τὸ . . . εἰς ἀναγέννησιν λουτρόν). W. acc. of pers. (Just., A II, 12, 4 συκοφαντίᾳ τῇ εἰς ἡμᾶς; Tat. 17, 3 τὴν εἰς τοὺς μεμηνότας βοήθειαν) ἡ εἰς ὑμᾶς χάρις *the grace meant for you* **1 Pt 1:10.** διδόναι εἴς τι *pay out for someth.*, money for a field **Mt 27:10.**

ⓔ w. the result of an action or condition indicated *into, to, so that:* αὐξάνειν εἰς ναόν *grow into a temple* **Eph 2:21.** πληροῦσθαι εἴς τι **3:19.** λυπηθῆναι εἰς μετάνοιαν *be grieved so that repentance takes place* **2 Cor 7:9.** Of prayer ἀναβαίνειν εἰς μνημόσυνον **Ac 10:4.** ὁμολογεῖν εἰς σωτηρίαν *confess to salvation = so as to receive salvation* **Ro 10:10;** cp. **1:16; 1 Pt 2:2;** εἰς ἔπαινον κτλ. *to praise* etc. **1 Pt 1:7;** εἰς βοήθειαν (1 Ch 12:17; Jdth 6:21; JosAs 23:4) **Hb 4:16;** cp. **10:39; Rv 13:3; Ro 6:16; 8:15; 13:4, 14; 1 Cor 11:34; 2 Cor 2:16** al.; εἰς κενόν (s. κενός 3) **2 Cor 6:1; Gal 2:2; Phil 2:16; 1 Th 3:5.** σχίζειν εἰς δύο *tear in two* **Mt 27:51; Mk 15:38.** Cp. GPt 5:20 (cp. Polyb. 2, 16, 11; Lucian, Symp. 44, Tox. 54; 1 Km 15:29; Tob 5:3 S; 1 Macc 9:11; Ath. 18, 3 ᾠὸν . . . εἰς δύο ἐρράγη). W. subst. inf. foll. *so that* **Ro 1:20; 3:26; 4:18; 6:12; 7:4; 1 Th 3:13; 2 Th 2:10f; Hb 11:3** al.

ⓕ to denote purpose *in order to, to* (Appian, Liby. 101 §476 ἐς ἔκπληξιν=in order to frighten; Just., A I, 21, 4 εἰς προτροπήν 'to spur on') εἰς ἄγραν *in order to catch someth.* **Lk 5:4.** εἰς ἀπάντησιν, συνάντησιν, ὑπάντησίν τινι (s. these 3 entries) *to meet someone, toward someone* **Mt 8:34; 25:1; J 12:13.** εἰς μαρτύριον αὐτοῖς *as a witness,* i.e. *proof, to them* **Mt 8:4; 10:18; 24:14** al. εἰς ἄφεσιν ἁμαρτιῶν *for forgiveness of sins, so that sins might be forgiven* **Mt 26:28;** cp. **Mk 1:4; Lk 3:3; Ac 2:38.** εἰς μνημόσυνόν τινος *in memory of someone* **Mt 26:13; Mk 14:9;** cp. **Lk 22:19** al. (εἰς μνημόσυνον En 99:3). εἰς ὅ *for which purpose* (Hdt. 2, 103, 1) **Col 1:29;** otherw. **2 Th 1:11** *with this in view;* εἰς τί; *why?* (Wsd 4:17; Sir 39:16, 21) **Mt 14:31; Mk 14:4; 15:34;** Hm 2:5; D 1:5. εἰς τοῦτο *for this reason* or *purpose* **Mk 1:38; Lk 4:43 v.l.; J 18:37; Ac 9:21; 26:16; Ro 9:17; 14:9; 2 Cor 2:9; 1J 3:8;** Hs 1:9 (Just., A I, 13, 3). εἰς αὐτὸ τοῦτο *for this very reason* **2 Cor 5:5; Eph 6:22; Col 4:8.** W. subst. inf. foll. (X., Ages. 9, 3, Mem. 3, 6, 2; Just., A I, 9, 5) *in order to* (oft. LXX; neg. μή *in order not to;* s. B-D-F §402, 2) **Mt 20:19; 26:2; 27:31; Mk 14:55** and oft.—εἰς ὁδόν *for the journey* **6:8.**

ⓖ As in Mod. Gk., it is used for the dat., esp. the dat. of advantage, but also=*for* in general (X., An. 3, 3, 19 τ. ἵππους εἰς ἱππέας κατασκευάσωμεν; Lycurg. 85 διεκαρτέρουν εἰς τ. πατρίδα; UPZ 180a I, 7 [113 BC] τὸν εἰς Τάγην οἶκον ᾠκοδομημένον; BGU 37, 4f [51 AD] ξύλα εἰς τοὺς ἐλαιῶνάς μου wood for my olive orchards; PLond I, 43, 9 p. 48 [II BC]; PTebt 5, 77; POxy 37 I, 9; EpJer 9; Sir 37:7, cp. vs. 8; Jdth 14:2; Bel 3 Theod., vs. 22 LXX) εἰς πάντα τ. λαόν **Lk 9:13;** cp. **3J 5.** εἰς ἡμᾶς **Eph 1:19;** cp. **Col 1:25; 1 Th 4:10; Ro 10:12.** χρείαν ἔχειν εἰς τ. ἑορτήν **J 13:29;** cp. **Mk 8:19f; Gal 2:8; 1 Th 2:9; 5:15** et al.—εἰς is commonly used in speaking of the person *for* whom a payment etc. is made (Dssm., B 113–15; NB 23 [BS 117f; 194f]) **1 Cor 16:1; 2 Cor 8:4; 9:1, 13; Ro 15:26;**

Ac 24:17. εἰς λόγον τινός *in an account for someth.* (POxy 275, 19; 21 [66 AD]; 496, 10; 530, 15) **Phil 4:15;** cp. vs. **17.** εἰς Χριστόν **Phlm 6** prob. *in honor of Christ* (Tetrast. Iamb. 1, 7, 4 p. 266 εἰς θεούς; Pla., Lysis 205d ᾄδεις εἰς σαυτὸν ἐγκώμιον; Ps.-Pla., Minos 319c; Athen. 15, 667c; Synes., Ep. 75 p. 222b).

❺ **marker of a specific point of reference,** ***for, to, with respect to, with reference to*** (Arrian, Anab. 6, 26, 3 τοῦτο τὸ ἔργον εἰς καρτερίαν ἐπαινῶ Ἀλεξάνδρου=I praise this deed with regard to Alexander's endurance; Ath. 31, 1 οὐδὲν χείρους εἰς ἀρετῆς λόγον 'none the worse in respect to excellence') εὔθετος εἴς τι *fit, suitable for someth.* **Lk 14:35;** also εὔχρηστος **2 Ti 4:11.** ἡτοιμασμένος *ready for* **2:21.** εὐκαιρέω εἴς τι **Ac 17:21.** ἱκανόω **Col 1:12.** ἰσχύω **Mt 5:13.** περισσεύω **2 Cor 9:8.** συνεργέω **Ro 8:28.** τοῦτο οὐκ εἰς ταύτας τ. ἡμέρας λέγω *I say this not with reference to these days* Hs 9, 26, 6.—After the verbs ἀπορέομαι, διακρίνομαι, καυχάομαι, παρρησίαν ἔχω, s. these entries. After the adj. ἄκαρπος, ἀκέραιος, βραδύς, σοφός, συνεργός, ὑπήκοος, φρόνιμος, s. these entries. W. acc. of pers. ἀσθενεῖν εἴς τινα *be weak toward someone* **2 Cor 13:3.** εὐδοκεῖν **2 Pt 1:17.** λέγειν εἴς τινα *say w. reference to someone* (Diod. S. 11, 50, 4; Just., D. 77, 1 εἰς Χριστὸν . . . εἰρῆσθαι) **Ac 2:25.**—On **Ro 6:17** s. παραδίδωμι 1b end. δέχομαί τινα εἰς ὄνομά τινος **Mt 10:41f;** s. ὄνομα 1dγℵ.

❻ **marker of a guarantee,** ***by*** ὀμνύναι εἴς τι *swear by someth.* **Mt 5:35** (cp. PGiss 66, 8f [early II AD] ἐρωτῶ εἰς τὴν τ. θεῶν εὐσέβειαν; but the sole use of εἰς in a series of datives w. ἐν may reflect bilingualism; for prob. Hb. perspective, s. M'Neile, comm. ad loc).

❼ **distributive marker:** w. numbers εἰς is distributive '-fold' (cp. ἐστρίς 'until three times' Pind., O. 2, 68; GDI IV p. 884, ⁿ62, 36 [IV BC]) **Mk 4:8 v.l.** (otherw. ἐς τετρακοσίους, ἐς ὀγδοήκοντα about 400, about 80: Arrian, Anab. 5, 15, 2; 6, 2, 4; 7, 20, 3).

❽ The predicate nom. and the predicate acc. are somet. replaced by εἰς w. acc. under Semitic influence, which has strengthened Gk. tendencies in the same direction:

ⓐ predicate nom.—**α.** w. γίνεσθαι (PFay 119, 34 [100 AD] ἵνα μὴ εἰς ψωμίον γένηται; Wsd 14:11; 1 Macc 1:36; 10:70; Jdth 5:10, 18 al.) **Mt 21:42** (Ps 117:22). ἐγένετο εἰς δένδρον **Lk 13:19;** cp. **J 16:20; Ac 5:36; Rv 8:11; 16:19.**

β. w. εἶναι (Bar 2:23; Jdth 5:21, 24; Sir 31:10 et al.) **Mt 19:5** (Gen 2:24); **Lk 3:5** (Is 40:4); **2 Cor 6:18; Hb 1:5; 8:10** (in the last 3 pass. OT expressions are also reproduced). Not fr. the OT: **1J 5:8.**

γ. λογίζεσθαι εἰς (Wsd 2:16; 1 Macc 2:52) **Ro 4:3** (Gen 15:6); cp. **2:26; 9:8.** λ. εἰς οὐθέν (Is 40:17; Wsd 3:17; cp. 9:6) **Ac 19:27.**

ⓑ predicate acc. (Heliod. 6, 14, 1 τ. πήραν εἰς καθέδραν ποιησαμένη=she used the knapsack as a seat; Vett. Val. 59, 7; 1 Macc 10:54; 11:62; Jdth 5:11 al.; JosAs 13:12 παράθου με αὐτῷ εἰς παιδίσκην) ἐγείρειν τινὰ εἰς βασιλέα **Ac 13:22** (cp. 1 Km 13:14). ἀνατρέφεσθαί τινα εἰς υἱόν **7:21** (cp. Ex 2:10). τέθεικά σε εἰς φῶς ἐθνῶν **13:47** (cp. Is 49:6). Cp. **Mt 21:46;** 1 Cl 42:4.—B-D-F §145; 157, 5; Rdm.² 20f; Mlt. 71f; Mlt-H. 462. Johannessohn, Kasus 4f.

❾ **marker of instrumentality,** ***by, with*** (Arrian, Anab. 5, 12, 3 ἐς ἀκρίβειαν=with care; Vi. Aesopi I G 7 P. νικᾶν εἰς εὐσέβειαν πάντα ψόγον=overcome all censure with piety) εἰς διαταγὰς ἀγγέλων **Ac 7:53** (=ἐν διαταγαῖς, B-D-F §206, 1). Sim. ὕπαγε εἰς εἰρήνην (1 Km 1:17) **Mk 5:34; Lk 7:50; 8:48** (=ἐν εἰρήνῃ). Mlt-Turner 254f.

❿ Other uses of εἰς—ⓐ *at, in the face of* μετανοεῖν εἰς τὸ κήρυγμα *repent at the proclamation* **Mt 12:41; Lk 11:32;** cp. **Ro 4:20** and perh. **Mt 3:11.** JMantey, JBL 70, '51, 45–48, 309–11 argues for a causal use here *because of the proclam.*, with reff.; against him RMarcus, ibid. 129f; 71, '52, 43f; JDavis, Restoration Qtrly 24, '81, 80–88.

ⓑ for βαπτίζω εἰς s. βαπτίζω 2c.

ⓒ μένειν εἰς *remain with* (PFay 111, 12 [95/96 AD]) so perh. **J 6:27.**

ⓓ in pregnant constructions: σῴζειν εἰς *bring safely into* **2 Ti 4:18** (cp. X., An. 6, 4, 8; Diod. S. 2, 48; Cebes 27; SIG 521, 26 [III BC], OGI 56, 11; 4 Macc 15:3). διασῴζειν **1 Pt 3:20** (cp. Gen 19:19). μισθοῦσθαι ἐργάτας εἰς τ. ἀμπελῶνα *to go into the vineyard* **Mt 20:1.** ἐλευθεροῦσθαι εἰς *be freed and come to* **Ro 8:21.** ἀποδιδόναι τινὰ εἰς Αἴγυπτον **Ac 7:9** (cp. Gen 37:28). ἔνοχος εἰς τ. γέενναν **Mt 5:22;** cp. **10:9; Mk 6:8; J 20:7.**—DELG. M-M. TW.

εἷς, μία, ἕν, gen. **ἑνός, μιᾶς, ἑνός** a numerical term, 'one' (Hom.+)

❶ **a single pers. or thing, with focus on quantitative aspect,** ***one***—ⓐ in contrast to more than one—**α.** adj. μίλιον ἕν **Mt 5:41;** cp. **20:12; 25:15, 24; Ac 21:7; 28:13; 2 Pt 3:8.** Opp. πάντες **Ro 5:12** (εἷς ἄνθρωπος as Hippocr., Ep. 11, 2 [IX p. 326]; SHanson, Unity of the Church in the NT, '46, 65–73 [lit.]). Opp. the nation **J 11:50; 18:14** (cp. Oenom. in Eus., PE 5, 25, 5 μεῖον εἶναι ἕνα ἀντι πάντων πεσεῖν τὸν βασιλέα=it is a lesser evil when one, instead of all the citizens, falls, namely, the king).

β. noun, **Lk 23:16 (17) v.l.** w. partitive gen. (Diod. S. 1, 91, 5 αὐτῶν εἷς; Jos., Vi. 204; Just., A I, 1, 1 al.) **Mt 5:19; 6:29; 18:6; Mk 9:42; Lk 12:27; 15:21 v.l.; 17:2, 22; 23:39; J 19:34** or w. ἐκ (Maximus Tyr. 1, 6 ab ἐκ πολλῶν εἷς; Lucian, Somn. 9; Jos., Bell. 7, 47) **Mt 18:12; 22:35; 26:21; Mk 14:18; J 1:40; 6:8; Ac 11:28** al. ὁ εἷς τῶν δώδεκα *one of the twelve* **Mk 14:10** is a peculiar expr. (cp. BGU 1145, 25 [18 BC] ὁ εἷς αὐτῶν Ταυρῖνος; UPZ 161, 50; 54; PTebt 138; 357, 10).

ⓑ in contrast to the parts, of which a whole is made up (Theophr. in Apollon. Paradox. 16 τὰ πολλὰ ἓν γίγνεσθαι; Stephan. Byz. s.v. Ὠκεανός: γίγνεται ἐκ δύο εἰς ἕν; Just., D. 103, 5 ἐξ ἀμφοτέρων . . . ἓν ὄνομα). ἔσονται οἱ δύο εἰς σάρκα μίαν **Mt 19:5; Mk 10:8; 1 Cor 6:16** (all three Gen 2:24). οἱ πολλοὶ ἓν σῶμά ἐσμεν *we, though many, form one body* **Ro 12:5;** cp. **1 Cor 12:12, 20; Eph 2:15.** πάντες εἷς ἐστε *you are all one* **Gal 3:28.** ἕν εἰσιν **1 Cor 3:8;** cp. **J 10:30; 17:11, 21–23** (cp. 1QS 5, 2; Just., D. 42, 3 ἓν ὄντες πρᾶγμα). Also εἰς τὸ ἕν **1J 5:8** (Appian, Iber. 66 §280 ἐς ἕν=together, as a unity). εἰς ἓν **J 11:52** (cp. 1QS 5, 7). ὁ ποιήσας τὰ ἀμφότερα ἓν *who has united the two divisions* **Eph 2:14.**—MAppold, The Oneness Motif (John) '76.

ⓒ w. negative foll. εἷς . . . οὐ (μή), stFonger than οὐδείς (Aristoph., Eccl. 153, Thesm. 549; X., An. 5, 6, 12; Demosth. 30, 33 ἡ γυνὴ μίαν ἡμέραν οὐκ ἐχήρευσεν; Dionys. Hal., Comp. Verb. 18) ἓν ἐξ αὐτῶν οὐ πεσεῖται *not one of them will fall* **Mt 10:29** (Lucian, Herm. 28 ἓν ἐξ ἁπάντων); cp. **5:18; Mk 8:14; Lk 11:46; 12:6.** The neg. rarely comes first **Mt 5:36.**

❷ **a single entity, with focus on uniformity or quality,** ***one***

ⓐ ***one and the same*** (Pind., N. 6, 1 ἓν ἀνδρῶν, ἓν θεῶν γένος· ἐκ μιᾶς δὲ πνέομεν ἀμφότεροι; Dio Chrys. 19 [36], 6; Maximus Tyr. 19, 4a; cp. OGI 383, 59 [I BC, the ruler's statue is to be made of the type of stone used for statues of the gods]; Gen 11:1; 40:5; Lev 22:28; Wsd 7:6; Ar. 13, 5 μία φύσις τῶν θεῶν) ἐν ἑνὶ οἴκῳ *in one and the same house* **Lk 12:52** (Diod. S. 14, 43, 1 ἐν ἑνὶ τόπῳ). Expressing unanimity ἐν ἑνὶ στόματι

w. *one voice* **Ro 15:6;** τοῦ ἑνὸς ἄρτου *one and the same loaf* **1 Cor 10:17;** εἷς ὁ θεός *one and the same God* (Amphitheos of Heracleia: 431 fgm. 1b Jac. Διόνυσος κ. Σαβάζιος εἷς ἐστι θεός; difft. Ath. 10, 2 ἑνὸς ὄντος τοῦ πατρὸς καὶ τοῦ υἱοῦ) **Ro 3:30;** cp. **9:10; 1 Cor 6:16f; 12:9, 13.** εἷς κύριος, μία πίστις, ἓν βάπτισμα· εἷς θεός κτλ. (cp. the three genders of εἷς consecutively in Simonides 97 Diehl[2] ἓν πέλαγος, μία ναῦς, εἷς τάφος [of shipwrecked pers.]; Just., D. 63, 5 μιᾷ ψυχῇ . . . συναγωγῇ . . . ἐκκλησίᾳ) **Eph 4:5f** (NJklA 35, 1915, 224ff. The repetition of εἷς is like Herm. Wr. 11, 11; Epict. 3, 24, 10ff).—**Rv 9:13; 18:8; Ac 17:26.** ἐν ἑνὶ πνεύματι, μιᾷ ψυχῇ **Phil 1:27;** cp. **Ac 4:32** (cp. Aristot., EN 9, 8, 2; Plut., Mor. 478c). τὸ ἓν φρονεῖν *be of one mind* **Phil 2:2.** συνάγειν εἰς ἕν *unite, bring together* (Pla., Phileb. 23e; Dionys. Hal. 2, 45, 3 συνάξειν εἰς ἓν τὰ ἔθνη; POxy 1411, 3 τῶν δημοσίων εἰς ἓν συναχθέντων; TestJob 28:5 τὰ χρήματα ἐὰν συναχθῇ εἰς ἓν ἐπὶ τὸ αὐτό 'if all [our] valuables were brought together at one place'; Jos., Bell. 3, 518) **J 11:52.** τὸ ἓν καὶ τὸ αὐτό *one and the same* **1 Cor 12:11** (cp. Diod. S. 11, 47, 3; 17, 104, 6; Epict. 1, 11, 28; 1, 19, 15; Just., D. 123, 1 ἑνὸς καὶ τοῦ αὐτοῦ . . . νόμου); cp. ἓν καὶ αὐτό τινι **11:5.**—εἰς ἕνα τόπον *in a place by itself* (Jos., Ant. 6, 125) **J 20:7.**

ⓑ *(a) single, only one* (Diod. S. 16, 11, 2; Appian, Bell. Civ. 2, 44 §180 εἷς ἀνήρ; Maximus Tyr. 11, 6c μαντεῖον ἕν al.; Just., D. 141, 3 τὴν μίαν τοῦ Δαυείδ . . . παράπτωσιν) λόγον ἕνα **Mt 21:24** (GrBar 5:1); **Gal 5:14.** ἕνα ἄρτον **Mk 8:14.** εἷς ἄρτος **1 Cor 10:17a** (εἷς ἄ. is also the symbol of the unity of the Pythagorean fellowship: Diog. L. 8, 35; here Diog. L. adds that οἱ βάρβαροι hold the same view ἔτι καὶ νῦν). πῆχυν ἕνα **Mt 6:27** (s. πῆχυς); ἓν μέλος **1 Cor 12:26;** ἓν ἔργον **J 7:21** (here, following ἕν, καί adds an indication of the greatness of the accomplishment, as Appian, Bell. Civ. 2, 133 §555 ἓν ἐκ τῶν Καίσαρος ἔργων προὔθηκα . . . , καί). εἷς ἐστιν ὁ ἀγαθός **Mt 19:17;** ποιῆσαι ἕνα προσήλυτον **23:15;** ἕνα εἶχεν υἱὸν ἀγαπητόν *he had an only son, whom he loved dearly* **Mk 12:6** (εἷς υἱ. as Phalaris, Ep. 18). ὁ δὲ θεὸς εἷς ἐστιν **Gal 3:20;** cp. **Mk 12:32; 1 Cor 8:4, 6** (v.l. adds to God the Father and Jesus Christ ἓν πνεῦμα ἅγιον κτλ. Cp. also Maximus Tyr. 11, 5a θεὸς εἷς . . . κ. πατήρ, κ. θεοὶ πολλοί and as early as Xenophanes, fgm. 19 Diehl[3] εἷς θεὸς ἔν τε θεοῖσι κ. ἀνθρωποῖσι μέγιστος [= fgm. 23 Diels]); **Js 2:19;** PtK 3 p. 15, 20 (Herm. Wr. 11, 11; 14 εἷς ὁ θεός; POxy 1382, 20 εἷς Ζεὺς Σάραπις; Sb 159, 1 εἷς θεὸς ὁ βοηθῶν ὑμῶν; Philo, Spec. Leg. 1, 67; Jos., Ant. 5, 97 θεός τε εἷς; 8, 343, C. Ap. 2, 193; SibOr 4, 30 and fgm. 1, 7; Ath. 6, 1 μονάς ἐστιν ὁ θεός, τοῦτ' ἔστιν εἷς; 6, 4 ὁ θεὸς εἷς; s. EPeterson, Εἷς Θεός 1926; D. Monotheismus als polit. Problem '35; additional reff. Horst, Ps.-Phoc. p. 151f). εἷς ἐστιν ὑμῶν ὁ διδάσκαλος **Mt 23:8;** cp. vs. **9.** μιᾶς γυναικὸς ἀνήρ *a husband married only once* (numerous sepulchral ins celebrate the virtue of a surviving spouse by noting that he or she was married only once, thereby suggesting the virtue of extraordinary fidelity, e.g. CIL VI, 3604; 723; 12405; 14404; cp. Horace, Odes 3, 14, 4; Propertius 4, 11, 36; Valerius Maximus 4, 3, 3; and s. esp. CIL VI, 1527, 31670, 37053=ILS 8393 [text and Eng. tr.: EWistrand, The So-Called Laudatio Thuriae, '76]; s. GWilliams, JRS 48, '58 16–29. For the use of μία in ref. to a woman: Ael. Aristid. 46 p. 346 D.: ὑπὲρ μιᾶς γυναικός=for only one woman; μία γυνή quite freq.: Diod. S. 17, 72, 6; cp. 1, 80, 3, where the phrase γαμοῦσι μίαν simply means that the priests married only once, not that they lead a strictly moral life, a concept for which Greeks never use the expression μιᾶς γυναικὸς ἀνήρ or anything like it; Hippostratus [III BC]: 568 fgm. 1 Jac.; Appian, Bell. Civ. 4, 95 §402; Ath. 33, 2 ἐφ' ἑνὶ γάμῳ: Ath. terms a second marriage εὐπρεπὴς μοιχεία veiled adultery) **1 Ti 3:2, 12; Tit 1:6;** others render *husband of one wife* (e.g. RSV in later printings; REB). Correspondingly ἑνὸς ἀνδρὸς γυνή (cp. the exemplary conduct of Hannah [Anna] Lk 2:36; Paus. 7, 25, 13 the priestess of the earth goddess must be a woman who, before she became a priestess, was not πλέον ἢ ἑνὸς ἀνδρὸς ἐς πεῖραν ἀφιγμένη) **1 Ti 5:9.**—Abs. **1 Cor 9:24; 2 Cor 5:14.** μεσίτης ἑνός *an intermediary for one alone* **Gal 3:20;** cp. **Js 4:12.** οὐδὲ εἷς *not even a single* (X., Mem. 1, 6, 2, Cyr. 1, 3, 10 et al.; Sir 42:20; 49:14 v.l.; 1 Macc 11:70) **Mt 27:14; Ac 4:32.** Freq. at the end of a sentence or clause (ref. fr. comedy in ESchwartz, NGG 1908, p. 534, 3. Also Hermocles [IV–III BC] p. 174, 17 Coll. Alex.; Dio Chrys. 21 [38], 23; Ael. Aristid. 28, 156 K.=49 p. 542 D.; 53 p. 617 D.; Epict. 2, 18, 26, Enchir. 1, 3; Philonides in Stob. 3, 35, 6 ed. Hense III p. 688; Mitt-Wilck. I/2, 59, 5 [39 AD]; Bel 18 Theod.; 1 Macc 7:46) **Ro 3:10;** οὐδὲ ἓν foll. by ἐὰν μή **J 3:27.** This is a good reason for placing the period after οὐδὲ ἕν **J 1:3** (s. GBergh van Eysinga, PM 13, 1909, 143–50. EHennecke, Congr. d' Hist. du Christ. I 1928, 207–19; Md'Asbeck, ibid. 220–28; REisler, Revue de Philol. 3 sér. 4, 1930, 350–71; BVawter, CBQ 25, '63, 401–6; KAland, ZNW 59, '68, 174–209; Metzger 195f; γίνομαι 2a), but the lack of inner punctuation in the older mss. validates consideration of alternative punctuation. οὐκ ἔστιν ἕως ἑνός *there is not even one* **Ro 3:12** (Ps 13:3; Just., D. 103, 2 οὐδὲ μέχρις ἑνὸς ἀνθρώπου 'not a single person'). μία εἴσοδος *the only entrance* Hs 9, 12, 6.—ἕν *only one thing:* ἔτι ἕν σοι λείπει *you still lack only one thing* (Jos., Bell. 4, 257) **Lk 18:22.** ἕν σε ὑστερεῖ *you lack only one thing* **Mk 10:21;** cp. **Lk 10:42.** ἓν οἶδα *at least this one thing I know* **J 9:25.** ἓν δὲ τοῦτο *this one thing* (Porphyr., Vi. Plot. 19; Just., D. 115, 6 ἓν δὲ μικρὸν ὁτιοῦν) **2 Pt 3:8.**—ἓν δέ is a short interjectional sentence (like Xenophon Eph. 1, 5, 3 τοσοῦτο δέ·) *just one thing!* **Phil 3:13** (AFridrichsen, ConNeot 9, '44, 31f).—**Gal 5:14** commercial imagery εἷς λόγος *(just) one entry, one heading* (cp. BGU 831, 13).

ⓒ *alone* (οὐδεὶς) . . . εἰ μὴ εἷς ὁ θεός **Mk 2:7** (in the parallel Lk 5:21 μόνος ὁ θεός, cp. Herm Wr. 11, 11 εἰ μὴ εἷς ὁ θεός . . . εἰ μὴ μόνῳ τῷ θεῷ); **10:18; 12:29** (Dt 6:4); **Mt 23:10; Lk 18:19.**—EBishop, ET 49, '38, 363–66.

❸ **an unspecified entity, some/one**=τις, whereby εἷς can mean exactly the same thing as the indef. art. (Aristoph. et al. [Av. 1292 εἷς κάπηλος]; Περὶ ὕψους 33, 4 p. 62, 18 V. [the rdg. of cod. Paris], εἷς ἕτερος w. μή 'for no other reason'; Strabo 5, 3, 2, 230c ἐπηγγείλατο ἕνα ἀγῶνα ἱππικόν; Syntipas p. 29, 3 μία γαλῆ; Appian, Liby. 117 §554 νυκτὸς μιᾶς=one night; Marc. Diac. 27, 5 ἐν μιᾷ ἡμέρᾳ=on a certain day; SIG 1170, 15 [160 AD] μιᾷ ἡμέρᾳ; UPZ 162 I, 27 [117 BC]; PAmh 30, 28 [II BC] Κονδύλου ἑνὸς τῶν ἁλιείων; BGU 1044, 6; Gen 21:15; Jdth 14:6; 1 Esdr 3:5. B-D-F §247, 2; Mlt. 96f; Rob. 674f; Mlt-Turner 195f; EBruhn, RhM 49, 1894, 168–71; JWackernagel, Syntax II[2] 1928, 151; MBlack, An Aramaic Approach[3], '67, 104–6).

ⓐ ***someone, anyone*** **Mt 18:24; 19:16; Mk 10:17;** εἷς ὀνόματι Κλεοπᾶς **Lk 24:18.** Oft. w. partitive gen. foll. (Alexis 220, 5; Diod. S. 20, 107, 5 εἷς τῶν φίλων; Epict. 4, 2, 9; Dio Chrys. 71 [21], 15 εἷς τῶν Σπαρτῶν; TestJob 26:6 μίαν τῶν . . . γυναικῶν; Jos., Ant. 9, 106) ἕνα τῶν προφητῶν (some) *one of the prophets* **Mt 16:14** (a diminishing term? s. Reader, Polemo p. 257). ἕνα τ. συνδούλων **18:28.** ἐν μιᾷ τ. πόλεων **Lk 5:12.** ἐν μιᾷ τ. ἡμερῶν *on one of the days* vs. **17;** cp. **15:19, 26; 22:47.**

ⓑ as indef. art. (s. at 3 above beg.) εἷς γραμματεύς *a scribe* **Mt 8:19.** συκῆν μίαν *a fig tree* **Mt 21:19;** cp. **26:69; Mk 12:42.** παιδάριον ἓν **J 6:9 v.l.;** ἑνὸς ἀετοῦ **Rv 8:13;** cp. **18:21; 19:17;** ἄρχων εἷς ἐλθών **Mt 9:18.** εἷς στέφανος ApcPt 3:10; ἓν σῶμα AcPlCor 2:26.

ⓒ used w. τὶς (Pla., Thu., et al.; Jdth 2:13) εἷς τις νεανίσκος *a certain young man* **Mk 14:51 v.l.** W. partitive gen. foll. (Trypho

Alex. [I BC] in Athen. 3, 78a ἕνα τινὰ τ. Τιτάνων; Aesop, Fab. 300 H.//30 P. and H-H.; Hierocles 27, 484; IG XII/5, 445, 12 [III BC] ἕνα τινὰ αὐτῶν; Ael. Aristid. 29, 14 K.=40 p. 755D.: εἷς τις τ. χορευτῶν) εἷς τις τῶν παρεστηκότων *a certain one of the bystanders* vs. **47** (on the v.l. without τις s. PDickerson, JBL 116, '97, 302); also εἷς τις ἐξ αὐτῶν (Jos., Vi. 290) **Lk 22:50; J 11:49.**

❹ **marker of someth. that is first, *the first*—ⓐ** perh. Hebraistic (cp. Num 1:1 ἐν μιᾷ τοῦ μηνὸς τ. δευτέρου; 2 Esdr 10:17; Esth 1:1a; Jos., Ant. 1, 29.—But s. also Lydus, Mens. 3, 4 W. τὴν κεφαλὴν τ. χρόνου οἱ Πυθαγόρειοι οὐχὶ πρώτην ἀλλὰ μίαν ὠνόμασαν; Callim., fgm. 550 P. [482 Schneider] πρὸ μιῆς ὥρης=before the first hour of the day) is its use w. expressions denoting time instead of the ordinal number εἰς μίαν σαββάτων *on the first day of the week* **Mt 28:1;** cp. **Lk 24:1; Mk 16:2; J 20:1, 19; Ac 20:7;** also κατὰ μίαν σαββάτου **1 Cor 16:2** (cp. Just., D. 41, 4 τῇ μιᾷ τῶν σαββάτων ἡμέρᾳ; 27, 5 [here w. πρό and μετά resp., in accordance with Latin usage]).

ⓑ not Semitic (Hdt. 4, 161 μία, ἄλλη, τρίτη; Ael. Aristid. 36, 40 K.=48 p. 453 D.: ἕν, δεύτερον, τρίτον, τέταρτον; JosAs 2:17) εἷς καὶ δεύτερος *a first and second* **Tit 3:10** (cp. Alciphron, Ep. 1, 9, 2; Galen XII 746 K.: ὕδωρ ὄμβριον ἔγχριε μέχρι μιᾶς καὶ δευτέρας ἡμέρας; Maximus Tyr. 28, 2h μία-δευτέρα; EpArist 143; Jos., Ant. 11, 150; 16, 350 πεσόντος ἑνὸς καὶ δευτέρου). S. also ἡ οὐαὶ ἡ μία **Rv 9:12.**—ἓν τριάκοντα **Mk 4:8, 20** is prob. to be considered an Aramaism *thirtyfold* (B-D-F §248, 3; EKautzsch, Gramm. d. bibl. Aram. 1884 §66, 2; JHudson, ET 53, '41/42, 266f).

❺ special combinations:—ⓐ εἷς . . . εἷς (Hom. et al. εἷς μὲν . . . εἷς δέ: X., Cyr. 1, 2, 4; Aristot., Rhet. 2, 20, 1393a; pap in Mitt-Wilck. I/2, 50, 11 and 13 [III BC] ἓν μὲν . . . ἓν δέ; II/2, 372 V, 14 [II AD] ὁ εἷς . . . ὁ εἷς; POxy 1153, 14 [I AD] ἓν μὲν . . . καὶ ἕν; 2 Km 12:1; Sir 34:23f εἷς . . . καὶ εἷς; Esth 10:3g δύο, ἕνα τῷ λαῷ . . . καὶ ἕνα τ. ἔθνεσιν; TestJob 51:3 μιᾶς ὑποσειμιούσης τῇ μιᾷ) *(the) one . . . the other* **Mt 20:21; 24:40f; 27:38; J 20:12; Gal 4:22;** B 7:6f. εἷς τὸν ἕνα *one another* (=ἀλλήλους) **1 Th 5:11** (cp. Theocr. 22, 65 εἷς ἑνί; TestJob 27:3 εἷς τόν ἕνα κατέρραξαν 'threw each other to the ground').

ⓑ εἷς . . . εἷς . . . εἷς *one . . . another . . . a third* **Mt 17:4** (cp. 1 Km 10:3; 13:17, 18).

ⓒ εἷς ἕκαστος *every single,* strengthening ἕκαστος, adj. **Eph 4:16.** Mostly subst.; s. ἕκαστος b.

ⓓ ὁ εἷς . . . ὁ ἕτερος *the one . . . the other* (Aristot., De Rep. Ath. 37, 1; Hyperid. 5, 14f; UPZ 161, 39; 43; 46 [119 BC]; PGen 48, 6ff μίαν μὲν . . . τὴν δὲ ἑτέραν; BGU 194, 15f; Esth 5:1a; TestAbr A 11 p. 88, 29 [Stone p. 24]; Just. D. 49, 2 al.) **Mt 6:24; Lk 7:41; 16:13; 17:34f; 18:10** al.; also ὁ εἷς . . . ὁ ἄλλος **Rv 17:10.**

ⓔ distrib. (1 Ch 24:6 εἷς εἷς; AscIs 3:27 εἷς καὶ εἷς καὶ εἷς ἐν τόποις καὶ τόποις) καθ' ἕνα, καθ' ἕν (Hdt., Pla. et al.; 1 Esdr 1:31; 4 Macc 15:12, 14; Jos., Bell. 4, 240, Ant. 12, 191; Ath. 25, 3 καθ' ἕνα καὶ κατὰ ἔθνη) ITr 12:2; καθ' ἕνα πάντες *all, one by one* **1 Cor 14:31** (cp. Ps.-Xenophon, Cyn. 6, 14). ὑμεῖς οἱ καθ' ἕνα ἕκαστος *each one of you* **Eph 5:33.** καθ' ἕν *one after the other* (hence τὸ καθ' ἕν 'a detailed list': PLille 11, 8 [III BC]; PTebt 47, 34; 332, 16) **J 21:25.** Also καθ' ἓν ἕκαστον (X., Cyr. 1, 6, 22, Ages. 7, 1; EpArist 143) **Ac 21:19.** ἓν καθ' ἕν (Aesop, Fab. 274 P.; PLeid II, X 1, 22) *each one* **Rv 4:8.** In this pass. the second ἕν could be an undeclined nom. as in εἷς κατὰ εἷς (cp. Lucian, Sol. 9; 3 Macc 5:34. Other exx. in W-S. §26, 9; 11 and Wetstein I 627) *one after the other* **Mk 14:19; J 8:9.** τὸ καθ' εἷς opp. οἱ πολλοί *individually* **Ro 12:5;** but κατὰ ἕνα = ἕκαστον Hs 9, 3, 5; 9, 6, 3 (B-D-F §305). ἀνὰ εἷς ἕκαστος *each one* **Rv 21:21.**

ⓕ ἀπὸ μιᾶς s. ἀπό 6 (as idiom w. noun to be supplied Mitt-Wilck. I/2, 46, 15 [338 AD] μίαν ἐκ μιᾶς, i.e. ἡμέραν=day after day).—B. 937; 1007f. DELG. M-M. EDNT. TW. Sv.

εἰσάγω fut. εἰσάξω LXX; 2 aor. εἰσήγαγον GJs 10:1; pf. 2 pl. εἰσαγειόχατε 1 Km 21:16; aor. pass. εἰσήχθην LXX (Hom.+) ***bring or lead in/into*** τινά *someone* **J 18:16;** GJs 18:1; **Lk 2:27.** τινὰ εἴς τι *someone into someth.* (X., An. 1, 6, 11; 4 Km 9:2; Jos., Ant. 1, 38; Just., D. 113, 3; Ar. 15, 7 ὑπὸ στέγην) into a city **Ac 9:8;** barracks **21:37; 22:24;** arena MPol 6:2; house **Lk 22:54;** B 3:3 (Is 58:7); temple **Ac 21:28f** (on the implications of alleged violation of temple sanctity s. Boffo, Iscrizioni no. 32 p. 283f [lit.]); cp. B 16:9; Ox 840, 8; ἐν τῷ ναῷ GJs 10:1; the Kingdom MPol 20:2 (cp. TestJob 47:3 εἰς τὸν μείζονα αἰῶνα); the world 1 Cl 38:3; cp. B 6:16; a tomb GPt 6:24. τὸν πρωτότοκον εἰς τὴν οἰκουμένην *firstborn son into the world* **Hb 1:6.** ὧδε **Lk 14:21.**—τὶ **Ac 7:45.**—M-M.

εἰσακούω fut. εἰσακούσομαι; 1 aor. εἰσήκουσα; pf. εἰσακήκοα. Pass. 1 fut. εἰσακουσθήσομαι; 1 aor. εἰσηκούσθην (s. ἀκούω; Hom. et al.; SEG VIII, 551, 35; 715, 14; LXX; PsSol 6:5; TestSol 1:1 C; TestAbr A; JosAs 15:2 cod. A; ParJer 7:32; ApcMos, GrBar 16:4; Just., D. 28, 2; 72:1 [unknown quot.]; cp. D 14, 4; 37, 4; 64, 4f; ἐπ- LXX) gener. 'listen to'

❶ **to obey on the basis of having listened carefully, *obey*** (Soph., Thu. et al.; PSI 377, 20; Dt 1:43; 9:23; Sir 3:6; 39:13) τινός **1 Cor 14:21;** 1 Cl 8:4 (Is 1:19f).

❷ **to listen, with implication of heeding and responding, *hear*** (oft. LXX of God listening to petitions)—ⓐ w. ref. to the pers. making the request (Quint. Smyrn. 12, 154 the deity hears [w. gen. as Just.]) 1 Cl 22:7 (Ps 33:18); 57:5 (Pr 1:28). Pass. **Mt 6:7; Hb 5:7** (s. ἀπό 5a).

ⓑ w. ref. to a prayer (Ps 4:2; Bar 2:14; Sir 34:26; Ps 6:5; PsSol 6:5; Jos., Ant. 1, 190; TestLevi 4:2) **Lk 1:13** (cp. Sir 51:11); **Ac 10:31;** GJs 20:3 (v.l. ἐπ-).—CCox, Biblica 62, '81, 251–58 usage in Gk. Psalter.—M-M.

εἰσδέχομαι fut. εἰσδέξομαι; 1 aor. εἰσεδεξάμην LXX, ptc. εἰσδεξάμενος. Pass. aor. 3 sg. εἰσεδέχθη 2 Macc 4:22 (s. δέχομαι; Pind., Hdt. et al.; ins, pap, LXX; EpArist 103)

❶ **to receive graciously into one's presence, *receive, welcome*** **2 Cor 6:17** (Ezk 20:34).

❷ **to grant admittance, *take in*** 1 Cl 12:3 (cp. Jos., Ant. 14, 285 'admit').—M-M. TW.

εἴσειμι (εἰς + εἶμι) inf. εἰσιέναι, ptc. εἰσιών; impf. εἰσῄειν (Hom. et al.; ins, pap, LXX, Joseph., Just. A I, 47, 6) **to enter an area, *go in/into*** εἴς τι *someth.* (SIG 982, 3 εἰς τὸν ναόν; UPZ 162 VIII, 19 [117 BC]; Ex 28:29; Jos., Bell. 3, 325, Ant. 3, 269 εἰς τὸ ἱερόν): the temple **Ac 3:3; 21:26;** cp. **Hb 9:6;** MPol 9:1. εἰς τὸν οἶκον GJs 11:1. πρός τινα *to someone* (Soph., Phil. 953; X., Cyr. 2, 4, 5; TestJos 3:6) **Ac 21:18.**—Frisk s.v. εἶμι. M-M.

εἰσέρχομαι fut. εἰσελεύσομαι (En 25:6; TestJob 40:4; Just., A I, 35, 10; M. Ant. 10, 8); 2 aor. εἰσῆλθον (also εἰσῆλθα, B-D-F §81, 3; Mlt-H. 208; **Mt 7:13; Lk 11:52;** impv. εἰσελθάτω **Mk 13:15**); pf. εἰσελήλυθα LXX; ptc. εἰσεληλυθώς Hs 9, 12, 4; 9, 13, 4; plpf. εἰσεληλύθει 2 Macc 9:2 (Hom.+)

❶ **to move into a space, *enter*—ⓐ** of geographical and other types of localities and areas as goal

α. cities and villages w. specific names (Jos., Ant. 9, 122): into Jerusalem **Mt 21:10** (Just., D. 88, 6). εἰς Ἱεροσόλυμα εἰς τὸ ἱερόν *into Jerusalem and into the temple* **Mk 11:11.** Caesarea **Ac 10:24; 23:33.** Capernaum **Mt 8:5; Mk 2:1; Lk 7:1.**

β. the world gener. εἰς τὸν κόσμον *come into the world* (Philo, Op. M. 78) in var. mngs.: of first appearance, of sin and death **Ro 5:12;** 1 Cl 3:4 (cp. Wsd 2:24); of birth (M. Ant. 6, 56) 1 Cl 38:3; of the incarnation of Christ **Hb 10:5.**

γ. structural areas and establishments: into the sanctuary **Hb 9:12, 24f;** temple (Jos., Ant. 3, 319) **Lk 1:9; Rv 15:8;** house **Mt 10:12; 12:29; 17:25 v.l.; Mk 7:17; Lk 1:40; 8:41; Ac 11:12; 16:15; 21:8;** synagogue (unless the sense 'gathering' applies in certain pass., s. συναγωγή 4) **Mk 1:21; 3:1; Lk 4:16; 6:6; Ac 13:14; 14:1; 18:19;** cp. **Js 2:2;** city **Mt 10:11; 27:53; Mk 1:45; Lk 10:8, 10; 22:10; Ac 9:6; 14:20** al.; village **Mk 8:26; Lk 9:52; 17:12;** barracks **Ac 23:16;** praetorium **J 18:28; 19:9;** cp. **Ac 25:23; Mt 6:6; J 18:1; Mk 16:5; J 20:6; 10:1; Mt 24:38; Lk 17:27;** 1 Cl 9:4. εἰς τ. νεφέλην **Lk 9:34** (cp. Ex 24:18).—W. indication of place from which, εἰ. ἔκ τινος: ἐξ ἀγροῦ *come in from the field* **Lk 17:7** (cp. PEleph 13, 6 [223/22 BC] οὔπω εἰσελήλυθεν ἐξ ἀγροῦ; Gen 30:16).—W. indication of place through which, διά τινος (2 Ch 23:20; Jo 2:9; Jer 17:25; Jos., Ant. 13, 229 εἰ. δι' ἄλλης πύλης) **Mt 7:13; 19:24 v.l.; Lk 13:24; 18:25a; J 10:1, 2** (ἐρχόμενος P^{75}), **9.**—W. ὑπό: τὴν στέγην *under the roof,* i.e., *enter* the house (Gen 19:8 v.l.) **Mt 8:8; Lk 7:6.**—W. adv. εἰ. ἔσω *go inside* (2 Ch 29:18; Bel 19 Theod.) **Mt 26:58;** AcPl Ha 4, 3. ὧδε *come in here* (Zech 7:3; Ezk 40:4) **22:12.** ὅπου ἐὰν εἰσέλθῃ *wherever he goes in* **Mk 14:14; Hb 6:20.**—Without emphasis on the preposition **Mt 9:18 v.l.** (s. on εἰς 3b; προσέρχομαι 1a).

δ. Freq. the 'place to which' is not mentioned, but can be inferred fr. the context (Tob 5:9; 8:13; Jdth 14:14; 1 Macc 7:36; 2 Macc 1:15 al.; PTebt 418, 6ff): εἰσελθὼν διήρχετο τὴν Ἰεριχώ *he entered Jericho and was passing through it* **Lk 19:1.** καὶ ὅτε εἰσῆλθον (sc. εἰς τ. οἶκον) *and when they had entered* **Ac 1:13.** μὴ εἰσελθάτω (sc. εἰς τὴν οἰκίαν) **Mk 13:15,** also εἰσελθοῦσα **7:25 v.l.;** εἰσελθών **Mt 9:25;** cp. **Ac 5:7, 10; 10:25; 1 Cor 14:23f;** AcPl Ha 3, 13. But the idea of destination can be so unimportant that εἰ. comes to mean simply *come, go* **Lk 18:25a;** cp. **Mt 19:24** (s. 1aγ above).—Of things *go (in, into), come (in, into), enter* of food: into the mouth (Ezk 4:14; Da 10:3) **Mt 15:11** (cp. Sextus 110; TestJob 38:3 διὰ στόματος τροφὴ εἰσέρχεται); **Ac 11:8.**

ⓑ of being(s) as goal—**α.** to come or go to πρός τινα *come* or *go to someone* (X., Mem. 3, 10, 1; Cebes, Tab. 29; Jos., Ant. 8, 235; Gen 16:4; Ps 50:2; Jdth 12:13; 15:9) **Mk 15:43; J 14:23 v.l.; Ac 10:3; 11:3; 16:40; Rv 3:20;** 1 Cl 12:4.

β. to come or go in among εἴς τινα *come* or *go in among* εἰς τὸν δῆμον *the crowd* **Ac 19:30.** εἰς ὑμᾶς **20:29.** ἐπί τινα *come to someone* (cp. Ezk 44:25) ἐν παντὶ χρόνῳ ᾧ εἰσῆλθεν καὶ ἐξῆλθεν ἐφ' ἡμᾶς *went in and out among us = associated with us* **Ac 1:21** (on εἰ. καὶ ἐξέρχ. cp. Eur., Phoen. 534 ἐς οἴκους . . . εἰσῆλθε κἀξῆλθ' [καὶ ἐξῆλθε]; Num 27:17; 2 Ch 1:10; **J 10:9**).

γ. to enter into persons or animals *enter into someone* (Wsd 1:4 of wisdom; Jos., Ant. 4, 121 of the divine spirit entering into prophets) esp. of hostile spirits which take possession of someone's body as their dwelling **Mk 9:25; Lk 8:30** (Lucian, Philops. 16: the exorcist asks the spirits ὅθεν [οἱ δαίμονες] εἰσεληλύθασιν εἰς τὸ σῶμα; ApcSed 5:5 [διάβολος] ὡς καπνὸς εἰσέρχεται εἰς τὰς καρδίας τῶν ἀνθρώπων). Of hostile spirits: into the swine **Mk 5:12f; Lk 8:32f.** Of Satan: into Judas **22:3; J 13:27;** into a person Hm 12, 5, 4. For this εἰ. ἔν τινι (s. ἐν 3) εἰσῆλθεν ἐν αὐτοῖς **Rv 11:11;** cp. **Lk 9:46;** 1 Cl 48:2 (Ps 117:19).

❷ **to enter into an event or state,** of pers.: ***come into someth.*** = *share in someth., come to enjoy someth.* (Jos., C. Ap. 2, 123 εἰς τοὺς ἡμετέρους νόμους) εἰς τὴν βασιλείαν τ. θεοῦ (τ. οὐρανῶν) **Mt 5:20; 7:21; 19:24; Mk 9:47; 10:15, 23ff; Lk 18:17, 25; J 3:5;** 2 Cl 6:9 al. (cp. Da 11:9). For this εἰς τὴν ζωήν *enter into eternal life*=attain it **Mt 18:8f; 19:17; Mk 9:43, 45.** HWindisch, D. Sprüche v. Eingehen in d. Reich Gs.: ZNW 27, 1928, 163–92.—εἰς τὴν κατάπαυσιν *enter into rest* **Hb 3:11, 18; 4:1, 3, 5f, 10f** (all Ps 94:11). μέχρι δουλείας εἰσελθεῖν *even to the extent of slavery* 1 Cl 4:9. Of Christ εἰ. εἰς τ. δόξαν αὐτοῦ *into his glory* **Lk 24:26.** Of temptations εἰ. εἰς πειρασμόν *come into temptation* **Mt 26:41; Lk 22:40, 46;** εἰς χαράν **Mt 25:21, 23;** Pol 1:3. εἰς τὸν κόπον τινός *enter into someone's labor,* i.e. enjoy the fruit of another's labor **J 4:38** (cp. Pr 23:10).—W. this usage, too (s. 1aδ above), the goal need not be mentioned, but can be implied **Mt 7:13; 23:13; Lk 11:52** (cp. 3 Macc 1:12); **Ro 11:25.**

❸ **to happen, with focus on initial aspect, *happen, develop,*** of thoughts: εἰσῆλθεν δὲ διαλογισμὸς ἐν αὐτοῖς *an argument arose among them* **Lk 9:46.** εἰς τὰ ὦτά τινος *come to someone's ears* (Ps 17:7) **Js 5:4;** *reach into* **Hb 6:19.**—M-M. TW.

εἰσηγαγον s. εἰσάγω.

εἰσηγέομαι 1 aor. εἰσηγησάμην (Simonides, in Athen. 15, 680d cod. A [s. Diehl fgm. 71 with Wilamowitz's correction ἁγεῖται]; Hdt. et al.; pap; Ps 63:6 Sym.; Pseudo-Eupolemus, p. 198, 14f Denis [in Eus. PE 9, 17, 8]; Joseph., Philo, Tat.; gener. 'lead in, introduce') **to bring to bear on a matter, *display, apply*** πᾶσαν εἰσήγησαι σπουδήν *make every effort, lose no time* AcPlCor 1:16.—DELG s.v. ἡγέομαι.

εἰσῄει s. εἴσειμι.

εἰσήκω fut. εἰσήξω (no certain evidence of use in literary texts before imperial times: Aeschyl., Ag. 1181 [mss. FTr; Fraenkel reads ἐσάιξειν w. Bothe; s. F.'s comm. ad loc.]; Aristoph., Vesp. 606; and Dio Cassius 37, 32 all have been emended by scholars; BCH 6, 18 [II BC]; Sb 631d, 1) **to arrive on a scene, *enter*** the kgdm. of God 2 Cl 11:7.—DELG s.v. ἥκω.

εἰσήνεγκον s. εἰσφέρω.

εἰσιέναι s. εἴσειμι.

εἰσκαλέομαι 1 aor. εἰσεκαλεσάμην in our lit. only mid. (so Hippocr., Progn. 1 [II p. 112]; Polyb. 21, 22, 2; PPetr II, 12(3), 10 [214 BC]; III, 29(h), 5.—Pass., Jos., Vi. 221; act., Ant. 11, 252) **to invite in as a guest, *invite in*** τινά *someone* **Ac 10:23.**—M-M. TW.

εἴσοδος, ου, ἡ (Hom. et al.; ins, pap, LXX, TestSol; GrBar 4:15 [Christ.]; Just., Mel.)

❶ **place of entering, *entrance*** (Od. 10, 90 et al.; Herm. Wr. 1, 22. So mostly ins, pap; Judg 1:24f; 4 Km 23:11; Jos., Bell. 5, 220, Ant. 15, 347) of Christ μία εἴσοδός ἐστι πρὸς τὸν κύριον (this) *is the only entrance to the Lord* Hs 9, 12, 6 (εἴσ. πρός w. acc. as Philo, Fuga 183).

❷ **act of arriving at a destination, *entrance, access*** (Hdt. 1, 118; X., Hell. 4, 4, 7; EpArist 120; Philo, Deus Imm. 132; Jos., Bell. 5, 346; 1 Km 29:6; Ps 120:8; PsSol) τῶν ἁγίων (s. ἅγιος 2b) *(in) to the sanctuary* **Hb 10:19.** As festive metaphor, εἰς τὴν αἰώνιον βασιλείαν **2 Pt 1:11.** Abs. πρὸ προσώπου τῆς εἰσόδου αὐτοῦ *before his coming* **Ac 13:24** (cp. Mal 3:1).

❸ **act of finding acceptance, *acceptance*** εἴσοδον ἔχειν πρός τινα *receive a welcome fr. someone* **1 Th 1:9;** cp. **2:1** (cp. the Lat. pap POxy 32, 14 [II AD] ideo peto a te ut habeat introitum at te=therefore I ask that he be granted the right of admittance to you; Dssm., LO 164 [LAE 198] and M-M. s.v.; M.

Ant. 5, 19 τὰ πράγματα . . . οὐδ. ἔχει εἴσοδον πρὸς ψυχήν); but εἴ. can also mean *visit* (Eur., Andr. 930, 952) here.—M-M. TW.

εἰσπηδάω 1 aor. εἰσεπήδησα (s. πηδάω; Hdt. 4, 132 et al.; SIG 372, 9; POxy 37 I, 16; 1120, 14; Am 5:19; JosAs 5:1 cod. A; Jos., Ant. 5, 46 al.) **a rapid motion forward into, *leap in, rush in*** abs. (Menand., Sam. 564 S. [219 Kö.]; Herodian 7, 5, 3; PTebt 304, 10 [167/68 AD]; Sus 26 Theod.; TestJob 40:10; TestJos 8:3 πρός με) **Ac 16:29.** W. εἰς (X., An. 1, 5, 8; PHal 1, 169 [III BC]) **14:14 v.l.**—M-M.

εἰσπορεύομαι (s. πορεύομαι) impf. εἰσεπορευόμην; fut. 1 pl. εἰσεπορευσόμεθα Dt 1:22; aor. εἰσεπορεύθην LXX; pf. εἰσπεπόρευμαι LXX; in our lit. only mid. (as since X. Cyr. 2, 3, 21; ins, pap, LXX, En 7:1; PsSol 2:11) **to enter into an area, *go into, enter.*** W. εἴς τι *into someth.* foll. (Cebes 4, 2; Gen 23:10; Ex 1:1 al.) εἰς Καφαρναούμ *come to Capernaum* **Mk 1:21;** into villages **6:56; 11:2;** the temple (cp. Ex 28:30; 30:20f) **Ac 3:2;** a house **Lk 22:10; Ac 18:4** D; εἰς τ. βασιλείαν τ. θεοῦ **Lk 18:24** (s. εἰσέρχομαι 2). W. attraction of the relative ἐν ᾗ εἰσπορευόμενοι εὑρήσετε *in which, when you enter, you will find* **19:30.** W. the 'place where' expr. by a clause: εἰσπορεύεται ὅπου ἦν τὸ παιδίον *he went in where the child was* **Mk 5:40.** κατὰ τοὺς οἴκους εἰσπορευόμενος *going into one house after the other* **Ac 8:3.** W. πρός τινα foll. (Cebes 29, 3; SIG[2] 491, 17; POxy 717, 7 [I BC]; Gen 44:30; Esth 2:13f; Da 11:16 Theod.) *come to someone* **28:30.** Abs. οἱ εἰσπορευόμενοι (cp. Zech 8:10) *those who enter* **Lk 8:16; 11:33.** ἦν μετ' αὐτῶν εἰσπορευόμενος καὶ ἐκπορευόμενος εἰς Ἰερουσαλήμ *he went in and out among them at Jerusalem* **Ac 9:28** (cp. Tob 5:18; PsSol 2:11). Of the devil, who enters a pers. and takes possession Hm 12, 5, 4. Of foods εἰ. εἰς τὸ στόμα *go into the mouth* **Mt 15:17;** into a person **Mk 7:15, 18f.**—In imagery *come in, enter* εἴς τινα *someone:* grief Hm 10, 2, 2f. Abs. of desires **Mk 4:19.**—M-M. TW.

εἰστήκειν s. ἵστημι.

εἰστρέχω 2 aor. εἰσέδραμον, ptc. εἰσδραμών (s. τρέχω; since Thu. 4, 67, 5; 111, 1; Jos., Ant. 7, 359 al.; 2 Macc 5:26) **to make a quick visit in an area, *run in*** **Ac 12:14.**

εἰσφέρω fut. εἰσοίσω LXX; aor. εἰσήνεγκα and εἰσήνεγκον (B-D-F §81, 2; W-S. §13, 13; Mlt-H. 263) pf. pass. ptc. εἰσενηνεγμένος 2 Macc 14:38; aor. εἰσηνέχθην LXX (Hom.+) gener. 'bring in, carry in'.

❶ **to bring into an area, *bring in*** τινά: μὴ εὑρόντες ποίας (sc. ὁδοῦ) εἰσενέγκωσιν αὐτόν (i.e., εἰς τ. οἶκον) *since they found no way to bring him in* **Lk 5:19;** cp. vs. **18.** οὐδὲν εἰσηνέγκαμεν εἰς τ. κόσμον *we have brought nothing into the world* (Philo, Spec. Leg. 1, 294f τὸν μηδὲν εἰς τ. κόσμον εἰσενηνοχότα; cp. Cicero, Tusc. 1, 38 [91]) **1 Ti 6:7;** Pol 4:1. Pass. τὸ αἷμα εἰσφέρεται . . . εἰς τὰ ἅγια *the blood is brought into the sanctuary* **Hb 13:11** (cp. Lev 4:5; 16:27 [pass.]). Also forcefully *drag in* (PAmh 77, 22 [139 AD]) **Lk 12:11.** On **J 18:16 v.l.** s. RBorger, TRu, '87, 35f.

❷ **to cause someone to enter into a certain event or condition, *bring in,*** fig. ext. of 1: εἰ. τινὰ εἰς πειρασμόν *bring* or *lead someone into temptation* **Mt 6:13; Lk 11:4;** D 8:2; Pol 7:2. τὶ εἰς τὰς ἀκοάς τινος *bring someth. to someone's ears* **Ac 17:20** (cp. Soph., Aj. 149 εἰς ὦτα φέρει πάντων Ὀδυσσεύς); *introduce* ξένας διδαχάς *strange teachings* Hs 8, 6, 5 (cp. POxy 123, 13 συνείδησιν εἰσήνεγκαν=they sent a report; also X., Mem. 1, 1, 2 καινὰ δαιμόνια εἰσφέρειν [s. Just., A I, 5, 3; A II, 10, 5]).—M-M. TW.

εἶτα adv. (Soph., Thu.+; loanw. in rabb.).—❶ **pert. to being next in order of time, *then, next*** (placed first) εἶτα γενομένης θλίψεως *then when oppression comes* **Mk 4:17;** cp. **8:25; Lk 8:12; J 2:3 v.l.; 11:7 v.l.; 13:5; 19:27; 20:27; Js 1:15;** 1 Cl 25:3; 56:13; B 8:2; 12:2; 13:2; Hv 3, 7, 3 al.; GPt 11:47. In enumerations: πρῶτον . . . εἶτα (X., An. 1, 3, 2; Philo Mech. 71, 26f; Epict. 1, 15, 7; 1, 26, 3 al.; BGU 665, 10 [I AD]; EpArist 77; Jos., Ant. 15, 149; Just., D. 8, 4 al.) *first . . . then* **1 Ti 2:13; 3:10; 1 Cor 12:28 v.l.;** 1 Cl 23:4; 2 Cl 11:3; B 6:17. ἔπειτα . . . εἶτα *after that . . . then* (Galen XIII 740 K.) **1 Cor 15:7, 24;** also εἶτα . . . ἔπειτα (Galen XIII 743 K.) vs. **5f.** Since in enumerations εἶ. oft. serves to put things in juxtaposition without reference to chronological sequence, it becomes in general

❷ **a transition word to mark an addition to someth. just stated, *furthermore, then, next*** (Wsd 14:22; Ar. 10:3; Tat. 4:2) B 6:3; 11:10; 13:2; Dg 11:6, introducing a new argument in a demonstration **Hb 12:9.**—The Ionic-Hellenistic form εἶτεν (Phryn. 124 Lob.; SIG 972, 150 [175–172 BC]; 736, 30f [92 BC]; PGM 13, 400; Mayser 14; s. B-D-F §35, 3; Rob. 119, 160; M-M εἶτεν) is found as v.l. **Mk 4:28.**—DELG. M-M.

εἴτε s. εἰ 6o.

εἶτεν s. εἶτα end.

εἶχον s. ἔχω end.

εἴωθα pf. of an obsolete pres. ἔθω; plpf. εἰώθειν; verbal adj. εἰωθός **to maintain a custom or tradition, *be accustomed*** (so Hom. et al.; pap, LXX, Philo; Jos., Ant. 11, 37; Tat.; Ath., R. 76, 29) **Mt 27:15; Mk 10:1;** B 7:8; IEph 7:1. ὡς εἰώθειν *as I have been accustomed to do* Hs 5, 1, 2. ἃ εἰώθεσαν ποιεῖν αἱ γυναῖκες GPt 12:50. τὸ εἰωθός (Jos., Ant. 17, 150): κατὰ τὸ εἰωθὸς αὐτῷ *according to his custom* **Lk 4:16.** κατὰ τὸ εἰ. τῷ Παύλῳ *as was Paul's custom* **Ac 17:2** (cp. PSI 488, 19 [258 BC] κατὰ τὸ εἰωθός; Num 24:1; Sus 13).—DELG. M-M. s.v. ἔθω.

εἴων s. ἐάω.

ἐκ, before vowels **ἐξ,** prep. w. gen. (Hom.+; s. lit. s.v. ἀνά and εἰς beg.)

❶ **marker denoting separation, *from, out of, away from***

ⓐ w. the place or thing fr. which separation takes place. Hence esp. w. verbs of motion ἀναβαίνω, ἀναλύω, ἀνίστημι, ἐγείρομαι, εἰσέρχομαι, ἐκβάλλω, ἐκπορεύομαι, ἐξέρχομαι, ἔρχομαι, ἥκω, καταβαίνω, μεταβαίνω, ῥύομαι, συνάγω, φεύγω; s. these entries. καλεῖν ἐξ Αἰγύπτου **Mt 2:15** (Hos 11:1); ἐκ σκότους **1 Pt 2:9.** αἴρειν ἐκ τ. κόσμου **J 17:15.** ἐξαλείφειν ἐκ τῆς βίβλου **Rv 3:5** (Ex 32:32f; Ps 68:29). ἀποκυλίειν τ. λίθον ἐκ τ. θύρας **Mk 16:3;** cp. **J 20:1; Rv 6:14;** σῴζειν ἐκ γῆς Αἰγ. **Jd 5;** διασῴζειν ἐκ τ. θαλάσσης **Ac 28:4.** παραγίνεσθαι ἐξ ὁδοῦ *arrive on a journey* (lit. from, i.e. interrupting a journey) **Lk 11:6;** fig. ἐπιστρέφειν ἐξ ὁδοῦ *bring back fr. the way* **Js 5:20;** cp. **2 Pt 2:21.** ἐκ τῆς χειρός τινος (Hebraistically מִיַּד פּ, oft. LXX; s. B-D-F §217, 2; Rob. 649) *from someone's power* ἐξέρχεσθαι **J 10:39;** ἁρπάζειν 10:28f (cp. Plut., Ages. 615 [34, 6] ἐκ τῶν χειρῶν τῶν Ἐπαμινώνδου τ. πόλιν ἐξαρπάσας; JosAs 12:8 ἅρπασόν με ἐκ χειρὸς τοῦ ἐχθροῦ); ἐξαιρεῖσθαι **Ac 12:11** (cp. Aeschin. 3, 256 ἐκ τ. χειρῶν ἐξελέσθαι τῶν Φιλίππου; Sir 4:9; Bar 4:18, 21 al.); ῥύεσθαι **Lk 1:74;** cp. vs. **71** (Ps 105:10; Wsd 2:18; JosAs 12:10); εἴρυσταί σε κύριος ἐκ χειρὸς ἀνόμου AcPlCor 1:8 (cp. ἐκ τούτων ἅπαντων PsSol 13:4).—After πίνειν, of the object fr. which one drinks (X., Cyr. 5, 3, 3): ἐκ τ. ποτηρίου **Mt 26:27;**

Mk 14:23; 1 Cor 11:28; cp. **10:4; J 4:12.** Sim. φαγεῖν ἐκ τ. θυσιαστηρίου **Hb 13:10.**

ⓑ w. a group or company fr. which separation or dissociation takes place (Hyperid. 6, 17 and Lucian, Cyn. 13 ἐξ ἀνθρώπων) ἐξολεθρεύειν ἐκ τοῦ λαοῦ **Ac 3:23** (Ex 30:33; Lev 23:29). συμβιβάζειν ἐκ τ. ὄχλου **19:33;** ἐκλέγειν ἐκ τ. κόσμου **J 15:19;** cp. **Mt 13:41, 47; Ac 1:24; 15:22; Ro 9:24.** For ἐκ freq. ἐκ μέσου **Mt 13:49; Ac 17:33; 23:10; 1 Cor 5:2; 2 Cor 6:17** (cp. Ex 31:14).—ἀνιστάναι τινὰ ἔκ τινων **Ac 3:22** (Dt 18:15); ἐκ νεκρῶν **17:31.** ἐγείρειν τινὰ ἐκ νεκρῶν **J 12:1, 9, 17; Ac 3:15; 4:10; 13:30; Hb 11:19;** AcPlCor 2:6; ἀνίστασθαι ἐκ νεκρῶν **Ac 10:41; 17:3;** ἀνάστασις ἐκ νεκρ. **Lk 20:35; 1 Pt 1:3;** cp. **Ro 10:7.** Also s. ἠρεμέω.

ⓒ of situations and circumstances out of which someone is brought, *from:* ἐξαγοράζειν ἔκ τινος *redeem fr. someth.* **Gal 3:13;** also λυτροῦν (cp. Sir 51:2) **1 Pt 1:18;** σῴζειν ἔκ τινος *save fr. someth.* **J 12:27; Hb 5:7; Js 5:20** (Od. 4, 753; MLetronne, Recueil des Inscr. 1842/8, 190; 198 σωθεὶς ἐκ; SIG 1130, 1f; UPZ 60:6f [s. διασῴζω]; PVat A, 7 [168 BC]=Witkowski 36, 7 διασεσῶσθαι ἐκ μεγάλων κινδύνων; Sir 51:11; EpJer 49; JosAs 4:8 ἐκ τοῦ … λιμοῦ); ἐξαιρεῖσθαι **Ac 7:10** (cp. Wsd 10:1; Sir 29:12). τηρεῖν ἔκ τινος *keep from someth.* **Rv 3:10;** μεταβαίνειν ἔκ τινος εἴς τι **J 5:24; 1J 3:14;** μετανοεῖν ἔκ τινος *repent and turn away fr. someth.* **Rv 2:21f; 9:20f; 16:11.** ἀναπαύεσθαι ἐκ τ. κόπων *rest fr. one's labors* **14:13.** ἐγείρεσθαι ἐξ ὕπνου *wake fr. sleep* (Epict. 2, 20, 15; Sir 22:9; cp. ParJer 5:2 οὐκ ἐξυπνίσθη ἐκ τοῦ ὕπνου αὐτοῦ) **Ro 13:11.** ζωὴ ἐκ νεκρῶν **11:15.** ζῶντες ἐκ νεκρῶν *people who have risen fr. death to life* **6:13** (cp. Soph., Oed. R. 454; X., An. 7, 7, 28; Demosth. 18, 131 ἐλεύθερος ἐκ δούλου καὶ πλούσιος ἐκ πτωχοῦ γεγονώς; Palaeph. 3, 2). S. ἀνάστασις 2b.

ⓓ of pers. and things with whom a connection is severed or is to remain severed: τηρεῖν αὐτοὺς ἐκ τοῦ πονηροῦ *keep them fr. the evil one* **J 17:15;** cp. **Ac 15:29.** Pregnant constr.: ἀνανήφειν ἐκ τῆς τοῦ διαβόλου παγίδος **2 Ti 2:26.** νικᾶν ἔκ τινος *free oneself from … by victory* **Rv 15:2** (for possible Latinism s. reff. to Livy and Velleius Paterculus in OLD s.v. 'victoria'; but s. also RCharles, ICC Rv II, 33). ἐλεύθερος ἐκ **1 Cor 9:19** (cp. Eur., Herc. Fur. 1010 ἐλευθεροῦντες ἐκ δρασμῶν πόδα 'freeing our feet from flight' [=we recovered from our flight]). καθαρός εἰμι ἐγὼ ἐξ αὐτῆς *I practiced abstinence with her* GJs 15:4.

❷ **marker denoting the direction fr. which someth. comes,** ***from*** καταβαίνειν ἐκ τοῦ ὄρους (Il. 13, 17; X., An. 7, 4, 12; Ex 19:14; 32:1 al.; JosAs 4:1 ἐκ τοῦ ὑπερῴου) **Mt 17:9.** θρὶξ ἐκ τῆς κεφαλῆς ὑμῶν οὐ μὴ ἀπόληται **Lk 21:18.** ἐκπίπτειν ἐκ τ. χειρῶν **Ac 12:7.** διδάσκειν ἐκ τοῦ πλοίου **Lk 5:3.** ἐκ τῆς βάτου χρηματισμοῦ διδομένου 1 Cl 17:5 (cp. Just., A I, 62:3). ἐκ τῆς πρύμνης ῥίψαντες τὰς ἀγκύρας **Ac 27:29.** κρέμασθαι ἔκ τινος (Hom. et al.; 1 Macc 1:61; 2 Macc 6:10; Jos., Ant. 14, 107) **28:4.** ἐκ ῥιζῶν *to* (lit. from) *its roots* (Job 28:9; 31:12) **Mk 11:20;** B 12:9.—Since the Greek feeling concerning the relation betw. things in this case differed fr. ours, ἐκ could answer the question 'where?' (cp. Soph., Phil. 20; Synes., Ep. 131 p. 267a ἐκ τῆς ἑτέρας μερίδος=on the other side; BGU 975, 11; 15 [45 AD]; PGM 36, 239; LXX; JosAs 16:12 εἱστήκει … ἐξ εὐωνύμων; 22:7) ἐκ δεξιῶν *at (on) the right* (δεξιός 1b) **Mt 20:21, 23; 22:44** (Ps 109:1); **25:33; Lk 1:11; Ac 2:25** (Ps 15:8), **34** (Ps 109:1); **7:55f;** B 11:10. ἐξ ἐναντίας *opposite* **Mk 15:39** (Hdt. 8, 6, 2; Thu. 4, 33, 1; Mitt-Wilck. I/2, 461, 6; Sir 37:9; Wsd 4:20 al.); ὁ ἐξ ἐναντίας *the opponent* (Sext. Emp., Adv. Phys. 1, 66 [=Adv. Math. 9, 66]; 2, 69 [=Adv. Math. 10, 69], Adv. Eth. 1, 25; Bias in Diog. L. 1, 84) **Tit 2:8.**—ἐκ τοῦ κατωτάτου ᾅδου … προσευχομένου Ἰωνᾶ AcPlCor 2:30.

❸ **marker denoting origin, cause, motive, reason,** ***from, of***

ⓐ in expr. which have to do w. begetting and birth *from, of, by:* ἐκ introduces the role of the male (Ps.-Callisth. 1, 9 ἐκ θεοῦ ἔστι; JosAs 21:8 συνέλαβεν Ἀσενὲθ ἐκ τοῦ Ἰωσήφ; Tat. 33, 3 συλλαμβάνουσιν ἐκ φθορέως; Ath. 22, 4 ἐκ τοῦ Κρόνου; SIG 1163, 3; 1169, 63; OGI 383, 3; 5 [I BC]) ἐν γαστρὶ ἔχειν ἔκ τινος **Mt 1:18.** κοίτην ἔχειν ἔκ τινος **Ro 9:10;** also of the female (SIG 1160, 3; PEleph 1, 9 [311/10 BC] τεκνοποιεῖσθαι ἐξ ἄλλης γυναικός; PFay 28, 9 γεννᾶσθαι ἐκ; Demetr.: 722 fgm. 1, 14 Jac.; Jos., Ant. 1, 191; Ath. 20, 3 ἐξ ἧς παῖς Διόνυσος αὐτῷ) γεννᾶν τινα ἐκ *beget someone by* (a woman; s. γεννάω 1a) **Mt 1:3, 5,** etc. ἐκ Μαρίας ἐγεννήθη AcPlCor 1:14; 2:5; γίνεσθαι ἐκ γυναικός (Jos., Ant. 11, 152; Ar. 9, 7) **Gal 4:4;** cp. vs. **22f.**—γεννᾶσθαι ἐξ αἱμάτων κτλ. **J 1:13;** ἐκ τ. σαρκός **3:6;** ἐκ πορνείας **8:41.** ἐγείρειν τινὶ τέκνα ἐκ **Mt 3:9; Lk 3:8.** (τὶς) ἐκ καρποῦ τ. ὀσφύος αὐτοῦ **Ac 2:30** (Ps 131:11). γεννᾶσθαι ἐκ τ. θεοῦ **J 1:13; 1J 3:9; 4:7; 5:1, 4, 18** (Just., A I, 22, 2); ἐκ τ. πνεύματος **J 3:6** (opp. ἐκ τ. σαρκός). εἶναι ἐκ τοῦ θεοῦ (Menand., Sam. 602 S. [257 Kö.]) **J 8:47; 1J 4:4, 6; 5:19;** opp. εἶναι ἐκ τ. διαβόλου **J 8:44; 1J 3:8** (cp. OGI 90, 10 of Ptolemaeus Epiphanes ὑπάρχων θεὸς ἐκ θεοῦ κ. θεᾶς).

ⓑ to denote origin as to family, race, city, people, district, etc.: ἐκ Ναζαρέτ **J 1:46.** ἐκ πόλεως vs. **44.** ἐξ οἴκου **Lk 1:27; 2:4.** ἐκ γένους (Jos., Ant. 11, 136) **Phil 3:5; Ac 4:6.** ἐκ φυλῆς (Jos., Ant. 6, 45; 49; PTebt I, 26, 15) **Lk 2:36; Ac 13:21; 15:23; Ro 11:1.** Ἑβρ. ἐξ Ἑβραίων *a Hebrew, the son of Hebrews* **Phil 3:5** (Goodsp., Probs., 175f; on the connotation of ancestral ἀρετή **Phil 3:5** cp. New Docs VII 233, no. 10, 5). ἐκ σπέρματός τινος **J 7:42; Ro 1:3; 11:1.** ἐξ ἐθνῶν **Ac 15:23;** cp. **Gal 2:15.** Cp. **Lk 23:7; Ac 23:34.** ἐκ τ. γῆς **J 3:31.** For this ἐκ τῶν κάτω **J 8:23** (opp. ἐκ τ. ἄνω). ἐκ (τούτου) τ. κόσμου **15:19ab; 17:14; 1J 2:16; 4:5.** ἐξ οὐρανοῦ ἢ ἐξ ἀνθρώπων **Mt 21:25; Mk 11:30.**—To express a part of the whole, subst.: οἱ ἐξ Ἰσραήλ *the Israelites* **Ro 9:6.** οἱ ἐξ ἐριθείας *selfish, factious people* **2:8.** οἱ ἐκ νόμου *partisans of the law* **4:14;** cp. vs. **16.** οἱ ἐκ πίστεως *those who have faith* **Gal 3:7, 9;** cp. the sg. **Ro 3:26; 4:16.** οἱ ἐκ περιτομῆς *the circumcision party* **Ac 11:2; Ro 4:12; Gal 2:12.** οἱ ἐκ τῆς περιτομῆς **Tit 1:10.** For this οἱ ὄντες ἐκ περιτομῆς **Col 4:11.** οἱ ἐκ τ. συναγωγῆς *members of the synagogue* **Ac 6:9.** οἱ ἐκ τῶν Ἀριστοβούλου **Ro 16:10f.** οἱ ἐκ τῆς Καίσαρος οἰκίας **Phil 4:22** (s. Καῖσαρ and οἰκία 3). In these cases the idea of belonging, the partisan use, often completely overshadows that of origin; cp. Dg 6:3.

ⓒ to denote derivation (Maximus Tyr. 13, 3f φῶς ἐκ πυρός; Ath. 18:3 γένεσιν … ἐξ ὕδατος) καπνὸς ἐκ τ. δόξης τ. θεοῦ **Rv 15:8** (cp. EpJer 20 καπνὸς ἐκ τ. οἰκίας). ἡ σωτηρία ἐκ τ. Ἰουδαίων ἐστίν **J 4:22.** εἶναι ἔκ τινος *come, derive from someone* or *someth.* (Jos., Ant. 7, 209) **Mt 5:37; J 7:17, 22; 1J 2:16, 21;** εἶναι is oft. to be supplied **Ro 2:29; 11:36; 1 Cor 8:6** (Plut., Mor. 1001c); **11:12; 2 Cor 4:7; Gal 5:8.** ἔργα ἐκ τοῦ πατρός **J 10:32.** οἰκοδομὴ ἐκ θεοῦ **2 Cor 5:1;** χάρισμα **1 Cor 7:7;** δικαιοσύνη **Phil 3:9.** φωνὴ ἐκ τ. στόματος αὐτοῦ **Ac 22:14.** Here belongs the constr. w. ἐκ for the subj. gen., as in ἡ ἐξ ὑμῶν (v.l.) ἀγάπη **2 Cor 8:7;** ὁ ἐξ ὑμῶν ζῆλος **9:2 v.l.; Rv 2:9** (cp. Vett. Val. 51, 16; CIG II 3459, 11 τῇ ἐξ ἑαυτῆς κοσμιότητι; pap. [Rossberg 14f]; 1 Macc 11:33 χάριν τῆς ἐξ αὐτῶν εὐνοίας; 2 Macc 6:26). ἐγένετο ζήτησις ἐκ τ. μαθητῶν Ἰωάννου *there arose a discussion on the part of John's disciples* **J 3:25** (Dionys. Hal. 8, 89, 4 ζήτησις πολλὴ ἐκ πάντων ἐγένετο; Appian, Bell. Civ. 2, 24 §91 σφαγή τις ἐκ τῶν στρατιωτῶν ἐγένετο).

ⓓ of the effective cause *by, because of* (cp. the 'perfectivizing' force of ἐκ and other prepositions in compounds, e.g. **Mt 4:7; Mk 9:15.** B-D-F §318, 5) α. personal in nature, referring to originator (X., An. 1, 1, 6; Diod. S. 19, 1, 4 [saying of Solon]; Arrian, Anab. 3, 1, 2; 4, 13, 6 of an inspired woman κατεχομένη ἐκ τοῦ θείου; Achilles Tat. 5, 27, 2; SibOr 3, 395; Just.: A I, 12, 5 ἐκ δαιμόνων φαύλων . . . καὶ ταῦτα . . . ἐνεργεῖσθαι, also D. 18, 3; Nicetas Eugen. 7, 85 H. ἐκ θεῶν σεσωσμένη; Ps.-Clem., Hom. p. 7, 19 Lag. τὸν ἐκ θεοῦ σοι ἀποδιδόμενον μισθόν): ὠφελεῖσθαι ἔκ τινος **Mt 15:5; Mk 7:11.** ζημιοῦσθαι **2 Cor 7:9.** λυπεῖσθαι **2:2.** εὐχαριστεῖσθαι **1:11.** ἀδικεῖσθαι **Rv 2:11.** ἐξ ἐμαυτοῦ οὐκ ἐλάλησα **J 12:49** (cp. Soph., El. 344 οὐδὲν ἐξ σαυτῆς λέγεις).

β. impersonal in nature (Arrian, Anab. 3, 21, 10 ἀποθνήσκειν ἐκ τ. τραυμάτων; 6, 25, 4; JosAs 29:8 ἐκ τοῦ τραύματος τοῦ λίθου; POxy 486, 32 τὰ ἐμὰ ἐκ τ. ἀναβάσεως τ. Νίλου ἀπολωλέναι): ἀποθανεῖν ἐκ τ. ὑδάτων **Rv 8:11.** πυροῦσθαι **3:18.** σκοτοῦσθαι **9:2.** φωτίζεσθαι **18:1.** κεκοπιακὼς ἐκ τῆς ὁδοιπορίας **J 4:6** (Aelian, VH 3, 23 ἐκ τοῦ πότου ἐκάθευδεν). ἔκαμον ἐκ τῆς ὁδοῦ GJs 15:1.

ⓔ of the reason which is a presupposition for someth.: *by reason of, as a result of, because of* (X., An. 2, 5, 5; Appian, Bell. Civ. 1, 42 §185 ἐκ προδοσίας; POxy 486, 28f ἐκ τῆς ἐπιστολῆς; Just., A I, 68, 3 ἐξ ἐπιστολῆς; numerous examples in Mayser II/2 p. 388; Philo, De Jos. 184 ἐκ διαβολῆς; Jos., Vi. 430; JosAs 11 παραλελυμένη . . . ἐκ τῆς πολλῆς ταπεινώσεως; Ar. 8, 6 ἐκ τούτων . . . τῶν ἐπιτηδευμάτων τῆς πλάνης; Just., A I, 4, 1 ἐκ τοῦ . . . ὀνόματος; also inf.: 33, 2 ἵνα . . . ἐκ τοῦ προειρῆσθαι πιστευθῇ 68, 3 al.): δικαιοῦσθαι ἔκ τινος **Ro 4:2; Gal 2:16; 3:24;** cp. **Ro 3:20, 30** (cp. εἴ τις ἐκ γένους [δίκαι]ος=has the right of citizenship by descent [i.e. has the law on his side]: letter of MAurelius 34, ZPE 8, '71, 170); οὐκ . . . ἡ ζωὴ αὐτοῦ ἐστιν ἐκ τῶν ὑπαρχόντων αὐτῷ *he does not live because of his possessions* **Lk 12:15.** ἐκ ταύτης τ. ἐργασίας **Ac 19:25.** ἐξ ἔργων λαβεῖν τὸ πνεῦμα **Gal 3:2, 5;** cp. **Ro 11:6.** ἐξ ἀναστάσεως λαβεῖν τ. νεκρούς **Hb 11:35.** ἐσταυρώθη ἐξ ἀσθενείας **2 Cor 13:4.** τὸ ἐξ ὑμῶν *as far as it depends on you* **Ro 12:18.**—ἐκ τοῦ πόνου *in anguish* **Rv 16:10;** cp. vs. **11; 8:13.**—ἐκ τούτου *for this reason, therefore* (SIG 1168, 47; 1169, 18; 44; 62f; BGU 423, 17=Mitt-Wilck. I/2, 480, 17) **J 6:66; 19:12.**

ⓕ Sim. ἐκ can introduce the means which one uses for a definite purpose, *with, by means of* (Polyaenus 3, 9, 62 ἐξ ἱμάντος=by means of a thong) ἐκ τοῦ μαμωνᾶ **Lk 16:9** (X., An. 6, 4, 9; PTebt 5, 80 [118 BC] ἐκ τ. ἱερῶν προσόδων; ParJer 1:7 [of Jerusalem] ἐκ τῶν χειρῶν σου ἀφανισθήτω; Jos., Vi. 142 ἐκ τ. χρημάτων); cp. **8:3.**

ⓖ of the source, fr. which someth. flows or comes:

α. λαλεῖν ἐκ τ. ἰδίων **J 8:44.** ἐκ τοῦ περισσεύματος τ. καρδίας **Mt 12:34.** τὰ ἐκ τ. ἱεροῦ *the food from the temple* **1 Cor 9:13.** ἐκ τ. εὐαγγελίου ζῆν *get one's living by proclaiming the gospel* vs. **14.**

β. information, insight, etc. (X., An. 7, 7, 43 ἐκ τῶν ἔργων κατέμαθες; Just., A I, 28, 1 ἐκ τῶν ἡμετέρων συγγραμμάτων . . . μαθεῖν 34, 2 al.) κατηχεῖσθαι ἐκ **Ro 2:18.** ἀκούειν ἐκ **J 12:34.** γινώσκειν **Mt 12:33; Lk 6:44; 1J 3:24; 4:6.** ἐποπτεύειν **1 Pt 2:12.** δεικνύναι **Js 2:18** (cp. ἀποδεικνύναι Just., D. 33, 1).

γ. of the inner life, etc., fr. which someth. proceeds (since Il. 9, 486): ἐκ καρδίας **Ro 6:17; 1 Pt 1:22 v.l.** (cp. Theocr. 29, 4; M. Ant. 3, 3). ἐκ ψυχῆς **Eph 6:6; Col 3:23** (X., An. 7, 7, 43, Oec. 10, 4; Jos., Ant. 17, 177; 1 Macc 8:27). ἐκ καθαρᾶς καρδίας **1 Ti 1:5; 2 Ti 2:22; 1 Pt 1:22.** ἐξ ὅλης τ. καρδίας σου καὶ ἐξ ὅλης τ. ψυχῆς σου καὶ ἐξ ὅλης τ. διανοίας σου καὶ ἐξ ὅλης τ. ἰσχύος σου **Mk 12:30;** cp. **Lk 10:27** (Dt 6:5; cp. Wsd 8:21; 4 Macc 7:18; Epict. 2, 23, 42 ἐξ ὅλης ψυχῆς). ἐκ πίστεως **Ro 14:23;** cp. **2 Cor 2:17.** Also of circumstances which accompany an action without necessarily being the source of it: γράφειν ἐκ πολλῆς θλίψεως *write out of great affliction* **2 Cor 2:4; Phil 1:17.**

ⓗ of the material out of which someth. is made (Hdt. 1, 194; Pla., Rep. 10, 616c; OGI 194, 28 [42 BC] a statue ἐκ σκληροῦ λίθου; PMagd 42, 5 [221 BC]=PEnteux 83, 5; POxy 707, 28; PGM 13, 659; Wsd 15:8; 1 Macc 10:11; Jdth 1:2; En 99:13; JosAs 3:9; Just., A I, 59, 1) *of, from* στέφανος ἐξ ἀκανθῶν **Mt 27:29; J 19:2;** cp. **2:15; 9:6; Ro 9:21; 1 Cor 15:47; Rv 18:12; 21:21;** perh. also **1 Cor 11:12** ἡ γυνὴ ἐκ τοῦ ἀνδρός.

ⓘ of the underlying rule or principle *according to, in accordance with* (Hdt., Pla. et al. [Kühner-G. I 461g], also OGI 48, 12 [III BC] ἐκ τ. νόμων; PEleph 1, 12 [312/11 BC] ἐκ δίκης; PPetr III, 26, 9 ἐκ κρίσεως; LXX, e.g. 1 Macc 8:30; Jos., Ant. 6, 296 ἐκ κυνικῆς ἀσκήσεως πεποιημένος τὸν βίον) ἐκ τ. λόγων **Mt 12:37** (cp. Wsd 2:20). ἐκ τ. στόματός σου κρινῶ σε *by what you have said* **Lk 19:22** (cp. Sus 61 Theod.; also X., Cyr. 2, 2, 21 ἐκ τ. ἔργων κρίνεσθαι). ἐκ τῶν γεγραμμένων *on the basis of things written* **Rv 20:12.** ἐκ τ. καλοῦντος **Ro 9:12.** ἐκ τ. ἔχειν *in accordance w. your ability* **2 Cor 8:11.** ἐξ ἰσότητος *on the basis of equality* vs. **13.**

❹ **marker used in periphrasis,** ***from, of***—ⓐ for the partitive gen. (B-D-F §164, 1 and 2; 169; Rob. 599; 1379).

α. after words denoting number εἷς, μία, ἕν (Hdt. 2, 46, 2 ἐκ τούτων εἷς; POxy 117, 14ff [II/III AD] δύο . . . ἐξ ὧν . . . ἓν ἐξ αὐτῶν; Tob 12:15 BA; Sir 32:1; Jos., Bell. 7, 47; JosAs 20:2 ἐκ τῶν παρθένων μία Just., D. 126, 4) **Mt 10:29; 18:12; 22:35; 27:48; Mk 9:17** al.; εἷς τις **J 11:49;** δύο **Mk 16:12; Lk 24:13; J 1:35; 21:2.** πέντε **Mt 25:2.** πολλοί (1 Macc 5:26; 9:69) **J 6:60, 66; 7:31; 11:19, 45.** οἱ πλείονες **1 Cor 15:6.** οὐδείς (Epict. 1, 29, 37; 1 Macc 5:54; 4 Macc 14:4; Ar. 13, 6; Just., D. 16, 2) **J 7:19; 16:5.** χιλιάδες ἐκ πάσης φυλῆς **Rv 7:4.**

β. after the indef. pron. (Plut., Galba 1065 [27, 2]; Herodian 5, 3, 9; 3 Macc 2:30; Jos., Vi. 279) **Lk 11:15; J 6:64; 7:25, 44, 48; 9:16; 11:37, 46** al. Also after the interrog. pron. **Mt 6:27; 21:31; Lk 11:5; 12:25; 14:28** al.

γ. the partitive w. ἐκ as subj. (2 Km 11:17) εἶπαν ἐκ τ. μαθητῶν αὐτοῦ **J 16:17.**—**Rv 11:9.** As obj., pl. **Mt 23:34; Lk 11:49; 21:16; 2J 4** (cp. Sir 33:12; Jdth 7:18; 10:17 al.).

δ. used w. εἶναι *belong to someone* or *someth.* (Jos., Ant. 12, 399) καὶ σὺ ἐξ αὐτῶν εἶ *you also belong to them* **Mt 26:73;** cp. **Mk 14:69f; Lk 22:58; J 7:50; 10:26; Ac 21:8;** cp. 2 Cl 18:1. οὐκ εἰμὶ ἐκ τ. σώματος *I do not belong to the body* **1 Cor 12:15f;** cp. 2 Cl 14:1.

ε. after verbs of supplying, receiving, consuming: ἐσθίειν ἔκ τινος (Tob 1:10; Sir 11:19; Jdth 12:2; JosAs 16:8) **1 Cor 9:7; 11:28; J 6:26, 50f; Rv 2:7.** πίνειν **Mt 26:29; Mk 14:25; J 4:13f; Rv 14:10;** χορτάζειν ἔκ τινος *gorge w. someth.* **19:21** (s. ζ below); μετέχειν **1 Cor 10:17;** λαμβάνειν (1 Esdr 6:31; Wsd 15:8) **J 1:16; Rv 18:4;** Hs 9, 24, 4. τὸ βρέφος . . . ἔλαβε μασθὸν ἐκ τῆς μητρὸς αὐτοῦ *the child took its mother's breast* GJs 19:2; διδόναι (Tob 4:16; Ezk 16:17) **Mt 25:8; 1J 4:13.** διαδιδόναι (Tob 4:16 A) **J 6:11.**

ζ. after verbs of filling: ἐπληρώθη ἐκ τῆς ὀσμῆς *was filled w. the fragrance* **J 12:3** cp. **Rv 8:5.** χορτασθῆναι ἔκ τινος *to be satisfied to the full w. someth.* **Lk 15:16.** γέμειν ἐξ ἁρπαγῆς *be full of greed* **Mt 23:25.**

ⓑ in periphrasis for the gen. of price or value *for* (Palaeph. 45; PFay 111, 16 [95/96 AD]; 119, 5 [c. 100 AD]; 131, 5; PLond II, 277, 9 p. 217 [23 AD]; BGU III, 916, 19 [I AD]; PAmh II, 133, 19 [II AD]; Jos., Ant. 14, 34; B-D-F §179) ἀγοράζειν τι ἔκ τινος **Mt 27:7** (POxy 745, 2 [c. 1 AD] τ. οἶνον ἠγόρασας ἐκ δραχμῶν ἕξ; EpJer 24); cp. **Ac 1:18; Mt 20:2.**

❺ **marker denoting temporal sequence,** ***from***—ⓐ of the time when someth. begins *from, from . . . on, for,* etc. ἐκ κοιλίας μητρός *from birth* (Ps 21:11; 70:6; Is 49:1) **Mt 19:12** al.; also ἐκ γενετῆς **J 9:1** (since Il. 24, 535; Od. 18, 6; s. also γενετή). ἐκ νεότητος (since Il. 14, 86; Ps 70:5; Sir 7:23; Wsd 8:2; 1 Macc 2:66; JosAs 17:4) **Mk 10:20; Lk 18:21.** ἐξ ἱκανῶν χρόνων *for a long time* **23:8.** ἐκ πολλῶν χρόνων *a long time before* 1 Cl 42:5 (cp. Epict. 2, 16, 17 ἐκ πολλοῦ χρόνου. Cp. ἐκ πολλοῦ Thu. 1, 68, 3; 2, 88, 2; ἐξ ὀλίγων ἡμερῶν Lysias, Epitaph. 1). ἐκ γενεῶν ἀρχαίων **Ac 15:21** (cp. X., Hell. 6, 1, 4 ἐκ πάντων προγόνων). ἐκ τ. αἰῶνος *since the world began* **J 9:32** (cp. ἐξ αἰῶνος Sext. Emp., Adv. Math. 9, 76; Diod. S. 4, 83, 3; Aelian, VH 6, 13; 12, 64; OGI 669, 61; Sir 1:4; 1 Esdr 2:17, 21; Jos., Bell. 5, 442). ἐξ ἐτῶν ὀκτώ *for eight years* **Ac 9:33;** cp. **24:10.** ἐξ ἀρχῆς (PTebt 40, 20 [117 BC]; Sir 15:14; 39:32; Jos., C. Ap. 1, 225; Ath. 8, 1) **J 6:64.** ἐκ παιδιόθεν *fr. childhood* **Mk 9:21** (s. παιδιόθεν. Just., A I, 15, 6 ἐκ παίδων. On the use of ἐκ w. an adv. cp. ἐκ τότε POxy 486 [II AD]; ἐκ πρωΐθεν 1 Macc 10:80).

ⓑ of temporal sequence—**α.** ἡμέραν ἐξ ἡμέρας *day after day* **2 Pt 2:8;** 2 Cl 11:2 (cp. Ps.-Eur., Rhes. 445; Henioch. Com. 5:13 K.; Theocr. 18, 35; Gen 39:10; Num 30:15; Sir 5:7; Esth 3:7; En 98:8; 103:10).

β. ἐκ δευτέρου *for the second time, again,* s. δεύτερος 2. ἐκ τρίτου **Mt 26:44** (ParJer 7:8; cp. PHolm 1, 32 ἐκ τετάρτου).

❻ various uses and units—ⓐ blending of constructions, cp. Rob. 599f: ἐκ for ἐν (Hdt., Thu. et al., s. Kühner-G. I 546f; LXX, e.g. Sus 26 Theod.; 1 Macc 11:41; 13:21; Jdth 15:5) ὁ πατὴρ ὁ ἐξ οὐρανοῦ δώσει **Lk 11:13.** μὴ καταβάτω ἆραι τὰ ἐκ τῆς οἰκίας αὐτοῦ **Mt 24:17.** τὴν ἐκ Λαοδικείας (ἐπιστολὴν) ἵνα καὶ ὑμεῖς ἀναγνῶτε **Col 4:16.**

ⓑ like the OT use of מִן: ἔκρινεν ὁ θεὸς τὸ κρίμα ὑμῶν ἐξ αὐτῆς *God has pronounced judgment for you against her* **Rv 18:20** (cp. Ps 118:84; Is 1:24; En 100:4; 104:3). ἐξεδίκησεν τὸ αἷμα τ. δούλων αὐτοῦ ἐκ χειρὸς αὐτῆς **19:2,** cp. **6:10** (both 4 Km 9:7).

ⓒ adv. expressions (Just., A I, 2, 1 ἐκ παντὸς τρόπου 'in every way'): ἐξ ἀνάγκης (ἀνάγκη 1). ἐκ συμφώνου *by mutual consent* (BGU 446, 13=Mitt-Wilck. II/2, 257, 13; CPR I, 11, 14 al. in pap; cp. Dssm., NB 82f [BS 225]) **1 Cor 7:5.** ἐκ λύπης *reluctantly* **2 Cor 9:7.** ἐκ περισσοῦ *extremely* (Dio Chrys. 14 [31], 64; Lucian, Pro Merc. Cond. 13; Da 3:22 Theod.; Galen, CMG V/10/2/2 p. 284, 17 [-ττ]) **Mk 6:51; 1 Th 5:13 v.l.;** ἐκ μέτρου *by measure = sparingly* **J 3:34.** ἐκ μέρους (Galen, CMG V/10/2/2 p. 83, 24) *part by part = as far as the parts are concerned, individually* **1 Cor 12:27** (distributive; cp. PHolm 1, 7 ἐκ δραχμῶν ϛ′=6 dr. each); mostly in contrast to 'complete', *only in part* **13:9** (BGU 538, 35; 574, 10; 887, 6; 17 al. in pap; EpArist 102). ἐξ ὀνόματος *individually, personally, by name* IEph 20:2; IPol 4:2; 8:2.

ⓓ ἐκ . . . εἰς w. the same word repeated gives it special emphasis (Plut., Galba 1058 [14, 2] ἐκ προδοσίας εἰς προδοσίαν; Ps 83:8) ἐκ πίστεως εἰς πίστιν **Ro 1:17.—2 Cor 2:16** (twice).—The result and goal are thus indicated **Ro 11:36; 1 Cor 8:6; Col 1:16.** AFridrichsen, ConNeot 12, '48, 54.—DELG s.v. ἐξ. M-M.

ἕκαστος, η, ον (Hom.+) **one of an aggregate in a distributive sense, *each, every,*** distributive pronoun—ⓐ As adj. ἕκαστον δένδρον *every tree* (perh. *both kinds of trees,* good and bad, w. ἕκαστος=ἑκάτερος, as in late H. Gk.; s. HSahlin, Zwei Lukas-Stellen, '45, 5 w. ref. there; L-S-J-M s.v. ἕκαστος IV) **Lk 6:44.** ἑκάστῳ στρατιώτῃ **J 19:23.** καθ' ἑκάστην ἡμέραν *every day* (Thu. 6, 63, 2; X., Mem. 4, 2, 12 et al.; PAmh 136, 7 al. in pap; Ex 5:8; Esth 2:11; 3:4 al.; TestAbr A 86, 22f [Stone p. 20] καθεκάστην) **Hb 3:13;** B 19:10; also ἑκάστης ἡμέρας AcPl Ha 6, 8 (Just., D. 2, 6) κατὰ μῆνα ἕκαστον (Lucian, Nav. 24; BGU 86, 36 al. in pap) **Rv 22:2,** but ἕκ. may refer to ξύλον.

ⓑ As subst. *each one, every one* **Mt 16:27; J 6:7; Ac 4:35; Ro 2:6; 12:3.** W. partitive gen. foll. **Lk 13:15; Ac 2:38; Ro 14:12; 1 Cor 15:38; 16:2;** 1 Cl 24:5; 41:1; B 2:8 (cp. Just., A I, 18, 1 ἑκάστου τῶν . . . βασιλέων). Followed by ἴδιος (1 Esdr 5:8; Job 2:11; 3 Macc 5:21, 34): ἑκάστῳ κατὰ τὴν ἰδίαν δύναμιν **Mt 25:15.** Cp. **Lk 6:44; Ac 2:8; Ro 14:5;** Papias (2:16) al.—ἕ. *every one* (has or does someth., but one does one thing, another someth. else) **1 Cor 1:12; 14:26.**—Strengthened εἷς ἕκαστος *every single one* (Hdt. 6, 128; Thu. 1, 77, 6; 2, 60, 4 et al.; PTebt 397, 1; 4 Macc 13:13; 15:19; Jos., Ant. 19, 305; JosAs 2:10; Ath. 4:1 πρὸς ἓν ἕκαστον; also ἕ. . . . τις Just., A II, 13, 3 and D. 134, 2). **Mt 26:22; Ac 2:6; 20:31;** Dg 8:3; Hs 8, 1, 5; 8, 11, 2 al. W. part. gen. foll. (X., An. 6, 6, 12; Ptolem., Apotel. 1, 2, 11 εἷς ἕκαστος τῶν ἀνθρώπων; 4 Macc 8:5, 9; 13:18; 16:24; 27:5 JosAs 27:5) **Lk 4:40; 16:5; Ac 2:3; 17:27; 21:26; 1 Cor 12:18; Eph 4:7; 1 Th 2:11; 2 Th 1:3.** ἀνὰ εἷς ἕκαστος *every single one* (ἀνά 3) **Rv 21:21.** καθ' ἓν ἕκαστον *one after the other = in detail* (Hyperid. 3, 14; Dionys. Hal., Comp. 3; 23; PHal 1, 223 [III BC]) **Ac 21:19;** 1 Cl 32:1. For this καθ' ἕκαστα (PCairGoodsp 15, 14; Just., D. 1, 4; Tat. 12, 3; καθ' ἕκαστος Ar. [Milne 74, 21]; καθ' ἕκαστον Tat. 41, 2; Ath. 28, 4) B 1:7.—The sg. is used w. pron. or verbs in the pl. (Hom. et al.; LXX; Jos., Bell. 6, 19) ὑμῖν ἑκάστῳ **Rv 2:23;** cp. **6:11.** ἵνα σκορπισθῆτε ἕκαστος **J 16:32;** cp. **Mt 18:35; Lk 2:3** (Appian, Liby. 39 §164 ἀνεζεύγνυον ἑκάτερος ἐς τὸ αὑτοῦ στρατόπεδον); **Ac 11:29; Eph 4:25; Hb 8:11** (Jer 38:34); **Rv 5:8; 20:13.**—The pl. ἕκαστοι is extremely rare (Polyb. 1, 12, 9; Diod. S. 14, 5, 4; Phlegon: 257 fgm. 36, 3, 14 Jac.; Lucian, Herm. 68; Ath. 18, 2; 22, 5; UPZ 110, 47; 53; 152 [164 BC]) **Phil 2:4; Rv 6:11** t.r. (Erasmian rdg.); Hs 5, 6, 2.—S. πᾶς and ref. to Schmidt, Syn. IV 547. DELG. M-M. TW.

ἑκάστοτε adv. of time, preferred by Atticists: Phryn. 103 Lob. (Pre-Socr., Hdt.+; SIG 107, 44 and 45; 114, 20; 578, 60; PAmh 78, 4; PFlor 367, 20; TestSol 13:14 C; Just.) ***at any time, always*** **2 Pt 1:15.**—DELG s.v. ἕκαστος. M-M.

ἑκάτερος, α, ον (Pind. et al.; pap, LXX; En 24:2; Test12Patr; ApcrEzk [Epiph. 70, 16]; EpArist; Philo, Sacr. Abel. 138; Jos., Ant. 12, 239; Tat.; Mel. P. 48, 341 [Christ.]; Ath.) ***each of two, both*** Dg 12:4; Agr 2.—DELG s.v. ἕκαστος.

ἑκατέστησας s. καθίστημι.

ἑκατόν indecl. (Hom.+; Just., D. 32, 4 as round number) ***one hundred*** **Mt 13:8, 23; 18:12, 28; Lk 15:4; 16:6f; 24:13 v.l.** (ἑκ. ἑξήκοντα); **J 19:39; 21:11; Ac 1:15; Rv 7:4; 14:1, 3; 21:17;** Hv 4, 1, 6 as a numerical symbol (s. entry ρ′; Lghtf. records the full form).—**Mk 4:8, 20** ἓν ἑ. is prob. the correct rdg. (εἷς 4b); κατὰ ἑ. *by hundreds* **6:40.**—DELG. M-M.

ἑκατονταετής, ές (so rightly L., W-H. [s. B-D-F §13; Lob., Phryn. p. 406f]; mostly [all oth. edd.] accented ἑκατονταέτης) ***a hundred years old*** (since Pind., P. 4, 502; Gen 17:17; Philo, Mut. Nom. 1) ἑ. που ὑπάρχων *about* 100 *yrs. old* **Ro 4:19.**—DELG s.v. ἑκατόν.

ἑκατονταπλασίων, ον (ἑκατόν + -πλασιών) ***a hundred times as much, a hundredfold*** (X., Oec. 2, 3; 2 Km 24:3; GrBar 15:2.—Neut. pl. as adv. Strabo 3, 1, 5) **Lk 8:8.** ἑκατονταπλασίονα λαμβάνειν (Georg. Mon. 678, 60 ἔλαβον τὸ χρέος ἑκατονταπλασίονα) **Mt 19:29; Mk 10:30; Lk 18:30 v.l.** (s. JLebreton, RSR 20, 1930, 42–44).—S. DELG s.v. -πλάσιος.

ἑκατοντάρχης, ου, ὁ (Aeschyl. fgm. 304 M.=182 N. [in Athen. 1, 11 D.]; Hdt. 7, 81 et al.; Dionys. Hal.; Plut.; Vett. Val.

p. 78, 26; Herodian 5, 4, 7; OGI 665, 23 [49 AD]; PRyl 141, 2 [37 AD]; 4 Km 11:10, 15; s. Thackeray 156; Jos., Bell. 2, 63) **a Roman officer commanding about a hundred men** (subordinate to a tribune), ***centurion, captain*** **Mt 8:13; Lk 7:6; 23:47; Ac 10:1, 22; 21:32; 22:26; 24:23; 27:1, 6, 11, 31, 43.** For this ἑκατόνταρχος (X., Cyr. 5, 3, 41; Plut., Lucull. 515 [35, 2]; Herodian 5, 4, 12; Sb 599; PRein 26, 4; 30, 2 et al. pap; LXX; Philo, Mos. 1, 317; Jos., Bell. 3, 124, Ant. 17, 282; Just.—Both forms in the same pass.: Jos., Ant. 14, 69) **Mt 8:5, 8** (s. χιλίαρχος and PZuntz in JTS 46, '45, 183); **27:54** (in all these pass. ἑκατοντάρχης is v.l.); **Ac 22:25; 28:16 v.l.;** 1 Cl 37:3.—**Lk 7:2** can be either form, as well as the gen. pl. in **Ac 23:17, 23,** since the placing of the accents in the editions is not definitive (Mayser 256f).—Schürer I 362–72 (lit.); CCichorius, Cohors: Pauly-W. IV 1901, 231–56; AvDomaszewski, D. Rangordnung d. röm. Heeres 1908, 2d ed. BDobson '67; ABludau, D. Militärverhältnisse in Cäsarea im apost. Zeitalter: Theol.-prakt. Monatsschr. 17, 1906, 136–43; FLundgreen, D. paläst. Heerwesen in d. ntl. Zeit: Pj 17, 1921, 46–63; TBroughton, The Rom. Army: Beginn. I/5, 427–41; GZuntz, The Centurion of Capernaum, etc.: JTS 46, '45, 183–90.—DELG s.v. ἑκατόν. M-M.

ἑκατόνταρχος s. ἑκατοντάρχης.

ἐκβαίνω 2 aor. ἐξέβην (Hom. et al., pap, LXX, EpArist, Philo) ***go out, come from*** w. ἀπό (PGen 54, 25 ἀπὸ τ. κώμης; Sir 38:18) **Hb 11:15.**—M-M.

ἐκβάλλω fut. ἐκβαλῶ; 2 aor. ἐξέβαλον; plpf. ἐκβεβλήκειν **Mk 16:9.** Pass.: 1 fut. ἐκβληθήσομαι; aor. ἐξεβλήθην; pf. 3 sg. ἐκβέβληται (Just.), ptc. ἐκβεβλημένος (Hom.+) gener. 'to throw out', then

❶ **force to leave, *drive out, expel,*** τινά (SIG 1109, 95; PTebt 105, 31; Gen 3:24 al.; Jos., Bell. 1, 31, Ant. 1, 58) **Mt 21:12** (Chariton 3, 2, 12 πάντας ἐ. fr. the temple of Aphrodite; Lysimachus: 621 fgm. 1, 306 Jac. [in Jos., C. Ap. 1, 306] God demands that the Egyptian king ἐκβάλλειν ἐκ τῶν ἱερῶν those who are unclean; CRoth, Cleansing of the Temple and Zech 14:21: NovTest 4, '60, 174–81; for lit. on Jesus' action s. DSeeley, CBQ 55, '93, 263 n. 1); **Mk 1:12** is perh. to be understood in this sense, cp. Gen 3:24, but s. 2 below; **Mk 5:40; 11:15; Lk 19:45; 20:12.** Pass. **Mt 9:25;** Hs 1, 4; 9, 14, 2. τινὰ or τὶ ἔκ τινος (Dio Chrys. 49 [66], 3; SIG 317, 12; PLond III, 887, 6 p. 1 [III BC]; PMagd 12, 11=PEnteux 54, 11; Ex 6:1; Num 22:6 al.; Philo, Cher. 10) **J 2:15;** Hs 8, 7, 5. ἀπό τινος (Ex 23:31; Num 22:11; 2 Ch 11:16; Philo, Det. Pot. Ins. 163; Jos., Ant. 13, 352; Just., D. 92, 2 ἀπὸ τῆς Ἰερουσαλήμ) **Ac 13:50.** ἔξω τινός *out of someth.* (Lev 14:40; 1 Macc 13:47 v.l.): a city (Hyperid. 5:31) **Lk 4:29; Ac 7:58;** cp. Hs 1:6; ἐ. ἔξω (without amplification as 2 Ch 29:16) **J 6:37; 9:34f** (s. below); **Ac 9:40.** Pass. **Lk 13:28; J 12:31** (βάλλω P[66] et al.). W. the destination given ἐ. εἴς τι *drive someone out into someth.* (Dt 29:27; 2 Ch 29:16; Jer 22:28; Mel., P. 48): into the darkness outside (cp. En 10:4) **Mt 8:12; 22:13; 25:30.**—From a vineyard **Mt 21:39; Mk 12:8; Lk 20:15;** in these three passages *throw out, toss out* is prob. meant.—Mid., throw someth. overboard to save oneself: **Ac 27:38** grain (the act. in this sense Diod. S. 3, 40, 5; τὰ ὑπάρχοντα En 101:5; Jos., Bell. 1, 280).—Used esp. of the expulsion of spirits who have taken possession of a pers. (Jos., Ant. 6, 211; Just. A II, 10, 6 δαίμονας … ἐκβαλὼν τῆς πολιτείας; PGM 4, 1227 πρᾶξις γενναία ἐκβάλλουσα δαίμονας; 1252; 1254) **Mt 8:31; 9:33f; 10:1, 8; 12:26; 17:19; Mk 1:34, 39, 43; 3:15, 23; 6:13; 7:26** (ἔκ τινος); **9:18, 28; 16:9** (παρά τινος); **Lk 9:40; 11:14; 13:32.** W. the means given (Lucian-Epigr. in Anth. Pal. 11, 427 δαίμονα ἐ. δυνάμει) τῷ σῷ ὀνόματι *by your name* **Mt 7:22.** λόγῳ *with a word* **8:16.** For this ἔν τινι *by someone* or *someth.* by the ruler of the evil spirits **9:34; Mk 3:22;** by Beelzebul **Mt 12:24, 27; Lk 11:15, 18f;** by the name of Jesus **Mk 9:38; 16:17; Lk 9:49;** by the finger of God **Lk 11:20;** cp. vs. **19;** ἐν πνεύματι θεοῦ **Mt 12:28.**—GSterling, Jesus as Exorcist: CBQ 55, '93, 467–93.—*Expel someone fr. a group, repudiate someone* (Pherecyd. 83 Zeus expels insolent deities) a servant girl **Gal 4:30** (Gen 21:10); a wife (Demosth. 59, 63; 83; Diod. S. 12, 18, 1; BGU 1050, 15; PGiss 2, 23; Lev 21:7; Pr 18:22a; Sir 7:26; Jos., Ant. 16, 215; 17, 78) Agr 18; ἐκ τ. ἐκκλησίας ἐ. **3J 10** (cp. POxy 104, 17; Jos., Bell. 2, 143). Vss. **J 9:34f,** referred to above, prob. belong here too, since the Johannine love of multiple meaning has combined the mngs. *drive out of the audience-room* and *expel from the synagogue.*—Idiom: λόγους ἐ. εἰς τὰ ὀπίσω *cast words behind oneself*=pay no attention to them 1 Cl 35:8 (Ps 49:17); ἐ. τὸ ὄνομα *disdain, spurn the name* **Lk 6:22** (cp. Pla., Crito 46b and Rep. 2, 377c; Soph., Oed. Col. 636; 646); difft., Wlh. ad loc.; s. Black, An Aramaic Approach[3], '67, 135f, w. special ref. to Dt 22:14, 19.

❷ **to cause to go or remove from a position (without force), *send out/away, release, bring out*** (PRyl 80, 1 [I AD] ἐκβάλετε … ὑδροφύλακας; 1 Macc 12:27) workers **Mt 9:38; Lk 10:2** (cp. PMich 618, 15f [II AD]); *send away* **Js 2:25;** *release* **Ac 16:37;** *lead out* (Μαρτύριον τῆς ἁγ. Αἰκατερίνας 18 p. 17 Viteau: ἐκέλευσεν ὁ βασ. ἐκβληθῆναι αὐτὴν ἐκ τ. φυλακῆς; Theophanes, Chron. 388, 28) **Mk 1:12** (but s. 1 above); *bring out* of sheep **J 10:4** (cp. Hs 6, 2, 6; Longus 3, 33, 2 προσέβαλλε ταῖς μητράσι τοὺς ἄρνας; BGU 597, 4 ἵνα βάλῃ τὸν μόσχον πρὸ τ. προβάτων).

❸ **to cause someth. to be removed from someth., *take out, remove*** (1 Macc 13:48; Diosc. 1, 50; s. Rydbeck 155–58; 184) a beam or splinter ἐκ τ. ὀφθαλμοῦ **Mt 7:4f; Lk 6:42;** Ox 1 verso, 2 (ASyn. 68, 44) (cp. GTh 26; Aesop. p. 28 Ursing ἐκβάλλεις ἄκανθα[ν] ἐκ ποδῶν μου); *bring out* τὶ *someth.* (Horapollo 2, 105; TestAbr A 6, p. 83, 23 [Stone p. 14] ἐκ τοῦ κόλπου '[pearls] out of the purse') ἐκ τοῦ ἀγαθοῦ θησαυροῦ ἐ. τὰ ἀγαθά *out of the good treasure* (=the tr. of the good) *that which is good* **Mt 12:35; 13:52;** *take out* a sum of money **Lk 10:35.** Of an eye, tear *out* and *throw* away **Mk 9:47** (Syntipas p. 101, 2; cp. La 3:16 ἐ. ὀδόντας). Of material in the body (Ps.-Plut., Hom. 205; schol. on Nicander, Alexiph. 485; cp. Ps.-Aristot., Mirabilia 6 οἱ κυνηγοὶ εἰς ἀγγεῖον αὐτὴν [=τὴν τοῦ ἀνθρώπου κόπρον] ἐμβάλοντες=the hunters let their excrement fall into a pot.—ἐκβ. τι=let someth. fall Diog. L. 6, 35) *evacuate* **Mt 15:17.**

❹ **to pay no attention to, *disregard*** τὴν αὐλὴν τὴν ἔξωθεν τοῦ ναοῦ ἔκβαλε ἔξωθεν *leave out* (of consideration) *the outer court of the temple* **Rv 11:2** (Epicurus in Diog. L. 10, 147 ἐ. τι=disregard someth.; M. Ant. 12, 25 βάλε ἔξω τὴν ὑπόληψιν=do not concern yourself about … ; Mitt-Wilck. II/2, 372 VI, 22f [II AD] τὸ ἀναγνωσθὲν δάνειον ἐκβάλλω=I pass over, omit. On the belief of Jerusalem's inhabitants that the temple could be saved, while the beleagured city was ruined, s. Jos., Bell. 5, 459).

❺ **to bring someth. about, *cause to happen, bring*** ἐ. εἰς νῖκος τὴν κρίσιν *lead justice on to victory* **Mt 12:20** (s. κρίσις 3).—B. 713. M-M. TW.

ἔκβασις, εως, ἡ (s. ἐκβαίνω; Hom. et al.; pap, LXX; Jos., Ant. 1, 91; Mel., P. 58, 427 [ἐμ- Ch.])

❶ **end point of a duration, *end*** ἐ. τῆς ἀναστροφῆς **Hb 13:7** can mean *the end of one's life* (cp. Marinus, Vi. Procli 26 ἐ. τοῦ βίου; Wsd 2:17), but can also be understood as

❷ **outcome of an event or state, *outcome*** (cp. PRyl 122, 5 [II AD]=produce [τῶν ἐδαφῶν]; Wsd 11:14) as result of one's way of life, w. implication of success **Hb 13:7.**

❸ **way out of some difficulty,** ***a way out, end*** (Comp. II 107f J. [Menand., fgm. 696 Kock III 200] τ. κακοῦ; Polyb. 3, 7, 2; Epict. 2, 7, 9, Ench. 32, 3; Vett. Val. 180, 14f ἡ ἔκβασις τ. πραγμάτων; cp. 186, 24; PFlor 74, 16 τ. ἑορτῆς) **1 Cor 10:13** (s. WGauld, ET 52, '40/41, 337–40).—DELG s.v. βαίνω. M-M. TW.

ἐκβλαστάνω 1 aor. ἐξεβλάστησα (s. βλαστάνω; Hippocr., Alim. 6 ed. Litt. IX p. 100; Lucian, Ver. Hist. 2, 41) **to spring up as a sprout, of seed,** ***sprout up*** (so lit., Theophr., CP 1, 3, 5; 3, 23, 1; Num 17:20; Job 38:27; TestJos 19:6 [A]) **Mk 4:5 v.l.**

ἐκβολή, ῆς, ἡ (s. ἐκβάλλω; Aeschyl. et al.; pap, LXX; Jos., Ant. 17, 86, C. Ap. 1, 294 al.) gener. 'to throw out of an area or object'; in our lit., as nautical t.t. ***jettisoning,*** of a ship's cargo to save the vessel in a storm (cp. Aeschyl., Sept. 769; Aristot., EN 3, 1, 5, 1110a, 9; Lucian, De Mer. Cond. 1): ἐκβολὴν ποιεῖσθαι *jettison* (Pollux 1, 99; Jon 1:5) **Ac 27:18.**—DELG s.v. βάλλω. M-M.

ἔκβολος, ον (Eur. et al.; Jdth 11:11) **pert. to being cast off as unwanted,** ***rejected, excluded*** ἔσονται ἔκβολοι *they will be excluded* Hv 3, 5, 5.—S. DELG s.v. βάλλω. M-M.

ἐκγαμίζω (Rhet. Gr. IV 247, 14.—Eustath. in Il. 9, 384 p. 758, 54 ἐγγαμίζειν οἱ ὕστερον λέγουσιν) **to arrange marriage for someone,** ***give in marriage,*** as v.l. in **Mt 24:38** and **1 Cor 7:38** (here twice). Pass. *be given in marriage* **Mt 22:30; Lk 17:27; 20:35,** everywhere as v.l. Except for the Mt passages, most edd. read γαμίζω (q.v. 1).—M-M.

ἔκγονος, ον prim. sense 'born of, sprung from'; usu. subst. ὁ, ἡ ἔκγονος (ἐκγίγνομαι 'be born of'; Hom. et al.; ins, pap; JosAs 29:11 cod. Ἀτῷ ἐ. [p. 85, 15 Bat.]; s. Mayser 228; Orpheus 10 Denis p. 165) τὰ ἔκγονα gener. ***descendants*** (Diod. S. 4, 82, 4; Diog. L. 3, 81; LXX, Philo; Jos., Ant. 11, 2; 111) spec. *grandchildren* (Hesych. τέκνα τέκνων; OGI 740, 4f [I BC] τ. τέκνων καὶ τ. ἐκγόνων; Dio Chrys. 21 [38], 21; Chariton 2, 9, 2; Herm. Wr. 10, 14b; Ath., R. 611, 18 ἐγγόνων; s. L-S-J-M entry ἔγγονος). The ancient versions understand it in the latter sense **1 Ti 5:4.** Hm 9, 9 v.l. for θυγάτηρ.—B. 112; 121. DELG s.v. γίγνομαι B 223. M-M. TW. Sv.

ἐκδαπανάω 1 fut. pass. ἐκδαπανηθήσομαι ***spend, exhaust*** (s. δαπανάω; Polyb. 24, 7, 4 τὰς προσόδους; Jos., Ant. 15, 117 τὰς προθυμίας; Galen freq.; PBad 19, 19; GrBar 9:8; Tat. 6, 2) (orig. to spend completely, use up, as of funds in Polyb. above) in our lit. only fig. in pass. *be spent* of the sacrifice of one's own life ὑπέρ τινος *for someone* **2 Cor 12:15** (ZNW 18, 1918, 201).—DELG s.v. δάπτω.

ἐκδέχομαι impf. ἐξεδεχόμην; fut. ἐκδέξομαι; 1 aor. ἐξεδεξάμην (both LXX); pf. 3 sg. ἐκδέδεκται Gen 44:32 (Hom. et al.; pap, LXX; TestSol D 7:4; TestAbr A 16 p. 97, 15 [Stone p. 42]; TestJob; TestGad 7:4; TestIss 4:3; ParJer 2:9; GrBar; EpArist 205; Philo, Op. M. 34; Joseph., Just.; intr.: Ath. 12, 2 τὸν ἐκδεχόμενον βίον 'the life to come') 'take, receive'; in our lit. **to remain in a place or state and await an event or the arrival of someone,** ***expect, wait*** (Soph. et al.; pap) τινά *(for) someone* (Soph., Philoct. 123; Polyb. 3, 45, 6; BGU 892, 6 ἐκδεχόμενός σε) **Ac 17:16;** συνερχόμενοι εἰς τὸ φαγεῖν ἀλλήλους ἐκδέχεσθε *when you come together to eat, wait for one another* **1 Cor 11:33; 16:11.** τὶ *(for) someth.* (Plut., Mar. 414 [17, 1]; Ps.-Apollod. 1, 9, 27, 3; POxy 724, 12; 939, 27; PFlor 332, 5 σου τὴν παρουσίαν; Jos., Ant. 11, 328; TestGad 7:4; TestIss 4:3) the movement of the water **J 5:3 v.l.;** the reign of God 2 Cl 12:1 (Lucian, Nav. 28 ἐ. τὴν βασιλείαν); τ. ἅγιον αἰῶνα B 10:11; fruit **Js 5:7;** 2 Cl 20:3; the heavenly city **Hb 11:10.** Foll. by ἕως *wait until* (Dionys. Hal. 6, 67 ἕως ἂν γένηταί τι) **Hb 10:13.** W. acc. and ἕως foll. ἐκδέξομαι αὐτὸν ἕως ὀψέ *I will wait for him until evening* Hs 9, 11, 2. ἔκδεξαί με ὧδε, ἕως *wait here for me, until* Hs 9, 10, 5.—S. ἐκδοχή.—M-M. TW.

ἔκδηλος, ον ***quite evident, plain*** (Hom. et al.; Demosth. 24, 10; Vett. Val. 92, 10; SIG 695, 63 [II BC]; OGI 665, 13 [49 AD]; PHerm 6, 3=Stud. Pal. V, 6, 3; 3 Macc 3:19; 6:5; EpArist 85; Philo; Joseph.) **2 Ti 3:9;** AcPlCor 1:16.—M-M.

ἐκδηλόω 1 aor. impv. ἐκδήλωσον (Theophr., CP 2, 18, 4 al.) ***show plainly*** εἰ πονε[ῖ]ς ἐκδ[ήλωσον] *if you are troubled, tell me* AcPl Ha 7, 30.

ἐκδημέω 1 aor. inf. ἐκδημῆσαι—❶ orig. of movement from a geographical area, 'leave one's country, take a long journey' (Soph., Oed. R. 114; Hdt. 1, 30; Pla., Leg. 12, 952d; Epict. 1, 4, 22; BGU 1197, 7 [4 BC]; pap since III BC incl. PTebt 316, 20; POxy 59, 16; TestAbr A; Jos., Ant. 9, 88) then fig. (cp. ἐκδημία of death Anth. Pal. 3, 5) ἐκ τοῦ σώματος ***leave, get away fr., the body*** **2 Cor 5:8** (TestAbr A 15 p. 95, 24 [Stone p. 38]; cp. Plut., Mor 943a–c, s. GSoury, La Démonologie de Plutarque '42; lit. on γυμνός 1b).

❷ 'be in a strange land' (opp. ἐνδημέω, as Philo, Spec. Leg. 4, 142; pap, e.g. PMichZen 80, 4) fig. ***be away*** abs. **2 Cor 5:9** (cp. Pla., Leg. 9, 864e ἐκδημῶν abs.=living in exile); w. ἀπὸ τ. κυρίου vs. **6.**—DELG s.v. δῆμος. M-M. TW. Spicq.

ἐκδίδωμι (s. δίδωμι; Hom. et al.; ins, pap, LXX, TestSol 13:9 C; TestAbr A 12 p. 91, 25 [Stone p. 30]; 14 p. 93, 24 [St. p. 34]; Philo, Joseph.) fut. ἐκδώσω; aor. ἐξέδωκα LXX; in our lit. only mid.; fut. ἐκδώσομαι; 2 aor. ἐξεδόμην, 3 sg. ἐξέδετο (on this form s. B-D-F §94, 1; W-S. §14, 11; Mlt-H. 212; it is also found PSI 288, 8 [II AD]); pf. ἐκδέδομαι LXX, pass. ptc. ἐκδεδομένος LXX ***let out for hire, lease*** (so the act. in earlier Gk.: Hdt. et al.; Pla., Leg. 7 p. 806d; the mid. Polyb. 6, 17, 2; of hiring out a son as apprentice POxy 275, 6 [66 AD]; PTebt 385, 3) τὶ a vineyard **Mt 21:33, 41; Mk 12:1; Lk 20:9;** 1 Cl 55:2 v.l. (for παραδίδωμι).—B. 810. M-M.

ἐκδιηγέομαι fut. ἐκδιηγήσομαι; aor. inf. ἐκδιηγήσασθαι (s. διηγέομαι; Hippocr., Progn. II p. 110; Aristot., Rhet. 23 p. 1434b, 4; Galen; LXX; ParJer 4:12; Philo, Mos. 1, 235; Jos., Bell. 5, 567, Ant. 5, 279; Just., D. 22:9 [for διηγῇ Ps 49, 16 w. cod. A]) **to provide detailed information when telling someth.,** ***tell (in detail)*** τὶ *someth.* **Ac 15:3.** Abs. w. dat. of pers. **13:41** (Hab 1:5); 1 Cl 35:7 v.l. (for διηγέομαι).—S. DELG s.v. ἡγέομαι.

ἐκδικέω (s. ἐκδίκησις, ἔκδικος) fut. ἐκδικήσω; 1 aor. ἐξεδίκησα, impv. ἐκδίκησον. Pass.: fut. ἐκδικηθήσομαι; aor. ἐξεδιχήθην; pf. 3 sg. ἐκδεδίκηται LXX (Diod. S., Plut., Herodian, ins, pap, LXX; En 20:4; TestSol 20:2; TestJud 23:3 [not A]; JosAs, Philo, Joseph., Just.; Ath. 32, 1; s. Anz 364).

❶ **to procure justice for someone,** ***grant justice*** (Plut., Ag. et Cleom. 845 [5, 5]; PAmh 134, 10; PStras 41, 9; 1 Macc 6:22; Jos., Ant. 6, 303) τινά **Lk 18:5;** taking justice into one's own hands ἐκ. ἑαυτόν *take one's revenge* **Ro 12:19** (cp. POxy 937, 7 ἐκδικήσω ἐμαυτόν). ἐ. με ἀπὸ τ. ἀντιδίκου μου *see to it that I get justice against my opponent* **Lk 18:3** (cp. TestLevi 2:2).—On the parable, GDelling, ZNW 53, '62, 1–25=Studien zum NT, '70, 203–25.

❷ **to inflict appropriate penalty for wrong done** (of special significance in an honor/shame-oriented society) ***punish, take vengeance for*** τὶ (Ctesias, fgm. 37=688 fgm. 13a p. 459, 20 Jac.

φόνον; Plut., Ant. 67, 2 τ. τοῦ πατρὸς θάνατον; Herodian 2, 6, 9; Jos., Ant. 9, 171; Just., A I, 68, 10 [Hadrian]) **2 Cor 10:6.** τὸ αἷμα (Dt 32:43; 4 Km 9:7; prayers for vengeance fr. Rheneia: Dssm., LO 353f, 359 [LAE 424f, 431f]; cp. SIG 1181, 11), w. the pers. *on* whom vengeance is taken, or who is punished, designated by ἐκ (Num 31:2; 1 Km 24:13; ApcPl 40 Tdf.) **Rv 6:10,** or ἐκ χειρός τινος (4 Km 9:7) **19:2.**

❸ **to carry out one's obligations in a worthy manner,** ***do justice to*** ἐ. τὸν τόπον *do justice to one's official position* IPol 1:2 (cp. Cornelius in Eus., HE 6, 43, 9 and 11; Origen, In Mt. bk.12, 14 p. 98, 28ff ed. EKlostermann '35: οἱ τ. τόπον τῆς ἐπισκοπῆς ἐκδικοῦντες χρῶνται τῷ ῥητῷ ὡς Πέτρος). S. ἐκδίκησις.—DELG s.v. δίκη. M-M. TW.

ἐκδίκησις, εως, ἡ ***vengeance, punishment*** (s. ἐκδικέω, ἔκδικος; Polyb. 3, 8, 10 ἐ. ποιεῖσθαι; SIG 563, 14 [III BC]; LXX, En; TestSol 22:4 H; Test12Patr, Philo)

❶ **meting out of justice,** ***giving of justice*** ἐ. ποιεῖν *see to it that justice is done,* w. gen. of the person for whom it is done (Num 31:2; 1 Macc 2:67) **Lk 18:7f;** also w. the dat. of the pers. for whom it is done (Judg 11:36; TestSol 22, 4) **Ac 7:24.**

❷ **retaliation for harm done,** ***vengeance*** (s. ἐκδικέω 2) ἐμοὶ ἐκδίκησις *vengeance belongs to me* **Ro 12:19; Hb 10:30.**

❸ **penalty inflicted on wrongdoers,** abs. ***punishment*** (of Paul's opponent) **2 Cor 7:11.** Of the final judgment ἡμέραι ἐκδικήσεως **Lk 21:22** (cp. Dt 32:35; En 25:4; Philo, Leg. All. 3, 106). W. gen. of the pers. being punished (Ezk 9:1; Jdth 8:35; 9:2 εἰς ἐ. ἀλλογενῶν) εἰς ἐ. κακοποιῶν *for pun. of the evildoers* **1 Pt 2:14.** W. the dat. to denote the pers. being punished διδόναι ἐκδίκησίν τινι **2 Th 1:8** (cp. Sir 12:6 τ. ἀσεβέσιν ἀποδώσει ἐ.).—GBjörck, PUps 8, p. 81ff.—DELG s.v. δίκη. M-M. TW.

ἔκδικος, ον (s. prec. two entries; trag. et al.; ins, pap, LXX; JosAs 28:3; SibOr 3, 365; Tat.) **pert. to justice being done so as to rectify wrong done to another,** ***punishing,*** subst. ***one who punishes*** (Plut., Mor. 509f; Herodian 2, 14, 3; 7, 4, 5; Sir 30:6; Wsd 12:12; 4 Macc 15:29) of God: (Appian, Bell. Civ. 2, 85 §360; Jos., Bell. 5, 377) ἔ. περὶ πάντων τούτων **1 Th 4:6.** Of civil authority: διάκονος ἔκδικος *agent of punishment* **Ro 13:4.**—ἕως ἔλθῃ ἔ. *until an avenger comes* (for the murder of Zachariah) GJs 24:2.—DELG s.v. δίκη. M-M. TW.

ἐκδιώκω fut. ἐκδιώξω; 1 aor. ἐξεδίωξα LXX, ptc. ἐκδιώξας. Pass.: fut. 3 pl. ἐκδιωχθήσονται Ps 36:28; 3 sg. ἐξεδιώχθη Da 4:33; 5:21 Theod. (s. διώκω; since Thu. 1, 24, 5; of a dream in UPZ 81 IV, 18; POxy 2410, 9; LXX=drive away; likew. En 23:4; Jos., C. Ap. 1, 292; TestJud 18:4; Just., A II, 6, 6).

❶ **to use tactics that cause the departure of someone from a place,** ***drive out*** **1 Th 2:15** (so REB, NRSV) but s. 2. **Lk 11:49 v.l.** is prob. also to be so understood.

❷ **to annoy persistently,** ***persecute severely*** (so perh. Demosth. 32, 5; certainly BGU 836, 5; Ps 118:157; Sir 30:19) τινά *someone* **1 Th 2:15** ('persecute' Goodsp.; 'harass' Moffatt).—M-M.

ἔκδοτος, ον (s. ἐκδίδωμι; since Hdt. 3, 1, 1; Polyb.; Palaeph. 41, 2; Vett. Val.; PGrenf I, 1 [1], 7 [II BC]; Jos., Ant. 6, 316 al.; Sym.; Theod.) **pert. to being handed over,** ***given up, delivered up*** **Ac 2:23** (of delivery to an enemy Hdt. 3, 1, 1; Aeschin. 3, 142). ἑαυτὸν ἔ. δέδωκα τῷ θανάτῳ *I have delivered myself up to death* ISm 4:2 (διδόναι τινὰ ἔ. as Demosth. 23, 85; Polyb. 20, 10, 5; 28, 4, 11; SIG 372, 13 [III BC]; Bel 22 Theod.; cp. Vett. Val. 106, 24; 220, 16).—DELG s.v. δίδωμι A2. M-M.

ἐκδοχή, ῆς, ἡ (ἐκ + δέχομαι; Aeschyl. et al.; Philo; pap in var. mngs.: PMichZen 28, 21; Sb 9220 [a], 8; UPZ 110, 86) found nowhere else (except Hesych.: ἐκδοχή· προσδοκία) in the mng. which it must have in its only occurrence in OT and our lit.: ***expectation*** φοβερὰ ἐ. τῆς κρίσεως *a fearful ex. of judgment* **Hb 10:27.**—Frisk s.v. δέχομαι. M-M.

ἐκδύω fut. ἐκδύσω LXX; 1 aor. ἐξέδυσα; fut. mid. ἐκδύσομαι LXX; aor. mid. ἐξεδυσάμην (δύω, 'get into'; Hom. et al.; ins, pap, LXX, Test12Patr, JosAs, Philo)

❶ **to remove clothing from the body,** ***strip, take off.*** Act., w. acc. of pers. (SIG 1169, 47 [IV BC]; PMagd 6, 13=PEnteux 75, 13 [221 BC]; 1 Ch 10:9; Hos 2:5) **Mt 27:28; Lk 10:30.** W. acc. of pers. and thing (Gen 37:23; TestJud 3:5; TestZeb 4:10) **Mt 27:31; Mk 15:20.**—Mid., *strip, undress (oneself)* abs., lit. (as X., Hell. 3, 4, 19 et al.; Is 32:11) POxy 655, 22 (ASyn. 67, 35=GTh 37). Fig., of the body as a garment (Artem. 5, 40 ἐκ τῶν σαρκῶν ἐκδύνειν) οὐ θέλομεν ἐκδύσασθαι *we do not want to strip ourselves* **2 Cor 5:4;** cp. vs. **3.**—Lit. on γυμνός 1.

❷ **to remove by force,** ***plunder,*** fig. ext. of 1: B 10:4.—M-M. TW.

ἐκεῖ adv. of place (Aeschyl.+)—❶ **in ref. to a position in the immediate vicinity,** ***there, in that place*** (the static aspect) **Mt 2:13, 15; 5:24; 8:12; 12:45** al. Somet. more definitely ἐκεῖ πρὸς τῷ ὄρει **Mk 5:11.** W. the art. οἱ ἐκεῖ *those who were there* (X., Hell. 1, 6, 4; Celsus 2, 43; PRyl 239, 9 [III AD] ἐπίμινον τοῖς ἐκεῖ; Jos., Ant. 1, 243; 9, 114) **Mt 26:71.** τὰ δὲ ἐκεῖ θαυμάσσια *the marvelous things there* (in heaven) AcPl Ha 2, 23 (cp. Just., A I, 29, 2 οἱ ἐκεῖ ἰατροί; 62, 3 al.). Corresp. to the relatives οὗ, ὅπου . . . ἐκεῖ *where . . . there* (Epict. 4, 4, 15; Jos., C. Ap. 1, 32) **Mt 6:21; 18:20; Mk 6:10; Lk 12:34.** Pleonastic after ὅπου (B-D-F §297; cp. Gen 13:4; Ex 20:24) **Mk 6:55 v.l.; Rv 12:6, 14.**—ISm 8:2.

❷ **in ref. to a position relatively distant,** ***there, to that place*** (the directional aspect)=ἐκεῖσε 1 (since Hdt. 1, 209; Thu. 3, 71, 2; Epict. 1, 27, 18; PMeyer 20, 46 ἐκεῖ πέμπω τ. ἐπιστολάς; PFlor 125, 7; 133, 9; Gen 19:22; 2 Km 2:2; Tob 7:16 al.; Jos., Ant. 18, 327; 20, 212; Just., D. 92, 2 εἰσελθεῖν ἐκεῖ) ἐκεῖ ἀπέρχεσθαι *go there* (thither) **Mt 2:22;** cp. **26:36.** βάλλειν **Lk 21:2.** ἔρχεσθαι (Hdt. 1, 121; Jos., Ant. 6, 83) **J 18:3.** προπέμπεσθαι **Ro 15:24.** συνάγεσθαι **Mt 24:28; J 18:2.** συντρέχειν **Mk 6:33.** ὑπάγειν **J 11:8;** ἀποφέρειν AcPt Ox 849 verso, 10. μετάβα ἔνθεν ἐκεῖ *move from here to there* **Mt 17:20.**—Hv 3, 1, 3.—DELG. M-M. S. entry κἀκεῖ 1 and ὧδε 1.

ἐκεῖθεν adv. of place (trag., Thu.+; pap, LXX, En; JosAs 16:2 cod. A [p. 63, 5 Bat]; ViEzk 15 [Sch. 75, 14]; Jos., Bell. 7, 96; Ant. 8, 303; Just., A I, 50, 12; Ath, R. 69, 30) ***from there*** **Mt 4:21; 5:26,** cited D 1:5; **9:9, 27; 11:1; 12:9, 15; 13:53; 14:13** al. οἱ ἐ. (Thu. 1, 62, 4) **Lk 16:26 v.l.**—S. κἀκεῖθεν. DELG s.v. ἐκεῖ. M-M.

ἐκείνης adverbial gen. of ἐκεῖνος (sc. τῆς ὁδοῦ) ***there*** **Lk 19:4** (here D has the st. dat. form ἐκείνῃ Hdt. 8, 106; Thu. 4, 77 et al.; s. B-D-F §186, 1; Rdm. 2^2 135, 2; Rob. 494).—WHavers, IndogF 19, 1906, 83ff. Frisk s.v. ἐκεῖνος. S. entry κἀκεῖνος.

ἐκεῖνος, η, ο demonstr. pron. (Hom.+) **pert. to an entity mentioned or understood and viewed as relatively remote in the discourse setting,** ***that person, that thing, that*** ('that over there'; opp. οὗτος 'this')

ⓐ abs.—**α.** denoting contrast to another entity **Lk 18:14** (Just., A I, 43, 2, D. 85, 1). τοῦτο ἢ ἐκεῖνο *this or that* **Js 4:15.** ἡμῖν . . . ἐκείνοις **Mt 13:11; Mk 4:11;** cp. **2 Cor 8:14.** ἐκεῖνον

. . . ἐμέ **J 3:30.** ἐκεῖνοι . . . ἡμεῖς **1 Cor 9:25; Hb 12:25; 1J 4:17.** ἄλλοι . . . ἐκεῖνος **J 9:9.** Opp. a certain pers.: Jesus **Mk 16:19f;** the Judeans **J 2:20f** et al.

β. referring back to and resuming a word immediately preceding, oft. weakened to *he, she, it* (X., An. 4, 3, 20; Just., D. 1, 3 al.) **Mk 16:10f.** Esp. oft. so in J: **5:37; 8:44; 10:6; 11:29; 12:48; 13:6 v.l.; 14:21, 26; 16:14** al. Hence **19:35** perh. the eyewitness (just mentioned) is meant, who then, to be sure, would be vouching for his own credibility and love of the truth (s. aγ).—Interchanging w. αὐτός (cp. Thu. 1, 32, 5; X., Cyr. 4, 5, 20; Lysias 14, 28; Kühner-G. I 649) ἐζωγρημένοι ὑπ᾽ αὐτοῦ εἰς τὸ ἐκείνου θέλημα *under the spell of his will* **2 Ti 2:26.** ἐκεῖνος for αὐτός **Lk 9:34 v.l.; 23:12 v.l.** Used to produce greater emphasis: ἐκεῖνον λαβών *take that one* **Mt 17:27;** cp. **J 5:43.** τῇ ἐκείνου χάριτι *by his grace* **Tit 3:7.** Sim. after a participial subj. (X., Cyr. 6, 2, 33 ὁ γὰρ λόγχην ἀκονῶν, ἐκεῖνος καὶ τὴν ψυχήν τι παρακονᾷ=the one who sharpens his spear, he is the one who sharpens his inner self) τὸ ἐκπορευόμενον ἐκεῖνο κοινοῖ **Mk 7:20.** ὁ πέμψας ἐκεῖνος **J 1:33;** cp **5:37 v.l.** (for αὐτός) ὁ ποιήσας με ὑγιῆ ἐκεῖνος **5:11.** ὁ λαλῶν ἐκεῖνός ἐστιν **9:37.** ὁ εἰσερχόμενος ἐκεῖνος κλέπτης ἐστίν **10:1.** τῷ λογιζομένῳ . . . ἐκείνῳ κοινόν **Ro 14:14** al.

γ. w. ref. to well-known or notorious personalities (Just., A I, 4 ὡς ἐκεῖνος [Πλάτων] ἔφη; Kühner-G. I 650; Arrian, Periplus 1, 1 ὁ Ξενοφῶν ἐκεῖνος) Jesus (cp. Mel., P. 80, 593 σὺ ἐχόρευες, ἐκεῖνος δὲ ἐθάπτετο): **J 7:11; 9:12, 28; 1J 2:6; 3:3, 5, 7, 16; 4:17.** The ἐ. **J 19:35** appears to refer to ὁ ἑωρακώς, the eyewitness mentioned at the beginning of the vs. (Some scholars refer to the Johannine writer [cp. Jos., Bell. 3, 7, 16–202], who allegedly seeks to corroborate another's statement, and support has been offered in the use of ἐ. in indirect discourse in which speakers refer to themselves as ἐ. [Isaeus 8, 22a; Polyb. 3, 44, 10; 12, 16, 5] on the ground that the narrator of the 4th Gospel could no more use the I-form than could the speaker in indirect discourse. But contexts of the passages cited contain some indication of the referent. Some refer to Jesus [Erasmus, Zahn; ESchwartz, NGG 1907, 361; Lagrange; others cited RBrown, comm. ad loc.—Acc. to Iambl., Vi. Pyth. 35, 255, as well as Aristoxenus, fgm. 33 p. 17, 3 οἱ Πυθαγόρειοι παρ᾽ ἐκείνου μαθόντες, the Pythagoreans called their master after his death simply ἐκεῖνος]. Yet how much more clearly this idea might have been conveyed in J by simply using ὁ κύριος!). S. FBlass, StKr 75, 1902, 128–33.—W. an unfavorable connotation (Themistocles, Ep. 16 p. 755, 14; 27; Lucian, Pereg. 13 of Jesus; Julian, Letter 60 p. 379a of the Christians; Just., D. 67, 2 of Jews by Hellenes) of the Jews B 2:9; 3:6; 4:6; 8:7 al.

δ. w. relative foll. (cp. Just., D. 128, 4 ἀναλυόμενοι εἰς ἐκεῖνο ἐξ οὗπερ γεγόνασιν): ἐκεῖνός ἐστιν ᾧ ἐγὼ βάψω **J 13:26.** ἐκεῖνον . . . ὑπὲρ οὗ **Ro 14:15.** ἐκείνης ἀφ᾽ ἧς **Hb 11:15.** W. ὅτι foll. (Ael. Aristid. 39 p. 747 D.; Just., A I, 19, 5) **Mt 24:43.**

ⓑ used w. nouns—**α.** to differentiate pers. or things already named, fr. others: τῇ οἰκίᾳ ἐκείνῃ *that* (particular) *house* **Mt 7:25;** cp. vs. **27.** τῇ πόλει ἐκείνῃ *that city* (just mentioned) **10:15; 18:32; Mk 3:24f; Lk 6:48f; J 18:15; Ac 1:19; 3:23** (Dt 18:19); **8:8; 14:21; 16:3** and oft. (cp. Just., D. 4, 2 αὐτοῦ ἐκείνου τοῦ βασιλικοῦ νοῦ μέρος 'a portion of that same governing mind').

β. of time—**א.** of the past, when the time cannot (or is not to) be given w. exactness: ἐν τ. ἡμέραις ἐκείναις *in those days* (Ex 2:11; Judg 18:1; 1 Km 28:1; Jdth 1:5; PsSol 17:44; 18:6; AscIs 3, 20; 23; 27) **Mt 3:1,** cp. **24:38; Mk 1:9; 8:1; Lk 2:1.** Of a definite period (1 Macc 1:11; 9:24; 11:20) **Lk 4:2; 9:36.**

ב. of the future (ἐκείνη ἡ ἡμέρα; Plut., Gai. Marc. 231 [35, 6]; Epict. 3, 17, 4; Ael. Aristid. 19, 8 K.=41 p. 765 D.) **Mt 24:22ab, 29;** ἐν ἐκ. τ. ἡμέραις **24:19; Ac 2:18** (Jo 3:2); **Rv 9:6.** Also in sg. ἐν ἐκείνῃ τ. ἡμέρᾳ (Jdth 11:15) **Lk 17:31; J 16:23, 26;** AcPlCor 2:32; esp. of God's climactic judgment day **Mt 7:22; Lk 6:23; 10:12; 2 Th 1:10; 2 Ti 1:12, 18;** cp. **Rv 16:14 v.l.** ὁ αἰὼν ἐ. (opp. αἰὼν οὗτος) *the age to come* **Lk 20:35** (s. αἰών 2b).

ג. of a period ascertainable fr. the context **Mt 13:1; Mk 4:35; J 1:39** (Jos., Ant. 7, 134 μεῖναι τὴν ἡμέραν ἐκείνην) al. ἀπ᾽ ἐκείνης τ. ἡμέρας (Jos., Bell. 4, 318, Ant. 7, 382; Mel. HE 4, 26, 3 ἐν ἐκείναις ταῖς ἡμέραις) **Mt 22:46.** κατὰ τὸν καιρὸν ἐ. *at that time* **Ac 19:23.** κατ᾽ ἐ. τὸν καιρόν (Jos., Ant. 1, 171 al.; Just., A I, 26, 3 al.: κατ᾽ ἐκεῖνο τοῦ καιροῦ, D. 103, 3 ἐκείνου τοῦ καιροῦ) **12:1.** ἐν ἐ. τῇ ὥρᾳ **Rv 11:13.**

ⓒ For ἐκείνης, the adverbial gen. of ἐκεῖνος, s. the preceding entry.—IndogF 19, 1906, 83ff. S. κἀκεῖνος. M-M.

ἐκεῖσε adv. of place (Aeschyl., Hdt.+).—❶ **in ref. to attention directed toward a remote place or other side,** ***there, to that place, thither*** (Hdt. et al.; Hom. in the Ionic form κεῖσε) prob. pregnant construction ἐκεῖσε γὰρ τὸ πλοῖον ἦν ἀποφορτιζόμενον τὸν γόμον *there the ship was (heading) to unload her cargo* **Ac 21:3,** but s. 2; as v.l. in the phrase ὧδε κἀκεῖσε (Lucian, Hermotim. 1; Polyaenus, Exc. 57, 5) *here and there* (hither and thither): Hm 5, 2, 7; s 6, 1, 6; 6, 2, 7; 9, 3, 1.

❷ **in ref. to a position established by a shift of view**=ἐκεῖ 1 ***there, at that place*** (Hippocr. et al.; Chrysipp.: Stoic. II 244; Polyb. 5, 51, 3; POxy 60, 9; 1204, 6; PSI 162, 11; Job 39:29; TestAbr A 14 p. 94, 6 [Stone p. 36]; Jos., Ant. 3, 40; 8, 350) ApcPt 5:18; perh. **Ac 21:3;** τοὺς ἐ. ὄντας **22:5.**—B-D-F §103. DELG s.v. ἐκεῖ. M-M.

ἐκέκραξα s. κράζω.

ἐκέρασα s. κεράννυμι.

ἐκέρδησα s. κράζω.

ἐκζητέω fut. ἐκζητήσω; 1 aor. ἐξεζήτησα. Pass.: 1 fut. ἐκζητηθήσομαι; 1 aor. ἐξεζητήθην; pf. pass. ptc. ἐξεζητημένα Ps 110, 2. (Ael. Aristid. 38 p. 726 D.; ins, pap, LXX; En 104:7; TestAsh; Just., D. 95, 4).

❶ **to exert effort to find out or learn someth.,** ***seek out, search for*** w. acc. of pers. or thing sought (POxy 1465, 11 [I BC] τοὺς αἰτίους; LXX; EpArist 24) τὶ (Aelian, NA 15, 1 p. 356, 24; TestAsh 5:4) **Hb 12:17;** B 21:8. ἐ. τὰ δυνάμενα ἡμᾶς σῴζειν *seek out the things that can save us* 4:1. τὰ δικαιώματα κυρίου *seek out the Lord's requirements* 2:1. κρίσιν *search for justice* 1 Cl 8:4 (Is 1:17). τὰ εὐάρεστα 35:5. τόπον 1 Cl 14:5 (Ps 36:36). τὰ πρόσωπα τῶν ἁγίων *seek the faces of the saints* i.e. associate w. them, attend their meetings D 4:2; B 19:10. τινά: (παρθένους) GJs 10:1. ἐ. τὸν κύριον *seek the Lord* to serve him (Ps 33:5; 68:33; Dt 4:29 al.) **Ac 15:17** (Am 9:12); cp. **Ro 3:11** (Ps 13:2; 52:3); **Hb 11:6;** 1 Cl 13:1.—περί τινος *seek for someth.* **1 Pt 1:10** (w. ἐξεραυνάω as 1 Macc 9:26 A). Foll. by an indirect question instead of an obj. B 10:4; 21:6. Abs. (BGU 1141, 41 [14 BC]; IGR IV, 834, 5) ἐ. ἐπιμελῶς *search carefully* Hv 3, 3, 5.

❷ **to look for someth. with a view to securing it,** ***desire, seek to get*** (1 Macc 7:12) ἐ. τι ἐκ τ. χειρῶν τινος B 2:5 (Is 1:12).

❸ **to look for someone with a view to some kind of association,** ***seek out, visit*** τινά: τοὺς πεινῶντας Hv 3, 9, 5.

❹ **to look for in expectation of fixing blame,** ***look for, seek,*** in the judicial sense *charge (to, with)* τὸ αἷμα (Gen 9:5; 42:22; 2 Km 4:11; Ezk 3:18; Jo 4:21 v.l.) ἀπό τινος **Lk 11:50f;** Pol 2:1.—M-M.

ἐκζήτησις, εως, ἡ (only in Christian wr.) ***useless speculation*** **1 Ti 1:4** (v.l. ζητήσεις).—TW.

ἐκθαμβέω (s. ἔκθαμβος; Orph., Arg. 1217 [tmesis]; PGrenf I 53, 18=Mitt-Wilck. I/2, 131, 18 [IV AD]; TestAbr B 13 p. 118, 11 [Stone p. 84]) fut. 3 sg. ἐκθαμβήσει Sir 30:9; 1 aor. pass. ἐξεθαμβήθην, in our lit. only in Mk and only pass. in active sense: **to be moved to a relatively intense emotional state because of someth. causing great surprise or perplexity,** ***be very excited*** **Mk 9:15** (the presence of Jesus suggests possible resolution of a dispute; but consideration of Mark's larger narrative structure leads some scholars to prefer the sense *be amazed* [as in Galen: CMG V 9, 2 p. 5, 12=XVI 493 K.], which lacks immediate motivation in the scene at hand); *be overwhelmed, be alarmed* **16:5f;** *be distressed* w. ἀδημονεῖν **14:33.**—Cp. θαμβέω in **1:27; 10:32.**—DELG s.v. θάμβος. M-M. TW.

ἔκθαμβος, ον s. ἐκθαμβέω; ***utterly astonished*** (so Polyb. 20, 10, 9; IDefixAudollent 271, 20 [III AD]; 1 Km 4:13 Sym.; but = terrible Da 7:7 Theod.; TestSol) **Ac 3:11.** εἶδον αὐτὸν (τὸν ἀέρα) ἔκθαμβον *I noticed that it* (the air) *was astonished* (i.e. amazement brought it to a standstill) GJs 18:2 (not pap). ἔκθαμβον γενέσθαι πρός τινα *be greatly astonished at someone* ApcPt 4:11. Abs. ἔ. γενέσθαι Hv 3, 1, 5.—M-M. TW.

ἐκθαυμάζω impf. ἐξεθαύμαζον; fut. 3 sg. ἐκθαυμάσει Sir 27:23; 43:18; aor. 3 pl. ἐξεθαύμασαν 4 Macc 17:17 (Dionys. Hal., De Thu. Jud. 34 et al.; LXX; EpArist 312; Philo, Somn. 2, 70) ***be utterly amazed*** ἐπί τινι *at someone* **Mk 12:17** (here in the sense of grudging admiration; cp. Sir 27:23 ἐπί τινος).—M-M. TW.

ἔκθετος, ον (Eur., Andr. 70; Vett. Val. 106, 14; Sb 5252, 19 [I AD]) ***exposed, abandoned*** of infants (Manetho, Apot. 6, 52) βρέφη **Ac 7:19.**—S. ἐκτίθημι 1. DELG s.v. τίθημι. M-M.

ἐκκαθαίρω fut. ἐκκαθαρῶ Judg 7:4 (cod. B); 1 aor. ἐξεκάθαρα (Hom. et al.; ins; PCairZen 729, 10 [III BC]; PTebt 908, 1 [II BC]; LXX, Philo; Jos., Ant. 3, 227; Ath. 11, 2; 12,1)

❶ **to remove as unclean,** ***clean out*** (Pla., Euth. 3a; Aristot., HA 9, 40 et al.; Philo, Mos. 1, 303) ἐ. τὴν παλαιὰν ζύμην *clean out the old yeast* **1 Cor 5:7.**

❷ **to rid of someth. unclean,** ***cleanse,*** w. acc. of what is cleansed (Hom. et al.; Philostrat., Vi. Apoll. 5, 7 p. 169, 32; OGI 483, 158; Jos., Bell. 4, 323) fig. (Plut., Mor. 64f λογισμόν; Epict. 2, 23, 40; Vett. Val. 242, 15; Ath. 12, 1 ἑαυτούς) ἑαυτὸν ἐ. *cleanse oneself* ἀπό τινος (Epict. 2, 21, 15) **2 Ti 2:21.**—DELG s.v. καθαρός. M-M. TW.

ἐκκαίω fut. ἐκκαύσω LXX; 1 aor. ἐξέκαυσα. Pass.: fut. ἐκκαυθήσομαι and ἐκκαήσομαι LXX; aor. ἐξεκαύθην LXX and ἐξεκάην LXX; pf. 3 sg. ἐκκέκαυται; ptc. ἐκκεκαυμένη LXX (Hdt. et al.; LXX; SibOr 4, 178; Sir 28:8) gener. 'kindle'. In our lit. only fig. (Jos., Vi. 134 αὐτούς).

❶ **to instigate someth. destructive,** ***kindle, start:*** *a schism* (Diod. S. 20, 33, 7 στάσιν ἐξέκαυσαν) 1 Cl 1:1 (cp. Polyb. 2, 1, 3 πόλεμον; Diod. S. 15, 92, 3; Sir 28:8).

❷ **to have a strong desire for,** ***be inflamed:*** with sensual desire—pass. w. act. sense (Chariton 5, 9, 9; Longus 3, 13, 3) ἐξεκαύθησαν εἰς ἀλλήλους *toward each other* **Ro 1:27** (Alciphron 3, 31, 1 ἐξεκαύθην εἰς ἔρωτα. Cp. Plut., Tib. Gracch. 830 [13, 4], Alex. 582 [31, 3]; Sir 16:6 al.; Jos., Vi. 263).—M-M.

ἐκκακέω 1 aor. ἐξεκάκησα (ἐκ + κακός; Vett. Val. 201, 15; Herm. Wr., fgm. XXIII 46 [484, 3 Sc.]; Hesych.; Sym. Jer 18:12; TestJob 24:10; Philo, Conf. Lingu. 51 codd.) ***lose heart*** (w. διψυχέω.—Astrampsychus p. 31 Dec. 61, 3) Hm 9:8. V.l. for ἐγκακέω q.v.: **Lk 18:1; 2 Cor 4:1, 16; Gal 6:9; Eph 3:13; 2 Th 3:13.**—M-M. s.v. ἐνκακέω.

ἐκκεντέω 1 aor. ἐξεκέντησα. Pass.: aor. ἐξεκεντήθη (Just., D. 32, 2); pf. ptc. ἐκκεκεντημένος LXX (the word since Aristot.) ***pierce*** (so Polyb. 5, 56, 12; Polyaenus 5, 3, 8; LXX; PsSol 2:26) τινά *someone* (=kill him: Num 22:29; 2 Macc 12:6) **Rv 1:7.** ὄψονται εἰς ὃν ἐξεκέντησαν *they will look at him whom they have pierced* **J 19:37** (Zech 12:10 [Aq., Theod.], cp. Just., A I, 52, 12, D. 14, 8; 32, 2; 64, 7; 118, 1); s. PapHeid I 66ff; ARahlfs, ZNW 20, 1921, 182ff.—S. Frisk s.v. κεντέω. TW.

ἐκκλάω fut. 3 sg. ἐκκλάσει Lev 1:17; 1 aor. pass. ἐξεκλάσθην (since Pla., Rep. 10, 611d; Paus. 8, 40, 2) **to separate someth. from someth. with force,** ***break off*** (PTebt 802, 12 and19 [135 BC]) of branches **Ro 11:17, 19, 20.**

ἐκκλείω 1 aor. ἐξέκλεισα, inf. ἐκκλεῖσαι; pass. ἐξεκλείσθην; 1 fut. ἐκκλεισθήσομαι (Eur., Hdt. et al.; pap; LXX rarely and as v.l.)

❶ **to exclude or withdraw from fellowship,** ***shut out, exclude*** τινά *someone* (Hdt. 1, 144 et al.; PMagd 10, 6 [III BC] =PEnteux 53, 6) **Gal 4:17** (s. MHitchcock, JTS 40, '39, 149–51). Pass. ἐ. ἀπὸ πόλεως *be excluded fr. one's home city* Hs 1:5. ἔξω τῆς θύρας τοῦ πύργου *be shut outside the door of the tower* v 3, 9, 6 (cp. Jos., Vi. 294).

❷ **to make no room for,** ***exclude, shut out*** someth. = make it impossible, fig. ext. of 1 (Polyb. 17 [18], 8, 2; Diod. S. 3, 16, 6; 18, 3, 1 Lucian, Pseudolog. 11; PMagd 12, 4 [III BC]=PEnteux 54, 4) of boasting ἐξεκλείσθη *it is excluded* (*shut out* Goodsp.) **Ro 3:27.**—DELG s.v. κλείς. M-M.

ἐκκλησία, ας, ἡ (ἐκ + καλέω; Eur., Hdt.+)—❶ **a regularly summoned legislative body,** ***assembly,*** as gener. understood in the Gr-Rom. world (Jos., Ant. 12, 164; 19, 332, Vi. 268) **Ac 19:39** (on '[regular] statutory assembly', s. ἔννομος and IBM III/2, p. 141. The term ἐννόμη ἐ. here contrasts w. the usage vss. **32** and **40,** in which ἐ. denotes simply 'a gathering'; s. 2 below. On the ἐ. in Ephesus cp. CIG III, 325; IBM III/1, 481, 340; on the ἐ. in the theater there s. the last-named ins ln. 395; OGI 480, 9).—Pauly-W. V/2, 1905, 2163–2200; RAC IV 905–21 (lit.).

❷ **a casual gathering of people,** ***an assemblage, gathering*** (cp. 1 Km 19:20; 1 Macc 3:13; Sir 26:5) **Ac 19:32, 40.**

❸ **people with shared belief,** ***community, congregation*** (for common identity, cp. the community of Pythagoras [Hermippus in Diog. L. 8, 41]. Remarkably, in Himerius, Or. 39 [Or. 5], 5 Orpheus forms for himself τὴν ἐκκλησίαν, a group of wild animals, who listen to him, in the Thracian mountains where there are no people), in our lit. of common interest in the God of Israel.

ⓐ of OT Israelites *assembly, congregation* (Dt 31:30; Judg 20:2; 1 Km 17:47; 3 Km 8:14; PsSol 10:6; TestJob 32:8 τῆς εὐώδους ἐ.; Philo; Jos., Ant. 4, 309; Diod. S. 40, 3, 6) **Hb 2:12** (Ps 21:23); e.g. to hear the law (Dt 4:10; 9:10; 18:16) **Ac 7:38.**

ⓑ of Christians in a specific place or area (the term ἐ. apparently became popular among Christians in Greek-speaking areas for chiefly two reasons: to affirm continuity with Israel through use of a term found in Gk. translations of the Hebrew Scriptures, and to allay any suspicion, esp. in political circles, that Christians were a disorderly group).

α. of a specific Christian group *assembly, gathering* ordinarily involving worship and discussion of matters of concern to the community: **Mt 18:17;** συνερχομένων ὑμῶν ἐν ἐ. *when you come together as an assembly* **1 Cor 11:18;** cp. **14:4f, 12, 19, 28,**

35; pl. vs. **34.** ἐν ἐ. ἐξομολογεῖσθαι τὰ παραπτώματα *confess one's sins in assembly* D 4:14; cp. **3J 6** (JCampbell, JTS 49, '48, 130–42; for the Johannines s. ESchweizer below). In **Ac 15:22** the 'apostles and elders' function in the manner of the βουλή or council, the committee of the whole that was responsible in a Gr-Rom. polis for proposing legislation to the assembly of citizens.—Of Christians gathering in the home of a patron *house-assembly* ('house-church') Πρίσκαν καὶ Ἀκύλαν … καὶ τὴν κατ' οἶκον αὐτῶν ἐ. **Ro 16:5;** cp. **1 Cor 16:19.** Νύμφαν καὶ τὴν κατ' οἶκον αὐτῆς ἐ. **Col 4:15;** ἡ κατ' οἶκόν σου ἐ. **Phlm 2.**—FFilson, JBL 58, '39, 105–12; other reff. οἶκος 1aα.—Pl. ἐ. τῶν ἁγίων **1 Cor 14:33;** ἐ. τῶν ἐθνῶν **Ro 16:4.—1 Ti 5:16** prob. belongs here, s. βαρέω b.

β. *congregation* or *church* as the totality of Christians living and meeting in a particular locality or larger geographical area, but not necessarily limited to one meeting place: **Ac 5:11; 8:3; 9:31** (so KGiles, NTS 31, '85, 135–42; s. c below), **11:26; 12:5; 15:3; 18:22; 20:17;** cp. **12:1; 1 Cor 4:17; Phil 4:15; 1 Ti 5:16** perh., s. α above; **Js 5:14; 3 J 9f;** 1 Cl 44:3; Hv 2, 4, 3. More definitely of the Christians in Jerusalem **Ac 8:1; 11:22;** cp. **2:47 v.l.; 15:4, 22;** Cenchreae **Ro 16:1;** cp. vs. **23;** Corinth **1 Cor 1:2; 2 Cor 1:1;** 1 Cl ins; 47:6; AcPlCor 1:16; Laodicea **Col 4:16; Rv 3:14;** Thessalonica **1 Th 1:1; 2 Th 1:1;** Colossae **Phlm subscr. v.l.** Likew. w. other names: **Rv 2:1, 8, 12, 18; 3:1, 7;** IEph ins; 8:1; IMg ins; ITr ins; 13:1; IRo 9:1; IPhld ins; 10:1; ISm 11:1; Pol ins. Plural: **Ac 15:41; 16:5; Ro 16:16; 1 Cor 7:17; 2 Cor 8:18f, 23f; 11:8, 28; 12:13; Rv 2:7, 11, 17, 23, 29; 3:6, 13, 22; 22:16;** the Christian community in Judea **Gal 1:22; 1 Th 2:14;** Galatia **Gal 1:2; 1 Cor 16:1;** Asia vs. **19; Rv 1:4,** and cp. vss. **11** and **20;** Macedonia **2 Cor 8:1.** κατ' ἐκκλησίαν *in each individual congregation* or *assembly* **Ac 14:23** (on the syntax cp. OGI 480, 9 [s. 1 above]: ἵνα τιθῆνται κατ' ἐκκλησίαν in order that they [the statues] might be set up at each [meeting of the] ἐ.). On κατὰ τ. οὖσαν ἐ. **Ac 13:1** cp. εἰμί 1 end.

ⓒ **the global community of Christians, *(universal) church*** (s. AvHarnack, Mission I[4] 420 n. 2 on Ac 12:1): **Mt 16:18** (OBetz, ZNW 48, '57, 49–77: Qumran parallels; s. HBraun, Qumran I, '66, 30–37); **Ac 9:31** (but s. 3bβ); **1 Cor 6:4; 12:28; Eph 1:22; 3:10, 21; 5:23ff, 27, 29, 32** (HSchlier, Christus u. d. Kirche im Eph 1930; also ThBl 6, 1927, 12–17); **Col 1:18, 24; Phil 3:6;** B 7:11; Hv 2, 2, 6; 2, 4, 1 (with the depiction of the church as an elderly lady cp. Ps.-Demetr. 265 where Hellas, the homeland, is represented as λαβοῦσα γυναικὸς σχῆμα); 3, 3, 3; IEph 5:1f and oft.—The local assembly or congregation as well as the universal church is more specif. called ἐ. τοῦ θεοῦ or ἐ. τ. Χριστοῦ. This is essentially Pauline usage, and it serves to give the current Gk. term its Christian coloring and thereby its special mng.:

α. ἐ. τοῦ θεοῦ (Orig., C. Cels. 1, 63, 22) **1 Cor 1:2; 10:32; 11:16, 22; 15:9; 2 Cor 1:1; Gal 1:13; 1 Th 2:14; 2 Th 1:4; 1 Ti 3:5, 15; Ac 20:28;** ITr 2:3; 12:1; IPhld 10:1; ISm ins al.

β. ἐ. τοῦ Χριστοῦ (Orig., C. Cels. 5, 22, 14) **Ro 16:16.**

γ. both together ἐ. ἐν θεῷ πατρὶ καὶ κυρίῳ Ἰησοῦ Χριστῷ **1 Th 1:1.**

δ. ἡ ἐ. ἡ πρώτη ἡ πνευματική *the first, spiritual church* (conceived in a Platonic sense as preexistent) 2 Cl 14:1; ἐ. ζῶσα *the living church* the body of Christ vs. 2; ἡ ἁγία ἐ. Hv 1, 1, 6; 1, 3, 4; ἡ καθολικὴ ἐ. ISm 8:2; ἡ ἁγία καὶ καθολικὴ ἐ. MPol ins; ἡ κατὰ τὴν οἰκουμένην καθολικὴ ἐ. 8:1; 19:2; ἓν σῶμα τῆς ἐ. ISm 1:2.—The literature before '32 is given in OLinton, D. Problem der Urkirche in d. neueren Forschung (s. esp. 138–46) '32 and AMedebielle, Dict. de la Bible, Suppl. II '34, 487–691; before '60, s. RAC; also s. TW, Sieben, and JHainz, Ekklesia '72. Esp. important: EBurton, Gal (ICC) 1921, 417–20; KHoll, D. Kirchenbegriff des Pls usw.: SBBerlAk 1921, 920–47=Ges. Aufs. II 1928, 44ff; FKattenbusch, D. Vorzugsstellung d. Petrus u. d. Charakter d. Urgemeinde zu Jerusalem: KMüller Festschr. 1922, 322–51; KLSchmidt, D. Kirche des Urchristentums: Dssm. Festschr. 1927, 259–319, TW III 502–39. S. also: EPeterson, D. Kirche aus Juden u. Heiden '33; KLSchmidt, D. Polis in Kirche u. Welt '39; WBieder, Ekkl. u. Polis im NT u. in d. alten Kirche '41; OMichel, D. Zeugnis des NTs v. d. Gemeinde '41; NDahl, D. Volk Gottes '41; RFlew, Jesus and His Church[2], '43; GJohnston, The Doctrine of the Church in the NT '43; WKümmel, Kirchenbegriff u. Geschichtsbewusstsein in d. Urg. u. b. Jesus '43; DFaulhaber, D. Johev. u. d. Kirche '38; AFridrichsen, Kyrkan i 4. ev.: SvTK 16, '40, 227–42; ESchweizer, NT Essays (Manson memorial vol.) '59, 230–45; EWolf, Ecclesia Pressa—eccl. militans: TLZ 72, '47, 223–32; SHanson, Unity of the Church in the NT '46; HvCampenhausen, Kirchl. Amt u. geistl. Vollmacht in den ersten 3 Jahrh. '53; EKäsemann, Sätze hlg. Rechtes im NT, NTS 1, '55, 248–60; AGeorge, ET 58, '46/47, 312–16; in ATR: JBernardin 21, '39, 153–70; BEaston 22, '40, 157–68; SWalke 32, '50, 39–53 (Apost. Fath.); JMurphy, American Ecclesiastical Review 140, '59, 250–59; 325–32; PMinear, Images of the Church in the NT, '60; BMetzger, Theology Today 19, '62, 369–80; ESchweizer, Church Order in the NT, tr. FClarke '61; RSchnackenburg, The Church in the NT, tr. WO'Hara '65; LCerfaux, JBL 85, '66, 250–51; AHilhorst, Filología Neotestamentaria 1, '88, 27–34. S. also ἐπίσκοπος 2 end; Πέτρος; πέτρα 1.—B. 1476f. DELG s.v. καλέω. M-M. EDNT. TW. Sv.

ἐκκλησιάζω (s. ἐκκλησία; Aristoph., Thu. et al.; LXX, Philo, Joseph.) 1 aor. impv. ἐκκλησίασον **to hold an assembly, *convene, assemble*** τινά (in this sense X. et al., Aeneas Tact. 263; Diod. Sic. 21, 16, 4) ἐκκλησίασον τοὺς χηρεύοντας τοῦ λαοῦ *convene the widowers of the people* GJs 8:3 (cp. Esth 4:16 τοὺς Ἰουδαίους).—DELG s.v. καλέω.

ἐκκλησιαστικός, ή, όν (Demosth. et al.) *pert. to the (universal) church* (Cat. Cod. Astr. VII 216) ὁ ἐ. κανὼν καὶ καθολικός *the generally accepted rule of the church* EpilMosq 2 (fr. Irenaeus 3, 3, 4).

ἐκκλίνω fut. ἐκκλινῶ LXX; 1 aor. ἐξέκλινα; 3 sg. pf. ἐκκέκλικεν Hos 5:6 v.l. (Thu.+; ins, pap, LXX; ParJer 7:11; Jos., Ant. 13, 14; Anz 319; Test12Patr. Intr. B-D-F §308).

❶ **to keep away from, *steer clear of*—ⓐ** pers. *stay away from, avoid* ἀπ' αὐτῶν (Thu. 5, 73, 3; Sir 7:2; 22:13; 1 Macc 6:47) **Ro 16:17.** W. acc. (Polyb. 1, 34, 4; Aelian, VH 4, 28) τινά (Appian, Bell. Civ. 4, 129 §542 τὸν ἐχθρόν; Jos., Vi. 304) *avoid someone* IEph 7:1.

ⓑ way of life or engagement in someth., abs. *turn aside (from)* (Polyaenus 3, 10, 12 naval engagement; Socrat., Ep. 1, 9 engaging with the enemy; Appian, Bell. Civ. 5, 16 §66 a body; M. Ant. 8, 50, 1 ἔκκλινον=turn aside!—here of staying clear of prickly shrubs) of those who turn away from seeking God's interests **Ro 3:12** (Ps 13:3; 52:4). This sense is closely allied to

❷ **to stop doing someth., *cease*** ἀπό τινος *fr. someth.*, fr. evil **1 Pt 3:11;** 1 Cl 22:4 (both Ps 33:15).—M-M.

ἐκκολάπτω 1 aor. ἐξεκόλαψα LXX; pf. pass. ptc. ἐκκεκολαμμένος (ins: Sb 7259, 34 [95/94 BC]) (κολάπτω 'peck', then 'engrave', s. next entry; Thu. [1, 132, 3] et al.; SIG 543, 27; 1047, 44; Ex 36:13) **to chip material off a stone surface, *chisel out*** λίθος ὡς ἐκ πέτρας ἐ. *a stone apparently chiseled out of a rock* (i.e. it appeared to be a fashioned monolith) Hs 9, 9, 7.—DELG s.v. κολάπτω.

ἐκκόλαψις, εως, ἡ (s. ἐκκολάπτω; Aristot., HA 561b, 29) ***chiseling out*** an opening for a door Hs 9, 2, 2.

ἐκκολυμβάω 1 aor. ἐξεκολύμβησα (s. κολυμβάω; Eur., Hel. 1609; Diod. S. 20, 86, 4; 20, 88, 6; Dionys. Hal. 5, 24) ***(dive overboard and) swim away*** (Anticleides [III BC]: 140 fgm. 4 Jac.; Diod. S. 14, 73, 4) **Ac 27:42.**—DELG s.v. κόλυμβος.

ἐκκομίζω impf. pass. ἐξεκομιζόμην (s. κομίζω; Hdt. et al.; ins, pap, Joseph.) ***carry out*** of a corpse being taken to a burial place outside a town (Polyb. 35, 6, 2; Plut., Agis 804 [21, 1]; Herodian 2, 1, 2; Sb 7630, 20 [II AD]; BGU 326 II, 1=Hunt-Edgar 85 II, 1 [II AD]; Philo, Mos. 1, 100; Jos., Bell. 5, 567) **Lk 7:12.**—M-M.

ἐκκοπή, ῆς, ἡ s. ἐγκοπή.

ἐκκόπτω fut. ἐκκόψω; 1 aor. ἐξέκοψα, impv. ἔκκοψον. Pass. 2 fut. ἐκκοπήσομαι **Ro 11:22;** 2 aor. pass. ἐξεκόπην; pf. pass. ptc. ἐκκεκομμένος LXX (Hdt.+; ins, pap, LXX, En, Joseph., SibOr; Just., A I, 27, 2, D. 72, 3; on A I, 15, 2 cp. **Mt 5:29** ἔξελε)

❶ to cut so as to sever, *cut off/down:* of a tree *cut down* (Hdt. 9, 97; SIG 966, 33f; 41; PFay113, 10; Dt 20:19f; En 26:1; PsSol 12:3; Jos., Ant. 10, 52) **Mt 3:10; 7:19; Lk 3:9** (Harpocration s.v. ὀξυθυμία: ἐκκόπτοντες . . . καίουσι useless trees); **13:7, 9.** Of a branch *cut off* **Ro 11:24,** cp. vs. **22;** of a hand **Mt 5:30; 18:8** (cp. Philo, Sp. Leg. 3, 179 'does not mean that the body is to be deprived of a necessary part through mutilation'; cp. ὀφθαλμούς PsSol 4:20; Aeschines 1, 172 τοὺς ὀφθαλμούς; Maximus Tyr. 32, 10g; Syntipas p. 107, 2 γλῶτταν; Jos., Ant. 10, 140 τ. ὀφθαλμούς). Of a door, *hew out* of rock Hs 9, 2, 2 (cp. SibOr 5, 218 ἐ. πέτρην).

❷ to do away with, *exterminate* fig. ext. of 1: of pers. (Hdt. 4, 110; Lysias 28, 6; Lucian, Jupp. Tr. 21; Jos., Vi. 193; Just., A I, 27, 2) ἐκ ῥιζῶν *root and branch* B 12:9. Of things (Epict. 2, 22, 34; Vett. Val. 268, 6; Herm. Wr. 1, 22; OGI 669, 64; Sb 4284, 8 τὰ βίαια καὶ ἄνομα; Job 19:10; 4 Macc 3:2, 3, 4) τὴν ἀθέμιτον ὀργήν *root out the lawless anger* 1 Cl 63:2. τὴν ἀφορμήν *remove the occasion* (=stop them from) **2 Cor 11:12** (s. ἀφορμή).—M-M. p. xxxii. TW.

ἐκκρεμάννυμι impf. mid. ἐξεκρεμάμην (vernac. form ἐξεκρεμόμην, 3 sg. ἐξεκρέμετο B-D-F §93; W-S. §14, 17; Mlt-H. 206); fem. ptc. ἐκκρεμαμένην (Just., D. 96, 1)

❶ to suspend someth. out from an area, *hang out* act. (Jos., Bell. 7, 429) τὶ ἔκ τινος *someth. fr. someth.* (Aristoph., Eq. 1363) lit. 1 Cl 12:7.

❷ The mid. (Eur., Thu. et al.; Gen 44:30) is used in a fig. sense **to pay close attention to someone or someth., *hang on*** (cp. Philo, Abr. 170 of Abraham's devotion to Isaac. Ext. of the lit. sense Jos., Bell. 5, 433 of children clinging to morsels) ὁ λαὸς ἐξεκρέματο αὐτοῦ ἀκούων *the people hung upon his words* **Lk 19:48** (cp. Eunap., Vi. Soph. p. 29 τῆς φωνῆς ἐξεκρέμαντο κ. τῶν λόγων); or, *the people kept listening to him.*—TW.

ἐκλαλέω 1 aor. ἐξελάλησα (Eur.; Demosth.; Jdth 11:9; Philo, Mos. 1, 283, Vi. Cont. 26; Jos., Ant. 16, 375) **to speak out about or publicize something, *tell*** τινί *someone* (Ps.-Apollod., Epit. 2, 1; Philo, Sacr. Abel. 60) w. ὅτι foll. **Ac 23:22.**—M-M.

ἐκλάμπω fut. ἐκλάμψω; 1 aor. ἐξέλαμψα (s. λάμπω; Aeschyl., Hdt. et al.; Albinus, Didasc. 10 p. 165, 28 H.; Herm. Wr. 10:4b; horoscope in PLond I, 130, 95 p. 135 [I/II AD]; LXX; Philo) **to emit rays of light, *shine (out)*** of the sun (X., Hell. 1, 1, 16; Diod. S. 3, 48, 2; Lucian, Ver. Hist. 1, 6; Sir 50:7; Jos., Ant. 9, 225) μικρὸν ἐξέλαμψεν Hv 4, 1, 6. Of the sun also **Mt 13:43,** where its radiance is compared to that of the righteous (cp. Da 12:3 Theod.; EpJer 66 v.l.; of a beautiful woman's face: Chariton 5, 3, 9). Of a flame *blaze up* (Diod. S. 1, 57, 7 τοῦ πυρὸς ἐκλάμψαντος; Appian, Syr. 56 §284; Jos., Ant. 4, 55) MPol 15:1.—M-M. TW.

ἐκλανθάνομαι pf. ἐκλέλησμαι (Hom. et al.; Philo, Leg. All. 3, 92) ***forget (altogether)*** τινός (Polyb. 5, 48, 6; POxy 1203, 8 [I AD]; Ps 12:2 Sym.; Philo, De Jos. 99; Jos., Ant. 4, 53; 7, 318) τῆς παρακλήσεως **Hb 12:5.**—M-M s.v. ἐκλανθάνω.

ἐκλέγομαι impf. ἐξελεγόμην; fut. ἐκλέξομαι LXX; 1 aor. ἐξελεξάμην. Pass. 2 aor. ἐξελέγην; pf. pass. ἐκλέλεγμαι, ptc. ἐκλελεγμένος **Lk 9:35** (Hdt.+; ins, pap, LXX; En 6:2; 7:1; TestJob 9:4; Test12Patr; JosAs cod. A [p. 68, 20 and 71:15 Bat.]; EpArist; Joseph., Just.; Mel., P. 83, 622 [B]; the act. does not occur in our lit.)

❶ to pick out someone or someth., *choose (for oneself)* τινά (τί) *someone* (*someth.*) w. indication of that from which the selection is made τινὰ ἔκ τινος (Isocr. 9, 58; 2 Km 24:12; 2 Ch 33:7; Sir 45:4; Demetr.: 722 fgm. 1, 16 and18 Jac.; ἐκ τῶν γραφῶν Iren. 1, 19, 1 [Harv. I 175, 9; of the 'eclecticism' of dissidents]) *choose someone fr. among a number* πάντων 1 Cl 59:3; of two **Ac 1:24.** ὑμᾶς ἐκ τοῦ κόσμου **J 15:19.** ἐξ αὐτῶν Hs 9, 9, 3. ἐκλεξαμένους ἄνδρας ἐξ αὐτῶν πέμψαι *to choose men fr. among them and to send them* **Ac 15:22,** cp. **25.** For this τινὰ ἀπό τινος (Dt 14:2; Sir 45:16; Just. D. 27, 1 ἀπὸ τῶν προφητικῶν λόγων): ἀπ' αὐτῶν δώδεκα *twelve of them* **Lk 6:13.**

❷ to make a choice in accordance with significant preference, *select someone/someth. for oneself,* w. simple acc.

ⓐ w. acc. of pers. (Jo 2:16; Bar 3:27; 1 Macc 10:32; Jos., Ant. 7, 372 God chooses Solomon; Just., D. 17, 1 ἄνδρας; Mel., P. 83 [Bodm.] σέ): **Mk 13:20; J 13:18; 15:16;** GEb 19, 85 and 34, 60. Jesus 1 Cl 64. The twelve **J 6:70;** PtK 3 p. 15, 17. The apostles **Ac 1:2;** B 5:9. Stephen **Ac 6:5.** A faithful slave Hs 5, 2, 2. Of God: the ancestors (as God's own) **Ac 13:17** (oft. LXX, cp. Dt 4:37; 10:15).

ⓑ w. acc. of thing (X., Mem. 1, 6, 14; Pla., Leg. 2, 670d, Tim. p. 24c; Demosth. 18, 261 et al.; PMagd 29, 4 [III BC]=PEnteux 66, 4 τ. βέλτιστον τόπον; Is 40:20; 1 Macc 7:37; 2 Ch 35:19d; Jos., Bell. 2, 149 τόπους; Just., A I, 43, 7 τὰ καλά; Hippol., Ref. 5, 9, 20): B 21:1; good part **Lk 10:42;** places of honor **14:7;** a good place Hv 3, 1, 3; a fast B 3:1, 3 (Is 58:5f).

ⓒ w. indication of the purpose for which the choice is made: α. εἴς τι *for someth.* (Ps 32:12; Just., D. 67, 2 ἐκλεγῆναι εἰς Χριστόν) eternal life Hv 4, 3, 5. εἰς τὸ ἱερατεύειν *to be priest* 1 Cl 43:4.

β. w. ἵνα foll. **1 Cor 1:27f.**

γ. w. inf. foll. (1 Ch 15:2; 28:5; 1 Esdr 5:1) ἐξελέξατο ἡμᾶς εἶναι ἡμᾶς ἁγίους *he has chosen us that we might be holy* **Eph 1:4.** Without obj. ἐν ὑμῖν ἐξελέξατο ὁ θεὸς διὰ τοῦ στόματός μου ἀκοῦσαι *in your presence God chose that (they) were to hear through my mouth* **Ac 15:7.** W. ellipsis of the inf. ἐξελέξατο τοὺς πτωχοὺς (sc. εἶναι) πλουσίους *(God) chose the poor that they might be rich* **Js 2:5.**

δ. abs.: ἐκλελεγμένος *chosen* of Jesus, as God's child **Lk 9:35** (cp. ὃν ὁ πατὴρ . . . ἐξελέξατο διὰ λόγου εἰς ἐπίγνωσιν αὐτοῦ Iren. 1, 15, 3 [Harv. I 150, 6]; ἀγαπητός is found in the parallels Mt 17:5; Mk 9:7, and in Lk as v.l.; it = ἐκλελεγμένος also Vett. Val. 17, 2). Of Christians 1 Cl 50:7; cp. Pol 1:1. Of the church IEph ins.

❸ **gather in a crop,** ***gather*** ἐξ ἀκανθῶν ἐκλέγονται σῦκα **Lk 6:44** D; s. συλλέγω.—HRowley, The Biblical Doctrine of Election, '50.—DELG s.v. λέγω. M-M s.v. ἐκλέγω. TW.

ἐκλείπω fut. ἐκλείψω; 2 aor. ἐξέλιπον; pf. ἐκλέλοιπα LXX; pf. pass. ptc. ἐκλελειμμένος LXX. In our lit. only intr. (so trag., Thu., et al.; ins, pap, LXX; En 10:16; 15:5; 100:5; TestSol, TestAbr A, Test12Patr; JosAs 13:8 [also cod. A p. 53, 8; 64, 19 Bat.]; GrBar 4:6f; Joseph.; Ar. 6, 2; Just., A I, 32, 2 [after Gen 49:2])

❶ **to be no longer in existence,** ***fail, give out, be gone*** of money (X., Hell. 1, 5, 3 v.l.; PSI 495, 16 [258 BC] ἡμῖν τὸ ἐφόδιον ἐγλέλοιπεν=our travel money is all gone; 1 Macc 3:29) **Lk 16:9,** practically equivalent to 'when you go bankrupt' (on v.l. s. 3 below).

❷ **to go away from a place,** ***depart*** (Hdt. et al.) κἀκείνους κατέλειπεν ἐκεῖ καὶ ἔκλειπεν a questionable rdg. of **Ac 18:19** minuscule 104 (XI AD).

❸ **to cease as state or event,** ***fail, die out*** (JosAs 13:8 οἱ ὀφθαλμοί μου ἐξέλιπον; Plut., Lycurgus 31, 8 of a race) of faith **Lk 22:32.** ὅταν ἐκλίπητε *when you die* **Lk 16:9 v.l.** (for this mng. of ἐ. cp. Pla., Leg. 6, 759e; 9, 856e; X., Cyr. 8, 7, 26; Arrian, Anab. 6, 10, 2; POxy 497, 15 [II AD]; Gen 49:33; Ps 17:38; Tob 14:11; Wsd 5:13; Jos., Bell. 4, 68, Ant. 2, 184; TestReub 1:4; TestAbr A 19 p. 102, 18 [Stone p. 52]). Cp. *come to an end*=you will never grow old **Hb 1:12** (Ps 101:28). Of the sun *cease to shine* **Lk 23:45;** Luke's diction is standard for description of an eclipse *be eclipsed* (Thu. 2, 28; 7, 50, 4; X., Hell. 1, 6, 1; FGrH 239 B, 16 [III BC]=Marm. Par., Jac. p. 22; Dio Chrys. 57 [74], 28; Plut., Pelop. 295 [31, 3]; Sir 17:31; Philo, Mos. 2, 271; Ar. 6, 2; s. JSawyer, JTS 23, '72, 124–28; for the phenomenon as portent marking the death of an exceptional person of merit s. σκότος 1).

❹ **to be deficient in one's appearance,** ***be inferior*** εἶδος ἐκλεῖπον παρὰ τὸ εἶδος τ. ἀνθρώπων *an appearance inferior to that of humans* 1 Cl 16:3 (cp. Is 53:3).—M-M.

ἐκλεκτός, ή, όν (ἐκ +λέγω; since Pla., Leg. 12, 946d+).

❶ **pert. to being selected,** ***chosen*** gener. of those whom God has chosen fr. the generality of mankind and drawn to himself **Mt 20:16 v.l.; 22:14** (B 4:14; KStendahl, The Called and the Chosen: The Root of the Vine, ed. AFridrichsen '53, 63–80). Hence of Christians in particular (as in the OT of the Israelites 1 Ch 16:13; Ps 88:4; 104:6, 43; Is 65:9, 15, 23 al.—PAltmann, Erwählungstheol. u. Universalismus im AT, Beih. 92, ZAW, '64) *chosen* **24:22, 24, 31; Mk 13:20, 22, 27; 1 Pt 1:1; 2 Ti 2:10;** 1 Cl 6:1; 58:2; Hv 2, 4, 2. ἐ. τοῦ θεοῦ (cp. En 1:8) **Lk 18:7** (cp. 1QS 8:6; 1QH 2:13); **Ro 8:33** (cp. the Qumran passages just cited); **16:13** (s. 3 below); **Col 3:12; Tit 1:1;** 1 Cl 1:1; 2:4; 46:3f, 8; 49:5; 59:2; 2 Cl 14:5; Hv 1, 3, 4; 2, 1, 3; 2, 2, 5; 2, 4, 2; 3, 5, 1; 3, 8, 3; 3, 9, 10; 4, 2, 5; 4, 3, 5; EpilMosq 5. W. κλητοί ApcPt Rainer 2 and 5. W. κλητοί and πιστοί (SibOr 3, 69 w. πιστοί) **Rv 17:14.** γένος ἐκλεκτόν **1 Pt 2:9** (Is 43:20; TestJob 1:5). Of a Christian assembly or congregation **2J 1, 13** (w. personification of the assembly); ITr ins. Opp. ἄπιστοι MPol 16:1; ἅγιοι ἐ. 22:1.

❷ **pert. to being esp. distinguished,** ***elect***—ⓐ gener. of angels **1 Ti 5:21** (after En 39:1).

ⓑ of the Messiah ὁ ἐ. τοῦ θεοῦ (cp. En 39:6f; 40:5; 45:3–5; 49:2–4 al.) **Lk 23:35** (cp. 9:35); **J 1:34 v.l.** (AvHarnack, SBBerlAk 1915, 552–56=Studien I '31, 127–32; GDelling, Jüd. Lehre u. Frömmigkeit in den ParJer, Berlin '67, 18f).

ⓒ of David 1 Cl 52:2 (Ps 88:20; cp. Sir 47:22).

❸ **pert. to being considered best in the course of a selection,** ***choice, excellent*** (PRein 43, 9; BGU 603, 18 and 38; Ps 17:27; Sir 24:15; Bar 3:30; Wsd 3:14) ἀνὴρ ἐ. (EpArist 13; SibOr 3, 521) IPhld 11:1. Perh. **Ro 16:13** ὁ ἐ. ἐν κυρίῳ *the outstanding Christian.* In imagery of a *picked* or *elite* stone (cp. Strabo 1, 3, 18 after Ibycus [fgm. 21 Diehl] λίθος, ὃν καλεῖ ἐκλεκτόν = λόγαιον 'picked'; En 8:1) **1 Pt 2:4, 6;** B 6:2 (both Is 28:16); here a connection w. sense 2 is readily perceived.—DELG s.v. λέγω. M-M. EDNT. TW.

ἐκλελεγμένος s. ἐκλέγομαι.

ἐκλέλησμαι s. ἐκλανθάνομαι.

ἐκλήθην s. καλέω.

ἐκλιπαρέω 1 aor. ἐξελιπάρησα (λιπαρέω 'persevere'; Strabo et al.; Apollon. Paradox. 3; Philostrat., Vi. Apoll. 4, 1 p. 125, 17; Philo, In Flacc. 31; Jos., Ant. 5, 260) **to plead with so as to persuade,** ***beg, entreat*** πολλά *earnestly* (Diog. L. 4, 7) MPol 4.—DELG s.v. λίπτω.

ἐκλογή, ῆς, ἡ (ἐκ + λέγω)—❶ **a special choice,** ***selection, choice, election*** act. sense (s. ἐκλέγομαι 2; Pla., Rep. 3, 414a; PTebt 5, 166 [118 BC]; POxy 496, 15; BGU 1158, 13; Mitt-Wilck. II/2, 234; al. pap; PsSol 9:4; EpArist 33; Jos., Bell. 2, 165, Ant. 8, 24; Just., Mel.) σκεῦος ἐκλογῆς (Hebraistic= σ. ἐκλεκτόν) *a chosen instrument* **Ac 9:15.** Esp. of God's selection of Christians **2 Pt 1:10; 1 Th 1:4.** κατ' ἐκλογήν (Polyb. 6, 10, 9; Alciphron 2, 36, 1; Just., D. 49, 1. The expression is capable of various interpretations, either='by choice' as Apollon. Rhod. 2, 16b or adjectivally, as Diod. S. 13, 72, 4 ὁπλῖται κατ' ἐκλογήν=picked, select, crack hoplites): κατ' ἐκλογὴν χάριτος *acc. to selection out of generosity* = *selected out of generosity* or *by grace* **Ro 11:5.** ἡ κατ' ἐ. πρόθεσις τ. θεοῦ *the purpose of God which operates by selection* **9:11.** κατὰ τὴν ἐ. ἀγαπητοί *as far as (their) selection* or *election (by God) is concerned, beloved* **11:28** (cp. Dt 7:7 κύριος . . . ἐξελέξατο ὑμᾶς). μαρτύριον ἐκλογῆς Dg 4:4. ἐκλογὰς ποιεῖν ἀπό τινων *make a selection from among some people* MPol 20:1 (cp. Antig. Car. 26 ποιεῖσθαι τ. ἐκλογὴν ἔκ τινος=make a selection from).

❷ ***that which is chosen/selected,*** pass. sense (Polyb. 1, 47, 9 ἡ ἐ. τῶν ἀνδρῶν; Athen. 14 p. 663c; Phryn. 1; Philo, Spec. Leg. 4, 157) of pers. *those selected* (ἐκλογή collect.) **Ro 11:7;** 1 Cl 29:1.—AvHarnack, TU 42, 4, 1918 app.: Z. Terminologie der Wiedergeburt usw.—DELG s.v. λέγω B2a. M-M. TW. Sv.

ἐκλύω 1 aor. ἐξέλυσα LXX; pf. ptc. ἐκλελυκότα 2 Macc 12:18. Pass.: 1 fut. ἐκλυθήσομαι; 1 aor. ἐξελύθην; pf. ἐκλέλυμαι LXX (Hom. et al.; pap, LXX; TestSol 18:5 P, ἔγκλυσον for ἔγκλεισον; TestJob 30:1; TestZeb 2:4 v.l.; JosAs 10:16 cod. A and Pal. 364 for ἀπεβάλετο). In lit. freq. in the sense 'loose from someth., set free', also 'relax'. In our lit. only in the pass. w. act. sense: **be exhausted in strength,** ***become weary, give out*** (Hippocr., X. et al.; Epict. 2, 19, 20; Phlegon: 257 fgm. 36, I, 2 Jac.; Vett. Val. 18, 23; 126, 28; LXX; Philo, Virt. 88; Jos., Ant. 5, 134; 13, 233): fr. hunger (Diod. S. 19, 49, 2; PTebt 798, 7 [II BC] 2 Km 16:2; 17:29; La 2:19; 1 Macc 3:17) **Mt 15:32; Mk 8:3.** Of the waist *be ungirded* D 16:1. θερίσομεν μὴ ἐκλυόμενοι *we will reap if we do not give out* **Gal 6:9;** *lose courage* (Dt 20:3; 1 Macc 9:8) μηδὲ ἐκλύου *do not lose heart* **Hb 12:5** (Pr 3:11); fully ἐ. ταῖς ψυχαῖς (Polyb. 20, 4, 7; 29, 17, 4; cp. Diod. S. 20, 1, 4) vs. **3.**—M-M. TW. Spicq.

ἐκμάσσω impf. ἐξέμασσον; 1 aor. ἐξέμαξα; pf. ptc. ἐκμεμαχώς Sir 12:11 (μάσσω 'knead, mold'; trag., Pre-Socr. et al.; Epict. 1, 19, 4; ins; Sir 12:11; EpJer 11, 23; JosAs 13:5 cod. A [p. 57, 11 Bat.]) **to cause to become dry by wiping with**

a substance, ***wipe*** τί τινι *someth. w. someth.* (Plut., Artax. 10, 20 [19, 5]; Artem. 5, 4) feet, with one's hair **Lk 7:38, 44; J 11:2; 12:3;** feet, with a towel *dry* **13:5.**—DELG s.v. μάσσω. M-M.

ἐκμυκτηρίζω impf. ἐξεμυκτήριζον; fut. 3 sg. ἐκμυκτηριεῖ Ps 2:4 (LXX; TestJos 2:3) (the simplex μυκτηρίζω [fr. μυκτήρ 'nostril'] refers to using the nose as a means to ridicule) ***ridicule, sneer,*** τινά *(at) someone* (Ps 2:4; 34:16) **Lk 16:14;** 1 Cl 16:16 (Ps 21:8). Abs. **Lk 23:35.** V.l. for μυκτηρίζω GJs 3:1 codd. (not pap).—S. DELG s.v. μύσσομαι. TW. Spicq.

ἐκνεύω (νεύω 'nod') fut. 3 sg. ἐκνεύσει (Mi 6:14); 1 aor. ἐξένευσα (Eur., X. et al.) 'turn' (4 Km 2:24; 23:16; 3 Macc 3:22) **to draw away from, *turn aside, withdraw*** (Plut., Mor. 577b; Philo, Mos. 2, 251; Jos., Ant. 7, 83; 9, 120; Just. D. 9, 3=ὑποχωρέω) **J 5:13** (cp. BGU 1189, 7 [I BC / I AD] ἐκνεύειν τὴν ἐμφάνειαν=make oneself invisible).—M-M.

ἐκνήφω fut. ἐκνήψω LXX; 1 aor. ἐξένηψα 'become sober' (Lynceus in Athen. 4, 5 p. 130b; LXX) lit. of one recovering from a drunken revel, 'sober up' (Anth. Pal. 5, 135, 6); in our lit., only fig. ***come to one's senses*** (Plut., Demosth. 20, 3; Aretaeus p. 41, 10; SibOr fgm. 3, 41) ἐκνήψατε δικαίως *sober up for uprightness* ('come to a sober and right mind' NRSV) **1 Cor 15:34.**—ELövestam, Über die ntl. Aufforderung zur Nüchternheit, StTh '58, 83f (on gnostic connection); AMalherbe, JBL 87, '68, 78 (on connection w. Epicurus).—M-M. TW.

ἑκούσιος, ία, ιον (s. next; Soph., Thu. et al.; ins, pap, LXX; TestLevi 9:7; Philo) **pert to doing someth. of one's own volition, *voluntary, as a volunteer*** of backsliders MPol 4 (Zahn's cj. for ἑαυτοῖς or ἑαυτούς). κατὰ ἑκούσιον (opp. κατὰ ἀνάγκην) *of one's own free will* **Phlm 14** (Num 15:3 καθ' ἑκούσιον; Thu. 8, 27, 3 καθ' ἑκουσίαν [sc. γνώμην]; as opposed to legal compulsion, cp. Plut., Mor. 446e).—DELG s.v. ἑκών. M-M. TW. Sv.

ἑκουσίως adv. of ἑκούσιος (s. prec.; Eur., Thu. et al.; ins, pap, LXX, Philo; TestDan 4:6; SibOr 11, 78) ***willingly*** ποιμαίνειν (opp. ἀναγκαστῶς) **1 Pt 5:2;** *without compulsion,* i.e. *deliberately, intentionally* ἁμαρτάνειν (Ps.-Demetr., Form. Ep. p. 5, 17) **Hb 10:26.**—DELG s.v. ἑκών. M-M.

ἔκπαλαι adv. (s. πάλαι; Plut., Themist. 127 [30, 1] and Aristid. 17, 2; Arrian, Exp. Alex. 1, 9, 8 Roos; OGI 584, 5 [II AD]; POxy 938, 3; Philo, Agr. 152; Jos., Bell. 7, 159, Ant. 16, 244; Lob., Phryn. p. 45ff)

❶ **pert. to a point of time long before a current moment, *long ago* 2 Pt 3:5.**

❷ **pert. to a relatively long interval of time since a point of time in the past, *for a long time* 2 Pt 2:3.**—DELG s.v. πάλαι. M-M.

ἐκπειράζω fut. ἐκπειράσω; 1 aor. ἐξεπείρασα (s. πειράζω; LXX; TestSol 12, 1 C; as quot. fr. Dt 8:2 in Philo, Congr. Erud. Grat. 170)

❶ **to subject to test or proof, *tempt*** τινά *someone* the Lord God **Mt 4:7; Lk 4:12** (both Dt 6:16); of a midwife who checked Mary's virginity and was dismayed that she had put God to proof GJs 20:1; *test* **Lk 10:25,** but mng. 2 is also prob.

❷ **to entrap someone into giving information that will jeopardize the person, *entrap*** Jesus **Lk 10:25** (s. 1); **J 8:4 v.l.;** τὸν χριστόν **1 Cor 10:9.**

❸ **to entice to do wrong by offering attractive benefits, *tempt,*** of the devil Hm 12, 5, 4; of one erroneously thought to be an evil being ἐκπειράζων με Hv 5:3. Pass. ἐκπειρασθεὶς ὑπὸ τ. διαβόλου *tempted by the devil* m 4, 3, 6.—TW.

ἐκπέμπω fut. 3 sg. ἐκπέμψει Eccl 17:11; 1 aor. ἐξέπεμψα. Pass.: 1 aor. pass. ἐξεπέμφθην, ptc. ἐκπεμφθείς (s. πέμπω; Hom.+) **to cause someone to go away (for a purpose), *send out*** (Jos., Ant. 2, 11) spies 1 Cl 12:2. ἐκπεμφθέντες ὑπὸ τοῦ ἁγίου πνεύματος *sent out by the Holy Spirit* **Ac 13:4.** προφήτας ἐξέπεμψεν (God) *sent out prophets* AcPl Ha 8, 17 (s. καταπέμπω). Of Christ ἀπὸ τ. θεοῦ ἐξεπέμφθη 1 Cl 42:1; *send away* (Jos., Ant. 1, 216, Vi. 332 εἰς τὰ Ἱερ.) εἰς Βέροιαν **Ac 17:10.**—M-M.

ἐκπέπτωκα s. ἐκπίπτω.

ἐκπερισσοῦ s. περισσός.

ἐκπερισσῶς adv. **pert. to being beyond normal limits, *extraordinarily*** ἐ. λαλεῖν *say with great emphasis* **Mk 14:31** (PJoüon, RSR 29, '39, 240f).—S. DELG s.v. περί.

ἐκπεσεῖν s. ἐκπίπτω.

ἐκπετάννυμι fut. ἐκπετάσω LXX; 1 aor. ἐξεπέτασα; plpf. ἐκπεπετάκειν; 1 aor. pass. ἐξεπετάσθην LXX (πετάννυμι 'spread out'; Eur. et al.; Polyb., Plut., Lucian; Kaibel 779, 2; LXX; En 14:8; TestSol 2:1 L; JosAs 12:1; Jos., Ant. 3, 128; Just., D. 90, 4.—Anz 286) **to cause an object to extend in space, *spread/hold out*** τὰς χεῖρας *the hands* in an imploring gesture (cp. JosAs 12:1) **Ro 10:21;** B 12:4 (both Is 65:2); Hs 9, 3, 2.—M-M.

ἐκπέτασις, εως, ἡ (s. prec. entry; Plut., Mor. 564b) ***spreading out, opening*** σημεῖον ἐκπετάσεως ἐν οὐρανῷ *a sign,* (consisting of) *an opening in the heavens* D 16:6 (EStommel, Röm. Quartalschrift 48, '53, 21–42; Wengst, Didache p. 99f, n. 139: celestial sign of the cross).—DELG s.v. πετάννυμι.

ἐκπέτομαι 2 aor. ἐξέπτην (Sir 43:14, otherw. in LXX ἐξεπετάσθην) (Hes. et al.; LXX) lit. to fly out or away; in out lit. only fig. ***fly out/away*** ἐξέπτη ἡ λύπη αὐτοῦ *his grief left him* AcPl Ha 3, 17.

ἐκπηδάω 1 aor. ἐξεπήδησα; pf. inf. ἐκπεπηδηκέναι Sus 39 Theod. (Soph., Hdt. et al.; pap, LXX, JosAs)

❶ **to move forward with haste, *rush*** (lit. 'leap') ***out*** (so Menand., Peric. 527 S. [277 Kö.]; UPZ 170b, 28 [127/126 BC]) εἰς τὸν ὄχλον *into the crowd* **Ac 14:14** (cp. Jdth 14:17 ἐξεπήδησεν εἰς τ. λαόν; Jos., Ant. 6, 191).

❷ **to make a quick movement from a position, *get up quickly*** (X., Cyr. 1, 4, 8; Appian, Bell. Civ. 2, 36 §142; Polyaenus 8, 2; Mitt-Wilck. I/2, 1 II, 13 [c. 246 BC]; Jos., Ant. 8, 273) **Ac 10:25** D.

❸ **spend time in, *live*** λάβετε τὸ φῶ[ς οἱ ἐ]ν σκοτίᾳ θαν[άτου ἐκ]|πεπηδημένοι *you who move around* (?) *in fatal darkness take the light* AcPl BMM verso 4f//AcPl Ha 8, 32f (in the latter Schmidt proposed [καθήμ]ενοι, but s. Sander's note in HTR 3, '38, 86f on the two rdgs., with his rendering, 'those who are living [sinfully] in the darkness of death', and his ref. to fig. usage in PGrenf I, 53, 24, where, he observes, two women are represented as 'living in harlotry' or 'in sin'; s. Borger, GGA 134 on the problem relating to addition of ἐκ).—S. πεδάω, πηδάω.—M-M.

ἐκπίπτω fut. inf. ἐκπεσεῖσθαι (Ath 18, 4); 1 aor. ἐξέπεσα (B-D-F §81, 3; W-S. §13:13; Mlt-H. 208); 2 aor. ἐξέπεσον; pf. ἐκπέπτωκα (s. πίπτω; Hom.+; ins, pap, LXX, TestSol 20:16;

TestJud 21:4; EpArist, Philo, Joseph.; Ath. 18, 4; 25, 1) gener. 'fall off/from' (as pass. of ἐκβάλλω 'be thrown out, banished'; Ath. 18, 4 ἐκπεσεῖσθαι . . . ὑπὸ τῶν παίδων)

❶ **to fall from some point, *fall:*** lit., of withered flowers that fall to the ground (but ἐ. also means 'fall'=perish: X., Hell. 1, 1, 32; Lucian, Merc. Cond. 42, end) **Js 1:11; 1 Pt 1:24** (both Is 40:7). ἔκ τινος *from something* (Is 6:13; 14:12) chains from hands **Ac 12:7.** εἴασαν αὐτὴν ἐκπεσεῖν *they let it* (the boat) *fall* **27:32,** but s. 2 below; **Mk 13:25 v.l.**

❷ **to drift or be blown off course and run aground, *drift off course, run aground,*** nautical term, εἴς τι *on someth.* (Eur., Hel. 409 εἰς γῆν; Thu. 2, 92, 3; Diod. S. 1, 31, 5; 2, 60, 1) on the Syrtis **Ac 27:17;** on an island vs. **26.** κατὰ τραχεῖς τόπους *the rocks* vs. **29.** Abs. perh. vs. **32,** s. 1 above.

❸ **to change for the worse from a favorable condition, *lose*** fig. (Hdt. 3, 14; Thu. 8, 81, 2) τινός *someth.* (Plut., Tib. Gracch. 834 [21, 7]; OGI 521, 2; PTebt 50, 14; Philo, Leg. All. 3, 183; Jos., Ant. 7, 203 βασιλείας) grace, favor **Gal 5:4;** one's own stability **2 Pt 3:17.**

❹ **become inadequate for some function, *fail, weaken*** fig. (Pla., Ep. 2 p. 314b; Diod. S. 14, 109, 5; PTebt 27, 26; Plut., Mor. 9b; Sir 34:7) of God's word **Ro 9:6** (on the probability of commercial metaphor, FDanker, Gingrich Festschr. '72, 107). Of love **1 Cor 13:8 v.l.** (acc. to AHarnack, SBBerlAk 1911, p. 148, 1, original). ὥστε καὶ Παῦλον ἐκπεσεῖν τῆς προσευχῆς *so that even Paul ceased praying* AcPl Ha 2, 8.—M-M. TW.

ἐκπλέκω 1 aor. ἐξέπλεξα (πλέκω 'twist', opp. ἐμπλέκω; BGU II, 665 II, 5 [I AD]; PTebt 315, 21; 29 [II AD]; POxy 1490, 6 et al. pap) ***disentangle (oneself)*** ὥστε ἀπὸ τ. ἀκανθῶν . . . μὴ δύνασθαι ἐκπλέξαι τὰ πρόβατα *so that the sheep could not disentangle themselves fr. the thorn-bushes* Hs 6, 2, 6 (cp. Artem. 4, 57 ἄκανθαι . . . τὰς ἐμπλοκάς).

ἐκπλέω 1 aor. ἐξέπλευσα (s. πλέω; Soph., Hdt. et al.; SIG 454, 13 [III BC]; OGI 69, 5; PSI 444, 1 [III BC]; BGU V §64 and 66–68; POxy 1271, 3; Jos., Ant. 18, 247 al.) ***sail away*** εἴς τι *to a place* (X., Hell. 4, 8, 32; Diod. S. 14, 99, 4; Jos., Bell. 1, 481) **Ac 15:39; 18:18** (prob. in both pass. in sense of *sail back;* on ἐκπλέω signifying return to point of origin s. Renehan '82, 64, w. citation of Isocr. 17, 19 and 37). ἀπό τινος *fr. a place* **20:6.**—M-M.

ἔκπληκτος, ον ***shocking, frightful*** in act. sense (s. πλήσσω and next entry; so Hero I, 338, 5; 342, 4; Lucian, Herm. 18; Orph. Hymn. 39, 10) βουλή (w. πονηρά) Hv 1, 2, 4.—S. DELG s.v. πλήσσω.

ἔκπληξις, εως, ἡ (s. preceding entry; Hippoc., Aeschyl, Thu. et al.; 1 Km 14:15 Aq; Job 4:13 Sym.; Ps 30:23 al. Sym.; EpArist 96:99; Joseph.) **state or condition of being astonished, *amazement*** GJs 18:3 v.l. (s. Strycker 151, note).—S. DELG s.v. πλήσσω.

ἐκπληρόω pf. ἐκπεπλήρωκα (s. πληρόω; trag., Hdt.+; ins, pap, LXX, TestSol; TestGad 5:1; Philo; Jos., Ant. 19, 193) **cause to happen, with implication that someth. is brought to fruition, *fulfill*** of promises **Ac 13:33** (cp. Hdt. 8, 144; Polyb. 1, 67, 1 τ. ἐλπίδας καὶ τ. ἐπαγγελίας; Ael. Aristid. 51, 46 K.=27 p. 545 D.: ἐνύπνιον; PTebt 10, 7; 48, 12; 3 Macc 1:2, 22); *bring to completion* (Hdt. 8, 82; PRyl 66, 8; 2 Macc 8:10) ἐ. τὰς ἡμέρας τῶν ἁμαρτιῶν *fill up the days of the sins,* i.e., in this pass., *atone fully* for them Hv 3, 7, 6 (with ἐ. τὰς ἡμέρας cp. Diod. S. 2, 57, 5 τὸν χρόνον ἐκπληρώσαντες).—S. DELG s.v. πίμπλημι. M-M. TW.

ἐκπλήρωσις, εως, ἡ (s. prec. entry; Dionys. Hal. 6, 86; Epict. 4, 1, 175; BGU 1825, 23 [I BC]; 2 Macc 6:14; Philo, Op. M. 146, Leg. All. 3, 34; 145) **a process viewed in its entirety with focus on its being brought to a proper conclusion, *completion*** διαγγέλλων τὴν ἐ. τῶν ἡμερῶν τοῦ ἁγνισμοῦ *giving notice that the days of purification would be completed* **Ac 21:26** (cp. Strabo 17, 1, 46 ἐκπλ. τ. ἐνιαυτοῦ).—DELG s.v. πίμπλημι. TW.

ἐκπλήσσω Att. ἐκπλήττω MPol 7:3; 1 aor. ἐξέπληξα; in NT (and LXX) only in pass.—impf. ἐξεπλησσόμην; 2 aor. ἐξεπλάγην (Hom. et al.; LXX, TestSol; TestAbr A 3 p. 80, 13 [Stone p. 8]; TestJob; ApcrEzk [Epiph. 70, 12]) **to cause to be filled with amazement to the point of being overwhelmed, *amaze, astound, overwhelm*** (lit. strike out of one's senses), act. τινά *someone* (Appian, Mithrid. 116 §566; Ammonius Hermiae in Aristotle, Lib. de Interpr. p. 66, 6 Busse τὸν ἀκροατήν; Jos., Bell. 7, 419) B 1:3 (Himerius, Or. 39 [=Or. 5], 7 of an 'overwhelming' sight). —Pass. in act. sense ***be amazed, overwhelmed*** w. fright (Dio Chrys. 80 [30], 12) οἱ μαθηταὶ ἐξεπλήσσοντο σφόδρα *the disciples were terribly shocked* **Mt 19:25; Mk 10:26;** or wonder (Dio Chrys. 71 [21], 14; SIG 1168, 46 [IV BC]; Jos., Ant. 8, 168; 17, 110;142) **Mt 13:54; Mk 6:2; 7:37; Lk 2:48** the parents of Jesus *were dumbfounded;* MPol 7:3. W. the reason given: ἐπί τινι *at someth.* or *someone* (X., Cyr. 1, 4, 27 ἐπί τῷ κάλλει; Dio Chrys. 29 [46], 1; Aelian, VH 12, 41) **Mt 7:28; 22:33; Mk 1:22; 11:18; Lk 4:32; 9:43; Ac 13:12;** B 7:10; 16:10.—M-M.

ἐκπλοκή, ῆς, ἡ s. πλοκή.

ἐκπνέω (s. πνέω) 1 aor. ἐξέπνευσα **breathe out one's life/soul, *expire,*** euphem. for *die* **Mk 15:37, 39; Lk 23:46** (without obj. since Soph., Aj. 1026; Plut., Mor. 597f; M. Ant. 4, 33, 2; Jos., Ant. 12, 357; PHolm ι [10],18. W. βίον or ψυχήν since Aeschyl.).—TW.

ἐκπορεύομαι (s. πορεύομαι) impf. ἐξεπορευόμην; fut. ἐκπορεύσομαι; pf. ἐκπεπόρευμαι LXX (mid. since X.; ins, pap, LXX, En; GrBar 6:1; Just., D. 31, 2 ποταμὸς εἷλκεν ἐκπορευόμενος [Da 7:10 LXX and Theod.])

❶ **to be in motion from one area to another, *go***—ⓐ abs. (UPZ 5, 11; 78, 44; BGU 1078, 4 [39 AD] al.) *go away* **Ac 3:11** D. ὄχλοι ἐκπορευόμενοι *crowds* or *people that came out* **Lk 3:7;** *go out* **Ac 25:4.** εἰσπορεύεσθαι καὶ ἐ. *go in and out* **9:28** (cp. Dt 31:2; Tob 5:18; 1 Macc 3:45). Esp. of hostile spirits *come out* **Mt 17:21; Ac 19:12.**

ⓑ w. indication of the place fr. which: ἔκ τινος (Polyb. 6, 58, 4; Mi 1:3; Ezk 47:12 al.) out of the sanctuary **Mk 13:1.** ἐκ γῆς Αἰγύπτου B 2:7 (cp. Dt 25:17). Of a bride *come out of the bridal chamber* Hv 4, 2, 1. ἔξω τῆς πόλεως *outside the city* **Mk 11:19.** ἀπό τινος (Jer 5:6; Sir 42:13) from Jericho **Mt 20:29; Mk 10:46.** ἐκεῖθεν **6:11** (cp. 2 Km 16:5). Cp. παρά τινος *proceed from someone* (Ezk 33:30) of the Spirit ὃ παρὰ τοῦ πατρὸς ἐκπορεύεται **J 15:26.**

ⓒ w. the goal indicated: εἴς τι (X., An. 5, 6, 33; Jer 6:25; Ezk 44:19) εἰς ὁδόν *set out on a journey* **Mk 10:17.** εἰς ἀφεδρῶνα **7:19** (s. ἀφεδρών). ἐ. εἰς ἀνάστασιν ζωῆς *come out* (of the graves) *to a resurrection that brings life* (opp. κρίσεως) **J 5:29.** ἐπί τινα *to someone* (cp. Zech 6:6, 8) **Rv 16:14.** πρός τινα *to someone* (Judg 9:33; Is 36:16) **Mt 3:5; Mk 1:5.**

❷ **to come forth from, *come/go out, proceed,*** in imagery, of things, words, or thoughts τὸ ἐκπορευόμενον ἐκ τοῦ στόματος *what comes out of the mouth* (cp. Pr 3:16a) **Mt 15:11,** cp. vs. **18; Lk 4:22; Eph 4:29.** For this τὰ ἐκ τοῦ ἀνθρώπου ἐκπορευόμενα *what comes out of a pers.* **Mk 7:15,** cp. vs. **20.**

ἔσωθεν ἐκ τ. καρδίας vs. **21**, cp. vs. **23.** ῥῆμα ἐκπορευόμενον διὰ στόματος θεοῦ (διά A1a) **Mt 4:4** (Dt 8:3). Of truth ἐ. ἐκ τοῦ στόματος Hm 3:1. Of fire, lightning, etc. (Job 41:12): lightning (Ezk 1:13) **Rv 4:5;** fire **9:17f; 11:5;** fiery locusts Hv 4, 1, 6. Of streams of water *flow out* (Ezk 47:1, 8, 12) ἐκ τ. θρόνου τ. θεοῦ **Rv 22:1** (ὑποκάτω τοῦ θρόνου ἐξεπορεύοντο ποταμοὶ πυρὸς En 14:19). Of a sword *project* ἐκ τ. στόματος **1:16; 19:15;** ἐ. ἦχος περὶ αὐτοῦ εἰς πάντα τόπον *reports about him spread into every place* **Lk 4:37.**—M-M. TW.

ἐκπορνεύω 1 aor. ἐξεπόρνευσα; pf. 3 sg. ἐκπεπόρνευκε Gen. 38:24 (Poll. 6, 30; TestDan 5:5; LXX) ***indulge in illicit sexual relations/debauchery*** **Jd 7.**—DELG s.v. πέρνημι. TW.

ἐκπρεπής, ές (s. πρέπω; Hom. et al.; LXX) **to be extraordinarily appropriate or fitting, *remarkable, outstanding,*** God's created works Hv 1, 1, 3. Superlative (Aesop, Fab. 349 P.=Babr. 114 Cr. and L-P.) κάλλει ἐκπρεπεστάτη *most distinguished for her beauty = exceptionally beautiful* (a woman; cp. Parthenius 29:1; Philo, Congr. Erud. Gr. 124; Jos., Ant 3, 78) 3, 10, 5.—DELG s.v. πρέπω.

ἐκπτύω 1 aor. ἐξέπτυσα (Hom. et al.; Plut., Mor. p. 328c; Epict. 3, 12, 17) orig. of spitting motion 'spit, spit out', then metaph. to eject saliva as an expression of contempt (s. ἐξουθενέω 1 and 2) or to ward off hostile spirits (s. βασκαίνω 1 and Theocr. 6, 39 the herder Damoctas spits three times on his chest to avoid the evil eye; 20, 11 in expression of contempt; Lucian, Navig. 15, Apologia 6; Theophr., Char. 16, 14 μαινόμενον ἰδὼν ἢ ἐπίληπτον φρίξας εἰς κόλπον πτύσαι 'he shudders when he sees someone who is mad or has fits and he spits on his chest'), hence ***disdain*** **Gal 4:14** (ἐ. is omitted by P^{46}).—Ltzm. ad loc.; SSeligmann, D. böse Blick I 1910, 293–98; JHElliott, The Fear of the Leer: Forum IV/4, '88, 42–71 (lit.). S. also πτύσμα.—M-M. TW.

ἐκπυρόω 1 fut. pass. ἐκπυρωθήσομαι (ἐκ + πῦρ; Eur. et al.; Cornutus 17 p. 27, 10; 2 Macc 7:3f) ***set on fire, destroy by fire*** of the end of the world (Heraclitus, fgm. B 31 γῆ κ. οὐρανὸς πάλιν ἐκπυροῦται; A 1, 8 [I 141, 21] and 10 [146, 18]; Stoics since Zeno: Stoic. I p. 27, 15; 114, 36; II 182, 16; Plut., Mor. 1067a; MPohlenz, Stoa '49, I 486 index: ἐκπύρωσις) **2 Pt 3:10** as conjectured, w. numerous other conjectures, s. var. editions of the Nestle NT.; FOlivier, RTP 1920, 237ff, Religio 11, '35, 481–89.—DELG s.v. πῦρ.

ἐκριζόω 1 aor. ἐξερίζωσα, pass. ἐξεριζώθην, 1 fut. ἐκριζωθήσεται (ἐκ + ῥίζα; Aesop 179 H.; Babrius 36, 8 L-P.; Geopon. 3, 5, 8; SIG 889, 9f; 1239, 16f; PapRyl 583, 15; Sb 7188, 25 [both II BC]; PCairMasp 87, 9; LXX; TestAsh 1:7; 4:2; SibOr, fgm. 3, 21)

❶ **pull up or out by the roots, *uproot,*** of vegetation (Wsd 4:4; TestSol 6:1 D McCown) grain w. weeds **Mt 13:29.—15:13;** a tree (SIG 889, 9f; Da 4:14, 26) ἐκριζώθητι *be uprooted* **Lk 17:6.** δένδρα ἐκριζωθέντα *uprooted trees* **Jd 12.**

❷ **to destroy from the bottom up, *uproot, utterly destroy*** fig. ext. of 1 (SIG 1239, 16f; Sir 3:9; Zeph 2:4 al.) a people 1 Cl 6:4. Of doubt: πολλοὺς ἐκριζοῖ ἀπὸ τῆς πίστεως *it uproots many fr. the faith* Hm 9:9.—DELG s.v. ῥίζα. M-M. TW.

ἐκρίπτω impf. ἐξερρίπτουν 2 Macc 10:30; fut. 3 sg. ἐκρίψει Sir 10:9; 1 aor. ἐξέριψα LXX. Pass.: 2 fut. 3 sg. ἐξεριφήσεται Zeph 2:4; 2 aor. ἐξερίφην; pf. ptc. ἐξερριμμένος LXX (s. ῥίπτω; trag. et al.; UPZ 151, 12 [259 BC]; PLond I, 106, 13 p. 61 [II BC]; LXX; TestSol 16:2 P).

❶ **to remove with force from an area, *drive away*** of chaff blown by the wind B 11:7 (Ps 1:4).

❷ **to cause to be deprived of, *to drive out fr.,*** fig. ext. of 1 ἐκριφῆναι ἐκ τῆς ἐλπίδος *be driven out fr. the hope = be deprived of the hope* 1 Cl 57:2 (cp. Pr 5:23).

ἔκρυσις, εως, ἡ (ἐκ + ῥέω; Hippocr., Aristot. et al.; IG XI/2, 144 A, 73 [ἐγρ-], IV/III BC; Ezk 40:38) **someth. given off as in a stream, *outflow, efflux,*** in description of the miserable death of Judas Papias (3:3).—JKürzinger, Papias v. Hierap. u. d. Evgg. des NT, 1883, p. 104f.—DELG s.v. ῥέω.

ἔκστασις, εως, ἡ (s. ἐξίστημι; Hippocr.+)—❶ **a state of consternation or profound emotional experience to the point of being beside oneself** ('distraction, confusion, perplexity, astonishment' in var. aspects: Menand., fgm. 149 Kock [=136, 2 Kö.] πάντα δὲ τὰ μηδὲ προσδοκώμεν' ἔκστασιν φέρει; Περὶ ὕψους 1, 4; SIG 1240, 14; 1 Km 11:7; 2 Ch 14:13; Ps 30:23) ***amazement/astonishment*** ἐξέστησαν μεγάλῃ ἐκστάσει *they were quite beside themselves w. amazement* **Mk 5:42** (cp. Gen 27:33; Ezk 26:16; 27:35 al.); ἔ. ἔλαβεν ἅπαντας **Lk 5:26.** [κατ]εῖχεν αὐτὰς ἔκστασις [μεγάλη] AcPl Ha 5, 29. W. τρόμος **Mk 16:8.** W. θάμβος **Ac 3:10.**

❷ **a state of being in which consciousness is wholly or partially suspended, freq. associated with divine action, *trance, ecstasy*** (Galen XIX 462 K. ἔ. ἐστιν ὀλιγοχρόνιος μανία; Philo, Rer. Div. Her. 257; 258; 264; 265 [after Gen 2:21; 15:12], Vi. Cont. 40; Plotinus 6, 9, 11; PGM 4, 737; Just., D. 115, 3 ἐν ἐκστάσει [opp. ἐν καταστάσει]; Orig., C. Cels. 7, 3, 39) γενέσθαι ἐν ἐκστάσει *fall into a trance* **Ac 22:17;** ἐγένετο (ἐπέπεσεν v.l.) ἐπ' αὐτὸν ἔ. *a trance came over him* **10:10.** Cp. **11:5.**—ERohde, Psyche[3] II 18ff; WInge, Ecstasy: EncRelEth V 157–59; ASharma, Ecstasy: EncRel V 11–17.—RAC IV 944–87. B. 1094. DELG s.v. ἵστημι. M-M. EDNT. TW. Sv.

ἐκστρέφω 1 aor. ἐξέστρεψα LXX; pf. pass. ἐξέστραμμαι (στρέφω; Hom. et al.; LXX; Just., A I, 38, 8 τὰ χείλη 'purse' or 'pucker the lips') **to cause to turn aside from what is considered true or morally proper, *turn aside, pervert*** τινά *someone* (Aristoph., Nub. 554 ἐκστρέψας τοὺς ἱππέας) Hs 8, 6, 5. Pass. ἐξέστραπται ὁ τοιοῦτος *such a man is perverted= he has gone the wrong way* **Tit 3:11** (cp. Dt 32:20).

ἐκσφενδονάω (σφενδόνη 'sling') 1 aor. ἐξεσφενδόνησα (Suda) **to cast someth. with a slinging motion, *hurl away*** (Heliod. 9, 5) in fig. ext. of mng. *hurl away* τινὰ ἀπό τινος *someone fr. someth.* B 2:10.—DELG s.v. σφενδόνη. TW.

ἐκσῴζω 1 aor. ἐξέσωσα (s. σῴζω; Aeschyl., Hdt. et al.; Sb 8671, 4 hymn to Isis; IK Ephesos V, 1628, 9) **to keep safe from injury in perilous circumstance, *bring safely*** ἐκσῶσαι, v.l. for ἐξῶσαι, because of similarity of sound (s. ἐξωθέω) **Ac 27:39.**—DELG s.v. σῶς.

ἐκταράσσω 1 aor. ἐξετάραξα LXX (s. ταράσσω; Isocr. et al.; pap, LXX) **to cause to be in uproar, *agitate, cause trouble to, throw into confusion*** τινά *someone* **Ac 15:24** D; τὴν πόλιν **16:20** (cp. Plut., Coriol. 223 [19, 2]; Cass. Dio [oft.]; PGen 1, 12; Jos., Bell. 7, 41, Ant. 17, 253).—M-M. TW.

ἐκτείνω fut. ἐκτενῶ; 1 aor. ἐξέτεινα; pf. ἐκτέτακα 1 Km 1:16. Pass.: 1 fut. 3 sg. ἐκταθήσεται Zech 1:16; 1 aor. 3 sg. ἐξετάθη 1 Macc 6:40; pf. ptc. ἐκτεταμένος LXX (τείνω 'stretch'; Aeschyl., Hdt.+)

❶ **to cause an object to extend to its full length in space, *stretch out*** ἐ. ἑαυτό *stretch itself out* Hv 4, 1, 9. Of nets *spread* *out* B 5:4 (Pr 1:17). ἀγκύρας ἐκτείνειν *put out* or *lay out anchors* **Ac 27:30;** s. ἄγκυρα.—Esp. in the expr. ἐ. τὴν χεῖρα (τὰς χεῖρας) *hold out* or *extend the hand(s)* (class.; Diod. S. 13, 15, 1; oft. LXX; JosAs 8:4 al.; Jos., Ant. 8, 233, cp. 13, 14; Just., D. 111, 1) of a man w. a disabled hand: **Mt 12:13; Mk 3:5; Lk 6:10.** To grasp someth. (Gen 22:10 al.) **Mt 26:51;** D 4:5; B 19:9. To take hold of someone **Mt 14:31.** To heal someone (by touch; s. OWeinreich, Antike Heilungswunder 1909, 15ff; 51ff; JBehm, D. Handauflegung 1911, 102ff) **Mt 8:3; Mk 1:41; Lk 5:13.** W. εἰς to indicate purpose **Ac 4:30.** ἐ. τὴν χεῖρα *lay a hand on someone* (Diog. L. 6, 29 τὰς χεῖρας ἐπὶ τοὺς φίλους ἐ.) w. hostile intent (Jer 6:12; 1 Macc 6:25; 12:42; 2 Macc 15:32; cp. Jos., Ant. 7, 327) **Lk 22:53.** To point at someone **Mt 12:49.** As a gesture in prayer (1 Esdr 8:70; 4 Macc 4:11; Agatharchides: 86 fgm. 20, 209 Jac. [in Jos., C. Ap. 1, 209].—Earlier writers would have said ἀνατείνω τὰς χεῖρας: Pind., O. 7, 65; [Ps.-]Plut., Mor. 774b) 1 Cl 2:3; B 12:2. Gesture of a speaker **Ac 26:1** (cp. Quintilian 9, 3, 84ff; Apuleius, Metam. 2, 21; KSittl, D. Gebärden d. Griechen u. Römer 1890, 350ff). Of one who is crucified (Epict. 3, 26, 22 ἐκτείνας σεαυτὸν ὡς οἱ ἐσταυρωμένοι; Jos., Ant. 19, 94) **J 21:18;** B 12:2 (Just., A I, 35, 6 ἐξετάθη τὰς χεῖρας).

❷ **to extend in time beyond normal expectation,** ***draw out at length.*** fig. ext. of 1 λόγους ἐ. (Pla., Leg. 10, 887a ὁ λόγος ἐκταθείς, others sim.) *speak at length, be long-winded* (Polyb. 12, 26b, 4) 1 Cl 57:4 (Pr 1:24).—M-M. TW.

ἐκτελέω 1 aor. ἐξετέλεσα; pf. ptc. ἐκτετελεκότες 2 Macc 15:9 (s. τελέω; Hom. et al.; ins, pap, LXX; TestJob 1:2 οἰκονομίαν; 11:2 διακονίαν; ParJer 9:29; GrBar 4:14 τὴν εὐχήν; Jos. Bell. 2, 313; 7, 395; Just., D. 9, 2) **bring to completion with implication of a job well done,** ***finish*** of a building **Lk 14:29f** (cp. 2 Ch 4:5).—DELG s.v. τέλος. M-M.

ἐκτένεια, ας, ἡ (late word [Phryn. p. 311 Lob.]; Molpis: 590 fgm. 2b Jac. [in Athen. 4, 141e]; oft. in ins [s. Thieme 27; Rouffiac 40]; PPetr III, 144 IV, 17 [=Mitt-Wilck. I/2, 1 IV, 17 III BC]; UPZ 110, 12; LXX; Jos., Ant. 7, 231) **a state of persistence in an undertaking or enterprise, with implication of exceptional interest or devotion,** ***perseverance, earnestness*** ἐν ἐ. *earnestly* (=ἐκτενῶς) **Ac 12:5** D; **26:7** (cp. Jdth 4:9). Also μετὰ ἐκτενείας 1 Cl 33:1; μετὰ πάσης ἐκτενείας 37:1 (IGR IV, 984, 6 μετὰ πάσης ἐ. καὶ λαμπρότητος; 2 Macc 14:38).—IMg 14 cj. Lghtf.—DELG s.v. τανυ- etc. E p. 1092. M-M. TW. Spicq.

ἐκτενής, ές (Aeschyl.; Polyb. 22, 5, 4; ins [s. on ἐκτένεια]; PTebt 24, 45; 3 Macc 3:10; 5:29; Philo; Just., D. 107, 2 ἐκτενοῦς ὀλολυγμοῦ) **pert. to being persevering, with implication that one does not waver in one's display of interest or devotion,** ***eager, earnest,*** comp. ἐκτενέστερος (IGR IV, 293 II, 38) **Ac 12:5 v.l.** ἐκτενῆ τὴν δέησιν ποιεῖσθαι *make earnest supplication* 1 Cl 59:2 (UPZ 110, 46 [164 BC] τὴν ἐκτενεστάτην ποιήσασθαι πρόνοιαν). ἐκτενῆ ὑπὸ πάντων προσευχὴν γενέσθαι AcPl Ha 6, 6f. τὴν ἀγάπην ἐκτενῆ ἔχειν *keep affection constant* **1 Pt 4:8.** μετ' ἐκτενοῦς ἐπιεικείας *w. constant gentleness* 1 Cl 58:2; 62:2.—DELG s.v. τανυ- etc. E p. 1092. M-M. TW. Spicq.

ἐκτενῶς adv. of ἐκτενής (q.v.; Aristot.+; Polyb. 31, 14, 12; Diod. S. 2, 24, 3; M. Ant. 1, 4; Vett. Val. p. 187, 5; ins [s. ἐκτένεια]; POxy 2228, 40; PMichael 20, 2; LXX; Jos., Ant. 6, 341) **pert. to being persevering,** ***eagerly, fervently, constantly*** ἀγαπᾶν **1 Pt 1:22.** Of prayer (as always in LXX: Jon 3:8; 3 Macc 5:9 al.) προσευχὴ ἐ. γινομένη **Ac 12:5.** βοᾶν πρὸς τὸν θεὸν ἐ. 1 Cl 34:7.—Neut. of the comp. of ἐκτενής as adv. ἐκτενέστερον (Agatharchides: 86 fgm. 6 Jac [in Athen. 12, 527c]; SIG 695, 66): ἐ. προσεύχεσθαι prob. elative *very fervently* **Lk 22:44.**—M-M. Spicq.

ἐκτίθημι fut. 3 sg. ἐκθήσει Job 36:15; aor. ἐξέθηκα LXX; impf. mid. ἐξετιθέμην; fut. ἐκθήσομαι (Tat. 4, 3). Pass.: fut. 3 sg. ἐκτεθήσεται Zech 1:16; 1 aor. ἐξετέθην. In our lit. not in the act. (s. τίθημι; Hom.+) 'to set outside' (a bed Od. 23, 179), then

❶ **withdraw support or protection from,** ***expose, abandon*** (Hdt. 1, 112; Jos., C. Ap. 1, 308) of children (so act. and mid. since Hdt. 1, 112; Diod. S. 2, 4, 3 παιδίον; 3, 58, 1; 4, 64, 1 τὸ βρέφος; Aelian, VH 2, 7; Lucian, Sacr. 5; BGU 1104, 24 [8 BC] τὸ βρέφος ἐκτίθεσθαι; Wsd 18:5; Just., A I, 27, 1 τὰ γεννώμενα; Ath. 35:2 τὸ γεννηθέν) **Ac 7:21** (of Moses also Philo, Mos. 1, 12; Mel., P. 59, 433 and 69, 502); ApcPt fgm. 3, p. 12, 37 (εἰς θάνατον indicates the normal result of the exposure); cp. fgm. 1, p. 12, 12.—On exposure of infants in antiquity s. P van der Horst, The Sentences of Pseudo-Phocylides '78, 233f; MHuys; ἔκθεσις and ἀπόθεσις—The Terminology of Infant Exposure in Greek Antiquity: AntCl 58, '89, 190–97. S. also ῥίπτω 1.

❷ **to convey information by careful elaboration,** ***explain, expound,*** fig. ext. of mng. 1, cp. our 'fill someone in on someth.' (Aristot. et al.; Diod. S. 12, 18, 4; Athen. 7, 278d; PHib 27, 24 τὴν ἀλήθειαν; 2 Macc 11:36; EpArist 1; 161; Jos., Ant. 1, 214; Ar. 8, 2 [w. acc. and inf.]; Tat.) τί τινι *someth. to someone* (PMeyer 1, 13 [II BC] ᾧ καὶ τὰ καθ' ἑαυτοὺς ἐκτεθειμένων ἡμῶν; Jos., Ant. 2, 11) **Ac 18:26; 28:23.** ApcPt Rainer 14f. τινί w. λέγων foll. **11:4.**—M-M.

ἐκτίλλω impf. ἐξέτιλλον; fut. 3 sg. ἐκτιλεῖ (3 Km 14:15); 1 aor. ἐξέτιλα. Pass.: fut. ἐκτιλήσομαι LXX; 2 aor. 3 sg. pass. ἐξετίλη (Da 7:4 Theod.) (s. τίλλω; since Anacr. 54, 9 Diehl[2] [388, 9 Page]; BGU 1818, 15 [I BC]; LXX; PsSol 14:4) **to extract someth.,** ***pull out*** τὶ (Aristot., HA 8, 21 [603b, 22] τρίχας; Aëtius 160, 19) sticks Hs 8, 4, 3; weeds (Aristot., Mirabil. 11 [831a, 30]; Antig. Car. 34) s 5, 2, 4f; 5, 4, 1; 5, 5, 3.

ἐκτινάσσω fut. ἐκτινάξω LXX; 1 aor. ἐξετίναξα, mid. ἐξετιναξάμην; pf. pass. ptc. ἐκτιναχθήσομαι Judg 16:20 (τινάσσω 'shake'; Hom. et al.; pap, LXX; SibOr 5, 152).

❶ **to dislodge or remove someth. with rapid movements,** ***shake off*** τὶ (Is 52:2 τὸν χοῦν) τὸν κονιορτὸν τῶν ποδῶν *the dust that clings to one's feet* (AMerx, D. vier kanon. Ev. II/1, 1902, 178f takes the words to mean the dust which is raised by the feet and settles in the clothes; but s. Cadbury, Beginn., V 270) **Mt 10:14;** cp. **Mk 6:11; Lk 9:5** D. For this the mid. ἐκτινάσσεσθαι τὸν κονιορτὸν ἐπί τινα **Ac 13:51,** a symbolic act denoting the breaking off of all association (difft. EBöklen, Deutsch. Pfarrerbl. 35, '31, 466ff).

❷ **to agitate someth. with forceful jerky motions,** ***shake out clothes*** **Ac 18:6** (here mid., but act. sense e.g. BGU 827, 22 ἐκτίνασσε τὰ ἱμάτια; PAthen 60, 6f cushions; Sb 7992, 17.—UPZ 6, 10f, ἐκτινάσσειν is a gesture protesting innocence; s. GGA 1926, 49; Cadbury, Beginn. V 269–77. The precise meaning of the action cannot be established with certainty; nor is it clear whether something is shaken from the garments or whether they are simply shaken).—M-M.

ἐκτιτρώσκω 1 aor. ἐξέτρωσα (Hdt. 3, 32; PCairGoodsp 15, 15; Job 21:10 Sym.) ***cause an abortion*** ApcPt 11:26.

ἕκτος, η, ον (s. ἕξ; Hom.+) *sixth* Hs 9, 1, 7; 9, 23, 1; month **Lk 1:26, 36;** GJs 13:1 (numerical sign); seal **Rv 6:12;** cp. **9:13f; 16:12; 21:20;** hour (=12 if Jewish reckoning is used; Jos., Vi.

279) **Mt 20:5; 27:45; Mk 15:33; Lk 23:44; J 4:6; 19:14; Ac 10:9.**—DELG s.v. ἕξ. M-M.

ἐκτός adv. (s. ἐξ; Hom.+; ins, pap, LXX, TestJob 21:1; TestNapht 6:2; ParJer 7:1; EpArist, Philo; Jos., Ant. 14, 471)

❶ τὸ ἐκτός (sc. μέρος) **the outside surface of someth.,** ***the outside*** **Mt 23:26** (cp. PTebt 316, 95 [99 AD] ἐν τῷ ἐ.; Sir Prol. ln. 5 οἱ ἐ.; Lucian, Vit. Auct. 26 and Proclus on Pla., Cratyl. p. 23, 12 P. τὰ ἐ.).

❷ **a position not contained within a specific area,** ***outside,*** here ἐ. functions as prep. w. gen. (s. ἀνά, beg.) (Parthenius 9, 4 ἐκτὸς ἐγένετο αὑτοῦ=he was beside himself) ἐ. τοῦ σώματος *outside the body* **2 Cor 12:2;** cp. vs. **3 v.l.** Of sin in general, apart from fornication ἐ. τοῦ σώματός ἐστιν *remains outside the body,* since sexual immorality pollutes the body itself **1 Cor 6:18.** ταῦτα ἐ. τῆς ἐκείνου μεγαλειότητος *these things lie outside the divine majesty* Dg 10:5. ποιεῖν τι ἐ. τῆς ἐντολῆς τ. θεοῦ *do someth.* (good) *apart fr. God's commandment,* i.e. beyond what is commanded Hs 5, 3, 3. *Outside* the altar area ITr 7:2 v.l.

❸ **marker of an exception,** ***except***—ⓐ ἐκτὸς εἰ μή *unless, except* (post-class., in Dio Chrys., Plut., Lucian [Nägeli 33]; Vett. Val. index III; LBW 1499, 23; CIG 2825; Lyc. ins: JHS 34, 1914, p. 31 no. 44, 6; B-D-F §376; Rob. 640) **1 Cor 14:5; 15:2; 1 Ti 5:19.**

ⓑ functions as prep. w. gen. οὐδὲν ἐ. ὧν *nothing except what* (cp. 1 Ch 29:3; 2 Ch 17:19; TestNapht 6:2) **Ac 26:22;** ἐ. τοῦ ὑποτάξαντος *except the one who subjected* **1 Cor 15:27.**—DELG s.v. ἐξ. M-M.

ἐκτρέπω 2 aor. pass. ἐξετράπην; 2 fut. ἐκτραπήσομαι (s. τρέπω; trag., Hdt.+; PRyl 133, 22 [I AD]; Sb 9136, 8; Am 5:8; OdeSol 11:9; Just.). In our lit., as it seems, only pass. with intr. sense

❶ ***turn, turn away*** (Hdt. et al.) w. that to which one turns indicated by εἰς (Diod. S. 16, 12, 3; 17, 108, 4 εἰς ὕβρεις; Epict. 1, 6, 42; Philo, Spec. Leg. 2, 23; Jos., Ant. 8, 251 εἰς ἀσεβεῖς ἐξετράπη πράξεις) **1 Ti 1:6.** ἐπὶ τοὺς μύθους **2 Ti 4:4** (cp. Pla., Soph. 222a ἀπὸ … ἐπί; OdeSol 11:9 ἐξετράπην τῶν ματαίων ἐπὶ τὸν ὕψιστον θεόν; Galen XI 792 K. Πάμφιλος εἰς μύθους γραῶν ἐξετράπετο; Just., D 24, 1 ἐπ' ἄλλους … λόγους). ὀπίσω τοῦ Σατανᾶ *to follow Satan* **1 Ti 5:15.**—W. acc. *turn away from* or *avoid someth.* (Demosth. 19, 225; Polyb. 35, 4, 14; Musonius p. 26, 4 H.; Diog. Oen. fgm. 28 II, 7f Ch. ἐ. δεῖ τοὺς σοφιστικοὺς λόγους; Jos., Ant. 4, 290) **6:20.** W. gen. (Ps.-Aristot., Mirabilia 137 [844b, 4] ἐκτρέπεσθαι τῆς ὁδοῦ; Lucian, Dial. Deor. 25, 2; Jos., Ant. 6, 34 τῶν τοῦ πατρὸς ἐπιτηδευμάτων ἐκτραπόμενοι; Just, D. 8, 2 τῆς ὀρθῆς ὁδοῦ). τῆς ἐλπίδος *let oneself be turned aside* IMg 11.—ἵνα μὴ τὸ χωλὸν ἐκτραπῇ **Hb 12:13** is difficult. In line w. the previous senses one possibility is: *turn* from the way (abs. as X., An. 4, 5, 15), but ἐ. is oft. taken here, because of the context, in the sense of

❷ **to be wrenched,** ***be dislocated:*** a medical t.t. (Hippocr., κατ' ἰητρ. 14 Kühlewein; Diosc., Mat. Med. 2, 15 W.; Hippiatr. 26, 6 p. 126, 24 ἐὰν ἵππος ὦμον ἐκτραπῇ) *in order that what is lame may not be dislocated* (as in the expression 'twist' or 'sprain one's ankle'). Less probable, in view of the contrasting phrase ἰαθῇ δὲ μᾶλλον, is: *that what is lame might not be avoided* (Lucian, Pseudolog. 17 ἡμεῖς τοὺς χωλοὺς ἐκτρεπόμεθα=we go out of the lame men's way).—M-M. Spicq.

ἐκτρέφω fut. ἐκθρέψω LXX; 1 aor. ἐξέθρεψα; 2 aor. ptc. pass. ἐκτραφείς LXX (s. τρέφω; trag., Hdt. et al.; ins, pap, LXX; TestNapht 8:5; Jos., C. Ap. 2, 139).

❶ **to provide food,** ***nourish*** w. acc. (Plut., Lycurg. 16, 4; PRyl 178, 14 [I AD]; Gen 47:17; Mel., P. 52, 383 [Bodm.] μαστοῖς) w. θάλπειν *nourish and cherish* (Vi. Aesopi I c. 9 p. 250, 13 Eberh. τρέφει κ. θάλπει) **Eph 5:29.**

❷ **to bring up from childhood,** ***rear, bring up*** τινά (X., An. 7, 2, 32; Polyb. 6, 6, 2; Epict. 2, 22, 10; SIG 709, 34; oft. LXX) **Eph 6:4;** Hv 3, 9, 1.—M-M.

ἐκτρίβω (Soph., Hdt. et al.; Sb 6796, 194; LXX; En 99:16; PsSol 17:23; JosAs 24:9 cod. A for ἐκθλίψω; Just.)

❶ **to cause removal by irritation,** ***wear out, drive out*** τί (in imagery of wearing someth. out by rubbing; cp. PCorn 1, 194 [258/257 BC] of removing grime from silverware by polishing) the Holy Spirit (i.e, as the context indicates, causes it so much grief that it departs) Hm 10, 1, 2f; 10, 2, 1f (Appian, Bell. Civ. 2, 98 §409 τὸ πνεῦμα [=breath] ἐκτρῖψαι).

❷ **to obliterate (as by rubbing),** ***ruin, destroy*** (Hdt.; Plut., Mor. 529c; Ael. Aristid. 19, 1 K.=41 p. 762 D.; oft. LXX) τινά *someone* (cp. our colloq. 'rub out' or 'wipe out' of pers.) Hs 6, 1, 4. τ. ψυχάς 6, 2, 1.

ἔκτρομος, ον ***trembling*** (ins fr. Hadrumetum in Dssm. B p. 29 ln. 26 [BS 273ff]; cp. p. 44 [BS 290]=IDefixWünsch 5, 26; PGM 4, 3076 [LAE 254]) in our lit. only as v.l. ἔκφοβός εἰμι καὶ ἔ. *I am full of fear and trembling* **Hb 12:21** (for ἔντρομος; cp. Ps 17:8; 76:19).—M-M.

ἔκτρωμα, ατος, τό (Aristot., De Gen. An. 4, 5, 4 [773b, 18]; PTebt III, 800, 30 [142 BC], on this s. New Docs 2, 82, prob. 'miscarriage'; Num 12:12; Job 3:16; Eccl 6:3; Philo, Leg. All. 1, 76; Phryn. p. 208f Lob., w. preference for ἄμβλωμα 'abortion') a birth that violates the normal period of gestation (whether induced as abortion, or natural premature birth or miscarriage [cp. Hesych. ἐκ.=παιδίον νεκρὸν ἄωρον; also the verb ἐκτιτρώσκειν PCairGoodsp 15, 15f of a mother who miscarried because of violence done to her], or birth beyond term) ***untimely birth.*** So Paul calls himself, perh. taking up an insult (ἔ. as a term of contempt in Tzetzes [XII AD], Hist. Var. 5, 515 Kiessl.; Straub 48f) hurled at him by his opponents **1 Cor 15:8** (in any case the point relates to some deficiency in the infant [cp. Hos 13:13, MSchaefer, ZNW 85, '94, 207–17, not an insult]: Paul confesses himself to be unworthy of being called a full-fledged apostle); imitated IRo 9:2. ESchwartz, NGG 1907, 276 refers to Eus., HE 5, 1, 45. Cp. AvHarnack, SBBerlAk 1922, p. 72, 3; AFridrichsen, Paulus abortivus: Symb. Philol. f. ODanielsson '32, 78–85; JMunck, NT Essays: memorial vol. for TManson, '59, 180–93; PvonderOsten-Sacken, ZNW 64, '73, 245–62 esp. 250–57 ('miscarriage' among the apostles).—Acc. to GBjörck, ConNeot 3, '39, 3–8 'monster', 'horrible thing'.—M-M. EDNT. TW. Spicq.

ἐκτυπόω fut. 2 sg. ἐκτυπώσεις. Pass.: aor. ἐξετυπώθην; pf. ptc. ἐκτετυπωμένος LXX (s. τύπος; Hippoc., Pla., X. et al.; LXX; JosAs 3:10; EpArist 98; Philo, Somn. 2, 191; Mel., fgm. 12, 8) **to follow a pattern in forming someth.,** ***to shape*** εἰς τ. μορφὴν τούτων ἐκτυπωθῆναι *be shaped in their form* Dg 2:3 (Cos. and Dam. 13, 23 ἐν ᾧ ἐκτυποῦνται σχήματι).—DELG s.v. τύπτω.

ἐκφέρω fut. ἐξοίσω LXX; 1 aor. ἐξήνεγκα, inf. ἐξενεγκεῖν (ἐξενέγκαι LXX). Pass.: fut. 2 pl. ἐξενεχθήσεσθε Am 4:3; 1 aor. inf. ἐξενεχθῆναι Bar 2:24 (s. φέρω; Hom.+)

❶ **to convey someth. out of a structure or area,** ***carry/bring out*** lit. τί (opp. εἰσφέρω) **1 Ti 6:7,** sim. Pol 4:1; a corpse for burial (Il. 24, 786 and oft. in later auth. as Epict. 2, 22, 10; Jos., Ant. 15,

46) **Ac 5:6, 9f;** στολήν (cp. 4 Km 10:22, w. ref. to a στολιστής, who brings out ἐνδύματα; of various items brought out Cyr. 5, 2, 7 and Herodian 2, 1, 2) **Lk 15:22** (v.l. ἐνέγκατε P[75] et al.); sick people into the streets **Ac 5:15.**

❷ **to conduct out of a structure or area, with implication of assistance, *bring/lead out,*** lit., with ἔξω (Leontius 13 p. 27, 8) ἔξω τ. κώμης **Mk 8:23.**

❸ **to cause to grow, *produce*** fig. of everything that nature causes to grow: plants and their products (Hdt. 1, 193; X., Oec. 16, 5; Polyb. 36, 16, 8; Plut., Mor. 2e [937d]; Epict. 4, 8, 36; IAndrosIsis, Kyme 18 p. 122 P.; Gen 1:12; Hg 1:11; SSol 2:13; Tat. 2:1 τί γὰρ σεμνὸν . . . ἐξηνέγκατε) fruit 1 Cl 24:5; thorns and thistles **Hb 6:8;** even κέρατα ἐ. *grow horns* 1 Cl 52:2 (Ps 68:32).—M-M.

ἐκφεύγω fut. ἐκφεύξομαι; 2 aor. ἐξέφυγον; 2 pf. ἐκπέφευγα (s. φεύγω; Hom. et al.; pap, LXX; En 10:3, 17; PsSol 15:8; TestAbr A 8 p. 85, 28 [Stone p. 18]; GrBar 7:5; Just.).

❶ **to seek safety in flight, *run away*** (2 Km 17:2 A) **Ac 16:27;** ἐκ τ. οἴκου **Ac 19:16.**

❷ **to become free from danger by avoiding some peril, *escape*—ⓐ** abs. (Hdt. 5, 95, 1 φεύγων ἐκφεύγει=he escapes by flight; Lucian, Alex. 28; ViEzk 10 [p. 75, 3 Sch.]; Jos., Bell. 1, 65, Ant. 2, 341) fig. (Sir 16:13) **1 Th 5:3; Hb 2:3; 12:25.**

ⓑ w. acc. of that which one escapes—**α.** lit., a monster (Artem. 4 p. 200, 25 θηρίον ἐ.) Hv 4, 2, 3.

β. fig. (Diod. S. 5, 59, 2 τὸ μύσος ἐ.; 17, 112, 3 τὸν κίνδυνον; Ael. Aristid. 34 p. 656 D.: τὴν αἰσχύνην; EpArist 268; Philo, Leg. All. 3, 93 λήθην) tribulations **Lk 21:36;** Hv 4, 2, 4b and 5; judgment (κρίσιν: 2 Macc 7:35; Just., A I, 68, 2 al.; cp. PRyl 28, 164ff ἐν κρίσει βαρηθεὶς ἔσται καὶ ἐκφεύξεται) τὸ κρίμα τοῦ θεοῦ **Ro 2:3.** τὰς χεῖράς τινος (Phalaris, Ep. 92; Sus 22; Tob 13:2) **2 Cor 11:33.** τὸ ἀποθανεῖν (Pla., Apol. 39a) ITr 2:1.

ⓒ καλῶς ἐξέφυγες *you have made good your escape* or *you deserved to escape* Hv 4, 2, 4a.

❸ **to be aware of a peril and take measures to avoid it, *shun, avoid*** τὶ (Epict. 4, 5, 2 Σωκράτης πανταχοῦ ἐξέφυγεν μάχην; Diog. L. 10, 117; Philo, Leg. All. 3, 236 κακίαν) *the world* Hv 4, 3, 4.—M-M.

ἐκφοβέω 1 aor. ἐξεφόβησα; pf. pass. ptc. ἐκπεφοβημένος LXX (s. φοβέομαι and next entry; trag., Thu. et al.; PLond II, 342, 9 p. 174 [185 AD]; Sb 4284, 10 ἐκφοβῶν ἡμᾶς; LXX; En; TestAbr A 16 p. 97, 5 [Stone p. 42]; Jos., Bell. 1, 492, Ant. 2, 82) **to cause to be intensely afraid, *frighten, terrify*** τινὰ διά τινος *someone w. someth.* **2 Cor 10:9.**—DELG s.v. φέβομαι II. M-M.

ἔκφοβος, ον pert. to being intensely afraid, *terrified* (s. ἐκφοβέω; Aristot., Physiogn. 6 p. 812b, 29; Plut., Fab. 178 [6, 8]) ἔκφοβοι ἐγένοντο *they became terrified* **Mk 9:6;** w. ἔντρομος **Hb 12:21** (cp. Dt 9:19).—S. Frisk s.v. φέβομαι. TW.

ἔκφρικτος, ον (s. φρίκη, φρίσσω) **pert. to being enough to make one tremble/shudder, *frightening*** (opp. ἥμερος), of words, to the extent of being unbearable Hv 1, 3, 3; for ἔκπληκτος Hv 1, 2, 4 cod. Athous.—DELG s.v. φρίξ.

ἐκφύω 1 aor. ἐξέφυσα (s. φύω; Hom. et al.; Ps 103:14 Sym.; Philo; Joseph.) **to give rise to someth. by a physical process, *put forth,*** trans. lit. 'cause to grow' (cp. Jos., Ant. 10, 270) τὰ φύλλα (the branch) *puts forth leaves* (ἐκφύῃ pres. subj.) **Mt 24:32; Mk 13:28** (cp. Artem. 5, 63; 65; EpArist 70; Philo, Sacr. Abel. 25; Ps.-Clem., Hom. 2, 45; 19, 14). The accentuation ἐκφυῇ (B-D-F. §76, 2; W-S. §13, 11; Mlt-H. 264), which is freq. preferred (but rejected by Jülicher, Gleichnisreden, II 4) would make the form a 2 aor. pass. subj., used intr., and make τὰ φύλλα the subj.: *the leaves sprout* (cp. Jos., Ant. 2, 83). Of pers. ποία δὲ μήτρα ἐξέφυσέν με; *what womb bore me?* GJs 3:1.—DELG s.v. φύομαι. M-M.

ἐκφωνέω (s. φωνέω, φωνή; Dionys. Hal., Comp. Verb. 14 et al.; Just., D. 97, 1?; Tat., Ath.; magic pap: PWarr 21, 32) 1 aor. ἐξεφώνησα; pf. ἐκπεφώνηκα (Tat., Ath.); pf. pass. 3 sg. ἐκπεφώνηται (Ath. 24, 5); plpf. 3 sg. ἐκπεφώνητο (Just., D. 97, 1 as corrected in cod. Paris) *cry out* (so Plut., Caes. 739 [66, 8]; Philo, De Jos. 51) **Lk 16:24 v.l.**—DELG s.v. φωνή.

ἐκχέω (Hom.+; also Mel., P. 74, 542 [Jer 7:6]) fut. ἐκχεῶ; 1 aor. ἐξέχεα; pf. ἐκκέχυκα Ezk 24:7. Beside it the H. Gk. form **ἐκχύν(ν)ω** (W-S. §15; B-D-F §73; 74, 2; 101; Mlt-H. 195; 215; 265) 1 fut. ἐκχυθήσομαι; 1 aor. ἐξεχύθην; pf. pass. ἐκκέχυμαι.

❶ **cause to be emitted in quantity, *pour out*—ⓐ** of liquids: water D 7:3. αἷμα ἐ. *shed blood=commit a murder* (αἷμα 2a) **Ac 22:20; Ro 3:15** (Is 59:7; Ps 13:3); **Rv 16:6;** GJs 23:3 (1 Km 25:31); cp. AcPl Ha 11, 8. αἷμα ἐκχυννόμενον (Jos., Ant. 19, 94 αἷμα πολὺ ἐκκεχυμένον) **Mt 23:35;** cp. **Lk 11:50;** in the cultic sense *pour out* (cp. Lev 4:7), esp. of Jesus' death (Orig., C. Cels. 8, 42, 33) 1 Cl 7:4. αἷμα ἐ. περὶ πολλῶν εἰς ἄφεσιν ἁμαρτιῶν *blood shed for* (the benefit of) *many, for the forgiveness of sins* **Mt 26:28** (w. purpose indicated by εἰς as Lucian, Tim. 5 εἰς εὐεργεσίαν); αἷ. ἐ. ὑπὲρ πολλῶν **Mk 14:24;** cp. **Lk 22:20.** Wine ἐκχεῖται *is spilled (out)* (cp. Gen 38:9) **Mt 9:17;** cp. **Mk 2:22 v.l.;** cp. **Lk 5:37;** ἐ. φιάλην, as we say, *pour out a bowl* (i.e. its contents) **Rv 16:1ff, 8, 10, 12, 17.**

ⓑ of solid objects (Lev 4:12) ἐξεχύθη πάντα τὰ σπλάγχνα *all his bowels gushed out* **Ac 1:18** (cp. Quint. Smyrn. 8, 302 ἔγκατα πάντ' ἐχύθησαν; 9, 190; 2 Km 20:10; Jos., Bell. 7, 453; AcThom 33 [Aa II/2, 150, 19]). Of coins *scatter* on the ground **J 2:15.**

❷ **cause to fully experience, *pour out*** fig. ext. of 1 (cp. Lycophron 110 πόθον; Ps.-Demetr., Eloc. 134 τοῦ λόγου τὴν χάριν; Aelian, NA 7, 23 θυμόν; τὴν ὀργήν PsSol 2:24; ψυχὴν εἰς θάνατον 16:2; Philo, Spec. Leg. 1, 37 of light; Jos., Ant. 6, 271 φόνον) of the Holy Spirit which, acc. to Joel's prophecy, is to pour down on people like rain (Jo 2:23; cp. 1QS 4:21): *pour out* (Iren. 5, 12, 2 [Harv II 351, 2]) **Ac 2:33.** ἐπί τινα (after Jo 3:1) **2:17f; 10:45; Tit 3:6;** B 1:3; 1 Cl 46:6. The ref. to the Holy Spirit has perh. brought the idea of outpouring into **Ro 5:5** ἡ ἀγάπη τ. θεοῦ ἐκκέχυται ἐν ταῖς καρδίαις ἡμῶν διὰ πνεύματος ἁγίου τοῦ δοθέντος ἡμῖν. But gener., whatever comes from above is connected w. this verb (Ps 44:3 χάρις; Sir 18:11 ἔλεος; Hos 5:10 ἐπ' αὐτοὺς ἐκχεῶ ὡς ὕδωρ τὸ ὅρμημά μου; Philo, Aet. M. 147 ἄνωθεν ἐ.; TestLevi 18:5; ἐκχεῖσθαι . . . ὁ λόγος ἐπὶ πᾶσαν τὴν οἰκουμένην Orig., C. Cels. 6, 78, 26).

❸ **to give oneself totally in commitment, *give oneself up to, dedicate oneself,*** pass. (Polyb. 31, 25, 4 εἰς ἑταίρας; Plut., Anton. 21, 1; Philo, Op. M. 80; TestReub 1:6; εἰς πράγματα ἀφροδισιακὰ Hippol., Ref. 4, 19, 2) w. dat. (Alciphron 3, 34, 1 τῷ γέλωτι) τῇ πλάνῃ τ. Βαλαὰμ **Jd 11.** λίαν ἐ. ἀγαπῶν ὑμᾶς *I am totally consumed w. affection for you= my affection for you streams out of me.* IPhld 5:1.—M-M. TW.

ἐκχύν(ν)ω s. ἐκχέω.

ἔκχυσις, εως, ἡ (s. ἐκχέω; Aristot. et al.; PTebt 86, 9 [II BC]; PLond III, 1177, 84 p. 183 [113 AD]; LXX; En 17:7) 'outflow' (as of bodies of water Aristot. Mete. 354a, 26; cp. Theophr., Vent. 50) in our lit. only fig. ***outpouring*** of the Holy Spirit 1 Cl 2:2 (w. ἐπί τινα as 3 Km 18:28).—Frisk s.v. χέω C4.

ἐκχωρέω 1 aor. ἐξεχώρησα (Soph., Hdt. et al.; ins, pap, LXX; Tat. 24, 1 ἡμῖν ἐκχωρήσατε) **to leave a certain area, *go out, go away, depart*** abs. (PLond I, 106, 16 p. 61 [III BC]; Jos., Bell. 1, 137) **Lk 21:21;** 1 Cl 54:2. W. gen. foll. (PMagd 20, 7=PEnteux 10, 7 [221 BC] τῆς οἰκίας) τῆς γῆς (Diod. S. 5, 15, 4; Jos., Ant. 1, 74) 31:4. ἰδίων πόλεων 55:1. For this ἔκ τινος (PAmh 30, 42 [II BC] ἐκ τ. οἰκίας) ἐκ τῆς χώρας (as SIG 679, 53) Hs 1:4.—DELG s.v. χώρα. M-M.

ἐκψύχω 1 aor. ἐξέψυξα (ψύχω, var. 'breathe, make cool'; s. ψύχος; Epicharmus, Hippocr., Herodas [in tmesis], LXX) gener. 'to lose one's life energy' ('dry up, wither' Epicharmus, POxy 2427 [fgm. 27, 6=CGFP no. 85, 245]; 'faint' Hippocr., e.g. Morb. 1, VI p. 146 [s. Hobart 37]; Ezk 21:12), then, by ext. of mng., **to lose one's life energy completely, *breathe one's last, die*** (Herodas 4, 29; Babrius 115, 11; Judg 4:21 A) **Ac 5:5, 10; 12:23.**—Frisk s.v. ψυχή. M-M. Spicq.

ἑκών, οῦσα, όν (Hom. et al.; ins, pap, LXX, Philo; Jos., Vi. 347; 351; Just, D. 5, 5) **pert. to being favorably disposed to do someth. without pressure, *willing(ly), glad(ly)*** Dg 2:9; IRo 4:1. Opp. force 5:2; MPol 4:1; *of one's own free will* (cp. Epict. 3, 5, 9; 4, 3, 9; Lucian, Herm. 77; SIG 1176, 4) ἑ. τοῦτο πράσσω **1 Cor 9:17** (w. ἄκων, extension of the usual pairing ἑκών . . . ἄκων, s. Reader, Polemo p. 337; cp. GRickert, ΕΚΩΝ and ΑΚΩΝ in Early Gk. Thought [American Classical Studies 20] '89). ὑπετάγη οὐχ ἑκοῦσα *it was subjected against its own will* (v.l. οὐ θέλουσα) **Ro 8:20** (cp. Philo, Ebr. 122).—DELG. M-M. TW.

ἔλαθον s. λανθάνω.

ἐλαία, ας, ἡ—❶ tree that produces olives, *olive tree* (Hom.+) **Ro 11:17, 24** (a variety of Olea Europaea, Zohary 56f; on the imagery s. Straub 74f); pl. **Rv 11:4** (cp. Zech 4:3, 11). τὸ ὄρος τῶν ἐλαιῶν (Zech 14:4; ParJer 9:20; cp. Jos., Bell. 2, 262, Ant. 20, 169; Just., D. 103, 1; 2; 7 [**Mt 26:30** par.]) *the Mount of Olives,* a hill east of Jerusalem and known for its olive trees (Dalman, Orte[3] 277ff [Eng. tr. 320–27]) **Mt 21:1; 24:3; 26:30; Mk 11:1; 13:3; 14:26; Lk 19:37; 22:39; J 8:1.** For **Lk 19:29; 21:37** s. ἐλαιών.

❷ **fruit of the olive tree, *olive*** (Aristoph., Pla.+; Diosc.; Plut.; PHib 49, 8 [257 BC]; PFay 130, 16; POxy 1494, 16) **Js 3:12.**—Lit., s. ἀγριέλαιος.—B. 380. OEANE IV 179–84. DELG and Frisk. M-M.

ἔλαιον, ου, τό (Hom.+)—❶ **oil extracted from the fruit of the olive tree, *olive oil*—ⓐ** the general term: **Lk 16:6;** w. wine and flour (cp. Dt 7:13; 11:14; 28:51; 2 Ch 31:5; Ezk 16:19 al.) **Rv 18:13;** w. wine Hm 11:15; D 13:6.—For illumination: in lamps (Philo, Aet. M. 91) **Mt 25:3f, 8.**—For treating of wounds (Is 1:6) **Lk 10:34** (used w. wine, as e.g. Theophr., HP 9, 12 ἐν οἴνῳ καὶ ἐλαίῳ; Hobart 28f) and otherw. for healing **Mk 6:13; Js 5:14** (on kind of oil New Docs 4, 248; s. on ἀλείφω 1 and cp. SIG 1170, 27.—Artem. 4, 82 a seemingly dead man is brought back to life by being anointed with warm oil).

ⓑ esp. used for anointing (Posidon.: 87 fgm. 10 Jac.; Jos., Bell. 5, 565) **Lk 7:46** (cp. 4 Km 9:6; Ps 22:5). Fig. ἔχρισέν σε ὁ θεὸς ἔ. ἀγαλλιάσεως *God anointed you w. the oil of gladness* **Hb 1:9** (Ps 44:8). ἔ. ἁμαρτωλῶν *oil of sinners* 1 Cl 56:5 (Ps 140:5).

❷ the effect for the cause: ***olive orchard*** τὸ ἔ. καὶ τὸν οἶνον μὴ ἀδικήσῃς *do not harm the olive orchard and the vineyard* **Rv 6:6** (s. SReinach, RevArch 3d s. 39, 1901, 350–74; JMoffatt, Exp. 7th ser. 6, 1908, 359–69; SKrauss, ZNW 10, 1909, 81–89; AvHarnack, Erforschtes u. Erlebtes 1924, 53ff).—Dalman, Arbeit, under ἄρτος 1a. BHHW II 1336–39.—B. 380. Frisk. M-M. TW.

ἐλαιών, ῶνος, ὁ a site consisting primarily of olive trees, *olive grove, olive orchard* (oft. in pap since III BC [Dssm., NB 36ff=BS 208ff; BOlsson, Aegyptus 13, '33, 327ff]; Strabo 16, 4, 14; LXX; Philo, Spec. Leg. 2, 105). This word, which has become a proper name, is surely to be read **Ac 1:12** ἀπὸ ὄρους τ. καλουμένου Ἐλαιῶνος *from the hill called* or *known as 'The Olive Grove' = the Mount of Olives,* s. ἐλαία 1 (cp. Jos., Ant. 7, 202 διὰ τοῦ Ἐλαιῶνος ὄρους; PLond II, 214, 9f p. 161 [III AD] εἰς ἀμπελικὸν χωρίον καλούμενον, Ἐλαιῶνα; TestNapht 5:1; ἐν τῷ ὄρει τοῦ Ἐλαιῶνος; Just., D. 99, 2 τὸ ὄρος τὸ λεγόμενον Ἐλαιών). Therefore it is also prob. to be so understood **Lk 19:29; 21:37,** where the accentuation ἐλαιῶν cannot be ruled out absolutely (B-D-F §143; W-S. §10, 4; Mlt. 49; 235; Rob. 154 n. 2; 267). The name Olivet is fr. Lat. olivetum = olive grove.—GDalman, Jerusalem 1930, 21–55: Orte[3] 277–85 [Eng. tr 261–68]: WSchmauch, Der Oelberg: TLZ 77, '52, 391–96; BCurtis, HUCA 28, '57, 137–80; BHHW II 1139–40; s. also entry ἐλαία.—DELG. EDNT. M-M.

Ἐλαμ(ε)ίτης, ου, ὁ (Αἰλαμῖται Is 21:2 for the usual Ἐλυμαῖος; on the spelling s. B-D-F §38) ***an Elamite,*** inhabitant of Elam, a district north of the Persian Gulf, east of the lower Tigris valley **Ac 2:9**—OEANE II 228–34.

ἐλάσσων, ἔλασσον (ἐλαχύς 'small, little'; s. ἐλαττόω; Hom. et al.; ins, pap, LXX [Thackeray 121, 2; 122]; Just., D. 88, 2; Att. ἐλάττων [Gignac I 147] **Hb 7:7; 1 Ti 5:9;** Hv 3, 7, 6; s 9, 28, 4; apolog. exc. Mel. See B-D-F §34, 1; Mlt-H. 107)

❶ **relatively small in quantity on any dimension, *less*** οὐκ ἐ. w. gen. foll. *not less than* (2 Macc 5:5) Hs 2:4; 9, 11, 7. Adv. ἔλαττον *less* ἔ. ἐτῶν ἑξήκοντα *less than 60 years* **1 Ti 5:9** (cp. Pla., Ep. 2, 314b οὐκ ἐλάττω τριάκοντα ἐτῶν; adjectivally: Just., D. 88, 2 τριάκοντα ἔτη ἢ πλείονα ἢ καὶ ἐλάσσονα μείνας, μέχρις οὗ etc.—Kühner-G. II 311f).

❷ **situated lower in status or quality, *inferior,*** opp. κρεῖττον **Hb 7:7** (the neut. [Mussies 124] sg. for more than one pers. as Περὶ ὕψους 36, 1 [p. 56, 13 Vahlen] τὸ θνητόν; Plut., Mor. 160d τὸ παρόν = οἱ παρόντες); in imagery τόπος ἐ. *an inferior place* Hv 3, 7, 6.—Of quality *inferior* (cp. PRyl 77, 39) wine **J 2:10;** fruit Hs 9, 28, 4; opp. μεῖζον (Ael. Aristid. 29 p. 561 D.; Jos., Ant. 15, 226) **Mt 20:28** D.

❸ used as comp. of μικρός 'smaller' in age=***younger*** (opp. μείζων) **Ro 9:12;** B 13:2 (both Gen 25:23), 5.—DELG s.v. ἐλαχύς. M-M. TW. Spicq.

ἐλαττονέω fut. 3 sg. ἐλαττονήσει LXX; 1 aor. ἠλαττόνησα, pass. 3 sg. ἠλαττονήθη 3 Km 17:16 cod. A (Aristot., Plant. 2, 3 [825a, 23]; BGU 1195, 19; LXX) **to be in possession of relatively less, *have less, have too little*** abs. (PEnteux 34, 9 and 12 [217 BC]) **2 Cor 8:15** (Ex 16:18).—DELG s.v. ἐλαχύς. M-M. Spicq.

ἐλαττόω (fr. ἐλαχύς via ἐλάσσων) fut. ἐλαττώσω LXX; 1 aor. ἠλάττωσα. Pass. ἐλαττωθήσομαι LXX; aor. ἠλαττώθην LXX; pf. ptc. ἠλαττωμένος (Thu.+; ins, pap, LXX; TestSol 18:11 PL; TestLevi 18:9; EpArist, Philo, Joseph., Just., Tat.; Ath., R. 58, 27; the pass. predominates, s. 2 and 3 below)

❶ **to cause to be lower in status, *make lower, inferior*** (Jos., C. Ap. 2, 202) τινά *someone,* παρά w. acc. shows the pers. or thing in comparison w. whom, or w. what, the subj. is made inferior (cp. for grammar PTebt 19, 11 [114 BC] σὺ δὲ ὀρθῶς ποιήσεις τὸ προσάγγελμα μὴ ἐλαττώσας παρὰ τὸ πρῶτον=you will do right in not diminishing the report relative to the first) **Hb 2:7, 9** (both Ps 8:6).

❷ **to be in possession of less relative to another, *be worse off, be in need,*** pass. (1 Km 2:5; 21:15; 2 Km 3:29; Ps 33:11 al.) **2 Cor 12:13 v.l.;** Dg 10:6.

❸ **to become less important, *diminish, become less,*** pass. intr. sense (Peripl. Eryth. c. 45; Philo, Leg. All. 2, 3, Virt. 46, Gig. 27, Aet. M. 65; 120; Jos., Ant. 7, 31. Of persons: Thu. 4, 59, 2; OGI 139, 10 [II BC]; PTebt 382, 13 [I BC]; TestLevi 18:9 ὁ Ἰσραήλ) **J 3:30** (opp. αὐξάνω q.v.; perh. the diminution of light is spec. in mind here: Cass. Dio 45, 17: τὸ φῶς τοῦ ἡλίου ἐλαττοῦσθαί τε καὶ σβέννυσθαι ἐδόκει).—M-M. Spicq.

ἐλάττωμα, ατος, τό (Polyb., Dionys. Hal.; Diod. S. 11, 62, 2; 12, 4, 4; Vett. Val. 265, 5; Philostrat., Vi. Apoll. 8, 7 p. 310, 31; ins; PTebt 97, 1 [118 BC]; BGU 1060, 26; LXX; TestJos 17:2; Jos., C. Ap. 1, 256; Ar. 7:3; Tat. 11:1) **pert. to deficiency in quality, *defect*** Hs 9, 9, 6.—DELG s.v. ἐλαχύς.

ἐλάττων s. ἐλάσσων.

ἐλαύνω fut. 2 sg. ἐλάσεις Ex 25:12; pf. ἐλήλακα; impf. pass. ἠλαυνόμην (Hom.+) **to urge or propel along, *drive*** of the wind (Jos., Bell. 7, 317, Ant. 5, 205), which drives clouds **2 Pt 2:17** or ships **Js 3:4** (Aristaen., Ep. 2, 11; Sb 997 καταπλέων ὑπὸ χειμῶνος ἐλασθείς; 998, 3). Cp. **Jd 23** as a cj. by Wohlenberg. Of a spirit who drives a possessed pers. (cp. Appian, Macedon. 18 §2 αὐτὸν ἐλαύνοντος θεοῦ=since a god drove him on) w. εἰς **Lk 8:29.** Of shepherds εἶδον ἐλαυνόμενα πρόβατα *I saw sheep driven on* GJs 18:3 (not pap). Abs. intr. either *advance, make progress* (Il. 13, 27; Soph., El. 734; Hdt. 1, 60, 4; Apollon. Rhod. 3, 1238; Polyaenus 3, 10, 17; Aesop, Fab. 21 P. and H-H.=22 Ch.; Is 33:21 οὐδὲ πορεύσεται πλοῖον ἐλαῦνον) or *row* (Od. 3, 157; Ps.-Demosth. 50, 53 ἄσιτοι δὲ οὐκ ἂν ἐδύναντο ἐλαύνειν; Isocr., Areop. 20) **Mk 6:48; J 6:19** (on the pf. ptc. s. Soph., Lex. I 46)—B. 713; 715. DELG. M-M.

ἐλαφρία, ας, ἡ (s. ἐλαφρός 3; Aretaeus p. 162, 10; Hesych.) **condition of treating a matter frivolously, as by irresponsible change of mind, *vacillation, levity*** τῇ ἐ. χρᾶσθαι *be vacillating, fickle* **2 Cor 1:17.**

ἐλαφρός, ά, όν (Hom. et al.; ins, pap, LXX) comp. ἐλαφρότερος (Il. 22, 287; Hdt 3, 23, 3; Crinagoras no. 47, 6=Anth. Pal. 11, 42, 6; Philo, Leg. All. 1, 42; Jos., Ant. 2, 61)

❶ **having little weight, *light*** in weight (Hom. et al.; Lucian, Merc. Cond. 13 φέρειν τὸν ζυγὸν ἐλαφρόν; PGiss 47, 7): a burden **Mt 11:30.** Fig. *easy to bear, insignificant* (Hdt. 7, 38, 1; Plut.; Ex 18:26) τὸ ἐ. τῆς θλίψεως *insignificant affliction* **2 Cor 4:17;** comp. adv. ἐλαφροτέρως *more lightly* θλίβειν τινά Hs 7:6.

❷ From the time of Homer, ἐ. has the mng. 'quick, nimble'. A transfer is readily made to impulsive behavior. Hence of ill temper (Crinagoras loc. cit. of the θυμός) ***impetuous*** Hm 5, 2, 4.

❸ **pert. to shallowness of character, *frivolous, fickle, vacillating*** (s. ἐλαφρία; Polyb. 6, 56, 11) Hm 11:6; 12, 4, 5.—B. 1073. Schmidt, Syn. II 136–39. DELG. M-M. TW.

ἔλαχε s. λαγχάνω.

ἐλάχιστος, ίστη, ον (ἐλαχύς 'small, little'; since Hom. Hymns, Merc. 573 and Hdt.; ins, pap, LXX; Test12Patr; JosAs 1:13 codd. AHPal. 364 for χεῖρον; ApcMos 16; Just., Ath.) used as superl. of μικρός. From it a vernac. comp. ἐλαχιστότερος is formed (B-D-F §61, 2; W-S. §11, 4; Mlt. 236; M-M. s.v. ἐλαχιστότερος).

❶ **pert. to being the lowest in status, *least.*** In our lit. only rarely as a true superl. (Jos., Bell. 6, 198) *smallest, least* (PTebt 24, 67 [117 BC]; Josh 6:26) ὁ ἐ. τῶν ἀποστόλων *the least of the apostles* **1 Cor 15:9.** Otherwise elative (s. B-D-F §60, 2; Mlt. 236) in this mng. and the succeeding ones,οὐδαμῶς ἐ. εἶ ἐν τ. ἡγεμόσιν Ἰούδα *you are by no means least among the leaders of Judah* **Mt 2:6.** Of pers. *unimportant* (SIG 888, 58; PsSol 2:26; TestJos 17:8) **Mt 5:19b; 25:40, 45** (WBrandt, D. geringsten Brüder: Jahrb. d. Theol. Schule Bethel 8, '37, 1ff; on the disguised beggar theme cp. Od. 14, 55ff and s. Od. 17, 485–87 [Old Testament, cp. 3 Km 17:8ff]; s. DFlückiger-Guggenheim, Göttliche Gäste '84 [Gk. Mythology]; ABurnett, ClPh 65, '70, 124–25 [lit]); comp. w. same sense as the superlative ἐμοὶ τῷ ἐλαχιστοτέρῳ *to me, the very least* **Eph 3:8.**

❷ **pert. to being relatively the smallest in a specific class or group, *very small/short*** (TestJud 15:6; Jos., Bell. 6, 330 ἐ. μέρος) ἐ. πηδάλιον *very small rudder* **Js 3:4;** ἐ. κοκκάριον *a very small grain* Hm 11:20, cp. 21; of animals *the smallest* 1 Cl 20:10.—Neut. as adv. in this sense (Polyaenus 8, 7, 2) ἐ. βασανίζεσθαι *be tortured (punished) a very short time* Hs 6, 4, 2 (restored fr. Lat. texts)=*for too short a time.* W. ref. to number *very few* (Diod. S. 1, 71, 3 ἐλάχιστα ἀγνοήματα=fewest mistakes [in contrast to many failures of others]) Hs 8, 5, 4 people; 9, 8, 7 stones. τὸ ἐ. ἀψίνθιον *very little wormwood* Hm 5, 1, 5. ἐ. τῶν ῥάβδων *a very small section* (w. ref. to being partially verdant or dry) *of the sticks* Hs 8, 1, 14f; 8, 5, 5f; 8, 10, 1 and 3.

❸ **pert. to being considered of very little importance, *insignificant, trivial*** (also elative). Of commandments *(relatively) insignificant* **Mt 5:19a** (FDibelius, ZNW 11, 1910, 188–90; GDalman, Jesus 1929, 62–65 [tr. PLevertoff]). Of parts of the body 1 Cl 37:5. κριτήρια ἐ. *trivial cases* **1 Cor 6:2.** ἐλάχιστον *a very little thing* **Lk 12:26;** (opp. τὸ πολύ) **16:10; 19:17;** 2 Cl 8:5 (on ἐν ἐ. cp. Mitt-Wilck. II/2, 372 V, 23f). ἐμοὶ εἰς ἐ. ἐστιν **1 Cor 4:3** (s. εἰμί 2cβ). Adv. ἐλάχιστον ἐξαμαρτεῖν *sin a little* Hs 8, 10, 1.—DELG s.v. ἐλαχύς. M-M. EDNT. TW.

Ἐλδάδ, ὁ indecl. *Eldad,* a Hebrew prophet who, w. Modad, prophesied in camp during the journey through the desert (Num 11:26–29: Ἐλδὰδ καὶ Μωδάδ 27). Ἐ. καὶ Μ. is the title of a lost apocalyptic book, which is quoted as an authority Hv 2, 3, 4.—Schürer III/2, 783.

Ἐλεάζαρ, ὁ indecl. (Ex 6:23 al.; Philo, Somn. 2, 186.—EpArist; Joseph.: Ἐλεάζαρος, ου [Ant. 4, 152] -αζάρ N^{25}.) *Eleazar,* in the genealogy of Jesus **Mt 1:15; Lk 3:23ff** D.—BHHW I 390–91. M-M.

ἐλεάω (IKyme 41, 37; Pr 21:26; 4 Macc 9:3; TestAbr A 10 p. 88, 21 [Stone p. 24, 21]) the forms which grammatically belong to such a present derive from a mixture of the inflectional types -ᾶν and -εῖν (B-D-F §90; W-S. §13, 26; Mlt-H. 195ff) ***have mercy on*** of people: ἐλεᾶτε **Jd 22; 23** (both w. -εῖτε and ἐλέγχετε as vv.ll.); 1 Cl 13:2; Pol 2:3. Of God: ἐλεῶντος θεοῦ **Ro 9:16** (s. ἐλεέω).—DELG s.v. ἔλεος.

ἐλεγμός, οῦ, ὁ (s. three next entries; LXX; PsSol 10:1) =ἔλεγξις; the LXX exhibits various mngs: 'testing' of an accused pers. through trial by ordeal (Num 5:18ff), also 'reproof, correction' (Sir 21:6; 32:17; 48:7) and 'discipline, punishment' (4 Km 19:3; Jdth 2:10; 1 Macc 2:49) in our lit. **expression of strong disapproval, *reproach, rebuke, reproof*** w. διδασκαλία and ἐπανόρθωσις **2 Ti 3:16** (v.l. ἔλεγχον).—DELG s.v. ἐλέγχω. TW.

ἔλεγξις, εως, ἡ (Acta Alex. VII B 43; Philod., Rhet. I p. 134, 8 Sudh.; Philostrat., V. Apoll. 2, 22; Job 21:4; 23:2; En 14:1; Hesych.)=ἐλεγμός **expression of strong disapproval,** ***reproach, rebuke, reproof*** ἔ. ἔσχεν ἰδίας παρανομίας *he received a rebuke for his transgression* **2 Pt 2:16.**—GJs 16:1 (Num 5:18 τοῦ ἐλεγμοῦ).—DELG s.v. ἐλέγχω. TW.

ἔλεγχος, ου, ὁ (Pind., Pre-Socr. et al.; pap, LXX; PsSol tit. [no. 9]; TestJos 6:6; Philo [s. CBarrett, JTS n.s. 1, '50, 9], Joseph., Just., Tat., Ath.)

❶ **the act of presenting evidence for the truth of someth.,** ***proof, proving*** (Pla., Gorg. 471e; Demosth. 44, 15 τὸ πρᾶγμα τὸν ἔλεγχον δώσει; Epict. 3, 10, 11; POxy 237 VIII, 17; PStras 41, 6 ὁ ἔλ. δεικνύσει; Job 23:7, cp. vs. 4; Philo, Praem. 4 ἔ. τ. ἀληθείας; Jos., Bell. 1, 626; 628, C. Ap. 2, 17) ἔ. πραγμάτων οὐ βλεπομένων faith is *a proving* (or *conviction about*) *unseen things*=faith means to be sure about things unseen (in contrast to confidence in the temporal) **Hb 11:1.**

❷ **the act of charging a pers. with wrongdoing,** ***accusation*** σύ μου ἔ. εἶ; *will you accuse me?* Hv 1, 1, 6 (other interpretations: *complaint* [Hab 2:1]: *will you lodge a complaint against me?; conviction* [BGU 1138, 13=Mitt-Wilck. II/2, 100, 13 (19/18 BC)]; Kaibel 814 of a monument that serves as a touchstone to identify either those well-disposed toward the dead or the impious; cp. TestJos 6:6).

❸ **expression of strong disapproval,** ***reproof, censure, correction*** (Job 6:26; 13:6; Wsd 2:14; Philo, Rer. Div. Her. 76) 1 Cl 57:4f (Pr 1:25, 30); **2 Ti 3:16 v.l.**—DELG s.v. ἐλέγχω. M-M. TW.

ἐλέγχω fut. ἐλέγξω; 1 aor. ἤλεγξα LXX, impv. ἔλεγξον, inf. ἐλέγξαι; pass. ἠλέγχθην (Hom.+)

❶ **to scrutinize or examine carefully,** ***bring to light, expose, set forth*** (Aristoph., Eccl. 485; Herodian 3, 12, 4; PHib 55, 3 [250 BC] τὸν ποιμένα τ. ἐλέγξοντα περὶ ὧν μοι εἶπας) **J 3:20; Eph 5:11, 13** (the darkness-light theme suggests exposure, with implication of censure); Dg 2:8. τὰ κρυπτά (Artem. 1, 68) IPhld 7:1. ταῦτα ἔλεγχε *declare this* **Tit 2:15** (but s. 3 below); τ. ἁμαρτίας τινὸς πρὸς τὸν κύριον *expose someone's sins before the Lord* Hv 1, 1, 5 (Jos., Vi. 339 τὰς πονηρίας ἐ.); *demonstrate, prove* (POxy 237 VIII, 40; Wsd 2:11; Ath. 30, 4) τὶ *someth.* Dg 9:6; οὐκ ἐλέγχετε=*disprove* 2:9.

❷ **to bring a pers. to the point of recognizing wrongdoing,** ***convict, convince*** someone of someth., *point someth. out to someone* (PAmh 33, 34 [157 BC]; BGU 1138, 13=Mitt-Wilck. II/2, 100, 13 [19/18 BC]; POxy 1032, 30; PStras 41, 31; Jos., Ant. 4, 219; SibOr 5, 34; Just., A I, 4, 6 αὐτὸν … ἁμαρτάνοντα; Ath. 2, 1 ἡμᾶς … ἀδικοῦντας; Just., D. 67, 2 ὅπως μήτε … μωραίνειν ἐλέγχησθε) τινά **Tit 1:9, 13; Jd 22 v.l.** (COsburn, ZNW 63, '72, 139–44 [text]); **23 v.l.;** περί w. gen. introduces the thing of which one is convicted or convinced (Aristoph., Plut. 574; Jos., C. Ap. 2, 5; PLips 43, 11 μάρτυρας τοὺς ἐλέγχοντας Θαῆσιν περὶ ἀφαιρέσεως βιβλίων χρειστιακῶν) **J 8:46; 16:8** (s. δικαιοσύνη 3a end); **Jd 15** (En 1:9). Pass. ἐ. ὑπό τινος **Ac 6:10 v.l.; 1 Cor 14:24;** ὑπὸ τ. συνειδήσεως ἐλεγχόμενοι **J 8:9 v.l.** (cp. Philo, De Jos. 48 ὑπὸ τοῦ συνειδότος ἐλεγχόμενος, Spec. Leg. 3, 54 al.); ἀπὸ τῆς ὀσμῆς ἐλέγχεσθαι *be convicted* (perh. *tested*) *by the odor* IMg 10:2. ἐλεγχόμενοι ὡς παραβάται *convicted as transgressors* **Js 2:9;** ἵνα … ὁ πόνηρὸς … ἐλεγχθῇ[το] μὴ ὢν θεός AcPlCor 2:15.

❸ **to express strong disapproval of someone's action,** ***reprove, correct*** (Aelian, VH 13, 25; Sir 20:2; 31:31; Pr 9:7f al.; Just. D. 107, 3) **2 Ti 4:2;** τινά **1 Ti 5:20;** D 2:7. W. the connotation of refuting (Diod. S. 13, 90, 4; Appian, Bell. Civ. 5, 28, end; PGM 4, 2620; Just., A I, 64, 6 al.; Ath. 18, 1 τὰ εἴδωλα; Tat. 8, 4 τὴν μαντικήν) πᾶσαν αἵρεσιν Epil Mosq 2.—τινὰ περί τινος **Lk 3:19.** τινὰ ἐπί τινι B 19:4. ἔλεγξον αὐτὸν μεταξὺ σοῦ καὶ αὐτοῦ μόνου *show him his fault while you are alone w. him* **Mt 18:15** (cp. CD 9, 6–8 and s. Lev 19:17). Perh. **Tit 2:15** belongs here (s. 1 above).

❹ **to penalize for wrongdoing,** ***punish, discipline*** (Wsd 1:8; 12:2; Job 5:17 al.) **Hb 12:5** (Pr 3:11); (w. παιδεύειν, as Sir 18:13) **Rv 3:19.**—LLutkemeyer, CBQ 8, '46, 221–23.—B. 1442. DELG. M-M. TW.

ἐλεεινός, ή, όν (s. ἔλεος; Hom. et al.; Diod. S. 13, 28, 3; Dio Chrys. 33 [50], 3 and 4; Ael. Aristid. 34, 47 K.=50 p. 564 D.; Philostrat., Imag. 1, 4 p. 300, 6; POxy 130, 3; 131, 2; TestSol 2:13 D; ApcEsdr 2:30 p. 26, 24 Tdf.; ApcSed; Jos., Ant. 4, 133, Vi. 138; Mel., P. 27, 192 [Ch.; ἐλεινόν PBodm for Att. ἐλεινός; so W-H.].—B-D-F §31, 3; Rob. 204; Mussies 24) **pert. to being deserving of sympathy for one's pathetic condition,** ***miserable, pitiable*** (w. ταλαίπωρος) **Rv 3:17.** Comp. ἐλεεινότεροι πάντων ἀνθρώπων as superl. (s. B-D-F §60; Mlt. 78f) *most miserable of all* **1 Cor 15:19.**—DELG s.v. ἔλεος. M-M.

ἐλεέω fut. ἐλεήσω; 1 aor. ἠλέησα, impv. ἐλέησον. Pass.: 1 fut. ἐλεηθήσομαι; 1 aor. ἠλεήθην; pf. pass. ptc. ἠλεημένος (s. ἔλεος; Hom.+) **to be greatly concerned about someone in need,** ***have compassion/mercy/pity*** τινά *on* or *for someone* (Diod. S. 12, 30, 4; 20, 4, 6 τοὺς πολίτας; PCairZen 145, 12 [256 BC]; UPZ 78, 24 [159 BC]; PFay 106, 16 [II AD] ἀξιῶ σε ἐλεῆσαί με; PFlor 378, 3; TestJob; Philo) Hv 1, 3, 2. τὸν σύνδουλον **Mt 18:33.** Abs. *feel pity* MPol 2:2. Esp. *show mercy to someone, help someone (out of compassion)* **Mt 9:27; 15:22; 17:15; 20:30f** (on κύριε ἐλέησον cp. Epict. 2, 7, 12 [TZahn, D. Stoiker Epikt. u. s. Verh. z. Christentum[2] 1895, 46f; FDölger, Sol salutis 1920, 62f]; Ps 6:3; 9:14 al.; EPeterson, Εἷς θεός 1926, 164–67; Achilles Tat. 3, 5, 4 ἐλέησον δέσποτα Πόσειδον; Jos., Ant. 9, 64 δέσποτα ἐλέησον); **Mk 10:47f; Lk 16:24; 17:13; 18:38f;** D 2:7; *do acts of compassion* **Ro 12:8;** τινά *to someone* (Chariton 1, 9, 5; Celsus 2, 71) ApcPt 15:30; B 20:2; D 5:2. Of God's mercy (Epici p. 43 B.=p. 20 K.: Cypria fgm. 1, 3 Ζεὺς ἐλέησε; Hes., astron. fgm. 182 Rz.: Ἥφαιστος; Phanodemus [IV BC]: 325 fgm. 14b Jac.: Artemis; Menand., Epitr. 855, 874 S. [535, 554 Kö.] θεῶν τις ὑμᾶς ἠλέησε; Diod. S. 24, 12, 2 δαιμονίου ἐλεήσαντος; UPZ 78, 24 [159 BC] of Isis, the θεὰ θεῶν: ἐλέησον τὰς διδύμας; Jos., Ant. 11, 1; SibOr 3, 628); **Mk 5:19; Phil 2:27; Ro 9:15** (Ex 33:19), **16, 18; 11:32;** 1 Cl 18:2 (Ps 50:3); 59:4; 2 Cl 1:7; B 3:5 (on the acc. of the thing cp. Diod. S. 18, 25, 2); Dg 9:2; AcPlCor 1:6. Pass. *find* or *be shown mercy* (PsSol 7:6; 15:13; ὑπὸ κυρίου 16:15; Appian, Hann. 28 §119 ἐλεεῖσθαι ὑπό τινος, Bell. Civ. 4, 13 §52) **Mt 5:7; Ro 11:30f; 1 Ti 1:13, 16;** IEph 12:1; 1 Cl 56:16. οἱ οὐκ ἠλεημένοι νῦν δὲ ἐλεηθέντες *who once had not found mercy, but now have found it* **1 Pt 2:10.** Of a congregation ἠλεημένη *that has found mercy* (cp. Hos 1:6) IRo ins; IPhld ins; ISm ins; *receive as a gracious gift, be favored with* ἠλεημένος ὑπὸ κυρίου πιστὸς εἶναι (Herm. Wr. 13, 7 ἐλεηθεὶς ὑπὸ τ. θεοῦ) **1 Cor 7:25;** cp. **2 Cor 4:1;** IRo 9:2; IPhld 5:1. Also s. ἐλεάω.—DELG s.v. ἔλεος. M-M. EDNT. TW. Spicq.

ἐλεημοσύνη, ης, ἡ (s. ἔλεος; Callim. 4, 152 w. mng. 'compassion'; PAbinn 19, 25f; PGen 51, 26; LXX; TestJob) gener. 'kind deed', then

❶ **exercise of benevolent goodwill,** ***alms, charitable giving*** w. focus on attitude and action as such (so Diog. L. 5, 17; Da 4:27; Tob; Sir) **Mt 6:4;** D 15:4. ποιεῖν ἐ. *give alms* (Tob 1:3, 16; 4:7f; Sir 7:10) **Mt 6:2f; Ac 9:36** (JJeremias, ZNW 44, '53, 103f);

10:2; 24:17; διδόναι ἐ. (Diog. L., loc. cit. πονηρῷ ἀνθρώπῳ ἐλεημοσύνην ἔδωκεν) **Lk 11:41** (s. Black, Aramaic Approach, 2); **12:33.** Alms ascend to God **Ac 10:4;** they are remembered before God vs. **31;** cp. 2 Cl 16:4.

❷ **that which is benevolently given to meet a need,** ***alms*** w. focus on material as such αἰτεῖν ἐ. *ask for alms* **Ac 3:2** (TestJob 9:8); λαμβάνειν *receive alms* vs. **3;** πρὸς τὴν ἐ. καθήμενος (the one who) *sat begging* vs. **10.** ἱδρωσάτω ἡ ἐ. εἰς τὰς χεῖράς σου *let your alms sweat in your hands,* i.e., do not give them hastily D 1:6 (cp. SibOr 2, 79f).—Billerb. IV 536–58: D. altjüd. Privatwohltätigkeit; HBolkestein, Wohltätigkeit u. Armenpflege im vorchristl. Altertum '39; Dodd 59–62; LCountryman, The Rich Christian in the Church of the Early Empire, '80, RAC I 301–7.—DELG s.v. ἔλεος. M-M. TW.

ἐλεήμων, ον gen. **-ονος** (s. ἔλεος; Hom.+) **pert. to being concerned about people in their need,** ***merciful, sympathetic, compassionate*** of God (so predom. LXX; EpArist 208; TestJud 19:3; Philo, Somn. 1, 93; PLond VI, 1917, 25 [c. 330–40]; Just. D. 107, 2.—Sb 8266, 19 [261/260 BC] of the god Amenophis; Apollod. [II BC]: 244 fgm. 121 Jac. of Leto; IAndrosIsis 128; also of Isis: SEG VIII, 550, 34 [I BC]) w. οἰκτίρμων (as Ex 34:6 al. LXX; PLond VI, 1917, 20 and 22) 1 Cl 60:1. Of Christ (PGM 13, 290) **Hb 2:17.** Of people (Epict. 2, 21, 3; 5; 6; Ptolem., Apotel. 3, 14, 33; Herm. Wr. 1, 22; Ps 111:4; Pr 11:17; 20:6; TestSol 22:1 B; TestAbr A 4 p. 81, 3 [Stone p. 10]; TestSim 4:4; JosAs 8:9; Jos., Ant. 10, 41) **Mt 5:7;** 2 Cl 4:3; D 3:8. εἰς πάντας *toward everyone* Pol 6:1.—DELG s.v. ἔλεος. M-M. TW.

ἔλεος, ους, τό (Hom.+, but in later Gk. almost always ὁ ἔλεος; so also in Diod. S. 12, 18, 4; Herm. Wr. 13, 3; SIG 814, 21 [67 AD]; PMagd 18, 6=PEnteux 43, 6 [III BC]; Is 64:3; En 12:6; ApcMos13; ApcrEzk P 1 recto 9; EpArist 208; Philo; Jos., Bell. 1, 560, Ant. 4, 239 ἐξ ἐλέου; POxy 2754, 5 [111 AD].—Neut., Polyb. 1, 88, 2 and Diod. S. 3, 18, 5 [v.l. in latter pass.]; Ps.-Callisth. 1, 46a, 2; Herm. Wr. 13, 8a; gravestone: Sb 6650, 4; pap; Just.; sim. predom. in LXX [Thackeray 158; Helbing 47]; En 5:6; 27:4; TestAbr A 14 p. 94, 11 and 15 [Stone p. 36]; TestJob; Test12Patr; JosAs 23:4; ApcEsdr 2, 8 p. 25, 29 Tdf. [pl.]; ApcSed 5:8 [pl.]; and always in our lit. [B-D-F §51, 2; W-S. §8, 11; Mlt. 60; for the Apost. Fathers s. Reinhold 54], where the masc. appears now and then as v.l.: **Mt 9:13; 12:7; 23:23; Tit 3:5; Hb 4:16) kindness or concern expressed for someone in need,** ***mercy, compassion, pity, clemency***

ⓐ of humans toward humans (Did., Gen. 180, 2) *mercy* **Mt 9:13; 12:7** (both Hos 6:6); **23:23; Js 3:17;** ποιεῖν ἔ. *show mercy* (Gen 24:44, 49; 1 Km 15:6 al.) **Js 2:13;** *show compassion, do good* μετά τινος *to someone* (Judg 1:24; 8:35; 1 Km 20:8 al.) **Lk 10:37.**

ⓑ of God toward humans (Timocles Com. [IV BC] 31 τοῖς τεθνεῶσιν ἔλεος ἐπιεικὴς θεός; LXX), gener. **Lk 1:50** (cp. Ps 102:17), 54 (cp. Ps 97:3); (w. εἰρήνη as En 5:5) **Gal 6:16;** B 15:2; Hv 3, 9, 8; s 4:2. ἔλεος κυκλώσει τινά *compassion will surround someone* (for protection) 1 Cl 22:8 (Ps 31:10). In greetings (w. εἰρήνη; cp. Tob 7:12 S) Pol ins; (w. χάρις [cp. Wsd 3:9; 4:15], εἰρήνη) **1 Ti 1:2; 2 Ti 1:2; 2J 3;** cp. ISm 12:2; (w. εἰρήνη, ἀγάπη [cp. PsSol 18:3]) **Jd 2;** MPol ins; ἐν παντὶ ἐ. IPhld ins. Hebraistic: ἐμεγάλυνεν κύριος τὸ ἔ. αὐτοῦ μετ' αὐτῆς *the Lord had showed great kindness to her* **Lk 1:58.** δῴη ἔ. ὁ κύριος τῷ Ὀνησιφόρου οἴκῳ *may the Lord show kindness to the house of Onesiphorus* **2 Ti 1:16.** ἔχειν ἔ. *find mercy* Hv 2, 2, 3. Cp. also 1 Cl 9:1; 28:1; 50:2; 56:5 (Ps 140:5); ITr 12:3.—Esp. the mercy shown by God in Christ to humans **Ro 15:9; Tit 3:5;** Hv 3, 9, 1. πλούσιος ἐν ἐλέει *rich in mercy* **Eph 2:4.** κατὰ τὸ πολὺ αὐτοῦ ἔ. *acc. to his great mercy* **1 Pt 1:3** (cp. Ps 50:3; 24:7.—κατ' ἔλεον of Zeus: Lucian, Deor. 13, 1; of Hera: Παραδοξογράφοι ed. AWestermann 1839 p. 222, 7; of Athena ibid. 227, 17 and 19); cp. 1 Cl 18:2 (Ps 50:3); λαμβάνειν ἔ. (TestLevi 15:4) *receive mercy* **Hb 4:16;** εὑρίσκειν ἔ. *find mercy* **2 Ti 1:18;** ποιεῖν ἔ. μετά τινος *show kindness to someone* **Lk 1:72.** σπλάγχνα ἐλέους *merciful heart* vs. **78** (TestZeb 7:3; 8:2). σκεύη ἐλέους *vessels of mercy* (opp. σκεύη ὀργῆς; s. σκεῦος 3) **Ro 9:23.** τῷ ὑμετέρῳ ἐλέει *because of the mercy shown to you* (dat. of cause; s. ἀπιστία 1) **11:31.**—of Christ toward humans τὸ ἔλεος τοῦ κυρίου ἡμῶν Ἰησοῦ Χριστοῦ **Jd 21.**—AKlocker, Wortgeschichte von ἔλεος u. οἶκτος, etc., diss. Innsbruck, '53; NGlueck, Das Wort Ḥesed im AT, Beih. ZAW, '61.—S. ἐλεέω end.—Schmidt, Syn. III 572–83. DELG. M-M. TW. Spicq.

ἐλευθερία, ας, ἡ (Pind., Hdt.; ins, pap, LXX, Philo, Joseph.; Just., D. 1, 5; Tat. 7, 1; Mel., P. 49, 353; 68, 490) **the state of being free,** ***freedom, liberty*** (for a Hellenic perspective Dio Chrys. 30 and 80; opp. δουλεία: Jos., Bell. 7, 255) **2 Pt 2:19;** IPol 4:3; Hs 5, 2, 7. Esp. of freedom which stands in contrast to constraint of the Mosaic law, looked upon as slavery **Gal 2:4; 5:1** (τῇ ἐ. dat. of advantage *for freedom.* KRengstorf, TLZ 76, '51, 659–62). In contrast to legal serfdom, **Js 1:25** refers to νόμος τ. ἐλευθερίας (FNötscher, Vom AT zum NT, '62, 80–122 [Qumran]); **2:12** (on both Js-passages s. EStauffer, TLZ 77, '52, 527–32).—In gener. of the liberty of a Christian (cp. Philo, Conf. Lingu. 94, Migr. Abr. 25, Rer. Div. Her. 124; 273; 275) **1 Cor 10:29; 2 Cor 3:17.** ἐπ' ἐλευθερίᾳ καλεῖσθαι *be called for freedom* (=to be free; cp. Plut., Sulla 9, 14; SIG[2] 845, 4; 8; BGU 1141, 24 [14 BC].—Lucian, Sat. 9 ἐπὶ τῇ ἐλευθερίᾳ ζῶμεν) **Gal 5:13a** (s. καλέω 4). This freedom must not degenerate into license (Iren. 4, 37, 4 [Harv. II 288, 11]; cp. 4, 39, 3 [Harv. II 300, 4]) vs. **13b; 1 Pt 2:16.** In contrast to the slavery of corruption stands the ἐ. τῆς δόξης τῶν τέκνων τοῦ θεοῦ *the glorious freedom of God's children* **Ro 8:21.**—JWeiss, D. christl. Freih. nach der Verkünd. des Ap. Pls 1902; ABonhöffer, Epiktet u. d. NT 1911, 164; RBultmann, ZNW 13, 1912, 97ff; 177ff (esp. 100ff), Theol. des NT '48, 326–48, Theology of the NT, tr. KGrobel '51, I 330–45; OSchmitz, D. Freiheitsged. b. Epikt. u. d. Freiheitszeugnis d. Pls 1923; Mich. Müller, Freiheit: ZNW 25, 1926, 177–236; KDeissner, Autorität u. Freiheit im ältesten Christentum '31; WBrandt, Freiheit im NT '32; EGulin, D. Freiheit in d. Verk. d. Pls.: ZST 18, '41, 458–81; EFuchs, D. Freiheit des Glaubens (Ro 5–8) '49; HWedell, Idea of Freedom . . . in Paul: ATR 32, '50, 204–16; AWilder, Eleutheria in the NT, Ecumenical Review (Geneva) 13, '61, 409–20; KNiederwimmer, D. Begriff d. Freiheit im NT, '66; idem, EDNT I 432–34; DNestle, Eleutheria, I: Die Griechen, '67; MPohlenz, Freedom in Greek Life and Thought, 1900, esp. 170–74.—RAC VIII 269–306.—DELG s.v. ἐλεύθερος. M-M. TW. Sv.

ἐλευθέριος, (α), ον (since Theognis 538; Democr. 282 Diels; Pla.; EpArist 246; Philo, Joseph.) ***appropriate for a free pers.*** ἐπιθήσει σοι ἐ. στέφανον. *he* (Christ) *will place on you a freedom wreath* (cp. Simonides 94a, 2; b, 2 Diehl[2] στέφανος ἐλευθερίας) AcPl Ha 2, 31.—DELG s.v. ἐλεύθερος.

ἐλεύθερος, έρα, ον (Hom.+; Just., A I, 43, 3 προαιρέσει ἐλευθέρᾳ al.) in our lit. used as adj. and subst.—❶ **pert. to being free socially and politically,** ***free*** (Jos., C. Ap. 2, 134. Cp. the pride of the Indians in freedom: Arrian, Ind. 10, 8 πάντας Ἰνδοὺς εἶναι ἐλευθέρους, οὐδέ τινα δοῦλον εἶναι Ἰνδόν) **J 8:33;** (opp. slave) **1 Cor 7:21; 12:13; Gal 3:28** (Just., D. 139, 5; cp. the temple law fr. Philadelphia [I BC]: SIG 985, 4ff πρόσοδον . . . ἀνδράσι κ. γυναιξίν, ἐλευθέροις κ. οἰκέταις=access . . . to men and women, free and slave; 67th letter of Apollonius of Tyana [Philostrat. I 363, 31]: the temple of Artemis at Eph. is open to all, Ἕλλησι, βαρβάροις, ἐλευθέροις, δούλοις); **4:22f; 30f** (oft. in marriage contracts since PEleph 1, 4 [311 BC]); **Eph 6:8; Col 3:11; Rv 6:15; 13:16; 19:18;** Hs 5, 2, 2. Paradox: the free pers. a slave of Christ **1 Cor 7:22,** which infl. IRo 4:3. Sim. in reference to way of life (Heraclid. Crit., fgm. 1, 30 [Ps.-Dicaearch. p. 146 F.] τοῖς τρόποις ὄντες ἐλεύθεροι=free people, judging by their customs; πράσσειν ὅσα βούλονται ὡς ἐ. [of Simon Magus's followers] Iren. 1, 23, 3 [Harv. I 193, 12]) **1 Pt 2:16.**

❷ **pert. to being free from control or obligation, *independent, not bound*** οὐκ εἰμὶ ἐ.; (cp. Epict. 3, 22, 48) **1 Cor 9:1;** *free* fr. the tax **Mt 17:26;** ἐ. τῇ δικαιοσύνῃ *independent as far as righteousness is concerned* **Ro 6:20;** ἐ. ἀπό τινος (Pla., Leg. 8, 832d; X., Cyr. 3, 2, 23; Jos., Ant. 5, 34): ἐ. ἀπὸ τ. νόμου *no longer bound by the law* which joined her to her husband (cp. Dt 21:14) **Ro 7:3;** ἐ. ἔκ τινος *independent of someone* **1 Cor 9:19** (cp. Eur., Herc. Fur. 1010). W. inf. ἐ. ἐστὶν . . . γαμηθῆναι **7:39.**—Of the freedom of the heavenly Jerusalem, in contrast to Judean thinking **Gal 4:26.** Of the true freedom of one set free by Christ **J 8:36.**—B. 1336. CManning, Stoicism and Slavery in the Rom. Empire: ANRW II Principat 36/3, '89, 1518–43. DELG. M-M. EDNT. TW. Sv.

ἐλευθερόω fut. ἐλευθερώσω; 1 aor. ἠλευθέρωσα; pf. inf. ἠλευθερωκέναι (Just., D. 41, 1). Pass.: 1 fut. ἐλευθερωθήσομαι; 1 aor. ἠλευθερώθην; pf. pass. ἠλευθέρωμαι (s. ἐλεύθερος; Aeschyl., Hdt.+) **to cause someone to be freed from domination, *free, set free,*** lit. (Appian, Hann. 27 §116; TestJos 1:5) ἀπὸ τ. κοινοῦ ἐλευθεροῦσθαι (of slaves) *be freed at the church's expense* IPol 4:3.—Elsewh. in our lit. only w. ref. to spiritual and moral matters (Epict. 4, 7, 17 ἠλευθέρωμαι ὑπὸ τοῦ θεοῦ . . . , οὐκέτι οὐδεὶς δουλαγωγῆσαί με δύναται; Maximus Tyr. 36, 5a ἄνδρα ἐλευθερωθέντα ὑπὸ τοῦ Διός; Iren., Hippol.; VLeinieks, The City of Dionysos, '96, 303–25, on Dionys. as liberator). τινά *someone* **J 8:32, 36.** πᾶσαν σάρκα διὰ τῆς ἰδίας σαρκός AcPlCor 2:6. ἀπὸ τ. ἁμαρτίας *fr. sin* **Ro 6:18, 22** (Just., D. 41, 1 ἀπὸ τῆς κακίας). ἀπὸ τ. νόμου τ. ἁμαρτίας **8:2;** ἀπὸ τ. δουλείας τ. φθορᾶς **Ro 8:21.** τῇ ἐλευθερίᾳ *for freedom* (fr. the Mosaic law, w. implication of God as patron) **Gal 5:1.** ἐν ᾧ ἠλευθερώμεθα *whereby* (Christ's body) *we have been liberated* AcPlCor 2:18. JFrame, Paul's Idea of Deliverance: JBL 49, 1930, 1–12.—DELG s.v. ἐλεύθερος. M-M. TW.

ἔλευσις, εως, ἡ (fr. ἐλεύσομαι, s. ἔρχομαι; Dionys. Hal. 3, 59, 1 ed. JReiske 1774 [ed. CJacoby 1885ff has ἔλασις]; Cornutus 28 p. 54, 11; Cass. Dio 8, 10, 7; Syntipas p. 23, 28; Cat. Cod. Astr. XII 157, 1; Hesych.; Etym. Gud. 454, 9; TestSol; TestAbr A 16 p. 97, 15 [Stone p. 42]) **the act of reaching a point with implication of determined objective, *coming, arrival*** (Lat.: adventus) of the first coming of Christ: ἐ. τοῦ δικαίου **Ac 7:52;** ἔ. τοῦ κυρίου ἡμῶν Pol 6:3; ἡ ἔ. τοῦ Χριστοῦ 1 Cl 17:1.—Of Christ's second coming (AcThom 28 [Aa II/2 p. 145, 7]) **Lk 21:7** D; **23:42** D (in Irenaeus 1, 10 of both). ὁ κύριος . . . εἰς ταχεῖαν ποιήσεται τὴν ἔ. *the Lord . . . will soon make his appearance* or *advent* AcPlCor 2:3.—GKilpatrick, JTS 46, '45, 136–45. DELG s.v. ἐλεύσομαι. TW.

ἐλεύσομαι s. ἔρχομαι.

ἐλεφάντινος, η, ον (ἐλέφας 'ivory'; Alcaeus+; Epict. 2, 19, 26; SIG[2] 586: 47, 55, 75, 80; Sb 7181 B 12; LXX, Joseph.) **pert. to being made of ivory, *of ivory*** σκεῦος *articles made of ivory* **Rv 18:12.** Of a couch (cp. Appian, Liby. 32 §137, 4=a chair for a king; Bell. Civ. 2, 106 §442; Jos., Bell. 7, 126.—Ant. 8, 140 Solomon's ivory throne) Hv 3, 1, 4.—BHHW I 393f. DELG s.v. ἐλέφας. M-M.

ἐλήλακα s. ἐλαύνω.

ἐλήλυθα s. ἔρχομαι.

ἐλθεῖν s. ἔρχομαι.

Ἐλιακίμ, ὁ indecl. (אֶלְיָקִים) *Eliakim* (cp. 4 Km 18:18; 23:34 al.—In Jos., Ant. 10, 82 Ἐλιάκ[ε]ιμος), in the genealogy of Jesus **Mt 1:13; Lk 3:30,** also **3:23ff** D.

ἕλιγμα, ατος, τό (fr. ἕλιξ 'spiral', s. ἑλίσσω; Soranus 155, 5; Athen.; Hesych.) ***package, roll*** σμύρνης καὶ ἀλόης **J 19:39 v.l.,** certainly erroneous (for μίγμα).—S. GRudberg, Eranos 15, 1915, 67. S. μίγμα and σμῆγμα.—DELG s.v. ἕλιξ.

Ἐλιέζερ, ὁ indecl. (אֱלִיעֶזֶר) *Eliezer* (cp. Gen 15:2; Ex 18:4 al.; Philo), in the genealogy of Jesus **Lk 3:29.**—BHHW I 399.

Ἐλιούδ, ὁ indecl. *Eliud,* in the genealogy of Jesus **Mt 1:14f; Lk 3:23ff** D.

Ἐλισάβετ, ἡ indecl. (אֱלִישֶׁבַע; s. EKönig, ET 21, 1910, 185–87; LKöhler, AKaegi Festschr. 1919, 186.—SEG VIII, 202 [I BC/I AD, ossuary fr. Jerus.] Ἐλισάβη) *Elizabeth* (cp. Ex 6:23; Philo, Poster. Cai. 76), wife of Zacharias the priest, mother of John the Baptist **Lk 1:5, 7, 13, 24, 36, 40f, 57;** GEb 13, 75; GJs 12:2 and 3; 22:3 (Just., D. 84, 4). According to a few witnesses also **Lk 1:46** (on this s. Harnack, SBBerlAk 1900, 538ff=Studien I '31, 62ff; Zahn, Lk: Exkurs III p. 745ff [older lit. here]; ENorden, D. Geburt d. Kindes 1924, 76ff; RHarris, ET 41, 1930, 266f; 42, '31, 188–90). Acc. to vs. **36** and GJs 12:2 Mary, the mother of Jesus, was related to her.—UMittman-Richert, Magnifikat u. Benediktus '96, 94–97. BHHW I 401.

Ἐλισαιέ, ὁ indecl. (3 Km 19:16f, 19; 4 Km 2–8; Sir 48:12) 1 Cl 17:1, and

Ἐλισαῖος, ου, ὁ (Ἑλισαῖος Tdf. Sod. Vog. Ἐλισσαῖος t.r. [the Lat. Vulg. Eliseus follows the Gk. form]; EpArist 47 al.; Jos., Ant. 8, 352–54; 9, 28; Just., D. 86, 6) **Lk 4:27;** AcPlCor 2:32 (Ἐλεισαίου) *Elisha* (אֱלִישָׁע), the Hebrew prophet.—BHHW I 399–401.

ἑλίσσω fut. ἑλίξω. Pass. 1 aor. opt. 3 sg. ἑλιχθείη Job 18:8; 1 fut. ἑλιχθήσομαι; 2 fut. 3 sg. ἑλιγήσεται Is. 34:4 (s. ἕλιγμα; Hom. et al.; predom. poet., but also Philo Mech. 76, 8; Lucian.—IAndrosIsis 172; POxy 1679, 10; LXX; Ath. 20, 1) **to cause someth. to take the shape of a roll, *roll up*** τὶ *someth.* ὡσεὶ περιβόλαιον ἑλίξεις αὐτούς *you will roll them up like a cloak* **Hb 1:12** (Ps 101:27 v.l.). Of the heaven (cp. SEG VII, 14, 8 [I AD] Hymn to Apollo: οὐρανὸν διελίσσει; PGM 12, 241 ἡ γῆ ἑλίσσεται) ὡς βιβλίον ἑλισσόμενον *like a scroll that is rolled up* (Aeneas Tact. 1553 ἑ. τὸ βιβλίον; Vit. Hes. p. 48, 8; PGM 36, 234 of rolling up an inscribed lead tablet) **Rv 6:14;** cp. ἑλιχθήσεται ὡς βιβλίον ApcPt fgm. 5, p. 13, 10 (Is 34:4).—DELG s.v. ἕλιξ. M-M.

ἕλκος, ους, τό (s. ἑλκόω; Hom.+) ***wound*** (so Il. 4, 190; Antig. Car. 36) or ***sore, abscess, ulcer*** (so Thu., Theophr., Polyb., also SIG 1168, 114; 1169, 38; SEG XLII, 818, 3; LXX; TestSol 9:6; Just., D. 115, 5). The latter seems to be implied **Lk 16:21,** for the narrative indicates that the beggar desires food, not medical attention (also s. next entry). ἕ. κακὸν καὶ πονηρόν (cp. Dt 28:35; Job 2:7) *a foul and vile sore* **Rv 16:2.** ἐβλασφήμησαν ἐκ τῶν ἕ. αὐτῶν *they reviled (God) because of their sores* vs. **11.**—B. 304. Schmidt, Syn. III 297–302. DELG. M-M.

ἑλκόω (s. ἕλκος; trag. et al., esp. in medical wr. [Hippocr.: CMG I 1 p. 49, 23; Galen: CMG V 4, 1, 1 p. 80, 13; Hobart 31f; in a letter to a physician: PMerton 12, 20], also Aristeas Hist.: 725 fgm. 1, 3 Jac [in Eus., PE 9, 25, 3]) ***cause sores/ulcers*** pf. pass. ptc. εἱλκωμένος (ἡλ- t.r.; on the reduplication s. B-D-F §68; Rob. 364) *covered w. sores* (X., De Re Equ. 1, 4; 5, 1; Plut., Phoc. 742 [2, 3]; Artem. 1, 23; 28; 41) **Lk 16:20**—DELG s.v. ἕλκος.

ἑλκύω s. ἕλκω fut. and aor.—M-M.

ἕλκω impf. εἷλκον, ἧλκον (ApcMos; GJs, s. deStrycker 241f); fut. ἑλκύσω; 1 aor. εἵλκυσα; aor. pass. 3 sg. εἱλκύσθη Da 4:17a; for the forms w. -υ- s. Mlt-H. 236; B-D-F §101 p. 45 (Hom.; Pherecyd. 26; ins, pap, LXX; TestSol 26:9 H; JosAs; ParJer 4:6; ApcMos 38; Joseph., Just., Mel., P. 56, 409) gener. 'pull, drag, draw'.

❶ **to move an object from one area to another in a pulling motion, *draw,*** with implication that the object being moved is incapable of propelling itself or in the case of pers. is unwilling to do so voluntarily, in either case with implication of exertion on the part of the mover τὶ *someth.* a sword (Soph., Ant. 1233; Libanius, Or. 13 p. 73, 5 F. ξίφος) **J 18:10;** *haul* a net **21:6, 11.** ἧλκεν τὴν πορφύραν (Mary) *stretched* (i.e. in a tugging motion) *the purple (garment)* GJs 11:1; ἔστρωσεν τὸν ὄνον ... καὶ ἧλκεν ὁ υἱὸς αὐτοῦ (Joseph) *saddled the ass ... and his son guided it* 17:2. τινά *someone* (Diod. S. 34 + 35 fgm. 2, 14 τινὰ εἰς; Achilles Tat. 7, 15, 4 εἷλκόν με εἰς τὸ δεσμωτήριον, with ref. in the context to resistance; Jos., Bell. 1, 591 τινὰ εἰς.—Also Clearchus, fgm. 73; Diod. S. 14, 5, 3 ἕ. τινὰ ἐπὶ τὸν θάνατον) ἔξω τ. ἱεροῦ *drag someone out of the temple* **Ac 21:30;** εἰς τ. ἀγορὰν ἐπὶ τ. ἄρχοντας **16:19** (on the judicial implication s. Reader, Polemo 370); εἰς κριτήρια *hale into court* **Js 2:6** (Herodas 5, 59 ἕ. τινὰ εἰς τὰς ἀνάγκας=to punishment; Just., A II, 12, 4 εἰς βασάνους). οἱ ἕλκοντες ἡμᾶς Ox 654, 10, [οἱ ἕλκον]τες ὑμᾶς 14 (cp. GTh 3; *those who mislead us* line10, is expanded by Dssm. [LO 365=LAE 427] w. εἰς τὰ κριτήρια; difft. by others. Actually nothing need be supplied, since ἕ. τινά means *pull* or *tug someone back and forth, mistreat someone* [Libanius, Or. 58 p. 183, 20 F. ἕλκων κάπηλον; cp. Jos., Bell. 1, 338 εἷλκεν τοὺς ἔνδοθεν]). Of stones ἐκ τοῦ βυθοῦ ἑλκομένους *which were dragged out of the deep* Hv 3, 2, 6; 3, 5, 2.

❷ **to draw a pers. in the direction of values for inner life, *draw, attract,*** an extended fig. use of mng. 1 (Pla., Phdr. 238a; Epict. 2, 20, 15 ἡ φύσις ἕλκει; Aelian, NA 4, 13; Porphyr., Marc. 16 μόνη ἡ ἀρετὴ τ. ψυχὴν ἄνω ἕλκει καὶ πρὸς τὸ συγγενές; Jer 38:3; SSol 1:4; 4 Macc 14:13; 15:11; Jos., Ant. 15, 27; Ath. 26, 1 περὶ τὰ εἴδωλα) **J 6:44.** ἑλκ. πρός with acc. (Hierocles 25 p. 477 it is said of God ἑλκύσαι πρὸς τὴν ἀλήθειαν τοὺς ἀνθρώπους; Ath., R. 75, 20 ἑλκούσης ... ἐπιθυμίας πρὸς τροφήν): πρὸς ἐμαυτόν **12:32.**

❸ **to appear to be pulled in a certain direction, *flow*** an ext. fig. use intr. *flow along* of a river ἦν ποταμὸς ἕλκων ἐκ δεξιῶν *a river flowed along on the right* B 11:10 (cp. Da 7:10 Theod.; TestSol 26:9 H).—B. 571. DELG. M-M. TW.

Ἑλλάς, άδος, ἡ ***Greece*** (Hes. et al.; ins; 1 Macc 8:9; Philo; Joseph.; SibOr index; Just, D. 1, 3); in popular usage it could also designate the Rom. province officially known as Achaia (s. Ἀχαΐα; Paus. 7, 16) **Ac 20:2.**—Frisk. DELG s.v. Ἕλληνες. M-M. TW.

ἐλλείπω (s. next entry; Hom. Hymns, trag. et al.; also Aristarch. Sam. 382, 10; ins, pap; En 23:2; EpArist; Philo; Jos., Ant. 17, 110, C. Ap. 2, 206) **to be deficient or inadequate in respect to someth., *leave off*** ἀπό τινος *fr. someth.* (= perh. *leave out of consideration*) B 4:9. μὴ ἐλλείπητε μηδενὶ ἑαυτῶν *do not fail, as far as you are concerned, in any respect* 21:8. Abs. μὴ ἐλλείπητε *do not fail* 21:2.—S. DELG s.v. λείπω.

ἔλλειψις, εως, ἡ (s. prec. entry; since Democr. fgm. 102 and Pla.; Philo; Just., A II, 1, 2) **falling short of someth., *failing*** δίχα ἐλλείψεως *without failing* 1 Cl 20:10.—S. DELG s.v. λείπω.

Ἕλλην, ηνος, ὁ (s. Ἑλλάς; Hdt.+)—❶ **a pers. of Greek language and culture, *Greek*** (opp. βάρβαρος [ANikolaidis, Ἑλληνικός–βαρβαρικός, Plutarch on Greek and Barbarian Characteristics: WienerStud n.s. 20, '86, 229–44] as Thu. 1, 1, 2 et al.; TestSol 6:8 PL; Philo, Ebr. 193 al.; Jos., Ant. 4, 12 al.; Just., D. 117, 5; Tat. 21, 3; s. UWilcken, Hellenen u. Barbaren: NJklA 17, 1906, 457–71; JJüthner, Hell. u. Bar. 1923; HRiesenfeld, ConNeot 9, '44, 1ff) **Ro 1:14** (cultured Romans affected interest in things Greek and would therefore recognize themselves under this term).

❷ in the broader sense, **all persons who came under the influence of Greek, as distinguished from Israel's, culture**

ⓐ ***gentile, polytheist, Greco-Roman*** (2 Macc 4:36; 11:2; 3 Macc 3:8; 4 Macc 18:20; ViJon 1 [p. 82, 15 Sch.]; SibOr 5, 265; Praxagoras [hist. IV AD]: 219 T 1, 8 [Phot., Bibl. 62, 8:219] Jac. τὴν θρησκείαν Ἕλλην; apolog.) **J 7:35; Ac 9:29 v.l.** and **11:20 v.l.** (both for Ἑλληνιστάς); **16:1, 3; 21:28; 1 Cor 1:22; Gal 2:3;** PtK 2 p. 14, 1 and 7; p. 15, 7; Dg 1; 3:3; 5:17. The expr. Ἰουδαῖοι καὶ Ἕλληνες, which clearly indicates Israel's advantages fr. Judean perspective, embraces a broad range of nationalities, with Ἕλλην focusing on the polytheistic aspect: **Ac 14:1; 18:4; 19:10, 17; 20:21; Ro 1:16; 2:9f; 3:9; 10:12; 1 Cor 1:24; 10:32; 12:13; Gal 3:28; Col 3:11** (CPJ 33, 6f=Mitt-Wilck. 55, 6 [III BC] παρὰ τῶν Ἰουδαίων καὶ τῶν Ἑλλήνων does not mean to indicate that Judeans have any special privilege [despite the fact that Ἰ. comes before Ἑ.]. Here the expression expresses gentile perspective. Cp. also Epict. 2, 9, 19 τί ὑποκρίνῃ Ἰουδαῖον ὢν Ἕλλην=why do you play the part of a Judean, when you are actually a Greek?).

ⓑ used of non-Israelites/gentiles who expressed an interest in the cultic life of Israel (cp. Jos., Bell. 7, 45) **J 12:20.** οἱ σεβόμενοι Ἕλληνες *God-fearing gentiles* **Ac 17:4.**—On the use of the art. s. B-D-F §262, 2=Rehkopf §262, 3.—LWeniger, Jesus u. d. Griechen: NJklA 41, 1918, 477–80; JLeipoldt, Jesu Verh. zu Griech. u. Juden '41; B. 1489.—Frisk s.v. Ἑλλάς. DELG s.v. Ἕλληνες. M-M. EDNT. TW. Sv.

Ἑλληνικός, ή, όν (Aeschyl., Hdt. et al.; ins; UPZ 108, 30; PVindobBosw 7, 17; LXX; EpArist 38; Philo; Jos., Ant. 12, 240; 263) **pert. to being Greek in nature, *Greek*** **Lk 23:38 v.l.;** ἐν τῇ Ἑ. (sc. γλώσσῃ) *in the Greek language* **Rv 9:11.**—Frisk s.v. Ἑλλάς. DELG s.v. Ἕλληνες. TW. Sv.

Ἑλληνίς, ίδος, ἡ (Pind., trag., Thu. et al.; ins; PGiss 36, 10; 2 Macc 6:8)—❶ **Greek in language and culture, *Greek*** as adj. (opp. βάρβαρος) πόλις (Nicol. Dam.: 90 fgm. 136, 10 Jac.; Ael. Aristid. 24, 29 K.=44 p. 833 D.; Jos., Ant. 17, 320; 18, 377 al.; Just., A I, 33, 7 τῇ Ἑ. διαλέκτῳ; Tat. 37, 1 εἰς Ἑ. ... φώνην; contrast Just., A I, 31, 4 Ἑλλάδα φ.) *with Greek heritage* Dg 5:4.—γυνή **Ac 17:12.;** the woman mentioned **Mk 7:26** may be in this same category, but s. 2.

❷ **a Greek-oriented woman alien to Israel's life, *Greek (polytheist),*** subst. ἡ Ἑ. *Greek* (from Israel's perspective) **Mk**

7:26, w. focus on the woman's religious interest, but s. 1.—S. Συροφοινίκισσα and Χαναναῖος. Frisk s.v. Ἑλλάς. DELG s.v. Ἕλληνες. M-M. TW.

Ἑλληνιστής, οῦ, ὁ one who uses the Greek language, *Hellenist,* spec. a Greek-speaking Israelite in contrast to one speaking a Semitic lang. (TestSol 6:8 A; Chrysost., Hom. 14 on Ac 6:1 and Hom. 21 on Ac 9:29 ed. Montf. IX 111 and 169) **Ac 6:1; 9:29; 11:20.**—Zahn, Einl. I 41; 51; GWetter, ARW 21, 1922, 410ff; HCadbury: Beginn. I/5, '33, 59–74; EBlackman, ET 48, '37, 524f; CMoule, ET 70, '58/59, 100–102; MSimon, St. Stephen and the Hellenists in the Primitive Church, '58; Haenchen ad loc. S. Ἕλλην 2.—Frisk s.v. Ἑλλάς. DELG s.v. Ἕλληνες. TW.

Ἑλληνιστί adv., **pert. to using the Greek language, *in Greek, in the Greek language*** (X., An. 7, 6, 8; pap [Mayser 457; PGiss 36, 6]; Philo; Joseph.; loanw. in rabb.) (w. Ἑβραϊστί, Ῥωμαϊστί; cp. Jos., Ant. 14, 191) **J 19:20.** Ἑ. γινώσκειν *understand Greek* **Ac 21:37.** Schürer III 142–44.—Frisk s.v. Ἑλλάς. DELG s.v. Ἕλληνες. M-M. TW.

ἐλλογέω (ἐν+λέγω; this is the regular form [s. Nägeli 48: exx. fr. ins, pap]; formations like ἐλλόγα **Phlm 18** and ἐλλογᾶται **Ro 5:13 v.l.** arose through confusion of the inflectional types -εῖν and -ᾶν [B-D-F §90; Mlt-H. 196; 198; 307]) **to charge with a financial obligation, *charge to the account of someone*** τινί, commercial t.t. (=ἐν λόγῳ τιθέναι 'to put into an account', s. λόγος 2a; PRyl 243, 11 [II AD]; BGU 140, 31f; PStras 32, 10 ἵνα οὕτως αὐτῷ ἐνλογηθῇ) **Phlm 18.** Sin οὐκ ἐλλογεῖται **Ro 5:13.**—S. DELG s.v. λέγω B2. M-M. TW.

ἐλλόγιμος, ον (s. prec. entry; Hdt. et al.) prim. 'pert to someth. being taken into account or special consideration', hence

❶ ***included*** ἐντεταγμένος καὶ ἐ. εἰς τ. ἀριθμὸν τῶν σῳζομένων *enrolled and included in the number of those who are saved* 1 Cl 58:2. μικροὶ καὶ ἐλλόγιμοι *small, but included* 57:2.

❷ ***reputable, eminent*** (SIG 803, 8; OGI 56, 9; Philo, Mos. 1, 266) ἄνδρες ἐ. (Philostrat., Vi. Apoll. p. 50, 31; Herm. Wr. 12, 6; Celsus 1, 21) 1 Cl 44:3. Superl. ἐλλογιμώτατος *highly regarded* ἄνδρες (in sg. Philostrat., Vi. Apoll. p. 106, 32; 112, 26; honorific in Byz. pap) 62:3.—DELG s.v. λέγω B2. Sv.

Ἐλμαδάμ, ὁ and v.l. Ἐλμωδάμ (also Ἐλμασάμ indecl.) ***Elmadam,*** in the genealogy of Jesus **Lk 3:28.**

ἑλόμενος s. αἱρέω.

ἐλπίζω Att. fut. ἐλπιῶ; 1 aor. ἤλπισα; pf. ἤλπικα (B-D-F §341) (s. ἐλπίς; trag., Hdt.+)

❶ **to look forward to someth., with implication of confidence about someth. coming to pass, *hope, hope for*** (cp. Judg 20:36; PsSol 17:33. both in the sense 'rely on, trust')

ⓐ abs. *hope (for)* (Philo, Det. Pot. Ins. 138 τὸ ἐλπίζειν) **2 Cor 8:5;** B 12:7; 2 Cl 11:5; pres. pass. ptc. ἐλπιζόμενα *what we hope for* (Polyaenus 3, 9, 11 τὰ ἐλπιζόμενα) **Hb 11:1.**

ⓑ w. indication of what is hoped for: in acc. (Is 38:18; Wsd 2:22) πάντα **1 Cor 13:7.** ὃ γὰρ βλέπει τις ἐλπίζει **Ro 8:24;** cp. vs. **25.** (W. εἰς: Sir 2:9 εἰς ἀγαθά; PsSol 15:1 εἰς βοήθειαν . . . τοῦ θεοῦ.) W. perf. inf. **2 Cor 5:11;** B 17:1. W. ὅτι foll. (Polyb. 3, 63, 7; Arrian, Alex. An. 1, 4, 7; POxy 1672, 7 [c. 40 AD]; Philo, Leg. All. 3, 85) the deliverer of Israel **Lk 24:21.** W. acc. and pres. inf. (Just., D. 32, 2 ἐλπίζων τινὰ ἐξ ὑμῶν δύνασθαι εὑρεθῆναι) Hm 12, 6, 4. W. the connotation of desire (Appian, Bell. Civ. 2, 1 §3 ἐ. περὶ ἁπάντων) ἤλπιζέν τι σημεῖον ἰδεῖν *he was hoping to see a sign* **Lk 23:8.** ἐλπίζει καταντῆσαι *hopes to attain* **Ac 26:7.**

ⓒ w. indication of the pers. or thing on whom (which) hope is based *put one's confidence in someone or someth.*: τινί *in someth.* (Thu. 3, 97, 2 τῇ τύχῃ) τῷ ὀνόματι **Mt 12:21;** εἴς τι (Is 51:5): εἰς τ. οἰκοδομήν *put one's hope* (or, *confidence*) in the building (the temple) B 16:1. εἴς τινα *in someone* (Herodian 7, 10, 1; cp. Ps 118:114; Just., D., 8, 3 εἰς ἄνθρωπον): Moses **J 5:45;** PEg[2] 14. εἰς θεόν (Ps 144:15; PIand 11, 2; SibOr 5, 284; cp. Jos., Bell. 6, 99) **1 Pt 3:5.** εἰς Χριστόν IPhld 11:2; cp. 5:2. εἴς τινα w. ὅτι foll. **2 Cor 1:10.** For this, ἔν τινι (Ps 55:5 B; Judg 9:26 B; 4 Km 18:5; Did., Gen. 98, 5) **Mt 12:21 v.l.; 1 Cor 15:19.** For this, ἐπί τινα: ἐπὶ τ. θεόν (Ps 41:6, 12 al.; Philo; Just., D. 101, 1) **1 Ti 5:5;** cp. D 4:10; 1 Cl 11:1; 12:7; B 6:3; 19:7; Hm 12, 5, 2 (Just. D. 102, 6 ἐπὶ θεόν). ἐπὶ κύριον 1 Cl 16:16 (Ps 21:9); 22:8 (Ps 31:10). ἐπὶ θεόν . . . ἐπὶ Χριστόν AcPl Ha 2, 29f. ἐπὶ Ἰησοῦν B 6:9; 8:5 (cp. Just., D. 47, 2 ἐπὶ τοῦτον τὸν Χριστόν). ἐπί τι (Ps 51:10; Synes., Ep. 58 p. 202d ἐπὶ τὴν ἐκκλησίαν ἤλπισε): ἐπὶ τὴν χάριν **1 Pt 1:13.** ἐπὶ τὸ ὄνομα θεοῦ 1 Cl 59:3; B 16:8. ἐπὶ τὸν σταυρόν 11:8. For this, ἐπί τινι (pers.: Ps 7:2; 15:1; 21:5 al.; as v.l. TestJob 37:1 and 5; also ἐπί τινος 37:1; thing: Appian, Maced. 9 §7 ἐπὶ τῷδε=on this account; Ps 12:6; Is 26:8; 42:4) **1 Ti 4:10; 6:17; Ro 15:12** (Is 11:10); B 12:2f.

❷ **to look forward to someth. in view of the measures one takes to ensure fulfillment, *expect,*** w. aor. inf. foll. (Thu. 2, 80, 1; Agathias Hist. 3, 5 p. 243f D.; En 103:11; Philo, Migr. Abr. 195) παρ' ὧν ἐλπίζετε λαβεῖν *from whom you expect to receive again* **Lk 6:34;** cp. 2 Cl 1:2. **Ro 15:24; 1 Cor 16:7; Phil 2:19, 23; 1 Ti 3:14; 2J 12; 3J 14;** IEph 1:2; IRo 1:1; B 1:3; Hs 8, 9, 4; 8, 11, 2. W. ὅτι foll. (cp. reff. in 1b) **Ac 24:26; 2 Cor 1:13; 13:6; Phlm 22;** Hs 8, 2, 9. (W. fut. inf. Just., D. 2, 6.) (Besides the mngs. 'hope, expect' as positive aspect, Gk. lit. also includes the corresp. neg. aspect 'foresee, fear, anticipate', e.g. punishment: Diod. S. 13, 43, 1 the Aegestaeans, anticipating punishment [ἤλπιζον . . . τιμωρίαν δώσειν] from the Sicilian Greeks, resolved to withdraw from disputed territory; contempt: Chion, Ep. 9; sorrow: Procop. Soph., Ep. 140; a misfortune: Lucian, Dial. Deor. 25, 1, Gall. 25, end).—DELG s.v. ἔλπομαι. M-M. TW. Spicq.

ἐλπίς, ίδος, ἡ (s. ἐλπίζω; Hom.+ 'expectation, hope', also 'foreboding' Aeschyl. et al.)

❶ **the looking forward to someth. with some reason for confidence respecting fulfillment, *hope, expectation:***

ⓐ gener. *hope, expectation, prospect* ἐπ' ἐλπίδι (for the spelling s. 1bα below) *in hope* (Ps.-Pla., Alc. 1, 105a ἐπὶ τίνι ἐλπίδι ζῇς; Eur., Herc. Fur. 804; X., Mem. 2, 1, 18; Diod. S. 13, 21, 7; Jos., Ant. 4, 36) **1 Cor 9:10a** in a quotation (source unknown; cp. Sir. 6:19). παρ' ἐλπίδα *contrary to* (all human) *expectation* (Aeschyl., Ag. 899; Aeneas Tact. 1020; Lycophron vs. 535; Dionys. Hal. 6, 25; Appian, Bell. Civ. 3, 22 §85; Philo, Mos. 1, 250; Jos., Bell. 3, 183, Vi. 380; Just., D. 2, 5) **Ro 4:18.** W. objective gen. (Diod. S. 16, 55, 4 τῆς εὐεργεσίας ἐλπίς; Appian, Celt. 1 §9 ἐλπὶς ἀναβιώσεως; Jos., Vi. 325 ἐ. κέρδους; Just., D. 8, 3 ἐ. . . . ἀμείνονος μοίρας) ἐλπὶς τ. ἐργασίας *hope of gain* **Ac 16:19;** μετανοίας IEph 10:1; Hs 6, 2, 4; 8, 7, 2; 8, 10, 2. W. gen. of the inf. (Dositheus 19, 6 ἐ. τοῦ δύνασθαι; Ath. 33, 1 τοῦ συνέσεσθαι θεῷ) τοῦ σῴζεσθαι **Ac 27:20;** τοῦ μετέχειν **1 Cor 9:10b.** ἐλπίδα ἔχειν (oft. LXX and non-bibl. wr.) w. gen. of the inf. τοῦ μετανοῆσαι Hs 8, 6, 5. τῇ ἐ. ἐσώθημεν *we are saved* (or *possess salvation*) *only in hope/anticipation* (not yet in reality) **Ro 8:24** (Diod. S. 20, 40, 1 περιεβάλετο ταῖς ἐλπίσι μείζονα δυναστείαν=he entertained prospects of control over a larger realm). ἡ ἐ. ἡμῶν βεβαία ὑπὲρ ὑμῶν *our expectations* *involving you are well founded* (Paul is confident that the Cor. will hold out under oppression in the future as they have in the past) **2 Cor 1:7.** Of the confidence that the Jews placed in their temple ματαία ἡ ἐ. αὐτῶν B 16:2 (on empty hope, s. Reader, Polemo 313).

ⓑ esp. pert. to matters spoken of in God's promises, *hope*

α. without specif. ref. to Christian hope ἐπ' ἐλπίδι (for the spelling ἐφ' ἐλπίδι s. B-D-F §14; Rob. 224 and cp. an ins fr. Asia Minor: PASA II, 1888, p. 89 ln. 15 ἐπ' ἐλπίδος and ln. 26 ἐφ' ἐλπίδος) *in (the) hope* (Diod. S. 13, 21, 7 ἐπ' ἐλπίδι [σωτηρίας]) **Ro 8:20** (B-D-F §235, 2); cp. **Tit 1:2.** ἐπ' ἐλπίδι ἐπίστευσεν *full of hope he believed* (in God) **Ro 4:18.** The ἐπ' ἐ. of **Ac 2:26** could also be understood in this way, but it is also prob. that in this quot. fr. Ps 15:9 the OT mng. *in safety* (Judg 18:7 B, 27 B; Hos 2:20; Pr 1:33) is correct, as 1 Cl 57:7 (Pr 1:33), unless, with Lat., Syr., and Copt. transl. and Clem. Al., Strom. 2, 22 πεποιθώς is to be added. Of Israel's messianic hope **Ac 23:6** (ἐ. καὶ ἀνάστασις for ἐ. τῆς ἀν. [obj. gen.] as 2 Macc 3:29 ἐ. καὶ σωτηρία); **26:6; 28:20.** In imagery of one who combines γνῶσις with interest in ζωή Dg 12:6.

β. of Christian expectation: abs. **Ro 5:4f; 12:12; 15:13; 1 Cor 13:13** (cp. Pol. 3:3; on the triad: faith, hope, love s. on ἀγάπη 1aα; s. also WWeis, ZNW 84, '93, 196–217); **Hb 3:6; 6:11; 10:23; 1 Pt 3:15;** Agr. 7; 2 Cl 17:7; IEph 1:2; IMg 7:1; expectation of resurrection 1 Cl 27:1. ἐ. ἀγαθή (Pla., Phd. 67c; X., Mem. 2, 1, 18 et al.; FCumont, Lux Perpetua '49 p. 401–5 with numerous reff., including some from the mystery religions [IG V/2 p. 63: 64/61 BC]; μετὰ ἀγαθῆς ἐ. Hippol., Ref. 4, 49, 3; cp. ἐ. ἔχειν . . . ἀρίστας Orig., C. Cels. 4, 27, 14) **2 Th 2:16** (POtzen, ZNW 49, '58, 283–85); ἐ. κρείττων **Hb 7:19;** ἐ. ζῶσα **1 Pt 1:3;** cp. εἰς ἐ. B. 11:8. τὸ κοινὸν τῆς ἐ. *the common hope* 1 Cl 51:1; cp. κοινὴ ἐ. IPh 5:2; καινότης ἐλπίδος *new hope* IMg 9:1. W. subj. gen. **Phil 1:20;** ἐ. τῶν ἐκλεκτῶν 1 Cl 58:2; cp. 57:2. W. obj. gen., which designates the obj. of the hope (Ps.-Callisth. 1, 18, 1 ἱλαρὸς ἐπὶ τῇ τοῦ τέκνου ἐλπίδι=glad because of hope for the son; τῆς ἀναστάσεως Iren. 4, 18, 5 [Harv. II 208, 2]; Orig., C. Cels. 3, 3, 9; Did., Gen. 216, 16) ἐπ' ἐ. τῆς ἐπαγγελίας *because of hope in the promise* **Ac 26:6,** cp. vs. **7;** ἐ. ζωῆς αἰωνίου **Tit 1:2; 3:7** (Ath. 33, 1); cp. B 1:4, 6; Hs 9, 26, 2; ἐ. τῆς δόξης τ. θεοῦ **Ro 5:2;** cp. **Col 1:27;** ἐ. σωτηρίας (cp. Aeneas Tact. ln. 14; Lucian, Abdic. 31; En 98:14; Philo, Leg. ad Gai. 329; Jos., Bell. 3, 194) **1 Th 5:8;** 2 Cl 1:7. ἐλπίδα δικαιοσύνης ἀπεκδεχόμεθα **Gal 5:5** is also obj. gen., since it is a blending of the two expressions 'we await righteousness' and 'we have expectation of righteousness' (cp. Job 2:9a προσδεχόμενος τὴν ἐλπίδα τῆς σωτηρίας μου); ἐ. τοῦ κυρίου ἡμῶν **1 Th 1:3** prob. belongs here also: *hope in our Lord.*—The gen. can also give the basis for the expectation: ἐ. τοῦ εὐαγγελίου *hope that is based on the gospel* **Col 1:23;** ἐ. τῆς κλήσεως *the hope that is given w. the calling* **Eph 1:18; 4:4;** ἐ. τῆς πίστεως *hope that faith affords* B 4:8; ὁ θεὸς τῆς ἐ. **Ro 15:13.** Sim. ἐ. εἰς (Plut., Galba 1061 [19, 6]; Achilles Tat. 6, 17, 5): ἐ. εἰς θεόν (εἰς τὸν θεόν Did., Gen. 150, 26) *hope in God* or *directed towards God* **1 Pt 1:21** (cp. AcThom 28 [Aa II/2, 145, 4]); εἰς τ. Ἰησοῦν B 11:11; cp. ἐ. ἐν (αὐτῷ Diod. S. 17, 26, 2): ἐν τῷ ὀνόματι αὐτοῦ **Mt 12:21 v.l.** ἐπὶ λίθον ἡ ἐ.; *is (our) hope based on a stone?* (w. ref. to Is 28:16) B 6:3.—As obj. of ἔχω: ἔχειν ἐλπίδα **Ro 15:4; 2 Cor 3:12** (cp. Just., D. 141, 3); ἐ. μὴ ἔχοντες (Diod. S. 21, 12, 1 μηδεμίαν ἔχειν ἐλπίδα σωτηρίας) **Eph 2:12; 1 Th 4:13;** Hv 3, 11, 3; s 9, 14, 3; οὐκ ἔχουσιν ἐλπίδα (Wsd 3:18) Hv 1, 1, 9; ἀπώλεσάς σου τὴν πᾶσαν ἐ. 33, 7. W. ἐπί τινι *in someone* **1J 3:3** (cp. Appian, Bell. Civ. 3, 86 §354 ἐφ' ἑνί; Lucian, Somn. 2; Ps 61:8; Is 26:3f; ἐπὶ τῇ μετανοίᾳ Orig., C. Cels. 3, 65, 17); likew. εἴς τινα (Thu. 3, 14, 1;—Appian, Liby. 51 §223 ἐλπίδα τῆς σωτηρίας ἔχειν ἔν τινι=place a hope of safety in someone) **Ac 24:15;** πρός τινα ibid. v.l. The obj. of the hope follows in the aor. inf. **2 Cor 10:15;** in the acc. w. inf. **Ac 24:15;** w. ὅτι **Ro 8:20f** (v.l. διότι [q.v. 4]); **Phil 1:20.**

❷ **that which is the basis for hoping,** ***(foundation of) hope*** (ἐλπὶς . . . σύ, ὁ θεός PsSol 15:1; Thu. 3, 57, 4 ὑμεῖς, ὦ Λακεδαιμόνιοι, ἡ μόνη ἐλπίς; Plut., Mor. 169c; Oenom. in Eus., PE 5, 23, 5: for the Athenians in the Persian Wars, σωτηρίας ἐλπὶς μόνος ὁ θεός=God was their only hope for deliverence; IG III, 131, 1; Jer 17:7) of a Christian community **1 Th 2:19;** of Christ, our hope **1 Ti 1:1** (sim. POxy 3239 [II AD] of Isis; New Docs 2, 77; EJudge, TynBull 35, '84, 8); cp. **Col 1:27;** IEph 21:2; IPhld 11:2; IMg 11; ISm 10:2; ITr ins; 2:2; Pol 8:1.

❸ **that for which one hopes,** ***hope, something hoped for*** (Vi. Aesopi G 8 P. ἀπὸ θεῶν λήμψεσθαι ἐλπίδας) ἐ. βλεπομένη οὐκ ἔστιν ἐ. *something hoped for, when it is seen, is no longer hoped for*=one cannot hope for what one already has **Ro 8:24.** διὰ τ. ἐλπίδα τὴν ἀποκειμένην ὑμῖν ἐν τ. οὐρανοῖς *because of what you hope for, which is stored up for you in the heavens* **Col 1:5;** προσδεχόμενοι τ. μακαρίαν ἐ. *waiting for the blessed hope* **Tit 2:13** (cp. 2 Macc 7:14 τὰς ὑπὸ τοῦ θεοῦ προσδοκᾶν ἐλπίδας and Aristot. EN 1, 9, 10 οἱ δὲ λεγόμενοι διὰ τὴν ἐλπίδα μακαρίζονται of children who may be called fortunate in the present only because of latent promise). ἡ προκειμένη ἐ. **Hb 6:18** (cp. Just., D. 35, 2 ἐν τῇ ἐ. κατηγγελμένῃ ὑπ' αὐτοῦ).—PVolz, D. Eschatol. der jüd. Gemeinde '34, 91ff; JdeGuibert, Sur l'emploi d' ἐλπίς et ses synonymes dans le NT: RSR 4, 1913, 565–96; APott, D. Hoffen im NT 1915; WGrossouw, L'espérance dans le NT: RB 61, '54, 508–32; DDenton, SJT 34, '81, 313–20 (link w. ὑπομονή).—B. 1164. Schmidt, Syn. III 583–90. DELG s.v. ἔλπομαι. M-M. EDNT. TW. Spicq. Sv.

Ἐλύμας, α, ὁ *Elymas* (PKatz recommends Ἐλυμᾶς. In Diod. S. [20, 17, 1; 18, 3] as name of a Libyan king Αἰλύμας) a magician of Cyprus **Ac 13:8,** who was also called Barjesus acc. to vs. 6. Ac obviously considers the two names to be linguistically equiv. to each other; it is hardly correct to assume, w. some, that vs. **8** means to say that the word Elymas=μάγος (but s. Haenchen, Acts, ad loc.). Wendt, e.g., holds that the Arab. verb ᶜ*alima*=recognize, gain insight into someth., whence ᶜ*alîm*=magician, one who tries to see into the future. Dalman (Gramm.[2] 162) finds in Ἐ. Ἐλυμαῖος=Ἐλαμίτης; Grimme interprets it as 'astrologer', Burkitt as ὁ λοιμός *pestilence* (s. λοιμός II, 2), Harris, Zahn, Clemen and Wlh. prefer the rdg. Ἕτοιμας, from D, and identify the magician w. the sorcerer Ἄτομος in Jos., Ant. 20, 142. See RHarris, Exp. 1902, I 189ff; FBurkitt, JTS 4, 1903, 127ff; CClemen, Paulus 1904, I 222f; TZahn, NKZ 15, 1904, 195ff, D. Urausgabe der AG des Luk. 1916, 149f; 350ff; HGrimme, OLZ 12, 1909, 207ff; Wlh., Kritische Analyse der AG 1914, 24.—M-M.

ἐλωΐ (אֱלָהִי; Ἐλωΐ TestSol 6:8) Aram. for ἠλί, ἠλ(ε)ί ***my God*** **Mt 27:46 v.l.; Mk 15:34.** Cp. EKautzsch, Gramm. d. Bibl.-Aram. 1884, 11; Wlh. on Mk; Dalman, Jesus 184–87; FDanker, ZNW 61, '70, 52f (lit.). BHHW I, 395f.—M-M.

ἔμαθον s. μανθάνω.

ἐμαυτοῦ, ῆς reflexive pron. of the first pers. (on the origin and use of this word, found also in ins, pap, LXX; TestJud 19:4; Jos., Vi. 361; Just., Tat., Ath. s. Kühner-Bl. I 596ff; also B-D-F §283; W-S. §22, 11; Rob. 687–90). In gen., dat., acc. ***myself***

ⓐ as possessive gen. w. a noun τὸ ἐμαυτοῦ σύμφορον *my own advantage* (opp. τὸ τῶν πολλῶν) **1 Cor 10:33.**

ⓑ w. a verb ἐμφανίσω ἐμαυτόν **J 14:21.** οὐδὲ ἐμαυτὸν ἠξίωσα *I did not consider myself worthy* **Lk 7:7.** συγχαίρω ἐμαυτῷ *I rejoice with (=congratulate) myself* B 1:3. δοξάσω ἐμαυτόν **J 8:54.** ἁγιάζω ἐμαυτόν **17:19.** μετρῶ ἐμαυτόν ITr 4:1. ἥγημαι ἐμαυτὸν μακάριον **Ac 26:2.** ἔδοξα ἐμαυτῷ (Aristoph., Vesp. 1265; Demosth. 18, 225) *I once believed* vs. **9;** σύνοιδά τι ἐμαυτῷ *I am aware of someth.* **1 Cor 4:4;** cp. B 1:4. πᾶσιν ἐμαυτὸν ἐδούλωσα *I made myself a slave to all* **1 Cor 9:19.**

ⓒ freq. used w. prep. ἀπ᾿ ἐμαυτοῦ *of my own accord, on my own authority* **J 5:30; 7:17, 28; 8:28, 42; 14:10;** *of my own free will* **10:18.** ἐξ ἐμαυτοῦ *on my own authority* **12:49.** εἰς ἐμαυτόν for εἰς ἐμέ **1 Cor 4:6.** ἐν ἐμαυτῷ *to myself* Hv 1, 2, 1; 3, 1, 5; 4, 1, 4. περὶ ἐμαυτοῦ **J 8:14, 18; Ac 24:10.** πρὸς ἐμαυτόν **J 12:32; 14:3;** *with me* (Aristoph., Ran. 53) **Phlm 13.** ὑπὲρ ἐμαυτοῦ **2 Cor 12:5.** ὑπ᾿ ἐμαυτόν *under my authority* **Mt 8:9; Lk 7:8.**

ⓓ referring back to the subj. of the governing clause θέλω πάντας ἀνθρώπους εἶναι ὡς καὶ ἐμαυτόν *I wish that everyone were as I am* **1 Cor 7:7.**—M-M.

ἐμβαίνω 2 aor. ἐνέβην, ptc. ἐμβάς (s. βαίνω; Hom.+; ins, pap, LXX, TestJud 9:6 v.l.; ApcSed, Joseph.; Just., A I, 61, 5 εἰς τὰς μήτρας) gener. 'to step into an area'; in our lit. mostly of boarding water transport ***embark*** (Ael. Aristid. 46 p. 228 D.; Mitt-Wilck. I/2, 1 II, 17f [III BC] εἰς ναῦς; Jos., Vi. 164; 304) εἰς (τὸ) πλοῖον (X., An. 1, 4, 7; 1 Macc 15:37) **Mt 8:23; 9:1; 13:2; 14:22; 15:39; Mk 4:1; 5:18; 6:45; 8:10** (cp. vs. **13,** where εἰς [τὸ] πλοῖον is to be supplied, and is found as v.l.—Similar expansion Dio Chrys. 2, 22); **Lk 8:22** (v.l. ἀνέβη P[75] et al.), **37;** cp. **5:3; J 6:17; 21:3; Ac 21:6 v.l.;** AcPl Ha 7, 18; εἰς τὰ πλοιάρια **J 6:24** (X., An. 1, 3, 17 εἰς τὰ πλοῖα). After an omission ὁ κύριος ἐμβαίνει AcPl Ha 7, 22.—Of entry into a pool *go in, step in* (cp. Jos., Ant. 5, 18) **J 5:3 (4) v.l.**—M-M.

ἐμβάλλω fut. ἐμβαλῶ; 2 aor. ἐνέβαλον, inf. ἐμβαλεῖν. Pass.: fut. ἐμβληθήσομαι LXX; pf. ἐμβέβληται Job 18:8 (Hom.+) **to cause to be put in a specific area, freq. in the sense of enforced movement, *throw*** (in, into) τινά *someone* εἰς τὴν γέενναν **Lk 12:5;** εἴς τινα τόπον κρημνώδη *drove (the sheep) toward some craggy place* Hs 6, 2, 6 (UPZ 70, 8 [152/151 BC] ἐνβέβληκαν [sc. οἱ θεοί] ὑμᾶς εἰς ὕλην μεγάλην; Just. A II, 2, 10 εἰς δεσμά. But ἐ. can also be used without connotation of pressure *send somewhere* PPetr II, 41, 2 [III BC]; BGU 1209, 14 [I BC]; Jos., C. Ap. 1, 257).—*Put* or *set* (in, into) (Didymus [I BC / I AD] ed. Schmidt p. 258, 58; Leo 1, 10 conceal a message; SIG 1170, 16 μέλι ἐ. εἰς τὸ γάλα) *set a stone into the foundations* B 6:2 (Is 28:16). καρδίας σαρκίνας 6:14. Pass. *be set* εἰς τὸν τόπον *in the place* Hs 9, 6, 5f.—M-M.

ἐμβαπτίζω (s. βαπτίζω; Nicander [II BC] fgm. 70, 12 [in Athen. 4, 11, 133d]; Plut., Sulla 466 [21, 8]) = next entry, **to immerse or plunge partially in a liquid for a brief time, *dip in/into.*** Mid. *dip* for oneself (s. ἐμβάπτω) **Mk 14:20** D.—S. DELG s.v. βάπτω.

ἐμβάπτω 1 aor. ἐνέβαψα (s. βάπτω; Hipponax 36; Aristoph., X. et al.; Hymn to Demeter in PSI 1282, 60; TestZeb 4:9)=prec. entry ***dip*** (in, into) τὶ ἔν τινι **Mt 26:23;** cp. **J 13:26b** P[66] et al. Mid. *dip* for oneself (Aristoph. fgm. 151 [in Athen. 9, 367b]) abs. (sc. the hand, or what the hand holds) **Mk 14:20** (cp. Athen. 6, 345e). βάψας τὸ ψώμιον . . . ἐμβάψας τὸ ψωμίον **J 13:26 v.l.**

ἐμβατεύω (ἐν + βαίνω; Aeschyl. et al.; ins; pap; LXX; TestSol 1, 1 D ἐμβαπτεύσας) is found in our lit. only **Col 2:18** ἃ ἑόρακεν ἐμβατεύων, a passage whose interpr. is much disputed. The word ranges in mng. as follows:

❶ **set foot upon, *enter, visit*** (since Aeschyl, Pers. 449; Jos., Ant. 2, 265; 1 Macc 12:25; 13:20 al.) e.g., an oracular chamber, s. FFrancis, The Background of EMBATEUEIN (Col 2:18) in Legal Papyri and Oracle Inscriptions: Conflict at Colossae, ed., FFrancis and WMeeks '73, 197–207, esp. 201. S. 4 below. The phrase ἃ ἑόρακεν ἐμβατεύων could then =*entering an oracle for interpretation of what he has seen.*

❷ **come into possession of, *acquire*** (Eur., Demosth., pap), even by force (Jos 19:49, 51).

❸ **investigate closely, *enter into*** a subj., to investigate it closely, ***go into detail*** (2 Macc 2:30; Philo, Plant. 80 Wendl. v.l.), hence in **Col 2:18** prob. *entering at length upon the tale of what one has seen* in a vision (ANock, JBL 52, '33, 132) and thus justifying the approach taken to heavenly messengers.

❹ Three ins of Asia Minor [II AD], which refer to the Apollo of Klaros (the wording in question is found in MDibelius, D. Isisweihe bei Apuleius=SAHeidelberg 1917, 4 p. 33f; one of these ins also in OGI 530; cp. ln. 15), show that ἐ. was applied to aspects of the mystery religions. Various views have been presented: *one who enters* (the sanctuary) *which he saw* (in ecstasy) (s. also Clemen 340f) or *taking his stand on what he has seen* in the mysteries (M-M). AFridrichsen, ZNW 21, 1922, 135–37 connects the words w. what follows: *puffed up without reason by what he saw when he was initiated* (but s. VLeinieks, The City of Dionysos, '96, 145: ἐνεβάτευσεν in the Klaros ins does not mean 'entered the mysteries' but rather 'entered the oracular chamber for consultation' [citing Francis, s. 1 above]; s. also Nock, cited in 3). Cp. RYates, ET 97, '85, 12–15 (participation in angelic liturgy).—Field, Notes 197f; SEitrem, Studia Theologica 2, '48, 90–94; SLyonnet, Col 2:18 et les mystères de Apollon Clarien, Biblica 43, '62, 417–35: 'investigate, examine thoroughly'. For a summary of views s. Hermeneia comm., Col. and Phlm, '71, 118–21.—The conviction that the text must be corrupt led to var. conjectures (their history in RHarris, Sidelights on NT Research 1909, 198f).—DELG s.v. βαίνω p. 157. M-M. TW.

ἐμβιβάζω 1 aor. ἐνεβίβασα (causal of ἐμβαίνω q.v.; Thu. et al.; ins, pap, LXX; Jos., Vi. 168) ***put in*** τινὰ εἴς τι *someone* (into) *something* εἰς πλοῖον *cause someone to embark, put someone on board ship* **Ac 27:6.**—S. DELG s.v. βαίνω 3 p. 156. M-M.

ἐμβλέπω impf. ἐνέβλεπον; 1 aor. ἐνέβλεψα; fut. mid. ἐμβλέψομαι LXX (Soph. et al.; pap, LXX, TestSol 5:2 P; JosAs 4:11 cod. A for ἀνέβλεψε; Philo, Joseph.; Just., A I, 15, 1 [for βλέπων **Mt 5:28**]).

❶ **to look at someth. directly and therefore intently, *look at, gaze on*** τινί (Pla., Rep. 10, 608d; Polyb. 15, 28, 3; Sir 42:12; Jos., Bell. 3, 385; 7, 341) *someone* **Mk 10:21, 27; 14:67; Lk 20:17; 22:61; J 1:36, 42;** Hv 3, 8, 2 (most of these pass. read: ἐμβλέψας αὐτῷ or αὐτοῖς λέγει or εἶπεν; cp. X., Cyr. 1, 3, 2 ἐμβλέπων αὐτῷ ἔλεγεν; Syntipas p. 106, 10). ἔμβλεπε τοῖς λοιποῖς *look at the rest* Hs 9, 2, 7. εἴς τι *look at someth.* (Ps.-Pla., Alc. 1, 132e; Ps-Demosth. 34 p. 913, 4; Comp. II 167 J. [Menander, fgm. 538, 2 Kock]; LXX) **Mt 6:26,** if ἐ. is to be taken literally here (s. 2 below); **Ac 1:11;** MPol 9:2. Abs. (X., Mem. 3, 11, 10; Herodas 5, 40; Bel 40 Theod.) **Mt 19:26** (cp. Job 2:10); B 5:10. Abs. also **Ac 22:11,** if the rdg. οὐκ ἐνέβλεπον is tenable. The v.l. οὐδὲν ἔβλεπον has 9:8 in its favor, as well as the fact that the verbs ἐμβ. and β. are not infreq. interchanged in the mss. (cp. **Ac 1:11;** Sir 51:7), and the observation that ἐμβ. **22:11** would have to mean *be able to see;* the latter mng. cannot be established beyond all doubt by ἐνέβλεπεν τηλαυγῶς ἅπαντα **Mk 8:25,** since for this pass. *he could see everything plainly* is no more likely than *he had a clear view of everything* (on the acc. cp. Herodas 6, 44; Anth. Pal. 11, 3; Judg 16:27; SibOr 7, 124).

❷ to give serious thought to something, ***look at, consider,*** fig. ext. of 1, εἴς τι (PSI 542, 16 [III BC]; UPZ 162 III, 7 [117 BC]; PTebt 28, 15 [114 BC]; Is 51:1f; Sir 2:10 al.) ἐ. τοῖς ὄμμασιν τῆς ψυχῆς εἰς τὸ μακρόθυμον αὐτοῦ βούλημα 1 Cl 19:3 (Philo, Sobr. 3 τὸ ψυχῆς ὄμμα … ἐμβλέπον). So perh. also **Mt 6:26** (s. 1 above). W. obj. τοῖς τῆς καρδίας ὀφθαλμοῖς ἐνέβλεπον τὰ … ἀγαθά MPol 2:3.—M-M.

ἐμβριθής, ές (βρίθω 'be heavy'; Hdt.+; BGU 1769, 4 [I BC]; Philo) 'pert. to being weighty', then by ext. of mng. ***dignified, serious*** (Philostrat., Vi. Soph. 2, 14; Damasc., Vi. Isid. 16) ἐμβριθεῖ τῷ προσώπῳ *w. a serious face* MPol 9:2 (Himerius, Or. 48 [=Or. 14], 13 πρόσωπον ἐμβριθές).—DELG s.v. βριαρός.

ἐμβριμάομαι, also ἐμβριμόομαι **Mk 14:5 v.l.; J 11:33 v.l., 38** (s. B-D-F §90; Mlt-H. 198; 201.) fut. 3 pl. ἐμβριμήσονται Da (LXX) 11:30; 1 aor. ἐνεβριμησάμην, pass. ἐνεβριμήθην (βρίμη 'strength', also 'bellowing'; Aeschyl. et al. in the sense 'snort').

❶ insist on someth. sternly, ***warn sternly*** **Mk 1:43** (s. KLake, HTR 16, 1923, 197f); **Mt 9:30.**

❷ As an expr. of anger and displeasure in (Lucian, Necyomant. 20; Ps.-Libanius, Declam. 40 Förster VII p. 336; Ps 7:12 Aq.; Is 17:13 Sym.; cp. LXX La 2:6 ἐμβριμήματι ὀργῆς; ἐμβριμήσεως En 101:7; MartMt 21 [Aa II/1, 247, 3f]) w. dat. of pers. ***scold, censure*** (Da 11:30) **Mk 14:5.** ἐμβρειμ[ησάμενος]| εἶπεν α[ὐτοῖς] *he said to them indignantly* PEg[2] 51f (=ASyn. 27, 40; 83, 26; 150, 106; 254, 79; 257, 22; 280, 45).

❸ to feel strongly about someth., ***be deeply moved*** ἐν ἑαυτῷ **J 11:38** (ἐβριμήσατο P[75]); for this τῷ πνεύματι vs. **33** (on the apparent harshness of expression: MBlack, An Aramaic Approach[3], '67, 240–43).—CBonner, Traces of Thaumaturgic Technique in the Miracles: HTR 20, 1927, 171–81; EBevan, JTS 33, '32, 186–88.—DELG s.v. βρίμη. M-M. TW.

ἐμβριμῶς ***ferociously, furiously*** adv. not otherw. attested, restored ἐμβρ[ιμῶς], w. πικρῶς AcPl Ha 2, 7 (s. ὠρύομαι).—S. DELG s.v. βρίμη.

ἐμβροχή, ῆς, ἡ fig. as medical t.t. ***wet application, cold compress*** (Plut., Mor. p. 42c; Soranus p. 36, 21; Galen: CMG V/9, 1 p. 375, 17; Oribasius, Ecl. 89, 7: CMG VI/2, 2 p. 268, 1) τοὺς παροξυσμοὺς ἐμβροχαῖς παῦε *quiet the attacks of fever w. cold compresses* IPol 2:1.—DELG s.v. βρέχω.

ἐμέω 1 aor. ἤμεσα (Hom. et al.; SIG 1169, 126; Is 19:14) ***vomit, throw up*** (contrasted w. πτύω=spit out: Artem. 1, 33 p. 35, 8) metaph. (Herm. Wr. 7, 1a) τινὰ ἐκ τοῦ στόματος *spew someone from one's mouth* like undrinkable water (cp. TestAsh 7:2 καὶ ἔσεσθε … ὡς ὕδωρ ἄχρηστον; on the emetic character of some Laodicean water supplies s. MRudwick-EGreen, ET 69, '57/58, 176–78; PWood, ibid. 73, '61/62, 263–64; also CHemer, The Letters to the Seven Churches etc. '86, 186–91; s. χλιαρός) **Rv 3:16.**—B. 265. DELG. M-M.

ἐμμαίνομαι to be filled with such anger that one appears to be mad, ***be enraged*** τινί *against someone* (Jos., Ant. 17, 174) περισσῶς ἐμμαινόμενος αὐτοῖς *being furiously enraged at them* **Ac 26:11.**—DELG s.v. μαίνομαι. M-M.

Ἐμμανουήλ, ὁ indecl. (עִמָּנוּ אֵל Is 7:14; 8:8 both MT; Is 7:14 LXX; TestSol; GrBar 4:15 (Christ). Greek Christians spell it Ἐμμανουήλ: Recueil des inscriptions grecques chrétiennes d'Égypte, ed. GLefebvre 1907, 214; 222; POxy 1162, 14 [IV AD]; PUps 8 verso) ***Emmanuel.*** In a quot. of Is 7:14 applied to Jesus **Mt 1:23** and defined as μεθ' ἡμῶν ὁ θεός *God w. us.*—HWildberger, Jesaja I, '72, 263 (lit.); BHHW II 761. DDD 'Emmanuel' 572f.

Ἐμμαοῦς, ἡ (Ἐμμαούς oth. edd.) ***Emmaus,*** a village (κώμη) in Judea 60 stades (c. 11.5 km.) fr. Jerusalem **Lk 24:13.** The site cannot be determined w. certainty. Three are proposed: 1. The old Emmaus of Maccabaean times, not infreq. mentioned by Joseph. (Niese edition, index), later Nicopolis, and now ᶜAmwâs; so Eusebius-Jerome, Onomastikon p. 90 Kl.; JBoehmer (Studierstube 6, 1908, 285–89; ET 20, 1909, 186–89; 429); Dalman (Orte[3] 240–49=Engl. tr. 226–32); LPirot (Dict. de la Bible, Suppl. II '34, 1049–63); EBishop, ET 55, '43/44, 152f, et al.; CKopp, The Holy Places of the Gospels, tr. RWalls, '63, 396–400. It is located rather far fr. Jerusalem for the 60 stades of vs. 13; but F-MAbel (RB 34, 1925, 347–67) prefers to take the v.l. 160 stades as the original (but s. Metzger 184).—2. Since the middle ages some have thought of present-day el-Kubêbe (65 stades fr. Jerusalem; Baedeker, Plummer, Zahn et al., later PViaud, Qoubeibeh Emm. évangélique 1930 [against this HVincent, RB 40, '31, 57–91]; AdeGuglielmo, CBQ 3, '41, 293–301).—3. The military colony of Vespasian, about 34 stades west of Jerusalem, called Ἀμμαοῦς in Jos. (Bell. 7, 217, where a v.l. has ἑξήκοντα for τριάκοντα: an assimilation to **Lk 24:13**?) and presumably identical w. present-day Kaloniye (Buhl 166; 186; Schürer I 512–13, details n. 142; Wlh. et al.). S. also M-JLagrange, Luc 1921, 617ff; HVincent and F-MAbel, Emmaüs, sa Basilique et son Histoire '32; Geographie II,[3] '67, 314–16; BHHW I 404.—JWanke, Die Emmauserzählung '73 (lit.). OEANE II 240f.

ἐμμένω fut. ἐμμενεῖ LXX; 1 aor. ἐνέμεινα (s. μένω beg.; Aeschyl., Hdt.+; ins, pap, LXX, En; TestSol 18:18; Philo, Joseph.)

❶ to stay in the same place over a period of time, ***stay/remain (in)*** w. ἐν (Thu. 2, 23, 3; X., An. 4, 7, 16)

ⓐ lit. (PTebt 230 descr. [II BC] ἐ. μέχρι νυκτός 'remained [in the shop] until evening') ἐν ἰδίῳ μισθώματι **Ac 28:30.**

ⓑ metaph. αἱ πονηρίαι αὐτῶν ἐν τ. καρδίαις ἐμμένουσι Hv 3, 6, 3.

❷ to persist in a state or enterprise, ***persevere in, stand by*** τινί *someth.* (Attic wr., also Diod. S. 15, 19, 4; Plut., Ages. 608 [23, 5]; SIG 1219, 20 [III BC]; POxy 138, 36; Sir 11:21; 1 Macc 10:26; Philo, Congr. Erud. Gr. 125; Jos., C. Ap. 2, 257) τῇ ἁπλότητι Hv 3, 1, 9; τῇ πίστει (Jos., Ant. 19, 247, Vi. 34) **Ac 14:22;** Hs 8, 9, 1. πᾶσιν τοῖς γεγραμμένοις ἐν τῷ βιβλίῳ *abide by everything written in the book* **Gal 3:10** (Dt 27:26 underlies this. But the change of [ἐν] πᾶσι τοῖς λόγοις τ. νόμου there into πᾶσιν τ. γεγραμμ. ἐν τ. β. here seems to have been caused by the infl. [prob. unconscious] of a common legal formula of the official style, which uses ἐ. followed by the dat. of a ptc., mostly in pl., w. or without ἐν; s. Dssm., NB 76f [BS 248f]; ABerger, D. Strafklauseln in den Pap.-urkunden 1911, 3f; OEger, ZNW 18, 1918, 94.—The legal formula also influences religious language in Alex. Aphr., Fat. 17, II/2 p. 188, 15 ἐμμένειν τοῖς ὑπὸ τῶν θεῶν προαγορευομένοις); τῇ πρὸς τὸν πατέρα κλήσει AcPl Ha 7, 33. For this ἔν τινι (Thu. 4, 118, 14; Polyb. 3, 70, 4 ἐν τ. πίστει; Sir 6:20) ἐν τ. διαθήκῃ μου **Hb 8:9** (Jer 38:32); ἐν τοῖς ἔργοις Hm 4, 1, 9; ἐν ταῖς πράξεσιν s 8, 7, 3. ἐπί τινι (Is 30:18 v.l.): ἐφ' οἷς ἐπιστεύσαμεν *remain true to the things we have* *believed* 2 Cl 15:3. Abs. (En 5:4; SibOr 5, 524) *persevere, stand firm* Hv 2, 2, 7; 2, 3, 2.—DELG s.v. μένω. M-M. TW.

ἐμμέσῳ some edd. **Rv 1:13; 2:1; 4:6; 5:6; 6:6; 22:2** for ἐν μέσῳ (s. B-D-F §19).—M-M.

Ἐμμώρ, ὁ some edd. -όρ; indecl. (חֲמוֹר) (LXX.; JosAs 23:13.—Theodot. [II BC]: 732 fgm. 1, 2 Jac [in Eus., PE 9, 22, 2] and Philo, Migr. Abr. 224 Ἑμώρ.—In Jos., Ant. 1, 337 Ἕμμωρος, ου) ***Hamor,*** from whose sons (TestLevi 5:4; 6:3; Demetr.: 722 fgm. 1, 9 Jac.), living near Shechem, Abraham bought a burial-place (Josh 24:32 Aq., Sym., cp. Gen 33:19; 34:2) **Ac 7:16;** BHHW II 692.

ἐμνήσθην s. μιμνῄσκομαι.

ἐμοί s. ἐγώ.

ἐμός, ή, όν possess. pron. (via ἐμέ; Hom.+; s. B-D-F §285; W-S. §22; Rob. 684; 770) **pert. to me (the speaker), esp. as possessor, agent, or object of an action,** ***my, mine***

ⓐ as adj.—**α.** in attrib., often without special emphasis, freq. used—**א.** for the possess. gen., where μου could be used in nearly all cases **Mt 18:20; J 3:29; 10:27; 15:11; Ro 10:1;** with emphasis τῇ ἐμῇ χειρί *w. my own hand* (cp. PSI 223, 6 ὁλόγραφον χειρὶ ἐμῇ) **1 Cor 16:21; Gal 6:11; Col 4:18; 2 Th 3:17; Phlm 19.** ὁ ἐμὸς καιρός *my time*=the time when I am to be fully revealed **J 7:6, 8.** ἡ ἡμέρα ἡ ἐμή **8:56** and sim.—IRo 7:2; 9:3; Hs 5, 3, 3.

ב. for the obj. gen. (Aeschyl., Pers. 699 τὴν ἐμὴν αἰδῶ respect for me; X., Cyr. 3, 1, 28; 8, 3, 32; Antiphon 5, 41; Jos., Ant. 1, 100) εἰς τὴν ἐμὴν ἀνάμνησιν *in memory of me* (but s. PSchorlemmer, Die Hochkirche 1925, nos. 4; 5; ELohmeyer, JBL 56, '37, 244f) **1 Cor 11:24f; Lk 22:19.** πίστις ἐμή *faith in me* PtK 3 p. 15, 21.

β. pred. **J 7:16; 14:24; 16:15.** οὐκ ἔστιν ἐμὸν τοῦτο δοῦναι *it is not for me to give* **Mt 20:23; Mk 10:40** (Pla., Leg. 2, 664b ἐμὸν ἂν εἴη λέγειν; Lucian, Jupp. Conf. 10 οὐκ ἐμὸν τοῦτο; Jos., Ant. 2, 335 σόν ἐστι ἐκπορίζειν).

ⓑ subst. τὸ ἐμόν *my property* (cp. Jos., Ant. 18, 199) **Mt 25:27; J 16:14f.** For this τὰ ἐμά (cp. Phalaris, Ep. 16; Jos., Ant. 13, 57; ApcSed 6:4; Tat. 26, 2) **Mt 20:15** (perh. *on my own premises* WHatch, ATR 26, '44, 250–53); **Lk 15:31** (Ps.-Callisth. 1, 38, 5 τὰ σὰ ἡμέτερα γενήσ.); **J 17:10.**—οἱ ἐμοί (Ael. Aristid. 50, 5 K.=26 p. 503 D.; Sb 1911 [ins]; POslo 25, 10 [217 AD] et al. s. Pres.; Jos., Vi. 291) **Rv 13:14 v.l.**—GKilpatrick, The Poss. Pron. in the NT: JTS 42, '41, 184–86.—DELG s.v. ἐγώ. M-M.

ἐμπαιγμονή, ῆς, ἡ (hapax leg.; s. ἐμπαίζω) **an act of ridicule or derision,** ***mocking*** ἐλεύσονται ἐν ἐ. ἐμπαῖκται *mockers will come w. their mocking* **2 Pt 3:3.** S. ἐμπαίζω.—DELG s.v. παῖς p. 849. TW.

ἐμπαιγμός, οῦ, ὁ (s. ἐμπαίζω; Herodian, Gr. I 166, 7; II 119, 6; PsSol 2, 11) **derisive expression of contempt,** ***scorn, mocking*** (so Ezk 22:4; Sir 27:28; Wsd 12:25; PsSol) w. μάστιγες as experienced by heroic believers **Hb 11:36** (cp. 2 Macc 7:7, derision of an esp. painful kind).—M-M (no documentary sources). TW.

ἐμπαίζω fut. ἐμπαίξω; 1 aor. ἐνέπαιξα; pf. ἐμπέπαιχα LXX. Pass.: 1 fut. ἐμπαιχθήσομαι; 1 aor. ἐνεπαίχθην; pf. pass. ptc. ἐμπεπαιγμένος (s. παίζω; trag. et al.; pap, LXX; TestSol 2:3 B; Anz 288).

❶ **to subject to derision,** ***ridicule, make fun of, mock*** (in word and deed) τινί *someone* (Hdt. 4, 134, 2; Epict. 1, 4, 10; oft. LXX) **Mt 27:29, 31; Mk 10:34; 15:20; Lk 14:29; 22:63** (DMiller, JBL 90, '71, 309–13); **23:36.** Abs. **Mt 20:19; 27:41; Mk 15:31; Lk 23:11.** Pass. (2 Macc 7:10) **18:32.**—For lit. on the mocking of Jesus s. on στέφανος 1.

❷ **to trick someone so as to make a fool of the person,** ***deceive, trick*** (Anth. Pal. 10, 56, 2 τοῖς ἐμπαιζομένοις ἀνδράσι ταῦτα λέγω. Cp. Vett. Val. p. 16, 14; also prob. Epict. 2, 7, 9; 2, 19, 28; 4, 1, 134; Vi. Aesopi W 129 P.; Jer 10:15) **Mt 2:16** (=GJs 22:1). V.l. for ἐμπτύω B 7:9.—DELG s.v. παῖς p. 849. M-M. EDNT. TW.

ἐμπαίκτης, ου, ὁ (Is 3:4) (s. preceding cognate entries) ***mocker*** **Jd 18; 2 Pt 3:3.**—TW.

ἐμπέμπω (apparently hapax leg.) ***send (in)*** **Lk 19:14 v.l.**

ἐμπεπλησμένος s. ἐμπίμπλημι.

ἐμπεριέχω (s. περιέχω; Aristot., Theophr. et al.; TestSol 11:9 C [Tdf.]; Jos., Ant. 14, 422) **to encompass,** ***embrace*** of God ὁ τὰ πάντα ἐμπεριέχων *the One who embraces all things* 1 Cl 28:4 (Herm. Wr. fgm. 26 p. 542 Sc. of God: πάντα ἐμπεριέχει cp. PMich XIII, 659, 286 and 295 [VI AD] of an agreement w. all provisions 'embraced' in it. S. Knopf, Hdb. ad loc.).

ἐμπεριπατέω fut. ἐμπεριπατήσω Lev 26:12; 1 aor. ἐνεπεριπάτησα (s. περιπατέω; Plut., Lucian, Achilles Tat.; PSI 413, 20 [III BC]; LXX, Philo, Joseph.) fig. extension of mng. of ἐ. 'to walk about in an area': ***walk about, move*** ἐν αὐτοῖς *among them* (w. ἐνοικεῖν) **2 Cor 6:16** (Lev 26:12).—TW.

ἐμπερίτομος, ον (s. περιτέμνω) ***circumcised*** B 9:6 v.l. (found elsewh. only in Ps.-Clem., Hom. p. 4, 22 Lag., and Philostorg., HE 3, 4).

ἐμπί(μ)πλημι alternate form ἐμπι(μ)πλάω in ptc.; ἐμπιπλῶν **Ac 14:17;** fut. ἐμπλήσω LXX; 1 aor. ἐνέπλησα. Pass.: impf. 3 sg. ἐνεπίμπλατο MPol 12:1; fut. ἐμπλησθήσομαι; 1 aor. ἐνεπλήσθην; pf. ἐμπέπλησμαι, ptc. ἐμπεπλησμένος; B-D-F §93; 101, p. 48; Mlt-H. 205; 384 (Hom.+; ins, pap, LXX, TestSol 20:3 P; TestJob, Test12Patr; ParJer 9:20; JosAs 15:4 cod. A; Philo, Joseph., Just.; Tat. 30, 1).

❶ **to completely take up the space of someth.,** ***fill*** ὅλην τὴν πέτραν *cover the entire rock* Hs 9, 4, 2 (cp. Ezk 35:8). Fig. (cp. Himerius, Or. 47 [=Or. 3], 4 μουσικῆς ἐμπ.=fill with song; Is 29:19; Jer 15:17; Sir 4:12) τινά or τί τινος *someone* or *someth. w. someth.* (Pla., 7th Letter, 350e πάντα κακῶν ἐμπεπλήκασιν; Jos., Ant. 3, 99) **Ac 14:17** (s. 2 below). Pass. w. gen. (Socrat., Ep. 13, 1; Appian, Bell. Civ. 2, 77 §324 μετανοίας; Heliod. 7, 27, 4 ὀργῆς; Jos., Ant. 5, 146 ὕβρεως) ἐ. θάρσους καὶ χαρᾶς MPol 12:1 (Diod. S. 20, 8, 6 ἐνέπλησε τὴν δύναμιν θάρσους=he filled the army w. courage). πεινῶντας ἐνέπλησεν ἀγαθῶν (cp. Ps 106:9 ψυχὴν πεινῶσαν ἐνέπλησεν ἀγαθῶν; Jer 38:25.—Eutecnius 4 p. 41, 26 of Dionysus: σύμπασαν γῆν ἐμπιπλάντα τ. ἀγαθῶν; Appian, Hann. 60 p. 251 ἄνδρας ἐμπλήσας κακῶν=overwhelm with evils) *he has filled the hungry w. good things* **Lk 1:53** leads over to

❷ **to provide a sufficient amount,** ***satisfy*** (Diod. S. 5, 39, 4 ἀπὸ λαχάνων ἐμπίμπλανται; oft. LXX; Jos., Ant. 4, 234 al.) τινά τινος *someone w. someth.* **Ac 14:17** (s. 1); ἐ. τὴν ἑαυτοῦ ψυχήν *satisfy oneself* Hs 5, 3, 7. Abs. (Dio Chrys. 57 [74], 11; Appian, Bell. Civ. 2, 64 §268) ὡς ἐνεπλήσθησαν *when they had eaten their fill* **J 6:12.** μετὰ τὸ ἐμπλησθῆναι D 10:1. οἱ ἐμπεπλησμένοι *those who have plenty to eat* **Lk 6:25.** Cp. B 3:5 v.l. (Funk; Is 58:10).

❸ ἐμπλησθῆναί τινος 'have one's fill of someth.', in the sense *enjoy someth.* (cp. 'looking one's fill' Od. 11, 451; Socrat., Ep. 27, 5; Sus 32; Philo, Deus Imm. 151) ὑμῶν *your company* **Ro 15:24.**—DELG s.v. πίμπλημι. M-M. TW.

ἐμπί(μ)πρημι fut. ἐμπρήσω LXX; 1 aor. ἐνέπρησα, pass. ἐνεπρήσθην LXX (Hdt. et al.; B-D-F §93; 101 p. 54 [πιμπλάναι]; Mlt-H. 207)

❶ **to initiate a process of burning,** ***set on fire, burn*** πόλιν (OGI 8, 11; Judg 18:27; 2 Macc 8:6; Philo, Aet. M. 20; Jos., Bell. 5, 411) **Mt 22:7** (KRengstorf, D. Stadt der Mörder [Mt 22:7], Beih. ZNW 26, '60, 106–29). ναόν (Appian, Celt. 6 §2; Jos., Bell. 5, 405) GPt 7:26.

❷ **to experience burning sensation as the result of a physical malady,** ***become feverish*** **or** ***swell up*** ἐμπιπρᾶσθαι **Ac 28:6 v.l.;** Tdf. text; s. πίμπρημι.—DELG s.v. πίμπρημι. M-M.

ἐμπίπτω fut. ἐμπεσοῦμαι; 2 aor. ἐνέπεσον; pf. ptc. ἐμπεπτωκότας 4 Km 25:11 (Hom.+)

❶ **to fall into a particular physical area,** ***fall (in, into)*** (Dio Chrys. 57 [74], 22 εἰς βόθρον; Jos., Ant. 4, 284 εἰς ὄρυγμα ἐ. βόσκημα) εἰς βόθυνον *into a pit* (Is 24:18; Jer 31:44) **Mt 12:11; Lk 6:39.** ἐ. ἐπὶ πῦρ *fall into the fire* Hv 3, 2, 9.

❷ **to experience a state or condition,** ***fall (into/among)*** in imagery (SIG 1170, 3 εἰς νόσους; PTebt 17, 8f [114 BC] εἰς δαπάνας; Just., D. 23, 1 εἰς ἄτοπα … νοήματα; temp. Mel., HE 4, 26, 3 τοῦ πάσχα ἐμπεσόντος … ἐν ἐκείναις ταῖς ἡμέραις) εἰς τοὺς λῃστάς *among robbers* (Epict. 3, 13, 3 εἰς λῃστὰς ἐμπ.; Porphyr., Vi. Pyth. 15; cp. Socrat., Ep. 1, 9 εἰς τ. ἱππέας) **Lk 10:36;** εἰς τὰ ἄγκιστρα τῆς κενοδοξίας ἐ. *be caught on the fishhooks of false doctrine* IMg 11 (cp. schol. on Pla. 190e ἐμπεσούμεθα εἰς τὸ Πρωταγόρειον δόγμα); ἐ. εἰς χεῖράς τινος *fall into someone's hands* (Chariton 8, 3, 7; Alciphron 3, 36, 1; Sir 38:15; Sus 23) GPt 11:48; θεοῦ **Hb 10:31** (cp. 2 Km 24:14; 1 Ch 21:13; Sir 2:18; Jos., Ant. 7, 323). εἰς πειρασμόν **1 Ti 6:9** (cp. Diod. S. 17, 105, 6 ἐνέπεσε εἰς λύπην καὶ φροντίδα; Pr 17:20 εἰς κακά; 1 Macc 6:8 εἰς ἀρρωστίαν). εἰς κρίμα τοῦ διαβόλου **3:6.** εἰς ὀνειδισμὸν καὶ παγίδα τοῦ διαβόλου vs. **7** (cp. **6:9** and Pr 12:13; Sir 9:3). εἰς ταύτας τὰς πράξεις τὰς πολλάς *get into these many activities* Hm 10, 1, 5. εἰς ἐπιθυμίαν 12, 1, 2 (cp. **1 Ti 6:9.**—X., Hell. 7, 5, 6 εἰς ἀθυμίαν; Ael. Aristid. 37 p. 701 D.).

❸ **to originate and so come to attention,** ***set in, arise*** abs. (Pla., Rep. 8, 545d στάσις; Epict. 2, 5, 10 χειμὼν ἐμπέπτωκε) ζήλου ἐμπεσόντος περί τινος *when jealousy arose about someth.* 1 Cl 43:2.—M-M. Spicq.

ἔμπλαστρος, ου, ἡ (Philumen. p. 12, 22; 14, 28 al.; Galen XII 688; 690 K.; Oribas., Ecl. 89, 4: CMG VI/2, 2 p. 267, 28; Geopon. 12, 12, 2; Cos. and Dam. 47, 65; PStras 647, 2 [II AD]) ***a plaster*** used for healing wounds IPol 2:1.—DELG s.v. πλάσσω.

ἐμπλέκω pf. pass. ptc. ἐμπεπλεγμένος; 2 aor. pass. ἐνεπλάκην; fut. ἐμπλακήσομαι LXX (TestSol 5:8 εἰς φόνους) (Aeschyl. et al.; PTebt 39, 17; PRein 7, 18 [both II BC]; LXX) in gener. to interconnect closely, with var. mngs. in lit.: 'intertwine, braid, entangle, be caught in' (opp. ἐκπλέκω) in our lit. only pass. in act. sense.

❶ **to be involuntarily interlaced to the point of immobility,** ***be entangled,*** lit. of sheep whose wool is caught in thorns Hs 6, 2, 6f (Arrian, Anab. 6, 22, 8 of hares who are caught in thorns; Aesop, Fab. 74 P.=128 H.; 76 H-H.).

❷ **to become involved in an activity to the point of interference with other activity or objective,** ***be involved in,*** fig. ext. of mng. 1 ταῖς τοῦ βίου πραγματείαις *become entangled in civilian pursuits* **2 Ti 2:4** (cp. Epict. 3, 22, 69; Polyb. 24, 11, 3 τ. Ἑλληνικοῖς πράγμασιν ἐμπλεκόμενος). Of defilements of the world *be involved in* **2 Pt 2:20.**—M-M.

ἐμπλοκή, ῆς, ἡ (Polyb. 18, 18, 11; 15; Plut., Mor. 916d; PRyl 124, 28; 150, 12 [both I AD]) (s. preceding entry) ***braiding, braid*** τριχῶν (fashionable or elaborate) *braiding of hair* (Nicol. Dam.: 90 fgm. 2 Jac.; Strabo 17, 3, 7 ἐ. κόμης) **1 Pt 3:3** (v.l. ἐμπλοκῆς or ἐκ πλοκῆς).—M-M.

ἐμπνέω (also ἐν-) 1 aor. ptc. ἐμπνεύσαντα Wsd 15:11, 3 sg. opt. ἐμπνεύσαι (Ath. 9, 1); pf. pass. ptc. ἐμπεπνευσμένων (Just., A I, 36, 1) (s. πνέω; Hom. et al.; LXX; Kaibel 562, 9 [ἐς δ' ὅσον ἐνπείει 'as long as he draws breath']; TestSol; TestJob 41:5; Philo; Jos., Bell. 5, 458, Ant. 12, 256; Just., A I, 36, 1; Ath. 9, 1) gener. in lit. in ref. to blowing or breathing.

❶ **to emit breath,** ***breathe*** (Kaibel above) fig. in the idiom ἀπειλῆς καὶ φόνου *he breathed murderous threats* **Ac 9:1** (B-D-F §174; for its use w. gen. cp. Perictione in Stob. 4, 28, 19 Ἀραβίης ὀδμῆς ἐμπνέοντα; Josh 10:40. Cp. Chion, Ep. 3, 3 Ἄρεος πνέω=breathe the lust of war; Theocr. 22, 82 the two opponents φόνον ἀλλήλοισι πνέοντες).

❷ **to give another a share in one's breath and thus have influence,** ***inspire*** (Hes., Theogony 31 the Muses ἐνέπνευσαν δέ μ' ἀοιδὴν θέσπιν, ἵνα κτλ.; Plut., Mor. 421b; PGM 2, 84) of prophets ἐνπνεόμενοι ὑπὸ τῆς χάριτος αὐτοῦ IMg 8:2 (cp. TestJob 41:5 Ἐλίους ἐμπνευσθεὶς ἐν τῷ Σατανᾷ; Περὶ ὕψους 16:2 ἐμπνευσθεὶς ὑπὸ θεοῦ; Lucian, Phal. 2, 12 of the Pythia: ἐμπνεῖται; schol. on Apollon. Rhod. 4, 1381f: the poet ἐμπέπνευσται by the Muses; Just., A I, 36, 1 προφητῶν … ἐμπεπνευσμένων; Ath. 9, 1 ὡς εἰ καὶ αὐλητὴς αὐλὸν ἐμπνεύσαι).—DELG s.v. πλέκω. M-M. TW.

ἐμποδίζω 1 aor. ἐνεπόδισα. Pass. aor. ἐνεποδίσθην LXX; pf. ptc.. ἐμπεποδισμένον (Mel., fgm. 11) (ποδίζω 'tie the feet', also s. πούς; Soph., Hdt. et al.; ins, pap, LXX, TestSol; TestJud 18:5; Jos., Ant. 19, 226, Vi 48; Tat. 16, 1) (orig. 'put feet in bonds', hence 'fetter' Hdt. 4, 69, then gener. to be obstructive) ***hinder*** τινί *someone* (Aristot.; Polyb.; Epict. 2, 22, 15; 17; 3, 4, 6) w. inf. foll. ζῆσαι *from living* IRo 6:2. μηδὲν ἀλλήλοις *without hindering each other* 1 Cl 20:2.—B. 1355. DELG s.v. πούς.

ἐμπολιτεύω (s. πολιτεύομαι; Thu., Isocr. et al.; Joseph.) in lit. to have civil rights in a place 'be a citizen', mid. 'become a citizen'; in our lit. mid. ***take control, carry out one's designs*** AcPlCor 2:15 in a bad sense of Satan.—DELG s.v. πόλις.

ἐμπορεύομαι (s. three next entries) fut. ἐμπορεύσομαι; in gener lit. both in the sense of travel and of traveling for business reasons, but in our lit. only in commercial sense

❶ **to carry on an activity involving buying and selling,** ***be in business*** intr. *carry on business* (since Thu. 7, 13, 2; SIG 1166, 1; Sb 9066 I, 12; Ezk 27:13; TestJob) **Js 4:13.**

❷ **to engage w. someone in a business transaction,** ***buy and sell, trade in*** (oft. w. acc. of thing as obj. [Philo, Vi. Cont. 89; Jos., Bell. 1, 514, Ant. 4, 134]; rarely w. acc. of pers., cp. Achilles Tat. 8, 10, 11; Athen. 13, 25, 569f Ἀσπασία [a procurer] ἐνεπορεύετο πλήθη καλῶν γυναικῶν; Pr 3:14) in a neg. sense of misrepresentation of merchandise ὑμᾶς ἐμπορεύσονται *they will exploit you* **2 Pt 2:3** (cp. vs. 1 τὸν ἀγοράσαντα αὐτοὺς δεσπότην; on the theme of clever use of words s. Thu. 38, 12, 10).—B. 819. DELG s.v. ἔμπορος. M-M.

ἐμπορία, ας, ἡ (s. prec. and two next entries; Hes., Hdt. et al.; SIG 185, 32 [IV BC]; OGI 629, 164; SEG XXVI, 1392, 47; PTebt 6, 25 [II BC]; PGiss 9, 3; POxy 76, 10; CPJ 4526, 14 ἐ.

Ἰουδαίων; LXX; EpArist 114; Jos., C. Ap. 1, 60; 61; TestJos 11:5; TestAbr A 2 p. 79, 10 [Stone p. 6]; loanw. in rabb.) the business or work in which one engages ***business, trade*** **Mt 22:5.** ἐμπορίαν ἀσκεῖν *engage in business* 2 Cl 20:4 (the verb also governs θεοσέβειαν).—DELG s.v. ἔμπορος. M-M.

ἐμπόριον, ου, τό (s. two prec. entries; Hdt. et al.; ins, pap [Mayser 93, 2]; LXX; Jos., Ant. 9, 17) **place where business is carried on, *market*** οἶκος ἐμπορίου (epexeg. gen.) *marketplace* **J 2:16.**—DELG s.v. ἔμπορος. M-M.

ἔμπορος, ου, ὁ (s. three prec. entries; Hom. et al.) Od. 2, 319 'one who boards a ship as passenger', then, esp. **one who travels by ship for business reasons, *merchant*** (Hdt., Thu. et al.; ins, pap, LXX; Philo, Op. M. 147; Jos., Ant. 2, 32; 20, 34; TestZeb 4:6; loanw. in rabb.) denotes *wholesale dealer* in contrast to κάπηλος 'retailer' (for the contrast cp. Pla., Rep. 2, 371d) **Mt 13:45 v.l.; Rv 18:3, 11, 15, 23.** For this pleonast. ἄνθρωπος ἔ. **Mt 13:45.**—B. 821. DELG. M-M. TW.

ἔμπροσθεν (also ἐνπ-; Hdt.+; also in OT quotes w. and against LXX; Mel., P. 61, 444 [ἀπέναντι Dt 28:66]) ἔμπροσθε (SIG 371, 13 [289/288 BC]; 915, 27) ApcPt 3:6; orig. adv. of place, then used as prep. (B-D-F §104, 2; 214, 1; 6; Mlt-H. 329).

❶ **pert. to a position in front of an object**—ⓐ gener. adv. as marker of something that is relatively removed in distance ***in front, ahead*** (opp. ὄπισθεν, as X., Equ. 1, 3; Polyb. 12, 15, 2; Aelian, VH 12, 21; Palaeph. 29, 2; 2 Ch 13:14; Ezk 2:10) **Rv 4:6.** As subst.: εἰς τὸ ἔ. *toward the front* (Diod. S. 11, 18, 5; 19, 26, 10; 19, 83, 2; Jos., C. Ap. 1, 203) προδραμὼν εἰς τὸ ἔ. *he ran ahead* **Lk 19:4** (where εἰς τὸ ἔ. is pleonast., as Artem. 2, 9 p. 93, 2 προϊέναι εἰς τοὔμπροσθεν; B-D-F §484; Semitism [?]: MBlack, An Aramaic Approach[3], '67, 116); τὰ ἔ. (sc. ὄντα; cp. X., An. 6, 3, 14; 1 Macc 13:27; TestJob 27:1; location in a dialogue Just., D. 126, 6; 140, 4) *what lies ahead* (as a goal) **Phil 3:13.**—*Forward, ahead* πορεύεσθαι ἔ. (X., Cyr. 4, 2, 23) **Lk 19:28.** αἱ ἔ. ἐκκλησίαι *the congregations/churches farther on* or *principal churches* (s. JKleist, tr., '46, ad loc. w. note) IPol 8:1.

ⓑ indicating more immediate presence of the object that is in front, with ἔ. functioning as prep. w. gen. (s. on ἀνά, beg.) ***in front of, before*** in a variety of aspects

α. purely local (X., Cyr. 3, 2, 5; Jos., Bell. 6, 366) Hs 9, 2, 7 (opp. ὀπίσω); ἔ. τοῦ ναοῦ *before the shrine* (Cebes, Tab. 1, 1) 1 Cl 41:2; ἔ. τοῦ θυσιαστηρίου **Mt 5:24;** ἔ. τοῦ βήματος **Ac 18:17;** ἔ. τοῦ Ἰησοῦ **Lk 5:19;** cp. **14:2;** ApcPt 3:6; GPt 4:12. γονυπετεῖν ἔ. τινος *kneel before someone* **Mt 27:29;** πίπτειν ἔ. τῶν ποδῶν τινος *fall at someone's feet* **Rv 19:10; 22:8;** βάλλειν ἔ. τινος **Mt 7:6** (PGM 4, 1229 βάλε ἔ. αὐτοῦ κλῶνας ἐλαίας). μαστιγοῦντες ἑαυτοὺς ἔ. τούτων τῶν εἰδώλων *flagellating themselves before these images* ApcPt Bodl. (as restored by EWinstedt, s. MJames, JTS 1910, 12, 157).

β. of position without ref. to motion toward, *before, in the presence of* (Gen 45:5) ὁμολογεῖν and ἀρνεῖσθαι **Mt 10:32f; 26:70; Lk 12:8;** cp. **Gal 2:14.** Esp. of appearance before a judge **Mt 27:11;** also before the divine judge **25:32; Lk 21:36; 1 Th 2:19; 3:13;** GPt 11:48; cp. **2 Cor 5:10.** But the judicial element is not decisive in all the pass. in which pers. stand or come ἔ. τοῦ θεοῦ or ἔ. τ. χυρίου; cp. **1 Th 1:3; 3:9; 1J 3:19.**

γ. of appearance before a large assemblage to discharge an obligation, *before, in the sight of* (SIG 1173, 14 [138 AD] the man who was healed through the intervention of Asklepios ηὐχαρίστησεν ἔμπροσθεν τοῦ δήμου) **Mt 5:16; 6:1; 17:2; 23:13** *in the face of;* **Mk 2:12; 9:2; Lk 19:27; J 12:37; Ac 10:4.**

δ. as a reverential way of expressing oneself, when one is speaking of an eminent pers., and esp. of God, not to connect the subject directly w. what happens, but to say that it took place 'before someone' (s. Dalman, Worte 171–74): ἐπακοῦσαι ἔ. αὐτοῦ ἔθνη *that the nations should give heed* (or *obey*) *(before) God* B 12:11 (Is 45:1). ποιεῖν τὸ πονηρὸν ἔ. τοῦ κυρίου Hm 4, 2, 2 (cp. Judg 2:11; 3:12; 4:1). εὐδοκία ἔ. σου *pleasing to you* **Mt 11:26; Lk 10:21;** θέλημα ἔ. τ. πατρὸς ὑμῶν **Mt 18:14.**

ε. *before, ahead of,* w. motion implied ἔ. τινος (UPZ 78, 15 [159 BC] ἔμπροσθεν αὐτῶν ἐπορευόμην) **J 10:4;** B 11:4 (Is 45:2); προπορεύεσθαι ἔ. τινος 3:4 (Is 58:8); cp. 4:12; ἀποστέλλεσθαι ἔ. τινος (Gen 24:7; 32:4) **J 3:28;** σαλπίζειν ἔ. τινος *blow a trumpet before someone* **Mt 6:2;** τὴν ὁδὸν κατασκευάζειν ἔ. τινος **Mt 11:10; Lk 7:27.**

ζ. of rank (Pla., Leg. 1, 631d; 5, 743e; 7, 805d; Demosth. 56, 50 εἶναι ἔ. τινος; Gen 48:20) ἔ. τινος γίνεσθαι *rank before* (i.e. *higher than*) *someone* **J 1:15, 30** (Plut., Pericl. 158 [11, 1] οἱ ἀριστοκρατικοὶ . . . Περικλέα . . . πρόσθεν ὁρῶντες γεγονόντα τῶν πολιτῶν). If ἔ. τινος γ. is to be understood temporally here (as 3 Km 3:12; 16:25, 33; 4 Km 18:5; Eccl 1:16; 2:7, 9; Jos, Ant. 1, 109; cp. Demetr.: 722 fgm. 1, 12 Jac. ἔτει ἑνὶ ἔμπροσθεν)='be earlier than someone', the foll. ὅτι πρῶτός μου ἦν, which gives the reason for it, would simply be an instance of tautology (but s. OCullmann, ConNeot 11, '47, 31, who holds that the ὅτι- clause refers to the absolute time of the Prologue while the preceding words merely give the order in which the ministries of John and Jesus began). S. on ὀπίσω 2b.

❷ **on the front surface of someth., *in front*** (opp. ὄπισθεν, as cp. Ezk 2:10) **Rv 4:6.**—DELG s.v. πρόσθε(ν). M-M.

ἐμπτύω fut. ἐμπτύσω; 1 aor. ἐνέπτυσα; 1 fut. pass. ἐμπτυσθήσομαι (s. πτύω; Hdt. et al.; pap, LXX) ***spit on/at*** τινί *someone* (cp. Aristot. in Aelian, VH 1, 15; Nicol. Dam.: 90 fgm. 103g, 2 Jac.; Ps.-Callisth. 1, 18, 9) **Mk 10:34; 14:65; 15:19.** ταῖς ὄψεσί τινος *spit in someone's face* GPt 3:9. εἴς τινα **Mt 27:30.** εἰς τὸ πρόσωπόν τινος (Herodas 5, 76; Plut., Mor. 189a; PMagd 24, 7 [=PEnteux 79, 7; 218 BC]; Num 12:14; TestZeb 3:4) **Mt 26:67.** Abs. *spit upon* of a scapegoat B 7:8f. Pass. *be spit upon* (Musonius 10 p. 52 H.) **Lk 18:32.**—DELG s.v. πτύω. TW. M-M.

ἐμφανής, ές (s. ἐμφαίνω, φαίνω; Aeschyl. et al.; ins, pap, LXX; Philo, Aet. M. 56; Joseph.)

❶ **capable of being seen, *visible*** ἐμφανῆ γενέσθαι *become visible* (Jos., Ant. 15, 52; Just., D. 110, 1) τινί *to someone* (Aelian, VH 1, 21) **Ac 10:40** of the resurrected Lord (Ps.-Pla., Alc. 2, 141a θεὸς ἐμφανὴς γίγνεται; POxy 2754, 4 [111 AD] of the emperor). W. the same mng. ἐ. εἶναί τινι (POxy 260, 11 [59 AD]; cp. Mi 4:1) Ox 655, 19f=Kl. Texte 8[3], p. 23, 20f (cp. GTh 37); Ox 1081, 2=Kl. Texte[3] p. 25, 2 (s. Coptic text SJCh 88, 19).

❷ **pert. to being known, *known,*** ext of mng. 1 (cp. Hdt 3, 150, 2) ἐ. ἐγενόμην *I have made myself known* (i.e. *revealed myself*) **Ro 10:20** (Is 65:1).—M-M.

ἐμφανίζω fut. ἐμφανίσω; 1 aor. ἐνεφάνισα; 1 aor. pass. ἐνεφανίσθην (s. ἐμφαίνω; Eur., Pla., X., et. al.; ins, pap, LXX, En; TestSol 3:7; TestAbr B 4 p. 109, 1 [Stone p. 66]; Philo, Joseph.) 'make apparent'

❶ **to lay open to view, *make visible*** ἐ. σεαυτόν τινι **J 14:22** (cp. Ex 33:13, [18] ἐμφάνισόν μοι σεαυτόν). Pass. w. act. sense *become visible, appear* τινί *to someone* (Diog. L., Prooem. 7 αὐτοῖς θεοὺς ἐμφανίζεσθαι λέγοντες; Philo, Leg. All. 3, 101; Jos., Bell. 6, 47, Ant. 1, 223; Wsd 17:4; τοῖς μὴ ἀπιστοῦσιν αὐτῷ Did., Gen. 248, 19) πολλοῖς **Mt 27:53.** σοί Hv 3, 1, 2; cp. 3, 10, 2. τῷ προσώπῳ τοῦ θεοῦ *before God's face* (of Christ's appearance before God in heaven) **Hb 9:24.**

❷ **to provide information, *make clear, explain, inform, make a report*** (Hippol., Ref. 8, 9, 8) esp. of an official report to the authorities (as PMagd 11, 9 [= PEnteux 27, 9; 221 BC]; UPZ 42, 18 [162 BC]; PEleph 8, 3; 2 Macc 11:29) τὶ πρός τινα *someth. to someone: inform* **Ac 23:22;** w. ὅτι foll. (X., Cyr. 8, 1, 26) *make clear* **Hb 11:14.**—τινί w. ὅπως foll. **23:15** (cp. PSI 442, 23 [III BC] ταῦτα δὲ ἐνεφάνισά σοι, ὅπως ἂν μηδείς σε παρακρούηται). Fig. extension: of matters that transcend physical sight or mere verbal statement *reveal, make known* (cp. Wsd 1:2; Philo, Leg. All. 3, 27) ἐμφανίσω αὐτῷ ἐμαυτόν *I will reveal myself to that person* **J 14:21.**

❸ **to convey a formal report about a judicial matter, *present evidence, bring charges*** τινί τι (X., Mem. 4, 3, 4; Diod. S. 14, 11, 2; Esth 2:22; Jos., Ant. 4, 43) GPt 11:43. ἐ. τινὶ κατά τινος *bring formal charges against someone* (Jos., Ant. 10, 166) **Ac 24:1; 25:2;** ἐ. περί τινος *concerning someone* **25:15** (cp. PHib 72, 4 [III BC]; PSI 400, 2; 2 Macc 3:7; En 22:12; Jos., Ant. 14, 226).—DELG s.v. φαίνω B. M-M. TW.

ἔμφοβος, ον (='terrible' in Soph., Oed. C. 39) **pert. to being in a state of fear, *afraid, startled, terrified*** (Theophr., Char., 25, 1; Vett. Val. 59, 7; PGM 13, 873; Sb 7452, 13; Sir 19:24) ἔ. γίνεσθαι *be afraid,* etc. (cp. Aesop 49 P.=83 H.=H-H. 40 III) **Lk 24:5, 37; Ac 10:4; 22:9 v.l.; 24:25** (s. Field, Notes 139); **Rv 11:13.**—DELG s.v. φέβομαι. M-M.

ἐμφράσσω 1 aor. ἐνέφραξα (s. φράσσω; Thu. et al.; POslo 111, 130; 169 [235 AD]; LXX; Jos., Ant. 9, 36; 12, 346) **to bar passage, *stop (up), shut,*** τὸ στόμα *stop the mouth* (Demosth. 19, 208; Esth 4:17o; Job 5:16; Ps 62:12) of a monster (Da 6:23 Theod.; cp. Aelian, NA 14, 8 p. 345, 7) Hv 4, 2, 4.—DELG s.v. φράσσω.

ἐμφύρω pf. pass. ptc. ἐμπεφυρμένος (φύρω 'mix', s. φύραμα; Aeschyl., fgm. 446 Mette [=38 N.] ἵπποι δ᾽ ἐφ᾽ ἵπποις ἐμπεφυρμένοι in descr. of a confused battle scene; Lycophron 1380; Ezk 22:6 v.l.) **to put together/combine in a mass, *mix up, knead in*** ἐμπεφυρμένος τινί *mixed up w. someth.=involved* (in earthly pursuits) Hm 10, 1, 4; s 8, 8, 1; 9, 20, 1f. W. the world m 12, 1, 2. DELG s.v. φύρω.

ἐμφυσάω fut. ἐμφυσήσω Ezk 21:36; 1 aor. ἐνεφύσησα (φυσάω 'to blow'; Aristoph., Hippocr. et al.; POxy 1088, 25 [I AD]; LXX; TestSol 7, 6 D; ApcMos 33; Philo) ***breathe on*** τινί *someone* 1 Cl 39:6 (Job 4:21). Abs. (unless αὐτοῖς also belongs to ἐνεφύσ.), for the purpose of transmitting the Holy Spirit **J 20:22** (cp. Gen 2:7; Wsd 15:11; Philo, Op. M. 135 ὃ ἐνεφύσησεν, οὐδὲν ἦν ἕτερον ἢ πνεῦμα θεῖον; PGM 13, 762f ὁ ἐνφυσήσας πνεῦμα ἀνθρώποις εἰς ζωήν=12, 238, but πνεύματα; Stephan. Byz. s.v. Ἰκόνιον: the deluge at the time of Deucalion destroyed everyone [πάντας]. When the earth had dried out, ὁ Ζεὺς ἐκέλευσε τῷ Προμηθεῖ καὶ τῇ Ἀθηνᾷ εἴδωλα διαπλάσαι ἐκ τοῦ πηλοῦ, καὶ προσκαλεσάμενος τοὺς ἀνέμους ἐμφυσῆσαι πᾶσιν ἐκέλευσε καὶ ζῶντα ἀποτελέσαι 'Zeus ordered P. and A. to shape images out of clay, and then summoned the winds to breathe on all of them and so make them live'.).—DELG s.v. φυσάω. M-M. TW.

ἔμφυτος, ον (ἐμφύω 'to implant'; since Pre-Socr., trag., Hdt.; ins, pap; Wsd 12:10; Ps.-Phoc. 128; Philo; Jos., Bell. 1, 88, Ant. 16, 232; Just. Ath., R. 63, 19 al.; ABurger, Les mots de la famille de φύω en grec ancien 1925) in gener. lit. mostly in the sense 'implanted by natural process, inborn' (Hdt. 9, 94, 3 ἔμφυτον αὐτίκα μαντικὴν εἶχε) in our lit. only in fig. extension of mng., with ref. to subsequent implantation but with connotation of quality (in contrast to someth. that is developed, e.g., through personal effort Pla., Eryxias 398c; cp. Pind., N. 3, 40f) ***implanted*** λόγος ἔ. *the word* of the gospel *implanted* in you **Js 1:21** (as someth. implanted the word is permanently established in the individual and like inborn assets functions in an exceptional manner; s. WKnox, JTS 46, '45, 14f). ἡ ἔ. δωρεὰ τῆς διδαχῆς αὐτοῦ *the implanted gift of his teaching* B 9:9. οὕτως ἔ. τῆς δωρεᾶς πνευματικῆς χάριν εἰλήφατε *so implanted have you received the benefit of the spiritual gift* 1:2 (i.e. God's beneficence is productive, as attested by the illustrious spiritual character of the recipients, vs. 2a; οὗ τό v.l.: *whose implanted blessing, the favor of the spiritual gift, you have received;* s. Windisch, Hdb. ad loc.).—DELG s.v. φύομαι. M-M. TW.

ἐν prep. w. dat. (Hom.+). For lit. s. ἀνά and εἰς, beg. For special NT uses s. AOepke, TW II 534–39. The uses of this prep. are so many and various, and oft. so easily confused, that a strictly systematic treatment is impossible. It must suffice to list the main categories, which will help establish the usage in individual cases. The earliest auditors/readers, not being inconvenienced by grammatical and lexical debates, would readily absorb the context and experience little difficulty.

❶ **marker of a position defined as being in a location, *in, among*** (the basic idea, Rob. 586f)—ⓐ of the space or place within which someth. is found, *in:* ἐν τῇ πόλει **Lk 7:37.** ἐν Βηθλέεμ **Mt 2:1.** ἐν τῇ ἐρήμῳ **3:1** (Just., D. 19, 5, cp. A I, 12, 6 ἐν ἐρημίᾳ) ἐν τῷ ἱερῷ **Ac 5:42.** ἐν οἴκῳ **1 Ti 3:15** and very oft. ἐν τοῖς τοῦ πατρός μου *in my Father's house* **Lk 2:49** and perh. **Mt 20:15** (cp. Jos., Ant. 16, 302, C. Ap. 1, 118 ἐν τοῖς τοῦ Διός; PTebt 12, 3; POxy 523, 3; Tob 6:11 S; Goodsp., Probs. 81–83). ἐν τῇ ἀγορᾷ **Mt 20:3.** ἐν (τῷ) οὐρανῷ *in heaven* (Arat., Phaen. 10; Diod. S. 4, 61, 6; Plut., Mor. 359d τὰς ψυχὰς ἐν οὐρανῷ λάμπειν ἄστρα; Tat. 12, 2 τὰ ἄστρα τὰ ἐν αὐτῷ) **Ac 2:19** (Jo 3:3); **Rv 12:1;** IEph 19:2.—W. quotations and accounts of the subject matter of literary works: *in* (Ps.-Demetr. c. 226 ὡς ἐν τῷ Εὐθυδήμῳ; Simplicius in Epict. p. 28, 37 ἐν τῷ Φαίδωνι; Ammon. Hermiae in Aristot. De Interpret. c. 9 p. 136, 20 Busse ἐν Τιμαίῳ παρειλήφαμεν=we have received as a tradition; 2 Macc 2:4; 1 Esdr 1:40; 5:48; Sir 50:27; Just., A I, 60, 1 ἐν τῷ παρὰ Πλάτωνι Τιμαίῳ) ἐν τῇ ἐπιστολῇ **1 Cor 5:9.** ἐν τῷ νόμῳ **Lk 24:44; J 1:45.** ἐν τοῖς προφήταις **Ac 13:40.** ἐν Ἠλίᾳ *in the story of Elijah* **Ro 11:2** (Just., D. 120, 3 ἐν τῷ Ἰούδα). ἐν τῷ Ὡσηέ **9:25** (Just., D. 44, 2 ἐν τῷ Ἰεζεκιήλ). ἐν Δαυίδ *in the Psalter* (*by David* is also prob.: s. 6) **Hb 4:7.** ἐν ἑτέρῳ προφήτῃ *in another prophet* B 6:14. Of inner life φανεροῦσθαι ἐν ταῖς συνειδήσεσι *be made known to* (your) *consciences* **2 Cor 5:11.** ἐν τῇ καρδίᾳ **Mt 5:28; 13:19; 2 Cor 11:12** et al.

ⓑ *on* ἐν τῷ ὄρει (X., An. 4, 3, 31; Diod. S. 14, 16, 2 λόφος ἐν ᾧ=a hill on which; Jos., Ant. 12, 259; Just., D. 67, 9 ἐν ὄρει Χωρήβ) **J 4:20f; Hb 8:5** (Ex 25:40). ἐν τῇ ἀγορᾷ *in the market* **Mt 20:3.** ἐν τῇ ὁδῷ *on the way* **Mt 5:25.** ἐν πλαξίν *on tablets* **2 Cor 3:3.** ἐν ταῖς γωνίαις τῶν πλατειῶν *on the street corners* **Mt 6:5.**

ⓒ *within the range of, at, near* (Soph., fgm. 37 [34 N.^{2}] ἐν παντὶ λίθῳ=near every stone; Artem. 4, 24 p. 217, 19 ἐν Τύρῳ=near Tyre; Polyaenus 8, 24, 7 ἐν τῇ νησῖδι=near the island; Diog. L. 1, 34; 85; 97 τὰ ἐν ποσίν=what is before one's feet; Jos., Vi. 227 ἐν Χαβωλώ) ἐν τῷ γαζοφυλακείῳ (q.v.) **J 8:20.** ἐν τῷ Σιλωάμ *near the pool of Siloam* **Lk 13:4.** καθίζειν ἐν τῇ δεξιᾷ τινος *sit at someone's right hand* (cp. 1 Esdr 4:29) **Eph 1:20; Hb 1:3; 8:1.**

ⓓ *among, in* (Hom.+; PTebt 58, 41 [111 BC]; Sir 16:6; 31:9; 1 Macc 4:58; 5:2; TestAbr B 9 p. 13, 27 [Stone p. 74]; Just., A I, 5, 4 ἐν βαρβάροις) ἐν τῇ γενεᾷ ταύτῃ *in the generation now living* **Mk 8:38.** ἐν τῷ γένει μου *among my people* **Gal 1:14** (Just., D. 51, 1 al. ἐν τῷ γένει ὑμῶν). ἐν ἡμῖν **Hb 13:26.** ἐν τῷ ὄχλῳ *in the crowd* **Mk 5:30** (cp. Sir 7:7). ἐν ἀλλήλοις *mutually* (Thu. 1, 24, 4; Just., D. 101, 3) **Ro 1:12; 15:5.** ἐν τοῖς ἡγεμόσιν (=among the commanding officers: Diod. S. 18, 61, 2; Appian, Bell. Civ. 5, 21 §84) Ἰούδα **Mt 2:6** et al. ἐν ἀνθρώποις *among people* (as Himerius, Or. 48 [14], 11; Just., A I, 23, 3, D. 64, 7) **Lk 2:14;** cp. **Ac 4:12.**

ⓔ *before, in the presence of,* etc. (cp. Od. 2, 194; Eur., Andr. 359; Pla., Leg. 9, 879b; Demosth. 24, 207; Polyb. 5, 39, 6; Epict. 3, 22, 8; Appian, Maced. 18 §2 ἐν τοῖς φίλοις=in the presence of his friends; Sir 19:8; Jdth 6:2; PPetr. II, 4 [6], 16 [255/254 BC] δινὸν γάρ ἐστιν ἐν ὄχλῳ ἀτιμάζεσθαι=before a crowd) σοφίαν λαλοῦμεν ἐν τοῖς τελείοις *in the presence of mature* (i.e. spiritually sophisticated) *adults* **1 Cor 2:6** (cp. Simplicius in Epict. p. 131, 20 λέγειν τὰ θεωρήματα ἐν ἰδιώταις). ἐν τ. ὠσὶν ὑμῶν *in your hearing* **Lk 4:21** (cp. Judg 17:2; 4 Km 23:2; Bar 1:3f), where the words can go linguistically just as well w. πεπλήρωται as w. ἡ γραφὴ αὕτη (this passage of scripture read in your hearing). ἐν ὀφθαλμοῖς τινος *in someone's eyes,* i.e. *judgment* (Wsd 3:2; Sir 8:16; Jdth 3:4; 12:14; 1 Macc 1:12) **Mt 21:42** (Ps 117:23). ἔν τινι in the same mng. as early as trag. (Soph., Oed. C. 1213 ἐν ἐμοί=in my judgment, Ant. 925 ἐν θεοῖς καλά; also Pla., Prot. 337b; 343c) ἐν ἐμοί **1 Cor 14:11;** possibly **J 3:21** (s. 4c below) and **Jd 1** belong here.—In the 'forensic' sense ἔν τινι can mean *in someone's court* or *forum* (Soph., Ant. 459; Pla., Gorg. 464d, Leg. 11, 916b; Ael. Aristid. 38, 3 K.=7 p. 71 D.; 46 p. 283, 334 D.; Diod. S. 19, 51, 4; Ps.-Heraclit., Ep. 4, 6; but in several of these pass. the mng. does not go significantly beyond 'in the presence of' [s. above]) ἐν ὑμῖν **1 Cor 6:2** (*by you* is also tenable; s. 6 below).

ⓕ esp. to describe certain processes, inward: ἐν ἑαυτῷ *to himself,* i.e. in silence, διαλογίζεσθαι **Mk 2:8; Lk 12:17;** διαπορεῖν **Ac 10:17;** εἰδέναι **J 6:61;** λέγειν **Mt 3:9; 9:21; Lk 7:49;** εἰπεῖν **7:39** al.; ἐμβριμᾶσθαι **J 11:38.**

❷ **marker of a state or condition,** ***in***—ⓐ of being clothed and metaphors assoc. with such condition *in, with* (Hdt. 2, 159; X., Mem. 3, 11, 4; Diod. S. 1, 12, 9; Herodian 2, 13, 3; Jdth 10:3; 1 Macc 6:35; 2 Macc 3:33) ἠμφιεσμένον ἐν μαλακοῖς *dressed in soft clothes* **Mt 11:8.** περιβάλλεσθαι ἐν ἱματίοις **Rv 3:5; 4:4.** ἔρχεσθαι ἐν ἐνδύμασι προβάτων *come in sheep's clothing* **Mt 7:15.** περιπατεῖν ἐν στολαῖς *walk about in long robes* **Mk 12:38** (Tat. 2, 1 ἐν πορφυρίδι περιπατῶν); cp. **Ac 10:30; Mt 11:21; Lk 10:13.** ἐν λευκοῖς *in white* (Artem. 2, 3; 4, 2 ἐν λευκοῖς προϊέναι; Epict. 3, 22, 1) **J 20:12;** Hv 4, 2, 1. Prob. corresp. ἐν σαρκί *clothed in flesh* (cp. Diod. S. 1, 12, 9 deities appear ἐν ζῴων μορφαῖς) **1 Ti 3:16; 1J 4:2; 2J 7.** ἐν πάσῃ τῇ δόξῃ αὐτοῦ *in all his glory* **Mt 6:29** (cp. 1 Macc 10:86). ἐν τ. δόξῃ τοῦ πατρός *clothed in his Father's glory* **16:27;** cp. **25:31; Mk 8:38; Lk 9:31.**

ⓑ of other states and conditions (so freq. w. γίνομαι, εἰμί; Attic wr.; PPetr II, 11 [1], 8 [III BC] γράφε, ἵνα εἰδῶμεν ἐν οἷς εἶ; 39 [g], 16; UPZ 110, 176 [164 BC] et al.; LXX; Just., A I, 13, 2 πάλιν ἐν ἀφθαρσίᾳ γενέσθαι; 67, 6 τοῖς ἐν χρείᾳ οὖσι; Tat. 20, 1f οὐκ ἔστι γὰρ ἄπειρος ὁ οὐρανός, . . . πεπερασμένος δὲ καὶ ἐν τέρματι; Mel., HE 4, 26, 6 ἐν . . . λεηλασίᾳ 'plundering'): ὑπάρχων ἐν βασάνοις **Lk 16:23.** ἐν τῷ θανάτῳ **1J 3:14.** ἐν ζωῇ **Ro 5:10.** ἐν τοῖς δεσμοῖς **Phlm 13** (Just., A II, 2, 11 ἐν δ. γενέσθαι). ἐν πειρασμοῖς **1 Pt 1:6;** ἐν πολλοῖς ὢν ἀστοχήμασι AcPlCor 2:1. ἐν ὁμοιώματι σαρκός **Ro 8:3.** ἐν πολλῷ ἀγῶνι **1 Th 2:2.** ἐν φθορᾷ *in a state of corruptibility* **1 Cor 15:42.** ἐν ἑτοίμῳ ἔχειν **2 Cor 10:6** (cp. PEleph 10, 7 [223/222 BC] τ. λοιπῶν ἐν ἑτοίμῳ ὄντων; PGen 76, 8; 3 Macc 5:8); ἐν ἐκστάσει *in a state of trance* **Ac 11:5** (opp. Just., D, 115, 3 ἐν καταστάσει ὤν). Of qualities: ἐν πίστει κ. ἀγάπῃ κ. ἁγιασμῷ **1 Ti 2:15;** ἐν κακίᾳ καὶ φθόνῳ **Tit 3:3;** ἐν πανουργίᾳ **2 Cor 4:2;** ἐν εὐσεβείᾳ καὶ σεμνότητι **1 Ti 2:2;** ἐν τῇ ἀνοχῇ τοῦ θεοῦ **Ro 3:26;** ἐν μυστηρίῳ **1 Cor 2:7;** ἐν δόξῃ **Phil 4:19.**

❸ **marker of extension toward a goal that is understood to be within an area or condition,** ***into:*** ἐν is somet. used w. verbs of motion where εἰς would normally be expected (Diod. S. 23, 8, 1 Ἄννων ἐπέρασε ἐν Σικελίᾳ; Hero I 142, 7; 182, 4; Paus. 7, 4, 3 διαβάντες ἐν τῇ Σάμῳ; Epict. 1, 11, 32; 2, 20, 33; Aelian, VH 4, 18; Vett. Val. 210, 26; 212, 6 al., s. index; Pel.-Leg. 1, 4; 5; 2, 1; PParis 10, 2 [145 BC] ἀνακεχώρηκεν ἐν Ἀλεξανδρείᾳ; POxy 294, 4; BGU 22, 13; Tob 5:5 BA; 1 Macc 10:43; TestAbr B 2 p. 106, 23=Stone p. 60 [s. on the LXX Thackeray 25]; πέμψον αὐτοὺς ἐν πολέμῳ En 10:9; TestAbr A 6 p. 83, 22 [Stone p. 14] δάκρυα . . . ἐν τῷ νιπτῆρι πίπτοντα): εἰσέρχεσθαι **Lk 9:46; Rv 11:11;** ἀπάγειν GJs 6:1; ἀνάγειν 7:1; εἰσάγειν 10:1; καταβαίνειν **J 5:3 (4) v.l.;** ἀναβαίνειν GJs 22:13; ἀπέρχεσθαι (Diod. S. 23, 18, 5) Hs 1:6; ἥκειν GJs 5:1; ἀποστέλλειν 25:1. To be understood otherwise: ἐξῆλθεν ὁ λόγος ἐν ὅλῃ τῇ Ἰουδαίᾳ *the word went out = spread in all Judaea* **Lk 7:17;** likew. **1 Th 1:8.** The metaphorical expr. ἐπιστρέψαι ἀπειθεῖς ἐν φρονήσει δικαίων *turn the disobedient to the wisdom of the righteous* **Lk 1:17** is striking but consistent w. the basic sense of ἐν. S. also γίνομαι, δίδωμι, ἵστημι, καλέω, and τίθημι. ἐν μέσῳ *among* somet. answers to the question 'whither' (B-D-F §215, 3) **Mt 10:16; Lk 10:3; 8:7.**

❹ **marker of close association within a limit,** ***in***—ⓐ fig., of pers., to indicate the state of being filled w. or gripped by someth.: *in someone*=in one's innermost being ἐν αὐτῷ κατοικεῖ πᾶν τὸ πλήρωμα *in him dwells all the fullness* **Col 2:9.** ἐν αὐτῷ ἐκτίσθη τὰ πάντα (prob. to be understood as local, not instrumental, since ἐν αὐ. would otherwise be identical w. δι' αὐ. in the same vs.) *everything was created in association with him* **1:16** (cp. M. Ant. 4, 23 ἐν σοὶ πάντα; Herm. Wr. 5, 10; AFeuillet, NTS 12, '65, 1–9). ἐν τῷ θεῷ κέκρυπται ἡ ζωὴ ὑμῶν *your life is hid in God* **3:3;** cp. **2:3.** Of sin in humans **Ro 7:17f;** cp. κατεργάζεσθαι vs. **8.** Of Christ who, as a spiritual being, fills people so as to be in charge of their lives **8:10; 2 Cor 13:5,** *abides* **J 6:56,** *lives* **Gal 2:20,** and *takes form* **4:19** in them. Of the divine word: οὐκ ἔστιν ἐν ἡμῖν **1J 1:10;** μένειν ἔν τινι **J 5:38;** ἐνοικεῖν **Col 3:16.** Of God's spirit: οἰκεῖν (ἐνοικεῖν) ἔν τινι **Ro 8:9, 11; 1 Cor 3:16; 2 Ti 1:14.** Of spiritual gifts **1 Ti 4:14; 2 Ti 1:6.** Of miraculous powers ἐνεργεῖν ἔν τινι *be at work in someone* **Mt 14:2; Mk 6:14;** ποιεῖν ἔν τινι εὐάρεστον **Hb 13:21.** The same expr. of God or evil spirits, who somehow work in people: **1 Cor 12:6; Phil 2:13; Eph 2:2** al.

ⓑ of the whole, w. which the parts are closely joined: μένειν ἐν τῇ ἀμπέλῳ *remain in the vine* **J 15:4.** ἐν ἑνὶ σώματι μέλη πολλὰ ἔχομεν *in one body we have many members* **Ro 12:4.** κρέμασθαι ἔν τινι *depend on someth.* **Mt 22:40.**

ⓒ esp. in Paul. or Joh. usage, to designate a close personal relation in which the referent of the ἐν-term is viewed as the controlling influence: *under the control of, under the influence of, in close association with* (cp. ἐν τῷ Δαυιδ εἰμί 2 Km 19:44): of Christ εἶναι, μένειν ἐν τῷ πατρί (ἐν τῷ θεῷ) **J 10:38; 14:10f** (difft. CGordon, 'In' of Predication or Equivalence: JBL 100, '81, 612f); and of Christians **1J 3:24; 4:13, 15f;** *be* or *abide in Christ* **J 14:20; 15:4f;** μένειν ἐν τῷ υἱῷ καὶ ἐν τῷ πατρί **1J 2:24.** ἔργα ἐν θεῷ εἰργασμένα *done in communion with God* **J 3:21** (but s. 1e above).—In Paul the relation of the individual to Christ is very oft. expressed by such phrases as ἐν Χριστῷ, ἐν κυρίῳ etc., also vice versa (FNeugebauer, NTS 4, '57/58, 124–

38; AWedderburn, JSNT 25, ’85, 83–97) ἐν ἐμοὶ Χριστός **Gal 2:20,** but here in the sense of a above.—See, e.g., Dssm., D. ntl. Formel ‘in Christo Jesu’ 1892; EWeber, D. Formel ‘in Chr. Jesu’ u. d. paul. Christusmystik: NKZ 31, 1920, 213ff; LBrun, Zur Formel ‘in Chr. Jesus’ im Phil: Symbolae Arctoae 1, 1922, 19–37; MHansen, Omkring Paulus-Formeln ‘i Kristus’: TK 4/10, 1929, 135–59; HBöhlig, Ἐν κυρίῳ: GHeinrici Festschr. 1914, 170–75; OSchmitz, D. Christusgemeinschaft d. Pls[2] ’56; AWikenhauser, D. Christusmystik d. Pls[2] ’56; KMittring, Heilswirklichkeit b. Pls; Beitrag z. Verständnis der unio cum Christo in d. Plsbriefen 1929; ASchweitzer, D. Mystik d. Ap. Pls 1930 (Eng. tr., WMontgomery, The Myst. of Paul the Ap., ’31); WSchmauch, In Christus ’35; BEaston, Pastoral Ep. ’47, 210f; FBüchsel, ‘In Chr.’ b. Pls: ZNW 42, ’49, 141–58. Also HKorn, D. Nachwirkungen d. Christusmystik d. Pls in den Apost. Vätern, diss. Berlin 1928; EAndrews, Interpretation 6, ’52, 162–77; H-LParisius, ZNW 49, ’58, 285–88 (10 ‘forensic’ passages); JAllan, NTS 5, ’58/59, 54–62 (Eph), ibid. 10, ’63, 115–21 (pastorals); FNeugebauer, In Christus, etc. ’61; MDahl, The Resurrection of the Body (1 Cor 15) ’62, 110–13.—Paul has the most varied expressions for this new life-principle: life in Christ **Ro 6:11, 23;** love in Christ **8:39;** grace, which is given in Christ **1 Cor 1:4;** freedom in Chr. **Gal 2:4;** blessing in Chr. **3:14;** unity in Chr. vs. **28.** στήκειν ἐν κυρίῳ *stand firm in the Lord* **Phil 4:1;** εὑρεθῆναι ἐν Χ. *be found in Christ* **3:9;** εἶναι ἐν Χ. **1 Cor 1:30;** οἱ ἐν Χ. **Ro 8:1.—1 Pt 5:14;** κοιμᾶσθαι ἐν Χ., ἀποθνήσκειν ἐν κυρίῳ **1 Cor 15:18.—Rv 14:13;** ζῳοποιεῖσθαι **1 Cor 15:22.**—The formula is esp. common w. verbs that denote a conviction, hope, etc. πεποιθέναι **Gal 5:10; Phil 1:14; 2 Th 3:4.** παρρησίαν ἔχειν **Phlm 8.** πέπεισμαι **Ro 14:14.** ἐλπίζειν **Phil 2:19.** καύχησιν ἔχειν **Ro 15:17; 1 Cor 15:31.** τὸ αὐτὸ φρονεῖν **Phil 4:2.** ὑπακούειν **Eph 6:1.** λαλεῖν **2 Cor 2:17; 12:19.** ἀλήθειαν λέγειν **Ro 9:1.** λέγειν καὶ μαρτύρεσθαι **Eph 4:17.** But also apart fr. such verbs, in numerous pass. it is used w. verbs and nouns of the most varied sort, often without special emphasis, to indicate the scope within which someth. takes place or has taken place, or to designate someth. as being in close assoc. w. Christ, and can be rendered, variously, *in connection with, in intimate association with, keeping in mind* ἁγιάζεσθαι **1 Cor 1:2,** or ἅγιος ἐν Χ. **Phil 1:1;** ἀσπάζεσθαί τινα **1 Cor 16:19.** δικαιοῦσθαι **Gal 2:17.** κοπιᾶν **Ro 16:12.** παρακαλεῖν **1 Th 4:1.** προσδέχεσθαί τινα **Ro 16:2; Phil 2:29.** χαίρειν **3:1; 4:4, 10.** γαμηθῆναι ἐν κυρίῳ *marry in the Lord*=marry a Christian **1 Cor 7:39.** προϊστάμενοι ὑμῶν ἐν κυρίῳ *your Christian leaders (in the church)* **1 Th 5:12** (but s. προΐστημι 1 and 2).—εὐάρεστος **Col 3:20.** νήπιος **1 Cor 3:1.** φρόνιμος **4:10.** παιδαγωγοί vs. **15.** ὁδοί vs. **17.** Hence used in periphrasis for ‘Christian’ οἱ ὄντες ἐν κυρίῳ **Ro 16:11;** ἄνθρωπος ἐν Χ. **2 Cor 12:2;** αἱ ἐκκλησίαι αἱ ἐν Χ. **Gal 1:22; 1 Th 2:14;** νεκροὶ ἐν Χ. **4:16;** ἐκλεκτός **Ro 16:13.** δόκιμος vs. **10.** δέσμιος **Eph 4:1.** πιστὸς διάκονος **6:21;** ἐν Χ. γεννᾶν τινα *become someone’s parent in the Christian life* **1 Cor 4:15.** τὸ ἔργον μου ὑμεῖς ἐστε ἐν κυρίῳ **9:1.**—The use of ἐν πνεύματι as a formulaic expression is sim.: ἐν πν. εἶναι *be under the impulsion of the spirit,* i.e. the new self, as opposed to ἐν σαρκί *under the domination of the old self* **Ro 8:9;** cp. ἐν νόμῳ **2:12.** λαλεῖν *speak under divine inspiration* **1 Cor 12:3.** ἐγενόμην ἐν πνεύματι *I was in a state of inspiration* **Rv 1:10; 4:2;** opp. ἐν ἑαυτῷ γενόμενος *came to himself* **Ac 12:11** (cp. X., An. 1, 5, 17 et al.).—The expr. ἐν πν. εἶναι is also used to express the idea that someone is under the special infl. of a good or even an undesirable spirit: **Mt 22:43; Mk 12:36; Lk 2:27; 1 Cor 12:3; Rv 17:3; 21:10.** ἄνθρωπος ἐν πν. ἀκαθάρτῳ (ὤν) **Mk 1:23** (s. GBjörck, ConNeot 7, ’42, 1–3).—ἐν τῷ πονηρῷ κεῖσθαι *be in the power of the evil one* **1J 5:19.** οἱ ἐν νόμῳ *those who are subject to the law* **Ro 3:19.** ἐν τῷ Ἀδὰμ ἀποθνήσκειν *die because of a connection w. Adam* **1 Cor 15:22.**—On the formula ἐν ὀνόματι (Χριστοῦ) s. ὄνομα 1, esp. dγℶ. The OT is the source of the expr. ὀμνύναι ἔν τινι *swear by someone* or *someth.* (oft. LXX) **Mt 5:34ff; 23:16, 18ff; Rv 10:6;** παραγγέλλομέν σοι ἐν Ἰησοῦ **Ac 19:14 v.l.** The usage in ὁμολογεῖν ἔν τινι *acknowledge someone* **Mt 10:32; Lk 12:8** (s. ὁμολογέω 4b) is Aramaic.

❺ marker introducing means or instrument, ***with,*** a construction that begins w. Homer (many examples of instrumental ἐν in Radermacher’s edition of Ps.-Demetr., Eloc. p. 100; Reader, Polemo p. 258) but whose wide currency in our lit. is partly caused by the infl. of the LXX, and its similarity to the Hebr. constr. w. בְּ (B-D-F §219; Mlt. 104; Mlt-H. 463f; s. esp. M-M p. 210).

ⓐ it can serve to introduce persons or things that accompany someone to secure an objective: ‘along with’

α. pers., esp. of a military force, w. blending of associative (s. 4) and instrumental idea (1 Macc 1:17; 7:14, 28 al.): ἐν δέκα χιλιάσιν ὑπαντῆσαι *meet, w. 10,000 men* **Lk 14:31** (cp. 1 Macc 4:6, 29 συνήντησεν αὐτοῖς Ἰούδας ἐν δέκα χιλιάσιν ἀνδρῶν). ἦλθεν ἐν μυριάσιν αὐτοῦ **Jd 14** (cp. Jdth 16:3 ἦλθεν ἐν μυριάσι δυνάμεως αὐτοῦ).

β. impers. (oft. LXX; PTebt 41, 5 [c. 119 BC]; 16, 14 [114 BC]; 45, 17 al., where people rush into the village or the house ἐν μαχαίρῃ, ἐν ὅπλοις). (Just., D. 86, 6 τῆς ἀξίνης, ἐν ᾗ πεπορευμένοι ἦσαν … κόψαι ξύλα) ἐν ῥάβδῳ ἔρχεσθαι *come with a stick* (as a means of discipline) **1 Cor 4:21** (cp. Lucian, Dial. Mort. 23, 3 Ἑρμῆν καθικόμενον ἐν τῇ ῥάβδῳ; Gen 32:11; 1 Km 17:43; 1 Ch 11:23; Dssm., B 115f [BS 120]). ἐν πληρώματι εὐλογίας *with the full blessing* **Ro 15:29.** ἐν τῇ βασιλείᾳ αὐτοῦ **Mt 16:28.** ἐν αἵματι **Hb 9:25** (cp. Mi 6:6). ἐν τῷ ὕδατι καὶ ἐν τῷ αἵματι **1J 5:6.** ἐν πνεύματι καὶ δυνάμει τοῦ Ἠλίου *equipped w. the spirit and power of Elijah* **Lk 1:17.** φθάνειν ἐν τῷ εὐαγγελίῳ *come with the preaching of the gospel* **2 Cor 10:14.** μὴ ἐν ζύμῃ παλαιᾷ *not burdened w. old leaven* **1 Cor 5:8.**

ⓑ it can serve to express means or instrumentality in terms of location for a specific action (cp. TestAbr A 12 p. 91, 5f [Stone p. 30] κρατῶν ἐν τῇ χειρὶ αὐτοῦ ζυγόν; Tat. 9, 2 οἱ ἐν τοῖς πεσσοῖς ἀθύροντες ‘those who play w. gaming pieces’ [as, e.g., in backgammon]): κατακαίειν ἐν πυρί **Rv 17:16** (cp. Bar 1:2; 1 Esdr 1:52; 1 Macc 5:5 al.; as early as Il. 24, 38; cp. POxy 2747, 74; Aelian, HA 14, 15. Further, the ἐν **Rv 17:16** is not textually certain). ἐν ἅλατι ἁλίζειν, ἀρτύειν **Mt 5:13; Mk 9:50; Lk 14:34** (s. M-M p. 210; WHutton, ET 58, ’46/47, 166–68). ἐν τῷ αἵματι λευκαίνειν **Rv 7:14.** ἐν αἵματι καθαρίζειν **Hb 9:22.** ἐν ῥομφαίᾳ ἀποκτείνειν *kill with the sword* **Rv 6:8** (1 Esdr 1:50; 1 Macc 2:9; cp. 3:3; Jdth 16:4; ἀπολεῖ ἐν ῥομφαίᾳ En 99:16; 4 [6] Esdr [POxy 1010] ἐν ῥ. πεσῇ … πεσοῦνται ἐν μαχαίρῃ; cp. Lucian, Hist. Conscrib. 12 ἐν ἀκοντίῳ φονεύειν). ἐν μαχαίρῃ πατάσσειν **Lk 22:49** (διχοτομήσατε … ἐν μ. GrBar 16:3); ἐν μ. ἀπόλλυσθαι *perish by the sword* **Mt 26:52.** ποιμαίνειν ἐν ῥάβδῳ σιδηρᾷ **Rv 2:27; 12:5; 19:15** (s. ποιμαίνω 2aγ and cp. PGM 36, 109). καταπατεῖν τι ἐν τοῖς ποσίν *tread someth. w. the feet* **Mt 7:6** (cp. Sir 38:29). δύο λαοὺς βλέπω ἐν τοῖς ὀφθαλμοῖς μου *I see two peoples with my eyes* GJs 17:2 (ἐν ὀφθαλμοῖσιν ὁρᾶν=see with the eyes: cp. Il. 1, 587; Od. 8, 459; Callinus [VII BC], fgm. 1, 20 Diehl[2]). ποιεῖν κράτος ἐν βραχίονι *do a mighty deed w. one’s arm* **Lk 1:51** (cp. Sir 38:30); cp. **11:20.** δικαιοῦσθαι ἐν τῷ αἵματι *be justified by the blood* **Ro 5:9.** ἐν ἁγιασμῷ πνεύματος **2 Th 2:13; 1 Pt 1:2;** ἐν τ. παρακλήσει **2 Cor 7:7.** εὐλογεῖν ἐν εὐλογίᾳ **Eph 1:3.** λαλοῦντες ἑαυτοῖς ἐν ψαλμοῖς **5:19.** ἀσπάσασθαι … ἐν εὐχῇ *greet w. prayer* GJs 24:1. Of intellectual process γινώσκειν ἔν τινι *know* or *recognize by someth.* (cp. Thuc. 7, 11, 1 ἐν ἐπιστολαῖς ἴστε; Sir 4:24; 11:28; 26:29) **J 13:35; 1J 3:19;** cp. ἐν τῇ κλάσει τοῦ ἄρτου *in the breaking of bread* **Lk 24:35** (s. 10c).— The ἐν which takes the place of the gen. of price is also instrumental ἠγόρασας ἐν τῷ αἵματί σου **Rv 5:9** (cp. 1 Ch 21:24 ἀγοράζω ἐν ἀργυρίῳ).—ἐν ᾧ *whereby* **Ro 14:21.**—The idiom ἀλλάσσειν, μεταλλάσσειν τι ἔν τινι *exchange someth. for someth. else* **Ro 1:23, 25** (cp. Ps 105:20) is not un-Greek (Soph., Ant. 945 Danaë had to οὐράνιον φῶς ἀλλάξαι ἐν χαλκοδέτοις αὐλαῖς=change the heavenly light for brass-bound chambers).

❻ marker of agency: *with the help of* (Diod. S. 19, 46, 4 ἐν τοῖς μετέχουσι τοῦ συνεδρίου=with the help of the members of the council; Philostrat., Vi. Apoll. 7, 9 p. 259, 31 ἐν ἐκείνῳ ἑαλωκότες) ἐν τῷ ἄρχοντι τ. δαιμονίων ἐκβάλλει τὰ δαιμόνια **Mt 9:34.** ἐν ἑτερογλώσσοις λαλεῖν **1 Cor 14:21.** κρίνειν τ. οἰκουμένην ἐν ἀνδρί **Ac 17:31** (cp. SIG[2] 850, 8 [173/172 BC] κριθέντω ἐν ἄνδροις τρίοις; Synes., Ep. 91 p. 231b ἐν ἀνδρί); perh. **1 Cor 6:2** (s. 1e); ἀπολύτρωσις ἐν Χρ. *redemption through Christ* **Ro 3:24** (cp. ἐν αὐτῷ σωθήσεσθε Just., A I, 60, 3).

❼ marker of circumstance or condition under which someth. takes place: ἐν ᾧ κρίνεις **Ro 2:1** (but s. B-D-F §219, 2); ἐν ᾧ δοκιμάζει **14:22;** ἐν ᾧ καυχῶνται **2 Cor 11:12;** ἐν ᾧ τις τολμᾷ **11:21;** ἐν ᾧ καταλαλοῦσιν *whereas they slander* **1 Pt 2:12,** cp. **3:16** (on these Petrine pass. s. also ὅς 1k); ἐν ᾧ ξενίζονται *in view of your changed attitude they consider it odd* **4:4.** ἐν ᾧ in **3:19** may similarly refer to a changed circumstance, i.e. from death to life (WDalton, Christ's Proclamation to the Spirits, '65, esp. 135–42: 'in this sphere, under this influence' [of the spirit]). Other possibilities: *as far as this is concerned:* πνεῦμα· ἐν ᾧ *spirit; as which* (FZimmermann, APF 11, '35, 174 'meanwhile' [indessen]; BReicke, The Disobedient Spirits and Christian Baptism, '46, 108–15: 'on that occasion'=when he died).—Before a substantive inf. (oft. LXX; s. KHuber, Unters. über den Sprachchar. des griech. Lev., diss. Zürich 1916, 83): *in that* w. pres. inf. (POxy 743, 35 [2 BC] ἐν τῷ δέ με περισπᾶσθαι οὐκ ἠδυνάσθην συντυχεῖν Ἀπολλωνίῳ; Just., D. 10, 3 ἐν τῷ μήτε σάββατα τηρεῖν μήτε …) βασανιζομένους ἐν τῷ ἐλαύνειν as *they were having rough going in the waves*=having a difficult time making headway **Mk 6:48.** ἐθαύμαζον ἐν τῷ χρονίζειν … αὐτόν *they marveled over his delay* **Lk 1:21.** ἐν τῷ τὴν χεῖρα ἐκτείνειν σε *in that you extend your hand* **Ac 4:30;** cp. **3:26; Hb 8:13.** W. aor. inf. ἐν τῷ ὑποτάξαι αὐτῷ τὰ πάντα **Hb 2:8.** Somet. the circumstantial and temporal (s. 7 and 10) uses are so intermingled that it is difficult to decide between them; so in some of the pass. cited above, and also Hv 1, 1, 8 et al. (B-D-F §404, 3; Rob. 1073).—WHutton, Considerations for the Translation of ἐν, Bible Translator 9, '58, 163–70; response by NTurner, ibid. 10, '59, 113–20.—On ἐν w. article and inf. s. ISoisalon-Soininen, Die Infinitive in der LXX, '65, 80ff.

❽ marker denoting the object to which someth. happens or in which someth. shows itself, or by which someth. is recognized, ***to, by, in connection with:*** ζητεῖν τι ἔν τινι *require someth. in the case of someone* **1 Cor 4:2;** cp. ἐν ἡμῖν μάθητε *so that you might learn in connection w. us* vs. **6.** Cp. **Phil 1:30.** ἵνα οὕτως γένηται ἐν ἐμοί *that this may be done in my case* **1 Cor 9:15** (Just., D. 77, 3 τοῦτο γενόμενον ἐν τῷ ἡμετέρῳ Χριστῷ). ἐδόξαζον ἐν ἐμοὶ τὸν θεόν perh. *they glorified God in my case* **Gal 1:24,** though *because of me* and *for me* are also possible. μήτι ἐν ἐμοὶ ἀνεκεφαλαιώθη ἡ ἱστορία GJs 13:1 (s. ἀνακεφαλαιόω 1). ποιεῖν τι ἔν τινι *do someth. to (with) someone* (Epict., Ench. 33, 12; Ps.-Lucian, Philopatr. 18 μὴ ἑτεροῖόν τι ποιήσῃς ἐν ἐμοί; Gen 40:14; Jdth 7:24; 1 Macc 7:23) **Mt 17:12; Lk 23:31.** ἐργάζεσθαί τι ἔν τινι **Mk 14:6.** ἔχειν τι ἔν τινι *have someth. in someone* **J 3:15** (but ἐν αὐτῷ is oft. constr. w. πιστεύων, cp. v.l.); cp. **14:30** (s. BNoack, Satanas u. Soteria '48, 92). ἵνα δικαιοσύνης ναὸν ἐν τῷ ἰδίῳ σώματι ἀναδείξῃ AcPlCor 2:17 (s. ἀναδείκνυμι 1).—For the ordinary dat. (Diod. S. 3, 51, 4 ἐν ἀψύχῳ ἀδύνατον=it is impossible for a lifeless thing; Ael. Aristid. 49, 15 K.=25 p. 492 D.: ἐν Νηρίτῳ θαυμαστὰ ἐνεδείξατο=[God] showed wonderful things to N.; 53 p. 629 D.: οὐ γὰρ ἐν τοῖς βελτίστοις εἰσὶ παῖδες, ἐν δὲ πονηροτάτοις οὐκέτι=it is not the case that the very good have children, and the very bad have none [datives of possession]; 54 p. 653 D.: ἐν τ. φαύλοις θετέον=to the bad; EpJer 66 ἐν ἔθνεσιν; Aesop, Fab. 19, 8 and 348a, 5 v.l. Ch.) ἀποκαλύψαι τὸν υἱὸν αὐτοῦ ἐν ἐμοί **Gal 1:16.** φανερόν ἐστιν ἐν αὐτοῖς **Ro 1:19** (Aesop 15c, 11 Ch. τ. φανερὸν ἐν πᾶσιν=evident to all). ἐν ἐμοὶ βάρβαρος (corresp. to τῷ λαλοῦντι βάρβ.) **1 Cor 14:11** (Amphis Com. [IV BC] 21 μάταιός ἐστιν ἐν ἐμοί). δεδομένον ἐν ἀνθρώποις **Ac 4:12.** θεῷ … ἐν ἀνθρώποις **Lk 2:14.**—Esp. w. verbs of striking against: προσκόπτω, πταίω, σκανδαλίζομαι; s. these entries.

❾ marker of cause or reason, ***because of, on account of*** (PParis 28, 13=UPZ 48, 12f [162/161 BC] διαλυόμενοι ἐν τῷ λιμῷ; Ps 30:11; 1 Macc 16:3 ἐν τῷ ἐλέει; 2 Macc 7:29; Sir 33:17)

ⓐ gener. ἁγιάζεσθαι ἔν τινι **Hb 10:10; 1 Cor 7:14.** ἐν τ. ἐπιθυμίαις τῶν καρδιῶν **Ro 1:24;** perh. ἐν Ἰσαὰκ κληθήσεταί σοι σπέρμα **9:7; Hb 11:18** (both Gen 21:12). ἐν τῇ πολυλογίᾳ αὐτῶν *because of their many words* **Mt 6:7.** ἐν τούτῳ πιστεύομεν *this is the reason why we believe* **J 16:30;** cp. **Ac 24:16; 1 Cor 4:4** (Just., D. 68, 7 οὐχὶ καὶ ἐν τούτῳ δυσωπήσω ὑμᾶς μὴ πείθεσθαι τοῖς διδασκάλοις ὑμῶν='surely you will be convinced by this [argument] to lose confidence in your teachers, won't you?'); perh. **2 Cor 5:2.** Sim., of the occasion: ἔφυγεν ἐν τῷ λόγῳ τούτῳ *at this statement* **Ac 7:29;** cp. **8:6.** W. attraction ἐν ᾧ = ἐν τούτῳ ὅτι *for the reason that = because* **Ro 8:3; Hb 2:18; 6:17.**

ⓑ w. verbs that express feeling or emotion, to denote that toward which the feeling is directed; so: εὐδοκεῖν (εὐδοκία), εὐφραίνεσθαι, καυχᾶσθαι, χαίρειν et al.

❿ marker of a period of time, ***in, while, when***

ⓐ indicating an occurrence or action within which, at a certain point, someth. occurs **Mt 2:1.** ἐν ταῖς ἡμέραις ἐκείναις **3:1.** ἐν τῷ ἑξῆς *afterward* **Lk 7:11.** ἐν τῷ μεταξύ *meanwhile* (PTebt 72, 190; PFlor 36, 5) **J 4:31.** *in the course of, within* ἐν τρισὶν ἡμέραις (X., Ages. 1, 34; Diod. S. 13, 14, 2; 20, 83, 4; Arrian, Anab. 4, 6, 4 ἐν τρισὶν ἡμέραις; Aelian, VH 1, 6; IPriene 9, 29; GDI 1222, 4 [Arcadia] ἰν ἀμέραις τρισί; EpArist 24; Demetr.: 722 fgm. 1:3 Jac.) **Mt 27:40; J 2:19f.**

ⓑ point of time when someth. occurs ἐν ἡμέρᾳ κρίσεως **Mt 11:22** (En 10:6; Just., D. 38, 2; Tat. 12, 4). ἐν τῇ ἐσχάτῃ ἡμέρᾳ **J 6:44; 11:24; 12:48;** cp. **7:37.** ἐν ἐκείνῃ τῇ ὥρᾳ **Mt 8:13; 10:19;** cp. **7:22; J 4:53.** ἐν σαββάτῳ **12:2; J 7:23.** ἐν τῇ ἡμέρᾳ **J 11:9** (opp. ἐν τῇ νυκτί vs. **10**). ἐν τῷ δευτέρῳ *on the second visit* **Ac 7:13.** ἐν τῇ παλιγγενεσίᾳ *in the new age* **Mt 19:28.** ἐν τῇ παρουσίᾳ **1 Cor 15:23; 1 Th 2:19; 3:13; Phil 2:12** (here, in contrast to the other pass., there is no reference to the second coming of Christ.—Just., D. 31, 1 ἐν τῇ ἐνδόξῳ γινομένῃ αὐτοῦ παρουσίᾳ; 35, 8; 54, 1 al.); **1J 2:28.** ἐν τῇ ἀναστάσει *in the resurrection* **Mt 22:28; Mk 12:23; Lk 14:14; 20:33; J 11:24** (Just., D. 45, 2 ἐν τῇ τῶν νεκρῶν ἀναστάσει). ἐν τῇ ἐσχάτῃ σάλπιγγι *at the last trumpet-call* **1 Cor 15:52.** ἐν τῇ ἀποκαλύψει *at the appearance of Jesus/Christ* (in the last days) **2 Th 1:7; 1 Pt 1:7, 13; 4:13.**

ⓒ to introduce an activity whose time is given *when, while, during* (Diod. S. 23, 12, 1 ἐν τοῖς τοιούτοις=in the case of this kind of behavior) ἐν τῇ προσευχῇ *when (you) pray* **Mt 21:22.** ἐν τῇ στάσει *during the revolt* **Mk 15:7.** ἐν τῇ διδαχῇ *in the course of his teaching* **Mk 4:2; 12:38.** If **Lk 24:35** belongs here, the sense would be *on the occasion of, when* (but s. 5b). ἐν αὐτῷ *in it* (the preaching of the gospel) **Eph 6:20.** γρηγοροῦντες ἐν αὐτῇ (τῇ προσευχῇ) *while you are watchful in it* **Col 4:2.** Esp. w. the pres. inf. used substantively: ἐν τῷ σπείρειν *while (he) sowed* **Mt 13:4; Mk 4:4;** cp. **6:48** (s. 7 above and βασανίζω); ἐν τῷ καθεύδειν τοὺς ἀνθρώπους *while people were asleep* **Mt 13:25;** ἐν τῷ κατηγορεῖσθαι αὐτόν *during the accusations against him* **27:12.** W. the aor. inf. the meaning is likewise *when.* Owing to the fundamental significance of the aor. the action is the focal point (s. Rob. 1073, opp. B-D-F §404) ἐν τῷ γενέσθαι τὴν φωνήν **Lk 9:36.** ἐν τῷ ἐπανελθεῖν αὐτόν **19:15.** ἐν τῷ εἰσελθεῖν αὐτούς **9:34.**—W. ἐν ᾧ *while, as long as* (Soph., Trach. 929; Cleanthes [IV/III BC] Stoic. I p. 135, 1 [Diog. L. 7, 171]; Demetr.: 722 fgm. 1, 11 Jac.; Plut., Mor. 356c; Arrian, Anab. 6, 12, 1; Pamprepios of Panopolis [V AD] 1, 22 [ed. HGerstinger, SBWienAk 208/3, 1928]) **Mk 2:19; Lk 5:34; 24:44** D; **J 5:7.**

⓫ **marker denoting kind and manner,** esp. functioning as an auxiliary in periphrasis for adverbs (Kühner-G. I 466): ἐν δυνάμει *w. power, powerfully* **Mk 9:1; Ro 1:4; Col 1:29; 2 Th 1:11;** ἐν δικαιοσύνῃ *justly* **Ac 17:31; Rv 19:11** (cp. Just., A II, 4, 3 and D. 16, 3; 19, 2 ἐν δίκῃ). ἐν χαρᾷ *joyfully* **Ro 15:32.** ἐν ἐκτενείᾳ *earnestly* **Ac 26:7.** ἐν σπουδῇ *zealously* **Ro 12:8.** ἐν χάριτι *graciously* **Gal 1:6; 2 Th 2:16.** ἐν (πάσῃ) παρρησίᾳ *freely, openly* **J 7:4; 16:29; Phil 1:20.** ἐν πάσῃ ἀσφαλείᾳ **Ac 5:23.** ἐν τάχει (PHib 47, 35 [256 BC] ἀπόστειλον ἐν τάχει) **Lk 18:8; Ro 16:20; Rv 1:1; 22:6.** ἐν μυστηρίῳ **1 Cor 2:7** (belongs prob. not to σοφία, but to λαλοῦμεν: in *the form of a secret;* cp. Polyb. 23, 3, 4; 26, 7, 5; Just., D. 63, 2 Μωυσῆς … ἐν παραβολῇ λέγων; 68, 6 εἰρήμενον … ἐν μυστηρίῳ; Diod. S. 17, 8, 5 ἐν δωρεαῖς λαβόντες=as gifts; 2 Macc 4:30 ἐν δωρεᾷ=as a gift; Sir 26:3; Polyb. 28, 17, 9 λαμβάνειν τι ἐν φερνῇ). Of the norm: ἐν μέτρῳ ἑνὸς ἑκάστου μέρους *acc. to the measure of each individual part* **Eph 4:16.** On **1 Cor 1:21** s. AWedderburn, ZNW 64, '73, 132–34.

⓬ **marker of specification or substance:** w. adj. πλούσιος ἐν ἐλέει **Eph 2:4;** cp. **Tit 2:3; Js 1:8.**—of substance *consisting in* (BGU 72, 11 [191 AD] ἐξέκοψαν πλεῖστον τόπον ἐν ἀρούραις πέντε) τὸν νόμον τῶν ἐντολῶν ἐν δόγμασιν **Eph 2:15.** ἐν μηδενὶ λειπόμενοι **Js 1:4** (contrast Just., A I, 67, 6 τοῖς ἐν χρείᾳ οὖσι). **Hb 13:21a.**—*amounting to* (BGU 970, 14=Mitt-Wilck. II/2, 242, 14f [177 AD] προσηνενκάμην αὐτῷ προοῖκα ἐν δραχμαῖς ἐννακοσίαις) πᾶσαν τὴν συγγένειαν ἐν ψυχαῖς ἑβδομήκοντα πέντε **Ac 7:14.**—Very rarely for the genitive (Philo Mech. 75, 29 τὸ ἐν τῷ κυλίνδρῳ κοίλασμα; EpArist 31 ἡ ἐν αὐτοῖς θεωρία = ἡ αὐτῶν θ.; cp. 29; Tat. 18, 1 πᾶν τὸ ἐν αὐτῇ εἶδος) ἡ δωρεὰ ἐν χάριτι *the free gift in beneficence* or *grace* **Ro 5:15.**—DELG. LfgrE s.v. ἐν col. 569 (lit. esp. early Greek). M-M. TW.

ἐναγκαλίζομαι 1 aor. ptc. ἐναγκαλισάμενος; pf. ptc. ἐνηγκαλισμένον (TestAbr B 2 p. 105, 10 [Stone p. 58]) (Meleager [I BC]: Anth. Pal. 7, 476, 10; Plut., Mor. 492d; Alciphron 4, 19, 5; IG XII/7, 395, 25 ὧν τέκνα ἐνηνκαλίσατο; Pr 6:10; 24:33; TestJob 52:10; JosAs 19:3; Mel., P. 24, 164 [B]) ***take in one's arms, hug*** τινά *someone* **Mk 9:36; 10:16** (Diod. S. 3, 58, 2f: Cybele takes little children into her arms [ἐναγκ.] and cures them [σῴζω] when they are sick; hence she is commonly called 'mother of the mountain' [ὀρεία μήτηρ]).—M-M. DELG s.v. ἀγκ-.

ἐνάλιος, ον (Pind. et al.; as εἰνάλιος as early as Homer, also Philo, Decal. 54) ***belonging to the sea*** (τὰ) ἐνάλια *sea creatures* **Js 3:7.**—DELG s.v. ἅλς.

ἐναλλάξ adv. (Pind. et al.; SIG 963, 7; 969, 15; Sb 7350, 4; PGM 4, 145; Gen 48:14; Just., D. 87, 4) **in the opposite direction, *crosswise,*** ὑποδεικνύουσα αὐτοῖς ἐ. *as she pointed in the wrong direction* 1 Cl 12:4. ποιεῖν τὰς χεῖρας *place one's hands crosswise* B 13:5 (Gen 48:14).—DELG s.v. ἄλλος.

ἐνάλλομαι fut. ἐναλοῦμαι Job 16:4; 3 sg. aor. ἐνήλατο LXX **to move in springing motion on an object, *leap upon*** (Aeschyl., Pers. 516; Soph., Oed. R. 1261; Job 6:27 [ἐπί τινι]; Mitt-Wilck. I/2, 11, 43 [II BC]) **Ac 19:16** D.—DELG s.v. ἅλλομαι.

ἐνανθρωπέω (Heliod. 2, 31, 1 ψυχὴ ἐνανθρωπήσασα; Etym. Gud. 467, 2; patristic usage, Lampe s.v.) ***take on human form*** **1J 4:17 v.l.**—DELG s.v. ἄνθρωπος.

ἔναντι adv., functions as prep. w. gen. (SIG 646, 52 [170 BC] ἔναντι Γαΐου; POxy 495, 5 [181/89 AD]; 2343, 9; oft. LXX; PsSol 3:4; Just., D. 77, 2 [here under the influence of Is 8:4; but Just., D. 56, 2 (Gen 19:27) and 18 (Gen 18:22) ἔ. for LXX ἐναντίον]; JWackernagel, Hellenistica 1907, 1ff)

❶ **pert. to being in front of an object, *opposite, before*** ἔ. τοῦ θεοῦ *before God,* i.e. in the temple (Ex 28:29) **Lk 1:8.**

❷ **pert. to someone's perspective or perception of someth.,** ***before*** fig. *in the eyes, in the judgment* ἔ. τοῦ θεοῦ **Ac 8:21;** 1 Cl 39:4 (Job 4:17 v.l.); ἔ. Φαραώ **Ac 7:10 v.l.**—DELG s.v. ἄντα 2.

ἐναντίον neut. of ἐναντίος—❶ **pert. to being in front of, *in the sight of, before,*** functions as prep. w. gen. (Hom. et al.; ins, pap, LXX, En; PsSol 8:8; TestSol 22:2 HP; TestJob 15:8; JosAs 23:11; ParJer; ApcMos 32; Jos., Ant. 16, 344).

ⓐ *before* ἐ. τοῦ θεοῦ *before God* 2 Cl 11:7; ἐ. τοῦ λαοῦ *in public* (Ex 19:11) **Lk 20:26;** ἐ. πάντων **Mk 2:12 v.l.;** ἐ. τοῦ κείραντος *before the shearer* **Ac 8:32;** 1 Cl 16:7; B 5:2 (all three Is 53:7). ἀναγγέλλειν ἐ. τινός *proclaim before someone* 1 Cl 16:3 (Is 53:2).

ⓑ *in the sight* or *judgment (of)* (cp. our 'before the court'; cp. Gen 10:9; Sir 39:20; 1 Macc 3:18; 7:25) δίκαιος ἐ. τοῦ θεοῦ **Lk 1:6** (s. ἐνώπιον 3); δυνατὸς ἐ. τοῦ θεοῦ **24:19.** ἔδωκεν αὐτῷ χάριν καὶ σοφίαν ἐ. Φαραώ **Ac 7:10** (Gen 39:21).

❷ adv. w. art. τοὐναντίον *on the other hand* (X., Pla. et al.; 3 Macc 3:22; Philo, Op. M. 2; Jos., Ant. 1, 270; 18, 24) **2 Cor 2:7; Gal 2:7; 1 Pt 3:9;** MPol 12:1.—DELG s.v. ἄντα. M-M. s.v. ἐναντίος.

ἐναντιόομαι aor. inf. ἐναντιωθῆναι 3 Macc 3:1; fut. ptc. ἐναντιωθησόμενα 4 Macc 5:26 (s. next entry; Aeschyl.+; ins, pap, LXX; EpArist 254; Manetho 609: fgm. 10a, 240 Jac. [in Jos., C. Ap. 1, 240]; Jos., Ant. 14, 309; Just., D. 27, 2) **to be in opposition to, *oppose (oneself)*** w. dat. (Diod. S. 16, 74, 2; ins; Sb 8393, 10; UPZ 144, 22 [164 BC]; Mitt-Wilck. II/2, 242, 12f [177 AD=BGU 970, 12] τοῖς διατεταγμένοις) **Ac 13:45 v.l.;** τῷ θελήματι θεοῦ *the will of God* 1 Cl 61:1 (cp. PGM 12, 262).—DELG s.v. ἄντα.

ἐναντίος, α, ον (Hom. et al.; ins, pap, LXX; PsSol 8:8; Test12Patr, EpArist, Philo, Joseph.; apolog. except Ar.)

❶ **pert. to being opposite in terms of direction,** ***opposite, against, contrary*** of the wind (X., An. 4, 5, 3; Dio Chrys. 17 [34], 19; Jos., Bell. 3, 421) **Mt 14:24; Mk 6:48; Ac 27:4.**—ἐξ ἐναντίας (earlier Gk. [Hdt., Thuc.], oft. LXX; B-D-F §241, 1) ἐξ ἐ. τινός *opposite someone* παρεστηκέναι **Mk 15:39** (cp. Sir 37:9).

❷ **pert. to being in opposition,** ***opposed, contrary*** τινί *to someone* (Pr 14:7) Ἰουδαίων . . . πᾶσιν ἀνθρώποις ἐναντίων *who oppose all people* **1 Th 2:15.** ἐναντίον εἶναί τινι *be opposed to someone* τῷ θεῷ B 16:7; ISm 6:2. ἐναντίον ποιεῖν τί τινι (PSI 282, 13 [183 AD] μηδὲ ποιῆσαι ἐναντίον τι τῇ αὐτῇ ὑπογραφῇ; Jos., Ant. 2, 43; 5, 169; Just., A II, 4, 3) **Ac 28:17.** ἐναντία πράσσειν πρὸς τὸ ὄνομά τινος **26:9** (ἐν. πράσσειν as Jos., Ant. 18, 279; 19, 305). ἐν τούτοις τοῖς ἔργοις . . . καὶ μὴ ἐν τοῖς ἐναντίοις *in the contrary (evil) works* 2 Cl 4:3 (cp. TestLevi 14:4 ἐναντίας ἐντολὰς διδάσκοντες τοῖς τοῦ θεοῦ δικαιώμασιν).—τὰ ἐναντία *the opposite,* ἀπολαμβάνειν τὰ ἐναντία παρά τινος *receive the opposite fr. someone* Hv 5:7 (cp. POxy 1258, 10f [45 AD] εὐορκοῦντι μέν μοι εὖ εἴη, ἐπιορκοῦντι δὲ τὰ ἐναντία. Likew. SIG 914, 45; 921, 113; Jos., C. Ap. 2, 37; Just. A I, 43, 5ff; Ath. 3, 2).—ὁ ἐξ ἐναντίας (s. 1 above) *the opponent* **Tit 2:8** (cp. Sext. Emp., Phys. 1, 66 οἱ ἐξ ἐ.; 2, 69, Eth. 125 ; Diog. L. 1, 84; Mitt-Wilck. I/2, 461, 1 πρὸς τὸν ἐξ ἐναντίας; Philo, Aet. M. 7).—DELG s.v. ἄντα. M-M. Sv.

ἐναργής, ές (ἀργής 'bright'; Hom.+; ins, pap, EpArist, Philo; Jos., Ant. 14, 266, C. Ap. 2, 190; Ath., R. 77, 25; ἐναργῶς Just., D. 54, 1; 114, 1; Ath., R. 65, 1 al.) **pert. to being readily perceived,** ***clear, evident, visible*** **Hb 4:12 v.l.** (for ἐνεργής). For the ἐνεργής of the Gk. text in **1 Cor 16:9** and **Phlm 6** some Lat. mss. have 'evidens' or 'manifesta'.—Frisk s.v. ἀργής. B. 1233.

ἐνάρετος, ον **pert. to being exceptional in character or performance,** ***first-rate, high-class, exceptional, virtuous*** (a favorite word of Stoics [s. ἀρετή; Phryn. 328f Lob.]; Chrysipp.: Stoic. III 72; 4 Macc 11:5; TestAbr A 20 p. 104, 7 [Stone p. 56]; Philo, Deus Imm. 11; Jos., Bell. 6, 89; OGI 485, 2; 505, 8; pap; T. Kellis 22, 56 [of God], 60 [of powers in the heavenly luminaries]; Just., A I, 4, 3 al.; ἐναρέτως A I, 21, 6; A II, 9, 1) *virtuous* βίος (=*life that meets the highest standard*) 1 Cl 62:1. Perh. subst. ἐνάρετον κ. τέλειον (τέλειος 1aα) IPhld 1:2.—τὸ σημεῖον τὸ ἐ. *miraculous sign* AcPl Ha 3, 16 (s. ἀρετή 2).—DELG s.v. ἀρετή.

ἐναρμόνιος, ον (ἁρμονία 'means of joining', ἁρμόζω 'fit together'; Pla. et al.; Philo) ***harmonious*** ἄστρων ἐναρμόνιον κίνησιν Hs 12, 4, 1 v.l.—DELG s.v. ἅρμα.

ἐνάρχομαι 1 aor. ἐνηρξάμην; plpf. 3 sg. ἐνῆρκτο Num 17:12 (s. ἄρχομαι; since Eur., who uses it as a sacrificial t.t., construed w. acc.) ***begin*** (so, without further connotation, in later wr., Polyb. et al.; PTebt 24, 34; 36 [117 BC]; LXX; TestAsh 1:9; EpArist 129) τὶ *someth.* (opp. ἐπιτελεῖν, ἐπιτελεῖσθαι) ἐν ὑμῖν ἔργον ἀγαθόν **Phil 1:6.** Abs. (Sb 4369b, 23 [III BC]) ἐναρξάμενοι πνεύματι *you who have made a beginning* (in your Christian life) *spirit-wise* (or, *in spirit-fashion*) (opp. σαρκί 'flesh-wise', 'in the mode of the old self') **Gal 3:3** (s. πνεῦμα 5dβ).—M-M.

ἔνατος, η, ον (Hom.+; for the spelling ἔνν- B-D-F §11, 2; Rob. 213) ***ninth*** θεμέλιος **Rv 21:20;** ὄρος Hs 9, 1, 9; 9, 26, 1. ὥρα (=3 p.m.; TestAbr B 12 p. 117, 2 [Stone p. 82]) **Mt 20:5; 27:45f; Mk 15:33f; Lk 23:44; Ac 10:3, 30;** GPt 6:22. As a time for prayer **Ac 3:1** (s. Elbogen[2] 98; Billerb. II 696–702 and προσεύχομαι end). GJs 2:4 (numerical sign Θ̄).—DELG s.v. ἐννέα. M-M. TW.

ἐναφίημι (s. ἀφίημι; Hdt. et al.; pap; Ezk 21:22; Jos., Bell, 6, 336) (primary mng., to let drop into) ***let, permit,*** **Mk 7:12 v.l.** (cp. Oribasius, Fgm. 37).

ἐνγ- s. ἐγγ-.

ἐνδεής, ές (s. δέησις, δέομαι; Soph., Hdt. et al.; ins, pap, LXX, Philo; Jos., Ant. 17, 175 al.; Ar. 11, 1; Just.; Tat. 5, 2; Ath., R. 61, 12 al.)

❶ **pert. to being in need of material possessions,** ***poor, impoverished,*** **Ac 4:34** (cp. Dt 15:4).

❷ **pert. to being relatively deficient in someth., such as knowledge,** ***poorly instructed*** Hv 3, 1, 2. Comp. ἐνδεέστερος: ἐνδεέστερον γίνεσθαί τινος *become needier than someone* perh. in ref. to need of knowledge of the kind that the Shepherd provides m 8:10; apparently with the same theme ἑαυτὸν ἐ. ποιεῖν τινος 11:8 (as the context indicates, one who has the spirit from above does not parade knowledge but waits for the Holy Spirit to provide insight and then speaks).—DELG s.v. 2 δέω. M-M. TW.

ἔνδειγμα, ατος, τό (s. δεῖγμα, ἐνδείκνυμι; Pla., Critias, 110b; Demosth. 19, 256) **the proof of something,** ***evidence, plain indication*** ἔ. τῆς δικαίας κρίσεως τ. θεοῦ *of God's righteous judgment* **2 Th 1:5.**—DELG s.v. δείκνυμι.

ἐνδείκνυμι fut. ptc. ἐνδειξόμενος 2 Macc 13:9; in our lit. only in mid. 1 aor. ἐνεδειξάμην (s. prec. entry and δείκνυμι; Hom. et al.; ins, pap, LXX; TestJob 50:2; TestZeb 3:8 v.l.; ApcEsdr 3:15 p. 27, 29 Tdf.; EpArist, Philo; Jos., Bell. 2, 109, Ant. 19, 33 al.).

❶ **to direct attention to or cause someth. to become known,** ***show, demonstrate,*** τὶ *someth.* (X., An. 6, 1, 19 εὔνοιαν; Wsd 12:17) τὴν ὀργήν **Ro 9:22.** πᾶσαν πίστιν ἀγαθήν **Tit 2:10;** cp. **3:2. Hb 6:11;** 1 Cl 21:7. τὶ εἴς τινα or εἴς τι *show someth. toward someone* or *someth.* οἱ εἰς τὰ κωφὰ τὴν αὐτὴν ἐνδεικνύμενοι φιλοτιμίαν *those who show the same respect to the mute (cult images)* Dg 3:5. (ἀγάπην) εἰς τὸ ὄνομα αὐτοῦ *show love for God's name* (ἧς for ἥν by attraction) **Hb 6:10.** τὴν ἔνδειξιν ἐνδείκνυσθαι (as Pla., Leg. 12, 966b) εἴς τινα *give proof to someone* **2 Cor 8:24.** *Appoint, designate* **Lk 10:1** P[75]. Used w. double acc. (Jos. Bell. 2, 109) ἐ. τὸ ἔργον τοῦ νόμου γραπτόν *show that what the law demands is written* **Ro 2:15;** cp. Dg 5:4. τὶ ἔν τινι *show someth. in someone* **Ro 9:17** (Ex 9:16); cp. **1 Ti 1:16;** *someth. in* or *by someth.* τὴν σοφίαν ἐν ἔργοις ἀγαθοῖς 1 Cl 38:2. τὸ πλοῦτος τ. χάριτος ἐν χρηστότητι **Eph 2:7.**

❷ **to display conduct that affects another,** ***show*** τί τινι *someth. to someone, accord, do to* (Vett. Val. 200, 19; Gen 50:17; 2 Macc 13:9; TestZeb 3:8 v.l. ἐνεδείξαντο αὐτῷ κακά) πολλά μοι κακὰ ἐνεδείξατο *he showed (=did) me a great deal of harm* **2 Ti 4:14.** The mng. of ἐ. is sharpened for the Gr-Rom. ear and mind by the cultural expectation that exemplary conduct is to be rewarded by a recipient. The reciprocal system is freq. expressed with the verbs ἐνδείκνυμι (e.g. SIG 347, 34f ἐνδεικνύωνται τὴν εὔνοιαν τῶ[ι] δήμωι) and ἀποδίδωμι (e.g. χάριν ἀξίαν ἀποδιδοὺς τῶν εὐεργεσίων 'expressing appropriate appreciation for the benefactions' SIG 547, 10). Alexander the coppersmith is cast in an especially bad light through the use of diction that characterizes him as one at odds not only with Paul but Gr-Rom. culture. Instead of εὔνοια or the like, Alexander 'displays' or 'shows' a base character in his dealings w. the apostle and will receive an appropriate requital from the Lord.—M-M.

ἔνδειξις, εως, ἡ (s. prec. entry; Pla. et al.; IG[2] 1128, 35 [in a special legal sense]; PPrinc 119, 3; Philo; Jos., Ant. 19, 133)

❶ **someth. that points to or serves as an indicator of someth.,** ***sign, omen*** ἐστὶν αὐτοῖς ἔ. ἀπωλείας *a sign of destruction for them* **Phil 1:28.**

❷ **someth. that compels acceptance of someth. mentally or emotionally,** ***demonstration, proof*** (Polyb. 3, 38, 5; cp. PPrinc 119, 3 [IV AD]) εἰς ἔνδειξίν τινος (Philo, Op. M. 45; 87) **Ro 3:25;** for this πρὸς τὴν ἔ. τινος (Plut., Pericl. 169 [31, 1]) vs. **26;** ἔ. ἐνδείκνυσθαι **2 Cor 8:24** (ἐνδείκνυμι 1). WKümmel, πάρεσις und ἔνδειξις, ZTK 49, '52, 154–67 favors 'demonstration' for the above passages.—DELG s.v. δείκνυμι. M-M. TW.

ἕνδεκα indecl. (Hom. et al.; pap, LXX; TestJob 22:1; TestGad 5:11) ***eleven*** οἱ ἕ. μαθηταί *the eleven disciples* (without Judas) **Mt 28:16.** ἀπόστολοι **Ac 1:26.** For this οἱ ἕ. (already established as the name of a board in Athens: Lysias 10, 10; Antiphon 5, 70; X.; Pla.; Alciphron 2, 19, 2) **Mk 16:14; Lk 24:9, 33; Ac 2:14; 1 Cor 15:5 v.l.** JPlevnik, CBQ 40, '78. 205–11.—M-M.

ἑνδέκατος, η, ον (Hom. et al.; POslo 141, 2 [50 AD] al.; LXX; EpArist; Jos., Ant. 14, 150; Tat. 41, 3) ***eleventh*** **Rv 21:20;** Hs 9, 1, 10; 9, 28, 1. περὶ τὴν ἑ. ὥραν *at the eleventh hour* (=5 p.m.) **Mt 20:9** (cp. Sb 19, 10 [25 AD] ὅρᾳ [sic] ἑνδεκάτῃ τ. ἡμέρας). Without ὥρα (like our *at 5*) vs. **6.**—M-M.

ἐνδελεχισμός, οῦ, ὁ (=ἐνδελέχεια 'continuity'; Philumen. the physician in Oribasius 45, 29, 21 [CMG VI/2/1 p. 186, 26]; LXX; Jos., Bell. 6, 94, Ant. 11, 77) **a scheduled practice maintained without interruption,** ***continuity*** θυσίαι ἐνδελεχισμοῦ *perpetual sacrifices* (תָּמִיד) 1 Cl 41:2, i.e. the daily burnt offerings; cp. Ex 29:38f; Num 28:3ff.—Schürer II 299–301; OHoltzmann, Tamid (=Mishna 5, 9) 1928.—DELG s.v. δολιχός.

ἐνδέχομαι (s. δέχομαι; 'receive', trag., Hdt. et al.) in our lit. only impers. ἐνδέχεται, **to be acceptable to one's way of thinking,** ***it is possible*** (Thu. et al.; PPetr II, 45; III, 8 [246 BC]; Sb 5249, 2 and 9 [III BC]; PGiss 48, 6; POxy 237 VIII, 31; cp. 2 Macc 11:18; Jos., Ant. 9, 210; Just., D. 135, 5) ὃ ἐὰν ἐνδέχηται *whatever is possible* or *permitted* Hv 3, 3, 4 (Philo, Sacr. Abel. 31 ὅσα ἂν ἐνδέχηται). W. acc. and inf. foll. (Artem. 4, 47 p. 228, 24; Phlegon: 257 fgm. 36, 2, 4 Jac. οὐκ ἐνδέχεται with acc. and inf.; Philo, Cher. 51; Ar. 4, 4 al.) οὐκ ἐνδέχεται *it is impossible that* **Lk 13:33;** Hm 11:12.—M-M.

I. ἐνδέω fut. ἐνδήσω pf. pass. 2 sg. ἐνδέδεσαι Ezk 28:13; ptc. ἐνδεδεμένος LXX (Hom. et al.; LXX, Philo; Jos., Ant. 4, 123; 12, 194)

❶ **to make secure by close connection,** ***bind to,*** 'leopards' (=soldiers), of Paul bound to soldiers who took turns in guarding him IRo 5:1 (s. δέω 2).

❷ **to be intricately linked with someth.,** ***entangle, involve,*** fig. extension of mng. 1 ἑαυτόν *oneself* τινί: οὐ μικρῷ κινδύνῳ *in no little danger* 1 Cl 59:1.—DELG s.v. 1 δέω.

II. ἐνδέω fut. ἐνδεήσω (Eur., Hdt. et al.) in our lit. only mid. (X., Pla. et al.; pap, LXX; Tat. 41, 3 τὸ μέχρι νῦν ἐνδέον 'what is still lacking') ***be in want*** (PAmh 81, 14 εἰς τὸ μηδὲν ἐνδεῖσθαι) ὁ ἐνδεόμενος *the needy one* D 4:8; 5:2; B 20:2.—DELG s.v. 2 δέω.

ἐνδημέω 1 aor. ἐνεδήμησα (ἔνδημος 'at home'; Lysias 9, 5; Plut., Gen. Socr. 6, 578e; ins, pap; Jos., Ant. 3, 262) **to be in a familiar place,** ***to be at home,*** in our lit. only fig. (Chariton 6, 3, 2 the god Eros ἐνδεδήμηκεν εἰς τ. ἐμὴν ψυχήν) ἐ. ἐν τῷ σώματι *be at home in the body*=phys. life **2 Cor 5:6;** ἐ. πρὸς τὸν κύριον *be at home w. the Lord* of the afterlife in heaven after departure fr. the body vs. **8.** Abs. in the same sense (opp. ἐκδημεῖν or ἀποδημεῖν, q.v., as vss. 6 and 8) vs. **9.**—RBerry, SJT 14, '61, 60–76.—S. γυμνός 1b.—DELG s.v. δῆμος. M-M. TW.

ἐνδιδύσκω impf. mid. ἐνεδιδυσκόμην (Delph. ins in SIG[2] 857, 13 [156/151 BC]; LXX; Jos., Bell. 7, 29) **to put on clothing,** ***dress, put on,*** τινά τι *someone w. someth.* (2 Km 1:24) αὐτὸν πορφύραν *dress him in a purple* (=royal) *garment* **Mk 15:17.** Mid. *dress oneself* τὶ *in someth.* (Jdth 9:1 v.l.; 10:3 v.l.; TestLevi app. III 19 p. 248 Charles) **Lk 8:27 v.l.; 16:19.** Fig. (Cleopatra 146f ἐξήνεγκεν αὐτοὺς . . . ἐκ θανάτου εἰς ζωὴν κ. ἐνέδυσεν αὐτοὺς θείαν δόξαν πνευματικήν, ἣν οὐκ ἐνεδιδύσκοντο τὸ πρίν) τὰ πνεύματα ταῦτα Hs 9, 13, 5 (cp. also ἐνδύσασθαι Χριστόν Ro 13:14, s. ἐνδύω 2b).—M-M.

ἔνδικος, ον (s. δίκη; Pind. et al.; ILegGort passim [V BC]; Philo) 'based on what is right', hence ***just, deserved*** ὧν τὸ κρίμα ἔνδικόν ἐστιν *their condemnation is deserved* **Ro 3:8.** μισθαποδοσία *a just penalty* **Hb 2:2.**—DELG s.v. δίκη. M-M.

ἔνδοθεν adv. of place (Hom. et al.; Sb 6997, 4 [III BC]; PErl 21, 17; LXX; TestJob 25 ἔ. θυρῶν; Philo, Det. Pot. Ins. 127; Jos., Ant. 11, 108; SibOr 5, 232; Mel., P. fgm. 8b, 26 and 29, p. 230 and 232 P.) **pert. to space inside,** ***within*** ἔνδοθεν δὲ ἐκεῖ[ναι πεπλ]ήρω‹ν›ται σκορπίων *within they are filled with scorpions* Ox 840, 39f (the contrast here 35 [τὸ ἐκτός] and 39 as Appian, Hann. 32 §134 ἔνδοθεν . . . τὰ ἐκτός).—DELG s.v. ἔνδον.

ἐνδόμησις rdg. of the t.r. for ἐνδώμησις, q.v.—M-M.

ἐνδοξάζομαι 1 aor. pass. ἐνεδοξάσθην; fut. ἐνδοξασθήσομαι (s. δοξάζομαι, δόξα) **to be held in high esteem,** ***be glorified, honored*** (LXX; TestSim 6:5; PGM 13, 448 διά σε ἐνεδοξάσθη) of the name of the Lord Jesus **2 Th 1:12.** ἐν τοῖς ἁγίοις αὐτοῦ *among his holy ones* vs. **10.**—M-M. TW.

ἔνδοξος, ον (s. prec. entry; X., Pla.+; Ath., R. 58, 5 'plausible').—❶ **pert. to being held in high esteem,** ***honored, distinguished, eminent*** (Pla., Sophist. 223b; ins; LXX; Jos., Bell. 5, 287, Ant. 6, 180) cp. **Mt 20:28** D=Agr 22. διακονία esteemed by God Hm 2:6. Opp. ἄτιμος **1 Cor 4:10.** Opp. ἄδοξος (as Teles p. 52, 3; Philo, Ebr. 195) 1 Cl 3:3; MPol 8:1; cp. ἐ. παρὰ τῷ θεῷ *more honorable in the sight of God* Hs 5, 3, 3. ἀνὴρ ἔ. τῇ ὄψει *of distinguished appearance* Hv 5:1.

❷ **pert. to possessing an inherent quality that is not ordinary,** ***glorious, splendid*** ἔ. ἄγγελος Hs 7:1; 9, 1, 3; cp. 9, 7, 1. Of clothing **Lk 7:25** (cp. TestLevi 8:5 στολὴν ἁγίαν καὶ ἔ.; Herodian 1, 16, 3 τὴν ἔνδοξον πορφύραν περιτίθενται but here w. focus on the esteem in which purple is held; s. πορφύρα and lit. on the sheen of royal purple garments; cp. New Docs 3, 53f). Of the church, brilliant in purity **Eph 5:27;** τὰ ἔ. *splendid deeds* **Lk 13:17** (cp. Ex 34:10; Job 5:9; 9:10; 34:24; Aeschin. 3, 231 ἔνδοξα κ. λαμπρὰ πράγματα; Mel., HE 4, 26, 8).—Much used in this sense as a favorable epithet: ἀρετή Hm 6, 2, 3; ἐντολή 12, 3, 4; πολυσπλαγχνία s 8, 6, 1; (w. μέγας; Dt 10:21) πράξεις 1 Cl 19:2; ἐπαγγελίαι 34:7; (w. μεγαλοπρεπής; cp. OGI 513, 11; En 32:3) βούλησις 9:1; θρησκεία 45:7; (w. μακάριος) πνεύματα B 1:2. βουλή Hv 1, 3, 4; δύναμις Hm 7:2; δωρεαί

1 Cl 23:2; πράγματα Hv 4, 1, 4; s 9, 2, 5; φόβος m 7:4. Of names, esp. divine (Tob 8:5 BA; Prayer of Manasseh [=Odes 12] 3; PGM 12, 257) ἔ. ὄνομα 1 Cl 43:2. μέγα καὶ ἔ. ὄνομα Hv 4, 1, 3; s 9, 18, 5. πανάγιον καὶ ἔ. ὄνομα 1 Cl 58:1; παντοκράτορι καὶ ἔ. ὀνόματι 60:4; cp. Hv 3, 3, 5.—DELG s.v. δοκέω. M-M. TW.

ἐνδόξως adv. of ἔνδοξος (s. prec. entry; ins [e.g. SIG index]; pap, LXX; En 103:6; SibOr 2, 153) **pert. to being splendid or glorious, *in splendor*** οἰκοδομεῖσθαι B 16:6, 8 (cp. Tob 14:5); ἐ. πάντα ἔχει *all is so glorious* Hs 5, 5, 4; s 9, 18, 4; τίθησιν ἐ. *he gave it* (the elevated serpent) *a place of honor* B 12:6.

ἔνδυμα, ατος, τό (s. ἐνδύω; since V BC [SIG 1218, 3]; Polyb. 38, 20, 7; Strabo 3, 3, 7; Plut., Sol. 8, 5; SIG 1179, 7; PFay12, 20 [103 BC]; LXX; PsSol 2:20; OdeSol 11:11; JosAs 20:5 cod. A; GrBar 9:7; AscIs 3:25; Philo, Spec. Leg. 1, 85; Jos., Bell. 5, 231, Ant. 3, 153)

❶ **material of any kind manufactured to cover the body, *garment, clothing,* Mt 6:25, 28; Lk 12:23;** Ox 840, 19f; 27; also Ox 655, 11f, 16 (=ASyn. 67, 34; Unknown Sayings 86f; Fitzmyer, Oxy p. 545); GPt 4:12; ApcPt 5:17; 6:21 τὸ ἔ. αὐτοῦ λευκὸν ὡς χιών **Mt 28:3** (cp. Da 7:9 Theod.); ἔ. ἀπὸ τριχῶν καμήλου *clothing made of camel's hair* **Mt 3:4;** GEb 13, 78; ἔ. γάμου *a wedding robe* **Mt 22:11f** ([JosAs 20:5 cod. A for γάμου στολήν] on the lack of a festal robe cp. Lucian, Nigr. 14; cp. Acta Alex. VII A, 100–104; Suetonius, Nero 32, 3); τὸ τῆς αἰσχύνης ἔ. *the garment worn for modesty's sake* (Pythagoreans in Diog. L. 8, 43) GEg 252, 57 (cp. Esth 4:17k ἱμάτια στενοχωρίας).

❷ **covering in ref. to one's inner life, *covering.***—Hermas is esp. fond of this transferred use (cp. OdeSol 11:11) ἔχειν ἔ. τῆς ἐπιθυμίας τῆς ἀγαθῆς *clothe oneself in the garment of good desire* m 12, 1, 2. Sim. of Christian virtues as the clothing of the spiritual maidens: ἐνδύειν τὸ ἔ. αὐτῶν s 9, 13, 2; ἀποδύσασθαι τὸ ἔ. *take off the clothing*=renounce the virtues 9, 13, 8; cp. vs. 7.—Idiom: of specious goodness that is fraught with hazard *to come in sheep's clothing* ἔ. προβάτων (cp. Dox. Gr. 573, 21 τὸ ἐκ τῶν προβάτων ἔ.) *sheep's clothing,* disguising a wolf **Mt 7:15.**—B. 395. DELG s.v. δύω. M-M. TW.

ἐνδυναμόω (δυναμόω 'strengthen'; s. δύναμις) 1 aor. ἐνεδυνάμωσα, pass. ἐνεδυναμώθην; pf. pass. ptc. ἐνδεδυναμωμένος Hs 5, 4, 4 (Judg 6:34 B; Ps 51:9 v.l. [ARahlfs, Psalmi cum Odis '31 and Swete]; 1 Ch 12:19 v.l.; Gen 7:20 Aq.; Just., D. 88, 5).

❶ **to cause one to be able to function or do someth., *strengthen*** τινά *someone* or τὶ *someth.* (Cat. Cod. Astr. XI/2 p. 166, 22) of God or Christ, who give power (Herm. Wr. 1, 32 ἐνδυνάμωσόν με) **Phil 4:13; 2 Ti 4:17;** Hs 7:4 v.l. Of Christ **1 Ti 1:12;** ISm 4:2; ἐ. τινὰ ἔν τινι *make someone strong in someth.* Hs 6, 1, 2 v.l.

❷ **to become able to function or do someth., *become strong*** pass. w. act. sense (Plotinus 4, 9, 5; Achmes 37, 2)**—ⓐ** of one who is physically weak ἀπὸ ἀσθενείας **Hb 11:34 v.l.;** so perh. **Ac 9:22** (cp. vs. **19**).

ⓑ usu. of inner or moral strength: ἐ. τῇ πίστει *grow strong in faith* **Ro 4:20.** ἐν τῇ πίστει Hv 3, 12, 3. ἐν ταῖς ἐντολαῖς *in keeping the commandments* m 12, 5, 1; cp. 5, 2, 8 below. ἐν πᾶσι τοῖς δικαιώμασι τοῦ κυρίου Hm 12, 6, 4. ἐν κυρίῳ καὶ ἐν τῷ κράτει **Eph 6:10.** διὰ τοῦ πνεύματος Hs 9, 1, 2; cp. 9, 13, 7. Of women ἐνδυναμωθεῖσαι διὰ τῆς χάριτος τ. θεοῦ 1 Cl 55:3. ἐνδυναμοῦ *be strong* ἐν τ. χάριτι **2 Ti 2:1.** Abs. Hm 5, 2, 8. RAC IV 415–58.—DELG s.v. δύναμαι. M-M. (ref. to Soph., Lex. for the adj. ἐνδύναμος). TW.

ἐνδύνω (epic, Ionic, poet. form beside ἐνδύω, as early as Hom.; Aelian, VH 4, 22; PGM 7, 271; LXX [Helbing 83; 92], in var. senses 'go into [freq. of clothes], enter, creep')

❶ **to enter into an area through devious means or pretense, *slip in*** (Antig. Car. 172: slip εἰς τοὺς κόλπους) εἰς τὰς οἰκίας *worm their way into houses* **2 Ti 3:6.**

❷ **to become introspective, *retire within*** fig. ext. of 1 μὴ καθ' ἑαυτοὺς ἐνδύνοντες μονάζετε *do not retire within yourselves and live alone* B 4:10.—M-M.

ἔνδυσις, εως, ἡ (s. ἐνδύω; Pla. et al.; LXX; Sb 7607, 22; TestJob)—❶ **the act of putting on, *putting on*** ἐνδύσεως ἱματίων κόσμος *adornment that consists in putting on robes* **1 Pt 3:3** (cp. Laudatio Turiae 31 [ed. EWikstrand, The So-Called L.T., '76] of a beloved spouse who attired herself unobtrusively 'ornatus non conspiciendi').

❷ **that which is put on, *clothing*** (Athen. 12, 550c; Cass. Dio 78, 3; Job 41:5; Esth 5:1a; EpArist 96) Dg 9:6.—M-M. TW.

ἐνδύω fut. ἐνδύσω LXX; 1 aor. ἐνέδυσα, pf. ptc. ἐνδεδυκώς LXX; plpf. inf. ἐνδεδύκειν LXX. Mid.: fut. ἐνδύσομαι LXX; 1 aor. ἐνεδυσάμην; pf. ptc. ἐνδεδυμένος (δύω 'get into, put on'; Hom. et al.; pap, LXX; PsSol 11:7; TestJob, Test12Patr, JosAs; ApcMos 20; Philo, Joseph.; Just., A I, 52, 3 [cp. citations below under 2a]).

❶ act. **to put clothing or apparel on someone, *dress, clothe*** τινά *someone* (Appian, Bell. Civ. 5, 99 §411; PGiss 77, 8; Gen 3:21; Ex 29:5; Num 20:26) ἐνδύσατε αὐτόν *dress him* **Lk 15:22.** τινά τι *put someth. on someone* (class.; Diod. S. 2, 27, 3; Gen 41:42; Ex 40:13; 1 Macc 10:62 al.; Just., A I, 52, 3; Mel., P. 17, 116): **Mt 27:28 v.l., 31;** ἐνέδυσαν αὐτὸν τὰ ἱμάτια αὐτοῦ **Mk 15:20;** αὐτὸν ἐ. τὸ ἔνδυμα αὐτῶν *clothe him w. their clothing* Hs 9, 13, 2 (s. ἐνδιδύσκω).

❷ mid. **to put any kind of thing on oneself, *clothe oneself in, put on, wear*** τί *someth.***—ⓐ** lit. (PsSol 11:7; TestJob 39:5; Philo, Somn. 1, 214) **Mt 6:25; Lk 12:22;** Ox 655, 6f (ASyn. 67, 33; cp. GTh 36); ἱμάτιον **Lk 8:27;** cp. Hs 9, 13, 8; 9, 15, 1; GJs 2:4. ἱματισμόν Hs 9, 13, 3. δύο χιτῶνας **Mk 6:9.** ἐσθῆτα βασιλικήν **Ac 12:21.** σάκκον B 3:2 (cp. Ps 34:13; Jon 3:5; Jos., Ant. 8, 385; 11, 256). τὰ ὅπλα **Ro 13:12.** τὴν πανοπλίαν *put on the whole armor* (Jos., Ant. 13, 309) **Eph 6:11;** cp. vs. **14.** θώρακα πίστεως **1 Th 5:8** (cp. Wsd 5:18 [esp. the rdg. of S]; Is 59:17; TestLevi 8:2 ἔνδυσαι τὸ πέταλον τῆς πίστεως; Jos., Ant. 7, 283 θώρακα ἐνδεδυμένος; on this matter s. MDibelius, Hdb. on Eph 6:11; cp. Reader, Polemo p. 366). ἐνδεδυμένος (POxy 285, 11 [c. 50 AD] ἐνδεδυμένος χιτῶνα λεινοῦν; 2 Ch 5:12; Da 10:5) *clothed* ἔνδυμα *in a garment* (Zeph 1:8) AcPt 5:17; Ox 840, 27f. ἔνδυμα γάμου **Mt 22:11.** τρίχας καμήλου **Mk 1:6.** χιτῶνας Hs 9, 2, 4. βύσσινον *a fine linen garment* **Rv 19:14.** ποδήρη *a long robe* **1:13.** λίνον καθαρόν **15:6.** σύνθεσιν ἱματίων Hs 6, 1, 5; μέλανα 9, 9, 5. ῥάκη ῥυπαρά ApcPt 15:30 (δέρματα προβάτων Just., A I, 16, 13 and D. 35, 3 [for **Mt 7:15** ἐν ἐνδύμασι]).—Abs. **2 Cor 5:3 v.l.** (for ἐκδυσάμενοι); here it is uncertain whether an obj. is to be supplied, or whether we might transl.: *when we have dressed ourselves* (cp. Aristot., Anima 1, 3, 407b, 23 ψυχὴν . . . ἐνδύεσθαι σῶμα; Herm. Wr. 10, 18). ApcPt 6:21. Lit. on γυμνός 1b.

ⓑ metaph., very oft., of the taking on of characteristics, virtues, intentions, etc. (LXX; PGM 11a, 19 πάλιν θεὸς ἐνδύσεται τὸ ἑαυτῆς κάλλος ὅπερ ἐξεδύσατο; Iren. 1, 9, 3 [Harv. I 85, 1] τὸν σωτῆρα ἐνδύσασθαι σῶμα ψυχικόν [heretical teaching]). Esp. in the usage of Hermas, upon which the use of Lat. 'induere' in the same sense has prob. had its infl. (exx. in Wetstein on Lk 24:49). The mid. sense is not always clearly right; the pass. is somet. better. ἀφθαρσίαν **1 Cor 15:53f** (cited in Ath., R. 71, 16). ἐξ ὕψους δύναμιν *be clothed w. power fr. above* **Lk 24:49;** cp. Hs 9, 13, 8 (cp. Ps 92:1). δόξαν ApcPt 3, 7. ἰσχύν (Is 51:9; 52:1; Pr 31:26) Hv 3, 12, 2. σπλάγχνα οἰκτιρμοῦ *compassion* **Col 3:12.** ἀκακίαν Hs 9, 29, 3. ἀλήθειαν m 11:4. ἀρετήν 1:2; s 6, 1, 4. ἀφροσύνην 6, 5, 3. ἐπιθυμίαν m 12, 1, 1; 12, 2, 4. ἱλαρότητα 10, 3, 1 and 4. μακροθυμίαν 5, 2, 8. πίστιν (Philo, Conf. Lingu. 31) v 4, 1, 8; m 9:7; s 6, 1, 2. σεμνότητα m 2:4. ὑπερηφανίαν s 8, 9, 1. ὁμόνοιαν 1 Cl 30:3. χάριν IPol 1:2. Note the bold figure τὸν κύριον Ἰησοῦν Χριστὸν ἐ. *clothe oneself in the Lord Jesus Christ* (cp. Dionys. Hal. 11, 5 Ταρκύνιον ἐνδύεσθαι; Ephippus [after 323 BC: 126 fgm. 5 Jac. in Athen. 12, 53, 537e]: Alex. the Great liked to put on the ἱερὰς ἐσθῆτας of the gods, and so became Ammon, Artemis, Hermes, Heracles; Artem. 3, 14 θεοῦ σκευὴν ἔχειν καὶ περικεῖσθαι of the incarnation Mel., P. 66, 468; 100, 767) **Ro 13:14;** cp. **Gal 3:27** (s. Apuleius, Metamorph. 11 and also MDibelius, Die Isisweihe etc., Botschaft u. Geschichte 2, '56, 30–79). Sim. Hs 9, 24, 2 says τὸ πνεῦμα τὸ ἅγιον ἐ., which expresses the same idea as τὸν καινὸν ἄνθρωπον *put on the new* (i.e. spiritual) *person* **Eph 4:24; Col 3:10.** For the fig. s. FDölger, ΙΧΘΥΣ I 1910, 116ff; WStraub, D. Bildersprache des Ap. Pls '37, 24f, 84f.—B. 393. DELG s.v. δύω. M-M. TW.

ἐνδώμησις, εως, ἡ (δωμάω 'to build') (-δό- as v.l. **Rv 21:18;** used of a bldg. for cultic purposes SIG 996, 31 [I AD?]; found also in an ins fr. Tralles: BCH 28, 1904, 78, ln. 9; Jos., Ant. 15, 335 has ἐνδόμησις in most mss. [one reads ἐνδώμησις] mng. a mole in a harbor) primary mng. 'interior structure'; in our lit. prob.=***construction*** hence *material* τοῦ τείχους **Rv 21:18.**—DELG s.v. δέμω. M-M. s.v. -δομ-.

ἐνεγκ- s. φέρω.

ἐνέδρα, ας, ἡ (s. next entry; Thu. et al.; Philo, Spec. Leg. 4, 67; Jos., Vi. 216 al.; pap, LXX; JosAs 8:5; 26:5) primary mng. 'sitting in', hence as **act of concealment for surprise attack, *ambush*** ἐ. ποιεῖν (Thu. 3, 90, 2 ἐνέδραν πεποιημένοι; Palaeph. 1 p. 4, 16; 4 p. 11, 18) *arranging for an ambush* **Ac 25:3;** cp. **23:16** (v.l. τὸ ἔνεδρον); *entrapments* αἱ ἐ. τοῦ διαβόλου ITr 8:1; cp. IPhld 6:2.—B. 1417. DELG s.v. ἕζομαι B2 p. 314. M-M.

ἐνεδρεύω (s. prec. entry) fut. 3 sg. ἐνεδρεύσει Sir 27:28; 1 aor. ἐνήδρευσα LXX (ἔνεδρα 'sitting in'; Thu. et al.; ins, pap, LXX; JosAs)

❶ **to conceal oneself in a suitable position for surprise attack, *lie in wait*** τινά *for someone* (Ps.-Demosth. 40, 10; Diod. S. 19, 69, 1; SIG 730, 19 [I BC]; PRein 7, 26 [II BC]; Dt 19:11; Wsd 2:12; Jos., Bell. 2, 595, Ant. 5, 172) **Ac 23:21.**

❷ **to use intrigue, *plot*** w. inf. foll. (cp. Jos., Ant. 6, 331) **Lk 11:54.**—M-M.

ἔνεδρον, ου, τό (Herodian Gramm. I 378, 2; =deceit POxy 892, 11 [338 AD]. In LXX it has almost driven out the older form ἐνέδρα; s. Thackeray 156f) =ἐνέδρα (q.v.) **Ac 23:16 v.l.**—M-M.

ἐνειλέω 1 aor. ἐνείλησα (Ps.-Aristot., De Mundo 4, 396a, 14; Artem. 1, 54 et al.; PTebt 24, 62 [117 BC]; PRyl 144, 19f [38 AD]; 1 Km 21:10; TestJud 3:6).

❶ **to envelop an object by wrapping it in someth., *wrap (up) in*** τινί *someth.* (Aeneas Tact. 1346; Plut., Brut. 1005 [45, 4]; Dio Chrys. 73 [23], 3 σπαργάνοις; Philostrat., Her. 12, 1 p. 187, 2 βρέφος τῇ λεοντῇ=the child in the lion-skin) τῇ σινδόνι *in the linen cloth* (Diosc. 5, 72 τὶ ὀθονίῳ) **Mk 15:46;** GPt 6:24 (so Gebhardt, Blass; s. εἰλέω).

❷ **to encircle an object with confining material, *confine in,*** w. dat. of the confining medium, extended use of mng. 1 ἐνειλημένος τοῖς δεσμοῖς *confined in chains* Pol 1:1 (-λημμ- cod. Vat.; s. ἐνελίσσω).—DELG s.v. 1 εἰλέω. M-M.

ἔνειμι ptc. ἐνών; impf. 3 pl. ἐνῆσαν 3 Km 10:17 (s. εἰμί 1, in sense of 'be, exist'; Hom. et al.; pap, LXX; TestSol 13:3 P; EpArist 285; Joseph.)

❶ **to be inside an area or object, *be in*** 2 Cl 19:2. τὰ ἐνόντα *what is inside, the contents* (Thu. 4, 57, 3 et al.; PTebt 414, 20 [II AD] τὸ σφυρίδιν [= -ιον] μετὰ τῶν ἐνόντων; Jos., Bell. 6, 183; Just., A II, 13, 5; Ath., R. 75, 24 al.) **Lk 11:41.**

❷ **to be within the limits of realization, *it is possible*** ἔνεστι impers. (Polyb. 21, 4, 14; 22, 14, 2; 4 Macc 4:22; Philo, Migr. Abr. 189: ὡς ἔνι μάλιστα=as much as is possible; Phalaris, Ep. 88 ὡς ἐνῆν; Jos., Ant. 1, 244; Just., D. 46, 2; Tat. 19, 2; Ath. 31, 2) IRo 4:1; Hs 8, 10, 2 v.l. Shortened to ἔνι, q.v.—M-M.

ἕνεκα (Attic; PLond I, 42, 14 p. 30 [172 BC]; POxy 533, 25; 1293, 16f [other exx. in Mayser 242]; LXX [Thackeray 135]; OdeSol 11:17; Jos., Ant. 3, 107; this form **Ac 26:21; Mt 19:5; Lk 6:22; Ac 19:32,** but unanimously attested only in **Ac 26:21.** Also **Mt 5:10, 19:29; Mk 13:9; Lk 21:12; Ro 8:36** [all only in some mss.]; 2 Cl 1:2; MPol 17:3; Hv 1, 3, 1; m 12, 4, 2), **ἕνεκεν** (increasingly prominent fr. III BC on: it is the prevailing form in ins [Meisterhans[3]-Schw. 217; Threatte II 666–68; Thieme 8; Hauser 21]; pap [Mayser 241]; LXX [Thackeray 82]; TestAbr A 17 p. 99, 10 [Stone p. 46]; EpArist; Ar. [Milne 74, 24]; Tat.; Ath., R.; and our lit.; Just. has this form, but only in citations), **εἵνεκεν** q.v. (Sb 1568, 7 [II BC]; PGiss 40 II, 21; PGM 5, 385; ins since 161 AD [Meisterhans[3]-Schw. 216]; LXX [Thackeray 82f]; **Lk 4:18** [Is 61:1]; **18:29 v.l.; Ac 28:20 v.l.; 2 Cor 3:10; 7:12 v.l.;** Hv 3, 2, 1), **εἵνεκα** (O. Wilck II 1148 [II BC]; En 101:2; later exx. in Crönert 114; Hv 3, 1, 9; Reinhold 39f). B-D-F §30, 3; 35, 3; W-S. §5, 20c; Mlt-H. 67f; 329f; Rob. index.

❶ functions as prep. w. gen. to indicate **cause of or reason for someth., *because of, on account of, for the sake of,*** **Mt 5:10f; 10:18, 39; 16:25; 19:29; Mk 8:35; 10:29; 13:9; Lk 6:22; 9:24; 18:29; 21:12; Ac 28:20; Ro 8:36** (Ps 43:23); **14:20; 2 Cor 3:10; 7:12;** 2 Cl 1:2; ITr 12:2; IPol 3:1; Pol 2:3; MPol 13:2; 17:3; Hv 1, 1, 6; 3, 1, 9; 3, 5, 2; m 5, 2, 2; 12, 4, 2; s 1:5; 9, 28, 5f; D 10:3; B 14:9; ἕ. τούτου *for this reason* (Lucian, D. Deor. 23, 2) **Mt 19:5; Mk 10:7** (Gen 2:24); Hv 1, 3, 1; also ἕ. τούτων **Ac 26:21** (PsSol 2:4). Used w. a rel. οὗ εἵ. (Musonius, Ep. 1, 11; Quint. Smyrn. 12, 227; PGiss 27 [117 AD]) **Lk 4:18** (Is 61:1); τίνος ἕ.; *why?* (Demosth.; Menand., Epitr. 547 S. [371 Kö.]; Dio Chrys. 14 [31], 84; Tat. 9, 3) **Ac 19:32;** ἕ. τοῦ w. inf. foll. (Menand., fgm. 358, 2 Kö.; Am 1:6; 2:4; 1 Esdr 8:21; Jos., Ant. 11, 293).

❷ **marker of objective or purpose, *in order that*** ἕ. τοῦ φανερωθῆναι τὴν σπουδὴν ὑμῶν *in order that your zeal might be made known* **2 Cor 7:12** (B-D-F §403; Rob. 1073).—DELG. M-M.

ἐνέκρυψα s. ἐγκρύπτω.

ἐνελίσσω pf. pass. ἐνείλιγμαι (s. ἐνειλέω; Hdt. et al.) *wrap (up) in* τινί *someth.* (POxy 1153, 23 [I AD]) in our lit. only as a conjecture by Zahn: ἐνειλιγμένος τοῖς δεσμοῖς *bound in chains* Pol 1:1.

ἐνέμεινα s. ἐμμένω.

ἐνενήκοντα indecl. (Hom. et al.; pap, LXX; TestAbr A 1 p. 77, 2 [Stone p. 2]; ApcSed 12:4; Philo; Jos., Ant. 18, 365; Tat. 31, 3 v.l.; on spelling s. B-D-F §11, 2; Mayser 214) ***ninety*** **Mt 18:12f; Lk 15:4, 7.**—M-M.

ἐνεός, ά, όν (ἐννεός t.r.) (Pla. et al.; LXX; Jos., Ant. 4, 276) primary mng., pert. to lacking ability to speak, 'mute'; then by extension ***speechless*** (EpJer 40 ἐνεὸν οὐ δυνάμενον λαλῆσαι) οἱ ἄνδρες εἱστήκεισαν ἐνεοί *the men stood speechless* fr. fright **Ac 9:7** (cp. Apollon. Paradox. 6: Pythagoras ἤκουσε φωνὴν μεγάλην ὑπὲρ ἄνθρωπον 'Πυθαγόρα χαῖρε.' τοὺς δὲ παρόντας περιδεεῖς γενέσθαι; Quint. Smyrn. 8, 250f: the Trojans ἐθάμβεον when they heard the voice of Ares commanding them, but could not see the form of the god).—DELG. M-M.

ἐνέπαιξα, ἐνεπαίχθην s. ἐμπαίζω.

ἐνέπεσον s. ἐμπίπτω.

ἐνέπλησα, ἐνεπλήσθην s. ἐμπίμπλημι.

ἐνέπρησε s. ἐμπίμπρημι.

ἐνέργεια, ας, ἡ (s. ἐνεργής, ἐνεργέω; Pre-Socr. et al.; ins, pap, LXX, TestSol, EpArist, Philo, Just., Ath., Hippol.) **the state or quality of being active, *working, operation, action,*** so in NT, and always of transcendent beings (cp. Chrysipp.: Stoic. II 115; Diod. S. 15, 48, 1 θεία ἐ.; likew. Orig., C. Cels. 3, 14, 7; Ps.-Callisth. 1, 30, 4 τὴν τοῦ θεοῦ ἐ.; Sallust. 3 p. 4, 8; 4 p. 4, 27; OGI 262, 4 [III AD] περὶ τῆς ἐνεργείας θεοῦ Διός; Herm. Wr. 10, 22b; 16, 13 δαίμονος γὰρ οὐσία ἐνέργεια; PGM 3, 290; Wsd 7:26; 13:4; 2 Macc 3:29; 3 Macc 4:21; 5:12, 28; EpArist 266; Aristobulus in Eus., PE 8, 10, 12 [p. 142 Holladay] ἐ. τοῦ θεοῦ; Did., Gen. 247, 11 τὸ ἄγγελος ὄνομα ἐνεργείας καὶ οὐκ οὐσίας ἐστίν) ἐ. πλάνης *a deluding influence* **2 Th 2:11.** πίστις τῆς ἐνεργείας τ. θεοῦ *faith in God's (productive) power* **Col 2:12;** cp. **Ac 4:24** D; **1 Cor 12:10 v.l.** Mostly in the expr. κατὰ (τὴν) ἐνέργειαν: κ. τ. ἐ. τοῦ κράτους *according to the manifestation of his power* **Eph 1:19** (for the genitival constr. cp. 1QS 11, 19f; 1QH 4, 32); cp. **3:7; 4:16; Col 1:29;** κ. τ. ἐ. τοῦ δύνασθαι αὐτόν *through the power that enables him* **Phil 3:21.** κατ' ἐνέργειαν τοῦ Σατανᾶ *by the activity of Satan* **2 Th 2:9.**—ἐνεργείᾳ τοῦ πονηροῦ *by urging of the wicked one* AcPl Ha 9, 19 (cp. ὄφεως Just., D. 39, 6; αἱ τῶν δαιμόνων ἐ. Orig., C. Cels. 1, 60, 6).—W. ref. to mode of operation *way of working* τῆς ὀξυχολίας Hm 5, 1, 7; 5, 2, 1. W. δύναμις (Aristot. p. 23a, 10ff; Philo, Rer. Div. Her. 110 al.; Ath. 10, 3; 26, 1) 6, 1, 1a. Pl. (Epict. 2, 16, 18; 4, 11, 33; Philo; Ath.) 6, 1, 1b; 6, 2, 2 and 6. The pl. also v 3, 8, 3, where the word refers to what someth. is equipped to do and may be rendered *function.*—DELG s.v. ἔργον. RAC V 4–51. M-M. TW.

ἐνεργέω 1 aor. ἐνήργησα; pf. ἐνήργηκα; aor. pass. inf. ἐνεργηθῆναι; ptc. ἐνεργηθέντα (s. ἐνέργεια; Just., D. 78, 6, A I, 26, 4) (Aristot.+).

❶ intr. **to put one's capabilities into operation, *work, be at work, be active, operate, be effective*—ⓐ** act. (Philo Mech. 59, 48; 96, 12; Vett. Val. 226, 2; Herm. Wr. 12, 11ab; PGiss 78, 4 [II AD] καλῶς δὲ ποιήσεις καὶ περὶ τὰ λοιπὰ ἐνεργήσασα; Wsd 15:11; 16:17; Jos., Ant. 15, 290, Vi. 156) τὸ θέλειν καὶ τὸ ἐ. *the will and the action* **Phil 2:13b.** Used w. ἐν and dat. of pers. (TestDan 5:5 ἐνεργούντων ἐν ὑμῖν τῶν πνευμάτων; TestSim 4:8; without ἐν Ath. 10, 3) αἱ δυνάμεις ἐνεργοῦσιν ἐν αὐτῷ *miraculous powers are at work in him* **Mt 14:2; Mk 6:14;** cp. **Eph 2:2.** Of God (Julian 4, 142d ἐνεργεῖν ἐθέλει) ὁ ἐνεργῶν B 2:1 (s. HWindisch, Hdb. ad loc.). W. dat. of advantage (cp. Pr 31:12) ὁ ἐνεργήσας Πέτρῳ *the one who was at work for Peter* **Gal 2:8** (the εἰς foll. supplies the goal of the activity, as **Ro 7:5;** s. b below).

ⓑ mid., in our lit. always w. impers. subj. (Diod. S. 13, 85, 2 the siege 'went into effect', 'began'; Herm. Wr. 12, 11c τὰ ἀσώματα) τὰ παθήματα ἐνηργεῖτο ἐν τ. μέλεσιν *the passions were at work in our members* **Ro 7:5** (the εἰς foll. introduces the goal; s. a above on Gal 2:8). ἡ παράκλησις ἡ ἐνεργουμένη ἐν ὑπομονῇ *consolation that functions in (the act of) enduring* **2 Cor 1:6.** ὁ θάνατος ἐν ἡμῖν ἐνεργεῖται *death is at work in us* **4:12** (Lucian, Charon 2 ἐνεργεῖν τὰ τοῦ θανάτου ἔργα). Of God's word **1 Th 2:13.** δύναμις ἐνεργουμένη ἐν ἡμῖν *the power that works in us* **Eph 3:20;** cp. **Col 1:29.** πίστις δι' ἀγάπης ἐνεργουμένη *faith working* (=expressing itself) *through love* **Gal 5:6.** τὸ μυστήριον ἐνεργεῖται τῆς ἀνομίας *the secret force of lawlessness is at work = is in operation* **2 Th 2:7.** δέησις ἐνεργουμένη *effective prayer* **Js 5:16.** τὰ ἐνεργούμενα *the forces at work* 1 Cl 60:1. τὰ καθ' ἕκαστα βλέποντες ἐνεργούμενα *we see how one thing after the other works itself out = comes to pass* B 1:7.—JRoss, ἐνεργεῖσθαι in the NT: Exp. 7th ser., 7, 1909, 75–77; JMayor, ibid. 191f; AGarvie, ET 55, '43/44, p. 97. For the view that the passages in b are passive, not mid., s. the art. by Clark below, p. 98ff and ref. there.

❷ trans. **to bring someth. about through use of capability, *work, produce, effect*** w. acc. (of pers. Just., A I, 26, 4; Ath. 9, 1 al.) of thing (Philo Mech. 59, 48; Polyb. 3, 6, 5; Diod. S. 13, 85, 2; POxy 1567; Pr 21:6; 31:12; Jos., Ant. 3, 155; 15, 283; Just., A I, 12, 5 ταῦτα; 23, 3 ἀσεβῆ ἔργα al.; Iren. 3, 21, 2 [Harv. II 114, 6]; δαίμονες ἐ. λοιμούς Orig., C. Cels. 1, 31, 27; ἡ 'Ιησοῦ δύναμίς ἐστιν ἐνεργοῦσα τὴν ἐπιστροφήν 1, 43, 39; Hippol.) τί *someth.*: of God ὁ τὰ πάντα ἐνεργῶν **Eph 1:11** (cp. EpArist 210). Of the Spirit **2:2.** τὶ ἔν τινι *produce someth. in someone* ὁ ἐνεργῶν τὰ πάντα ἐν πᾶσιν **1 Cor 12:6;** cp. vs. **11.** ὁ ἐνεργῶν ἐν ὑμῖν τὸ θέλειν *the one who produces the will in you* **Phil 2:13a.** οὐδὲ ἐνεργῆσαι δύναται εἰς αὐτούς *it cannot influence them* Hm 5, 2, 1 (cp. Just., D. 18, 3 τὰ ἐξ ἀνθρώπων . . . ἐνεργούμενα εἰς ἡμᾶς); δυνάμεις ἐ. **Gal 3:5** (Just., D. 7, 3); ἐνέργειαν ἐ. **Eph 1:20.** (W. acc. and inf.: Just., A I, 62, 1 al.)—GWhitaker, ET 26, 1914/15, 474–76; KClark, The Mng. of ἐνεργέω and καταργέω in the NT: JBL 54, '35, 93–101.—M-M. TW.

ἐνέργημα, ατος, τό (s. ἐνέργεια, ἐνεργέω; since Epicurus p. 4, 10 Us.)—❶ **activity as expression of capability, *activity*** (Polyb. 2, 42, 7; 4, 8, 7; Diod. S. 4, 51, 6; Vett. Val. 264, 13; EpArist 156; Philo, Det. Pot. Ins. 114; PGM 1, 194; 12, 317) ἐνεργήματα δυνάμεων *activities that express themselves in miracles = miraculous powers* **1 Cor 12:10** (ἐνέργεια, -αι vv.ll.). διαιρέσεις ἐνεργημάτων vs. **6.** Cp. Ox 850, 34 of a transcendent hostile power.

❷ **activity as someth. that impacts on another, *experience*** (Plut., Mor. 899d; Herm. Wr. 1, 22) τὰ συμβαίνοντά σοι ἐνεργήματα *the experiences that befall you* D 3:10; B 19:6.—M-M. TW.

ἐνεργής, ές (s. ἐνέργεια, ἐνεργέω; Aristot. et al.; Polyb. 11, 23, 2; Plut., Sol. 96 [31, 2] v.l.; Diosc., Mat. Med. 1, 18; Vett. Val. 276, 11; Herm. Wr. 10, 23; POxy 1088, 56 [I AD]; Just.) **pert. to practical expression of capability, *effective, active, powerful,*** κοινωνία τῆς πίστεως **Phlm 6.** ὁ λόγος τοῦ θεοῦ **Hb 4:12.** Of a door (fig.), the opening of which promises a rich field of labor **1 Cor 16:9.**—M-M. TW.

ἐνερείδω (Hom. et al.; grave ins Sb 5909) **to cause to enter by exerting force, *thrust in*** pf. pass. ἐνήρεισμαι *be thrust in, become fixed* (cp. Plut., Mor. 327b; 344c) ἔρις ἐνήρεισται (gener. accepted conjecture of Zahn for the impossible ἐνείρισται of the mss.) ἐν ὑμῖν *is firmly rooted among you* IEph 8:1.—DELG s.v. ἐρείδω.

ἐνεστηκώς, ἐνεστώς s. ἐνίστημι.

ἐνευλογέω (s. εὐλογέω; LXX) **to confer special benefits, *act kindly, bless,*** in our lit. only 1 fut. pass. ἐνευλογηθήσομαι **Ac 3:25** (Gen 22:18; s. εὐλογέω 3); **Gal 3:8** (Gen 12:3 v.l.; Just., D. 34, 6 al. for εὐλογηθήσονται Ps 71:17).—DELG s.v. λέγω B1.

ἐνεχθείς s. φέρω.

ἐνέχω impf. ἐνεῖχον; pf. pass. 3 sg. ἐνέσχηται 3 Macc 6:10 (Pind. et al.; ins, pap, LXX; TestGad, s. 1; Jos., Ant. 16, 214; Just., D. 17, 1).

❶ act. **have a grudge against someone, *bear ill-will,*** τινί (ellipt. for χόλον ἐ. τινί: so Hdt. 1, 118, 1; cp. Gen 49:23; TestGad 5:11 v.l.; cp. our colloq. 'have it in for someone') **Mk 6:19.** Abs. δεινῶς ἐ. *be very hostile* **Lk 11:53.**

❷ pass. **to experience constraint, *be subject to, be loaded down with,*** w. dat. (oft. since Pind., P. 8, 69 and Hdt. 2, 121, β 2; PTebt 5, 5 [118 BC]; BGU 1051, 34 al.; 3 Macc 6:10; EpArist 16; Jos., Ant. 18, 179; εἰς . . . ἀδικίαν Just., D. 17, 1) ζυγῷ δουλείας **Gal 5:1.** θλίψεσιν **2 Th 1:4 v.l.**—Field, Notes 28f; 64.—M-M. TW. Spicq.

ἔνθα adv. (Hom. et al.; pap, LXX, pseudepigr., Philo, Joseph., apolog.; Mel., P. 19, 128f) **pert. to a position in an area that is relatively distant fr. the speaker, *there*** MPol 18:3 ; Mel., P. 19, 128f.—Relat. ***where*** (TestAbr A 5 p. 82, 13 [Stone p. 12]; Test12Patr; GrBar 11:9 *whither;* Mel., P. 45, 321 [Ch.]; Parthenius 5, 5; 8, 4; Appian, Iber. 89 §387; Jos., Ant. 14, 5, C. Ap. 2, 282; Just.; Mel., HE 44, 26, 14) GPt 13:56. τὸν τόπον . . . , ἔνθα ἐτάφη *where* (Judas) *was buried* Papias (3:3e). V.l. for ὁπόθεν Papias (3:2g).—M-M.

ἐνθάδε adv., in our lit. only of place (so Hom.+; ins, pap; JosAs 9:5 [16:3, cod. A and Pal. 364]) **pert. to a position relatively near the speaker, *here***

ⓐ w. verbs expressing movement *here, to this place* (3 Macc 6:25; Jos., Ant. 4, 134) ἔρχεσθαι ἐ. (Herodas 2, 97; PCairPreis 48, 6; POxy 967) **J 4:15 v.l., 16;** Hs 9, 5, 5. διέρχεσθαι **J 4:15.** συνέρχεσθαι **Ac 25:17.** παραγένεσθαι AcPlCor 1:16.

ⓑ in ref. to the area in which someth. is located *here, in this place* (Lucian, Dial. Mort 20, 3; En 19:1; 2:13; TestSol; Jos., Bell. 1, 633, Ant. 1, 343; Just.; Ath. 31, 3) **Lk 24:41; Ac 10:18; 16:28; 17:6; 25:24;** τὰ ἐ. *the things that are here* (POxy 1154, 9f [I AD] εἰμὶ ξένος τῶν ἐ.; Jos., Ant. 16, 322) 2 Cl 6:6. ἡ ἐ. ἀπόλαυσις *enjoyment here and now* (Herm. Wr. 6, 3a τὸ ἐ. ἀγαθόν; POxy 1296, 5 [III AD] οἱ ἐ. θεοί) 10:3f. ὁ δοκῶν ἐ. θάνατος *what seems to be death here* (on earth) Dg 10:7.—DELG s.v. ἔνθα. M-M.

ἔνθεν adv. (Hom.+; PFuad I Univ. no. XLI recto, 11; LXX; causal Just. A I, 6, 1; Ath.)

❶ **extension from a source relatively near the speaker, *from there, from here*** (Demetr.: 722 fgm. 1, 10 Jac.; TestSol ἔνθεν καὶ ἔ.; JosAs 24:21 cod. A ἔ. κακεῖθεν for ἔμπροσθεν; ApcEsdr 6:6 p. 31, 11 Tdf. al.; Jos., Ant. 4, 323) μετάβα ἔ. (v.l. ἐντεῦθεν) ἐκεῖ *move fr. this place to that* **Mt 17:20;** διαβαίνειν ἔ. **Lk 16:26.**

❷ **duration measured fr. a point of time, *from then on*** (Apollon. Rhod. 1, 1138; 2, 713; SibOr 1, 387) 2 Cl 13:3; IEph 19:3.—DELG s.v. ἔνθα.

ἔνθεος, ον (s. θεός; trag., X., Pla.+; GDI 805d [Boeotia]; Sb 9217, 4; 9253, 6 [both beg. IV AD]; PGM 1, 21; 160; 13, 144; Philo; Jos., Bell. 3, 353, Ant. 9, 35; SibOr 3, 295; 5, 263; Ath. 7, 2) ***inspired by God,*** in our lit. only as a rdg. of the Sacra Parallela (KHoll, Fgmte. vornic. Kirchenväter aus den Sacr. Par. 1899, p. 22) on ITr 8:2 τὸ ἔ. πλῆθος (Lghtf. has it in the text for ἐν θεῷ).—TW. Sv.

ἐνθυμέομαι dep.; fut. 3 sg. ἐνθυμηθήσεται or ἐνθυμήσεται LXX; 1 aor. ἐνεθυμήθην; pf. ptc. ἐντέθυμημένης 3 Macc 1:25 (s. ἐνθύμησις; Aeschyl., Pre-Socr. et al.; pap, LXX; JosAs 23:7 cod. A; ApcSed 10:5) **to process information by thinking about it carefully, *reflect (on), consider, think,*** w. acc. of thing (Thu. 5, 32, 1; Celsus 7, 18; Sir 16:20; Bar 3:31; 4 Macc 8:27; TestJob 49:1; Philo, Mut. Nom. 240; Jos., Bell. 1, 232, Ant. 11, 155; Just., D. 65, 2) ταῦτα **Mt 1:20.** πονηρά (Wsd 3:14; TestSim 2:14 πονηρὸν πρᾶγμα; TestBenj 3:6) ἐν ταῖς καρδίαις *think evil in your hearts* **9:4.** περί τινος (Pla., Rep. 10, 595a; Isocr. 15, 199, Ep. 9, 8 Blass; Appian, Bell. Civ. 2, 5 §18; Wsd 6:15; TestBenj 3:6) **Ac 10:19 v.l.** (s. διενθυμέομαι).—DELG s.v. θυμός. M-M. TW.

ἐνθύμησις, εως, ἡ (s. prec. entry; since Eur.; Thu. 1, 132, 5; Ps.-Lucian, Salt. 81; Vett. Val. 301, 8; Herm. Wr. 1, 22; PGM 5, 328; BGU 1024 IV, 12; Sym. Job 21:27 and Ezk 11:21; TestJob 47:10; TestJud 13:2; JosAs 23:8) **the process of considering someth., *thought, reflection, idea*** **Mt 9:4; 12:25;** Hm 4, 1, 3. ἡ ἐ. ἀναβαίνει ἐπὶ τὴν καρδίαν *the idea arises in the heart* m 4, 1, 2; 6, 2, 7. χαράγματι τέχνης καὶ ἐνθυμήσεως ἀνθρώπου, τὸ θεῖον εἶναι ὅμοιον *that the divine nature is like something fashioned by human skill and thought* **Ac 17:29.** κριτικὸς ἐνθυμήσεων καὶ ἐννοιῶν *passing judgment on reflections and thoughts* **Hb 4:12;** cp. 1 Cl 21:9.—DELG s.v. θυμός. M-M. TW.

ἐνί poet. form of ἐν IEph 11:2 (cod. Laur.).

ἔνι (for ἔνεστιν [s. ἔνειμι and B-D-F §98; Mlt-H. 306; Rob. s.v. εἰμί p. 313] Hom. [Il. 18, 53; Od. 21, 288]+; ins, pap; Philo; SibOr 3, 39.—On the LXX s. PKatz and ADebrunner, MusHelv 11, '54, 57–64) **to be or exist in a certain context, *there is,*** in our lit. only w. a negative οὐκ ἔνι *there is not* or *no* (Vi. Aesopi I c. 17 p. 270, 6 Ebh.) ἐν ὑμῖν οὐδεὶς σοφός; *is there no wise man among you?* **1 Cor 6:5.** Ἰουδαῖος οὐδὲ Ἕλλην *there is neither Jew nor Gentile* **Gal 3:28; Col 3:11.** παρ' ᾧ οὐκ ἔ. παραλλαγή *with whom there is no variation* **Js 1:17.** οὐκ ἔ. τόπος ἀπόκρυφος *there was no place to hide* GJs 22:3 (s. deStrycker p. 250).—DELG s.v. εἰμί. M-M.

ἐνιαυτός, οῦ, ὁ (Hom.+; ins, pap, LXX, En; TestJud, EpArist, Philo; Jos., Ant. 15, 378, C. Ap. 1, 157; Just., A I, 57, 2; Theoph. Ant. I, 4 [p. 64, 19])

❶ **a period of one year, *year*** **Rv 9:15;** ἐ. καὶ μῆνας ἕξ *a year and a half* **Ac 18:11;** cp. **Js 5:17** (GKittel, Rabbinica 1920, 31–35). ἀρχιερεὺς τοῦ ἐ. ἐκείνου *high priest for that year* **J 11:49, 51; 18:13** (s. UHolzmeister, ZKT 44, 1920, 306–12.—The supposition that there was a different high priest every year holds good for Asia Minor [IBM III, 498; s. CBrandis, Pauly-W. II 475] and for Syria [Lucian, Syr. D. 42], but not for Jerusalem). ποιεῖν ἐ. *spend a year* **Js 4:13** (cp. Pr 13:23; TestJud 10:4). πρῶτος ἐ. *first year of* one's *life* GJs 6:2.—In acc. in answer to the question 'how long?' (Thu. et al.): ὅλον ἐ. *for a whole year* **Ac 11:26;** Hs 6, 4, 4; ὅλον τὸν ἐ. *the whole year through* s 6, 5, 4; ἅπαξ τοῦ ἐ. *once a year* **Hb 9:7** (Ex 30:10; Lev 16:34; cp. Philo, Leg. ad Gai. 306). μέχρι ἐνιαυτοῦ *for as long as a year* Hs 6, 5, 3. κατ' ἐνιαυτόν *every year, annually* (Thu. 1, 93, 3 al.; oft. ins; UPZ 122, 6 [157 BC] of an annual pilgrimage; LXX; EpArist 180) **Hb 9:25; 10:1, 3;** B 10:6. Also παρ' ἐνιαυτόν B 10:7 (Diod. S. 4, 65, 1; SIG 193, 14 [IV BC] παρὰ τὸν ἐ. ἕκαστον).

❷ more gener. **a period of time other than a calendar year,** ***year*** (Aristoph., Ran. 347; Pla., Leg. 10, 906c; Diod. S. 38 + 39 fgm. 5: God has ordained eight ages; each one is an ἐνιαυτὸς μέγας; Jos., Ant. 1, 106 ὁ μέγας ἐνιαυτός consists of 600 years), of the age of salvation brought by the Messiah ἐ. κυρίου δεκτός **Lk 4:19;** B 14:9 (both Is 61:2.—Cp. also Phlegon: 257 fgm. 1, 9 Jac., where Pythia announces the coming of a rather long period of time as φιλόφρων ἐνιαυτός).

❸ The mng. of ἐ. in the combination καιροὶ καὶ ἐνιαυτοί **Gal 4:10** is not certain. It could be an allusion to the so-called 'sabbatical years' (Lev 25), but it may also signify certain *days of the year* (SIG[2] 438, 162 [c. 400 BC]), such as the New Year festival. GBarton, JBL 23, 1914, 118–26.—B. 1012. DELG. M-M. EDNT. Sv.

ἐνιδρύω 1 aor. ἐνίδρυσα (Hdt.+; ins, pap; Philo, De Prov. in Eus., PE 8, 14, 63) ***to place/establish in,*** τινί *someone* τὸν λόγον ἀνθρώποις Dg 7:2 (Plut., Mor. 1008a τῇ κεφαλῇ τὸν λογισμόν).—DELG s.v. ἱδρύω.

ἔνιοι, αι, α (Orph., Aristoph., Hdt. et al.; ins, pap; 3 Macc 2:31; 3:4; Jos., Ant. 1, 121; 18, 45; Just., A I, 20, 3; Tat., Ath.) **pert. to plural but undetermined number,** ***some, several,*** 1 Cl 44:6; 2 Cl 19:2 v.l.; Dg 5:3; ἔνια γράψας Papias (2:15); ἐνίοις δὲ αὐτῶν (2:4).—DELG.

ἐνίοτε adv. (Eur., Hippocr. et al.; PCairZen 362, 25 [242 BC]; Sir 37:14; TestJob) ***sometimes*** **Mt 17:15 v.l.;** 2 Cl 19:2 (based on Syr. tr.)—B. 987. DELG s.v. ἔνιοι.

ἐνίστημι 2 aor. ἐνέστην, ptc. ἐνστάς; pf. ἐνέστηκα, ptc. ἐνεστηκώς and ἐνεστώς; mid. fut. ἐνστήσομαι (Eur., Hdt.+; also Just., D. 142, 2 'begin, enter upon'; pf. ptc.: Tat. 26, 1; Ath. 27, 2). In our lit. only intr. and esp. in ref. to circumstances prevailing or impending, with contextual stress on the temporal feature of someth. taking place in a sequence.

❶ **to take place as an event,** ***be here, be at hand, arrive, come.*** **2 Ti 3:1;** in past tenses *be present, have come* ἐνέστηκεν ἡ ἡμέρα τοῦ κυρίου *the day of the Lord has come* **2 Th 2:2** (cp. Phlegon: 257 fgm. 36, 6 Jac, ἐνστάσης τῆς ἡμέρας τοῦ γάμου=when the wedding day came; PGM 13, 364 ὅταν ἐνστῇ ἡ ἡμέρα; Jos., Ant. 12, 175 ἐνστάσης τῆς ἡμέρας=when the day came; s. Goodsp., Probs. 179f; but BWarfield, Exp. 3d ser., 4, 1886, 37 and AOepke, TW II, 540 favor mng. 2).

❷ **to be present as condition or thing at the time of speaking,** ***be now, happen now*** ὁ καιρὸς ὁ ἐνεστηκώς (Polyb. 1, 60, 9; 21, 3, 3; Jos., Ant. 16, 162; pap) *the present time* **Hb 9:9;** cp. 1 Cl 55:1. ὁ αἰὼν ὁ ἐνεστώς *the present age* **Gal 1:4.** ἡ ἐνεστῶσα ἀνάγκη *the present* or *current distress* **1 Cor 7:26** (so REB; NRSV mg.; for a difft. view s. 3 below). ἐνεστώς fairly oft. in contrast to μέλλων (Sext. Emp., Adv. Math. 2, 193; Philo, Plant. 114; Tat. 26, 1; Ath. 27, 2) ἡ ἐ. χάρις IEph 11:1. ἐνεστῶτα, μέλλοντα **Ro 8:38; 1 Cor 3:22;** B 1:7; 4:1; 5:3; 17:2.—EBurton, Gal. ICC, 432f.

❸ **to be about to occur, w. connotation of threatening,** ***be imminent, be impending*** (Hdt.; Polyb. 3, 97, 1 'press hard'; PGM 13, 1049; LXX; Jos., Ant. 4, 209) ἡ ἐ. ἀνάγκη *the impending distress* **1 Cor 7:26** ('impending crisis' NRSV); B 17:2 (but for both of these s. 2; for **2 Ti 3:1** s. 1).—DELG s.v. ἵστημι. M-M. TW.

ἐνισχύω fut. ἐνισχύσω LXX; 1 aor. ἐνίσχυσα, pass. ἐνισχύθην—❶ intr. (Aristot., Theophr., Diod. S. 18, 61, 3, LXX; PMerton 12, 10 [58 AD]; TestJob 47:7) **to recover from loss of strength,** ***grow strong, regain one's strength*** (cp. Epict. 3, 24, 108; Gen 48:2; TestJob, TestSim; ApcMos 10) ἐνίσχυσεν **Ac 9:19** (v.l. ἐνισχύθη). Cp. **19:20** D.

❷ trans. (Hippocr. et al. [Hobart 81]; 2 Km 22:40; Sir 50:4; PsSol 16:12f; TestSol 26:8 H [without obj.]; TestDan 6:5; Jos. Ant. 7, 269), **to cause to recover from loss of strength,** ***strengthen*** τινά **Lk 22:43;** B 14:7 (Is 42:6). τὶ *urge someth. insistently* MPol 17:2.—DELG s.v. ἰσχύς. M-M.

ἐνκ- s. ἐγκ-.

ἐννέα indecl. (Hom.+) ***nine*** **Mt 18:12f; Lk 15:4, 7;** IRo 10:3; οἱ ἐ. *the (other) nine* **Lk 17:17** (B-D-F §306, 5; 480, 1).—M-M.

ἐννεός s. ἐνεός.

ἐννεύω impf. ἐνένευον (νεύω 'nod'; Aristoph., fgm. Babyl. 58 Dind.=75 K.; Lucian, Dial. Meretr. 12, 1; Jos., Ant. 8, 97; Pr 6:13; 10:10) **to signify by bodily movement,** ***nod, make signs*** τινί *to someone* **Lk 1:62.** ἐ. τινὶ τῇ χειρί *motion to someone w. the hand* Hv 3, 1, 9 (cp. Pr 6:13; 10:10 ὀφθαλμῷ).—DELG s.v. νεύω.

ἐννοέω 1 aor. ptc. ἐννοήσας (s. νοέω; trag., Hdt.+) ***have in mind, consider*** τὶ someth. ἐ. ἔννοιαν *conceive a plan* Dg 8:9.—DELG s.v. νόος. TW.

ἔννοια, ας, ἡ **the content of mental processing,** ***thought, knowledge, insight,*** (so esp. in the philosophers: Pla., Phd. 73c; Aristot., EN 9, 11, 1171a, 31f; 10, 10, 1179b, 13f; Epict. 2, 11, 2 and 3 al.; Plut., Mor. 900a; Diog. L. 3, 79; T. Kellis 22, 4; Herm. Wr. 1, 1; Philo; but also outside philosophic contexts: X., An. 3, 1, 13; Diod. S. 20, 34, 6; PRein 7, 15 [II BC]; UPZ 19, 111; 110, 32 [all II BC]; Pr 1:4; 2:11 al.; Jos., Bell. 2, 517 and Ant. 14, 481; Test12Patr; TestSol 20:5 εἰς ἔννοιαν ἐλθεῖν; Just. Tat.; Ath.; ἐ. ἔχειν τοῦ θεοῦ Orig., C. Cels. 4, 96, 3; περὶ τοῦ δημιουργοῦ ἐ. 4, 26, 46; ἔ. τῶν νόμων Did., Gen. 113, 1) κ. ὑμεῖς τ. αὐτὴν ἔννοιαν ὁπλίσασθε *arm yourselves also w. the same way of thinking* **1 Pt 4:1;** ἐννοεῖν ἔ. Dg 8:9. ἐδόκει γ[ὰρ ἑτε]ρογνωμονεῖν τῇ ἐκ[ε]ίν[ου ἐν]νοίᾳ (what was said) *appeared to differ in sense from what he* (the Redeemer) *had in mind* GMary 463, 9–11.—αὕτη ἡ ἀπό[ρ]ροια τῆ[ς ἐ]ννοίας, *this emanation of the* (divine) *mind* Ox 1081, 30f=SJCh 90, 7f; cp. Just., A I, 64, 5 πρώτην ἔννοιαν ἔφασαν τὴν Ἀθηνᾶν 'they called Athena the first thought [of Zeus]', sim. Helen as wife of Simon Magus 26, 3. Pl. (Jos., Ant. 6, 37; Just., D. 93, 1; Tat., Ath.) w. διαλογισμοί 1 Cl 21:3. W. ἐνθυμήσεις (Job 21:27 Sym.) **Hb 4:12;** 1 Cl 21:9. W. λογισμοί Pol 4:3.—B. 1212. DELG s.v. νόος. M-M. TW. Sv.

ἔννομος, ον (s. νόμος; Pind., Aeschyl. et al.; ins, pap, Sir prol. ln. 14; Philo, Abr. 242, Poster. Cai. 176; Jos., Ant. 19, 302; SibOr 3, 246; Just., D. 47, 4 ἔ. πολιτείαν; Ath., R. 70, 23 al.) **pert. to being in accordance with law,** ***legal, lawful.*** ἔ. ἐκκλησία **Ac 19:39** could, acc. to the context, mean a legally convened assembly in contrast to a mob, but certain features of the word's usage

(Lucian, Deor. Conc. 14; SIG 672, 37 [II BC] ἐν τᾷ ἐννόμῳ ἐκκλησίᾳ) suggest the interpr. *regular assembly* in contrast to one called for a special occasion (s. IBM III/2, p. 141; WRamsay, Pauline and Other Studies[3] n.d. [1906] 203–15).—*Subject to law, obedient to law* (Aelian, VH 2, 22 v.l.): ἔ. Χριστοῦ *subject to the jurisdiction of Christ* **1 Cor 9:21** as opposed to Mosaic jurisdiction (B-D-F §182, 3; Rob. 504—Proclus on Pla., Crat. p. 93, 5 P., the contrast ἔ. and ἔκνομος). The entire vs. can be rendered: 'I identified as one outside Mosaic jurisdiction with those outside it; not, of course, being outside God's jurisdiction, but inside Christ's'. Fr. a purely linguistic point of view one can also transl. ἔννομος *true to the law, upright, in the right* (so ἔ. in Aeschyl., Suppl. 404; Pla., Rep. 4, 424e) *acc. to the judgment of Christ.*—CDodd, Studia Paulina (JdeZwaan Festschr.) '53, 96–110.—M-M. EDNT. TW.

ἐννόμως adv. (s. prec. entry; =in accordance w. law: Lysias 9, 12; 30, 35; Lucian, Symp. 32; Cass. Dio 56, 7, 2; Pr 31:25; Just., D. 67, 2 and 4) **Ro 2:12 v.l.** as substitute for and in the sense of ἐν νόμῳ ***subject to*** or ***in possession of the law*** (opp. ἀνόμως, which prob. gave rise to the v.l.).

ἔννυχος, ον pert. to the period between sunset and sunrise, *at night* (s. νύξ; Il. 11, 716; Pind., trag., then Aesop, Fab. 55 v.l. P. [=110 H.; H-H. 55a; Ch. 89a]; IG VII, 584, 5; Sb 6699, 6 [early Ptolem.]; 3 Macc 5:5; SibOr 3, 293) acc. neut. pl. as adv. (cp. Soph., Ajax 930 πάννυχα) ἔννυχα (v.l. ἔννυχον) *at night-time* πρωῒ ἔ. λίαν *in the early morning, when it was still quite dark* **Mk 1:35.**—Frisk s.v. νύξ. M-M.

ἐνοικέω fut. ἐνοικήσω; 1 aor. ἐνῴκησα (3 sg. ἐνοίκησεν TestSim 5:1) (Eur., Hdt.+) ***live, dwell (in)*** in our lit.—except for **Lk 13:4 v.l.**—always w. ἔν τινι (PEnteux 14, 4f [III BC]; UPZ 162 II, 18f [II BC] and s. pap [e.g. BASP XXXII p. 124 ln. 7]) and of God or of nonphysical entities that 'make their home' in or among people: ἐνοικήσω ἐν αὐτοῖς *I will live among them* **2 Cor 6:16.** Of the Holy Spirit, which makes its home in people **Ro 8:11; 2 Ti 1:14.** Of the word of Christ **Col 3:16.** Of faith **2 Ti 1:5.** Of sin **Ro 7:17 v.l.** (cp. TestSim 5:1). V.l. for κατοικέω B 16, 10.—DELG s.v. οἶκος IIc. M-M.

ἐνοξίζω (ὀξίζω 'taste or smell like vinegar') 1 aor. ἐνώξισα (hapax leg.) **to have the taste of fermentation, *become sour*** IMg 10:2.—DELG s.v. ὀξύς.

ἔνοπλος, ον (trag. et al.; PMG: Carmina popularia no. 11 [=857] p. 455 Page; pap; PGM 13, 197; PGurob 1, 7 [mystery text]; LXX; JosAs 2:18; Philo, Aet. M. 57; Jos., Bell. 2, 444, Ant. 14, 294) ***armed*** Judaicon, ASyn. 351, 14=GHb 20b.—DELG s.v. ὅπλον.

ἐνοπτρίζομαι (Plut., Mor. 696a; Porphyr., Ad Marcellam 13 twice [s. PCorssen, ZNW 19, 1920, 2f]; Philo, Migr. Abr. 98) ***see (as) in a mirror*** τὴν ὄψιν 1 Cl 36:2. Another possibility is the simple mng. *look at, see* (Hierocles 1, 416: 'as it is impossible for an impure eye to contemplate radiant objects, so it is for a soul without virtue to see the beauty of truth', τῆς ἀληθείας ἐνοπτρίσασθαι κάλλος).—DELG s.v. ὄπωπα.

ἐνοράω 2 aor. ἐνεῖδον, ptc. ἐνιδών (Hdt., Aristoph. et al.; Philo, Op. M. 15) **to be observant about someth., *see, perceive,*** δύναμιν Dg 12:5.

ἐνορκίζω 1 aor. ἐνώρκισα 2 Esdr 23:25 cod. A (act. CIG IV, 9288, 6; IG XII/3, 1238, 7; MAMA III, 77, 1) **to put someone under oath, *adjure,*** *cause someone* (τινά) *to swear* τι *by someth.* w. acc. and inf. foll. ὑμᾶς τὸν κύριον *you by the Lord* **1 Th 5:27** (B-D-F §149; 155, 7; 392, 1d; Rob. 484; 1085).—DELG s.v. ὅρκος. M-M. TW.

ἑνότης, ητος, ἡ (Aristot. et al.; Epicurus p. 13, 14 Us.; Plut., Mor. 95a; 416e al.; TestZeb 8:6; Ath.) **a state of oneness or of being in harmony and accord, *unity*** τηρεῖν τὴν ἑ. τοῦ πνεύματος *maintain the unity of the spirit* **Eph 4:3.** ἑ. τῆς πίστεως *unity in the faith* vs. **13;** σύνδεσμος τῆς ἑ. *bond of unity* **Col 3:14 v.l.** SHanson, The Unity of the Church in the NT: Col, Eph, '46, esp. 122, 138f, 158.—Esp. common in Ign.: ἐν ἑ. IEph 4:2. ἐν ἑ. γίνεσθαι *become a unity* 14:1. ἐν ἑ. σύμφωνα εἶναι *sound together in unison* 5:1. ἐν τῇ ἑ. ὑμῶν IPhld 2:2. ἑ. τῆς ἐκκλησίας 3:2. (Cp. ἑ. τῆς κατὰ τὸ εὐαγγέλιον πολιτείας Did., Gen. 182, 19.) Esp. also of the unity of Christians w. God and Christ ἐν ἑ. Ἰησοῦ Χριστοῦ ὄντες 5:2; ἑ. θεοῦ 8:1; 9:1; ISm 12:2 (here ἐν should be placed before ἑνότητι, Hdb. ad loc.); IPol 8:3.—DELG s.v. εἷς. M-M. TW. Sv.

ἐνοχλέω 1 aor. inf. ἐνοχλῆσαι 1 Esdr 2:24; aor. pass ἠνωχλήθην 1 Kgm 30:13 (Aristoph., Hippocr.; Menand., Thrasonides: CGFP no. 151, 189 et al.; ins, pap, LXX, pseudepigr.) **to interfere or bother to the point of causing discomfort, *trouble, annoy,*** τοὺς ἡμετέρους ἐνοχλεῖν ἐπειρῶντο Qua (1; cp. TestJos 7:4 τὸ πνεῦμα τοῦ βελίαρ ἐνοχλεῖ αὐτήν; contrast w. dat.: TestJos 3:6; Ath. 12, 3; 22, 5). Pass. (Memnon [I BC/I AD]: no. 434 fgm. 1, 29, 6 Jac. ἐνοχλεῖσθαι ὑπό τινος; Dio Chrys. 3, 57; POxy 899, 44; Jos., Vi. 159, Ant. 12, 153; Ath., R. 74, 12 al.) εἰ ἡ τοιαύτη παρθένος χαλεπῶς ἐνοχλεῖται *that a young woman such as she* (Thecla) *is so profoundly disturbed* (by Paul's words) AcPl Ox 6, 15–17 (cp. Aa I 241, 15f). οἱ ἐνοχλούμενοι ἀπὸ πνευμάτων ἀκαθάρτων *those who were troubled by unclean spirits* **Lk 6:18** (cp. Galen XIX 171 K.; Lucian, Philops. 31 οἰκία ἐνοχλουμένη ὑπὸ τῶν φασμάτων; Appian, Bell. Civ. 3, 61 §252 τοῦ δαιμονίου ἐνοχλοῦντος=the [evil] divinity causing unrest). Abs. *cause trouble* **Hb 12:15** (Dt 29:17 v.l.). S. χολή (PKatz).—New Docs 3, 67. M-M. TW.

ἔνοχος, ον (Pla.+; ins, pap, LXX; EpArist 25; Philo; Jos., Ant. 17, 127) =ἐνεχόμενος 'caught in'.—**❶ pert. to being held in or constrained, *subject to,*** w. gen. (Sir prol. ln. 13) ἔ. δουλείας *held in slavery* **Hb 2:15.**

❷ pert. to being required to give an account for someth. held against one, *liable, answerable, guilty.*—ⓐ w. dat. to denote the tribunal to which one is answerable, τ. κρίσει, τ. συνεδρίῳ **Mt 5:21, 22ab** (sim. datives are not uncommon, e.g. X., Mem. 1, 2, 64; IAsMinLyk II 1889, 166 no. 193 ἔνοχος ἔστω πᾶσι θεοῖς; POxy 275, 32 [66 AD]).

ⓑ w. gen. (s. Mlt. 39; Wilcken, APF 1, 1901, 170, n. 3; ENachmanson, Eranos 11, 1911, 232)**—α.** to denote the punishment θανάτου *deserving of death* (Diod. S. 27, 4, 7; Gen 26:11; Ar. 13, 7) **Mt 26:66; Mk 14:64.** αἰωνίου κρίσεως **3:29 v.l.** (for ἁμαρτήματος [see ἁμάρτημα])

β. to denote the crime (Antiphon 6, 46 τοῦ φόνου; Lysias 14, 5; Pla., Leg. 11, 914e τῶν βιαίων; Vett. Val. 117, 10 ἔ. μοιχείας; 2 Macc 13:6; Philo, Decal. 133) *guilty* αἰωνίου ἁμαρτήματος **Mk 3:29.** τῆς ἁμαρτίας τοῦ καταλαλοῦντος *involved in the sin of the slanderer* Hm 2:2; cp. 4, 1, 5. ἔνοχοι γείν[ονται τούτου τοῦ| αἵ[μ]ατος s 10, 4, 3 (Gk. text POxy 404, 41f; Lat.: reus fit sanguinis eius).

γ. to denote the pers. (or thing) against whom the sin has been committed (Is 54:17 ἔνοχοί σου those who wrong you; s. Dssm. LO 91f [LAE 116]) ἔ. τοῦ σώματος καὶ τοῦ αἵματος *sin* *against the body and the blood* **1 Cor 11:27;** γέγονεν πάντων ἔ. *has sinned against all* (the commandments) **Js 2:10.**

ⓒ ἔ. εἰς τ. γέενναν τοῦ πυρός is to be explained as brachylogy *guilty enough to go into the hell of fire* **Mt 5:22c** (εἰς τὸ πύρ quot. Just., A I, 16, 2).—RBagnall, BASP 6, '69, 91f.—B. 1445. DELG s.v. 1 ἔχω 4. M-M. EDNT. TW.

ἑνόω 1 aor. pass. ἡνώθην; pf. pass. ptc. ἡνωμένος (s. εἷς; Aristot. et al.; Sb 2034, 5; 4832, 5; Sym.; TestNapht; Philo, Migr. Abr. 220, Mut. Nom. 200; Jos., Bell. 3, 15; Ath.) **to cause to be unified, *unite,*** in our lit. only pass. Of a congregation ἡνωμένη *united* IEph ins. Of prayer ἡ ἡνωμένη ὑμῶν ἐν θεῷ προσευχή *your united prayer in God* IMg 14. Of the Lord ἡνωμένος ὤν 7:1. Here τῷ πατρί is to be supplied; it actually occurs ISm 3:3, *united w. the father.* The dat. is also used elsewh. to indicate that w. which (or whom) the unification takes place (TestNapht 8:2 τῷ Λευί; Herm. Wr. 1, 10; Proclus on Pla., Cratyl. p. 59, 23; 83, 27 P.) τῷ ἐπισκόπῳ IMg 6:2. πάσῃ ἐντολῇ IRo ins.—B. 844. DELG s.v. εἷς.

ἐνπ- s. ἐμπ-.

ἐνσκιρόω pf. pass. ptc. ἐνεσκιρωμένος (σκιρόομαι 'become hard'; X., De Re Equ. 4, 2; Stoic. III p. 102, 38; Is 27:1 Theod.; Etym. Mag. p. 344, 30) prim. mng. 'to cause to become hard'; in our lit. of moral insensitivity, ***harden, make callous*** Hv 3, 9, 8.—DELG s.v. σκῖρος.

ἐνστερνίζομαι pf. mid. ptc. ἐνεστερνισμένος (late word, only in Christian wr., usu. in mid.; Hesych.; Suda; Psellus p. 72, 17; B-D-F §123, 2) ***to store away within oneself*** ἐπιμελῶς ἐ. ἦτε τοῖς σπλάγχνοις (sc. τ. λόγους) *you had carefully stored away in the depths of your being* 1 Cl 2:1.—DELG s.v. στέρνον.

ἔνταλμα, ατος, τό (s. ἐντέλλω; LXX; PLond IV, 1384, 55 [VIII AD]; Just., D. 46, 5; 67, 10) **that which is commanded as officially binding, *commandment*** (w. διδασκαλία) ἐ. ἀνθρώπων **Mt 15:9; Mk 7:7; Col 2:22** (all three Is 29:13); τὰ τοῦ κυρίου ἐ. 2 Cl 17:3.—DELG s.v. τέλλω.

ἐντάσσω 1 aor. ἐνέταξα; pf. pass. 3 sg. ἐντέτακται Job 15:22 cod. A, ptc. ἐντεταγμένος (s. τάσσω; X., An. 3, 3, 18 v.l.; ins, pap, LXX; Jos., C. Ap. 1, 172) **to cause to be put on an official register, *enroll*** εἴς τι *in someth.* εἰς τὸν ἀριθμὸν τῶν σῳζομένων 1 Cl 58:2.—DELG s.v. τάσσω.

ἐνταῦθα adv. (Hom.+) **pert. to a position relatively near the speaker, *here*** Ox 840, 23.—DELG s.v. ἔνθα.

ἐνταφιάζω fut. 3 sg. ἐνταφιάσει (TestJud 26:3) (s. next entry and τάφος; Anth. Pal. 11, 125, 5; Plut., Mor. 995c; SIG 1235, 5 [I AD]; Gen 50:2; AssMos fgm. g; TestJud 26:3) ***prepare for burial, bury,* J 19:40.** πρὸς τὸ ἐνταφιάσαι με *to prepare me for burial* **Mt 26:12.**—DELG s.v. θάπτω. M-M.

ἐνταφιασμός, οῦ, ὁ (s. prec. entry; schol. on Eur., Phoen. 1654 and on Aristoph., Plut. 1009.—ἐνταφιαστής as early as PParis 7, 6 [100 BC]; Gen 50:2) **the performance of what is customary for burial, *preparation for burial*** or ***burial*** itself **Mk 14:8; J 12:7.**—Field, Notes 98.—DELG s.v. θάπτω. M-M.

ἐντέλλω (s. ἔνταλμα; Pind. et al.) but usu., and in our lit. exclusively, mid. dep. (oft. Hdt.+; ins, pap, LXX, pseudepigr., Joseph., Just.; Mel., P. 11, 73) fut. ἐντελοῦμαι (**Mt 4:6; Lk 4:10**); 1 aor. ἐνετειλάμην; pf. ἐντέταλμαι (in our lit. only w. act. sense as Polyb. 17, 2, 1; Herodian 1, 9, 9; Tob 5:1; 2 Macc 11:20; Jos., Vi. 318 [plpf.]), 2 sg. ἐντέταλσαι Hm 12, 6, 4; 3 sg. plpf. ἐνετέταλτο (Just.); 1 aor. pass. subj. 3 sg. ἐνταλθῇ (TestJob 20:9) **to give or leave instructions, *command, order, give orders,*** abs. **Mt 15:4 v.l.** (w. λέγων foll.); Pol 6:3; B 7:3. τινί *to someone* **Mt 17:9; J 14:31; Ac 1:2; 13:47;** τί *someth.* (Herodian 1, 9, 10; Sir 48:22) IRo 3:1; Hm 12, 6, 4. τινί τι *someone someth.* (Hdt. 1, 47; Diog. Oenoand. [II AD] fgm. 50, 3 [=66 William] of testamentary instructions φίλοις τάδε ἐντέλλομαι; Jos., Vi. 242) **Mt 28:20; Mk 10:3; J 15:14;** περί τινος *concerning someth.* (1 Macc 9:55) **Hb 11:22.** τινὶ περί τινος (UPZ 61, 9 [161 BC]; APF 8 p. 212 no. 14, 12; BGU 1755, 14 [I BC]; Sir 17:14; 1 Macc 3:34; Jos. Ant. 7, 358) **Mt 4:6; Lk 4:10** (both Ps 90:11). W. inf. foll. (Gen 42:25; 2 Ch 36:23; Manetho: 609 fgm. 9a, 98 Jac. [in Jos., C. Ap. 1, 98]; Just., D. 22, 11 al.) **Mt 19:7; J 8:5;** Hv 5: 7; m 4, 1, 1. W. acc. and inf. ἐντέταλται τῷ Ἰσραὴλ προσφέρειν δάμαλιν τοὺς ἄνδρας B 8:1. W. gen. of the inf. foll. **Lk 4:10** (Ps 90:11). W. ὅτι foll. *say emphatically* IRo 4:1. W. ἵνα foll. (Jos., Ant. 8, 375; 7, 356) **Mk 13:34; J 15:17.**—τ. διαθήκης ἧς (by attraction for ἥν) ἐνετείλατο πρὸς ὑμᾶς ὁ θεός *of the decree which God has ordained for you* **Hb 9:20.**—DELG s.v. τέλλω. M-M s.v. ἐντέλλομαι. TW.

ἔντερον, ου, τό (Hom. et al., mostly pl., as also Artem. 1, 33 p. 35, 15 [where a distinction is made between ἔντερα and σπλάγχνα]; PGM 4, 2596; 2658; Gen 43:30; 2 Macc 14:46) 'intestine(s)' then also ***entrails*** (so in the sg. Hippocr., π. νουσ. 3, 14 vol. VII 134; Diocles 43 p. 136, 33; Sir 31:20) φαγεῖν τὸ ἔ. ἄπλυτον μετὰ ὄξους *eat the entrails unwashed, with vinegar* B 7:4 (quot. of uncertain orig.).—DELG s.v. ἐν.

ἐντεῦθεν adv.—❶ (Hom. et al.; ins, pap, LXX; JosAs 24:5; ParJer 7:32; Just., D. 6, 1; Tat. 20, 2; τοὐντεῦθεν Just., D. 4:2) **pert. to extension from a source near the speaker, *from here*** (En 22:13; Jos., Bell. 6, 299; 7, 22) **Lk 4:9; 13:31; J 7:3; 14:31;** 1 Cl 53:2 (Ex 32:7). ἄρατε ταῦτα ἐ. *take these things away from here* **J 2:16.** κατάβηθι ἐ. *go home from here* GJs 4:2. ἐντεῦθεν (for ἔνθεν) ἐκεῖ *fr. here to there* **Mt 17:20 v.l.** ἐντεῦθεν καὶ ἐντεῦθεν *fr. here and fr. there = on each side* (cp. Num 22:24) **J 19:18.** For this ἐντεῦθεν κ. ἐκεῖθεν **Rv 22:2;** ἡ βασιλεία ἡ ἐμὴ οὐκ ἔστιν ἐ. *my kingdom is not from here*=ἐκ. τ. κόσμου τούτου **J 18:36.**

❷ **pert. to the reason for, or source of, someth., *fr. this*** (cp. Thu. 1, 5, 1; 1 Esdr 4:22; Jos., Ant. 4, 225, C. Ap. 2, 182; Just., D. 6, 1 μάθοις δ' ἂν ἐντεῦθεν) ἐ., ἐκ τῶν ἡδονῶν *fr. this, namely your passions* **Js 4:1.**—DELG s.v. ἔνθα. M-M.

ἔντευξις, εως, ἡ (Pla. et al.; ins, pap [s. esp. PEnteux]; 2 Macc 4:8; TestSol D 2:5), in our lit.

❶ **a formal request put to a high official or official body, *petition, request,*** an administrative t.t. (Polyb. 5, 35, 4; Diod. S. 16, 55, 3; Plut., Tib. Gracch. 829 [11, 6]; EpArist 252; Jos., Ant. 15, 79; Just., A I, 1, 1; ins, pap [Mitteis, Grundzüge 13ff; RLaqueur, Quaestiones epigraph., diss. Strassb. 1904, 8ff; Wilcken, APF 4, 1908, 224; OGI 138 n.10; Dssm., B 117f; 143f (BS 121; 146); OGuéraud, Enteux. Cavassini, Aegyptus 35, '55, 299ff; ESeidl, Ptolem. Rechtsgesch '62, 65; HWolff, D. Justizwesen der Ptolem. '62, 127ff]); the letter fr. the church at Rome to the church at Corinth calls itself a *petition, appeal* 1 Cl 63:2; so does the sermon known as 2 Cl (19:1).—Since a petition denoted by ἔ. is preferably directed to a king, the word develops the mng.

❷ ***prayer*** (Plut., Numa 70 [14, 12] ποιεῖσθαι τὰς πρὸς τὸ θεῖον ἐντεύξεις; En 99:3; TestSol D 2:5), and chiefly

ⓐ *intercessory prayer* (w. προσευχή, the general word for prayer, and εὐχαριστία, a prayer of thanksgiving; s. Elbogen[2] 4ff; 73) **1 Ti 2:1;** cp. Hs 2:5ab; Hs 5, 4, 3.

ⓑ gener. *prayer* Hm 5, 1, 6; 10, 3, 2f; 11:9, 14; s 2:5c, 6, 7.

ⓒ It can even approach the sense *prayer of thanksgiving* **1 Ti 4:5** (=εὐχαριστία vss. 3, 4).

ⓓ The context requires the sense *power of intercession* Hm 10, 3, 3 end; Hs 5, 4, 4.—New Docs 4, 104. DELG s.v. τυγχάνω. M-M. TW. Spicq.

ἐντίθημι 3 sg. aor. ἐνέθηκεν (Mel.), ptc. ἐντιθείς, ptc. pl. ἐνθέντες 2 Macc 3:27; pf. ptc. pl. ἐντεθεικότες 3 Macc 5:28; mid. aor. impv. 2 pl. ἔνθεσθε Pr 8:5 (Hom. et al.; Lucian, Alex. 47 ἀλήθειαν; ins, pap, LXX; TestJob 53:7 ἐνέθεντο εἰς τὸν τάφον; TestNapht 2:2; Jos., Ant. 11, 239; Mel., P. 20, 138 [B]) ***put in, implant,*** *implant* τὸ ὄνομα τ. κυρίου Ἰησοῦ **Ac 18:4** D.—DELG s.v. τίθημι.

ἔντιμος, ον (s. τιμή; Soph. et al.; ins, pap, LXX, En, TestJob; AssMos fgm. k; Jos., Ant. 15, 243).

➊ **pert. to being highly regarded because of status or personal quality, *honored, respected*—ⓐ** of rank *distinguished* ἐντιμότερός σου *someone more distinguished than you* (cp. Num 22:15) **Lk 14:8** (ἔ. at a banquet: Lucian, Merc. Cond. 26).

ⓑ esp. for one's qualities *esteemed, highly honored* (opp. ἄτιμος) 1 Cl 3:3; ἔ. ἔχειν τινά *hold someone in esteem* (Pla.; Diod. S.) **Phil 2:29.**

➋ **pert. to being esteemed as someth. of considerable worth, *valuable, precious*** (Ps.-Demosth. 56, 9; PLond V, 1708, 33 [VI AD]) of slaves **Lk 7:2;** Hs 5, 2, 2 v.l. Of stones (Diod. S. 2, 50, 1; Tob 13:17 BA; cp. Job 28:10) **1 Pt 2:4, 6;** B 6:2 (in both cases Is 28:16).—DELG s.v. τιμή. M-M.

ἐντολή, ῆς, ἡ (s. ἐντέλλω; Pind., Hdt.+; also Mel., P. 7, 48; 48, 343)—➊ **an order authorizing a specific action, *writ, warrant,*** perh. **J 11:57** (ἐντολὰς διδόναι ἵνα, as OGI 441, 59 [81 BC]).

➋ **a mandate or ordinance, *command*—ⓐ** of commands by pers. in high position (JRS 66 '76, 106–31, line 31 [18–19 AD] by a legate of Tiberius): father (Tob 4:19) **Lk 15:29.** Apostles **Ac 17:15; Col 4:10.** Judean-type (s. Ἰουδαϊκός and Ἰουδαῖος 2) instruction of a sectarian nature and without divine sanction ἐντολαὶ ἀνθρώπων **Tit 1:14.** Papias (2:3) distinguishes ἀλλοτρίας ἐ. from the Lord's instruction.

ⓑ of commands given by divine authorities (cp. SIG 888, 51 [238 AD] of imperial decrees: ταῖς θείαις ἐντολαῖς).

α. of commandments of OT law.

א. The sg. takes in all the commandments as *the law* (4 Macc 13:15; 16:24) κατὰ τ. ἐντολήν *according to the law* **Lk 23:56;** cp. **Ro 7:8ff; Hb 7:18; 9:19.** κατὰ νόμον ἐντολῆς σαρκίνης *acc. to a legal system which demands that one meets a (specific) physical standard* (i.e. Levitical descent) **7:16; Mt. 15:6 v.l.** (for λόγον). In contrast to God's ἐ. is the παράδοσις of the Pharisees **15:3;** cp. **Mk 7:8f.**

ב. More freq. the pl. stands for the totality of legal ordinances (Epict. 4, 7, 17 ἔγνωκα τοῦ θεοῦ τὰς ἐντολάς; SEG VIII, 170, 5; Just., D. 10, 3; Orig., C. Cels. 1, 4, 13; Theoph. Ant. 3, 11 [p. 226, 28]) **Mt 5:19; 19:17; Mk 10:19; Lk 1:6** (also s. β below); **18:20.**

ג. of specific commandments **Mt 22:36, 38** (cp. EpArist 228 ὁ θεὸς πεποίηται ἐ. μεγίστην.—HHunt, The Great Commandment: ET 56, '44, 82f; CBurchard, Das doppelte Liebesgebot, JJeremias Festschr., '70, 39–62.—Just., D. 40, 1 αὕτη ἡ ἐ. al. παραβάται τῆς τοῦ θεοῦ ἐντολῆς [of Adam and Eve] Did., Gen. 84, 27), **40; Mk 10:5; 12:28, 31; Ro 13:9; Eph 6:2;** B 7:3; 9:5. ὁ νόμος τῶν ἐντολῶν **Eph 2:15.**—Of Levites ἐντολὴν ἔχουσιν ἀποδεκατοῦν τὸν λαόν *they have the legal right to take tithes from the people* **Hb 7:5.**

β. of divine commandments gener. (Julian, Caesares 336c: Mithras gave ἐντολαί to his initiates), as they concern people **Lk 1:6** (also s. αב above); **1 Cor 7:19; 1J 3:22–24;** ISm 8:1. λαμβάνειν **2J 4.** φυλάσσειν *observe* (Jos., Ant. 7, 384) B 4:11. τηρεῖν **1J 5:3; Rv 12:17; 14:12.** ποιεῖν **1J 5:2.** ἐ. καινήν . . . παλαιάν **1J 2:7f; 2J 5.** ἐ. ἔχομεν. . . ἵνα **1J 4:21;** cp. **2J 5.** κατορθώσασθαι τὰς ἐ. τοῦ κυρίου *preserve the Lord's commandments* Hv 3, 5, 3. αἱ ἐ. αὐτοῦ βαρεῖαι οὐκ εἰσίν **1J 5:3.** περιπατεῖν κατὰ τὰς ἐ. αὐτοῦ **2J 6.**

γ. of God's commands to Christ **J 10:18** (λαμβάνειν as Jos., Bell. 4, 498); **12:49f; 14:31 v.l.; 15:10b;** B 6:1.

δ. of the precepts of Jesus **J 13:34; 14:15, 21; 15:10a, 12** (w. ἵνα foll.); **1 Cor 14:37; Rv 22:14 v.l.;** 2 Cl 3:4; 6:7; 17:3. Applied to God as well as Christ τὰς ἐ. αὐτοῦ **1J 2:3f.** Of the commands in the Sermon on the Mount 1 Cl 13:3. ποιεῖν τὰς ἐντολάς μου 2 Cl 4:5 (fr. an unknown gospel). ἐ. Ἰησοῦ Χριστοῦ 17:6 (cp. κατὰ τὴν ἐ. τοῦ Ἰησοῦ Orig., C. Cels. 6, 7, 29); IEph 9:2; cp. Pol 2:2; IRo ins; φυλάσσειν τὰς ἐ. τοῦ κυρίου *observe the Lord's commandments* 2 Cl 8:4 (cp. Just., D. 134, 4 τοὺς φυλάσσοντας τὰς ἐ. αὐτοῦ).

ε. of commands of the angel of repentance Hv 5:5; s 10, 3, 4 (Gk. text from POxy 404, 17); cp. the title of the second part: ἐντολαί, also m 1:2; 2:7 al.

ζ. of God's expectation of Christians, with special ref. to their ethical decisions ἐντολή **1 Ti 6:14; 2 Pt 2:21.** ἡ τ. ἀποστόλων ὑμῶν ἐ. τοῦ κυρίου κ. σωτῆρος *the command of the Lord and Savior (given) through your apostles* **3:2;** cp. ITr 13:2.—DELG s.v. τέλλω. M-M. EDNT. TW. Sv.

ἐντόπιος, ία, ιον (s. τόπος; Pla. et al.; Dionys. Hal. 8, 83; ins, pap; the anti-Semite Molon [I BC] in Eus., PE 9, 19, 2) **pert. to belonging to a certain place, *local,*** subst. οἱ ἐ. *the local residents* (OGI 194, 11 [42 BC]; PLond II 192, 94 p. 225 [I AD]) **Ac 21:12** (opp. Paul's companions).—DELG s.v. τόπος. M-M.

ἐντός adv. of place (Hom.+; ins, pap, LXX, JosAs 2:4; EpArist, Philo, Joseph., Just.. D 2, 6) in our lit. functions only as prep. w. gen.

➊ **pert. to a specific area inside someth., *inside, within, within the limits of*** (Lucian, Dial. Mort. 14, 5; JosAs 2:4 ἐ. τοῦ θαλάμου; Jos., Bell. 3, 175 τ. πόλεως ἐντός; 7, 26; Just., D. 2, 6 ὀλίγου . . . ἐ. χρόνου) τοῦ θυσιαστηρίου *within the sanctuary* IEph 5:2; ITr 7:2. ἐάν τις τούτων ἐ. ᾖ *if anyone is in their company* (i.e. the comp. of faith, hope, and love) Pol 3:3.—In ἡ βασιλεία τοῦ θεοῦ ἐντὸς ὑμῶν ἐστιν **Lk 17:21** (cp. Ox 654, 16=GTh 3=JBL 65, '46, 177; also s. WSchubart, ZNW 20, 1921, 215–23), ἐ. ὑμῶν is probably patterned after ἐν σοί (=[God] is among you) Is 45:14, but with Lk preferring ἐντός in the sense *among you, in your midst,* either now or suddenly in the near future (cp. X., Hell. 2, 3, 19 ἐ. τούτων, An. 1, 10, 3 ἐ. αὐτῶν [on the relevance of the second X. passage, s. Field, Notes 71 and s. Roberts below]; POxy 2342, 8 [102 AD], of a woman who keeps a supply of wine ἐντὸς αὐτῆς 'under her own control'; Ps 87:6 Sym.; cp. Jos., Ant. 6, 315; Arrian, Anab. 5, 22, 4 ἐ. αὐτῶν=in their midst; so NRSV text, and s. Noack and Bretscher below). The sense *within you, in your hearts* has linguistic support in Ps 38:4; 102:1; 108:22, all ἐντός μου; s. also Jos., Ant. 5, 107, but Lk generally avoids ref. to God's reign as a psychological reality. The passage has invited much debate: AWabnitz, RTQR 18, 1909, 221ff; 289ff; 456ff; CBruston, ibid. 346ff; BEaston, AJT 16, 1912, 275–83; KProost, TT 48, 1914, 246ff; JHéring, Le royaume de Dieu et sa venue '37; PAllen, ET 50, '39, 233–35; ASledd, ibid. 235–37; WKümmel, Verheissung u. Erfüllung '45, 17ff; BNoack, D. Gottesreich bei Lk (17:20–24) '48; CRoberts, HTR 41, '48, 1–8, citing PRossGeorg III, 1, 9: ἵνα ἐντός μου αὐτὸ εὕρω; HCadbury, Christian Century 67, '50, 172f (*within your possession* or *reach;* cp. Tertullian, Adv. Marc. 4, 35), cp. Pol 3:3 above and JGriffiths, ET 63, '51/52, 30f; HRiesenfeld, Nuntius 2, '49, 11f; AWikgren, ibid. 4, '50, 27f; PBretscher, CTM 15, '44, 730–66; 22, '51, 895–907. W. stress on the moral implications, RFrick, Beih. ZNW 6, 1928, 6–8, s. ARüstow, ZNW 51, '60, 197–224; JZmijewski, D. Eschatologiereden d. LkEv, '72, 361–97.

❷ **pert. to what is inside an area,** ***content*** τὸ ἐ. τοῦ ποτηρίου *the inside of the cup*=what is in the cup (cp. τὰ ἐ. τοῦ οἴκου 1 Macc 4:48, also schol. on Nicander, Alexiph. 479 τὰ ἐντός=the inside; Is 16:11) **Mt 23:26.**—DELG s.v. ἐν. M-M.

ἐντρέπω pass.: 2 fut. ἐντραπήσομαι; 2 aor. ἐνετράπην; pf. ἐντέτραμμαι 1 Esdr 8:71 (s. τρέπω; Hom. et al.; pap, LXX, Joseph.) prim. 'turn about'; in our lit. metaph.

❶ **to cause to turn (in shame),** ***to shame*** (τινά) (Diog. L. 2, 29; Aelian, VH 3, 17; Sext. Emp., Psych. 3, 16) οὐκ ἐντρέπων ὑμᾶς γράφω ταῦτα *I write this not to make you ashamed* **1 Cor 4:14.** Pass. *be put to shame, be ashamed* (UPZ 62, 29 [161/160 BC]; 70, 4; Ps 34:26; Is 44:11) **2 Th 3:14; Tit 2:8;** IMg 12.

❷ **to show deference to a pers. in recognition of special status,** ***turn toward someth./someone, have regard for, respect*** τινά 1 Cl 38:2 v.l. Pass. w. mid. sense (Alexis Com. 71 ed. Kock II 320; Polyb. 9, 36, 10; 30, 9, 2; Diod. S. 19, 7, 4 θεούς; Ex 10:3; Wsd 2:10; 6:7; Jos., Bell. 7, 362) τὸν υἱόν μου **Mt 21:37; Mk 12:6; Lk 20:13.** ἄνθρωπον μὴ ἐντρεπόμενος *who showed deference to no human* (paralleling the judge's attitude toward God vs. 3a) **18:2,** cp. vs. **4** (cp. Pla., Laws 11, 917b). ὡς ἀδελφήν *respect someone as a sister* Hv 1, 1, 7. τὸν κύριον Ἰησοῦν 1 Cl 21:6. τὸν ἰσχυρόν 38:2 (s. also v.l. above). ἀλλήλους IMg 6:2. τοὺς διακόνους ὡς Ἰησοῦν ITr 3:1; cp. ISm 8:1; ITr 3:2. W. αὐτούς to be supplied fr. the context: ἐντρεπόμεθα **Hb 12:9.**—DELG s.v. τρέπω. M-M.

ἐντρέφω (s. τρέφω; Eur. et al.; mid. since Hes., Op. 781) prim. 'bring up, rear', then ***train in*** τινί *someth.* (Pla., Leg. 7, 798a; Epict. 4, 4, 48; Philo, Spec. Leg. 1, 314, Leg. ad Gai. 195 τ. ἱεροῖς γράμμασιν; Jos., Bell. 6, 102, C. Ap. 1, 269) ἐντρεφόμενος τοῖς λόγοις τῆς πίστεως **1 Ti 4:6** (Ath. 11, 1 οἱ λογοι οἷς ἐντρεφόμεθα; on the imagery s. Straub 24).—DELG s.v. τρέφω. M-M.

ἔντρομος, ον (Plut., Fab. Max. 175 [3, 1]; Meleager [I BC]: Anth. Pal. 5, 204, 8; schol. on Eur., Phoen. 1284–87; LXX; JosAs ch. 18 cod. A [p. 68, 17 Bat.]; Just., D. 103, 8) **pert. to being in a quivering condition because of exposure to an overwhelming or threatening circumstance,** ***trembling*** **Lk 8:47** D. ἔ. γενόμενος (cp. Soranus p. 68, 7f; Ps 17:8; 76:19); **Ac 7:32; 16:29;** GJs 11:1; ἔκφοβος καὶ ἔ. (as 1 Macc 13:2) *full of fear and trembling* **Hb 12:21.**—DELG s.v. τρέμω. M-M.

ἐντροπή, ῆς, ἡ s. ἐντρέπω; as in Gk. lit. gener. only metaph.

❶ **the state of being ashamed,** ***shame, humiliation*** (Diod. S. 40, 5a; schol. on Apollon. Rhod. 3, 656–63a; Ps 34:26; 68:8, 20) πρὸς ἐντροπήν τινι *to put someone to shame* **1 Cor 6:5; 15:34.**

❷ **deference to a pers. in recognition of special status,** ***respect, regard*** (Soph. et al.; Polyb. 4, 52, 2; Dio Chrys. 29 [46], 4; OGI 323, 7 [II BC]; PGM 5, 17; Jos., Ant. 2, 46; 14, 375) πᾶσαν ἐ. τινι ἀπονέμειν *pay someone all the respect due him* IMg 3:1.—B. 1141. M-M.

ἐντρυφάω (via τρυφή) fut. ἐντρυφήσω; 1 aor. ἐνετρύφησα LXX (s. τρυφάω; Eur. et al.)

❶ **to take exuberant delight in,** ***delight in*** τινί *someth.* ἐντρύφα ἐν αὐτῇ (i.e. ἱλαρότητι) *indulge in it* Hm 10, 3, 1.

❷ **to engage in self-indulgent behavior,** ***revel, carouse, cavort,*** ext. of mng. 1 (X., Hell. 4, 1, 30; Diod. S. 19, 71, 3; LXX; Philo, Spec. Leg. 3, 27; Tat. 12, 4) ἔν τινι *in someth.* (Is 55:2 ἐν ἀγαθοῖς, also Cass. Dio 65, 20) ἐν ταῖς ἀπάταις *revel in their lusts* **2 Pt 2:13** (v.l. ἀγάπαις and ἀγνοίαις).—DELG s.v. θρύπτω III. M-M.

ἐντυγχάνω fut. 2 pl. ἐντεύξεσθε (Just., A I, 45, 6); 2 aor. ἐνέτυχον; 1 aor. subj. mid. ἐντεύξωμαι Hm 10, 2, 5 (cp. the simplex 2 Macc 15:7) in various senses: 'meet, turn to, approach, appeal, petition' (s. τυγχάνω; Soph., Hdt.+).

❶ **to make an earnest request through contact with the pers. approached**—ⓐ ***approach*** or ***appeal*** *to someone,* τινί (Polyb. 4, 30, 1; Diod. S. 19, 60, 1; OGI 664, 10; 669, 46; SIG 820, 13 [I AD]; PTebt 58, 43; Da 6:13 LXX; Jos., Ant. 16, 170; Just., D. 2, 6 τοῖς Πλατωνικοῖς) MPol 17:2. τινὶ περί τινος (Polyb. 4, 76, 9; PSI 410, 14 [III BC] περὶ Ὥρου ἐντυχεῖν Ἀμμωνίῳ; PAmh 142, 10) περὶ οὗ ἅπαν τὸ πλῆθος ἐνέτυχόν μοι *concerning whom all the people appealed to me* **Ac 25:24** (En 22:7 Ἄβελ ἐντυγχάνει περὶ αὐτοῦ [τοῦ Κάϊν]. Of things: Jos., Ant. 12, 18 περὶ ὧν ἐντυγχάνειν μέλλει τῷ βασιλεῖ; Plut, Alex. 692 [49, 4] ὡς περὶ ἀναγκαίων ἔχοντας ἐντυχεῖν καὶ μεγάλων, Them. 125 [27, 2] [s. Field, Notes 140f]). ὑπέρ τινος *plead for someone* (Aelian, VH 1, 21; PAmh 35, 20; PTebt 183 [II BC]) of intercession by the Holy Spirit κατὰ θεὸν ἐ. ὑπὲρ ἁγίων **Ro 8:27.** Of Christ's intercession **Ro 8:34; Hb 7:25.** τινὶ κατά τινος *appeal to someone against a third person* (cp. PGiss 36, 15 [161 BC] ἐνετύχομεν καθ' ὑμῶν; PAmh 134, 10; 1 Macc 8:32; 11:25; En 7:6 ἡ γῆ ἐνέτυχεν κατὰ τῶν ἀνόμων; TestJob 17:5 καθ' ἡμῶν) **Ro 11:2;** Hm 10, 2, 5.—DCrump, Jesus the Intercessor '92.

ⓑ Since petitions are also directed toward God, ἐ. can be rendered ***pray*** (Maximus Tyr. 10, 1b ἐντυχεῖν θεοῖς; BGU 246, 12 [c. 200 AD] ἰδότες ὅτι νυκτὸς καὶ ἡμέρας ἐντυγχάνω τῷ θεῷ ὑπὲρ ὑμῶν; Wsd 8:21; 16:28; En 9:3 and 10 al.; Philo, Mos. 1, 173) w. dat. of the one being prayed to τῷ κυρίῳ (w. ἐξομολογεῖσθαι) Hm 10, 3, 2; τῷ θεῷ *to God* s 2:6. Also πρὸς τὸν κύριον (cp. Plut., Fab. 185 [20, 2]) Hs 2:8. περί τινος *for someone* 1 Cl 56:1; Pol 4:3.

❷ From the idea of 'coming across' or 'encountering' a book (Plato et al.) derives the sense ***read*** (Polyb. 1, 3, 10; Plut., Rom. 24 [12, 6]; Vett. Val. 358, 25; 2 Macc 2:25; 15:39; Jos., Ant. 1, 15; 12, 226; Just., A I, 26, 8 al.; Philo, Spec. Leg. 4, 161 [a book] ἐντυγχάνειν κ. ἀναγινώσκειν 'read and attend to') Dg 12:1.—RLaqueur, Quaestiones Epigr., diss. Strassb. 1904, 15ff.—DELG s.v. τυγχάνω. M-M. TW. Spicq. Sv.

ἐντυλίσσω 1 aor. ἐνετύλιξα; pf. pass. ptc. ἐντετυλιγμένος (Aristoph., Plut. 692, Nub. 987; Epict. 1, 6, 33; Athen. 3, 69, 106e; PSI 1082, 16).

❶ **to wrap someth. around an object,** ***wrap (up),*** σῶμα σινδόνι *a body in a linen cloth* **Lk 23:53;** w. ἐν **Mt 27:59** (cp. PGM 7, 826 ἐντύλισσε τὰ φύλλα ἐν σουδαρίῳ; but the Matthean verse has strong attestation for the simple dat.).

❷ *fold up* of a σουδάριον **J 20:7.**—DELG s.v. τύλη. M-M.

ἐντυπόω pass.: 1 fut. 3 sg. ἐντυπωθήσεται; pf. ptc. ἐντετυπωμένα (Ex 36:37 cod. A; TestSol) (s. τύπος; Ps.-Aristot., Mirabilia 155; Ps.-Aristot., De Mundo 6; Cass. Dio; Plut.; Philostrat., Vi. Apoll. 3, 42 p. 117, 13; Ex 36:37 v.l.; TestSol 13, 12 C; EpArist 67; Philo, Leg. All. 3, 95 τῇ ψυχῇ; Jos., Bell. 2, 120) **to form letters or designs by incision,** ***carve, impress,*** ἐν γράμμασιν ἐντετυπωμένη λίθοις *carved in letters on stone* **2 Cor 3:7** (Istros [III BC]: 334 fgm. 53 Jac. ἐντετύπωται τῷ λίθῳ ἀνθρωποειδὴς εἰκών=a human figure was chiseled in the stone).—DELG s.v. τύπτω. M-M.

ἐνυβρίζω 1 aor. ἐνύβρισα (s. ὑβρίζω; Soph. et al.; Polyb.; Diod. S.; Kaibel 195, 1; POxy 237 VI, 17; TestSol 4, 2 D; JosAs 23:4 [ἐνυβρίσθην]; Jos., Ant. 20, 117 al.; Ath. 2, 2 εἰς τὸ ὄνομα; 24, 4 τῇ ἀρχῇ) ***to insult, outrage*** τὶ (Jos., Ant. 1, 47 μου τὴν γνώμην=God's command) τὸ πνεῦμα **Hb 10:29.**—DELG s.v. ὕβρις. M-M. TW.

ἔνυδρος, ον (since Hes. fgm. 27 of things that contain water; since Soph. also of entities that live in or by water, so also Wis 19:10, 19; 4 Macc 1:34; Hes. 19:3; Philo; Jos., Ant. 16, 142; Ar. 12, 3) ***(living) in water*** ζῷα … ἔ. Hm. 12, 4, 1 v.l.—DELG s.v. ὕδωρ.

ἐνυπνιάζομαι (s. ὕπνος) 1 fut. ἐνυπνιασθήσομαι; 1 aor. ἐνυπνιάσθην Gen 28:12 al. and ἠνυπνιάσθην Da (Theod.) 2:3; 1 aor. mid. ἠνυπνιασάμην Jer 23:25 (as dep. Hippocr. et al.; Plut., Brut. 995 [24, 3]; Jo. Lydus, De Ostentis p. 76, 21; Philo, Somn. 2, 105, and always in OT and NT) ***to dream*** ἐνυπνίοις ἐ. *have visions in dreams* **Ac 2:17** (Jo 3:1). Of factious pers. ἐνυπνιαζόμενοι **Jd 8.**—M-M. TW.

ἐνύπνιον, ου, τό (s. prec. entry; Pind., Aeschyl., Hdt. et al.; Arrian, Alex. An. 2, 18, 1; ins, pap, LXX, En; PsSol 6:3; Philo; Jos., C. Ap. 1, 207; 211; Test12Patr) ***a dream*** **Ac 2:17** (Jo 3:1).—B. 269. DELG s.v. ὕπνος. M-M. TW.

ἐνφωνέω (not found elsewhere) **Lk 16:24** D (Tdf. app. for φωνέω). S. also ἐκφωνέω.

ἐνών s. ἔνειμι.

ἐνώπιον prop. neut. of ἐνώπιος, functioning as a prep. (s. on ἀνά beg.) w. gen. (as SIG[2] 843, 7 [Trajan] ἐνώπιον τῶν προγεγραμμένων θεῶν, cp. Plut. Mor. 274b, 3; PCairZen 73, 14 [257 BC]; PLond II, 35, 6 p. 25 [161 BC] restored; PGrenf I 38, 11; POxy 658, 9; LXX, pseudepigr.; Just., A I, 50, 5 [for ἐνάντιον Is 53:12, so also in 4 other LXX quot.]) esp. in Lk (22 times), Ac (13 times) and Rv (32 times); 9 times in 1 Cl; once each in J, 1J, 3J, Js, 1 Pt; not at all in Mt, Mk, 2 Pt, 2J, Jd.

❶ **pert. to a position in front of an entity,** ***before*** *someone* or *someth.* εἶναι ἐ. τινος **Rv 7:15;** usu. εἶναι must be supplied **1:4; 4:5f; 8:3; 9:13.** After 'stand', 'place', 'step', etc. (schol. on Apollon. Rhod. 4, 1043b of suppliants: ὥσπερ ἐνώπιον τῶν θεῶν ἱστάμενοι): στῆναι **Ac 10:30;** GJs 11:2; ἑστηκέναι **Rv 7:9; 8:2** (RCharles, ICC Rv ad loc.: *attend upon, be in the service of*); **11:4; 12:4; 20:12;** παρεστηκέναι (cp. 3 Km 12:6; Judg 20:28) **Lk 1:19; Ac 4:10;** ἱστάναι **6:6;** καθῆσθαι **Rv 11:16.** θύρα ἠνεῳγμένη ἐ. τινος *a door that stands open before someone* **3:8.** After verbs of motion: τιθέναι **Lk 5:18;** βάλλειν **Rv 4:10;** ἀναβαίνειν **8:4;** πίπτειν of worshippers or admirers falling down before someone (1 Km 25:23) **4:10; 5:8;** cp. **7:11;** προσκυνεῖν (Ps 21:28, cp. 30) **Lk 4:7; Rv 3:9; 15:4** (cp. 22:8; on this Hebraism s. προσκυνέω a). Of a forerunner or herald: after προέρχεσθαι (cp. 2 Ch 1:10; 1 Km 12:2ab) **Lk 1:17;** προπορεύεσθαι vs. **76.** σκάνδαλα βάλλειν ἐ. τινος **Rv 2:14.**

❷ **pert. to being present or in view,** ***in the sight of, in the presence of, among***—ⓐ lit. φαγεῖν ἐ. τινος **Lk 24:43; 13:26** (cp. 2 Km 11:13; 3 Km 1:25). σημεῖα ποιεῖν **J 20:30.** ἀνακρίνειν **Lk 23:14;** cp. **5:25; 8:47; Ac 19:9, 19; 27:35; Rv 13:13; 14:3, 10; 3J 6;** ἐ. πολλῶν μαρτύρων **1 Ti 6:12.** ἐ. πάντων **5:20;** cp. **Lk 11:53** D; βαπτισθῆναι ἐ. αὐτοῦ **3:7** D (s. 4b below); χορεύσασα ἐ. τῶν ἀγγέλων GJs 15:3.

ⓑ nonliteral ἡμεῖς ἐ. τοῦ θεοῦ πάρεσμεν **Ac 10:33.** Also after verbs of motion βαστάζειν τὸ ὄνομα ἐ. τ. ἐθνῶν **Ac 9:15.** After ἀρνεῖσθαι **Lk 12:9;** ὁμολογεῖν **Rv 3:5;** 2 Cl 3:2 (ἔμπροσθεν **Mt 10:32**); κατηγορεῖν **12:10;** καυχᾶσθαι **1 Cor 1:29;** δικαιοῦν ἑαυτόν **Lk 16:15.** πίστιν κατὰ σεαυτὸν ἔχε ἐ. τοῦ θεοῦ *keep (your) conviction to yourself in the sight of God* (=*keep … between yourself and God*) **Ro 14:22** (s. πίστις 2dε); cp. **2 Cor 4:2;** MPol 14:1f. Also a favorite expr. in assertions and oaths which call upon God, as the One who sees all: **Gal 1:20; 1 Ti 5:21; 6:13; 2 Ti 2:14; 4:1.**—Such renderings as *among, before, in the presence of* are also appropriate for the following: γίνεται χαρὰ ἐ. τῶν ἀγγέλων **Lk 15:10.** ἔσται σοι δόξα ἐ. πάντων **14:10.** εὑρίσκειν χάριν ἐ. τοῦ θεοῦ **Ac 7:46** (cp. Gen 6:8 v.l. [ARahlfs, Genesis 1926, 61] al.). ἐ. τοῦ πάντων δεσπότου GJs 11:2.—προορώμην τ. κύριον ἐ. μου **Ac 2:25** (Ps 15:8).—After verbs of remembering and forgetting: μνησθῆναι ἐ. τοῦ θεοῦ **Ac 10:31; Rv 16:19.** ἐπιλελησμένον ἐ. τοῦ θεοῦ **Lk 12:6** (cp. ἐρωτηθῆναι ἐνώπιον τῆς ἁγίας δόξης σου TestAbr B 4 p. 108, 22 [Stone p. 64]).—For dat. auctoris: εἰσηκούσθη ἡ δέησις σου ἐ. κυρίου τοῦ θεοῦ GJs 20:3 (cp. PsSol 1:2; GrBar 1:5).

❸ **pert. to exposure to value judgment,** ***in the opinion/judgment of*** ἐ. ἑαυτῶν B 4:11 (Is 5:21); ἐ. ἀνθρώπων **Ro 12:17; 2 Cor 8:21b;** Pol 6:1 (cp. Pr 3:4). As a rule (as **2 Cor 8:21a**) of θεός or κύριος; so after τὰ ἀρεστά **1J 3:22;** βδέλυγμα **Lk 16:15;** δίκαιος **1:6 v.l.; Ac 4:19;** δικαιοσύνη **Lk 1:75;** δικαιοῦσθαι **Ro 3:20;** εὐάρεστος **Hb 13:21;** 1 Cl 21:1; 60:2 (cp. Dt 13:19); καλός, ἀπόδεκτος **1 Ti 2:3; 5:4;** μέγας (4 Km 5:1) **Lk 1:15;** πολυτελής **1 Pt 3:4;** πεπληρωμένος **Rv 3:2.** The combinations ἀρεστός and εὐάρεστος ἐ. τινος cited above form a transition to combinations in which ἐ. w. gen. stands simply for the dative: ἤρεσεν ὁ λόγος ἐ. παντὸς τ. πλήθους **Ac 6:5** (cp. Dt 1:23 v.l.; 2 Km 3:36). φανεροῦσθαι ἐ. τοῦ θεοῦ **2 Cor 7:12;** cp. **Lk 24:11; Hb 4:13.**—Prob. this is the place also for ἡ ἁμαρτία μου ἐνώπιόν μου ἐστίν 1 Cl 18:3 (Ps 50:5); ταπεινώθητε ἐ. κυρίου *humble yourselves before the Lord* **Js 4:10.**

❹ special uses—ⓐ *in relation to* ἁμαρτάνειν ἐ. τινος *sin against someone* **Lk 15:18, 21** (cp. Jdth 5:17; 1 Km 7:6; 20:1).

ⓑ *by the authority of, on behalf of* **Rv 13:12, 14; 19:20.** Also simply *by* **Lk 3:7** D (but s. 2a).—Johannessohn, Präpositionen 194–97; 359–61; AWikenhauser, Ἐνώπιος–ἐνώπιον–κατενώπιον: BZ 8, 1910, 263–70.—DELG s.v. ἐνῶπα. M-M.

ἐνωρίστερον adv. of ἔνωρος (Phylarch: 81 fgm. 44 Jac.) ***earlier, ahead of time*** AcPl Ha 3, 4.—DELG s.v. ὥρα.

Ἐνώς, ὁ indecl. (אֱנוֹשׁ) ***Enos,*** son of Seth (Gen 4:26; Philo, Det. Pot. Ins. 138f.—In Jos., Ant. 1, 79; 83 Ἄνωσος [v.l. Ἔνωσος], ου), in the genealogy of Jesus **Lk 3:38.**—BHHW I 413.

ἔνωσις, εως, ἡ (Pre-Socr. et al.; Aristot., Phys. 222a, 20; M. Ant. 6, 38; Herm. Wr. 1, 6; 14, 6 al.; Philo, Leg. All. 1, 8; Ar. 13,

5; Ath.) **the quality or state of being in complete accord (as opposed to discord or dissidence),** ***union, unity,*** IMg 13:2; ITr 11:2. σαρκὸς καὶ πνεύματος *with flesh and spirit* IMg 1:2. ἕ. τοῦ αἵματος *unity in his blood* (capable of more than one interpr., but the main thing is the idea of union through the *one* blood) IPhld 4. τὴν ἕ. ἀγαπᾶν 7:2. τῆς ἑ. φροντίζειν *be intent on unity* IPol 1:2. ἄνθρωπος εἰς ἕ. κατηρτισμένος *a man with designs on unity* IPhld 8:1. τὴν ἕ. ποιεῖσθαι *enter into a union* (in marriage) IPol 5:2.—ThPreiss, La mystique de l'imitation du Christ et de l'unité chez Ign. d'Ant.: RHPR 18, '38, 197–241.—DELG s.v. εἷς. M-M. Sv.

ἐνωτίζομαι 1 aor. ἐνωτισάμην LXX, 2 pl. ἠνωτίσασθε Jer 44:8 **to listen carefully to what is said,** ***give ear, pay attention to*** (s. οὖς 2; Hesych.; Doukas 84, 19 IBekker [1834]) τὶ *someth.* (Syntipas p. 12, 6 al.; Psellus p. 77, 6; Gen 4:23; Job 33:1; TestReub 1:5, Iss 1:1) τὰ ῥήματα **Ac 2:14** (cp. Ps 5:2). Abs. B 9:3 (Is 1:2).—On the form, s. B-D-F §123, 2.—M-M. TW.

Ἑνώχ, ὁ some edd. Ἐνώχ; indecl. (חֲנוֹךְ) (LXX; En; ApcEl [PSI I, 7 verso, 4 restored]; TestAbr B; ApcEsdr 5:2 p. 30, 23 Tdf.; Philo; Test12Patr; Just., D. 23, 1 al.—In Jos., Ant. 1, 79; 85; 9, 28, Ἄνωχος [v.l. Ἔνωχος], ου) ***Enoch,*** son of Jared, father of Methuselah (Gen 5:18ff). In the genealogy of Jesus **Lk 3:37.** As an example of faith and obedience toward God, and therefore translated to heaven (Gen 5:22, 24; Sir 44:16; Jos., Ant. 1, 85) **Hb 11:5;** 1 Cl 9:3. Prophetic word fr. Enoch **Jd 14f** (=En 1:9). Here he is called ἕβδομος ἀπὸ Ἀδάμ (cp. Diog. L. 3, 1 Plato is ἕκτος ἀπὸ Σόλωνος in the line of Solon's descendants; Athen. 13, 555d says of Socrates' father-in-law Aristides: οὐ τοῦ δικαίου καλουμένου … ἀλλὰ τοῦ τρίτου ἀπ' ἐκείνου).—The quot. fr. Enoch in B 4:3 cannot be identified w. certainty. Enoch is introduced by conjecture **1 Pt 3:19** (ἐν ᾧ καί; following others by FSpitta 1890 and JHarris, Exp. 6th ser., 4, 1901, 346–49; 5, 1902, 317–20; Moffatt; so Goodsp., Probs. 195–98, JBL 73, '54, 91f, but against it ESelwyn, 1 Pt, '46, 197f).—PKatz, Gnomon 26, '54, 226; HJansen, D. Hen. gestalt. E. vergleich. rel. gesch. Untersuchung '39; RAC V 461–76; BHHW II, 692.—TW.

ἐξ prep. s. ἐκ.

ἕξ indecl. (Hom. et al.; pap, LXX, pseudepigr., Philo, Joseph.; Just., D. 132, 1; Mel., HE 4, 26, 4) ***six*** **Mt 17:1; Mk 9:2; Lk 4:25; 13:14; J 2:6, 20** al. πρὸ ἓξ ἡμερῶν τοῦ πάσχα *six days before the Passover* **12:1.**—MPol 9:3; Hv 3, 2, 5.—DELG. M-M.

ἐξαγγέλλω fut. ἐξαγγελῶ LXX; 1 aor. ἐξήγγειλα, 3 sg. pass. ἐξηγγέλθη (Just., D. 75, 1) (s. ἀγγέλλω; Hom. et al.; Philo; Jos., Vi. 357 al.) ***proclaim, report*** (so trag., Hdt.+; ins [OGI 266, 34, s. note]; PGM 5, 294; LXX; Philo, Plant. 128; Joseph.; TestJos 5:2, 3; Just.) **short ending of Mk.** τὰς ἀρετάς **1 Pt 2:9.**—M-M. TW.

ἐξαγοράζω (s. ἀγοράζω) 1 aor. ἐξηγόρασα. The commercial associations of the vb. 'buy, buy up' τὶ 'someth.' (Polyb. 3, 42, 2; Plut., Crass. 543 [2, 5]) or 'redeem' (lit. 'buy back'), 'deliver' τινά 'someone' (Diod. S. 15, 7, 1; 36, 2, 2; not in LXX) invite a variety of extended usage:

➊ **to secure deliverance of,** ***deliver, liberate*** τοὺς ὑπὸ νόμον *those who are subject to the law* **Gal 4:5.** The thing from which deliverance is obtained is added with ἐκ: ἡμᾶς ἐκ τῆς κατάρας τοῦ νόμου **3:13** (Dssm., LO 270–78 [LAE 322–34]; w. ἀπό Ar. 11, 3).

➋ **to gain someth., esp. advantage or opportunity,** ***make the most of.*** The sense of the act. in Da 2:8 (καιρὸν ὑμεῖς ἐξαγοράζετε) is 'gain' or 'buy time': the king's oneiromancers face an hour of peril in which there are no options except to deliver what the monarch requests. The mid. ἐξαγοράζεσθαι τ. καιρόν **Col 4:5; Eph 5:16** appropriately expresses choice in perilous times (ὅτι αἱ ἡμέραι πονηραί εἰσιν) *make the most of the time* or *opportunity* in the sense 'take advantage of any opportunity that comes your way'. (The context of **Col. 4:5** relates to opportunity for evangelism; **Eph 5:16** to avoidance of anything that inteferes with understanding of the Lord's will.) S. also καιρός 1b; cp. Plut., Sert. 571 [6, 6] καιρὸν ὠνεῖσθαι, Phil. 364 [15] ἁρπάσας τὸν καιρόν; cp. OED s.v. redeem 8, 'save (time) fr. being lost'.—RPope, ET 22, 1911, 552–54. For other interpretations, s. the lit. and 3 below.

➌ The earliest occurrence of ἐ. suggests a further sense for the verb when used with the acc. ***buy off*** (Heraclides [III BC], Reisebilder 1951 §22 p. 82 FPfister: τὸν ἀδικηθέντα ἐξαγοράζειν=buy off the claims of the injured man, satisfy the one who has been wronged). So also the mid. διὰ μιᾶς ὥρας τὴν αἰώνιον κόλασιν ἐξαγοραζόμενοι *with a single hour* (of torment) *buying off* (avoiding) *eternal punishment* MPol 2:3 v.l. (cp. Iren., 5, 1, 2 [Harv. II 316, 8]). ἐ. in Col and Eph (s. 2 above) can be understood from this perspective, if 1 Cor 7:29–32 is taken into account (the καιρός is συνεσταλμένος and its 'evil' days present wrathful demands which must be satisfied).—Some mss. of MPol 2:3 read ζωήν instead of κόλασιν; in that case ἐ. would mean *purchase* (s. KLake, transl. ad loc., n. 2, also transll. of Kleist and Goodsp.).—SLyonnet, Biblica 42, '61, 85–89, Sin, Redemption and Sacrifice, '70, 104–19.—M-M. TW. Sv.

ἐξάγω fut. ἐξάξω LXX; 2 aor. ἐξήγαγον. Pass.: 2 fut. 3 sg. ἐξαχθήσεται Sir 23:24; aor. ἐξήχθην LXX (s. ἄγω; Hom.+)

➊ **to conduct from an area,** ***lead out, bring out.,*** lit. τινά *someone* 1 Cl 10:6 (Gen 15:5); 12:4 (Jos 2:3); (out) of a country (Just., D. 120, 3) **Ac 7:36, 40** (Ex 32:1); **13:17** (cp. Dt 4:37); **Hb 8:9** (Jer 38:32); 1 Cl 53:2; B 4:8; 14:3 (the three last Ex 32:7ff; Dt 9:12); (out) of prison (PTebt 15, 13 [114 BC]; Gen 40:14; Ps 141:8; JosAs 4:14) **Ac 5:19; 12:17; 16:37, 39;** (out) of the river Hv 1, 1, 2; sheep fr. the fold (Pollux 1, 250; cp. Philo, Agr. 44) **J 10:3.** W. indication of the destination: into the desert (Ex 16:3) **Ac 21:38.** W. ἵνα foll. **Mk 15:20.** ἔξω (τινός) **Mk 8:23 v.l.** ἔξω w. destination given ἕως πρὸς (εἰς v.l.) Βηθανίαν *as far as Bethany* **Lk 24:50** (cp. Gen 15:5; 19:17).

➋ **to remove from a state or condition,** ***free,*** fig. ext. of mng. 1 (Diod. S. 3, 33, 6 ἐξάγειν ἐκ τοῦ ζῆν=remove from life, put to death; Mel., P. 24, 163 ὑπὸ τοῦ ἀγγέλου [B; θανάτου Ch.] ἐξήγετο) ἐ. ἐκ δεσμῶν *free from bonds* B 14:7 (Is 42:7).—M-M.

ἐξαίρετος, ον (Hom. et al.) prim. mng. 'taken out', hence

➊ **pert. to being selected and taken out from a whole,** ***excepted, separated*** (Thu. et al.) ἔκ τινος *from someth.* ἐκ κακῶν οὐκ ἐ. ἔσονται *they will not be delivered fr. evils* 1 Cl 39:9 (Job 5:5). That which is chosen or separated receives special attention, hence

➋ **pert. to being exceptional,** ***chosen, excellent, remarkable*** (Hom. et al.; OGI 503, 9; pap, LXX; TestJob 15:9; 52:7; Philo, Abr. 7; Joseph.; Just., Tat. 26, 2) τὸ εὐαγγέλιον ἐ. τι ἔχει *has someth. distinctive* (cp. Epict. 1, 2, 17; 3, 1, 25; Philo, Leg. All. 3, 86; TestJob 52:7 ἐν τῇ ἐξαιρέτῳ διαλέκτῳ; Just., D. 2:4 τὸ ἴδιον καὶ τὸ ἐξαίρετον τῆς φιλοσοφίας) IPhld 9:2.—M-M.

ἐξαιρέτως adv. (s. prec. entry; Philo Bybl. [100 AD]: 790 fgm. 1, 29 Jac. [in Eus., PE 1, 9, 29]; Plut., Mor. 667f; Epict. 1, 6, 12;

Lucian; Herodian; Vett. Val. et al.; OGI 603, 6; PAmh 136, 11; BGU 168, 4; PLips 64, 3; Dt 32:12 Aq.; Philo, Plant. 21; Jos., Bell. 2, 125, Ant. 19, 335; Just., D. 142, 1) ***especially*** ITr 12:2; ISm 7:2; Dg 4:4.

ἐξαιρέω fut. ἐξελῶ LXX (s. B-D-F §74, 3); 2 aor. ἐξεῖλον, impv. ἔξελε. Mid.: fut. ἐξελοῦμαι; 2 aor. ἐξειλάμην (-όμην v.l.; s. αἱρέω), inf. ἐξελέσθαι **Ac 7:34** (=Ex 3:8; s. B-D-F §81, 3); pf. 2 sg. ἐξῄρησαι Ezk 33:9. Pass.: 1 fut. 3 sg. ἐξαιρεθήσεται Eccl 7:26, 3 pl. ἐξαιρεθήσονται Job 5:5 cod. A ; pf. ptc. ἐξῃρημένης (Ath., R. 75, 29), inf. ἐξῃρῆσθαι (Ath., R. 77, 28) (Hom.+).

➊ **to remove someth. from its place, *take out, tear out,*** act., τὶ *someth.* an eye (Heliod. 2, 16, 1 τ. ὀφθαλμὸν ἐξεῖλε τὸν δεξιόν; Heraclid., Pol. 30; Phalaris, Ep. 147, 3; Plut., Mor. 373e) **Mt 5:29; 18:9** (cp. Just. A I, 15, 1 ἔκκοψον; on the topic Jos., Ant. 6, 71). τί τινος *someth. fr. someone* B 6:14.

➋ **to deliver someone from peril or confining circumstance, *set free, deliver, rescue,*** mid. (Aeschyl., Suppl. 924; Polyb. 1, 11, 11; LXX), τινά *someone* **Ac 7:34; 23:27;** 1 Cl 52:3 (Ps 49:15). τινὰ ἔκ τινος *someone fr. someth.* (Demosth. 18, 90; PPetr III, 36 [a] recto, 21 ἐξελοῦ με ἐκ τῆς ἀνάγκης; Wsd 10:1; Sir 29:12; Bar 4:18, 21 al.) **Ac 7:10; 12:11** (ἐκ χειρός Ex 18:4 and oft. in OT, but also Aeschin. 3, 256; see on ἐκ 1a); **Gal 1:4;** 1 Cl 56:8 (Job 5:19). Abs. 1 Cl 39:9 (Job 5:4).—**Ac 26:17** is also prob. to be rendered *deliver, save* (w. HHoltzmann, Wendt, Preuschen, Zahn, Steinmann, Eng. trs., against Overbeck, Knopf, Beyer who render 'select, choose out [for oneself]' as Od. 14, 232; Hdt. 3, 150; LXX) τινὰ ἔκ τινος (cp. X., An. 2, 5, 20).—M-M. TW. Spicq.

ἐξαίρω (s. αἴρω) fut. ἐξαρῶ LXX; 1 aor. ἐξῆρα, impv. 2 pl. ἐξάρατε. Pass.: 1 fut. ἐξαρθήσομαι; aor. 3 sg. ἐξήρθη Da 8:11; pf. 3 sg. ἐξῆρται LXX, ptc. acc. pl. ἐξηρμένους Sir 16:9 **to exclude or remove someone from a group, *remove, drive away*** (so Soph. et al.; PRyl 133, 19 [33 AD]; PLond II, 177, 21 p. 169; PGM 7, 367; LXX; En 1:1; JosAs ch. 29 end cod. A, p. 86 Bat.; Philo; Jos., C. Ap. 1, 81; Test12Patr; Just., D. 102, 3) τὸν πονηρὸν ἐξ ὑμῶν *drive out the evil man fr. among you=put the evil man out* **1 Cor 5:13** (Dt 24:7 al. [formulaic: PZaas, JBL 103, '84, 259–61]); pass. vs. **2 v.l.** ἐξάρωμεν τοῦτο *let us put an end to this* 1 Cl 48:1.—DELG s.v. αἴρω. M-M.

ἐξαιτέω 1 aor. mid. ἐξῃτησάμην (Soph., Hdt. et al.; SIG 326, 29 [IV BC]; BGU 944, 8; PMich 506, 7) in our lit. only mid.

➊ **to ask for with emphasis and with implication of having a right to do so, *ask for, demand,*** τινά *someone* (X., An. 1, 1, 3; Demosth. 29, 14; Plut., Per. 169 [32, 5]; Palaeph. 40 p. 61, 1; Jos., Ant. 16, 277; 18, 369; Just., D. 140, 3 υἱούς 'pray for sons') ὁ σατανᾶς ἐξῃτήσατο ὑμᾶς τοῦ σινιάσαι *Satan asked for you, to sift you* **Lk 22:31** (cp. Plut., Mor. 417d βίαιοι δαίμονες ἐξαιτούμενοι ψυχὴν ἀνθρωπίνην; TestBenj 3:3; s. Field, Notes 76, 'obtain by asking').

➋ **to make an earnest request of someone, *ask*** τινά *someone, plead* (Eur., Hec. 49) w. ἵνα foll. MPol 7:2.—M-M. TW.

ἐξαίφνης adv. (s. ἄφνω; Hom. et al.; OGI 56, 48; UPZ 78, 7 [159 BC]; PSI 184, 5; LXX; JosAs 26:5; Jos., Ant. 12, 362; Just.) **pert. to a very brief period of time between two states or events, *suddenly, unexpectedly*** **Mk 13:36; Lk 2:13; 9:39; Ac 9:3; 22:6;** 1 Cl 23:5; IPol 8:1; Hv 2, 1, 4; 3, 12, 2; s 6, 1, 2. (W-H. ἐξέφνης except for Ac 22:6; some mss. spell it so in this pass. also.)—S. εὐθέως and ἐξάπινα. DDaube, The Sudden in the Scriptures, '64. 30f.—Schmidt, Syn. II 164–67. DELG s.v. αἶψα. M-M. Spicq. Sv.

ἑξάκις (Pind. et al.; Sb 1838; PSI 1235, 16; LXX) ***six times*** 1 Cl 56:8 (Job 5:19).

ἑξακισχίλιοι, αι, α (Hdt. 1, 192; Thu. 2, 13, 3 al.; ins, pap [s. Preis. III 275], LXX; Jos., Bell. 4, 115, Ant. 14, 33) ***six thousand*** B 15:4.

ἐξακολουθέω fut. ἐξακολουθήσω; 1 aor. ἐξηκολούθησα (Epicurus p. 156, 6 Us.; Philo Mech. 58, 5; Polyb.; Dionys. Hal., Comp. Verb. 24; Epict. 1, 22, 16; Plut.; ins, pap, LXX, Test12Patr, Joseph., Just.; Mel., P. 93, 704)

➊ **to accept as authoritative determiner of thought or action, *obey, follow,*** w. dat., an authority that may be personal 1 Cl 14:1 (cp. Leo 20, 12 ἐξ. τινί a pers. authority; Am 2:4; TestZeb 9:5, TestNapht 3:3 πνεύμασι πλάνης) or impersonal: σεσοφισμένοις μύθοις **2 Pt 1:16** (cp. Jos., Ant. 1, 22 τοῖς μύθοις ἐξακολουθήσαντες; Just., A I, 2, 1 δόξαις). ταῖς ἀσελγείαις **2:2** (cp. TestIss 6:2 τοῖς πονηροῖς διαβουλίοις).

➋ **to imitate behavior, *follow, pursue,*** a way τῇ ὁδῷ τοῦ Βαλαάμ **2 Pt 2:15** (cp. Is 56:11 ταῖς ὁδοῖς αὐτῶν ἐξηκολούθησαν).—M-M. TW.

ἐξακοντίζω (Eur., X. et al.) ***hurl out*** as a javelin, fig. (TGF, adespota 529 γλώσσῃ ματαίους ἐ. λόγους) w. no object expressed, perh. *aim (at)* or *plunge (into)* εἰς ἔριν 1 Cl 14:2.—DELG s.v. ἀκ-.

ἑξακόσιοι, αι, α (Hdt. 1, 51 al.; pap, LXX; JosAs; Jos., Vi. 200; 241; Tat. 19, 1) ***six hundred*** **Rv 13:18; 14:20;** 1 Cl 43:5.

ἐξακριβάζομαι aor. 3 sg. ἐξηκριβάσατο Num 23:10; inf. ἐξακριβάσασθαι Da 7:19 (the act. Jos., Ant. 19, 332) **to make detailed inquiry, *ask*** or ***inquire exactly*** τὶ *about someth.* (Num 23:10) Hm 4, 3, 3 . τὶ παρά τινος *of someone about someth.* 4, 2, 3.—DELG s.v. ἀκριβής.

ἐξαλείφω fut. ἐξαλείψω LXX; 1 aor. ἐξήλειψα. Pass.: 1 fut. 3 sg. ἐξαλειφθήσεται LXX; Hs 9, 24, 4; 1 aor. ἐξηλείφθην, inf. ἐξαλειφθῆναι LXX; **Ac 3:19;** 1 Cl 53:5 and 2 aor. ἐξαλιφῆναι 1 Ch 29:4 cod. B (s. ἀλείφω; Aeschyl., Hdt. et al.; ins, pap, LXX, En; TestJud 22:3 v.l.; ApcEsdr 3:6 p. 27, 14).

➊ in accordance w. the prim. mng. **to cause to disappear by wiping—ⓐ *wipe away*** πᾶν δάκρυον ἐκ (v.l. ἀπό) τῶν ὀφθαλμῶν **Rv 7:17; 21:4.**

ⓑ ***wipe out, erase*** (X., Hell. 2, 3, 51 τινὰ ἐκ τ. καταλόγου; Anaxippus Com. [IV BC] 1, 5 ἐκ τ. βυβλίων; SIG 921, 19 ἐξαλειψάτω τὸ ὄνομα ὁ ἱερεύς, OGI 218, 129; Ps 68:29 ἐ. ἐκ βίβλου ζώντων; Jos., Ant. 6, 133 τὸ ὄνομα ἐ.) τὸ ὄνομα ἐκ τῆς βίβλου τῆς ζωῆς *the name fr. the book of life* **Rv 3:5;** 1 Cl 53:4 (Ex 32:32).

➋ Certain expr. show the infl. of the transition (s. the graffito in Rdm.[2] 228 [ref. to p. 219]: Ὁ ἐξαλίψον ταῦτα τὰ γράμματα, ἐξαλίψουσιν τὸ γένος αὐτοῦ=let the one who obliterates these letters be assured that his posterity will be obliterated) to the more general mng. **to remove so as to leave no trace, *remove, destroy, obliterate*** (Philostrat., Vi. Apoll. 8, 7 p. 313, 4; Κυπρ. I p. 58 no. 1; Jos., Ant. 17, 335), insofar as the removal results fr. the *blotting out* of a written record (t.t. in the papyri for washing out a papyrus sheet, s. M-M s.v.; Preis., Fachw. s.v. ἀπαλείφω; s. also Dio Chrys. 14 [31], 86; Jos., Ant. 4, 210); among the expressions are the foll.: ἐ. τὸ καθ' ἡμῶν χειρόγραφον **Col 2:14.** τὸ ἀνόμημά μου 1 Cl 18:2 (Ps 50:3). τὰς ἀνομίας 18:9 (Ps 50:11; EDalglish, Ps 51 in the Light of Near East, etc., '62, 86–89 [Semitic background]). τὰς ἁμαρτίας **Ac 3:19** (cp. Ps 108:14; 3 Macc 2:19; En 10:20; PsSol 13:10). Only the more general sense is pertinent (as Diod. S. 3, 40, 7 ἐ. τὰς ἐλπίδας; TestJud 22:3) for 1 Cl 53:3. ἐξαλείψωμεν ἀφ' ἡμῶν τὰ πρότερα ἁμαρτήματα *let us remove fr. ourselves our former sins* 2 Cl 13:1 (ἐξ. ἀπό as Gen 7:23; PsSol 2, 17). Pass. (Lucian, Pro Imag. 26; Jos., Ant. 4, 210) 1 Cl 53:5; Hs 9, 24, 4. οὐκ ἐξαλειφθήσεται τὸ αἷμα αὐτοῦ *no one will be able to wipe away his* (Zacharias's) *blood* GJs 24:2.—M-M.

ἐξάλλομαι fut. 3 pl. ἐξαλοῦνται LXX; 1 aor. 3 sg. ἐξήλατο Na 3:17 (s. ἅλλομαι; Hom. et al.; LXX)

❶ **to spring free from a place,** ***leap out*** (Hom. et al.; Mi 2:12 ἐξ ἀνθρώπων) ἐξαλοῦνται ἐκ τ. μνημείων οἱ νεκροί GNaass 141, 85 (=347, 57).

❷ **to spring up to a standing position,** ***leap up*** (so Aristoph., Vesp. 130; X., Cyr. 7, 1, 27; Jos., Bell. 1, 443; Is 55:12; cp. Demetr.: 722 fgm. 1, 9 Jac. 'fly off') ἐξαλλόμενος ἔστη **Ac 3:8** (Hobart 36f). Cp. **14:10 v.l.**—DELG s.v. ἅλλομαι. M-M.

ἐξαμαρτάνω fut. 2 pl. ἐξαμαρτήσετε (Ath. 2, 4); 2 aor. ἐξήμαρτον, inf. ἐξαμαρτεῖν or ἐξαμαρτῆσαι Eccl 5:5 (trag., Hdt. et al.; PsSol 5:16; ApcMos 13; LXX, Philo; Jos., Ant. 12, 278; 13, 71; Just., Ath. 2, 4) **to miss the mark of a standard of obligation,** ***violate a law or command, commit an offence, do wrong, sin*** ἐ. τι (Soph., Phil. 1012; Hdt. 3, 145 al.) Hm 6, 2, 7; ἐλάχιστον ἐ. *miss the mark (of God's expectation) by a very little* s 8, 10, 1 (the use of the adv. ἐλάχιστον points to imagery of 'missing the mark'; the offender or sinner comes so very close to divine approval for uprightness, but because of deficient self-control fails to hit the mark; cp. Lucian, Jupp. Trag. 20 τὰ τοιαῦτα ἐ. of deities guilty of misdeeds).

ἐξαμβλόω 1 aor. pass. ἐξημβλώθην (Eur. et al.; Philo, Det. Pot. Ins. 147; Jos., Ant. 4, 278) ***cause to miscarry*** τὰ βρέφη τὰ ἐξαμβλωθέντα ApcPt 2 (Ps.-Apollod. 3, 4, 3 W. βρέφος ἐξαμβλωθέν).—DELG s.v. ἀμβλίσκω.

ἐξαμηνιαῖος, α, ον (s. μήν 'month'; PCairZen 340, 5 and 27f [III BC] ἔριφοι ἑξαμηνιεῖοι) ***of six months*** GJs 6:1 v.l. (for ἑξάμηνος).

ἑξάμηνος, ον (s. prec. entry; Hdt. et al.; 4 Km 15:8; 1 Ch 3:4) ***of six months*** γεναμένης αὐτῆς ἑξαμήνου (de Strycker) *when* (Mary) *was six months old* GJs 6:1.

ἐξανάστασις, εως, ἡ (intr.='getting up' in Hippocr.; Polyb. 3, 55, 4 al.; fig. perh. BGU 717, 11) **the state or condition of coming up from among the dead,** ***resurrection*** ἡ ἐ. ἡ ἐκ νεκρῶν *resurrection fr. the dead* **Phil 3:11** (the compound in contrast to the simplex ἀνάστασις that precedes connotes a coming to fullness of life, as vss. 12–21 indicate).—M-M.

ἐξανατέλλω fut. ἐξανατελῶ Ps 131:17; 1 aor. ἐξανέτειλα (intr. in Empedocles [V BC] fgm. B 62, 4; Moschus 2, 58; Ps 111:4) ***spring up*** of a quick-growing plant **Mt 13:5; Mk 4:5.**—TW.

ἐξανίστημι (s. ἀνίστημι) fut. ἐξαναστήσω; 1 aor. ἐξανέστησα; 2 aor. ἐξανέστην; pf. 3 sg. ἐξανέστηκεν Ezk 7:10.

❶ **to cause to stir from a position,** ***raise up, awaken*** (Soph., Hdt. et al.; LXX; Jos., Ant. 5, 46) τινά *someone* 1 Cl 26:2 (quot. of uncertain orig.; possibly Ps 70:21f LXX?). τοὺς ἀσθενοῦντας *raise up the weak* 59:4.

❷ **to beget progeny,** ***raise up offspring*** fig. ext of mng. 1, ἐ. σπέρμα (Gen 19:32, 34) **Mk 12:19; Lk 20:28.**

❸ **to come to the fore,** intr. in mid. and 2 aor. act. (Pind., Hdt. et al.; Jos., Bell. 2, 279, Ant. 17, 132 al.; LXX; PsSol 6:4; JosAs 16:14 cod. A and Pal. 364)

ⓐ ***stand up*** (distinct from others) to speak (X., An. 6, 1, 30) **Ac 15:5.**

ⓑ ***rise up*** of one who appears on the scene and becomes an object of special attention (Judg 5:7 A; En 15:12) B 4:4.—M-M. TW.

ἐξανοίγω 1 aor. ptc. ἐξανοίξαντες (s. ἀνοίγω; Aristoph. et al.; Diod. S. 1, 33, 11; Strabo 16, 1, 10) ***to open (fully)*** **Ac 12:16** D.—DELG s.v. ἵστημι.

ἐξαπατάω 1 aor. ἐξηπάτησα; pf. 3 pl. ἐξηπατήκασιν (Tat. 14, 1); aor. pass. inf. ἐξαπατηθῆναι (Just., D. 8, 3) (s. ἀπατάω; Hom. et al.) **to cause someone to accept false ideas about someth.,** ***deceive, cheat,*** τινά *someone* (Jos., Ant. 10, 111) **Ro 7:11; 2 Th 2:3;** IEph 8:1. Of the serpent's deception of Eve (cp. Gen 3:13) **2 Cor 11:3; 1 Ti 2:14;** GJs 13:1, in the first and third pass.=*lead astray* (Hdt. 2, 114, 2). τὰς καρδίας τῶν ἀκάκων *the hearts of the unsuspecting* **Ro 16:18** (Philo, Leg. All. 3, 109 τ. αἴσθησιν). ἑαυτὸν ἐ. *deceive oneself* (Ael. Aristid. 24, 35 K.=44 p. 835 D.; Lucian, Merc. Cond. 5, end; Jos., Ant. 13, 89; Just., D. 34, 1 al.; cp. Epict. 2, 20, 7; 2, 22, 15 μὴ ἐξαπατᾶσθε) **1 Cor 3:18;** τινά τινι ἐ. *deceive someone w. someth.* τῇ ὕλῃ IRo 6:2.—M-M. TW. Sv.

ἐξάπινα adv. (ins: Sb 7792, 4; pap, e.g. PGiss 68, 6 [II AD]; Iambl., Protr. 20; Zonaras 7, 25; 10, 37; LXX; PsSol 1:2; TestSol 20:17 P)

❶ **pert. to someth. brought about in a very brief time,** ***suddenly*** **Mk 9:8.**

❷ **pert. to someth. happening unexpectedly and without time for preparation,** ***unexpectedly*** ἔρχεσθαι Hs 9, 7, 6. S. also εὐθέως, ἐξαίφνης.—DELG s.v. ἐξαπίνης. M-M.

ἐξαπλόω pf. pass. ptc. ἐξηπλωμένος **to lay out in such a way that no part is concealed,** ***unfold, spread out*** (ἁπλόω 'make single, spread out', s. ἁπλοῦς; Ps.-Lucian, Philopatr. 17; Galen, De Temper. 1 p. 552 [p. 27, 12 Helmr.]; Herm. Wr. p. 436, 9 Sc.; Suda) a linen cloth Hv 3, 1, 4.—DELG s.v. ἁπλόος.

ἐξαπορέω (s. ἀπορέω) 1 aor. ἐξηπορήθην, in our lit. only pass. dep. ἐξαπορέομαι (this in Diod. S., Plut. et al.; SIG 495, 12 [III BC]; PEleph 2, 10 [285/284 BC]) **to be at a loss psychologically,** ***be in great difficulty, doubt, embarrassment*** w. gen. of that in respect to which this occurs (Dionys. Hal. 7, 18 τοῦ ἀργυρίου) τοῦ ζῆν *despair of living* **2 Cor 1:8.** Abs. (Ps 87:16) ἀπορούμενοι ἀλλ' οὐκ ἐξαπορούμενοι *perplexed, but not despairing* ('sometimes at a loss, but not a loser') **4:8.**—M-M.

ἐξαποστέλλω fut. ἐξαποστελῶ; 1 aor. ἐξαπέστειλα; pf. ἐξαπέσταλκα LXX. Pass.: 2 fut. 3 sg. ἐξαποσταλήσεται Sir 28:23 cod. B; 2 aor. ptc. n. ἐξαποσταλέν EpJer 61:2; pf. ἐξαπέσταλμαι 1 Esdr 1:25; ptc. n. pl. ἐξαπεσταλμένα Esth 8:5 v.l. (since Ep. Phil. in Demosth. 18, 77=Hercher no. 3 p. 465; ins, pap, LXX, pseudepigr.; Jos., Ant. 18, 201; Just., D. 83, 4 [on Ps 109:2]; Mel., P. 85, 640 προφήτας. S. Anz 356f; OGlaser, De ratione, quae intercedit inter sermonem Polybii et eum, qui in titulis saec. III, II, I apparet 1894, 33f).

❶ **to send someone off to a locality or on a mission,** ***send away, send off, send out*** (Polyb. 4, 11, 6)—ⓐ of removal fr. a place, without indication of purpose: **Ac 17:14** (w. inf. foll. as EpArist 13). εἰς Ταρσόν (cp. PSI 384, 4 ἐ. αὐτὸν... εἰς

Φιλαδέλφειαν; 1 Macc 11:62; 2 Macc 14:27; PsSol 17:12 ἕως ἐπὶ δυσμῶν) **9:30.**

ⓑ for fulfillment of a mission in another place (GNachtergall, Les Galates etc. '77, no. 80, 1 and 4 [II BC]; Diod. S. 17, 2, 5 τινὰ εἰς; Ps.-Callisth. 3, 26, 5; JosAs 1:1) **Ac 7:12.** Βαρναβᾶν διελθεῖν ἕως Ἀντιοχείας **11:22.** Of the sending out of apostles **22:21.** Of higher beings sent by God (cp. Wsd 9:10): angels (Gen 24:40; Ps 151:4; TestAbr A 8 p. 86, 5 [Stone p. 20]; JosAs 15:13; PFouad 203, 2ff [I–II AD]) **12:11;** Hs 8, 6, 3; 9, 14, 3; Jesus: ἐξαπέστειλεν ὁ θεὸς τὸν υἱὸν αὐτοῦ (sc. ἐξ οὐρανοῦ, cp. Ps 56:4) **Gal 4:4.** ὁ ἐξαποστείλας ἡμῖν τὸν σωτῆρα 2 Cl 20:5. Of the Spirit (Ps 103:30) ἐ. ὁ θεὸς τὸ πνεῦμα τοῦ υἱοῦ αὐτοῦ εἰς τὰς καρδίας ἡμῶν **Gal 4:6.**

❷ **to send off as an act of dismissal,** ***send away*** (Ps.-Callisth. 3, 26, 6; w. double acc. Polyb. 15, 2, 4) τινὰ κενόν *someone empty-handed* (Gen 31:42; Job 22:9) **Lk 1:53; 20:10f.**

❸ **to send someth. off in an official sense,** ***send, dispatch***

ⓐ in relation to the mission of Jesus ἡμῖν ὁ λόγος τ. σωτηρίας ταύτης ἐξαπεστάλη **Ac 13:26.** S. also the **short ending of Mk** ἐξαπέστειλεν . . . τὸ ἱερὸν καὶ ἄφθαρτον κήρυγμα τῆς αἰωνίου σωτηρίας.—ἐ. τὴν ἐπαγγελίαν τ. πατρός μου ἐφ᾽ ὑμᾶς *I will send the promise of my Father* (=what my Father has promised) *upon* or *to* (PRyl 127, 22 [29 AD] τοὺς αἰτίους ἐξαποστεῖλαι ἐπὶ σέ) *you* **Lk 24:49 v.l.** (for ἀποστέλλω).

ⓑ of punishments: ἐξαποστέλλει μάστιγας ὑμῖν *God sends out plagues on you* Hv 4, 2, 6 (cp. GrBar 16:3 ἐξαποστείλατε κάμπην καὶ βροῦχον, ἐρυσίβην καὶ ἀκρίδα, χάλαζαν).—New Docs 2, 82–83. M-M. EDNT. TW.

ἐξάπτω (s. ἅπτω) 1 aor. ἐξῆψα. Pass.: 1 aor. ἐξήφθην LXX; pf. 3 sg. ἐξῆπται Pr 22:15, inf. ἐξῆφθαι (Just. 42, 1) **to cause to glow or catch fire,** ***light, kindle*** (so in lit. sense Tim. Locr. 7, 97e; Aeneas Tact. 1698; Hero Alex. I p. 214, 12; Aelian, VH 5, 6 τὴν πυράν; PGM 13, 12; Ex 30:8; 1 Macc 4:50; Philo, Gig. 25.—Fig. Jos., Vi. 105; 123; Just., D. 42, 1; Mel., fgm. 8b 23; Ath., R. 62, 12) τὸ πῦρ (Aristot., Part. An. 2, 9, 655a, 15) MPol 15:1.

ἐξάρατε, ἐξαρθῇ s. ἐξαίρω.

ἐξαριθμέω (s. ἀριθμέω) fut. ἐξαριθμήσω LXX; 1 aor. ἐξηρίθμησα; fut. pass. 3 sg. ἐξαριθμηθήσεται LXX ***count*** (so Hdt. et al.; ins, pap, LXX; ApcEsdr 4:2 p. 27, 1 Tdf. al.) τὶ *someth.* (Lycophron v. 1255) τὴν ἄμμον τῆς γῆς *the sand of the earth* 1 Cl 10:5a (Gen 13:16). τοὺς ἀστέρας 10:6 (Gen 15:5). Pass. 10:5b (on the figure cp. Ael. Aristid. 46, 3 K.=3 p. 30 D.: ἐξαρ. τοὺς χόας τ. θαλάττης).

ἐξαρπάζω 1 aor. inf. ἐξαρπάσαι 1 Macc 7:29 (Hom., Hdt. Joseph.) **to carry off, with connotation of suddenness,** ***snatch away, abduct*** ἐξαρπάσαντες αὐτόν **Ac 23:25 v.l.**

ἐξαρτάω pf. pass. ptc. ἐξηρτημένος (ἀρτάω 'fasten to, hang'; Eur. et al.; Polyb. 18, 1, 4; Hero Alex. I p. 434, 16; PTebt 769, 1 [III BC]).

❶ **to cause to be suspended by attachment to someth.,** ***hang up*** τινός *by someth.* (Proclus on Pla., Cratyl. p. 89, 11 Pasqu.) τῶν πλοκάμων *by the braids of their hair* ApcPt 9:24.

❷ pass. (Eur., X. et al.; POxy 471, 83 [II AD]; Ex 28:7) **to be closely associated with someone,** ***be attached to, be an adherent of,*** τινός *someone* (Eur., Suppl. 735; Plut., Galb. 1056 [8, 2], Arat. 1047 [42, 1], Gracchi 837 [27, 4] ἐξηρτημένον αὐτοῦ πλῆθος) **Mk 3:21 v.l.**—DELG s.v. 2 ἀείρω.

ἐξαρτίζω (s. ἄρτιος) 1 aor. ἐξήρτισα; pf. pass. ptc. ἐξηρτισμένος (late; Ex 28:7 v.l.).

❶ **to bring someth. to an end,** ***finish, complete*** (IG XII/2, 538; POxy 296, 7 [I AD] of documents; Jos., Ant. 3, 139) ἐ. ἡμᾶς τ. ἡμέρας *our time was up* **Ac 21:5** (cp. Hippocr., Epid. 2, 180 ἀπαρτίζειν τὴν ὀκτάμηνον).

❷ **to make ready for service,** ***equip, furnish*** (Diod. S. 14, 19, 5 Vogel v.l.; Lucian; Arrian; Jos., Ant. 3, 43 v.l.; CIG II, 420, 13; Mitt-Wilck. I/2, 176, 10 [I AD]; pap, e.g. PAmh 93, 8; PTebt 342, 17) πρὸς πᾶν ἔργον ἀγαθὸν ἐξηρτισμένος *for every good deed* **2 Ti 3:17** (with ἐξηρτισμένος πρός τι cp. Diod. S. 19, 77, 3 ναῦς ἐξηρτισμένας πρὸς τὸν πόλεμον πρὸς τὴν τῶν Ἑλλήνων ἐλευθέρωσιν).—DELG s.v. ἀραρίσκω, s. also ἄρτι. M-M. TW. Spicq.

ἐξασθενέω fut. ἐξασθενήσω; aor. 3 pl. ἐξησθένησαν Ps 63:9; pf. ptc. ἐξησθενηκότας (PsSol 17:31) (s. ἀσθενέω; Hippocr. et al.; Plut.; Aelian, NA 16, 27; Vett. Val. 125, 11; 139, 29; BGU 903, 15; PTebt 50, 33) in our lit. only fig. (cp. Diod. S. 20, 78, 1 τοῖς λογισμοῖς; Philo; Agatharchides: 86 fgm. 20 [in Jos., C. Ap. 1, 211] Jac.) ***become quite weak*** ἐν τῇ ἀγάπῃ IPhld 6:2 (for the constr. w. ἐν cp. Vett. Val. 59, 13).—DELG s.v. σθένος.

ἐξαστράπτω (s. ἀστράπτω; Pollux 1, 117; Zosimus the alchemist 111 Berthelot; Rhet. Gr. I 640, 31; Tryphiodorus [V AD] vs. 103 [ed. Weinberger 1896]; Leontius 44b p. 91, 12; Na 3:3; Ezk 1:4, 7; TestSol 21, 2; TestAbr A 90, 22 [Stone p. 28]; TestJob 46:8; JosAs 22 cod. A [p. 73, 2 Bat.]; GrBar 7:4) ***flash/gleam like lightning*** fig. of a white garment **Lk 9:29.**—DELG s.v. ἀστεροπή (cp. ἀστήρ and ὀπή 'opening, hole'). M-M. TW.

ἐξαυτῆς (=ἐξ αὐτῆς τ. ὁδοῦ [DELG s.v. αὐτός; also Frisk s.v. ἐξαυτῆς]; ἐξ αὐτῆς **Mk 6:25 v.l.;** cp. Philo, Mut. Nom. 142) adv. ***at once, immediately, soon thereafter*** (since Theognis 1, 231 Diehl v.l.; Cratinus [V BC], fgm. 34 [I 22 Kock]; Polyb.; Jos., Ant. 7, 122; 15, 186; En 31:2 [corrupt]. Written as one word PLond 893, 6 [40 AD]; PRyl 236, 22; PTebt 421, 2; POxy 64, 3 et al.) **Mk 6:25; Ac 10:33; 11:11; 21:32; 23:30** (v.l. ἐξ αὐτῶν); **Phil 2:23.**—M-M.

ἐξαφίημι aor. inf. ἐξαφεῖναι 2 Macc 12:24; aor. pass. inf. ἐξαφεθῆναι (ἀφίημι; Soph. et al., in various senses; 2 Macc 12:24; Joseph.; pap; pass. PMerton 79, 8 [II BC]) **to set free from restraint,** ***let loose, release*** ἐκέλευσεν αὐτῷ ἐξαφεθῆναι λέοντα *he gave the order to have a lion released against (Paul)* AcPl 4:19.

ἐξέβαλον s. ἐκβάλλω.

ἐξέβην s. ἐκβαίνω.

ἐξεγείρω fut. ἐξεγερῶ; 1 aor. ἐξήγειρα. Pass.: 1 fut. ἐξεγερθήσομαι; aor. ἐξηγέρθην LXX; pf. 3 sg. ἐξεγήγερται Zech 2:17 (s. ἐγείρω; trag., Hdt. et al.; LXX; Joseph.; SibOr 3, 767; PLond 1912, 100; Mel., P. 85, 641 [B]).

❶ **to awaken someone fr. sleep,** ***awaken*** (trag. et al.; Epict. 2, 20, 17; SIG 1168, 118; Sir 22:9; 1 Esdr 3:13) 1 Cl 26:2 (Ps 3:6). Pass. w. intr. sense *wake up* (Hdt. 1, 34 al.) εὐθὺς ἐξεγερθείς *as soon as he had awakened* (or *risen*) **Mk 6:45** D.

❷ **to raise up fr. the dead,** ***raise*** (cp. Aeschyl., Choëph. 495; Da 12:2 Theod.; the awakening of the spirits of the dead IDefixWünsch 5, 21 p. 24) **1 Cor 6:14** (perh. of rising to the new resurrection life in Christ; cp. Phil 3:11 ἐξανάστασις); AcPlCor 2:31.

❸ **to bring to a sitting position,** ***raise up*** τινὰ τῆς χειρός *someone by the hand* Hv 3, 1, 7. Pass. w. act. sense *rise up* 3, 12, 2.

❹ **cause to appear,** ***bring into being*** (Cantharus Com. [V BC], fgm. 1; PLond 1912, 100; Zech 11:16; Jos., Ant. 8, 271; Mel., P. 85 τοὺς βασιλεῖς [Bodm.]) **Ro 9:17,** unless this is to be interpreted as in 5.

❺ **give one higher status,** ***elevate*** **Ro 9:17,** but s. 4.—M-M. TW.

ἐξέδετο, ἐξεδόμην s. ἐκδίδωμι.

ἐξειλάμην, ἐξείλατο, ἐξεῖλον s. ἐξαιρέω.

I. ἔξειμι fr. εἶμι; inf. ἐξιέναι, ptc. ἐξιών; impf. ἐξῄειν, 3 pl. ἐξῄεσαν (Hom. et al.; ins, pap, LXX, Joseph.) **to depart from an area,** ***go out, go away*** without further indication of place (Herodian 7, 9, 4; Jos., C. Ap. 1, 231) **Ac 13:42; 17:15;** MPol 8:1. τινός (since Hom.) ἐξῄει τοῦ στεινοῦ καὶ σκοτεινοῦ τόπου *he left the narrow and dark place* (of the prison) AcPl Ha 3, 19. ἔκ τινος (Hdt. 1, 94, 4; ViDa 12 [p. 78, 9 Sch.]; Lucian, Eunuch. 6) **Ac 13:42 v.l.;** *go on a journey* (Ael. Aristid. 51, 1 K.=27 p. 534 D.) **Ac 20:4** D, 7. ἐπὶ τὴν γῆν *get to land* **Ac 27:43** (cp. PLips 110, 5 ἐ. ἐπὶ τὴν Καπαδοκίαν; Jos., Vi. 289).—M-M.

II. ἔξειμι fr. εἰμί s. ἔξεστιν.

ἐξεῖπον supplies aor. for ἐξαγορεύω, which is not used in our lit. (s. εἶπον; trag.; Thu. 7, 87, 4 al.; En 14:16; TestJob 41:5; TestZeb 1:6; Jos., Vi. 204; Just.; Tat. 23:1; Ath. 23:4f) **to make a statement w. a relatively wide audience envisaged,** ***express, proclaim*** ('say out') τὶ 1 Cl 49:3. γνῶσιν 48:5. ὅσα Dg 11:8. W. relative clause as obj. 2 Cl 14:5.

ἔξελε, ἐξελέσθαι s. ἐξαιρέω.

ἐξελέγχω fut. 3 sg. ἐξελέγξει LXX; 1 aor. subj. 3 sg. ἐξελέγξῃ Pr 30:6 v.l.; inf. ἐξελέγξαι ([strengthened for ἐλέγχω] Heraclitus, Pind., trag. et al.; Thu. 3, 64, 4; SIG 417, 8; OGI 669, 58; PEdg 33 [=PCairZen 202, Sb 6739], 5; PTebt 25, 14; UPZ 113, 13 al.; LXX; Philo; Jos., C. Ap. 1, 105; 2, 138; Tat. 12, 3) **to expose someone's errors in devastating fashion:** only **Jd 15** as v.l. for ἐλέγξαι ***convict.***—M-M.

ἐξελήλυθα s. ἐξέρχομαι.

ἐξελίσσω (s. ἑλίσσω; Eur. et al.; SEG VIII, 464, 32; 3 Km 7:45) **to move forward in a manner that suggests an unrolling process,** ***unroll,*** of heavenly bodies that τοὺς ἐπιτεταγμένους αὐτοῖς ὁρισμούς *roll on* or *travel through their appointed courses* 1 Cl 20:3 (Plut., Mor. 368a of the σελήνη: τὸν αὑτῆς κύκλον ἐξελίσσει; Heliod. 5, 14, 3).—DELG s.v. ἕλιξ.

ἐξέλκω fut. 3 sg. ἐξελκύσει; aor. 3 pl. ἐξείλκυσαν LXX, subj. 2 sg. ἐξελκύσῃς Job 36:20, pass. 3 pl. ἐξειλκύσθησαν Judg 20:31 cod. A (Hom. et al.; LXX) **to drag away, with connotation of initial reluctance,** ***drag away*** ὑπὸ τῆς ἰδίας ἐπιθυμίας ἐξελκόμενος *taken in tow by his own desire(s)* **Js 1:14** (cp. Pla., 7th Letter, 325b εἷλκεν δέ με ἡ ἐπιθυμία; X., Cyr. 8, 1, 32 μὴ . . . ἑλκόμενος ὑπὸ τῶν ἡδονῶν=not drawn away [from the good] by pleasures at hand; Aelian, HA 6, 31 ὑπὸ τ. ἡδονῆς ἑλκόμενοι).—DELG s.v. ἕλκω. M-M.

ἐξέμασα s. ἐκμάσσω.

ἐξεμπλάριον, ίου, τό (Lat. loanw., 'exemplarium'; occurs in the so-called 'confession ins' fr. Phrygia and Lydia [s. FSteinleitner, D. Beicht 1913, 130a, index; Ramsay, CB I/1, 151 no. 47, also 46 and 48]; POxy 1066; also s. Lampe s.v. The material in JHS 7, 1887, 385ff is doubtful. For various spellings s. Ramsay, CB I/1, 149–51, nos. 41, 46, 47, 48.) ***(living) example, embodiment,*** τῆς ἀγάπης IEph 2:1; ITr 3:2. θεοῦ διακονίας *of God's ministry* ISm 12:1.

ἐξενεγκ- s. ἐκφέρω.

ἐξέπεσα s. ἐκπίπτω.

ἐξεπέτασα s. ἐκπετάννυμι.

ἐξεπλάγην s. ἐκπλήσσω.

ἐξέπλευσα s. ἐκπλέω.

ἐξέπνευσα s. ἐκπνέω.

ἐξέραμα, ατος, τό (ἔραμα Diosc., De Venen. 19) **what has been vomited,** ***vomit,*** of a dog (Philumen. p. 8, 30) **2 Pt 2:22.**—DELG s.v. ἐξεράω; Frisk s.v. ἀπεράω; cp. ἔρα 'earth'. M-M.

ἐξεραυνάω fut. ἐξερευνήσω LXX; 1 aor. ἐξηραύνησα, aor. pass. 3 sg. ἐξηρευνήθη LXX (H. Gk. substitute for ἐξερευνάω [var. edd.], which is found Soph. et al.. On the sound-change s. on ἐραυνάω. The compound form also in Polyb.; Plut.; Vett. Val. 267, 5; LXX; PsSol 17, 9; Philo, Plant. 141; Jos., Bell. 4, 654; Mel., P. 23, 160) **to make careful inquiry,** ***try to find out*** περί τινος *concerning someth.* **1 Pt 1:10.**—DELG s.v. ἐρέω. M-M. TW.

ἐξερευνάω s. ἐξεραυνάω.

ἐξερίζω 1 aor. ἐξήρισα (s. ἐρίζω, ἔρις; Plut., Pomp. 649 [56, 3]; Appian, Bell. Civ. 2, 151 §634) ***be factious, contentious*** ἐξήρισαν εἰς τοσοῦτο θυμοῦ *carried their factiousness to such a pitch of fury* 1 Cl 45:7.—DELG s.v. ἔρις.

ἐξέρχομαι fut. ἐξελεύσομαι (this fut. form M. Ant. 10, 36); 2 aor. ἐξῆλθον (but ἐξῆλθα [as e.g. 2Km 11:23] **J 21:3** D; **Ac 16:40; 2 Cor 6:17** [Is 52:11]; **1J 2:19; 3J 7 v.l.; Rv 18:4.**—For ἐξήλθοσαν s. Josh 8:19; 1 Ch 2, 53; Jdth 10:6; **Mk 8:11** D, cp. schol. on Lycophron vs. 252 ἤλθοσαν); pf. ἐξελήλυθα (s. ἔρχομαι; Hom. et al.; ins, pap, LXX; pseudepigr.; Jos., Bell. 2, 480; Just.; Ar. [JTS 25, 1924, 76 ln. 41]).

❶ **to move out of or away from an area—ⓐ** of animate entities ***go out, come out, go away, retire*—α.** of humans

א. freq. w. indication of the place from which, with or without mention of destination ἔκ τινος (Hdt. 8, 75, 1; 9, 12) ἐκ τ. μνημείων **Mt 8:28; 27:53.** ἐκ γῆς Χαλδαίων **Ac 7:4;** cp. **Mk 7:31; J 4:30** (ἐκ τ. πόλεως as X., Hell. 6, 5, 16); **Ac 22:18; Hb 3:16;** 1 Cl 10:2. ἐκ τοῦ πλοίου *get out* **Mk 5:2;** cp. **Rv 14:15, 17f.** ἐκ τοῦ σταδίου AcPl Ha 5, 14 (Just., A I, 45, 5 ἀπὸ Ἰ.).—ἀπό τινος (Ps.-Heraclitus, Ep. 5, 3 [=Malherbe p. 196]; Aesop, Fab. 141 P. [248b H.; 202 Ch.; 146a H-H.]; POxy 472, 1; 528, 7; LXX; JosAs 23:16 ἀπ' αὐτου; Jos., Ant. 12, 407 ἀ. τ. Ἱεροσ.; Just., A I, 60, 2 ἀπὸ Αἰγύπτου, D. 91, 3 al.) ἀπὸ Βηθανίας **Mk 11:12;** cp. **Lk 17:29; Phil 4:15.** ἀπὸ τ. πόλεως **Lk 9:5;** cp. **Mt 24:1; Ac 16:40.** ἀπ' ἐμοῦ *leave me* **Lk 5:8;** ἐξ. ἀπὸ τ. ἀνδρός *leave her husband* **Mk 10:12** D.—ἔξω τινός **Mt 10:14** (cp. Jdth 14:2); foll. by εἰς w. acc. of place **Mt 21:17; Mk 14:68;** foll. by παρά w. acc. of place **Ac 16:13;** foll. by πρός w. acc.

of pers. **Hb 13:13.**—W. εἰς alone ἐξελεύσονται εἰς τὸ σκότος *they will have to go out into the darkness* **Mt 8:12 v.l.**—W. gen. alone (Hom. et al.; Longus 4, 23, 2; POxy 942, 4) τ. οἰκίας **Mt 13:1** (vv.ll. ἐκ and ἀπό).—ἐκεῖθεν **15:21; Mk 6:1, 10; Lk 9:4; 11:53; J 4:43.** οὐ μὴ ἐξέλθῃς ἐκεῖθεν *you will never be released from there* **Mt 5:26; Lk 12:59;** D 1:5. ὅθεν ἐξῆλθον **Mt 12:44; Lk 11:24b.**—εἰσέρχεσθαι καὶ ἐ. **J 10:9; Ac 1:21.**—Cp. **Ac 15:24.**

ב. Somet. the place fr. which is not expressly named, but can be supplied fr. the context *go away* fr. region or house, *get out (of), disembark (fr.)* a ship, etc. **Mt 9:31f; 12:14; 14:14; 18:28; Mk 1:35, 45; Lk 4:42; 5:27; J 8:9; 11:31, 44; 13:30f; 18:1, 4; Ac 12:9f, 17; 16:3** *(go out);* **Hb 11:8;** D 11:6; AcPl Ha 3, 26; 7, 36; AcPl Ant 13, 2 (=Aa I 236, 6). ἐ. ἔξω (cp. Gen 39:12ff) **Mt 26:75; Lk 22:62; J 19:4f; Rv 3:12.** Sim. to leave a place and make an appearance at another: *appear* (Aristoph., Av. 512, Ach. 240) ἐξῆλθον οἱ Φ. *the Pharisees appeared* **Mk 8:11** (so LKoehler, TZ 3, '47, 471; also KSchmidt and ADebrunner, ibid. 471–73).

ג. indication of goal *(get up and) go out, get ready* of a servant, to fulfill a mission (Mitt-Wilck. II/2, 89, 36) οἱ ἄγγελοι **Mt 13:49.** Freq. w. εἴς τι (X., Hell. 7, 4, 24 al.) εἰς τὰς ὁδούς *into the streets* **Mt 22:10.** εἰς τὸν πυλῶνα **26:71;** cp. **Mk 14:68.** εἰς τὴν ἔρημον **Mt 11:7.** εἰς τὸ ὄρος τῶν ἐλαιῶν *to the Mount of Olives* **26:30; Mk 14:26.** εἰς τὴν Γαλιλαίαν **J 1:43.** εἰς Μακεδονίαν **Ac 16:10; 2 Cor 2:13.** εἰς τὸν λεγόμενον κρανίου τόπον **J 19:17.** εἰς τὸν κόσμον **1J 4:1; 2J 7** (Just., A I, 39, 3; cp. D. 53, 3 εἰς τὴν οἰκουμένην). εἰς ὑπάντησίν τινι *to meet someone* (Jdth 2:6 v.l. w. gen.; cp. ἐ. εἰς ἀπάντησίν τινι 1 Esdr 1:23; 1 Macc 12:41; TestJob 9:7; or εἰς συνάντησίν τινι Tob 11:16 BA; Jdth 2:6; 1 Macc 3:11, 16; 10:2, 86; JosAs 5:3 [cod. B]; 25:8) **Mt 8:34; J 12:13;** also εἰς ὑπάντησίν τινος (cp. εἰς ἀπάντησίν τινος 2 Ch 19:2; Tob 11:16 S; 1 Macc 12:41 v.l. [ed. WKappler '36]; εἰς συνάντησίν τινος 3:11 v.l. [ed. Kappler]) **Mt 25:1** (EPeterson, ZST 7, 1930, 682–702); also ἀπάντησιν αὐτου **25:6;** cp. **Ac 28:15 v.l.** πρός τινα (cp. 1 Macc 9:29; Tob 11:10 BA) *to someone* **J 18:29, 38; 2 Cor 8:17.** ἐπί τινα *go out against someone* (PTebt 283, 9 [I BC] ἐξελήλυθεν ἐπὶ τ. μητέρα μου; Jdth 2:7) **Mt 26:55; Mk 14:48.** ἐπὶ τ. γῆν *step out on the land* **Lk 8:27.**

ד. w. purpose expressed by the inf. **Mt 11:8; 20:1; Mk 3:21; 4:3; Lk 7:25f; 8:35; Ac 20:1; Rv 20:8;** GJs 11:1; 18:1; w. gen. of the inf. τοῦ σπείρειν *to sow* **Mt 13:3; Lk 8:5;** by the ptc. **Rv 6:2;** 1 Cl 42:3; w. ἵνα **Rv 6:2.**

β. of transcendent beings—**א.** in Johannine usage of Jesus, who comes forth from the Father: ἐκ τοῦ θεοῦ ἐξῆλθον **J 8:42.** ἀπὸ θεοῦ ἐξῆλθεν καὶ πρὸς τὸν θεὸν ὑπάγει **13:3.** παρὰ τοῦ θεοῦ ἐξῆλθον **16:27;** cp. **17:8** (for ἐξ. παρά τινος cp. Num 16:35). ἐξῆλθον παρὰ (v.l. ἐκ) τοῦ πατρός **16:28.** ἀπὸ θεοῦ ἐξῆλθες vs. **30.**

ב. of spirits that *come* or *go out* of persons (Damasc., Vi. Isid. 56 οὐκ ἐπείθετο τὸ δαιμόνιον τῆς γυναικὸς ἐξελθεῖν; PGM 4, 1243f ἔξελθε, δαῖμον, . . . καὶ ἀπόστηθι ἀπὸ τοῦ δεῖνα) ἔκ τινος **Mk 1:25f; 5:8; 7:29; 9:25; Lk 4:35** twice as v.l.; ἀπό τινος (cp. En 22:7 τὸ πνεῦμα . . . τὸ ἐξελθὸν ἀπὸ Ἄβελ) **Mt 12:43; 17:18; Lk 4:35 twice, 41; 8:29, 33, 35, 38; 11:24; Ac 16:18.** Abs. **Mk 5:13; 7:30; 9:26, 29; Lk 4:36; Ac 8:7** (text prob. damaged or perh. anacoluthon).

γ. an animal: a snake *come out* **Ac 28:3.**

ⓑ of inanimate entities ***go out.***—**α.** of liquid *come out, flow out* (Judg 15:19; ViIs 3 [p. 69, 7 Sch.]) **J 19:34; Rv 14:20;** AcPl Ha 11, 2 (s. γάλα a).

β. of noise, a message, etc.: a voice *rings out* **Rv 16:17; 19:5** (SyrBar 13:1). The sound of proclamation *goes out* (cp. Mi 4:2) **Ro 10:18** (Ps 18:5); also rumors and reports **Mt 9:26; Lk 4:14; 7:17; Mk 1:28; J 21:23;** ἡ πίστις τινός *the news of someone's faith* **1 Th 1:8;** cp. B 11:8; 19:4. A decree *goes out* (Da 2:13 Theod.) **Lk 2:1.** ἀφ' ὑμῶν ὁ λόγος τ. θεοῦ ἐξῆλθεν; *did the word of God* (Christian proclamation) *originate fr. you?* **1 Cor 14:36.**

γ. with the source or place of origin given, of lightning ἐ. ἀπὸ ἀνατολῶν *goes out fr. the east* **Mt 24:27.** Of words ἐκ τοῦ αὐτοῦ στόματος ἐ. εὐλογία καὶ κατάρα *fr. the same mouth come blessing and cursing* **Js 3:10.** ἐκ τῆς καρδίας ἐ. διαλογισμοὶ πονηροί *evil thoughts come* **Mt 15:19;** cp. vs. **18.** Of a sword ἐ. ἐκ τ. στόματος *came out of the mouth* **Rv 19:21.**

δ. of time or a condition *be gone, disappear* (Hippocr. of diseases; X., An. 7, 5, 4 of time; Gen 47:18) ἐξῆλθεν ἡ ἐλπὶς τ. ἐργασίας αὐτῶν *their hope of gain was gone* **Ac 16:19;** cp. **Mk 5:30.**

❷ **to depart in death, *die*** ἐ. ἐκ τοῦ κόσμου *leave the world* as a euphemism for *die* (so as a Jewish expr. אֲזַל מִן עָלְמָא Targ. Koh. 1:8; TestAbr A 1 p. 78, 8: Stone p. 4 [τὸν κόσμον B 4 p. 109, 6: Stone p. 66]; ParJer 4:10; s. Dalman, Worte 141. S. also HKoch, ZNW 21, 1922, 137f.—The Greeks say ἐξέρχ. τοῦ σώματος: Iambl., Myst. in Stob. 1, 49, 67 p. 457, 9; Sallust. 19, 2 p. 34, 20; also TestAbr B 7 p. 112, 7 [Stone p. 72] and ParJer 6:20 ἐκ τοῦ σώματος; or τοῦ βίου: Himerius, Or. [Ecl.] 2, 14; TestAbr B 1 p. 105, 4 [Stone p. 58]; abs. Ar. [Milne, 76, 41]) **1 Cor 5:10;** 2 Cl 5:1; 8:3; AcPl Ha 6, 32. Also ἀπὸ τ. κ. ApcPt 2:5.

❸ **to come fr. by way of ancestry, *go out, proceed*** ἐκ τῆς ὀσφύος τινός *fr. someone's loins = be descended fr. him* (Gen 35:11; 2 Ch 6:9) **Hb 7:5.** W. gen. of source **Mt 2:6** (Mi 5:1).

❹ **to discontinue an association, *depart*** ἐξέλθατε ἐκ μέσου αὐτῶν *come away from among them* **2 Cor 6:17** (Is 52:11). Leave a congregation **1J 2:19.**

❺ **to get away fr. or out of a difficult situation, *escape,*** ἐξῆλθεν ἐκ τ. χειρὸς αὐτῶν *he escaped fr. them* **J 10:39.**—M-M. EDNT. TW.

ἐξεστακέναι s. ἐξίστημι.

ἔξεστιν impers. verb, 3 sg. of the unused ἔξειμι; fut. ἐξέσται LXX (Eur., Hdt. et al.; LXX; ParJer 5:20; Just., A I, 66, 1; Ath.)

❶ **to be authorized for the doing of someth., *it is right, is authorized, is permitted, is proper.***—ⓐ w. pres. inf. foll. (Lucian, Jud. 3; Esth 8:12g; 4 Macc 1:12; Ath. 32, 2 al.). **Mt 12:2, 12; 14:4.** W. aor. inf. foll. (X., An. 4, 3, 10; Ath. 6:3 al.) **Mt 12:10; 15:26 D; 19:3; 22:17; 27:6; Mk 3:4** (ἔξεστιν . . . ἤ); **12:14; Lk 6:9; 14:3.** Without inf., which is easily supplied fr. the context (cp. PRyl 77, 43 τοῦτο δὲ οὐκ ἐξῆν; Ath. 16, 3) **Mk 2:24; Lk 6:2; Ac 8:36 [37] v.l.; 1 Cor 10:23.**

ⓑ foll. by dat. of pers. and pres. inf. (X., Hiero 1, 26; BGU 1127, 20 [18 BC]; PSI 203, 7; Jos., Ant. 13, 252) **Mk 6:18; Ac 16:21; 22:25;** GJs 2:2. Foll. by dat. of pers. and aor. inf. (2 Esdr 4:14; 1 Macc 14:44) **Mt 20:15; Mk 10:2; J 5:10; 18:31** (JAllen, Why Pilate?: CMoule Festschr., '70, 78–83; on the legal issues s. also SSafrai, CRINT I/1, 397–400); **Ac 21:37;** GJs 1:2; 2:2.—Foll. by dat. of pers. without the necessity of supplying an inf. (PRyl 62, 16 πάντα τὰ ἄλλα ἔξεστί μοι) **1 Cor 6:12.**

ⓒ foll. by acc. w. inf. (Pla., Pol., 290d al.) **Mk 2:26; Lk 6:4** (s. B-D-F §409, 3; Rob. 1084f); **20:22.**

ⓓ the ptc. of ἐ. is ἐξόν; by the addition of the copula, which must oft. be understood (as Isaeus 6, 50; Jos., Ant. 8, 404), it comes to mean the same as ἔξεστιν: w. pres. inf. foll. ISm 8:2; foll. by dat. of pers. and aor. inf. **2 Cor 12:4;** PEg[2] 48 (cp. Just.,

A I, 66, 1). ἐ. ἦν w. dat., and aor. inf. (Esth 4:2; Jos., Ant. 20, 202) **Mt 12:4.** W. dat., and inf. to be supplied μὴ εἶναι ἐ. αὐτῷ *he had no authority* MPol 12:2.

❷ **to be within the range of possibility, *it is possible*** the ptc. of ἐ. (s. above) w. aor. inf. foll. **Ac 2:29**—B. 647. M-M. TW.

ἐξετάζω fut. ἐξετάσω LXX; 1 aor. ἐξήτασα; pf. 1 pl. ἐξητάκαμεν (Ath. 23, 1). Pass.: aor. 3 sg. ἐξητάσθη (Just., A II, 2, 12); pf. ptc. ἐξητασμένος (Ath., R. 64, 6 al.) (ἐτάζω 'examine, test'; s. also next entry; since Theognis 1, 1016; Soph., Thu. et al., also ins, pap, LXX; pseudepigr., Philo, Joseph., Just., Tat., Ath.).

❶ **try to find out by use of careful methods, which may include pers. inquiry, *scrutinize, examine, inquire*** (Thu. et al.; Wsd 6:3; Sir 3:21; Just. A I, 7, 2 al.; Tat. 30, 2; Ath. 24, 1 al.) ἀκριβῶς ἐ. (Lucian, Dial. Mort. 30, 3; POxy 237 VI, 31 τὸ πρᾶγμα ἀκρειβῶς ἐξητασμένον; Dt 19:18; TestJob; Philo, Somn. 1, 228; Jos., Ant. 3, 70; Just. A I, 32, 2) τὶ *someth.* (Dionys. Hal., Ep. ad Pomp. 1, 16 τὴν ἀλήθειαν; Dio Chrys. 17 [34], 26; Philo, Migr. Abr. 185; Just., D. 112, 1 τὴν δύναμιν … τῶν εἰρημένων) Hs 9, 13, 6; περί τινος *make a careful search for someone* **Mt 2:8** (on ἐ. περί τινος cp. Pla., Leg. 3, 685a; PGen 54, 30; BGU 380, 5; Jos., C. Ap. 2, 237; Just., D. 1, 3 περὶ τοῦ θείου). W. indir. quest. foll. (cp. Thu. 7, 33, 6; Epicrates Com. [IV BC] 11, 17 vol. II p. 287 Kock; Aelian, VH 1, 28; Just., A I, 14, 4 al.) **Mt 10:11.**

❷ **to inquire intensively, *question, examine,*** τινά *someone* (Soph., Oed. Col. 211; X., Mem. 1, 2, 36; BGU 372 II 13; PGrenf I 53, 22; Just., D. 92, 2 al.)

ⓐ gener. **J 21:12;** Ox 654, 32 [ἐξ]ετάζουσιν=ASyn. 60, 7 (w. dir. quest. foll.; otherw. ἐρωτάω and ἐπερωτάω; s. M-EBoismard, RB 54, '47, 491). περὶ τοιούτων πραγμάτων ἐξεταζόμενος ὁ σωτήρ *when the Savior was questioned about such matters* GMary 463, 12.

ⓑ As legal t.t. *question* judicially, esp. in connection w. torture (Polyb. 15, 27, 7; Herodian 4, 5, 3; 4; SIG 780, 11 [6 BC]; Dt 19:18; Esth 1:1o; Sir 23:10; Jos., Ant. 18, 183; Just., A I, 39, 3) pass. Hs 9, 28, 4; w. relative clause foll. περὶ ὧν ἔπραξε D 1:5 (cp. PGM 7, 331 περὶ ὧν σε ἐξετάζω).—DELG s.v. ἐτάζω. M-M.

ἐξετασμός, οῦ, ὁ (s. prec. entry; Demosth. 18, 16; Diod. S. 11, 3, 7; 9; Plut., Mor. 1068b; IG II^2, 500, 12; LXX) **a systematic investigation of facts, *examination, inquiry*** of God's judgment (Wsd 4:6) ἐ. ἀσεβεῖς ὀλεῖ *a searching inquiry shall destroy the godless* 1 Cl 57:7 (Pr 1:32).

ἐξεταστικῶς adv. (s. ἐξετάζω; Demosth. 17, 13) ***with probing inquiry*** PEg^2 43–44 (as restored by the ed. ἐξ[ετασ]τικῶς).

ἐξέφνης s. ἐξαίφνης.

ἐξεχύθην s. ἐκχέω.

ἐξέχω (s. ἔχω; Aristoph. et al.; SIG 827 III, 11 [116/17 AD]; LXX; ViDa 1 [p. 76, 13 Sch.]; cp. 2 Esdr 13:25, 27 ὁ πύργος ὁ ἐξέχων ἐκ τοῦ οἴκου τ. βασιλέως; Just., D. 91, 2) **to be readily noticeable, *stand out, be prominent,*** of raised places as places of honor οἱ ἐξέχοντες τόποι **Mt 20:28 v.l.**=ASyn. 216, 38 [Agr 22].

ἐξηγέομαι (s. next entry) mid. dep. fut. 3 pl. ἐξηγήσονται; Job 12:8; 1 aor. ἐξηγησάμην. Pass.: aor. 3 sg. ἐξηγήθη (Just., D. 68, 6); inf. ἐξηγηθῆναι (Just., D. 55, 3); pf. ptc. ἐξηγημένα (Just., D. 79, 1; 126, 5) (Hom. et al.) prim. mng. 'lead' (s. ἡγέομαι 1), but never so in our lit.

❶ **to relate in detail, *tell, report, describe,*** chiefly narrative (so Hdt.; ins, pap, LXX, EpArist; Philo, Leg. All. 3, 21; Berosus: 680 fgm. 8a 140 Jac. [in Jos., C. Ap. 1, 140]; Just., D. 58, 4; but 112, 1 'interpret', 68, 7 'translate') τὶ *someth.* τὰ ἐν τῇ ὁδῷ *their experiences on the way* **Lk 24:35.** πάντα GPt 11:45. τ. δεσμὸν τ. ἀγάπης τ. θεοῦ *describe the bond of the love of God* 1 Cl 49:2. τί τινι *relate someth. to someone* (Judg 7:13) **Ac 10:8;** Hv 4, 2, 5; GJs 19:3. καθ' ἓν ἕκαστον *one by one* **Ac 21:19.** ἐ. καθὼς ὁ θεὸς ἐπεσκέψατο **15:14.** ὅσα ἐποίησεν ὁ θεός vs. **12.** ἐξηγουμένου Παύλου ἃ πέπονθεν ἐν Φιλίπποις AcPl Ha 6, 4.

❷ **to set forth in great detail, *expound.*** Oft. as t.t. for the activity of priests and soothsayers who impart information or reveal divine secrets; also used w. ref. to divine beings themselves (Pla., trag., Thu., X.; Wetstein on **J 1:18.**—Arrian, Anab. 2, 3, 3 of soothsayers: τὰ θεῖα ἐξηγεῖσθαι; 6, 2, 3; Ael. Aristid. 13 p. 219 D.: τὰ μέλλοντα ὥσπερ μάντις ἐξηγεῖτο, 45, 30 K. of the proclamation of the Sarapis-miracles; Pollux 8, 124 ἐξηγηταὶ δ' ἐκαλοῦντο οἱ τὰ περὶ τῶν διοσημιῶν καὶ τὰ τῶν ἄλλων ἱερῶν διδάσκοντες=they are termed interpreters/expounders who teach things about portents and other sacred matters; Jos. of the interpr. of the law: Bell. 1, 649; 2, 162, Ant. 18, 81; Lucian, Peregr. 11 τῶν βίβλων τὰς μὲν ἐξηγεῖτο καὶ διεσάφει). ἐκεῖνος ἐξηγήσατο *he has made known* or *brought news of* (the invisible God) **J 1:18** (so also JMichael, JTS 22, 1921, 14–16 against RHarris, The Origin of the Prologue 1917, 35; s. Hdb.^{3} ad loc.; APersson, D. Exegeten u. Delphi 1918).—B. 1238. M-M. TW. Spicq.

ἐξήγησις, εως, ἡ—❶ **narration that provides a detailed description, *narrative, description*** (s. prec. entry; Thu. et al.; Pla., Leg. 1, 631a; Polyb. 6, 3, 1; Judg 7:15 B; Sir 21:16; Just., A I, 68, 3 al.; Tat. 35, 2) τῆς τελειότητος αὐτῆς οὐκ ἔστιν ἐ. *its perfection cannot be fully described* 1 Cl 50:1. κατὰ πᾶσαν ἐ. *in every report* AcPl Ha 6, 13.

❷ **setting forth someth. in great detail, *explanation, interpretation*** (Pla. et al.; Diod. S. 2, 29, 3; Dionys. Hal., De Thu. Jud. 54, 3; Philo, Vi. Cont. 78; Jos., Ant. 11, 192; Just., D. 79, 2; 115, 2 al. 'exposition'; 124, 3 al. 'translation') τοῦ πύργου Hv 3, 7, 4. According to Eusebius, the work of Papias was titled λογίων κυριακῶν ἐξήγησις Papias (2:1) or, according to Apollinarius, ἐ. τῶν κυριακῶν λόγων (3:1); s. also (3:8, 9). S. κυριακός.—TW. Sv.

ἐξῄειν, ἐξῄεσαν impf. of ἔξειμι.

ἑξήκοντα indecl. (Hom. et al.; pap, LXX, pseudepigr., Philo; Jos., Ant. 11, 18) ***sixty*** **Mt 13:8, 23; Mk 4:8, 20; Lk 24:13** (Strabo 16, 2, 36: 60 stades fr. Jerus.; Jos., Vi. 115 ἀπέχειν ἑ. σταδίους); **1 Ti 5:9; Rv 11:3; 12:6; 13:18.**—DELG s.v. ἕξ. M-M.

ἑξῆς adv. (Hom.+) **next in a series, *in the next place*** (Dionys. Hal. 1, 71, 2; Philo, Op. M. 131 al.; Just., D. 42, 2 al. in quot. and certain lines of argument) Dg 3:1. Of time, so always in NT—τῇ ἑ. ἡμέρᾳ (SIG 1170, 24; SIG^2 680, 4; Jos., Ant. 4, 302) *on the next day* **Lk 9:37.** Freq. the noun must be supplied τῇ ἑξῆς (EpArist 262; Jos., Bell. 2, 430; POxy 1063, 6) **Ac 21:1; 25:17; 27:18.** W. ἐν τῷ ἑξῆς **Lk 7:11** χρόνῳ is to be supplied *(soon) afterward.*—DELG. M-M.

ἐξηχέω (s. ἠχέω) fut. 3 sg. ἐξηχήσει Sir 40:13; aor. 3 pl. ἐξήχησαν Jer 3:14; pf. pass. ἐξήχημαι (mostly act. intr. 'sound forth': Jo 3:14; Sir 40:13; Philo, In Flacc. 39, Rer. Div. Her. 15, Dec. 46) trans., 'cause to resound or be heard' (Polyb. 30, 4, 7; Philo, Abr. 180) pass. **be caused to sound forth,** ***ring out*** (3 Macc 3:2) ἀφ' ὑμῶν ἐξήχηται ὁ λόγος τοῦ κυρίου *the word of the Lord has sounded forth fr. you* **1 Th 1:8.**—DELG s.v. ἠχή.

ἔξιημι (s. ἵημι) aor. inf. ἐξεῖναι **to clear the way for someone to go to a destination,** ***let (one) go out, send out*** ἐξεῖναι Παῦλον εἰς τὴν Ῥώμην *send Paul to Rome* AcPl Ha 6, 15f.

ἐξιλάσκομαι (s. ἱλάσκομαι) fut. ἐξιλάσομαι; 1 aor. ἐξιλασάμην; fut. pass. 3 sg. ἐξιλασθήσεται LXX. When one endeavors to attain the goodwill of another, the word can be rendered ***appease*** (a pers. PTebt 750, 16 [II BC]); in this sense ἐ. is akin to θεραπεύειν as in Thu 1, 137, 3 τινὰ χρημάτων δόσει. Throughout Greek lit., deity is the most freq. obj. (as early as the oracle in Hdt. 7, 141 Δία; X., Cyr. 7, 2, 19 Ἀπόλλωνα; Menand., fgm.754, 6 Kö. [=544, 6 p. 164 Kock] τὸν θεόν; Polyb. 3, 112, 19; Diod. S. 1, 59, 2 θυσίαις τὸ θεῖον; 14, 77, 4 τ. θεούς; 20, 14, 3; Strabo 4, 1, 13; Dio Chrys. 15 [32], 77; Ael. Aristid. 46, 3 K.=3 p. 30 D.; Zech 7:2; 8:22; Ezk 16:63; PsSol 3:8; TestLevi 3:5 πρὸς κύριον; JosAs 28:5; EpArist 316; Philo, Poster. Cai. 72 [after Lev 16:10]; Jos., Bell. 5, 19; SibOr 7, 30.—S. ἱλάσκομαι and ἵλεως). In 1 Cl 7:7; Hv 1, 2, 1 sin necessitates appeasement of God (cp. IG II^2, 1366, 15f=SIG 1042 [II/III AD] ἁμαρτίαν ὀφειλέτω Μηνὶ Τυράννῳ, ἣν οὐ μὴ δύνηται ἐξειλάσασθαι [= let such a one be liable to Sovereign Men for an offense for which there is no expiation]; s. also Just., A I, 50, 2 τοῖς ἀνόμοις ἐξιλάσεται [for Is 53:12]).—TW.

ἕξις, εως, ἡ (Pre-Socr. et al., Iasos 98, 16 [I BC]; POxy 2190, 16 [I AD]; LXX; in var. mngs. 'physical/mental state, proficiency, skill') in the only place in which it is used in our lit. it refers to **a state of maturity,** ***maturity*** (cp. 'characteristic' Philo, Leg. All. 1, 10, 3; 'skill, proficiency': Polyb. 10, 47, 7; 21, 9, 1; Diod. S. 2, 29, 4; Sir prol 1:11; Iasos s. above; EpArist 121) αἰσθητήρια διὰ τὴν ἕ. γεγυμνασμένα (solid food is for adults who) *because of their mature state* (have) *their senses trained* (to distinguish between good and evil) **Hb 5:14** (so JLee, NovT 39, '97, 151–76, esp. p. 166; MKiley, CBQ 42, '80, 501–3: 'characteristic state [as adults]'). With the exception of ASouter, A Pocket Lexicon to the Gk. NT 1916 (s. s.v. 'condition, state'), lexicons of NT Gk., as well as versions and translations of the NT, gener. render ἕξ. in our pass. w. 'exercise, practice'.—DELG s.v. 1 ἔχω. TW. Sv.

ἐξίστημι w. the Koine by-form **ἐξιστάνω** (B-D-F §93; Mlt-H. 241) **Ac 8:9** (v.l. ἐξιστῶν fr. ἐξιστάω) fut. ἐκστησῶ LXX; 1 aor. ἐξέστησα; 2 aor. ἐξέστην; pf. ἐξέστακα, ptc. [intr.] ἐξεστώς (Judg 4:21 B) and ἐξεστηκυῖα 1 Km 4:13; plpf. 2 sg. ἐξεστηκεῖς (TestJob 39:13). Mid.: impf. ἐξιστάμην; pf. ἐξίσταμαι. Pass.: aor. 3 sg. ἐξεστάθη (Judg 5:4 A). In both trans. and intr. usage the main idea is involvement in a state or condition of consternation.

❶ trans.: primary sense 'change, displace' (Aristot. et al.; Just., D. 67, 3 οὐκ ἐκστήσετε με τῶν προκειμένων 'you won't budge me from my position on these matters') then **to cause to be in a state in which things seem to make little or no sense,** ***confuse, amaze, astound*** (so oft. w. added words τινὰ φρενῶν Eur., Bacch. 850; τινὰ τοῦ φρονεῖν X., Mem. 1, 3, 12; τινὰ ταῖς διανοίαις Polyb. 11, 27, 7, but also w. simple acc., as in the foll.) τινά *someone* (Musonius p. 35, 12 τὰ ἐξιστάντα τοὺς ἀνθρώπους; Lucian, Dom. 19; Stob., Ecl. III 517, 15 οἶνος ἐξέστησέ με; Josh 10:10; Judg 4:15; 2 Km 22:15 al.; Jos., Bell. 3, 74; TestBenj 3:3 v.l.; Hippol., Ref. 6, 40, 2; 9, 11, 1) **Lk 24:22.** Of a sorcerer τὸ ἔθνος τῆς Σαμαρείας **Ac 8:9, 11.**

❷ intr. (2 aor. and pf. act.; all of the mid.). Out of the sense 'to become separated from someth. or lose someth.' (Empedocles et al.) emerges the psychological sense (the only sense of the intr. in our lit.; for physical disturbance s. TestZeb 2:5; cp. Orig., C. Cels. 3, 70, 20) **be out of one's normal state of mind.**

ⓐ of inability to reason normally ***lose one's mind, be out of one's senses*** (so Eur. [e.g. Bacch. 359 al. in the sense 'step out of one's mind' VLeinieks, The City of Dionysos '96, 111], Isocr. et al., mostly [as Jos., Ant. 10, 114] w. τῶν φρενῶν, τοῦ φρονεῖν, or sim. addition. Without such addition e.g. Aristot., HA 6, 22 p. 577a, 12 ἐξίσταται καὶ μαίνεται; Menand., Sam. 279 S. [64 Kö.] ἐξέστηχ' ὅλως; Dio Chrys. 80 [30], 6; Is 28:7; TestJob 35f and 39; Philo, Ebr. 146; Orig., C. Cels. 7, 4, 14 [of the Pythia]; Did., Gen. 230, 14) ἔλεγον ὅτι ἐξέστη *they said, 'He has lost his senses'* **Mk 3:21** (cp. Irish Eccl. Record 64, '44, 289–312; 65, '45, 1–5; 6–15; JSteinmueller, CBQ 4, '42, 355–59; HWansbrough, NTS 18, '71/72, 233–35; lit. also on παρά A 3b end). Prob. ironical εἴτε ἐξέστημεν… εἴτε σωφρονοῦμεν *if we were out of our senses …; if we are in our right mind* **2 Cor 5:13** (CBruston, RTQR 18, 1908, 344ff). But more freq. in our lit. is the weakened sense

ⓑ ***be amazed, be astonished,*** of the feeling of astonishment mingled w. fear, caused by events which are miraculous, extraordinary, or difficult to understand (Philippides Com. [IV/III BC] fgm. 27 K. ἐγὼ ἐξέστην ἰδών=I was astounded when I saw [the costly vessels]; Gen 43:33; Ruth 3:8; 1 Km 14:15 al.; ApcSed 10:6; cp. Iren. 1, 2, 3 [Harv. I 17, 11]) MPol 12:1. ἐξίσταντο πάντες οἱ ὄχλοι (cp. Ex 19:18; Lev 9:24) **Mt 12:23;** cp. **Mk 2:12.** ἐξέστησαν ἐκστάσει μεγάλῃ (cp. Gen 27:33) *they were utterly astonished* **5:42.** λίαν ἐν ἑαυτοῖς ἐξίσταντο *they were utterly astounded within them* **6:51.—Lk 8:56; Ac 2:7** (w. θαυμάζω), **12** (w. διαποροῦμαι); **8:13; 9:21; 10:45** (w. ὅτι foll.); **12:16.** ἐξίσταντο ἐπὶ τῇ συνέσει αὐτοῦ *they were amazed at his intelligence* **Lk 2:47** (ἐπί τινι as Wsd 5:2; Hos 3:5). Of heaven B 11:2 (Jer 2:12). (S. ἵστημι).—M-M. EDNT. TW. Spicq.

ἐξισχύω (s. ἰσχύω) fut. 2 sg. ἐξισχύσεις Sir 7:6 cod. B; 1 aor. ἐξίσχυσα (Strabo 17, 1, 3; Vett. Val. 288, 12) **to be fully capable of doing or experiencing someth.,** ***be able, be strong enough, be in a position*** w. inf. foll. (Proclus on Pla., Cratyl. p. 65, 19 Pasqu.; POxy 1120, 7; BGU 275, 11; PAnt 35 II, 13; Sir 7:6 v.l.; Jos., Bell. 1, 451) **Eph 3:18.**—DELG s.v. ἰσχύς. M-M.

ἔξοδος, ου, ἡ (s. ὁδός; 'going out, going away' trag. et al.; ins, pap, LXX; PsSol 4:14; TestSol 25:5; Philo, Joseph., Test-12Patr; Just.; Mel., P. 1, 3).

❶ **movement from one geographical area to another,** ***departure, path, course***—ⓐ of the mass departure or exodus fr. Egypt (Ps 104:38; 113:1; Philo, Mos. 2, 248; Jos., Ant. 5, 72, C. Ap. 223; TestSim 9; Mel., P. 1:3) *the (well-known) departure/exodus* **Hb 11:22.**

ⓑ of stones and their fortunes in the course of movement fr. one place to another *course, fate, destination,* in apocalyptic imagery Hv 3, 4, 3 (the Shepherd's question: Where are the stones headed?).

❷ **departure from among the living,** euphemism (the one who dies has the illusion of a choice, and the mourner finds consolation in the theme) for ***death*** (Soph., Oed. Rex 959, 1372, Tr. 4; Wsd 3:2; 7:6; Philo, Virt. 77; Jos., Ant. 4, 189 ἐ. τοῦ ζῆν; TestNapht 1:1. Cp. Epict. 4, 4, 38; Just., D. 105, 3; 5) μετὰ τὴν ἐμὴν ἔ. *after my death* **2 Pt 1:15** (cp. the last will and test. of Abraham, bishop of Hermonthis, PLond I, 77, 57 p. 234 κελεύω μετὰ τ. ἐμὴν ἔξοδον τ. βίου). τὴν ἔ., ἣν ἤμελλεν πληροῦν *his departure, which he was to carry out* **Lk 9:31.**—M-M. TW.

ἐξοιδέω 1 aor. inf. ἐξοιδῆσαι (οἰδέω 'swell'; Eur., Polyb., et al.) ***swell, be swollen up*** τὰ βλέφαρα τῶν ὀφθαλμῶν αὐτου φασί τοσοῦτον ἐξοιδῆσαι, ὡς . . . *it was said that his eyelids became so swollen, that* Papias (3:2).—DELG s.v. οἰδέω.

ἐξοίσουσι s. ἐκφέρω.

ἐξολεθρεύω fut. ἐξολεθρεύσω LXX; 1 aor. ἐξωλέθρευσα. Pass.: 1 fut. ἐξολεθρευθήσομαι; aor. ἐξωλεθρεύθην LXX (Crito [early II AD]: 200 fgm. 2 Jac.; TestSol 6:2 D ἐξολόθρευσον; JosAs ch. 11 cod. A [p. 53, 19 Bat.] ἐξολοθρευθῆναι; SibOr 5, 454; 12, 102; 14, 107; Just., D. 131, 5 ἐξολοθρευθήσεσθαι τὰ δαιμόνια; Test12Patr; Pel.-Leg. p. 23, 15; 24, 18; PCairMasp 2 III, 28 [VI AD].—As v.l. in Plut., Dio 965 [18, 9] Ziegler, Jos., Ant. 8, 270 N., and SibOr 3, 309 G. On the spelling of the word [ἐξολο-] s. B-D-F §32, 1; Thackeray p. 87f; Mlt-H. 71) **to eliminate by destruction, *destroy utterly, root out*** τινά 1 Cl 53:3 (Dt 9:14). τὶ: πάντα τὰ χείλη τὰ δόλια *all lying lips* 15:5 (Ps 11:4). τὶ ἔκ τινος *someth. fr. someth.* 22:6 (Ps 33:17). Pass. B 7:3 (Lev 23:29). ἐκ τοῦ λαοῦ **Ac 3:23** (Lev 23:29). ἀπό τινος 1 Cl 14:4 (Ps 36:38, but without ἀπό τ. For the combination ἐ. ἀπὸ τ. γῆς cp. 1 Macc 2:40; Jdth 6:2). ἐκ γῆς **1 Pt 3:12 v.l.** (Ps 33:17).—DELG s.v. ὄλλυμι. M-M. TW.

ἐξομοιόω aor. ptc. ἐξομοιωθέντες (Just., D. 44, 2; 45, 4) 'to make just like or similar' (Hdt. et al.; Sextus 381). Pass. in act. sense ***become just like/similar, resemble fully*** (trag. et al.; 2 Macc 4:16; Philo, Aet. M. 44; Just.); τινί *someone* (Epict. 1, 2, 18; 2, 14, 12; Socrat., Ep. 6, 4; Just., D. s. above, also 122, 2) τέλεον αὐτοῖς ἐξομοιοῦσθε *finally you become quite like them* Dg 2:5.—DELG s.v. ὁμός.

ἐξομολογέω (s. next entry and ὁμολογέω) 1 aor. ἐξωμολόγησα; fut. mid. ἐξομολογήσομαι; aor. mid. ἐξωμολογησάμην LXX (quotable since III BC—Mitt-Wilck. II/2, 20, 18; 37, 17—PHib 30, 18 [300–271 BC]; also LXX, pseudepigr., Philo, Joseph.).

❶ **to indicate acceptance of an offer or proposal, *promise, consent,*** act., abs. **Lk 22:6** (the act. is found as rarely [perh. Alex. Aphr., An. Mant. II 1 p. 168, 15] as the pass. [perh. SIG 685, 95]).

❷ **to make an admission of wrong-doing/sin, *confess, admit,*** mid. (Plut., Eum. 594 [17, 7], Anton. 943 [59, 3] τ. ἀλήθειαν, Stoic. Repugn. 17 p. 1042a; Sus 14; Jos., Bell. 1, 625, Ant. 8, 256) τὶ *someth.* (POslo 17, 14 [136 AD] τὸ ἀληθές; Cyranides p. 100, 18 πάντα ὅσα ἔπραξεν; Orig., C. Cels. 2, 11, 30 τὸ ἡμαρτημένον) τὰς ἁμαρτίας (Jos., Ant. 8, 129; s. the ins in Steinleitner, nos. 13, 5; 23, 2; 24, 11; 25, 10) **Mt 3:6; Mk 1:5** (cp. 1QS 1:24–26); **Js 5:16** (s. PAlthaus, Zahn Festgabe 1928, 1ff); Hv 1, 1, 3; s 9, 23, 4. τὰς ἁ. τῷ κυρίῳ *confess sins to the Lord* Hv 3, 1, 5, cp. 6. τὰ παραπτώματα ἐν ἐκκλησίᾳ *confess transgressions in the congregation* D 4:14. περὶ τῶν παραπτωμάτων *make a confession of transgressions* 1 Cl 51:3. ἐπὶ τ. ἁμαρτίαις *for sins* B 19:12. Abs. *make a confession of sins* **Ac 19:18;** 2 Cl 8:3. W. dat. of the one to whom sins are confessed 1 Cl 52:1, 2 (w. similarity in form to Ps 7:18; 117:19 and sim. Ps passages, but not=*praise* because of 1 Cl 51:3 [s. 4 below]).—JSchnitzer, D. Beichte im Lichte d. Religionsgesch.: Ztschr. f. Völkerpsychol. 6, 1930, 94–105; RPettazzoni, La confessione dei Peccati II '35.

❸ **to declare openly in acknowledgment, *profess, acknowledge,*** mid. (PHib 30, s. above; POxy 1473, 9; Lucian, Herm. 75) w. ὅτι foll. **Phil 2:11** (Is 45:23; s. 4 below).—Nägeli 67.

❹ fr. the mngs. 'confess' and 'profess' there arose, as Rtzst., Erlösungsmyst. 252 shows, the more general sense ***to praise,*** in acknowledgment of divine beneficence and majesty (so mostly LXX; TestJob 40:2 πρὸς τὸν πατέρα) w. dat. of the one praised (oft. LXX; TestSol 1:5; Philo, Leg. All. 1, 80) σοί (2 Km 22:50; 1 Ch 29:13; Ps 85:12; 117:28 al.; Did., Gen. 60, 20) **Mt 11:25=Lk 10:21** (s. Norden, Agn. Th. 277–308; JWeiss, GHeinrici Festschr. 1914, 120ff; TArvedson, D. Mysterium Chr. [Mt 11:25–30] '37; NWilliams, ET 51, '40, 182–86; 215–20; AHunter, NTS 8, '62, 241–49); **Ro 15:9** (Ps 17:50); 1 Cl 26:2; 61:3; B 6:16 (cp. Ps 34:18). τῷ θεῷ (Tob 14:7; Philo, Leg. All. 2, 95) **Ro 14:11** (Is 45:23); τῷ κυρίῳ (fr. Gen 29:35 on, oft. in LXX) 1 Cl 48:2 (Ps 117:19); Hm 10, 3, 2.—DELG s.v. ὁμός. M-M. EDNT. TW. Sv.

ἐξομολόγησις, εως, ἡ (Dionys. Hal., Plut., JosAs; Philo, Leg. All. 1, 82; Jos., Bell. 5, 435; Theoph. Ant. 2, 29 [p. 170, 17; w. μετάνοια]) s. preceding entry 4, ***praise*** of God (so LXX; 'acknowledgment, profession' PsSol; JosAs title and 15:2): by rich men λίαν μικρὰν ἔχει τὴν ἐ. Hs 2:5; because of the nearness of ἔντευξις='intercessory prayer' perh. ἐ. here acquires the more specialized sense 'prayer of thanksgiving' (s. MDibelius, Hdb. on Hs 2:5 [cp. m 10, 3, 2 ἐξομολογούμενος]).—TW.

ἐξόν s. ἔξεστιν 4.

ἐξορίζω 1 aor. ἐζώρισα; pass. 1 pl. ἐζωρίσθημεν 1 Macc 1:11 v.l. (Eur., Pla.; ICypr 135, 11; PRyl 75, 33 and 37; also 2 Km 8:4 Aq; TestGad 6:3; GrBar 4:10; ApcSed 5:3; 6:7; Philo, Det. Pot. 142; Joseph.; Tat. 20, 1) ***exclude, ban*** ἐ. με ἐκ ναοῦ *me from the temple* GJs 3:1.

ἐξορκίζω fut. ἐξορκιῶ and ἐξορκίσω Gen 24:3; 1 aor. 2 sg. ἐξώρκισας Judg. 17:2 A (s. ὁρκίζω; Demosth. et al.; ins, pap; TestSol; PFouad 203, 16; Jos., Ant. 2, 200; 11, 145, mostly= ἐξορκόω 'cause someone to swear')

❶ **to compel someone to do someth. by invoking a transcendent power, *solemnly command*** (so POslo 148, 10 [II/I BC] ἐξορκίζω; IDefixWünsch 4, 1ff [III AD]; PGM 3, 10; 119; 4, 1239 ἐξορκίζω σε δαῖμον κατὰ τούτου τ. θεοῦ; 12, 137; amulet in BGU 956, 1 [III AD] ἐ. ὑμᾶς κατὰ τ. ἁγίου ὀνόματος; cp. 3 Km 22:16; Just., D. 85, 3 κατὰ παντὸς ὀνόματος . . . κατὰ τοῦ θεοῦ Ἀβραάμ al.) of expulsion of an evil spirit *exorcise* an evil spirit **Ac 19:13 v.l., 14 v.l.**

❷ **to put someone under oath to warrant the truth of what is said, *put under oath, adjure*** τινά *someone* ἐ. σε κατὰ τοῦ θεοῦ (w. κατά as above) *I adjure you by God* **Mt 26:63** (w. ἵνα foll. as Cyranides p. 120, 3; on adjuration in Jewish tradition s. Mishna: Shebuoth).—DELG s.v. ὅρκος. M-M. TW.

ἐξορκιστής, οῦ, ὁ one who drives out evil spirits by invocation of transcendent entities, *exorcist* (so an epigr. of Lucian in Anth. Pal. 11, 427; Ptolem., Apotelesm. 4, 4, 10 Boll-B.) of wandering Judean exorcists **Ac 19:13.** For the idea cp. Jos., Ant. 8, 42ff, esp. 45: Solomon as the author of τρόποι ἐξορκώσεων, which drive out evil spirits.—WHeitmüller, 'Im Namen Jesu' 1903 index III.—DELG s.v. ὅρκος. TW.

ἐξορύσσω 1 aor. ἐξώρυξα (s. ὀρύσσω; Hdt. et al.; PHal 1, 100 and 109 [III BC]; LXX, Philo, Joseph.) **to extract someth. out of an area by force—ⓐ** of eyes ***tear out*** (so Hdt. 8, 116; Plut., Artox. 1018 [14, 10]; Lucian, D. Deor. 1, 1; Jos., Ant. 6, 71; 1 Km 11:2; Judg 16:21 A) **Gal 4:15** (the eye as a precious member: Aeschyl., Sept. 530; Moschus 4, 9; Callim., H. 3, 211; Artem. 1, 25; Heliod. 2, 16, 4 the beloved is ὀφθαλμὸς κ. ψυχὴ κ. πάντα ἐμαυτῆς; Eustath. Macremb. 6, 10 Ζεῦ Πάτερ, μή μου τοὺς ὀφθαλμοὺς ἐκκόψῃς. On the theme of sacrifice of eyes for others s. Lucian, Tox.; Betz, Hermeneia Gal. ad loc.).—JBligh, TU 102, '68, 382f.

ⓑ of a roof ***dig through*** **Mk 2:4,** prob. in ref. to making an opening by digging through the clay of which the roof was made (ABertholet, Kulturgesch. Israels 1920, 122; CMcCown, JBL 58, '39, 213–16; BHHW I 311), and putting the debris to one side (ἐ. of debris that has been dug out Hdt. 2, 150; 7, 23), so that it does not fall on the heads of those in the house.—S. στέγη.—M-M.

ἐξουδενέω/ἐξουδενόω fut. ἐξουδενήσω, -ώσω LXX; 1 aor. ἐξουδένησα, ἐξουδένωσα; pf. ἐξουδένηκα, -ωκα LXX. Pass.: fut. 3 pl. ἐξουδενωθήσονται Ps 57:8; 1 aor. ἐξουδενήθην (ἐξουδενώθην); pf. ἐξουδένωμαι LXX. (**ἐξουδενέω:** Vi. Aesopi W 77b p. 96, 37 P.; BGU 1117, 31f [13 BC]=Mitt-Wilck. II/2, 107, 31f; PMich 477, 23 [II AD]. **ἐξουδενόω:** Job 30:1; PsSol 2:26 ἐξουδενωμένον; Test12Patr; JosAs 6:6 [also cod. A]; Just., D. 101, 2 [cod. A, -θένω—Otto]; Sb 7524, 11 [249 BC?]; pap: APF 11, '35, 125 [II BC]; Syntipas p. 78, 15; schol. on Lucian p. 279, 10 Rabe). The NT mss. vary (on the spelling s. Phryn. p. 182 Lob.; B-D-F §33 and 108, 2 app.; Mlt-H. 111f; 310; 396. For LXX Thackeray 105). Lit. 'to make an οὐδείς/οὐδέν of someone/someth.', ***treat with contempt/scorn*** ἐξουδενέω (4 Km 19:21) **Mk 9:12; 2 Cor 10:10 v.l.;** ἐξουδενόω **Mk 9:12 v.l.,** s. ἐξουθενέω.—DELG s.v. ὀρύσσω. M-M.

ἐξουθενέω/ἐξουθενόω (s. prec. entry) fut. ἐξουθενήσω, -ωσω LXX; 1 aor. ἐξουθένησα, -ωσα; pf. ἐξουθένηκα, -ωκα LXX. Pass.: 1 aor. ἐξουθενήθην, -ώθην; pf. ἐξουθένημαι, ptc. ἐξουθηνημένος LXX, ἐξουθενωμένοι (only TestAsh 7:2 w. ἐξουδενωμένοι) (**ἐξουθενέω:** Herodian Gr. II 508, 10; Just.; Cass. Dio 7, 8, 8; En 99:14 [pres. ptc.]; Vi. Aesopi G 80 p. 60, last two lines P. ἐξουθενηθείς; Vi. Aesopi W 77b p. 97, 2 P. ἐξουθένησας [beside p. 96, 37 ἐξουδενῆσαι]; schol. on Pla., Gorg. 483b; TestSol 22:5 P ἐξουθενημένην; JosAs 13:10 ἐξουθένηκα; 2:1 [pres. ptc.]. **ἐξουθενόω:** Rhet. Gr. I 623, 27; PsSol 2:5 and 27; En 99:14 pres. ptc.; TestLevi 16:2; TestAsh 7:2; **Mk 9:12 v.l.;** 1 Cl 18:17=Ps 50:19. For the spelling s. New Docs 2, 83 and the reff. s.v. ἐξουδενέω.)

➊ **to show by one's attitude or manner of treatment that an entity has no merit or worth,** ***disdain*** τινά *someone* (Ps.-Callisth. p. 72, 19; Achmes 128, 10; schol. on Soph., Ajax 368 p. 36 Papag. [1888]) **Lk 18:9** (Field, Notes 72); **Ro 14:3, 10; 1 Cor 16:11;** σὺ τίς εἶ ἐξουθενῶν αὐτήν *who in the world are you to disdain her?* GMary 463, 23; τὶ *someth.* (Jos., Bell. 6, 315. Pass.: Philo, Leg. All. 2, 67) 1 Cl 18:17 (Ps 50:19). ἐξουθενημένος *despised, of no account* οἱ ἐ. (Philo, Mos. 2, 241; Just., D. 121, 3 παρουσίᾳ; 131, 2 μυστηρίου) **1 Cor 6:4;** τὰ ἐ. **1:28.** Of the speaking ability of the apostle when he appears in person (parall. ἀσθενής): *it amounts to nothing* **2 Cor 10:10.** The expr. τ. πειρασμὸν ὑμῶν ἐν τ. σαρκί μου οὐκ ἐξουθενήσατε **Gal 4:14** contains two major components: 'My physical weakness did indeed distress you' and 'You did not despise me because of it'. The acc. in the phrase τ. πειρασμὸν ὑμῶν is prob. temporal, and the concluding verb is abs.; the thought can be rendered *during your time of trial in connection with my physical disability, you showed no disdain.* (See 2.)

➋ **to have no use for someth. as being beneath one's consideration,** ***reject disdainfully*** (1 Km 8:7; PsSol 2:5; En 99:14). So **1 Th 5:20; Ac 4:11.**—Bauer observed that at least for διαπτύω τι the mng. 'reject someth.' is well established (Dositheus, Ars Gramm. 68, 10 Tolk.: διέπτυσεν αὐτοῦ τὰς ἱκετείας) and likewise for περιπτύω (Simplicius in Epict. p. 58, 8; 61, 20; 98, 36; 119, 18). He suggested that **Gal 4:14** might be translated: 'You neither treated me w. contempt nor did you turn away from the temptation that my physical appearance might have become to you.' (See 1.)

➌ **to regard another as of no significance and therefore worthy of maltreatment** (=ἐξουδενέω), ***treat w. contempt*** (Just., A I, 63, 16 ἐξουθενηθῆναι καὶ παθεῖν) τινά **Lk 23:11;** B 7:9. Pass. **Mk 9:12 v.l.**—DELG s.v. οὐ. M-M.

ἐξουθένημα, ατος, τό (s. prec. two entries) ***a despised thing*** ἐγώ εἰμι ἐ. λαοῦ *I am an object of contempt for the people* 1 Cl 16:15 (Ps 21:7 v.l. [ARahlfs, Psalmi cum Odis '31 ad loc.]).

ἐξουσία, ας, ἡ (Soph., Thu.+; ins, pap, LXX, En, pseudepigr., Philo, Joseph., Just.; Tat. 30, 1; Mel., P. 104, 810 [Bodm.]) from ἔξεστιν.

➊ **a state of control over someth.,** ***freedom of choice, right*** (e.g., the 'right' to act, decide, or dispose of one's property as one wishes: BGU 1158, 13 [9 BC] = Mitt-Wilck. II/2, 234, 13 legal t.t., esp. in wills: POxy 272, 13; BGU 183, 25 ἔχειν αὐτὴν τὴν ἐ. τῶν ἰδίων πάντων; PTebt 319, 21.—Sir 30:11) ἐξουσίαν ἔχειν *have the right* **2 Th 3:9** (Just., D 16, 4). W. inf. foll. (Teles p. 23, 14; 24, 11; Tob 2:13 S; 7:10 S) **J 10:18; 1 Cor 9:4ff; Hb 13:10; Rv 13:5;** B 4:2. W. obj. gen. foll. (τίς οὖν ἔτι ἔχει μου ἐξουσίαν; Epict. 3, 24, 70; διδόναι ἐξουσίαν τῶν πετεινῶν Did., Gen. 61, 24) εἰ ἄλλοι τῆς ὑμῶν ἐ. μετέχουσι **1 Cor 9:12.** Also ἐ. ἐπὶ τὸ ξύλον τῆς ζωῆς *the right to the tree of life* **Rv 22:14.** W. verbs of two constr. ἔχει ἐ. ὁ κεραμεὺς τοῦ πηλοῦ ἐκ τοῦ αὐτοῦ φυράματος *the potter has a right over the clay, to make fr. the same lump* **Ro 9:21.** ἐ. ἔχειν περί τινος (4 Macc 4:5) *be at liberty w. regard to a thing* (opp. ἀνάγκην ἔχειν) **1 Cor 7:37; cp. 8:9;** ἐ. ἐν τ. εὐαγγελίῳ *a right in the gospel* **9:18.** ἐν τῇ σῇ ἐ. ὑπῆρχεν *was at your disposal* **Ac 5:4** (Esth 4:17b; Appian, Liby. 52 §226 ἐν ἐ. εἶναί τί τινι=someth. is at someone's disposal, is within one's power).

➋ **potential or resource to command, control, or govern,** ***capability, might, power*** (on capacity for someth. cp. Did., Gen. 162, 5: ἡ προσαιρέσεως ἐξουσία; cp. 1 Esdr 4:28, 40; 2 Macc 7:16 the king can do what he pleases because he has the capability for doing so) ἡ ἐ. τ. ἵππων ἐν τ. στόματι αὐτῶν ἐστιν **Rv 9:19;** cp. vs. **3; 13:2, 4; 18:1; Mt 9:8; Ac 8:19.** W. inf. foll. to indicate the thing that one is able to do (En 25:4 ἅψασθαι; Diod. S. 4, 52, 4 ἀμύνασθαι εἶχεν ἐξουσίαν; Mel., P. 104 [B] πάντα κρίνει); ἐκβάλλειν τ. δαιμόνια **Mk 3:15.** ἐμβαλεῖν εἰς τ. γέενναν **Lk 12:5;** cp. **J 1:12; 7:1 v.l.; Rv 9:10; 11:6.** W. gen. of the inf. foll. τοῦ πατεῖν ἐπάνω ὄφεων **Lk 10:19;** ποιεῖν ἐ. *exercise power* **Rv 13:12.** ἐ. ἔχειν τινός *have power over someone* (Epict. 4, 12, 8) GPt 3:7; ἑαυτοῦ IPol 7:3; also ἐ. ἔχειν ἐπί τινος **Rv 20:6;** cp. AcPl Ha 1, 3. Esp. of God's power (Theodor. Prodr. 5, 313 ἡ θεῶν ἐ.; Da 4:17; Jos., Ant. 5, 109; 18, 214) **Lk 12:5** (cp. 2 Cl 5:4); **Ac 1:7; Jd 25;** Hs 9, 23, 4. πάντων τ. ἐξουσίαν *power over all* Hm 4, 1, 11; s 9, 28, 8. πᾶσα ἡ ἐ. 5, 7, 3 (En 9:5). τὴν κατὰ πάντων ἐ. MPol. 2:1. τέλους ἐ. *power over the end* PtK 2 p. 13, 22. ἐ. ἐπὶ τ. πληγάς *control over the plagues* **Rv 16:9.** Also of Satan's power **Ac 26:18; ending of Mk** in the Freer ms.; B 2:1.—The power that comes fr. God can involve transcendent knowledge, and both may be expressed by ἐ. (Herm. Wr. 1, 13; 14; 32). So his hearers conclude fr. Jesus' teaching that he must have ἐ. (i.e. it is not necessary for him to first ask what the traditional practice or interpretation requires) **Mk**

1:22 ('license' of a Jewish teacher L-S-J-M suppl., '68; against this AArgyle, ET 80, '68/69, 343); cp. **Mt 7:29** (Rtzst., Poim. 48, 3, Mysterienrel.[3] 302; 363; JStarr, HTR 23, 1930, 302–5; HWindisch, Pls. u. Christus '34, 151ff; DDaube, JTS 39, '38, 45–59; HFlowers, ET 66, '55, 254 ['like a king']; DHudson, ET 67, '55/56, 17; JCoutts, JTS 8, '57, 111–18 [Jesus and the 12]). The prep. expr. κατ' ἐξουσίαν *in accordance w. knowledge and power* **Mk 1:27** and ἐν ἐ. **Lk 4:32** belong to this classification; cp. **4:36.** The close relation of ἐ. w. 'gnosis' and teaching also B 18:1.—But it is not always possible to draw a hard and fast line betw. this sense and

❸ **the right to control or command, *authority, absolute power, warrant*** (Sextus 36: the πιστός has ἐ. fr. God) ἐ. καὶ ἐπιτροπή (cp. Ps.-Pla., Defin. p. 415c ἐξουσία, ἐπιτροπὴ νόμου) *authority and commission* **Ac 26:12.** ἐν ποίᾳ ἐξουσίᾳ ταῦτα ποιεῖς; *by whose authority are you doing this?* **Mt 21:23, 24, 27; Mk 11:28, 29, 33; Lk 20:2, 8.** ἐ. διδόναι τινί *put someone in charge* (Diod. S. 13, 36, 2; 14, 81, 6; cp. Vi. Aesopi G 11 p. 39, 6 P.; En 9:7; TestJob 3:6; Jos., Ant. 2, 90; 20, 193) **Mk 13:34;** PtK 2 p. 14, 13. οἷς ἔδωκεν τοῦ εὐαγγελίου τὴν ἐ. *to whom he gave rights over the Gospel* (for its proclamation) B 8:3. ὅτι τὸ ἄρχειν ἐξουσίας ἐστίν *that ruling depends on authority* 6:18. Of apostolic authority **2 Cor 10:8; 13:10;** ISm 4:1. Of Jesus' total authority **Mt 28:18** (cp. Herm. Wr. 1, 32; Da 7:14; DStanley, CBQ 29, '67, 555–73); Hs 5, 6, 1. W. gen. of the one who has authority ἐ. τοῦ Χριστοῦ **Rv 12:10** (Just., A I, 40, 7). W. gen. of that over which the authority is exercised (Diod. S. 2, 27, 3; IDefixWünsch 4, 21; Ps 135:8, 9; Wsd 10:14; Sir 17:2; Jos., Vi. 190) ἐ. πνευμάτων ἀκαθάρτων *over the unclean spirits* **Mt 10:1; Mk 6:7;** cp. **J 17:2;** Hm 4, 3, 5; PtK 2 p. 14, 13; 1 Cl 61:2; ISm 4:1; τούτου τοῦ λαοῦ Hs 8, 3, 3. Also ἐπί w. acc. (cp. Sir 33:20) **Lk 9:1;** cp. **Rv 6:8; 13:7.** Likew. ἐπί w. gen. (cp. Da 3:97) **Rv 2:26; 11:6b; 14:18.** παρά τινος (also ἀπό τινος Orig., C. Cels. 2, 13, 56) indicates the source of the authority (s. παρά A3b) **Ac 9:14; 26:10;** Hs 5, 6, 4 (restored from the Lat.; ἐ. λαμβάνειν as Diod. S. 11, 42, 6; TestJob 8:2f; 16:4; Vi. Aesopi G 11 p. 39, 4 P.) and κατά τινος the one against whom it is directed (TestJob 16:2 κατ' ἐμοῦ; 8:2 κατὰ τῶν ὑπαρχόντων μου 'over my possessions'; Sb 8316, 6f κύριε Σάραπι δὸς αὐτῷ κατεξουσίαν κατὰ τῶν ἐχθρῶν αὐτοῦ; Orig., C. Cels. 7, 43, 25) **J 19:11** (HvCampenhausen, TLZ 73, '48, 387–92); B 4:13. W. pres. inf. foll. (cp. X., Mem. 2, 6, 24 and 35; Diod. S. 12, 75, 4; 1 Macc 10:35; 11:58; Jos., Ant. 4, 247) **Mt 9:6; Mk 2:10; Lk 5:24; J 5:27.** W. aor. inf. foll. (Jdth 8:15; 1 Esdr 8:22; 1 Macc 1:13) **19:10.** Foll. by gen. of the pres. inf. (4 Macc 5:15) Hm 12, 4, 2.—RDillon, 'As One Having Authority' (Mark 1:22): CBQ 57, '95, 92–113.

❹ **power exercised by rulers or others in high position by virtue of their office, *ruling power, official power*** (Ps.-Pla., Alc. 1, 135b al.; LXX; Jos., Bell. 2, 140, Vi. 80) ἐ. ὡς βασιλεύς **Rv 17:12f** (Diod. S. 2, 45, 1 βασιλικὴν ἐ. ἔχειν; 14, 32, 5 ἐ. λαμβάνειν); ἐ. τοῦ ἡγεμόνος **Lk 20:20;** cp. **J 19:10f,** s. 3 above. ἐ. ἐπάνω δέκα πόλεων **Lk 19:17.** ἄνθρωπος ὑπὸ ἐξουσίαν τασσόμενος *a man under authority* **7:8** (MFrost, ET 45, '34, 477f); cp. **Mt 8:9;** Hs 1:3.—The power of a particular office (Diod. S. 1, 70, 1; 14, 113, 6 ἡ ὑπατικὴ ἐξουσία; Plut., Mar. 406 [2, 1], Caes. 734 [58, 1]) ἐπαρχικὴ ἐ. *the power of prefect* **Phlm subscr.**

❺ **bearer of ruling authority**—ⓐ human ***authorities, officials, government*** (Dionys. Hal. 8, 44; 11, 32; POxy 261, 15) **Lk 12:11** (here and elsewh. in NT w. ἀρχή, as also in Pla.); **Ro 13:1, 2, 3** (with **13:1b** cp. the express. 'ancient saying' [s. Hes., Theogony 96 ἐκ δὲ Διὸς βασιλῆες. On this HFränkel, Dichtung u. Philos. des frühen Griechentums '62, 111 n. 6] in Artem. 2, 36 p. 135, 24; 2, 69 p. 161, 17 τὸ κρατοῦν δύναμιν ἔχει θεοῦ=the ruling power has its authority from God; Wsd 6:3; Jos., Bell. 2, 140 οὐ δίχα θεοῦ περιγενέσθαι τινὶ τὸ ἄρχειν . . . ἐξουσίαν); **Tit 3:1.** For the view that the ἐ. of **Ro 13** are spirit powers, as b below, s. OCullmann, Christ and Time (tr. Filson) '50, 191–210.—On the subj. in gener. s. LGaugusch, D. Staatslehre d. Ap. Pls nach Ro 13: ThGl 5, '34, 529–50; JUitman, Onder Eig. Vaandel 15, '40, 102–21; HvCampenhausen, ABertholet Festschr. '50, 97–113; OCullmann, Zur neuesten Diskussion über die ἐξουσίαι in Rö 13:1: TZ 10, '54, 321–36, D. Staat im NT '61[2] (Eng. tr.: The State in the NT '56, 93–114); against him AStrobel, ZNW 47, '56, 67–93.—GCaird, Princip. and Powers '56; RMorgenthaler TZ 12, '56, 289–304; CMorrison, The Powers That Be '60; EBarnikol, Rö 13. Der nichtpaulinische Ursprung der absoluten Obrigkeitsbejahung v. Rö 13:1–7 '61, 65–133; HSchlier, Principalities and Powers in the NT '61 (Eng. tr.); MBorg, NTS 19, '72/73, 205–18. οἱ ἐπ' ἐξουσίαν ἀχθέντες *those who are brought before the authorities* Hs 9, 28, 4.

ⓑ of transcendent rulers and functionaries: powers of the spirit world (TestLevi 3:8; TestSol 20:15 B), sg. (w. ἀρχή and δύναμις) **1 Cor 15:24; Eph 1:21; Col 2:10.** Pl. (w. ἀρχαί as Just., D. 41, 1; cp. Orig., C. Cels. 4, 29, 22) **Eph 3:10; 6:12; Col 1:16; 2:15;** (w. ἄγγελοι, δυνάμεις) **1 Pt 3:22.** Cp. the v.l. for ἄρχειν Papias (4).

❻ **the sphere in which power is exercised, *domain*** (4 Km 20:13; Ps 113:2) **Lk 4:6.** ἐκ τ. ἐξουσίας Ἡρῴδου ἐστίν *he comes fr. Herod's jurisdiction* **23:7.** ἐ. τοῦ σκότους *domain of darkness* **22:53; Col 1:13** (opp. the βασιλεία of Christ). Hence ἐ. τοῦ ἀέρος simply *domain of the air* **Eph 2:2;** s. ἀήρ 2b.

❼ Various opinions are held about the mng. of **1 Cor 11:10** ὀφείλει ἡ γυνὴ ἐξουσίαν ἔχειν ἐπὶ τῆς κεφαλῆς διὰ τοὺς ἀγγέλους. Many now understand it as ***a means of exercising power*** (cp. δύναμις 1b.—It is abstract for concrete, as βασιλεία [1] in Diod. S. 1, 47, 5: a stone figure ἔχουσα τρεῖς βασιλείας ἐπὶ τῆς κεφαλῆς=that wears three symbols of royal power [diadems] on its head), that is to say, the *veil* (κάλυμμα is v.l. for ἐ. here; s. critical apparatus in N.) by which women at prayer (when they draw near to the heavenly realm) protect themselves fr. the amorous glances of certain angels. But the veil may also have been simply a symbol of womanly dignity, esp. befitting a Christian woman, and esp. in the presence of holy angels (s. Cadbury below).—WWeber, ZWT 46, 1903, 487–99; Dibelius, Geisterwelt 12–23 al.; EFehrle, Die kultische Keuschheit im Altertum 1910, 39; RPerdelwitz, StKr 86, 1913, 611–13; LBrun, ZNW 14, 1913, 298–308; GKittel, Rabbinica 1920, 17ff; Billerb. III 423–35; KBornhäuser, NKZ 41, 1930, 475–88; WFoerster, ZNW 30, '31, 185f; MGinsburger, RHPR 12, '32, 245–47; OMotta, ET 44, '33, 139–41; CSpicq, RB 48, '39, 557–62; EBlakeney, ET 55, '44, 138; SLösch, TQ 127, '47, 216–61; JFitzmyer, NTS 3, '57, 48–58; HCadbury, HTR 51, '58, 1f (Qumran parallels); MHooker, NTS 10, '64, 410–16; AIsaksson, Marriage and Ministry in the NT '65, 176–81; GSchwartz, ZNW 70, '79, 249 (Aramaic background).—LCerfaux et JTondriau, Un Concurrent du Christianisme, '57. S. on ἄγγελος 2c.—V.l. for ἄρχειν Papias (4).—DELG s.v. εἰμί. New Docs 2, 83f. M-M. EDNT. TW. Sv.

ἐξουσιάζω (s. prec. entry) 1 fut. ἐξουσιάσω LXX; TestSol 1:5; 1 aor. 3 sg. ἐξουσίασεν Eccl 5:18; fut. pass. ἐξουσιασθήσομαι (Aristot., Eth. Eud. 1, 5 p. 1216a, 2; Dionys. Hal. 9, 44, 6; ins, only late pap, LXX; TestSol 1:5) **to have the right of control, *have the right/power*** *for someth.* or *over someone* ὁ ἐξουσιάζων *one who is in authority* (Eccl 10:4, 5; TestSol C 9:8) **Lk 22:25.** Specif. the *right* or *power* to do with someth. as one sees fit (IG XIV, 79, 4) w. gen. of that over which one has the power (CIG III, 4584, 4 θυγατέρα αὐτῶν μὴ ἐξουσιάζειν τοῦ μνήματος) of husband and wife w. ref. to their marital duties ἐ. τοῦ ἰδίου σώματος *have power over her (his) own body* **1 Cor 7:4.** Paul uses the pass. in wordplay w. ἔξεστιν: οὐκ ἐξουσιασθήσομαι ὑπό τινος *I will not be mastered/authorized by anything* **6:12.**—M-M. TW.

ἐξουσιαστικός, ή, όν (Eccl 8, 4 Sym; Vett. Val. 6, 3, Iamblichus. -ώτερον Polyb. 5, 26, 3) **pert. to being free from external approval, *authoritative*** **Mk 1:27 v.l.** (cp. doctrina inpotentabilis It. cod. e).

ἐξοχή, ῆς, ἡ (ἐξέχω 'stand out, project from') from 'someth. that projects from a surface' (e.g. Diod. S. 5, 30 embossed figures on shields; Theod. Job 39:28; Sym. SSol 2:14 and Jer 13:4; Jos., Ant. 3, 135; 231) it is a short step to the idea of **having special status, *prominence*** (cp. the sense 'excellence, advantage' Cicero, Ad Att. 4, 15, 7; Vett. Val. 17, 23 and κατ᾽ ἐξοχήν *'par excellence'* Strabo 1, 2, 10; Philo, Leg. All. 1, 106; SIG 810, 16 [55 AD]; OGI 764, 52 [II BC]) ἄνδρες οἱ κατ᾽ ἐ. τῆς πόλεως *the most prominent men of the city* **Ac 25:23.**—DELG s.v. 1 ἔχω 4. M-M.

ἔξοχος, ον (s. prec. entry; Hom. et al. in poetry; in prose in Cornutus 16 p. 20, 21, Plut., Lucian, Herodian and other late wr., incl. Vett. Val. 16, 1) ***prominent*** (SibOr 5, 284) μάρτυς *a prominent confessor to the death = distinguished martyr* MPol 19:1. Superl. (Ps.-Lucian, Asin. 2; OGI 640, 16; POxy 1469, 1) τὸ ἐξοχώτατον *the most preëminent thing* 1 Cl 33:4.—M-M.

ἐξυπνίζω fut. ἐξυπνίσω. Pass.: fut. 3 sg. ἐξυπνισθήσεται (SyrBar 12:4), 3 pl. ἐξυπνισθήσονται Job 14:12; 1 aor. 3 sg. ἐξυπνίσθη LXX (s. ὕπνος; Plut., Mor. 979d; 1044d; M. Ant. 6, 31; Judg 16:14 B, 20 B; 3 Km 3:15; pseudepigr.; Hellenist. substitute for ἀφυπνίζω: Phryn. p. 96 and 224 Lob.) ***wake up, arouse*** τινά *someone* of sleeping persons (Chrysipp.: Stoic. II 334, 25) τὸν κεντυρίωνα GPt 10:38. In wordplay w. κοιμάω (for both words used of death s. Job 14:12, but in our pass. the wordplay nuances the idea that raising of the dead is as easy for Jesus as awakening one from sleep. On death as 'sleep' s. RLattimore, Themes in Greek and Latin Epitaphs '62, 164f; cp. Il. 16, 672 'sleep and death twin brothers'; Soph., Ajax 832, Electra 509.) **J 11:11.**—M-M. TW.

ἔξυπνος, ον (s. prec. entry; PGiss 19, 4; LXX, En) ***awake, aroused*** ἔ. γίνεσθαι (Syntipas p. 58, 5; 117, 2; 1 Esdr 3:3; En 13:9; Jos., Ant. 11, 34) *awaken* ἔ. γενόμενος (Leontius 8 p. 15, 14; TestLevi 5:7) **Ac 16:27.**—DELG s.v. ὕπνος. M-M. TW.

ἔξω adv. of place (s. ἔξωθεν; Hom.+).**—❶ pert. to a position beyond an enclosure or boundary, *outside*—ⓐ** funct. adverbially**—α.** w. a verb not signifying motion δεδεμένον πρὸς θύραν ἔ. *tied at the door outside* **Mk 11:4.** ἔ. εἶναι (X., An. 2, 6, 3; 7, 2, 29) ἔ. ἐπ᾽ ἐρήμοις τόποις ἦν **1:45;** ἑστάναι ἔ. *stand outside* (Gen 24:31; Dt 24:11; Sir 21:23) **Mt 12:46f; Mk 3:31** (cp. vs. **32**); **Lk 8:20; 13:25;** GEb 121, 33; w. πρός and dat. πρὸς τ. θύρᾳ ἔ. **J 18:16;** πρὸς τ. μνημείῳ ἔ. **20:11;** καθῆσθαι ἔ. **Mt 26:69;** προσεύχεσθαι ἔ. *pray outside* **Lk 1:10;** ἔ. ἔχειν τι *have someth. free* of uncovered shoulders Hs 9, 2, 4; 9, 9, 5; 9, 13, 8. The verb is to be supplied in pass. like **Rv 22:15.**

β. as a substitute for an adj. *outer, outside* (Pla., Phdr. 248a ὁ ἔξω τόπος. The same expr. BGU 1114, 5 [4 BC]; cp. POxy 903, 20 τὰς ἔξω θύρας). αἱ ἔ. πόλεις *the foreign* (lit. 'outside', i.e. non-Jewish) *cities* **Ac 26:11;** Hv 2, 4, 3. ὁ ἔ. ἡμῶν ἄνθρωπος *our outer being* (i.e. the body, as Zosimus 13: Hermet. IV p. 107, 16) **2 Cor 4:16** (s. ἄνθρωπος 5a); differently οἱ ἔ. ἄνθρωποι 2 Cl 13:1 (s. 3 below). τὸ ἔ. (opp. τὸ ἔσω) *the outside* (Thu. 7, 69, 4) 2 Cl 12:2, cp. vs. 4 (apocryphal saying of Jesus).

ⓑ funct. as prep. w. gen. in answer to the question 'where?' *outside* (Thu. 8, 67, 2 al.; Num 35:5, 27; Jdth 10:18; 13:3; TestJob 28:8 ἔ. τῆς πόλεως; Jos., Ant. 13, 91; 101; Tat. 2, 1 ἀλαζονείας ἔ.) **Lk 13:33.** ἔ. τῆς παρεμβολῆς *outside the camp* **Hb 13:11;** 1 Cl 4:11 (cp. Ex 29:14 al.); **Ac 28:16 v.l.;** ἔ. τ. πύλης **Hb 13:12** (Jos., Bell. 4, 360 ἔ. τῶν πυλῶν); ἔ. τῆς θύρας Hv 3, 9, 6; ἔ. τῆς οἰκίας 1 Cl 12:6 (cp. Josh 2:19).

❷ pert. to a position outside an area or limits, as result of an action, *out* (Hom. et al.)**—ⓐ** ἐξέρχεσθαι ἔ. *go out(side)* (Jos 2:19; cp. Ps 40:7) **Mt 26:75; Lk 22:62; J 19:4, 5; Rv 3:12;** ἐξῆλθεν ἔ. εἰς τὸ προαύλιον **Mk 14:68.** ἐξῆλθεν ἔ. πρὸς αὐτούς (cp. Gen 24:29; Judg 19:25) **J 18:29.** ἔ. ποιεῖν τινα *take someone out* **Ac 5:34.** ἄγειν **J 19:4, 13.** ἐξάγειν (Gen 15:5; Judg 19:25) **Mk 8:23 v.l.; Lk 24:50;** προάγειν **Ac 16:30.** βάλλειν (M. Ant. 12, 25 βάλε ἔξω) **Mt 5:13; 13:48; Lk 14:35; J 12:31 v.l.; 15:6; 1J 4:18.** ἐκβάλλειν (2 Ch 29:16) **Lk 13:28; J 6:37; 9:34f; 12:31; Ac 9:40; Rv 11:2 v.l.** δεῦρο ἔ. *come out!* **J 11:43** (δεῦρο 1).

ⓑ funct. as prep. w. gen in answer to the question 'whither?' *out* (fr. within), *out of* (Hom. et al.) ἀπελθεῖν ἔ. τ. συνεδρίου **Ac 4:15.** Likew. after ἐξέρχεσθαι (Polyaenus 3, 7, 3; cp. Jos., Ant. 8, 399) **Mt 10:14; 21:17; Ac 16:13; Hb 13:13** (ἐξέρχ. ἔ. τ. παρεμβολῆς as Num 31:13); ἐκπορεύεσθαι **Mk 11:19;** ἀποστέλλειν τινά **5:10;** ἐκφέρειν τινά (Lev 4:12) **8:23;** βάλλειν τινά 2 Cl 7:4; ἐκβάλλειν τινά (Lev 14:40) **Mt 21:39; Mk 12:8; Lk 4:29; 20:15;** w. acc. to be supplied, **Ac 7:58;** ἀπορρίπτειν τινά Hv 3, 5, 5; σύρειν τινά **Ac 14:19;** ἕλκειν τινά **21:30;** προπέμπειν τινά **21:5** (on ἕως ἔ. cp. 1 Km 9:26).

❸ pert. to noninclusion in a group, *on the outside,* as subst. w. art. ***outsider*** οἱ ἔξω *those who are outside* (2 Macc 1:16; Petosiris, fgm. 6 l. 206=the foreigners; fig. Thu. 5, 14, 3) of those who did not belong to the circle of the disciples **Mk 4:11.** Of non-Christians gener. (Iambl., Vi. Pyth. 35, 252 of non-Pythagoreans; Simplicius in Epict. p. 132, 6 those who are not ascetics) **1 Cor 5:12f; Col 4:5; 1 Th 4:12.** οἱ ἔ. ἄνθρωποι *those on the outside* (as Lucian, De Merc. Cond. 21) 2 Cl 13:1.—DELG s.v. ἐξ. M-M. TW.

ἔξωθεν adv. of place (s. prec. entry; Aeschyl., Hdt.+).

❶ pert. to derivation from a source that is outside, *from outside*—ⓐ used as adv. (Hierocles 7 p. 430 ἡ ἔ. βία=force from the outside; Judg 12:9; Jdth 13:1; Ath., R. 53, 8 τῆς ἔ. ἀνάγκης) τὸ ἔ. εἰσπορευόμενον *what goes into* (a person) *fr. the outside* **Mk 7:18.**

ⓑ funct. as prep. w. gen. (trag., X. et al.) *from outside* ἔ. τ. ἀνθρώπου εἰσπορευόμενον εἰς αὐτόν **Mk 7:15.**

❷ pert. to a position that is beyond a particular area, *outside*—ⓐ (Dio Chrys. 17 [34], 21; 67 [17], 1; PFlor 50, 99; Ex 26:35 al.; Jos., Bell. 5, 201, Vi. 118 ἔ. τῆς κώμης; TestZeb 3:6) ἔ. τῆς πόλεως (Aeneas Tact. 951; TestJob 24:1) **Rv 14:20.** ἡ αὐλὴ ἡ ἔ. τοῦ ναοῦ *the court outside the temple* **11:2a.** οὐθὲν ἔ. ἐστιν τῆς ἀληθείας *nothing is apart fr. the truth* Hv 3, 4, 3.

ⓑ as contrast to ἔσωθεν (Aeneas Tact. 1331; Diocles 141 p. 178, 13; Gen 6:14; Ex 25:11 al.; PGM 5, 307; Just., A I, 16, 13 and D. 35, 3 [cp. Mt 7:15]; Tat. 22, 1; Ath. 25, 3) **Mt 23:27f; 2 Cor 7:5; Rv 5:1 v.l.** (Plut., Dio 972 [31, 2] μία [sc. ἐπιστολή] δ᾽ ἦν ἐπιγεγραμμένη); IRo 3:2; Agr 25b.

❸ pert. to a position located on a surface, *having to do w. the outside, the external,* as substitute for an adj. (Demosth. 18, 9 οἱ ἔ. λόγοι; 4 Macc 6:34; 18:2; Jos., Ant. 14, 477) ὁ ἔ. κόσμος *external adornment* **1 Pt 3:3;** ἡ ἔ. ἐπιφάνεια *the outer* *surface* of the eyes of Judas, which were obscured by his swollen features Papias (3:2).—As subst. w. art. τὸ ἔξωθεν *the outside* (SIG 813a, 6; Ezk 41:17) **Mt 23:25; Lk 11:39f.**

❹ pert. to a position outside an area or limits as result of an action, *outward, out* ἔκβαλε ἔ. *throw out=leave out* (ἐκβάλλω 4) **Rv 11:2b.**

❺ pert. to noninclusion in a group, *on the outside,* as subst. w. art. οἱ ἔ. *those on the outside* i.e. non-Christians **1 Ti 3:7; Mk 4:11 v.l.** (cp. Hdt. 9, 5; Diod. S. 19, 70, 3; Himerius, Or. [Ecl.] 5, 18; Celsus 3, 14; Jos., Bell. 4, 179, Ant. 15, 316).—M-M.

ἐξωθέω (s. ὠθέω) fut. ἐξώσω LXX; 1 aor. ἐξῶσα (Tdf. has the older form ἐξέωσα **Ac 7:45;** so also Polyaenus 8, 46 p. 408, 17; Sb 7205, 13; PSI 41, 16; PFlor 58, 9), 3 sg. ἐξέωσεν 4 Km 17, 21. Pass.: fut. 3 pl. ἐξωσθήσονται LXX; aor. 3 pl. ἐξώσθησαν; pf. ptc. ἐξωσμένος LXX and ἐξεωσμένον 2 Km 14:14 v.l. (Hom., Il. 14, 494 ἐκ δ' ὦσε γλήνην, trag., Hdt. et al.; pap, LXX; TestGad 5:2; Philo, Poster. Cai. 55; Jos., Bell. 5, 338; 342)

❶ to force to leave an area, *push out* τινά *drive someone out* fr. a place, *expel* (Thu., X., Polyb. et al.) ἐξῶσεν (-έωσεν t.r. Tdf.) ἀπὸ προσώπου τινός *before someone* **Ac 7:45.**

❷ to run or drive ashore, *beach, run ashore,* a mariner's t.t. (so Thu., X. et al.) τὸ πλοῖον εἰς τὸν αἰγιαλόν **Ac 27:39.**—M-M.

ἐξώτερος, α, ον (Strabo; PFlor 100, 11 and 27; POxy 896, 14; PSI IV, 284, 2 [VI AD]; LXX) adjectival comparison of the adv. ἔξω (B-D-F §62; Rob. 298).

❶ pert. to an area outside a particular boundary, *outside* (in contrast to inside or in the middle; cp. 3 Km 6:29f) ἐξώτεροι τεθήσονται *they* (the stones) *will be placed outside* Hs 9, 7, 5; cp. 9, 8, 3; 5; 7. τὰ ἐξώτερα μέρη τ. οἰκοδομῆς *the outside of the building* 9, 9, 3.

❷ as superl. ***farthest, extreme*** (Ex 26:4) τὸ σκότος τὸ ἐ. *the darkness farthest out* **Mt 8:12; 22:13; 25:30** (ApcEsdr 4:37 p. 29, 16 Tdf.; Just., D. 76, 5 on **Mt 25:41**).—DELG s.v. ὠθέω. M-M.

ἔοικα (Hom. et al.; in the mng. 'seem' also Job 6:3, 25; Jos., C. Ap. 2, 175; Just., Tat.) old pf. of εἴκω ***be like, resemble,*** τινί *someone* or *someth.* (Hes., fgm. 263 Rz. ποταμῷ ῥέοντι ἐοικώς) κλύδωνι θαλάσσης **Js 1:6.** ἀνδρί vs. **23.**—DELG. M-M.

ἑορτάζω fut. ἑορτάσω; 1 aor. impv. 2 pl. ἑορτάσατε, inf. ἑορτάσαι LXX (s. next entry; Eur., Hdt. et al.; Plut., Mor. 378b; Paus. 2, 11, 3; OGI 194, 28 [restored]; 493, 26; PSI 1242, 8 [I BC / I AD]; Mitt-Wilck. I/2, 490, 6 and 11= BGU 646, 6; 11; LXX, Ath. 14, 1) ***celebrate a festival,*** of the Passover (Jos., Ant. 5, 20) as a figure of the Christian life **1 Cor 5:8** (Philo, Sacr. Abel. 111 ἑορτὴ ψυχῆς ἡ ἐν ἀρεταῖς … μόνος ἑορτάζει ὁ σοφός).—DELG s.v. ἑορτή. M-M.

ἑορτή, ῆς, ἡ (s. prec. entry; Hom.+; ins, pap, LXX; ParJer 7:31; EpArist, Philo, Joseph.; Ar. 10:8; Just., Mel.; Ath. 26, 3) **a day or series of days marked by a periodic celebration or observance, *festival, celebration*** ἐν μέρει ἑορτῆς *with regard to a festival* **Col 2:16.** More specif. defined ἡ ἑ. τοῦ πάσχα *the Passover festival* (Ex 34:25) **Lk 2:41; J 13:1.** τὸ πάσχα ἡ ἑ. τῶν Ἰουδαίων **6:4.** ἡ ἑ. τῶν ἀζύμων *the festival of unleavened bread* **Lk 22:1;** cp. GPt 2:5 (Mel., P. 93, 695). ἡ ἑ. τῶν Ἰουδαίων ἡ σκηνοπηγία *the Judeans' festival of Tabernacles* or *Booths* **J 7:2;** ἡ ἑ. *the festival* is shown by the context to be a particular one: Passover **Mt 26:5; Lk 2:42; J 4:45; 11:56; 12:12, 20** al.; the festival of Tabernacles **7:8, 10f, 14, 37.—5:1** the witnesses and editions vary betw. the indefinite ἑ. *a festival* and ἡ ἑ. *the festival* (for the attestation and interpr. s. Hdb. ad loc.; JUbbink, NThSt 5, 1922, 131–36). Simply ἑ. of the feast of Tabernacles PtK 2 p. 14, 29.—ἐν τ. ἑ. *during the festival* (Jos., Bell. 2, 89, Ant. 20, 109 ἐν ἑ.) **Mt 26:5; Mk 14:2; J 4:45; 7:11; 12:20;** εἶναι ἐν τ. ἑορτῇ *take part in the festival* **2:23** (CBurchard, ZNW 61, '70, 157–88—also Mk 14:2, Mt 26:5, J 7:11). εἰς τ. ἑορτήν *for the festival* **13:29** (cp. BGU 596, 7 [84 AD] ὅπως εἰς τ. ἑορτὴν περιστερείδια ἡμεῖν ἀγοράσῃ). ἀναβαίνειν (i.e. to Jerusalem) εἰς τ. ἑ. **7:8, 10** (cp. BGU 48, 18 ἐὰν ἀναβῇς τῇ ἑορτῇ); ἔρχεσθαι εἰς τ. ἑ. (Jos., Bell. 1, 73; 6, 300) **4:45; 11:56; 12:12.** τ. ἑορτῆς μεσούσης *when the festival was half over* **7:14.** τ. ἑορτῆς παυσαμένης GPt 14:58. κατὰ ἑορτήν *at each* (Passover) *festival* **Mt 27:15; Mk 15:6; Lk 23:17 v.l.** (should it be limited to the Passover? Any festival at all could be the proper occasion to free a prisoner. Cp. Heliod. 8, 7 p. 227, 6ff Bekker: ἡ δέσποινα … τήμερον ἀφήσειν ἐπηγγείλατο [Theagenes], ἑορτήν τινα πάτριον εὐωχεῖν μέλλουσα 'the mistress has promised to release [Theagenes], out of intention to celebrate some traditional festival'). κατὰ τὸ ἔθος τ. ἑορτῆς *acc. to the custom of the feast* **Lk 2:42.** τ. ἑορτὴν ποιεῖν *keep the festival* (Ael. Aristid. 29, 4 K.=40 p. 752 D.; Vi. Aesopi G 123 P.; Ex 23:16) **Ac 18:21** D. Of *a joyous festival* (contrast πένθος *time of sorrow)* Dg 4:5.—DELG. M-M.

ἐπαγγελία, ας, ἡ (s. ἀγγέλλω; Demosth. et al.; Aristot., EN 10, 1 p. 1164a, 29; ins, pap, LXX, pseudepigr., Philo, Joseph.) in many authors ἐ. refers to the act of making someth. known publicly, but in our lit. it most often bears the sense of

❶ declaration to do someth. with implication of obligation to carry out what is stated, *promise, pledge, offer* (Polyb. 1, 43, 6; 7, 13, 2; 18, 11, 1 al.; Diod. S. 1, 5, 3; 4, 16, 2; Epict. 1, 4, 3 ἡ ἀρετὴ ταύτην ἔχει τὴν ἐπαγγελίαν εὐδαιμονίαν ποιῆσαι; Michel 473, 10; IPriene 123, 9; 1 Macc 10:15; Philo, Mut. Nom. 201; Jos., Ant. 5, 307).

ⓐ of humans ὅπως ἀποδῶμεν τὴν ἐ. ἣν ἐπειγγειλάμεθα *so that we might keep our promise* GJs 7:1. Of one who lays claim to being a Christian IEph 14:2.

ⓑ in our lit. more generally of divine promises (Herm. Wr. in Stob. I 387, 15 W.; fgm. XXIII 8 v.l.; cp. Herm. Wr. 18, 14; Jos., Ant. 2, 219; Prayer of Manasseh [=Odes 12] 6; PsSol 12:6; perh. Ps 55:9).

α. God's *promise* sg. **Ac 2:39; Ro 4:13f, 16; 9:9** (where λόγος is to be supplied w. the gen. ἐπαγγελίας: *this word is a word of promise*); **Gal 3:17; 2 Pt 3:9;** 1 Cl 26:1; 2 Cl 15:4; B 5:7; 16:9. Pl. **Ro 9:4; 2 Cor 7:1; Gal 3:16; Hb 7:6; 8:6; 11:17;** 1 Cl 27:1; H 3, 4; ApcPt Rainer (figura etymol.; cp. 1a and 1bβ). Prep. phrases: δι' ἐπαγγελίας *by* or *because of a promise* **Gal 3:18b; 4:23;** also ἐξ ἐπαγγελίας **3:18a.** ἐν ἐπαγγελίᾳ *with promise* **Eph 6:2.** κατ' ἐπαγγελίαν *in accordance w. the promise* (PSI 281, 58 κατὰ τ. ἐπανγελίας αὐτου; sim. IK IX–X/2: Nikaia II/1, 702, 6; 1 Esdr 1:7; Orig., C. Cels. 1, 68, 43) **Ac 13:23; Gal 3:29;** cp. **2 Ti 1:1** (on these three s. New Docs 4, 147).—For var. reasons the gen. is used w. ἐ.: to denote the one fr. whom the promise comes (τ.) θεοῦ **Ro 4:20; 2 Cor 1:20; Gal 3:21;** 2 Cl 11:1; **1 Ti 1:1 v.l.;** to denote the thing promised (Jos., Ant. 3, 77 τ. ἀγαθῶν) ἐ. τ. αἰωνίου κληρονομίας **Hb 9:15.** τ. ζωῆς **1 Ti 4:8;** τ. παρουσίας **2 Pt 3:4;** to denote the one(s) for whom the promise is intended τ. πατέρων **Ro 15:8** (TestJob 20:1; on βεβαιῶσαι τὰς ἐ. cp. InsPriene 123, 9 ἐβεβαίωσεν τ. ἐπαγγελίαν).—On the other hand, τῆς ἐπαγγελίας is oft. added, as a kind of gen. of quality, to indicate the relation of the noun in question to the promise: γῆ τ. ἐ. *the promised land* **Hb 11:9** (TestAbr A 8 p. 85, 16 [Stone p. 18] al).; τέκνα τ. ἐ. *children of the promise,* i.e. those born because of the promise **Ro 9:8; Gal 4:28;** πνεῦμα τ. ἐ. **Eph 1:13;** διαθῆκαι τ. ἐ. **2:12.** As an obj. gen. in πίστις τῆς ἐ. *faith in the promise* B 6:17.—ἐ. w. inf. foll. εἰσελθεῖν *to enter* **Hb 4:1.**—ἐ. γενομένη πρὸς τ. πατέρας *a promise made to the fathers* **Ac 13:32;** also εἰς τ. πατ. **26:6** (Diod. S. 2, 60, 4 γεγενημένη ἐ.=a promise given).—Of Christ's promise (Orig., C. Cels. 2, 2, 43) 2 Cl 5:5.

β. w. specification of *what was promised* (Vi. Aesopi G 79 P.; PsSol 12:6) **1J 2:25** (figura etymol. as Hs 1, 7). Hv 3, 2, 1 (ἐπαγγελίαι w. δῶρα). δεκτὸς τῆς ἐ. *recipient of the promised benefit* ApcPt Rainer 20. W. epexeg. gen. foll. ἡ ἐ. τοῦ πνεύματος *what was promised, namely the Spirit* **Ac 2:33; Gal 3:14.** Foll. by gen. of the one who promises ἐ. τοῦ πατρός **Lk 24:49; Ac 1:4;** κομίσασθαι τὴν ἐ. **Hb 10:36; 11:13 v.l., 39.** λαβεῖν **Hb 11:13;** 2 Cl 11:7; ἀπολαβεῖν B 15:7; Hv 2, 2, 6; ἡ μέλλουσα ἐ. 2 Cl 10:3f.

γ. It is not always poss. to draw a hard and fast line betw. α and β (cp. Hippol., Ref. 5, 7, 19: ἐ. τοῦ λουτροῦ): **Ac 7:17; Gal 3:22; Eph 3:6; Hb 6:12, 15, 17; 11:9b, 33;** 1 Cl 10:2; 34:7.—FBaumgärtel, Verheissung: Zur Frage des evang. Verständnisses des AT '52.

❷ The pregnant use of ἐ. **Ac 23:21** is in effect an extension of mng. 1 and involves two major components: entertainment of a request and approval of it ***assurance of agreement*** προσδέχεσθαι τὴν ἀπό τινος ἐ. *wait for assurance fr. someone* or *consent* (namely, to do what has been proposed).—DELG s.v. ἄγγελος. M-M. EDNT. TW.

ἐπαγγέλλομαι (s. prec. entry; freq. 'announce, proclaim'; the act. since Hom.; the mid., which alone occurs in our lit., since Soph., Hdt., Thu.; ins, pap, LXX, TestSol 3:7; 20:2 P; TestAbr A 3 p. 79, 31 [Stone p. 6]; ApcMos 41; EpArist, Philo, Joseph., Just., Tat.) 1 aor. ἐπηγγειλάμην; pf. ἐπήγγελμαι, the latter also w. pass. mng. (cp. Kühner-G. I 120; s. 1b)

❶ **to declare to do someth. with implication of obligation to carry out what is stated, *promise, offer*—**ⓐ of human promises and offers τινί τι *promise someth. to someone* (PTebt. 58, 32 [III BC]; 1 Macc 11:28; 2 Macc 4:8) ἐλευθερίαν τινί Hs 5, 2, 7; **2 Pt 2:19;** ἐπαγγελίαν GJs 7:1.—Of the Sybil ὃ ἐπηγγείλατο ὅραμα Hv 3, 2, 3. W. dat. and inf. foll. (cp. Polyb. 1, 46, 4; PTebt 411, 9; 3 Macc 1:4; Jos., C. Ap. 1, 57). ἐπηγγείλαντο αὐτῷ ἀργύριον δοῦναι *they promised to give him money* **Mk 14:11** (cp. 2 Macc 4:27).

ⓑ of God: *promise* (2 Macc 2:18; 3 Macc 2:10; PsSol) τί *someth.* **Ro 4:21; Tit 1:2;** ITr 11:2; τινί τι (Sb 7172, 27f. [217 BC] ἃ ἐπηγγείλαντο [the gods] αὐτῷ) Hv 5:7; Dg 10:2. στέφανον τῆς ζωῆς τοῖς ἀγαπῶσιν **Js 1:12;** cp. **2:5** (ἧς ἐπηγγείλατο w. attraction of the relative=ἣν ἐ.). τὸ ποτήριον ὃ ἐπηγγειλάμην σοι ApcPt Rainer 11. γῆν Χαναναίων AcPl Ha 8, 14. ἡ ἐπαγγελία, ἣν αὐτὸς ἐ. ἡμῖν *what he himself has promised us* **1J 2:25** (ἡ ἐπαγγελία, ἣν ἐ. τινι as Esth 4:7. Cp. also Diod. S. 15, 6, 5 ἐπηγγείλατο ἐπαγγελίαν); cp. **Ac 7:17 v.l.;** Hv 1, 3, 4 (s. Joly ad loc. on the punctuation); s 1:7. W. inf. foll. (Jos., Ant. 3, 23; Just. A I, 40, 7) **Ac 7:5;** 2 Cl 11:6; Hv 3, 1, 2. W. ὅτι foll. 1 Cl 32:2. W. λέγων foll. **Hb 12:26.** Abs. (the abs. use also PPetr I, 29, 12 [III BC]) *make a promise* τινί **Hb 6:13.** God is described as ὁ ἐπαγγειλάμενος **10:23; 11:11** (a Phrygian ins [IGR IV, 766] calls aspirants for a city office, who make all kinds of promises, οἱ ἐπανγειλάμενοι; Larfeld I 494).—Of faith πάντα ἐπαγγέλλεται Hm 9:10.—Pass. (Just., D. 106, 3 τὴν ἐπηγγελμένην ... γῆν) τὸ σπέρμα, ᾧ ἐπήγγελται *the offspring for whom the promise was intended* **Gal 3:19.** ἐπηγγελμέναι δωρεαί *promised gifts* 1 Cl 35:4.

❷ **to claim to be well-accomplished in someth., *profess, lay claim to, give oneself out as an expert in*** *someth.* w. acc. (X., Mem. 1, 2, 7 τ. ἀρετήν, Hell. 3, 4, 3 στρατιάν; Diog. L., prooem. 12 σοφίαν; Lucian, Vit. Auct. 7 τ. ἄσκησιν; Philo, Virt. 54 θεοῦ θεραπείαν; Tat. 23, 2; 36, 1; 42, 1) θεοσέβειαν *devotion* **1 Ti 2:10.** γνῶσιν **6:21.** πίστιν IEph 14:2; here also w. inf. foll. (cp. Wsd 2:13 γνῶσιν ἔχειν θεοῦ) Χριστοῦ εἶναι.—M-M. TW.

ἐπάγγελμα, ατος, τό (s. prec. entry; Pla., Demosth. al.; Philo; Jos., C. Ap. 1, 24) in our lit. only of God

❶ **a declaration to do someth. with implication of obligation to carry out what is stated, *promise*** κατὰ τὸ ἐ. *according to the promise* **2 Pt 3:13.**

❷ **the content of what is promised, *the thing promised*** (Ael. Aristid. 52 p. 599 D.; Philo, Mut. Nom. 128) τὰ μέγιστα ἐ. ἡμῖν δεδώρηται *(God) promised very great things and has granted them to us* **1:4.**—TW.

ἐπάγω (s. ἄγω) fut. ἐπάξω; 1 aor. ptc. ἐπάξας (B-D-F §75; W-S. §13, 10; Mlt-H. 226; Rob. 348); 2 aor. ἐπήγαγον. Pass.: aor. subj. 3 sg. ἐπάχθῃ Sir 2:4, impv. ἐπάχθητι (Mel., fgm. 8b 14), ptc. ἐπαχθείς 4 Macc 4:13 (cod. A for ὑπ-); pf. ptc. ἐπηγμένην 2 Macc 7:38 (Hom.+; also Just., A I, 3, 1, D. 39, 2 al., and 129, 4 ἐπήγαγον of words 'I added') **to cause a state or condition to be or occur, *bring on,*** *bring someth. upon someone,* mostly someth. bad, τινί τι (Hes., Op. 240 πῆμά τινι ἐ. al.; OGI 669, 43 πολλοῖς ἐ. κινδύνους; PRyl 144, 21 [38 AD] . . . μοι ἐ. αἰτίας; Bar 4:9, 10, 14, 29; Da 3:28, 31; TestJud 22:1; Philo, Mos. 1, 96; Jos., Vi. 18; SibOr 7, 154; Just., D. 39, 2 τὴν κρίσιν, 55, 2 κατάραν al.) κατακλυσμὸν κόσμῳ ἐπάξας **2 Pt 2:5** (cp. Gen 6:17; 3 Macc 2:4 of the deluge ἐπαγαγὼν αὐτοῖς ἀμέτρητον ὕδωρ). λύπην τῷ πνεύματι *bring grief upon the spirit* Hm 3:4. ἑαυτοῖς ταχινὴν ἀπώλειαν *bring swift destruction upon themselves* **2 Pt 2:1** (cp. ἑαυτοῖς δουλείαν Demosth. 19, 259). Also ἐπί τινά τι (Ex 11:1; 33:5; Jer 6:19; Ezk 28:7 al.; TestJud 23:3; ApcEsdr 2:20 p. 26, 12 Tdf.) ἐφ' ἡμᾶς τὸ αἷμα τ. ἀνθρώπου τούτου *bring this man's blood upon us* **Ac 5:28** (cp. Judg 9:24 B ἐπαγαγεῖν τὰ αἵματα αὐτῶν, τοῦ θεῖναι ἐπὶ 'Αβιμελεχ, ὃς ἀπέκτεινεν αὐτούς). ἐ. τισὶ διωγμὸν κατά τινος *stir up, within a group, a persecution against someone* **Ac 14:2** D.—M-M.

ἐπαγωνίζομαι (Dionys. Hal., Plut et al.; ins, Philo) **to exert intense effort on behalf of someth., *contend.*** When used in athletic imagery, the dat. dependent on it indicates for the most part either the one against whom one is contending (Plut., Fab. 187 [23, 2]), or the pers. or thing upon whom (which) one depends for support in rivalry (Plut., Numa 65 [8, 16] ἑτέροις τεκμηρίοις, of engagement in literary one-upmanship). τῇ πίστει **Jd 3,** fr. the context, can only mean *for the faith* (cp. Plut., Mor. 1075d; Michel 394, 19 [I BC] ἐπηγωνίσατο τῇ πρὸς τ. πόλιν εὐνοίᾳ). The primary semantic component in the use of this verb in Jd 3 is the effort expended by the subject in a noble cause; as such it is the counterpart of the author's πᾶσαν σπουδὴν ποιούμενος and a manifestation of ἀρετή, giving expression to the Gr-Rom. ideal of dedication to the welfare of the larger group.—DELG s.v. ἄγω. M-M. TW.

ἐπαθροίζω **to gather together in addition or besides, *increase,*** pass. in act. sense (Plut., Anton. 936 [44, 1] ἅμα δ' ἡμέρᾳ πολὺ πλείονας ἐπηθροίζοντο=as soon as it was day they teemed in greatly increased numbers to mount an attack) τῶν ὄχλων ἐπαθροιζομένων *when the crowds increased in numbers* **Lk 11:29.**—DELG s.v. ἄθρόος.

Ἐπαίνετος, ου, ὁ ***Epaenetus*** one of the first Christians in Asia **Ro 16:5.** For the name s. Diod. S. 19, 79, 2; SIG 43, 39; 585, 250; 944, 26; 1174, 4.—LGPN I. M-M.

ἐπαινέω fut. ἐπαινέσω; 1 aor. ἐπῄνεσα; 1 fut. pass. ἐπαινεσθήσομαι LXX (s. next entry; Hom.+; ins [esp. in honorific decrees], pap, LXX, EpArist; JosAs 24:11; Philo, Joseph., Test12Patr; Tat.; Ath. 15, 2) **to express one's admiration for or approval of a pers., object, or event,** ***praise*** τινά *someone* (Jos., Vi. 232 ἐμέ; 279; Tat.; Ath. 15, 2) **1 Cor 11:22a;** IMg 12; ISm 5:2; MPol 4. ἑαυτὸν ἐ. *praise oneself* Hs 9, 22, 2. τὶ *someth.* (Aelian, VH 2, 12; Jos., Ant. 14, 293 τ. ἔργον; Ar. 13, 7; Just., D 2:5) 1 Cl 33:6. Abs. **1 Cor 11:22b,** unless ὑμᾶς is to be supplied, cp. ibid. a. W. acc. and ὅτι foll. *praise someone because* or *in that* **Lk 16:8** (s. the lit. on οἰκονόμος 1; JDerrett, NTS 7, '60/61, 210 n. 3 'sanction'); **1 Cor 11:2.** τοῦτο … οὐκ ἐπαινῶ ὅτι *this is someth. I cannot praise* (approve of), *namely that* **11:17** (for the sense 'approve of': Appian, Bell. Civ. 3, 14 §49; Ael. Aristid. 24, 22 K.=44 p. 831 D.; Aelian, fgm. 235 p. 263, 17 τὸ θεῖον οὐκ ἐπῄνει τὰ ὑπὸ τ. βασιλέως πραττόμενα. Oft. Philostrat. [Schmid IV 294]; Jos., Ant. 14, 293. Other exx. in AFridrichsen, Horae Soederblomianae I/1, '44, 28–32. On the contrast between what can be commanded and what cannot cp. SIG 22, 10–26.). Pass. ἡ γῆ τοῦ Ἰακὼβ ἐπαινουμένη παρὰ πᾶσαν τὴν γῆν *praised above every land* B 11:9 (quot. fr. an unknown prophet). Also in relig. usage: *praise* God (Philo) **Ro 15:11** (Ps 116:1 v.l.); GJs 8:1.—DELG s.v. αἶνος. M-M. TW.

ἔπαινος, ου, ὁ (s. prec. entry; Simonides, Pind., Hdt.+).

❶ **the act of expressing admiration or approval,** ***praise, approval, recognition*****—ⓐ** toward humans (freq. in honorific ins)**—α.** from humans ἔκ τινος 1 Cl 30:6; **Ro 2:29; 13:3.** εἰς ἔπαινόν τινος *to give recognition to someone* **1 Pt 2:14** (WvanUnnik, NTS 2, '55, 198–202, w. ref. to Diod. S. 15, 1, 1). ὁ ἀδελφός, οὗ ὁ ἔ. ἐν τ. εὐαγγελίῳ διὰ πασῶν τῶν ἐκκλησιῶν *the brother whose fame in connection with the gospel has gone through all the churches* **2 Cor 8:18.**

β. from God (cp. Wsd 15:19; Just., D. 123, 4) 1 Cl 30:6; **Ro 2:29** (AFridrichsen, Symbolae Arctoae 1, 1922, 39–49). ὁ ἔ. γενήσεται ἑκάστῳ ἀπὸ τ. θεοῦ **1 Cor 4:5** (on ἔ. γίνεταί τινι cp. SIG 304, 24).—εἰς ἔ. καὶ δόξαν (for the combination of the two nouns cp. IPriene 53, 15 [II BC] ἀξίως ἐπαίνου καὶ τιμῶν ποιεῖσθαι τ. κρίσεις; 199, 9 [I BC]; Dio Chrys. 14 [31], 111 δόξα κ. ἔ. 1 Ch 16:27; s. b below) **1 Pt 1:7** (w. τιμή and δόξα; for the honorific aspect, cp. IPriene 53, 15 ἐ. w. τιμή; 119, 9 ἐ. w. δόξα).

ⓑ toward God (cp. Ps 21:26; 34:28; Sir 39:10; concrete 'song of praise' in God's honor: Diod. S. 3, 73, 5; Arrian, Anab. 7, 3, 3 ἔπαινοι θεῶν) εἰς δόξαν καὶ ἔ. (s. aβ above) θεοῦ **Phil 1:11;** cp. **Eph 1:6, 12, 14.**

❷ ***a thing worthy of praise*** (Sir 39:10 ἔ. αὐτοῦ='what is praiseworthy in him/his praiseworthy deeds') **Phil 4:8.** B. 1189.—DELG s.v. αἶνος. M-M. EDNT. TW. Sv.

ἐπαίρω (s. αἴρω) 1 aor. ἐπῆρα, inf. ἐπᾶραι, impv. 2 sg. ἔπαρον (JosAs 17:6), ptc. ἐπάρας; pf. ἐπῆρκα **J 13:18 v.l.** Pass.: 1 fut. ἐπαρθήσομαι LXX; 1 aor. ἐπήρθην; pf. ptc. ἐπηρμένος LXX (trag., Hdt.+).

❶ **to cause to move upward,** ***lift up, hold up*** τὶ *someth.* ῥάβδον *a staff* (Ex 10:13) Hv 3, 2, 4. τὸν ἀρτέμωνα **Ac 27:40** s. on ἀρτέμων. ἐπῆρεν ὁ ποιμὴν τὴν χεῖρα αὐτοῦ GJs 8:3 (not pap). Esp. in the expr. ἐ. χεῖρας *lift up, raise the hands* in prayer (Aesop, Fab. 49 P.=83 H./74 Ch./49 H-H.; Horapollo 1, 15 τ. χεῖρας εἰς οὐρανὸν ἐπαίροντα … προσευχόμενος τῇ θεῷ; 2 Esdr 18:6; Ps 133:2; for the idea cp. LvSybel, Christl. Antike I 1906, 256; 258; GAppel, De Romanorum Precationibus 1909, 194. Cp. also ἐκτείνω 1) **1 Ti 2:8,** or in blessing (Sir 50:20; JosAs 8:9 τὴν χεῖρα) **Lk 24:50.** ἐ. τὰς κεφαλάς (w. ἀνακύπτειν) *raise (your) heads* (Philo, Op. M. 158; Jos., Bell. 1, 629; cp. ἐ. τὸ πρόσωπον 4 Km 9:32; αὐχένα Philo, Fug. 107) of people who regain their courage **Lk 21:28.** ἐ. τοὺς ὀφθαλμούς (Gen 13:10; 1 Ch 21:16 al.) *look up* **Mt 17:8; Lk 16:23; J 4:35; 6:5;** εἴς τινα **Lk 6:20;** εἰς τὸν οὐρανόν *to heaven* **Lk 18:13** (En 13:5 οὐκέτι δύνανται … ἐπᾶραι τ. ὀφθ. εἰς τ. οὐρ. ἀπὸ αἰσχύνης περὶ ὧν ἡμαρτήκεισαν); **J 17:1.** ἐ. τὴν πτέρναν *raise one's heel* to tread on someone **13:18** (ἐπί τινα as 1 Km 20:33). ἐ. τὴν φωνήν *raise one's voice* (Demosth. 18, 291; Chariton 5, 7, 10; Philostrat., Vi. Apollon. 5, 33 p. 190, 21; Judg 2:4; 9:7; 2 Km 13:36) **Lk 11:27; Ac 2:14; 14:11; 22:22.**—Pass. *be taken up* **Ac 1:9.** Of the exaltation to heaven of those who endured 1 Cl 45:8.

❷ **to offer resistance to,** ***be in opposition, rise up*** ext. of mng. 1 (cp. in a difft. sense Just., A I, 58, 3 τῆς γῆς 'from the earth') ἐπί τινα or τι *against* or *to someone* or *someth.* (as 2 Esdr 4:19; 1 Macc 8:5; 10:70 TestJob 34:4 καθ' ἡμῶν) ἐπὶ τὸ ποίμνιον 1 Cl 16:1. κατά τινος: πᾶν ὕψωμα ἐπαιρόμενον κατὰ τ. γνώσεως τ. θεοῦ **2 Cor 10:5** (ὕψωμα 2).

❸ **to suggest that one is better than one really is,** ***be presumptuous, put on airs,*** abs. (Aristoph., Nub. 810; Thu. 4, 18, 4; Aeschin. 87, 24; Sir 11:4; 32:1; 1 Macc 2:63; Jos., Vi. 24) **2 Cor 11:20;** 1 Cl 21:5. W. ὑπερυψοῦσθαι 14:5 (Ps 36:35). W. the dat. to denote the basis for the presumption (Hdt. 9, 49; Thu. 1, 120, 3; X., Cyr. 8, 5, 24; Appian, Bell. Civ. 5, 118 §489 ταῖς ναυσὶν ἐπαιρόμενος=proud of his fleet; Zeph 1:11; Philo, Mos. 1, 70; Jos., Ant. 9, 193) ἑαυτοὺς βουλόμενοι ἐπαίρεσθαι τ. διανοίαις αὐτῶν *want to put on airs w. their imaginations* 1 Cl 39:1 (cp. Appian, Liby. 111 §522 ἐπήρθησαν τοῖς φρονήμασι=they became presumptuous in their self-reliance).—DELG s.v. 1ἀείρω. M-M. TW.

ἐπαισχύνομαι 1 aor. ἐπαισχύνθην **2 Ti 1:16;** 1 fut. ἐπαισχυνθήσομαι (s. αἰσχύνη; Aeschyl., Hdt. et al.; LXX; TestJos 2:5) **to experience a painful feeling or sense of loss of status because of some particular event or activity,** ***be ashamed.***

ⓐ w. acc. of pers. *of someone* (X., Hell. 4, 1, 34; Lucian, Dem. 46b) **Mk 8:38; Lk 9:26;** ISm 10:2b. W. acc. of thing (Pla., Soph. 247c; Diod. S. 1, 83, 4; Job 34:19) τοὺς λόγους *of the words* **Mk 8:38; Lk 9:26.** τὸ εὐαγγέλιον *of the gospel* **Ro 1:16** (OMichel, GWehrung Festschr. '40, 36–53). τὸ ὄνομα τοῦ κυρίου Hs 8, 6, 4; 9, 21, 3. τὸ μαρτύριον τοῦ κυρίου ἡμῶν *of witnessing to our Lord* **2 Ti 1:8.** τὴν ἅλυσίν μου *of my chains* vs. **16;** cp. ISm 10:2 (w. ὑπερηφανεῖν).

ⓑ w. ἐπί τινι *of a thing* (Is 1:29; cp. Aristot., De Rhet. 2, 2) ἐφ' οἷς νῦν ἐπαισχύνεσθε *of which you are now ashamed* **Ro 6:21**

ⓒ w. inf. foll. (Aeschyl., Ag. 1373; Lucian, Dem. 46a) οὐκ ἐ. ἀδελφοὺς αὐτοὺς καλεῖν *he is not ashamed* (i.e. is not too proud) *to call them brothers* **Hb 2:11;** Hs 9, 14, 6. W. acc. of the pers. and inf. **Hb 11:16.**

ⓓ abs. (Pla., Rep. 9, 573b; TestJos 2:5) **2 Ti 1:12;** GJs 17:1.—DELG s.v. αἶσχος. TW.

ἐπαιτέω 1 aor. impv. 3 pl. ἐπαιτησάτωσαν Ps 108:10 (Hom. et al. in sense 'ask for more'; pap, LXX) ***beg*** as a mendicant (so Soph., O. C. 1364; Cat. Cod. Astr. VIII/4 p. 140, 9; Ps 108:10;

Sir 40:28; Jos., Bell. 2, 295) **Lk 16:3; 18:35; Mk 10:46 v.l.**—M-M.

ἐπακολουθέω fut. ἐπακολουθήσω LXX; 1 aor. ἐπηκολούθησα (Aristoph., Thu.+; ins, pap, LXX; TestNapht 3:3; Philo, Joseph.; Just., D. 65, 2 λόγους ἐπακολουθοῦντας; Ath., R. 78, 29)

❶ **to use someone as a model for doing someth.,** ***follow*** τοῖς ἴχνεσιν αὐτοῦ *follow in (Christ's) footsteps* (Philo, Virt. 64) **1 Pt 2:21.** ἐπηκολούθησάν μοι εἰς λόγον θεοῦ *they followed me in God's cause* ISm 10:1 (cp. Philo, Leg. ad Gai. 185). Of the prophets, who followed Moses in time 1 Cl 43:1.

❷ **to happen as result or appropriate event in connection with someth.,** ***follow.*** In contrast to προάγω: Pol 3:3; **1 Ti 5:24.**—τὰ ἐπακολουθοῦντα σημεῖα **Mk 16:20** are not only the *following* or *accompanying signs,* but also *authenticating* (for this mng. of ἐ. cp. PTebt 100, 20f [117/116 BC]; PEleph 10, 8 [223 BC]; PGen 22, 1).

❸ **to apply oneself to someth. with eager dedication,** ***follow after,*** i.e. *devote oneself to* someth., w. dat. (cp. Pla., Rep. 2, 370c; Josh 14:14 τῷ προστάγματι κυρίου; Jos., C. Ap. 1, 6) παντὶ ἔργῳ ἀγαθῷ ἐ. *devote oneself to every good work* **1 Ti 5:10.**—DELG s.v. ἀκόλουθος. M-M. TW.

ἐπακούω fut. ἐπακούσομαι; 1 aor. ἐπήκουσα; pf. 3 sg. ἐπακήκοε LXX; inf. ἐπακηκοέναι (Just., D. 137, 4); 1 aor. pass. 3 sg. ἐπηκούσθη 2 Ch 30:27 (s. ἀκούω; Hom. [Il. 2, 143 in the sense 'hear about']+; Tat. 30, 2 'understand' a foreign tongue). On LXX s. JBarr, JTS 31, '80, 67–72.

❶ **to pay close attention to what one is told w. implication of being responsive,** ***hear, listen to*** (Aeschyl., Choëph. 725; Lucian, Tim. 34 τ. εὐχῶν; Mitt-Wilck. I/2, 478, 6=BGU 1080, 6; IMaronIsis 7; PGM 13, 207 μοι; LXX; τῆς φωνῆς ἡμῶν En 103:14; 106:8; Jos., Ant. 9, 10) τινός *someone* (Lucian, Pseudolog. 23; UPZ 78, 24 [159 BC] Isis, ἐπάκουσόν μου; PGM 3, 497; Gen 17:20 al.; TestAbr A 14 p. 94, 2 [Stone p. 36]; JosAs 14:2) 1 Cl 8:3 (quot. of unknown orig.; cp. Is 65:24); B 3:5; ἐπήκουσά σου **2 Cor 6:2** (Is 49:8; CCox, Biblica 62, '81, 251–58); τῆς δεήσεως GJs 2:4; 4:1f; 20:3 (last not pap); προσευχομένου Ἰωνᾶ AcPlCor 2:30.—OWeinreich, Θεοὶ ἐπήκοοι: MAI 37, 1912, 1–68.

❷ **to act appropriately in response to what one hears,** ***heed, obey*** (Hes., Op. 275; Hdt. 4, 141; Pla., Soph., 227c; Vett. Val. 67, 16; Judg 2:17 A; 1 Macc 10:38 v.l.) abs. πρέπον ἐστὶν ἐ. κατὰ μηδεμίαν ὑπόκρισιν *it is fitting to be obedient without hypocrisy* IMg 3:2. ἔμπροσθέν τινος *before someone = obey someone* B 12:11 (Is 45:1).—New Docs 1, 15. M-M. TW. Spicq. Sv.

ἐπακροάομαι impf. ἐπηκροώμην (Menand., Epitr. 934 S. [614 Kö.]; Plato Com. [V/IV BC], fgm. 16 al.; Hobart 234 [Hippocr.]) ***listen to*** τινός *someone* (Lucian, Icar. 1; Philostrat., Vi. Apoll. 4, 36 p. 154, 13; TestJos 8:5) in the sense of overhearing **Ac 16:25.**—DELG s.v. ἀκούω. M-M.

ἐπάλληλος, ον **pert. to someth. happening again and again,** ***in rapid succession*** (Polyb., Diod. S. Plut. et al.; PFamTebt 15, 68 and 90) esp. of misfortunes (Plut., Pomp. 632 [25, 10]; Philo, Mos. 2, 263, In Flacc. 121 τὰς συνεχεῖς κ. ἐπαλλήλους κακώσεις; Jos., Bell. 5, 32) *happening repeatedly* ἐ. γενόμεναι συμφοραί 1 Cl 1:1.—DELG s.v. ἄλλος.

ἐπάν temporal conj. used w. subj. (X. et al.; ins, pap; Bel 11. As ἐπήν Hom. et al.; LXX; Just., D. 69, 3) ***when, as soon as*** w. pres. subj. ἐ. πονηρὸς ᾖ *when it is unsound* **Lk 11:34.** W. aor. subj., like the Lat. fut. exactum (Jos., Ant. 8, 302) ἐ. εὕρητε *when you have found* (him) **Mt 2:8.** ἐ. νικήσῃ αὐτόν lit. *when he will have overcome him* **Lk 11:22.**—M-M.

ἐπάναγκες (s. ἀνάγκη) neut. of ἐπανάγκης, which occurs only in the neut. ('compulsory' Andoc, 1, 12; Pla. Leg. 878e et al.) and in our lit. only as adv. (Hdt. et al.; Epict. 2, 20, 1; M. Ant. 1, 16, 8; ins, pap; Jos., Ant. 16, 365) **pert. to being essential in connection w. someth.,** ***of a necessary nature*** τὰ ἐπάναγκες *the necessary things = the things necessarily (to be imposed)* **Ac 15:28.**—DELG s.v. ἀνάγκη. M-M.

ἐπανάγω (s. ἀνάγω) aor. ἐπανήγαγον; pass. ptc. ἐπαναχθέντας 2 Macc 12:4 (ἀχθέντας cod. A) (Hdt. et al.; ins, pap, LXX, EpArist; Jos., Ant. 12, 128; 345) 'lead' or 'bring up', in our lit. only intrans.

❶ **to leave the shore so as to get into open water,** ***go out, put out*** to sea ἠρώτησεν αὐτὸν ἀπὸ τῆς γῆς ἐ. ὀλίγον *he asked him to push off a bit from shore* **Lk 5:3** (trans.='put out' ships and men at sea X., Hell. 6, 2, 28 ἀπὸ τῆς γῆς; 2 Macc 12:4). εἰς τὸ βάθος *to the deep water* vs. **4.**

❷ **to go back toward some point or area,** ***return*** (X., Cyr. 4, 1, 3; Diod. S. 16, 26 al.; 2 Macc 9:21) εἰς τὴν πόλιν **Mt 21:18.**—M-M.

ἐπανακάμπτω 1 aor. ἐπανέκαμψα (Aristot.; Aq., Sym., Theod. Is 35:10) **to come back to a place or person,** ***return*** (Syntipas p. 14, 8 al.) εἰς τὴν πόλιν Hs 1:2, 5. ἐπὶ τὰς παρθένους *to the virgins* s 9, 14, 1.—DELG s.v. κάμπτω.

ἐπαναμιμνῄσκω (also -ήσκω) 1 aor. pass. ἐπανεμνήσθην **to cause to remember,** ***remind someone*** (τινά) *of someth. again* (Pla., Leg. 3, 688a; Demosth. 6, 35) **Ro 15:15.** Pass. *call to mind, remember* someth. *again* τοῦ ῥήματος Hv 4, 1, 7.—DELG s.v. μιμνήσκω.

ἐπαναπαύομαι (found in act. in Aelian, NA 5, 56 and Judg 16:26 A; the mid. occurs in Hero Alex. I p. 424, 12; Epict.; Artem.; Herodian 2, 1, 2; Jos., Ant. 8, 84, almost always in LXX, once TestSol 7:7 P, and without exception in our lit.) fut. ἐπαναπαύσομαι; 1 aor. ἐπανεπαυσάμην LXX; pf. 3 sg. ἐπαναπέπαυται 4 Km 2:15; **1 Pt 4:14 v.l.** Pass.: 2 fut. 3 sg. ἐπαναπαήσεται **Lk 10:6** (-παύσεται v.l.); 2 aor. ἐπανεπάην D 4:2.

❶ **to be in a state or condition of repose,** ***rest, take one's rest*** GHb 70, 18=Ox 654, 8f (but the latter text in fragmentary state, s. editor's note); B 4:13. With implication of benefits bestowed in the process ἐπί τινα *rest upon someone* ἐπ᾽ αὐτὸν ἡ εἰρήνη ὑμῶν *your peace will rest upon him* **Lk 10:6** (Num 11:25, 26 ἐπανεπαύσατο τ. πνεῦμα ἐπ᾽ αὐτούς; 4 Km 2:15; cp. **1 Pt 4:14 v.l.**)

❷ **to find well-being or inner security,** ***find rest, comfort, support*** τινί *in someth.* and ἐπί τινα *on someone* (LXX) fig. (Herm. Wr. 9, 10 τῇ πίστει ἐ.) τοῖς λόγοις τ. ἁγίων D 4:2. ἐπὶ τὸν πένητα Hs 1, 2, 5 (s. ἀναπαύω). In the sense *rely on* (Trypho Gr. 194 [I BC]; Artem. 4, 65; Epict. 1, 9, 9; Mi 3:11; 1 Macc 8:11) νόμῳ **Ro 2:17.**—M-M. TW.

ἐπανατρέχω (ἀνατρέχω 'run back') 2 aor. ἐπανέδραμον (Philod., De Ira p. 63 W.; Lucian, Merc. Cond. 36; PLond III, 1044, 14 p. 254 [VI AD]; V, 1727, 46; Jos., Ant. 18, 361) **to run toward someth.,** ***race,*** in imagery of a runner who makes the turn on the track and heads for the goal, but prob. without pressing details *run, hasten on* ἐπὶ τὸν σκοπόν *toward the goal* 1 Cl 19:2 ('run again to the goal'; s. UWickert, ZNW 49, '58, 270–75; recurramus cod. Namurc.).

ἐπανέρχομαι (s. ἀνέρχομαι) fut. ἐπανελεύσομαι LXX; 2 aor. ἐπανῆλθον; pf. ἐπανελήλυθεν (Just., D. 56, 8) (Eur., Hdt. et al.) **to come back to a point or area,** ***return*** (so Thu., X., Pla.; SIG 591, 7 [c. 195 BC]; PLond III, 904, 23f p. 125 [104 AD]; POxy 933, 17; PTebt 333, 10; Pr 3:28; 2 Macc 4:36; Jos., Bell. 7, 106, Ant. 1, 91; Just., D 56, 6 al.; 56:1 ἐπὶ τὰς γραφὰς ἐπανελθών 'come back to the Scriptures') abs. ἐν τῷ ἐπανέρχεσθαί με *when I return* **Lk 10:35;** cp. **19:15;** Hs 8, 2, 9.—M-M.

ἐπανήκω (ἀνήκω 'to have come up to a point') fut. ἐπανήξω ***come back again*** (since Eur., Iph. A. 1628, also Polyb. 6, 58, 3; SIG 730, 6; PAmh 50, 5; Sb 9123, 4 [both II BC]; PGron 18, 8; LXX; EpArist 8; Jos., Ant. 12, 179; 191) Hs 9, 11, 2.

ἐπανίστημι (s. ἀνίστημι) 'set up, cause to arise'; fut. mid. ἐπαναστήσομαι. Also 1 aor. act. ptc. ἐπαναστήσας (Mel., P. 82, 609 cj. Bonner); 2 aor. act. ἐπανέστην; pf. ptc. ἐπανεστηκότων Dt 33:11; **to become active in forceful resistance or expression of hostility,** ***rise up, rise in rebellion*** (so since Il. 2, 85; Hdt., Thu., Aristoph., LXX, TestJob; ApcEsdr 3:13 p. 27, 25 Tdf.; ApcMos 24; Philo, Spec. Leg. 3, 17; SibOr 11, 175; PHib 249, 5; Sb 9302, 7 [both III BC]; Tat. 7, 2; Ath. 21, 3; Mel., fgm. 5) τινί *against someone* (so Hdt., Thu. et al.; Dt 33:11; Jdth 5:11; 16:17; PsSol; Jos., Bell. 1, 24; 2, 443; Tat., Ath.) ἐπανέστησάν μοι *have risen against me* B 5:13 (Ps 26:12). Also ἐπί τινα (LXX) **Mt 10:21; Mk 13:12** (cp. Mi 7:6).—M-M.

ἐπανόρθωσις, εως, ἡ 'correcting, restoration' (cp. e.g. ISardGauthier 3, 1 'restoration' of a city; 1 Esdr 8:52; 1 Macc 14:34) then in transf. sense ***improvement*** (Ps.-Pla., Tim. L., 104a; Heraclid. Lembus, Pol. 14 [Aristot., fgm. 611, 14 Rose]; Plut., Mor. 22a; 46d al.—ἐ. τοῦ βίου: Polyb. 1, 35, 1; cp. the verb ἐπανορθόω Strabo 9, 1, 20; Epict. 3, 21, 15 οὕτως ὠφέλιμα γίνεται τὰ μυστήρια . . . , ὅτι ἐπὶ ἐπανορθώσει τ. βίου κατεστάθη πάντα . . . , cp. Enchir. 51, 1; Iambl., Vi. Pyth. 6, 30; 21, 96 πρὸς ἐ.; POxy 78, 29; 237 VIII, 30; EpArist 130; 283 πρὸς ἐ.; Philo, Ebr. 91 πρὸς ἐ., Conf. Lingu. 182, Leg. All. 1, 85; cp. 2 Macc 2:22) ὠφέλιμος πρὸς ἐ. *useful for improvement* **2 Ti 3:16.**—B. 751. New Docs 2, 84. DELG s.v. ὀρθός. TW. Spicq.

ἐπάνω adv. (s. ἄνω; Hdt.+)—**❶ marker of a position relatively higher whether contiguous or not,** ***above, over***—ⓐ as adv. (Gen 7:20; Bar 2:5; Jos., C. Ap. 1, 33) *over, above, on* of place (En 18:5) οἱ ἄνθρωποι οἱ περιπατοῦντες ἐ. οὐκ οἴδασιν *the people who walk over (them) know nothing (about them)* **Lk 11:44.** In ref. to text previously cited προείρηκε δὲ ἐ. *(God) stated it above* B 6:18. τὰ ἐ. (cp. SIG 972, 74; 82; POxy 502, 54 τὰ ἐ.=what has been mentioned above) *the upper parts* (PGM 2, 157 τὰ ἐ. τῆς θύρας) of plants Hs 9, 1, 6; 9, 21, 1. Of couch covering ἐ. κεῖσθαι v 3, 1, 4.

ⓑ as prep. w. gen. (SIG 1173, 3 ἐ. τ. βήματος POxy 495, 8; PFlor 50, 32; LXX; En 32:2 ἐ. τῆς Ἐρυθρᾶς θαλάσσης; Jos., Bell. 2, 344, Ant. 6, 274; Just., A I, 60, 6 ἐ. τῶν ὑδάτων) ἐ. ὄρους *on (the top of) a hill* **Mt 5:14;** ἐ. τῆς πύλης Hs 9, 4, 2; ἐ. αὐτῶν **Mt 21:7;** cp. **23:18, 20, 22; 27:37; 28:2; Rv 6:8; 20:3.** ἐ. αὐτῆς prob. *at her head* **Lk 4:39** (perh. also poss.: bending *over her*) πατεῖν ἐ. ὄφεων *tread on snakes* **Lk 10:19** (cp. PGM 13, 282 ἐὰν θέλῃς ἐπάνω κροκοδείλου διαβαίνειν). ἐ. τῶν ὀρέων *over the mountains* D 9:4. ἐ. τῶν νεφελῶν τοῦ οὐρανοῦ 16:8 (cp. Mt 24:30; 26:64); ἐ. τῆς πέτρας Hs 9, 3, 1. ἐστάθη ἐ. οὗ ἦν τὸ παιδίον *stopped over the place where the child was* **Mt 2:9.**

❷ pert. to exceeding someth. in amount, ***more than,*** as adv. w. numbers (colloq. B-D-F §185; s. Rob. 666; cp. Lev 27:7) ὤφθη ἐ. πεντακοσίοις ἀδελφοῖς *he appeared to more than 500 of our fellowship* ('brothers'; s. ἀδελφός 2a) **1 Cor 15:6.** πραθῆναι ἐ. δηναρίων τριακοσίων *be sold for more than 300 denarii* **Mk 14:5.**

❸ pert. to being superior in status, ***above, over,*** *someth.* fig. (Socrat., Ep. 20 ὧν ἐ. πλούτου [p. 268 Malherbe]), funct. as prep. w. gen., of authority (Da 6:3 Theod.) ἐξουσία ἐ. δέκα πόλεων **Lk 19:17,** cp. **19.** ἐ. πάντων ἐστίν *is above all* **J 3:31** (Cebes 26, 3 ἐ. πάντων ἐστί; Jos., Ant. 4, 216 τὸ δίκαιον ἐπάνω πάντων).—DELG s.v. ἀνά. M-M.

ἐπάνωθεν adv. (s. prec. entry; Eur., Thu., Pla.+; LXX; EpArist 105) ***from above*** αὐτοὶ περιεσχίσαντο ἐ. ἕως κάτω *they* (themselves) *tore* (their garments) *from top to bottom* GJs 24:3 (v.l. ἀπὸ ἄνωθεν; cp. Mt. 27:51; Mk 15:38).

ἐπάξας s. ἐπάγω.

ἐπαοιδός, οῦ, ὁ (Ionic form, dominant in the Koine [Manetho, Apot. 5, 138; Epict. 3, 24, 10; LXX; Philo, Migr. Abr. 83; SibOr 225] for the Attic ἐπῳδός; s. Lob., Phryn. p. 243) **one who uses charms or incantations to get what one desires,** ***enchanter*** D 3:4.—GWalsh, The Varieties of Enchantment '84 (early Gk views of the function of poetry).—DELG s.v. ἀείδω.

ἐπᾶραι, ἔπαρον, ἐπάρας s. ἐπαίρω.

ἐπάρατος, ον (ἐπαράομαι 'imprecate'; Thu. et al.; Cass. Dio; SIG 799, 23 [38 AD]; Philo; Jos., Ant. 1, 58; 6, 117; 7, 208) **pert. to being pronounced outside the realm of the sacred, with implication of being under divine condemnation,** ***accursed*** **J 7:49.** On this subject s. Billerb. II 494–519.—DELG s.v. ἀρά. M-M. TW.

ἐπαρκέω fut. ἐπαρκέσω LXX; 1 aor. ἐπήρκεσα; aor. mid. impv. 3 sg. ἐπαρκείσθω (Hom. et al.; pap; 1 Macc 8:26; 11:35; Jos., Ant. 8, 113) **to come to the aid of someone,** ***help, aid*** (Jos., Ant. 15, 119) τινί *someone* (Hdt.; Aristoph., Plut. 830; X., Mem. 2, 7, 1 ἀλλήλοις ἐ.; Aristot., EN 4, 2 [1120a 3]; 8, 14 and 16 [1162a 23; 1163a 34]; Polyb. 1, 51, 10; Lucian, Nigr. 26 τ. δεομένοις; Jos., Ant. 1, 247) θλιβομένοις **1 Ti 5:10;** *provide for* χήραις vs. **16** (v.l. ἐπαρκείσθω).—DELG s.v. ἀρκέω. M-M.

ἐπαρχεία, ας, ἡ (s. next entry; -ία Ar. 15, 2; on the spelling s. B-D-F §23; Mlt-H. 315) **a Roman administrative area ruled by an ἔπαρχος or prefect,** ***province*** (Polyb. 1, 15, 10; 2, 19, 2 al.; OGI index VIII p. 657; POxy 471, 22; 1410, 3; cp. Preis. III 112; LXX only as v.l.; PsSol 22, 5 P; Jos., Bell. 5, 520; Ar. 15, 2; loanw. in rabb.) **Ac 23:34; 25:1** (Mlt-H. 157). See ἔπαρχος and ref. to Mason, but s. also New Docs 2, 85; JBertrand, Cités et royaumes du monde grec '92, 461f, n. 14.—DELG s.v. ἄρχω. M-M.

ἐπάρχειος, ον pert. to being governed by an ἔπαρχος or prefect, ***provincial*** ἡ ἐπάρχειος (sc. χώρα) *province* (s. prec. entry; OGI 549, 2; IG XIV, 911): ἐπιβὰς τῇ ἐ. *after he had arrived in the province* **Ac 25:1 v.l.** (s. ἐπαρχεία).

ἐπαρχικός, ή, όν pert. to an ἔπαρχος or prefect, ***prefectural*** (see next entry) (lit.; ins, e.g. OGI 578, 14) ἐπαρχικὴ ἐξουσία *with authority of a prefect* (Cass. Dio 75, 14, 1) **Phlm subscr. v.l.** (s. N.[25] or earlier). This refers to an office in Rome, that of the 'praefectus urbi', the governor of the capital city.

ἔπαρχος, ου, ὁ (s. prec. three entries; Aeschyl. et al.; ins [incl. Boffo, Iscrizioni no. 30, 4], pap, LXX; Jos., Ant. 20, 193 al.)

prefect, commanding officer (s. Hahn 118, 8; MMentz, De Magistratuum Romanorum Graecis Appellationibus, diss. Jena 1904, 46f). w. other military officers 1 Cl 37:3.—Mason 45, 138–40.

ἔπαυλις, εως, ἡ (s. αὐλή; Hdt. et al.; ins, pap, LXX; ἐπαύλη 'stall' TestJob 40, 5; 8) **property that serves as a dwelling place whether personally owned or by contract, *farm, homestead, residence*** (Diod. S. 12, 43, 1; 12, 45, 1; Plut., Per. 170 [33, 3]; Cato Maior 337 [2]; Sulla 466 [22] al.; SIG 364, 13 [III BC]; PTebt 120, 130; POxy 248, 28 and other pap; LXX; Philo, Abr. 139, Spec. Leg. 2, 116, Mos. 1, 330 al.; Jos., Bell. 2, 57 al.) **Ac 1:20** (Ps 68:26).—DELG s.v. αὐλή. M-M. TW.

ἐπαύριον (s. αὔριον) adv. 'tomorrow' (Polyb. 8, 15, 6; PLille 15, 2 [242 BC]; PTebt 119, 17; LXX; on the sp. ἐφ- s. deStrycker, Protevangile, p. 230) in our lit. almost exclusively (as Polyb. 3, 53, 6; PHamb 27, 4 [III BC] and mostly LXX; TestSol; TestIss 3:4; GrBar 9:3) τῇ ἐ. (sc. ἡμέρᾳ) ***on the next day*** **Mt 27:62; Mk 11:12; J 1:29, 35, 43; 6:22; 12:12; Ac 10:9, 23f; 14:20; 20:7; 21:8; 22:30; 23:32; 25:6, 23;** GJs 5:1; AcPl Ha 7, 12. εἰς τὴν ἐ. (Polyb. 8, 13, 6) *until the next day* **Ac 4:3 v.l.**—M-M.

ἐπαφίημι fut. ἐπαφήσω; 2 aor. subj. ἐπαφῶ (s. ἀφίημι; X. et al.; pap, LXX; Jos., Ant. 19, 175) **to remove retraints from someth. and permit it to do what it wishes, *let loose upon*** τινά τινι (Paus. 1, 12, 3 ἐλέφαντάς τινι) τῷ Πολυκάρπῳ λέοντα MPol 12:2.

Ἐπαφρᾶς, ᾶ, ὁ (GDI 1489, 1 [Locris]; CIG I, 268, 37; II, 1963, 1; 2248, 4; SIG 1112, 26; 1243, 34) ***Epaphras*** (prob. short form of Ἐπαφρόδιτος q.v.; s. W-S. §16, 9; B-D-F §125, 1; Mlt-H. 119; 314) a Christian of Colossae **Col 4:12,** founder of the church there **1:7;** cp. **Phlm 23.**—LGPN I. M-M.

ἐπαφρίζω (Moschus 5, 5 intr. 'foam up') trans.: **to cause to splash up like froth, *cause to foam*** τὶ fig. κύματα ἐπαφρίζοντα (ἀπαφρ. v.l.) τὰς ἑαυτῶν αἰσχύνας *waves casting up their own shameless deeds like (dirty) foam,* perh. imaging the dirty appearance of foam created under certain conditions **Jd 13.**—DELG s.v. ἀφρός.

Ἐπαφρόδιτος, ου, ὁ (very common, also in ins and pap; s. also Schürer I 48, 9) ***Epaphroditus,*** messenger sent by the Phil. church to Paul **Phil 2:25; 4:18; subscr.**—RHarris, Ep., Scribe and Courier: Exp., 5th ser., 8, 1898, 101–10.—LGPN I. M-M.

ἐπέβην s. ἐπιβαίνω.

ἐπεγείρω fut. ἐπεγερῶ LXX; 1 aor. ἐπήγειρα. Pass.: 1 fut. ἐπεγερθήσομαι LXX; 1 aor. ἐπηγέρθην (s. ἐγείρω; Hom. et al.; LXX; En 99:16; TestLevi 10:2; SibOr 3, 153; Philo, Mos. 1, 297; Jos., Ant. 8, 371) 'rouse up, awaken'; in our lit. only fig., **to cause an activity to begin through provocation, *arouse, excite, stir up*** τὶ *someth.* (Maximus Tyr. 23, 6b; Jos., Ant. 14, 442 τὸ φρόνημα) τὰς ψυχὰς τ. ἐθνῶν (κατά τινος) **Ac 14:2.** ἐ. διωγμὸν ἐπί τινα *stir up a persecution against someone* **13:50** (TestLevi 10:2 ἐπεγ. ἐπ᾽ αὐτὸν κακά). Pass. in act. sense ἐπεγείρεσθαι ἐπί τινα *be aroused against someone,* also *rise up, revolt against someone* 1 Cl 3:3 (cp. SIG 730, 10 [I BC]; Is 19:2; Jer 29:7; Mi 5:4).—M-M.

ἐπεί conj. (Hom.+. For early Gk. s. lit. LfgrE s.v. ἐπεί 626.).

❶ **marker of time at which, *when, after*** (Diod. S. 3, 35, 1; Ps.-Callisth. 3, 34, 4 ἐπεὶ ἦλθον=when they had come; Just., A II, 2, 2 [ἐπειδή v.l.]; Ath. 4:2) in NT only as a v.l. in **Lk 7:1** for ἐπειδή (B-D-F §455, 1; Rob. 971); Dg 8:11; 9:2; MPol 8:1.

❷ **marker of cause or reason, *because, since, for*** **Mt 18:32; 21:46; 27:6; Mk 15:42; Lk 1:34; J 13:29; 19:31; Ac 13:46 v.l.; 1 Cor 14:12; 2 Cor 11:18; 13:3; Hb 5:2, 11; 6:13; 9:17; 11:11;** 2 Cl 2:3; B 6:2f, 11 al.; cp. Hs 5, 5, 1; 6, 5, 1; AcPt Ox 849, 28; AcPl Ha 8, 13. ἐπεὶ καί *since indeed* (as Appian, Bell. Civ. 5, 71 §302; Ar., Oxy 1778, 33; Just., D. 112, 2; 122, 3 al.) B 7:3; GPt 2:5; MPol 6:2. ἐ. οὖν inferential *since, then* (X., Mem. 3, 9, 5; Job 35:7; 4 Macc 4:26) **Hb 2:14; 4:6;** B 12:10; IEph 1:3; IMg 2; 5:1; 6:1; IPol 8:1. οὐκ ἐπεί *not that* IMg 11:1; ITr 8:1. ἐ. οὐχ ὅτι IMg 3:2 (see ὅτι 2b). W. ellipsis *for* (if it were different), *for otherwise* (also earlier Gk.: Pla., Euthyphro 9b; X., Cyr. 2, 2, 31; Aristot., EN 2, 2, 1 [1103b 28]. Also Plut., Agis 795 [2, 5]; Epict., Ench. 33, 9; BGU 530, 30; 4 Macc 1:33; 2:7, 19 al.; B-D-F §456, 3; Rob. 1025f) **Ro 3:6; 11:6, 22; 1 Cor 14:16; 15:29; Hb 10:2;** AcPlCor 2:9 (cp. UPZ 110, 204 [164 BC] ἐπεὶ οὐκ ἂν οὕτως ἀλόγητοι ἦτε='for otherwise you would not be so unreasonable'). In an anacolouthon IRo 1:1. ἐ. ἔδει αὐτὸν πολλάκις παθεῖν *for otherwise he would have had to suffer many times* **Hb 9:26.** ἐ. ἄρα *for otherwise, you see* **1 Cor 5:10; 7:14.**—ἐπείπερ (Aeschyl. et al.; pap; Jos., Ant. 18, 296; 19, 268) *inasmuch as, seeing that* **Ro 3:30 v.l.** (for εἴπερ; s. also ἐπειδήπερ).—DELG. M-M.

ἐπείγω 1 aor. pass. ἠπείχθην Jer 17:16 Sym; Hos 6:3 Quinta (Joseph.) (in var. mgs. since Hom.; LXX; TestJos 2:2; Joseph.; Just., A I, 46, 6) **to exert pressure against, *press hard*** τὸ ἐν ἐμοὶ ἐπείγει με προελθεῖν *what is in me presses hard to come forth = my baby is about to come* GJs 17:3.—DELG.

ἐπειδή conj. (Hom.+)—❶ **marker of time at which, *when, after*** (Pherecyd. 14; Demosth. 18, 42; 213; Arrian, Anab. 5, 20, 1; Jos., Bell. 1, 231, Ant. 2, 334 al.; Just., A II, 2, 5f, D. 17, 1 al.; Ath. 6, 2) **Lk 7:1** (v.l. ἐπεὶ δέ).

❷ **marker of cause or reason,** *(just) because* (Diod. S. 19, 100, 7; cp. Just., D. 125, 2 ἐπειδή γε) **Lk 11:6; Ac 13:8** D, **46; 14:12; 15:24; 1 Cor 1:22; 14:16; Phil 2:26;** GPt 6:23; ApcPt 4:11; D 3:4; 5:6; 1 Cl 57:4 (Pr 1:24); 62:3; 2 Cl 12:1; B 7:5, 9; 12:5; IPhld 10:1; IPol 7:1; Hs 9, 13, 6; Dg 1:1; MPol 4:1; 12:2. ἐπειδὴ γάρ *for since* (Hero I p. 32, 20; Philo, Aet. M. 121; Just., D. 36, 6) **1 Cor 1:21; 15:21;** Hs 9, 1, 2.—M-M.

ἐπειδήπερ conj., intensified form of ἐπειδή (Thu. 6, 18, 3 and other Attic wr.; Aristot., Phys. 8, 5 p. 256b, 25; Dionys. Hal. 2, 72; ins; PFlor 118, 5; PRyl 238, 10; PStras 5, 10; Philo, In Flacc. 32, Leg. ad Gai. 164, Vi. Cont. 10; Jos., Bell. 7, 102, Ant. 1, 34; 5, 74) **a marker of cause or reason, *inasmuch as, since*** ('w. ref. to a fact already known' B-D-F §456, 3) **Lk 1:1** (Diod. S. 4, 7, 1: 'since we have referred to the Muses in connection with Dionysus, it is appropriate to recount the main facts about them'; Jos., Bell. 1, 17. The freq. inscriptional use of the simplex ἐπειδή in the protasis of preambles of official documents, w. the verb δοκέω foll. (as in **Lk 1:3**) in the apodosis, suggests that Luke enriches the mng. of his own preamble with a solemn tone); **Ro 3:30 v.l.;** cp. ἐπείπερ (ἐπεί end).—M-M.

ἐπεῖδον 2 aor. of ἐφοράω, impv. ἔπιδε, inf. ἐπιδεῖν (s. εἶδον; Hom.+; pap, LXX; TestSol C prol. 2; for Just. s. ἐπιβλέπω; Jos., Bell. 1, 76, Ant. 2, 346; SibOr 5, 329) **to fix one's glance upon, *look at, concern oneself with*** (of God's concern w. human things: Aeschyl.; Jos., C. Ap. 2, 181) ἐπί τι (1 Macc 3:59; 3 Macc 6:3) **Ac 4:29.** ἐπί τινι *look with favor on someone* or *someth.* 1 Cl 4:2 (Gen 4:4). W. inf. foll. ἀφελεῖν ὄνειδός μου *to take away my reproach* **Lk 1:25.** S. ἐφοράω.—HMiddendorf, Gott sieht, diss. Freiburg '35.—M-M.

ἔπειμι (fr. εἶμι) ***come upon, come near;*** ptc. ἐπιών, οῦσα, όν; this is the only form used in our lit., nearly always in the fem., and of time τῇ ἐπιούσῃ ἡμέρᾳ *on the next day* (Hdt. et al.; also Jos., C. Ap. 1, 309; in other mgs. Just., A I, 62, 1 [for ἀπ-]; Tat. 16, 3; Ath. 10, 2) **Ac 7:26.** Also simply τῇ ἐ. (Polyb. 2, 25, 11; 5, 13, 10; Appian, Mithrid. 99 §458; PPetr III, 56b, 12; Pr 3:28; 27:1; Jos., Ant. 3, 30; 4, 64) **16:11; 20:15; 21:18.** τῇ ἐπιούσῃ νυκτί *the next night* (Ael. Aristid. 48, 75 K.=24 p.485 D.) **23:11.** τῷ ἐπιόντι σαββάτῳ **18:19** D.—S. ἐπιούσιος (Hultgren). M-M.

ἐπείπερ conj. (Aeschyl. et al.; pap; Jos., Ant. 18, 296; 19, 268) **in view of the fact that, *since indeed* Ro 3:30 v.l.**—New Docs 2, 135. M-M.

ἐπεισαγωγή, ῆς, ἡ (since Thu. 8, 92, 1) **the process of causing someth. to be present, *bringing in (besides), introduction*** (Hippocr., Praec. 7; CMG I/1 p. 32, 23; Dionys. Hal., Veterum Cens. 2, 2, 10; Jos., Ant. 11, 196 ἑτέρας [of an additional wife] ἐ.) γίνεται ἐ. κρείττονος ἐλπίδος *a better hope is introduced* **Hb 7:19.**—DELG s.v. ἄγω. M-M (on cognates).

ἐπεισέρχομαι fut. ἐπεισελεύσομαι; 2 aor. 3 pl. ἐπεισῆλθον (-θόσαν v.l. 1 Macc 16:16); pf. 3 sg. ἐπεισελήλυθεν (Just., D. 53, 2) (Hdt. et al.; pap; Philo, Op. M. 119) 'rush in suddenly and forcibly' (UPZ 13, 19 [160 BC]; 1 Macc 16:16; Jos., Ant. 11, 265) ***come*** ἐπί τινα *upon someone* of the Day of Judgment ἐπὶ πάντας τοὺς καθημένους ἐπὶ πρόσωπον πάσης τῆς γῆς **Lk 21:35.**—M-M. Lit. s. ἐπέρχομαι.

ἔπειτα adv. (Hom.+)—❶ **being next in order of time, *then, thereupon.***—ⓐ without specific indication of chronological sequence **Mk 7:5 v.l.; Lk 16:7; Gal 1:21; Js 4:14;** 2 Cl 11:4; 13:3; D 12:1. Pleonast. ἔ. μετὰ τοῦτο (Pla., Lach. 190d; Sosipater 16 [in Athen. 9, 378b]) **J 11:7** (εἶτα v.l.). ἔ. μετὰ τρία ἔτη **Gal 1:18;** cp. **2:1.**

ⓑ together w. indications of chronological sequence πρῶτον … ἔ. *first … then* (X., An. 3, 2, 27; Diod. S. 16, 69, 4; Ael. Aristid. 23, 6 K.=42 p. 769 D.; 4 Macc 6:3; Jos., Ant. 12, 92) **1 Cor 15:46; 1 Th 4:17;** Pol 4:2. πρότερον … ἔπειτα **Hb 7:27;** ἀπαρχή … ἔ. *as first-fruit … next* **1 Cor 15:23.** ἔ … ἔ. *thereupon … then* (Ael. Aristid. 48, 38 K.=24 p. 475 D.) **15:6f.**

❷ **being next in position of an enumeration of items, *then*** πρῶτον… ἔ. (POxy 1217, 5 πρῶτον μὲν ἀσπαζομένη σε, ἔπειτα εὐχομένη …; Jos., Ant. 20, 13, C. Ap. 1, 104) **Hb 7:2; Js 3:17.** As fourth and fifth member in a list **1 Cor 12:28.**—DELG s.v. εἶτα. M-M.

ἐπέκεινα (=ἐπ' ἐκεῖνα) adv. **at a more advanced point, *farther on, beyond*** (Hdt. et al.; LXX w. and without gen.; En, Just.; Tat. 20, 2; temporal Just., D. 88, 1; Ath., R. 68, 16) οἱ ἐ. ἀδελφοί *the brothers farther on* MPol 20:1 (Appian, Hann. 6 §21 τοῖς ἐπέκεινα Κέλτοις; Herodian 4, 15, 3 οἱ ἐ. βάρβαροι). W. gen. (En 24:2; Chares [after 323 BC] : 125 fgm. 5 Jac. [in Athen. 13, 35, 575b]; Arrian, Anab. 5, 5, 3 ἐπ. Καυκάσου; Maximus Tyr. 11, 10e τούτων ἐπ. ἐλθεῖν; Synes., Ep. 148 p. 285b ἐ. Θούλης) Βαβυλῶνος *beyond Babylon* **Ac 7:43** (Am 5:27).—Sv.

ἐπεκλήθην s. ἐπικαλέω.

ἐπεκτείνομαι (as act. in Aristot., Strabo, Vett. Val. 362, 20) in our lit. only mid. (Theophr., HP 6, 8, 4; Cass. Dio 45, 1, 3; Cos. and Dam. 2, 6) **to exert oneself to the uttermost, *stretch out, strain*** τινί *toward someth.* (Galen, De Usu Part. II 388, 9 Helmr.) τοῖς ἔμπροσθεν *toward the (goal) that lies before (me)* **Phil 3:13.**—DELG s.v. τανυ- E, cp. Frisk τείνω.

ἐπελαβόμην s. ἐπιλαμβάνομαι.

ἐπελαθόμην s. ἐπιλανθάνομαι.

ἐπελεύσομαι s. ἐπέρχομαι.

ἐπέλθοι s. ἐπέρχομαι.

ἐπενδύομαι (s. ἐνδύω; the act. Hdt. 1, 195; Jos., Ant. 5, 37) in our lit. only mid. **to put a garment on over an existing garment, *put on (in addition)*** (Plut., Pelop. 283 [11, 1]; Jos., Ant. 3, 159) τὶ *someth.* of the heavenly, glorious body **2 Cor 5:2** (LBelleville [CBQ 58, '96, 287] interprets as full payment corresponding to an ἀρραβών). Abs. vs. **4.**—S. γυμνός 1b.—DELG s.v. δύω. TW.

ἐπενδύτης, ου, ὁ (s. prec. entry; Soph., fgm. no. 406 TGF; Ael. Dion. χ, 11; Pollux 7, 45; Sb 9026, 12f; 1 Km 18:4; 2 Km 13:18; AcPh 6 [Aa II/2 4, 6]) **a garment put on over another garment, *outer garment, coat*** (Suda: τὸ ἐπάνω ἱμάτιον in contrast to ὑποδύτης, the ἐσώτερον ἱμάτιον) τὸν ἐ. διεζώσατο *put on his outer garment* **J 21:7.**

ἐπενεγκεῖν s. ἐπιφέρω.

ἐπένειμα s. ἐπιμένω.

ἐπεξεργάζομαι aor. inf. ἐπεξεργάσασθαι (ἐξεργάζομαι 'work out, accomplish'; Soph. et al.; Just., D. 137, 4 '[accomplish] what has been discussed') **to cause or effect in addition, *cause besides*** ὥστε … ἑαυτοῖς κίνδυνον ἐπεξεργάζεσθαι *besides you are causing danger for yourselves* 1 Cl 47:7.—DELG s.v. ἔργον.

ἐπεποίθειν s. πείθω.

ἐπέρχομαι fut. ἐπελεύσομαι; 2 aor. ἐπῆλθον (3 pl. ἐπῆλθαν **Ac 14:19;** B-D-F §81, 3; W-S. §13, 13; Mlt-H. 208); plpf. 3 sg. ἐπεληλύθει 2 Macc 9:18 (Hom.+).

❶ **to move to or upon**—ⓐ ***come, arrive,*** abs. (Just., D. 51, 2) Agr 22=**Mt 20:28** D. ἀπό τινος (1 Macc 8:4) ἐπῆλθαν ἀπὸ Ἀντιοχείας Ἰουδαῖοι *Judeans came fr. Antioch* **Ac 14:19;** AcPl Ha 5, 21 (s. entry ἥττων).

ⓑ of the Holy Spirit ***come upon,*** from a superior position ἐπί τινα **Lk 1:35** (FSteinmetzer, 'Empfangen v. Hl. Geiste' 1938); **Ac 1:8** (cp. Is 32:15; for movement from a transcendent realm, cp. Biogr. p. 448 of an inspiration: τοῦτο ἐπελθὸν αὐτῷ πράττειν ἐκ τοῦ θείου).

❷ **to occur as an event or process *happen, come about***

ⓐ of a period of time (Jos., Ant. 6, 305 ἡ ἐπερχομένη ἡμέρα) νύξ 1 Cl 24:3. ὁ αἰὼν ὁ ἐπερχόμενος *the coming age* Hv 4, 3, 5. ἐν τοῖς αἰῶσι τοῖς ἐπερχομένοις *in the ages to come* **Eph 2:7.** τῷ σαββάτῳ ἐπερχομένης τῆς κυριακῆς, ἐν ἡμέρα, ᾗ ἔμελλεν θηριουμαχεῖν ὁ Παῦλος *on the Sabbath before the Lord's Day (Sunday) on which Paul was to fight the wild beasts* AcPl Ha 3, 8.

ⓑ of what happens in the course of time; in our lit. exclusively of someth. unpleasant.

α. *come (on), approach* κακὰ ἐπερχόμενα 1 Cl 56:10 (Job 5:21). ἐπὶ ταῖς ταλαιπωρίαις ὑμῶν ταῖς ἐπερχομέναις *over the miseries that are coming upon you* **Js 5:1.** In the same eschatological sense (cp. Is 41:22f; τέλος ἐπερχόμενον En 10:2) κρίσιν τὴν ἐπερχομένην Hv 3, 9, 5 (Just., D. 138, 3); θλῖψις ἐ. v 4, 1, 1; s 7:4; cp. τὰ λοιπὰ … τὰ ἐ. s 9, 5, 5. τὰ ἐπερχόμενα (cp. Is 41:4, 22f; Jdth 9:5): τὰ ἐ. τῇ οἰκουμένῃ *what is coming upon the world* **Lk 21:26.**

β. in related vein, abs. (Horapollo 2, 25 ὁ θάνατος; Pr 27:12; Jos., Ant. 2, 86) *come about* **Ac 13:40.** ἐπί τινα (Gen 42:21; Wsd 12:27; EpJer 48; 2 Macc 9:18) *come upon someone* ὅπως μηδὲν ἐπέλθῃ ἐπ᾽ ἐμὲ ὧν εἰρήκατε *that none of the things you have spoken of may come upon me* **Ac 8:24.**—Possibly to be restored in AcPl Ha 6, 25f (s. Schmidt's transcription and note).—**Lk 21:35 v.l.**

❸ **to come against someone with force,** ***attack*** (Hom. et al.; ins, pap; 1 Km 30:23; ViEz 9 [p. 75, 1 Sch.]; Jos., Ant. 5, 195; 6, 23; Just., D. 139, 3 τῇ γῇ) abs. **Lk 11:22** (v.l. ἐλθών).—DDaube, The Sudden in the Scriptures '64, 34ff.—M-M. TW.

ἐπερωτάω (s. ἐρωτάω); impf. ἐπηρώτων; fut. ἐπερωτήσω; 1 aor. ἐπηρώτησα. Pass.: 1 aor. subj. 2 sg. ἐπερωτηθῇς Sir 32:7; Just., D. 50, 1; ptc. ἐπερωτηθείς (Hdt., Thu.+).

❶ **to put a question to,** ***ask***—ⓐ gener. τινά **Mk 9:32; 12:34; Mt 22:46; Lk 2:46; 1 Cor 14:35.** τινά τι *someone about someth.* (Aeschines 1, 79) αὐτὸν τὴν παραβολήν *they asked him about the parable* **Mk 7:17**; cp. **11:29; Lk 20:40;** Hm 4, 1, 4. τινὰ περί τινος (Hdt. 1, 32; Demosth. 43, 66; PFlor 331, 3) **Mk 10:10; J 16:19** D. W. acc. of pers. and foll. by a question introduced by λέγων (TestJos 11:2) **Mt 12:10; 17:10; 22:23; Mk 9:11; 12:18; Lk 3:10** al. Foll. by εἰ and a dir. question εἴ τι βλέπεις; *do you see someth.?* **Mk 8:23** or an indirect question (PHib 72, 15 [241 BC]; Jos., Ant. 12, 163) **Mk 10:2; 15:44; Lk 6:9; 23:6** (ἐρωτάω P[75] but s. ed. note); **Ac 5:8** D. Followed by other questions, direct **Mk 5:9; 7:5; 9:16, 28** al. and indirect (X., Hell. 6, 4, 2; Oec. 6, 6) **Lk 8:9; 17:20; Ac 23:34;** 2 Cl 12:2. τί ἄρα ἔσται αὐτοῖς *what will happen to them* Hm 11:2. Abs. Ox 654, 23 (=GTh 4; ASyn. 256, 54; context mutilated, s. Fitzmyer, Oxy 523).

ⓑ of a judge's questioning (interrogation) in making an investigation (cp. PYadin 17, 38 of contractual process) **Mt 27:11; Mk 14:60f; 15:2, 4; J 9:19 v.l., 23; 18:21 v.l.; Ac 5:27.**

ⓒ The usage of the word w. regard to questioning deities (Hdt. 1, 53, 1 and oft.; SIG 977, 24; 1160; 1168, 16; Jos., Ant. 6, 123) approaches the mng. in the LXX: ἐ. τὸν θεόν, τὸν κύριον etc. *inquire after God,* i.e. after the thought, purpose, or will of God **Ro 10:20** (Is 65:1).

❷ **to make a request,** ***ask for*** τινά τι *ask someone for someth.* (Ps 136:3) αὐτὸν σημεῖον ἐκ τοῦ οὐρανοῦ **Mt 16:1.**—DELG s.v. ἐρέω. M-M. TW.

ἐπερώτημα, ατος, τό (s. prec. entry; Hdt. et al.; ins, pap; Da 4:17 Theod.; Just., D. 45, 1).

❶ **the content of asking,** ***question*** (Hdt. 6, 67; Thu. 3, 53, 2; 3, 68, 1; Sir 33:3 v.l.; Just., D. 45, 1) ξένον ἐ. *strange question* PEg[2] 64. λαλεῖ αὐτοῖς κατὰ τὰ ἐ. αὐτῶν *according to their questions* Hm 11:2.

❷ **a formal request,** ***appeal*** (ἐπερωτάω 2) συνειδήσεως ἀγαθῆς ἐ. εἰς θεόν *an appeal to God for a clear conscience* **1 Pt 3:21.** But cp. *a pledge* (s. L-S-J-M s.v. 3 with pap ref.; also the vb. in PYadin 17, 38) *to God proceeding fr. a clear conscience* (so GRichards, JTS 32, '31, 77 and ESelwyn, 1 Pt ad loc.); cp. also BReicke, The Disobed. Spirits and Christian Baptism '46, 182–86; NClausen-Bagge, Eperotaema '41. DTripp, ET 92, '81, 267–70, argues for a liturgical 'stipulatio' or injunction urging the baptismal candidate to turn sincerely to God's way.—M-M. TW. Spicq.

ἔπεσα, ἔπεσον s. πίπτω.

ἐπέστειλα s. ἐπιστέλλω.

ἐπέστην s. ἐφίστημι.

ἐπεστράφην s. ἐπιστρέφω.

ἐπετίθεσαν s. ἐπιτίθημι.

ἐπετράπην s. ἐπιτρέπω.

ἐπέτυχον s. ἐπιτυγχάνω.

ἐπεφάνην s. ἐπιφαίνομαι.

ἐπέχω impf. ἐπεῖχον; fut. 3 sg. ἐφέξει Sir 15:4; 2 aor. ἐπέσχον; pf. 3 sg. ἐπέσχηκεν **J 1:13 v.l.;** pf. pass. ptc. ἐπεσχημένας (Just., D. 93, 1) (s. ἔχω; Hom.+).

❶ **to maintain a grasp on someone or someth.,** ***hold fast*** τινά *someone* (TestJos 15:3 ἐπέσχον ἐμαυτόν, ἵνα μή . . .) **Lk 4:42** D. τὶ *someth.* (Diod. S. 12, 27, 3 ταραχῇ τ. πόλιν ἐπεῖχε; Plut., Otho 1074 [17, 6] τ. πόλιν ἐπεῖχε κλαυθμός; Jos., Bell. 1, 230; SibOr 3, 340; Ath. 8:2 τὸν κόσμον al.) λόγον ζωῆς **Phil 2:16.**

❷ **to be mindful or especially observant,** ***hold toward, aim at,*** intr., fig. of mental processes (Hdt., Thu.) τινί *someone* (PFay 112, 11 [99 AD] ἐπέχον τῷ δακτυλιστῇ. W. dat. of thing Polyb. 3, 43, 2; BGU 827, 21; Sir 34:2; 2 Macc 9:25) ἐπεῖχεν αὐτοῖς *he fixed his attention on them* **Ac 3:5.** ἔπεχε σεαυτῷ *take pains with yourself* **1 Ti 4:16.** W. indir. quest. foll. ἐπέχων πῶς . . . ἐξελέγοντο *he noticed how . . . they sought out* **Lk 14:7.**

❸ **to remain at a place for a period of time,** ***stop, stay,*** intr. (Soph. et. al.; PTebt 12, 8; Gen 8:10; Philo, De Jos. 96 ἐ. ταύτας [=three days]; Jos., Bell. 6, 354; Just., D. 142, 1) ἐπέσχεν χρόνον εἰς τὴν Ἀσίαν *he stayed for a while in Asia* **Ac 19:22.**—M-M. TW.

ἐπηγγειλάμην, ἐπήγγελμαι s. ἐπαγγέλλομαι.

ἐπήγειρα s. ἐπεγείρω.

ἐπῆλθον s. ἐπέρχομαι.

ἐπήλυτος, ον (s. ἔρχομαι, one of whose aor. poetic forms is ἤλυθον) (Dionys. Hal. 3, 72; Job 20:26; Philo, Cher. 120f; SibOr 7, 85) ***come lately, come after*** in imagery descriptive of one who is new to a thing B 3:6 (so Sin.—v.l. προσήλυτοι; s. Bihlmeyer ad loc.). The point seems to be that Barnabas endeavors to provide correct understanding of the Sinaitic law so that his readers do not encounter it as newcomers or neophytes.—DELG s.v. ἐλεύσομαι.

ἐπήνεσα s. ἐπαινέω.

ἔπηξα s. πήγνυμι.

ἐπῆρα s. ἐπαίρω.

ἐπηρεάζω (s. next entry; Hdt.+; ins, pap; Philo, Mos. 2, 199, De Jos. 71; Just. A I, 1, 1) **to treat someone in a despicable manner,** ***threaten, mistreat, abuse*** usu. w. dat. (as Ael. Aristid. 23, 28 K.=42 p. 777 D.; PFlor 99, 10 [I/II AD]; Jos., Bell. 1, 13); τινά (OGI 484, 26 [II AD]): περὶ τῶν ἐπηρεαζόντων ὑμᾶς *for those who mistreat you* (in something they do, as PFay 123, 7; PLond II, 157, 4f p. 255 [II AD?]) **Lk 6:28,** cp. **Mt 5:44 v.l.** (Just., A I, 15, 9). τὴν ἀγαθὴν ἀναστροφήν *disparage/malign (your) good conduct* **1 Pt 3:16.**—Schmidt, Syn. IV 275—78. DELG s.v. ἐπήρεια. M-M.

ἐπήρεια, ας, ἡ (s. prec. entry; Thu. et al.; OGI 262, 23f; 669, 6; BGU 340, 21; PRyl 28, 139; Sym.; Philo, In Flacc. 103; 179; Jos., Ant. 13, 382; 15, 23; Ath.) ***abuse, ill-treatment*** ἐ.

τοῦ ἄρχοντος τοῦ αἰῶνος τούτου IMg 1:3 (Lucian, Laps. 1 δαίμονος ἐπήρεια. S. Dssm., LO 398, 7 [LAE 454, 7] ἐ. τ. ἀντικειμένου).—DELG.

ἐπήρθην s. ἐπαίρω.

ἐπί prep. w. gen., dat., or acc.; s. the lit. on ἀνά, beg. (Hom.+). The basic idea is 'upon' (opp. ὑπό) Kühner-G. I 495; s. also Rob 600–605. (In the foll. classifications case use is presented seriatim; in earlier editions of this lexicon all sections, except 13, 17, and 18 [of time], were included under the general rubric 'Place'.)

➊ **marker of location or surface, answering the question 'where?'** ***on, upon, near***—ⓐ w. gen., marking a position on a surface ἐ. (τῆς) γῆς *on (the) earth* (cp. En 9:1; 98:1; ἐ. γῆς 25:6; PsSol 17:2) **Mt 6:10, 19; 9:6; 23:9; Mk 6:47** al. (Ar. 12, 1; Just., A I, 54, 7 al.). ἐ. τῆς θαλάσσης *on the sea* (cp. Job 9:8; Dio Chrys. 10 [11], 129 βαδίζειν ἐ. τῆς θαλ.; Lucian, Philops. 13 βαδίζειν ἐφ' ὕδατος, VH 2, 4; Artem. 3, 16 ἐ. τ. θαλάσσης περιπατεῖν; schol. on Nicander, Ther. 15 p. 5, 26ff relying on the testimony of Hesiod: Orion was given a gift [δωρεά] by the gods καὶ ἐ. κυμάτων πορεύεσθαι καὶ ἐ. τῆς γῆς) **Mt 14:26; Mk 6:48f; J 6:19** (w. acc. P[75]; s. 4bβ below). ἐ. τῶν νεφελῶν *on the clouds* **Mt 24:30; 26:64** (Da 7:13; cp. Philo, Praem. 8). ἐ. κλίνης **9:2; Lk 17:34.** ἐ. τοῦ δώματος *on the roof* vs. **31; Mt 24:17; 10:27** foll. by pl. W. verbs: κάθημαι ἐ. τινος *sit on someth.* (Job 2:8; ἐ. τοῦ ἅρματος GrBar 6:2; cp. JosAs 27:1 ἐ. τοῦ ὀχήματος καθεζόμενος; Just., D. 90, 5 ἐ. λίθου καθεζόμενος) **Mt 24:3; 27:19; Ac 8:28; Rv 6:16; 9:17** (the same prep. used in Rv w. κάθημαι and dat. s. bα below, and w. acc. cα). ἑστηκέναι ἐ. τινος *stand on someth.* **Ac 21:40; Rv 10:5, 8** (Just., D. 86, 2 ἐστηρίχθαι). With parts of the body: ἐ. χειρῶν αἴρειν *carry on* (i.e. *in/with*) *their hands* **Mt 4:6; Lk 4:11** (both Ps 90:12). ἐ. κεφαλῆς *on the head* (Hdt. 5, 12, 4) **J 20:7; 1 Cor 11:10; Rv 12:1.** ἐ. τοῦ μετώπου **Rv 7:3; 9:4.** ἐ. γυμνοῦ *on the naked body* **Mk 14:51.** Cp. use of ἐπί w. καθίζω and gen., and ἐπί w. κάθημαι and acc. **Mt 19:28.**—In a gener. and fig. sense **Ac 21:23.**

ⓑ w. dat., gener. suggesting contiguity *on, in, above.*

α. answering the question 'where?' (Hom. et al.; ins, pap, LXX; Just., D. 105, 5 ἐ. τῷ σταυρῷ; Tat., 9:1 ἐ. τοῖς ὄρεσι; Ath. 20, 1 ἐ. τῷ μετώπῳ; Mel., P. 19, 131 ἐ. σάκκῳ καὶ σποδῷ) ἐ. πίνακι *on a platter* **Mt 14:8, 11; Mk 6:25, 28.** ἀνακλῖναι ἐ. τῷ χλωρῷ χόρτῳ *on the green grass* **6:39.** ἐ. τοῖς κραβάττοις vs. **55.** ἐπέκειτο ἐπ' αὐτῷ *lay on it* (or *before it*) **J 11:38.** καθήμενος ἐ. τῷ θρόνῳ **Rv 4:9** (cp. gen. w. καθ. 1a above, and acc. cα below) **5:13; 7:10** and oft. ἐφ' ἵπποις λευκοῖς *on white horses* **19:14.** ἐ. σανίσιν *on planks* **Ac 27:44.** ἐ. τῇ στοᾷ *in the colonnade* **3:11.** τὰ ἐ. τοῖς οὐρανοῖς *what is above* (or *in*) *the heavens* **Eph 1:10.** ἐπ' αὐτῷ *above him, at his head* **Lk 23:38** (=Mt 27:37 ἐπάνω τ. κεφαλῆς αὐτοῦ).

β. answering the question 'whither?' *on, upon* (Hom. et al.) w. verbs that indicate a direction: οἰκοδομεῖν ἐ. τινι *build upon someth.* **Mt 16:18.** ἐποικοδομεῖν **Eph 2:20.** ἐπιβάλλειν ἐπίβλημα ἐ. ἱματίῳ παλαιῷ *put a patch on an old garment* **Mt 9:16.** ἐπιπίπτειν ἐ. τινι **Ac 8:16.** ἐκάθισεν ἐ. τῷ θρόνῳ *he sat down on the throne* GJs 11:1. λίθον ἐπ' αὐτῇ βαλέτω **J 8:7 v.l.** (cp. 12a below).

ⓒ w. acc., answering the question 'where?' (Hom. et al.; LXX; JosAs 29:2 φορῶν ἐ. τὸν μηρὸν αὐτοῦ ῥομφαίαν; Just., D. 53, 1 ζυγὸν ἐ. αὐχένα μὴ ἔχων)

α. *on, over someth.* καθεύδειν ἐ. τι *sleep on someth.* **Mk 4:38.** καθῆσθαι ἐ. τι *sit on someth.* **Mt 19:28** (in the same vs. καθίζω w. gen., s. a above) **J 12:15; Rv 4:4; 6:2; 11:16** al.; cp. **Lk 21:35b;** κεῖσθαι ἐ. τι *lie upon someth.* **2 Cor 3:15.** κατακεῖσθαι **Lk 5:25.** ἑστηκέναι ἐ. τὸν αἰγιαλόν *stand on the shore* **Mt 13:2;** cp. **Rv 14:1.** ἑστῶτας ἐ. τὴν θάλασσαν *standing beside the sea* **15:2.** ἔστη ἐ. τὴν κεφαλὴν τοῦ παιδίου (the star) *remained stationary over the head of the child* GJs 21:3. σκηνοῦν ἐ. τινα *spread a tent over someone* **Rv 7:15.** ἐ. τὴν δεξιάν *at the right hand* **5:1.** λίθος ἐ. λίθον *stone upon stone* **Mt 24:2.**

β. ἐ. τὸ αὐτό *at the same place, together* (Ps.-X., Respublica Athen. [The Old Oligarch] 2, 2; Pla., Rep. 329a; SIG 736, 66 [92 BC]. In pap='in all': PTebt 14, 20 [114 BC]; PFay 102, 6.—2 Km 2:13; En 100:2) εἶναι ἐ. τὸ αὐτό *be together* **Lk 17:35; Ac 1:15; 2:1, 44.** In **1 Cor 7:5** it is a euphemistic expr. for sexual union. κατοικεῖν ἐ. τὸ αὐτό *live in the same place* (Dt 25:5) Hm 5, 1, 4. Also w. verbs of motion (Sus 14 Theod.) συνέρχεσθαι ἐ. τὸ αὐτό *come together to the same place* **1 Cor 11:20; 14:23;** cp. B 4:10 (Just., A I, 67, 3 συνέλευσις γίνεται). συνάγεσθαι (Phlegon of Tralles [Hadr.]: 257 fgm. 36 III 9 Jac.; PsSol 2:2; TestJob 28:5 Jos., Bell. 2, 346) **Mt 22:34; Ac 4:26** (Ps 2:2); 1 Cl 34:7. ἐ. τὸ αὐτὸ μίγνυσθαι *be mixed together* Hm 10, 3, 3. προσετίθει ἐ. τὸ αὐτό *added to their number* **Ac 2:47.**

γ. *at, by, near someone* or *someth.* καθῆσθαι ἐ. τὸ τελώνιον *sit at the tax-office* **Mt 9:9** (ἐ. τὰς ὡραίας πύλας GrBar prol. 2); **Mk 2:14.** ἑστηκέναι ἐ. τὴν θύραν *stand at the door* **Rv 3:20.** σὺ ἔστης ἐ. τὸ θυσιαστήριον *you are standing* (ἕστηκας deStrycker) *as priest at the altar* GJs 8:2. ἐφ' ὑμᾶς *among you* **2 Th 1:10;** cp. **Ac 1:21.**—Of pers., *over* whom someth. is done ὀνομάζειν τὸ ὄνομα Ἰησοῦ ἐ. τινα *speak the name of Jesus over someone* **Ac 19:13.** ἐπικαλεῖν τὸ ὄνομά τινος ἐ. τινα=*to claim someone for one's own* (Jer 14:9; 2 Ch 7:14; 2 Macc 8:15) **Ac 15:17** (Am 9:12); **Js 2:7;** Hs 8, 6, 4. προσεύχεσθαι ἐ. τινα *pray over someone* **Js 5:14.**

➋ **marker of presence or occurrence near an object or area,** ***at, near***—ⓐ w. gen., of immediate proximity to things *at, near* (Hdt. 7, 115; X., An. 4, 3, 28 al.; LXX, Just.) ἐ. τ. θυρῶν *at the gates* (Plut., C. Gracch. 841 [14, 3]; PRyl 127, 8f [29 AD] κοιμωμένου μου ἐ. τῆς θύρας; 1 Macc 1:55; Just., D. 111, 4) **Ac 5:23** (s. b below for dat. in **5:9**). ἐ. τῆς θαλάσσης *near the sea* (Polyb. 1, 44, 4; Ex 14:2; Dt 1:40; 1 Macc 14:34) **J 21:1.** ἐ. τῆς ὁδοῦ *by the road* **Mt 21:19.** ἐσθίειν ἐ. τῆς τραπέζης τινός *eat at someone's table* **Lk 22:30** (cp. POxy 99, 14 [55 AD] τράπεζα, ἐφ' ἧς Σαραπίων καὶ μέτοχοι; Da 11:27 LXX ἐ. μιᾶς τραπέζης). ἐ. τοῦ (τῆς) βάτου *at the thornbush* = *in the passage about the thornbush* (i.e. Ex 3:1ff) **Mk 12:26; Lk 20:37.**

ⓑ with dat., of immediate proximity *at, near by* (Hom.+) ἦν ἔτι ἐ. τῷ τόπῳ ὅπου *was still at the place, where* **J 11:30 v.l.** (for ἐν; cp. Just., D. 402). ἐ. τῇ θύρᾳ (ἐ. θύραις) *at the door* (Hom. et al.; Wsd 19:17; Jos., Ant. 17, 90; Just., D. 32, 3) **Mt 24:33; Mk 13:29; Ac 5:9** (s. a above). ἐ. τοῖς πυλῶσιν **Rv 21:12.** ἐ. τῇ πηγῇ **J 4:6** (Jos., Ant. 5, 58 ἐ. τινι πηγῇ; Just., A I, 64, 1 ἐ. ταῖς . . . πηγαῖς). ἐ. τῇ προβατικῇ (sc. πύλῃ) *near the sheepgate* **5:2;** cp. **Ac 3:10.** ἐ. τῷ ποταμῷ *near the river* (since Il. 7, 133; Jos., Ant. 4, 176 ἐ. τ. Ἰορδάνῳ) **Rv 9:14.**—Of pers. (Diod. S. 14, 113, 6; Just., A I, 40, 7) ἐφ' ὑμῖν *among you* **2 Cor 7:7;** cp. **Ac 28:14 v.l.**

➌ **marker of involvement in an official proceeding,** ***before,*** w. gen., of pers., esp. in the language of lawsuits (Pla., Leg. 12, 943d; Isaeus 5, 1 al.; UPZ 71, 15; 16 [152 BC]; POxy 38, 11; Mitt-Wilck. I/2, 382, 23=BGU 909, 23; Jos., Vi. 258; Just., A II, 1, 1 ἐ. Οὐρβίκου). ἐ. τοῦ ἡγεμόνος *in the governor's presence* **Mt 28:14.** ἐ. ἡγεμόνων καὶ βασιλέων **Mk 13:9.** ἐ. σου *before you* (the procurator) **Ac 23:30.** ἐ. Τερτούλλου **Phlm subscr. v.l.;** στάντος μου ἐ. τοῦ συνεδρίου **Ac 24:20** (cp. Diod. S. 11, 55, 4 ἐ. τοῦ κοινοῦ συνεδρίου τ. Ἑλλήνων). γυναικὸς . . .

διαβληθείσης ἐ. τοῦ κυρίου Papias (2:17). κρίνεσθαι ἐ. τῶν ἀδίκων *go to law before the unrighteous* **1 Cor 6:1.** κριθήσεται ἐφ' ὑμῶν *before your tribunal* D 11:11. μαρτυρεῖν ἐ. Ποντίου Πιλάτου *testify before Pontius Pilate* **1 Ti 6:13** (s. μαρτυρέω 1c). ἐ. τοῦ βήματος (POxy 37 I, 3 [49 AD]) ἑστὼς ἐ. τοῦ βήματος Καίσαρός εἰμι *I am standing before Caesar's tribunal* **Ac 25:10** (Appian says Prooem. c. 15 §62 of himself: δίκαις ἐν Ῥώμῃ συναγορεύσας ἐ. τῶν βασιλέων=I acted as attorney in lawsuits in Rome before the emperors).—Gener. *in someone's presence* (Appian, Syr. 61 §324 ἐφ' ὑμῶν=in your presence) ἐ. Τίτου *before Titus* **2 Cor 7:14.** Cp.10 below.

❹ **marker of movement to or contact w. a goal,** ***toward, in direction of, on***—ⓐ w. gen., marking contact with the goal that is reached, answering the question 'whither?' *toward, on, at* w. verbs of motion (Appian, Iber. 98 §427 ἀπέπλευσεν ἐπ' οἴκου=he sailed [toward] home; PGM 4, 2468f ἀναβὰς ἐ. δώματος; JosAs 27:1 ἀνέδραμε . . . ἐ. πέτρας; Jos., Ant. 4, 91 ἔφευγον ἐ. τ. πόλεων; Tat. 33:3 Εὐρώπην ἐ. τοῦ ταύρου καθιδρύσαντος) βάλλειν τὸν σπόρον ἐ. τῆς γῆς **Mk 4:26;** also σπείρειν vs. **31.** πίπτειν (Wsd 18:23; TestAbr A 3 p. 80, 11 [Stone p. 8]; JosAs 9:1) **9:20; 14:35.** καθιέναι **Ac 10:11.** τιθέναι (Sir 17:4) **Lk 8:16; J 19:19; Ac 5:15.** ἔρχεσθαι **Hb 6:7; Rv 3:10;** γίνεσθαι ἐ. *reach, be at* **J 6:21.** γενόμενος ἐ. τοῦ τόπου *when he reached the place* **Lk 22:40.** καθίζειν *take one's seat* ἐ. θρόνου (JosAs 7:1 al.) **Mt 19:28** (s. 1a end); **23:2; 25:31; J 19:13** (ἐ. βήματος of Pilate as Jos., Bell. 2, 172; of Jesus Just., A I, 35, 6). κρεμαννύναι ἐ. ξύλου *hang on a tree* (i.e. cross) (Gen 40:19; cp. Just., D. 86, 6 σταυρωθῆναι ἐ. τοῦ ξύλου) **Ac 5:30; 10:39;** cp. **Gal 3:13** (Dt 21:23).

ⓑ w. acc.—**α.** specifying direction (En 24:2 ἐ. νότον 'southward' of position of the mountain) of motion that takes a particular direction, *to, toward* ἐκτείνας τ. χεῖρα ἐ. τοὺς μαθητάς **Mt 12:49;** cp. **Lk 22:53** (JosAs 12:8). πορεύεσθαι ἐ. τὸ ἀπολωλός *go after the one that is lost* **15:4.** ἐ. τὴν Ἄσσον *in the direction of Assos* **Ac 20:13.** ἐπιστρέφειν ἐ. τι *turn to someth.* **2 Pt 2:22** (cp. Pr 26:11; En 99:5). ὡς ἐ. λῃστήν *as if against a robber* **Mt 26:55; Mk 14:48; Lk 22:52.**

β. from one point to another *across, over* w. motion implied (Hom.+; LXX) περιπατεῖν, ἐλθεῖν ἐ. τ. θάλασσαν or ἐ. τ. ὕδατα **Mt 14:25, 28f; J 6:19** P^{75}. Of spreading *across the land* (PsSol 17:10): famine **Ac 7:11; 11:28;** darkness **Mt 27:45; Lk 23:44.** ἐ. σταδίους δώδεκα χιλιάδων *across twelve thousand stades* **Rv 21:16 v.l.** (Polyaenus 5, 44, 4 ἐ. στάδια δέκα); ἐ. πλεῖον *further* (1 Esdr 2:24; 2 Macc 10:27) **Ac 4:17.**

γ. of goal attained (Hom. et al.; LXX) *on, upon someone or someth.* πέσατε ἐφ' ἡμᾶς **Lk 23:30** (Hos 10:8). ἔπεσεν ἐ. τὰ πετρώδη **Mt 13:5;** cp. **Lk 13:4.** ἔρχεσθαι ἐ. τινα *come upon someone* **Mt 3:16;** also καταβαίνειν *fr. above* **J 1:33;** cp. **Rv 16:21.** ἀναβαίνειν (Jos., Ant. 13, 138; Just., A II, 12, 7) **Lk 5:19.** ἐπιβαίνειν **Mt 21:5** (Zech 9:9).—**Ac 2:3; 9:4** al.; διασωθῆναι ἐ. τ. γῆν *be brought safely to the land* **27:44;** cp. vs. **43; Lk 8:27.** ἐ. τὸ πλοῖον *to the ship* **Ac 20:13.** ἀναπεσεῖν ἐ. τὴν γῆν *lie down* or *sit down on the ground* **Mt 15:35.** ἔρριψεν αὐτὸν χαμαὶ ἐ. τὸν σάκκον *he threw himself down on the sackcloth* GJs 13:1. τιθέναι τι ἐ. τι *put someth. on someth.* (JosAs 16:11) **Mt 5:15; Lk 11:33; Mk 8:25 v.l.;** likew. ἐπιτιθέναι (JosAs 29:5) **Mt 23:4; Mk 8:25; Lk 15:5; J 9:6, 15; Ac 15:10.** ἐπιβάλλειν τ. χεῖρας ἐ. τινα (Gen 22:12 al.) **Mt 26:50; Lk 21:12; Ac 5:18.** Mainly after verbs of placing, laying, putting, bringing, etc. *on, to:* ἀναβιβάζω, ἀναφέρω, βάλλω, γράφω, δίδωμι, ἐγγίζω, ἐπιβιβάζω, ἐπιγράφω, ἐποικοδομέω, ἐπιρ(ρ)ίπτω, θεμελιόω, ἵστημι, κατάγω, οἰκοδομέω, σωρεύω; s. these entries. Sim. βρέχειν ἐ. τινα *cause rain to fall upon someone* **Mt 5:45** (cp. PsSol 17:18); also τ. ἥλιον ἀνατέλλειν ἐ. τινα *cause the sun to rise* so that its rays fall *upon someone* **ibid.** τύπτειν τινὰ ἐ. τὴν σιαγόνα *strike on the cheek* **Lk 6:29.** πίπτειν ἐ. (τὸ) πρόσωπον (Jdth 14:6) *on the face* **Mt 17:6; 26:39; Lk 5:12; 17:16; 1 Cor 14:25; Rv 7:11.**—*To, upon* w. acc. of thing πορεύεσθαι ἐ. τὴν ὁδόν *go to the road* **Ac 8:26;** cp. **9:11.** ἐ. τὰς διεξόδους **Mt 22:9.** ἵνα μὴ πνέῃ ἄνεμος ἐ. πᾶν δένδρον *so that no wind should blow upon any tree* **Rv 7:1.**

δ. of closeness to someth. or someone *to, up to, in the neighborhood of, on* ἐ. τὸ μνημεῖον *up to the tomb* **Mk 16:2; Lk 24:1 v.l., 22, 24;** cp. ἐ. τὸ μνῆμα **Mk 16:2 v.l.; Lk 24:1.** ἔρχεσθαι ἐ. τι ὕδωρ *come to some water* **Ac 8:36.** ἐ. τὴν πύλην τὴν σιδηρᾶν *to the iron gate* **12:10.** καταβαίνειν ἐ. τὴν θάλασσαν *go down to the sea* **J 6:16.** ἐ. τὸν Ἰορδάνην **Mt 3:13** (Just., D. 88, 3 al.). ἀναπίπτειν ἐ. τὸ στῆθος *he leaned back on* (Jesus') *breast* **J 13:25; 21:20.** πίπτειν ἐ. τοὺς πόδας *fall at* (someone's) *feet* **Ac 10:25** (JosAs 14:10 ἔπεσεν ἐ πρόσωπον ἐ. τοὺς πόδας αὐτοῦ). ἐ. τ. ἀκάνθας *among the thorns* **Mt 13:7.**—W. acc. of pers. *to someone* ἐ. τὸν Ἰησοῦν ἐλθόντες *they came to Jesus* **J 19:33;** cp. **Mt 27:27; Mk 5:21.**

ε. in imagery of goal or objective *to, toward* (Just., A II, 7, 6 ἐπ' ἀμφότερα τρέπεσθαι) ἐπιστρέφειν, ἐπιστρέφεσθαι ἐ. τινα *turn to* (Dt 30:10; 31:20 al.; Ar. 2, 1 ἔλθωμεν καὶ ἐ. τὸ ἀνθρώπινον γένος 'let us now turn to . . .'; Just., D. 56, 11 ἐ. τὰς γραφὰς ἐπανελθών) **Lk 1:17; Ac 9:35; 11:21; 14:15; 26:20; Gal 4:9; 1 Pt 2:25.**

❺ **marker of manner,** corresponding to an adv., w. dat. (Aeschyl., Suppl. 628 ἐπ' ἀληθείᾳ; UPZ 162 VI, 3 [117 BC] κακοτρόπως καὶ ἐ. ῥᾳδιουργίᾳ; POxy 237 VI, 21 ἐ. τῇ τῶν ἀνθρ. σωτηρίᾳ; ἐφ' ὁράσει En 14:8; Just., A I, 9, 3 ἐφ' ὕβρει; 55, 7 ἐ. τούτῳ τῷ σχήματι 'in this form'; Tat. 17, 1 ἐπ' ἀκριβείᾳ; Ath. 33, 2 ἐφ' ἑνὶ γάμῳ) ὁ σπείρων ἐπ' εὐλογίαις (in contrast to ὁ σπείρων φειδομένως *one who sows sparingly*) *one who sows in blessing* (i.e. *generously*) **2 Cor 9:6.** ἐπ' εὐλογίαις θερίζειν *reap generously* **ibid.**

❻ **marker of basis for a state of being, action, or result,** ***on,*** w. dat. (Hom. et al.)—ⓐ ἐπ' ἄρτῳ ζῆν *live on bread* **Mt 4:4; Lk 4:4** (both Dt 8:3. cp. Ps.-Pla., Alcib. 1, 105c; Plut., Mor. 526d; Alciphron 3, 7, 5; SibOr 4, 154). ἐ. τῷ ῥήματί σου *depending on your word* **Lk 5:5.** οὐ συνῆκαν ἐ. τοῖς ἄρτοις *they did not arrive at an understanding (of it) (by reflecting) on (the miracle of) the loaves* **Mk 6:52** (cp. Demosth. 18, 121 τί σαυτὸν οὐκ ἐλλεβορίζεις ἐ. τούτοις [sc. λόγοις];=why do you not come to an understanding concerning these words?). ἐ. τῇ πίστει *on the basis of faith* **Ac 3:16; Phil 3:9.** ἐπ' ἐλπίδι *on the basis of hope, supporting itself on hope* **Ac 2:26** (? s. ἐλπίς 1bα); **Ro 4:18; 8:20; 1 Cor 9:10; Tit 1:2.**—**Ac 26:6** ἐπ' ἐλπίδι gives the basis of the trial at law, as does ἐ. εὐεργεσίᾳ **4:9.** ἀπολύειν τ. γυναῖκα ἐ. πορνείᾳ **Mt 19:9** (cp. Dio Chrys. 26 [43], 10 ἀπολύειν ἐπ' ἀργυρίῳ; Ath. 2, 3 κρίνεσθαι . . . μὴ ἐ. τῷ ὀνόματι, ἐ. δὲ τῷ ἀδικήματι). γυναικὸς ἐ. πόλλαις ἁμαρτίαις διαβληθείσης Papias (2:17). *On the basis of the testimony of two witnesses* (cp. Appian, Iber. 79 §343 ἤλεγχον ἐ. μάρτυσι) **Hb 10:28** (Dt 17:6); sim. use of ἐ. τινί *on the basis of someth.:* **8:6; 9:10, 15** (here it may also be taken in the temporal sense; s. 18 below), **17.** ἁμαρτάνειν ἐ. τῷ ὁμοιώματι τ. παραβάσεως Ἀδάμ **Ro 5:14** (ὁμοίωμα 1). δαπανᾶν ἐ. τινι *pay the expenses for someone* **Ac 21:24.** ἀρκεῖσθαι ἐ. τινι *be content w. someth.* **3J 10.**

ⓑ w. verbs of believing, hoping, trusting: πεποιθέναι (Wsd 3:9; Sus 35; 1 Macc 10:71; 2 Macc 7:40 and oft.) **Lk 11:22; 18:9; 2 Cor 1:9; Hb 2:13** (2 Km 22:3). πιστεύειν **Lk 24:25; Ro 9:33; 10:11; 1 Pt 2:6** (the last three Is 28:16). ἐλπίζειν (2 Macc

2:18; Sir 34:7) **Ro 15:12** (Is 11:10); **1 Ti 4:10; 6:17;** cp. **1J 3:3.** παρρησιάζεσθαι **Ac 14:3.**

ⓒ after verbs which express feelings, opinions, etc.: *at, because of, from, with* (Hom. et al.) διαταράσσεσθαι **Lk 1:29.** ἐκθαυμάζειν **Mk 12:17.** ἐκπλήσσεσθαι **Mt 7:28; Mk 1:22; Lk 4:32; Ac 13:12.** ἐξίστασθαι (Jdth 11:16; Wsd 5:2 al.) **Lk 2:47.** ἐπαισχύνεσθαι (Is 1:29) **Ro 6:21.** εὐφραίνεσθαι (Sir 16:1; 18:32; 1 Macc 11:44) **Rv 18:20.** θαμβεῖσθαι **Mk 10:24;** cp. **Lk 5:9; Ac 3:10.** θαυμάζειν (Lev 26:32; Jdth 10:7 al.; Jos., Ant. 10, 277) **Mk 12:17 v.l.** μακροθυμεῖν (Sir 18:11; 29:8; 35:19) **Mt 18:26, 29; Lk 18:7; Js 5:7.** μετανοεῖν (Plut., Ag. 803 [19, 5]; Ps.-Lucian, Salt. 84; Prayer of Manasseh [=Odes 12] 7; Just., A I, 61, 10; D. 95, 3 al.) **2 Cor 12:21.** ὀδυνᾶσθαι (cp. Tob 6:15) **Ac 20:38.** ὀργίζεσθαι **Rv 12:17.** σπλαγχνίζεσθαι **Mt 14:14; Lk 7:13.** συλλυπεῖσθαι **Mk 3:5.** στυγνάζειν **10:22.** χαίρειν (PEleph 13, 3; Jos., Ant. 1, 294; Tob 13:15; Bar 4:33; JosAs 4:2; Ar. 15, 7) **Mt 18:13; Lk 1:14; 13:17; Ro 16:19** al. χαρὰν καὶ παράκλησιν ἔχειν **Phlm 7.** χαρὰ ἔσται **Lk 15:7;** cp. vs. **10** (Jos., Ant. 6, 116 ἡ ἐ. τῇ νίκῃ χαρά). Also w. verbs that denote aroused feelings παραζηλοῦν and παροργίζειν *make jealous* and *angry at* **Ro 10:19** (Dt 32:21). παρακαλεῖν **1 Th 3:7a** (cp. Just., D. 78:8 παράκλησιν ἐχουσῶν ἐ.), as well as those verbs that denote an expression of the emotions ἀγαλλιᾶσθαι (cp. Tob 13:15; Ps 69:5) **Lk 1:47;** Hs 8, 1, 18; 9, 24, 2. καυχᾶσθαι (Diod. S. 16, 70; Sir 30:2) **Ro 5:2.** κοπετὸν ποιεῖν (cp. 3 Macc 4:3) **Ac 8:2.** ὀλολύζειν **Js 5:1.** αἰνεῖν (cp. X., An. 3, 1, 45 al.) **Lk 2:20.** δοξάζειν (Polyb. 6, 53, 10; cp. Diod. S. 17, 21, 4 δόξα ἐ. ἀνδρείᾳ=fame because of bravery) **Ac 4:21; 2 Cor 9:13.** εὐχαριστεῖν *give thanks for someth.* (s. εὐχαριστέω 2; UPZ 59, 10 [168 BC] ἐ. τῷ ἐρρῶσθαί σε τ. θεοῖς εὐχαρίστουν) **1 Cor 1:4;** cp. **2 Cor 9:15; 1 Th 3:9.**—ἐφ' ᾧ = ἐπὶ τούτῳ ὅτι *for this reason that, because* (Diod. S. 19, 98; Appian, Bell. Civ. 1, 112 §520; Ael. Aristid. 53 p. 640 D.; Synes., Ep. 73 p. 221c; Damasc., Vi. Isid. 154; Syntipas p. 12, 9; 127, 8; Thomas Mag. ἐφ' ᾧ ἀντὶ τοῦ διότι; cp. W-S. §24, 5b and 12f. S. WKümmel, D. Bild des Menschen im NT '48, 36–40) **Ro 5:12** (SLyonnet, Biblica 36, '55, 436–56 [denies a causal sense here]. On the probability of commercial idiom s. FDanker, FGingrich Festschr. '72, 104f, also Ro 5:12, Sin under Law: NTS 14, '68, 424–39; against him SPorter, TynBull 41, '90, 3–30, also NTS 39, '93, 321–33; difft. JFitzmyer, Anchor Bible Comm.: Romans, ad loc. 'w. the result that all have sinned'); **2 Cor 5:4; Phil 3:12;** *for, indeed* **4:10.**

❼ **marker of addition to what is already in existence,** ***to, in addition to.*** W. dat. (Hom. et al.; PEleph 5, 17 [284/283 BC] μηνὸς Τῦβι τρίτῃ ἐπ' εἰκάδι; Tob 2:14; Sir 3:27; 5:5) προσέθηκεν τοῦτο ἐ. πᾶσιν *he added this to everything else* **Lk 3:20** (cp. Lucian, Luct. [On Funerals], 24). ἐ. τ. παρακλήσει ἡμῶν *in addition to our comfort* **2 Cor 7:13.** λύπη ἐ. λύπῃ *grief upon grief* **Phil 2:27 v.l.** (cp. Soph., Oed. C. 544, also Polyb. 1, 57, 1 πληγὴ ἐ. πληγῇ; Plut., Mor. 123f; Polyaenus 5, 52 ἐ. φόνῳ φόνον; Quint. Smyrn. 5, 602 ἐ. πένθει πένθος=sorrow upon sorrow; Sir 26:15). ἐ. τῇ σῇ εὐχαριστίᾳ *to your prayer of thanks* **1 Cor 14:16.** So perh. also **Hb 8:1.** ἐ. πᾶσι τούτοις *to all these* **Col 3:14; Lk 16:26 v.l.** (X., Mem. 1, 2, 25 al.; Sir 37:15; cp. 1 Macc 10:42; Just., D. 133, 1 ἐ. τούτοις πᾶσι).—W. acc.: addition to someth. of the same kind **Mt 6:27; Lk 12:25; Rv 22:18a.** λύπην ἐ. λύπην *sorrow upon sorrow* **Phil 2:27** (cp. Is 28:10, 13; Ezk 7:26; Ps 68:28).

❽ **marker of perspective,** ***in consideration of, in regard to, on the basis of, concerning, about,*** w. gen. (Antig. Car. 164 ἐ. τῶν οἴνων ἀλλοιοῦσθαι; 4 Macc. 2:9 ἐ. τῶν ἑτέρων . . . ἔστιν ἐπιγνῶναι τοῦτο, ὅτι . . .; Ath. 29, 2 τὰ ἐ. τῆς μανίας πάθη) ἐ. δύο ἢ τριῶν μαρτύρων *on the evidence of two or three witnesses* **1 Ti 5:19** (cp. TestAbr A 13 p. 92, 22ff. [Stone p. 32]). Sim. in the expr. ἐ. στόματος δύο μαρτύρων (Dt 19:15) **Mt 18:16; 2 Cor 13:1.** ἐπ' αὐτῆς *on the basis of it* **Hb 7:11.** ἐπ' ἀληθείας *based on truth = in accordance w. truth, truly* (Demosth. 18, 17 ἐπ' ἀληθείας οὐδεμιᾶς εἰρημένα; POxy 255, 16 [48 AD]; Da 2:8; Tob 8:7; En 104:11) **Mk 12:14, 32; Lk 4:25; 20:21; Ac 4:27.** ἐφ' ἑαυτοῦ *based on himself = to* or *by himself* (X., An. 2, 4, 10; Demosth. 18, 224 ἐκρίνετο ἐφ' ἑαυτοῦ; Dionys. Hal., Comp. Verb. 16 ἐ. σεαυτοῦ. Cp. Kühner-G. I 498e) **2 Cor 10:7.**—To introduce the object which is to be discussed or acted upon λέγειν ἐ. τινος *speak of, about someth.* (Pla., Charm., 155d, Leg. 2, 662d; Isocr. 6, 41; Aelian, VH 1, 30; Jer 35:8; EpArist 162; 170; Ath. 5:1 ἐ. τοῦ νοητοῦ . . . δογματίζειν) **Gal 3:16.** *Do someth. on, in the case of* (cp. 1 Esdr 1:22) σημεῖα ποιεῖν ἐ. τῶν ἀσθενούντων *work miracles on the sick* **J 6:2.**—On B 13:6 s. τίθημι 1bζ.—In ref. to someth. (Aristot., Pol. 1280a, 17; 4 Macc 12:5 τῶν ἐ. τῆς βασιλείας . . . πραγμάτων; Just., A I, 5, 1 ἐφ' ἡμῶν 'in our case', D. 131, 4; Ath. 15, 3 ἐ. τῆς ὕλης καὶ τοῦ θεοῦ 'as respects God and matter, so . . .') ἐ. τινων δεῖ ἐγκρατεύεσθαι *in certain matters one must practice self-control* Hm 8:1. οὔτε . . . οἴδασι τὸν ἐ. τοῦ πυροῦ σπόρον *nor do they comprehend* (the figurative sense of) *the sowing of wheat* AcPlCor 2:26 (cp. 1 Cor 15:36f).

❾ **marker of power, authority, control of or over someone or someth.,** ***over***—ⓐ w. gen. (Hdt. 5, 109 al.; Mitt-Wilck. I/1, 124, 1=BGU 1120, 1 [5 BC] πρωτάρχῳ ἐ. τοῦ κριτηρίου; 287, 1; LXX; AscIs 2:5 τοῦ ἐ. τῶν πραγματε[ι]ῶν=Denis p. 109) βασιλεύειν ἐ. τινος (Judg 9:8, 10; 1 Km 8:7) **Rv 5:10.** ἔχειν βασιλείαν ἐ. τῶν βασιλέων **17:18.** ἐξουσίαν ἔχειν ἐ. τινος *have power over someone* **20:6.** διδόναι ἐξουσίαν ἐ. τινος **2:26.** καθιστάναι τινὰ ἐ. τινος *set someone over, put someone in charge, of someth.* or *someone* (Pla., Rep. 5, 460b; Demosth. 18, 118; Gen 39:4f; 1 Macc 6:14; 10:37; 2 Macc 12:20 al.; EpArist 281; τεταγμένος En 20:5) **Mt 24:45; Lk 12:42; Ac 6:3.** εἶναι ἐ. τινος (Synes., Ep. 79 p. 224d; Tob 1:22; Jdth 14:13; 1 Macc 10:69) ὃς ἦν ἐ. πάσης τῆς γάζης αὐτῆς *who was in charge of all her treasure* **8:27.** Of God ὁ ὢν ἐ. πάντων (Apollonius of Tyana [I AD] in Eus., PE 4, 13) **Ro 9:5;** cp. **Eph 4:6.** ὁ ἐ. τινος w. ὤν to be supplied (Demosth. 18, 247 al.; Diod. S. 13, 47, 6; Plut., Pyrrh. 385 [5, 7], Aemil. Paul. 267 [23, 6]; PTebt 5, 88 [118 BC] ὁ ἐ. τ. προσόδων; 1 Macc 6:28; 2 Macc 3:7; 3 Macc 6:30 al.; EpArist 110; 174) ὁ ἐ. τοῦ κοιτῶνος *the chamberlain* **Ac 12:20.**

ⓑ w dat. (X., Cyr. 1, 2, 5; 2, 4, 25 al., An. 4, 1, 13; Demosth. 19, 113; Aeschines 2, 73; Esth 8:12e; Just., A II, 5, 2 ἀγγέλοις οὓς ἐ. τούτοις ἔταξε; cp. Ath. 24, 3; Ath. 6, 4 τὸν ἐ. τῇ κινήσει τοῦ σώματος λόγον) **Mt 24:47; Lk 12:44.**

ⓒ w. acc. (X., Hell. 3, 4, 20 al.; Dionys. Byz. §56 θεῷ ἐ. πάντα δύναμις; LXX; PsSol 17:3, 32) βασιλεύειν ἐ. τινα *rule over someone* (Gen 37:8; Judg 9:15 B al.) **Lk 1:33; 19:14, 27; Ro 5:14.** καθιστάναι τινὰ ἐ. τινα *set someone over someone* (X., Cyr. 4, 5, 58) κριτὴν ἐφ' ὑμᾶς *as judge over you* **Lk 12:14;** ἡγούμενον ἐπ' Αἴγυπτον **Ac 7:10;** cp. **Hb 2:7 v.l.** (Ps 8:7); **3:6; 10:21.** ἐξουσίαν ἔχειν ἐ. τι **Rv 16:9.** ἐξουσίαν διδόναι ἐ. τι (Sir 33:20) **Lk 9:1; 10:19; Rv 6:8;** cp. **22:14.** φυλάσσειν φυλακὰς ἐ. τι **Lk 2:8** (cp. En 100:5). ὑπεραίρεσθαι ἐ. τινα *exalt oneself above someone* **2 Th 2:4** (cp. Da 11:36); but here the mng. *against* is also poss. (s. 12b below). πιστὸς ἐ. τι *faithful over someth.* **Mt 25:21, 23.**

❿ **marker of legal proceeding,** ***before,*** w. acc. in the lang. of the law-courts ἐ. ἡγεμόνας καὶ βασιλεῖς ἄγεσθαι *be brought before governors and kings* **Mt 10:18;** cp. **Lk 21:12** (cp. BGU 22, 36 [114 AD] ἀξιῶ ἀκθῆναι [=ἀχθῆναι] τ. ἐνκαλουμένους ἐ. σὲ πρὸς δέουσαν ἐπέξοδον; Just., A II, 2, 12 ἐ. Οὔρβικον). ὑπάγεις ἐπ᾽ ἄρχοντα *you are going before the magistrate* **Lk 12:58;** cp. **Ac 16:19.** ἤγαγον αὐτὸν ἐ. τὸν Πιλᾶτον **Lk 23:1.** ἐ. τοὺς ἀρχιερεῖς **Ac 9:21.** ἐ. Καίσαρα πορεύεσθαι *come before the emperor* **25:12.** ἐ. τὰς συναγωγάς **Lk 12:11.** ἐ. τὸ βῆμα **Ac 18:12.** Cp. 3 above. Here the focus is on transfer to the judiciary.

⓫ **marker of purpose, goal, result,** ***to, for,*** w. acc. (Demetr.: 722 fgm. 2, 3 Jac. ἐ. κατοικίαν) ἐ. τὸ βάπτισμα *for baptism*=to have themselves baptized **Mt 3:7** (cp. Just., A I, 61, 10 ἐ. τὸ λουτρόν; D. 56, 1 ἐ. τὴν . . . κρίσιν πεμφθεῖσι). ἐ. τὴν θεωρίαν ταύτην *for* (i.e. to see) *this sight* **Lk 23:48** (sim. Hom. et al.; POxy 294, 18 [22 AD]; LXX; Tat. 23, 2 ἐ. τὴν θέαν). ἐ. τὸ συμφέρον *to (our) advantage* **Hb 12:10** (cp. Tat. 6, 1; 34, 2 οὐκ ἐ. τι χρήσιμον 'to no purpose'). ἐ. σφαγήν **Ac 8:32** (Is 53:7); cp. **Mt 22:5;** ἐ. τ. τελειότητα **Hb 6:1.** ἐ. τοῦτο *for this* (X., An. 2, 5, 22; Jos., Ant. 12, 23) **Lk 4:43.** ἐφ᾽ ὅ; *for what (reason)?* **Mt 26:50 v.l.** (s. ὅς 1bα and 1iβ). Cp. 16.

⓬ **marker of hostile opposition,** ***against***—ⓐ w. dat. (Hom. et al.; 2 Macc 13:19; Sir 28:23 v.l.; fig. Ath. 22, 7 τοὺς ἐπ᾽ αὐτοῖς λόγους 'counter-evidence') **Lk 12:52f** (s. use of acc. b below); **Ac 11:19.** Cp. **J 8:7 v.l.** (1bβ above).

ⓑ w. acc. (Hdt. 1, 71; X., Hell. 3, 4, 20 al.; Jos., Ant. 13, 331; LXX; En; TestJud 3:1 al.; JosAs 19:2; Just., D. 103, 7; Tat. 36, 2) ὥρμησαν ἐ. αὐτόν **Ac 7:57.** ἔρχεσθαι **Lk 14:31.** ἐπαναστήσονται τέκνα ἐ. γονεῖς **Mt 10:21; Mk 13:12;** cp. ἔθνος ἐ. ἔθνος **Mt 24:7; Mk 13:8.** ἐφ᾽ ἑαυτόν divided *against himself* **Mt 12:26; Mk 3:24f, 26; Lk 11:17f;** cp. **J 13:18** (s. Ps 40:10); **Ac 4:27; 13:50** al.—**Lk 12:53** (4 times; the first and third occurrences w. the acc. are prob. influenced by usage in Mic 7:6; the use of the dat. **Lk 12:52f** [s. a above] w. a verb expressing a circumstance is in accord with older Gk. [Il. et al.], which prefers the acc. with verbs of motion in ref. to hostility). Cp. 15.

⓭ **marker of number or measure,** w. acc. (Hdt. et. al.; LXX; GrBar 3:6) ἐ. τρίς (CIG 1122, 9; PHolm α18) *three times* **Ac 10:16; 11:10.** So also ἐ. πολύ *more than once* Hm 4, 1, 8. ἐ. πολύ (also written ἐπιπολύ) in a different sense *to a great extent, carefully* (Hdt., Thu. et al.; Lucian, D. Deor. 6, 2; 25, 2; 3 Macc 5:17; Jos., Ant. 17, 107) B 4:1. ἐ. πλεῖον *to a greater extent, further* (Hdt., Thu. et al.; Diod. S. 11, 60, 5 al.; prob. 2 Macc 12:36; TestGad 7:2; Ar. 4, 3; Ath. 7, 1 ἐ. το πλεῖστον) **2 Ti 3:9;** 1 Cl 18:3 (Ps 50:4). ἐ. τὸ χεῖρον **2 Ti 3:13.** ἐφ᾽ ὅσον *to the degree that, in so far as* (Diod. S. 1, 93, 2; Maximus Tyr. 11, 3c ἐφ᾽ ὅσον δύναται; Hierocles 14 p. 451) **Mt 25:40, 45;** B 4:11; 17:1; **Ro 11:13.**

⓮ **marker indicating the one to whom, for whom, or about whom someth. is done,** ***to, on, about***—ⓐ w. dat. πράσσειν τι ἐ. τινι *do someth. to someone* **Ac 5:35** (thus Appian, Bell. Civ. 3, 15 §51; cp. δρᾶν τι ἐ. τινι Hdt. 3, 14; Aelian, NA 11, 11); *about* γεγραμμένα ἐπ᾽ αὐτῷ **J 12:16** (cp. Hdt. 1, 66). προφητεύειν ἐ. τινι **Rv 10:11.** μαρτυρεῖν *bear witness about* **Hb 11:4; Rv 22:16.** ἐ. σοὶ . . . φανερώσει κύριος τὸ λύτρον *the Lord will reveal the salvation to you* GJs 7:2.

ⓑ w. acc.—**α.** ὁ ἄνθρωπος ἐφ᾽ ὃν γεγόνει τὸ σημεῖον *the man on whom the miracle had been performed* **Ac 4:22** (cp. Just., D. 128, 1 κρίσεως γεγενημένης ἐ. Σόδομα). ἐφ᾽ ὃν λέγεται ταῦτα *the one about whom this was said* **Hb 7:13** (cp. ἐ. πόρρω οὖσαν [γενεὰν] ἐγὼ λαλῶ En 1:2). γέγραπται ἐπ᾽ αὐτόν **Mk 9:12f;** cp. **Ro 4:9; 1 Ti 1:18;** βάλλειν κλῆρον ἐ. τι *for someth.* **Mk 15:24; J 19:24** (Ps 21:19). ἀνέβη ὁ κλῆρος ἐ. Συμεών *the lot came up in favor of Simeon* GJs 24:4.

β. of powers, conditions, etc., which come upon someone or under whose influence someone is: *on, upon, to, over* ἐγένετο ῥῆμα θεοῦ ἐ. Ἰωάννην *the word of God came to John* **Lk 3:2** (cp. Jer 1:1). Of divine blessings (cp. En 1:8; ParJer 5:28) **Mt 10:13; 12:28; Lk 10:6; 11:20;** cp. **10:9; Ac 10:10.** ἵνα ἐπισκηνώσῃ ἐπ᾽ ἐμὲ ἡ δύναμις τ. Χριστοῦ *that the power of Christ may rest upon me* **2 Cor 12:9.** χάρις θεοῦ ἦν ἐπ᾽ αὐτό **Lk 2:40.** Various verbs are used in ref. to the Holy Spirit, either in pass. or act. role, in connection w. ἐ. τινα: ἐκχεῖν **Ac 2:17f** (Jo 3:1f); cp. **10:45; Tit 3:6.** ἀποστέλλειν (ἐξαποστέλλειν v.l.) **Lk 24:49.** ἐπέρχεσθαι **1:35; Ac 1:8** (Just., D. 87, 3; cp. ἔρχεσθαι A I, 33, 6; D. 49, 7 ἀπὸ τοῦ Ἠλίου ἐ. τὸν Ἰωάννην ἐλθεῖν). ἐπιπίπτειν **10:44.** καταβαίνειν **Lk 3:22; J 1:33.** τίθεσθαι **Mt 12:18** (cp. Is 42:1). Also εἶναι **Lk 2:25.** μένειν **J 1:32f.** ἀναπαύεσθαι **1 Pt 4:14.** Of unpleasant or startling experiences **Lk 1:12, 65; 4:36; Ac 13:11; 19:17; Rv 11:11.—Lk 19:43; 21:35,** cp. vs. **34; J 18:4; Eph 5:6;** cp. **Rv 3:3.—Ro 2:2, 9; 15:3** (Ps 68:10). Of the blood of the righteous, that comes *over* or *upon* the murderers **Mt 23:35; 27:25; Ac 5:28.** Of care, which one casts *on* someone else **1 Pt 5:7** (Ps 54:23).

⓯ **marker of feelings directed toward someone,** ***in, on, for, toward,*** w. acc., after words that express belief, trust, hope: πιστεύειν ἐ. τινα, w. acc. (Wsd 12:2; Just., D. 16:4 al.) **Ac 9:42; 11:17; 16:31; 22:19; Ro 4:24.** πίστις **Hb 6:1.** πεποιθέναι (Is 58:14) **Mt 27:43; 2 Th 3:4; 2 Cor 2:3.** ἐλπίζειν (1 Ch 5:20; 2 Ch 13:18 al.; PsSol 9:10; 17:3; Just., D. 16:4 al.) **1 Pt 1:13; 1 Ti 5:5.** After words that characterize an emotion or its expression: *for* κόπτεσθαι (Zech 12:10) **Rv 1:7; 18:9.** κλαίειν **Lk 23:28; Rv 18:9** (cp. JosAs 15:9 χαρήσεται ἐ. σέ). σπλαγχνίζεσθαι **Mt 15:32; Mk 8:2; 9:22;** Hm 4, 3, 5; s 9, 24, 2. χρηστός *toward* **Lk 6:35.** χρηστότης **Ro 11:22; Eph 2:7;** cp. **Ro 9:23.** Esp. also if the feelings or their expressions are of a hostile nature: *toward, against* (cp. λοιδορεῖν Just., D. 137, 2) ἀποτομία **Ro 11:22.** μαρτύριον **Lk 9:5.** μάρτυς ἐ. τ. ἐμὴν ψυχήν *a witness against my soul* (cp. Dssm., LO 258; 355 [LAE 304; 417]) **2 Cor 1:23.** ἀσχημονεῖν **1 Cor 7:36.** μοιχᾶσθαι **Mk 10:11.** τολμᾶν **2 Cor 10:2** (En 7:4). βρύχειν τ. ὀδόντας **Ac 7:54.** Cp. 12.

⓰ **marker of object or purpose,** with dat. in ref. to someth. (Hom., Thu. et al.; SIG 888, 5 ἐ. τῇ τῶν ἀνθρ. σωτηρίᾳ; PTebt 44, 6 [114 BC] ὄντος μου ἐ. θεραπείᾳ ἐν τῷ Ἰσιείῳ; LXX; TestJob 3:5 ὁ ἐ. τῇ σωτηρίᾳ τῆς ἐμῆς ψυχῆς ἐλθών; Jos., Ant. 5, 101; Just., A I, 29, 1 ἐ. παίδων ἀναστροφῇ; D. 91, 4 ἐ. σωτηρίᾳ τῶν πιστευόντων) καλεῖν τινα ἐ. τινι *call someone for someth.* **Gal 5:13** (on ἐπ᾽ ἐλευθερίᾳ cp. Demosth. 23, 124; [59], 32); ἐ. ἀκαθαρσίᾳ *for impurity,* i.e. so that we should be impure **1 Th 4:7.** κτισθέντες ἐ. ἔργοις ἀγαθοῖς *for good deeds* **Eph 2:10.** λογομαχεῖν ἐ. καταστροφῇ τῶν ἀκουόντων *for the ruin of those who hear* **2 Ti 2:14** (cp. Eur., Hipp. 511; X., Mem. 2, 3, 19 ἐ. βλάβῃ; Hdt. 1, 68 ἐ. κακῷ ἀνθρώπου; Polyb. 27, 7, 13 and PGM 4, 2440 ἐπ᾽ ἀγαθῷ='for good'). Cp. 11.

⓱ **marker in idiom of authorization,** w. dat.: the formula **ἐ. τῷ ὀνόματί τινος,** ***in the name of someone,*** used w. many verbs (Just., D. 39, 6 w. γίνεσθαι, otherw. ἐ. ὀνόματος, e.g. A I, 61, 13; w. διὰ τοῦ ὀ. and in oaths κατὰ τοῦ ὀ. A II, 6, 6, D. 30, 3; 85, 2.—Ath. 23, 1 ἐ. ὀνόματι εἰδώλων.— ἐν τῷ ὀνόματι LXX; JosAs 9:1), focuses on the authorizing function of the one named in the gen. (cp. WHeitmüller ['Im Namen Jesu' 1903, 13ff], 'in connection with, or by the use of, i.e. naming, or calling out, or calling upon the name' [88]): βαπτίζειν **Ac 2:38.** δέχεσθαί τινα **Mt 18:5; Mk 9:37; Lk 9:48.** διδάσκειν **Ac 4:18; 5:28.** δύναμιν ποιεῖν **Mk 9:39.** ἐκβάλλειν δαιμόνια **Lk 9:49 v.l.** ἔρχεσθαι **Mt 24:5; Mk 13:6; Lk 21:8.** κηρύσσειν **24:47.** λαλεῖν **Ac 4:17; 5:40.** Semantically divergent from the preceding, but formulaically analogous, is καλεῖν τινα ἐ. τῷ ὀν. τινος *name someone after someone* (2 Esdr 17:63) **Lk 1:59.**—ὄνομα 1dγ**ɔ**.—M-M.

⑱ **marker of temporal associations,** ***in the time of, at, on, for***—ⓐ w. gen., time within which an event or condition takes place (Hom.+) *in the time of, under* (kings or other rulers): *in the time of Elisha* **Lk 4:27** (cp. Just., D. 46, 6 ἐ. Ἠλίου). ἐ. τῆς μετοικεσίας *at the time of the exile* **Mt 1:11.** *Under*=during the rule or administration of (Hes., Op. 111; Hdt. 6, 98 al.; OGI 90, 15; PAmh 43, 2 [173 BC]; UPZ 162 V, 5 [117 BC]; 1 Esdr 2:12; 1 Macc 13:42; 2 Macc 15:22; Jos., Ant. 12, 156 ἐ. ἀρχιερέως Ὀ.) ἐ. Ἀβιαθὰρ ἀρχιερέως *under, in the time of, Abiathar the high priest* **Mk 2:26.** ἐ. ἀρχιερέως Ἅννα καὶ Καιάφα **Lk 3:2.** ἐ. Κλαυδίου **Ac 11:28** (Just., A I, 26, 2). ἐ. τῶν πατέρων *in the time of the fathers* 1 Cl 23:3. ἐπʼ ἐσχάτων τῶν ἡμερῶν *in the last days* (Gen 49:1; Num 24:14; Mi 4:1; Jer 37:24; Da 10:14) **2 Pt 3:3;** Hs 9, 12, 3; cp. **Hb 1:2.** ἐπʼ ἐσχάτου τοῦ χρόνου *in the last time* **Jd 18.** ἐπʼ ἐσχάτου τῶν χρόνων *at the end of the times/ages* **1 Pt 1:20.** ἐ. τῶν προσευχῶν μου *when I pray, in my prayers* (cp. PTebt 58, 31 [111 BC] ἐ. τ. διαλόγου, 'in the discussion'; 4 Macc 15:19 ἐ. τ. βασάνων 'during the tortures'; Sir 37:29; 3 Macc 5:40; Demetr.: 722, fgm. 1, 14 Jac. ἐ. τοῦ ἀρίστου; Synes., Ep. 121 p. 258c ἐ. τῶν κοινῶν ἱερῶν) **Ro 1:10; Eph 1:16; 1 Th 1:2; Phlm 4.**

ⓑ w. dat., time at or during which (Hom. et al.; PTebt 5, 66 [118 BC]; PAmh 157; LXX; Just., A I, 13, 3 ἐ. χρόνοις Τιβερίου) *at, in, at the time of, during:* ἐ. τοῖς νῦν χρόνοις *in these present times* 2 Cl 19:4. ἐ. τῇ πρώτῃ διαθήκῃ *at the time of the first covenant* **Hb 9:15.** ἐ. συντελείᾳ τ. αἰώνων *at the close of the age* **9:26** (Tat. 13, 1 ἐ. σ. τοῦ κόσμου; cp. Sir 22:10 and PLond III, 954, 18 p. 154 [260 AD] ἐ. τέλει τ. χρόνου; POxy 275, 20 [66 AD] ἐ. συνκλεισμῷ τ. χρόνου; En 27:3 ἐπʼ ἐσχάτοις αἰῶσιν). ἐ. τῇ θυσίᾳ *at the time of, together with, the sacrifice* **Phil 2:17.** ἐ. πάσῃ τῇ μνείᾳ ὑμῶν *at every remembrance of you* **Phil 1:3.** ἐ. παροργισμῷ ὑμῶν *during your wrath,* i.e. *while you are angry* **Eph 4:26.** ἐ. πάσῃ τῇ ἀνάγκῃ *in all (our) distress* **1 Th 3:7b.** ἐ. πάσῃ τῇ θλίψει **2 Cor 1:4.** ἐ. τούτῳ *in the meanwhile* **J 4:27** (Lucian, Dial. Deor. 17, 2, cp. Philops. 14 p. 41; Syntipas p. 76, 2 ἐφʼ ἡμέραις ἑπτα; 74, 6).

ⓒ w. acc.—**α.** answering the question 'when?' *on:* ἐ. τὴν αὔριον (Sb 6011, 14 [I BC]; PRyl 441 ἐ. τὴν ἐπαύριον) *(on) the next day* **Lk 10:35; Ac 4:5.** ἐ. τὴν ὥραν τ. προσευχῆς *at the hour of prayer* **3:1** (Polyaenus 8, 17 ἐ. ὥραν ὡρισμένην).

β. answering the qu. 'how long?' *for, over a period of* (Hom. et al.; Mitt-Wilck. II/2, 170, 8=BGU 1058, 9 [13 BC]; POxy 275, 9; 15 ἐ. τὸν ὅλον χρόνον; PTebt 381, 19 ἐφʼ ὃν χρόνον περίεστιν ἡ μήτηρ; LXX; En 106:15; TestJob 30:2 ἐ. ὥρας τρεῖς; TestJud 3:4; TestGad 5:11; Jos., Ant. 11, 2; Just., D. 142, 1 ἐ. ποσόν 'for awhile') ἐ. ἔτη τρία *for three years* (Phlegon: 257 fgm. 36, 2, 1 Jac.) **Lk 4:25.** ἐ. τρεῖς ἡμέρας *for three days* (Diod. S. 13, 19, 2; Arrian, Anab. 4, 9, 4; GDI 4706, 119 [Thera] ἐπʼ ἁμέρας τρεῖς) GPt 8:30 al. ἐ. ἡμέρας πλείους *over a period of many days* (Jos., Ant. 4, 277) **Ac 13:31.**—**16:18** (ἐ. πολλὰς ἡμέρας as Appian, Liby. 29 §124; cp. Diod. S. 3, 16, 4); **17:2; 19:8, 10, 34; 27:20; Hb 11:30.** ἐ. χρόνον *for a while* (cp. Il. 2, 299; Hdt. 9, 22, 1; Apollon. Rhod. 4, 1257; Jos., Vi. 2) **Lk 18:4.** ἐ. πλείονα χρόνον (Diod. S. 3, 16, 6; Hero Alex. I p. 344, 17) **Ac 18:20.** ἐφʼ ὅσον χρόνον *as long as* **Ro 7:1; 1 Cor 7:39; Gal 4:1.** Also ἐφʼ ὅσον *as long as* **Mt 9:15; 2 Pt 1:13** (for other mngs. of ἐφʼ ὅσον s. above under 13). ἐφʼ ἱκανόν (sc. χρόνον) *for a considerable time* (EpArist 109) **Ac 20:11.** ἐ. χρόνον ἱκανόν Qua. ἐ. πολύ *for a long time, throughout a long period of time* (Thu. 1, 7; 1, 18, 1; 2, 16, 1 al.; Appian, Liby. 5 §21; Arrian, Cyneg. 23, 1; Lucian, Toxar. 20; Wsd 18:20; Sir 49:13; JosAs 19:3; Jos., Vi. 66: Just., A I, 65, 3) **Ac 28:6.** ἐ. πλεῖον the same (schol. on Pind., N. 7, 56b; PLille 3, 16 [III BC]; Jdth 13:1; Sir prol. l. 7; Jos., Ant. 18, 150) **Ac 20:9;** *any longer* (Lucian, D. Deor. 5, 3; Appian, Hann. 54 §227; 3 Macc 5:8; Wsd 8:12; Ath. 12, 3) **Ac 24:4;** 1 Cl 55:1.

ἐπιβαίνω fut. ἐπιβήσομαι LXX; 2 aor. ἐπέβην; pf. ἐπιβέβηκα (s. βαίνω; Hom.+; also Tat. 39, 1 [w. gen.]).

❶ **to move up onto someth.,** ***go up/upon, mount, board*** ἐπί τι (Hdt. 8, 120; Thu. 1, 111, 2; 7, 69, 4; X., Hell. 3, 4, 1; SIG 709, 36 [107 BC]; in all these passages the boarding of ships is involved. Gen 24:61 ἐπὶ τὰς καμήλους. 1 Km 25:20, 42 ἐπὶ τὴν ὄνον. Jos., Ant. 11, 258 ἐπὶ τ. ἵππον) ἐπὶ ὄνον **Mt 21:5** (Zech 9:9; cp. Just., A I, 32, 6). ἐπὶ τὸ θυσιαστήριον GJs 5:1. πλοίῳ (cp. Thu. 7, 70, 5 ταῖς ναυσίν) **Ac 27:2;** cp. Ac 21:6 v.l. Abs. *go on board, embark* (Thu. 7, 62, 2) **21:1** D, **2.**—So perh. also ἐ. εἰς Ἱεροσόλυμα *embark for Jerusalem* (i.e. to the seaport of Caesarea) vs. **4.** But this pass. may also belong to

❷ **to move to an area and be there,** ***set foot in*** (Hom. et al.) εἰς τ. Ἀσίαν *set foot in Asia* **Ac 20:18** (cp. Diod. S. 14, 84, 1 εἰς τ. Βοιωτίαν; POxy 1155, 3f [104 AD] ἰς Ἀλεξάνδρηαν; PFlor 275, 22; ViJer 7 ἐν Αἰγύπτῳ; Just., D. 16, 2 εἰς τὴν Ἰερουσαλήμ). W. dat. (Diod. S. 16, 66, 6) τῇ ἐπαρχείᾳ (v.l. ἐπαρχείῳ) *the province* **25:1** (s. ἐπάρχειος; cp. SIG 797, 16 [37 AD] ἐπιβὰς τῇ ἐπαρχείᾳ).—M-M.

ἐπιβάλλω (s. βάλλω) fut. ἐπιβαλῶ LXX; 2 aor. ἐπέβαλον, 3 pl. ἐπέβαλαν **Mk 14:46 v.l.; Ac 21:27 v.l.** (W-S. §13, 13; Mlt-H. 208); pf. 2 sg. ἐπιβέβληκας Ex 20:25. Pass.: fut. 3 sg. ἐπιβληθήσεται LXX; aor. 3 sg. ἐπεβλήθη LXX (Hom.+).

❶ **to put on,** trans., act.—ⓐ ***throw over*** τί τινι *someth. on someone:* βρόχον *a noose* **1 Cor 7:35** (perh. w. ref. to a halter that would help keep the wearers in check: 'keep you on a tight rein' REB). τί ἐπί τι **Rv 18:19 v.l.**

ⓑ ***lay on, put on*** ἱμάτιόν τινι (Lev 19:19.—Od. 14, 520 χλαῖναν) **Mk 11:7;** without the dat. **10:50 v.l.** τὴν χεῖρα *lay the hand* (Dt 15:10) ἐπί τι *on someth.* **Lk 9:62.** τὰς χεῖρας *hands* τινί *on someone* violently (Polyb. 3, 2, 8; 3, 5, 5; Lucian, Tim. 4; UPZ 106, 19 [99 BC]; Jos., Bell. 2, 491; Esth 6:2; Just., D. 95, 4) **Mk 14:46; Ac 4:3.** Also ἐπί τινα (PLeid G 19 [II BC], H 26) **Mt 26:50; Lk 20:19; 21:12; J 7:44** (ἔβαλεν v.l.); **Ac 5:18; 21:27** (Just., D. 93, 4 μέχρις … τοῦ Χριστοῦ 'even on the Messiah'). The sing. τ. χεῖρα in this connection is rare (Aristoph., Nub. 933, Lysistr. 440; Gen 22:12; 2 Km 18:12) *no one laid a hand on him* **J 7:30.** ἐ. τὰς χεῖρας foll. by inf. of purpose **Ac 12:1;** ἐπίβλημα ἐπὶ ἱματίῳ **Mt 9:16;** ἐπὶ ἱμάτιον **Lk 5:36.**

❷ **set to,** intr., act.—ⓐ ***throw oneself or beat upon*** (Pla., Phdr. 248a; Polyb. 5, 18, 3; 1 Macc 4:2) *break over* τὰ κύματα εἰς τὸ πλοῖον *the waves broke over the boat* **Mk 4:37.**

ⓑ The mng. of καὶ ἐπιβαλὼν ἔκλαιεν **Mk 14:72** is in doubt. Theophylact. offers a choice betw. ἐπικαλυψάμενος τ. κεφαλήν (so ASchlatter, Zürcher Bibel '31; Field, Notes 41–43; but in that case τὸ ἱμάτιον could scarcely be omitted) and ἀρξάμενος, which latter sense is supported by the v.l. ἤρξατο κλαίειν and can mean ***begin*** (PTebt 50, 12 [112/111 BC] ἐπιβαλὼν συνέχωσεν='he set to and dammed up' [Mlt. 131f]; Diogen. Cyn. in Diog. L. 6, 27 ἐπέβαλε τερετίζειν). The transl. would then be *and he began to weep* (EKlostermann; OHoltzmann; JSchniewind; CCD; s. also B-D-F §308). Others (BWeiss; HHoltzmann; 20th Cent.; Weymouth; L-S-J-M) proceed fr. the expressions ἐ. τὸν νοῦν or τὴν διάνοιαν (Diod. S. 20, 43, 6) and fr. the fact that ἐ. by itself, used w. the dat., can mean *think of* (M. Ant. 10, 30; Plut., Cic. 862 [4, 4]; Ath. 7, 1 'deal with a problem'), to the mng. *and he thought of it,* or *when he reflected on it.,* viz. Jesus' prophecy. Wlh. ad loc. has urged against this view that it is made unnecessary by the preceding ἀνεμνήσθη κτλ. Least probable of all is the equation of ἐπιβαλών with ἀποκριθείς (HEwald) on the basis of Polyb. 1, 80, 1; 22, 3, 8; Diod. S. 13, 28, 5 ἐπιβαλὼν ἔφη. Both REB ('he burst into tears') and NRSV ('he broke down and wept') capture the sense. Prob. Mk intends the reader to understand a wild gesture connected with lamentation (s. EdeMartino, Morte e pianto rituale nel mondo antico, '58, esp. 195–235).

❸ **to be scheduled for someone's possession,** ***fall to, belong to,*** intr., act. an extension of mng. 2, τὸ ἐπιβάλλον μέρος *the part that falls* to someone (Diod. S. 14, 17, 5; SIG 346, 36; 546 B, 19; 1106, 80; POxy 715, 13ff; PFouad 25 verso I, 12f; PFay 93, 8; cp. Tob 6:12; Ath., R. 49, 2 τῆς ἐπιβαλλούσης ἑκάστῳ χώρας 'the place appropriate to each'—Dssm., NB 57 [BS 230]) **Lk 15:12** (JDerrett, Law in the NT '70, 106). Impers. ἐπιβάλλει τινί *someone has opportunity* or *it is proper for someone* (Polyb. 18, 51, 1; OGI 443, 10; UPZ 110, 10 [164 BC] πᾶσιν ἐπιβάλλει; Tob 3:17; Jos., Bell. 1, 434, Ant. 19, 6) Pol 1:1. **Lk 15:12** that which belongs to me, 'is coming to me'.

❹ **to apply oneself earnestly to someth.,** ***take someth. upon oneself, undertake*** (lit. 'throw oneself upon'), mid. w. acc. (Thu. 6, 40, 2; UPZ 41, 26 [161/160 BC] πᾶν ὃ ἂν ἐπιβάλλησθε; Just., D. 68, 1 w. inf.) πρᾶξιν Hm 10, 2, 2. πολλά s 6, 3, 5.—M-M. TW.

ἐπιβαρέω 1 aor. ἐπεβάρησα **to be a burden to,** ***weigh down, burden*** (Dionys. Hal. 4, 9; 8, 73; Appian, Bell. Civ. 4, 15 §60; 4, 31 §133; Cyr. Ins. 8f; SIG 807, 16 [c. 54 AD]; POxy 1481, 12 [II AD]; POslo 60, 8) τινά *someone* πρὸς τὸ μὴ ἐπιβαρῆσαί τινα ὑμῶν *that I might not be a burden to any of you* **1 Th 2:9; 2 Th 3:8** (cp. 2 Cor 11:9 and s. ἀβαρής, καταβαρέω; Paul emulates civic-minded pers. who did not wish the public to be burdened, s. SIG citation above; cp. IGR III, 739, 30, 57f of the billionaire Opramoas μηδὲ ἐν τούτῳ βουλόμενος βαρεῖν τὸ ἔθνος 'not wishing in this matter to burden the people'). ἵνα μὴ ἐπιβαρῶ **2 Cor 2:5** seems to have the mng. 'in order not to heap up too great a burden of words'= *in order not to say too much* (Heinrici, Schmiedel, Ltzm., H-DWendland), although there are no exx. of it in this mng. Other possibilities are *exaggerate, be too severe with.* On the rhetorical aspect s. CClassen, WienerStud 107/108, '94/95, 333.—DELG s.v. βαρύς. M-M.

ἐπιβιβάζω fut. ἐπιβιβῶ LXX; 1 aor. ἐπεβίβασα put someone (τινά) on someth. *cause someone to mount* (βιβάζω 'cause to mount'; Thu. et al.; PCairZen 805, 4 [III BC]; BGU 1742, 12; 1743, 9; Sb 9754, 12 [all I BC]; LXX) ***put on, put Jesus*** ἐπὶ τ. πῶλον **Lk 19:35** (cp. ET 42, '31, 236f; 288; 381f; 382f; 526f); cp. **Ac 23:24.** τινὰ ἐπὶ τὸ ἴδιον κτῆνος *on his own animal* **Lk 10:34** (cp. 3 Km 1:33; but ἐ. ἐπί can also mean *load upon* [2 Km 6:3], assuming that the man was unconscious).—DELG s.v. βαίνω.

ἐπιβλέπω fut. ἐπιβλέψω, -ομαι LXX; 1 aor. ἐπέβλεψα (TestJud 17:1; Just., D. 19:3 ἐπέβλεψεν for ἐπεῖδεν [Gen. 4:4]) (Soph., Pla. et al.; LXX; PsSol 18:2; JosAs; ParJer 6:8; EpArist; Jos., Ant. 12, 58; Test12Patr; UPZ 78, 38 [159 BC]; Sb 7600, 5 [16 AD]).

❶ **to look intently,** ***look, gaze*** of God ἐν ταῖς ἀβύσσοις *look into the depths* 1 Cl 59:3 (cp. Sir 16:19; Da 3:55 Theod.) ἐπὶ τὴν γῆν, τὸν χείμαρρον GJs 18:2 (not pap).—V.l. for ἐπισκέπτομαι GJs 1:4.

❷ **to pay close attention to, with implication of obsequiousness,** ***show special respect for, gaze upon*** **Js 2:3.**

❸ **to look attentively at, with implication of personal concern for someone,** ***look upon.*** Of God's loving care, that looks upon someone or someth. (Ps.-Lucian, Astrol. 20; LXX; cp. Jos., Ant. 1, 20; PGM 13, 621) ἐπί τινα 1 Cl 13:4 (Is 66:2); GJs 6:2. ἐπί τι: ἐπὶ τὴν ταπείνωσιν *upon the humble station* **Lk 1:48** (cp. 1 Km 1:11; 9:16). Also of Jesus *look at* i.e. take an interest in ἐπὶ τὸν υἱόν μου *take a look at* (w. implication to help) **Lk 9:38.**—M-M.

ἐπίβλημα, ατος, τό (s. βάλλω; Nicostr. Com. 15; Plut., Arrian et al.; as a piece of clothing used as a covering as early as SIG 1218, 4 [c. 420 BC], also Is 3:22; lit. 'that which is thrown over') **a piece of cloth used to repair a hole in clothing,** ***a patch*** **Mt 9:16; Mk 2:21; Lk 5:36.** B-D-F §272.—M-M.

ἐπιβοάω (s. βοάω) fut. 1 pl. ἐπιβοήσομεν (Just.) (act. Aeschyl., Thu. et al.; IG IV^2/1, 742, 6 [II/III AD]; 4 Macc 6:4; Just. A I, 68, 2; mid. BGU VIII, 1762, 3 [I BC]) **to make a loud utterance,** ***cry out loudly*** (Heraclit. Sto. 6 p. 9, 15) of an aroused mob (Jos., Bell. 4, 283 ἐπεβόα πλῆθος, Ant. 11, 57) *yell, shout* **Ac 25:24 v.l.;** MPol 3:2; 12:2f.—DELG s.v. βοή. M-M.

ἐπιβουλή, ῆς, ἡ (s. βουλή; Hdt., Thu. et al.; UPZ 8, 14 [161 BC]; BGU 1816, 12 [60/59 BC]; POxy 237 VI, 6; 31; Sb 7464, 16; 9534, 5; LXX; TestBenj 3:5; ApcrEzk [Epiph. 70, 7]; Philo, Joseph.) **a secret plan to do someth. evil or cause harm,** ***a plot*** εἴς τινα *against someone* (Jos., Ant. 2, 197; 16, 319) **Ac 23:30.** Also τινί **20:3.** ἡ ἐ. αὐτῶν *their plot* **9:24.** Pl. (Epict. 1, 22, 14; 1 Esdr 5:70; 2 Macc 8:7 v.l.) ἐν ταῖς ἐ. τῶν Ἰουδαίων *through the plots of the Judeans* **20:19.**—DELG s.v. βούλομαι. M-M.

ἐπιγαμβρεύω (γαμβρεύω 'form connection by marriage') fut. ἐπιγαμβρεύσω; 1 aor. ἐπεγάμβρευσα **to become related by marriage** (schol. on Eur., Orest. 585–604, Phoen. 347; LXX), then ***marry as next of kin,*** usu. brother-in-law of levirate marriage γυναῖκα **Mt 22:24** (Dt 25:5 Aq.; cp. Gen 38:8 v.l. [ARahlfs, Genesis 1926, 159]; TestJud 10:4 'give her brother-in-law as husband to the widow'; reversed in the Armenian version). For the word s. Anz 378; for the idea KRengstorf, Jebamot 1929.—DELG s.v. γαμβρός. M-M.

ἐπίγειος, ον (Pla. et al.; TestSol; TestAbr A 4, 81, 18 [Stone p. 10]; Philo; Jos., Ant. 6, 186; 8, 44; Just., A II, 5, 2; Tat. 32, 1; Mel., P. 39; Ath.)

❶ **pert. to what is chacteristic of the earth as opposed to heavenly,** ***earthly***—ⓐ as adj. (Plut., Mor. 566d; M. Ant. 6, 30, 4 ἐ. ζωή; pap; TestJud 21:4; Ath. 31, 3 βίον) σῶμα **1 Cor 15:40** (opp. ἐπουράνιος; on this contrast s. below 1bα and MDahl, Resurrection of the Body '62, 113–16). Of the body οἰκία ἐ. *earthly dwelling* (cp. Philo, Cher. 101) **2 Cor 5:1** (EEllis, Paul and His Recent Interpreters '61, 40–43). W. the connotation of weakness (Lucian, Icarom. 2): σοφία *earthly wisdom*=human philosophy **Js 3:15** (cp. Ath. 24, 5 [mutilated context]) cp. εὕρημα ἐ. *an earthly* (i.e. *purely human*) *discovery* Dg 7:1. πνεῦμα ἐ. *earthly spirit* of the spirit in false prophets Hm 9:11; 11:6, 11f, 14, 17, 19 (cp. Tat. 32, 1 λόγου τοῦ . . . ἐ.).

ⓑ as subst.—α. τὰ ἐ. (M. Ant. 7, 48; Philo, Op. M. 101; 113; Just., A II, 5, 2; Ath. 27, 1 [both opp. τὰ ἐπουράνια].—Opp. τὰ ἐπουράνια as Herm. Wr. fgm. 26 p. 544, 1 Sc. Cp. Philo, Op. M. 117; Mel., P. 39.) *earthly things* **J 3:12** (LBrun, SymbOsl 8, 1929, 57–77); cp. Pol 2:1; Dg 7:2.

β. οἱ ἐ.: in the expr. πᾶν γόνυ ἐπουρανίων καὶ ἐπιγείων καὶ καταχθονίων **Phil 2:10** the second of the three main concepts is not confined to human beings (cp. PGM 4, 225f; 3038ff, esp. 3042f πᾶν πνεῦμα δαιμόνιον . . . ἐπουράνιον ἢ ἀέριον εἴτε ἐπίγειον εἴτε ὑπόγειον ἢ καταχθόνιον. 5, 166f πᾶς δαίμων οὐράνιος κ. αἰθέριος κ. ἐπίγειος κ. ὑπόγειος. 12,

67 θεοὶ οὐράνιοι κ. ἐπίγειοι κ. ἀέριοι κ. ἐπιχθόνιοι. 17a, 3 Ἄνουβι, θεὲ ἐπίγειε κ. ὑπόγειε κ. οὐράνιε. IDefixWünsch 4, 11; TestSol); cp. ITr 9:1.—IEph 13:2 it is impossible to say w. certainty from which nom. ἐπιγείων is derived, ἐπίγειοι or ἐπίγεια.

❷ **pert. to earthly things, with implication of personal gratification,** subst. ***worldly things*** τὰ ἐ. φρονεῖν *think only of worldly things* **Phil 3:19.**—DELG s.v. γῆ. M-M. TW.

ἐπιγελάω fut. ἐπιγελάσομαι (s. γελάω; Pla., X. et al.; LXX; Just., D. 139, 1) ***laugh at*** τινί *someth.* (Jos., Bell. 1, 233 ταῖς ἐλπίσιν) ἐ. τῇ ὑμετέρᾳ ἀπωλείᾳ *at your destruction* 1 Cl 57:4 (Pr 1:26).

ἐπιγίνομαι 2 aor. ἐπεγενόμην (s. γίνομαι; in var. mngs., but gener. of someth. happening next, Hom. et al.; ins, pap, LXX; TestSol 9:8 L for παραγίνομαι; Philo, Aet. M. 20 al.) **to happen, with implication of existence of a new condition,** ***come to pass,*** of wind *come up* (Thu. 3, 74, 2; 4, 30, 2; Diod. S. 18, 20, 7 ἐπιγενομένου μεγάλου πνεύματος; Jos., Ant. 9, 209) **Ac 28:13.** Of the night *come on* (Hdt. 8, 70 al.; Arrian, Anab. 1, 2, 7 νὺξ ἐπιγενομένη; 2, 11, 5; Polyaenus 3, 7, 3 al.; Jos., Ant. 1, 301) **27:27 v.l.**—DELG s.v. γίγνομαι. M-M.

ἐπιγινώσκω fut. ἐπιγνώσομαι; 2 aor. ἐπέγνων; pf. ἐπέγνωκα; 1 aor. pass. ἐπεγνώσθην (Hom.+) gener. 'know, understand, recognize'.

❶ **to have knowledge of someth. or someone,** ***know***

ⓐ with the prep. making its influence felt, *know exactly, completely, through and through* τὶ *someth.* (Jos., Ant. 20, 128 τ. ἀλήθειαν) τ. ἀσφάλειαν **Lk 1:4.** τ. δικαίωμα τ. θεοῦ **Ro 1:32.** τ. χάριν τ. θεοῦ **Col 1:6** (here ἐ. is the second stage after ἀκούειν; cp. IEph 4:2). Abs. **1 Cor 13:12a** (opp. γινώσκειν ἐκ μέρους); PtK 3 p. 15, 27. W. relat. clause foll. Dg 11:7. Pass. **1 Cor 13:12b; 2 Cor 6:9.**

ⓑ with no emphasis on the prep., essentially=γινώσκειν (X., Hell. 5, 4, 12, cp. 6, 5, 17; Thu. 1, 132, 5; SIG 741, 21; 747, 30; PFay 112, 14; PTebt 297, 9 al.; EpArist 246; SibOr 3, 96) *know* abs. Dg 10:3; 12:6. τινά **Mt 11:27** (the par. Lk 10:22 has the simple verb γιν.), s. on παραδίδωμι 3 end; **14:35; Mk 6:54;** Hv 5:3. EpilMosq 3, s. 4 below. Dg 10:1 (cj. Nock; s. Marrou ed.). τὸν κύριον B 10:3 (Is 1:3). ὁ δὲ θεὸν ἐπιγνούς Hs 9, 18, 1. τί **Ac 27:39.** τὴν ἀλήθειαν **1 Ti 4:3;** cp. 1 Cl 32:1 (Just., D. 110, 6); Hs 8, 6, 3; 8, 11, 2; Dg 10:8. τινὰ ἀπό τινος *someone by someth.* (cp. Sir 19:29) **Mt 7:16, 20** (the par. Lk 6:44 has the simplex). ἐ. μέλη ὄντας *recognize that you are members* IEph 4:2. ἐπιγνοὺς ἐνάρετον … οὖσαν *as I perceive how noble is* (the overseer's/bishop's mind) IPhld 1:2 (sim. w. ptc. Just., D. 58, 3 αὐτὸν ὑπηρετοῦντα). W. ὅτι foll. **Ac 19:34** (En 98:8; Just., D. 51, 3 al.). W. acc. and ὅτι foll. **1 Cor 14:37; 2 Cor 13:5;** Hv 5:4. Pass. w. indir. quest. foll. Hs 4:3.

❷ **to ascertain or gain information about someth.,** with no emphasis on the prep.—ⓐ ***learn, find out*** (Jos., Vi. 181) abs. **Mk 6:33** (v.l. ἔγνωσαν). W. ὅτι foll. (1 Macc 6:17) **Lk 7:37; 23:7; Ac 22:29; 28:1.**

ⓑ ***learn to know*** abs. **2 Pt 2:21b.** τὶ *someth.* (Herodian 2, 1, 10) **2:21a;** Hm 6, 2, 6; s9, 16, 7; PtK 4 p. 16, 1. περί τινος *someone* IRo 10:2.

ⓒ ***notice, perceive, learn of, ascertain*** abs. **Ac 9:30** (Field, Notes 117f). τὶ **Lk 5:22.** τὶ ἐν ἑαυτῷ *perceive someth. (in oneself)* **Mk 5:30** (the parallel Lk 8:46 has the simplex). W. ὅτι foll. **Lk 1:22.** ἐ. τῷ πνεύματι, ὅτι *perceive (in one's own mind) that* **Mk 2:8.** Also as legal t.t. *ascertain* (2 Macc 14:9) τὶ **Ac 23:28;** cp. **24:8.** W. ὅτι foll. **24:11.** W. relat. clause foll. **22:24.**

❸ **to connect present information or awareness with what was known before,** ***acknowledge acquaintance with, recognize, know again*** τινά *someone,* with the prep. making its influence felt **Lk 24:16, 31** (TestJob 28:3; Just., D. 40, 4; on self-disclosure in Gk. culture cp. GMost, JHS 109, '89, 114–33). τὶ *someth.* **Ac 12:14** (τ. φωνήν τινος as 1 Km 26:17; Judg 18:3 A). W. acc. of pers. and ὅτι foll. **3:10; 4:13.**

❹ **to indicate that one values the person of another,** ***acknowledge, give recognition to*** τινά *someone,* with the prep. making its influence felt (Chion, Ep. 6; Ruth 2:10, 19) **Mt 17:12** (mng. 3 is also prob.); **1 Cor 16:18** (Just., D. 29, 2; 45, 4 al.). EpilMosq 3 (in wordplay, w. Polycarp's answer to be understood in the sense of 1b).

❺ **to come to an understanding of,** ***understand, know*** τὶ or τινά **2 Cor 1:13f** (here the intensfying ἕως τέλους causes ἐ. to equal the simple verb γιν.; note also the qualifiers in the pass. that follow). τὸ ἀληθῶς ζῆν *know the true life* Dg 10:7. σὺ κάλλιον ἐπιγινώσκεις *you know very well* **Ac 25:10** (the influence of the adverb causes the compound to sink to the level of the simplex, as PLond II, 354, 24 p. 165 [c. 10 BC] ἐπιγνόντα ἀκρειβῶς ἕκαστα; Just., D. 96, 2 μᾶλλον).—DELG s.v. γιγνώσκω. M-M. TW.

ἐπίγνωσις, εως, ἡ (s. γνῶσις and prec. entry; Philo Mech. 59, 2; Polyb. 3, 7, 6; 3, 31, 4; Diod. S. 3, 38, 2; Epict. 2, 20, 21; Plut., Mor. 1145a; Herodian 7, 6, 7; pap [Mayser 438; UPZ 118, 16: 136 BC?; BGU 1873, 20f; PTebt 28, 11: c. 114 BC]; LXX, EpArist, Philo, Just., Tat.; καιρῶν ἐ. Did., Gen. 195, 28) ***knowledge, recognition*** in our lit. limited to transcendent and moral matters (Hierocles 22 p. 467). W. gen. of the thing known (Diod. S. 3, 56, 5 τῶν ἄστρων ἐ.) δόξης ὀνόματος αὐτοῦ 1 Cl 59:2 (here ἀγνωσία as contrast to ἐπίγν.). (τῆς) ἀληθείας *a knowledge of the truth* (Epict. 2, 20, 21; Philo, Omn. Pr. L. 74; τοῦ ἀληθοῦς Just., D. 3, 4.—MDibelius, Ἐπίγνωσις ἀληθείας: GHeinrici Festschr. 1914, 178–89) **1 Ti 2:4; 2 Ti 2:25; 3:7; Tit 1:1; Hb 10:26** (for the expr. εἰς ἐπίγνωσιν ἔρχεσθαι in **1 Ti 2:4; 2 Ti 3:7** cp. 2 Macc 9:11). ἁμαρτίας *consciousness of sin* **Ro 3:20.** τοῦ μυστηρίου τ. θεοῦ **Col 2:2.** τοῦ θελήματος αὐτοῦ **1:9.** παντὸς ἀγαθοῦ **Phlm 6** (cp. Herm. Wr. 3, 3b ἀγαθῶν ἐ.; EpArist 139; ἐ. τοῦ καλοῦ Did., Gen. 72, 17). W. gen. of the pers. known ἐ. τοῦ θεοῦ *knowledge of God* (Pr 2:5; Hos 4:1; Just., A II, 10, 6; Tat. 13, 1) **Col 1:10; 2 Pt 1:2;** cp. **Eph 1:17; 2 Pt 1:3;** Dg 10:1. Also ἡ περί σου ἐ. MPol 14:1; ἐ. τοῦ υἱοῦ τοῦ θεοῦ **Eph 4:13;** cp. **2 Pt 1:8; 2:20.** Knowledge of God and Christ **2 Pt 1:2;** but legal terminology may be reflected here (=cognitio, cp. PTebt 28, 11 πρὸς τὸ μὴ ἕκαστα ὑπ' ἐπίγνωσιν ἀχθῆναι [114 BC]; SIG 826d, 16f). Abs. (cp. Hos 4:6) θεὸν ἔχειν ἐν ἐ. *to recognize God* **Ro 1:28;** (w. αἴσθησις) **Phil 1:9;** ἀνακαινούμενος εἰς ἐ. *renewed in knowledge* **Col 3:10.** κατ' ἐπίγνωσιν *in accordance w. (real) knowledge* **Ro 10:2.**—DELG s.v. γιγνώσκω. M-M. TW.

ἐπιγραφή, ῆς, ἡ (s. γραφή; Thu. et al.; ins, pap; TestSol 18:22 P; Philo; Jos., Ant. 15, 272; Just., A I, 26, 2) ordinarily of a document incised on stone, but also of identifying notices on any kind of material: ***inscription, superscription*** of the 'titulus' fastened to a cross (cp. Sueton., Calig. 32, Domit. 10; Cass. Dio 54, 3; Eus., HE 5, 1, 44) ἐ. τῆς αἰτίας **Mk 15:26.** ἦν ἐ. ἐπ' αὐτῷ **Lk 23:38.** Of legends on coins **Mt 22:20; Mk 12:16; Lk 20:24.**—DELG s.v. γράφω. M-M.

ἐπιγράφω fut. ἐπιγράψω; 1 aor. ἐπέγραψα LXX. Pass.: 2 aor. ἐπεγράφην; pf. ἐπιγέγραμμαι; plpf. pass. ἐπεγεγράμμην (s. prec. entry; Hom.+)

❶ **to form letters or words on any kind of surface, *write on/in***—ⓐ lit., ὀνόματα ἐπιγεγραμμένα **Rv 21:12** (cp. εἰς χάρτην TestSol 18:25 P and cp. Sig T). ἦν ἡ ἐπιγραφὴ . . . ἐπιγεγραμμένη *the inscription (=identifying notice) . . . placed over him* **Mk 15:26;** cp. GPt 4:11 (cp. Ael. Aristid. 50, 46 K.=26 p. 516 D.: ἐπίγραμμα ἐπιγέγραπται). Of a dedicatory ins incised on an altar βωμὸς ἐν ᾧ ἐπεγέγραπτο (for ἐ. ἐν cp. SIG 89, 24 ἐν τῇ στήλῃ; 27; SIG[2] 588, 139; POxy 886, 16) **Ac 17:23** (cp. SIG 814, 48 . . . βωμόν, ἐπιγράφοντας . . .). ῥάβδους ἐπιγεγραμμένας ἑκάστης φυλῆς κατ᾿ ὄνομα *rods marked w. the name of each tribe* 1 Cl 43:2 (for the constr. ἐ. τί τινος cp. Plut., Mor. 400e; for the idea Num 17:16ff.—Diod. S. 13, 106, 9 a staff with an ἐπιγραφή).

ⓑ fig. *write in* or *on* ἐπί τι (cp. SIG 957, 68; 82; 1168, 7) ἐπὶ καρδίας **Hb 8:10** (Jer 38:33 v.l.; cp. Pr 7:3). ἐπὶ τὴν διάνοιαν **10:16.**

❷ **to enter a name into a record, *to record*** (Dem. 43, 15 'entered as guardian'; POxy 231, 52 [I AD]) fig. ἔργῳ ἐπιγράφεσθαι *be engaged in a work* (Socrat., Ep. 7, 2 μου εἰπόντος, ὡς οὐκ ἂν . . . ἔργῳ ἐπιγραφείην ἀδίκῳ; Appian, Bell. Civ. 1, 70 §323 ἔργοις ἐπιγράφεσθαι=take part in) οὔτε . . . κρείττονι ἔργῳ ἔχετε ἐπιγραφῆναι *and you can* (s. ἔχω 5) *not be identified with any better work* IRo 2:1. *Enroll* εἰς τὰς βίβλους τῶν ζώντων Hs 2:9.—M-M.

ἔπιδε s. ἐπεῖδον.

ἐπιδείκνυμι fut. ἐπιδείξω; 1 aor. ἐπέδειξα; pf. ptc. ἐπιδεδειχώς (Ath. 20, 1); pass. ptc. ἐπιδεδειγμένους 3 Macc 6:26 v.l. (Pind., Hdt.+)

❶ **to cause to be seen, *show, point out*** τινί τι *someth. to someone* (IAndrosIsis, Kyme 22 Ἐγὼ μυήσεις ἀνθρώποις ἐπέδειξα I [Isis] made humans acquainted w. initiations [into mystery rites]; Jos., Ant. 10, 31) **Mt 22:19; 24:1.** τὰς χεῖρας καὶ τοὺς πόδας **Lk 24:40 v.l.;** μαρτύριον MPol 1:1. ἐ. ἑαυτόν τινι *show oneself to someone* **Lk 17:14** (Appian, Mithrid. 89 §407 Ἀλέξανδρος αὑτὸν ἐπέδειξεν). ἐ. τινὶ σημεῖον ἐκ. τ. οὐρανοῦ *show someone* (=do in someone's presence) *a sign from heaven* **Mt 16:1;** cp. GJs 8:3. ἵνα μοι ἐπιδείξῃ ὃ ἐπηγγείλατο ὅραμα *so that you may grant me sight of the promised vision* Hv 3, 2, 3. Without dat. ὅλον ἑαυτὸν ἐπιδίξας *revealing himself completely* (a lion) AcPl Ha 4, 29. Also the mid. in the same mng. *show* τ. φυλάρχοις τὰς σφραγῖδας (cp. SIG 1157, 46f) 1 Cl 43:5. The mid. is found in a special sense **Ac 9:39** ἐπιδεικνύμεναι χιτῶνας, where the women *show* the garments *on themselves,* i.e. as they are wearing them (Socrat., Ep. 23, 3 τοιαῦτα ἐπιδεικνύμενοι=show such things on oneself).

❷ **to claim a characteristic or quality for someth., *represent,*** fig. extension of mng. 1 (Pla.; X., Symp. 3, 3 al.) τὸ ψεῦδός μου ἀληθὲς ἐπέδειξα *my lies I represented as truth* Hm 3:3.

❸ **to demonstrate that someth. is true, *demonstrate, show*** (Aristoph., Pla. et al.; Herm. Wr. 4, 7; PEleph 1, 7; PGiss 2 I, 24; LXX, esp. 4 Macc; Just., D. 24, 1) τί *someth., give proof* **Hb 6:17.** ἐ. ἑαυτόν *reveal oneself* Dg 8:5; cp. vs. 6. τινί w. indir. quest. foll. B 6:13. W. ὅτι foll. (Philo, Agr. 22) 5:7. W. διά τινος (Jos., C. Ap. 2, 1 διὰ τοῦ βιβλίου) θεὸς . . . διὰ γνώσεως ζωὴν ἐπιδεικνὺς *showing that life depends on knowledge* Dg 12:3 and acc. foll. **Ac 18:28.** Likew. the mid. (oft. Philo) 1 Cl 24:1. W. ὅτι foll. MPol 2:2.—M-M. TW.

ἐπιδέομαι 2 aor. sg. ἐπεδεήθης Dt 2:7 (s. δέομαι; Hdt. et al.; LXX; TestJob; Jos., C. Ap. 2, 192) ***need, be in need*** τινός *(of) a thing* (Alex. Aphr., An. Mant. II 1 p. 163, 1 οὐδενὸς ἐπιδεῖται=needs nothing; UPZ 59, 22 [108 BC] πάντων; Job 6:22) τῆς προσευχῆς καὶ ἀγάπης IMg 14. Of God οὗ τὰ πάντα ἐπιδέεται *of whom everything is in need* PtK 2. οἱ ἐπιδεόμενοι *those in need* (Sir 34:21; TestJob 9:6) Dg 10:6.—DELG s.v. 2 δέω.

ἐπιδέχομαι fut. 3 sg. ἐπιδέξεται Sir 36:21; 1 aor. ἐπεδεξάμην LXX; pf. ptc. ἐπιδεδεγμένος 2 Macc 2:26; 3 Macc 6:26(?) (Hdt. et al.; ins [freq. as t.t. for acceptance of a liturgy, but also of honorees; s. Mitchell, below], pap, LXX, TestIss 4:4, 6; EpArist, Philo; Jos., Vi. 218).

❶ **to receive into one's presence in a friendly manner, *receive, welcome*** τινά *someone* (Polyb. 21, 18, 3; Sb 12084 [I AD]; POxy 281, 9 [20–50 AD]; 1 Macc 10:1; 12:8, 43 al.) w. nuance of diplomatic courtesy **3J 9** and **10** of Diotrephes, who refuses to recognize emissaries; cp. the pass. from Polyb. and 1 Macc cited above.—Sim. in the sense *receive* **Ac 15:40** D (of Paul's reception of envoy Silas [s. vs. 27], not a misreading of ἐπιλεξάμενος).

❷ **to acknowledge receptively, *accept***=not reject (Polyb. 6, 24, 7; UPZ 110, 161 [164 BC]; 1 Macc 10:46; Sir 51:26) τινά *acknowledge someone's authority* **3J 9** (NRSV, w. many interpreters and versions; but the idea of 'authority' is not lexically defensible, s. 1 and MMitchell's refutation of this rendering, in JBL 117, '98, 299–320).—M-M.

ἐπιδημέω (s. δῆμος) 1 aor. ἐπεδήμασα (Thu. et al.; ins, pap, Philo, Joseph., Just.) the main idea in the use of this verb is the fact that the subject is in transit w. regard to a place to stay, hence it can be used both for a stay away from home as well as for a return home.

❶ **to stay in a place as a stranger or visitor, *be in town, stay*** (X., Pla. al.; Jos., Vi. 200 Γαλιλαῖον ἐπιδημοῦντα τοῖς Ἱεροσολύμοις; UPZ 42 I, 4 ἐν Μέμφει; cp. Wilcken, APF 4, 1908, 374; 422) οἱ ἐπιδημοῦντες Ῥωμαῖοι **Ac 2:10.** οἱ ἐ. ξένοι **17:21** (IPriene 108, 286; 111, 187 [I BC] τοὺς ἐπιδεδημηκότας ξένους). ἐν τῇ Ἐφέσῳ ἐπιδημοῦντές τινες Κορίνθιοι *some Corinthians were staying at Ephesus* **18:27** D. ἐπιδημοῦντος . . . σωτῆρος (opp. ἀπαλλαγέντος) *when the Redeemer was (on the earth)* Qua.

❷ **to go to the place where one normally lives, *return home*** (X., Pla.) ὅταν ἐπιδημήσῃς εἰς αὐτήν *when you go home to it* Hs 1:9.—DELG s.v. δῆμος. M-M.

ἐπιδημία, ας, ἡ (s. prec. entry; X., Pla. et al.; ins, pap; Philo, In Flacc. 33; Jos., Ant. 8, 102) **the state or condition of remaining in an area, *stay, sojourn*** of earthly life ἐ. τῆς σαρκὸς ἐν τῷ κόσμῳ τούτῳ *our stay* (lit. 'the sojourn of our flesh') *in this world* 2 Cl 5:5 (cp. Plut., Mor. 117f).—Sv.

ἐπιδιατάσσομαι (s. διατάσσω; only in Christian wr.; s. OEger, ZNW 18, 1918, 92f) **to add to, with implication of supplementary or modifying instructions,** legal t.t. ***add a codicil*** to a will **Gal 3:15.**—MConrat, ZNW 5, 1904, 215f.—TW.

ἐπιδίδωμι impf. 3 sing. ἐπεδίδου, 3 pl. ἐπεδίδουν; ἐπέδοσαν Hs 8, 5, 4; fut. ἐπιδώσω; 1 aor. ἐπέδωκα; 2 aor. ptc. ἐπιδούς; pf. ἐπιδέδωκα. Pass.: 1 aor. ἐπεδόθην; pf. ptc. ἐπιδεδομένος (s. δίδωμι; Hom.+).

❶ **to make a transfer of someth., *give, hand over, deliver*** τινί τι *someth. to someone* (for a meal: Lucian, Symp. 36; Aberciusins. 15) a stone **Lk 11:11 v.l.; Mt 7:9;** a snake vs. **10; Lk 11:11;** cp. a scorpion vs. **12;** a serving of fish **24:42;** bread vs. **30;** cp. ψωμίον **J 13:26 v.l.;** a letter **Ac 15:30** (cp. Diod. S. 14, 47, 2; Plut., Alex. 675 [19, 6]; PParis 20, 5; PEleph 15, 3; Jos., Ant. 15, 170); land of Canaan AcPl Ha 8, 13. Abs. *give* **Ac 27:35 v.l.**—Hv 3, 2, 5; s 8, 1, 2 and oft. τινὶ τ. χεῖρα Hv 1, 1, 2. Pass. ἐπεδόθη αὐτῷ βιβλίον τοῦ προφήτου Ἠσαΐου *the book of* *the prophet Isaiah was handed to him* **Lk 4:17** (cp. Jos., Vi. 361 ἐ. τὰ βιβλία). λίθοι ἦσαν ἀπὸ τῶν παρθένων ἐπιδεδομένοι Hs 9, 4, 6.

❷ **to yield control of someth.,** ***give up/over, surrender*** (Thu. 4, 11, 4; Plut., Mor. 319d; Athen. 12, 29, 525e εἰς τρυφήν) ἑαυτόν τινι (Polyaenus 4, 6, 1; Alex. Aphr., Fat. 32, II/2 p. 204, 27; OGI 730, 7 [s. also Larfeld I 494]; Jos., Bell. 6, 56, Ant. 4, 42; ὑπὲρ ἀληθείας … τὰς ψυχάς Ath. 3, 2) 1 Cl 14:2; 2 Cl 9:7. Abs. ἐπιδόντες ἐφερόμεθα *we gave* (ourselves) *up* (to the wind) *and let ourselves be driven* **Ac 27:15** (cp. Lucian, Hermot. 28 ἐ. ἑαυτὸν τῇ πνεούσῃ; s. also Alciphron 1, 10, 2).—M-M.

ἐπιδιορθόω (GDI 5039, 9 [Crete, II BC]; Themist., Or. 7 p. 113, 14; usu. in Christian wr.). In the only place where it occurs in our lit., both the 1 aor. subj. mid. ἐπιδιορθώσῃ and the 1 aor. subj. act. ἐπιδιορθώσῃς (v.l.) are attested; ***set right*** or ***correct in addition*** (to what has already been corrected) τὰ λείποντα *what remains* **Tit 1:5** (cp. Philo, In Flacc. 124 ἡ τῶν λειπομένων ἐπανόρθωσις). Simply *correct* is also prob. (Philopon., In Aristot., An. p. 525, 26; 28; 30 Hayduck).—DELG s.v. ὀρθός. M-M.

ἐπιδύω (δύω 'sink', s. δύσις) fut. mid. 3 sg. ἐπιδύσεται Dt 24:15; 2 aor. 3 sg. ἐπέδυ Jer 15:9 (w. tmesis Il. 2, 413; otherw. LXX; Philo, Spec. Leg. 3, 152 μὴ ἐπιδυέτω ὁ ἥλιος) **to sink down,** ***set (upon),*** esp. of the apparent movement of the sun when it 'sets' **Eph 4:26** (Plut., Mor. 488c πρὶν ἢ τὸν ἥλιον δῦναι τὰς δεξιὰς ἐμβαλόντες ἀλλήλοις 'before the sun went down they joined their right hands' and parted friends [the practice of Pythagoreans when they had altercations]; s. ἐπί 18b).—DELG s.v. δύω.

ἐπιείκεια, ας, ἡ (s. next entry; W-H. ἐπιεικία; cp. Gignac I 297; Mlt-H. 348) **the quality of making allowances despite facts that might suggest reason for a different reaction,** ***clemency, gentleness, graciousness, courtesy, indulgence, tolerance*** (Thu.; Aristot., EN 5, 14; Ps.-Pla., Def. 412b; Polyb. 1, 14, 4; Herodian 5, 1, 6; ins, pap, LXX; En 5:6; Philo, Mos. 1, 198; Jos., Ant. 6, 144; 15, 48) IPhld 1:1. τῇ σῇ ἐ. *with your (customary) indulgence* **Ac 24:4.** τῇ ἐπιεικείᾳ *by gentleness* IEph 10:3. W. πραΰτης (Plut., Pericl. 173 [39, 1], Sertor. 581 [25, 6]; Appian, Basil. 1 §5; Philo, Op. M. 103) **2 Cor 10:1;** Dg 7:4; 1 Cl 30:8; w. μακροθυμία 13:1; w. ταπεινοφροσύνη 30:8; 56:1. μετ' ἐκτενοῦς ἐπιεικείας *w. constant forbearance* 58:2; 62:2. ἐν πάσῃ ἐ. θεοῦ ζῶντος *w. all the courtesy of the living God* IPhld 1:2 (ἐ. as attribute of God, Dio Chrys. 80 [30], 19; Wsd 12:18; Bar 2:27; Da 3:42; 2 Macc 2:22; EpArist 192; 207).—AvHarnack, 'Sanftmut, Huld u. Demut' in d. alten Kirche: JKaftan Festschr. 1920, 113ff; LMarshall, Challenge of NT Ethics '47, 305–8; CSpicq, RB 54, '47, 333–39; FAgostino, Epieikia 1973, esp. 100–137. S. πραΰτης end.—DELG s.v. ἔοικα. M-M. TW. Spicq. Sv.

ἐπιεικής, ές (s. prec. entry; Hom.+; ins, pap [Mayser 92, 6]; LXX; PsSol 5:12; TestSol 1:1 VW; JosAs1:5; cod. A 15:8 al.; EpArist, Philo; Jos., C. Ap. 2, 211; Ar. 15, 5; Ath.; s. Mlt-H. 89; 314; 348) **not insisting on every right of letter of law or custom,** ***yielding, gentle, kind, courteous, tolerant*** (so Thu. et al.; s. esp. Aristot., EN 5, 10 [1137b] on relation of ἐ. to δίκαιος) w. ἄμαχος **1 Ti 3:3; Tit 3:2.** W. ἀγαθός prob.=*right-minded* (as Diod. S. 16, 30, 2, since in 16, 32, 2 ἀσεβής is in contrast to ἐπιεικής) **1 Pt 2:18.** W. εἰρηνικός **Js 3:17.** W. σώφρων (Hyperid. 6, 5) 1 Cl 1:2. W. εὔσπλαγχνος 29:1 (of God, as EpArist 211).—τὸ ἐπιεικές=ἡ ἐπιείκεια (Thu., Pla. et al.; POxy 1218, 5; EpArist 188; Philo, Somn. 295 τὸ τῶν δεσποτῶν ἐ.) τὸ ἐ. ὑμῶν *your forbearing spirit* **Phil 4:5.** τὸ ἐ. τῆς γλώσσης αὐτῶν *the gentleness of their tongue* 1 Cl 21:7.—Neut. of the comp. as adv. (PTebt 484 [c. 14 AD]; Esth 3:13b; Jos., Ant. 15, 14) ἐπιεικέστερον λαλεῖν *speak more gently* Hm 12, 4, 2.—M-M. TW. Spicq. Sv.

ἐπιεικία s. ἐπιείκεια.

ἐπιζητέω impf. ἐπεζήτουν; fut. ἐπιζητήσω LXX; 1 aor. ἐπεζήτησα; aor. pass. ἐπεζητήθην Tobit 2:8 S (s. ζητέω; Hdt.+).

❶ **to try to find out someth.,** ***search for, seek after***—ⓐ lit. τινά *someone* (PHamb 27, 4 [250 BC] αὐτὸν ἐπεζήτουν καὶ οὐχ ηὕρισκον; Jos., Ant. 17, 295) **Lk 4:42; Ac 12:19.**

ⓑ *inquire, want to know* περὶ τῆς θεότητος *inquire about the Godhead* Hm 10, 1, 4 (w. ἐρευνᾶν). περὶ τῶν μορφῶν ὧν ἐπιζητεῖς *about the forms of which you made inquiry* v 3, 11, 1; *want to know someth.* (Philo, Spec. Leg. 1, 46) **Ac 19:39;** Hs 6, 4, 1; 9, 16, 1.

ⓒ *discuss, debate, dispute* (Aristot., EN 9, 9, 2 [1169b, 13] ἐπιζητεῖται πότερον … ἤ='it is debated whether … or') τὰ ἐπιζητούμενα παρ' ὑμῖν πράγματα *the matters that are in dispute* (or *being discussed*) *among you* 1 Cl 1:1.

❷ **to be seriously interested in or have a strong desire for** ⓐ ***wish, wish for*** abs. Dg 11:5. τί (Diod. S. 17, 101, 6; Jos., Ant. 6, 149; 14, 407) **Mt 6:32; Lk 12:30; Ro 11:7; Phil 4:17; Hb 11:14.** τὴν μέλλουσαν πόλιν **13:14** (cp. Is 62:12). ζωήν Dg 12:6. W. inf. foll. (Polyb. 3, 57, 7; Diod. S. 19, 8, 4; PTebt 314, 6; TestJob 44:2) **Ac 13:7;** Dg 11:2. τί ἐπιζητεῖς; *what do you want?* Hs 7:1.

ⓑ ***desire, want*** (Theophr. et al.; PLille 7, 6 [III BC]; 1 Macc 7:13) σημεῖον of people who *want a sign* **Mt 12:39; 16:4; Lk 11:29 v.l.**—M-M. TW.

ἐπιθανάτιος, ον (s. θάνατος; Dionys. Hal. 7, 35; Bel 31; Etym. Mag. p. 457, 40) **pert. to being condemned to death,** ***sentenced to death*** **1 Cor 4:9.**—TW.

ἐπιθεῖναι, ἐπιθείς, ἐπίθες s. ἐπιτίθημι.

ἐπίθεσις, εως, ἡ (Pla., X.+; ins, pap, LXX, EpArist, Philo; Jos., Ant. 18, 7, Vi. 293) **the superimposing of someth. on someth.,** ***laying on*** (so Plut.) τῶν χειρῶν *the laying on of hands* (Philo, Leg. All. 3, 90, Spec. Leg. 1, 203) **Ac 8:18; 1 Ti 4:14; 2 Ti 1:6; Hb 6:2.**—JBehm, D. Handauflegung im Urchristentum 1911; HSmith, AJT 17, 1913, 47ff; JCoppens, L'Imposition des mains et les Rites connexes dans le NT 1925; FCabrol, Impos. des mains: Dict. d'Arch. VII, 1, 1926, 391ff; NAdler, Taufe u. Handauflegung (Ac 8:14–17) '51; ELohse, D. Ordination im Spätjudentum u. im NT '51; Billerb. II, '56, 647–61; DDaube, The NT and Rabbinic Judaism '56, 244–46; JJeremias, ZNW 52, '61, 101–4.—DELG s.v. τίθημι. M-M. TW. Spicq. Sv.

ἐπιθυμέω impf. ἐπεθύμουν; fut. ἐπιθυμήσω; 1 aor. ἐπεθύμησα (θυμέομαι 'set one's heart on a thing'; Aeschyl., Hdt.+).

❶ **to have a strong desire to do or secure someth.,** ***desire, long for*** w. gen. of the thing desired (Hdt. 2, 66; X., Mem. 1, 6, 5; Ex 34:24; Ps 44:12; Pr 23:3, 6; EpArist 223; TestSol 16:2; ApcMos 6; Jos., Ant. 12, 309) silver, gold, clothing **Ac 20:33;** a good work **1 Ti 3:1;** earthly things 2 Cl 5:6; someth. that belongs to another Hs 1:11. W. acc. of thing (Teles p. 42, 12; Diod. S. 37, 29, 2 τὸν πλοῦτον; Tetrast. Iamb. 2, 22, 1 p. 292; Mi 2:2; Wsd 16:3; Sir 1:26; 16:1; 40:22; EpArist 211) τὰ τοῦ πλησίον D 2:3; cp. B 19:6 (Ar. 15, 4 τὰ ἀλλότρια). τὴν οἰκοδομὴν αὐτοῦ Hs 9, 9, 7. μηδέν IRo 4:3. κόσμον 7:1. πονηρὸν ἔργον Hv 1, 2, 4. W. inf. foll. (Soph., Hdt. al.; POxy 963; Is 58:2; Sus 15 Theod.;

TestSol 9:2; TestJob 11:1; ApcSed 2:1; Jos., Bell. 6, 112; Just., D. 126, 6; Ath. 11, 2) **Mt 13:17; Lk 15:16; 16:21; 17:22; 1 Pt 1:12; Rv 9:6;** B 16:10; Hs 9, 1, 10; 2 Cl 5:7; Pol 1:3; MPol 17:1; 19:1; AcPl Ha 2, 12. Foll. by acc. and inf. **Hb 6:11.** Abs. (Is 58:11; 4 Macc 2:6; JosAs 24:18) **Ro 7:7; 13:9** (SLyonnet, OCullmann Festschr., '62, 157–65) (both Ex 20:17); **1 Cor 10:6; Js 4:2.**—ἐπιθυμίᾳ ἐπιθυμεῖν *eagerly desire* (Gen 31:30; cp. Diod. S. 16, 61, 3 νόσῳ νοσεῖν=be very ill) **Lk 22:15;** GEb 308, 32; s. B-D-F §198, 6; Rob. 531; Mlt-H. 443f. ἐ. κατά τινος *desire against* or *rise in protest against someth.* **Gal 5:17.**

❷ **to have sexual interest in someone,** ***desire,*** w. acc. of pers. (referring to γυναῖκα; cp. En 6:2) αὐτήν (not in ancient Gk., but used in Ex 20:17; cp. Sir 1:26. It is lacking in some witnesses; others have αὐτῆς, which corresponds to X., An. 4, 1, 14; Dt 21:11; Sus 8; Philo, Spec. Leg. 3, 66; Just., D 134, 1) *with a strong desire for her, with lust for her* (i.e., someone else's wife; s. Betz, SM ad loc.) **Mt 5:28** (cp. Ex 20:17; Dt 5:21; 4 Macc 2:5; lead tablet fr. Hadrumetum lines 44f: Dssm., B 31 [BS 274ff, s. p. 277] and IDefixWünsch 5 p. 25f μηδεμίαν ἄλλην γυναῖκα μήτε παρθένον ἐπιθυμοῦντα). Cp. Hv 1, 1, 4. W. gen. of pers. Hs 9, 13, 8—B. 1162. DELG s.v. θυμός. M-M. TW.

ἐπιθυμητής, οῦ, ὁ (s. prec. entry; Hdt. 7, 6 et al.; LXX; Jos., C. Ap. 2, 45; Ar.) ***one who desires,*** also in a pejorative sense (BGU 531 II, 22 [I AD] οὔτε εἰμὶ ἄδικος οὔτε ἀλλοτρίων ἐπιθυμητής [for ἀλλοτρ. ἐπιθυμ. s. Vett. Val. index III p. 397]; Pr 1:22) κακῶν *desirous of evil* **1 Cor 10:6** (Num 11:34). μὴ γίνου ἐ. *do not be lustful* D 3:3.—M-M. TW.

ἐπιθυμία, ας, ἡ (s. ἐπιθυμέω; Pre-Socr., Hdt.+)—❶ **a great desire for someth.,** ***desire, longing, craving***—ⓐ as a neutral term, in Hdt., Pla., Thu. et al. αἱ περὶ τὰ λοιπὰ ἐ. *desires for other things* **Mk 4:19.** ἐ. πράξεων πολλῶν *desire for much business* Hm 6, 2, 5 (but mng. 2 below is also poss.). ἐ. τῆς ψυχῆς *desire of the soul* **Rv 18:14.**

ⓑ of desire for good things (Diod. S. 11, 36, 5 ἐπιθ. τῆς ἐλευθερίας=for freedom; Pr 10:24 ἐ. δικαίου δεκτή; ἄνερ ἐπιθυμιῶν GrBar 1:3; Jos., C. Ap. 1, 111) ἐπιθυμίαν ἔχειν εἴς τι *have a longing for someth.* **Phil 1:23** (ἐ. ἔχειν as Jos., C. Ap. 1, 255; ἐ. εἰς as Thu. 4, 81, 2). ἐπιθυμίᾳ ἐπιθυμεῖν (Gen 31:30) *eagerly desire* **Lk 22:15** (s. on ἐπιθυμέω); ἐν πολλῇ ἐ. *w. great longing* **1 Th 2:17.** ἐλπίζει μου ἡ ψυχὴ τῇ ἐπιθυμίᾳ μου μὴ παραλελοιπέναι τι *I hope that, in accordance with my desire, nothing has been omitted* B 17:1. ἡ ἐ. καὶ ἡ ἀγρυπνία 21:7. ε. ἀγαθὴν καὶ σεμνήν Hm 12, 1, 1.

❷ **a desire for someth. forbidden or simply inordinate,** ***craving, lust*** (as early as Plato, Phd. 83b ἡ τοῦ ὡς ἀληθῶς φιλοσόφου ψυχὴ οὕτως ἀπέχεται τ. ἡδονῶν τε καὶ ἐπιθυμιῶν κτλ.; Polystrat. p. 30; Duris [III BC]: 76 fgm. 15 Jac.; then above all, the Stoics [EZeller, Philos. d. Griechen III/1[4], 1909, 235ff], e.g. Epict. 2, 16, 45; 2, 18, 8f; 3, 9, 21 al.; Maximus Tyr. 24, 4a μέγιστον ἀνθρώπῳ κακὸν ἐπιθυμία; Herm. Wr. 1, 23; 12, 4, also in Stob. p. 444, 10 Sc.; Wsd 4:12; Sir 23:5; 4 Macc 1:22; 3:2 al.; ApcMos 19 ἐ. . . . κεφαλὴ πάσης ἁμαρτίας; Philo, Spec. Leg. 4, 93, Leg. All. 2, 8, Vi. Cont. 74; Jos., Bell. 7, 261, Ant. 4, 143) **Ro 7:7f; Js 1:14f; 2 Pt 1:4.** ἐ. πονηρά (X., Mem. 1, 2, 64; Ar. 8, 4) Hv 1, 2, 4; 3, 7, 3; 3, 8, 4; m 8:5. ἐ. κακή (Pla., Leg. 9, 854a; Pr 12:12; 21:26; Just., A I, 10, 6) **Col 3:5.**—Of sexual desire (as early as Alcaeus [acc. to Plut., Mor. 525ab]; lead tablet fr. Hadrumetum 7 in Dssm., B 28 [BS 273ff] and IDefixWünsch no. 5 p. 23; PGM 17a, 9; 21; Sus Theod. 8; 11; 14 al., LXX 32; Jos., Ant. 4, 130; 132; Ath. 33, 1 μέτρον ἐπιθυμίας ἡ παιδοποιία; Did., Gen. 151, 27 ἄλογος ἐ.) D 3:3. πάθος ἐπιθυμίας **1 Th 4:5.** κατ' ἐπιθυμίαν (cp. Epict. 3, 15, 7; M. Ant. 2, 10, 1; 2; 3; Just., A II, 5, 4; Ath. 21, 1) *in accordance with physical desire alone* IPol 5:2. πρὸς ἐπιθυμίαν τ. ἀνθρώπων Ox 840, 38 (Ps.-Pla., Eryx. 21, 401e πρὸς τὰς ἐπιθυμίας τοῦ σώματος=to satisfy the desires of the body; cp. 405e: gambling, drunkenness and gluttony are called ἐπιθυμίαι.—In Ox 840, 38, since the ν in ἐπιθυμίαν is missing and restored, the word might also be ἐπιθυμίας.). ἐ. γυναικός (Da 11:37) Hm 6, 2, 5; 12, 2, 1. Pl. (oft. LXX; EpArist 256; Philo) w. παθήματα **Gal 5:24.** In a list of vices (cp. Philo, Congr. Erud. Grat. 172, Migr. Abr. 60, Vi. Cont. 2) **1 Pt 4:3;** D 5:1. ἐ. πολλαὶ ἀνόητοι *many foolish desires* **1 Ti 6:9;** νεωτερικαὶ ἐ. *youthful desires* **2 Ti 2:22** (WMetzger, TZ 33, '77, 129–36); κατὰ τὰς ἰδίας ἐ. *in accordance w. their own desires* **4:3;** cp. πρὸς τὰς ἰ. ἐ. Pol. 7:1; κατὰ τὰς ἐ. αὐτῶν AcPl Ha 8, 20 (for this: ἀνομίας AcPl BMM recto, 26, restored after Ox 1602, 27). αἱ πρότερον ἐν τῇ ἀγνοίᾳ ἐ. *the desires that ruled over you formerly, when you were ignorant* **1 Pt 1:14.**—W. gen.: subjective gen. ἐ. ἀνθρώπων **1 Pt 4:2;** τοῦ πατρὸς ὑμῶν **J 8:44;** gen. of quality ἐ. μιασμοῦ *defiling passion* **2 Pt 2:10;** cp. μιαρὰς ἐ. 1 Cl 28:1; βδελυκτὰς ἐ. 30:1. ἐ. τῆς ἀπάτης *deceptive desires* **Eph 4:22.** τῶν ἐ. τῶν ματαίων 2 Cl 19:2; cp. Hm 11, 8. ἐ. τῶν ἀσεβειῶν **Jd 18.** ἐ. τῆς πονηρίας *evil desire* Hv 1, 1, 8. ἐ. τῆς ἀσελγείας 3, 7, 2; the gen. can also indicate the origin and seat of the desire ἐ. τῶν καρδιῶν *of the hearts* (Sir 5:2) **Ro 1:24.** τῆς καρδίας . . . τῆς πονηρᾶς 1 Cl 3:4. ἐ. τοῦ θνητοῦ σώματος **Ro 6:12** (Ps.-Pla., Eryx. 21, 401e, s. above; Sextus 448 ἐπιθυμίαι τοῦ σώματος). τῆς σαρκός **Eph 2:3; 1J 2:16; 2 Pt 2:18;** B 10, 9. τῶν ὀφθαλμῶν **1J 2:16;** to denote someth. to which desire belongs gener. vs. **17;** σαρκικαὶ ἐ. (Hippol., Ref. 5, 9, 22; Did., Gen. 62, 3) **1 Pt 2:11;** D 1:4; σωματικαὶ ἐ. (4 Macc 1:32) ibid.; κοσμικαὶ ἐ. *worldly desires* **Tit 2:12;** 2 Cl 17:3; ἐ. τῶν ἐν τῷ κόσμῳ Pol 5:3; εἰς ἐ. *to arouse desires* **Ro 13:14;** ποιεῖν τὰς ἐ. *act in accordance w. the desires* **J 8:44.** τελεῖν ἐ. σαρκός *gratify the cravings of the flesh* **Gal 5:16;** ὑπακούειν ταῖς ἐ. *obey the desires* **Ro 6:12;** δουλεύειν ἐ. *be a slave to the desires* **Tit 3:3;** cp. δοῦλος ἐπιθυμίας IPol 4:3. ἄγεσθαι ἐπιθυμίαις *be led about by desires* **2 Ti 3:6.** πορεύεσθαι κατὰ τὰς ἐ. **Jd 16; 18; 2 Pt 3:3;** ἐν ἐπιθυμίαις (Sir 5:2) **1 Pt 4:3;** ταῖς ἐ. τοῦ αἰῶνος τούτου Hs 6, 2, 3; 6, 3, 3; 7:2; 8, 11, 3. ἀναστρέφεσθαι ἐν ταῖς ἐ. **Eph 2:3.**—BEaston, Pastoral Ep. '47, 186f; RAC II 62–78. S. πόθος.—Schmidt, Syn. III 591–601. M-M. TW. Sv.

ἐπιθύω 1 aor. ἐπέθυσα (s. θύω; Aeschyl. et al.; OGI 222, 37; 332, 29; pap [Mayser 33]; LXX; En 19:1) **to make an offering** (to a deity), ***offer a sacrifice*** (w. ὀμνύναι) as a patriotic gesture MPol 4; 8:2; **Ac 14:13 v.l.**—DELG s.v. 2 θύω.

ἐπικαθίζω fut. ἐπικαθιῶ Ezk 32:4 v.l.; 1 aor. ἐπεκάθισα LXX (s. καθίζω; in var. senses Thu et al.; also Jos., Ant. 18, 57)

❶ ***sit*** or ***sit down (on)*** intr. (Plut., Them. 118 [12, 1]; Gen 31:34; 2 Km 13:29; TestSol 6:1 P) ἐπάνω τινός *on someth.* **Mt 21:7** (ἐπικαθίσας Just., D. 53, 2). The rdg. ἐπεκάθισαν ἐπάνω αὐτόν (א [corr. for ἐκάθισαν] al.) would give the verb the trans. meaning

❷ ***set*** or ***put upon*** (Hippocr., Art. 78 τινὰ ἐπί τι, likew. 3 Km 1:38, 44; Ezk 32:4).—DELG s.v. ἕζομαι A. M-M.

ἐπικαθυπνόω (hapax leg.) ***fall asleep over*** τινί *someth.* ταῖς ἁμαρτίαις B 4:13.

ἐπικαίω (s. καίω) plpf. ἐπεκεκαύκειν (found in tmesis as early as Hom.; Sb 6720, 4) in Hom. 'burn'; in our lit. only in the sense **to burn surface area,** ***scorch,*** of the sun (Pla., Ep. 7, 340d οἱ τὰ σώματα ὑπὸ τ. ἡλίου ἐπικεκαυμένοι, likew. Dio Chrys. 53 [70], 2; cp. Polyb. 38, 8, 7) abs. *scorch* Hs 9, 1, 6.

ἐπικαλέω (s. καλέω) 1 aor. ἐπεκάλεσα; fut. mid. ἐπικαλέσομαι; 1 aor. mid. ἐπεκαλεσάμην. Pass.: 1 fut. 3 sg. ἐπικληθήσεται; 1 aor. ἐπεκλήθην; pf. ἐπικέκλημαι, ptc. ἐπικεκλημένος; plpf. 3 sg. ἐπεκέκλητο (in tmesis as early as Hom., otherw. Hdt. et al.; ins, pap, LXX, pseudepigr., Joseph.).

❶ **to call upon deity for any purpose** ('invoke' Hdt. 2, 39; 3, 8) ***to call upon, call out*** 1 Cl 39:7 (Job 5:1). In the mid. *to call on, invoke for* someth. (ἐ. τοὺς θεούς Hdt. et al.; X., Cyr. 7, 1, 35; Pla., Tim. 27c; Polyb. 15, 1, 13; Diod. S. 5, 49, 5 calling on the gods by the initiates; Epict. 2, 7, 12; 3, 21, 12 al.; Herm. Wr. 16, 3; OGI 194, 18 [I BC]; prayers for vengeance fr. Rheneia 1 [Dssm., LO 352ff/LAE 424ff; SIG 1181]; POxy 1380, 153 [early II AD]; 886, 10 [III AD]; PGM 3, 8; 43; 4, 1182; 1217; 1345; 13, 138; 270; LXX; PsSol 2:36 al.; JosAs 25:7; EpArist 17; 193; 226; Jos., Ant. 4, 222 al.) ἐπικαλεῖσθαι τ. κύριον (1 Km 12:17f; 2 Km 22:7; PsSol 9:6) **Ro 10:12; 2 Ti 2:22;** 1 Cl 52:3 (Ps 49:15); 57:5 (Pr 1:28); 60:4. Also ἐπικαλεῖσθαι τὸ ὄνομα κυρίου (Gen 13:4; 21:33 al.; Jos., Bell. 5, 438; PGM 1, 161; 4, 1209; 1609; 1811; 13, 871) **Ac 2:21** (Jo 3:5); **9:14, 21; 22:16; Ro 10:13** (Jo 3:5); **1 Cor 1:2;** 1 Cl 64:1. Abs. (Ps 4:2) **Ro 10:14; Ac 7:59.** εἰ πατέρα ἐπικαλεῖσθέ τινα *if you invoke someone as Father* **1 Pt 1:17** (P^{72} καλεῖτε, which may be classed under 2).—JTyrer, JTS 25, 1924, 139–50; reply by RConnolly, ibid. 337–68; FNötscher, Epiklese, Biblica 30, '49, 401–4=Vom A zum NT, '62, 221–25.

❷ **to address or characterize someone by a special term, *call, give a surname*** (X., Pla. et al.; OGI 603, 10; PFay 12, 1; PTebt 399, 15 al.; 1 Macc 2:2) τινά τι: τὸν οἰκοδεσπότην Βεελζεβοὺλ *call the master of the house Beelzebul* **Mt 10:25.** Pass. ὁ ἐπικαλούμενος *who is also called* (Socrat., Ep. 21, 3; Diod. S. 3, 84, 1; Diog. L. 4, 18; Jos., Ant. 18, 206; PYadin 5a I, 5 al.) **Ac 10:18; 11:13; 12:12.** With Συμεὼν ὁ ἐπικαλούμενος Νίγερ **Ac 13:1** D (cp. Diod. S. 17, 20, 7 Κλεῖτος ὁ Μέλας ἐπικαλούμενος). **Lk 22:3 v.l.; Ac 15:22 v.l.** Also ὁ ἐπικληθείς (Diog. L. 5, 58 of Strato of Lamps.: φυσικὸς ἐπικληθείς; Jos., Bell. 1, 60, Ant. 13, 103; Just., D. 106, 3; Ath. 28, 4) **Mt 10:3 v.l.; Ac 4:36; 12:25;** GEb 34, 59. ὃς ἐπικαλεῖται **Ac 10:5, 32.** ὃς ἐπεκλήθη (Jos., Ant. 13, 218; 271) **1:23;** cp. Papias (2:9). οὐκ ἐπαισχύνεται θεὸς ἐπικαλεῖσθαι αὐτῶν *to be called their God* **Hb 11:16.** The pass. is used w. ὄνομα, as in the OT, in ἐπικαλεῖται τὸ ὄνομά τινος ἐπί τινα *someone's name is called over someone* to designate the latter as the property of the former (KGalling, TLZ 81, '56, 65–70; of God's name 2 Km 6:2; 3 Km 8:43; Jer 7:30; 14:9 and oft.) **Ac 15:17** (Am 9:12, also 2 Ch 7:14). τὸ καλὸν ὄνομα τὸ ἐπικληθὲν ἐφ' ὑμᾶς **Js 2:7;** cp. Hs 8, 6, 4. Sim. οἱ ἐπικαλούμενοι τ. ὀνόματι αὐτοῦ *those who are called by his name* 9, 14, 3 (cp. Is 43:7).

❸ **a request put to a higher judicial authority for review of a decision in a lower court, *appeal*** mid., legal t.t. τινά *to someone* the Lat. 'provocatio' against the 'coercitio' of a provincial governor (cp. Plut., Marcell. 299 [2, 7], Tib. Gracch. 832 [16, 1]) Καίσαρα *appeal to Caesar* **Ac 25:11f; 26:32; 28:19.** Also τὸν Σεβαστόν **25:25.** W. inf. foll. τοῦ δὲ Παύλου ἐπικαλεσαμένου τηρηθῆναι αὐτὸν εἰς τὴν τοῦ Σεβαστοῦ διάγνωσιν *when Paul appealed to be held in custody for the Emperor's decision* **25:21.**—ASherwin-White, Rom. Society and Law in the NT '63, 57–70; AHMJones, Studies in Rom. Govt. and Law '60, 53ff; BAFCS III, index.

❹ **to invoke in an oath, *call on someone as a witness*** mid. τινὰ μάρτυρα legal t.t. (Pla., Leg. 2, 664c) **2 Cor 1:23** (θεοὺς ἐπικαλεῖσθαι μάρτυρας: Polyb. 11, 6, 4; Heliod. 1, 25, 1; Jos., Ant. 1, 243).—M-M. TW. Spicq.

ἐπικάλυμμα, ατος, τό (s. next entry; 'a covering' Aristot. et al.; LXX) **a stratagem for concealing someth., *cover, veil*** ἐ. τῆς κακίας *a covering for evil* **1 Pt 2:16** (Menand., fgm. 90 Kock πλοῦτος δὲ πολλῶν ἐπικάλυμμ' ἐστὶ κακῶν=wealth is a cover-up for many evils; Iren. s.v. κακία 1).—DELG s.v. καλύπτω.

ἐπικαλύπτω fut. ἐπικαλύψω; 1 aor. ἐπικάλυψα LXX. Pass.: 1 aor. ἐπεκαλύφθην; pf. ptc. ἐπικεκαλυμμένος 2 Km 5:30 (s. prec. entry; Hes. et al.; Just., D. 68, 6 and 130, 1 ἐπικεκαλυμμένως) 'to hide from view by covering', then by fig. extension as synonym for 'forgive' ***cover up*** ὧν ἐπεκαλύφθησαν αἱ ἁμαρτίαι *whose sins are put out of sight* **Ro 4:7;** 1 Cl 50:6 (both Ps 31:1).

ἐπικαταλλάσσομαι 2 aor. ἐπικατηλλάγην (hapax leg.) τινί ***be reconciled to someone*** 1 Cl 48:1.—DELG s.v. ἄλλος.

ἐπικατάρατος, ον (s. καταράομαι; ins fr. Euboea SIG 1240, 2 [II AD] and Halicarnassus CIG 2664 [II/III AD]; Vi. Aesopi G 3 P. ἐπικατάρατε; schol. on Soph., Ant. 867 p. 258 Papag. [1888]; LXX; Philo, Leg. All. 3, 111; 113; En 102:3; TestSol 20:6 P; ApcMos; Dssm., LO 74f [LAE 93f]) **pert. to being under divine condemnation, *cursed*** ἐ. πᾶς ὃς . . . *cursed be every one, who* . . . **Gal 3:10** (Dt 27:26; Just., D 89, 2; 96, 1), **13.** (W. παραβάτης τοῦ νόμου; opp. μακάριος) **Lk 6:4** D. ἐ. ὁ εἷς B 7:7; cp. 9. Of fish who are *cursed* and must live in the depths of the sea 10:5.—M-M.

ἐπίκειμαι impf. ἐπεκείμην (Hom.+).—❶ **to be at or in a place in contact with a surface, *lie upon*** ἐπί τινι *someth.* (Paus. 5, 10, 2) of a stone **J 11:38** (JSwetnam, CBQ 28, '66, 155–73). ἐπί τινος *on someth.* (Cass. Dio 67, 16; Herm. Wr. 1, 13b) of the brass serpent B 12:7. τὰ στόματα αὐτῶν ἐπικείμενα τῷ ὕδατι καὶ μὴ πίνοντα (I saw how) *their* (the goats') *mouths were at the water but not drinking* GJs 18:3. Abs. ὀψάριον ἐπικείμενον *fish lying on it* **J 21:9** (cp. PTebt 47, 25 [113 BC]; PGrenf II, 57, 9 τ. ἐπικειμένην σποράν; 2 Macc 1:21).—In imagery *be on* of the image on a coin IMg 5:2.

❷ **to act upon through force or pressure**—ⓐ of personal force, act of pushing ***press around, press upon, be urgent*** w. dat. of pers. (X., An. 4, 3, 7; Arrian, An. 1, 14, 5; Aesop, fab. 140 P.= 249 H.; Job 19:3; 21:27; Jos., Ant. 6, 334 al.) **Lk 5:1.**

ⓑ of impersonal force ***confront*** χειμῶνος ἐπικειμένου *since a storm lay upon us* **Ac 27:20** (cp. Plut., Timol. 250 [28, 7]; Wsd 17:20 v.l.). ἀνάγκη μοι ἐπίκειται *necessity is laid upon me* **1 Cor 9:16** (cp. Il. 6, 459; SibOr 3, 572). ἀγὼν ἡμῖν ἐπίκειται *a conflict confronts us* 1 Cl 7:1; μέγας ἐπίκειται πιρασμός *a serious temptation confronts* (Paul) AcPl Ha 8, 22. In a somewhat weakened sense *stand before* (Achilles Tat. 2, 16, 2) ὁ τοκετός μοι ἐπίκειται *the pains of birth* (typical of the tortures to come) *are upon me* IRo 6:1.

❸ **to have the force of obligation, *be imposed, be incumbent*** (Lucian, Cal. 17; Ar. 7:3 θάνατος; 1 Macc 6:57; Just., D. 53, 4 τὸν . . . νόμον ἐπικείμενον ἔχετε; TestJob 15:3 and Just., A I, 12, 3 τὰ ἐπικείμενα) δικαιώματα ἐπικείμενα *regulations imposed* **Hb 9:10.** διακονίαι ἐπίκεινταί τινι *duties are imposed on someone* 1 Cl 40:5. ἵνα μὴ κατέξω τὰ [προσ]|τεταγμένα καὶ ἐπεικίμ[εν]α *so that I do not default on my assignments and obligations* AcPl Ha 7, 15.

❹ **keep on doing someth., *be urgent about*** ἐπέκειντο αἰτούμενοι *they urgently demanded* **Lk 23:23** (cp. Hdt. 5, 104; Jos., Ant. 18, 184 πολλῷ μᾶλλον ἐπέκειτο ἀξιῶν; also 20, 110).

❺ **exist as possibility,** ***be open*** τούτοις ἐπίκειται μετάνοια *repentance is open to them* Hs 8, 7, 2 v.l.—M-M. TW.

ἐπικέλλω 1 aor. ἐπέκειλα nautical t.t. ('bring [a ship] to shore' Apollon. Rhod. 1, 1362; 2, 352 al.) ***run aground*** ἐ. τὴν ναῦν (cp. Od. 9, 148; 546) *run the ship aground* **Ac 27:41** (v.l. ἐπώκειλαν).—DELG s.v. κέλλω. M-M.

ἐπικερδαίνω (Plut., Flam. 370 [3, 2]; Cass. Dio 36, 12; Sb IV, 7464, 15 [III AD]) ***gain in addition*** **Mt 25:20 v.l.; 22 v.l.**—DELG s.v. κέρδος.

ἐπικεφάλαιον, ου, τό *poll tax* (Aristot., Oec. 2, 1346a, 4; pap) **Mk 12:14 v.l.** (for κῆνσον).—DELG s.v. κεφαλή. M-M.

Ἐπικούρειος, ου, ὁ (Numenius [s. on στρεβλόω 2] 1, 3 p. 63; Alciphron 3, 19, 3; Diog. L. 10, 3; 31; SIG 1227 φιλόσοφος Ἐπικούρειος; IGR IV, 997; Jos., Ant. 10, 277; 19, 32; Just., A II, 15, 3. For the spelling [-ριος Tdf., W-H., Sod.] W-S. §5, 13e; cp. Philo, Poster. Cai. 2) ***an Epicurean,*** a follower of Epicurus **Ac 17:18** (s. comm.).—RHicks, EncRelEth V 324–30; WdeWitt, E. and His Philosophy '54; WBarclay, ET 72, '60, 78–81; 72, '61, 101–4; 146–49; EAsmis, Epicurus' Scientific Method '84; RAC V 681–819.—M-M.

ἐπικουρία, ας, ἡ (ἐπικουρέω 'serve as ally, aid'; trag., Hdt. et al.; Diod. S. 1, 90, 2; Appian, Syr. 37 §192 θεῶν ἐ.; SIG 1015, 24 [III BC]; PFlor 382, 40; Wsd 13:18; Philo, Spec. Leg. 1, 298 τοῦ θεοῦ; Jos., Ant. 1, 281 ἡ ἐμὴ [=θεοῦ] ἐ.; 20, 56.) ***help*** ἐπικουρίας τυχὼν τῆς ἀπὸ θεοῦ *I have had help fr. God* **Ac 26:22** (Jos., Ant. 2, 94 ἐπικουρίας τυγχάνειν); in Il 5, 514 the verb ἐπικουρέω refers to service as an ally (cp. Isocr. 4, 168), and it is prob. that our passage refers to God as coming to the rescue with auxiliary aid (for other reff. s. L-S-J-M s.v. ἐπικουρέω and cognates).—B. 1354, the verb. New Docs 3, 67f. DELG s.v. ἐπίκουρος. M-M.

ἐπικράζω (Lucian, Anach. 16; Pollux 5, 85; TestSol 26:9 H ['call to']) ***shout threats*** κατά τινος *against someone* **Ac 16:39 v.l.** W. direct discourse foll. **28:19 v.l.**

ἐπικρίνω 1 aor. ἐπέκρινα, aor. pass. ptc. 1 fem. ἐπικριθεῖσαν 3 Macc 4:2 (s. κρίνω; Pla. et al.; ins, pap, LXX, Philo; Jos., Bell. 6, 416, Ant. 14, 192) **to come to a decision in a matter,** *decide, determine* foll. by acc. and inf. (SIG 1109, 71) ἐπέκρινεν γενέσθαι τὸ αἴτημα αὐτῶν *he decided that their demand should be granted* **Lk 23:24.**—For ἐπίκριμα 'decree' s. Cyr. Ins. 68.—M-M. TW.

ἐπιλαμβάνομαι (s. λαμβάνω) fut. ἐπιλήψομαι LXX; 2 aor. ἐπελαβόμην; pf. ptc. fem. ἐπειλημμένη Gen 25:26 (in our lit., as well as LXX and TestJos 8:2, only in the mid., which is used since Hdt.; also ins, pap; Philo, Somn. 2, 68; Jos., Bell. 6, 232; Just.).

❶ **to make the motion of grasping or taking hold of someth.,** ***take hold of, grasp, catch,*** sometimes w. violence, w. gen. foll. (Hdt. 6, 114 al.; LXX) of pers. (Laud. Therap. 24 ἐπιλαμβάνονται τοῦ ἀνδρός; 2 Km 13:11; Is 3:6) **Mt 14:31; Lk 23:26 v.l.; Ac 17:19; 21:30, 33** (s. 2 below); of thing (LXX) τῆς χειρός τινος (cp. Pla., Prot. 335c; Zech 14:13; Jos., Ant. 9, 180) **Mk 8:23; Ac 23:19;** fig. **Hb 8:9** (Jer 38:32). Foll. by gen. of pers. and of thing by which the person is grasped (X., An. 4, 7, 12 ἐ. αὐτοῦ τῆς ἴτυος 'his shield'; Diod. S. 17, 30, 4; Epict. 1, 29, 23; Bel 36 LXX; TestJos 8:2) μου τῆς χειρός *me by the hand* Hv 3, 2, 4 (Plut., Mor. 207c ἐπιλαβόμενος αὐτοῦ τῆς χειρός). αὐτοῦ τῆς πήρας *him by the knapsack* s 9, 10, 5. W. acc. of pers. (cp. Pla., Leg. 6, 779c) **Lk 9:47;** *press into service* **23:26** (for the loanw. ἀγγαρεύω, q.v.). Freq., where ἐ. seems to govern the acc., that case is actually the object of the finite verb upon which ἐ. depends: **Lk 14:4; Ac 9:27; 16:19; 18:17.**

❷ **to take into custody,** ***arrest*** (cp. Demosth. 33, 9) **Ac 21:33.**

❸ **to pounce on someth. compromising,** ***catch,*** fig. ext. of 1, w. double gen. (cp. 1 above) *someone in someth.* αὐτοῦ λόγου *him in someth. he said* **Lk 20:20;** also αὐτοῦ ῥήματος vs. **26**

❹ **take hold of in order to make one's own,** ***take hold of,*** fig. ext. of 1 (Hdt. 1, 127; 5, 23; Polyb. 6, 50, 6; 15, 8, 12; Pr 4:13) τῆς αἰωνίου ζωῆς **1 Ti 6:12;** cp. vs. **19.**

❺ **be concerned with/about.** The context of ἀγγέλων, σπέρματος Ἀβραάμ **Hb 2:16** suggests the rendering *take an interest in,* prob. in the sense *help* (schol. on Aeschyl., Pers. 742 [but s. KDolfe, ZNW 84, '93, on the textual problem]; Sir 4:11). This may be the place for the variant reading ἐπιλαβών (but the act. is otherw. never used in LXX or NT) **Mk 14:72.**—M-M. TW.

ἐπιλάμπω 3 sg. fut. ἐπιλάμψει Is 4:2; 1 aor. ἐπέλαμψα (Hom. +; ins; PGM 3, 135; LXX, Philo) **to cause emission of strong rays of light,** ***shine out, shine forth*** lit. (Dio Chrys. 71 [21], 14) **Ac 12:7** D (IGUR 1287, 8; of a divine light Jambl., Myst. 3, 2 φωτὸς ἐπιλάμψαντος). Fig., of God's mercy ὅταν ἐπιλάμψῃ τὸ ἔλεος τοῦ κυρίου *when the mercy of the Lord will shine forth* Hs 4:2 (Is 4:2 of God; Wsd 5:6 of righteousness; Proclus, Theol. 185 p. 162, 4 τὸ θεῖον φῶς ἄνωθεν ἐπιλάμπον. In ins t.t. for the 'shining forth' of the ruler who is given divine honors: SIG 814, 34; 900, 26; OGI 669, 7. Likewise POslo 126, 5 [161 AD]).—New Docs 4, 36.

ἐπιλανθάνομαι mid.: fut. ἐπιλήσομαι LXX; 2 aor. ἐπελαθόμην; pf. (also w. pass. mng., Kühner-G. I p. 120) ἐπιλέλησμαι. Pass: fut. ἐπιλησθήσομαι LXX (s. λανθάνω; Hom.+).

❶ **to not have remembrance of someth.,** ***forget*** w. gen. (Hom. et al., also LXX, Philo, Joseph.) of the pers. (cp. also PSI 353, 16; Gen 40:23; Dt 6:12 al.; ApcMos 31) 1 Cl 35:11 (Ps 49:22); B 10:3; Hs 6, 4, 2; GJs 13:2; 15:3. W. gen. of thing (Diod. S. 4, 61, 6; OGI 116, 15; Herm. Wr. 10, 6; Ps 105:13; 118:16; 1 Macc 1:49; 2 Macc 2:2; Jos., Bell. 6, 107, Ant. 2, 327; 10, 195) Hv 3, 13, 2; GJs 12:2. Foll. by acc. of thing (Hdt. 3, 46 al.; UPZ 61, 10 [161 BC]; PLond III, 964, 9 p. 212 [II/III AD]; POxy 744, 12; 1489, 3; LXX) τὰ ὀπίσω *what lies behind,* perh. in the sense *disregard, put out of mind* (s. 2) **Phil 3:13;** τὰς ἐντολάς Hs 6, 2, 2. W. inf. foll. (Hyperid. 2, 8; Aelian, VH 3, 31) **Mt 16:5; Mk 8:14.** W. ὅτι foll. (Jos., C. Ap. 1, 230) 1 Cl 46:7. W. indir. quest. foll. ὁποῖος ἦν *what sort of person he was* **Js 1:24.**—Hs 6, 5, 3.

❷ **to be inattentive to,** ***neglect, overlook, care nothing about*** w. gen. of thing (Diod. S. 4, 64, 1 ἐπιλαθόμενος τοῦ χρησμοῦ=he disregarded the oracle; Ps 9:13; 73:19, 23) τοῦ ἔργου ὑμῶν **Hb 6:10.** ἐπιλάθου τοῦ πλούτου καὶ τοῦ κάλλους σου *no longer give thought to your wealth or beauty* AcPl Ha 2, 21. W. neg. (X., Ages. 2, 13 τοῦ θείου) τῆς φιλοξενίας **13:2.** τῆς εὐποιΐας, κοινωνίας vs. **16.** Pass. (cp. Is 23:16) ἓν ἐξ αὐτῶν οὐκ ἔστιν ἐπιλελησμένον ἐνώπιον τοῦ θεοῦ *not one of them has escaped God's notice* **Lk 12:6.**—DELG s.v. λανθάνω. M-M.

ἐπιλέγω fut. ἐπιλέξω; 1 aor. ἐπέλεξα LXX, mid. ἐπελεξάμην. Pass.: aor. inf. ἐπιλεχθῆναι (Ath. 22:6); pf. ptc. ἐπιλελεγμέναις 1 Macc 12:41 (s. λέγω; Hdt.+)

❶ **to add someth. by way of identification,** ***call/name (in addition)*** act. and pass. (Pla., Leg. 3, 700b). Pass. (ApcMos 2 Ἀμιλαβὲς τοῦ ἐπιλεγομένου Ἄβελ; Jos., Ant. 13, 285 Πτολεμαῖον τὸν Λάθουρον ἐπιλεγόμενον) Ῥαὰβ ἡ ἐπιλεγομένη πόρνη *who is called a prostitute* 1 Cl 12:1 (on the rdg. s. Knopf, Hdb. ad loc.). κολυμβήθρα ἡ ἐπιλεγομένη Ἑβραϊστὶ βηθζαθά *is called B. in Hebrew* **J 5:2.** ὁ εἰρήναρχος . . . Ἡρώδης ἐπιλεγόμενος Herod MPol 6:2 (cp. TestAbr A 13 p. 92, 6 [Stone p. 32] υἱὸς Ἀδὰμ . . . ὁ ἐ. Ἄβελ).

❷ ***choose, select*** τινά *someone,* mid. **Ac 15:40** (cp. Hdt. 3, 157; Thu. 7, 19, 3; Diod. S. 3, 74, 2; 14, 12, 3; 1 Esdr 9:16; 1 Macc 12:45; ParJer 9:20; EpArist 39; 46; Jos., Ant. 4, 28; Tat. 12:3 τῆς ὕλης . . . τὸ ἔλλατον). ὡς ἐπιλέξαι αὐτον ἐκ τῶν φυλῶν ιβʹ ἄνδρας AcPl Ha 8, 34 (AcPl BMM verso 6).—M-M. Sv.

ἐπιλείπω fut. ἐπιλείψω (Theognis, Hdt. et al. [Od. 8, 475 not strictly an instance of tmesis]) 'leave behind', hence w. acc. as obj. also w. the mng. **to not be enough,** ***fail*** ἐπιλείψει με ὁ χρόνος *time would fail me* **Hb 11:32** (Isocr. 1, 11 ἐπιλίποι δ' ἂν ἡμᾶς ὁ πᾶς χρόνος; 6, 81; 8, 56; Demosth. 18, 296; Dionys. Hal., Comp. Verb. 4; Athen. 5, 220f; Philo, Sacr. Abel. 27; Jos., Ant. 8, 323 al.; Ath. 14, 2).—M-M.

ἐπιλείχω (λείχω 'lick up, lick'; cp. ἀπο-, περιλείχω) impf. ἐπέλειχον (Longus, Past. 1, 24, 4 ἐπιλείχω is a conjectural rdg.) ***lick*** τὰ ἕλκη *the sores* **Lk 16:21** (cp. 3 Km 22:38 ἐξέλειξαν οἱ κύνες τὸ αἷμα).—M-M.

ἐπιλελησμένος s. ἐπιλανθάνομαι.

ἐπιλησμονή, ῆς, ἡ (s. λανθάνω; Cratinus Com. [V BC], fgm. 410 K.; ins: WFerguson, The Legal Terms Common to the Macedon. Inscr. and the NT 1913, 57, of the building of a tomb in awareness of the 'forgetfulness' of one's heirs; Sir 11:27) ***forgetfulness*** ἀκροατὴς ἐπιλησμονῆς *a forgetful hearer* **Js 1:25** (on the constr. s. Mlt-H. 440; Rob. 496f; s. B-D-F §165).—DELG s.v. λανθάνω.

ἐπίλοιπος, ον (s. λοιπός; Pind., Hdt.+; ins, pap, LXX; Just.) **pert. to a part that remains from a whole,** ***left, remaining*** τὸν ἐ. χρόνον *the remaining time* (Hdt. 2, 13; Theopomp.: 115 fgm. 287 Jac. et al.) **1 Pt 4:2** (cp. 3 Macc 3:26; PPetr II, 13, 19, 4 τὸν ἐ. βίον).—Subst. τὰ ἐπίλοιπα *the rest* (Hdt. 4, 154; Da 7:7, 19 Theod.; Just.) **Lk 24:43 v.l.**—DELG s.v. λείπω. M-M.

ἐπίλυσις, εως, ἡ (Aeschyl. et al. w. var. mngs.; ins, pap) 'a setting free from someth.', then **the act or process of explaining,** ***explanation, interpretation*** (so Sext. Emp., Pyrrh. 2, 246; Vett. Val. 221, 9; 330, 10; Heliod. 1, 18, 2 ὀνειράτων ἐπίλυσις; Gen 40:8 Aq.; Philo, Vi. Cont. 75, ln. 8 v.l.; Clem. Alex., Paed. 2, 1, 14) πᾶσα προφητεία ἰδίας ἐπιλύσεως οὐ γίνεται **2 Pt 1:20** (γίνομαι 9c and ἴδιος 6.—Ps.-Callisth. 2, 1, 5 Stasagoras complains about the unfavorable interpretation of an omen by a prophet in these words: σὺ σεαυτῇ ἐπέλυσας τὸ σημεῖον=you gave the omen your own interpretation.—S. also WArndt, CTM 7, '36, 685–91). Of the interpretation of a parable (cp. 4 Esdr 12:10) Hs 5, 5, 1; 5, 6, 8; 5, 7, 1; 8, 11, 1; 9, 13, 9; 9, 16, 7.—DELG s.v. λύω. M-M. TW.

ἐπιλύω impf. ἐπέλυον; 1 fut. pass. ἐπιλυθήσομαι (s. prec. entry; Pla.+; IG IV^2/1, 77, 18; pap) the common use of this term in ref. to physical separation 'untie, loose, set free, release' does not appear in our lit., which focuses on noetic signification.

❶ **to clarify something,** ***explain, interpret*** (Sext. Emp., Pyrrh. 2, 246; Vett. Val. 173, 6; Athen. 10, 449e; Aq. Gen 40:8; 41:8, 12; Philo, Agr. 16; Jos., Ant. 8, 167 [mid.]) τινί τι *someth. to someone* parables **Mk 4:34;** Hs 5, 3, 1f; 5, 4, 2f; 5, 5, 1; 9, 10, 5; 9, 11, 9.

❷ **to come to a conclusion about a difficult matter,** ***resolve, decide, settle*** pass., of a dispute **Ac 19:39.**—M-M. TW.

ἐπιμαρτυρέω **to affirm that someth. is true,** ***bear witness, attest*** (s. μαρτυρέω; Pla., Crat. 397a; Lucian, Alex. 42; Plut., Lys. 445 [22, 9] al.; PLond 1692a, 19 [VI AD]; Cat. Cod. Astrol. IX/1 p. 182, 27f; Jos., Ant. 7, 349; Tat. 3:3 'endorse'; Ath., R. 77, 21) foll. by acc. and inf. **1 Pt 5:12.**—New Docs 2, 85f. M-M. TW.

ἐπιμέλεια, ας, ἡ (s. ἐπιμελής and next entry; Hdt. et al. The ἐπιμ- family is especially common in administrative documents.) **careful attention displayed in discharge of obligation or responsibility,** ***care, attention,*** of care received ἐπιμελείας τυχεῖν *be cared for* (Isocr. 6, 154; 7, 37; Athen. 13, 56 p. 589c; POxy 58, 22 αἱ ταμιακαὶ οὐσίαι τῆς προσηκούσης ἐπιμελείας τεύξονται; Philo, Spec. Leg. 3, 106; Jos., Ant. 2, 236) **Ac 27:3.**—Of exercise of diligence ἐν πάσῃ ἐ. σαρκικῇ καὶ πνευματικῇ *w. all diligence, both of the body and of the spirit* IPol 1:2 (cp. Diod. S. 14, 84, 2 ἐπιμέλεια τοῦ σώματος=care for the body).—DELG s.v. μέλω. Larfeld I 494. M-M. TW. Spicq.

ἐπιμελέομαι pass. dep., fut. ἐπιμελήσομαι; 1 aor. ἐπεμελήθην, impv. ἐπιμελήθητι (s. prec. entry; Hdt.+; ins, pap, LXX; TestSol 4:15 D; Just., D. 1:4; Ath. 23:5 [Pla., Phdr. 246e]) ***care for, take care of*** w. gen. (Hdt. et al.; Herm. Wr. 10, 22b; Gen 44:21; Sir 30:25; Philo; Jos., Ant. 1, 53; 8, 297; Just., D. 1, 4) τινός *someone or someth.* **Lk 10:34f; 1 Ti 3:5.** πίστεως, ἐλπίδος, whereby love for God and humans is generated and redounds to eternal life Agr 7.—DELG s.v. μέλω. M-M. Spicq.

ἐπιμελής, ές (s. prec. entry) ***careful, attentive*** (so act. in Aristoph., X., Pla., et al.; ins, pap, TestSol 5:6; EpArist 93; Philo; Jos., C. Ap. 1, 163) Pol 5:2.—DELG s.v. μέλω.

ἐπιμελῶς adv. (s. ἐπιμελέομαι; X., Pla.+; ins, pap, LXX; ViIs [p. 70, 2 Sch.]; EpArist 81; Philo; Jos., Ant. 12, 318; 17, 12) ***carefully, diligently*** ζητεῖν *hunt carefully* **Lk 15:8;** ἐκζητεῖν ἐ. Hv 3, 3, 5; πυνθάνεσθαι Dg 1. κατανοεῖν *consider, look at carefully* Hs 8, 2, 5; καθαρίζειν ἐ. s 9, 7, 2. ἐνστερνίζεσθαι 1 Cl 2:1; cp. 40:2 cj. Lghtf.; φυλάσσειν ἐ. Dg 7:1. τελεῖν διακονίαν ἐ. *perform a service carefully* Hm 12, 3, 3.—M-M. Spicq.

ἐπιμένω impf. ἐπέμενον; fut. ἐπιμενῶ; 1 aor. ἐπέμεινα (s. μένω; Hom.+)

❶ **to remain at or in the same place for a period of time,** ***stay, remain.*** Lit. ἐν Ἐφέσῳ **1 Cor 16:8** (cp. PLond III, 897, 12 p. 207 [84 AD] ἐν Ἀλεξανδρείᾳ ἐπιμένειν; PFay 296). αὐτοῦ *there* **Ac 21:4;** cp. **15:34 v.l.** W. the time more definitely given (Jos., Bell. 2, 545 ἔνθα δύο ἡμέρας ἐ., Vi. 47) **21:4;** ἐ. ἡμέρας τινάς *stay there for several days* **10:48.** ἡμέρας πλείους (Jos., Ant. 16, 15) **21:10.** ἡμέρας τρεῖς **28:12.** ἡμέρας ἑπτά vs. **14.** ἡμέρας δεκαπέντε **Gal 1:18.** ἐ. χρόνον τινά *for some time* **1 Cor 16:7.** πρός τινα *with someone* **ibid.; Gal 1:18.** παρά τινι **Ac 28:14.** ἐπί τινι (X., An. 7, 2, 1) **ibid. v.l.** W. dat. (PRyl 153, 3 [II AD]; 239, 9) ἄσκυλτον ἐ. τῇ πυρᾷ *remain unmoved on the pyre* MPol 13:3. ἐν τῇ σαρκί *remain in the body* **Phil 1:24.**

❷ **to continue in an activity or state,** ***continue, persist (in), persevere*** w. dat., transf. sense of 1 (X., Oec. 14, 7 τῷ μὴ ἀδικεῖν, Hell. 3, 4, 6; Aelian, VH 10, 15; SIG 1243, 26 ἐ. τῇ αὐθαδίᾳ; POxy 237 VI, 18 τῇ αὐτῇ ἀπονοίᾳ; PTebt 424, 4; Jos., Vi. 143; TestLevi 4:1 τ. ἀδικίαις; cp. Just., A II, 68, 2 τῇ ἀδικίᾳ; JosAs 23:12 τῇ βουλῇ) τῇ ἁμαρτίᾳ *in sin* **Ro 6:1.** τῇ πίστει **Col 1:23.** τῇ ἀπιστίᾳ **Ro 11:23.** ταῖς ἡδοναῖς Hs 8, 8, 5; 8, 9, 4. ταῖς πράξεσι s 9, 20, 4; τῇ ἐπιθυμίᾳ 9, 26, 2. αὐτοῖς (w. ref. to ταῦτα, τούτοις 1 Ti 4:15; cp. Jos., Ant. 8, 190) **1 Ti 4:16.** ἐ. τῇ χρηστότητι *continue in the sphere of* (God's) *goodness* **Ro 11:22.** τῇ πορνείᾳ Hm 4, 1, 5; cp. 6. ἐν τῇ ἀληθείᾳ Hv 3, 6,

2. W. ptc. foll. *keep on, persist* (stubbornly) *in doing someth.* (Pla., Meno 93d; Menand., Her. 35 J. and Kö. ἐπιμένει τὸ χρέος ἀπεργαζόμενος; Cornutus 17 p. 31, 11; POxy 237 VI, 18 [186 AD] ἐπιμένει ἐνυβρίζων μοι; 128, 7 ἐ. λέγων) ἐ. κρούων **Ac 12:16.** ἐπέμενον ἐρωτῶντες αὐτόν *they persisted in questioning him* **J 8:7;** cp. 2 Cl 10:5. ἐ. ἕως τέλους λειτουργοῦντες Hs 9, 27, 3. But ἐπιμένοντος πάλιν αὐτοῦ καὶ λέγοντος *when he insisted again and said* MPol 10:1. Without ptc. in the same mng. 8:2. Likew. abs. *persist* Hs 6, 5, 7. ἐπιμενόντων τῶν ζητούντων αὐτόν *when those who were looking for him did not give up (the search)* MPol 6:1.—M-M.

ἐπίμονος, ον (ἐπιμονή 'delay', μονή 'tarrying', s. μένω; Clearchus, fgm. 24 p. 17, 15; Polyb. 6, 43, 2 ἀκμαί; Plut., Mor. 166c κολαστήριον; SIG 679, 80 [143 BC]; Dt 28:59 Sym.; Philo, Ebr. 21) **pert. to continuing for a relatively long time,** ***lasting*** ἡ στάσις *the rebellion continues* 1 Cl 46:9. ἡ ἐ. κόλασις *continuous torture* MPol 2:4.—DELG s.v. μένω.

ἐπινεύω 1 aor. ἐπένευσα (s. νεύω; Hom. et al.; ins, pap, LXX; Ath. 37, 1) ***give consent (by a nod)*** οὐκ ἐπένευσεν *he did not give his consent* (PRyl 119, 21 [I AD]; cp. Philo, Migr. Abr. 111; Jos., Vi. 124) **Ac 18:20.**—M-M.

ἐπινοέω 1 aor. ἐπενόησα, pass. 3 sg. ἐπενοήθη Wsd 14:14 (s. νοέω; Hdt., Aristoph. et al.; ins, pap, LXX; TestSol 20:10 P.; ApcrEzk [Epiph. 70, 7]; EpArist, Philo; Jos., Bell. 3, 190, Ant. 17, 37) **to take notice of,** ***notice*** someth. undesirable κατά τινος *against someone=in someone* 1 Cl 39:4 (Job 4:18). τὶ περί τινος *someth. about someth.* οὐδὲν ἐπινοεῖς περὶ αὐτῶν; *do you not notice anything about them?* Hs 9, 9, 1.—EOwen, ἐπινοέω, ἐπίνοια and Allied Words: JTS 35, '34, 368–76.—DELG s.v. νόος. Sv.

ἐπίνοια, ας, ἡ (s. prec. entry; trag., Pre-Socr., Thu.+; SIG 902, 5; OGI 580, 7; POxy 237 VII, 35; 1468, 5; LXX; EpArist, Philo; Jos., Bell. 4, 356, Vi. 223 al.; TestJos 5:2, 3; SibOr 5, 81; Tat.) **the result of a thought process,** ***thought, conception*** (Thu. 3, 46, 6 al.; Wsd 6:16; 9:14; 2 Macc 12:45) θνητὴ ἐ. Dg 7:1 (cp. Philo, Mut. Nom. 219 ἀνθρωπίνη ἐ.); *inventiveness* (X., Cyr. 2, 3, 19 al.) w. φροντίς 5:3; *intent* (Aristoph., Thesm. 766; 4 Macc 17:2) ἡ ἐ. τῆς καρδίας σου *the intent of your heart* **Ac 8:22.**—DELG s.v. νόος. M-M. Sv.

ἐπινομή, ῆς, ἡ (elsewh. only in the mngs. 'spread' of fire, etc. [Plut., Alex. 685 (35, 4); Aelian, NA 12, 32], 'pasturage' [pap, s. νομή], and in medical wr. 'final turns of a bandage') μεταξὺ ἐπινομὴν δεδώκασιν (v.l. ἔδωκαν) prob. ***rule*** 1 Cl 44:2 *afterward they laid down a rule.* This takes for granted that ἐπινομή, which is the rdg. of the Codex Alexandr., is derived fr. ἐπινέμω 'distribute', 'allot' (s. Knopf, Hdb. ad loc.; also KLake ad loc., who compares ἐπινομίς, 'supplement, codicil'). The Latin translator (who rendered it 'legem') seems to have read and understood it so. The later Gk. ms. has ἐπιδομήν. The Syriac presupposes ἐπὶ δοκιμήν; the Coptic is as much at a loss as many modern interpreters admittedly are. Lghtf. proposes ἐπιμονήν. S. also RSohm, Kirchenrecht 1892 p. 82, 4.—DELG s.v. νέμω.

ἐπιορκέω (s. ὅρκος, ὁρκίζω) fut. ἐπιορκήσω (Hom. et al.; ins, pap, LXX, Philo; TestAsh 2:6.—On the spelling ἐφιορκέω s. B-D-F §14; Mlt-H. 99; 314f).

❶ **to swear that someth. is true when one knows it is false,** ***swear falsely, perjure oneself*** the context favors this sense for D 2:3 in which malicious speech about one's neighbor is castigated in various terms. It is prob. that also **Mt 5:33** belongs here, but 2 is favored by many.

❷ **to fail to do what one has promised under oath,** ***break one's oath*** (Il. 19, 188 note the fut ἐπιορκήσω; Chrysipp.: Stoic. II 63, 28; Herodian 3, 6, 7; Procop. Soph., Ep. 61; 1 Esdr 1:46) **Mt 5:33** (s. 1 above).—DELG s.v. ὅρκος. M-M. TW.

ἐπίορκος, ον (s. prec. entry; Hom. et al.) of persons (Hes. et al.; Jos., Vi. 102; Just., D. 12, 3; on the spelling ἐφί- s. B-D-F §14; Mlt-H. 99; 314f) **pert. to falseness in oath-taking,** subst. (Zech 5:3; Philo, Decal. 88) ***perjurer*** **1 Ti 1:10** (w. ψευσταί).—TW.

ἐπιοῦσα, ης, ἡ *the next day* s. ἔπειμι.

ἐπιούσιος, ον according to Origen, De Orat. 27, 7, coined by the evangelists. Grave doubt is cast on the one possible occurrence of ἐ. which is independent of our lit. (Sb 5224, 20), by BMetzger, How Many Times Does ἐ. Occur Outside the Lord's Prayer?: ET 69, '57/58, 52–54=Historical and Literary Studies, '68, 64–66; it seems likely that Origen was right after all. Found in our lit. only w. ἄρτος in the Lord's Prayer **Mt 6:11; Lk 11:3;** D 8:2. Variously interpreted: Sin. Syr. (on Lk) and Cur. Syr. אמינא *continual* (DHadidian, NTS 5, '58/59, 75–81); Peshitta דסונקנן *for our need;* Itala 'panis quotidianus', 'daily bread'; Jerome 'panis supersubstantialis' (on this JHennig, TS 4, '43, 445–54); GHb 62, 42 מָחָר = Lat. 'crastinus' *for tomorrow.* Of modern interpretations the following are worth mentioning:

❶ deriving it fr. ἐπί and οὐσία ***necessary for existence*** (in agreement w. Origen, Chrysostom, and Jerome are e.g. Beza, Tholuck, HEwald, Bleek, Weizsäcker, BWeiss, HCremer; Billerb. I 420; CRogge, PhilolWoch 47, 1927, 1129–35; FHauck, ZNW 33, '34, 199–202; RWright, CQR 157, '56, 340–45; HBourgoin, Biblica 60, '79, 91–96; Betz, SM p. 398f, with provisional support).

❷ a substantivizing of ἐπὶ τὴν οὖσαν sc. ἡμέραν ***for the current day, for today*** (cp. Thu. 1, 2, 2 τῆς καθ' ἡμέραν ἀναγκαίου τροφῆς; Vi. Aesopi W. 110 p. 102 P. τὸν καθημερινὸν ζήτει προσλαμβάνειν ἄρτον καὶ εἰς τὴν αὔριον ἀποθησαύριζε. Cp. Pind., O. 1, 99.—Acc. to Artem. 1, 5 p. 12, 26–28 one loaf of bread is the requirement for one day. S. ἐφήμερος.)—ADebrunner, Glotta 4, 1912, 249–53; 13, 1924, 167–71, SchTZ 31, 1914, 38–41, Kirchenfreund 59, 1925, 446–8, ThBl 8, 1929, 212f, B-D-F §123, 1; 124, PhilolWoch 51, '31, 1277f (but s. CSheward, ET 52 '40/41, 119f).—AThumb, Griechische Grammatik 1913, 675; ESchwyzer II 473, 2.

❸ ***for the following day*** fr. ἡ ἐπιοῦσα sc. ἡμέρα (cp. schol. Pind., N. 3, 38 νῦν μὲν ὡς ἥρωα, τῇ δὲ ἐπιούσῃ ὡς θεόν=today viewed as a hero, on the morrow a god; s. ἔπειμι): Grotius, Wettstein; Lghtf., On a Fresh Revision of the English NT[3] 1891, 217–60; Zahn, JWeiss; Harnack, SBBerlAk 1904, 208; EKlostermann; Mlt-H. p. 313f; PSchmiedel: W-S. §16, 3b note 23, SchTZ 30, 1913, 204–20; 31, 1914, 41–69; 32, 1915, 80; 122–33, PM 1914, 358–64, PhilolWoch 48, 1928, 1530–36, ThBl 8, 1929, 258f; ADeissmann, Heinrici Festschr. 1914, 115–19, RSeeberg Festschr. 1929, I 299–306, The NT in the Light of Modern Research, 1929, 84–86; AFridrichsen, SymbOsl 2, 1924, 31–41 (GRudberg ibid. 42; 3, 1925, 76); 9, 1930, 62–68; OHoltzmann; ASteinmann, D. Bergpredigt 1926, 104f; FPölzl-TInnitzer, Mt[4] '32, 129f; SKauchtschischwili, PhilolWoch 50, 1930, 1166–68.—FStiebitz, ibid. 47, 1927, 889–92, w. ref. to Lat. 'diaria'=the daily ration of food, given out for the next day; someth. like: *give us today our daily portion*—acc. to FDölger, AC 5, '36, 201–10, one loaf of bread (likew. WCrönert, Gnomon 4, 1928, 89 n. 1). S. also s.v. σήμερον.

❹ deriving it fr. ἐπιέναι 'be coming'—ⓐ on the analogy of τὸ ἐπιόν='the future', *bread for the future;* so Cyrillus of Alex. and Peter of Laodicea; among the moderns, who attach var. mngs. to it, esp. ASeeberg, D. 4te Bitte des V.-U., Rektoratsrede Rostock 1914, Heinrici Festschr. 1914, 109; s. LBrun, Harnack-Ehrung 1921, 22f.

ⓑ in the mng. 'come to': *give us this day the bread that comes to it,* i.e. *belongs to it;* so KHolzinger, PhilolWoch 51, '31, 825–30; 857–63; 52, '32, 383f.

ⓒ equal to ἐπιών=*next* acc. to TShearman, JBL 53, '34, 110–17.

ⓓ *the bread which comes upon (us)* viz. from the Father, so AHultgren, ATR 72, '90, 41–54.

ⓔ The petition is referred to the *coming* Kingdom and its feast by: REisler, ZNW 24, 1925, 190–92; JSchousboe, RHR 48, 1927, 233–37; ASchweitzer, D. Mystik des Ap. Pls 1930, 233–35; JJeremias, Jesus als Weltvollender 1930, 52; ELittmann, ZNW 34, '35, 29; cp. EDelebecque, Études grecques sur l'évangile de Luc '76, 167–81.—S. also GLoeschcke, D. Vaterunser-Erklärung des Theophilus v. Antioch. 1908; GWalther, Untersuchungen z. Gesch. d. griech. Vaterunser-Exegese 1914; DVölter, PM 18, 1914, 274ff; 19, 1915, 20ff, NThT 4, 1915, 123ff; ABolliger, SchTZ 30, 1913, 276–85; GKuhn, ibid. 31, 1914, 33ff; 36, 1919, 191ff; EvDobschütz, HTR 7, 1914, 293–321; RWimmerer, Glotta 12, 1922, 68–82; EOwen, JTS 35, '34, 376–80; JHensler, D. Vaterunser 1914; JSickenberger, Uns. ausreichendes Brot gib uns heute 1923; PFiebig, D. Vaterunser 1927, 81–83; GDalman, Worte[2] 1930, 321–34; HHuber, D. Bergpredigt '32; GBonaccorsi, Primi saggi di filologia neotest. I '33, 61–63; 533–39; JHerrmann, D. atl. Urgrund des Vaterunsers: OProcksch Festchr. '34, 71–98; MBlack, JTS 42, '41, 186–89, An Aramaic Approach[3], '67, 203–7, 299f, n. 3; SMowinckel, Artos epiousios: NorTT 40, '42, 247–55; ELohmeyer, D. Vaterunser erkl. '46.—Lit.: JCarmignac, Recherches sur le 'Notre Père', '69; CHemer, JSNT 22, '84, 81–94; Betz, SM 396–400.—M-M. EDNT. TW. Spicq. Sv.

ἐπιπέτομαι 2 aor. ἐπέπτην, ptc. ἐπιπτάς (s. πέτομαι; Hom. et al.) ***fly upon*** (ἐπί τι: Pla., Rep. 2, 365a; Dio Chrys. 70 [20], 12. ἐπί τινα: Just., D. 88, 3; τινί: ibid. 88, 8 [Mk 1:10 par.]) ἐ. ἐπὶ τὸν τοῦ ἡλίου βωμόν *light on the altar of the sun-god* 1 Cl 25:4.

ἐπιπίπτω 2 aor. ἐπέπεσον (-σα v.l. **Ro 15:3**); pf. ἐπιπέπτωκα (s. πίπτω; Hdt. et al.; ins, pap, LXX; pseudepigr.; Philo, De Jos. 256; Jos., Ant. 6, 23; 8, 377) gener. 'fall upon'.

❶ **to cause pressure by pushing against or falling on, *fall on, press*—**ⓐ to fall on, with implication of damage caused *fall upon someth.* ἐπί τι (X., Oec. 18, 7) of a hailstone *on a man's head* Hm 11:20.

ⓑ to make contact *approach impetuously/eagerly* τινί (Syntipas p. 11, 12) ἐπέπεσεν αὐτῷ *he threw himself upon him* **Ac 20:10.** ὥστε ἐπιπίπτειν αὐτῷ (w. ἵνα foll.) *so that they pressed about him (in order that)* **Mk 3:10** (cp. Thu. 7, 84, 3 ἀθρόοι ἀναγκαζόμενοι χωρεῖν ἐπέπιπτον ἀλλήλοις; JosAs 27:6 ἐπέπεσαν αὐτοῖς ἄφνω). ἐπί τι (Gen 50:1) ἐπὶ τὸν τράχηλόν τινος *fall on someone's neck (=embrace someone)* (Gen 45:14 [s. MWilcox, The Semitisms of Ac, '65, 67]; Tob 11:9, 13) **Lk 15:20; Ac 20:37.** ἐπιπεσὼν ἐπὶ τὸ στῆθος τοῦ Ἰησοῦ *he pressed close to Jesus' breast* **J 13:25 v.l.**

❷ **to happen to, *befall,*** of extraordinary events and misfortunes: *come upon* ἐπί τινα *someone.* ὀνειδισμοί *reproaches have fallen upon someone* **Ro 15:3** (Ps 68:10). φόβος ἐ. ἐπί τινα *fear came upon someone* (Josh 2:9; Jdth 14:3; Job 4:13) **Lk 1:12; Ac 19:17,** cp. **Rv 11:11.** φόβ. ἐ. τινί (Da 4:5; Job 13:11.—ἐ. τινί also Memnon [I BC/I AD]: 434 fgm. 1, 28, 3 Jac.; Synes., Kingship 16 p. 18c δέος ἐπιπεσεῖν ἅπασιν) 1 Cl 12:5. Abs. ἐπέπεσεν στάσις τῶν Φαρισαίων καὶ Σαδδουκαίων *a quarrel broke out betw. the Ph. and S.* **Ac 23:7 v.l.** Of the Holy Spirit: *comes upon someone* ἐπί τινι **8:16.** ἐπί τινα (cp. Ezk 11:5) **8:39 v.l.; 10:44; 11:15; 19:6** D. Of a trance ἔκστασις ἐ. ἐπί τινα (Da 10:7 Theod.) **10:10 v.l.**—M-M.

ἐπιπλήσσω (s. πλήσσω); 1 aor. ἐπέπληξα; prim. sense 'strike at' (since Hom.), also ***rebuke, reprove*** (Hom. et al.; Pla., Polyb.; BGU 1138, 22 [19 BC]) τινί *someone* (Il. 12, 211; Epict., Ench. 33, 16; Appian, Liby. 65 §291, Bell. Civ. 5, 13 §51; Philo, Leg. All. 2, 46; Jos., Ant. 1, 246; 19, 346) **1 Ti 5:1.** Also τινά ('the tragedy' in Simplicius in Epict. p. 95, 43 ἐπιπλήττουσί με; Lucian, Herm. 20; UPZ 15, 32 [156 BC]) πάντας δὲ οὓς ἐθεράπευσεν ἐπέπληξεν *all whom he healed he rebuked* **Mt 12:15f v.l.** (ASyn. 113, mg.). Abs. (X., Oec. 13, 12) **Lk 23:43** D (where ἐπλήσοντι is to be corrected to ἐπιπλήσσοντι).— M-M.

ἐπιποθέω fut. ἐπιποθήσω; 1 aor. ἐπεπόθησα (ποθέω 'long for', s. next entry; Hdt. et al.; LXX, Philo) **to have a strong desire for someth., with implication of need, *long for, desire*** τὶ *someth.* (Pla., Protag. 329d; Plut., Agis 798 [6, 2]; Lucian, D. Deor. 4, 3; Ps 118:131, 174; Tat. 20, 1) γάλα *milk* **1 Pt 2:2.** τινά *someone* (Hdt. 5, 93; Diod. S. 17, 101, 6; Epict. 3, 24, 53; Sir 25:21) πάντας ὑμᾶς **Phil 1:8; 2:26** (v.l. π. ὑ. ἰδεῖν). ὑμᾶς **2 Cor 9:14.** W. inf. foll. (Philo, Abr. 87 ἐ. θεὸν ἀνευρεῖν) τὸ οἰκητήριον ἐπενδύσασθαι **2 Cor 5:2.** ἰδεῖν τινα **Ro 1:11; 1 Th 3:6; 2 Ti 1:4.** πρὸς φθόνον ἐπιποθεῖ τὸ πνεῦμα **Js 4:5** is difficult because of the problem posed by uncertainty in the tradition concerning the correct reading of the verb: κατοικίζω text (causative) and κατοικέω v.l. (intr.), but the mng. of the verb is clear; if κατῴκισεν is read, one can render either *the spirit that (God) has caused to dwell in us yearns jealously* or (God) *yearns jealously over the spirit that he has put in us;* if κατῴκησεν *the spirit that has taken up abode in us yearns jealously.* See MDibelius ad loc. (w. lit.). AMeyer, D. Rätsel des Jk 1930, 258f; ASchlatter, D. Brief d. Jak. '32, 248–53.—CSpicq, RB 64, '57, 184–95. B. 1162. TW. Spicq. Sv.

ἐπιπόθησις, εως, ἡ (s. prec. entry; Appian, Gall. 5 §2; Ezk 23:11 Aq.; Clem. Alex., Strom. 4, 21, 131; Damascius, De Princ. 38; Etym. Mag. p. 678, 39) **yearning desire for, *longing*** **2 Cor 7:7, 11.**

ἐπιπόθητος, ον (s. ἐπιποθέω; Appian, Iber. 43 §179) **pert. to being earnestly desired, *longed for, desired*** ἀδελφοὶ ἀγαπητοὶ καὶ ἐ. **Phil 4:1.** εἰρήνη *peace that we desire* 1 Cl 65:1. ἡ ἐ. ὄψις ὑμῶν *the longed-for sight of you* B 1:3.

ἐπιποθία, ας, ἡ (s. ἐπιποθέω; Suda) ***longing, desire*** ἐπιποθίαν ἔχων τοῦ ἐλθεῖν *having a desire to come* **Ro 15:23; 2 Cor 7:11 v.l.**—TW.

ἐπιπολύ B 4:1 s. ἐπί 13.

ἐπιπορεύομαι 1 aor. ptc. fem. ἐπιπορευσαμένη 3 Macc 1:4 **be on one's way to, *go/journey to*** (s. πορεύομαι; Ephorus Cumanus [IV BC]: 70 fgm. 5 Jac.; Philo Mech. 90, 19; Polyb. 4, 9, 2; PLille 3, 78 [241 BC]; Mitt-Wilck. I/2, 116, 3 [II/III AD]; 3 Macc 1:4; Jos., Ant. 12, 400) πρός τινα *to someone* (Jos., Bell. 2, 481) **Lk 8:4.**—DELG s.v. πόρος. M-M.

ἐπιπρέπω (s. πρέπει; Hom. et al.) **to be appropriate to, *be becoming, suit, go well with*** τινί *someone* or *someth.* (X., Cyr. 7, 5, 83; Lucian, D. Mar. 1, 1 ὁ ὀφθαλμὸς ἐπιπρέπει τῷ προσώπῳ) ἡ κόμη ἐπιπρέπουσα τῷ προσώπῳ *the hair went well with the face* ApcPt 3:10.

ἐπι(ρ)ράπτω for the spelling s. W-S. §5, 26b; B-D-F §11, 1 (the word: Galen 18, p. 579 Kühn; Nonnus, Dionys. 9, 3; 42, 315) ***sew (on)*** ἐπί τι *on someth.* a patch on a garment **Mk 2:21.** JSpringer, The Marcan ἐπιράπτει: Exp. 8th ser., 21, 1921, 79f.

ἐπι(ρ)ρίπτω fut. ἐπιρρίψω LXX; 1 aor. ἐπέριψα; pf. ἐπέρριφα Josh 23:4; 2 aor. pass. ἐπερίφην (s. ῥίπτω; Hom. et al.; PTebt 5, 183; 185; 249 [118 BC]; LXX; En; TestSol 16, 2 P. On the spelling s. W-S. §5, 26b)

❶ **to propel someth. from one place to another,** ***throw*** τὶ ἐπί τι *someth. on someth.* (Cleopatra ln. 112; LXX). Lit., of clothes, on an animal used for riding **Lk 19:35** (cp. 2 Km 20:12; 3 Km 19:19=Jos., Ant. 8, 353). Pass. of a vine ὅταν ἐπιρριφῇ ἐπὶ τὴν πτελέαν *when it is attached to the elm* Hs 2:3.

❷ **to transfer one's concerns,** ***cast upon,*** fig. ext. of 1: τ. μέριμναν ἐ. ἐπὶ θεόν *cast one's care upon God* **1 Pt 5:7** (ἀπορ(ρ)ίπτω P[72]; Ps 54:23); Hv 3, 11, 3; 4, 2, 4f (in all these pass. Ps 54:23 is in the background). A fig. application of 4 Km 13:21 is made AcPlCor 2:32 τὸ σῶμα καὶ τὰ ὀστᾶ καὶ τὸ πνεῦμα χριστοῦ ἐπιριφέντες . . . ἀναστήσεσθε *you, who have been thrown upon the body, bones, and spirit of Christ . . . shall rise* AcPlCor 2:32.—M-M. TW.

ἐπιρρώννυμι impf. ἐπερρώννυον; aor. pass. 3 pl. ἐπερρώσθησαν (s. ῥώννυμι; Soph., Hdt. et al.; PSI 452, 26; 2 Macc 11:9) **to cause to be emboldened,** ***strengthen, encourage*** τὴν δειλίαν τινός *strengthen someone, fearful though the person may be* MPol 3, 1.

ἐπισείω 1 aor. ἐπέσεισα; pf. ptc. ἐπισεσεικώς 2 Macc 4:1 (s. σείω; Hom. et al; JosAs [p. 62, 21 Bat.]; Jos., Bell. 1, 215; 2, 412).

❶ **to brandish someth. at or against someone,** ***shake at/against*** τινὶ τὴν χεῖρα *shake one's hand at someone* (in a threatening gesture) MPol 9:2 (Artem. 5, 92 αὐτῷ χεῖρα ἐπισεῖσαι; Ael. Aristid. 39 p. 747 D.: ὑμῖν τὰ ὅπλα ἐπισείων).

❷ **to cause people to riot against,** ***urge on, incite*** τοὺς ὄχλους **Ac 14:19** D.

ἐπίσημος, ον (σῆμα, 'sign'; trag., Hdt.+).—❶ **of exceptional quality,** ***splendid, prominent, outstanding*** (Hdt., trag. et al.; pap, LXX, EpArist, Philo; Joseph.) κριὸς ἐ. ἐκ ποιμνίου *a splendid ram fr. the flock* MPol 14:1. Of pers. (Diod. S. 5, 83, 1; Jos., Bell. 6, 201; 3 Macc 6:1; Just., A II, 12, 5) ἐ. ἐν τοῖς ἀποστόλοις *outstanding among the apostles* **Ro 16:7.** διδάσκαλος MPol 19:1.

❷ Also in a bad sense: ***notorious*** (trag. et al.; Plut., Fab. Max. 182 [14, 2]; Jos., Ant. 5, 234) δέσμιος **Mt 27:16.**—DELG s.v. σῆμα. M-M. TW.

ἐπισήμως adv. (s. prec. entry; Polyb. 6, 39, 9; Jos., Bell. 6, 92; Ps 73:4 Sym.) ***in an outstanding manner*** θηριομαχεῖν MPol 3:1.

ἐπισιτισμός, οῦ, ὁ ***provisions*** (as stock of food, so X., An. 7, 1, 9; Polyb. 2, 5, 3; Herodian 6, 7, 1; OGI 200, 15; Sb 6949, 15; LXX; Jos., Bell. 3, 85) εὑρίσκειν ἐ. *find* or *get some provisions* **Lk 9:12.**—DELG s.v. σῖτος. M-M.

ἐπισκέπτομαι mid. dep., fut. ἐπισκέψομαι LXX; 1 aor. ἐπεσκεψάμην; pf. ἐπέσκεμμαι LXX. Pass.: fut. 3 sg. ἐπισκεπήσεται 1 Km 20:18; aor. ἐπεσκέπην LXX; on the other hand, fut. 3 sg. ἐπισκεφθήσεται Jer 3:16; aor. subj. 3 sg. ἐπισκεφθῇ 1 Esdr 2:16 (s. σκοπέω; trag., Hdt.+; s. B-D-F §101 p. 48 s.v. σκοπεῖν; Mlt-H. 258 s.v. -σκέπτομαι).

❶ **to make a careful inspection,** ***look at, examine, inspect*** (Hdt. 2, 109, 2 et al.) w. acc. (Diod. S. 12, 11, 4; Num 1:3; 1 Km 13:15; 2 Km 18:1) Hs 8, 2, 9; 8, 3, 3; 9, 10, 4; 1 Cl 25:5. Also *look for* with interest in selection, *select* w. acc. (PPetr II, 37, 2b verso 4 [III BC] ἐπισκεψάμενος ἐν ἀρχῇ ἃ δεῖ γενέσθαι ἔργα) ἄνδρας **Ac 6:3.**

❷ **to go to see a pers. with helpful intent,** ***visit*** τινά *someone* (Demosth. 9, 12; PLille 6, 5 [III BC] διαβάντος μου . . . ἐπισκέψασθαι τ. ἀδελφήν; Judg 15:1) ἀνέβη ἐπὶ τὴν καρδίαν αὐτοῦ ἐπισκέψασθαι τοὺς ἀδελφοὺς αὐτοῦ *(Moses) felt strongly about visiting his people* **Ac 7:23** (for the note of solicitude cp. X., Mem. 3, 11, 10 φροντιστικῶς); **15:36.** ἀλλήλους Hv 3, 9, 2. Esp. of visiting the sick (X., Mem. 3, 11, 10; Plut., Mor. 129c; Lucian, Philops. 6; Herodian 4, 2, 4; Sir 7, 35; TestJob 28:2; Jos., Ant. 9, 178) **Mt 25:36, 43;** Pol 6:1. W. special suggestion in the context on care to be bestowed: *look after* widows and orphans ἐν τῇ θλίψει αὐτῶν *in their distress* **Js 1:27;** cp. Hs 1:8. ὀρφανοὺς καὶ ὑστερουμένους Hm 8:10.

❸ **to exercise oversight in behalf of,** ***look after, make an appearance to help,*** of divine oversight (Gen 21:1; 50:24f; Ex 3:16; 4:31; Sir 46:14; Jdth 8:33; En 25:3; TestLevi 16:5; PsSol 9:4; JosAs 7:35; Just. D. 29, 1) **Lk 1:68.** ἐπισκέψεται ἡμᾶς ἀνατολὴ ἐξ ὕψους vs. **78** (here the imagery is of dawning light that makes inspection possible, the divine inspection being for the benefit of the oppressed; NRSV 'break upon' shifts the imagery); τὸν λαόν **7:16** (cp. Ruth 1:6). Of the orphaned Joachim ἐπισκέψηταί με κύριος ὁ θεός μου GJs 1:4; ὅπως ἐπισκέψηταί με *so that (God) might come to my aid* 2:4 (sc. cod. A, s. Tdf.); ὅτι ἐπεσκέψατό με καὶ ἀφεῖλεν . . . ὀνειδισμόν 6:3.—**Hb 2:6** (Ps 8:5); *be concerned about* w. inf. foll. (s. B-D-F §392, 3) ὁ θεὸς ἐπεσκέψατο λαβεῖν ἐξ ἐθνῶν λαόν *God concerned himself about winning a people fr. among the nations* **Ac 15:14.**—M-M. TW. Sv.

ἐπισκευάζομαι (s. σκεῦος) 1 aor. ἐπεσκευασάμην; pass. inf. ἐπισκευασθῆναι 1 Km 3:3 (as a rule—Aristoph., Thu. et al.; ins, pap, LXX—act. In our lit. only mid. as Jos., Bell. 1, 297) **to prepare for some activity or objective,** ***get ready*** (Thu. 7, 36, 2) **Ac 21:15.**—DELG s.v. σκεῦος. M-M s.v. ἐπισκευάζω.

ἐπισκηνόω 1 aor. ἐπεσκήνωσα (σκηνόω 'pitch tents', s. σκηνή) **to use a place for lodging,** ***take up quarters, take up one's abode*** w. ἐπί and acc. of the place where one takes up quarters (Polyb. 4, 18, 8 ἐπὶ τὰς οἰκίας of troops quartered in houses) ἵνα ἐπισκηνώσῃ ἐπ' ἐμὲ ἡ δύναμις τ. Χριστοῦ *that the power of Christ may dwell in me* **2 Cor 12:9.**—DELG s.v. σκηνή. M-M. TW.

ἐπισκιάζω fut. 3 sg. ἐπισκιάσει Ps 90:4; 1 aor. ἐπεσκίασα (σκιάζω 'overshadow, darken', s. σκιά; Hdt. et al.; Philo, Deus Imm. 3 and oft.; LXX; Just. A I, 33, 6; Ath. 30, 2)

❶ **to cause a darkened effect by interposing someth. between a source of light and an object,** ***overshadow, cast a shadow*** (Aristot., Gen. An. 5, 1; Theophr., C. Pl. 2, 18, 3) τινί *upon someone* (Theophr., De Sens. 79) ἵνα κἂν ἡ σκιὰ ἐπισκιάσῃ τινὶ αὐτῶν *that at least his shadow might fall on one of them* **Ac 5:15.**

❷ **to cause a darkening,** ***cover*** (Hdt. 1, 209 τῇ πτέρυγι τὴν Ἀσίην; Aelian, VH 3, 3) w. acc. of pers., mostly used in our lit. for ref. to divine activity such as a cloud that indicates the presence of God (cp. Ex 40:35; OdesSol 35, 1) **Mt 17:5; Lk 9:34.** W. dat. (Ps 90:4) **Mk 9:7.** W. acc. of thing ἦν νεφέλη σκοτεινὴ ἐπισκιάζουσα τὸ σπήλαιον *a dark cloud was hovering over* *the cave* (in which Jesus was born) GJs 19:2. This perspective is present in the account of Mary's unique conception δύναμις ὑψίστου ἐπισκιάσει σοι **Lk 1:35** (for the imagery of overshadowing involving the divine and the human cp. Philo, Rer. Div. Her. 265 M 511, De Somniis 1, 119 M 638, s. Leisegang [below] 25f; but against L's suggestion of polytheistic content s. RBrown, The Birth of the Messiah '77, 290); GJs 11:3; but Just., A I, 33, 4, D. 100, 5 αὐτήν. S. on this passage JHehn, BZ 14, 1917, 147–52; AAllgeier, ibid. 338ff, Byz.-Neugriech. Jahrb. 1, 1920, 131–41, Histor. Jahrbuch 45, 1925, 1ff; HLeisegang, Pneuma Hagion 1922, 24ff; ENorden, D. Geburt des Kindes 1924, 92–99; LRadermacher: PKretschmer Festschr. 1926, 163ff; AFridrichsen, SymbOsl 6, 1928, 33–36; MDibelius, Jungfrauensohn u. Krippenkind: SBHeidAk. 1931/32, 4. Abh. '32, 23f; 41; HvBaer, D. Hl. Geist in d. Lkschriften 1926, 124ff; KBornhäuser, D. Geburts- u. Kindheitsgesch. Jesu 1930, 81ff; SLösch, Deitas Iesu u. antike Apotheose '33, 101; RBrown, The Birth of the Messiah '77, 290f, 292–309.—DELG s.v. σκιά. M-M. EDNT. TW. Sv.

ἐπισκοπέω fut. ἐπισκοπήσω; 1 aor. ἐπεσκόπησα; pf. pass. ptc. ἐπεσκοπημένος (s. σκοπέω and next entry; Aeschyl. et al.).

❶ to give attention to, *look at, take care, see to it* w. μή foll. (Philo, Decal. 98) with implication of hazard awaiting one **Hb 12:15.**

❷ to accept responsibility for the care of someone, *oversee, care for* (Pla., Rep. 6 p. 506a τὴν πολιτείαν; Dio Chrys. 8 [9], 1 of Diogenes the Cynic's mission in life; LBW 2309; 2412e; pap [Witkowski 52, 12; cp. 63, 18; 71, 43]; 2 Ch 34:12), hence in a distinctively Christian sense of the activity of church officials **1 Pt 5:2,** esp. of one entrusted with oversight: *be an overseer* τινά *over someone* of Jesus, the ideal overseer/supervisor IRo 9:1. In a play on words w. ἐπίσκοπος: ἐπισκόπῳ μᾶλλον ἐπισκοπημένῳ ὑπὸ θεοῦ *the overseer/supervisor, who is rather overseen/supervised by God*='the bishop who has God as his bishop' IPol ins (ἐπισκοπέω of God: Jos., C. Ap. 2, 160). Abs. *serve as overseer* Hv 3, 5, 1.—DELG s.v. σκέπτομαι. M-M. TW.

ἐπισκοπή, ῆς, ἡ (s. prec. entry; Lucian, D. Deor. 20, 6='visit'; OGI 614, 6 [III AD]='care, charge'; Etym. Gud. 508, 27=πρόνοια; LXX; TestBenj 9:2; JosAs 29, end cod. A ἐπισκοπῇ ἐπισκέπτεσθαί τινα of God; Just., D. 131, 3).

❶ the act of watching over with special ref. to being present, *visitation,* of divine activity—ⓐ of a salutary kind (so Gen 50:24f; Ex 3:16; Wsd 2:20; 3:13; Job 10:12; 29:4 al.) καιρὸς τῆς ἐ. *the time of your gracious visitation* (Wsd 3:7) **Lk 19:44.** ἐν ἐ. τῆς βασιλείας τοῦ Χριστοῦ *when the kingdom of Christ visits us* 1 Cl 50:3. ἡμέρα ἐπισκοπῆς **1 Pt 2:12** is understood in this sense by the majority (e.g. Usteri, BWeiss, Kühl, Knopf, Windisch, FHauck, et al.). S. also b below.—The gracious visitation can manifest itself as *protection, care* (Job 10:12; Pr 29:13; 3 Macc 5:42; Just., D. 131, 3; Orig., C. Cels. 6, 71, 8 [as providential care w. πρόνοια]) ἐν ἑνότητι θεοῦ καὶ ἐπισκοπῇ *in unity w. God and under God's care* IPol 8:3.

ⓑ of an unpleasant kind (Hesych.= ἐκδίκησις; Jer 10:15; Sir 16:18; 23:24; Wsd 14:11; Theoph. Ant. 2, 35 [p. 188, 26]); ἡμέρα ἐ. (cp. Is 10:3) **1 Pt 2:12** is so understood by the minority (e.g. HvSoden, Bigg, Goodsp.; Danker, ZNW 58, '67, 98f, w. ref. to Mal 3:13–18). S. a above.

❷ position of responsibility, *position, assignment* (Num 4:16) of Judas' position as an apostle τὴν ἐ. λαβέτω ἕτερος *let another take over his work* (not an office as such, but activity of witnessing in line with the specifications in Ac 1:8, 21f) **Ac 1:20** (Ps 108:8).

❸ engagement in oversight, *supervision,* of leaders of Christian communities (a Christian ins of Lycaonia [IV AD] in Ramsay, CB I/2 p. 543; Iren. 3, 3, 3 [Harv. II 10, 2] al.; Orig., C. Cels. 3, 48, 20) **1 Ti 3:1** (s. UHolzmeister, Biblica 12, '31, 41–69; CSpicq, RSPT 29, '40, 316–25); 1 Cl 44:1, 4.—DELG s.v. σκέπτομαι. M-M. EDNT. TW.

ἐπίσκοπος, ου, ὁ (s. prec. entry; Hom. et al.; Diod. S. 37, 28, 1 [of a king w. synonym θεατής], ins, pap, LXX; JosAs 15:7 cod. A [p. 61, 16 Bat.] μετάνοια ... ἐπίσκοπος πάντων τῶν παρθένων; Philo, Joseph.—LPorter, The Word ἐπίσκοπος in Pre-Christian Usage: ATR 21, '39, 103–12) gener. 'one who watches over, guardian'. BThiering, 'Mebaqqer' and 'Episkopos' in the Light of the Temple Scroll: JBL 100, '81, 59–74 (office of 'bishop' adopted fr. Essene lay communities; cp. CD 14, 8–12; בקר Ezk 34:11 [LXX ἐπισκέπτειν]).

❶ one who has the responsibility of safeguarding or seeing to it that someth. is done in the correct way, *guardian* (so Il. 22, 255, deities are guardians of agreements, i.e. they 'see to it' that they are kept; Aeschyl., Sept. 272; Soph., Ant. 1148; Pla., Leg. 4, 717d; Plut., Cam. 5, 6 θεοὶ χρηστῶν ἐπίσκοποι καὶ πονηρῶν ἔργων; Maximus Tyr. 5, 8e ὦ Ζεῦ κ. Ἀθηνᾶ κ. Ἄπολλον, ἐθῶν ἀνθρωπίνων ἐπίσκοποι; Babrius 11, 4 P. '84=L-P.; Herodian 7, 10, 3. Oft. Cornutus, ed. Lang, index; SIG 1240, 21; UPZ 144, 49 [164 BC]; PGM 4, 2721; Job 20:29; Wsd 1:6; Philo, Migr. Abr. 115 al.; SibOr, fgm. 1, 3) παντὸς πνεύματος κτίστης κ. ἐπίσκοπος *creator and guardian of every spirit* 1 Cl 59:3.—Of Christ (w. ποιμήν) ἐ. τῶν ψυχῶν *guardian of the souls* **1 Pt 2:25.** The passages IMg 3:1 θεῷ τῷ πάντων ἐ.; cp. 6:1 show the transition to the next mng.

❷ In the Gr-Rom. world ἐ. freq. refers to one who has a definite function or fixed office of guardianship and related activity within a group (Aristoph., Av. 1023; IG XII/1, 49, 43ff [II/I BC], 50, 34ff [I BC]; LBW 1989; 1990; 2298; Num 31:14 al.; PPetr III, 36a verso, 16 [III BC]; Jos., Ant. 10, 53; 12, 254), including a religious group (IG XII/1, 731, 8: an ἐ. in the temple of Apollo at Rhodes. S. Dssm., NB 57f [BS 230f]. Cp. also Num 4:16. On the Cynic-Stoic preacher as ἐπισκοπῶν and ἐπίσκοπος s. ENorden, Jahrb. klass. Phil Suppl. 19, 1893, 377ff.—Philo, Rer. Div. Her. 30 Moses as ἐ.). The term was taken over in Christian communities in ref. to one who served as ***overseer*** or ***supervisor,*** with special interest in guarding the apostolic tradition (Iren., Orig., Hippol.). **Ac 20:28** (RSchnackenburg, Schriften zum NT, '71, 247–67; ELöwestam, Paul's Address at Miletus: StTh 41, '87, 1–10); (w. διάκονοι) **Phil 1:1** (JReumann, NTS 39, '93, 446–50); D 15:1; **1 Ti 3:2; Tit 1:7** (s. BEaston, Pastoral Epistles '47, 173; 177; 227). ἀπόστολοι, ἐ., διδάσκαλοι, διάκονοι Hv 3, 5, 1; (w. φιλόξενοι) s 9, 27, 2. Esp. freq. in Ignatius IEph 1:3; 2:1f; 3:2; 4:1; 5:1f and oft.; **2 Ti subscr.:** Tim., overseer of the Ephesians; **Tit subscr.:** Titus overseer of the Cretan Christians. The ecclesiastical loanword 'bishop' is too technical and loaded with late historical baggage for precise signification of usage of ἐπίσκοπος and cognates in our lit., esp. the NT.—EHatch-AHarnack, D. Gesellschaftsverf. d. christ. Kirchen im Altert. 1883; Harnack, D. Lehre d. 12 Apostel 1884, 88ff, Entstehung u. Entwicklung der Kirchenverfassung u. des Kirchenrechts in d. zwei ersten Jahrh. 1910; ELoening, D. Gemeindeverf. d. Urchristent. 1888; CWeizsäcker, D. apost. Zeitalter[2] 1892, 613ff; RSohm, Kirchenrecht I 1892; JRéville, Les origines de l'épiscopat 1894; HBruders, D. Verf. d. Kirche bis z. J. 175, 1904; RKnopf, D. nachapostl. Zeitalter 1905, 147ff; PBatiffol-FSeppelt, Urkirche u. Katholicismus 1910, 101ff; OScheel, Z. urchristl. Kirchen- u. Verfassungsproblem: StKr 85, 1912, 403–57; HLietzmann, Z. altchr. Verfassungsgesch.: ZWT 55, 1913, 101–6 (=Kleine Schriften I,

’58, 144–48); EMetzner, D. Verf. d. Kirche in d. zwei ersten Jahrh. 1920; KMüller, Beiträge z. Gesch. d. Verf. in d. alten Kirche: ABA 1922, no. 3; HDieckmann, D. Verf. d. Urkirche 1923; GvHultum, ThGl 19, 1927, 461–88; GHolstein, D. Grundlagen d. evangel. Kirchenrechts 1928; JJeremias, Jerusalem II B 1, 1929, 132ff (against him KGoetz, ZNW 30, ’31, 89–93); BStreeter, The Primitive Church 1929; OLinton, D. Problem d. Urkirche usw. ’32 (lit. from 1880); JLebreton-JZeiller, L’Eglise primitive ’34; HBeyer, D. Bischofamt im NT: Deutsche Theologie 1, ’34, 201–25; HGreeven, Propheten, Lehrer, Vorsteher bei Pls: ZNW 44, ’52/53, 1–43 (lit.); HvCampenhausen, Kirchl. Amt u. geistl. Vollmacht in den ersten 3 Jahrhunderten ’53; WMichaelis, Das Ältestenamt der christlichen Gemeinde im Lichte der Hl. Schrift ’53; RBultmann, Theol. of the NT (tr. KGrobel) ’55, II, 95–111; TManson, The Church’s Ministry ’56; FNötscher, Vom Alten zum NT ’62, 188–220; DMoody, Interpretation 19, ’65, 168–81; HBraun, Qumran u. das NT ’66, II 326–42; RGG³ I 335–37 (lit.); JFitzmyer, PSchubert Festschr., ’66, 256f, n. 41 (lit.); RAC II 394–407; RBrown, TS 41, ’80, 322–38 (rev. of NT data).—Poland 377. M-M. EDNT. TW. Sv.

ἐπισκοτέω (s. σκοτ- entries; Hippocr., Pla. et al.; Jos., Bell. 5, 343, C. Ap. 1, 214; Ath.) gener. ‘darken, obscure’.

❶ **to put someth. in the way so that one cannot see properly,** ***block from seeing*** ἐπισκοτεῖσθαι ὑπὸ πράξεων *be prevented by* (these) *occupations fr. seeing* Hm 10, 1, 4 (cp. Philo, De Jos. 147).

❷ **to put someth. in the way so that an object cannot be clearly discerned,** ***to obscure*** (Menand., fgm. 48 Kock and Kö.) pass. *be obscured* (Polyb. 2, 39, 12 ἐπισκοτεῖσθαι κ. κωλύεσθαι, of pers. whose qualifications are not recognized; Heraclit. Sto. 19 p. 29, 15) of the Spirit μὴ ἐπισκοτούμενον ὑπὸ ἑτέρου πονηροῦ πνεύματος Hm 5, 1, 2 (the imagery is one of contrast between a bright and open [καθαρόν] spirit and a base spirit that darkens; cp. Diog. L. 5, 76 ἐπεσκοτήθη ὑπὸ τοῦ φθόνου).—DELG s.v. σκότος.

ἐπισπάω (σπάω) in our lit. ἐ. only mid. (which is found Hdt.+; Herm. Wr., ins, pap, LXX; TestReub 5:1; JosAs 5:9 cod. A [p. 46, 2 Bat.]; Philo; Jos., Ant. 14, 424, C. Ap. 2, 31) fut. 3 pl. ἐπισπάσονται (TestReub 5:1); 1 aor. ἐπεσπασάμην LXX.

❶ **to cause to come to oneself,** ***draw to oneself*** lit. τινί τι an animal MPol 3:1 (cp. Diod. S. 17, 13, 2 ἐπισπᾶσθαι πληγάς=draw the blows [of the enemies] to oneself [in order to die more quickly]).

❷ **to be responsible for bringing someth. on oneself,** ***bring upon,*** fig. ext. of 1 (Hdt. 3, 7, 72; Polyb. 3, 98, 8; Anth. Pal. 11, 340, 2 ἔχθραν; OGI 13, 6 τ. κρίσιν; Wsd 1:12) τί τινι *someth. (on) someone* αἰχμαλωτισμὸν ἑαυτοῖς *bring captivity on themselves* Hv 1, 1, 8. ἀσθένειαν τῇ σαρκὶ αὐτῶν v 3, 9, 3. μεγάλην ἁμαρτίαν ἑαυτῷ m 4, 1, 8. ἑαυτῷ λύπην s 9, 2, 6.

❸ medical t.t. **to pull the foreskin over the end of the penis,** ***pull over the foreskin*** (Soranus, Gynaec. 2, 34 p. 79, 1 of a nurse: ἐπισπάσθω τὴν ἀκροποσθίαν) to conceal circumcision **1 Cor 7:18** (this special use of the word is not found elsewh., not even 4 Macc 5:2, where ἐπισπᾶσθαι means ‘drag up’, as 10:12). On epispasm [rabbinic מָשַׁךְ], as done by Hellenizing Israelites, esp. ephebes, to undo their circumcision s. 1 Macc 1:15; Jos., Ant. 12, 241; Billerb. IV 33f; MHengel, Judaism and Hellenism ’74, I 74, II 51f, n. 138 [lit.]; RHall, Epispasm—Circumcision in Reverse: BR 18/4, ’92, 52–57.—M-M.

ἐπισπείρω 1 aor. ἐπέσπειρα (s. σπείρω; since Pind., N. 8, 39; Hdt.; Ath. 33, 1) **to sow on top of a crop,** ***sow afterward,*** agricultural t.t. (Theophr., HP 7, 1, 3 of celery seed on top of any other crop that has been put in; 5, 4 sow bitter vetch to protect a crop of radishes against spiders, al.) τι *someth.* ζιζάνια ἀνὰ μέσον τοῦ σίτου *weeds among the wheat* **Mt 13:25.**—M-M.

ἐπισπουδάζω (s. σπουδάζω, σπουδή; Lucian, Pisc. 2; PHib 49, 3 [III BC]; PLille 3, 27; LXX) **to be zealous in addition,** ***be more zealous*** περί τινος *for someone;* but the text is prob. corrupt; ἐπί may be repeated from the preceding ἔτι Hs 2:6 v.l. (cp. the sound of the words in POxy 1172 ἔτι καὶ ἔτι ἐπισπουδάζει and s. MDibelius, Hdb. ad loc.). S. Whittaker mg.—DELG s.v. σπεύδω.

ἐπίσταμαι pass. dep.; impf. ἠπιστάμην Dg 8:1 (s. ἐπιστήμη; Hom.+; ins, pap, LXX, pseudepigr., Philo, Joseph.; Just.; Mel., HE 4, 26, 13).

❶ **to gain a firm mental grasp of someth.,** ***understand*** τὶ *someth.* (X., Symp. 3, 6; Wsd 8:8; Just., A I, 60, 11) μηδὲν ἐπιστάμενος *without understanding anything* **1 Ti 6:4.** Abs. (w. οἶδα) w. relative clause foll. σὺ τί λέγεις **Mk 14:68.**

❷ **to acquire information about someth.,** ***know, be acquainted with*** τινά (Aristoph., Eq. 1278 ’Αρίγνωτον; Musonius 3 p. 12, 5H.; Plut., Cic. 883 [44, 5]; Lucian, Dial. Mort. 9, 3; PGM 13, 844; Wsd 15:3; Jos., C. Ap. 1, 175; Just., A I, 63, 15) τὸν Παῦλον **Ac 19:15.** τὸν θεόν PtK 2 p. 14, 11. τὶ *someth.* (Hom., Hdt. et al., also Lucian, D. Deor. 25, 2; PRyl 243, 6; Num 32:11; 1 Esdr 8:23 al.; PsSol 14:8; ApcSed 8:11; Jos., C. Ap. 1, 15; Just., A I, 58, 2; 60, 5 al.; Mel., HE 4, 26, 13) **Jd 10.** πολλά B 1:4. τὸ βάπτισμα ’Ιωάννου **Ac 18:25.** τὸ τῆς αὔριον *what will happen tomorrow* **Js 4:14.** τὰς γραφάς 1 Cl 53:1 (cp. Just., D. 70, 5 τὰ γράμματα τῶν γραφῶν). περί τινος *know about someth.* (Thu. 6, 60, 1; Pla., Euthyphr. 4e) ἐπίσταται περὶ τούτων ὁ βασιλεύς *the king knows about this* **Ac 26:26.** W. ὅτι foll. (X., An. 1, 4, 8 al.; Ex 4:14; Tob 11:7; TestSol 5:11; TestJob 12:3; Just., A I, 26, 7 al.) **Ac 15:7; 19:25; 22:19;** 1 Cl 45:3. Also ὡς (Soph., Aj. 1370; X., Cyr. 2, 3, 22) **Ac 10:28.** W. indir. quest. foll.: πῶς ἐγενόμην **20:18** (cp. PTebt 408, 3 [3 AD] ἐπιστάμενος πῶς σε φιλῶ; Just., A I, 21, 2 πόσους . . . υἱοὺς φάσκουσι τοῦ Διός=[you know] how many . . . claim to be sons of Zeus) ποῦ ἔρχεται **Hb 11:8.** πῶς νοήσω αὐτόν Hm 6, 2, 5. W. acc. and ptc. (X., An. 6, 6, 17; Jos., Vi. 142; Just., D. 49, 1 and 3 al.) ὄντα σε κριτήν *that you have been a judge* **Ac 24:10.** πολλοὺς παραδεδωκότας ἑαυτούς 1 Cl 55:2. W. inf. (Just., A I, 68, 3 ἐπίστασθαι δίκαια ἀξιοῦν; w. acc. and inf. Just., A I, 5, 2 μὴ ἐπιστάμενοι δαίμονας εἶναι φαύλους=not knowing that [the gods they fear] are in fact bad spirits) **1 Th 5:3 v.l.** (s. ἐφίστημι).—B. 1210. DELG. M-M. TW. Sv.

ἐπιστάς s. ἐφίστημι.

ἐπίστασις, εως, ἡ (s. ἐφίστημι and next entry; Soph. et al. in var. mngs.; PAmh 134, 9 al. in pap; 2 Macc; EpArist; Philo, Leg. All. 3, 49; Jos., Ant. 16, 395; Just.) in our lit., both times w. the v.l. ἐπισύστασις (q.v.).

❶ **responsibility for a matter,** ***pressure, care.*** For ἡ ἐ. μοι ἡ καθ’ ἡμέραν **2 Cor 11:28** *pressure,* in the sense of anxiety caused by a heavy sense of responsibility is prob.: *the daily pressure on me.* Alternatives include: *attention* or *care daily required of me* (ἐ.=*attention, care:* Aristot., Phys. 196a, 38; Polyb. 2, 2, 2; 11, 2, 4; Diod. S. 29, 32 end; EpArist 256; Just., D. 28, 1); *superintendence, oversight* (X., Mem. 1, 5, 2 codd.; s. also L-S-J-M s.v. II 3) *the burden of oversight, which lies upon me day in and day out;* finally, ἐ. can also mean *stopping, hindrance, delay* (BGU 1832, 16; 1855, 19; Polyb. 8, 28, 13); then: *the hindrances* *that beset me day by day.* Cp. the role of the ἐπιστάτης next entry.

❷ **the act of bringing someth. to a stop, *stopping*** (X., An. 2, 4, 26; Polyb. 8, 28, 13) ἐ. ποιεῖν ὄχλου *to cause a crowd to gather* **Ac 24:12.** The phrase indicates that people stop with the result that a crowd develops; any first-century reader or auditor of Ac would prob. be aware that if Paul were responsible for collecting a mob around himself he would be at grave risk under the eyes of Roman authorities who were responsible for maintaining the peace. Hence the rendering 'stirring up a crowd' NRSV correctly assesses the mng of the text (cp. 2 Macc 6:3 'onslaught' NRSV).—DELG s.v. ἵστημι. M-M.

ἐπιστάτης, ου, ὁ (s. prec. entry; Hom. et al., freq. as an administrative t.t.; used for var. officials in lit., ins, pap, LXX; Jos., Ant. 8, 59, C. Ap. 2, 177) in Lk six times in the voc. ἐπιστάτα as a title addressed to Jesus, nearly always by the disciples (the synopt. parallels have διδάσκαλε [cp. Ammonius, 100 AD, p. 45 Valck. and Philo, Poster. Cai. 54 ἐπ. κ. διδάσκαλοι], κύριε, ῥαββί) ***master*** (cp. IG XII/1, 43, 21f ἐπιστάταν τῶν παιδῶν; IPriene 112, 73ff [after 84 BC] ἐ. τῶν ἐφήβων *whose task* was τὰς ψυχὰς πρὸς ἀρετὴν προάγεσθαι; Rouffiac p. 56f.—Diod. S. 3, 72, 1 Aristaeus the tutor of Dionysus; 3, 73, 4 Olympus the tutor of Zeus; and 10, 3, 4 Pherecydes the teacher of Pythagoras are all called ἐπιστάτης) **Lk 5:5; 8:24, 45; 9:33, 49; 17:13.**—OGlombitza, ZNW 49, '58, 275–78.—DELG s.v. ἵστημι. M-M. TW.

ἐπιστέλλω (s. ἐπιστολή, στέλλω) 1 aor. ἐπέστειλα; pf. 2 sg. ἐπέστακλας 3 Km 5:22 cod. A **to send someth. to, *inform/instruct by letter*** also simply *write* (so Hdt. et al.; SIG 837, 14; pap, LXX) w. dat. of pers. (PFay 133, 12; Jos., Ant. 4, 13; 14, 52) διὰ βραχέων ἐπέστειλα ὑμῖν *I have written to you briefly* **Hb 13:22** (cp. Herm. Wr. 14, 1 σοι δι' ὀλίγων ἐ.). ἱκανῶς ἐ. τινὶ περί τινος *sufficiently to someone about someth.* 1 Cl 62:1 (cp. Ps.-Aeschin., Ep. 12, 14; Jos., Ant. 12, 50). περί τινος (cp. UPZ 110, 185 [164 BC]; Jos., Ant. 18, 300) *concerning someone* **Ac 21:25.** τινὶ περί τινος (BGU 1081, 5) 1 Cl 47:3. W. subst. inf. foll. τοῦ ἀπέχεσθαι *to abstain* **Ac 15:20.** Abs. 1 Cl 7:1.—M-M. TW.

ἐπιστῇ, ἐπίστηθι s. ἐφίστημι.

ἐπιστήμη, ης, ἡ (s. ἐπίσταμαι; Soph., Thu.+; Epict.; Vett. Val. 211, 18; Herm. Wr. 4, 6; 10, 9 ἐπιστήμη δῶρον τ. θεοῦ; PFay 106, 22; POxy 896, 5; LXX, En; PsSol 2:33; JosAs 4:9; AssMos fgm. e; Philo; Just., Tat., Ath.) **the possession or gaining of knowledge with focus on understanding aspects of the knowledge acquired, *understanding, knowledge*** (w. σοφία, σύνεσις, γνῶσις [Aeneas Tact. 580 μετὰ ξυνέσεως κ. ἐ.]; Just., D. 3, 5 ἐ. τίς ἐστιν ἡ παρέχουσα αὐτῶν τῶν ἀνθρωπίνων καὶ τῶν θείων γνῶσιν;) B 2:3; 21:5. As a Christian virtue Hv 3, 8, 5; 7 (cp. Cebes 20, 3.—For the relationship between πίστις and ἐπιστήμη s. Simplicius in Epict. p. 110, 35ff τὸ ἀκοῦσαι παρὰ θεοῦ ὅτι ἀθάνατός ἐστιν ἡ ψυχή, πίστιν μὲν ποιεῖ βεβαίαν, οὐ μέντοι ἐπιστήμην. εἰ δέ τις ἀξιοῦται παρὰ θεοῦ καὶ τὰς αἰτίας μανθάνειν . . . =when someone hears from God [through the mediation of a μάντις] that the soul is immortal, that creates, to be sure, a firm faith, but not knowledge. But when someone is considered worthy by God of learning the causes as well . . . [then ἐπιστήμη puts in its appearance]). ἔπαινος ἐπιστήμης **Phil 4:8 v.l.**—DELG s.v. ἐπίσταμαι. M-M. TW.

ἐπιστήμων, ον gen. ονος (s. ἐπίσταμαι; Hom. et al.; Epict. 2, 22, 3; POxy 1469, 12; LXX; En 5:8; Philo; Just., D. 8, 5; Ath. 9:1 ἐπιστημονεστάτους) **pert. to being knowledgeable in a way that makes one effectual in the exercise of such knowledge, *expert, learned, understanding*** (w. σοφός, as Dt 1:13; 4:6; Da 5:11; Philo, Migr. Abr. 58) **Js 3:13** the expert in σοφία will be verified by quality of performance; B 6:10; (w. συνετός, as Da 6:4) οἱ ἐνώπιον ἑαυτῶν ἐ. *those who are experts in their own estimation* 4:11 (Is 5:21).—DELG s.v. ἐπίσταμαι (lit.). M-M.

ἐπιστηρίζω fut. ἐπιστηριῶ Ps 31:8; 1 aor. ἐπεστήριξα, 2 sg. ἐπεστήρισας Ps 37:3. Pass.: fut. ἐπιστηριχθήσομαι Judg 16:26; aor. ἐπεστηρίχθην LXX, subj. 3 sg. ἐπεστηρισθῇ; pf. 3 sg. ἐπεστήρικται Jdth 8:24 v.l. (for -ισται); plpf. 3 sg. ἐπεστήρικτο LXX (s. στηρίζω; Aristot. et al.; LXX) **to cause someone to become stronger or more firm, *strengthen,*** in our lit. of believers in connection with their commitment and resolve to remain true, esp. in the face of troubles: τινά or τί the brothers **Ac 11:2** D; cp. **18:23.** Souls (=hearts as center of personal feeling and psychic response) **14:22;** congregations or churches **15:41.** Abs. vs. **32** (sc. ἀδελφούς).—TW.

ἐπιστολή, ῆς, ἡ (s. ἐπιστέλλω) ***letter, epistle*** (so Eur., Thu.+; loanw. in rabb.) **2 Cor 7:8; 2 Th 3:17;** 1 Cl 47:1; 63:2; IEph 12:2; ISm 11:3; Pol 13:2b. δι' ἐπιστολῆς (Diod. S. 19, 48, 1; Polyaenus 7, 39; 53rd letter of Apollonius of Tyana [Philostrat. I 358, 9]; Ps.-Demetr., Form. Ep. p. 5, 10; BGU 884, 6; 1046 II, 5) *by a letter* **2 Th 2:2** (Vi. Aesopi W 104 P. ἐ. ὡς ἐκ τοῦ Αἰσώπου; Polyaenus 8, 50 of two dead persons ὡς ἔτι ζώντων ἐπιστολή), vs. **15**, cp. **3:14.** γράφειν ἐπιστολήν (Diod. S. 17, 39, 2; Philo, Leg. ad Gai. 207) **Ac 15:23** D; **23:25** (on the specific type of administrative communication s. Taubenschlag, OpMin II 722, w. ref. to PTebt 45, 27); **Ro 16:22;** ἐν τῇ ἐ. **1 Cor 5:9** (ἐν τῇ ἐ.='in the letter known to you' [s. ὁ 2a] as ChronLind B 14 ἐν τᾷ ἐπιστολᾷ; Hyperid. 3, 25 ἐν τ. ἐπιστολαῖς; Pla., Ep. 7, 345c ἡ ἐ.=the letter [known to you]). ταύτην δευτέραν ὑμῖν γράφω ἐ. **2 Pt 3:1** (cp. BGU 827, 20 ἰδοὺ τρίτην ἐπιστολήν σοι γράφω. PMich 209, 5 δευτέραν ἐπιστολὴν ἔπεμψά σοι). ἀπὸ τῆς Ἰωάννου προτέρας ἐ. Papias (2:17); αἱ δύο ἐπιστολαὶ αἱ μικραί Papias (11:1); ἀναδιδόναι τὴν ἐπιστολήν τινι *deliver the letter to someone* **Ac 23:33.** Also ἐπιδιδόναι **15:30.** διαπέμπεσθαι *send* MPol 20:1. διακονεῖν *care for* **2 Cor 3:3.** ἀναγινώσκειν (X., An. 1, 6, 4; 1 Macc 10:7; Jos., C. Ap. 2, 37) **3:2; Col 4:16; 1 Th 5:27.** In all probability the plur. in our lit.—even **Ac 9:2;** Pol 3:2—always means more than one letter, not a single one (as Eur., Iph. A. 111; 314; Thu. 1, 132, 5; 4, 50, 2, also M. Iulius Brutus, Ep. 1, 1 [fr. Mithridates]; 1 Macc 10:3, 7; Jos., Ant. 10, 15; 16): δι' ἐπιστολῶν *with letters* **1 Cor 16:3.** τῷ λόγῳ δι' ἐπιστολῶν ἀπόντες (do someth.) *through word by means of letters, when we are absent* **2 Cor 10:11** (cp. UPZ 69, 3 [152 BC] ἀπόντος μου . . . διὰ τοῦ ἐπιστολίου); vs. **9;** ἐ. βαρεῖαι καὶ ἰσχυραί *the letters are weighty and powerful* vs. **10.** ἔγραψεν ὑμῖν ὡς καὶ ἐν πάσαις ἐ. **2 Pt 3:16.** ἐ. συστατικαί *letters of recommendation* **2 Cor 3:1** (s. on συστατικός). ἐπιστολὰς πέμπειν (Ps.-Demosth. 11, 17; Diod. S. 17, 23, 6 ἔπεμψεν ἐπιστολάς=letters; OGI 42, 6; 2 Macc 11:34) IPol 8:1; cp. Pol 13:2a. ἐπιστολὴ πρός τινα *a letter to someone* (2 Esdr 12:7; 2 Macc 11:27; Jos., C. Ap. 1, 111) **Ac 9:2; 22:5** (letters empowering someone to arrest people and deliver them to the authorities in the capital city, as PTebt 315, 29ff [II AD]); **2 Cor 3:1** (πρὸς ὑμᾶς ἢ ἐξ ὑμῶν).—Later epistolary subscriptions to the NT letters, as well as B, 1 Cl, 2 Cl.—GBahr, Paul and Letter Writing in the First Century, CBQ 28, '66, 465–77; JWhite, Light fr. Ancient Letters '86, 3–20, 221–24 lit. Lit. on χαίρω 2b. B. 1286; RAC II 564–85.—DELG s.v. στέλλω. M-M. EDNT. TW.

ἐπιστομίζω 'to put someth. on the mouth', fig. (s. στόμα; Aristoph., Eq. 845; Pla., Gorg. 482e al.; Plut., Mor. 156a; 810e), ***to silence*** τινά *someone* (Demosth. 7, 33; Libanius, Or. 2 p. 243, 20 F.) οὓς δεῖ ἐπιστομίζειν *who must be silenced* **Tit 1:11.** The mng. *bridle, hinder, prevent* (Lucian, Pro Im. 10, Calumn. 12; Philo, Det. Pot. Insid. 23; Jos., Ant. 17, 251) is also prob., esp. **ibid. v.l.,** an addendum in minuscule 460: τὰ τέκνα . . . ἐπιστόμιζε *silence the children.*—DELG s.v. στόμα. M-M. Spicq.

ἐπιστρέφω fut. ἐπιστρέψω; 1 aor. ἐπέστρεψα. Pass.: fut. ἐπιστραφήσομαι; 2 aor. pass. ἐπεστράφην (s. next entry and στρέφω; Hom.+) gener. 'to turn to'

❶ **to return to a point where one has been, *turn around, go back*—ⓐ** act. intr. (X., Hell. 4, 5, 16; Polyb. 1, 47, 8; Aelian, VH 1, 6; LXX; En 99:5f; ParJer 7:31) abs. **Lk 8:55** (cp. Judg 15:19); **Ac 15:36; 16:18; Rv 1:12b;** εἴς τι (SIG 709, 11 [c. 107 BC]; 2 Km 15:27; 1 Esdr 5:8; 1 Macc 5:68; 3 Macc 7:8 εἰς τὰ ἴδια ἐ.) **Mt 12:44** (exorcism of evil spirits so that they never return: Jos., Ant. 8, 45; 47 μηκέτ' εἰς αὐτὸν ἐπανήξειν); **Lk 2:39.** εἰς τὰ ὀπίσω **Mk 13:16; Lk 17:31;** also ἐ. ὀπίσω **Mt 24:18.** ἐπί τι (SIG 709, 20) **2 Pt 2:22.** ἐπί τινα **Lk 10:6** D. πρός τινα *to someone* **Lk 17:4.** W. inf. foll. to denote purpose (Jdth 8:11 v.l.; ApcMos 31 ἐπιστρέψῃ τοῦ ἐλεῆσαι ἡμᾶς) βλέπειν **Rv 1:12a** (s. φωνή 2e). Also simply *turn* πρὸς τὸ σῶμα **Ac 9:40** (for ἐ. πρός w. acc. cp. Aesop, Fab. 141 P.=248 H., Ch. 202, H.H. 146 I and III [ἐστράφη II]; 1 Macc 7:25; 11:73).

ⓑ aor. pass. in act. sense (Eur., Alc. 188; 1 Macc 4:24) εἰς τὰ ὀπίσω (Lucian, Catapl. 14) Hv 4, 3, 7. Of a greeting, which is to return unused **Mt 10:13.**

❷ **to change direction, *turn around,*** aor. pass. in act. sense (Hdt. 3, 156; X., Cyr. 6, 4, 10, Symp. 9, 1 al.; Jos., Ant. 7, 265; 16, 351) ἐπιστραφεὶς ἐν τῷ ὄχλῳ *he turned around in the crowd* **Mk 5:30.** ἐπιστραφεὶς καὶ ἰδών **8:33** (Jos., Bell. 2, 619 ἐπιστραφεὶς κ. θεασάμενος).—**J 21:20** (the only occurrence in J; s. M-EBoismard, Le chapitre 21 de StJean: RB 54, '47. 488). MPol 12:3. μὴ ἐπιστραφείς *without turning about=without troubling himself (about it)* 8:3.

❸ **to cause a pers. to change belief or course of conduct, with focus on the thing to which one turns, *turn*** act. trans., in a spiritual or moral sense (Plut., Mor. 21c ἐ. τινὰ πρὸς τὸ καλόν; Jos., Ant. 10, 53) τινὰ or τὶ ἐπί τινα *someone* or *someth. to someone* (2 Ch 19:4; Jdth 7:30; PsSol 8:27) πολλοὺς ἐπὶ κύριον **Lk 1:16.** καρδίας πατέρων ἐπὶ τέκνα vs. **17** (cp. Sir 48:10 and s. Hes., Op. 182). τινὰ ἔκ τινος *turn someone fr. someth.* (cp. Mal 2:6) **Js 5:20;** cp. vs. **19.** Of God τοὺς πλανωμένους ἐπίστρεψον *bring back those who have gone astray* 1 Cl 59:4; cp. Hm 8:10. Sim. of presbyters Pol 6:1; cp. 2 Cl 17:2. ὅταν τις ἡμᾶς . . . ἐπιστρέψῃ ἀπὸ τῆς ἀδικίας εἰς τὴν δικαιοσύνην 2 Cl 19:2. τὸν οἶκον. . . εἰς τὸν κύριον Hv 1, 3, 1. Cp. Ox 850, 7.

❹ **to change one's mind or course of action, for better or worse, *turn, return*—ⓐ** intr. act. (Ps 77:41; 2 Esdr 19:28; ApcSed 12:4f) *turn back, return* **Ac 15:16** D. *Repent* Hs 9, 26, 2. ἐπί τι *to someth.* 1 Cl 9:1; Pol 7:2; **Gal 4:9.** ἔκ τινος *from someth.* (cp. 3 Km 13:26) **2 Pt 2:21 v.l.** Esp. of a change in a sinner's relation with God *turn* (oft. LXX) ἐπί w. acc.: ἐπὶ κύριον τὸν θεόν Theoph. Ant. 3, 11 [p. 226, 25]) ἐπὶ τὸν κύριον **Ac 9:35; 11:21;** Hs 9, 26, 3. ἐπὶ τὸν θεόν **26:20;** cp. 1 Cl 18:13; 2 Cl 16:1. πρὸς (τὸν) κύριον (1 Km 7:3; Hos 5:4; 6:1; Am 4:6 al. LXX) **2 Cor 3:16;** Hm 6, 1, 5; Hm 12, 6, 2. πρὸς τὸν θεόν **1 Th 1:9** (non-Pauline terminology for conversion, acc. to GFriedrich, TZ 51, '65, 504). Here and occasionally elsewh. the thing from which one turns is added, w. ἀπό and the gen. (2 Ch 6:26; Bar 2:33 v.l. ἀπὸ πασῶν τῶν ἁμαρτιῶν Theoph. Ant. 3, 11 [p. 228, 10]) **Ac 14:15;** perh. **15:19.** ἐ. ἀπὸ σκότους εἰς φῶς καὶ τῆς ἐξουσίας τ. σατανᾶ ἐπὶ τ. θεόν **26:18.** Abs. **Mt 13:15; Mk 4:12; Ac 28:27** (all three Is 6:10); **Lk 22:32** (s. CPickar, CBQ 4, '42, 137–40); (w. μετανοεῖν) **Ac 3:19.**

ⓑ aor. pass. in act. sense, *turn to* ἐπὶ τὰ εἴδωλα *to images (of deities)* B 4:8; εἰς τὴν διχοστασίαν *toward disunity* Hs 8, 7, 5; in good sense *turn (about)* (Ps.-Demosth. 10, 9; Epict. 2, 20, 22 οἱ πολῖται ἡμῶν ἐπιστραφέντες τιμῶσι τὸ θεῖον; Dt 30:10; Jer 3:14; Ps 7:13 al.; ApcSed 14:6 πρὸς τὸν ἐμὸν βάπτισμα) ἐ. ἐπί τινα (Is 55:7) **1 Pt 2:25.** ἐπὶ τὸν δεσπότην 1 Cl 7:5. πρός τινα (Diog. L. 3, 25 all Greeks to Pla.; Synes., Provid. 1, 9, 97c πρὸς τὸν θεόν) πρὸς τ. κύριον (Hos 14:2f; Jo 2:13 al.) Hm 12, 6, 2. πρός με (Am 4:8; Jo 2:12 al.) 1 Cl 8:3 (scripture quot. of unknown orig.). Abs. *be converted* **J 12:40 v.l.;** Hm 12, 4, 6. ἐγγὺς κύριος τοῖς ἐπιστρεφομένοις *the Lord is near to them who turn (to him)* v 2, 3, 4.—ANock, Conversion '33; EDietrich, Die Umkehr (Bekehrung u. Busse im AT u. Judentum) '36.—M-M. TW. Sv.

ἐπιστροφή, ῆς, ἡ (s. prec. entry; trag., Thu.+; ins, pap, LXX, Joseph.; Just. D. 30, 1; var. senses) in our lit. only intr. 'turning (toward)'

❶ **turning one's attention to someth., *attention*** (Soph. et al.; ἡ πρὸς ἀνθρώπους ἐ. τοῦ θεοῦ Orig., C. Cels. 4, 5, 26) ἐ. ποιεῖσθαι *give attention, concern oneself* (Demosth. 12, 1; 19, 306; Appian, Bell. Civ. 4, 35 §148; Michel 543, 3; PPetr II, 19 [2], 2; Jos., Ant. 9, 237) w. περί τινος (Chrysipp.: Stoic. III 187; SIG 685, 128 [139 BC]) 1 Cl 1:1.

❷ **change of one's way of thinking or believing, *conversion*** (Sir 18:21; 49:2; PsSol 16:11; Jos., Ant. 2, 293; Just., D. 30, 1; Orig., C. Cels. 1, 43, 39; Porphyr., Ad Marcellam 24 μόνη σωτηρία ἡ πρὸς τ. θεὸν ἐπιστροφή; Hierocles 24 p. 473; Simplicius p. 107, 22 ἡ ἐπὶ τὸ θεῖον ἐπιστροφή) τῶν ἐθνῶν **Ac 15:3.** εἶναι εἰς ἐ. τινι *be a means of conversion for someone* B 11:8.—PAubin, Le problème de la 'conversion' '63. DELG s.v. στρέφω. M-M. TW.

ἐπισυνάγω fut. ἐπισυνάξω; 1 aor. inf. ἐπισυνάξαι **Lk 13:24** as well as 2 aor. inf. ἐπισυναγαγεῖν **Mt 23:37** (W-S. §13, 10; Mlt-H. 226). Pass.: 1 fut. ἐπισυναχθήσομαι; 1 aor. ἐπισυνήχθην; pf. 3 sg. ἐπισυνῆκται 1 Macc. 15:12, ptc. ἐπισυνηγμένος (s. next entry; Polyb.; Plut., Mor. 894a al.; ins, pap, LXX, En; TestSol D 3, 3f; Test12Patr; GrBar 15:2; ApcMos 29; EpArist, Joseph.) in our lit. always=συνάγω (cp. **Lk 17:37**=Mt 24:28) **to bring together, *gather (together)*** τινά *someone* (3 Km 18:20 [συναγ. v.l.]; Ps 105:47 al.; TestNapht 8:3) τὰ τέκνα **Mt 23:37a; Lk 13:34.** Of a hen that gathers her brood **Mt 23:37b.** τοὺς ἐκλεκτοὺς ἐκ τῶν τεσσάρων ἀνέμων *the chosen people from the four winds* **24:31; Mk 13:27.** Pass. *be gathered* (OGI 90, 23; SIG 700, 21 [117 BC]; 2 Ch 20:26; 1 Esdr 9:5 al.; En 22:3; Philo, Op. M. 38) of birds of prey around a dead body **Lk 17:37.** Of a crowd gathering (Jos., Ant. 18, 37) **12:1.** ὅλη ἡ πόλις **Mk 1:33.**—DELG s.v. ἄγω. M-M.

ἐπισυναγωγή, ῆς, ἡ (s. prec. entry; scarcely to be differentiated fr. συναγωγή: IG XII/3 suppl. no. 1270, 11f [II BC] and s. Dssm., LO 81; LAE 101ff]; 2 Macc 2:7).

❶ **a gathering together to or toward at some location, *meeting,*** of a Christian group ἐγκαταλείπειν τὴν ἐ. ἑαυτῶν *neglect their own meeting(s)* **Hb 10:25.**

❷ **the action of ἐπισυνάγεσθαι, *assembling*** ἐπί τινα *with someone* **2 Th 2:1.**—M-M. TW. Spicq.

ἐπισυντρέχω (hapax leg.; συντρέχω 'run together') ***run together*** of crowds **Mk 9:25.**

ἐπισυρράπτω for ἐπι(ρ)ράπτω (q.v.) **Mk 2:21** D.

ἐπισύστασις, εως, ἡ a gathering together against established authority, *uprising, disturbance, insurrection* (σύστασις 'bringing together'; Sext. Emp., Eth. 127; Berosus: 680 fgm. 9 [in Jos., C. Ap. 1, 149]; SIG 708, 27 [I BC]; PEnteux 86, 5 [221 BC]; Num 17:5; 26:9; 1 Esdr 5:70; Artapanus: 726 fgm. 2 [in Eus., PE 9, 23, 1] Jac.) **Ac 24:12 v.l.** (for ἐπίστασις). On **2 Cor 11:28 v.l.** s. ἐπίστασις.—DELG s.v. ἵστημι. M-M.

ἐπισφαλής, ές (Hippocr., Pla. et al.; Diod. S. 13, 77, 2; POxy 75, 20; Wsd 9, 14; Philo, Praem. 33; Jos., Ant. 5, 52; 139) **pert. to causing mishap, *unsafe, dangerous*** of a voyage in autumn **Ac 27:9.**—DELG s.v. σφάλλω. M-M.

ἐπισφραγίζω (s. σφραγίζω) 1 aor. ἐπεσφράγισα (Diod. S. 14, 55, 1 βιβλίον ἐπεσφραγισμένον; pap; 2 Esdr 20:1; TestSol 7:8 ἐπεσφράγισα; the mid. in Pla. et al.; Philo and Mel. P. 57, 415) **to put a seal on someth., *seal,*** τ. διωγμόν *the persecution,* thereby bringing it to an end, as a letter MPol 1:1.—DELG s.v. σφραγίς.

ἐπισχύω impf. ἐπίσχυον; aor. 3 pl. ἐπίσχυσαν 1 Macc 6:6 (s. ἰσχύς; X. et al.; BGU 1761, 3 [I BC]) from the trans. 'make strong' it is but a short step to the intr. ***grow strong*** in the sense of having additional resources or being persistent in doing someth. (Theophr. et al.; Vett. Val. 48, 6 τῶν δὲ τοιούτων καὶ ὁ λόγος ἐπισχύσει πρὸς συμβουλίαν ἢ διδαχήν; 1 Macc 6:6) *persist* ἐπίσχυον λέγοντες *they insisted and said* **Lk 23:5** (MBlack, An Aramaic Approach³, '67, 255 [Old Syriac]). ἀπέρχομαι εἰς κάμινον πυρὸς ... καὶ οὐκ ἐπισχύω, ἐὰν μὴ *I am entering a fiery furnace ... but cannot hold out, unless* AcPl Ha 6, 19–21.—DELG s.v. ἰσχύς. M-M.

ἐπισωρεύω (σωρεύω 'heap one thing upon another'; Epict. 1, 10, 5; Vett. Val. 332, 24; 344, 13 al.; Job 14:17 Sym.; SSol 2:4) 'to pile up in addition', then by fig. extension ***heap up*** διδασκάλους *accumulate a great many teachers* **2 Ti 4:3.** τινί *(in addition) to* (Athen. 3, 123e) ἐ. ταῖς ἁμαρτίαις ὑμῶν *heap sin upon sin* B 4:6.—DELG s.v. σωρός. M-M. TW.

ἐπιταγή, ῆς, ἡ (s. τάσσω and next entry; Polyb. et al.; Diod. S. 1, 70, 1 νόμων ἐπιταγή; ins; PFlor 119, 5; LXX, En; PsSol 18:12; EpArist)

❶ **authoritative directive, *command, order, injunction*** ἐπιταγὴν ἔχειν *have a command* **1 Cor 7:25.** κατ' ἐπιταγήν *in accordance w. the command=by command* (SIG 1153; 1171, 3; IG XII/1, 785; JHS 26, 1906, p. 28 no. 6 κατ' ἐ. τ. θεοῦ; PGM 12, 62; 1 Esdr 1:16; En 5:2) **Ro 16:26; 1 Ti 1:1; Tit 1:3;** Hv 3, 8, 2.—But κατ' ἐ. bears another sense κατ' ἐ. λέγειν *say as a command;* **1 Cor 7:6; 2 Cor 8:8.**

❷ **right or authority to command, *authority,*** μετὰ πάσης ἐ. *with all* or *full authority* **Tit 2:15.**—DELG s.v. τάσσω. New Docs 2, 86. M-M. TW.

ἐπιτάσσω 1 aor. ἐπέταξα. Pass.: 2 aor. ἐπετάγην LXX; pf. 3 sg. ἐπιτέτακται 1 Esdr 5:50; Ar. 4, 2; ptc. ἐπιτεταγμένος (s. prec. entry; trag., Hdt. et al.; ins, pap, LXX, pseudepigr., Joseph.; Ar. 4, 2; Tat. 16, 1) **to command with authority, *order, command*** τινί *someone* (Soph., Ant. 664; X., Cyr. 4, 2, 33; SIG 83, 33; PTebt 59, 9; Gen 49:33; Esth 1:1q, 8) B 19:7; D 4:10. τοῖς πνεύμασι (cp. PGM 12, 316a τῷ θεῷ) **Mk 1:27; Lk 4:36;** cp. **Mk 9:25;** the wind and waves (cp. 2 Macc 9:8) **Lk 8:25.** τί τινι (Hdt.; SIG 748, 25 [71 BC]; Jos., Ant. 1, 172): τινὶ τὸ ἀνῆκον *order someone* (to do) *his duty* **Phlm 8.** τινί w. inf. foll. (Hdt. et al.): the pres. (X., An. 2, 3, 6; 1 Macc 4:41) **Ac 23:2;** Hs 9, 4, 4; 9, 5, 1; w. aor. inf. (X., Cyr. 7, 3, 14; SIG 683, 37 [140 BC]; OGI 443, 2) **Mk 6:39; Lk 8:31.** ἐ. foll. by aor. inf. without dat. (earlier Gk,, also oft. LXX) ἐπέταξεν ἐνέγκαι τὴν κεφαλὴν αὐτοῦ *he gave orders to bring his head* **Mk 6:27.** Abs. (Thu. 1, 140, 2; POxy 294, 21 [22 AD] ὡς ἐπέταξεν ὁ ἡγεμών; Esth 8:8; 1 Macc 10:81; PGM 12, 316b) **Lk 14:22;** B 6:18.—Pass. ἐξελίσσειν τοὺς ἐπιτεταγμένους αὐτοῖς ὁρισμούς *roll on in their appointed courses* 1 Cl 20:3. τὰ ἐπιτασσόμενα (SIG 742, 2; POxy 275, 11) ὑπὸ τοῦ βασιλέως *the king's commands* 37:3 (cp. SIG 748, 18 τὰ ἐπιτασσόμενα ὑπ' αὐτῶν; Herm. Wr. 16, 10b ὑπὸ τ. θεῶν).—M-M. TW.

ἐπιτελέω fut. ἐπιτελέσω; 1 aor. ἐπετέλεσα. Pass.: 1 fut. ἐπιτελεσθήσομαι LXX; aor. ἐπετελέσθην (Hdt.+; freq. in civic decrees).

❶ **to finish someth. begun, *end, bring to an end, finish*** (1 Km 3:12; 1 Esdr 4:55; 6:27) τί *someth.* **Ro 15:28; Phil 1:6; 2 Cor 8:6, 11a.** Abs. vs. **11b.** So also **Gal 3:3,** either as mid.: *you have begun in the Spirit; will you now end in the flesh?* or, less prob., as pass. *will you be made complete in the flesh?* w. ref. to the Judaizers.

❷ **to bring about a result according to plan or objective, *complete, accomplish, perform, bring about*** (IMagnMai 17, 25) τί *someth.* πάντα (1 Esdr 8:16) 1 Cl 1:3; 2:8; 48:4. πᾶν ἔργον ἀγαθόν 33:1 (POslo 137, 9 [III AD] ἐ. τὰ καθήκοντα ἔργα). τὰ ἀνήκοντα τῇ βουλήσει 35:5 (PTebt 294, 11 τὰ τῇ προφητείᾳ προσήκοντα ἐπιτελεῖν). τά διατασσόμενα *carry out the commands* or *instructions* (PGM 4, 1539f τ. ἐντολάς) 37:2f; cp. 40:1f. τ. λειτουργίαν *perform a service* (Philo, Somn. 1, 214; s. below for this t.t., frequently used in recognition of civic-minded pers., and s. lit. s.v. λειτουργέω 2) 1 Cl 20:10; **Lk 13:32 v.l.** τὰς θεραπείας GJs 20:2 (not pap). τὰ κυνήγια *the animal-combat* AcPl Ha 3, 4. ἁγιωσύνην *bring about sanctification* **2 Cor 7:1** (cp. EpArist 133 κακίαν; 166 ἀκαθαρσίαν). τὴν σκηνήν *erect the tent,* i.e. carry out specifications for construction of a tent **Hb 8:5** (s. Ex. 26). Esp. of the performance of rituals and ceremonies (Hdt. et al.; SIG 1109, 111 ἐ. τὰς λιτουργίας; UPZ 43, 20 [162/161 BC]; 106, 21 [99 BC]; PTebt 292, 20f; Mitt-Wilck. I/2, 70, 9–11; EpArist 186; Philo, Ebr. 129; Jos., C. Ap. 2, 118) τ. λατρείας ἐ. *perform the rituals* (Philo, Somn. 1, 214) **Hb 9:6.** θυσίας *bring sacrifices* (Hdt. 2, 63; 4, 26; Diod. S. 17, 115, 6; Herodian 1, 5, 2; SIG index; IPriene 108, 27; JosAs 2:5; Philo, Somn. 1, 215; Jos., Ant. 4, 123; 9, 273; POxy 2782, 6–8 [II/III AD]) Dg 3:5. The pass. (IMagnMai 17, 25f) in this sense 1 Cl 40:3. τὴν ἡμέραν γενέθλιον ἐ. *celebrate the birthday* MPol 18:2 (Epici p. 39, 19f B.=p. 18, 3 K. γάμους ἐπετέλεσεν; Ammonius, Vi. Aristot. p. 11, 23 Westerm. ἑορτὴν ἐ.).—Mid. (=act., as Polyb. 1, 40, 16; 2, 58, 10; Diod. S. 3, 57, 4 πρᾶξιν ἐπιτελέσασθαι) γυναῖκες ἐπετελέσαντο ἀνδρεῖα *women have performed heroic deeds* 1 Cl 55:3.

❸ **to cause someth. to happen as fulfillment of an objective or purpose, *fulfill*** (PsSol 6:6 πᾶν αἴτημα; Lucian, Charon 6 τ. ὑπόσχεσιν) of a saying of scripture, pass. 1 Cl 3:1. Apparently in ref. to divine purpose *lay someth. upon someone, accomplish someth. in the case of someone* τινί τι (Pla., Leg. 10, 910d δίκην τινί) pass. τὰ αὐτὰ τῶν παθημάτων τῇ ἀδελφότητι ἐπιτελεῖσθαι *the same kinds of sufferings are laid upon the fellowship* or *are accomplished in the case of the fellowship* **1 Pt 5:9.**—DELG s.v. τέλος. M-M. TW.

ἐπιτήδειος, εία, ον adj. (Hom.: ἐπιτηδές 'appropriate for the situation', also s. next entry; Eur., Hdt. et al.; Ath., R. 52, 12 al.; gener. 'necessary, proper') **pert. to being made for an end or purpose, *fit for, necessary*** καιρῷ ἐπιτηδείῳ *at a suitable* *time* **Ac 24:25 v.l.** (καιρὸς ἐ. as Jos., Vi. 125; 176).—Subst. τὰ ἐ. *what is necessary* (Hdt. 2, 174, 1; Thu. 2, 23, 3; ins, pap, LXX; TestSol 3:1 D; Jos., Bell. 3, 183, Ant. 2, 326; 12, 376) w. τοῦ σώματος added *what is necessary for the body,* i.e. *for life* **Js 2:16.**—B. 644. DELG s.v. ἐπιτηδές. M-M. Sv.

ἐπιτήδευμα, ατος, τό (s. prec. entry; Thu. et al.; Diod. S. 3, 70, 7; Epict. 3, 23, 5 al.; Vett. Val. 73, 20; SIG 703, 15; 721, 12, 42; 766, 5; pap; LXX; Philo, Op. M. 80; Jos., Ant. 15, 368, C. Ap. 2, 123, 181 in var. senses; Ar. 8, 6; Just., D. 3, 3; Tat.) **that which one does with consistent purpose or habit,** ***pursuit, way of living*** (Hippocr., Epid. 1, 23; Menand., Kith., fgm. 4, 2 J. ἐ. τῷ βίῳ; Oenomaus in Eus., PE. 5, 34, 10 θεῖόν τι ἐ.= a sort of divine way of life) of Christian piety Dg 1 (s. EBlakeney, The Epistle to Diognetus '43, 33).—DELG s.v. ἐπιτηδές. TW.

ἐπιτηδεύω fut. 2 sg. ἐπιτηδεύσεις Jer 2:33; 1 aor. ἐπετήδευσα (s. prec. entry; Soph., Hdt. et al.; Diod. S. 1, 70, 2; Epict. 3, 1, 15; 3, 5, 8; BGU 1253, 11 [II BC]; LXX; En 9:6; Jos., Ant. 18, 66, C. Ap. 2, 189; Tat.; Ath., R. 48, 18 al.) **to make someth. an object of one's purpose,** ***take care*** w. ὡς foll. MPol 17:1.—DELG s.v. ἐπιτηδές.

ἐπιτηρέω (s. τηρέω; Hom. Hymns, Thu. et al.; ins [Sb 8304, 8]; pap; Jdth 13:3) **to look out for or watch for,** ***watch carefully, lie in wait*** B 10:4.

ἐπιτίθημι 3 pl. ἐπιτιθέασιν **Mt 23:4,** impv. ἐπιτίθει **1 Ti 5:22;** impf. 3 pl. ἐπετίθεσαν **Ac 8:17** (ἐπετίθουν v.l.); fut. ἐπιθήσω; 1 aor. ἐπέθηκα; 2 aor. ἐπέθην, impv. ἐπίθες, ptc. ἐπιθείς. Mid. fut. ἐπιθήσομαι; 2 aor. ἐπεθέμην (s. τίθημι; Hom.+).

❶ **to place someth. on or transfer to (a place or object)**

ⓐ *lay/put upon*—α. lit.: act., of placing of a physical thing τὶ (which somet. is to be supplied fr. the context; cp. Esth 5:2) ἐπί τι or τινα (X., Cyr. 7, 3, 14; SIG 1173, 9; cp. 1169, 4; PSI 442, 13 [III BC]; Gen 22:9; 42:26 al.; JosAs 29:5 αὐτὸν ἐπὶ τὸν ἵππον; ParJer 2:1 χοῦν ἐπὶ τὴν κεφαλήν) *someth. upon someth.* or *someone* **Mt 23:4; Lk 15:5; J 9:6 v.l.** (most mss. read ἐπέχρισεν), **15; Ac 15:10; 28:3;** B 7:8. χεῖρα (χεῖρας) ἐπί τινα or τι *lay hand(s) on someone* or *someth.* (SIG 1173, 4; Ex 29:10; Lev 1:4; 4:4 al.—KSudhoff, Handanlegg. des Heilgottes: Archiv f. Gesch. d. Med. 18, 1926, 235–50) **Mt 9:18; Mk 8:25** (v.l. ἔθηκεν); **16:18; Ac 8:17; 9:17** (cp. 1QapGen and s. SKotlek, ANRW II Principat 37/3, 2859). Also τινὶ τὰς χεῖρας (Jos., Ant. 9, 268; 16, 365) **Mt 19:13, 15; Mk 5:23; 6:5; 8:23; Lk 4:40; 13:13** (v.l. ἐπ' αὐτῇ); **Ac 6:6; 8:19; 9:12; 13:3; 19:6; 28:8** (s. χείρ end [Coppens]); of authorization as an elder **1 Ti 5:22** (Goodsp., Probs. 181f; cp. 1QapGen 20, 29); cp. τὴν χεῖρα **Mk 7:32;** AcPl Ha 3, 31; 4, 34. ἐπὶ τὴν κεφαλήν B 13:5 (Gen 48:18). S. on ἐπίθεσις.—In other combinations ἐ. τί τινι (X., Oec. 17, 9; Esth 2:17; 1 Esdr 4:30; TestJob 7:1; JosAs 10:5; Jos., Ant. 9, 149 ἐπέθεσαν αὐτῷ τ. στέφανον) αὐτῷ τὸν σταυρόν **Lk 23:26;** στέφανον … αὐτοῦ τῇ κεφαλῇ **J 19:2.** ἐπειθήσι (=ἐπιθήσει) σοι ἐλευθέριον στέφανον AcPl Ha 2, 31. τοὺς λίθους ἐπετίθουν ἀλλήλαις *they placed the stones on one another's shoulders* Hs 9, 3, 5.—τὶ ἐπί τινος (Hdt. 1, 121, 4 al.; 1 Km 6:18; Sus 34; ParJer 5:7; Just., D. 132, 2) **Mt 21:7; Lk 8:16 v.l.** ἐπέθηκαν ἐπὶ τ. κεφαλῆς αὐτοῦ *they placed* (the crown of thorns) *on his head* **Mt 27:29.** ἐπάνω τ. κεφαλῆς *put above (his) head* vs. **37.**—τῷ μνημείῳ λίθον *a stone at the grave* **Lk 23:53 v.l.** (λίθοι) ἐπιτιθέμενοι εἰς τ. οἰκοδομήν *stones put into the building* Hv 3, 5, 2.

β. fig.: act. (except **Ac 15:28,** below) ἐ. πληγάς τινι *inflict blows upon someone* (BGU 759, 13 [II AD] πληγὰς πλείστας ἐπέθηκάν μοι) **Ac 16:23;** cp. **Lk 10:30.** Differently ἐπιθήσει ὁ θεὸς ἐπ' αὐτὸν τ. πληγάς *God will bring upon him the plagues* **Rv 22:18b** (cp. δίκην τινί Hdt., Pla. et al., also UPZ 1, 13 [IV BC] ὁ θεὸς αὐτῷ τὴν δίκην ἐ. Dt 26:6; τειμωρίαν τινί IAndrosIsis, Kyme 20; 35); s. BOlsson, D. Epilog der Offb. Joh.: ZNW 31, '32, 84–86.—Pass. **Ac 15:28.**—ἐ. τινὶ ὄνομα *give a surname to someone* (cp. Hdt. 5, 68 al.; BGU 1139, 7 [I BC]; 2 Esdr 19:7) **Mk 3:16f** (on the giving of new names to disciples cp. Diog. L. 5, 38: Theophrastus' name was Τύρταμος; his teacher, Aristotle, μετωνόμασεν and gave him the name Theophrastus because of his god-like eloquence). B 12:8f ἐ. τὸ ἔλεος ἐπί τινα *bestow mercy upon someone* 15:2.

ⓑ *give* τινί τι *someth. to someone,* mid. (BGU 1208 1, 4 [27 BC]; PRyl 81, 9 τὴν ὅλου τ. πράγματος ἐξουσίαν τοῖς κατασπορεῦσι ἐπεθέμην) ἀναγομένοις τὰ πρὸς τὰς χρείας *when we sailed they gave us what we needed* **Ac 28:10;** unless the verb is to rendered here *put on board* the needed supplies (so NRSV, REB).

ⓒ *add* ἐπί τι, act. (Hom., et al.) ἐπ' αὐτά **Rv 22:18a.**

❷ **to set upon,** ***attack, lay a hand on,*** mid. (Jos., Ant. 1, 328) τινί (Hdt., Aristoph. et al.; Appian, Liby. 102 §482; PTebt 15, 11 [114 BC]; PFlor 332, 7; LXX; Philo, Leg. ad Gai. 371; Jos., Ant. 4, 96) foll. by subst. inf. of purpose in gen. (Gen 43:18) οὐδεὶς ἐπιθήσεταί σοι τοῦ κακῶσαί σε *in order to harm you* **Ac 18:10.**—M-M. TW.

ἐπιτιμάω impf. 3 sg. ἐπετίμα, 3 pl. ἐπετίμων; fut. 2 pl. ἐπιτιμήσετε Ruth 2:16; 1 aor. ἐπετίμησα; pass. ptc. ἐπιτιμηθείς 3 Macc 2:24; cp. Just., D. 116, 13 on Zech 3:2 (s. τιμάω; Hdt. [-έω] Thu., Pla.+).

❶ **to express strong disapproval of someone,** ***rebuke, reprove, censure*** also ***speak seriously, warn*** in order to prevent an action or bring one to an end. Abs. (Thu. 4, 28, 1; Demosth. 1, 16 et al.; SIG 344, 55 [?]; Sir 11:7; Jos., Ant. 5, 105) **Lk 4:41; 2 Ti 4:2.** τινί (X., Pla.; Epict. 3, 22, 10 al.; Lucian, Dial. Mort. 1, 8; PMagd 24, 5 [218 BC]; UPZ 64, 7; Gen 37:10 al.; Philo, De Jos. 74; Jos., C. Ap. 2, 239) **Mt 8:26; 17:18; 19:13; Mk 4:39** (cp. Ps 105:9); **8:32f; 10:13; Lk 4:39; 8:24; 9:21, 42, 55; 17:3; 18:15; 19:39; 23:40.**—Foll. by ἵνα or ἵνα μή to introduce that which the censure or warning is to bring about or prevent **Mt 12:16; 16:20 v.l.** (for διαστέλλω, q.v.); **20:31; Mk 3:12** (for the phrase πολλὰ ἐπετίμα cp. Ps.-Xenophon, Cyn. 12, 16); **8:30** (on Mk 3:12, 8:30 s. GBarton, JBL 41, 1922, 233–36); **10:48; Lk 18:39.** Foll. by λέγων and dir. discourse **Mt 16:22; Mk 1:25; 9:25** (for the terminology of exorcism in Mk s. HKee, NTS 14, '68, 232–46); **Lk 4:35.** In **Jd 9** ἐ. could =*rebuke* as a contrast to defame, avoided by the archangel (on the pass. cp. AssMos fgm. j [Denis p. 67]; s. JTromp, The Assumption of Moses '93, 272f). But the next mng. is also prob. here.

❷ ***punish*** (Diod. S. 3, 67, 2 πληγαῖς ἐπιτιμηθείς; 3 Macc 2:24; En 98:5; ParJer 6:17; Jos., Ant. 18, 107).—DELG s.v. τιμή. M-M. TW.

ἐπιτιμία, ας, ἡ (s. prec. entry; Demosth. et al.; Philo.—In Jos., C. Ap. 2, 199 ἐπιτίμιον) ***punishment*** (so OGI 669, 43 [I AD]; PLond I, 77, 53 p. 234 [VIII AD]; Wsd 3:10; Ath. 1, 4) **2 Cor 2:6.**—DELG s.v. τιμή. M-M. TW.

ἐπιτοαυτό s. ἐπί 1cβ.

ἐπιτρέπω 1 aor. ἐπέτρεψα. Pass.: fut. inf. ἐπιτραπήσεσθαι (Just., A I, 47, 5); 2 aor. pass. ἐπετράπην; pf. ἐπιτέτραμμαι (τρέπω 'turn/direct toward'; Hom.+).

❶ **to allow someone to do someth.,** *allow, permit* (so Pind. et al.) τινί *someone* w. inf. foll. (X., An. 1, 2, 19, Hell. 6, 3, 9; Epict. 1, 10, 10; 2, 7, 12; PMagd 2, 7 [221 BC]; 12, 11; PRyl 120, 16; Job 32:14; 4 Macc 4:18; ParJer 1:4; Jos., Ant. 8, 202; Just., Ath.) **Mt 8:21; 19:8; Mk 10:4; Lk 8:32a; 9:59, 61; Ac 21:39; 27:3; 1 Ti 2:12;** Dg 10:2; IEph 10:1; IRo 6:3; Hm 4, 1, 4; D 10:7; Ox 840, 12. Without inf. (Pind., O. 3, 36; SIG 260, 16; 360, 15; 34; Just., D. 141, 2; Tat. 20, 1; Ath. 1, 2; 2, 4): ἐπέτρεψεν αὐτοῖς *he gave them permission* **Mk 5:13; Lk 8:32b.** ᾧ ἂν αὐτὸς ἐπιτρέψῃ *whomever he permits = appoints* ISm 8:1. οὐκ ἐμαυτῷ ἐπιτρέψας *not on my own initiative* Pol 3:1. Abs. (Pind., O. 6, 21; X., Cyr. 5, 5, 9; SIG 490, 10; 591, 36) ἐπέτρεψεν ὁ Πιλᾶτος *P. gave his permission* **J 19:38;** cp. **Ac 21:40;** MPol 7:2. Of God (BGU 451, 10 [I/II AD] θεῶν ἐπιτρεπόντων; 248, 15 [cp. Dssm., NB 80=BS 252]; Jos., Ant. 20, 267 κἂν τὸ θεῖον ἐπιτρέπῃ) **1 Cor 16:7; Hb 6:3.**—Pass. (SIG 1073, 44; 52; POxy 474, 40) ἐπιτρέπεταί τινι *someone is permitted* w. inf. foll. (Jos., Ant. 5, 3) **Ac 26:1; 28:16; 1 Cor 14:34.** Abs. ἐκείνῳ ἐπιτέτραπται *it is entrusted to him = it is his duty* Hv 2, 4, 3.

❷ *order, instruct* (X., An. 6, 5, 11; Arrian, Ind. 23, 5 ἐ. τινί; Cass. Dio, fgm. 40, 5 Boiss. Cod.; PLond 1173, 3; Jos., Vi. 138) w. dat. of pers. and inf. 1 Cl 1:3.—B. 1340. Freq. as v.l. for ἐπιστρέφω.—M-M.

ἐπιτροπεύω (s. next entry and ἐπιτρέπω; Hdt.+; ins, pap, Philo; Jos., Bell. 7, 9, Ant. 10, 278; Ath. 25, 1) **to hold the office of an ἐπίτροπος,** *be a procurator* (Plut., Mor. 471a; IG XIV, 911) τινός *of a country* (Hdt. 3, 15) ἐπιτροπεύοντος Ποντίου Πιλάτου τῆς Ἰουδαίας *while P.P. was procurator of Judea* **Lk 3:1** D (for ἡγεμονεύοντος; the term in ms. D is inexact, for Pilate was a prefect; s. under ἐπίτροπος and cp. ἡγεμονεύω).—Mason s.v. ἐπίτροπος.—DELG s.v. τρέπω. M-M.

ἐπιτροπή, ῆς, ἡ (s. prec. entry; Thu. et al.; ins, pap, 2 Macc 13:14) **authorization to carry out an assignment,** ***permission, a commission, full power*** (Polyb. 3, 15, 7; Diod. S. 17, 47, 4; Dionys. Hal. 2, 45; POxy 743, 32 [2 BC] περὶ πάντων αὐτῷ τ. ἐπιτροπὴν δέδωκα; Philo, Poster. Cai. 181; Jos., Ant. 8, 162; Just., A I, 29, 2) μετ᾽ ἐπιτροπῆς (w. ἐξουσία) **Ac 26:12.**—M-M. Sv.

ἐπίτροπος, ου, ὁ (s. prec. entry; Pind., Hdt. et al.; ins, pap, LXX; ParJer 4:5; Philo, Joseph., Just.; loanw. in rabb.) a term applied to various officials and functionaries

❶ ***manager, foreman, steward*** (Hdt. et al.; Philo, Omn. Prob. Lib. 35; Jos., Ant. 7, 369) **Mt 20:8.** So also **Lk 8:3** (Jos., Ant. 18, 194) of Chuza, a highly placed official in Herod's retinue, perh. head of his estate. The term is also used of governors and procurators (Hdt. et al.; Jos., Ant. 15, 406 al.; cp. OGI index VIII; Magie 162f; Hahn 118; 224, 2; Rouffiac 46; Preisigke, Fachw. p. 93) but Chuza has lesser political status.

❷ ***guardian*** (Hdt. 9, 10; Thu. 2, 80, 6; Diod. S. 11, 79, 6; SIG 364, 53; 1014, 122 al.; POxy 265, 28; PRyl 109, 18; 2 Macc 11:1; 13:2; 14:2; Philo, Somn. 1, 107) **Gal 4:2.**—OEger, ZNW 18, 1918, 105–8; SBelkin, JBL 54, '35, 52–55; for the use of ἐ. in the sense of 'tutor' s. FX 7, '81, 254f and Betz, Gal. 203.—Schürer I 357–60. Mason 49. DELG s.v. τρέπω. M-M. TW.

Ἐπίτροπος, ου, ὁ (rare; SIG 957, 34) ***Epitropus,*** whose wife is addressed IPol 8:2; s. Hdb. ad loc.

ἐπιτυγχάνω fut. 3 sg. ἐπιτεύξεται Pr 12:27; 2 aor. ἐπέτυχον (s. τυγχάνω; Pre-Socr., Hdt.+; ins, pap, LXX, pseudepigr.; Jos., Ant. 5, 288; Philo; Just.; Ath., R. 57, 16 al.) **to be successful in achieving or gaining what one seeks,** ***obtain, attain to, reach*** w. gen. of what is reached (Aristoph., Plut. 245; Thu. 3, 3, 3; BGU 113, 3; 522, 8; Jos., Ant. 18, 279) of a thing (GrBar 4:13 ὀργῆς θεοῦ; ApcEsdr 6:22 στεφάνου; Appian, Iber. 48 §200 εἰρήνης) Hm 10, 2, 4; 2 Cl 5:6. τῆς ἐπαγγελίας **Hb 6:15;** cp. **11:33.** τοῦ κλήρου ITr 12:3. χάριτος IRo 1:2a.—θεοῦ *attain to God,* specif. Ignatian expr., meant to designate martyrdom as a direct way to God: IEph 12:2; IMg 14; ITr 12:2; 13:3; IRo 1:2; 2:1; 4:1; 9:2; ISm 11:1; IPol 2:3; 7:1. Also ἐ. Ἰησοῦ Χριστοῦ IRo 5:3. Without obj. IPhld 5:1.—W. acc. *obtain* (X., Hell. 4, 5, 19; 4, 8, 21; 6, 3, 16; UPZ 41, 26 [161/160 BC] πᾶν ἐπιτυγχάνειν; TestSol 9:3 προδότην) **Ro 11:7.** οὐδέν τ. αἰτημάτων *none of the things requested* Hm 9:5.—W. inf. foll. (Lucian, Necyom. 6; Jos., Bell. 1, 302; Just.) IRo 1:1. Abs. (Pla., Men., 97c; SIG 736, 79 [92 BC]) **Ac 13:29** D; **Js 4:2;** IEph 1:2; IRo 8:3.—M-M. Sv.

ἐπιφαίνω 1 aor. ἐπέφανα, inf. ἐπιφᾶναι, impv. ἐπίφανον; fut. mid. ἐπιφανοῦμαι Jer 36:14. Pass.: fut. 3 sg. ἐπιφανήσεται Zeph 2:11 (s. next entry and φαίνω; Theognis, Hdt. et al.; ins, pap, LXX, Philo, Joseph.).

❶ **to cause someth. to be seen,** ***show*** act. trans. ἐπίφανον τὸ πρόσωπόν σου 1 Cl 60:3 (Ps 79:4, 8, 20; Da 9:17 Theod.).

❷ **to provide illumination,** ***give light to,*** act., ext. of mng. 1: **Lk 1:79.** There is a slight diff. between this apparently intr. use and the next, which is clearly trans. (On the theme of divine consideration in providing light in darkness s. X. Mem. 4, 3, 4.)

❸ **to make one's presence known,** ***become apparent,*** act., ext. of mng. 1 (Theocr. 2, 11 of stars; Polyb. 5, 6, 6 of daylight; Dt 33:2; Ps 117:27) of sun and stars **Ac 27:20.** Cp. 2 above.

❹ ***show oneself, make an appearance,*** pass. (Hdt., Thu. et. al.; LXX) of God (cp. Chariton 1, 14, 1 Ἀφροδίτην ἐπιφαίνεσθαι; schol. on Apollon. Rhod. 2, introd. ἐπεφάνη αὐτοῖς ὁ Ἀπόλλων; SIG 557, 6 ἐπιφαινομένης αὐτοῖς Ἀρτέμιδος; 1168, 26; Sb 6152, 5 [96 BC] Isis; 6153, 6; Gen 35:7; 2 Macc 3:30; 3 Macc 6:9; Philo; Jos., Ant. 5, 277; 8, 240; 268) τοῖς δεομένοις 1 Cl 59:4. Of God's grace **Tit 2:11;** of God's love **3:4.**—M-M. TW. Spicq.

ἐπιφάνεια, ας, ἡ (s. prec. entry; Pre-Socr.; Polyb. et al.; ins, pap (s. under 2), LXX, ApcEsdr 3:3 p. 27, 7 Tdf.; EpArist, Philo, Joseph., Just.) gener. 'appearing, appearance', esp. also the splendid appearance, e.g., of the wealthy city of Babylon (Diod. S. 2, 11, 3). As a t.t. relating to transcendence it refers to a visible and freq. sudden manifestation of a hidden divinity, either in the form of a personal appearance, or by some deed of power or oracular communication by which its presence is made known (OGI 233, 35f [III/II BC] Artemis; Dionys. Hal. 2, 68; Diod. S. 1, 25, 3 and 4; 2, 47, 7 [the appearance of Apollo]; in 5, 49, 5 τῶν θεῶν ἐπιφάνεια to help humans; Plut., Them. 127 [30, 3]; Ael. Aristid. 48, 45 K.=24 p. 477 D.; Polyaenus 2, 31, 4 Διοσκούρων ἐ.; oft. ins, and in LXX esp. 2 and 3 Macc.; Aristobul. in Eus., PE 8, 10, 3 [p. 136, 25 Holladay]; EpArist 264; Jos., Ant. 1, 255; 2, 339; 3, 310; 9, 60; 18, 75; 286. For material and lit. s. FPfister, Epiphanie: Pauly-W. Suppl. IV 1924, 277–323; MDibelius, Hdb. exc. on 2 Ti 1:10; OCasel, D. Epiphanie im Lichte d. Religionsgesch.: Benedikt. Monatsschr. 4, 1922, 13ff; RHerzog, Die Wunderheilungen v. Epidauros '31, 49; BEaston, Pastoral Epistles '47, 171f; CWestermann, Das Loben Gottes in den Psalmen '54, 70; ESchnutenhaus, Das Kommen u. Erscheinen Gottes im AT: ZAW 76, '64, 1–21; EPax, Ἐπιφάνεια '55; DLührmann, KKuhn Festschr., '71; RAC V, 832–909). In our lit., except for Papias, only of Christ's appearing on earth.

❶ **act of appearing,** ***appearance*** in our lit. that of Jesus, of his—ⓐ first appearance on earth **2 Ti 1:10** (Just., A I, 14, 3 al.; Diod. S. 3, 62, 10 the mythographers speak of two appearances of Dionysus: δευτέραν ἐπιφάνειαν τοῦ θεοῦ παρ' ἀνθρώποις).—ALaw, Manifest in Flesh '96.

ⓑ appearance in judgment **1 Ti 6:14; 2 Ti 4:1, 8.** ἐ. τ. δόξης **Tit 2:13** (for this combination cp. OGI 763, 19f; Epict. 3, 22, 29). ἐ. τῆς παρουσίας **2 Th 2:8** *the appearance of his coming;* the combination is not overly redundant, for ἐ. refers to the salvation that goes into effect when the π. takes place. ἡμέρα τῆς ἐ. *the day of the appearing* 2 Cl 12:1; 17:4.

❷ **that which can ordinarily be seen,** ***surface appearance*** (Democr., Aristot. et al.) τοσοῦτον βάθος εἶχον ἀπὸ τῆς ἔξωθεν ἐπιφανείας *the eyes* (of Judas) *lay so deep behind* (the swollen) *facial skin* Papias (3:2). For the use of ἐ. in description of symptoms s. EGoodspeed, A Medical Papyrus Fragment: AJP 24, 1903, 328 ln. 5; cp. Gal. 16, 530.—DELG s.v. φαίνω. New Docs 4, 80f. M-M. TW. Spicq.

Ἐπιφάν(ε)ιος, ου (freq. since IV AD; OGI 688, 1; pap) ***Epiphanius,*** Christian in Corinth AcPl Ha 6, 1.

ἐπιφανής, ές (s. ἐπιφ- entries; Pind., Hdt.+; ins, pap, LXX, Philo; Jos., Ant. 4, 200 al.; Just. A I, 68, 3 [superl.]) **pert. to being resplendent,** ***splendid, glorious, remarkable,*** prob. suggesting light whose impact is esp. striking in its sudden appearance, of the day of God's judgment (Mélanges GGlotz '32, 290, 28: ins [II BC] ἡμέραι ἐ.) ἡμέρα κυρίου μεγάλη καὶ ἐ. **Ac 2:20** (Jo 3:4).—New Docs 4, 148. M-M. TW. Spicq.

ἐπιφαύσκω fut. ἐπιφαύσω (Hesychius=ἀνατέλλω, φαίνω.—mid. Job 41:10) **to shine out on,** ***arise, appear, shine*** (of heavenly bodies Job 25:5; 31:26; of the day Cass. Dio 9, 12, 8 and Act. Thom. 34 [Aa II /2 p. 151, 12]) τινί *for* or *upon someone* (Orph. Hymn. 50, 9 Q. of Bacchus θνητοῖς ἢ ἀθανάτοις ἐπιφαύσκων) of Christ ἐπιφαύσει σοι **Eph 5:14** (v.l. ἐπιψαύσεις τοῦ Χριστοῦ, to be rejected, w. Chrysost.) The origin of the quot. has not been established w. certainty.—Rtzst., Erlösungsmyst. 6; 136; KKuhn, NTS 7, '61, 334–46 (Qumran). S. also on ἐπιφώσκω.—Frisk s.v. φάος; cp. DELG s.v. φάε. TW.

ἐπιφέρω fut. ἐποίσω LXX; 2 aor. ἐπήνεγκον, inf. ἐπενεγκεῖν; mid. 3 sg. ἐπηνέγκατο (Mel., P. 51, 371); pf. inf. ἐπενηνοχέναι (Just., D. 60, 5); aor. pass. ptc. sg. gen. ἐπενεχθέντος 2 Macc 12:35 (s. φέρω; Hom.+).

❶ **to bestow someth. on someone,** ***bring, give, grant*** w. acc. of thing and dat. of pers. μετανοίας χάριν ἐπήνεγκεν 1 Cl 7:4 v.l.

❷ **bring someth. over and put it on someone,** ***take to*** τὶ ἐπί τινα of articles that were put in contact with St. Paul's body **Ac 19:12 v.l.**

❸ **to cause someone or someth. to undergo someth. adverse,** ***bring (on/about), inflict,*** τί τινι (EpArist 206 αἰσχύνην ἀνθρώποις; TestJob 7:13 ὑποστῆναι ἅπερ ἐπιφέρεις μοι; Philo, Leg. ad Gai. 133) ἁμαρτίαν 1 Cl 47:4 v.l.; Hv 1, 2, 4; m 11:4. βλασφημίας τῷ ὀνόματι *denigrations on the name* 1 Cl 47:7.—Of things that serve as punishment (EpArist 253 θάνατον; Jos., Ant. 2, 296 πληγὴν τ. Αἰγυπτίοις; cp. also PTebt 331, 10; Just. 39, 2) τὴν ὀργήν *wrathful punishment* **Ro 3:5.**

❹ **to add someth. on top of someth.,** ***add*** (Aristot., Rhet. 3, 6; Philo, Leg. ad Gai. 125) trouble **Phil 1:17 v.l.**

❺ **to bring charges or make accusations,** ***bring, pronounce*** (since Hdt. 1, 26, also Polyb. 5, 41, 3; 38, 18, 2; PRainer 232, 11 ψευδεῖς αἰτίας τινὶ ἐ.; Jos., Ant. 2, 130; 4, 248; 11, 117; Just., D. 9, 1) αἰτίαν **Ac 25:18 v.l.** κρίσιν βλασφημίας *pronounce a reviling judgment* **Jd 9.**—M-M.

ἐπιφράσσω 1 aor. ἐπέφραξα (s. φράσσω; Theoph. et al.) ***to close:*** because of the stench caused by the putrefying Judas, one could not come near the place where he died *without holding one's nose shut with one's hands* Papias (3:3) (cp. Theophr., De Sens. 85).

ἐπιφωνέω impf. ἐπεφώνουν; aor. ἐπεφώνησα LXX (s. φωνέω; Soph. et al.; ins, pap, LXX, TestJob 43:3; EpArist, Philo) ***cry out (loudly)*** τινί *against someone* (cp. Plut., Alex. 665 [3, 6]) **Ac 22:24.** ἄλλο τι *someth. different* **21:34** (s. ἄλλος 1c end). W. direct discourse foll. (OGI 595, 35; PRyl 77, 33; 1 Esdr 9:47) **Lk 23:21; Ac 12:22.**—DELG s.v. φωνή. M-M.

ἐπιφώσκω (Poeta De Herb. 25; pap; mid. Job 41:10 v.l.) **to grow towards or become daylight,** ***shine forth, dawn, break,*** perh. ***draw on*** (PLond I, 130, 39 p. 134 [I/II AD]; PGrenf II, 112, 15 τῇ ἐπιφωσκούσῃ κυριακῇ; Ps.-Clem., Hom. 3, 1 p. 36, 23 Lag.) σάββατον ἐπέφωσκεν *the Sabbath dawned* or *drew on* **Lk 23:54;** cp. GPt 2:5. ἐπιφώσκοντος τοῦ σαββάτου 9:34; cp. vs. 35. τῇ ἐπιφωσκούσῃ εἰς μίαν σαββάτων *as the first day of the week dawned* or *drew near* **Mt 28:1.** See GMoore, JAOS 26, 1905, 323–29; CTurner, JTS 14, 1913, 188–90; FBurkitt, ibid. 538–46; PGardner-Smith, ibid. 27, 1926, 179–81; MBlack, An Aramaic Approach^3, '67, 136–38. S. also on ἐπιφαύσκω.—M-M.

ἐπιχειρέω impf. ἐπεχείρουν; fut. 2 sg. ἐπιχειρήσεις TestJob 4:4; 1 aor. ἐπεχείρησα (Hom.; Hippocr. VM 1 et al.; ins, pap, LXX) **set one's hand to,** ***endeavor, try*** w. inf. foll. (Hdt., Aristoph. et al.; LXX; TestJob 4:4; Philo; Jos., Ant. 4, 310; 8, 3; Just.; Tat. 21, 2) ἀνελεῖν αὐτόν **Ac 9:29.** ὀνομάζειν ἐπί τινα τὸ ὄνομα **19:13.** W. acc. *attempt someth.* (unless νοῆσαι is to be understood w. it) Hs 9, 2, 6. Of literary composition (Hippocr., Περὶ ἀρχαίης ἰητρικῆς prol.: ὁπόσοι μὲν ἐπεχείρησαν περὶ ἰητρικῆς λέγειν ἢ γράφειν; Galen, Foet. Format. Prooem.; Thessalus of Trall.: Cat. Cod. Astr. VIII/3 p. 134 πολλῶν ἐπιχειρησάντων … παραδοῦναι; Polyb. 2, 37, 4; 3, 1, 4; 12, 28, 3; Diod. S. 4, 1, 2; Jos., Vita 40; 338, C. Ap. 2, 222) ἀνατάξασθαι διήγησιν **Lk 1:1.**—HCadbury, Comm. on the Preface of Luke: Beginn. I/2, 1922, 489–510; LAlexander, The preface to Luke's Gospel '93, 109f.—DELG s.v. χείρ. M-M.

ἐπιχείρησις, εως, ἡ (s. χείρ; Hdt. et al.; Jos., Ant. 15, 103; 16, 188) **the act of putting one's hand to (with implication of forceful gesture),** ***attempt, attack*** ἐπί τινα **Ac 12:3** D.

ἐπιχέω fut. 2 and 3 sg. ἐπιχεεῖς, -χεεῖ LXX; aor. 3 sg. ἐπέχεεν LXX. Pass.: 1 fut. 3 pl. ἐπιχυθήσονται Job 36:27; aor. ἐπεχύθην LXX; pf. ptc. ἐπικεχυμένος LXX (s. χέω; Hom. et al.; pap, LXX; JosAs 4:11 [codd. AB for περιεχύθη]; Jos., Ant. 2, 343 al.)

❶ **to cause to pour on or flow on,** ***pour over, pour on, apply*** τὶ *someth.* oil and wine (Hippocr., Mul. 2, 133 vol. VIII 296, 15 L.; Hippiatr. I 9, 4) **Lk 10:34.**

❷ **to cause to flow into someth.,** ***pour in*** (Pla., Rep. 407D; PGM 13, 12; EpArist 293) *pour in* τὶ εἴς τι *someth. into a vessel* Hm 5, 1, 5 here in the sense of *add* to someth. already contained in a vessel.—M-M.

ἐπιχορηγέω 1 aor. ἐπεχορήγησα; 1 fut. pass. ἐπιχορηγηθήσομαι. For the interpretation of passages using this verb and cognates it is well to explore the possibility of connection with the Gr-Rom. cultural background of generous public service that finds expression in the χορηγ- family.

❶ **to convey as a gift, *give, grant*** (Dionys. Hal. 1, 42; Diog. L. 5, 67; Phalaris, Ep. 50; Alex. Aphr., Probl. 1, 81. In marriage contracts ἐ. τὰ δέοντα: BGU 183, 6; POxy 905, 10; CPR I, 27, 12; cp. Strabo 11, 14, 16) τί τινι *someth. to someone* Hs 2:5, 7. σπέρμα τῷ σπείραντι *give seed to the sower* **2 Cor 9:10.** ὑμῖν τὸ πνεῦμα *he who gives you the Spirit* **Gal 3:5.** αὐτῷ τ. ἐγκράτειαν 1 Cl 38:2, end.—Pass. ἐπιχορηγηθήσεται ὑμῖν ἡ εἴσοδος *you will be granted an entrance* **2 Pt 1:11.** Without an acc. to denote what is given (En 7:3), ἐ. comes to mean

❷ **to provide (at one's own expense), *supply, furnish*** (SEG XXXIX, 605, 2 [205/204 BC?]; Dionys. Hal. 10, 54) fig. extension of mng. 1 ἐ. τὴν ἀρετήν **2 Pt 1:5** (within a variation of the rhetorical form κλῖμαξ).

❸ **to provide what is necessary for the well-being of another, *support*** (Sir 25:22; En 7:3; Ar. 15, 7; s. ἐπιχορηγία) ὁ πλούσιος ἐπιχορηγείτω τῷ πτωχῷ *let the rich person support the indigent one* 1 Cl 38:2 (Ar. 15, 7). Pass. ὁ πένης ἐπιχορηγούμενος ὑπὸ τοῦ πλουσίου *the poor person, who is supported by the rich* Hs 2:6. πᾶν τὸ σῶμα διὰ τῶν ἁφῶν καὶ συνδέσμων ἐπιχορηγούμενον καὶ συμβιβαζόμενον *the whole body supported and held together by sinews and ligaments* **Col 2:19** (for the pass. of the simplex the mng. *be supported, receive help* is well attested [Ps.-X., Respubl. Athen. (the 'Old Oligarch') 1, 13; Polyb. 3, 75, 3; 4, 77, 2; 9, 44, 1; Sir 44:6; 3 Macc 6:40], and in Hs 2:5 the simplex and the compound appear to be used w. the same value, but the compound may here mean *help afterwards,* for a wealthy individual is here obligated to a poor one).—Danker, Benefactor 331f.—DELG s.v. χορός. M-M. S. also next entry.

ἐπιχορηγία, ας, ἡ *assistance, support* (s. prec. entry; SIG 818, 9 [79 AD] of 'provision' out of temple proceeds 'for' repair of a fortification; Theoph. Ant. 2, 14 [p. 136, 2]; s. ἐπιχορηγέω 3) τοῦ πνεύματος **Phil 1:19;** ἁφὴ τῆς ἐ. *a ligament that serves for support* (cp. Col 2:19) **Eph 4:16.**—M-M.

ἐπιχρίω 1 aor ἐπέχρισα (s. χρίω; Hom. et al.; Sym. Ezk 13:10; 22:28; TestSol 18:20) **to apply a viscous substance, *anoint, spread/smear (on)*** (Soranus p. 75, 7; Galen: CMG V 9, 1 p. 136, 30; Diosc. 3, 25; PLeid X VII, 36; cp. Od. 21, 179 of a bow being prepared for service by rubbing with fat; Lucian, Hist. Conscrib. 62 of an inscription covered w. gypsum; Galen: CMG V 4, 2 p. 246, 20) τὶ ἐπί τι *spread on* or *smear on someth.* πηλὸν ἐπὶ τοὺς ὀφθαλμούς *spread the moistened mud on the man's eyes=(Jesus) anointed the man's eyes with the moistened mud* **J 9:6** (v.l. ἐπέθηκεν, s. ἐπιτίθημι 1aα; cp. SIG 1173, 17=Dssm., LO 108 [LAE 135] in a report of a healing κολλύριον ἐπιχρεῖσαι ἐπὶ τ. ὀφθαλμούς). Without ref. to what was put on, in Eng. the customary rendering is *anoint* ἐ. τοὺς ὀφθαλμούς *anoint the eyes* **J 9:11** (referring to the procedure vs. 6).—Of the stone that closed the entrance to the tomb of Jesus ἐπέχρισαν ἑπτὰ σφραγῖδας *they applied seven seals* i.e. wax that receives an impression fr. a seal GPt 8:33.—M-M.

ἐπιχωρέω 1 aor. 3 sg. ἐπεχώρησεν 2 Macc 12:12 (Soph., Thu., et al.; also Polyb., ins, pap, Joseph.; in var. senses) ***move over (towards)*** ὁ λίθος ἐπεχώρεσε (=ἐπεχώρησεν) παρὰ μέρος *the stone moved over to the side* GPt 9:37 (for emendations s. ἀποχωρέω and ὑποχωρέω).

ἐπιψαύω fut. ἐπιψαύσω (Hom. et al.; Diod. S. 3, 28, 3; 17, 20, 6; Hero Alex. I p. 6, 11ff; Heraclit. Sto. 44 p. 66, 12) **to make contact with, *touch, grasp, attain to*** τινός *someone* (Arrian, Cyneg. 9, 2 ἀλλήλων) **Eph 5:14** D, s. ἐπιφαύσκω.

ἔπλησα s. πίμπλημι.

ἐποικοδομέω 1 aor. ἐποικοδόμησα (on the lack of augment s. Mlt-H. 191); 1 aor. pass. ἐποικοδομήθην (s. οἰκοδομέω Thu. et al.; ins, pap, Philo, Joseph.) Used in imagery in our lit.

❶ **to build someth. on someth. already built, *build on to*** (X.; Pla., Leg. 5 p. 736e; ins; PGiss 67, 12; Jos., Ant. 12, 253).

ⓐ of stones to become part of a tower ἔμελλε πάλιν ἐποικοδομεῖσθαι *the building was to be continued* Hs 9, 5, 1; cp. v 3, 8, 9.

ⓑ of building on someth. or someone. In ref. to the beginnings of a congregation (w. θεμέλιον τιθέναι; cp. Jos., Ant. 11, 79.—Philo, Somn. 2, 8: θεμελίων τρόπον . . . ἄλλα . . . σοφῆς ἀρχιτέκτονος . . . ἐποικοδομῶμεν) **1 Cor 3:10;** cp. vs. **14.** ἐ. ἐπί τι *build upon someth.* (OGI 483, 117 ἐπὶ τοὺς τοίχους ἐ.) vs. **12.** ἐποικοδομηθέντες ἐπὶ τῷ θεμελίῳ τῶν ἀποστόλων *built on the foundation of the apostles* **Eph 2:20** (ἐπί w. dat. as X., An. 3, 4, 11); cp. **1 Pt 2:5 v.l.** in 2. This mng leads naturally to

❷ **to engage in a building process of personal and corporate development, *edify, build up/on,*** w. imagery less strong than in 1b (Epict. 2, 15, 8) **Ac 20:32 v.l.** ἐποικοδομούμενοι ἐν αὐτῷ *built upon him* (i.e. Christ; the prep. is explained by the preceding ἐρριζωμένοι) **Col 2:7.** ὡς λίθοι ζῶντες ἐποικοδομεῖσθε οἶκος πνευματικός *let yourselves be built on (him) into a spiritual house* **1 Pt 2:5 v.l.** (the compound connects God's people with Christ 'the living stone' vs. 4). Sim. **Jd 20** ἐ. (ἀνοικ. P[72]) ἑαυτοὺς τῇ πίστει *build each other up on the basis of the faith* (ἐ. w. dat. as Epict. loc. cit.; Philo, Gig. 30, Conf. Lingu. 5).—DELG s.v. οἶκος. M-M. TW.

ἐποκέλλω 1 aor. ἐπώκειλα (Hdt. 6, 16; 7, 182; Thu. 4, 26, 6; Arrian, Anab. 5, 20, 9 a ship) ***run aground*** τὴν ναῦν **Ac 27:41 v.l.** (for ἐπέκειλαν; s. ἐπικέλλω [κέλλω= 'put to shore']).

ἐπονομάζω aor. ἐπωνόμασα LXX; pf. 1 pl. ἐπωνομάκαμεν (Ath. 16, 3 [Pla., Rep. 269d]); aor. pass. ἐπωνομάσθην (Just.) (s. ὀνομάζω; trag., Hdt. et al.; LXX; Jos., Ant. 17, 14) ***call, name*** pass. σὺ Ἰουδαῖος ἐπονομάζῃ *you call yourself a Judean (Jew)* **Ro 2:17** (ἐπι- without special mng. as Maximus Tyr. 39, 4a; 5c; Appian, Basil. 1 §1; Dionys. Byz. §35; Himerius, Or. 48 [=Or. 14], 13; TestJud 1:3).—DELG s.v. ὄνομα. M-M. TW.

ἐποπτεύω 1 aor. ἐπώπτευσα (s. next entry and ὁράω; Hom.+; Sym. Ps 9:35; 32:13; Jos., C. Ap. 2, 294; Ath. 13, 2) **to pay close attention to, *watch, observe, see*** τὶ *someth.* (Polyb. 5, 69, 6; 31, 15, 10; Heraclit. Sto. 53 p. 75, 19) τὴν ἀναστροφήν *conduct* **1 Pt 3:2.** Abs. ptc. (ἐκ τ. καλῶν ἔργων is to be taken w. δοξάσωσιν: BWeiss, Kühl, HermvSoden, Knopf; differently Wohlenberg, Vrede) ἐποπτεύοντες *when they observe* them (sc. τ. ἔργα) **2:12** (s. ἐκ 3gβ) s. HMeecham, ET 65, '53, 93f.—DELG s.v. ὄπωπα. M-M. TW.

ἐπόπτης, ου, ὁ (s. prec. entry; Pind., Aeschyl. et al.; ins, pap [occasionally ἐφόπτης, e.g. SIG 1053, 3—I BC], LXX, EpArist; Jos., C. Ap. 2, 187; Just., A II, 12, 6 θεὸν τῶν πάντων ἐ.)

❶ **one who sees to or attends to, with implication of careful scrutiny, *a watchful observer,*** of God (Pind., N. 9, 5 al.; Cornutus 9 p. 9, 20; OGI 666, 25 [Nero] τ. Ἥλιον ἐ. καὶ σωτῆρα; Sb 1323 of the sun-god θεῷ ὑψίστῳ κ. πάντων ἐπόπτῃ; PGM 12, 237; Esth 5:1a; 2 Macc 3:39; 7:35; 3 Macc 2:21; EpArist 16. Also of emperors, e.g. IPerg 381; s. CBurk, De Chionis Epistulis, diss. Giessen 1912, 11) τὸν ἐ. ἀνθρωπίνων ἔργων *the one who oversees* or *watches over the deeds of humans,* the implication being that nothing escapes God's notice 1 Cl 59:3 (Diod. S. 16, 49, 5 τοὺς θεοὺς ἐπόπτας τῶν ὅρκων).

❷ **to have first-hand acquaintance with someth., with implication of special privilege,** ***eyewitness*** (esp. as t.t. of the mysteries, to designate those who have been initiated into the highest grade of the mysteries; s. SIG 42, 50 [c. 460 BC]; 1052, 4 Ῥοδίων ἱεροποιοὶ μύσται κ. ἐπόπται εὐσεβεῖς; 1053, 3; Michel 1141, 1 [II BC]; Plut., Alc. 202 [22, 4]; Himerius, Or. [Ecl.] 10, 4; PGM 7, 572) **2 Pt 1:16.**—SCole, Theoi Megaloi, '84, 46–48. New Docs 2, 87. DELG s.v. ὄπωπα. M-M. TW.

ἔπος, ους, τό (Hom. et al.; ins, pap; Sir 44:5) ***word*** ὡς ἔ. εἰπεῖν (Pla. et al., also Philo and Jos., Ant. 15, 387) to qualify speech that might sound too assertive *so to speak, one might almost say;* or perh. to effect a climax *to use just the right word* (for both senses see the many exx. in FBleek comm. Hb ad loc.; s. also POxy 67, 14) **Hb 7:9.**—B. 1261f. DELG. M-M. Sv.

ἐπουράνιος, ον (s. οὐρανός; Hom. et al.; Kaibel 261, 10; LXX; pseudepigr.; Philo, Leg. All. 3, 168; Tat., Ath.; Mel.. P. 39, 272) gener. 'heavenly'

❶ **pert. to being in the sky or heavens as an astronomical phenomenon,** ***celestial, heavenly*** σώματα ἐ. (opp. ἐπίγεια) *celestial bodies* **1 Cor 15:40** (acc. to vs. 41 the sun, moon, and stars are thought of, and are represented fig., as living beings clothed in light; s. Wendland, Kultur 158).

❷ **pert. to being associated with a locale for transcendent things and beings,** ***heavenly, in heaven*****—ⓐ** as adj.**—α.** of God (Od. 17, 484; Il. 6, 131; Sb 4166 Ζεὺς ἐπουράνιος [s. also IK IX–X/2: Nikaia II/1, 1114 and 1115]; Herm. Wr. 434, 9 Sc.; 3 Macc 6:28; 7:6; TestAbr, A 2 p. 78, 23 [Stone p. 4]; GrBar 11:9; SibOr 4, 51; 135; Theosophien 56, 39 p. 182 Erbse [=p. 148, 48 Holladay]) πατὴρ ἐ. **Mt 18:35 v.l.;** δεσπότης ἐ. 1 Cl 61:2.

β. of Christ ἐ. (ἄνθρωπος) **1 Cor 15:48f;** ἐ. ἀρχιερεὺς Ἰ. Χ. MPol 14:3.

γ. οἱ ἐ. (ἄνθρωποι) **1 Cor 15:48.** Ἰερουσαλὴμ ἐ. **Hb 12:22** (TestSol C prol. 2 Σιών; for the idea s. πόλις 2); βασιλεία ἐ. **2 Ti 4:18;** Epil Mosq 5 (Ath. 18, 1); MPol 20:2 v.l.; (πατρὶς) ἐ. **Hb 11:16.**—ζωὴ ἐ. 2 Cl 20:5 (cp. Ath. 31, 3 βίον). κλῆσις ἐ. **Hb 3:1.** δωρεὰ ἐ. **6:4.**

ⓑ as subst., of things or entities**—α.** neut. pl. τὰ ἐπουράνια (of things in heaven: Pla., Ap. 19b; Sext. Emp., Astrol. 44; ApcSed 7:2).

א. as periphrasis for *heaven* καθίσας ἐν τοῖς ἐ. *sitting in heaven* **Eph 1:20;** cp. **2:6.** ἐξουσίαι ἐν τοῖς ἐ. *the powers in heaven* of angelic beings **3:10.** Since there is more than one heaven (cp. 2 Cor 12:2), τὰ ἐ. can be the dwelling place of evil spirits **6:12.** Even **1:3** ὁ εὐλογήσας ἐν τοῖς ἐ. is, acc. to the usage of Eph, to be understood locally *in heaven* (s. RPope, ET 23, 1912, 365–68).—ALincoln, NTS 19, '73, 467–83.

ב. *the heavenly things* (Philo, Gig. 62; TestJob 36:3; 38:5) **J 3:12** (ἐπίγειος 2a).—**Hb 8:5; 9:23;** *heavenly goods* αἰτεῖν τὰ ἐ. Agr 10; τὰ ἐ. γράψαι *write about heavenly things* ITr 5:1. νοεῖν τὰ ἐ. *understand the heavenly things* 5:2. τὰ πάντα divided into ἐ. and ἐπίγεια Pol 2:1; *heavenly entities* ISm 6:1 (cp. TestAbr A 4 p. 81, 15 [Stone p. 10] τὰ ἐ. πνεύματα).

β. masc. pl. οἱ ἐπουράνιοι (as a designation of the gods Theocr. 25, 5; Moschus 2, 21; Lucian, Dial. Deor. 4, 3; TestSol 6:10 [hostile spirits]) *heavenly beings* **Phil 2:10** (s. on ἐπίγειος 1bβ); ITr 9:1.—IEph 13:2.—DELG s.v. οὐρανός. New Docs 4, 149. EDNT. M-M. TW.

ἐπράθην s. πιπράσκω.

ἐπρήσθησαν, ἐπρίσθησαν s. πρίζω.

ἑπτά indecl. (Hom.+; loanw. in rabb.) ***seven*** in dating an event MPol 21. As a sacred number (WRoscher, D. Sieben- u. Neunzahl in Kultus u. Mythus der Griechen 1904; JGraf, D. Zahl 'Sieben' 1917; JHehn, Z. Bed. der Siebenzahl: Marti Festschr. [=Beih. ZAW 41] 1925, 128–36; RGordis, JBL 62, '43, 17–26.—Jos., Bell. 7, 149 παρὰ τ. Ἰουδαίοις ἑβδομάδος ἡ τιμή), perhaps at times determining the choice of a number (Pla., Theaet. 174e τὶς ἑπτὰ πάππους πλουσίους ἔχων; Diod. S. 4, 27, 2 ἑπτὰ θυγατέρας; 4, 61, 3f): seven spirits **Mt 12:45; Mk 16:9; Lk 8:2; 11:26;** loaves of bread **Mt 15:34, 36f; 16:10; Mk 8:5f, 20;** baskets **Mt 15:37; Mk 8:8;** brothers **Mt 22:25f, 28; Mk 12:20, 22f; Lk 20:29, 31, 33;** sons **Ac 19:14;** nations **13:19** (Dt 7:1); years **Lk 2:36;** days **20:6; 21:4, 27; 28:14; Hb 11:30.** Seven church officials (PGaechter, Petrus u. seine Zeit '58, 106–35) **Ac 6:3;** cp. **21:8,** where οἱ ἑπτά 'the seven', corresp. to οἱ δώδεκα, designates a definite fixed group (οἱ ἑπτά=the seven wise men: Diog. L. 1, 40; 82;=the seven against Thebes: Aeschyl.; Diod. S. 4, 64, 1; 4, 66, 1). Esp. in Rv: seven churches **1:4, 11, 20;** lampstands vss. **12, 13 v.l., 20; 2:1;** stars **1:16, 20; 2:1; 3:1;** torches **4:5;** horns, eyes **5:6;** seals **5:1; 6:1** (cp. GPt 8:33); angels **8:2, 6; 15:1, 6–8; 17:1; 21:9** (cp. En 20:8); trumpets **8:2, 6;** thunders **10:3f;** heads **12:3; 13:1; 17:3, 7, 9;** crowns **12:3;** bowls **15:7; 16:1; 17:1; 21:9;** heads of state **17:9;** cp. v. **11;** plagues **15:1, 6, 8; 21:9; 22:18 v.l.;** mountains **17:9** (En 18:6; 24:2). Seven virtues Hv 3, 8, 2 al. χιλιάδες ἑ. *seven thousand.* **Rv 11:13.** On ἑβδομηκοντάκις ἑπτά **Mt 18:22** s. ἑβδομηκοντάκις.—BHHW III 1785. On ἕβδομας s. the entry; cp. ζ'.—DELG. M-M. EDNT. TW.

ἑπτάκις adv. (Pind., Aristoph. et al.; SIG 1068, 8 [Patmos III–II BC] ἑπτάκι; IG V/I, 213, 16 [V BC] ἑπτάκιν; PGM 4, 1272; 1, 143 [ἑπτάκις ἑπτά]; LXX; EpArist 177; Philo, Op. M. 91; Jos., Ant. 3, 242) ***seven times*** (as a relatively large number, cp. Diod. S. 4, 16, 2: the brave Amazon was victorious seven times) **Lk 17:4b;** 1 Cl 5:6; ἕως ἑ. *as many as seven times* **Mt 18:21f;** ἑ. τῆς ἡμέρας *seven times a day* **Lk 17:4a** (cp. Lucian, Jupp. Trag. 49 πεντάκις τῆς ἡμ.; Jos., Ant. 3, 199 δὶς τῆς ἡμ.; Horapollo 1, 8 p. 9 τριακοντάκις τῆς ἡ.).—New Docs 4, 149. M-M. TW.

ἑπτακισχίλιοι, αι, α (s. prec. entry and χίλιοι; Hdt. et al.; GDI IV, 1210, ⁿ3 II, 25 [I BC, Sicily]; LXX) ***seven thousand*** **Ro 11:4** (Just., D. 39, 1 al.; after 3 Km 19:18 ἑπτὰ χιλιάδας).—TW.

ἑπταπλασίων, ον, gen. **ονος** (s. next entry; Oribasius, Ecl. 89, 22: CMG VI 2, 2 p. 269, 9; 2 Km 12:6; Ps 78:12; TestAbr B 8 p. 112, 24 [Stone p. 72]; ApcZeph; Jos., Ant. 1, 77; AcPh 20 [Aa II/2, 11, 1f]) ***sevenfold*** ἑπταπλασίονα (ἀπο)λαμβάνειν *receive sevenfold in return* **Lk 18:30** D (cp. Sir 35:10; s. GKilpatrick in: Neotestamentica et Semitica '69, 203).—Cp. διπλάσιος: DELG.

ἑπταπλασίως adv. (s. prec. entry; LXX; the adj. Pla., Ep. 7, 332a; Eutocius [Archimed., Op. Omn. ed. JHeiberg III 1915] p. 244, 24) ***sevenfold*** Hs 6, 4, 2.

Ἔραστος, ου, ὁ ***Erastus*** (the name is found in lit. and ins; s. SIG 838, 6).**—❶** a Christian at Corinth, designated as οἰκονόμος τῆς πόλεως *city treasurer* **Ro 16:23.** A Lat. ins fr. Corinth, published in the lit. quoted below, mentions an official named Erastus.

❷ a companion of Paul **Ac 19:22; 2 Ti 4:20.**—FdeWaele, Erastus: Mededeelingen van het Nederlandsch Hist. Inst. te Rome

9, 1929, 40–48; HCadbury, E. of Cor.: JBL 50, '31, 42–58; WMiller, Who was E.?: BiblSacra 88, '31, 342–46; Hemer, Acts 235, 260 n. 32; Boffo, Iscrizioni no. 43; BHHW I 422.—LGPN I. M-M.

ἐραυνάω (s. next entry; later form, in ins since the time of Pompey [IG XII/5, 653, 21] and in pap since 22 AD [POxy 294, 9f] for the earlier ἐρευνάω) (Hom.+; s. B-D-F §30, 4; W-S. §5, 21 a; Mlt-H. 86; Thumb 176 f; ENachmanson, Eranos 11, 1911, 239; JWackernagel, TLZ 33, 1908, 37; for the LXX s. Thackeray 79; Helbing 7) **to make a careful or thorough effort to learn someth.,** ***search, examine, investigate*** τὶ *someth.* τὰς γραφάς **J 5:39** (HBell, ZNW 37, '39, 10–13). καρδίας **Ro 8:27.** νεφροὺς καὶ καρδίας *minds* (lit. *kidneys*) *and hearts* **Rv 2:23;** τὴν φύσιν αὐτῆς GJs 19:3; 20:1. Of the Spirit πάντα *fathoms everything* **1 Cor 2:10** (Horapollo 1, 34 πάντα ἐξερευνᾷ ὁ ἥλιος). πνεῦμα κυρίου λύχνος ἐραυνῶν τ. ταμιεῖα τῆς γαστρός *a lamp that illuminates the storehouses of the inward parts (=the inner life)* 1 Cl 21:2 (Pr 20:27). περί τινος *examine someth.* B 4:1; Hm 10, 1, 4; 6. With indir. quest. foll. **1 Pt 1:11.** Abs. ἐραύνησον κ. ἴδε (4 Km 10:23) **J 7:52.** ἠραύνησεν GJs 1:3.—DELG s.v. ἐρέω. M-M. TW.

ἐραυνητής, οῦ, ὁ (s. prec. entry; this spelling PFay 104 [III AD]; in the form ἐρευνητής Clearch. fgm. 19f [in Athen. 6, 256a]; Jos., Ant. 17, 110 al., also UPZ 149, 15 [c. 200 BC]) **one who makes careful or thorough inquiry,** ***searcher, examiner,*** of God ἐ. ἐννοιῶν κ. ἐνθυμήσεων 1 Cl 21:9.

ἐράω impv. ἐράτω (Pind., Hdt. et al.; PSI 406, 36 [III BC]; Philo, Just., Tat., Ath.; the noun ἔρως Just., D. 8, 1 of affection for prophets and 'friends of Christ'). From ἔραμαι (Hom. et al.; e.g. 1 aor. mid. ἠρασάμην Il. 14, 316b; Ath. 21, 4) 1 aor. pass. ἠράσθην. Freq. of sexual attraction, as Hdt. 9, 108; X., Cyr. 5, 1, 10; then, as in our lit., **to feel passionately about,** ***have a longing for, feel fervently about*** τινός *someth.* (Aeschyl., Eum. 852 γῆς; Herm. Wr. 6, 4b; Pr 4:6; Philo, Spec. Leg. 2, 258 ἀληθείας) τῆς σαρκός IRo 2:1. *Desire, yearn* (Il. 9, 64) ἐ. τοῦ ἀποθανεῖν 7:2. W. inf. foll. (Pind. et al.) ἀπὸ τοῦ κοινοῦ ἐλευθεροῦσθαι *have a desire to be freed* (fr. slavery) *at the expense of the church* IPol 4:3 (in view of the subtle wordplay suggested by the purpose clause, the writer evidently projects the sensual connotation that the word has in some contexts outside our lit.; s. above).—BWarfield, The Terminology of Love in the NT, PTR 16, 1918, 1–45; 153–203.—DELG s.v. ἔραμαι. TW. Sv.

ἐργάζομαι impf. ἠργαζόμην (εἰργ- edd., **Ac 18:3**); fut. 2 sg. ἐργᾷ; 3 sg.; ἐργᾶται and 3 pl. ἐργῶνται (all LXX); 1 aor. εἰργασάμην (**2J 8;** other edd. ἠρ.); pf. 3 sg. εἴργασται LXX; ptc. εἰργασμένος (for augment s. Mayser 332; Meisterhans[3]-Schw. 171; B-D-F §67, 3; Moulton, ClR 15, 1901, p. 35f; Mlt-H. 189f); pass. fut. 3 sg. ἐργασθήσεται Ezk 36:34; En 10:18 (s. ἔργον and next entry; Hom.+).

❶ **to engage in activity that involves effort,** ***work,*** intr. *work, be active* (Hes., Hdt. et al.) D 12:3. ταῖς χερσίν *work w. one's hands* **1 Cor 4:12** (ἐ. ἰδίαις χερσίν as Biogr. p. 253; on depreciation of manual labor cp. Jos., Ant. 17, 333); **1 Th 4:11** (s. ἴδιος 3a). Also διὰ τῶν χειρῶν B 19:10. νυκτὸς καὶ ἡμέρας *work night and day* **1 Th 2:9; 2 Th 3:8.** ἐν τῷ ἀμπελῶνι in the vineyard **Mt 21:28.** Abs. **Lk 13:14; J 9:4b; Ac 18:3; 1 Cor 9:6; 2 Th 3:10, 12.** τῷ ἐργαζομένῳ *to the worker* **Ro 4:4;** cp. vs. **5** (ἐργαζόμενοι καλοί, OdeSol 11:20) and **Lk 6:5** D (Unknown Sayings 49–54). Of God and Christ: *work, be busy* **J 5:17** (cp. Maximus Tyr. 15, 6ef: Heracles must work without ceasing, since Zeus his father does the same).—Of financial enterprise: a sum of money (five talents) ἐ. ἐν αὐτοῖς *do business/trade with them* (Demosth. 36, 44 ἐ. ἐν ἐμπορίῳ καὶ χρήμασιν) **Mt 25:16.**—MBalme, Attitudes to Work and Leisure in Ancient Greece: Greece and Rome 2d ser. 31, '84, 140–52.

❷ **to do or accomplish someth. through work,** trans.

ⓐ ***do, accomplish, carry out*** w. acc. (Ael. Aristid. 42, 13 K.=6 p. 69 D.: ταῦτα ἐργαζομένου σου τοῦ κυρίου [Asclepius]) ἔργον (X., An. 6, 3, 17 κάλλιστον ἔργον ἐ.; Pla., Polit. 1, 346d; Appian, Celt. 18 §2, Bell. Civ. 2, 58 §238 al.; Arrian, Anab. 7, 17, 3; PPetr II, 9 [2], 4 [III BC]; Sir 51:30; TestSol D 4:8 τὸ ἐ. ὑμῶν; Just. D. 88, 8 τεκτονικὰ ἔργα) **Ac 13:41** (Hab 1:5); 1 Cl 33:8. τὰ ἔργα τοῦ θεοῦ *do the work of God* (cp. Num 8:11) **J 6:28; 9:4.** τὸ ἔργον κυρίου *the Lord's work* **1 Cor 16:10.** ἐ. τι εἴς τινα *do someth. to someone* (Ps.-Demosth. 53, 18): ἔργον καλὸν εἴς τινα *do a fine thing to someone* **Mt 26:10;** cp. B 21:2; **3J 5.** Also ἔν τινι **Mk 14:6.** In a different sense ἔργα ἐν θεῷ εἰργασμένα *deeds performed in God* **J 3:21.** ἐ. τὸ ἀγαθόν *do what is good* (cp. Dio Chrys. 16 [33], 15; GrBar 11:9; and Jos., Ant. 6, 208 ἀγαθά) **Ro 2:10; Eph 4:28;** Hm 2:4. Opp. ἐ. πονηρόν (Lucian, Catapl. 24) m 10, 2, 3. ἐ. ἀγαθὸν πρὸς πάντας *do good to all people* **Gal 6:10.** κακὸν ἐ. (Dio Chrys. 13 [7], 33; Palaeph. 1 and 3; Just., D. 95, 1 κακά; Ath. 11, 2 ἀεί τι ἐ. . . . κακόν): κακὸν τῷ πλησίον ἐ. *do wrong to one's neighbor* **Ro 13:10** (cp. Pr 3:30; EpArist 273). Gener. *someth.* **Col 3:23; 2J 8;** μηδὲν ἐ. *do no work* **2 Th 3:11.** οὐδὲν τῇ δικαιοσύνῃ *do nothing for righteousness* Hs 5, 1, 4 (Ps.-Aristot., Mirabilia 142 οὐδὲν ἐργ.=accomplish nothing).—Also used with attributes, etc. (in Isocr. w. ἀρετήν, σωφροσύνην; Philo, Gig. 26 τελειότητα) δικαιοσύνην (Ps 14:2) *do what is right* **Ac 10:35; Hb 11:33;** Hv 2, 2, 7; m 5, 1, 1; s 9, 13, 7. ἐ. δικαιοσύνην θεοῦ *do what is right in God's sight* **Js 1:20** (but s. c below; v.l. κατεργάζεσθαι, q.v.). τὴν ἀνομίαν (Ps 5:6; 6:9 al.) **Mt 7:23.** ἁμαρτίαν *commit sin* **Js 2:9** (Jos., Ant. 6, 124 τὸ ἁμάρτημα). Of the effect: τί ἐργάζῃ; *what work are you doing?* **J 6:30** (cp. Philo, Leg. All. 3, 83; Tat. 25, 1 τί μέγα . . . ἐ. φιλόσοφοι;).

ⓑ *practice, perform, officiate at* (τέχνην, etc., X., Pla. et al.) τὰ ἱερά *the temple rites* **1 Cor 9:13** (cp. Num 8:11).

ⓒ *bring about, give rise to* as proceeds from work (s. next entry 4; Soph., Ant. 326; Epict., fgm. Stob. 14 πενία λύπην ἐργάζεται; Just., A I, 45, 6 ὅπερ . . . κόλασιν διὰ πυρὸς αἰωνίαν ἐργάζεται). μετάνοιαν **2 Cor 7:10.** ἐ. δικαιοσύνην θεοῦ *bring about the righteousness that will stand before God* (but s. a above) **Js 1:20.** θάνατον ἑαυτοῖς ἐ. *bring death on themselves* Hs 8, 8, 5 (Just., D. 124, 4).

ⓓ *work (on)* (τὴν γῆν Gen 2:5; En 10:18; ApcMos 24) τὴν θάλασσαν *work on the sea for a livelihood* (Aristot., Probl. 38, 2, 966b, 26; Dionys. Hal. 3, 46; Appian, Liby. 2 §5; 84 §397; Lucian, Electr. 5) **Rv 18:17** (s. CLindhagen, ΕΡΓΑΖΕΣΘΑΙ, '50: Uppsala Univ. Årsskrift '50, 5, 5–26).

ⓔ *work for/earn food* (Hes., Op. 43 βίον ἐ.; Hdt. 1, 24 χρήματα; cp. Pla., Hipp. Mai. 282d, Laches 183a; X., Mem. 2, 8, 2; Theod. Pr 21:6. Also βρῶμα: Palaeph. p. 28, 10) ἐ. τὴν βρῶσιν **J 6:27:** in this context βρῶσις appears to be the free gift of the Human One (Son of Man).—As in the similar case of the Samaritan woman (cp. J 6:35 w. 4:14) hearers are simply prepared for the statement that they are to accept what is freely given. But ἐργάζεσθαι can also mean, when used w. food, *prepare for use, digest, assimilate* sc. τὴν τροφήν (Aristot., De Vita et Morte 4; Maximus Tyr. 15, 5a [ἐργ. τὴν τροφήν of the activity of the jaws]; more often ἐργασία τ. τροφῆς). The compound κατεργάζεσθαι is more common in this sense, but it is avoided in this passage for the sake of wordplay w. ἐργάζεσθαι in vs. 28.—DELG s.v. ἔργον. M-M. EDNT. TW.

ἐργασία, ας, ἡ (s. prec. entry; Pind.+; ins, pap, LXX, En 8:1; TestSol, Joseph., Just.).

❶ **engagement in some activity or behavior with sustained interest, *practice, pursuit*** τινός *of someth.* (Pla., Gorg., 450c τ. τεχνῶν; Ps.-Pla., Eryx., 404b; Sir 6:19; 38:34) εἰς ἐ. ἀκαθαρσίας πάσης *for the practice of all kinds of sinful things* **Eph 4:19.** πολλαπλασιάζειν τὴν ἐ. *do many kinds of work* GHb 297, 21 (s. also 4 below).

❷ **manner of activity, *working, function*** (Pla., Prot., 353d τῆς ἡδονῆς) τῶν ἀγγέλων Hm 6, 2, 6 cj. Gebhardt-Harnack-Zahn on basis of Lat. and Ethiopic mss. (Whittaker: ἐνέργεια).

❸ **business activity, *trade, business*** (X., Oec. 6, 8; Diod. S. 1, 80, 1; PLond III, 906, 6 p. 108 [128 AD]; PFay 93, 7; Sir 7:15) **Ac 19:25** (Arrian, Peripl. 21, 1 ξόανον τῆς παλαιᾶς ἐργασίας).

❹ **proceeds of work or activity *profit, gain*** (X., Mem. 3, 10, 1; Polyb. 4, 50, 3; Artem. 4, 57 ἔχειν . . . ἐργασίαν=have profits or wages; PGM 4, 2438; Wsd 13:19; Jos., Bell. 2, 109) **Ac 16:19.** παρέχειν ἐργασίαν τινί *bring profit to someone* vs. **16; 19:24** (cp. the litotes Aesop, Fab. 112 H.=56 P. of a μάγος οὐ μικρὸν βίον πορίζουσα). πολλαπλ. τ. ἐ. *multiply the gains* GHb 297, 21 (s. 1 above).

❺ For δὸς ἐργασίαν **Lk 12:58** s. δίδωμι 17a (ἐ.=*pains:* Jos., Ant. 3, 35 μὴ σὺν πόνῳ μηδ᾽ ἐργασίᾳ).—DELG s.v. ἔργον. M-M.

ἐργαστήριον, ίου, τό (s. next entry and ἔργον; Hdt., Aristoph. et al.; ins; PLond III, 897, 18 p. 207 [84 AD]; POxy 1455, 9; PYadin 5a I, 10. Cat. Cod. Astr. IX/2 p. 134, 19 al.; Philo) ***workshop*** MPol 13:1.

ἔργαστρα, ων, τά (s. prec. entry; pl. in var. mngs. since IV BC; also Sb 6771, 89 'wages') ***workshops*** ἃ πέπονθεν ἐν φιλίπποις ἐν τοῖς ἐ. *what he (Paul) suffered in the workshops of Philippi* ('in the workhouse' [tr. CSchmidt]) AcPl Ha 6, 5.

ἐργάτης, ου, ὁ (s. prec. three entries; trag., Hdt.+; loanw. in rabb.).—❶ **one who is engaged in work, *worker, laborer***

ⓐ of pers. engaged in physical labor **Mt 10:10; Lk 10:7; 1 Ti 5:18;** D 13:2; ὁ ἀγαθὸς ἐ. 1 Cl 34:1. Esp. of agricultural laborers (Soph., Oed. R. 859 al.; Wsd 17:16; Philo, Agr. 5 al. γῆς ἐ.) **Mt 9:37f; Lk 10:2; Js 5:4;** GJs 18:2 (not pap). Of workers in a vineyard **Mt 20:1f, 8;** ὁ περί τι ἐ. (Ps.-Demosth. 35, 32 οἱ περὶ τὴν γεωργίαν ἐργάται) *workers engaged in someth.* **Ac 19:25.**

ⓑ in transf. sense, of apostles and teachers: ἐργάται δόλιοι *deceitful workers* **2 Cor 11:13;** κακοὶ ἐ. **Phil 3:2;** ἐ. ἀνεπαίσχυντος **2 Ti 2:15.**—THaraguchi, ZNW 84, '93, 178–95.

❷ **one who effects someth. through work, *a doer*** w. gen. (X., Mem. 2, 1, 27 τ. καλῶν κ. σεμνῶν; Aristoxenus, fgm. 43 ἐ. φιλίας; Dio Chrys. 53 [70], 1 τ. ἀργῶν; Sextus 384 ἀληθείας; GrBar 13:4 τῶν τοιούτων; EpArist 231 ἀγαθῶν; Philo, Leg. All. 1, 54 τ. ἀρετῶν) ἐ. ἀδικίας *one who does what is wrong, an evildoer* **Lk 13:27** (PHoffmann, ZNW 58, '67, 188–214). ἐ. ἀνομίας (1 Macc 3:6; ἐ. τῆς ἀ. Just., A I, 16, 11) **13:27 v.l.;** 2 Cl 4:5.—DELG s.v. ἔργον. M-M. EDNT. TW.

ἔργον, ου, τό (Hom.+) *work.*—❶ **that which displays itself in activity of any kind, *deed, action***—ⓐ in contrast to rest **Hb 4:3, 4** (Gen 2:2), **10.** In contrast to word: freq. used to describe people of exceptional merit, esp. benefactors (X., Hier. 7, 2, Cyr. 6, 4, 5; Cebes 2, 2 λόγῳ καὶ ἔργῳ Πυθαγόρειος; Lucian, Tox. 35. Oft. in Epict.; GDI 5039, 20 [Crete] οὔτε λόγῳ οὔτε ἔργῳ; Sir 3:8; 16:12; 4 Macc 5:38; En 14:22 πᾶς λόγος αὐτοῦ ἔργον; TestAbr A 9 p. 86, 26 [Stone p. 20] ἐν παντὶ ἔργῳ καὶ λόγῳ; Philo; Jos., Ant. 17, 220, C. Ap. 2, 12; Larfeld I 497f) δυνατὸς ἐν ἔργῳ καὶ λόγῳ *mighty in word and deed* **Lk 24:19;** cp. **Ac 7:22;** ἐν λόγῳ ἢ ἐν ἔ. *in word and deed* **Col 3:17;** cp. **Ro 15:18; 2 Cor 10:11; 2 Th 2:17; Tit 1:16a; 1J 3:18;** 2 Cl 17:7, also 4:3. A similar contrast betw. the ποιητὴς ἔργου *doer who acts* and the forgetful hearer **Js 1:25,** and betw. ἔργα and a πίστις that amounts to nothing more than a verbal statement **2:14–26** (s. JRopes, Exp. 7th ser., 5, 1908, 547–56 and his comm. 1916 ad loc.; HPreisker, ThBl 4, 1925, 16f; ETobac, RHE 22, 1926, 797–805; AMeyer, D. Rätsel des Jk 1930, 86ff; ASchlatter, D. Brief des Jak. '32, 184–207).

ⓑ *manifestation, practical proof* τὸ ἔ. τῆς πίστεως **1 Th 1:3; 2 Th 1:11.** ἔ. διακονίας **Eph 4:12.** τὸ ἴδιον ἔργον τῆς προσευχῆς AcPl Ha 4, 27. τὸ ἔ. τοῦ νόμου *acting in accordance with the law* **Ro 2:15** (perh. also *the bringing of the law into effect,* as Polyaenus 1, 19 τοῦ λογίου τὸ ἔργον=realization or fulfilment of the oracular response). ἡ ὑπομονὴ ἔ. τέλειον ἐχέτω *let endurance show itself perfectly in practice* **Js 1:4.**

ⓒ *deed, accomplishment*—**α.** of the deeds of God and Jesus, specif. miracles (Epict. 3, 5, 10 ἰδεῖν ἔργα τὰ σά [=τοῦ θεοῦ]; Ael. Aristid. 50, 17 K.=26 p. 506 D.: ἔργον τοῦ θεοῦ θαυμαστόν; Quint. Smyrn. 9, 481 ἔργον ἀθανάτων of the healing of Philoctetes; Josh 24:29; Ps 45:9; 65:5; 85:8; JosAs 9:5; Jos., Bell. 5, 378 τ. ἔργα τοῦ θεοῦ, C. Ap. 2, 192) **Mt 11:2; J 5:20, 36; 7:3, 21** (Diod. S. 5, 33, 5 ἓν ἔργον=just one practice); **9:3; 10:25, 37f; 14:10, 11, 12; 15:24; Ac 13:41** (Hab 1:5); **15:18 v.l.; Hb 3:9** (Ps 94:9); **Rv 15:3.** On **Mt 11:19** s. δικαιόω 2bα.

β. of the deeds of humans, exhibiting a consistent moral character, referred to collectively as τὰ ἔργα (Ps 105:35; Job 11:11; Jon 3:10) **J 3:20 f; 7:7; Js 3:13; 1J 3:12; Rv 2:2, 19; 3:1, 8, 15.** σωτῆρος ἡμῶν τὰ ἔ. Qua. τὰ πρῶτα ἔ. **Rv 2:5.** πάντα τὰ ἔργα (Am 8:7; Mi 6:16) **Mt 23:5.** κατὰ τὰ ἔργα *in accordance w. the deeds* (Ps 27:4; 61:13; Pr 24:12; En 100:7; PsSol 2:16) **Mt 23:3; Ro 2:6; 2 Ti 1:9; 4:14; Rv 2:23; 20:12f.** Also κατὰ τὸ ἔργον **1 Pt 1:17.** The collective τὸ ἔργον is used for the pl. (Sir 11:20) **Gal 6:4; Hb 6:10; Rv 22:12.** The ἔργον or ἔργα is (are) characterized by the context as good or bad **Lk 11:48; 1 Cor 5:2; 2 Cor 11:15; 2 Ti 4:14; Js 2:25; 3J 10; Rv 14:13; 16:11; 18:6** (since in all these passages except **Rv 14:13** ἔ. refers to something bad, it is well to point out that ἔργον when used alone also means *an evil* or *disgraceful deed,* e.g., Appian, Bell. Civ. 2, 22 §83 ἔργον οὐδὲν αὐτοῖς ἀπῆν=they abstained from no shameful deed; Apollon. Rhod. 4, 476; 742; Arrian, Anab. 3, 21, 4). Or they are characterized by an added word: ἔ. ἀγαθόν **Ro 2:7; 13:3; 2 Cor 9:8; Phil 1:6; Col 1:10; 1 Ti 5:10; 2 Ti 2:21; 3:17; Tit 1:16b; 3:1; Hb 13:21 v.l.** Pl. **Eph 2:10** (misunderstood by JSanders, Ethics in the NT, '75, 78; cp. **Phil 1:6**); **1 Ti 2:10.** πλήρης ἔργων ἀγαθῶν *rich in good deeds* **Ac 9:36.** ἔ. καλόν **Mt 26:10; Mk 14:6; J 10:33.** Pl. (GrBar 15:2; Dio Chrys. 3, 52) **Mt 5:16; J 10:32; 1 Ti 5:10a, 25; 6:18; Tit 2:7, 14; 3:8, 14, Hb 10:24; 1 Pt 2:12** (WvanUnnik, NTS 1, '54/55, 92–110; cp. Diod. S. 16, 1, 1); 2 Pt 1:10 v.l.; 2 Cl 12:4. ἔργα ὅσια, δίκαια 6:9. ἔ. δικαιοσύνης B 1:6 (PsSol 18:8). ἐξ ἔργων τῶν ἐν δικαιοσύνῃ *righteous deeds* **Tit 3:5.** τὰ ἔ. τοῦ θεοῦ *the deeds that God desires* (Jer 31:10; 1 Esdr 7:9, 15) **J 6:28;** cp. vs. **29.** τὰ ἔ. μου (i.e. Χριστοῦ) **Rv 2:26.** ἔργα πεπληρωμένα ἐνώπιον τ. θεοῦ **3:2.** ἔ. ἄξια τ. μετανοίας **Ac 26:20.** ἔ. τῆς πίστεως *the deeds that go with faith* Hs 8, 9, 1. ἔ. αἰώνιον *an imperishable deed* IPol 8:1. τὰ ἔ. τοῦ Ἀβραάμ *deeds like Abraham's* **J 8:39.** τὰ ἔ. τ. πέμψαντός με **9:4.**—ἔργα πονηρά *evil deeds* (1 Esdr 8:83; En 98:6; Tat. 23:2) **Col 1:21; 2J 11;** cp. **J 3:19; 7:7; 1J 3:12** and ἀπὸ παντὸς ἔ. πονηροῦ **2 Ti 4:18.** Also ἔ. τῆς πονηρᾶς ὁδοῦ B 4:10. νεκρά *dead works,* i.e. those that lead to death **Hb 6:1; 9:14.** ἄκαρπα *unfruitful actions* **Eph 5:11.** ἄνομα *lawless deeds* **2 Pt 2:8.** Also ἔ. τῆς ἀνομίας B 4:1; Hs 8, 10, 3. ἔργα ἀσεβείας *impious deeds* **Jd 15** (ἀσεβῆ ἔ. Just., A I, 23, 3). τοῦ σκότους *deeds of darkness* (i.e. unbelief) **Ro 13:12;** cp. **Eph 5:11.** ἔ. τῆς σαρκός *deeds that originate in the flesh* (i.e. sin) **Gal 5:19.** τὰ ἔ. τοῦ πατρὸς ὑμῶν *deeds such as your father* (the devil) *commits* **J 8:41.** τῶν Νικολαϊτῶν **Rv 2:6.**—κρύφια, φανερὰ ἔ. *secret, open deeds* 2 Cl 16:3. Freq. in Paul ἔργα νόμου *deeds that the law commands you to do* **Ro 3:20, 28;** cp. **27; Gal 2:16; 3:2, 5, 10** (cp. 4Q MMT 3, 27 [=A Facsimile Edition of the Dead Sea Scrolls, ed. REisenman/JRobinson, I '91, xxxi, fig. 8, c line 29]; MAbegg, Paul, 'Works of the Law' and MMT: BAR 20/6, '94, 52–55; JDunn, NTS 43, '97, 147–53). Also simply ἔργα, w. the same meaning **Ro 4:2, 6; 9:12, 32; 11:6; Eph 2:9;** s. ELohmeyer, ZNW 28, 1929, 177–207.—S. δικαιοσύνη 3 end.

❷ **that which one does as regular activity,** ***work, occupation, task*** (cp. Aristoph., Av. 862; X., Mem. 2, 10, 6; Arrian, Anab. 5, 23, 1; Epict. 1, 16, 21; Sir 11:20; TestSol 1:2 al.; Just., A II, 3, 5 βασιλικόν) w. gen. of the one who assigns the task τοῦ κυρίου **1 Cor 15:58; 16:10; Phil 2:30.** διδόναι τινὶ τὸ ἔ. αὐτοῦ *assign his task to someone* **Mk 13:34;** πληροῦν ἔ. *accomplish a task* **Ac 14:26.** τ. ἔ. τελειοῦν *finish the work* (Dionys. Hal. 3, 69, 2 τ. οἰκοδομῆς τ. πολλὰ εἰργάσατο, οὐ μὴν ἐτελείωσε τὸ ἔργον; 2 Esdr 16:3, 16) **J 17:4;** cp. **4:34.** ἡ κυρίου τοῦ ἔργου *shop superintendent* GJs 2:2 (s. deStrycker ad loc.) Of the task and work of the apostles **Ac 13:2; 15:38.** οἱ πιστευθέντες παρὰ θεοῦ ἔργον τοιοῦτο *those who were entrusted by God with so important a duty* 1 Cl 43:1. καρπὸς ἔργου *fruit of work* **Phil 1:22.** To love someone διὰ τὸ ἔ. αὐτοῦ *because of what the person has done* **1 Th 5:13.** Of an office **1 Ti 3:1** (4 is also poss.). ἔ. ποιεῖν εὐαγγελιστοῦ *do the work of an evangelist* **2 Ti 4:5.**—ἔ. συγγενικὸν ἀπαρτίζειν *accomplish a proper, natural task* IEph 1:1.

❸ **that which is brought into being by work,** ***product, undertaking, work*** (Hom. et al.; Gen 2:2; 3 Km 7:15, 19; Jer 10:3; 1 Esdr 5:44; TestAbr A 13 p. 93, 11 [Stone p. 34] εἴ τινος κατακαύσει τὸ πῦρ; Just., D. 88, 8; Mel., P. 36, 244) *work* in the passive sense. W. special ref. to buildings (Aristoph., Av. 1125; Polyb. 5, 3, 6; Diod. S. 1, 31, 9; Appian, Mithrid. 30 §119; Arrian, Anab. 6, 18, 2; Dionys. Byz. §27; IG IV^2/1, 106, 56; 114, 31 al.; PPetr III, 43 [2] I, 2 [III BC] εἰς τὰ ἔργα=for the buildings al.; 1 Macc 10:11; SibOr 4, 59; EPeterson, Biblica 22, '41, 439–41) **1 Cor 3:13, 14, 15.** Perh. a building is also meant in **1 Cor 9:1** and **Ro 14:20** (s. καταλύω 2b). γῆ κ. τὰ ἐν αὐτῇ ἔ. **2 Pt 3:10** (FDanker, ZNW 53, '62, 82–86, would read καὶ γῆ κατὰ τὰ ἐν αὐτῇ ἔργα). Images of deities as ἔργα ἀνθρώπων 2 Cl 1:6 (Herodas 4, 26 ἔργα καλά of works of sculpture; Ath. 17:3f); sim. in the formulation ἔργον χειρός (cp. En 98:5; ApcEsdr 1:10; Herodas 7, 2f τῶν σῶν . . . χειρέων νοηρες ἔργον; Epict. 3, 7, 24 τὰ χειρὸς ἔργα; Jos., Bell. 3, 268 of courageous deeds χειρῶν ἔργα; cp. Just., D. 23, 5 of circumcision not as ἔργον δικαιοσύνης) τὸ ἔ. τῶν χειρῶν τινος *the work of someone's hands*=what someone has made **Ac 7:41; Rv 9:20** (cp. Is 17:8; Just., A I, 20, 5 al.). Of the world as created by God (Celsus 4, 99) **Hb 1:10** (Ps 101:26; Ar 4:24 al.); **2:7 v.l.;** B 5:10; 15:3. τὰ ἔ. τοῦ διαβόλου *the devil's undertakings* or *enterprises* (Arrian, Anab. 1, 11, 7 Τρωικὸν ἔ.=the Trojan undertaking, of the Trojan War) **1J 3:8.** τὰ ἔργα τῆς θηλείας *the works of the female* (w. ref. to sensual desire like Horapollo 1, 11 p. 18 θηλείας ἔργον and Longus 4, 19, 5 ἔργα γυναικῶν) GEg 252, 56. Of adultery **Rv 2:22.**

❹ **someth. having to do with someth. under discussion,** ***thing, matter*** (Hom. et al.) **Ac 5:38.** κρεῖττον IRo 2:1 (cp. GrBar 5:3 μείζονα τούτων ἔργα). ἔ. εὐφροσύνης *a joyful thing* B 10:11; οὐ πεισμονῆς τὸ ἔ. *not a matter of persuasion* IRo 3:3. οὐ νῦν ἐπαγγελίας τὸ ἔ. *it is not a matter of what we now profess* IEph 14:2. Perh. also **1 Ti 3:1** (s. 2 above).—JKleist, 'Ergon' in the Gospels: CBQ 6, '44, 61–68. DELG. M-M. EDNT. TW. Sv.

ἐργοπαρέκτης, ου, ὁ (s. ἔργον and παρέχω; hapax leg.) lit. 'one who gives work', ***employer*** 1 Cl 34:1.

ἐρεθίζω 1 aor. ἠρέθισα; aor. pass. ptc. ἐρεθισθείς 2 Macc 14:27; fut. pass. 3 sg. ἐρεθισθήσεται Da 11:10, 25 (s. ἔρις; Hom. et al.; Epict., Ench. 20; LXX; TestSol 4:6; 8:5 PC; TestDan 4:4) **to cause someone to react in a way that suggests acceptance of a challenge,** ***arouse, provoke*** mostly in bad sense *irritate, embitter,* as τὰ τέκνα **Col 3:21** (cp. Epict., loc. cit., where ἐ. takes up the preceding λοιδορεῖν and τύπτειν; 1 Macc 15:40; Philo, Ebr. 16; Jos., Bell. 2, 414, Ant. 4, 169; 20, 175; Ath., R. 75, 22). In a good sense of an encouraging example (Ael. Aristid. 28, 75 K.=49 p. 516 D.; Appian, Iber. 26 §103) **2 Cor 9:2.**—DELG s.v. ἐρέθω. M-M. EDNT. Spicq.

ἐρείδω fut. ἐρείσω Pr 3:26; TestSol 6:10; 1 aor. ἤρεισα (Hom. et al.; LXX; Jos., Bell. 7, 283, Ant. 8, 133; SibOr 4, 106) **to stick in someth.,** ***jam fast, become fixed*** (Aeschyl., Ag. 976; Plut., Numa 60 [2, 2], Crass. 554 [19, 4]) of the bow of a ship **Ac 27:41** (cp. Pind., P. 10, 51f ταχὺ δ' ἄγκυραν ἔρεισον χθονὶ πρῴραθε=quickly drop the anchor fr. the prow and let it grapple the bottom).—DELG. M-M.

ἐρεύγομαι fut. ἐρεύξομαι (Hom. et al.; LXX; SibOr 4, 81) orig. 'belch', then **to express forcefully someth. intelligible,** ***utter, proclaim*** (cp. the imagery Callimachus: POxy 1011 fol. 1 verso, 7=fgm. 75, 7 Pf. I 77, but ἐξερυγάννω here in tmesis and said satirically 'belch out their story') τὶ *someth.* κεκρυμμένα **Mt 13:35** (cp. Ps 77:2 φθέγξομαι; for the imagery of forceful utterance cp. Job 32:19f). ῥῆμα *a word* 1 Cl 27:7 (Ps 18:3).—DELG 1. M-M.

ἐρευνάω s. ἐραυνάω.

ἐρευνητής s. ἐραυνητής.

ἐρημία, ας, ἡ uninhabited or lonely region, normally with sparse vegetation, ***desert*** (s. next entry; so Aeschyl., Hdt. et al.; BGU 888, 15 [II AD]; PGrenf II, 84, 4; LXX; Philo; Jos., Bell. 3, 515 [near the Jordan]; Just., A I, 12, 6; Mel. P. 94, 722; loanw. in rabb.) **Mt 15:33; Mk 8:4;** (w. ὄρη) **Hb 11:38.** In contrast to πόλις (as Ezk 35:4; Jos., Ant. 2, 24, Vi. 11) **2 Cor 11:26.** GJs 16:2b (hill-country).—DELG s.v. ἐρῆμος. M-M. TW.

ἔρημος, ον (s. prec. and next entry; Hom.+; on the accent s. B-D-F §13; Mlt-H. 58).

❶ as adj. **pert. to being in a state of isolation,** ***isolated, desolate, deserted***—ⓐ of an area *isolated, unfrequented, abandoned, empty, desolate* τόπος (Diod. S. 15, 49, 1 ἐν ἐ. τόπῳ; Plut., Numa 61 [4, 1]; Arrian, Ind. 22, 4; OGI 580, 7; En 18:12; TestAbr B 12 p. 116, 24 [Stone p. 80]; ParJer; AscIs 2:8; Philo, Spec. Leg. 4, 141; Jos., C. Ap. 1, 308; Just., A I, 53, 9 χώραν ἔ.) **Mt 14:13, 15; Mk 1:35, 45; 6:31f, 35; Lk 4:42; 9:10 v.l., 12.** οἶκος (Artem. 2, 33 p. 130, 10; Philo, Spec. Leg. 2, 133; Jos., Vi. 376) **Mt 23:38.** ἔπαυλις **Ac 1:20.** ὁδός *lonely* **8:26** (Arrian, Anab. 3, 3, 3 ἐρήμη ἡ ὁδός; 3, 21, 7; s. on Γάζα). χωρίον Papias (3).

ⓑ of pers. *desolate, deserted* (trag., Thu.; JosAs 12:11 'orphaned'; Just., D. 69, 4; τοῖς ἐ. γνώσεως θεοῦ) a childless woman (Chariton 3, 5, 5) **Gal 4:27;** 2 Cl 2:1 (both Is 54:1; cp. Philo, Exsecr. 158). ἔ. ἀπὸ τ. θεοῦ *deserted by God* 2:3 (cp.

Appian, Bell. Civ. 4, 30 §130 ἔ. ἐκ παραπομπῆς=deserted by his escort).

❷ as subst. ἡ ἔ. (Hdt. 3, 102 al.; LXX; En 10:4; TestAbr B 12 p. 116, 26; 28 [Stone p. 80]; ParJer 7:20; Jos., C. Ap. 1, 89; sc. χώρα) **an uninhabited region or locality, *desert, grassland, wilderness*** (in contrast to cultivated and inhabited country) **Mt 24:26; Rv 12:6, 14; 17:3.** Pl. *lonely places* (cp. PTebt 61a, 151 [118 BC]; PsSol 5:9) **Lk 1:80; 5:16; 8:29.** *Steppe, grassland* as pasture **15:4.** Of the Judean wilderness, the stony, barren eastern declivity of the Judean mountains toward the Dead Sea and lower Jordan Valley (1 Macc 2:29; 5:24, 28; 2 Macc 5:27) **Mt 3:1** (ἡ ἔ. τῆς Ἰουδαίας); **4:1; 11:7; Mk 1:4 12f; Lk 3:2; 4:1; 7:24; J 11:54.** Here also belong the reff. to Is 40:3 (cp. 1QS 8, 12–14 w. ref. to Is 40:3 and s. HRüger, ZNW 60, '69, 142–44; GNebe, ibid. 63, '72, 283–89): **Mt 3:3; Mk 1:3; Lk 3:4; J 1:23;** GJs 16:2ab v.l. (s. ἐρημία). Gathering-place of an aroused band of Judean patriots **Ac 21:38** (on the language cp. Jos., Bell. 7, 438; on the Egyptian, Bell. 2, 261f ἐκ τῆς ἐρημίας, Ant. 20, 169; Schürer I 463, 33; 464). Of the Arabian desert (LXX; Just.) ἡ ἔ. τοῦ ὄρους Σινᾶ (Ex 19:1f; cp. vs. 3 al.) **Ac 7:30;** cp. **J 3:14; 6:31, 49; Ac 7:36, 38, 42** (Am 5:25),**44; 13:18; 1 Cor 10:5; Hb 3:8** (Ps 94:8), **17;** AcPl Ha 8, 16. As the place where the prophets Eldad and Modat preached Hv 2, 3, 4.—AJonsen, Die bibl. Wüste, diss. Würzb. 1923; UMauser, Christ in the Wilderness (Mk) '63; RFunk, JBL 78, '59, 205–14.—DELG s.v. ἐρῆμος (the accented form in Hom. et al.). M-M. TW. Sv.

ἐρημόω fut. ἐρημώσω; 1 aor. ἠρήμωσα LXX; pf. ptc. acc. ἠρημωκότας 1 Macc 15:4. In our lit. only pass.: fut. ἐρημωθήσομαι LXX; 1 aor. ἠρημώθην; pf. 3 sg. ἠρήμωται Is 1:7; ptc. ἠρημμωμένος; plpf. ἠρήμωτο (Just., A I, 47, 4) (s. prec. two entries; Pind., Hdt.+) **to make uninhabitable, *lay waste, depopulate*** a city (Thu., also PSI 71, 11; Cat. Cod. Astr. VIII/3, p. 169, 14; 1 Esdr 2:17; 2 Esdr 12 [Neh 2]: 3; Is 6:11 al.; Jos., Bell. 2, 279, Ant. 11, 24) **Rv 18:19;** fig. **17:16.** βασιλεία *a kingdom depopulated* by civil war (Philo, Decal. 152) **Mt 12:25; Lk 11:17.** Of a vineyard ἐρημοῦται ὑπὸ τῶν βοτανῶν *is laid waste by weeds* Hs 9, 26, 4.—*Ruin* (Sir 16:4) of wealth associated with Babylon (Sir 21:4) **Rv 18:17.** On the contrast in fortunes cp. the fate of Persepolis Diod. S. 17, 70, 5.—DELG s.v. ἐρῆμος. M-M. TW.

ἐρημώδης, ες (s. prec. three entries; hapax leg.) ***desert-like*** of a mountain Hs 9, 1, 9; 26, 1. Of persons 9, 26, 3.

ἐρήμωσις, εως, ἡ state of being made uninhabitable, *devastation, destruction, depopulation* (s. prec. four entries; Arrian, Anab. 1, 9, 7; 5, 1, 5; Cat. Cod. Astr. VIII/3 p. 136, 25 τόπων ἐνδόξων ἐρημώσεις; LXX; En 98:3;TestLevi 17:10; ParJer; JosAs 11 cod. A [p. 54, 13 Bat.]; Jos., Ant. 12, 322; Just.) of Jerusalem **Lk 21:20.** On τὸ βδέλυγμα τῆς ἐ. **Mt 24:15; Mk 13:14** s. βδέλυγμα 2 and HBévenot, RB 45, '36, 53–65.—TW.

ἐρίζω fut. 3 sg. ἐρίσει (Just., D. 123, 8 [cp. Is 42:2]); aor. subj. 2 pl. ἐρίσητε 1 Km 12:14f (Hom.+; Lucian; Plut.; BGU 1043, 5; PGM 13, 202; LXX; TestSol 8:6; Jos., Bell. 4, 396; 5, 414) ***quarrel, wrangle*** abs. (Epict. Schenkl fgm. 25 fr. Stob.) **Mt 12:19** (w. κραυγάζειν; MBlack, An Aramaic Approach, '67, 257).—Schmidt, Syn. IV, 197–204. DELG s.v. ἔρις. M-M. Spicq.

ἐριθεία, ας, ἡ (W-H. ἐριθία; s. Mlt-H. 339) found before NT times only in Aristot., Polit. 5, 3 p. 1302b, 4; 1303a, 14, where it denotes a self-seeking pursuit of political office by unfair means. Its meaning in our lit. is a matter of conjecture. A derivation fr. ἔρις is not regarded w. favor by recent NT linguistic scholarship and some consider it also unlikely for the sources fr. which Paul possibly derived the lists of vices in **2 Cor 12:20; Gal 5:20,** since ἔρις and ἐριθεῖαι are both found in these lists; yet for Paul and his followers, the mng. ***strife, contentiousness*** (so Ltzm., MDibelius, JSickenberger) cannot be excluded (cp. Phil 1:17 w. 15 and s. Anecd. Gr. p. 256, 17 ἐρ.= φιλον[ε]ικία). But ***selfishness, selfish ambition*** (PAlthaus on Ro 2:8; M-M.) in all cases gives a sense that is just as prob. W. ζῆλος **Js 3:14, 16.** κατὰ ἐριθείαν **Phil 2:3;** IPhld 8:2; ἐξ ἐ. **Phil 1:17;** οἱ ἐξ ἐ. **Ro 2:8** (s. Rdm.[2] p. 26; 217 n. 4). Pl. *disputes* or *outbreaks of selfishness* (B-D-F §142) **2 Cor 12:20; Gal 5:20.** KFritzsche, Comm. in Ep. ad Rom. 1836 on 2:8 pp. 143–48; CBruston, RTP 41, 1909, 196–228.—DELG s.v. ἔριθος. M-M. EDNT. TW. Spicq.

ἔριον, ου, τό (Hom. et al.; ins, pap, LXX, En; ParJer 9:18; Philo; Jos., Ant. 4, 80; 208 al.) ***wool*** B 7:11; 8:5f. λευκόν *white wool* (PGM 2, 70f; Da 7:9; En 106:2, 10; cp.; ParJer 9:18 ὡς ἔριον λευκόν) **Rv 1:14;** cp. 1 Cl 8:4 (Is 1:18). κόκκινον *red* **Hb 9:19;** B 7:8; 8:1 ab (Num 19:6). Pl. (Il., Pla. et al.; ins, pap, LXX) a large white chair ἐξ ἐρίων χιονίνων γεγονυῖα *cushioned with snow-white woolen cloth* Hv 1, 2, 2.—B. 400. DELG s.v. εἶρος. M-M.

ἔρις, ιδος, ἡ (s. next entry; Hom. et al.; Aelian, VH 2, 21; PEdg 48 [=Sb 6754], 16; PGrenf I, 1, 21; LXX; EpArist 250; Philo; Jos., Ant. 14, 470; SibOr 3, 640) acc. ἔριν (Od. 3, 136 al.; TestSol 4, 1 D; JosAs 1:10) **Phil 1:15; Tit 3:9 v.l.** Pl. ἔριδες **1 Cor 1:11** or ἔρεις (GrBar 8:5 [acc.]; 13:4 [nom.]) 1 Cl 35:5; 46:5 (Ps 138:20 Swete). W-S. §9, 8; B-D-F §47, 3; Mlt-H. 131. **Engagement in rivalry, esp. w. ref. to positions taken in a matter, *strife, discord, contention* Tit 3:9;** IEph 8:1. In a list of vices **Ro 1:29;** (w. ζῆλος) **13:13; 1 Cor 3:3;** cp. **2 Cor 12:20; Gal 5:20;** 1 Cl 5:5; 6:4; 9:1; (w. φθόνος as Appian, Bell. Civ. 2, 2 §6) **Phil 1:15; 1 Ti 6:4;** (w. στάσις as Appian, Bell. Civ. 3, 86 §357) 1 Cl 3:2; 14:2; 54:2. ἔ. ἐστὶν ἐπί τινος *there is strife about someth.* 44:1. Pl. *quarrels* (Maximus Tyr. 22, 3f; Philo) **Ro 13:13 v.l.** (w. ζήλοις); **1 Cor 1:11; Tit 3:9;** 1 Cl 35:5; 46:5.—B. 1360. DELG. M-M. TW. Spicq. Sv.

ἐριστικός, ή, όν *contentious, quarrelsome* (s. prec. entry; Pla., Lys. 211b; Aristot., Rhet. 1, 11; Lucian, Herm. 16; Herm. Wr. 12, 9; Philo) in a list of vices D 3:2.

ἐρίφιον, ου, τό (s. next entry; Athen. 14, 661b; PThéad 8, 11 al.; Tob 2:13) dim. of ἔριφος, properly 'kid' but also ***goat*** (cp. the interchange betw. ἐ. and ἔριφος Tob 2:12, 13) **Lk 15:29 v.l.; Mt 25:33** the imagery here relates to the fact of a separation, not an evaluation of goats as such (cp. vs. 32 ἔριφος).—DELG s.v. ἔριφος. M-M.

ἔριφος, ου, ὁ (s. prec. entry; Hom.+) ***kid, he-goat.*** Pl. w. πρόβατα prob. simply *goats* (cp. ἄρνας κ. ἐρίφους POxy 244, 10 [23 AD]; Molpis: 590 fgm. 2c [in Athen. 4, 141e] ἄρνες, ἔριφοι; Longus 3, 33, 2; EpArist 146) **Mt 25:32;** GJs 18:3 (not pap).—*Kid* **Lk 15:29** (as a roast: Alcaeus 44 Diehl[2]; Maximus Tyr. 30, 5a).—B. 166. DELG.

Ἑρμᾶς, ᾶ, ὁ *Hermas* (OGI 48, 1; SEG XL, 1034, 1; BGU 79, 8; 11; 264, 5; PLond III, 1178, 14 p. 216 [194 AD]; PMich 157, 18 [250 AD]; s. Rouffiac p. 91; MDibelius on Hv 1, 1, 4) short form of a name beg. w. Ἑρμ- (B-D-F §125, 1; Rob. 172).

❶ receiver of a greeting **Ro 16:14.**

❷ author of the Shepherd of Hermas, acc. to the Muratorian Fgm. (lines 73ff) brother of the Roman bishop Pius Hv 1, 1, 4; 1, 2, 2–4; 1, 4, 3; 2, 2, 2; 2, 3, 1; 3, 1, 6; 9; 3, 8, 11; 4, 1, 4; 7. BHHW II 694–95.—DELG s.v. Ἑρμῆς. LGPN I. M-M.

ἑρμηνεία, ας, ἡ (s. next entry; since Pre-Socr., X., Pla.; Vett. Val. p. 4, 5; Philo, Just., Mel.) ἑρμηνία W-H.; Mlt-H. 339.

❶ **capacity of doing translation,** ***translation*** (BGU 326 I, 1; II, 15; POxy 1466, 3; Sir prol. 20; EpArist 3; 11 al.; Just.) γλωσσῶν **1 Cor 12:10;** cp. **14:26.**

❷ **product of interpretive procedure,** ***interpretation, exposition*** of words of Jesus Papias (2:3), on this cp. Mel., P. 41, 282; 42, 296.—DELG s.v. ἑρμηνεύς. M-M. TW. Spicq. Sv.

ἑρμηνευτής, οῦ, ὁ (s. prec. entry; Pla., Pol. 290c; Ar 10:3) **one who helps someone to understand thoughts expressed in words,** ***translator*** (Gen 42:23) **1 Cor 14:28 v.l.** (for διερμηνευτής). Mark is called the ἑ. *interpreter* of Peter, Papias (2:15).—DELG s.v. ἑρμηνεύς. M-M. TW.

ἑρμηνεύω (s. prec. two entries) aor. 3 sg. ἡρμήνευσεν (Papias [2:15]); pf. inf. ἑρμηνευκέναι Esth 10:31; pf. pass. ptc. ἡρμηνευμένην 2 Esdr 4:7 (trag. et al.)

❶ **to help someone understand a subject or matter by making it plain,** ***explain, interpret*** (Pla., Ion, 535a al.; BGU 140, 20 [201/2 AD]; Philo) τινί τι *someth. to someone* **Lk 24:27 v.l.** Ἰουδαϊσμὸν ἑ. ὑμῖν *propound the Judean way (Judaism) to you* (w. the implication that interpretation has first been done) IPhld 6:1 (ἑρμ. also means simply *proclaim, discourse on,* without the idea of interpreting: Soph., Oed. C. 399; Philostrat., Vi. Soph. 2, 14; 2, 22 al.; Celsus 3, 55; SIG 1168, 88 [IV BC]; SEG VIII, 551, 39 [I BC]).

❷ **to render words in a different language,** ***translate*** (so the act. and mid., X., An. 5, 4, 4; BGU 326 II, 22; PRyl 62; 2 Esdr 4:7; Job 42:17b; TestSol 13:6 P.; EpArist 39; Philo; Jos., Ant. 6, 156, C. Ap. 2, 46) **J 1:38 v.l., 42; 9:7** (Stephan. Byz. s.v. Ἰστός: κέλλα ῥαρσάθ, ὃ ἑρμηνεύεται ἱστὸς νηός). Μελχισέδεκ is ἑρμηνευόμενος βασιλεὺς δικαιοσύνης **Hb 7:2.**—Of translation of Matthew's work Papias (2:15).—DELG s.v. ἑρμηνεύς. M-M. EDNT. TW. Spicq.

Ἑρμῆς, οῦ, ὁ ***Hermes*****—❶** the Greek god (SEitrem, Hermes: Pauly-W. VIII 1, 1912, 738–92; LFarnell, The Cults of the Gk. States V, 1909, 1–84; also LfgrE s.v. Ἑρμείας col. 708 (lit.)) **Ac 14:12** (s. the lit. on Λύστρα and cp. Ael. Aristid. 46 p. 135 D.: Ἑρμῆν ῥητορικὴν ἔχοντα; 46 p. 398 D. of Demosth., ὃν ἐγὼ φαίην ἂν Ἑρμοῦ τινος λογίου τύπον εἰς ἀνθρώπους κατελθεῖν; Orph. Hymn. 28, 4 Q: Hermes as λόγου θνητοῖσι προφήτης; Ar. 10:3 λόγων ἑρμηνευτήν; Just., Ath.).

❷ receiver of a greeting **Ro 16:14** (H. as a man's name [cp. OGI 481, 4; 597, 4; PVindBosw 6, 2 (250 AD); 4, 2; Jos., Ant. 14, 245] is either simply the name of the god [HMeyersahm, Deorum nomina hominibus imposita, diss. Kiel 1891; HUsener, Götternamen 1896, 358] or a short form like Ἑρμᾶς [q.v.]; a slave's name SEG XLI, 1414, 1; CIL 6, 8121; B-D-F §125, 1; Rob. 172).—DELG. M-M.

Ἑρμογένης, ους, ὁ also Ἑρ- Tdf. (SIG² and OGI ind.; POxy 1292, 1 [30 AD]; Jos., C. Ap. 1, 216) ***Hermogenes,*** a Christian fr. Asia **2 Ti 1:15.**—LGPN I. M-M.

ἑρπετόν, οῦ, τό (Hom. et al.; PGM 1, 116; LXX, En, EpArist, Philo, Joseph.; SibOr fgm. 3, 8; Tat. 9, 1; Ath., R. 62, 13) ***reptile*** (w. τετράποδα and πετεινά; cp. Palaeph. p. 50, 8) **Ac 10:12; Ro 1:23;** (w. τετρ., πετ. and θηρία) **Ac 11:6;** (w. still others, as Herm. Wr. 1, 11b) PtK 2 p. 14, 18; (w. θηρία) Hs 9, 26, 1 (s. below); θηρία, πετεινά, ἑ., ἐνάλια *fourfooted animals, birds, reptiles, fish* **Js 3:7** (cp. Gen 1:25f; 9:2f; En 7:5; Philo, Spec. Leg. 4, 110–16; PGM 1, 118f). ἑ. in a recital praising the Creator Hm 12, 4, 1 v.l. Esp. of a *snake* (Eur., Andr. 269; Theocr. 24, 56; Jos., Ant. 17, 109) ἑ. θανατώδη *deadly snakes* Hs 9, 1, 9; cp. also 9, 26, 1 (s. above).—DELG s.v. ἕρπω. M-M.

ἐρρέθην s. εἶπον.

ἔρρηξα s. ῥήγνυμι.

ἐρρίζωμαι s. ῥιζόω.

ἔρριμαι, ἐ(ρ)ριμμένος s. ῥίπτω.

ἐρρυσάμην, ἐρρύσθην s. ῥύομαι.

ἔρρωσθε, ἔρρωσο s. ῥώννυμι.

ἐρυθρός, ά, όν ***red*** (Hom. [color of wine or blood] et al.; ins, LXX, En, TestSol; JosAs 4:11 ἵδρως ἐ.) of roses ApcPt 3:8. ἡ ἐρυθρὰ θάλασσα *the Red Sea* (Aeschyl., Hdt. et al.) **Ac 7:36; Hb 11:29;** 1 Cl 51:5. MCopisarow, VetusT 12, '62, 1–14; NSnaith, ibid. 15, '65, 395–98.—B. 1056. Schmidt, Syn. III 41f. DELG s.v. ἐρεύθω. M-M.

ἔρχομαι impv. ἔρχου, ἔρχεσθε; impf. ἠρχόμην; fut. ἐλεύσομαι; 2 aor. ἦλθον, and the mixed forms ἦλθα (W-S. §13, 13; B-D-F §81, 3; Mlt-H. 208f), ἤλθοσαν (LXX; TestAbr A 20 p. 103, 12 [Stone p. 54]), ἤλθωσαν (GJs 21:1; ἤλθωσιν17:3; s. deStrycker p. 246f); pf. ἐλήλυθα; plpf. 3 sg. ἐληλύθει 3 Km 10:10, 12 (Hom.+). This multipurpose marker is not readily susceptible to precise classification, but the following outline of usage covers the principal lines:

❶ **of movement from one point to another, with focus on approach from the narrator's perspective,** ***come*****—ⓐ** of movement itself**—α.** abs. ἔρχου καὶ ἔρχεται **Mt 8:9; Lk 7:8;** cp. **Mt 22:3; Lk 14:17; J 5:7; Ac 10:29; 1 Cor 11:34; Rv 8:3** al. κραυγὴ γέγονεν· ἰδοὺ ὁ νυμφίος ἔρχεται **Mt 25:6 v.l.** (Jos., Bell. 5, 272 βοῶντες· ὁ υἱὸς ἔρχεται). οἱ ἐρχόμενοι καὶ οἱ ὑπάγοντες **Mk 6:31.** ἦλθε δρομέως *came on the run* AcPl Ha 4, 30 (TestAbr A 5 p. 82, 24 [Stone p. 12] ἦλθεν δρομαία ἐπ' αὐτούς=Sarah came to them on the run). Also w. the specif. mng. *come back, return* (Hom. et al.; Bar 4:37; 1 Esdr 5:8; Tob 2:3 BA) **J 4:27; 9:7; Ro 9:9;** of Joseph GJs 16:2 (foll. by κατέβη of Mary; both Joseph and Mary 'return' from an uninhabited area). *Come* before the judgment-seat of God 2 Cl 9:4. *Come* in a hostile sense **Lk 11:22** P^{75} et al. (cp. X., Hellenica 6, 5, 43).

β. used w. prepositions: ἀπό w. gen. of place (Herodian 1, 17, 8 ἀ. τοῦ λουτροῦ; ἀ. βορρᾶς PsSol 11:3; ἀ. τῆς μεγάλης πόλεως TestAbr A 2 p. 78, 30 [Stone p. 4]) **Mk 7:1; 15:21; Ac 18:2; 2 Cor 11:9;** w. gen. of pers. **Mk 5:35; J 3:2b; Gal 2:12.**—ἐκ w. gen. of place **Lk 5:17; J 3:31b.**—εἰς w. acc. of place *into* **Mt 2:11; 8:14; 9:1; Mk 1:29; 5:38; Lk 23:42** (cp. 1bα below, end); **J 11:30;** εἰς Κόρινθον AcPl Ha 6, 2 (εἰς τὸν παράδεισον TestAbr A 11 p. 90, 1 [Stone p. 28]). *to, toward* **J 11:38; 20:3.** εἰς τὸ πέραν **Mt 8:28; 16:5.** εἰς τ. ἑορτήν *to the festival,* i.e. to celebrate it **J 4:45b; 11:56.** ἐκ . . . εἰς **J 4:54.**—διά w. gen. of place and εἰς **Mk 7:31;** ὁ . . . ἐρχόμενος διὰ τῆς θύρας *one who enters by the gate* **10:2** (P^{75}).— μετά w. gen. of pers. ἵνα ἔλθω μετ' αὐτοῦ ἐν τῇ δόξῃ τοῦ πατρὸς αὐτοῦ *so that I might return with him in the glory of his Father* AcPl Ha 10, 8. ἐν w. dat. of the thing w. which one comes **Ro 15:29.** ἐν ῥάβδῳ **1 Cor 4:21,** also to denote the state of being in which one comes ἐν πνεύματι **Lk 2:27;** cp. **Ro 15:32;** w. dat. of the pers. who accompanies someone **Jd 14.**—ἐπί w. acc. of place *over* **Mt 14:28,** *to* (JosAs 26:5; ParJer 8:4; Jos., Ant. 7, 16; Just., D. 88, 3) **Lk 19:5; Ac 12:10, 12;** w. acc. of thing *to* (PTor I, 1; II, 29 [116 BC] ἔρχεσθαι ἐπὶ τὸ κριτήριον; Jos., Ant. 12, 395) **Mt 3:7; Mk 11:13b;** w. acc. of pers. *to* (ἐπὶ γυναῖκας Just., A I, 33,

3) **J 19:33; Ac 24:8 v.l.;** *against* **Lk 14:31** (1 Macc 5:39 ἔρχ. ἐπί τινα εἰς πόλεμον; Jos., Ant. 7, 233; Mel., P. 17, 114).—κατά w. acc. of place *to* **Lk 10:33; Ac 16:7;** AcPl Ha 2, 5.—παρά w. acc. of place *to* **Mt 15:29;** w. gen. of pers. *from* **Lk 8:49.**—πρός w. acc. of pers. *to* (X., Mem. 1, 2, 27; En 106:4; JosAs 3:6; Jos., Ant. 2, 106; 11, 243; Just., D. 77, 4) **Mt 3:14; 7:15; Mk 9:14; Lk 1:43; J 1:29, 47; 2 Cor 13:1** and oft. ἀπό τινος (gen. of pers.) πρός τινα **1 Th 3:6.**

γ. w. an adverb of place ἄνωθεν ἔ. **J 3:31.** ἐκεῖ **18:3.** ἐνθάδε **4:16.** ὄπισθεν **Mk 5:27.** πόθεν (Jdth 10:12) **J 3:8; 8:14; Rv 7:13.** ποῦ **Hb 11:8.** ὧδε **Mt 8:29; Ac 9:21** (ApcEsdr 5:10; ApcSed 9:4; cp. ParJer 7:16 ἐνταῦθα. The adv. w. a case funct. as prep. ἄχρι τινός **Ac 11:5.** ἐγγύς τινος Hv 4, 1, 9. ἕως τινός **Lk 4:42** (ApcMos 34 ἐλθὲ ἕως ἐμοῦ).

δ. w. a case, without a prep.: dat. of pers. *come to someone* (Aeschyl., Prom. 358; Thu. 1, 13, 3; X., An. 7, 7, 30; BGU 1041, 16 [II AD] ὅτι ἔρχομαί σοι) **Mt 21:5** (Zech 9:9); **Rv 2:5, 16.**

ε. The purpose of coming is expressed by an inf. (Eur., Med. 1270, also Palaeph. p. 62, 12; 1 Macc 16:22; Bel 40 Theod.; 1 Esdr 1:23; 5:63; TestSol 5 D ἦλθε θεάσασθαι; TestAbr B 5 p. 109, 21 [Stone p. 66] ἔρχομαι … κοιμηθῆναι; Just., D. 78, 7 ὃν ἐληλύθεισαν προσκυνῆσαι) **Mt 2:2; 12:42; Mk 15:36; Lk 1:59; 3:12** al.; by a fut. ptc. (Hom. et al.) **Mt 27:49; Ac 8:27;** by a pres. ptc. **Lk 13:6** (TestJob 9:8 αἰτοῦντες); by ἵνα **J 10:10; 12:9b** (TestJob 34:5; ApcMos 29); εἰς τοῦτο ἵνα **Ac 9:21;** διά τινα **J 12:9a.**

ζ. Single forms of ἔ. are used w. other verbs to denote that a person, in order to do someth., must first come to a certain place: in parataxis ἔρχεται καί, ἦλθεν καί etc. (Ex 19:7; 2 Km 13:36; 2 Esdr 5:16; JosAs 10:6; TestJob 8:3; ApcMos 37) **Mt 13:19, 25; Mk 2:18; 4:15; 5:33; 6:29; 12:9; 14:37; Lk 8:12, 47; J 6:15; 11:48; 12:22; 19:38; 20:19, 26; 21:13; 3J 3; Rv 5:7; 17:1; 21:9.** ἔρχου καὶ ἴδε **J 1:46; 11:34.** ἔρχεσθε καὶ ὄψεσθε **1:39.** A ptc. of ἔ. followed by a finite verb ἐλθών (Hdt. 2, 115; LXX; TestJob 7:1; Just., D. 8, 4 al.) **Mt 2:8; 8:7; 9:10, 18** (cp. εἰς 3b; προσέρχομαι 1a); **12:44; 14:12; 18:31; 27:64; 28:13; Mk 7:25; 12:14, 42; 14:45; 16:1; Ac 16:37, 39.** ἐρχόμενος **Lk 13:14; 16:21; 18:5.** The participial constr. is best transl. *come and.* In some pass. ἐλθών is to be rendered *when (someone) has come* **J 16:8; 2 Cor 12:20; Phil 1:27** (opp. ἀπών).—Instead of the transcription]λη λυθεισα POxy 1081, 3, read after the Coptic SJCh 88, 19–89, 1: ἐ]ληλύθεισαν.

ⓑ of making an appearance *come before the public, appear* (cp. ἦλθον εἰς τόνδε τὸν κόσμον 'I was born' Ar. 1, 1).

α. of Jesus as Messiah **Lk 3:16; J 4:25; 7:27, 31,** who for this reason (on the basis of pass. like Ps 117:26; Hab 2:3; Da 7:13 Theod.) is called ὁ ἐρχόμενος **Mt 11:3; Lk 7:19f; Hb 10:37** (Hab 2:3), or ὁ ἐρχόμενος ἐν ὀνόματι κυρίου **Mt 21:9; 23:39; Mk 11:9; Lk 13:35; 19:38; J 12:13** (in all cases Ps 117:26); also in John, in whose writings the idea of Jesus having come heaven-sent to the earth is of considerable importance **J 16:28:** (ὁ προφήτης) ὁ ἐρχόμενος εἰς τ. κόσμον **J 6:14; 11:27** (cp. ἐρχόμενος εἰς τ. κόσμον ἐπὶ τὸ ὄρος τῶν ἐλαιῶν ParJer 9:20). Of the appearance of Jesus among humans (s. Harnack, 'Ich bin gekommen': ZTK 22, 1912, 1–30; AFrövig, D. Sendungsbewusstsein Jesu u. d. Geist 1924, 129ff) **Mt 11:19; Lk 7:34; J 5:43; 7:28; 8:42.** Foll. by the inf. of purpose **Mt 5:17; 10:34f; Lk 19:10.** W. ἵνα foll. **J 10:10b** (ἦλθον, as here, Herm. Wr. 1, 30). W. εἰς τ. κόσμον and ἵνα foll. **12:46; 18:37;** εἰς κρίμα, ἵνα **9:39;** w. inf. foll. **1 Ti 1:15.** ἔ. ἐν σαρκί *come in the flesh* **1J 4:2; 2J 7;** B 5:10f. εἰς σάρκα AcPlCor 1:14. ἔ δι' ὕδατος καὶ αἵματος **1J 5:6** w. the continuation ἐν τ. ὕδατι καὶ ἐν τ. αἵματι (on the mng. of the prep. s. B-D-F §223, 3; 198, 4). ὀπίσω w. gen. *come after* of Christ in relation to his forerunner **Mt 3:11; Mk 1:7; J 1:15, 27, 30.** The idea of coming is even plainer in connection w. the coming of the Human One (Son of Man), the return of Jesus fr. his heavenly home **Mt 10:23; Ac 1:11** (opp. πορεύεσθαι); **1 Cor 4:5; 11:26; 2 Th 1:10** (Just., D. 28, 2 al.). W. ἐν τῇ δόξῃ **Mt 16:27; 25:31; Mk 8:38; Lk 9:26** (cp. ἔνδοξος … ἐλεύσεται Just., D. 49, 2). ἐπὶ τ. νεφελῶν μετὰ δυνάμεως καὶ δόξης **Mt 24:30** (Just., D. 31, 1). ἐν νεφέλαις, νεφέλῃ etc. **Mk 13:26; Lk 21:27.** ἐν τ. βασιλείᾳ αὐτοῦ *in his kingdom* **Mt 16:28; Lk 23:42 v.l.**

β. of forerunners of the Messiah and those who identify themselves as such: Elijah **Mt 11:14; 17:10, 11, 12; Mk 9:11, 12, 13** (Just., D. 49, 1); John the Baptist **Mt 11:18; Lk 7:33; J 1:31;** w. εἰς μαρτυρίαν *for testimony* **1:7.** Others, including false messiahs, false teachers, and an antichrist **Mt 24:5; Mk 13:6; Lk 21:8** (ἐπὶ τ. ὀνόματί μου *calling on my name*); **J 10:8; 2 Cor 11:4; 2 Pt 3:3; 1J 2:18.**

❷ **to proceed on a course, with destination in view,** ***go*** (Hom. et al.; LXX) ὀπίσω τινός *go with* (lit. 'after') *someone* fig., of a disciple **Mt 16:24; Mk 8:34 v.l.; Lk 9:23; 14:27.** ἐπί τι *go to someth.* **Mt 21:19; Mk 11:13a** (w. indir. quest. foll.). πρός τινα **Lk 15:20.** σύν τινι **J 21:3.** ἔ. ὁδόν *go on a journey* (Hom. et al.) **Lk 2:44.** S. also 1bα above.

❸ **to change place or position, with implication of being brought,** ***be brought*** (Hom. et al.; Thu. 6, 71, 2 χρήματα; Arrian, Anab. 2, 13, 5 ἀγγελία et al.) ὁ λύχνος *the lamp is brought* **Mk 4:21.** Sim. ἐλθούσης τ. ἐντολῆς *when the commandment came* **Ro 7:9.**

❹ **to take place,** ***come***—ⓐ of time—**α.** of temporal increments ἔρχονται ἡμέραι in future sense (1 Km 2:31; Am 8:11) **Lk 23:29; Hb 8:8** (Jer 38:31); ἐλεύσονται ἡμ. **Mt 9:15; Mk 2:20; Lk 5:35; 17:22; 21:6** (TestSol 13:7 C; Just., D. 40, 2). ἦλθεν ἡ ἡμέρα **22:7; Rv 6:17.**—ἔρχεται ὥρα ὅτε *the time is coming when* **J 4:21, 23; 5:25; 16:25;** also ἔ. ὥρα ἐν ᾗ **J 5:28;** ἔ. ὥρα ἵνα **16:2, 32.** ἦλθεν ἡ ὥρα *the hour has come=the hour is here* **Mk 14:41b; J 16:4; Rv 14:7, 15;** w. ἵνα foll. **J 13:1** (ἥκω P66). ἐλήλυθεν ἡ ὥ. ἵνα **12:23; 16:32;** without ἵνα **17:1;** cp. **7:30; 8:20.**—ἔρχεται νύξ **9:4** (Appian, Bell. Civ. 2, 40 §159 νυκτὸς ἐρχομένης). ἡμέρα κυρίου **1 Th 5:2.** καιροί **Ac 3:20** (GrBar 8:1 ὁ καιρός). τὸ πλήρωμα τ. χρόνου **Gal 4:4.**

β. of events and situations that are connected w. a certain time ὁ θερισμός **J 4:35.** ὁ γάμος τ. ἀρνίου **Rv 19:7.** ἡ κρίσις **18:10.** So also the ptc. ἐρχόμενος *coming, future, imminent:* αἰὼν ἔ. (=הָעוֹלָם הַבָּא) *the age to come* **Mk 10:30; Lk 18:30;** ἑορτὴ ἔ. *the coming festival* **Ac 18:21 v.l.;** σάββατον ἔ. **13:44;** ὀργὴ ἔ. *the wrath which will be revealed* (at the Judgment) **1 Th 1:10.** τὰ ἐρχόμενα *what is to come* (Is 44:7 τὰ ἐπερχόμενα) **J 16:13.** Of God in **Rv** ὁ ὢν κ. ὁ ἦν κ. ὁ ἐρχόμενος **1:4, 8; 4:8.**

ⓑ of events and circumstances—**α.** of natural or sensory phenomena (Hom. et al.; also TestAbr A 19 p. 102, 10 [Stone p. 52]; βροντῆς … καὶ ἀστραπῆς ἐλθούσης; ApcEsdr 5:7 νεφέλη) ποταμοί **Mt 7:25, 27.** κατακλυσμός **Lk 17:27.** λιμός **Ac 7:11.** Of rain ἔ. ἐπὶ τῆς γῆς *come upon the earth* **Hb 6:7.** Sim. of the coming down of birds fr. the air **Mt 13:4, 32; Mk 4:4;** of a voice resounding fr. heaven ἦλθεν φωνὴ ἐκ τ. οὐρανοῦ **J 12:28** (Test Abr A 10 p. 88, 15 and 14 p. 94, 25 [Stone p. 24; p. 36]; Just., D. 88, 8; cp. Il. 10, 139; En 13:8; TestSol 1:3 VW; TestJob 3:1; ParJer 9:12; ApcEsdr 7:13).

β. of transcendent and moral-spiritual phenomena: of spiritual coming of God *come, appear* **J 14:23;** of Christ **ibid.** and vss. **3, 18, 28;** of the Paraclete **15:26; 16:7, 13.**—ἡ ἀποστασία **2 Th 2:3.** ἡ βασιλεία τ. θεοῦ **Mt 6:10; Lk 11:2** (MBurrows, JBL 74, '55, 1–8); **17:20; 22:18** al.; 1 Cl 42:3.—τ. σκάνδαλα **Mt 18:7; Lk 17:1.** τὰ ἀγαθά **Ro 3:8** (cp. Jer. 17:6). τὸ τέλειον **1 Cor 13:10.** ἡ πίστις **Gal 3:23, 25.**

❺ ἐ. in var. prepositional combinations ἔ. ἐκ τ. θλίψεως *have suffered persecution* **Rv 7:14.** ἔ. εἰς τὸ χεῖρον **Mk 5:26** (Witkowski no. 36, 12=White no. 35 τοῦ παιδίου εἰς τὰ ἔσχατα ἐληλυθότος of a child in desperate circumstances; TestAbr A 20 p. 102, 27 [Stone p. 52] εἰς θάνατον ἔρχονται). εἰς τοσαύτην ἀπόνοιαν, ὥστε 1 Cl 46:7 (Hyperid. 2, 5 εἰς τοῦτο ἀπονοίας ἔ., ὥστε). εἰς πειρασμόν **Mk 14:38** (cp. Himerius, Or. 48 [Or. 14], 19 εἰς ἐπιθυμίαν ἐλθεῖν). εἰς ἀπελεγμόν **Ac 19:27.** εἰς τὴν ὥραν ταύτην **J 12:27.** ἔ. εἰς κρίσιν *submit to judgment* (letter of Philip in Demosth. 12, 11; 16; ApcEsdr 2:26 ἔλθωμεν ὁμοῦ εἰς κρίσιν) **5:24.** εἰς ἐπίγνωσιν **1 Ti 2:4; 2 Ti 3:7** (Polyb. 6, 9, 12; Appian, Mithr. 31 §123 ἔρχεσθαι ἐς γνῶσίν τινος; Cebes 12, 3 εἰς τὴν ἀληθινὴν παιδείαν ἐλθεῖν; TestSol 20:5 εἰς ἔννοιαν ἐλθεῖν; Just., D. 90, 1 οὐδ' εἰς ἔννοιαν τούτου ἐλθεῖν). ἵνα ἔλθω εἰς τὴν ἐκ νεκρῶν ἀνάστασιν *so that I might realize the resurrection of the dead* (cp. ApcMos 10 εἰς τὴν ἡμέραν τῆς ἀναστάσεως) AcPlCor 2:35. εἰς φανερόν *come to light* **Mk 4:22; Lk 8:17.** εἰς προκοπὴν *result in furthering* **Phil 1:12** (cp. Wsd 15:5). ἔ. εἴς τι of the writer of a letter *come to,* i.e. *deal with someth.* (a new subject) **2 Cor 12:1** (cp. w. ἐπὶ Ar. 2:1 al.; Just., D. 42 ἐπὶ τὸν λόγον). εἰς ἑαυτόν *come to oneself* (=to one's senses) (Diod. S. 13, 95, 2; Epict. 3, 1, 15; TestJos 3:9; GrBar 17:3; Sb 5763, 35) **Lk 15:17.** ἐπί τινα of serious misfortunes *come over someone* (Dt 28:15; Jos., Ant. 4, 128) **J 18:4** (cp. PIand 21, 2 ἡμῶν τὰ ἐρχόμενα οὐκ οἶδα); tortures IRo 5:3; blood upon the murderers **Mt 23:35;** the Holy Spirit comes down upon someone (cp. Ezk 2:2; Just., D. 49, 7; 88, 1 ἐλεύσεσθαι ἐπ' αὐτὸν τὰς δυνάμεις) **Mt 3:16; Lk 11:2 v.l.; Ac 19:6;** peace **Mt 10:13;** the wrath of God **Eph 5:6;** cp. **Col 3:6;** ἡ βασιλεία **Lk 11:2** D; ἔ. πρὸς τ. Ἰησοῦν *come to Jesus= become disciples of Jesus* **J 5:40; 6:35, 37, 44f, 65;** πρὸς τ. πατέρα **14:6.** ἔ. ὑπὸ τὸν ζυγόν 1 Cl 16:17 (cp. PsSol 18, 7f. ὑπὸ ῥάβδον παιδείας Χριστοῦ).—Not infreq. the pres. ἔρχομαι has the mng. of the fut.: **Mt 17:11; Lk 12:54** (corresp. to καύσων ἔσται vs. 55); **19:13; J 14:3.** Esp. also ἕως ἔρχομαι *until I shall come* **J 21:22f; 1 Ti 4:13;** Hs 5, 2, 2; 9, 10, 5; 6; 9, 11, 1. S. B-D-F §323; 383, 1; Rob. 869. S. also 4αα above.—B. 696. DELG. M-M. EDNT. TW.

ἐρῶ s. εἶπον.—M-M.

ἔρως, ωτος, ὁ (s. ἐράω; Hom. et al.; Herm. Wr., pap; Pr 7:18; 30:16; Philo; Jos., Ant. 1, 302, C. Ap. 2, 244; Just. D. 8, 1 of Justin's passionate interest in the prophets and Christ's friends; Tat. 1:3; Ath. 30:3) ***ardor, fondness*** ὁ ἐμὸς ἔ. ἐσταύρωται *my ardor* (for the world) *has been crucified* (cp. Gal 6:14) IRo 7:2.—S. ἀγάπη 1 end.—B. 1110. DELG s.v. ἔραμαι. Sv.

ἐρωτάω fut. ἐρωτήσω; 1 aor. ἠρώτησα; 2 aor. ἠρόμην, fr. ἔρομαι, s. Schwyzer I 746, 7 (Just., D. 3, 5; Ath. 35, 1). Pass.: 1 aor. 3 sg. ἠρωτήθη 2 Km 20:18, inf. ἐρωτηθῆναι (TestAbr B 4 p. 108, 22 [Stone p. 64]), ptc. ἐρωτηθείς (TestSol 11, 1 C); pf. ptc. ἠρωτημένος 2 Km 20:18.

❶ **to put a query to someone, *ask, ask a question*** (Hom.+) abs. (Da 2:10; 1 Macc 10:72) **Lk 22:68.** τινά *someone* (Lucian, D. Deor. 7, 1; Gen 24:47; 40:7; Ex 13:14 al.; En 22:6; TestSol 7:4 al.; TestJob 47:5; Just., D. 3, 5) **J 1:25; 8:7; 9:21; 16:19, 30** al. τινά τι *someone about someth.* (X., Mem. 3, 7, 2, Cyr. 3, 3, 48; Job 21:29; TestSol 3:6 D; Jos., Ant. 6, 48; Just., D. 68, 4) ὑμᾶς λόγον ἕνα *ask you one question* **Mt 21:24=Lk 20:3** (cp. Pla., Leg. 10, 895e; Jer 45:14; ApcSed 8:5 al.; TestJob 36:5); αὐτὸν τὰς παραβολάς *ask him about the parables* **Mk 4:10.** Certainly **J 16:23** belongs here too. τινὰ περί τινος *someone about someth.* (2 Esdr 11:2; Is 45:11; Just., D. 94, 4) **Mt 19:17; Lk 9:45; J 18:19.** W. τινά and direct question (X., An. 1, 6, 7; TestSol 15:2 al.; TestAbr A 10 p. 87, 30 [Stone p. 22]; GrBar 9:5 al.; Just., D. 99, 3) **Mk 8:5; Lk 19:31; J 1:19, 21; 5:12; 16:5;** the direct quest. introduced by λέγων or λέγοντες (En 23:3; TestSol 7:3 al.; TestJob 44:4; ParJer 2:4) **Mt 16:13; J 9:2, 19.** W. τινά and indir. quest. foll. (X., Cyr. 8, 5, 19; Just., A I, 17, 2, D. 64, 3) **9:15.** Cp. **Lk 23:6** P[75] (s. ed. note and s.v. ἐπερωτάω 1a; ἐρωτ. εἰ also Thu. 1, 5, 2).

❷ **to ask for someth., *ask, request*** (Babrius 42, 3; 97, 3; Apollon. Dysc., Synt. 3, 167 Uhlig ἐρωτῶ σε νῦν ἐν ἴσῳ τῷ παρακαλῶ σε, λιτανεύω, ἱκνοῦμαι; SIG 705, 56 [112 BC]; 741, 5 [after 88 BC]; POxy 744, 6; 13 [1 BC]; 292, 7 [c. 25 AD]; 110; 111; 113; 269; 745; 746 al.; Jer 44:17; Jos., Ant. 7, 164; TestSim 4:1.—Dssm., B 30; 31; 45, NB 23f [BS 195f; 290f]) τὶ *for someth.* **Lk 14:32** (s. εἰρήνη 1 a). περί τινος *for someth.* Hv 3, 1, 6b (w. ἵνα foll.). τὶ περί τινος *for someth. concerning a thing* 3, 1, 6a. W. acc. of pers.: τινά *someone* **J 14:16** (Field, Notes 101f). τ. κύριον Hv 2, 2, 1 (Jos., Ant. 5, 42 ἐ. τ. θεόν; SibOr 2, 309). Foll. by λέγων, which introduces the request in direct discourse **Mt 15:23; Lk 7:4 v.l.; J 4:31; 12:21.** W. impv. foll. (BGU 423, 11 ἐρωτῶ σε οὖν, γράψον μοι ἐπιστόλιον; POxy 745, 7; 746, 5) **Lk 14:18f; Phil 4:3.** τινὰ περί τινος *beseech someone on someone's behalf* (JosAs 15:7 περὶ τῶν μετανοούντων ἐρωτᾷ αὐτόν [about the topic Μετάνοια]) **Lk 4:38; J 16:26; 17:9, 20;** *concerning someth.* **1J 5:16,** sim. ὑπέρ τινος **2 Th 2:1** (on the interchange of περί and ὑπέρ s. B-D-F §229, 1; 231; Rob. 629; 632). τινὰ κατὰ τοῦ κυρίου *beseech someone by the Lord* Hv 3, 2, 3 (B-D-F §225). W. ἵνα foll. (POxy 744, 13 [1 BC]) **Mk 7:26; Lk 7:36; 16:27; J 4:47; 17:15; 19:31, 38; 2J 5.** W. ὅπως foll. (SIG 741, 5 [after 88 BC]; PTebt 409, 4; 6; En 13:4) **Lk 7:3; 11:37; Ac 23:20.** W. inf. foll. (Chariton 8, 7, 3; PTebt 410, 11; PRyl 229, 8 [38 AD]; POxy 292, 7 [c. 25 AD]; Jos., Ant. 6, 328) **Lk 5:3; 8:37; J 4:40; Ac 3:3; 10:48; 16:39; 18:20; 1 Th 5:12.** Foll. by εἰς and subst. inf. **2 Th 2:1.**—ἐ. and παρακαλέω together (POxy 744, 6; 294, 28 [22 AD]. S. the quot. fr. Apollon. Dysc., above) **1 Th 4:1.** —*Urge* w. inf., impv. et al. B 4:6; 21:2, 4, 7.—B. 1264; 1271. DELG s.v. ἐρέω. M-M. TW.

ἐρώτησις, εως, ἡ (='question' Hippocr. et al.; OGI 508, 10; PSI X, 1179, 48 [II/III AD, lit.]; En; ParJer 4:4f cod. C; Philo, Rer. Div. Her. 18; Just., A II, 3, 4ff) ***request*** (so prob. Syntipas 105, 30) of a prayer Hv 3, 10, 6. S. prec. entry.—DELG s.v. ἐρέω.

ἔσβεσα s. σβέννυμι.

ἐσήμανα s. σημαίνω.

Ἐσθήρ, ἡ (אֶסְתֵּר) (indecl. in the book of Esther; in Jos., Ant. 11, 199; 225; 227 al. Ἐσθήρ, ῆρος) ***Esther,*** hero of the book named after her 1 Cl 55:6.

ἐσθής, ῆτος, ἡ (ἕννυμι 'put clothing on'; Hom.+) ***clothing*** **Lk 23:11; 24:4; Ac 10:30** (cp. SIG 1157, 39; OGI 332, 38 ἐν ἐσθῆσιν λαμπραῖς); **12:21** (=Jos., Ant. 19, 344 στολὴν ἐνδὺς ἐξ ἀργύρου πεποιημένην πᾶσαν); **Js 2:2f;** Dg 5:4. The dat. pl. form ἐσθήσεσι, which is not unanimously attested either in **Ac 1:10** or **Lk 24:4** (but found 2 Macc 3:33; 3 Macc 1:16; Philo, Vi. Mos. 2, 152; BGU 16, 12 [159/60 AD]; PLond I, 77, 20, 32 p. 233 [VIII AD]. S. also Crönert 173, 1. The form ἐσθῆσιν Jos., Bell. 2, 176 becomes ἐσθήσεσιν in Eus., HE 2, 6, 7.), does not come from a word ἔσθησις, for which there is no reliable evidence in the sing., nor in the pl. except for the dative (s. L-S-J-M), but belongs to ἐσθής; it is the result of an attempt to make the dat. ending more conspicuous by doubling it (WSchulze, ZVS 42, 1909, 235, 2; Schwyzer I, 604). ἔσθεσι Dg 5:1 was in the original, glossed w. ἱματίοις; s. the ed. of Marrou ad loc.

B-D-F §47, 4; Mlt-H. 133.—B. 395. DELG s.v. ἕννυμι. M-M. TW.

ἐσθίω (Hom.+) and, mainly in the ptc., **ἔσθω** (Hom., also in other poets, rare in prose [Plut., Mor. p. 101d]; Coan ins, III BC: RHerzog, ARW 10, 1907, 400ff; 23; 27; 42; POslo 153, 15 [beg. II AD]; PGiss 80, 5; ostraca [BGU 1507, 14; 1508, 3; 4: III BC]; LXX; En 98:11 [?]. ἔσθων Lev 17:14; 1 Km 14:30; Sir 20:17; **Mk 1:6; Lk 7:33f, 10:7** [the three last v.l.]; μὴ ἔσθετε Lev 19:26. ὅταν ἔσθητε Num 15:19. ἵνα ἔσθητε **Lk 22:30.** B-D-F §101; W-S. §15; Mlt-H. 238; Schwyzer, I 704 n. 1). Impf. ἤσθιον; fut. ἔδομαι LXX (Mel, P. 12, 80; 13, 83; 93, 697; 1 Cl 39:9; 57:6); 2 aor. ἔφαγον, w. extension of 1 aor. endings (B-D-F §84, 2; Rob. 333; cp. Schwyzer I 753f): 3 pl. ἐφάγοσαν Ps 77:29, 1 pl. ἐφάγαμεν 2 Km 19:43; fut. φάγομαι (B-D-F §74, 2; Mlt-H. 238), 2 sing. φάγεσαι **Lk 17:8;** Ruth 2:14 (W-S. §13, 6 and 17; B-D-F §87; Mlt-H. 198); pf. pass. ptc. acc. ἐδηδεμένους (Ath., R. 52, 20); pres. 3 sg. ἔσθεται Lev 11:34; Dt 12:22.

❶ **to take someth. in through the mouth, usually solids, but also liquids,** ***eat.***—ⓐ w. acc. of thing (Hom. et al.) τί φάγωσιν (after neg.) *anything to eat* **Mt 15:32; Mk 6:36; 8:1f;** cp. **Mt 6:25, 31; Lk 12:22** (s. Epict. 1, 9, 8; 19). τοὺς ἄρτους τῆς προθέσεως *the consecrated bread* **Mt 12:4; Mk 2:26; Lk 6:4.** Locusts and wild honey **Mk 1:6.** Manna (Ps 77:24) **J 6:31, 49** (Just., D. 20, 4). Vegetables **Ro 14:2b.** Meat **14:21; 1 Cor 8:13;** GEb 308, 31f; 34f (τὰς σάρκας αὐτῶν 'one's own flesh' 4 [6] Esdr; POxy 1010). τὰ εἰδωλόθυτα **1 Cor 8:10;** cp. vs. **7; Rv 2:14, 20** (Just., D. 34, 8; 35, 1). τὰς θυσίας (Sir 45:21; Ps 105:28) **1 Cor 10:18.** τὰ ἐκ τοῦ ἱεροῦ *food from the temple* **9:13.** τὴν σάρκα τ. υἱοῦ τ. ἀνθρώπου **J 6:53** (which passage many interpret as referring to the Eucharist while others explain it as speaking of receiving Christ spiritually through faith). πάντα *all kinds of food* **Ro 14:2a** (μὴ πάντα ἐσθίοντες Just., 20, 3). τὰ παρατιθέμενα *the food that is set before (one)* **Lk 10:8; 1 Cor 10:27.** τὸ ἐν μακέλλῳ πωλούμενον **10:25.** τὸ βιβλαρίδιον **Rv 10:10** (cp. Ezk 2:8; 3:3). τὸ πάσχα *the Passover meal,* esp. *the Passover lamb* (2 Esdr 6:21; 2 Ch 30:18; ESchürer, Über φαγεῖν τὸ πάσχα 1883; Dalman, Jesus 81f) **Mt 26:17; Mk 14:12, 14; Lk 22:8, 11, 15; J 18:28.** κυριακὸν δεῖπνον φαγεῖν **1 Cor 11:20.** ἄρτον ἐσθίειν *eat a meal,* w. bread as its main part (Ex 2:20; 1 Km 20:34; 2 Km 9:7; 3 Km 13:15 al.) **Mt 15:2; Mk 3:20; 7:2, 5; Lk 14:1** (s. Billerb. IV 611–39: E. altjüd. Gastmahl); of the end-time banquet **Lk 14:15** (cp. ἄρτον ζωῆς JosAs 15:4). τὸν ἑαυτοῦ ἄρτον ἐ. *eat one's own bread* **2 Th 3:12.** ἄρτον φαγεῖν παρά τινος *eat someone's bread* vs. **8.** τὰ παρά τινος *what someone provides* **Lk 10:7.** Neg. οὐκ ἔφαγεν οὐδέν *he ate nothing at all* **Lk 4:2** (cp. Job 21:25 οὐ φαγὼν οὐδὲν ἀγαθόν; En 15:11 πνεύματα … μηδὲν ἐσθίοντα). Of complete abstinence μὴ ἐσθίων ἄρτον μήτε πίνων οἶνον **7:33.** οὔτε ἐπὶ τὸ φαγεῖν οὔτε ἐπὶ τὸ πεῖν AcPl Ox 6, 7=Aa 241, 12f. οὐδέποτε ἔφαγον πᾶν κοινόν *I have never eaten anything common at all* **Ac 10:14** (cp. 1 Macc 1:62; Just., D. 20, 3). Allegorical interpretation of Mosaic laws against eating forbidden foods B 10 (cp. Hierocles 26 p. 480 reinterpretation of the Pythagorean laws against forbidden foods as moral laws).—Of animals (Hom. et al.; Aelian, VH 1, 1; 2, 40; 3 Km 13:28; Is 65:25; Da 4:33 Theod.; GrBar 4:5 [δράκων]; 6:11 [Φοῖνιξ): birds τὰς σάρκας τινός *eat someone's flesh* (Gen 40:19) **Rv 17:16; 19:18.** Swine **Lk 15:16** (ὧν here is for ἅ by attraction, not a gen. dependent on ἐ., as it prob. is in X., Hell. 3, 3, 6; Ps.-Lucian, Asin. 21; such a constr. would be unique in our lit.).

ⓑ w. prepositions, to denote the thing of which one partakes: α. w. ἀπό τινος (Lev 22:6; Num 15:19; Dt 14:12, 19; Pr 13:2; Da 4:33a; ApcSed 4:5; ApcMos 17 al.) dogs: ἐ. ἀπὸ τῶν ψιχίων *eat the crumbs* **Mt 15:27; Mk 7:28** (on the pl. ἐσθίουσιν after the neut. κυνάρια cp. Lk 11:7; 1 Cl 42:2; B-D-F §133; s. Rob. 403f). ἀπὸ τραπέζης *partake of a meal* D 11:9. ἀπὸ τῆς εὐχαριστίας 9:5.

β. w. ἔκ τινος *of/from someth.* (Jdth 12:2; Sir 11:19; JosAs 16:7f; ApcMos 16f) ἐκ τοῦ ἄρτου *eat (some of) the bread* (2 Km 12:3; Tob 1:10; TestJob 7:10 ἐκ τῶν ἄρτων μου) **1 Cor 11:28;** cp. **J 6:26, 50f.** ἐκ τῶν καρπῶν αὐτῶν Hs 9, 1, 10. ἐκ τοῦ γάλακτος τῆς ποίμνης *get sustenance fr. the milk of the flock* **1 Cor 9:7.** ἐκ τ. θυσιαστηρίου **Hb 13:10.** ἐκ τ. ξύλου τ. ζωῆς *from the tree of life* **Rv 2:7** (s. En 32:6); cp. μηκέτι ἐκ σοῦ μηδεὶς καρπὸν φάγοι (v.l. φάγῃ) **Mk 11:14.**

ⓒ used with other prep. expressions ἐ. μετά τινος *eat w. someone* (1 Km 9:19; Jdth 12:11; Job 1:4; Ezk 47:22; TestAbr B 4 p. 109, 10 [Stone p. 66]) **Mt 9:11; 24:49; Mk 2:16; 14:18** (cp. Ps 40:10); **Lk 5:30; 7:36.** ἐνώπιόν τινος *in someone's presence* (cp. ἐναντίον τ. θεοῦ Ex 18:12; Ezk 44:3) **13:26; 24:43.** ἐπὶ τ. τραπέζης τινός *at someone's table* (2 Km 9:11; cp. vs. 13; Da 11:27) **Lk 22:30.** διὰ προσκόμματος ἐ. *eat with offense* (i.e. so that one takes offense in doing so; perh. also so that one gives offense) **Ro 14:20.**

ⓓ abs. **Mt 12:1; 14:20; 26:21, 26; Mk 7:3f; 14:18a, 22; Ac 27:35;** D 12:3; B 7:5 al. Used w. λαμβάνειν (Gen 3:22) λάβετε φάγετε **Mt 26:26b;** οἱ ἐσθίοντες **14:21; 15:38.** φάγωμεν κ. πίωμεν *let us eat and drink* **1 Cor 15:32** (Is 22:13; Ath., R. 72, 11). φάγε, πίε, εὐφραίνου **Lk 12:19** (Aristobulus of Cass. [III BC]: 139 fgm. 9 Jac. [cited in Strabo 14, 5, 9], statue of Sardanapalus w. the ins ἔσθιε, πῖνε, παῖζε· ὡς τἆλλα τούτου οὐκ ἄξια='Eat, drink, have fun. There's nothing like it.' This saying of Sardanapalus is also found in Arrian, Anab. 2, 5, 4. A similar thought in the Phrygian grave-ins: IGal 78, 11ff). τὸ φαγεῖν *eating* **Mt 15:20; 1 Cor 11:21.** διδόναι τινὶ φαγεῖν *give someone someth. to eat* (Ex 16:8, 15; Num 11:18, 21) **Mt 14:16; 25:35, 42; Mk 5:43; 6:37; Lk 8:55; 9:13; J 6:52; Rv 2:7.** φέρειν τινὶ φαγεῖν (cp. 2 Km 17:29) **J 4:33.** εὐκαιρέω φαγεῖν *I find time to eat* **Mk 6:31.** ἔχω βρῶσιν φαγεῖν *I have food to eat* **J 4:32.**—With the principle stated in **2 Th 3:10** cp. Lucian, Par. 13: when a pupil progresses well δότε αὐτῷ φαγεῖν; when he does not, μὴ δῶτε.

ⓔ ἐ. and πίνω are freq. found together, as in some pass. already quoted (Hom. et al.; very oft. LXX; En 102:9; 4 [6] Esdr [POxy 1010]; TestAbr A 4 p. 81, 16 [Stone p. 10]; B 5 p. 109, 16 [Stone p. 66]; JosAs 9:3 al.; Philo, Det. Pot. ins 113; Jos., C. Ap. 2, 234).

α. = receive support **1 Cor 9:4.**—**β.** = eat a meal **Lk 5:30; 17:8; 1 Cor 11:22;** AcPl Ox 6, 7. Of a festive sacrificial meal **1 Cor 10:7** (Ex 32:6).

γ. in contrast to fasting—the latter expressed by ἐ. and πίνω w. a neg. (Iambl., Vi. Pyth. 28, 141 οὔτε πίνων οὔτε ἐσθίων) **Mt 11:18; Lk 4:2 v.l.; 7:33; Ac 9:9; 23:12, 21—Mt 11:19; Lk 5:33; 7:34;** B 7:5.

δ. of ordinary daily activities **Lk 17:27f.**

ε. of carefree, even luxurious or dissipated living **Mt 24:49; Lk 12:19, 45; 1 Cor 15:32** (cp. Is 22:13).—HRiesenfeld, ConNeot 9, '44, 10f.

❷ **to do away with completely,** fig. extension of mng. 1 (Hom. et al.; LXX) ***consume, devour*** (of fire Il. 23, 182; Is 10:17; 26:11) πυρὸς ἐσθίειν μέλλοντος τ. ὑπεναντίους *fire, which is about to consume the adversaries* **Hb 10:27** (Is 26:11). ὁ ἰὸς … φάγεται τ. σάρκας ὑμῶν ὡς πῦρ *the rust will eat your flesh like fire* **Js 5:3** (cp. Aeschyl., fgm. 253 φαγέδαινα [an ulcer] σάρκας ἐσθίει ποδός; Is 30:27 ἡ ὀργὴ τοῦ θυμοῦ ὡς πῦρ ἔδεται). B. 327.—DELG s.v. ἔδω. M-M. EDNT. TW.

ἔσθω s. ἐσθίω.

Ἑσλί, ὁ (Ἐσλί t.r. Merk., Bov.; Ἐσλεί Tdf., W-H., Sod., Vog.) indecl. ***Esli,*** in the genealogy of Jesus **Lk 3:25.**

ἐσόμενος s. εἰμί.

ἔσοπτρον, ου, τό (Pind., N. 7, 14 [20]; Anacreontea 7, 3; 22, 5 Pr.; Plut., Mor. 139e; Epict. 2, 14, 21; 3, 22, 51; Proclus on Plato, Timaeus 33b Diehl II p. 80, 20; CPR I, 27, 10 [190 AD]; ins s. New Docs 4, 149f; POxy 978; 1449, 19 ἔσοπτρον ἀργυροῦν; Wsd 7:26; Sir 12:11; TestJob 33:8; Philo, Migr. Abr. 98; Jos., Ant. 12, 81; ὁρᾶσθαι τὸ πρόσωπον τοῦ ἀνθρώπου ἐν τῷ ἐ. Theoph. Ant. 1, 2 [p. 60, 23]) ***mirror*** κατανοεῖν τὸ πρόσωπον ἐν ἐ. *look at one's face in a mirror* **Js 1:23.** δι' ἐσόπτρου βλέπειν ἐν αἰνίγματι *see indirectly in a mirror* (because one sees not the thing itself, but its mirror-image; cp. Herm. Wr. 17) **1 Cor 13:12.** On this s. Straub 44–46; RSeeberg: D. Reformation 10, 1911, 137–39; Rtzst., Hist. Mon. 238–55; HAchelis, Bonwetsch Festschr. 1918, 56ff; PCorssen, ZNW 19, 1920, 2–10; SBassett, 1 Cor 13:12: JBL 47, 1928, 232ff; JBehm, D. Bildwort v. Spiegel 1 Cor 13:12: RSeeberg Festschr. I 1929, 315–42; WKnox, St. Paul and the Church of the Gentiles '39, 121 n. 4; APerry, ET 58, '46/47, 279; NHugedé, La Métaphore du miroir dans 1 et 2 Cor. '57; FDanker, CTM 30, '60, 428f. S. the lit. on 1 Cor 13 s.v. ἀγάπη 1aα, esp. HRiesenfeld, ConNeot 5. At Ox 1081, 43 [. . . . . .]ρω must certainly be read ἐσόπτρῳ after the Coptic (s. WTill, TU 60/5 ['55] 223).—New Docs 4, 149f. DELG s.v. ὄπωπα. M-M. TW. Spicq.

ἑσπέρα, ας, ἡ (Pind., Hdt.+) ***evening*** **Ac 4:3;** τῇ ἑ. *in the evening* **20:15 v.l.** ἕως ἑσπέρας (Jos., Ant. 6, 364; also μέχρις ἑ. Just.): ἀπὸ πρωῒ ἕως ἑσπέρας *from morning till evening* (3 Km 22:35) **28:23.** Also ἀπὸ προΐθεν ἕως ἑσπέρας (Ex 18:13; Sir 18:26) 1 Cl 39:5 (Job 4:20). ἀφ' ἑσπ[έρας| ἕως π]ρωῒ (Lev 24:3) Ox 655, 2 (GTh 36; Kl. Texte 8^3 p. 23 ln. 15; Fitzmyer, Oxy. 544). πρὸς ἑ. ἐστίν *it is getting toward evening* **Lk 24:29** (X., Hell. 4, 3, 22 ἐπεὶ πρὸς ἑσπέραν ἦν; Hierocles 27 p. 484; Ex 12:6; Jos., Ant. 5, 195; cp. πρὸς ἑσπέρᾳ ἐστίν TestSol B 2 p. 106, 7).—B. 997. DELG s.v. ἕσπερος. M-M.

ἑσπερινός, ή, όν (s. prec. entry; since X., Resp. Lac. 12, 6; POxy 901, 5; BGU 1024 VI, 6; LXX) **pert. to the evening,** ***of evening*** φυλακή the first watch of the night, six to nine p.m. **Lk 12:38 v.l.**—M-M.

Ἑσρώμ, ὁ (also Ἐ-, Ἑσρών, Ἐσρών) indecl. *Hezron,* in the genealogy of Jesus (1 Ch 2:5 v.l., 9; in Ruth 4:18f v.l.) **Mt 1:3; Lk 3:33.**

ἑσσόομαι 1 aor. ἡσσώθην (Ionic for ἡσσάομαι—Hdt. 1, 82, 3; 2, 169, 1; 8, 130, 2; s. JWackernagel, Hellenistica 1907, 17–19; B-D-F §34, 1; Mlt-H. 107; 240; 396; difft. W-S. §15, p. 127) **to be put in lesser or worse circumstances or status,** ***be inferior to*** or ***be worse off than*** τί γάρ ἐστιν ὃ ἡσσώθητε ὑπὲρ τὰς λοιπὰς ἐκκλησίας; *in what respect, then, are you being made to feel less important than the other congregations?* **2 Cor 12:13** (ἡττήθητε v.l.).—FZorell, BZ 9, 1911, 160f. DELG s.v. ἧκα.

ἑστάθην, ἑστάναι, ἕστηκα, ἕστην, ἕστησα s. ἵστημι.

ἐστράφην s. στρέφω.

ἐστρωμένος, ἔστρωσαν s. στρώννυμι.

ἔστω s. εἰμί.

ἑστώς s. ἵσταμαι.

ἔστωσαν s. εἰμί.

ἐσφάγη s. σφάζω.

ἔσχατος, η, ον (Hom.+) gener. 'last'—**❶ pert. to being at the farthest boundary of an area,** ***farthest, last*** ὁ ἔσχατος τόπος, perh. to be understood locally of the place in the farthest corner **Lk 14:9f** (but s. 2 below).—Subst. τὸ ἔσχατον *the end* (schol. on Apollon. Rhod. 4, 1515a p. 319, 19 εἰς τὸ ἔσχατον τῆς νήσου; PTebt 68, 54 [II BC] of a document) ἕως ἐσχάτου τῆς γῆς *to the end of the earth* (Is 48:20; 62:11; 1 Macc 3:9; PsSol 1:4; εἰς τὸ ἔ. τῆς γῆς TestSol 7:6 D) **Ac 1:8** (CBurchard, D. Dreizehnte Zeuge, '70, 134 n. 309; EEllis, 'The End of the Earth', Acts 1:8: Bulletin for Biblical Research 1, '91, 123–32, tr. of his text in: Der Treue Gottes Trauen, Beiträge . . . für Gerhard Schneider, ed. CBussmann and WRadl '91, 277–86 [Luke wrote in mid-60's and Paul reached Gades in Spain]; BBecking, DDD 573–76); **13:47;** B 14:8 (the two last Is 49:6). Pl. (Hes., Theog. 731 and an oracle in Hdt. 7, 140 ἔσχατα γαίης; X., Vect. 1, 6; Diod. S. 1, 60, 5; Ael. Aristid. 35, 14 K.=9 p. 103 D.: ἐσχ. γῆς; Crates, Ep. 31 and Demosth., Ep. 4, 7 ἐπ' ἔσχατα γῆς) τὰ ἔ. τῆς γῆς *the ends of the earth* 1 Cl 28:3 (Theocr. 15, 8; schol. on Apollon. Rhod. 2, 413–18b. With εἰς before it Ps 138:9).

❷ pert. to being the final item in a series, ***least, last*** in time

ⓐ coming last or the last of someth. that is left w. ref. to its relation with someth. preceding **Mt 20:12, 14; Mk 12:6, 22; J 8:9 v.l.** Opp. πρῶτος (2 Ch 9:29 al.; Sir 24:28; 41:3): ἀπὸ τῶν ἐ. ἕως τῶν πρώτων **Mt 20:8;** cp. **27:64; 1 Cor 15:45** (ἔ. also the later of two, as Dt 24:3f ἔ. . . . πρότερος; hence 1 Cor 15:47 replaced by δεύτερος). Cp. **Mt 21:31 v.l.** ὁ. ἔ. *the latter*. Of things τὰ ἔσχατα **Rv 2:19;** Hv 1, 4, 2. τὰ ἔσχατα (in contrast to τὰ πρῶτα as Job 8:7; TestSol 26:8) *the last state* **Mt 12:45; Lk 11:26; 2 Pt 2:20.** Of the creation in the last days ποιῶ τ. ἔσχατα ὡς τ. πρῶτα (apocryphal quot.; cp. Hippolytus, Comm. on Daniel 4:37) B 6:13.

ⓑ w. ref. to a situation in which there is nothing to follow the ἔ. (Diod. S. 19, 59, 6 κρίσιν ἐσχάτην τῆς περὶ Δημήτριον βασιλείας=the last [final] crisis in the reign of Demetrius; TestAbr B 3 p. 108, 3 [Stone p. 64] ἐσχατός μού ἐστιν): ἡ ἐ. ἡμέρα τ. ἑορτῆς (cp. 2 Esdr 18:18) **J 7:37.** τὴν ἐ. ἡμέραν τῆς ζωῆς Hv 3, 12, 2; ἐν τῇ ἐσχάτῃ αὐτοῦ ἡμέρᾳ *in the last days of his life* GJs 1:3 (cp. ApcEsd 7:10 ὥσπερ καὶ τὰ ἔσχατα τοῦ Ἰωσήφ). ὁ ἔ. κοδράντης (cp. 2 Esdr 15:15) **Mt 5:26; Lk 12:59 v.l.;** D 1:5; cp. **1 Cor 15:26, 52; Rv 15:1; 21:9.** τὴν . . . ἐ. ῥάβδον GJs 9:1. τὰ ἔ. ῥήματα *the last words* (of a speech) Hv 1, 3, 3. As a self-designation of the Risen Lord ὁ πρῶτος καὶ ὁ ἔ. *the first and the last* **Rv 1:17; 2:8; 22:13.** Esp. of the last days, which are sometimes thought of as beginning w. the birth of Christ, somet. w. his second coming ἡ ἐ. ἡμέρα *the last day* (PViereck, Sermo Gr., quo senatus pop. Rom. magistratusque . . . usi sunt 1888 ins 29, 9 [116 BC] εἰς ἐσχάτην ἡμέραν=forever) **J 6:39f, 44, 54; 11:24; 12:48** (ApcMos 41; BAebert, D. Eschatol. des J, diss. Bres. '36); Hv 2, 2, 5. Pl. (Is 2:2) **Ac 2:17; 2 Ti 3:1; Js 5:3;** D 16:3; B 4:9. ἐπ' ἐσχάτου τῶν ἡμερῶν τούτων (Num 24:14; Jer 23:20; 25:19) *in these last days* **Hb 1:2.** ἐπ' ἐσχάτων τ. ἡμερῶν (Hos 3:5; Jer 37:24; Ezk 38:16) **2 Pt 3:3** (cp. ἐπ' ἐσχάτων χρόνων **1 Pt 1:20 v.l.**); 2 Cl 14:2; B 12:9; 16:5; Hs 9, 12, 3; GJs 7:2.—ἐπ' ἐσχάτου τοῦ χρόνου **Jd 18;** ἐπ' ἐσχάτου τ. χρόνων **1 Pt 1:20.**—ἔ. καιρός vs. **5;** D 16:2. Pl. (TestIss 6:1 ἐν ἐσχάτοις καιροῖς) IEph 11:1. ἐπ' ἐ. [κα]ιρ[ῶ]ν AcPl Ha 8, 25 (Ox 1602, 39f reads ἐπ' ἐ|σχάτῳ τῶν καιρῶν, cp. BMM recto 33; ApcMos 13).—ἐ. ὥρα (Teles p. 17, 5) **1J 2:18.**—The neut. ἔσχατον as adv. *finally* (SIG 1219, 11 [III BC]; POxy 886, 21; Num 31:2; Pr 29:21; Tat. 35, 1) ἔ. πάντων *last of all* **Mk 12:22; 1 Cor 15:8** (PJones, TynBull 36, '85, 3–34). S. lit. s.v. παρουσία.

❸ **pert. to furthest extremity in rank, value, or situation,** ***last:*** *last, least, most insignificant* (opp. πρῶτος as Hierocles 23 p. 468: a human is ἔσχατος μὲν τῶν ἄνω, πρῶτος δὲ τῶν κάτω): (οἱ) πρῶτοι ἔσχατοι καὶ (οἱ) ἔσχατοι πρῶτοι **Mt 19:30; 20:16; Mk 9:35** (πάντων ἔσχατος as Appian, Bell. Civ. 2, 77 §322); **10:31; Lk 13:30;** Ox 654, 25 (restored); 26 (=ASyn. 256, 55; GTh 4; Fitzmyer, Oxy. p. 523). τὸν ἔ. τόπον κατέχειν *take the poorest place* (in this sense the ἔ. τόπος would be contrasted with the ἐνδοξότερος, as Diog. L. 2, 73) **Lk 14:9;** cp. vs. **10** (but s. 1 above). Of the apostles, whom God has exhibited as the *least* among humans, by the misfortunes they have suffered (Diod. S. 8, 18, 3 the ἔσχατοι are the people living in the most extreme misery; Dio Chrys. 21 [38], 37 the tyrants treat you as ἐσχάτους; Cass. Dio 42, 5, 5 Πομπήιος . . . καθάπερ τις τῶν Αἰγυπτίων ἔσχατος) **1 Cor 4:9.** ἔ. τῶν πιστῶν IEph 21:2; cp. ITr 13:1; IRo 9:2; ISm 11:1. Of a very hazardous situation *extreme* εἰς . . . ἔ. κίνδυνον *in extreme danger* AcPl Ha 4, 15f (cp. Just., D. 46, 7 ὑπομένομεν τὰς ἐ. τιμωρίας).—In a positive sense, ***utmost, finest*** εὐλόγησον αὐτὴν ἐσχάτην εὐλογίαν *bless her with the ultimate blessing* GJs 6:2 (s. de Strycker ad loc.; cp. Just., D. 32, 1 τῇ ἐ. κατάρᾳ *w. the worst curse*).—B. 940. Cp. τελευταῖος Schmidt Syn. IV 524–34. DELG. M-M. EDNT. TW. Sv.

ἐσχάτως adv. (s. prec. entry; Hippocr. et al.; X., An. 2, 6, 1) **pert. to being at the very end,** ***finally*** ἐ. ἔχειν (cp. Lat. 'in extremis esse') *be at the point of death* (Artem. 3, 60; the topic of 'being at the point of death' appears in honorary ins relating to physicians, to memorialize their skill and dedication; see, e.g., ZPE 25, '77, 270–72, no. 2) **Mk 5:23.**—M-M.

ἔσω adv. of place (Hom. et al. in the form εἴσω, and predom. so in later times. In our lit., as in the LXX [Thackeray 82]; TestSol; JosAs 2:19; ApcMos 19, only ἔσω, likew. SIG 989, 2 [II BC]; UPZ 13, 17 [160 BC]; BGU 1127, 9 [18 BC].—Jos., Bell. 6, 265 εἴσω, but Ant. 15, 398 ἔσω)

❶ **a position within an area,** ***inside.*** When used with verbs of motion, the preferred Eng. rendering is *in, into* εἰσελθὼν ἔ. *he went in* (Bel 19 Theod.) **Mt 26:58;** AcPl Ha 4, 3. ἕως ἔ. εἰς τὴν αὐλὴν *right into the courtyard* **Mk 14:54** (ἔσω εἰς τὴν αὐλὴν as PBas I, 19 [c. 600 AD]; ἔσω εἰς τὸν παράδεισον ApcMos 19). W. gen. of place (already Hom.) ἔ. τῆς αὐλῆς *into the palace* **15:16** (JosAs 2:19 'within').

❷ When used without a verb of motion the customary rendering is ***inside, within*** as opp. to outside **Ac 5:22** D, **23;** ἦσαν ἔ. *they were inside* **J 20:26.** αἱ ἔ. φλέβες *the inner veins* MPol 2:2. ὁ ἔ. ἄνθρωπος *the inner being* **Ro 7:22; Eph 3:16.** Also ὁ ἔ. ἡμῶν ἄ. **2 Cor 4:16** (s. ἄνθρωπος 5a and ἔξω 1aβ).—οἱ ἔ. *those within (the Christian community)* (Aeneas Tact. 1312 of those in the city) **1 Cor 5:12;** τὸ ἔ. *the inside* (Lucian, Nav. 38, Sacr. 13.—Opp. τὸ ἔξω; s. ἔξω 1aβ)=the soul 2 Cl 12:2, 4 (a saying of Jesus, and an explanation of it).—DELG s.v. εἰς. M-M. EDNT. TW. Sv.

ἔσωθεν adv. of place (Aeschyl., Hdt. et al.; pap, LXX; TestSol; TestAbr A 12 p. 90, 20 [Stone p. 28]; JosAs 10:8).

❶ **extension from a source that is inside,** ***from inside*** (Hdt. 7, 36, 2; Aeneas Tact. 1636; Ath., R. 22 p. 75, 21) **Lk 11:7.** ἔ. ἐκπορεύεσθαι *come fr. within* **Mk 7:23;** fuller ἔ. ἐκ τῆς καρδίας vs. **21.**

❷ **pert. to the inner part of an object,** ***inside, within*** (Hdt. et al.; Epict.; POxy 1449, 44; LXX; TestAbr A 12 p. 90, 20 [Stone p. 28]; EpArist 89; Jos., Ant. 14, 477; 15, 424; Tat. 22, 1) **Mt 7:15; 23:25, 27f;** IRo 7:2. αὐλὴν τὴν ἔ. **Rv 11:2 v.l.** Used w. ἔξωθεν (Epict. 4, 11, 18; Gen 6:14; Ex 25:11) **2 Cor 7:5.** ἔ. καὶ ἔξωθεν *inward and outward* IRo 3:2; **Rv 5:1 v.l.** (for ἔσωθεν κ. ὄπισθεν, s. γράφω 2b). κυκλόθεν καὶ ἔ. *all around and within* **4:8.**—τὸ ἔ. ὑμῶν (ὑμῖν P[75]) *your inner nature* **Lk 11:39.** τὸ ἔξωθεν κ. τὸ ἔ. vs. **40.** οἱ ἔσωθεν=οἱ ἔσω (s. ἔσω 2) **1 Cor 5:12 v.l.**—M-M. TW. Sv.

ἐσώτερος, α, ον (s. prec. entry; PMagd 29, 10 [218 BC]; Mayser 14; 301; PRyl III, 478, 120 ὁ οἶκος ὁ ἐσώτερος; LXX) comp. of ἔσω; ***inner*** ἡ ἐ. φυλακή *the inner prison* **Ac 16:24** (on the topic s. Mommsen, Röm. Strafrecht 1899, 302).—In τὸ ἐσώτερον τοῦ καταπετάσματος, ἐ. funct. as prep. w. gen. (cp. 1 Km 24:4) *what is inside* (=behind) *the curtain,* the Holy of Holies **Hb 6:19** (Lev 16:2, 12, 15).—DELG s.v. εἰς. M-M.

ἑταῖρος, ου, ὁ (Hom.+; also Ath. 31, 1 [v.l. ἑτέροις]) **a person who has someth. in common with others and enjoys association, but not necessarily at the level of a φίλος** or **φίλη,** ***comrade, companion,*** of a member of one's group *fellow-member* D 14:2. Of playmates **Mt 11:16 v.l.** Of Jesus' disciples (X., Mem. 2, 8, 1 al. Socrates refers to his pupils as ἑ.; Ael. Aristid. 47 p. 421 D. οἱ Πλάτωνος ἑ.; Porphyr., Vi. Pythag. 55 of Pythag.—Philo, Vi. Cont. 40 of Odysseus' companions) **Mt 26:50** (ἑταῖρε; cp. Jos., Ant. 12, 302 ὦ ἑταῖροι); GPt 7:26. Παπίας . . . ὁ Πολυκάρπου ἑ. γενόμενος Papias (1:2; cp. 11:1). As a general form of address to someone whose name one does not know: ἑταῖρε *my friend* (Theognis 753 Diehl; Aristoph., Pla., et al.) **Mt 20:13; 22:12.**—Instead of being an itacized variant of ἕτερος, the reading ἑταῖροι **Lk 23:32** P[75] may well imply *political partisans* (cp. Lysias 43, 28).—JErnstman, Οἰκεῖος, Ἑταῖρος, Ἐπιτήδειος, Φίλος, diss. Utrecht '32.—Schmidt, Syn. III 463–71. DELG. LfgrE s.v. ἑ. (lit. col. 743). M-M. TW. Spicq. Sv.

ἐταράχθην s. ταράσσω.

ἐτάφη s. θάπτω.

ἐτέθην s. τίθημι.

ἔτεκον s. τίκτω.

ἑτερόγλωσσος, ον (s. ἕτερος, γλῶσσα; Polyb. 23, 13, 2; Strabo 8, 1, 2; Philo, Conf. Lingu. 8; Aq Ps 113:1 and Is 33:19) ***speaking a foreign language*** ἐν ἑτερογλώσσοις λαλεῖν *speak through people who use strange languages* **1 Cor 14:21** (after Is 28:11, where Aq. seems to have written ἑτερόγλ.). Paul interprets it as having to do w. speaking w. tongues.—M-M. TW.

ἑτερογνωμονέω (s. ἕτερος, γνώμη, and next entry; Cyr. Al.; s. Lampe s.v.) ***be of a different opinion, not be in agreement with*** ἐδόκει γ[ὰρ ἑτε]||ρογνωμονεῖν τῇ ἐκ[ε]ίν[ου ἐν]||νοίᾳ *for* (Mary Magdalene's) *words did not appear to agree with* (Christ's) *way of thinking* GMary 463, 9–11.—DELG s.v. γιγνώσκω.

ἑτερογνώμων, ον, gen. **ονος** (s. prec. entry; Vett. Val. 79, 18; Agathias 4, 2.—ἑτερογνωμοσύνη; Jos., Ant. 10, 281) ***of a different opinion*** γυναικὸς ἑτερογνώμονος ὑπαρχούσης *the woman* (Lot's wife) *who was of a different opinion* 1 Cl 11:2.—M-M. s.v. ἑτερόγλωσσος.

ἑτεροδιδασκαλέω (s. ἕτερος, διδασκαλία; only in Christian wr.) **to teach contrary to standard instruction,** ***give divergent,*** i.e. ***divisive, instruction*** **1 Ti 1:3; 6:3** (cp. 1QH 4, 16); IPol 3:1.—DELG s.v. διδάσκω. TW.

ἑτεροδοξέω (s. ἕτερος, δοκέω and next entry; Pla., Theaet. 190e; Philo, Rer. Div. Her. 247.—Jos., Bell. 2, 129 ἑτερόδοξος of those who do not belong to the Essenes) ***hold different,*** i.e. ***divisive*** or ***sectarian, opinions*** ISm 6:2.—TW.

ἑτεροδοξία, ας, ἡ (s. prec. entry; Pla., Theaet. 193d; Philo, fgm. 72 Harris) **expression of thought that differs from accepted views or teachings, with implication of being divisive,** ***strange, erroneous opinion*** IMg 8:1.—TW.

ἑτεροζυγέω (s. ἕτερος, ζυγός; κτήνη ἑτερόζυγα=draft animals that need different kinds of yokes, because they are of different species [e.g., an ox and a donkey]: Lev 19:19; Philo, Spec. Leg. 4, 203; cp. Jos., Ant. 4, 228.—ἑτερόζυγος is found in a different sense in Ps.-Phoc. 15, and generally = 'not belonging together' as early as PCairZen 38, 11 [257 BC]) ***be unevenly yoked, be mismated*** τινί *with someone* μὴ γίνεσθε ἑτεροζυγοῦντες ἀπίστοις **2 Cor 6:14** (JFitzmyer, Qumran and 2 Cor 6:14–7:1: CBQ 23, '61, 271–80, yoking associated with instruction; Straub 6).—DELG s.v. ζεύγνυμι. M-M. TW. Spicq.

ἑτεροκλινής, ές, gen. **οῦς** (s. ἕτερος, also κλινέω 'lean' Hippocr. et al.) gener. pert. to being inclined away from the perpendicular, of buildings 'leaning to one side', then transf. to the mental realm ***inclined to, having a propensity for*** (Epict. 3, 12, 7 ἑτεροκλινῶς ἔχω πρὸς ἡδονήν; the adv. also 1 Ch 12:34) *having other allegiance,* of the rebellious or apostate 1 Cl 11:1; 47:7.—DELG s.v. κλίνω.

ἕτερος, α, ον (Hom.+; in the NT it is entirely lacking in 1 and 2 Pt; 1, 2, and 3J; Rv; found in Mk only in the bracketed ending **16:12;** in J only **19:37**) as adj. and subst., gener. 'other'

❶ pert. to being distinct from some other item implied or mentioned, ***other***—ⓐ *other* of two, contrasting a definite person or thing w. another (Appian, Hann. 43 §185 Ἄννων ἕτερος=the other of the two Hannos; of an eye ApcEsdr 4:29; Ath. 17, 4; cp. θάτερος Just., D. 1, 2 al.; Tat. 8, 1 al.) ἐν τῷ ἑτέρῳ πλοίῳ *in the other boat* **Lk 5:7;** cp. **23:40.** ὁ ἕ. in contrast to ὁ πρῶτος (X., An. 3, 4, 25) **Mt 21:30;** ὁ εἷς ... ὁ ἕ. (s. εἷς 5d) **6:24; Lk 7:41; 16:13; 17:34 f; 18:10; Ac 23:6; 1 Cor 4:6.** ἕ. βασιλεύς *another king* (of two mentioned) **Lk 14:31.** The usage Hv 3, 8, 4 is colloq., for seven women are referred to; the narrator describes the first two, but anticipates Hermas' interrupting inquiry about the identity of the other five and therefore treats the first two as a complete series.—1 Cl 38:2.

ⓑ of more than two—**α.** *another* ἕ. τῶν μαθητῶν **Mt 8:21;** cp. **Gal 1:19.** ἕ. προσδοκῶμεν; *are we to look for someone else?* **Mt 11:3; Lk 7:19 v.l.** ἐν ἑ. σαββάτῳ **Lk 6:6.** ἑτέρα γραφή *another Scripture passage* **J 19:37;** 2 Cl 2:4; cp. **Lk 9:56, 59, 61; 16:18** (cp. Job 31:10); **Ac 1:20** (Ps 108:8); **7:18** (Ex 1:8); **Ro 7:3.** ἕτερον παράδοξον *a further wonder* Papias (2:9). ἕ. τις *someone else, any other* **Ac 8:34; Ro 8:39; 13:9** (cp. Cicero, Tusc. 4, 7, 16); **1 Ti 1:10;** ἤ τις ἕ. Papias (2:4) (cp. οὐδεὶς ἕ. En 24:4; Just., D. 49, 3).

β. likew. in the pl. ἕτεροι *other(s)* **Ac 2:13** (ἕτεροι δέ joins the opinion of other people to an opinion previously expressed, as schol. on Pind., P. 9, 183), 40; **Lk 10:1.** ἕτεραι γενεαί *other generations* (cp. Ps 47:14; 77:4, 6 al.) **Eph 3:5.** ἑτέρους διδάσκειν (Da 11:4) **2 Ti 2:2.** At the end of lists ἕτεροι πολλοί (cp. Demosth. 18, 208 and 219; 19, 297; Appian, Bell. Civ. 2, 62 §260) **Mt 15:30; Ac 15:35;** ἕ. πολλαί **Lk 8:3;** ἕ. πολλά (TestSol 8:9; Jos., Vi. 39; 261) **22:65.** πολλὰ κ. ἕτερα **3:18.** περὶ ἑτέρων **Ac 19:39 v.l.** τινὲς ἕ. (Jos., Vi. 15; Ar. 10, 7 ἑτέρων τινῶν) **Ac 27:1.** ἑπτὰ ἕ. πνεύματα an evil spirit takes *seven other evil spirits* with it **Mt 12:45; Lk 11:26** (cp. TestSol 15:1 ἑτέρας δύο κεφαλάς; TestAbr B 10 p. 114, 24 [Stone p. 76] τῶν ἑτέρων δύο στεφανῶν). Differently, to indicate a difference in kind, καὶ ἕ. (ἑταῖροι P[75]; s. s.v. ἑταῖρος) κακοῦργοι δύο *also two others, who were criminals* **23:32** (cp. TestJud 9:6; PTebt 41, 9 [c. 119 BC] τινῶν ἡμῶν [men] καὶ ἑτέρων γυναικῶν; Dio Chrys. 30 [47], 24 ἑτέραν γυναῖκα Σεμίρ.=and in addition, a woman, Semiramis). οἱ ἕ. *the others, the rest* **Mt 11:16; Lk 4:43.**

γ. used interchangeably w. ἄλλος, which is felt to be its equivalent (Ps.-Pla., Alcib. I 116e; Apollon. Rhod. 4, 141; Dio Chrys. 57 [74], 22; Arrian, Anab. 5, 21, 2; 3; Herm. Wr. 11, 12a; CPR I, 103, 21 ἀπό τε ἄλλων πρασέων ἢ ἑτέρων οἰκονομιῶν; 3, 19; 6, 17. Cp. also POxy 276, 11 σὺν ἄλλοις σιτολόγοις w. PGen 36, 10 σὺν ἑτέροις ἱερεῦσι; POslo 111, 246 μηδένα ἄλλον with ln. 292 μηδένα ἕτερον; and **Mt 10:23** with v.l.; Mlt-Turner 197f): εἰς ἕ. εὐαγγέλιον ὃ οὐκ ἔστιν ἄλλο *to another gospel, which is no (other) gospel at all* **Gal 1:6f** (ἄλλος 2b). For another view cp. 2 below. ἄλλον Ἰησοῦν ... πνεῦμα ἕ. ... εὐαγγέλιον ἕ. **2 Cor 11:4.** S. also δ.

δ. In lists (Ath. 4, 1 ἕ. μὲν ... ἄλλο δὲ; 26, 2 ἄλλους μὲν ... ἐφ' ἑτέρων δέ) ὃ μὲν ... καὶ ἕτερον ... καὶ ἕ. ... καὶ ἕ. *some ... some* etc. **Lk 8:(5), 6, 7, 8.** ὃς μὲν ... ἄλλος δὲ ... ἕτερος ... ἄλλος δὲ ... ἄλλος δὲ ... ἕτερος ... **1 Cor 12:(8), 9, 10;** τὶς ... ἕ. **3:4;** τὶς ... ἕ. ... ἄλλος τις **Lk 22:(56), 58, (59).** πρῶτος ... ἕ. **16:(5), 7;** πρῶτος ... και ἕ. **14:(18), 19f.** ὁ πρῶτος ... ὁ δεύτερος ... ὁ ἕ. *the first ... the second ... the third* **19:(16, 18), 20;** δοῦλος ... ἕ. δοῦλος ... τρίτος **20:(10), 11, (12).** Pl. τινὲς ... ἕτεροι **11:(15), 16.** ἄλλοι ... ἕ. (PParis 26, 31 [163/162 BC]) **Hb 11:(35), 36.** οἱ μὲν ... ἄλλοι δὲ ... ἕ. δὲ ... **Mt 16:14.**

ε. ὁ ἕτερος *one's neighbor* (the contrast here is w. αὐτός: Demosth. 34, 12 ἕ. ἤδη ἦν καὶ οὐχ ὁ αὐτός; cp. Is 34:14) **Ro 2:1; 13:8** (WMarxsen, TZ 11, '55, 230–37; but s. FDanker, FGingrich Festschr. '72, 111 n. 2); **1 Cor 6:1; 10:24, 29; 14:17; Gal 6:4.** Without the article διδάσκων ἕτερον σεαυτὸν οὐ διδάσκεις; **Ro 2:21** (cp. Ael. Aristid. 28, 1 K.=49 p. 491 D.: νουθετεῖν ἑτέρους ἀφέντες ἑαυτούς). Pl. **Phil 2:4.**

ζ. τῇ ἑτέρᾳ (sc. ἡμέρᾳ) *on the next day* (X., Cyr. 4, 6, 10) **Ac 20:15; 27:3.**—ἐν ἑτέρῳ *in another place* (in Scripture; cp. Jos., Ant. 14, 114; Just., D. 58, 8 ἐν ἑτέροις etc.) **13:35; Hb 5:6.** εἰς οὐδὲν ἕτερον ... ἤ **Ac 17:21** (CPR I, 32, 15 οὐδὲν δὲ ἕτερον; Jos., Ant. 8, 104; Tat. 14, 2 οὐδὲν ... ἕτερον ἤ).

❷ pert. to being dissimilar in kind or class from all other entities, ***another, different*** fr. what precedes, externally or internally (cp. Pla., Symp. 186b ἕτερος καὶ ἀνόμοιος al.; OGI 458, 8 [c. 9 BC] ἑτέραν ὄψιν; POxy 939, 18; Wsd 7:5; Jdth 8:20 al.; TestSol 11:3 ἑτέραν πρᾶξιν; Just., D. 6, 1 ἕ. ... τι τὸ μετέχον τινὸς ἐκείνου οὗ μετέχει; 55, 1 ἕ. θεὸς παρὰ τὸν ποιητὴν τῶν ὅλων; 119, 3 ἡμεῖς λαὸς ἕ. ἀνεθήλαμεν, καὶ ἐβλαστήσαμεν στάχυες καινοί): ἐν ἑ. μορφῇ *in a different form* **Mk 16:12** (cp. Ath. 26, 3 εἰς ἕ. σχῆμα). εἶδος ἕτερον **Lk 9:29** (TestSol 15:3). ἑτέρα ... δόξα, ἑτέρα ... *glory of one kind, ... of a different kind* **1 Cor 15:40.** ἕ. νόμος **Ro 7:23.** ἑ. γνῶσις B 18:1. ἑ. ὁδός **Js 2:25.** ἑ. διδαχή Hs 8, 6, 5 (v.l. ξένος). On ἕ. in this sense in **Gal 1:6** s. M-M. s.v. Also in the sense *strange* ἐν χείλεσιν ἑτέρων *through the lips of strangers* **1 Cor 14:21** (cp. Is 28:11). λαλεῖν ἑτέραις γλώσσαις **Ac 2:4** may mean either *speak with different* (even *other* than their own) *tongues* or *speak in foreign languages* (cp. Is 28:11; Sir prol. ln. 22; 1QH 4, 16). S. γλῶσσα 3.—JKElliott, ZNW 60, '69, 140f.—Schmidt, Syn. IV 559–69. DELG. M-M. EDNT. TW.

ἑτέρως adv. (s. prec. entry; Hom. et al., more common Pla. et al.; SIG 851, 10; POxy 34, 15 [II AD]; Philo, Aet. M. 28; Jos., C. Ap. 1, 26; Ath. 19, 1, R. 54, 13) ***differently, otherwise*** ἑ. φρονεῖν **Phil 3:15.**—M-M.

ἔτι adv. (Hom.+)—**❶ pert. to continuance,** ***yet, still*** (contrast ἤδη 'already'–ἔτι 'still' Chariton 49).—**ⓐ** in positive statements, to denote that a given situation is continuing *still, yet.*

α. of the present **Lk 14:32; Hb 11:4.** ἔ. σαρκικοί ἐστε **1 Cor 3:3.** ἔ. ἐστὲ ἐν ταῖς ἁμαρτίαις **15:17.** ἔ. ὑπὸ κίνδυνόν εἰμι ITr 13:3. εἰ ἔτι ἀνθρώποις ἤρεσκον *if I were still trying to please people* **Gal 1:10; 5:11a.** καὶ τούτοις ἔτι κεῖται μετάνοια *the possibility of repentance is also open to these* Hs 6, 7, 2. ἔτι καὶ νῦν *even now* Dg 2:3 (Just., D. 7, 2; cp. A I, 26, 5 καὶ νῦν ἔτι; A II, 6, 6 καὶ ἔτι νῦν).

β. of the past, w. the impf. (Arrian, Anab. 6, 13, 2 ἔτι ἠπίστουν=they still disbelieved) ἔ. ἐν τῇ ὀσφύϊ ἦν *he was still in the loins* (i.e. not yet begotten) **Hb 7:10;** cp. **J 11:30.** Oft. w. the pres. ptc., which stands for the impf. (Diog. L. 9, 86 ἔτι ὁ ἥλιος ἀνίσχων) ἔ. αὐτοῦ λαλοῦντος *while he was still speaking* (cp. Job 1:16, 17, 18; TestAbr A 12 p. 90, 14 [Stone p. 28]; Jos., Ant. 8, 282) **Mt 12:46; 17:5; 26:47; Mk 5:35a; 14:43; Lk 8:49; Ac 10:44** al. εἶπεν ἔτι ζῶν *he said while he was still living* **Mt 27:63** (Jos., Ant. 4, 316; 8, 2 ζῶν ἔ.). ἔ. προσερχομένου αὐτοῦ *while he was still approaching* **Lk 9:42.** ἔ. αὐτοῦ μακρὰν ἀπέχοντος *while he was still a long way off* **15:20.** σκοτίας ἔ. οὔσης *while it was still dark* **J 20:1.** ἔ. ὢν πρὸς ὑμᾶς *when I was still with you* **2 Th 2:5;** cp. **Lk 24:6, 41, 44; Ac 9:1; Ro 5:6, 8; Hb 9:8.** ὄντος ἔτι ἐν σαρκί σου *while you are still alive* AcPlCor 1:6 (TestAbr A 9 p. 87, 3 [Stone p. 22] ἔτι ἐν τούτῳ τῷ σώματι ὤν; Just., D. 49, 7 ἔτι ὄντος τότε ἐν ἀνθρώποις Μωυσέως).

γ. of the future πλησθήσεται ἔ. ἐκ κοιλίας *he will be filled while he is still in his mother's womb* **Lk 1:15** (ἔ. ἐκ κοι. Is 48:8; cp. 43:13 and Anth. Pal. 9, 567, 1 ἔ. ἐκ βρέφεος; Ps.-Plut., Mor. 104d). καὶ ἔ. ῥύσεται *and he will deliver us again* **2 Cor 1:10** (PsSol 9:11 εἰς τὸν αἰῶνα καὶ ἔτι al.).

ⓑ in neg. statements—**α.** οὐδὲ ἔ. νῦν *not even yet* **1 Cor 3:2** (s. νῦν 1aβℶ).—**β.** to denote that someth. is stopping, has stopped, or should stop *no longer* (PsSol 3:12 al.; TestSol D 4:9 τέθνηκεν καὶ οὐκ ἔτι ἴδῃς αὐτόν; ApcMos 13; Arrian, Anab. 5, 25, 3 and 6; 6, 29, 2a οὐ ἔτι=not any longer; Aesop, Fab. 243 H.=Ch. 200 p. 333, 52 μὴ ἔτι=no longer; Jos., C. Ap. 1, 72; Just., D. 5, 4 al.) οὐ δύνῃ ἔ. *you can no longer* **Lk 16:2;** cp. **Mt 5:13; Lk 20:36; Rv 12:8** al.; οὐ μὴ ἔ. *never again* **Hb 8:12; 10:17** (both Jer 38:34; En 5:8; TestAbr B 3 p. 107, 21 [Stone p. 62]; GrBar 1:7); **Rv 18:21, 22, 23.** Sim. in rhetorical questions τί ἔ. σκύλλεις τ. διδάσκαλον; *why should you bother the Teacher any further?*= you should not bother him any further **Mk 5:35b.** Cp. *what further need have we of witnesses?* **Mt 26:65; Mk 14:63; Lk 22:71.**—**Ro 6:2.**

ⓒ of time not yet come ἔ. (χρόνον) μικρόν *a little while longer* **J 7:33; 12:35; 13:33; 14:19; Hb 10:37** (TestJob 24:1) ἔ. τετράμηνός ἐστιν καί *there are still four months before* **J 4:35** (PParis 18 ἔ. δύο ἡμέρας ἔχομεν καὶ φθάσομεν εἰς Πηλοῦσι).

❷ pert. to number—ⓐ ***what is left or remaining*** (TestAbr A 14 p. 93, 26 [Stone p. 34] τί ἔτι λείπεται;) ἔ. ἕνα εἶχεν υἱόν **Mk 12:6.** τί ἔ. ὑστερῶ; *what do I still lack?* **Mt 19:20;** cp. **Lk 18:22; J 16:12; Rv 9:12.**

ⓑ ***that which is added to what is already at hand*** (GrBar 16:3 ἔ. σὺν τούτοις; Just., D. 8, 1 ἔ. ἄλλα πολλά; Tat. 20, 1 κόσμος . . . ἡμᾶς ἔ. καθέλκει) *in addition, more, also, other* ἔ. ἕνα ἢ δύο *one or two others* **Mt 18:16;** ἔ. τοῦτο . . . δεῖ τελεσθῆναι **Lk 22:37 v.l.;** ἔ. προ[σθείς] *while he added* Ox 1081 (SJCh) 9, after Wessely. ἔ. δέ (X., Mem. 1, 2, 1; Diod. S. 1, 74, 1; 13, 81, 3; Strabo 10, 3, 7; Dio Chrys. 36 [53], 1; 2 Macc 6:4) **Hb 11:36.** ἔ. δὲ καί *furthermore* (X., An. 3, 2, 28 al.; UPZ 61, 10 [161 BC]; PMich 174, 7 [146 AD]; 2 Esdr 19:18; EpArist 151; Jos., Bell. 2, 546, Ant. 7, 70; Ar. 4:3 al.; Just., D. 34, 1; Tat. 29, 1 al.; Mel., HE 4, 26, 13; Ath. 13, 1) **Ac 2:26** (Ps 15:9); 1 Cl 17:1, 3; Hs 5, 2, 5; B 4:6; AcPl Ox 6, 20 (= Aa I 242, 2) al. ἔ. τε καί (Jos., Ant. 14, 194) **Lk 14:26; Ac 21:28.** ἔ. ἄνω, ἔ. κάτω *farther up, farther down* **Mt 20:28** D. ἔ. ἅπαξ *once again* (2 Macc 3:37; TestAbr A 9 p. 86, 24 [Stone p. 20] al.; ApcSed 12:2) **Hb 12:26f** (Hg 2:6). W. a comp. ἔ. μᾶλλον (Hom. et al.; POxy 939, 3; Jos., Ant. 20, 89) **Phil 1:9;** περισσότερον ἔ. **Hb 7:15.** ἔ. καί ἔ. *again and again* B 21:4; Hs 2:6.

❸ in logical inference, in interrog. sentences (Just., D. 7, 1, 151 τίνι οὖν . . . ἔ. τις χρήσαιτο διδασκάλῳ;) τίς ἔ. χρεία; *what further need would there be?* **Hb 7:11.** τί ἔ. μέμφεται; *why, then, does (God) still find fault?* **Ro 9:19;** cp. **3:7; Gal 5:11b.**—DELG. M-M.

ἑτοιμάζω fut. ἑτοιμάσω; 1 aor. ἡτοίμασα; pf. ἡτοίμακα. Pass.: fut. ἑτοιμασθήσομαι LXX; 1 aor. ἡτοιμάσθην; pf. pass. ἡτοίμασμαι (s. ἑτοιμασία, ἕτοιμος; Hom.+) **to cause to be ready,** ***put/keep in readiness, prepare***

ⓐ of things that are being put in readiness τὶ *someth.: prepare* a way **Mt 3:3; Mk 1:3; Lk 3:4** (all three Is 40:3; cp. J 1:23 εὐθύνω [q.v.]; **1:76; Rv 16:12;** a pyre MPol 13:2; a meal (Gen 43:16; EpArist 181; TestAbr B 4 p. 108, 14f [Stone p. 64]; JosAs 3:6) **Mt 22:4; Lk 17:8;** cp. 1 Cl 39:9; τὸ πάσχα (q.v.) **Mt 26:19; Mk 14:16; Lk 22:13;** cp. GEb 308, 31.—**Mk 15:1 v.l.; Lk 23:56; 24:1.** ἃ ἡτοίμασας *what you have prepared* **12:20.** Of possessions Hs 1:1, 2, 4.—τινί τι *someth. for someone* Hs 1:6. θηρίων τῶν ἐμοὶ ἡτοιμασμένων *the beast held in readiness for me* IRo 5:2. Of the preparations for receiving and entertaining someone (PTebt 592 . . . σοῦ ταχὺ ἐρχομένου . . . ἡτοιμάκειν σοι πάντα; POxy 1299, 9; 1490, 7; TestAbr A 4 p. 80, 19 and 28 [Stone p. 8]) ἑτοίμαζέ μοι ξενίαν **Phlm 22.** ἑ. τινὶ τόπον **J 14:2, 3** (cp. Appian, Bell. Civ. 2, 53 §219 of those who go before, who ἀσφαλῆ τὰ ἐκεῖ προετοιμάσαι=prepare a safe place there [for those who follow]; 1 Ch 15:1). So also without an object acc. ἑ. τινί *make preparations for someone* **Lk 9:52.** In a different sense *prepare (a meal)* **Mk 14:15.** Abs. (1 Esdr 1:4; Jer 26:14; Job 28:27) **Lk 12:47; 22:9, 12.** ὁλοκαύτωμα δεκτὸν τῷ θεῷ ἡτοιμασμένον MPol 14:1. τινί w. inf. foll. **Mt 26:17.** W. ἵνα foll. **Mk 14:12.** τινί τι w. ἵνα foll. **Lk 22:8.**—ἡτοιμασμένος *ready, prepared* εἴς τι *for someth.* (3 Macc 6:31) of a vessel **2 Ti 2:21;** of horses εἰς πόλεμον **Rv 9:7** (cp. Pr 21:31 ἵππος ἑτοιμάζεται εἰς ἡμέραν πολέμου, also 1 Macc 13:22; 12:27; TestLevi 3:2 v.l.; fig. of building stones IEph 9:1.).—S. also pass. in b end, beg. w. **Mk 10:40.**

ⓑ Of pers. (En 99:3; TestJob 43:14; Jos., Vi. 203) ἑ. στρατιώτας **Ac 23:23** (AMeuwese, De rer. gest. Divi Augusti vers. graeca 1920, 82). Of a bride **Rv 21:2.** ἑ. ἑαυτόν *prepare oneself* (Ezk 38:7; ParJer 6:6; 9:11; cp. POslo 88, 13 ἑτοιμάζεσθαι ἑαυτόν) **19:7;** w. ἵνα foll. **8:6.** Ἰωσὴφ ἡτοιμάσθη τοῦ ἐξελθεῖν *Joseph prepared to leave* GJs 21:1. W. εἰς foll. (Appian, Mithrid. 26 §103; PsSol 10:2 νῶτον εἰς μάστιγας). Of angels ἡτοιμασμένοι εἰς τ. ὥραν *held in readiness for that hour* **Rv 9:15.** Of Jesus, ὃς εἰς τοῦτο ἡτοιμάσθη, ἵνα B 14:5. God comes ἐφ' οὓς τ. πνεῦμα ἡτοίμασεν *to those whom the Spirit has prepared* D 4:10; B 19:7. Of a people that is made ready (2 Km 7:24) B 3:6; 5:7; 14:6; τῷ κυρίῳ (Sir 49:12) **Lk 1:17.** Here God is referred to several times as the one who brought the preparation about, and in the following pass. God appears explictly as subject: w. pers. or thing as obj. (Ex 23:20; En 25:7; PsSol 5:10; χορτάσματα . . . παντὶ ζῶντι;

JosAs 8:11 κατάπαυσιν ... τοῖς ἐκλεκτοῖς; ApcEsdr 6:17 and 21 ὁ στέφανός σοι ἡτοίμασται) **Mt 20:23;** βασιλείαν **25:34;** D 10:5. πῦρ **Mt 25:41.**—**Mk 10:40; Lk 2:31; 1 Cor 2:9**=1 Cl 34:8 (quot. of unknown orig.); cp. 2 Cl 14:5; **Hb 11:16** (πόλιν ἑ. as Hab 2:12); **Rv 12:6;** 1 Cl 35:3; Dg 8:11.—M-M. TW.

Ἕτοιμας s. Ἐλύμας.

ἑτοιμασία, ας, ἡ (s. next entry; Hippocr.; BGU 625, 17; PHerm 95, 20; LXX) ***readiness, preparation*** (so Hippocr., Decent. 12 vol. IX 240 L.; Ps 9:38; EpArist 182; Jos., Ant. 10, 9 v.l.) τοῦ εὐαγγελίου τῆς εἰρήνης *for the gospel of peace* **Eph 6:15.** The mng. *equipment* (here specif. 'boots'), as in Mod. Gk., is favored by ABuscarlet, ET 9, 1897/98, 38f; EBlakeney, ET 55, '43/44, 138; JGregg, ET 56, '44, 54; L-S-J-M. W. ἄσκησις MPol 18:3.—M-M. TW.

ἕτοιμος, η, ον (s. ἑτοιμάζω, ἑτοιμασία, ἑτοίμως; an adj. of two endings in pl. according to Jdth 9:6; **Mt 25:10;** B-D-F §59, 2; Mlt-H. 157) ***ready***

ⓐ (loanw. in rabb.) of things designed to serve a purpose (Hom.+; ins, pap, LXX, Philo; Jos., Ant. 7, 339 πάντα), of an altar IRo 2:2. Of preparations for a meal (cp. Dt 32:35) **Mt 22:4** (Appian, Bell. Civ. 1, 56 §246 πάντα ἕτοιμα; BGU 625, 13 [III AD] πάντα ἕ.), vs. **8; Lk 14:17** (of a meal, 'served': Ps.-Clem., Hom. 5, 30.—A call to a meal just before it is to be served, as Esth 6:14; Philo, Op. M. 78; Lucian, Merc. Cond. 14). Of a dining room: *put in readiness* **Mk 14:15.** Of a collection for the saints **2 Cor 9:5.** τὰ ἕ. *what has been accomplished* (by someone else) **10:16.** καιρός *the time is ready=is here* **J 7:6.** W. inf. of purpose (Esth 1:1e) σωτηρία ἑ. ἀποκαλυφθῆναι *ready to be revealed* **1 Pt 1:5.**

ⓑ of pers. (Pind.+; PHib 44, 7 [253 BC]; LXX; PsSol 6:1; TestJob 7:13; TestLevi 3:2; JosAs 15:10; Philo; Joseph.; Ar. 15:10; Just., Tat. Of a human embryo that is ready to become a living being at the sixth month ἕτοιμον γίνεται καὶ λαμβάνει τὴν φυχήν ApcEsdr 5:13.) *ready, prepared* **Mt 25:10.** ἕ. εἰμι *I am ready* (Thu. et al.; PTebt 419, 10; LXX) **Ac 23:21;** Hs 9, 2, 4; w. inf. foll. (Diod. S. 13, 98, 1 ἕτοιμός εἰμι τελευτᾶν; 1 Macc 7:29; 2 Macc 7:2; 4 Macc 9:1; PsSol 6:1; TestJob 7:13; Jos., Ant. 10, 9; Ar. 15:10; Just., A II, 3, 5) **Lk 22:33;** w. τοῦ and inf. foll. (Mi 6:8; 1 Macc 13:37) **Ac 23:15;** Hs 8, 4, 2. ἕ. γίνεσθαι *be ready, prepare oneself* (Diod. S. 4, 49, 5 ἑτοίμους γενομένους; Ps.-Callisth. 2, 11, 1; 6; Ex 19:15; Num 16:16) **Mt 24:44; Lk 12:40;** D 16:1; w. ἵνα foll. Hs 1:6. ἕ. πρός τι (X., Mem. 4, 5, 12; Aelian, VH 14, 49; BGU 1209, 17 [23 BC]; Tob 5:17 BA; Just., D. 56, 16; Tat. 42, 1) **Tit 3:1; 1 Pt 3:15.** Also εἴς τι (Hdt. 8, 96 et al.; 1 Macc 4:44; 12:50 al.; JosAs 15:10; Jos., Ant. 15, 357) 1 Cl 2:7; ISm 11:3; IPol 7:3.—ἐν ἑτοίμῳ *in readiness* (Epicurus in Diog. L. 10, 127; Theocr. 22, 61 and Epigr. 16, 5; Dionys. Hal. 8, 17; 9, 35; PGen 76, 8; PGM 13, 375; 3 Macc 6:31) ἐν ἑτοίμῳ ἔχειν *be ready* (Polyb. 2, 34, 2; Philo, Leg. ad Gai. 259) w. inf. foll. **2 Cor 10:6.**—Comp. ἑτοιμότερος (Agatharchides [II BC]: 86 fgm. 6 Jac.; PFlor 123, 4) *more ready, more willing* 2 Cl 15:4.—M-M. TW.

ἑτοίμως adv. (s. prec. entry; Aeschyl.+; ins, pap, LXX; Philo, Spec. Leg. 1, 49) ***readily*** ἑ. ἔχειν *be ready, be willing* w. inf. foll. (Aeneas Tact. 582; Diod. S. 16, 28, 2; PAmh 32, 6 [II BC]; BGU 80, 17; POxy 1469, 21; Da 3:15 LXX; Jos., Ant. 12, 163; Just., D. 50, 1) **2 Cor 12:14; 13:1 v.l.; 1 Pt 4:5.** ἀποθανεῖν **Ac 21:13** (cp. Jos., Ant. 13, 6 ἀποθνήσκειν).—DELG s.v. ἑτοῖμος (the Homeric form). M-M.

ἔτος, ους, τό (Hom.+) *year* **Ac 7:30; 13:21; Hb 1:12** (Ps 101:28); **3:10, 17** (Ps 94:10); **2 Pt 3:8** (Ps 89:4); **Rv 20:3–7;** 1 Cl 25:5 al.—ἔτη ἔχειν *be* x *years old* (Jos., Ant. 1, 198) **J 8:57;** differently w. the addition ἐν τ. ἀσθενείᾳ αὐτοῦ *be ill for* x *years* **5:5** (cp. TestJob 26:1 ἐν ταῖς πληγαῖς). εἶναι, γίνεσθαι ἐτῶν w. a numeral to indicate age (X., Mem. 1, 2, 40 al.; Gen 7:6; 12:4 and oft.; Demetr.: 722 fgm. 1, 1 al. Jac.; Jos., Ant. 10, 50) **Mk 5:42; Lk 2:42; Ac 4:22; 1 Ti 5:9** (Cyr. Ins. 16 μηδένα νεώτερον πέντε κ. εἴκοσι ἐτῶν); ὡς or ὡσεὶ ἐτῶν w. numeral *about* x *years old* (X., An. 2, 6, 20 ἦν ἐτῶν ὡς τριάκοντα; PTebt 381, 4f [123 BC]; s. Dssm. in PMeyer, Griech. Texte aus Ägypt. 1916, p. 26, 48; for use of round numbers s. Meyer 47, no. 7, 5 and 7; 67, no. 12, 12) **Lk 3:23; 8:42;** GJs 12:3.—Acc. to denote duration of time in answer to the quest.: how long? (X., Cyr. 1, 2, 9; SIG 1168: 3, 8, 14, 95; SIG[2] 847, 4; 850, 6 al.; 2 Km 21:1; EpJer 2; Jdth 8:4; 1 Macc 1:7, 9 al.; Demetr.: 722 fgm. 1, 6 Jac.; Just., D. 88, 2) δώδεκα ἔτη *for twelve years* **Mt 9:20;** cp. **Mk 5:25; Lk 2:36; 13:7f, 11, 16; 15:29; Ac 7:6** (Gen 15:13), 36, 42 (Am 5:25); B 10:6; MPol 9:3 al. The dat. is also used in almost the same sense (Appian, Illyr. 25 §71 ἔτεσι δέκα=for ten years; Polyaenus 1, 12; Lucian, Dial. Meretr. 8, 2 et al.; SIG 872, 17; 898, 28; 966, 17; ins concerning a Lycaon. bishop [Exp. 7th ser., 6, 1908, 387, 12] εἴκοσι πέντε ὅλοις ἔτεσιν τ. ἐπισκοπὴν διοικήσας; B-D-F §201; Rob. 523) of the temple τεσσεράκοντα καὶ ἓξ ἔτεσιν οἰκοδομήθη *it was under construction for forty-six years* **J 2:20;** cp. **Ac 13:20.** Likew. ἐπί w. acc. (SIG 1219, 27 ἐπὶ δέκα ἔτη; Mitt-Wilck. 327, 16 [107 BC]; Jos., Ant. 5, 211) **Lk 4:25; Ac 19:10.**—Other prep. combinations: ἀπὸ (SIG 762, 14; 820, 8) ἐτῶν δώδεκα *for twelve years* **Lk 8:43;** ἀπὸ πολλῶν ἐ. **Ro 15:23.** Also ἐκ πολλῶν ἐ. **Ac 24:10;** cp. **9:33.** δι' ἐ. πλειόνων *after several years* **24:17;** cp. **Gal 2:1.** εἰς ἔ. πολλά *for many years to come* **Lk 12:19** (cp. SIG 707, 19f; 708, 43). ἐν ἔτει πεντεκαιδεκάτῳ **3:1** (cp. SIG 736: 11, 52, 54, 90; 3 Km 6:1; 15:1 al.). ἕως ἐτῶν ... *until* x *years* of age (cp. Jo 2:2; Jos., Ant. 5, 181) **Lk 2:37.** κατ' ἔτος *every year* (GDI 4195, 30f [Rhodes]; PAmh 86, 11 [78 AD]; POxy 725, 36; 2 Macc 11:3; Jos., Ant. 7, 99) **2:41;** μετὰ τρία ἔ. *after three years* **Gal 1:18; 3:17** (cp. SIG 708, 26; Tob 14:2 BA; Is 23:15; Da 4:33a; 1 Macc 1:29; Tat. 31, 3). πρὸ ἐτῶν δεκατεσσάρων *fourteen years ago* **2 Cor 12:2** (as Just., A I, 46, 1). χιλιάδα τινὰ ... ἐτῶν Papias (2:12). *fourteen years ago.*—B. 1011f. DELG. M-M.

εὖ adv. (Hom.+; ins, pap, LXX; TestJob 44:3; ParJer 7:9; EpArist, Philo, Joseph.; Ar. [Milne, p. 74 ln. 1]; Just.; Tat. 17, 3; Ath. καλῶς becomes the more usual word: JLee, NovT 27, '85, 11f.)

❶ **pert. to that which is good or beneficial, as applied to interpersonal relationship or experience, *well*** εὖ ποιεῖν *do good, show kindness* (X., Cyr. 1, 6, 30, Oec. 2, 5; Demosth. 20, 37; POxy 1292, 3 [c. 30 AD]; LXX; TestJob 44:3f [εὐποιεῖν]; Jos., Ant. 14, 378; Just., A I, 28, 3, D. 118, 5) τινί (Ex 1:20; Sir 12:2, 5. Usu. the acc. follows) **Mk 14:7.** εὖ δουλεύειν 1 Cl 16:12 (Is 53:11). εὖ πράσσειν (ποιεῖν) means as a rule *get along well, be prosperous* (Pind.; X., Mem. 1, 6, 8; 2, 4, 6; 4, 2, 26, Oec. 11, 8; Pla., Prot. 333d; Ps.-Pla., Alc. I, 116b; Diog. L. 3, 61; Philo, Virt. 170, Decal. 43; Jos., Ant. 12, 156 al.; cp. Ath. 25, 2. As epistolary formula *farewell* in POxy 115, 12; 120, 27; 527, 9; 822; PGen 59, 24; 2 Macc 9:19). This sense is poss. in **Ac 15:29,** but *do well,* i.e. *act correctly* or *rightly* gives a better sense and is supported by the Vulgate, Armenian and Coptic transl. (so Simonides, fgm. 4, 10 D.[2]; X., Mem. 3, 9, 14; Ps.-Pla., Eryx. 393e; Epict. 4, 6, 20; Artem. 2, 3 p. 86, 13; M. Ant. 3, 13; Philo, Mut. Nom. 197; Jos., Ant. 4, 286; Just., A I, 28, 3. Further support is gained from recognition of the appropriateness of the phrase in Ac 15:23–29 as an official document transmitted from one group to another in the diplomatic format used, e.g., in IMagnMai 91d, which concludes 8–10 with a related grammatical structure: εὖ οὖν ποιήσετε [τ]ὸν [ἔπαινον|Σωσικλείου]ς καὶ τὰς δεδομένας αὐτῷ τιμὰς εὐνόως ἀποδεξά[μενοι ἔρρω|σθε]='you will do well in receiving the commendation of Sosicles and the honors awarded him. Farewell.' εὖ πράσσειν thus expresses a fundamental feature in the reciprocity system that ran through Gr-Rom. society: recipients of a benefit 'act correctly' by reciprocating in some way); sim. IEph 4:2 and ISm 11:3 require some such rendering as *do right*. ἵνα εὖ σοι γένηται *that you may prosper* **Eph 6:3** (cp. Ex 20:12; Dt 5:16—Gen 12:13; Dt 4:40; TestJob 46:9; ParJer 7:9). εὖ ἔχειν πρός τινα *be well-disposed* or *gracious to someone* Hs 9, 10, 7.

❷ **pert. to meeting a standard of performance, *well done! excellent!*** abs. as interjection (Ps.-X., Cyneg. 6, 20 Rühl v.l.) **Mt 25:21, 23; Lk 19:17 v.l.** (for εὖγε).—DELG s.v. ἐύς. M-M.

Εὕα, ας, ἡ (חַוָּה; Εὔα Tdf. S. Vog.—Schmiedel prefers Ἕυα) ***Eve*** (Gen 4:1; Tob 8:6; TestAbr A 8 p. 85, 26 [Stone p. 18]; ApcEsdr 2:16; ApcMos; SibOr 1, 29; Philo, Leg. All. 2, 81; Jos., Ant. 1, 49; Just.) **1 Ti 2:13.** Deception of Eve by the serpent **2 Cor 11:3;** B 12:5; Dg 12:8; GJs 13:1 (cp. Just., D. 79, 4 al.).—WStaerk, Eva-Maria: ZNW 33, '34, 97–104. BHHW I 499.

εὐαγγελίζω (s. next entry) fut. εὐαγγελιῶ 2 Km 18:19; 1 aor. εὐηγγέλισα. The act., found in our lit. only **Rv 10:7; 14:6; Ac 16:17 v.l.,** belongs to later Gk. (Polyaenus 5, 7; Cass. Dio 61, 13, 4; PGiss 27, 6 [II AD]; PAmh 2, 16; 1 Km 31:9; 2 Km 18:19f; cp. Phryn. 268 Lob.), and does not differ in mng. (s. B-D-F §309, 1) from the much more common mid. in earlier Gk. εὐαγγελίζομαι (Aristoph., Demosth. et al.; Philo, Joseph.; predom. in LXX; likewise PsSol 11:1; ParJer; Just.; pass. JosAs 19:2) impf. εὐηγγελιζόμην; fut. εὐαγγελιοῦμαι 2 Km 18:20; Is 60:6; 1 aor. εὐηγγελισάμην (on the augment s. B-D-F §69, 4; Rob. 367). The foll. tenses are used in a passive sense: pres.; 1 aor. εὐηγγελίσθην; pf. εὐηγγέλισμαι.

❶ gener. ***bring good news, announce good news*** τί τινι (Jos., Bell. 3, 503, Ant. 7, 250) **Lk 1:19** (ταῦτα εὐ. of the announcement by an angel of the impending birth of a much-desired child Jos., Ant. 5, 282; cp. 277 εὐ. αὐτῇ παιδὸς γονήν; Just., D. 56, 5 εὐ. τῇ Σάρρᾳ ὅτι τέκνον ἕξει); **2:10; 1 Th 3:6.** τὶ ἐπί τινα **Rv 14:6.** τινά *to someone* (pass. w. pers. subj. JosAs 19:2 ἐγὼ εὐηγγελίσθην περὶ σοῦ ἐξ οὐρανοῦ; for the usage s. 2 below) **10:7.**

❷ mostly specif. **proclaim the divine message of salvation, *proclaim the gospel*** (cp. Is 60:6; Ps 67:12; PsSol 11, 1; ParJer 5:19 εὐαγγελίσασθαι αὐτοῖς καὶ καταχρῆσαι αὐτοὺς τὸν λόγον al. S. also PGM 5, 142 εὐάγγελος τ. θεοῦ=a glad messenger of God) *proclaim, preach*.

ⓐ mid.—**α.** w. mention of the thing proclaimed, as well as of the pers. who receives the message τί τινι **Lk 4:43; Ac 8:35** (τὸν Ἰησοῦν); **Gal 1:8b; Eph 2:17; 3:8;** B 8:3; 14:9. τὸ εὐαγγέλιον εὐ. τινι **1 Cor 15:1; 2 Cor 11:7.** τί τινα *someth. to someone* (on the constr. s. below) **Ac 13:32.** εὐ. τὸν υἱὸν τ. θεοῦ ἐν τ. ἔθνεσιν *proclaim the Son of God among the nations* **Gal 1:16**

β. w. mention of the object of the proclamation τὶ (Lucian, Tyrannic. 9 τὴν ἐλευθερίαν; Synes., Prov. 1. 7 p. 96a [the heavenly σημεῖα] τὴν βασιλείαν Αἰγυπτίοις εὐηγγελίζετο [mid.]=brought the Egyptians news of the fortunate reign; Ps 39:10; 95:2) **Lk 8:1; Ac 8:4; 10:36; 15:35; 17:18; Ro 10:15** (Is 52:7); **Gal 1:23.** Also w. pers. obj. in acc. to denote the object of the proclamation τινά *someone* τ. Χριστὸν Ἰ. **Ac 5:42;** τ. κύριον Ἰ. **11:20;** cp. **17:18.** εὐ. περὶ τῆς βασιλείας **8:12** (Jos., Ant. 15, 209 περὶ τούτων εὐηγγελίζετο). W. acc. and inf. foll. (Plut., Mar. 22 [22, 4]; Jos., Ant. 6, 56) **Ac 14:15;** 1 Cl 42:3.

γ. w. mention of the one who receives the message τινί (Aristoph., Eq. 643 al.; Jer 20:15; ParJer 3:15; Philo, De Jos. 250; Jos., Ant. 5, 24) **Lk 4:18** (Is 61:1); **Ro 1:15; 1 Cor 15:2; Gal 1:8a; 4:13; 1 Pt 1:12** P[72]. εἰς τ. ὑπερέκεινα ὑμῶν εὐ. *proclaim the gospel in lands beyond you* **2 Cor 10:16** (cp. **1 Pt 1:25**). τινά (Alciphron 2, 9, 2 v.l.; Heliod. 2, 10, 1 ed. IBekker [acc. to mss.]; Jos., Ant. 18, 228; Eus., HE 3, 4) **Lk 1:28 v.l.; 3:18; Ac 8:25, 40; 14:21; 16:10; Gal 1:9; 1 Pt 1:12;** Pol 6:3; PtK 3 p. 15, 19.

δ. abs. *proclaim* (ParJer 9:20 ἀποστόλους ἵνα εὐαγγελίζονται ἐν τοῖς ἔθνεσιν) **Lk 9:6; 20:1; Ac 14:7; Ro 15:20; 1 Cor 1:17; 9:16, 18.**

ⓑ pass.—**α.** w. a thing as subj. *be proclaimed* **Lk 16:16; Gal 1:11** (τὸ εὐαγγέλιον); **1 Pt 1:25.** Impers. νεκροῖς εὐηγγελίσθη **1 Pt 4:6** (cp. Just., D. 72, 4).

β. w. a pers. as subj. of one receiving a message of deliverance *have good news announced to one* (2 Km 18:31; Jo 3:5) of the gospel **Mt 11:5; Lk 7:22; Hb 4:2, 6.** Of apostles receiving the gospel in behalf of others ἀπό τινος *fr. someone* 1 Cl 42:1.—B. 1478. DELG s.v. ἄγγελος. M-M. EDNT. TW. Spicq.

εὐαγγέλιον, ου, τό (s. prec. entry; Hom. et al.; LXX, TestSol D 1:13; ApcSed 14:9; Joseph., Just., Mel.) orig. 'a reward for good news', then simply 'good news' (so Plut., Sertor. 573 [11, 8]; 582 [26, 6], Phoc. 749 [16, 8]; 752 [23, 6] al.; Appian, Bell. Civ. 3, 93 §384; 4, 20 §78; Ps.-Lucian, Asin. 26; Jos., Bell. 2, 420; 4, 618; 656; IG III, 10 = II², 1077 [OWeinreich, ARW 18, 1915, p. 43, 3]; papyrus letter [after 238 AD] in Dssm., LO 313f [LAE 371]=Sb 421.—Also in sacral use: Diod. S. 15, 74, 2 Διονύσιος τοῖς θεοῖς εὐαγγέλια θύσας=offered a sacrifice for good news to the gods; OGI 458=IPriene 105, 40f ἦρξεν δὲ τῷ κόσμῳ τῶν δι' αὐτὸν εὐανγελίων ἡ γενέθλιος τοῦ θεοῦ [s. AHarnack, Red. u. Aufs. I² 1906, 310ff; PWendland, ZNW 5, 1904, 335ff, D. urchristl. Literaturformen 1912, 409f]; Philostrat., Vi. Apollon. 1, 28 of the appearing of Apollon.; Ael. Aristid. 53, 3 K.=55 p. 708 D.: Ζεὺς Εὐαγγέλιος) in our lit. only in the sense of good news relating to God's action in Jesus Christ.

❶ **God's good news to humans, *good news*** as proclamation

ⓐ abs.—**α.** τὸ εὐαγγέλιον **Mk 1:15; 8:35; 10:29; Ro 1:16; 10:16; 11:28; 1 Cor 4:15; 9:18, 23; 2 Cor 8:18; Gal 2:2; Eph 3:6; Phil 1:5; 2:22; 4:3; 1 Th 2:4; 2 Ti 1:8, 10;** IPhld 5:1, 2; 8:2; 9:2; ISm 5:1; 7:2; MPol 1:1; 22:1.

β. in gen., dependent on another noun ὁ λόγος τοῦ εὐ. **Ac 15:7;** τὸ μυστήριον τ. εὐ. **Eph 6:19;** cp. vs. **15; Phil 1:7, 12, 16;** ἡ ἀλήθεια τοῦ εὐ. **Gal 2:5, 14; Col 1:5** (but the last passage can also be transl. *the true message of the gospel*). ἡ ἐλπὶς τοῦ εὐ. *the hope that is kindled by the gospel* vs. **23;** ἡ πίστις τοῦ εὐ. *faith in the gospel* **Phil 1:27;** ἐν τ. δεσμοῖς τοῦ εὐ. **Phlm 13;** ἡ ἐξουσία τοῦ εὐ. *authority over* (i.e. *to proclaim*) *the gospel* B 8:3; ἀρχὴ τοῦ εὐ. *beginning* (of the proclaiming) *of the gospel* **Phil 4:15;** cp. 1 Cl 47:2 (s. on this WHartke, D. Sammlung u. d. ältesten Ausgaben der Paulusbriefe 1917, 55); **Mk 1:1** (s. 3 below).

γ. in certain combinations w. verbs τὸ εὐ. κηρύσσειν **Mt 26:13; Mk 13:10; 14:9** (JJeremias, ZNW 44, '53, 103–7: apocalyptic proclamation); **16:15;** cp. **Mt 4:23; 9:35; 24:14; Mk 1:14; Ac 1:2** D; B 5:9; GMary 463, 29; 33. καταγγέλλειν **1 Cor 9:14.** γνωρίζειν **15:1.** εὐαγγελίζεσθαι **Gal 1:11** (cp. **2 Cor 11:7**).

ⓑ in combination—**α.** w. adj. εὐ. αἰώνιον **Rv 14:6.** ἕτερον **2 Cor 11:4; Gal 1:6** (EGrässer, ZTK 66, '69, 306–44). ἅγιον AcPlCor 2:36.

β. w. gen. (s. OSchmitz, D. Christusgemeinschaft des Pls im Lichte seines Genetivgebrauchs 1924, 45–88).

א. objective genitive εὐ. τῆς βασιλείας **Mt 4:23; 9:35; 24:14.** τ. θεοῦ **Mk 1:14.** τ. χάριτος τ. θεοῦ *of God's grace* **Ac 20:24.** τ. εἰρήνης **Eph 6:15.** τ. σωτηρίας **1:13.** τ. δόξης τ. Χριστοῦ *of the glory of Christ* **2 Cor 4:4;** cp. **1 Ti 1:11** (τὸ Ἰησοῦ Χριστοῦ εὐ. Orig., C. Cels. 2, 13, 62). εὐ. τ. Χριστοῦ is usu. interpr. as the *gospel* (*good news*) *about Christ* (because of **Ro 1:1–3; 2 Cor 4:4; 1 Th 3:2,** cp. **Ro 15:16**) **Ro 15:19; 1 Cor 9:12; 2 Cor 2:12** (here and **Ro 1:1** εἰς εὐαγγέλιον=for the purpose of bringing the good news, as Appian, Bell. Civ. 4, 113 §474). **2 Cor 9:13; 10:14; Gal 1:7; Phil 1:27; 1 Th 3:2;** cp. **Ro 1:9; 2 Th 1:8;** B 5:9; MPol 19:1. εὐ. τῆς ἀκροβυστίας *the gospel for the uncircumcised* **Gal 2:7.**

ב. Subjective genitive (τοῦ) θεοῦ **Ro 1:1; 15:16; 2 Cor 11:7; 1 Th 2:2, 8, 9; 1 Pt 4:17.** The one who is commissioned to do the proclaiming can be mentioned in the subj. gen. εὐ. μου, ἡμῶν **Ro 2:16; 16:25; 2 Cor 4:3; 1 Th 1:5; 2 Th 2:14; 2 Ti 2:8.** S. LBaudiment, 'L'Évangile' de St. Paul 1925; Molland (3 below) 83–97.

❷ details relating to the life and ministry of Jesus, ***good news of Jesus*** D 8:2; 11:3; 15:3f; 2 Cl 8:5; MPol 4:1; perh. also **Mk 1:1** (LKeck, The Introduction to Mark's Gospel, NTS 12, '66, 352–70; DDormeyer, NTS 33, '87, 452–68); IPhld 8:2; ISm 7:2. This usage marks a transition to

❸ a book dealing with the life and teaching of Jesus, a ***gospel account*** that deals w. the life and teaching of Jesus (Just., A I, 66, 3 al.) Dg 11:6 (ἐν τοῖς εὐ.; TestSol 1:13 D; Orig., C. Cels. 1:9, 19 [w. ἐν τοῖς προφήταις]) τὸ καθ' Ἑβραίους εὐ.—Papias (2:17).—(Cp. ὁ τὸ εὐ. γράψας Ἰωάννης Orig., C. Cels. 5, 12, 13).—ASeeberg, D. Evangelium Christi 1905; Harnack, Entstehg. u. Entwicklg. d. Kirchenverfassung 1910, 199–239; PZondervan, Het woord 'Evangelium': TT 48, 1914, 187–213; MBurrows, The Origin of the Word 'Gospel': JBL 44, 1925, 21–33; JSchniewind, Euangelion 1; 2; 1927, '31, Die Begriffe Wort u. Evglm. b. Pls, diss. Halle 1910; AFridrichsen, Τὸ εὐαγγέλιον hos Pls: NorTT 13, 1912, 153–70; 209–56, Der Begriff Evgl. b. Irenäus, Hippolyt, Novatian: ibid. 1917, 148–70; AOepke, D. Missionspredigt des Ap. Pls. 1920, 50ff; EBurton, ICC Gal 1921, 422f; EMolland, D. Paulin. Euangelion; D. Wort u. d. Sache '34; RAsting, D. Verkündigung im Urchristentum '39 (on Word of God, Gospel, Witness); GFriedrich, TW II 705–35; KRengstorf, ZNW 31, '32, 54–56; MAlbertz, D. Botschaft des NT, vols. I and II, '47–'57; JvDodewaard, Biblica 35, '54, 160–73; HKoester, TU 65, '57, 6–12; JBowman, 'Gospel' and Its Cognates in Palestinian Syriac, NT Essays (TManson memorial), ed. Higgins '59, 54–67; HFrankemölle, Evangelium '88; HKoester, From the Kerygma to the Written Gospels: NTS 35, '89, 361–81; RAC VI 1107–60.—DELG s.v. ἄγγελος. M-M. On εὐαγγελ- terms s. New Docs 3, 12–14. EDNT. TW. Spicq. Sv.

εὐαγγελιστής, οῦ, ὁ (s. prec. two entries; acc. to ADieterich ZNW 1, 1900, 336–38, title of polytheistic priests: IG XII/1, 675.—GDI 5702, 22; 37 [Ionic] εὐαγγελίς is the official title of the priestess of Hera) ***proclaimer of the gospel, evangelist*** (ApcSed 15:4 [of Matthew]) **Eph 4:11** (DHadidian, CBQ 28, '66, 317–21: gospel writer). Acc. to **Ac 21:8** a designation of Philip (s. Ac 6:5). **2 Ti 4:5** Timothy is so called.—Harnack, Mission u. Ausbreitung[4] 1924, 334, 6 al. (p. 983 index).—M-M. TW. Spicq.

εὐανθής, ές, gen. οῦς (ἄνθη, 'full bloom'; Hom. et al.; Plut., Lucian, Aelian et al.; SEG VIII, 548, 8 [I BC]; Philo, Somn. 1, 205) ***beautifully blooming*** φυτά *beautifully blooming plants* ApcPt 5:15.—DELG s.v. ἄνθος.

εὐαρεστέω (s. ἀρεστός and εὐάρεστος) fut. εὐαρεστήσω Ps 114:9; 1 aor. εὐηρέστησα; pf. εὐηρέστηκα; on the augment s. B-D-F §69, 4.

❶ to do someth. or act in a manner that is pleasing or satisfactory, ***please, be pleasing*** τινί *to someone* (SIG 611, 19 [189 BC]; Diod. S. 14, 4, 2; Plut., Mor. 121f; Epict. 1, 12, 8; 2, 23, 42; LXX; Just.; Tat. 9:2) τῷ θεῷ (Gen 6:9; Philo, Abr. 35, Exsecr. 167; cp. TestGad 7:6) 1 Cl 41:1; Hv 3, 1, 9. Of Enoch, who pleased God (Gen 5:22, 24; Sir 44:16) **Hb 11:5** (PKatz, Kratylos 5, '60, 160f), and in the same context vs. **6,** where the verb stands abs.; τῷ παντοκράτορι θεῷ ὁσίως εὐ. 1 Cl 62:2. Of Jesus εὐηρέστησεν τῷ πέμψαντι αὐτόν IMg 8:2; *please* the Lord (Christ) Pol 5:2.

❷ to experience pleasure, ***be pleased, take delight***—**ⓐ** act. (Lysippus Com. [V BC] 7 ed. Kock I 702) τινί *with* or *in someth.* (Dionys. Hal. 11, 60, 1; EpArist 286; cp. Ps 25:3) τῷ νόμῳ *with the law* Hs 8, 3, 5 (but here mng. 1 cannot be totally ruled out).

ⓑ the pass. is mostly used in this sense (prob. POxy 265, 43 [I AD] καὶ εὐαρ[εστοῦμαι?]) εὐαρεστοῦμαί τινι *be satisfied w. someth.* (Diod. S. 3, 55, 9; 20, 79, 2; Diog. L. 10, 137). τοιαύταις θυσίαις *with such sacrifices* **Hb 13:16.**—DELG s.v. ἀρέσκω. M-M. TW.

εὐαρέστησις, εως, ἡ (s. prec. entry; Diod. S. 26, 1, 1; Dionys. Hal.; Plut., Mor. 574f; Epict. 1, 12 tit.; Aq., Sym., Theod. Ex 29:18; Sym. Ezk 20:41; Theod. Lev 1:9; TestIss 4:1; Philo, Deus Imm. 116; Jos., Ant. 12, 269) **the experience of being pleased because of what another does,** ***being pleased*** εἰς εὐ. τῷ ὀνόματι αὐτοῦ *that they may be well-pleasing to (God's) name* (i.e., to God) 1 Cl 64.

εὐάρεστος, ον ***pleasing, acceptable*** (s. εὐαρεστέω; in the Gr-Rom. world commonly said of things and esp. of pers. noted for their civic-minded generosity and who endeavor to do things that are pleasing: Diod. S. 15, 46, 5; IPriene 114, 15 [after 84 BC]; ins of Nisyros: MAI 15, 1890, p. 134, 11f; PFay 90, 17; PFlor 30, 30; PStras 1, 9; Wsd; Philo, De Jos. 195; Just.) τινί *to someone.* In our lit. gener. w. ref. to God, to whom someth. is acceptable τῷ θεῷ (Wsd 4:10; Philo, Spec. Leg. 1, 201, Virt. 67; TestDan 1:3; Just., D. 45, 4; Theoph. Ant. 2, 29 [p. 170, 12]) **Ro 12:1; 14:18; 2 Cor 5:9** (prob. w. Christ as referent) w. φιλοτιμέομαι, q.v.; **Phil 4:18;** 1 Cl 49:5; ISm 8:2. τῷ κυρίῳ **Eph 5:10;** Hs 5, 3, 2. ἐνώπιον τοῦ θεοῦ **Hb 13:21;** cp. 1 Cl 21:1; 60:2; 61:2. ἐν κυρίῳ **Col 3:20.** εὐ. δοῦλος τ. θεοῦ Hm 12, 3, 1. Of the content of the divine will τὰ εὐάρεστα (καὶ εὐπρόσδεκτα) αὐτῷ 1 Cl 35:5. Abs. τὸ εὐάρεστον (w. ἀγαθόν, τέλειον) *what is acceptable* to God **Ro 12:2.** Of slaves εὐ. εἶναι *give satisfaction* to their masters **Tit 2:9** (the choice of diction prob. designed to elevate their status). In a parable *well thought of,* i.e. the master was quite satisfied with his performance Hs 5, 2, 2.—M-M. TW.

Εὐάρεστος, ου, ὁ (in ins of Smyrna CIG 3148; 3152; 3162 and also found elsewh., e.g. Ael. Aristid. 50, 23 K.=26 p. 508 D.; Sb 3988; Jos., Ant. 19, 145) ***Evarestus,*** a Christian of Smyrna, writer of the church's letter about the martyrdom of Polycarp MPol 20:2.

εὐαρέστως adv. (s. εὐαρεστός; X., Mem. 3, 5, 5; Epict. 1, 12, 21, fgm. 34 Sch.; CIG 2885, 20; SIG 587, 10; 708, 20 [II BC]; Just., D. 45, 4; 49, 4) ***in an acceptable manner*** εὐ. λατρεύειν τῷ θεῷ **Hb 12:28.**—M-M. TW.

Εὐβούλα, ας (so also IGLSyria 931, otherwise Εὐβούλη [s. WRoscher I 1396 and Aa I 63, 2 al.] as Sb 8954 [Ptolemaic])

Eubula, wife of the freedman Diophantos (s. Διόφαντος) AcPl Ha 2, 13; 17; 35; 3, 3; 11; 4, 15; 5, 19.

Εὔβουλος, ου, ὁ (Diod. S. 16, 66, 1; freq. in ins [cp. SIG[2] index I] and pap [s. Preisigke, Namenb.]) ***Eubulus,*** a Christian in Rome **2 Ti 4:21.** A presbyter in Corinth AcPl Ha 1, 1.—LGPN I.

εὖγε adv. (εὖ + γέ; Aristoph., Pla.; Arrian, Cyneg. 18, 1; Lucian, LXX) ***well done! excellent!*** **Lk 19:17** (v.l. εὖ, q.v.).—DELG s.v. ἐύς.

εὐγενής, ές, gen. οῦς (s. γένος; trag.+; loanw. in rabb.) comp. εὐγενέστερος (Mitt-Wilck. I/2 131, 33f [IV AD]).

❶ pert. to being of high status, ***well-born, high-born*** (X., Hell. 4, 1, 7; Philo, De Jos. 106; Jos., Ant. 10, 186; Just.) **1 Cor 1:26.** ἄνθρωπός τις εὐ. *a certain nobleman* **Lk 19:12.**

❷ pert. to having the type of attitude ordinarily associated with well-bred persons, ***noble-minded, open-minded*** οὗτοι ἦσαν εὐγενέστεροι τῶν ἐν Θεσσαλονίκῃ *these were more open-minded than those in Th.* **Ac 17:11** (cp. Menand. Dysc. 723 [FDanker, NTS 10, '64, 366f; Cicero, Ad Att. 13, 21, 7; Jos., Ant. 12, 255).—EbNestle, ZNW 15, 1914, 91f.—DELG s.v. γίγνομαι. M-M. TW. Spicq.

εὐγλωττία, ας, ἡ (s. γλῶσσα; Eur. et al; Maximus Tyr. 25, 2d) **smoothness of tongue, with implication of ingratiating manner,** ***glibness, fluency of speech*** **Ro 16:18 v.l.** (on this rdg. JNorth, NTS 42, '96, 600f; cp. εὐλογία).—DELG s.v. γλῶχες.

εὐδαιμονέω aor. inf. εὐδαιμονῆσαι (Just., A I, 3, 3 [Pla., Rep. 5, 473de]) a person who prospers or experiences some good fortune appears to be enjoying special favor from a divinity [δαίμων], hence ***be happy, fortunate*** (trag., Hdt. et al.; Epict.; POxy 1593, 2; Philo; Jos., C. Ap. 1, 224; Just.) Dg 10:5.—Schmidt, Syn. IV 394–407, esp. 398–402. DELG s.v. δαίμων.

εὐδία, ας, ἡ (εὔδιος 'calm, clear' [the early gen. of Ζεύς is Διός])—**❶** ***fair weather*** (X., Pla. et al.; Plut., Mor. 8c; POxy 1223, 12; Sir 3:15; Philo, Gig. 51) **Mt 16:2.**

❷ oft. in imagery, to represent peace and rest (opp. χειμών: Pind., al.; X., An. 5, 8, 20; Epict. 2, 18, 30), then in the mng. ***tranquillity, peace*** (Herodas 1, 28; OGI 90, 11 [196 BC] τ. Αἴγυπτον εἰς εὐδίαν ἀγαγεῖν; Philo, Spec. Leg. 1, 69; Jos., Ant. 14, 157) ISm 11:3.—DELG. M-M. Spicq.

εὐδίδακτος, ον (s. διδακτός, διδάσκω; Diod. S. 2, 29, 4) ***docile,*** of a lion: ὡς ἀμνὸς εὐ. καὶ ὡς δοῦλος αὐτοῦ *like a docile lamb and as (Paul's) servant* AcPl Ha 4, 31.—DELG s.v. διδάσκω.

εὐδοκέω impf. ηὐδόκουν (on **1 Th 2:8** and the form εὐδοκοῦμεν [v.l. ηὐδοκοῦμεν] s. W-S. §12, 5b; B-D-F §67, 1; Rob. 1215); fut. εὐδοκήσω LXX; 1 aor. εὐδόκησα and ηὐδόκησα (s. δοκέω and two next entries; gener. 'to be content, be well pleased': Polyb., Diod. S., Dionys. Hal.; ins, pap, LXX; PsSol 2:4; Test12Patr, Just.; Anz 358)

❶ to consider someth. as good and therefore worthy of choice, ***consent, determine, resolve*** w. inf. foll. (Polyb. 1, 78, 8; PGrenf I, 1, 17 [II BC] εὐδοκῶ ζήλῳ δουλεύειν; PTebt 591; Esth 4:17d; 1 Macc 6:23; 14:46f. Of God Ps 67:17) **Lk 12:32; 1 Cor 1:21; Gal 1:15; 1 Th 2:8; 3:1.** ἐν αὐτῷ εὐδόκησεν πᾶν τὸ πλήρωμα κατοικῆσαι *all the fullness willed to dwell in him* **Col 1:19.** εὐ. μᾶλλον w. inf. *wish rather, prefer* (cp. Polyb. 18, 35, 4; Sir 25:16) **2 Cor 5:8.** W. acc. and inf. (Polyb. 1, 8, 4; 2 Macc 14:35) **Ro 15:26.** Abs. (SIG 683, 59; SIG[2] 853, 2; PRyl 120, 24; 155, 17; 1 Macc 11:29) vs. **27.**

❷ to take pleasure or find satisfaction in someth., ***be well pleased, take delight***—ⓐ w. pers. obj. ἔν τινι *with* or *in someone* (of God's delight in someone 2 Km 22:20; Is 62:4 v.l.; Mal 2:17; Ps 43:4) **Mt 3:17; 17:5; Mk 1:11** (on the aor. s. BBacon, JBL 20, 1901, 28–30); **Lk 3:22; 1 Cor 10:5; Hb 10:38** (Hab 2:4); GEb 18, 37; 39. Also ἐπί τινα (Is 54:17 v.l.) ibid. εἴς τινα (cp. Just., D. 29, 1 εἰς τὰ ἔθνη) **2 Pt 1:17.** τινά (SIG 672, 27 [162/160 BC]; Gen 33:10) **Mt 12:18 v.l.** (for εἰς ὅν). Abs. **Ro 9:16 v.l.**

ⓑ w. impers. obj., also *delight in, like, approve* τί (Eccl 9:7; Sir 15:17) **Hb 10:6, 8;** 1 Cl 18:16 (on all three pass. cp. Ps 50:18). τινί (Polyb. 2, 38, 7; Diod. S. 14, 110, 4; PLond III, 1168, 15 p. 136 [18 AD]; POxy 261, 17 [55 AD]; 1 Esdr 4:39; 1 Macc 1:43) **2 Th 2:12.** ἔν τινι (Polyb. 2, 12, 3; Sb 4512, 57 [II BC] συγχώρησιν, ἐν ᾗ οὐκ εὐδοκεῖ ὁ πατήρ; Hg 1:8; Sir 34:19; Just., D. 12, 3) **2 Cor 12:10; 2 Th 2:12 v.l.**—DELG s.v. δοκάω II. M-M. TW. Spicq.

εὐδόκησις, εως, ἡ (s. prec. and next entry; Polyb. 16, 20, 4; Diod. S. 15, 6, 4; Dionys. Hal. 3, 13; SIG 685, 108 [139 BC], OGI 335, 122 [II BC]; PLond II, 289, 35 p. 185 [91 AD]; POxy 1200, 35) **the quality or state of being satisfied,** ***approval, satisfaction, good pleasure*** γίνεσθαι ἐν εὐ. 1 Cl 40:3.

εὐδοκία, ας, ἡ (s. εὐδοκέω; Hippocr.: CMG I 1 p. 32, 7 εὐδοκίη; Philod., π. εὐσεβ. 25, 5 [TGomperz, Herculan. Studien II 1866 p. 145]; FJacobs, Anth. Gr. II 1814 p. 815 no. 179; IG XIV 102*. Elsewh. only in Jewish lit.—LXX; PsSol 3:4; 8:33; En; TestSol D 8:4; TestBenj 11:2; Philo, Somn. 2, 40 v.l.—and Christian wr.; Hesychius; Suda).

❶ state or condition of being kindly disposed, ***good will*** of humans δι' εὐδοκίαν *from good will* **Phil 1:15;** ὑπὲρ τῆς εὐ. *above and beyond good will* or *in his* (God's) *good will* (in which case s. 2 below) **2:13.** εὐ. ἀγαθωσύνης *good will of uprightness* (subj. gen. like the foll. ἔργον πίστεως) or *desire for/interest in goodness* (obj. gen.), as 3 below, **2 Th 1:11. Lk 2:14** ἐν ἀνθρώποις εὐδοκίας has frequently been interpreted *among men characterized by good will* (on the text s. AMerx, D. vier kanon. Ev. II 2, 1905, 198–202; on the content, w. varying views on the source [human or divine] of εὐ., GAicher, BZ 9, 1907, 381–91; 402f; Harnack, SBBerlAk 1915, 854–75 [=Studien I '31, 153–79], s. JRopes, HTR 10, 1917, 52–56; JJeremias, ZNW 28, 1929, 13–20; GvRad, ibid. 29, 1930, 111–15; EBöklen, Deutsches Pfarrerblatt 36, '32, 309f; JWobbe, BZ 22, '34, 118–52; 224–45; 23, '36, 358–64; ESmothers, RSR 24, '34, 86–93; FHerklotz, ZKT 58, '34, 113f; Goodsp, Probs. 75f; CHunzinger, ZNW 44, '52f, 85–90; JFitzmyer, TS [Baltimore] 19, '58, 225–27=Essays 101–4 [Qumran parallels]). But evidence from Qumran (1QH 4:32f; see Hunzinger above) and recent literary analysis of Lk points to mng. 2 below, whether εὐδοκία or εὐδοκίας is the rdg. preferred.

❷ state or condition of being favored, ***favor, good pleasure*** this would refer to the persons upon whom divine favor rests (so oft. LXX; En 1:8; TestSol D 8:4; s. Jeremias and Fitzmyer w. Qumran ref. cited in 1), and the mng. (w. the rdg. εὐδοκίας) would be *people to whom (God) shows good will* or *whom (God) favors* (B-D-F §165). On οὕτως εὐ. ἐγένετο ἔμπροσθέν σου **Mt 11:26; Lk 10:21** s. ἔμπροσθεν 1bδ; κατὰ τὴν εὐ. τ. θελήματος αὐτοῦ **Eph 1:5;** cp. vs. **9.**—The mng. 'favor' is close to

❸ desire, usually directed toward someth. that causes satisfaction or favor, ***wish, desire*** (cp. Ps 144:16 ἐμπιπλᾷς πᾶν ζῷον εὐδοκίας=you give freely to every living thing whatever it desires; Sir 39:18; also 1:27; 35:3) εὐ. τῆς ἐμῆς καρδίας *the*

desire of my heart **Ro 10:1;** cp. **2 Th 1:11,** and s. 1 above.—M-M. EDNT. TW. Spicq. Sv.

εὐειδής, ές, gen. **οῦς** (s. εἶδος; Hom. et al.; LXX; En 24:2; Ath. 34, 1) comp. εὐειδέστερος, superl. εὐειδέστατος ***well-formed, beautiful,*** of women (Hom. et al.) εὐειδέσταται τῷ χαρακτῆρι *very beautiful in outward appearance* Hs 9, 9, 5. Of a young person (Cornutus 32 p. 66, 16; Da 1:4) *handsome* Hv 2, 4, 1. Also παῖς λίαν εὐειδὴς ἐν χάριτι=*a boy of unusual charm* AcPl Ha 3, 13. Of fruits *more beautiful* Hs 9, 28, 3.

εὐείκτως adv. of εὔεικτος (Etymol. Magn. 390, 33 εὔεικτον; Cass. Dio 69, 20) *tractably* 1 Cl 37:2 cj. (Tdf. for εἰκτικῶς).

εὐεργεσία, ας, ἡ (s. two next entries; Hom.+) in the Gr-Rom. world freq. used of performance by civic-minded pers.

❶ **the doing of that which is beneficial,** ***doing of good*** (Diod. S. 20, 25, 2) or ***service*** (Herm. Wr. 1, 30; Wsd 16:11; EpArist 205) τῆς εὐ. ἀντιλαμβάνεσθαι *devote oneself to* or *benefit by service* (in the second interp. a slave's obligatory action is transmuted into extraordinary service; s. ἀντιλ. 2 and 4) **1 Ti 6:2.**

❷ **the content of beneficial service,** ***good deed, benefit, a kindness*** (Jos., Ant. 6, 211; 11, 213) w. the obj. gen. of the one who benefits by it (Pla., Leg. 850b εὐ. πόλεως) εὐ. ἀνθρώπου ἀσθενοῦς *a good deed to a sick man* **Ac 4:9.** Pl. *good deeds* (Appian, Bell. Civ. 5, 60 §255; Chion 16, 7; ins, pap; 2 Macc 9:26; TestJob 44:2; ParJer 3:12; Jos., Ant. 16, 146) of God's doing (Diod. S. 2, 25, 8 ἡ τῶν θεῶν εὐ.; 3, 56, 5; Ael. Aristid. 50, 68 K.=26 p. 522 D.: εὐ. τοῦ θεοῦ; Ps 77:11; Philo) 1 Cl 19:2; 21:1; 38:3; Dg 8:11; 9:5.—DELG s.v. ἔργον. M-M. TW. Spicq.

εὐεργετέω aor. εὐεργέτησα; aor. pass. 3 pl. εὐεργετήθησαν Wsd 11:5; fut. 3 pl. εὐεργετηθήσονται Wsd 3:5 (s. prec. entry; trag+; esp. freq. in ins and pap) **to render exceptional service, esp. to a community,** ***do good to, benefit*** τινά *someone* (Aeschyl. et al.; Philo, Mut. Nom. 18) τὰ πάντα *do good to all things* 1 Cl 20:11 (cp. EpArist 210). τὸν ἐλαττούμενον Dg 10:6. Abs. (Soph. et al.) **Ac 10:38.** Pass. *be treated well* (X., Pla. et al.; ins, POxy 899, 45; LXX; TestJob 16:5; SyrBar 13:12; Philo; Jos., Ant. 14, 370) εὐεργετούμενοι χείρους γίνονται *when they are well treated, they become even worse* IRo 5:1.—HBolkestein, Wohltätigkt. u. Armenpflege im vorchr. Altertum '39; s. other lit. next entry.—M-M. EDNT. TW. Spicq.

εὐεργέτης, ου, ὁ (s. prec. two entries; Pind. et al.; ins, pap, LXX; Tat. 18:12) ***benefactor*** as a title of princes and other honored pers., esp. those recognized for their civic contributions (Hdt. 8, 85; X., Hell. 6, 1, 4 al.; esp. ins [SIG² index III 5 p. 175, VI p. 321; also SIG index IV]; POxy 38, 13 [I AD]; 486, 27. Coins [Dssm., LO 215, 4/LAE 249, 1]. Esth 8:12n; 2 Macc 4:2; 3 Macc 3:19; Philo, Omn. Prob. Lib. 118, In Flacc. 81; Jos., Bell. 3, 459. S. JOehler, Pauly-W. VI 978–81; Magie 67f) **Lk 22:25** (on the thought cp. Aeschin. 3, 248–50; s. also DLull, NovT 29, '86, 289–305). Of God (Ael. Aristid. 43, 29 K.=1 p. 11 D. of Zeus; Plut., Mor. 355e Osiris μέγας βασιλεὺς εὐ.; Philo of Byblus in Eus., PE 1, 9, 29; CIG 5041=Mitt-Wilck. I/2, 116, 6 Isis and Sarapis as εὐεργέται; Philo, Spec. Leg. 1, 209, Congr. Erud. Grat. 171 and oft.; PGM 4, 992; 1048.—Wendland, Kultur 103; 121f; RKnopf on 1 Cl 19:2) εὐ. πνευμάτων 1 Cl 59:3.—ESkard, Zwei relig.-politische Begriffe: Euergetes-Concordia '32; ANock, Soter and Euergetes: The Joy of Study (FGrant Festschr.) '51, 127–48; A Passoni dell' Acqua, Aegyptus 76, 177–91; FDanker, Proclamation Commentaries: Luke, '87, 28–46, Benefactor, '82, 323–25; The Endangered Benefactor in Luke-Acts: SBLSP 20, '81, 39–48; on philosophical perspectives s. CManning, Liberalitas, The Decline and Rehabilitation of a Virtue: Greece and Rome 2d ser. 32, '85, 73–83; RAC VI 848–60.—Larfeld I 495. M-M. EDNT. TW. Spicq. Sv.

εὐεργετικός, ή, όν (s. prec. three entries; Aristot. et al.; Diod. S. 6, 1, 8; Vett. Val. 9, 18; 11, 8f; OGI 90, 11; 34; Mitt-Wilck. 352, 11; Wsd 7:22; Jos., Ant. 16, 150) ***beneficent*** of God (Antipat. of Tarsus [c. 150 BC] in Plut., Stoic. Repugn. 38 p. 1051e; Arius Didym. [c. birth of Christ] in Eus., PE 15, 15, 5; Diod. S. 1, 25, 3: τὸ εὐεργετικόν=the will to do good, of Isis; Musonius 90, 11 H.; Philo, Plant. 90) 1 Cl 23:1.—M-M.

εὐθαλέω (s. next entry; Nicander, fgm. 74, 16; Plut. et al.; Da 4:4 Theod.) ***flourish, thrive*** of trees (POxy 729, 22 [137 AD]; PVindBosw 8, 22) Dg 12:1.—DELG s.v. θάλλω.

εὐθαλής, ές (s. prec. entry) ***flourishing, thriving,*** of plants

ⓐ lit. (Moschus 3, 107; Dio Chrys. 13 [7], 15; Plut., Mor. 409a; Da 4:21 Theod.; TestJos 19:3 [Armenian vers., s. Charles] τόπον εὐθαλῆ.—Philo, Rer. Div. Her. 270]; Just., D. 110, 4; 119, 3 [both fig.]) Hs 9, 1, 7; 9, 24, 1. Of vines in a well-kept vineyard 5, 2, 4f.

ⓑ in imagery (Aeschyl., fgm. 290, 5d al.; POxy 902, 15) Hs 4:3.

εὔθετος, ον (s. τίθημι; Aeschyl., Hippocr. et al.; Polyb. 26, 5, 6; Diod. S.; SIG 736, 74; 148; 154; PTebt 27, 44 [113 BC]; PFlor 3, 8; LXX; EpArist 122) orig. 'well-placed', then in ref. to **that which is well suited for someth.,** ***fit, suitable, usable, convenient*** τινί *for someth.* (Nicol. Com. [IV BC], fgm. 1, 40 [in Stob., Flor. 14, 7 vol. III p. 471, 14 H.] ἐμαυτὸν εὔ. τῷ πράγματι . . . γεγονέναι) τῇ βασιλείᾳ τοῦ θεοῦ **Lk 9:62** (vv.ll. ἐν τῇ β., εἰς τὴν β.); *for someone* **Hb 6:7.** εἴς τι *for someth.* (Diod. S. 2, 57; Dionys. Hal., Comp. Verb. 1; Diosc. 2, 65) of salt οὔτε εἰς γῆν οὔτε εἰς κοπρίαν *of no use either for the soil or for the dunghill* **Lk 14:35** (on the difficult εἰς γῆν s. FPerles, ZNW 19, 1920, 96). καιρὸς εὔ. *a convenient time* or *opportunity* (Diod. S. 14, 80, 1; Ps 31:6; Artapanus: 726 fgm. 3, 7 [in Eus., PE 9, 27, 7]) καιρὸν εὔ. λαμβάνειν (Diod. S. 5, 57, 4 οἱ Αἰγύπτιοι καιρ. εὔ. λαβόντες) Pol 13:1.—DELG s.v. τίθημι. M-M. B. 644.

εὐθέως adv. of εὐθύς (Soph.+; in H. Gk., including LXX [Helbing 23], pseudepigr.; Just., D. 10, 4, more common than the adv. εὐθύς and εὐθύ. In Philo and Jos. [Bell. 1, 527, Ant. 19, 362] less freq. than the adv. εὐθύς. Mayser 245; WSchmid, Der Atticismus III 1893, 126; loanw. in rabb. In mss. and edd., esp. t.r., instead of adv. εὐθύς q.v.) ***at once, immediately*** **Mt 4:20, 22; 8:3; 13:5; 14:31** (quick rescue from danger at sea; cp. BGU 423, 8 [II AD] of Sarapis: ἔσωσε εὐθέως) and oft. (acc. to N. 13 times in Mt; 1 in Mk; 6 in Lk; 3 in J; 9 in Ac. Also **Gal 1:16; Js 1:24; 3J 14; Rv 4:2;** 7 times in Apostolic Fathers, e.g. 1 Cl 12:4; MPol 6:1; Hm 6, 2, 3). On the difference betw. εὐθέως and εὐθύς s. HvSoden, D. Schriften d. NT I/2, 1911, §314 p. 1391; HPernot, Études sur la langue des Évangiles 1927, 181ff; DDaube, The Sudden in the Scriptures '64, 46–72; LRydbeck, Fachprosa 167–76. S. also παραχρῆμα.—DELG s.v. εὐθύς. M-M.

εὐθηνέω (s. next entry; epic, Ionic, and later by-form for Att. εὐθενέω) impf. 3 pl. εὐθηνοῦσαν La 1:5; aor. inf. εὐθηνῆσαι PsSol 1:3 **to be abundant in growth,** ***thrive, flourish, be in good condition***

ⓐ act. (Aeschyl. et al.; SIG 526, 42; 46; BGU 1122, 23 al.; LXX; PsSol 1:3; JosAs cod. A 12:7; 18:7; Philo, Det. Pot. ins 106; Jos., Ant. 7, 297) ὅλον τὸ ὄρος εὐθηνοῦν ἦν *the whole mountain was flourishing* Hs 9, 1, 8; 9, 24, 1 (cp. Da 4:4 Theod. ἐγὼ εὐθηνῶν ἤμην).

ⓑ mid., w. aor. pass. (Hdt. 1, 66 al.; POxy 1381, 238 [II AD]; Ps 72:12), w. sim. mng., of patience εὐθηνουμένη ἐν πλατυσμῷ μεγάλῳ *thrives in a spacious area* Hm 5, 2, 3 (cp. 1:2).—DELG s.v. εὐθενέω.

εὐθηνία, ας, ἡ (s. prec. entry; in var. senses 'well-being, prosperity, good condition' Aristot.; OGI 90, 13 [196 BC]; 669, 4; Sb 7027, 3; PTebt 788, 23 [II BC]; LXX; JosAs 1, 1; 22, 1; Philo, Congr. Erud. Grat. 173, Abr. 1; Jos., Bell. 4, 88; 6, 216) **state of favorable circumstances, *rapport, well-being,*** εὐθηνίαν πάντοτε ἕξεις μετὰ πάντων *you will enjoy a good relation with everyone* Hm 2:3 (εὐ. ἔχειν also Philo, Mut. Nom. 260). ἔχειν τὴν εὐ. ἐν ἑαυτῷ m 5, 1, 2. The older Lat. transl. (the so-called Vulgate) of Hermas renders the word in both pass. 'pax', *peace,* prob. rightly.

εὐθής, ές (s. τίθημι; LXX; Philo, Leg. All. 3, 309 codd.; TestAsh 1:2; Georg. Mon. 58, 21; 213, 8 deBoor [1892]; Chron. Pasch. 186, 18) by-form in H. Gk. for the adj. εὐθύς ***upright*** 1 Cl 18:10 (Ps 50:12).—DELG s.v. τίθημι.

εὐθίνη, ης s. Ἰουθίνη.

εὐθυδρομέω 1 aor. εὐθυδρόμησα of a ship ***run a straight course*** (s. εὐθύς, δρόμος; Philo, Agr. 174 πνεῦμα εὐθυδρομοῦν τὸ σκάφος ἀνέωσεν, Leg. All. 3, 223 ναῦς εὐθυδρομεῖ) εἰς Σαμοθρᾴκην **Ac 16:11** (w. εἰς as Agathias Hist. 2, 21 [VI AD]: HGM II 71). Abs. (Laud. Therap. 28 εὐθυδρομήσας διέφυγεν) εὐθυδρομήσαντες ἤλθομεν *we ran a straight course and came* **21:1** (εὐθυδρόμος in Polyb. 34, 4, 5; Orph. Hymns 21, 10 Qu.).—DELG s.v. δραμεῖν.

εὐθυμέω (s. θυμός and next entry; trans. = 'cheer, delight' Aeschyl. et al.; mid. = 'be cheerful' X., Pla. et al.) in our lit. only intr. ***be cheerful*** (Eur., Cycl. 530; Plut., Mor. 465c; 469f; PAmh 133, 4 [beg. II AD]; PLips 111, 5 al. in letters; Pr 15:15 Sym.; TestSol 25:9 B; TestJob 40:6; Jos., Ant. 18, 284) **Js 5:13;** *cheer up, keep up one's courage* **Ac 27:22, 25.**—DELG s.v. θυμός. M-M. Spicq.

εὔθυμος, ον (s. prec. and next entry; Hom. et al.) ***cheerful, in good spirits*** (Pind., Pla. et al.; Sb 6222, 10; 2 Macc 11:26; Jos., Bell. 1, 272, Ant. 14, 369) εὔθυμοι γενόμενοι πάντες *they were all encouraged* **Ac 27:36.** εὔθυμόν τινα ποιεῖν *encourage someone* Hm 8:10. Comp. εὐθυμότερος (OGI 669, 7 [I AD]; POxy 939, 19; Philo, De Jos. 162; 198) εὐθυμότερον γίνεσθαι IPol 7:1.—M-M.

εὐθύμως adv. (s. prec. two entries; Aeschyl., X. et al.; M. Ant. 3, 16, 4; OGI 669, 4 [I AD]; Jos., Ant. 10, 174; 258) ***cheerfully*** ἀπολογεῖσθαι *make one's defence cheerfully* **Ac 24:10** (v.l. εὐθυμότερον, cp. X., Cyr. 2, 2, 27; PGiss 41 II, 12).—M-M. Spicq.

εὐθύνω fut. 2 sg. εὐθυνεῖς PsSol 9:7; 1 aor. εὔθυνα (W-S. §13, 13); aor. pass. ηὐθύνθην LXX; 3 sg. εὐθύνθη 1 Km 18:26 (s. εὐθύς; trag.+; Cyr. Ins. 68–71 al.; BGU V [Gnomon], 220 [II AD]; LXX; PsSol 9:7; TestSol 19:1; TestJob 36:4; TestSim 5:2; Philo; Jos., Ant. 15, 76; Just., A I, 4, 6; Ath. 2, 3).

➊ **to cause someth. to be in a straight or direct line, *straighten, make straight*** **J 1:23** (for ἑτοιμάζω Is 40:3 [cp. Mt 3:3; Mk 1:3; Lk 3:4; s. MMenken, Biblica 66, '85, 190–205]; cp. Sir 2:6; 37:15; 49:9, but here εὐ. τ. ὁδούς is fig., as TestSim 5:2).

➋ **to keep someth. on course, *guide straight*** (cp. Num 22:23), of a ship *steer* (so Eur., Cycl. 15; Appian, Bell. Civ. 2, 89 §374; Philo, Abr. 70, Leg. All. 3, 224, Conf. Lingu. 115) ὁ εὐθύνων *the pilot* **Js 3:4.**—DELG s.v. εὐθύς. M-M.

εὐθύς, εῖα, ύ gen. **έως** (Pind. et al.; ins, pap, LXX; TestSol 8, 11 C; ApcMos 17) 'straight'.

➊ **pert. to being in a straight or direct line, *straight,*** lit., of a way (Thu. 2, 100, 2; Arrian, Anab. 3, 4, 5; Vi. Aesopi W 4 P. εὐθεῖα ὁδός; TestSol 8:11 C; Philo, Deus Imm. 61 [metaph.]; Jos., Ant. 19, 103) εὐθείας ποιεῖν τὰς τρίβους *make the paths straight* (and thus *even*) **Mt 3:3; Mk 1:3; Lk 3:4** (all 3 Is 40:3; cp. Diod. S. 14, 116, 9 εὐθείας ποιῆσαι τὰς ὁδούς; Carmina Pop. 851 PMG [47 Diehl] εὐρυχωρίαν ποιεῖτε τῷ θεῷ). τὴν ὁδὸν τὴν εὐθεῖαν τιθέναι *take the straight road* 2 Cl 7:3. As the name of a street ἡ ῥύμη ἡ καλουμένη Εὐθεῖα *the street called 'Straight (Street)'* **Ac 9:11.** ἡ εὐθεῖα w. ὁδός to be supplied (so in earlier Gk., e.g. Pla., Leg. 4, 716a; also Sallust. 7 p. 14, 5; Ps 142:10 v.l.) **Lk 3:5** (Is 40:4).

➋ ***proper, right,*** fig. extension of mng. 1 (since Pind., trag., Thu.)—ⓐ of a way in fig. sense (Tob 4:19 BA; Ps 106:7; Pr 20:11 al.) αἱ ὁδοὶ τ. κυρίου αἱ εὐ. **Ac 13:10** (cp. Hos 14:10; Sir 39:24). καταλείποντες εὐ. ὁδὸν *forsaking the straight way* (=teaching) **2 Pt 2:15** (cp. Pr 2:13).

ⓑ of the καρδία: *right, upright* (Ps 7:11; 10:2 al.) ἔναντι τοῦ θεοῦ *before God* **Ac 8:21.** Also εὐ. μετ' αὐτοῦ 1 Cl 15:4 (Ps 77:37).—DELG. M-M.

εὐθύς adv. (developed fr. the nom. masc. sg. of εὐθύς)

➊ ***immediately, at once*** (so Pind.; Thu. 2, 93, 4 +; Epict.; pap [Mayser 244; also POxy 744, 7 [1 BC]; PRyl 234, 4]; LXX; TestSol 18:5, 37; TestAbr [παρ' εὐθύς A 19 p. 102, 20/Stone p. 52]; Test12Patr; ParJer 5:20; Philo; Jos., Ant. 11, 236 al.; Just.; s. Phryn. 144f Lob.; WSchmid, D. Atticismus I 1887, 121; 266; II 1889, 113; in the mss. and edd., esp. t.r., freq. the form εὐθέως, q.v.) **Mt 3:16; 13:20f; 14:27; 21:3** (but εὐθέως vs. 2); oft. in **Mk** e.g. **1:10, 12** (on the originality of the word, not the form, in Mk s. JWeiss, ZNW 11, 1910, 124–33); **Lk 6:49; J 13:30, 32; 19:34; Ac 10:16;** ISm 3:2; Hv 3, 13, 2; 5:2, 4; m 5, 1, 3; 11:12; s 7:4.

➋ For the inferential use, weakened to ***then, so then*** e.g. in **Mk 1:21, 23, 29** s. Mlt-H. 446f.—PVannutelli, Synoptica 1, '38, cxiv–cxxvi; GRudberg, ConNeot 9, '44, 42–46. Mlt-Turner 229. S. on εὐθέως. DDaube, The Sudden in the Scriptures '64, 46–72; LRydbeck, 167–176, 184.—M-M. EDNT. TW.

εὐθύτης, ητος, ἡ 'straightness' (Aristot. et al.) in our lit. only fig. (LXX; PsSol 2:15; TestIss 3:1; TestGad 7:7; ApcMos 27; Syntipas 125, 8; Psellus p. 238, 1 with δικαιοσύνη and φιλανθρωπία) ***righteousness, uprightness*** ἡ ῥάβδος τῆς εὐθύτητος (gen. of quality) *the righteous scepter* **Hb 1:8** (Ps 44:7); 1 Cl 14:5 (Ps 36:37). πορεύεσθαι ἐν τῇ εὐ. τοῦ κυρίου *walk in the uprightness of the Lord* Hv 3, 5, 3.—DELG s.v. εὐθύς.

εὐκαιρέω impf. εὐκαίρουν **Mk 6:31** and ηὐκαίρουν **Ac 17:21** (s. W-S. §12, 5b; B-D-F §67, 1); 1 aor. subj. εὐκαιρήσω (s. two next entries and καιρός; Polyb. et al.; ins, pap) **to experience a favorable time or occasion for some activity, *have time, leisure, opportunity*** (Phryn. 125 Lob. οὐ λεκτέον, ἀλλ' εὖ σχολῆς ἔχειν) abs. (Polyb. 20, 9, 4; pap) ἐλεύσεται ὅταν εὐκαιρήσῃ *as soon as he finds an opportunity* **1 Cor 16:12** (cp. PEleph 29, 7 [III BC] ἐὰν δὲ μὴ εὐκαιρῇς τοῦ διαβῆναι; UPZ 71, 18 [152 BC]). W. inf. foll. (Plut., Mor. 223; Ps.-Lucian, Amor. 33) φαγεῖν *have time to eat* **Mk 6:31** (cp. PSI 425, 29 [III BC] εἰ δὲ μὴ εὐκαιρεῖ τις τῶν παρά σοι γραμματέων, ἀπόστειλόν μοι κτλ.). W. εἴς τι and inf. foll. εἰς οὐδὲν ἕτερον ηὐκαίρουν ἢ λέγειν *used to spend their time in nothing else than telling* **Ac 17:21.**—DELG s.v. καιρός. M-M. TW. Spicq.

εὐκαιρία, ας, ἡ (s. prec. and two next entries) ***favorable opportunity, the right moment*** (so since Pla., Phdr. 272a, also BGU 665 II, 4 [I AD] al.; TestJos 7:3 and s. Ps 144:15; 1 Macc 11:42) ζητεῖν εὐκαιρίαν *watch for a favorable opportunity* (Jos., Ant. 20, 76) w. ἵνα foll. **Mt 26:16.** Foll. by gen. of the inf. w. the art. (cp. BGU 46, 18 [193 AD] ἐὰν εὐκαιρίας τύχω τοῦ εὑρεῖν) **Lk 22:6.** S. B-D-F §400, 1; Mlt. 216–18; Mlt-H. 448–50.—M-M. TW. Spicq.

εὔκαιρος, ον (s. prec. two entries; Soph., Hippocr.+; also Aesop., Fab. 248b H.//141 v.l. P.//146 H-H.) in our lit. only **pert. to time that is considered a favorable occasion for some event or circumstance, *well-timed, suitable*** ἡμέρα *a suitable day* **Mk 6:21** (Herodian 1, 9, 6 καιρὸς εὔκαιρος; 2 Macc 14:29; JGreig, ET 65, '53/54, 158f) *coming at the right time* (Plut., Mor. 10e εὔκαιρος σιγή; Ps 103:27) βοήθεια *help in time of need* **Hb 4:16** (OGI 762, 4 βοηθείτω κατὰ τὸ εὔκαιρον; cp. Cat. Cod. Astr. XII 168, 2).—M-M. TW. Spicq.

εὐκαίρως adv. (s. prec. three entries; since X., Ages. 8, 3; SIG 495, 43; PHal 17, 6 [III BC]; PLond I, 33, 23 p. 20 [161 BC]; Sir 18:22; Philo, Somn. 2, 252; Jos., Ant. 14, 323) ***conveniently*** παραδιδόναι **Mk 14:11.** εὐ. ἀκαίρως *in season and out of season,* i.e. *when it is convenient and when it is inconvenient* **2 Ti 4:2** (on the asyndeton s. Kühner-G. II 346d; rhetorical exx. AMalherbe, JBL 103, '84, 235–43; Reader, Polemo p. 361; s. ἀκαίρως). εὐκαίρως ἔχειν *have leisure* (Polyb. 5, 26, 10; pap) **Mk 6:31** D.—M-M. Spicq.

εὐκατάλλακτος, ον (Aristot., Rhet. 2, 4, 1831b 5) ***easily placated, favorable*** of God (3 Macc 5:13) Hv 1, 1, 8.—DELG s.v. ἄλλος. Frisk s.v. ἀλλάσσω.

εὐκλεής, ές, gen. **οῦς** (s. next entry; Hom. et al.; Wsd 3:15; Jer 31:17; Philo; Jos., Bell. 4, 250, Ant. 19, 240) **pert. to being generally well-spoken of, *famous, renowned*** (w. σεμνός) κανὼν τῆς παραδόσεως *renowned standard given us by tradition* 1 Cl 7:2.—DELG s.v. κλέος.

εὐκλεῶς adv. (s. prec. entry; Aeschyl. et al.) **pert. to being generally well-spoken of, *gloriously*** φέρειν, of such as suffered in a manner that brought them renown 1 Cl 45:5.

εὐκόλως adv. (opp. δυσκόλως; since X., Mem. 4, 8, 2; Herm. Wr. 13, 16; PCairMasp 2 III, 23; 4, 19) **pert. to being easy, with implication of causing no imposition, *easily*** Hm 12, 3, 5 v.l. (for εὐκόπως).—DELG s.v. κόλον.

εὔκοπος, ον (s. κόπος and next entry; Polyb. 18, 18, 2; LXX) ***easy*** in our lit. only in comp. εὐκοπώτερος (Diosc. I 39 W.) Hm 12, 4, 5. In the NT always in the expr. εὐκοπώτερόν ἐστιν *it is easier* w. inf. foll. (cp. Sir 22:15) **Mt 9:5; Mk 2:9; Lk 5:23.** W. acc. foll. and inf. (cp. 1 Macc 3:18) **Mt 19:24; Mk 10:25; Lk 16:17; 18:25.**—DELG s.v. κόπτω. M-M.

εὐκόπως adv. (s. prec. entry; Hippocr., Aristoph., Diod. S.; Plut., Mor. 726e; POxy 1467, 14; EpArist 208; 250) ***easily*** φυλάσσειν Hm 12, 3, 5.

εὐκταῖος, α, ον pert. to being an object of petition, *prayed for,* and what is prayed for may be said to be ***wished for*** (so Aeschyl., Pla.+; PGiss 68, 3 [II AD]; Philo; Jos., Ant. 1, 292 al.; Mel., HE 4, 26, 7) εἰρήνη 1 Cl 65:1 (w. ἐπιπόθητος).—DELG s.v. εὔχομαι.

εὐλάβεια, ας, ἡ (s. two next entries; [εὐλαβίη Theognis 1, 118] trag., Pla. et al.; OGI 315, 69; UPZ 42, 22 [162 BC]; LXX, Philo, Joseph.) the primary mng. relates to exercise of caution; in dealing with the transcendent realm one must be esp. cautious about giving offense to deities, hence 'reverence, piety', and in our lit. prob. only of **reverent awe in the presence of God, *awe, fear of God*** (Diod. S. 13, 12, 7 ἡ πρὸς τὸ θεῖον εὐ.; Plut., Camill. 139 [21, 2], Numa 75 [22, 7], Aemil. Paul. 256 [3, 2], Mor. 549e, 568c ['hesitation']; UPZ [s. above]; Pr 28:14; Philo, Cherub. 29 εὐ. θεοῦ, Rer. Div. Her. 22; 29) μετὰ εὐ. καὶ δέους *with awe and reverence* **Hb 12:28** (s. δέος and cp. Epicharmos 221 Kaibel) μετὰ φόβου καὶ πάσης εὐ. *with fear and all reverence* Pol 6:3. So prob. also εἰσακουσθεὶς ἀπὸ τῆς εὐ. **Hb 5:7** (ἀπό 5a; s. JJeremias, ZNW 43, '52/53, 107–11; AStrobel, ZNW 45, '54, 252–66) *heard because of his piety.* But others (e.g. Harnack, SBBerlAk 1929, 69–73=Studien I 245–52; HStrathmann[4] '47 ad loc.) prefer to take the word here in the sense *fear, anxiety* (as Demosth. 23, 15; Plut., Fab. 174 [1, 2]; Herodian 5, 2, 2; Wsd 17:8; Philo, Leg. All. 3, 113, Virt. 24; Jos., Ant. 11, 239; 12, 255) *heard* (and rescued) *from his anxiety.* εὐ. has the sense *scruple, hesitation* in Plut., Mor. 568c.—DELG s.v. λαμβάνω. M-M. TW. Sv.

εὐλαβέομαι pass. dep.; impf. 3 sg. εὐλαβεῖτο LXX, 2 pl. ηὐλαβεῖσθε (Just., D. 123, 3); 1 fut. εὐλαβηθήσομαι LXX; 1 aor. εὐλαβήθην LXX; ptc. εὐλαβηθείς (s. prec. entry; trag., Pla.+; ins, pap, LXX, En, Philo, Joseph.; Just., D. 7, 1; 123, 3).

❶ **to be concerned about a matter, *be concerned, be anxious*** (Soph., Oed. R. 47 al.; Polyb. 18, 23, 5; Diod. S. 4, 73, 2; 16, 22, 2; UPZ 119, 5 [156 BC]; LXX; Jos., Ant. 1, 283) w. μή foll. *lest, that* (Polyb. 3, 111; Diod. S. 2, 13, 4; Epict. 4, 13, 4; 1 Macc 12:40; En 106:6; Jos., Ant. 6, 157; 8, 333) **Ac 23:10 v.l.;** 1 Cl 44:5. So perh. also Νῶε … εὐλαβηθεὶς κατεσκεύασεν κιβωτόν *Noah … became apprehensive and built an ark* **Hb 11:7;** or *Noah took care* (cp. Pla., Gorg. 519a ἐὰν μὴ εὐλαβῇ; Sb 4650, 13 εὐλαβήθητι μήπως μὴ καταλάβουσίν σε; Sir 18:27; EpJer 4). But many prefer the next mng.

❷ **to show reverent regard for, *reverence, respect*** (Pla., Leg. 9 p, 879e τ. ξενικὸν θεόν; Pr 2:8; 30:5; Na 1:7 al.; Philo, Rer. Div. Her. 29; Jos., Ant. 6, 259 τὸ θεῖον) εὐλαβηθείς (sc. θεόν) *out of reverent regard* (for God's command).—KKerényi, Εὐλάβεια: Byz.-Neugr. Jahrb. 8, 1930, 306–16; WSchmid, PhilolWoch 51, '31, 708f; JvanHerten, Θρησκεία, Εὐλάβεια, Ἱκέτης, diss. Utrecht '34.—M-M. TW.

εὐλαβής, ές, gen. **οῦς** comp. εὐλαβέστερος (s. two prec. entries; Pla. et al.; ins, pap, LXX, Philo; Jos., Ant. 2, 217; 6, 179 al.; Just., D. 79, 2 τὸ εὐ. τοῦτο; comp. adv. Eur., Iph. T. 1375) in our lit. only of relig. attitudes, ***devout, God-fearing*** (cp. Demosth. 21, 61 εὐλαβῶς w. εὐσεβῶς; Mi 7:2 the same two words occur in the text and as v.l.) κατὰ τὸν νόμον *by the standard of the law* **Ac 22:12;** (w. δίκαιος, as Pla., Pol. 311b) **Lk 2:25;** ἄνδρες εὐ. *devout men* **Ac 2:5; 8:2.** εὐλαβέστερος emphatic *reverent enough* MPol 2:1.—M-M. TW.

εὔλαλος, ον (s. λαλέω; 'sweetly speaking', Anth. Pal. 5, 148, 1 [Meleager I BC]; 9, 525, 6; 570, 2; Orph., Argon. 244; Achmes 39, 27; LXX) **pert. to speaking in a manner that creates favorable surface impressions, *talkative, glib*** (Cat. Cod. Astr. XI/2 p. 125, 5); subst. ὁ εὐ. *the glib person* 1 Cl 30:4 (Job 11:2).—DELG s.v. λαλέω.

εὐλογέω impf. ηὐλόγουν and εὐλόγουν (W-S. §12, 5b; Rob. 367); fut. εὐλογήσω; 1 aor. εὐλόγησα (also ηὐ- LXX); pf. εὐλόγηκα. Pass.: 1 fut. pass. εὐλογηθήσομαι; pf. ptc.

εὐλογημένος (also ηὐ- Is 61:9) (s. next entry; trag.+; Ps.-Pla., Min. 320e; Isocr., Archid. 43; Ps.-Aristot., Rhet. ad Alex. 4, 1426a, 3ff; Polyb. 1, 14, 4; Cass. Dio 42, 28; Herm. Wr.; ins; PSI 405, 5 [III BC]; LXX, pseudepigr.; Philo, Joseph., Just.; Ath. 11, 2; Christian pap).

❶ **to say someth. commendatory,** ***speak well of, praise, extol*** (so quite predom. outside our lit.; cp. ins Pfuhl-Möbius II, 1606, 2 [II AD] in sense of 'speak well of someone') τὸν θεόν (cp. CIG 4705b, 2 εὐλογῶ τὸν θεόν, i.e. Pan; 4706c, 2 τὴν Εἶσιν. Within Israelite tradition: εὐ. τὸν θεόν OGI 73, 1 [III BC]; PGM 4, 3050f; LXX; En 106:11; PsSol 2:33; TestSol 7:1 al.; Jos., Ant. 7, 380; SibOr 4, 25; Just., A I, 67, 2) **Lk 1:64; 2:28; 24:53** (v.l. αἰνοῦντες); **Js 3:9;** MPol 14:2f. Christ as object οἱ ἰχθύες . . . σε εὐλογοῦσιν GJs 3:3; ἡ γῆ . . . σε εὐλογεις MPol 19:2; cp. per me dominum benedic Papias (1:3). τὴν σὴν οἰκονομίαν AcPl Ha 3, 22. Also abs. *give thanks and praise* (TestAbr A 5 p. 82, 8 [Stone p. 12]) **Mt 14:19; 26:26; Mk 6:41; 14:22; Lk 24:30; 1 Cor 14:16** (beside εὐχαριστέω as Herm. Wr. 1, 27. S. also the confession ins in FSteinleitner, D. Beicht 1913, 112). ἐπ᾽ αὐτούς *over them* **Lk 9:16** D.

❷ **to ask for bestowal of special favor, esp. of calling down God's gracious power,** ***bless*** (LXX)—ⓐ upon pers. τινά *bless someone* **Mk 10:16 v.l.** (for κατευλογέω). **Lk 24:50f; Hb 7:1, 6f** (cp. Gen 14:19; Demetr.: 722 fgm. 1, 1 and 19; GJs 12:2, twice). Opp. καταρᾶσθαι (Gen 12:3; EpJer 65; Philo, Fuga 73, Mos. 2, 196; Jos., Bell. 6, 307) 1 Cl 15:3 (Ps 61:5). εὐ. τοὺς καταρωμένους *those who curse* **Lk 6:28;** D 1:3. τοὺς διώκοντας ὑμᾶς *your persecutors* **Ro 12:14a.** Of paternal blessings by Isaac (Gen 27) and Jacob (Gen 48) **Hb 11:20f;** B 13:4f. Priestly blessing GJs 7:2; 12:1 (for 6:2 s. 3 below). Abs. (Philo, Migr. Abr. 113 opp. καταρᾶσθαι) λοιδορούμενοι εὐλογοῦμεν *when we are reviled we bless* **1 Cor 4:12;** cp. **Ro 12:14b; 1 Pt 3:9** (on kind treatment of the unkind cp. Plut., Mor. 88–89); Dg 5:15.—Of the word of blessing w. which one greets a person or wishes the person well (4 Km 4:29; 1 Ch 16:43) **Lk 2:34.** Also the acclamation εὐλογημένος ὁ ἐρχόμενος ἐν ὀνόματι κυρίου (Ps 117:26) **Mt 21:9; 23:39; Mk 11:9; Lk 13:35; J 12:13;** cp. **Lk 19:38; Mk 11:10.**

ⓑ upon things, which are thereby consecrated τὶ *bless, consecrate* (Ex 23:25; 1 Km 9:13; cp. Jos., Bell. 5, 401) **Mk 8:7; Lk 9:16.** In the language of the Eucharist **1 Cor 10:16.** Probably **Mt 26:26; Mk 14:22** also belong here, in which case the obj. is to be supplied fr. the context; likew. **Mt 14:19; Mk 6:41** (s. 1 above).

❸ **to bestow a favor,** ***provide with benefits:*** w. God or Christ as subj. (Eur., Suppl. 927; PGM 4, 3050a; LXX; En 1:8; TestAbr A 1 p. 77, 15 [Stone p. 2] al.; Just., D. 123, 6) τινά *someone* **Ac 3:26;** 1 Cl 10:3 (Gen 12:2); 33:6 (Gen 1:28); ἐκκλησίαν Hv 1, 3, 4. εὐλογῶν εὐλογήσω σε *surely I will bless you* **Hb 6:14** (Gen 22:17). W. God as implied subj. GJs 6:2; εὐλόγησον αὐτὴν ἐσχάτην εὐλογίαν (the infant Mary) *with the ultimate/finest blessing* ibid. τινὰ ἔν τινι *someone with someth.* (Ps 28:11; TestJos 18:1 v.l.) ἐν πάσῃ εὐλογίᾳ **Eph 1:3** (cp. TestIss 5:6 ἐν εὐλογίαις τῆς γῆς.—On the form cp. BGU βεβαιώσει πάσῃ βεβαιώσει). Pass. **Gal 3:9;** 1 Cl 31:2; GJs 15:4 (Just.). ἐν τῷ σπέρματί σου εὐλογηθήσονται **Ac 3:25 v.l.** (Gen 12:3). Pf. ptc. εὐλογημένος *blessed* (LXX; Ps 5:19; Just., D. 121, 1 al.) 1 Cl 30:5 (Job 11:2), 8. σῶμα . . . εὐ. AcPlCor 2:27. Of a child (Dt 28:4) **Lk 1:42b.** εὐλογημένη ἐν γυναιξίν *among women* vs. **28 v.l.; 42a.** GJs 11:1; 12:1; cp. εὐλόγησόν με 2:4 (in Anna's prayer for a child); 4:4. ἐν πᾶσιν *in every respect* IEph 2:1. ἐν μεγέθει θεοῦ πατρὸς πληρώματι IEph ins. ἐν χάριτι θεοῦ *by the grace of God* IMg ins. εὐλογημένοι τοῦ πατρός *those blessed by the Father* **Mt 25:34;** τοῖς ηὐλογημένοις ὑπὸ τοῦ θεοῦ 1 Cl 30:8 (cp. Is 61:9 σπέρμα ηὐλογημένον ὑπὸ θεοῦ).—Lit. on εὐλογέω and εὐλογία in TSchermann, Allg. Kirchenordnung 1914/16 II 640, 4. Also JHempel, D. israel. Ansch. v. Segen u. Fluch im Lichte d. altoriental. Parallelen: ZDMG n.F. 4, 1925, 20–110; EMaass, Segnen, Weihen, Taufen: ARW 21, 1922, 241–81; LBrun, Segen u. Fluch im Urchristentum '32; JZdevsar, Eulogia u. Eulogein im NT, diss. Rome '54; AMurtonen, VetusT 9, '59, 158–77; EKleszmann, Monatsschr. für Past.-Theol., 48, '59, 26–39. BWestcott, Hebrews, 1889, 203–10.—B. 1479. New Docs 4, 151f. M-M. EDNT. TW.

εὐλογητός, ή, όν (s. prec. and next entry) in our lit. only (as predom. LXX; cp. also En 22:14; TestSol, JosAs, ParJer; Herm. Wr. 1, 32 εὐλογητὸς εἶ πάτερ) of God (and Christ) εὐ. κύριος ὁ θεὸς τ. Ἰσραήλ (3 Km 1:48; 2 Ch 2:11; 6:4; Ps 71:18), ***blessed, praised*** **Lk 1:68** (PVielhauer, ZTK 49, '52, 255–72; AVanhoye, Structure du 'Benedictus', NTS 12, '66, 382–89; UMittman-Richert, Magnifikat und Benediktus '96). εὐ. εἰς τ. αἰῶνας (Ps 88:53; 40:14) **Ro 1:25; 9:5; 2 Cor 11:31;** cp. **1:3; Eph 1:3; 1 Pt 1:3;** B 6:10; IEph 1:3 (on formulation of praise s. Elbogen 4f and PSchorlemmer, 'Die Hochkirche' 1924, 110ff; 151). Of Christ MPol 14:1. ὁ εὐ. as periphrasis for the name of God, which is not mentioned out of reverence **Mk 14:61** (Dalman, Worte 163f).—EBishop, IGoldziher Memorial I '49, 82–88; SEsh, Der Heilige (Er Sei Gepriesen) '57.—DELG s.v. λέγω. TW.

εὐλογία, ας, ἡ (s. prec. two entries; Pind.+).—❶ **act of speaking in favorable terms,** ***praise*** (Pind., Thu. et al.; OGI 74 [III BC] θεοῦ εὐλογία. Θεύδοτος Ἰουδαῖος σωθεὶς ἐκ πελάγους; Sb 317; 1117; T. Kellis 22, 11f; Herm. Wr. 1, 30 εὐ. τ. πατρὶ θεῷ; 2 Esdr 19:5; Sir 50:20; Jos., Ant. 11, 80 εἰς θεόν) **Rv 5:12f; 7:12.**

❷ in an extended sense of 'fine speaking' (Pla., Rep. 3, 400d; Lucian, Lexiph. 1), ἐ. is used in a pejorative sense (Aesop 274 and 274b H.=155 P., 222 Ch., 160 H-H. uses the adj. εὔλογος of an argument that sounds good but is false; cp. Lucian, Abdic. 22) and specifically of **words that are well chosen but untrue,** ***false eloquence, flattery*** **Ro 16:18** (v.l. εὐγλωττίας).

❸ **act or benefit of blessing,** ***blessing***—ⓐ by which persons call down God's grace upon other persons (opp. κατάρα, as Gen 27:12; Sir 3:9; Philo, Mos. 1, 283; Jos., Ant. 4, 302; TestBenj 6:5; JosAs 9:1) **Js 3:10.** Often the explanation of **Hb 12:17** is thought to be given in Gen 27:38. Others place the passage under bα. ἡ εὐ. τοῦ Ζαχαρίου GJs 24:1.

ⓑ of God's activity in blessing (Wsd 15:19; Sir 11:22 al.) 1 Cl 31:1. ὁδοὶ τ. εὐλογίας *the ways of blessing* i.e. those which God blesses, ibid.

α. as benefit bestowed by God or Christ (Gen 49:25; Ex 32:29; Lev 25:21 al.; PsSol 5:17; JosAs 24:6) μεταλαμβάνει εὐλογίας *shares the blessing* **Hb 6:7** (but s. 4 below). εὐ. πνευματική *spiritual blessing* **Eph 1:3.** εὐ. Χριστοῦ **Ro 15:29;** κληρονομεῖν τὴν εὐ. **Hb 12:17** (s. a above); **1 Pt 3:9.** εὐ. τοῦ Ἀβραάμ **Gal 3:14** (cp. Gen 28:4). ἐσχάτην εὐ. *ultimate/finest blessing* GJs 6:2 (cp. Just., D. 91, 1 εὐλογίᾳ, ἣν εὐλόγει τὸν Ἰωσήφ; also s. εὐλογέω 3).

β. in a special sense of divine benefit bestowed in the Eucharist: *blessing* (εὐλογέω 2b) τὸ ποτήριον τῆς εὐ. *the cup that conveys blessing,* defined as 'sharing in the blood of Christ' **1 Cor 10:16** (JosAs 8:11 καὶ πιέτω ποτήριον εὐλογίας σου; here a technical term for the cup of wine drunk at the close of an Israelite's meal; HGressmann, Sellin Festschr. 1927, 55ff; ROtto, The Kingdom of God and the Son of Man, tr. FFilson and BLee-Woolf, '57, 265ff).

ⓒ as benefit brought by humans (Gen 33:11; 1 Km 25:27; 4 Km 5:15.—Cyr. Scyth. uses εὐλογία='gift, bounty' [from humans] without biblical influence: 68, 17 and 28; 217, 16; 238, 12; also εὐλογέω=bestow 137, 9) **2 Cor 9:5a;** mng. 4 is in favor with some interpreters.

❹ Since the concept of blessing connotes the idea of bounty, εὐ. also bears the mng. ***generous gift, bounty*** (opp. πλεονεξία) **2 Cor 9:5b;** perh. also **5a,** s. 3c above. ἐπ᾽ εὐλογίαις (opp. φειδομένως) *bountifully* **9:6ab** (Philo, Leg. All. 3, 210: ἐπ᾽ εὐλογίαις=in order that blessed influence might be felt). This may perh. be the place for **Hb 6:7** (s. 3bα above) γῆ . . . μεταλαμβάνει εὐλογίας ἀπὸ τ. θεοῦ *the earth receives rich bounty from God.* RAC VI 900–928. JMateos, Análisis de un campo lexematico—Εὐλογία en el NT: Filología Neotestamentaria 1, '88, 5–25; cp. Betz, 2 Cor 96–99, 103.—Renehan '85, 73f. M-M. TW.

εὔλογος, ον (s. prec. three entries; Aeschyl. et al.; OGI 504, 9; 669, 10; UPZ 162 V, 2 [117 BC]; Philo; Jos., C. Ap. 1, 259; Just., D. 56, 10; Tat. 9:1; Ath., R. 49, 23) **pert. to making good sense,** ***reasonable, right*** IMg 7:1. εὔλογόν ἐστιν *it is reasonable* w. inf. foll. (Pla., Crat. 396b; cp. Philo, Deus Imm. 127) ISm 9:1.

εὐμετάδοτος, ον (s. μεταδίδωμι; M. Ant. 1, 14, 4; 6, 48, 1; Vett. Val. 7, 13; 11, 7 al.; Vi. Aesopi I c. 26 p. 289, 1) ***generous*** **1 Ti 6:18.**—M-M. Spicq.—DELG s.v. δίδωμι.

εὔμορφος, ον (Sappho 82a [comp.]; trag., Hdt. et al.; POxy 471, 79; 109) ***well-formed, beautiful*** of women (Artem. 1, 78 p. 73, 9 al.; Xenophon Eph. 1, 4, 3; Sir 9:8; Philo, Virt. 110; TestJud 13:3; TestSol; TestAbr A; Just., D. 134, 1.—εὐμορφία Jos., Ant. 15, 23) Hs 9, 13, 8.—DELG s.v. μορφή.

Εὐνίκη, ης, ἡ (name of mythological figures in Hes., Theogon. 246 Rz.; Theocr. 13, 45; Ps.-Apollod. 1, 2, 7; CIG IV, 8139.—Gr-Rom. women bear this name: GDI 4033 [Rhodes]; Κυπρ. I p. 93 no. 40; PFay 130, 18) ***Eunice,*** mother of Timothy **2 Ti 1:5.**

εὐνοέω (s. next entry; trag., Hdt. et al.; ins, pap, LXX) ***be well-disposed, make friends*** τινί *to* or *with someone* (Soph., Aj. 689 al.; Polyb. 3, 11, 7; Herodian 8, 8, 5; SIG 524, 17; 985, 23; 1268, 15; OGI 532, 9 [3 BC]; PRyl 153, 10; POxy 494, 9; Da 2:43; Jos., Bell. 4, 214, C. Ap. 1, 309; 2, 121) ἴσθι εὐνοῶν τῷ ἀντιδίκῳ σου ταχύ *make friends quickly with your opponent = settle the case quickly w. your plaintiff* **Mt 5:25** (εὔνοια appears in a comparable passage Plut., Mor. 489c; for the constr. cp. PHolm 5, 16 ἔστω κρεμάμενα=they are . . . to hang. B-D-F §353, 6; Rob. 375).—DELG s.v. νόος. M-M. TW. Spicq.

εὔνοια, ας, ἡ (s. prec. entry; Aeschyl., Hdt.+; also Aristot. EN 1166ab; ins, pap, LXX, EpArist, Philo; Jos., Ant. 2, 161; Ath., R. 48, 22) gener. 'goodwill'.

❶ **a kindly supportive feeling,** ***favor, affection, benevolence*** (Diod. S. 1, 51, 5; 1, 54, 1; Jos., Bell. 4, 213, Ant. 11, 132; 18, 376) ἡ κατὰ θεὸν εὐ. (your) *godly benevolence* ITr 1:2. εὐ. εἴς τινα *affection for* someone (Thu. 2, 8, 4 al.; SIG 390, 18; 2 Macc 9:26; 11:19) MPol 17:3. ἐπὶ εὐνοίᾳ τῶν ἀδελφῶν *upon the affection of the members (of the gathered group = fellowship)* AcPl Ha 6, 10. Abstr. for concr. παρακαλῶ ὑμᾶς, μὴ εὐ. ἄκαιρος γένησθέ μοι *I beg of you, do not show* (lit. *be to*) *me an unseasonable kindness* IRo 4:1 (cp. the proverb ἄκαιρος εὔνοι᾽ οὐδὲν ἔχθρας διαφέρει [Zenob., Paroem. 1, 50]). ὀφειλομένη εὐ. (s. ὀφείλω 2aα) **1 Cor 7:3 v.l.**

❷ **a positive attitude exhibited in a relationship,** ***good attitude, willingness*** (common term in diplomatic documents in ref. to positive attitudes displayed by a person, city, or state: SIG 799, 27 σπουδὴ καὶ εὐ. 'readiness and goodwill'; BGU 1121, 19 [5 BC]; s. also, e.g., the numerous reff. in IPriene, index VIII p. 277) as a virtue of slaves (POxy 494, 6 [156 AD]; cp. Lucian, Bis Accus. 16) μετ᾽ εὐνοίας δουλεύοντες **Eph 6:7** (on μετ᾽ εὐ. cp. Pla., Phdr. 241c; Demosth. 18, 276; SIG 330, 8; Sir prol. 1:16).—ESkard, Zwei Religiös-Politische Begriffe, Euergetes-Concordia '32, 29–35. Larfeld I 495–99. M-M. TW. Spicq. Sv.

εὐνουχία, ας, ἡ (s. two next entries; so far found only in Christian wr., e.g. Athenagoras, Legat. 33) ***state of being unmarried*** Agr 18 (=Clem. Al., Strom. 3, 15, 97).—DELG s.v. εὐνή.

εὐνουχίζω (s. prec. and next entry; Clearchus, fgm. 49; Appian, Bell. Civ. 3, 98 §409; Lucian, Sat. 12; Archigenes [II AD] in Oribas. 8, 2, 8; Galen: CMG V/4/2 p. 334, 8; 335, 4; Cass. Dio 68, 2, 4; Jos., Ant. 10, 33.—Fig., Philostrat., Vi. Apoll. 6, 42 p. 252, 27 τὴν γῆν; Just., A I, 15, 4) **to cause someone to be a eunuch,** ***castrate, emasculate, make a eunuch of*** ἑαυτόν *oneself* **Mt 19:12b;** pass., **12a.** From ancient times it has been disputed whether the word is to be taken literally in both occurrences, fig. in both, or fig. in the first and lit. in the second (s. WBauer, Heinrici Festschr. 1914, 235–44). The context requires the fig. interp. (s. εὐνουχία) for the second occurrence, and the lit. for the first (s. JKleist, CBQ 7, '45, 447–49).—ANock, Eunuchs in Anc. Rel.: ARW 23, 1925, 25–33 (=Essays in Religion and the Anc. World I, '72, 7–15); LGray, Eunuch: EncRelEth V 579–85; JBlinzler, BRigaux Festschr., '70, 45–55 (Justin).—DELG s.v. εὐνή. TW.

εὐνοῦχος, ου, ὁ (s. prec. entry; Hdt., Aristoph. et al.; Vett. Val. 18, 19; 86, 34; BGU 725, 14; 29; LXX, Test12Patr; AscIs 3:11; Philo; Jos., Bell. 1, 488, Ant. 17, 44; Ath. 34, 1)

❶ **a castrated male person,** ***eunuch.*** **Mt 19:12b.** Eunuchs served, esp. in the orient, as keepers of a harem (Esth 2:14) and not infreq. rose to high positions in the state (Hdt. 8, 105; AscIs 3:11 τῶν εὐνούχων καὶ τῶν συμβούλων τοῦ βασιλέως): the εὐ. δυνάστης of Queen Candace **Ac 8:27, 34, 36, 38f.**—S. on Κανδάκη.—Diod. S. 11, 69, 1 Mithridates is physically a εὐνοῦχος and holds the position of κατακοιμιστής (=the chamberlain; note the etymology of εὐ.: εὐνή 'bed' + ἔχω) τοῦ βασιλέως (Xerxes). In 17, 5, 3 Βαγώας as χιλίαρχος bears the title of a high official at the Persian court (18, 48, 4f). Since he is also described as εὐνοῦχος, the word must be understood literally. Similarly in Ac 8:27ff, the man baptized by Philip performs the function of δυνάστης Κανδάκης βασιλίσσης. Here also 'eunuch' refers primarily to his physical state, but Luke's interest in showing the broad outreach of the Gospel, esp. through the arrival of an important personage from a distant locality, prob. comes into play (for OT perspectives contrast Dt 23:1 MT and Is 56:3). FSpencer, The Ethiopian Eunuch and His Bible—A Social-Science-Analysis: BTB 22, '92, 155–65.

❷ **a human male who, without a physical operation, is by nature incapable of begetting children,** ***impotent male*** (Wsd 3:14) εὐ. ἐκ κοιλίας μητρός **Mt 19:12a.**

❸ **a human male who abstains fr. marriage, without being impotent,** ***a celibate*** **Mt 19:12c** (cp. Ath. 34, 1).—s. εὐνουχίζω.—JBlinzler, ZNW 48, '57, 254–70; Pauly-Wiss. Suppl. III/2, 1772f; B. 141. New Docs 3, 41. Schmidt, Syn. IV 35–37. DELG s.v. ἐυνή. M-M. EDNT. TW.

Εὐοδία, ας, ἡ (SIG² 868, 19; OGI 77; Κυπρ. I p. 46 no. 72 Greek grave ins from Cyprus; BGU 550, 1) ***Euodia,*** a Christian **Phil 4:2.**—M-M.

εὐοδόω fut. εὐοδώσω; 1 aor. εὐώδωσα LXX; pf. 3 sg. εὐόδωκεν Gen 24:21, 27; Tob 10:14 S. Pass.: fut. εὐοδωθήσομαι; aor. εὐοδώθην and εὐωδώθην LXX (s. ὁδός; Soph., Hdt. et al.; pap, LXX; on the latter Anz 290; Just., A II, 7, 8) in our lit. only the pass. is used, and not literally 'be led along a good road', but in the sense: **have things turn out well,** ***prosper, succeed*** of pers., abs. (Josh 1:8; Pr 28:13; 2 Ch 18:11; En 104:6; TestGad 7:1) εὔχομαί σε εὐοδοῦσθαι κ. ὑγιαίνειν *I pray that all may go well with you and that you may be in good health* **3J 2;** cp. εὐοδοῦταί σου ἡ ψυχή *it is well with your soul* **ibid.**; εὐ. ἔν τινι *succeed in someth.* (2 Ch 32:30; Sir 41:1; Jer 2:37; Da 6:4) Hs 6, 3, 5f. W. inf. foll. (cp. 1 Macc 16:2) εἴ πως ἤδη ποτὲ εὐοδωθήσομαι ἐλθεῖν πρὸς ὑμᾶς *whether I will finally succeed in coming to you* **Ro 1:10.** θησαυρίζων ὅ τι ἐὰν εὐοδῶται *save as much as he gains* **1 Cor 16:2.** Yet, in this pass. the subj. may be a thing (Hdt. 6, 73 τῷ Κλεομένεϊ εὐωδώθη τὸ πρῆγμα; 2 Esdr 5:8; Tob 4:19 BA; 1 Macc 3:6) understood, such as business or profit.—DELG s.v. ὁδός. M-M. TW.

εὐοικονόμητος, ον (s. οἰκονομία; since Diphilus [IV/III BC] in Athen. 2, 54d) **pert. to someth. well arranged,** of a beginning: ***well-ordered*** IRo 1:2 (the adv. εὐοικονομήτως, 'suitably' in Eustath.).—DELG s.v. οἶκος.

εὐπάρεδρος, ον (s. παρεδρεύω; Hesych.: εὐπάρεδρον· καλῶς παραμένον) **pert. to being in constant attendance,** ***constantly in service*** πρὸς τὸ εὐ. τῷ κυρίῳ *that you might be devoted to the Lord* **1 Cor 7:35** (v.l. εὐπρόσεδρος).—DELG s.v. ἕζομαι.

εὐπειθής, ές gen. οῦς (s. πείθω; Aeschyl., X., Pla.+; Musonius 83, 19; Epict. 3, 12, 13; Plut., Mor. 26d; SEG XXIX, 116, 9 [III BC]; BGU 1104, 23; 1155, 17; POxy 268, 6; 4 Macc 12:6; Philo, Virt. 15) ***compliant, obedient*** **Js 3:17.**—DELG s.v. πείθομαι. New Docs 4, 152. M-M. Spicq.

εὐπερίσπαστος, ον (s. περισπάω and next entry; Ps.-X., Cyn. 2, 7 'easy to pull away'; the verbal in -τος is indifferent as to voice, Mlt. 221) ***easily distracting*** (cp. ἀπερίσπαστος 'not distracted' Polyb., Plut.; Sir 41:1; its adv. 1 Cor 7:35) **Hb 12:1 v.l.** (FBeare, JBL 63, '44, 390f).—DELG s.v. σπάω.

εὐπερίστατος, ον (s. prec. entry; Hesychius=εὔκολον, εὐχερῆ; Suda=μωρόν, ταχέως περιτρεπόμενον; Mlt-H. 282) ***easily ensnaring, obstructing, constricting,*** of sin **Hb 12:1.** S. εὐπερίσπαστος.—FBeare, JBL 63, '44, 390f.—M-M. Spicq.

Εὔπλους, ου, ὁ (CIG 1211; 2072; IHierapJ 194; 270; IPont-Eux I, 58; 61; 63; CIL III, 2571; Suppl. 9054; IX, 4665; X, 7667; 7700; BGU 665 II, 7 [I AD]) ***Euplus,*** a Christian IEph 2:1.

εὐποιΐα, ας, ἡ—❶ rendering of service, with implication of being generally recognized as laudable, ***well-doing*** (Epict. in Stob., fgm. 45 Schenkl; Arrian, Anab. 7, 28, 3; Polyaenus, Exc. 1 τῶν πλησίον; Lucian, Abdic. 25; Diog. L. 10, 10; in public documents in ref. to exceptional public service InsPerg 333; IPriene 112, 19; 113, 76 [both in the form εὐποΐα]; IG III, 1054; not approved by Pollux 5, 140) **Hb 13:16.**

❷ **the content of well-doing,** ***a good deed*** (Chion, Ep. 7, 3; Syntipas p. 24, 7; SEG XXVIII, 1217, 5; POxy 1773, 34; PLond III, 1244, 8 p. 244 [IV AD]; Philo, Mut. Nom. 24; Jos., Ant. 2, 261; 19, 356; Just., A II, 6, 2 [pl.]) IPol 7:3—S. on εὐεργετέω.—Larfeld I 494f. DELG s.v. ποιέω. New Docs 3, 68. M-M. Spicq.

εὐπορέω (s. next entry, also εὔπορος 'well off') aor. 3 sg. εὐπόρησεν Wsd 10:10; impf. mid. 3 sg. εὐπορεῖτο (ηὐ- v.l.; on the augm. s. W-S. §12, 5b; B-D-F §67, 1); aor. pass. subj. 3 sg. εὐπορηθῇ; ptc. εὐπορηθείς LXX; **to prosper financially,** ***have plenty, be well off*** (the mid. is used now and then in this sense, which usu. belongs to the active [TestJob 12:1; 24:4]: e.g. the mid. is found Aristot., Oec. 2, 23; Polyb. 1, 66, 5; 5, 43, 8; Jos., Ant. 17, 214, Vi. 28; cp. Lev 25:26, 49) abs. (as Theopomp.: 115 fgm. 36 Jac. [in Athen. 6, 275c]; Lucian, Bis Acc. 27; SIG 495, 66; PGM 4, 3125; Just., A I, 67, 6) καθὼς εὐπορεῖτό τις *according to each one's* (financial) *ability* **Ac 11:29.**—DELG s.v. πόρος. M-M. TW. Spicq.

εὐπορία, ας, ἡ (s. prec. entry; Thu. et al. in var. mngs.; LXX 4 Km 25:10 v.l. Oft. Aq., Philo, Joseph.) having the means for someth., 'means', then abundant means, ***prosperity*** (X., Demosth. et al.; cp. POxy 71 I, 17 οὐδεμία δέ μοι ἑτέρα εὐπορία ἐστὶν ἢ τὰ χρήματα ταῦτα; Jos., Bell. 7, 445; ἐν εὐ. βίου πολλοῦ TestAbr A 1 p. 78, 2 [Stone p. 4]) ἡ εὐ. ἡμῖν ἐστιν *we get our prosperity* **Ac 19:25;** another prob. mng. is *easy means of earning a living.*—M-M. Spicq.

εὐπραγέω 1 aor. εὐπράγησα (=εὖ πράσσω, s. πρᾶγμα; Thu. et al., mostly='be well off'; so also Jos., Ant. 13, 284; TestGad 4:5) ***do what is right*** (cp. Ps 35:4 Sym.) 2 Cl 17:7.—DELG s.v. πράσσω.

εὐπράσσω s. εὖ.

εὐπρέπεια, ας, ἡ (s. two next entries and πρέπω; Thu.+; Epict. 1, 8, 7; SIG 358; 880, 17; LXX; TestSol; TestAbr A 16 p. 98, 1 [Stone p. 44]; TestJob; TestNapht 2:8; Philo, Aet. M. 126; Jos., Ant. 4, 131; Tat 1:2) ***fine appearance, beauty,*** ApcPt 3:10. ἡ εὐ. τοῦ προσώπου αὐτοῦ *the beauty of its* (i.e. the flower's) *appearance* **Js 1:11.** περιτιθέναι τὴν εὐ. τινι *clothe someth. w. beauty* Hv 1, 3, 4.—DELG s.v. πρέπω. M-M. Spicq.

εὐπρεπής, ές gen. οῦς (s. prec. entry and πρέπω; Aeschyl., Hdt.+; Diod. S. 1, 45, 4 Vogel v.l. [the text has ναοῖς ἐκπρεπέσι]; Epict. 1, 2, 18 al.; ins; POxy 1380, 130 [II AD]; LXX; TestAbr A; JosAs; Philo; Jos., Ant. 6, 160; Ath. 33, 2). Comp. εὐπρεπέστερος (Aeschyl. et al.; Wsd 7:29) Dg 2:2; Hs 5, 2, 4. Superl. εὐπρεπέστατος (Hdt. et al.; TestAbr A 2 p. 78, 18 [Stone p. 4]; Jos., Ant. 1, 200) Hs 2:1; 9, 1, 10; 9, 10, 3.

❶ **pert. to having an attractive appearance,** ***looking well*** of a vineyard carefully dug and weeded εὐπρεπέστερος ἔσται *it will look better* Hs 5, 2, 4. Of a white mountain εὐπρεπέστατον ἦν ἐν ἑαυτῷ τὸ ὄρος *the mountain by itself* (without any trees) *was most beautiful* 9, 1, 10. Of a place that has been cleaned *very attractive* 9, 10, 3. Of a building *magnificent* 9, 9, 7. οὐδὲν εὐπρεπέστερον w. gen. *no better to look at than* Dg 2:2.

❷ **pert. to being compatible or harmonious,** ***suited*** τινί *to someth.* of the elm and the vine εὐπρεπέσταταί εἰσιν ἀλλήλαις *they are very well suited to each other* Hs 2:1.

εὐπρεπῶς adv. of εὐπρεπής (s. prec. two entries; Aeschyl. et al.; SIG 1109, 110; 1 Esdr 1:10; Wsd 13:11; Jos., Ant. 13, 31)

❶ **pert. to making a fine appearance,** ***attractively*** Hs 5, 2, 5. This mng. has also been suggested for 9, 2, 4, but the context seems to require the sense

❷ **pert. to being in accordance w. what is expected,** ***fittingly, appropriately,*** of women περιεζωσμέναι ἦσαν εὐ.

εὐπρόσδεκτος, ον '(easily) acceptable, pleasant, welcome' (s. προσδέχομαι; Plut., Mor. 801c)

❶ **pert. to being capable of eliciting favorable acceptance,** ***acceptable***—ⓐ of things: of offerings (schol. on Aristoph., Pax 1054 εὐπρόσδεκτος ἡ θυσία) προσφορά **Ro 15:16;** of pers. 1

Cl 40:4. Of willingness to give, which is said to be acceptable **2 Cor 8:12.** W. the dat. of the one to whom someth. is acceptable: to people **Ro 15:31;** to God θυσίαι εὐ. τῷ θεῷ **1 Pt 2:5** (cp. Vi. Aesopi W 8 P. εὐπρόσδεκτον παρὰ τῷ θεῷ τὸ ἀγαθοποιεῖν; Cat. Cod. Astr. VII 178, 6 εὐ. αἱ εὐχαὶ πρὸς θεόν; SIG 1042, 8 ἀπρόσδεκτος ἡ θυσία παρὰ τ. θεοῦ). ἱλαρότης Hm 10, 3, 1. λειτουργία s 5, 3, 8. εὐ. τῷ θελήματι αὐτοῦ *acceptable to his will* 1 Cl 40:3; τὰ εὐ. *what is acceptable* to God 35:5.

ⓑ of pers. 1 Cl 40:4.

❷ **pert. to being welcome in a situation,** ***favorable,*** of a time that is favorable for bringing God's grace to fruition καιρὸς εὐ. **2 Cor 6:2.**—DELG s.v. δέχομαι. M-M. TW. Spicq.

εὐπρόσεδρος, ον (προσεδρεύω 'attend to') **pert. to being in constant attendance,** ***constantly in service, constant*** **1 Cor 7:35 v.l.** (s. εὐπάρεδρος).—DELG s.v. ἕζομαι.

εὐπροσωπέω 1 aor. εὐπροσώπησα (εὐπρόσωπος 'fair of face', s. πρόσωπον; PTebt 19, 12 [114 BC] ὅπως εὐπροσωπῶμεν) ***make a good showing*** ἐν σαρκί *before people* **Gal 6:12.**—DELG s.v. ὄπωπα. M-M. TW.

εὐρακύλων, ωνος, ὁ (CIL VIII, 26652 'euroaquilo'; a hybrid formation of Lat.-Gk. sailor's language, made fr. εὖρος and Lat. aquilo, B-D-F §5, 1d; 115, 1; Rob. 166) **the northeast wind, Euraquilo,** ***the northeaster*** **Ac 27:14** (v.l. εὐροκλύδων, q.v.). JSmith, The Voyage and Shipwreck of St. Paul[4] 1880, 119ff; 287ff; Hemer, Acts 141f; Warnecke, Romfahrt 37–39.—M-M.

εὑρετέος, α, ον (Thu 3, 45, 4) ***to be discovered / found out*** πῶς πίστ[ις] εὑρ[ετ]έ[α] *how faith is to be discerned* Ox 1081, 32f (cp. SJCh 90, 9–11, w. difft. syntax).—DELG s.v. εὑρίσκω.

εὕρημα, ατος, τό (s. next entry; trag., Hdt. et al.; POxy 472, 33 [II AD]; Philo; Jos., C. Ap. 2, 148; the LXX has the later form εὕρεμα [Phryn. p. 445f Lob.; Dio Chrys. 59 (76), 1]; s. Thackeray p. 80) ***discovery, invention*** Dg 7:1.—DELG s.v. εὑρίσκω.

εὑρίσκω (s. prec. entry; Hom.+) impf. εὕρισκον (also ηὕρισκον Ex 15:22; Da 6:5 LXX; Mel., P. [consistently]); fut. εὑρήσω; 2 aor. εὗρον, and mixed forms 1 pl. εὕραμεν (BGU 1095, 10 [57 AD]; Sb 6222, 12 [III AD]) **Lk 23:2,** 3 pl. εὕροσαν LXX, -ωσαν GJs 24:3 (s. deStrycker p. 247), εὕρησαν 10:1 (s. deStrycker p. 245); pf. εὕρηκα. Mid. 2 aor. εὑράμην **Hb 9:12** (B-D-F §81, 3; s. Mlt-H. 208). Pass.: pres. εὑρίσκομαι; impf. 3 sg. ηὑρίσκετο; 1 fut. εὑρεθήσομαι (W-S. §15 s.v.); 1 aor. εὑρέθην (also ηὑ- LXX); perf. εὕρημαι LXX.

❶ **to come upon someth. either through purposeful search or accidentally,** ***find***—ⓐ after seeking, *find, discover, come upon,* abs. (opp. ζητεῖν, Pla., Gorg. 59 p. 503d; Epict. 4, 1, 51 ζήτει καὶ εὑρήσεις; PTebt 278, 30 [I AD] ζητῶι καὶ οὐχ εὑρίσκωι) **Mt 7:7f; Lk 11:9f;** Ox 654 (=ASyn. 247, 20) preface 5 (restored Fitzmyer); GHb 70, 17; τινὰ ζητεῖν κ. εὑ. (3 Km 1:3) **2 Ti 1:17.** τινά or τὶ ζητεῖν κ. οὐχ εὑ. (PGiss 21, 5; Sextus 28; 4 Km 2:17; 2 Esdr 17:64; Ps 9:36; Pr 1:28; SSol 5:6; Ezk 22:30; TestJob 40:7 ἐπιζητήσας αὐτὴν καὶ μὴ εὑρών) **Mt 12:43; 26:60; Mk 14:55; Lk 11:24; 13:6f; J 7:34, 36; Rv 9:6.** εὑ. τινά **Mk 1:37; Lk 2:45; 2 Cor 2:13.** τὶ **Mt 7:14; 13:46; 18:13; Lk 24:3.** νομήν *pasture* **J 10:9** (cp. La 1:6); **Ac 7:11;** σπήλαιον GJs 18:1; τὸ πτῶμα 24:3. The obj. acc. can be supplied fr. the context **Mt 2:8; Ac 11:26;** GJs 21:2 (not pap). W. the place given ἐν τῇ φυλακῇ **Ac 5:22.** πέραν τῆς θαλάσσης **J 6:25.** Pass. w. neg. εἴ τις οὐχ εὑρέθη ἐν τῇ βίβλῳ τῆς ζωῆς γεγραμμένος *if anyone('s name) was not found written in the book of life* **Rv 20:15** (cp. PHib 48, 6 [255 BC] οὐ γὰρ εὑρίσκω ἐν τοῖς βιβλίοις; 2 Esdr 18:14). The pass. w. neg. can also mean: no longer to be found, despite a thorough search=*disappear* (PRein 11, 11 [III BC]) of Enoch οὐχ ηὑρίσκετο **Hb 11:5** (Gen 5:24). ὄρη οὐχ εὑρέθησαν **Rv 16:20;** cp. **18:21.** The addition of the neg., which is actually found in the Sahidic version, would clear up the best-attested and difficult rdg. of **2 Pt 3:10** καὶ γῆ καὶ τὰ ἐν αὐτῇ ἔργα εὑρεθήσεται; other proposals in Nestle. See also Danker 2 below.

ⓑ accidentally, without seeking ***find, come upon*** τινά *someone* (PGen 54, 31 εὑρήκαμεν τὸν πραιπόσιτον; Gen 4:14f; 18:28ff; 1 Km 10:2; 3 Km 19:19; Sir 12:17; TestSol 18:21; Just., A II, 11, 3) **Mt 18:28; 27:32; J 1:41a** (Diog. L. 1, 109 τὸν ἀδελφὸν εὑρών=he came upon his brother), **43, 45; 5:14; 9:35; Ac 13:6; 18:2; 19:1; 28:14.** Foll. by ἐν w. dat. to designate the place (3 Km 11:29; 2 Ch 21:17; 1 Macc 2:46; Herodian 3, 8, 6) **Mt 8:10; Lk 7:9; J 2:14;** τὶ *someth.* (Gen 11:2; 26:19; Judg 15:15; 4 Km 4:39 al.; Just., D. 86, 5) **Mt 13:44** (Biogr. p. 324 εὑρὼν θησαυρόν); **17:27; Lk 4:17; J 12:14** (Phot., Bibl. 94 p. 74b on Iambl. Erot. [Hercher I 222, 38] εὑρόντες ὄνους δύο ἐπέβησαν); **Ac 17:23.** Pass. *be found, find oneself, be* (Dt 20:11; 4 Km 14:14; 1 Esdr 1:19; 8:13; Bar 1:7; TestSol 7:6; GrBar 4:11) Φ. εὑρέθη εἰς Ἄζωτον *Philip found himself* or *was present at Azotus* **Ac 8:40** (cp. Esth 1:5 τοῖς ἔθνεσιν τοῖς εὑρεθεῖσιν εἰς τ. πόλιν; also s. 4 Km 2), on the other hand, a Semitic phrase . . . אִשְׁתְּכַח בְּ=to arrive in, or at, may underlie the expr. here and in εὑρεθῆναι εἰς τ. βασιλείαν Hs 9, 13, 2 (s. MBlack, Aramaic Studies and the NT, JTS 49, '48, 164). οὐδὲ τόπος εὑρέθη αὐτῶν ἔτι ἐν τ. οὐρανῷ *there was no longer any place for them in heaven* **Rv 12:8** (s. Da 2:35 Theod.); cp. **18:22, 24.** οὐδὲ εὑρέθη δόλος ἐν τ. στόματι αὐτοῦ **1 Pt 2:22;** 1 Cl 16:10 (both Is 53:9); cp. **Rv 14:5** (cp. Zeph 3:13). ἵνα εὑρεθῶ ἐν αὐτῷ (i.e. Χριστῷ) *that I might be found in Christ* **Phil 3:9** (JMoffatt, ET 24, 1913, 46).

ⓒ w. acc. and ptc. or adj., denoting the state of being or the action in which someone or someth. is or is involved (B-D-F §416, 2; s. Rob. 1120f) *discover*

α. w. ptc. (Thu. 2, 6, 3; Demosth. 19, 332; Epict. 4, 1, 27; PTebt 330, 5 [II AD] παραγενομένου εἰς τ. κώμην εὗρον τ. οἰκίαν μου σεσυλημένην; Num 15:32; Tob 7:1 S; 8:13; Da 6:14; 6:12 Theod.; TestSol 1:5 D; TestAbr A 5 p. 82, 25 [Stone p. 12], B 2 p. 109, 15 [Stone p. 60]; TestJob 37:8; ParJer 7:29 al.; Jos., Bell. 6, 136 τ. φύλακας εὗρον κοιμωμένους; Ath. 33, 1) εὑρίσκει σχολάζοντα *he finds it unoccupied* (that gives the condition for his return: HNyberg, ConNeot 2, '36, 22–35) **Mt 12:44.** εὗρεν ἄλλους ἑστῶτας *he found others standing there* **20:6** (cp. Jdth 10:6); cp. **21:2; 24:46; 26:40, 43; Mk 11:2; 13:36; 14:37, 40; Lk 2:12; 7:10; 8:35; 11:25; 12:37, 43; 19:30; Ac 5:23; 9:2; 10:27; 27:6;** 2 Cl 6:9; ITr 2:2 and oft. εὗρεν αὐτὴν ὀγκωμένην GJs 13:1a; 15:2; εὗρον τὸ αἷμα (πτῶμα pap) αὐτοῦ λίθον γεγενημένον 24:3; εὗρον αὐτὸν ἔτι ζῶντα AcPl Ha 10, 12; εὑρήσετε δύο ἄνδρας προσευχομένους ibid. 19. W. ellipsis of the ptc. εὑρέθη μόνος (sc. ὤν) **Lk 9:36.** ὁ ὄφις . . . εὗρεν τὴν Εὔαν μόνην GJs 13:1b; οὐδὲν εὑρίσκω αἴτιον (ὄν) **Lk 23:4;** cp. vs. **22.**

β. w. adj. (TestAbr A 12 p. 91, 24 [Stone p. 30] εὗρεν αὐτῆς ζυγίας τὰς ἁμαρτίας; ApcMos 16) εὗρον αὐτὴν νεκράν **Ac 5:10** (TestJob 40:11). εὕρωσιν ὑμᾶς ἀπαρασκευάστους **2 Cor 9:4.**

γ. elliptically w. a whole clause οὐχ οἵους θέλω εὕρω ὑμᾶς *I may find you not as I want* (to find you) **2 Cor 12:20.** Several times w. καθώς foll.: εὗρον καθὼς εἶπεν αὐτοῖς *they found it just as he had told them* **Mk 14:16; Lk 19:32;** GJs 15:2; cp. **Lk 22:13.** ἵνα . . . εὑρεθῶσιν καθὼς καὶ ἡμεῖς *that they may be found* (leading the same kind of life) *as we* **2 Cor 11:12.**

❷ **to discover intellectually through reflection, observation, examination, or investigation,** ***find, discover,*** transf. sense of 1 (X., Hell. 7, 4, 2; M. Ant. 7, 1; Wsd 3:5; Da 1:20 Theod.; Jos., Ant. 10, 196; Just., A I, 31, 7 al.; Ath. 17, 2 'create' an artistic work) τὶ *someth.*: *I find it to be the rule* **Ro 7:21.** ὧδε εὑ. ἐντολήν *here I find a commandment* B 9:5. τινά w. ptc. foll. *find someone* doing someth. (Anonymi Vi. Platonis p. 7, 18 Westerm.) **Lk 23:2; Ac 23:29.** Likew. τὶ w. ptc. foll. **Rv 3:2.** τινά w. adj. foll. **2:2.** W. ὅτι foll. B 16:7. (TestSol 22:11). Of the result of a judicial investigation εὑ. αἰτίαν θανάτου *find a cause for putting to death* **Ac 13:28.** εὑ. αἰτίαν, κακόν, ἀδίκημα ἔν τινι **J 18:38; 19:4, 6; Ac 23:9.** εἰπάτωσαν τί εὗρον ἀδίκημα *let them say what wrong-doing they have discovered* **24:20.** ποιεῖτε ἵνα εὑρεθῆτε ἐν ἡμέρᾳ κρίσεως *act in order that you may pass muster in the day of judgment* B 21:6. Cp. **2 Pt 3:10** w. an emendation of καὶ γῆ κατὰ τὰ (for καὶ γῆ καὶ τὰ) ἐν αὐτῇ ἔργα εὑρεθήσεται (cp. PsSol 17:8) *and the earth will be judged according to the deeds done on it* (FDanker, ZNW 53, '62, 82–86).—W. acc. of a price or measure calculated εὗρον *they found* **Ac 19:19; 27:28.** W. indir. quest. foll. **Lk 5:19** which, by the use of the article, can become an object acc.: εὑ. τὸ τί ποιήσωσιν **19:48.** τὸ πῶς κολάσωνται αὐτούς **Ac 4:21.** W. inf. foll. ἵνα εὕρωσιν κατηγορεῖν αὐτοῦ *in order to find a charge against him* **Lk 6:7; 11:54** D (but there is no accusative with εὕρωσιν; cp. PParis 45, 7 [153 BC] προσέχων μὴ εὕρῃ τι κατὰ σοῦ ἰπῖν=εἰπεῖν. For this reason it is perhaps better to conclude that εὑρίσκω with inf.=*be able:* Astrampsychus p. 5 ln. 14 εἰ εὑρήσω δανείσασθαι ἄρτι=whether I will be able to borrow money now; p. 6 ln. 72; p. 42 Dec. 87, 1. Then the transl. would be: *so that they might be able to bring an accusation against him*). Of seeking and finding God (Is 55:6; Wsd 13:6, 9; cp. Philo, Spec. Leg. 1, 36, Leg. All. 3, 47) **Ac 17:27.** Pass. εὑρέθην τοῖς ἐμὲ μὴ ζητοῦσιν *I have let myself be found by those who did not seek me* **Ro 10:20** (Is 65:1).—As נִמְצָא *be found, appear, prove, be shown* (to be) (Cass. Dio 36, 27, 6; SIG 736, 51; 1109, 73; 972, 65; POxy 743, 25 [2 BC]; ParJer 4:5; Jos., Bell. 3, 114; Just., A I, 4, 2; Tat. 41:3; Mel., P. 82, 603; Ath. 24, 4) εὑρέθη ἐν γαστρὶ ἔχουσα *it was found that she was to become a mother* **Mt 1:18.** εὑρέθη μοι ἡ ἐντολὴ εἰς θάνατον (sc. οὖσα) *the commandment proved to be a cause for death to me* **Ro 7:10.** οὐχ εὑρέθησαν ὑποστρέψαντες; *were there not found to return?* **Lk 17:18;** cp. **Ac 5:39; 1 Cor 4:2** (cp. Sir 44:20); **15:15; 2 Cor 5:3; Gal 2:17; 1 Pt 1:7; Rv 5:4;** 1 Cl 9:3; 10:1; B 4:14; Hm 3:5 and oft. ἄσπιλοι αὐτῷ εὑρεθῆναι *be found unstained in his judgment* **2 Pt 3:14.** σχήματι εὑρεθεὶς ὡς ἄνθρωπος *when he appeared in human form* **Phil 2:7.** εὑρεθήσομαι μαχόμνενος τῷ νόμῳ κυρίου . . . εὑρεθήσομαι παραδιδοὺς ἀθῷον αἷμα GJs 14:1.

❸ **to attain a state or condition,** ***find (for oneself), obtain.*** The mid. is used in this sense in Attic wr. (B-D-F §310, 1; Rob. 814; Phryn. p. 140 Lob.); in our lit. it occurs in this sense only **Hb 9:12.** As a rule our lit. uses the act. in such cases (poets; Lucian, Lexiph. 18; LXX; Jos., Ant. 5, 41) τὴν ψυχήν **Mt 10:39; 16:25.** ἀνάπαυσιν (Sir 11:19; 22:13; 28:16; 33:26; ἄνεσιν ApcEsdr 5:10) ταῖς ψυχαῖς ὑμῶν *rest for your souls* **11:29.** μετανοίας τόπον *have an opportunity to repent* or *for changing the (father's) mind* **Hb 12:17.** σκήνωμα τῷ θεῷ Ἰακώβ *maintain a dwelling for the God of Jacob* **Ac 7:46b** (Ps 131:5). χάριν *obtain grace* (SSol 8:10 v.l.) **Hb 4:16.** χάριν παρὰ τῷ θεῷ *obtain favor with God* **Lk 1:30;** also ἐνώπιον τοῦ θεοῦ **Ac 7:46a;** GJs 11:2 (LXX as a rule ἐναντίον w. gen.; JosAs 15:14 ἐνώπιόν σου). ἔλεος παρὰ κυρίου *obtain mercy from the Lord* **2 Ti 1:18** (cp. Gen 19:19; Da 3:38).—The restoration [πίστιν εὑρ]ίσκομεν Ox 1081, 26 is not valid; on basis of the Coptic SJCh 90, 2 read w. Till p. 220 app.: [ταῦτα γιγν]ῴσκομεν.—B. 765; RAC VI, 985–1052. DELG. M-M. EDNT. TW.

εὐροκλύδων, ωνος, ὁ ***Euroclydon,*** explained as the *southeast wind, that stirs up waves;* another form is εὐρυκλύδων=the wind that stirs up broad waves; only **Ac 27:14 v.l.,** where εὐρακύλων (q.v.) is the correct rdg., and the two other forms are prob. to be regarded as scribal errors (but s. Etym. Magn. 772, 30 s.v. τυφών: τυφὼν γάρ ἐστιν ἡ τοῦ ἀνέμου σφόδρα πνοή, ὃς καὶ εὐρυκλύδων καλεῖται).—εὐροκλύδων favored by AAcworth, JTS n.s. 24, '73, 190–92, but without external evidence; against him CHemer, ibid. 26, '75, 100–111; s. also Warnecke 37f n. 17.

εὐρυκλύδων s. εὐροκλύδων.

εὐρύχωρος, ον **pert. to having ample room,** ***broad, spacious, roomy*** (Aristot., HA 10, 5 p. 637a, 32; Diod. S. 19, 84, 6; LXX; TestAbr A 88, 30 [Stone p. 24]; JosAs 24:21 [cod. A and Pal. 364]; Philo, Sacr. Abel. 61; Jos., Ant. 1, 262; SibOr 3, 598) of a road *spacious* **Mt 7:13;** τὸ εὐ. *a large room* (Appian, Bell. Civ. 4, 41 §171; 2 Ch 18:9; 1 Esdr 5:46), in which one can live comfortably and unmolested (cp. Ps 30:9 ἐν εὐρυχώρῳ; Hos 4:16) Hm 5, 1, 2.—DELG s.v. χώρα. M-M. TW.

εὐσέβεια, ας, ἡ (s. next entry and σέβομαι; Pre-Socr., Aeschyl. et al.; ins, pap as 'piety, reverence, loyalty [exhibited towards parents or deities], fear of God'; opp. πονηρός Diod. S. 5, 79, 2; cp. Diog. L. 3, 83: the pious follow sacrificial custom and take care of temples; hence Aeneas is repeatedly called 'pius' in Vergil's Aeneid, s. AMichels, ClJ 92, '97, 399–416) in our lit. and in the LXX only of **awesome respect accorded to God,** ***devoutness, piety, godliness*** (Pla., Rep. 10, 615c εἰς θεούς [w. γονέας]; X., Cyr. 8, 1, 25; Posidon. 87 fgm. 59, 107 περὶ τὸ δαιμόνιον; Diod. S. 4, 39, 1 εἰς τὸν θεόν; 7, 14, 6; 19, 7, 3; Epict., Ench. 31, 1 περὶ τ. θεούς; Herm. Wr. 4, 7 πρὸς τ. θεόν; ins [SIG and OGI indices]; UPZ 41, 10 [161/160 BC] πρὸς τὸ θεῖον; PHerm 52:19; PTebt 298, 45; PGiss 66, 10; LXX, esp. 4 Macc.; TestSol 8:9; TestJud 18:5; TestIss 7:5; EpArist 2; 42 πρὸς τ. θεὸν ἡμῶν al.; Philo, Deus Imm. 17 πρὸς θεόν; 69, Poster. Cai. 181; Jos., Ant. 18, 117, C. Ap. 1, 162 περὶ τὸ θεῖον [Ath. 28, 2; cp. 30, 3 περὶ αὐτούς]; Just., Ath. W. ἀνδρεία and σοφία Orig., C. Cels. 8, 17, 16; Theoph. Ant., Hippol.) ἰδίᾳ εὐσεβείᾳ *by our own piety* **Ac 3:12;** cp. διὰ τ. ἡμετέρας εὐ. 1 Cl 32:4. ἐν πάσῃ εὐ. *in all piety* **1 Ti 2:2;** cp. **4:7f; 6:5f, 11.** μετ' εὐσεβείας *in godliness* (cp. 2 Macc 12:45) 1 Cl 15:1. τὰ πρὸς εὐσέβειαν *what belongs to piety* **2 Pt 1:3** (cp. Jos., Ant. 11, 120 τὰ πρὸς τ. θρησκείαν). ἔχειν μόρφωσιν εὐσεβείας *have the outward form of godliness*=be devout only in appearance **2 Ti 3:5** (cp. Philo, Plant. 70 εἰσί τινες τῶν ἐπιμορφαζόντων εὐσέβειαν). W. φιλοξενία 1 Cl 11:1. *Godliness* as a result of steadfastness and cause of brotherly love **2 Pt 1:6f** (on the list of virtues cp. Lucian, Somn. 10; OGI 438, Dssm. LO 270 [LAE 322]). ἡ ἐν Χριστῷ εὐ. *Christian piety* 1 Cl 1:2. περὶ τὴν εὐ. φιλοπονεῖν *show a concern for piety* 2 Cl 19:1.—*Respect for deity, devotion* (Diod. S. 16, 60, 3; Jos., C. Ap. 1, 60) ἡ κατ' εὐσέβειαν διδασκαλία *teaching that is in accordance with godliness* **1 Ti 6:3;** ἡ ἀλήθεια ἡ κατ' εὐ. **Tit 1:1.** τὸ τῆς εὐ. μυστήριον *the key to our piety* or *the secret of our devotion to God* **1 Ti 3:16** (s. MMassinger, Biblioth. Sacra 96, '40, 479–89).—Pl. *godly acts* **2 Pt 3:11** (cp. PGM 13, 717; Just., D. 47, 2).—OKern, D. Rel. der Griechen I 1926, 273–90; FBräuninger, Unters. zu d. Schriften des Hermes Trismeg., diss. Berlin 1926, esp. on εὐσέβεια and γνῶσις; FTillmann, Past. Bonus 53, '42, 129–36; 161–65 ('Frömmigkeit' in den Pastoralbr.); WFoerster, NTS 5, '59, 213–18 (Pastorals). S. ὅσιος, end.—B. 1462. Larfeld I 496. DELG s.v. σέβομαι. M-M. TW. Sv.

εὐσεβέω fut. 3 pl. εὐσεβήσουσι Sus 64 LXX; aor. 3 pl. εὐσέβησαν 4 Macc 9:6 (s. prec. entry; Theognis, trag. et al.; ins, pap, LXX, Just., Orig.) 'be reverent, respectful, devout' (w. εἰς, πρός, περί τινα) in our lit. only w. acc. **to show uncommon reverence or respect,** ***show profound respect for someone*** (trag. et al.; ins, LXX). εὐ. refers to a sense of awesome obligation arising within a system of reciprocity in which special respect is showed to those who have the greatest investment in one's well-being, such as deities and parental figures.

ⓐ Of divine beings *show exceptional devotion to, worship* (Aeschyl., Ag. 338 τοὺς θεούς; SIG 814, 36 εὐσεβῶν τ. θεούς; Sb 6828, 7; 4 Macc 11:5; Philo, Spec. Leg. 1, 312, Praem. 40; Jos., Ant. 10, 45, C. Ap. 2, 125 τὸν θεόν) ὃ οὖν ἀγνοοῦντες εὐσεβεῖτε **Ac 17:23.** There is here no ref. to a formal cult but to a desire to ensure that transcendent power is appropriately recognized, as attested by the word δεισιδαιμονέστερος vs. 22; the Athenians manifest a kind of 'wild-card' theology through erection of a special altar.

ⓑ Of humans, esp. toward parents or ancestors τὸν ἴδιον οἶκον εὐ. *show special respect for the members of one's own household* **1 Ti 5:4.**—M-M. TW.

εὐσεβής, ές (s. prec. entry; Theognis, Pind. et al.; ins, pap, LXX) **pert. to being profoundly reverent or respectful,** ***devout, godly, pious, reverent*** in our lit. only of one's relation to God (Pla., Euthyphr. 5c, Phlb. 39e; X., Apol. 19, Mem. 4, 6, 4; 4, 8, 11; Epict. 2, 17, 31; Lucian, De Calumn. 14; SIG 821c, 3; 1052, 5 μύσται καὶ ἐπόπται εὐ.; LXX; En; EpArist 233; Philo, Leg. All. 3, 209 al.; Jos., Ant. 9, 236; Ar. [Milne 76, 36]; Just.; Mel., HE 4, 26, 10) στρατιώτης εὐ. **Ac 10:7.** W. φοβούμενος τ. θεόν vs. **2.** πεποίθησις *devout confidence* 1 Cl 2:3.—Subst. ὁ. εὐ. *godly* or *devout pers.* (X., Mem. 4, 6, 2, Cyr. 8, 1, 25; Diod. S. 1, 92, 5 οἱ εὐσεβεῖς; SEG VIII, 550, 4 [I BC] pl.= devotees of Isis; Sir 12:4; 39:27; Pr 13:19; Eccl 3:16 v.l.; En 102:4; 103:3; PsSol 13:5; TestLevi 16:2; Just., A I, 2, 1 τοὺς κατὰ ἀλήθειαν εὐ.) **2 Pt 2:9;** 2 Cl 19:4. χῶρος εὐσεβῶν *a place among the godly* (s. χῶρος I) 1 Cl 50:3; τὸ εὐ. (contrast τὸ κερδαλέον) *piety* (Soph., Oed. Col. 1127 al.; Epict. 1, 29, 52; Philo, Agr. 128; Jos., Ant. 12, 43; Just., D. 98, 1) 2 Cl 20:4. The moral dimension is indicated by the subsequent ref. to an 'unjust spirit'.—BEaston, Pastoral Epistles, '47, 218. S. also ὅσιος, end.—M-M. TW.

εὐσεβῶς adv. of εὐσεβής (Pind., X., Pla. et al.; ins, pap, LXX) in our lit. of one's relation to God ***in a godly manner*** (oft. ins [SIG index]; 4 Macc 7:21 v.l.; EpArist 37 and 261; Philo, Aet. M. 10; Ath. 1:3 εὐσεβέστατα διακειμένους) 1 Cl 61:2 (cp. X., Mem. 4, 3, 16: 'Can there be any better or more reverent way to honor the gods than by doing what they command?'); ζῆν **2 Ti 3:12; Tit 2:12** (s. βιοῦν εὐ.: Ps.-Pla., Axioch. 372a). W. δικαίως (SIG 772; Jos., Ant. 8, 300; ABurk, Die Pädagogik des Isokrates . . . '23, 173 n. 2) 1 Cl 62:1. W. δικ. and σωφρόνως (Socrat., Ep. 15, 1 ἐβίωσε σωφρόνως κ. ὁσίως κ. εὐ.) **Tit 2:12.**—M-M.

εὔσημος, ον (σῆμα 'sign', s. σημαίνω, σημεῖον; trag., Hippocr. et al.; ins, pap; Ps 80:4) **readily recognizable,** ***clear, distinct*** (Aeschyl., Suppl. 714; Theophr., Caus. Pl. 6, 19, 5; Artem. 2, 44 εὐσήμου ὄντος τ. λόγου; Porphyr., Abst. 3, 4 of speech; OGI 90, 43; 665, 13) εὐ. λόγον διδόναι *utter intelligible speech* **1 Cor 14:9.**—DELG s.v. σῆμα. M-M. TW.

εὐσπλαγχνία, ας, ἡ (s. next entry and σπλάγχνα; Ps.-Eur., Rhes. 192; Theod. Prodr. 8, 317; Nicetas Eugen. 8, 238; PLond 1916, 31, [IV AD, Christ.]; PCairMasp 97 verso D, 69; TestZeb 5:1 al.; ApcSed 5:8 al.) ***tenderheartedness, benevolence*** w. γλυκύτης (as Theoph. Ant., Ad Autol. 2, 14) 1 Cl 14:3.—DELG s.v. σπλήν. M-M.

εὔσπλαγχνος, ον (s. prec. entry; in the mng. 'with healthy intestines': Hippocr., Prorrh. 2, 6; Hesych.) **pert. to having tender feelings for someone,** ***tenderhearted, compassionate*** (so Prayer of Manasseh [=Odes 12]: 7; TestZeb 9:7; JosAs ch. 13 cod. A [p. 57, 25 Bat. w. φιλάνθρωπος]; ApcEsdr 1:10 p. 25, 2 Tdf. [w. πολυέλεος, so also Cat. Cod. Astr. IX/2 p. 165, 4 of the goddess Selene]; ApcSed 15:1 [w. ἀναμάρτητος]; PGM 12, 283; Just., D. 108, 3) of God (as in the pass. already given) w. ἐπιεικής 1 Cl 29:1.—Of humans (TestSim 4:4; Syntipas p. 106, 23; Leontios 46 p. 99, 15; Nicetas Eugen. 6, 193 H.) 54:1. (W. φιλάδελφος, ταπεινόφρων) **1 Pt 3:8.** W. numerous other qualifications: of deacons Pol 5:2 and elders 6:1 (for the mng. *good-hearted* in **1 Pt 3:8** and Pol 6:1 s. ESelwyn, First Peter '46, 188f). εὐ. εἴς τινα *toward someone* **Eph 4:32.**—DELG s.v. σπλήν. TW.

εὐστάθεια, ας, ἡ (s. two next entries; Epicurus in Plut., Mor., 135c; Epict. 2, 5, 9; Vett. Val. 183, 3; SIG 1109, 15; OGI 669, 4 and 45; PGiss 87, 18; LXX; EpArist 216 and 261; Philo; Jos., Ant. 18, 207) a favorite term for describing stable political conditions, then **state or condition of being free from internal agitation,** ***good disposition, tranquility, stability, firmness*** 1 Cl 61:1 (w. εἰρήνη as Philo, De Jos. 57, In Flacc. 135); 65:1.—DELG s.v. στάθμη.

εὐσταθέω impv. εὐστάθει; impf. 3 pl. εὐσταθοῦσαν (Mlt-H. 194f); fut. inf. εὐσταθήσειν 3 Macc 7:4; aor. 3 sg. εὐστάθησεν 2 Macc 14:25; impv. 2 sg. εὐστάθησον (Mel., P. 24, 174) **to be free from inner or outward disturbance,** ***be stable, be tranquil, be at rest*** (Ps.-Eur., Rhesus 317; Dionys. Hal., Plut., Lucian, Epict.; Vett. Val. 42, 21; Herm. Wr. 466, 22 Sc.; OGI 54, 19; SIG 708, 35; IMaronIsis 30; BGU 1764, 14 [I BC]; 2 Macc 14:25; TestJob 36:5; Jos., Ant. 15, 137 περὶ τ. βίον; Mel., P. 24, 174) *lead a quiet life* Hm 5, 2, 2; *be at rest* (in contrast to affliction) s 7:3; *be calm* (Epict. 1, 29, 61), or *stand firm* εὐστάθει IPol 4:1. Of sheep οὐκ εὐσταθοῦσαν *they had no peace* Hs 6, 2, 7.—DELG s.v. στάθμη.

εὐσταθής, ές (s. prec. two entries; Hom. et al.; LXX; adv. εὐσταθῶς TestJob 36:6) ***stable, firm, calm*** τὸ εὐσταθές *calmness, composure* (Epict., Ench. 33, 11; Philo, Conf. Lingu. 43) MPol 7:2.—DELG s.v. στάθμη.

εὐσυνείδητος, ον (s. συνείδησις) ***with a good conscience*** (M. Ant. 6, 30, 15) εὐσυνείδητον εἶναι *have a good conscience* IMg 4. ἔν τινι *about someone* IPhld 6:3. Cp. εὐσυνείδητον πρᾶγμα ποιῶν Sb I, 4426, 12 (III AD).—DELG s.v. οἶδα.

εὐσχημονέω (s. three next entries; Pla., Leg. 732c; Menand.; Philod.; PSI V 541, 5; not LXX; Joseph.) gener. 'behave with dignity/decorum': in our lit. only as rdg. of P[46] in **1 Cor 13:5** for ἀσχημονεῖ. If it is not a scribal error here, it must have the sense ***be pretentious, be pompous*** as outward display of goodness (s. εὐσχήμων 2), which is not found elsewh., but cp. εὐσχημῶν 'specious' Eur., Med. 584. S. ADebrunner, ConNeot XI, '47, 37–41.—DELG s.v. 1 ἔχω 3.

εὐσχημόνως adv. (s. prec. entry; Aristoph., Vesp. 1210; X., Mem. 3, 12, 4, Cyr. 1, 3, 8 al.; Epict. 2, 5, 23; SIG 598e, 5 al.; 717, 14; TestSol 8:7; Jos., Ant. 15, 102)

❶ **pert. to being proper in behavior, *decently, becomingly*** εὐ. περιπατεῖν *behave decently* **Ro 13:13** (as of one properly attired; s. εὐσχημοσύνη); **1 Th 4:12** (SIG 1019, 7ff ἀναστρέφεσθαι εὐ.).

❷ **pert. to being appropriate, *correctly*** πάντα εὐ. καὶ κατὰ τάξιν γινέσθω *everything is to be done in the right way and in order (orderly sequence?)* **1 Cor 14:40** (SIG 736, 42 εὐ. πάντα γίνηται; Ael. Aristid. 46 p. 364 D.: εὐ. καὶ τεταγμένως [i.e. ταῦτα ἐπράττετο]).—New Docs 2, 86. M-M. Spicq.

εὐσχημοσύνη, ης, ἡ (s. prec. two entries; Hippocr., Pla., X.+; Diod. S. 5, 32, 7; Epict. 4, 9, 11; OGI 339, 32; Michel 545, 8f [II BC]; 4 Macc 6:2; EpArist 284) **the state of being appropriate for display, *propriety, decorum, presentability,*** of clothing (cp. Maximus Tyr. 15, 3b; SIG 547, 37; 4 Macc 6:2) of modest concealment τὰ ἀσχήμονα ἡμῶν εὐ. περισσοτέραν ἔχει *our unpresentable* (parts) *receive greater presentability* (=are treated with greater modesty) **1 Cor 12:23.**—M-M. TW. Spicq.

εὐσχήμων, ον, gen. ονος (Eur., Hippocr. et al.; ins, pap; Pr 11:25; TestJob 21:2)

❶ **pert. to being appropriate for display, *proper, presentable*** τὰ εὐ. (sc. μέλη) *the presentable parts* **1 Cor 12:24** (cp. Socrat., Ep. 31 tongue and head τὸ θειότατον . . . τῶν μερῶν ἁπάντων; Diod. S. 20, 63, 3 head and face τὰ κυριώτατα μέρη τοῦ σώματος; Maximus Tyr. 40, 2f κεφαλή and ὄμματα are nobler than μηροί and σφυρά). τὸ εὐ. *good order* (cp. Epict. 4, 1, 163; 4, 12, 6) **7:35.**

❷ **pert. to being considered especially worthy of public admiration, *prominent, of high standing/repute, noble*** (Plut., Mor. 309c; Vett. Val. index; PFlor 61, 61 [85 AD]; 16, 20; PHamb 37, 7; OGI 485, 3 ἄνδρα ἀπὸ προγόνων εὐσχήμονα; Jos., Vi. 32; Phryn. p. 333 Lob.) **Ac 13:50** (on influence of women for personal interest cp. Theopomp. of Chios: fgm. 121 Jac.); **17:12** (*well-to-do:* VVanderlip, ASP 12, '72, 25), **34** D. εὐ. βουλευτής *a prominent counsellor* (Joseph of Arimathaea) **Mk 15:43.**—M-M. TW. Spicq.

εὐτάκτως adv. (s. next entry and τάσσω; since Aeschyl., Pers. 399; Hippocr.; X., Cyr. 2, 2, 3; Epict. 3, 24, 95; SIG 717, 25; 736, 42; ISardGauthier 3, 6 p. 81; SEG XLIII, 1322 [reff.]; PTebt 5, 55; BGU 1147, 12; Pr 30:27; 3 Macc 2:1; Ath. 25:3) ***in good order*** ἐγένοντο ἀμφότερα εὐ. *both originated in good order* 1 Cl 42:2 (on the pl. of the verb w. the neut. pl. s. ἐσθίω 1bα). As a military t.t.: of soldiers εὐ. ἐπιτελεῖν τὰ διατασσόμενα *carry out orders with good discipline* 37:2.—DELG s.v. τάσσω.

εὐταξία, ας, ἡ (s. prec. entry; Thu.+) gener. 'good order' esp. also (military t.t.) ***good discipline*** (Thu. 6, 72, 4; Ps.- Pla., Alc. 1 p. 122c al.; Jos., Bell. 2, 529) IEph 6:2.

εὔτεκνος, ον (s. τέκνον; Eur. et al.; Philo). In ISm 13:2 the word is understood by Zahn and Hilgenfeld as an adj., in which case any of the var. mngs. found in other lit. is applicable: ***with many children, w. good children, fortunate because of children.*** Other scholars, including Lghtf., Funk, Krüger, Bihlmeyer, treat εὔ. as a proper name, because εὔ. as an adj. seems not to fit well into the context. On the other hand, Εὔ. as a name is unattested to date; but s. OGI 53 and the grammarian Εὐτέκνιος in Pauly-W. VI 1492.—DELG s.v. τίκτω.

εὐτόνως adv. (τείνω 'stretch'; Aristoph., Plut. 1095; X., Hier. 9, 6 al.; Josh 6:8; Philo, Agr. 70; Jos., Bell. 4, 423; Just., A I, 65, 1) **pert. to expression of intense emotion, *vigorously, vehemently*** εὐ. κατηγορεῖν τινος *accuse someone vehemently* **Lk 23:10.** εὐ. διακατελέγχεσθαί τινι *refute someone vigorously* **Ac 18:28.**—M-M.

εὐτραπελία, ας, ἡ (s. τρέπω; Hippocr. et al., mostly in a good sense: 'wittiness', 'facetiousness' [cp. our 'turn a phrase']; so also Posidipp. Com. fgm. 28, 5; Diod. S. 15, 6, 5; Philo, Leg. ad Gai. 361; Jos., Ant. 12, 173; 214. Acc. to Aristot., EN 2, 7, 13 it is the middle term betw. the extremes of buffoonery [βωμολοχία] and boorishness [ἀγροικία]; acc. to Aristot., Rhet. 2, 12 it is πεπαιδευμένη ὕβρις) in our lit. only in a bad sense ***coarse jesting, risqué wit*** (for sim. sense cp. εὐτράπελος Isocr. 7, 49) **Eph 5:4.**—HRahner, LexThK III 1212. PvanderHorst, Is Wittiness Christian? A Note on εὐτραπελία in Eph 5:4: Miscellanea Neotestamentica, ed. AKlÿn/WvanUnnik '78, 163–77.—DELG s.v. τρέπω. M-M. TW. Spicq. Sv.

Εὔτυχος, ου, ὁ (IG III, 1095; 1113; 1122; SEG XLI, 1700, 4 [I/II AD] al.; CIL III 2784; 3028 al.; PPetr I, 12, 8; Preisigke, Namenbuch; Joseph.; Hemer, Acts 237) ***Eutychus,*** a young Christian in Troas **Ac 20:9.**—M-M.

εὐφημία, ας, ἡ (s. next entry and φήμη; Pind. et al. in var. mngs.; Sym.; EpArist 191; Philo; Jos., Ant. 16, 14; 17, 200) **favorable expression about someth., *good report, good repute*** (so Diod. S. 1, 2, 4; Aelian, VH 3, 47; OGI 339, 30; SIG 711 L, 11; Michel 394, 39; PLond III, 981, 8–10 p. 242 [IV AD] ἡ εὐφημία σου περιεκύκλωσεν τ. κόσμον ὅλον; M. Ant. 6, 18) opp. δυσφημία **2 Cor 6:8.**—DELG s.v. φημί. M-M. TW. Sv.

εὔφημος, ον (s. prec. entry; Aeschyl. et al. in var. mngs.; ins; Sym. Ps 62:6; Philo; Jos., C. Ap. 2, 248) the basic idea: 'pert. to what is being said with cautious reserve' (in deference to the transcendent or out of respect for those of high status, words ought to be carefully chosen, for one might utter someth. that is unlucky; s. the reff. in L-S-J-M under the various terms in the εὐφημ- family), in a transf. sense ***praiseworthy, commendable,*** ὅσα εὔφημα **Phil 4:8** (M. Ant. 6, 18; Dibelius, Hdb. ad loc.; CClassen, WienerStud 107/108, '94/95, 329; for the formulation s. ὅσος 2).—M-M.

εὐφορέω 1 aor. εὐφόρησα **to produce unusually well, *bear good crops, yield well, be fruitful*** (s. φέρω; Hippocr. et al.; Philo, De Jos. 159; Jos., Bell. 2, 592) of farm land (Philostrat., Vi. Apoll. 6, 39 p. 251, 8 of γῆ) **Lk 12:16.**—DELG s.v. φέρω. M-M.

εὐφραίνω fut. εὐφρανῶ LXX; 1 aor. εὔ- and ηὔφρανα LXX; inf. εὐφρᾶναι Hm 12, 3, 4; B 21:9. Pass.: 1 fut. εὐφρανθήσομαι; 1 aor. ηὐφράνθην (also εὐ- LXX) (s. φρήν; Hom.+).

❶ **to cause to be glad, *gladden, cheer (up)*** τινά *someone* act. (Hom.+; OGI 504, 10 εὐφρᾶναι ὑμᾶς; PFlor 154 II, 12; LXX; En 107:3; Philo, Spec. Leg. 3, 186; Jos., Ant. 4, 117) τίς ὁ εὐφραίνων με; *who makes me glad?* **2 Cor 2:2.** εἰς τὸ εὐφρᾶναι ὑμᾶς *to cheer you* B 21:9. Of the commandments of the angel of repentance δυνάμεναι εὐφρᾶναι καρδίαν ἀνθρώπου *be able to gladden the heart of a person* Hm 12, 3, 4 (cp. Ps 18:9; 103:15 εὐφραίνει καρδίαν ἀνθρώπου; Pr 23:15; Sir 40:20; PsSol 5:12 εὐφρᾶναι ψυχὴν ταπεινοῦ; Aelian, VH 1, 32; Ramsay, CB I/2 386 no. 232, 19 τὴν ψυχὴν εὐφραίνετε πάντοτε).

❷ **to be glad or delighted, *be glad, enjoy oneself, rejoice, celebrate*** pass. w. act. sense (Hom.+; also OdeSol 11:15; Ar. [Milne 76, 30]; Just., D. 80, 1 al; Mel., P. 16, 103 al.) ἐπί τινι

(Aristoph., Acharn. 5; X., Symp. 7, 5; Epict. 4, 4, 46; BGU 1080, 7; Sir 16:1, 2; 18:32; 1 Macc 11:44; 12:12; Philo, Mos. 1. 247; TestLevi 18:13) **Rv 18:20;** B 10:11. ἐπί τινα (Is 61:10; Ps 31:11) **Rv 18:20 v.l.** ἔν τινι *in, about,* or *over someone* or *someth.* (X., Hier. 1, 16; BGU 248, 28; Sir 14:5; 39:31; 51:15, 29; PsSol 5:18; ApcMos 43; Philo, Spec. Leg. 2, 194) Hs 9, 18, 4; **Rv 18:20 v.l.** ἐν τοῖς ἔργοις τῶν χειρῶν **Ac 7:41** (s. 3 below); ἐν τοῖς δικαιώμασιν αὐτοῦ εὐ. *take delight in God's ordinances* B 4:11 (cp. Ps 18:9). διά τινος *be gladdened by someth.= rejoice in someth.* (X., Hier. 1, 8; Philo, Spec. Leg. 2, 194) 1:8. Abs. (PGM 3, 24; 4, 2389; En 25:6; TestSol 1:1 A; 1:10 D; ParJer 6:6; Philo, Cher. 86; SibOr 3, 785) **Lk 15:32** (but s. 3 below); **Ac 2:26** (Ps 15:9); **Ro 15:10** (Dt 32:43); **Gal 4:27** (Is 54:1); **Rv 11:10; 12:12;** 1 Cl 52:2 (Ps 68:32); 2 Cl 2:1 (Is 54:1); 19:4; Dg 12:9; Hv 3, 4, 2; m 5, 1, 2; s 5, 7, 1; 9, 11, 8; ApcPt 4:18. Esp. of the joys of dining (Od. 2, 311; X., Cyr. 8, 7, 12; Dt 14:26; 27:7; TestAbr 4 p. 80, 25 [Stone p. 8], B 5 p. 109, 16 [Stone p. 66]) φάγε, πίε, εὐφραίνου *eat, drink, be merry* **Lk 12:19** (cp. Eccl 8:15; Eur., Alcest. 788; for the theme cp. Is 22:13; 1 Cor 15:32 and s. ἐσθίω 1d); cp. **15:23f, 29** and s. 3 below; **16:19.** τελεσθέντος τοῦ δείπνου κατέβησαν εὐφρανόμενοι GJs 6:3.

❸ **to observe a special occasion with festivity,** ***celebrate*** pass., in this sense prob. **Lk 15:23, 29, 32; Ac 7:41** (s. 2 above).—DELG s.v. φρήν. M-M. EDNT. TW.

εὐφρασία, ας, ἡ (s. prec. entry; Epict., Gnomolog. 19 'cheerfulness'; TestAbr B 3 p. 107, 15/Stone p. 62 [in conn. w. a feast]; ParJer 3:21 [= 3:15 Harris] εὐ. τοῦ κυρίου 'favor'; Ar. [Milne 75, 30]) ***cheerfulness, joy*** ἀτενίζουσα ὡς πρὸς εὐ. οὕτως πρόσκειται ἀνδρὶ ξένῳ of Thecla *gazing intently, as though enraptured, she devotes herself to the strange man* AcPl Ox 6:9f (= Aa 1, 241, 13).—GDelling, Jüdische Lehre und Frömmigkeit in den ParJer '67, 28f.

Εὐφράτης, ου, ὁ (פְּרָת; Hdt.+; OGI 54, 13f; 17; Gen 2:14 al.; LXX; Philo; Joseph.; SibOr) ***the Euphrates,*** the westernmost of the two rivers that include Mesopotamia betw. them. ὁ ποταμὸς ὁ μέγας Εὐ. *the great river Euphrates* (Gen 15:18; Ex 23:31.—Cp. Diod. S. 17, 75, 2 μέγας ποταμὸς . . . Στιβοίτης) **Rv 9:14; 16:12.**—OEANE II 287–90.

εὐφροσύνη, ης, ἡ (εὔφρων 'cheerful'; Hom. et al.; also PLips 119 II, 1) ***joy, gladness, cheerfulness*** **Ac 2:28** (Ps 15:11); **14:17** (cp. Sir 30:22 and PsSol 15:3 εὐφροσύνη καρδίας, and s. καί 1aδ). W. ἀγαλλίασις 1 Cl 18:8 (Ps 50:10); B 1:6. ἀγάπη εὐφροσύνης *love that goes with joy* ibid. τέκνα εὐφροσύνης *children of gladness*=children for whom gladness is in store 7:1. ἔργον εὐφροσύνης *a work of gladness* 10:11; ἡμέραν ἄγειν εἰς εὐ. *celebrate a day with gladness* 15:9 (s. Jdth 12:13 and Esth 9:18).—DELG s.v. φρήν. New Docs 4, 152–54. M-M. TW. Sv.

εὐχαριστέω (s. χάρις) 1 aor. εὐχαρίστησα (ηὐχ- **Ro 1:21** [edd. exc. t.r.] s. W-S. §12, 5b; Mlt-H. 191f); 1 aor. pass. subj. 3 sg. εὐχαριστηθῇ; ptc. εὐχαριστηθείς (Just.)

❶ **to show that one is under obligation,** ***be thankful, feel obligated to thank.*** This mng. is common in diplomatic documents in which the recipient of a favor reciprocates with assurance of goodwill (e.g. decrees of the Byzantines in Demosth. 18, 91f, concluding: οὐκ ἐλλείψει εὐχαριστῶν καὶ ποιῶν ὅ τι ἂν δύνηται ἀγαθόν =the people of the Chersonesus 'will never stop being grateful and doing whatever they can' (for the people of Athens); cp. OGI 730, 11; IPriene 44, 8 et al.). In this sense ἐ. = χάριν διδόναι (in contrast to χάριν εἰδέναι, s. Phryn. p. 18 Lob.). This mng. has been suggested for **Lk 18:11** (the Pharisee is interpreted as making requital in fasting and tithing vs. 12) and **Ro 16:4** (in sense of indebtedness; this pass. is the only one in the NT that deals w. thankfulness toward humans [as 2 Macc. 12:31]), but both pass. fit equally well in 2.

❷ **to express appreciation for benefits or blessings,** ***give thanks, express thanks, render/return thanks*** (as 'render thanks' since Polyb. 16, 25, 1; Posidon. 87, fgm. 36 [in Athen. 5, 213e]; Diod. S. 20, 34, 5; Plut., Mor. 505d; Epict., ins, pap, LXX, Philo; Jos., Ant. 20, 12; cp. Phryn. p. 18 Lob.). Except for **Ro 16:4** (cp. 2 Macc 12:31) εὐ. is used w. God as object (Diod. S. 14, 29, 4; 16, 11, 1 τοῖς θεοῖς περὶ τῶν ἀγαθῶν; Epict. 1, 4, 32; 1, 10, 3; 2, 23, 5 τῷ θεῷ; Artem. 4, 2 p. 206, 4 θῦε καὶ εὐχαρίστει; Herm. Wr. 1, 29 τ. θεῷ; SIG 995, 11 τ. θεοῖς; 1173, 9f; UPZ 59, 10 [168 BC] τ. θεοῖς; PTebt 56, 9; BGU 423, 6 τ. κυρίῳ Σεράπιδι; PGM 13, 706 [w. δέομαι]; Jdth 8:25; 2 Macc 1:11; 10:7; 3 Macc 7:16; EpArist 177 ὑμῖν, . . . τῷ θεῷ; Philo, Spec. Leg. 2, 204; 3, 6 θεῷ; TestSol 7:4 and Jos., Ant. 1, 193 τ. θεῷ; TestJos 8:5 τῷ κυρίῳ; TestAbr A 15 p. 95, 14 [Stone p. 38]; Ar. 15, 10 al.; Just., Orig., Hippol., Did.) αὐτῷ (of Jesus, who reveals himself as God in a miracle) **Lk 17:16.** τῷ θεῷ (μου) **Ac 28:15; Ro 7:25 v.l.; 1 Cor 14:18; Phil 1:3; Col 1:3, 12; 3:17; Phlm 4;** 1 Cl 38:4; 41:1 v.l.; B 7:1; IEph 21:1; Hv 4, 1, 4. εὐχαριστῶ σοι=God **Lk 18:11** (cp. 1QH 2:20 al. אוֹדְכָה אֲדוֹנָי 'I praise you, O Lord'). Elliptically **Ro 1:21,** where τῷ θεῷ is to be understood fr. the preceding ὡς θεόν (though εὐ. occasionally is used w. the acc. *praise someone w. thanks* SIG 1172, 3 εὐχαριστεῖ Ἀσκληπιόν; Cat. Cod. Astr. VII 177, 17); **1 Th 5:18;** 2 Cl 18:1.—Esp. of thanksgiving before meals, w. dat. added τῷ θεῷ **Ac 27:35; Ro 14:6** (cp. Ar. 15, 10); σοι D 10:3; ᾧ B 7:1. Abs. **Mt 15:36; 26:27; Mk 8:6, 7 v.l.; 14:23; Lk 22:17, 19; J 6:11, 23; 1 Cor 11:24** (cp. Just., A I, 65, 5). W. mention of the obj., for which one gives thanks τινί τι *(to) someone for someth.* Hs 7:5 (εὐ. τι='thank for someth.', a rare usage [Hippocr., Ep. 17, 46], s. **2 Cor 1:11** below; cp. Just., A I, 65, 5 τοῦ εὐχαριστηθέντος ἄρτου). περί τινος *for someone, because of someone* (Philo, Spec. Leg. 1, 211) **1 Th 1:2;** for someth. Hs 5, 1, 1; also foll by ὅτι *because* (Ps.-Callisth. 2, 22, 11; Berl. pap: APF 12, '37, 247; TestAbr A 15 p. 95, 14 [Stone p. 38]) **Ro 1:8; 1 Cor 1:4f; 2 Th 1:3; 2:13.** ὑπέρ τινος w. gen. of the pers. on whose behalf one thanks **2 Cor 1:11; Eph 1:16;** Hs 2:6; also foll. by ὅτι *because* IPhld 11:1; ISm 10:1. ὑπέρ τινος w. gen. of thing *for someth.* (Philo, Congr. Erud. Gr. 96) **1 Cor 10:30; Eph 5:20;** D 9:2f; 10:2. W. ἐπί τινι *because of, for* (IPergamon 224a, 14; Sb 7172, 25 [217 BC] εὐχαριστῶν τοῖς θεοῖς ἐπὶ τῷ συντελέσαι αὐτοὺς ἃ ἐπηγγείλαντο αὐτῷ; UPZ 59, 10f [168 BC]; Philo, Spec. Leg. 1, 67; TestGad 7:6 v.l. ἐπὶ πᾶσι τῷ κυρίῳ; Jos., Ant. 1, 193) **1 Cor 1:4;** Hs 9, 14, 3. W. (τινί and) ὅτι foll. **Lk 18:11** (cp. 1QH 2:20 al.); **J 11:41; 1 Cor 1:14; 1 Th 2:13; Rv 11:17;** 1 Cl 38:2; IPhld 6:3; D 10:3, 4. W. acc. of content εὐχαριστεῖν ὅσα θέλουσιν *do the eucharistic prayer (in as many words as) the prophets choose* D 10:7. Abs. σὺ εὐχαριστεῖς *you offer a prayer of thanksgiving* **1 Cor 14:17;** in wordplay *do the Eucharist* οὕτως εὐχαριστήσατε D 9:1; εὐχαριστήσατε 14:1; cp. 10:1. As a parenthetical clause εὐχαριστῶ τῷ θεῷ *thanks be to God* **1 Cor 14:18.** Pass. (cp. Dssm., B 119 [BS 122]; Philo, Rer. Div. Her. 174 ἵνα ὑπὲρ τ. ἀγαθῶν ὁ θεὸς εὐχαριστῆται) ἵνα ἐκ πολλῶν προσώπων τὸ εἰς ἡμᾶς χάρισμα διὰ πολλῶν εὐχαριστηθῇ ὑπὲρ ἡμῶν *in order that thanks may be given by many persons on our behalf for the blessing granted to us* **2 Cor 1:11** (on εὐ. τι s. above).—PSchubert, Form and Function of the Pauline Thanksgivings '39. In a few passages the word could also mean

❸ ***pray*** gener. (PTebt 56, 9 [II BC] εὐχαριστῆσαι τοῖς θεοῖς; PLond II, 413, 3 p. 301 and II, 418, 3 p. 303 [both Christ., c. 346

AD]; BGU 954, 4).—1 Cl 62:2 v.l. (for εὐαριστεῖν).—FHort, Εὐχαριστία, εὐχαριστεῖν (in Philo): JTS 3, 1902, 594–98; TSchermann, Εὐχαριστία and εὐχαριστεῖν: Philol 69, 1910, 375–410; GBoobyer, 'Thanksgiving' and the 'Glory of God' in Paul, diss. Heidelb. 1929; JMRobinson, Die Hodajot-Formel in Gebet und Hymnus des Frühchristentums, in: Apophoreta (Festschr. EHaenchen) '64, 194–235; HPatsch, ZNW 62, '71, 210–31; RAC VI, 900–928.—B. 1166. DELG s.v. χάρις. New Docs 127–29. M-M. EDNT. TW.

εὐχαριστία, ας, ἡ (s. prec. entry; since Hippocr. Comp. II 87f. Ps.-Menand. fgm. 693 Kock; ins; PLond III, 1178, 25 p. 216 [194 AD]; LXX; Philo, Joseph., Just., Did.).

❶ **the quality of being grateful, with implication of appropriate attitude, *thankfulness, gratitude*** (an important component of Gr-Rom. reciprocity; s. decrees of the Byzantines in Demosth. 18, 91 [s. εὐχαριστέω 1]; Polyb. 8, 12, 8; Diod. S. 17, 59, 7; OGI 227, 6; 199, 31 [I AD] ἔχω πρὸς τ. μέγιστον θεόν μου Ἄρην εὐχαριστίαν; BGU 1764, 21 [I BC]; 2 Macc 2:27; Esth 8:12d; Philo, Leg. All. 1, 84) μετὰ πάσης εὐ. (cp. Orig., C. Cels. 7, 46, 8) *with all gratitude* **Ac 24:3.**

❷ **the expression or content of gratitude, *the rendering of thanks, thanksgiving*** (SIG 798, 5 [c. 37 AD] εἰς εὐχαριστίαν τηλικούτου θεοῦ εὑρεῖν ἴσας ἀμοιβάς; Wsd 16:28; Sir 37:11; Philo, Spec. Leg. 1, 224; Jos., Ant. 1, 156; 2, 346; 3, 65; 4, 212) abs. **Eph 5:4** (s. OCasel, BZ 18, 1929, 84f, who, after Origen, equates εὐχαριστία w. εὐχαριτία='the mark of fine training'). τῷ θεῷ *toward God* **2 Cor 9:11.** μετὰ εὐχαριστίας *with thanksgiving* (Philo, Spec. Leg. 1, 144) **Phil 4:6; 1 Ti 4:3f;** ἐν εὐ. **Col 4:2.** περισσεύειν ἐν εὐ. *overflow w. thanksg.* **2:7;** περισσεύειν τὴν εὐ. *increase the thanksg.* **2 Cor 4:15.** εὐχαριστίαν τῷ θεῷ ἀνταποδοῦναι περὶ ὑμῶν *render thanks to God for you* **1 Th 3:9.** Also εὐ. διδόναι (Theodor. Prodr. 8, 414 H. θεοῖς) **Rv 4:9.** Esp. *prayer of thanksgiving* (Herm. Wr. 1, 29) **1 Cor 14:16; Rv 7:12.** Pl. **2 Cor 9:12; 1 Ti 2:1.**

❸ **the observance and elements of the Eucharist, *Lord's Supper, Eucharist*** ποτήριον τῆς εὐχ. **1 Cor 10:16 v.l.**—D 9:1, 5 JClabeaux, in: Prayers fr. Alexander to Constantine, ed. MKiley, '97, 260–66; IEph 13:1; IPhld 4; ISm 8:1. W. προσευχή 7:1. Cp. Just., A I, 65, 3; 66, 1; Orig., C. Cels. 57, 20; RKnopf, Hdb. on D 9:1.—JRéville, Les origines de l'Eucharistie 1908; MGoguel, L'Euch. des origines à Justin mart. 1909; FWieland, D. vorirenäische Opferbegriff 1909; GLoeschcke, Zur Frage nach der Einsetzung u. Herkunft der Eucharistie: ZWT 54, 1912, 193–205; ALoisy, Les origines de la Cène euch.: Congr. d'Hist. du Christ. I 1928, 77–95. GMacGregor, Eucharistic Origins 1929; KGoetz, D. Ursprung d. kirchl. Abendmahls 1929; HHuber, D. Herrenmahl im NT, diss. Bern 1929; WGoossens, Les origines de l'Euch. '31; RHupfeld, D. Abendmahlsfeier, ihr ursprüngl. Sinn usw., '35; JJeremias, D. Abendmahlsworte Jesu '35, [2]'49, [3]'60 (Eng. tr., The Eucharistic Words of Jesus, AEhrhardt '55; s. also KKuhn, TLZ 75, '50, 399–408), D. paul. Abdm.—eine Opferdarbietung?: StKr 108, '37, 124–41; AArnold, D. Ursprung d. Chr. Abdmahls '37, [2]'39; LPoot, Het oudchristelijk Avondmaal '36; ELohmeyer, D. Abdm. in d. Urgem.: JBL 56, '37, 217–52; EKäsemann, D. Abdm. im NT: Abdm. gemeinschaft? '37, 60–93; HSasse, D. Abdm. im NT: V. Sakr. d. Altars '41, 26–78; EGaugler, D. Abdm. im NT '43; NJohansson, Det urkristna nattvardsfirandet '44; ESchweizer, D. Abdm. eine Vergegenwärtigung des Todes Jesu od. e. eschatalogisches Freudenmahl?: TZ 2, '46, 81–101; TPreiss, TZ 4, '48, 81–101 (Eng. tr., Was the Last Supper a Paschal Meal? in Life in Christ, chap. 5, '54, 81–99); F-JLeenhardt, Le Sacrement de la Sainte Cène, '48; GWalther, Jesus, das Passalamm des Neuen Bundes usw., '50; RBultmann, Theol. of the NT (tr. KGrobel), '51, I, 144–52; AHiggins, The Lord's Supper in the NT, '52; OCullmann, Early Christian Worship (transl. ATodd and JTorrance), '53; HLessig, D. Abendmahlsprobleme im Lichte der NTlichen Forschung seit 1900, diss. Bonn, '53; ESchweizer, TLZ 79, '54, 577–92 (lit.); GBornkamm, Herrenmahl u. Kirche bei Paulus, NTS 2, '55/56, 202–6; CMoule, The Judgment Theme in the Sacraments, in Background of the NT and Its Eschatology (CDodd Festschr.) '56, 464–81; MBlack, The Arrest and Trial of Jesus and the Date of the Last Supper, in NT Essays (TManson memorial vol.) '59, 19–33; PNeuenzeit, Das Herrenmahl, '60; The Eucharist in the NT, five essays tr. fr. French by EStewart, '64; EKilmartin, The Eucharist in the Primitive Church, '65; BIersel, NovT 7, '64/65, 167–94; HBraun, Qumran II, '66, 29–54; JAudet, TU 73, '59, 643–62; HSchürmann, D. Paschamahlbericht, '53, D. Einsetzungsbericht, '55, Jesu Abschiedsrede, '57 (all Lk 22); HPatsch, Abendmahl u. Historischer Jesus, '72; FHahn RGG[4], I, 10–15 (NT); CMarkschies, ibid., 15–21 (early church). S. also the lit. on ἀγάπη 2.—M-M. TW.

εὐχάριστος, ον (s. prec. two entries; Hdt. et al.; ins, pap, Pr 11:16; Philo) **pert. to being grateful, *thankful*** (cp. the first mng. of εὐχαριστέω and εὐχαριστία; so X., Cyr. 8, 3, 49; OGI 267, 36; 339, 60 and oft. in ins of cities and their people who are grateful to their benefactors; Jos., Ant. 16, 162; Ar. [Milne, 76, 49]) εὐχάριστοι γίνεσθε **Col 3:15** (IPriene 103, 8 [c. 100 BC] γενόμενος ὁ δῆμος εὐ.; Philo, Spec. Leg. 2, 209; Just., A I, 13, 2 εὐ. ὄντας).—M-M. TW.

εὐχερής, ές, gen. ους (s. χείρ; Soph., Hippocr. et al.; ins; UPZ 162 VIII, 13 [117 BC] εὐχερῶς; LXX).

❶ **pert. to having a tendency or inclination to, with implication of feeling relatively free from restraint, *easily inclined, prone, reckless*** (Demosth. 21, 103; Aristot., Metaph. 1025a, 2; PGM 4, 2504 εὐχερῶς; Philo, Somn. 1, 13; Jos., Vi. 167; Just., D. 20, 1 and 67, 8 πρός; A II, 2, 7 εὐχερῶς) ἐν καταλαλιᾷ *prone to slander* B 20:2.

❷ **pert. to requiring little effort, *easy*** εὐχερές ἐστιν w. inf. foll. *it is easy* (Batr. 62; SIG 674, 65; Jdth 7:10) ὑμῖν εὐχερές ἐστιν ποιῆσαι *it is easy for you to do* IRo 1:2.—DELG s.v. χείρ.

εὐχή, ῆς, ἡ (s. εὔχομαι; Hom.+; Mel., HE 4, 26, 8 'wish')

❶ **speech or petition directed to God, *prayer*** (X., Symp. 8, 15; Diod. S. 20, 50, 6 εὐχὰς τοῖς θεοῖς ἐποιοῦντο; Dio Chrys. 19 [36], 36; OGI 383, 233 [I BC]; BGU 531 I, 5 [I AD]; PGiss 23, 5 [II AD]; LXX; TestAbr A, TestJob, Test12Patr; ParJer 9:3; GrBar 4:14; Philo, Sacr. Abel. 53 and oft. [on Philo: CLarson, JBL 65, '46, 185–203]; Jos., Bell. 7, 155, Ant. 15, 52; Just., Iren., Orig.) ἡ εὐ. τῆς πίστεως *the prayer offered in faith* **Js 5:15;** πληρῶσαι τὴν εὐ. *finish a prayer* MPol 15:1; also τελέσας … τὴν εὐ. GJs 9:1. μου ἡ εὐ. *my prayer* 1:4. ἐν εὐχῇ 24:1 (v.l. εὐχαῖς). Pl. D 15:4. νήφειν πρὸς τὰς εὐ. *be watchful in prayer(s)* Pol 7:2.

❷ **a solemn promise with the understanding that one is subject to penalty for failure to discharge the obligation, *vow*** (X., Mem. 2, 2, 10; Diod. S. 1, 83, 2; Jos., Bell. 2, 313) **Ac 18:18; 21:23** (JUbbink, NThSt 5, 1922, 137–39). θυσίαι εὐχῶν *votive offerings* (cp. Lev 22:29.—Diod. S. 3, 55, 8 θυσίαι as the result of εὐχαί) 1 Cl 41:2. ἀποδιδόναι τῷ ὑψίστῳ τὰς εὐ. (ἀποδίδωμι 2c) 52:3 (Ps 49:14).—AWendel, D. israel.-jüd. Gelübde '31. HSalmanowitsch, D. Nasiräat nach Bibel u. Talmud, diss. Giessen '31; HGowen, The Hair-Offering: JSOR 11, 1927, 1–20; RAC VIII 1134–1258; IX 1–36.—DELG s.v. εὔχομαι. M-M. TW. Spicq.

εὔχομαι impf. εὐχόμην **Ac 27:29** (Tdf., s. Proleg. p. 121) and ηὐχόμην **Ro 9:3; Ac 27:29;** fut. εὔξομαι LXX; 1 aor. εὐξάμην (also ηὐ- LXX); pf. ptc. ηὐγμένος Num 6:20 (s. prec. entry; Hom.+).

❶ **to speak to or to make requests of God,** ***pray*** abs. (LXX; TestSol 26:8 A 5 p. 81, 33; Just., D. 90, 5; 103, 8) τῷ θεῷ (Hom.; Thu. 3, 58, 5; X., Cyr. 7, 1, 1; Plut., Pericl. 156 [8, 6]; Epict. 1, 29, 37; OGI 219, 21; POxy 1298, 4; PRyl 244, 3; Sir 38:9; ApcMos 5:31; Philo, Ebr. 125; Jos., Ant. 14, 22; 18, 211; Just., D. 1:4; Orig., C. Cels. 8, 37, 12 al.—On εὐχ. τ. θεοῖς s. GGhedini, Aegyptus 2, 1921, 191ff) **Ac 26:29;** IRo 1:1. πρὸς τ. θεόν *to God* (X., Mem. 1, 3, 2, Symp. 4, 55; 2 Macc 9:13; 15:27; TestSol 18:42; EpArist 305) **2 Cor 13:7.** That which is requested of God is expressed either by the simple acc. *pray for someth.* (Pind. et al.; Jos., Ant. 12, 98) **2 Cor 13:9;** by the acc. w. inf. (Hom. et al.; TestSol 18:42; Did., Gen 73, 10) **Ac 26:29; 2 Cor 13:7;** or by prepositional phrases: εὐ. περί τινος GJs 8:3; 13:1; εὐ. περί τινος πρὸς τὸν κύριον Hs 5, 3, 7; εὐ. ὑπέρ τινος *for someone* (X., Mem. 2, 2, 10; Aeschin. 3:18 ὑπέρ τινος πρὸς τοὺς θεούς; Longus 2, 24, 2; Diog. L. 8, 9 εὐ. ὑπὲρ ἑαυτῶν; PMeyer 24, 4; TestGad 7:1; TestJos 18:2; ParJer 2:3; ApcMos 35; Jos., Ant. 11, 119; Just., D. 96, 3 al.) w. ὅπως foll. (ParJer 2:3 [cod. C]; Epict. 2, 16, 13; Polyaenus 1, 26 εὐ. Δὶ ὅπως; PRyl 244, 3 εὔχομαι θεοῖς πᾶσιν ὅπως ὑγιαίνοντας ὑμᾶς ἀπολάβω; Jos., Ant. 11, 17) **Js 5:16;** also ἵνα (cp. Dionys. Hal. 9, 53; Epict. 2, 6, 12; EpArist 45; Just., D. 35, 8 al.) Hs 5, 2, 10.—For lit. s. προσεύχομαι, end.

❷ ***wish*** (Pind. et al.; ins, pap, Philo; perh. Jos., Ant. 12, 98; cp. Mel., HE 4, 26, 8 εὐχή=wish) τὶ *for someth.* (X., Hell. 5, 1, 3) IMg 1:2. W. inf. foll. (Περὶ ὕψους 9, 10; Alexandr. graffito in UvWilamowitz, SBBerlAk 1902, 1098 εὔχομαι κἀγὼ ἐν τάχυ σὺν σοὶ εἶναι; SibOr 4, 111; Just., A I, 15, 6) ITr 10:1. Foll. by acc. and inf. (X., An. 1, 4, 7; Ep. 46 of Apoll. of Ty.: Philostrat. I 355, 24 K.; Just., D. 79, 2 al.) **Ac 27:29; 3J 2** (cp. POxy 292, 11 [perh. 25 AD] πρὸ δὲ πάντων ὑγιαίνειν σε εὔχομαι; PFay 117, 27; PMich 203, 2); IEph 1:3; 2:1; ITr 12:3; IRo 5:2; ISm 11:1; 13:2; IPol 8:3; MPol 22:1. Foll. by nom. and inf. **Ro 9:3,** on the analogy of θέλω w. inf. (cp. Aeschyl., Eum. 429; TestReub 1:7)=opt. w. ἄν. Foll. by ἵνα μή IPhld 6:3. As a greeting formula εὐ. πλεῖστα χαίρειν IMg ins; ITr ins.—AAdkins, ClQ 19, '69, 20–33 (Hom.).—M-M. EDNT. TW. Spicq. Sv.

εὔχρηστος, ον (s. χρηστός; Hippocr. et al.; ins, pap, LXX; EpArist 136; Joseph.; Mel., P. 94, 723) **pert. to being helpful or beneficial,** ***useful, serviceable*** (a common term in Gr-Rom. lit. in description of service that has special social value), abs. (opp. ἄχρηστος) Hv 3, 6, 7. Of gold Hv 4, 3, 4. τινί *to* or *for someone* or *someth.*: w. dat. of pers. (PPetr III, 53 [n], 5) σκεῦος εὐ. τ. δεσπότῃ *a vessel that is useful to the master* **2 Ti 2:21.** W. a play on the name Onesimus (opp. ἄχρηστος) σοὶ κ. ἐμοὶ εὐ. **Phlm 11.**—Hv 3, 6, 6b; m 5, 1, 6; s 9, 26, 4. Of members εὐ. ὅλῳ τ. σώματι 1 Cl 37:5. εὐ. γίνεσθαι w. dat. of pers. (IPriene 102, 5 [c. 100 BC] προγόνων γεγενημένων εὐχρήστων τῷ δήμῳ) Hv 3, 6, 6c; 7b; m 5, 1, 5; s 9, 15, 6. εὐ. εἴς τι *for someth.* (Diod. S. 5, 40, 1; IGR IV, 818, 23 εἰς χρίας κυριακὰς εὔχρηστον γενόμενον; Wsd 13:13; Jos., Ant. 4, 281) **2 Ti 4:11;** Hv 3, 5, 5; 3, 6, 1; 6a.—DELG s.v. χρή. Larfeld I 497. M-M.

εὐψυχέω (s. ψυχή; BGU 1097, 15 [I AD] ἐγὼ εὐψυχοῦσα παραμένω; POxy 115, 1; Poll. 3, 28, 135; Jos., Ant. 11, 241) **to be heartened,** ***be glad, have courage*** **Phil 2:19,** with implication of release from anxiety; impv. εὐψύχει (on grave ins='farewell': CIG 4467 and very oft. in Sb [II Allgem. Wörterliste p. 404]) *have courage* Hv 1, 3, 2.—DELG s.v. ψυχή. M-M. TW. Spicq.

εὐωδία, ας, ἡ (s. ὄζω; X., Pla.+; LXX; pseudepigr.; Philo; Ath. 13, 1) ***aroma, fragrance*** ὀσμὴ εὐωδίας (=רֵיחַ הַנִּיחֹחַ Gen 8:21; Ex 29:18 al. of the fragrance fr. a sacrifice, pleasing to God) *a fragrant odor* w. θυσία (TestLevi 3:6) **Phil 4:18; Eph 5:2;** B 2:10. Of the apostles Χριστοῦ εὐ. ἐσμὲν τῷ θεῷ *we are the aroma of Christ for God* **2 Cor 2:15** (ἐν εὐωδίᾳ χρηστότητος κυρίου OdeSol 11:15). When Polycarp was burned at the stake, a *fragrance* was noted MPol 15:2 (s. Diod. S. 3, 46, 4 θεία εὐωδία κτλ.).—ELohmeyer, Vom göttl. Wohlgeruch: SBHeidAk 1919, Abhdlg. 9; Rtzst., Erlösungsmyst. 34; 143ff, Mysterienrel.^{3} 82f; 393ff; HKees, Totenglauben u. Jenseitsvorstellungen d. alt. Ägypter 1926, 148; HVorwahl, ARW 31, '34, 400f; PDeBoer, Studies in the Religion of Anc. Israel, '72, 37–47 (fragrance).—DELG s.v. ὄζω. EDNT. M-M. TW.

εὐώνυμος, ον (s. ὄνομα; Hes., Pind. et al.) **as point of reference opposite of 'right',** ***left*** (Aeschyl., Hdt. et al.; SIG 827 III, 9; 16; 1167; PRyl 63, 4; LXX; JosAs; ApcrEzk [Epiph 70, 10]; Philo; Jos., Ant. 12, 429) **Rv 10:2.** καταλιπόντες αὐτὴν (i.e. τὴν Κύπρον) εὐώνυμον *leaving it on the left* **Ac 21:3.** ἐξ εὐωνύμων *at the left* (Diod. S. 4, 56, 3; Ex 14:22, 29; 2 Ch 4:8 al.) **Mt 20:23; 25:33, 41; 27:38** (cp. 2 Ch 3:17); **Mk 10:40;** Hv 3, 2, 4. ἐξ εὐωνύμων τινός *at someone's left* (2 Km 16:6; 3 Km 22:19 al.) **Mt 20:21; Mk 15:27.** A quite isolated use: εὐώνυμα *on the left* (w. δεξιά='on the right') Hs 9, 12, 8.—B. 866. DELG s.v. ὄνομα. M-M.

εὐωχέω (s. ἔχω and Boisacq 300, also next entry; Hdt. et al.; Philo; Joseph.; pap; mid. since Alcaeus, fgm. 70, 5 L-P.; Jdth 1:16; 3 Macc 6:40; pap; εὐωχηθείς OGI 168, 11) in Gk. lit. the act. of ε. refers to provision of sumptuous entertainment (Hdt. et al.); the mid. εὐωχεῖσθαι ***to feast*** (Alcaeus, above, et al.) is also used, as AcPl Ha 7, 10 (prob. in ref. to an Agape celebration after the Eucharist, s. Schubart p. 51, n. 10; in ref. to cultic festivities IGLSyria 1, 157f [I BC]; s. HDörrie, GGAbh 60, '64, 81).

εὐωχία, ας, ἡ (s. prec. entry; Aristoph., Hippocr. et al.; Diod. S. 2, 26, 4; ins, pap, LXX; TestJob 44:2; Philo; Jos., Ant. 6, 163, C. Ap. 2, 138) ***banquet, feasting*** **Jd 12 v.l.**

ἔφαγον s. ἐσθίω.

ἐφάλλομαι fut. 3 sg. ἐφαλεῖται 1 Km 10:6; 2 aor. ἐφαλόμην; 3 sg. ἐφήλατο 1 Km 11:6; 16:13 (s. ἅλλομαι; Hom. et al.; ins,, pap, LXX) ***leap upon*** ἐπί τινα *someone* (1 Km 10:6; 16:13 of the coming of the Spirit of God upon a pers.) of a 'possessed' man **Ac 19:16.**—DELG s.v. ἅλλομαι. M-M.

ἐφάπαξ (s. ἅπαξ) adv.—❶ **pert. to being simultaneous,** ***at once, at one time*** (PLond II, 483, 88 p. 328 [616 AD]; V, 1708, 242; PFlor 158, 10) ἐπάνω πεντακοσίοις ἀδελφοῖς ἐ. *to more than 500 fellow-believers at once* **1 Cor 15:6.**

❷ **taking place once and to the exclusion of any further occurrence,** ***once for all, once and never again*** (Eupolis Com. [V BC] 175 Kock) **Ro 6:10; Hb 7:27; 9:12; 10:10.**—M-M. TW. Spicq.

'Εφέσινος, η, ον Rv 2:1 v.l. (Erasmian rdg.); s. Ἔφεσος.

'Εφέσιος, ία, ιον ***Ephesian*** οἱ Ἐ. *the Ephesians* (oft. ins; Philo, Leg. ad Gai. 315; Jos., Ant. 14, 224; Tat 33, 2; Ath. 31, 1) **Ac 18:27** D; **19:28, 34; 20:4** D; **21:29; Eph subscr.** IEph 8:1; 11:2; IMg 15; ITr 13:1; IRo 10:1; IPhld 11:2; ISm 12:1. ἄνδρες Ἐ. (as Achilles Tat. 7, 9, 2) **Ac 19:35a;** AcPl Ha 1, 24. ἡ Ἐφεσίων πόλις (cp. ἡ τῶν Ἱεροσολυμιτῶν π. Jos., Ant. 5, 82; 10, 109 al.) **Ac 19:35b;** ἡ Ἐφεσίων ἐκκλησία **2 Ti subscr.**

(lit. on the Letter to the Eph s. SHanson, The Unity of the Church in the NT, '46, 173–90) (s. the foll. entry).

Ἔφεσος, ου, ἡ ***Ephesus*** (s. prec. entry; Hdt. et al.; oft. in ins; Joseph., SibOr; Ath. 17, 3), a seaport of Asia Minor in the plain of the Caÿster River. Famous for its temple of Artemis (s. Ἄρτεμις). The Christian congregation at Ephesus was either founded by Paul, or its numbers greatly increased by his ministry (GDuncan, St. Paul's Ephesian Ministry 1929). **Ac 18:19, 21, 24, 27** D; **19:1, 17, 26; 20:16f** (on Ephesian setting of Paul's speech Ac 20:17–38, s. DWatson, in Persuasive Artistry [GAKennedy Festschr.] '91, 185–86, n. 3); **1 Cor 15:32; 16:8; subscr. v.l.; Eph 1:1** (here it is lacking in P^{46} Sin. B Marcion [who has instead: to the Laodiceans]; s. Harnack, SBBerlAk 1910, 696ff; JSchmid, D. Eph des Ap. Pls 1928; Goodsp., Probs. 171–73); **1 Ti 1:3; 2 Ti 1:18; 4:12; Rv 1:11** (the order Eph., Smyrna, Perg., Sardis also in an official ins, fr. Miletus [56–50 BC]: TWiegand, Milet Heft 2 [city hall] p. 101f); **2:1.**—OBenndorf, Z. Ortskunde u. Stadtgesch. von Eph. 1905; LBürchner, Ephesos: Pauly-W. V 1905, 2773–822; Österr. Archäol. Institut: Forschungen in Ephesos Iff, 1906ff, preliminary reports in the 'Jahreshefte' 1922ff; JKeil, Ephesos[2] 1930; WRamsay, The Church in the Roman Empire before AD 170 1912, 135–39; JBakhuizenvdBrink, De oudchristelijke monumenten van Ephesus 1923; VSchultze, Altchr. Städte u. Landsch. II/2, 1926, 86–120; Dssm., D. Ausgrabungen in Eph. 1926: ThBl 6, 1927, 17–19, The Excav. in Eph.: Biblical Review 15, 1930, 332–46; RTonneau, E. au temps de S. Paul: RB 38, 1929, 5–34; 321–63; PAntoine, Dict. de la Bible, Suppl. II '34, 1076–1104; FRienecker, Der Eph. (w. illustrated supplement) '34; BA 8, '45, 61–80; FMiltner, E., Stadt d. Artemis u. d. Joh. '54; HKoester, Ephesos, Metropolis of Asia '66; SFriesen, BAR 19, '93, 24–37. S. Δημήτριος 2.—OEANE II 252–55. Die Inschriften von Ephesos, 8 vols. '79–84. GHorsley, NovT 34, '92, 105–68.

ἐφευρετής, οῦ, ὁ (σ. εὑρίσκω; Anacreontea 38, 3 Preisend.; Porphyr., Against the Chr. [ABA 1916] 15, 1; Etym. Mag. p. 435, 28) **one who forms strategies or tactics to effect someth.,** ***inventor, contriver*** ἐφευρεταὶ κακῶν *contrivers of evil* **Ro 1:30** (cp. Theophyl. Sim., Ep. 29 p. 772 H. κακῶν ἐφευρετικόν; Philo, In Flacc. 20 κακῶν εὑρεταί; 73; 2 Macc 7:31; Vergil, Aen. 2, 164 scelerum inventor Ulixes; Tacit., Annal. 4, 11 Seianus facinorum omnium repertor=Sejanus, contriver of all kinds of crimes).—DELG s.v. εὑρίσκω. M-M.

Ἔφηβος, ου, ὁ (cp. e.g. Ins. Hisp. Lat. ed. Huebner 1869 no. 4970, 172; Ins. Pariet. Pomp. ed. KZangemeister 1871 no. 1478; SEG XXVI, 184; XXXIX, 1205 [proper name, or ἔφηβος as age category?]) ***Ephebus,*** whose first name is Claudius, a Roman Christian 1 Cl 65:1.

ἐφήδομαι (s. ἥδομαι; X. et al.) ***(take) delight in,*** mostly in a bad sense 'delight in someone's misfortune' or 'enjoy bad things' (Dio Chrys. 3, 103; 10 [11], 64; Ael. Aristid. 36 p. 690 D.; Jos., C. Ap. 2, 5); τινί *(in) someth.* (X., Hell. 4, 5, 18; Jos., Ant. 16, 127) τοῖς ἁμαρτήμασιν Dg 9:1.

ἐφημερία, ας, ἡ (s. ἡμέρα and next entry; SEG VII 29 [I BC]) **a class of priests who performed daily** (hence the name) **duties for a fixed period in the temple at Jerusalem,** ***division*** (LXX; cp. Jos., Ant. 12, 265). There were 24 such divisions, each one of which took care of the temple duties for one week (1 Ch 23:6; 28:13 al.). Schürer II 245–50; Billerb. II 55ff. The ἐ. Ἀβιά **Lk 1:5** was the eighth division. ἐν τῇ τάξει τ. ἐφημερίας αὐτοῦ *in the order of his division* vs. **8.**—DELG s.v. ἦμαρ. M-M. TW.

ἐφήμερος, ον (s. prec. entry; Pind., Thu. et al.; Philo; ApcrEzk P 1 recto 9) ***for the day*** ἡ ἐ. τροφή *food for the day, daily food* (Diod. S. 3, 32, 3; Dionys. Hal. 8, 41, 5; Ael. Aristid. 28, 139 K.=49 p. 537 D.; Stob. 1, 1, 13 [I p. 27 W.]; Vett. Val. p. 62, 17 ἐνδεεῖς τῆς ἐ. τροφῆς; PCairZen 4, 647, 20 [III BC]; PSI 685, 9) **Js 2:15.**—HFränkel, TAPA 77, '46, 131–45.—M-M. Sv.

ἐφικνέομαι 2 aor. ἐφικόμην (ἱκνέομαι 'come'; Hom. et al.; IPriene 105, 47; Sir 43:27 cod. C; SibOr 11, 215; Just., D. 4, 2 ἐφικτόν) **to arrive at or come to someth.,** ***come to, reach*** εἴς τινα *someone* **2 Cor 10:14.** ἄχρι τινός *as far as someone* vs. **13.**—DELG s.v. ἵκω.

ἔφιππος, ον (s. ἵππος; Soph. et al.; PLond 1912, 44; 2 Macc 11:8 ἔ. ἐν λευκῇ ἐσθῆτι; 12:35 τὶς … ἔ. ἀνήρ; 4 Macc 4:10 ἔ. … ἄγγελοι; pap) **pert. to being on a horse,** ***mounted, on horseback;*** subst. *rider* **Rv 19:14 v.l.**

ἐφίστημι (s. ἵστημι; Hom. et al.; ins, pap, LXX; TestJob 17:2; EpArist, Joseph.; Just. ['pay attention' D. 28, 1]; Ath.) fut. ἐπιστήσω; 1 aor. ἐπέστησα LXX; 2 aor. ἐπέστην, impv. ἐπίστηθι, ptc. ἐπιστάς; pf. ἐφέστηκα LXX, ptc. ἐφεστώς; plpf. 3 sg. ἐφειστήκει LXX; mid. 3 sg. indic. ἐπίσταται **1 Th 5:3 v.l.** (on the form s. W-S. §5, 10c); 1 aor. pass. ἐπεστάθην 1 Cl 12:4; Hv 3, 1, 6. This aor. pass. can have mid. mng. (Eur., Iph. T. 1375 al.) and as a rule the mid. has, like the 2 aor., pf. and plpf. act., intransitive sense; it is only this intr. sense that is found for ἐφίστημι in our lit.

❶ **to stand at or near a specific place,** ***stand at/near,*** of living entities and oft. w. connotation of suddenness, pres. and aor. w. dat. of pers. **Lk 2:9; 24:4** (of angels, as Diod. S. 1, 25, 5 of Isis in a dream; Lucian, Dial. Deor. 17, 1 of Hephaestus; SIG 1168, 37 ὁ θεὸς ἐπιστάς; TestSol 1:8 ἐν ᾗ ἂν ὥρᾳ ἐπιστῇ σοι τὸ δαιμόνιον; Jos., Ant. 3, 188. Of a figure in a dream Hdt. 5, 56); **Ac 4:1; 12:7** D; **23:11.** ἐπεστάθη μοι *she approached me* Hv 3, 1, 6. ἐπί τι *approach* or *stand by someth.* (Sir 41:24) **Ac 10:17; 11:11.** ἐπάνω τινός *stand at someone's head* **Lk 4:39** (cp. 2 Km 1:9). περιστερὰ … ἐπεστάθη ἐπὶ τὴν κεφαλὴν τοῦ Ἰωσήφ *a dove … perched on the head of Joseph* GJs 9:1 (ἐπετάσθη v.l.). Abs. (EpArist 177) **Lk 2:38; 10:40; 20:1; Ac 6:12; 12:7; 22:13; 23:27;** 1 Cl 12:4; MPol 6:1; GJs 4:1 v.l.; AcPl Ha 4, 8.—Perf. *stand by, be present* αὐτὸς ἤμην ἐφεστώς *I (myself) was standing by* **Ac 22:20** (cp. Jos., Vi. 294).

❷ **to happen, esp. of misfortunes, which (suddenly) come upon someone,** ***happen to, overtake, befall*** (Soph., Oed. R. 777; Thu. 3, 82, 2; LXX) w. dat. of pers. (cp. Cornutus 10 p. 11, 17; Wsd 6:8; 19:1) αἰφνίδιος αὐτοῖς ἐφίσταται ὄλεθρος **1 Th 5:3.** ἐπί τινα **Lk 21:34.**—DDaube, The Sudden in the Scriptures '64, 36.

❸ **to come near with intention of harming,** ***attack*** w. dat. of thing τῇ οἰκίᾳ Ἰ. **Ac 17:5.**

❹ **to be present to begin someth.,** ***begin, come on*** perf. διὰ τ. ὑετὸν τὸν ἐφεστῶτα *because it had begun to rain* **Ac 28:2** (Polyb. 18, 20, 7 διὰ τὸν ἐφεστῶτα ζόφον). But the mng. here could also be *because it threatened to rain* (s. 6).

❺ **to be present in readiness to discharge a task,** ***fix one's mind on, be attentive to*** (Eur., Andr. 547; Demosth. 18, 60) ἐπίστηθι *stand by=be ready, be on hand, be persistent* **2 Ti 4:2.**

❻ **to be before one as an event about to occur,** ***be imminent*** perf. (Il. 12, 326; Demosth. 18, 176; Jos., Ant. 13, 241, Vi. 137 al.) ὁ καιρὸς τῆς ἀναλύσεώς μου ἐφέστηκεν *the time of my departure is imminent* **2 Ti 4:6.** For **Ac 28:2** s. 4.

❼ **to stand over someth. as leader or overseer,** ***be over, be in charge of*** perf. (Eur., Aristoph. et al.: Jdth 8:10; 12:11; Synes.,

Ep. 140 p. 276b ὁ ἐφεστὼς θεός; Just., D. 36, 6; Ath. 12, 1; 31, 2) εἴς τι: οἱ ἄνδρες οἱ εἰς τὴν οἰκοδομὴν ἐφεστῶτες *the men who were in charge of the construction* Hs 9, 6, 2.—M-M. TW.

ἐφόδιον, ου, τό (s. ὁδός) ***travel allowance, provisions for a journey*** (used Aristoph., Hdt. et al. in sg. and pl.; ins, pap; Dt 15:14; Jos., Vi. 224 al.) fig. of the provisions which Christ gives his followers for the journey of life 1 Cl 2:1 (for the fig. mng. cp. Menand., fgm. 407, 2 Kö. ἐ. βίῳ; Epict. 3, 21, 9 ἔχοντάς τι ἐ. τοιοῦτον εἰς τὸν βίον; Plut., Mor. 160b; Sextus 551; Philo, Rer. Div. Her. 273; Jos., Bell. 1, 463; 6, 80).—DELG s.v. ὁδός.

ἐφοράω fut. ἐπόψομαι LXX (s. ὁράω; Hom. et al.; ins,, pap, LXX; Philo, Aet. M. 83; Jos., Bell. 1, 630; SibOr fgm. 3, 42; Just., D. 127, 2) ***gaze upon*** τὶ *someth.* ApcPt 10:25. S. also ἐπεῖδον.—DELG s.v. ὁράω. TW.

Ἐφραίμ, ὁ indecl. (-άιμ Bov. N.[25]—אֶפְרַיִם; LXX; JosAs 21:8; Philo.—Translit. into Gk. var. ways: Jos., index) ***Ephraim.***

❶ son of Joseph, blessed by Jacob in place of his older brother Manasseh (cp. Gen 48:14, 17ff; Demetr.: 722, fgm. 1, 12) B 13:5.

❷ name of a city, 'near the desert', to which, acc. to **J 11:54**, Jesus retired for a short time toward the end of his life. On the location of this place acc. to ancient and modern concepts s. Hdb. ad loc. Ms. D has εἰς τὴν χώραν Σαμφουριν (=Sepphoris) ἐγγὺς τῆς ἐρήμου εἰς Ἐφραὶμ λεγομένην πόλιν.—TZahn, NKZ 19, 1908, 31–39; SCase, Jesus and Sepphoris: JBL 45, 1926, 14–22; BHHW 1, 420f.

εφφαθα Aram. word, translated διανοίχθητι ***be opened*** **Mk 7:34.** It is understood as a contraction of the form of the ethpeel (אֶתְפְּתַח); s. Wlh. ad loc.—Dalman, Gramm.[2] 278; IRabinowitz, ZNW 53, '62, 229–38; JEmerton, JTS 18, '67, 427–31; but s. MBlack, BRigaux Festschr., '70, 57–60.—Hott, NovT 9, '67.

ἐχθές adv. (Soph. et al.; also found in Attic prose; it is the proper Koine form: PEleph 29, 6 [III BC]; PSI 442, 21 [III BC]; PLips 105, 1 [I/II AD]; PFay 108, 7 [II AD]; LXX [Thackeray 97]; Jos., C. Ap. 2, 14 al.; χθές as v.l. in many NT mss., and always in t.r.)

❶ **the day preceding today, *yesterday*** **J 4:52; Ac 16:35** D; **7:28;** 1 Cl 4:10 (the two last pass. Ex 2:14). More gener. it can mean

❷ **time that is past as opposed to now, *yesterday*** (Soph., Ant. 456 νῦν κἀχθές; Ael. Aristid. 53 p. 623 D.: χθὲς κ. πρῴην; cp. Jos., C. Ap. 2, 154) w. σήμερον=the present (Sir 38:22; Himerius, Ecl. 31, 1 W.) **Hb 13:8.** S. χθές.—DELG s.v. χθές. M-M.

ἔχθρα, ας, ἡ (s. next entry; Pind., Thu. et al.; ins, pap, LXX; ApcMos 25f; Just., D. 1023, 3 [Gen 3:15]) ***enmity*** Dg 5:17; **Eph 2:14, 16** (opp. φιλία, as Hyperid., fgm. 209; Ael. Aristid. 38 p. 713 D.; SIG 826c, 10; PHib 170 [247 BC]). ἔ. τοῦ θεοῦ *enmity toward God* **Js 4:4.** Also ἔ. εἰς θεόν **Ro 8:7.** ἐν ἔ. εἶναι (cp. 1 Esdr 5:49) πρός τινα *live at enmity w. someone* **Lk 23:12** (ἔ. πρός τινα as Demetr.: 722, fgm. 1, 1 Jac.; Lucian, Hermot. 85; Philo, Spec. Leg. 1, 108; Jos., Ant. 4, 106). Pl. of hostile feelings and actions (Pla., 7th Epistle 337b; Philo, Sacr. Abel. 96) **Gal 5:20.**—B. 1132f. DELG s.v. ἔχθος. M-M. TW.

ἐχθρός, ά, όν (s. prec. entry; Hom.+) 'hostile'—❶ **pert. to being subjected to hostility, *hated,*** pass. (Hom.; θεοῖς ἐ. since Hes., Theog. 766, also Pla., Rep. 1, 23, 352b; Epict. 3, 22, 91; Ael. Aristid. 28, 15 K.=49 p. 495 D.; Alciphron 3, 12, 5; Athen. 6, 225c; Achilles Tat. 7, 6, 3, likew. X., Cyr. 5, 4, 35 καὶ θεοῖς ἐ. καὶ ἀνθρώποις.—Philo, Spec. Leg. 3, 88 πᾶς ἐ. θεῷ) **Ro 11:28,** where the pass. sense becomes at least quite probable because of the contrast w. ἀγαπητός, otherwise the passage belongs in 2bα.

❷ **pert. to being hostile, *hating, hostile,*** act. (Pind., Hdt. et al.; LXX)—ⓐ adj. (X., An. 1, 3, 12; 20; PGM 36, 144; Sir 36:9; Jos., Ant. 11, 27; Just., D. 93, 2 ἐν συνειδήσεσιν ἐ.; Mel., P. 16, 110 al.) ἐ. ἄνθρωπος (Horapollo 2, 35) **Mt 13:28.** The position of ἐ. before ἄ. (difft. Esth 7:6) suggests that ἐ. is an adj. here, giving the sense *hostile person;* but ἄ. by itself could also serve to emphasize indefiniteness: *some enemy = any enemy at all* (s. EKlostermann, Hdb. ad loc.). Then this example would also belong to b.

ⓑ subst. (Hes., Pind.; PEdg 14 [=Sb 6720], 18 [257/256 BC]; LXX, En 103:12; Test12Patr, EpArist, Philo, Joseph.; SibOr 3, 727) ὁ ἐ. *the (personal) enemy.*

α. abs. 2 Cl 6:3. Enemies of humans (PsSol 17:13; Ar. 15:5; Just., A I, 68, 1 al; Mel., P. 24, 175 al.) **Lk 1:74; 2 Th 3:15;** D 1:3b; B 16:4; 2 Cl 13:4. Enemies of God or Christ (Just., A I, 51, 1) **Ro 5:10; 11:28** (but s. 1 above); **1 Cor 15:25; Col 1:21;** 1 Cl 36:6. Death as the last enemy **1 Cor 15:26.** The devil as enemy (cp. TestSol 1:2 D; TestJob 47:10; TestDan 6:3f; JosAs 12:8; GrBar 13:2; ApcMos 2:7 al. Mel., P. 102, 783) **Lk 10:19;** cp. **Mt 13:39.**

β. w. gen. of the pers. who is the obj. of the enmity: people **Mt 5:43f; Lk 6:27, 35** (cp. Ox 1224 fgm. 2 recto I, 2; Delph. commands: SIG 1286 I, 15; 16 [III BC] φίλοις εὐνόει, ἐχθροὺς ἀμύνου; Sextus 213 εὔχου τοὺς ἐχθροὺς εὐεργετεῖν; Pittacus in Diog. L. 1, 78 φίλον μὴ λέγειν κακῶς, ἀλλὰ μηδὲ ἐχθρόν; Epict. 3, 22, 54 as a principle of the Cynic philosopher: δερόμενον φιλεῖν [δεῖ] αὐτοὺς τοὺς δέροντας . . . ὡς ἀδελφόν 'while enduring a flogging he must think as a brother and love his very floggers'; Vi. Aesop. G 110 P.; Hierocles 7 p. 430 οὐδεὶς ἐχθρὸς τῷ σπουδαίῳ . . . μισεῖ οὐδένα ἄνθρωπον . . . φιλία πρὸς πάντας ἀνθρώπους.—HHaas, Idee u. Ideal d. Feindesliebe in d. ausserchr. Welt 1927; MWaldmann, D. Feindesliebe in d. ant. Welt u. im Christent. 1902; TBirt. Chr. Welt 29, 1915, 475–83; FKattenbusch, StKr 89, 1916, 1–70; PFiebig, ibid. 91, 1918, 30–64; 305f; JYates, Theology 44, '42, 48–51; Betz, SM 301–13); **Mt 10:36; 13:25; Lk 1:71; 19:27; Ro 12:20** (Pr 25:21); **Gal 4:16; Rv 11:5, 12;** GJs 6:3. God or Christ as the object of enmity **Mt 22:44; Mk 12:36; Lk 20:43; Ac 2:35; Hb 1:13; 10:13;** B 12:10; 1 Cl 36:5 (all Ps 109:1). ἐχθρὸς τ. θεοῦ **Js 4:4** (cp. Aeschyl., Prom. 120 ὁ Διὸς ἐ.; Just. D. 93, 4 ὡς ἐ. θεοῦ).

γ. w. gen. of that which is the obj. of the enmity (Demosth. 45, 66; Philo, Conf. Lingu. 48 ἀληθείας ἐ., Somn. 2, 90 λογισμοῦ; Jos., C. Ap. 2, 291 ἀδικίας) ἐ. πάσης δικαιοσύνης *enemy of all righteousness* **Ac 13:10.** ἐ. τοῦ σταυροῦ τ. Χριστοῦ **Phil 3:18** (OLinton, ConNeot 4, '36, 9–21).—B. 1345. Schmidt, Syn. III 496–506. EDNT. M-M. TW.

ἔχιδνα, ης, ἡ (Hes.; Hdt.+; Aq. Is 59:5; TestAbr A; Just., A I, 60, 2; Tat. 18, 2; Ath. 20, 3; loanw. in rabb.) ***snake,*** our texts do not permit identification of species, but the term ordinarily suggests a poisonous one: prob. vipera ammodytes, commonly known as sandviper (Diod. S. 4, 38, 2; Conon [I BC/I AD] fgm. 1, 8 ; Lucian, Alex. 10; Artem. 2, 13) **Ac 28:3** (present-day Malta has no poisonous snakes, but Kephallenia, the site of Paul's shipwreck as determined by HWarnecke [Romfahrt 145–56], has the species vip. ammod., Romfahrt 108–10; 152–54).—Fig. of persons (Aeschyl., Choeph. 994; Eur., Ion 1262) γεννήματα ἐχιδνῶν *brood of vipers* (cp. Theophyl. Sim., Ep. 73 τὰ τῆς ἐχίδνης κυήματα; AcPlCor 2:38) **Mt 3:7; 12:34; 23:33; Lk 3:7.**—OKeller, Die antike Tierwelt II, 1913, 284–557; NHenkel,

Studien zum Physiologus im Mittelalter '76, 181–85 (ancient sources); Pauly-W. III A 1, 1927, 494–57.—B. 194. M-M. TW.

ἔχω (Hom.+) impf. εἶχον, 1 pl. εἴχαμεν and 3 pl. εἶχαν (both as vv.ll.; Mlt-H. 194; B-D-F §82) **Mk 8:7; Rv 9:8** or εἴχοσαν (B-D-F §84, 2; Mlt-H. 194; Kühner-Bl. II p. 55) **J 15:22, 24;** 2 aor. ἔσχον; mixed aor. forms include ἔσχαν Hv 3, 5, 1, ἔσχοσαν 1 Esdr 6:5; 1 Macc 10:15 (ἔσχον, εἶχον vv.ll.); pf. ἔσχηκα; plpf. ἐσχήκειν.—In the following divisions: act. trans. 1–9; act. intr. 10; mid. 11.

❶ **to possess or contain, *have, own*** (Hom.+)—ⓐ to possess someth. that is under one's control—**α.** *own, possess* (s. esp. TestJob 9f) κτήματα πολλά *own much property* **Mt 19:22; Mk 10:22.** πρόβατα **Lk 15:4; J 10:16.** θησαυρόν **Mt 19:21; Mk 10:21b.** βίον *living* **Lk 21:4; 1J 3:17.** δραχμὰς δέκα **Lk 15:8.** πλοῖα **Rv 18:19.** κληρονομίαν **Eph 5:5.** θυσιαστήριον **Hb 13:10a;** μέρος ἔ. ἔν τινι *have a share in someth.* **Rv 20:6.** Gener. μηδὲν ἔ. *own nothing* (SibOr 3, 244) **2 Cor 6:10.** ὅσα ἔχεις **Mk 10:21;** cp. **12:44; Mt 13:44, 46; 18:25.** τί ἔχεις ὃ οὐκ ἔλαβες; *what do you have that you have not been given?* **1 Cor 4:7.** The obj. acc. is often used w. an adj. or ptc.: ἔ. ἅπαντα κοινά *have everything in common* **Ac 2:44** (cp. Jos., Ant. 15, 18). ἔ. πολλὰ ἀγαθὰ κείμενα *have many good things stored up* **Lk 12:19.—Hb 12:1.** Abs. ἔ. *have (anything)* (Soph.et al.; Sir 13:5; 14:11) **Mt 13:12a; Mk 4:25a; Lk 8:18a.** ἐκ τοῦ ἔχειν *in accordance w. what you have* **2 Cor 8:11.** ἔ. εἰς ἀπαρτισμόν *have (enough) to complete* **Lk 14:28.** W. neg. ἔ. *have nothing* **Mt 13:12b; Mk 4:25b; Lk 8:18b.**—ὁ ἔχων *the one who has, who is well off* (Soph., Aj. 157; Eur., Alc. 57; X., An. 7, 3, 28; Ar. 15:7). πᾶς ὁ ἔχων *everyone who has (anything)* **Mt 25:29a; Lk 19:26a.** ὁ μὴ ἔχων *the one who has nothing* (X., An. 7, 3, 28; 1 Esdr 9:51, 54; 2 Esdr 18:10) **Mt 25:29b; Lk 19:26b; 1 Cor 11:22.**

β. *have = hold in* one's *charge* or *keeping* ἔ. τὰς κλεῖς *hold the keys* **Rv 1:18;** cp. **3:7.** τὸ γλωσσόκομον *the money-box* **J 12:6; 13:29.**

ⓑ to contain someth. *have, possess,* of the whole in relation to its parts

α. of living beings, of parts of the body in men and animals μέλη **Ro 12:4a;** cp. **1 Cor 12:12.** σάρκα καὶ ὀστέα **Lk 24:39** (Just., A I, 66, 2 καὶ σάρκα καὶ αἷμα) ἀκροβυστίαν **Ac 11:3.** οὖς **Rv 2:7, 11.** ὦτα **Mt 11:15; Mk 7:16; Lk 8:8.** χεῖρας, πόδας, ὀφθαλμούς **Mt 18:8f; Mk 9:43, 45, 47.** Of animals and animal-like beings ἔ. πρόσωπον **Rv 4:7.** πτέρυγας vs. **8.** κέρατα **5:6.** ψυχάς **8:9.** τρίχας **9:8.** κεφαλάς **12:3** (TestAbr B 14 p. 118, 19 [Stone p. 84]) al. ἔχοντες ὑγιῆ τὴν σάρκα AcPlCor 2:32 (Just., D. 48, 3 σάρκα ἔχων). Of plants (TestAbr B 3 p. 107, 6 [Stone p. 62] εὗρον δένδρον … ἔχον κλάδους) ῥίζαν ἔ. **Mt 13:6; Mk 4:6.**

β. of inanimate things: of cities τ. θεμελίους ἔ. **Hb 11:10;** cp. **Rv 21:14.** Of a head-covering χαρακτῆρα ἔχει βασιλικόν *has a royal emblem* GJs 2:2.

ⓒ to have at hand, have at one's disposal *have* ἄρτους **Mt 14:17;** cp. **15:34; J 21:5,** where the sense is prob. 'Did you catch any fish for breakfast?'. οὐκ ἔχω ὃ παραθήσω αὐτῷ *I have nothing to set before him* **Lk 11:6.** μὴ ἐχόντων τί φάγωσι *since they had nothing to eat* **Mk 8:1;** cp. **Mt 15:32** (Soph., Oed. Col. 316 οὐκ ἔχω τί φῶ). οὐκ ἔχω ποῦ συνάξω *I have no place to store* **Lk 12:17.** ἄντλημα *a bucket* **J 4:11a.** οἰκίας ἔ. *have houses (at one's disposal)* **1 Cor 11:22.** Of pers.: *have (at one's disposal)* (PAmh 92, 18 οὐχ ἕξω κοινωνόν and oft. in pap) Moses and the prophets **Lk 16:29.** παράκλητον *an advocate, a helper* **1J 2:1.** οὐδένα ἔ. ἰσόψυχον **Phil 2:20.** ἄνθρωπον οὐκ ἔ. **J 5:7.**

ⓓ to have within oneself *have* σύλλημα ἔχει ἐκ πνεύματος ἁγίου *she has something conceived through the Holy Spirit* GJs 18:1. Var. constr. w. ἐν: of women ἐν γαστρὶ ἔ. *be pregnant* (γαστήρ 2) **Mt 1:18, 23** (Is 7:14); **24:19; Mk 13:17; Lk 21:23; 1 Th 5:3; Rv 12:2.** ἔ. τινὰ ἐν τῇ καρδίᾳ *have someone in one's heart* **Phil 1:7** (Ovid, Metam. 2, 641 aliquem clausum pectore habere). ἔ. τι ἐν ἑαυτῷ (Jos., Ant. 8, 171; cp. TestAbr A 3 p. 80, 14 [Stone p. 8] ἔκρυψεν τὸ μυστήριον, μόνος ἔχων ἐν τῇ καρδίᾳ αὐτοῦ): ζωήν **J 5:26.** τὴν μαρτυρίαν **1J 5:10;** τὸ ἀπόκριμα τοῦ θανάτου *have a sentence of death within oneself* **2 Cor 1:9.**

ⓔ to have with oneself or in one's company *have* μεθ' ἑαυτοῦ (X., Cyr. 1, 4, 17) τινά *someone* **Mt 15:30; 26:11; Mk 2:19; 14:7; J 12:8;** AcPl Ha 8, 35; σὺν αὐτῷ 4:18.—The ptc. w. acc. = *with* (Diod. S. 12, 78, 1 ἔχων δύναμιν with a [military] force; 18, 61, 1 ὁ θρόνος ἔχων τὸ διάδημα the throne with the diadem; JosAs 27:8 ἔχοντες ἐσπασμένας τὰς ῥομφαίας 'with their swords drawn') ἀνέβησαν ἔχοντες αὐτόν *they went up with him* **Lk 2:42** D.

❷ **to stand in a close relationship to someone, *have, have as***—ⓐ of relatives πατέρα ἔ. **J 8:41.** ἀδελφούς **Lk 16:28.** ἄνδρα (Aristot., Cat. 15b, 27f λεγόμεθα δὲ καὶ γυναῖκα ἔχειν καὶ ἡ γυνὴ ἄνδρα; Tob 3:8 BA) *be married* (of the woman) **J 4:17f; 1 Cor 7:2b, 13; Gal 4:27** (Is 54:1). γυναῖκα of the man (cp. Lucian, Tox. 45; SIG 1160 γυναικὸς Αἴ., τῆς νῦν ἔχει; PGM 13, 320; 1 Esdr 9:12, 18; Just., D. 141, 4 πολλὰς ἔσχον γυναῖκας. As early as Od. 11, 603 Heracles ἔχει Ἥβην) **1 Cor 7:2a, 12, 29** (for the wordplay cp. Heliod. 1, 18, 4 in connection w. the handing over of a virgin: σὺ ἔχων οὐκ ἕξεις; Crates, 7th Ep. [p. 58, 8 Malherbe] πάντ' ἔχοντες οὐδὲν ἔχετε). τέκνα **Mt 21:28; 22:24; 1 Ti 3:4; 5:4; Tit 1:6.** υἱούς (Artem. 5, 42 τὶς τρεῖς ἔχων υἱούς; cp. θυγατέρα TestAbr B 10 p. 114, 17 [Stone p. 76]) **Lk 15:11; Gal 4:22.** σπέρμα *have children* **Mt 22:25.** W. acc. as obj. and in predicate (Ar. 8, 4 τούτους συνηγόρους ἔχοντες τῆς κακίας; 11, 3 ἔσχε μοιχὸν τὸν Ἄρην; Ath. 7, 2 ἔχομεν προφήτας μάρτυρας) ἔ. τινὰ πατέρα *have someone as father* **Mt 3:9.** ἔ. τινὰ γυναῖκα (w. γυναῖκα to be understood fr. the context) **14:4;** cp. **Mk 6:18;** ὥστε γυναῖκά τινα τοῦ πατρὸς ἔ. *that someone has taken his father's wife* (as his own wife: the simple ἔχειν in this sense as Plut., Cato Min. 21, 3; Appian, Bell. Civ. 3, 10 §34; Jos., C. Ap. 1, 147. Perh. an illicit relationship is meant, as Longus 4, 17; Hesychius Miles. [VI AD], Viri Ill. 4 JFlach [1880] ἔχω Λαΐδα) **1 Cor 5:1** (Diod. S. 20, 33, 5 of a man who had illicit relations with his stepmother: ἔχειν λάθρᾳ τοῦ πατρὸς τὴν Ἀλκίαν).

ⓑ more gener. φίλον *have a friend* **Lk 11:5.** ἀσθενοῦντας *have sick people* **Lk 4:40** and χήρας *widows* **1 Ti 5:16** to care for; παιδαγωγοὺς ἔ. **1 Cor 4:15.** δοῦλον **Lk 17:7.** οἰκονόμον **16:1;** κύριον ἔ. *have a master,* i.e. be under a master's control **Col 4:1;** δεσπότην ἔ. **1 Ti 6:2;** βασιλέα **J 19:15.** ἀρχιερέα **Hb 4:14; 8:1.** ποιμένα **Mt 9:36.** ἔχων ὑπ' ἐμαυτὸν στρατιώτας *I have soldiers under me* **Lk 7:8.** W. direct obj. and predicate acc. ἔ. τινὰ ὑπηρέτην *have someone as an assistant* **Ac 13:5** (Just., A I, 14, 1) ἔ. τινὰ τύπον *have someone as an example* **Phil 3:17.**—Of the relation of Christians to God and to Jesus ἔ. θεόν, τὸν πατέρα, τὸν υἱόν *have God, the Father, the Son,* i.e. be in communion w. them **1J 2:23; 2J 9;** AcPl Ha 4, 7.—HHanse, at end of this entry.

❸ **to take a hold on someth., *have, hold (to), grip***—ⓐ of holding someth. in one's hand ἔ. τι ἐν τῇ χειρί *have someth. in one's hand* (since Il. 18, 505) **Rv 1:16; 6:5; 10:2; 17:4.** Of holding in the hand without ἐν τῇ χειρί (Josh 6:8; JosAs 5:7) ἔ. κιθάραν **5:8.** λιβανωτὸν χρυσοῦν **8:3,** cp. vs. **6; 14:17** and s. ἀλάβαστρον **Mt 26:7** and **Mk 14:3.**

ⓑ of keeping someth. safe, a mina (a laborer's wages for about three months) in a handkerchief *keep safe* **Lk 19:20.**

ⓒ of holding fast to matters of transcendent importance, fig. τὴν μαρτυρίαν **Rv 6:9; 12:17; 19:10;** the secret of Christian piety **1 Ti 3:9;** an example of sound teaching **2 Ti 1:13;** *keep* (Diod. S. 17, 93, 1 τὴν βασιλείαν ἔχειν=keep control) **Mk 6:18.**

ⓓ of states of being *hold, hold in its grip, seize* (Hom. et al.; PGiss 65a, 4 παρακαλῶ σε κύριέ μου, εἰδότα τὴν ἔχουσάν με συμφορὰν ἀπολῦσαί μοι; Job 21:6; Is 13:8; Jos., Ant. 3, 95 δέος εἶχε τοὺς Ἑβρ.; 5, 63; Just., D. 19, 3) εἶχεν αὐτὰς τρόμος καὶ ἔκστασις *trembling and amazement had seized them* **Mk 16:8.**

❹ **to carry/bear as accessory or part of a whole,** ***have on, wear,*** of clothing, weapons, etc. (Hom. et al.; LXX; TestAbr B p. 114, 22 [Stone p. 76]) τὸ ἔνδυμα **Mt 3:4; 22:12** (cp. ἔνδυσιν TestJob 25:7). κατὰ κεφαλῆς ἔχων w. τὶ to be supplied *while he wears (a covering) on his head* **1 Cor 11:4.** ἔ. θώρακας **Rv 9:9, 17.** ἔ. μάχαιραν *wear a sword* (Jos., Ant. 6, 190) **J 18:10.** Sim. of trees ἔ. φύλλα *have leaves* **Mk 11:13** (ApcSed. 8:8).

❺ **be in a position to do someth.,** ***can, be able,*** ἔ. w. inf. foll. (Hom. et al.; cp. Eur., Hec. 761; Hdt. 1, 49; Pla., Phd. p. 76d; Demosth., Ep. 2, 22; Theocr. 10, 37 τὸν τρόπον οὐκ ἔχω εἰπεῖν=I cannot specify the manner; Lucian, Dial. Mort. 21, 2, Hermot. 55; Epict. 1, 9, 32; 2, 2, 24 al.; Ael. Aristid. 51, 50 K.=27 p. 546 D.: οὐκ ἔχω λέγειν; PPetr II, 12, 1, 16; PAmh 131, 15; Pr 3:27; ApcEsdr 2:24; 3:7; 6:5; TestAbr A 8, p. 86, 13 [Stone p. 20]; Jos., Ant. 1, 338; 2, 58; Just., A I, 19, 5, D. 4, 6 οὐκ ἔχω εἰπεῖν) ἔ. ἀποδοῦναι *be able to pay* **Mt 18:25a; Lk 7:42; 14:14.** μὴ ἔ. περισσότερον τι ποιῆσαι *be in a position to do nothing more* **12:4.** οὐδὲν ἔ. ἀντειπεῖν *be able to make a reply* **Ac 4:14;** cp. **Tit 2:8.** ἔ. κατηγορεῖν αὐτοῦ **J 8:6** (cp. 9a below, end). ἀσφαλές τι γράψαι οὐκ ἔχω *I have nothing definite to write* **Ac 25:26a;** cp. **26b.** ἔ. μεταδιδόναι **Eph 4:28a.** ἔ. τὴν τούτων μνήμην ποιεῖσθαι *be able to recall these things to mind* **2 Pt 1:15.** κατ' οὐδενὸς εἶχεν μείζονος ὀμόσαι *he could swear by no one greater* **Hb 6:13.** In the same sense without the actual addition of the inf., which is automatically supplied fr. context (X., An. 2, 1, 9) ὃ ἔσχεν (i.e. ποιῆσαι) ἐποίησεν *she has done what she could* **Mk 14:8.**

❻ **to have an opinion about someth.,** ***consider, look upon, view*** w. acc. as obj. and predicate acc. (POxy 292, 6 [c. 25 AD] ἔχειν αὐτὸν συνεσταμένον=look upon him as recommended; 787 [16 AD]; PGiss 71, 4; Job 30:9; Ps.-Clem., Hom. 16, 19; Ath. 32, 3 τοὺς μὲν υἱοὺς . . . νοοῦμεν, τοὺς δὲ ἀδελφοὺς ἔχομεν) ἔχε με παρῃτημένον *consider me excused* (= don't expect me to come) **Lk 14:18b, 19** (cp. Martial 2, 79 excusatum habeas me). τινὰ ἔντιμον ἔ. *hold someone in honor* **Phil 2:29.** ἔ. τινὰ ὡς προφήτην *consider someone a prophet* **Mt 14:5; 21:26, 46 v.l.** (cp. GNicod 5 [=Acta Pilati B 5 p. 297 Tdf.] ἔχειν [Jannes and Jambres] ὡς θεούς; Just., D. 47, 5 τὸν μετανοοῦντα . . . ὡς δίκαιον καὶ ἀναμάρτητον ἔχει). ἔ. τινὰ εἰς προφήτην *consider someone a prophet* **Mt 21:46** (cp. Duris [III BC]: 76 fgm. 21 Jac. ὃν εἰς θεοὺς ἔχουσιν). εἶχον τ. Ἰωάννην ὄντως ὅτι προφήτης ἦν *they thought that John was really a prophet* **Mk 11:32.**

❼ **to experience someth.,** ***have*** (freq. in auxiliary capacity CTurner, JTS 28, 1927, 357–60)—ⓐ of all conditions of body and soul (Hom. et al.; LXX)—**α.** of illness, et al. (ApcMos 6 νόσον καὶ πόνον ἔχω; Jos., C. Ap. 1, 305) ἀσθενείας *have sicknesses/diseases* **Ac 28:9.** μάστιγας *physical troubles* **Mk 3:10.** πληγὴν τῆς μαχαίρης **Rv 13:14.** θλῖψιν **J 16:33b; 1 Cor 7:28; Rv 2:10.** Esp. of possession by hostile spirits: δαιμόνιον ἔ. *be possessed by an evil spirit* **Mt 11:18; Lk 7:33; 8:27; J 7:20; 8:48f, 52; 10:20.** Βεελζεβούλ **Mk 3:22.** πνεῦμα ἀκάθαρτον vs. **30; 7:25; Ac 8:7.** πνεῦμα δαιμονίου ἀκαθάρτου **Lk 4:33.** πνεῦμα πονηρόν **Ac 19:13.** πνεῦμα ἄλαλον **Mk 9:17.** πνεῦμα ἀσθενείας *spirit of sickness* **Lk 13:11.** τὸν λεγιῶνα (the evil spirit called) *Legion* **Mk 5:15.**

β. gener. of conditions, characteristics, capabilities, emotions, inner possession: ἀγάπην ἔ. *have love* (cp. Diod. S. 3, 58, 3 φιλίαν ἔχειν; Just., D. 93, 4 φιλίαν ἢ ἀγάπην ἔχοντες) **J 5:42; 13:35; 15:13; 1J 4:16; 1 Cor 13:1ff; 2 Cor 2:4; Phil 2:2; 1 Pt 4:8.** ἀγνωσίαν θεοῦ *fail to know God* **1 Cor 15:34.** ἁμαρτίαν **J 9:41; 15:22a.** ἀσθένειαν **Hb 7:28.** γνῶσιν **1 Cor 8:1, 10** (Just., A II, 13, 1; D. 28, 4). ἐλπίδα **Ac 24:15; Ro 15:4; 2 Cor 3:12; 10:15; Eph 2:12; 1J 3:3** (Ath. 33, 1). ἐπιθυμίαν **Phil 1:23.** ἐπιποθίαν **Ro 15:23b;** ζῆλον ἔ. *have zeal* **Ro 10:2.** *Have jealousy* **Js 3:14.** θυμόν **Rv 12:12.** λύπην (ApcMos 3 p. 2, 16 Tdf.) **J 16:21f; 2 Cor 2:3; Phil 2:27;** μνείαν τινὸς ἔ. *remember someone* **1 Th 3:6.** παρρησίαν **Phlm 8; Hb 10:19; 1J 2:28; 3:21; 4:17; 5:14.** πεποίθησιν **2 Cor 3:4; Phil 3:4.** πίστιν **Mt 17:20; 21:21; Mk 4:40; Ac 14:9; Ro 14:22; 1 Cor 13:2; 1 Ti 1:19** al. (Just., A I, 52, 1). προφητείαν *have the gift of prophecy* **1 Cor 13:2.** σοφίαν (X., Mem. 2, 3, 10) **Rv 17:9.** συνείδησιν ἁμαρτιῶν **Hb 10:2.** καλὴν συνείδησιν **13:18;** ἀγαθὴν σ. **1 Ti 1:19; 1 Pt 3:16;** ἀπρόσκοπον σ. **Ac 24:16;** ὑπομονήν **Rv 2:3.** φόβον **1 Ti 5:20.** χαράν **Phlm 7.** χάριν ἔ. τινί *be grateful to someone* **Lk 17:9; 1 Ti 1:12; 2 Ti 1:3;** σιγὴν ἔ. *be silent* Hs 9, 11, 5. ἀνάγκην ἔσχον *I felt it necessary* **Jd 3** (HKoskenniemi, Studien zur Idee und Phraseologie des Griechischen Briefes bis 400 n. Chr. '56, 78–87).

γ. of advantages, benefits, or comforts that one enjoys: ἔ. τὰ αἰτήματα *to have been granted the requests* **1J 5:15;** ἀνάπαυσιν ἔ. *have rest* **Rv 4:8; 14:11;** ἀπόλαυσιν τινος ἔ. *enjoy someth.* **Hb 11:25.** βάθος γῆς **Mt 13:5b; Mk 4:5b;** γῆν πολλήν **Mt 13:5a; Mk 4:5a.** τὴν προσέλευσιν τὴν πρὸς τὸν κύριον AcPl Ha 8, 22f; εἰρήνην **Ro 5:1.** ἐλευθερίαν **Gal 2:4.** S. ἐξουσία, ἐπαγγελία, ἔπαινος, ζωή, ἰκμάς, καιρός, καρπός, καύχημα, καύχησις, λόγος, μισθός, νοῦς, πνεῦμα, προσαγωγή, πρόφασις, τιμή, χάρις (=favor), χάρισμα.

δ. of a sense of obligation in regard to someth.—W. dir. object *have = have someth. over one, be under someth.*: ἀνάγκην ἔχειν *be under necessity* **1 Cor 7:37a;** w. inf. foll. *have a need* (ἀνάγκη 1) **Lk 14:18; 23:16 v.l.; Hb 7:27;** χρείαν ἔ. *be in need* abs. **Eph 4:28b;** τινός *need someth.* (Aeschyl. et al.; SIG 333, 20; 421, 35 al.; PPetr III, 42 G 9, 7 [III BC] ἐάν τινος χρείαν ἔχῃς; Ath. 13, 2 ποίας ἔτι χρείαν ἑκατόμβης ἔχει;) **Mt 6:8; 9:12a; Mk 11:3; Lk 19:31, 34; J 13:29; 1 Cor 12:21; Hb 10:36** al.; w. inf. foll. (TestSol 13:2) **Mt 3:14; 14:16; J 13:10; 1 Th 1:8; 4:9; 5:1.** νόμον **J 19:7.** ἐπιταγήν **1 Cor 7:25.** ἐντολήν (SIG 559, 9 ἔ. τὰς ἰντολάς; 1 Esdr 4:52; 2 Macc 3:13; Jos., Bell. 1, 261) **Hb 7:5; 1J 2:7; 4:21; 2J 5;** cp. **J 14:21.** διακονίαν **2 Cor 4:1.** ἀγῶνα **Phil 1:30; Col 2:1.** πρᾶξιν **Ro 12:4b.** ἔγκλημα **Ac 23:29.** κόλασιν ApcPt Bodl. (ApcEsdr 1:22 p. 25, 17 Tdf.).

ε. of a sense of inevitability in respect to some action.—W. inf. foll. *one must* (Ps.-Callisth. 2, 1, 3 καθαιρεθῆναι ἔχεις=you must be deposed; Porphyr., Against the Christians 63 Harnack [ABA 1916] παθεῖν; Gen 18:31; Jos., Ant. 19, 348 τοῦ τεθνάναι; TestSol 5:12 σίδηρα ἔχεις φορέσαι; TestAbr A 18 p. 100, 22 [Stone p. 48] τοῦ βίου τούτου ἀπαλλάξαι εἶχες; Just., D. 51, 2 ἔργῳ πεισθῆναι ὑμῶν ἐχόντων) βάπτισμα ἔχω βαπτισθῆναι *I must undergo a baptism* **Lk 12:50.** ἔχω σοί τι εἰπεῖν *I have someth. to say to you* (Lucian, Philops. 1 ἔχεις μοι εἰπεῖν. Without dat. Aelian, VH 2, 23; Jos., Ant. 16, 312) **7:40.** καινόν σοι θέαμα ἔχω ἐξηγήσασθαι *I have a wonderful new* *thing to tell you*=‘I must tell you about something wonderful that I’ve just seen’ GJs 19:3. ἀπαγγεῖλαι **Ac 23:17, 19;** cp. vs. **18.** πολλὰ γράφειν **2J 12; 3J 13.**

ⓑ of temporal circumstances w. indications of time and age: πεντήκοντα ἔτη οὔπω ἔχεις *you are not yet fifty years old* **J 8:57** (cp. Jos., Ant. 1, 198). τριάκοντα κ. ὀκτὼ ἔτη ἔχων ἐν τῇ ἀσθενείᾳ αὐτοῦ *who had been sick for 38 years* **5:5** (Cyranides p. 63, 25 πολὺν χρόνον ἔχων ἐν τῇ ἀρρωστίᾳ. W. cardinal numeral TestJob 26:1 δέκα ἑπτὰ ἔτη ἔχω ἐν ταῖς πληγαῖς; POxy 1862, 17 τέσσαρες μῆνας ἔχει. Mirac. S. Georgii 44, 7 [JAufhauser 1913] ἔσχεν … ἔτη ἑπτά); cp. **Mt 9:20 v.l.** τέσσαρας ἡμέρας ἔ. ἐν τῷ μνημείῳ *have lain in the grave for four days* **J 11:17** (Jos., Ant. 7, 1 αὐτοῦ δύο ἡμέρας ἔχοντος ἐν τῇ Σεκέλλᾳ). πολὺν χρόνον ἔ. *be* (somewhere or in a certain condition) *for a long time* **5:6.** ἡλικίαν ἔχειν *be of age* (Pla., Euthyd. 32, 306d; Plut., Mor. 547a; BGU 168 τοῖς ἀτελέσι ἔχουσι τὴν ἡλικίαν) **9:21, 23.** τέλος ἔχειν *have an end, be at an end* (Lucian, Charon 17; UPZ 81 III, 20 [II AD] τέλος ἔχει πάντα; Ar. 4:2 ἀρχὴν καὶ τέλος) **Mk 3:26; Lk 22:37** (on the latter pass. s. τέλος 2); cp. **Hb 7:3.**

❽ **as connective marker,** ***to have*** or ***include in itself, bring about, cause*** w. acc. (Hom. et al.; Wsd 8:16) of ὑπομονή: ἔργον τέλειον **Js 1:4.** Of πίστις: ἔργα **2:17.** Of φόβος: κόλασιν **1J 4:18.** Of παρρησία: μεγάλην μισθαποδοσίαν **Hb 10:35.** Of πολυτέλεια: λύπην, χαράν Hs 1, 10. ἐσχάτην εὐλογίαν, ἥτις διαδοχὴν οὐκ ἔχει *ultimate blessing, which has no successor* GJs 6:2.

❾ special combinations—ⓐ w. prep. ἐν: τὸν θεὸν ἔ. ἐν ἐπιγνώσει *acknowledge God* **Ro 1:28** (cp. ἐν ὀργῇ ἔ. τινά=‘be angry at someone’, Thu. 2, 18, 5; 2, 21, 3; ἐν ὀρρωδίᾳ ἔ. τ. 2, 89, 1; ἐν ἡδονῇ ἔ. τ.=‘be glad to see someone’ 3, 9, 1; ἐν εὐνοίᾳ ἔ. Demosth. 18, 167). ἐν ἑτοίμῳ ἔ. **2 Cor 10:6** (ἕτοιμος b). ἐν ἐμοὶ οὐκ ἔχει οὐδέν *he has no hold on me* **J 14:30** (Appian, Bell. Civ. 3, 32 §125 ἔχειν τι ἔν τινι=have someth. [hope of safety] in someone). κατά τινος: on **1 Cor 11:4** s. above 4. ἔ. τι κατά τινος *have someth. against someone* **Mt 5:23; Mk 11:25;** w. ὅτι foll. **Rv 2:14.** ἔ. κατά τινος w. sim. mng. Hm 2:2; s 9, 23, 2; w. ὅτι foll. **Rv 2:4, 20.** ἔ. τινὰ κατὰ πρόσωπον *meet someone face to face* **Ac 25:16.** μετά: ἔ. τι μετά τινος *have someth. w. someone* κρίματα *lawsuits* **1 Cor 6:7.** περί: ἔ. περί τινος *have* (a word, a reference, an explanation) *about someth.* B 12:1; with adv. τελείως 10:10. πρός τινα *have someth. against someone* (Ps.-Callisth. 2, 21, 21 ὅσον τις ὑμῶν ἔχει πρὸς ἕτερον) **Ac 24:19.** ζητήματα ἔ. πρός τινα *have differences w. someone (on points in question)* **25:19.** λόγον ἔ. πρός τινα **19:38.** πρᾶγμα (=Lat. causa, ‘lawsuit’: BGU 19 I, 5; 361 II, 4) ἔ. πρός τινα (POxy 743, 19 [2 BC] εἰ πρὸς ἄλλους εἶχον πρᾶγμα; BGU 22:8) **1 Cor 6:1.** ἵνα ἔχωσιν κατηγορίαν αὐτοῦ **J 8:4** D (cp. 5 above). πρός τινα ἔ. μομφήν *have a complaint against someone* **Col 3:13.**

ⓑ τοῦτο ἔχεις ὅτι *you have this* (in your favor), *that* **Rv 2:6.** ἔ. ὁδόν *be situated* (a certain distance) *away* (cp. Peripl. Eryth. 37: Ὡραία ἔχουσα ὁδὸν ἡμερῶν ἑπτὰ ἀπὸ θαλάσσης) of the Mt. of Olives ὅ ἐστιν ἐγγὺς Ἰερουσαλὴμ σαββάτου ἔχον ὁδόν **Ac 1:12.**—ἴδε ἔχεις τὸ σόν *here you have what is yours* **Mt 25:25.** ἔχετε κουστωδίαν *there you have a guard* (=you can have a guard) **27:65** (cp. POxy 33 III, 4).

❿ **to be in some state or condition,** act. intr. (spatially: Ath. 25, 1 οἱ ἄγγελοι … περὶ τὸν ἀέρα ἔχοντες καὶ τὴν γῆν) w. adv. (Hom. et al.; ins, pap, LXX).

ⓐ impers. ***it is, the situation is*** (Himerius, Or. 48 [=Or. 14], 10 πῶς ὑμῖν ἔχειν ταῦτα δοκεῖ; =how does this situation seem to you? Just., D. 3, 5 τὸ … ὡσαύτως ἀεὶ ἔχων) ἄλλως **1 Ti 5:25.** οὕτως (Antig. Car. 20; Cebes 4, 1; POxy 294, 11 [22 AD] εἰ ταῦτα οὕτως ἔχει; TestSol 20:8; Jos., Ant. 15, 261; Just., D. 3:5 οὐχ οὕτως ἔχει) **Ac 7:1; 12:15; 17:11; 24:9.** τὸ καλῶς ἔχον *what is right* 1 Cl 14:2 (Michel 543, 12 [c. 200 BC] καλῶς ἔχον ἐστὶ τιμᾶσθαι τοὺς εὔνους ἄνδρας). τὸ νῦν ἔχον *for the present* **Ac 24:25** (cp. Plut., Mor. 749a; Lucian, Anachars. 40, Catapl. 13 τὸ δὲ νῦν ἔχον μὴ διάτριβε; Tob 7:11).

ⓑ pers. ***be (in a certain way)*** πῶς ἔχουσιν *how they are* **Ac 15:36** (cp. Gen 43:27; Jos., Ant. 4, 112). ἑτοίμως ἔ. *be ready, hold oneself in readiness* w. inf. foll. (BGU 80, 17 [II AD] ἡ Σωτηρία ἑτοίμως ἔχουσα καταγράψαι; Da 3:15 LXX; Jos., Ant. 13, 6; Just., D. 50, 1) **21:13; 2 Cor 12:14; 1 Pt 4:5.** Also ἐν ἑτοίμῳ ἔ. **2 Cor 10:6** (s. ἕτοιμος b end). εὖ ἔ. *be well-disposed* πρός τινα *toward someone* Hs 9, 10, 7 (cp. Demosth. 9, 63 ἥδιον ἔχειν πρός τινα; SIG 1094, 4 φιλανθρώπως ἔχει πρὸς πάντας). κακῶς ἔ. *be sick* (Aristoph. et al.; POxy 935, 15; Ezk 34:4) **Mt 4:24; 8:16; 9:12b; 17:15 v.l.** (see πάσχω 2). καλῶς ἔ. *be well, healthy* (Epict. 1, 11, 4; PGen 54, 8; PFlor 230, 24) **Mk 16:18;** ἐσχάτως ἔ. (s. ἐσχάτως) **5:23;** κομψότερον ἔ. *feel better* (κομψῶς ἔ.: Epict. 2, 18, 14; 3, 10, 13; PParis 18; PTebt 414, 10 ἐὰν κομψῶς σχῶ) **J 4:52.**

⓫ **to be closely associated,** in a variety of renderings, ***hold fast, be next to, be next,*** mid. (Hom. et al.) in NT only ptc.

ⓐ of proper situation or placement, esp. of inner belonging *hold fast, cling to.* The ‘to’ of belonging and the ‘with’ of association are expressed by the gen. (Theognis 1, 32 ἀεὶ τῶν ἀγαθῶν ἔχεο=ever hold fast to the good people; X., Oec. 6, 1; Pla., Leg. 7, 811d; Lucian, Hermot. 69 ἐλπίδος οὐ μικρᾶς ἐχόμενα λέγεις; Sallust. 14 p. 26, 24 τ. θεῶν; Philo, Agr. 101 τὰ ἀρετῆς ἐχόμενα; Jos., Ant. 10, 204 οὐδὲν ἀνθρωπίνης σοφίας ἐχόμενον, C. Ap. 1, 83 παλαιᾶς ἱστορίας ἐχόμενον; Just., A I, 68, 1 λόγου καὶ ἀληθείας ἔχεσθαι; Tat. 33, 1 μανίας ἔχεται πολλῆς; Ath., R. 48, 3 λόγῳ … ἀληθείας ἐχομένῳ) τὰ ἐχόμενα σωτηρίας *things that belong to salvation* **Hb 6:9.**

ⓑ of proximity—**α.** spatial, to be next to someth: ἐχόμενος *neighboring* (Isocr. 4, 96 νῆσος; Hdt. 1, 134 al. οἱ ἐχόμενοι=‘the neighbors’; Diod. S. 5, 15, 1; Appian, Bell. Civ. 2, 71 §294; Arrian, Peripl. 7, 2; PParis 51, 5 and oft. in pap; 1 Esdr 4:42; Jos., Ant. 6, 6 πρὸς τὰς ἐχομένας πόλεις; 11, 340) κωμοπόλεις **Mk 1:38.**

β. temporal, to be next, *immediately following* (Thu. 6, 3, 2 τ. ἐχομένου ἔτους al.; SIG 800, 15; PRev 34, 20; PAmh 49, 4; PTebt 124, 43; LXX) τῇ ἐχομένῃ (sc. ἡμέρᾳ, as Polyb. 3, 112, 1; 5, 13, 9; 2 Macc 12:39; Jos., Ant. 6, 235; 7, 18 al.; cp. εἰς τὴν ἐχομένην [i.e. ἡμέραν] PMich 173, 16 [III BC]) *on the next day* **Lk 13:33** (v.l. ἐρχομένῃ); **Ac 20:15;** w. ἡμέρᾳ added (PAmh 50, 17) **21:26.** τῷ ἐχομένῳ σαββάτῳ **13:44 v.l.** (for ἐρχομένῳ; cp. 1 Macc 4:28, where the witnesses are similarly divided).—On the whole word HHanse, ‘Gott Haben’ in d. Antike u. im frühen Christentum ’39.—B. 641; 740. EDNT. M-M. TW. Sv.

ἕως (Hom.+)—❶ **to denote the end of a period of time,** ***till, until.***—ⓐ as conjunction—**α.** w. the aor. ind. (Lysias 25, 26; Ps.-Demosth. 47, 58; Wsd 10:14; 1 Macc 10:50; Jdth 10:18; En 13:7; 102:10; PsSol 2:26; 4:10; SibOr 5, 528; Ar. 12, 2) ἕως ἐστάθη *until it stood still* **Mt 2:9.** ἕως ἦλθεν ὁ κατακλυσμός *until the flood came* **24:39.**—**Ac 19:10** D.

β. w. the aor. subj. and, as the rule requires (s. AFuchs, D. Temporalsätze mit d. Konj. ‘bis’ u. ‘so lange als.’ 1902), ἄν (X., An. 5, 1, 11; SIG 966, 11; 1207, 10; PPetr II, 40a, 28; POxy 1124, 7; Gen 24:14; 49:10; Ex 33:22; Lev 22:4 and oft. LXX; TestAbr B 7 p. 112, 2 [Stone p. 72]; TestJob 21:2; ParJer 2:3; ApcMos 26 p. 14, 7 Tdf.; Jos., Ant. 13, 400; Just., A I, 45, 1), to denote that the commencement of an event is dependent on circumstances: ἕως ἂν εἴπω σοι *until I tell you* **Mt 2:13.—5:18** (AHoneyman, NTS 1, '54/55, 141f), **26** (cp. SIG 731, 16ff ἕως ἂν ἀποδῷ); **10:23; 22:44** (Ps 109:1); **Mk 6:10; 9:1; 12:36** (Ps 109:1); **Lk 20:43** (Ps 109:1); **21:32; Ac 2:35** (Ps 109:1); **1 Cor 4:5; Hb 1:13;** B 12:10 (the two last Ps 109:1).—Without ἄν (Soph., Aj. 555, Phil. 764; Polyb. 35, 2, 4; SIG 976, 79; UPZ 18, 10 [II BC]; PGrenf II, 38, 16 [I BC]; POxy 531, 6; 1125, 15; 1159, 21; Sir 35:17; Tob 14:5 BA; En 10:12, 17; TestSol 15:10; ParJer 5:14; GrBar 11:2; SibOr 5, 217; Just. D. 39, 6): **Mt 10:23 v.l.; 18:30; Mk 14:32; Lk 15:4** and **22:34** (both v.l. ἕως οὗ); **2 Th 2:7; Js 5:7; Hb 10:13; Rv 6:11.**

γ. w. the pres. ind. (cp. Plut., Lycurg. 29, 3) ἕως ἔρχομαι *until I come* **J 21:22f; 1 Ti 4:13;** Hs 5, 2, 2; 9, 10, 5f; cp. 9, 11, 1.

δ. w. the fut. ind. (cp. PHolm 26, 7; Jdth 10:15) in a text-critically doubtful pass. (B-D-F §382, 2; Rob. 971f; 976) ἕως ἥξει ὅτε εἴπητε (ἥξει ὅτε is lacking as v.l.) *until (the time) comes when you say* **Lk 13:35.**

ⓑ used as prep. (appears first at the end of the IV cent. BC [Schwyzer II 550]) *until, up to* (Aristot. et al.; ins, pap, LXX; pseudepigr., also SibOr 5, 57; 118)

α. w. gen. of a noun or an equivalent expr. (SIG 588, 64 [196 BC] ἕ. τοῦ τ. συνθήκης χρόνου; OGI 90, 16 ἕ. τοῦ πρώτου ἔτους; BGU 1128, 8 [14 BC]; oft. LXX; TestAbr A 20 p. 103, 23 [Stone p. 54]) ἕ. τῆς ἡμέρας (Jdth 12:14; 1 Esdr 4:55; 1 Macc 13:39) **Mt 27:64; Lk 1:80.** ἕ. τῆς ἡμέρας ἐκείνης (Jdth 1:15) **Mt 26:29; Mk 14:25.** ἕ. τ. ἡμ. ταύτης (4 Km 17:23; 1 Macc 8:10; 13:30; 1 Esdr 8:73; Bar 1:13; ApcMos 13 p. 7, 1 Tdf.) 1 Cl 11:2. ἕ. ὥρας ἐνάτης **Mk 15:33; Lk 23:44.** ἕ. τῆς πεντηκοστῆς **1 Cor 16:8.** ἕ. τῆς σήμερον (sc. ἡμέρας) **Mt 27:8** (Just., D. 134, 5). ἕ. τέλους *until the end* **1 Cor 1:8** (JosAs 12:3); ἕ. αἰῶνος *forever* (1 Ch 17:16; Sir 24:9; 44:13; Jdth 13:19; 1 Esdr 8:82; PsSol 18:11; TestJob 34:4) Hv 2, 3, 3. Of someone's age or a period of life ἕ. ἐτῶν ὀγδοήκοντα τεσσάρων *until the age of 84,* prob.=*until she was now 84 years old* (so Goodsp., Probs. 79–81) **Lk 2:37** (cp. Jos., Ant. 5, 181). Used w. proper names (Polyb. 2, 41, 5; Diod. S. 1, 50, 6) ἕ. Ἰωάννου *up to the time of John* **Mt 11:13.** ἕ. Σαμουήλ **Ac 13:20.** In such cases, as well as in others, ἕ. often looks back to a preceding ἀπό: *from ... to* (Bar 1:19; 1 Esdr 8:73; Sir 40:1; 1 Macc 16:2; 3 Macc 6:38 al.; Demetr.: 722 fgm. 1, 18 Jac.): ἀπὸ Ἀβραὰμ ἕ. Δαυίδ **Mt 1:17a.** ἀπὸ τ. βαπτίσματος Ἰωάννου ἕ. τῆς ἡμέρας **Ac 1:22.** ἀπὸ τ. ἕκτης ὥρας ἕ. ὥρας ἐνάτης **Mt 27:45** (cp. SIG 736, 109 [92 BC] ἀπὸ τετάρτας ὥρας ἕ. ἑβδόμας; 1 Esdr 9:41). ἀπὸ πρωῒ ἕ. ἑσπέρας **Ac 28:23** (cp. Jos., Ant. 6, 364).—ἕ. τοῦ νῦν *until now* (Ps.-Lucian, Halc. 4; SIG 705, 44f [112 BC]; UPZ 122 [157 BC]; Gen 15:16; 18:12; Num 14:19; 1 Macc 2:33) after ἀπ' ἀρχῆς **Mt 24:21; Mk 13:19** (cp. BGU 1197, 8 [4 BC] ἕως τ. νῦν ἀπὸ τοῦ ἐννεακαιδεκάτου ἔτους Καίσαρος; Ezk 4:14). ἀπὸ Δαυὶδ ἕ. τ. μετοικεσίας Βαβυλῶνος *to the Babylonian exile* **Mt 1:17b.**—As here, a historical event forms the boundary (cp. 1 Esdr 5:71; ParJer 3:11) in ἕ. τ. τελευτῆς Ἡρῴδου **2:15.**—W. the articular inf. (on the acc. with it s. B-D-F §406, 3) ἕ. τοῦ ἐλθεῖν αὐτὸν εἰς Καισάρειαν *until he came to Caesarea* **Ac 8:40** (s. SIG 588, 93f; Gen 24:33; 28:15; 1 Macc 3:33; 5:19; Polyb., Joseph. [B-D-F, §403]); but s. also 3a below.

β. w. gen. of the relative pron. (οὗ or ὅτου) in the neut.

ℵ. ἕ. οὗ *until* (Hdt. 2, 143; Plut. et al.; LXX; En; TestAbr; TestJob 24:4; in local mng. SIG 495, 101) w. aor. ind. (Judg 3:30; 4:24 B; 4 Km 17:20; Tob 1:21; 2:4, 10; Jdth 10:10; 15:5; JosAs 10:2, 19; Jos., Ant. 10, 134) **Mt 1:25; 13:33; Lk 13:21; Ac 21:26.** W. aor. subj. (BGU 1209, 8 [23 BC]; PRyl 229, 14 [38 AD]; Judg 5:7 B; Ps 71:7; Jdth 6:5, 8; TestAbr B 2 p. 107, 3 [Stone p. 62]; ParJer 9:3; GrBar 13:5; ApcMos 31 p. 17, 10 Tdf.) **Mt 18:34; Lk 15:4 v.l., 8; 22:18; 24:49; Ac 25:21; 2 Pt 1:19.** After neg.=*until, before* **Mt 17:9; J 13:38; Ac 23:12, 14, 21.**

ב. ἕ. ὅτου *until* w. aor. ind. (Diod. S. 19, 108, 3; 3 Km 10:7; 11:16; Da 2:34; 7:4) **J 9:18.** W. aor. subj. (POxy 1061, 16 [22 BC]; 1 Km 22:3; 2 Esdr 14:5) **Lk 12:50; 13:8; 15:8 v.l.; 22:16, 18 v.l.**

γ. w. adv. of time (JosAs 10:17 ἕ. πρωΐ; Ath. 22, 6 ἕ. νῦν) ἕ. ἄρτι *until now* (s. ἄρτι 3), **Mt 11:12; J 2:10; 5:17; 16:24; 1J 2:9; 1 Cor 4:13; 8:7; 15:6.** ἕ. σήμερον (Sir 47:7) **2 Cor 3:15.** ἕ. πότε; *how long?* (Ps 12:2, 3; 2 Km 2:26; 1 Macc 6:22; ApcSed 12:1f) **Mt 17:17ab; Mk 9:19ab; Lk 9:41; J 10:24; Rv 6:10.**

❷ **to denote contemporaneousness, *as long as, while***

ⓐ conj. w. ind. (Hom.+; Jdth 5:17) in our lit. only the pres. (Appian, Bell. Civ. 2, 53 §218 ἕως χειμάζουσιν and ibid. ἕως Πομπήιος ἡγεῖται=while Pompey imagines; Jos., Bell. 7, 347; Just., D. 4, 4 ἕ. ἐν τῷ σώματί ἐστιν ἡ ψυχή) ἕ. ἡμέρα ἐστίν *while it is day* **J 9:4** (v.l. ὡς. On this interchange s. LRadermacher, Philol. 60, 1901, 495f; B-D-F §455, 3); **12:35f v.l.;** ἕ. αὐτὸς ἀπολύει τ. ὄχλον *while he himself dismissed the crowd* **Mk 6:45.** ἕ. ὑπάγουσιν *while they were on their way* **Mt 25:10** D; ἕ. ἔτι ἔχομεν *while we still have* 2 Cl 16:1 (cp. Pla., Phd. 89c ἕ. ἔτι φῶς ἐστιν, Parmen. 135d ἕ. ἔτι νέος εἶ; Appian, Bell. Civ. 3, 32 §127 ἕως ἔτι δύνασαι; PEleph 14, 24 [223 BC]; Sir 33:21 ἕως ἔτι ζῇς).

ⓑ conj. w. subjunctive (PTebt 6, 42 [140 BC] ἕως ... μένωσι; Dio Chrys. 27 [44], 5 ἕως ἂν ... φέρῃ='as long as'; Appian, Numid. 4 §2) **Mk 14:32; Lk 17:8.**

ⓒ in a few cases ἕως also has this sense when functioning as prep. with the gen. of the rel. pronoun in the neut. *while* ἕ. οὗ (Jos., Ant. 3, 279 [ἔχουσι]) w. subj. **Mt 14:22; 26:36** (but s. Burton, MT §325 and Zwaan §314).—ἕ. ὅτου (SSol 1:12) w. ind. **Mt 5:25.**

❸ **marker of limit reached, *as far as, to,*** funct. as prep.

ⓐ w. gen. of place *as far as, to* (Polyb. 3, 76, 2; Diod. S. 1, 27, 5; SIG 588, 32 [196 BC] ἕ. θαλάσσης; 1231, 12 ἀπὸ ... ἕως; PTebt 33, 5 [112 BC]; LXX; En 21:1; 22:6; PsSol 15:10; TestAbr A 5 p. 82, 12f [Stone p. 12]; TestJob 20:6; GrBar 2:5; 11:8; JosAs 16:14; Jos., Bell. 1, 512; Mel., HE 4, 26, 14 ἕ. τοῦ τόπου ..., ἔνθα) ἕ. Φοινίκης **Ac 11:19.** ἕ. Ἀντιοχείας vs. **22;** ἕ. Βηθλεέμ **Lk 2:15.** ἕ. οὐρανοῦ, ᾅδου **Mt 11:23; Lk 10:15** (ApcEsdr 4:32 p. 29, 8 Tdf.). ἕ. τῆς αὐλῆς **Mt 26:58;** cp. **Lk 4:29.** ἕ. ἐσχάτου τ. γῆς (Is 48:20; 62:11; 1 Macc 3:9; PsSol 1:4) **Ac 1:8.** ἕ. τρίτου οὐρανοῦ **2 Cor 12:2** (ApcSed 2:4). ἀπὸ ... ἕ.: ἀπὸ ἀνατολῶν ἕ. δυσμῶν **Mt 24:27.** ἀπ' ἄκρων οὐρανῶν ἕ. ἄκρων αὐτῶν vs. **31** (cp. Dt 30:4). ἀπ' ἄκρου γῆς ἕ. ἄκρου οὐρανοῦ **Mk 13:27** (cp. Jdth 11:21).—Also w. gen. of a pers., who is in a certain place (Aelian, VH 3, 18 ἕ. Ὑπερβορέων; 4 Km 4:22; 1 Macc 3:26) ἦλθον ἕ. αὐτοῦ **Lk 4:42.** διελθεῖν ἕ. ἡμῶν **Ac 9:38.** Prob. **Ac 8:40** also belongs here (s. above 1bα end); then a pass. like Gen 10:19 would be comparable.

ⓑ w. adv. of place (LXX) ἕ. ἄνω (2 Ch 26:8) *to the brim* **J 2:7.** ἕ. ἔσω *right into* **Mk 14:54.** ἕ. κάτω (Ezk 1:27; 8:2 looking back to ἀπό) ἀπ' ἄνωθεν ἕ. κάτω *fr. top to bottom* **Mt 27:51; Mk 15:38** (cp. ἀπὸ ἔσω ἕως ἔξω TestSol 18:15 P). ἕ. ὧδε (Gen 22:5; 2 Km 20:16; 3 Km 18:45; Ar. 17, 1) ἀρξάμενος ἀπὸ τ. Γαλιλαίας ἕ. ὧδε **Lk 23:5.**

ⓒ w. a prep. or another adv. ἕ. πρός (Polyb. 3, 82, 6; 12, 17, 4; Gen 38:1; Ezk 48:1) ἕ. πρὸς Βηθανίαν *as far as B.* **Lk 24:50** (for the v.l. ἕ. εἰς B. cp. Polyb. 1, 11, 14; Diod. S. 1, 27, 5; Aelian, VH 12, 22; Dt 31:24; 4 Km 2:6; PsSol 2:5; Jos., Ant. 16, 90). ἕ.

καὶ εἰς *even into* **Ac 26:11.** ἕ. ἔξω τῆς πόλεως **21:5.** ἕ. ἐπὶ τὴν θάλασσαν **Ac 17:14** (cp. 1 Macc 5:29; 3 Macc 7:18 A; PsSol 17:12; ἕ. ἐπὶ πολύ TestSol 7:2).

❹ **marker of order in a series, *up to*** ἀρξάμενος ἀπὸ τῶν ἐσχάτων ἕ. πρώτων **Mt 20:8.** ὁ δεύτερος καὶ ὁ τρίτος ἕ. τῶν ἑπτά **22:26.** ἀπὸ μικροῦ ἕ. μεγάλου *small and great* (Bar 1:4; 1 Macc 5:45; Jdth 13:4) **Ac 8:10; Hb 8:11** (Jer 38:34).—**J 8:9 v.l.**

❺ **marker of degree and measure, denoting the upper limit, *to the point of*** ἕ. ἑπτάκις (4 Km 4:35; cp. TestSol 5:8 ἕ. ἑπτά; ApcSed 16:4 ἕ. εἴκοσι) *as many as seven times* **Mt 18:21f;** cp. vs. **22.** ἕ. ἡμίσους τῆς βασιλείας μου (Esth 5:3; 7:2) **Mk 6:23.** οὐκ ἔστιν ἕ. ἑνός (cp. PTebt 56, 7 [II BC] οὐκ ἔχομεν ἕ. τῆς τροφῆς τῶν κτηνῶν ἡμῶν='we do not even have enough to feed our cattle'; Leontios, Vi. Joh. [ed. HGelzer 1893] 66, 21ff οὐ … ἕως ἑνὸς νομίσματος='not even a single coin'; cp. PRossGeorg III, 3, 22 ἕως δραχμῶν ἕκατον) *there is not even one* **Ro 3:12** (Ps 13:3). ἐᾶτε ἕ. τούτου *stop! No more of this* **Lk 22:51** (ἕ. τούτου='to this point' Aristot., HA 9, 46; Polyb. 9, 36, 1; cp. 2 Km 7:18). ἕ. θανάτου *unto death* (Antig. Car. 16; Sir 34:12; 51:6; 4 Macc 14:19; JosAs 29:3): *contend* (Sir 4:28; cp. OGI 266, 29 [III BC] μαχοῦμαι ἕως ζωῆς καὶ θανάτου) 1 Cl 5:2. περίλυπός ἐστιν ἡ ψυχή μου ἕ. θανάτου **Mt 26:38; Mk 14:34** (cp. Jon 4:9 σφόδρα λελύπημαι ἐγὼ ἕ. θανάτου).—DELG s.v. 2 ἕως. EDNT. New Docs 4, 154. M-M.

ἑωσφόρος, ου, ὁ (fr. ἕως, Attic form of Ionic ἠώς 'dawn, morning', and φέρω; Hom., Hes.+; LXX, Philo) ***morning star*** **2 Pt 1:19 v.l.**—DELG s.v. 1 ἕως.

ϛ

ϛ The stigma or vau (cp. Semitic waw [ו]), sixth letter of the oldest Gk. alphabets. It is used to express the numeral *6* in the form ϛ′ (one of the earlier forms is ϝ; s. Schwyzer III 110 index; L-S-J-M s.v. F): ***six*** or ***sixth*** in the titles of Hm 6 and s 6. Cp. the entry χξϛ′ **Rv 13:18 v.l.**

Z

ζ′ numerical sign = *7* (ἑπτά) **Ac 12:10** D; GJs 10:1 (SyrBar 12:5); or *7th* (ἑβδόμη) Hm 7; [s 7] in the superscriptions (Apollon. Paradox. 33: Θεόφραστος ἐν τῷ ζ′ περὶ φυτῶν).

Ζαβουλών, ὁ indecl. (זְבוּלוּן) (LXX; JosAs 27:6; Demetr.: 722 fgm. 1, 5 Jac.; Philo, Fuga 73; Test12Patr. Joseph. acc. to his ordinary usage would prob. decline Ζαβουλών [Ant. 1, 308; 2, 179] -ῶνος) ***Zebulun*** (Gen 30:20), an Israelite tribe **Rv 7:8;** its territory (beside Naphtali) **Mt 4:13, 15; Lk 4:31** D.

Ζακχαῖος, ου, ὁ (זַכַּי) (in this form also in WCrum, Coptic Ostraca [1902] 435, 7 acc. to Wilcken's restoration: APF 2, 1903, p. 174, 3; 2 Macc 10:19. In the form Σακχαῖος Jos., Vi. 239. On Ζαχαῖος s. Preisigke, Namenbuch) ***Zacchaeus,*** a chief tax-collector of Jericho **Lk 19:2, 5, 8.**—M-M.

Ζάρα, ὁ (-ρά edd.; Ζάρε v.l.— זֶרַח) ***Zerah*** in the genealogy of Jesus **Mt 1:3** (cp. 1 Ch 2:4).

ζαφθάνι is the rdg. of Cod. D in **Mt 27:46** and **Mk 15:34** for σαβαχθάνι; it is a scholarly correction based on the Hebr. (read ἀζαφθάνι=עֲזַבְתָּנִי and s. Dalman, Worte 43; Wlh., Mk[2] 1909 on **15:34;** AMerx, D. vier kanon. Ev. II/1, 1902, 424).

Ζαχαρίας, ου, ὁ (זְכַרְיָה, 'Zechariah') ***Zacharias*** (freq. name: OT; EpArist; Joseph., index Niese; Preisigke, Namenbuch).

❶ a priest, father of John the Baptist **Lk 1:5, 12f, 18, 21, 40, 59, 67; 3:2;** GEb 13, 75; GJs (as high priest; s. EAmann, Le Protévangile de Jacques et ses remaniements latines 1910, 213) 10:2; 23:1, 3; 24:1 (twice), 2–4.

❷ *Z.* **Lk 11:51,** designated as son of Barachias (q.v.) in **Mt 23:35** (EbNestle, ZNW 6, 1905, 198–200). In GJs identical w. 1.

❸ In **Mt 27:9** *Z.* (meaning the prophet [always so in Justin]) is v.l. for Jeremiah (on confusion w. Jer, e.g. Orig., In Matt., GCS 38 p. 249, 16ff).—BHHW III, 2199.

[ζάω] contr. ζῶ (Hom.+) impf. ἔζων (**Ro 7:9** B ἔζην; on this form s. Schwyzer I 675; B-D-F §88; Mlt-H. 194, both w. ref.); fut. ζήσω (uniformly attested **Ro 6:2; Hb 12:9**); the later (since Hippocr. VII p. 536 L.; LXX; AscIs 3:9; Jos., Ant. 1, 193 al.) form ζήσομαι (B-D-F §77; Rob. 356) is more common (on the fut. forms s. JLee, NovT 22, '80, 289–98; GKilpatrick, ibid. 25, '83, 146–51); 1 aor. ἔζησα. On the LXX usage s. Thackeray 269; for forms in pap, Gignac II 370.

❶ **to be alive physically, *live***—ⓐ of physical life in contrast to death—**α.** gener. **Ac 22:22; Ro 7:1, 2, 3; 14:8ac; 1 Cor 7:39; 2 Cor 5:15a; 6:9; Hb 9:17.** ψυχὴ ζῶσα *a living soul* (Gen 1:20 al.; Just., D. 6, 1 ζῇ ψυχῇ) **1 Cor 15:45** (Gen 2:7); **Rv 16:3 v.l.** ὅσα ἔτη ζῇ *as many years as he lives* B 10:6 (cp. SIG 663, 6; Sb 173, 6 Αὐρήλιος ζήσας ἔτη νε′; En 10:10). τὸ ζῆν *life* (Attic wr., ins, pap, LXX) ὥστε ἐξαπορηθῆναι ἡμᾶς καὶ τοῦ ζῆν *so that* *we even despaired of life* **2 Cor 1:8.** διὰ παντὸς τοῦ ζῆν *during the whole lifetime* **Hb 2:15** (cp. Diod. S. 1, 74, 3 διατελεῖν πάντα τὸν τοῦ ζῆν χρόνον; 4, 46, 4). ἔτι ζῶν *while he was still living*= before his death **Mt 27:63** (Ramsay, CB I/2 660 no. 618 Ζώσιμος ἔτι ζῶν κατεσκεύασεν; 3 Km 12:6). ζῶντες ἐβλήθησαν . . . εἰς τὴν λίμνην τοῦ πυρός *they were thrown alive into the lake of fire* **Rv 19:20.** ζῶσα τέθνηκεν *though alive she is dead* **1 Ti 5:6** (cp. Sextus 7). ἡμεῖς οἱ ζῶντες *we during our (earthly) life* **2 Cor 4:11;** the same phrase=*we who are still living* **1 Th 4:15, 17.** Here the opp. is νεκροί, as in **Mt 22:32; Mk 12:27; Lk 20:38a.** ζῶντες καὶ νεκροί *the living and the dead* **Ac 10:42; Ro 14:9b; 2 Ti 4:1; 1 Pt 4:5;** 2 Cl 1:1; B 7:2.—Occasionally the contrast betw. νεκρός and ζῆν is used fig. with ref. to the realm of religion and ethics **Lk 15:24 v.l., 32.**

β. of dead persons who return to life *become alive again:* of humans in general (3 Km 17:23) **Mt 9:18; Ac 9:41; 20:12; Rv 20:4, 5;** AcPl Ha 11, 7. Of Jesus **Mk 16:11; Lk 24:5, 23; Ac 1:3; 25:19; Ro 14:9a; 2 Cor 13:4a; Rv 1:18b; 2:8** (Just., D. 69, 6 νεκροὺς . . . ζῆν ποιήσας).

γ. of sick persons, if their illness terminates not in death but in recovery *be well, recover* (Artem. 4, 4 ἔζησεν ὁ παῖς=became well; 5, 71; 72; PGM 1, 188; 4 Km 1:2; 8:8 εἰ ζήσομαι ἐκ τῆς ἀρρωστίας μου ταύτης; Jos., Vi. 421) **Mk 5:23; J 4:50, 51, 53.**—Of removal of anxiety **1 Th 3:8.**

δ. also of healthy persons *live on, remain alive* (X., An. 3, 2, 39 ὅστις δὲ ζῆν ἐπιθυμεῖ πειράσθω νικᾶν; Ep. 56 of Apollonius of Tyana [Philostrat. I 359, 14]; ApcMos 31 διὰ τί σὺ ἀποθνήσκεις καγὼ ζῶ;) **Ac 25:24; 28:4.** ἐὰν ὁ κύριος θελήσῃ ζήσομεν **Js 4:15.** ὃς ἔχει τὴν πληγὴν τῆς μαχαίρης καὶ ἔζησεν **Rv 13:14.**

ε. of beings that in reality, or as they are portrayed, are not subject to death: of Melchizedek **Hb 7:8** (opp. ἀποθνήσκοντες ἄνθρωποι). Jesus as everlasting high priest πάντοτε ζῶν **7:25.**—In this sense it is most comprehensively applied to God (s. CBurchard, Untersuch. zu JosAs p. 103) (ὁ) θεὸς (ὁ) ζῶν (cp. 4 Km 19:4, 16; Is 37:4, 17; Hos 2:1; Da 6:21 Theod.; 3 Macc 6:28; TestAbr A 17 p. 99, 10 [Stone p. 46]; TestJob 37:2; JosAs 49:3 al.; SibOr 3, 763; POxy 924, 11 [IV AD, Gnostic]; PGM 4, 1038 ὁ μέγας ζῶν θεός; 7, 823; 12, 79; Philo, Decal. 67 ὁ ζῶν ἀεὶ θεός; Orig., C. Cels. 8, 59, 18.—The phrase 'the living God' is not found in Joseph.) **Mt 16:16; 26:63; J 6:69 v.l.; Ac 14:15; Ro 9:26** (Hos 2:1); **2 Cor 3:3; 6:16; 1 Th 1:9; 1 Ti 3:15; 4:10; 6:17 v.l.; Hb 3:12; 9:14; 10:31; 12:22; Rv 1:18a; 4:10; 7:2; 10:6;** 2 Cl 20:2; GJs 20:1; AcPl Ha 2, 32; also ὁ ζῶν πατήρ **J 6:57.** W. the addition εἰς τοὺς αἰῶνας τῶν αἰώνων **Rv 15:7;** cp. **4:9** (cp. Tob 13:2; Sir 18:1). God takes a sovereign oath in the words ζῶ ἐγώ *as surely as I live* (Num 14:28 al.) **Ro 14:11** (Is 49:18; classical parallels GStählin, NovT 5, '62, 142 n. 2). ζῇ κύριος ὁ θεός [μου] *as surely as the Lord my God lives* GJs 4:1; 6:1; 13:3; 15:3; 19:3 (Judg 8:19; 1 Km 25:34 al; GrBar 1:7; cp. ApcEsdr 2:7); in expanded form καὶ ζῇ ὁ Χριστὸς αὐτοῦ 15:4 (s. deStrycker ad loc.).—Christ lives διὰ τὸν πατέρα *because of the Father* **J 6:57b** (s. Bultmann, comm. ad loc.).

ⓑ w. mention of that upon which life depends ἐπί τινι *on the basis of someth.* (Andoc. 1, 100; Isocr. 10, 18; Ael. Aristid. 28, 103 K.=49 p. 525 D.) ζ. ἐπ' ἄρτῳ *live on bread* **Mt 4:4; Lk 4:4** (both Dt 8:3). ζ. ἔκ τινος obtain *one's living fr. someth.* (Aristoph., Eccl. 591; Demosth. 57, 36; POxy 1117, 19; 1557, 12; TestJob 47:1f) **1 Cor 9:14.**

ⓒ w. more precise mention of the sphere (Artem. 3, 62 ἐν ἀγορᾷ ζ.=spend his life in the marketplace) ζ. ἐν σαρκί *live in the flesh* in contrast to the heavenly life **Phil 1:22; Gal 2:20c;** ζ. ἐν κόσμῳ *live in the world* **Col 2:20.** ζ. ἐν θεῷ, *live in God* (as the Being who penetrates and embraces everything) **Ac 17:28** (s. κινέω 3). For AcPl Ha 1, 15 s. 2a end.

❷ **to live in a transcendent sense, *live,*** of the sanctified life of a child of God (ζῆν in the sense of a higher type of life than the animal: X., Mem. 3, 3, 11; Cass. Dio 69, 19: after years of public service, Similis retires and prepares this epitaph: Σίμιλις ἐνταῦθα κεῖται βιοὺς μὲν ἔτη τόσα, ζήσας δὲ ἔτη ἑπτά=Here lies Similis, existing for so many years, but alive for only seven.).

ⓐ in the world ἐγὼ ἔζων χωρὶς νόμου ποτέ *I was once* (truly) *alive without law* (this has been interpr. to mean *when no law existed;* Paul is then regarded as speaking fr. the viewpoint of humanity in paradise before the command Gen 2:16 f; 3:3. Another interpr. thinks of Paul as referring to the period in his life when he was not conscious of the existence and significance of the law. In view of Paul's climactic affirmation in Ro 7:25, Paul probably illustrates in the first person the perils of a Christian who succumbs to the illusion that moral action is connected with law rather than with the 'spirit of life in Christ' Ro 8:2) **Ro 7:9.** Even now those who listen to the voice of the Son of God enjoy this life **J 5:25;** cp. **11:26;** likew. those who receive him into their being ὁ τρώγων τὸν ἄρτον **6:57c;** cp. **Ro 6:11, 13** (ἐκ νεκρῶν ζῶντας); **Gal 2:19; Rv 3:1.** This heavenly life on earth is a ζ. πνεύματι **Gal 5:25** or a life not of mere human achievement, but of Christ who lives in Christians **2:20ab.** Also of the superhuman power of the apostle ζήσομεν σὺν αὐτῷ ἐκ δυνάμεως θεοῦ εἰς ὑμᾶς *we shall live with him* (Christ) *through God's power in our dealings with you* **2 Cor 13:4.** ὁ κύριος βούλεται ζῆν ἡμᾶς ἐν θεῷ=*the Lord wills that we live under God's direction* AcPl Ha 1, 15 (opp. ἀποθανεῖν ἐν ἁμαρτίαις; s. 1c end)

ⓑ in the glory of the life to come (Sir 48:11; cp. Dt 4:1; 8:1; 30:16).—**α.** abs. **Lk 10:28; J 11:25; 14:19; Ro 8:13b; Hb 12:9.** ἐμοὶ τ. ζῆν Χριστός=*life is possible for me only where Christ is* (hence death is gain) **Phil 1:21** (s. OSchmitz, GHeinrici Festschr. 1914, 155–69). Another common interpr. is *for me to live is Christ,* i.e. while I am alive I experience real life in connection with Christ; w. death comes life in all fullness in the presence of Jesus.

β. More specifically εἰς τὸν αἰῶνα *have eternal life* (Ps.-Lucian, Philopatr. 17 ζῆν εἰς τὸν αἰῶνα; PsSol 14:2) **J 6:51, 58** (in J the blessed life which the follower of Jesus enjoys here and now in the body is simply continued in the heavenly life of the future. In other respects also the dividing line betw. the present and the future life is somet. nonexistent or at least not discernible); B 6:3; 8:5; 9:2; 11:10f; ἅμα σὺν αὐτῷ (i.e. Χριστῷ) ζ. *live together with Christ* **1 Th 5:10;** ζ. δι' αὐτοῦ (i.e. Chr.) **1J 4:9;** ζ. κατὰ θεὸν πνεύματι *live, as God (lives), in the Spirit* **1 Pt 4:6.** ὁ δίκαιος ἐκ πίστεως ζήσεται (cp. Hab 2:4) *he that is just through faith will have life* **Ro 1:17** (AFeuillet, NTS 6, '59, 52–80; but s. Fitzmyer, Ro [AB] ad loc.); **Gal 3:11; Hb 10:38.** This life is τὸ ἀληθινὸν ζῆν ITr 9:2; IEph 11:1. Christ is called τὸ ἀδιάκριτον ἡμῶν ζῆν *our unshakable* or *inseparable life* 3:2. τὸ διὰ παντὸς ἡμῶν ζῆν *our total life* 1 Mg 1:2—The law-directed pers. believes concerning legal performance: ὁ ποιήσας αὐτὰ ζήσεται ἐν αὐτοῖς (Lev 18:5) **Gal 3:12;** cp. **Ro 10:5** (cp. Dio Chrys. 58 [75], 1 οἱ τοῦτον [= τ. νόμον] φυλάττοντες ἔχονται τῆς σωτηρίας=those who observe law have a firm grip on security).

❸ **to conduct oneself in a pattern of behavior, *live*** (Hom. et al.)—ⓐ used w. adverbs or other modifiers: adv. (Sallust. 19 p. 34, 25 κακῶς ζῆν [Just., A I, 4, 7]; SIG 889, 13ff; Wsd 14:28; Philo; Jos., Ant. 12, 198; Ath. 3, 1 δίκην θηρίων) ἀσώτως **Lk 15:13.** ἐθνικῶς and ἰουδαϊκῶς **Gal 2:14.** εὐσεβῶς **2 Ti 3:12.** πανούργως Hm 3, 3. σωφρόνως κ. δικαίως κ. εὐσεβῶς **Tit 2:12** (Plut., Mor. 1108c ζῆν σωφρόνως κ. δικαίως; cp. Diog. L. 10, 132; 140; Ar. 15, 10).—Φαρισαῖος *live as a Pharisee* **Ac**

26:5. ἐν πίστει **Gal 2:20d.** ἐν ἁμαρτίᾳ **Ro 6:2;** ζ. ἐν τούτοις *live in these* (sins) **Col 3:7.** κατὰ ἀλήθειαν *in keeping w. the truth* IEph 6:2 (cp. Philo, Post. Cai. 73 κατὰ βούλημα τὸ τοῦ θεοῦ ζ.; Jos., Ant. 4, 302 κατὰ τ. νόμους ζ.; Just., D. 47, 4 κατὰ τὸν νόμον; Orig., C. Cels. 7, 12, 7 κατὰ τὰς θείας γραφάς). κατὰ θεόν 8:1 (cp. SIG 910 A and B). κατὰ Ἰησοῦν Χριστόν IPhld 3:2. κατὰ Χριστιανισμόν *live in accordance w. (our) commitment to Christ* IMg 10:1. κατὰ σάρκα **Ro 8:12f;** Dg 5:8; κατὰ κυριακὴν ζ. (opp. σαββατίζειν) *include the observance of the Lord's day in one's life* IMg 9:1. Of a married woman ζ. μετὰ ἀνδρός *live w. her husband* **Lk 2:36** (for the added acc. of extent of time cp. Ael. Aristid. 46 p. 332 D.; Pr 28:16; ἥτις ἔζησεν καλῶς μετ' ἐμοῦ ἔτη 28, μῆνας 4, ἡμέρας 5: SEG II, 384, 6–8 [restored]; s. also FDanker, Jesus and the New Age '88, 71).

ⓑ τινί *live for someone* or *someth., for the other's benefit* (Hom. et al.; Demosth. 7, 17 οἳ οὐκ αἰσχύνονται Φιλίππῳ ζῶντες καὶ οὐ τῇ ἑαυτῶν πατρίδι; Dionys. Hal. 3, 17 . . . παῖδες, τῷ πατρὶ ζῶντες) ζ. τῷ θεῷ (4 Macc 7:19; 16:25; Philo, Mut. Nom. 13, Rer. Div. Her. 111; s. SAalen, NTS 13, '67, 10) **Lk 20:38b** (cp. Soph., Ajax 970); **Ro 6:10, 11; Gal 2:19;** Hm 3:5; AcPl Ha 10, 7; τῷ κυρίῳ **Ro 14:8b** (cp. Plut., Cleom. 819 [31, 5]). For Christ **2 Cor 5:15;** τῷ ἐμῷ βασιλεῖ AcPl Ha 9, 26 (restored after Aa I 112, 14) τῇ δικαιοσύνῃ ζ. **1 Pt 2:24;** ἑαυτῷ ζ. *live for oneself* (Menand., fgm. 646 Kö. οὐχ ἑαυτῷ ζῆν μόνον; Diod. S. 10, 33, 2 ζ. ἑαυτοῖς=live for themselves) **Ro 14:7.**

❹ **to be full of vitality,** ***be lively*** the ptc. is used fig. w. respect to things (cp. τῶν δένδρων τῶν ζώντων ParJer 9:3), of spring water in contrast w. cistern water ὕδωρ ζῶν (Gen 26:19; Lev 14:5; Jer 2:13 v.l.; Zech 14:8.—Stagnant water is called ὕ. νεκρόν: Synes., Ep. 114, 254d) **J 4:10f** (Hdb. exc. on J 4:14); **7:38;** D 7:1f (Wengst p. 77 n. 57). ζώσας πηγάς **Rv 7:17 v.l.**

❺ **to be life-productive,** ***offer life*** ptc. used w. respect to things (SIG 1173 [138 AD], 5 ζῶσαι ἀρεταὶ ἐγένοντο=miracles full of divine life occurred) λόγια ζῶντα *words that meant life* **Ac 7:38.** λόγος ζῶν θεοῦ **1 Pt 1:23;** cp. **Hb 4:12.** ὁδὸς ζῶσα *a living way* **10:20.** ἐλπὶς ζῶσα *a living hope* **1 Pt 1:3.**—ζ. is also used of things which serve as descriptions of pers. who communicate divine life: of Christ ὁ ἄρτος ὁ ζῶν **J 6:51a.** λίθος ζῶν **1 Pt 2:4.** Of Christians: θυσία ζῶσα *a living sacrifice* **Ro 12:1.** λίθοι ζῶντες **1 Pt 2:5.**—τὰ παρὰ ζώσης φωνῆς καὶ μενούσης *the (words) of a living and abiding voice* Papias (2:4) (opp. ἐκ τῶν βιβλίων).—Lit. s. ζωή end. DELG s.v. ζώω.M-M. TW.

ζβέννυμι (PGM 7, 364 in the ms.; **1 Th 5:19 v.l.**) s. σβέννυμι.—M-M.

Ζεβεδαῖος, ου, ὁ (זַבְדִּי; Jos., Ant. 5, 33; PGrenf II, 113, 42; Just., D. 106, 3) ***Zebedee,*** father of the apostles John and James, **Mt 4:21; 10:2; 20:20; 26:37; 27:56; Mk 1:19f; 3:17; 10:35; Lk 5:10; J 21:2.**—BHHW III, 2205.

ζεστός, ή, όν (mng. 'boiled, cooked' in Appian; of 'boiling' water in Nicander, fgm. 70, 11f ζεστὸν ὕδωρ; Strabo; Soranus p. 37, 2 al.; Diosc., Sext. Emp.; SibOr 3, 461) ***hot;*** in **Rv 3:15f** the underlying idea is that the membership at Laodicea is as ineffective spiritually as its water (for the most part undesirable for drinking purposes) in pleasing one's palate (on the application to pers. cp. Etym. Mag. 413, 23 ζεστὸν ἄνθρωπον φαμὲν τὸν εὐκίνητον κ. θερμόν). MRudwick and EGreen, ET 69, '57/58, 176–78; CHemer, The Letters to the Seven Churches of Asia in Their Local Setting 1989 (1986) 186–91. S. χλιαρος, ψυχρός.—DELG s.v. ζέω. TW.

ζεύγνυμι (Hom. et al.; ins, LXX; JosAs; ApcrEzk [Epiph. 70, 15]; Just., D. 132, 2; Tat. 15, 1) aor. ἔζευξα LXX. Pass.: aor. 3 pl. ἐζεύχθησαν 1 Macc 1:15 v.l; pf. ptc. ἐζευγμένος 2 Km 20:8 (JosAs 5:5) ***connect, join*** (with a yoke) **Mk 10:9 v.l.** for συνέζευξεν (of marital union also Parthenius 17, 3; Appian, Basil. 1 §1, Bell. Civ. 2, 14 §50; Athen. 12, 554b; Sb 6647, 5; Jos., Ant. 16, 11).—B. 843. DELG.

ζεῦγος, ους, τό—❶ a team of two draft animals joined by a common frame, ***yoke, team,*** ζεῦγος βοῶν (Hom. et al.; Diod. S. 14, 18, 5; Arrian, Anab. 2, 3, 2; PPetr III, 31, 5 [240 BC]; 3 Km 19:21; Job 1:3, 14; 42:12; TestAbr A 2 p. 78, 14 [Stone p. 4]; TestJob 10:5 al.; cp. Jos., Ant. 8, 353; 12, 192) **Lk 14:19.** Unless the author intends to emphasize that the ten oxen (ζεύγη πέντε) were being sold as well-trained working animals, the term can also have the more general mng. 2 (in both senses it is a loanw. in rabb.).

❷ ***pair*** (Aeschyl., Ag. 44; Hdt. 3, 130; X., Oec. 7, 18; OGI 533, 6; 47; POxy 267, 6 [36 AD] ἐνωτίων ζ.; BGU 22, 31 [114 AD] ζ. ψελλίων) ζ. τρυγόνων *a pair of turtle doves* **Lk 2:24** (Lev 5:11. Of doves also Sb 7814, 21; 24 [256 AD]).—DELG s.v. ζεύγνυμι II; Frisk s.v. ζεῦγος. M-M. TW.

ζευκτηρία, ας, ἡ (s. ζεύγνυμι) **someth. used to link things (usually two) together,** ***bands,*** the *ropes* that tied the rudders (the nautical t.t. is 'pendant' or 'pennant' [s. OED s.v. 'pennant']: LCasson, Ships, etc. in the Ancient World '71, 228) **Ac 27:40** (the adj. ζευκτήριος since Aeschyl., Pers. 736. The subst. neut. = 'yoke' in sg. in Aeschyl., Ag. 515; PHerm 95, 18, in pl. τὰ ζευκτήρια. PLond III, 1177, 167 [113 AD] p. 185 σχοινίων καὶ ζευκτηρίων; POxy 934, 5; PFlor 16, 26 al. in pap; for the procedure cp. Eur., Hel. 1552 πηδάλια ζεύγλαισι παρακαθίετο, Breusing 102–3).—DELG s.v. ζεύγνυμι I.

Ζεύς, Διός, acc. **Δία** (Hom. et al.; ins; 2 Macc 6:2; EpArist 16; Philo, Joseph., SibOr, apolog. exc. Mel.) ***Zeus,*** king of the Greek gods, thought by the people of Lystra to have appeared in the pers. of Barnabas **Ac 14:12.** His role as benefactor to those engaged in agricultural pursuits (cp. Hymn to Zeus Diktaios in AnthLG, Diehl^2 II, 279–81) prob. serves as a motivational component that accounts for the counter-description of 'the living God' (vss. 15–17) and the extraordinary response of the audience (vs. 18). ὁ ἱερεὺς τ. Διὸς τ. ὄντος πρὸ τ. πόλεως *the priest of (the temple/shrine of) Zeus located before the city* vs. **13** (cp. Chariton 4, 4, 9 εἰς Ἀφροδίτην βαδίζειν; Philostrat. I 363, 17 ἐν Ἀρτέμιδι=in the temple of Artemis; CBreytenbach, NTS 39, '93, 396–413 [ins.]).—Lit. LfgrE 860 s.v. Ζεύς; also SEG XLIII, 1311. DDD 1758–71. S. entry Λύστρα.

ζέω ptc. ζέων (lit. 'boil, seethe' Hom.+; GDI p. 1034 no. 3 [Crete, II BC] religious regulation καταχέαι τινὶ ὕδωρ ζέον; pap; Job 32:19; Jos., Bell. 3, 271, Ant. 13, 345; Ath.) fig. of emotions, anger, love, eagerness to do good or evil, **to be stirred up emotionally,** ***be enthusiastic/excited/on fire*** (trag.; Pla., Rep. 440c; Chariton 1, 5, 1; Plut., Mor. 1088 f; 4 Macc 18:20; Philo, Mos. 2, 280) ζέων τῷ πνεύματι of Apollos before he became a full-fledged member of the Christian community *with burning zeal* **Ac 18:25** (cp. Eunap. p. 82 ζέοντος δαίμονος, i.e. of the orator.—S. also HPreisker, ZNW 30, '31, 301–4; RStrelan, Paul, Artemis, and the Jews in Ephesus: BZNW 80, '96, 216–29). The admonition to Christians to be τῷ πνεύματι ζέοντες **Ro 12:11** directs them to *maintain the spiritual glow* (Moffatt).—B. 676. Straub 20. DELG. M-M. TW.

ζηλεύω (cp. ζηλόω and s. next entry; Democrit. fgm. B 55 v.l.; Simplicius in Epict. p. 56d; Leontius 44a p. 89, 2; Cat. Cod. Astr. X 219, 8) abs. **to be intensely serious about someth.,** ***be eager, earnest*** **Rv 3:19.**—DELG s.v. ζῆλος.

ζῆλος, ου, ὁ and **ζῆλος, ους, τό** in NT masc. sg. exc. **2 Cor 9:2; Phil 3:6** (both masc. as v.l.); n. gen. only **Ac 5:17 v.l.;** masc. pl. only **Rom 13:13 v.l.; 2 Cor 12:20 v.l.; Gal 5:20 v.l.;** in Apost. Fathers most oft. masc., but n. sg. ITr 4:2 and 1 Cl 4:8; 9:1; 11:13; 14:1; 63:2. For LXX usage s. Thackeray 158, 5; cp. ἐν ζήλει PsSol 2:24; 4:3; τὸ ζῆλος TestGad 5:3 (μῖσος v.l.); in Test12Patr ὁ ζῆλος, but w. n. in variants. Pl. ζήλη (GrBar 8:5). S. prec. entry and ζηλόω.

❶ **intense positive interest in someth.,** ***zeal, ardor,*** marked by a sense of dedication (since Soph., Aj. 503; Aristot., Rhet. 2, 11, 1; LXX; TestAsh 4:5) **2 Cor 9:2.** W. σπουδή (Dio Chrys. 17 [34], 48) **7:11;** κατὰ ζ. *as far as zeal is concerned* **Phil 3:6.** W. obj. gen. (Soph., Oed. Col. 943; Strabo 13, 2, 4; Plut., Cor. 215 [4, 3]; Lucian, Adv. Ind. 17; 1 Macc 2:58. Oft. Philo; Jos., C. Ap. 2, 271) ζ. θεοῦ *zeal for God* (Jdth 9:4; cp. ἐν ζήλῳ κυρίου TestAsh 4:5) **Ro 10:2.** ζ. τοῦ οἴκου σου *zeal for your house* **J 2:17** (Ps 68:10). In the same sense ὑπέρ τινος: τὸν ὑμῶν ζ. ὑπὲρ ἐμοῦ *your ardor on my behalf* **2 Cor 7:7.** ἔχει . . . ζῆλον ὑπὲρ ὑμῶν **Col 4:13 v.l.** W. gen. of quality θεοῦ ζῆλος *an ardor like that of God* or *divine ardor* **2 Cor 11:2** (cp. Is 9:6; Philo, Post. Cai. 183; on the idea FKüchler, ZAW 28, 1908, 42ff; BRenaud, Je suis un Dieu jaloux, '63). Of the fire of judgment which, with its blazing flames, appears like a living being intent on devouring God's adversaries πυρὸς ζῆλος ἐσθίειν μέλλοντος τ. ὑπεναντίους **Hb 10:27** (cp. Is 26:11; Zeph 1:18; 3:8; Ps 78:5).

❷ **intense negative feelings over another's achievements or success,** ***jealousy, envy*** (Hes., Op. 195; Lysias 2, 48 w. φθόνος; Plut., Thes. 6, 9, Lycurg. 41 [4, 3]; PGrenf I, 1, 13 [II BC]; Eccl 4:4; 9:6; Sir 30:24; 40:4 [both w. θυμός]; Test12Patr [exc. TestAsh 4:5]; AscIs 3:30; Jos., Ant. 14, 161; cp. Cicero, Tusc. Disp. 4, 8, 17) 1 Cl 3:2; 4:7ff; 5:2, 4f; 6:1ff; 43:2; 63:2. W. ἔρις **Ro 13:13;** 1 Cl 5:5; 6:4; cp. **1 Cor 3:3; 2 Cor 12:20; Gal 5:20** (in the three last passages ζῆλος seems to be coördinate with ἔρις in the sense 'rivalry' or 'party-attachment'; cp. GrBar 8:5; 13:4). W. ἐριθεία **Js 3:14, 16.** W. φθόνος (Democr. fgm. B191; Lysias 2, 48; Pla., Phlb. 47e; 50c; 1 Macc 8:16) 1 Cl 3:2; 4:7 al. πλησθῆναι ζήλου *become filled w. jealousy* **Ac 5:17; 13:45.** ζ. leads to death 1 Cl 9:1; 39:7 (Job 5:2). ζ. ἄδικον καὶ ἀσεβῆ 3:4; μυσερὸν ζ. 14:1; μιαρὸν κ. ἄδικον ζ. 45:4. ἔχειν ζῆλόν τινα ἐν ἀλλήλοις περί τινος *be jealous of one another because of someth.* Hs 8, 7, 4. The pl. ζῆλοι found as v.l. **Ro 13:13** (s. beg. of this entry); **2 Cor 12:20; Gal 5:20** denotes the var. outbreaks of jealousy and the forms it takes (cp. Pla., Leg. 3, 679c ζῆλοί τε καὶ φθόνοι); ζήλη in vice list GrBar 8:5.—BReicke, Diakonie, Festfreude u. Zelos . . . , '51, 231–393.—DELG. M-M. EDNT. TW. Sv.

ζηλοτυπία, ας, ἡ (Aeschines et al.; Polyb. 4, 87, 4; Plut.; Dio Chrys. 14 [31], 99 al.; Lucian; Num 5:15, 18, 25, 29; Philo; Jos., Ant. 7, 386, C. Ap. 2, 123) ***jealousy*** D 5:1.—B. 1139. DELG s.v. ζῆλος.

ζηλόω (s. ζῆλος) fut. ζηλώσω Ezk 39:25 (TestReub 6:5 ζηλώσετε [-σατε v.l.]); 1 aor. ἐζήλωσα; pf. ἐζήλωκα LXX (-σα v.l.) (s. ζῆλος; Hom. Hymns, Hesiod et al.; ins, pap; Thu. 2, 64, 4 'emulate, vie with'; Tat. 25, 1 ζηλῶν . . . τὸν κύνα 'emulating the dog [the Cynic]').

❶ **be positively and intensely interested in someth.,** ***strive, desire, exert oneself earnestly, be dedicated***—ⓐ w. a thing as obj. τὶ *(for) someth.* (Eur., Hec. 255; Thu. 2, 37; Demosth. 20, 141; Polyb. 6, 25, 11 τὸ βέλτιον; Diod. S. 1, 95, 4; PSI 94, 9 ζηλοῖ τ. μάθησιν; Wsd 1:12; Sir 51:18 τὸ ἀγαθόν; Jos., C. Ap. 2, 261) ζ. τὰ χαρίσματα τὰ μείζονα *strive for the more valuable spiritual gifts* **1 Cor 12:31** (JSmit, NTS 39, '93, 246–64 [ironical]). τὸ προφητεύειν **14:39.** τὰ πνευματικά vs. **1** (where beside the acc. a ἵνα-clause depends on ζ.).

ⓑ w. a personal obj. τινά *be deeply interested in someone, court someone's favor, make much of,* with implication of desiring the other to be on one's own side (Περὶ ὕψους 13, 2 οἱ ζηλοῦντες ἐκείνους; Pr 23:17; 24:1; pass. Jos., C. Ap. 1, 225) **Gal 4:17ab; 2 Cor 11:2.** μηδέν με ζηλώσαι *let nothing attract me* (and turn me away fr. my purpose) IRo 5:3.—Abs. *manifest zeal* (Thu. 2, 64, 4) ζήλωσον *take a stand, decide* **Rv 3:19 v.l.** Laodicea is indecisive and is invited to show that the congregation is zealous about the Lord's interests. Pass. καλὸν ζηλοῦσθαι ἐν καλῷ πάντοτε *it is fine to be zealously courted at all times in what is fine* **Gal 4:18.**

❷ **to have intense negative feelings over another's achievements or success,** ***be filled w. jealousy, envy*** τινά *toward someone* (Hes., Op. 23; Hom. Hymns, Cer. 168; 223; Gen 26:14; 30:1; Demetr.: 722 fgm. 1, 3 Jac.) τὸν Ἰωσήφ **Ac 7:9** (cp. Gen 37:11). Abs. **Ac 17:5; 1 Cor 13:4; Js 4:2;** 2 Cl 4:3; AcPl Ha 2, 11; 6, 31.—M-M. TW.

ζηλωτής, οῦ, ὁ (Isocr., Pla. et al.; ins, LXX; JosAs 11 cod A [p. 53, 25 Bat.]; ApcSed 6:8; Philo, Joseph., Ar.)

❶ **one who is earnestly committed to a side or cause,** ***enthusiast, adherent, loyalist.***—ⓐ w. gen.—**α.** of pers. (Dio Chrys. 38 [55], 6 Ὁμήρου ζ.; SIG 717, 33; OGI 339, 90; Jos., Vi. 11) ζ. τοῦ θεοῦ *one who is loyal to God* **Ac 22:3** (Musonius 37, 3 ζ. τοῦ Διός; Epict. 2, 14, 13).

β. of thing (Diod. S. 1, 73, 9 τ. πολεμικῶν ἔργων; 2, 1, 4 ζ. τῆς ἀρετῆς; Epict. 2, 12, 25; 3, 24, 40; SIG 675, 27f ζ. τῆς αὐτῆς αἱρέσεως; 756, 32; Philo, Praem. 11 ἀρετῆς, Spec. Leg. 1, 30, Virt. 175; Jos., C. Ap. 1, 162) ζ. ἐστε πνευμάτων *you are eager to possess spirits* (i.e., spiritual gifts) **1 Cor 14:12.** ζ. καλῶν ἔργων *eager to perform good deeds* **Tit 2:14.** τοῦ ἀγαθοῦ **1 Pt 3:13.** τοῦ νόμου *an ardent observer of the law* **Ac 21:20** (cp. 2 Macc 4:2; Philo, Spec. Leg. 2, 253; Jos., Ant. 12, 271). ζ. τ. πατρικῶν μου παραδόσεων **Gal 1:14** (Thrasyllus [I AD] in Diog. L. 9, 38: Democritus as ζ. τῶν Πυθαγορικῶν; Philo, Mos. 2, 161 ζ. τῶν Αἰγυπτιακῶν πλασμάτων).—Also rather in the sense of an *enthusiastic adherent* of a person or a cause (Strabo 10, 5, 6 p. 486 τοῦ Βίωνος ζηλωτής; Appian, Bell. Civ. 2, 2 §4 Σύλλα φίλος καὶ ζ.; Polyaenus 5, 2, 22; Diog. L. 2, 113; Memnon [I BC/I AD]: 434 fgm. 1, 35, 1 Jac. ζ. τῆς Λαμάχου προαιρέσεως=of the party of L.).—Abs. (Iambl., Vi. Pyth. 5, 29; Marinus, Vi. Procli 38 Boiss.; Ar. 7, 3 al.), in a bad sense *jealous* (w. ἐριστικός, θυμικός) D 3:2.

ⓑ w. περί to introduce a thing—**α.** w. gen. 1 Cl 45:1—**β.** w. acc. Pol 6:3.

❷ **an ultranationalist,** ***patriot, zealot*** (ὁ) ζηλωτής is the cognomen of one of the Twelve, called Simon the Patriot (Zealot) to distinguish him fr. Simon Peter **Lk 6:15; Ac 1:13;** GEb 34, 61 (cp. Jos., Bell. 2, 651; 4, 160 and s. Καναναῖος. WFarmer, Maccabees, Zealots and Josephus '56; MHengel, Die Zeloten [Herod I to 70 AD][2], '76; MSmith, HTR 64, '71, 1–19; SBrandon, Jesus and the Zealots, '67; s. Brandon's answer to criticism NTS 17, '70/71, 453 and s. JGriffiths, ibid. 19, '73, 483–89; HKingdon, ibid. 19, '72, 74–81).—DELG s.v. ζῆλος. M-M. EDNT. TW. Sv.

ζημία, ας, ἡ (Epicharm. 148 [Doric ζαμία]; Soph., Hdt.+; loanw. in rabb. In Hdt., Thu. et al. usu. 'punishment') in our lit. only having to do with suffering the loss of someth., with implication of sustaining hardship or suffering, ***damage, disadvantage, loss, forfeit*** (Philo, Somn. 1, 124 al.; Jos., Ant. 4, 211) Hs 6, 3, 4. μετὰ πολλῆς ζ. τινός *with heavy loss of someth.* **Ac 27:10;** κερδῆσαι τὴν ζ. *avoid, save oneself damage* vs. **21.** ἡγοῦμαί τι ζημίαν *I consider someth. (a) loss* (X., Mem. 2, 4, 3; cp. 2, 3, 2; Epict. 2, 10, 15; 3, 26, 25 [opp. κέρδος, as Lysias 7, 12; Pla., Leg. 835b al.]) **Phil 3:8;** cp. vs. **7.** —B. 809. DELG. M-M. TW. Spicq. Sv.

ζημιόω fut. 3 pl. ζημιώσουσιν Dt 22:19; 1 aor. 3 sg. ἐζημίωσεν 1 Esdr 1:34. Pass.: 1 fut. ζημιωθήσομαι; 1 aor. ἐζημιώθην, subj. ζημιωθῶ, ptc. ζημιωθείς (Eur., Hdt. et al.; ins, pap, LXX, Philo, Joseph., Test12Patr) gener. 'to cause injury or inflict punishment', in our lit. only pass.

❶ **to experience the loss of someth., with implication of undergoing hardship or suffering, *suffer damage/loss, forfeit, sustain injury*** (PFlor 142, 8 of a sale ὥστε μήτε τὸν πιπράσκοντα ζημιοῦσθαι; Pr 22:3) w. acc. τὶ *suffer loss w. respect to someth., forfeit someth.* (Thu. 3, 40, 3; Pla., Leg. 916e; Philo, Spec. Leg. 3, 143 τ. τιμήν; Jos., Ant. 11, 214; s. B-D-F §159, 2; Rob. 485) τὴν ψυχήν **Mt 16:26; Mk 8:36;** cp. **Lk 9:25;** 2 Cl 6:2. ἐν μηδενὶ ζ. ἔκ τινος *in no way suffer loss through someone* **2 Cor 7:9;** permit oneself (permissive pass. Gildersleeve, Syntax I §167) to *sustain loss* w. acc. δι' ὃν τὰ πάντα ἐζημιώθην *for whose sake I forfeited everything* **Phil 3:8.**

❷ ***be punished*** (Lysias 31, 26 al.; OGI 669, 40; PTebt 5, 92; Pr 19:19; Jos., Ant. 15, 16) **1 Cor 3:15.**—DELG s.v. ζημία. M-M. TW. Spicq.

Ζηνᾶς, acc. -ᾶν, ὁ (IMagnMai 323; Preisigke, Namenbuch) ***Zenas,*** a Christian and νομικός (q.v. 2) **Tit 3:13.**—LGPN I. M-M.

Ζήνων, ωνος, ὁ (freq. in lit. [incl. Joseph.], ins and pap; Tat. 3:1) *Zeno* **2 Ti 4:19 v.l.;** AcPl Ant 13, 5 (//Aa I 236, 7, here as son of Onesiphorus and Lectra).—LGPN I.

ζητέω impf. ἐζήτουν; fut. ζητήσω; 1 aor. ἐζήτησα. Pass.: impf. sg. ἐζητεῖτο **Hb 8:7;** 1 fut. ζητηθήσομαι; aor. ἐζητήθην (LXX; AcPlCor 2:8; 1) (s. two next entries; Hom.+).

❶ **try to find someth.,** ***seek, look for*** in order to find (s. εὑρίσκω 1a)—ⓐ what one possessed and has lost, w. acc. τινά **Mt 28:5; Mk 1:37; Lk 2:48f; J 6:24, 26; 7:34, 36.** τί **Mt 18:12; Lk 19:10;** AcPlCor 2:8 (ParJer 5:12). Abs. **Lk 15:8.**

ⓑ what one desires somehow to bring into relation w. oneself or to obtain without knowing where it is to be found τινά **2 Ti 1:17; J 18:4, 7f; Ac 10:19, 21.** ζητεῖν τ. θεόν, εἰ ἄρα γε αὐτὸν εὕροιεν *search for God, in the hope that they may find him* **17:27** (cp. Wsd 1:1; 13:6; Philo, Spec. Leg. 1, 36; Tat. 13, 2); **Ro 10:20** (Is 65:1). τί **Mt 2:13; 12:43; 13:45** (in the special sense *seek to buy* as X., Cyr. 2, 2, 26; Theophr., Char. 23, 8 ἱματισμὸν ζητῆσαι εἰς δύο τάλαντα); **Lk 11:24.** τὶ ἔν τινι *someth. on someth.* fruit on a tree **13:6f.** Abs. **Mt 7:7f; Lk 11:9f** (ζήτει καὶ εὑρήσεις Epict. 4, 1, 51).

ⓒ be on the search for *look for, search out* τινά *someone* **Mk 3:32; Ac 9:11;** IPol 4:2. For the purpose of arrest, pass. GPt 7:26; MPol 3:2.

❷ **to seek information, *investigate, examine, consider, deliberate*** (X., Cyr. 8, 5, 13; Lucian, Hermot. 66; Aelian, VH 2, 13; 4 Macc 1:13; Just., D. 28, 1 τὸ ζητούμενον 'question, problem'; cp. דרשׁ in post-bibl. Hebr. and Aram.: Dalman, Aram.-neuhebr. Handwörterbuch[2] 1922; HStrack, Einleitg. in Talmud u. Midraš[5] 1921, 4) παραλόγως ζ. *engage in irrational investigations* Dg 11:1. ἐν ἑαυτῷ ζ. περί τινος *ponder someth.* Hs 2:1. περὶ τούτου ζητεῖτε μετ' ἀλλήλων ὅτι; *are you deliberating with each other on the fact that?* **J 16:19** (Just., D. 19, 1 al.). W. indir. discourse foll. *consider* (Diod. S. 1, 51, 6 πόσαι . . .; Tat. 26, 1 τίς ὁ θεός; 29, 1 ὅτῳ τρόπῳ) πῶς **Mk 11:18; 14:1, 11.** τί **Lk 12:29.** τὸ πῶς **22:2.** εἰ B 11:1.—As legal t.t. *investigate* (Dinarchus 1, 8; POxy 237 VI, 41; 726, 16; O. Theb 134, 4; EBickermann, RHR 112, '35, 214f) ἔστιν ὁ ζητῶν κ. κρίνων *there is one who investigates and judges* **J 8:50b** (cp. Philo, De Jos. 174). **J 11:56** may also have this technical sense.

❸ **to devote serious effort to realize one's desire or objective, *strive for, aim (at), try to obtain, desire, wish (for)***

ⓐ *desire to possess* τὶ *someth.* (Lucian, Hermot. 66 τ. εὐδαιμονίαν; Just., D. 102, 6 σωτηρίαν καὶ βοήθειαν) τ. βασιλείαν **Mt 6:33; Lk 12:31.** εὐκαιρίαν **Mt 26:16; Lk 22:6.** ψευδομαρτυρίαν **Mt 26:59;** cp. **Mk 14:55.** τὴν δόξαν **J 5:44; 7:18; 8:50a.** τιμὴν κ. ἀφθαρσίαν **Ro 2:7;** cp. **1 Cor 7:27b; 2 Cor 12:14; Col 3:1; 1 Pt 3:11** (Ps 33:15).

ⓑ *wish for, aim at* τὶ *someth.* τὸν θάνατον **Rv 9:6.** λύσιν **1 Cor 7:27a.** τὸ θέλημά τινος *be intent on someone's will*=aim to satisfy it **J 5:30.** τὸ σύμφορόν τινος *someone's benefit* (Hermogenes 283 p. 301, 11 R. v.l. ἐμοῦ . . . οὐ τὸ Φιλίππου συμφέρον ζητοῦντος [a citation of Dem. 18, 30, which reads Φιλίππῳ]) **1 Cor 10:33;** τὰ (τὸ) ἑαυτοῦ ζητεῖν *strive for one's own advantage* **10:24; 13:5; Phil 2:21.**

ⓒ w. interrog. pron. τί ζητεῖτε; (cp. Gen 37:15) *what do you want?* **J 1:38;** cp. **4:27** (JFoster, ET 52, '40/41, 37f).

ⓓ w. inf. foll. (Hdt. 3, 137) mostly aor. (Plut., Thes. 35, 6; SIG 372, 7; Wsd 8:2; Sir 7:6; 27:1; Tob 5:14 BA; TestSol 15:7; Jos., Ant. 11, 174; 13, 7) **Mt 12:46; 21:46; Mk 12:12; Lk 5:18; 9:9; 11:54 v.l.; 17:33; J 5:18; 7:1; Ac 13:7** D, **8; 16:10** (cp. 3 Km 11:22); **Ro 10:3; Gal 2:17.** Rarely the pres. inf. (X., An. 5, 4, 33; Esth 8:12c) **Lk 6:19; Gal 1:10** (ζ. ἀρέσκειν as Ael. Aristid. 34, 39 K.=50 p. 560 D.)—ἵνα for the inf. **1 Cor 14:12.**

ⓔ OT lang. apparently is reflected in ζ. τὴν ψυχήν τινος *seek the life of someone* **Mt 2:20** (cp. Ex 4:19); **Ro 11:3** (3 Km 19:10); cp. also 3 Km 19:14; Sir 51:3; Ps 34:4; 37:13; 39:15; 53:5; 62:10; 85:14.

❹ ***ask for, request, demand*** τὶ *someth.* σημεῖον **Mk 8:12.** σοφίαν **1 Cor 1:22.** δοκιμὴν **2 Cor 13:3.** τινά **J 4:23.** τὶ παρά τινος *demand someth. fr. someone* (Demosth. 4, 33; Sir 7:4; 28:3; 1 Esdr 8:50; Tob 4:18) **Mk 8:11; Lk 11:16; 12:48.** Also τὶ ἀπό τινος B 21:6. ζητεῖται ἐν τ. οἰκονόμοις ἵνα *it is required of managers that* **1 Cor 4:2** (AFridrichsen, ConNeot 7, '42, 5).—B. 655; 764. DELG. M-M. EDNT. TW. Sv.

ζήτημα, ατος, τό (s. prec. entry; Soph., Hippocr.+; ins, pap; Ezk 36:37 v.l.; Just., D. 123, 7; loanw. in rabb.) in our lit. only in Ac, w. the mng. it still has in Mod. Gk. ***(controversial) question, issue, argument*** (Epict. 2, 11, 8) **Ac 15:2; 26:3.** ζ. περί τινος *questions about someth.* (Pla., Leg. 10, 891c) **18:15; 25:19.**—In **23:29,** since περί had already been used, the subj. of the discussion is added in the gen., ζ. τοῦ νόμου αὐτῶν.—DELG s.v. ζητέω. M-M.

ζήτησις, εως, ἡ (s. prec. two entries; Soph., Hdt. et al.; ins, pap, Philo, Joseph.; Just.; Mel., HE 4, 26, 3)

❶ **a search for information, *investigation*** (Pla. et al.; Jos., Vi. 302, esp. as legal t.t.: Dinarchus 1, 10; OGI 629, 9; POxy 237 VIII, 39; 513, 45 ζ. περὶ τούτου) ἀπορούμενος ἐγὼ τὴν περὶ τούτων ζ. *because I was at a loss concerning the investigation of these things* **Ac 25:20.** In the Past. Epistles it may denote the investigation of relig. and theol. problems (Alex. Aphr., Fat. 2, II 2 p. 166, 14 ζήτησις περὶ τῆς εἱμαρμένης; cp. Philo, Migr.

Abr. 76; Just., D. 1, 3): **1 Ti 6:4; 2 Ti 2:23; Tit 3:9.** But here the context permits other interpr. as well, namely

❷ matter for dispute, *controversial question, controversy* (Jos., Ant. 15, 135, C. Ap. 1, 11) for **2 Ti 2:23; Tit 3:9** and

❸ engagement in a controversial discussion, *discussion, debate, argument* (Diod. S. 15, 48, 4; Just., D. 68, 4; 80, 1) for **1 Ti 6:4** (w. λογομαχία); **Ac 15:2, 7.** ἐγένετο ζ. ἐκ τ. μαθητῶν Ἰωάννου μετὰ Ἰουδαίου περὶ καθαρισμοῦ *there arose a debate betw. the disciples of John and a Judean on purification* **J 3:25** (cp. Hdt. 5, 21 ζ. τῶν ἀνδρῶν τούτων μεγάλη ἐκ τ. Περσέων ἐγίνετο; Dionys. Hal. 8, 89, 4 ζ. πολλὴ ἐκ πάντων ἐγίνετο.—ζ. περί τινος as Athen. 3, 83a; Jos., Ant. 14, 195; ζ. betw. Christians and Jews Orig., C. Cels. 3, 1, 16).—DELG s.v. ζητέω. M-M. TW. Sv.

ζιζάνιον, ου, τό (ApcMos, ch. 16; Geopon.; Etym. Mag. p. 411, 47) prob. (Suda: ζιζάνιον: ἡ ἐν τῷ σίτῳ αἶρα) **troublesome weed in grainfields, *darnel, cheat*** (Geopon. 2, 43 τὸ ζιζάνιον, τὸ λεγόμενον αἶρα, φθείρει τὸν σῖτον. Concerning αἶρα [without ζ.] the same statement in Theophr., HP 8, 8, 3, CP 4, 4, 8); resembling wheat, in our lit. only pl. (Geopon. 10, 87, 1; 14, 1, 5) in Mt in the parable of the 'weeds (tares) among the wheat' (cp. also Psellus p. 268, 17 οἱ τὰ ζιζάνια ἐπισπείροντες) **Mt 13:25ff, 29f, 36, 38, 40** (s. RLiechtenhan, Kirchenblatt 99, '43, 146–49; 167–69). The word is supposedly Semitic: ILöw, Aramäische Pflanzennamen 1881, 133; HLewy, D. semit. Fremdwörter im Griech. 1895, 52. On the subj. s. LFonck, Streifzüge durch die bibl. Flora 1900, 129f; Sprenger, Pj 9, 1913, 89ff; HGuthe, ZDPV 41, 1918, 164f; ILöw, D. Flora d. Juden I 1928, 723–29; AMoldenke, Plants of the Bible, '52; Zohary, Plants 161.—DELG. M-M.

Ζμύρνα (OGI 458, 41 [c. 9 BC]; PRyl 153, 18 [II AD]; coins of Smyrna since the time of Trajan) v.l. for Σμύρνα, q.v.—M-M.

Ζοροβαβέλ, ὁ also -βάβελ; (זְרֻבָּבֶל) indecl. (in Joseph. Ζοροβάβηλος, ου [Ant. 11, 95]) ***Zerubbabel*** (Zech 4:6, 9f; Hg 1:1; 2:21, 23; 1 Ch 3:19; 1 Esdr 4:13; 5:5, 8 al.; 2 Esdr 2:2; 3:8; 17:7; Sir 49:11; ViZech 3 [p. 88, 7 Sch.]), descendant of David, Persian governor of Jerusalem after the return of the first exiles (ESellin, Serubbabel 1899), in the genealogy of Jesus **Mt 1:12f; Lk 3:27.**

ζόφος, ου, ὁ (Hom., trag. et al.; Plut., Lucian; Epict., fgm. p. 487, 2 Sch.; Sym., Philo; Ath., R. 19 p. 71, 30).

❶ darkness ranging from partial to total state, with suggestion of foreboding, *darkness, gloom* Hb 12:18.

❷ esp. **darkness of the nether regions, *gloom*** (Od. 20, 356), and these regions themselves (Il. 15, 191; 21, 56; Od. 11, 57) ὁ ζόφος τοῦ σκότους either *black darkness* or *the darkest nether regions* **2 Pt 2:17; Jd 13** (the juxtaposition of ζ. and σκότος as Ael. Aristid. 24, 44 K.=44 p. 838 D.; Lucian, Catapl. 2); σειραὶ ζόφου *chains of hell* **2 Pt 2:4.** ὑπὸ ζόφον *in* (lit. 'under') *darkness* (cp. Aeschyl., Pers. 839; Eur., Hipp. 1416.—Quint. Smyrn. 2, 619 ὑπὸ ζ. of the underworld) **Jd 6.** S. ταρταρόω.—DELG. M-M. TW.

ζυγός, οῦ, ὁ (Hom. Hymns, Cer. 217 and prose since Pla., Tim. 63b; Polyb., Epict.; PFay 121, 4 εἰς τὸν ζ.; PStras 32, 12; LXX [Thackeray p. 154]; En 103:11; PsSol 7:9 [acc. without art.]; 17:30; TestAbr A 12f [Stone p. 30, 6 al.]; Just., D. 53, 1; Ath., R. 58, 22 [? acc. without art.]) for Attic **τὸ ζυγόν** (Hom. et al.; pap; Gignac II 97; Jos., Ant. 12, 194; Just., D. 88, 8 [but ζυγούς GThGk A 13, 1: Ea 152]).

❶ a frame used to control working animals or, in the case of humans, to expedite the bearing of burdens, *yoke* in our lit. only fig. of any burden: ζ. δουλείας *yoke of slavery* (Soph., Aj. 944; cp. Hdt. 7, 8, γ3; Pla., Leg. 6, 770e; Demosth. 18, 289; Gen 27:40) **Gal 5:1.** ὑπὸ ζυγὸν δοῦλοι *slaves under the yoke* (i.e. under the y. of sl.) **1 Ti 6:1.** ζυγὸς ἀνάγκης *yoke of necessity* (Eur., Or. 1330) B 2:6. Of the teaching of Jesus **Mt 11:29f** (cp. Sir 51:26, also 6:24–28; THaering, Mt 11:28–30: ASchlatter Festschr. 1922, 3–15; TArvedson, D. Mysterium Christi '37, 174–200; HBetz, JBL 86, '67, 10–24); D 6:2. ὑπὸ τὸν ζυγὸν τῆς χάριτος ἔρχεσθαι *come under the yoke of grace* 1 Cl 16:17 (opp. ViDa 7 [p. 77, 12 Sch.] ὑπὸ ζ. γίνονται τοῦ Βελίαρ). ἐπιθεῖναι ζυγὸν ἐπὶ τ. τράχηλόν τινος *put a yoke on the neck of someone* **Ac 15:10** (sim. expr. have become formal since Hes., Op. 815; Orph. Hymns 59, 5; Zosimus, Hist. 2, 37, 8; SibOr 3, 448). From this mng. it is a short step to application of such a balancing structure to

❷ an instrument for determining weight, *scale.* The context of **Rv 6:5** requires this mng., even though the gender of ζ. cannot be definitely determined. In older Gk. the neuter and apparently preferred form τὸ ζυγόν refers to the 'lever of a balance' (Aeschyl., Suppl. 822), then 'balance, pair of scales' (Pla. et al.; s. LXX in Thackeray, loc. cit.; Michel 1222, 4 [II BC]; but masc. TestAbr A).—B. 726. DELG s.v. ζεύγνυμι III. Frisk s.v. ζυγόν. M-M. TW.

ζύμη, ης, ἡ ('yeast, leaven' Aristot., Gen. An. 3, 4, 755a, 18ff; Plut., Mor. 289f; PTebt 375, 27; LXX; Philo, Spec. Leg. 1, 291; 2, 182; Jos., Ant. 3, 252; Just., D. 14, 3; cp. 14, 2 [1 Cor 5:8?])

❶ fermented dough, *leaven* (the rendering 'yeast' [as NRSV gener., REB Mt 13:33, Lk 13:21] popularly suggests a product foreign to ancient baking practice), lit. **Mt 13:33; Lk 13:21.** More fully ζ. τῶν ἄρτων **Mt 16:12.** μικρὰ ζύμη ὅλον τὸ φύραμα ζυμοῖ *a little leaven ferments the whole lump of dough* **1 Cor 5:6** (Cyranides p. 64, 22 μετὰ ζύμης μικρᾶς)=**Gal 5:9,** shown by its repeated use to be a proverbial saying, serves to picture the influence of apparently insignificant factors in the moral and relig. sphere (on neg. aspect s. HBetz, Gal., Hermeneia 266 n. 125).

❷ that which negatively permeates attitude or behavior, *leaven* fig. ext. of 1: ζ. is used of the attitudes of Pharisees and of Herod **Mk 8:15.** Of the pretense of Pharisees **Lk 12:1.** Of the teaching of Pharisees and Sadducees **Mt 16:6, 11.** In IMg 10:2 the *leaven that has grown old and sour* means a life regulated by Judean cultic instruction. It is contrasted w. Jesus Christ, the νέα ζ., ibid. Employing the language of the Passover rules (Ex 12:15, 19; 13:7; Dt 16:3f), Paul admonishes ἐκκαθάρατε τ. παλαιὰν ζ. **1 Cor 5:7** and explains that *the old leaven* is ζ. κακίας κ. πονηρίας vs. **8** (on problems connected w. the imagery s. Straub 80f).—RAC I 1056–62.—DELG. M-M. EDNT. TW.

ζυμόω (Hippocr. et al.; Plut., Mor. 659b; LXX) ***to ferment, leaven* 1 Cor 5:6; Gal 5:9.** Pass. (Philo, Vi. Cont. 81) **Mt 13:33; Lk 13:21.**—DELG s.v. ζύμη. TW.

ζῶ s. [ζάω] ζῶ.

ζωγρέω (ζωός, ἀγρέω) fut. 2 pl. ζωγρήσετε Dt 20:16; aor. ἐζώγρησα LXX; pf. pass. ptc. ἐζωγρημένος (Hom. et al.; Kaibel 841, 7; LXX) ***capture alive*** (Suda: ζωγρεῖ· ζῶντας λαμβάνει. So as early as Hom.; also Hdt. 1, 86, 1; X., An. 4, 7, 22; Polyb. 3, 84, 10; Num 31:18; 2 Ch 25:12; Philo, Virt. 43; Jos., Bell. 2, 448, Ant. 9, 194; 20, 210; Tat. 18, 3) fig. ἀνθρώπους ἔσῃ ζωγρῶν *you will catch people* i.e., win them for God's kgdm. **Lk 5:10** (on the metaphor of fishing cp. Aristaen., Ep. 2, 23 ἀντὶ ἰχθύων παρθένους ζ.). ἐζωγρημένοι ὑπ᾽ αὐτοῦ εἰς τὸ ἐκείνου θέλημα *held captive by him* (the devil) *to perform* *his* (the devil's; s. B-D-F §291, 6; Rob. 707; on the thought cp. Vi. Aesopi W 106 P. εἱμαρμένη ἐζώγρησεν *fate caught* [me] to destroy [Aesop]) *will* **2 Ti 2:26** (differently LBunn, ET 41, 1930, 235–37).—DELG s.v. ζωάγρια. M-M. Spicq.

ζωή, ῆς, ἡ (Hom.+; in Hom. 'living'='substance, property', without which there would not be life; after Hom. 'life, existence' opp. death, then 'way of life' Hdt. 4, 112)

❶ **life in the physical sense,** *life* ἐν σαρκὶ ζ. Orig., C. Cels. 6, 59, 8)—ⓐ opp. θάνατος (Pind. et al.; Lucian, Tox. 38; Sir 37:18; Pr 18:21; Philo; Just., A I, 57, 3; Mel., P. 49, 355) **Ro 8:38; 1 Cor 3:22; Phil 1:20.** ἐν τῇ ζωῇ σου *during your life* **Lk 16:25** (s. Sir 30:5); cp. **12:15; Ac 8:33** (Is 53:8); **Js 4:14;** 1 Cl 16:8 (Is 53:8); 17:4 (cp. Job 14:5); 20:10; Hm 3:3. πᾶς χρόνος τῆς ζωῆς ἡμῶν B 4:9 (cp. PsSol 17:2; JosAs 13:12). πάσας τὰς ἡμέρας τῆς ζωῆς αὐτῶν Hs 9, 29, 2; cp. GJs 4:1; τὰς λοιπὰς τῆς ζωῆς ἡμέρας Hv 4, 2, 5; cp. v 5, 2; m 12, 2; s 6, 3, 6. τὴν ἐσχάτην ἡμέραν τῆς ζωῆς αὐτοῦ Hv 3, 12, 2. ἐν τῇ ζ. ταύτῃ *in this life* **1 Cor 15:19;** also ζ. ἡ νῦν (opp. ἡ μέλλουσα) **1 Ti 4:8** (Tat. 14, 2). τέλος ζωῆς *end of life* **Hb 7:3** (TestAbr A 1 p. 78, 5 [Stone p. 4]). ζωὴ κ. πνοή *life and breath* **Ac 17:25** (cp. Gen 2:7; 7:22). πνεῦμα ζωῆς *breath of life* **Rv 11:11** (cp. Gen 6:17; 7:15; TestAbr A 18 p. 100, 31 [Stone p. 48]). ψυχὴ ζωῆς *living thing* **16:3** (cp. Gen 1:30; Just., D. 6, 1 ἡ ψυχὴ ἤτοι ζωή ἐστιν ἢ ζωὴν ἔχει). πρὸς ζωῆς *necessary for life* 1 Cl 20:10. Of the indestructible life of those clothed in the heavenly body **2 Cor 5:4.** The life of the risen Christ also has this character **Ro 5:10; 2 Cor 4:10f;** ζ. ἀκατάλυτος **Hb 7:16.** ὁδοὶ ζωῆς **Ac 2:28** (Ps 15:11). Christ is ἐν θανάτῳ ζ. ἀληθινή IEph 7:2.

ⓑ *means of sustenance, livelihood* (Hdt. et al.; Sir 4:1; 29:21) Hs 9, 26, 2.

ⓒ *the course or mode of one's life* (cp. βίος 1) Hm 8, 4 and 9; 11, 7 and 16; s 9, 16, 2 al. In some of these pass. a transition to the moral aspect is apparent.

❷ **transcendent life,** ***life***—ⓐ God and Christ—α. God as ζωή Dg 9:6b; as ζωὴ αἰώνιος **1J 5:20.** Of the cross IEph 18:1. It is true of God that ἔχει ζωὴν ἐν ἑαυτῷ **J 5:26a.** God's commandment is eternal life **12:50** (cp. Philo, Fug. 198 God is the πρεσβυτάτη πηγὴ ζωῆς; Herm. Wr. 11, 13; 14; 12, 15 God the πλήρωμα τ. ζωῆς; PGM 3, 602 [s. Rtzst., Mysterienrel.[3] 286, ln. 11]; the deity called Νοῦς as ζωή and φῶς Herm. Wr. 1:9, 12, 17, 21, 32; 13:9, 18, 19. Cp. also Ps 35:10; 55:14; SibOr fgm. 3, 34; JosAs 8:10f al.).

β. of Christ, who received life fr. God **J 5:26b** (ἡ ζωὴ τῆς πίστεως ParJer 9:14). ἐν αὐτῷ ζ. ἦν **1:4a;** cp. **1J 5:11b.** He is the ἀρχηγὸς τ. ζωῆς **Ac 3:15,** the λόγος τ. ζωῆς **1J 1:1;** cp. vs. **2,** the ἄρτος τ. ζωῆς **J 6:35, 48;** cp. vs. **33** (EJanot, Le pain de vie: Gregorianum 11, 1930, 161–70), also simply ζωή **11:25; 14:6** or ἡ ζ. ὑμῶν **Col 3:4;** cp. B 2, 10; IMg 9:1. Since the life in him was τὸ φῶς τ. ἀνθρώπων **J 1:4b,** people through following him obtain τὸ φῶς τ. ζωῆς **8:12** (on the combination of light and life cp. 1QS 3, 7 and the Orph. Hymns to Helios no. 8, 18 Qu. ζωῆς φῶς, as well as Christian ins of Rome [Ramsay, Luke the Physician 1908 p. 375, 238 AD], where a father calls his dead son γλυκύτερον φωτὸς καὶ ζωῆς; s. also α above).—SBartina, La vida como historia en J 1:1–18, Biblica 49, '68, 91–96.

ⓑ The discussion now turns naturally to the life of the believers, which proceeds fr. God and Christ.

α. without (clear) eschatol. implications, of the life of grace and holiness ἐν καινότητι ζωῆς περιπατεῖν *walk in* (i.e. *live*) *a new life* **Ro 6:4;** cp. IEph 19:3. ἀπηλλοτριωμένοι τ. ζωῆς τ. θεοῦ *estranged fr. the life of God* **Eph 4:18** (cp. Philo, Post. Cai. 69 τῆς θεοῦ ζωῆς ἀπεσχοινίσθαι). ἡ ζωὴ τ. ἀνθρώπων *the* (true) *life of persons* (in God) Hm 2:1.—Of the life of salvation and of glory. It is ζ. κυρίου B 1:4 (cp. PGM 12, 255 κύριε τ. ζωῆς; 13, 783) or ζ. ἐν Χρ. Ἰησοῦ **2 Ti 1:1;** cp. ζωὴν ὑμῖν ὁ κύριος χαρίζεται Hs 9, 28, 6; effected by his words or by the proclamation of the gospel: ῥήματα ζ. αἰωνίου **J 6:68;** cp. vs. **63.** τὰ ῥήματα τῆς ζ. ταύτης **Ac 5:20.** λόγος ζωῆς *word of life* **Phil 2:16;** cp. **2 Ti 1:10; 2 Cor 4:12.** Hence the apostle, proclaiming the gospel, can term himself the bearer of the 'fragrance of Christ', leading those appointed to this bliss, the rescued ἐκ ζωῆς εἰς ζωήν *from life to life* (i.e., as it seems, ever more deeply into the divine life) **2 Cor 2:16.**—The Spirit stands w. Christ as the power of life πνεῦμα τῆς ζωῆς ἐν Χρ. Ἰησοῦ *the spirit of life in Chr. J.* **Ro 8:2;** cp. vss. **6, 10** and **J 6:63.**—Like the words of Christ, the divine ἐντολή is also to bring life **Ro 7:10;** Hm 7:5; s 8, 7, 6. This ζ. is regarded as God's gift ζ. ἐν ἀθανασίᾳ 1 Cl 35:2. W. ἀφθαρσία **2 Ti 1:10;** 2 Cl 14:5; IPol 2:3. W. γνῶσις D 9:3; Dg 12:3–7. W. εὐσέβεια **2 Pt 1:3.** W. εἰρήνη **Ro 8:6.** W. σωτηρία 2 Cl 19:1. ἀγάπην ἥτις ἐστὶν ἀρχὴ ζωῆς καὶ τέλος IEph 14:1. Christians, who truly belong to the ἐκκλησία τῆς ζωῆς 2 Cl 14:1, are heirs of life, the gift of grace **1 Pt 3:7.** This life, as long as they are in the body, κέκρυπται σὺν τ. Χριστῷ ἐν τῷ θεῷ *is hidden with Christ in God* **Col 3:3.** Those who forfeit their ζ. (=their real life in contrast to their physical existence as ψυχή) are excluded fr. the life of glory Hv 1, 1, 9; s 6, 2, 3; 8, 6, 4; 6; 8, 8, 2f; 5; 9, 21, 4.—Cp. also **Ac 11:18** (s. 1QS 3, 1); **13:46, 48.** ἡ ὁδὸς τῆς ζ. D 1:2; 4:14. τὰς τρίβους τῆς ζ. Hs 5, 6, 3. Esp. in Johannine usage the term ζ. is copiously employed, as a rule to designate the result of faith in Christ; in most cases it is stated expressly that the follower of Jesus possesses life even in this world: ἔχειν ζωήν (Theophr. in a scholion on Pla. 631c εἰ ζωὴν εἶχεν ὁ πλοῦτος='had life, were alive') **J 3:15f, 36a; 5:24a, 40; 6:40, 47, 51, 53f; 10:10; 20:31; 1J 3:15; 5:12ab, 13.** διδόναι ζωήν (cp. Sb 8202, 3 [105 BC]) **J 10:28; 17:2; 1J 5:11.**—Cp. **5:16.** ὁρᾶν ζωήν **J 3:36b.** μεταβεβηκέναι ἐκ τ. θανάτου εἰς τ. ζωήν *to have passed fr. death into life* **J 5:24; 1J 3:14.** Hence in the eschatol. pass. **J 5:29** ἀνάστασις ζωῆς means not a resurrection to enter life (cp. 2 Macc 7:14 and MPol 14:2, where ἀνάστασις ζωῆς αἰ., it seems, is *res. to everlasting life*), but a resurrection which corresponds to the Christian's possession of life here and now, a *resurrection proceeding from life.* J is fond of calling this Life ζ. αἰώνιος, as in many pass. just cited (s. αἰώνιος 3) **J 3:15f, 36; 4:14, 36; 5:24, 39; 6:27, 40, 47, 54, 68; 10:28; 12:25, 50; 17:2f; 1J 1:2; 2:25; 3:15; 5:11, 13, 20.** But the use of this expr. in our lit. is by no means limited to J and 1J; it is also found in Mt, Mk, Lk, Ac, Ro, Gal, 1 Ti, Tit, Jd, 2 Cl, Ign, MPol, Hermas, Didache (Just., Mel., Ath.; Orig., C. Cels. 2, 77, 31 [w. ἀνάστασις]; cp. ἀΐδιος ζ. Tat. 14, 2) w. unmistakable eschatol. connotation.

β. ζ. (and ζ. αἰώνιος; cp. 1QS 4:7 and s. **J 3:15** al.; opp. ἀπώλεια TestAbr B 8 p. 113, 2 [Stone p. 74]) is used of life in the blessed period of final consummation, in the foll. pass.: ἐν τῷ αἰῶνι τῷ ἐρχομένῳ ζ. αἰ. *in the coming age eternal life* **Mk 10:30; Lk 18:30;** cp. **Mt 19:29** (Ar. 15, 3 ζ. τοῦ μέλλοντος αἰῶνος). τί ποιήσω ἵνα ζ. αἰ. κληρονομήσω; **Mk 10:17;** cp. **Lk 18:18; 10:25; Mt 19:16f** (PsSol 14:10). As a result of the Last Judgment ἀπελεύσονται οἱ δίκαιοι εἰς ζ. αἰ. **Mt 25:46** (cp. PsSol 13:11); s. also **Ro 2:7** (cp. 1QS 4:6–8).—Cp. also **Mt 7:14; 18:8f; Mk 9:43, 45; Ro 5:17f, 21; 6:22f;** ζ. ἐκ νεκρῶν *life for those who have come out of the state of death* **11:15.—Gal 6:8; 1 Ti 1:16; 6:12, 19; 1 Pt 3:10** (Ps 33:13); **Jd 21;** 2 Cl 8:4, 6; Dg 9:1, 6a. For **2 Cor 5:4** s. 1a. Of martyrs τὴν αἰώνιον ζ. ἐξαγοραζόμενοι *purchasing eternal life for themselves* MPol 2:3 (Mosquensis, other Gk. codd. κόλασιν). W. ἀνάπαυσις τ.

μελλούσης βασιλείας 2 Cl 5:5. This life is called ἡ ὄντως ζ. *the real, true life* (the redundancy may derive from awareness of a distinction sometimes made in the Gr-Rom. world between real living ζωή and biological existence βίος; s., e.g., IPriene 105, 10=OGI 458, 10; cp. Cass. Dio 69, 19) **1 Ti 6:19;** ζωῆς ἀληθοῦς Dg 12:4; ἡ ἐπουράνιος ζ. 2 Cl 20:5; ἀΐδιος ζ. IEph 19:3 (s. ἀΐδιος). Hope is directed toward it, ζωῆς ἐλπίς B 1:6; cp. **Tit 1:2; 3:7;** Hs 9, 26, 2.—The references to future glory include the foll. expressions: βίβλος or βιβλίον (τῆς) ζωῆς (s. βίβλος 2) **Phil 4:3; Rv 3:5; 13:8; 17:8; 20:12, 15; 21:27;** Hv 1, 3, 2. τὸ ξύλον (τῆς) ζωῆς *the tree of life* (4 Macc 18:16; cp. Pr 3:18; Gen 2:9; PsSol 14:3; ParJer 9:16 [δένδρον]; ApcEsdr 2:11; ApcMos 19 al.; Philo.—ξύλον 3) **Rv 2:7; 22:2, 14, 19;** Dg 12:3f. στέφανος τ. ζωῆς (s. Bousset, Rel.[3] 277f; MDibelius on **Js 1:12;** FCumont, Études syriennes 1917, 63–69; s. στέφανος) **Js 1:12; Rv 2:10.** ὕδωρ (τῆς) ζωῆς (Just., D. 19, 2 βάπτισμα; cp. ὕδωρ 2) **21:6; 22:1, 17.** πηγὴ ζωῆς B 11:2 (cp. Jer 2:13; Ps 35:10; OdeSol 11:6). ζωῆς πηγαὶ ὑδάτων *springs of living water* **Rv 7:17.** For ἄρτος τῆς ζωῆς s. ἄρτος 2 end.—FBurkitt, ZNW 12, 1911, 228–30; RCharles, A Critical Hist. of the Doctrine of a Fut. Life in Israel, in Judaism and in Christianity[2] 1913; FLindblom, D. ewige Leben 1914; Bousset, Rel.[3] 269–95; JFrey, Biblica 13, '32, 129–68.—EvDobschütz, D. Gewissheit des ew. Leb. nach d. NT: 'Dienet einander' 29, 1920/21, 1–8; 43–52; 65–71; 97–101; JUbbink, Het eeuwige leven bij Pls 1917; ESommerlath, D. Ursprung d. neuen Lebens nach Pls[2] 1926; JMüller, D. Lebensbegr. d. Hl. Pls '40; NvArseniew, D. neue Leben nach dem Eph: Internat. Kirchl. Ztschr. 20, 1930, 230–36; EvSchrenk, D. joh. Anschauung vom 'Leben' 1898; JFrey, 'Vie' dans l'Év. de St. Jean: Biblica 1, 1920, 37–58; 211–39; RBultmann, D. Eschatol. d. Joh Ev.: Zwischen d. Zeiten 6, 1928, 1ff; HPribnow, D. joh. Anschauung v. 'Leben' '34; DLyons, The Concept of Eternal Life in J '38; JKoole, Diorama Johanneum. Ζωή: GereformTT 43, '42, 276–84; FMussner, ΖΩΗ (Joh. lit.), diss. Munich '52; DHill, Gk. Words and Hebrew Mngs. '67, 163–201.—B. 285. S. βίος and Schmidt, Syn. IV 40–53. DELG s.v. ζώω 1. EDNT. M-M. TW. Sv.

ζώνη, ης, ἡ (Hom. et al.; Kaibel 482, 3; pap, LXX, EpArist, Philo, Joseph., Test12Patr, JosAs; Mel., fgm. 8b 24 'zone', loanw. in rabb.) ***belt, girdle,*** in our lit. only of a man's belt or girdle, unless the ref. is to heavenly beings (Rv). Of the Baptist ζ. δερματίνη (4 Km 1:8= Jos., Ant. 9, 22) **Mt 3:4; Mk 1:6;** GEb 13, 79 (s. DBuzy, Pagne ou ceinture?: RSR 23, '33, 589–98 and on Ἰωάννης 1). Of Paul **Ac 21:11ab.** Of the Human One (Son of Man) περιεζωσμένος πρὸς τ. μαστοῖς ζ. χρυσᾶν **Rv 1:13;** sim. of angels περιεζωσμένοι περὶ τὰ στήθη ζ. χρυσᾶς **15:6** (cp. 4 Km 3:21 περιεζωσμένοι ζ.—The golden belt or girdle as Ps.-Callisth. 2, 21, 17). λύειν τὴν ζ. *loose,* i.e. *remove the belt* (Hyperid., fgm. 67) MPol 13:2. This belt is also used to hold money (Plut., Mor., 665b ἀνθρώπου … ζώνην δὲ χαλκοῦς ἔχουσαν ὑπεζωσμένου; PRyl 127, 32 [29 AD] ζ. ἐν ᾗ κέρματος (δραχμαὶ) δ′; 141, 22) **Mt 10:9; Mk 6:8.**—B. 434. DELG s.v. ζώννυμι. M-M. TW.

ζώννυμι by-form **ζωννύω** impf. 2 sg. ἐζώννυες (B-D-F §92; Mlt-H. 202f); fut. ζώσω; 1 aor. ἔζωσα; 1 aor. mid. impv. ζῶσαι; pf. ptc. ἐζωσμένος LXX (Hom. et al.; ins, LXX; TestJob 47:5; JosAs) ***gird*** τινά *someone* **J 21:18ab.** Mid. *gird oneself* (Jos., Bell. 2, 129) **Ac 12:8.**—DELG. TW.

ζωογονέω (N. text ζῳογ-, but correct is ζωογ- fr. the adj ζωός 'living' + γενέσθαι, cp. ζωοποιέω, s. B-D-F §26; difft. ζῷον, s. DELG s.v. ζώω) fut. ζωογονήσω; 1 aor. ἐζωογόνησα LXX; plpf. 2 pl. ἐζωοκονήκειτε Judg 8:19 v.l. (Aristot., Theophr. et al.; Herm. Wr. 9, 6; LXX; JosAs 12:2 cod. A [p. 12, 22 Bat.]; Philo; Mel., P. 101, 776 v.l. [for ἐζωοποίησα, s. Ch.]).

❶ **to cause to be alive, *give life to, make alive*** (Theophr., CP 4, 15, 4; Athen. 7, 298c; 1 Km 2:6) τὶ *someth.* (s. Theophr. and Athen., loc. cit.) τὰ πάντα **1 Ti 6:13.**

❷ **to cause to remain alive, *keep/preserve alive*** (Diod. S. 1, 23, 4; Ex 1:17f; Judg 8:19; 1 Km 27:9, 11; 3 Km 21:31; Philopon. in Aristot., An. p. 332, 9 Hayduck; Theophanes Conf. 337, 31; 379, 21 de Boor; Georg. Mon. 166, 9 de B.) τὴν ψυχήν **Lk 17:33.** Pass. **Ac 7:19.**—M-M. TW. Spicq.

ζῷον, ου, τό (also ζῶον; for sp. B-D-F §26, Mlt-H. §36, L-S-J-M s.v.; cp. Rob. 194f; Pre-Socr., Hdt.+).

❶ **a living creature, wild or domesticated, but not including plants, *animal*** in our lit. exclusive of human beings (Diod. S. 3, 31, 2; 5, 45, 1; Epict. 3, 1, 1; Jos., Ant. 3, 228; apolog. [Tat. 15, 2 Περὶ ζῴων] as book title) **Hb 13:11;** 1 Cl 20:4, 10; 33:3; B 10:7f; Ox 840, 4 (s. JJeremias, ConNeot 11, '48, 98); Hm 12, 4, 1 v.l.; GJs 3:2 (tame animals, s. deStrycker ad loc. [opp. τὸ … λογικὸν ζῷον, ὁ ἄνθρωπος Just., D. 93, 3]). ἄλογα ζῷα (s. ἄλογος 1) **2 Pt 2:12; Jd 10.**

❷ **a creature that transcends normal descriptive categories and is freq. composite, *living thing/being*** (cp. Diod. S. 4, 47, 3 of a dragon; OGI 90, 31 τῷ τε Ἄπει καὶ τῷ Μνεύει … καὶ τοῖς ἄλλοις ἱεροῖς ζῴοις τοῖς ἐν Αἰγύπτῳ; PTebt 5, 78 [118 BC]; 57, 12; POxy 1188, 4; Herm. Wr. 11, 7; Ath. 18, 3; God no σύνθετον ζῷον 'composite animal' Just., D. 114, 3; Ath. 6, 3; of an embryo Ath. 35, 2) of the miraculous bird, the phoenix 1 Cl 25:3. Of the four peculiar beings at God's throne, whose description **Rv 4:6–9** reminds one of the ζῷα in Ezk 1:5ff, the cherubim. S. also **Rv 5:6, 8, 11, 14; 6:1, 3, 5–7; 7:11; 14:3; 15:7; 19:4.**

❸ One isolated pass. in our lit. has ζῶα in the sense ***living creatures,*** including both humans and animals (Cornutus 16 p. 20, 20; Ael. Aristid. 45, 32 K.; Jos., Ant. 1, 41; Just., D. 4, 2; 107, 2) 1 Cl 9:4.—SLongsdale, Attitudes towards Animals in Ancient Greece: Greece and Rome, 2d ser. 26, '79, 146–59 (lit.).—B. 137. DELG s.v. ζώω. M-M. TW.

ζωοποιέω (ζωός + ποιέω; N. reads w. iota subscr., but ζωοπ- is correct; s. B-D-F §26 and s. on ζῷον beg.) fut. ζωοποιήσω; 1 aor. ἐζωοποίησα (LXX; Mel., P, 101, 776), inf. ζωοποιῆσαι, pass. ἐζωοποιήθην Hm 4, 3, 7, ptc. ζωοποιηθείς (AcPlCor 2:8) (Aristot. and Theophr. et al.; Herm. Wr.; LXX; TestGad 4:6; JosAs 8:2, 10; EpArist 16; Mel.; Ath., R. 51, 22; ψυχὴ ζ. καὶ κινεῖ τὸ σῶμα Orig., C. Cels. 6, 48, 17). In other lit. (e.g., Aristot., Theophr.) ζ.=ζωογονέω in the sense of 'propagate living creatures'. In LXX and NT

❶ **to cause to live, *make alive, give life to,*** esp. in a transcendent sense—ⓐ subj. God, Christ, and Spirit; of God (ὁ θεραπεύων καὶ ζ. Theoph. Ant. 1, 7 [p. 72, 17]), who ζ. τὰ πάντα *gives life to all things* **1 Ti 6:13 v.l.** (for ζῳογονοῦντος; cp. 2 Esdr 19:6). Esp. of dead persons who are called to life τοὺς νεκρούς (TestGad 4:6) *bring the dead to life* **J 5:21a** (cp. ins in MSchwabe, Israel Exploration Journ. 4, '54, 249–61); cp. **21b; Ro 4:17.** τὰ θνητὰ σώματα ὑμῶν **8:11.** θανατοῦνται καὶ ζωοποιοῦνται Dg 5:12 (on the contrast betw. the two verbs cp. 4 Km 5:7). Christ θανατωθεὶς μὲν σαρκὶ ζωοποιηθεὶς δὲ πνεύματι **1 Pt 3:18.** Through his suffering (='death'; s. πάσχω 3aα) Christ gives life to the believers B 12:5 (for 7:2 s. b below). ἐν τ. Χριστῷ πάντες ζωοποιηθήσονται **1 Cor 15:22.**

The Spirit is called life-giving **J 6:63;** (contrasted w. the letter) **2 Cor 3:6.** So Christ, ὁ ἔσχατος Ἀδάμ, ἐγένετο εἰς πνεῦμα ζῳοποιοῦν **1 Cor 15:45.** ὑπὸ τοῦ πατρός . . . ἐζητήθη ἵνα ζωοποιηθῇ διὰ τῇ υἱοθεσίας (humanity) *was sought* (by its Father) *so that it might be restored to life through adoption* AcPlCor 2:7f.

ⓑ of things, circumstances, words. The law cannot do so **Gal 3:21.** τῷ λόγῳ ζωοποιούμενοι ζήσομεν *through the word we shall be kept alive and shall (really) live* B 6:17b; through the Shepherd's word ἐζωοποιήθην *I feel new life* Hm 4, 3, 7. ἵνα ἡ πληγὴ αὐτοῦ ζωοποιήσῃ ἡμᾶς *so that his wound might give life to us* B 7:2. αὐτὸς ὢν νεκρὸς δύναται ζωοποιῆσαι *although it* (the serpent Num 21:8f) *is dead it can bestow life* in typification of Christ 12:7. Baptism makes alive Hs 9, 16, 2; cp. 9, 16, 7. κολαζόμενοι χαίρουσιν ὡς ζωοποιούμενοι *when they are punished they rejoice in awareness of being awakened to life* Dg 5:16 (s. ὡς 3aβ).—Cp. Paul's illustration of sprouting seed ὃ σπείρεις οὐ ζῳοποιεῖται ἐὰν μὴ ἀποθάνῃ **1 Cor 15:36** (Geopon. 9, 11, 7; Herm. Wr. 9, 6).

❷ **to keep alive,** ***sustain life*** of nourishing milk for a child γάλακτι ζωοποιεῖται *it is kept alive with milk* B 6:17a (illustrative of the divine word, s. 1b).—DELG s.v. ζώω. M-M. TW. Sv.

Ζώσιμος, ου, ὁ (ins, pap [Preisigke, Namenbuch]), ***Zosimus,*** a martyr Pol 9:1 (with Rufus as here CIG 192; 244; 1969; 3664).

Ζωτίων, ωνος, ὁ (usu. [ins, pap] spelled Σωτίων elsewh.) ***Zotion,*** an eccl. assistant in Magnesia IMgMai 2.

H

η′ numerical sign = ***8*** (ὀκτώ; Jos., C. Ap. 1, 126) B 9:8; or ***8th*** (ὀγδόη [ἐπιστολή]) Hm 8; [s 8] in superscriptions (Apollon. Paradox. 41 Θεόφραστος ἐν τῷ η′ περὶ φυτῶν).

ἤ particle (Hom.+).—❶ **marker of an alternative,** ***or,*** disjunctive particle (B-D-F §446; Rob. 1188f)—ⓐ separating—**α.** opposites, which are mutually exclusive λευκὴν ἢ μέλαιναν **Mt 5:36.** ἰδοὺ ἐκεῖ [ἤ] ἰδοὺ ὧδε **Lk 17:23.** ψυχρὸς ἢ ζεστός **Rv 3:15.** ἐξ οὐρανοῦ ἢ ἐξ ἀνθρώπων *from God or fr. humans* **Mt 21:25.** δοῦναι ἢ οὔ *to give or not* (to give) **22:17;** cp. **Mk 12:14.** ἀγαθὸν ποιῆσαι ἢ κακοποιῆσαι **3:4.** Cp. **Lk 2:24; Ro 14:4; 1 Cor 7:11** (cp. Ath. 2:4 ἀγαθὸς ἢ πονηρός).

β. related and similar terms, where one can take the place of the other or one supplements the other τὸν νόμον ἢ τοὺς προφήτας **Mt 5:17** (JosAs 2:11 ἀνὴρ . . . ἢ παιδίον ἄρρεν; Just., D. 93, 4 φιλίαν ἢ ἀγάπην; schol. on Soph., Oed. Col. 380 Papag. ἢ ἀντὶ τοῦ καὶ ἐστί) πόλιν ἢ κώμην **10:11.** ἔξω τ. οἰκίας ἢ τ. πόλεως ἐκείνης vs. **14.** πατέρα ἢ μητέρα vs. **37.** τέλη ἢ κῆνσον **17:25.** οὐ μὴ ἀποκριθῆτέ μοι ἢ ἀπολύσητε **Lk 22:68 v.l.** πρόσκομμα ἢ σκάνδαλον **Ro 14:13;** cp. **vs. 21 v.l.** εἰς τίνα ἢ ποῖον καιρόν **1 Pt 1:11.** νοῆσαι ἢ συνιέναι B 10:12. Cp. **Mk 4:17; 10:40; Lk 14:12; J 2:6; Ac 4:34; 1 Cor 13:1;** AcPlCor 2:26. In enumerations as many as six occurrences of ἤ are found: **Mk 10:29; Ro 8:35;** cp. **Mt 25:44; Lk 18:29; 1 Cor 5:11; 1 Pt 4:15** (Just., A II, 1, 2).—ἤτε . . . ἤτε (Hom. et al.; PRossGeorg III, 2, 4 [III AD]) ἤτε ἄρσενα ἤτε θήλειαν *whether it is a boy or a girl* GJs 4:1 pap (εἴτε . . . εἴτε codd.).—ἢ καί *or (even, also)* (PLond III, 962, 5 p. 210 [254/61 AD]; EpJer 58) ἢ καὶ ὡς οὗτος ὁ τελώνης **Lk 18:11;** cp. **11:12; 12:41; Ro 2:15; 4:9; 14:10; 1 Cor 16:6; 2 Cor 1:13b.**—ἤ for καί **Mk 3:33 v.l.; Col 2:16 v.l.**

ⓑ ἢ . . . ἢ *either . . . or* **Mt 6:24; 12:33; Lk 16:13;** AcPlCor 1:7f. ἢ . . . ἢ . . . ἢ *either . . . or . . . or* (Philod., οἰκ. col. 22, 41 Jensen; Just., A I, 28, 4 al; Mel., P. 36, 246f) **1 Cor 14:6** (ἤ four times as Libanius, Or. 28 p. 48, 15 F and Or. 31 p. 130, 7; Just., D. 85, 3). **Eph 5:4 v.l.** ἤτοι. . . ἢ (Hdt., Thu. et al. [s. Kühner-G. II 298]; PTebt 5, 59; PRyl 154, 25; Wsd 11:18; TestSol 10:28 C [without ἤ]; Philo, Op. M. 37; Jos., Ant. 18, 115; Just., D. 6, 1; 100, 3; Ath. 8, 1 and R. 52, 26) *either . . . or* **Ro 6:16.**

ⓒ In neg. statements ἤ comes to mean *nor, or,* when it introduces the second, third, etc., item ἰῶτα ἓν ἢ μία κεραία οὐ μὴ παρέλθῃ **Mt 5:18.** πῶς ἢ τί *how or what* **10:19;** cp. **Mk 7:12; J 8:14; Ac 1:7.** οὐκ ἐδόξασαν ἢ ηὐχαρίστησαν **Ro 1:21.** διαθήκην οὐδεὶς ἀθετεῖ ἢ ἐπιδιατάσσεται **Gal 3:15.** ἵνα μή τις δύνηται ἀγοράσαι ἢ πωλῆσαι *so that no one can either buy or sell* **Rv 13:17.**—**Phil 3:12.**—Likew. in neg. rhetorical questions; here present-day English idiom, making the whole sentence neg., requires the transl. *or* **Mt 7:16;** cp. **Mk 4:21; 1 Cor 1:13; Js 3:12.**

ⓓ Gener., ἤ oft. occurs in interrog. sentences—**α.** to introduce and to add rhetorical questions (Just., D 2, 4 al.; Ath. 8:3 al.) ἢ δοκεῖς ὅτι; *or do you suppose that?* **Mt 26:53.** ἢ Ἰουδαίων ὁ θεὸς μόνον; *or is God the God of the Judeans alone?* **Ro 3:29.** ἢ ἀγνοεῖτε; *or do you not know?* **6:3; 7:1;** also ἢ οὐκ οἴδατε; **11:2; 1 Cor 6:9, 16, 19;** cp. **10:22; 2 Cor 11:7.**

β. to introduce a question which is parallel to a preceding one or supplements it **Mt 7:10;** οὐκ ἀνέγνωτε . . .; ἢ οὐκ ἀνέγνωτε . . .; *have you not read . . . ? Or have you not read . . . ?* **Mt 12:(3), 5;** cp. **Lk 13:4; Ro 2:4; 1 Cor 9:6** (cp. Just., D. 27, 5 al.; Mel., P. 74, 541 ἢ οὐ γέγραπταί σοι . . .;)—**Mt 20:15; 1 Cor 11:22; 2 Cor 3:1.**

γ. in the second member of direct or indir. double questions: πότερον . . . ἤ (Aeschyl., Hdt. et al.) *whether, if . . . or* **J 7:17;** B 19:5; D 4:4; Hs 9, 28, 4. ἢ . . . ἢ . . . ἢ . . . ἢ *whether . . . or . . . or . . . or* (Hom.; Theognis 913f; oracle in Hdt. 1, 65, 3; Theocr. 25, 170f et al.; s. Kühner-G. II 530, 12) **Mk 13:35.** Usu. the first member is without the particle **Mt 27:17; J 18:34; Ac 8:34; Ro 4:10; 1 Cor 4:21; Gal 1:10; 3:2, 5.**

δ. used w. an interrog. word, mostly after another interrog. sentence ἢ τίς; **Mt 7:9; Mk 11:28; Lk 14:31; 20:2; J 9:21; Ro 3:1;** 2 Cl 1:3; 6:9. τίς . . .; τίς . . .; ἢ τίς . . .; **1 Cor 9:7.** τί . . .; ἢ τί . . .; *what . . . ? Or what?* **Mt 16:26; 1 Cor 7:16.**—ἢ πῶς: ἢ πῶς ἐρεῖς; *or how can you say?* **Mt 7:4;** cp. **12:29; Lk 6:42 v.l.** (cp. JosAs 6:2; Tat. 17, 3 al.).

❷ **a particle denoting comparison,** ***than, rather than***

ⓐ after a comparative before the other member of the comparison ἀνεκτότερον . . . ἢ *more tolerable . . . than* **Mt 10:15;** cp.

11:22, 24; Lk 10:12. εὐκοπώτερον . . . ἤ Mt 19:24; Mk 10:25; cp. Lk 9:13; J 4:1. μᾶλλον ἤ *more, rather . . . than* Mt 18:13; J 3:19; Ac 4:19; 5:29; 1 Cor 9:15; 1 Cl 2:1a; 14:1; 21:5. For numerals without ἤ after πλείων and ἐλάσσων, e.g. Mt 26:53 (πλείους ἤ v.l. and var. edd.), s. B-D-F §185, 4 (cp. comp. Ath. 16, 8 μηδὲν πλέον [ἤ corr.] ὅσον ἐκελεύσθησαν).

ⓑ also without a preceding comp. (Kühner-G. II 303; B-D-F §245, 3).

α. w. verbs without μᾶλλον (Job 42:12) χαρὰ ἔσται ἐπὶ ἑνὶ ἢ ἐπὶ ἐνενήκοντα ἐννέα *there will be more joy over one than over 99* **Lk 15:7.** λυσιτελεῖ . . . ἤ *it would be better . . . than* **17:2** (cp. Andoc. 1, 125 τεθνάναι νομίσασα λυσιτελεῖν ἢ ζῆν; Tob 3:6 BA). θέλω . . . ἤ *I would rather . . . than* **1 Cor 14:19** (cp. Epict. 3, 1, 41; BGU 846, 16 [II AD] θέλω πηρὸς γενέσται [= γενέσθαι], εἴ [= ἢ] γνοῦναι, ὅπως ἀνθρόπῳ ἔτι ὀφείλω ὀβολόν 'I had rather become maimed than know that I still owe someone an obol' [1/6 of a drachma]; Hos 6:6; 2 Macc 14:42; Jos., Ant. 18, 59; Just., A I, 15, 8. βούλομαι . . . ἤ *I had rather . . . , than* as early as Hom., e.g. Il. 1, 117).

β. after the positive degree (as early as Hdt. 9, 26) καλόν ἐστιν . . . ἤ *it is better . . . than* **Mt 18:8, 9; Mk 9:43, 45, 47;** 1 Cl 51:3 (Gen 49:12; Ps 117:8f; Sir 20:25; 22:15; Jon 4:3, 8; 4 Macc 9:1. Cp. Polyaenus 8, 49 καλὸν ἀποθανεῖν ἢ ζῆν; Philemon Com. no. 203 θανεῖν κράτιστόν [=far better] ἐστιν ἢ ζῆν ἀθλίως).

γ. ἤ is used in comparison, w. the idea of exclusion (Ps.-Callisth. 1, 37, 4 μέμφεσθε τὸν ἑαυτῶν βασιλέα ἢ ἐμέ='blame your own king, not me'; Gen 38:26 δεδικαίωται Θαμαρ ἢ ἐγώ; 2 Km 19:44; Just., A I, 15, 8 on Lk 5:32 θέλει ὁ πατὴρ τὴν μετάνοιαν ἢ τὴν κόλασιν) δεδικαιωμένος ἢ ἐκεῖνος *rather than* (=*and not*) *the other man* **Lk 18:14 v.l.**

ⓒ οὐδὲν ἕτερον ἤ *nothing else than* (cp. X., Cyr. 2, 3, 10; 7, 5, 41; Jos., Ant. 8, 104; Tat. 15, 2; cp. οὐδὲν ἄλλο . . . ἤ Just., A I, 33, 6 al.; Ath. 18, 1 μὴ εἶναι . . . ἕτερον τρόπον . . . ἢ τοῦτον) **Ac 17:21.** τί . . . ἤ *what other . . . than* (X., Oec. 3, 3; TestJob 42:5; s. Kühner-G. II 304, 4) **24:21.**

ⓓ πρὶν ἤ *before* (Ionism, very rare in Attic wr., but common in the Koine [e.g. Nicol. Dam.: 90 fgm. 130, 14 p. 397, 9 Jac.; Diod. S. 1, 64, 7; 1, 92, 4; Jos., Ant. 8, 345; Just., A I, 12, 10 al.; Tat. 6:1 al.]: ATschuschke, De πρίν particulae apud scriptores aetatis Augusteae prosaicos usu, diss. Bresl. 1913, 31; 33. S. also πρίν a).

α. w. aor. inf. foll. (Aelian, VH 1, 5; Herodian 2, 3, 2; Wsd 2:8; Sir 11:8 al.) and accompanying acc. (Nicol. Dam.: 90 fgm. 128, 14 [Βίος] p. 397, 9 Jac.; Aelian, VH 1, 21; PSI 171, 25 [II BC]; Sir 48:25; Tob 2:4; 3:8; 8:20; TestReub 1:1) **Mt 1:18; Mk 14:30; Ac 7:2.**

β. foll. by aor. subj. and ἄν **Lk 2:26** (without ἄν Jos., Ant. 4, 10).

γ. foll. by pres. opt. **Ac 25:16.**

ⓔ used w. other particles—**α.** ἀλλ' ἤ s. ἀλλά 1a.—**β.** ἤπερ *than* (Hom., Il. 1, 260; 9, 26, 7; Hdt.; Polyb. 2, 51; 61; 2 Macc 14:42; 4 Macc 15:16; Jos., Bell. 5, 10, Ant. 18, 62; Just., A I, 29, 1) after μᾶλλον **J 12:43** (cp. Tob 14:4 S ἐν τ. Μηδίᾳ ἔσται σωτηρία μᾶλλον ἤπερ ἐν Ἀσσυρίοις; Tat. 13, 3; 14, 1; without μᾶλλον 40, 1; Diod. S. 13, 60, 3 πλείονα ἤπερ); after πλέον IEph 6:2 (Lat.).—ἢ γάρ **Lk 18:14 v.l.** may derive from ἤ + παρ'.—DELG. M-M. EDNT.

ἦ adv. ***truly;*** the word is perh. so to be accented 1 Cor 9:10, 15 (Just.; also Ath., R. 53, 7 al.). **Hb 6:14 v.l.** ἦ μήν (Hom. et al.; Jos., Ant. 15, 368; 17, 72) *indeed* (for similar sounding εἰ μήν). Hs 9, 17, 5 Funk writes μᾶλλον δὲ ἦ χείρονες. The right rdg. prob. is μ. δ. καὶ χ. GJs 19:3 pap οὐ μὴ πιστεύσω η (interrog. ἦ B-D-F §440, 3) παρθένος ἐγέννησεν (opp. codd. . . . πιστεύσω ‹ὅτι› ἡ παρθένος ἐγ. [on this pass. s. deStrycker]).—Denniston 279–88. DELG. M-M.

ἤγαγον s. ἄγω.

ἡγεμονεύω (ἡγεμών; Hom.+; SIG 877, 5; OGI 493, 24; PTebt 302, 7; PRyl 113, 20; PStras 41, 17; Philo, Joseph., Just.; SibOr 5, 348) **to exercise an administrative position, *be leader, command, rule, order,*** of the administration of imperial legates (governors; s. ἡγεμών 2; the verb in this mng. POslo 99, 3 [160/61 AD]; Jos., Ant. 15, 345; Just., A I, 29, 2) ἡγεμονεύοντος τῆς Συρίας Κυρηνίου *while Quirinius was governor of Syria* **Lk 2:2.** On the governorship of Quirinius s. FBleckmann, Klio 17, 1920, 104–12; HDessau, ibid. 252–58; RBrown, The Birth of the Messiah '77, 547–56. S. also on ἀπογραφή and Κυρήνιος.—Of Pontius Pilate ἡγεμονεύοντος Π. Π. τῆς Ἰουδαίας *while P.P. was prefect of Judaea* **Lk 3:1** (for this D has the less precise ἐπιτροπεύω).—DELG s.v. ἡγέομαι. M-M.

ἡγεμονία, ας, ἡ (ἡγεμών; Hdt.+; loanw. in rabb.) **state of being in control over others in official capacity, *chief command, direction, management*** of any high office.

ⓐ of the imperial government (of the royal dignity Hdt. 1, 7; 7, 2; EpArist 219; Jos., Ant. 2, 348; ins fr. the age of Augustus: ZNW 22, 1923, 16. Of Nero, SIG 810, 16; of Gaius [Caligula], Philo, Leg. ad Gai. 8; 168; of Vespasian, Jos., Vi. 423) **Lk 3:1;** 1 Cl 61:1.

ⓑ of the office of governor (Jos., Ant. 18, 88 of Syrian legates; OGI 614, 4 of the propraetor of Arabia; POxy 59, 10; 237 V, 6; PRyl 77, 36) ἐν καιρῷ τῆς ἡ. Ποντίου Πιλάτου *at the time when P.P. was prefect* IMg 11.—DELG s.v. ἡγέομαι. M-M. TW.

ἡγεμονικός, ή, όν (s. prec. two entries and next entry; X., Pla.; UPZ 144, 28 [164 BC]; LXX; Philo; Jos., Bell. 2, 305, C. Ap. 2, 125) **pert. to being in a supervisory capacity, *guiding, leading*** πνεῦμα ἡγ. *the guiding Spirit* 1 Cl 18:12 (Ps 50:14). On πνεῦμα ἡγ. and its philosophical presuppositions s. Knopf, Hdb. ad loc., exc.; JSchneider, ZNW 34, '35, 62–69.—Sv.

ἡγεμών, όνος, ὁ (Hom.+; loanw. in rabb.).—❶ **one who rules, esp. in a preeminent position, *ruler*** (Soph., Oed. R. 103; SIG 814, 25; Ex 15:15; Job 42:17d; Jos., Ant. 19, 217. Perh. 'chieftain' Gen 36:15ff; 1 Ch 1:51ff) ἐν τοῖς ἡγεμόσιν Ἰούδα *among the rulers of Judah* **Mt 2:6** (after Mi 5:1; the rendering ἐν τ. ἡγεμόσιν instead of the LXX ἐν χιλιάσιν, following rabbinic methods of interpretation, is suggested by ἡγούμενον in 2 Km 5:2, cited in the last part of **Mt 2:6.** On the view that a misunderstanding of the original text or a variant in the LXX tradition underlies the text, s. comm.).

❷ **head imperial provincial administrator, *governor*** in the provinces (Dio Chrys. 31 [48], 1; Ael. Aristid. 50, 12 K.= 26 p. 505 D.; OGI index; pap; Jos., Ant. 15, 405) **Mt 10:18; 27:23 v.l.; Mk 13:9; Lk 21:12; 1 Pt 2:14.** Esp. of the *procurators* or *prefects* in Judaea: Pontius Pilate (Jos., Ant. 18, 55 Πιλᾶτος δὲ ὁ τ. Ἰουδαίας ἡγεμών; JVardaman, A New Inscr. [Lat.] which Mentions Pilate as 'Prefect', JBL 81, '62, 70f; Boffo, Iscrizione no. 25) **Mt 27:2, 11, 14 f, 21, 27; 28:14; Lk 20:20;** Felix **Ac 23:24, 26, 33; 24:1, 10;** Festus **26:30.**—Jerome (in Epheus) AcPl Ha 1, 23. WLiebenam, Beiträge z. Verwaltungsgesch. d. röm. Reiches I 1886, 1ff; Pauly-W. XXIII, 1, 1240–79. GBurton, Provincial Procurators and the Public Provinces: Chiron 23, '93, 13–28.—LRobert, AntCl 62, '60, 329. DELG s.v. ἡγέομαι. EDNT. M-M.

ἡγέομαι fut. ἡγήσομαι LXX; 1 aor. ἡγησάμην; pf. ἥγημαι (s. prec. four entries; Hom.+).

❶ **to be in a supervisory capacity, *lead, guide;*** in our lit. only pres. ptc. (ὁ) ἡγούμενος of men in any leading position (Soph., Phil. 386; freq. Polyb.; Diod. S. 1, 4, 7; 1, 72, 1; Lucian, Alex. 44; 57; ins, pap, LXX, EpArist; TestZeb 10:2; ViEzk 2 [p. 74, 7 Sch.]; Just., A II, 1, 1; Tat.; Mel., HE 4, 26, 10; Ath. 1, 2) *ruler, leader* (opp. ὁ διακονῶν *the servant*) **Lk 22:26.** Of princely authority (Ezk 43:7; Sir 17:17; 41:17) **Mt 2:6;** 1 Cl 32:2; 60:4.—Of high officials **Ac 7:10;** MPol 9:3 (read by Eus. for ἀνθυπάτου); 1 Cl 5:7; 51:5; 55:1. Of military commanders (Appian, Iber. 78 §333, Bell. Civ. 3, 26 §97; 1 Macc 9:30; 2 Macc 14:16) 37:2f. Also of leaders of religious bodies (PTebt 525 Παεῦς ἡγούμενος ἱερέων; PLond II, 281, 2 p. 66 [66 AD]; PVindBosw 1, 31 [87 AD] τῶν τ. ἱεροῦ ἡγουμένων κ. πρεσβυτέρων. Cp. also Sir 33:19 οἱ ἡγούμενοι ἐκκλησίας; Sb 7835 [I BC], 10; 14 the [monarchic] ἡγούμενος of the cultic brotherhood of Zeus Hypsistos) of heads of a Christian congregation **Hb 13:7, 17, 24;** 1 Cl 1:3. ἄνδρας ἡγουμένους ἐν τοῖς ἀδελφοῖς *leading men among the brothers/members* **Ac 15:22.** FBüchsel, TW II 909f.—Of Paul taken to be Hermes ὁ ἡγούμενος τοῦ λόγου *the chief speaker* **14:12** (Cyranides p. 15, 30 Hermes as λόγων ἡγούμενος; Iambl., Myst. [Herm. Wr. IV p. 28, 4 Sc.] Hermes ὁ τῶν λόγων ἡγεμών; s. also Ἑρμῆς 1).

❷ **to engage in an intellectual process, *think, consider, regard*** (trag., Hdt.+) ἀναγκαῖον w. inf. foll. (s. ἀναγκαῖος 1 and cp. BGU 824, 4; PRyl 235, 4) **2 Cor 9:5; Phil 2:25.** δίκαιον w. inf. foll. *I consider it my duty to* **2 Pt 1:13** (Just., A I, 4, 2 and D. 125, 1). περισσὸν ἡγεῖσθαι w. articular inf. foll. *consider superfluous* (POxy 1070, 17 τὸ μὲν οὖν γράφειν . . . περιττὸν νῦν ἡγησάμην) Dg 2:10. Foll. by acc. w. inf. (Hdt. 3, 8, 3; SIG 831, 13; Philo, Agr. 67; Jos., Ant. 19, 107; Just., A I, 9, 1 al.) **Phil 3:8a** (s. also ζημία); ἀποστόλους πιστοὺς ἡγησάμενος εἶναι PtK 3 p. 15, 18.—W. double acc. *look upon, consider someone* or *someth. (as) someone* or *someth.* (Aeschyl., Hdt. et al.; Wsd 1:16; 7:8; Philo, Cher. 70; Jos., Ant. 7, 51; Just., A I, 9, 3 and D. 12, 1 al.) **Ac 26:2** (the perf. ἥγημαι w. pres. mng., as Hdt. 1, 126; Pla., Tim. 19e; POslo 49, 3 [c. 100 AD]; Job 42:6); **Phil 2:3, 6; 3:7, 8b** (=AcPl Ha 2, 23); **1 Ti 1:12; 6:1** (Job 30:1; JosAs 3:4 cod. A [p. 42, 20 Bat.]); **Hb 10:29; 11:11, 26; 2 Pt 2:13; 3:15;** in vs. **9** one acc. is supplied by the context; Hv 2, 1, 2; Dg 2:6; 9:6. Also τινὰ ὥς τινα **2 Th 3:15;** cp. 2 Cl 5:6; Hv 1, 1, 7 (ὡς as Philo, Agr. 62; cp. Job 19:11; 33:10; Tat. 34, 1) πᾶσαν χαρὰν ἡγήσασθε, ὅταν . . . *deem it pure joy, when* . . . **Js 1:2** (cp. POxy 528, 8 πένθος ἡγούμην; Just., D. 14, 2 ἡγεῖσθε εὐσέβειαν, ἐάν . . .). μωρίαν μᾶλλον εἰκὸς ἡγοῖντ' ἄν, οὐ θεοσέβειαν *ought consider it folly rather than reverence for God* Dg 3:3; cp. 4:5. Also pass. ἐκείνη βεβαία εὐχαριστία ἡγείσθω *let (only) that observance of the Eucharist be considered valid* ISm 8:1. In **1 Th 5:13** there emerges for ἡ. the sense *esteem, respect* (s. Mitt-Wilck. I/2, 116, 4f [II/III AD] ἡγοῦ μάλιστα τοὺς πατρῴους καὶ σέβου Ἶσιν).—B. 711; 1204. DELG. M-M. TW. Spicq.

ᾔδειν s. οἶδα.

ἡδέως adv. of ἡδύς (Soph., Hippocr.+) **pert. to being pleased in connection with someth., *gladly*** (Aristoph., Thu. et al.) λαμβάνειν (Aristoph., Equ. 440) ITr 6:2. ἡδ. ἀκούειν *like to hear* (Jos., Ant. 3, 191; Just., D. 10, 4; 59, 1) **Mk 6:20; 12:37;** Hm 2:2. ἀνέχεσθαι *gladly tolerate* **2 Cor 11:19.** ἡδ. ποιεῖν (Ps.-Menand., Dist. fgm. 704 Kock; POxy 113, 30; PGrenf II, 73, 20) *do gladly* Hs 6, 5, 5. βαστάζειν 8, 10, 3; 9, 14, 6. ὑποδέχεσθαι 8, 10, 3; 9, 27, 2. Ἰσαὰκ ἡδ. προσήγετο θυσία. *I. gladly let himself be led as a sacrifice* 1 Cl 31:3. ὃν καὶ ὁ βασιλεὺς ἡδέως ἔχει (the child) *of whom even Caesar is fond* Ox 849, 16f. Restored text: [ἡδέως θλείβον]ται Hs 8, 10, 4f (s. Bonner 113, 18f, based on Lat. libenter patiuntur).—Comp. ἥδιον (Lysias 7, 40; IPriene 105, 19 [c. 9 BC]; BGU 372 I, 15; Sir 22:11; Just., D. 29, 1) *more gladly* ἥδ. διδόναι 1 Cl 2:1 (cp. μακάριος 2bγ). ὑπομιμνῄσκειν 62:3. Superl. as elative (B-D-F §60, 2; Rob. 278f; 670; M-M s.v.) ἥδιστα *very gladly* (Pla., Theaet. 183d; Lucian, Scyth. 8; POxy 1061, 21 [22 BC]; 933, 5; PLond III, 897, 8 p. 207 [84 AD]; Jos., Vi. 365) **2 Cor 12:15; Ac 13:8** D. ἥδιστα μᾶλλον καυχήσομαι *I will rather boast all the more gladly* **2 Cor 12:9** (s. B-D-F §246).—B. 1032. DELG s.v. ἥδομαι B (ἡδύς). M-M. Spicq.

ἤδη adv. (Hom.+; contrast ἤδη 'already' and ἔτι 'still' Chariton 49).—❶ **a point of time prior to another point of time, w. implication of completion, *now, already, by this time.***

ⓐ w. pres. tense: **Mt 3:10; 15:32; Mk 4:37; 8:2; 11:11; Lk 7:6; 21:30** (w. ἐγγὺς εἶναι as Jos., Ant. 6, 223); **J 4:36** (if ἤδη belongs to the preceding sentence vs. **35,** cp. on its position Tob 3:6 BA; Jos., Ant. 3, 48); **11:39** al. *now* (Appian, Bell. Civ. 5, 21 §82 ἤδη λέγουσα; Just., D. 43, 3), ἤδη καί *even now* (3 Macc 3:10; 6:24; Jos., Ant. 16, 100) **Lk 3:9.** Sim. νῦν ἤδη **1J 4:3** (Just., D. 137, 4 καὶ νῦν ἤδη; cp. 55, 1 τὰ νῦν δὲ ἤδη).—*at once* (Polyaenus 6, 8) γινώσκεται ἤδη=*we know at once* **Lk 21:30** D.

ⓑ w. a past tense (Just., A I, 42, 1 ὡς ἤδη γενόμενα al.): **Mt 14:15, 24; 17:12; Mk 6:35; 13:28; 15:42, 44 v.l.; Lk 12:49** al. σῶμα ἤδη νενεκρωμένον **Ro 4:19.** διὰ τὸ ἤδη πεφημίσθαι *because the rumor had already spread far and wide* AcPl Ha 4, 17f al.

❷ **marker of culmination, *now at length*** in the phrase ἤδη ποτέ (Heraclit. Sto. 62 p. 82, 14; Epict. 3, 24, 9; Just., D. 32, 5; 75, 2; ostracon fr. Thebes in Dssm., LO 167 [LAE 186]), somet. used w. a past tense **Phil 4:10;** 2 Cl 13:1, somet. w. the fut. (Jos., Ant. 3, 300): εἴ πως ἤδη ποτὲ εὐοδωθήσομαι ἐλθεῖν *whether now at last I may perh. succeed in coming* **Ro 1:10.**

❸ **marker of logical proximity and immediateness, *in fact*** (so also Ath.) ἤδη ἐμοίχευσεν **Mt 5:28.** ἤδ. κέκριται **J 3:18.** ἤδ. ἥττημα ὑμῖν ἐστιν **1 Cor 6:7.**

❹ **marker of intensification:** in **Mt 5:28** and **1 Cor 6:7** ἤδη approaches the sense ***really*** or our colloq. 'you see'.—DELG. M-M. TW.

ἥδιον, ἥδιστα s. ἡδέως.

ἥδομαι 1 aor. ἥσθην (Just., D. 142, 1; Ath. 17, 2) (cp. ἡδονή, ἡδύς; Hom.+) ***be pleased with, delight in*** τινί *someth.* (Hdt. et al.; PGM 13, 657) τροφῇ φθορᾶς *perishable food* IRo 7:3.—B. 1099. DELG. TW.

ἡδονή, ῆς, ἡ (s. prec. entry; Pre-Socr., trag., Hdt.+).

❶ **state or condition of experiencing pleasure for any reason, *pleasure, delight, enjoyment, pleasantness*** (Diod. S. 3, 10, 2; Pr 17:1; Jos., Ant. 3, 19; 4, 88) ἡδονὴν ἡγεῖσθαί τι *consider someth. pleasure* **2 Pt 2:13.** ἡδονὴν ἔχει τί τινι *someth. causes pleasure to someone* 2 Cl 15:5. Of a *desire* to do good (Pla., Aristot.; Jos., C. Ap. 2, 189) Hs 6, 5, 7.—Usu. in a bad sense: *(evil) pleasure, (illicit) desire* (Demosth. 18, 138 ἐπὶ τ. λοιδορίαις ἡδ. 'delight in reviling'; Musonius 89, 16f: opp. ἀρετή. Oft. Philo, Herm. Wr.; Ath. 34, 1 πάσης αἰσχρᾶς ἡδονῆς) more fully ἡδ. κακή ITr 6:2; IPhld 2:2. Usu. pl. (Vett. Val. 76, 1; 4 Macc 5:23; 6:35; Just., A I, 21, 5) τοῦ βίου *pleasures of life* **Lk 8:14;** IRo 7:3. Abs. (w. ἐπιθυμίαι, as Dio Chrys. 32 [49], 9; Ael. Aristid. 35, 27 K.=9 p. 108 D.; 4 Macc 5:23; Philo, Agr. 83; 84 al.; Mel., P. 50, 361) **Tit 3:3;** Dg 9:1.—**Js 4:1, 3;** Dg 6:5; Hs 8, 8, 5; 8, 9,

4. πρὸς ἡδονὴν ἐδέσμευεν *the devil bound humanity to its lust* AcPlCor 2:11.

❷ **pleasurable experience of sensation,** ***agreeable taste*** (Sopater in Athen. 14, 649a ἡδ. τραγημάτων al.; Num 11:8; Wsd 16:20; Jos., Ant. 3, 28) ἡδονὴν ἔχειν *have a pleasant taste* Hm 10, 3, 3. ἡδονὴ τοῦ οἴνου 12, 5, 3.—Renehan '75, 100. DELG s.v. ἥδομαι A. M-M. TW. Sv.

ἡδύοσμον, ου, τό (ἡδύς, ὀσμή; Theophr., HP 7, 7, 1; Strabo 8, 3, 14; Diosc. 3, 34; Galen XI 882, 16 K.; XII 928, 9) ***mint*** (garden plant; Zohary, Plants 88: a perennial herb, mentha longifolia, the most common species of mentha) ἀποδεκατοῦν τὸ ἡδ. *pay tithes of mint* **Mt 23:23; Lk 11:42** (w. πήγανον as Hippiatr. I p. 12, 15).—DELG s.v. ἥδομαι B. M-M.

ἡδυπάθεια, ας, ἡ (ἡδύς + πάθη, 'experience of someth. pleasant'; X., Cyr. 7, 5, 74; Cebes 9, 3; 28, 1; Plut., Mor. 132c; 4 Macc 2:2, 4) **experience of a luxurious mode of life,** ***enjoyment, comfort;*** pl. (Athen. 4, 165e) ἀποτάσσεσθαι ταῖς ἡδ. *renounce the enjoyments* 2 Cl 16:2. μισεῖν τὰς ἡδ. τῆς ψυχῆς *hate the evil pleasures of the soul* 17:7. Cp. DELG s.v. ἥδομαι B.

ἡδύς, εῖα, ύ (cp. ἥδομαι; Hom. et al.; ins, pap, LXX, En, ParJer 5:3; EpArist, Philo; Jos., Ant. 12, 47 ἡδὺ τῷ θεῷ; Ath. 33, 1 [pl. subst.]; orig. of someth. pleasant to one of the senses, then anyth. that pleases or is welcome) ***pleasant*** αὕτη ἡ ὁδὸς ἡδυτέρα αὐτοῖς ἐγένετο *this way became more suitable to them* Hs 8, 9, 1 (Ps.-Dicaearchus p. 140 F. ὁδὸς ἡδεῖα).—B. 1032. DELG s.v. ἥδομαι B. Spicq. Sv.

ἦθος, ους, τό (Hom. et al.) **a pattern of behavior or practice that is habitual or characteristic of a group or an individual,** ***custom, usage, habit*** (so Hes., Hdt. et al.) τῆς ἁγνείας *the habit of purity* 1 Cl 21:7. τῆς φιλοξενίας 1:2. Pl. τὰ ἤθη *habits,* ἤθη χρηστά *good habits* (cp. Philo, Spec. Leg. 2, 104.—EpArist 290 and POxy 642 [II AD] ἦθος χρηστόν) **1 Cor 15:33** (φθείρουσιν ἤθ. χρ. ὁμιλίαι κακαί is a proverb, occurring in Menander's comedy Thais [fgm. 218 Kock, 187 Körte] and perh. as early as Eur. [PHib 7, 94—III BC; Socrates, HE 3, 6]. According to Diod. S. 12, 12, [3] 4 Charondas the lawgiver [V BC] champions the principle that good men would easily have their characters ruined by association with evil men [τὰ ἤθη πρὸς κακίαν]. In 16, 54, 4 it is said of a tyrant: πονηραῖς ὁμιλίαις διέφθειρε τὰ ἤθη τῶν ἀνθρώπων 'he corrupted people's morals through base speech'.—S. also χρηστός 3a. Similar ideas as early as Theognis 1, 35f; 305–8). Of Judean laws as v.l. **Ac 16:21** and **26:3** (s. ἔθος 2).—DELG. M-M. TW. Sv.

ἥκω (Hom.+; ins, pap, LXX, pseudepigr.; Jos., Ant. 16, 329; 341 al.; Just., A II, 2, 5; for ἔρχεσθαι Just., D. 49, 3 and 88, 7 [**Mt 3:11f**], D. 53, 3 [Zech 9:9]); for ἤχθη (A I, 51, 1 [Is 53:8]; D. 13, 6 [Is 53:8]) since it has the mng. of a perf., its conjugation somet. has perf. forms (as in pap [Mayser I 2^2 '38, 148]; LXX [Helbing 104]; JosAs 3:7f; Joseph. [WSchmidt 470]) ἥκασι(ν) **Mk 8:3** (v.l. ἥκουσιν); 1 Cl 12:2. Impf. ἧκον; fut. ἥξω; 1 aor. ἧξα (POxy 933, 13).

❶ **to be in a place as the result of movement to,** ***have come, be present,*** of persons—ⓐ w. mention of the starting point ἀπό τινος **Mt 8:11; Lk 13:29.** ἔκ τινος **J 4:47; Ro 11:26.** μακρόθεν **Mk 8:3** (cp. Josh 9:6, 9; Is 60:4, FDanker, JBL 82, '63, 215f).

ⓑ w. mention of the goal εἴς τι **J 4:47** (s. a above); ἥ. εἰς θάνατον *go to one's death* 1 Cl 16:9. ἥ. εἰς τὴν πύρωσιν τῆς δοκιμασίας D 16:5. ἐν τῷ οἴκῳ αὐτοῦ *at home* GJs 5:1. πρός τινα (PSI 326, 4 [261 BC]; En 106:8) **Ac 28:23 v.l.;** GJs 9:3. ἐπί τινα *have come to someone* (UPZ 78, 44 [159 BC]), also w. hostile intent (Pla., Rep. 336b et al.; 2 Ch 20:2) **Rv 3:3b.** ἐπί τι (Lucian, Jupp. Tr. 24; Achilles Tat. 5, 10, 1) B 4:3. W. inf. foll. 1 Cl 12:2. ἕως ὧδε 20:7. ἐκεῖ *there* (POslo 58, 5) Hv 3, 1, 3.

ⓒ abs. **Mt 24:50; Lk 12:46; 15:27; J 8:42; Hb 10:7, 9** (both Ps 39:8), 37 (Hab 2:3); **1J 5:20; Rv 2:25; 3:3a, 9;** 1 Cl 23:5 (Mal 3:1); D 16:7. ἰδοὺ ἥκει Ἰωακεὶμ μετὰ τῶν ποιμνίων αὐτοῦ *there came Joachim with his flocks* GJs 4:4.

ⓓ of the coming of a worshiper to a deity (OGI 186, 6 ἥκω πρὸς τὴν κυρίαν Ἶσιν; 196, 2; Sb 1059, 8402 [I BC], 8411 [79 BC], 8412 [66 BC] al.; 3 Km 8:42; Jer 27:5; ἐπὶ σὲ ἥξομεν PsSol 5:7) **J 6:37; Rv 15:4** (Ps 85:9).

ⓔ of a solemn appearance *be here* (of a deity PGM 1, 26; 29; Zosimus: Herm. Wr. IV p. 111, 5 θεὸς ἥξει πρός σε; 111, 9; Synes., Provid. 2, 2 p. 118b; SibOr 3, 49) expressed w. special force by ἥκω (PGiss 3, 2 [ἄγνωστος, beg.]; s. OWeinreich, ARW 18, 1915, 38ff) **J 8:42.**

❷ **to make an appearance or come to pass,** ***come,*** impers. (Demosth. 23, 12; Diod. S. 18, 58, 2 ἧκε γράμματα='a letter came'; Plut., Philop. 366 [21, 1]; Epict. 2, 2, 20; Ael. Aristid. 48, 13 K.=24 p. 468 D.) of time (Ezk 7:12 ἥκει ὁ καιρός; Ps 101:14) or of events **Mt 24:14; J 2:4; 13:1 v.l.; 2 Pt 3:10; Rv 18:8.** Of information, reports ὡς ἐκ παραδόσεως ἀγράφου εἰς αὐτὸν ἥκοντα *as coming to him from an unwritten tradition* Papias (2:11). Of the reign of God 2 Cl 12:2. ἕως ἥξει ὅτε *until the time comes when* **Lk 13:35.** ἐπί τινα *upon someone* (Is 47:9; cp. τὰ ἀγαθὰ ἥξεις . . . ἐπ' αὐτούς En 107:1) of the final tribulations **Mt 23:36; Lk 19:43.**—DELG. M-M. TW.

ἡλάμην s. ἅλλομαι.

ἠλέγχθην s. ἐλέγχω.

ἦλθα, ἦλθον s. ἔρχομαι.

ἠλί (v.l. ἐλωί; other spellings ἠλι, ἠλει, ἡλει)=אֵלִי ***my God*** (Hebr. Ps 22:2) **Mt 27:46.**—GDalman, Jesus-Jeshua, 1929 [tr. PLevertoff], 204–7; FBuckler, AJSL 55, '38, 378–91; WKenneally, CBQ 8, '46, 124–34; FZimmerman, JBL 66, '47, 465f.

Ἠλί, ὁ (edd. also Ἡλί, Ἡλεί; עֵלִי; cp. e.g. 1 Km 1:3; 2:12, 20, 22; 3 Km 2:27.—In Jos., Ant. 5, 340f al. Ἠλ[ε]ίς, gen. Ἠλεῖ 5, 341; 350) ***Eli (Heli),*** the father (or, acc. to some, the grandfather) of Joseph, in the genealogy of Jesus **Lk 3:23.**—M-M. s.v. Ἠλεί.

Ἠλίας, ου, ὁ (edd. also -είας, Ἡλείας, Ἡλίας; אֵלִיָּה or אֵלִיָּהוּ) ***Elijah*** (or, following the Gk., Elias) the Tishbite, a prophet (3 Km 17–20; 4 Km 1f; 2 Ch 21:12; Mal 3:22; Sir 48:1, 4, 12; ApcEl [PSI 7 verso, 4]; AscIs 2:14; SibOr 2, 247; Joseph., ApcEsdr, Just.), whose life and deeds were invested w. great importance by the compatriots of Jesus (Schürer II 515f; 604f; Billerb. IV 764–98) **Mt 11:14; 16:14; 17:3f** (PDabeck, Biblica 23, '42, 175–89), **10ff; 27:47, 49; Mk 6:15; 8:28; 9:4f, 11ff; 15:35f; Lk 1:17; 4:25f; 9:8, 19, 30, 33, 54 v.l.; J 1:21, 25; Js 5:17;** 1 Cl 17:1. ἐν Ἠλίᾳ *in the story of Elijah* **Ro 11:2.**—JRobinson, Elijah, John and Jesus: 12 NT Studies '62, 28–52; GFohrer, Elia '68.[2]—EDNT. TW.

ἡλικία, ας, ἡ (Hom.+)—❶ **the period of time that one's life continues,** ***age, time of life***—ⓐ gener. of time that is past. **Mt 6:27=Lk 12:25** προσθεῖναι ἐπὶ τ. ἡλικίαν αὐτοῦ πῆχυν ἕνα, where acc. to the context the ref. is to someth. insignificant (Lk 12:26 has expressly ἐλάχιστον.—Paus. Attic. σ, 22 evaluates as τὸ ἐλάχιστον the expression σπιθαμὴ τοῦ βίου=a span [the distance between thumb and little finger of the extended hand] of life), may refer to length of life (so Goodsp. Probs. 24–26, following Wetstein), not to bodily size, and πῆχυς is then a measure of time (cp. Hebr. Ps 39:6 and s. πῆχυς). Likew. perh. in the par. Ox 655, 13–15 (GTh 67, 34; Fitzmyer 544) τίς ἂν προσθ‹εί›η| ἐπὶ τὴν εἱλικίαν| ὑμῶν; 'who could add to your time of life?' On the other hand, the context also speaks of nourishment and growth, and the saying may be one of the typically bold dominical sayings w. the sense: 'Who grows by worrying about one's height?' (s. 3 below).—Fr. the context, ἡλ. in the sense of 'age' can be more closely defined as *youthfulness* (4 Macc 8:10, 20) IMg 3:1; MPol 3:1, or *old age* 7:2; 9:2 (cp. 4 Macc 5:6, 11, 36).

ⓑ of age gener., including the years lying ahead προκόπτειν ἐν (missing in many mss.) τ. ἡλικίᾳ *increase in years* (but s. 3 below) **Lk 2:52** (cp. SIG 708, 17–19: ins in honor of a young man of Istropolis [II BC] [τῇ] τε ἡλικίᾳ προκόπτων καὶ προαγόμενος εἰς τὸ θεοσεβεῖν ὡς ἔπρεπεν αὐτῷ πρῶτον μὲν ἐτείμησεν τοὺς θεοὺς 'advancing in years and growing in piety as became him, he showed honor first to the gods'; Biogr. p. 266.—On σοφία, ἡλικία, χάρις: AFridrichsen, SymbOsl 6, 1928, 33–38).

❷ **the age which is sufficient or requisite for certain things,** ***maturity*** (Jos., Ant. 1, 68; 2, 230a).—ⓐ the age of strength (2 Macc 5:24; 7:27; En 106:1), also of women (αἱ ἐν ἡλ. παρθένοι or γυναῖκες in Hippocr., Pla., Plut.) παρὰ καιρὸν ἡλικίας *past the normal age* (παρά C3) **Hb 11:11** (s. καταβολή 1 and 2 and s. Philo, Abr. 195). Thus fig. **Eph 4:13:** εἰς ἄνδρα τέλειον, εἰς μέτρον ἡλικίας τοῦ πληρώματος τ. Χριστοῦ, ἵνα μηκέτι ὦμεν νήπιοι *to the measure of the full maturity of Christ,* who is a mature person (τέλειος), not a (νήπιος) minor (cp. Diod. S. 18, 57, 2 εἰς ἡλικίαν ἔρχεσθαι); but s. 3 below.

ⓑ the age of legal maturity, majority (oft. in pap) ἡλικίαν ἔχειν *be of age* (Pla., Euthd. 306d; Plut., Mor. 547a; BGU 168, 5 τοῖς ἀτελέσι ἔχουσι τ. ἡλικίαν) **J 9:21, 23.**

❸ ***bodily stature*** (Hdt. 3, 16; Pla., Euthd. 271b; Demosth. 40, 56; Diod. S. 3, 35, 6; Plut., Philop. 362 [11, 2]; Lucian, Ver. Hist. 1, 40; Jos., Ant. 2, 230b) τῇ ἡλικίᾳ μικρὸς ἦν *small of stature* **Lk 19:3.** Some scholars hold that **Mt 6:27; Lk 12:25** should be listed here (s. Field, Notes, 6f); many would prefer *stature* for **Lk 2:52; Eph 4:13.**—B. 956. DELG s.v. ἧλιξ. M-M. TW. Sv.

ἡλίκος, η, ον (Soph. et al.) ***how great*** (Aristoph., Pla. et al.; SIG 850, 11; PTebt 27, 78 [123 BC]; Jos., Bell. 1, 626, Ant. 8, 208) ἡλίκον ἀγῶνα ἔχω *how great a struggle I have* **Col 2:1.** ἡλίκην ἔχει βάσανον *what great torment someth. causes* 2 Cl 10:4. ἡλίκοις γράμμασιν **Gal 6:11 v.l.:** here ἡλ. may also mean *how small* (Antiphanes Com. 166, 6; Lucian, Herm. 5; Epict. 1, 12, 26). In a play on words ἰδοὺ ἡλίκον πῦρ ἡλίκην ὕλην ἀνάπτει *see how large a forest a little fire sets ablaze* **Js 3:5.**—DELG. M-M.

ἥλιος, ου, ὁ (Hom.+; loanw. in rabb.) ***the sun*** (with and without art.: B-D-F §253, 1; PBerl 11710, 4 w. art. [Otero p. 84 no. 4]; pl. TestAbr A 7 p. 84, 4 [Stone p. 16]) **Mt 13:43; 17:2** (cp. OdeSol 11:13); **Lk 21:25; Ac 2:20** (Jo 3:4); **26:13; 27:20; 1 Cor 15:41; Rv 1:16; 6:12; 8:12; 10:1; 12:1** (cp. Athena associated w. the sun: Ptocheia or Odysseus in Disguise at Troy—PKöln VI, 245 [=ASP 31] '91, 41–44; sim. Isis lines 13–16 of the poem; cp. IMaronIsis 9 [ὅτ]αν οἷς ἔβλεψα τὸν ἥλιον [corrected restoration of ed. pr.]=whenever, with what [eyes] I have seen the sun); **16:8; 19:17; 21:23;** 1 Cl 20:3; B 5:10; 15:5; Dg 7:2; IEph 19:2; Hm 12, 4, 1 (addition cod. A); s 9, 2, 2; 9, 17, 4; 9, 21, 1; 3. ἥλ.=*heat of the sun* (Polyaenus 8, 10, 3; Is 49:10; Jon 4:8b) **Rv 7:16;** =*light of the sun* **Ac 13:11** (cp. Diod. S. 10, 20, 3 ἐφορᾶν τὸν ἥλιον; 18, 27, 2; Maximus Tyr. 27, 3d ἥλιος for ἐξ ἡλίου αὐγή; Ps 57:9; Jos., Ant. 16, 204 τ. ἥλιον βλέπ.; Ath. 17, 2 ἐν ἡλίῳ). ἀνατέλλειν (cp. ἀνατέλλω 1 and 2) **Mt 5:45; 13:6; Mk 4:6; 16:2; Js 1:11.** λάμπειν GPt 6:22. ἐκλάμπειν *shine forth* Hv 4, 1, 6. ἐπικαίειν s 9, 1, 6. δύνειν (q.v.) **Mk 1:32; Lk 4:40;** GPt 2:5; 5:15. ἐπιδύειν **Eph 4:26.** σκοτίζεσθαι *be darkened* **Mt 24:29; Mk 13:24; Lk 23:45 v.l.** σκοτοῦσθαι **Rv 9:2.** ἐκλείπειν *be in eclipse* (Ps.-Lucian, Philopatris 24) **Lk 23:45.** ἀνατολὴ ἡλίου *east* (ἀνατολή 2a) **Rv 7:2; 16:12.** φῶς ἡλίου *sunlight* (Lycurgus the orator, fgm. 77; Ael. Aristid. 45, 29 K.; Just., D. 128, 24) **22:5.** πρὸ ἡλίου κ. σελήνης *before the creation of sun and moon* 2 Cl 14:1. ὁ τοῦ ἡλίου βωμός *the altar of the sun* or *of Helios* 1 Cl 25:4 (ἥλ. as a deity: Dio Chrys. 3, 73; Maximus Tyr. 19, 3d [Pythag.]; Jos., C. Ap. 2, 265; Ar. 6, 1ff; Ath. 28, 4).—FBoll, D. Sonne im Glauben u. in d. Weltanschauung d. alten Völker 1922; KSchauenburg, Helios '55; GHalsberghe, The Cult of Sol Invictus '72.—B. 54. DELG. LfgrE 894 (lit.). DDD s.v. Helios. M-M. TW.

Ἡλιούπολις, εως, ἡ (s. ἥλιος, πόλις; Socrat., Ep. 26, 1 [Ἡλίου πόλις]; Arrian, Anab. 3, 1, 3 [Ἡλιούπολις]; Ex 1:11 [Ἡλίου πόλις]; TestJos 18:3; JosAs; Demetr.: 722 fgm. 1:12 Jac.; Philo, Somn. 1, 77; Jos., C. Ap. :1, 250, 261, 265; Ath. 28, 1) ***Heliopolis,*** a city of Lower Egypt w. a temple of the sun god; it plays a role in the legend of the bird Phoenix 1 Cl 25:3.

ἧλος, ου, ὁ (Hom. et al.; ins, pap, LXX; Jos., Ant. 5, 208; Just., Mel.—In crucifixion: Asclepiades Junior [physician I/II AD] in Alexander Trallianus 1, 15) ***nail*** GPt 6:21; MPol 13:3. ὁ τύπος τῶν ἥλων *the imprint of the nails* **J 20:25ab.** Also ὁ τόπος τ. ἥλων *the place of the nails* vs. **25b.**—JHewitt, HTR 25, '32, 29–45.—B. 597. DELG. M-M.

Ἠλύσιον πεδίον, τό (s. DELG and Frisk on etym.; since Hom. Od. 4, 563; also SibOr 2, 338) ***Elysian Field(s), Elysium*** also called *Isles of the Blest* ApcPtRainer 2, 1.—JKroll, Elysium '53. S. Ἀχερούσιος.

ἡμεῖς s. ἐγώ.

ἡμέρα, ας, ἡ (Hom.+; loanw. in rabb.)—❶ **the period betw. sunrise and sunset, *day***—ⓐ lit. (opp. νύξ; e.g. Ath. 24, 2 ἀντιδοξοῦντι . . . ὡς . . . τῇ ἡμέρᾳ νύξ) **Mt 4:2** (fasting for 40 days and 40 nights as Ex 34:28. S. νύξ 1d.—Cp. JosAs 13:8 ἑπτὰ ἡμέρας καὶ ἑπτὰ νύκτας; Lucian, Ver. Hist. 1, 10 ἑπτὰ ἡμέρας κ. τὰς ἴσας νύκτας); **12:40** and oft. ἡμέρα γίνεται *day is breaking* (X., An. 2, 2, 13; 7, 2, 34; Appian, Iber. 74 §315; Jos., Ant. 10, 202, Vi. 405) **Lk 4:42; 6:13; 22:66; Ac 12:18; 16:35; 27:29, 39.** ἡμέρα διαυγάζει *the day dawns* **2 Pt 1:19.** κλίνει *declines, evening approaches* **Lk 9:12; 24:29** (cp. Just., D. 56, 16 ἡμέρα προκόπτει). φαίνει *shines* **Rv 8:12.** In the gen. to denote a point of time ἡμέρας *in daylight* (Hippocr., Ep. 19, 7; Arrian, Ind. 13, 6; Lucian, Ver. Hist. 1, 10) 1 Cl 25:4. ἡμέρας μέσης *at midday, noon* (Lucian, Nigr. 34; cp. Jos., Ant. 5, 190) **Ac 26:13.** But also, as in Thu. et al., of time within which someth. occurs, ἡμέρας *during the day* **Rv 21:25.** ἡμέρας καὶ νυκτός *(by) day and night* (Appian, Liby. 121, §576; Arrian, Anab. 7, 11, 4; Jos., Ant. 11, 171; Just., D. 1, 4 δι' ὅλης νυκτὸς καὶ ἡμέρας; also in reverse order as Is 34:10) **Mk 5:5; Lk 18:7; Ac 9:24; 1 Th 2:9; 3:10; 2 Th 3:8;** AcPl Ha 2, 10; 3, 2. The acc. of time νύκτα καὶ ἡμέραν (in this sequence Dio Chrys. 7 [8], 15; Ael. Aristid. 51, 1 K.=27 p. 534 D.; Esth 4:16; cp. νύκτωρ καὶ μεθ' ἡμέραν Mel., HE 4, 26, 5; Ath. 34, 3) *(throughout the) day and (the) night* **Mk 4:27; Lk 2:37; Ac 20:31; 26:7.** τὰς ἡμέρας *every day* (opp. τὰς νύκτας; cp. Dio Chrys. 4, 36; Jos., C. Ap. 1, 199) **Lk 21:37;** cp. πᾶσαν ἡμέραν *(throughout) every day* **Ac 5:42** (cp. Hdt. 7, 203, 1). τὴν ἡμέραν ἐκείνην *(throughout) that day* (Ael. Aristid. 49, 45 K.) **J 1:39.** ὅλην τ. ἡμ. (Jos., Ant. 6, 22) **Mt 20:6.** The acc. in a distributive sense συμφωνεῖν ἐκ δηναρίου τὴν ἡμέραν *on a denarius a day* **Mt 20:2** (s. Meisterhans^3-Schw. 205; pap in Mlt., ClR 15, 1901, 436; 18, 1904, 152). ἡμέρας ὁδός *a day's journey* **Lk 2:44** (cp. X., An. 2, 2, 12; Gen 31:23; 1 Macc 5:24; Jos., C. Ap. 2, 21; 23). Daylight lasts for twelve hours, during which a person can walk without stumbling **J 11:9ab.** ἡ ἐν ἡμέρᾳ τρυφή *reveling in broad daylight* **2 Pt 2:13.**

ⓑ fig. (SibOr 5, 241) Christians as υἱοὶ φωτὸς καὶ υἱοὶ ἡμέρας *children of light and of the day* **1 Th 5:5;** cp. vs. **8** (in contrast, Aristoph., fgm. 573 K. calls Chaerephon, the friend of Socrates νυκτὸς παῖδα, in a derogatory sense). In **J 9:4** day denotes the period of human life; cp. **Ro 13:12f.**

❷ civil or legal day, including the night, ***day*** **Mt 6:34; 15:32; Mk 6:21; Lk 13:14;** B 15:3ff. Opp. hours **Mt 25:13;** hours, months, years **Rv 9:15;** cp. **Gal 4:10.**

ⓐ In the gen., answering the question, how long? (Nicostrat. Com., fgm. 5 K. ἡμερῶν τριῶν ἤδη=now for three days; Porphyr., Vi. Plotini 13 W. τριῶν ἡμ.; BGU 37, 7 [50 AD]; 249, 11 [70–80 AD] ἡμερῶν δύο διαμένομεν) τεσσεράκοντα ἡμερῶν *during 40 days* **Ac 1:3** D*. ἑκάστης ἡμέρας *each day* AcPl Ha 6, 8 (cp. ILegGort 1, 9 of a fine τᾶς ἁμέρας ϝεκάστας 'for each day', on the gen. Buck, Dialects §170; Just., D. 2, 6 al.)—In the dat., answering the quest., when? (X., An. 4, 7, 8; Jdth 7:6; Esth 7:2; Bel 40 Theod.; JosAs 11:1; Just., A I, 67, 7 al.) τῇ τρίτῃ ἡμέρᾳ (cp. Arrian, Anab. 6, 4, 1 τρίτῃ ἡμ.; AscIs 3:16 τῇ τρίτῃ ἡμ.; JosAs 29:8; Just., D. 100, 1 al., cp. D. 85, 6 τῇ δευτέρᾳ ἡμ.) **Mt 16:21; 17:23; Lk 9:22; 24:7, 46; 1 Cor 15:4.** ᾗ δὲ ἡμέρᾳ *on the day on which* (PLille 15, 1 [242 BC] ᾗ ἡμέρᾳ; 1 Esdr 1:49; Jos., Ant. 20, 26) **Lk 17:29;** cp. vs. **30.** μιᾷ ἡμέρᾳ *in (the course of) one day* (Appian, Iber. 58 §244) **1 Cor 10:8.**

ⓑ In the acc., usu. answering the quest., how long? (X., An. 4, 7, 18; Nicol. Dam.: 90 fgm. 130, 26 p. 410, 30 Jac. τὴν ἡμέραν ἐκείνην=throughout that day; Polyaenus 6, 53 τρεῖς ἡμέρας; Arrian, Anab. 6, 2, 3; Lucian, Alex. 15 ἡμέρας=several days; Philo, Vi. Cont. 30 τὰς ἓξ ἡμέρας; JosAs 10:20 τὰς ἑπτὰ ἡμέρας) ὅλην τ. ἡμέραν *the whole day long* **Ro 8:36** (Ps 43:23), **10:21** (Is 65:2). ἡμέραν μίαν *for one day* **Ac 21:7** (Just., D. 12, 3). ἔμειναν οὐ πολλὰς ἡμέρας **J 2:12;** cp. **4:40; 11:6; Ac 9:19; 10:48; 16:12; 20:6c; 21:4, 10; Gal 1:18; Rv 11:3, 9.** ἡμέραν ἐξ ἡμέρας *day after day* (Ps.-Euripides, Rhes. 445f, Henioch. 5, 13 Kock; Gen 39:10; Num 30:15; Is 58:2; Ps 95:2; Sir 5:7; En) **2 Pt 2:8;** 2 Cl 11:2 (quot. of unknown orig.; s. also e below, end). Only rarely does the acc. answer the quest., when? (Antiphanes Com. [IV BC] fgm. 280; Ps.-Lucian, Halc. 3 τρίτην ἡμ.) τὴν ἡμέραν τῆς πεντηκοστῆς *on the Day of Pentecost* **Ac 20:16.** Peculiar is the expr. τεσσαρεσκαιδεκάτην σήμερον ἡμέραν προσδοκῶντες *this is the fourteenth day you have been waiting* **Ac 27:33** (cp. X., An. 4, 5, 24 ἐνάτην ἡμέραν γεγαμημένην).—ἑπτάκις τῆς ἡμέρας *seven times a day* **Lk 17:4.**

ⓒ Used w. prep.: ἀπό w. gen. *from ... (on)* **Mt 22:46; J 11:53; Ac 20:18.** ἀφ' ἧς ἡμέρας (PRev 9, 1 [258 BC]; PsSol 18:11f; EpArist 24) **Col 1:6, 9;** Hm 4, 4, 3. ἀπὸ ... ἄχρι ... **Phil 1:5.** ἀπὸ ... μέχρι ... **Ac 10:30.** ἄχρι w. gen. *until* **Mt 24:38b; Lk 1:20; 17:27; Ac 1:2; 2:29.** ἄχρι ἡμερῶν πέντε *five days later* **Ac 20:6b.** μέχρι τῆς σήμερον (ἡμέρας) *up to the present day* (1 Esdr 8:74) **Mt 28:15.** ἕως τ. ἡμέρας **Mt 27:64; Ac 1:22; Ro 11:8** (Dt 29:3; Just., D. 134, 5 ἕως τῆς σήμερον ἡμ.; for this Ath. 2, 1 εἰς ... τὴν σήμερον ἡμ.). δι' ἡμερῶν *after (several) days* **Mk 2:1** (cp. Hdt. 6, 118, 3 δι' ἐτέων εἴκοσι; Thu. 2, 94, 3; Pla., Hipp. Maj. 281a διὰ χρόνου=after a [long] time). διὰ τριῶν ἡμερῶν *within three days* (PPetr II, 4 [6], 8 δι' ἡμερῶν ε'=in the course of 5 days) **Mt 26:61; Mk 14:58.** δι' ἡμερῶν τεσσεράκοντα **Ac 1:3** (s. διά A 2a). διὰ τ. ἡμέρας *in the course of the day* **Lk 9:37** D εἰς τ. ἡμέραν *for the day* (PPetr III, 95 col. 2, 6 [III BC]) **J 12:7; Rv 9:15;** εἰς ἡμέρας μ' *40 days long* AcPl Ha 6, 11. ἐν τῇ ἡμ. *in the daytime* **J 11:9b.** ἐν μιᾷ τῶν ἡμερῶν *one day* **Lk 5:17; 8:22; 20:1.** ἐν *on* w. dat. sing. **Mt 24:50; Lk 1:59; 13:31 v.l.** (Just., D. 29, 3 ἐν ταύτῃ τῇ ἡμ.; 111, 3 ἐν ἡμ. τοῦ πάσχα); **J 5:9; Hb 4:4** (cp. Gen 2:2); AcPl Ha 3, 9. *In, within* w. dat. pl. (Alexis Com. 246, 2 K. ἐν πένθ' ἡμέραις; Philo, Somn. 2, 112; TestJob 30:4; JosAs 21:7 ἐν ταῖς ἑπτὰ ἡμέραις τοῦ γάμου) ἐν τρισὶν ἡμέραις (PTebt 14, 5 [114 BC]; Porphyr., Vi. Plot. 17 p. 111, 26 W.; TestJob 24:9; EpArist 24) **Mt 27:40; Mk 15:29; J 2:19f.**—ἐπί w. acc. *over a period of* ἐπὶ ἡμέρας πλείους *over a period of many days* (PTurin I, 2, 15 [116 BC] ἐφ' ἱκανὰς ἡμ.; Jos., Ant. 4, 277) **Ac 13:31;** cp. **27:20;** ἐπὶ πολλὰς ἡμ. (Jos., Ant. 18, 57) **16:18;** cp. **Hb 11:30.** καθ' ἡμέραν *every day* (Hyperid. 6, 23; 26; Polyb. 1, 57, 7; 4, 18, 2 al.; Diod. S. 1, 36, 7 and 8; 2, 47, 2 al.; SIG 656, 22; UPZ 42, 13 [162 BC]; PGiss 17, 1; Tob 10:7; Sus 8 and 12 Theod.; 1 Macc 8:15; EpArist 304; Jos., Bell. 2, 265, Ant. 20, 205; Ar. [POxy 1778, 27]; Just., D. 39, 2 al.) **Mt 26:55; Mk 14:49** ('by day': AArgyle, ET 63, '51/52, 354); **Lk 16:19; 22:53; Ac 2:46f; 3:2; 16:5; 17:11; 19:9; 1 Cor 15:31; 2 Cor 11:28; Hb 7:27; 10:11.** Also (w. optional art., s. B-D-F §160; Rob. 766) τὸ καθ' ἡμ. (Aristoph., Equ. 1126; Pla.; Polyb. 4, 18, 2; POxy 1220, 4; TestJob 14:2; but simply καθ' ἡμ. **Ac 2:45** D) **Lk 11:3; 19:47; Ac 17:11 v.l.;** καθ' ἑκάστην ἡμ. *every day* (X., Mem. 4, 2, 12, Equ. 5, 9; PTebt 412, 2; Mitt-Wilck. I/2, 327, 18; Ex 5:8; Esth 2:11; Job 1:4; Bel 4:6; PsSol 18:11; GrBar 8:4) **Hb 3:13.** κατὰ πᾶσαν ἡμ. w. same mng. (Jos., Ant. 6, 49) **Ac 17:17.** μεθ' ἡμέρας ἓξ *six days later* (PSI 502, 16 [257 BC] μεθ' ἡμέρας ιβ'; 436, 3 [Just., D. 27, 5 μετὰ μίαν ἡμ. al.]) **Mt 17:1;** cp. **26:2; 27:63; Mk 8:31; Lk 1:24; J 4:43; 20:26; Ac 1:5; 15:36; 24:1; 28:13;** AcPl Ha 1, 33; 11, 8; AcPlCor 2:30. πρὸ ἓξ ἡμερῶν τοῦ πάσχα *six days before the Passover* **J 12:1** (not a Latinism, since it is found as early as Hippocr. πρὸ τριῶν ἡμερῶν τῆς τελευτῆς [WSchulze, Graeca Latina 1901, 15; Rydbeck 64f]; cp. Plut., Symp. 8, 717d; Lucian, De Morte Peregr. 1; Aelian, HA 11, 19; mystery ins of Andania [SIG 736, 70 πρὸ ἁμερᾶν δέκα τῶν μυστηρίων]; PFay 118, 15; PHolm 4, 23; PGM 13, 26; 671; Am 1:1; 2 Macc 15:36; Jos., Ant. 15, 408; Just., D. 27, 5; s. WSchmid, D. Attizismus III 1893, 287f; IV 1897, 629; Mlt. 100f; B-D-F §213).—It is striking to find the nom. denoting time in the expression ἤδη ἡμέραι τρεῖς προσμένουσίν μοι **Mt 15:32; Mk 8:2;** cp. **Lk 9:28** (s. B-D-F §144; Rob. 460).

ⓓ Of festive days: ἡ ἡμέρα τῶν σαββάτων (σάββατον 1bβ) or τοῦ σαββάτου (σάββ. 1a) **Lk 4:16; 13:14b, 16; J 19:31; Ac 13:14** (Just., D. 27, 5). ἡ ἡμέρα or αἱ ἡμέραι τ. ἀζύμων **Lk 22:7; Ac 12:3; 20:6.** ἡ ἡμέρα τ. πεντηκοστῆς **Ac 2:1; 20:16.** μεγάλη ἡμέρα *the great day* (of atonement) PtK 2 p. 14, 29. In gen. of a Judean festival GJs 1:2; 2:2 (the author no longer has a clear understanding of the precise festival signified by the term; s. Amann and deStrycker on 1:2). ἡ κυριακὴ ἡμέρα *the Lord's Day, Sunday* **Rv 1:10** (cp. Just. A I, 67, 7 τὴν ... τοῦ ἡλίου ἡμέραν). Festive days are spoken of in the foll. passages: ὃς μὲν κρίνει ἡμέραν παρ' ἡμέραν, ὃς δὲ κρίνει πᾶσαν ἡμέραν *one person considers one day better than another, another considers every day good* **Ro 14:5.** φρονεῖν τ. ἡμέραν *concern oneself w. (=observe) the day* vs. **6.** ἡμέρας παρατηρεῖσθαι *observe days* **Gal 4:10.**—Used w. gen. to denote what happens or is to be done on the day in question ἡμ. τοῦ ἁγνισμοῦ **Ac 21:26.** τ. ἐνταφιασμοῦ *day of burial* **J 12:7.** ἕως ἡμέρας ἀναδείξεως αὐτοῦ πρὸς τὸν Ἰσραήλ **Lk 1:80** (s. ἀνάδειξις).

ⓔ OT terminology is reflected in the expr. *fulfilling of the days* (Ex 7:25; 1 Ch 17:11; Tob 10:1b; cp. מָלֵא) ἐπλήσθησαν αἱ ἡμ.

τῆς λειτουργίας αὐτοῦ *the days of his service came to an end* **Lk 1:23.** ἐπλήσθησαν ἡμ. ὀκτὼ τοῦ περιτεμεῖν αὐτόν *the eighth day, on which he was to be circumcised, had come* **2:21;** cp. vs. **22.** S. ἐκπλήρωσις, συμπληρόω, συντελέω, τελέω, τελειόω. The Hebr. has also furnished the expr. ἡμέρᾳ καὶ ἡμέρᾳ *day after day* (Esth 3:4 יוֹם וָיוֹם=LXX καθ' ἑκάστην ἡμέραν; יוֹם יוֹם Ps 68:20=LXX 67:20 ἡμέραν καθ' ἡμέραν) **2 Cor 4:16;** GJs 6:1.—ἡμέραν ἐξ ἡμέρας (rather oft. in the OT for various Hebr. expressions, but also in Henioch. Com. 5, 13 K.) *day after day* **2 Pt 2:8;** prophetic quot. of unknown origin 2 Cl 11:2. ἡμέρᾳ ἀφ' ἡμέρας GJs 12:3.

❸ **a day appointed for very special purposes,** *day* (UPZ 66, 5 [153 BC] ἡ ἡμ.=the wedding day; ins in ÖJh 64, '95, p. 74 of a commemorative day for the founder of Ephesus τῇ τοῦ 'Ανδρόκλου ἡμέρᾳ), e.g. of childbirth **J 16:21 v.l.**

ⓐ τακτῇ ἡμέρᾳ **Ac 12:21.** ἡμέραν τάξασθαι (Polyb. 18, 19, 1) **28:23.** στῆσαι (Dionys. Hal. 6, 48) **17:31.** ὁρίζειν (Polyb., Dionys. Hal.; Epict., Ench. 51, 1) **Hb 4:7;** Hv 2, 2, 5. Of the day of the census (s. Lk 2:1) αὕτη ἡ ἡμέρα κυρίου GJs 17:1. ἐν ἡμέρᾳ, ᾗ ἔμελλεν θηριομαχῖν ὁ Παῦλος AcPl Ha 3, 9.

ⓑ esp. of a day of judgment, fixed by a judge—**α.** ἀνθρωπίνη ἡμ. *a day appointed by a human court* **1 Cor 4:3** (cp. the ins on a coin amulet [II/III AD] where these words are transl. 'human judgment' by CBonner, HTR 43, '50, 165–68). This expr. is formed on the basis of ἡμ. as designating

β. the day of God's final judgment (s. ὥρα 3). ᾗ ἡμ. ὁ υἱὸς τοῦ ἀνθρώπου ἀποκαλύπτεται *the day on which the Human One (Son of Man) reveals himself* **Lk 17:30;** ἡ τοῦ θεοῦ ἡμ. **2 Pt 3:12.** ἡ ἡμέρα ἡ μεγάλη τοῦ θεοῦ τ. παντοκράτορος **Rv 16:14.** ἡμ. κυρίου (Jo 1:15; 2:1, 11; Is 13:6, 9 al.) occurring only once in the NT of the day of *God,* the Lord, in an OT quot. πρὶν ἐλθεῖν ἡμ. κυρίου τ. μεγάλην κ. ἐπιφανῆ **Ac 2:20** (Jo 3:4; cp. JosAs 14:2). Otherw. Jesus Christ is the Lord of this day: **1 Cor 5:5; 1 Th 5:2** (P-ÉLangevin, Jesus Seigneur, '67, 107–67; GHolland, SBLSP 24, '85, 327–41); **2 Th 2:2; 2 Pt 3:10.** He is oft. mentioned by name or otherw. clearly designated, e.g. as υἱὸς τ. ἀνθρώπου, **Lk 17:24; 1 Cor 1:8; 2 Cor 1:14; Phil 1:6, 10; 2:16.** ἡ ἐσχάτη ἡμ. *the last day* (of this age) (s. ἔσχατος 2b) **J 6:39f, 44, 54; 11:24; 12:48;** Hv 2, 2, 5. ἡμ. (τῆς) κρίσεως (Pr 6:34; Jdth 16:17; PsSol 15:12; En; GrBar 1:7; cp. TestLevi 3:2, 3; Just., D. 38, 2; Tat. 12, 4) **Mt 10:15; 11:22, 24; 12:36; 2 Pt 2:9; 3:7; 1J 4:17;** 2 Cl 17:6; B 19:10. ἐν ἡμέρᾳ ὅτε κρίνει ὁ θεὸς διὰ Χρ. 'Ι. *the day on which . . .* **Ro 2:16** (RBultmann, TLZ 72, '47, 200f considers this a gloss). ἡμ. ὀργῆς καὶ ἀποκαλύψεως δικαιοκρισίας τοῦ θεοῦ **2:5** (ἡμ. ὀργῆς as Zeph 1:15, 18; 2:3; Ezk 7:19 v.l.; cp. **Rv 6:17**). ἡ ἡμ. ἡ μεγάλη (Jer 37:7; Mal 3:22) **Rv 6:17; 16:14.** ἡμ. μεγάλη καὶ θαυμαστή B 6:4. ἡμ. ἀπολυτρώσεως **Eph 4:30.** ἡμ. ἐπισκοπῆς (s. ἐπισκοπή 1a and b) **1 Pt 2:12.** ἡμ. ἀνταποδόσεως B 14:9 (Is 61:2); ἐκείνη ἡ ἡμ. (Zeph 1:15; Am 9:11; Zech 12:3f; Is 10:20; Jer 37:7f) **Mt 7:22; Lk 6:23; 10:12; 21:34; 2 Th 1:10; 2 Ti 1:12, 18; 4:8;** AcPlCor 2:32. Perh. ἡμ. σφαγῆς (cp. Jer 12:3; En 16:1) **Js 5:5** belongs here (s. σφαγή). Abs. ἡμ. **1 Cor 3:13; Hb 10:25;** B 7:9; 21:3; cp. **1 Th 5:4.**—ἡμέρα αἰῶνος (Sir 18:10) *day of eternity* **2 Pt 3:18** is also eschatological in mng.; it means the day on which eternity commences, or the day which itself constitutes eternity. In the latter case the pass. would belong to the next section.

❹ **an extended period,** *time* (like יוֹם, but not unknown among the Greeks: Soph., Aj. 131; 623; Eur., Ion 720; Aristot., Rhet. 2, 13, 1389b, 33f; PAmh 30, 43 [II BC] ἡμέρας αἰτοῦσα='she asked for time', or 'a respite')

ⓐ in sg. ἐν τ. ἡμέρᾳ τ. πονηρᾷ *when the times are evil* (unless the ref. is to the final judgment) **Eph 6:13.** ἐν ἡμ. σωτηρίας of the salutary time that has come for Christians **2 Cor 6:2** (Is 49:8). Of the time of the rescue fr. Egypt ἐν ἡμέρᾳ ἐπιλαβομένου μου τ. χειρὸς αὐτῶν *at the time when I took them by the hand* **Hb 8:9** (Jer 38:32; on the constr. cp. Bar 2:28 and B-D-F §423, 5; Rob. 514). ἐν ἐκείνῃ τ. ἡμέρᾳ *at that time* **Mk 2:20b; J 14:20; 16:23, 26.** τ. ἡμέραν τ. ἐμήν *my time* (era) **8:56.** ἐν τῇ ἐσχάτῃ αὐτοῦ ἡμέρᾳ *in his* (Abraham's) *last days* GJs 1:3.

ⓑ chiefly in the pl. αἱ ἡμέραι of time of life or activity, w. gen. of pers. (1 Km 17:12 A; 2 Km 21:1; 3 Km 10:21; Esth 1:1s; Sir 46:7; 47:1; ἡμέραι αὐτοῦ En 12:2; ἡμέραι ἃς ἦτε 102:5 and oft.) ἐν ἡμέραις Ἡρῴδου **Mt 2:1; Lk 1:5;** Νῶε **17:26a; 1 Pt 3:20;** Ἠλίου **Lk 4:25.** ἐν ταῖς ἡμ. τοῦ υἱοῦ τ. ἀνθρώπου **17:26b;** cp. **Mt 23:30.** ἀπὸ τ. ἡμερῶν Ἰωάννου **Mt 11:12.** ἕως τ. ἡμερῶν Δαυίδ **Ac 7:45;** cp. **13:41** (Hab 1:5). W. gen. of thing ἡμέραι ἐκδικήσεως *time of vengeance* **Lk 21:22;** τ. ἀπογραφῆς **Ac 5:37;** cp. **Rv 10:7; 11:6.** ἐν τ. ἡμέραις τῆς σαρκὸς αὐτοῦ *in the time of his appearance in the flesh* **Hb 5:7.**—ἡμέραι πονηραί *corrupt times* **Eph 5:16;** cp. B 2:1; 8:6. ἡμ. ἀγαθαί *happy times* (Artem. 4, 8) **1 Pt 3:10** (Ps 33:13). ἀφ' ἡμερῶν ἀρχαίων **Ac 15:7;** αἱ πρότερον ἡμ. **Hb 10:32.** πάσας τὰς ἡμέρας *all the time, always* **Mt 28:20** (cp. Dt 4:40; 5:29; PsSol 14:4). νῦν τ. ἡμέραις *at the present time* Hs 9, 20, 4. ἐν (ταῖς) ἐσχάταις ἡμ. **Ac 2:17; 2 Ti 3:1; Js 5:3;** B 4:9; D 16:3. ἐπ' ἐσχάτου τ. ἡμερῶν τούτων **Hb 1:2;** cp. **2 Pt 3:3;** GJs 7:2. ἐν τ. ἡμέραις ἐκείναις *at that time* **Mt 3:1; 24:19, 38; Mk 1:9; Lk 2:1; 4:2b; 5:35b.** ἐν τ. ἡμ. ταύταις *at this time* **Lk 1:39; 6:12; Ac 1:15.** εἰς ταύτας τ. ἡμέρας *w. respect to our time* (opp. πάλαι) Hs 9, 26, 6. πρὸ τούτων τ. ἡμερῶν *before this (time)* **Ac 5:36; 21:38;** πρὸς ὀλίγας ἡμ. *for a short time* **Hb 12:10;** ἐλεύσονται ἡμ. *there will come a time:* w. ὅταν foll. **Mt 9:15; Mk 2:20a; Lk 5:35a;** w. ὅτε foll. **Lk 17:22** (Just., D. 40, 2). ἥξουσιν ἡμέραι ἐπί σε καί *a time is coming upon you when* **Lk 19:43.** ἡμ. ἔρχονται καί **Hb 8:8** (Jer 38:31). ἐλεύσονται ἡμ. ἐν αἷς **Lk 21:6; 23:29.**—Esp. of time of life πάσαις τ. ἡμέραις ἡμῶν *for our entire lives* **Lk 1:75.** πάσας τὰς ἡμέρας τῆς ζωῆς αὐτοῦ *all his life* GJs 4:1 (cp. En 103:5; TestJob 46:9). μήτε ἀρχὴν ἡμερῶν μήτε ζωῆς τέλος ἔχων *without either beginning or end of life* **Hb 7:3.** προβεβηκὼς ἐν ταῖς ἡμ. *advanced in years* **Lk 1:7, 18;** cp. **2:36** (s. Gen 18:11; 24:1; Josh 13:1; 23:1; 3 Km 1:1; προβαίνω 2).—B. 991. DELG s.v. ἦμαρ. EDNT. M-M. TW. Sv.

ἥμερος, ον (s. next entry; ranging in mng. from 'tame' or 'gentle' of animals to 'civilized' or 'gentle' of humans: Hom. et al.; LXX; TestAbr A 2 p. 79, 5 [Stone p. 6]; EpArist; Philo; Jos., C. Ap. 2, 137; 212. Loanw. in rabb.) ***gentle, kind***

ⓐ of pers. who do not cause someone to feel intimidated because of their behavior (Pind. et al.; SIG 932, 7; OGI 116, 7; Philo, Leg. ad Gai. 243, Mos. 2, 279; Ath.1, 2 and R. 49, 8) *gentle, mild-mannered* opp. ἄγριος (cp. Dio Chrys. 11 [12], 28) IEph 10:2.

ⓑ of words *kind* (opp. ἔκφρικτος 'frightening') Hv 1, 3, 3. Comp. ἡμερώτερος (since Aeschyl., Ag. 1632) of commandments Hm 12, 4, 5.—DELG. TW.

ἡμερόω (s. prec. entry; Aeschyl., Hdt. et al.; PPrinc 119, 12 [IV AD] of land cleared for crops; Wsd 16:18; TestJud 2:3; Philo) ***to tame*** fig. of wicked desires Hm 12, 1, 2.—DELG s.v. ἥμερος.

ἡμέτερος, α, ον (s. ἡμεῖς; Hom.+) *our* used w. nouns **Ac 2:11; 19:35** D; **24:6 v.l.; 26:5; Ro 15:4; 2 Ti 4:15; 1J 1:3; 2:2;** 1 Cl 7:4; 32:4; 33:5; B 5:5; 7:3; Dg 9:2, 6; ISm 5:1; Hs 9, 11, 3; 9, 24, 4; MPol 12:2; Qua.—τὸ ἡμ. *what is ours* (=the real riches vs. 11) **Lk 16:12 v.l.** (opp. τὸ ἀλλότριον, q.v., 1bα, and s. SAntoniadis, Neotestamentica: Neophilologus 14, 1929, 129–35). οἱ ἡμ. *our people* (cp. Leo 4, 8; PGiss 84 II, 7f; Jos., Ant. 14, 228, Vi. 401; 406; Just., A I, 29, 2 al.)=the Christians **Tit 3:14;** MPol 9:1; Qua (1). S. ἐμός b.—DELG s.v. ἡμεῖς. M-M.

ἦ μήν s. ἤ.

ἡμιθανής, ές (ἡμι-, prefix used in compounds, 'half' + θνήσκω; Dionys. Hal. 10, 7; Diod. S. 12, 62, 5; Strabo 2, 3, 4; Anth. Pal. 11, 392, 4; Chariton 3, 3, 16; PAmh 141, 13; PLips 37:21; 4 Macc 4:11; JosAs 27:3 [Bat. p. 81, 9f]) ***half dead*** **Lk 10:30** (on the penalty in Egyptian law for not aiding a victim of violence, s. Diod. S. 1, 77, 3).—DELG s.v. ἡμι- and θάνατος. M-M.

ἡμίξηρος, ον (ἡμι- + ξηρός; PFlor 118, 3 [III AD]; TestSim 2:12; Etym. Mag. p. 535, 23) ***half dry, half withered*** of branches Hs 8, 1, 8f; 8, 4, 6; 8, 5, 2ff; 8, 7, 1f. Of vegetation 9, 1, 6.

ἥμισυς, εια, υ gen. **ἡμίσους** (Dssm., NB 14 [BS 186]) **Mk 6:23;** neut. pl. ἡμίση (Theophr., Char. 11, 5; Polyaenus 6, 15); the spelling ἡμίσια is also used **Lk 19:8** (Rdm.[2] 63) ('half' as adj. and subst. Hom. et al.; ins, pap, LXX, pseudepigr., Philo, Joseph.)

❶ ***half*** adj. (ῥάβδους) ἡμίσους ξηρούς (ἡμιξήρους v.l.) Hs 8, 4, 6; (λίθους) τοὺς ἡμίσεις λευκούς, ἡμίσεις δὲ μέλανας 9, 8, 5.

❷ ***the half*** subst. (Thu. 5, 31, 2 ἡ ἡμίσεια τῆς γῆς; X., Cyr. 4, 5, 1 τοῦ σίτου ὁ ἥμισυς; 2, 3, 17 οἱ ἡμίσεις τῶν ἀνδρῶν; 4, 5, 4 τῶν ἄρτων οἱ ἡμίσεις; Demosth. 4, 16 οἱ ἡμίσεις τῶν ἱππέων; 1 Macc 3:34, 37; Jos., Bell. 6, 290) (τὸ) ἥμ. *one half* (Hom. et al.; TestJob 31:2; Jos., Ant. 7, 275) **Rv 12:14** (Da 12:7); Hs 8, 1, 11; 8, 5, 2; 8, 8, 1; ApcPt 12:27. τὰ ἡμίσια τῶν ὑπαρχόντων (Tob 10:10 BA v.l.) **Lk 19:8.** ἕως ἡμίσους τῆς βασιλείας μου *up to one half of my kingdom* (Esth 5:3; 7:2) **Mk 6:23.** ἡμέρας τρεῖς καὶ ἥμισυ *three and one-half days* **Rv 11:9, 11** (transition to numeral [indecl., s. Mussies 220] cp. ἥμισυ **Lk 19:8 v.l.;** τὰς ἐννέα ἥμισυ φυλάς AscIs 3:2; Athen. 6, 274c τῶν δυοῖν δραχμῶν καὶ ἡμίσους; Ex 25:17; 26:16. Without καί Plut., Mar. 34, 4).—GKittel, Rabbinica 1920, 39ff.—B. 935. DELG s.v. ἡμι-. M-M.

ἡμιώριον, ου, τό or ἡμίωρον **Rv 8:1** N.[25] (Menand. fgm. 850 Kö.; Strabo 2, 5, 36; Archigenes [II AD] in Aëtius p. 160, 13. On the development of both forms s. Kühner-Bl. II 323; s. Mlt-H. 176; 280; 341; cp. DELG s.v. ὥρα) (ἡμι- + ὥρα) *a half hour* **Rv 8:1.**—M-M s.v. ἡμίωρον.

ἤνεγκα s. φέρω.

ἠνεῳγμένος, ἠνεῴχθην s. ἀνοίγω.

ἡνίκα particle denoting time (Hom.+; ins, pap, LXX, pseudepigr., Philo; Jos., Ant. 12, 138 al.; Just., D. 105, 3) ***when, at the time when*** w. pres. subj. and ἄν *whenever* **2 Cor 3:15;** *when, as soon as* 1 Cl 57:4 (Pr 1:26). W. aor. subj. and ἐάν *(at the time) when, every time that* (POxy 104, 26 [96 AD] ἡνίκα ἐὰν ἀπαλλαγῇ τ. ἀνδρός; PTebt 317, 18 ἡνίκα ἐὰν εἰς τὸν νόμον παραγένηται; Gen 27:40) **2 Cor 3:16** (Ex 34:34, but w. ἄν and impf.).—DELG. M-M.

ἤπερ s. ἤ 2eβ.

ἤπιος, α, ον (since Hom., also Empedokles; Vorsokr. 17, 18 [the rdg. in Ath. 22, 1], Epict.p. 487, 3; grave ins APF 5, 1913, 166 no. 17, 4 the deceased is decribed as ἤπιον ἀνθρώποισι; POxy 1380, 11; 86; 155; Philo, Mos. 1, 72; cp. DELG s.v.) *gentle* **1 Th 2:7 v.l.** (for νήπιοι q.v.). ἤπ. πρός τινα *kind toward someone* **2 Ti 2:24** (v.l. νήπιον).—DELG. M-M. Spicq. Sv.

ἠπίως adv. of ἤπιος (since Soph., El. 1439; Hdt. 7, 105; also Paus. 10, 11, 4) ***kindly*** 1 Cl 23:1.

Ἤρ, ὁ indecl. (עֵר) ***Er*** (Gen 38:3; TestJud 8:3; 10:1, 3; Philo, Poster. Cai. 180), in the genealogy of Jesus **Lk 3:28.**

ἦρα s. αἴρω.

ἠρεμέω 1 aor. ἠρέμησα (since Hippocr., Pla., Aristot., pap [II AD]; Job 38:19 Sym. al., Philo, Joseph.) ***be quiet, hold one's peace*** τὰ πετεινὰ . . . ἠρεμοῦντα GJs 18:2 (not pap). Ἰωσὴφ ἠρέμησεν ἐξ αὐτῆς *Joseph let her alone* (he left Mary's presence for the time being and ceased to upbraid her) 14:1 (s. deStrycker p. 304f). (Jos., Bell. 5, 388 ἀπὸ τῶν ὅπλων ἠρεμοῦσαι [χεῖρες] parallels grammar but not the thought.)—DELG s.v. ἠρέμα (adv.).

ἤρεμος, ον (Lucian, Tragodop. 207; OGI 519, 10 [III AD] ἤρεμον καὶ γαληνὸν τὸν βίον διαγόντων; Paroem. Gr.: Zenob. 2, 65 [Hadrian] βίον ἄλυπον καὶ ἤρ. ἔχειν; Esth 3:13b acc. to cod. A; Hesychius) ***quiet, tranquil,*** of life: ἵνα ἤρεμον κ. ἡσύχιον βίον διάγωμεν **1 Ti 2:2** (cited in Ath. 37, 1).—B. 840f. DELG and Boisacq s.v. ἠρέμα. M-M.

ἤρθην s. αἴρω.

Ἡρῴδης, ου, ὁ (freq.; also in ins [OGI index I] and pap [Preisigke, Namenbuch], where it is not infrequently found in the correct [B-D-F §26; Mlt-H. 84] spelling with ι; s. Schürer I 294, 20) ***Herod,*** name of Idumaean princes forming a dynasty, whose rule in Palestine was established through the favor of Mark Antony and Octavian toward 1; the dynasty continued to rule, though in varied forms, until after the death of 3.—WOtto, Herodes. Beiträge z. Gesch. d. letzten jüd. Königshauses 1913; HWillrich, D. Haus des H. zwischen Jerusalem u. Rom 1929; MStern, in CRINT I/1 216–307; Pauly-W. Suppl. II 1-191. BHHW II 696–763.

❶ Herod I, the Great (41 [37]–4 BC) **Mt 2:1–22; Lk 1:5;** GJs 21:2; 22:1; 23:1f; 25:1 (Just., A I, 31, 2 al.). A palace built by him and named after him is mentioned **Ac 23:35.**—Schürer I 287–329; EMeyer II 322–27; ASchalit, König Herodes '69 (transl. by JAmir from the Hebr. of '60).; MGrant, Herod the Great '71; EncJud VIII 375–87; ABD III 161–69.

❷ the son of 1, Herod Antipas (4 BC–39 AD), tetrarch of Galilee and Perea (Jos., Ant. 17, 318), mentioned in the NT because of (among other things) his clash w. John the Baptist, whom he had executed (s. Ἰωάννης 1). The synoptics state that John raised objections to the tetrarch's marriage to Herodias (q.v.), who forsook one of his brothers to marry him. Acc. to Lk (and GPt) this Herod played a role in the passion story (AVerrall, JTS 10, 1909, 322–53; MDibelius, ZNW 16, 1915, 113–26; KBornhäuser, NKZ 40, 1929, 714–18; JBlinzler, Her. Ant. u. Jes. Chr. '47; VHarlow, The Destroyer of Jesus. The Story of Herod Antipas '54; HHoehner, Herod Antipas '72). **Mt 14:1, 3, 6; Mk 6:14–22; 8:15; Lk 3:1, 19; 8:3; 9:7, 9; 13:31; 23:7–15; Ac 4:27; 13:1;** ISm 1:2; GEb 13, 74; GPt 1:1f; 2:4f. Called βασιλεύς **Mk 6:14;** cp. **Mt 14:9;** GEb 13, 74; GPt 1:2 (ApcEsdr 4:11 p. 28, 11 Tdf.; Just., D. 103, 3f al.; Mel., P. 93, 704).—Schürer I 340–53.

❸ Herod Agrippa I (s. Ἀγρίππας 1) **Ac 12:1, 6, 11, 19, 21.**

❹ a police magistrate in Smyrna (s. εἰρήναρχος) MPol 6:2; 8:2; 17:2, 21.—SPerowne, The Later Herods '58.—ISBE II 688–98. M-M. EDNT.

Ἡρῳδιανοί, ῶν, οἱ (on the sp. s. Ἡρῴδης) ***the Herodians,*** partisans of Herod the Great and his family (Jos., Ant. 14, 450 οἱ τὰ Ἡρῴδου φρονοῦντες; cp. Appian, Bell. Civ. 3, 82 §334 οἱ Πομπηιανοί; 3, 91 §376 Καισαριανοί) **Mt 22:16; Mk 3:6; 8:15 v.l.; 12:13.**—BBacon, JBL 39, 1920, 102–12; EBickermann, RB 47, '38, 184–97; PJoüon, RSR 28, '38, 585–8; HRowley, JTS 41, '40, 16–27; WOtto, Pauly-W. Suppl. II 200–202; WBennet, NovT 17, '75, 9–14 (Mk); WBraun, Were the Herodians Essenes? A Critique of an Hypothesis: RevQ 14, '89, 75–88.—TW.

Ἡρῳδιάς, άδος, ἡ (for the sp. s. Ἡρῴδης) ***Herodias,*** granddaughter of Herod the Great (Ἡρῴδης 1), daughter of his son Aristobulus, mother-in-law of Philip the tetrarch who married her daughter Salome (q.v.), and, before her marriage to Herod Antipas, the wife of another Herod, the son of Herod the Great and Mariamne II (Jos., Ant. 17, 14; Schürer I 321) and half-brother of Herod Antipas (Jos., Ant. 18, 109f). In **Mk 6:17** and **Mt 14:3** (except D) this first husband of Herodias is called (some hold erroneously) Philip; cp. **Mt 14:6; Mk 6:19; Lk 3:19.** In **Mk 6:22** Ἡ. is a daughter of Herod; on the problem of the rdg. in N. s. RBorger, TRu 52, '87, 25–27. S. also HHoehner, Herod Antipas '72, 110–71.—Schürer I 344–50; WLillie, Salome or Herodias?: ET 65, '53f, 251; MStern, The Jewish People in the First Century '74, 284ff; HHoehner, ISBE II, '82, 695.

Ἡρῳδίων, ωνος, ὁ (for the sp. s. Ἡρῴδης; grave-ins fr. Kom-el-Gadi: Sb 351 [6/7 AD]. S. also Preisigke, Namenbuch) ***Herodion,*** a Jewish Christian, greeted **Ro 16:11.**

Ἠσαΐας, ου, ὁ (also Ἡσαΐας and Ἰησαΐας; יְשַׁעְיָהוּ) ***Isaiah*** (Tyndale's 'Esaias' follows the Gk. form), the prophet (LXX; ParJer 9:21; AscIs, Joseph., Just., Mel.; Ath. 9, 1) **Mt 3:3; 4:14; 8:17; 12:17; 13:14, 35 v.l.; 15:7; 27:9; Mk 7:6; Lk 3:4; 4:17; J 1:23; 12:38f, 41; Ac 28:25; Ro 9:27, 29; 10:16, 20; 15:12;** B 12:11. Of the book of Isaiah γέγραπται ἐν τῷ Ἠ. *it is written in I.* **Mk 1:2;** ἀνεγίνωσκεν τ. προφήτην Ἠ. **Ac 8:28,** cp. vs. **30;** λέγει ἐν τῷ Ἠ. *he* (the preëxistent Christ) *says in I.* 2 Cl 3:5.

Ἠσαῦ, ὁ (Ἡσαῦ; עֵשָׂו) indecl. (LXX; TestJob 1:6; Test12Patr; Philo; Just.; in Joseph. Ἠσαῦς, αῦ [Ant. 2, 5]) ***Esau*** **Hb 11:20.** 'Dis-favored' by God **Ro 9:13** (Mal 1:2f). Typical of an immoral and vulgar person (on Esau in this light cp. Book of Jubilees 35, 13f; Philo, Virt. 208; s. Gen 27:41; 28:7f) **Hb 12:16.** The flight of Jacob fr. Esau (Gen 27:41ff) 1 Cl 4:8.—TW.

ἦσθα s. εἰμί.

ἥσσων (cp. the deriv. ἡττάομαι; Hom. et al.; ins [SIG 709, 3]; pap [UPZ 113, 12: 156 BC; PTebt 105, 36]; LXX [Thackeray 122]), **ἥττων** (Aristoph., Pla. et al.; ins [SIG 851, 10]; pap [PPetr II, 47, 26: 208 BC; PTebt 329, 29] s. Gignac I 147; LXX; TestNapht 2:7 [?]; EpArist 257; Joseph.; Just.; Ath. 24, 5), ον, gen. ονος. Comp. without a positive: **pert. to being less on a scale of evaluation,** ***lesser, inferior, weaker*** ἥσ. ἁμαρτία *a lesser sin* 1 Cl 47:4. ἥσ. κίνδυνος 55:6 v.l. ἥσ. τόπος **Mt 20:28** D=Agr 22.—Subst. ὁ ἥσ. **Mt 20:28 v.l.;** οἱ ἥσ. 1 Cl 39:9 (Job 5:4). τὸ ἧσσον (opp. τὸ κρεῖσσον): εἰς τὸ ἧσ. συνέρχεσθε *(when) you come together (it is) for the worse* (but the comp. sense is no longer strongly felt: AFridrichsen, Horae Soederblom. I/1, '44, 30f) **1 Cor 11:17.**—The neut. as adv. *less* (M. Ant. 3, 2, 6; Jos., Ant. 4, 194; 5, 206; Just., A I, 18, 6 and D. 95, 1) εἰ περισσοτέρως ὑμᾶς ἀγαπῶν ἧσσον ἀγαπῶμαι; *if I love you much more, am I on that account to be loved less?* **2 Cor 12:15.** οὐχ ἧττον (v.l. ἥττονι) 1 Cl 55:6 *no less, just so* (Just., A I, 18, 6).—DELG s.v. ἦκα (adv.). M-M.

ἡσυχάζω fut. ἡσυχάσω LXX; 1 aor. ἡσύχασα, impv. ἡσύχασον (s. three next entries; Solon, fgm. 4c, 1 West=4, 5 Diehl; Aeschyl.,Thu. et al.; pap, LXX, Philo, Joseph., Test12Patr) in our lit. only intrans.

❶ **to relax from normal activity,** ***rest*** (Appian, Bell. Civ. 4, 72 §306; JosAs 10:8 ἐν τῇ κλίνῃ μοὺ; Jos., Ant. 18, 354) 1 Cl 4:5 (Gen 4:7); *abstain fr. work* (Herodian 7, 5, 3) of the conduct prescribed in the law for the sabbath **Lk 23:56** (Neptunianus [II AD] ed. WGemoll, Progr. Striegau 1884, 53 the ants are said τὸ σάββατον ἡσυχάζειν κ. σχολὴν ἄγειν).

❷ **to live a quiet life or refrain from disturbing activity,** ***be peaceable/orderly*** (Thu. 1, 120, 3 w. εἰρήνη as synonym and opp. πολεμεῖν; BGU 372 II, 14; PSI 41, 23 σωφρονῖν καὶ ἡσυχάζειν; Philo, Abr. 27). Of conduct that does not disturb the peace. Christian leaders endeavored to keep their members free of anything that might be construed as disturbance of public order: **1 Th 4:11.** In a semantically dense statement: w. gen. (for the gen. in connection with verbs expressing cessation, s. Kühner-Gerth II/1, 396) *cease from* (cp. Job 32:6) τῆς ματαίας στάσεως (here στάσις 'disorder' is opp. of ἡσυχία 'order', in ref. to corporate congregational life) 1 Cl 63:1.

❸ **to be free from being disturbed,** ***have rest*** (Diog. L. 3, 21) ἀπό τινος *from someth., remain undisturbed* 1 Cl 57:7 (Pr 1:33), unless the ἀπό-clause goes w. ἀφόβως, in which case this pass. belongs under mng. 1. False v.l. cod. a ἡσύχαζον for ἀπηλαύνετο GJs 18:3.

❹ **to refrain from saying someth.,** ***be quiet, remain silent*** (Aeschyl., Prom. 327; ViAesopi G 38; Job 32:1; 2 Esdr 15:8; Philo, Somn. 2, 263; Jos., Bell. 3, 263, Ant. 1, 339) **Lk 14:4; Ac 11:18; 21:14; 22:2** D (for ἡσυχία).—DELG s.v. ἥσυχος. M-M. TW. Spicq.

ἡσυχία, ας, ἡ (s. prec. entry; Hom.+).—❶ **state of quietness without disturbance,** ***quietness, rest*** (Diod. S. 4, 2, 2 opp. to accompaniment of thunder and lightning; 16, 13, 2 without any fanfare; 18, 9, 3 without experiencing disturbance; Diog. L. 9, 21 of a quiet scholar's life w. implied contrast of being engaged in public affairs; Pind., P. 1, 70 σύμφωνον ἐς ἀσυχίαν 'to harmonious peace' among citizens; Jos., Ant. 18, 245 opp. bustle of city life) w. πραότης Hm 5, 2, 6 (TestAbr A 1 p. 77, 3 [Stone p. 2]). Of living in a way that does not cause disturbance (Mel., HE 4, 26, 6) **2 Th 3:12** (cp. ἀτάκτως vs. 11 and juxtaposition of ἀτακτεῖν and ἡσυχία Sotades 6, 8f [Coll. Alex. p. 241]; μετὰ ἡσυχίας as in Diod. S. [s. above] and SIG 1109, 64f of an injunction to bit-players in a cultic drama not to overplay or 'ham it up'; UPZ 8, 17 [161 BC]; BGU 614; Sir 28:16). ἡσυχίαν ἔχειν ἀπό τινος *have respite from someth.* ApcPt 17:32.

❷ **state of saying nothing or very little,** ***silence*** (Pla., Ep. 2, 312c; Pr 11:12; Philo, Rer. Div. Her. 14; Jos., Ant. 3, 67) IEph 15:2. ἐν ἡσ. *in silence* (Philo, Somn. 2, 263) **1 Ti 2:11f;** IEph 19:1. παρέχειν ἡσυχίαν *quiet down, give a hearing* (cp. Jos., Ant. 5, 235; cp. Just., D. 115, 5 ἡσυχίαν ἠγάγετε) **Ac 22:2** (is it prob. that here such concepts as 'reverence', 'devotion', 'respect' may have some influence? Cp. Dio Chrys. 68 [18], 10: Herodotus should be read μετὰ πολλῆς ἡσυχίας 'with much respect'). ἡσυχίας γενομένης **21:40** D (cp. Dio Chrys. 13 [7], 26; Philo, Vi. Cont. 75).—Schmidt, Syn. IV 248–64. DELG s.v. ἥσυχος. M-M. TW. Spicq. Sv.

ἡσύχιος, ον (s. prec. two entries and ἡσύχως; Hom. et al.; ins, pap; Is 66:2; PsSol 12:5; Joseph.) ***quiet, well-ordered*** D 3:8. W. πραΰς 1 Cl 13:4; B 19:4 (both Is 66:2); Hm 5, 2, 3; 6, 2, 3; 11:8. Again w. πραΰς: πνεῦμα **1 Pt 3:4** (cp. PsSol 12, 5 ψυχὴ ἡσ.). βίος (Pla., Demosth.; SIG 866, 15; POxy 129, 8 [VI AD]) εἰρηνικὸν καὶ ἡσύχιον βίον διάξαι *lead a peaceable and quiet life* (thus lightening the task of the heads of state; Jos., Ant. 13, 407 βίος ἡσύχιος, but in a difft. sense; cp. Thu. 1, 120, 3) **1 Ti 2:2.** Here ἡσ. prob.= *without turmoil.* ἡσύχιον εἶναι Hm 8:10.—B. (ἥσυχος) 840. DELG s.v. ἥσυχος. M-M. Spicq.

ἡσύχως adv. of ἥσυχος 'quiet' (s. prec. entry; trag. et al.; TestAsh 6:6; JosAs 10:9; also 23:9 cod. A [p. 74, 20 Bat.]) **pert. to being quietly efficient,** ***quietly*** λειτουργεῖν=to carry out responsibility without commotion 1 Cl 44:3.

ἦτα, τό indecl. (Hippocr.; Pla. Cratyl. 418c; BGU 153, 16 and 34 [II AD]; Philo, Leg. Alleg. 121; Schwyzer I 140) ***eta*** seventh letter of the Gk. alphabet, as numeral=***eight.*** In a context of numerical symbolism τὸ δεκαοκτώ· ἰῶτα δέκα, ἦτα ὀκτώ· ἔχεις Ἰησοῦν *the Eighteen: Iota* (is) *ten, eta* (is) *eight: thus you have Jesus* B 9:8.—S. the numeral η΄.

ἤτε . . . ἤτε s. ἤ 1aβ.

ἥτις s. ὅστις.

ἤτοι s. ἤ 1b.

ἡττάομαι (ἥσσων, cp. next entry) in our lit. only in pass. (so Soph., Hdt. et al.; pap, LXX [Thackeray 122]; TestSol 17:4 P [act.]; Test12Patr; Jos., Bell. 1, 57 al.; Just. On the spelling w. ττ s. B-D-F §34, 1; Mlt-H. 107; JWackernagel, Hellenistica 1907, 12ff); 1 fut. ἡττηθήσομαι LXX; 1 aor. ἡττήθην; perf. ἥττημαι

❶ **to be vanquished,** ***be defeated, succumb*** τινί *to/by a pers.* or *thing* (Plut., Cato Min. 16, 7; Is 51:7; Jos., Ant. 1, 288; TestReub 5:3; Just., A II, 5, 3) **2 Pt 2:19;** cp. vs. **20.**

❷ **to be made to feel less important,** ***be treated worse*** ὑπέρ τι *to someth.* **2 Cor 12:13 v.l.;** s. ἑσσόομαι.—DELG s.v. ἧκα. M-M.

ἥττημα, ατος, τό (s. prec. entry) (Is 31:8) ***loss*** **Ro 11:12.** ὅλως ἥτ. ὑμῖν ἐστιν *it is an utter loss for you* **1 Cor 6:7** (Field, Notes 160f).—M-M.

ἥττων s. ἥσσων.

ἤτω s. εἰμί.

ηὐξήθην, ηὔξησα s. αὐξάνω.

ηὐφράνθην s. εὐφραίνω.

ἤφιε s. ἀφίημι.

ἠχέω fut. ἠχήσω LXX; aor. ἤχησα LXX (s. next entry; Hes. et al.) in our lit. only intr. (cp. 3 Km 1:41; Is 16:11; Mel., fgm. 8b, 28) ***sound, ring out*** of brass instruments χαλκὸς ἠχῶν (cp. Hdt. 4, 200; Pla., Prot. 329a) **1 Cor 13:1.** ἤχησεν σάλπιγξ Κυρίου GJs 8:3 (cp. PsSol 8:1 σάλπιγγος ἠχούσης σφαγὴν καὶ ὄλεθρον). *Roar, thunder* of the sea (cp. Himerius, Or. 40 [=Or. 6], 1 ἠχοῦσα θάλασσα; Ps 45:4; Jer 5:22) **Lk 21:25 v.l.** (on the Peshitta here, s. MBlack, An Aramaic Approach[3], '67, 261f).—DELG s.v. ἠχή.

ἦχος, ου, ὁ (masc. doublet of ἠχή, cp. prec. entry; Pre-Socr. et al.; Herm. Wr. 1, 4; Sb 8339, 8 [ins 123 AD] τοῦ θεοῦ τὸν ἦχον; PGM 13, 399; 401; 532; LXX; En 102:1; TestSol 4:8 ἤχου; GrBar 6:13 [nom., perh. neuter]; ApcSed 11:19 p. 135, 1 Tdf. [nom.]; EpArist 96; Philo; Jos., Bell. 4, 299 al.; SibOr 5, 253).

❶ **auditory impression of varying degrees of loudness,** ***sound, tone, noise*** **Ac 2:2.** σάλπιγγος (Diod. S. 3, 17, 3; Achilles Tat. 3, 2, 3; 3, 13, 1; Ps 150:3; Jos., Ant. 11, 83) **Hb 12:19.** φωνῆς (Lucian, Nigr. 7) Hv 4, 1, 4.

❷ **information that is spread far and wide,** ***report, news*** ἐξεπορεύετο ἦχ. περὶ αὐτοῦ *a report about him went out* **Lk 4:37.**—This pass., as well as **Ac 2:2** and Hv 4, 1, 4, may also belong to the following entry.—B. 1037. DELG s.v. ἠχή. M-M.

ἦχος, ους, τό (w. doublet of ἠχή, cp. prec. entry; Ps.-Callisth. p. 61, 2; 9; PGM 13, 201; 204; 394; 545 ἐκ τοῦ ἤχους. In the LXX only the acc. ἦχος Jer 28:16 can w. certainty be listed here; ἦχος βροντῆς [acc.] TestAbr A 17 p. 99, 25 [Stone p. 46]; cp. nom. GrBar 6:13; s. also Reinhold 54) ***sound, tone, noise*** ἐν ἀπορίᾳ ἤχους θαλάσσης **Lk 21:25** (v.l. ἠχούσης; s. entries ἠχέω and ἠχώ; Nymphis [III BC]: 432 fgm. 3, 32 Jac., where the masc. pl. [s. preceding entry] refers to the roar of the waves, as well as the masc. sing.; Dio Chrys. 13 [7], 5 ὁ ἦχος τῆς θαλ.; Ps 64:8).—If, with some edd., we accentuate ἠχοῦς, this pass. must be assigned to the next entry.—DELG s.v. ἠχή. M-M. Schmidt, Syn. III 313–17, ψόφος.

ἠχώ, οῦς, ἡ (s. prec. three entries; trag. et al.; Philostrat., Vi. Soph. 2, 3, 1; Herm. Wr. 444, 19 Sc.; Job 4:13; Wsd 17:18) ***sound,*** fig. πάλιν ἔσομαι ἠχ. *I shall again be nothing but a sound* IRo 2:1 (but ἠχώ in this pass. is only a conjecture by Bunsen, Zahn et al.). On Lk 21:25 s. ἦχος and ἠχέω.—DELG s.v. ἠχή.

ϑ΄ numerical sign = ***9*** (ἐννέα; Jos., C. Ap. 1, 122) or ***9th*** (ἐνάτη) Hm 9 and s 9 (sc.) in superscriptions; GJs 2:4; AcPl Ha 11, 3.

ϑάβιτα **Mk 5:41** D; s. ῥαβιθά.

Θαβώρ, ὁ indecl. (תָּבוֹר) ***Tabor,*** a mountain on the south border of the Galilean highland (Judg 4:6ff; Ps 88:13) GHb 20, 61 (Orig., in Joh 2, 12, 87).—JBoehmer, ARW 12, 1909, 313–21, D. Name Th.: Ztschr. f. Semitistik 7, 1929, 161–69; CKopp, The Holy Places of the Gospels (tr. RWalls) '63, 242–47; BHHW III 1962f.

Θαδδαῖος, ου, ὁ (תַּדַּי, Talmud. תַּדַּאי. S. MLidzbarski, Handbuch d. nordsem. Epigr. 1898, 388; DDiringer, Le Iscrizioni antico-ebraiche palestinesi '34, 183; prob.=Θεόδοτος or a sim. form, MLidzbarski, Ephemeris für semit. Epigr. II 1908, 16) ***Thaddaeus*** **Mt 10:3; Mk 3:18.** In both pass. Λεββαῖος is found as v.l. It has been suggested that originally one of these names was found in one gospel, and the other name in the other, and that the variants in both cases are to be explained as an attempt to bring the lists of apostles into agreement. In Lk (**6:16**=**Ac 1:13**) Ἰούδας Ἰακώβου occurs in place of these names. BHHW III 1963. S. entry Λεββαῖος.

θάλασσα, ης, ἡ (Hom.+)—❶ ***sea***—ⓐ gener. (Hom. et al.) **Mk 9:42; 11:23; Lk 17:2, 6;** θαλάσσης καὶ σάλου **21:25** (σάλῳ θαλασσῶν PsSol 6:3); **Rv 8:8f;** 1 Cl 33:3. W. γῆ (Epict. 3, 26, 1; Michel 521, 10; SIG 4, 260b: index IV; PsSol 2:26, 29; Philo; Jos., Ant. 1, 282) **Rv 7:1–3** (cp. Artem. 1, 2 p. 6, 8–10 [=Pack p. 7, 11–13] ἡλίου δὲ καὶ σελήνης καὶ τῶν ἄλλων ἄστρων ἀφανισμὸν ἢ τελείαν ἔκλειψιν γῆς τε καὶ θαλάσσης).—W. ἡ ξηρά, the dry land **Mt 23:15** (Jon 1:9; En 97:7). W. γῆ and οὐρανός to denote the whole universe (Ex 20:11; Hg 2:6, 21; Ps 145:6; Jos., Ant. 4, 40, C. Ap. 2, 121; Ar. 1, 1al.) **Ac 4:24; 14:15; Rv 5:13; 10:6; 14:7; 21:1.** W. γῆ and ἀήρ PtK 2 p. 14, 17. κίνδυνοι ἐν θαλάσσῃ **2 Cor 11:26** (cp. BGU 423, 7; Jos., Vi. 14 πολλὰ κινδυνεύσας κατὰ θάλασσαν). τὴν θ. ἐργάζεσθαι *have work on the sea* **Rv 18:17** (s. ἐργάζ. 2d and Polyaenus 6, 24 θαλασσουργέω of a fisher). The sand of the seashore as symbol of numberlessness **Ro 9:27** (Is 10:22); **Hb 11:12** (Gen 22:17). Waves of the sea **Js 1:6; Jd 13.** τὸ πέλαγος τῆς θ. *the high seas* **Mt 18:6** (cp. Apollon. Rhod. 2, 608); ἡ ἄπειρος θ. 1 Cl 20:6.

ⓑ of specific seas—**α.** of the Red Sea ἡ ἐρυθρὰ θ. (s. ἐρυθρός) **Ac 7:36; Hb 11:29.** Without adj., but w. ref. to the same sea **1 Cor 10:1f** (s. FDölger, Antike u. Christent. II '31, 63–79; Just., D. 131, 3 al.).

β. of the Mediterranean Sea (Hdt. et al.) **Ac 10:6, 32; 17:14; 27:30, 38, 40;** AcPl Ha 3, 6; 33; 7, 27; 34 (Just., D. 3, 1 al.)

❷ ***lake*** (a Semitic usage, s. the expl. in Aristot., Meteor. 1, 13 p. 351a, 8 ἡ ὑπὸ τὸν Καύκασον λίμνη ἣν καλοῦσιν οἱ ἐκεῖ θάλατταν; cp. Num 34:11) of Lake Gennesaret ἡ θ. τῆς Γαλιλαίας *the Lake* (or *Sea;* OED s.v. 'sea', I 3) *of Galilee* **Mt 4:18; 15:29; Mk 1:16; 7:31.** For the same lake ἡ θ. τῆς Τιβεριάδος **J 21:1.** Both together **6:1** ἡ θ. τῆς Γαλιλαίας τῆς Τιβεριάδος *the Galilean Lake of Tiberias.* Simply θάλασσα **Mt 8:24** (Jesus addressed as κύριος vs. 25; cp. IAndrosIsis, Kyme 39: Isis is κυρία τῆς θ.; also IMaronIsis 39); **13:1; 14:24ff** (on walking on the θ. cp. Dio Chrys. 3, 30); **Mk 2:13; 3:7** al. RKratz, Rettungswunder '79; EStruthersMalbon, The Jesus of Mark and the Sea of Galilee: JBL 103, '84, 363–77.—B. 36. DELG. M-M. EDNT. TW.

θάλλω impf. ἔθαλλον; pf. ptc. τεθηλώς (Just.) (Hom. Hymns and Hes. et al.; ins, pap, LXX; OdeSol 11:12; SibOr 5, 400; Just., D. 9, 1) ***grow up, flourish*** of plants (Diog. L. 7, 86 θάλλει τὰ φυτά='the plants flourish') Hs 9, 1, 8.—DELG.

θάλπω fut. 3 sg. θάλψει Job 39:14 (Hom. et al.; ins, pap, LXX; TestJos 5:4; Ath. R. 56, 9) in Gk. lit. freq. in the sense 'make warm' (Jos., Ant. 7, 343 of a young woman who provided warmth for King David); in our lit. usage is limited to the fig. ext. ***cherish, comfort*** (Theocr. 14, 38; M. Ant. 5, 1, 1; Alciphron 4, 19, 9; OGI 194, 5 [42 BC] τὴν πόλιν ἔθαλψε), of children whom a mother cherishes **1 Th 2:7.** Of a wife, whom her husband is to care for as his own σάρξ (CPR I, 30, 20 of the husband to his wife ἀγαπᾶν καὶ θάλπειν καὶ θεραπεύειν; Sb 4658, 12) **Eph 5:29.**—DELG. M-M. Spicq.

Θαμάρ, ἡ also Θάμαρ. (תָּמָר) indecl. (LXX, Philo, TestJud; Just., D. 86, 6.—Jos. Ant. 7, 162; 178 has the same name, of David's daughter, as Θαμάρα, ας [s. BHHW III 1964]) ***Tamar,*** daughter-in-law of Judah and mother of his twin sons Perez and Zerah (Gen 38:6, 29f). In the genealogy of Jesus **Mt 1:3.**—TW.

θαμβέω 1 aor. ἐθάμβησα; impf. pass. ἐθαμβούμην. Pass.: 1 fut. θαμβηθήσομαι; 1 aor. ἐθαμβήθην, also ἐθαμβώθην ApcPt 3:8 (s. two next entries; Hom. et al.; pap, LXX; TestSol 7:2)

❶ ***be astounded*** (this is the orig. sense), intr. τρέμων κ. θαμβῶν *trembling and astounded* **Ac 9:6** t.r. (Erasmian rdg.).

❷ elsewh. in our lit. only trans. 'astound, amaze' and only in the pass. w. act. sense ***be astounded, amazed*** (Plut., Caes. 729 [45, 7], Brut. 993 [20, 9]; PGM 13, 527; Wsd 17:3; 1 Macc 6:8; TestSol 7:2; JosAs 18 cod. A [p. 68, 13 Bat.] and Pal. 364) **Mk 1:27; 10:32; Ac 3:11** D; ApcPt 3:8. ἐπί τινι *at someth.* **Mk 10:24.**—W. less force, *wonder, be surprised* GHb 187, 17 cp. Ox 654, 7f (ASyn. 187, 19–20). S. also GThGk 2:5.—DELG s.v. θάμβος. M-M. TW.

θάμβος, ους, τό (s. prec. entry; Hom. et al.; LXX) so certainly **Ac 3:10,** and **θάμβος, ου, ὁ** (Simonides 620, also LXX) so certainly **Lk 5:26 v.l.; Ac 3:10 v.l.** θ. μέγας **Lk 4:36** D (Jos., Bell. 5, 324; 7, 30 the gender cannot be determined) **a state of astonishment brought on by exposure to an unusual event, *amazement, awe*** (in the Gr-Rom. world freq. associated with activity of transcendent forces or beings [Od. 3, 372 et al.]) ἐγένετο ἐπὶ πάντας *came upon them all* **Lk 4:36.** περιέσχεν αὐτόν *had seized him* **5:9.** ἐπλήσθησαν θάμβους **Ac 3:10.**—B. 1093. DELG. M-M. EDNT. TW.

θαμβόω (Lucian, Syr. Dea 25) s. θαμβέω 2.

Θάμυρις, ιδος (Hom., Il. 2, 595; Tat. 41, 1f; Θαμύρις BGU 1074, 2 [I AD]) ***Thamyris,*** engaged to Thecla AcPl Ox 6, 19 (=Aa I, 241, 11; 242, 1).

θανάσιμος, ον (s. θάνατος; Aeschyl. et al.) ***deadly*** θ. φάρμακον (Eur., Ion 616; Diod. S. 4, 45, 2; Diosc. 2, 24; SIG 1180, 2; Philo, Plant. 147; Jos., Ant. 4, 279; 17, 69) *deadly poison* ITr 6:2. θηρία ἑρπετὰ θ. *death-dealing vermin* Hs 9, 1, 9 (λάχανα … θ. Just., D. 20, 3).—Subst. (so the pl. Diosc. 2, 19; 2, 81, 1; Jos., Ant. 14, 368) θανάσιμόν τι **Mk 16:18.**—DELG s.v. θάνατος. M-M. Spicq.

θανατηφόρος, ον (s. θάνατος, φέρω; Aeschyl., Hippocr. et al.; Diod. S. 3, 3, 6; 3, 5, 3; Vett. Val. 225, 7; 237, 7; 9 al.; Cyr.-Ins 9; 21; pap; LXX; TestAbr A 8 p. 86, 1 [Stone p. 20]; 17 p. 100, 1 [Stone p. 48]) ***death-dealing*** ἰὸς *poison* (SibOr, fgm. 3, 33 p. 231 G.) **Js 3:8;** καρπὸς θ. (Artem. 4, 57) ITr 11:1.—M-M.

θάνατος, ου, ὁ (Hom.+)—❶ **the termination of physical life, *death***—ⓐ natural death **J 11:4, 13; Hb 7:23; 9:15f; Rv 18:8** (s. also 1d); 1 Cl 9:3. Opp. ζωή (Mel., P. 49, 355; cp. 2a.) **Ro 7:10; 8:38; 1 Cor 3:22; 2 Cor 1:9** (s. also 1bα); **Phil 1:20.** γεύεσθαι θανάτου *taste death = die* (γεύομαι 2) **Mt 16:28; Mk 9:1; Lk 9:27; J 8:52; Hb 2:9b.** Also ἰδεῖν θάνατον (Astrampsychus p. 26 Dec. 48, 2. Also θεάομαι θ. p. 6 ln. 53) **Lk 2:26; Hb 11:5;** ζητεῖν τὸν θ. **Rv 9:6** (where follows φεύγει ὁ θ. ἀπ' αὐτῶν). θανάτου καταφρονεῖν *despise death* ISm 3:2; Dg 10:7a (Just., A II, 10, 8 al.; Tat. 11, 1 al.). περίλυπος ἕως θανάτου *sorrowful even to the point of death* (Jon 4:9 σφόδρα λελύπημαι ἕως θανάτου; Sir 37:2) **Mt 26:38; Mk 14:34;** ἄχρι θ. *to the point of death* of a devotion that does not shrink even fr. the sacrifice of one's life **Rv 2:10; 12:11** (TestJob 5:1; cp. Just., D. 30, 2 μέχρι θ. al.); διώκειν ἄχρι θανάτου *persecute even to death* **Ac 22:4.** Also διώκειν ἐν θανάτῳ B 5:11. διώκειν εἰς θ. AcPl Ha 11, 20 (opp. εἰς ζωήν). εἰς θ. πορεύεσθαι *go to one's death* **Lk 22:33.** [ἀναβῆναι] εἰς τὸν τοῦ θανάτου [τόπον] AcPl Ha 6, 30. ἀσθενεῖν παραπλήσιον θανάτῳ *be nearly dead with illness* **Phil 2:27;** ἐσφαγμένος εἰς θ. *receive* *a fatal wound* **Rv 13:3a.** ἡ πληγὴ τοῦ θανάτου *a fatal wound* **13:3b, 12.** φόβος θανάτου **Hb 2:15.**

ⓑ of death as a penalty (Thu. et al.; Diod. S. 14, 66, 3: the tyrant is μυρίων θανάτων τυχεῖν δίκαιος='worthy of suffering countless deaths'; Just., A I, 45, 5 θανάτου ὁρισθέντος κατὰ . . . τῶν ὁμολογούντων τὸ ὄνομα τοῦ Χριστοῦ al.).

α. as inflicted by secular courts ἔνοχος θανάτου ἐστίν *he deserves death* (ἔνοχος 2bα) **Mt 26:66; Mk 14:64;** παραδιδόναι εἰς θ. *betray, give over to death* **Mt 10:21; Mk 13:12** (ApcEsdr 3:12 p. 27, 23 Tdf.). θανάτῳ τελευτᾶν *die the death = be punished w. death* **Mt 15:4; Mk 7:10** (both Ex 21:17). ἄξιον θανάτου, *deserving death* (the entire clause οὐδὲν . . . αὐτῷ=*he is not guilty of any capital crime;* cp. Jos., Ant. 11, 144) **Lk 23:15** (s. αἴτιος 2); **Ac 23:29; 25:11, 25.** αἴτιον θανάτου **Lk 23:22** (s. αἴτιος 2). Also αἰτία θανάτου (Lucian, Tyrannic. 11) **Ac 13:28; 28:18;** κρίμα θ. *sentence of death:* παραδιδόναι εἰς κρίμα θ. *sentence to death* **Lk 24:20;** fig. ἐν ἑαυτοῖς τὸ ἀπόκριμα τοῦ θ. ἐσχήκαμεν **2 Cor 1:9.** κατακρίνειν τινὰ θανάτῳ (εἰς θάνατον v.l.) *condemn someone to death* **Mt 20:18.**—Several of the pass. just quoted refer to the death sentence passed against Christ; sim., θάνατος is freq. used

β. of the death of Christ gener. (Just., D. 52, 4 al.; ἀνθρώπου θ. ἀποθανεῖν Orig., C. Cels. 1, 61, 40): **Ro 5:10; 6:3–5; 1 Cor 11:26; Phil 2:8a; 3:10; Col 1:22; Hb 2:14a;** IEph 7:2; 19:1; IMg 9:1; ITr 2:1. τὸ πάθημα τ. θανάτου *the suffering of death* **Hb 2:9.** ἕως θανάτου καταντῆσαι *even to meet death* Pol 1:2.—GWiencke, Pls über Jesu Tod '39.—The expr. ὠδῖνες τοῦ θανάτου, used **Ac 2:24** in a passage referring to Christ, comes fr. the LXX, where in Ps 17:5 and 114:3 it renders חֶבְלֵי־מָוֶת (cp. 1QH 3, 7–12). This would lit. be 'bonds of death'. But an interchange of חֶבֶל 'bond' and חֵבֶל 'pain', specif. 'birth-pangs', has made of it *pangs of death* (cp. a sim. interchange in 2 Km 22:6 al. LXX, and the expr. in Pol 1:2 λύσας τ. ὠδῖνας τοῦ ᾅδου after **Ac 2:24 v.l.**). This results in a remarkably complex metaphor (s. BGildersleeve, Pindar 1885, 355 on 'telescoped' metaphor) **Ac 2:24,** where death is regarded as being in labor, and unable to hold back its child, the Messiah (s. Beginn. IV ad loc.; Field, Notes 112).

γ. of natural death as divine punishment (Did., Gen. 148, 25; 171, 9) **Ro 5:12ab; 21; 1 Cor 15:21;** B 12:2, 5.

ⓒ of the danger of death (2 Ch 32:11) σῴζειν τινὰ ἐκ θανάτου *save someone fr. death* (PsSol 13:2 [ἀπὸ . . . θ.]; Ael. Aristid. 45 p. 120 D.; Just., D. 98, 1 σωθῆναι ἀπὸ τοῦ θ.) **Hb 5:7.** Also ῥύεσθαι ἐκ θ. **2 Cor 1:10** (Just., D. 111, 3). θάνατοι *danger(s)/perils of death* (Epict. 4, 6, 2; Ptolem., Apotel. 2, 9, 5; Ael. Aristid. 46 p. 307 D.: ὥσπερ 'Οδυσσεὺς θ.; Maximus Tyr. 15, 8a; Philo, In Flacc. 175 προαποθνήσκω πολλοὺς θανάτους) **11:23.** μέχρι θανάτου ἐγγίζειν *come close to dying* **Phil 2:30. 2 Cor 4:11,** cp. vs. **12,** is reminiscent of the constant danger of death which faced the apostle as he followed his calling.

ⓓ of the manner of death (Artem. 1, 31 p. 33, 10; 4, 83 p. 251, 16 μυρίοι θ.='countless kinds of death'; TestAbr A 20 p. 102, 25 [Stone p. 52] ἑβδομήκοντα δύο εἰσὶν θ.; ParJer 9:22; Ps.-Hecataeus: 264 fgm. 21, 191 Jac. [in Jos., C. Ap. 1, 191]) ποίῳ θ. *by what kind of death* **J 12:33; 18:32; 21:19.** θ. σταυροῦ **Phil 2:8b.**

ⓔ death as personified **Ro 5:14, 17; 6:9; 1 Cor 15:26** (cp. Plut., Mor. 370c τέλος ἀπολεῖσθαι [for ἀπολείπεσθαι] τὸν "Αιδην); vss. **54–56** (s. on κέντρον 1); **Rv 1:18; 6:8a; 20:13f; 21:4;** B 5:6; 16:9 (this concept among Jews [Hos 13:14; Sir 14:12; 4 Esdr 8, 53; SyrBar 21, 23; TestAbr A 16ff; Bousset, Rel.^{3} 253, 2] and Greeks [ERohde, Psyche1903, II 241; 249; CRobert, Thanatos 1879].—JKroll, Gott u. Hölle '32; Dibelius, Geisterwelt 114ff; JUbbink, Paulus en de dood: NThSt 1, 1918, 3–10 and s. on ἁμαρτία 3a).

❷ **death viewed transcendently in contrast to a living relationship with God,** ***death*** extension of mng. 1 (Philo)

ⓐ of spiritual death, to which one is subject unless one lives out of the power of God's grace. θάνατον οὐ μὴ θεωρήσῃ **J 8:51.** Opp. ζωή **5:24; 1J 3:14; Ro 7:10; 8:6.** This death stands in the closest relation to sin: **Ro 7:13b; Js 1:15; 5:20;** 2 Cl 1:6; Hv 2, 3, 1; also to the flesh: Paul thinks of the earthly body as σῶμα τ. θανάτου **Ro 7:24.** In contrast to the gospel the law of Moses engraved on stone διακονία τοῦ θανάτου *service that leads to death* **2 Cor 3:7** (cp. Tat. 14, 1 θανάτου . . . ἐπιτηδεύματα). The νόμος, which is τὸ ἀγαθόν, proves to be θάνατος *death = deadly* or *cause of death* **Ro 7:13a.** The unredeemed are ἐν χώρᾳ καὶ σκιᾷ θανάτου **Mt 4:16;** cp. **Lk 1:79** (both Is 9:2). ἐν σκοτίᾳ θανάτου AcPl Ha 8, 32 (=BMM verso 4). This mng. of θάνατος cannot always be clearly distinguished fr. the foll., since spiritual death merges into

ⓑ eternal death. θαν. αἰώνιος B 20:1. This kind of death is meant **Ro 1:32; 6:16, 21, 23; 7:5; 2 Cor 7:10; 2 Ti 1:10; Hb 2:14b;** B 10:5; 2 Cl 16:4; Dg 10:7b; Hv 1, 1, 8; m 4, 1, 2. ἁμαρτία πρὸς θάνατον **1J 5:16f** (Polyaenus 8, 32 bravery πρὸς θ.='to the point of death'; s. ἁμαρτάνω e and TestIss 7:1 ἁμαρτία εἰς θάνατον). ὀσμὴ ἐκ θανάτου εἰς θάνατον *a fragrance* that comes *from death* and leads *to death* **2 Cor 2:16.** In **Rv** this (final) death is called *the second death* (ὁ δεύτερος θ. also Plut., Mor. 942f) **2:11; 20:6, 14b; 21:8** (s. TZahn, comm. 604–8).—GQuell, Die Auffassung des Todes in Israel 1926; JLeipoldt, D. Tod bei Griechen u. Juden '42; TBarrosse, Death and Sin in Ro: CBQ 15, '53, 438–59; ELohse, Märtyrer u. Gottesknecht '55 (lit.); SBrandon, The Personification of Death in Some Ancient Religions, BJRL 43, '61, 317–35.

❸ **a particular manner of death,** ***fatal illness, pestilence*** and the like, as established by context (Job 27:15; Jer 15:2: θάνατος . . . μάχαιρα . . . λιμός) **Rv 2:23.** ἀποκτεῖναι ἐν ῥομφαίᾳ κ. ἐν λιμῷ κ. ἐν θανάτῳ **6:8b; 18:8** (cp. PsSol 13:2; 15:7; Orig., C. Cels. 5, 37, 10).—JToynbee, Death and Burial in the Roman World '71; SHumphreys, The Family, Women, and Death '83.—B. 287. DELG. BHHW III 1999–2001. DDD 1609–13. M-M. TW. Sv.

θανατόω fut. θανατώσω; 1 aor. ἐθανάτωσα. Pass.: 1 fut. θανατωθήσομαι; 1 aor. ἐθανατώθην; pf. τεθανάτωμαι LXX (s. prec. entry; Aeschyl., Hdt. et al.; LXX; TestSol 20:5; 22:20 P; Philo, Joseph., Test12Patr, Just.)

❶ **to cause cessation of life,** ***put to death*** lit. τινά *kill someone, hand someone over to be killed,* esp. of the death sentence and its execution (as X., An. 2, 6, 4; Pla., Leg. 9, p. 872c; Aelian, VH 5, 18; Ex 21:12ff; Sus 28; 1 Macc 1:57; 4 Macc 8:25) **Mt 10:21; 26:59; 27:1; Mk 13:12; 14:55.** The obj. acc. is easily supplied in θανατώσουσιν ἐξ ὑμῶν *they will put some of you to death* **Lk 21:16.** Pass. **2 Cor 6:9** (for the wordplay ἀποθνήσκοντες . . . καὶ μὴ θανατούμενοι *dying . . . but not under penalty of death* cp. Ps.-Callisth. 1, 33, 11 p. 36, 21 θανὼν καὶ μὴ θανών); **1 Pt 3:18;** 1 Cl 12:2; B 12:2; Dg 5:12. *Be in danger of death* **Ro 8:36** (Ps 43:23.—Vi. Aesopi W 9 P. of ill treatment over a period of time: κατὰ πᾶσαν ἀποκτείνεις ἡμέραν).

❷ **to cause total cessation of an activity,** ***put to death, extirpate*** (Lycurgus 61 πολεώς ἐστι θάνατος ἀνάστατον=destruction spells a city's death) fig. ext. of 1 τὶ *someth.* τὰς πράξεις τοῦ σώματος **Ro 8:13.**

❸ **to cause death that transcends the physical,** ***bring death***

ⓐ of spiritual or eternal death 1 Cl 39:7 (Job 5:2); Hs 9, 20, 4. θ. τινὰ ἔν τινι *bring death to someone by someth.* m 12, 1, 3; cp. 12, 2, 2.

ⓑ of the death that the believer dies through mystic unity w. the body of the crucified Christ; τῷ νόμῳ (dat. of disadvantage) **Ro 7:4** (on rabb. associations s. WDiezinger, NovT 5, '62, 268–98).—DELG s.v. θάνατος. EDNT. TW.

θανατώδης, ες (s. θάνατος, -ώδης; Hippocr.+) ***deadly, fatal*** (so Aelian, NA 7, 5; Polyaenus 4, 3, 28; SEG VIII 549, 7 [I BC]; Philo, Abr. 46) of desires Hm 12, 2, 3.

θάπτω impf. ἔθαπτον; fut. θάψω LXX; 1 aor. ἔθαψα. Pass.: 2 fut. ταφήσομαι LXX; 2 aor. ἐτάφην; pf. 3 sg. τέθαπται 3 Km 18:31 (Hom. et al.; ins, pap, LXX, pseudepigr., Joseph., Ar. [Milne 74, 22f], Just., Mel., Ath.) ***bury*** τινά *someone* (Jos., Bell. 4, 317, Ant. 4, 78) **Mt 8:21f; 14:12; Lk 9:59f** (νεκρός B2); **Ac 5:9;** GPt 2:5. τὶ *someth.* τὸ σῶμα 6:23. W. obj. acc. to be supplied **Ac 5:6, 10** (cp. Polyb. 12, 26, 7 τοὺς πρεσβυτέρους ὑπὸ τῶν νέων θάπτεσθαι). Pass. (Jos., Ant. 4, 202; Just., D. 78, 8; 118, 1; Mel., P. 8, 56 al.) **Lk 16:22; Ac 2:29; 1 Cor 15:4.** τὸν τόπον . . . , ἔνθα ἐτάφη Papias (3:3; for the rdg. s. EPreuschen, Antilegomena 1905, 98, 20 app.).—PHeinisch, Die Trauergebräuche bei den Israeliten (Biblische Zeitfragen 13) '31, 70–100; DKurtz/JBoardman, Greek Burial Customs '71.—B. 291f. DELG. M-M.

Θάρα, ὁ (also Θαρά) indecl. (תֶּרַח) (LXX; Philo [Θάρρα].—In Joseph. Θέρρος [v.l. Θάρρος], ου [Ant. 1, 252]) ***Terah,*** father of Abraham (Gen 11:24ff; Josh 24:2; 1 Ch 1:26); in the genealogy of Jesus **Lk 3:34.**—BHHW III 1964f.

θαρρέω 1 aor. impv. 2 pl. θαρρήσατε (Bar 4:27 cod. B); inf. θαρρῆσαι (Attic [Pla.], and increasing in frequency beside θαρσέω [q.v.] in the Koine [Schwyzer I 285], occurring also in ins, pap, LXX [Thackeray 123]. Likew. Philo; Jos., Ant. 6, 181; 20, 175; Vi. 143; Just., D. 89, 3; Ath. 2, 2.—Thumb 77. On associations of this term in the Eleusinian Mysteries s. RJoly, RevÉtGr 68, '55, 164–70.) **to have certainty in a matter, *be confident, be courageous* 2 Cor 5:6, 8.** ὥστε θαρροῦντας (IMaronIsis 11f) ἡμᾶς λέγειν *so that we can say w. confidence* **Hb 13:6.** θ. ἔν τινι *be able to depend on someone* **2 Cor 7:16;** *be bold* εἴς τινα *toward someone* **10:1;** cp. vs. **2** (s. δέομαι aβ). εἰ ἄρα . . . θαρρεῖς τῷ Πέτρου θεῷ *if then . . . you really do believe the God of Peter* (AcPt Ox 849, 7; 'credis' cod. Vercellensis).—DELG s.v. θάρσος A. M-M. TW. Spicq. Sv.

θαρσέω (Hom. et al.; ins, pap, LXX; En, JosAs; Jos., Ant. 1, 187; 8, 293; 11, 334) in the NT (and quite predom. in LXX) only impv. θάρσει, θαρσεῖτε. 1 aor. ἐθάρσησα **to be firm or resolute in the face of danger or adverse circumstances, *be enheartened, be courageous*** ApcPt 2:5; Hv 4, 1, 8. θάρσει *have courage! don't be afraid!* (Il. 4, 184 al.; Gen 35:17; Zeph 3:16) **Mt 9:2, 22; Mk 10:49; Lk 23:43** D; **Ac 23:11** (on Homeric assoc. s. Warnecke 57, 12). Pl. (Ex 14:13) **Mt 14:27; Mk 6:50; J 16:33.** MParca, ASP 31, '91, 55f (reff.)— B. 1149. DELG s.v. θάρσος A. M-M. TW. Spicq.

θάρσος, ους, τό (Hom. et al.; Epict. 1, 24, 8; 2, 13, 3; SIG 709, 25; PCairMasp 158, 16; LXX, Philo, Joseph.; SibOr 1, 241) ***courage*** θ. λαμβάνειν *take courage* (Jos., Ant. 9, 55) **Ac 28:15** (for assoc. w. deity cp. Plut., Mor. 34a); Hv 3, 1, 5. W. χαρά MPol 12:1.—Schmidt, Syn. III 543–50, cp. ἀνδρεῖος. TW. Spicq.

θᾶττον s. ταχέως 1b.

θαῦμα, ατος, τό (Hom. et al.; ins, LXX; TestSol 3:8 D; TestAbr A 3 p. 80, 12 [Stone p. 8]; 7 p. 84, 26f [Stone p. 16f]; JosAs 28:1; Jos., Ant. 15, 395).

❶ **an object of wonder, *wonder*** (Herm. Wr. 1, 16; PMich 149 III, 19 [II AD]; Philo, Plant. 3).—ⓐ gener. *a wonder, marvel* (Bacchylides 17, 123 of a divine miracle; Appian, Bell. Civ. 1, 16, §67; Philostrat., Imag. 2, 12 p. 358, 1; 2, 18 p. 371, 6; Himerius, Or. 6 [=Or. 2], 25: Xerxes penetrates the strait; SibOr 3, 281) **2 Cor 11:14.**

ⓑ *wonder* in special sense, *portent, miracle* (Philostrat., Vi. Apoll. 1, 39 p. 41, 5; SEG VIII, 551, 35 [I BC]) ἰδεῖν θ. *see a wonder, miracle* MPol 15:1 (cp. Henioch. Com. 3 ὁρῶ θαῦμ' ἄπιστον; Lucian, Adv. Ind. 8 θ. μέγα τοῖς ὁρῶσιν); TestSol 3:8 D.

❷ **a state of wondering because one is extraordinarily impressed by someth., *wonder, amazement*** (Hom. et al.; Plut., Timol. 241 [12, 9] μετὰ θαύματος; Job 18:20) ἐθαύμασα ἰδὼν αὐτὴν θαῦμα μέγα *when I saw her I wondered in great amazement* **Rv 17:6.** θ. ἐγένετο μέγα AcPl Ha 4, 25.—B. 1093f. DELG. M-M. Schmidt, Syn. IV 179–88. TW. Sv.

θαυμάζω (s. prec. entry and three next entries; Hom.+) impf. ἐθαύμαζον; fut. θαυμάσομαι (θαυμάσω LXX; PsSol 2:18); 1 aor. ἐθαύμασα; pf. 2 sg. τεθαύμακας Job 41:1. Pass.: 1 fut. θαυμασθήσομαι; 1 aor. ἐθαυμάσθην.

❶ **to be extraordinarily impressed or disturbed by someth.,** act.—ⓐ intr. *wonder, marvel, be astonished* (the context determines whether in a good or bad sense)

α. abs. (X., Cyr. 7, 1, 6; Herm. Wr. 14, 4; Jos., Ant. 6, 56; Just., D. 89, 3; Tat. 22, 1; Ath. 11, 1; 24, 5) **Mt 8:10; 15:31; 22:22; 27:14; Mk 5:20; 15:5** (on silence evoking a sense of wonder cp. Plut., Marc. 224 [23]; TDwyer, The Motif of Wonder in the Gospel of Mark [JSNT Suppl. 128], '96); **Lk 1:63; 8:25; 11:14; 24:41; J 5:20; 7:21; Ac 4:13; 13:12 v.l., 41; Rv 17:7** (New Docs 5, 35); GJs 8:1; AcPl Ha 10, 29; 11, 2.—Somet. the expr. of amazement is added w. λέγων, λέγοντες **Mt 8:27; 9:33; 21:20; J 7:15; Ac 2:7.**—θ. θαῦμα μέγα **Rv 17:6,** s. θαῦμα 2.

β. used w. prep. expr.: διά τι *wonder at someth.* (Isocr. 4, 59; Strabo 17, 1, 5; Aelian, VH 12, 6; 14, 36) **Mk 6:6.** W. same mng. ἔν τινι (En 25:1) at someth.: ἐν τῷ χρονίζειν αὐτόν *that he stayed, at his delay* **Lk 1:21** (for this sense cp. Sir 11:21 μὴ θαύμαζε ἐν ἔργοις ἁμαρτωλοῦ; Is 61:6; En 25:1), but the words may also be taken in the sense: *during his stay* (s. B-D-F §404, 3; Rob. 1073). On the other hand θ. ἐν ἑαυτῷ *wonder to oneself* Hs 8, 1, 4; 9, 2, 5. ἐπί τινι *at someth.* (X., Mem. 1, 4, 2; 4, 2, 3; Diod. S. 2, 33, 1; Dio Chrys. 7 [8], 27; 62 [79], 1; 6; Job 41:1; 42:11; Jdth 11:20) **Lk 2:33; 4:22** (JNolland, JBL 98, '79, 219–29); **9:43; 20:26; Ac 3:12;** Hs 9, 2, 2. περί τινος **Lk 2:18.**

γ. w. ὅτι foll. (freq. w. πῶς in the pap, cp. POxy 2728, 5f; 2729, 4 et al.). *wonder, be surprised that* (Ps.-X., Cyn. 1, 3; Philo, Somn. 2, 183 μὴ θαυμάσῃς ὅτι; Jos., Vi. 339; Just., D. 3, 2; POxy 1348 [III AD]; 2783, 6 [III AD]) **Lk 11:38; J 3:7; 4:27; Gal 1:6** (cp. Demosth. 18, 159); GJs 16:2; AcPl BMM verso 37. Also w. εἰ foll. (s. εἰ 2 and cp. Hyperid. 3, 1; Philo Mech. 77, 41; Polyb. 3, 33, 17; PHib 159 [III BC] θαυμάζω εἰ πιστεύεις. Philo, Migr. Abr. 26; Jos., C. Ap. 1, 68, Ant. 1, 57 al.) **Mk 15:44; 1J 3:13;** Dg 10:4; MPol 7:2; 16:1; AcPl Ox 6, 15 (πῶς Aa I, 241, 15); AcPlCor 2:2.

ⓑ trans. *admire, wonder at, respect (persons)* w. acc.

α. τὶ *someth.* (Diod. S. 3, 56, 5; Alciphron 4, 6, 3; Herm. Wr. 4, 5; Da 8:27 Theod.; Philo, Abr. 103 al.; Jos., Vi. 222; Ar. 1, 1; Just., A I, 47, 1 al.; Mel., P. 22, 148; Ath. 1, 2 al.) **Lk 24:12; J 5:28; Ac 7:31** (but here θ. in the impf. is probably rather='wish to learn to know [about]', as Chion, Ep. 9 θ. τὴν συντυχίαν='wish to know what happened'); 1 Cl 1:2; 2 Cl 13:4, cp. vs. 3; MPol 2:2; 3:2; 7:2.—The expression θαυμάζειν πρόσωπα **Jd 16** (s. PKatz, Kratylus, 5, '60, 161), like πρόσωπον λαμβάνειν (cp.

D 4:3; B 19:4), is found in the LXX (Lev 19:15; Dt 10:17; Job 22:8 al.; PsSol 2:18) and prob. has the same sense as found there: *show partiality, respect persons* (cp. TestMos 5:5).

β. τινά *someone* (Diod. S. 1, 93, 2; Diog. L. 9, 4; Himerius, Or. [Ecl.] 3, 20; Jos., C. Ap. 2, 125; Mel., P. 92, 691) **Lk 7:9;** Dg 10:7f.—Pass. *be marvelled at* (Hdt 3, 82; SIG 1073, 41; PGiss 47, 5 ὡς καὶ ὑπὸ πάντων τῶν ἰδόντων θαυμασθῆναι; LXX; Tat. 32, 2 'Νέστορα . . . θαυμάζεσθαι; Ath., R. 51, 31 τῶν ἐπὶ σοφίᾳ θαυμαζομένων) **2 Th 1:10** (or as 2 below?).

❷ ***wonder, be amazed,*** as dep. w. 1 aor. and 1 fut. pass. (Kühner-Bl. II 439f. Once thus in LXX, Esth 4:17p [Thackeray 240, 1]) **Rv 17:8.** In pregnant constr. ἐθαυμάσθη ὅλη ἡ γῆ ὀπίσω τ. θηρίου *the whole world followed the beast, full of wonder* **13:3** (here wonder becomes worship: cp. Ael. Aristid. 13 p. 290 D.; 39 p. 747 of Dionysus and Heracles, οἳ ὑφ' ἡμῶν ἐθαυμάσθησαν. Sir 7:29; Jos., Ant. 3, 65.—The act. is also found in this sense: Cebes 2, 3 θ. τινά='admire' or 'venerate' someone; Epict. 1, 17, 19 θ. τὸν θεόν).—DELG s.v. θαῦμα. M-M. EDNT. TW. Sv.

θαυμάσιος, α, ον later also, though rarely, w. two terminations (s. prec. entry and two next entries; since Hom. Hymns and Hes.; ins, pap, LXX; TestAbr A; TestSim 6:7; Philo, Joseph., Just.; Tat. 18, 2) **pert. to being a cause of wonder or worthy of amazement, *wonderful, remarkable, admirable.***

ⓐ of things (EpArist 89; Jos., Vi. 208) διήγησιν . . . θαυμασίαν Papias (2:9), subst. τὰ θαυμάσια *wonderful things, wonders* (Hdt. 2, 35; Ex 3:20 and oft.; TestAbr A 6 p. 83, 26 [Stone p. 14]; TestSim 6:7; Philo; Just.) **Mt 21:15;** Hv 4, 1, 3. AcPl Ha 8, 33=BMM verso 6f Jesus ἐποίει μεγάλα καί θαυμάσια; also τὰ . . . ἐκῖ θαυμάσια *the marvels there* AcPl Ha 2, 23f.

ⓑ of pers. (TestSol 1, 13 D; TestAbr A 11 p. 89, 9 and 12 [Stone p. 26]. SIG 798, 11 [37 AD] θαυμασιώτερος; OGI 504, 12 θαυμασιώτατος. Superl. also POxy 940 verso; PGiss 57 verso; Philo, Abr. 38; Jos., C. Ap. 1, 51; Tat. 18, 2) ὁ θαυμασιώτατος Π. MPol 5:1; 16:2.—DELG s.v. θαῦμα. M-M. TW.

θαυμαστός, ή, όν (s. next entry; Hom. Hymns +) **pert. to being a cause of wonder or worthy of amazement, *wonderful, marvelous, remarkable*** (Diod. S. 1, 36, 7 θ. is heightened to παντελῶς ἄπιστον), in our lit. not of human personalities, but of God (Da 9:4 Theod.; Ps 92:4b) 1 Cl 60:1 and of things which are often related to God: name (Ps 8:2, 10) Hs 9, 18, 5; D 14:3; light **1 Pt 2:9,** cp. 1 Cl 36:2; glory Hm 12, 4, 2; course of action (the fem. for the neuter as a result of literal transl. fr. the Hebr.; s. B-D-F §138, 2; Rob. 254) **Mt 21:42; Mk 12:11** (both Ps 117:23); the judgment day B 6:4; the deeds of God **Rv 15:3** (cp. Tob 12:22 BA; Sir 11:4; Ael. Aristid. 48, 30 K.=24 p. 473 D.).—W. μέγας (as in some of the pass. already mentioned; cp. also SIG 1073, 26 μέγα τι καὶ θαυμαστόν; LXX; Philo, Mos. 2, 10; Just., D 10, 2; Tat. 25, 1) **Rv 15:1;** 1 Cl 26:1; 50:1; 53:3; 2 Cl 2:6; 5:5; Hv 1, 3, 3 cj. Joly. W. μέγας and ἰσχυρός Hm 12, 4, 2. W. μακάριος 1 Cl 35:1. W. παράδοξος (Menand., fgm. 466 Kö.; Just., D. 133, 1) Dg 5:4.—τί θαυμαστὸν εἰ; *what wonder is it, if?* (Epict. 1, 25, 33; 2, 9, 9; 4 Macc 2:1; Philo, Aet. M. 137; w. acc. and inf. Ath. 30, 1) 1 Cl 43:1. ἐν τούτῳ τὸ θαυμαστόν ἐστιν *the remarkable thing about it is this* **J 9:30.—2 Cor 11:14 v.l.**—DELG s.v. θαῦμα. M-M. TW.

θαυμαστῶς adv. (s. prec. entry; Pla. et al.; SIG 796a, 8; Herm. Wr. 506, 17 Sc.; LXX) ***wonderfully*** ἤκουσα μεγάλως καὶ θ. *I have heard great and wonderful things* Hv 1, 3, 3 (the mng. is unmistakable, but the text is prob. damaged; s. MDibelius, Hdb. ad loc.; difft. Joly, s. θαυμαστός). μεγάλως καὶ θαυμαστῶς πάντα ἐστί s 5, 5, 4. μεγάλως καὶ θ. ἔχει τὸ πρᾶγμα τοῦτο *this is a great and wonderful thing* v 3, 4, 1 (θ. ἔχειν as EpArist 58).—DELG s.v. θαῦμα.

θεά, ᾶς, ἡ (Hom.+; ins, pap; TestSol 15:3; Ar.) **a transcendent being conceived of as female and ordinarily understood as tutelary or source of special benefits to her devotees and therefore worthy of highest admiration and respect, *god/goddess,*** of Artemis ἡ μεγάλη θεά (cp. IBM III, 481, 324f τῇ μεγίστῃ θεᾷ Ἐφεσίᾳ Ἀρτέμιδι.—θεὰ μεγάλη of Isis: OGI 92, 3 [about 200 BC]; θεὰ μήτηρ [of Rhea] Orig., C. Cels. 4, 48, 11) **Ac 19:27, 37 v.l.** ὡς θεάν σε ἡγησάμην *I have regarded you as a goddess* Hv 1, 1, 7 (ὡς θεὰ λεγομένη TestSol 15:3); Hermas insists that he has nothing but the highest regard for Rhoda, whose beauty he had admired.—DELG s.v. θεός. M-M. TW.

θέαμα, ατος, τό (s. next entry; Semonides, fgm. 7, 67; Aeschyl.; Strabo 14, 2, 5 of the seven 'wonders' of the world; CPJ 519, 60 [II/III AD]; Ex 3:3 Sym.; Philo; Joseph.; Mel., P. 19, 127; 29, 197) **someth. notable exhibited to view, *a sight, spectacle*** GJs 19:2f.—DELG s.v. θέα.

θεάομαι fut. θεάσομαι TestSol D 4, 9; 1 aor. ἐθεασάμην; pf. τεθέαμαι; 1 aor. pass. (w. pass. mng) ἐθεάθην (Att. [Kühner-Bl. II 441]+)

❶ **to have an intent look at someth., to take someth. in with one's eyes, with implication that one is esp. impressed, *see, look at, behold***

ⓐ quite literally (POxy 963; Sb 1800; Jos., Ant. 3, 132; 6, 340) interchanging w. ὁρᾶν Hv 3, 8, 1. W. acc. as obj. (Hom., Il. 7, 444; Hes., Works 482; PSI 41, 19; Tob 2:2 BA; 2 Macc 2:4; En 6:2; 21:2) **Mt 11:7; Lk 7:24; J 8:10 v.l.; Ac 21:27; 22:9; 1J 1:1** (τοῖς ὀφθαλμοῖς ἡμῶν; cp. Philo, Mos. 1, 278 θ. αὐτοὺς ὀφθαλμοῖς); **4:12** (PvanderHorst, ZNW 63, '72, 280–82 [wordplay]). The obj. acc. is oft. found w. a ptc. that indicates what has been observed in the pers. or thing seen (En 9:1; 23:2; Philo, Vi. Cont. 89; Jos., Vi. 28; 281; B-D-F §416, 1): **Mk 16:14.** ἐθεάσατο τελώνην καθήμενον **Lk 5:27; 6:4** D (Unknown Sayings 49–54). Cp. **J 1:38; Ac 1:11.** W. ὅτι foll. **J 6:5.** W. acc. and ὅτι: θεάσασθε τ. χώρας, ὅτι λευκαί εἰσιν *see that the fields are white* **4:35.** W. acc. and ὡς: ἐθεάσαντο τὸ μνημεῖον καὶ ὡς ἐτέθη τὸ σῶμα αὐτοῦ **Lk 23:55.** W. acc. and εἰ *see/determine whether* GJs 1:3 (codd. not pap). W. acc. and ὅπως in an interlocking constr. ὅταν θεάσωνται τοὺς ἀρνησαμένους ὅπως κολάζονται *when they see how those who have denied are punished* 2 Cl 17:7. W. relative clause foll. **J 11:45** (ὁράω $P^{45, 66}$). θεασάμενος ἦν ὅσα ἀγαθὰ ἐποίησεν *he* (Joseph) *had seen all the good things that he* (Jesus) *had done* GPt 6:23.

ⓑ The passive means either—**α.** *be seen* ὑπό τινος *by someone* **Mk 16:11,** or—**β.** *be noticed, attract attention* τινί *by* or *of someone* **Mt 6:1; 23:5** (s. B-D-F §191, 1; Rob. 542, s. also 534).

❷ **to see for the purpose of visiting, *come to see, visit*** (Appian, Samn. 7, §1 θ. τὴν Ἑλλάδα) τινά *someone* (2 Ch 22:6; Jos., Ant. 16, 6) **Ro 15:24** (St. Paul compliments the congregation as one of the noteworthy 'sights' on his projected trip). Here belongs also εἰσελθὼν ὁ βασιλεὺς θεάσασθαι τ. ἀνακειμένους *the king went in to see his guests* **Mt 22:11** (the implication being that he went in to 'look them over').

❸ **to perceive someth. above and beyond what is merely seen with the eye, *see, behold, perceive***—ⓐ w. physical eyes, receive an impression of someth. transcendent *see, behold* (cp. PParis 51, 38 [160 BC] of a vision in the temple of Sarapis at Memphis τὸ ὅραμα τοῦτο τεθήαμαι; SIG 730, 20; 2 Macc 3:36; Tob 13:7; Jdth 15:8; En 106:13) τεθέαμαι τὸ πνεῦμα καταβαῖνον ὡς περιστερὰν **J 1:32** (he sees the dove and also becomes aware that it is the Spirit); ἐθεασάμεθα τ. δόξαν αὐτοῦ **1:14** (we saw the person and work of Christ and perceived in them the divine glory; cp. Tob 13:16 BA θεασάμενοι πᾶσαν τ. δόξαν σου). Cp. **1J 4:14.**

ⓑ of perception that is wholly nonsensual=*see, perceive* (X., Hiero 2, 5. W. ὅτι foll. Pla., Prot. p. 352a; Demosth. 4, 3; θεὸν θ. Theoph. Ant. 1, 2 [s. 60, 12]) Dg 10:7. θεασάμενος ἐν ἡμῖν πολλὴν πλάνην *he perceived much error in us* 2 Cl 1:7.—DELG s.v. θέα. M-M. TW.

θεατρίζω (ins fr. Gerasa: JRS 18, 1928, 144ff, no. 14, 18 [c. 102–14 AD], where the word certainly appears, though its mng. is uncertain; s. HCadbury, ZNW 29, 1930, 60–63; Achmes 21, 5 ἀτίμως θεατρισθήσεται; 51, 11; Suda II 688, 26; Byz. Chron. in Psaltes p. 328; ἐκθεατρίζω in Polyb. 3, 91, 10 and Diod. S. 34+35 fgm. 2, 46) ***put to shame, expose publicly*** ὀνειδισμοῖς τε καὶ θλίψεσιν θεατριζόμενοι *publicly exposed to reproach and affliction* **Hb 10:33** (Posidon.: 87 fgm. 108 [app.] Jac. ἐξεθεάτριζον ὀνειδίζοντες).—DELG s.v. θέα. TW.

θέατρον, ου, τό (s. prec. two entries; Thu. et al.; ins, pap, Philo, Joseph.; Just., D. 122, 4; Tat. 8, 1; loanw. in rabb.) 'a place for seeing', esp. dramatic productions (Hdt. 6, 67, 3); then

❶ **a place for public assemblies, *theater*** (Diod. S. 16, 84, 3 δῆμος ἅπας συνέδραμεν εἰς τὸ θέατρον; Chariton 8, 7, 1; Polyaenus 8, 21; IBM III, 481, 395 φερέτωσαν κατὰ πᾶσαν ἐκκλησίαν εἰς τὸ θέατρον [Ephesus]. Ins fr. the theater at Ephesus [103/4 AD] in Dssm., LO 90f [LAE 114]=OGI 480, 9. S. also SIG index; Jos., Bell. 7, 47; 107, Ant. 17, 161) **Ac 19:29, 31;** AcPl Ha 1, 24.

❷ **what one sees at a theater, *a play, spectacle*** (Ps.-Pla., Axioch. 371c; Achilles Tat. 1, 16, 3) fig. θ. ἐγενήθημεν τῷ κόσμῳ *we have become a spectacle for the world* **1 Cor 4:9** (Synes., Prov. 1, 10 p. 100c θεαταὶ δὲ ἄνωθεν οἱ θεοὶ τῶν καλῶν τούτων ἀγώνων; Sallust, Jugurtha 14, 23; Pliny the Younger, Panegyricus 33, 3; s. HConzelmann, 1 Cor [Hermeneia] ad loc.).—DELG s.v. θέα. M-M. TW.

Θεγρί, ὁ indecl. ***Thegri*** Hv 4, 2, 4, an angel in charge of animals. On him and his name s. MDibelius, Hdb., exc. ad loc., and s. Σεγρί.

θεῖον, ου, τό (since Homer [θέειον and θήιον]; pap, LXX; Jos., Bell. 7, 189; SibOr 3, 691; Just., A I, 53, 8) ***sulphur*** **Lk 17:29** (Gen 19:24); **Rv 9:17f** (w. καπνός and πῦρ as Philo, Mos. 2, 56); **14:10; 19:20; 20:10; 21:8;** 1 Cl 11:1.—DELG s.v. θεός.

θεῖος, θεία, θεῖον (Hom.+.; adv. θείως Just., A I, 20, 3.—RMuquier, Le sens du mot θεῖος chez Platon 1930; JvanCamp and PCanart, Le sens du mot *theios* chez Platon '56).

❶ **pert. to that which belongs to the nature or status of deity, *divine*—**ⓐ adj. *divine* δύναμις (Pla., Leg. 3, 691e φύσις τις ἀνθρωπίνη μεμιγμένη θείᾳ τινὶ δυνάμει; Dio Chrys. 14 [31], 95; decree of Stratonicea CIG II 2715ab [Dssm., B 277ff-BS 360ff]; EpArist 157 al.; Philo, Det. Pot. Ins. 83 al.; SibOr 5, 249; Just., A I, 32, 9) **2 Pt 1:3.** φύσις (Diod. S. 5, 31, 4; Dio Chrys. 11 [12], 29; Ael. Aristid. 37, 9 K.=2 p. 16 D.; Manetho: 609 fgm. 10 p. 92, 16 Jac. [Jos., C. Ap. 1, 232]; SIG 1125, 8; Philo, Decal. 104 τῶν θείας φύσεως μετεσχηκότων; Jos., Ant. 8, 107) vs. **4.** κρίσις (Simplicius in Epict. p. 20, 30; Philo, Spec. Leg. 3, 12, 1) 2 Cl 20:4. γνῶσις (cp. 4 Macc 1:16) 1 Cl 40:1. πνεῦμα (Menand., fgm. 417, 3 Kö. [=482, 3 Kock]; PGM 4, 966; Aristobulus p. 218, 5 Denis [Eus., PE 8, 10, 4=Holladay p. 136 ln. 28]; ApcSed 14:6; Philo; Jos., Ant. 6, 222; 8, 408; 10, 239; Just., A I, 32, 2 al.; Tat. 13, 2; cp. 4:2 θειοτέρου) Hm 11:2, 5, 7ff, 12, 21 (TestSol 1:10 L). ἔργα of the deeds of the Virtues v 3, 8, 7.

ⓑ subst. τὸ θεῖον *divine being, divinity,* freq. simply = 'the numinous' (Hdt. 3, 108; Thu. 5, 70; X., Cyr. 4, 2, 15, Hell. 7, 5, 13, Mem. 1, 4, 18; Pla., Phdr. p. 242c; Polyb. 31, 15, 7; Diod. S. 1, 6, 1; 13, 3, 2; 16, 60, 2; Epict. 2, 20, 22; Lucian, e.g. De Sacrif. 1, Pro Imag. 13; 17; 28; Herm. Wr. 11, 21b codd.; ins [SIG index p. 377f]; UPZ 24, 11; 36, 13 and 22; 39, 5; Mitt-Wilck. I/2, 70, 14; 116, 2 σέβου τὸ θεῖον; PGM 3, 192.—Philo, Op. M. 170, Agr. 80, Leg. ad Gai. 3; Jos., Ant. 1, 85 and 194; 2, 275; 5, 133; 11, 127; 12, 281 and 302; 13, 242 and 300; 14, 183; 17, 41, Bell. 3, 352; 4, 190; Just., D. 3, 7 al.; Tat. 16, 2; Ath. 1, 2 al.—LXX, En, EpArist, SibOr and other pseudepigr. do not have τὸ θεῖον) **Ac 17:27** D, **29; Tit 1:9 v.l.**—New Docs 3, 68 (ins).

❷ **of persons who stand in close relation to, or reflect characteristics of, a deity, including esp. helpfulness to one's constituencies, *divine*** (Diog. L. 7, 119: the Stoa says of the σοφοί: θείους εἶναι· ἔχειν γὰρ ἐν ἑαυτοῖς οἱονεὶ θεόν; cp. Pla., Rep. 366c.—Cp. on ἄνθρωποι θεῖοι Rtzst., Mysterienrel.[3] 25f; 237ff; 298; HWindisch, Pls u. Christus '34, 1–114; BGildersleeve, Essays and Studies 1896, 251–96 [Apollonius of Tyana]; LBieler, Θεῖος Ἀνήρ I '35; II '36; CHolladay, Theios Aner in Hellenistic Judaism '72; JKingsbury, Int 35, '81, 243–57 [Mark's Christology]; EKoskenniemi, Apollonios von Tyana in der neutestamentlichen Exegese '94) in the superl. (Oenomaus in Eus., PE 5, 28, 2 Lycurgus as ὁ θειότατος ἀνθρώπων; Iambl., Vi. Pyth. 29, 161 ὁ θειότατος Πυθαγόρας; used of the emperors in ins [SIG index p. 378a] and pap [PLond III, 1012, 4 p. 266]) οἱ θειότατοι προφῆται *the prophets, those people so very near to God* IMg 8:2 (cp. TestSol 1:4 C ὦ θεῖε βασιλεῦ; Philo, Mos. 2, 188; Jos., Ant. 10, 35 ὁ προφήτης θεῖος, C. Ap. 1, 279 [Moses]). Of angels Papias (4).

❸ **gener., of that which exceeds the bounds of human or earthly possibility, *supernatural*** (Lucian, Alex. 12 θεῖόν τι καὶ φοβερόν) of a monster ὑπενόησα εἶναί τι θεῖον *I suspected that it was some other-worldly thing* Hv 4, 1, 6.—RAC XIII 155–366. DELG s.v. θεός. M-M. TW. Sv.

θειότης, ητος, ἡ (s. prec. entry; of a divinity: the term in such description is not tautologous but usually refers to performance that one might properly associate w. a divinity: Plut., Mor. 398a; 665a; Lucian, Calumn. 17; Herm. Wr. 9, 1c; SIG 867, 31 of Artemis, who made Ephesus famous διὰ τῆς ἰδίας θειότητος, i.e. through manifestations of her power, s. ln. 35; POxy 1381, 165 πληρωθεὶς τ. σῆς [Imouthes-Asclepius] θειότητος namely manifestations of healing; PGM 7, 691; Wsd 18:9; EpArist 95; ApcSed 14:8; 15:2; Philo, Op. M. 172 v.l.; Just., D. 3:5.—Of persons who stand in close relation to a divinity: Heraclit. Sto. 76 p. 102, 4 Homer; Jos., Ant. 10, 268 Daniel; ins, pap, princes and emperors. So of Augustus, e.g. SEG XXVI, 1392, 31 [18–19 AD].—Of the Christian proclamation θ. τοῦ παρ' ἡμῖν λόγου Theoph. Ant. 3, 29 [p. 264, 16]) **the quality or characteristic(s) pert. to deity, *divinity, divine nature, divineness*** **Ro 1:20.**—HNash, θειότης-θεότης Ro 1:20, Col 2:9: JBL 18, 1899, 1–34.—New Docs 3, 68. DELG s.v. θεός. Lampe s.v. M-M. TW. Sv.

θειώδης, ες (θεῖος + -ώδης; Diod. S. 2, 12, 2; Strabo 1, 3, 18; Hero Alex. I p. 12, 8; III p. 214, 7; Aretaeus 170, 12; Galen: CMG V 4, 2 p. 107, 33; 186, 5 al.) ***sulphurous*** **Rv 9:17.**

Θέκλα, ης, ἡ ***Thecla*** (so far found only as a Christian name: CIG 8683; 9138; 9139; PBodl uncatal.: JEA 23, '37, 10f [gen. Θέκλας]; AcPlTh [Aa I 235–72] passim) **2 Ti 3:11** gloss; AcPl Ox 6 (twice).

θέλημα, ατος, τό (s. two next entries; Antiphon Soph. 58; Aristot., De Plant. 1, 1 p. 815b, 21; Aeneas Tact. 2, 8; 18, 19; POxy 924, 8 [IV AD]; LXX; PsSol 7:3; OdeSol 11:21; TestSol, Test12Patr, JosAs; ParJer 1:7; ApcEsdr 4:24 p. 28, 2 Tdf.; ApcSed, Just., Tat., Mel., P. 76, 552)

❶ **what one wishes to happen, objective sense,** ***what is willed***—ⓐ gener. ἐὰν θ. ᾖ *if it is his* (God's or Christ's) *will* IEph 20:1; IRo 1:1 (θέλημα abs.=*God's will* also ISm 11:1; IPol 8:1 and in Paul **Ro 2:18;** s. also b below). γενηθήτω τὸ θέλημά σου **Mt 6:10; 26:42; Lk 11:2 v.l.;** D. 8:2; τὸ θ. τοῦ θεοῦ γενέσθω MPol 7:1. τοῦτό ἐστιν τὸ θ. τ. πέμψαντός με **J 6:39f.** μὴ τὸ θ. μου ἀλλὰ τὸ σὸν γινέσθω **Lk 22:42.** Cp. **Ac 21:14; Col 4:12; Hb 10:10** (only here in the NT w. ἐν; cp. AcPlCor 2:26). οὕτως οὐκ ἔστιν θέλημα ἔμπροσθεν τοῦ πατρὸς ἵνα *so it is not the Father's will that* **Mt 18:14** (οὐκ ἔστιν θ. as Mal 1:10; Eccl 5:3; 12:1).

ⓑ what one wishes to bring about by one's own action, since one has undertaken to do what one has willed οὐ ζητῶ τὸ θ. τὸ ἐμόν *I do not aspire (to do) my own will* **J 5:30a; 6:38.** τὸ μυστήριον τοῦ θελήματος αὐτοῦ *the secret purpose of God's will,* i.e. the carrying out of God's plan of salvation **Eph 1:9.** οὐκ ἦν θ., ἵνα ἔλθῃ *he was not willing to come* **1 Cor 16:12** (but this passage could also belong under the abs. use of 1a).

ⓒ what one wishes to bring about by the activity of others, to whom one assigns a task.

α. of persons ὁ δοῦλος ὁ γνοὺς τὸ θ. τοῦ κυρίου αὐτοῦ *what his master wants* **Lk 12:47** (in a parable). τὸ θ. τοῦ πατρός **Mt 21:31.**

β. of the devil εἰς τὸ ἐκείνου θ. *to do his will* **2 Ti 2:26.**

γ. predom. of God (or Christ) τὸ θέλημα τοῦ θεοῦ (cp. Herm. Wr. 5, 7; 13, 2; Philo, Leg. All. 3, 197; TestIss 4:3, TestNapht 3:1; Just., A I, 63, 10 al.) **Ro 12:2; Eph 5:17; 1 Th 4:3; 5:18; 1 Pt 2:15; 4:2;** cp. **J 5:30b;** 1 Cl 40:3; 56:2. θελήματι τοῦ κελεύοντος λόγου Dg 11:8. γινώσκειν τὸ θέλημα *know the will* **Ro 2:18; Ac 22:14.** ἡ ἐπίγνωσις τοῦ θ. αὐτοῦ **Col 1:9;** ποιεῖν τὸ θ. (1 Esdr 9:9; 4 Macc 18:16; JosAs 12:3) **Mt 7:21; 12:50; Mk 3:35; J 4:34; 6:38b; 7:17; 9:31; Eph 6:6; Hb 10:7, 9** (both Ps 39:9), **36; 13:21; 1J 2:17;** 2 Cl 5:1; 6:7; 8:4; 9:11; 10:1; 14:1; Pol 2:2. Also ποιεῖν τὰ θελήματα (Ps 102:21; Is 44:28; 2 Macc 1:3) GEb121, 34; **Mk 3:35 v.l.; Ac 13:22.** μὴ λειποτακτεῖν (q.v.) ἀπὸ τοῦ θελήματος αὐτοῦ 1 Cl 21:4. προσέλθωμεν τῷ θ. αὐτοῦ *let us heed the (Lord's) will* 33:8. ὑποτασσώμεθα τῷ θ. αὐτοῦ 34:5 (opp. ἀντιτασσόμενος 36:6; ἐναντιουμένους 61:1). εἶξαι . . . τῷ θ. τοῦ θεοῦ 56:1.

δ. ποιεῖν τὰ θελήματα τ. σαρκός *do what the flesh desires* **Eph 2:3.**

❷ **the act of willing or desiring, subjective sense,** ***will***

ⓐ of the human will (Ps 1:2) θελήματι ἀνθρώπου *by an act of the human will* **2 Pt 1:21.** ἐὰν . . . ἐπιδῶμεν ἑαυτοὺς τοῖς θελήμασιν τῶν ἀνθρώπων 1 Cl 14:2 *if we heedlessly permit ourselves to be controlled by the will of humans* ἐξουσίαν ἔχειν περὶ τ. ἰδίου θ. *have control over one's desire* **1 Cor 7:37;** here θ. acc. to many has the connotation of sexual desire, as **J 1:13** (θ. σαρκός, θ. ἀνδρός; cp. PGM 4, 1430; 1521; 1533). Of the will of an assembled crowd, directed toward the death of Jesus **Lk 23:25.**

ⓑ as a rule of the will of God (or Christ) ἡ βουλὴ τοῦ θ. **Eph 1:11;** ἡ εὐδοκία τοῦ θ. vs. **5** (cp. CD 3, 15). εἰ θέλοι τὸ θ. τοῦ θεοῦ *if the will of God should so decree* **1 Pt 3:17** (cp. Just., D. 119, 1 θελήματι τοῦ θελήσαντος). θελήματι θεοῦ *by God's will* ITr 1:1; Pol 1:3. Also διὰ θελήματος θεοῦ **Ro 15:32; 1 Cor 1:1; 2 Cor 1:1; 8:5; Eph 1:1; Col 1:1; 2 Ti 1:1;** 1 Cl 32:3f; Χριστοῦ AcPl Ha 5, 35; also διὰ τὸ θέλημα **Rv 4:11** or ἐν τ. θελήματι τ. θεοῦ **Ro 1:10;** ἐν θ. θεοῦ 1 Cl 49:6; AcPl Ha 7, 13; AcPlCor 2:26; cp. 1 Cl ins; IEph ins, or ἐκ θελήματος θεοῦ (cp. Ps 27:7) 1 Cl 42:2; πρὸς τὸ θ. *according to (the master's) will* Hs 9, 5, 2. Also κατὰ τὸ θ. (1 Esdr 8:16) **Gal 1:4; 1J 5:14; 1 Pt 4:19;** IPhld ins; ISm 1:1; 1 Cl 20:4; Hm 12, 6, 2; MPol 2:1 (Just., D. 85, 4 al.).—DELG s.v. ἐθέλω. M-M. TW.

θέλησις, εως, ἡ (s. prec. and next entry; acc. to Pollux 5, 47 an ἰδιωτικόν 'vulgar word'; cp. Phryn. p. 353 Lob. But also found Stoic. III 41; Philod., Rhet. II 297 Sudh.; PGM 4, 1429 θέλησις τῶν θελημάτων; Ezk 18:23; 2 Ch 15:15; Pr 8:35 al.; TestSol D; AcThom 169 [Aa II/2, 284, 6]; Just., D. 60, 2; 61, 1. The Doric pl. θελήσιες='wishes': Melissa, Epist. ad Char. p. 62 Orell.) **the act of willing,** ***will,*** of God (Herm. Wr. 4, 1a; 10, 2; Iambl., De Myst. 2, 11 p. 97, 15 Parthey ἡ θεία θ.) κατὰ τὴν αὐτοῦ θ. *according to God's will* **Hb 2:4;** τῇ αὐτοῦ θ. *by God's will* (Tob 12:18; 2 Macc 12:16) 2 Cl 1:6.—DELG s.v. ἐθέλω. TW.

θέλω (s. prec. two entries; on its relation to the Attic ἐθέλω, which is not found in NT, LXX, En, TestSol, TestAbr, TestJob, Test12Patr, GrBar, JosAs, ParJer, ApcEsdr, ApcMos, AscIs, s. Kühner-Bl. I 187f; II 408f; B-D-F §101 p. 45; Mlt-H. 88; 189; Rob. 205f. θέλω is found since 250 BC in the Attic ins [Meisterhans^3-Schw. p. 178; Threatte II 637f], likew. quite predom. in the pap [Mayser I^2/2, '38, 119]; LXX, En, TestSol, TestAbr, TestJob, Test12Patr; GrBar 13:1; JosAs 23:7; ApcSed; AscIs 3:23; Jos., Ant. 18, 144, C. Ap. 2, 192; apolog., exc. Mel. [but s. ἐθέλω]) impf. ἤθελον; fut. θελήσω **Rv 11:5 v.l.;** 1 aor. ἠθέλησα ([ἤθελα TestAbr A 5 p. 82, 2: Stone p. 12] on the augment s. B-D-F §66, 3; Mlt-H. 188); pf. 2 sg. τεθέληκας Ps 40:11; 1 aor. pass. subj. θεληθῶ IRo 8:1. 'Wish'.

❶ **to have a desire for someth.,** ***wish to have, desire, want*** τὶ *someth.* (on the difference betw. θ. and βούλομαι s. the latter) (Diogenes the Cynic, fgm. 2: Trag. Gr. p. 809 Nauck^2; Sotades [280 BC: not the comic poet] in Stob. 3, 1, 66 t. III p. 27, 5 H.; πάντα θέλων Theocr. 14, 11 πάντα, πᾶν ὃ ἐὰν θελήσωμεν, ποιήσωμεν En 97:9) **Mt 20:21; Mk 14:36** (DDaube, A Prayer Pattern in Judaism, TU 73, '59, 539–45); **Lk 5:39; J 15:7; 1 Cor 4:21; 2 Cor 11:12.** W. pres. inf. foll. τί πάλιν θέλετε ἀκούειν; *why do you want to hear (it) again?* **J 9:27a.** εἰ θέλεις τέλειος εἶναι **Mt 19:21** (Lucian, Dial. Deor. 2, 2 εἰ ἐθέλεις ἐπέραστος εἶναι). ἤθελεν ἀπολογεῖσθαι *wished to make a defense* **Ac 19:33.** ἤθελον παρεῖναι πρὸς ὑμᾶς ἄρτι *I wish I were with you now* **Gal 4:20.** ἤθελον *I would like* w. aor. inf. (Epict. 1, 29, 38; PLond III, 897, 20 p. 207 [84 AD]); Hv 3, 8, 6; 3, 11, 4 (s. B-D-F §359, 2; cp. Rob. 923). θέλω w. aor. inf. foll. also occurs **Mt 5:40; 12:38; 16:25; 19:17; Mk 10:43; Lk 8:20; 23:8; J 12:21** (Diog. L. 6, 34 ξένων δέ ποτε θεάσασθαι θελόντων Δημοσθένην); **Ac 25:9b; 2 Cor 11:32 v.l.; Gal 3:2; Js 2:20** (cp. Seneca, Ep. 47, 10: vis tu cogitare); **1 Pt 3:10;** B 7:11 (Ar. 13:5; Just., D. 8:4; Tat. 19, 2; Ath. 32, 1). Abs., though the inf. is to be supplied fr. the context: **Mt 17:12** (sc. ποιῆσαι); **27:15; Mk 9:13; J 21:18.** Foll. by acc. w. inf. **Mk 7:24; Lk 1:62; J 21:22f; Ac 16:3; Ro 16:19; 1 Cor 7:7, 32; 14:5; Gal 6:13** (Just., D. 6, 2; Tat. 19, 3). Negative οὐ θέλω (other moods take μή as neg.) *I do not wish, I am not willing, I will not* foll. by acc. (Just., D. 28, 4 περιτομήν) and aor. inf. **Mt 23:4; Lk 19:14, 27; 1 Cor 10:20;** IRo 2:1. οὐ θέλω (θέλομεν) ὑμᾶς ἀγνοεῖν *I do not wish you to be ignorant = I want you to know* (BGU 27, 5 and PGiss 11, 4 [118 AD] γινώσκειν σε θέλω ὅτι) **Ro 1:13; 11:25; 1 Cor 10:1; 12:1; 2 Cor 1:8; 1 Th 4:13.** W. ἵνα foll. (Epict. 1, 18, 14; 2, 7, 8) **Mt 7:12; Mk 6:25; 9:30; 10:35; Lk 6:31; J 17:24** (on **Mt 7:12=Lk 6:31** [w. inf. αὐτοῖς γίνεσθαι Ar. 15, 5] s. LPhilippidis, D. 'Goldene Regel' religionsgesch. untersucht 1929, Religionswissensch. Forschungsberichte über die 'goldene Regel'

'33; GKing, The 'Negative' Golden Rule, JR 8, 1928, 268–79; ADihle, D. Goldene Regel, '62; Betz, SM ad loc.). Foll. by aor. subj. (deliberative subj.; s. Kühner-G. I 221f; B-D-F §366, 3; 465, 2; Rob. 935; Epict. 3, 2, 14 θέλεις σοι εἴπω;='do you wish me to tell you?'; Mitt-Wilck. I/2, 14 III, 6 καὶ σοὶ [=σὺ] λέγε τίνος θέλεις κατηγορήσω) θέλεις συλλέξωμεν αὐτά; *do you want us to gather them?* **Mt 13:28;** θέλις χαλκέα ἄγωμεν; *do you want us to bring a smith?* AcPl Ha 3, 5. τί θέλετε ποιήσω ὑμῖν; *what do you want me to do for you?* **Mt 20:32** (cp. Plautus, Merc. 1, 2, 49 [ln. 159]: quid vis faciam?); cp. **26:17; 27:17, 21; Mk 10:36** (CTurner, JTS 28, 1927, 357; AHiggins, ET 52, '41, 317f), **51; 14:12; 15:9, 12 v.l.; Lk 9:54; 18:41; 22:9.** W. ἤ foll.: *I would rather* ... *than* ... or *instead of* (Trypho Alex. [I BC], fgm. 23 [AvVelsen 1853] = Gramm. Gr. II/2 p. 43, 10 περιπατεῖν θέλω ἤπερ ἑστάναι; Epict. 3, 22, 53; BGU 846, 15 [II AD] θέλω πηρὸς γενέσθαι, ἢ γνῶναι, ὅπως ἀνθρώπῳ ἔτι ὀφείλω ὀβολόν; 2 Macc 14:42; Just., A I, 15, 8) **1 Cor 14:19.** W. εἰ foll. (Is 9:4f; Sir 23:14) τί θέλω εἰ ἤδη ἀνήφθη *how I wish it were already kindled!* **Lk 12:49.**

❷ **to have someth. in mind for oneself, of purpose, resolve, *will, wish, want, be ready*** (cp. Pla., Ap. 41a) *to do* τὶ *someth.* **Ro 7:15f, 19f** (Epict. 2, 26, 1 of one who errs ὃ μὲν θέλει οὐ ποιεῖ what he resolves he does not do; cp. also 2, 26, 2; 4 and s. on ποιέω 2e; Ar. 9, 1 εἰ θελήσομεν ἐπεξελθεῖν τῷ λόγῳ; Just., D. 2, 2 θέλω εἰπεῖν); **1 Cor 7:36; Gal 5:17.** W. aor. inf. foll. (Judg 20:5) **Mt 11:14; 20:14; 23:37; 26:15.** ἤθελεν παρελθεῖν αὐτούς *he was ready to pass by them* **Mk 6:48** (CTurner, JTS 28, 1927, 356). Ἡρῴδης θέλει σε ἀποκτεῖναι *Herod wants to kill you* **Lk 13:31.** Cp. **J 1:43.** ὑμεῖς δὲ ἠθελήσατε ἀγαλλιασθῆναι *you were minded to rejoice* **5:35; 6:21; 7:44; Ac 25:9a; Gal 4:9; Col 1:27; 1 Th 2:18; Rv 11:5.** Also pres. inf. (2 Esdr 11:11) **J 6:67; 7:17; 8:44; Ac 14:13; 17:18; Ro 7:21;** 2 Cl 6:1; B 4:9. Abs., but w. the inf. supplied fr. the context **Mt 8:2** (cp. what was said to the physician in Epict. 3, 10, 15 ἐὰν σὺ θέλῃς, κύριε, καλῶς ἕξω); **Mk 3:13; 6:22; J 5:21; Ro 9:18ab; Rv 11:6.** τί οὖν θέλετε, κρίνατε AcPl Ha 1, 26. W. acc. and inf. foll. 1 Cl 36:2.—Abs. ὁ θέλων *the one who wills* **Ro 9:16.** τοῦ θεοῦ θέλοντος *if it is God's will* (Jos., Ant. 7, 373; PMich 211, 4 τοῦ Σεράπιδος θέλοντος; PAmh 131, 5 ἐλπίζω θεῶν θελόντων διαφεύξεσθαι; PGiss 18, 10; BGU 423, 18 τῶν θεῶν θελόντων; 615, 4f; Ar. 7, 1 μὴ θέλοντος αὐτοῦ) **Ac 18:21.** Also ἐὰν ὁ κύριος θελήσῃ (Pla., Phd. 80d; Ps.-Pla., Alcib. 1 p. 135d; Demosth. 4, 7; 25, 2 ἂν θεὸς θέλῃ; Ps.-Demetr., Form. Ep. 11, 12 ἐὰν οἱ θεοὶ θ.; PPetr I, 2, 3; Just., D. 5, 3 ἔστ' ἂν ὁ θεὸς θέλῃ) **1 Cor 4:19;** cp. **Js 4:15;** 1 Cl 21:9. ὅτε θέλει καὶ ὡς θέλει 27:5 (cp. BGU 27, 11 ὡς ὁ θεὸς ἤθελεν). καθὼς ἠθέλησεν (i.e. ὁ θεός) **1 Cor 12:18; 15:38** (Hymn to Isis: SEG VIII, 549, 19f [I BC] πᾶσι μερίζεις οἷσι θέλεις). Cp. εἰ θέλοι τὸ θέλημα τοῦ θεοῦ=*if God so wills it* **1 Pt 3:17** (v.l. θέλει; on fluctuation of opt. and ind. in the ms. tradition, cp. Soph., Antig. 1032). οὐ θέλω *I will not, do not propose, am not willing, do not want* w. pres. inf. foll. (Gen 37:35; Is 28:12; Tat. 4:2 al.) **J 7:1; 2 Th 3:10;** 2 Cl 13:1. W. aor. inf. foll. (2 Km 23:16; Jer 11:10) **Mt 2:18** (cp. Jer 38:15); **15:32; 22:3; Mk 6:26; Lk 15:28; J 5:40; Ac 7:39; 1 Cor 16:7;** Dg 10:7 al. Abs., but w. the inf. to be supplied fr. the context **Mt 18:30; Lk 18:4.** οὐ θέλω *I prefer not to* **Mt 21:29.** AcPl Ha 3, 6; 7, 3.—Of purpose, opp. ἐνεργεῖν **Phil 2:13.** Opp. κατεργάζεσθαι **Ro 7:18.** Opp. ποιεῖν **2 Cor 8:10** (s. Betz, 2 Cor 64). Opp. πράσσειν **Ro 7:15, 19.**

❸ **to take pleasure in, *like*—ⓐ** w. inf. foll.: to do someth. **Mk 12:38** (later in the same sentence w. acc.; cp. b τὶ); **Lk 20:46** (w. φιλεῖν).

ⓑ τινά (Gorgias: Vorsokr. 82 fgm. 29 [in the Gnomolog. Vatic. 166, s. WienerStud. 10, p. 36] τοῖς μνηστῆρσιν, οἳ Πηνελόπην θέλοντες ...; Vi. Aesopi W 31 P. θέλω αὐτήν; Ps 40:12; Tob 13:8; ParJer 8:2 ὁ θέλων τὸν κύριον) **Mt 27:43** (Ps 21:9); IMg 3:2. τὶ (Epict. 1, 4, 27; Ezk 18:32) **Mt 9:13; 12:7** (both Hos 6:6); **Hb 10:5, 8** (both Ps 39:7). ἔν τινι (neut.: TestAsh 1:6 v.l. ἐὰν ἡ ψυχὴ θέλῃ ἐν καλῷ; Ps 111:1; 146:10; masc.: 1 Km 18:22; 2 Km 15:26; 3 Km 10:9) θέλων ἐν ταπεινοφροσύνῃ *taking pleasure in humility* **Col 2:18** (Augustine, Ep. 149, 27 [MPL 33, 641f]; AFridrichsen, ZNW 21, 1922, 135f; s. B-D-F §148, 2 and R. §148, 2).

ⓒ abs. *feel affection* perh. w. obj. *for me* understood (opp. μισεῖν) IRo 8:3.

❹ **to have an opinion, *maintain*** contrary to the true state of affairs (Paus. 1, 4, 6 Ἀρκάδες ἐθέλουσιν εἶναι; 8, 36, 2; Herodian 5, 3, 5 εἰκόνα ἡλίου ἀνέργαστον εἶναι θέλουσιν) λανθάνει αὐτοὺς τοῦτο θέλοντας *in maintaining this it escapes them (=they forget)* **2 Pt 3:5.** Of the devil [θεὸς] θέλων εἶναι AcPlCor 2:11.—HRiesenfeld, Zum Gebrauch von θέλω im NT: Arbeiten ... aus dem neutestamentlichen Seminar zu Uppsala 1, '36, 1–8; AWifstrand, Die griech. Verba für 'wollen': Eranos 40, '42.

❺ τί θέλει τοῦτο εἶναι; *what can this mean?* **Ac 2:12;** cp. **17:20; Lk 15:26** D.—B. 1160. DELG s.v. ἐθέλω. EDNT. TW. Sv.

θέμα, ατος, τό (s. τίθημι; Cebes; Plut.; ins, pap, LXX; SibOr 2, 46; 49) orig. 'deposit of money'; in our lit. specif. ***a prize*** offered contestants, in so far as it consists of money, not a wreath (SIG 1063, 21 w. note 4; OGI 339, 81f; 566, 28) θ. ἀφθαρσία *the prize is immortality* IPol 2:3 (Zahn in his edition unnecessarily changed ἀφθαρσία, which is the rdg. of the mss., to the gen.). θέμα λίαν καλόν exceptionally fine prize **1 Tim 6:19** cj.—DELG s.v. τίθημι.

θεμέλιον, ου, τό (s. two next entries; designated by Moeris p. 185, together w. its pl. θεμέλια, as the real Attic form. But this is not in agreement w. what is found in literature. We have the neut. e.g. in Aristot., Phys. Auscult. 2, 9 p. 200a, 4; Heraclit. Sto. 38 p. 55, 20; Paus. 8, 32, 1; Vett. Val. index; Ps.-Lucian, Salt. 34, also in pap [Mayser 289]; LXX [Thackeray 154]) ***foundation, basis.*** In our lit. only the pl. is found **Ac 16:26;** B 6:2 (Is 28:16); Hs 9, 5, 4; 9, 15, 4; 9, 21, 2, in literal as well as fig. mng. of the double-minded depicted as plants with green foliage but dry roots. In other passages either the gender cannot be determined or the words in question belong to the following entry, where the ambiguous pass. are also given. But the dat. τοῖς θεμελίοις Hs 9, 4, 3 is not to be classed w. the latter, since H always uses the neut. elsewh.—TW. DELG s.v. θεμός (cp. τίθημι).

θεμέλιος, ου, ὁ (s. prec. and next entry; Thu. 1, 93, 2; Polyb. 1, 40, 9; Lucian, Calum. 20; Macho Com., fgm. 2 V. 2 K. [in Athen. 8, 346a]; Epict. 2, 15, 8; SIG 888, 55; 70; LXX [s. Thackeray 154]; En 18:1; TestSol 8:12 τοὺς θ. τοῦ ναοῦ; JosAs 15:13 cod. A [p. 62, 12 Bat.] ἀπὸ τῶν θεμελίων τῆς ἀβύσσου; Philo, Cher. 101, Spec. Leg. 2, 110; Jos., Bell. 5, 152, Ant. 5, 31; 11, 19; loanw. in rabb. In our lit. the masc. is certainly sg. in **1 Cor 3:11f; 2 Tim 2:19; Rv 21:19b;** 1 Cl 33:3; Hs 9, 4, 2; 9, 14, 6; pl. in **Hb 11:10; Rv 21:14, 19a**)

❶ **the supporting base for a structure, *foundation*—ⓐ** of a stone that constitutes a foundation (cp. Aristoph., Aves 1137 θεμέλιοι λίθοι: here θεμέλιος is an adj.) θεμελίους **Rv 21:14;** οἱ θ. **19a;** ὁ θ. **19b.**

ⓑ of the structural base for a building (Diod. S. 11, 63, 1 ἐκ θεμελίων; Philo, Exsecr. 120 ἐκ θεμελίων ἄχρι στέγους οἰκίαν; TestSol 8:12 ὀρύσσειν τοὺς θ. τοῦ ναοῦ) χωρὶς θεμελίου **Lk 6:49.** τιθέναι θεμέλιον (cp. Hyperid. 6, 14) **14:29;**

ἐπί τι *on someth.* **6:48.** The foundations of the heavenly city built by God τοὺς θ. **Hb 11:10** (s. RKnopf, Heinrici Festschr. 1914, 215; LMuntingh, Hb 11:8–10 in the Light of the Mari Texts: AvanSelms Festschr. '71, 108–20 [contrasts 'tents of Abraham' w. the city]).

❷ **the basis for someth. taking place or coming into being,** ***foundation,*** fig. extension of mng. 1—ⓐ of the elementary beginnings of a thing; of the founding of a congregation ἐπ' ἀλλότριον θ. **Ro 15:20;** θεμέλιον ἔθηκα **1 Cor 3:10;** οἰκοδομεῖν ἐπὶ τὸν θ. **12.** Of elementary teachings θεμέλιον καταβάλλεσθαι *lay a foundation* (Dionys. Hal. 3, 69; cp. the lit. use Jos., Ant. 11, 93; 15, 391) **Hb 6:1.** θεμέλιος τῆς οἰκοδομῆς Hs 9, 4, 2; of Christ s. 2b.

ⓑ of the indispensable prerequisites for someth. to come into being: God's will is the foundation of an orderly creation ἐπὶ τὸν ἀσφαλῆ … θ. 1 Cl 33:3. The foundation of the Christian church or congregation: Christ θ. … ἄλλον … θεῖναι **1 Cor 3:11** (AFridrichsen, TZ 2, '46, 316f); αὐτὸς θεμέλιος αὐτοῖς ἐγένετο *he* (God's son) *became its foundation* Hs 9, 14, 6; the apostles and prophets ἐπὶ τῷ θ. **Eph 2:20;** cp. ὁ … στερεὸς … θ. **2 Ti 2:19.**

ⓒ a foundation provides stability, therefore *treasure, reserve* (Philo, Sacr. Abel. 81 θεμέλιος τῷ φαύλῳ κακία, Leg. All. 3, 113) **1 Ti 6:19** θεμέλιον καλὸν εἰς τὸ μέλλον = 'something fine to build on for the future'.—DELG s.v. θεμός. Frisk s.v. θέμεθλα. M-M. TW.

θεμελιόω (s. θεμέλιος) fut. θεμελιώσω; 1 aor. ἐθεμελίωσα. Pass.: 1 aor. 3 sg. ἐθεμελιώθη LXX; pf. τεθεμελίωμαι; plpf. 3 sg. τεθεμελίωτο (on the missing augment s. B-D-F §66, 1; W-S. §12, 4; Mlt-H. 190) (X., Cyr. 7, 5, 11; SIG 1104, 15; synagogue ins fr. Jerus.: SEG VIII, 170, 9 [before 70 AD]; LXX; En; TestSol; JosAs 12:3 [cod. A ch. 19 p. 69, 18 Bat.]; Philo, Op. M. 102)

❶ **to provide a base for some material object or structure,** ***lay a foundation, found,*** lit. τὶ *someth.* τὴν γῆν (Job 38:4; Pr 3:19; En 18:12; 21:2; JosAs 12:3) **Hb 1:10;** Hm 12, 4, 1 v.l. (Ps 101:26). θεμελιώσας τ. γῆν ἐπὶ ὑδάτων (who) *founded the earth upon the waters* Hv 1, 3, 4 (cp. Ps 23:2). In the same sense ἐπί w. acc. τεθεμελίωτο ἐπὶ τὴν πέτραν **Mt 7:25; Lk 6:48 v.l.**

❷ **to provide a secure basis for the inner life and its resources,** ***establish, strengthen,*** fig. ext. of mng. 1 (Diod. S. 11, 68, 7 βασιλεία καλῶς θεμελιωθεῖσα; 15, 1, 3).

ⓐ of believers, whom God establishes **1 Pt 5:10,** or to whom he gives a secure place Hv 1, 3, 2. Pass. **Eph 3:17; Col 1:23;** Hv 3, 13, 4; 4, 1, 4.

ⓑ of revelations that H. receives: πάντα τεθεμελιωμένα ἐστίν *they are all well-founded* Hv 3, 4, 3.—Of the church viewed as a tower: τεθεμελίωται τῷ ῥήματι τοῦ παντοκράτορος καὶ ἐνδόξου ὀνόματος *it has been established by the word of the almighty and glorious name* (of God) Hv 3, 3, 5.—DELG s.v. θεμός. M-M. TW.

θεμιτός, ή, όν (θέμις 'law as established by custom'; Hom. Hymns, Hdt. et al.; ins, pap; Jos., Bell. 6, 432) **pert. to being appropriate or right, with implication that the thing so described is not a matter of codified law but unwritten procedure based on custom and awareness of the transcendent,** ***allowed, permitted, right*** θεμιτόν ἐστιν *it is right* w. inf. foll. (Sext. Emp., Adv. Gramm. 81; SIG 965, 16f) 1 Cl 63:1. Mostly w. neg. (Hdt. 5, 72 al.; Ael. Aristid. 45 p. 25 D.; Tob 2:13 BA; Philo, Op. M. 17 οὐ θ.; Jos., Ant. 14, 72) οὐ θ. *it is not right* (without copula as Hyperid. 6, 27; Just., D. 134, 3; Ath., R. 77, 29) Dg 6:10.—HVos, ΘΕΜΙΣ '56; LfgrE col. 991 (lit.) s.v. θέμις. DDD 1613f. DELG s.v. θέμις.

θεοδίδακτος, ον (Prolegomenon Syll. p. 91, 14 [used by John Doxopatres, rhetorician, XI AD, in a comm. on the Progymnasmata of Aphthonius] θεοδίδακτος ἡ ῥητορική; but not a rhetorician's term as such, s. CClassen, WienerStud 107/8, '94/95, 332f. Elsewh. in eccl. wr., s. Lampe s.v.; s. also our entry διδακτός 1; Maximus Tyr. 26, 1c 'Απόλλωνος διδάγματα; Ps.-Callisth. 1, 13, 5 ὑπὸ θεοῦ τινος διδασκόμενος; Damascius, Princ. 111 p. 229 R. παρ' αὐτῶν τ. θεῶν διδαχθέντες; Theoph. Ant. 2, 9 [p. 120, 3 w. ὅσιος and δίκαιος]) ***taught/instructed by God*** **1 Th 4:9** (JKloppenberg, NTS 39, '39, 281–89, in allusion to the Dioscuri as paradigms of φιλαδελφία); B 21:6.—DELG s.v. διδάσκω. M-M. TW. Spicq.

θεοδρόμος, ου, ὁ *God's runner* (s. θεός, δρόμος; prob. a new word formed by Ignatius; he may have based it on pass. like Gal 5:7; 1 Cor 9:24–26; 2 Ti 4:7) IPhld 2:2; IPol 7:2.—Cp. DELG s.v. δραμεῖν.

θεολόγος, ου, ὁ (s. θεός, λόγος; Aristot.+; Diod. S. 5, 80, 4; Philod.; Plut., Mor. 417f; Sext. Emp., Math. 2, 31; Diog. L. 1, 119; Porphyr., Abst. 2, 36–43 ἅ τε λέγει ὁ θεολόγος [Orpheus]; ins, esp. w. ref. to the emperor cult in Asia Minor [OGI 513 w. note 4; III AD]; PGM 13, 933 ὡς ὁ θεολόγος 'Ορφεὺς παρέδωκεν διὰ τῆς παραστιχίδος; Apollon. Paradox. 4 of Abaris; Philo, Praem. 53 [Moses]) **one who speaks of God or divine things,** ***God's herald*** eccl. by-name for John (later also for others) Rv ins v.l.—Dssm., NB 58f (BS 231f), LO 297 (LAE 353, n. 1); Rtzst., Hist. Mon. 135ff; FKattenbusch, D. Entstehung e. christl. Theologie. Z. Gesch. der Ausdrücke θεολογία, θεολογεῖν, θεολόγος: ZTK n.s. 11, 1930, 161–205.—M-M. Sv.

θεομακάριστος, ον ***blessed by God*** of Polycarp θεομακαριστότατος IPol 7:2. Also of Christ's passion θ. … πάθους ISm 1:2. S. next entry.—DELG s.v. μάκαρ.

θεομακαρίτης, ου, ὁ (hapax leg.; the noun μακαρίτης ='one blessed', i.e. 'dead, lately dead' [Aeschyl. et al.]). As adj. (like μακαρίτης Aristoph., Pl. 555) ***divinely blessed*** of Christ's passion ISm 1:2 v.l. (s. θεομακάριστος).—DELG s.v. μάκαρ.

θεομαχέω (s. next entry; Eur., Iph. A. 1409; X., Oec. 16, 3; Menand., fgm. 162 Kö.=187 p. 54 Kock [μὴ θεομάχει; Manetho: 609 fgm. 10, p. 95, 7 Jac. [in Jos., C. Ap. 1, 246]; Jos., C. Ap. 1, 263; Diod. S. 14, 69, 2; Epict. 3, 24, 21; 24; 4, 1, 101, s. MAdinolfi, in Atti del IV Simposio di Tarso su S. Paola Apostolo, ed. LPadovese '96, 63f; Philostrat., Vi. Apoll. 4, 44; 2 Macc 7:19) ***fight against God, oppose God*** and God's works **Ac 23:9 v.l.**—WNestle, Philologus 59, 1900, 48–50 (Eur. and Ac); OWeinreich, Gebet u. Wunder 1929, 172f; Pauly-W. Suppl. IV, 1924, 290f.—DELG s.v. μάχομαι. M-M.

θεομάχος, ον (s. prec. entry; Scymnus the geographer [II BC] 637 CMüller; Heraclit. Sto. 1 p. 1, 7; Lucian, Jupp. Tr. 45; Vett. Val. 331, 12; Sym. Job 26:5; Pr 9:18; 21:16; cp. Jos., Ant. 14, 310; Tat. 13, 3) ***fighting against God*** **Ac 5:39.**—AVögeli, Lk and Eur.: TZ 9, '53, 415–38.—DELG s.v. μάχομαι. M-M. TW.

Θεονόη, ης, ἡ (Roscher V 631f; pap since VI AD) ***Theonoe*** a Christian in Corinth ὡς ἀπεκαλύφθη Θεονόῃ AcPlCor 1:8.

θεόπνευστος, ον (s. θεός, πνέω; Ps.-Phocyl. 129 τῆς θεοπνεύστου σοφίης λόγος ἐστὶν ἄριστος [s. Horst 201f]; Plut., Mor. 904f; Vett. Val. 330, 19; Ps.-Callisth. 1, 25, 2; SibOr 5, 308; 406; TestAbr A 20 p. 103, 22 [Stone p. 54] μυρίσμασι θ.; for the idea, cp. θεία ἐπίπνοια SIG 695, 12; on these texts and others, s. BWarfield, Revelation and Inspiration 1927, 229–59;

New Docs 3, 30; also 1, 15) ***inspired by God*** **2 Ti 3:16** (MAustin, ET 93, '81, 75–79 'expiration').—DELG s.v. πνέω. M-M. TW. Spicq.

θεοπρεπής, ές (s. θεός, πρέπω; Pind., N. 10, 2; also Diod. S. 3, 69, 2; 11, 89, 5; 8; Plut., Dio 970 [28, 4]; Philo, Mos. 2, 15; OGI 383, 57) **pert. to being fit for God, *worthy of God, revered, venerable, godly,*** superl. θεοπρεπέστατος (Plut., Mor. 780f; cp. PGM 1, 178 ὡς πρέπον θεῷ).

ⓐ of pers. (Lucian, Alex. 3) θ. πρεσβύτης MPol 7:2. Also of a group of pers.: θ. πρεσβυτέριον ISm 12:2. συμβούλιον ἄγειν θεοπρεπέστατον *call a council in every way worthy of God* IPol 7:3. ἐκκλησία θεοπρεπεστάτη ISm ins.

ⓑ of things: Ignatius is proud to have ὄνομα θεοπρεπέστατον *a name that most redounds to the glory of God* IMg 1:2 (cp. Maximus Tyr. 35, 2e θεοπρεπῆ ὀνόματα in contrast to ἀνθρωπικὰ ὀν.; cp. also the use of the verb πρέπω in the sense 'be appropriate, be worthy of' Just., A II, 2, 16). He uses θ. also of his bonds ISm 11:1.—ODreyer, Untersuchungen zum Begriff des Gottgeziemenden in der Antike '70. DELG s.v. πρέπω. TW. Sv.

θεοπρεσβευτής, οῦ, ὁ one commissioned or empowered by God, *an ambassador of God* (cp. also IPhld 10:1) ISm 11:2 (θεοπρεσβύτης v.l., Lightfoot, Funk; s. πρεσβύτης).—DELG s.v. πρέσβυς.

θεός, οῦ (Hom.+; Herm. Wr.; ins, pap, LXX, pseudepigr., Philo, Joseph.) **ὁ** and **ἡ,** voc. θεέ (Pisidian ins [JHS 22, 1902, 355] θέ; PGM 4, 218 θεὲ θεῶν; 7, 529 κύριε θεὲ μέγιστε; 12, 120 κύριε θεέ; 13, 997; LXX [Thackeray 145; PKatz, Philo's Bible '50, 152f]; ApcMos 42; Jos., Ant. 14, 24 ὦ θεὲ βασιλεῦ τ. ὅλων; SibOr 13, 172 βασιλεῦ κόσμου θεέ) **Mt 27:46,** more frequently (s. 2 and 3c, h below) ὁ θεός (LXX; ParJer 6:12; ApcEsdr 7:5; ApcMos 32; B-D-F §147, 3m; JWackernagel, Über einige antike Anredeformen 1912; Mlt-H. 120). On the inclusion or omission of the art. gener. s. W-S. §19, 13d; B-D-F §254, 1; 268, 2; Rob. 758; 761; 780; 786; 795; Mlt-Turner 174; BWeiss, D. Gebr. des Artikels bei den Gottesnamen, StKr 84, 1911, 319–92; 503–38 (also published separately). The sg. article freq. suggests personal claim on a deity. 'God, god'.

❶ In the Gr-Rom. world the term θεός primarily refers to a **transcendent being who exercises extraordinary control in human affairs or is responsible for bestowal of unusual benefits, *deity, god, goddess*** (s. on θεά) **Ac 28:6; 2 Th 2:4** (cp. SibOr 5, 34 ἰσάζων θεῷ αὐτόν; Ar. 4, 1 οὐκ εἰσὶ θεοί; Tat. 10, 1 θεὸς . . . κύκνος γίνεται . . .; Ath. 18, 3 θεός τις δισώματος); θεὸς Ῥαιφάν **Ac 7:43** (Am 5:26; s. entry Ῥαιφάν). οὐδεὶς θεὸς εἰ μὴ εἷς *there is no god but one* **1 Cor 8:4** (cp. AcPl Ha 1, 17 restored). θεοῦ φωνὴ καὶ οὐκ ἀνθρώπου **Ac 12:22.**—ἡ θεός *the (female) god, goddess* (Att., later more rarely; Peripl. Eryth. c. 58; Lucian, Dial. Deor. 17, 2; SIG 695, 28; ins, one of which refers to Artemis, in Hauser p. 81f; Jos., Ant. 9, 19; Ar. 11, 2 [Artemis]; Ath. 29, 2 [Ino]) **Ac 19:37.**—Pl. **Ac 7:40** (Ex 32:1). Cp. **14:11; 19:26;** PtK 2 p. 14, 21. εἴπερ εἰσὶν λεγόμενοι θεοί *even if there are so-called gods* **1 Cor 8:5a;** s. vs. **5b** (on θεοὶ πολλοί cp. Jos., Ant. 4, 149.—Maximus Tyr. 11, 5a: θ. πολλοί w. εἷς θ. πατήρ). οἱ φύσει μὴ ὄντες θεοί *those who by nature are not really gods* **Gal 4:8b** (cp. Ar. 4, 2 μὴ εἶναι τὸν οὐρανὸν θεόν al.). θεοὶ . . . λίθινοι etc. AcPl Ha 1, 18 (cp. JosAs 10:13 τοὺς χρυσοῦς καὶ ἀργυροῦς). Of the devil μὴ ὢν θεός AcPlCor 2:15.

❷ Some writings in our lit. use the word θ. w. ref. to Christ (without necessarily equating Christ with the Father, and therefore in harmony w. the Shema of Israel Dt 6:4; cp. Mk 10:18 and 4a below), though the interpretation of some of the pass. is in debate. In Mosaic and Gr-Rom. traditions the fundamental semantic component in the understanding of deity is the factor of performance, namely saviorhood or extraordinary contributions to one's society. Dg. 10:6 defines the ancient perspective: ὃς ἃ παρὰ τοῦ θεοῦ λάβων ἔχει, ταῦτα τοῖς ἐπιδεομένοις χορηγῶν, θεὸς γίνεται τῶν λαμβανάντων *one who ministers to the needy what one has received from God proves to be a god to the recipients* (cp. Sb III, 6263, 27f of a mother). Such understanding led to the extension of the mng. of θ. to pers. who elicit special reverence (cp. pass. under 4 below; a similar development can be observed in the use of σέβομαι and cognates). In **Ro 9:5** the interpr. is complicated by demand of punctuation marks in printed texts. If a period is placed before ὁ ὢν κτλ., the doxology refers to God as defined in Israel (so EAbbot, JBL 1, 1881, 81–154; 3, 1883, 90–112; RLipsius; HHoltzmann, Ntl. Theol.[2] II 1911, 99f; EGünther, StKr 73, 1900, 636–44; FBurkitt, JTS 5, 1904, 451–55; Jülicher; PFeine, Theol. d. NTs[6] '34, 176 et al.; RSV text; NRSV mg.). A special consideration in favor of this interpretation is the status assigned to Christ in 1 Cor 15:25–28 and the probability that Paul is not likely to have violated the injunction in Dt 5:7.—If a comma is used in the same place, the reference is to Christ (so BWeiss; EBröse, NKZ 10, 1899, 645–57 et al.; NRSV text; RSV mg. S. also εἰμί 1.—Undecided: THaering.—The transposition by the Socinian scholar JSchlichting [died 1661] ὧν ὁ='to whom belongs' was revived by JWeiss, D. Urchristentum 1917, 363; WWrede, Pls 1905, 82; CStrömman, ZNW 8, 1907, 319f). In **2 Pt 1:1; 1J 5:20** the interpretation is open to question (but cp. ISmyrna McCabe .0010, 100 ὁ θεὸς καὶ σωτὴρ Ἀντίοχος). In any event, θ. certainly refers to Christ, as one who manifests primary characteristics of deity, in the foll. NT pass.: **J 1:1b** (w. ὁ θεός 1:1a, which refers to God in the monotheistic context of Israel's tradition. On the problem raised by such attribution s. J 10:34 [cp. Ex 7:1; Ps 81:6]; on θεός w. and without the article, acc. to whether it means God or the Logos, s. Philo, Somn. 1, 229f; JGriffiths, ET 62, '50/51, 314–16; BMetzger, ET 63, '51/52, 125f), **18b.** ὁ κύριός μου καὶ ὁ θεός μου *my Lord and my God!* (nom. w. art.=voc.; s. beg. of this entry.—On a resurrection as proof of divinity cp. Diog. L. 8, 41, who quotes Hermippus: Pythagoras returns from a journey to Hades and appears among his followers [εἰσέρχεσθαι εἰς τὴν ἐκκλησίαν], and they consider him θεῖόν τινα) **J 20:28** (on the combination of κύριος and θεός s. 3c below). **Tit 2:13** (μέγας θ.). **Hb 1:8, 9** (in a quot. fr. Ps 44:7, 8). S. TGlasson, NTS 12, '66, 270–72. **Jd 5** P[72]. But above all Ignatius calls Christ θεός in many pass.: θεὸς Ἰησοῦς Χριστός ITr 7:1; Χριστὸς θεός ISm 10:1. ὁ θεὸς ἡμῶν IEph ins; 15:3; 18:2; IRo ins (twice); 3:3; IPol 8:3; τὸ πάθος τοῦ θεοῦ μου IRo 6:3. ἐν αἵματι θεοῦ IEph 1:1. ἐν σαρκὶ γενόμενος θεός 7:2. θεὸς ἀνθρωπίνως φανερούμενος 19:3. θεὸς ὁ οὕτως ὑμᾶς σοφίσας ISm 1:1.—Hdb. exc. 193f; MRackl, Die Christologie d. hl. Ign. v. Ant. 1914. ὁ θεός μου Χριστὲ Ἰησοῦ AcPl Ha 3, 10; Χριστὸς Ἰησοῦς ὁ θ[εός] 6, 24; cp. ln. 34 (also cp. Just., A I, 63, 15, D. 63, 5 al.; Tat. 13, 3; Ath. 24, 1; Mel., P. 4, 28 al.).—SLösch, Deitas Jesu u. antike Apotheose '33. Cp. AWlosk, Römischer Kaiserkult '78.

❸ **God in Israelite/Christian monotheistic perspective, *God*** the predom. use, somet. with, somet. without the art.

ⓐ ὁ θεός **Mt 1:23; 3:9; 5:8, 34; Mk 2:12; 10:18; 13:19** (cp. TestJob 37:4); **Lk 2:13; J 3:2b; Ac 2:22b; Gal 2:6** al. With prep. εἰς τὸν θ. **Ac 24:15.** ἐκ τοῦ θ. **J 8:42b, 47; 1J 3:9f; 4:1ff, 6f; 5:1, 4; 2 Cor 3:5; 5:18** al.; ἐν τῷ θ. **Ro 5:11; Col 3:3** (Ath. 21,

1). ἔναντι τοῦ θ. **Lk 1:8;** ἐπὶ τὸν θ. **Ac 15:19; 26:18, 20** (Just., D. 101, 1); ἐπὶ τῷ θ. **Lk 1:47** (Just., D. 8, 2); παρὰ τοῦ θ. **J 8:40** (Ar. 4, 2; Just., A I, 33, 6 al.; without art. Just., D. 69, 6 al.). παρὰ τῷ θ. **Ro 2:13; 9:14** (Just., A I, 28, 3; Tat. 7, 1; Ath. 31, 2 al.); πρὸς τὸν θ. **J 1:2; Ac 24:16;** AcPl Ha 3, 8 (Just., D. 39, 1 al.; Mel., HE 4, 26, 13 al.); τὰ πρὸς τὸν θ. **Hb 2:17; 5:1; Ro 15:17** is acc. of respect: *with respect to one's relation to God* or *the things pert. to God, in God's cause* (s. B-D-F §160; Rob. 486. For τὰ πρὸς τ. θ. s. Soph., Phil. 1441; X., De Rep. Lac. 13, 11; Aristot., Pol. 1314b, 39; Lucian, Pro Imag. 8; Mitt-Wilck. I/2, 109, 3 [III BC] εὐσεβὴς τὰ πρὸς θεούς; Ex 4:16; 18:19; Jos., Ant. 9, 236 εὐσεβὴς τὰ πρὸς τ. θεόν). τὰ πρὸς τ[ὸν] θεὸν ἐτήρουσαν, *when they were observant of matters pert. to God* AcPl Ha 8, 13 (=τα προς θ̅ν̅| ἐτήρουσαν Ox 1602, 10f=BMM recto 16 restored after the preceding).

ⓑ without the art. **Mt 6:24; Lk 2:14; 20:38; J 1:18a; Ro 8:8, 33b; 2 Cor 1:21; 5:19; Gal 2:19; 4:8f; 2 Th 1:8; Tit 1:16; 3:8; Hb 3:4;** AcPl Ha 8, 20=BMM recto 25 (s. also HSanders' rev. of Ox 1602, 26, in HTR 31, '38, 79, n. 2, Ghent 62 verso, 6); AcPlCor 1:15; 2:19, 26. W. prep. ἀπὸ θεοῦ **J 3:2a; 16:30** (Just., A II, 13, 4 τὸν . . . ἀπὸ ἀγεννήτου . . . θεοῦ λόγον). εἰς θεόν IPhld 1:2. ἐκ θεοῦ (Pind., O. 11, 10, P. 1, 41; Jos., Ant. 2, 164; Just., A I, 22, 2; Mel., P. 55, 404) **Ac 5:39; 2 Cor 5:1; Phil 3:9.** ἐν θεῷ **J 8:21; Ro 2:17; Jd 1;** AcPl Ha 1, 15; 2, 35. ἐπὶ θεόν AcPl Ha 2, 29 (cp. πρὸς θεόν Just., D. 138, 2). κατὰ θεόν *acc. to God's will* (Appian, Iber. 19 §73; 23 §88; 26 §101, Liby. 6 §25, Bell. Civ. 4, 86 §364) **Ro 8:27; 2 Cor 7:9ff;** IEph 2:1. ἡ κατὰ θ. ἀγάπη *godly love* IMg 1:1; cp. 13:1; ITr 1:2. παρὰ θεῷ (Jos., Bell. 1, 635) **Mt 19:26; Lk 2:52.**

ⓒ w. gen. foll. or w. ἴδιος to denote a special relationship: ὁ θ. ᾿Αβραάμ **Mt 22:32; Mk 12:26; Lk 20:37; Ac 3:13; 7:32** (all Ex 3:6). ὁ θ. (τοῦ) ᾿Ισραήλ (Ezk 44:2; JosAs 7:5) **Mt 15:31; Lk 1:68;** cp. **Ac 13:17; 2 Cor 6:16; Hb 11:16.** ὁ θ. μου **Ro 1:8; 1 Cor 1:4; 2 Cor 12:21; Phil 1:3; 4:19; Phlm 4.** OT κύριος ὁ θ. σου (ἡμῶν, ὑμῶν, αὐτῶν) **Mt 4:7** (Dt 6:16); **22:37** (Dt 6:5); **Mk 12:29** (Dt 6:4); **Lk 1:16; 4:8** (Dt 6:13); **10:27** (Dt 6:5); **Ac 2:39.** ὁ κύριος καὶ ὁ θ. ἡμῶν **Rv 4:11** (Just., D. 12, 3; the combination of κύριος and θεός is freq. in the OT: 2 Km 7:28; 3 Km 18:39; Jer 38:18; Zech 13:9; Ps 29:3; 34:23; 85:15; 87:2; TestAbr A 3 p. 79, 19 [Stone p. 6]; JosAs 3:4; 12:2 κύριε ὁ θ. τῶν αἰώνων. But s. also Epict. 2, 16, 13 κύριε ὁ θεός [GBreithaupt, Her. 62, 1927, 253–55], Herm. Wr.: Cat. Cod. Astr. VIII/2, p. 172, 6 κύριε ὁ θεὸς ἡμῶν, the PGM ref. at the beg. of this entry, and the sacral uses τ. θεῷ κ. κυρίῳ Σοκνοπαίῳ [OGI 655, 3f—24 BC]; PTebt 284, 6; τῷ κυρίῳ θεῷ ᾿Ασκληπίῳ [Sb 159, 2]; deo domino Saturno [ins fr. imperial times fr. Thala in the prov. of Africa: BPhW 21, 1901, 475], also Suetonius, Domit. 13 dominus et deus noster [for the formulation s. 4a: PMich 209]; Ar. 15, 10; Just., D. 60, 3 al.) τὸν ἴδιον θ. AcPl Ha 3, 22.—ὁ θ. τοῦ κυρίου ἡμῶν ᾿Ι. Χ. **Eph 1:17.**

ⓓ used w. πατήρ (s. πατήρ 6a) ὁ θ. καὶ πατὴρ τοῦ κυρίου ἡμῶν ᾿Ιησοῦ Χριστοῦ **Ro 15:6; 2 Cor 1:3; Eph 1:3; Col 1:3; 1 Pt 1:3.** ὁ θ. καὶ πατὴρ ἡμῶν **Gal 1:4; Phil 4:20; 1 Th 1:3; 3:11, 13.** ὁ θ. καὶ πατήρ **1 Cor 15:24; Eph 5:20; Js 1:27.** θ. πατήρ **Phil 2:11; 1 Pt 1:2;** cp. **1 Cor 8:6.** ἀπὸ θεοῦ πατρὸς ἡμῶν **Ro 1:7b; 1 Cor 1:3; 2 Cor 1:2; Gal 1:3; Eph 1:2; Phil 1:2; Col 1:2; Phlm 3;** ἀπὸ θ. π. **Gal 1:3 v.l.; Eph 6:23; 2 Th 1:2; 2 Ti 1:2; Tit 1:4;** παρὰ θεοῦ π. **2 Pt 1:17; 2J 3.**

ⓔ w. gen. of what God brings about, in accordance w. the divine nature: ὁ θ. τῆς εἰρήνης **Ro 15:33; 1 Th 5:23.** τῆς ἐλπίδος *the God fr. whom hope comes* **Ro 15:13.** πάσης παρακλήσεως **2 Cor 1:3b.** ὁ θ. τῆς ἀγάπης **13:11.** ὁ θ. πάσης χάριτος **1 Pt 5:10.** In οὐ γάρ ἐστιν ἀκαταστασίας ὁ θεός **1 Cor 14:33,** θεός is to be supplied before ἀκατ.: *for God is not a God of disorder.*

ⓕ The gen. (τοῦ) θεοῦ is—**α.** subj. gen., extremely freq. depending on words like βασιλεία, δόξα, θέλημα, ἐντολή, εὐαγγέλιον, λόγος, ναός, οἶκος, πνεῦμα, υἱός, υἱοί, τέκνα and many others. Here prob. (s. β) belongs τὸ μωρὸν τ. θ. *the (seeming) foolishness of G.* **1 Cor 1:25** (s. B-D-F §263, 2).

β. obj. gen. ἡ ἀγάπη τοῦ θ. *love for God* **Lk 11:42; J 5:42;** ἡ προσευχὴ τοῦ θ. *prayer to God* **Lk 6:12.** πίστις θεοῦ *faith in God* **Mk 11:22.** φόβος θεοῦ *fear of, reverence for God* **Ro 3:18** al. (s. φόβος 2bα) If **1 Cor 1:25** is to be placed here (s. α above), τὸ μωρὸν τ. θ. refers to apostolic allegiance to God, which is viewed by outsiders as folly.

γ. τὰ τοῦ θεοῦ *the things, ways, thoughts,* or *secret purposes of God* **1 Cor 2:11.** φρονεῖν τὰ τ. θ. **Mt 16:23; Mk 8:33** s. φρονέω 2b (ἀτιμάζοντας τὰ τοῦ θ. Just., D. 78, 10 al.). ἀποδιδόναι τὰ τ. θ. τῷ θεῷ *give God what belongs to God* **Mt 22:21; Mk 12:17; Lk 20:25.**

δ. Almost as a substitute for the adj. *divine* IMg 6:1f; 15 (cp. Ath. 21, 4 οὐδὲν ἔχων θεοῦ [of Zeus]).

ⓖ The dat. τῷ θεῷ (s. B-D-F §188, 2; 192; Rob. 538f; WHavers, Untersuchungen z. Kasussyntax d. indogerm. Sprachen 1911, 162ff) is

α. dat. of advantage (cp. e.g. Ath. 26, 3 ὡς ἐπηκόῳ θεῷ) *for God* **2 Cor 5:13.** Perh. (s. β) ὅπλα δυνατὰ τῷ θ. **10:4.** The dat. of **Ro 6:10f** rather expresses the possessor.

β. ethical dat. *in the sight of God,* hence w. superl. force (s. Beginn. IV, 75, on **Ac 7:20**) *very:* μεγάλοι τῷ θ. B 8:4 (cp. Jon 3:3). ἀστεῖος τῷ θ. **Ac 7:20.** Perh. (s. α) ὅπλα δυνατὰ τ. θ. *weapons powerful in the sight of God* **2 Cor 10:4.** This idea is usu. expressed by ἐνώπιον τοῦ θ.

ⓗ ὁ θ. is used as a vocative **Mk 15:34** (Ps 21:2. θεός twice at the beginning of the invocation of a prayer: Ael. Dion. θ, 8; Paus. Attic. θ, 7 'θεὸς θεός' ταῖς ἀρχαῖς ἐπέλεγον ἐπιφημιζόμενοι); **Lk 18:11; Hb 1:8** (Ps 44:7; MHarris, TynBull 36, '85, 129–62); **10:7** (Ps 39:9); AcPl Ha 3, 10; 5, 12; 31. S. also 2 and 3c and the beg. of this entry.

ⓘ θ. τῶν αἰώνων s. αἰών 3 and 4; θ. αἰώνιος s. αἰώνιος 2; θ. ἀληθινός s. ἀληθινός 3b; εἷς ὁ θεός s. εἷς 2b; (ὁ) θ. (ὁ) ζῶν s. [ζάω] 1aε.—ὁ μόνος θεός *the only God* (4 Km 19:15, 19; Ps 85:10; Is 37:20; Da 3:45; Philo, Leg. All. 2, 1f; s. Norden, Agn. Th. 145) **J 5:44** (some mss. lack τοῦ μόνου); **1 Ti 1:17.**—ὁ μόνος ἀληθινὸς θ. (Demochares: 75 fgm. 2 p. 135, 7 Jac. [in Athen. 6, 62, 253c] μόνος θ. ἀληθινός) **J 17:3.** cp. the sim. combinations w. μόνος θ. **Ro 16:27; Jd 25.** μόνος ὁ θεὸς μένει AcPl Ha 2, 27.—θ. σωτήρ s. σωτήρ 1.—OHoltzmann, D. chr. Gottesglaube, s. Vorgesch. u. Urgesch.1905; EvDobschütz, Rationales u. irrat. Denken über Gott im Urchristent.: StKr 95, 1924, 235–55; RHoffmann, D. Gottesbild Jesu '34; PAlthaus, D. Bild Gottes b. Pls: ThBl 20, '41, 81–92; Dodd 3–8; KRahner, Theos im NT: Bijdragen (Maastricht) 11, '50, 212–36; 12, '51, 24–52.

❹ **that which is nontranscendent but considered worthy of special reverence or respect, *god*** (Artem. 2, 69 p. 161, 17: γονεῖς and διδάσκαλοι are like gods; Simplicius in Epict. p. 85, 27 acc. to ancient Roman custom children had to call their parents θεοί; s. 2 above and note on σέβομαι).

ⓐ of humans θεοί (as אֱלֹהִים) **J 10:34f** (Ps 81:6; humans are called θ. in the OT also Ex 7:1; 22:27; cp. Philo, Det. Pot. Insid. 161f, Somn. 1, 229, Mut. Nom. 128, Omn. Prob. Lib. 43, Mos. 1, 158, Decal. 120, Leg. All. 1, 40, Migr. Abr. 84). θ. γίνεται τῶν λαμβανόντων (a benefactor) *proves to be a god to recipients* Dg 10:6 (cp. Pliny, NH 2, 7, 18; s. 2 above, beg.— Aristot., Pol. 3, 8,

1, 1284a of the superior pers. as a god among humans; Arcesilaus [III BC] describes Crates and Polemo as θεοί τινες='a kind of gods' [Diog. L. 4, 22]; Antiphanes says of the iambic poet Philoxenus: θεὸς ἐν ἀνθρώποισιν ἦν [Athen. 14, 50, 643d]; Diod. S. 1, 4, 7 and 5, 21, 2 of Caesar; for honors accorded Demetrius, s. IKertész, Bemerkungen zum Kult des Demetrios Poliorketes: Oikumene 2, '78, 163–75 [lit.]; Dio Chrys. 30 [47], 5 Πυθαγόρας ἐτιμᾶτο ὡς θεός; Heliod. 4, 7, 8 σωτὴρ κ. θεός, addressed to a physician; BGU 1197, 1 [4 BC] a high official, and 1201, 1 [2 BC] a priest θεός and κύριος; PMich 209, 11f [II/III AD] οἶδας ἄδελφε, ὅτει οὐ μόνον ὡς ἀδελφόν σε ἔχω, ἀλλὰ καὶ ὡς πατέρα κ. κύριον κ. θεόν; Just., A I, 26, 2 [Σίμων] θεὸς ἐνομίσθη καὶ . . . ὡς θεὸς τετίμηται; Tat. 3, 2 μὴ θεὸς ὢν [Empedocles]; Ath. 30, 2 Ἀντίνους . . . ἔτυχε νομίζεσθαι θεός of benefactors in gener. AcJ 27 [Aa II/1, 166, 4]).—JEmerton, JTS 11, '60, 329–32.

ⓑ of the belly (=appetite) as the god of certain people **Phil 3:19** (cp. Athen. 3, 97c γάστρων καὶ κοιλιοδαίμων. Also Eupolis Com. [V BC] fgm. 172 K. [in Athen. 3, 100b]; on the use of θ. in ref. to impersonal entities [e.g. Eur., Cyclops 316 of wealth as a god] s. DDD 693f).

❺ of the devil ὁ θ. τοῦ αἰῶνος τούτου **2 Cor 4:4** (s. αἰών 2a and WMüllensiefen, StKr 95, 1924, 295–99).—DDD 668–99. RAC XI 1202–78; XII 81–154; B. 1464. LfgrE s.v. θεός col. 1001 (lit.). Schmidt, Syn. IV 1–21. DELG. M-M. TW. Sv.

θεοσέβεια, ας, ἡ (s. two next entries; X., An. 2, 6, 26; Pla., Epin. p. 985d; 989e; Gen 20:11; Job 28:28; Sir 1:25; Bar 5:4; Philo, Just.; Tat. 17, 3; Ath. 4, 2; Theoph. Ant. 3, 15 [p. 234, 16].—The word is found as a title in Christian ins; cp. PLond 1924, 4; 1925, 3f; 1929, 3 [all IV AD].) **reverence for God or set of beliefs and practices relating to interest in God, *piety, godliness* 1 Ti 2:10;** *religion* 2 Cl 20:4; Dg 1; 3:3; 4:5; Qua (1); ἀόρατος θ. *invisible worship* (i.e., without images, sacrifices, or elaborate ceremonies, and with stress on the inner life, s. vss. 5–7) Dg 6:4. τὴν ἀπλανῆ θεοσέβειαν *inerrant worship,* as urged by the prophets of Israel, apparently w. ref. to emphasis on inner attitudes AcPlCor 2:10. τὸ τῆς θ. μυστήριον Dg 4:6 (Wengst 343 n. 34).—DELG s.v. σέβομαι. M-M. TW. Spicq.

θεοσεβέω (s. prec. entry; Pollux 1, 22; Cass. Dio 54, 30, 1; SIG 708, 18 [II BC]; TestJos 6:7; Just., D. 46, 6; Ath.) **to have reverence for God, *worship God*** κατὰ τὰ αὐτὰ Ἰουδαίοις *in the same way as the Jews* Dg 3:1.—LFeldman, BAR 12, '86, 58–63 (ins). DELG s.v. σέβομαι.

θεοσεβής, ές (s. two prec. entries; Soph., Hdt.+; Vett. Val. 17, 1; 19; 18, 16; Herm. Wr. 9, 4b; IG XIV, 1325; Kaibel 729, 2; PGiss 55, 1; UPZ 14, 20 [158 BC], on which s. the editor's note p. 159; LXX; TestAbr A 4, p. 81, 4 [Stone p. 10]; TestNapht 1:10; JosAs; EpArist 179; Philo, Mut. Nom. 197; Jos., C. Ap. 2, 140; Just. [D. 118, 3 θεοσεβέστεροι]; Tat. 13, 3; Ath. 37, 1. cp. also Jos., Ant. 12, 284; 20, 195, and the Jewish ins in the theater at Miletus in Dssm., LO 391f [LAE 446f] and Schürer III 164–72, SAB 1897, 221ff; ins BWander, Gottesfürchtige und Sympathisanten [WUNT 104] '98, 87–137, w. caution concerning relevance for biblical data) ***god-fearing, devout* J 9:31.** W. θεοφιλής: γένος τῶν Χριστιανῶν MPol 3:2. Of Job 1 Cl 17:3 (Job 1:1).—Lampe s.v. DELG s.v. σέβομαι. S. SEG XLII, 726 and 1226. M-M. TW. Spicq. Sv.

θεοστυγής, ές quotable fr. earlier times only in the pass. sense 'god-detested' (Eur., Tro. 1213, Cycl. 396; 602; Soph., Inachus [POxy 2369]; Neophron TrGF I, 2, 4; Ath. 30, 1), then 'godforsaken'. In the list of vices **Ro 1:30** the act. mng. ***hating God*** seems preferable (ADebrunner, Griech. Wortbildungslehre, 1917, 52 §105). It is obviously act. in Ps.-Clemens, Hom. 1, 12 ἄδικοι κ. θεοστυγεῖς. The noun θεοστυγία 1 Cl 35:5 is also to be taken as act. In favor of the pass. sense: Goodsp. ('abhorrent to God'); Mft. ('loathed by God'); NRSV mg.; Lat. Vulg.; s. Rob 232.—CFritzsche (1836) on Ro 1:30. CCranfield, Ro (ICC) ad loc. (lit.). DELG s.v. στυγέω. TW.

θεοστυγία, ας, ἡ hapax leg. ***hatred/enmity toward God*** 1 Cl 35:5 (s. θεοστυγής).

θεότης, ητος, ἡ (Plut., Mor. 415bc οὕτως ἐκ μὲν ἀνθρώπων εἰς ἥρωας, ἐκ δὲ ἡρώων εἰς δαίμονας αἱ βελτίονες ψυχαὶ τὴν μεταβολὴν λαμβάνουσιν. ἐκ δὲ δαιμόνων ὀλίγαι μὲν ἔτι χρόνῳ πολλῷ δι' ἀρετῆς καθαρθεῖσαι παντάπασι θεότητος μετέσχον=so from humans into heroes and from heroes into demi-gods the better souls undergo their transition; and from demi-gods, a few, after a long period of purification, share totally in divinity; Lucian, Icarom. 9; ApcSed 2:4 al.; Tat. 12, 4; 21, 2; Mel., fgm. 6; Herm. Wr. 12, 1; 13, 7a; Proclus, Theol. 137 p. 122, 5 al.; Cleopatra 62; 117; 137; οἱ αἱρετικοὶ διαφόρους εἰσάγοντες θεότητας Did., Gen. 184, 28; θ. τοῦ Ἰησοῦ Orig., C. Cels. 2, 36, 17) **the state of being god, *divine character/nature, deity, divinity,*** used as abstract noun for θεός (Orig., C. Cels. 7, 25, 9): τὸ πλήρωμα τῆς θ. *the fullness of deity* **Col 2:9** (s. Nash s.v. θειότης). ἐπιζητεῖν περὶ τῆς θ. *inquire concerning the deity* Hm 10, 1, 4; cp. 5f. δύναμις τῆς θ. *power of the deity* 11:5; πνεῦμα (τῆς) θ. 11:10, 14.—DELG s.v. θεός. TW. Sv.

θεοφιλής, ές *(be)loved by God* (so Pind., Hdt. et al.; Diod. S. 5, 34, 1; Dio Chrys. 16 [33], 21; OGI 383, 42 [I BC]; PGM 13, 225; EpArist 287; Jos., Ant. 1, 106; 14, 22; 455; Just., D. 7, 1; Tat. 12, 3), also act. ***loving God*** (Isocr. 4, 29; Philo, Praem. 43) w. θεοσεβής MPol 3:2.—DELG s.v. θεός. TW.

Θεόφιλος, ου, ὁ (in lit. [e.g. Diod. S. 16, 53, 1] as well as [since III BC] in ins and pap for Jews [EpArist 49; Joseph.] and Gentiles) ***Theophilus***

❶ a Christian of prominence, to whom **Lk (1:3)** and **Ac (1:1)** are dedicated.

❷ an elder in Corinth AcPlCor 1:1.—Haenchen on Ac 1:1. Cp. DELG s.v. θεός. M-M.

θεοφόρος, ον ***god-bearing, inspired,*** *inspired* (Aeschyl., fgm. 225; Philod., π. θεῶν 1 col. 4, 12 Diels: 'bearing the divine spirit within oneself'; Leontios 12 p. 22, 14; 15 p. 30, 15; AJA 37, 244 [ins II AD; Bacchic mysteries].—Heraclitus, Ep. 8, 2 the Σίβυλλα as θεοφορουμένη γυνή); subst. ὁ θ. *the God-bearer* IEph 9:2 (s. the foll. entry and cp. the v.l. for 1 Cor 6:20 in Lat. mss. 'portate [=ἄρατε] deum in corpore vestro').—Cp. DELG s.v. θεός. TW. Sv.

Θεοφόρος, ου, ὁ (not found as proper name before Ign., and perh. coined by him or for him; on the word and name s. Hdb., Ergänzungsband 1923, 189–91.—Ael. Aristid., because of his close relationship to Asclepius, receives the surname Θεόδωρος: 50, 53f K.=26 p. 518 D.) ***Theophorus,*** surname of Ignatius: IEph ins; IMg ins; ITr ins; IRo ins; IPhld ins; ISm ins; IPol ins—DELG s.v. θεός. TW. Sv.

θεραπεία, ας, ἡ (s. two next entries; Eur., Hdt.+; ins, pap, LXX, TestJob 38:8; JosAs, EpArist, Philo, Joseph.; Just., A I, 9, 3; Ath., R. 49, 10 al.; Just., A I, 12, 5 and Tat. 34, 2 'cultic service') gener. 'serving, service, care' bestowed on another.

❶ **the use of medical resources in treating the sick,** ***treatment,*** esp. ***healing*** (Hippocr. et al.; PTebt 44, 6–9 [114 BC] ὄντος μου ἐπὶ θεραπείᾳ ἐν τῷ . . . Ἰσιείῳ χάριν τ. ἀρρωστίας 'when I was in the . . . shrine of Isis for treatment of a malady'; Sb 159, 4f; 1537b; TestJob 38:8).

ⓐ lit. (Diod. S. 1, 25, 7 [pl.]; 17, 89, 2; Lucian, Abdic. 7; Philo, Deus Imm. 63; Jos., Vi. 85) **Lk 9:11.** θεραπείας ποιεῖν *perform healings* Ox 1 recto, 12f (ASyn. 33, 85; cp. GTh 31); τὰς θ. ἐπετέλουν GJs 20:2 (codd. not pap).

ⓑ fig., w. obj. gen. (cp. Pla., Prot. 345a τ. καμνόντων; Sb 1537b; θ. ὅλου σώματος; SIG 888, 125; Philo, Spec. Leg. 1, 191 θ. ἁμαρτημάτων) θ. τῶν ἐθνῶν **Rv 22:2.**

❷ =οἱ θεράποντες ***servants*** (Hdt. et al.; Gen 45:16; Esth 5:2b; JosAs; Philo, In Flacc. 149; Jos., Bell. 1, 82, Ant. 4, 112) καταστῆσαί τινα ἐπὶ τῆς θ. *put someone in charge of the servants* (cp. Polyb. 4, 87, 5 ὁ ἐπὶ τῆς θ. τεταγμένος) **Lk 12:42; Mt 24:45 v.l.**—DELG s.v. θεράπων. M-M. TW.

θεραπεύω impf. ἐθεράπευον; fut. θεραπεύσω; 1 aor. ἐθεράπευσα. Pass.: impf. ἐθεραπευόμην; 1 aor. ἐθεραπεύθην; perf. ptc. τεθεραπευμένος (s. prec. and next entry; Hom.+; ins, pap, LXX; TestSol 9:7 P; TestJos 7:2; JosAs 29:4; ApcrEzk P 1 verso 2 [restored]; Philo; apolog. exc. Ar.)

❶ **to render service or homage,** ***serve*** a divinity (Hes., Hdt.+; Diod. S. 5, 44, 2 οἱ θεραπεύοντες τοὺς θεοὺς ἱερεῖς; Arrian, Anab. 7, 2, 4; OGI 90, 40; SIG 663, 6; 996, 30; 1042, 10; Michel 982, 14; PGiss 20, 20; LXX [Thackeray p. 8]; EpArist 256; Philo, Spec. Leg. 2, 167; Jos., Bell. 7, 424, Ant. 4, 67; Ath. 16, 1 and 3; Orig., C. Cels. 8, 12, 17) pass. ὑπό τινος: οὐδὲ ὑπὸ χειρῶν ἀνθρωπίνων θεραπεύεται *nor is he served by human hands* **Ac 17:25** (Field, Notes 127).

❷ ***heal, restore*** (Athen. 12 p. 522b; SIG 1004, 21; 1168, 126; 1170, 20; 1171, 7; 1172, 5; Tob 12:3; Sir 38:7; JosAs; apolog. exc. Ar.; Hippol., Ref. 4, 44, 2; a ready transference is made to this mng. from the use of θ. in the var. senses of 'care for, wait upon, treat medically') τινά *someone* (Jos., Bell. 1, 272; of Jesus Orig., C. Cels. 2, 64, 17) **Mt 4:24; 8:7, 16; 10:8; 12:15, 22; 14:14; 15:30; 17:16, 18; 19:2; 21:14; Mk 1:34; 3:2, 10; 6:13; Lk 4:23** (Horapollo 2, 76 ὑφ' ἑαυτοῦ θεραπευθείς), **40; 10:9; 13:14b; J 5:10; Ac 4:14; 5:16; 8:7; 28:9;** Qua; AcPl Ha 5, 36; 8, 36=AcPl BMM verso 10 (blind). τινὰ ἀπό τινος *heal* or *cure someone from an illness* (BGU 956, 2 ἐξορκίζω ὑμᾶς κατὰ τοῦ ἁγίου ὀνόματος θεραπεῦσαι τὸν Διονύσιον ἀπὸ παντὸς ῥίγου [= ῥίγους] καὶ πυρετοῦ) **Lk 7:21.** Pass. **5:15; 6:18; 8:2** (Tat. 16:3 al.). ἀπό τινος has a different mng. in **vs. 43** οὐκ ἴσχυσεν ἀπ' οὐδενὸς θεραπευθῆναι *she could not be healed by anybody.*—θ. νόσον καὶ μαλακίαν (cp. Philo, Det. Pot. ins 43; Jos., Ant. 17, 150) **Mt 4:23; 9:35; 10:1;** (τὰς) νόσους **Mk 3:15 v.l.; Lk 9:1** (Just., A I, 48, 1; cp. 54, 10). Of wounds pass. (cp. Iren. 1, 3, 3 [Harv. I 27, 4]) **Rv 13:3, 12;** wounds healed by a plaster IPol 2:1. AcPl BMM verso 14 θ̣ερα[πεύων] (because of a lacuna the obj. cannot be determined). Abs. **Mt 12:10; Mk 6:5; Lk 6:7; 9:6; 13:14; 14:3;**—Fig. in isolated instances (e.g., Vi. Aesopi I c. 98 τὴν ὀργὴν ὁ λόγος θεραπεύσει): of God (Wsd 16:12) ὁ θεραπεύων θεός *God, who can heal* 2 Cl 9:7 (ὁ θεός, ὁ θεραπεύων καὶ ζωοποιῶν Theoph. Ant. 1, 7 [p. 72, 17]; of Christ Did., Gen. 105, 16; cp. Shmone Esre 8 אֵל . . . רוֹפֵא).—JHempel, Heilung als Symbol u. Wirklichkeit '58; JDewey, Jesus' Healings of Women, BTB 24, '94, 122–31; JCarroll, Sickness and Healing in the NT Gospels: Int 49, '95, 130–42.—On medical practice in the Gr-Rom. world, s. ANRW II/37/1–3, '93–96. B. 306. DELG s.v. θεράπων. M-M. EDNT. TRE XIV 763–68. TW.

θεράπων, οντος, ὁ (s. two prec. entries; Hom.+; Alciphron 4, 19, 9 Διονύσου θ. καὶ προφήτης; SIG 219, 12; 1168, 114f οἱ θεράποντες of the temple of Asclepius; BGU 361 III, 18; LXX [Thackeray p. 7f]; TestSol, TestJob; TestLevi 4:2; ApcMos prol.; Philo) **one who renders devoted service, esp. as an attendant in a cultic setting,** ***attendant, aide, servant,*** servant in our lit. only of Moses (as Ex 4:10; 14:31; Num 12:7 [in Just., D. 46, 3 al.]; Wsd 10:16; Theoph. Ant. 3, 18 [p. 240, 13]) **Hb 3:5;** 1 Cl 4:12; 43:1; 51:3; cp. vs. 5; 53:5; B 14:4.—B. 1334. DELG. M-M. TW. Sv.

θερεία, ας, ἡ (subst. from the fem. form of the adj. θέρειος [sc. ὥρα]; Pind. et al.; Aristot.; Diod. S.; pap; En 2:3; Jos., C. Ap. 1, 79) ***summertime*** Hs 4:2 (v.l. θρόνος), 3 and 5 (v.l. θέρος).—DELG s.v. θέρομαι 2.

θερίζω fut. θερίσω, but 3 pl. θεριοῦσι Job 4:8; Ps 125:5; 1 aor. ἐθέρισα. Pass. 1 aor. ἐθερίσθην; perf. pass. ptc. n. pl. τεθερισμένα Jdth 4:5 (s. θερισμός; Pre-Socr., trag.+; ins, pap, LXX, TestLevi 13:6; Philo; Jos., Ant. 3, 251 al.; Hippol., Ref. 5, 8, 39; Did., Gen. 33, 2).

❶ **to harvest a grain crop by reaping,** ***reap, harvest.*** **Mt 6:26; Lk 12:24;** 1 Cl 56:15 (Job 5:26) ὁ θερίσας *the harvester* **Js 5:4** (cp. BGU 349, 10 ἐμοῦ τοῦ μισθωσαμένου θερίζοντος τῷ μισθῷ); cp. **J 4:36.**—Dalman, Arbeit III.

❷ **to gain results or benefits,** ***reap,*** fig. extension of mng. 1

ⓐ esp. in proverbial expr. (Paroem. Gr.: Diogenian. 2, 62) ἄλλος ἐστὶν ὁ σπείρων καὶ ἄλλος ὁ θερίζων *one sows, and another reaps* **J 4:37,** cp. vs. **38.** ὃ γὰρ ἐὰν σπείρῃ ἄνθρωπος, τοῦτο καὶ θερίσει *whatever a man sows he will also reap* **Gal 6:7** (cp. Aristot., Rhet. 3, 3, 4 [1406b 9f] quoting Gorgias σὺ δὲ ταῦτα αἰσχρῶς μὲν ἔσπειρας κακῶς δὲ ἐθέρισας; Pla., Phdr. 260d; Philo, Leg. ad Gai. 293). θερίζων ὅπου οὐκ ἔσπειρας *reaping where you did not sow* **Mt 25:24, 26; Lk 19:21f.** Of a reward gener. (TestLevi 13:6 ἐὰν σπείρητε πονηρά, πᾶσαν ταραχὴν καὶ θλῖψιν θερίσετε; Philo, Conf. Lingu. 152; Jer 12:13; Pr 22:8) φθοράν, ζωὴν αἰώνιον **Gal 6:8.** τὰ σαρκικὰ ὑμῶν *reap* (=lay claim to) *your material benefits* **1 Cor 9:11.** Abs. **Gal 6:9; 2 Cor 9:6.**

ⓑ of the harvest of the Last Judgment, which brings devastation **Rv 14:15.** ἐθερίσθη ἡ γῆ vs. **16** (cp. Plut., Mor. 182a θερίζειν τὴν Ἀσίαν).—B. 506.—DELG s.v. θέρομαι 2. M-M. EDNT. TW.

θερινός, ή, όν (Pind. et al.; Sb 358, 7; 14 [ins III BC]; BGU 1188, 9 [I BC]; POxy 810; LXX; Philo; Jos., Ant. 15, 54) ***of summer*** καιροί *seasons of summer* 1 Cl 20:9.—DELG s.v. θέρομαι 2.

θερισμός, οῦ, ὁ (s. θερίζω; X., Oec. 18, 3; Polyb. 5, 95, 5; PLille 1 verso, 9 [III BC]; PHib 90, 5; BGU 594, 5; LXX; JosAs 2:19 καιρὸς . . . θερισμοῦ; EpArist 116; Philo, Somn. 2, 23)

❶ **the process (and time) of harvesting,** *harvest.* ἕως τ. θερισμοῦ **Mt 13:30a.** ἐν καιρῷ τ. θερισμοῦ vs. **30b** (cp. Jer 27:16 ἐν καιρῷ θ.); **Mk 4:29.** In these parables, θερισμός serves to explain procedures in the reign of God, as **Mt 13:39** plainly shows. Harvest-time as background for discussion of the apostolic mission and approaching judgment **J 4:35a** (s. 2b).

❷ **crop to be harvested,** ***harvest*** fig. extension of mng. 1

ⓐ of persons to be won **Mt 9:37f; Lk 10:2.** In **J 4:35b** the evangelist may be combining an agricultural observation with a statement about the apostolic mission πρὸς θερισμόν in pass. sense of *undergoing a reaping.*

ⓑ of the approaching judgment ἐξηράνθη ὁ θ. τῆς γῆς *the earth's harvest is dry* (=fully ripe) **Rv 14:15.**—DELG s.v. θέρομαι 2. M-M. TW.

θεριστής, οῦ, ὁ (θερίζω; X., Hier. 6, 10 al.; Plut.; Philostrat., Her. 158, 31; PHib 44, 4; PFlor 80, 6; Bel 33; ViHab 5 [p. 86, 6 Sch.]; Philo, Virt. 90) ***reaper, harvester*** **Mt 13:30, 39.**—DELG s.v. θέρομαι 3. M-M.

θερμαίνω (θερμός; Hom. et al.; LXX; TestSol 18:18 P; Ar. 6, 1; POxy 1778, 30) 1 aor. impv. θέρμανον Sir 38:17; subj. 2 sg. θερμάνῃς TestSol 18:18 P; in our lit. only **θερμαίνομαι** (PSI 406, 37 [III BC]; Jos., Bell. 3, 274) impf. ἐθερμαινόμην; 1 aor. ἐθερμάνθην LXX ***warm** oneself* at a fire (Is 44:16) **Mk 14:67; J 18:18ab, 25.** πρὸς τὸ φῶς *at the fire* **Mk 14:54.** Of clothing (Hg 1:6; Job 31:20) θερμαίνεσθε *dress warmly! keep warm!* **Js 2:16.**—DELG s.v. θέρομαι 3.

θέρμη (also in the form **θέρμα;** s. Phryn. 331 Lob.; WRutherford, New Phryn. 1881, 198; 414; Frisk s.v. θερμός. The word since Aristoph., fgm. 690; Thu.+; ins, pap; Job 6:17; Ps 18:7; Sir 38:28; GrBar 9:8; Jos., Bell. 3, 272), **ης, ἡ** (der. fr. θερμός) ***heat*** ἀπὸ τῆς θ. *because of the heat* **Ac 28:3.**—DELG s.v. θέρομαι 3 (θερμός). M-M.

θερμός, ή, όν (Hom.+; LXX; En 14:13; ApcSed 14:3 p. 136, 2 Ja.; Jos., Vi. 85; Just., D. 29, 3) ***warm*** of water for baptism ὕδωρ (cp. Soranus p. 41, 8; Philumen. p. 23, 17; 26, 12; SIG 1170, 12; Philo, Mos. 1, 212) D 7:2.—B. 1077. DELG s.v. θέρομαι 3.

θέρος, ους, τό (Hom.+; OGI 56, 41; PHib 27, 33; LXX, TestSol, Test12Patr, Philo; Jos., Ant. 5, 190; 212; Ar. 4:2 θέρη) ***summer*** **Mt 24:32; Mk 13:28; Lk 21:30** (ZNW 10, 1909, 333f; 11, 1910, 167f; 12, 1911, 88). Fig. for heavenly bliss Hs 4:3 and 5 v.l. for θερεία.—B. 511; 1014f. DELG s.v. θέρομαι 2 (θέρος). M-M.

θέσις, εως, ἡ (Pind. et al.; ins, pap, LXX, EpArist, Philo; Tat. 27, 3 ἄστρων θέσεις; 28, 1 τῶν νόμων θέσεις; Ath., R. 67, 2 νόμων θέσις) ***position*** ἰσχυρὰ ἡ θέσις *the position is secure* Hv 3, 13, 3.—DELG s.v. τίθημι. TW. Sv.

Θεσσαλία, ας, ἡ (Hdt. et al.; ins; Philo, Leg. ad Gai. 281; SibOr) ***Thessaly,*** a region in northeast Greece **Ac 17:15** D.

Θεσσαλονικεύς, έως, ὁ (Mel., HE 4, 26, 10; Steph. Byz. s.v. Θεσσαλονίκη) ***Thessalonian,*** an inhabitant of Thessalonica **Ac 20:4; 27:2; 1 Th 1:1,** ins; **2 Th 1:1,** ins.

Θεσσαλονίκη, ης, ἡ (Polyb. 22, 11, 2; Strabo 7 fgm. 24; Ps.-Lucian, Asin. 46; anon. De Historia Diadochorum [time unknown]: 155 fgm. 2, 3 Jac.; ins [SIG index vol. IV 94]) ***Thessalonica,*** a city in Macedonia on the Thermaic Gulf. Paul founded a congregation here **Ac 17:1, 11, 13; Phil 4:16; 2 Ti 4:10.**—BHHW III 1968; DACL XV 1 and 624–713; Kl. Pauly V 761–63.

Θευδᾶς, ᾶ, ὁ (CIG 2684; 3563; 5689; BCH 11, 1887, 213–15) ***Theudas,*** the short form of a name compounded w. θεός, but perh. not Θεόδωρος, since in CIG 3920=SIG 1229 two brothers Theodore and Theudas are mentioned (s. B-D-F §125, 2; Mlt-H. 88; 91). **Ac 5:36** mentions a Jewish insurrectionist named Theudas; the only such pers. known to history revolted and was killed in the time of the procurator Cuspius Fadus, 44 AD and later (Jos., Ant. 20, 97–99). For the grave chronological difficulties here s. the comm., e.g. Haenchen and Beginn. IV ad loc.—Schürer I 456 (lit. here, note 6); JSwain, HTR 37, '44, 341–49.—New Docs 4, 183–85 (ins w. numerous orthographic variations). M-M.

θέω (Hom.+) ***run*** w. acc. of place (Ps.- X., Cyneg. 4, 6 τὰ ὄρη) θ. τὴν ὁδὸν τὴν εὐθεῖαν *run the straight course* 2 Cl 7:3. DELG s.v. 1 θέω.

θεωρέω impf. ἐθεώρουν; 1 aor. ἐθεώρησα, 1 aor. pass. ἐθεωρήθην (Aeschyl., Hdt.+).

❶ **to observe someth. with sustained attention,** ***be a spectator, look at, observe, perceive, see*** (w. physical eyes) abs. (2 Macc 3:17) **Mt 27:55; Mk 15:40; Lk 14:29; 23:35** (cp. Ps 21:8). οἱ θεωροῦντες AcPl Ha 1, 34. W. indir. quest. foll. **Mk 12:41; 15:47.** W. acc. foll. τινά **J 6:40; 12:45; 14:19a; 16:10, 16f, 19; Ac 3:16; 25:24; Rv 11:11f;** 1 Cl 16:16 (Ps 21:8); 35:8 (Ps 49:18). W. acc. of pers. and a ptc. (TestSol 20:6; JosAs 4:2; Just., D. 101, 3) **Mk 5:15; Lk 10:18; 24:39; J 6:19, 62; 10:12; 20:12, 14; 1J 3:17.** W. acc. of pers. and ὅτι **J 9:8.** τὶ *someth.* (X., Cyr. 4, 3, 3; TestSol 19:2 τὸν ναόν; Jos., Ant. 12, 422) **Lk 21:6; 23:48.** πνεῦμα *a ghost* **24:37.—J 2:23; 6:2; 7:3.** ἔν τινί τι *see someth. in someone:* the whole church in the envoys IMg 6:1; cp. ITr 1:1. W. acc. of thing and ptc. foll. **J 20:6; Ac 7:56; 8:13; 10:11; 17:16.** W. ἀκούειν **Ac 9:7** (Apollon. Rhod. 4, 854f: when a deity [in this case Thetis] appears, only those who are destined to do so can see and hear anything; none of the others can do so). θεωρεῖν καὶ ἀκούειν ὅτι **19:26.**—Pass. *was exposed* MPol 2:2.—Rather in the sense *view* (Cebes 1, 1 ἀναθήματα) τὸν τάφον **Mt 28:1.**—*Catch sight of, notice* **Mk 3:11.** τὶ *someth.* θόρυβον **5:38.** W. ὅτι foll. **Mk 16:4.**—The expr. *see someone's face* for *see someone in person* is due to OT infl. (cp. Jdth 6:5; 1 Macc 7:28, 30) **Ac 20:38.**

❷ **to come to the understanding of someth.,** ***notice, perceive, observe, find***—ⓐ esp. on the basis of what one has seen and heard τὶ *someth.* (Apollod. Com., fgm. 14 K. θ. τὴν τοῦ φίλου εὔνοιαν='become aware of the friend's goodwill by the actions of the doorkeeper and the dog'; Sallust. 4 p. 4, 24 τὰς οὐσίας τ. θεῶν θ.=perceive the true nature of the gods; τὰ ἀδικήματα ὑμῶν En 98:7; τὰ πράγματα Just., A II, 10, 4; τὸ θεῖον … νῷ μόνῳ καὶ λόγῳ θεωρούμενον; Ath. 4, 1) **Ac 4:13.** W. acc. of the thing and ptc. (EpArist 268) **28:6.** W. acc. of the pers. and predicate adj. (cp. Diod. S. 2, 16, 8) δεισιδαιμονεστέρους ὑμᾶς θ. *I perceive that you are very devout people* **Ac 17:22.** W. ὅτι foll. (2 Macc 9:23) **J 4:19; 12:19.** Foll. by ὅτι and inf. w. acc. (B-D-F §397, 6; Mlt. 213) **Ac 27:10.** W. indir. quest. foll. **21:20; Hb 7:4.**

ⓑ of the spiritual perception of the one sent by God, which is poss. only to the believer (s. Herm. Wr. 12, 20b; En 1:1 al.; Philo, e.g. Praem. 26) *see* **J 14:17, 19b;** cp. also **17:24** (θ. τὸν θεόν Theoph. Ant. 1, 2 [p. 60, 25]).

ⓒ *undergo, experience* θάνατον (OT expr.; cp. Ps 88:49; also Lk 2:26; Hb 11:5; s. ὁράω A3) **J 8:51** (εἶδον v.l.).—HKoller, Theoros u. Theoria: Glotta 36, '58, 273–86; RRausch, Theoria '82. DELG s.v. θεωρός. M-M. EDNT. TW. Sv.

θεώρημα, ατος, τό (in var. mngs. since Pla., Aristot., Demosth., also En 19:3 ['vision']; Philo) **someth. seen,** ***a sight*** καινόν σοι ἔχω εἰπεῖν θ. *I want to tell you about someth. unusual that I saw* AcPl Ox 6, 1f (διήγημα Aa I, 241, 11).—DELG s.v. θεωρός.

θεωρία, ας, ἡ (Aeschyl., Hdt. +) **that which one looks at,** ***spectacle, sight*** (so mostly of public spectacles, religious festivals, processions, etc., s. DHagedorn and LKoenen, ZPE 2, '68, 74) συνπαραγενόμενοι ἐπὶ τὴν θ. ταύτην *who had gathered for this spectacle* **Lk 23:48** (w. sim. mng. IG IV[2]/1, 123, 26 θ.

for the ὄχλος; 3 Macc 5:24.—Mitt-Wilck. I/2, 3, 6 [112 BC] ἐπὶ θεωρίαν a Rom. senator goes sightseeing in Egypt. ἄγωμεν ἐπὶ τὴν θεωρίαν *let us be off for the show* AcPl Ha 4, 7).—DELG s.v. θεωρός. M-M. TW.

θήκη, ης, ἡ gener. 'receptacle' (Aeschyl., Hdt.+; ins, pap, LXX; En 17:3; Test12Patr; JosAs, Joseph., Ar. 4, 3; loanw. in rabb.).

❶ ***grave*** (trag., Hdt. et al.; SIG 1233, 1; POxy 1188, 4; 21 [13 AD]; PGM 4, 2215; Jos., Ant. 8, 264; 16, 181; Ar. 4, 3) 1 Cl 50:4.

❷ ***sheath*** for a sword (Posidon.: 87 fgm. 15, 1 Jac.; Pollux 10, 144; PPetr III, 140a, 4; Jos., Ant. 7, 284) **J 18:11.**—DELG (w. some relation to the root of τίθημι). M-M.

θηλάζω fut. θηλάσω LXX; 1 aor. ἐθήλασα—❶ **to breast-feed an infant, *nurse*** (Lysias, Aristot. et al.; pap, LXX; En 99:5) abs. **Mt 24:19; Mk 13:17; Lk 21:23; 23:29 v.l.** Ἄννα θηλάζει GJs 6:3 (once in pap, twice in codd.)

❷ **to receive nourishment at the breast, *suck, nurse*** (Hippocr., Aristot.+; PRyl 153, 18; LXX; TestSol 1:2 [cod B] and 4; TestAbr A 6 p. 83, 13 [Stone p. 14]; TestBenj 1:3; ApcEsdr 5:2 p. 29, 25 Tdf.; Philo, Det. Pot. Ins. 118) μαστοὶ οὓς ἐθήλασας *the breasts you have sucked* **Lk 11:27** (cp. SSol 8:1; Job 3:12; Hippocr. VIII 594 L. θ. τὸν μαστόν; Theocr. 3, 16 μασδὸν ἐθήλαξεν). οἱ θηλάζοντες or τὰ θηλάζοντα if the pl. of βρέφος is implied in the gen. pl. θηλαζόντων *nursing babies* **Mt 21:16** (Ps 8:3).—B. 334.—DELG s.v. θηλή. M-M. TW.

θηλυκός, ή, όν (Aristot. et al.; PLille 10, 5 [III BC]; POxy 1458, 11; PGM 4, 2518; Num 5:3; Dt 4:16; TestSol; Philo, Deus Imm. 141) **pert. to being female, *female*** ἵνα ἀδελφὸς ἰδὼν ἀδελφὴν οὐδὲν φρονῇ περὶ αὐτῆς θηλυκόν *that a male member when he sees a female member should not think of her as a female* 2 Cl 12:5.—DELG s.v. θηλή.

θῆλυς, εια, υ (Hom.+) ***female*** ἡ θ. *woman* (Hdt. 3, 109; X., Mem. 2, 1, 4 et al.; Lev 27:4–7; En 15:5 and 7; TestJob 46:2f; Just., A I, 27, 1 al.) **Ro 1:26f;** 1 Cl 55:5; 2 Cl 12:2, 5 (both the latter pass. are quot. fr. an apocryphal gospel, presumably GEg); GEg 54, 21; *girl* εἴτε ἄρσενα εἴτε θηλείαν GJs 4:1; cp. 5:2 (TestJob 46:2f; Just., A II, 5, 5). Also τὸ θ. (PTebt 422, 18 'daughter') ἄρσεν καὶ θ. *male and female* (LXX; Philo; Jos., Ant. 1, 32; cp. Pla., Rep. 454d; Aristot., Metaph. 988a, 5; Ath. 22, 4 and R. 76, 20) **Mt 19:4; Mk 10:6;** 1 Cl 33:5; 2 Cl 14:2 (all Gen 1:27); **Gal 3:28.**—GNaass 252, 60; GEg 252, 57f; 2 Cl 12:2 (s. above); cp. B 10:7.—B. 84f.—DELG s.v. θηλή. M-M.

θημωνιά, ᾶς, ἡ (θημών 'heap'; LXX; Just., D. 113, 6; Etym. Mag. p. 451, 8; Anecd. Gr. p. 264, 18=σωρὸς καρπῶν) ***heap (of sheaves)*** θ. ἅλωνος *a heap on the threshing-floor* 1 Cl 56:15 (Job 5:26).—DELG s.v. τίθημι.

θῆξις, εως, ἡ (patristic wr., lexicographers, glossarists) lit. someth. very small 'point', then ***moment*** (s. deStrycker, GJs, p. 300f) πάντα θήξει ὑπὸ τοῦ δρόμου ἀπηλαύνετο *in a moment everything went back to normal* GJs 18:3 (not pap).—DELG s.v. θήγω.

θήρ, ός, ὁ (Hom. et al.; Sb 4011, 4; LXX; ViDa 7 [p. 77, 13 Sch.]; Ath., R. 56, 20) ***(wild) animal*** 1 Cl 20:4. θῆρες ἄγριοι *wild animals* 56:12 (Job 5:23).—Schmidt, Syn. II 432–36. DELG.

θήρα, ας, ἡ (s. θήρ; Hom.+; ins, pap, LXX; TestZeb; Philo, Mos. 1, 298; Jos., Ant. 1, 274; 18, 45, usu. in the mng. 'hunt' or 'prey') ***net, trap*** (so Horapollo 2, 26 w. παγίς; Ps 34:8; Pr 11:8) **Ro 11:9.**—DELG s.v. θήρ. M-M.

θηρεύω 1 aor. ἐθήρευσα (s. θήρ; Hom. et al.; ins, pap, LXX; TestZeb 5:5; Ar. 11, 2) ***to hunt, catch*** fig. (so in many ways Pind. et al.; Diod. S. 2, 5, 1; Ps 139:12; Philo; Jos., Ant. 19, 308) θ. τι ἐκ τοῦ στόματος αὐτοῦ *catch him in someth. he might say* **Lk 11:54** (Pla., Gorg. 489b ὀνόματα θηρεύειν='to hunt for the words [of other people] to see whether they might perhaps commit errors' [ἐάν τις ῥήματι ἁμάρτῃ].—θ.=catch by treachery: Ps.-Clemens, Hom. 8, 22). τίς ὁ θηρεύσας με; *Who has deceived me?* GJs 13:1.—DELG s.v. θήρ. M-M.

θηριομαχέω (s. θηρίον, μάχομαι) 1 aor. ἐθηριομάχησα

❶ **be forced to fight with wild animals as a punishment, *fight with wild animals*** (Diod. S. 3, 43, 7; Artem. 2, 54; 5, 49; Ptolem., Apotel. 4, 9, 10; Vett. Val. 129, 33; 130, 21; Jos., Bell. 7, 38) IEph 1:2; ITr 10; ἐπισήμως θ. MPol 3, 1. For **1 Cor 15:32** s. 2.

❷ **to be in a position of having to contend with adversaries, *struggle with, contend with.*** It is uncertain whether θ. is used lit. or fig. in **1 Cor 15:32.** It is quite unlikely that Paul could have engaged in a real struggle w. wild animals (but. s. Bowen below). He says nothing about such an experience in 2 Cor 11:23–29, and Ac does not mention it (but Ac is silent about many matters). Also the apostle could not have been sentenced 'ad bestias' without losing his Roman citizenship, which he still held at a later date, and which formed the basis for his appeal to the emperor. If, nevertheless, the verb is to be taken as lit., the expr. is to be considered (w. JWeiss on 1 Cor 15:32 and WMichaelis, Die Gefangenschaft d. Paulus in Ephesus 1925, 118ff) a contrary to fact (unreal) conditional sentence: 'if I had fought w. wild animals' (against this JSchmid, Zeit u. Ort d. paul. Gefangenschaftsbr. '31, 39–60; WKümmel, Hdb. '49). But the expr. can also be fig. (freq. in Cynic-Stoic diatribe; AMalherbe, JBL 87, '68, 71–80), as it certainly is in IRo 5:1 ἀπὸ Συρίας μέχρι Ῥώμης θηριομαχῶ . . . δεδεμένος δέκα λεοπάρδοις, ὅ ἐστι στρατιωτικὸν τάγμα *from Syria to Rome I am fighting with wild animals, bound to ten leopards, that is, a detachment of soldiers* (cp. OGI 201, 16 ἐπολέμησα ἀπὸ Π. ἕως Τ.); here Ign. describes the sufferings of his journey as a prisoner with a word that suggests a struggle w. wild animals (cp. Appian, Bell. Civ. 2, 61 §252, where Pompey says in sim. fig. language: οἵοις θηρίοις μαχόμεθα; Philo, Mos. 1, 43f. Ignatius longed to have actual wild beasts consume him IRo 4:1f; 5:2.). In AcPl Ha 3, 9; 4, 8; 5, 13 actual fights with wild beasts (Lat. venationes) are meant.—CBowen, JBL 42, 1923, 59–68; CCoffin, ibid. 43, 1924, 172–76; JHunkin, ET 39, 1928, 281f; R Osborne, JBL 85, '66, 225–30; lit. s.v. ἀγών.—DELG s.v. θήρ. M-M.

θηριομαχίον, ου, τό (s. prec. and next entry; TAM II, 508, 12) pl. τὰ θ. (cp. Cic. Ep. 70, 20; 22 ludus bestiarius. The combat usu. pitted the condemned pers. against lions, tigers, leopards, wolves, or dogs.) ***fight with beasts*** AcPl Ha 2, 11; 36, 3 and 17.—Cp. DELG s.v. θήρ.

θηριομάχος, ον (M. Ant. 10, 87 et al.) ***fighting with wild beasts*** τῷ θ. ἀνθρώπῳ AcPl Ha 5, 30. Subst. τοῦ θ. λόγον 2, 14.—DELG s.v. θήρ.

θηρίον, ου, τό (Hom.+), in form, but not always in mng., dim. of θήρ.

❶ **any living creature, excluding humans, *animal, beast***

ⓐ of real animals—α. gener. **Hb 12:20.** τὰ θ. τῆς γῆς (Gen 1:24, 25, 30) B 6:12; cp. vs. 18; GJs 3:2; τῆς θαλάσσης B 4:5 (Da 7:7). W. adj. θ. ἄγρια (X., An. 1, 2, 7; TestSol 10, 3 C) 1 Cl 56:11 (Job 5:22).

β. of animals of a particular kind.—א. quadrupeds as such (Ps.-Clemens, Hom. 3, 36): **Js 3:7;** φυλακὴ παντὸς θηρίου ἀκαθάρτου *cage for every kind of unclean animal* **Rv 18:2.**

ב. wild animals (Diod. S. 1, 87, 3; Jos., Bell. 3, 385, Ant. 9, 197) **Mk 1:13** (FSpitta, ZNW 5, 1904, 323ff; 8, 1907, 66ff.—Himerius, Or. 39 [=Or. 5], 5: Orpheus in the Thracian mountains, where he has no one to listen to him θηρίων τὴν ἐκκλησίαν ἐργάζεται=forms a community for himself from the wild animals); so perh. **Ac 11:6** (s. Hs 9, 26, 1 below).—DDD 1689–92.

ג. w. emphasis on aspect of danger: gener. (Antig. Car. 29 [wolf]; Diod. S. 17, 92, 2 and 3 [lion]; Maximus Tyr. 20, 2b; Jos., Ant. 2, 35) **Rv 6:8** (cp. Hdt. 6, 44, 3); IEph 7:1.

ד. a reptile *snake* (Diod. S. 20, 42, 2, alternating with ὄφις; Polyaenus 2, 3, 15 with ἔχις; Aretaeus 159, 8 τὸ διὰ τ. θηρίων φάρμακον; 163, 2; Just., A I, 60, 2; Galen IV 779 K.; θήρ=snake: Simias [III BC], Coll. Alex. fgm. 26, 17 p. 119) **Ac 28:4f;** Hs 9, 26, 7b; so also ibid. 7a and prob. 9, 26, 1 w. ἑρπετά (cp. **Ac 11:6;** Jos., Ant. 17, 117). Cp. PtK 2 p. 14, 18.

γ. oft. of *wild animals* in a controlled setting, namely of fighting w. animals in an arena (Diod. S. 36, 10, 3; Artem. 2, 54; Jos., Bell. 7, 38) IRo 4:1f; 5:2f; ISm 4:2a, b; MPol 3:1; 4; 11:1f; Dg 7:7; Hv 3, 2, 1; AcPl Ha 1, 28; 2, 4; 5, 5 and 9. εἰς τὰ θηρία κατακρίνεσθαι *be condemned to fight w. wild animals* MPol 2:4. κατέκρινεν αὐτὸν εἰς θηρία AcPl Ha 1, 29.

ⓑ of animal-like beings of a transcendent kind (Paus. 1, 24, 6 griffins; 2, 37, 4 the hydra; cp. Da 7:3ff) B 4:5 (Da 7:7). Of a monstrous dragon (schol. on Apollon. Rhod. 4, 156–66a the guardian of the golden fleece; Damascius, Vi. Isid. 140) Hv 4, 1, 6; 4, 1, 8; 4, 1, 10; 4, 2, 1; 4, 2, 3ff; 4, 3, 1 and 7 (on the monster in H, s. Joly p. 113 n. 2). The 'beasts' or 'animals' of **Rv: 11:7; 13:1ff, 11f, 14f, 17f; 14:9, 11; 15:2; 16:2, 10, 13; 17:3, 7f, 11ff, 16f; 19:19f; 20:4, 10.**—Lit. s.v. δράκων. BMurmelstein, StKr 101, 1929, 447–57; RSchütz, D. Offb. d. Joh. u. Kaiser Domitian '33; PMinear, JBL 72, '53, 93–101.

❷ **wicked person, someone w. a 'bestial' nature,** ***beast, monster,*** fig. ext. of mng. 1 (Aristoph., Equ. 273, Plutus 439, Nub. 184; Appian [s. θηριομαχέω, end]; Alciphron 2, 17, 4 al.; Achilles Tat. 6, 12, 3; Jos., Bell. 1, 624; 627, Ant. 17, 117 and 120; cp. Vett. Val. 78, 9; BGU 1024 IV, 5ff) **Tit 1:12** (Damascius, Vi. Isid. 301 the wife of Isid. is called a κακὸν θ.). θ. ἀνθρωπόμορφα *beasts in human form* (Philo, Ab. 33) ISm 4:1.—B. 137. DELG s.v. θήρ. DDD 1689–92. M-M. EDNT. TW.

θησαυρίζω 1 aor. ἐθησαύρισα; pf. pass. ptc. τεθησαυρισμένος (s. next entry; Hdt. et al.; SIG 954, 80; LXX; En 97:9; PsSol 9:5; Philo)

❶ **to keep some material thing safe by storing it,** ***lay up, store up, gather, save*** τὶ *someth.* (Diod. S. 5, 21, 5; 20, 8, 4) ὅ τι ἐὰν εὐοδῶται *in keeping with his gains* **1 Cor 16:2.** τί τινι *someth. for someone* θησαυροὺς ἑαυτῷ *store up treasures for oneself* **Mt 6:19** (citation Just., A I, 15, 11). Abs. (Philod., Oec. p. 71 Jensen; Ps 38:7; Just., A I, 15, 12 [on Mt 6:20?]) *store up treasure* **Js 5:3.** τινί *for someone* **Lk 12:21; 2 Cor 12:14.**

❷ **to do someth. that will bring about a future event or condition,** ***store up,*** fig. extension of mng. 1 (Diod. S. 9, 10, 3 words ἐν ταῖς ψυχαῖς τεθησαυρισμέναι; Philostrat., Vi. Soph. 2, 1, 2 θ. ἐν ταῖς γνώμαις=in the hearts)

ⓐ of treasures in heaven (cp. Tob 4:9; PsSol 9:5 θ. ζωὴν αὐτῷ παρὰ κυρίῳ) **Mt 6:20** (citation Just., A I, 15, 11; cp. 12 [citation?]).

ⓑ *store up* (plentifully) ὀργὴν ἑαυτῷ *anger for oneself* **Ro 2:5** (cp. Diod. S. 20, 36, 4 φθόνος; Appian, Samn. 4, 3; Vi. Aesopi G 107 P. κακά; IPriene 112, 15 ἐθησαύρισεν ἑαυτῷ παρὰ μὲν τ. ζώντων ἔπαινον, παρὰ δὲ τ. ἐπεσομένων μνήμην 'he stored up praise for himself fr. the living, and remembrance fr. those yet to be born'; Pr 1:18 κακά. S. also ὀργή 2b; on θ. ἐν ἡμ. cp. Tob 4:9).

ⓒ *save up, reserve* (4 Macc 4:3; Philo, Sacr. Abel. 62, Deus Imm. 156) heaven and earth τεθησαυρισμένοι εἰσίν *are reserved* **2 Pt 3:7.**—DELG s.v. θησαυρός. M-M. TW.

θησαυρός, οῦ, ὁ (s. prec. entry; Hes., Hdt.+; loanw. in rabb.; τὴν θ. TestSol 13:2 C).

❶ **a place where someth. is kept for safekeeping,** ***repository*** (Theoph. Ant. 2, 35 [p. 188, 16])—ⓐ of repositories for material things—α. *treasure box* or *chest* (cp. X., An. 5, 4, 27; Diod. S. 17, 71, 1; PTebt 6, 27; PAmh 41, 8; En 97:9; Jos., Ant. 9, 163) **Mt 2:11.**

β. *storehouse, storeroom* (Appian, fgm. 6; PRyl 231, 8; PFay 122, 4; POxy 101, 29; Am 8:5; Pr 8:21) **Mt 13:52** (with ἐκβάλλειν ἐκ τοῦ θ. cp. Arrian, Cyneg. 34, 1 ἐμβάλλειν ἐς τὸν θ.).

ⓑ of repositories for transcendent things (TestAsh 1:9) of the heart as the treasury for heavenly possessions θ. τῆς καρδίας **Lk 6:45;** cp. **Mt 12:35** (on ἀγαθὸς θ. s. Dt 28:12).—GKaminski, JDAI 106, '91, 63–181 (ins); s. SEG XLI, 1846.

❷ **that which is stored up,** ***treasure*** **Mt 6:21; Lk 12:34** (cp. Just., A I, 15, 16).—ⓐ of material things (TestSol C 10, 21 al.; Diod. S. 17, 71, 1) **Mt 6:19; 13:44** (for θ. buried in the ground: Maximus Tyr. 15, 5h; Artem. 2, 58; Philostrat., Vi. Apoll. 6, 39 p. 250, 4ff; JDerrett, Law in the NT, '70, 1–16). The treasures of Egypt **Hb 11:26.**

ⓑ of transcendent things (Iren. 4, 26, 1 [Harv. II 235, 9]; on θ. that is dug up in metaph. sense cp. Philemo Com. 169 K. ἐὰν γυνὴ γυναικὶ κατ' ἰδίαν ὁμιλεῖ, μεγάλων κακῶν θησαυρὸς ἐξορύσσεται. Metaph. use also by end)

α. of the treasures in heaven **Mt 6:20.** θ. ἀνέκλειπτος ἐν τ. οὐρανοῖς **Lk 12:33.** θησαυρὸν ἔχειν ἐν οὐρανῷ *have treasure in heaven* the treasure is, in effect, deposited there and becomes available to people after death **Mt 19:21; Mk 10:21; Lk 18:22.**—WPesch, Biblica 41, '60, 356–78 (Mt 6:19–21; Lk 12:33f).

β. θησαυροὶ σκοτεινοί *treasures lying in darkness* B 11:4 (Is 45:3).

γ. of the gospel and its glory **2 Cor 4:7.** Of Christ: ἐν ᾧ εἰσιν πάντες οἱ θησαυροὶ τῆς σοφίας καὶ γνώσεως ἀπόκρυφοι *in whom all the treasures of wisdom and knowledge lie hidden* **Col 2:3** (ἐν θησαυροῖς σοφίας Sir 1:25; cp. X., Mem. 1, 6, 14; 4, 2, 9 θησαυροὶ σοφίας; Pla., Phileb. 15e; Diod. S. 9, 10, 3 κάλλιστος θ.; Himerius, Or. [Ecl.] 3, 20 θ. ἀθάνατος of the possession of virtue; Pr 2:3ff; Philo, Congr. Erud. Gr. 127).—B. 777; BHHW III 1686. DELG. M-M. EDNT. TW.

θιγγάνω 2 aor. ἔθιγον (trag. et al. but not in Attic prose [WRutherford, New Phryn. 1881, 169f; 391]; Hippocr. [Anz 293]; ins, pap; Ex 19:12; JosAs16 [p. 64, ln. 20 Bat.] cod. A [ἔθηξε fr. the by-form θίγω]) ***touch*** τινός *someth.* (Aeschyl. et al.; EpArist 106) **Hb 12:20** (cp. Dio Chrys. 31, 10). In a hostile sense τινός *someone* (Eur., Iph. A. 1351; of what is morally harmful AcThom 12 [Aa II/2, 118, 5] παῖδες, ὧν αἱ βλάβαι αὗται οὐ θιγγάνουσι) **Hb 11:28.** Abs. **Col 2:21** (IG XII/3, 451 μὴ θίγγανε); but s. ἅπτω 3.—Cp. ψηλαφάω, s. Schmidt, Syn. I, 228–43. DELG. M-M.

θλάω impf. 3 pl. ἔθλων PsSol 13:3; fut. θλάσω; 1 aor. ἔθλασα; pf. τέθλακα. Pass.: aor. 2 sg. ἐθλάσθης Ezk 29:7; pf. ptc. τεθλασμένος LXX (Hom. et al; PFay 112, 20 [99 AD]; PsSol 13:3; Jos., Ant. 10, 7=4 Km 18:21) ***break*** a seal (which in this case is not a natural, purposeful act, but one greatly to be regretted, since the seal appears as a means of protection, whose destruction is followed by dire consequences) Hs 8, 6, 3.—DELG.

θλίβω fut. θλίψω; 1 aor. ἔθλιψα. Pass.: fut. 3 sg. θλιβήσεται Job 20:22; 2 aor. ἐθλίβην; pf. ptc. τεθλιμμένος (s. next entry; Hom.+; ins, pap, LXX, pseudepigr.; Philo; Jos., Bell. 3, 330, Ant. 20, 111; SibOr; Mel., P. 80, 587).

❶ **to press or crowd close against, *press upon, crowd*** τινά *someone* (Sir 16:28 v.l.; JosAs 23:8 τὸν πόδα) **Mk 3:9** (cp. Appian, Bell. Civ. 4, 45, §194 ἐπιθλίβω τινά=crowd around someone).

❷ **to cause someth. to be constricted or narrow, *press together, compress, make narrow*** (Dionys. Hal. 8, 73 βίοι τεθλιμμένοι, provisions that have become scarce; ὁ θεὸς ἔθλιψεν τὴν σελήνην GrBar 9:7); pass. of space that is limited (of small living quarters Theocr. 21, 18 θλιβομένα καλύβα= tight quarters; Lucian, Alex. 49 τ. πόλεως θλιβομένης ὑπὸ τ. πλήθους =the city jammed full w. a multitude) ἔν τινι τόπῳ τεθλιμμένῳ καὶ πεπληρωμένῳ ἑρπετῶν πονηρῶν *a tight place and full of bad snakes = a place jammed full with bad snakes* ApcPt 10:25 (the misery is twofold: tight quarters to begin with and being totally surrounded by snakes). Of a road (w. a corresp. στενὴ πύλη) ὁδὸς τεθλιμμένη *a narrow, confined road* and therefore a source of trouble or difficulty to those using it **Mt 7:14** (TestAbr A 11 p. 88, 30 [Stone p. 24]; s. KBornhäuser, Die Bergpredigt 1923, 177ff); on the imagery s. AMattill, JBL 98, '79, 531–46; Betz, SM 527: "The chances of failure are greater than the chances of success, a sobering message."

❸ **to cause to be troubled, *oppress, afflict*** τινά *someone* (Dt 28:53; Lev 19:33; SibOr 3, 630) **2 Th 1:6.** τὸ πνεῦμα τὸ ἅγιον *oppress the Holy Spirit* Hm 10, 2, 5; χρεώστας θ. *oppress debtors* 8:10.—Pass. *be afflicted, distressed* (UPZ 42, 22 [162 BC]; PsSol 1:1 al.) **2 Cor 1:6; 4:8; 7:5; Hb 11:37;** Hm 2:5. θλιβείς *by suffering* B 7:11. θλιβεὶς τῇ γνώμῃ τινός *distressed by someone's scheming* IPhld 6:2. ψυχὴ θλιβομένη *distressed soul* Hs 1:8 (PGM 1, 213 θλίβεταί[?] μου ἡ ψυχή; TestSol 1:4 θλιβομένης μου τῆς ψυχῆς; Mel., P. 80, 587; Proclus on Pla., Crat., 72, 3 Pasqu. δαίμονες θλίβουσι τ. ψυχάς; Nicetas Eugen. 2, 27 H. ψυχὴ τεθλιμμένη; cp. Philo, De Ios. 179). On Hs 8, 10, 4 s. Bonner 113 note.—Subst. ὁ θλιβόμενος *the oppressed (one)* (TestSol D 4, 11 παραμυθία των θ.; JosAs 12:11 τῶν θλιβομένων βοηθός; Diod. S. 13, 109, 5 οἱ θλιβόμενοι=those who were hard pressed) **1 Ti 5:10;** ISm 6:2; B 20:2; D 5:2. Esp., as in some of the aforementioned pass., of the persecution of Christians **1 Th 3:4; 2 Th 1:7.** θλιβῆναι πάσῃ θλίψει *suffer every kind of affliction* Hs 6, 3, 6; cp. 7:1ff; 8, 10, 4. ὑπὲρ τοῦ νόμου θλιβέντες *persecuted for the law* (i.e., for the way of life that is in accordance with the instructions of Jesus) 8, 3, 7.—DELG. M-M. EDNT. TW.

θλῖψις, εως, ἡ (s. θλίβω; on the accent s. B-D-F §13; W-S. §6, 3c; Mlt-H. 57.—KLipsius, Grammat. Untersuchungen über d. bibl. Gräz. 1863, 34f, prefers to write θλίψις; so also W-H.) rare in extra-Biblical Gk., and there lit., 'pressing, pressure' (Aristot., Meterol. 4, 4, 383a, 13; Epicurus p. 45, 9 Us.; Ps.-Aristot., De Mundo 4, 394a, 29; Strabo, Galen).

❶ in our lit. (as in LXX, En, Test12Patr, JosAs cod. A; Just., D. 116, 2; Mel.) freq. and in the metaph. sense **trouble that inflicts distress, *oppression, affliction, tribulation*** (so Vett. Val. 71, 16; Cat. Cod. Astr. VIII/3 p. 175, 5; 178, 8; pl. 169, 2 [s. Boll 134f]; OGI 444, 15 [II or I BC] διὰ τὰς τ. πόλεων θλίψεις; BGU 1139, 4 [I BC]; POxy 939, 13; PAmh 144, 18). Of distress that is brought about by outward circumstances (Jos., Ant. 4, 108; En, PsSol, Mel.; Did., Gen. 116, 10), in sg. and pl. **Ac 11:19; Ro 5:3b; 12:12; 2 Cor 1:8; 6:4; 8:2; Rv 1:9; 2:9, 22;** 1 Cl 22:7 (Ps 33:18); 59:4; 2 Cl 11:4 (quot. of unknown orig.); Hs 7:4ff. ἐπὶ πάσῃ τῇ θ. ἡμῶν **2 Cor 1:4a; 7:4; 1 Th 3:7;** ἐν πάσῃ θ. (TestGad 4:4) **2 Cor 1:4b;** ἐν (τ.) θ. **Ro 5:3a; Eph 3:13; 1 Th 1:6; 3:3.** ἐν πολλαῖς θ. καὶ ποικίλαις Hs 7, 4. θ. μεγάλη *great tribulation* (SibOr 3, 186) **Mt 24:21** (1 Macc 9:27); **Ac 7:11;** Hv 4, 2, 4. Plural Hv 3, 2, 1. ἡ θ. ἡ μεγάλη *the great tribulation* **Rv 7:14;** τὸ ἐλαφρὸν τῆς θ. *slight affliction* **2 Cor 4:17.** ἀνταποδοῦναί τινι θλῖψιν *repay someone w. affliction* **2 Th 1:6.** W. ἀνάγκη (q.v. 2) **1 Th 3:7.** W. διωγμός **Mt 13:21; Mk 4:17; Ac 8:1** D; **13:50** D; pl. **2 Th 1:4.** W. δεσμά (TestJos 2:4) **Ac 20:23.** W. ὀνειδισμός **Hb 10:33.** W. στενοχωρία (q.v.) **Ro 2:9.** W. στενοχωρία and διωγμός **8:35** (w. λιμός and στενοχωρία Hippol., Ref. 5, 26, 12).—On the catalogue of hardships (peristasis) cp. 1 Cor 4:9–13; 2 Cor 4:8f; 6:4–10; 11:23–28; 12:10; Phil 4:11; s. FDanker, Augsburg Comm. 2 Cor '89, 89–91; 180f; idem, The Endangered Benefactor in Luke-Acts: SBLSP '81, 39–48; JFitzgerald, Cracks in an Earthen Vessel '88; MFerrari, Die Sprache des Leids in den paulinischen Persistasen-katalogen '91; MEbner, Leidenslisten u. Apostelbrief '91.—ἡμέρα θλίψεως *day of affliction* (Gen 35:3; 2 Km 22:19; cp. En 103:9; TestLevi 5:5) 1 Cl 52:3 (Ps 49:15).—Of the tribulations of the last days (as Da 12:1) **Mt 24:21, 29; Mk 13:19, 24.** ἡ θ. ἡ ἐρχομένη ἡ μεγάλη *the great tribulation to come* Hv 2, 2, 7; cp. 2, 3, 4; 4, 1, 1; 4, 2, 5; 4, 3, 6.—Distress caused by war 1 Cl 57:4 (Pr 1:27). θ. θανάτου *affliction of death* B 12:5. *Difficult circumstances* **2 Cor 8:13; Js 1:27;** συγκοινωνεῖν τῇ θ. *show an interest in (someone's) distress* **Phil 4:14.** Of a woman's birth-pangs **J 16:21.**—ὅταν γένηται θ. *when persecution comes* Hv 3, 6, 5. θλῖψιν ἀκούειν *hear of persecution* Hs 9, 21, 3. θλῖψιν ἔχειν **J 16:33; 1 Cor 7:28; Rv 2:10;** Hv 2, 3, 1; s 7:3. ἐὰν ὑπενέγκῃ τὰς θλίψεις τὰς ἐπερχομένας αὐτῷ Hs 7:4; cp. 7:6. ἐξείλατο αὐτὸν ἐκ πασῶν τῶν θλίψεων αὐτοῦ **Ac 7:10.** διὰ πολλῶν θ. εἰσελθεῖν εἰς τ. βασιλείαν **14:22.** τότε παραδώσουσιν ὑμᾶς εἰς θλῖψιν **Mt 24:9;** cp. B 12:5. ἀποστήσεται πᾶσα θ. ἀπὸ σοῦ . . . ἀπὸ πάντων ἀποστήσεται ἡ θ. Hs 7, 7.—Of the sufferings of Christ θλίψεις τοῦ Χριστοῦ **Col 1:24** (s. on ἀνταναπληρόω and πάθημα 1).

❷ **inward experience of distress, *affliction, trouble*** (Gen 35:3; 42:21 θ. τῆς ψυχῆς) θ. καὶ συνοχὴ καρδίας *trouble and anguish of heart* **2 Cor 2:4.** θλῖψιν ἐγείρειν τοῖς δεσμοῖς μου *cause trouble for me in my imprisonment* **Phil 1:17.** Ἄννα . . . περιείλατο πᾶσαν θλῖψιν ἀπ' αὐτῆς GJs 2:4 (cod. A, not pap; s. περιαιρέω 1).—DELG s.v. θλίβω. M-M. TW.

θνῄσκω (s. next entry and ἀποθνῄσκω; Hom.+. On the spelling s. Kühner-Bl. I 133; II 442; B-D-F §26 and 27; W-S. §5, 11b; Mlt-H. 84) fut. 3 sg. θανεῖται Pr 13:14; 2 aor. ἔθανον LXX; pf. τέθνηκα, inf. τεθνηκέναι (**Ac 14:19** τεθνάναι v.l. as Jos., Vi. 59); ptc. τεθνηκώς (LXX; τεθνεώς Tat.; τεθνηῶτες Job 39:30); analogous formations: 3 fut. mid. 1 pl. τεθνηξόμεθα 4 Macc. 8:21 (on this fut. s. Schwyzer I 783, esp. n. 3) and aor. ptc. acc. pl. τεθνήξαντας (TestAbr A 18 p. 100, 27 [Stone p. 48]); plpf. 3 sg. ἐτεθνήκει **J 11:21 v.l.,** 2 pl. τεθνήκειτε Hs 9, 28, 6. Gener. 'die', pf. 'to have died, be dead'.

❶ **to pass from physical life, *die,* Mt 2:20; Mk 15:44; Lk 8:49; J 19:33; Ac 14:19; 25:19.** Subst. perf. ptc. *have died, be dead* (ὁ) τεθνηκώς *the man who had died* (class.; LXX) **Lk 7:12; J 11:44; 12:1 v.l.**

❷ **to lose one's relationship w. God, *die,*** fig. extension of mng. 1 (w. ζῆν: Chariton 7, 5, 4) of spiritual death (Ael. Aristid. 52, 2 K.=28 p. 551 D.: τὸ τεθνηκὸς τῆς ψυχῆς; Bar 3:4; Philo, Fug. 55 ζῶντες ἔνιοι τεθνήκασι καὶ τεθνηκότες ζῶσι) ζῶσα τέθνηκεν *she is dead though she is still alive* **1 Ti 5:6.** (Timocles

Com. [IV BC] 35 οὗτος μετὰ ζώντων τεθνηκώς=dead among the living) οὔτε ζῶσιν οὔτε τεθνήκασιν Hs 8, 7, 1; 9, 21, 2; cp. 9, 21, 4. διὰ τὰς ἁμαρτίας ὑμῶν τεθνήκειτε [ἂν] τῷ θεῷ *because of your sins you would have died to God* 9, 28, 6.—DELG s.v. θάνατος. TW.

θνητός, ή, όν (s. prec. entry and ἀποθνήσκω; Hom. et al.; SIG 798, 10 [37 AD] ; LXX; TestSol 4, 11 D; ApcEsdr 6:19 p. 31, 29 Tdf.; SibOr 3, 236; Ar. 9, 6; Just., D. 14, 8; Tat., Mel., Ath.) pert. to being subject to death (in the Gr-Rom. world the basic difference between humans and deities relates to the mortality of the former and the immortality of the latter) ***mortal*** opp. ἀθάνατος (Dio Chrys. 20 [37], 30; Plut., Mor. 960b; Herm. Wr. 1, 15; Philo, Rer. Div. Her. 265; Jos., Ant. 11, 56) D 4:8; Dg 6:8. σάρξ (Heraclit. Sto. 74, 1 p. 98, 7 θνητὴ σάρξ of humankind) **2 Cor 4:11.** σῶμα (Hyperid. 6, 24; Ps-Pla., Axioch. 11, 370c; Philo, Mut. Nom. 36; Jos., Bell. 7, 344; Orig., C. Cels. 4, 15, 19; 4, 17, 15) **Ro 6:12; 8:11.** θ. ἐπίνοια Dg 7:1. ὁ θ. *the mortal = mere human* (Empedocles: Vorsokrat. 31 B 112, 4 ὁ θ.='human' in contrast to θεός; Job 30:23; Pr 3:13; 20:24; Philo, Praem. 87) 1 Cl 39:2; οἱ θ. *mortals* (Hom. et al.; Sb 4456, 4; 5829, 14; Wsd 9:14) Dg 9:2 (opp. ὁ ἀθάνατος). τὸ θ. (oft. Philo; Did., Gen. 148, 27) **1 Cor 15:53f** (opp. ἀθανασία as Philo, Aet. M. 46); **2 Cor 5:4** (opp. ἡ ζωή).—DELG s.v. θάνατος II (cp. the pf. τέθνηκα). M-M [Syll. 365, 10 refers to SIG^2=SIG 798, 10 above]. TW.

θορυβάζω pres. pass. 2 sg. θορυβάζῃ (s. two next entries; Dositheus 71, 16; En 14:8; Etym. Mag. p. 633, 34; also Eus. Al. [MPG LXXXVI/1, 444c]) act. 'cause trouble'; in our lit. only pass. w. intr. sense ***be troubled/distracted*** περί τι *by* or *about someth.* of a busy housewife **Lk 10:41** (v.l. τυρβάζῃ, q.v.).—DELG s.v. θόρυβος.

θορυβέω impf. ἐθορύβουν; aor. ptc. θορυβήσαντος Wsd 18:19. Pass.: impf. ἐθορυβούμην; fut. 3 pl. θορυβηθήσονται Na 2:4; 1 aor. ἐθορυβύθην Da 8:17 LXX; pf. ptc. τεθορυβημένος Sir 40:6 (s. prec. and next entry; Soph., Hdt. et al.; ins, pap, LXX; TestJos 7:5; Joseph.; Just., D. 9, 2 θορυβείτωσαν).

❶ ***throw into disorder,*** act. and w. acc. (cp. Wsd 18:19; Jos., Vi. 401, Ant. 18, 65) πόλιν *set the city in an uproar, start a riot in the city* **Ac 17:5.**

❷ **to cause emotional disturbance, *disturb, agitate,*** act. in **Ac 21:13** D (but here θ. may also be used abs). Mostly pass. w. intr. sense: *be troubled, distressed, aroused* (Chariton 5, 8, 3; Appian, Bell. Civ. 1, 25 §110; Polyaenus 8, 23, 19; Jos., Ant. 17, 251) GPt 5:15. μὴ θορυβεῖσθε **Mk 13:7** D; **Ac 20:10** (PTebt 411, 12 μηδὲν μέντοι θορυβηθῇς). τί θορυβεῖσθε; **Mk 5:39.** Of an ὄχλος: θορυβούμενος *aroused, in disorder* **Mt 9:23** (Appian, Bell. Civ. 5, 10 §42 ἡ χώρα θορυβουμένη).—DELG s.v. θόρυβος. M-M.

θόρυβος, ου, ὁ (s. prec. two entries; Pind., Hdt. et al.; OGI 48, 9; IMagnMai 114, 3; pap, LXX, Philo, Joseph.; loanw. in rabb.).

❶ **a raising of voices that contributes to lack of understanding, *noise, clamor*** **Ac 21:34;** MPol 8:3; 9:1 (for the expr. μέγας θ. s. Hs 9, 3, 1 in 3a below; Jos., Ant. 17, 184); AcPl Ha 1, 28 (sc.).

❷ **a state of confusion, *confusion, unrest*** 1 Cl 57:4 (Pr 1:27).

❸ **a state or condition of varying degrees of commotion, *turmoil, excitement, uproar*** (X., An. 3, 4, 35; Appian, Bell. Civ. 2, 118, §494)

ⓐ of the milling about of a throng: of mourners **Mk 5:38** (though mngs. 1 and 2 are also poss.); of a crowd of workers Hs 9, 3, 1

ⓑ of the noise and confusion of excited crowds (Philo, In Flacc. 120; Jos., Bell. 1, 201; 2, 611) **Mk 14:2; Ac 20:1;** γίνεται θ. (cp. PTebt 15, 3 [114 BC] θορύβου γενομένου ἐν τῇ κώμῃ) **Mt 26:5; 27:24;** GJs 21:1, foll. by ἕως παύσηται ὁ θ. in 25:1. μετὰ θορύβου (Polyaenus 6, 41, 1; Ezk 7:11; Jos., Ant. 5, 216) *with a disturbance* **Ac 24:18.**—DELG. M-M. TW.

θράσος, ους, τό (s. next entry; Hom. et al.; LXX, EpArist, Philo; Jos., Ant. 16, 66, Vi. 120) in a good sense 'courage', but when a pers. is undisciplined an impulse for bold action can deteriorate into 'recklessness' or 'rashness' and one projects the impression of lacking regard for the feelings, concerns, or thoughts of others, hence ***arrogance, shamelessness*** 1 Cl 30:8. οὐ δώσεις τῇ ψυχῇ σου θράσος *you must not give (=admit) arrogance to your soul, you must not become arrogant* B 19:3; D 3:9 (cp. Diod. S. 5, 29, 3 τὸ θράσος τῆς ψυχῆς).—JWackernagel, Hellenistica, 1907, 15f.—DELG s.v. θάρσος B.

θρασύτης, ητος, ἡ (s. prec. entry; Thu. et al.) ***boldness, arrogance*** (Dio Chrys. 48 [65], 5; Sb 6026, 1 [III AD]; Philo, Spec. Leg. 3, 175 al.) B 20:1; D 5:1.—DELG s.v. θάρσος B.

θραυματίζω ***break*** **Lk 4:18** D, s. θραύω 3.

θραύω fut. θραύσω LXX; 1 aor. ἔθραυσα. Pass.: fut. 3 sg. θραυσθήσεται LXX; 1 aor. ἐθραύσθην; pf. ptc. τεθραυσμένος (s. prec. entry; Pind., Hdt. et al.; Vett. Val.; ins, pap, LXX; PsSol 17:22. Fig. usage in some of the preceding, but also s. Maximus Tyr. 14, 6e; Cat. Cod. Astr. VIII p. 147, 12; Jos., Bell. 1, 323) gener. 'break in pieces'.

❶ **to cause someth. to be broken into pieces, *break*** (Diod. S. 20, 93, 2; SIG^2 588, 27 [II BC]; Kaibel 1003, 3; Jos., Ant. 8, 390) **Mk 14:3 v.l.** Of pottery Hm 11:13.

❷ **to cause someth. to lose its validity, *break,*** fig. extension of mng. 1 Dg 11:5.

❸ **to cause to be oppressed, *break, weaken, oppress,*** fig. extension of mng. 1 (Orph. Hymns 87, 3 ψυχήν; Plut., Anton. 923 [17, 4] θραυόμενος τὸν λογισμόν; M. Ant. 4, 49, 2) Hv 3, 11, 3. τεθραυσμένοι *the downtrodden* **Lk 4:18;** B **3:3** (both Is 58:6).—DELG. M-M.

θρέμμα, ατος, τό (s. τρέφω; trag. et al.) ***(domesticated) animal*** esp. a sheep or goat (X., Oec. 20, 23 al.; SIG 636, 26; 826g, 20; OGI 200, 11; 629, 175; POxy 246, 16; BGU 759, 11; PAmh 134, 5; TestSol 9:9 C [ms. V]; TestAbr B; TestJob 16:6; TestGad 1:6; Philo; Jos., Ant. 7, 148; Ar. 10, 7; Just., D. 134, 5) **J 4:12** (Timaeus Hist. [IV/III BC]: 566 fgm. 56a Jac. αὐτοὶ καὶ τὰ θρέμματα αὐτῶν).—DELG s.v. τρέφω A. M-M.

θρηνέω impf. ἐθρήνουν; fut. θρηνήσω; 1 aor. ἐθρήνησα; fut. pass. 3 sg. θρηνηθήσεται Mi 2:4 (s. next entry; Hom. et al.; LXX; TestSol 1:6 D; TestAbr B 6 p. 110, 1 [Stone p. 68]; TestZeb 4:5; ApcEsdr 5:27 p. 31, 1 Tdf.; Ar.; Just.) gener. 'to express oneself in grief', freq. in sounds and rhythms established by funereal custom in various regions of the ancient world (cp. Il. 24, 722; Od. 24, 61).

❶ **to express oneself in sorrowful tones, *mourn, lament*** intr. (w. κλαίειν Just., D. 141, 3; cp. Jo 1:5) **J 16:20.**

❷ **to express oneself in a song or hymn of grief, *sing a dirge*** intr. (Aesop., Fab. 369 H. [female mourners]; LXX) **Mt 11:17; Lk 7:32.** As v.l. ἐθρήνησε for ἐποίησεν θρῆνον GJs 3:1 (cod. A).

❸ **to mourn for someone in ritual fashion, *mourn for, lament*** τινά *someone* (Herodian 3, 4, 6; Nicetas Eugen. 7, 182 H.; LXX; Philo, Leg. All. 3, 231; Jos., Bell. 3, 436; Ar. 8, 2; Just., D. 95, 2 ἑαυτούς) **Lk 23:27** (w. κόπτεσθαι as Xenophanes: Vorsokr. 21 Testimon. A 13; Mi 1:8; Jos., Ant. 6, 377;

s. EMartino, Morte e pianto rituale nel mondo antico, '58, 195–235). δύο θρήνους ἐθρήνει GJs 2:1. S. κόπτω 2.—PHeinisch, Die Totenklage im AT, '31; CWestermann, Struktur u. Geschichte der Klage im AT: ZAW 66, '54, 44–80; PFerris, The Genre of Communal Lament in the Bible and the Ancient Near East, '92 (OT); CBuresch, Consolationum a Graecis Romanisque scriptarum historia critica 1886; EReiner, Die Rituelle Totenklage der Griechen '38; MAlexiou, The Ritual Lament in Greek Tradition '74. Add. reff. Betz, SM 120.—DELG s.v. θρῆνος. On the semantic field s. Schmidt, Syn. III 378ff. M-M. TW.

θρῆνος, ου, ὁ (s. prec. entry; Hom. et al.)—❶ **ritual expression of lament for the dead,** ***a dirge,*** **Mt 2:18 v.l.** (Jer 38:15).

❷ **expression of grief,** ***lamentation,*** in a general sense Ἄννα δύο θρήνους ἐθρήνει GJs 2:1. ἐποίησεν θρῆνον 3:1 (s. θρηνέω 2).—DELG. TW.

θρησκεία, ας, ἡ (also -ία; Hdt.+; ins, pap, LXX, Philo, Joseph., Tat., Mel., HE 4, 26, 7; Theoph. Ant. 3, 29 [p., 266, 24]; not limited to deities, s. Boffo, Iscrizioni no. 39, 3; s. next entry) **expression of devotion to transcendent beings, esp. as it expresses itself in cultic rites,** ***worship,*** the being who is worshiped is given in the obj. gen. (Aelian, NA 10, 28 τοῦ Σαράπιδος; Herodian 4, 8, 7 τοῦ θεοῦ; Delph. ins in SIG 801d, 4 τοῦ Ἀπόλλωνος; Wsd 14:27 τ. εἰδώλων; Philo, Spec. Leg. 1, 315 τῶν θεῶν; Jos., Ant. 1, 222; 12, 271 τοῦ θεοῦ) θρησκεύειν τὴν θρησκείαν τοῦ ὑψίστου 1 Cl 45:7. θ. τῶν ἀγγέλων **Col 2:18** (MDibelius, Hdb. exc. 2:23 [lit.; also AWilliams, JTS 10, 1909, 413–38].—Ramsay, CB I/2 p. 541 no. 404 and p. 741 no. 678 testify to the worship of angels in Phrygia. The Council of Laodicea, Can. 35 rejects it; Theodoret III 490 [on Col 2:16] deplores its tenacious survival in Phrygia and Pisidia). Of Judean cultic tradition ἡμετέρα θ. *our religion* **Ac 26:5** (cp. 4 Macc 5:7 and Jos., Ant. 12, 253 Ἰουδαίων [subj. gen] θ.; Ps.-Clemens, Hom. 5, 27). Of Christianity τὰ ἀνήκοντα τῇ θ. ἡμῶν *the things that befit our religion* 1 Cl 62:1. τὴν θ. προσάγειν θεῷ *offer service to God* Dg 3:2. **Js** contrasts the μάταιος θ. **1:26** w. vs. **27,** the θ. καθαρὰ καὶ ἀμίαντος παρὰ τ. θεῷ, which consists in good deeds (Herm. Wr. 12, 23 θρησκεία τ. θεοῦ μία ἐστί, μὴ εἶναι κακόν).—JvanHerten, Θρησκεία, εὐλάβεια, ἱκέτης, diss. Utrecht '34; cp. LRobert, Études épigraphiques et philologiques '38, 226–35. S. on εὐλαβέομαι.—B. 1463. DELG sv. θρησκεύω. M-M. EDNT. TW. Spicq. Sv.

θρησκεύω (s. prec. entry; Hdt. et al.; SIG 783, 42f [27 BC] τοὺς θεοὺς ἐθρήσκευσεν εὐσεβῶς; Sb 991, 7 [III AD]; Herm. Wr. 12, 23 τοῦτον τὸν λόγον, ὦ τέκνον, προσκύνει καὶ θρήσκευε; Wsd 11:15; 14:17; TestJob 2:2; Just., A I, 62, 2) **practice cultic rites,** ***worship,*** w. the acc. of that which is worshiped or served (Dionys. Hal. 2, 23, 1 τοὺς θεούς; Celsus 8, 66; SIG [s. above]; Herm. Wr. [s. above]; Wsd 11:15; Jos., Ant. 8, 248; 9, 289; SibOr 5, 77; but cp. Theoph. Ant. 2, 35 [p. 186, 18] w. the dat., perh. influenced by the related terms προσκυνέω and λατρεύω) πῶς θρησκεύοντες αὐτόν (i.e. τ. θεόν) *how you worship him* Dg 1. τινά τινι *serve* or *worship someone by means of someth.* 2:8; θ. θρησκείαν *engage in worship* 1 Cl 45:7.—DELG.

θρησκός, όν (s. prec. two entries; Hesych.; Etym. Mag. p. 455, 9; θρῆσκος, L-S-J-M [lex.]; Soph., Lex.) ***religious*** **Js 1:26.**—B. 1463. DELG s.v. θρησκεύω. TW. Spicq. Sv.

θριαμβεύω 1 aor. ἐθριάμβευσα (Ctesias; Polyb.; Diod. S. 16, 90, 2; Dionys. Hal.; Epict. 3, 24, 85 al.; not a Lat. loanw.—s. B-D-F §5, 1 and L-S-J-M s.v. θρίαμβος II). The verb θ. appears only in **2 Cor 2:14** and **Col 2:15.** The principal interpretations follow:

❶ ***lead in a triumphal procession,*** in imagery (cp. Seneca, On Benefits 2, 11, 1) of the Roman military triumph (Lat. triumphare; Plut., Rom. 33, 4; Arat. 1052 [54, 8]; Appian, Mithrid. 77 §338; 103 §482; Jos., Bell. 7, 123–57; cp. Theophyl. Sim., Ep. 68), w. acc. τινά *someone* as a captive.

ⓐ of Paul τῷ θεῷ χάρις τῷ πάντοτε θριαμβεύοντι ἡμᾶς ἐν τ. Χριστῷ *thanks be to God, who continually leads us as captives in Christ's triumphal procession* (REB) **2 Cor 2:14.** The rhetorical pattern of the ep. appears to favor this interpr.

ⓑ of God's victory over hostile forces θριαμβεύσας αὐτοὺς ἐν αὐτῷ *in connection with him* (Christ) *God exhibits them* (the hostile transcendent powers) *in triumph* **Col 2:15.**

❷ ***to lead in triumph,*** in imagery of Roman generals leading their troops in triumph (s. Jos., Bell.7, 5, 4–6), so numerous scholars and versions **2 Cor 2:14** τῷ θεῷ χάρις κτλ. *thanks be to God, who always leads us as partners in triumph in Christ.* Since there is no lexical support for this interpr. (L-S-J-M cites the pass. but without external support), others see a shift of mng. from 'lead in triumph' to the sense

❸ ***cause to triumph.*** This interpr. (KJV, Beza, Calvin, Klöpper, Schmiedel, Belser, GGodet, Sickenberger ad loc.; sim. Weizsäcker.) remains unexampled in Gk. usage (appeal to Ctesias: 688 fgm. 13 [Pers. 13] p. 461, 8 Jac. in this sense is very questionable, s. 6 below).

❹ ***triumph over*** is preferred by many for **Col 2:15** (Mel., P. 102, 781 of Christ ἐγὼ ὁ καταλύσας τὸν θάνατον καὶ θριαμβεύσας τὸν ἐχθρόν.—Pass.: δι' . . . σταυροῦ . . . ἐθριαμβεύθη σατανᾶς Serap. of Thmuis, Euch. 25, 2).

❺ ***expose to shame*** (Marshall; s. also Lietzmann, HNT ad loc. and app.; cp. Ctesias [s. 3 above; the textual sequence is in question] θριαμβεύσας τὸν μάγον 'after he had publicly unmasked the magician'), in which case the triumphal aspect is submerged in a metaphor expressing the low esteem in which God permits the apostle's office to be held. **Col 2:15** can also be understood in this way. (The idea that the term θρ. itself expresses the paradox of a disgraced apostle and a victorious mission [Williamson s. 6 below] is semantically untenable.) ἀναστενάζων, ὅτι ἐθριαμβεύετο ὑπὸ τῆς πόλεως, *groaning that he had become the city's object of ridicule* AcPl Ha 4, 12f.

❻ ***display, publicize, make known*** (Ctesias: 688 fgm. 16 [Pers. 58 of the head and right hand of a slain enemy] p. 472, 30 Jac.; s. Ltzm., Hdb. ad loc.; ἐκθριαμβίζω BGU 1061 [14 BC]), a semantic shift affirmed by Egan for both NT pass (παύσασθε λόγους ἀλλοτρίους θριαμβεύοντες 'cease [openly] expressing these strange opinions' Tat. 26, 1).—Windisch leaves the choice open between 3 and 6.—LWilliamson, Jr., Int 22, '68, 317–32; REgan, NovT 19, '77, 34–62; Field, Notes 181f; RPope, ET 21, 1910, 19–21; 112–14; AKinsey, ibid. 282f; FPrat, RSR 3, 1912, 201–29; HVersnel, Triumphus '70; PMarshall, NovT 25, '83, 302–17; CBreytenbach, Neot. 24, '90, 250–71; JScott, NTS 42, '96, 260–81; cp. TSchmidt, NTS 41, '95, 1–18, on Mk 15:16–32.—Against triumphal imagery, JMcDonald, JSNT 17, '83, 35–50.—DELG s.v. θρίαμβος. M-M. EDNT. TW.

θρίξ, τριχός, ἡ (Hom.+) ***hair***—ⓐ of animals τρίχες καμήλου *camel's hair:* ἔνδυμα ἀπὸ τρ. κ. *a garment of camel's hair* **Mt 3:4.** So **Mk 1:6** says of John the Baptist that he was ἐνδεδυμένος τρίχας κ. *dressed in camel's hair.*—Of apocalyptic animals w. long hair **Rv 9:8** (JMichl, BZ 23, '36, 266–88; Biblica 23, '42, 192f).

ⓑ of human hair (Jos., Ant. 15, 86, C. Ap. 1, 282): white, black hair **Mt 5:36;** cp. **Rv 1:14.** τρίχες πρεσβύτεραι *belonging to an* *older person,* i.e. *gray* Hv 3, 10, 4f; 3, 12, 1. τρ. λευκαί 4, 2, 1. οὐδὲν . . . οὔτε θρὶξ οὔτε βλέφαρον *nothing, neither a hair nor an eyelash* (βλ. apparently=βλεφαρίς by synecdoche) AcPlCor 2:30. Coming out easily (ἐκ or ἀπὸ τ. κεφαλῆς) **Lk 21:18; Ac 27:34** (cp. 1 Km 14:45). αἱ τρίχες τῆς κεφαλῆς πᾶσαι *all the hairs of the head* **Mt 10:30; Lk 12:7** (Alcaeus 39, 10 [80, 10 D.[2]] παρὰ μοῖραν Διὸς οὐδὲ τρίχες [here the text breaks off]='against the will of Zeus not even the hairs are' . . .—The hair as someth. quite worthless: Paroem. Gr. Zen. [time of Hadrian] 2, 4 ἡ θρὶξ οὐδενὸς ἀξία); cp. **7:38** (αἱ τρ. τῆς κεφαλῆς as Jdth 10:3; Ps 39:13; Philo, Leg. ad Gai. 223), **44; J 11:2; 12:3.** ἐμπλοκὴ τριχῶν *braiding the hair* **1 Pt 3:3.** τρίχας λελυμένη *with the hair loose* Hs 9, 9, 5; cp. 9, 13, 8. λαμβάνειν τινὰ ἐν μιᾷ τῶν τρ. αὐτοῦ *take someone by a single hair* GHb 20, 61. τρίχες ὀρθαί *hair standing on end* (Il. 24, 359; Lucian, Philops. 22) Hv 3, 1, 5.—DELG. M-M.

θροέω 1 aor. pass. ptc. θροηθείς (trag. et al., in act. and mid. w. the mng.: 'cry out, tell out, speak, announce', etc.—act.: Jos., Ant. 18, 234; 19, 137) in the NT only pass. in the sense ***be inwardly aroused*** (cp. Tetrast. Iamb. 2, 1, 4 p. 286; Malalas 41, 12; SSol 5:4), *be disturbed* or *frightened* (TestAbr B 111, 7 [Stone p. 70]) **2 Th 2:2.** μὴ θροεῖσθε **Mt 24:6; Mk 13:7;** AcPl Ha 5, 25. θροηθέντες καὶ ἔμφοβοι γενόμενοι **Lk 24:37 v.l.**—DELG s.v. θρέομαι.

θρόμβος, ου, ὁ (trag., Hdt. et al.) ***drop*** θ. αἵματος (Aeschyl., Choëph. 533; 546; Pla., Critias p. 120a; also medical wr. [Hobart 82f]) *small amount of* (flowing) *blood, clot of blood* **Lk 22:44** (Just., D. 103, 8).—WSurbled-Sleumer, D. Moral in ihren Beziehungen z. Medizin u. Hygiene II[2] 1919, 183ff.—DELG. M-M.

θρόνος, ου, ὁ (Hom.+; ins, pap, LXX, pseudepigr.; Jos., Ant. 7, 353; 8, 399; Mel., P. 83, 620 [B]; loanw. in rabb.).

❶ ***chair, seat***—ⓐ gener. ἐκάθισεν ἐπὶ τοῦ θρόνου (Mary) *sat down on her chair* GJs 11:1 (JosAs 7:1 Ἰωσὴφ ἐκάθισεν ἐπὶ θρόνου *sat on a chair*).

ⓑ specif. a chair set aside for one of high status, *throne.*

α. of human kings and rulers (Hdt. 1, 14, 3; X., Cyr. 6, 1, 6; Herodian 1, 8, 4) καθελεῖν ἀπὸ θρόνων *dethrone* **Lk 1:52.** The throne of David (2 Km 3:10; PsSol 17:6), the ancestor of the Messiah **1:32; Ac 2:30.**

β. of God (Soph., Ant. 1041; OGI 383 [ins of Antiochus of Commagene] 41f πρὸς οὐρανίους Διὸς Ὠρομάσδου θρόνους; Ps 46:9; Ezk. Trag. vs. 68 [in Eus., PE 9, 29, 5]; TestSol 13:5 C) **Hb 12:2; Rv 7:15; 12:5; 22:1, 3;** cp. **1:4; 3:21b; 4:2ff, 9; 5:1, 6f, 11, 13** al. (s. Cat. Cod. Astr. IX/2 p. 118f, notes w. lit.).—ὁ θρόνος τ. χάριτος **Hb 4:16;** τ. μεγαλωσύνης **8:1.**—Of heaven as God's throne (after Is 66:1) **Mt 5:34; 23:22; Ac 7:49;** B 16:2 (the two last pass. are direct quot. of Is 66:1.—Cp. Theosophien 56, 33f. For heaven as the throne of Zeus s. Orpheus: Hymn. 62, 2f Q. and Demosth. 25, 11).

γ. of Christ, who occupies the throne of his ancestor David (s. α above). It is a θ. δόξης αὐτοῦ **Mt 19:28a; 25:31** (PsSol; 2:19); an eternal throne **Hb 1:8** (Ps 44:7), which stands at the right hand of the Father's throne Pol 2:1 or is even identical w. it **Rv 22:1, 3;** cp. **3:21b.** His own are to share this throne w. him vs. **21a.**

δ. of the 12 apostles as judges (Philochorus [IV/III BC]: 328 fgm. 64bβ Jac. the νομοφύλακες . . . ἐπὶ θρόνων ἐκάθηντο; Plut., Mor. 807b; Paus. 2, 31, 3; Ps 121:5; Jos., Ant. 18, 107) or rulers in the time of the final consummation **Mt 19:28b** (Galen X 406 K. Θέσσαλος ἅμα τοῖς ἑαυτοῦ σοφισταῖς ἐφ' ὑψηλοῦ θρόνου καθήμενος); **Lk 22:30;** cp. **Rv 20:4.**

ε. of the 24 elders of **Rv 4:4; 11:16.**—Rv also mentions thrones of infernal powers; the throne of the dragon, which the 'beast' receives **13:2;** cp. **16:10.**—ὁ θ. τοῦ Σατανᾶ **2:13** in the letter to Pergamum is freq. (e.g. Dssm., LO 240, 8 [LAE 280, 2]; Lohmeyer ad loc.; Boll 112, 4) taken to be the famous Altar of Zeus there (cp. En 25:3 the mountain whose peak is like a throne); others (Zahn; JWeiss, RE X 551) prefer to think of the temple of Asclepius, and Bousset of Perg. as the center of the emperor-cult.—TBirt, D. Thron d. Satans: PhilologWoch 52, '32, 259–66.

❷ **supreme power over a political entity, *dominion, sovereignty,*** fig. extension of mng. 1 (a semantic component prob. present in some of the aforementioned passages, for the idea of authority is intimately associated with the chair that is reserved for an authority figure) θ. αἰώνιος of Jesus Christ 1 Cl 65:2; MPol 21.

❸ **name of a class of powerful beings, earthly or transcendent, *the enthroned,*** pl. (TestLevi 3:8; cp. the astrol. PMich 149 XVI, 23 and 24 [II AD].—Kephal. I 117, 24–26, personification of the one who sits on the throne, the judge) perh. of transcendent beings **Col 1:16** (cp. Mel., P. 83, 620; DSanger, in EDNT s.v.), but in view of the ref. to things 'seen and unseen' in the same vs. it is probable that the author thinks also of earthly rulers (s. 2 above).—B. 481. DELG. DDD 1628–31. M-M. TW.

θρύπτω (Pla. et al.; POxy 471, 80 [II AD]; Ps 57:8 Sym.; Philo; Jos., Bell. 4, 563) ***break in (small) pieces*** θρυπτόμενον as a supplement to τὸ σῶμα τὸ ὑπὲρ ὑμῶν **1 Cor 11:24** in D (cp. Dio Chrys. 60 + 61 [77 + 78], 41; Soranus p. 34, 10 θρυπτόμενον τὸ σῶμα; Nicander, Ther. 108 ἂν σάρκες θρύπτωνται; Galen: CMG V/4, 2 p. 148, 23 θρύμμα ἄρτου; Diod. S. 1, 83, 3 καταθρύπτοντες τοὺς ἄρτους).—DELG.

Θυάτειρα (-ιρα), ων, τά (Polyb. 16, 1, 7; 32, 27, 10; Strabo 13, 4, 4; Ptolem. 5, 2, 14; Appian, Syr. 30 §150; ins. On the acc. in -αν **Rv 1:11 v.l.,** s. B-D-F §57; Mlt-H. 128) ***Thyatira,*** a city in Lydia in Asia Minor, on the Lycus R. betw. Pergamum and Sardis, founded by Macedonian Greeks (s. Strabo loc. cit.; OGI 211 w. note 2). Its busy industrial life included notably the dyeing of purple cloth. There was in Th. a guild of dyers (βαφεῖς), the existence of which is attested by numerous ins (CIG 3497–98 [=IGR IV, 1213; 1265]; 3496; other ins in WBuckler, Monuments de Thyatire: Rev. de philol. 37, 1913, 289–331. Also the ins that the guild of purple-dyers in Thessalonica dedicated to a certain Menippus of Thyatira: LDuchesne and ChBayet, Mission au Mont Athos 1876, p. 52 no. 83). **Ac 16:14; Rv 1:11; 2:18, 24.**—EZiebarth, RhM 51, 1896, 632ff; AWikenhauser, Die Ap-Gesch. 1921, 410f (lit.); CHemer, The Letters to the Seven Churches of Asia in Their Local Setting '86, 106–28 (for epigraphic sources, s. p. 244f); Kraft, Hdb. '74, 67ff; BHHW III 1981; Pauly-W. VI/1, 657–59.—M-M.

θυγάτηρ, τρός, ἡ (Hom.+) voc. θύγατερ (B-D-R 147, 3) for which the nom. without the art. is also used (**Mk 5:34; Lk 8:48; J 12:15;** W-S. §29, 4; Mlt-H. 136); pl. θυγατέρες etc.

❶ **a human** (θ. is used in lit. also of offspring of animals, e.g. Simonides of Ceos 7 of mules) **female in relation of child to parent, *daughter*** (Epict. 4, 11, 35; Paus. 8, 20, 3) **Mt 10:35, 37; Lk 8:42; 12:53.** Foll. by gen. of father or mother **Mt 9:18; 14:6; 15:22, 28; Mk 5:35; 6:22; 7:26, 29; Lk 2:36; 8:49; Ac 2:17** (Jo 3:1); **7:21; Hb 11:24;** B 19:5; D 4:9; cp. **Ac 21:9;** GJs 17:1; Papias (2:9; 11:2). τὰς θυγατέρας τῶν Ἑβραίων τὰς ἀμιάντους, *the undefiled daughters of the Hebrews.* GJs 6:1 (s. deStrycker ad loc.; s. also the lit. s.v. γαμίζω 1bγ).

❷ **someone treated as one's daughter,** ***daughter*** (for such extended use of θ. cp. Paradoxogr. Vat. 60 Keller; Phalaris, Ep. 142, 3 θ.=girl) voc. in a friendly greeting to girls or women **Mt 9:22; Mk 5:34; Lk 8:48.** Sim. of God's daughters as children in a transcendent sense **2 Cor 6:18** (cp. Is 43:6; Wsd 9:7); in personal address υἱοὶ καὶ θυγατέρες B 1:1 (cp. Ath. 32, 2).

❸ **female members of an ancestral group, political entity, or specific class of persons,** ***daughters,*** θυγατέρες Ἀαρών *the female descendants of Aaron,* i.e., the women of priestly families **Lk 1:5.** θ. Ἀβραάμ **13:16** (cp. 4 Macc 15:28). Of women who are readers of B, and are therefore his pupils B 1:1 (but s. 2 above). θυγατέρες Ἰερουσαλήμ **Lk 23:28** is an OT expr. to designate the individual female inhabitants of the city (cp. SSol 2:7; 3:5; Is 3:16; 4:4; PsSol 2:6, 13). But the situation is different from the usage θυγάτηρ Σιών in 4.

❹ **someth. personified as female,** ***daughter*** (Procop. Soph., Ep. 93 the letters are θυγατέρες of their writers), of doubt θ. ἐστὶ τοῦ διαβόλου *the devil's daughter* Hm 9:9; cp. 12, 2, 2 (Pind., O. 10, 3f ἀλάθεια as θυγάτηρ Διός). Of virtues, one of which is the daughter of the other in turn Hv 3, 8, 4f.—Of special interest is the sing. θυγάτηρ Σιών, as in OT fashion (cp. Zech 2:14; 9:9; Jer 4:31 al.—SibOr 3, 324 θυγατέρες δυσμῶν=peoples of the west) this term denotes the city of Zion and its inhabitants **Mt 21:5; J 12:15** (both w. combination of Is 62:11 and Zech 9:9). B. 106; BHHW III 1999. JLeipoldt, Die Frau in der antiken Welt u. im Urchristentum '62; BRawson, The Roman Family: The Family in Ancient Rome, ed. BRawson '86, 1–57.—DELG. M-M. EDNT.

θυγάτριον, ου, τό (s. prec.; Strattis Com. [c. 400 BC], fgm. 63 Kock; Menand., fgm. 361 Kö.; Machon vs. 348 [in Athen. 13, 581c]; Plut., Mor, 179e; Epict. 1, 11, 4; Dio Chrys. 10 [11], 54; SIG 364, 55; PPetr III, 53 r, 2; PLond I, 24, 6 p. 32 [163 BC]; Jos., Ant. 19, 200.—WSchmid, D. Attizismus IV 1897, 305) dim. of θυγάτηρ ***little daughter*** (though the word can denote one who is marriageable: Lucian, Tox. 22), **Mk 5:23** here perh., in view of the dialogue, as term of endearment; **7:25.**—DELG s.v. θυγάτηρ. M-M.

θύελλα, ης, ἡ (Hom. et al.; Ps.-Aristot., De Mundo 4 p. 395a, 6: θύελλα πνεῦμα βίαιον κ. ἄφνω προσαλλόμενον; Jos., Bell. 2, 396; 3, 368; SibOr 4, 115) **atmospheric disturbance marked by violent gusts of wind,** ***storm, whirlwind*** **Hb 12:18** (cp. Dt 4:11; 5:22).—DELG s.v. 1 θύω. TW.

θύϊνος, η, ον (Strabo 4, 6, 2 al., perh. also PLond III, 928, 20 p. 191 [II BC]) ***from the citron tree*** ξύλον *citron wood* (Diosc. 1, 22; 3 Km 10:11 Sym.) =*scented* **Rv 18:12.**—DELG s.v. 2 θύω A2. M-M. TW.

θῦμα, ατος, τό (s. θύω; trag., Thu.+; OGI 332, 40 [II BC] al. ins; Mitt-Wilck. I/2, 1 III, 3 [III BC]; oft. LXX; Just., A I, 12, 5; A II, 5, 4) ***sacrifice, offering*** PtK 2 p. 14, 20.—DELG s.v. 2 θύω B1.

θυμίαμα, ατος, τό (s. next entry; Soph., Hdt.+; ins, pap, LXX, pseudepigr., Philo, Joseph.; Just.; Ath. 13, 1).

❶ **aromatic substance used in cultic ritual,** ***incense***

ⓐ sing. (Hdt. 1, 198; PTebt 112, 22 [112 BC]; Jos., Ant. 3, 197) B 2:5 (Is 1:13). More often

ⓑ in the pl. (Soph., Oed. R. 4; Hdt. 2, 86, 4; Pla., Rep. 2, 373a; SIG 999, 16f; LXX, Philo; Jos., Ant. 4, 32) **Rv 5:8; 8:3f; 18:13.**

❷ **cultic burning of incense,** ***incense burning, incense offering*** (LXX) τὸ θυσιαστήριον τοῦ θ. *the incense altar* (Ex 30:1, 27; 2 Macc 2:5) **Lk 1:11;** ἡ ὥρα τοῦ θ. *the hour of the incense offering* vs. **10.**—DELG s.v. 2 θύω A4. M-M.

θυμιατήριον, ου, τό (s. prec. entry; Hdt., Thu. et al.; ins, pap, LXX; TestJob 32:8 al.; ApcMos) gener. a place or vessel for the burning of incense (Kühner-Bl. II p. 281, 5), usu. a 'censer' (Hdt. 4, 162, 3; Thu. 6, 46, 3; Aelian VH 12, 51; POxy 521, 19 [II AD]), but **Hb 9:4 incense altar** (as SIG 996, 12 [I AD?]; esp. of the incense altar in the Jewish temple: Philo, Rer. Div. Her. 226, Mos. 2, 94; Jos., Bell. 5, 218, Ant. 3, 147; 198).—New Docs 3, 69. DELG s.v. 2 θύω A4. M-M (w. rev. of Dittenberg's interpr. of SIG^2 583, 12=SIG above).

θυμιάω fut. θυμιάσω; 1 aor. ἐθυμίασα (both LXX), inf. θυμιᾶσαι. Pass. aor. ἐθυμιάθην LXX; pf. ptc. τεθυμιαμένη SSol 3:6 (s. prec. two entries; Pind., Hdt. et al.; Diod. S. 16, 11, 1; OGI 352, 37 [II BC]; pap [Kl. T. 135 no. 5, 46]; LXX; TestSol 6:10; TestAbr A 4 p. 80, 22 [Stone p. 8]; Philo; Jos., Ant. 3, 199 al.) ***make an incense offering*** ἔλαχεν τοῦ θυμιᾶσαι *it fell to his lot to make the incense offering* **Lk 1:9** (for the construction cp. 1 Km 14:47).—DELG s.v. 2 θύω A4. M-M.

θυμικός, ή, όν (s. θυμός; Aristot. et al.; Philo) ***hot-tempered, irascible*** (so Aristot., Rhet. 2, 14 p. 1389a, 9; Cornutus 20 p. 39, 16; Athen. 2, 45 p. 55f; Tat. 9, 1) D 3:2.—DELG s.v. θυμός.

θυμομαχέω (s. θυμός, μάχομαι) ***be very angry*** τινί *at someone* (Polyb. 27, 8, 4 ἐπί τινι) **Ac 12:20.**

θυμός, οῦ, ὁ (Hom. +).—❶ **intense expression of the inner self, freq. expressed as strong desire,** ***passion, passionate longing*** (Hom. et al.; Pla., Cratyl. 419e θυμὸς ἀπὸ τῆς θύσεως κ. ζέσεως τ. ψυχῆς) ἐκ τ. οἴνου τοῦ θυμοῦ τῆς πορνείας αὐτῆς πεπότικεν τ. ἔθνη *she has caused the nations to drink the wine of her passionate immorality* **Rv 14:8;** cp. **18:3.** τὸ ποτήριον τ. οἴνου τ. θυμοῦ τ. ὀργῆς αὐτοῦ *the wine-cup of God's passionate wrath* **16:19;** cp. **19:15.** But in all these cases mng. 2 may be the correct one; for the other pass. in Rv where θ. occurs, mng. 2 is prob. the only one possible.

❷ **a state of intense displeasure,** ***anger, wrath, rage, indignation*** **Rv 12:12** (θυμὸν ἔχειν as Theognis 748 Bergk). ὁ οἶνος τ. θυμοῦ τ. θεοῦ *the wine of God's wrath* or *indignation* (s. ἄκρατος) **14:10;** cp. vs. **19; 15:1, 7; 16:1** (the figure of the outpouring of wrath freq. in OT). If this mng. holds true for all the Rv pass., the combination of genitives of θυμός and ὀργή in **16:19; 19:15** is to be taken as a strengthening of the thought (cp. Ex 32:12; Jer 32:37; 37:24; La 2:3; CD 10, 9; En 5:9; PsSol 2:23; Ath. 21, 1), and in **14:8; 18:3** we have a complex metaphor (cp. Pind., P. 10, 51–54 and BGildersleeve's comment on 'telescoped' metaphor [Pindar: The Olympian and Pythian Odes 1885, 355]): the wine of harlotry, w. which Babylon intoxicates the nations, becomes the wine of God's wrath for them.—In the other occurrences of θ. in our lit., the same mng. is indicated: of God (w. ὀργή; both words are oft. used together thus in the LXX) **Ro 2:8;** 1 Cl 50:4. Of humans **Hb 11:27;** (w. ὀργή, as Aelian, VH 15, 54; Ael. Aristid. 35, 10 K.=9 p. 101 D.; Herodian 8, 4, 1; Sir 45:18; Jos., Bell. 2, 135, Ant. 20, 108) **Col 3:8;** (w. πικρία and ὀργή) **Eph 4:31;** cp. Hm 5, 2, 4 and Js 3:11 P^{74}. ἐξερίσαι εἰς τοσοῦτο θυμοῦ *reach such a pitch of fury* 1 Cl 45:7; ἀκατάσχετος θ. MPol 12:2. πλησθῆναι θυμοῦ *be filled w. anger* **Lk 4:28;** cp. **Ac 19:28.**—Pl. θυμοί (Herm. Wr. 12, 4; Philo, Rer. Div. Her. 64; Jos., Bell. 4, 314) *outbursts of anger* **2 Cor 12:20; Gal 5:20;** 1 Cl 46:5.—JIrmscher, Götterzorn bei Homer '50. SSullivan, Glotta

59, '81, 147–55 (Hesiod and Gk. lyric poets). B. 1087; 1134. DELG. M-M. TW.

θυμόω 1 aor. 3 sg. ἐθύμωσεν Hos 12:15; pass. ἐθυμώθην; fut. θυμωθήσομαι LXX (s. θυμός; Aeschyl., Hdt. et al.; Dio Chrys. 10 [11], 20; LXX; TestSol 20:6; JosAs; ParJer 6:23 [cod. C]; EpArist 254; Jos., Bell. 1, 221, Ant. 12, 270) ***make angry;*** pass. *become angry.* Abs. (Polyb. 5, 16, 4; TestDan 4:4; TestSol 20:6) ἐθυμώθη λίαν **Mt 2:16.** In GJs 22:1 v.l. for ὀργισθείς.—DELG s.v. θυμός.

θύρα, ας, ἡ (Hom.+) 'door'. As is oft. the case in earlier lit. (e.g. Il. and Od. passim), the pl. can be used of one door (Phlegon: 257 fgm. 36, 1, 3 Jac.; Philo, Ebr. 49; cp. Jos., C. Ap. 2, 119.—B-D-F §141, 4; Rob. 408).

❶ ***door***—ⓐ of habitable quarters ἀνοίγειν *open the door* (LXX; JosAs 10:9; Jos., Vi. 246) **Ac 5:19;** B 16:9. Pass. **Ac 16:26f** (Achilles Tat. 7, 13, 1 Λευκίππη τὰς θύρας ἀνεῳγμένας ὁρῶσα). (ἀπο)κλείειν *shut* **Mt 6:6; Lk 13:25a.** Pass (LXX; JosAs 10:6; 14:5; Jos., Ant. 18, 74) **Mt 25:10; Lk 11:7; J 20:19, 26; Ac 21:30;** κρούειν τὴν θ. *knock at the door* **12:13; Lk 13:25b;** also πρὸς τὴν θ. GJs 12:2; ἔδραμεν πρὸς τήν θ. ibid. διὰ τῆς θ. **J 10:1f.** ἐπὶ τ. θυρῶν *before the door(s)* **Ac 5:23.** Also ἐπὶ θύραις (LXX; Aesop, Fab. 466 P.; Jos., Ant. 17, 90. Also with art.: Clearchus, fgm. 24 p. 17, 21; Appian, Bell. Civ. 3, 93 §385) 1 Cl 39:9 (Job 5:4); ἐπὶ τῇ θ. **Ac 5:9.** πρὸ τῆς θύρας **12:6** (schol. on Nicander, Ther. 860 πρὸ τ. θυρῶν); so also JosAs 5:1. πρὸς (τὴν) θ. *at the door* (Hegesippus Com. [III BC] 1, 24 K.) **Mk 1:33; 11:4;** τὰ πρὸς τὴν θ. *the place near the door* **2:2** (TestAbr A 6 p. 83, 6 [Stone p. 14]). πρὸς τῇ θ. ἔξω *outside the door* **J 18:16** (cp. Lucian, Herm. 7, 7 ὁ παρὰ τὴν θύραν ἔξω ἑστώς).—θ. τοῦ πύργου Hv 3, 9, 6.—On the θύρα ὡραία **Ac 3:2** s. ὡραῖος 2.—1 Cl 43:3 v.l.

ⓑ fig. (Maximus Tyr. 19, 5d ὁ ἔρως ἔστη ἐπὶ θύραις τ. ψυχῆς; Iambl., Myst. 10, 5 [Herm. Wr. IV p. 39, 5ff Sc.] ἡ ἱερατικὴ δόσις καλεῖται 'θύρα πρὸς θεόν').

α. ἐγγύς ἐστιν ἐπὶ θύραις *he is near, at your very door* (cp. X., An. 6, 5, 23; Just., D 32, 3) **Mt 24:33; Mk 13:29.** Also πρὸ τῶν θυρῶν ἕστηκεν **Js 5:9;** cp. also **Ac 5:9.** ἕστηκα ἐπὶ τ. θύραν καὶ κρούω **Rv 3:20a;** s. also vs. **20b.**

β. of the door to the kgdm. of heaven: εἰσελθεῖν διὰ τῆς στενῆς θύρας *come in through the narrow door* **Lk 13:24.** Perh. the same door is meant in δέδωκα ἐνώπιόν σου θύραν ἠνεῳγμένην **Rv 3:8.** But here sense

γ. is also prob., acc. to which the opening of the door represents something made possible or feasible: θύρα μοι ἀνέῳγεν μεγάλη **1 Cor 16:9** (HNie, Vox Theologica 10, '40, 185–92); cp. **2 Cor 2:12; Col 4:3.** Sim. ὁ θεὸς . . . ἤνοιξεν τοῖς ἔθνεσιν θύραν πίστεως **Ac 14:27** (πίστις 2dα).

❷ **a passage for entering a structure, *entrance, doorway, gate***—ⓐ of the door-like opening of a cave-tomb (cp. Od. 9, 243; SEG VIII, 200, 3 [I AD, Jerus.]) ἡ θ. τοῦ μνημείου **Mt 27:60; Mk 15:46; 16:3.** θ. τοῦ μνήματος GPt 8:32; cp. 9:37; 12:53f.—The firm vault of heaven has a 'door' (cp. Ps 77:23), which opens to admit favored ones **Rv 4:1** (difft., GRinaldi, CBQ 25, '63, 336–47).

ⓑ In John Jesus calls himself ἡ θύρα **J 10:9,** thus portraying himself as an opening that permits passage: *the gate for* the sheep; ἡ θύρα (ὁ ποιμήν P^{75} et al.) τῶν προβάτων vs. **7,** however, has the sense which is prominent in the context, *the gate to the sheep* (s. Hdb. ad loc.; EFascher, Ich bin d. Thür! Deutsche Theologie '42, 34–57; 118–33).—Jesus as the θύρα τοῦ πατρός *the door to the Father* IPhld 9:1.—B. 466. DELG. M-M. EDNT. TW.

θυρεός, οῦ, ὁ (Polyb. 6, 23, 2; Diod. S. 5, 18, 3; 5, 33, 4 al.; PSI 428, 36 [III BC]; LXX; Jos., Ant. 8, 179; SibOr 3, 729; loanw. in rabb.) prop. 'a long, oblong shield' (shaped like a door: s. θύρα) ***shield,*** in imagery θ. τῆς πίστεως *shield of faith* **Eph 6:16.** ABotuno, La metafora della porta: RivB 39, '91, 207–15.—B. 1402. DELG s.v. θύρα. M-M. TW.

θυρίς, ίδος, ἡ (s. θύρα) ***window*** (so Aristot.+; ins, pap, LXX; En 101:2; TestJos 14:1; JosAs; Philo, Plant. 169; Joseph.; loanw. in rabb.) καθέζεσθαι ἐπὶ τῆς θ. *sit at (in) the window* **Ac 20:9.** διὰ θυρίδος *through the window* **2 Cor 11:33** (Palaeph. p. 20, 5; UPZ 15, 7; 53, 5; Josh 2:15; 1 Km 19:12; Jos., Bell. 6, 252, Ant. 6, 217; for related incidents, s. Wetstein: Athen. 5, 52, p. 214a and Plut., Aemil. Paul. 26, 269a). ἀπὸ ταύτης τῆς θυρίδος AcPl Ox 6 recto, 5f (=Aa I 241, 12).—DELG s.v. θύρα. M-M. TW.

θυρωρός, οῦ ***doorkeeper, gatekeeper*** **ὁ** of a man (s. θύρα; Sappho et al.; pap, LXX; TestJob 43:6; Jos., Ant. 11, 108) *doorkeeper* **Mk 13:34;** *gatekeeper* **J 10:3. ἡ** of a woman *doorkeeper* (BGU 1061, 10 [14 BC]; PRyl 36, 6 [34 AD]; PStras 24:17; 2 Km 4:6; TestJob; JosAs 10:3; Jos., Ant. 7, 48) **J 18:16f** (MBlack, An Aramaic Approach[3], '67, 258f [Sin. Syriac]).—DELG s.v. θύρα. M-M.

θυσία, ας, ἡ (s. θύω and next entry; Pind., Hdt.+).—❶ **act of offering, *offering*** fig. ἐπὶ τῇ θυσίᾳ τ. πίστεως ὑμῶν *as you offer your faith* **Phil 2:17** (though mng. 2b is not impossible for the complex set of imagery in this pass.; s. below).

❷ **that which is offered as a sacrifice, *sacrifice, offering***

ⓐ lit.—**α.** (stated gener. Dg 3:5; Just., D. 43, 1 al.; Ath. 26, 3) **Mt 9:13; 12:7** (both Hos 6:6); **Mk 9:49 v.l.,** s. ἁλίζω; **Hb 10:5** (Ps 39:7), **26.** Pl. **Mk 12:33; Lk 13:1** (cp. Jos., Bell. 2, 30 παρὰ ταῖς ἰδίαις θυσίαις ἀπεσφάχθαι); **Hb 10:1, 8;** 1 Cl 4:2 (Gen 4:5; cp. Diod. S. 12, 20, 2 τῶν θεῶν οὐ χαιρόντων ταῖς τῶν πονηρῶν θυσίαις); B 2:4, 5 (Is 1:11), 7 (Jer 7:22). The various kinds are specified 1 Cl 41:2. ἀνάγειν θυσίαν *bring an offering* **Ac 7:41** (ἀνάγω 3). Also ἀναφέρειν θ. **Hb 7:27** (ἀναφέρω 3); δοῦναι θ. **Lk 2:24.** προσφέρειν (Ex 32:6; Lev 2:1, 8 and oft.; Just., D. 41, 3 al.) **Ac 7:42** (Am 5:25); **Hb 5:1; 8:3; 10:11; 11:4;** 1 Cl 10:7. Pass. **Hb 9:9.** φέρειν θ. (2 Ch 29:31, Jer 17:26; Just. A I, 24, 2 al.) 1 Cl 4:1 (Gen 4:3). προσάγεσθαι θ. (cp. 1 Esdr 1:16) *be led as a sacrifice* 1 Cl 31:3.

β. of a sacrificial meal (Polycrates: 588 fgm. 1 Jac. equated w. θοίνη ['feast']; Ps.-Callisth. 3, 29, 9 τὴν θυσίαν ἐποιησάμεθα τῶν Σωτηρίων=the meal to celebrate deliverance) ἐσθίειν τὰς θ. *eat the sacrifices* (Ps 105:28; Num 25:2) **1 Cor 10:18.** The Eucharist is spoken of as a *sacrifice* or *offering* and sacrificial meal D 14:1ff (s. Knopf, Hdb. exc. on D 9 and 10, p. 24f).

γ. of the sacrificial death of Christ which, in contrast to the earthly sacrifices, is to be classed among the κρείττονες θυσίαι **Hb 9:23; 10:12.** διὰ τῆς θυσίας αὐτοῦ **9:26.** παρέδωκεν ἑαυτὸν ὑπὲρ ἡμῶν θυσίαν τ. θεῷ **Eph 5:2** (Diod. S. 4, 82, 2 τὴν θυσίαν ὑπὲρ ἁπάντων τ. Ἑλλήνων).—B 7:3.—Of aspiration to martyrdom ἵνα διὰ τῶν ὀργάνων τούτων θεοῦ θυσία εὑρεθῶ IRo 4:2. προσδεχθείην . . . σήμερον ἐν θυσίᾳ πίονι καὶ προσδεκτῇ MPol 14:2.

ⓑ fig. (Sextus 47: the doing of good as the only θυσία pleasing to God; sim. Persius 2, 73–75, a pure heart is the appropriate sacrifice in temples: compositum ius fasque animo . . . haec cedo ut admoveam templis) a broken spirit designated as θ. 1 Cl 18:16f; 52:4; B 2:10 (all three Ps 50:19). θ. αἰνέσεως *praise-offering* (s. on αἴνεσις) is used fig. in our lit. of spiritual sacrifice 1 Cl 35:12 (Ps 49:23); 52:3 (Ps 49:14). It is explained **Hb 13:15** as καρπὸς χειλέων ὁμολογούντων τῷ ὀνόματι αὐτοῦ (=τ. θεοῦ).—εἰ σπένδομαι ἐπὶ τῇ θυσίᾳ τῆς πίστεως ὑμῶν *even if I must pour out my blood over the sacrifice of your faith* (i.e., consisting in your faith) **Phil 2:17** (cp. Arrian, Anab. 6, 19, 5 σπείσας ἐπὶ τῇ θυσίᾳ τὴν φιάλην; but s. 1 above). θ. δεκτή *an acceptable sacr.* (s. δεκτός 2) **Phil 4:18;** Hs 5, 3, 8; cp. **Hb 13:16** and 2aγ end. πνευματικαὶ θ. *spiritual sacrifices* **1 Pt 2:5** (cp. Herm. Wr. 13, 18; 19; 21 λογικαὶ θυσίαι; s. on this Rtzst., Mysterienrel.[3] 38; 328f.—SibOr 8, 408 ζῶσα θυσία). παρακαλῶ ὑμᾶς παραστῆσαι τὰ σώματα ὑμῶν θυσίαν ζῶσαν *I appeal to you to present your bodies as a living sacrifice* **Ro 12:1** (παριστάναι θυσίαν is a t.t. of sacrificial procedure: OGI 332, 17 and 42; 456, 20f; 764, 23 and 33 al., SIG[2] 554, 6; SIG[3] 694, 50.—PSeidensticker, Lebendiges Opfer Röm 12:1, diss. Münster, '54).—OSchmitz, Die Opferanschauung d. spät. Judentums u. die Opferaussagen d. NTs 1910; HWenschkewitz, D. Spiritualisierung der Kultusbegriffe Tempel, Priester u. Opfer im NT '32; WvLoewenich, Z. Verständnis d. Opfergedankens im Hb: ThBl 12, '32, 167–72; JBrinktrine, D. Messopferbegr. in den ersten 2 Jahrh. 1918; RYerkes, ATR 29, '47, 28–33; RdeVaux, Les Sacrifices de l'Ancien Testament '64. BHHW II 1345–52; Pauly-W. XVIII 579–627; JCasabona, Recherches sur le vocabulaire des Sacrifices en Grec '66.—B. 1467. DELG s.v. 2 θύω B6. TRE XXV esp. 253–78. M-M. Sv. S. also εὐχαριστία 3.

θυσιαστήριον, ου, τό (s. prec. entry; LXX; pseudepigr; Philo, Mos. 2, 105; Jos., Ant. 8, 88; 105; Just., D. 118, 2; gener. 'altar')

❶ **a structure on which cultic observances are carried out, including esp. sacrifices, *altar*—ⓐ** of the altar of burnt offering in the inner forecourt of the temple at Jerusalem (s. Schürer II 298f) **Mt 5:23f; 23:18–20, 35; Lk 11:51; Hb 7:13; Rv 11:1;** 1 Cl 41:2; B 7:9 (cp. Lev 16:7–9, 18). λειτουργεῖν τῷ θ. *serve at the altar* 1 Cl 32:2; παρεδρεύειν τῷ θ. (s. παρεδρεύω) **1 Cor 9:13a;** συμμερίζεσθαι τῷ θ. (s. συμμερίζω) vs. **13b;** κοινωνοὶ τοῦ θ. *partners, sharers in the altar*=closely united w. the altar (=w. God; s. 10:20) **10:18** (s. κοινωνός 1bα; but s. GJourdan, JBL 67, '48, 122f). **Mt 23:35** and therefore prob. also GJs 5:1; 7:3; 8:2; 23:1; 24:2.

ⓑ of the incense altar—**α.** in the temple at Jerusalem τὸ θ. τοῦ θυμιάματος (Ex 30:1, 27) **Lk 1:11.**

β. the heavenly altar of **Rv** also seems to be thought of as an incense altar: **6:9; 8:3, 5; 9:13; 14:18; 16:7.** Hermas also speaks of a θ. τοῦ θεοῦ in heaven Hm 10, 3, 2f; s 8, 2, 5.

ⓒ of an *altar* gener.: the one erected by Abraham (Gen 22:9) **Js 2:21;** B 7:3. Pl. **Ro 11:3** (3 Km 19:10).

ⓓ various other referents, esp. fig. extensions of those above

α. IRo 2:2 Ign. speaks of the altar that is ready to receive his death as a martyr.

β. Pol 4:3 the Christian widows are called a θυσιαστήριον θεοῦ, since they are to bring to God none but perfect gifts (cp. Sextus 46b, the pure heart as a θ. for God).

γ. The pass. ἔχομεν θ. ἐξ οὗ φαγεῖν οὐκ ἔχουσιν ἐξουσίαν οἱ τῇ σκηνῇ λατρεύοντες *we have an altar, from which those who serve the tabernacle have no right to eat* **Hb 13:10** is difficult. Scholars such as FBleek, ASeeberg and BHaensler, BZ 11, 1913, 403–9, interpret the θ. as the cross of Christ, others (e.g. THaering, Der Brief an die Hebr. 1925, 103) as the communion table. HWindisch rejects both these interpr. BWeiss and ERiggenbach[2, 3] 1922 give up the attempt to understand it. S. also JCreed, ET 50, '38, 13–15; JWilson, ibid. 380f; JOulton, ibid. 55, '44, 303–5.—προσέρχεσθαι ἐν τῷ θ. λειτουργεῖν τὸ θεῖον **Tit 1:9 v.l.** is also to be interpr. fr. the viewpoint of Christian institutions.

❷ **the people of God as cultic entity, *sanctuary,*** in imagery ἐντὸς (τοῦ) θ. εἶναι *be inside the sanctuary* (θ. in this mng. perh. also **Rv 14:18** and Procop., Aed. 1, 65; ins Ἀρχαιολογικὸν Δελτίον 12, 1927, 69), i.e. the Christian community or church, under the care and control of its constituted authorities IEph 5:2; ITr 7:2 (opp. ἐκτὸς θ.). This is in accord w. Ignatius' emphatic assertion that there is only one θ. IMg 7:2; IPhld 4.—B. 1467. DELG s.v. 2 θύω B6. EDNT. TW.

θύω impf. ἔθυον; fut. θύσω LXX; 1 aor. ἔθυσα; pf. τέθυκα LXX. Pass.: 1 aor. ἐτύθην, ptc. τυθείς (Just. D. 111, 3), θυθείς (Mel., P. 71, 516 [B]); pf. ptc. τεθυμένος (Hom.+).

❶ **to make a cultic offering, *sacrifice*** (this is the primary mng. and the one most commonly found) τινί τι *someth. in honor of someone* (Diod. S. 16, 18, 5; 17, 100, 1; Lucian, Dial. Deor. 2, 4; SIG 589, 48; 993, 11f; Gen 46:1; Jos., Bell. 2, 214 τῷ θεῷ χαριστήρια; SibOr 3, 626) **1 Cor 10:20** (Dt 32:17). τ. θεῷ θυσίαν *offer a sacr. to God* 1 Cl 52:3 (Ps 49:14). τινί *in honor of someone* (X., Cyr. 8, 7, 3; Mitt-Wilck. I/2, 116, 2 θύε πᾶσι τοῖς θεοῖς; BGU 287, 7; LXX; EpArist 138; Jos., Bell. 1, 56 τῷ θεῷ; Just., D. 46, 7; 136, 3 τῇ Βάαλ; Ath. 1, 1 Ποσειδῶνι) **Ac 14:18;** 2 Cl 3:1. Abs. (Lucian, Jupp. Trag. 22, beg.; PHib 28, 7; LXX; Ath. 13, 1; 26, 2) **Ac 14:13;** MPol 12:2. (Used also of human sacrifice: Apollodorus [II BC]: 244 fgm. 125 Jac.=Porph., De Abst. 2, 55; Ar. 9, 1 τὰ ἴδια τέκνα to Cronos; Just., D. 19, 6 τὰ τέκνα ὑμῶν ἐθύετε τοῖς δαιμονίοις al.)

❷ **to take life, *kill, slaughter,*** in a gener. sense—ⓐ humans (Eur., Iph. T. 621; Sir 34:20; 1 Macc 7:19) abs. in agricultural imagery **J 10:10,** which also requires placement in b.

ⓑ animals **J 10:10** (GKilpatrick, BT 12, '61, 130–32, kill for food; in this sense also the killing of a rooster by thieves Aesop, Fab. 122 P.=195 H.; sheep 143 P.=262 H.; oxen [subject to slaughtering instead of professional butchering] 290 P.=Babr. 21. S. also Tob 7:8; Jos., Ant. 1, 197 μόσχον; Tat. 23, 2 ζῶα); calf **Lk 15:23, 27, 30;** pass. **Mt 22:4.**

❸ **to kill ceremonially, *slaughter sacrifically*** (on the close relation betw. sacrifice and slaughter s. Ltzm., Hdb. on 1 Cor 10:25) τὸ πάσχα *the Passover lamb* (Ex 12:21; Dt 16:2, 5f; 1 Esdr 1:6; 7:12) **Mk 14:12.** Pass. **Lk 22:7;** hence τὸ πάσχα ἡμῶν ἐτύθη Χριστός **1 Cor 5:7** (Just., D. 111, 3; Mel., P. 71, 516 B.; θύω of the sacrifice of a person, s. 1 above). Abs. **Ac 10:13; 11:7**

❹ ***celebrate,*** but perh. only when an animal is slaughtered in connection with a celebration (Polyaenus 1, 44. θ. εὐαγγέλια='a joyous festival'; Appian, Syr. 4 §17; 16 §69 γάμους both times; Athen. 12, 43, 532e θ. τὰ ἐπινίκια; Achilles Tat. 8, 19, 3 θ. τοὺς γάμους.—Philochorus no. 328 fgm. 65 Jac. uses θυσία of domestic family festivals) **Mk 14:12; Lk 22:7** (s. 3 above).—DELG s.v. 2 θύω B1. TRE XXV 253–71. M-M. EDNT. TW.

θῶ s. τίθημι. DELG.

Θωμᾶς, ᾶ, ὁ (the Aram. תְּאוֹמָא='twin', which was never used simply as a surname [MLidzbarski, Handb. der nordsem. Epigraphik 1898, 383], came to coincide in Gk.-speaking regions w. the Gk. name Θωμᾶς [RHerzog, Philol 56, 1897, 51]; s. Dalman, Gramm.[2] 145, 6; Wuthnow 55; B-D-F §53, 2d; 125, 2) ***Thomas,*** one of the 12 apostles (s. Δίδυμος) **Mt 10:3; Mk 3:18; Lk 6:15; J 11:16; 14:5; 20:24, 26–28; 21:2; Ac 1:13;** Ox 654, 3 (GTh 1)=ASyn. 247, 19; Papias (2:4).—BHHW III 1974.—M-M. EDNT.

θώραξ, ακος, ὁ—❶ protective covering for the chest in combat, *breastplate* (so Hom.+; ChronLind 36; 41; 47; PPetr III, 6a, 28 [237 BC]; PGiss 47, 6; LXX; TestJud 3:5; Philo, Leg.

All. 3, 115; Jos., Ant. 8, 414, Vi. 293; loanw. in rabb.) **Rv 9:9b, 17.**—Fig. ἐνδύεσθαι τὸν θώρακα τῆς δικαιοσύνης *put on the breastplate of righteousness* **Eph 6:14** (cp. Is 59:17; Wsd 5:18). θ. πίστεως **1 Th 5:8.**

❷ **the part of the body covered by the breastplate,** ***the chest*** (Eur.; Pla., Tim. 69e; Aristot., Hist. An. 1, 7; Diod. S. 15, 87, 1; 5; Polyaenus 3, 9, 22) **Rv 9:9a** (though mng. 1 is not to be excluded).—B. 1399. DELG. M-M. TW.

I

ι´ numerical sign = ***10*** (δέκα: Jos., C. Ap. 1, 157; cp. SibOr 5, 14) B 9:8 (ἰῶτα codd. HV); Hs 9, 3, 3; 9, 4, 2; 3; 9, 5, 4; 9, 15, 4; or ***10th*** (δεκάτη) Hm 10 superscr.

ια´ numerical sign = ***11th*** (ἑνδεκάτη) Hm 11 superscr.

Ἰάϊρος, ου, ὁ, Ἰάειρος W-H. (=יָאִיר ‘he enlightens’ or rarely [1 Ch 20:5]=יָעִיר ‘he arouses’) ***Jairus*** (Ἰαΐρ Num 32:41; Dt 3:14; 1 Ch 2:22f al. Ἰάϊρος 1 Esdr 5:31; Esth 1:1a; Jos., Bell. 2, 447; s. PThomsen, Inschr. d. Stadt Jerusalem [=ZDPV 43, 1920, 138ff] no. 190; O. Wilck II, 1231) a synagogue official **Mk 5:22; Lk 8:41** (on his title, s. SEG XLIII, 1297 [lit.]).—M-M.

Ἰακώβ, ὁ indecl. (יַעֲקֹב) ***Jacob.*** This, the un-Grecized form of the OT, is reserved for formal writing, and esp. for the patriarch (so also pseudepigr.; Philo, e.g. Leg. Alleg. 3, 18, Sacrif. Abel. 5, Ebr. 82, Migr. Abr. 200; SibOr 2, 247; Just.; Mel.; also in magic: PGM 4, 1736; 1803, and in the spelling Ἰακούβ [IDefixWünsch 3, 2]. Differently Josephus, s. Ἰάκωβος; s. Dssm. B 184, 3 [BS 282]; for exceptions s. Ἰάκωβος 4).

❶ son of Isaac (husband of Leah and Rachel) **Mt 1:2; Lk 3:34; J 4:5f, 12; Ac 7:8, 12, 14f, 46** (but s. below); **Ro 9:13** (Mal 1:2f); **Hb 11:9, 20f;** 1 Cl 4:8; 31:4; B 11:9 (quot. of unknown orig.); 13:4f. Of the nation of Israel, *the descendants of Jacob* (Num 23:7; Sir 23:12; Is 9:7; 40:27 al.; Just., D. 11, 5 γένος, cp. 26:1 ὅσοι ἀπὸ Ἰ. γεγέννηνται) **Ro 11:26** (Is 59:20); so perh. also in οἶκος Ἰ. **Ac 7:46.** Also (Ex 19:3; Is 2:5; PsSol 7:10; Just., D. 53, 4) **Lk 1:33;** cp. 1 Cl 29:2 (Dt 32:9). The triad Abraham, Isaac, and Jacob (also in magic [s. Ἀβραάμ] and grave ins Sb 2034, 11; 3901, 12) **Mt 8:11; Lk 13:28;** B 8:4; IPhld 9:1; GJs 20:2 (not pap) σπέρμα (Just., D. 135, 5 τὸ ἐξ Ἰ. σπέρμα). Esp. the God of Abraham, Isaac, and Jacob (Ex 3:6; Just., D. 11, 1 al.; also in magic: PGM 4, 1231f; IDefixWünsch 5, 2; 37) **Mt 22:32; Mk 12:26; Lk 20:37; Ac 3:13; 7:32.**—Cp. B 6:8 (Ex 33:1).

❷ the father of Joseph, in the genealogy of Jesus **Mt 1:15f; Lk 3:23** D.—M-M. TW.

Ἰάκωβος, ου, ὁ (Grecized form of the preceding, W-S. §10, 3; EpArist 48; 49. Oft. in Joseph., even for the patriarch [s. Ἰακώβ]. In the spelling Ἰάκουβος: POxy 276, 5 [77 AD]; BGU 715 II, 11; 1 Esdr 9:48) ***James*** (for the history of this name s. OED s.v. James).

❶ son of the Galilean fisherman Zebedee, brother of John, member of the Twelve, executed by Herod Agrippa I not later than 44 AD: **Mt 4:21; 10:2; 17:1; Mk 1:19, 29; 3:17; 5:37; 9:2; 10:35, 41; 13:3; 14:33; Lk 5:10; 6:14; 8:51; 9:28, 54; Ac 1:13a; 12:2;** GEb 34, 60; Papias (2:4).—ESchwartz, Über d. Tod der Söhne Zeb. 1904; JBlinzler and ABöhling, NovT 5, ’62, 191–213.

❷ son of Alphaeus (s. Ἁλφαῖος) also belonged to the Twelve **Mt 10:3; Mk 2:14 v.l.** (s. 6 below); **3:18; Lk 6:15; Ac 1:13b.** This James is perh. identical with

❸ son of Mary **Mt 27:56; Mk 16:1; Lk 24:10** (s. B-D-F §162, 3), who is called **Mk 15:40** Ἰ. ὁ μικρός, *James the small* or *the younger* (μικρός 1ab.—TZahn, Forschungen VI 1900, 345f; 348ff).

❹ the Lord’s brother (Jos., Ant. 20, 200), later head of the Christian community at Jerusalem, confused w. 2 at an early date; **Mt 13:55; Mk 6:3; 1 Cor 15:7; Gal 1:19; 2:9, 12; Ac 12:17; 15:13; 21:18;** GHb 361, 7 (Lat.); probably Papias 2:4. This J. is certainly meant **Js 1:1** (MMeinertz, D. Jk u. sein Verf. 1905; AMeyer, D. Rätsel des Jk 1930); **Jd 1;** and perh. GJs 25:1 in title and subscr.—GKittel, D. Stellg. des Jak. zu Judentum u. Heidenchristentum: ZNW 30, ’31, 145–57, D. geschichtl. Ort des Jk: ibid. 41, ’42, 71–105; KAland, D. Herrenbr. Jak. u. Jk: Neut. Entwürfe ’79, 233–45; GKittel, D. Jak. u. die Apost. Väter: ZNW 43, ’50/51, 54–112; WPrentice, in Studies in Roman Economic and Social Hist. in honor of AJohnson ’51, 144–51; PGaechter, Petrus u. seine Zeit ’58, 258–310; DLittle, The Death of James: The Brother of Jesus, diss. Rice Univ. ’71; WPratscher, Der Herrenbruder Jakobus u. die Jakobustradition ’87.

❺ father of an apostle named Judas, mentioned only by Luke: **Lk 6:16a; Ac 1:13c.**

❻ **Mk 2:14 v.l.** (s. 2 above) the tax-collector is called James (instead of Levi; s. FBurkitt, JTS 28, 1927, 273f).—HHoltzmann, Jak. der Gerechte u. seine Namensbrüder: ZWT 23, 1880, 198–221; FMaier, Z. Apostolizität des Jak. u. Jud.: BZ 4, 1906, 164–91; 255–66; HKoch, Z. Jakobusfrage Gal 1:19: ZNW 33, ’34, 204–9.—EDNT. M-M.

ἴαμα, ατος, τό (Hdt. et al. w. the mng. ‘remedy’) ***healing*** (Pla., Leg. 7 p. 790d; Lucian, Calumn. 17; SIG 1168, 2 ἰάματα τ. Ἀπόλλωνος καὶ τ. Ἀσκλαπιοῦ; 24; 35; IGUR IV, 1702; cp. Jer 40:6; also ApcSed 10:6b p. 134, 7 Ja.) χαρίσματα ἰαμάτων *(spiritual) gifts of healing* **1 Cor 12:9, 28, 30;** cp. ἰάματα B 3:4 v.l. (for ἱμάτια; s. ἱμάτιον end) Funk.—M-M. TW.

Ἰαμβρῆς, ὁ ***Jambres,*** **2 Tim 3:8;** s. Ἰάννης.

Ἰανναί, ὁ indecl. ***Jannai,*** in the genealogy of Jesus **Lk 3:24** (Ἰαννά v.l.).

Ἰάννης, ὁ ***Jannes,*** named w. Jambres as one of the Egyptian sorcerers who (Ex 7:11ff) opposed Moses before Pharaoh **2 Ti 3:8.** The names go back to Jewish tradition (Schürer III 781–83; MDibelius, Hdb. ad loc.; TestSol 25:4, whence Numenius of Apamea [II AD] in Eus., PE 9, 8, 1 got them). Μαμβρῆς appears as v.l. for Ἰαμβρῆς, reflecting variation in the mss. A Jewish apocryphal work bearing both names has disappeared except for the title (Schürer, loc. cit.).—RJames, JTS 2, 1901, 572ff; The

Damascus Document (Kl. T. 167) 5, 19f (cp. CD 5, 18f and S-Schechter, Fragments of a Zadokite Work 1910, pp. xxxvii and lixf); Billerb. III 660–64; LGrabbe, The Jannes-Jambres Tradition in Targum Pseudo-Jonathan and Its Date: JBL 98, 79, 393–401; APietersma, The Apochryphon of Jannes and Jambres the Magician—PChesterBeatty XVI (EPROR 119) '94.—BHHW II, 802. TW.

ἰάομαι mid. dep., impf. ἰώμην; fut. ἰάσομαι; 1 aor. ἰασάμην. Pass. forms w. pass. mng.: 1 fut. ἰαθήσομαι; 1 aor. ἰάθην, impv. ἰαθήτω; pf. ἴαμαι (B-D-F §311, 1) (Hom.+; SIG 1168, 108; 113; 117; 1169, 7; PSI 665, 5 [III BC]; BGU 1026 XXII, 15; LXX, En, TestSol; ApcrEzk P 1 verso 12; Philo; Jos., Ant. 9, 105; Just., Tat., Ath.)

➊ **to restore someone to health after a physical malady, *heal, cure*** lit. τινά *someone* **Lk 5:17; 6:19; 9** (in vs. **2** τοὺς ἀσθενεῖς is omitted in v.l.), **11, 42; 14:4; 22:51; J 4:47; Ac 9:34; 10:38; 28:8;** 1 Cl 59:4; AcPl BMM verso 11.—Pass. **Mt 8:8, 13; 15:28; Lk 7:7; 8:47; 17:15; J 5:13; Ac 5:16** D; GJs 20:2 (4 in the expanded vers., s. deStrycker); very questionable is AcPl BMM verso 18 (corrupt, Sander's text: καὶ οὐκ εἰ αθι[lacuna]). ἰαθῆναι ἀπό τινος *be cured of an illness:* ἀπὸ τῆς μάστιγος *of the terrible suffering* **Mk 5:29.** ἀπὸ τῶν νόσων αὐτῶν **Lk 6:18.** ἰᾶσθαι διά τινος *be cured by someth.* B 8:6.

➋ **to deliver from a variety of ills or conditions that lie beyond physical maladies, *restore, heal,*** fig. ext. of 1 (Ael. Aristid. 13 p. 273 D.; Julian, Ep. 61, 424a, fr. the evils of ignorance; Sallust. 14 p. 28, 3 κακίαν; Jos., Ant. 2, 119 λύπην)

ⓐ *restore* (ἰαθήσεται ἡ γῆ En 10:7) τινά *someone* fr. sin and its consequences **Mt 13:15; J 12:40; Ac 28:27** (all three Is 6:10); the brokenhearted **Lk 4:18 v.l.;** B 14:9 (both Is 61:1).

ⓑ τὶ *someth.* (Philostrat., Vi. Soph. 1, 22 p. 38, 9) *heal* (cp. the proverb in Hdt. 3, 53, 4; Thu. 5, 65, 2; Apollon. Rhod. 4, 1081; Appian, Ital. 5 §10, Bell. Civ. 1, 3 §9; Prov. Aesopi 91 P.: κακὸν κακῷ ἰᾶσθαι) τὰ ἁμαρτήματα Hv 1, 1, 9 (Appian, Hann. 31 §131 ἁμάρτημα ἰ.). τὰ ἀγνοήματα Hs 5, 7, 4. τὰ προγεγονότα πονηρά *all the past evils* v 1, 3, 1; cp. s 9, 23, 5. Abs. of the results of divine punishment, which God brings to an end 1 Cl 56:7 (Job 5:18).—Pass. of sin **Js 5:16;** 2 Cl 9:7; Hs 9, 28, 5. The figure of sin as a wound or disease is also plain in ἵνα τὸ χωλὸν ἰαθῇ **Hb 12:13,** and τῷ μώλωπι αὐτοῦ ἡμεῖς ἰάθημεν 1 Cl 16:5; B 5:2; cp. **1 Pt 2:24** (all three Is 53:5; cp. Tat. 43, 3).—DELG. M-M. TW.

Ἰάρετ, ὁ (also Ἰαρέδ, Ἰάρεδ, Ἰάρεθ; indecl.; יֶרֶד, in pause יָרֶד) ***Jared,*** father of Enoch (Gen 5:15, 18; 1 Ch 1:2; En 106:13; Ἰάρεδ in all these, but Ἰάρετ as v.l. in Gen 5:18 [ARahlfs, Genesis 1926].—Jos., Ant. 1, 79; 84 Ἰάρεδος, ου), in the genealogy of Jesus **Lk 3:37.**

ἴασις, εως, ἡ (ἰάομαι; Archilochus [VII BC] et al.; SIG 244 I, 53; LXX; En 10:7; TestJob 38:8; TestZeb 9:8; ApcSed 10:6; Philo, Joseph.; Just., A II, 13, 4; also [for ἰάθημεν Is 53:5] D. 17, 1; 95, 3 and [on Is 11:2] D. 39, 2).

➊ **restoration to health after a physical malady, *healing, cure*** lit. (Hippocr., Pla. et al.; LXX; Jos., Ant. 7, 294) **J 5:7 v.l.** εἰς ἴασιν *for healing = to heal* **Ac 4:30;** τὸ σημεῖον τῆς ἰ. *the miracle of healing* vs. **22.** ἰάσεις ἀποτελεῖν (s. Vett. Val. on 2) *perform cures* **Lk 13:32;** δέησις περὶ τῆς ἰ. *prayer for healing* B 12:7.

➋ **deliverance from a variety of ills or conditions that lie beyond physical maladies, *cure, deliverance,*** fig. extension of mng. 1 (Pla., Leg. 9, 862c ἴασις τῆς ἀδικίας; Lucian, Jupp. Trag. 28; Alciphron 3, 13, 2; Vett. Val. 190, 30 τῶν φαύλων ἴασιν ἀποτελεῖ; Sir 43:22; Philo, Leg. All. 2, 79 ἴ. τοῦ πάθους; Jos., Ant. 5, 41) of *forgiveness of sins* (Arrian, Anab. 7, 29, 2 μόνη ἴασις ἁμαρτίας ὁμολογεῖν τε ἁμαρτόντα καὶ δῆλον εἶναι ἐπ' αὐτῷ μεταγινώσκοντα='the only cure for a sin is for the sinner to confess it and to show repentance for it'; Hierocles 11, 441 ἰ. γίνεται τῶν προημαρτημένων; Sir 28:3; s. also ἰάομαι 2) ἴασιν δοῦναι *grant forgiveness* Hm 4, 1, 11; s 5, 7, 3f. ἴασιν δοῦναί τινι s 7:4. ποιεῖν ἴασιν τοῖς ἁμαρτήμασίν τινος *forgive someone's sins* m 12, 6, 2. λαμβάνειν ἴασιν παρὰ τοῦ κυρίου τῶν ἁμαρτιῶν *receive forgiveness of sins fr. the Lord* s 8, 11, 3 (λαμβ. ἴ. as Philo, Post. Cai. 10).—DELG s.v. ἰάομαι. M-M. TW.

ἴασπις, ιδος, ἡ (Pla. et al.; SIG[2] 587, 87f [IV BC]; PGM 12, 203 ἴασπιν; LXX; TestSol; Jos., Bell. 5, 234, Ant. 3, 168. Occasionally also masc., e.g., Petosiris, fgm. 29) ***jasper,*** a precious stone found in various colors, mostly reddish, somet. green (Cyranides p. 23, 22 λίθος χλωρός), brown, blue, yellow, and white. In antiquity the name was not limited to the variety of quartz now called jasper, but could designate any opaque precious stone. **Rv 21:18f.** W. λίθος **4:3** (TestSol C 11:8). λίθος ἴασπις κρυσταλλίζων *a stone of crystal-clear jasper* **21:11** (cp. Is 54:12); perh. the opal is meant here; acc. to some, the diamond. S. on ἀμέθυστος.—DELG. M-M.

Ἰάσων, ονος, ὁ (freq. found, also in LXX; EpArist 49; Joseph. It was a favorite practice among Jews to substitute the purely Gk. name Ἰάσων for the Hebrew-Gk. Ἰησοῦς: Dssm., B 184, 1 [BS 315, 2]; B-D-F §53, 2d) ***Jason.***

➊ host of Paul and Silas in Thessalonica **Ac 17:5–7, 9.**

➋ one who sends a greeting **Ro 16:21,** hardly the same as 1.

➌ Ἰάσονι is found for Μνάσωνι **Ac 21:16 v.l.**—LGPN I. M-M.

ἰατρός, οῦ, ὁ (s. ἰάομαι; Hom.+)—➊ **one who undertakes the cure of physical ailments, *physician*** **Mt 9:12; Mk 2:17; Lk 5:31** (cp. on these pass. Plut., Mor. 230f, Phocion 746 [10, 5]; Stob., Floril. III p. 462, 14 H. οὐδὲ γὰρ ἰατρὸς ὑγιείας ὢν ποιητικὸς ἐν τοῖς ὑγιαίνουσι τὴν διατριβὴν ποιεῖται=no physician who can produce cures wastes time among the healthy); Ox 1 recto, 9–14 (ASyn. 33, 85, s. GTh 31; cp. Dio Chrys. 8 [9], 4 νοσοῦντες ἐπιδημοῦντος ἰατροῦ μὴ προσῄεσαν said in irony, of sick people unwilling to consult a resident physician); **Mk 5:26** (Sb 8266, 13ff [161/160 BC] when physicians refuse to help, the god Amenothis intervenes with a miracle). ἰατροῖς προσαναλίσκειν ὅλον τὸν βίον *spend all of one's money on physicians* **Lk 8:43 v.l.** (PStras 73, 18f, a physician's fee of 20 drachmas; Diod. S. 32, 11, 3 a physician διπλοῦν ἀπῄτει τὸν μισθόν. But some physicians are honored for accepting no remuneration, s. FKudlien, in Sozialmassnahmen und Fürsorge, ed. HKloft, '88, 90–92; s. also Danker, Benefactor, nos. 1–4 for positive view). Given as the profession of one named Luke **Col 4:14** (Heraclid. Pont., fgm. 118 W. Ἀσκληπιάδης ὁ ἰ.; Strabo 10, 5, 6 p. 486 Ἐρασίστρατος ὁ ἰ.; Sb 8327 [ins II AD] Ἀπολλώνιος ἰατρός). In a proverb (s. Jülicher, Gleichn. 172f; EKlostermann and FHauck ad loc.) ἰατρὲ θεράπευσον σεαυτόν *physician, heal yourself* **Lk 4:23** (Eur., fgm. 1086 Nauck[2] ἄλλων ἰατρὸς αὐτὸς ἕλκεσιν βρύων. Aesop, Fab. 289 P.=H. 78 and 78b=Babr. 120 πῶς ἄλλον ἰήσῃ, ὃς σαυτὸν μὴ σῴζεις).—Papias (3:2); AcPl Ha 5, 34. For IEph 7:2 s. 2.

➋ **one who undertakes the healing of supra-physical maladies, *physician (of the soul)*** (Diog. L. 3, 45 an epigram calls Plato the ἰητὴρ ψυχῆς; schol. on Pla. 227a ὁ Σωκράτης ἰατρὸς περὶ ψυχήν; Diod. S. 34+35 fgm. 17, 1 τῆς λύπης ὁ κάλλιστος ἰατρὸς χρόνος; Philo, Spec. Leg. 2, 31 ἰ. ἁμαρτημάτων) of God (s. DRahnenführer, Das Testament des Hiob, ZNW 62, '71, 76;

I

Aristoph., Av. 584 and Lycophron 1207; 1377 of Apollo; Simplicius in Epict. p. 41, 51 God as ἰατρός; Ael. Aristid. 47, 57 K.=23 p. 459 D.: Asclepius as ἀληθινὸς ἰατρός) Dg 9:6. Of Jesus Christ ἰ. σαρκικὸς καὶ πνευματικός *physician of body and soul* (or *ph. who is flesh and spirit*) IEph 7:2. s. JOtt, D. Bezeichnung Christi als ἰατρός in d. urchristl. Literatur: Der Katholik 90, 1910, 457f; AvHarnack, Mission[4] I 1923, 129ff; RAC I 720–25. On medical practice in the Gr-Rom. world s. ANRW II Principat 37, 1–3, 93–96.—B. 308. DELG s.v. ἰάομαι. M-M. SEG XXXIX, 1804. TW.

Ἰαχίν, ὁ indecl. ***Jachin,*** in the genealogy of Jesus, **Lk 3:23ff** D.

ιβʹ numeral *12* (in mss. for δώδεκα as Jos., C. Ap. 1, 122; Mel., P. 83, 627 [B]) **Mk 6:7** D. Postscript to Mk in the Ferrar group (s. Ῥωμαϊστί): ἐγράφη ιβʹ ἔτη τῆς ἀναλήψεως τ. κυρίου; **Ac 1:26** D; GJs 1:1; 6:3; 8:2f; ***twelfth*** (δωδεκάτη) Hm 12 superscr.

Ἰγνάτιος, ου, ὁ (on the name s. Hdb., Ergänzungsband 1923, 189. In addition to the examples given there of the name in this spelling see also Sb 8802b, 6 [82/83 AD]; 7662, 23 [II AD]) ***Ignatius,*** eccl. supervisor (bishop) of Antioch IEph IMg ITr IRo IPhld ISm IPol ins; Pol 9:1; 13:1f.

ἴδε (on the accentuation s. εἶδον beg.) properly impv. of εἶδον, but stereotyped as a particle, and hence used when more than one pers. is addressed, and when that which is to be observed is in the nom. (B-D-F §144; this use of the impv. [LXX; Just., A I, 50, 3 for ἰδού Is 52:13] begins in Hom.; s. Kühner-G. I 84, 4) *(you) see,* mostly at the beginning of a sentence, but somet. in the middle (**J 3:26**). It serves

❶ to point out someth. to which the speaker wishes to draw attention, ***look! see!***(Gen 27:6; Sir 28:24) **Mt 25:20, 22; Mk 2:24; 11:21; 13:1; J 5:14; 18:21;** B 8:1; 12:10. ἴ. οὖν B 6:14; 15:7 v.l. W. indir. quest. foll. **J 11:36;** cp. **16:29; 19:4; Gal 5:2;** B 12:11. For εἰ δέ **Ro 2:17 v.l.; Js 3:3 v.l.** (s. BMetzger, A Textual Commentary '71, 507, 681f).W. εἰ foll. *see whether* Hm 11:18ab.

❷ to introduce someth. unexpected, ***take notice*** **J 3:26; 7:26; 11:3; 12:19.**

❸ to indicate a place or individual, ***here is (are)*** (like French voici) ἴ. ὁ τόπος *here is the place* **Mk 16:6.** ἴ. ἡ μήτηρ μου καὶ οἱ ἀδελφοί μου *here are my mother and my brothers* (or *brothers and sisters?* s. ἀδελφός 1; cp. ἴδε τὰ τέκνα σου PsSol 11:1) **3:34;** cp. **Mt 25:20, 22; Mk 11:21; J 1:29, 36, 47; 19:14, 26** s. GDalman, Jesus-Jeshua (tr. PLevertoff) 1929, 201–3. W. adv. of place ἴδε ὧδε … ἴ. ἐκεῖ *here is … there is* **Mk 13:21.**

❹ w. obvious loss of its fundamental mng. as in our colloquial speech, ***see! pay attention!***—ⓐ (schol. on Pla. 130c: Ἀλκιβιάδης, ἴδε, τί λέγει='hear') ἴ. νῦν ἠκούσατε *see, now you have heard=there, now you have heard* **Mt 26:65.** ἴδε πόσα σου κατηγοροῦσιν *see* (listen to) *how many charges they bring against you* **Mk 15:4;** ἴ. Ἠλίαν φωνεῖ *listen, he's calling Elijah* vs. **35.** ἴδε, ὅτι ἄρα τότε καλῶς καταπαυόμενοι ἁγιάσομεν αὐτήν, ὅτε … *pay attention* (to what this means)! *We shall only be able to sanctify (the sabbath) in true rest, when* B 15:7.

ⓑ simply *here* ἴ. ἔχεις τὸ σόν *here, you have what is yours* **Mt 25:25.** S. bibliog. s.v. ἰδού 2, esp. Fiedler; s. also ὁράω.—M-M.

ἰδέα, ας, ἡ (the form εἰδέα is freq. in later Gk.; Pind., Hdt. et al.; pap, LXX, TestAbr; TestBenj 10:1 [deJonge; εἰδέαν Ch.]; AscIs 3:13 [pap col. IX, 3 ἡ εἰδέα]; 4:4 [pap col. XIV, 13f ἐν τῇ εἰδέᾳ]; Philo, Joseph., Just., Ath.—CRitter on εἶδος).

❶ **outward look of someth.,** ***appearance,*** w. focus on physical features (as distinct fr. μορφή, which is freq. used e.g. in assoc. w. suggestion of status or the impression made by it, such as μορφὴ θεοῦ and μορφὴ δούλου Phil 2:6f) (Theognis, Pind. et al.; Artem. 2, 44 φαίνονται οἱ θεοὶ ἐν ἀνθρώπων ἰδέᾳ [v.l. εἰδέᾳ] τε καὶ μορφῇ=the gods show themselves in the semblance and aspect of humans; POxy 1277, 10; Gen 5:3; EpJer 62; 2 Macc 3:16; TestAbr A 11 p. 89, 4 [Stone p. 26]; TestBenj 10:1; Jos., Bell. 3, 508, Ant. 8, 177; Just., A I, 62, 3 ἐν ἰδέᾳ πυρός al.) Hs 9, 17, 1f; ἡ ἰ. αὐτοῦ ἱλαρὰ ἦν *his appearance was pleasant* 6, 1, 6. κατηφὴς τῇ ἰ. *downcast in appearance* Hv 1, 2, 3; cp. s 6, 2, 5; 9, 3, 1. ἠλλοιώθη ἡ ἰ. αὐτοῦ *his appearance changed* v 5:4; cp. **Lk 9:29** D. ἄλλην ἰ. ἔχειν Hs 9, 1, 4. The rendering *face* (cp. Diod. S. 3, 8 of Ethiopians ταῖς ἰδέαις σίμοι; perh. Plut., Flamin. 369 [1, 1]; Field, n. 22) prob. fits **Mt 28:3 v.l.** (for εἰδέα) and Hv 1, 2, 3; s 6, 1, 6; s. εἰδέα.

❷ **a variety of someth.,** ***form, kind*** (Aristoph., Ran. 384 ἑτέρα ὕμνων ἰδέα; Thu. 1, 109, 1; 3, 102, 7; Appian, Mithrid. 22 §87 συμφορῶν ἰδέαι ποικίλαι=various kinds of misfortune, Bell. Civ. 4, 14 §53; 4 Macc 1:14, 18; Philo, Op. M. 22, Praem. 90; Jos., Ant. 15, 416) ἄλλαις βασάνων ἰδέαις *with other kinds of torture(s)* MPol 2:4 (cp. Thu. 3, 81, 5 πᾶσα ἰ. θανάτου).—S. also εἰδέα.—B. 1212. DELG s.v. ἰδεῖν. M-M. TW. Sv.

ἴδιος, ία, ον (Hom.+; s. B-D-F §286; W-S. §22, 17; Rob. 691f; Mlt-Turner 191f.—For the spelling ἴδιος s. on ὀλίγος.)

❶ **pert. to belonging or being related to oneself,** ***one's own*** ⓐ in contrast to what is public property or belongs to another: *private, one's own (exclusively)* (opp. κοινός, as Pla., Pol. 7, 535b; Appian, Bell. Civ. 5, 41 §171; Ath. 25, 4) οὐδὲ εἷς τι τῶν ὑπαρχόντων αὐτῷ ἔλεγεν ἴδιον εἶναι *nor did anyone claim that anything the person had was private property* or *nor did anyone claim ownership of private possessions* **Ac 4:32;** cp. D 4:8.

ⓑ in respect to circumstance or condition *belonging to an individual* (opp. ἀλλότριος) κατὰ τὴν ἰδίαν δύναμιν *according to each one's capability* (in contrast to that of others) **Mt 25:15.** τὴν δόξαν τὴν ἰ. ζητεῖ **J 7:18;** cp. **5:18, 43.** ἕκαστος εἰς τὴν ἰδίαν πόλιν **Lk 2:3 v.l.** (for ἑαυτοῦ); sim. **Mt 9:1** (noting the departure of Jesus to his home territory); cp. Dg 5:2. Christ ἐλευθερώσῃ πᾶσαν σάρκα διὰ τῆς ἰδίας σαρκός AcPlCor 2:6; cp. vs. 16 ἕκαστος τῇ ἰ. διαλέκτῳ ἡμῶν **Ac 2:8;** cp. **1:19** τῇ ἰ. διαλέκτῳ αὐτῶν, without pron. **2:6** (Tat. 26, 1 τὴν ἰ. αὐτῆς … λέξιν); ἰδίᾳ δυνάμει **3:12;** cp. **28:30;** τὴν ἰ. (δικαιοσύνην) **Ro 10:3;** cp. **11:24; 14:4f.** ἕκαστος τ. ἴ. μισθὸν λήμψεται κατὰ τ. ἴ. κόπον *each will receive wages in proportion to each one's labor* **1 Cor 3:8.** ἑκάστη τὸν ἴδιον ἄνδρα *her own husband* **7:2** (Diog. L. 8, 43 πρὸς τὸν ἴδιον ἄνδρα πορεύεσθαι). ἕκαστος ἴδιον ἔχει χάρισμα **7:7.** ἕκαστος τὸ ἴδιον δεῖπνον προλαμβάνει (s. προλαμβάνω 1c) **1 Cor 11:21** (Eratosth.: 241 fgm. 16 Jac. of the festival known as Lagynophoria τὰ κομισθέντα αὐτοῖς δειπνοῦσι κατακλιθέντες … κ. ἐξ ἰδίας ἕκαστος λαγύνου παρ' αὐτῶν φέροντες πίνουσιν 'they dine on the things brought them … and they each drink from a flagon they have personally brought'. Evaluation: συνοίκια ταῦτα ῥυπαρά· ἀνάγκη γὰρ τὴν σύνοδον γίνεσθαι παμμιγοῦς ὄχλου 'that's some crummy banquet; it's certainly a meeting of a motley crew'); cp. **1 Cor 9:7; 15:38.** ἕκαστος τὸ ἴ. φορτίον βαστάσει **Gal 6:5.—Tit 1:12; Hb 4:10; 7:27; 9:12; 13:12.—J 4:44** s. 2 and 3b.

❷ **pert. to a striking connection or an exclusive relationship,** ***own*** (with emphasis when expressed orally, or italicized in written form) κοπιῶμεν ταῖς ἰ. χερσίν *with our own hands* **1 Cor 4:12** (first pers., cp. UPZ 13, 14 [158 BC] εἰμὶ μετὰ τ. ἀδελφοῦ ἰδίου=w. my brother; TestJob 34:3 ἀναχωρήσωμεν εἰς τὰς ἰδίας χώρας). ἐν τῷ ἰ. ὀφθαλμῷ *in your own eye* **Lk**

6:41; 1 Th 2:14; 2 Pt 3:17 (here the stability of the orthodox is contrasted with loss of direction by those who are misled by error). **Ac 1:7** (God's authority in sharp contrast to the apostles' interest in determining a schedule of events). ἰ. θέλημα *own will* and ἰδία καρδία *own heart* or *mind* **1 Cor 7:37ab** contrast with μὴ ἔχων ἀνάγκην 'not being under compulsion'; hence ἰ. is not simply equivalent to the possessive gen. in the phrase ἐν τῇ καρδίᾳ αὐτοῦ. **1 Cor 6:18,** ἰ. heightens the absurdity of sinning against one's own body. **Lk 10:34** (apparently the storyteller suggests that the wealthy Samaritan had more than one animal, but put his own at the service of the injured traveler). ἐπὶ τὸ ἴδιον ἐξέραμα **2 Pt 2:22** (cp. ἐπὶ τὸν ἑαυτοῦ ἔμετον Pr 26:11), with heightening of disgust. Some would put **J 4:44** here (s. 1 end). εἰς τὸν ἴδιον ἀγρόν **Mt 22:5** (the rude guest prefers the amenities of his own estate). **Mk 4:34b** (Jesus' close followers in contrast to a large crowd). **Ac 25:19** (emphasizing the esoteric nature of sectarian disputes). **Js 1:14** (a contrast, not between types of desire but of sources of temptation: those who succumb have only themselves to blame). διὰ τοῦ αἵματος τοῦ ἰδίου *through his own blood* **Ac 20:28** (so NRSV mg.; cp. the phrase SIG 547, 37; 1068, 16 ἐκ τῶν ἰδίων commonly associated with the gifts of generous officials, s. 4b. That the 'blood' would be associated with Jesus would be quite apparent to Luke's publics).

❸ pert. to a person, through substitution for a pronoun, *own.* Some of the passages cited in 2 may belong here. ἴ. is used for the gen. of αὐτός or the possess. pron., or for the possess. gen. ἑαυτοῦ, ἑαυτῶν (this use found in Hellenistic wr. [Schmidt 369], in Attic [Meisterhans³-Schw. 235] and Magnesian [Thieme 28f] ins; pap [Kuhring—s. ἀνά beg.—14; Mayser II/2, 73f]. S. also Dssm., B 120f [BS 123f], and against him Mlt. 87–91. LXX oft. uses ἴ. without emphasis to render the simple Hebr. personal suffix [Gen 47:18; Dt 15:2; Job 2:11; 7:10, 13; Pr 6:2 al.], but somet. also employs it without any basis for it in the original text [Job 24:12; Pr 9:12; 22:7; 27:15]. Da 1:10, where LXX has ἴ., Theod. uses μου. 1 Esdr 5:8 εἰς τὴν ἰδίαν πόλιν=2 Esdr 2:1 εἰς πόλιν αὐτοῦ; **Mt 9:1** is formally sim., but its position in the narrative suggests placement in 1)

ⓐ with the second pers. (Jos., Bell. 6, 346 ἰδίαις χερσίν=w. your own hands). **Eph 5:22** (cp. vs. 28 τὰς ἑαυτῶν γυναῖκας); **1 Th 4:11; 1 Pt 3:1.**

ⓑ with the third pers. ἐν τῇ ἰδίᾳ πατρίδι **J 4:44** (cp. ἐν τῇ πατρίδι αὐτοῦ: Mt 13:57; Mk 6:4; Lk 4:24, but **J 4:44** is expressed in a slightly difft. form and may therefore belong in 1b above); **Mt 25:14; 15:20 v.l.; J 1:41** (UPZ 13, s. 2 above: ἀδ. ἴ.); **Ac 1:19; 24:24; 1 Ti 6:1; Tit 2:5, 9; 1 Pt 3:5;** MPol 17:3; AcPl Ha 3, 21; 4, 27 (context uncertain); τὸ ἴδιον πλάσμα AcPlCor 2:12, 1; ἴδιον χωρίον Papias (3:3).

❹ as subst., **person or thing associated with an entity**

ⓐ ***associates, relations*** οἱ ἴδιοι (comrades in battle: Polyaenus, Exc. 14, 20; SIG 709, 19; 22; 2 Macc 12:22; Jos., Bell. 1, 42, Ant. 12, 405; compatriots: ViHab 5 [p. 86, 7 Sch.]; Philo, Mos. 1, 177) fellow-Christians **Ac 4:23; 24:23** (Just., D. 121, 3). The disciples (e.g., of a philosopher: Epict. 3, 8, 7) **J 13:1.** Relatives (BGU 37; POxy 932; PFay 110; 111; 112; 116; 122 al.; Vett. Val. 70, 5 ὑπὸ ἰδίων κ. φίλων; Sir 11:34; Just., A II, 7, 2 σὺν τοῖς ἰδίοις . . . Νῶε and D. 138, 2 Νῶε . . . μετὰ τῶν ἰδίων) **1 Ti 5:8; J 1:11b** (the worshipers of a god are also so called: Herm. Wr. 1, 31).—Sg. τὸν ἴδιον **J 15:19 v.l.** (s. b below).

ⓑ ***home, possessions*** τὰ ἴδια *home* (Polyb. 2, 57, 5; 3, 99, 4; Appian, Iber. 23; Peripl. Eryth. 65 εἰς τὰ ἴδια; POxy 4, 9f ἡ ἀνωτέρα ψυχὴ τ. ἴδια γεινώσκει; 487, 18; Esth 5:10; 6:12; 1 Esdr 6:31 [τὰ ἴδια αὐτοῦ=2 Esdr 6:11 ἡ οἰκία αὐτοῦ]; 3 Macc 6:27, 37; 7:8; Jos., Ant. 8, 405; 416, Bell. 1, 666; 4, 528) **J 16:32** (EFascher, ZNW 39, '41, 171–230); **19:27; Ac 5:18** D; **14:18 v.l.; 21:6;** AcPl Ha 8, 5. Many (e.g. Goodsp, Probs. 87f; 94–96; Field, Notes 84; RSV; but not Bultmann 34f; NRSV) prefer this sense for **J 1:11a** and **Lk 18:28;** another probability in both these pass. is *property, possessions* (POxy 489, 4; 490, 3; 491, 3; 492, 4 al.). ἐκ τῶν ἰδίων *from his own well-stocked supply* (oft. in ins e.g. fr. Magn. and Priene, also SIG 547, 37; 1068, 16 [in such ins the focus is on the generosity of public-spirited officals who use their own resources to meet public needs]; Jos., Ant. 12, 158) **J 8:44.** The sg. can also be used in this way τὸ ἴδιον (SIG 1257, 3; BGU 1118, 31 [22 BC]) **J 15:19** (v.l. τὸν ἴδιον, s. a above).—τὰ ἴδια *one's own affairs* (X., Mem. 3, 4, 12; 2 Macc 9:20; 11:23 v.l., 26, 29) **1 Th 4:11,** here πράσσειν τὰ ἴδια=*mind your own business.*—**Jd 6** of one's proper sphere.

❺ pert. to a particular individual, *by oneself, privately,* adv. ἰδίᾳ (Aristoph., Thu.; Diod. S. 20, 21, 5 et al.; ins, pap, 2 Macc 4:34; Philo; Jos., Bell. 4, 224, C. Ap. 1, 225; Ath. 8, 1f) **1 Cor 12:11;** IMg 7:1.—κατ' ἰδίαν (Machon, fgm. 11 vs. 121 [in Athen. 8, 349b]; Polyb. 4, 84, 8; Diod. S. 1, 21, 6; also ins [SIG 1157, 12 καὶ κατὰ κοινὸν καὶ κατ' ἰδίαν ἑκάστῳ al.]; 2 Macc 4:5; 14:21; JosAs 7:1; Philo, Sacr. Abel. 136; Just., D. 5, 2) *privately, by oneself* (opp. κοινῇ: Jos., Ant. 4, 310) **Mt 14:13, 23; 17:1, 19; 20:17; 24:3; Mk 4:34a; 6:31f; 7:33** (Diod. S. 18, 49, 2 ἕκαστον ἐκλαμβάνων κατ' ἰδίαν='he took each one aside'); **9:2** (w. μόνος added), **28; 13:3; Lk 9:10; 10:23; Ac 23:19; Gal 2:2** (on the separate meeting cp. Jos., Bell. 2, 199 τ. δυνατοὺς κατ' ἰδίαν κ. τὸ πλῆθος ἐν κοινῷ συλλέγων; Appian, Bell. Civ. 5, 40 §170); ISm 7:2.

❻ pert. to being distinctively characteristic of some entity, *belonging to/peculiar to an individual* ἕκαστον δένδρον ἐκ τ. ἰδίου καρποῦ γινώσκεται *every tree is known by its own fruit* **Lk 6:44.** τὰ ἴδια πρόβατα *his (own) sheep* **J 10:3f.** εἰς τὸν τόπον τ. ἴδιον *to his own place* (*=the place where he belonged*) **Ac 1:25;** cp. **20:28.** The expression τοῦ ἰδίου υἱοῦ οὐκ ἐφείσατο **Ro 8:32** emphasizes the extraordinary nature of God's gift: *did not spare his very own Son* (Paul's association here with the ref. to pandemic generosity, ὑπὲρ ἡμῶν πάντων παρέδωκεν αὐτόν, contributes a semantic component to ἰ. in this pass.; for the pandemic theme see e.g. OGI 339, 29f; for donation of one's own resources, ibid. 104; IGR 739, II, 59–62. For the term ὁ ἴδιος υἱός, but in difft. thematic contexts, see e.g. Diod. S. 17, 80, 1 of Parmenio; 17, 118, 1 of Antipater. In relating an instance in which a son was not spared Polyaenus 8, 13 has υἱὸς αὐτοῦ, evidently without emphasis, but Exc. 3, 7 inserts ἴδιος υἱός to emphasize the gravity of an officer's own son violating an order.). **1 Cor 7:4ab.** ἕκαστος ἐν. τ. ἰδίῳ τάγματι *each one in his (own) turn* **15:23** (cp. En 2:1 τ. ἰ. τάξιν). καιροὶ ἴδιοι *the proper time* (cp. Diod. S. 1, 50, 7 ἐν τοῖς ἰδίοις χρόνοις; likew. 5, 80, 3; Jos., Ant. 11, 171; Ps.-Clemens, Hom. 3, 16; TestSol 6:3 ἐν καιρῷ ἰ.; Just., D. 131, 4 πρὸ τῶν ἰ. καιρῶν; Mel., P. 38, 258ff) **1 Ti 2:6; 6:15; Tit 1:3;** 1 Cl 20:4; cp. **1 Ti 3:4f, 12; 4:2; 5:4.** ἴδιαι λειτουργίαι . . . ἴδιος ὁ τόπος . . . ἴδιαι διακονίαι in each case *proper: ministrations, . . . place, . . . services* 1 Cl 40:5.—In ἰδία ἐπίλυσις **2 Pt 1:20** one's *own private interpretation* is contrasted with the meaning intended by the author himself or with the interpretation of another person who is authorized or competent (s. ἐπίλυσις and WWeeda, NThSt 2, 1919, 129–35).—All these pass. are close to mng. 3; it is esp. difficult to fix the boundaries here.—DELG. M-M. EDNT. TW. Spicq. Sv.

ἰδίως adv. of ἴδιος (Pla. et al.; Hero Alex. I p. 432, 4; SIG 1002, 13; Wsd 17:10 v.l.; Philo, Plant. 13, Migr. Abr. 50; Just., A I, 22, 2 al. [opp. κοινῶς]; Ath., R. 70, 15 al.) ***in a special way,***

especially ἀγαπᾶν B 4:6; perh. ἰ. is intended to form a contrast to πάντας, in which case it could mean *individually.*

ἰδιώτης, ου, ὁ (s. ἴδιος; Hdt.+; loanw. in rabb.).—❶ **a person who is relatively unskilled or inexperienced in some activity or field of knowledge,** ***layperson, amateur*** in contrast to an expert or specialist of any kind (the uncrowned person in contrast to the king [Hdt. 2, 81; 7, 199; EpArist 288f; Philo, Decal. 40; Jos., Bell. 1, 665]; private soldier in contrast to an officer [Polyb. 1, 69, 11]; in contrast to a physician [Thu. 2, 48, 3; Philo, Conf. Lingu. 22], philosopher [Plut., Mor. 776e; Epict., index Sch.; Philo, Omn. Prob. Lib. 3; Just., A II, 10, 8], orator [Isocr. 4, 11; Lucian, Jupp. Trag. 27], the μάντις [Paus. 2, 13, 7], poet [Alexis Com. 269; Pla., Laws 890a], priest [OGI 90, 52; Philo, Spec. Leg. 3, 134], educated person [Lucian, Lexiph. 25]: any person who does not belong to any one of these groups. Civilian in contrast to soldier [Jos., Bell. 2, 178], private citizen in contrast to an official [Sb 3924, 9; 25; POxy 1409, 14]) ἰ. τῷ λόγῳ *unskilled in speaking* (cp. Jos., Ant. 2, 271 of Moses: ἰ. . . . λόγοις) **2 Cor 11:6** (WGemoll, PhilolWoch 52, '32, 28; cp. WRoberts, Longinus on the Sublime 1899, 200 s.v. ἰδιώτης). (W. ἄνθρωπος ἀγράμματος) *an untrained person* **Ac 4:13** (Just., A I, 39, 3; 60, 11; Ath. II, 3).

❷ **one who is not knowledgeable about some particular group's experience,** ***one not in the know, outsider.*** In **1 Cor 14:23f** ἰδιῶται and ἄπιστοι together form a contrast to the Christian congregation. The ἰ. are neither similar to the ἄπιστοι (against Ltzm., Hdb. ad loc.), nor are they full-fledged Christians, but stand betw. the two groups, prob. as prospects for membership and are therefore relatively outsiders (ἰδιώτης as a t.t. of religious life e.g. OGI 90, 52 [196 BC], SIG 1013, 6; mystery ins fr. Andania [92 BC]: SIG 736, 16–19 αἱ μὲν ἰδιώτιες . . . αἱ δὲ ἱεραί. In relig. associations the term is used for nonmembers who may participate in the sacrifices: FPoland, Gesch. des griech. Vereinswesens 1909, 247*; 422.—Cp. also Cratin. Iun. Com. [IV BC] fgm. 7 vol. II 291 K. of the Pythagoreans: ἔθος ἐστὶν αὐτοῖς, ἂν τιν' ἰδιώτην ποθὲν λάβωσιν εἰσελθόντα κτλ.). The closer relation which they, in contrast to the ἄπιστοι, held w. the Christian group (so as early as Severian of Gabala [died after 409 AD]: KStaab, Pauluskommentare aus. d. griech. Kirche '33, p. xxxv; 268) is clearly shown by the fact that they had a special place in the room where the Christians assembled **1 Cor 14:16** (PTomson, Paul and the Jewish Law [CRINT III/1] '90, 142–44; ἀναπληρόω 4).—DELG s.v. ἴδιος. M-M. TW. Spicq. Sv.

ἰδιωτικός, ή, όν (s. ἴδιος; Hdt. et al.; ins, pap; 4 Macc 4:3, 6; Philo, In Flacc. 133 πράγματα [opp. δημόσια]; Jos., Bell. 5, 228; Just., A II, 3, 3) ***private*** θλίψεις ἰ. *troubles of one's own* Hv 2, 3, 1.—DELG s.v. ἴδιος. M-M. s.v. ἰδιώτης.

ἰδού demonstrative or presentative particle that draws attention to what follows (Soph.+). It is actually the aor. mid. impv. of εἶδον, ἰδοῦ, except that it is accented w. the acute when used as a particle (Schwyzer I 799) '(you) see, look, behold' (for var. renderings see e.g. ESiegman, CBQ 9, '47, 77f, fr. RKnox's transl.).

❶ **prompter of attention,** ***behold, look, see.*** Like הִנֵּה it somet. serves to enliven a narrative—ⓐ by arousing the attention of hearers or readers (in 1 Cl, 2 Cl, and B only in quots. fr. the OT) **Lk 22:10; J 4:35; 1 Cor 15:51; 2 Cor 5:17; Js 5:9; Jd 14; Rv 1:7; 9:12; 11:14;** Hv 1, 3, 4 al.

ⓑ by introducing someth. new or unusual—**α.** after a gen. abs., in order to introduce someth. new, which calls for special attention in the situation generally described by the gen. abs.: **Mt 1:20; 2:1, 13; 9:18; 12:46; 17:5; 26:47; 28:11.**

β. with other constructions: καὶ ἰδού **Mt 2:9; 3:16; 4:11; 8:2, 24, 29, 32, 34; 9:2, 3, 20** al.; **Lk 1:20, 31, 36; 2:25; 9:30, 38; 10:25** al.; **Ac 12:7; 16:1;** PEg[2] 32. Also someth. quite extraordinary *and yet* ὡς ἀποθνῄσκοντες κ. ἰδοὺ ζῶμεν **2 Cor 6:9;** cp. **Mt 7:4; Ac 27:24** (contrary to all appearances).

γ. introducing whole stories: **Mt 13:3.**

δ. in the middle of a statement, and at the same time enlivening it **Mt 23:34; Ac 2:7; 13:11; 20:22, 25.**

ε. w. emphasis on the size or importance of someth. (freq. omitted in transl., but w. some loss of mng.) ἰ. ἡμεῖς ἀφήκαμεν πάντα **Mt 19:27; Mk 10:28.** ἰ. δέκα κ. ὀκτὼ ἔτη *eighteen long years* **Lk 13:16** (cp. BGU 948, 6 ἡ μήτηρ σου ἀσθενεῖ, ἰδοὺ δέκα τρεῖς μῆνες; Dt 8:4); vs. **7; 15:29; 19:8; 2 Cor 12:14.**—καὶ ἰ. ἐγὼ μεθ' ὑμῶν εἰμι πάσας τὰς ἡμέρας **Mt 28:20;** cp. **20:18; 23:38; Lk 2:34; 6:23; 13:30** al.

ⓒ as a call to closer consideration and contemplation *remember, consider,* etc. **Mt 10:16; 11:8; 22:4; Mk 14:41; Lk 2:48; 7:25;** Hv 2, 3, 4. Likew. ἰδοὺ γάρ **Lk 1:44, 48; 2:10; Ac 9:11; 2 Cor 7:11;** AcPl Ha 6, 19. The citing of examples **Js 3:4f; 5:4, 7, 11** belongs here. Variants in **3:3** include ἴδε (q.v.) and ἰδοῦ; the text has εἰ δέ.

❷ **marker of strong emphasis,** ***see*** used w. a noun without a finite verb, as in our colloquial 'see!' 'what do you know!' 'of all things!' 'wonder of wonders!' The term can be rendered *here* or *there is (are), here* or *there was (were)* or *there comes (came),* but oral rendition requires emphasis so as to express the nuance in the source text (old Attic ins in Meisterhans[3]-Schw. p. 203 ἰδοὺ χελιδών; Epict. 4, 11, 35; UPZ 78, 25 [159 BC]; LXX) καὶ ἰ. φωνὴ ἐκ τ. οὐρανῶν *and, see, a voice came from heaven* or *and a voice came right from heaven* **Mt 3:17.** καὶ ἰ. ἄνθρωπος *and there was a man* **Mt 12:10.** ἰ. ἄνθρωπος φάγος *Look! A glutton!* **11:19; Lk 7:34;** cp. **5:12, 18; 7:37; 11:31; 13:11; 17:21a; 19:2, 20; 22:38, 47; 23:50; Ac 8:27** (WCvanUnnik, ZNW 47, '56, 181–91), **36; 2 Cor 6:2; Rv 12:3; 21:3.** ἰ. ὁ νυμφίος *here is the bridegroom* **Mt 25:6.** ἰ. ὁ ἄνθρωπος *here is the man* **J 19:5.** In **Rv** as a formula εἶδον κ. ἰδού **4:1; 6:2, 5, 8; 7:9; 14:14;** cp. **19:11.** The godly pers. answers ἰ. ἐγώ *here I am* to the divine call, in order to signify willingness to obey God's command (1 Km 3:4; TestJob 3:2) **Ac 9:10.** (In Mt ἰ. is found 62 times, in Mk 7 times [and also as **v.l. Mk 13:23** and **15:35**], in Lk 57 times, in J 4 times [including once in a quot.], in Ac 23 times, in Paul 9 times [including once in a quot.], Hb 4 times in quotations, Js 6 times, Jd once, 1 Pt once in a quot., Rv 26 times; it is not found at all in 1–3J, 2 Pt, Eph, Phil, Col, 1 and 2 Th, Pastorals, Phlm, Dg, Ign, Pol). S. Mlt. 11, w. note 1; MJohannessohn, ZVS 64, '37, 145–260; 66, '39, 145–95; 67, '40, 30–84 (esp. on καὶ ἰδού); PVannutelli, Synoptica 2, '38, xlvi–lii: ἰδού in the Syn. Gosp.; PFiedler, D. Formel 'Und Siehe' im NT: Studien z. A. u. NT 20, '69; AVargas-Machucha, (καὶ) ἰδού en el estilo narrativo de Mt, Biblica 50, '69, 233–44. See ἴδε.—DELG s.v. ἰδεῖν. M-M.

Ἰδουμαία, ας, ἡ *Idumea,* Grecized form (Diod. S. 19, 95, 2 al.; Appian, Mithrid. 106 §499; LXX; Joseph.) of אֱדוֹם (Edom); a mountainous district south of Judea **Mk 3:8.**

ἱδρόω 1 aor. impv. ἱδρωσάτω (s. ἱδρώς; Hom. et al.; POxy 1242, 52; 4 Macc 3:8; 6:11) ***sweat, perspire*** fig. ἱδρωσάτω ἡ ἐλεημοσύνη σου εἰς τὰς χεῖράς σου *let your alms sweat in your hands,* i.e., do not give alms without due consideration D 1:6 (quot. of unknown orig.; cp. SibOr 2, 79; Mt 7:6.—S. ἐλεημοσύνη 2.).—DELG s.v. ἱδρώω.

ἱδρύω pf. pass. ptc. ἱδρυμένος (Hom.+; ins [e.g. IAndrosIsis, Kyme 24]; PGiss 99, 16; 4 Macc 17:3; TestJob 10:1; 32:7; Philo; Jos., Ant. 1, 60, C. Ap. 2, 36; Just.; Ath. 14, 1) act. 'cause to sit down', in our lit. only pass. ***be seated, sit, be established.*** Perf. pass. *be established* of faith ἵδρυται *it is established* Dg 11:6. ὁ ἱδρυμένος αὐτοῖς τόπος *the place established for them* 1 Cl 44:5.—DELG.

ἱδρώς, ῶτος, ὁ (s. ἱδρόω; Hom.+; PGM 5, 152 ἱ. ... ἐπὶ τ. γῆν; LXX; JosAs; Philo; Jos., Bell. 3, 5, Ant. 7, 282) ***sweat, perspiration*** **Lk 22:44** (Just., D. 103, 8. On this LBrun, ZNW 32, '33, 265–76.—Bloody sweat [JosAs 4:11] as an extraordinary phenomenon: Apollon. Rhod. 4, 1284 of images; Appian, Bell. Civ. 4, 4 §14).—διὰ κόπου καὶ ἱδρῶτος (cp. Philo, Leg. All. 3, 251) B 10:4. RBrown, SPSBL '92, 158f.—B. 264. DELG s.v. ἱδρώω. M-M.

Ἰεζάβελ, ἡ (also Ἰεζαβήλ) indecl. (אִיזֶבֶל; 3 Km 16:31 al.—In Joseph. Ἰεζαβέλη, ης [Ant. 8, 356]) ***Jezebel,*** Ahab's queen, who favored the cult of the Phoenician Baal in Israel and persecuted the prophets of Yahweh (3 Km 16– 4 Km 9), and who was also addicted to whoredom and magic (4 Km 9:22). Hence the name was applied to a woman who endangered orthodox teaching within the Christian community at Thyatira **Rv 2:20.** ESchürer (Weizsäcker Festschr. 1892, 39–58) considers that the name refers to a prophetess of the temple of the Chaldaean Sibyl in that city. Zahn, in Einl.[3] II 620ff and in his comm., prefers the rdg. γυναῖκά σου and takes it to mean the bishop's wife.—S. Kraft, Hdb. '74 ad loc.; on alleged assoc. of J. w. witchcraft, s. PDuff, NTS 43, '97, 116–33; Mussies 889–92; DDD s.v. Jezebel.—M-M. TW.

Ἰεζεκιήλ, ὁ indecl. (יְחֶזְקֵאל; Just.; Mel., HE 4, 26, 14; in Joseph. Ἰεζεκίηλος) ***Ezekiel,*** OT prophet (Ezk 1:3) 1 Cl 17:1. λέγει ἡ γραφὴ ἐν τῷ Ἰεζεκιήλ 2 Cl 6:8 (on the quot. fr. Ezk 14:14, 16, 18 s. Knopf, Hdb. ad loc.).

Ἱεράπολις, εως, ἡ (also Ἱερὰ Πόλις; B-D-F §115, 2 advance the sp. Ἱερᾷ πόλει; s. Mlt-H. 278) ***Hierapolis,*** a city in Phrygia in Asia Minor, on the Lycus R. (Antig. Car. 174 ἐν Ἱεραπόλει; SibOr 5, 318; 12, 280; Altertümer v. Hierap.: Jahrb. d. Deutsch. Arch. Inst., Ergänzungsheft 4, 1898; SJohnson, BA 13, '50, 12–18) **Col 4:13;** s. νέος 5 and Ἡλιούπολις; Papias (2 and 9). Παπίας Ἱεραπόλεως ἐπίσκοπος Papias (11:1); cp. (9; 12:2).—BHHW II 717f; Kl. Pauly II 1129f; PECS 390f.—M-M.

Ἱεραπολίτης, ου, ὁ (Aa 1, 90, 1 v.l.) ***inhabitant of Hierapolis*** Παπίας ... ὁ Ἱεραπολίτης Papias (6 and 7). S. Ἱεράπολις.

ἱερατεία, ας, ἡ (s. two next entries; Aristot., Pol. 7, 8 p. 1328b, 12f; Dionys. Hal. 2, 73; ins fr. before 335 BC [IPriene 139, 7], cp. OGI 90, 52; SIG index IV p. 390a; PTebt 298, 14; LXX, Test12Patr) ***priestly office/service*** κατὰ τὸ ἔθος τῆς ἱ. *according to the custom of the priestly office* **Lk 1:9.** τὴν ἱ. λαμβάνειν *receive the priestly office* (cp. Dionys. Hal. loc. cit. παραλαμβάνει τὴν ἱερατείαν ὁ δοκιμασθείς) **Hb 7:5.**—*Priesthood* **Rv 5:10 v.l.**—Frisk s.v. ἱερός. M-M. TW.

ἱεράτευμα, ατος, τό (s. next entry; only in the Gk. of Bibl. wr. and others dependent on them) ***priesthood*** οἰκοδομεῖσθαι εἰς ἱ. ἅγιον *be built up into a holy priesthood* **1 Pt 2:5;** βασίλειον ἱ. *a priesthood of royal rank* or *in royal service* vs. **9** (Ex 19:6; 23:22; cp. Mel., P. 68, 494 [Christ.]). PDabin, Le sacerdoce royal des fidèles dans l. livres saints '41, 179–97; WArndt, CTM 19, '48, 241–49; JBlinzler, Episcopus [Faulhaber Festschr.] '49, 49–65; JElliott, The Elect and the Holy (1 Pt 2:4–10) '66, A Home for the Homeless '81, esp. p. 168: ἱ. focuses on the dedication of God's people to ἀγαθοποιΐα.—Frisk s.v. ἱερός. M-M. TW.

ἱερατεύω fut. ἱερατεύσω; 1 aor. sg. ἱεράτευσα TestLevi 12:5 (s. ἱερός and prec. two entries; late Gk. word: Herodian 5, 6, 3; Heliod. 10, 40 al.; ins fr. II BC: OGI 90, 51 [196 BC]; IMagnMai 178, 6 [II BC]; other exx. fr. ins in Dssm., NB 43 [BS 215f]; PGiss 11, 10 [118 AD]; PKöln 81 [105/104 BC] of a priesthood held by queen Cleopatra; LXX; Test12Patr; Jos., Ant. 3, 189; 15, 253; Just., A I, 62, 2) ***hold the office*** or ***perform the service of a priest*** **Lk 1:8.** W. λειτουργεῖν 1 Cl 43:4.—Frisk s.v. ἱερός. New Docs 4, 156 (ins). M-M. TW.

Ἰερεμίας, ου, ὁ (also Ἱερ-; יִרְמְיָה, יִרְמְיָהוּ; LXX; ParJer; EpArist 50; Philo, Cher. 49; Joseph., Just., Mel.; Ath. 9, 1) ***Jeremiah,*** prophet at the time of the fall of the Judean state ῥηθὲν διὰ Ἰερεμίου τοῦ προφήτου (cp. Jos., Ant. 11, 1; Just., A I, 51, 8 and D. 72, 2) **Mt 2:17; 27:9** (v.l. Ἠσαΐου). Some of Jesus' compatriots considered that he was Jeremiah come again (s. Billerb. I 730) **Mt 16:14.**—HSparks, JTS n.s. 1, '50, 155f; JCarmignac, KKuhn Festschr., '71, 283–98.—TW.

ἱερεύς, έως, ὁ (Hom.+; acc. -έαν GJs 15:2) ***priest*****—ⓐ** lit., w. focus on cultic function**—α.** of Gr-Rom. priests (Demetr.: 722 fgm. 1, 12 Jac.; Tat. 36, 1 Βηρωσσός al.; Ath. 28, 1) **Ac 14:13;** 1 Cl 25:5. οἱ ἱερεῖς τ. εἰδώλων B 9:6.

β. of Israel's priests (Diod. S. 40, 3, 4 and 5); ordinary: ὁ ἱερεύς *the priest* who officiates in a given situation (Lev 13:2ff; Just., D. 115, 3 al.) **Mt 8:4; Mk 1:44; Lk 5:14.** Otherwise of an individual priest **1:5; 10:31; Hb 8:4; 10:11** (v.l. ἀρχι-). Pl. **Mt 12:4f; Mk 2:26; Lk 6:4; 17:14; 20:1 v.l.; J 1:19; 8:4** D; **Ac 4:1** (v.l. ἀρχι-); **6:7; Hb 7:14f, 20, 23; 9:6;** GPt 7:25; B 7:4 (quot. of unknown orig.; s. Windisch ad loc.), vs. 6 (cp. Lev. 16:5). IPhld 9:1; GJs 4:3; 6:2 (twice); 8:2 (twice); 10:1; 24:1 (twice), 2, 4. W. Λευῖται 1 Cl 32:2 (cp. **Lk 10:31** and 32: Named before the Levites as Jos., Ant. 11, 80f and oft. in Joseph. [Schmidt 358]). W. the Lev. and the ἀρχιερεύς 40:5. οἱ ἱ. τοῦ ναοῦ B 7:3.—Of the high priest (Diod. S. 34 + 35 fgm. 1, 3; 3 Km 1:8; Bar 1:7; 1 Macc 15:1) **Ac 5:27** D. Ἀαρὼν ὁ ἱερεύς (cp. Ex 35:19; Lev 13:2.—ἱ. also of Gr-Rom. high priests in Mayser II/2 p. 465; Appian, Bell. Civ. 4, 134 §562 Caesar, the Pontifex Maximus, is called a ἱ.; Synes., Prov. 2, 3 p. 122a) GEb 13, 75 (s. GHb 361, 7 servus sacerdotis); GJs 5:1 (twice); 7:2; 8:3; 9:1 (three times), 2; 10:1 (three times); 12:1 (twice); 15:2 (foll. by ἀρχιερεύς, q.v.; s. also HGreeven, NTS 6, '60, 295f).

ⓑ fig. ext. of a**—α.** of Christ, who is called in **Hb** ἱερεύς (in sense aβ; s. 5:5f; Just., D. 34, 2 al.) εἰς τὸν αἰῶνα κατὰ τὴν τάξιν Μελχισέδεκ (Ps 109:4) **5:6; 7:17, 21;** also ἱερεὺς μέγας (1 Macc 12:20; cp. Sir 50:1; Jdth 4:6, 8, 14; Philo, Spec. Leg. 1, 161 al.=ἀρχιερεύς) **10:21.** Cp. also **7:1, 3, 11** and s. ἀρχιερεύς 2a; CSpicq, MGoguel Festschr. '50, 258–69.

β. of the Christians ἱερεῖς τοῦ θεοῦ *priests of God* **Rv 20:6;** cp. **1:6; 5:10** (Diog. L. 7, 119: acc. to the Stoa the σοφοί are the only real priests).—AGunneweg, Leviten u. Priester '65; B. 1472.—Frisk s.v. ἱερός. M-M. EDNT. TW. Sv.

Ἰεριχώ, ἡ (also Ἱερ-, Ἰερειχώ, Ἱερειχώ) indecl. (יְרִיחוֹ; LXX; Just., D. 111, 4. On the word s. W-S. §10, 1a. Joseph. varies betw. Ἱεριχώ, gen. -οῦς and Ἱεριχοῦς, gen. -οῦντος; s. Niese index. Ἱεριχοῦς, -οῦντος also Galen XI 693 K. and Steph. Byz. s.v., but in Strabo 16, 2, 41 Ἱερικοῦς. On the spelling s. B-D-F §38) ***Jericho,*** a city in Judea, not far from the ford across the Jordan just north of the Dead Sea **Mt 20:29; Mk 10:46; Lk 18:35; Hb 11:30;** 1 Cl 12:2. Since a much-traveled road led to Jerusalem, 150 stades (Jos., Bell. 4, 474) or about 30 km. away, a customs house was located here **Lk 19:1.** The road fr. Jerusalem to Jericho, which leads through desolate mountainous country

(Jos., loc. cit. ἔρημον κ. πετρῶδες), was notoriously unsafe **Lk 10:30** (AvVeldhuizen, TSt 25, 1907, 41–43).—ESellin and CWatzinger, Jericho 1913; Dalman, Orte[3] 257ff; PThomsen, Jericho: Reallex. d. Vorgesch. VI 196, 153ff; JPritchard, The 1951 Campaign at Herodian Jer.: BASOR no. 123, '51, 8–17; JKelso, NT Jericho: BA 14, '51, 34–43; LMowry, ibid. 15, '52, 26–42.—BHHW II 816–19. OEANE III 220–24.

ἱερόθυτος, ον (s. ἱερός, θύω; Pind., fgm. 66 [OxfT=78 S-M.] refers to death for one's homeland as ἱερόθυτος θάνατος; this is one of the earliest extant occurrences of the word; SIG 624, 43; 736, 23; PGM 4, 2899) ***devoted/sacrificed to a divinity,*** subst. τὸ ἱ. *meat sacrificed to idols* (Ps.-Aristot., Mirabilia 123 p. 824b, 1f; Plut., Mor. 729c ἐγεύοντο τῶν ἱεροθύτων) **1 Cor 10:28.**—M-M. TW.

ἱερόν, οῦ, τό (subst. neut. of the adj. ἱερός, q.v.) ***sanctuary, temple*** (so Hdt.+)—ⓐ of Gr-Rom. temples (Diod. S. 13, 7, 6 τ. Διὸς ἱερόν; Appian, Liby. 81 §383 al.; Bel 22 Theod.; 1 Macc 10:84; Philo, Leg. ad Gai. 139 al.; Jos., Ant. 18, 65; Just., A I, 9, 5; Ath. 14, 2) the temple of Artemis at Ephesus (s. b end, below) **Ac 19:27.**

ⓑ of the temple at Jerusalem, including the whole temple precinct w. its buildings, courts, etc. (LXX; Ezk 45:19; 1 Ch 29:4 and oft. in the Apocrypha; TestSol; EpArist; Philo, Joseph.; Just., A I, 32, 6 τὸ μέγιστον ἱ. . . . τῶν Ἰουδαίων; Polyb. 16, 39, 4; Diod. S. 40, 3, 3; Strabo 16, 2, 34; OGI 598, 3; PGM 13, 233) **Mt 12:6; 21:23; 24:1b; Mk 11:27; 12:35; 13:3; Lk 2:46; 20:1; 21:5; J 8:20; 11:56; 18:20; Ac 24:6; 25:8;** Ox 840, 9. στρατηγὸς τ. ἱεροῦ *captain of the temple* (Jos., Bell. 6, 294) **Ac 4:1; 5:24;** pl. **Lk 22:52.** ἀναβαίνειν εἰς τὸ ἱ. **Lk 18:10; J 7:14; Ac 3:1.** εἰσάγειν εἰς τὸ ἱ. **21:28f.** (εἰσ)ελθεῖν εἰς τὸ ἱ. **Mt 21:12a, 23; Mk 11:11, 15a; Lk 2:27; 19:45; Ac 3:8; 5:21.** εἰσιέναι εἰς τὸ ἱ. **3:3; 21:26.** εἰσπορεύεσθαι εἰς τὸ ἱ. **3:2b.** παραγίνεσθαι εἰς τὸ ἱ. **J 8:2.** ἐξελθεῖν ἀπὸ τοῦ ἱ. **Mt 24:1a;** ἐκ τοῦ ἱ. **J 8:59;** ἐκπορεύεσθαι ἐκ τοῦ ἱ. **Mk 13:1.** Cp. **Mt 26:55; Mk 14:49; Lk 19:47; 21:37; 22:53; 24:53; J 5:14; 7:28; Ac 2:46; 3:2a; 5:20, 25, 42; 21:27; 22:17; 24:12, 18; 26:21.** ἔξω τοῦ ἱ. **Ac 21:30.** As the place where the priests worked **Mt 12:5.** Provided w. porticoes **J 10:23.** Even when the action takes place in the Court of the Gentiles, where merchants and money-changers had their places **Mt 21:12** (s. also vss. **14** and **15); Mk 11:15f; Lk 19:45; J 2:14f,** or in the Court of Women **Lk 2:37,** the choice of the word ἱ. emphasizes the fact that the holy precinct is the scene of the action (τὸ ἱ. w. ὁ ναός the temple bldg: Jos., Bell. 2, 400. On the cleansing of the temple s. ACaldecott, JTS 24, 1923, 382ff; FBurkitt, ibid. 25, 1924, 386ff; FBraun, RB 38, 1929, 178–200; ELohmeyer, ThBl 20, '41, 257–64.—Appian, Bell. Civ. 2, 120 §507 ἐν τοῖς ἱεροῖς robbers encamp in the temples; Ep. 65 of Apollonius of Tyana [Philostrat. I 363, 23] the ἱερόν of Artemis at Ephesus as τῶν ἀποστερούντων μυχός=hideaway for robbers). On τὸ πτερύγιον τοῦ ἱεροῦ (**Mt 4:5; Lk 4:9;** PEg[3] 8 [πτερύγιον restored]) s. πτερύγιον. On ἐπὶ τῇ ὡραίᾳ πύλῃ τοῦ ἱ. **Ac 3:10** s. ὡραῖος 2.

ⓒ in a gener. sense, whether polytheistic or monotheistic: τὰ ἐκ τοῦ ἱ. ἐσθίειν **1 Cor 9:13** (s. JMoffatt, Comm.).—PJoüon, Les mots employés pour désigner 'le temple' dans AT, NT et Josèphe: RSR 25, '35, 329–43; OWolf, D. Tempel v. Jerus. '31; ELohmeyer, Kultus u. Evglm, '42; GMay, ET 62, '50f, 346f; CKopp, The Holy Places in the Gospels (tr. RWalls) '63, 283–304; RClements, God and Temple, '65; SSafrai, The Temple: CRINT I/2, 865–907.—B. 1465. M-M. EDNT. TW. Sv.

ἱεροπρεπής, ές (ἱερός, πρέπω; on the termination s. DELG s.v. πρέπω) ***reverent, venerable*** (X., Symp. 8, 40; Pla., Theag. 122d; Cass. Dio 56, 46; Lucian, Sacrif. 13; Plut., Lib. Educ. 14 p. 11c; 4 Macc 9:25; 11:20; Philo, Abr. 101, Decal. 60, Leg. All. 3, 204; Jos., Ant. 11, 329) of the conduct of the older women of the congregation **Tit 2:3.** The more specialized mng. *priestlike* (so Dibelius), resulting fr. the use of the word in describing the conduct of a priest (Michel 163, 21; IPriene 109, 216; SIG 708, 24; Philo, Omn. Prob. Lib. 75) is less prob. here.—M-M. TW. Spicq. Sv.

ἱερός, ά, όν (Hom.+)—**❶ pert. to being of transcendent purity, *holy,*** adj. (Jos., Ant. 16, 27; 28; Just., A I, 1, 1 ἱερᾷ . . . συγκλήτῳ; D. 52, 3 τῶν ἱερῶν σκευῶν ἀρθέντων) [τὰ] ἱερὰ γράμματα (γράμμα 2c) **2 Ti 3:15.** Also ἱεραὶ βίβλοι (βίβλος 1) 1 Cl 43:1. ἱ. γραφαί (γραφή 2bα) 45:2; 53:1. (On 'sacred' writings s. New Docs 3, 64.) ἱ. κήρυγμα short ending of Mk; of God ἱ. χεῖρες *holy hands,* that touch nothing profane 1 Cl 33:4; τῶν ἱ. ἀποστόλων Papias (2:2). αὕτη ἡ πολυτέλεια καλὴ καὶ ἱερά Hs 1:10 v.l. (s. ἱλαρός).

❷ belonging to the temple and its service, *holy thing,* subst. τὰ ἱερά (Demosth. 57, 3 τῶν ἱερῶν καὶ κοινῶν μετέχειν; Philo, Spec. Leg. 3, 40; Jos., Ant. 14, 214) τὰ ἱερὰ ἐργάζεσθαι *perform the holy services in the temple* (cp. Ael. Aristid. 51, 66 K.=27 p. 550 D.: ἱερὰ ποιεῖν) **1 Cor 9:13a.**—Ἱερᾷ πόλει s. Ἱεράπολις.—B. 1475. LfgrE s.v. (lit. col. 1139). M-M. Schmidt, Syn. IV 321–45. DELG. TW. Sv.

Ἱεροσόλυμα, τά and **ἡ** (also Ἰερ-, Ἱεροσάλημα [GJs 20:4 pap]) and **Ἰερουσαλήμ, ἡ** indecl. (also Ἱερ-; יְרוּשָׁלַםִ ,יְרוּשָׁלֵם) ***Jerusalem.*** On the breathing s. B-D-F §39, 1; Mlt-H. 101; on the form of the name s. B-D-F §56, 1 and 4; W.-S. §10, 3; Mlt-H. 147f; Ramsay, Exp. 7th ser., 3, 1907, 110ff, 414f; Harnack, D. Apostelgesch. 1908, 72ff; RSchütz, ZNW 11, 1910, 169–87; JJeremias, ZNW 65, '74, 273–76; GKilpatrick, NovT 25, '83, 318–26; DSylva, ZNW 74, '83, 207–21.—τὰ Ἱεροσόλυμα (Polyb. 16, 39, 4; Diod. S. 34 + 35, fgm. 1, 1; 2; 3; 5; Strabo 16, 2, 34; 36; 40; Appian, Syr. 50 §252; Cass. Dio 37, 15; 17; Timochares [II BC]: 165 fgm. 1 Jac. [in Eus., PE 9, 35]; Ps.-Hecataeus: 264 fgm. 21, 197 Jac. [in Jos., C. Ap. 1, 197]; Agatharchides [II BC]: 86 fgm. 20a, 209 Jac. [in Jos., C. Ap. 1, 209]; Manetho [III BC]: 609 fgm. 10 a, 241 Jac. [in Jos., C. Ap. 1, 241 al.]; Lysimachus [I BC – I AD]: 621 fgm. 1, 311 Jac. [in Jos., C. Ap. 1, 311]; PGM 13, 997; LXX in Apocr. [Thackeray 168]; EpArist 32; 35; 52; Philo, Leg. ad Gai. 278; Joseph. [Niese index]; Just. [9 times]) is the form found in Mt (the sole exception **23:37** is fr. a quot.), Mk and J; it is also found in Lk and Ac, as well as **Gal 1:17f; 2:1;** PtK 4 p. 15, 35.—πᾶσα Ἱεροσόλυμα **Mt 2:3;** GEb 13, 78; seems to go back to a form ἡ Ἱεροσόλυμα, ης (cp. Pel.-Leg. 14, 14 πᾶσα [ἡ] Ἱεροσόλυμα; Tob 14:4; s. B-D-F §56, 4.—S. also PGM 4, 3069 ἐν τῇ καθαρᾷ Ἱεροσολύμῳ and 13, 233 ἐν Ἱερωσολύμῳ).—ἡ Ἰερουσαλήμ (predom. in LXX; pseudepigr.; Philo, Somn. 2, 250; Just. [22 times apart from quot.]; Mel. [consistently].—Jos., C. Ap. 1, 179 Clearchus [fgm. 7] is quoted as reporting remarks of his teacher Aristotle in which the latter uses the form Ἱερουσαλήμη [doubted by Niese; Eus., PE 9, 5, 6 has the same quot. fr. Clearchus w. the form Ἱερουσαλήμ]) besides **Mt 23:37** (s. above) in Lk, Ac (s. PLCouchoud/RStahl, RHR 97, 1928, 9–17), predom. in Paul, **Hb 12:22;** Rv; 1 Cl 41:2; Judaicon 20, 71; GPt; εἰς Ἱερουσαλήμ AcPl Ha 8, 30 (Ἱεροσόλυμα BMM verso 1).—Mostly without the art. (PsSol; GrBar prol. 2; AscIs), s. B-D-F §261, 3; 275, 2; W-S. §18, 5e; w. the art. only **J 2:23; 5:2; 10:22; 11:18;** cp. **Ac 5:28; Gal 4:25f; Rv 3:12.** No certain conclusions can be drawn concerning the use of the two forms of the name (they are used in the same immediate context by Hecataeus [264 fgm. 21

Jac., in Eus., PE 9, 4, 2 v.l.]); the mss. vary considerably in their practice.

❶ **the city of Jerusalem,** ***Jerusalem*** **Mt 2:1** and oft.; **Mk 3:8** and oft.; **Lk 2:25, 41; J 1:19; Ro 15:19, 25f; Gal 1:17f; 2:1** al. ἀναβαίνειν εἰς Ἱεροσόλυμα **Mt 20:17f; Mk 10:32f; Lk 19:28; J 2:13; 5:1; 11:55; Ac 21:15; 25:1;** Ἰερουσαλήμ **Lk 18:31; Ac 11:2; 21:12.** καταβαίνειν ἀπὸ Ἱεροσολύμων **Mk 3:22; Ac 11:27; 25:7;** καταβαίνειν ἀπὸ Ἰερουσαλήμ **Lk 10:30; Ac 8:26.** θυγατέρες Ἰερουσαλήμ **Lk 23:28,** s. θυγάτηρ 3.

❷ **Jerusalem as collective for its inhabitants,** ***Jerusalem*** πᾶσα Ἱ. *the whole city of Jerusalem* (Caecilius Calactinus, fgm. 75 p. 57, 8 says πᾶσα ἡ Ἑλλάς [Thu. 1, 6, 1] stands ἀντὶ τῶν Ἑλλήνων; Pla., Ep. 7, 348a πᾶσα Σικελία; Demosth. 18, 18; Psellus p. 43, 12 πᾶσα ἡ Πόλις='all Byzantines') **Mt 2:3;** cp. **3:5;** Ἰερουσαλὴμ Ἰερουσαλήμ **23:37** (Aeschines, Ctesiph. 133 Θῆβαι, Θῆβαι; Ps.-Demetr. in Eloc. 267 adds to this Aeschines passage the comment, 'The repetition of the name produces a powerful effect'; sim. Lk 10:41; 22:31; Ac 9:4.—HvanderKwaak, NovT 8, '66, 56–70); **Lk 2:38; 13:34** (Jerusalem is here viewed as dead; such personal address is normal in the ancient world: HJahnow, Das hebräische Leichenlied 1923, 50f; 100; s. for the Hellenic world Il. 18, 333; 19, 287; 315); **Ac 21:31.**—For a geographical and historical treatment HGuthe, RE VIII 666ff; XXIII 671f; HVincent and F-MAbel, Jérusalem I 1912; II 1926; GDalman, J. u. s. Gelände 1930; MJoin-Lambert, Jerusalem (tr. CHaldane) '58; PWinter, 'Nazareth' and 'Jer.' in Lk 1 and 2, NTS 3, '56/57, 136–42 (lit.); CKopp, The Holy Places of the Gospels '63 (tr. RWalls), 283–417. On its cultural history JJeremias, Jerus. in the Time of Jesus (tr. FH and CHCave) '69; BLifshitz, Jérusalem sous la domination romaine: ANRW II/8, 77, 444–89; MPorthuis/CSafrai, eds., The Centrality of Jerusalem '96. For its theol. significance, JBlinzler in Wikenhauser Festschr. '52, 20–52; JSchneider, ibid., 207–29. BHHW II 820–50 (lit.). OEANE III 224–38.

❸ **transcendent Jerusalem,** ***Jerusalem,*** fig. and eschatol. usage ἡ νῦν Ἰ. *the present J.* is contrasted w. the ἄνω Ἰ. *the heavenly J.* **Gal 4:25f.** For the latter also Ἰ. ἐπουράνιος **Hb 12:22** and ἡ καινὴ Ἰ. *the new J.* **Rv 3:12; 21:2,** also ἡ ἁγία Ἰ. **21:10;** cp. vs. **2.** On the theol. usage s. JdeYoung, Jerus. in the NT '60.—For lit. s. on πόλις 2.—M-M. EDNT. TW.

Ἱεροσολυμίτης, ου, ὁ (also -είτης, Ἰεροσολυμίτης, Ἰεροσολυμείτης; Sir 50:27; 4 Macc 4:22; 18:5; Joseph. [Niese index]) ***an inhabitant of Jerusalem*** **Mk 1:5; J 7:25.**—TW.

ἱεροσυλέω (s. ἱερός, συλάω, and next entry; on the terminal formation s. DELG s.v. συλάω; Aristoph. et al.; Polyb. 30, 26, 9; Artem. 3, 3; Heraclitus, Ep. 7, 4H.; SIG 417, 8; 10 [273/272 BC; cp. ἱεροσυλία 1017, 18; in tales of Alexander: PSI II, 1285 col. I, 38; col. III, 42; col. IV, 9 [II AD]; 2 Macc 13:6; ἱεροσύλημα 4:39; ἱερόσυλος 4:42]; 2 Macc 9:2; Philo; Jos., C. Ap. 1, 249, Ant. 17, 163)

❶ **to take objects from a temple by force or stealth,** ***rob temples*** (Manetho: 609 fgm. 10a, 249 Jac. [=Jos., C. Ap. 1, 249], w. vandalism against sacred images) prob. to be taken literally of temple plundering **Ro 2:22** (w. κλέπτω and μοιχεύω as Philo, Conf. Lingu. 163; cp. also Herm. Wr. 12, 5; JDerrett, NTS 40, '94, 558–71 w. focus on violation of conscience). Some interpret ἱ. in this pass. as meaning

❷ **to commit irreverent acts,** ***commit sacrilege*** (in Isaeus 8, 39 ἱεροσυλία is used of conduct relating to burial rites).—EKrentz, The Name of God in Disrepute—Romans 2:17–29: CTM 17, '90, 429–39.—DELG s.v. συλάω. M-M. TW.

ἱερόσυλος, ον (s. prec. entry; Aristoph. et al.; Aristot., Pol. 5, 4 p. 1304a, 3f; Diod. S. 16, 25, 2; Plut., Sol. 17, 1; ins; 2 Macc 4:42; Jos., Bell. 1, 654, Ant. 16, 164)

❶ **pert. to a temple robber,** subst. ὁ ἱ. *temple robber* (Draco in Plut., Solon 17, 2; Dio Chrys. 31 [14], 82; Alciphron 3, 7, 5; Philo, De Jos. 84; Jos., Ant. 16, 168) **Ac 19:37.** Some (e.g., KLatte, Hlg. Recht 1920, 83ff) interpret ἱ. in this pass. to mean

❷ **pert. to being sacrilegious,** transf. sense of 1, subst. ***a sacrilegious person,*** i.e. the equivalent of a temple plunderer (SIG 578, 47ff [II BC] ὁ δὲ εἴπας ἢ πρήξας τι παρὰ τόνδε τὸν νόμον . . . ἔστω ἱερόσυλος; 1016, 8; SIG[2] 680, 10. S. also Menand., Dyscolus 640 ἱερόσυλε σύ=you rogue!, Epitr. 1100 S. [=742 Kö.]).—DELG s.v. συλάω. M-M. TW.

ἱερουργέω (ἱερουργός 'sacrificing priest'; Plut., Num. 14, 1, Alex. 31, 4; Herodian 5, 6, 1; 5, 5, 9; Philostrat., Vi. Soph. 2, 10, 2 p. 91, 25; CIG add. to 4528 [III p. 1175]; IG[2] I, 4, 4f; 8 [V BC]; 4 Macc 7:8 v.l.; Philo, Mos. 1, 87 al.; Jos., Ant. 6, 102; 7, 333) **to act in some cultic or sacred capacity,** ***perform holy service, act as a priest*** τὶ *w. regard to someth.* τὸ εὐαγγέλιον *serve the gospel as a priest* (perh. w. emphasis on sacrifice; Field, Notes 165) **Ro 15:16.**—DELG s.v. ἱερός. M-M. TW.

Ἰερουσαλήμ s. Ἱεροσόλυμα.

Ἱερώνυμος, ου, ὁ (Hdt. 9:33, 2; Joseph.) *Jerome* proconsul in Ephesus AcPl Ha 1, 30; 33; 2, 9; 12; 3, 1; 4; 4, 5; 8; 16; 5, 4; 10; 22.

ἱερωσύνη, ης, ἡ ***priestly office, priesthood*** (s. ἱερός; Hdt.+; Pla., Demosth.; Diod. S. 5, 58, 2; Plut. et al.; ins; PBrem 70, 6; LXX; Test12Patr; Philo; Jos., Ant. 2, 216, C. Ap. 1, 31; Ath. 28, 3. On the word-formation s. Mayser 15; 154, 11 [lit.]; Mlt-H. 358.) 1 Cl 43:2; ἡ Λευιτικὴ ἱ. *the Levitic priesthood* **Hb 7:11;** μετατιθεμένης τῆς ἱ. *when the priesthood changes* vs. **12;** ἀπαράβατον ἔχειν τὴν ἱ. vs. **24** (Ps.-Aristot., Mirabilia 137 τ. ἱερωσύνην ἔχειν='hold the priestly office').—DELG s.v. ἱερός. M-M.

Ἰεσσαί, ὁ indecl. (יִשַׁי; in Joseph. Ἰεσσαῖος, ου [Ant. 6, 162]; Just.) ***Jesse,*** David's father (1 Km 16:1, 10; 17:12; 20:27; TestSol 26:9 H) **Ac 13:22;** 1 Cl 18:1. In the genealogy of Jesus (cp. Ruth 4:22) **Mt 1:5f; Lk 3:32;** ἡ ῥίζα τοῦ Ἰ. *the Scion of Jesse* of the Messianic king **Ro 15:12** (Is 11:10).

Ἰεφθάε, ὁ indecl. (יִפְתָּח; in Joseph. Ἰαφθᾶς [v.l. Ἰεφθάς], α [Ant. 5, 271]) ***Jephthah,*** son of Gilead, one of the judges of Israel (Judg 11f) **Hb 11:32.**

Ἰεχονίας, ου, ὁ (יְכָנְיָהוּ=יְהוֹיָכִין) ***Jechoniah,*** a king of Judah (Jos., Bell. 6, 103, Ant. 10, 229f). Acc. to the genealogy **Mt 1:11f** he was a son of Josiah and had brothers. In 1 Ch 3:15f Ἰεχονία is the son of Ἰωακίμ and the grandson of Josiah, and only one brother is mentioned. 1 Ch 3:17; **Mt 1:12** and **Lk 3:23ff** D agree that he was the father of Salathiel.

ιϛʹ numeral ***16*** GJs 12:3.

Ἰησαΐας s. Ἠσαΐας.

Ἰησοῦς (יֵשׁוּעַ Jeshua, later form for יְהוֹשׁוּעַ Joshua; s. MLidzbarski, Handb. d. nordsem. Epigr. 1898, 291; FPraetorius, ZDMG 59, 1905, 341f; FSteinmetzer, BZ 14, 1917, 193ff; FWaele, Wetenschappelijke Tijdingen 5, '42, 177–81), gen. **οῦ,** dat. **οῦ,** acc. **οῦν,** voc. **οῦ, ὁ** ***Joshua/Jesus.*** This name, common among Jews (several persons w. it in LXX and Joseph. [Niese, index]; EpArist 48; 49; ins fr. the time of Augustus [RevÉpigr n.s. 1, 1913 no. 12]; POxy 816 [I BC]; PLond III, 1119a, 2 p. 25 [105 AD]. Ostraca: Sb 5812; 5817; 5820; 5822), usu. takes the article in the gospels (in J the nom. freq. appears without the art.: RNevius, NTS 12, '65, 81–85; GFee, NTS 17, '71, 168–83) except when it is accompanied by a word in apposition w. the art.; in the epistles and Rv it does not regularly take the art. (B-D-F §260, 1; W-S, §18, 6; HvSoden, D. Schriften des NTs I/2, 1911, 1406–9).

❶ ***Joshua, successor of Moses,*** military leader of the people when they entered Canaan (Josh; 1 Macc 2:55; 2 Macc 12:15; Philo, Joseph., Just.; Mel., HE 4, 26, 14; SibOr 2, 247) **Ac 7:45; Hb 4:8.** Fully Ἰ. υἱὸς Ναυή (Josh 1:1; cp. Sir 46:1; AssMos fgm f; Just., D. 113, 2; 115, 4) B 12:8f or Ἰ. ὁ τοῦ Ναυή 1 Cl 12:2 (AssMos fgm a; Just., D. 49, 6 al.; cp. 111, 4 ἀπὸ Ἰ. τοῦ Ναυῆ).

❷ ***Jesus, son of Eliezer,*** in the genealogy of Jesus **Lk 3:29** (Ἰωσή v.l.).

❸ ***Jesus Christ,*** more definitely designated as Ἰ. Χριστός, Χριστὸς Ἰ., ὁ κύριος Ἰ. (Χριστός [so also TestSol D 1, 12]), ὁ σωτὴρ Ἰ. Χριστός etc. **Mt 1:1, 21, 25** and oft. S. Χριστός, κύριος, σωτήρ. On the use of the names in Paul s. EvDobschütz, D. Th.-Briefe in Meyer[7] 1909, 60f.—Two times by Ar. (15, 1; 3), 5 times by Mel., freq. by Just.—On the abbreviation of the names in mss. s. LTraube, Nomina sacra 1907, 113ff; EbNestle, ZNW 9, 1908, 248ff.—The older lit. on Jesus in ASchweitzer, Gesch. der Leben-Jesu-Forschung[2] 1913. Further RGG III[3], '59, 619–53 (bibliog. 651–53); MVeit, D. Auffassung v. d. Pers. Jesu im Urchristent. nach d. neuesten Forschungen, diss. Marburg '46; REisler, Ἰησοῦς βασιλεύς 1928–1930; RBultmann, Jesus[2] 1929 (reprinted '51), D. Urchristentum '49; PFeine, Jesus 1930; FPrat, Jésus-Christ '33; JKlausner, J. von Nazareth[2] '34 (Eng. tr. 1926); MGoguel, La Vie de J. '32 (Eng. tr. '44); KAdam, Jes. Christus[4] '35; FWillam, D. Leben J. im Lande u. Volke Israel[4] '34; JPickl, Messiaskönig J. in d. Auffassung seiner Zeitgenossen[3] '39; RGuardini, D. Herr '37; MDibelius, Jesus '39 ([3]'60) (Eng. tr. '49); ALoisy, Hist. et mythe à propos de J-Ch. '38; HFelder, Jes. v. Naz.[2] '39; CNoel, The Life of J. '39; VGrÿnbech, J. d. Menschensohn '41; RMeyer, D. Proph. aus Galil. '40; CCadoux, The Hist. Mission of J. '41; AOlmstead, J. in the Light of History '42; WManson, J. the Messiah '43, 6th impr. '52; ARawlinson, Christ in the Gospels '44; GRicciotti, Life of Christ '47; FBüchsel, Jesus '47; HCadbury, J.: What Manner of Man '47; GDuncan, J., Son of Man '47; JHoffmann, Les Vies de Jésus et le Jésus de l'Histoire '47; WKümmel, Verheissung u. Erfüllung[2] '53; GBornkamm, J. von Nazareth '56 (Eng. tr. '60); JKnox, Jesus, Lord and Christ '58; HRistow u. KMatthiae, ed., D. historische Jesus u. d. kerygmatische Christus '60; ESchweizer, Jesus (Eng. tr. DGreen) '71; HBraun, Qumran u. d. NT II '66, 54–118 (lit.); WKümmel in TRu 31, '65/66; 40, '75; 41, '76 etc.; GSchneider, EDNT II 180–84; JMeier, A Marginal Jew—Rethinking the Historical Jesus, 2 vols. '91–'94 (lit.). For more recent studies, see the standard bibliographic aids.—On the name: WLowrie, Theol. Today 8, '51, 11–19; VTaylor, Names of Jesus '53.

❹ ***Jesus Barabbas*** **Mt 27:16f;** s. Βαραββᾶς.

❺ ***Jesus/Justus*** Ἰ. ὁ λεγόμενος Ἰοῦστος *Jesus who is called Justus* (on the double name s. Dssm., B 183f [BS 315]), συνεργὸς ἐκ περιτομῆς **Col 4:11.** It has been conjectured (Zahn, Einl. I 321, 4; EAmling, ZNW 10, 1909, 261f) that this Jesus is referred to again in **Phlm 23.** On this ADeissmann, D. Name J.: Mysterium Christi '31, 13–41.—M-M. EDNT. TW.

ἱκανός, ή, όν (s. three next entries; trag., Hdt.+; ins, pap, LXX; PsSol 5:17; TestNapht 2:4; JosAs 28:11; ParJer 6:6 [שַׁדַּי]; ApcSed 2:3; EpArist, Philo, Joseph., Just.; Tat. 36, 2 ἱκανώτατος; loanw. in rabb.).

❶ **sufficient in degree, *sufficient, adequate, large enough*** ἱκανόν ἐστιν *it is enough* (Epict. 1, 2, 36; 3 Km 16:31; the copula is oft. omitted: Gen 30:15; Ezk 34:18; Just., D. 13, 1) **Lk 22:38** (WWestern, ET 52, '40/41, 357 'large' or 'long enough'). εἴ τινι μὴ δοκοίη κἂν ταῦτα ἱκανά *if this should seem insufficient to anyone* Dg 2:10. Latinism (B-D-F §5, 3b; Mlt. 20f) τὸ ἱκανὸν ποιεῖν τινι satisfacere alicui=*satisfy* (Polyb. 32, 3, 13; Appian, Lib. 74; BGU 1141, 13 [14 BC] ἐάν σοι Ἔρως τὸ ἱκανὸν ποιήσῃ γράψον μοι; POxy 293, 10; PGiss 40 I, 5); also possible is *do someone a favor* (so plainly Diog. L. 4, 50 = grant your request) **Mk 15:15** (cp. χαρίζομαι PFlor I, 61, 61 [85 AD]=Mitt-Wilck. II/2, 80 II, 61, of one 'worthy to be flogged' ἄξιος . . . μαστιγωθῆναι ln. 59f); Hs 6, 5, 5; τὸ ἱ. *pledge, security, bond* (POxy 294, 23 [22 AD]; BGU 530, 38; PStras 41, 51) λαμβάνειν τὸ ἱ. satis accipere=*take bail* (OGI 484, 50; 629, 101 [both II AD]) **Ac 17:9.**

❷ **pert. to meeting a standard, *fit, appropriate, competent, qualified, able,*** w. the connotation *worthy, good enough* (Thu.; Diod. S. 13, 106, 10; POxy 1672, 15; Ex 4:10) πρός τι *for someth.* (Pla., Prot. 322b; 2 Macc 10:19; EpArist 211) **2 Cor 2:16** (FFallon, HTR 76, '83, 369–74, 'divine man' motif). W. inf. foll. (Hdt. 8, 36; Jos., Ant. 1, 29; 5, 51; Just., D. 8, 2; B-D-F §393, 4; Rob. 658) **Mt 3:11; Mk 1:7; Lk 3:16; 1 Cor 15:9; 2 Cor 3:5** (Dodd 15f); **2 Ti 2:2** (Jos., Ant. 3, 49 εἰπεῖν ἱ.); 1 Cl 50:2. Also w. ἵνα foll. (B-D-F §393, 4; Rob. 658; cp. PHolm 4, 23) **Mt 8:8; Lk 7:6; J 1:27 v.l.**—S. ITr 3:3 cj. Lghtf.

❸ **pert. to being large in extent or degree, *considerable***

ⓐ of pers. ὄχλος *a large crowd* **Mk 10:46; Lk 7:12; Ac 11:24, 26; 19:26** (SIG 569, 14 πλῆθος ἱ.; PPetr II, 20; II, 7; PLille 3, 76 [III BC]; Jos., Ant. 5, 250). λαὸν ἱ. *large following* **5:37 v.l.**

ⓑ of things κλαυθμός *weeping aloud* **Ac 20:37** (=*there was quite a bit of crying*). φῶς *a very bright light* **Ac 22:6.**—ἱκανὸν ἡ. ἐπιτιμία *the punishment is severe enough* **2 Cor 2:6** (on the lack of agreement in gender s. B-D-F §131; Rob. 411).—ἀργύρια *a rather large sum of* (lit. 'enough', i.e. 'substantial bribe' REB) *money* **Mt 28:12** (cp. SIG 1106, 74; 77).—Esp. of time ἐξ ἱκανοῦ *for a long time* **Lk 23:8 v.l.** ἐφ' ἱκανόν *enough, as long as one wishes; for a long time* (Polyb. 11, 25, 1; Diod. S. 11, 40, 3; 13, 100, 1; SIG 685, 34; 2 Macc 7:5; 8:25; EpArist 109) **Ac 20:11.** ἱ. χρόνος *a considerable time* (Aristoph.; Pla., Leg. 5 p. 736c; SIG 665, 12; UPZ 161, 29 [119 BC] ἐφ' ἱ. χρόνον; Jos., Ant. 7, 22, C. Ap. 1, 237) ἱ. χρόνον διέτριψαν **Ac 14:3** (Just., D. 2, 3). ἱ. χρόνου διαγενομένου **27:9.** ἱκανῷ χρόνῳ *for a long time* **Lk 8:27; Ac 8:11** (on the dat. s. B-D-F §201; Rob. 527). Pl. **Lk 20:9** (B-D-F §201; Rob. 470). ἐξ ἱ. χρόνων *for a long time* **23:8;** ἐκ χρόνων ἱ. **Mt 8:27 v.l.;** for this ἀπὸ χρόνων ἱ. **Lk 8:27** D. ἐπὶ ἱ. χρόνον Qua.

❹ **in relatively large numbers, *many, quite a few*—ⓐ** of pers. abs. ἱκανοί *many, quite a few* (Mitt-Wilck. I/2, 11 B Fr. (a), 10 [123 BC]; PTebt 41, 13 ἱκανῶν ἡμῶν; 1 Macc 13:49; Jos., Ant. 14, 231) **Ac 12:12; 14:21; 19:19; 1 Cor 11:30** (*quite a few,* contrast πολλοί as Ac 19:18f); cp. μαθηταί **Lk 7:11 v.l.**

ⓑ of things λαμπάδες *a good many lamps* **Ac 20:8.** ἀγέλη χοίρων ἱκανῶν **Lk 8:32.** ἐν λόγοις ἱ. *w. many words = at length* **Lk 23:9.** Superl. κεράμια ἱκανώτατα *a large number of jars* Hm 12, 5, 3 (SIG 736, 108 ξύλα ἱ.).

ⓒ of periods of time ἀπὸ ἱ. ἐτῶν *for many years* **Ro 15:23 v.l.** (cp. 2 Macc 1:20). ἡμέραι ἱ. (UPZ 162 II, 15 [117 BC] ἐφ' ἱκανὰς ἡμέρας) **Ac 9:23;** ἡμέρας ἱ. *for many days* **9:43; 18:18.** Also ἐν ἱ. ἡμέραις **27:7.**—B. 927. DELG s.v. ἵκω. M-M. TW. Spicq.

ἱκανότης, ητος, ἡ state of being qualified or adequate for someth., ***fitness, capability, qualification*** (s. ἱκανός Lysias, fgm. 211 Sauppe [in Pollux 4, 23]; Pla., Lysis 11 p. 215a; Stoic. III 68, 3) **2 Cor 3:5.**—DELG s.v. ἵκω. TW. Spicq.

ἱκανόω (s. ἱκανός) 1 aor. ἱκάνωσα, impv. 2 sg. ἱκάνωσον ('be satisfied [with]' PsSol 2:22), pass. ἱκανώθην LXX (outside the NT the pass. is used: Teles p. 39, 6; 42, 4; Dionys. Hal. 2, 74; PTebt 20, 8; LXX [mostly pres. impv. 3 sg. ἱκανούσθω 'let it suffice']; TestIss 1:7; s. Anz 353) **to cause to be adequate,** ***make sufficient, qualify*** (perh. shading into the sense *empower, authorize* [PTebt 20, 8]) w. double acc. *someone for someth.* **2 Cor 3:6.** τινὰ εἴς τι *someone for someth.* **Col 1:12** (s. καλέω 4).—DELG s.v. ἵκω. M-M. TW. Spicq.

ἱκανῶς adv. of ἱκανός (Soph., Hdt.+; PPetr III, 53n, 3; POxy 1088, 56; PTebt 411, 6; Job 9:31; 3 Macc 1:4; Philo, Op. M. 90; Jos., C. Ap. 1, 58; 287, Ant. 2, 31; Just.; Ath. 10, 1)

❶ ***sufficiently,*** of number ἱ. ἐπεστείλαμεν 1 Cl 62:1.

❷ ***capably*** ἱ. ἐλέγχειν *ably refute* Epil Mosq 2.

ἱκεσία, ας, ἡ (s. three next entries; Eur.+; ins, pap; 2 Macc 10:25; 12:42; TestSol 22:5; ApcMos 13; Philo; Jos., Ant. 11, 326; 12, 300; Just., D. 107, 2) **prayer of a suppliant,** ***supplication*** ἱ. ποιεῖσθαι *make supplication* (Aeschin. 3, 121; Dionys. Hal. 8, 43, 5) ἐκτενῆ τὴν δέησιν καὶ ἱ. ποιεῖσθαι *pray w. eager supplication* 1 Cl 59:2 (ἱ. w. δέησις as OGI 569, 11; Mitt-Wilck. I/2, 6, 3).—DELG s.v. ἵκω.

ἱκετεύω 1 aor. ἱκέτευσα LXX (s. prec. and two next entries; Hom.+; ins, pap, LXX; Jos., C. Ap. 2, 213) ***supplicate, beseech*** θεόν (curse of Artemisia [pap in Sb 5103, III BC] 9f ἱκετεύουσα τοὺς θεούς; Appian, Bell. Civ. 2, 104 §431 θεοὺς πάντας ὁ Καῖσαρ ἱκέτευεν; Ps 36:7; 2 Macc 11:6; σοὶ ὅπως TestSol 13:7 C; TestAbr; EpArist 197; Philo, Cherub. 47; Jos., Ant. 3, 6) 1 Cl 7:7; 48:1. W. inf. foll. 2:3. V.l. ἱκέτευεν for ἐκάθισεν … ἐλιτάνευσεν GJs 2:4 (cod. E).—Schmidt, Syn. I 177–98. DELG s.v. ἵκω.

ἱκετηρία, ας, ἡ (actually the fem. of the adj. ἱκετήριος, w. ἐλαία or ῥάβδος to be supplied: the olive branch was the sign of a suppliant. As subst.='sign of a suppliant' Aeschyl., Hdt. et al.) ***supplication*** (so Isocr. et al.; POslo 148, 12 [II/I BC]; 2 Macc 9:18; Philo, Leg. ad Gai. 228) w. δέησις (Isocr. 8, 138 Blass v.l.; Job 40:27; Philo, Leg. ad Gai. 276). As a supplication made to God, *prayer* (Ael. Aristid. 49, 38 K.=25 p. 498 D.; Aelian, fgm. 304; Sb 5103, 9; 11 [s. ἱκετεύω above]) w. δέησις (Polyb. 3, 112, 8 θεῶν ἱκετηρίαι καὶ δεήσεις; Philo, Cher. 47 v.l.) δεήσεις κ. ἱκετηρίας πρὸς τὸν δυνάμενον σῴζειν αὐτὸν προσενέγκας **Hb 5:7.** CSpicq, RB 56, '49, 549f.—DELG s.v. ἵκω. M-M.

ἱκέτης, ου, ὁ (s. prec. three entries; Hom. et al.; ins, LXX; TestAbr A 2 p. 78, 27 [Stone p. 4]; Philo; Jos., C. Ap. 2, 207) ***suppliant*** ἱκέται γενόμενοι τοῦ ἐλέους αὐτοῦ *as suppliants of God's mercy* 1 Cl 9:1 (cp. Jos., Ant. 7, 361 ἱκέτης γίνεται τ. θεοῦ and the Delphic commands in SIG 1268, 24 ἱκέτας ἐλέει).—S. on εὐλαβέομαι.—DELG s.v. ἵκω. TW. Sv.

ἰκμάς, άδος, ἡ (Hom. et al.; LXX; Philo, Op. M. 38. Exx. fr. Joseph., Plut., Lucian in Cadbury, Style 43) ***moisture:*** of moisture in the soil, without which plants cannot live (Theophr., HP 6, 4, 8 ἰκμάδα ἔχειν in contrast to ξηραίνεσθαι; Jos., Ant. 3, 10; Jer 17:8) **Lk 8:6;** Hs 8, 2, 7; 9. Of juices secreted by decaying flesh 1 Cl 25:3 (on the medical use of the word s. Hobart 57f).—DELG. M-M.

Ἰκονιεύς, έως, ὁ ***inhabitant of Iconium*** τὴν Ἰκονιέων πόλιν AcPl Ox 6, 19 (=Aa I, 242, 1).—Pauly-W. IX/1, 990f.—S. Ἰκόνιον.

Ἰκόνιον, ου, τό (on the spelling s. B-D-F §42, 3; Rob. 197) ***Iconium*** (c. 140 km. fr. Antioch; acc. to X., An. 1, 2, 19 belonging to Phrygia, likew. Pliny, Nat. Hist. 5, 41; Acta Justini 4; Steph. Byz. s.v.; but Strabo 12, 6, 1 puts it in Lycaonia), visited by Paul several times **Ac 13:51; 14:1, 19, 21; 16:2; 2 Ti 3:11.** τὸ Ἰ. AcPl Ant 13, 2 (=Aa I, 236, 6).—Ramsay, Bearing 53ff [Phrygia], Cities 317–82; Bludau (s. Λύστρα); AWikenhauser, Die Apostelgesch. 1921, 336f; VSchultze, Altchr. Städte u. Landschaften II 2, 1926; BHHW II 760; Conzelmann, Acts (Hermeneia) 107f.—M-M.

ἰκτῖνος, ου, ὁ (metaplastic acc. ἰκτῖνα [Cyranides p. 24, 8]) ***hawk, kite*** (Semonides, Theognis, Hdt., X., Pla. et al.), whose flesh Israelites were forbidden to eat (Lev 11:14; Dt 14:13) B 10:4.—DELG.

ἱλαρός, ά, όν (Aristoph., X.+; ins, pap, LXX, En; TestJos 8:5; JosAs 23:10; EpArist; Philo; Jos., Bell. 6, 364, Ant. 18, 291; Tat. 26, 4 ἱλαρώτερον) **pert. to being full of cheer,** ***cheerful, glad, happy*** of things (Appian, fgm. 7 βοὴ ἱλαρά; Aesop, Fab. 314 P.=Babr. 24 Cr.//L-P. ἱ. κῶμοι; Synes., Kingship 1 p. 1c λόγοι ἱ.; En 32:4 βότρυες … ἱλαροὶ λίαν; Philo, Spec. Leg. 2, 48 ἱ. βίος) πάντα ὁμαλὰ κ. ἱλαρά *everything is smooth and cheerful* Hm 2:4; ὄψιν … ἱλαρωτέραν 3:1; μακροθυμία 5, 2, 3; πνεῦμα τὸ ἅγιον … ἱλαρόν 10, 3, 2; ἐντολαί s 6, 1, 1; βοτάνας ἱ. 9, 1, 8; ἐγένετο ὁ τόπος ἱ. 9, 10, 3; αὕτη ἡ πολυτέλεια καλὰ καὶ ἱλαρά *such expenditure is noble and joyful* s 1, 10; λειτουργία καλὴ καὶ ἱλαρά *a fine and joyful service* s 5, 3, 8; ἰδέα … ἱλαρά joyful face (of the shepherd) 6, 1, 6b.—Of animals (Philostrat., Imag. 1, 15): sheep s 6, 1, 6a.—Of humans (TestJob 12:1; Diod. S. 4, 5, 3) v 1, 2, 3; 1, 4, 3; 3, 3, 1; 3, 9, 10 al. δότης *one who gives cheerfully, gladly* (=*without reluctance*) **2 Cor 9:7** (cp. Pr 22:8a). But here some entertain the sense *kind, gracious* (s. Nägeli 65f and Artem. 1, 5 θεοί; POxy 1380, 127 the ἱλαρὰ ὄψις of Isis; Philo, Spec. Leg. 4, 74 ἱ. μεταδόσεις=gracious gifts).—DELG s.v. ἱλάσκομαι 2. M-M.

ἱλαρότης, ητος, ἡ (s. ἱλαρός; Diod. S. 3, 17, 1; 4, 86, 6 Cornutus 24 p. 45, 11; Plut., Ages. 596 [2, 4]; Alciphron 3, 43; Vita Philonidis 21, 4 Crönert [SBBerlAk 1900, II 942ff]; PLond 1917, 4 [IV AD] and PAnt 44, 6 [IV/V AD]; Pr 18:22; PsSol 4:5; 16:12; TestAbr A 20 p. 103, 16 [Stone p. 54]; TestNapht 9:2; Philo, Plant. 166) **quality or state of cheerfulness, opp. of an attitude suggesting being under duress,** ***cheerfulness, gladness, wholeheartedness, graciousness*** **Ro 12:8;** Hm 5, 1, 2 (contrast ὀξυχολία); 10, 3, 1 (contrast λύπηρος ἀνήρ 'morose person'); 4 (opp. 'moroseness'); s 9, 15, 2 (personified in the last pass.).—DELG s.v. ἱλάσκομαι. M-M. TW.

ἱλάσκομαι (s. two next entries) mid. dep.; fut. ἱλάσομαι LXX; 1 aor. pass. impv. ἱλάσθητι (in mid. mng. ἱλάσθην LXX) (Hom. et al.; ins; LXX [Thackeray 270f]; s. also Dodd and Hill, below).

❶ **to cause to be favorably inclined or disposed,** ***propitiate, conciliate*** (Il. 1, 100 Apollo; Hdt. 5, 47, 2 an offended Olympic victor; 8, 112, 3 Themistocles; Strabo 4, 4, 6 τὸν θεόν; Cornutus 34 p. 73, 5; Heraclit. Sto. 16 p. 24, 9 τὸν Ἥλιον; Appian, Samn. 12 §6, Hann. 27 §115 θυσίαις κ. εὐχαῖς ἱ. τ. θεούς; Herm. Wr. 1, 22; Philo, Spec. Leg. 1, 116; Jos., Ant. 6, 124 τὸν θεὸν ἱ.; 8, 112, C. Ap. 1, 308 ἱ. τοὺς θεούς; SibOr 3, 625; 628). Pass.: of one addressed in prayer, to act as one who has been conciliated, but with focus on the initiative of the one who functions thus: *be propitiated, be merciful* or *gracious* (4 Km 24:4; La 3:42; Da 9:19 Theod.) w. dat. (of advantage, Esth 4:17h ἱλάσθητι τ. κλήρῳ σου; cp. also Ps 78:9) ἱλάσθητί μοι τῷ ἁμαρτωλῷ (dat. of advantage) *have mercy on me, sinner that I am* **Lk 18:13** (Sb 8511, 7 [ins, imperial times] ἵλαθί μοι, Μανδοῦλι [a divinity]); GJs 5:1 (twice; in the first instance perh. with inf. foll., s. deStrycker 289 n. 2).—B-D-F §314.

❷ **to eliminate impediments that alienate the deity,** ***expiate, wipe out,*** of Christ as high priest εἰς τὸ ἱλάσκεσθαι τὰς ἁμαρτίας τοῦ λαοῦ *to expiate the sins of the people* **Hb 2:17** (so Mft. [NRSV 'make a sacrifice of atonement'] cp. SIG 1042, 15f [=IG II², 1366; II/III AD] ἁμαρτίαν ὀφιλέτω Μηνὶ Τυράννῳ ἣν οὐ μὴ δύνηται ἐξειλάσασθαι 'let him be liable to Men Tyrranos for a sin he can have no hope of expiating' [cp. 1Km 3:14; on this ins s. New Docs 3, no. 6]; Ps 64:4 τὰς ἀσεβείας ἱ.; Dssm., NB 52 [BS 225]; Breytenbach 98).—CDodd, JTS 32, '31, 352–60; also Dodd 82–95 on ἱ. and related words (against Dodd: LMorris, ET 62, '51, 227–33; RNicole, WTJ 17, '55, 117–57; in support: NYoung, EvQ 55, '83, 169–76); SLyonnet, Verbum Domini 37, '59, 336–52, Sin, Redemption and Sacrifice, '70, 120–66, 256–61; DHill, Gk. Words and Hebrew Mngs. '67, 23–48; KGraystone, Ἱλάσκεσθαι and Related Words in the LXX: NTS 27, '81, 640–56; GHorsley, New Docs, 3, 25 (on Graystone and Hill); JFitzmyer, 'Reconciliation' in Pauline Theology, in: No Famine in the Land (McKenzie Festschr.) '75, 155–77; JLunceford, An Historical and Exegetical Inquiry into the NT Meaning of the ἹΛΑΣΚΟΜΑΙ Cognates, diss. Baylor '79; CBreytenbach, Versöhnung '89.—DELG. M-M. TW. Sv.

ἱλασμός, οῦ, ὁ (s. prec. and next entry)—❶ **appeasement necessitated by sin,** ***expiation*** (τῶν θεῶν Orph., Arg. 39; Plut., Fab. 18, 3; cp. Plut., Sol. 12, 5. In these cases we have the pl., prob. referring to the individual actions to be expiated. But also sg.: Plut., Mor. 560d, Camill. 7, 5; Lev 25:9; Ps 129:4; Philo, Leg. All. 3, 174) εἰς ἱ. ἐμοί *for my expiation* GJs 1:1; so perh. abstr. for concr. of Jesus as the ἱ. περὶ τ. ἁμαρτιῶν ἡμῶν **1J 2:2; 4:10.** But mng. 2 has been popular.

❷ **instrument for appeasing,** ***sacrifice to atone, sin-offering*** (Ezk 44:27 προσοίσουσιν ἱ. cp. Num 5:8; 2 Macc 3:33) s. above.—S. also lit. cited s.v. ἱλάσκομαι. DELG s.v. ἱλάσκομαι 1. M-M. TW.

ἱλαστήριον, ου, τό (subst. neut. of ἱλαστήριος, ον [PFay 337 I, 3ff—II AD; 4 Macc 17:22; Jos., Ant. 16, 182]; s. prec. two entries). In Gr-Rom. lit. that which serves as an instrument for regaining the goodwill of a deity; concr. a 'means of propitiation or expiation, gift to procure expiation' (IKosPH, 81, 347 ὁ δᾶμος ὑπὲρ τᾶς Αὐτοκράτορος Καίσαρος θεοῦ υἱοῦ Σεβαστοῦ σωτηρίας θεοῖς ἱλαστήριον; ChronLind B 49 Ἀθάναι ἱλατήριον; Dio Chrys. 10 [11], 121. The mng. is uncertain in POxy 1985, 11).

❶ ***means of expiation,*** of Christ, ὃν προέθετο ὁ θεὸς ἱλαστήριον *whom God set forth as a means of expiation* **Ro 3:25** (so REB; cp. CBreytenbach, Versöhnung, '89, 168 [s. below]; difft. GFitzer, TZ 22, '66, 161–83 and NRSV 'sacrifice of atonement'). The unique feature relative to Gr-Rom. usage is the initiative taken by God to effect removal of impediments to a relationship with God's self. In this pass. ἱ. has also been taken to mean

❷ ***place of propitiation*** (as Ezk 43:14, 17, 20; cp. also Luther's 'Gnadenstuhl', and s. on **Hb 9:5** below). For this view of ἱ. **Ro 3:25** s. TManson, JTS 46, '45, 1–10 (against him Breytenbach 167f.)—S. also Dssm., ZNW 4, 1903, 193–212 (s. EncBibl III, 3027–35); PFiebig and GKlein ibid. 341–44; SFraenkel, ibid. 5, 1904, 257f; CBruston, ibid. 7, 1906, 77–81; GottfKittel, StKr 80, 1907, 217–33; EdaSMarco, Il piano divino della salute in Ro 3:21–26: diss. Rome '37; VTaylor, ET 50, '39, 295–300; GBarton, ATR 21, '39, 91f; WDavies, Paul and Rabbinic Judaism² '55, 227–42; ELohse, Märtyrer u. Gottesknecht '55; LMorris, NTS 2, '55/56, 33–43; DWhiteley, JTS n.s. 8, '57, 240–55; DBailey, Jesus as the Mercy Seat: diss. Cambridge '99 (ins).—The LXX uses ἱ. of the lid on the ark of the covenant, כַּפֹּרֶת, which was sprinkled w. the blood of the sin-offering on the Day of Atonement (Ex 25:16ff al. Likew. TestSol 21:2; Philo, Cher. 25, Fuga 100, Mos. 2, 95.—JStelma, Christus' offer bij Pls [w. Philo] '38). So **Hb 9:5,** transl. *mercy-seat;* for the history of this word s. OED s.v.—DELG s.v. ἱλάσκομαι 1. M-M s.v. ἱλαστήριος. EDNT. TW. Sv.

ἱλατεύομαι (on the formation s. DELG s.v. ἱλάσκομαι) 1 aor. ἱλατευσάμην (the act. Jdth 16:15 v.l.; Da 9:19) ***be gracious*** τινί *to someone* Hv 1, 2, 1.

ἵλεως, ων (B-D-F §44, 1; W-S. §8, 8; Rdm. 62; Mlt. 240; Mlt-H. 121.—Hom. et al. as ἵλαος; ἵλεως is the Attic form. Also ins, pap, LXX, JosAs, Philo, Joseph.) **pert. to being favorably disposed, with implication of overcoming obstacles that are unfavorable to a relationship,** ***gracious, merciful,*** in the wider lit. mostly—in our lit. and in LXX always—of God (also Diod. S. 4, 24, 4; Lucian, Pro Imag. 12; Oenomaus [time of Hadrian] in Eus., PE 5, 19, 1 θεὸς ἵ. ἔσται; 6, 7, 42; M. Ant. 12, 36; Philo; Jos., Ant. 4, 222; 7, 290; SibOr 1, 161) ἵ. ἔσομαι τ. ἀδικίαις αὐτῶν *I will be merciful toward their iniquities* **Hb 8:12** (Jer 38:34). ἵλεώ τινος τυγχάνειν *find someone merciful = find mercy in someone's sight* (Herm. Wr. 5, 2; Philo, De Jos. 104) 1 Cl 61:2. ἵ. γενέσθαι τινί *be gracious* or *forgiving to someone* (Archilochus, fgm. 75 Ἥφαιστε, ... μοὶ, ... ἵλαος γενεῦ; Sallust. 4 p. 10, 4; Num 14:19; Dt 21:8; 2 Macc 2:22) Hv 2, 2, 8. Abs. ἵ. γενέσθαι (Alciphron 4, 18, 17; UPZ 78, 24 [159 BC]; Ezk. Trag. vs. 124 [in Eus., PE 9, 29, 11]; TestSol 20:4) 1 Cl 2:3; 48:1; Hs 9, 23, 4.—ἵλεώς σοι, κύριε (sc. εἴη ὁ θεός, as, in a related way, Herodas 4, 25; Plut., Mor. 983e ἵλεως ὁ θεὸς εἴη) *may God be gracious to you, Lord,* i.e. may God in mercy spare you this, *God forbid!* **Mt 16:22** (cp. IGR, 107, 10 ἵλεώς σοι=may [Sarapis] help you; OGI 721, 10; Gen 43:23; 2 Km 20:20; 1 Ch 11:19; JosAs 6:4; ViDa 18 [p. 79, 8 Sch.].—Difft. PKatz, TLZ 82, '57, 113f (s. also Kratylos 5, '60, 159) and B-D-F §128, 5. S. Rob. 395f; HMaehler, ZPE 4, '69, 99f).—DELG s.v. ἱλάσκομαι 1. M-M. TW.

Ἰλλυρικόν, οῦ, τό (the adj. Ἰλλυρικός, ή, όν in Apollon. Rhod. 4, 516; Strabo) ***Illyricum,*** a district across the Adriatic Sea fr. Italy, in official usage Dalmatia (Illyris Superior) and Pannonia (I. Inferior). **Ro 15:19** ἀπὸ Ἰερουσαλὴμ καὶ κύκλῳ μέχρι τοῦ Ἰ. is the only reference extant to missionary activity of Paul in this part of the world. Yet in view of the close connection of Illyricum with Macedonia (Appian, Bell. Civ. 3, 63 §258; 4, 75 §317 τῆς Ἰλλυρίδος ἐπὶ τῇ Μακεδονίᾳ; 5, 145 §602) there is no difficulty in assuming that Paul visited Ill. from Mac.—WWeber, Untersuchungen z. Gesch. des Kaisers Hadrianus 1907, 55.—Is Paul perh. using the expression also to indicate the vast area he traversed (as one might say: 'from Dallas, Texas, all the way to Anchorage, Alaska')?—S. Δαλματία. Kl. Pauly II 1367–69. M-M.

ἱμάς, άντος, ὁ (Hom. et al.; ins, pap, LXX; Jos., Ant. 12, 192–94; Just., D. 131, 6) leather ***strap*** or ***thong,*** on sandals (X., An. 4, 5, 14; Menand., fgm. 97, 3 Kö. [no. 109, 2 Kock]; Plut.,

Mor. 665b; Is 5:27) **Mk 1:7; Lk 3:16; J 1:27.** The interpr. of ὡς προέτειναν αὐτὸν τ. ἱμᾶσιν **Ac 22:25** is in doubt. It can be instrumental dat., *with the thongs,* used for tying him to the post, but is better taken as a dat. of purpose *for the thongs,* in which case οἱ ἱμάντες=*whips* (Posidonius: 87 fgm. 5 Jac.; POxy 1186, 2 τὴν διὰ τῶν ἱμάντων αἰκείαν.—Antiphanes 74, 8, Demosth. 19, 197 and Artem. 1, 70 use the sing. in this way).—DELG. M-M.

ἱματίζω pf. pass. ptc. ἱματισμένος (s. two next entries; PLond I, 24 recto, 14 p. 32 [163 BC]; BGU 1125, 8; PTebt 385, 15, al. in pap) ***dress, clothe*** **Mk 5:15; Lk 8:35.**—DELG s.v. ἕννυμι. M-M.

ἱμάτιον, ου, τό (s. prec. and next entry; since Hipponax 70, Hdt., Aristoph.+) prim. 'a piece of clothing'

❶ ***clothing, apparel,*** gener. of any garment (PRyl 154, 8; PPetr II, 32, 18; PSI 94, 16; LXX) sg. **Mt 9:16; Mk 2:21; 5:27; Lk 5:36; 8:27; Hb 1:11f** (Ps 101:27); B 6:2 (Is 50:9) al. Pl. *clothing* (Philo, Leg. All. 3, 239) **Mt 11:8 v.l.; 27:31, 35; Mk 5:28, 30; 9:3; 15:20, 24** al.; **Lk 7:25; 23:34; J 19:23f; Rv 16:15.** The pl. in the foll. pass. is explained by the fact that each one of a number of persons contributed one piece of clothing: **Mt 21:7, 8; Mk 11:7, 8; Lk 19:35, 36** (on these pass. s. Plut., Cato Min. 764 [12, 1]); **Ac 9:39** (Paradoxogr. Vat. 26 Keller ἱμάτια ἐπιδεικνύναι); Hs 9, 13, 5. ἡ τῶν ἱματίων ἀλαζών *she who prides herself on her apparel* AcPl Ha 2, 20.—ἀποθέσθαι ἑαυτῷ πάντα τὰ ἱ. *take off all one's (own) clothes* MPol 13:2. περιαιρεῖσθαι τὰ ἱ. *take off* GJs 2:4. ἱ. μαλακά *soft clothing* **Lk 7:25.** λευκά *white clothing* **Rv 3:4f, 18; 4:4;** cp. **Mt 17:2; Mk 9:3.** μέλανα ἱ. Hs 9, 15, 1; 3 (in such cases ἱ. can be omitted, as we say 'dressed in white' or 'in black': J 20:12; Hv 4, 2, 1. Cp. B-D-F §241, 7 and λευκός 2 end). πενθικά ... νυμφικά GJs 2:4 (Mel., P. 19, 132 ἱ. πενθικόν). σκυθροπότερα *clothing fit for mourners* AcPl Ha 2, 16. Ruined by moths **Js 5:2.** ἱ. κατατρίβεται *wear out* AcPl Ha 2, 25; 9, 9 (restored). σύνθεσις ἱματίων Hs 6, 1, 5. ἔνδυσις ἱματίων *putting on clothing* **1 Pt 3:3.**

❷ of outer clothing *cloak, robe* (Lucian, Alex. 11) **Mt 9:20f; 23:5 v.l.; 24:18; Mk 5:27; 6:56; 10:50; 13:16; Lk 8:44; 22:36; J 19:2, 5; Rv 19:16.** W. χιτών, the undergarment (Diod. S. 4, 38, 1; Dio Chrys. 13 [7], 61; Diogenes, Ep. 30, 3; Diog. L. 6, 6; SIG 736, 17 [92 BC]; PEdg 11=Sb 6717, 9 [257 BC]) **Ac 9:39;** D 1:4; **Mt 5:40** (here the order is χιτ. ... ἱ.; the situation is that of a lawsuit, in which the defendant is advised to give up not only the indispensable χιτών demanded by the opponent, but the ἱ. as well); **Lk 6:29** (here the order is ἱ. ... χ., a sequence that suggests highway robbery, in which the robber first deprives a victim of the outer garment. Cp. UPZ 122, 14 [157 BC], the report of a robbery: βουλόμενός μου περιελέσθαι τὸ ἱμάτιον. Also PLille 6, 9 ἐξέδυσαν χιτῶνα ... ἱμάτιον.—But Lk may have had Dt 24:10–13 in mind [ἱ. as a pledge]. Through nonretaliation the debtor shows the shamelessness of the creditor: FDanker, Jesus and the New Age, '88, 145). ἱ. περιβάλλειν, περιβάλλεσθαι (PFay 12, 19 [c. 103 BC]; Gen 28:20; 1 Km 28:8 al.) **J 19:2; Ac 12:8; Rv 19:13.** The outer garment was laid off in order to leave the arms free **Ac 7:58; 22:20;** so perh. also vs. **23.** It was torn as a sign of grief (oft. LXX) **14:14,** and removed from a person who was to be flogged **16:22.**

❸ Certain pass. fall betw. 1 and 2; they speak of τὰ ἱμάτια, but involve only one person, who obviously is doing someth. to one outer garment (Mussies 83): ὁ ἀρχιερεὺς διέρρηξεν τὰ ἱ. αὐτοῦ **Mt 26:65** (cp. Gen 37:29, 34; Josh 7:6; Jdth 14:16 al.). Cp. **J 13:4, 12; Ac 18:6.**—B 3:4 ἱμάτια is an uncertain rdg.: v.l. ἰάματα; it is a quot. fr. Is 58:8 (s. the variants there, ed. JZiegler).—Dalman, Arbeit V '37. BHHW II 962–65. B. 395; 416. DELG s.v. ἕννυμι. M-M. TW.

ἱματισμός, οῦ, ὁ (s. prec. two entries; Theophr., Char. 23, 8; Polyb. 6, 15, 4; Diod. S. 17, 94, 2; Plut., Alex. 39, 10; SIG 999, 5; 1015, 36; PHib 54, 16 [c. 245 BC]; PTebt 381, 13; 384, 19; LXX; JosAs 2:7; Philo, Migr. Abr. 105) ***clothing, apparel*** **Lk 9:29; J 19:24** (Ps 21:19); **Ac 20:33;** D 13:7; B 6:6 (Ps 21:19); Hs 9, 13, 3. ἱ. ἔνδοξος *fine clothing* **Lk 7:25.** ἱ. πολυτελής *expensive apparel* (Pel.—Leg. p. 4, 8; cp. Plut., Mor. 229a ἱμάτια πολυτελῆ) **1 Ti 2:9.** ἱ. λαμπρότατος *shining apparel* Hv 1, 2, 2. White clothing (Aeneas Tact. 1488 ἱ. λευκός) **Lk 9:29;** Hs 8, 2, 3f.—DELG s.v. ἕννυμι. M-M. TW.

ἱμείρομαι s. ὁμείρομαι and Frisk s.v. ἵμερος. M-M. s.v. ἱμείρω.

ἵνα (Hom.+) conjunction, the use of which increased considerably in H. Gk. as compared w. earlier times because it came to be used periphrastically for the inf. and impv. B-D-F §369; 379; 388–94 al.; Mlt. index; Rob. index.

❶ **marker to denote purpose, aim, or goal,** ***in order that, that,*** final sense—ⓐ w. subjunctive, not only after a primary tense, but also (in accordance w. Hellenistic usage) after a secondary tense (B-D-F §369, 1; Rob. 983; Mlt-Turner 100–102; JKnuenz, De enuntiatis Graecorum finalibus 1913, 15ff):

α. after a present tense **Mk 4:21; 7:9; Lk 6:34; 8:16; J 3:15; 5:34; 6:30; Ac 2:25** (Ps 15:8); **16:30; Ro 1:11; 3:19; 11:25; 1 Cor 9:12; Gal 6:13; Phil 3:8; Hb 5:1; 6:12; 1J 1:3** and oft.

β. after a perfect **Mt 1:22; 21:4; J 5:23, 36; 6:38; 12:40, 46; 14:29; 16:1, 4; 17:4; 1 Cor 9:22b** al.

γ. after a pres. or aor. impv. **Mt 7:1; 14:15; 17:27; 23:26; Mk 11:25; J 4:15; 5:14; 10:38; 1 Cor 7:5; 11:34; 1 Ti 4:15; Tit 3:13.** Likew. after the hortatory subj. in the first pers. pl. **Mk 1:38; Lk 20:14; J 11:16; Hb 4:16.**

δ. after a fut. **Lk 16:4; 18:5; J 5:20; 14:3, 13, 16; 1 Cor 15:28; Phil 1:26.**

ε. after a secondary tense: impf. **Mk 3:2; 6:41; 8:6; Lk 6:7; 18:15** al.—Plpf. **J 4:8.**—Aor. **Mt 19:13; Mk 3:14; 11:28; 14:10; Lk 19:4, 15; J 7:32; 12:9; Ro 7:4; 2 Cor 8:9; Hb 2:14; 11:35; 1J 3:5.**

ⓑ w. fut. ind. (LXX e.g. Sus 28; En 15:5; TestSol 13:7; SIG 888, 87ff; OGI 665, 35; POxy 299; 1071, 5 ἵνα ποιήσουσιν καὶ πέμψουσιν; Gen 16:2 [Swete; ARahlfs, Genesis 1926 v.l.] al.; Just., D. 115, 6), beside which the aor. subj. is usu. found in the mss. (B-D-F §369, 2; Rob. 984; Mlt-Turner 100) ἵνα σταυρώσουσιν **Mk 15:20 v.l.** ἵνα ἐρεῖ σοι **Lk 14:10.** ἵνα δώσουσιν **20:10.** ἵνα θεωρήσουσιν **J 7:3.** ἵνα δώσει **17:2 v.l.; Rv 8:3.** ἐπισκιάσει **Ac 5:15 v.l.;** ξυρήσονται **21:24.** κερδανῶ **1 Cor 9:21 v.l.;** καυθήσομαι **13:3 v.l.** καταδουλώσουσιν **Gal 2:4.** κερδηθήσονται **1 Pt 3:1.** ἵνα ... δηλώσεις Hv 3, 8, 10. The fut. ind. is also used oft. when ἵνα has no final mng., esp. in Rv: **1 Cor 9:18** (ἵνα as answer, as Epict. 4, 1, 99); **Rv 6:4, 11; 9:4, 5, 20; 13:12; 14:13; 22:14.** Occasionally the fut. ind. and aor. subj. are found in the same sentence **Rv 3:9;** cp. also **Phil 2:10f v.l.** (on this interchange s. Reinhold 106; JVogeser, Zur Sprache d. griech. Heiligenlegenden, diss. Munich 1907, 34f; Knuenz, op. cit. 23ff; 39; Dio Chrys. 26 [43], 7 ἵνα μὴ παρῶ ... μηδὲ ἕξουσιν; POxy 1068, 5 ἵνα διαπέμψεται, ἵνα δυνηθῶ ...).—On the interchange of pres. subj. and fut. ind. in **J 15:8** s. GLee, Biblica 51, '70, 239f.

ⓒ ἵνα is found w. the pres. ind. only in passages where the subj. is also attested in the mss.; its presence is prob. due to corruption of the text (B-D-F §369, 6; Rob. 984f; Mlt-Turner 100f. But see the clear instance in PAnt III, 188, 15: ἵνα μὴ ἔσμεν, and cp. BGU 1081, 3 ἐχάρην, ἵνα σὲ ἀσπάζομαι; TestNapht 8:2; PassPtPl 60 [Aa I, 170, 8] ἵνα κατευθύνει; AcPtPl 58 [Aa I, 203, 17]; AcPlTh 11 [Aa I, 243, 11 v.l.]). φυσιοῦσθε **1 Cor 4:6** and ζηλοῦτε **Gal 4:17** could be subj. (B-D-F §91; Rob. 984). But **Gal 6:12 v.l.** διώκονται; **Tit 2:4 v.l.** σωφρονίζουσιν; **J 5:20 v.l.** θαυμάζετε; **17:3 v.l.** γινώσκουσιν; **1J 5:20 v.l.** γινώσκομεν; **Rv 12:6 v.l.** τρέφουσιν; **13:17 v.l.** δύναται; ἵνα σύνετε B 6:5 v.l. (in text συνιῆτε; v.l. συνῆτε); ἵνα . . . ᾄδετε IEph 4:2 (Lghtf. ᾄδητε); μετέχετε ibid. (v.l. μετέχητε).διατάσσομαι ITr 3:3 (v.l. διατάσσωμαι). βλασφημεῖται 8:2 v.l.

ⓓ The opt. after ἵνα is not used in our lit. (B-D-F §369, 1; 386, 3; Rob. 983). **Mk 12:2 v.l.** ἵνα λάβοι (for λάβῃ). **Eph 1:17** ἵνα δῴη (v.l. δῷ) is certainly subj., and δώῃ is the correct rdg. (B-D-F §95, 2; Mlt. 196f). Likew. ἵνα παραδοῖ **J 13:2.**

ⓔ after a demonstrative (Epict. 2, 5, 16 ἐν τούτῳ . . . ἵνα) εἰς τοῦτο *for this (purpose, namely) that* **J 18:37; 1J 3:8; Ro 14:9; 2 Cor 2:9; 1 Pt 3:9; 4:6;** B 5:1, 11; 14:5. εἰς αὐτὸ τοῦτο *for this very purpose, that* **Eph 6:22; Col 4:8.** διὰ τοῦτο *for this reason . . . that* (Himerius, Or. 14, 3) **2 Cor 13:10; Phlm 15; 1 Ti 1:16;** the ἵνα clause can also precede διὰ τοῦτο **J 1:31.** τούτου χάριν . . . ἵνα *for this reason . . . that* **Tit 1:5.**

ⓕ ἵνα with 'I should like to say this' supplied is found also in earlier Gk (Soph. Ph. 989) **Mk 2:10** (B-D-F §470, 3. Differently [a virtual impv.] DSharp, ET 38, 1927, 427f). The necessary supplement precedes in ἵνα δείξῃ (he said this), *in order to show* B 7:5.—Cp. **J 15:13.**

❷ **marker of objective, *that.*** Very oft. the final mng. is greatly weakened or disappears altogether. In this case the ἵνα-constr. serves as a substitute for an inf. that supplements a verb, or an acc. w. inf. (cp. Od. 3, 327 and a spurious document in Demosth. 18, 155. Later very common, also in ins, pap [Rdm.[2] 191ff]; LXX).

ⓐ after verbs w. the sense—**α.** 'wish, desire, strive' (PGiss 17, 5 [II AD] ἠγωνίασα . . . ἵνα ἀκούσω; BGU 1081, 3 ἐχάρην, ἵνα σὲ ἀσπάζομαι) θέλειν ἵνα (TestAbr A 19, 101, 9 [Stone p. 50]) **Mt 7:12; Mk 9:30; 10:35; Lk 6:31; J 17:24; 1 Cor 14:5.** βουλεύεσθαι **J 11:53; 12:10.** συμβουλεύεσθαι **Mt 26:4.** συντίθεσθαι **J 9:22.** ἀγαλλιᾶσθαι joyfully strive after **8:56** (s. ἀγαλλιάω). ζητεῖν **1 Cor 4:2; 14:12;** AcPlCor 2:8. ζηλοῦν **14:1.** εὔχεσθαι 'wish' IPhld 6:3.

β. 'take care, be ashamed, be afraid' φυλάσσεσθαι **2 Pt 3:17.** προσέχειν take care that B 16:8. βλέπειν see to it, that **1 Cor 16:10.**

γ. 'request, demand': δεῖσθαι request (Dionys. Hal. 4, 12, 1; Lucian, Dom. 9; Jos., Ant. 6, 321; 12, 125 al.) **Lk 9:40; 21:36; 22:32;** B 12:7; Pol 6:2; Hv 3, 1, 2; s 5, 4, 1. ἐρωτᾶν request (s. ἐρωτάω 2) **Mk 7:26; Lk 7:36; 16:27; J 4:47; 17:15** al. (JEarwaker, ET 75, '64, 316f so interprets the third ἵνα in **17:21**). παρακαλεῖν request, exhort (EpArist 318; 321, Jos., Ant. 14, 168) **Mt 14:36; Mk 5:18; 6:56; 7:32; 8:22; Lk 8:32; 1 Cor 1:10** al. αἰτεῖσθαι **Col 1:9** (Just., D. 30, 2 αἰτοῦμεν). προσεύχεσθαι **Mt 24:20; 26:41; Mk 14:35; Lk 22:46; 1 Cor 14:13** al. εὔχεσθαι pray (s. εὔχομαι 1 end) Hs 5, 2, 10. εὐχαριστεῖν **Eph 1:16f.** ἀξιοῦν demand, request (CIG 4892, 13 [III AD]; Jos., Ant. 14, 22) Hv 4, 1, 3. καταξιοῦν ISm 11:1; IPol 7:2.

δ. 'summon, encourage, order' (Epict, 4, 11, 29; 1 Esdr 8:19; EpArist 46) ἀπαγγέλλειν **Mt 28:10.** παραγγέλλειν (CIG 4957, 48 [68 AD] restored) **Mk 6:8.** διαμαρτύρεσθαι **1 Ti 5:21.** ἐντέλλεσθαι (Jos., Ant. 7, 356) **Mk 13:34; J 15:17.** κηρύσσειν **Mk 6:12.** διαστέλλεσθαι **Mt 16:20; Mk 5:43; 7:36; 9:9.** ἐπιτιμᾶν warn **Mt 16:20; 20:31; Mk 8:30; 10:48; Lk 18:39.** ἐξορκίζειν **Mt 26:63.** ὁρκίζειν Hs 9, 10, 5. λέγειν order **Mt 4:3; 20:21; Mk 3:9; 9:18; Lk 4:3; 10:40;** Hv 2, 2, 6. γράφειν write (Jos., Ant. 11, 7; 127) **Mk 9:12; 12:19; Lk 20:28.** ἀποστέλλειν **Ac 16:36.**

ε. 'cause, bring about' πείθειν **Mt 27:20.** ποιεῖν **J 11:37; Col 4:16;** cp. **Rv 3:9; 13:16.** τιθέναι appoint **J 15:16.** ἀγγαρεύειν **Mt 27:32; Mk 15:21.**

ζ. 'permit, grant' ἀφιέναι **Mk 11:16.** On **J 12:7** s. CBarrett, The Gospel According to St. John[2], '78, 413–14. διδόναι **10:37; Rv 9:5.**

η. συνευδοκεῖν Hs 5, 2, 8.

ⓑ after impers. expr.: ἀρκετόν (ἐστι) *it is sufficient* **Mt 10:25.** λυσιτελεῖ (εἰ . . . ἢ ἵνα) **Lk 17:2.** συμφέρει **Mt 5:29f; 18:6; J 11:50.** ἐμοὶ εἰς ἐλάχιστόν ἐστιν *it is a matter of little consequence to me* **1 Cor 4:3.** ἔδει B 5:13. πολλὰ λείπει Hv 3, 1, 9.

ⓒ after nouns and adjs., esp. when they are parts of fixed expressions:—**α.** χρείαν ἔχειν **J 2:25; 16:30; 1J 2:27.** ἔστιν συνήθεια **J 18:39.** θέλημά ἐστιν **Mt 18:14; J 6:40; 1 Cor 16:12b.** βουλὴ ἐγένετο **Ac 27:42.** ἐντολή (cp. Polyb. 36, 17, 10 νόμος) **J 15:12; 11:57; 13:34; Ac 17:15; 2J 6.** δέησις **Eph 6:19.** ἐξουσία **Ac 8:19.** ἐμὸν βρῶμά ἐστιν **J 4:34.** τίς ἐστιν ὁ μισθός; ἵνα . . . **1 Cor 9:18.**

β. οὐκ εἰμὶ ἱκανός **Mt 8:8; Lk 7:6.** οὐκ εἰμὶ ἄξιος **J 1:27;** cp. Hs 9, 28, 5. S. B-D-F §379; Rob. 996.

ⓓ after nouns mng. time: χρόνον διδόναι, ἵνα *give time* **Rv 2:21.** ἔρχεται ἡ ὥρα *the time comes* (Aesop, Fab. 242 H. ἡ ἡμέρα, ἵνα=the day on which) **J 12:23; 13:1; 16:2, 32.** S. B-D-F §382, 1; 393.

ⓔ ἵνα can also take the place of the explanatory inf. after a demonstrative (B-D-F §394; Rdm.[2] 192.—Wsd 13:9; Just., D. 14, 2 τοῦτο γάρ ἐστι τὸ σύμβολον τῶν ἀζύμων, ἵνα μὴ . . .) **Mk 11:28.** πόθεν μοι τοῦτο ἵνα ἔλθῃ (for τὸ ἐλθεῖν τὴν κτλ.) **Lk 1:43** (cp. GJs 12:2). τοῦτο προσεύχομαι ἵνα **Phil 1:9.** cp. **1 Cor 9:18.** This is a favorite usage in **J:** τοῦτό ἐστιν τὸ ἔργον τοῦ θεοῦ ἵνα πιστεύητε (for τὸ πιστεύειν ὑμᾶς) **6:29;** cp. vs. **50.** μείζονα ταύτης ἀγάπην οὐδεὶς ἔχει ἵνα . . . θῇ (for τοῦ θεῖναι) **15:13;** cp. **3J 4.—J 6:39; 17:3; 1J 3:11, 23; 4:21; 5:3; 2J 6a.** ἐν τούτῳ: ἐν τούτῳ ἐδοξάσθη ὁ πατήρ μου ἵνα . . . φέρητε (for ἐν τῷ φέρειν ὑμᾶς ἐδοξάσθη) **J 15:8;** cp. **1J 4:17.**—S. also Hs 9, 28, 4, and ποταπὴν ἀγάπην ἵνα **1J 3:1.**

ⓕ ἵνα is used elliptically ἀλλ' ἵνα *but this has happened that,* where the verb to be supplied must be inferred fr. the context (Epict. 1, 12, 17): ἀλλ' ἵνα μαρτυρήσῃ (sc. ἦλθεν) **J 1:8.** ἀλλ' (ἐγένετο ἀπόκρυφον) ἵνα ἔλθῃ εἰς φανερόν *but it was hidden that it might be revealed* **Mk 4:22** (but cp. CCadoux, JTS 42, '41, 169 n. 3). ἀλλ' (κρατεῖτέ με) ἵνα πληρωθῶσιν *but you are holding me (prisoner), that* **14:49.** ἀλλ' (ἐγένετο τυφλὸς) ἵνα φανερωθῇ **J 9:3.** ἀλλ' (ἀποθνήσκει) ἵνα . . . συναγάγῃ **11:52.—13:18;** Hv 3, 8, 10 (cp. 1b above).

ⓖ ἵνα w. subjunctive as a periphrasis for the impv. (B-D-F §387, 3; Mlt. 178; 210f; 248; Rob. 994; Mlt-Turner 94f; FSlotty, D. Gebr. des Konj. u. Opt. in d. griech. Dialekten I 1915, 35; CCadoux, The Impv. Use of ἵνα in the NT: JTS 42, '41, 165–73; in reply HMeecham, JTS 43, '42, 179f, also ET 52, '40/41, 437; AGeorge, JTS 45, '44, 56–60. Goodsp., Probs. 57f.—Soph., Oed. Col. 155; Epict. 4, 1, 41, Enchir. 17; PTebt 408, 17 [3 AD]; BGU 1079, 20; PFay 112, 12; POxy 299, 5 ἵν' εἰδῇς 'know'; PGM 4, 2135; Tob 8:12 BA; 2 Macc 1:9. ἵνα πρὶν τούτων ἴδητε τὴν ἀπώλειαν τῶν υἱῶν 'before these events, you shall behold the destruction of your sons' En 14:6. κύριε, ἵνα γινώσκῃ τὸ σὸν κράτος ὅτι 'Lord, may you in your majesty know, that . . . ' TestAbr A 4 p. 80, 35f [Stone pp. 8 and 10]). ἵνα ἐπιθῇς τὰς χεῖρας αὐτῇ *please lay your hands on her* **Mk 5:23.** ἡ δὲ γυνὴ ἵνα φοβῆται τ. ἄνδρα *the wife is to respect her husband* **Eph 5:33.** Cp. **Mt 20:33; Mk 10:51; 1 Cor 7:29; 16:16; 2 Cor 8:7; Gal 2:10.** ἵνα ἀναπαήσονται *let them rest* **Rv 14:13.** W. θέλω: θέλω ἵνα δῷς **Mk 6:25** (=δός **Mt 14:8.**).—On **Mk 2:10** s. 1f above.

ⓗ ἵνα without a finite verb, which can be supplied fr. the context (Epict. 3, 23, 4 ἵνα ὡς ἄνθρωπος, i.e. ἐργάζῃ) ἵνα ἡμεῖς εἰς τὰ ἔθνη, αὐτοὶ δὲ εἰς τὴν περιτομήν (i.e. εὐαγγελιζώμεθα and εὐαγγελίζωνται) **Gal 2:9.** ἵνα κατὰ χάριν (γένηται) **Ro 4:16.** ἵνα ἄλλοις ἄνεσις (γένηται) **2 Cor 8:13.** ἵνα (γένηται) καθὼς γέγραπται **1 Cor 1:31** (B-D-F §481; Rob. 1202f).

❸ **marker serving as substitute for the inf. of result,** ***so that*** ('ecbatic' or consecutive use of ἵνα: B-D-F §391, 5; Mlt. 206–9; Rob. 997–99 and in SCase, Studies in Early Christianity [Porter-Bacon Festschr.] 1928, 51–57; EBlakeney, ET 53, '41/42, 377f, indicating that the result is considered probable, but not actual. But this distinction is not always strictly observed. Cp. Epict. 1, 24, 3; 25, 15; 27, 8 al.; 2, 2, 16 οὕτω μωρὸς ἦν, ἵνα μὴ ἴδῃ; Vett. Val. 185, 31; 186, 17; 292, 20; Jos., Bell. 6, 107; Just., D. 112, 5; PLond III, 964, 13 p. 212 [II/III AD]. Many exx. in AJannaris, An Historical Greek Grammar 1897 §1758 and 1951) ἦν παρακεκαλυμμένον ἀπ' αὐτῶν ἵνα μὴ αἴσθωνται αὐτό *it was concealed from them, so that they might not comprehend it* **Lk 9:45.** τίς ἥμαρτεν, ἵνα τυφλὸς γεννηθῇ; *Who sinned, so that he was born blind?* **J 9:2.** Cp. **2 Cor 1:17; Gal 5:17; 1 Th 5:4; 1J 1:9; Rv 9:20; 13:13;** Hs 7:2; 9, 1, 10.—In many cases purpose and result cannot be clearly differentiated, and hence ἵνα is used for the result that follows according to the purpose of the subj. or of God. As in Semitic and Gr-Rom. thought, purpose and result are identical in declarations of the divine will (Ps.-Callisth. 2, 16, 10 the rule of the Persian king is being overthrown by the deity ἵνα Δαρεῖος … φυγὰς γενόμενος κτλ. Here ἵνα means both 'in order that' and 'so that'): **Lk 11:50; J 4:36; 12:40; 19:28; Ro 3:19; 5:20; 7:13; 8:17; 11:31f** al. (ESutcliffe, Effect or Purpose, Biblica 35, '54, 320–27). The formula ἵνα πληρωθῇ is so to be understood, since the fulfillment is acc. to God's plan of salvation: **Mt 1:22; 2:15; 4:14; 12:17; 21:4; 26:56; J 12:38; 17:12; 19:24, 36.**—The ἵνα of **Mk 4:12=Lk 8:10,** so much in dispute, is prob. to be taken as final (w. AvVeldhuizen, NTS 8, 1925, 129–33; 10, 1927, 42–44; HWindisch, ZNW 26, 1927, 203–9; JGnilka, Die Verstockung Israels '61, 45–48; B-D-F §369, 2 [here, and B-D-R p. 386f n. 2, the lit. on 'causal' ἵνα, which is allowed at least for **Rv 22:14** and perh. **14:13,** where P[47] has ὅτι; see 2g]. S. also FLaCava, Scuola Cattol. 65, '37, 301–4; MBlack, An Aramaic Approach[3], '67, 211–16; ISluiter, Causal ἵνα, Sound Greek: Glotta 70, '92, 39–53. On **J 12:7** s. τηρέω 2a).

❹ **marker of retroactive emphasis,** ***that.*** At times, contrary to regular usage, ἵνα is placed elsewhere than at the beginning of its clause, in order to emphasize the words that come before it (B-D-F §475, 1; cp. the position of ὅτι Gal 1:11): τὴν ἀγάπην ἵνα γνῶτε **2 Cor 2:4.** εἰς τὸν ἐρχόμενον μετ' αὐτὸν ἵνα πιστεύσωσιν **Ac 19:4.** τῷ ὑμετέρῳ ἐλέει ἵνα **Ro 11:31.** Cp. **J 13:29; 1 Cor 7:29; Gal 2:10; Col 4:16b.**—EStauffer, Ἵνα u. d. Problem d. teleol. Denkens b. Pls: StKr 102, 1930, 232–57; JGreenlee, ἵνα Substantive Clauses in the NT: Asbury Seminarian 2, '47, 154–63; HRiesenfeld, Zu d. johanneischen ἵνα-Sätzen, StTh 19, '65, 213–20; MBlack, An Aramaic Approach[3], '67, 76–81.—Frisk. M-M. EDNT. TW.

ἱνατί (oft. written separately; for ἵνα τί γένηται; 'to what end?' B-D-F §12, 3; W-S. §5, 7e; Rob. 739) ***why, for what reason?*** (Aristoph., Nub. 1192; Pla., Apol. 14 p. 26d, Symp. 205a; Epict. 1, 29, 31; LXX; PsSol 3:1; 4:1; TestAbr A 8 p. 85, 24 [Stone p. 18]; 86, 10f [St. p. 20]; TestJos 7:5; GrBar 1:2; Jos., Bell. 6, 347) **Mt 9:4; 27:46** (Ps 21:2); **Lk 13:7; Ac 4:25** (Ps 2:1); **7:26; 1 Cor 10:29;** 1 Cl 4:4 (Gen 4:6); 35:7 (Ps 49:16); 46:5, 7; B 3:1 (Is 58:4). W. εἰς τί *why and for what?* D 1:5. B-D-F §299, 4.—M-M. s.v. ἵνα.

ἰνδάλλομαι (etym. connection w. εἶδος, οἶδα; Hom. et al.; SibOr 13, 71) ***form false ideas, entertain strange notions*** (Dio Chrys. 11 [12], 53; Sext. Emp., Adv. Math. 11, 122 ὁ τὸν πλοῦτον μέγιστον ἀγαθὸν ἰνδαλλόμενος; Clem. Alex., Protr. 10, 103, 2) ἐπί τινι *about someth.* 1 Cl 23:2 (s. Harnack, Lghtf., Knopf ad loc.).—DELG.

Ἰόππη, ης, ἡ (Antig. Car. 151; Diod. S. 19, 59, 2; 19, 93, 7; Strabo 16, 2, 28; 34; Dionys. Perieg. in GGM II 160; OGI 602, 2; 1 Esdr 5:53; 1 Macc 10:75 al.; 2 Macc 4:21; EpArist 115; Joseph.; SibOr 5, 251. On the sp. w. one π or two [so Bibl. mss. throughout] s. B-D-F §40; W-S. §5, 26, n. 54; Mlt-H. 102; Rob. 214; Schürer II 110f, 193 n. 35) ***Joppa,*** modern Jaffa, seaport and city on the Philistine coast northwest of Jerusalem **Ac 9:36, 38, 42f; 10:5, 8, 23, 32; 11:5, 13.**—Schürer II 110–14 (lit.); FScholten, Palästina I: Jaffa '31. BHHW II 803f.—M-M.

Ἰορδάνης, ου, ὁ (יַרְדֵּן) (Strabo 16, 2, 16; Galen XI 693 K.; Tacitus, Hist. 5, 62; LXX, ParJer; ApcSed 8:3 p. 133, 1 Ja.; EpArist, Philo, Joseph.; Just.; Mel., fgm. 8b, 42; SibOr 7, 67 [Ἰόρδανος, also found in Joseph. and Paus. 5, 7, 4]; on the use of the art. w. it s. B-D-F §261, 8) ***the Jordan,*** chief river of Palestine (EpArist 116). It arises at the foot of Mt. Hermon, flows through the Sea of Galilee, and empties into the Dead Sea **Mt 3:5f, 13; 4:15** (Is 8:23), **25; 19:1; Mk 1:5, 9; 3:8; 10:1; Lk 3:3; 4:1; J 1:28; 3:26; 10:40;** GEb 13, 74; PEg[2] 66; HGuthe, RE XIV 573ff, Palästina[2] 1927; Dalman, Orte[3], index; OWaser, V. Flussgott J.: AKaegi Festschr. 1919, 191–217; WvSoden, ZAW n.s. 16, '39, 153f; NGlueck, The River Jordan [2] '54.—TW.

ἰός, οῦ, ὁ (Pind. et al.; pap, LXX; TestJob 43:8; TestReub 5:6; ApcMos 19)

❶ ***poison, venom***—ⓐ lit. ἰὸν ἐχίδνης Papias (11:2) and ἰὸς ἀσπίδων (TestJob 43:12; cp. Appian, Mithr. 88 §490 ἰὸς ὄφεων; Philo, Leg. ad Gai. 166; Jos., Bell. 1, 601; Constant. Manasses 4, 39 H.) **Ro 3:13** (Ps 13:3; 139:4). Of animal (i.e. snake; s. θηρίον 1aβ) poison also Hs 9, 26, 7. These passages, as well as Hv 3, 9, 7 and ITr 6:2 v.l., show that the transition to the fig. use was easy.

ⓑ fig. (Aeschyl., Eum. 730 al.; Herm. Wr. p. 480, 15 Sc.; Test Reub 5:6) **Js 3:8.**

❷ ***corrosion, rust*** (Theognis 451; Pla., Tim. 59c, Rep. 10, 609a; Theocr. 16, 17 et al.; SIG[2] 587, 310 [329 BC] σίδηρος καταβεβρωμένος ὑπὸ τοῦ ἰοῦ; SIG 284, 15; Herm. Wr. 14, 7; Ezk 24:6, 11f; EpJer 10 and 23; Philo, Div. Rer. Her. 217 [χρυσὸς] ἰὸν οὐ παραδέχεται, gold is praised for being rust-proof; sim. Theognis 449–52; but if not adequately refined or subject to chemical pollution some metals in a gold object would be subject to oxidation) **Js 5:3;** Dg 2:2.—DELG ἰός (3). M-M. TW.

Ἰουδαία, ας, ἡ (יְהוּדָה; but the word is to be derived fr. Aram. יְהוּדָי; fr. the adj. Ἰουδαῖος with γῆ or χώρα supplied, as Philo, Leg. ad Gai. 281) 'Judea' (since Clearchus, the pupil of Aristotle: fgm. 6 [in Jos., C. Ap. 1, 179]; ins [Schürer II 1 n. 2]; PRyl 189, 5; LXX; Philo).

❶ **the southern part of Palestine in contrast to Samaria, Galilee, Perea and Idumea,** ***Judea*** (s. **Mk 3:7f; Ac 9:31;** so LXX and oft. Joseph., Just. Also Strabo 16, 2, 34 w. Galil. and

Samar.) **Mt 2:1, 5, 22; 3:1; 4:25; 24:16; Mk 3:7; 13:14; Lk 1:65; 2:4; 3:1; 5:17; 6:17; 21:21; J 4:3, 47, 54; 7:1, 3; 11:7; Ac 1:8; 8:1; 9:31; 12:19; 15:1; 21:10; 28:21; Ro 15:31; 2 Cor 1:16; Gal 1:22;** AcPl Ha 8, 29f=BMM verso 2. Metaph. of the inhabitants **Mt 3:5** (Ἰ. χώρα **Mk 1:5;** see Ἰουδαῖος 1).—Buhl 64–75; HGuthe, RE IX 556–85; XXIII 713f (lit.); BHHW II 901; YAharoni, The Land of the Bible[2] '79; MStern, in CRINT I/1, 308–76.

❷ **Judea, broadly understood as the region occupied by the people of Israel, *Judea*** ='land of the Judeans (Jews)', i.e. Palestine (Nicol. Dam. [I BC]: 90 fgm. 96 Jac. [in Jos., Ant. 14, 9]; Diod. S. 40, 3, 2; Strabo 16, 2, 34; Memnon [I BC / I AD]: 434 fgm. 1, 18, 9 Jac.; Ptolem. 5, 16, 1; cp. 15, 6–8 and Apotelesmatica 2, 3, 29 and 31. Cass. Dio 37, 16; 47, 28; Tacitus, Hist. 5, 9, 1; LXX; EpArist 4 and12; Philo, Leg. ad Gai. 200; Joseph.; Just., D. 32, 4.—On the NT: ELevesque, Vivre et Penser 3, '43/44, 104–11 denies the wider use) **Lk 1:5; 4:44** (v.l. Γαλιλαίας, s. the entry, end); **7:17; 23:5; Ac 10:37; 11:1, 29; 1 Th 2:14.** πᾶσα ἡ χώρα τῆς Ἰ. *the whole Judean (Jewish) country* **Ac 26:20.** εἰς τὰ ὅρια τῆς Ἰ. πέραν τοῦ Ἰορδάνου *into the Judean (Jewish) territory beyond the Jordan* **Mt 19:1;** cp. **Mk 10:1.** On the mention of Judea **Ac 2:9** cp. the variants and conjectures in Nestle; EvDobschütz, ZWT 45, 1902, 407–10; Harnack, AG 1908, 65f; SKrauss, ZDPV 33, 1910, 225; OLagercrantz, Eranos 10, 1910, 58–60; LKöhler, ET 22, 1911, 230f. Also BZ 1, 1903, 219; 7, 1909, 219; 9, 1911, 218; ZNW 9, 1908, 253f; 255f; Haenchen ad loc.; TRE XXV 591–96.—OEANE III 253–57. M-M. EDNT. TW.

ἰουδαΐζω **live as one bound by Mosaic ordinances or traditions, *live in Judean or Jewish fashion*** (so Plut., Cic. 864 [7, 6]; Esth 8:17; Jos., Bell. 2, 454 μέχρι περιτομῆς ἰ.; s. also 463; Acta Pilati A 2, 1) **Gal 2:14;** BWander, Gottesfürchtige und Sympathisanten (WUNT 104) '98, 212–18; IMg 10:3.—TW.

Ἰουδαϊκός, ή, όν (Artem. 4, 24 p. 217, 11; OGI 543, 16; 586, 7; Cleomedes [II AD] in DDurham, The Vocabulary of Menander 1913, 27; 2 Macc 8:11 v.l.; 13:21; EpArist 28; 121; Philo, In Flacc. 55; Jos., Ant. 12, 34; 14, 228; 20, 258 al.; Just. A I, 53, 4 w. Σαμαρειτικός) ***Judean (Jewish)*** Ἰ. μῦθοι **Tit 1:14.** Τὸ Ἰ. title of a Judeo-Christian Gospel in some mss. (see e.g. ASyn. 333, 51; also Hennecke-Schneemelcher [Wils.] I 136).—M-M. TW.

Ἰουδαϊκῶς adv. (Jos., Bell. 6, 17) ***in a Judean (Jewish) manner,*** Ἰ. ζῆν **Gal 2:14.**—M-M. TW.

Ἰουδαῖος, αία, αῖον (Clearchus, the pupil of Aristotle, fgm. 6 [in Jos., C. Ap. 1, 179]; Theophr., fgm. 151 W. [WJaeger, Diokles v. Karystos '38, 134–53: Theophrastus and the earliest Gk. report concerning the Judeans or Jews]; Hecataeus of Abdera [300 BC] : 264 fgm. 25, 28, 2a Jac. [in Diod. S. 1, 28, 2] al.; Polyb.; Diod. S.; Strabo; Plut.; Epict. 1, 11, 12f, al.; Appian, Syr. 50 §252f, Mithrid. 106 §498, Bell. Civ. 2, 90 §380; Artem. 4, 24 p. 217, 13; Diog. L. 1, 9; OGI 73, 4; 74, 3; 726, 8; CIG 3418; Ramsay, CB I/2, 538 no. 399b τ. νόμον τῶν Εἰουδέων [on Ἰ. in ins s. RKraemer, HTR 82, '89, 35–53]; Mitt-Wilck. I/2, 55; 56 [both III BC]; 57 [II BC]; BGU 1079, 25 [41 AD]; PFay 123, 16 [100 AD]; POxy 1189, 9; LXX; TestSol; AscIs 2:7; EpArist; SibOr; Philo, Joseph., Ar., Just., Tat. For a variety of synonyms s. Schürer III 87–91.). Gener. as description of 'one who identifies with beliefs, rites, and customs of adherents of Israel's Mosaic and prophetic tradition' (the standard term in the Mishnah is 'Israelite'). (Since the term 'Judaism' suggests a monolithic entity that fails to take account of the many varieties of thought and social expression associated with such adherents, the calque or loanword 'Judean' is used in this and other entries where Ἰ. is treated. Complicating the semantic problem is the existence side by side of persons who had genealogy on their side and those who became proselytes [on the latter cp. Cass. Dio 37, 17, 1; 67, 14, 2; 68, 1, 2]; also of adherents of Moses who recognized Jesus as Messiah [s. **Gal 2:13** in 2d below; s. also 2eα] and those who did not do so. Incalculable harm has been caused by simply glossing Ἰ. with 'Jew', for many readers or auditors of Bible translations do not practice the historical judgment necessary to distinguish between circumstances and events of an ancient time and contemporary ethnic-religious-social realities, with the result that anti-Judaism in the modern sense of the term is needlessly fostered through biblical texts.)

❶ **pert. to being Judean (Jewish), with focus on adherence to Mosaic tradition, *Judean,*** as a real adj. (Philo, In Flacc. 29; Jos., Ant. 10, 265) ἀνὴρ Ἰ. (1 Macc 2:23; 14:33) *Judean* **Ac 10:28; 22:3.** ἄνθρωπος **21:39.** ἀρχιερεύς **19:14.** ψευδοπροφήτης **13:6.** ἐξορκισταί **19:13.** γυνή (Jos., Ant. 11, 185) **16:1.** χώρα **Mk 1:5.**—But γῆ **J 3:22** is to be taken of Judea in the narrower sense (s. Ἰουδαία 1), and means *the Judean countryside* in contrast to the capital city. Of Drusilla, described as οὖσα Ἰουδαία *being Judean* or *Jewish,* but for the view that Ἰ. is here a noun s. 2b.

❷ **one who is Judean (Jewish), with focus on adherence to Mosaic tradition, *a Judean,*** Ἰουδαῖος as noun (so predom.). Since Jerusalem sets the standard for fidelity to Israel's tradition, and since Jerusalem is located in Judea, Ἰ. frequently suggests conformity to Israel's ancestral belief and practice. In turn, the geographical name provided outsiders with a term that applied to all, including followers of Jesus, who practiced customs variously associated with Judea (note the Roman perception **Ac 18:15** ['Judeans' at Corinth]; **23:28**).

ⓐ (ὁ) Ἰ. *Judean* (w. respect to birth, nationality, or cult) **J 3:25;** (Mitt-Wilck. I/2, 57, 5 [II BC] παρ' Ἰουδαίου=from a Judean) **4:9; 18:35; Ac 18:2, 24; 19:34; Ro 1:16; 2:9f, 17, 28f** (on the 'genuine' Judean cp. Epict. 2, 9, 20f τῷ ὄντι Ἰουδαῖος . . . λόγῳ μὲν Ἰουδαῖοι, ἔργῳ δ' ἄλλο τι); **10:12; Gal 2:14; 3:28; Col 3:11.**—Collective sing. (Thu. 6, 78, 1 ὁ Ἀθηναῖος, ὁ Συρακόσιος; EpArist 13 ὁ Πέρσης; B-D-F §139; Rob. 408) **Ro 3:1.**

ⓑ of Drusilla οὖσα Ἰουδαία *being a Judean* **Ac 24:24,** but for the simple adjectival sense s. 1 end.

ⓒ (οἱ) Ἰουδαῖοι (on the use of the art. B-D-F §262, 1; 3) *the Judeans* οἱ Φαρισαῖοι κ. πάντες οἱ Ἰ. **Mk 7:3;** τὸ πάσχα τῶν Ἰ. **J 2:13;** cp. **5:1; 6:4; 7:2;** ὁ βασιλεὺς τῶν Ἰ. (Appian, Mithrid. 117 §573 Ἰουδαίων βασιλεὺς Ἀριστόβουλος) **Mt 2:2; 27:11, 29** (in these three last pass., Ἰ. is used by non-Israelites; Mt's preferred term is Ἰσραήλ); **Mk 15:2** and oft. πόλις τῶν Ἰ. **Lk 23:51;** ἔθνος τῶν Ἰ. **Ac 10:22;** λαὸς τῶν Ἰ. **12:11.** χώρα τῶν Ἰ. **10:39** (Just., A I, 34, 2; cp. A I, 32, 4 ἡ γῆ Ἰουδαίων). ἄρχων τῶν Ἰ. **J 3:1;** συναγωγὴ τῶν Ἰ. **Ac 14:1a.** Cp. **J 2:6; 4:22; 18:20.** Ἰ. καὶ Ἕλληνες (on the combination of the two words s. B-D-F §444, 2: w. τε . . . καί) *Judeans and Hellenes* **Ac 14:1b; 18:4; 19:10; 20:21; 1 Cor 1:24; 10:32; 12:13;** PtK 2 p. 15, 7; ἔθνη τε καὶ Ἰ.=*non-Judeans and Judeans* **Ac 14:5;** cp. ISm 1:2. Ἰ. τε καὶ προσήλυτοι *Judeans and proselytes* **Ac 2:11;** cp. **13:43;** οἱ κατὰ τὰ ἔθνη Ἰ. *the Judeans who live among the nations* (in the Diaspora) **21:21.** Judeans and non-Judeans as persecutors of Christians MPol 12:2; cp. also 13:1; 17:2; 18:1; **1 Th 2:14** (Polytheists, Jews, and Christians Ar. 2, 1).—Dg 1.—Without the art. (cp. 19:3 φαρισαῖοι) **Mt 28:15,** suggesting that not all 'Judeans' are meant, and without ref. to Israel, or Jews, as an entity.

ⓓ a Mosaic adherent who identifies with Jesus Christ *Judean* **Gal 2:13;** cp. **Ac 21:20** and εα below. On **Rv 2:9; 3:9** s. Mussies 195.

ⓔ in J Ἰουδαῖοι or 'Judeans' for the most part (for exceptions s. a and c) constitute two groups

α. those who in various degrees identify with Jesus and his teaching **J 8:52; 10:19–21; 11:45; 12:11** al.

β. those who are in opposition to Jesus, with special focus on hostility emanating from leaders in Jerusalem, center of Israelite belief and cult; there is no indication that John uses the term in the general ethnic sense suggested in modern use of the word 'Jew', which covers diversities of belief and practice that were not envisaged by biblical writers, who concern themselves with intra-Judean (intra-Israelite) differences and conflicts: **1:19; 2:18, 20; 5:10, 15f; 6:41, 52** (a debate); **7:1, 11, 13; 9:18, 22; 10:24, 31, 33** (in contrast to the πολλοί from 'beyond the Jordan', 10:40–42, who are certainly Israelites) **11:8; 13:33; 18:14.** S. Hdb. exc. on **J 1:19** and, fr. another viewpoint, JBelser, TQ 84, 1902, 265ff; WLütgert, Heinrici Festschr. 1914, 147ff, Schlatter Festschr. 1922, 137–48; GBoccaccini, Multiple Judaisms: BRev XI/1 '95, 38–41, 46.—**J 18:20** affirms that Jesus did not engage in sectarian activity. Further on anti-Judean feeling in J, s. EGraesser, NTS 11, '64, 74–90; DHare, RSR, July, '76, 15–22 (lit.); Hdb. exc. on **J 1:19;** BHHW II 906–11, 901f, 905.—LFeldman, Jew and Gentile in the Ancient World '93.—MLowe, Who Were the Ἰουδαῖοι?: NovT 18, '76, 101–30; idem Ἰουδαῖοι of the Apocrypha [NT]: NovT 23, '81, 56–90; UvonWahlde, The Johannine 'Jews'—A Critical Survey: NTS 28, '82, 33–60; JAshton, ibid. 27, '85, 40–75 (J).—For impact of Ἰουδαῖοι on gentiles s. ESmallwood, The Jews under Roman Rule fr. Pompey to Diocletian '81; SCohen, Crossing the Boundary and Becoming a Jew: HTR 82, '89, 13–33; PvanderHorst, NedTTs 43, '89, 106–21 (c. 200 AD); PSchäfer, Judeophobia, Attitudes toward the Jews in the Ancient World '97.—On the whole word s. Ἰσραήλ end. For Ἰουδαῖοι in ins s. SEG XXXIX, 1839. M-M. EDNT. TW.

Ἰουδαϊσμός, οῦ, ὁ ***Judeanism/Judaism***=the Judean way of belief and life (2 Macc 2:21; 8:1; 14:38; 4 Macc 4:26; synagogue ins at Stobi ln. 8: ZNW 32, '33, 93f) **Gal 1:13f.** Contrasted w. Χριστιανισμός IMg 10:3; IPhld 6:1. κατὰ (νόμον is prob. a gloss) Ἰουδαϊσμὸν ζῆν *live in accordance w. the Judean way (Judaism)* IMg 8:1.—TW.

Ἰούδας, α, ὁ (יְהוּדָה Judah, etym. unknown; LXX; TestSol 1:12 D; Test12Patr; JosAs 27:6; AscIs, EpArist, Philo, Joseph., Just., Mel., P. 93, 703.—The indecl. form Ἰουδά, which occasionally occurs in the LXX [e.g. Gen 29:35; 2 Macc 14:13 Swete; Thackeray 163] is not to be postulated for our lit., not even **Mt 2:6; Lk 1:39**) ***Judas, Judah*** (Hebr., the Engl. sp. conventionally used for 1 and 2), *Judas* (Gk., conventional sp. for nos. 3–7), *Jude* (s. 8 below); cp. B-D-F §53, 1; 55, 1a; Mlt-H, 143f.

❶ *Judah,* son of the patriarch Jacob—ⓐ in pers.: in the genealogy of Jesus **Mt 1:2f; Lk 3:33.** κατὰ τὸν Ἰούδαν *through Judah* 1 Cl 32:2.—ⓑ the tribe of Judah (Judg 1:2) ἐξ Ἰούδα ἀνατέταλκεν ὁ κύριος **Hb 7:14.** Also φυλὴ Ἰούδα **Rv 5:5; 7:5** (Just., D. 43, 1).

ⓒ the country belonging to the tribe of Judah (Josh 11:21; 2 Ch 28:18) Βηθλέεμ γῆ Ἰούδα **Mt 2:6a;** cp. **Lk 2:4** D; ἡγεμόνες Ἰ. **Mt 2:6b;** πόλις Ἰ. (2 Ch 23:2) **Lk 1:39** (cp. CTorrey, HTR 17, 1924, 83–91). ὁ οἶκος Ἰ. (w. ὁ οἶκος Ἰσραήλ) the inhabitants of the land **Hb 8:8** (Jer 38:31).

❷ *Judah,* a pers. in the genealogy of Jesus—ⓐ Ἰ. son of Ἰωσήφ 2: **Lk 3:30.**—ⓑ Ἰ. son of Ἰωανάν: **Lk 3:26 v.l.**

❸ *Judas,* called ὁ Γαλιλαῖος, a revolutionary in the time of Quirinius 'in the days of the census' (cp. Jos., Ant. 18, 4–10, 23–25; 20, 102, Bell. 2, 118; 433; 7, 253.—Schürer I 381f; 414; 417f; 425; II 599–606) **Ac 5:37.**—WLodder, J. de Galileër: NTS 9, 1926, 3–15.

❹ *Judas* of Damascus, Paul's host **Ac 9:11.**

❺ *Judas,* an apostle, called Ἰ. Ἰακώβου *son of Jacob* or *James* (linguistically speaking, ἀδελφός might also be supplied: Alciphron 4, 17, 10 Τιμοκράτης ὁ Μητροδώρου, i.e. his brother), to differentiate him fr. the informer. He is mentioned in lists of apostles only in the writings of Luke, where two men named Judas are specifically referred to **Lk 6:16** and presupposed **Ac 1:13;** cp. **J 14:22.**

❻ *Judas,* several times called Ἰσκαριώθ or (ὁ) Ἰσκαριώτης (q.v.), the one who turned in Jesus **Mt 10:4; 26:14, 25, 47; 27:3; Mk 3:19; 14:10, 43; Lk 6:16** (προδότης 'traitor'); **22:3, 47f; J 12:4; 13:29; 18:2f, 5; Ac 1:16, 25;** GEb 34, 61; Agr 23b; MPol 6:2 (also Mel., P. 93, 703). His father was Simon **J 13:2,** and this Simon is also called Ἰσκαριώτης **6:71; 13:26** (v.l. described him as Ἰσκαρ.). On Judas himself and the tradition concerning him, incl. the manner of his death, s. Papias (1:5 Lat. [cp. Hippolytus in Da 60 p. 338, 3 Bonwetsch]; 3:1, 2).—Cp. EPreuschen, Antileg.[2] 1905, 98. Lit. in Hennecke-Schneemelcher (Wils.) II 62–64 (s. also I 313f) as well as GMarquardt, D. Verrat des J. Isch.—eine Sage 1900; WWrede, Vorträge u. Studien 1907, 127–46; FFeigel, D. Einfluss d. Weissagungsbeweises 1910, 48ff; 95; 114; WSmith, Ecce Deus 1911, 295–309; KWeidel, StKr 85, 1912, 167–286; GSchläger, Die Ungeschichtlichkeit des Verräters J.: ZNW 15, 1914, 50–59; MPlath, ibid. 17, 1916, 178–88; WCadman, The Last Journey of Jesus to Jerus. 1923, 129–36; JRobertson, Jesus and J. 1927; DHaugg, J. Isk. in den ntl. Berichten 1930 (lit.); JFinegan, D. Überl. d. Leidens- u. Auferstehungsgesch. Jesu '34; FDanker, The Literary Unity of Mk 14:1–25: JBL 85, '66, 467–72. Esp. on the death of J.: RHarris, AJT 4, 1900, 490–513; JBernard, Exp. 6th ser., 9, 1904, 422–30; KLake, Beginn. V '33, note 4, 22–30; PBenoit, La mort de Judas, AWikenhauser Festschr. '53, 1–19; KLüthi, Judas Iskarioth in d. Geschichte d. Auslegung von d. Reformation bis zur Gegenwart '55; idem, D. Problem d. Judas Iskarioth neu untersucht: EvTh 16, '56, 98–114; MEnslin, How the Story Grew: Judas in Fact and Fiction: FGingrich Festschr., ed. Barth and Cocroft, '72, 123–41; and s. παραδίδωμι and πρηνής.—JBrownson, Neutralizing the Intimate Enemy—The Portrayal of Judas in the Fourth Gospel: SPSBL '92, 49–60; WKlassen, Judas—Betrayer or Friend of Jesus? '96; s. also WVogler, Judas Iskarioth '83.

❼ *Judas,* called Βαρσαββᾶς (s. the entry), a Christian prophet in a leading position in the Jerusalem congregation **Ac 15:22, 27, 32.** His name also appears in the interpolated vs. **34.**

❽ *Judas,* a brother of Jesus **Mt 13:55; Mk 6:3.** Prob. the same man is meant by the *Jude* of **Jd 1.**—M-M. EDNT.

Ἰουδίθ, ἡ indecl. (יְהוּדִית) ***Judith***—❶ a heroic Israelite (Jdth 8–16) 1 Cl 55:4.—❷ a servant of Anna GJs 2:2 v.l.; 2:3 v.l.

Ἰουθίνη, ης (an unusual nominal formation, also transmitted as Εὐθίνη; cp. Εὐθήνη prob. PLond 261, 178 col. 12 p. 58 [I AD]; s. deStrycker p. 313ff) ***Juthine*** name of Anna's servant GJs 2:2f (v.l. Ἰουδίθ).

Ἰουλία, ας, ἡ ***Julia,*** a common name—❶ recipient of a greeting **Ro 16:15** (Ἀουλία P[46]). The name is found even among slave women in the imperial household. GMilligan, The NT Documents 1913, 183.

❷ The name Ἰ. is read also as v.l. in vs. 7 (for Ιουνιαν; s. Ἰουνιᾶς and Ἰουνία).—M-M.

Ἰούλιος, ου, ὁ ***Julius,*** a common name (also in Joseph.), borne by a centurion of the imperial cohort **Ac 27:1, 3** (v.l. Ἰουλιανός, also the name of a ἑκατοντάρχης Jos., Bell. 6, 81).

Ἰουνία, ας, ἡ (SEG XVIII, 143 [c. 43 AD]; on the form s. Mlt-H. 155) ***Junia,*** compatriot or relative of Paul, one who like Paul suffered imprisonment, and distinguished among the apostles **Ro 16:7 v.l.** Ancient commentators took Andr. and Junia as a married couple. Some patristic identification (JFitzmyer, Anchor Bible: Romans, '93, 737f) favors the reading of her name in the text (so NRSV, REB; RCervin, NTS 40, '94, 464–70); in opposition to this identification Ltzm. (Hdb. ad loc.), who offers no evidence to support his statement that the context appears to exclude her from consideration. Moreover, unlike Ἰουνιᾶν (s. next entry), the form Ἰουνίαν is actually found so accented in some mss. (s. N. app.). For apostolic prestige accorded a woman s. Aa I, 235 app. ln. 2: ἰσαπόστολος of Thecla.

Ἰουνιᾶς, ᾶ, ὁ ***Junias*** (not found elsewh., could be a short form of the common Junianus; s. B-D-F §125, 2; Rob. 172) according to the rdg. of the N. text a Judean Christian, who was imprisoned w. Paul or shared a similar experience **Ro 16:7;** s. on Ἀνδρόνικος. But the accented form Ἰουνιᾶν has no support as such in the ms. tradition; for critique of B-D-R §125, 2, 6 in connection w. the N. rdg. s. UPlisch, NTS 42, '96, 477f, n. 2. For the strong probability that a woman named *Junia* is meant s. prec. entry.—M-M.

Ἰοῦστος, ου, ὁ (Κυπρ. I p. 42 no. 27 name of the ἀρχιερεὺς τῆς νήσου [Cyprus]; PWarr 16, 4 [III AD]), a name commonly borne by Judeans and proselytes (s. Lghtf. on **Col 4:11**) ***Justus,*** surname

❶ of Joseph Barsabbas, one of the two candidates in the election for apostle **Ac 1:23;** Papias (2:9; 11:2).

❷ of Titius, a Corinthian proselyte **Ac 18:7.** s. Goodsp. s.v. Τίτιος.

❸ of a Jewish Christian named Jesus, who supported the prisoner Paul in his work **Col 4:11.** Deissmann on Ἰησοῦς 5.—On the double name s. Dssm., B 183f (BS 315f).

ἱππεύς, έως, ὁ (s. two next entries; Hom. et al.; ins, pap, LXX, Philo; Jos., Vi. 157 al.; SibOr 3, 612; 805) acc. pl. τοὺς ἱππεῖς (Polyaenus 1, 29, 1; 8, 23, 12; SIG 502, 9 [228/225 BC]; 627, 15 [183 BC]) ***horse rider, cavalryman*** **Ac 23:23, 32;** MPol 7:1.—DELG s.v. ἵππος. M-M.

ἱππικός, ή, όν (s. prec. and next entry; Aeschyl. et al.; ins, pap; 1 Macc 15:38; 3 Macc 1:1; TestSol 11:6 C; Philo; Jos., Bell. 2, 117; 308) ***pert. to a rider of horses,*** τὸ ἱ. ***the cavalry*** (Hdt. 7, 87 al.; SIG 697e, 5 Diocles, of the στρατηγῶν ἐπὶ τὸ ἱππικόν) τὰ στρατεύματα τοῦ ἱ. *the troops of cavalry* **Rv 9:16.**—DELG s.v. ἵππος. M-M.

ἵππος, ου, ὁ (s. two prec. entries; Hom.+) ***horse, steed*** **Js 3:3; Rv 9:9; 14:20; 18:13; 19:18.** Horses of var. colors play a large role in **Rv** (s. on πυρρός): a white *horse* (Aeneas Tact. 1488) **6:2; 19:11, 14;** cp. vss. **19, 21;** fiery red **6:4;** black vs. **5;** pale, dun vs. **8.** Grasshoppers like horses **9:7;** horses w. lions' heads vs. **17;** cp. **19.** S. MMüller, D. apokal. Reiter: ZNW 8, 1907, 290ff; GHoennicke, D. apokal. Reiter: Studierstube 19, 1921, 3ff; AvHarnack, D. apokal. Reiter: Erforschtes u. Erlebtes 1923, 53ff; LKöhler, D. Offenb. d. Joh. 1924, 59–68; Boll 78ff, agreeing w. him GBaldensperger, RHPR 4, 1924, 1ff, against him JFreundorfer, Die Apk. des Ap. Joh. 1929, 67–123; FDornseiff, ZNW 38, '39, 196f; B. 167f; BHHW III 1438f; Pauly-W. XIX 2, 1430–44; Kraft, Hdb. '74, 114–18.—DELG. M-M. TW.

ἶρις, ιδος, ἡ (also ἴρεως as gen.)—❶ ***rainbow*** (Hom. et al.): ApcPt 3:10 (Mel., fgm, 8b 11); **Rv 4:3; 10:1.**

❷ **an arc or circle of light, whether colored or not,** ***halo, radiance*** (Aristot., Meteor. 3, 4; 5; Theophr., Ostent. 1, 13; Lucian, Dom. 11) ἶρις ὅμοιος ὁράσει σμαραγδίνῳ *a halo that was like an emerald (in appearance)* some have proposed this mng. for **Rv 4:3,** but the reminiscence of Ezk 1:27f is decisively supportive of 1 above.—M-M. DELG. TW.

Ἰσαάκ, ὁ (יִצְחָק; v.l. Ἰσάκ [B-D-F §39, 3]) indecl. (LXX, TestAbr, Test12Patr, ParJer; ApcrEzk P 1 verso 11; SibOr 2, 247; Philo; Just., Mel.—Joseph. and EpArist 48 Ἴσακος, ου [Ant. 1, 227]; EpArist 49 Ἴσαχος) ***Isaac,*** son of Abraham (Gen 21:3ff) **Ac 7:8a;** GJs 1:3. Father of Jacob, **Ac 7:8b.** Named w. him and Abraham (s. Ἀβραάμ and Ἰακώβ) **Mt 8:11; Lk 13:28;** B 8:4; IPhld 9:1; GJs 20:2 (not pap). God as the God of Abr., Is., and Jac. (Ex 3:6) **Mt 22:32; Mk 12:26; Lk 20:37; Ac 3:13; 7:32;** B 6:8. Bearer of the promises **Ro 9:7** (Gen 21:12), **10; Gal 4:28;** cp. **Hb 11:9, 18** (Gen 21:12), **20.** Husband of Rebecca **Ro 9:10;** B 13:2 (Gen 25:21), 3. Sacrifice of Isaac (Gen 22:1ff) **Hb 11:17; Js 2:21;** 1 Cl 31:3; B 7:3. In the genealogy of Jesus **Mt 1:2; Lk 3:34.**—HSchoeps, The Sacrifice of Isaac in Paul's Theology: JBL 65, '46, 385–92.—M-M. TW.

ἰσάγγελος, ον (s. ἴσος, ἄγγελος; Iambl. in Stob., Ecl. I 457, 9 W.; Hierocles 4, 425 ἀνθρώπους σέβειν . . . τοὺς ἰσοδαίμονας καὶ ἰσαγγέλους. Christian grave-ins: Kaibel 542, 7 ἰσαγ[γέλου τύχης]; cp. Philo, Sacr. Abel. 5 ἴσος ἀγγέλοις γεγονώς) ***like an angel*** of the glorified ones **Lk 20:36** (cited Just., D. 81, 4).—M-M. TW.

ἴσθι s. εἰμί.

Ἰσκαριώθ indecl. (**Mk 3:19; 14:10; Lk 6:16; 22:47** D), and **Ἰσκαριώτης, ου, ὁ** (so all other passages and always t.r.; D mostly Σκαριώθ, Σκαριώτης, q.v. On the suffix YArbeitmann, JBL 99, '80, 122–24) ***Iscariot,*** surname of Judas the informer, as well as of his father (s. Ἰούδας 6). The mng. of the word is obscure; s. Wlh. on **Mk 3:19;** Dalman, Jesus 26 (Eng. tr. 51f). It is usu. taken to refer to the place of his origin, *from Kerioth* (in southern Judea; Buhl 182) אִישׁ קְרִיּוֹת (agreeing w. this we have the v.l. ἀπὸ Καρυώτου **J 6:71; 12:4** D; **13:2** D, **26** D; **14:22** D). Another interpr. connects it w. σικάριος (q.v.), 'assassin, bandit' (among others FSchulthess, D. Problem der Sprache Jesu 1917, 41; 55, ZNW 21, 1922, 250ff). S. also CTorrey, HTR 36, '43, 51–62 ('false one'). **Mt 10:4; 26:14; Mk 14:43 v.l.; Lk 22:3; J 6:71; 12:4; 13:2, 26; 14:22;** GEb 34, 61.—HIngholt, Iscariot: JPedersen Festschr. '53; BGärtner, D. rätselhafte Termini Nazaräer u. Iskarioth '57, 37–68; OCullmann, RHPR 42, '62, 133–40; KLüthi, J. Isk. in d. Geschichte der Auslegung (Reformation to present) '55.—M-M.

Ἰσοκράτης, ους, ὁ (lit., ins, pap) ***Isocrates,*** a Christian scribe EpilMosq 5ab.

ἴσος, η, ον (s. three next entries; Hom.+) **pert. to being equivalent in number, size, quality,** ***equal*** τράγοι B 7:10. τὸ μῆκος καὶ τὸ πλάτος καὶ τὸ ὕψος αὐτῆς ἴσα ἐστίν **Rv 21:16.** ἡ ἴ. δωρεά *the same gift* **Ac 11:17.** τὴν ἀγάπην τινὶ ἴ. παρέχειν *show the same* (degree of) *love* 1 Cl 21:7. Of testimony given by witnesses *consistent* **Mk 14:56, 59.** ἴσον ποιεῖν τινά τινι *treat someone equally w. someone else* (Polyb. 2, 38, 8; 2 Macc 9:15 αὐτοὺς ἴσους Ἀθηναίοις ποιήσειν) **Mt 20:12.** ἑαυτὸν τῷ θεῷ *make oneself equal to God* **J 5:18** (cp. Philo, Leg. All. 1, 49 ἴσος θεῷ).—Subst. τὰ ἴσα *an equal amount* (PRyl 65, 7 [I BC] εἰς τὸ βασιλικὸν τὰ ἴσα) ἀπολαβεῖν τὰ ἴ. *receive an equal amount in return* **Lk 6:34.**—The neut. pl. ἴσα (like the neut. sing. ἴσον; TestAbr A 1 p. 77, 8 [Stone p. 2]) functions as an adv. (Hom. et al.; Diod. S. 1, 89, 1; Wsd 7:3) w. dat. (Demosth. 19, 314; oft. Philostrat. [Schmid IV 48]; Himerius, Or. 20, 4 W. ἴσα ποιηταῖς; PTebt 278, 33 [I AD]; Job 11:12; 30:19) ἴσα εἶναί τινι *be equal with someone* **Phil 2:6** (=PEg[3] 86f; ἴσα εἶναι as Thu. 3, 14, 1; ἴσα θεῷ as Dionys. Byz. §24 p. 12, 14; §41 p. 17, 12; Himerius, Or. [Ecl.] 3, 20; s. W-S. §28, 3; B-D-F §434, 1; Aeschyl., Pers. 856 ἰσόθεος of a king; so also Philod., Rhet. II p. 57, 11 Sudh. of a philosopher; Nicol. Dam.: 90 fgm. 130, 97 Caesar τὸν ἴσα κ. θεὸν τιμώμενον; 117 Jac.; Ael. Aristid. 46 p. 319 D.: ἐξ ἴσου τοῖς θεοῖς ἐθαυμάζετο; TestAbr 12 p. 91, 24f [Stone p. 30]; other reff. SLösch, Deitas Jesu und Antike Apotheose '33, 124f; for critique of vainglorious quest for divine honors s. Plut., Mor. 360c). ἐξ ἴσου (Soph., Hdt. et al.; SIG 969, 84; pap; Tat. 4, 2 ἐπ' ἴσης τῷ . . . θεῷ; Ath., R. 49, 20) *equally, alike* Pol 4:2.—B. 910. Larfeld I 497. LfgrE s.v. ἴσος col. 1227 (lit.). Cp. ὅμοιος Schmidt, Syn. IV 472–87. DELG. M-M. TW. Spicq. Sv.

ἰσότης, ητος, ἡ (s. prec. entry; Eur.et al.; oft. Philo; only twice LXX; EpArist 263).

➊ **state of matters being held in proper balance, *equality*** (Ps.-Phoc. 137) ἐξ ἰσότητος *as a matter of equality* **2 Cor 8:13;** also ὅπως γένηται ἰ. *that there may be equality* vs. **14.**

➋ **state of being fair, *fairness*** extension of mng. 1 (Menand., Monost., 259 Mei.; Polyb. 2, 38, 8 ἰ. κ. φιλανθρωπία; Diod. S. 5, 71, 2 [=362 J.]; Vett. Val. 332, 34) w. τὸ δίκαιον (cp. Diog. L. 7, 126; Philo, Spec. Leg. 4, 231 ἰσότης μήτηρ δικαιοσύνης) *justice and fairness* **Col 4:1.** On fair treatment of slaves s. Pl. Leges 5, 776d–788a; Aristot. Politica 1260b, 6; Seneca, Letter 47.—On the topic: PvanderHorst, The Sentences of Pseudo-Phocyclides '78, 205 (reff.); RHirzel, Themis, Dike u. Verwandtes 1907; Betz, 2 Cor (Hermeneia) 67f.—DELG s.v. ἴσος. M-M. TW. Spicq.

ἰσότιμος, ον (s. ἴσος, τιμή; Strabo 15, 3, 20; Dio Chrys. 24 [41], 2; Plut. et al.; OGI 234, 25 [c. 200 BC]; 544, 33 [adv.]; PRyl 253; Mitt-Wilck. I/2, 13, 10; Philo; Jos., Ant. 12, 119; Ath. 22, 2) gener. 'equal in honor/value', also simply ***equal, like, of the same kind/value*** (Aelian, NA 10, 1; Herodian 2, 3, 6; Herm. Wr. 12, 12; Jos., Ant. 12, 3, 1 'equally privileged') ἰσότιμον ἡμῖν πίστιν *a faith of the same kind as ours = faith w. the same privilege as ours* (i.e. the recipients are not less advantaged than the apostles) **2 Pt 1:1.** Cp. SJCh 92, 1–3.—M-M. TW. Spicq.

ἰσόχρονος, ον (in var. senses since the astronomer Eudoxus IV BC) ***contemporary*** SJCh 91, 14; 92, 2.

ἰσόψυχος, ον (s. ἴσος, ψυχή; Aeschyl., Agam. 1470; schol. on Eur., Andr. 419; Ps 54:14) ***of like soul/mind*** **Phil 2:20** (AFridrichsen, SymbOsl 18, '38, 42–49 would supply ὑμῖν: *having much in common with you.* The same scholar ConNeot 7, '42, 3, w. ref. to the adv. ἰσοψύχως in AcPl Ha 6, 8; PChristou, JBL 70, '51, 293–96: 'confidant').—M-M. Sv.

ἰσοψύχως adv. of ἰσόψυχος; AcPl Ha 6, 8.—Lit. s. ἰσόψυχος.

'Ισραήλ, ὁ indecl. (יִשְׂרָאֵל. For the sp. 'Ιστραήλ s. B-D-F 39, 5; on the mng. Just., D. 125, 1ff; Mel., P. 82, 603 w. note p. 185 Perler) (LXX, pseudepigr., Philo, Just., Mel.; PGM 4, 3034; 3055 al.—Jos., Ant. 1, 333 'Ισράηλος).

➊ **the patriarch Jacob, *Israel;*** οἱ ἐξ 'I. *the descendants of Israel* **Ro 9:6a.** Also ἐκ γένους 'I. **Phil 3:5** (cp. 1 Esdr 1:30; Jdth 6:2); οἶκος 'I. *the house of Israel*=all the descendants of the patr. (cp. Jdth 14:5; 3 Macc 2:10) **Mt 10:6; 15:24; Ac 2:36; 7:42** (Am 5:25); **Hb 8:10** (Jer 38:33); 1 Cl 8:3 (quot. of unknown orig.; AcPlCor 2:10). Also υἱοὶ 'I. (Mi 5:2; Sir 46:10; 47:2 and oft.) **Mt 27:9; Lk 1:16; Ac 5:21; 7:23, 37; 9:15; 10:36; Ro 9:27b; 2 Cor 3:7, 13; Hb 11:22; Rv 2:14; 7:4; 21:12;** AcPlCor 2:32 (also in sense of 2). On the other hand, ὁ οἶκος 'I. **Hb 8:8** in contrast to οἶκος 'Ιούδα (after Jer 38:31) means the people of the Northern Kingdom. Some of the pass. mentioned here may belong under

➋ **the people/nation of Israel, *Israel*** (Just., A I, 53, 4 τὸ δὲ 'Ιουδαικὸν καὶ Σαμαρειτικὸν φῦλον 'I. κέκληνται 'the Judean and Samaritan peoples are called Israel') τὸν λαόν μου τὸν 'I. **Mt 2:6;** ἄκουε 'I. **Mk 12:29** (Dt 6:4).—**Lk 1:54; Ro 9:27a, 31; 10:19; 11:7, 25f;** 1 Cl 29:2 (Dt 32:9); 43:5; ἐν τῷ 'I. **Mt 8:10; 9:33; Lk 2:34; 4:25, 27; 7:9;** 1 Cl 43:6; B 4:14; κατὰ τοῦ 'I. **Ro 11:2;** πρὸς τὸν 'I. **Lk 1:80; Ro 10:21;** B 5:2; τὶς τοῦ 'I. PtK 3; βασιλεὺς τοῦ 'I. **Mt 27:42; Mk 15:32; J 1:49; 12:13;** GPt 3:7; 4:11; 1 Cl 4:13; βασιλείαν τοῦ 'I. **Ac 1:6;** διδάσκαλος τοῦ 'I. **J 3:10;** πολιτεία τοῦ 'I. **Eph 2:12;** πόλεις τοῦ 'I. **Mt 10:23.** ὁ θεὸς (τοῦ) 'I. **15:31; Lk 1:68** (TestSol); ὁ θεὸς τοῦ λαοῦ τούτου 'I. **Ac 13:17;** γῆ 'I. **Mt 2:20f;** ὁ λαὸς 'I. **Lk 2:32; Ac 4:10; 13:24.** The pl. λαοὶ 'I. vs. **27** because of the quot. Ps 2:1 in vs. **25.** πρεσβύτεροι τοῦ 'I. **Ac 4:8 v.l.** αἱ φυλαὶ τοῦ 'I. *the tribes of Israel* (CIG IV 9270 [Iconium; prob. Judean] ὁ θεὸς τ. φυλῶν τοῦ 'Ισραήλ) **Mt 19:28; Lk 22:30;** cp. **Rv 7:4; 21:12.** τὸ δωδεκάφυλον τοῦ 'I. *the twelve tribes of Israel* 1 Cl 55:6. τὸ δωδεκάσκηπτρον τοῦ 'I. 31:4; ἡ ἐλπὶς τοῦ 'I. **Ac 28:20;** παράκλησιν τοῦ 'I. **Lk 2:25;** λύτρωσιν 'I. vs. **28 v.l.;** cp. λυτροῦσθαι τὸν 'I. **24:21;** ἐρύσατο τὸν 'I. AcPl Ha 8, 10. ἵνα φανερωθῇ τῷ 'I. **J 1:31.** δοῦναι μετάνοιαν τῷ 'I. **Ac 5:31.** ἤγαγεν τῷ 'I. σωτῆρα 'Ιησοῦν **13:23.**—'I. is the main self-designation of God's ancient people; fr. this as a starting-point it is also used of

➌ **Christians as entitled to the term Israel, *Israel*** (e.g. Just., D. 123, 7 Trypho asks ὑμεῖς 'I. ἐστε; 135, 3 Justin's answer καὶ ἡμεῖς ἐκ τῆς κοιλίας τοῦ Χριστοῦ λατομηθέντες 'Ισραηλιτικὸν τὸ ἀληθινόν ἐσμεν γένος; cp. Plut., Mor. 352c 'Ισιακός ἐστιν ὡς ἀληθῶς of a genuine worshiper of Isis) in contrast to ὁ 'I. κατὰ σάρκα *Israel in the physical sense* **1 Cor 10:18.** ὁ 'I. τοῦ θεοῦ *the* (true) *divine Israel* **Gal 6:16.** οὐ γὰρ πάντες οἱ ἐξ 'I. οὗτοι 'I. *not all who are descended fr. Israel* (=Jacob), or *who belong to the Israelite nation, are really Israelites* **Ro 9:6.**—FMaier, I. in d. Heilsgesch. nach Rö 9–11, 1929.—JJocz, A Theology of Election: Israel and the Church '58; JMunck, Paul and the Salvation of Mankind (tr. GClarke) '59; WTrilling, Das Wahre Israel (Mt)[3] '64; JvanGoudoever, NovT 8, '66, 111–23 (Lk); GStrecker, D. Weg d. Gerechtigkeit, '66, esp. 99–118.—EDNT. TW.

'Ισραηλίτης, ου, ὁ (fr. יִשְׂרְאֵלִי; also -είτης [as Boffo, Iscrizioni, ins p. 48 no. 2, 1=SEG XXXII, 809, cp. -ῖται no. 810]; LXX, Test12Patr; Joseph. index; Just.—As a fem.: Inschrift 44 of the Villa Torlonia in Rome, ed. HBeyer and HLietzmann 1930; 'Ισραηλῖτις Mel., P. 96, 737) ***Israelite*** **J 1:47** (cp. Plut., Mor. 352c 'Ισιακός ἐστιν ὡς ἀληθῶς of a genuine worshiper of Isis); **Ro 9:4; 11:1; 2 Cor 11:22.** As a form of address ἄνδρες 'Ισραηλῖται *men of Israel* (Jos., Ant. 3, 189) **Ac 2:22; 3:12; 5:35; 13:16; 21:28.**—M-M. TW.

'Ισσαχάρ, ὁ (also -άχαρ, 'Ισαχάρ t.r.; יִשָּׂשכָר) indecl. (LXX; Test12Patr ['Ισαχάρ]; Philo.—Jos., Ant. 1, 308 'Ισσαχάρης; 2, 178 'Ισακχάρου) ***Issachar,*** a son of the patriarch Jacob (Gen

30:18; Demetr.: 722 fgm. 1, 4 al. Jac.), and hence an Israelite tribe Gen 49:14; Num 1:26 al.) **Rv 7:7** (v.l. Ἰσαχάρ; so Test12Patr and variants in Philo).

ἴστε s. οἶδα.

ἵστημι (Hom.+, ins, pap [Mayser 353]; LXX [Thackeray 247f]; pseudepigr., Philo, Joseph., apolog. exc. Ar.) and also **ἱστάνω** (since I BC SIG 1104, 26 ἱστανόμενος; pap [Mayser, loc. cit., with ἀνθιστάνω documented here as early as III BC]; Epict. 3, 12, 2; LXX [Ezk 17:14; Thackeray, loc. cit.]; later wr. in Psaltes 236) **Ro 3:31;** Hs 8, 1, 10 (s. Whittaker on 8, 1, 8; s. B-D-F §93; Mlt-H. 202). Fut. στήσω; 1 aor. ἔστησα; 2 aor. ἔστην, impv. στῆθι, inf. στῆναι, ptc. στάς; pf. ἕστηκα (*I stand*), ptc. ἑστηκώς, ός and ἑστώς En 12:3; JosAs 7:2; **J 12:29,** -ῶσα **J 8:9 v.l.,** neut. ἑστώς **Rv 14:1 v.l.** (s. B-D-F §96; W-S. §14, 5; Mlt-H. 222) and ἑστός, inf. always ἑστάναι; plpf. εἱστήκειν (*I stood*) or ἱστήκειν GPt 2:3, third pl. εἱστήκεισαν **Mt 12:46; J 18:18; Ac 9:7; Rv 7:11** (W-H. spell it ἱστ. everywhere); ἑστάκαμεν w. act. mng. 1 Macc 11:34; fut. mid. στήσομαι **Rv 18:15.** Pass.: 1 fut. σταθήσομαι; 1 aor. ἐστάθην (PEg[2] 65). S. στήκω. Trans.: A. Intr.: B, C, D.

A. trans. (pres., impf., fut., 1 aor. act.; s. B-D-F §97, 1; Mlt-H. 241) gener. 'put, place, set'.—**❶ to cause to be in a place or position, *set, place, bring, allow to come*** τινά *someone,* lit. ἐν τῷ συνεδρίῳ **Ac 5:27.** εἰς αὐτούς *before them* **22:30.** ἐκ δεξιῶν τινος *at someone's right (hand)* **Mt 25:33.** ἐν μέσῳ *in the midst, among* **18:2; Mk 9:36; J 8:3.** ἐνώπιόν τινος *before someone* **Ac 6:6.** Also κατενώπιόν τινος **Jd 24.** ἐπί τι *upon someth.* **Mt 4:5; Lk 4:9.** παρά τινι *beside someone* **9:47.**

❷ to propose someone for an obligation, *put forward, propose,* lit. (e.g. Just., A I, 60, 3 Μωυσέα … τύπον σταυροῦ … στῆσαι ἐπὶ τῇ ἁγίᾳ σκηνῇ) τινά for a certain purpose: the candidates for election to the apostleship **Ac 1:23.** μάρτυρας ψευδεῖς **6:13** (cp. Mel., P. 93, 700 ψευδομάρτυρες).

❸ to set up or put into force, *establish,* fig. ext. of 1 (cp. Gen 26:3 τὸν ὅρκον; Ex 6:4) τὴν ἰδίαν δικαιοσύνην **Ro 10:3.** τὸ δεύτερον (opp. ἀναιρεῖν τὸ πρῶτον, a ref. to sacrificial system) **Hb 10:9.**—Of legal enforcement κύριε, μὴ στήσῃς αὐτοῖς ταύτην τ. ἁμαρτίαν *Lord, do not hold this sin against them* **Ac 7:60** (contrast ἀφίημι 1 Macc 13:38f; 15:5; Stephen's expression=ἄφες **Lk 23:34;** s. Beginn. IV, ad loc.).

❹ to validate someth. that is in force or in practice, *reinforce validity of, uphold, maintain, validate* τὶ *someth.* fig. ext. of 1 (1 Macc 2:27 τὴν διαθήκην) τὴν παράδοσιν ὑμῶν *validate* or *maintain your own tradition* **Mk 7:9.** νόμον ἱστάνομεν *we uphold (the) law* **Ro 3:31** (s. καταργέω 2).

❺ to cause to be steadfast, *make someone stand* δυνατεῖ ὁ κύριος στῆσαι αὐτόν **Ro 14:4.**

❻ to specify contractually—ⓐ *set/fix a time* a period of time ἡμέραν (s. ἡμέρα 3a) Ac 17:31.

ⓑ ***determine a monetary amount*** οἱ δὲ ἔστησαν αὐτῷ τριάκοντα ἀργύρια **Mt 26:15** (=Zech 11:12 ἔστησαν τὸν μισθόν μου τριάκοντα ἀργύρους), presents a special problem for interpreters because of the author's theological and narrative interests, which prompt him to connect an allusion here to Zech 11:12 in anticipation of a fulfillment statement at **Mt 27:9f,** which in haggadic fashion draws on Zech 11:13 in the longer form of the MT and Jer 32 (MT 39):7–9 (s. JDoeve, Jewish Hermeneutics in the Synoptic Gospels and Acts, '54, 185–87). Jer 39:9 and Zech 11:12 use the verb ἵ. in the sense *weigh out* on scales (Hom.; X., Cyr. 8, 2, 21, Mem. 1, 1, 9 al.; GDI p. 870, ^{n}49 A [Ephesus VI BC] 40 minas ἐστάθησαν; Is 46:6; Jer 39:9; 2 Esdr 8:25), and some (e.g. BWeiss, HHoltzmann, JWeiss; FSchulthess, ZNW 21, 1922, 227f; Field, Notes 19f) interpret **Mt 26:15** in this sense. Of course Mt's readers would know that coinage of their time was not 'weighed out' and would understand ἵ. in the sense of striking a bargain (ἵστημι=set a price, make an offer, close a bargain: Herodas 7, 68 pair of shoes; BGU 1116, 8 [I BC]; 912, 25 [I AD]; PRainer 206, 10 [II AD] κεφάλαιον), *they set out (=offered, allowed) for him (=paid him) 30 silver coins* (Wlh., OHoltzmann, Schniewind), but the more sophisticated among them would readily recognize the obsolete mng. **Ac 7:60** is sometimes interpreted in a related sense, but the absence of a direct object of amount paid suggests that the pass. is better placed in 3 above.

B. intr., aor. and fut. forms—**❶ to desist from movement and be in a stationary position, *stand still, stop*** (Hom., Aristot.; Philostrat., Ep. 36, 2 ὁ ποταμὸς στήσεται; TestSol 7:3 οὕτως ἔστη ἡ αὔρα) **Lk 24:17.** στὰς ὁ Ἰησοῦς ἐφώνησεν αὐτούς **Mt 20:32.—Mk 10:49; Lk 7:14; 17:12; 18:40.** στῆναι τὸ ἅρμα **Ac 8:38.** ἀπὸ μακρόθεν ἔστησαν **Rv 18:17;** cp. vs. **15.** ἔστησαν ἐν τῷ τόπῳ τοῦ σπηλαίου GJs 19:2. ἔστη ἐπὶ τόπου πεδινοῦ *he took his stand on a level place* **Lk 6:17.** Of a star ἐστάθη ἐπάνω οὗ ἦν τὸ παιδίον **Mt 2:9;** also ἐπὶ τὴν κεφαλὴν τοῦ παιδίου GJs 21:3. Of a flow of blood *come to an end* ἔστη ἡ ῥύσις τ. αἵματος **Lk 8:44** (cp. Ex 4:25 [though HKosmala, Vetus Test. 12, '62, 28 renders it as an emphatic εἶναι] Heraclid. Pont., fgm. 49 W.; POxy 1088, 21 [I AD]; Cyranides p. 117 note γυναικὶ … αἷμα ἵστημι παραχρῆμα). στῆθι *stand* **Js 2:3.** ἡ χεὶρ αὐτοῦ ἔστη ἄνω *his hand remained* (motionless) *upraised* GJs 18:3 (not pap).

❷ to come up in the presence of others, *come up, stand, appear* ἔμπροσθέν τινος *before someone* **Mt 27:11; Lk 21:36.** Also ἐνώπιόν τινος **Ac 10:30;** GJs 11:2 (κατενώπιον TestSol 22:13; Just., D. 127, 3) or ἐπί τινος: σταθήσεσθε *you will have to appear* **Mt 10:18 v.l.; Mk 13:9;** ἐπὶ τοῦ παλατίου AcPl Ha 9, 20. στῆθι εἰς τὸ μέσον **Lk 6:8;** cp. vs. **8b; J 20:19, 26** (Vi. Aesopi I c. 6 p. 243, 15 Αἴσωπος στὰς εἰς τὸ μέσον ἀνέκραξεν). Also ἐν μέσῳ **Lk 24:36; Ac 17:22;** Ox 1 verso, 11 (s. Unknown Sayings, 69–71). ἔστη εἰς τὸ κριτήριον *she stood before the court* GJs 15:2. Cp. **J 21:4; Rv 12:18; Lk 7:38.** *Step up* or *stand* to say someth. or make a speech **Lk 18:11.** Cp. **19:8; Ac 2:14; 5:20; 11:13** al. ἔστησαν … προσδοκῶντες τὸν Ζαχαρίαν *they stood waiting for Z.* GJs 24:1. Pract. in the sense of the pf. δυνάμενοι … ἀλλ' οὐδὲ στῆναι (the cult images) *which could not remain standing* AcPl Ha 1, 20 (cp. ἵστατο δένδρον κυπάρισσος TestAbr A 3 p. 79, 17 [Stone p. 6]; ὁ τόπος ἐν ᾧ ἱστάμεθα GrBar 6:13).

❸ to stand up against, *resist,* w. πρὸς and acc. *offer resistance* (Thu. 5, 104) **Eph 6:11;** abs. *resist* (Ex 14:13) vs. **13.** (Cp. the term στάσις in the sense of 'rebellion'.)

❹ stand firm so as to remain stable, *stand firm, hold one's ground* (Ps 35:13) in battle (X., An. 1, 10, 1) **Eph 6:14.** σταθήσεται *will stand firm* **Ro 14:4a.** τίς δύναται σταθῆναι; **Rv 6:17.** εἰς ἣν στῆτε *stand fast in it* (Goodsp., Probs. 198) **1 Pt 5:12.** Of house, city, or kingdom **Mt 12:25f; Mk 3:24f; Lk 11:18.** Cp. **Mk 3:26.** The OT expr. (Dt 19:15) ἵνα ἐπὶ στόματος δύο μαρτύρων ἢ τριῶν σταθῇ πᾶν ῥῆμα **Mt 18:16; 2 Cor 13:1.**

❺ come to a standing position, *stand up* ἐπὶ τοὺς πόδας *on one's feet* (Ezk 2:1) **Ac 26:16; Rv 11:11.** Abs. **Ac 3:8.**

C. intr., perf. and plupf.—**❶ to be in a standing position, *I stand, I stood*** of bodily position, e.g. of a speaker **J 7:37; Ac 5:25,** of hearers **J 12:29** or spectators **Mt 27:47; Lk 23:35; Ac 1:11,** of accusers **Lk 23:10.** Cp. **J 18:5, 16, 18ab, 25; 19:25; Ac 16:9** al.

❷ to be at a place, *stand (there), be (there),* w. the emphasis less on 'standing' than on 'being, existing'.—ⓐ position indicated by adv. of place ἔξω **Mt 12:46f; Lk 8:20; 13:25.** μακρόθεν

Lk 18:13. ἀπὸ μακρόθεν *at a distance* **23:49; Rv 18:10.** ἐκεῖ **Mk 11:5.** ὅπου **13:14.** ὧδε **Mt 16:28; 20:6b.** αὐτοῦ **Lk 9:27;** ἀπέναντι AcPl Ha 3, 30.

ⓑ w. place indicated by a prep. ἐκ δεξιῶν τινος *at the right (hand) of someone or someth.* **Lk 1:11; Ac 7:55f** (HOwen, NTS 1, '54/55, 224–26). ἐν αὐτοῖς *among them* **Ac 24:21;** w. ἐν and dat. of place **Mt 20:3; 24:15; J 11:56; Rv 19:17.** ἐν μέσῳ **J 8:9 v.l.** μέσος ὑμῶν **1:26** (v.l. στήκει). ἐπί w. gen. (X., Cyr. 3, 3, 66; Apollodorus [II BC]: 244 fgm. 209 Jac. ἐπὶ τ. θύρας) **Ac 5:23; 21:40; 24:20; 25:10; Rv 10:5, 8;** AcPl Ha 7, 37; w. dat. **Ac 7:33;** w. acc. **Mt 13:2; Rv 3:20; 7:1; 14:1; 15:2;** GJs 5:2 (ἕστηκας codd., ἕστης pap). παρά w. acc. of place **Lk 5:1f.** πέραν τῆς θαλάσσης **J 6:22.** πρό w. gen. of place **Ac 12:14.** πρός w. dat. of place **J 20:11.** σύν τινι **Ac 4:14.** μετά τινος AcPl Ha 11, 3. κύκλῳ τινός *around someth.* **Rv 7:11.** W. ἐνώπιον (functioning as prep.) ἐνώπιόν τινος **Rv 7:9; 11:4; 12:4; 20:12.**

ⓒ abs. (Epict. 4, 1, 88 ἑστῶσα of the citadel, simply standing there; Tat. 26, 2 παρατρέχοντας μὲν ὑμᾶς, ἑστῶτα δὲ τὸν αἰῶνα) **Mt 26:73; J 1:35; 3:29; 20:14; Ac 22:25.** τὰ πρόβατα εἱστήκει *the sheep stood still* GJs 18:2 (not pap). The verb standing alone in the sense *stand around idle* (Eur., Iph. Aul. 861; Aristoph., Av. 206, Eccl. 852; Herodas 4, 44) **Mt 20:6a.** ἀργός can be added (Aristoph., Eccl. 879f, Pax 256 ἕστηκας ἀργός) vs. **6a v.l., 6b** (w. the question cp. Eubulus Com., fgm. 15, 1 K. τί ἕστηκας ἐν πύλαις; Herodas 5, 40). W. modifying words (Pla., Phdr. 275d ἕστηκε ὡς ζῶντα τὰ ἔκγονα) εἱστήκεισαν ἐνεοί *they stood there speechless* **Ac 9:7.** ὡς ἐσφαγμένον **Rv 5:6.** cp. **Ac 26:6.** εἱστήκει ἀπεκδεχόμενος AcPl Ant 13, 22 (=Aa I, 237, 5).

❸ **to stand in attendance on someone,** ***attend upon, be the servant of*** Rv 8:2 (RCharles, Rv ICC vol. 1, p. 225).

❹ **stand firm in belief,** ***stand firm*** of personal commitment in gener. (opp. πεσεῖν), fig. ext. of 1, **1 Cor 10:12;** 2 Cl 2:6. τ. πίστει ἕστηκας *you stand firm because of your faith* **Ro 11:20;** cp. **2 Cor 1:24.** ὃς ἕστηκεν ἐν τ. καρδίᾳ αὐτοῦ ἑδραῖος *one who stands firm in his heart* **1 Cor 7:37.** ὁ θεμέλιος ἕστηκεν *the foundation stands (unshaken)* **2 Ti 2:19** (Stob. 4, 41, 60 [vol. V, p. 945]: Apelles, when he was asked why he represented Tyche [Fortune] in a sitting position, answered οὐχ ἕστηκεν γάρ=because she can't stand, i.e. has no stability; Hierocles 11, 441 ἑστῶτος τοῦ νόμου=since the law stands firm [unchanged]; Procop. Soph., Ep. 47 μηδὲν ἑστηκὸς κ. ἀκίνητον; 75).

❺ **to be in a condition or state,** ***stand*** or ***be in someth.,*** fig. ext. of 1; grace (Hierocles 12, 446 ἐν ἀρετῇ) **Ro 5:2;** within the scope of the gospel **1 Cor 15:1;** in truth **J 8:44.**

D. intr., pres. mid. **to have a beginning,** ***begin,*** calendaric expression (as old as Hom.) μὴν ἱστάμενος *the month just beginning* (oft. ins) MPol 21—B. 835. DELG. M-M. TW.

ἱστίον, ου, τό ***a sail*** (so, mostly in pl., Hom. et al.; also ins, pap; Is 33:23; Just., A I, 55, 3) συστέλλειν τὰ ἱ. *shorten the sails* or *furl them* altogether **Ac 27:15 v.l.**—B. 736. DELG s.v. ἱστός.

ἱστορέω (s. next entry) fut. ἱστορήσω; 1 aor. ἱστόρησα; pf. ptc. gen. pl. ἱστορηκότων (Ath. 30, 3); pf. pass. 3 sg. ἱστόρηται 1 Esdr 1:31 (Aeschyl., Hdt. et al. in the sense 'inquire', etc.; ins, pap, 1 Esdr, Just., Ath.) ***visit*** (for the purpose of coming to know someone or someth.: Plut., Thes. 30, 3, Pomp. 640 [40, 2], Lucull. 493 [2, 9], Mor. 516c; Epict. 2, 14, 28; 3, 7, 1; OGI 694; Sb 1004; PLond III, 854, 5 p. 206 [I AD]; Jos., Bell. 6, 81, Ant. 1, 203 a monument) ἱστορῆσαι Κηφᾶν *to make the acquaintance of Cephas* **Gal 1:18** (GKilpatrick, TManson memorial vol., ed. AHiggins '59, 144–49 'to get information from'; against him OHofius, ZNW 75, '84, 73–85 [reff.]; but s. JDunn, ibid. 76, '85, 138f. Cp. Ac 17:23 v.l. [Clem. Al., Strom. 1, 19 p. 58, 20 St.]).—DELG s.v. οἶδα. M-M. TW. Sv.

ἱστορία, ας, ἡ (s. prec. entry; Hdt.+) prim. 'inquiry', then the results of inquiry: 'story, account, recital'

❶ ***account, story,*** in a gener. sense ἐν ταῖς ἱ. τῶν ιβʹ φυλῶν *in the 'accounts of the 12 Tribes'* GJs 1:1; γράψας τὴν ἱ. ταύτην 25:1a; cp. γράψαι τ. ἱ. 25:1b. Of a specific account ἱστορίαν περὶ γυναικὸς ἐπὶ πολλαῖς ἁμαρτίαις διαβληθείσης ἐπὶ τοῦ κυρίου, ἣν τὸ καθ' Ἑβραίους εὐαγγέλιον περιέχει *a story, recorded by the Gospel of the Hebrews, about a woman who was accused of many sins in the Lord's presence* Papias (2:17).

❷ **story as personal experience,** ***story*** μήτι ἐν ἐμοὶ ἀνεκεφαλαιώθη ἡ ἱ. τοῦ Ἀδάμ; *has the story of Adam been recapitulated with me?* (cp. ApcMos 7) GJs 13:1.—DELG s.v. οἶδα. TW.

ἱστός, οῦ, ὁ (Hom. et al.; pap, LXX; TestSol 12:6 C; EpArist 320 [prob. 'bolts' of cloth]) lit. 'someth. set upright' ***mast*** **Ac 27:38 cj.** by SNaber, Mnemosyne n.s. 23 1895, 267ff (but s. Bruce, Acts ad loc.); s. also DELG and Frisk.

ἰσχνόφωνος, ον (ἰσχνός 'weak' + φωνή q.v.; Hdt. et al.; Ex; Ezk. Trag. 114 [in Eus., PE 9, 29, 9]) ***weak-voiced*** but also ***having an impediment in one's speech*** 1 Cl 17:5 (Ex 4:10).

ἰσχυροποιέω (ἰσχυρός + ποιέω) fut. ἰσχυροποιήσω; 1 aor. ἰσχυροποίησα; pres. pass. impv. ἰσχυροποιοῦ (Polyb. et al.; Ezk 27:27 Aq.) ***strengthen*** Diod. S. 17, 65; Herm. Wr. 16, 12) τινά *someone* Hv 1, 3, 2; 4, 1, 3. τινὰ ἐν τῇ πίστει *strengthen someone in the faith* Hm 12, 6, 1. Pass. (Antig. Car. 175; Epict. 2, 18, 7; 4, 9, 15; Vett. Val. 333, 7; 347, 5 al.) s 6, 3, 6. εἰς τὸ ἀγαθόν *to do good* v 3, 13, 2. ἐν ταῖς ἐντολαῖς *in keeping the commandments* 5:5.

ἰσχυροποίησις, εως, ἡ (s. prec. entry; Clem. Al., Strom. 4, 12, 85; Aëtius 12, 21) ***strengthening*** Hv 3, 12, 3.

ἰσχυρός, ά, όν (s. ἰσχύς, ἰσχύω; Aeschyl.+) comp. ἰσχυρότερος (Hdt.+; ins, pap, LXX; Ar. 1, 2; Just., D. 103, 3; Ath. 34, 2) gener. 'strong, mighty, powerful'.

❶ **pert. to being strong physically, mentally, or spiritually,** ***strong,*** of living beings—ⓐ of transcendent beings: of God (SIG 216, 1 [IV BC] ἰσχυρῷ θειῷ [=θεῷ s. note 4] Σανέργει; Dt 10:17; 2 Macc 1:24 and oft.; TestSol C 12, 3; Philo, Spec. Leg. 1, 307; PGM 10, 11; 12, 374; 36, 105; Just., D. 103, 3) **Rv 18:8.** Of angels (PGM 3, 71f ἄγγελος κραταιὸς κ. ἰσχυρός) **5:2; 10:1; 18:21.** Of Christ **1 Cor 10:22;** cp. also **Lk 11:22** (s. below on **Lk 11:21**). Of the one to come after John the Baptist ἰσχυρότερός μου (cp. Judg 5:13 A; PGM 13, 202) **Mt 3:11; Mk 1:7; Lk 3:16.** τὸ ἀσθενὲς τ. θεοῦ ἰσχυρότερον τ. ἀνθρώπων **1 Cor 1:25** (cp. Philo, Ebr. 186 τὸ ἀσθενές . . . τὸ ἰ.). Of Satan, who may be the ἰσχυρός of the parable **Mt 12:29; Mk 3:27; Lk 11:21** (cp. PGM 5, 147 the δαίμων, who calls himself ἰσχυρός, and the ἰσχυρός of 13, 203 who, acc. to 197 is ἔνοπλος, as well as the Φόβος καθωπλισμένος 528 fighting the ἰσχυρότερος 543; Mel., P. 102, 783). In case Satan is not meant, these passages, together w. **Lk 11:22** (s. above) belong under b below.

ⓑ of human beings (opp. ἀσθενής as Philo, Somn. 1, 155; Tat. 32, 2f) **1 Cor 4:10;** Agr. 4.—**1J 2:14;** Hs 9, 15, 1. ἰ. ἐν πολέμῳ *mighty in war* **Hb 11:34.** ἐν τῇ πίστει Hv 3, 5, 5; m 11, 4. οἱ ἰσχυροί (Ps.-X., Constitution of Athens 1, 14; 4 Km 24:15 codd.; Da 8:24 Theod.) **Rv 6:15; 19:18.** ὁ ἰ. 1 Cl 13:1 (Jer 9:22); 38:2. Even the neut. τὰ ἰσχυρά refers to persons **1 Cor 1:27.**

❷ **pert. to being high on a scale of extent as respects strength or impression that is made,** ***violent, loud, mighty,*** etc., of things (cp. IAndrosIsis, Kyme 16 of justice) ἄνεμος *violent* (TestSol 6:1 D; Dio Chrys. 60 and 61 [77 and 78], 7 χειμὼν ἰ.) **Mt 14:30 v.l.;** βροντή *loud* **Rv 19:6.** κραυγή **Hb 5:7.** φόβος Hm 7:4 (=the fear of the Lord is very productive). πίστις 9:7, 10. μετάνοια s 7:6. λίθος *solid, mighty* (Sir 6:21) B 6:2. πέτρας ἰ. B 11:5 (Is 33:16). λιμός *a severe famine* **Lk 15:14** (cp. Petosiris, fgm. 6, ln. 49 λιμὸς ἰ.; Hdt. 1, 94; SIG 495, 59 [c. 230 BC] σιτοδείας γενομένης ἰσχυρᾶς; Gen 41:31). πόλις *mighty* (Is 26:1 v.l.; TestJud 5:1) **Rv 18:10** (cp. also τεῖχος X., Cyr. 7, 5, 7; 1 Macc 1:33 v.l. Kappler; πύργος Judg 9:51 B). φωνή *loud* (Aesop. Fab. 420 P. ἰσχυρᾷ τῇ φωνῇ; Ex 19:19; Da 6:21 Theod.) **Rv 18:2;** παράκλησις ἰ. *strong encouragement* **Hb 6:18.** ἰσχυροτέρας ἀποκαλύψεις *more meaningful revelations* Hv 3, 10, 8. ῥῆμα *mighty* 1, 3, 4. (W. βέβαια and τεθεμελιωμένα) πάντα ἰσχυρά *everything is secure* 3, 4, 3. θέσις Hv 3, 13, 3. (W. βαρεῖαι, as TestJud 9:2) ἐπιστολαί *weighty and strong* (cp. X., Cyr. 3, 3, 48; Wsd 6:8) *letters* **2 Cor 10:10.** Avoided in J (s. MBoismard, Le chaiptre 21 de StJean: RB 54, '47, 491).—B. 295. DELG s.v. ἰσχύς. M-M. TW.

ἰσχυρότης, ητος, ἡ (s. prec. and next entry; Dionys. Hal. 3, 65, 2 Jac. v.l.; Philo, Leg. All. 3, 204) ***power, (inward) strength*** προσῆλθεν ὑμῖν ἰ. *you received power* Hv 3, 12, 3. Of stones: *solidity, strength* (cp. Job 6:12 ἰσχὺς λίθων) s 9, 8, 7.—DELG s.v. ἰσχύς.

ἰσχυρόω (s. two prec. entries; 1 aor. 3 pl. ἰσχύρωσαν Is 41:7) ***strengthen,*** pass. in act. sense ἰσχυροῦ ἐν αὐταῖς *be strong in them* (the commandments) Hm 5, 2, 8.

ἰσχυρῶς adv. of ἰσχυρός (Hdt. et al.; LXX; JosAs; Philo, Aet. M. 21; Jos., Ant. 12, 368, C. Ap. 1, 127; Just., D. 63, 1) ***strongly, dependably*** (w. ἀνδρείως) ἀναστρέφεσθαι *conduct oneself dependably and courageously* Hs 5, 6, 6. ὑποφέρειν *bear bravely* 7:5. ἀνθεστηκέναι m 12, 5, 4. ἑστάναι *stand firmly* v 3, 13, 3. ταπεινοφρονῆσαι *be extremely humble* s 7:4 (simply='very much': Antig. Car. 35; Appian, Liby. 96, §454; Diog. L. 1, 75 ἰ. ἐτίμησαν).

ἰσχύς, ύος, ἡ (s. ἰσχυρός, ἰσχύω; Hes.+; rare in later times and in ins and pap [e.g. PMich 156—II AD], but oft. LXX; pseudepigr.; Philo; Jos., C. Ap. 1, 19 al.; Just., Ath., Iren.) **capability to function effectively, *strength, power, might*** 1 Cl 13:1 (Jer 9:22); 39:2; B 6:3; 12:11 (Is 45:1); Hv 3, 12, 2; ἐξ ἰ. *by the strength* **1 Pt 4:11.** ἐξ ὅλης τῆς ἰ. *with all one's strength* **Mk 12:30, 33** (ψυχῆς v.l.); 1 Cl 33:8; cp. **Lk 10:27** (s. Herm. Wr. 1, 30 ἐκ ψυχῆς κ. ἰσχύος ὅλης); ἰσχύειν τῇ ἰ. Hs 9, 1, 2. (W. δύναμις, as Dio Chrys. 14 [31], 11; 30 [47], 3; Appian, Bell. Civ. 4, 71 §302; PLond III, 1319, 5 p. 272 [544/45 AD]; cp. Thu. 7, 66, 3; 2 Ch 26:13; Jos., Ant. 11, 44) ἄγγελοι ἰσχύϊ κ. δυνάμει μείζονες **2 Pt 2:11.** Used w. δύναμις and sim. words as attributes of God (ἰ. as divine attribute in trag. and oft. LXX; cp. τοῦ λόγου ἰ. Orig., C. Cels. 1, 62, 71) **Rv 5:12; 7:12.** cp. also 1 Cl 60:1; Dg 9:6. Of God κράτος τῆς ἰ. (cp. Job 12:16 παρ' αὐτῷ κράτος καὶ ἰσχύς.; En 1:4 ἐν τῇ δυνάμει τῆς ἰσχύος αὐτοῦ; Philo, De Prov. in Eus., PE 8, 14, 38; Ath. 24, 2) **Eph 1:19; 6:10** (for the Eph passages cp. the Qumran parallels noted by KKuhn, NTS 7, '61, 335, e.g. 1QH 4, 32; 18, 8; 1QS 11, 19f); 1 Cl 27:5. Of the Lord ἀπὸ τῆς δόξης τῆς ἰ. αὐτοῦ (Is 2:10, 19, 21) **2 Th 1:9.** Of the *power* of prayer IEph 5:2 (cp. ἐν ἰσχύι λόγου PsSol 17:36; Lucian, Hist. Conscr. 43 τῆς ἑρμηνείας ἰσχύς; Alex. Aphr., Fat. 16, II 2 p. 186, 23 of the power of truth; Phalaris, Ep. 70, 1). Of generative power ἐκ καρποῦ τῆς ἰσχύος AcPl Ox 1602, 12f (AcPl Ha 8, 14 ὀσφύος)=BMM recto 17.—DELG. M-M. TW.

ἰσχύω fut. ἰσχύσω; 1 aor. ἴσχυσα; pf. ptc. sg. n. ἰσχυκός (Da 4:20 Theod.) (s. ἰσχύς; Pind.+ in sense 'be strong, prevail')

❶ **be in possession of one's physical powers, *be in good health*** οἱ ἰσχύοντες *those who are healthy* (Soph., Tr. 234; X., Cyr. 6, 1, 24, Mem. 2, 7, 7) **Mt 9:12; Mk 2:17.**

❷ **to have requisite personal resources to accomplish someth., *have power, be competent, be able*—ⓐ** πολύ *be able to do much* (cp. Diod. S. 1, 60, 2 πλέον ἰ.; 4, 23, 3; Appian, Bell. Civ. 2, 88 §371 τοσοῦτον ἰ.; Jos., C. Ap. 1, 77 μεῖζον ἰ., Ant. 15, 88 πλεῖστον ἰ.) **Js 5:16.** τί ταπεινοφροσύνη . . . ἰσχύει *what strength humility has* 1 Cl 21:8; πάντα **Phil 4:13.** εἰς οὐδέν *be good for nothing* **Mt 5:13.** ὅτε . . . ἴσχυσας τῇ ἰσχύι σου, ὥστε δύνασθαι Hs 9, 1, 2.

ⓑ w. inf. foll. (Diod. S. 1, 83, 8; Plut., Pomp. 58, 6; PEleph 17, 23; POxy 396; 533, 16; 1345 οὐκ ἴσχυσα ἐλθεῖν σήμερον; LXX; TestSol 22:8; JosAs 10:8; Philo, Leg. All. 3, 27; Jos., Bell. 6, 367, Ant. 2, 86; Just., A I, 44, 12 al.; Tat. 15, 3) **Mt 8:28; 26:40; Mk 5:4; 14:37; Lk 6:48; 8:43; 14:6, 29f; 20:26; J 21:6** (the only instance in J; s. JBoismard); **Ac 6:10; 15:10; 25:7; 27:16;** 2 Cl 18:2; Hv 1, 3, 3. *Be strong enough* σκάπτειν *to dig* **Lk 16:3;** cp. Hv 3, 8, 8. εἰς τὰς ἀκτίνας . . . ἀντοφθαλμῆσαι *gaze at the (sun's) rays* B 5:10. Abs., though the inf. can easily be supplied fr. the context (as Sir 43:28) οὐκ ἴσχυσαν (ἐκβαλεῖν) **Mk 9:18.** οὐκ ἰσχύσουσιν (εἰσελθεῖν) **Lk 13:24.**

❸ **to be in control, *have power, be mighty*** (Diod. S. 11, 23, 3; PPetr II, 18, 12; Just., D. 90, 4) ὁ λόγος ηὔξανεν κ. ἴσχυεν **Ac 19:20.** μέχρι πότε θάνατος ἰσχύσει; *how long will death hold its power?* GEg 252, 50. ἰ. ἐν αὐταις (ταῖς ἐντολαῖς)=*be strong in keeping the commandments* Hm 5, 2, 8 v.l. *Win out, prevail* (Thu. 3, 46, 3; Dio Chrys. 17 [34], 19; ParJer 1:6 ἴσχυσα ἐπὶ τὴν ἱερὰν πόλιν) ὁ δράκων οὐκ ἴσχυσεν **Rv 12:8.** κατά τινος *over, against someone* **Ac 19:16.** MPol 3:1; cp. 9:1 ἴσχυε . . . καὶ ἀνορίζου *be strong and brave* (in faith).

❹ ***have meaning, be valid, be in force,*** esp. as legal t.t. (Diod. S. 2, 33, 1; Aelian, VH 2, 38 νόμον ἰσχύειν; SIG 888, 59; 151 ἴσχυσεν τὰ προστάγματα; PTebt 286, 7 νομὴ ἄδικος οὐδὲν εἰσχύει; Ath. 2, 2) of a will μήποτε ἰσχύει ὅτε ζῇ ὁ διαθέμενος **Hb 9:17.** οὔτε περιτομή τι ἰσχύει, οὔτε ἀκροβυστία *neither circumcision nor uncircumcision means anything* **Gal 5:6.**—*Have the value of* (IGR IV, 915a, 12 ἡ δραχμὴ ἰσχύει ἀσσάρια δέκα; Jos., Ant. 14, 106) ὅλον ἐνιαυτὸν ἰσχύει ἡ ἡμέρα *the day is equal to a whole year* Hs 6, 4, 4.—DELG s.v. ἰσχύς. M-M. TW.

ἴσως adv. of ἴσος (Alcaeus, fgm. 89, 2 Diehl [=344, 2 L.-P.]='probably'; Sappho, fgm. 98, 11 [= 96, 11 L.-P.]='equally'; Theognis; ins, pap, LXX; as Alcaeus and Sappho exhibit, usage fluctuated [cp. English usage] between comparison [equal, alike] and probability [likely, probable]), in our lit. ***perhaps, probably*** (Attic wr., also PAmh 135, 16; PTebt 424, 3; POxy 1681, 4 ἴσως με νομίζετε, ἀδελφοί, βάρβαρόν τινα εἶναι; 4 Macc 7:17; Philo, Aet. M. 60; 134; Jos., Bell. 4, 119, Ant. 4, 11; Just., Ath.) **Lk 20:13;** GJs 17:2.—M-M.

'Ιταλία, ας, ἡ (Soph., Ant. 1119; Hdt. 1, 24 al.; SIG 1229, 2 πλεύσας εἰς 'Ιταλίαν; Philo; SibOr; oft. Joseph.) always w. the art. (B-D-F §261, 6) ***Italy* Ac 18:2** (Jos., Ant. 16, 7 ἧκον ἀπὸ τῆς 'Ιτ.); **27:1, 6;** Hb subscr. (no art.). οἱ ἀπὸ τ. 'Ιταλίας **Hb 13:24;** s. ἀπό 3b.—Kl.-Pauly II, 1479–85 (lit.).

'Ιταλικός, ή, όν (Pla. et al.; SIG 726, 4 [97/96 BC]; 746, 19; 1171, 10; Philo, Vi. Cont. 48; Jos., Ant. 9, 85; 18, 44; loanw. in rabb.) ***Italian*** σπεῖρα 'Ι. *the Italian cohort* (Arrian, Alan. 13 ed. ARoos II 1928 p. 181, 6 ἡ σπεῖρα ἡ 'Ιλταλική) **Ac 10:1.**—Lit. on ἑκατοντάρχης.—M-M.

ἰταμός, ή, όν (since Aeschyl., fgm. 282; Aristoph.; Demosth. et al.; Lucian; Aelian; Ael. Aristid. 31, 5 K.=11 p. 128 D.; Jer 6:23; 27:42) ***bold, impetuous*** Hm 11:12.—DELG s.v. εἶμι.

ἰτέα, ας, ἡ (Hom. et al.; Diod. S. 5, 41, 5; PTebt 703, 195 [III BC]; LXX; Jos., Ant. 3, 245; Just., D. 86, 5 ἰτέας [for στελέχη φοινίκων Ex 15:27]) ***willow tree*** Hs 8, 1, 1f; 8, 2, 7.—DELG.

'Ιτουραῖος, αία, αῖον (since Eupolemus [II BC] 723 fgm. 2 Jac. [in Eus., PE 9, 30, 3], mostly in the pl. of the subst. masc. 'Ιτουραῖοι [Appian, Mithrid. 106 §499, Bell. Civ. 5, 7, §31; Arrian, Alans 1 and 18; Jos., Ant. 13, 318]. Schürer 561–67) ἡ 'I. χώρα ***Ituraea,*** a region along the Lebanon and Anti-Lebanon ranges belonging to the Tetrarchy of Philip, w. Chalcis as its capital city **Lk 3:1.** S. Schürer loc. cit. for sources and lit.—M-M.

ἰχθύδιον, ου, τό (s. next entry; Aristoph.et al.; also pap) dim. of ἰχθύς ***little fish*** (Aelian, NA 6, 24 p. 150, 11) **Mt 15:34; Mk 8:7.** Obviously without diminutive sense *fish* (PFay 117, 7 [108 AD]; PFlor 119, 7 [254 AD]; Synes., Ep. 4 p. 166a) B 10:5 (=ἰχθύς 10:10).—DELG s.v. ἰχθῦς. M-M.

ἰχθύς (Herodian 2, 936 prefers ἰχθῦς; s. Schwyzer I 350; DELG and Frisk s.v. ἰχθῦς; B-D-F §13; Mlt-H. 141f), **ύος, ὁ** (Hom.+; ins, pap, LXX; En 7:5; 101:7; PsSol 5:9; TestSol; also PVindob 18:38 superscr.; Test12Patr; JosAs 10:14; Philo, Joseph., Just., Ath.) acc. pl. ἰχθύας (Epict. 4, 1, 30; Arrian, Anab. 5, 4, 3; PFay 113, 13 [100 AD].—The acc. form ἰχθῦς [Athen. 7 p. 327b] is not found in our lit.) ***fish,*** as food **Mt 7:10; 14:17, 19; 15:36; 17:27** (s. RMeyer, OLZ 40, '37, 665–70; JDerrett, Law in the NT, '70, 258–60); **Mk 6:38, 41, 43; Lk 5:6, 9; 9:13, 16; 11:11; 24:42; J 21:6, 8, 11** (Jos., Bell. 3, 508 the γένη ἰχθύων in the Lake of Gennesaret.—TestZeb 6:6 extraordinary catches of fish caused by divine intervention). The flesh of fishes **1 Cor 15:39.** ἰχθύες τ. θαλάσσης B 6:12 (Gen 1:26, 28); cp. vs. 18; 10:10. οἱ ἰ. αὐτῶν (τῶν ὑδάτων) GJs 3:3. Fish that by nature have no scales may not be eaten by Jews B 10:1 (s. Lev 11:9–12; Dt 14:9f).—RAC VII 959–1097 (lit.); D'Arcy Thompson, A Glossary of Greek Fishes '47. B. 184. M-M.

ἴχνος, ους, τό (Hom.+)—**❶** ***footprint,*** in our lit. only in fig. sense (as Appian, Bell. Civ. 2, 148 §617; Sir 21:6; Philo, Op. M. 144; Mel., P. 54, 398) and in ref. to exceptional performance περιπατεῖν τοῖς ἴ. *walk in the footsteps* **2 Cor 12:18.** στοιχεῖν τοῖς ἴ. τινος **Ro 4:12** (SIG 708, 6 αὐτὸς στοιχεῖν βουλόμενος καὶ τοῖς ἴ. ἐκείνων ἐπιβαίνειν; Philo, Gig. 58). ἐπακολουθεῖν τοῖς ἴ. τινος *follow in someone's footsteps* **1 Pt 2:21.** πρὸς τὰ ἴ. τινὸς εὑρεθῆναι *be found in someone's footsteps* MPol 22:1.

❷ ***sole,*** of the foot itself or of the footwear, both of which as a whole can be referred to as ἴχνος (Eur., Bacch. 1134; Hippocr., Art. 62 vol. IV p. 266 L.; Herodas 7, 12; 113; 119; Arrian, Ind. 16, 5; Galen X p. 876 K.; Anth. Pal. 9, 371, 2; POxy 1449, 51 [III AD]; 2130, 18 [267 AD]; Dt 11:24). Then the expression ὑπὸ τὰ ἴ. τινὸς εὑρεθῆναι IEph 12:2 would belong to the excessively humble sayings of Ign., to which later pap (Preis. I 706) offer comparable examples: *under* or *below, at the soles* or *the feet.*—DELG. M-M. TW.

ἰχώρ, ῶρος, ὁ (Hom. et al.) ***serum,*** of blood (so in Pythagoras, acc. to Diog. L. 8, 28; Pla. et al.; PGM 4, 2577; 2645; 4 Macc 9:20; Philo, Spec. Leg. 4, 119), also ***serious discharge, pus*** (Memnon [I BC / I AD]: 434 fgm. 1, 2, 4 Jac.; Job 2:8; 7:5; TestJob; Jos., Ant. 2, 296) ApcPt 11:26; Papias (3:2).—Frisk.

'Ιωαθάμ, ὁ indecl. (also 'Ιωάθαμ; יוֹתָם; 1 Ch 3:12 Ιωαθαν) ***Jotham,*** in the genealogy of Jesus **Mt 1:9; Lk 3:23ff** D ('Ιωαθάν).

'Ιωακίμ, ὁ (יְהוֹיָקִים; -κείμ GJs, cp. 'Ελιακίμ) indecl. (also JosAs 1:14, s. 'Ιεχονίας) ***Joachim/Jehoiakim*** **Mt 1:11 v.l.; Lk 3:23ff** D.—Father of Mary GJs 1:1, 4 (twice); 4:2 (three times); 4:3f (four times); 5:1 (twice); 6:2 (twice); 7:1 (twice); 7:2.

'Ιωανάν, ὁ indecl. ('Ιωαννᾶς v.l.; יוֹחָנָן; B-D-F §53, 2—2 Esdr [Ezra] 10:6; 22:22f; 2 Ch 17:15; 23:1) ***Joanan,*** in the genealogy of Jesus **Lk 3:27.**

'Ιωάν(ν)α, ας, ἡ (on the spelling s. B-D-F §40; 53, 3) ***Joanna*** **Lk 8:3; 24:10.**

'Ιωάν(ν)ης, ου, ὁ (on the spelling s. W-S. §5, 26c; FBlass, Philology of the Gospels 1898, 75f; 81; B-D-F §40; 55, 1c; Mlt-H. 102; Rob. 194; 214; GRudberg, Ntl. Text u. Nomina sacra 1915, 13f.—The name is also found 1 Macc 2:1f; 9:36, 38; 13:53; 1 Esdr 8:38; 9:29; ApcEsdr 1:19 p. 25, 13 Tdf. [Christian addition]; EpArist 47; 49; 50 and in Joseph. and Just.) ***John.***

❶ the Baptizer/Baptist (Jos., Ant. 18, 116–19; Just.) **Mt 3:1, 4, 13; 4:12** al.; **Mk** (s. JStarr, JBL 51, '32, 227–37) **1:4, 6, 9, 14; 2:18; 6:14, 16ff; 8:28; 11:30, 32; Lk 1:13, 60, 63; 3:2, 15f, 20** al.; **J 1:6, 15, 19, 26, 28, 32, 35** al.; **Ac 1:5, 22; 10:37; 11:16; 13:24f; 18:25; 19:3f;** GEb 13, 74 and 77f; 18, 36 and 38f; PEg^3 67; ISm 1:1.—Schürer II 345–48; JThomas, Le mouvement baptiste en Palest. et Syrie '35; MDibelius, Die urchr. Überlieferung von Joh. d. Täufer 1911; CBernoulli, J. der Täufer und die Urgemeinde 1918; CBowen: Studies in Early Christianity, ed. SCase (Porter-Bacon Festschr.) 1928, 127–47; E Parsons: ibid. 149–70; WMichaelis, Täufer, Jesus, Urgemeinde 1928; MGoguel, Jean-Baptiste 1928; ELohmeyer, Joh. d. T. '32; WHoward, J. the Bapt. and Jesus: Amicitiae Corolla, '33, 118–32; PGuénin, Y a-t-il conflit entre Jean B. et Jésus? '33; GMacgregor, John the Bapt. and the Origins of Christianity: ET 46, '35, 355–62; CKraeling, John the Bapt. '51; WWink, John the Bapt. in the Gosp. Trad. '68; JRife, The Standing of the Baptist: Gingrich Festschr., 205–8. JBecker, Joh. d. T. u. Jesus v. Nazareth '72.—HWindisch, D. Notiz üb. Tracht u. Speise d. Täuf. Joh.: ZNW 32, '33, 65–87; PJoüon, Le costume d'Élie et celui de J. Bapt.: Biblica 16, '35, 74–81. Esp. on his baptism: JJeremias, ZNW 28, 1929, 312–20; KAland, Z. Vorgeschichte d. christlichen Taufe, Neutest. Entwürfe '79, 183–97; his death: HWindisch, ZNW 18, 1918, 73–81; PZondervan, NThT 7, 1918, 131–53; 8, 1919, 205–40; 10, 1921, 206–17; DVölter, ibid. 10, 1921, 11–27; his disciples: HOort, TT 42, 1908, 299–333; WMichaelis, NKZ 38, 1927, 717–36.—JDoeve, NedTTs 9, '55, 137–57; DFlusser, Johannes d. Täufer '64; AGeyser, The Youth of J. the Bapt., NovT 1, '56, 70–75; CScobie, John the Bapt. '64; JMeier, John the Baptist in Matthew's Gospel: JBL 99, '80, 383–405.—HBraun, Qumran u. d. NT '66, II, 1–29. On the Mandaeans s. RGG^3 IV '60. 709–12 (lit.).

❷ son of Zebedee, one of the 12 disciples, brother of James (s. 'Ιάκωβος 1) **Mt 4:21; 10:2; 17:1; Mk 1:19, 29; 3:17; 5:37; 9:2, 38; 10:35, 41; 13:3; 14:33; Lk 5:10; 6:14; 8:51; 9:28, 49, 54; 22:8; Ac 1:13; 3:1, 3f, 11; 4:13, 19; 8:14; 12:2; Gal 2:9:** GEb 34, 60; Papias (2:4). Cp. Papias (1:4; 2:17; 3:1; 7:11f). Title of the Fourth Gospel κατὰ 'Ιωάννην.—WThomas, The Apostle John '46; cp. JKügler, Der Jünger den Jesus liebte '88.

❸ Tradition equates J., son of Zebedee (2), w. the *John* of **Rv 1:1, 4, 9; 22:8** (Just., D. 81, 4).—On 2 and 3 cp. the comm. on the Johannine wr., also Zahn, RE IX 272ff, Forsch. VI 1900, 175–217; Harnack, Die Chronologie der altchristl. Lit. 1897, 320–81;

ESchwartz, Über d. Tod der Söhne Zebedäi 1904; WHeitmüller, ZNW 15, 1914, 189–209; BBacon, ibid. 26, 1927, 187–202.—S. survey of lit. HThyen, in TRu 39, '75 (other installments 43, '78; 44, '79); also in EDNT II 211.

❹ father of Peter **J 1:42; 21:15–17;** Judaicon 158, 74 (s. Ἰωνᾶς 2 and cp. 1 Esdr 9:23 with its v.l.).

❺ an otherw. unknown member of the high council **Ac 4:6** (v.l. Ἰωνάθας). Schürer II 233f.

❻ surnamed Mark, son of Mary. His mother was a prominent member of the church at Jerusalem. He was a cousin of Barnabas and accompanied Paul and Barn. on the first missionary journey **Ac 12:12, 25; 13:5, 13; 15:37;** s. Μᾶρκος and BHolmes, Luke's Description of John Mark: JBL 54, '35, 63–72.

❼ Ἀριστίων καὶ ὁ πρεσβύτερος Ἰ., *Aristion and John the Elder* Pa (2:4) distinguished from the sons of Zebedee Eus. HE 3, 39, 5ff.—M-M. TW.

Ἰωάς, ὁ indecl. (יוֹאָשׁ 2 Kings [=4 Km] 14:1) ***Joash,*** king of Judah (Joseph.: Ἰώασος, ου [Ant. 9, 158]) **Mt 1:8 v.l.; Lk 3:23ff** D.

Ἰώβ, ὁ indecl. (אִיּוֹב; LXX; TestAbr A 15 p. 96, 13 [Stone p. 40]; TestJob; Philo, Mut. Nom. 48.—Cp. Jos., Ant. 2, 178 Ἴωβος, the son of Issachar) ***Job,*** hero of the book of the same name, example of patient suffering **Js 5:11;** 1 Cl 17:3 (Job 1:1); 26:3; 2 Cl 6:8 (Ezk 14:14).

Ἰωβήδ, ὁ indecl. (עוֹבֵד) ***Obed,*** David's grandfather (1 Ch 2:12 v.l. Likew. as v.l. in the book of Ruth 4:21f [D. Buch Ruth griech., ed. ARahlfs 1922, 28]), in the genealogy of Jesus **Mt 1:5; Lk 3:32** (v.l. Ἰωβήλ, Ὠβήδ.—Jos., Ant. 5, 336; 6, 157 Ὠβήδης, ου).

Ἰωδά, ὁ indecl. ***Joda*** (1 Esdr 5:56), in the genealogy of Jesus **Lk 3:26** (v.l. Ἰούδας).

Ἰωήλ, ὁ indecl. (יוֹאֵל) ***Joel,*** the OT prophet. τὸ εἰρημένον διὰ τοῦ προφήτου Ἰωήλ (i.e. Jo 3:1–5a) **Ac 2:16.**

Ἰωνάθας, ου, ὁ (PPetr III, 7, 15 [236 BC]; 1 Esdr 8:32; EpArist 48 and 49; 50 has Ἰωνάθης, like Joseph. [gen. -ου: Ant. 6, 234]) ***Jonathas*** **Ac 4:6** D instead of Ἰωάννης (s. Ἰωάν(ν)ης 5; Jos., Ant. 18, 95a Ἰωνάθης is mentioned, a son of Annas, who followed Caiaphas as high priest).—M-M.

Ἰωνάμ, ὁ indecl. ***Jonam,*** in the genealogy of Jesus **Lk 3:30** (v.l. Ἰωνάν as 1 Esdr 9:1 v.l.).

Ἰωνᾶς, ᾶ, ὁ (יוֹנָה) ***Jonah*—❶** the OT prophet (4 Km 14:25; Book of Jonah; Tob 14:4, 8 BA; 3 Macc 6:8; Jos., Ant. 9, 206–14; Just.; SibOr 2, 248). He is meant by the enigmatic saying about the 'sign of Jonah' **Mt 12:39–41; 16:4; Lk 11:29f, 32** (**Mt 12:40** and AcPlCor 2:29f the sign consists in Jonah's stay inside the monster for three days and nights. Lk thinks perh. of the preaching of the prophet to the Ninevites; s. on σημεῖον 1 and AVögtle, Synoptische Studien [Wikenhauser Festschr.] '53, 230–77); 1 Cl 7:7.

❷ a Galilean fisher, father of Simon Peter and Andrew **Mt 16:17 v.l.** βὰρ Ἰωνᾶ (for Βαριωνᾶ); **J 1:42 v.l.; 21:15–17 v.l;** GHb 254, 70 (Lat.). Acc. to J 1:42; 21:15–17 his name was Ἰωάν(ν)ης (s. Ἰωάν(ν)ης 4); the J pass. all have Ἰωνᾶ as v.l., cp. Βαριωνᾶς and s. B-D-F §53, 2; W-S. §5, 26c.—On 1 and 2 HGale, JBL 60, '41, 255–60; OGlombitza, NTS 8, '61/62, 359–66.—REdwards, The Sign of Jonah in the Theology of the Evangelists and Q, '71.—TW.

Ἰωράμ, ὁ indecl. (יְהוֹרָם; in Joseph. Ἰώραμος, ου [Ant. 9, 58]) ***Joram*** (=*Jehoram*), king of Judah (4 Km 8:16ff; 2 Ch 21:3ff.—The name also 1 Esdr 1:9); in the genealogy of Jesus **Mt 1:8; Lk 3:23ff** D.

Ἰωρίμ, ὁ (also -ρείμ) indecl. ***Jorim,*** in the genealogy of Jesus **Lk 3:29.**

Ἰωσαφάτ, ὁ indecl. (יְהוֹשָׁפָט; in Joseph. Ἰωσάφατος, ου [Ant. 8, 399]) ***Josaphat*** (=*Jehoshaphat*), king of Judah (3 Km 22:41ff; 2 Ch 17–20; κοιλὰς Ἰ. Jo 4:12; ApcEsdr 3:6 [27, 13 Tdf.]); in the genealogy of Jesus **Mt 1:8; Lk 3:23ff** D w. final δ.

Ἰωσῆς, ῆ or **ῆτος** (s. Mayser 274), **ὁ** (the name is found IG XIV [Sic. It. 949] Κλαύδιος Ἰωσῆς; ins fr. Cyrene: Sb 1742. S. ibid. 3757 [I AD]; BGU 715 I, 4 [CPJ II, 428; s. Schürer III 55] Ἰ. ὁ καὶ Τεύφιλος; Jos., Bell. 4, 66 v.l. S. B-D-F §53, 2; 55, 2; Rob. 263; Wuthnow 60) ***Joses***

❶ name of a brother of Jesus **Mk 6:3; Mt 13:55 v.l.;** s. Ἰωσήφ 5.

❷ son of a Mary and brother of James the younger **Mk 15:40, 47; Mt 27:56 v.l.** (for Ἰωσήφ, q.v. 9; on the text s. AMerx, D. Vier kanon. Ev. II 1, 1902, 430ff).

❸ name of a member of the early church better known as Barnabas **Ac 4:36 v.l.** (s. Ἰωσήφ 7).

❹ S. Ἰησοῦς 2.—M-M.

Ἰωσήφ, ὁ indecl. (יוֹסֵף; Apollonius Molon [I BC] : 728 fgm. 1, 3 Jac. [in Eus., PE 9, 19, 3]; Sb II 250, word-list; LXX; Test12Patr; JosAs; ApcEsdr p. 7, 10 and p. 32, 24 Tdf.; Philo; Just.; Mel., P. 59, 432.—EpArist: Ἰώσηφος; Jos. Ant. 2, 17; also C. Ap. 1, 92 Ἰώσηπος, ου) ***Joseph.***

❶ the patriarch (Gen 30:24 and oft.; Test12Patr; JosAs; Demetr.: 722 fgm. 1, 5 al. Jac; Philo, Mut. Nom. 90f and oft.; Just., D. 100, 1 al.; Mel., P. 59, 432) **J 4:5; Ac 7:9, 13f, 18; Hb 11:21f;** 1 Cl 4:9; B 13:4f; φυλὴ Ἰ. in **Rv 7:8** stands for the half-tribe Ephraim which, w. its other half Manasseh vs. **6** brings the number of the tribes to twelve once more, after the loss of the tribe of Dan, to which acc. to tradition the Antichrist belongs (WBousset, Der Antichrist 1895, 112f).

❷ son of Jonam, in the genealogy of Jesus **Lk 3:30.**

❸ son of Mattathias **Lk 3:24.**

❹ husband of Mary the mother of Jesus (Just., D. 102, 2f; 103, 3) **Mt 1:16** (BHHW II 886–89 [lit.]; PSchmiedel, PM 6, 1902, 88–93, SchTZ 31, 1914, 69–82; ibid. 32, 1915, 16–30; ERiggenbach, ibid. 31, 1914, 241–49; GKuhn, NKZ 34, 1923, 362–85; UHolzmeister, De S. Jos. Quaestiones Biblicae '45), **18–20, 24; 2:13, 19; Lk 1:27; 2:4, 16, 33 v.l.; 3:23** (a genealogy in which the first name is given without the article, and all subsequent names have the article, as Theopomp. [IV BC]: 115 fgm. 393 Jac.: in ascending order to Heracles; Diod. S. 5, 81, 6 Λέσβος ὁ Λαπίθου τοῦ Αἰόλου τοῦ Ἱππότου; Nicol. Dam.: 90 fgm. 30 p. 343, 30 Jac. Δηιφόντῃ τῷ Ἀντιμάχου τοῦ Θρασυάνορος τοῦ Κτησίππου τοῦ Ἡρακλέους. Other exx. in Klostermann ad loc.; B-D-F §162, 2); **4:22; J 1:45; 6:42** (PMenoud, RTP 63, 1930, 275–84). GJs 9:1ff; 13:1ff; 14:1f; 15:1f, 4; 16:1ff; 17:1ff; 18:1; 19:1 (not pap); 21:1.

❺ a brother of Jesus **Mt 13:55.** Cp. Ἰωσῆς 1.

❻ *Joseph* of Arimathaea, member of the Sanhedrin, in whose tomb Jesus was buried **Mt 27:57, 59; Mk 15:43, 45; Lk 23:50; J 19:38;** GPt 6:23. Acc. to GPt 2:3 he was a friend of Pilate.—EvDobschütz, ZKG 23, 1902, 1–17.

❼ *Joseph,* surnamed Barnabas **Ac 4:36.** S. Ἰωσῆς 3.

❽ *Joseph,* surnamed Barsabbas (s. Βαρσαβ[β]ᾶς 1), also called Justus (s. Ἰοῦστος 1) **Ac 1:23.**

❾ son of a certain Mary **Mt 27:56** (s. Ἰωσῆς 2).

❿ son of Joda **Lk 3:26 v.l.** (s. Ἰωσήχ).—M-M.

Ἰωσήχ, ὁ indecl. (Mlt-H. 108f) ***Josech,*** son of Joda, in the genealogy of Jesus **Lk 3:26** (v.l. Ἰωσήφ, q.v. no. 10).

Ἰωσίας, ου, ὁ (also -είας; יֹאשִׁיָּהוּ) ***Josiah,*** king of Judah (4 Km 22f; 2 Ch 34f; Sir 49:1, 4; Bar 1:8; 1 Esdr 1:1–32; Jos., Ant. 10:48, 67–77); in the genealogy of Jesus **Mt 1:10f; Lk 3:23ff** D (here the gen. Ἰωσία).—EDNT.

ἰῶτα, τό indecl. (written out as a word Plato, Cratyl. 418b; Aeneas Tact. 1506; Scholiast on Nicander, Ther. 950; Sb 358, 12; 20 [III BC]) ***iota.*** In **Mt 5:18** it is evidently the Gk. equivalent of the Aram. yod which, in the orig. form of the saying, represented the smallest letter of the alphabet (s. MLidzbarski, Handb. d. nordsemit. Epigraphik 1898, 190ff; ESutcliffe, Biblica 9, 1928, 458–62). As numeral=***ten*** B 9:8. S. ι´ as numeral.—DELG. M-M. TW.

K

κ´ numerical sign = ***20*** (εἴκοσι: the textual tradition varies between κ´ and κε´ [=25]) Hs 9, 4, 3; 9, 5, 4.

κάβος, ου, ὁ (Semitic loanword [קַב; s. Masson 84] Geopon. 7, 20, 1; 4 Km 6:25) **a measure (usu. for grain, etc.) equal to approx. two liters,** ***cab*** **Lk 16:6 v.l.;** s. κάδος.—DELG.

κἀγώ (since Il. 21, 108, also ins [Meisterhans³-Schw. 72]; pap [Mayser 159 w. exx. for all cases; s. also UPZ 78, 15 [159 BC]; PSI 540, 17; PTebt 412, 4 καἰγώ]; LXX [Thackeray 137f]; pseudepigr.; Jos., Ant. 7, 212; Just.; Tat. 5:2. Formed by crasis, as found in most edd., fr. καὶ ἐγώ) dat. κἀμοί, acc. κἀμέ. S. B-D-F §18; W-S. §5, 9; Mlt-H. 84.

❶ ***and I*** ὁ πατήρ σου κἀγώ **Lk 2:48;** cp. **Mt 11:28; J 6:57; 7:28; 8:26; 10:28; 17:22;** IPhld 11:1 al.—In a narrative told in the first pers. sg. it connects one member w. another **J 1:31, 33, 34.** It oft. expresses a reciprocal relation *and I, as I* ἐν ἐμοὶ μένει κἀγὼ ἐν αὐτῷ **J 6:56.** μείνατε ἐν ἐμοὶ κἀγὼ ἐν ὑμῖν **15:4;** cp. **10:15, 38; 14:20;** also **2 Cor 12:20; Gal 6:14.**

❷ ***but I:*** Jesus in contrast to the prince of this world **J 12:32;** cp. **Ac 22:19.** ὑμεῖς . . . κἀμοί *you . . . but to me* **10:28.** σὺ πίστιν ἔχεις, κἀγὼ ἔργα ἔχω *you have faith, but I have deeds* **Js 2:18a.**

❸ ***I also, I too***—ⓐ = I, as well as others δοκῶ κἀγὼ πνεῦμα θεοῦ ἔχειν *I believe that I, too, have the Spirit of God* **1 Cor 7:40.** κἀγὼ προσκυνήσω αὐτῷ **Mt 2:8.** Cp. **Lk 1:3; Ac 8:19.**—*I, too* **J 5:17; 2 Cor 11:21, 22abc.**—καθὼς . . . κἀγώ *just as . . . I also* **J 15:9; 17:18; 20:21.**

ⓑ *I for my part, I in turn* **Mt 10:32f; 26:15** (s. 5 below);**18:33; 21:24; Lk 22:29;** B 1:4; ISm 4:2. ὅτι ἐτήρησας . . . κἀγώ σε τηρήσω *because you have kept . . . I, in turn, will keep you* **Rv 3:10.**—Introducing the moral of a parable κἀγὼ ὑμῖν λέγω *I, for my part, say to you* **Lk 11:9** (cp. **16:9**).—κἀγὼ δέ *but I, for my part* **Mt 16:18.**

ⓒ The καί in κἀγώ is redundant in comparison τοιούτους ὁποῖος κἀγώ εἰμι *such as I am* **Ac 26:29 v.l.** ἐὰν μείνωσιν ὡς κἀγώ *if they remain as I am* **1 Cor 7:8;** cp. **10:33; 11:1.** Sim. διὰ τοῦτο κἀγὼ οὐ παύομαι *for that reason I do not cease* **Eph 1:15;** cp. **1 Th 3:5.**

❹ ***I in particular*** or *I, for instance* τί ἔτι κἀγὼ ὡς ἁμαρτωλὸς κρίνομαι; **Ro 3:7.**

❺ ***if I,*** as introduction to what is in effect a conditional clause κἀγὼ ὑμῖν παραδώσω αὐτόν *if I hand him over to you* **Mt 26:15** (cp. SIG 1168, 69f τί μοι δωσεῖς, αἴ τύ κα ὑγιῆ ποιήσω; *What will you give me, if I make you well?* For interpr. of κἀγώ as introd. to a protasis s. Rob. 951.)—M-M.

κάδος, ου, ὁ (Semitic word, s. Masson 42–44; since Archilochus Lyr., Anacr., Hdt.; GDI 5220 [Sicily: 18 times]; pap; Is 40:15; 2 Ch 2:9 v.l., ἐλαίου κάδ.) ***jar, container*** **Lk 16:6 v.l.** (for βάτος II); s. κάβος.—DELG.

καθά conj. or adv. (since Polyb. 3, 107, 10 [FKälker, Quaest. de elocut. Polyb. 1880, 300]; Diod. S. 4, 81, 3; 19, 48, 2; 19, 71, 7; ins [Meisterhans³-Schw. 257; SIG index]; PRyl 160 II, 18; POxy 1473, 10; LXX; PsSol 2:12; TestAbr B 5 p. 109, 19 [Stone p. 66]; TestJob 17:4; JosAs 24:10f; ParJer 3:22 [AB]; Jos., Ant. 19, 96; 298; 20, 6; Ar. 4, 2; Just.; Tat. 1, 2; Ath. 20, 2) ***just as*** **Mt 27:10; Lk 1:2** D (s. B-D-F §453); IMg 10:1; Hs 1:8; AcPl Ha 5, 18.—*how, the way in which* ἄκουε . . . , καθὰ δῖ (=δεῖ) σε σωθῆναι AcPl Ha 1, 5; Hs 8, 7, 1 v.l.—M-M.

καθαίρεσις, εως, ἡ (s. καθαιρέω; Thu. et al.; ins, pap, LXX; Jos., Ant. 14, 437) gener. 'tearing down, destruction'.

❶ **causing destruction by tearing down,** ***tearing down, destruction*** lit. (τ. τειχῶν X., Hell. 2, 2, 15; 5, 1, 35; Polyb. 23, 7, 6 v.l.; SIG² 587, 76; PMagd 96 [III BC] demolition of a temple; Ex 23:24 καθαιρέσει καθελεῖς τ. στήλας αὐτῶν; Jos., Ant. 17, 163) in illustrative discourse (cp. Philo, Conf. Lingu. 130 πρὸς τὴν τοῦ ὀχυρώματος τούτου καθαίρεσιν) πρὸς καθαίρεσιν ὀχυρωμάτων *for the tearing down of bulwarks* **2 Cor 10:4.**

❷ **causing weakening of capability,** ***disabling,*** fig. extension of mng. 1 (Diod. S. 34 + 35, fgm. 7, 1 of removal from office; Philo; opp. οἰκοδομή [q.v.]='edification') εἰς οἰκοδομὴν καὶ οὐκ εἰς καθαίρεσιν **2 Cor 13:10.** W. obj. gen. of the pers. εἰς καθαίρεσιν ὑμῶν **10:8** (cp. 1 Macc 3:43 καθ. τοῦ λαοῦ).—DELG s.v. αἱρέω. M-M. TW.

καθαιρέτης, ου, ὁ (s. καθαιρέω; since Thu. 4, 83, 5; BGU 14 V, 12 [255 AD]) ***destroyer*** ὁ τῶν ἡμετέρων θεῶν κ. MPol 12:2.—DELG s.v. αἱρέω.

καθαιρέω 2 fut. καθελῶ **Lk 12:18;** 1 aor. impv. 2 pl. καθαιρήσατε (Just., A I, 56, 4); 2 aor. καθεῖλον, ptc. καθελών. Pass.: fut. καθαιρεθήσομαι LXX; 1 aor. καθῃρέθην; pf. ptc. καθῃρημένος LXX; plpf. 3 sg. καθῄρητο Judg 6:28 B (Hom.+).

❶ **to bring down from one level to another,** ***take down, bring down, lower*** (Demetr. [?]: 722 fgm. 7 Jac.) τινά or τι *someone* or *someth.*: someone fr. a carriage MPol 8:3. Judas fr. a tree Papias

(3:1). Of raised hands *let (them) drop* B 12:2 (w. τὰς χεῖρας to be supplied); the body fr. the cross (Polyb. 1, 86, 6; Philo, In Flacc. 83; Jos., Bell. 4, 317) **Mk 15:36, 46; Lk 23:53.** ἀπὸ τοῦ ξύλου (Josh 8:29; 10:27) **Ac 13:29.** δυνάστας ἀπὸ θρόνων *bring down the rulers fr. their thrones* **Lk 1:52** (κ. abs. in this mng.: Hdt. 7, 8, 1; Aelian, VH 2, 25; Jos., Ant. 8, 270; for the theme cp. 3 Macc 2:2–20).

❷ **to destroy by tearing down, *tear down, destroy, overpower*** ⓐ lit.—**α.** of buildings *tear down* (X., Hell. 4, 4, 13 τῶν τειχῶν=a part of the walls; SIG 826e, 31 τ. οἰκίαν; PAmh 54, 3; Is 5:5; 22:10; Jos., Vi. 65; Just., A I, 56, 4 τὸν ἀνδριάντα) in contrast to οἰκοδομέω (Jer 49:10; 51:34; Ezk 36:36): the temple B 16:3 (cp. Diod. S. 20, 93, 1 ἱερά; Is 49:17). Barns **Lk 12:18.** Pass. B 16:4.

β. *conquer, destroy* (Thu. 1, 4; 1, 77, 6 al.; Aelian, VH 2, 25; POxy 1408, 23 τοὺς λῃστάς; EpArist 263; Philo, Agr. 86; Jos., Ant. 10, 209; δαίμονας κ. Orig., C. Cels. 8, 73, 29) ἔθνη **Ac 13:19.** Pass. καθαιροῦνται αἱ δυνάμεις τοῦ σατανᾶ IEph 13:1.

ⓑ fig. (Epict. 1, 28, 25 τὰ δόγματα τὰ ὀρθὰ κ.; Zech 9:6 καθελῶ ὕβριν ἀλλοφύλων; Jos., Ant. 6, 179 τ. ἀλαζονείαν; Tat. 26, 3 πολεμοῦντες . . . ἑαυτοῖς ἀλλήλους καθαιρεῖτε; Iren. 1, 15, 2 [Harv. I 149, 8] κ. τὸν θάνατον) λογισμούς *destroy sophistries* **2 Cor 10:4.** Pass. ἄγνοια IEph 19:3. καθαιρεῖσθαι τῆς μεγαλειότητος αὐτῆς *suffer the loss of her magnificence* **Ac 19:27** (cp. Achmes 13, 22 ὁ κριτὴς . . . καθαιρεῖται τῆς ἀξίας αὐτοῦ=the judge suffers the loss of his dignity; B-D-F §180, 1; Rob. 518. Field, Notes 129f would supply τὶ and transl. *diminish*).—DELG s.v. αἱρέω. M-M. TW.

καθαίρω 1 aor. ptc. καθάρας; mid. aor. ptc. καθηράμενος (Just., D. 4, 3); pf. pass. 3 sg. κεκάθαρται Hs 9, 10, 4; ptc. κεκαθαρμένος (Hom.+)

❶ **to cause someth. to become clean, *make clean,*** lit., of a place that has been swept (cp. Diod. S. 19, 13, 4 τόπον ἀνακαθαίρειν=clear [out] a place): πάντα κεκάθαρται *everything is clean* Hs 9, 10, 4. Fig. (Diod. S. 4, 31, 4; 4, 69, 4; Dio Chrys. 60 + 61 [77 + 78], 40 τὴν αὑτοῦ διάνοιαν καθαίρει τῷ λόγῳ; Himerius, Or. 41 [=Or. 7], 1 Ἡλίῳ Μίθρᾳ ψυχὴν καθάραντες=after we have cleansed our souls by the agency of Helios Mithra; Philo, Somn. 1, 198 καθαίρει ψυχὴν ἁμαρτημάτων; Jos., Ant. 5, 42; Just., D. 4, 3 al.) οἱ κεκαθαρμένοι *those who are purified* Hs 9, 18, 3. καθᾶραι ἑαυτὸν ἀπὸ τῶν λογισμῶν *clear oneself from the thoughts* Dg 2:1 (κ. ἀπό as Appian, Bell. Civ. 2, 1 §2; Jos., Ant. 13, 34).

❷ **to remove superfluous growth from a plant, *clear, prune*** of a vine (cp. Philo, Agr. 10, Somn. 2, 64) **J 15:2.**—DELG s.v. καθαρός. M-M. TW.

καθάπερ conj. or adv. (Attic wr.; ins, pap; LXX; TestJud 21:6[a]; ApcMos 17; EpArist 11; Philo; Jos., Bell. 4, 406, C. Ap. 1, 74; 130 and oft. [BBrüne, Josephus 1912, 34]; Just., D. 29, 3; Tat; Mel., fgm. 8b, 26) ***just as,*** in our lit. only Paul, Hb, Dg. κ. γέγραπται (the formulation contributes a solemn official tone to the text, cp. ὅπως συντελεσθῇ ὁ ὅρκος καθάπερ γέγραπται SIG 1007, 35 [II BC]; sim. καθάπερ Ἴωνες δεδώκασι καὶ ἐν τῆι στήλῃ ἀναγέγραπται IPriene 201, 8f [restored]) as **v.l. Ro 3:4; 9:13; 10:15; 11:8** (always for καθώς; cp. Philod., εὐσεβ. 60 Gomp. καθάπερ ἐν Ἠοίαις=as it says in the Eoiai [a work of Hesiod lost except for fragments]).—**1 Cor 10:10; 2 Cor 3:13, 18** (v.l. καθώσπερ); **1 Th 2:11.** *As it were* (Diod. S. 14, 1, 4a) Dg 3:3. καθάπερ καί *as also* **Ro 4:6; 2 Cor 1:14; 1 Th 3:6, 12; 4:5;** Dg 2:1 (Just., D. 29, 3; Tat. 5, 3). It is oft. used elliptically, as **Hb 4:2,** but the verb can easily be supplied fr. the context: οὐ κ. . . . οὕτως ἀλλά *not as . . . but* Dg 7:2; κ. . . . οὕτως *just as . . . so* (Diod. S. 23, 14, 3; 23, 15, 11; 27, 18, 2; Ps.-Demetr. 186; 2 Macc 2:29; 6:14; 15:39; 4 Macc 15:31f; Tat. 8, 3) **Ro 12:4; 1 Cor 12:12;** without a verb **2 Cor 8:11; Hb 5:4 v.l.** (for καθώσπερ); s. also καθώς.—FDanker, Gingrich Festschr., '72, 99f.—M-M.

καθάπτω (s. κατά, ἅπτω) 1 aor. καθῆψα (in mid. Hom. et al.; in act. trag. et al.) ***take hold of, seize*** (it is usu. the mid., found here as a v.l., that has this mng. [cp. Jos., Bell. 3, 319; 385; of the sun SSol 1:6 Sym. 'burn']; Just., D. 137, 2, ὁ τοῦ ἠγαπημένου καθαπτόμενος, but the act. also has it [Ps.-Xenophon, Cyneg. 6, 9; Polyb. 8, 8, 3]) τινός *someth.* (quot. in Pollux 1, 164; Epict. 3, 20, 10 ὁ τοῦ τραχήλου καθάπτων) of a snake καθῆψεν τ. χειρὸς αὐτοῦ *it fastened on his hand* **Ac 28:3.**—DELG s.v. ἅπτω. M-M.

καθαρεύω (s. καθαρός; Aristoph., Pla.+; pap, Philo; TestReub 6:1, 2; Just., D. 49, 7) ***be pure, clean*** Ox 840, 23 and 24. κ. τινός *be free fr. someth.* (Pla., Ep. 8 p. 356e; Plut., Phoc. 37, 2 φόνου, Cato Min. 24, 6 ἁμαρτημάτων; Ael. Aristid. 44 p. 828 D. τῶν αἰσχρῶν; Herm. Wr. 6, 3 τ. κακίας; CPR I, 232, 34 πάσης αἰτίας; Philo, Rer. Div. Her. 7 ἁμαρτημάτων; Jos., Ant. 1, 102 φόνου, Vi. 79) τοῦ αἵματός τινος *free fr. someone's blood* GPt 11:46.—DELG s.v. καθαρός.

καθαρίζω (s. next entry; also καθερίζω; s. B-D-F §29, 1; W-S. §5, 20c; Mlt-H. 67) Attic fut. καθαριῶ (**Hb 9:14; J 15:2** D; B-D-F §101 s.v. καθαίρειν; s. Mlt-H. 218); 3 sg. -ίσει (Num 30:13 cod. B; Mal 3:3) 1 aor. ἐκαθάρισα, impv. καθάρισον. Pass.: fut. καθαρισθήσομαι LXX; 1 aor. ἐκαθαρίσθην (also ἐκαθερίσθην: **Mt 8:3b v.l.; Mk 1:42 v.l.**), impv. καθαρίσθητι; pf. 3 sg. κεκαθάρισται (1 Km 20:26; TestJob 43:17), ptc. κεκαθαρισμένος. See Reinhold 38f; Thackeray 74. (H. Gk. substitute for the st. καθαίρω: as agricultural t.t. PLond I 131 recto, 192 p. 175 [78/79 AD]; PStras 2, 11; PLips 111, 12. In the ritual sense, mystery ins fr. Andania=SIG 736, 37; likew. 1042, 3; Jos., Ant. 10, 70; 11, 153; 12, 286; Just., Mel., P. 72, 526. The word is also found BGU 1024 IV, 16; EpArist 90 and in var. mngs. in LXX; En 10:20, 22; TestJob; TestReub 4:8; TestLevi 14:6.—Dssm., NB 43f [BS 216f]; in var. senses 'cleanse, clear [as of an area], purify')

❶ **to make physically clean, *make clean, cleanse*** τί *someth.* **Mt 23:25f; Lk 11:39.** The much-discussed passage καθαρίζων πάντα τὰ βρώματα **Mk 7:19** may belong here (so BWeiss; HHoltzmann; Schniewind), but s. 3a below.

❷ **to heal a person of a disease that makes one ceremonially unclean, *make clean, heal*** esp. leprosy—ⓐ τινά *make someone clean* **Mt 8:2; 10:8; Mk 1:40; Lk 5:12;** AcPl Ha 8, 36//BMM verso 10; s. also BMM verso 12 and 39 (Mel., P. 72, 526 τοὺς λεπρούς). Pass. (Lev 14:7 al.) **Mt 11:5; Mk 1:42; Lk 4:27; 7:22; 17:14, 17;** PEg[2] 37; καθαρίσθητι (cp. 4 Km 5:13) *be clean!* **Mt 8:3a; Mk 1:41; Lk 5:13; 17:14 v.l.;** PEg[2] 38.

ⓑ τί *remove someth. by* or *for the purpose of purification* (cp. Od. 6, 93 καθαίρειν ῥύπα; Epict. 2, 16, 44; 3, 24, 13) pass. ἐκαθαρίσθη αὐτοῦ ἡ λέπρα *his leprosy disappeared* **Mt 8:3b.**

❸ **to purify through ritual cleansing, *make clean, declare clean***—ⓐ a Levitical cleansing of foods *make clean, declare clean* (cp. Lev 13:6, 23) ἃ ὁ θεὸς ἐκαθάρισεν **Ac 10:15; 11:9.** Many (Origen; Field, Notes 31f; et al.) prefer to take καθαρίζων πάντα τ. βρώματα **Mk 7:19** (s. 1 above) in this sense, regarding the words as an observation of the evangelist or a marginal note by a reader: *he* (Jesus) (*hereby*) *declares all foods clean.*—WBrandt, Jüd. Reinheitslehre u. ihre Beschreibung in den Evang. 1910.

ⓑ of moral and cultic cleansing—**α.** *cleanse, purify* fr. sin (LXX) τινά or τί: (τὰς ψυχάς Hippol., Ref. 10, 14, 10) τὴν καρδίαν Hs 6, 5, 2. τὰς καρδίας v 3, 9, 8. χεῖρας **Js 4:8;** ἑαυτούς Hs 8, 7, 5; τὸ ἐντὸς τ. ποτηρίου *the contents of the cup,* which must not be acquired in a sinful manner, nor used for a sinful purpose **Mt 23:26.** ἐλθέτω τὸ ἅγ. πνεῦμά σου ἐφ' ἡμᾶς κ. καθαρισάτω ἡμᾶς *let your Holy Spirit come upon us and make us pure* **Lk 11:2 v.l.** In parable τοὺς λίθους Hs 9, 7, 2 and 6; 9, 8, 4.—Pass. Hv 4, 3, 4. ἅπαξ κεκαθαρισμένους **Hb 10:2.** καθαρισθήσεται ἡ ἐκκλησία Hs 9, 18, 2; cp. 3. καθαρισθήσομαι 1 Cl 18:7 (Ps 50:9).—τινὰ (τὶ) ἀπό τινος (on the constr. w. ἀπό s. the two pass. fr. SIG at the beg. of that entry; Lev 16:30 καθαρίσαι ὑμᾶς ἀπὸ τ. ἁμαρτιῶν; Ps 18:14; 50:4; Sir 23:10; 38:10 and oft.; En 10:20, 22; PsSol 10:1; 17:22; Jos., Ant. 12, 286; TestReub 4:8; Just., D. 116, 2) κ. τινὰ ἀπὸ πάσης ἁμαρτίας **1J 1:7;** cp. vs. **9;** 1 Cl 18:3 (Ps 50:4). κ. ἑαυτὸν ἀπὸ μολυσμοῦ σαρκός *cleanse oneself from defilement of the body* **2 Cor 7:1.** ἀπὸ τῆς λύπης Hm 10, 3, 4. ἀπὸ πάσης ἐπιθυμίας Hs 7:2. τῶν πονηριῶν 8, 11, 3; ἀπὸ τούτου τοῦ δαιμονίου 9, 23, 5. κ. τὴν καρδίαν ἀπὸ τῆς διψυχίας *cleanse the heart of doubt* m 9:7. ἀπὸ τῶν ματαιωμάτων *from vanities* 9:4. κ. ἑαυτῶν τὰς καρδίας ἀπὸ τῶν ἐπιθυμιῶν 12, 6, 5. κ. τὴν συνείδησιν ἡμῶν ἀπὸ νεκρῶν ἔργων **Hb 9:14.** Pass. καθαρίζεσθαι ἀπὸ τ. ἁμαρτιῶν Hv 2, 3, 1; ἀπὸ τ. ὑστερημάτων 3, 2, 2a; cp. b and 3, 8, 11.—κ. τινά (τί) τινι (dat. of instr.): τῇ πίστει καθαρίσας (i.e. God) τὰς καρδίας αὐτῶν **Ac 15:9.** Of Christ and the community of Christians καθαρίσας τῷ λουτρῷ τοῦ ὕδατος ἐν ῥήματι **Eph 5:26** (OCasel, Jahrb. für Liturgiewiss. 5, 1925, 144ff). Of Christ and baptism ἵνα τῷ πάθει τὸ ὕδωρ καθαρίσῃ *so that through (his) suffering he might purify the water* IEph 18:2.—καθάρισον ἡμᾶς τὸν καθαρισμὸν τῆς σῆς ἀληθείας *purify us w. the cleansing of your truth* 1 Cl 60:2.—Of Christ and Christians κ. ἑαυτῷ λαὸν περιούσιον **Tit 2:14.**—PEg[3] 57f.

β. *remove by* or *for the purpose of purification* τὶ *someth.* (s. 2b and cp. Dt 19:13; κεκαθάρισται ἡμῶν ἡ ἀνομία TestJob 43:17) τὰς ἁμαρτίας τινός Hs 5, 6, 2f.

ⓒ **Hb 9:22f** occupies an intermediate position, since ceremon. purification and moral purification merge, and the former becomes the shadow-image of the latter.

ⓓ *set free* τινά τινος *someone from someth.* 1 Cl 16:10 (Is 53:10).—DELG s.v. καθαρός. M-M. EDNT. TW.

καθαρισμός, οῦ, ὁ (fr. καθαρίζω; occurs as an agricultural t.t. [s. καθαρίζω, beg.] PMich 185, 16 [122 AD]; PLond II, 168, 11 p. 190 [162 AD]; in the sense 'propitiation' in Ps.-Lucian, Asin. 22; found also in LXX; TestLevi 14:6 and in Achmes 92, 19 v.l. It replaces the much more common καθαρμός)

❶ **cleansing from cultic impurity,** ***purification*** (2 Macc 2:16 of the dedication of a temple) **J 3:25.** W. subj. gen. κ. τῶν Ἰουδαίων **2:6.** W. obj. gen. of the pers.: **Mk 1:44; Lk 5:14** (Manetho in Jos., C. Ap. 1, 282 deals with the ceremonies that a person who has been healed of leprosy undergoes). αἱ ἡμέραι τ. καθαρισμοῦ αὐτῶν (cp. Ex 29:36) **Lk 2:22** includes Joseph in the purification, whereas only the woman was required to undergo purification (Aristot., HA 7, 10 p, 587b, 1ff this is called καθαρμός); the pronoun αὐτῶν perh. is colloq. usage to account for Joseph's presence in the process.

❷ **cleansing from inward pollution,** ***purify,*** fig. extension of 1 (TestLevi 14:6 v.l.) 1 Cl 60:2 (s. καθαρίζω 3bα). κ. τῶν ἁμαρτιῶν ποιεῖσθαι *bring about purification from sin* (cp. Job 7:21) **Hb 1:3.** Cp. **2 Pt 1:9.**—DELG s.v. καθαρός. M-M. TW.

κάθαρμα, ατος, τό (trag. et al.; of persons: Aristoph., Plutus 454; Demosth. 21, 185; Dio Chrys. 13 [7], 30; Diog. L. 6, 32 ἀνθρώπους ἐκάλεσα, οὐ καθάρματα; Philostrat., Vi. Apoll. 1, 12; Synes., Ep. 148 p. 288a [of the Cyclopes]; Philo, Virt. 174; Jos., Bell. 4, 241) ***refuse,*** for περικάθαρμα (q.v.) **1 Cor 4:13 v.l.**—DELG s.v. καθαρός. TW.

καθαρός, ά, όν (s. καθαρίζω; Hom.+)—❶ **pert. to being clean or free of adulterating matter,** ***clean, pure,*** of a cup **Mt 23:26.** σινδών *clean linen* (PGM 4, 1861; 2189; 3095; 5, 217) **Mt 27:59.** λίνον καθαρὸν λαμπρόν (v.l. λίθον; on this Philo, Mos. 2, 72) **Rv 15:6.** βύσσινον λαμπρὸν κ. **19:8;** cp. vs. **14;** ὠμόλινον κ. Hs 8, 4, 1. ὕδωρ *pure, clean water* (Eur., Hipp. 209; SIG 972, 169; PGM 4, 3252; Ezk 36:25; Philo, Spec. Leg. 3, 58; Mel., fgm. 8b, 17; 40 P.) **Hb 10:22.** Of metals (Hdt. 4, 166; Aristot., Meteor. 383b, 1; Theocr. 15, 36 ἀργύριον; Plut., Alex. 684 [32, 9] ἄργυρος; Sb 4481, 13 σίδηρος) χρυσίον κ. *pure gold* (Diod. S. 3, 14, 4; Ex 25:31; 2 Ch 3:5) **Rv 21:18a, 21;** ὕαλος κ. *clear crystal* vs. **18b.** In the fig. lang. of Ignatius, referring to martyrdom, we have the concept κ. ἄρτος (Hdt. 2, 40; Teles p. 40, 11; Dio Chrys. 13 [7], 76 al.; Jur. Pap. 36, 29; POxy 736, 26) *pure* (wheat) *bread,* without admixture IRo 4:1. κ. φῶς *pure light* IRo 6:2.—ὁ λελουμένος ἐστὶν καθαρὸς ὅλος *a person who has bathed is clean all over* **J 13:10a.**

❷ **pert. to being cultically/ceremonially pure,** ***ritually pure*** (ins; PGM 4, 3084; 3085; LXX; Iren. 3, 12, 7 [Harv. II 60, 3]; Did., Gen. 177, 13) of the temple τὸ ἱερὸν . . . καθαρόν Ox 840, 17f. πάντα καθαρά *everything is ritually pure,* hence fit for use **Ro 14:20; Tit 1:15ac.**

❸ **pert. to being free from moral guilt,** ***pure, free*** fr. sin (Pind., P. 5, 2; Pla., Rep. 6 p. 496d καθαρὸς ἀδικίας τε καὶ ἀνοσίων ἔργων, Crat. 403e; 405b al.; LXX; PsSol 17:36; EpArist, Philo, Joseph.; TestBenj 8:2f; ἔχειν κ. ψυχήν Theoph. Ant. 1, 2 [p. 60, 22]).

ⓐ of a pers. as entity οἱ καθαροί **Tit 1:15b;** cp. **J 13:10b, 11; 15:3.** Christendom is Christ's λαὸς κ. Hs 9, 18, 4. οἱ καθαροὶ τῇ καρδίᾳ (Ps 23:4) **Mt 5:8;** cp. PEg[3] 45 (τῇ καρδίᾳ restored), 47f (καρδίας restored). καθαρὸς τῇ συνειδήσει ITr 7:2b; *guiltless* **Ac 18:6.** καθαρά εἰμι ἐγὼ καὶ ἄνδρα οὐ γινώσκω *I am guiltless and still a virgin* GJs 13:3. ἀπό τινος *free from* (Ps.-Demosth. 59, 78; Cass. Dio 37, 24, 2. Exx. fr. pap and ins in Dssm., NB 24 [BS 196]; PGM 13, 648; 1004; Gen 24:8; Pr 20:9; Tob 3:14; PsSol 17:36; Jos., Ant. 4, 222; Ath. 12, 3; ἀπὸ ἁμαρτίας Orig., C. Cels. 7, 50, 6) ἀπὸ τ. αἵματος (Sus 46 Theod.) **Ac 20:26.** ἀπὸ ῥύπου 1 Cl 17:4 (Job 14:4). καθαρός εἰμι ἐγὼ ἐξ αὐτῆς *I am without guilt as respects her* GJs 15:4. Before God ἐνώπιον αὐτοῦ 15:3.—Also of the Holy Spirit Hm 5, 1, 2, imagery of brightness.

ⓑ of things related to a pers. as a morally or spiritually responsible being κ. καρδία (Lucian, Nigr. 14 κ. ἦθος; Simplicius in Epict. p. 93, 49 ζωὴ κ.; Gen 20:5; Ps 50:12; cp. κ. ψυχή: Pythagoras in Diog. L. 8, 31; Diod. S. 12, 20, 2; 13, 29, 6; πνεῦμα κ. Ath. 27:1) **1 Ti 1:5; 2 Ti 2:22; 1 Pt 1:22;** B 15:1; 1 Cl 18:10; Hv 3, 9, 8; σάρξ s 5, 7, 1; κ. συνείδησις (POslo 17, 10 [136 AD]) **1 Ti 3:9; 2 Ti 1:3;** 1 Cl 45:7 (cp. κ. συνειδός: Philo, Spec. Leg. 1, 203, Praem. 84); θρησκεία κ. **Js 1:27.** χεῖρες καθαραί (Aeschyl., Eum. 313, also Plut., Pericl. 8, 8; SIG 983, 5; Job 9:30; 22:30; Philo, Virt. 57; Jos., Bell. 5, 380, Ant. 4, 222; Just., D. 12, 3) B 15:1. μετάνοια κ. Hm 2:7; 12, 3, 2. διάνοια 1 Cl 1:8; Hs 4:7. τόπον κ. m 5, 1, 3. ἔντευξιν 10, 3, 3.

❹ **pert. to being pure ritually and morally,** ***pure,*** ritual and moral purity merge (Simplicius in Epict. p. 111, 18) **Lk 11:41.** After a confession of sins καθαρὰ ἡ θυσία ὑμῶν D 14:1, 3. ὁ ἐντὸς θυσιαστηρίου ὢν καθαρός ἐστιν ITr 7:2a.—TWächter, Reinheitsvorschriften im griech. Kult 1910; FPfister, Katharsis.—M-M. Pauly-W. Suppl. IV '35, 146ff.—DELG. EDNT. TW.

καθαρότης, ητος, ἡ (s. καθαρός; X., Mem. 2, 1, 22 al.; Caecilius the orator [I BC] p. 98, 7; 107, 1 EOfenloch [1907] of purity of speech; Epict. 4, 11, 5; POxy 67, 6; 904, 2; Ex 24:10 v.l.; Wsd 7:24; EpArist 234; TestNapht 3:1; τοῦ νοῦ κ. Did., Gen. 114, 10; Orig., C. Cels. 1, 26, 51 as quality of the pious) **state or condition of being ritually cleansed,** ***purity:*** τῆς σαρκός **Hb 9:13** (s. also Iambl., Vita Pyth. 24, 106 καθαρότης τῆς ψυχῆς; Did., Gen. 151, 11). ἐν καθαρότη[τι καταστήσει] *[will provide lodgings] in purity* (='will practice purity while providing lodgings [for the young women]') Hs 10, 3, 4 (POxy 404 recto, 118f).—DELG s.v. καθαρός. M-M. TW.

καθαρῶς adv. of καθαρός (Hes. and Hom. Hymns+; UPZ 144, 29 [164 BC]; 2 Macc 7:40 v.l.; Philo; Jos., Ant. 18, 100; Ath., R. 66, 13 al.) ***in purity*** fig. Dg 12:3.

καθέδρα, ας, ἡ (κατά + ἕδρα 'seat', s. next entry; Thu. et al.; ins, pap, LXX, En; Jos., Ant. 5, 130; 19, 100; loanw. in rabb.) ***chair, seat*** (so Polyb. 1, 21, 2; Herodian 2, 3, 7; Lucian, Jupp. Tr. 11; BGU 717, 14; LXX; κ. θρόνου En 24:3) Hv 1, 2, 2; 1, 4, 1 and 3; 3, 10, 3; 3, 11, 2 and 4. καθέδρα λοιμῶν B 10:10 (after Ps 1:1). *Seat* of those selling someth. (but s. Dalman, Arbeit VII 192) **Mt 21:12; Mk 11:15;** the *teacher's chair* (SIG 845, 2f ὁ ἐπὶ τῆς καθέδρας σοφιστής) Hm 11:1; ἡ Μωϋσέως κ. **Mt 23:2** (cp. Pj 23, 1927, 44; ill. NAvigad, Chorazin: Enc. of Arch. Excavations in the Holy Land I, 1975, 302; LRahmani, Israel Exploration Journal 40, '90, 192–214). κ. κρίσεως *judge's seat* GPt 3:7 (cp. Ps 106:32 ἐν καθέδρᾳ [καθέδραις SA] πρεσβυτέρων).—B. 482. DELG s.v. ἕζομαι B2. M-M. TW.

καθέζομαι (s. καθέδρα) impf. ἐκαθεζόμην; fut. καθεδοῦμαι and καθεσθήσομαι, 2 pl. καθεσθήσεσθε **Mt 19:28 v.l.** (s. κάθημαι, καθίζω); aor. ἐκαθέσθην (TestAbr A 5 p. 81, 31 [Stone p. 10]; AcPl Ha 4, 18); impv. 2 sg. καθέσθητι (TestSol 13:2); inf. καθεσθῆναι (Just., D. 83, 1) (Hom.+). In our lit., at least quite predom., it means

❶ **to be in a seated position,** ***sit*** (as Lysias 13, 37; Epict. 1, 29, 55; 3, 24, 18; Paus. 10, 5, 2; Vett. Val. 78, 24; OGI 201, 13; LXX; TestSol; Jos., Bell. 5, 73, Ant. 12, 171; Just., D. 90, 5 ἐπὶ λίθου) ἐν τῷ ἱερῷ of teachers **Mt 26:55.** Of pupils **Lk 2:46.** ἐν τῷ συνεδρίῳ *in the council* **Ac 6:15.** ἐπὶ τῆς θυρίδος **20:9** (Ael. Aristid. 47, 23 K.=23 p. 451 D.: κ. ἐπὶ βήματος). ἐπὶ τῇ πύλῃ **3:10** D. ἐν τῷ οἴκῳ *sit, remain at home* **J 11:20.** Abs. *sit there* **20:12.** The more general *be, be situated* is also poss. in some pass. (Paus. Attic. σ, 8 ἐν νησίῳ καθεζόμεναι=stay; Stephan. Byz. s.v. Σκίρος: ἐν τῷ τόπῳ τούτῳ; Biogr. p. 265; Lev 12:5; Jos., Ant. 6, 32, Vi. 286; Just., D. 49, 3; 51, 2 al.).

❷ **to take a seated position,** ***sit down*** (Hom., trag. et al.; Jos., Vi. 222; SibOr 5, 460; TestSol 13:2; 18:24; TestJob 51:3; Just., D. 107, 3.—The impf. w. aor. nuance: 'I sat down'; B-D-F §101; s. Rob. 837ff; 882f) ἐκαθέζετο αὐτὴ ἐκ δεξιῶν *she herself sat down at the right* Hv 3, 2, 4. εἰς καθέδραν *on a chair* 3, 11, 4. Ἰησοῦς ἐκαθέζετο οὕτως ἐπὶ τῇ πηγῇ *Jesus sat down, just as he was, by the well* **J 4:6** (on the word and the idea s. Jos., Ant. 2, 257f and Marinus, Vi. Procli 10 Boiss. As early as Demosth. 21, 119 οὑτωσὶ καθεζόμενος). Cp. also **6:3 v.l.; Lk 22:30** D. ὡς . . . ἐκαθέσθη *as* (Jerome) *sat down* AcPl Ha 4, 18f.—DELG s.v. ἕζομαι B2. M-M. TW.

καθεῖλον, καθελεῖν, καθελῶ, καθελών s. καθαιρέω.

καθεῖς (καθ' εἷς) s. εἷς 5e.

καθεξῆς adv. less common than the earlier ἑξῆς and ἐφεξῆς (IGR IV, 1432, 9; Plut., Mor. 615b; Aelian, VH 8, 7; TestJud 25:1; ApcMos 8) **pert. to being in sequence in time, space, or logic,** ***in order, one after the other,*** διερχόμενος κ. τὴν Γαλατικὴν χώραν καὶ Φρυγίαν *one place after the other in Galatia and Phrygia* **Ac 18:23.** κ. τινί (τι) γράφειν *write someth. for someone in orderly sequence* **Lk 1:3** (s. PScheller, De hellenist. historiae conscr. arte, diss. Leipz. 1911, 45, in ref. to Polyb. 38, 5 [39, 1]; HConzelmann, Die Mitte der Zeit[3] '60, Eng. tr. GBuswell '60 [theology dominates the structure of Lk]; MVölkel, NTS 20, '74, 289–99; FMussner, in Jesus und Paulus, WKümmel Festschr. '75, 253–55; GSchneider, ZNW 68, '77, 128–31; DMoessner, in The Four Gospels, FNeirynck Festschr., ed. FvanSegbroeck et al. '92, II 1065–76; LAlexander, The Preface to Luke's Gospel '93, 131f). ἐκτίθεσθαι τινι κ. *explain to someone point by point* **Ac 11:4.**—W. the art. οἱ κ. *the successors* **Ac 3:24;** τὸ κ. *what follows:* ἐν τῷ κ. *in what follows* MPol 22:3; *afterward* **Lk 8:1.** τὸ κ. *and so forth* 1 Cl 37:3.—DELG s.v. ἑξῆς. M-M. TW.

καθερίζω s. καθαρίζω.

καθεύδω impf. ἐκάθευδον (Hom.+; SIG 1004, 44; BGU 1141, 32; PSI 94, 17; LXX; TestSol 13:3; Test12Patr; JosAs; Philo; Jos., Vi. 248; Just., D. 127, 2) impf. ἐκάθευδον.

❶ **to cease being awake,** ***to sleep,*** lit. **Mt 8:24; 13:25; 25:5; 26:40, 43, 45; Mk 4:27, 38; 13:36; 14:37, 40f; Lk 22:46; 1 Th 5:7.** The mng. is in doubt in **Mt 9:24; Mk 5:39** (RKer, ET 65, '53/54, 315f); **Lk 8:52;** in these pass. mng. 3 has won supporters.

❷ **to be spiritually indolent,** ***be indifferent,*** fig. ext. of 1 (cp. X., An. 1, 3, 11; Oenomaus in Eus., PE 5, 19, 2 of dull indifference) **1 Th 5:6.**—The word is also used fig. in the quot. fr. an unknown hymn: ἔγειρε ὁ καθεύδων *awake, O sleeper!* **Eph 5:14.**

❸ **to be dead,** ***sleep,*** fig. ext. of 1 (Ps 87:6; Da 12:2), a euphemistic expression (far more common in this sense is κοιμάω, q.v. 2; on the subject s. BLier, Topica carminum sepulcralium latinorum: Philol 62, 1903, 445–77, 563–603; 63, 1904, 54–65; MOgle, The Sleep of Death: MAAR 11, '33, 81–117; RLattimore, Themes in Greek and Latin Epitaphs '62; cp. εὕδειν Il. 14, 482; Soph., O.C. 621; Pind. fgm. 116, 3f [OxfT]; s. Schmidt, Syn. I 488f) and so, accord. to most scholars, **1 Th 5:10** (THoward, Grace Theological Journal 6, '85, 337–48; but MLautenschlager, ZNW 80, '89, 39–59, in sense 2); also s. **Mt 9:24; Mk 5:39; Lk 8:52** in 1 above.—B. 269. DELG s.v. εὕδω. M-M. TW.

καθήγησις, εως, ἡ (s. next entry; since I BC in the mng. 'rule, principle') prob. ***instruction*** με|γάλῃ καθ[ηγήσει] *with thorough instruction* (?) AcPl Ha 6, 31.—DELG s.v. ἡγέομαι.

καθηγητής, οῦ, ὁ (s. prec. entry) ***teacher*** (so Dionys. Hal., Jud. de Thu. 3, 4; Plut., Mor. 327f of Aristotle; Vett. Val. 115, 18; IG XIV, Suppl. 2454, 5, a memorial, s. New Docs 4, 156; FX 7, '81, 64, 3 and p. 158, n. 106 for other reff.; ARaubitschek, Hesperia 35, '66, 248f, no. 10; PGiss 80, 7; 11; POxy 930, 6; 20) **Mt 23:10.** This verse is deleted by Blass, Wlh., Dalman (Worte 279; 276) as a variant of vs. **8.** In the latter κ. is v.l.—DELG s.v. ἡγέομαι. M-M. Spicq.

καθῆκα s. καθίημι.

καθηκόντως adv. of the pres. ptc. of καθήκω (q.v.) ***as is fitting,*** in accordance w. obligation or duty (Polyb. 5, 9, 6; Plut., Mor. 448e; OGI 90, 28 [II BC]; PTebt 793 II, 15 [183 BC]; EpArist 181; Philo, Cher. 14) 1 Cl 1:3.—DELG s.v. ἥκω.

καθήκω impf. 3 sg. καθῆκεν Jdth 11:13 (Aeschyl., Hdt. et al.) **to be appropriate,** ***come/reach to, be proper/fitting*** καθήκουσα ἡ τιμή *the proper respect* 1 Cl 1:3. Usu. impers. **καθήκει** ***it comes (to someone)*** (X. et al., oft. ins, pap, LXX) foll. by acc. and inf. (Diod. S. 16, 1, 1; Jos., Ant. 7, 131) οὐ καθῆκεν αὐτὸν ζῆν *he should not be allowed to live* **Ac 22:22** (on the impf. s. B-D-F §358, 2; Rob. 886f).—τὸ καθῆκον *what is proper, duty* (Menand., fgm. 532, 2 Kö.; Stoic wr. since Zeno [s. Ltzm., Hdb. on Ro 1:28; GNebel, Her 70, '35, 439–60; MPohlenz, D. Stoa I /II 4th ed. '70/72: index]; Polyb. 6, 6, 7; pap and ins [on freq. in both s. M-M.]; EpArist 227; Philo, Leg. All. 2, 32a) πολιτεύεσθαι κατὰ τὸ κ. τῷ Χριστῷ *conduct oneself in a manner that enhances the prestige of Christ* (dat. of advantage) 1 Cl 3:4 (cp. IG[2] 1365, 15f). παρὰ τὸ κ. (Diog. L. 7, 108; SIG 643, 6 [171 BC]; POxy 1203, 3; Philo, Leg. All. 2, 32b; Jos., Ant. 13, 66): παρὰ τὸ κ. τῆς βουλήσεως αὐτοῦ ποιεῖν τι *do anything contrary to the duty imposed by his will* 1 Cl 41:3. Pl. τὰ κ. (X., Cyr. 1, 2, 5 al.; EpArist 245; Philo, Leg. All. 1, 56) τὰ μὴ καθήκοντα (UPZ 191, 8 [III BC]; 2 Macc 6:4; 3 Macc 4:16) ποιεῖν τὰ μὴ καθήκοντα *do what is improper* **Ro 1:28** (M-JLagrange, Le catalogue des vices dans Ro 1:28–31, RB 8, 1911, 534–49; against Stoic influence: M-M.).—On probability of a contractual metaphor **Ro 1:28** s. Danker, Gingrich Festschr., '72, 95f.—B. 643. DELG s.v. ἥκω. M-M. TW.

καθηλόω 1 aor. καθήλωσα; pf. pass. ptc. καθηλωμένος (κατά + ἧλος 'nail'; Polyb. 1, 22, 5; Diod. S. 20, 85, 2; Hero I 442, 10; Plut., Alex. 24, 7; SIG 969, 57; 84; PLond IV, 1384, 41; LXX) **to fasten w. nails,** ***nail on,*** of one condemned to be burned at the stake MPol 14:1 (cp. Ps.-Callisth. 2, 18, 2 ἐδέδεντο ἐν πέδαις καθηλωταῖς). Of Christ on the cross: τὰς σάρκας B 5:13 (Ps 118:120); ISm 1:2. Hence of Christians ὥσπερ καθηλωμένοι ἐν τῷ σταυρῷ τοῦ κυρίου Ἰ. Χρ. σαρκί τε καὶ πνεύματι *as if nailed to the cross of the Lord Jesus Christ in body and in spirit* 1:1.—DELG s.v. ἧλος.

κάθημαι (Hom.+; ins, pap, LXX, pseudepigr.; Jos., Ant. 5, 192; Ath. 17:3 [ptc. as name of an image of Athene]) 2 sg. κάθῃ (since Hyperid., fgm. 115 [OLautensach, Glotta 8, 1917, 186]; POxy 33 verso III, 13 [II AD]; TestJob 24:3) **Ac 23:3;** pl. κάθησθε **Lk 22:30 v.l.,** impv. κάθου (Moeris 215: κάθησο Ἀττικῶς, κάθου κοινῶς; later Attic [Lautensach, Glotta 9, 1918, 88; s. also AMaidhof, Z. Begriffsbestimmung der Koine 1912, 300]) twice in **Js 2:3** and seven times in a quot. fr. Ps 109:1 (B-D-F §100; Mlt-H. 206f; s. 3 below); impf. ἐκαθήμην (on the augment s. B-D-F §69, 1; Mlt-H. 192); fut. καθήσομαι (oft. LXX) **Mt 19:28; Lk 22:30.**

➊ **to be in a seated position,** ***sit***—ⓐ w. the place indicated by a prep. ἀπέναντί τινος *opposite someth.* **Mt 27:61.**—εἴς τι *on someth.* (Pel.-Leg. p. 4, 4 καθημένη εἰς βαδιστήν='sitting on a donkey'; cp. also Musonius 43, 18 H. καθῆσθαι εἰς Σινώπην) εἰς τὸ ὄρος τ. ἐλαιῶν **Mk 13:3;** cp. Hs 5, 1, 1.—ἐκ δεξιῶν τινος *at someone's right* (hand) **Mt 26:64; Mk 14:62; Lk 22:69.**—ἐν: **Mt 11:16; 26:69; Lk 7:32.** ἐν σάκκῳ κ. σποδῷ **10:13.** ἐν δεξιᾷ τινος *at someone's right* **Col 3:1.** ἐν τοῖς δεξιοῖς *on the right* (side) **Mk 16:5.**—ἐπάνω τινός *on* or *upon someth.* **Mt 23:22; Rv 6:8.**—ἐπί τινος on *someth.* (Babrius 57, 14; UPZ 79, 10 [160 BC]) **Mt 24:3.** ἐπὶ τοῦ θρόνου (Aeschines in Ps.-Demetr. 205; Cebes 21, 3 ἐπὶ θρόνου ὑψηλοῦ; Ex 11:5 al.; TestAbr A 12 p. 91, 9 [Stone p. 30]; B 8 p. 112, 21 [Stone p. 72]; Jos., Ant. 5, 192); **Rv 4:2 v.l.; 4:9f; 5:1, 7, 13 v.l.; 6:16; 7:10 v.l., 15; 19:4 v.l.; 20:11 v.l.; 21:5 v.l.** ἐπὶ θρόνων **Lk 22:30.** ἐπὶ τῆς νεφέλης (Is 19:1) **14:15f.** ἐπὶ τοῦ ἅρματος **Ac 8:28.** ἐπὶ τ. ἵππων **Rv 9:17; 19:18.** ἐπὶ τοῦ ἵππου vs. **19, 21** (cp. TestJud 3:2). Of judges (κ.='sit in judgment': Pla., Ap. 35c; Hyperid. 3, 6) ἐπὶ τοῦ βήματος **Mt 27:19.**—ἐπὶ τῇ ὡραίᾳ πύλῃ *at the 'Beautiful Gate'* **Ac 3:10.** ἐπὶ τῷ θρόνῳ **Rv 5:13; 6:16 v.l.; 7:10, 15 v.l.; 19:4; 21:5.**—ἐπί τι w. acc. of place (Lev 8:35) ἐπὶ τὸ τελώνιον **Mt 9:9; Mk 2:14; Lk 5:27;** ἐπὶ πῶλον ὄνου **J 12:15;** ἐπ' αὐτόν (horse) **Rv 6:2, 4f; 19:11, 18 v.l.;** ἐπὶ θηρίον **17:3;** ἐπὶ (τὸν) θρόνον, (τοὺς) θρόνους (3 Km 1:27; Jer 13:13 A; 43, 30 A; TestJob 20:4) **Mt 19:28; Rv 4:2, 4; 11:16; 20:11;** ἐπὶ τὴν νεφέλην **14:14, 16 v.l.**—παρά τι *beside someth.* παρὰ τὴν ὁδόν *at the side of the road* **Mt 20:30; Mk 10:46; Lk 18:35.**—περί τινα *around someone* **Mk 3:32, 34.**—πρὸς τὸ φῶς *by the fire* **Lk 22:56** (Aristoph., Vesp. 773 πρὸς τὸ πῦρ κ. Likewise Menand., fgm. 806 Kö.).

ⓑ w. the place indicated by an adv. of place: ἐκεῖ **Mk 2:6;** οὗ **Ac 2:2; Rv 17:15;** ὅπου vs. **9.**

ⓒ abs. *sit, sit there* (Epict. 2, 16, 13 εὔχου καθήμενος; 33) **Mt 27:36; Lk 5:17; J 2:14; 9:8; Ac 14:8; 1 Cor 14:30;** B 10:4.

ⓓ w. some indication of the state or characteristics of the pers. sitting (Ex 18:14 σὺ κάθησαι μόνος; κ. of a judge Ael. Aristid. 46 p. 318 D.; 327) σὺ κάθῃ κρίνων με; *do you sit there to judge me?* **Ac 23:3** (Ἄβελ . . . κάθηται ὧδε κρῖναι TestAbr A 13 p. 92, 7 [Stone p. 32]).

ⓔ in the special sense *sit quietly* **Mk 5:15; Lk 8:35.** *Be enthroned* in majesty (Od. 16, 264) κάθημαι βασίλισσα **Rv 18:7.**

➋ **to be a resident in a place,** ***stay, be, live, reside, settle,*** fig. ext of 1 (Hom. et al.; Hdt. 5, 63 ἐν Δελφοῖς; Musonius p. 59, 7 ἐν πόλει; Ael. Aristid. 50, 14 K.=26 p. 505 D.; Is 9:8 v.l.; 2 Esdr 21:6; Jdth 4:8; 5:3) **Lk 21:35; Rv 14:6** (cp. Jer 32:29); **17:1, 9** (s. 1b). πρός τινα *w. someone* D 12:3; 13:1. ἐν σκότει (σκοτίᾳ v.l.) . . . καὶ ἐν σκιᾷ θανάτου **Mt 4:16.** ἐν σκότει καὶ σκιᾷ θανάτου (Ps 106:10) **Lk 1:79** (cp. Pind., O. 1, 83 ἐν σκότῳ καθήμενος [=one who enters old age without accomplishments worthy of remembrance]; Ael. Aristid. 46 p. 272 D.: ἐν τ. στενοῖς τ. ἐλπίδων ἐκάθηντο). (The restoration [καθήμ]ε̣ν̣ο̣ι̣ AcPl Ha 8, 33 is questionable, s. the rdg. of BMM, s.v. πεδάω.)

➌ **to take a seated position,** ***sit down;*** the occurrence of this sense in our lit. can scarcely be disputed; the same is true of the LXX (W-S. §14, 3). It is to be assumed for the impv. in all its occurrences; seven of them are connected w. Ps 109:1: κάθου ἐκ δεξιῶν μου **Mt 22:44; Mk 12:36; Lk 20:42; Ac 2:34; Hb 1:13;** 1 Cl 36:5; B 12:10. The impv. has the same mng. twice in **Js 2:3.** But this sense is also quite probable for the foll. pass.: ἐν τῇ θαλάσσῃ **Mk 4:1.** ἐπάνω τινός **Mt 28:2.** μετά τινος **26:58; J 6:3** (καθίζω v.l.). παρὰ τὴν θάλασσαν **Mt 13:1.**—ἐκεῖ **Mt 15:29.**—μέσος αὐτῶν **Lk 22:55.**—Abs. **Mt 13:2.**—B. 455. DELG s.v. ἧμαι. M-M. EDNT. TW.

καθημέραν for καθ' ἡμέραν s. ἡμέρα 2e.

καθημερινός, ή, όν (s. κατά, ἡμέρα; Theophr. et al.; Plut., Lyc. 10, 1, Pyrrh. 14, 12; Polyaenus 4, 2, 10; Alciphron 1, 5, 2; Athen. 6 p. 259f; PTebt 275, 21; PGM 7, 218; Jdth 12:15; Jos., Ant. 3, 238; 11, 297) fr. καθ' ἡμέραν *daily* διακονία **Ac 6:1.** λόγος *the word repeated daily* Hv 1, 3, 2.—DELG s.v. ἦμαρ. M-M.

καθίζω (Hom. et al.; ins, pap, LXX; pseudepigr.; Joseph.; Just. [only in paraphrases]; Tat. 23, 1) fut. καθίσω **Mt 25:31** and καθιῶ Is 47:8; 1 aor. ἐκάθισα, impv. κάθισον **Mk 12:36 v.l.;** pf. 3 sg. κεκάθικεν (B-D-F §101; W-S. §14, 2, 15; Rob. 1216) **Hb 12:2,** 1 pl. κεκαθίκαμεν Hs 9, 5, 6; mid. fut. καθίσομαι and καθιοῦμαι Hv 3, 1, 9.

➊ **to cause to sit down,** ***seat, set,*** trans. καθίσας ἐν δεξιᾷ αὐτοῦ *(God) had* (him) *sit at his right hand* **Eph 1:20.** God swore to David ἐκ καρποῦ τῆς ὀσφύος αὐτοῦ καθίσαι ἐπὶ τὸν θρόνον αὐτοῦ *to set one of his descendants upon his throne* **Ac**

2:30 (cp. 2 Ch 23:20). ἐκάθισαν αὐτὸν ἐπὶ καθέδραν κρίσεως *they seated him on the judge's chair* GPt 3:7 (αὐτὸν ἐκάθισαν ἐπὶ βήματος Just., A I, 35, 6). **J 19:13** is probably to be understood in this sense, since the trial is evidently in progress (cp. Dio Chrys. 4, 67; Loisy; PCorssen, ZNW 15, 1914, 339f; IdelaPotterie, Biblica 41, '60, 217–47; s. CBQ 25, '63, 124–26); but also s. 3 below. ἐκάθισέ με ἐπὶ τὸ ἄκρον τοῦ ὄρους Hs 9, 1, 4. On an ass ἐκάθισεν αὐτήν GJs 17:2; ὄνῳ καθίσαντες αὐτόν MPol 8:1. ἐκάθισεν αὐτὴν ἐπὶ τρίτου βαθμοῦ τοῦ θυσιαστηρίου *on the third step of the altar* GJs 7:3.

❷ **to put in charge of someth.,** ***appoint, install, authorize,*** trans., fig. ext. of 1 (Pla., Leg. 9, 873e δικαστήν; Polyb. 40, 5, 3; Jos., Ant. 20, 200 καθίζει συνέδριον κριτῶν, Vi. 368; POxy 1469, 7) τοὺς ἐξουθενημένους ἐν τῇ ἐκκλησίᾳ καθίζετε; *do you appoint as judges persons who have no standing in the church?* **1 Cor 6:4** (on καθ.='appoint as judge' cp. Jos., Ant. 13, 75).

❸ **to take a seated position,** ***sit down,*** intr. (Hdt., Thu., ins, pap, LXX, pseudepigr.) abs. (Diod. S. 8, 10, 4; Polyaenus 2, 21; Just., A I, 32, 6) **Mt 5:1; 13:48; Mk 9:35; Lk 4:20; 5:3; 7:15 v.l.; 14:28, 31; 16:6; J 8:2; Ac 13:14; 16:13;** Hv 1, 2, 2. W. inf. foll. ἐκάθισεν φαγεῖν καὶ πεῖν **1 Cor 10:7** (Ex 32:6). W. an adv. of place ὧδε (Sb 4117, 5; Ruth 4:1, 2; 4 Km 7:4) **Mk 14:32** (perh. *stay here;* Hv 3, 1, 8). αὐτοῦ *here* (Gen 22:5) **Mt 26:36.** W. prep. εἰς τὸν ναὸν τοῦ θεοῦ *in the temple of God* (PSI 502, 21 [III BC] καθίσαντες εἰς τὸ ἱερόν) **2 Th 2:4.** εἰς τὴν κλίνην *on the bed* (cp. Dicaearchus, fgm. 20 W. εἰς θρόνον) Hv 5:1 (on sitting down after prayer cp. the Pythagorean precept: Philosoph. Max. 508, 60 καθῆσθαι προσκυνήσαντες=after prayer we should sit down. Similarly Numa: Plut., Numa 14, 7.—HLewy, Philol. 84, 1929, 378–80). εἰς τὸν τόπον τοῦ ἀγγέλου Hs 8, 4, 1. εἰς τὸ ἔδαφος AcPl Ha 2, 20. ἐκ δεξιῶν τινος *at someone's right* **Mt 20:21, 23; Mk 10:37, 40; 12:36 v.l.; 16:19;** Hv 3, 2, 2. Also ἐν δεξιᾷ τινος **Hb 1:3; 8:1; 10:12; 12:2.** ἐν τῷ θρόνῳ μου *on my throne* **Rv 3:21ab** (Hdt. 5, 25 ἐν τῷ κατίζων θρόνῳ). ἐπί τινος (3 Km 2:12 al. ἐπὶ θρόνου; Diod. S. 1, 92, 2; 17, 116, 3 ἐκάθισεν ἐπὶ τοῦ θρόνου=sat down on; Jos., Ant. 8, 344) **Mt 19:28a; 25:31;** ἐπὶ τῆς καθέδρας **23:2** (B-D-F §342, 1; cp. Rob. 837). ἐπὶ τῷ θρόνῳ (τοῦ θ. codd.) GJs 11:1. ἐπί τι (Thu. 1, 126, 10; Aesop, Fab. 393 H.; AscIs 3:17) θρόνους **Rv 20:4** (cp. 3 Km 1:46; 2 Ch 6:10); ἐπὶ καθέδραν B 10:10 (Ps 1:1); on an animal (TestAbr B 2 p. 106, 25 [Stone p. 60] ἐπὶ κτῆνος; Achilles Tat. 1, 12, 2 ἐπὶ τ. ἵππον) **Mk 11:2, 7; Lk 19:30; J 12:14.** Of the Holy Spirit as a flame of fire ἐκάθισεν ἐφ' ἕνα ἕκαστον αὐτῶν *it rested upon each one of them* **Ac 2:3;** κατέναντί τινος *opposite someth.* **Mk 12:41.** σύν τινι *sit down w. someone* **Ac 8:31.** Esp. of a judge (Pla., Leg. 2 p. 659b; Ps 9:5) κ. ἐπὶ (τοῦ) βήματος *sit down in the judge's seat* to open the trial (Jos., Bell. 2, 172 ὁ Πιλᾶτος καθίσας ἐπὶ βήματος, Ant. 20, 130) **J 19:13** (JBlinzler, Der Prozess Jesu^3 '60, 257–62; s. 1 above); **Ac 12:21; 25:6, 17.**—Under a tree GJs 2:4.—Mid. *sit down* (Pla. et al.; 3 Km 1:13; Da 7:26 [LXX]; Just., D. 109, 3 [for ἀναπαύσεται Mi 4:4]) **Mt 19:28b v.l.; J 6:3 v.l.;** s. καθέζομαι and κάθημαι.

❹ **to be or remain in a place,** intr. ***reside, settle, stay, live*** (Thu. 3, 107, 1; 4, 93, 1) ἐν τῇ πόλει **Lk 24:49** (cp. 1 Ch 19:5; 2 Esdr 21 [Neh 11]: 1f; Jos., Bell. 1, 46, Ant. 18, 86; SIG 685, 28 ἐν τῷ ἱερῷ). W. acc. of time **Ac 18:11.**—DELG s.v. ἕζομαι. M-M. EDNT. TW.

καθίημι 1 aor. καθῆκα (Hom.+; LXX; TestZeb 6:2; Tat. 19, 1 γένειον . . . καθειμένον wear a 'long beard') ***let down*** τινά *someone* διὰ κεράμων εἰς (cp. Jos., Ant. 2, 31; 35 κ. εἰς τὸν λάκκον) **Lk 5:19.** διὰ τοῦ τείχους **Ac 9:25** (Polyaenus 6, 49 αὐτοὺς ἀπὸ τῶν τειχῶν καθῆκαν; 8, 21). Pass. ἐπὶ τ. γῆς **10:11;** ἐκ τοῦ οὐρανοῦ **11:5.**—DELG s.v. ἵημι. M-M.

καθιστάνω s. καθίστημι.

καθίστημι/καθιστάνω (**Ac 17:15;** 1 Cl 42:4; EpArist 280; 281; Jos., Ant. 16, 129; POxf 16, 12). Pres. 3 sg. καθιστᾷ Da 2:21 Theod.; impf. καθίστα (Just., D. 52, 3); ptc. καθιστῶν LXX; fut. καταστήσω; 1 aor. κατέστησα; pf. καθέστακα LXX; intr. καθέστηκα LXX; plpf. -κεισαν (3 Macc 2:33). Pass.: 1 fut. κατασταθήσομαι; 1 aor. καθεστάθην; pf. ptc. καθεσταμένος (LXX; 1 Cl 54:2; Jos., Ant. 12, 268) (s. κατά, ἵστημι; Hom.+).

❶ **to take someone somewhere,** ***bring, conduct, take*** (Od. 13, 274; Thu. 4, 78, 6; X., An. 4, 8, 8; UPZ 78, 14 [159 BC]; BGU 93, 22 κατάστησον αὐτοὺς εἰς Μέμφιν; Josh 6:23; 1 Km 5:3; 2 Ch 28:15; Jos., Ant. 7, 279; oneself Tat. 2, 1 τίς . . . ἀλαζονείας ἔξω καθέστηκεν;=which one has been free of boastfulness?) **Ac 17:15.**

❷ **to assign someone a position of authority,** ***appoint, put in charge*** (Hdt. et al.)—ⓐ someone over (of) someth. or someone τινὰ ἐπί τινος (Arrian, Exp. Al. 3, 6, 6 ἐπὶ τ. χρημάτων; Gen 41:41; Num 3:10; Da 2:48; Jos., Ant. 2, 73) **Mt 24:45;** cp. **25:21, 23; Lk 12:42; Ac 6:3.** τινὰ ἐπί τινι *over someth.* (Jos., Ant. 12, 278) **Mt 24:47; Lk 12:44.** τινὰ ἐπί τι (Isocr. 12, 132; X., Cyr. 8, 1, 9; Da 3:12 Theod.) **Hb 2:7 v.l.** (Ps 8:7). W. acc. of pers. and inf. of purpose ὁ υἱὸς κατέστησε τ. ἀγγέλους ἐπ' αὐτοὺς τοῦ συντηρεῖν αὐτούς Hs 5, 6, 2.

ⓑ w. acc. *authorize, appoint* (Pla., Rep. 10, 606d ἄρχοντα; Vi. Aesopi W 15 p. 83 P.; 1 Macc 3:55; Jos., Ant. 9, 4 κρίτας; Just., D. 52, 3 βασιλεῖς) πρεσβυτέρους **Tit 1:5.** Cp. 1 Cl 42:5 (for δώσω Is 60:17; the latter rdg. Iren. 4, 26, 5 [Harv. II 238]); 43:1; 44:2. Pass. 44:3; 54:2; foll. by εἰς w. inf. of the high priest: εἰς τὸ προσφέρειν δῶρα καθίσταται *is appointed to offer gifts* **Hb 8:3.** Sim. ὑπὲρ ἀνθρώπων καθίσταται τὰ πρὸς τὸν θεόν, ἵνα προσφέρῃ *is appointed (to act) on behalf of people in matters relating to God, to bring* **Hb 5:1.**—A second acc. (predicate) can be added to τινά: *make* or *appoint someone someth.* (Hdt. 7, 105 al.; PHib 82 I, 14 [239/238 BC]; Sir 32:1; 1 Macc 9:25; 10:20; Jos., Ant. 12, 360) **Lk 12:14; Ac 7:10; Hb 7:28** (Diog. L. 9, 64 ἀρχιερέα κ. αὐτόν). τίς σε κατέστησεν ἄρχοντα; **Ac 7:27, 35;** 1 Cl 4:10 (all three Ex 2:14).—W. εἰς: εἰς ἐπισκόπους καὶ διακόνους 1 Cl 42:4 (Just., D. 65:7).

❸ **cause someone to experience someth.,** ***make, cause*** τινά τι (Eur., Androm. 635 κλαίοντά σε καταστήσει; Pla., Phlb. 16b ἐμὲ ἔρημον κατέστησεν; POxy 939, 19 σε εὐθυμότερον; Jos., Ant. 6, 92; 20, 18; Just., A I, 33, 6 τὴν παρθένον . . . ἐγκύμονα κατέστησε) ταῦτα οὐκ ἀργοὺς οὐδὲ ἀκάρπους καθίστησιν *this does not make (you) useless and unproductive* **2 Pt 1:8.**—Pass. *be made, become* (Menand., fgm. 769 K.=483 Kö. ἅπαντα δοῦλα τοῦ φρονεῖν καθίσταται; Herodas 1, 40 ἱλαρὴ κατάστηθι=be(come) cheerful; Diod. S. 17, 70, 3; Περὶ ὕψους 5; PRein 18, 40 [108 BC] ἀπερίσπαστος κατασταθήσεται='be left undisturbed'; EpArist 289 σκληροὶ καθίστανται; Philo, Aet. M. 133) ἁμαρτωλοὶ κατεστάθησαν . . . δίκαιοι κατασταθήσονται **Ro 5:19** (FDanker in Gingrich Festschr. '72, 106f, quoting POxy 281, 14–24 [20–50 AD] in possible legal sense; cp. PTebt 183; but cp. Cat. Cod. Astr. IX/2 p. 132, 12 of restoration to a healthy condition). The two pass. in **Js** where the word occurs prob. belong here also (φίλος τ. κόσμου) ἐχθρὸς τ. θεοῦ καθίσταται **4:4;** cp. **3:6,** where the text may not be in order.—JdeZwaan, Rö 5:19; Jk 3:6; 4:4 en de Κοινή: TSt 31, 1913, 85–94.—Restored text Hs 10, 3, 4 (POxy 404 recto, 19) (s. καθαρότης).—DELG s.v. ἵστημι. M-M. TW.

καθό adv. (Pla. et al.; ins, pap, LXX; Jos., Ant. 16, 26; Tat. 5:1; Mel., P. 9, lines 60–67; Ath.)=καθ' ὅ. (so, e.g., schol. to Pla. 181e='as well as')

➊ **marker of similarity,** ***as*** (Michel 731, 22 [II BC] καθὸ πάτριόν ἐστιν; EpArist 11) as κ. δεῖ *as is fitting, as one should* **Ro 8:26** (cp. Diod. S. 8, 15, 1 κατὰ τὴν ἀξίαν οὐδὲ θελήσαντες δυνάμεθα τιμῆσαι τὸ δαιμόνιον=we cannot honor deity in a worthy manner, even though we may wish [to do so]).

➋ **marker of degree,** ***in so far as, to the degree that*** καθὸ κοινωνεῖτε τοῖς τοῦ Χριστοῦ παθήμασιν *in so far as you share the sufferings of Christ* **1 Pt 4:13.** καθὸ ἐὰν ἔχῃ **2 Cor 8:12a;** cp. vs. **12b.**—M-M.

καθολικός, ή, όν (κατά + ὅλος; Hippocr. et al.; Polyb.; Dionys. Hal., Comp. Verb. 12; Iambl., Vi. Pyth. 15, 65; Porphyr., Vi. Pyth. 30; Ps.-Plut., Hom. 201 κ. λόγοι; SIG 785, 4 [6 BC]; OGI 668, 47; BGU 19 I, 5 [135 AD]; Philo; Just., D. 102, 4 καθολικὰς καὶ μερικὰς κρίσεις 'general and individual judgments'; Ath. 27, 1; κ. ἀνάστασις ἁπάντων ἀνθρώπων Theoph. Ant. 1, 13 [p. 86, 24]. Later a much-used title) ***general, universal*** ἡ κ. ἐκκλησία *the universal assembly/church* (in contrast to a single congregation [cp. the contrast μερικὰ κ. καθολικά in Zosimus 7: Hermetica IV p. 105, 24]; s. Hdb. on ISm 8:2) ISm 8:2; MPol ins; 8:1; 19:2. Not in contrast to a single congregation MPol 16:2; but the text is not certain. ὁ ἐκκλησιαστικὸς κανὼν καὶ κ. (Artem. 1, 2 p. 4, 23 ὅρος κ.=a generally valid definition; 4, 2 p. 205, 1 λόγος; Aëtius p. 30, 20 of a law of general validity; Herm. Wr. 2 ins v.l. Ἑρμοῦ ... λόγος καθολικός; Epict. 4, 4, 29; 4, 12, 7 τὰ καθολικά=the laws or truths of general validity) EpilMosq 2. Ἐπιστολὴ καθολικά (καθολικὴ ἐπιστολή first in the Antimontanist Apollonius [c. 197 AD] in Eus., HE 5, 18, 5. Eusebius himself speaks, as we do, of 'the' seven general epistles: 2, 23, 25) as v.l. in the ins of Js; 1 and 2 Pt; 1–3 J; and Jd.—M-M. TW. Sv.

καθόλου adv. (earlier Gk.: Demosth. et al. [B-D-F §225; also 12, 3]; ins, pap, LXX, EpArist; Jos., Bell. 4, 460; 5, 390, Ant. 4, 286; Just.) ***entirely, completely,*** μὴ κ. *not at all* (Sb 4369a, 36; Ex 22:10 v.l.) τὸ κ. μὴ φθέγγεσθαι *not to speak at all* **Ac 4:18** (s. B-D-F §399, 3; Ezk 13:3; TestGad 5:5. μηδὲν τὸ καθόλου λαβεῖν: BGU 1058, 25; 1106, 24; 1165, 24 [all I BC]). κ. τὸ φῶς μὴ βλέπειν Papias (3:2 [not g and h]).—M-M. Sv.

καθοπλίζω (s. ὁπλίζω, ὅπλον; Soph. et al.; the act. in the sense 'arm fully, equip' X. et al.; LXX; EpArist 14; Jos., Ant. 2, 341) in our lit. mid. καθοπλίζομαι 1 aor. ptc. καθοπλισάμενος; pf. pass. ptc. καθωπλισμένος (PGM 13, 528; 4 Macc 4:10; 7:11; Jos., Ant. 5, 244; Tat. 16:2 [on Eph 6:14]) **to arm oneself with weaponry,** ***arm, equip oneself*** (Polyb. 3, 62, 7 al.; 4 Macc 3:12).

ⓐ lit. ὁ ἰσχυρὸς καθωπλισμένος *the strong man in his armor* **Lk 11:21.**

ⓑ fig. (Diod. S. 9, 1, 4 of souls equipped w. [the] armor [of Solon's legislation]; 4 Macc 11:22) καθωπλίσασθαι τὸν φόβον κυρίου *arm oneself w. the fear of God* Hm 12, 2, 4. καθωπλισμένος τῷ φόβῳ τ. θεοῦ ibid.—DELG s.v. ὅπλον. M-M.

καθοράω fut. inf. κατόψεσθαι (Just.); aor. inf. κατιδεῖν (Just., D. 2, 4) (Hom. et al.; Abercius Ins. 5; PLond II, 342, 13 p. 174; LXX) ***perceive, notice,*** also of inward seeing (Pind., P. 9, 49; Aristot., Rhet. 3, 9 τὸ τέλος πάντες βούλονται καθορᾶν; Philostrat., Vi. Soph. 1, 22 p. 38, 10 al.; 3 Macc 3:11; Philo; Jos., Ant. 8, 168; Just.; Tat. 13, 2) τὰ ἀόρατα αὐτοῦ τ. ποιήμασι νοούμενα καθορᾶται *God's invisible attributes are perceived with the eye of reason in the things that have been made* **Ro 1:20** (on the wordplay cp. Ps.-Aristot., De Mundo 399b, 14ff ἀόρατος τοῖς ἔργοις ὁρᾶται; SibOr 4, 12 ὃς καθορῶν ἅμα πάντας ὑπ' οὐδενὸς αὐτὸς ὁρᾶται.—Philostrat., Ep. 41 νοῦς ὁρῇ).—DELG s.v. ὁράω. M-M. TW.

καθότι (Hdt., Thu.+; ins, pap, LXX; En 6:6 [Syncellus]; TestAbr A 2 p. 78, 19 [Stone p. 4]; 11 p. 89, 23 [Stone p. 26]; JosAs 2:1; 4:14; Joseph.) marker

➊ **of extent or degree,** ***as, to the degree that*** καθότι ἄν (Michel 534, 28 [III BC] καθότι ἂν δοκεῖ αὐτοῖς; Lev 25:16; 27:12) **Ac 2:45; 4:35.**

➋ **of rationale for someth.,** ***because, in view of the fact that*** (Polyb. 18, 21, 6; Jos., Ant. 18, 90) **Lk 1:7; 19:9; Ac 2:24; 17:31;** ITr 5:2; GJs 1:2; 2:2 and 3.

➌ **of an oath,** *(I swear)* ***as*** like ὅτι (e.g. 1 Km 26:16) ζῇ κύριος ὁ θεός μου κ. οὐ γινώσκω ... *as my God lives, I do not know* ... GJs 13:3; 15:3f.

➍ **of dir. speech,** ***in this matter*** (an approximation, but best left untransl.) λέγουσα κ. 13:3.—M-M.

καθώς adv. (its use strongly opposed by Phryn. p. 425 Lob.; Aristot.+; ins, pap, LXX, pseudepigr., Philo; Jos., Ant. 12, 158 al.; Ar.; Just., A I, 51, 6; Tat. 33, 3) marker

➊ **of comparison,** ***just as,*** w. οὕτως foll. *(just) as ... so* **Lk 11:30; 17:26; J 3:14; 2 Cor 1:5; 10:7; Col 3:13; 1J 2:6;** 1 Cl 20:6; Hs 9, 4, 1. κ. ... ὁμοίως *as ... so, likewise* **Lk 6:31.** κ. ... ταῦτα **J 8:28;** τὰ αὐτὰ ... κ. **1 Th 2:14.** κ. ... καί *as ... so* or *so also* **J 15:9; 17:18; 20:21; 1J 2:18; 4:17; 1 Cor 15:49.** οὕτως καθώς *just as* **Lk 24:24.** Freq. the demonstrative is omitted: ποιήσαντες κ. συνέταξεν αὐτοῖς ὁ Ἰησοῦς *they did as Jesus had directed them* **Mt 21:6;** cp. **28:6; Mk 16:7; Lk 1:2, 55, 70; 11:1; J 1:23; 5:23; Ac 15:8; Ro 1:13; 15:7; 1 Cor 8:2; 10:6; 2 Cor 1:14; 9:3; 11:12; Eph 4:17;** Hm 12, 2, 5; 1 Cl 16:2. As a formula κ. γέγραπται *as it is written* (cp. Sb 7532, 16 [74 BC] καθὰ γέγραπται) **Mt 26:24; Mk 1:2; 9:13; 14:21; Lk 2:23; Ac 15:15; Ro 1:17; 2:24; 3:4, 10; 4:17; 8:36** and very oft. in Paul. See s.v. καθάπερ and cp. κ. προείρηκεν **Ro 9:29.** κ. διδάσκω *as I teach* **1 Cor 4:17.** καθὼς εἶπον ὑμῖν **J 10:26 v.l.** καθὼς εἶπεν ἡ γραφή **J 7:38.** The accompanying clause is somet. to be supplied fr. the context: κ. παρεκάλεσά σε (POxy 1299, 9 καθὼς ἐνετειλάμην σοι= [act, do] as I have instructed you) **1 Ti 1:3;** cp. **Gal 3:6.** ἤρξατο αἰτεῖσθαι (ἵνα ποιήσῃ αὐτοῖς) κ. ἐποίει αὐτοῖς *as he was accustomed to do for them* **Mk 15:8.** ἰάθη Σαλώμη καθὼς προσεκύνησεν *Salome was healed in accordance with her prayer* GJs 20:3. In combination w. εἶναι: ὀψόμεθα αὐτὸν κ. ἐστιν *we will see him (just) as he is* **1J 3:2,** in the sense of ποῖος 'as' **J 6:58; 14:27** (s. HLjungvik, Eranos 62, '64, 34f). κ. ἀληθῶς ἐστιν *as it actually is* **1 Th 2:13.** Somet. an expression may be condensed to such an extent that opposites are compared ἀγαπῶμεν ἀλλήλους οὐ κ. Κάϊν **1J 3:11f.** οὗτός ἐστιν ὁ ἄρτος ... οὐ κ. ἔφαγον οἱ πατέρες *quite different from that which the fathers ate* **J 6:58.** In compressed speech, to introduce a quotation, e.g. εἰς τὴν κατάπαυσιν ..., κ. εἴρηκεν (after Ps 94:11) *in the rest ... of which God has said* **Hb 4:3; 8:5** (s. HLjungvik, Eranos 62, '64, 36f).

➋ **of extent or degree to which,** ***as, to the degree that*** (Num 26:54; Ar. 2, 1; 4, 1) κ. ἠδύναντο ἀκούειν *so far as they were able to understand* **Mk 4:33.** κ. εὐπορεῖτό τις *each according to each one's (financial) ability* **Ac 11:29.** κ. βούλεται *(just)* as *the Spirit chooses* (NRSV) **1 Cor 12:11;** cp. vs. **18.** κ. ἔλαβεν χάρισμα *to the degree that one has received a gift* **1 Pt 4:10.** Cp. **Ac 2:4; 1 Cor 15:38.**

❸ **of cause,** *since, in so far as,* esp. as a conjunction beginning a sentence (B-D-F §453, 2; Rob. 968; 1382) **J 17:2; Ro 1:28; 1 Cor 1:6; 5:7; Eph 1:4; 4:32; Phil 1:7.**

❹ **of temporality,** ***as, when.*** The temporal mng. of κ. is disputed, but seems well established (2 Macc 1:31; 2 Esdr 15:6; EpArist 310; s. ὡς 8); κ. (v.l. ὡς) ἤγγιζεν ὁ χρόνος *when the time came near* **Ac 7:17** (EpArist 236 καθὼς εὔκαιρον ἐγένετο).

❺ After verbs of saying it introduces indirect discourse (=ὡς, πῶς) Συμεὼν ἐξηγήσατο, κ. ὁ θεὸς ἐπεσκέψατο *S. has related how God visited* **Ac 15:14.** μαρτυρούντων σου τῇ ἀληθείᾳ, κ. σὺ ἐν τῇ ἀληθείᾳ περιπατεῖς *who testify to your truth, namely how you walk in the truth* **3J 3.**—M-M.

καθώσπερ adv.=καθώς (a redundant expr. like οἷον ὡς, οἷον ὥσπερ; Himerius, Or. 1, 20; Paroem. Gr. II p. 73, 11; 473, 13; Nicetas Eugen. 8, 106 H.) *(just) as* κ. καὶ Ἀαρών *just as Aaron also* (was) **Hb 5:4; 2 Cor 3:18 v.l.** (for καθάπερ).

καί conjunction (Hom.+), found most frequently by far of all Gk. particles in the NT; since it is not only used much more commonly here than in other Gk. lit. but oft. in a different sense, or rather in different circumstances, it contributes greatly to some of the distinctive coloring of the NT style.—HMcArthur, KAI Frequency in Greek Letters, NTS 15, '68/69, 339–49. The vivacious versatility of κ. (for earlier Gk. s. Denniston 289–327) can easily be depressed by the tr. 'and', whose repetition in a brief area of text lacks the support of arresting aspects of Gk. syntax.

❶ **marker of connections,** ***and***—ⓐ single words—**α.** gener. Ἰάκωβος καὶ Ἰωσὴφ καὶ Σίμων καὶ Ἰούδας **Mt 13:55.** χρυσὸν καὶ λίβανον καὶ σμύρναν **2:11.** ἡ ἐντολὴ ἁγία καὶ δικαία καὶ ἀγαθή **Ro 7:12.** πολυμερῶς κ. πολυτρόπως **Hb 1:1.** ὁ θεὸς κ. πατήρ *God, who is also the Father* **1 Cor 15:24;** cp. **2 Cor 1:3; 11:31; Eph 1:3; Js 1:27; 3:9** al.—Connects two occurrences of the same word for emphasis (OGI 90, 19 [196 BC] Ἑρμῆς ὁ μέγας κ. μέγας; pap in Mayser II/1, 54) μείζων κ. μείζων *greater and greater* Hv 4, 1, 6. ἔτι κ. ἔτι *again and again* B 21:4; Hs 2, 6 (B-D-F §493, 1; 2; s. Rob. 1200).

β. w. numerals, w. the larger number first δέκα καὶ ὀκτώ **Lk 13:16.** τεσσεράκοντα κ. ἕξ **J 2:20.** τετρακόσιοι κ. πεντήκοντα **Ac 13:20.**—The καί in **2 Cor 13:1** ἐπὶ στόματος δύο μαρτύρων καὶ τριῶν σταθήσεται πᾶν ῥῆμα='or' ([v.l. ἢ τριῶν for καὶ τριῶν as it reads **Mt 18:16**]; cp. **Js 4:13 v.l.** σήμερον καὶ αὔριον='today or tomorrow', but s. above all Thu. 1, 82, 2; Pla., Phd. 63e; X., De Re Equ. 4, 4 ἁμάξας τέτταρας καὶ πέντε; Heraclides, Pol. 58 τρεῖς καὶ τέσσαρας; Polyb. 3, 51, 12 ἐπὶ δυεῖν καὶ τρισὶν ἡμέραις; 5, 90, 6; Diod. S. 34 + 35 fgm. 2, 28 εἷς καὶ δύο=one or two; schol. on Apollon. Rhod. 4, 1091 p. 305, 22 W. τριέτης καὶ τετραέτης) *by the statement of two or three witnesses every charge must be sustained,* as explained by Dt 19:15.

γ. adding the whole to the part *and in general* (Aristoph., Nub. 1239 τὸν Δία καὶ τοὺς θεούς; Thu. 1, 116, 3; 7, 65, 1) Πέτρος καὶ οἱ ἀπόστολοι *Peter and the rest of the apostles* **Ac 5:29.** οἱ ἀρχιερεῖς κ. τὸ συνέδριον ὅλον *the high priest and all the rest of the council* **Mt 26:59.** Vice versa, adding a (specially important) part to the whole *and especially* (πᾶς Ἰουδὰ καὶ Ἰερουσαλήμ 2 Ch 35:24; cp. 32, 33; 1 Macc 2:6) τοῖς μαθηταῖς κ. τῷ Πέτρῳ **Mk 16:7.** σὺν γυναιξὶ κ. Μαριάμ **Ac 1:14.**

δ. The expr. connected by καί can be united in the form of a hendiadys (Alcaeus 117, 9f D.[2] χρόνος καὶ καρπός=time of fruit; Soph., Aj. 144; 749; Polyb. 6, 9, 4; 6, 57, 5 ὑπεροχὴ καὶ δυναστεία=1, 2, 7; 5, 45, 1 ὑπεροχὴ τῆς δυναστείας; Diod. S. 5, 67, 3 πρὸς ἀνανέωσιν καὶ μνήμην=renewal of remembrance; 15, 63, 2 ἀνάγκη καὶ τύχη=compulsion of fate; 16, 93, 2 ἐπιβουλὴ κ. θάνατος=a fatal plot; Jos., Ant. 12, 98 μετὰ χαρᾶς κ. βοῆς=w. a joyful cry; 17, 82 ἀκρίβεια κ. φυλακή) ἐξίσταντο ἐπὶ τῇ συνέσει καὶ ταῖς ἀποκρίσεσιν αὐτοῦ *they were amazed at his intelligent answers* **Lk 2:47.** δώσω ὑμῖν στόμα κ. σοφίαν *I will give you wise utterance* **21:15.** τροφὴ κ. εὐφροσύνη *joy concerning (your) food* **Ac 14:17.** ἐλπὶς κ. ἀνάστασις *hope of a resurrection* **23:6** (2 Macc 3:29 ἐλπὶς καὶ σωτηρία; s. OLagercrantz, ZNW 31, '32, 86f; GBjörck, ConNeot 4, '40, 1–4).

ε. A colloquial feature is the coordination of two verbs, one of which should be a ptc. (s. B-D-F §471; Rob. 1135f) ἀποτολμᾷ κ. λέγει = ἀποτολμῶν λέγει *he is so bold as to say* **Ro 10:20.** ἔσκαψεν κ. ἐβάθυνεν (=βαθύνας) **Lk 6:48.** ἐκρύβη κ. ἐξῆλθεν (=ἐξελθών) **J 8:59.** Sim. χαίρων κ. βλέπων *I am glad to see* **Col 2:5.** Linking of subordinate clause and ptc. Μαριὰμ ὡς ἦλθεν . . . καὶ ἰδοῦσα **J 11:32 v.l.** Cp. παραλαβών . . . καὶ ἀνέβη **Lk 9:28 v.l.**

ⓑ clauses and sentences—**α.** gener.: ἐν γαστρὶ ἕξει κ. τέξεται υἱόν **Mt 1:23** (Is 7:14). εἰσῆλθον . . . κ. ἐδίδασκον **Ac 5:21.** διακαθαριεῖ τὴν ἅλωνα αὐτοῦ κ. συνάξει τὸν σῖτον **Mt 3:12.** κεκένωται ἡ πίστις καὶ κατήργηται ἡ ἐπαγγελία **Ro 4:14** and very oft. Connecting two questions **Mt 21:23,** or quotations (e.g. **Ac 1:20**), and dialogue (**Lk 21:8**), or alternate possibilities (**13:18**).

β. Another common feature is the practice, drawn fr. Hebrew or fr. the speech of everyday life, of using κ. as a connective where more discriminating usage would call for other particles: καὶ εἶδον καὶ (for ὅτι) σεισμὸς ἐγένετο **Rv 6:12.** καὶ ἤκουσεν ὁ βασιλεὺς . . . καὶ (for ὅτι) ἔλεγον *and the king learned that they were saying* **Mk 6:14** (s. HLjungvik, ZNW 33, '34, 90–92; on this JBlinzler, Philol. 96, '43/44, 119–31). τέξεται υἱὸν καὶ καλέσεις τὸ ὄνομα αὐτοῦ (for οὗ τὸ ὄνομα καλ.) **Mt 1:21;** cp. **Lk 6:6; 11:44.** καλόν ἐστιν ἡμᾶς ὧδε εἶναι καὶ ποιήσωμεν σκηνάς **Mk 9:5.** Esp. freq. is the formula in historical narrative καὶ ἐγένετο . . . καί (like וְ . . . וַיְהִי) *and it happened* or *came about . . . that* **Mt 9:10; Mk 2:15; Lk 5:1 v.l.** (for ἐγένετο δὲ . . . καί; so also the text of **6:12**), **12, 17; 14:1; 17:11** al. (Gen 7:10 al.; JosAs 11:1; 22:1). S. MJohannessohn, Das bibl. Καὶ ἐγένετο u. seine Geschichte, 1926 (fr. ZVS 35, 1925, 161–212); KBeyer, Semitische Syntax im NT I, 1 '62, 29–62; Mlt-Turner 334f; ÉDelebecque, Études Grecques sur L'Évangile de Luc '76, 123–65; JVoelz, The Language of the NT: ANRW II/25/2, 893–977, esp. 959–64.—As in popular speech, κ. is used in rapid succession **Mt 14:9ff; Mk 1:12ff; Lk 18:32ff; J 2:13ff; 1 Cor 12:5f; Rv 6:12ff; 9:1ff.** On this kind of colloquial speech, which joins independent clauses rather than subordinating one to the other (parataxis rather than hypotaxis) s. B-D-F §458; Rdm.[2] p. 222; Rob. 426; Dssm., LO 105ff (LAE 129ff), w. many references and parallels fr. secular sources. This is a favorite, e.g., in Polyaenus 2, 3, 2–4; 2, 4, 3; 3, 9, 10; 3, 10, 2; 4, 6, 1; 7, 36 al.

γ. It is also coordination rather than subordination when κ. connects an expr. of time with that which occurs in the time (Od. 5, 362; Hdt. 7, 217; Thu. 1, 50, 5; Pla., Symp. 220c; Aeschin. 3, 71 νὺξ ἐν μέσῳ καὶ παρῆμεν; s. B-D-F §442, 4; KBrugmann[4]-AThumb, Griechische Gramm. 1913, 640*): ἤγγικεν ἡ ὥρα κ. παραδίδοται *the time has come when he is to be given up* **Mt 26:45.** κ. ἐσταύρωσαν αὐτόν *when they crucified him* **Mk 15:25.** κ. ἀνέβη εἰς Ἱεροσόλυμα *when he went up to Jerusalem* **J 2:13.** κ. συντελέσω *when I will make* **Hb 8:8** (Jer 38:31); cp. **J 4:35; 7:33; Lk 19:43; 23:44; Ac 5:7.**

δ. καί introducing an apodosis is really due to Hebr./LXX infl. (B-D-F §442, 7; Abel §78a, 6 p. 341; Mlt-H. 422; KBeyer, Semitische Syntax im NT I, 1 '62, 66–72; but not offensive to ears trained in good Gk.: s. Il. 1, 478; Hdt. 1, 79, 2; sim.Thu. 2, 93, 4 ὡς ἔδοξεν αὐτοῖς, καὶ ἐχώρουν εὐθύς; 8, 27, 5; Herm. Wr. 13, 1 . . . , καὶ ἔφης; Delebecque [s. above in β] 130–32) καὶ ὅτε ἐπλήσθησαν ἡμέραι ὀκτὼ . . . , κ. ἐκλήθη τὸ ὄνομα αὐτοῦ **Lk 2:21;** cp. **Rv 3:20.** Also κ. ἰδού in an apodosis **Lk 7:12; Ac 1:10.**

ε. connecting negative and affirmative clauses **Lk 3:14.** οὔτε ἄντλημα ἔχεις κ. τὸ φρέαρ ἐστὶ βαθύ *you have no bucket, and the well is deep* **J 4:11;** cp. **3J 10** (οὔτε . . . καί Eur., Iph. Taur. 591f; Longus, Past. 1, 17; 4, 28; Aelian, NA 1, 57; 11, 9; Lucian, Dial. Meretr. 2, 4 οὔτε πάντα ἡ Λεσβία, Δωρί, πρὸς σὲ ἐψεύσατο καὶ σὺ τἀληθῆ ἀπήγγελκας Μυρτίῳ 'It wasn't all lies that Lesbia told you, Doris; and you certainly reported the truth to Myrtium'). After a negative clause, which influences the clause beginning w. καί: μήποτε καταπατήσουσιν . . . κ. στραφέντες ῥήξωσιν ὑμᾶς **Mt 7:6;** cp. **5:25; 10:38; 13:15** (Is 6:10); **27:64; Lk 12:58; 21:34; J 6:53; 12:40** (Is 6:10); **Ac 28:27** (Is 6:10); **1 Th 3:5; Hb 12:15; Rv 16:15.**

ζ. to introduce a result that comes fr. what precedes: *and then, and so* **Mt 5:15; 23:32; Mk 8:34; 2 Cor 11:9; Hb 3:19; 1J 3:19.** καὶ ἔχομεν *and so we have* **2 Pt 1:19.** Esp. after the impv., or expr. of an imperatival nature (Soph., Oed. Col. 1410ff θέσθε . . . καὶ . . . οἴσει, El. 1207; Sir 2:6; 3:17) δεῦτε ὀπίσω μου καὶ ποιήσω *and then I will make* **Mt 4:19.** εἰπὲ λόγῳ, κ. ἰαθήσεται ὁ παῖς μου *speak the word, and then my servant will be cured* **Mt 8:8; Lk 7:7;** cp. **Mt 7:7; Mk 6:22; Lk 10:28; J 14:16; Js 4:7, 10; Rv 4:1.**—καί introduces a short clause that confirms the existence of someth. that ought to be: ἵνα τέκνα θεοῦ κληθῶμεν, καὶ ἐσμέν *that we should be called children of God; and so we really are* (καλέω 1d) **1J 3:1** (Appian, Bell. Civ. 2, 40 §161 they were to conquer Sardinia, καὶ κατέλαβον=and they really took it; 4, 127 §531 one day would decide [κρίνειν] the fate of Rome, καὶ ἐκρίθη).

η. emphasizing a fact as surprising or unexpected or noteworthy: *and yet, and in spite of that, nevertheless* (Eur., Herc. Fur. 509; Philostrat., Her. 11 [II 184, 29 Kayser] ῥητορικώτατον καὶ δεινόν; Longus, Past. 4, 17 βουκόλος ἦν Ἀγχίσης καὶ ἔσχεν αὐτὸν Ἀφροδίτη) κ. σὺ ἔρχῃ πρός μέ; *and yet you come to me?* **Mt 3:14;** cp. **6:26; 10:29; Mk 12:12; J 1:5, 10; 3:11, 32; 5:40; 6:70; 7:28; 1 Cor 5:2; 2 Cor 6:9; Hb 3:9** (Ps 94:9); **Rv 3:1.** So also, connecting what is unexpected or otherw. noteworthy with an attempt of some kind (JBlomqvist, Das sogenannte και adversativum '79): *but* ζητεῖ κ. οὐχ εὑρίσκει *but he finds none* (no resting place) **Mt 12:43.** ἐπεθύμησαν ἰδεῖν κ. οὐχ εἶδαν *but did not see (it)* **13:17;** cp. **26:60; Lk 13:7; 1 Th 2:18.** Cp. GJs 18:3 (not pap). Perhaps **Mk 5:20.** Introducing a contrasting response καὶ ἀποδώσεις μοι Hv 2, 1, 3.

θ. to introduce an abrupt question, which may often express wonder, ill-will, incredulity, etc. (B-D-F §442, 8. For older lit. exx. of this usage s. Kühner-G. II p. 247f; for later times EColwell, The Gk. of the Fourth Gospel '31, 87f): κ. πόθεν μοι τοῦτο; *how have I deserved this?* **Lk 1:43.** κ. τίς; *who then?* **Mk 10:26; Lk 10:29; J 9:36.** καὶ τί γέγονεν ὅτι . . . ; *how does it happen that . . . ?* **14:22.** καὶ πῶς σὺ λέγεις . . . ; *how is it, then, that you say* . . . **J 14:9 v.l.** W. a protasis εἰ γὰρ ἐγὼ λυπῶ ὑμᾶς, κ. τίς ὁ εὐφραίνων με; *for if I make you sad, who then will cheer me up?* **2 Cor 2:2** (cp. Ps.-Clem., Hom. 2, 43; 44 εἰ [ὁ θεὸς] ψεύδεται, καὶ τίς ἀληθεύει;). Thus **Phil 1:22** is prob. to be punctuated as follows (s. ADebrunner, GGA 1926, 151): εἰ δὲ τὸ ζῆν ἐν σαρκί, τοῦτο μοι καρπὸς ἔργου, καὶ τί αἱρήσομαι; οὐ γνωρίζω *but if living on here means further productive work, then which shall I choose? I really don't know.* καὶ πῶς αὐτοῦ υἱός ἐστιν; *how, then, is he his son?* **Lk 20:44** (cp. Gen 39:9).

ι. to introduce a parenthesis (Eur., Orest. 4, Hel. 393; X., Equ. 11, 2.—B-D-F §465, 1; Rob. 1182) κ. ἐκωλύθην ἄχρι τοῦ δεῦρο *but so far I have been prevented* **Ro 1:13.**

ⓒ oft. explicative; i.e., a word or clause is connected by means of καί w. another word or clause, for the purpose of explaining what goes before it *and so, that is, namely* (PPetr II, 18 [1], 9 πληγὰς . . . καὶ πλείους=blows . . . indeed many of them.—Kühner-G. II 247; B-D-F §442, 9; Rob. 1181; Mlt-Turner 335) χάριν κ. ἀποστολήν *grace, that is, the office of an apostle* **Ro 1:5.** ἀπήγγειλαν πάντα καὶ τὰ τ. δαιμονιζομένων *they told everything, namely what had happened to those who were possessed* **Mt 8:33.** καὶ χάριν ἀντὶ χάριτος *that is, grace upon grace* **J 1:16.** Cp. **1 Cor 3:5; 15:38.**—**Mt 21:5.**—Other explicative uses are καὶ οὗτος, καὶ τοῦτο, καὶ ταῦτα (the first and last are in earlier Gk.: Hdt., X. et al.; s. Kühner-G. I 647; II 247) *and,* also ascensive *and indeed, and at that* Ἰ. Χρ., καὶ τοῦτον ἐσταυρωμένον *J. Chr., (and) indeed him on the cross* **1 Cor 2:2.** καὶ τοῦτο **Ro 13:11; 1 Cor 6:6, 8; Eph 2:8.** καὶ ταῦτα w. ptc. *and to be sure* **Hb 11:12.** See B-D-F §290, 5; 425, 1; 442, 9.—The ascensive force of καί is also plain in Ῥωμαῖον καὶ ἀκατάκριτον *a Roman citizen, and uncondemned at that* **Ac 22:25.** ἔρχεται ὥρα καὶ νῦν ἐστιν an *hour is coming, indeed it is already here* **J 5:25.** προσέθηκεν καὶ τοῦτο ἐπὶ πᾶσιν καὶ κατέκλεισεν τὸν Ἰωάννην ἐν φυλακῇ *added this on top of everything else, namely to put John in prison* **Lk 3:20.**

ⓓ After πολύς and before a second adj. καί is pleonastic fr. the viewpoint of modern lang. (earlier Gk.: Hom. et al. [Kühner-G. II 252, 1]; cp. Cebes 1, 1 πολλὰ καὶ ἄλλα ἀναθήματα; 2, 3; B-D-F §442, 11) πολλὰ . . . κ. ἄλλα σημεῖα *many other signs* **J 20:30** (cp. Jos., Ant. 3, 318). πολλὰ κ. βαρέα αἰτιώματα *many severe charges* **Ac 25:7.** πολλὰ . . . καὶ ἕτερα **Lk 3:18** (cp. Himerius, Or. 40 [=Or. 6], 6 πολλὰ καὶ ἄλλα). πολλοὶ καὶ ἀνυπότακτοι **Tit 1:10.**

ⓔ introducing someth. new, w. loose connection: **Mt 4:23; 8:14, 23, 28; 9:1, 9, 27, 35; 10:1; 12:27; Mk 5:1, 21; Lk 8:26; J 1:19** and oft.

ⓕ καί . . . καί *both . . . and, not only . . . , but also* (Synes., Dreams 10 p. 141b καὶ ἀπιστεῖν ἔξεστι καὶ πιστεύειν.—B-D-F §444, 3; Rob. 1182; Mlt-Turner 335) connecting single expressions **Mt 10:28; Mk 4:41; Ro 11:33; Phil 2:13; 4:12.** κ. ἐν ὀλίγῳ κ. ἐν μεγάλῳ **Ac 26:29.** κ. ἅπαξ κ. δίς (s. ἅπαξ 1) **Phil 4:16; 1 Th 2:18.** Connecting whole clauses or sentences: **Mk 9:13; J 7:28; 9:37; 12:28; 1 Cor 1:22.** Introducing contrasts: *although . . . yet* (Anthol. VII, 676 Δοῦλος Ἐπίκτητος γενόμην καὶ σῶμ' ἀνάπηρος καὶ πενίην Ἶρος καὶ φίλος ἀθανάτοις 'I was Epictetus, a slave; crippled in body and an Iros [a beggar in Hom., Od.] in poverty, but dear to the Immortals') **J 15:24; Ac 23:3.** καὶ . . . κ. οὐ **Lk 5:36; J 6:36.** καὶ οὐ . . . καί **17:25;** κ. . . . κ. *now . . . now* **Mk 9:22.** On τὲ . . . καί s. τέ 2c. Somet. w. ἤ q.v. 1aβ.—HCadbury, Superfluous καί in the Lord's Prayer (i.e. Mt 6:12) and Elsewhere: Munera Studiosa (=WHatch Festschr.) '46.

❷ marker to indicate an additive relation that is not coordinate to connect clauses and sentences, *also, likewise,* funct. as an adv.

ⓐ simply κ. τὴν ἄλλην *the other one also* **Mt 5:39;** cp. vs. **40; 6:21; 12:45; Mk 1:38; 2:26; 8:7** and oft. Freq. used w. pronouns κἀγώ (q.v.). καὶ σύ **Mt 26:73.** κ. ὑμεῖς **20:4, 7; Lk 21:31; J 7:47** and oft. κ. αὐτός (s. αὐτός 1f).

ⓑ intensive: *even* **Mt 5:46f; 10:30; Mk 1:27; Lk 10:17; J 14:9 v.l.; Ac 5:39; 22:28; Ro 9:24** (ἀλλὰ καί); **1 Cor 2:10; 2 Cor 1:8; Gal 2:17; Eph 5:12; Phlm 21; Hb 7:25; 1 Pt 4:19** (but s. d below); **Jd 23;** Hs 5, 2, 10; 7:1; ἔτι καὶ νῦν Dg 2:3. CBlackman, JBL 87, '68, 203f would transl. **Ro 3:26b:** . . . *even in the act of declaring righteous* (cp. the gen. abs. Polemon Soph.

B 14 Reader καὶ Δάτιδος ἀποπλέοντος=even though Datis was sailing away). In formulas expressing a wish: ὄφελον καί *if only, would that* **Gal 5:12.** In connection w. a comparative: κ. περισσότερον προφήτου *one who is even more than a prophet* **Mt 11:9.** κ. μείζονα ποιήσει **J 14:12.**

ⓒ In sentences denoting a contrast καί appears in var. ways, somet. in both members of the comparison, and oft. pleonastically, to our way of thinking καθάπερ . . . , οὕτως καί *as . . . , thus also* **2 Cor 8:11.** ὥσπερ . . . , οὕτως καί (Hyperid. 1, 2, 5–8) **Ro 5:19; 11:30f; 1 Cor 11:12; 15:22; Gal 4:29.** ὡς . . . , οὕτως καί **Ro 5:15, 18.** ὃν τρόπον . . . , οὕτως καί **2 Ti 3:8.**—οὕτως καί *thus also* **Ro 6:11.** ὡσαύτως καί *in the same way also* **1 Cor 11:25.** ὁμοίως καί (Jos., Bell. 2, 575) **J 6:11; Jd 8.** ὡς καί **Ac 11:17; 1 Cor 7:7; 9:5.** καθὼς καί **Ro 15:7; 1 Cor 13:12; 2 Cor 1:14; Eph 4:17.** καθάπερ καί **Ro 4:6; 2 Cor 1:14.**—καί can also stand alone in the second member w. the mng. *so also, so.* ὡς . . . καί **Mt 6:10; Ac 7:51; Gal 1:9; Phil 1:20.** καθὼς . . . καί **Lk 6:31 v.l.; J 6:57; 13:15; 1 Cor 15:49.**—οἷος . . . , τοιοῦτος καί **1 Cor 15:48.** After a comp. ὅσῳ καί *by so much also* **Hb 8:6.** καί is found in both members of the comparison (s. Kühner-G. II 256; 2 Macc 2:10; 6:14) **Ro 1:13; 1 Th 2:14.** καθὼς καὶ . . . οὕτως καί **Col 3:13** (cp. Hyperid. 1, 40, 20–25 ὥσπερ καὶ . . . οὕτω καί; 3, 38).

ⓓ w. expressions that introduce cause or result, here also pleonastic to a considerable degree διὰ τοῦτο καί *for this reason (also)* **Lk 11:49; J 12:18.** διὸ καί **Lk 1:35; Ac 10:29; Ro 4:22; Hb 13:12.** εἰς τοῦτο καί **2 Cor 2:9.** ὥστε καί **1 Pt 4:19** (but this pass. may well fit in b). ὅθεν καί **Hb 7:25; 11:19.**

ⓔ after an interrogative (as Thu., X., et al.; s. Kühner-G. II 255. S. also B-D-F §442, 14) *at all, still* ἱνατί καὶ τ. γῆν καταργεῖ; **Lk 13:7.** τί καί; (Hyperid. 3, 14 τί καὶ ἀδικεῖ; what kind of wrong, then, is he committing?) τί καὶ ἐλπίζει; *why does he still* (need to) *hope?* **Ro 8:24. v.l.** τί καὶ βαπτίζονται; *why are they baptized (at all)?* **1 Cor 15:29;** cp. vs. **30.**

ⓕ used w. a relative, it oft. gives greater independence to the foll. relative clause: **Mk 3:14; Lk 10:30; J 11:2 v.l.; Ac 1:3, 11; 7:45; 10:39; 11:30; 12:4; 13:22; 28:10; Ro 9:24; 1 Cor 11:23; Gal 2:10; Col 1:29** al.

ⓖ used pleonastically w. prep.—**α.** μετά (BGU 412, 6 μετὰ καὶ τ. υἱοῦ) **Phil 4:3.**

β. σύν (ins in PASA III 612; PFay 108; BGU 179, 19; 515, 17) 1 Cl 65:1.—Dssm., NB 93 (BS 265f).

ⓗ w. double names ὁ καί *who is also called* . . . (the earliest ex. in a fragment of Ctesias: 688 fgm. 15, 51 p. 469, 23 Jac. Ὦχος καὶ Δαρειαῖος [s. Hatch 141]; OGI 565; 574; 583; 589; 603; 604; 620; 623; 636; POxy 45; 46; 54; 101; 485; 1279; PFay 30; BGU 22, 25; 36, 4; Jos., Ant. 1, 240; 5, 85; 12, 285; 13, 320; 18, 35. Further material in WSchmid, Der Atticismus III 1893, 338; Dssm., B 181ff [BS 313–17]. Lit. in B-D-F §268, 1) Σαῦλος, ὁ καὶ Παῦλος **Ac 13:9.** Ἰγνάτιος, ὁ καὶ Θεοφόρος ins of all the letters of Ign.

ⓘ with other particles—**α.** καὶ γάρ *for* (s. γάρ 1b).—καὶ γὰρ . . . ἀλλά (or *granted that . . . but*) **2 Cor 13:4; Phil 2:27.**—καὶ γὰρ οὐ(κ): *neither* **1 Cor 11:9;** *for even . . . not* **2 Cor 3:10.**

β. καί γε (without intervening word [opp. earlier Gk, e.g. Pla., Phd. 58d; Rep. 7, 531a]: Hippocr., Septim. 9, VII 450 Littré; Cornutus p. 40, 12; Περὶ ὕψους 13, 2; Rhetor Apsines [III AD] p. 332, 17 Hammer; TestReub 4:4 al.; for גַּם always in Theod. [DBarthélemy, Les devanciers d'Aquila '63, 31ff]), weakened force: *(if) only* or *at least* **Lk 19:42 v.l.;** intensive: *indeed* (Jos. Ant 29, 19) **Ac 2:18** (**J 3:2 v.l.;** Mel., P. 30, 207); Hm 8:5; 9:9. καί γε οὐ μακράν=*and indeed God is not far* **Ac 17:27.**— Kühner-G. II 176b; Schwyzer II 561; B-D-F §439, 2; Rdm.[2] 35–37.

γ. καὶ . . . δέ *and also, but also* (s. δέ 5b).

δ. καίτοι (Il. 13, 267 et al., ins, pap; 4 Macc 2:6; 5:18; 7:13; Ath. 8, 1 al.; Mel., P. 58, 422) particle (B-D-F §425, 1; 450, 3; Rob. 1129 and 1154) w. finite verb (Chion, Ep. 3, 1; Jos. Ant 5, 78) *yet, on the other hand* **Ac 14:17.** W. gen. abs. foll. (BGU 850, 4 [76 AD] καίτοι ἐμοῦ σε πολλὰ ἐρωτήσαντος; 898, 26; Philo, Vi. Mos. 1, 20; Jos., Ant. 2, 321; Ath. 19, 2; 25, 2) **Hb 4:3.**—καίτοι γε or καί τοι γε (since Aristoph., Ach. 611; but esp. in later Gk. [cp. Schwyzer II 561; MMeister, De Aiocho dial., Breslau diss. 1915 p. 31, 5]; Ps.-Pla., Axioch. 364b; Jos., Bell. 1, 7, Ant. 5, 36; Epict. 3, 24, 90; Just., A II, 11, 2; D. 7, 3; Ath. 3, 1; 22, 7; SIG 685, 76 and 82 [139 BC]) *although* **J 4:2; Ac 14:17 v.l.;** Dg 8:3. W. part. foll. (Jos., C. Ap. 1, 230; Mel., P. 58, 422) AcPt Ox 849, 18.—Kühner-G. II 151f; B-D-F §439, 1; 450, 3.—For ἀλλὰ κ., δὲ και, ἐὰν κ., εἰ κ., ἢ κ. s. ἀλλά, δέ, ἐάν, εἰ, ἤ.—ERobson, KAI-Configurations in the Gk. NT, 3 vols. diss. Syracuse '79. LfgrE s.v. καί col. 1273f (lit.). DELG. M-M. EDNT.

Καϊάφας, α, ὁ (also as v.l. Καϊαφᾶς and Καϊφᾶς) ***Caiaphas*** (Jos., Ant. 18, 35; 95; Mel., P. 93, 705 [Καιφας B]), high priest 18–36 AD who played an important role in the condemnation of Jesus. Cp. **Mt 26:3, 57; Lk 3:2; J 11:49; 18:13f, 24, 28; Ac 4:6;** GEb 13, 74. Acc. to **J 18:13** he was son-in-law to Annas (s. Ἅννας 1).—Schürer II 216, 230; MStern in CRINT I 349–53.—KRengstorf, Rabb. Texte, ser. 1, vol. 3, '33ff, p. 16f on Tos. Jeb. 1, 10. On the name s. B-D-F §37; Dalman, Gramm. 161, 2; EbNestle, Theol. Studien f. ThZahn, 1908, 251ff; FCBurkitt, The Syriac Forms of NT Proper Names (Proceed. of the Brit. Acad. 1911/12) 385; JJeremias, Jerusalem z. Zeit Jesu[3] '63, 218–23; PWinter, On the Trial of Jesus '61.—M-M. TW.

καίγε s. γέ bγ (cp. και 2iβ).

Κάϊν, ὁ indecl. (קַיִן; W-H. Καίν; LXX; En 22:7; Philo; TestBenj 7:5; TestAbr A 13 p. 92, 6 [Stone p. 32]; ApcMos, Philo; Just., D. 99, 3.—In Jos., Ant. 1, 52; 65f; 57 Κάις, Κάιος, Κάιν) ***Cain,*** Adam's son (Gen 4:1ff) **Hb 11:4; 1J 3:12; Jd 11;** 1 Cl 4:1ff.—NDahl, in Apophoreta (Haenchen Festschr.) '64, 70–84; PBretscher, Cain, Come Home! '76; JReeves, Heralds of That Good Realm '96, 1100f, n. 89 on Cain's patrimony in tradition. S. also Ἅβελ.—TW.

Καϊνάμ, ὁ indecl. (Καϊνάν, Hebr. קֵינָן Gen 5:9) ***Cainan,*** in the genealogy of Jesus.—❶ son of Arphaxad (LXX Gen 10:24; 11:12; 1 Ch 1:18) **Lk 3:36.** The name is lacking in P[75] D.

❷ son of Enos (Gen 5:9ff.—Jos., Ant. 1, 79; 84 Καινᾶς, ᾶ) **Lk 3:37.**

καινίζω (s. καινός; trag. et al.) ***make new*** B 6:11 v.l. (for ἀνακ.).

καινοποιέω (s. καινός, ποιέω; Soph., Polyb., Lucian, also Is 61:4 Sym; Jos, Just., A I, 61, 1) ***make new*** **Rv 21:5 v.l.**

καινός, ή, όν (Aeschyl., Hdt.+; ins, pap, LXX, TestSol; TestAbr A 7 p. 84, 27 [Stone p. 16]; Test12Patr; JosAs 14:13 and 15; Philo, Joseph., Just., Mel.) comp. καινότερος; prim. sense 'new'.

❶ **pert. to being in existence for a relatively short time,** ***new, unused*** (X., Hell. 3, 4, 28; PGM 36, 265; Judg 15:13; 2 Km 6:3; 4 Km 2:20) ἀσκοί *wineskins* (Josh 9:13) **Mt 9:17; Mk 2:22; Lk 5:38.** ἱμάτιον (Artem. 2, 3 p. 86, 3; 3 Km 11:29f) vs. **36.** μνημεῖον **Mt 27:60; J 19:41** (w. ἐν ᾧ οὐδέπω οὐδεὶς ἦν τεθειμένος added). τὸ κ. *the new* piece=πλήρωμα **Mk 2:21; Lk 5:36.** καινὰ καὶ παλαιά **Mt 13:52** (perh. with ref. to coins; cp. PGrenf II, 74, 9; 77, 7f).

❷ **pert. to being not previously present, *unknown, strange, remarkable,*** also w. the connotation of the marvelous or unheard-of (Pla., Apol. 24c; X., Mem. 1, 1, 1 ἕτερα καὶ καινὰ δαιμόνια; Just., A I, 15, 9; Orig., C. Cels. 1 58, 15) διδαχή **Mk 1:27; Ac 17:19.** ἐντολή (κ. νόμος: Menand., fgm. 238, 3 Kö.; Diod. S. 13, 34, 6) **J 13:34; 1J 2:7f** (Polyaenus 2, 1, 13 οὐ καινοὺς νόμους . . . ἀλλὰ τ. παλαιούς); **2J 5.** ὄνομα (Is 62:2; 65:15) **Rv 2:17** (here w. ὃ οὐδεὶς οἶδεν εἰ μὴ ὁ λαμβάνων, perh. as antidote to adversarial magic); **3:12.** ᾠδή **5:9** (Ps 143:9; cp. Is 42:10; Ps 32:3; 39:4.—Philo, Vi. Cont. 80 ὕμνος κ. [opp. ἀρχαῖος]); **14:3.** γλῶσσαι **Mk 16:17.** κ. γένος of Christians Dg 1. θεώρημα AcPl Ox 6, 1f (διήγημα Aa I, 241, 11). θέαμα GJs 19:2f (Mel., P. 19, 127). Christ as ὁ κ. ἄνθρωπος *the new kind of human being* IEph 20:1. ἢ λέγειν τι ἢ ἀκούειν τι καινότερον *either to hear or to say someth. quite new* (='the latest thing') **Ac 17:21** (s. Kühner-G. II 306f; Norden, Agn. Th. 333ff [but s. HAlmqvist, Plutarch u. d. NT '46, 79f, w. ref. to Plut.]; B-D-F §244, 2; Rdm. 70 and s. Demosth. 4, 10 ὦ ἄνδρες Ἀθηναῖοι . . . λέγεταί τι καινόν; γένοιτ' ἄν τι καινότερον . . . ; also Theophr., Char. 8, 2; BGU 821, 6 [II AD] ὅταν ᾖ τι καινότερον, εὐθέως σοι δηλώσω; Simplicius, Coroll. De Tempore, in Aristot., Phys. p. 788, 36ff καινοτέραν ἐβάδισεν ὁδόν=he traveled a rather new road [of interpretation]; Jos., Ant. 14, 104; Iren. 1, 18, 1 [Harv. I 169, 3]).

❸ **pert. to that which is recent in contrast to someth. old, *new***—ⓐ w. no criticism of the old implied (Herodas 4, 57 καινὴ Ἀθηναίη; Lucian, M. Peregr. 12 κ. Σωκράτης): of the Son of God or Logos, who is old and new at the same time Hs 9, 12, 1ff; Dg 11:4.

ⓑ in the sense that what is old has become obsolete, and should be replaced by what is new. In such a case the new is, as a rule, superior in kind to the old ἡ κ. διαθήκη *the new covenant* or *declaration* (Jer 38:31; Just., D. 11, 4 al.; Did., Gen. 46, 4; 156, 5) **Mt 26:28 v.l.; Mk 14:24 v.l.; Lk 22:20; 1 Cor 11:25; 2 Cor 3:6; Hb 8:8** (Jer 38:31), **13; 9:15.** κ. νόμος (Timocles Com. [IV BC] fgm. 32, 4 κατὰ τὸν νόμον τ. καινόν; Just., D. 12, 3; Mel., P. 7, 46) B 2:6. λαὸς κ. 5:7; 7:5; cp. 15:7.—Esp. in eschatol. usage κ. οὐρανοί, κ. γῆ (Is 65:17; 66:22) **2 Pt 3:13; Rv 21:1;** Ἰερουσαλὴμ καινή vs. **2; 3:12.** καινὰ πάντα ποιεῖν **21:5.** καινὸν πίνειν τὸ γένημα τῆς ἀμπέλου **Mt 26:29; Mk 14:25.**—Of the renewing of a pers. who has been converted κ. ἄνθρωπος **Eph 4:24;** Dg 2:1. κ. κτίσις *a new creature* **2 Cor 5:17a;** cp. **17b** (Ps.-Pla., Axioch. 11 p. 370e ἐκ τῆς ἀσθενείας ἐμαυτὸν συνείλεγμαι καὶ γέγονα καινός=out of weakness I have brought myself together and become new; cp. Orig., C. Cels. 6, 67, 33); **Gal 6:15;** cp. B 16:8. All the Christians together appear as κ. ἄνθρωπος **Eph 2:15.**—RHarrisville, The Concept of Newness in the NT, '60; GSchneider, Καινὴ Κτίσις (Paul and background), diss. Trier, '59, Neuschöpfung oder Wiederkehr? '61. Qumran: DSwanson, A Covenant Just Like Jacob's, The Covenant of 11QT 29 and Jeremiah's New Covenant: New Qumran Texts and Studies, ed. GBrooke/FMartínez '94, 273–86.—B. 957. Schmidt, Syn. II 94–123. DELG. M-M. EDNT. TW. S. νεός.

καινότης, ητος, ἡ (since Thu. 3, 38, 5; Plut., Pericl. 13, 5; Lucian, Tyrannic. 22; 3 Km 8:53a; Ezk 47:12; Philo, Vi. Cont. 63) ***newness*** w. connotation of someth. extraordinary (καινός 2) of a star IEph 19:2. Hebraistically, the noun for an adj. κ. πνεύματος = πνεῦμα καινόν *a new spirit* **Ro 7:6.** κ. ζωῆς *a new life* **6:4;** cp. IEph 19:3 (for lit. s. παλιγγενεσία 2). κ. ἐλπίδος *a new hope* IMg 9:1.—DELG s.v. καινός. TW.

καινοφωνία s. κενοφωνία.

καινῶς adv. of καινός (OGI 669, 46; 49; Mel., P. 57, 416) ***newly*** καὶ τοῦτο οὐ κ. (sc. ἐγένετο) *and this was nothing new* 1 Cl 42:5. καινῶς (τ. θεὸν) σεβόμενοι *worshiping God in a new way* PtK 2 p. 15, 3; cp. 8.

καίπερ conj. (since Od. 7, 224; SIG 709, 18; 1108, 8; PGiss 47, 22; PSI 298, 17; LXX, TestJos, Joseph., Just.) ***although*** w. ptc. (so usu., also Diod. S. 8, 9, 2; 10, 19, 2; 17, 114, 1; Wsd 11:9; Jos., Ant. 1, 319; 3, 280; TestJos 10:5; w. finite verb Just., A I, 4, 4) **Phil 3:4; Hb 5:8; 7:5; 12:17; 2 Pt 1:12.** Also 1 Cl 7:7; 16:2; ISm 3:3; MPol 17:1; Hv 3, 2, 9; s 8, 6, 4; 8, 11, 1 (B-D-F §425, 1; Rob. 1129; FScheidweiler, καίπερ nebst e. Exkurs zum Hb: Her 83, '55, 220–30).—M-M.

καιρός, οῦ, ὁ (Hes.+; loanw. in rabb.)—❶ **a point of time or period of time, *time, period,*** freq. with implication of being esp. fit for someth. and without emphasis on precise chronology

ⓐ gener. (cp. Just., D. 32, 4 τὸν γὰρ καιρὸν [Da 7:26] ἑκατὸν ἔτη ἐξηγεῖσθε λέγεσθαι) κ. δεκτός *a welcome time* **2 Cor 6:2a** (Is 49:8); cp. vs. **2b.** καιροὶ χαλεποί *difficult times* **2 Ti 3:1.** In ref. to times of crisis for the state λοιμικοῦ καιροῦ 1 Cl 55:1 (s. JFischer ad loc. note 322) καιροὶ καρποφόροι *fruitful times* or *seasons* (so Achmes 156, 15f: καρποφόρος is the καιρός in which the tree bears fruit, in contrast to late autumn, when there is no more) **Ac 14:17** (OLagercrantz, ZNW 31, '32, 86f proposes, on the basis of Mod. Gk., the mng., 'weather', but the pl. is against this mng.). καιροὶ ἐαρινοί 1 Cl 20:9.—ἔσται καιρὸς ὅτε *there will come a time when* **2 Ti 4:3;** εἰς τίνα ἢ ποῖον κ. *to what time or what sort of time* (some, e.g. NRSV, interpret τίνα=*the person,* but cp. PTebt 25, 18 [117 BC] καὶ διὰ τίνος καὶ ἀπὸ ποίου ἐπιδείγματος; s. ποῖος 1aα, also ποταπός) **1 Pt 1:11.** ἄχρι καιροῦ *until (another) time, for a while* **Lk 4:13; Ac 13:11;** ἐν καιρῷ ὀλίγῳ *in a little time* 1 Cl 23:4; ἐν παντὶ κ. *at all times, always* (Aristot. 117a, 35; Sir 26:4) **Lk 21:36; Eph 6:18;** Hm 5, 2, 3. κατὰ καιρόν *from time to time, regularly* (TestJob 36:4; Lucian, Hermot. 10; Plut., Mor. 984d) **J 5:4** (s. 2 also); 1 Cl 24:2; GJs 3:3; πρὸς κ. *for a limited time* (perh. also *for the present moment;* cp. Strabo 6, 2, 3; Ps.-Plut., Fluv. 23; BGU 265, 20 [II AD]; 618, 19; 780, 14; Wsd 4:4; Philo, Post. Cai. 121; Jos., Bell. 6, 190; Tat. 13, 1) **Lk 8:13; 1 Cor 7:5.** πρὸς καιρὸν ὥρας (a combination of πρὸς κ. and πρὸς ὥραν [2 Cor 7:8; Gal 2:5; Phlm 15; J 5:35]) *for a short time* (cp. our 'for a short space of time') **1 Th 2:17.**

ⓑ a moment or period as especially appropriate *the right, proper, favorable time* ἐν καιρῷ *at the right time* (X., An. 3, 1, 39; Diod. S. 36, 7, 2; Appian, Bell. Civ. 3, 8 §29; SIG 1268 [Praecepta Delphica II, 6; III BC]) **Mt 24:45; Lk 12:42** (cp. on both Ps 103:27, w. v.l.). καιρῷ (Thu. 4, 59, 3 v.l.; Diog. L. 1, 41) **Lk 20:10** (v.l. ἐν κ.). τῷ καιρῷ **Mk 12:2.** ὁ καιρὸς ὁ ἐμός, ὁ καιρὸς ὁ ὑμέτερος *the proper time for me (you)* **J 7:6, 8** (Eunap., Vi. Iambl. p. 459 Didot: the worker of miracles acts ὅταν καιρὸς ᾖ). νῦν κ. ταῦτα ὑμᾶς μαθεῖν οὐκ ἔστιν *now is not the time for you to learn this* AcPl Ha 1, 26 (Just., D. 8, 1 ἃ νῦν κ. οὐκ ἔστι λέγειν al.).—καιρὸν λαβεῖν *find a favorable time, seize the opportunity* (Lysias, C. Agor. 6; Cleanthes [III BC]: Stoic. I no. 573; Diod. S. 2, 6, 5; EpArist 248; Jos., Bell. 1, 527, Ant. 4, 10; cp. PTebt 332, 9). καιρὸν μεταλαβεῖν (s. μεταλαμβάνω 2) **Ac 24:25.** λαβεῖν κ. εὔθετον *find a convenient opportunity* Pol 13:1. κ. ἔχειν *have opportunity* (Thu. 1, 42, 3; Pla., Ep. 7, 324b; Plut., Lucull. 501 [16, 4]; PFlor 259, 3; 1 Macc 15:34; Jos., Ant. 16, 73; 335; Ath., R. 23 p. 77, 6; Did., Gen. 112, 10) **Gal 6:10; Hb 11:15;** 2 Cl 16:1; ISm 9:1; IRo 2:1. ὀλίγον καιρὸν ἔχειν **Rv 12:12.** ἐξαγοράζεσθαι τὸν κ. *make the most of the opportunity* **Col 4:5; Eph 5:16** (s. ἐξαγοράζω 2). On **Ro 12:11 v.l.** s. δουλεύω 2aβ and b. κατὰ κ. **Ro 5:6** is more naturally construed with ἀπέθανεν than with ἀσεβῶν (cp. κατὰ καιρὸν θεριζόμενος *reaped in its proper time* Job 5:26).—The concept of the appropriate time oft. blends with that of

❷ **a defined period for an event.** ***definite, fixed time.*** Abs. καιροί *festal seasons* (Ex 23:14, 17; Lev 23:4.—So perh. also beside θυσίαι in the Ins de Sinuri ed. LRobert '45 no. 42) **Gal 4:10** (κ. w. ἡμέρα as Polyaenus 8, 23, 17). τὰς τῶν καιρῶν ἀλλαγὰς καταδιαιρεῖν . . . ἃ μὲν εἰς ἑορτάς, ἃς δὲ εἰς πένθη *to set up periods of fasting and mourning in accord with changes in seasons* Dg 4:5.—Not infreq. w. a gen., which indicates the reason why the time is set apart (Pla., Leg. 4, 709c χειμῶνος καιρός; Aesop, Fab. 258 P.=255 H-H.//206 Ch. ἀπολογίας κ., also oft. LXX; Philo, Spec. Leg. 1, 191 κ. εὐφροσύνης; Jos., Ant. 18, 74; Tat. 36, 1 κατ' ἐκεῖνον αὐτὸν . . . τὸν τοῦ πολέμου κ.; Hippol., Ref. 9, 30, 27 κ. τῆς παρουσίας; Did., Gen. 175, 2 κ. τοῦ ἐξελθεῖν εἰς τὴν γῆν) κ. θερισμοῦ *time of harvest* **Mt 13:30** (JosAs 2:19). κ. τῶν καρπῶν *time when the fruit is ripe* **21:34;** cp. vs. **41.** κ. σύκων *time when the figs are ripe* **Mk 11:13** (ParJer 5:31; cp. Horapollo 2, 92 ὁ κ. τῶν ἀμπέλων). κ. μετανοίας *time for repentance* 2 Cl 8:2. κ. πειρασμοῦ **Lk 8:13b.** ὁ κ. τῆς ἀναλύσεως *the time of death* **2 Ti 4:6.** κ. ἐπισκοπῆς σου **Lk 19:44.** κ. διορθώσεως **Hb 9:10.** κ. ἡλικίας **11:11.** κ. τῆς ἡγεμονίας Ποντίου Πιλάτου *the time of the procuratorship of P. P.* IMg 11. κατὰ τὸν καιρὸν τοῦ μαρτυρίου *at the time of martyrdom* EpilMosq 2 (cp. Mel., HE 4, 26, 3 ᾧ Σάγαρις καιρῷ ἐμαρτύρησεν). ἐν τῷ ἑαυτοῦ καιρῷ (Num 9:7) **2 Th 2:6.** ὁ κ. αὐτῶν the time set for the fulfillment of Gabriel's words **Lk 1:20;** cp. Dg 11:5 (s. διαγγέλλω 2). ὁ κ. μου *my time*=the time of my death **Mt 26:18.** κ. τοῦ ἰαθῆναι *time to be healed* 2 Cl 9:7. κ. τοῦ ἄρξασθαι τὸ κρίμα **1 Pt 4:17;** cp. the extraordinary ἦλθεν ὁ κ. τῶν νεκρῶν κριθῆναι καὶ δοῦναι = ἵνα κριθῶσιν οἱ νεκροὶ καὶ δῷς **Rv 11:18.**—Pl. (Num 9:3 κατὰ καιρούς; Tob 14:4 S πάντα συμβήσεται τοῖς καιροῖς αὐτῶν; Heraclit. Sto. 11 p. 18, 18=the periods of time between; Maximus Tyr. 1, 2f πολλοὶ κ.; TestNapht 7:1 δεῖ ταῦτα πληρωθῆναι κατὰ τοὺς καιροὺς αὐτῶν; Ar. 4, 2 κατὰ καιρούς) καιροὶ ἐθνῶν *times of the Gentiles* (in which they may inflict harm on God's people or themselves be converted) **Lk 21:24.**—κατὰ καιρόν *at the appropriate time* (Arrian, Anab. 4, 5, 1; PSI 433, 4 [261 BC]; Just., A I, 19, 4; Mel., HE 4, 26, 3) **J 5:4;** 1 Cl 56:15 (Job 5:26). Also ἐν καιρῷ (Himerius, Or 13 [Ecl. 14], 3): ἐν καιρῷ αὐτοῦ B 11:6, 8 (Ps 1:3). καιρῷ ἰδίῳ *in due time* **Gal 6:9.** Pl. καιροῖς ἰδίοις *at the right time* **1 Ti 2:6; 6:15; Tit 1:3;** cp. 1 Cl 20:4 (Just., D. 131, 4 πρὸ τῶν ἰδίων κ.).—κατὰ τὸν ἴδιον καιρόν vs. 10.—πεπλήρωται ὁ κ. *the time* (determined by God) *is fulfilled* **Mk 1:15.** Pl. (cp. Ps 103:19) ὁρίσας προστεταγμένους καιρούς *he* (God) *has determined allotted times* (MDibelius, SBHeidAk '38/39, 2. Abh. p. 6f, 'seasons'; cp. 1QM 10, 12–15; FMussner, Einige Parallelen [Qumran and Areopagus speech], BZ 1, '57, 125–30) **Ac 17:26;** cp. κατὰ καιροὺς τεταγμένους 1 Cl 40:1; ὡρισμένοις καιροῖς καὶ ὥραις vs. 2; τοῖς προστεταγμένοις κ. vs. 4.

❸ **a period characterized by some aspect of special crisis, *time*—ⓐ** gener.: *the present (time)* **Ro 13:11; 12:11 v.l.** ὁ καιρός (i.e. the crisis involving Christians) ἀπαιτεῖ σε *the times call upon you* IPol 2:3 (Diod. S. 17, 27, 2 ὑπὸ τῶν καιρῶν προεκλήθησαν=they were called out by the [critical circumstances of the] times). Also ὁ νῦν κ. (PSI 402, 7 [III BC] ἐν τῷ νῦν καιρῷ) **Ro 3:26; 8:18; 11:5; 2 Cor 8:14;** B 4:1. κ. ὁ νῦν τῆς ἀνομίας *the present godless time* 18:2 (s. also b below). ὁ κ. ὁ ἐνεστηκώς (Polyb. 1, 60, 9; Jos., Ant. 16, 162) **Hb 9:9;** ἐν ἐκείνῳ τῷ κ. *at that time, then* (Gen 21:22; Is 38:1; τῷ κ. ἐκείνῳ TestSol D 8, 2) **Mt 11:25; 12:1; 14:1;** cp. **Eph 2:12.** Also κατ' ἐκεῖνον τὸν κ. (Jos., Ant. 1, 171, Vi. 49; GJs 10:2.—Diod. S. 2, 27, 1 and Vi. Aesopi G 81 P. κατ' ἐκείνους τοὺς καιρούς=at that time. Cp. κατ' ἐκεῖνο καιροῦ Hippol., Ref. 9, 12, 10.) **Ac 12:1; 19:23.** ἔτι κατὰ καιρὸν ὑπὲρ ἀσεβῶν *for those who at that time were still godless* **Ro 5:6,** though κατὰ κ. here prob.=*at the right time,* as in mng. 1b above (s. B-D-F §255, 3). τῷ τότε τῆς ἀδικίας καιρῷ . . . τὸν νῦν τῆς δικαιοσύνης Dg 9:1; cp. 9:2. Of the future κατὰ τ. καιρὸν τοῦτον *at this time* **Ro 9:9** (Gen 18:10, 14). Cp. EpilMosq 2 in 2 above. ἐν αὐτῷ τῷ κ. *just at that time* (2 Esdr 5:3) **Lk 13:1.** W. attraction of the relative ἐν ᾧ κ. *at that time, then* **Ac 7:20.** κατὰ τὸν καιρὸν ὃν καὶ πέρυσι *at the same time as in the year preceding* Hv 2, 1, 1.

ⓑ One of the chief terms relating to the endtime: ὁ καιρός *the time of crisis, the last times* (FBusch, Z. Verständnis d. synopt. Eschatol. Mk 13 neu untersucht '38; GDelling, D. Zeitverständn. des NTs '40; WMichaelis, D. Herr verzieht nicht d. Verheissung '42; WKümmel, Verheissung. u. Erfüllung '45,[3] '56; OCullmann, Christus u. d. Zeit '46 [tr. FFilson, Christ and Time '50, 39–45; 79; 121]) ὁ κ. ἤγγικεν **Lk 21:8.** ὁ κ. ἐγγύς **Rv 1:3; 22:10.** οὐκ οἴδατε πότε ὁ καιρός ἐστιν **Mk 13:33.** Cp. **Ro 13:11** (s. 3a above) if it is to be interpreted as eschatological (cp. Plut., Mor. 549f). πρὸ καιροῦ *before the endtime and the judgment* **Mt 8:29; 1 Cor 4:5.** ἐν καιρῷ **1 Pt 5:6.** Also ἐν καιρῷ ἐσχάτῳ **1:5;** D 16:2. Pl. πλήρωμα τῶν καιρῶν **Eph 1:10.** ἐπηρώτων . . . περὶ τῶν καιρῶν, εἰ ἤδη συντέλειά ἐστιν Hv 3, 8, 9. τὰ σημεῖα τ. καιρῶν *the signs of the (Messianic) times* **Mt 16:3.** τοὺς καιροὺς καταμάνθανε *learn to understand the times* IPol 3:2 (s. WBauer, Hdb. suppl. vol. ad loc.) The Messianic times described as καιροὶ ἀναψύξεως **Ac 3:20.**—ἔσχατοι καιροί (or ὕστεροι καιροί **1 Ti 4:1**) come before the ἔσχατος κ. IEph 11:1 (cp. ἐπ' ἐσχάτων κ. AcPl Ha 8, 26 [restoration is certain=Ox 1601, 40//BMM recto 34]); χρόνοι ἢ καιροί *times and seasons* (cp. Iren. 1, 17, 2 [Harv. I 168, 9] and καιρῶν κατὰ χρόνους ἀλλαγή Theoph. Ant. 1, 6 [p. 70, 1]; Artem. 4, 2 p. 203, 25f the χρόνος is divided into καιροὶ καὶ ὧραι), which must be completed before the final consummation **Ac 1:7** (Straton of Lamps. in FWehrli, Die Schule des Aristoteles, V fgm. 10, 32f κατὰ τοὺς καιροὺς καὶ τοὺς χρόνους; quoted in JBarr, Biblical Words for Time, '62, 33; see also Diog. L. 5, 64); cp. **1 Th 5:1.** συντέμνειν τοὺς καιρούς *shorten the (last) times* B 4:3. Sim. in sg. ὁ καιρὸς συνεσταλμένος ἐστίν **1 Cor 7:29.**—The expr. καιρὸν καὶ καιροὺς κ. ἥμισυ καιροῦ also belongs to the eschatol. vocab.; it means the apocalyptic time of $1 + 2 + 1/2 = 3\,1/2$ years, during which acc. to Da 12:7 (cp. 7:25) a tyrranical enemy of God and God's people is to reign on earth **Rv 12:14** (in imagery of a serpentine monster, δράκων)—ὁ κ. οὗτος *the present age* (cp. αἰών 2a) **Mk 10:30; Lk 12:56; 18:30.** Also ὁ νῦν κ. B 4:1. As ruled by the devil: ὁ ἄνομος κ. 4:9. καταργεῖν τὸν κ. τοῦ ἀνόμου *destroy the age of the lawless one* 15:5. The soul seeks και[ρο]ῦ χρόνου αἰῶνος ἀνάπαυσιν ἐ[ν] σιγῇ *peace in silence, at the time of the aeon crisis* GMary 463, 1.—On Dg 12:9 s. the editions of vGebh.-Harnack and Bihlmeyer.—JMánek, NTS 6, '59, 45–51; JBarr, Biblical Words for Time, '62.—B. 954. Schmidt, Syn. II 54–72. DELG. M-M. EDNT. TW. Sv.

Καῖσαρ, αρος, ὁ (=Lat. Caesar; on the distribution of this word, freq. found in lit., ins, pap s. Hahn [sources and lit. 123, 3] and Magie.—Philo, Joseph., Ar. [ins], Just., SibOr, loanw. in rabb.—In our lit. w. the art. only **Mt 22:21 v.l.; Lk 20:25 v.l.; J 19:12** [s. B-D-F §254, 1]; Just., A I, 17, 1) ***emperor, Caesar*** (orig. a proper name, then used as a title) **Mt 22:17, 21a; Mk 12:14, 16; Lk 20:22, 24; 23:2** (s. φόρος); **J 19:12b** (cp. Philo, In Flacc. 40), **15; Ac 17:7; 25:8, 10–12, 21; 26:32; 27:24; 28:19;** κύριος Κ. MPol 8:2. ὀμνύναι τὴν Καίσαρος τύχην (s. τύχη)

9:2; 10:1. τὰ Καίσαρος *what belongs to the emperor* **Mt 22:21b; Mk 12:17; Lk 20:25** (HWindisch, Imperium u. Evangelium im NT '31; KPieper ThGl 25, '33, 661–69; EStauffer, Gott u. Kaiser im NT '35; GKittel, Christus u. Imperator '39; JBenum, Gud och Kejsaren '40; HLoewe, 'Render Unto Caesar' '40; NHommes, God en Kejzer in het NT '41; OEck, Urgem. u. Imperium '41; MDibelius, Rom u. die Christen im 1. Jahrh. '42; JDerrett, Law in the NT, '70). φίλος τ. Καίσαρος *friend of the emperor* (as official title CIG 3499, 4; 3500, 4; Epict. 3, 4, 2; 4, 1, 8; 45–48; 95; 4, 4, 5; Jos., Ant. 14, 131) **J 19:12a** (EBamel, TLZ 77, '52, 205–10); AcPl Ha 11, 4. οἱ ἐκ τῆς Καίσαρος οἰκίας *those (slaves) who belong to the emperor's household* **Phil 4:22** (s. Lghtf., Phil 171ff; Dssm., LO 127, 1; 202, 3; 380 [LAE 382]; New Docs 3, 7–9; and s. οἰκία 3).—W. proper names Τιβέριος Κ. *Emperor Tiberius* **Lk 3:1** (Just., A I, 13, 3). ἐπὶ Κλαυδίου Κ. **Ac 11:28 v.l.** (cp. Just., A I, 26, 2; 56, 2). Κ. Νέρων **2 Ti subscr.;** without name AcPl Ha 9, 4; 14; 26. But Καῖσαρ Αὔγουστος Caesar Augustus **Lk 2:1,** since here K. is not a title, but a part of the name (Bl-D. §5, 3a).—Pauly-W. Suppl. IV 806–53; IX 1139–54; Kl. Pauly II 1110–122; IV 1135–40. B. 1324. M-M. TW.

Καισάρεια, ας, ἡ (Καισαρία a wrong accent; s. W-S. §5, 13c end) ***Caesarea.***—❶ Καισάρεια ἡ Φιλίππου *C. Philippi,* a city at the foot of Mt. Hermon, once known as Paneas, rebuilt by Philip the Tetrarch and made an important city; he named it Caesarea in honor of Tiberius Caesar (Jos., Ant. 18, 28, Bell. 2, 168) **Mt 16:13.** αἱ κῶμαι Κ. τῆς Φ. are villages near the city **Mk 8:27.**—Schürer II 169–71 (sources and lit.); Dalman, Orte[3] (index).

❷ Καισάρεια without further designation is *Caesarea* 'by the sea' (Philo, Leg. ad Gai. 305; Jos., Bell. 7, 23 [here both Caesareas together]), located south of Mt. Carmel, founded by Herod the Great on the site of the ancient Straton's Tower, named C. in honor of Augustus Caesar; later became the seat of the Roman procurators (Jos., Ant. 13, 313; 15, 293; 331ff; 19, 343, Bell. 1, 408–14, s. index). **Ac 8:40; 9:30; 10:1, 24; 11:11; 12:19; 18:22; 21:8, 16; 23:23, 33; 25:1, 4, 6, 13.**—Schürer II 115–18 (sources and lit.); LHaefeli, Caesarea am Meere 1923; CKopp, The Holy Places of the Gospels, tr. RWalls, '63, 231–35; ANeger, Encyclopedia of Archaeological Excavations in the Holy Land I, '75, 270–85; BHHW I 295f; Kl. Pauly III 48f; OEANE I 399–404.—M-M.

καίτοι, καίτοιγε s. καί 2iδ.

καίω (Hom.+) fut. καύσω LXX; 1 aor. ἔκαυσα. Pass. 1 aor. inf. καυθῆναι (MPol 5:2 v.l.) and 2 aor. (B-D-F §76, 1; Rob. 349f) καῆναι (MPol 5:2; 12:3); fut. καυθήσομαι (καυθήσωμαι **1 Cor 13:3 v.l.,** an impossible form, s. W-S. §13, 7; B-D-F §28; Mlt-H. 219) and καήσομαι (Hs 4, 4); pf. ptc. κεκαυμένος.

❶ **to cause to be lighted or be on fire, *to light, to have/keep burning*—ⓐ** lit. λύχνον *a lamp* (Posidon: 87 fgm. 94 Jac.; cp. Lev 24:2, 4; Jos., C. Ap. 1, 308; PGM 4, 2372) **Mt 5:15** (so act. καίω τι X., An. 4, 4, 12; 4, 1, 11; EpJer 18. But, in contrast to ἅπτω, κ. lays the emphasis less upon the act of lighting than on keeping a thing burning; s. Jülicher, Gleichn. 80.—Diod. S. 13, 111, 2 πυρὰ κάειν=keep fires burning). Pass. w. act. sense *be lit, burn* **Mk 4:21 v.l.** λύχνοι καιόμενοι (Artem. 2, 9; cp. Phlegon: 257 fgm. 36. 1, 1 Jac. καιομένου τοῦ λύχνου; Ex 27:20; Jos., Ant. 8, 90) **Lk 12:35; J 5:35;** λαμπάδες . . . καιόμεναι **Rv 4:5;** GJs 7:2; cp. ἀστὴρ . . . καιόμενος ὡς λαμπάς **Rv 8:10.** πῦρ καιόμενον (Hdt. 1, 86; Is 4:5; SibOr 7, 6) MPol 11:2a. κλίβανος καιόμενος *a burning* or *heated oven* (Hos 7:4) 2 Cl 16:3. W. πυρί added (Pla., Phd. 113a εἰς τόπον μέγαν πυρὶ πολλῷ καιόμενον) **Hb 12:18** (cp. Dt 4:11; 5:23; 9:15); **Rv 8:8.** πυρὶ καὶ θείῳ *w. fire and brimstone* (cp. Is 30:33) **21:8;** cp. **19:20.**

ⓑ fig. of emotional experience (schol. on Apollon. Rhod. 3, 762 ἡ ὀδύνη καίουσα; Philo, Decal. 49 καιόμενοι κ. κατακαιόμενοι ὑπὸ τ. ἐπιθυμιῶν) of the heart οὐχὶ ἡ καρδία ἡμῶν καιομένη ἦν; *were not our hearts burning?* **Lk 24:32** (cp. PGM 7, 472 καιομένην τὴν ψυχὴν κ. τὴν καρδίαν; TestNapht 7:4 ἐκαιόμην τοῖς σπλάγχνοις. PGrenf I, 1 I, 9 [II BC] συνοδηγὸν ἔχω τὸ πολὺ πῦρ τὸ ἐν τῇ ψυχῇ μου καιόμενον. Cp. Ps 38:4. On the variants s. in addition to the comm. WAllen, JTS 2, 1901, 299).

❷ **to cause someth. to burn so as to be consumed, *burn (up)*** act. trans. (Hom. et al.; Job 15:34; Just., A I, 53f) MPol 18:1. Pass. intr. *be burned* (Is 5:24; Jos., Ant. 4, 248 [ἡ παιδίσκη] καιέσθω ζῶσα) **Mt 13:40 v.l.** (for κατακαίεται, s. κατακαίω) **J 15:6;** Hs 4:4. The stones being burned Hv 3, 2, 9; 3, 7, 2 are to be understood as representing apostates: ApcPt Bodl. (restored by Bartlet).—MPol 12:3a. σὰρξ καιομένη 15:2. δεῖ με ζῶντα καυθῆναι *I must be burned alive* 5:2; cp. 12:3b (Ael. Aristid, 36, 67 K.=48 p. 465 D.: καυθήσεσθαι ζῶντες; 45 p. 74 D.; Appian, Hann. 31 §132 ζῶντας ἔκαυσε). The mng. is disputed in ἐὰν παραδῶ τὸ σῶμά μου ἵνα καυθήσομαι **1 Cor 13:3 v.l.** (for καυχήσωμαι; s. καυχάομαι 1). Most scholars in this connection think of martyrdom (e.g. Ltzm., JSickenberger, H-D Wendland.—Cp. e.g. Da 3:19f; 2 Macc 7:5; 4 Macc 6:26; 7:12; Jos., Ant. 17, 167. Also Dio Chrys. 7 [8], 16 μαστιγούμενον κ. τεμνόμενον κ. καόμενον).—JWeiss (in Meyer[9]) and FDölger (Antike u. Christentum I 1929, 254–70) prefer to interpret it as voluntary self-burning (Diod. S. 17, 107, 1–6 Κάλανος; Lucian, Peregr. 20 καύσων ἑαυτόν of Peregr.; RFick, D. ind. Weise Kalanos u. s. Flammentod: NGG, Phil.-hist. Kl. '38; NMacnicol, ET 55, '43/44, 50–52). KSchmidt (TW III 466–69) leaves the choice open betw. the two possibilities mentioned.—Preuschen (ZNW 16, 1915, 127–38) interprets it to mean *brand, mark as a slave by branding,* i.e. to sell oneself as a slave and present the purchase price to charity (for the idea s. 1 Cl 55:2).—B. 75. DELG. M-M. TW.

κἀκεῖ adv. (formed by crasis [on crasis in the NT s. HvSoden, D. Schriften d. NT I/2, 1911, 1380f] fr. καὶ ἐκεῖ; variously rendered in the mss.). Found Eratosth. p. 22, 11; 31, 10; Diod. S. 4, 34, 1; 4, 85, 5; Att. ins fr. I BC [Meisterhans[3]-Schw.]; 3 Macc 7:19; in other LXX pass. in individ. mss. [Thackeray 138]; En 10:4 al.; TestSol 8:5 P; GrBar; Jos., Ant. 16, 299; Just., D. 56, 6 al.; Mel. fgm. 8b [2], 15).

❶ **marker of addition of location, *and there* Mt 5:23; 10:11; 28:10** (v.l. καὶ ἐκεῖ); **Mk 1:35; 14:15 v.l.** (for καὶ ἐκεῖ); **J 11:54; Ac 14:7; 22:10; 25:20; 27:6;** ApcPt 18:33. ὧδε κἀκεῖ Hm 5, 2, 7; s 9, 3, 1 (κἀκεῖσε cod. A in both).

❷ **marker of location with emphasis on connection with earlier narrative matter, *there also* Mk 1:38 v.l.** (for καὶ ἐκεῖ); **Ac 17:13.** κἀκεῖ δέ *but there also* 1 Cl 41:2.

κἀκεῖθεν adv. (formed by crasis fr. καὶ ἐκεῖθεν. Ins fr. Athens in SIG 640, 8 [175/174 BC]; not LXX [Thackeray 138]).

❶ **extension of a source that is away fr. the speaker, *and from there*** (En 21:7 al.; JosAs 24:21 cod. A; Lucian, Dial. Deor. 7, 4; Jos., Ant. 14, 379) **Mk 9:30; Lk 11:53; Ac 7:4; 14:26; 16:12; 20:15; 21:1; 27:4; 28:15;** MPol 7:1.

❷ **a point of time subsequent to another point of time, *and then*** (ἐκεῖθεν in this mng. in Diod, S. and Cass. Dio) **Ac 13:21.**

κἀκεῖνος, η, ο (formed by crasis fr. καὶ ἐκεῖνος; variously rendered in the mss.; X., Cyr. 5, 5, 29 codd.; Diod. S. 3, 17, 5; 4, 84, 4; 11, 56, 8; PParis 2 col. 15 [before 165 BC]; Wsd 18:1; Is 57:6; 2 Macc 1:15 [s. Thackeray 138]; TestSol 9:7 P; TestReub 6:2; Just.; Ath., R. 19, p. 72, 6).

❶ **pert. to being relatively distant, in specification of narrative characters or items,** ***and that (one, thing)***—ⓐ *and that one, and he* or *she* **Lk 11:7** κ. ἔσωθεν *the other, namely the one inside;* **22:12; Ac 18:19; Hb 4:2.** After ταῦτα *this . . . and that, the one . . . and the other* **Mt 23:23** (par. **Lk 11:42**).

ⓑ *that one also, also he* or *she* (Lucian, Dial. Deor. 2, 2; 7, 3; Just., D. 17, 1; 122, 1; 123, 1) **J 10:16; 17:24; Ac 5:37; 15:11; 1 Cor 10:6; 2 Ti 2:12; Hb 4:2.** κἀκεῖνοι δέ **Ro 11:23.**

❷ **pert. to specification of an entity, w. ascensive force in ref. to what is highlighted**—ⓐ ***and he, and it (that)*** **Mt 15:18** κἀκεῖνα κοινοῖ *and that's what defiles;* **Mk 16:11** κἀκεῖνοι ἀκούσαντες *they in turn, on hearing;* **J 6:57** καὶ ὁ τρώγων με κἀκεῖνος ζήσει *so also the one who eats me is the one who will live;* **7:29** κἀκεῖνός με ἀπέστειλεν *and that's the one who sent me* (sim. **14:12**); **19:35 v.l.** (for καὶ ἐ.); sim.

ⓑ ***this one, that one*** (Jos., Ant, 14, 474) **Mk 12:4f** (par. **Lk 20:11**); **16:13.**

κἀκεῖσε adv. (formed by crasis fr. καὶ ἐκεῖσε; Appian, Iber. 26 §103; Herodian 4, 8, 6; Jos., Ant, 7, 327) ***and there, and thither,*** always w. ὧδε (Aesop 62) the rdg. of cod. A for καὶ ἐκεῖ Hs 6, 1, 6; 6, 2, 7; for κἀκεῖ m 5, 2, 7; s 9, 3, 1.

κακία, ας, ἡ (s. κακός; Theognis, Pre-Socr.+)—❶ **the quality or state of wickedness,** ***baseness, depravity, wickedness, vice.*** κ. is the opposite of ἀρετή and all virtue and therefore lacking in social value (X., Mem. 1, 2, 28; Aristot., Rhet. 2, 6; EN 2, 3–7; Cicero, Tusc. 4, 15; Appian, Bell. Civ. 4, 129 §544 κακία-ἀρετή; Just., A I, 28, 4 and Ath. 24, 4; R. 22 p. 75, 11; Herm. Wr. 9, 4b; SIG 1268, 18 κακίας ἀπέχου; Sb 4127, 6; Wsd 7:30; 12:2, 10; Sir 14:6, 7 al.; LXX; oft. Philo; Jos., Ant. 8, 252; Orig., C. Cels. 2, 76, 82; Did., Gen. 39, 24) 2 Cl 10:1. περισσεία κακίας *excess of wickedness* **Js 1:21.** δεσμὸς κακίας *fetter of wickedness* IEph 19:3. W. πονηρία in the same general mng. (cp. Ael. Aristid. 33 p. 625 D.; Sir 25:17, 19) **1 Cor 5:8.** πάσης κ. πλήρης 1 Cl 45:7. τῇ κακίᾳ νηπιάζειν *be a child as far as wickedness is concerned* i.e. have as little experience in wickedness as a child has **1 Cor 14:20;** cp. Hs 9, 29, 1; 3. μετανόησον ἀπὸ τ. κακίας σου ταύτης **Ac 8:22** (Just., D. 109, 1). ὡς ἐπικάλυμμα ἔχοντες τ. κακίας τὴν ἐλευθερίαν *use freedom as a cloak for wickedness* **1 Pt 2:16** (cp. ἵνα μὴ εἰς ἐπικάλλυμα κακίας καταχρησώμεθα τῇ ἐλευθερίᾳ Iren. 4, 37, 4 [Harv. II 288, 11]; s. ἐπικάλλυμα).

❷ **a mean-spirited or vicious attitude or disposition,** ***malice, ill-will, malignity*** (Diod. S. 1, 1; PRein 7, 15 [II BC]; POxy 1101, 7; Philo; Just., D. 65, 2 ἁπλῶς καὶ μὴ μετὰ κακίας εἰπών; 136, 2; Tat. 34, 1) w. other vices **Ro 1:29; Eph 4:31; Col 3:8; Tit 3:3; 1 Pt 2:1;** B 20:1; D 5:1. τὸ στόμα σου ἐπλεόνασεν κακίαν 1 Cl 35:8 (Ps 49:19). Cp. B 2:8 (Zech 8:17).

❸ **a state involving difficult circumstances,** ***trouble, misfortune*** (Thu. 3, 58, 1 opp. ἡδονή; 1 Km 6:9; Eccl 7:14 ἐν ἡμέρᾳ κακίας; 12:1; Sir 19:6; Am 3:6; 1 Macc 7:23; Jos., Ant. 1, 97; Just., D. 142, 3) ἀρκετὸν τῇ ἡμέρᾳ ἡ κ. αὐτῆς *each day has enough trouble of its own* **Mt 6:34**—GBaumbach, Das Verständnis des Bösen in den synopt. Evv., '63.—DELG s.v. κακός. M-M. TW. Sv.

κακοδιδασκαλέω (Sext. Emp., Adv. Math. 2, 42; s. κακοδιδασκαλία and καλοδιδάσκαλος) ***teach evil*** τινά *to someone* τὰς ἀναιτίους ψυχάς *to innocent souls* 2 Cl 10:5.

κακοδιδασκαλία, ας, ἡ ***evil/false teaching*** IPhld 2:1 (=κακὴ διδασκαλία IEph 16:2).

κακοήθεια, ας, ἡ (s. κακός, ἦθος; X., Pla. et al.; T. Kellis 22, 22) **a basic defect in character that leads one to be hurtful to others,** ***meanspiritedness, malice, malignity, craftiness*** (so Polyb. 5, 50, 5; Vett. Val. 44, 20; PGrenf I, 60, 13 [cp. Sb 5112, 15]; Esth 8:12f; 3 Macc 3:22; Jos., Ant. 1, 50; 16, 68, C. Ap. 1, 222 [w. φθόνος]; Tat. 16, 1) in a catalogue of vices (Apollonius of Tyana, Ep. 43 [Philostrat. I 354, 6]: φθόνου, κακοηθείας, μίσους, διαβολῆς, ἔχθρας) **Ro 1:29;** 1 Cl 35:5 (Aristot., Rhet. 2, 13 p. 1389b, 20f defines it thus: ἔστι κακοήθεια τὸ ἐπὶ τὸ χεῖρον ὑπολαμβάνειν ἅπαντα=malice means seeing the worst in everything; Ammonius [100 AD] p. 80 Valck. defines it as κακία κεκρυμμένη=baseness lurking in the shadows. Cp. 4 Macc 1:4; 3:4).—DELG s.v. ἦθος. M-M. TW. Spicq.

κακοήθης, ες (s. prec. entry; Pla., Menand. et al.; Vett. Val. 47, 2; 4; PGiss 40 II, 11; 4 Macc 1:25; 2:16; Philo, Somn. 2, 192; Jos., Ant. 1, 42; contrast καλοήθης in a list of virtues: Cat. Cod. Astr. XII 100, 9) ***malicious, spiteful*** D 2:6.—M-M. s.v. κακοήθεια.

κακολάλος s. κατάλαλος.

κακολογέω impf. 3 sg. ἐκακολόγει 2 Macc 4:1; 3 pl. ἐκακολόγουν Ezk 22:7; fut. 2 sg. οκακολογήσεις Ex 22:27 (κακολόγος 'slanderer'; Lysias 8, 5; Plut., Vett. Val. et al.; PFay 12, 15 [II BC]; PRyl 150, 9; SB V/2, 7835, 15f [I BC]; LXX) ***speak evil of, revile, insult*** τινά *someone* (Jos., Ant. 20, 180) **Mk 9:39.** πατέρα ἢ μητέρα **Mt 15:4; Mk 7:10** (both Ex 21:16; cp. Pr 20:9a: Ezk 22:7). τὶ *someth.* τὴν ὁδόν *the Way* (i.e. Christian way of life) **Ac 19:9.** Abs. D 2:3.—DELG s.v. λέγω B2b. New Docs 2, 88, w. critique of M-M. TW.

κακοπάθεια s. κακοπαθία.

κακοπαθέω (s. next entry) 1 aor. ἐκακοπάθησα, impv. κακοπάθησον.

❶ ***suffer misfortune*** (X., Mem. 1, 4, 11; Polyb. 3, 72, 5; Teles 61, 6; Musonius 28, 9; Vett. Val. 106, 10; PEdg 14, 17 [=Sb 6720–257/256 BC]; PLond I, 98 recto, 73 p. 130 [I/II AD]; PRyl 28, 84; Jon 4:10; EpArist 241; Philo, Somn. 2, 181; Jos., Ant. 12, 336, C. Ap. 2, 203) **2 Ti 2:9; Js 5:13;** 2 Cl 19:3. (On Ox 1602, 23f s. the editor's note on the correction of καλοπαθοῦντες in the pap; the duplicate AcPl Ha 8, 19 reads [π]ο̣λλὰ γὰρ παθόντες//BMM recto 24.)

❷ ***bear hardship patiently*** (Aristot., EN 10, 6, 1176b, 29; Appian, Bell. Civ. 5, 87 §364; Philo, Virt. 88; Jos., Ant. 10, 220) **2 Ti 4:5.**—DELG s.v. πάσχω. M-M. TW. Spicq.

κακοπαθία, ας, ἡ (this spelling in ins since III BC; also BGU 1209, 7 [23 BC]; alternate sp. in mss. κακοπάθεια [s. W-S. §5, 13c, p. 44f; B-D-F §23; s. prec. entry]) ***suffering.*** Both in the pass. sense as *suffering, misfortune, misery* that come to a person (Thu. 7, 77, 1 al.; Mal 1:13; 2 Macc 2:26f; EpArist 208; Philo, De Jos. 223; Ath., R. 18 p. 71, 10; R. 22, p. 75, 19), as well as in the active mng. *suffering* that a person endures, *a strenuous effort* that one makes, or *perseverance* that one practices (Polyb. 3, 42, 9; 4, 8, 3; Plut., Numa 3, 5; Vett. Val. 277, 16; 4 Macc 9:8; EpArist 92; 259. The ins since OGI 244, 12 [III BC], s. the editor's note. Also the pap [BGU] mentioned above; s. Dssm.,

NB 91f [BS 263f]; Thieme 29). The latter mng. is apparently the preferred one in later times, and is therefore to be accepted in **Js 5:10** (v.l. καλοκαγαθίας), where it has the further advantage of fitting better into the context. Differently GBjörck, ConNeot 4, '40, 3, who takes κ. w. μακροθ. as hendiadys.—DELG s.v. κακός, πάσχω 2. M-M. TW. Spicq.

κακοποιέω 1 aor. ἐκακοποίησα (s. next entry; Aeschyl. et al.; ins, pap, LXX; Test12Patr; Ar. 13, 5; Tat. 17, 4).

❶ **to do that which is evil or wrong,** ***do wrong, be an evil-doer/criminal,*** intr. (X., Oec. 3, 11; PHib 59, 10 [III BC]; Pr 4:16; TestAsh 2:8) **1 Pt 3:17; 3J 11.** Even **Mk 3:4=Lk 6:9** could belong here. But in these pass. the word may mean

❷ ***harm, injure*** (X., Mem. 3, 5, 26 al.; Musonius 32, 17; SIG 736, 103; 1243, 15; EpArist 164; 168; Gen 31:7; Num 35:23; TestJos 18:2; PFouad 203, 14 ψυχήν). In all four NT pass, it is contrasted w. ἀγαθοποιέω.—M-M. TW.

κακοποιός, όν (s. prec. entry; Pind. et al.; Hippol.) **pert. to doing evil** (Aristot., EN 4, 9 p. 1125a, 18f; Polyb. 15, 25, 1; Sallust. 9 p. 18, 19; Pr 12:4; AscIs 3:13; Ar. 13, 6 [fem.]) subst. ***evil-doer, criminal*** (schol. on Nicander, Alex. 569; PMich 149 [II AD], 10; 16 al.; Pr 24:19) **J 18:30 v.l.; 1 Pt 2:12; 3:16 v.l.; 4:15** (on support for the sense *sorcerer* s. ESelwyn comm. ad loc.). Opp. ἀγαθοποιός **2:14** (Artem. 4, 59 p. 238, 9; 11).—M-M. TW.

κακός, ή, όν (Hom.+; gener. pert. to not meeting accepted standards of behavior, 'bad, worthless, inferior').

❶ **pert. to being socially or morally reprehensible,** ***bad, evil*** (Hom.+; LXX)—ⓐ of pers. ὁ κ. δοῦλος *the bad slave* **Mt 24:48** (TestJob 7:7 κακὴ δούλη); κ. ἐργάτης *evil-doer* **Phil 3:2.** Subst. without art. (Sir 20:18) **Rv 2:2.** κακοὺς κακῶς ἀπολέσει **Mt 21:41** (cp. Hipponax [VI BC] 77, 3 D.[3]; Soph., Phil. 1369; Aristippus in Diog. L. 2, 76 κακοὶ κακῶς ἀπόλοιντο; Nicol. Dam.: 90 fgm. 66, 33 Jac.; Cebes 32, 5; Alciphron 2, 2, 1 κακὸς κακῶς ἀπόλοιτο; Jos., Ant. 2, 300; 7, 291; 12, 256; SIG 526, 46f [III BC] ἐξόλλυσθαι κακῶς κακούς; POxy 1238, 5 κακὸς κακῶς ἀπόλ.).—New Docs 4 p. 31 [lit.].

ⓑ of human characteristics, actions, emotion, plans, etc. (POxy 532, 22 [II AD] ὑπὸ κακοῦ συνειδότος κατεχόμενος; 2 Macc 5:8; 4 Macc 17:2; Just., D. 17, 1 κακῆς προλήψεως; 94, 2 κ. πράξεις; 121, 3 πολιτείας) διαλογισμοί *evil thoughts* **Mk 7:21.** ἐπιθυμία *base desire* (Menand., fgm. 718, 7 Kö.=535, 7 Kock; Pr 12:12; Just., A I, 10, 6) **Col 3:5;** ἔργον κ. *bad deed* **Ro 13:3.** ὁμιλίαι *bad company, evil associations* **1 Cor 15:33** (s. ἦθος). διδασκαλία IEph 16:2; cp. 9:1.

ⓒ neut. as subst. (Hom.+; ins, pap, LXX, TestAsh 1:5; 4:5; Philo; Just., D. 1, 5 al.) τὸ κακόν *evil, wrong* what is contrary to custom or law εἰ κακῶς ἐλάλησα, μαρτύρησον περὶ τοῦ κακοῦ *if I have said something in a wrong way, say what's wrong about it* **J 18:23; Ro 7:21** (opp. τὸ καλόν, the right, the fine, the admirable deed) (Maximus Tyr. 34, 2a: the soul falls victim to [the] κακόν, contrary to its own efforts and in spite of its struggles); **16:19; 1 Cor 13:5; Hb 5:14; 1 Pt 3:10f;** 1 Cl 22, 4 (both Ps 33:15); **3J 11.** Perh. also **Ro 14:20** (s. 2 below). οὐδὲν κ. *nothing wrong* **Ac 23:9.** Pl. *evil deeds* (Ael. Aristid. 45 p. 74 D.; TestSim 5:3; Ar. 13, 7; Just., A I, 28, 4) **Ro 1:30; 1 Cor 10:6; Js 1:13** (s. ἀπείραστος); πάντα τὰ κ. *all evils* **1 Ti 6:10.** μῆνις . . . ἐκ τοσούτων κακῶν συνισταμένη *vengefulness composed of so many evils* Hm 5, 2, 4.—κακὸν ποιεῖν *do (what is) evil* (Menand., Sam. 652 S. [307 Kö.]; Eccl 4:17; Plut., Mor. 523a) **Mt 27:23; Mk 15:14; Lk 23:22; J 18:30** (s. κακοποιός); **2 Cor 13:7; 1 Pt 3:12** (Ps 33:17). Also τὸ κ. ποιεῖν **Ro 13:4a;** τὰ κ. ποιεῖν (Pr 16:12) **3:8;** cp. GPt 4:13. (τὸ) κ. πράσσειν (TestAsh 6:2; only pl. Pr 10:23 and Just., D. 108, 1) **Ro 7:19; 9:11 v.l.; 13:4b; 2 Cor 5:10 v.l.** κατεργάζεσθαι τὸ κ. **2:9.**

❷ **pert. to being harmful or injurious,** ***evil, injurious, dangerous, pernicious,*** of things or conditions (Pr 16:9 ἡμέρα κ.; TestAbr B 4 p. 108, 12 [Stone p. 64] οὐδὲν κ.; Just., A I, 2, 3 φήμη κ.) ἕλκος κ. καὶ πονηρόν **Rv 16:2.** κ. θηρία **Tit 1:12** (cp. POxy 1060, 7 ἀπὸ παντὸς κακοῦ ἑρπετοῦ. On transfer to human beings s. θηρίον 2). θανάσιμον φάρμακον . . ., ὅπερ ὁ ἀγνοῶν ἡδέως λαμβάνει ἐν ἡδονῇ κακῇ *a deadly poison which the ignorant takes with perilous delight* ITr 6:2 (cp. Just., A I, 21, 5 κακῶν καὶ αἰσχρῶν ἡδονῶν). Subst. τὸ κακόν *(the) evil* (Susario Com. [VI BC] κακὸν γυναῖκες; AnthLG: fgm. iamb. adesp. 29 Diehl δῆμος ἄστατον κακόν; Ps.-Pla., Eryxias 8, 395e: opp. τὸ ἀγαθόν; Apollon. Rhod. 3, 129; Theocr. 14, 36; Plut., Lysander 18, 9 of ἄγνοια; Maximus Tyr. 24, 4a μέγιστον ἀνθρώπῳ κακὸν ἐπιθυμία 'desire for more is humanity's worst bane'; TestGad 3:1 [μῖσος]; Philo, Rer. Div. Her. 287 [λιμὸς] . . . κακὸν χεῖρον) of the tongue ἀκατάστατον κακόν **Js 3:8** (s. ἀκατάστατος). (τὰ) κακά *misfortunes* (Appian, Iber. 79, §338; Maximus Tyr. 41, 3aff; schol. on Soph., Trach. 112 p. 286 Papag.; Is 46:7; EpArist 197; 207; TestJob 23:6; TestLevi 10:2; Jos., Bell. 6, 213, Ant. 3, 86) **Lk 16:25; Ac 8:24** D; 2 Cl 10:1; AcPl Ha 3, 10; 11:7. κακόν τι πάσχειν *suffer harm* **Ac 28:5** (cp. EpJer 33; Jos., Ant. 12, 376; Just., A I, 2, 4; Ath. 12, 1). πράσσειν ἑαυτῷ κ. *do harm to oneself* **16:28.** τί κ. ἐστιν; w. inf. foll. *what harm is there?* MPol 8:2. Prob. **Ro 14:20** (s. 1c above) κ. τῷ ἀνθρώπῳ *harmful for the person* belongs here. ἡσυχάσει ἄφοβος ἀπὸ παντὸς κακοῦ *will have rest without fear of any evil* 1Cl 57:7 (Pr 1:33).

❸ Certain passages fall betw. 1 and 2; in them the harm is caused by evil intent, so that 1 and 2 are combined: ***evil, harm, wrong*** **Ro 12:21ab** (cp. the proverb s.v. ἰάομαι 2b. Also Polyaenus 5, 11 οὐ κακῷ κακὸν ἠμυνάμην, ἀλλ' ἀγαθῷ κακόν; but s. SRobertson, ET 60, '48/49, 322). κακά τινι ποιεῖν **Ac 9:13** (the dat. as 4Km 8:12; TestJud 7:8 οὐδὲν κακόν; Vi. Aesopi G 11 P.; Witkowski 64, 12 [95 BC]=PGrenf II, 36 ἡμῖν κακὸν ἐποίησεν; s. B-D-F §157). (διάβολος) ποιήσει τι κακὸν τοῖς δούλοις τοῦ θεοῦ (the devil) *will inflict some kind of harm on God's slaves* Hm 4, 3, 4. κακόν τινι ἐργάζεσθαι **Ro 13:10.** κακά τινι ἐνδείκνυσθαι **2 Ti 4:14** (cp. Da 3:44; TestZeb 3:8). (τινί) κακὸν ἀντὶ κακοῦ ἀποδιδόναι (cp. Paroem. Gr.: Apostol. 18, 33 χρὴ μὴ τὸ κακὸν διὰ κακοῦ ἀμύνασθαι; Mel., P. 90, 676 ἀνταποδοὺς . . . κακὰ ἀντὶ καλῶν) **Ro 12:17; 1 Th 5:15; 1 Pt 3:9;** Pol 2:2.—WLofthouse, Poneron and Kakon in O and NT: ET 60, '48/49, 264–68; s. κακία (GBaumbach).—B. 1177. DELG. M-M. TW.

κακοτεχνία, ας, ἡ (s. κακός, τέχνη; Pla. et al.; ins, pap) ***craftiness, deceit*** pl. *intrigues* (Lucian, Calumn. 12, Alex. 4) of the devil, w. ἐνέδραι IPhld 6:2.—At IPol 5:1, where there is no ref. to the devil, and where Polycarp is advised to make κακοτεχνίαι the subject of preaching, the word seems to mean *evil arts,* i.e. the arts and trades which are forbidden for a Christian, esp. magic. In favor of this interpr. is the fact that the context of this passage deals with conjugal relations in a manner that suggests a warning against recourse to magical formulae that feature erotic themes. S. Zahn, Ign. von Ant. 1873, 321; Lghtf. and Hdb. ad loc. For spells designed for lovers, s. HBetz, The Greek Magical Papyri in Translation including the Demotic Spells, I, '86.

κακουργέω (s. next entry; Eur., Thu. et al.; ins, pap; TestSol 7:7; EpArist 271) ***treat badly*** (Jos., Bell. 2, 277, Ant. 2, 101 al.) pass. of the soul κακουργουμένη σιτίοις καὶ ποτοῖς ἡ ψυχή *the soul when badly treated w. respect to food and drink,* i.e. *when stinted in food and drink* Dg 6:9.—M-M s.v. κακοῦργος.

κακοῦργος, ον (s. prec. entry; [in the form κακοεργός Od. 18, 54] Soph., Hdt.+; TestSol 4:6; SibOr 5, 386; 419; Just., A I, 7, 1, D. 22, 5 [s. Am 6:7]) usu. as subst. ὁ κ. ***criminal, evil-doer*** (Thu. 1, 134, 4 al.; Menand., Dyscolus 258; OGI 669 17 [I AD]; PLille 7, 20 [III BC]; PFay 108, 11; LXX; Philo, In Flacc. 75; Jos., Ant. 2, 59), one who commits gross misdeeds and serious crimes (Diod. S. 20, 81, 3 of pirates; Ep. Socr. 30, 6 w. παράνομος; Syntipas p. 61, 7; 114, 1 w. λῃστής; opp. of the εὐσεβής: Lycurgus, Contra Leocratem 93) **Lk 23:32f, 39** (Plut., Mor. 554b); **2 Ti 2:9;** GPt 4:10, 13; 7:26; Ox 840, 5.—DELG s.v. ἔργον I 1 p. 364. M-M. TW. Spicq.

κακουχέω (s. κακός, ἔχω; since Teles p. 34, 8; pap [in marriage contracts]) ***maltreat, torment*** pass. (Diod. S. 3, 23, 3; 19, 111, 4; Cass. Dio 35, 9; Plut., Mor. 114e; 3 Km 2:26) **Hb 11:37; 13:3.**—M-M.

κακόω fut. κακώσω; 1 aor. ἐκάκωσα; pf. 2 sg. κεκάκωκας 3 Km 17:20. Pass.: 1 aor. ἐκακώθην LXX; pf. inf. κεκακῶσθαι.

❶ **to cause harm to, *harm, mistreat*** w. acc. (Hom.+; PTebt 407, 9 [II AD]; LXX; TestSol 8:11; Test12Patr; Philo, Spec. Leg. 2, 135; Jos., Vi. 121; Just., D. 109, 3 [s. Mi 4:6]) **Ac 7:6** (Gen 15:13), **19; 12:1; 18:10; 1 Pt 3:13.** Pass. 1 Cl 16:7 (Is 53:7).

❷ **to cause someone to think badly about another, *make angry, embitter*** τὰς ψυχάς τινων κατά τινος *poison the minds of some persons against another* **Ac 14:2** (cp. Jos., Ant. 16, 10; pass., 16, 205; 262; Ps 105:32).—DELG s.v. κακός. M-M. TW.

κακῶς adv. of κακός (Hom.+) gener. 'badly'—❶ **pert. to experiencing harm in a physical sense, *bad, badly*—ⓐ** without expression of intensity in the idiom κ. ἔχειν *be ill/sick* (ἔχω 10b) **Mt 4:24; 8:16; 9:12b; 14:35; 17:15 v.l.; Mk 1:32, 34; 2:17; 6:55; Lk 5:31; 7:2.**

ⓑ with expression of intensity κ. πάσχειν (Aeschyl., Prom. 759; Polyb. 3, 90, 13) *suffer severely* **Mt 17:15.** δαιμονίζεσθαι *be severely tormented by a demon* **15:22.**—κακοὺς κ. ἀπολέσει (κακός 1a) **21:41.**

❷ **pert. to being bad in a moral sense, *wrongly, wickedly*** (as Just., A I, 4, 7 κ. ζῆν al.): κ. διακονεῖν Hs 9, 26, 2. κ. λαλεῖν *speak wrongly, wickedly* (1 Macc 7:42) **J 18:23.** Also κ. εἰπεῖν (Libanius, Or. 51 p. 9, 11 F. [opp. ἐπαινεῖν]; Jos., Ant. 6, 299) w. acc. *against* or *about someone* (Pittacus in Diog. L. 1, 78 φίλον μὴ λέγειν κακῶς; Diod. S. 27, 4, 4; Artem. 3, 48; Lucian, Pisc. 6; Procop. Soph., Ep. 161 p. 596) **Ac 23:5** (Ex 22:27; Is 8:21). κ. αἰτεῖσθαι *ask with wrong motives* **Js 4:3.**—M-M. TW.

κάκωσις, εως, ἡ (Thu. et al.; Vett. Val. index; PSI 158, 16; LXX, ParJer, Philo; Jos., Bell. 1, 444, Ant. 13, 151; TestNapht 4:2; difft. TestGad 8:2 πονηρίᾳ καὶ κακώσει 'baseness and wickedness') ***mistreatment, oppression*** (Appian, Samn. 2 §2; Sextus 96) **Ac 7:34** (Ex 3:7). W. πληγή 1 Cl 16:4 (Is 53:4).—M-M.

καλάμη, ης, ἡ (Hom. et al.; pap, LXX) ***stalk, straw*** as a building material (cp. Diod. S. 5, 21, 5 οἰκήσεις ἐκ τῶν καλάμων ἢ ξύλων) **1 Cor 3:12** (collective singular, as Arrian, Ind. 27, 9); the mng. *stubble* (Hom. et al., pap) is less probable.—DELG s.v. κάλαμος 2. M-M.

κάλαμος, ου, ὁ (Pind., Hdt. et al.; pap, LXX, TestSol 5:6 L; TestAbr; TestNaphth 2:8 [windpipe, trachea]; JosAs; ApcMos 29; Joseph.; loanw. in rabb.).

❶ ***reed*** (for detailed account s. Theophr., HP 4, 11 [also RStrömberg, Theophrastea '37, 100f]; 3 Km 14:15; Job 40:21; JosAs), swaying in the wind (Lucian, Hermot. 68 ἐοικὼς … καλάμῳ … πρὸς πᾶν τὸ πνέον καμπτομένῳ) **Mt 11:7; Lk 7:24;** easily broken κ. συντετριμμένος *a bent reed* **Mt 12:20** (cp. Is 42:3 and s. PvanDijk, Het gekrookte riet en de rookende vlaswiek [Mt 12:18 vv.ll.]: GereformTT 23, 1923, 155–72).

❷ ***stalk, staff*** (Artem. 2, 48 p. 150; cp. 4 Km 18:21 ἡ ῥάβδος ἡ καλαμίνη=Jos., Ant. 10, 7 κάλαμος; TestSol 5:6 L) **Mt 27:29f, 48** (acc. to Zohary, Plants 134, the Phragmitis Australis); **Mk 15:19, 36;** GPt 3:9.

❸ ***measuring rod*** (PRyl 64, 2; Ezk 40:3ff; 42:16ff) **Rv 11:1; 21:15f.**

❹ ***reed pen*** (Pla., Phdr. 61 p. 276c; Plut., Demosth. 29, 4; Lucian, Hist. Conscr. 38; Themist., In Constant. p. 31c ἐν καλάμῳ καὶ μέλανι; PGrenf II, 38, 7 [81 BC]; POxy 326; 521, 21; Ps 44:2; 3 Macc 4:20; TestAbr A 12 p. 91, 4 [Stone p. 30]) **3J 13.**—B. 1290. DELG. M-M. TW.

καλάνδαι, ῶν, αἱ (Lat. loanw.: calendae.—Dionys. Hal. 6, 48; 8, 55; 9, 67; 16, 3; Plut., Numa 61 [3, 6], Mar. 412 [12, 3]; ins [indices in SIG, OGI]; pap [Preis., III 90]; Jos., Ant. 14, 228; loanw. in rabb.) ***the calends,*** the first day of the month in the Roman calendar πρὸ ἐννέα καλανδῶν Σεπτεμβρίων=*on August 24* IRo 10:3. πρὸ ἑπτὰ καλ. Μαρτίων on *February 23* MPol 21.

καλέω impf. ἐκάλουν; fut. καλέσω (LXX; JosAs 17:5; 20:6; Jos., Ant. 11, 266.—W-S. §13, 5; B-D-F §74, 1; Mlt-H. 242); 1 aor. ἐκάλεσα; pf. κέκληκα. Mid.: fut. 3 sg. καλέσεται (Just., D. 43, 5). Pass. 1 fut. κληθήσομαι (W-S. §15); 2 fut. 3 sg. κεκλήσεται Lev 13:45; Hos 12:1; 1 aor. ἐκλήθην; pf. κέκλημαι (Hom.+).

❶ **to identify by name or attribute, *call, call by name, name***

ⓐ *call* (to someone) abs., with naming implied (opp. ὑπακούειν; cp. PHamb 29, 3 [89 AD] κληθέντων τινῶν καὶ μὴ ὑπακουσάντων; Just., D. 136, 2 οὔτε καλοῦντος αὐτοῦ ἀνέχεσθε οὔτε λαλοῦντος ἀκούετε) of God ἐκάλουν καὶ οὐχ ὑπηκούσατε 1 Cl 57:4 (Pr 1:24); w. obj. τὰ ἴδια πρόβατα καλεῖ κατ' ὄνομα **J 10:3 v.l.**

ⓑ *call, address as, designate as* w. double acc. (Just., D. 3, 5 θεὸν σὺ τί καλεῖς; Hippol., Ref. 6, 20, 1) αὐτὸν καλῶμεν κύριον 2 Cl 4:1; cp. **Mt 22:43, 45; 23:9** (here the sense supplies the second acc.: *you are to call no one your father*); **Lk 20:44; Ac 14:12; Ro 9:25; Hb 2:11; 1 Pt 1:17** P^{72}; **3:6.** A voc. can take the place of the second acc. τί με καλεῖτε κύριε, κύριε; **Lk 6:46.** Pass. καλεῖσθαι ὑπὸ τῶν ἀνθρώπων ῥαββί **Mt 23:7.** ὑμεῖς μὴ κληθῆτε ῥαββί *you are not to have people call you 'rabbi'* vs. **8;** vs. **10.** Cp. **Lk 22:25; Js 2:23.** ὁ οἶκός μου οἶκος προσευχῆς κληθήσεται **Mt 21:13; Mk 11:17** (both Is 56:7). κληθήσονται υἱοὶ θεοῦ **Ro 9:26** (Hos 2:1).

ⓒ *name, provide with a name* w. double acc. (Iren. 1, 1, 1 [Harv. I 8, 3]) ἐκάλουν αὐτὸ … Ζαχαρίαν *they were for naming him Z.* **Lk 1:59** (on ἐπὶ τῷ ὀνόματι τ. πατρός *after his father['s name]* cp. 1 Esdr 5:38; Sir 36:11 and s. Hs 9, 17, 4).—Pass. *be given a name, be named* (Jos., Ant. 1, 34) κληθήσεται Ἰωάννης *his name is to be John* **Lk 1:60;** cp. vs. **62.** σὺ κληθήσῃ Κηφᾶς **J 1:42.** Also of localities **Mt 27:8; Ac 1:19;** ApcPt Rainer (s. Ἀχερουσία).—*Have as a name, be called* (Lucian, Jud. Voc. 7 Λυσίμαχος ἐκαλεῖτο; Just., D. 1, 3 Τρύφων…καλοῦμαι; 63, 5 Χριστιανοὶ … καλούμεθα) ὃς καλεῖται τ. ὀνόματι τούτῳ *who bears this name* **Lk 1:61.** Also of localities (Appian, Bell. Civ. 3, 70 §289; 3, 91 §374; SIG 599, 5 τὸ φρούριον ὃ καλεῖται Κάριον; Just., A I, 59, 6 τὸ καλούμενον Ἔρεβος) πόλις Δαυὶδ ἥτις καλεῖται Βηθλέεμ **Lk 2:4.** Cp. **Ac 28:1; Rv 11:8.**—Lk, Ac, Rv, GPt add to a pers. or thing the name or surname which he, she, or it bears, by means of the pres. pass. ptc. (cp. SIG 685, 39 νῆσον τὴν καλουμένην Λεύκην; 826e 22; 1063, 5; PPetr II, 45 II, 20; BGU 1000, 6; PCairGoodsp 9, 4; O. Wilck II, 1210, 4). The name: ἀδελφὴ καλουμένη Μαριάμ *a sister named Mary* **Lk 10:39** (PCairMasp 23, 16 τ. ἀδελφὴν καλουμένην Πρόκλαν; TestJob 48:1 ἡ καλουμένη Ἡμέρα). Cp. **19:2; Ac 7:58; Rv 19:11,** also **12:9.** πόλις καλουμένη N. **Lk 7:11;** cp. **9:10; 19:29; 21:37; 23:33; Ac 1:12; 3:11; 8:10; 9:11; 10:1; 27:8, 14, 16; Rv 1:9; 16:16;** GPt 6:24. The surname (2 Macc 10:12 Πτολεμαῖος ὁ καλούμενος Μάκρων; 1 Macc 3:1; Jos., Ant. 13, 367; TestJob 1:1 Ιωβ τοῦ καλουμένου Ιωβαβ): Σίμων ὁ κ. ζηλωτής *Simon the Zealot* **Lk 6:15.** Cp. **1:36; 8:2; 22:3** (s. ἐπικαλέω 2); **Ac 1:23; 13:1; 15:22** (s. ἐπικαλέω), **37.**—The example of the OT (Gen 17:19; 1 Km 1:20; Hos 1:9; 1 Macc 6:17) has influenced the expr. καλεῖν τὸ ὄνομά τινος, w. the name added in the acc. καλέσεις τὸ ὄνομα αὐτοῦ Ἰησοῦν **Mt 1:21;** GJs 11:3; 14:2. Cp. **Mt 1:23** (Is 7:14), **25; Lk 1:13, 31.** Pass. **Lk 2:21; Rv 19:13.**

ⓓ Very oft. the emphasis is to be placed less on the fact that names are such and such, than on the fact that the bearers of the name actually are what the name says about them. The pass. *be named* thus approaches closely the mng. *to be,* and it must be left to the sensitivity of the interpreter whether this transl. is to be attempted in any individual case (Quint. Smyrn. 14, 434 οὔτ᾽ ἔτι σεῖο κεκλήσομαι=I do not wish any longer to be yours, i.e. your daughter). Among such pass. are these: Ναζωραῖος κληθήσεται *he is to be a Nazarene* **Mt 2:23.** υἱοὶ θεοῦ κληθήσονται **5:9;** cp. vs. **19ab.** υἱὸς ὑψίστου κληθήσεται (in parallelism w. ἔσται μέγας) **Lk 1:32;** so GJs 11:3, but without the ref. to greatness; cp. **Lk 1:35, 76; 2:23.** οὐκέτι εἰμὶ ἄξιος κληθῆναι υἱός σου **15:19, 21.** οὐκ εἰμὶ ἱκανὸς καλεῖσθαι ἀπόστολος **1 Cor 15:9.** ἵνα τέκνα θεοῦ κληθῶμεν, καί ἐσμέν *that we should be called children of God; and so we really are* **1J 3:1** (sim. Eur., Ion 309 τ. θεοῦ καλοῦμαι δοῦλος εἰμί τε; cp. Just., D. 123, 9; καλεῖσθαι beside εἶναι as Plut., Demetr. 900 [25, 6]). οἱ κεκλημένοι ἐν ὀνόματι κυρίου *those who are identified by the Lord's name* i.e. as Christians Hs 8, 1, 1. ἄχρις οὗ τὸ σήμερον καλεῖται *as long as it is called 'today', as long as 'today' lasts* **Hb 3:13** (WLorimer, NTS 12, '66, 390f, quoting Pla., Phd. 107c).—Here we may also class ἐν Ἰσαὰκ κληθήσεταί σοι σπέρμα *in (through) Isaac you are to have your descendants* **Ro 9:7** and **Hb 11:18** (Gen 21:12).

❷ **to request the presence of someone at a social gathering,** ***invite*** (Hom. et al.; pap; 2 Km 13:23; Esth 5:12; ISardRobert 1, '64, p. 9, lines 1–4) τινά *someone* εἰς (τοὺς) γάμους *to the wedding* (Diod. S. 4, 70, 3; POxy 1487, 1 καλεῖ σε Θέων εἰς τοὺς γάμους) **Mt 22:9; Lk 14:8,** cp. vs. **10** (syn. ἐρωτάω; s. three texts, invitations to the κλινή of Sarapis [ZPE 1, '67, 121–26], two w. ἐ. and one w. καλέω New Docs 1, 5–9; on Luke's compositional use of the meal context, s. XdeMeeûs, ETL 37, '61, 847–70; cp. **J 2:2; Rv 19:9.** Abs. *invite* τινά *someone* **1 Cor 10:27** (Diog. L. 7, 184 of Chrysippus: ἐπὶ θυσίαν [sacrificial meal] ὑπὸ τῶν μαθητῶν κληθῆναι); priests to a child's birthday GJs 6:2. Cp. **Lk 7:39; 14:9, 12f, 16.** οἱ κεκλημένοι *the invited guests* (Damox. Com. [IV/III BC] fgm. 2, 26 K. in Athen. 3, 59, 102c τ. κεκλημένον; Jos., Ant. 6, 48; 52); **Mt 22:3b** (οἱ κεκλημένοι εἰς τ. γάμους as Diphilus Com. [IV/III BC] fgm. 17, 1), **4, 8; Lk 14:7, 17;** cp. vs. **24.** ὁ κεκληκώς, *the host* **14:10** (s. above).—If αὐτοῦ **Mk 2:15** refers to Jesus' home, κ. in vs. **17** registers the double sense of an invitation to dinner and receipt of Messianic benefits, w. Jesus as host (s. AMcNeile, Mt '57, 118); difft. **Lk 5:27–32,** s. 4 below. Of a follow-up invitation to guests upon completion of banquet preparations **Mt 22:3a** (cp. 3b below).

❸ **to use authority to have a person or group appear,** ***summon***—ⓐ *call together* τινάς *people*: Workers to be paid **Mt 20:8.** Slaves to receive orders **25:14; Lk 19:13.** Shepherds GJs 4:3. τὰς θυγατέρας τῶν Ἑβραίων for Mary's diversion 6:1; 7:2. τὰς παρθένους Ox 404 recto, 21 (Hs 113, 5); GJs 10:1. Guests **Mt 22:3a** (s. 2 end).

ⓑ *summon* τινά *someone* (Appian, Bell. Civ. 4, 82 §347; 4, 86 §362; 1 Macc 1:6) ἀπέστειλαν πρὸς αὐτὸν καλοῦντες αὐτόν *they sent to him to summon him* **Mk 3:31.** Cp. **Mt 2:7; 22:3a.** Of Joseph ἐκάλεσεν αὐτήν GJs 13:2 (for the context cp. **Mt 1:18f**). Of God: the Israelites fr. Egypt (as a type of Christ) **Mt 2:15.**—*Call upon* (Himerius, Or. 48 [=Or. 14], 10; 4 Macc 3:19) **Hb 11:8.**

ⓒ a legal t.t. *call in, summon before a court* (oft. pap) τινά *someone* (Jos., Ant. 14, 169) **Ac 4:18; 24:2.**—The transition to mng. 4 is well illustrated by **Mt 4:21; Mk 1:20;** Papias (8), where the summons is also a call to discipleship.

❹ From the mngs. 'summon' and 'invite' there develops the extended sense **choose for receipt of a special benefit or experience,** ***call*** (Paus. 10, 32, 13 οὓς ἂν ἡ Ἶσις καλέσῃ δι᾽ ἐνυπνίων; Ael. Aristid. 30, 9 K.=10 p. 116 D.: ὑπὸ τοῦ θεοῦ κληθείς) καλούμενος ὑπὸ τοῦ θεοῦ **Hb 5:4.** τινὰ εἴς τι *someone to someth.*, in the usage of the NT, as well as that of the LXX, of the choice of pers. for salvation: God (much more rarely Christ) calls εἰς τὴν ἑαυτοῦ βασιλείαν καὶ δόξαν **1 Th 2:12;** εἰς τὴν αἰώνιον αὐτοῦ δόξαν **1 Pt 5:10.** εἰς ζωὴν αἰώνιον **1 Ti 6:12.** εἰς κοινωνίαν τοῦ υἱοῦ αὐτοῦ *to fellowship with his son* **1 Cor 1:9.** ἐκ σκότους εἰς τὸ αὐτοῦ φῶς *from darkness to his light* **1 Pt 2:9.** ἀπὸ σκότους εἰς φῶς 1 Cl 59:2. διὰ τ. χάριτος αὐτοῦ **Gal 1:15.** *for this God called you through our proclamation, namely to obtain the glory* **2 Th 2:14;** cp. **1 Th 2:12.** καλέσαντι ... εἰς τὴν μερίδα τοῦ κλήρους τῶν ἁγίων **Col 1:12 v.l.** (for ἱκανώσαντι). Without further modification **Ro 8:30; 9:24; 1 Cor 7:17f, 20–22, 24; Eph 1:11 v.l.;** 2 Cl 9:5; 10:1.—κ. κλήσει ἁγίᾳ *call with a holy calling* **2 Ti 1:9.** ἀξίως τῆς κλήσεως ἧς (attraction, instead of ἥν) ἐκλήθητε *worthily of the calling by which you were called* **Eph 4:1** (on the constr. s. W-S. §24, 4b; Rob. 478). Of God: ὁ καλῶν τινά **Gal 5:8; 1 Th 5:24.** Abs. ὁ καλῶν **Ro 9:12.** ὁ καλέσας τινά **Gal 1:6; 1 Pt 1:15; 2 Pt 1:3.** Likew. of Christ ὁ καλέσας τινά 2 Cl 5:1 (Just., A I, 15, 7). Pass. οἱ κεκλημένοι *those who are called* **Hb 9:15.** κεκλημένοι ὑπὸ τοῦ θεοῦ δι᾽ αὐτοῦ (=Ἰ. Χρ.) 1 Cl 65:2. οἱ κεκλημένοι ὑπ᾽ αὐτοῦ (=υἱοῦ τ. θεοῦ) Hs 9, 14, 5. οἱ κληθέντες Hm 4, 3, 4. S. also 1d.—More closely defined: ἐν δικαιοσύνῃ B 14:7 (Is 42:6). ἐπ᾽ ἐλευθερίᾳ (s. ἐλευθερία) **Gal 5:13.** οὐκ ἐπὶ ἀκαθαρσίᾳ ἀλλ᾽ ἐν ἁγιασμῷ *not for impurity, but in consecration* **1 Th 4:7.** ἐν εἰρήνῃ *in peace* **1 Cor 7:15.** ἐκλήθητε ἐν μιᾷ ἐλπίδι τῆς κλήσεως ὑμῶν *you were called in the one hope that you share in your call* **Eph 4:4.** ἡμεῖς διὰ θελήματος αὐτου (=θεοῦ) ἐν Χριστῷ Ἰησοῦ κληθέντες 1 Cl 32:4. εἰς εἰρήνην τοῦ Χριστοῦ ἐν ἑνὶ σώματι **Col 3:15.** ἐν τῇ σαρκί 2 Cl 9:4. ἐν Ἰσαάκ **Hb 11:18** (=**Ro 9:7**). πόθεν ἐκλήθημεν καὶ ὑπὸ τίνος καὶ εἰς ὃν τόπον 2 Cl 1:2. εἰς τοῦτο ἵνα *for this reason, that* **1 Pt 3:9;** cp. **2:21.** Of Christ: οὐκ ἦλθον καλέσαι δικαίους ἀλλὰ ἁμαρτωλούς (+ εἰς μετάνοιαν v.l.) **Mt 9:13; Mk 2:17** (on a prob. double sense in this pass. s. 2); 2 Cl 2:4; cp. vs. 7 (cp. Just., A I, 40, 7 εἰς μετάνοιαν καλεῖ πάντας ὁ θεός); **Lk 5:32** (ἐλήλυθα ... εἰς μετάνοιαν). Of God: ἐκάλεσεν ἡμᾶς οὐκ ὄντας *he called us when we did not exist* 2 Cl 1:8. ὁ καλῶν τὰ μὴ ὄντα ὡς ὄντα *the one who calls into being what does not exist* **Ro 4:17** (Philo, Spec. Leg. 4, 187 τὰ μὴ ὄντα ἐκάλεσεν εἰς τὸ εἶναι; cp. Is 41:4; 48:13).—Of the call to an office by God **Hb**

5:4.—JHempel, Berufung u. Bekehrung (also GBeer Festschr.) '35; HWildberger, Jahwes Eigentumsvolk '60.—B. 1276. DELG. EDNT. M-M. TW.

καλιά, ᾶς, ἡ (Hes. et al. ['wooden dwelling, hut']; beg. w. Theocr. 'bird's nest', also Gen 6:14 [Sym. for νοσσίας]; PSI 569, 2 'bird cage') ***bird's nest*** ἐν τῇ δαφνιδέᾳ *Anna saw a nest of sparrows in the laurel tree* GJs 3:1.—DELG.

καλλιέλαιος, ου, ἡ (s. καλός, ἐλαία) ***the cultivated olive tree*** (opp. ἀγριέλαιος wild olive tree; this contrast as early as Aristot., De Plant. 1, 6, 820b, 40) **Ro 11:24.**—OPlasberg, APF 2, 1903, 219ff; here, fr. a Strassburg pap the words εἰς καλλιελαίαν. The word as adj. also PEdg 21, 3=Sb 6727, 3 (257/256 BC). Cp. Nicetas Choniates, De Manuele Comneno 4, 4 (MPG CXXXIX 480) of a Hungarian son-in-law at the Byzantine court: μήτε τὸν ἐκ φυταλιᾶς ἑτεροφύλου ῥάδαμνον εἰς καλλιέλαιον μετεγκεντρίζειν πιότατον 'nor to take a scion from an alien orchard and transfer it into a very productive olive tree'. An expression very much like this Psellus p. 99, 17.—Lit. on ἀγριέλαιος and ἐλαία 2.—M-M.

κάλλιον s. καλῶς 7.

καλλονή, ῆς, ἡ (Eur., Hdt.+; SIG 783, 46; 51; PFlor 65, 12; PLond V, 1764, 4; LXX; En 24:2; PsSol 12:2 [καλάμην H]; JosAs 18 cod. A [p. 68, 18 Bat.] and Pal. 364; EpArist) ***beauty,*** of the future glory 1 Cl 35:3. τὸ μεγαλεῖον τῆς κ. τοῦ θεοῦ *great beauty* 49:3.—DELG s.v. καλός.

κάλλος, ους, τό (Hom.+; LXX; pseudepigr.; Philo; Jos., C. Ap. 1, 195; 2, 167; Just., A II, 11, 5; Tat. 2, 2; Ath.) ***beauty*** 1 Cl 16:3 (Is 53:2); Hv 1, 1, 2; 3, 10, 5; s 9, 13, 9; AcPl Ha 2, 21; 25, 9; 9, 10. κ. τῆς ὄψεως *of the face* ApcPt 3:7.—DELG s.v. καλός 2. TW.

καλλωπίζω (s. καλός, ὤψ 'face'; X., Pla.; LXX, TestAbr; JosAs cod. A [p. 43, 7 and 15 Bat.]; ApcSed 11:7 and 17 [p. 134, 19 and 37 Ja.]; Jos., Ant. 1, 121; Just., D. 29, 2 λόγοι ... τέχνῃ ἀνθρωπίνῃ κεκαλλωπισμένοι) aor. impv. καλλώπισον (TestAbr A 4 p. 80, 20 [Stone p. 8]); aor. 3 sg. mid. ἐκαλλιωπίσατο LXX; pf. pass. ptc. κεκαλλωπισμένος (LXX, Just.) 'beautify the face' (Galen, Protr. 10 p. 34, 2 J.=p. 15, 3 Kaibel=p. 121, 15 M.), also gener. ***adorn, beautify*** (Philostrat., Ep. 27 p. 239, 28 ἵππους; Theoph. Ant. 2, 12 [p. 130, 13]) Ox 840, 38.—DELG and Frisk s.v. ὄπωπα, also Frisk s.v. *ωψ.

καλοδιδάσκαλος, ον (s. καλός, διδάσκαλος, διδάσκω; not found elsewh.) ***teaching what is good,*** of elderly women **Tit 2:3.**—TW.

Καλοὶ λιμένες, Καλῶν λιμένων, οἱ *Fair Havens,* the name, not found elsewh. in ancient sources, of a bay on the south coast of Crete, near the city of Lasaea **Ac 27:8.** Diod. S. 3, 44, 7 describes a harbor named Charmuthas as λιμὴν κάλλιστος. In general καλός is not infrequently found as an adj. applied to a serviceable harbor: Diod. S. 5, 10, 1 λιμέσι καλοῖς; 5, 13, 3. καλὸς λιμήν is a coastal place on the Black Sea in Arrian, Peripl. 19, 5.—Breusing 158f. Maps in JSmith, Voyage and Shipwreck of St. Paul[4] 1880, 82f; HBalmer, D. Romfahrt d. Ap. Pls. 1905, 313f (lit.); Haenchen ad loc.; Warnecke, Romfahrt 19; Hemer, Acts 136.

καλοκἀγαθία, ας, ἡ (s. καλός, ἀγαθός; on the crasis s. Gignac I, 324; cp. Schwyzer 427; Aristoph., X. et al.; Diod. S. 1, 79; Epict. 1, 7, 8; 4, 1, 164; ins, pap, 4 Macc, EpArist. Oft. in Philo; the adj. combination καλὸς κἀγαθός in older usage denotes 'perfect gentleman', w. focus on social status superior to the general working class, Hdt. [1, 30, 4 the earliest use, in Solon's words to Croesus] et al., then a pers. of lofty moral character and civic-mindedness, for ins s., e.g., OGI index VIII) ***nobility of character, excellence*** **Js 5:10 v.l.;** IEph 14:1.—JBerlage, De vi et usu vocum καλὸς κἀγαθός, καλοκαγαθία: Mnemosyne 60, '33, 20–40; JJüthner, Rzach Festschr. 1930, 99–119; Danker, Benefactor 319f.—Larfeld I 497. DELG s.v. καλός. TW. Sv.

καλοποιέω (s. καλός, ποιέω; Etym. Mag. 189, 24; PLond IV, 1338, 28; Lev 5:4 v.l. Swete; cp. Philo, Somn. 2, 296 v.l.) ***do what is right, good*** **2 Th 3:13.**—M-M.

καλός, ή, όν (Hom.+; pert. to meeting high standards or expectations of appearance, kind, or quality) superl. κάλλιστος, η, ον (Diod. S. 5, 13, 1; JosAs 14:17 cod. A; ApcSed 11:4 p. 134, 14 Ja. καλλίστατε; Jos., Ant. 16, 142; Just., D. 20, 3; Tat. 28, 1).

❶ **pert. to being attractive in outward appearance, *beautiful, handsome, fine*** in outward appearance λίθοι κ. *beautiful stones* **Lk 21:5.** Of pers. (Lucian, Tim. 16, Dial. Mort. 1, 3) Hv 3, 13, 1; s 9, 3, 1.

❷ **pert. to being in accordance at a high level w. the purpose of someth. or someone, *good, useful.***—ⓐ of things τόπον καλὸν ἀνακεχωρηκότα *a beautiful remote place* Hv 3, 1, 3; in the phys. sense *free from defects, fine, precious* opp. σαπρός (PLond II, 356, 4ff p. 252 [I AD]; TestJob 7:5 ἄρτον [opp. κεκαιμένον]) of fish **Mt 13:48;** superl. τὰ κάλλιστα *the especially good ones* **vs. 48** D. Of a tree and its fruit **12:33; Lk 6:43.** Opp. πονηρός of fruits **Mt 7:17ff.** Otherw. of fruits (Menand., Mon. 303 Mei. [402 J.] καρπός) **3:10; Lk 3:9;** Hs 2, 4. ἀμπελῶνες m 10, 1, 5. τράγοι B 7:6, 10. γῆ *good soil* **Mt 13:8, 23; Mk 4:8, 20; Lk 8:15.** σπέρμα **Mt 13:24, 27, 37f.** οἶνος **J 2:10ab;** Hm 12, 5, 3. μαργαρῖται *fine pearls* **Mt 13:45.** Subst. (Epict. 1, 12, 12 καλόν τι ἐλευθερία ἐστί) καλὸν τὸ ἅλας *salt is a good thing* **Mk 9:50; Lk 14:34.** ἔργον *something useful* Hs 5, 2, 7.—Superl. of Polycarp's writings συγγράμματα κάλλιστα *most excellent writings* EpilMosq 2.

ⓑ of moral quality (opp. αἰσχρός IAndrosIsis, Kyme 32) *good, noble, praiseworthy, contributing to salvation* etc. ἔργον καλόν, ἔργα καλά (Hippocr., Ep. 27, 30; Athen. 1, 15 p. 8f ἐν τοῖς καλοῖς ἔργοις; SibOr 3, 220) **Mt 5:16; 26:10; Mk 14:6; J 10:32f; 1 Ti 5:10, 25; 6:18; Tit 2:7, 14; 3:8ab, 14; Hb 10:24; 1 Pt 2:12; 2 Pt 1:10 v.l.;** 2 Cl 12:4. λόγια τοῦ θεοῦ 2 Cl 13:3. καλόν: ἐν καλῷ **Gal 4:18b;** cp. Pol 6:3. (Opp. κακόν) διάκρισις καλοῦ τε καὶ κακοῦ **Hb 5:14** (Sext. Emp., Pyrrh. 3, 168 διάκρισις τῶν τε καλῶν κ. κακῶν). (τὸ) κ. (opp. κακ.) ποιεῖν (2 Ch 14:1; 31:20) **Ro 7:21; 2 Cor 13:7.** Without the contrast w. κακ. **Gal 6:9; Js 4:17;** 1 Cl 8:4 (Is 1:17); Dg 4:3. κατεργάζεσθαι **Ro 7:18.** ἐργάζεσθαι B 21:2. καλὰ προνοεῖσθαι ἐνώπιόν τινος (Pr 3:4) **Ro 12:17;** sim. **2 Cor 8:21.**—ἀναστροφή (cp. 2 Macc 6:23) **Js 3:13; 1 Pt 2:12.** συνείδησις **Hb 13:18** (cp. PRein 52, 5 οὐ καλῷ συνειδότι χρώμενοι); φόβος 1 Cl 21:8; νουθέτησις 56:2; νηστεία Hs 5, 3, 5; μαρτυρία κ. *a good reputation* **1 Ti 3:7.** ἐν καρδίᾳ καλῇ κ. ἀγαθῇ *in a noble and good heart* **Lk 8:15** (w. ἀγ., as freq. in Gr-Rom. wr. to characterize exceptional citizens [s. καλοκἀγαθία], also Jos., Ant. 4, 67; 10, 188 al.; Just., A II, 2, 7 al.). Of the law *morally unobjectionable* (Maximus Tyr. 20, 9a) **Ro 7:16;** cp. **1 Ti 1:8.** ἐντολαί Hm 12, 3, 4; s 6, 1, 1f. οὐ καλὸν τὸ καύχημα ὑμῶν **1 Cor 5:6.** τοῦτο καλὸν καὶ ἀπόδεκτον ἐνώπιον τ. θεοῦ **1 Ti 2:3; 5:4 v.l.;** cp. 1 Cl 7:3; 21:1; 60:2; 61:2; Pol 6:1 (Pr 3:4). πολυτέλεια καλὴ καὶ ἱλαρά Hs 1, 10. λειτουργία 5, 3, 8. Superl.: of martyrs ὑπόδειγμα κάλλιστον *finest example* 1 Cl 6:1.

ⓒ in any respect *unobjectionable, blameless, excellent.*—**α.** of pers. κύριος B 7:1; cp. 19:11 (καλός of God: Celsus 4, 14). μαθητής IPol 2:1. ἱερεῖς IPhld 9:1. διάκονος Χριστοῦ ᾿Ι. **1 Ti 4:6a.** οἰκονόμος **1 Pt 4:10.** στρατιώτης Χρ. ᾿Ι. **2 Ti 2:3.** ποιμήν **J 10:11ab, 14.** ἀνταποδότης D 4:7.

β. of things μέτρον *good, full measure* **Lk 6:38.** θεμέλιος **1 Ti 6:19.** βαθμός **3:13.** ἔργον *someth. helpful, beneficial* **3:1.** διδασκαλία **4:6b.** παραθήκη **2 Ti 1:14.** ὁμολογία **1 Ti 6:12b, 13.** ἀγών **6:12a; 2 Ti 4:7.** στρατεία **1 Ti 1:18.** κτίσμα (3 Macc 5:11) **4:4.** πλάσμα B 6:12. σκεῦος 21:8. βάπτισμα ApcPt Rainer 4. καλὸν θεοῦ ῥῆμα (cp. Josh 21:45; 23:15; Zech 1:13) **Hb 6:5.** τὸ καλὸν ὄνομα τὸ ἐπικληθὲν ἐφ᾿ ὑμᾶς **Js 2:7** (in a Pompeian graffito [Dssm., LO 237; LAE 277] a lover speaks of the καλὸν ὄνομα of his beloved). οὐδὲν φαινόμενον καλόν (ἐστιν) IRo 3:3. πάντα ὁμοῦ κ. ἐστιν IPhld 9:2. τὸ καλόν *what passes the test* **1 Th 5:21.**

ⓓ The term καλόν (ἐστιν) in the gener. sense *it is good* qualifies items that fit under one of the preceding clasifications (Pr 17:26.—כְּלַיִן=καλόν loanw. in rabb.).

α. *it is pleasant, desirable, advantageous* (Jos., Bell. 4, 163) **Mt 17:4; 18:8f; Mk 9:5; Lk 9:33.—1 Cor 7:26a.**

β. *it is morally good, pleasing to God, contributing to salvation* **1 Cor 7:1** (cp. Gen 2:18), **8, 26b; Hb 13:9.**—οὐ καλόν **Mt 15:26; Mk 7:27.**

γ. καλόν ἐστιν αὐτῷ μᾶλλον *it is better for him* **Mk 9:42;** cp. **1 Cor 9:15.** καλόν (σοί) ἐστιν . . . ἤ *it is a(n)* (greater) *advantage* (for you) . . . , *than* (cp. Jon 4:3; ApcEsdr 1:6 p. 24, 13) **Mt 18:8f; Mk 9:43, 45, 47** (s. B-D-F §190, 2). καλὸν ἦν αὐτῷ *it would have been better for him* **Mt 26:24; Mk 14:21 v.l.** (B-D-F §358, 1; 360, 1). Without copula **Mk 14:21;** 1 Cl 51:3; IRo 6:1; 2 Cl 16:4.—That which is good or better is added in the inf., which forms the subject of καλόν ἐστιν (Appian, Bell. Civ. 3, 13 §46 καλὸν εἴη τινὶ θνήσκειν; Polyaenus 8, 9, 2; Jos., Bell. 1, 650; 4, 163) **Mt 15:26; 18:8f; Mk 7:27; Gal 4:18a;** Hm 6, 2, 9; also the articular inf. (Menand., Monost. 283; 291 [396; 410 J.] καλὸν τὸ θνήσκειν al.). κ. τὸ μὴ φαγεῖν κρέα **Ro 14:21; 1 Cor 7:26b;** IEph 15:1; IRo 2:2; Pol 5:3; MPol 11:1; w. acc. and inf. ἡμᾶς ὧδε εἶναι **Mt 17:4; Mk 9:5; Lk 9:33;** cp. **Mk 9:43, 45, 47;** B 21:1; with εἰ (ApcSed 4:2) **Mt 26:24** (1Cl 46:8); **Mk 9:42; 14:21;** with ἐάν **1 Cor 7:8.** S. B-D-F §409, 3; KBeyer, Semitische Syntax im NT ’62, 76–78.—B. 1176; 1191. DELG. M-M. EDNT. TW. Sv.

κάλπις, ιδος, ἡ (Hom. et al.; 4 Macc 3:12 v.l.) ***pitcher*** GJs 11:1 (twice).—DELG.

κάλυμμα, ατος, τό (s. next entry; Hom. et al.; Delian ins [III BC]: BCH 32, 13 no. 3a, 42; LXX; Philo, Leg. All. 2, 53; TestJud 14:5) ***head-covering, veil*** lit., of the veil w. which Moses covered his face (Ex 34:33–35) **2 Cor 3:13.**—κ. is v.l. for ἐξουσία **1 Cor 11:10.**—Fig. *veil, covering* that prevents right understanding τὸ αὐτὸ κ. ἐπὶ τῇ ἀναγνώσει . . . μένει *the same veil remains when . . . is read* **2 Cor 3:14** (JCarmignac, NTS 24, ’77/78, 384–86). κ. ἐπὶ τὴν καρδίαν κεῖται *a veil lies* on the *mind* vs. **15;** περιαιρεῖται τὸ κ. *the cover is taken away* vs. **16** (cp. Ex 34:34).—JGöttsberger, D. Hülle des Mos. nach Ex 34 u. 2 Cor 3: BZ 16, 1924, 1–17; SSchulz, Die Decke des Moses (2 Cor 3:7–18): ZNW 49, ’58, 1–30; CHickling, The Sequence of Thought in 2 Cor 3: NTS 21, ’74/75, 380–95.—B. 436. M-M. TW.

καλύπτω fut. καλύψω; 1 aor. ἐκάλυψα; pf. 3 sg. κεκάλυφεν Num 22:11. Pass.: fut. 3 sg. καλυφθήσεται Eccl 6:4; pf. ptc. κεκαλυμμένος (s. prec. entry; in Hom., Pind., trag.; rare in Attic prose [X., Cyr. 5, 1, 4 κεκαλυμμένη, Equ. 12, 5]; but w. increasing frequency in Aristot., Plut., Paus., Ael. Aristid. [Anz 271], also ins; CPR 239, 5; LXX; pseudepigr.; Philo, Leg. All. 3, 158; Jos., Ant. 13, 208; SibOr 4, 53. Prob. passed into the Koine fr. Ionic [Nägeli 27]); gener. ‘cover, hide, conceal’.

❶ **to cause to be covered in some physical way, *cover someone (up)*** lit. τινά **Lk 23:30,** perh. in the special sense *bury* (exx. in HGüntert, Kalypso 1919, 31ff; also ins in Ramsay, CB I/2, 476 no. 342). τί τινι *cover someth. w. someth.* (Num 4:12) λύχνον σκεύει κ. *a lamp with a vessel* **8:16** (cp. Num 4:9). Of a boat καλύπτεσθαι ὑπὸ τῶν κυμάτων *be covered by the waves* **Mt 8:24** (Achilles Tat. 3, 2, 6; Ps 77:53; Ex 15:10).

❷ **to cause someth. not to be known, *hide, conceal, keep secret***—ⓐ *cover (up), remove from sight* πλῆθος ἁμαρτιῶν (cp. Ps 84:3; ApcSed 1:2; s. also Philosoph. Max. p. 490, 56 ἡ εὔνοια τὴν ἁμαρτίαν περιστέλλει; cp. Pind., N. 5, 16–18) **1 Pt 4:8; Js 5:20;** 1 Cl 49:5; 2 Cl 16:4 (for the last 4 cp. also Prov 10:12). ἁμαρτίας Dg 9:3.

ⓑ *hide* (Hos 10:8) pf. pass. *be hidden* (=unknown) of the gospel: κεκαλυμμένον τὸ εὐαγγέλιον ἡμῶν **2 Cor 4:3;** cp. **Mt 10:26** (Vi. Aesopi W 110 p. 102, 17 P. πάντα τὰ καλυπτόμενα ὁ χρόνος εἰς φῶς ἄγει).

ⓒ *veil* of the καρδία (q.v. 1bβ) of uncomprehending disciples: *was our heart not veiled?* **Lk 24:32** D.—B. 849. DELG. M-M. TW. Spicq. Sv.

καλῶς adv. of καλός (Hom.+; loanw. in rabb.; καλῶς overtakes εὖ: JLee, NovT 27, ’85, 11–13.) gener. ‘well, beautifully’.

❶ **pert. to meeting relatively high standards of excellence or expectation, *fitly, appropriately, in the right way, splendidly*** (Is 23:16) κ. πάντα πεποίηκεν *he has done everything very well, indeed* **Mk 7:37.** διὰ τὸ κ. οἰκοδομῆσθαι αὐτήν *because it was well built* **Lk 6:48;** καλῶς κτισθέντα (opp. ἄχρηστα) *created to good purpose* Dg 4:2. σὺ κάθου ὧδε κ. *be seated here in a good place = here’s a nice place for you* **Js 2:3** (=ἐν καλῷ, as Alciphron, Ep.3, 20 ἄγει μέ τις λαβὼν εἰς τὸ θέατρον, καθίσας ἐν καλῷ ‘someone took me to the theater and showed me to a good seat’; Lucian, Paras. 50 καλῶς κατακείμενος; other pass. Field, Notes 236), unless κ. here=*please* (so JRopes, ICC 1916 ad loc.; NRSV. Either rendering catches the deferential tone of κ.). σὺ κ. εὐχαριστεῖς *you may give thanks well enough* **1 Cor 14:17;** ἐτρέχετε κ. *you were running so well* **Gal 5:7.** Cp. **1 Ti 3:4, 12** (Diog. L. 1, 70 Chilon advises that one must μανθάνειν τῆς αὑτοῦ οἰκίας καλῶς προστατεῖν), **13; 5:17;** Papias (4). In these pass. the mng. approaches 2.

❷ **pert. to meeting expectations of personal excellence, *commendably, in a manner free from objection*** ζηλοῦσιν οὐ καλῶς **Gal 4:17.** κ. ἀναστρέφεσθαι (s. ἀναστρέφω 3a) **Hb 13:18.** πολιτεύεσθαι 1 Cl 44:6. κ. καὶ ἁγνῶς Hs 5, 6, 6; ἀγωνίζεσθαι 2 Cl 7:1 (cp. **1 Tim 6:12**). ἐργάζεσθαι Hm 7, 1. δουλεύειν s 5, 6, 5. κ. καὶ δικαίως παραδεδόσθαι 1 Cl 51:2. κ. καὶ ἀληθῶς φρονεῖν Hm 3, 4. κ. καὶ σεμνῶς ὁρᾶν s 9, 1, 2. τὸ κ. ἔχον *orderly behavior* 1 Cl 14:2. κ. ἔχει θεὸν καὶ ἐπίσκοπον εἰδέναι *it is commendable to honor God and (at the same time) the supervisor (bishop)* ISm 9:1.

❸ **pert. to being of advantage, *in a manner that is beneficial/acceptable, well*** κ. ποιεῖν *do good* (Lucian, Ep. Sat. 3, 31) **Mt 12:12.** W. dat. (Zeph 3:20) τοῖς μισοῦσιν ὑμᾶς **Mt 5:44 v.l.; Lk 6:27.** κ. λέγειν w. acc. *speak well of* **6:26.** S. B-D-F §151, 1. κ. ἔχειν *be well, in good health* **Mk 16:18** (ἔχω 10b). καλῶς λαμβάνειν *receive hospitably* Hs 9, 11, 8 (λαμβάνω 5).

❹ **pert. to being in accord w. a standard, *rightly, correctly***

ⓐ κ. ποιεῖν *do what is right, act rightly, do well* (Dio Chrys. 30 [47], 25; Ael. Aristid. 36 p. 685 D.) **1 Cor 7:37f; Js 2:8, 19;** Hv 2, 4, 2. W. ptc. (Appian, Bell. Civ. 3, 75 §305; Sb 5216,

7 [I BC]; 6265, 8 [I AD]; POslo 55, 7; Jos., Ant. 11, 279; B-D-F §414, 5; Rob. 1121) *be kind enough to do someth.* **Ac 10:33; Phil 4:14;** *do well in doing someth.* **2 Pt 1:19; 3J 6;** GEg 252, 53; ISm 10:1

ⓑ w. verbs of speaking, hearing, understanding κ. ἀποκρίνεσθαι *answer rightly, well* **Mk 12:28.** εἰπεῖν (Simplicius in Epict. p. 44, 50; 47, 51; Jos., Ant, 8, 380) **Lk 20:39; J 4:17;** B 10:11; AcPl Ha 1, 25. λαλεῖν **Ac 28:25.** λέγειν (TestJob 7:8; Epict. 1, 19, 6) **J 8:48; 13:13;** cp. **18:23.** μανθάνειν, μνημονεύειν Papias (2:3). προφητεύειν *prophesy rightly* **Mt 15:7; Mk 7:6;** PEg[2] 54; cp. κ. ἀκούειν *hear correctly* (Menand., fgm. 507 Kö.) Hm 4, 3, 2. κ. ἐπίστασθαί τι *know someth. well* 1 Cl 53:1 (Appian, Bell. Civ. 2, 98 §406 εἰδέναι κ.; Procop. Soph., Ep. 18 ἴσθι κ.=you may be quite sure).

ⓒ in general μισεῖν B 10:8; καταπαύεσθαι 15:5, 7; ἀξιοῦν Dg 3:2.—As exclamation καλῶς *Quite right! That is true! Well said!* (Arrian, Cyneg. 18, 1; Ael. Aristid. 33 p. 617 D.; 45 p. 44; Lucian, Dial. Deor. 20, 10; 3 Km 2:18) **Mk 12:32; Ro 11:20.**

❺ ***fortunately*** καλῶς ἐξέφυγες *fortunately you escaped* Hv 4, 2, 4.

❻ in irony (Soph., Ant. 739; Aelian, VH 1, 16 al.) κ. ἀνέχεσθε *you put up with it all right* **2 Cor 11:4** (Moffatt; s. PKirberg, Die Toleranz der Korinther 1910; JMachen, The Origin of Paul's Religion 1921, 131ff). κ. ἀθετεῖν **Mk 7:9.** But here perh. the καλῶς of vs. **6,** which is not ironic, may require a similar interpr., and the sentence should be a question: *are you doing the right thing in rejecting God's commandment?*

❼ comp. κάλλιον (for the superl., as Galen, Protr. 8 p. 24, 19 J.=p. 10, 31 Kaibel; s. B-D-F §244, 2) ὡς καὶ σὺ κ. ἐπιγινώσκεις *as also you know very well* **Ac 25:10.**—M-M.

καμάρα, ας, ἡ (Hdt. et al.; Diod. S. 3, 19, 2; 17, 82, 3; SIG 1243, 4; pap) ***arch, vault, vaulted room*** (Is 40:22) MPol 15:2 (on the mngs. of the Carian word fr. which it is said to be derived s. FSolmsen, BPhW 26, 1906, 853; cp. the cautionary note Boisacq 402).—DELG and Frisk.

κἀμέ s. κἀγώ.

κάμηλος, ου, ὁ and **ἡ** (of Semitic origin, cp. Hebr. גָּמָל; Aeschyl., Hdt.; ins, pap, LXX, TestSol, TestJob, Philo; Jos., Ant. 1, 252; 8, 167 al.; Ath., R. 12 p. 61, 11) ***camel*** τρίχες καμήλου *camel's hair* **Mt 3:4; Mk 1:6;** GEb 13, 79 (here there is naturally no thought of the soft τρίχες καμήλου from which the garments of distinguished people are made acc. to Ctesias [IV BC]: 688 fgm. 10 Jac.). Proverbially εὐκοπώτερόν ἐστιν κάμηλον διὰ τρυπήματος [vv.ll. τρήματος, τρυμαλίας] ῥαφίδος διελθεῖν *it is easier for a camel to go through a needle's eye* of someth. impossible, w. the contrast emphasized greatly, perh. also with a humorous twist because of the hump involved (for a proverb comparing someth. very small w. someth. very large, cp. Lucian, Ep. Sat. 1, 19 μύρμηξ ἢ κάμηλος): the largest animal and the smallest opening **Mt 19:24;** w. variations **Mk 10:25** and **Lk 18:25** (s. κάμιλος; GAicher, Kamel u. Nadelöhr 1908; ERostan, Les Paradoxes de Jésus 1908, 11ff; WBleibtreu [s. μισέω 2] 17f; RLehmann u. KLSchmidt, ThBl 11, '32, 336–40; EBöklen, Deutsches Pfarrerblatt 37, '33, 162–65; CLattey, Verb. Dom. 31, '53, 291f; EBest, ET 82, '70, 83–89; JDerrett, NTS 32, '86, 465–70). To strain out a gnat τὴν δὲ κ. καταπίνειν *but swallow a camel*=be over-zealous in small matters and careless in important ones **Mt 23:24** (s. κώνωψ.—The camel is contrasted w. the elephant in Phalaris, Ep. 86; Ps.-Libanius, Ep. 1597, 1 ed. F. XI p. 593, 1.—Artem. 4 p. 199, 9 explains that camel and elephant would have the same mng. in figurative interpretation).—JSauer, in Studies in the History and Archeology of Jordan V '95, 39–48.—BHHW II 923; Pauly-W. X 2, 1824–32; B. 189f. OEANE I 406–8. EDNT. DELG. M-M. TW.

κάμιλος, ου, ὁ ***rope, ship's cable*** is the rdg. of several mss., and of several versions (e.g. Armenian; FHerklotz, BZ 2, 1904, 176f) **Mt 19:24; Mk 10:25; Lk 18:25** instead of κάμηλος (q.v.). κάμιλος, found only in Suda 1967c and the scholia on Aristoph. (Vesp. 1035), may be ancient (B-D-F §24; Mlt-H. 72—'Byzantine invention'), but is secondary in the gospels.—Boisacq 403, n. 1; Bröndal, BPhW 38, 1918, 1081f; PHaupt, Camel and Cable: AJP 45, 1924, 238ff.—DELG. TW.

κάμινος, ου, ἡ (Aeschyl., Hdt. et al.; IG IV, 332; pap, LXX, TestSol 11:7; ParJer 6:23 [fig. for Egypt]; Joseph., loanw. in rabb. S. Schwyzer II 34 n. 2; B-D-F §49, 1) ***oven, furnace*** καπνὸς καμίνου (Ex 19:18; Job 41:12) **Rv 9:2.** κ. τοῦ πυρός *fiery oven, kiln* (Da 3:6, 11 al.) of potters' kilns (Sir 27:5) 2 Cl 8:2. Of smelters' furnaces (X., Vectig. 4, 49; Diod. S. 5, 13, 1; 5, 27, 2; Ezk 22:20, 22) **Rv 1:15;** MPol 15:2. κ. πυρός as the place of the fiery trial of the three young men (Da 3:20ff; 4 Macc 16:21; Jos., Ant. 10, 213) 1 Cl 45:7. AcPl Ha 6, 20 in imagery of Rome. Fig. of hell **Mt 13:42, 50.**—DELG. M-M. TW.

καμμύω fut. καμμύσω (LXX; TestJob 40:4); 1 aor. ἐκάμμυσα (contracted fr. καταμύω; censured by Phryn. 339f Lob., it spread fr. the poets [Batr. 191; Alexis Com. 319; Apollon. Dysc., Synt. 323, 22; 326, 9] into popular speech: X., Cyr. 8, 3, 27 codd.; Hero Alex. I p. 412, 5; PGM 4, 586; 958; 1057; 1069; 7, 855; 13, 945; LXX [Thackeray 99]; Philo [s. below].—W-S. §5, 22c; 12, 6; B-D-F §69, 1; Mlt-H. 92; 243; 398; Thumb 63f; Crönert 64, 4) ***close (the eyes)*** τοὺς ὀφθαλμούς (so Ps.-Callisth. 3, 33, 27 w. ref. to the dying Alexander) fig. (Philo, Somn. 1, 164 καμμύσαντες τὸ τ. ψυχῆς ὄμμα; La 3:45) of an attitude of hostility toward the gospel **Mt 13:15; Ac 28:27** (both Is 6:10).—DELG s.v. μύω. M-M.

κάμνω 2 aor. ἔκαμον; pf. κέκμηκα **Rv 2:3** t.r. (s. Tdf. app.), ptc. κεκμηκώς; fut. 2 sg. mid. καμῇ (ApcMos 24).

❶ ***be weary, fatigued*** (so Hom. et al.; PGiss 47, 8; PLond V, 1708, 50; 4 Macc 3:8; TestIss 3:6; JosAs 11 cod. A [p. 53, 8 Bat.] and Pal. 364; ApcMos) τῇ ψυχῇ *in spirit* Hm 8:10. Here we may think of a weariness of the soul (for weariness of this kind cp. Diod. S. 20, 96, 3 κάμνοντες ταῖς ψυχαῖς; Philo, Post. Cai. 31 [the wandering soul]; Jos., Ant. 2, 290; Just., D. 5, 6). But another interpretation may perh. be derived from Diod. S. 15, 38, 2: κάμνειν τῇ συνεχείᾳ τῶν πολέμων=be tired or weary of the continued succession of the wars. Then the κάμνοντες τῇ ψυχῇ would be not the weary in spirit but those who are tired of living (as Job 10:1).—**Hb 12:3** it may be abs. (as Jos., Vi. 209), i.e., if τ. ψυχαῖς ὑμῶν belongs w. ἐκλυόμενοι. ἔκαμνον ἐκ τῆς ὁδοῦ *I was weary from the trip* GJs 15:1. Of documents σχεδὸν ἐκ τοῦ χρόνου κεκμηκότα *almost worn out by time* MPol 22:3; EpilMosq 5 (Diog. L. 9, 113: in Timon's house the works of the poets lie about unprotected, many of them half eaten up [ἡμίβρωτα]). Weary with work (TestJob 39:11 μὴ κάμητε εἰκῇ; ApcMos 24) κεκοπίακας καί οὐ κέκμηκας **Rv 2:3,** an Erasmian rdg. (s. above).

❷ ***be ill*** (so Soph., Hdt. et al.) ὁ κάμνων *the sick man* (Strabo 8, 6, 15; Musonius 20, 8 θεραπείαν τῶν καμνόντων; Epict., fgm. 19; M. Ant. 6, 55; SIG 943, 9f ἐπιμέλεια τῶν καμνόντων; TestSol 18, 34 P; Philo, Omn. Prob. Lib. 12, Migr. Abr. 124 τὴν τῶν καμνόντων σωτηρίαν; Tat.) **Js 5:15.** Another possibility here is the mng. *be hopelessly sick, waste away* (schol. on Apollon. Rhod. 4, 1091 p. 306, 23 W.; Jos., Ant. 8, 266), or even

❸ *die* (Crinagoras, no. 25, 1; Diod. S. 14, 71, 1 and 4; Dionys. Byz. §109; 110; Kaibel 321, 8 καμών=dead; grave ins [ANock, Sallust. p. xxxiii, 94 ὅταν κάμῃς, τοῦτο τὸ τέλος=when you die, that's the end]; Wsd 4:16; 15:9; SibOr 3, 588).—B. 540. DELG. M-M. Spicq.

κἀμοί s. κἀγώ.

Καμπανός, ή, όν ***Campanian,*** belonging to the district of Campania in south central Italy (incl. Naples, Cumae) ἡ ὁδὸς ἡ Κ.=*Via Campana* (CIL VI 2107, 3; 14; 10250; 29772) Hv 4, 1, 2.—MDibelius, Hdb. ad loc.

κάμπτω fut. κάμψω; 1 aor. ἔκαμψα; aor. pass. 3 pl. ἐκάμφθησαν Job 9:13, inf. καμφθῆναι 4 Macc 3:4. (Hom. et al.; pap, LXX, Philo).

❶ trans. **to bend or incline some part of the body, *bend, bow*** freq. as gesture of respect or devotion: τὸν τράχηλον *the neck* (Aesop, Fab. 452 p. 501, 12f P. ἔκαμψα τὸν ἐμαυτοῦ τράχηλον) B 3:2 (Is 58:5). γόνυ (also pl.) *bend the knee* as a sign of (religious) devotion (LXX) τινί *before someone* (SibOr 3, 616f) τῇ Βάαλ **Ro 11:4** (3 Km 19:18). Also πρός τινα **Eph 3:14.** Fig. κ. τὰ γόνατα τῆς καρδίας (s. γόνυ) 1 Cl 57:1.

❷ intr. (Polyaenus 3, 4, 3 ἔκαμψεν=he bent inward) **to assume a bending posture, *bend (itself)*** ἐμοὶ κάμψει πᾶν γόνυ *every knee shall bend before me* **Ro 14:11** (Is 45:23). ἐν τῷ ὀνόματι Ἰησοῦ *when the name of Jesus is proclaimed* **Phil 2:10** (also infl. by Is 45:23).—B. 542. Renehan '75, 115f. DELG. M-M. TW.

κἄν (formed by crasis fr. καὶ ἐάν, quotable Hes. et al.; pap, LXX [Thackeray 138]; TestAbr; TestJob; TestReub; TestJud; Philo, Aet. M. 134 al.; Joseph.; SibOr 3, 18; Just., Tat., Ath.; W-S. §5, 8; B-D-F §18; 371; Rob. 208; w. variations in mss.) particle gener. w. subjunctive (w. ind. Hs 5, 5, 4; Just. A I, 11, 2).

❶ ***and if*** **Mt 10:23 v.l.; Mk 16:18; Lk 6:34** D; **13:9** (here the suppression of the first apodosis [καλῶς ἔχει] as quite freq. in Attic; B-D-F §454, 4; s. Rob. 1023); **J 8:55; Js 5:15;** κἂν λίαν συνετὸς ἦν τις Hs 5, 5, 4; κἂν μιάνῃς 5, 7, 2. κἂν … δέ *but if* IRo 5:2. κἂν … κἂν … κἂν *and if … and if … and if* **1 Cor 13:2f v.l.** κἂν … κἂν *and if … and if, whether … whether* (Demosth. 25, 15; TestJud 15:5, TestReub 4:7) **Lk 12:38.**

❷ ***even if, even though*** οὐ μόνον … ἀλλὰ κἂν εἴπητε *not only … but even if you say* **Mt 21:21.—26:35** (κἂν δέῃ ἀποθανεῖν as Jos., Ant. 6, 108; 11, 228); **J 8:14; 10:38; 11:25;** 2 Cl 19:3; *even if … just* **Hb 12:20.**

❸ ***(even) if only, at least*** (Soph., El. 1483; Lucian, Tim. 20 κἂν ὄνος 'at least a donkey'; PRein 52, 6; POxy 1593, 5ff κἂν νῦν 'now at least'; κἂν τοσοῦτον *at least so much* Ath. 20, 3) κἂν τῶν ἱματίων *just his clothes* **Mk 5:28;** cp. **6:56** (cp. TestJob 12:1 κἂν διακονῆσαι … σήμερον; Athen. 5, 212f ἑκάστου σπεύδοντος κἂν προσάψασθαι τῆς ἐσθῆτος). κἂν ἡ σκιά *at least his shadow* **Ac 5:15.** κἂν ὡς ἄφρονα δέξασθέ με *accept me at least as a fool* **2 Cor 11:16.**—2 Cl 18:2; IEph 10:1. In the apodosis of a conditional sentence 2 Cl 7:3; GPt 12:52, 54.—κἂν ταῦτα *even if this=this, little though it be* Dg 2:10 (cp. Lucian, Dial. Mar. 1, 3).—M-M.

Κανά, ἡ (also Κανᾶ, e.g. Tdf.) indecl. ***Cana,*** name of a city in Galilee (cp. Jos., Vi. 86), the location of which can no longer be determined. Among the possibilities are the sites now known as Khirbet Qana, c. 14 km. north of Nazareth (RMackowski, 'Scholars' Qanah.' A Re-examination of the Evidence in Favor of Khirbet Qanah: BZ 23, '79, 278–84; Dalman, Orte[3] 108–14 [Eng. tr. 112f]);Kafr Kanna, a.k.a. Kefr Kenna, c. 5 km. northeast of Naz. (TSoiron, D. Evangelium u. d. hl. Stätten in Palästina 1929), easily available to ancient pilgrims; and even ᶜAin Qana, $1^1/_2$ km. north of Naz. near Reina (s. WSanday, Sacred Sites of the Gospels 1903, 24, n.)—the first receives the most scholarly support. Place of Jesus' first miracle in **J 2:1, 11** (lit. in Hdb. exc. after J 2:12; CKopp, The Holy Places of the Gospels, tr. RWalls, '63, 143–54; RRiesner, Bibel u. Kirche 43, '88, 69–71); **4:46.** Home of Nathanael **21:2;** according to many, also of Simon Mt 10:4 (s. Καναναῖος).—Heinz Noetzel, Christus und Dionysus '60.—EDNT. BHHW II 926. M-M.

Καναναῖος, ου, ὁ ***Cananean,*** surname of the second Simon among the 12 disciples **Mt 10:4; Mk 3:18** (in both pass. without translation [so REB, per contra NRSV]; v.l. Κανανίτης in both pass.). Not a toponym *from Cana* (Jerome) nor *Canaanite,* but fr. Aram. קַנְאָן 'enthusiast, zealot' (cp. **Lk 6:15; Ac 1:13,** where he is called ζηλωτής), prob. because he had formerly belonged to the party of the 'Zealots' or 'Freedom Fighters' (Schürer I 382, 426, 439–41; II 598–606 [lit.]; JKlausner, Jesus v. Naz.[2] '34, 272ff [Eng. tr. 1926, 205f; 284f]; MHengel, D. Zeloten[2] '76 [Eng. tr. The Zealots '88]; against this view Bÿrge Salomonsen, NTS 12, '66, 164–76); s. FBurkitt, Syriac Forms of NT Proper Names 1912, 5, and Σίμων 2.—M-M.

Κανανίτης, ου, ὁ **man from Cana, *Cananite.*** Acc. to Strabo 14, 5, 14 one of the two Stoics named Athenodorus received this name to distinguish him fr. the other Ath.; ἀπὸ κώμης τινός (Cana near Tarsus) was added. Numerous mss. replace the apparently unintelligible Καναναῖος with this term in **Mt 10:4** and **Mk 3:18.** Surname of the apostle Judas in some Sahidic and Syriac versions of **J 14:22.**

Κανδάκη, ης, ἡ ***Candace*** (Bion of Soli [II BC], Aethiopica: 668 fgm. 1 Jac. [βασιλέως] μητέρα καλοῦσι Κ. 'they term the mother of a king Candace'; Strabo 17, 1, 54 p. 820; Ps.-Callisth. 3, 18; Cass. Dio 54, 5; Pliny, HN 6, 35, 7; Sb 8366 [ins 109 AD]) title of the queen of Ethiopia (on Egypt. monuments she is called k[e]nt[e]ky) **Ac 8:27.**—RPietschmann, Pauly-W. I 1894, 1095ff; Grohmann, ibid. X/2, 1919, 1858f; WMaxMüller, Aethiopien 1904; GRöder, Klio 12, 1912, 72ff; AWikenhauser, Die Apostelgesch. 1921, 361f; StLösch, TQ 111, 1930, 477–519; BHHW II 930; ADihle, Umstrittene Daten: Wiss. Abhdl. der Arbeitsgemeinschaft … Westfalen 32, '65, 65–79; IReimer, Women in the Acts of the Apostles '95.—M-M.

κανών, όνος, ὁ (Hom. et al.; ins, pap, LXX; TestNapht 2:3. For the mngs. of the word [primarily 'straight rod'] s. TZahn, Grundriss d. Gesch. d. ntl. Kanons[2] 1904, 1ff; HOppel, ΚΑΝΩΝ: Philol. Suppl. 30, 4, '37; LWenger, Canon: SBWienAk 220, 2, '42) the mngs. found in our lit. are

❶ **a means to determine the quality of someth., *rule, standard*** (Eur., Hec. 602; Demosth. 18, 296; Aeschin., In Ctesiph. 66; Sext. Emp., Log. 2, 3; Ps.-Plut., Consol. ad Ap. 103a; Epict., index Sch.; Lucian, Pisc. 30; UPZ 110, 58 [164 BC]; PLond I, 130, 12 p. 133 [I/II AD]; 4 Macc 7:21; EpArist 2; Philo; Jos., Ant. 10, 49, C. Ap. 2, 174; TestNapht 2:3) τῷ κανόνι τούτῳ στοιχεῖν **Gal 6:16; Phil 3:16 v.l.;** ἔλθωμεν ἐπὶ τὸν τῆς παραδόσεως ἡμῶν κανόνα 1 Cl 7:2 (cp. Epict. 1, 28, 28 ἔλθωμεν ἐπὶ τοὺς κανόνας; τὸν κ. ἀληθείας …, ὃν διὰ τοῦ βαπτίσματος εἴληφεν Iren. 1, 9, 4 [Harv. I 88, 1]).

❷ **set of directions or formulation for an activity, *assignment, formulation*** for public service (s. λειτουργία 1; ins New Docs 1, p. 37, ln. 29 κατὰ πόλιν καὶ κώμην ἔταξα κανόνα τῶν ὑπηρεσιῶν 'I have promulgated in the individual cities and villages a schedule of what I judge desirable to be supplied' [tr. Horsley]) ἐν τῷ κανόνι τῆς ὑποταγῆς ὑπάρχειν 1 Cl 1:3.

παρεκβαίνειν τὸν ὡρισμένον τῆς λειτουργίας κανόνα 41:1. Sim. of the mission assignment given to Paul, which included directions about geographical area **2 Cor 10:13, 15f** (s. FStrange, BA 46, '83, 167f; AdeOliveira, Die Diakonie der Gerechtigkeit und der Versöhnung in der Apologie des 2. Korintherbriefes '90, 141–42, n. 306: κ. signifies the apostle's mission assignment). Others (incl. NRSV, REB) emphasize the geographical component and render *sphere (of action), province, limit.*

❸ In the second century in the Christian church κ. came to stand for revealed truth, ***rule of faith*** (Zahn, RE VI 683ff.—Cp. Philo, Leg. All. 3, 233 ὁ διαφθείρων τὸν ὑγιῆ κανόνα τῆς ἀληθείας; Synes., Ad. Paeon. 4 p. 310d τῆς ἀληθείας κανών of mathematics; Hippol., Ref. 10, 5, 2). ἐκκλησιαστικὸς καὶ καθολικὸς κ. EpilMosq 2. ᾧ παρέλαβε κανόνι *by the rule that the person has received* AcPlCor 2:36.—The use of κανών as 'list' in ref. to the canonical scriptures, as well as in the sense of '(synodical-) canon', is late.—RGG^3 III, 1116–22. TRE XVII '88, 562–70. New Docs 2, 88f. DELG (lit.). M-M. TW. Sv.

Καπερναούμ s. Καφαρναούμ.

καπηλεύω (Aeschyl., Hdt. et al.; ins, pap; Philo, Virt. 112, Leg. ad Gai. 203; cp. Dio Chrys. 8, 9, subst; freq. of tavern-keeping) ***trade in, peddle, huckster*** (of retail trade; cp. the contrast καπηλεία–ἐμπορία Jos., C. Ap. 1, 61) τὶ *someth.*, also fig. (Pla., Prot. 5, 313d οἱ τὰ μαθήματα καπηλεύοντες. Sim., Nicol. Dam.: 90 fgm. 132, 2 Jac.; Iambl., Vi. Pyth. 34, 245; Philostrat., Vi. Apoll. 1, 13 τὴν σοφίαν καπηλεύειν) τὸν λόγον τ. θεοῦ **2 Cor 2:17** (Anon. Vi. Pla. p. 8, 48 Westerm. κάπηλος λόγων). Because of the tricks of small tradesmen (Dio Chrys. 14 [31], 37f; Lucian, Hermot. 59 φιλόσοφοι ἀποδίδονται τὰ μαθήματα ὥσπερ οἱ κάπηλοι, . . . δολώσαντες καὶ κακομετροῦντες; Is 1:22 οἱ κ. μίσγουσι τ. οἶνον ὕδατι) the word almost comes to mean *adulterate* (so Vulg., Syr., Goth.).—Pauly-W. X/2, 1888f.—B. 821. DELG s.v. κάπηλος. M-M. EDNT. TW. Spicq.

καπνός, οῦ, ὁ (Hom. et al.; BGU 1026 XXII, 17; LXX; ApcSed 5:5; Jos., Ant. 5, 284; 12, 310) ***smoke*** **Rv 9:2f; 18:9, 18.** ἀναβαίνει (Horapollo 2, 16 εἰς οὐρανόν; Ex 19:18; Josh 8:20; Is 34:10) **8:4; 9:2a; 14:11; 19:3.** καπνὸς καμίνου (Ex 19:18; Job 41:12) **9:2b.** Of the cloud of smoke in which God appears (Is 6:4) **15:8.** W. fire and brimstone (s. θεῖον) **9:17f.** W. fire and blood ἀτμὶς καπνοῦ *steaming smoke* **Ac 2:19** (Jo 3:3).—B. 73. DELG. M-M. Sv.

Καππαδοκία, ας, ἡ (Menand., Kolax fgm. 2, 2 S.; Strabo 11, 13, 15–12, 2, 11 al.; TestSim 6:3; Joseph., ind.; ins) ***Cappadocia***, a province in the interior of Asia Minor. Mentioned w. other parts of Asia Minor (Posidon.: 87 fgm. 36, 50 Jac.) **Ac 2:9; 1 Pt 1:1** (Ps.-Callisth. 2, 11, 1 Alexander sends a circular letter [ἐγκύκλιος ἐπιστολή] to five adjoining satrapies, among them Cappadocia).—JMarquardt, Röm. Staatsverwaltung I^2 1881, 365ff; Ramsay, Hist. Geogr. 281ff, Church 443ff; EKirsten, Kappadokia '55. OEANE I 419–22.

καραδοκία, ας, ἡ (κάρα 'head, peak' + a form der. fr. the root of δέχομαι; Aq Ps 38:8 and Pr 10:28.—καραδοκέω Eur., Hdt. et al.; Jos., Bell. 4, 305; 5, 28, Ant. 17, 86) ***eager expectation*** **Phil 1:20 v.l.** (for ἀποκαραδοκία).—DELG s.v. κάρα, δεχομαι B.

καρδία, ας, ἡ (since Hom. [καρδίη, κραδίη]. Rather rare in other wr. in the period of the Gk. Bible [s. Diod. S. 32, 20; Plut., Mor. p. 30a; 63a; Epict. 1, 27, 21; M. Ant. 2, 3, 3; 7, 13, 3; Ps.-Apollod. 1, 4, 1, 5; Lucian; pap, incl. PGM 5, 157; 13, 263; 833; 1066; s. below 1bη], but common LXX, pseudepigr.; Ar. 15, 3; Just., D. 39, 5; 46, 5 al.; Ath. 31, 3. On Philo and Joseph. s. ASchlatter, D. Theol. d. Judentums nach d. Bericht d. Jos. '32, 21).

❶ ***heart*** as seat of physical, spiritual and mental life (as freq. in Gk. lit.), fig. extension of 'heart' as an organ of the body (Il. 13, 282 al.), a mng. not found in our lit.

ⓐ as the center and source of physical life (Ps 101:5; 103:15) ἐμπιπλῶν τροφῆς . . . τὰς κ. satisfying *the hearts w. food* **Ac 14:17.** τρέφειν τὰς κ. *fatten the hearts* **Js 5:5.**

ⓑ as center and source of the whole inner life, w. its thinking, feeling, and volition (νοῦν κ. φρένας κ. διάνοιαν κ. λογισμὸν εἶπέ τις ποιητὴς [Hes., fgm. 247 Rz.] ἐν καρδίᾳ περιέχεσθαι=some poet said that the heart embraces perception, wit, intellect, and reflection), of humans whether in their pre-Christian or Christian experience

α. in an all-inclusive sense: said of God's or Christ's awareness about the inner life of humans γινώσκειν τὰς καρδίας (cp. 1 Km 16:7; 1 Ch 28:9; s. also Did., Gen. 170, 24) **Lk 16:15;** δοκιμάζειν **1 Th 2:4;** ἐρευνᾶν **Ro 8:27; Rv 2:23** (νεφροὺς κ. καρδίας as Ps 7:10; Jer 17:10; 20:12); κριτικὸς ἐνθυμήσεων καὶ ἐννοιῶν καρδίας **Hb 4:12;** τὰ κρυπτὰ τῆς κ. **1 Cor 14:25** (cp. TestReub 1:4). Generally, of human attitudes ὁ κρυπτὸς τῆς κ. ἄνθρωπος **1 Pt 3:4.** ἐκ καρδίας *from* (the bottom of) *the heart*=sincerely (Aristoph., Nub. 86) **Ro 6:17.** Also ἀπὸ τῶν καρδιῶν (M. Ant. 2, 3, 3 ἀπὸ καρδίας εὐχάριστος τ. θεοῖς; Lucian, Jupp. Tr. 19; Is 59:13; La 3:33) **Mt 18:35.** ἐκ καθαρᾶς καρδίας **1 Ti 1:5; 2 Ti 2:22; 1 Pt 1:22.** ἐξ ὅλης τ. καρδίας (TestLevi 13:1) **Ac 8:37 v.l.** Χριστὸν ἁγιάσατε ἐν ταῖς κ. ὑμῶν **1 Pt 3:15.** Opp. κοιλία **Mk 7:19.** Opp. πρόσωπον and καρδία externals and inner attitude of heart (cp. 1 Km 16:7 ἄνθρωπος ὄψεται εἰς πρόσωπον, ὁ δὲ θεὸς ὄψεται εἰς καρδίαν) **2 Cor 5:12.** The same contrast προσώπῳ οὐ καρδίᾳ *outwardly, not inwardly* **1 Th 2:17.** As seat of inner life in contrast to mouth or lips, which either give expression to the inner life or deny it **Mt 15:8; Mk 7:6** (both Is 29:13); **Mt 15:18; Ro 10:8** (Dt 30:14); vs. **9f; 2 Cor 6:11.** ψάλλοντες (+ ἐν v.l.) τῇ καρδίᾳ **Eph 5:19.** ᾄδειν ἐν ταῖς κ. **Col 3:16.**

β. of inner awareness (see the 'poet' under 1b above; Aesop, Fab. 254P.=232H//134b H-H.//184 Ch.; 3 Km 10:2; Job 12:3; 17:4): **2 Cor 4:6; Eph 1:18; 2 Pt 1:19.** τῇ κ. συνιέναι *understand* **Mt 13:15b; Ac 28:27b** (both Is 6:10). νοεῖν τῇ κ. *think* **J 12:40b.** ἐν τῇ κ. λέγειν (Dt 8:17; 9:4; Ps 13:1. Also Aesop Fab. 62 H.=283b 5 H-H.//179c Ch. βοῶν ἐν τῇ καρδίᾳ alternating w. ταῦτα καθ' ἑαυτὸν λέγοντος) *say to oneself,* i.e. think, reflect, without saying anything aloud **Mt 24:48; Lk 12:45; Ro 10:6; Rv 18:7;** διαλογίζεσθαι **Mk 2:6, 8; Lk 3:15; 5:22;** Hv 1, 1, 2; 3, 4, 3. The κ. as the source of διαλογισμοί **Mt 15:19; Mk 7:21; Lk 2:35; 9:47.** διαλογισμοὶ ἀναβαίνουσιν ἐν τῇ καρδίᾳ **Lk 24:38.** ἀναβαίνει τι ἐπὶ τὴν καρδίαν τινός *someth. enters someone's mind*=someone thinks of someth. (s. ἀναβαίνω 2) **Ac 7:23; 1 Cor 2:9;** Hv 3, 7, 2; m 12, 3, 5; s 5, 7, 2. Also of memory Hv 3, 7, 6; m 4, 2, 2; 6, 2, 8. θέσθαι ἐν τῇ καρδίᾳ **Lk 1:66.** διατηρεῖν ἐν τ. καρδίᾳ **Lk 2:51** (cp. TestLevi 6:2). συμβάλλειν vs. **19.** ἐνθυμεῖσθαι **Mt 9:4.** διακρίνειν Hv 1, 2, 2. πάντα τὰ ῥήματά μου ἐν καρδίᾳ λαμβάνων *taking all my words to heart* AcPl Ha 1, 6.—Likew. of a lack of understanding: ἡ ἀσύνετος κ. *the senseless mind* **Ro 1:21;** βραδὺς τῇ κ. *slow of comprehension* **Lk 24:25** (cp. Tetr. Iamb. 2, 31a, 6 the mocking words of the fox ὦ ἀνόητε κ. βραδὺ τῇ καρδίᾳ). ἐπαχύνθη ἡ κ. τοῦ λαοῦ **Mt 13:15a; Ac 28:27a** (both Is 6:10). πωροῦν τὴν κ. **J 12:40a;** κ. πεπωρωμένη **Mk 6:52; 8:17;** ἡ πώρωσις τῆς κ. **3:5; Eph 4:18.** ἀπατᾶν καρδίαν αὐτοῦ **Js 1:26;** cp. **Ro 16:18.** κάλυμμα ἐπὶ τὴν κ. κεῖται **2 Cor 3:15** (cp. ἐστί τι 'κάλλυμα' ἀγνοίας ἐν τῇ καρδίᾳ Orig., C. Cels. 4, 50, 5).—As the seat of thought, κ. is also the seat of doubt διακρίνεσθαι ἐν τῇ κ. **Mk 11:23.** διστάζειν Hm 9:5.—The gospel is sown in the heart **Mt 13:19 v.l.; Mk 4:15 v.l.; Lk 8:12, 15.** God opens the heart **Ac 16:14** or the eyes of the heart **Eph 1:18;** 1 Cl 59:3 to Christian knowledge.

γ. of the will and its decisions (Diod. S. 32, 20) ἕκαστος καθὼς προῄρηται τῇ κ. *each of you must give as you have made up your mind* **2 Cor 9:7** (NRSV) (cp. TestJos 17:3 ἐπὶ προαιρέσει καρδίας). θέτε ἐν ταῖς καρδίαις ὑμῶν (s. 1 Km 21:13) *make up your minds* **Lk 21:14;** cp. **Ac 5:4.** πρόθεσις τ. καρδίας **11:23.** βάλλειν εἰς τὴν κ. ἵνα *put it into someone's heart to* **J 13:2.** Also διδόναι εἰς τ. κ. (2 Esdr 17:5) w. inf. foll. **Rv 17:17,** or πληροῦν τὴν κ. w. inf. foll. **Ac 5:3.** Cp. **1 Cor 4:5; 7:37; 2 Cor 8:16;** in citation **Hb 3:8, 15; 4:7** (each Ps 94:8) al. πλανᾶσθαι τῇ κ. **3:10.** God's law written in human hearts **Ro 2:15; 2 Cor 3:2f.** In citation **Hb 8:10; 10:16** (both Jer 38:33). Stability in the face of dissident teaching **Hb 13:9.**

δ. of moral decisions, the moral life, of vices and virtues: ἁγνίζειν τὰς κ. **Js 4:8;** καθαρίζειν τὰς κ. **Ac 15:9;** Hv 3, 9, 8; w. ἀπό τινος Hm 12, 6, 5; καθαρὸς τῇ κ. *pure in heart* (Ps 23:4) **Mt 5:8;** καθαρὰ κ. (Sextus 46b) Hv 4, 2, 5; 5:7; m 2:7 cj.; s 7:6. ῥεραντισμένοι τὰς κ. ἀπὸ συνειδήσεως πονηρᾶς *with hearts sprinkled clean from a consciousness of guilt* **Hb 10:22.** κ. ἄμεμπτος **1 Th 3:13.** ἀμετανόητος **Ro 2:5.** κ. πονηρὰ ἀπιστίας **Hb 3:12;** λίθιναι κ. B 6:14 (Ezk 36:26). γεγυμνασμένη πλεονεξίας *trained in greediness* **2 Pt 2:14** (cp. κ. . . . ἐπὶ τὸ κακὸν ἔγκειται Did., Gen. 104, 14). Cp. **Lk 21:34; Ac 8:21f.** περιτομὴ καρδίας (cp. Jer 9:25; Ezk 44:7, 9) **Ro 2:29.**—B 9:1; 10:12. Cp. **Ac 7:51.**

ε. of the emotions, wishes, desires (Theognis 1, 366; Bacchylides 17, 18): ἐπιθυμίαι τῶν κ. *desires of the heart* **Ro 1:24.** ἐπὶ τὴν κ. σου ἀνέβη ἡ ἐπιθυμία τ. πονηρίας Hv 1, 1, 8; cp. s 5, 1, 5. ἐνθύμησις m 4, 1, 2; 6, 2, 7. μὴ ἀναβαινέτω σου ἐπὶ τὴν κ. περὶ γυναικός m 4, 1, 1; cp. Hv 1, 2, 4; **Mt 5:28.—6:21; 12:34f; Lk 6:45; 12:34; 24:32** (s. καίω 1b); **Js 3:14; 5:8.** Of joy: ηὐφράνθη ἡ κ. **Ac 2:26** (Ps 15:9). χαρήσεται ἡ κ. **J 16:22.** Of sorrow: ἡ λύπη πεπλήρωκεν τὴν κ. **16:6;** λύπη ἐγκάθηται εἰς τὴν κ. *grief sits in the heart* Hm 10, 3, 3. ἡ κ. ταράσσεται (Job 37:1; Ps 142:4) **J 14:1, 27;** ὀδύνη τῇ κ. **Ro 9:2.** συνοχὴ καρδίας *anguish of heart* **2 Cor 2:4;** διαπρίεσθαι ταῖς κ. **Ac 7:54;** κατανυγῆναι τὴν κ. **2:37;** συνθρύπτειν τὴν κ. **21:13.** κ. συντετριμμένη *a broken heart* B 2:10; 1 Cl 18:17b (Ps 50:19). συντετριμμένοι τὴν κ. **Lk 4:18 v.l.** παρακαλεῖν τὰς κ. **Eph 6:22; Col 2:2; 4:8; 2 Th 2:17.** Of hope (Ps 111:7) Hm 12, 5, 2. Of repentance ἐξ ὅλης κ. Hv 3, 13, 4; m 5, 1, 7; 12, 6, 1. Of sensitivity about doing what is right (1 Km 24:6; 2 Km 24:10) **1J 3:19, 20, 21** (s. ASkrinjar, Verb. Dom. 20, '40, 340–50). Of a wish εὐδοκία τῆς κ. (s. εὐδοκία 3) **Ro 10:1.** Of a longing for God τὴν κ. ἔχειν πρὸς κύριον Hm 10, 1, 6. ἐπιστρέφεσθαι πρὸς τὸν κύριον ἐξ ὅλης τῆς κ. 12, 6, 2 (cp. 3 Km 8:48). προσέρχεσθαι μετὰ ἀληθινῆς κ. *with sincere desire* (cp. Is 38:3; TestDan 5:3 ἀλ. κ.) **Hb 10:22.** Cp. the opposite **Ac 7:39.**—Also of the wish or desire of God ἀνὴρ κατὰ τὴν κ. (τοῦ θεοῦ) *after God's heart* i.e. *as God wishes him to be* **Ac 13:22** (cp. 1 Km 13:14).

ζ. esp. also of love (Aristoph., Nub. 86 ἐκ τῆς κ. φιλεῖν; M. Ant. 7, 13, 3 ἀπὸ κ. φιλεῖν τ. ἀνθρώπους) ἀγαπᾶν τινα ἐξ ὅλης τ. καρδίας **Mk 12:30, 33; Lk 10:27** (cp. Dt 6:5 and APF 5, 1913, 393 no. 312, 9 ἐκ ψυχῆς κ. καρδίας). ἐν ὅλῃ τ. καρδίᾳ **Mt 22:37;** ἐπιστρέψαι καρδίας πατέρων ἐπὶ τέκνα **Lk 1:17** (Mal 3:23); εἶναι ἐν τῇ κ. *have a place in the heart* **2 Cor 7:3;** ἔχειν τινὰ ἐν τῇ κ. **Phil 1:7;** Hm 12, 4, 3; s 5, 4, 3; cp. m 12, 4, 5; κατευθύνειν τὰς κ. εἰς τὴν ἀγάπην τοῦ θεοῦ **2 Th 3:5.**—The opp. κατά τινος ἐν τῇ κ. ἔχειν *have someth. against someone* Hv 3, 6, 3.

η. of disposition (TestJob 48:1 ἀνέλαβεν ἄλλην κ.) διάνοια καρδίας **Lk 1:51;** ἁπλότης (τ.) καρδίας (TestReub 4:1, Sim 4:5 al.) **Eph 6:5; Col 3:22;** ἀφελότης καρδίας **Ac 2:46.** κ. καὶ ψυχὴ μία **Ac 4:32** (cp. Iren. 1, 10, 2 [Harv. I 92, 5]; combination of ψυχή and καρδία as PGM 7, 472; IDefixWünsch 3, 15; Dt 11:18; 1 Km 2:35; 4 Km 23:3 and oft. LXX—on such combinations s. Reader, Polemo p. 260 and cp. Demosth. 18, 220 ῥώμη καὶ τόλμη). πραῢς καὶ ταπεινὸς τῇ κ. **Mt 11:29** (cp. TestReub 6:10). ἡ εἰρήνη τοῦ Χριστοῦ βραβευέτω ἐν ταῖς κ. ὑμῶν *let the peace of Christ control you* **Col 3:15;** cp. **Phil 4:7.**

θ. The human καρδία as the dwelling-place of heavenly powers and beings (PGM 1, 21 ἔσται τι ἔνθεον ἐν τῇ σῇ κ.): of the Spirit **Ro 5:5; 2 Cor 1:22; Gal 4:6;** of the Lord **Eph 3:17;** of the angel of righteousness Hm 6, 2, 3; 5.

❷ ***interior, center, heart,*** fig. ext. of 1 (Ezk 27:4, 25; Jon 2:4; Ps 45:3; EpJer 19) τῆς γῆς **Mt 12:40.**—S., in addition to works on Bibl. anthropology and psychology (πνεῦμα end): HKornfeld, Herz u. Gehirn in altjüd. Auffassung: Jahrb. für jüd. Gesch. u. Lit. 12, 1909, 81–89; ASchlatter, Herz. u. Gehirn im 1. Jahrh.: THaering Festschr. 1918, 86–94; RBultmann, Theologie des NT '48, 216–22 (Paul), tr., Theol. of the NT, KGrobel, '51, I, 220–27; RJewett, Paul's Anthropological Terms, '71, 305–33. For OT viewpoints s. RNorth, BRev 11/3, '95, 33 (lit.)—B. 251. EDNT. DELG. M-M. TW. Sv.

καρδιογνώστης, ου, ὁ (s. καρδία, γνώστης; only in Christian wr., e.g. Ps.-Clem., Hom. 10, 13; other reff. in Haenchen ad loc.) ***knower of hearts, one who knows the hearts,*** of God **Ac 1:24; 15:8** (on these pass. s. JBauer, BZ 32, '88, 114–17); Hm 4, 3, 4.—M-M. DELG s.v. γιγνώσκω. TW.

καροῦχα, ας, ἡ (Sym. Is 66:20; Chron. Pasch. 571, 7 LDind. [1832] and in Byz. wr.) ***carriage*** (actually a Celtic word, Lat. carruca) MPol 8:2f.—Pauly-W. III 1614f.

καρπάσινος, η, ον (Dionys. Hal. 2, 68, 5; Strabo 7, 2, 3; Esth 1:6) ***made of fine flax*** (Lat. carbasus; כַּרְפַּס) λέντιον κ. (v.l. καρπάσιον) *a fine linen cloth* Hv 3, 1, 4 (Tibullus 3, 2, 21 carbasea lina).—Pauly-W. III 1572ff. DELG s.v. κάρπασος.

Κάρπος, ου, ὁ (Artem. 3, 38; SIG² 438, 20; InsHierap 129; coin fr. Magnesia [Thieme 40]; pap [Preisigke, Namenbuch]) ***Carpus,*** a Christian in Troas **2 Ti 4:13.**—LGPN I. M-M.

καρπός, οῦ, ὁ (Hom.+) 'fruit' (the sing. used collectively: Diod. S. 3, 24, 1).

❶ product or outcome of someth., *fruit*—ⓐ in a physical sense—**α.** of plants: trees **Mt 12:33; 21:19; Mk 11:14; Lk 6:44; 13:6f;** IEph 14:2; Hs 1, 2, 1; 9, 1, 10; 9, 28, 1 and 3 (Did., Gen. 86, 3). Of the fruit of the vine (Jos., Ant. 2, 67; Ath 22:6) **Mt 21:34; Mk 12:2; Lk 20:10; 1 Cor 9:7;** 1 Cl 23:4; of a berry-bush B 7:8. Of field *crops* (Diod. S. 4, 4, 2; Ps.-Phoc. 38; SibOr 4, 16; Hippol., Ref. 7, 29, 5) **2 Ti 2:6;** 1 Cl 24:4; qualified by τῆς γῆς **Js 5:7a;** cp. vs. **7b v.l.;** 1 Cl 14:1 (Gen 4:3); GJs 3:3. συνάγειν τοὺς κ. (Lev 25:3) **Lk 12:17;** cp. **J 4:36;** ὅταν παραδοῖ ὁ κ. *when the* (condition of the) *crop permits* **Mk 4:29** ('fruit'=grain as Ps.-Scylax, Peripl. §93 p. 36 Fabr. [πυροὺς κ. κριθάς]). βλαστάνειν τὸν κ. *produce crops* **Js 5:18** (βλαστάνω 1). ποιεῖν κ. (=עָשָׂה פְּרִי) *bear* or *yield fruit* (Gen 1:11f; 4 Km 19:30; Ezk 17:23; ParJer 9:16, 19.—Diosc., Mat. Med. 2, 195) **Mt 3:10** (s. δένδρον); **7:17ff; 13:26; Lk 3:9; 6:43; 8:8; 13:9; Rv 22:2a.** Also διδόναι (=נָתַן פְּרִי; Lev 26:20; Dt 11:17; Ps 1:3; Zech 8:12) **Mt 13:8; Mk 4:7f;** B 11:6 (Ps 1:3); Hs 2:4; 5, 2, 4.

φέρειν (Apollon. Rhod. 4, 1396–99b; Jo 2:22; Hos 9:16; Jos., Ant. 3, 11; SibOr 2, 320; Did., Gen. 31, 3) **Mt 7:18a v.l.; J 12:24** (of the resurrection: ἐκφέρει 1 Cl 24:5); **15:2, 4;** Hs 2:3, 8a. ἡ γῆ προφέρει τοὺς κ. αὐτῆς GJs 8:3. ἀποδιδόναι *bear fruit* (Lev 26:4) **Rv 22:2b;** Hs 2:8b; cp. **Hb 12:11,** but *pay* a person a *portion of the fruit* **Mt 21:41.** γεννᾶν κ. θανατηφόρον *bear deadly fruit* ITr 11:1 (in imagery, s. b below). κ. ἔχειν of trees Hs 9, 28, 3; of staffs 8, 1, 18; 8, 2, 1; 8, 3, 7; 8, 4, 6; 8, 5, 6; of Aaron's staff (Num 17:23ff) 1 Cl 43:5.

β. of a human being: Hebraistically of offspring ὁ κ. τῆς κοιλίας *the fruit of the womb* (Gen 30:2; Ps 131:11; Mi 6:7; La 2:20; TestAbr A 6 p. 83, 14 [Stone p. 14]; Mel., P. 52, 384 [since the central mng. of κοιλία is someth. 'hollow', in the Ps and Mi pass. κοιλία is used in the general sense of 'body' as the cavity from which someth. emanates]) **Lk 1:42.** τοῦ μὴ δοῦναί σοι καρπόν=*to grant you no children* GJs 2:3; cp. 6:3 (s. b below). Fr. the standpoint of a father: ὁ κ. τῆς ὀσφύος *the fruit of his loins* **Ac 2:30;** AcPl Ha 8, 14 (ἰσχύος Ox 1602, 12f//BMM recto 17).

ⓑ fig., in the spiritual (opp. physical) realm; sometimes the orig. figure is quite prominent; somet. it is more or less weakened: *result, outcome, product* (cp. Epict. 2, 1, 21 τῶν δογμάτων καρπός; IPriene 112, 14 [I BC] μόνη μεγίστους ἀποδίδωσιν καρπούς; Dio Chrys. 23 [40], 34 τῆς ἔχθρας καρπός) κ. τοῦ πνεύματος **Gal 5:22** (a list of virtues following a list of vices as Cebes 19, 5; 20, 3; Ael. Aristid. 37, 27 K.=2 p. 27 D.). τοῦ φωτός **Eph 5:9;** κ. πολὺν φέρειν *be very fruitful* **J 15:5, 8, 16.** κ. δικαιοσύνης *fruit of righteousness* (cp. Epicurus, fgm. 519 δικαιοσύνης καρπὸς μέγιστος ἀταραξία; Am 6:12; Pr 11:30; 13:2; EpArist 232) **Phil 1:11; Js 3:18;** Hs 9, 19, 2a; cp. ἔδωκέν μοι κύριος . . . καρπὸν δικαιοσύνης αὐτοῦ GJs 6:3 (of the birth of Mary; s. β above); κ. εἰρηνικὸς δικαιοσύνης *peaceful fruit of righteousness* **Hb 12:11.** κ. ἀληθείας Hs 9, 19, 2b. The outcome of acting is a deed: ἀπὸ τῶν καρπῶν τινος ἐπιγινώσκειν τινά *know someone by the person's deeds,* as one knows a tree by its fruits **Mt 7:16, 20;** Hs 4:5 (Proverbia Aesopi 51 P.: Δῆλος ἔλεγχος ὁ καρπὸς γενήσεται | παντὸς δένδρου ἣν ἔχει φύσιν=its fruit will be for every tree a clear proof of its nature). γεννᾶν καρπὸν θανατηφόρον *bear deadly fruit* ITr 11:1 (s. 1aα); moral performance as fruit vs. 2 (accord. to the imagery, Christians are branches of the cross as their trunk and their deeds are the produce). Fruit of martyrdom Hs 9, 28, 4. ποιεῖν τοὺς καρποὺς αὐτῆς (=τῆς βασιλείας τ. θεοῦ) *prove fruitful for the kingdom* ποιεῖν καρπὸν ἄξιον τῆς μετανοίας **Mt 21:43.** *bear fruit consistent with repentance* **3:8;** the pl. in the parallel **Lk 3:8** is farther removed fr. the orig. picture: καρποί = ἔργα (cp. Pr 10:16). καρποὶ ἀγαθοί **Js 3:17.** Cp. Dg 12:1. τίνα καρπὸν ἄξιον . . . (δώσομεν); *what fruit (are we to bring to Christ that would be) worthy of what he has given us?* 2 Cl 1:3. Of the outcome of life in sin as well as in righteousness **Ro 6:21f** (of the results of evil e.g., Oenomaus fgm. 2m [in Eus., PE 5, 20, 10]); ταχὺς κ. (s. ταχ. 1a) 2 Cl 20:3. After an upright life καρπὸν προσδοκῶν Dg 12:6; cp. 12:8; resurrection as the reward after a miserable life ἔδονται τῆς ἑαυτῶν ὁδοῦ τοὺς κ. 2 Cl 19:3.—ἀφ' οὗ καρποῦ ἡμεῖς (the suffering of Jesus,) *the fruit from which we are,* i.e. from which we derive our identity as Christians (the cross is here viewed as a tree on which Jesus hangs as the fruit: Ignatius probably thinks of Christians as germinated seeds) ISm 1:2.—Of the proceeds of a collection **Ro 15:28.**

ⓒ Hebraistically, a praise-offering as καρπὸς χειλέων (Hos 14:3; Pr 18:20; 31:31 v.l.; PsSol 15:3) **Hb 13:15.**

❷ ***advantage, gain, profit*** (Polyaenus 3, 9, 1 κ. τῆς ἀνδραγαθίας; EpArist 260 σοφίας κ.; Philo, Fug. 176 ἐπιστήμης; Jos., Ant. 20, 48 εὐσεβείας) κ. ἔργου *gain from the labor* **Phil 1:22.** οὐ δόμα, ἀλλὰ τὸν καρπόν *not the gift, but the advantage* (accruing to the Philippians fr. their generous giving) **4:17;** κ. ἔχειν *have fruit* **Ro 1:13.**—B. 511. DELG 1 καρπός. EDNT. TW.

καρποφορέω (s. καρπός, φέρω) fut. καρποφορήσω; 1 aor. ἐκαρποφόρησα

❶ **to cause production of fruit or seeds, *bear fruit/crops*** lit. (X. et al.; Theophr., HP 3, 3, 7; Diod. S. 2, 49, 4; PMichZen106, 6 [III BC]; Wsd 10:7; Hab 3:17; En 5:1; Just., D. 110, 4) of land **Mk 4:28** (γῆ κ. as Jos., C. Ap. 1, 306; Did., Gen. 31, 14). Of a vine Hs 2:3.

❷ **to cause the inner life to be productive, *bear fruit*** (Philo, Cher. 84 κ. ἀρετάς; Did., Gen. 32, 24; for construction w. acc. cp. Hippol., Ref. 6, 46, 3; abs. OdeSol 11:23; cp. SEG XLII, 1193, 8 and 1421, 4 both Christian V AD) **Mt 13:23; Mk 4:20; Lk 8:15;** Hs 4:5, 8. κ. ἐν τῇ καρδίᾳ *bear fruit in the heart,* i.e. in a resolve to do what is right B 11:11; cp. ἐν σεαυτῷ Hs 4:5. Of faith τῆς πίστεως ῥίζα καρποφορεῖ εἰς τὸν κύριον ἡμῶν Ἰησοῦν Χριστόν *the root of faith yields fruit in* (or *to*) *our Lord Jesus Christ* Pol 1:2. W. dat. of advantage κ. τῷ θεῷ **Ro 7:4** (so OdeSol 11:1). Also τῷ θανάτῳ vs. **5.** κ. ἐν παντὶ ἔργῳ ἀγαθῷ *bear fruit in all kinds of good deeds* **Col 1:10.**—Mid. (IBM 918) *bear fruit* of itself **1:6.**—DELG s.v. φέρω p. 1190. M-M. TW.

καρποφόρος, ον (s. καρποφορέω; Pind., Hdt.+; ins; PSI 171, 40 [II BC]; Gk. Parchments fr. Avroman: JHS 35, 1915, 22ff, no. 1 A, 13 [88 BC]; Sb 991, 5; 6598, 7; LXX; OdeSol 11:16a; TestSol C prol. 3; JosAs 2:19; ch. 16 cod. A [p. 65, 17 Bat.]; Philo; Jos., Bell. 3, 44, Ant. 4, 85; Just., D. 110, 4; SibOr, fgm. 3, 5) ***fruitbearing, fruitful*** καιροὶ κ. (s. καιρός 1a) **Ac 14:17.** Cp. **J 15:2** D.—DELG s.v. φέρω p. 1190. M-M.

καρτερέω (s. κράτος) fut. καρτερήσω LXX; 1 aor. ἐκαρτέρησα (Soph., Thu. et al.; pap, LXX; TestJob 4:10; Jos., Ant. 11, 52) **to continue without wavering in a state or condition, *be strong, be steadfast, hold out, endure*** (Thu. 2, 44, 3; Pla., Theaet. 157d, Lach. 193a; Diod. S. 3, 5, 3 καρτερῆσαι μέχρι τῆς τελευτῆς; PGrenf I, 1, 19 [II BC]; PAmh 130, 6; Job 2:9; Sir 2:2; 12:15; 2 Macc 7:17 al.) τὸν ἀόρατον ὡς ὁρῶν ἐκαρτέρησεν *he persevered as if he saw him who is invisible* **Hb 11:27.** Cp. Windisch; Strathmann.—GWhitaker, in ET 27, 1916, 186 prefers the mng. *fix one's eyes upon,* on the basis of certain pass. in Plut.—But the proper understanding of this word must surely proceed from the fact that the ptc. with καρτερεῖν does not denote an accompanying circumstance, but rather the quality in which someone endures or is steadfast (Diod. S. 8, 18, 3 τοιοῦτον βίον ζῶντα καρτερεῖν=keep on living a life like this; 14, 65, 4 μέχρι τίνος καρτερήσομεν ταῦτα πάσχοντες;=how long will we continue to suffer this?; 18, 60, 1 καρτερεῖν δεσποζόμενος=allow oneself to be continually dominated; Arrian., Anab. 7, 8, 3 οὔκουν σιγῇ ἔχοντες ἐκαρτέρησαν=they did not continue, then, in silence; Ps.-Dicaearchus p. 141 ln. 11 F. ἀκούων καρτ.=listen continually). Accordingly **Hb 11:27,** giving the reason for Moses' fearlessness: *he kept the one who is invisible continually before his eyes* (i.e., in faith), *as it were.*—DELG s.v. κράτος. M-M. TW.

[ἀπὸ] Καρυώτου s. Ἰσκαριώθ.

κάρφος, ους, τό (Aeschyl., Hdt. et al.; Gen 8:11) **a small piece of straw, chaff, or wood, to denote someth. quite insignificant, *speck, splinter, chip*** (cp. the proverb κινεῖν μηδὲ κ. Aristoph., Lysias 474 and Herodas 1, 54; 3, 67.—Ion of Chios [V BC]: 392 fgm. 6 p. 280, 7 Jac. of a tiny foreign object in a wine cup. Grave ins, Kaibel 980, 9 [ὁ εὐσεβὴς] οὐδὲ κάρφος ἐβλάβη) **Mt 7:3ff; Lk 6:41f;** Ox 1 verso, 2 (ASyn. 68, 44)=GTh 26.—For lit. s. on δοκός.—DELG s.v. κάρφω. M-M.

καρχηδών s. χαλκηδών.

κατά (Hom.+) prep. (s. the lit. s.v. ἀνά beg., also LfgrE s.v. κατά 1346; with the gen. 74 times in NT; w. acc. 391 times in NT).

A. w. the gen.—**❶ marker of extension or orientation in space or specific area**—ⓐ of location that is relatively lower, ***down from*** *someth.* (Hom. et al.; LXX; Ath. 1, 4 κ. κόρρης προπηλακίζειν=to smack on one side of the head) ὁρμᾶν κ. τοῦ κρημνοῦ *rush down (from) the bank* (cp. Polyb. 38, 16, 7 κ. τῶν κρημνῶν ῥίπτειν; Jos., Bell. 1, 313) **Mt 8:32; Mk 5:13; Lk 8:33.** κ. κεφαλῆς ἔχειν *have someth. on one's head* (lit. hanging down fr. the head, as a veil. Cp. Plut., Mor. 200f ἐβάδιζε κ. τῆς κεφαλῆς ἔχων τὸ ἱμάτιον.; Mitt-Wilck. I/2, 499, 5 of a mummy ἔχων τάβλαν κ. τοῦ τραχήλου) **1 Cor 11:4.**

ⓑ of position relatively deep, ***into*** *someth.* (Od. 9, 330 κ. σπείους 'into the depths of the cave'; Hdt. 7, 235; X., An. 7, 1, 30) ἡ κ. βάθους πτωχεία *extreme* (lit. 'reaching down into the depths'; cp. Strabo 9, 3, 5 [419] ἄντρον κοῖλον κ. βάθους) or *abysmal poverty* **2 Cor 8:2.** This may perh. be the mng. of πλήσσειν τινὰ κ. τῶν ὀφθαλμῶν *strike someone deep into the eyes* ApcPt 11:26 (cp. Demosth. 19, 197 ξαίνει κ. τοῦ νώτου; PPetr II, 18 [2b], 15 [246 BC] ἔτυπτεν αὐτὸν κ. τοῦ τραχήλου).—κ. γαστρός Just., D. 78, 3 for ἐν γαστρί Mt 1:18 (cp. Ath. 35, 2 τὸ κ. γαστρὸς ζῷον εἶναι).

ⓒ extension in various directions within an area, ***throughout*** (so in Luke's writings; Polyb. 3, 19, 7 κ. τῆς νήσου διεσπάρησαν; PGiss 48, 8 κ. κυριακῆς γῆς; Jos., Ant. 8, 297; SibOr 3, 222; 4, 24; 5, 305) γνωστὸν γενέσθαι καθ' ὅλης Ἰόππης *become known throughout all Joppa* **Ac 9:42.** καθ' ὅλης τῆς Ἰουδαίας **9:31; 10:37; Lk 23:5.** φήμη ἐξῆλθεν καθ' ὅλης τῆς περιχώρου **4:14.**

❷ *down upon, toward, against someone or someth,* fig. ext. of 1.—ⓐ w. verbs of swearing, to denote what one swears by (Thu. 5, 47, 8; Lysias 32, 13; Isaeus 7, 28; Demosth. 21, 119; 29, 26; SIG 526, 4ff; 685, 25; UPZ 110, 39 [164 BC]; BGU 248, 13; Jdth 1:12; Is 45:23; 2 Ch 36:13) ***by*** ἐξορκίζειν (q.v.) **Mt 26:63.** ὀμνύναι (q.v.) **Hb 6:13, 16.** ὁρκίζειν (q.v.) Hs 9, 10, 5. Sim. ἐρωτᾶν κ. τινος *request, entreat by someone* Hv 3, 2, 3.

ⓑ in a hostile sense, ***against***—α. after verbs that express hostile action, etc. διχάζειν **Mt 10:35.** ἐπαίρεσθαι **2 Cor 10:5.** ἰσχύειν **Ac 19:16.** κακοῦν **14:2.** στρατεύεσθαι **1 Pt 2:11.** φυσιοῦσθαι **1 Cor 4:6**

β. after words and expressions that designate hostile speech, esp. an accusation ἔχειν (τι) κ. τινος *have* or *hold someth. against someone* **Rv 2:4, 14, 20.** φέρειν **J 18:29.** ἐγκαλεῖν **Ro 8:33.** ἐντυγχάνειν τινὶ κ. τινος **11:2** (TestJob 17:5). κατηγορεῖν **Lk 23:14.** ποιεῖν κρίσιν **Jd 15a.** τὸ κ. ἡμῶν χειρόγραφον *the bond that stands against us* **Col 2:14.** ἐμφανίζειν **Ac 24:1; 25:2.** αἰτεῖσθαί τι **25:3, 15.** αἱ κ. τινος αἰτίαι vs. **27.** εἰπεῖν πονηρόν **Mt 5:11** (cp. Soph., Phil. 65 κακὰ λέγειν κ. τινος. X., Hell. 1, 5, 2; Isocr., C. Nic. 13; Plut., Mor. 2a λέγειν κ.; SIG 1180, 1 λέγειν κ. τινος; Just., A I, 23, 3; 49, 6 κ. τῶν . . . ὁμολογούντων). λαλεῖν ῥήματα **Ac 6:13;** cp. **Jd 15b** (TestDan 4:3; JosAs 23:15). μαρτυρεῖν κ. τ. θεοῦ *give testimony in contradiction to God* **1 Cor 15:15.** ζητεῖν μαρτυρίαν κ. τινος *testimony against someone* **Mk 14:55.** ψευδομαρτυρεῖν **14:56f.** ψευδομαρτυρία **Mt 26:59.** γογγύζειν **20:11.** στενάζειν **Js 5:9.** διδάσκειν **Ac 21:28.** συμβούλιον διδόναι (ποιεῖν v.l.) **Mk 3:6;** σ. λαβεῖν **Mt 27:1.** ψεύδεσθαι **Js 3:14** (Lysias 22, 7; X., Ap. 13; Ath. 35, 1 καθ' ἡμῶν . . . κατεψεύσατο).

γ. after expressions that designate such a position or state of mind in a different way εἶναι κ. τινος *be against someone* (opp. ὑπέρ) **Mk 9:40** (WNestle, ZNW 13, 1912, 84–87; AFridrichsen, ibid., 273–80); **Ro 8:31;** (opp. μετά) **Mt 12:30; Lk 11:23.** δύνασθαί τι κ. τινος *be able to do someth. against someone* **2 Cor 13:8.** ἔχειν τι κ. τινος *have someth. against someone* (in one's heart) **Mt 5:23; Mk 11:25;** Hs 9, 24, 2; cp. ibid. 23, 2, where the acc. is to be supplied. ἐξουσίαν ἔχειν **J 19:11.** ἐπιθυμεῖν **Gal 5:17.** μερίζεσθαι καθ' ἑαυτῆς **Mt 12:25.** Cp. 1 Cl 39:4 (Job 4:18).—κατά prob. means *against* also in ἔβαλεν κατ' αὐτῆς ἄνεμος **Ac 27:14.** ἐτελείωσαν κ. τ. κεφαλῆς αὐτῶν τὰ ἁμαρτήματα *they completed the full measure of sins against their own head* GPt 5:17.

B. w. acc. (so in the NT 399 times [besides καθ' εἷς and κατὰ εἷς])—**❶ marker of spatial aspect**—ⓐ of extension in space, ***along, over, through, in, upon*** (Hom. et al.; OGI 90, 7 ἐκ τῶν κ. τ. χώραν ἱερῶν; PHib 82, 19; PTebt 5, 188; LXX; Just.; Mel., HE 4, 26, 5) **Ac 24:12.** καθ' ὅλην τ. πόλιν *throughout the city* **Lk 8:39** (cp. Diod. S. 4, 10, 6 καθ' ὅλην τὴν Ἑλλάδα). ἐγένετο λιμὸς κ. τὴν χώραν ἐκείνην **15:14.** κ. τὰς κώμας **9:6.** κ. πόλεις καὶ κώμας **13:22** (Appian., Maced. 9 §1 and 4 κ. πόλεις; Just., A I, 67, 3 κ. πόλεις ἢ ἀγρούς).—κ. τόπους *in place after place* **Mt 24:7; Mk 13:8; Lk 21:11** (Theophr., περὶ σημ. 1, 4 p. 389 W.; Cat. Cod. Astr. III 28, 11 ἐν μέρει τ. ἀνατολῆς κ. τόπους, VIII/3, 186, 1 λιμὸς καὶ λοιμὸς καὶ σφαγαὶ κ. τόπους). οἱ ὄντες κ. τὴν Ἰουδαίαν *those throughout Judea* or *living in Judea* **Ac 11:1.** διασπαρῆναι κ. τὰς χώρας τῆς Ἰουδαίας *be scattered over the regions of Judea* **8:1.** κ. τὴν οὖσαν ἐκκλησίαν *in the congregation there* **13:1.** τοῖς κ. τὴν Ἀντιόχειαν καὶ Συρίαν καὶ Κιλικίαν ἀδελφοῖς **15:23.** τοὺς κ. τὰ ἔθνη Ἰουδαίους *the Judeans (dispersed) throughout the nations* **21:21.** τοῖς κ. τὸν νόμον γεγραμμένοις *throughout the law = in the law* **24:14b.** κ. τὴν ὁδόν *along* or *on the way* (Lucian, Catapl. 4; Jos., Ant. 8, 404) **Lk 10:4; Ac 25:3; 26:13.** τὸ κ. Κιλικίαν καὶ Παμφυλίαν πέλαγος *the sea along the coast of Cilicia and Pamphylia* **27:5;** but the geographical designation τὰ μέρη τ. Λιβύης τῆς κ. Κυρήνην **2:10** prob. belongs to b: *the parts of Libya toward Cyrene.*

ⓑ of extension toward, ***toward, to, up to*** ἐλθεῖν (γίνεσθαι v.l.) κ. τὸν τόπον *come up to the place* (Jos., Vi. 283) **Lk 10:32.** ἐλθόντες κ. τὴν Μυσίαν *to Mysia* **Ac 16:7;** cp. **27:7.** πορεύεσθαι κ. μεσημβρίαν (s. μεσημβρία 2) *toward the south* **8:26** (cp. Jos., Bell. 5, 505). κ. σκοπὸν διώκειν *run* (over the course) *toward the goal* **Phil 3:14.** λιμὴν βλέπων κ. λίβα καὶ κ. χῶρον *a harbor open to the southwest and northwest* **Ac 27:12** (s. βλέπω 8).—κ. πρόσωπον *to the face* (cp. Jos., Ant. 5, 205) **Gal 2:11.** ἔχειν τινὰ κ. πρόσωπον *meet someone face to face* (Thieme 19 has reff. for the use of κατὰ πρόσωπον as a legal formula) **Ac 25:16.** κ. πρόσωπον ταπεινός *humble when personally present* **2 Cor 10:1.** κ. πρόσωπόν τινος *in the presence of someone* **Lk 2:31; Ac 3:13.** τὰ κ. πρόσωπον *what lies before one's eyes,* i.e. *is obvious* **2 Cor 10:7.** κ. ὀφθαλμοὺς προγράφειν *portray before one's eyes* **Gal 3:1.**

ⓒ of isolation or separateness, ***by*** (Thu. 1, 138, 6 οἱ καθ' ἑαυτοὺς Ἕλληνες 'the Greeks by themselves'; Polyb. 1, 24, 4; 5, 78, 3; 11, 17, 6; Diod. S. 13, 72, 8; Gen 30:40; 43:32; 2 Macc 13:13; Philo, Migr. Abr. 87; 90; Just., D. 4, 5 αὐτὴ καθ' ἑαυτὴν γενομένη; Tat. 13, 1 ἡ ψυχὴ καθ' ἑαυτήν; Ath. 15, 2 ὁ πηλὸς καθ' ἑαυτόν) ἔχειν τι καθ' ἑαυτόν *keep someth. to oneself* **Ro 14:22** (cp. Jos., Ant. 2, 255; Heliod. 7, 16, 1). καθ' ἑαυτὸν μένειν *live by oneself* of the private dwelling of Paul in Rome **Ac 28:16.** πίστις νεκρὰ καθ' ἑαυτήν *faith by itself is dead* **Js 2:17** (Simplicius in Epict. p. 3, 43 τὸ σῶμα καθ' αὑτὸ νεκρόν ἐστιν). ἡ κατ' οἶκον ἐκκλησία *the congregation in the* *house* **Ro 16:5; 1 Cor 16:19.** κατ᾽ ἰδίαν s. ἴδιος 5. κ. μόνας (Thu. 1, 32, 5; Menand., Epitr. 988 S. [658 Kö.], fgm. 146 Kö. [158 Kock]; Polyb. 4, 15, 11; Diod. S. 4, 51, 16; BGU 813, 15 [s. APF 2, 1903, 97]; LXX) *alone, by oneself* **Mk 4:10; Lk 9:18;** Hm 11:8 (here, as well as BGU loc. cit. and LXX, written as one word καταμόνας).

ⓓ of places viewed serially, distributive use w. acc., ***x by x*** (Arrian., Anab. 4, 21, 10 κ. σκηνήν=tent by tent) or ***from x to x:*** κατ᾽ οἶκον *from house to house* (PLond III, 904, 20 p. 125 [104 AD] ἡ κατ᾽ οἰκίαν ἀπογραφή) **Ac 2:46b; 5:42** (both in ref. to various house assemblies or congregations; w. less probability NRSV 'at home'); cp. **20:20.** Likew. the pl. κ. τοὺς οἴκους εἰσπορευόμενος **8:3.** κ. τὰς συναγωγάς **22:19.** κ. πόλιν (Jos., Ant. 6, 73) *from city to city* IRo 9:3, but *in every (single) city* **Ac 15:21; 20:23; Tit 1:5.** Also κ. πόλιν πᾶσαν (cp. Herodian 1, 14, 9) **Ac 15:36;** κ. πᾶσαν πόλιν **20:23** D. κ. πόλιν καὶ κώμην **Lk 8:1;** cp. vs. **4.**

❷ **marker of temporal aspect** (Hdt. et al.; ins, pap, LXX, apolog.)—ⓐ in definite indications of time: ***at, on, during*** (Hdt. 8, 17; Polemon Soph. B 43 Reader κατ᾽ ἐκείνην τὴν ἡμέραν 'in the course of that day') κατ᾽ ἀρχάς *in the beginning* (cp. ἀρχή 1b) **Hb 1:10** (Ps 101:26). κ. τὴν ἡμέραν τοῦ πειρασμοῦ *in the day of trial* **3:8** (Ps 94:8.—Cp. Antig. Car. 173 κ. τὸν σπόρου καιρόν). νεκροῦ … ἀνάστασιν κατ᾽ αὐτὸν γεγονυῖαν ἱστορεῖ (Papias) *reports that a resurrection from the dead occurred in his time* Papias (2, 9; so, with personal names, Hdt.; Just., D. 23, 1 τοῦ θεοῦ … τοῦ κ. τὸν Ἐνώχ; Tat. 31, 2 Θεαγένης … κ. Καμβύσην γεγονώς). Of the future: κ. τὸν καιρὸν τοῦτον *at that time, then* **Ro 9:9** (Gen 18:10). Of the past: κ. ἐκεῖνον τὸν καιρόν *at that time, then* (2 Macc 3:5; TestJos 12:1; Jos., Ant. 8, 266; cp. κατ᾽ ἐκεῖνο τοῦ καιροῦ Konon: 26 fgm. 3 p. 191, 25 Jac.; Just., A I, 17, 2; 26, 3 al.) **Ac 12:1; 19:23.** κ. καιρόν *at that time, then* **Ro 5:6** (Just., D. 132, 1; cp. OGI 90, 28 καθ᾽ ὃν καιρόν), unless καιρός here means *the right time* (s. καιρός 1b end). κατ᾽ ὄναρ (as καθ᾽ ὕπνον Gen 20:6; Just., D 60, 5 κ. τοὺς ὕπνους) *during a dream, in a dream* **Mt 1:20; 2:12** (s. s.v. ὄναρ for ins).

ⓑ with indefinite indications of time: ***toward, about*** κ. τὸ μεσονύκτιον *about midnight* **Ac 16:25;** cp. **27:27.—8:26** (s. μεσημβρία 1).

ⓒ distributively (cp. 1d): ***x period by x period:*** κατ᾽ ἔτος *every year* (s. ἔτος) **Lk 2:41.** Also κατ᾽ ἐνιαυτόν (s. ἐνιαυτός 1) **Hb 9:25; 10:1, 3.** καθ᾽ ἡμέραν *daily, every day* (s. ἡμέρα 2c) **Mt 26:55; Mk 14:49; Lk 16:19; 22:53; Ac 2:46f; 3:2; 16:5; 17:11; 19:9; 1 Cor 15:31; Hb 7:27; 10:11.** Also τὸ καθ᾽ ἡμέραν (s. ἡμέρα 2c) **Lk 11:3; 19:47; Ac 17:11 v.l.** ἡ ἐπίστασις ἡ καθ᾽ ἡμέραν (s. ἐπίστασις) **2 Cor 11:28.** κ. πᾶσαν ἡμέραν *every day* (Jos., Ant. 6, 49) **Ac 17:7.** Also καθ᾽ ἑκάστην ἡμέραν (s. ἡμέρα 2c) **Hb 3:13.** κ. μίαν σαββάτου *on the first day of every week* **1 Cor 16:2.** κ. πᾶν σάββατον *every Sabbath* **Ac 13:27; 15:21b; 18:4.** κ. μῆνα ἕκαστον *each month* **Rv 22:2** (κ. μῆνα as SIG 153, 65; POxy 275, 18; 2 Macc 6:7). κ. ἑορτήν *at each festival* **Mt 27:15; Mk 15:6.**

❸ **marker of division of a greater whole into individual parts, *at a time, in detail,*** distributive use apart from indications of place (s. above 1d) and time (s. 2c)

ⓐ w. numerals: κ. δύο ἢ τὸ πλεῖστον τρεῖς *two or, at the most, three at a time* (i.e. in any one meeting, cp. ἀνὰ μέρος) **1 Cor 14:27** (Dio Chrys. 80 [30], 42 κ. δύο καὶ τρεῖς; Jos., Ant. 3, 142 κ. ἕξ; 5, 172 κ. δύο καὶ τρεῖς).καθ᾽ ἕνα (on this and the foll. s. εἷς 5e) singly, *one after the other* vs. **31.** κ. ἕνα λίθον *each individual stone* Hs 9, 3, 5; καθ᾽ ἕνα λίθον 9, 6, 3. κ. ἓν ἕκαστον *one by one, in detail* **Ac 21:19;** 1 Cl 32:1 (Ath. 28, 4 καθ᾽ ἕκαστον). εἷς καθ᾽ εἷς **Mk 14:19; J 8:9;** cp. **Ro 12:5** (B-D-F §305; Rob. 460). κ. ἑκατὸν καὶ κ. πεντήκοντα *in hundreds and in fifties* **Mk 6:40.**

ⓑ περί τινος λέγειν κ. μέρος *speak of someth. in detail* **Hb 9:5** (s. μέρος 1c). κατ᾽ ὄνομα *(each one) by name* (ἀσπάζομαι … τοὺς ἐνοίκους πάντες κα[τ᾽] ὄνομα PTebt [III AD] 422, 11–16; Jos., Vi. 86) **J 10:3; 3J 15** (cp. BGU 27, 18); ISm 13:2.

❹ **marker of intention or goal, *for the purpose of, for, to*** (Thu. 6, 31, 1 κ. θέαν ἥκειν=to look at something; cp. Sb 7263, 6 [254 BC]; X., An. 3, 5, 2 καθ᾽ ἁρπαγὴν ἐσκεδασμένοι; Arrian, Anab. 1, 17, 12; 4, 5, 1; 21, 9; 6, 17, 6; 26, 2; Lucian, Ver. Hist. 2, 29; Anton. Lib., Fab. 24, 1 Δημήτηρ ἐπῄει γῆν ἅπασαν κ. ζήτησιν τῆς θυγατρός; 38; Jdth 11:19) κ. τὸν καθαρισμὸν τῶν Ἰουδαίων *for the Jewish ceremonial purification* **J 2:6.** κατὰ ἀτιμίαν λέγω *to my shame* **2 Cor 11:21** (cp. Jos., Ant. 3, 268 κ. τιμὴν τ. θεοῦ τοῦτο ποιῶν). ἀπόστολος … κ. πίστιν … καὶ ἐπίγνωσιν *an apostle … for the faith … and the knowledge* **Tit 1:1** (but the mng. 'in accordance with' is also prob.).

❺ **marker of norm of similarity or homogeneity, *according to, in accordance with, in conformity with, according to***

ⓐ to introduce the norm which governs someth.—**α.** the norm of the law, etc. (OGI 56, 33; Mitt-Wilck., I/2, 352, 11 κ. τὰ κελευσθέντα [as Just., D. 78, 7]; POxy 37 II, 8) κ. τὸν νόμον (Jos., Ant. 14, 173; 15, 51; Just., D. 10, 1 al.; Ath. 31, 1; κ. τοὺς νόμους Ἀρεοπαγείτης, letter of MAurelius: ZPE 8, '71, 169, ln. 27) **Lk 2:22; J 18:31; 19:7; Hb 7:5.** τὰ κ. τ. νόμον *what is to be done according to the law* **Lk 2:39** (cp. EpArist 32). κ. τὸ ὡρισμένον *in accordance w. what has been determined* **22:22.** Cp. **1:9; 2:24, 27, 42; Ac 17:2; 22:3.** κ. τὸ εὐαγγέλιόν μου **Ro 2:16; 16:25a; 2 Ti 2:8.** κ. τὸ εἰρημένον **Ro 4:18** (cp. Ath. 28, 1 κ. τὰ προειρημένα). κ. τὰς γραφάς (Just., D. 82, 4; cp. Paus. 6, 21, 10 κ. τὰ ἔπη=according to the epic poems; Just., A I, 32, 14 κ. τὸ λόγιον, D. 67, 1 κ. τὴν προφητείαν ταύτην) **1 Cor 15:3;** cp. **Js 2:8.** κ. τὴν παράδοσιν **Mk 7:5** (Tat. 39, 1 κ. τὴν Ἑλλήνων παράδοσιν).—κ. λόγον *as one wishes* (exx. in Dssm., B 209 [not in BS]; also PEleph 13, 1; 3 Macc 3:14) **Ac 18:14** (though 5bβ below is also prob.).—It can also stand simply w. the acc. of the pers. according to whose will, pleasure, or manner someth. occurs κ. θεόν (cp. Socrat., Ep. 14, 5 κ. θεόν; 26, 2; Nicol. Dam.: 90 fgm. 4 p. 332, 1 Jac. and Appian, Bell. Civ. 2, 84 §352 κ. δαίμονα; Jos., Ant. 4, 143 ὁ κ. τοῦτον[=θεόν] βίος; Just., D. 5, 1 κ. τινας … Πλατωνικούς; Tat. 1, 3 κ. … τὸν κωμικόν) **Ro 8:27; 2 Cor 7:9–11;** κ. Χριστὸν Ἰ. **Ro 15:5.** κ. κύριον **2 Cor 11:17.** Cp. **1 Pt 1:15.** κ. τ. Ἕλληνας *in the manner of the Greeks,* i.e. *polytheists* PtK 2, p. 14, 1; 7. κ. Ἰουδαίους ln. 25.

β. the norm according to which a judgment is rendered, or rewards or punishments are given ἀποδοῦναι τινι κ. τ. πρᾶξιν or ἔργα αὐτοῦ (Ps 61:13; Pr 24:12; Just., A I, 12, 1; 17, 4 al.; κατ᾽ ἀξίαν τῶν πράξεων) **Mt 16:27; Ro 2:6; 2 Ti 4:14; Rv 2:23.** μισθὸν λήμψεται κ. τ. ἴδιον κόπον **1 Cor 3:8.** κρίνειν κ. τι **J 7:24; 8:15; 1 Pt 1:17;** cp. **Ro 2:2.**

γ. of a standard of any other kind κ. τ. χρόνον ὃν ἠκρίβωσεν *in accordance w. the time which he had ascertained* **Mt 2:16.** κ. τ. πίστιν ὑμῶν *acc. to your faith* **9:29.** κ. τ. δύναμιν *acc. to his capability* **25:15** (Just., D. 139, 4; Tat. 12, 3; cp. Just., A II, 13, 6 κ. δύναμιν). Cp. **Lk 1:38; 2:29; Ro 8:4; 10:2; Eph 4:7.** ἀνὴρ κ. τ. καρδίαν μου **Ac 13:22** (καρδία 1bε).

δ. Oft. the norm is at the same time the reason, so that *in accordance with* and *because of* are merged: οἱ κ. πρόθεσιν κλητοί **Ro 8:28.** κατ᾽ ἐπιταγὴν θεοῦ **16:26; 1 Ti 1:1; Tit 1:3.** κ. ἀποκάλυψιν **Eph 3:3** (Just., D. 78, 2). οἱ καθ᾽ ὑπομονὴν ἔργου ἀγαθοῦ **Ro 2:7.** κατ᾽ ἐκλογήν **11:5** (Just., D. 49, 1). Cp. κ. τὴν βουλήν **Eph 1:11** (Just., A I, 63, 16 al.); **2 Th 2:9; Hb 7:16.** κ. τί γνώσομαι τοῦτο; *by what shall I know this?* (cp.

Gen 15:8) **Lk 1:18.**—Instead of 'in accordance w.' κ. can mean simply *because of, as a result of, on the basis of* (Ael. Aristid. 46 p. 219 D.: κ. τοὺς νόμους; Jos., Ant. 1, 259; 278; Just., A I, 54, 1 κατ' ἐνέργειαν τῶν φαύλων δαιμόνων; Ath. 7, 1 κ. συμπάθειαν τῆς παρὰ τοῦ θεοῦ πνοῆς; 32, 1 κ. χρησμόν). κ. πᾶσαν αἰτίαν *for any and every reason* (αἰτία 1) **Mt 19:3.** κ. ἀποκάλυψιν **Gal 2:2.** Cp. **Ro 2:5; 1 Cor 12:8** (κ. τ. πνεῦμα = διὰ τοῦ πν.); **Eph 1:5; 4:22b; Phil 4:11; 1 Ti 5:21; 2 Ti 1:9; Tit 3:5;** κ. ἀνάγκην **Phlm 14** (Ar. 1, 2; 4, 2 al.; Just., A I, 30, 1; 61, 10; Ath. 24, 2); IPol 1:3. ὁ κ. τὸ πολὺ αὐτοῦ ἔλεος ἀναγεννήσας ἡμᾶς **1 Pt 1:3.**—καθ' ὅσον (Thu. 4, 18, 4) *in so far as, inasmuch as* **Hb 3:3.** καθ' ὅσον . . . , κ. τοσοῦτο *in so far as . . . , just so far* (Lysias 31, 8; Galen, De Dignosc. Puls. 3, 2, VIII 892 K.) **7:20, 22.**

ⓑ as a periphrasis to express equality, similarity, or example *in accordance with, just as, similar(ly) to* (TestJob 32:6 τίς γὰρ κ. σε ἐν μέσῳ τῶν τέκνων σου; Tat. 25, 1 κ. . . . τὸν Πρωτέα like Proteus; schol. on Nicander, Ther. 50: sheep are not burden-bearers κ. τοὺς ὄνους=as donkeys are).

α. κ. τὰ ἔργα αὐτῶν μὴ ποιεῖτε *do not do as they do* **Mt 23:3.** κ. Ἰσαάκ *just as Isaac* **Gal 4:28.** κ. θεὸν κτισθείς **Eph 4:24** (Synes., Prov. 2, 2 p. 118c κ. θεόν=just as a god). Cp. **Col 3:10.** κ. τὸν τύπον **Hb 8:5** (Ex 25:40; Mel., P. 58, 424 [νόμον v.l.]). Cp. **5:6** (Ps 109:4); **8:9** (Jer 38: 32); **Js 3:9.**—κ. τὰ αὐτά *in (just) the same way* (OGI 56, 66; PEleph 2, 6; 1 Macc 8:27; 12:2; Just., D. 1, 2; 3, 5; 113, 3) **Lk 6:23, 26; 17:30;** Dg 3:1. On the other hand, the sing. κ. τὸ αὐτό **Ac 14:1** means *together* (marriage contract PEleph 1, 5 [IV BC] εἶναι ἡμᾶς κ. ταὐτό; 1 Km 11:11). καθ' ὃν τρόπον *just as* (2 Macc 6:20; 4 Macc 14:17) **Ac 15:11; 27:25.** καθ' ὅσον . . . , οὕτως *(just) as . . . , so* **Hb 9:27.** κ. πάντα τρόπον *in every way* (PSI 520, 16 [250 BC]; PCairZen 631, 2; 3 Macc 3:24) **Ro 3:2.** κ. μηδένα τρόπον (PMagd 14, 9 [221 BC]; PRein 7, 31; 3 Macc 4:13; 4 Macc 4:24; Just., D. 35, 7; s. Reader, Polemo 262) **2 Th 2:3.** Cp. Johannessohn, Kasus, 1910, 82. κατά w. acc. serves in general

β. to indicate the nature, kind, peculiarity or characteristics of a thing (freq. as a periphrasis for the adv.; e.g. Antiochus of Syracuse [V BC]: 555 fgm. 12 Jac. κ. μῖσος=out of hate, filled with hate) κατ' ἐξουσίαν *with authority* or *power* **Mk 1:27.** κ. συγκυρίαν *by chance* **Lk 10:31.** κ. ἄγνοιαν *without knowing* **Ac 3:17** (s. ἄγνοια 2a). κ. ἄνθρωπον **1 Cor 3:3** al. (s. Straub 15; Aeschyl., Th. 425; ἄνθρωπος 2b). κ. κράτος *powerfully,* **Ac 19:20** (κράτος 1a). κ. λόγον *reasonably, rightly* (Pla.; Polyb. 1, 62, 4; 5; 5, 110, 10; Jos., Ant. 13, 195; PYale 42, 24 [12 Jan., 229 BC]) **18:14** (but s. above 5aα). λέγειν τι κ. συγγνώμην οὐ κατ' ἐπιταγήν *say someth. as a concession, not as a command* **1 Cor 7:6;** cp. **2 Cor 8:8.** κ. τάξιν *in (an) order(ly manner)* **1 Cor 14:40** (τάξις 2). κατ' ὀφθαλμοδουλίαν *with eye-service* **Eph 6:6.** μηδὲν κατ' ἐριθείαν μηδὲ κ. κενοδοξίαν **Phil 2:3.** κ. ζῆλος *zealously* **3:6a,** unless this pass. belongs under 6 below, in its entirety. κ. σάρκα *on the physical plane* **Ro 8:12f; 2 Cor 1:17;** also **5:16ab,** if here κ. σ. belongs w. οἴδαμεν or ἐγνώκαμεν (as Bachmann, JWeiss, H-D Wendland, Sickenberger take it; s. 7a below). καθ' ὑπερβολήν (PTebt 42, 5f [c. 114 BC] ἠδικημένος καθ' ὑπερβολὴν ὑπό, Ἁρμιύσιος; 4 Macc 3:18) *beyond measure, beyond comparison* **Ro 7:13; 1 Cor 12:31; 2 Cor 4:17.** καθ' ὁμοιότητα (Aristot.; Gen 1:12; Philo, Fug. 51; Tat. 12, 4 κ. τὸ ὅμοιον αὐτῇ) *in a similar manner* **Hb 4:15b.** κ. μικρόν *in brief* B 1:5 (μικρός 1eγ).

❻ denoting relationship to someth., ***with respect to, in relation to*** κ. σάρκα *w. respect to the flesh, physically* of human descent **Ro 1:3; 4:1; 9:3, 5** (Ar. 15, 7 κ. σάρκα . . . κ. ψυχήν; Just., D. 43, 7 ἐν τῷ γένει τῷ κ. σάρκα τοῦ Ἀβραάμ al.). κ. τὸν ἔσω ἄνθρωπον **7:22** (cp. POxy 904, 6 πληγαῖς κατακοπτόμενον κ. τὸ σῶμα). Cp. **Ro 1:4; 11:28; Phil 3:5, 6b** (for vs. **6a** s. 5bβ above); **Hb 9:9b.** τὰ κ. τινα (Hdt. 7, 148; Diod. S. 1, 10, 73; Aelian, VH 2, 20; PEleph 13, 3; POxy 120, 14; Tob 10:9; 1 Esdr 9:17; 2 Macc 3:40; 9:3 al.) *someone's case, circumstances* **Ac 24:22** (cp. PEleph 13, 3 τὰ κ. σε; Just., A I, 61, 13 τὰ κ. τὸν Ἰησοῦν πάντα, D. 102, 2 τὰ κ. αὐτόν; Ath. 24, 4 τὸ κ. τοὺς ἀγγέλους); **25:14; Eph 6:21; Phil 1:12; Col 4:7.** κ. πάντα *in all respects* (since Thu. 4, 81, 3; Sb 4324, 3; 5761, 22; SIG 834, 7; Gen 24:1; Wsd 19:22; 2 Macc 1:17; 3 Macc 5:42; JosAs 1:7; Just., A II, 4, 4, D. 35, 8 al.); **Ac 17:22; Col 3:20, 22a; Hb 2:17** (Artem. 1, 13 αὐτῷ ὅμοιον κ. π.); **4:15a.**

❼ Somet. the κατά phrase, which would sound cumbersome in the rendering 'such-and-such', 'in line with', or 'in accordance with', is best rendered as an adj., a possessive pron., or with a genitival construction to express the perspective from which something is perceived or to be understood. In translation it thus functions as

ⓐ an adj. (Synes., Kingdom 4 p. 4d τὰ κατ' ἀρετὴν ἔργα i.e. the deeds that are commensurate with that which is exceptional = virtuous deeds; PHib 27, 42 ταῖς κ. σελήνην ἡμέραις; 4 Macc 5:18 κ. ἀλήθειαν=ἀληθής; Just., A I, 2, 1 τοὺς κ. ἀλήθειαν εὐσεβεῖς; Tat. 26, 2 τῆς κ. ἀλήθειαν σοφίας) οἱ κ. φύσιν κλάδοι *the natural branches* **Ro 11:21.** ἡ κατ' εὐσέβειαν διδασκαλία **1 Ti 6:3;** cp. **Tit 1:1b.** οἱ κ. σάρκα κύριοι *the earthly masters* (in wordplay, anticipating the κύριος who is in the heavens, vs. 9) **Eph 6:5.** Cp. **2 Cor 5:16b,** in case (s. 5bβ above) κ. σ. belongs w. Χριστόν (as the majority, incl. Ltzm., take it): *a physical Christ, a Christ in the flesh,* in his earthly relationships (σάρξ 5). Correspondingly in vs. **16a** κ. σ. would be taken w. οὐδένα: *no one simply as a physical being.*—JMartyn, JKnox Festschr., '67, 269–87.

ⓑ a possessive pron., but with limiting force (Demosth. 2, 27 τὰ καθ' ὑμᾶς ἐλλείμματα [i.e. in contrast to the activities of others: 'your own']; Aelian, VH 2, 42 ἡ κατ' αὐτὸν ἀρετή; 3, 36; OGI 168, 17 παραγεγονότες εἰς τοὺς καθ' ὑμᾶς τόπους; SIG 646, 6; 807, 15 al.; UPZ 20, 9 [II BC] ἐπὶ τῆς καθ' ἡμᾶς λειτουργίας; PTebt 24, 64; 2 Macc 4:21; Tat. 42, 1 τίς ὁ θεὸς καὶ τίς ἡ κατ' αὐτὸν ποίησις; Mel., HE 4, 26, 7 ἡ καθ' ἡμᾶς φιλοσοφία) τῶν καθ' ὑμᾶς ποιητῶν τινες *some of your (own) poets* **Ac 17:28.** ἡ καθ' ὑμᾶς πίστις **Eph 1:15.** ὁ καθ' ὑμᾶς νόμος **Ac 18:15.** τὸ κατ' ἐμὲ πρόθυμον *my eagerness* **Ro 1:15.**

ⓒ a gen. w. a noun (Polyb. 3, 113, 1 ἡ κ. τὸν ἥλιον ἀνατολή; 2, 48, 2; 3, 8, 1 al.; Diod. S. 14, 12 ἡ κ. τὸν τύραννον ὠμότης; Dionys. Hal. 2, 1; SIG 873, 5 τῆς κ. τ. μυστήρια τελετῆς; 569, 22; 783, 20; PTebt 5, 25; PLond III, 1164k, 20 p. 167 [212 AD] ὑπὸ τοῦ κ. πατέρα μου ἀνεψιοῦ) τὰ κ. Ἰουδαίους ἔθη *the customs of the Judeans* **Ac 26:3** (Tat. 12, 5 τῇ κ. Βαβυλωνίους προγνωστικῇ; 34, 2 ἡ κ. τὸν Ἀριστόδημον πλαστική). Cp. **27:2.** ἡ κ. πίστιν δικαιοσύνη *the righteousness of faith* **Hb 11:7.** ἡ κατ' ἐκλογὴν πρόθεσις *purpose of election* **Ro 9:11.**—Here also belong the titles of the gospels εὐαγγέλιον κατὰ Μαθθαῖον etc., where κατά is likew. periphrasis for a gen. (cp. JLydus, De Mag. 3, 46 p. 136, 10 Wünsch τῆς κ. Λουκανὸν συγγραφῆς; Herodian 2, 9, 4 of an autobiography ἐν τῷ καθ' αὑτὸν βίῳ; Jos., C. Ap. 1, 18 τ. καθ' αὑτὸν ἱστορίαν; 2 Macc 2:13. Cp. B-D-F §163; 224, 2; Zahn, Einleitung §49; BBacon, Why 'According to Mt'? Exp., 8th ser., 16, 1920, 289–310).—On the periphrasis of the gen. by κατά s. Rudberg (ἀνά beg.) w. many exx. fr. Pla. on. But it occurs as early as Thu. 6, 16, 5 ἐν τῷ κατ' αὐτοὺς βίῳ.—M-M. DELG. EDNT. TW.

καταβαίνω impf. κατέβαινον; fut. καταβήσομαι; 2 aor. κατέβην, impv. κατάβηθι and κατάβα (Diog. L. 2, 41) **Mk 15:30 v.l.;** pf. καταβέβηκα (Hom.+; gener. 'go/come down')

❶ **to move downward,** ***come/go/climb down*** lit.—ⓐ of pers.:—**α.** w. indication of the place fr. which one comes or goes down: ἀπό τινος (Pind., N. 6, 51; X., Cyr. 5, 5, 6; Ael. Aristid. 51, 22 K.=27 p. 538 D.: ἀπὸ τ. ὄρους; Gen 38:1; Ex 32:15 ἀπὸ τ. ὄρους; 4 Km 1:16; Na 3:7 v.l.; Ezk 47:1; JosAs 5:11 ἀπὸ τ. ἅρματος; Jos., Ant. 6, 108) **Mt 8:1; Mk 9:9 v.l.;** ἀπὸ ὀρινῆς GJs 18:1 (pap; 19:1 codd.). *Come down* fr. a cross (Chariton 4, 3, 6 κατέβαινε τοῦ σταυροῦ, after the command κατάβηθι) **Mt 27:40, 42; Mk 15:30, 32.** *Get out* of a boat (cp. Ezk 27:29) **Mt 14:29.** W. ἔκ τινος: ἐκ τ. ὄρους (Il. 13, 17; X., An. 7, 4, 12; Ex 19:14; 32:1; Dt 9:15; 10:5; Josh 2:23) **17:9; Mk 9:9.** ἐντεῦθεν 1 Cl 53:2 (Dt 9:12); GJs 4:2b. Abs., though it is clear fr. the context where the descent is from **Mk 13:15** (s. δ); **Lk 19:5f; J 5:7; Ac 20:10; 23:10;** B 4:8; 14:3 (the two last Ex 32:7, where ἐντεῦθεν is added); MPol 7:2. Of someone on an elevation GJs 1:4; 4:3; 16:2. W. inf. foll. (Gen. 11:5; 43:20; Ex 3:8) **Mt 24:17; Lk 17:31.** καταβὰς ἔστη **6:17.**—*Go, return, go back* κατέβησαν εὐφραινόμενοι GJs 6:3 *they returned (home) with joy.* Here the prep. functions as an auxiliary adv. (cp. Gen 43:13; Jer 43:14).

β. as in LXX (for יָרַד 3 Km 22:2; 4 Km 8:29; 10:13 al.) of going away fr. Jerusalem or Palestine: ἀπὸ Ἱεροσολύμων **Mk 3:22; Lk 10:30** (cp. 1 Macc 16:14); **Ac 25:7;** cp. **Lk 10:31; Ac 24:1, 22.** Of the temple GJs 5:1 s. under δ. W. geograph. reff. in general (oft. LXX; TestSim 4:3 εἰς Αἴγυπτον; Jos., Vi. 68 εἰς Τιβεριάδα) εἰς Αἴγυπτον **Ac 7:15** (also κ. ἐκεῖ Did., Gen. 227, 5). εἰς Ἀντιόχειαν **18:22.—14:25; 16:8; 25:6; Lk 2:51; J 2:12.** Abs. **J 4:47, 49, 51; Ac 8:15; 10:20.**

γ. of coming down fr. heaven (Maximus Tyr. 11, 12e κ. ἐκ τ. θεοῦ μέχρι γῆς) ἀπὸ τοῦ οὐρανοῦ (Diogenes, Ep. 38, 1; Da 4:13, 23 Theod.; Philo, Migr. Abr. 185; Ar. 15, 1) **J 6:38; 1 Th 4:16.** ἐξ οὐρανοῦ (Chariton 6, 3, 4 τις ἐξ οὐρ. καταβέβηκε. Of things Dt 28:24; 4 Km 1:10) **Mt 28:2; J 3:13** (for the contrast ἀναβαίνω εἰς τ. οὐρ. . . . καταβαίνω cp. Pr 30:4; PGM 4, 546f; cp. Iren. 1, 9, 3 [Harv. I 84, 5]); **6:33, 41f, 50f, 58; Rv 10:1; 18:1; 20:1.** Abs. (Aristob. in Eus., PE 8, 10, 13 [=Holladay p. 144 ln. 94]; PGM 4, 3024; 36, 299; Orig., C. Cels. 4, 3, 2; Did., Gen. 110, 17) **Ac 7:34** (Ex 3:8); **J 1:51; Eph 4:10.**

δ. w. indication of the place to which one goes or comes down εἰς τ. οἰκίαν **Mk 13:15 v.l.** (cp. α above). εἰς τὸν παράδεισον αὐτῆς *in her garden* GJs 2:4; εἰς τὴν ἄβυσσον **Ro 10:7.** εἰς ᾅδου (Ar. 11, 3; Diod. S. 4, 25, 4 and Artem. 2, 55 with ἀναβαίνειν ἐξ ᾅδου) 1 Cl 51:4 (Num 16:30; Ps 54:16). εἰς τὰ κατώτερα μέρη τῆς γῆς (s. κατώτερος) **Eph 4:9.** Esp. of baptism κ. εἰς (τὸ) ὕδωρ *go down into the water* **Ac 8:38;** B 11:8, 11; Hm 4, 3, 1; s 9, 16, 4 and 6a; cp. 6b. εἰς τὸν οἶκον αὐτοῦ (from the temple) *home(ward)* **Lk 18:14;** sim. ἐκ τοῦ ναοῦ . . . καὶ ἥκει ἐν τῷ οἴκῳ αὐτοῦ GJs 5:1; cp. 8:1. ἐπὶ τὴν θάλασσαν (X., Ages. 1, 18; cp. Gen 24:16, 45) **J 6:16.** ἐπὶ τὸν λιμένα AcPl Ha 5, 15; πρὸς τοὺς ἄνδρας (cp. 1 Km 10:8; 4 Km 1:15; 1 Macc 10:71) **Ac 10:21;** cp. **14:11** θεοὶ . . . κατέβησαν πρὸς ἡμᾶς. ἄγγελος . . . κυρίου κατέβη πρὸς Ἰωακείμ GJs 4:2a. ἄγγελος κατέβαινεν ἐν τ. κολυμβήθρᾳ *into the pool* **J 5:4** (cp. Judg 7:9f B κ. ἐν τ. παρεμβολῇ). Of the descent of the devil: πρός τινα **Rv 12:12** (cp. Philo, Gig. 12 [ψυχαὶ] πρὸς σώματα κατέβησαν).

ⓑ of things etc.: a sheet fr. heaven (cp. SibOr 2, 20) *come down* **Ac 10:11; 11:5.** Every good gift comes down ἀπὸ τοῦ πατρὸς τῶν φώτων **Js 1:17.** Of the New Jerusalem κ. ἐκ τ. οὐρανοῦ ἀπὸ τοῦ θεοῦ **Rv 3:12; 21:2, 10.** Of the Holy Spirit at the baptism of Jesus: καταβ. εἰς αὐτόν *come down* and enter *into him* **Mk 1:10.** ἐπ' αὐτόν *upon him* **Mt 3:16; Lk 3:22; J 1:32f.** Of rain (cp. Ps 71:6; Is 55:10; Jos., Ant. 2, 343) *fall* **Mt 7:25, 27.** Of a storm *come down* **Lk 8:23.** Of fire *fall down* ἀπὸ τοῦ οὐρανοῦ (cp. Jos., Ant. 2, 343) **9:54.** ἐκ τοῦ οὐρανοῦ εἰς τὴν γῆν **Rv 13:13.** ἐκ τ. οὐρανοῦ (4 Km 1:10, 14; 2 Macc 2:10) **20:9.** Of hail ἐκ τοῦ οὐρανοῦ ἐπί τινα *fall down fr. heaven upon someone* **16:21.** Of drops of blood ἐπὶ τὴν γῆν **Lk 22:44** (cp. Sir 35:15 δάκρυα ἐπὶ σιαγόνα). Of a road *lead away* ἀπὸ Ἰερουσαλήμ **Ac 8:26.**

❷ **to suffer humiliation,** fig. extension of mng. 1 ***be brought down*** ἕως ᾅδου (cp. Is 14:11, 15. ἕως as Ps 106:26; ApcEsdr 4:32 p. 29, 9 Tdf.) **Mt 11:23; Lk 10:15** (both w. καταβιβασθήσῃ as v.l.; s. καταβιβάζω).—M-M. TW.

καταβάλλω fut. καταβαλῶ LXX; 2 aor. κατέβαλον; pf. 3 sg. καταβέβληκε Pr 7:26. Pass.: aor. ptc. καταβληθείς 4 Macc 12:1; pf. ptc. καταβεβλημένη Pr 25:28 (s. βάλλω; Hom.+; ins, pap, LXX, En; TestSol 23:1; TestJob 18:1; ApcEsdr 5:12 p. 30, 6 [τὸν σπόρον . . . ἐν τῇ γῇ; cp. Ath. 33, 1]; EpArist, Philo, Joseph., Just., Tat., Ath.).

❶ **to strike with sufficient force so as to knock down,** ***throw down, strike down*** act. and pass. (X., Cyr. 1, 3, 14 et al.—'desist from, cease' Tat. 1, 2; 9, 3; Ath. 21, 3) τινά *someone* (Diod. S. 14, 17, 10; Appian, Liby. 111, §527; Lucian, Dial. Deor. 14, 2; Philo, Agr. 120; PsSol, TestSol, Just.; Tat. 20, 1) pass. καταβαλλόμενοι ἀλλ' οὐκ ἀπολλύμενοι *struck down, but not destroyed* **2 Cor 4:9;** cp. **Rv 12:10 v.l.**

❷ **to lay someth. down with implication of permanence,** ***found, lay (a foundation),*** θεμέλιον, mid. (Dionys. Hal. 3, 69 τοὺς θεμελίους; Porphyr., Abst. 8, 10; Jos., Ant. 11, 93; 15, 391; cp. 2 Macc 2:13 βιβλιοθήκην; EpArist 104) in imagery (so e.g. of the founding of a philos. school Plut., Mor. 329a) **Hb 6:1.**—M-M.

καταβαρέω 1 aor. κατεβάρησα (s. βαρέω; Polyb.; Diod. S. 19, 24, 5 et al.; Cyr. Ins. line 11; POxy 487, 10) ***burden, be a burden to*** τινά *someone* (Appian, Bell. Civ. 5, 67 §283) **2 Cor 12:16** (v.l. κατενάρκησα). Abs. αἱ ἁμαρτίαι ὑμῶν κατεβάρησαν *your sins weighed heavily* (the context supplies ὑμᾶς) *on you* Hs 9, 28, 6.—M-M.

καταβαρύνω pass. aor. subj. 1 pl. καταβαρυνθῶμεν 2 Km 13:25 (s. prec. entry; Theophr. et al.; LXX) ***weigh down, burden, oppress*** τὴν ζωήν *make someone's life hard* (cp. τὸν βίον Antip. in Stob. 4, 22, 25 vol. IV 511, 7 H.) Hm 12, 6, 2. Pass. (Herm. Wr. 2, 9) of the eyes ἦσαν καταβαρυνόμενοι *were heavy*=fell shut **Mk 14:40.**—DELG s.v. βαρύς.

κατάβασις, εως, ἡ (s. βαίνω; Hdt. et al.; ins, pap, LXX; AscIs 3, 13; Philo, Joseph.) **the way down,** ***descent*** (Polyb. 3, 54, 5; Diod. S. 4, 21, 2; 14, 28, 5; Jos., Bell. 2, 547), also ***slope, declivity*** (Ps.-Demetr., Eloc. §248; Josh 10:11) ἐγγίζειν πρὸς τῇ κ. τοῦ ὄρους τῶν ἐλαιῶν *come close to the slope of the Mount of Olives* **Lk 19:37.**—DELG s.v. βαίνω. M-M. Sv.

καταβῇ s. καταβαίνω.

καταβιβάζω (the causal of καταβαίνω) fut. καταβιβάσω LXX; aor. κατεβίβασα LXX. Pass.: fut. καταβιβασθήσομαι; aor. impv. καταβιβάσθητι Ezk 31:18 (βιβάζω 'cause to mount'; Hdt. et al.; PLond II, 130, 105f p. 136; LXX; TestSol 10:35 C τὴν σελήνην) ***bring down, drive down*** τινά *make someone come down* **Ac 19:33** D. Pass. (cp. Philo, Deus Imm. 120) ἕως ᾅδου **Mt 11:23 v.l.; Lk 10:15 v.l.** in both pass. for καταβήσῃ (s. καταβαίνω 2).—DELG s.v. βαίνω 3 p. 156. M-M.

καταβοάω fut. 3 sg. καταβοήσεται Dt 24:15; 1 aor. κατεβόησα LXX (Hdt. et al.; OGI 669, 5; 51; PSI 440, 19; 551, 2; 4; 6; LXX; Jos., Bell. 3, 410, Ant. 3, 307) **to make a loud**

outcry, ***cry out, bring charges, complain*** **Ac 18:13** D.—DELG s.v. βοή.

καταβολή, ῆς, ἡ (s. καταβάλλω; Hippocr., Demosth. et al.; ins, pap, 2 Macc 2:29; AssMos fgm. a=Tromp p. 272; EpArist, Philo, Joseph.; Just., D. 102, 4 τῇ ἐπὶ τοῦ πύργου καταβολῇ [s. καταβάλλω 2]; Ath., R. 17 p. 69, 6).

❶ **the act of laying someth. down, with implication of providing a base for someth.,** ***foundation.*** Readily connected with the idea of founding is the sense *beginning* (Jos., Bell. 2, 260 ἀποστάσεως καταβολή) τ. καταβολὴν τ. στάσεως ποιεῖν *be responsible for beginning the dissension* (cp. Polyb. 13, 6, 2 καταβολὴν ἐποιεῖτο τυραννίδος) 1 Cl 57:1. Esp. καταβολὴ κόσμου (Plut., Mor. 956a ἅμα τῇ πρώτῃ καταβολῇ τ. ἀνθρώπων): ἀπὸ καταβολῆς κόσμου *from the foundation of the world* (Theoph., Ant. 3, 26 [p. 258, 27]; difft., Polyb. 1, 36, 8; 24, 8, 9; Diod. S. 12, 32, 2—all three ἐκ καταβολῆς) **Mt 13:35; 25:34; Lk 11:50; Hb 4:3; 9:26; Rv 13:8; 17:8;** B 5:5. πρὸ καταβολῆς κόσμου (AssMos fgm. a) **J 17:24; Eph 1:4; 1 Pt 1:20.**—OHofius, ZNW 62, '71, 123–38. Also abs. (without κόσμου, s. κόσμος 3; cp. EpArist 129) **Mt 13:35 v.l.** This may be the mng. of **Hb 11:11,** where it is said of Sarah δύναμιν εἰς καταβολὴν σπέρματος ἔλαβεν *she received the ability to establish a posterity* (s. NRSV mg.). But

❷ κ., a t.t. for the ***sowing*** of seed, used of begetting (τοῦ σπέρματος [εἰς γῆν ἢ μήτραν M. Ant. 4, 36]: Plut., Mor. 320b σπορὰ κ. καταβολή of the procreation of Romulus by Ares and Silvia; 905e; Ps.-Lucian, Amor. 19; Galen, Aphorism. 4, 1, XVII/2, 653 K.; cp. Philo, Op. M. 132; Epict. 1, 13, 3; Herm. Wr. 9, 6; Ath., R. 17 p. 69, 6 σπερμάτων καταβολήν; s. Field, Notes 232). If this mng. is correct for **Hb 11:11,** there is prob. some error in the text, since this expression could not be used of Sarah, but only of Abraham (e.g. αὐτῇ Σάρρᾳ='together w. Sarah' is read by W-H. margin; Riggenbach; Michel; B-D-F §194, 1. This use of the dat. is found in Thu., X. et al., also Diod. S. 20, 76, 1; Appian, Samn. 7 §2; Polyaenus 6, 18, 2; 7, 15, 3; 8, 28; Theod. Prodr. 6, 148 H. αὐτῇ Ῥοδάνῃ). Windisch, Hdb. ad loc. and s. αἷμα 1a.—MBlack, An Aramaic Approach[3], '67, 83–89.—DELG s.v. βάλλω. M-M. EDNT. TW.

καταβραβεύω (s. βραβεύω; Demosth., 21, 93; Vett. Val. 344, 30; Sb 4512 B, 57 [II BC]) 'decide against' (as umpire), and so ***rob of a prize, condemn*** τινά (Didymus [I BC/I AD] p. 179 MSchmidt; s. Field, Notes 196f) **Col 2:18.**—DELG s.v. βραβεύς 'arbitrator, umpire'. M-M.

καταγγελεύς, έως, ὁ (s. next entry; OGI 456, 10 [I BC] 'proclaimer of the games'; IG XII/8, 190, 39f [I AD]; Pel.-Leg. 18, 21) ***proclaimer, preacher*** ξένων δαιμονίων of foreign divinities **Ac 17:18.**—DELG s.v. ἄγγελος. M-M. TW.

καταγγέλλω impf. κατήγγελλον; 1 aor. κατήγγειλα; pf. κατήγγελκα. Pass.: 2 aor. κατηγγέλην **Ac 17:13;** pf. ptc. κατηγγελμένος (Just.). (Since X., An. 2, 5, 38; ins [e.g. SIG 797, 6]; pap; 2 Macc; Philo, Op. M. 106; Joseph., Just., Tat.; freq. used of public decrees) **to make known in public, with implication of broad dissemination,** ***proclaim, announce***

ⓐ w. a thing as obj. τὶ *someth.*: the gospel **1 Cor 9:14;** customs **Ac 16:21.** τ. ἡμέρας ταύτας **3:24** (Jos., Ant. 3, 206 ἑορτήν). τὸν θάνατον τοῦ κυρίου καταγγέλλετε *you proclaim* (by celebrating the sacrament rather than w. words) *the Lord's death* **1 Cor 11:26.** τὸν λόγον τοῦ θεοῦ ἐν ταῖς συναγωγαῖς **Ac 13:5;** cp. **15:36.** Pass. **17:13.** ἐν τῷ Ἰησοῦ τὴν ἀνάστασιν τὴν ἐκ νεκρῶν *proclaim in the person of Jesus the resurrection from the dead* **4:2.** Pass. ἡ πίστις ὑμῶν καταγγέλλεται ἐν ὅλῳ τῷ κόσμῳ *your faith is well known throughout the world* **Ro 1:8;** cp. Pol 1:2.—τινί τι *someth. to someone* (Philo, Aet. M. 68; Jos., Ant. 2, 15) ἄφεσιν ἁμαρτιῶν **Ac 13:38;** ὁδὸν σωτηρίας **16:17.** τὸ μυστήριον (μαρτύριον v.l.) τοῦ θεοῦ *the secret purpose of God* **1 Cor 2:1.** φῶς τῷ τε λαῷ καὶ τοῖς ἔθνεσιν *proclaim light to the people (of Israel) and to the gentiles* **Ac 26:23;** cp. **17:23.** εἴς τι: εἰς τὸ εὐαγγέλιον *direct one's proclamation toward the gospel,* i.e. foreshadow the gosp. IPhld 5:2.

ⓑ w. personal obj.: τινά *someone* (Iren. 1, 19, 1 [Harv. I 175, 4]) τὸν Χριστόν **Phil 1:17;** cp. vs. **18; Col 1:28** (Just., D. 7, 3). τινά τινι *someone to someone* **Ac 17:3** (Iren. 1, 20, 2 [Harv. I 178, 10]). οἱ προφῆται κ. εἰς αὐτόν *the prophets directed their proclamation toward him* (Jesus) IPhld 9:2.—DELG s.v. ἄγγελος. M-M. TW.

καταγέλαστος, ον (s. next entry, also γελάω; Aristoph., Hdt. et al.; Dio Chrys. 57 [74], 12; Ael. Aristid. 43, 1 K.=1 p. 1 D.; Celsus 6, 78; Wsd 17:8; Philo; Jos., C. Ap. 1, 254) ***ridiculous*** Dg 4:1.—DELG s.v. γελάω.

καταγελάω impf. κατεγέλων; 1 aor. κατεγέλασα; fut. mid. καταγελάσομαι LXX; fut. pass. καταγελασθήσομαι LXX (s. prec. entry; Aeschyl., Hdt.+; SIG 1168, 122 [III BC]; BGU 814, 21; POxy 3313, 17 [II AD]; LXX; TestSol 4, 5f D; TestJob 32:11; Just.; Tat. 10, 2) ***laugh at, ridicule*** τινός *someone* (Hdt. 5, 68 al.; Achilles Tat. 1, 1, 13 [ed. SGaselee '47]; Philo, Omn. Prob. Lib. 156; Jos., Ant. 5, 144; ἡμῶν Just., A I, 58, 2) **Mt 9:24; Mk 5:40; Lk 8:53;** 1 Cl 56:11 (Job 5:22); 2 Cl 13:4.—DELG s.v. γελάω. M-M. TW.

καταγίνομαι (s. γίνομαι; Demosth., Teles et al.; ins, pap, LXX; Manetho: 609 fgm. 8, 77 Jac. [in Jos., C. Ap. 1, 77]) ἔν τινι ***busy oneself with, be taken up with someth.*** (Polyb. 31, 29, 6; Diog. L. 6, 70) ὁ νοῦς αὐτῶν περὶ τὴν πρᾶξιν καταγίνεται *their mind is taken up w. their own affairs* Hm 10, 1, 5.

καταγινώσκω fut. 3 sg. καταγνώσεται Pr 28:11; 2 aor. κατέγνων LXX. Pass.: fut. 3 sg. καταγνωσθήσεται Sir 19:5; aor. inf. καταγνωσθῆναι; pf. pass. ptc. κατεγνωσμένος (TestBenj 6:7) (s. κατάγνωσις; Aeschyl., Hdt.+ in various senses) ***condemn, convict*** (Thu. 6, 60, 4; Lysias 1, 32 al.; PYale 42, 24; of God's unfavorable judgment Jos., Bell. 7, 327) τινός *someone* or *someth.* (Ps.-Pla., Demod. 382e; OGI 691, 2; POxy 1062, 14; Dt 25:1; Philo, Omn. Prob. Lib. 79; Jos., Ant. 4, 5) κ. ἡμῶν ἡ καρδία **1J 3:20** (TestGad 5:3 οὐχ ὑπ᾽ ἄλλου καταγινωσκόμενος ἀλλ᾽ ὑπὸ τ. ἰδίας καρδίας; Sir 14:2; TestBenj 6:7 μὴ καταγνωσθῆναι ὑπὸ τῶν ἀνθρώπων, ὁμοίως καὶ ὑπὸ τοῦ θεοῦ); vs. **21** the obj. is to be supplied fr. what precedes; likew. **Mk 7:2** D; τ. ἀπάτης τοῦ κόσμου *condemn the deceit of the world* Dg 10:7.—κατεγνωσμένος ἦν *he stood condemned* (by his own actions or by his opinions publicly expressed, cp. Diod. S. 34+35 fgm. 29 κατεγνώσθη=he was condemned [by his outrageous deed or by his opinion publicly expressed], i.e. the faithless friend of Gracchus; Diog. L. 6, 33 καταγινωσκομένους [by their public opinions]; Jos., Bell. 2, 135) **Gal 2:11.**—FMozley, Exp. 8th Ser. IV 1912, 143–46.—DELG s.v. γιγνώσκω. M-M. TW.

κατάγνυμι fut. κατεάξω **Mt 12:20,** 2 sg. κατάξεις Hab 3:12; 1 aor. κατέαξα, ptc. κατάξας, impv. κάταξον LXX; 2 aor. pass. κατεάγην (W-S. §12, 2; 15 under ἄγνυμι; B-D-F §66, 2; 101 under ἄγνυμι; Mlt-H. 189; 226 under ἄγνυμι), 3 sg. κατεάχθη Jer 31:25 (ἄγνυμι 'break, shiver'; Hom.+; ins, pap, LXX, Philo; Jos., Bell. 6, 402, Ant. 5, 225) ***break*** a reed **Mt 12:20;** limbs of the body (Menand., Epitr. 1062 S.=704 Kö.;

Prov. Aesopi 10 P. λόγος καλὸς ὀστοῦν κατεάξει) τὰ σκέλη *the legs* **J 19:31, 32, 33** (Eus., HE 5, 21, 3 κατεάγνυται τὰ σκέλη; Philostorg. 3, 27 Ἀέτιον ἀμφοῖν τοῖν σκέλοιν κατεαγῆναι.—Pauly-W. IV 1731. Cp. σκελοκοπέω and s. σκέλος). DELG s.v. ἄγνυμι. M-M.

κατάγνωσις, εως, ἡ (s. καταγινώσκω; Thu. et al.; PStras 40, 29; Sb 4670, 5; 4681, 5; 4835, 5; Sir 5:14; Philo, Ebr. 205; Jos., Bell. 6, 34, Vi. 93) ***condemnation*** μᾶλλον ἑαυτῶν κ. φέρουσιν ἢ τῆς ὁμοφωνίας *they would rather bear condemnation of themselves than of the harmony* 1 Cl 51:2.—DELG s.v. γιγνώσκω.

καταγράφω impf. κατέγραφον; fut. καταγράψω Hos 8:12; aor. κατέγραψα LXX. Pass.: aor. κατεγράφην LXX; pf. ptc. καταγεγραμμένοι LXX (s. γράφω; Eur., Pla. et al.; ins, pap, LXX) ***write,*** also ***draw figures*** (so Paus. 1, 28, 2; Serenus Antinoensis [IV AD] p. 280, 13; 282, 22 al. [ILHeiberg 1896].—But καταγρ. also means 'write down an accusation': PCairZen 140, 17 [256 BC] κατὰ τούτων καταγέγραφέν σοι) εἰς τὴν γῆν *on the ground* **J 8:6** (v.l. ἔγραφεν), vs. **8** D. For ins s. KMiller, Apollo Lairbenos: Numen 32, '85, 46–70; e.g. MAMA IV, 275 B I, 4 (II AD).—On the subject matter s. Diog. L. 2, 127: Menedemus the philosopher (300 BC), in whose presence someone behaved improperly, διέγραφεν εἰς τοὔδαφος (=drew a cartoon on the ground [and thereby shamed him]).—M-M.

κατάγω fut. κατάξω LXX; 2 aor. κατήγαγον; 1 aor. pass. κατήχθην, ptc. καταχθείς (s. ἄγω; Hom.+) ***lead/bring down*** τινά *someone* κατάγαγέ με ἀπὸ τοῦ ὄνου GJs 17:3a; cp. 3b; w. the destination given (fr. Jerusalem) εἰς Καισάρειαν **Ac 9:30** (PCairZen 150, 2 [256 BC] εἰς Ἀλεξάνδρειαν; ApcEsdr 4:21 p. 28, 33 εἰς τὸ ἔδαφος τῆς ἀπωλείας; ApcMos 39 εἰς τὸν τόπον τοῦτον). (Fr. the barracks, located on higher ground) εἰς τὸ συνέδριον *into the council building* **23:20, 28** (s. συνέδριον 1c and 3); cp. vs. **15** (v.l. πρός); **22:30.** εἰς ᾅδου (1 Km 2:6; s. ᾅδης 1 end; TestAbr A 19 p. 101, 19 [Stone p. 50] εἰς ᾅδην) *into the underworld* 1 Cl 4:12. Χριστὸν κ. *bring Christ down* (fr. heaven) (Iambl., Vi. Pyth. 13, 62 an eagle fr. the air) **Ro 10:6.**—Of things: τὰ πλοῖα ἐπὶ τὴν γῆν *bring the boats to land* (fr. the 'high' seas) (cp. Hdt. 8, 4; Cass. Dio 50, 13, 2) **Lk 5:11.** Hence the pass., in act. sense, of ships and seafarers *put in* εἴς τι *at a harbor* (Jos., Ant. 13, 332; 14, 378) εἰς Σιδῶνα **Ac 27:3.** εἰς Συρακούσας **28:12;** εἰς Τύρον **21:3 v.l.** (for κατήλθομεν).—M-M. Spicq.

καταγωνίζομαι mid. dep. (since Polyb., also ins; PMich I, 80, 6 [III BC) 1 aor. κατηγωνισάμην (s. ἀγωνίζομαι) ***conquer, defeat, overcome*** (Polyb. 2, 42, 3; 2, 45, 4; 3, 4, 10 al.; Plut., Num. 19, 6; Aelian, VH 4, 8; Lucian, Dial. Deor. 13, 1; Alciphron 1, 20, 3; TestReub 5:2; Philo, Abr. 105; Jos., Ant. 4, 153; 7, 53; w. acc. in many of these pass.; OGI 553, 7 κ. τοὺς ὑπεναντίους) w. acc. of the pers. MPol 19:2. βασιλείας **Hb 11:33.**—DELG s.v. ἄγω. M-M. TW.

καταδέχομαι mid. dep.; 1 aor. κατεδεξάμην (s. δέχομαι; Hippocr., Pla. et al.; ins, pap, LXX; TestLevi 6:6; ApcEsdr 7:1 p. 32, 8 Tdf.; AssMos fgm. k p. 67 Denis; Jos., C. Ap. 1, 292) ***receive, accept*** τὶ *someth.* (Pla., Rep. 3, 401e τὶ εἰς τὴν ψυχήν) τὰ λόγια θεοῦ 1 Cl 19:1.

καταδέω 1 aor. κατέδησα (s. δέω; Hom. et al.; ins, pap, LXX; ApcrEzk P 1 verso 11; Jos., Ant. 5, 309 al.) ***bind up*** τὶ *someth.* (Hdt. 2, 122 τ. ὀφθαλμούς; Jos., Ant. 8, 390) τὰ τραύματα *bandage the wounds* (cp. Sir 27:21 and s. Hobart 27) **Lk 10:34.**—M-M.

κατάδηλος, ον (s. δῆλος; Soph., Hdt. et al.; PLips 64=Mitt-Wilck. I/2, 281, 28; 33; 37 τοῦτο κατάδηλον; 47; TestSol 13:5 P; Jos., Ant. 10, 191, Vi. 167) ***very clear, quite plain*** περισσότερον ἔτι κ. ἐστιν *it is clearer still* **Hb 7:15.**—M-M.

καταδιαιρέω aor. impv. 2 sg. καταδιέλε Ps 54:10; mid. aor. 3 pl. καταδιείλαντο Jo 4:2 (s. διαιρέω; Polyb. 2, 45, 1; Hero Alex. III p. 66, 2; Dionys. Hal. 4, 19; Sext. Emp., Math. 5, 23; Herm. Wr. 3, 1b; CPR I, 22, 25; 27, 21; Ps 54:10; 135:13) ***divide, make a distinction between*** τὰς τῶν καιρῶν ἀλλαγάς Dg 4:5.—DELG s.v. αἱρέω.

καταδικάζω 1 aor. κατεδίκασα, pass. κατεδικάσθην ***condemn, find/pronounce guilty*** (s. next entry, also δικάζω; Hdt.+, though mostly w. gen. of pers.; ins, pap, LXX; TestSol 4:2 D; TestAbr A 14 p. 93, 21 [Stone p. 34]; SyrBar 12:3; Philo; Jos., Bell. 4, 274; Ar. [Milne 74, 23]; Just.; Tat. 22, 1; Ath. 2, 3) τινά *someone* (so Diod. S. 14, 4, 2 τ. πονηροτάτους; 15, 40, 1; La 3:36; Jos., Ant. 7, 271; Just.) τοὺς ἀναιτίους *the innocent* **Mt 12:7.** τὸν δίκαιον **Js 5:6.** Abs. **Lk 6:37a.** Pass. (Polyb. 6, 37, 1; Artem. 2, 9 p. 95, 2; Herm. Wr. 2, 17a; En 10:14; Philo; Jos., Bell. 3, 391; Ar., Just., Tat.; Did. Gen. 97, 3) vs. **37b.** ἐκ τῶν λόγων σου *by, on the basis of your words* **Mt 12:37.**—DELG s.v. δίκη. M-M. TW.

καταδίκη, ης, ἡ (s. prec. entry; Thu.+; Herm. Wr. 10, 8a; ins, pap; Wsd 12:27; TestSol 13:4; GrBar 4:15 [Christian]; Philo; Jos., Ant. 17, 338; Just.; Tat. 29, 2; loanw. in rabb.) ***condemnation, sentence of condemnation, conviction, guilty verdict*** (so Epicharmus [V BC] Com. Graec. fgm. 148, 4 Kaibel [in Athen. 2, 3, 36d] restored; Polyb.; Plut.; Philo, Spec. Leg. 3, 116; Jos., Bell. 4, 317) αἰτεῖσθαι κατά τινος κ. *ask for a conviction of someone* **Ac 25:15.**—M-M. TW.

καταδιώκω fut. καταδιώξω LXX; 1 aor. κατεδίωξα; fut. mid. καταδιώξομαι LXX; aor. pass. 2 pl. κατεδιώχθητε Mi 2:11 (s. διώκω; Thu. et al.; pap, LXX; PsSol 15:8; TestSol 25:6; Test12Patr; JosAs; ApcEl [PSI 7 verso, 6] κατα[διώκουσιν], nearly always 'pursue' in a hostile sense; so also Theoph. Ant. 3, 21 [p. 246, 9] Φαραώ … κ. Ἑβραίους) ***search for eagerly, hunt for*** τινά *someone* **Mk 1:36** (in a good sense in Polyb. 6, 42, 1; Ps 37:21. W. acc. of the pers. Ps 22:6. κ. μετά τινος=go w. someone 1 Km 30:22. ὀπίσω τινός Sir 27:17).—M-M.

καταδουλόω fut. καταδουλώσω; aor. 3 sg. κατεδούλωσεν (TestJos 18:3); aor. mid. 3 sg. κατεδουλώσατο LXX (s. δουλόω; Hdt. et al.; ins; PGM 9, 4 καταδούλωσον πᾶν γένος ἀνθρώπων; 9; LXX, TestSol 2:13 D; Test12Patr; SibOr 2, 175; Philo) ***enslave, reduce to slavery,*** in our lit. only in fig. sense (the act. is so used in PGM 9 [s. above]; Menand., Mis. fgm. 3 Kö.=338, 1 Kock; Plut., Mor. 828c) τινά *someone* **2 Cor 11:20; Gal 2:4.**—DELG s.v. δοῦλος. M-M. TW.

καταδυναστεύω fut. 3 pl. καταδυναστεύσουσιν Ezk 45:8; 1 aor. κατεδυνάστευσα LXX, pass. inf. καταδυναστευθῆναι PsSol 17:41 (δυναστεύω 'hold power'; X.+; PPetr III, 36 (a) verso, 2 [pass.]; POxy 67, 15 [act.]; LXX; PsSol 17:41; EpArist; Jos., Ant. 12, 30) ***oppress, exploit, dominate*** τινός *someone* (Diod. S. 13, 73; EpArist 148 v.l.) of exploitation by the rich (oft. in LXX of outrages against the poor, widows, and orphans) **Js 2:6;** Dg 10:5.—Of the tyrannical rule of the devil (Plut., Mor. 367d of the evil spirit Typhon) Hm 12, 5, 1f; pass. *be dominated* **Ac 10:38** (ὑπό τινος as Strabo 6, 2, 4 p. 270; Horapollo 1, 6).—DELG s.v. δύναμαι. M-M.

κατάθεμα, ατος, τό (s. next entry; IDefixAudollent 22, 23; AcPh 28 [Aa II/2, 15, 12]) **that which is devoted** or **given over** to a deity, i.e. under a curse (חֵרֶם), hence ***accursed thing*** (s. ἀνάθεμα 2) **Rv 22:3** (Erasmian rdg.: κατανάθεμα). The passage D 16:5 is (perh. purposely) obscure: σωθήσονται ὑπ' αὐτοῦ τοῦ κ. *they will be saved by the accursed one himself* (i.e. by Christ who, in the minds of those offended by him, is accursed; cp. also Gal 3:13 κατάρα; Wengst, Didache p. 99 n. 138).—DELG s.v. τίθημι. M-M. Lampe. TW.

καταθεματίζω (s. prec. entry; AcPh [Aa II/2, 9, 23]; Just., D. 47, 4 καταθεματίσαντας [v.l. καταvα-]; Iren. 1, 13, 4 καταθεματίσασαι [Harv. I 119f]; 16, 3 [H. 163, 8] καταθεματίσαντας. See PGlaue, ZNW 45, '54, 94) ***curse*** **Mt 26:74** (v.l. καταναθεματίζειν).—DELG s.v. τίθημι. M-M. Lampe. TW.

καταιγίς, ίδος, ἡ (αἰγίς 'rushing storm'; Democr. 14; Ps.-Aristot., De Mundo 4, 15; Aelian, NA 15, 2 p. 367, 20; Herm. Wr. 16, 10b; LXX; PsSol 8:2; TestJob 20:8; TestJud 21:9; JosAs 12:10; Philo, Deus Imm. 60) ***a sudden blast of wind*** 1 Cl 57:4 (Pr 1:27).—DELG s.v. αἰγίς.

καταισχύνω (s. αἰσχύνω; Hom. et al.; LXX; TestJud 12:5; TestJos 17:1) fut. καταισχυνῶ 4 Macc 5:35; aor. κατῄσχυνα LXX. Pass.: impf. κατῃσχυνόμην; 1 aor. κατῃσχύνθην; pf. 3 pl. κατῄσχυνται Tob 10:2 BA; ptc. κατῃσχυμμένος Hm 12, 5, 2 (B-D-F §72).

❶ ***dishonor, disgrace*** (Diod. S. 11, 46, 2; 13, 106, 10; Epict. 2, 8, 21; Philo, Spec. Leg. 3, 14; Jos., Ant. 20, 89 σποδῷ τ. κεφαλήν) τὴν κεφαλήν **1 Cor 11:4f.**

❷ ***put to shame*** (Appian, Bell. Civ. 4, 126 §526) τινά *someone* of God τοὺς σοφούς, τὰ ἰσχυρά **1 Cor 1:27.** Pass. *be put to shame, be humiliated* (Diod. S. 19, 72, 7; LXX), also *be ashamed* (Diod. S. 2, 4, 3 καταισχυνθεῖσα=because she was ashamed) **Mt 20:28** D; **Lk 13:17; 2 Cor 7:14; 9:4; 1 Pt 3:16;** Hm 12, 5, 2.—*Humiliate* (TestJud 12:5) τοὺς μὴ ἔχοντας *those who have nothing* (cp. Ruth 2:15) **1 Cor 11:22.**

❸ ***disappoint,*** of the shame and disappointment that come to one whose faith or hope is shown to be vain.—ⓐ act. causative (anonymous iambic poet [III/II BC] AnthLG Κατὰ 'Αισχροκερδείας [In turpilucrum] ln. 101 ed. Diehl³ fasc. 3, p. 135 [=Diehl I 1925, p. 297, ln. 35]: a god τὸ θεῖον οὐ καταισχύνει=cause to be ruined or lost; Ps 118:31) ἡ ἐλπὶς οὐ καταισχύνει *hope does not disappoint* **Ro 5:5.**

ⓑ pass. *be disappointed* (anonymous iambic poet in Ps.-Callisth. 1, 46a, 9 τὸ θράσος κατῃσχύνθη=boldness has been put to shame; Is 50:7 v.l.; Ps 30:2; Sir 2:10) **Ro 9:33; 10:11; 1 Pt 2:6** (on all three cp. Is 28:16).—DELG s.v. αἶσχος. M-M. TW.

κατακαίω (s. καίω; Hom.+; ins, pap, LXX; En 10:14; TestSol, TestAbr A 13 p. 93, 11 [Stone p. 34]; ApcEsdr; Just., A II, 21, 3; Ath. 29, 1) impf. κατέκαιον; fut. κατακαύσω; 1 aor. κατέκαυσα; inf. κατακέαι (= -κῆαι?; AcPl Ha 1, 27). Pass.: 2 fut. κατακαήσομαι (Tobit 14:4 BA; **1 Cor 3:15; 2 Pt 3:10 v.l.** This form also Nicol. Dam.: 90 fgm. 68 p. 371, 32 Jac.; SibOr 3, 507) and 1 fut. κατακαυθήσομαι (LXX; **Rv 18:8;** Hs 4:4); 2 aor. κατεκάην (Da 3:94 LXX; Jos., Bell. 6, 191; Just. A I, 21, 3) and 1 aor. κατεκαύθην (LXX; MPol 12:3 v.l.; Jos., Bell. 7, 450); pf. κατακέκαυμαι LXX; s. B-D-F §76, 1; W-S. §13, 9f and 15; Mlt-H. 242 (s.v. καίω) ***burn down, burn up, consume*** by fire τὶ *someth.*: weeds **Mt 13:30;** books **Ac 19:19** (cp. PAmh 30, 36 [II BC] ἠναγκάσθην ἐνέγκαι τὰς συνγραφὰς καὶ ταύτας κατακαῦσαι. Acc. to Diog. L. 9, 52, books of Protagoras were burned by the Athenians in the marketplace); a heifer B 8:1 (cp. Num 19:5, 8).—Pass. ἔργον **1 Cor 3:15** (cp. TestAbr A 13 p. 93, 11 [Stone p. 34] εἴ τινος τὸ ἔργον κατακαύσει τὸ πῦρ); cp. γῆ καὶ τὰ ἐν αὐτῇ ἔργα κατακαήσεται **2 Pt 3:10 v.l.** (for εὑρεθήσεται). Bodies of animals **Hb 13:11.** A third of the earth w. its trees and grass **Rv 8:7abc.** ὡς ξύλα Hs 4:4. Of being burned at the stake as a martyr MPol 12:3 (Diod. S. 1, 59, 3; 12, 25, 3 [in Roman admin. of justice]; Dio Chrys. 9 [10], 26 κατεκαύθη ζῶν; 29 [46], 7; Artem. 2, 52 p. 183, 1 P. [cp. 2, 49 p. 182, 15 P.]; 2, 49 p. 151, 16; Jos., Bell. 7, 450 [in Roman admin. of justice]). AcPl Ha 1, 27 κατακέαι (κατάκαιε or κατακῆαι [s. above, beg.]?) αὐτόν (Ath. 29, 1).—W. the addition of πυρί *burn, consume someth. w. fire* (Ex 29:14, 34; Lev 9:11) chaff **Mt 3:12; Lk 3:17** (both π. ἀσβέστῳ); pass., weeds **Mt 13:40** (καίεται v.l.). W. ἐν πυρί added (oft. LXX) *someone:* κ. τινὰ ἐν π. **Rv 17:16.** Pass. **18:8;** but κατακαύσει ὑμᾶς πυρὶ ἀσβέστῳ AcPl Ha 1, 22.—Of a pillow ὑπὸ πυρὸς κατακαίεσθαι *be consumed by fire* MPol 5:2.—M-M.

κατακαλύπτω fut. κατακαλύψω; 1 aor. κατεκάλυψα LXX. Pass.: aor. 3 sg. κατεκαλύφθη Jer 28:42; pf. ptc. κατακεκαλυμμένος (s. next entry, also καλύπτω; Hom. et al.; ins, LXX; JosAs 3:11; 14:17 A for καλύπτω; 18:6 A for σκεπάζω) ***cover, veil***

ⓐ act. (Is 6:2) and pass. (Sus 32 Theod.) of a young woman κατακεκαλυμμένη ἕως τοῦ μετώπου *covered* or *veiled to the forehead* Hv 4, 2, 1. But here the form could also be

ⓑ mid. *cover oneself* w. a veil, abs. (s. Jos., Ant. 7, 254) **1 Cor 11:6ab.** W. acc. (either of the obj. or of specification, as Gen 38:15) τὴν κεφαλήν vs. **7** (Ps.-Dicaearchus p. 144 ln. 16ff F. of the Theban women: τὸ τῶν ἱματίων ἐπὶ τῆς κεφαλῆς κάλυμμα τοιοῦτόν ἐστιν, ὥσπερ προσωπιδίῳ δοκεῖν πᾶν τὸ πρόσωπον κατειλῆφθαι. In case the text is in order, it may be transl. about as follows: the covering of the clothes on the head is of such a kind that the whole face seems to be covered as with a mask).—AJeremias, D. Schleier v. Sumer bis heute '31; RdeVaux, RB 44, '35, 395–412.—M-M s.v. κατακαλύπτομαι. TW.

κατακάλυψις, εως, ἡ (s. prec. entry; Περὶ ὕψους 17, 3; Galen XIII 99 K.; XIX 445; Proclus, In Pla., Tim. III p. 149, 17 Diehl) ***covering*** ἐν μίτρᾳ ἦν ἡ κ. αὐτῆς *her head was covered with a snood* Hv 4, 2, 1.

κατάκαρπος, ον (s. καρπός; Aristodem. [II BC]: 383 fgm. 9 Jac. [in Athen. 11 p. 495f; Leontios, Prooem. p. 2, 16 and 21 of vine and olive tree; LXX; TestSol 17:2 P) ***very fruitful*** δένδρα Hs 9, 1, 10.

κατακαυχάομαι 2 sg. κατακαυχᾶσαι; fut. 3 pl. κατακαυχήσονται Zech 10:12 (Jer 27:11, 38; grave ins of Asia Minor: SBBerlAk '32, p. 855 κατακαυχᾶσθαι κατά τινος of a gladiator over his defeated foe).

❶ **to boast at the expense of another, *boast against, exult over*** τινός *someone* or *someth.* τῶν κλάδων the branches **Ro 11:18a.**—Abs. *boast, brag* **Ro 11:18b; Js 3:14; 4:16 v.l.** (for καυχᾶσθε).

❷ **to have a cause for boasting because of advantage in power, *triumph over*** τινός (Rhet. Gr. I 551, 13; 589, 23; Constan. Manasses 1, 59 Hercher; Psellus p. 183, 3 τῆς φύσεως κατεκαυχήσατο) κ. ἔλεος κρίσεως *mercy triumphs over judgment* **Js 2:13.**—DELG s.v. καυχάομαι. TW.

κατάκειμαι impf. κατεκείμην; fut. 2 sg. κατακείσῃ Pr 23:34 (s. κεῖμαι; Hom. et al.; grave ins: Sb 6089, 1; pap, LXX, TestSol 11:2; TestReub 3:13; Joseph.; Mel., P. 80, 594)

❶ **to be in a recumbent position free from any activity,** ***lie down***—ⓐ in a gener. sense *rest* (M. Ant. 5, 1, 1; TestReub; Mel.) MPol 7:1. Also of animals lying in the meadow Hs 9, 1, 9.
ⓑ of sick people (Hdt. 7, 229; Aristoph., Eccl. 313; Lucian, Icarom. 31; Plut., Cic. 43, 3; Jos., Ant. 6, 214; PRyl 68, 16 [89 BC]; PTebt 422, 19; TestSol) **J 5:3, 6.** W. the sickness given: **Ac 28:8.** κατέκετο πυρέσσουσα *she lay sick w. a fever* **Mk 1:30.** Also of one who has already died **5:40 v.l.** W. indication of the place where: ἐπί τινος *lie on someth.* ἐπὶ κραβάττου **Ac 9:33.** ἐπί τι *on someth.* **Lk 5:25;** cp. **Mk 2:4.**
❷ **to recline (on a couch) for the purpose of dining,** ***recline for a meal, dine*** (X., An. 6, 1, 4, Symp. 1, 14; Pla., Symp. 177d, Rep. 2, 372d) abs. (Dio Chrys. 31 [48], 3 οἱ κατακείμενοι; Jos., Vi. 222) **Mk 14:3; Lk 5:29.** W. ἐν foll. (Diog. L. 7, 1, 19 ἐν συμποσίῳ) **Mk 2:15; Lk 7:37;** ἐν εἰδωλείῳ κ. *dine in a temple* **1 Cor 8:10.** On this custom s. New Docs 1, 5–9 w. ins. reff. The sense 'couch' for the related noun (κλινή) does not appear in the NT. Cp. Horace, Satires 2, 8 for a Roman couch arrangement at a banquet.—M-M. TW.

κατακεντέω 1 aor. κατεκέντησα; pf. pass. ptc. κατακεκεντημένοι Jer 28:4 ***pierce, stab*** (κεντέω, 'to prick'; Pla., Tim. 76b; Diod. S. 3, 37, 6 et al.; Jdth 16:12; Ezk 23:47; Philo, Poster. Cai. 182; Jos., Ant. 14, 292 τ. ἄνδρα) w. acc. B 7:8, 9.

κατακλάω 1 aor. κατέκλασα; aor. pass. 3 sg. κατεκλάσθη Ezk 19:12 (s. κλάω; Hom. et al.; Philo, Somn. 2, 236; Jos., Bell. 7, 204, Ant. 2, 305) ***break in pieces*** τοὺς ἄρτους **Mk 6:41; Lk 9:16.**—M-M.

κατακλείω 1 aor. κατέκλεισα; aor. pass. κατεκλείσθην LXX; pf. ptc. κατακεκλεισμένους 3 Macc 3:25 (s. κλείω; Hdt., Thu.+; ins, pap, LXX; TestSol; Philo, Aet. M. 135 κ. ἐν; Jos., Bell. 4, 327, Ant. 13, 380 κ. ἐν; Mel., P. 55, 404 εἰς τὸν ᾅδην; Ath. 6, 2 εἰς μονάδα τὸν θεόν) ***shut up, lock up*** ἐν φυλακῇ *in prison* **Lk 3:20.** Also ἐν φυλακαῖς **Ac 26:10** (cp. Jer 39:2f ἐν αὐλῇ τ. φυλακῆς . . . , ἐν ᾗ κατέκλεισεν αὐτόν; OGI 669, 17 [I AD]).—DELG s.v. κλείς. M-M.

κατακληροδοτέω (s. κλῆρος, δίδωμι; Theophyl. Sim., Hist. 6, 7, 12; Dt 1:38 v.l. [Just., D. 132, 3]; 21:16; 1 Macc 3:36) ***parcel out by lot*** **Ac 13:19 v.l.** (s. κατακληρονομέω).—DELG s.v. κλῆρος. M-M.

κατακληρονομέω (s. κληρονομέω) fut. κατακληρονομήσω LXX for נָחַל, יָרַשׁ al.; 1 aor. κατεκληρονόμησα; aor. pass. κατεκληρονομήθην (s. κλῆρος; LXX; TestSol 9:5 P; TestBenj 10:5). The term κληρός primarily means a lot cast in a transaction, then that which is assigned by lot. The transferred sense 'inheritance' is readily derived from a testator's right to make an assignment, ordinarily of a portion of property. The verb κληρονομέω therefore refers to deeding of property. In the following passages the focus of the compound verb κ. is on the right of possession of a distributed portion:
❶ **to assign possession of,** ***give (over) as rightful possession*** (Dt 3:28; 12:10; 31:7 al.) τὶ *someth.* a country **Ac 13:19** (v.l. κατεκληροδότησεν).
❷ **to lay claim to someth. that has been assigned,** ***take possession of, occupy*** (Num 13:30; Dt 2:21; Ps 36:34) B 6:8.—DELG s.v. κλῆρος. TW.

κατακλίνω 1 aor. κατέκλινα, pass. κατεκλίθην; pf. pass. ptc. κατακεκλιμένος **Mk 5:40 v.l.** (s. κλίνω; Hom. et al.; ins, pap, LXX, EpArist; Philo, Op. M. 85; Joseph.). **to lay down**
ⓐ act. ***cause to lie down*** or ***sit down*** to eat; τινά *someone* (Hdt. 1, 126; X., Cyr. 2, 3, 21 ἐπὶ τὸ δεῖπνον; PGM 1, 168; Jos., Ant. 6, 52 κ. ἐπάνω τῶν κεκλημένων) κατακλίνατε αὐτοὺς κλισίας **Lk 9:14;** cp. vs. **15.**
ⓑ pass. in act. sense—α. Gener. *lie* of a dead person **Mk 5:40 v.l.**
β. ***recline at dinner*** (Aristoph., Vesp. 1208; 1210; X., Cyr. 5, 2, 15; SIG 1042, 25; Jdth 12:15; Jos., Ant. 6, 163) **Lk 7:36; 24:30.** εἰς τὴν πρωτοκλισίαν *in the place of honor* **14:8.**—M-M. TW.

κατακλύζω 1 aor. pass. κατεκλύσθην (s. next entry; Pind., Aeschyl., Hdt.+; ins, pap, LXX; SibOr 3, 690; Philo; Jos., Bell. 5, 566; Just., D. 138, 3) ***flood, inundate,*** pass. κόσμος ὕδατι κατακλυσθεὶς ἀπώλετο *the world was destroyed by being flooded w. water* **2 Pt 3:6.**—M-M.

κατακλυσμός, οῦ, ὁ (s. prec. entry; Pla.+; Marm. Par. [III BC]: 239 fgm. A 4 Jac. [Deucalion]; Celsus 1, 19; 4, 11; PMagd 28, 18 [III BC]; BGU 1121, 27; LXX; En; Test12Patr; GkBar 4:10; SibOr 3, 109; Philo, Joseph.; Just., A II, 7, 2; Tat. 39, 2) ***flood, deluge,*** in our lit. only of the flood in Noah's time (Gen 6–9; Jos., Ant. 1, 92f; 10, 147, C. Ap. 1, 130; Nicol. Dam.: 90 fgm. 72 Jac. [in Jos., Ant. 1, 95]; Berosus: 680 fgm. 6 Jac. [in Jos., Ant. 1, 158]; SibOr 4, 53; Iren., Hippol., Orig., Did.; Theoph. Ant. 2, 30 [p. 172, 4] πρὸ κ.; 3, 16 [p. 236, 18] ἀπὸ κ.) **Mt 24:38f; Lk 17:27.** κατακλυσμὸν ἐπάγειν *bring a flood* (Gen 6:17) τινί *upon someth.* **2 Pt 2:5.**—DELG s.v. κλύζω. M-M. Sv.

κατακολουθέω 1 aor. κατηκολούθησα (s. ἀκολουθέω; Teles p. 57, 10; Polyb.; Dio Chrys. 59 [76], 4; ins, pap, LXX, Tat.) ***follow*** (Longus 3, 15) τινί *someone* **Ac 16:17.** Abs. **Lk 23:55.** Fig. (so mostly, incl. EpArist; Jos., Ant. 6, 147, C. Ap. 2, 281 al.) τῇ σοφίᾳ τινός *approach* or *attain the wisdom of someone* Pol 3:2.—DELG s.v. ἀκόλουθος. M-M.

κατακόπτω impf. κατέκοπτον; fut. κατακόψω LXX; 1 aor. κατέκοψα LXX. Pass.: aor. κατεκόπην (LXX; JosAs 23:3); pf. ptc. κατακεκομμένος LXX (Hdt.+).
❶ **to cut in a rough manner,** ***lacereate, cut*** τινά τινι *someone w. someth.* ἑαυτὸν λίθοις *cut oneself w. stones* **Mk 5:5** (REB: 'gash himself'). Some prefer the sense *beat* (Kaibel 316, 3 of a wailing woman beating her breasts, s. κόπτω: PLips 37, 20 κατέκοψαν πληγαῖς αὐτόν; PSI 313, 10. S. other exx. in Field, Notes 27).
❷ ***break in pieces*** (Pla., Euthyd. 301c; 2 Ch 15:16; 34:7) of stones (Is 27:9) Hv 3, 2, 7; cp. 3, 6, 1.—M-M.

κατακρημνίζω 1 aor. κατεκρήμνισα; pass. inf. κατακρημνισθῆναι 4 Macc 4:25 (s. κρημνός; X., Cyr. 1, 4, 7; 8, 3, 41; Diod. S. 4, 31, 3; 2 Ch 25:12; Philo, Agr. 68; Jos., Bell. 4, 312, Ant. 6, 114) ***throw down (from) a cliff*** τινά *someone* (Phylarchus [III BC]: 81 fgm. 24 Jac.; Philod., Ira p. 56 W.; Jos., Ant. 9, 191) **Lk 4:29.**—DELG s.v. κρημνός.

κατάκριμα, ατος, τό (In this and the cognates that follow the use of the term 'condemnation' does not denote merely a pronouncement of guilt [s. κρίνω 5], but the adjudication of punishment.) **judicial pronouncement upon a guilty person,** ***condemnation, punishment, penalty*** (s. three next entries; freq. of fines: Dionys. Hal. 6, 61 κατακριμάτων ἀφέσεις; POxy 298, 4 [I AD]; CPR I, 1, 15ff; 188, 14f; Mitt-Wilck. I/2, 28, 12; Dssm., NB 92f [BS 264f]) οὐδὲν κ. τοῖς ἐν Χριστῷ Ἰησοῦ *there is no death-sentence for those who are in Christ Jesus* **Ro 8:1.** The context (esp. 7:24) qualifies the nature of the judicial sentence. εἰς πάντας ἀνθρώπους εἰς κ. (sc. ἐγένετο) (led) *to condemnation* or *doom for all humanity* **5:18.** In wordplay w. κρίμα vs. **16.**—FDanker in Gingrich Festschr. 105 (Ro).—DELG s.v. κρίνω. M-M. EDNT. TW.

κατακρίνω fut. κατακρινῶ; 1 aor. κατέκρινα. Pass.: fut. κατακριθήσομαι; 1 aor. κατεκρίθην; pf. κατακέκριμαι (s. prec. and two next entries; Pind., Hdt. et al.; ins, pap, LXX; En 10:14; 13:5; PsSol 4:2; TestSol; ApcMos 39; Jos., Ant. 3, 308; 10, 238; Ar. [Milne 74, 25]; Just., A II, 14, 2; Tat. 23, 2) **pronounce a sentence after determination of guilt,** ***pronounce a sentence on*** τινά *someone* (Wsd 4:16; Esth 2:1; Sus 53) **J 8:10f.** In wordplay w. κρίνω **Ro 2:1.** Pass. **Mt 27:3;** Dg 5:12; w. διακρίνομαι **Ro 14:23.** τινὰ θανάτῳ (s. θάνατος 1bα) *sentence someone to death* (Da 4:37a; Jos., Ant. 10, 124; Hippol. Ref., 8, 10, 7) **Mt 20:18** (cp. 26:66); **Mk 10:33** (cp. 14:64). Also κ. εἰς θάνατον (κ. εἰς=sentence someone to, as Artem. 1, 53 p. 50, 25; cp. κατακριθεὶς πρὸς θηρία Iren. 5, 28, 4 [Harv. II 403, 6]) **Mt 20:18 v.l.;** Hs 8, 11, 3 (for the reading also s. Bonner 155, n. on lines 23–28). εἰς τὰ θηρία MPol 2:4; εἰς θηρία AcPl Ha 1, 29; εἰς πῦρ αἰώνιον Dg 10:7. Of cities καταστροφῇ κ. *consign to destruction* **2 Pt 2:6** (on the dat. s. B-D-F §195, 2; Rob. 533; s. also SIG 736, 160ff τὸν μὴ ποιοῦντα κατακρινάτω εἴκοσι δραχμαῖς). W. acc. and inf. foll. (Sus 41 Theod. κατέκριναν αὐτὴν ἀποθανεῖν) κατέκριναν αὐτὸν ἔνοχον εἶναι θανάτου *they adjudged him liable to* or *subject to death* **Mk 14:64** (the actual sentence of course comes later). Abs. **Ro 8:34.** Of God's condemnation **Mk 16:16**=*will be under sentence,* i.e. of loss of salvation; **1 Cor 11:32**=*so that we might not be under sentence together with the world* (wordplay w. κρίνειν); **Js 5:9 v.l.** The conduct of one person, since it sets a standard, can result in the condemnation before God of another person whose conduct is inferior (Wsd 4:16; cp. Ro 2:27) **Mt 12:41f** (JJeremias, Jesus' Promise to the Nations, '58, 50 n. 3); **Lk 11:31f; Hb 11:7.** ὁ θεὸς … κατέκρινεν τὴν ἁμαρτίαν ἐν τῇ σαρκί *God has pronounced sentence on sin in the flesh* **Ro 8:3.**—M-M. TW.

κατάκρισις, εως, ἡ (s. two prec. entries and next; Vett. Val. 108, 4; 117, 35; Syntipas p. 43, 11 θεόθεν κ. AcThom 84 [Aa II/2 p. 200, 9]; 128 [p. 236, 20]; 135 [p. 242, 10]; τοῦ ὄφεως κ. Theoph. Ant. 2, 23 [p. 56, 10]; Iren.; Did.) **a judicial verdict involving a penalty,** ***condemnation*** κατάκρισιν ἔχειν τινί *bring condemnation for someone* 2 Cl 15:5. πρὸς κ. οὐ λέγω *I do not say this to condemn* **2 Cor 7:3.** Of Mosaic cult and legislation: ἡ διακονία τῆς κατακρίσεως *the ministry of condemnation* (s. διακονία 3) **3:9.**—DELG s.v. κρίνω. M-M. TW.

κατάκριτος, ον (s. three prec. entries; Diod. S. 33, 2; Plut., Mor. 188a; Ps.-Lucian, Am. 36; 52; SEG VIII, 13, 21 [=Boffo, Iscrizioni no. 39]; Philo, Virt. 139; Jos., Bell. 1, 639; 6, 108; AcJ 10 [Aa II/1, 157, 12]) **pert. to being subject to the carrying out of a sentence,** ***condemned*** abs. IEph 12:1; ITr 3:3; IRo 4:3.

κατακροάομαι mid. dep.; impf. 3 sing. κατηκροᾶτο (ἀκροάομαι 'listen to'; Eupolis Com. [V BC] fgm. 245 K.) ***listen attentively*** τινός *to someone* (Jos., Bell. 4, 38) προσευχομένου Hv 3, 1, 6.—DELG s.v. ἀκούω.

κατακύπτω 1 aor. κατέκυψα (s. κύπτω; Hom. et al.; Epict. 2, 16, 22; Lucian, Icarom. 15 al.; 4 Km 9:32; EpArist 91) ***bend down*** (Appian, Bell. Civ. 2, 62 §258 [ὑπ' αἰδοῦς=out of shame]; Jos., Bell. 2, 224) **J 8:8.**—M-M.

κατακυριεύω (κυριεύω 'to be lord or master of') fut. κατακυριεύσω; 1 aor. κατεκυρίευσα, impv. κατακυρίευσον; 1 aor. pass. κατεκυριεύθην.

❶ **to bring into subjection,** ***become master, gain dominion over, subdue*** (Diod. S. 14, 64, 1; Num 21:24; 32:22; Ps 9:26 al.) τινός (LXX; Test12Patr) **Ac 19:16.** Fig. *become master, gain power* τινός *over someone* (TestJud 15:5) or *someth.* τοῦ διαβόλου Hm 7:2; 12, 4, 7; 12, 6, 4. τῶν ἔργων τοῦ διαβόλου 12, 6, 2. τῶν πονηρῶν ἔργων 5, 1, 1. τῆς διψυχίας *master doubt* 9:10. τῆς ἐπιθυμίας τῆς πονηρᾶς κατακυριεῦσαι *to master base desire* 12, 2, 5. ἃ βλέπεις, ἐκείνων κατακυρίευε *what you see, strive to master that* s 9, 2, 7.—Pass. ὑπό τινος *let oneself be overcome by someth.* Hm 12, 2, 3.

❷ **to have mastery,** ***be master, lord it (over), rule*** τινός *of, over someone* or *someth.* (Ps 118:133; Gen 1:28; Sir 17:4; TestNapht 8:6; ApcMos 14; Ar.) **Mt 20:25; Mk 10:42.** τῆς γῆς B 6:13, 17. τῶν ὑπὸ τὸν οὐρανὸν πάντων *be master of everything under heaven* Hm 12, 4, 2; cp. 3. τῶν κλήρων **1 Pt 5:3.**—DELG s.v. κύριος. TW.

καταλαλέω fut. 3 pl. καταλαλήσουσιν Mi 3:7; 1 aor. κατελάλησα LXX (s. two next entries and λαλέω; Aristoph.+; Polyb.; Stoic. III 237, 6 al.; SIG 593, 6 [II BC]; PHib 151 [c. 250 BC]; LXX, En; TestAbr B 12 p. 116, 20 [Stone p. 80]; Test12Patr; Philo [only in connection w. the OT: Leg. All. 2, 66f=Num 12:8 and Leg. All. 2, 78=Num 21:7]) **speak ill of,** ***speak degradingly of, speak evil of, defame, slander*** τινός *someone* (Ps 77:19 τοῦ θεοῦ; 100:5 τοῦ πλησίον αὐτοῦ; TestIss 3:4, Gad 5:4; cp. Diod. S. 11, 44, 6; τῆς τοῦ θεοῦ δόξης Theoph. Ant. 3, 30 [p. 268, 28]) **Js 4:11ab;** 2 Cl 4:3; Hm 2:2a. ἵνα ἐν ᾧ καταλαλοῦσιν ὑμῶν **1 Pt 2:12** (cp. SIG loc. cit. ἵνα μηδ' ἐν τούτοις ἔχωσιν ἡμᾶς καταλαλεῖν οἱ …). Also κατά τινος (so mostly LXX, En) 1 Cl 35:8 (Ps 49:20). Pass. **1 Pt 3:16.**—Fig. (Ps.-Lucian, As. 12 τοῦ λύχνου) νόμου *speak against the law* **Js 4:11c.**—Abs. ὁ καταλαλῶν *one who speaks evil* Hm 2:2 (three times).—M-M. TW.

καταλαλιά, ᾶς, ἡ (s. prec. and next entry; Leontius 18 p. 36, 9; Wsd 1:11; TestGad 3:3; GrBar; AscIs 3, 26; AcPh 142 [Aa II/2, 81, 8].—The ancients preferred κατηγορία. Thus Thom. Mag.: καταλαλιὰ οὐδεὶς εἶπε τῶν ἀρχαίων ἀλλ' ἀντὶ τούτου κατηγορία) **the act of speaking ill of another,** ***evil speech, slander, defamation, detraction*** in lists of vices (s. on πλεονεξία) in sing. and pl. (to denote individual instances) **2 Cor 12:20;** 1 Cl 35:5; B 20:2; Pol 2:2; 4:3; Hm 8:3; s 9, 15, 3. ἀποτίθεσθαι πάσας καταλαλιάς *put away all slanders* **1 Pt 2:1.** φεύγειν καταλαλιάς *avoid evil speaking* 1 Cl 30:1; cp. vs. 3; πιστεύειν τῇ κ. *believe the slander* Hm 2:2; πονηρὰ ἡ κ. 2:3; κ. is injurious to faith s 9, 23, 2; cp. 3.—DELG s.v. λαλέω. TW.

κατάλαλος, ον (s. two prec. entries) **pert. to speaking ill of others,** ***slanderous*** w. δίψυχοι Hs 8, 7, 2. W. δόλιοι 9, 26, 7. Subst. ὁ κ. (POxy 1828 r, 3) *slanderer* (in a list of vices) **Ro 1:30** (κακολάλους D); Hs 6, 5, 5.—DELG s.v. λαλέω. TW.

καταλαμβάνω (s. λαμβάνω; Hom.+) 2 aor. κατέλαβον; pf. κατείληφα. Mid.: fut. καταλήψομαι LXX; 2 aor. κατελαβόμην. Pass.: fut. 3 pl. καταλη(μ)θήσονται (PsSol 15:9); 1 aor. κατελήμφθην **Phil 3:12** (B-D-F §101 p. 53 s.v. λαμβ.; Mlt-H. 246f s.v. λαμβ.; on the form κατειλήφθη **J 8:4** in the older NT editions s. W-S. §12, 1); pf. 3 sg. κατείληπται, ptc. κατειλημμένος. Gener. 'to seize, lay hold of' (of forceful seizure Plut., Cleom. 806 [4, 2]; POxy 1101, 26; PsSol 8:19)

❶ **to make someth. one's own,** ***win, attain,*** act. and pass. (Diog. L. 5, 12 καταλαμβάνω means 'come into possession of an inheritance'); abs. (though τὸ βραβεῖον is to be supplied fr. the context) of the winning of a prize **1 Cor 9:24.** As a result of διώκειν (cp. Diod. S. 17, 73, 3 ἐπιδιώκων … τὸν Δαρεῖον … καταλαβών; Sir 11:10 ἐὰν διώκῃς, οὐ μὴ καταλάβῃς; 27:8) **Phil 3:12a, 13:** Χριστόν, corresp. to κατελήμφθην ὑπὸ Χριστοῦ Ἰ. vs. **12b.** δικαιοσύνην **Ro 9:30.** ἐπίγνωσιν πατρός

Dg 10:1 cj (vGebhardt for καὶ λάβῃς). The pass. is found in the mng. *make one's own* in the **ending of Mark** in the Freer ms. 3 (KHaacker, ZNW 63, '72, 125–29).—This may also be the mng. of κ. in **J 1:5** ἡ σκοτία αὐτὸ (=τὸ φῶς) οὐ κατέλαβεν (-λαμβάνει Tat. 13, 1; cp. Arrian., An. Alex. 1, 5, 10 εἰ νὺξ αὐτοὺς καταλήψεται 'if the night would overtake them'; here preceded in 1, 5, 9 by k. in the sense 'occupy' of positions above a plain; s. Wetstein on J 1:5 and 2b below) *the darkness did not grasp it* (Hdb. ad loc.; so also Bultmann, and similarly JDyer, JBL 79, '60, 70f: *appreciate*), in which case *grasp* easily passes over to the sense *comprehend* (the act. [for the mid. in the same sense s. 4a below] has the latter sense in Pla., Phdr. 250d; Polyb. 8, 4, 6; Dionys. Hal. 5, 46, 3; PTebt 15, 5; 38, 18; EpArist 1; Aristobul. [Eus., PE 8, 10, 10 and 17=Denis 219, 18 and 221, 5/Holladay p. 140, 2f and 148, 3]; Philo, Mut. Nom. 4; Jos., Vi. 56). Most Greek commentators since Origen take κ. here as *overcome, suppress* (Hdt. 1, 46 κ. τινῶν αὐξανομένην τὴν δύναμιν; 1, 87 τὸ πῦρ; WNagel, ZNW 50, '59, 132–37). So Goodsp. *put out* (Probs. 93f). But perh. J intended to include both mngs. here (so FGingrich, ClW 37, '43, 77), and some such transl. as *master* would suggest this (so MSmith, JBL 64, '45, 510f).

❷ **to gain control of someone through pursuit, *catch up with, seize***—ⓐ of authority figures *catch up with, overtake* (Hdt. 1:63 τοὺς φεύγοντας; Polyb. 1:47; Gen. 31:23; Judg 18:22; PsSol 15:8) διωκόμενοι κατελήμφθησαν *they were pursued and overtaken* AcPl Ha 11, 18.

ⓑ mostly of varieties of evil *seize w. hostile intent, overtake, come upon* (Hom.+; oft. LXX; TestSol 2:4 D; Wetstein and Zahn [comm.] on **J 1:5** for other exx.; s. also SIG 434/5, 14) μὴ ἡμᾶς καταλάβῃ κακά *lest evil overtake us* (cp. Gen 19:19; Num 32:23) 2 Cl 10:1; cp. B 4:1. Of a hostile divinity ὅπου ἐὰν αὐτὸν καταλάβῃ *wherever it seizes him* (the sick man) **Mk 9:18.**

ⓒ esp. used of night, evening, darkness coming upon a pers. (Dionys. Hal. 2, 51, 3 ἑσπέρα γὰρ αὐτοὺς κατέλαβεν; Lucian, Tox. 31; 52; Philo, De Jos. 145; Jos., Ant. 5, 61 καταλαβοῦσα νύξ, Vi. 329 [GrBar 9:1]. But the thought in these instances is not necessarily always that of night as something hostile to humans in general. κ. can also mean simply 'arrive', 'come on', as in numerous exx. cited by Wetstein [above]; s. also Dionys. Hal. 10, 56, 1 ἐπεὶ κατέλαβεν ὁ τ. ἀρχαιρεσιῶν καιρός; Strabo 3, 1, 5; Jos., Ant. 4, 78) GJs 14:1 κατέλαβεν (-ἔβαλεν pap) αὐτὸν νύξ; **J 6:17 v.l.** σκοτία. In imagery, w. sugg. of sense in 2b: **12:35.**

❸ **to come upon someone, with implication of surprise, *catch***—ⓐ of moral authorities *catch, detect* (PLille 3, 58 [III BC]; Just., D. 47, 5 [noncanonical dominical saying]; PRyl 138, 15. Esp. of the detection of adultery Epict. 2, 4, 1; BGU 1024 III, 11; Sus 58) τινὰ ἐπί τινι *someone in someth.* ἐπὶ μοιχείᾳ in *adultery* (Diod. S. 10, 20, 2 ἐπὶ μοιχείᾳ κατειλημμένη) **J 8:3** a woman caught in the act of adultery. Pass. (Just., A I, 47, 6) w. ptc. indicating the punishable act ἐπ' αὐτοφώρῳ μοιχευομένη *in the act of committing adultery* vs. **4.**

ⓑ of a thief: in imagery of the coming of 'the day', unexpected by the 'children of darkness' and fraught w. danger for them **1 Th 5:4.**

❹ **to process information, *understand, grasp***—ⓐ learn about someth. through process of inquiry, mid. *grasp, find, understand* (Dionys. Hal. 2, 66, 6; Sext. Emp., Math. 7, 288; Vett. Val. 225, 8; TestJob 37:6 τὰ βάθη τοῦ κυρίου al.; Philo, Mos. 1, 278; Jos., Ant. 8, 167; Tat. 4:2 [on Ro 1:20]; Ath. 5, 2; 24, 2) w. acc. and inf. **Ac 25:25.** W. ὅτι foll. **4:13; 10:34.** W. indirect discourse foll. **Eph 3:18.**

ⓑ on **J 1:5** s. 1 and 2 above.—B. 701; 1207. M-M. TW.

καταλάμπω (s. λάμπω; Eur., Pla. et al.; PGM 7, 704; Philo; TestGad 7:3 v.l.) ***shine upon,*** pass. *be illuminated, be bright* (Eur., Tro. 1069, Ion 87; X., Mem. 4, 7, 7) τινί *by* or *with someth.* (Cebes 17, 1 φωτὶ καταλαμπόμενος; Wsd 17:19; Philo, Somn. 1, 218) ἀκτῖσιν ἡλίου ApcPt 5:15 (Dio Chrys. 19 [36], 45 τὸ καταλαμπόμενον Ἡλίῳ).

καταλέγω (Hom. et al. various mngs., but all marked by a quantitative component ranging from relation of details as in a story 'recount' to numerical calculation 'enumerate'; Dt 19:16 'reckon something against someone'='accuse' [cp. our colloq. 'keep score' of another's faults]; TestSol 8:2 D 'relate in full' [as Just., A I, 46, 3; Ath. 14:2]; Philo, Aet. M. 114; Jos., Ant. 19, 301, C. Ap. 1, 131 al.; Just. [freq. 'accuse']; Ath.) **to make a selection for membership in a group** (of soldiers Aristoph. et al.; Just., A I, 39, 5. Of reception into the circle of the 'Twelve Gods' Diod. S. 4, 39, 4; into the Senate, Plut., Pomp. 625 [13, 11]. Cp. Michel 165, 2; BGU 1073, 10) aor. ptc. καταλέξας (TestSol D 8:2), pass. inf. καταλεχθῆναι (Just., D. 17, 3). χήρα καταλεγέσθω μὴ ἔλαττον ἐτῶν ἑξήκοντα γεγονυῖα either gener. *be selected* or specif. *be enrolled* **1 Ti 5:9** (of reception into a religious body κ. is also used POxy 416, 4. On the constr. cp. the double acc. Pla., Leg. 742e κ. τινὰ πλούσιον.).—M-M. TW.

κατάλειμμα, ατος, τό (Galen; LXX; En 106:18) ***remnant*** (so Galen XIV p. 456, 13 K.) **Ro 9:27 v.l.** (Is 10:22); s. ὑπόλειμμα.—DELG. s.v. λείπω. TW.

καταλείπω (s. λείπω; Hom.+) alternate form καταλιμπάνω (LXX; TestIss 6:1; ApcEsdr 3:12 p. 27, 24 Tdf.) impf. κατέλειπον; fut. καταλείψω; 1 aor. κατέλειψα (**Ac 6:2;** Hs 8, 3, 5 v.l.; CPR I, 102; Jos., Bell. 1, 504, Ant. 10, 277); 2 aor. κατέλιπον (on the aor. forms s. B-D-F §75; W-S. §13, 10; Rob. 348; Helbing 90f; Thackeray 234; Dssm., NB 18 [BS 190]; Crönert 234, 6; KDieterich, Untersuchungen 1898, 238; Mayser 364); pf. καταλέλοιπα LXX. Pass.: fut. καταλειφθήσομαι LXX; 1 aor. κατελείφθην; pf. 3 sg. καταλέλειπται (LXX; JosAs 4:13), inf. καταλελεῖφθαι, ptc. καταλελειμμένος (W-S. §5, 13e) 'leave behind'.

❶ **to cause to be left in a place, *leave (behind)***—ⓐ of pers. τινά *someone*—**α.** by leaving a place (Diod. S. 1, 55, 4; 5, 51, 4; Da 10:13; ParJer 3:12; ApcMos 31; Just., D. 2, 3 al.) καταλείψει ἄνθρωπος τὸν πατέρα κτλ. **Mt 19:5; Mk 10:7; Eph 5:31** (all three Gen 2:24); **Mt 16:4; 21:17.** κἀκείνους κατέλιπεν αὐτοῦ **Ac 18:19.** κατέλιπόν σε ἐν Κρήτῃ, ἵνα **Tit 1:5 v.l.** (for ἀπολείπω). καταλείπω σε ἐν τῷ οἴκῳ μου GJs 9:3. ὁ Φῆλιξ κατέλιπεν τ. Παῦλον δεδεμένον **Ac 24:27** (the ptc. as TestReub 3:14); cp. the pass. *be left behind* (Hippol., Ref. 7, 25, 2) **25:14.**—Elsewh. the pass. has the mng. *remain behind* (X., An. 5, 6, 12) **J 8:9.** ἐν Ἀθήναις **1 Th 3:1.**

β. by dying *leave (behind)* (Hom. et al.; oft. pap and LXX) γυναῖκα **Mk 12:19.** σπέρμα *descendants* vs. **21** (s. ἀφίημι 4). τέκνα (Dt 28:54; cp. Pr 20:7; Jos., Ant. 12, 235) **Lk 20:31.**

ⓑ of things *leave (behind)* (s. β above) πρόβατα ἐν τῇ ἐρήμῳ **Lk 15:4.** πάντα ἐπὶ τ. γῆς *everything on land* **5:11** D. Of a youth fleeing fr. the police καταλιπὼν τὴν σινδόνα **Mk 14:52** (Aesop, Fab. 419 P.=196 H.//301 H-H.: κατέλιπε τὸν ἑαυτοῦ χιτῶνα; Gen 39:12; TestJos 8:3; cp. Mk 10:50, s. PDickerson, JBL 116, '97, 273–89).

❷ **to depart from a place, with implication of finality, *leave*** (Dio Chrys. 30 [47], 2 τ. πατρίδα; Just., D. 60, 2 τὰ ὑπὲρ οὐρανὸν πάντα) τὴν Ναζαρά **Mt 4:13.** Αἴγυπτον **Hb 11:27.** Fig. καταλείποντες εὐθεῖαν ὁδὸν ἐπλανήθησαν **2 Pt 2:15.** κ. ὁδὸν τοῦ θεοῦ ὅλως ApcPt Bodl.—*Leave someth.* as it is, located in its own place, of an island καταλιπόντες αὐτὴν εὐώνυμον **Ac 21:3.**

❸ **to cease from some activity,** ***leave to one side, give up*** of vice κακίαν 2 Cl 10:1 (ParJer 8:2 τὰ ἔργα τῆς Βαβυλῶνος). W. inf. foll. to denote purpose: *leave off from* τοῦ φυλάσσειν τὸν πύργον *cease to guard the tower* Hs 9, 5, 1 of young women who appeared to have ceased guarding a certain tower.

❹ **to cause someth. to remain in existence or be left over,** ***leave over*** (Alex. Aphr., Fat. 28, II 2 p. 199, 8) τὰ θηρία . . . ἵνα μηδὲν καταλίπωσι τῶν τοῦ σώματός μου *so that they don't leave a piece of my body* IRo 4:2. Pass. *remain* (Jos., Bell. 4, 338 σωτηρίας ἐλπίς; Iren. 1, 16, 1 [Harv. I 158, 12]; Hippol., Ref. 7, 31, 8), specif. in the sense *be incomplete, unfinished, open* (X., Cyr. 2, 3, 11 μάχη; PLond III, 1171, 43 [8 BC]) καταλειπομένη ἐπαγγελία *a promise that is still open* **Hb 4:1.**—*Leave over; see to it that* someth. *is left* (cp. Sir 24:33) κατέλιπον ἐμαυτῷ ἑπτακισχιλίους ἄνδρας *I have kept 7,000 men for myself* **Ro 11:4** (3 Km 19:18; here as in the Hebr. the first pers.).

❺ **to leave someth. with design before departing,** ***leave behind*** of an inheritance (Mel., P. 49, 347–79) Hv 3, 12, 2.

❻ **to cause to be left to one's own resources,** ***leave (behind)***

ⓐ by desertion or abandonment *leave behind, desert* MPol 17:2 Christ (Sir 28:23 κύριον; Just., D. 8, 3 θεόν).

ⓑ *leave without help* τινά w. the inf. of result (not of purpose; s. B-D-F §392, 1f; Rob. 1090, and cp. Il. 17, 151) ἡ ἀδελφή μου μόνην με κατέλιπεν διακονεῖν *my sister has left me without help, so that now I must serve alone* **Lk 10:40** (v.l. κατέλειπεν; for κ. ἐμὲ μόνον cp. Jos., Vi. 301).

❼ **to set someth. aside in the interest of someth. else,** ***leave***—ⓐ *abandon* ἀλήθειαν Hs 8, 9, 1.

ⓑ *give up* (e.g. schol. on Apollon. Rhod. 272–74 τὴν τέχνην give up one's trade); *lose* (Petosiris, fgm. 12 ln. 22 and 120 τὸν θρόνον) πάντα **Lk 5:28;** cp. 1 Cl 10:2; τὴν παροικίαν τ. κόσμου τούτου 2 Cl 5:1.

ⓒ *set to one side, neglect* (Ps.-X., Cyneg. 3, 10 τὰ αὑτῶν ἔργα; Dt 29:24 τ. διαθήκην; Jos., Ant. 8, 190 τ. τῶν πατρίων ἐθισμῶν φυλακήν; TestIss 6:1 τὴν ἁπλότητα) ἄμπελος ἐν φραγμῷ τινι καταλειφθεῖσα *just as a vine left to itself on some fence* Hs 9, 26, 4. τὸν λόγον τ. θεοῦ **Ac 6:2.**—DELG s.v. λίθος. M-M. TW.

καταλιθάζω (s. λιθάζω) fut. καταλιθάσω (only in Christian wr. But καταλιθοβολέω Ex 17:4; Num 14:10 and καταλιθόω in Paus.; Jos., Ant. 4, 282 al.) ***stone to death*** τινά *someone* **Lk 20:6.**—DELG s.v. λίθος. TW.

καταλλαγή, ῆς, ἡ (s. next entry) **reestablishment of an interrupted or broken relationship,** ***reconciliation*** (so Aeschyl., Sept. 767; Demosth. 1, 4) with God (2 Macc 5:20; Philo, Exs. 166 αἱ πρὸς τὸν πατέρα [=God] καταλλαγαί [in Philo always pl.]), which, acc. to Paul, is brought about by God alone (s. καταλλάσσω a). κ. κόσμου (opp. ἀποβολή) **Ro 11:15;** λόγος τῆς κ. *the word of reconciliation* **2 Cor 5:19** (cp. the function of judges [IPriene 53] and envoys [Dio Chrys. 38, 18], s. FDanker, Augsburg Comm: II Cor '89, 83; Breytenbach 64f; s. also διαλλασσομαι, πρεσβεύω) διακονία τῆς κ. *ministry of rec.* vs. **18.** Since humans are not active in this dispensation fr. God, they are said τ. καταλλαγὴν λαμβάνειν *to receive reconciliation* **Ro 5:11.**—EGvanLeeuwen, De καταλλαγή: ThSt 28, 1910, 159–71; ANygren, D. Versöhnung als Gottestat '32; CBreytenbach, Versöhnung, '89; idem NTS 39, '93, 59–79; AdeOliveira, Die Diakonie der Gerechtigkeit und der Versöhnung in der Apologie des 2 Korintherbriefes, '90.—EDNT. DELG s.v. ἄλλος. M-M. TW. Spicq.

καταλλάσσω (s. prec. entry and διαλλάσσω) 1 aor. κατήλλαξα; aor. mid. 3 aor. pl. κατηλλάξαντο (TestAbr A 8 p. 85, 30 [Stone p. 18]). Pass.: fut. 3 sg. καταλλαγήσεται 2 Macc 7:33; 2 aor. κατηλλάγην; ptc. καταλλαγείς; gener. 'exchange' one thing for another (TestJob 25:3 τρίχα . . . ἀντὶ ἄρτων); in our lit. only **the exchange of hostility for a friendly relationship,** ***reconcile*** (so Hdt. et al.; 2 Macc). Act. τινά (Hdt. 5, 29; 6, 108; Aristot., Oec. 2, 15) *someone* τινί *to someone.*

ⓐ act. of God, ἡμᾶς ἑαυτῷ διὰ Χριστοῦ *us to himself through Christ* **2 Cor 5:18**=ἐν Χριστῷ κόσμον ἑαυτῷ vs. **19.**

ⓑ pass.—**α.** *be reconciled, become reconciled* (BGU 1463, 3 [247 BC]; Philo, Leg. All. 3, 134) w. dat. of the pers. (cp. X., An. 1, 6, 2; Pla., Rep. 8, 566e; 2 Macc 1:5; 7:33; 8:29; Jos., Ant. 7, 184): of humanity's relation to God (Soph., Aj. 744; Jos., Ant. 6, 143 θεὸν καταλλάττεσθαι τῷ Σαούλῳ) καταλλαγῆναι τῷ θεῷ *be(come) reconciled to God* **Ro 5:10a; 2 Cor 5:20** (sim. formulation but difft. sense Vi. Aesopi G 100 P. Aesop pleads with the king καταλλάγηθι Σαμίοις; cp. Vi. Aesopi W 100 P. δέομαι σου, δέσποτα, διαλλάγηθι Σαμίοις, followed by the king's reply: κατήλλαγμαι; on the role of an envoy or meditator s. prec. entry). Abs. **Ro 5:10b.**

β. Of reconciliation betw. human beings **Ac 12:22** D. (γυνὴ) τῷ ἀνδρὶ καταλλαγήτω *let her become reconciled to her husband* **1 Cor 7:11** (cp. POxy 104, 27 [I AD]; the hypothesis, [summary] by Aristophanes the Grammarian, of Menander's Dyscolus, ln. 9: κατηλλάγη τῇ γυναικί).—DELG s.v. ἄλλος. M-M. TW. Spicq.

κατάλοιπος, ον (s. λοιπός; Pla. et al.; ins, pap, LXX) ***left, remaining*** οἱ κ. τῶν ἀνθρώπων *the rest of humanity* **Ac 15:17** (Am 9:12).—DELG s.v. λείπω. M-M.

κατάλυμα, ατος, τό (Polyb. 2, 36, 1; 32, 19, 2; Diod. S. 14, 93, 5; IG V/1, 869; SIG 609, 1; UPZ 120, 5 [II BC] al. in pap; LXX; TestLevi 3:4 v.l.; s. B-D-F §109, 2; Rob. 151) ***lodging place.*** The sense *inn* is possible in **Lk 2:7,** but in **10:34** Lk uses πανδοχεῖον, the more specific term for *inn.* κ. is therefore best understood here as *lodging* (PSI 341, 8 [256 BC]; EpArist 181) or *guest-room,* as in **22:11; Mk 14:14,** where the contexts also permit the sense *dining-room* (cp. 1 Km 1:18; 9:22; Sir 14:25). In further favor of this rendering is the contrast between two quarters: a φάτνη and a κατάλυμα. The latter could be a space in various types of structures. Cp. also the use of the cognate καταλύω (s. κ.4) **Lk 19:7** in ref. to hospitality.—PBenoit, BRigaux Festschr., '70, 173–86 (**Lk 2:7**); EPax, Bibel und Leben 6, '65, 285–98. DELG s.v. λύω. M-M. TW.

κατάλυσις, εως, ἡ (s. καταλύω 1–3; Thu.+; ins; PMagd 8, 10 [218 BC] κ. τοῦ βίου; LXX; En 5:6; Philo; Jos., Bell. 2, 594, Ant. 18, 55; 19, 301 al.; Just.) ***dissolution, abolition,*** also ***downfall*** (of a tyrant: Diod. S. 14, 64, 4; 14, 67, 1) θανάτου IEph 19:3.

καταλύω (s. prec. entry for mngs. 1–3, and κατάλυμα for mng. 4) fut. καταλύσω; 1 aor. κατέλυσα; pf. inf. καταλελυκέναι (Just., D. 41, 1). Pass.: 1 fut. καταλυθήσομαι; 1 aor. κατελύθην (Hom.+).

❶ **to detach someth. in a demolition process,** ***throw down, detach*** of a stone fr. a building **Mt 24:2; Mk 13:2; Lk 21:6.**

❷ **to cause the ruin of someth.,** ***destroy, demolish, dismantle***

ⓐ lit. of buildings (Hom. et al.; 2 Esdr 5:12; Jos., Ant. 9, 161 τ. ναοῦ [τ. θεοῦ] καταλυθέντος; SibOr 3, 459) τ. ναὸν τοῦ θεοῦ **Mt 26:61;** cp. **27:40; Mk 14:58; 15:29.** τὸν τόπον τοῦτον *this place* **Ac 6:14.**

ⓑ fig. (opp. οἰκοδομεῖν) *tear down, demolish* **Gal 2:18.** Of the body as an earthly tent ἐὰν ἡ ἐπίγειος ἡμῶν οἰκία τοῦ σκήνους καταλυθῇ *if the earthly tent we live in is destroyed* or *taken down* **2 Cor 5:1.** τὸ ἔργον τοῦ θεοῦ *tear down the work* (i.e. the Christian congregation which, because of vs. **19,** is prob. thought of as a *building of God*) **Ro 14:20.** On the contrary, the figure of the building is not present, and the gener. mng. *destroy, annihilate* (Strabo 13, 2, 3 p. 617; Ael. Aristid. 29 p. 570 D.: ἐλπίδας; TestBenj 3:8) is found in τὰ ἔργα τῆς θηλείας (s. ἔργον 3 end) GEg 252, 55.

❸ **to end the effect or validity of someth.,** ***put an end to***

ⓐ to cause to be no longer in force *abolish, annul, make invalid* (Hdt.+) κ. τὸν νόμον *do away with, annul* or *repeal the law* **Mt 5:17a** (cp. X., Mem. 4, 4, 14; Isocr. 4, 55; Diod. S. 34+35 fgm. 3 and 40, 2 [of the intention of the Seleucids against the Jews: καταλύειν τοὺς πατρίους νόμους]; Philostrat., Vi. Apoll. 4, 40; 2 Macc 2:22; Philo, Somn. 2, 123; Jos., Ant. 16, 35; 20, 81; Ath., R. 19 p. 72, 28). τ. νόμον κ. τ. προφήτας (sim. **Mt 5:17a) Lk 23:2** v.l. τὰς θυσίας *abolish sacrifices* GEb 54, 20. Abs. **Mt 5:17b** (opp. πληροῦν); D 11:2.

ⓑ to bring to an end, *ruin,* (Appian, Prooem. C. 10 §42 ἀρχάς=empires; Arrian, Anab. 4, 10, 3 τυραννίδα; 4 Macc 4:24 τὰς ἀπειλάς; Jos., Ant. 12, 1 τὴν Περσῶν ἡγεμονίαν) ἡ βουλὴ καταλυθήσεται *the plan will fail* **Ac 5:38.** Also of pers. (TestJob 34:5; Just., D. 100, 6 al.; Diod. S. 16, 47, 2 τοὺς μάγους; Appian, Bell. Civ. 1, 48 §210) *suppress, stop* vs. **39.** Of rulers who are *deposed* (Diod. S. 1, 66, 6; 9, 4, 2 [a tyrant]; 14, 14, 7 al.; Polyaenus 7, 3 and 10; 8, 29; IAndrosIsis, Kyme 25) καταλύεται ὁ ἄρχων τοῦ αἰῶνος τούτου *the ruler of this age is deposed* ITr 4:2.

❹ **to cease what one is doing,** ***halt*** (lit. 'unharness the pack animals'), *rest, find lodging* (Thu. et al.; SIG 978, 8; UPZ 12, 37 [158 BC]; 62, 34; BGU 1097, 5; Gen 19:2; 24:23, 25; Sir 14:25, 27; 36:27; JosAs 3:3; Jos., Vi. 248; Just., D. 78, 5 [ref. Lk 2:7]; cp. En 5:6) **Lk 9:12.** W. εἰσέρχεσθαι **19:7.**—B. 758. M-M. EDNT. TW.

καταμανθάνω 2 aor. κατέμαθον (s. μανθάνω; Hdt.+; ins, pap, LXX; En 3:1; Philo; Jos., Ant. 6, 230f, Vi. 10; Just., D. 120, 2; Tat.) ***observe (well), notice, learn*** τὶ *someth.* τοὺς καιρούς IPol 3:2. W. ὅτι foll. (Hippocr., Art. 8 p. 122, 2 Kühlewein) 1 Cl 7:5. W. acc. and ὅτι foll. (Aristot., Pol. 3, 14, 1285a, 1; Philo, Leg. All. 3, 183) 2 Cl 13:3. W. acc. and πῶς foll.: τὰ κρίνα τοῦ ἀγροῦ πῶς αὐξάνουσιν **Mt 6:28.** τοὺς ἑτεροδοξοῦντας … πῶς ἐναντίοι εἰσίν ISm 6:2.—M-M.

καταμαρτυρέω fut. καταμαρτυρήσω LXX; aor. κατεμαρτύρησα LXX (s. μαρτυρέω; Lysias, Demosth.; PPetr III, 17; I, 9; UPZ 162 V, 33 [117 BC]; LXX; Philo, Leg. All. 3, 199; Jos., Ant. 8, 358; 359) ***bear witness against, testify against*** τί τινος *testify someth. against someone* (Plut., Ages. 3, 9; Pr 25:18; Sus 43; 49 Theod.) **Mt 26:62; 27:13; Mk 14:60; 15:4 v.l.** —DELG s.v. μάρτυς. M-M. TW.

καταμένω fut. καταμενῶ; aor. κατέμεινα LXX (s. μένω; Hdt., Aristoph. et al.; ins, pap, LXX; TestLevi 9:5; EpArist, Philo; Jos., Ant. 6, 249; 7, 180) ***stay, live*** οὗ ἦσαν καταμένοντες *where they were staying* **Ac 1:13.** κ. πρός τινα *stay w. someone* **1 Cor 16:6 v.l.** (for παραμενῶ).—M-M.

καταμόνας t.r.; s. μόνος 3.

κατανάθεμα, ατος, τό (s. next entry, also κατάθεμα, ἀνάθεμα) **that which is devoted or given over to a deity,** ***accursed thing*** **Rv 22:3** t.r. (Erasmian rdg.; s. κατάθεμα).—DELG s.v. τίθημι.

καταναθεματίζω (s. prec. entry; Just., D. 47) ***curse*** **Mt 26:74 v.l.** (s. καταθεματίζω).

καταναλίσκω (s. ἀναλίσκω) fut. καταναλώσω LXX; 1 aor. κατηνάλωσα or κατανάλωσα LXX. Pass.: fut. 3 sg. καταναλωθήσεται LXX; aor. 3 sg. κατηναλώθη or καταναλώθη Is 59:14 (X., Pla.+; SIG 672, 39 [II BC]; PSI 41, 20; LXX; TestSol 2:4 D; Jos., Bell. 4, 242; Ath. 22, 4) ***consume*** of fire (Aristot., De Juv. 469b, 29): God is πῦρ καταναλίσκον *a consuming fire* **Hb 12:29** (Dt 4:24). Pass. πλοῦτος καταναλίσκεται *wealth is consumed* AcPl Ha 2, 24.—S. Frisk s.v. ἀναλίσκω and ἁλίσκομαι; DELG s.v. ἁλίσκομαι. M-M.

καταναρκάω (ναρκάω 'grow stiff/numb') fut. καταναρκήσω; 1 aor. κατενάρκησα (in Hippocr., Art. 48 p. 182, 18 Kühlewein, Epidem. 6, 7, 3 ed. Littré V 340='stupefy, disable'; Philod., παρρ. col. XIIb, 10 Oliv.—Jerome, Ep. 121, 10, 4 maintains that the Cilicians used it for Lat. gravare, 'weigh down, burden'. At any rate the Latin and Syriac versions understand it in that sense; Chrysostom and Theodoret take for granted that this is the mng.) ***burden, be a burden to*** τινός *someone* **2 Cor 11:9; 12:13, 16 v.l.** Abs. **12:14.** The Apostle's use of satire in the context suggests that in these pass. the mng. approaches our colloq. 'knock out' (s. 'disable' above), 'shake down'.—DELG s.v. νάρκη. M-M. Spicq.

κατανδραποδίζω (Justin., Nov. 42 preface, VI AD) ***enslave*** ἀπ̣α̣γ̣ο̣μ̣έ̣ν̣ο̣υ̣ς̣ κ̣α̣[ὶ κα]τανδρα̣π̣ο̣δ̣ι̣ζ̣ομένο̣υ̣ς̣ *led off and enslaved* AcPl Ha 1, 10.—DELG s.v. ἀνήρ A b. S. ἀνδραποδιστής.

κατανεύω 1 aor. κατένευσα (s. νεύω; Hom. et al.; BGU 1119, 24; 1120, 30 [I BC]; Philo, Post. Cai. 169; Jos., Vi. 156 al.) ***signal*** (usually by means of a nod) τινί *to someone.* The message to be given by the signal is added in the inf. (w. art.; s. B-D-F §400, 7; Rob. 1068) **Lk 5:7** (cp. Polyb. 39, 1, 3 κ. τινὶ προϊέναι).—M-M.

κατανοέω impf. κατενόουν; fut. κατανοήσω LXX; 1 aor. κατενόησα (s. νοέω; Hdt., Thu.+; ins, pap, LXX, En; TestAbr B 12 p. 116, 13 [Stone p. 80]; ParJer 5:14; ApcMos, EpArist, Philo, Joseph., Just.; Tat. 34, 1)

❶ ***notice, observe*** carefully τὶ *someth.* δοκόν **Mt 7:3; Lk 6:41.** πτελέαν καὶ ἄμπελον Hs 2:1. κόλπον **Ac 27:39.**

❷ **to look at in a reflective manner,** ***consider, contemplate*** τὶ *someth.* (Herm. Wr. 1, 13a; En 2:1; Philo, Leg. ad Gai. 358; Jos., Ant. 3, 302; 5, 5; Just., A I, 55, 2, with pers. pron. με D. 3, 2) κεράμια *pay attention to the jars* Hm 12, 5, 3ab. τὰ κρίνα **Lk 12:27.** τ. κόρακας **12:24.** τὸ ἑαυτοῦ σῶμα ἤδη νενεκρωμένον **Ro 4:19.** *Inspect* τ. ῥάβδους Hs 8, 1, 5; 8, 2, 5; 8, 3, 8; 8, 6, 1; τ. πύργον 9, 5, 6f. τὴν οἰκοδομήν 9, 6, 3. τοὺς λίθους 9, 7, 7 ; 9, 8, 1–7; 9. 9, 1. Abs., though the obj. is easily supplied fr. the context **Ac 7:31f; 11:6.** Also simply *look at, stare at* (Gen 3:6 the woman 'stared' at the tree) τὸ πρόσωπον **Js 1:23.** ἑαυτόν vs. **24.**

❸ **to think about carefully,** ***envisage, think about, notice*** extension of mng. 1 and 2 τινά *someone,* **Hb 3:1; 10:24;** *someth.* τὴν πανουργίαν *see through the trickery* **Lk 20:23** (cp. BGU 1011 II, 17 [II BC]; Jos., Ant. 14, 291, Vi. 72).—*Consider, contemplate* (Antig. Car. 31; Is 57:1; EpArist 3; Philo, Ebr. 137; Jos., Ant. 7, 204; Just., D. 17, 4 [ref. Mt 23:23 and par.]) τὶ *someth.* 1 Cl 32:1. W. indir. question foll. (Antiphanes [IV BC] Com.

fgm. 33, 1 K.) 24:1; 47:5. W. acc. and indir. question foll. 34:5; 37:2.—DELG s.v. νόος. M-M. TW.

καταντάω 1 aor. κατήντησα; pf. κατήντηκα **1 Cor 10:11** (ἀντάω 'come opposite to, meet'; Aristot., Polyb., Diod. S.; ins, pap, LXX; En 17:6; TestSol 1:12 D; Jos., Ant. 3, 246)

❶ **to get to a geographical destination,** ***come (to), arrive (at), reach,*** w. εἰς and acc. of place (Aristot., Dialog. fgm. 11 Rose εἰς τοὺς λιμένας; Diod. S. 3, 34, 7; 12, 55, 5; PTebt 59, 3 [99 BC] εἰς τ. πόλιν Σοκονώφεως; InsPriene 112, 97 [I BC]; 2 Macc 4:21, 44) εἰς Ἰκόνιον **Ac 13:51** D. εἰς Δέρβην **16:1.** Cp. **18:19, 24; 21:7; 25:13** (w. ἀσπάζω; cp. ἀπήντησεν αὐτῷ κ. ἠσπάσατο Plut., Mor. 488e); **27:12; 28:13.** ἄντικρυς Χίου *off Chios* **20:15.**

❷ **to reach a condition or goal,** fig. extension of 1 ***arrive at, attain, meet*** (cp. κατάντημα Ps 18:7)—ⓐ *arrive at someth.*, so that one comes to possess it, *attain (to) someth.* μέχρι καταντήσωμεν εἰς τ. ἑνότητα τ. πίστεως **Eph 4:13** (εἰς as Polyb. 6, 9, 10; BGU 1101, 5 εἰς τ. αὐτὸν βίον). W. εἴς τι also **Ac 26:7; Phil 3:11;** εἰς πέπειρον κ. *come to ripeness* 1 Cl 23:4. ἕως θανάτου καταντῆσαι *meet death* Pol 1:2. W. ἐπί τι (Epicurus p. 63, 3 Us.; Diod. S. 1, 79, 2; Ammon., In Int. [Aristot.] p. 264, 22 B. κ. ἐπὶ τὸ ἔσχατον) ἐπὶ τὸν σκοπὸν κ. *arrive at the goal, reach the goal* 1 Cl 63:1. Likew. ἐπὶ τὸν βέβαιον δρόμον κ. 6:2.

ⓑ The person does not come to someth., but someth. comes to the person (κ. εἰς as t.t. for the inheritance that comes to an heir: BGU 1169, 21 [10 BC]; POxy 75, 5; 248, 11; 274, 19. Cp. 2 Km 3:29). Of the word of God: ἢ εἰς ὑμᾶς μόνους κατήντησεν; *or has it come to you alone?* **1 Cor 14:36.** On εἰς οὓς τὰ τέλη τ. αἰώνων κατήντηκεν **10:11** s. αἰών 2b end.—DELG s.v. ἄντα. M-M. TW. Spicq.

καταντικρύ (s. ἄντικρυς; Hom. et al.) and **καταντικρύς** (late form, cp. Phryn. p. 444 Lob.; PGM 36, 3) *directly opposite* τινός *someth.* or *someone* (cp. Pla., Phd. 112e; X., Hell. 4, 8, 5; Arrian, Anab. 3, 16, 8; Eubul. Com. [IV BC], fgm. 80, 1 [in Athen. 11, 473d] κ. τῆς οἰκίας; PGM 4, 89) ApcPt 6:21; 14:29.

κατάνυξις, εως, ἡ (s. next entry; Cyr. Scyth. p. 19, 25; 34, 21; 97, 1; 206, 27 [=deep emotion]; Leontius 1 p. 6, 20; Pel.-Leg. p. 3, 7; LXX; Hesychius) ***stupefaction*** πνεῦμα κατανύξεως (Is 29:10) *a spirit of stupor* **Ro 11:8.**—DELG s.v. νύσσω. M-M. TW. Sv.

κατανύσσομαι (s. νύσσω and prec. entry) pass.: fut. κατανυγήσομαι LXX; 2 aor. κατενύγην and κατενύχθην LXX; pf. κατανένυγμαι LXX, TestJob (Pel.-Leg. 7, 16; LXX; TestSol 20:3 P; JosAs 6:1; Just., D. 91, 3; Hesychius.—The act. in Phlegon [II AD]: 257 fgm. 36 IV Jac.) ***be pierced, stabbed*** fig., of the feeling of sharp pain connected w. anxiety, remorse, etc. (Photius: κατανυγείς· λυπηθείς; Ps.-Callisth. 2, 36 Müller κατανυγεὶς ἐπὶ τοῖς λόγοις=stricken, taken aback; Cyr. Scyth. p. 53, 14; 96, 19; 108, 2 be deeply moved; Leontius 14 p. 30, 13 al.) κατενύγησαν τὴν καρδίαν *they were cut to the heart* **Ac 2:37** (v.l. κ. τῇ καρδίᾳ as Ps 108:16). τοῦ … Παύλου κατανυγέντος *since Paul was racked with pain* AcPl Ha 7, 36.—DELG s.v. νύσσω. M-M s.v. κατανύσσω. TW.

καταξαίνω fut. καταξανῶ Judg 8:7 A; aor. 3 sg. κατέξανεν Judg 8:16 A; 1 aor. pass. ptc. καταξανθείς (since Aeschyl. et al.) ***tear to shreds*** (lit. 'comb, card', as wool, s. ξαίνω) μάστιξιν καταξανθέντες *torn to shreds with whips* MPol 2:2.—DELG s.v. ξαίνω.

καταξιοπιστεύομαι (s. ἄξιος, πιστεύω and next entry) ***imposing by profession of honesty*** (so Lghtf., w. ref. to Polyb. 12, 17, 1: καταξιοπιστέομαι [Suda -εύομαι]) ITr 6:2.—DELG s.v. ἄξιος.

καταξιόω (s. ἀξιόω) 1 aor. κατηξίωσα. Pass.: aor. κατηξιώθην; pf. κατηξίωμαι (Papias 12:1 [?]; Just.) (Aeschyl. et al.; Polyb. 1, 23, 3; Diod. S. 2, 60, 3; ins, pap, LXX; TestSol 22:3; TestAbr A 86:21 [Stone p. 20]; TestJob; EpArist 175; Jos., Ant. 15, 76; Just.) **to consider someone worthy to receive some privilege, benefit, or recognition,** ***consider worthy.*** W. God or Jesus Christ as explicit or implied subj., act. τινά *someone* 1 Cl 50:2; IEph 20:1. W. inf. foll. IRo 2:2 (TestSol; TestAbr A; Just., D. 130, 4).—Pass. *be considered worthy* τινός *of a thing* (CIA III, 690, 9f; 4 Macc 18:3; Just., A I, 10, 2 al.) τῆς βασιλείας τοῦ θεοῦ **2 Th 1:5.** πλείονος γνώσεως 1 Cl 41:4. ὀνόματος θεοπρεπεστάτου (on the idea s. Hdb. ad loc.) IMg 1:2. τοῦ κλήρου ITr 12:3. τῆς τοιαύτης διακονίας *of such a service* IPhld 10:2: cp. IPol 1:1. μαρτυρίου Papias (12:1; but s. HNolter, TU 5, 1889, 178). W. inf. foll. (PAmh 145, 4; PGM 13, 707; Jos., Ant. 4, 281; Just., A I, 65, 1 al.) **Lk 20:35; 21:36 v.l.; Ac 5:41.** Also ἵνα ISm 11:1. W. a human subj., w. ἵνα foll. IPol 7:2. Pass. w. gen. 1:1. W. subst. inf. foll. (Just., D. 67, 2) τοῦ εἰς Συρίαν πορεύεσθαι 8:2.—DELG s.v. ἄξιος. M-M. TW.

καταπαλαίω 1 aor. κατεπάλαισα (s. παλαίω; Eur., Aristoph., Pla. et al.; 4 Macc 3:18; Philo, Vi. Cont. 43) ***win a victory over, defeat (in wrestling)*** abs. in wordplay w. ἀντιπαλαίειν Hm 12, 5, 2.

καταπατέω fut. καταπατήσω; 1 aor. κατεπάτησα. Pass.: fut. 3 sg. καταπατηθήσεται Is 25:10; 28:3; aor. κατεπατήθην; pf. 3 pl. καταπεπάτηνται 1 Macc 3:51 (s. πατέω; Hom., Hdt., Thu.+; SIG 1169, 115; pap, LXX; TestZeb 3:3; JosAs 29:3; SyrBar 13:11 [?]; Joseph.; Ar. 4, 3; Just., D. 76, 6 [for πατεῖν Lk 10:19]; Mel., P. 102, 782)

❶ **to tread so heavily as to injure,** ***trample under foot.***

ⓐ *trample* τὶ ἔν τινι *someth. with (under)someth.* **Mt 7:6** (of swine πατέω: Ananius Lyricus [VI BC]: fgm. 5, 4 AnthLG Diehl^3 [in Athen. 7, 282b]).—Pass. (Diod. S. 25, 3, 1) *be trampled under foot* **Mt 5:13; Lk 8:5.**

ⓑ *tread upon* of a milling crowd (Arrian, Anab. 2, 11, 3 ἀπ᾽ ἀλλήλων καταπατούμενοι=hard-pressed by each other, getting in each other's way; Polyaenus 4, 3, 21 ὑπ᾽ ἀλλήλων καταπατούμενοι) ὥστε καταπατεῖν ἀλλήλους *so that they stepped on one another* **Lk 12:1.**

❷ **to look on with scorn,** ***trample under foot, treat with disdain*** fig. extension of mng. 1 (Il. 4, 157 [in tmesis]; Pla., Leg. 4, 714a τοὺς νόμους, Gorg. 484a; Epict. 1, 8, 10; Lucian, Lexiph. 23; 2 Macc 8:2; Hos 5:11; Jos., Bell. 4, 386.—Cp. the underlying reality in Diod. S. 33, 5, 3 τὰ τῶν θεῶν ἀγάλματα ὑβριστικῶς κατεπάτησαν) τὸν υἱὸν τοῦ θεοῦ **Hb 10:29** (Artem. 4, 66 ἀνὴρ κατεπατήθη).—M-M. TW.

κατάπαυσις, εως, ἡ (s. next entry; Hdt. et al., but act. 'stopping, causing to rest'; also Jos., Ant. 17, 43)

❶ **state of cessation of work or activity,** ***rest*** (2 Macc 15:1 ἡ τῆς καταπαύσεως ἡμέρα of the Sabbath; sim. Orig., C. Cels. 6, 61, 12; esp. of the rest associated with the seventh day of creation Hippol., Ref. 8, 14, 1 and Did., Gen. 154, 23) τόπος τ. καταπαύσεως *place of rest,* i.e. where one rests and lives **Ac 7:49;** B 16:2 (both Is 66:1; cp. JosAs 22:9).

❷ ***place of rest*** abstract for concrete (Dt 12:9; Ps 131:14 al.; Did., Gen. 71, 4) εἰσελεύσονται εἰς τὴν κ. μου (Ps 94:11; cp.

JosAs 8:11); this OT pass. is typologically interpreted fr. a Christian viewpoint **Hb 3:11, 18; 4:1, 3, 5, 10f.**—GvRad, Zwischen den Zeiten 11, '33, 104–11; WHutton, ET 52, '41, 316f; OHofius, Katapausis '70.—DELG s.v. παύω. TW.

καταπαύω fut. καταπαύσω (LXX; JosAs cod. A) and καταπαύσομαι (B 15:5); 1 aor. κατέπαυσα (s. prec. entry; Hom.+; LXX; En 106:18; TestJob, Test12Patr; JosAs 28:5 cod. A; ApcMos, Philo, Joseph.; Anz 294f).

❶ **to cause to cease,** ***stop, bring to an end*** τὶ *someth.* (Hom.+; LXX; Philo, Leg. All. 1, 5; Jos., Vi. 422) τὸν διωγμόν MPol 1:1. τ. προσευχήν 8:1; AcPl Ha 10, 24 (cp. Aa I 115, 15 cod. A).

❷ **to cause persons to be at rest,** ***cause to rest*—ⓐ** by bringing to a place of rest (Ex 33:14; Dt 3:20; Josh 1:13; Sir 24:11) **Hb 4:8.**

ⓑ by causing to give up someth. they have begun to do with the result that they are quiet *restrain, dissuade someone fr. someth.* (cp. TestJob 14:5 τῆς ὀλιγωρίας; Jos., Ant. 3, 14 κ. τῆς ὀργῆς) κατέπαυσαν τ. ὄχλους τοῦ μὴ θύειν αὐτοῖς **Ac 14:18** (on the constr. s. B-D-F §400, 4; Rob. 1094; 1102).

ⓒ by simply causing rest τὶ *someth.* τὰ πάντα B 15:8.

❸ **to cease some activity,** ***stop, rest,*** intr.(Eur., Hec. 918; comic poet in Diod. S. 12, 14, 1 εὐημερῶν κατάπαυσον; Gen 2:2; Ex 31:18; TestJob 33:2; ApcMos 43) of God κατέπαυσεν ἐν τῇ ἡμέρᾳ τῇ ἑβδόμῃ *he rested on the seventh day* B 15:3, 5 (both Gen 2:2). κ. ἀπὸ τῶν ἔργων αὐτοῦ *from his work* **Hb 4:4, 10** (also Gen 2:2; cp. TestSim 6:4 γῆ ἀπὸ ταραχῆς). Mid. and pass. (B-D-F §309, 2; Aristoph. et al.; Appian, Bell. Civ. 5, 132 §548; Ex 16:13; Philo, Leg. All. 1, 18) B 15:5, 7; GJs 25:1 v.l. (for παύσηται; s. παύω).—M-M. TW.

καταπέμπω 1 aor. κατέπεμψα (Hes., Theog. 515; PEleph 10, 7 [III BC]; Joseph.; Just., D. 2, 1; Ath. 34, 2) ***send down, dispatch*** ὁ θεὸς … κατέπεμψε πνεῦμα διὰ πυρὸς εἰς Μαρίαν *God sent down the* (holy) *Spirit via fire into Mary* AcPlCor 2:13. πνεῦμα δυνάμεως … κατέπεμψεν εἰς σάρκα, τοῦτ' ἔστιν εἰς τὴν Μαρίαν (God) *sent down a spirit of power into* (human) *flesh, that is, into Mary* AcPl Ha 8, 25–27.

καταπέτασμα, ατος, τό (πετάννυμι 'spread out'; Heliod. 10, 28) ***curtain*** (ins of Samos of 346/345 BC, listing the furnishings of the Temple of Hera [in OHoffmann, D. griech. Dialekte III 1898, 72; Dssm., LO 80/LAE 101]; LXX; TestLevi 10:3; JosAs 10:4; EpArist 86; Philo; Joseph.). In the temple at Jerusalem one curtain separated the holy of holies fr. the holy place, and another covered the entrance fr. the forecourt to the temple proper. κ. means the latter in Ex 26:37; 38:18; Num 3:26; EpArist 86; Jos., Ant. 8, 75, Bell. 5, 212; the former in Ex 26:31ff; Lev 21:23; 24:3; Philo, Mos. 2, 86; 101; Jos., Ant. 8, 75. Our lit. knows only the inner curtain, τὸ δεύτερον κ. **Hb 9:3** (cp. Philo, Gig. 53 τὸ ἐσωτάτω καταπέτασμα). It is called simply τὸ κ. τοῦ ναοῦ. The priests have it woven by selected virgins ποιήσωμεν κ. τῷ ναῷ GJs 10:1. **Mt 27:51; Mk 15:38; Lk 23:45;** GPt 5:20 tell how it was torn at the death of Jesus. (EbNestle, NovT Suppl. 1896, 79[1], concludes, on the basis of GHb 347, 50 that פָּרֹכֶת 'curtain' was confused w. כַּפְתֹּר 'lintel', and thinks the lintel burst [but כַּפְתֹּר never means 'lintel'; rather 'capital of a column']; s. Zahn, NKZ 13, 1902, 729–56; HLaible, NKZ 35, 1924, 287–314; PFiebig, Neues Sächs. Kirchenbl. 40, '32, 227–36; ASchmidtke, Neue Fgmte u. Untersuchungen zu d. judenchristl. Evangelien: TU 37, 1, 1911 p. 257–64—GLindeskog, The Veil of the Temple: ConNeot 11, '47, 132–37; HSmid, diss. Groningen '65.)—τὸ ἐσώτερον τοῦ κ. (cp. Lev 16:2, 12) *the inner sanctuary behind the curtain, the holy of holies* as a figure for heaven **Hb 6:19.** κ. is used similarly in the fig. language of this epistle **10:20:** we have an εἴσοδος τ. ἁγίων, since Jesus has opened a ὁδὸς διὰ τοῦ καταπετάσματος *a way through the curtain.*—Billerbeck I 1043–46.—DELG s.v. πετάννυμι. M-M. TW.

καταπίμπρημι aor. 3 sg. κατέπρησεν (πίμπρημι 'burn, burn up'; Polyb., Polyaenus+; Philo, Div. Rer. Her. 296; Joseph.; Sb 8246, 46 [IV AD]; B-D-F §101, 69) ***burn to ashes*** κατέπ[ρ]ησεν as v.l. from P^{72} mg. in **2 Pt 2:6.**

καταπίνω fut. καταπίομαι (LXX; En 101:5); 2 aor. κατέπιον. Pass.: 1 aor. κατεπόθην; pf. 3 sg. καταπέποται (AcPlCor 2:29) (s. πίνω; Hes., Hdt.+; Ion of Chios fgm. 31 L. of Heracles' voracious appetite) in our lit. freq. in imagery, used both of liquids and solids

❶ **to drink down,** ***swallow, swallow up*** τὶ *someth.,* in imagery (of the earth, that drinks up water Pla., Critias 111d; Diod. S. 1, 32, 4) ἤνοιξεν ἡ γῆ τὸ στόμα αὐτῆς καὶ κατέπιεν τὸν ποταμόν **Rv 12:16** (Philostephanus Hist. [III BC], fgm. 23 [ed. CMüller III 1849 p. 32 ποταμὸς ὑπὸ γῆς καταπίνεται; Simplicius in Epict. p. 95, 35; cp. Num 16:30, 32). Δαθὰν καὶ Ἀβιρὼν καὶ Κόρε, πῶς … κατεπόθησαν ἅπαντες GJs 9:2 (cp. Num 16:32). τὴν κάμηλον κ. **Mt 23:24** (Just., D. 112, 4; on the camel s. κώνωψ.)

❷ **to destroy completely,** in the figure of one devouring or swallowing someth.**—ⓐ** ***devour*** (Hes., Theog. 459 υἱούς. Of animals that devour Tob 6:2; Jon 2:1; Jos., Ant. 2, 246; Ath. 34, 2) Ἰωνᾶς … εἰς κῆτος καταπέποται AcPlCor 2:29; the devil like a lion ζητῶν τίνα καταπιεῖν **1 Pt 5:8** (Damasc., Vi. Isid. 69 ὁ λέων καταπίνει τὸν ἄνθρωπον).

ⓑ of water, waves, ***swallow up*** (Polyb. 2, 41, 7 πόλις καταποθεῖσα ὑπὸ τ. θαλάσσης; Diod. S. 18, 35, 6; 26, 8; En 101:5; Philo, Virt. 201) pass. *be drowned* (Ex 15:4 v.l. κατεπόθησαν ἐν ἐρυθρᾷ θαλάσσῃ) **Hb 11:29.**—Transferred to mental and spiritual states (cp. Philo, Gig. 13, Deus Imm. 181) μή πως τ. περισσοτέρᾳ λύπῃ καταποθῇ *so that he may not be overwhelmed by extreme sorrow* **2 Cor 2:7** (TestAbr B 12 p. 117, 4 [Stone p. 82]).

❸ **to cause the end of someth.,** ***swallow up*** fig. (cp. PGM 12, 44 κατέπιεν ὁ οὐρανός; Ps 106:27; Philo, Leg. All. 3, 230; TestJud 21:7) pass. τὸ θνητὸν ὑπὸ τῆς ζωῆς *what is mortal may be swallowed up in life* **2 Cor 5:4.** ὁ θάνατος εἰς νῖκος *death has been swallowed up in victory* (after Is 25:8; s. also κέντρον 1 and ARahlfs, ZNW 20, 1921, 183f) **1 Cor 15:54.**—M-M. TW.

καταπίπτω 2 aor. κατέπεσον; pf. ptc. gen. pl. καταπεπτωκότων 3 Macc 2:20 (s. πίπτω; Hom.+) ***fall (down)*** εἰς τὴν γῆν *fall on the ground* **Ac 26:14** (TestJob 30:1; 40:4 ἐπὶ τὴν γῆν). ἐπὶ τὴν πέτραν (cp. Jos., Bell. 6, 64) **Lk 8:6.** Abs. (Jos., Ant. 5, 27) καταπίπτειν νεκρόν *fall down dead* **Ac 28:6** (cp. 4 Macc 4:11).—M-M. TW.

καταπιστεύω ***trust*** (s. πιστεύω; Polyb.; Plut., Lys. 8, 3; pap; Mi 7:5) w. dat. (Polyb. 2, 3, 3 al.) ἑαυτῷ *trust oneself* Hm 9:10.

καταπλέω 1 aor. κατέπλευσα (s. πλέω; Hom.+; ins, pap) ***sail down*** fr. the 'high seas' toward the coast, *sail toward* w. εἰς (X., Hell. 1, 7, 29 εἰς τ. γῆν; Appian, Basil. 1 §1 ἔς τινα αἰγιαλόν; OGI 344, 2 εἰς βιθυνίαν; Jos., Bell. 1, 610, Ant. 13, 86) εἰς τὴν χώραν τῶν Γερασηνῶν **Lk 8:26.** On the expr. κ. εἰς τοὺς ἀγῶνας *go to the contests* (κ. gener.='go through' SibOr 11, 203 κόσμον κ.) 2 Cl 7:1, 3 s. Harnack, Lghtf., Knopf ad loc.—M-M.

κατάπληξις, εως, ἡ (s. next entry; Thu. et al.; Diod. S. 17, 84, 3; Celsus 6, 75; BGU 1209, 16 [23 BC]; 2 Esdr 3:3; Philo; Jos., Bell. 6, 89; Just., D. 7, 3) ***terror*** Dg 7:3.—DELG s.v. πλήσσω.

καταπλήσσω mid. aor. 3 sg. κατεπλήξατο (Just., A I, 56, 2). Pass.: aor. κατεπλάγην LXX; perf. pass. ptc. καταπεπληγμένοι 3 Macc 2:23 (s. πλήσσω; Hom. et al.; ins, pap, LXX, Just.; variously 'strike down, terrify, amaze'). In a transf. sense from 'strike down' ***amaze, astound*** τινά *someone* (Philo, Omn. Prob. Lib. 100; Jos., Ant. 14, 370; Just., A I, 56, 2) IPol 3:1. Perf. pass. καταπέπληγμαι in act. sense *be amazed, astounded* τὶ *at someth.* (class.; PSI 502, 8 [III BC]; cp. 2 Macc 3:24; Philo, Post. Cai. 147; Jos., Vi. 120) οὗ καταπέπληγμαι τὴν ἐπιείκειαν *at whose gentleness I am amazed* IPhld 1:1.

καταπονέω aor. 3 pl. κατεπόνησαν (TestLevi 6:9) (s. πονέω; Hippocr.; Polyb., Diod. S. 11, 6, 3; pap, LXX; TestLevi 6:9; Joseph.) **to cause distress through oppressive means, *subdue, torment, wear out, oppress*** τινά *someone* B 20:2b; D 5:2b. In our lit. predom. in pres. pass. ptc. καταπονούμενος (Aelian, VH 3, 27 ὑπὸ πενίας καταπονούμενος; Jos., Bell. 2, 313, Ant. 7, 124) **Ac 4:2** D. Of Lot **2 Pt 2:7.**—Subst. ὁ καταπονούμενος *the one who is oppressed, mistreated, weary* (UPZ 110, 88 [164 BC]) ποιεῖν ἐκδίκησιν τῷ κ. *see to it that justice is done for the oppressed* **Ac 7:24;** πονεῖν ἐπὶ κ. *toil for one who is downtrodden* B 20:2a; D 5:2a.—M-M.

καταποντίζω fut. καταποντιῶ LXX; 1 aor. κατεπόντισα LXX; aor. pass. κατεποντίσθην (ποντίζω 'plunge/sink in the sea'; Epicharmus [ca. 480 BC]: Vorsokrat.[5] 23 B, 44a; Lysias, Demosth. et al.; Polyb., Diod. S. 14, 112, 1; PPetr II, 40 [a], 27 [III BC]; LXX; Jos., Ant. 10, 122, C. Ap. 2, 245) 'throw into the sea', then gener. ***drown,*** pass. *be sunk, be drowned* ἐν τῷ πελάγει τῆς θαλάσσης *be sunk* or *be drowned in the high seas* **Mt 18:6.** εἰς τὴν θάλασσαν 1 Cl 46:8 (Plut., Tim. 13, 10 εἰς τὸ πέλαγος; Ps.-Callisth. 1, 39, 5 εἰς βυθὸν θαλάσσης). Abs. ἀρξάμενος καταποντίζεσθαι *as he began to sink* **Mt 14:30.**—M-M.

κατάρα, ας, ἡ (s. next entry; Aeschyl. et al.; Ps.-Pla., Alc. 2, 143b; Polyb. 24, 8, 7; Diod. S. 1, 45, 2; Ael. Aristid. 33, 32 K.=51 p. 582 D.; SIG 1241, 1; PSI XI, 1219, 41 [II AD, schol. Callim.]; LXX, En, Test12Patr; GrBar 4:9, 15 [Christ.]; Philo; Jos., Ant. 4, 118; 307; Just.) ***curse, imprecation*** w. εὐλογία (as Dt 11:26; 30:1, 19; Sir 3:9; Philo, Det. Pot. Ins. 71) **Js 3:10.** ἀποδιδόναι κατάραν ἀντὶ κατάρας *repay a curse with a curse* Pol 2:2. Of infertile land, full of thorns and thistles κατάρας ἐγγύς *almost cursed* **Hb 6:8** (cp. Gen 3:17.—κ. ἐγγύς as Ael. Aristid. 26, 53 K.=14 p. 343 D.). Of the way of death κατάρας μεστή *full of cursing* B 20:1; D 5:1. Of persons κατάρας τέκνα (cp. Sir 41:9 ἐὰν γεννηθῆτε εἰς κατάραν γεννηθήσεσθε) *accursed* **2 Pt 2:14.**—In Paul of the adherents of Mosaic ordinances ὑπὸ κατάραν εἰσίν *they are under a curse* (this expr. corresponds to ἐξαποστελῶ [i.e., the κύριος] ἐφ' ὑμᾶς τ. κατάραν Mal 2:2; cp. Judg 9:57—κατάραν ὑφίστασθαι Did., Gen. 209, 24) **Gal 3:10** (ὑπὸ κ. φαίνονται εἶναι Just., D. 95, 1; ὑπὸ κ. γεγόνασιν Did, Gen. 211, 11). Of Christ: ἡμᾶς ἐξηγόρασεν ἐκ τῆς κ. τοῦ νόμου *he ransomed us from the curse of the law* vs. **13a.** Abstract for concrete γενόμενος ὑπὲρ ἡμῶν κ. *by becoming a curse-offering* (or *an object of a curse*) *in our behalf* vs. **13b.** So also ἐγὼ κατάρα ἐγεννήθην ἐνώπιον αὐτῶν πάντων *in the eyes of all I have been born to be cursed* GJs 3:1.—DELG s.v. ἀρά. M-M. TW.

καταράομαι mid. dep.; 1 aor. κατηρασάμην. Pass.: aor. 3 sg. κατηράθη (Just., D. 111, 2), opt. 3 sg. καταραθείη Job 3:6 and 24:1; pf. 3 pl. κεκατήρανται Num 22, 6 and 24:9; ptc. κεκατηραμένος or κατηραμένος LXX (s. prec. entry; Hom.+; LXX, En; PsSol 3:9; TestSol 20:6; TestAbr A 14 p. 94, 17 [Stone p. 36]; TestJob 13:5; GrBar 4:8; Philo, Joseph., Just.) ***to curse, execrate*** τινά *someone* (Plut., Cato Min. 774 [32, 4] v.l.; Ps.-Lucian, Asinus 27; Gen 12:3; 27:29 al.; Philo, Det. Pot. Ins. 103; Test12Patr; Just., D. 139, 1 al.) **Mt 5:44 v.l.; Lk 6:28; Js 3:9;** 1 Cl 10:3 (Gen 12:3); a tree **Mk 11:21.** W. dat. τινί (so Hdt. 4, 184; X., An. 7, 7, 48; Diod. S. 1, 45, 2; 14, 70, 2; EpJer 65; Philo, Fuga 73, Leg. All. 3, 65 τῷ ὄφει [but 75 τὸν ὄφιν]; Jos., Bell. 3, 297, C. Ap. 1, 204; Just., D. 133, 6) *curse someone* **Mt 5:44** D; **Lk 6:28 v.l.;** D 1:3. Abs. (Aristoph., Vesp. 614; Demosth. 18, 283) *curse* (w. εὐλογεῖν as Philo, Rer. Div. Her. 177) **Ro 12:14;** 1 Cl 15:3 (Ps 61:5); (w. ἀρνεῖσθαι and ὀμνύναι) Judaicon 333, 51=GHb 16—Perf. ptc. κατηραμένος w. pass. mng. (Plut., Lucull. 503 [18, 6]; 4 Km 9:34; Wsd 12:11; Just., D. 93, 4) οἱ κατηραμένοι *accursed ones* **Mt 25:41.** οἱ κ. ὑπὸ τοῦ θεοῦ (cp. Dt 21:23; Herm. Wr. 2, 17a) 1 Cl 30:8. κατηραμένην. . .τοῦ ὄφεως πίστιν *the cursed faith of* (i.e. associated w.) *the snake* AcPlCor 2:20 (cp. Gen. 3).—Lit. s. on εὐλογέω end; also KLatte, Heil. Recht 1920, 61–96; B. 1481. JPedersen, Der Eid bei den Semiten 1914; s. esp. the curse-laden inscriptions at Kommagene (I BC): OGI 383; and FDörner-TGöell, Arsameia am Nymphaios '63, pp. 40–59 text and tr. (lit.)—DELG s.v. ἀρά. M-M. TW.

καταργέω fut. καταργήσω; 1 aor. κατήργησα; pf. κατήργηκα. Pass.: 1 fut. καταργηθήσομαι; 1 aor. κατηργήθην; pf. κατήργημαι (s. ἀργέω; since Eur., Phoen. 753; Polyb.; POxy 38, 7 [49/50 AD]; PFlor 176, 7; 218, 13; PStras 32, 7; 2 Esdr; TestSol [also PVindobBosw for 18:38]; AscIs 3:31; Just.).

❶ **to cause someth. to be unproductive, *use up, exhaust, waste*** of a tree κ. τὴν γῆν **Lk 13:7** (cp. ἀργεῖ οὐδὲν ἀλλὰ καρποφορεῖ OdeSol 11:23).

❷ **to cause someth. to lose its power or effectiveness, *invalidate, make powerless*** fig. extension of 1 (so, above all, in Paul and the writings dependent on him; cp. Herm. Wr. 13, 7 κατάργησον τ. σώματος τὰς αἰσθήσεις; of the soul of Jesus: κ. τὰ ἐπὶ κολάσεσιν πάθη Iren. 1, 25, 1 [Harv. I 205, 4]) *make ineffective, nullify* τὴν πίστιν τοῦ θεοῦ *God's fidelity* **Ro 3:3.** ἐπαγγελίαν **Gal 3:17;** cp. **Ro 4:14;** τὰ ὄντα κ. *nullify the things that* (actually) *exist* **1 Cor 1:28.** τὸν νόμον *make the law invalid* **Eph 2:15;** cp. **Ro 3:31** (RThompson, ETh 63, '87, 136–48, on alleged rabbinic background; s. also ἵστημι A4). Also in B of the OT cultic ordinances, which have lost their validity for Christians 5:6; 9:4; 16:2.

❸ **to cause someth. to come to an end or to be no longer in existence, *abolish, wipe out, set aside*** τὶ *someth.* τὰ τοῦ νηπίου *set aside childish ways* **1 Cor 13:11.** Of God or Christ: God will *do away with* both stomach and food **6:13;** *bring to an end* πᾶσαν ἀρχήν, ἐξουσίαν, δύναμιν **15:24.** τὸν ἄνομον **2 Th 2:8.** τὸν καιρὸν τοῦ ἀνόμου *put an end to the time of the lawless one* (i.e., the devil) B 15:5. τὸν θάνατον *break the power of death* **2 Ti 1:10;** B 5:6; pass. **1 Cor 15:26** (MDahl, The Resurrection of the Body [1 Cor 15], '62, 117–19). τὸν τὸ κράτος ἔχοντα τοῦ θανάτου *destroy the one who has power over death* **Hb 2:14.** ἵνα καταργηθῇ τὸ σῶμα τ. ἁμαρτίας *in order that the sinful body may be done away with* **Ro 6:6.** In **2 Cor 3:14** the subject may be ἡ παλαιὰ διαθήκη or, more probably (despite some grammatical considerations), κάλυμμα; in the latter case the mng. is *remove.*—Pass. *cease, pass away* προφητεία, γνῶσις **1 Cor 13:8.** τὸ ἐκ μέρους *what is imperfect* vs. **10.** ἄρα κατήργηται τὸ σκάνδαλον τοῦ σταυροῦ *the cross has ceased to be an obstacle* **Gal 5:11.** πᾶς πόλεμος καταργεῖται *every war is brought to an end* IEph 13:2. καταργούμενος *doomed to* *perish* of the ἄρχοντες τοῦ αἰῶνος τούτου **1 Cor 2:6.** Of the radiance on Moses' face **2 Cor 3:7.** Subst. τὸ καταργούμενον *what is transitory* vss. **11, 13.**

❹ to cause the release of someone from an obligation (one has nothing more to do with it), ***be discharged, be released.*** In our lit. pass. καταργοῦμαι ἀπό τινος of a woman upon the death of her husband κατήργηται ἀπὸ τοῦ νόμου τοῦ ἀνδρός **Ro 7:2.** Of Christians κ. ἀπὸ τοῦ νόμου *be released fr. the law* **vs. 6.** Of those who aspire to righteousness through the law κ. ἀπὸ Χριστοῦ *be estranged from Christ* **Gal 5:4.**—Frisk s.v. 2 ἀργός; also DELG s.v. ἔργον. M-M. EDNT. TW.

καταριθμέω aor. inf. καταριθμῆσαι (Just., D. 132, 1). Pass.: aor. 3 pl. κατηριθμήθησαν Hos 4:14 Theod.; pf. pass. ptc. κατηριθμημένος (s. ἀριθμέω; Eur., Pla. et al.; ins, pap, LXX, Philo, Joseph., Just.).

❶ to enumerate, ***count*** (Jos., Ant. 11, 73; Just., A I, 9, 4 al.) ὁ ἀριθμὸς ὁ κατηριθμημένος τῶν ἐκλεκτῶν *the number of the chosen, that has been counted* 1 Cl 59:2.

❷ to include as an entity in a group, ***count among*** pass. *belong to* w. ἐν (Pla., Polit. 266a al.; Diod. S. 4, 85, 5; 16, 83, 3; SIG 810, 24 ἀνδρὸς παρ' ὑμεῖν ἐν τοῖς ἐπιφανεστάτοις καταριθμουμένου; UPZ 110, 99 [164 BC]; 2 Ch 31:19; Philo, Spec. Leg. 2, 118) of the traitor: κατηριθμημένος ἦν ἐν ἡμῖν *he belonged to our number* **Ac 1:17.**—DELG s.v. ἀριθμός. M-M.

καταρρέω impf. κατέρρεον; fut. 3 pl. καταρρεύσουσιν Jer 13:17 Sym.; aor. 3 pl. κατέρρευσαν Is 64:1 Aq; pf. 3 sg. κατερρύηκεν Jer 8:13 (s. ῥέω; Hom. et al.; PMagd 24, 5 [III BC]; LXX; TestSol 17:3; JosAs 29:1 cod. A for ἐρρύη; ApcMos 20; Joseph.) ***flow down*** of pus (Horapollo 2, 57) and foulness ApcPt 11:26.—DELG s.v. ῥέω.

καταρτίζω fut. καταρτίσω; 1 aor. κατήρτισα, mid. κατηρτισάμην, 2 sg. κατηρτίσω. Pass.: aor. κατηρτίσθην LXX; pf. pass. κατήρτισμαι (ἀρτίζω, 'get ready, prepare', s. next entry; Hdt. et al.; ins, pap, LXX; TestSol 5:12 H).

❶ to cause to be in a condition to function well, ***put in order, restore.***—ⓐ *restore to a former condition, put to rights* (since Hdt. 5, 28; 106; Dionys. Hal. 3, 10) τὶ *someth.* nets (by cleaning, mending, folding together) **Mt 4:21; Mk 1:19** (cp. GWynne, Exp. 7th ser., 8, 1909, 282–85). Fig. κ. τινά *restore someone* ἐν πνεύματι πραΰτητος *in a spirit of gentleness,* i.e. in a gentle manner **Gal 6:1.** Pass. καταρτίζεσθε *mend your ways* **2 Cor 13:11.**

ⓑ *put into proper condition* (cp. Epict. 3, 20, 10 of a trainer who adjusts parts of the body), *adjust, complete, make complete* τὶ *someth.* καταρτίσαι τὰ ὑστερήματα τ. πίστεως ὑμῶν *to fix up any deficiencies in your faith* or *to complete what is lacking in your faith* **1 Th 3:10.** τινά *someone:* ὑμᾶς ἐν παντὶ ἀγαθῷ *make you complete in every good thing* **Hb 13:21.** κατηρτισμένοι ἐν τῷ αὐτῷ νοῒ καὶ ἐν τῇ αὐτῇ γνώμῃ *adjusted / made complete in the same mind and the same conviction* **1 Cor 1:10.** ἐν μιᾷ ὑποταγῇ IEph 2:2. ἐν ἀκινήτῳ πίστει ISm 1:1. Abs. **1 Pt 5:10.** κατηρτισμένος *(fully) trained, practiced* (Polyb. 5, 2, 11 τ. εἰρεσίαις κατηρτισμένοι) κ. πᾶς (μαθητὴς) ἔσται ὡς ὁ διδάσκαλος αὐτοῦ *when fully trained, the pupil will be like the teacher* **Lk 6:40.** S. Betz, Gal. 297 n. 43.

❷ to prepare for a purpose, ***prepare, make, create, outfit.***

ⓐ act. and pass., of God (w. ποιεῖν) B 16:6. (W. κτίζειν) τὰ πάντα Hm 1:1. Pass. ὁ κόσμος κατηρτίσθη Hv 2, 4, 1; also οἱ αἰῶνες (s. αἰών 3) ῥήματι θεοῦ **Hb 11:3.** κατηρτισμένος εἴς τι *made, created for someth.*: σκεύη ὀργῆς κατηρτισμένα εἰς ἀπώλειαν *vessels of wrath, designed for destruction* **Ro 9:22.** ἄνθρωπος εἰς ἕνωσιν κατηρτισμένος *a man set on* (lit. *made for*) *unity* IPhld 8:1.

ⓑ mid. (PGM 4, 1147) καταρτίζεσθαί τί τινι *prepare someth. for someone* σῶμα **Hb 10:5** (Ps 39:7 codd.: BSA). W. reflexive mng.: *for oneself* κατηρτίσω αἶνον *you prepared praise for yourself* **Mt 21:16** (Ps 8:3).—DELG s.v. ἀραρίσκω. M-M. TW. Spicq.

κατάρτισις, εως, ἡ (s. prec. entry; Plut., Alex. 667 [7, 1] 'training'; cp. idem, κατάρτυσις Them. 112 [2, 7] w. παιδεία) **the process of perfecting,** ***maturation*** εὐχόμεθα τὴν ὑμῶν κ. *we pray for your maturation* (*for the perfecting of your characters* Goodsp.) **2 Cor 13:9.**—DELG s.v. ἀραρίσκω. TW.

καταρτισμός, οῦ, ὁ (s. prec. two entries; as medical term [Soranus 150, 8]: 'setting of a bone', etc. But more gener. PTebt 33, 12 [112 BC] 'preparation' αὐλῆς; cp. CMRDM 1, 121 s. New Docs 3, 70, no. 42; PRyl 127, 28; Sym. Is 38:12 'restoration') ext. fig. sense (not found in ins or pap) ***equipment, equipping*** εἴς τι *for someth.* πρὸς τὸν κ. τῶν ἁγίων εἰς ἔργον διακονίας *to equip God's people* (lit. 'the holy ones') *for service* **Eph 4:12,** though *training, discipline* (L-S-J-M) deserve consideration as glosses for κ.—DELG s.v. ἀραρίσκω. M-M. TW.

κατασβέννυμι fut. 3 sg. κατασβέσει Pr 15:18 and 28:2; 1 aor. 3 sg. κατέσβεσεν 4 Macc 16:4, inf. κατασβέσαι (s. σβέννυμι; Hom. et al.; PGM 12, 57 as restored by Dieterich; LXX; Philo, Aet. M. 91) ***put out, quench*** τὶ *someth.* τὸ πῦρ (Il. 21, 381) MPol 16:1.

κατασείω 1 aor. κατέσεισα (s. σείω; Thu. et al.; 1 Macc 6:38; Philo, Joseph.) in our lit. (Ac) always used w. χείρ 'make a motion'.

❶ to make rapid motions, ***shake, wave*** (rapidly) w. acc. τὴν χεῖρα (Vi. Aesopi W 87 P. τὴν χεῖρα τῷ ὄχλῳ κατασείσας; Philo, De Jos. 211, Leg. ad Gai. 181 τὴν δεξιὰν χεῖρα) **Ac 19:33,** in an effort to secure attention. It is an easy transition from this sense to

❷ to signal by a gesture, ***motion, make a sign*** w. dat. τῇ χειρί (Polyb. 1, 78, 3; Jos., Ant. 4, 323; 8, 275) **Ac 13:16.** Still another dat. can indicate the person(s) for whom the signal is intended (cp. X., Cyr. 5, 4, 4 κατασείω τινί; Jos., Ant. 17, 257. Sim. PGM 5, 453 κ. τῷ λύχνῳ='motion toward the lamp') κατέσεισεν τ. χειρὶ τ. λαῷ **21:40.** The purpose of the signal is given in the inf. (s. Appian, Bell. Civ. 4, 2 §5 ἥκειν and Jos. in the pass. quoted, but not Ant. 8, 275) κατασείσας αὐτοῖς τ. χειρὶ σιγᾶν *he motioned to them (with his hand) to be silent* **12:17.**—M-M.

κατασκάπτω (s. σκάπτω) fut. κατασκάψω LXX; 1 aor. κατέσκαψα. Pass.: fut. 3 sg. κατασκαφήσεται LXX; aor. κατεσκάφην; pf. ptc. κατεσκαμμένος LXX ***tear down, raze to the ground*** (so trag., Hdt. et al.; ins, LXX; Philo, Leg. ad Gai. 132; Ath., R. 19 p. 72, 29) τὶ *someth.* cities (Hdt. 7, 156; Ael. Aristid. 32 p. 604 D.; SIG 344, 7; Jos., Ant. 4, 313; 8, 128) 1 Cl 6:4 v.l. Altars **Ro 11:3** (3 Km 19:10). τὰ κατεσκαμμένα αὐτῆς *the parts of it that had been torn down* **Ac 15:16** (s. ἀνασκάπτω and καταστρέφω 2).—M-M.

κατασκευάζω fut. κατασκευάσω; 1 aor. κατεσκεύασα; pf. 3 sg. κατεσκεύακε (Aristobul. in Eus., PE 13, 12, 9 [=Denis 224; Holladay 176]); plpf. 3 sg. κατεσκευάκει (Tat. 17, 3). Pass.: 1 aor. κατεσκευάσθην; pf. ptc. κατεσκευασμένος (σκευάζω 'prepare, make ready', s. also σκεῦος; Anaxagoras, Hdt.+).

❶ to make ready for some purpose, ***make ready, prepare*** τὶ *someth.* τὴν ὁδόν (SIG 313, 22 [320 BC] of the ὁδοί along which the procession in honor of Zeus and Dionysus was to pass: ὅπως κατασκευασθῶσιν ὡς βέλτιστα) **Mt 11:10; Mk 1:2; Lk 7:27.**—Fig., in a mental or inward sense (Aristot., Rhet. 3, 19 κ. τὸν ἀκροατήν; Wsd 7:27; Jos., C. Ap. 2, 188 πλῆθος κατεσκευασμένον πρὸς τ. εὐσέβειαν) λαὸς κατεσκευασμένος *a people made ready* **Lk 1:17.**

❷ **to bring a structure into being,** ***build, construct, erect, create*** (Phylarchus [III BC]: 81 fgm. 29 Jac. ναούς; Plut., Mor. 189c, Num. 10, 9 οἶκος; Herodian 5, 6, 6; 9; SIG 495, 141 and 145; 1100, 21; 1229, 4; PAmh 64, 2 βαλανεῖον; POxy 892, 8; Philo, Rer. Div. Her. 112 σκηνήν; Jos., Bell. 6, 191, Vi. 65 οἶκος) κιβωτόν *construct an ark* (κ. is a favorite word for construction of ships: Diod. S. 1, 92, 2; 11, 62, 2; Palaeph. 29, 4; 31, 9; 1 Macc 15:3) **Hb 11:7.** Pass. **1 Pt 3:20.** οἶκον **Hb 3:3f.** Of God (Is 40:28; 45:7; ApcEsdr 5:19 p. 30, 19 Tdf. [πάντα διὰ τὸν ἄνθρωπον]; Philo, Aet. M. 39; 41; Aristob. in Eus., PE 13, 12, 9 [s. beg. of this entry]; Ath., R. 13 p. 63, 21 ζῷον) ὁ πάντα κατασκευάσας *the builder of all things* **Hb 3:4b** (cp. Epict. 1, 6, 7). Pf. pass. ptc. as subst. τὸ κατεσκευασμένον *what is produced* or *supplied* Dg 2:2.

❸ In addition to signifying the erection of a building it is also used in the sense ***furnish, equip*** (X., An. 4, 1, 8, Hiero 2, 2, Cyr. 5, 5, 2: σκηνή; Num 21:27) σκηνὴ κατεσκευάσθη ἡ πρώτη *the foremost tent* or *tabernacle was furnished* (an enumeration of its furnishings follows) **Hb 9:2.** τούτων δὲ οὕτως κατεσκευασμένων *such are the furnishings, and so* vs. **6.**—M-M. TW.

κατασκηνόω (s. next entry and σκηνόω; X. et al.; oft. in Polyb. and Plut.; LXX; PsSol 7:6; JosAs cod. A 15:6, 16 [p. 61, 11; 65, 17 Bat.]; Mel., P. 45, 321) inf. κατασκηνοῦν **Mt 13:32** and **Mk 4:32** (-σκηνοῖν v.l. in these two pass.; B-D-F §91; W-S. §13, 25; Rdm.[2] 95; Mlt. 53; Mlt-H. 197) fut. κατασκηνώσω; 1 aor. κατεσκήνωσα.; pf 3 sg. κατεσκήνωκεν (Mel., P. 45, 321f [Ch.; -σεν Bodm. p. 76, ln. 9])

❶ **to provide with an abode,** ***cause to dwell,*** trans. (Ps 22:2) of the name in the hearts D 10:2.

❷ **to take up an abode,** ***live, settle,*** intr. (so mostly; Philo, Leg. All. 3, 46; Jos., Ant. 3, 202) of birds (Ps 103:12): ἐν τοῖς κλάδοις *nest in the branches* (Da 4:21 Theod.) **Mt 13:32; Lk 13:19** (cp. JosAs 15). ὑπὸ τὴν σκιάν **Mk 4:32.**—Of humans *live, dwell* (Diod. S. 13, 96, 2; 14, 62, 3 ἐν τῷ νεῷ; 19, 94, 10 ἐν οἰκίαις; Ps 14:1; Jos., Ant. 9, 34) 1 Cl 58:1. ἡ σάρξ μου κατασκηνώσει ἐπ᾽ ἐλπίδι (Ps 15:9) *my flesh will dwell* ἐπ᾽ ἐλπίδι (ἐλπίς 1bα) **Ac 2:26;** cp. 1 Cl 57:7 (Pr 1:33). On a Christian gravestone (Sb 1540, 9 [408 AD]) κ. euphemistically means 'rest'.—New Docs 3, 106. DELG s.v. σκεῦος. M-M. TW.

κατασκήνωσις, εως, ἡ (s. prec. entry)—❶ **the act of taking up residence,** ***taking up lodging*** (so Polyb. 11, 26, 5; LXX) ἔχειν τόπον κατασκηνώσεως *have a place to dwell* Hs 5, 6, 7.

❷ **provision for shelter,** ***a place to live*** (so Diod. S. 17, 95, 2; OGI 229, 57 [III BC]) of birds: *nest* **Mt 8:20; Lk 9:58.**—DELG s.v. σκηνή. M-M. TW.

κατασκιάζω (s. next entry, also σκιάζω and σκιά; Hes. et al.; Kaibel 495; verbal adj. κατασκιαστός JosAs 5:5) ***overshadow*** of the winged cherubim in the sanctuary κατασκιάζοντα τὸ ἱλαστήριον **Hb 9:5** (TestSol 21:2; for the idea s. Ex 25:20: συσκιάζοντες ἐν ταῖς πτέρυξιν αὐτῶν ἐπὶ τ. ἱλαστηρίου).—DELG s.v. σκιά. M-M. TW.

κατάσκιος, ον (s. prec. entry; Hes., Hdt. et al.; Aelian, VH 12, 38; LXX; Philo, Aet. M. 63) ***shaded*** of a mountain covered w. trees (cp. Zech 1:8) Hs 9, 1, 9.—DELG s.v. σκιά.

κατασκοπεύω 1 aor. inf. κατασκοπεῦσαι (=next entry, s. σκοπέω; PTebt 230 [II BC]; LXX; TestSol 10:6; s. Anz 379) ***spy out*** τὴν χώραν (cp. τὴν γῆν Gen 42:30; Josh 2:2f; 14:7) 1 Cl 12:2.—DELG s.v. σκέπτομαι.

κατασκοπέω 1 aor. κατεσκόπησα (=prec. entry; Eur., Hel. 1607; 2 Km 10:3; 1 Ch 19:3. Elsewh. usu. in mid.) ***spy out, lie in wait for*** τὴν ἐλευθερίαν ἡμῶν *our freedom* **Gal 2:4.**—DELG s.v. σκέπτομαι. M-M. TW.

κατάσκοπος, ου, ὁ (s. two prec. entries; trag., Hdt. et al.; LXX; TestSim 4:3; Philo; Jos., Ant. 3, 302; 312; 16, 236; Just., D. 111, 4; 113, 1) ***a spy*** **Hb 11:31; Js 2:25 v.l.;** 1 Cl 12:2, 4 (cp. Josh 2:3) κ. τῆς γῆς B 12:9.—DELG s.v. σκέπτομαι. M-M. TW.

κατασοφίζομαι mid. dep.; 1 aor. κατεσοφισάμην (s. σοφίζω; Diod. S. 17, 116, 4; Lucian, LXX; TestSol, Philo; Jos., Ant. 6, 219; 8, 412. Anz 366) ***get the better of*** or ***take advantage of by cunning/trickery*** τινά *someone* (after Ex 1:10) τὸ γένος ἡμῶν **Ac 7:19.**—DELG s.v. σοφός. M-M.

κατασπείρω fut. κατασπερῶ, pass. κατασπαρήσομαι (LXX, TestSol) (s. σπείρω; Eur., Pla. et al.; LXX; TestSol 15:9) ***sow (upon)*** PEg[2] 69 (the Gk. proverbial expr. σπείρειν πόντον: Theognis 106 and 107; Ps.-Phocyl. 152, denoting an action that can hope for no results, may lie in the background here; cp. **J 12:24**).

κατάστασις, εως, ἡ (s. καθίστημι, στάσις; trag., Hdt. et al.; ins, pap; Wsd 12:12; Philo; Jos., C. Ap. 1, 58, Ant. 12, 267; Just., D. 115, 3 [opp. ἔκστασις]) ***state of being/character*** τῆς πολιτείας *of the way of life* Dg 5:4.—DELG s.v. ἵστημι.

καταστέλλω 1 aor. κατέστειλα, aor. pass. ptc. κατασταλείς (AcPl Ha 7, 9); pf. pass. ptc. κατεσταλμένος (s. στέλλω, καταστολή; Eur. et al.; pap, LXX) ***restrain, quiet*** w. acc. (Plut., Mor. 207e; 3 Macc 6:1; Jos., Bell. 2, 611; 4, 271, Ant. 20, 174) τὸν ὄχλον **Ac 19:35** (s. Mitt-Wilck. I/2, 10, 10f). κατασταλέντος τοῦ πνεύματος τοῦ ἐν Μύρτῃ *when the spirit in Myrte became calm* AcPl Ha 7, 9. κατεσταλμένος *calm, quiet* (Diod. S. 1, 76, 3; Epict. 4, 4, 10): δέον ἐστὶν ὑμᾶς κατεσταλμένους ὑπάρχειν *you must be calm* **Ac 19:36.**—M-M. TW.

κατάστημα, ατος, τό (Epicurus et al.) ***behavior, demeanor*** (Plut., Marcell. 311 [23, 6], Tib. Gracch. 824 [2, 2]; OGI 669, 3; 3 Macc 5:45 [κατάστεμα]; EpArist 122; 210; 278; Jos., Bell. 1, 40, Ant. 15, 236) ἐν κ. *in their behavior* **Tit 2:3.**—ITr 3:2.—DELG s.v. ἵστημι. M-M.

καταστολή, ῆς, ἡ (s. καταστέλλω; Hippocr.; Mitt-Wilck. I/2, 12, 15 [88 BC] 'subjugation'; Is 61:3; EpArist, Joseph.) Like the verb καταστέλλω, the basic idea is keeping something in check, hence the use of this term in the sense of 'reserve, restraint' (IPriene 109, 186f [120 BC] and EpArist 284f: both texts w. εὐσχημοσύνη; Epict. 2, 10, 15; 2, 21, 11: here personal deportment is certainly meant). The verb στέλλω means to 'furnish, equip', a sense that extends itself to the putting on of garments. Hence καταστολή readily serves to express outward attire, either the character one exhibits in personal deportment or someth. to cover the body, namely ***attire, clothing*** (Jos., Bell. 2, 126; cp. Is 61:3; Plut., 154 [Pericl. 5, 1] also appears to be used in this sense) ἐν κ. κοσμίῳ *dress in becoming manner* (REB; *dress modestly* NRSV) **1 Ti 2:9.** The writer skillfully moves from the lit. sense of garments to personal characteristics of 'modesty and self-control' as appropriate adornment.—DELG s.v. στέλλω. M-M. TW.

καταστρέφω 1 aor. κατέστρεψα. Pass.: fut. 3 sg. καταστραφήσεται LXX; aor. 3 sg. κατεστράφη; pf. 3 sg. κατέστραπται Mal 1:4, ptc. κατεστραμμένος, inf. κατεστράφθαι (Just., D. 107, 3) (s. καταστροφή and στρέφω; Hom. Hymns et al.; ins, LXX; TestSol 18:20 P; TestJob 20:5; JosAs 23:3; Jos., Bell. 1, 199, Ant. 8, 200 al.; Just.).

❶ **to cause to be overturned,** ***upset, overturn*** τὶ *someth.* (Diog. L. 5, 82 τὰς εἰκόνας) money-changers' tables **Mt 21:12; Mk 11:15; J 2:15 v.l.** (for ἀνατρέπω).

❷ **to cause someth. to be in total disarray,** ***destroy, ruin*** (Herodian 8, 4, 22; LXX; PGM 36, 299; Just., A I, 58, 3 al.) of God δύναται αὐτὰ (=τὰ πάντα) καταστρέψαι (cp. Job 11:10) 1 Cl 27:4. Of contentiousness πόλεις μεγάλας κατέστρεψεν 6:4 (v.l. κατέσκαψε). τὰ κατεστραμμένα *ruins* **Ac 15:16 v.l.** (for κατεσκαμμένα, cp. Am 9:11 with v.l.).

❸ **to upset in such a way that victims lose their bearings,** ***turn away, mislead, divert, ruin*** τινά *someone* Hm 6, 2, 4. τινὰ ἀπό τινος s 6, 2, 1. τινά τινι *someone by means of someth.* m 5, 2, 1 (s. καταστροφή 2).—M-M. TW.

καταστρηνιάω (στρηνιάω 'run riot/wild, become/wax wanton') 1 aor. κατεστρηνίασα ***be governed by strong physical desire*** (B-D-F §181; Mlt-H. 316) ὅταν καταστρηνιάσωσιν τοῦ Χριστοῦ *when they feel sensuous impulses that alienate them from Christ* **1 Ti 5:11** (cp. Ps.-Ignatius, Ad Antioch. 11).—DELG s.v. στρηνής. TW.

καταστροφή, ῆς, ἡ (s. καταστρέφω; Aeschyl., Hdt. et al.; LXX; En 102:10; TestJob 33:4; Jos., Ant. 15, 287; 376)

❶ **condition of total destruction, with the implication that nothing is in its customary place or position,** ***ruin, destruction*** gener. 1 Cl 57:4 (Pr 1:27). Of a city 7:7. καταστροφῇ κατακρίνειν *condemn to destruction* **2 Pt 2:6** (cp. Gen 19:29).

❷ **state of being intellectually upset to a ruinous degree,** ***ruin*** ἐπὶ καταστροφῇ τῶν ἀκουόντων *to the ruin of the hearers* (the opp. would be edification) **2 Ti 2:14** (s. καταστρέφω 3).—DELG s.v. στρέφω. M-M. TW.

καταστρώννυμι 1 aor. κατέστρωσα. Pass.: fut. 3 pl. καταστρωθήσονται Jdth 7:14; 1 aor. κατεστρώθην; pf. ptc. κατεστρωμένος (JosAs 2:3; 13:5) (s. στρώννυμι; Eur., Hdt. et al.; UPZ 77 II, 28 [II BC] al. pap; LXX) (primary mng. 'spread out')

❶ ***lay low, kill*** (the primary mng. 'spread out' offers the imagery in this transf. use of κ. Hdt. 8, 53; 9, 76; X., Cyr. 3, 3, 64; Jdth 7:14; 14:4; 2 Macc 5:26 al.) of the Israelites killed in the desert (cp. Num 14:16) **1 Cor 10:5.**

❷ ἐὰν καταστρώσω εἰς τὰς ἀβύσσους, a quot. of Ps 138:8f which differs considerably fr. the LXX, seems to presuppose for κ. the primary mng. 'spread out' someth., and so ***make a bed*** (cp. Hierocles in Stob., Flor. 85, 21 κλίνην; PTor I, 8, 17 [116 BC] κονίαν ἐπὶ τοῦ δρόμου=sand on the racecourse) *if I make my bed in the depths* 1 Cl 28:3.—DELG s.v. στόρνυμι. M-M.

κατασύρω fut. 3 sg. κατασυρεῖ Da 11:26 LXX; aor. κατέσυρα Jer 30:4 (s. σύρω; Hdt. et al.; LXX; Jos., Bell. 2, 190; Test12Patr) ***drag (away by force)*** (Parthenius 19; Dio Chrys. 1, 196; Philo, In Flacc. 174, Leg. ad Gai. 131) τινά *someone* πρὸς τὸν κριτήν *before the judge* **Lk 12:58.** DELG s.v. σύρω.

κατασφάζω (s. σφάζω; Jos., Ant. 6, 120) or **-σφάττω** (s. B-D-F §71) fut. 3 pl. κατασφάξουσιν Ezk 16:40; aor. κατέσφαξα LXX, pass. 3 pl. κατεσφάγησαν 2 Macc 10:31, subj. κατασφαγῶσιν (En 10:19) ***slaughter, strike down*** (trag., Hdt. et al.; Aelian, VH 13, 2; Herodian 5, 5, 8; PGiss 82, 11; LXX; En 10:12; Jos., Bell. 7, 362 al.) τινά *someone* ἔμπροσθέν τινος *before someone's eyes* **Lk 19:27.**—M-M.

κατασφραγίζω aor. pass. 3 sg. κατεσφραγίσθη Wsd 2:5; pf. pass. ptc. κατεσφραγισμένος (s. σφραγίζω; Aeschyl. et al.; ins, pap, LXX, TestSol) ***seal (up)*** of a scroll closed by a seal **Rv 5:1** (OGI 266, 42 [III BC] τά τε γράμματ' ἀνοίσω κατεσφραγισμένα, SIG 1157, 43; PSI 358).—DELG s.v. σφραγίς. M-M. TW.

κατάσχεσις, εως, ἡ (s. κατέχω; LXX; TestBenj 10:4; Philo, Rer. Div. Her. 194 [after Num 35:8]; Jos., Ant. 9, 9 v.l.; Just., D. 113, 4).

❶ ***possession, taking into possession*** (Memnon Hist. [I AD]: 434 fgm. 1, 36 Jac.) τὴν γῆν δοῦναι εἰς κ. *give the land as a possession* (as Gen 17:8; Ezk 33:24; 36:5; TestBenj 10:4) **Ac 7:5;** cp. **13:33** D and 1 Cl 36:4 (both Ps 2:8). W. gen. ἐν τῇ κ. τῶν ἐθνῶν prob. *when they took possession of* (the land of) *the Gentiles* **Ac 7:45.** S. Field, Notes 114; 116.

❷ ***holding back, restraining*** (Hippocr., κ. διαίτης 2, 64) μήποτε γενηθῇ αὐτῷ κατάσχεσίς τις *in order that he might experience no delay* **Ac 20:16** D.—DELG s.v. ἔχω. TW.

κατάσχωμεν s. κατέχω.

κατατίθημι fut. 2 sg. καταθήσεις (Jer 39:14 v.l.); 1 aor. κατέθηκα; 2 aor. mid. κατεθέμην; aor. pass. κατετέθην (ApcEsdr, Just.) (s. τίθημι; Hom.+; ins, pap, LXX; ApcEsdr 7:1 p. 32, 9 Tdf.; Just., D. 108, 2; Ath. 4, 1)

❶ ***lay (down), place*** τινὰ ἐν μνήματι *place* a body in a *tomb* (schol. on Apollon. Rhod. 4, 1091 p. 306, 24 W.) **Mk 15:46 v.l.** (ἐν τάφῳ ApcEsdr s. above).

❷ ***grant, give,*** mid. (EpArist 321; Jos., Ant. 6, 232; 11, 213) χάριτα κ. τινί *grant* or *do someone a favor* (X., Cyr. 8, 3, 26; BGU 596, 13 [84 AD] τοῦτο οὖν ποιήσας ἔσῃ μοι μεγάλην χάριτα κατατεθειμένος) **Ac 24:27.** Also χάριν κ. **25:9** (Philo, De Jos. 231.—τὴν χάριν καταθέσθαι Thu. 1, 33, 1; Hdt. 6, 41 means 'lay up a store of gratitude').—M-M.

κατατομή, ῆς, ἡ (s. τέμνω; Theophr., HP 4, 8, 12; Synes., Ep. 15 p. 272d; Eutecnius p. 23, 28; CIG I 160, 27f; Jer 48:37 Sym.; 'incision, notch', etc.) ***mutilation, cutting in pieces*** w. περιτομή in wordplay, prob. to denote those for whom circumcision results in (spiritual) destruction **Phil 3:2** (for similar wordplay cp. Diog. L. 6, 24 τ. μὲν Εὐκλείδου σχολὴν ἔλεγε χολήν, τ. δὲ Πλάτωνος διατριβὴν κατατριβήν).—DELG s.v. τέμνω. M-M. TW.

κατατοξεύω fut. κατατοξεύσω LXX; 1 aor. κατετόξευσα LXX; fut. pass. κατατοξευθήσομαι (τοξεύω 'shoot with a bow', s. τόξον; Hdt. et al.; LXX) ***shoot down*** βολίδι *with a missile* **Hb 12:20 v.l.** (Ex 19:13).—DELG s.v. τόξον.

κατατρέχω 2 aor. κατέδραμον ***run down*** (s. τρέχω; Hdt., Aristoph. et al.; ins, pap, LXX; En 17:5; Test12Patr; Jos., Ant. 8, 204 al.; Just., A II, 3, 3) w. ἐπί and acc. *run down to* (X., An. 7, 1, 20; Da 4:24; Job 16:10 v.l.) **Ac 21:32.**—M-M.

κατατρίβω fut. 3 sg. κατατρίψει Da 7:25; 2 aor. pass. κατετρίβην (in var. mngs. since Theognis 55; Aristoph., Pla., X.; ins, pap, LXX; Philo, Leg. Alleg. 2, 98; Jos., Bell. 4, 127) 'rub down' or 'away' hence ***wear out*** (s. τρίβω; Pla., Phd. 87c; Dt 8:4; cp. PPetr II, 32 [1] 21f [III BC]; PSI 527, 10 [III BC]) ἱμάτια κατατρίβεται *clothes wear out* AcPl Ha 2, 25; 9, 9f (restored).

καταυγάζω (s. αὐγάζω; Heraclid. Pont. [300 BC], fgm. 116 W. [pass.]; Apollon. Rhod. 4, 1248 [mid.]; Cornutus 32 p. 69, 10;

Sext. Emp.; Heliod. et al.; Herm. Wr. 10, 4b; PGM 13, 749 [pass.]; LXX; Philo, Cher. 62 [pass.]; Jos., Ant. 19, 344 [pass.]) ***shine upon, illuminate*** **2 Cor 4:4 v.l.** (for αὐγάσαι; but s. αὐγάζω and διαυγάζω 1).

καταφαγεῖν s. κατεσθίω.

καταφέρω 1 aor. κατήνεγκα. Pass.: fut. 3 sg. κατενεχθήσεται Eccl 10:18 Sym.; 1 aor. κατηνέχθην (s. φέρω; Hom.+; ins, pap, LXX, En; TestJob 5:2 ναὸν εἰς τὸ ἔδαφος 'demolish'; TestZeb 9:1 v.l.; Philo, Aet. M. 33; Joseph.).

❶ ***bring down*** abs. (sc. the tables of the law fr. the mountain) B 14:2.

❷ **to cause someth. to happen that is opposed to another's interest, *cast against,*** κατά='against' makes its influence felt in ψῆφον κ. τινός *cast one's vote against someone,* i.e. vote for someone's condemnation **Ac 26:10** (Aristot. 1437a, 19 τὴν διαβολὴν κ. τινός; cp. Jos., Ant. 10, 91 πάντες ἤνεγκαν τὰς ψήφους κατ' αὐτοῦ). αἰτιώματα κ. *bring charges* **25:7.**

❸ **to get into a state of being, *be brought into,*** pass. καταφέρεσθαί τινι ὕπνῳ βαθεῖ *sink into a deep sleep* (cp. Lucian, D. Mer. 2, 4; Herodian 2, 1, 2; 2, 9, 5; Jos., Ant. 2, 82 εἰς ὕπνον. καταφέρεσθαι abs. also has this mng.: Aristot. 456b, 31; 462a, 10) **Ac 20:9a.** κατενεχθεὶς ἀπὸ τοῦ ὕπνου *overwhelmed by sleep* vs. **9b.** S. also AcPl Ha 3, 26 βαθεῖ ὕπνῳ κατη[νέχ]θησαν.—Papias (3:1 mss. c d e for καθαιρεθείς).—M-M.

καταφεύγω fut. καταφεύξομαι LXX; 2 aor. κατέφυγον; aor. mixed 1 sg.κατέφυγα (JosAs 13:1) (s. φεύγω; Eur., Hdt.+).

❶ **to get away from an area, with implication of having a destination in mind, *flee*** εἰς τὰς πόλεις τῆς Λυκαονίας **Ac 14:6** (cp. κ. εἰς τ. πόλ. Aeneas Tact. 1794; Lev 26:25; Dt 4:42; TestJob 17:5.—Jos., Bell. 6, 201, Ant. 18, 373).

❷ **to gain shelter from danger, *take refuge*** (PSI 383, 15 [248 BC]; PMagd 25, 8; Alex. Aphr., Fat. 32, II 2 p. 204, 26 to Asclepius; Stephan. Byz. s.v. Σύβαρις: κ. ἐπὶ τὴν θεόν=to the deity; Philo; πρὸς σέ JosAs 13:1) w. inf. foll. οἱ καταφυγόντες κρατῆσαι τῆς προκειμένης ἐλπίδος *we who have taken refuge, to seize the hope that is placed before us* **Hb 6:18.**—M-M. Spicq.

καταφθείρω fut. καταφθερῶ 2 Ch 17:7; aor. κατέφθειρα LXX; pf. κατέφθαρκα LXX. Pass.: 2 fut. καταφθαρήσομαι; 2 aor. κατεφθάρην; pf. ptc. κατεφθαρμένος (s. next entry and φθείρω; Aeschyl., Pla., et al.; ins, pap, LXX; TestAsh 7:2; EpArist; Philo, Deus Imm. 141; 142; Just., D. 31, 5 [Da 7:19]).

❶ ***destroy*** (Aeschyl., LXX) pass. *be destroyed* (Polyb. 2, 64, 3; Lev 26:39; 2 Km 14:14 v.l.; 2 Macc 5:14) **2 Pt 2:12 v.l.** (cp. the portent Plut., Demetr. 894 [12, 3]).

❷ ***ruin, corrupt*** τινά *someone;* of grief παρὰ πάντα τὰ πνεύματα κ. τὸν ἄνθρωπον *it ruins a man more than all the (other) spirits* Hm 10, 1, 2. Pass. *be ruined, become useless* (SIG 1157, 74 [I BC] δένδρα; pap) ἀπό τινος *for someth.* ἀπὸ τῶν βιωτικῶν πράξεων *for the duties of everyday life* Hv 1, 3, 1b; cp. s 6, 2, 4. κ. ὑπό τινος εἴς τι: εἰς θάνατον *be injured by someone so that one dies* s 9, 26, 6. κατεφθαρμένος τὸν νοῦν *depraved in mind* **2 Ti 3:8** (Menand., Epitr. 692 S. p. 347 [502 Kö.] καταφθαρεὶς τὸν βίον). Abs. Hv 1, 3, 1a; m 10, 1, 4; s 9, 14, 3; 9, 26, 4.—M-M. TW. Spicq.

καταφθορά, ᾶς, ἡ (s. prec. entry; trag.; OGI 339, 5 [c. 120 BC]; UPZ 110, 126 [164 BC]; 162 III, 8; LXX) ***destruction, downfall, corruption*** παραδιδόναι τι εἰς κ. *give someth. up to destruction* of the Lord's 'flesh' B 5:1; 16:5 (quot. of uncertain origin). Somewhat difft. ἀπόλλυσθαι εἰς κ. *be destroyed* (by someone) *to the extent of corruption* Hs 6, 2, 2ff (w. θάνατος, as Sir 28:6; but H means that 'corruption' has a prospect of renewal, s 6, 2, 4).—DELG s.v. φθείρω.

καταφιλέω impf. κατεφίλουν; fut. καταφιλήσω LXX; 1 aor. κατεφίλησα (s. φιλέω; X., Cyr. 6, 4, 10; 7, 5, 32; Polyb. 15, 1, 7; Aelian, VH 13, 4; Plut., Brut. 991 [16, 5]; Lucian, Dial. Deor. 4, 5; 5, 3; M. Ant. 11, 34; PGrenf I, 1, 3 [II BC]; LXX; TestAbr B 6 p. 110, 1 [Stone p. 68]; Test12Patr, JosAs, ParJer; Jos., Ant. 7, 284; 8, 387; Ath. 32, 3 quot. of uncertain origin) ***kiss*** τινά *someone* in greeting or in farewell (Philo, Rer. Div. Her. 41) **Mt 26:49; Mk 14:45; Lk 15:20** (MDibelius, Judas u. der Judaskuss: Botschaft u. Geschichte, Gesammelte Aufsätze I, '53, 272–77); **Ac 20:37;** Hs 9, 6, 2; 9, 11, 4; GMary Ox 3525, 9. τὶ *someth.* (Menand., Epitr. 273 S. [97 Kö.]; Epict. 4, 10, 20 τὰς χεῖρας; PGM 4, 707) feet (Epict. 4, 1, 17; Sb 4323, 5 τοὺς πόδας) **Lk 7:38, 45.**—DELG s.v. φίλος. M-M. TW.

καταφρονέω fut. καταφρονήσω; 1 aor. κατεφρόνησα. Pass.: 1 aor. subj. 1 pl. καταφρονηθῶμεν 4 Macc 6:21 (s. next entry and φρονέω; Eur., Hdt.+).

❶ **to look down on someone or someth. with contempt or aversion, with implication that one considers the object of little value, *look down on, despise, scorn, treat with contempt*** τινός (X., Mem. 3, 4, 12; Menand., fgm. 301, 10 Kö. τῶν πτωχῶν; Diod. S. 1, 67, 7; PMagd 8, 11; 23, 4 [221 BC]; Jos., Bell. 1, 633; Iren. 1, 25, 1 [Harv. I 205, 2]; Did., Gen. 45, 24) *someone* or *someth.* (opp. ἀντέχεσθαι) **Mt 6:24; Lk 16:13.**—Dg 2:7. ἑνὸς τῶν μικρῶν τούτων **Mt 18:10** (difft. κ. τῶν μικρῶν [neut.]: Socrat., Ep. 29, 3); τῆς ἐκκλησίας τοῦ θεοῦ *God's congregation* (in contrast to isolationism, the partaking of τὸ ἴδιον δεῖπνον) **1 Cor 11:22;** doubt Hm 9:10; grief 10, 3, 1. κυριότητος **2 Pt 2:10.** μηδείς σου τῆς νεότητος καταφρονείτω *let no one look down on you because you are young* **1 Ti 4:12** (καταφρονήσας τῆς 'Αλεξάνδρου νεότητος Diod. S. 17, 7, 1 [Field, Notes 209]; Herodian 1, 3, 5; cp. PGen 6, 13 [146 AD]); cp. **Tit 2:15 v.l.** (for περιφρονείτω). Pass. Hm 7:2.—τοῦ πλούτου τῆς χρηστότητος *have little regard for God's goodness* **Ro 2:4** (s. Ltzm. ad loc.—Phylarchus [III BC]: 81 fgm. 24 Jac. οἱ πολλοὶ κ. τοῦ θείου). Abs. (sc. αὐτῶν) **1 Ti 6:2.**

❷ **to consider something not important enough to be an object of concern when evaluated against someth. else, *care nothing for, disregard, be unafraid of*** (Diod. S. 3, 50, 5; Epict. 4, 1, 70 τοῦ ἀποθανεῖν; 71; Arrian, Anab. 7, 4, 3; SIG 705, 36 [112 BC] καταφρονήσαντες τοῦ τῆς συγκλήτου δόγματος; EpArist 225; Joseph.) αἰσχύνης **Hb 12:2** (cp. Jos., Ant. 7, 313 τ. ὀλιγότητος=their small number); death (Just., A II, 10, 8; Tat. 11, 1; Diod. S. 5, 29, 2 τοῦ θανάτου κ.; on the topic cp. M. Ant. 11, 3) Dg 1:1; 10:7 (opp. φοβεῖσθαι); ISm 3:2; torture MPol 2:3; cp. 11:2.—DELG s.v. φρήν. M-M. TW. Spicq.

καταφρονητής, οῦ, ὁ (s. prec. entry; on a statement made by Duris: 76 fgm. 30 Jac.; Epict. 4, 7, 33; Plut., Brut. 988 [12, 1]; Vett. Val. 47, 33; LXX; GrBar 16:4; Philo, Leg. ad Gai. 322; Jos., Bell. 2, 122, Ant. 6, 347; Tat. 19, 2) ***despiser, scoffer*** **Ac 13:41** (Hab 1:5).—DELG s.v. φρήν. M-M. TW. Spicq.

καταφωνέω (s. φωνέω; Hesych.) impf. κατεφώνουν ***cry out against*** **Ac 22:24 v.l.** for ἐπιφωνέω (q.v.).

καταχαίρω fut. mid. καταχαροῦμαι (s. χαίρω; Hdt. et al.; IG XIV, 2410, 11; SEG II, 844 κατάχαιρε καὶ εὐφραίνου) ***rejoice*** at the misfortune of others 1 Cl 57:4 (Pr 1:26).

καταχέω 1 aor. 2 sg. κατέχεας Ps 88:46; 3 sg. κατέχεεν (χέω; Hom.+; also JosAs 10:15) ***pour out*** or ***down over*** w. gen.

of what the liquid is poured over (Hdt. 4, 62; Pla., Leg. 7, 814b; PMagd 24, 4; 9 [III BC]; Philo, Cher. 59; Jos., C. Ap. 2, 256 μύρον αὐτοῦ καταχέας) αὐτοῦ τῆς κεφαλῆς (Epict. 4, 5, 33; Jos., Ant. 9, 108; as early as Alcaeus 86, 1 D.[2]: Κὰτ τᾶς κεφάλας κακχεάτω μύρον=pour ointment on my head; cp. 50 Campbell) **Mk 14:3** (v.l. κατά or ἐπὶ τῆς κεφαλῆς). Also ἐπὶ τῆς κεφαλῆς αὐτοῦ **Mt 26:7.**—M-M.

καταχθόνιος, ον (χθών 'earth', i.e. the surface; Hom. et al.; Dionys. Hal. 2, 10; Strabo 6, 2, 11; Cornutus 34 p. 72, 18; IG III/2, 1423; 1424; XIV, 1660; OGI 382, 1; Sb 5762; PGM 4, 1918 mostly θεοὶ κ.; PGM 4, 2088 κ. δαίμων; IDefixAudollent 74, 1 ἄγγελοι κ.; TestSol 16:3 al. τῶν ἀερίων καὶ ἐπιγείων καὶ καταχθονίων πνευμάτων) ***under the earth, subterranean*** οἱ κ. *beings* or *powers under the earth* (w. ἐπουράνιοι, ἐπίγειοι) **Phil 2:10** (s. ἐπίγειος 2b).—DELG s.v. χθών. M-M. TW.

καταχορεύω (s. χορός; since II–III AD in the mng. 'dance in victory'; so Aelian, NA 1, 30) ***dance (for joy)*** κατεχόρευε τοῖς ποσὶν αὐτῆς (at three years of age, Mary) *danced for joy with her feet* GJs 7:3.—DELG s.v. χορός.

καταχράομαι fut. καταχρήσομαι (Tat.); 1 aor. κατεχρησάμην (s. χράομαι; Pla. et al.; ins, pap, LXX, Philo; Jos., Bell. 2, 109). As a rule the prep. gives the simple verb a special coloring ('make full use of', 'misuse', 'use up'); in the only two pass. where it occurs in our lit. (both 1 Cor), this word differs little, if at all, fr. the simple verb: ***use*** (Chariton 7, 1, 8; OGI 669, 19; SIG 736, 61 [92 BC] εἰς ἄλλο τι καταχρήσασθαι; PPetr III, 39; II, 15; 46 [3], 3; POxy 494, 20 καταχρᾶσθαι εἰς τὸ ἴδιον 'use for one's own needs' [fr. a will]; Jos., Ant. 3, 303) τινί *someth.* (Eunap. p. 61 παρρησίᾳ; Philo, Op. M. 171, Det. Pot. Ins. 101; Jos., Ant. 12, 184) τῇ ἐξουσίᾳ μου *to make use of my authority* **1 Cor 9:18.** Abs. οἱ χρώμενοι τὸν κόσμον ὡς μὴ καταχρώμενοι *using the world as though they had no use of it* **7:31** (in quite similar language, Plotin., Enn. 5, 3, 3 p. 498d interchanges προσχράομαι and χράομαι).—DELG s.v. χρή p. 1274 col. 2. M-M.

κατάχυμα, ατος, τό (Themist. 23 p. 354, 18; Suda. The form κατάχυσμα since Aristoph. et al.—Ammonius [100 AD] p. 78 Valck. and Thomas Mag. note a difference in the mng. of the two words) ***sauce, broth, soup*** ἐκ καταχύματος μεταλαμβάνειν *to fish out of the soup,* i.e. get everything for oneself Hv 3, 9, 2. The expr. seems to be proverbial. Dibelius, Hdb. ad loc., would prefer to take it as figurative, mng. *surplus, abundance,* though this sense has not been found elsewh.—S. DELG s.v. χυλός.

καταψεύδομαι aor. 3 sg. κατεψεύσατο (TestAbr B; Ath.) (s. ψεύδομαι; Eur. et al.; OGI 8, 14f; PFlor 382, 57; Wsd 1:11; Philo; Tat. 3, 2; Ath. 35, 1) ***tell lies (against)*** τινός *in contradiction* or *in opposition to someone* (Hyperid. 3, 18 τ. θεοῦ; Dio Chrys. 6, 17 τῆς θεοῦ; Chariton 5, 6, 10; Philostrat., Vi. Apoll. 5, 37 p. 198, 10; Sextus 367; En 104:9; TestAbr B 10 p. 114, 19 [Stone p. 76]; Jos., Bell. 6, 288) ITr 10. τινός w. ptc. foll. *say falsely about someone that* Dg 4:3. τινός τι *charge someone falsely w. someth.* (Pla., Phd. 85a, Euthyd. 283f, Rep. 2, 381d; 3, 391d al.; Philo, Op. M. 7 τοῦ θεοῦ ἀπραξίαν κ.) Hv 1, 1, 7.

καταψηφίζομαι (s. ψηφίζω; mid. dep., Thu. et al.; pap; Philo, Leg. All. 3, 74; Jos., Bell. 6, 250, Ant. 17, 153; Just.; the act. is rare and late) pass. ***be enrolled*** (as the result of a vote) **Ac 1:26 v.l.** (for συγκαταψηφίζομαι).—DELG s.v. ψῆφος. TW.

καταψύχω 1 aor. κατέψυξα (ψύχω 'make cold', s. ψύχος; Hippocr. et al.; PEdg 27 [=Sb 6733], 5 [256/255 BC]; Gen 18:4, but intr. here) ***cool off, refresh*** τὶ *someth.* (Theophr., C. Pl. 4, 12, 9; Philo, Migr. Abr. 210; Jos., Bell. 1, 66 τ. ὁρμήν) the tongue **Lk 16:24.**—DELG s.v. ψύχω p. 1295 col. 2. M-M. S. New Docs 4, 261f.

κατεάγην, -εαγῶσιν, -έαξα, -έαξω s. κατάγνυμι.

κατέβην s. καταβαίνω.

κατεγέλων s. καταγελάω.

κατέγνωσμαι s. καταγινώσκω.

κατέδραμον s. κατατρέχω.

κατείδωλος, ον (only in Christian wr.: Prochorus, AcJ 117, 4 Zahn; Georg. Syncell. [c. 900 AD] p. 177, 5) ***full of cult-images/idols,*** of Athens **Ac 17:16.**—DELG s.v. εἶδος. M-M. TW.

κατειλημμένος, κατείληφα s. καταλαμβάνω.

κάτειμι (fr. εἶμι; Hom. et al.; ins, pap; Philo, Aet. M. 58; Jos., Bell. 3, 343, Ant. 14, 50; Tat.) impf. 3 sg.κατῄει (TestJos 9:4; 12:1) ***come down, get down*** ἀπὸ τῆς καρούχας *from the carriage* MPol 8:3.

κατείργω 1 aor. pass. κατείρχθην (ἔργω 'bar one's way'; Eur., Hdt. et al.; Jos., Ant. 18, 322, C. Ap. 2, 241) ***shut up, enclose*** εἰς κάμινον πυρός 1 Cl 45:7.

κατεκάην s. κατακαίω.

κατεκρίθην s. κατακρίνω.

κατελαβόμην, κατέλαβον, κατελήμφθην s. καταλαμβάνω.

κατελθεῖν s. κατέρχομαι.

κατέλιπον s. καταλείπω.

κατέναντι adv. (JWackernagel, Hellenistica 1907, 3–6; JWaldis, Präpositionsadverbien mit d. Bedeutung 'vor' in d. LXX 1922; B-D-F §214, 4; Rob. 643) gener. 'opposite'.

❶ **marker of a position relative to someone who is viewed as having jurisdiction, whether visibly present or not, *in the sight of*** someone, ***before*** someone, funct. as prep. w. gen. (Sir 28:26; Jdth 12:15, 19) κ. θεοῦ ἐν Χριστῷ λαλοῦμεν *before God* (Sir 50:19; SibOr 3, 499) **2 Cor 2:17; 12:19** (both v.l. κατενώπιον). κ. οὗ ἐπίστευσεν θεοῦ (=κ. τοῦ θεοῦ ᾧ ἐπίστευσεν, W-S. §24, 4d; B-D-F §294, 2; Rob. 717) *before the God in whom he believed* **Ro 4:17.** GJs 1:2 v.l. (for κατενώπιον).

❷ **marker of position over against someth., *opposite***

ⓐ funct. as adv. εἰς τ. κατέναντι κώμην *into the village opposite* (us) **Lk 19:30** (cp. 2 Ch 4:10; Ezk 11:1; 40:10; AcPh 98: Aa II/2, 38, 23; s. also the formulation κατέναντι πρὸς ἀνατολάς *eastward* AcPlMart 5 [Aa I 115, 13; for which ἀπέν[αντι . . .] AcPl Ha 10, 21, with cod. A of AcPlMart]).

ⓑ funct. as prep. w. gen. of place or position (Lucian, Fug. 1; IPriene 37, 170 [II BC] κ. τοῦ ὄρευς; UPZ 79, 11 [159 BC]; LXX; En 14:5; Test12Patr; JosAs 28:3, 5; ParJer 7:15; Just., D. 62, 5 [for ἐναντίον Josh 5:13]) of place (En 14:15) κ. τοῦ ἱεροῦ *opposite the temple* **Mk 13:3.** κ. τοῦ γαζοφυλακείου **12:41.** κ. μου *opposite* or *before me* Hv 1, 2, 2 (Joly: κατενώπιον); cp. 3, 2, 4; 3, 9, 10. κ. αὐτῶν *before them* **Mk 6:41** D (MBlack, An Aramaic Approach[3], '67, 116). εἰς τὴν κώμην τὴν κ. ὑμῶν *into the village lying before you* **Mt 21:2; Mk 11:2.** κ. τοῦ ὄχλου *in* *the presence of the crowd* **Mt 27:24 v.l.** (for ἀπέναντι).—DELG s.v. ἄντα, 2 ἀντί. M-M.

κατενεχθείς s. καταφέρω.

κατενύγην s. κατανύσσομαι.

κατενώπιον (s. ἐνώπιον; Leo Gramm. 273, 18; Theodos. Melitenus 191 Tafel [1859]; Georg. Mon. 365, 21 de B. [1892]. Cp. Psaltes, Grammatik 337. For other lit. s. on κατέναντι, beg.; AWikenhauser, BZ 8, 1910, 263–70) adv., functions as prep. w. gen. (LXX [Johannessohn, Präp. 197]; TestSol 22:13; JosAs 23:12; Just., D. 127, 3; Christian amulet BGU 954, 6 [VI AD] κλίνω τ. κεφαλήν μου κ. σου) ἔστη κ. αὐτοῦ (sc. τοῦ Ἰωακείμ) Ῥουβήλ *R. stood before him* GJs 1:2 (v.l. κατεναντί[ον]). Otherw. in our lit. only in relation to God.

➊ **marker of a position in front of, *right opposite:*** *in the presence of God* (cp. Lev 4:17) on the day of judgment κ. τῆς δόξης αὐτοῦ **Jd 24** (cp. En 104:1).

➋ **marker of a position relative to someone who is viewed as having jurisdiction, whether visibly present or not, *before,*** funct. as prep. w. gen. κ. αὐτοῦ *before him* **Eph 1:4; Col 1:22;** κ. μου Hv 1, 2, 2 v.l. (Joly [in text]); κ. τοῦ θεοῦ **2 Cor 2:17 v.l.; 12:19 v.l.** ἡ δούλη κυρίου κ. αὐτοῦ GJs 11:3 (cp. **Lk 1:38**). κ. αὐτοῦ τῆς δικαιοσύνης Pol 5:2.—DELG s.v. ἐνῶπα. M-M.

κατεξουσιάζω (s. ἐξουσιάζω; scarcely to be found in other Gk.—though κατεξουσία occurs IG XIV, 1047, 5 and Sb 8316, 6f=CIG 4710, and the verb AcThom 45 [Aa II/2, 162, 24 v.l.]; 98 [p. 211, 2]; Tat. 15, 3; and Julian, C. Galil. 100c of the God of the Jews κ. τῶν ὅλων) ***exercise authority,*** perh. *tyrannize* τινός *over someone,* of the mighty ones of the earth **Mt 20:25; Mk 10:42.**—DELG s.v. εἰμί. M-M. TW.

κατέπεσον s. κατεπίπτω.

κατεπέστησαν s. κατεφίστημι.

κατεπιθυμέω (s. ἐπιθυμέω; otherw. found IV/V AD) ***be very eager*** κατεπιθυμεῖς καθίσαι ἐκ δεξιῶν μετ᾽ αὐτῶν Hv 3, 2, 2.

κατεπίθυμος, ον ***very eager, desirous*** (Jdth 12:16 κ. τοῦ συγγενέσθαι μετ᾽ αὐτῆς) w. inf. foll καθίσαι Hv 3, 2, 2 v.l. W. gen. τοῦ θεάσασθαι 3, 8, 1.

κατέπιον s. καταπίνω.

κατέπλευσα s. καταπλέω.

κατεπόθην s. καταπίνω.

κατέπρησα s. καταπίμπρημι.

κατεργάζομαι mid. dep., Att. fut. 2 sg. κατεργᾷ Dt 28:39; 1 aor. κατειργασάμην; perf. κατείργασμαι. Pass.: fut. 2 pl. κατεργασθήσεσθε Ezk 36:9; aor. κατειργάσθην (on κατηργασάμην and κατηργάσθην s. B-D-F §67, 3; W-S. §12, 1; Mlt-H. 189) (Soph., Hdt.+).

➊ **to bring about a result by doing someth., *achieve, accomplish, do*** τὶ *someth.* (Hdt. 5, 24 πρήγματα μεγάλα; X., Mem. 3, 5, 11; Jos., Vi. 289) **Ro 7:15, 17f, 20; 1 Cor 5:3;** 1 Cl 32:3f. τὴν ἀσχημοσύνην κατεργαζόμενοι *committing shameless acts* **Ro 1:27.** τὸ κακόν *do what is wrong* **2:9; 13:10 v.l.** τὸ βούλημα τῶν ἐθνῶν *do what the gentiles* (i.e. polytheists) *like to do* **1 Pt 4:3.** δικαιοσύνην θεοῦ *does what is right in the sight of God* or (s. ἐργάζεσθαι 2c) *achieves the uprightness that counts before God* **Js 1:20 v.l.** ἅπαντα κατεργασάμενοι *after you have done* or *accomplished everything* (in this case the reference would be to the individual pieces of armor mentioned in what follows, which the reader is to employ as is prescribed; but s. 4 below) **Eph 6:13.** ὧν οὐ κατειργάσατο Χριστὸς δι᾽ ἐμοῦ *of anything except what Christ has accomplished through me* **Ro 15:18.** Pass. τὰ σημεῖα τοῦ ἀποστόλου κατειργάσθη ἐν ὑμῖν *the signs by which an apostle demonstrates his authority have been done among you* **2 Cor 12:12.**

➋ **to cause a state or condition, *bring about, produce, create*** (Hdt. 7, 102 ἀρετὴ ἀπὸ σοφίης κατεργασμένη; Philo, Plant. 50; TestJos 10:1) τὶ *someth.* νόμος ὀργὴν **Ro 4:15.** θλῖψις ὑπομονὴν **5:3** (TestJos 10:1 πόσα κατεργάζεται ἡ ὑπομονή); cp. **Js 1:3.** λύπη μετάνοιαν **2 Cor 7:10a v.l.** (for ἐργάζεται). λύπη θάνατον vs. **10b;** cp. vs. **11** (where a dat. of advantage is added). φθόνος ἀδελφοκτονίαν 1 Cl 4:7. μνησικακία θάνατον Hv 2, 3, 1. ἡ ἁμαρτία κ. ἐν ἐμοὶ πᾶσαν ἐπιθυμίαν *sin called forth every desire within me* **Ro 7:8.** τινί τι *bring about someth. for someone* (Eur., Her. 1046 πόλει σωτηρίαν) μοι θάνατον **7:13.** αἰώνιον βάρος δόξης ἡμῖν **2 Cor 4:17.** εὐχαριστίαν τῷ θεῷ *bring about thankfulness to God* **9:11;** θάνατον ἑαυτῷ κ. *bring death upon oneself* Hm 4, 1, 2; cp. s 8, 8, 5 ἐργάζεσθαι.—*Work out* τὶ *someth.* (Pla., Gorg. 473d ὁ κατειργασμένος τὴν τυραννίδα ἀδίκως) τὴν ἑαυτῶν σωτηρίαν κατεργάζεσθε **Phil 2:12** (JMichael, Phil 2:12: Exp. 9th ser., 2, 1924, 439–50).

➌ **to cause to be well prepared, *prepare someone*** κ. τινα εἴς τι *prepare someone for someth.* (cp. Hdt. 7, 6, 1; X., Mem. 2, 3, 11) ἡμᾶς εἰς αὐτὸ τοῦτο *for this very purpose* **2 Cor 5:5.**

➍ **to be successful in the face of obstacles, *overpower, subdue, conquer*** (Hdt. 6, 2 νῆσον; Thu. 6, 11, 1 al. τινά; 1 Esdr 4:4; Philo, Sacr. Abel. 62; Jos., Ant. 2, 44) ἅπαντα κατεργασάμενοι στῆναι *after proving victorious over everything, to stand your ground* **Eph 6:13** (but s. 1 above).—M-M. TW.

κατέρχομαι 2 aor. κατῆλθον (κατῆλθα **Ac 27:5,** s. B-D-F §81, 3; W-S. §13, 13; cp. Mlt-H. 208f); pf. inf. κατεληλυθέναι (Tat. 27, 2) (s. ἔρχομαι; Hom.+; also Herm. 10, 25 οὐδεὶς τῶν οὐρανίων θεῶν ἐπὶ γῆν κατελεύσεται).

➊ **to move in a direction considered the opposite of up but not necessarily with suggestion of a gradient, *come down*** w. indication of the place fr. which ἀπό τινος: ἀπὸ τοῦ ὄρους (cp. Jos., Ant. 1, 109) **Lk 9:37.** ἀπὸ τῆς Ἰουδαίας **Ac 15:1; 21:10.—18:5.** ἐκεῖθεν GPt 9:36. The place from which is supplied fr. the context 11:44. W. indication of the place fr. which and the goal ἀπό τινος εἴς τι *from . . . to* **Ac 11:27; 12:19.** W. indication of the goal εἴς τι (TestJud 9:8 εἰς Αἴγυπτον; Jos., Ant. 8, 106 θεὸς κ. εἰς τὸ ἱερόν; Just., D. 56, 13 and 15 εἰς Σόδομα) **Lk 4:31; Ac 8:5; 13:4; 15:30; 19:1.** πρός τινα *to someone* **9:32.** Fig. (cp. Philo, Det. Pot. Ins. 117 ὅταν κατέρχηται [ἡ τῆς θείας σοφίας πηγή]) ἡ σοφία ἄνωθεν κατερχομένη *that comes from above* i.e. fr. God **Js 3:15.**

➋ **to arrive at a place, *arrive, put in,*** nautical t.t. of ships and those who sail in them, who 'come down' fr. the 'high seas' (Eustath. ad Hom. 1408, 29 [Od. 1, 182] κατελθεῖν, οὐ μόνον τὸ ἁπλῶς κάτω που ἐλθεῖν, ἀλλὰ καὶ τὸ ἐς λιμένα ἐλθεῖν, ὥσπερ καὶ καταβῆναι καὶ καταπλεῦσαι κ. καταχθῆναι κ. κατᾶραι, τὸ ἐλλιμενίσαι λέγεται=κ. does not only simply mean 'to come down somewhere', but also 'to come into a port', just as καταβῆναι etc. are used to refer to 'putting into port'; 1956, 35 [Od. 24, 115]) εἴς τι *at someth.* a harbor **Ac 18:22; 21:3; 27:5.**—M-M.

κατεσθίω/κατέσθω (**Mk 12:40;** PGM 5, 279 κατέσθεται; En 103:15; 104:3. S. on ἐσθίω, also B-D-F §101 and

Mlt-H. 238 under ἐσθίω) 2 aor. κατέφαγον; fut. καταφάγομαι (**J 2:17,** s. B-D-F §74, 2; W-S. §13, 6 and 17; Mlt-H. 198. S. also PIand 26, 23 [98 AD]; LXX) and κατέδομαι (1 Cl 8:4; LXX) (Hom. et al.; pap, LXX, TestSol, TestAbr, En, Test12Patr, JosAs, Philo; Jos., C. Ap. 1, 261; Just., D. 57, 2; Tat. 10, 2).

❶ **to eat up ravenously,** ***eat up, consume, devour, swallow*** lit. τὶ *someth.* (PFlor 150, 6 ἀπὸ τῶν μυῶν κατεσθιόμενα) of birds (SibOr 5, 471) **Mt 13:4; Mk 4:4; Lk 8:5** (τὰ πετεινὰ τ. οὐρανοῦ κ. as 3 Km 12:24m; 16:4). σάρκας (cp. Da 7:5) B 10:4. Of animals that are to devour Ignatius IRo 5:2 (cp. Babrius 103, 10 [lion] L-P. [cp. Aesop, Fab. 142 P.]; Gen 37:20, 33; SibOr 5, 470). Of the apocalyptic dragon τὸ τέκνον αὐτῆς *devour her child* **Rv 12:4.** A book **10:9f** (cp. Ezk 3:1 and BOlsson, ZNW 32, '33, 90f.—Artem. [of Ephesus] 2, 45 p. 149, 6 speaks of ἐσθίειν βιβλία, experienced in a dream, which is interpreted to mean a quick death). The moth that eats clothing, as a type σὴς καταφάγεται ὑμᾶς B 6:2 (Is 50:9).

❷ The extension of mng. 1 leads to a multifaceted imagery: ***devour*** as if by eating—ⓐ to destroy utterly, *destroy* (Heraclitus, Ep. 7, 10 τὰ ζῶντα κατεσθίετε. Pass. Diog. L. 6, 5 'the jealous ones by their own vileness') of fire: *consume* τινά *someone* (cp. Num 26:10; Job 20:26; Ps 77:63; TestAbr A 10 p. 88, 13 [Stone p. 24] al.; JosAs 25:7) **Rv 11:5; 20:9.** Of the sword (Jer 2:30; 2 Km 18:8) ὑμᾶς κατέδεται 1 Cl 8:4 (Is 1:20). Of zeal *consume* (TestSim 4:9; cp. Jos., Ant. 7, 163) **J 2:17** (Ps 68:10).

ⓑ to waste: τὸν βίον *devour property* (cp. Od. 3, 315; Hipponax 39 Diehl; Diog. L. 10, 8, τὴν πατρῴαν οὐσίαν, which was divided among the sons; Aesop., Fab. 169 P.=304 H./249 Ch./179 H-H.; POxy 58, 6; 10 [288 AD]; Gen 31:15) **Lk 15:30.**

ⓒ to rob: τὰς οἰκίας τῶν χηρῶν *eat up widows' houses* i.e. appropriate them in an unethical manner (cp. Od. 2, 237f κατέδουσι βιαίως οἶκον Ὀδυσσῆος; Alcaeus, fgm. 43, 7 D.[2]; Mnesimachus Com. [IV BC], fgm. 8 πόλιν; Jos., Bell. 4, 242) **Mk 12:40; Lk 20:47 (Mt 23:13 v.l.).**

ⓓ to engage in spiteful partisan strife: betw. δάκνω and ἀναλίσκω (q.v.), someth. like *tear to pieces* **Gal 5:15** (cp. Philo, Leg. All. 3, 230 the fig. triad κατεσθίει, βιβρώσκει, καταπίνει).

ⓔ to exploit, abs. εἴ τις κ. *if anyone devours* (you) (i.e. exploits, robs; cp. Ps 13:4; Is 9:12) **2 Cor 11:20.**—DELG s.v. ἔδω. M-M.

κατευθύνω fut. 3 sg. κατευθυνεῖ LXX; 1 aor. κατεύθυνα, opt. 3 sg. κατευθύναι, impv. κατεύθυνον, inf. κατευθῦναι. Pass.: fut. 3 sg. κατευθυνθήσεται LXX; aor. 3 sg. κατευθύνθη Sir 49:2 (s. εὐθύνω; Pla. et al.; Plut., LXX; TestJud 26:1; EpArist; Philo, Decal. 60; Jos., Bell. 3, 118) gener. 'make/keep straight', ***lead, direct*** τὶ εἴς τι *someth. to someth.* τοὺς πόδας εἰς ὁδὸν εἰρήνης *the feet in the way of peace* **Lk 1:79.** κ. τὰ διαβήματα *direct the steps* (Ps 39:3; 36:23 pass.) 1 Cl 60:2. τ. καρδίας (1 Ch 29:18 πρὸς σέ; 2 Ch 12:14; 19:3) *hearts* to the love of God **2 Th 3:5.** τ. ὁδόν *direct the way* (cp. Jdth 12:8) τὴν ὁδὸν ἡμῶν πρὸς ὑμᾶς *direct our way to you* **1 Th 3:11.** κ. τὴν πορείαν ἐν ὁσιότητι *direct their course in devoutness* 1 Cl 48:4.—DELG s.v. εὐθύς. M-M. TW.

κατευλογέω impf. κατευλόγουν (s. εὐλογέω; Plut., Mor. 66a; 1069c; Ps.-Plut., Amator. 750c; Tob 10:14; 11:17 BA) ***bless*** **Mk 10:16.**

κατευοδόω (=εὐοδέω, 'have free course or passage, prosper', s. ὁδός; LXX; TestJud 1:6; ParJer 7:24 κατευοδόσῃ [C; -εύσῃ AB]) fut. 3 sg. κατευοδώσει Ps 67:20; 1 aor. pass. κατευοδώθην. Pass. in act. sense ***prosper*** (Achmes 13, 14; 39, 16; Cat. Cod. Astr. XII 128, 14; 162, 15) πάντα … κατευοδωθήσεται *everything … will prosper* B 11:6 (Ps 1:3). The same Ps pass. influences IMg 13:1, where the Gk. tradition κατευοδωθῆτε is to be preferred w. Lghtf., Funk, Bihlmeyer (Zahn changes it to κατευοδωθῇ): *you prosper in everything you do, both in the flesh and in the spirit.*—TW.

κατευωχέω (εὐωχέομαι 'fare sumptuously'; Hdt. et al.; ins [KClinton, Hesperia 49, '80, p. 263 ln. 8, in a fragmentary context, IV BC]; Philo, Joseph.) ***to feast*** (mid.) κατευωχούμενοι **2 Pt 2:13 v.l.**

κατεφίσταμαι (s. ἐφίστημι) 2 aor. κατεπέστην (hapax leg.) ***rise up*** τινί *against someone* **Ac 18:12.**

κατέχω impf. κατεῖχον; fut. καθέξω LXX, 3 pl. κατασχήσουσι (JosAs 16 [p. 64, 18 Bat. and cod. A]); 2 aor. κατέσχον. Pass.: fut. 2 pl. κατασχεθήσεσθε Ruth 1:13; aor. 3 sg. κατεσχέθη LXX (s. ἔχω; Hom.+). Trans. in all mngs. below, except 7.

❶ **to prevent the doing of someth. or cause to be ineffective,** ***prevent, hinder, restrain***—ⓐ to hold someone back from going away *hold back, hinder, prevent from going away* (Hom. et al.; BGU 1205, 27 [28 BC]; 37, 6 [50 AD]; PFay 109, 11; Gen 24:56; cp. Jos., Ant. 7, 76; Just., A I, 45, 1) Hs 9, 11, 6. ὃν ἐβουλόμην πρὸς ἐμαυτὸν κ. *whom I wished to keep with me* **Phlm 13.** Foll. by gen. of the inf. w. article (B-D-F §400, 4) οἱ ὄχλοι κατεῖχον αὐτὸν τοῦ μὴ πορεύεσθαι ἀπ' αὐτῶν **Lk 4:42.**

ⓑ *hold down, suppress* τὶ *someth.* (γέλωτα X., Cyr. 2, 2, 1; Chariton 3, 7, 4 τ. λύπην; WCrum, Coptic Ostraca p. 4, 522=Dssm., LO 260 [LAE 306]=PGM II 233, no. O 1, 1–3 Κρόνος, ὁ κατέχων τὸν θυμὸν ὅλων τ. ἀνθρώπων, κάτεχε τ. θυμὸν Ὥρι; cp. II, 7, 935f, p 41; Jos., Vi. 233 τ. ὀργήν) τ. ἀλήθειαν ἐν ἀδικίᾳ *stifle the truth by unrighteousness/wickedness* **Ro 1:18** (cp. JFitzmyer, Ro [AB], '93, 278; but s. 6 below).

ⓒ to prevent someone from exercising power, *restrain, check* (Thu. 6, 29, 3; Appian, Bell. Civ. 2, 149 §622 τοῦ δαίμονος κατέχοντος τὸ πέλαγος=divine power held the sea back until Alexander reached the other shore; PGiss 70, 3 [II AD] ἡ ἀναγραφὴ κατέσχεν ἡμᾶς μέχρι ὥρας ἕκτης) ἵνα μὴ κατέξω τ̣ὰ̣ [προσ]|τεταγμένα καὶ ἐπεικίμ̣[εν]α *so that I might not delay* (carrying out) *the instructions and orders* AcPl Ha 7, 14f. τὸ κατέχον (Themistocl., Ep. 13, 4) **2 Th 2:6** and ὁ κατέχων vs. **7** mean *that which restrains* and *one who restrains,* i.e. what prevents God's adversary fr. coming out in open opposition to God, for the time being. In an effort to define κ. more specifically here, many interpreters have followed the exegesis of the ancient church (Tertullian) and taken τὸ κ. to be the Roman Empire and ὁ κ. the Emperor (OBetz, NTS 9, '63, 276–91). An alternative view, as old as Theodore of Mops., but without sustained acceptance, would make τὸ κ. the preaching of Christian missionaries and ὁ κ. the apostle Paul (so OCullmann, Dodd Festschr. '56, 409–21). These and other attempts to limit more precisely the mng. of these terms in 2 Th invite skepticism because of insufficient textual data (vs. 5 appears to imply in-house information). The concept of the temporary restraining of the forces of hell (cp. Rtzst., Poim. 27 late Egyptian prayer 6, 4 Horus as κατέχων δράκοντα=PGM 4, 994f; cp. 2770 Μιχαὴλ … κατέχων, ὃν καλέουσι δράκοντα μέγαν) does not appear to play any role here.—WBousset, D. Antichrist 1895; NFreese, StKr 93, 1921, 73–77; VHartl, ZKT 45, 1921, 455–75; WSchröder, D. 2. Thess. 1929, 8–15; DBuzy, RSR 24, '34, 402–31; OCullmann, RThAM 1, '38, 26–61; JSchmid, TQ 129, '49, 323–43; OBetz, NTS 9, '63, 276–91. Difft. CGiblin, Threat to Faith '67, 167–242, a hostile power. S. also JTownsend, SBLSP 19, '80, 233–46; RAus, JBL 96, '77, 537–53; New Docs 3, 28.

ⓓ to hold back with design *hold back* τὶ *someth.* κ. ἐν μυστηρίῳ τὴν σοφὴν αὐτοῦ βουλήν *hold back his wise plan as a secret* Dg 8:10.

❷ **to adhere firmly to traditions, convictions, or beliefs, *hold to, hold fast*** (cp. the lit. sense λαμπάδας ἐν ταῖς χερσίν ParJer 3:2)

ⓐ *keep in one's memory* (Theophr., Char. 26, 2, a word of Homer) εἰ κατέχετε *if you hold it fast* **1 Cor 15:2.**

ⓑ *hold fast, retain faithfully* (X., Symp. 8, 26 τ. φιλίαν; TestJud 26:1 τ. ὁδούς) τὸν λόγον **Lk 8:15.** τὰς παραδόσεις *guard the traditions* **1 Cor 11:2.** τὸ καλόν *hold fast what is good* **1 Th 5:21;** Agr 11. τὴν παρρησίαν βεβαίαν κ. *keep the confidence firm* **Hb 3:6;** cp. vs. **14.** κ. τὴν ὁμολογίαν ἀκλινῆ **10:23.**

❸ **to keep in one's possession, *possess*** (Ps.-Aristot., Mirabilia 159; 160; Polyb. 1, 2, 3; IMagnMai 105, 51 [II BC] ἵνα ἔχωσιν κατέχωσίν τε καρπίζωνταί τε; Ezk 33:24; Da 7:18, 22; Ath. 8:3) τὶ *someth.* **Mt 21:38 v.l.;** ὡς μηδὲν ἔχοντες καὶ πάντα κατέχοντες **2 Cor 6:10** (DMealand [ZNW 67, '76, 277–79] cites Ps.-Crates Ep. 7 Hercher=p. 58 no. 7, 8 Malherbe: ἔχοντες μηδὲν πάντ' ἔχομεν, ὑμεῖς δὲ πάντ' ἔχοντες οὐδὲν ἔχετε). Abs. **1 Cor 7:30.**

❹ **to keep within limits in a confining manner, *confine***

ⓐ in prison *keep, confine* (PFlor 61, 60; BGU 372 I, 16; Gen 39:20; Philo, Leg. All. 3, 21) pass. Χριστιανοὶ κατέχονται ὡς ἐν φρουρᾷ τῷ κόσμῳ *they are confined in the world as in a prison* Dg 6:7.

ⓑ by law: ἀποθανόντες ἐν ᾧ κατειχόμεθα *having died to that by which we were bound* **Ro 7:6** (cp. PAmh 97, 17 οὐ κατασχεθήσομαι τῇ ὑποσχέσει; PRyl 117, 13).

ⓒ by disease (Diod. S. 4, 14, 5; Philo, Op. M. 71, Congr. Erud. Grat. 138; PSI 299, 3 κατεσχέθην νόσῳ; act., Jer 13:21; Jos., Vi. 48) **Lk 4:38** D; **J 5:4 v.l.**

❺ **to have a place as one's own, *take into one's possession, occupy*** (Hdt. 5, 72 et al.; PAmh 30, 26 [II BC] τὴν οἰκίαν) τὸν ἔσχατον τόπον **Lk 14:9** (cp. Philosoph. Max. 491, 69 τὸν κάλλιστον κατέχουσι τόπον; Jos., Ant. 8, 104). Cp. GPt 5:15.—AcPl Ha 5, 28 [κατ]εῖχεν αὐτὰς ἔκστασις perh. means *astonishment overcame them.*

❻ ***lay claim to,*** legal t.t. **Ro 1:18** (the point is that a claim is made for truth, which is denied in practice, cp. vss. 22f; s. FDanker, in Gingrich Festschr. 93. For a difft. interpr. see 1b above).

❼ ***hold course,*** nautical t.t., intr. (Hdt. 7, 188 κατέσχε ἐς τὸν αἰγιαλόν; Dicaearchus, fgm. 85 W. εἰς Δῆλον κατέσχε; Polyb. 1, 25, 7; Philostrat., Vi. Apoll. 4, 13 p. 133, 5; 5, 18 p. 178, 13; cp. Jos., Ant. 1, 204) κατεῖχον εἰς τὸν αἰγιαλόν *they headed for the beach* **Ac 27:40.**

❽ Perh. in the sense of ***determine*** (cp. προσέχω 2c) κατεχόντων εἰ ἄρα ἀληθῶς ἀπέθανεν AcPt Ox 849, 2f; s. ed.'s notes.—M-M. EDNT. TW. Spicq.

κατηγορέω impf. κατηγόρουν; fut. κατηγορήσω; 1 aor. κατηγόρησα; aor. pass. 3 sg. κατηγορήθη (AscIs 3:5) (trag., Hdt. +; loanw. in rabb.) gener. 'speak against'

❶ nearly always as legal t.t.: ***bring charges*** in court

ⓐ before a human judge: *against someone* τινά *someone* **Mk 3:2 v.l.;** τινός (Hdt., Aristoph., Pla. et al., also SIG 173, 37; 780, 8; PPetr III, 21g, 14; PEdgar 33 [=Sb 6739], 4; AscIs 3:6) **Mt 12:10; Mk 3:2; Lk 6:7; 11:54 v.l.; 23:2, 10; J 8:6; Ac 25:5.** τί τινος *accuse someone of a thing* (trag., X., Demosth. et al., also 1 Macc 7:25) κατηγόρουν αὐτοῦ πολλά **Mk 15:3** (for πολλά cp. PLond 893, 12 [40 AD] πολλὰ κ.); cp. vs. **4.** οὐχ ὡς τοῦ ἔθνους μου ἔχων τι κατηγορεῖν *not that I had any charge to bring against my own people* **Ac 28:19.** This may also be the place for περὶ πάντων τούτων, ὧν ἡμεῖς κατηγοροῦμεν αὐτοῦ *of which we accuse him* **24:8;** sim. **25:11,** if this is a case of attraction of the relative ὧν = τούτων ἅ. But it is also poss. to take it as a double gen. (cp. Demosth. 21, 5 παρανόμων ἔμελλον αὐτοῦ κατηγορεῖν; Dositheus 68, 2 βίας σου κατηγορῶ).—Also τινὸς περί τινος (Thu. 8, 85, 2; X., Hell. 1, 7, 2; Jos., Ant. 13, 104) **Ac 24:13.** κατά τινος (X., Hell. 1, 7, 9) w. gen. or (in the case of attraction, s. above) acc. of thing **Lk 23:14.** Abs. (OGI 218, 95 [III BC]; POxy 237 VIII, 21) **Ac 24:2, 19.** Pass. *be accused* ὑπό τινος *by someone* (Thu. 1, 95, 3 ἀδικία κατηγορεῖτο αὐτοῦ ὑπὸ τ. Ἑλλήνων; 2 Macc 10:13; Philo, Mut. Nom. 206) **Mt 27:12.** τί κατηγορεῖται ὑπὸ τ. Ἰουδαίων **Ac 22:30.** ὁ κατηγορούμενος *the accused* (PCairMasp 63, 2) **25:16.**

ⓑ before God's tribunal κατηγορήσω ὑμῶν πρὸς τ. πατέρα **J 5:45a** (for the constr. w. πρός cp. 1 Macc 7:6; 2 Macc 10:13). ὁ κατήγωρ . . . ὁ κατηγορῶν αὐτοὺς ἐνώπιον τ. θεοῦ ἡμῶν **Rv 12:10** (for the acc. s. PLond I, 41, 10 p. 28 [161 BC] ὁ βουκόλος κατηγόρησεν αὐτάς). Subst. ὁ κατηγορῶν *the accuser* (cp. Jos., C. Ap. 2, 137) **J 5:45b.**

❷ without legal connotation ***accuse, reproach*** (X., Mem. 1, 3, 4; Aelian, VH 9, 17; Herodian 6, 9, 1; Philo, Plant. 80; SB V/2, 7835, 17 [New Docs 1, 28]) Job αὐτὸς ἑαυτοῦ κατηγορεῖ *he accuses himself* 1 Cl 17:4. Abs., of thoughts **Ro 2:15.**—B. 1439. DELG s.v. ἀγορά. M-M. TW.

κατηγορία, ας, ἡ (s. prec. and two next entries; Hdt.+; ins; POxy 237 VIII, 7; Mitt-Wilck II/2, 68, 19f [restored]: Philo; Jos., Ant. 2, 49, C. Ap. 2, 137; Just., A II, 2, 7; Ath.; on the correctness of this term s. καταλαλία; loanw. in rabb.) ***accusation*** τίνα κ. φέρετε κατὰ τοῦ ἀνθρώπου τούτου; *what accusation do you bring against this man?* **J 18:29.** κ. παραδέχεσθαι κατά τινος *entertain an accusation against someone* **1 Ti 5:19** (κατά τινος, as Isocr. 5, 147; SIG 704 F 7; 705, 32). ἔχειν κατηγορίαν κατά τινος **J 8:11 v.l.;** cp. ἔχειν κατηγορίαν τινός **8:4** D; εὑρεῖν κ. **Lk 6:7 v.l.** W. gen. of the content of the accusation (Demosth. 18, 279; Philo, Fuga 36) κ. ἀσωτίας *charge of profligacy* **Tit 1:6.**—DELG s.v. ἀγορά. M-M. TW. Sv.

κατήγορος, ου, ὁ (s. two prec. entries; Soph., Hdt.; ins, pap; Pr 18:17; 2 Macc 4:5; Philo; Jos., Bell. 4, 339, C. Ap. 2, 132; Tat.; Ath. 2:3; Hippol.; κ. τοῦ χριστιανισμοῦ Orig. C. Cels. 1, 64, 31) ***accuser*** **J 8:10 v.l.; Ac 23:30, 35; 24:8 v.l.; 25:16, 18; Rv 12:10 v.l.;** IMg 12 (Pr 18:17).—DELG s.v. ἀγορά. M-M. TW.

κατήγωρ, ορος, ὁ (s. three prec. entries; loanw. in rabb., and not a Hebr. [Bousset, Offb. Joh.[6] 1906, 342] or an Aram. [W-S. §8, 13 p. 85f] modification of the Gk. κατήγορος, but rather a colloquial formation starting fr. the fact that the gen. pl. is κατηγόρων whether the word belongs to the second or third declension. This form is found also PGM 10, 25. Cp. Dssm., LO 72f [LAE 90f]; Rdm.[2] 19; Mlt-H. 127f; B-D-F §52; Psaltes, 175; ADebrunner, GGA 1926, 137ff) ***accuser,*** designation of the devil (Billerb. I 141f) κ. τῶν ἀδελφῶν ἡμῶν **Rv 12:10.**—DELG s.v. ἀγορά. M-M. TW.

κατήφεια, ας, ἡ (s. next entry; Hom. et al.; Dionys. Hal.; Plut.; Philo, Spec. Leg. 3, 193; Jos., Ant. 13, 406; 19, 260) ***gloominess, dejection*** (Chariton 6, 8, 3; 7, 3, 3; cp. Plut., Mor. 528e τ. κατήφειαν ὁρίζονται λύπην κάτω βλέπειν ποιοῦσαν 'they define κ. as sorrow that makes one look down'. Sim., Etym. Mag. 496, 53) μετατραπήτω . . . ἡ χαρὰ εἰς κ. *let your joy be turned into gloominess* **Js 4:9.**—DELG s.v. κατηφής. M-M.

κατηφής, ές (s. prec. entry; Hom. et al.; POxy 471, 92; Acta Alex. VII A, 92f; Wsd 17:4; Jos., Ant. 2, 55) ***downcast*** τί οὕτως κ. τῇ ἰδέᾳ; *why do you look so downcast?* Hv 1, 2, 3; τί οὕτως στυγνὸς κ., κύριε; *why do you look so sad and downcast?* AcPl Ha 7, 30. This word is restored in 8, 8: [κατηφ]ὲς ἀποθέμενον, but τῆς λύπης, as in the duplicate AcPl BMM recto 7 (s. λύπη), fits just as well. Although κατηφής is used in the immediate context of Ha, the pap also uses λύπη.—DELG.

κατηχέω 1 aor. κατήχησα, pass. κατηχήθην; pf. pass. κατήχημαι (late word; PStras 41, 37 [III AD]; not LXX, but ParJer 5:19; Philo, Joseph.) gener. 'to communicate'.

➊ **to share a communication that one receives, *report, inform*** (Jos., Vi. 366 αὐτός σε πολλὰ κατηχήσω='I will personally give you much information') pass. *be informed, learn* (Philo, Leg. ad Gai. 198; Ps.-Plut., Fluv. 7, 2; 8, 1; 17, 1 κατηχηθεὶς περὶ συμβεβηκότων; PPrinc II, 20, 1 [II AD]) ἵνα ἐπιγνῷς περὶ ὧν κατηχήθης λόγων τὴν ἀσφάλειαν (=τὴν ἀ. τῶν λόγων περὶ ὧν κ.) *so that you may be certain about the things you have heard* or *been informed of* **Lk 1:4** (so, Zahn, JWeiss, EKlostermann; FVogel, NKZ 44, '33, 203–5; Beyer, RSV; prob. in ref. to variations in reports or stories relating to the career of Jesus; s. ἀσφάλεια 2; others prefer mng. 2a). In a forensic context κατηχήθησαν περὶ σοῦ ὅτι *they have been informed concerning you that* **Ac 21:21;** cp. vs. **24.**

➋ ***teach, instruct*** (Lucian, Jupp. Trag. 39; Ps.-Lucian, Asin. 48; in our lit. only of instruction in theological matters. The noun κατήχησις normally refers to 'instruction' [LAlexander, The Preface to Luke's Gospel '93, 139, s. also 141f]).

ⓐ gener. τινά *someone* **1 Cor 14:19.** ὁ κατηχῶν *the teacher* **Gal 6:6b.** Pass. (Ps.-Lucian, Philopatr. 17 of teaching about God: κατηχούμενος πείθου παρ' ἐμοῦ) κατηχούμενος ἐκ τοῦ νόμου *instructed in the law* **Ro 2:18.** W. acc. of what is taught κατηχημένος τὴν ὁδὸν τοῦ κυρίου *in the way of the Lord* **Ac 18:25** (cp. Iren. 3, 12, 7 [Harv. II 61, 2f]; Hippol., Ref. 6, 36, 2]). ὁ κατηχούμενος τὸν λόγον *in* (Christian) *teaching* **Gal 6:6a** (B-D-F §159, 1. BWeiss, HHoltzmann, FHauck, Rengstorf, Goodsp., NRSV, et al. prefer this mng. **Lk 1:4** [but s. 1 above]: *that you may know the truth about the things you have been taught.* S. on παρακολουθέω 3.).

ⓑ in the specif. sense of basic Christian instruction for new converts *give instruction* 2 Cl 17:1.—PCarrington, The Primitive Christian Catechism '40; CDodd in NT Essays (TWManson memorial vol.) '59, 106–18.—DELG s.v. ἠχή. M-M. EDNT. TW. Spicq. Sv.

κατήχθημεν s. κατάγω.

κατ' ἰδίαν s. ἴδιος 5.

κατιόω (s. ἰός 2; Sir 12:11) pf. pass. 3 sg. κατίωται; pass. in intr. sense ***become rusty, tarnished, corroded*** (Strabo 16, 2, 42; Epict. 4, 6, 14) of gold and silver (cp. EpJer 10) **Js 5:3.** —DELG 4 ἰός. TW.

κατισχύω (s. ἰσχύω) impf. κατίσχυον; fut. κατισχύσω; 1 aor. κατίσχυσα (in various senses relating to display of strength: 'be strong, powerful, gain the ascendancy': Soph.+; oft. in later wr. and in LXX; En 104:6; PsSol 2:7; Test12Patr, EpArist; Jos., Ant. 14, 357, but scarcely at all in ins, pap [PGM 13, 797]) intr.

➊ **to have the strength or capability to obtain an advantage, *be dominant, prevail*** abs. (Polyb. 11, 13, 3; Ex 17:11; En 104:6) κατίσχυον αἱ φωναὶ αὐτῶν *their voices prevailed* **Lk 23:23** (Antig. Car. 152 κατίσχυκεν ἡ φήμη). W. inf. foll. *be able, be in a position* **21:36.**

➋ **to have the capability to defeat, *win a victory over*** w. gen. (Dio Chrys. 12 [13], 4 al.; Aelian, HA 5, 19; Wsd 7:30; Jer 15:18; Jos., Bell. 2, 464 κατισχύσας πλειόνων=conqueror of a superior force; TestReub 4:11) πύλαι ᾅδου οὐ κατισχύσουσιν αὐτῆς (i.e. τῆς ἐκκλησίας) **Mt 16:18** (s. on πύλη a). πάσης πονηρίας Hv 2, 3, 2. κ. τῶν ἔργων τοῦ διαβόλου *win the victory over the works of the devil* Hm 12, 6, 4.—DELG s.v. ἰσχύς. M-M. TW.

κατοικέω (s. four next entries) fut. κατοικήσω; 1 aor. κατῴκησα; pf. inf. κατῳκηκέναι (Just., D. 79, 2); aor. pass. subj. κατοικηθῶ LXX (s. οἰκέω; Soph., Hdt.+).

➊ **to live in a locality for any length of time, *live, dwell, reside, settle (down)*** intr.—ⓐ w. the place indicated by ἔν τινι (X., An. 5, 3, 7; IHierapJ 212 τῶν ἐν Ἱεραπόλει κατοικούντων Ἰουδαίων; PMagd 25, 2 [221 BC]; PTebt 5, 180; Lev 23:42; Gen 14:12; Philo, Sobr. 68; Jos., Vi. 31; PMert 63, 9) **Lk 13:4 v.l.; Ac 1:20** (cp. Ps 68:26); **2:5 v.l.** (for εἰς s. below); **7:2, 4a, 48; 9:22; 11:29; 13:27; 17:24; Hb 11:9; Rv 13:12;** B 11:4; IEph 6:2; Hs 3:1. Also used w. εἰς and acc. (Ps.-Callisth. 1, 38, 3 εἰς φθαρτὰ σώματα ἀθανάτων ὀνόματα κατοικεῖ; schol. on Soph., Trach. 39 p. 281 Papag.; B-D-F §205; Rob. 592f) **Mt 2:23; 4:13; Ac 2:5; 7:4b.** εἰς τὰ τείχη Hs 8, 7, 3. εἰς τὸν πύργον 8, 8, 5. εἰς τὸν αἰῶνα τὸν ἐρχόμενον s 4:2. ἐπὶ τῆς γῆς *live on the earth* **Rv 3:10; 6:10; 8:13; 11:10ab; 13:8, 14ab; 14:6 v.l.; 17:8.** ἐπὶ παντὸς προσώπου τῆς γῆς *live on the whole earth* **Ac 17:26.** ἐπὶ ξένης (i.e. χώρας) Hs 1:6. ποῦ, ὅπου **Rv 2:13ab.** Abs. (Ramsay, CB I/2, 461 nos. 294 and 295 οἱ κατοικοῦντες Ῥωμαῖοι) ὑπὸ πάντων τῶν (sc. ἐκεῖ) κατοικούντων Ἰουδαίων *by all the Jews who live there* **Ac 22:12.**

ⓑ in relation to the possession of human beings by God, Christ, the Holy Spirit, and other transcendent beings, virtues, etc. (cp. Wsd 1:4; TestDan 5:1, TestJos 10:2f) ὁ θεὸς κ. ἐν ἡμῖν B 16:8. Of Christ **Eph 3:17;** cp. Hm 3:1. Of the Holy Spirit Hm 5, 2, 5; 10, 2, 5; s 5, 6, 5; ὁ κύριος ἐν τῇ μακροθυμίᾳ κ. m 5, 1, 3. ἐν αὐτῷ κ. πᾶν τὸ πλήρωμα τῆς θεότητος **Col 2:9;** cp. **1:19;** ἐν οἷς δικαιοσύνη κ. **2 Pt 3:13** (cp. Is 32:16). ἡ μακροθυμία κατοικεῖ μετὰ τῶν τ. πίστιν ἐχόντων *patience dwells with those who have faith* Hm 5, 2, 3. Of spirit control or possession **Mt 12:45; Lk 11:26** (κ. ἐκεῖ as Palaeph. 39 p. 44, 4).

➋ **to make something a habitation or dwelling by being there, *inhabit*** τὶ *someth.* (Demosth., Ep. 4, 7 τ. Ἰνδικὴν χώραν; Ps.-Aristot., Mirabilia 136; SIG 557, 17 τ. Ἀσίαν; PMagd 9, 1 [III BC]; PTor 4, 8 [117 BC] τὴν αὐτὴν πόλιν; Gen 13:7; Ezk 25:16; Philo, Leg. All. 3, 2; Jos., Vi. 27 Δαμασκόν) Ἰερουσαλήμ **Lk 13:4; Ac 1:19; 2:14; 4:16.** Cp. **2:9** (cp. Diod. S. 18, 11, 2 Μεσσήνιοι καὶ οἱ τὴν Ἀκτὴν κατοικοῦντες); **9:32, 35; 19:10, 17.** οἱ κατοικοῦντες τὴν γῆν *the inhabitants of the earth* **Rv 12:12 v.l.; 17:2.** κ. πόλεις (Hdt. 7, 164) Dg 5:2. οἰκίας πηλίνας 1 Cl 39:5 (Job 4:19). ὅλον τὸν κόσμον Hs 9, 17, 1. Of God ὁ κ. τὸν ναόν *the One who dwells in the temple* (cp. Jos., Bell. 5, 458f) **Mt 23:21;** cp. **Js 4:5 v.l.**—DELG s.v. οἶκος II C. M-M. TW.

κατοίκησις, εως, ἡ (s. prec. and three next entries; Thu. et al.; PLond 1708, 111; IMaronIsis 34; LXX; En; Jos., Ant. 6, 321, C. Ap. 2, 34; 35) ***living (quarters), dwelling*** κ. ἔχειν ἐν τοῖς μνήμασιν *live among the tombs* **Mk 5:3.** ἐν τῷ πύργῳ κ. ἔχειν Hv 3, 8, 8. ἐγένετο ἡ κ. αὐτῶν (cp. Gen 10:30) εἰς τὸν πύργον *they found a home in the tower* Hs 8, 7, 5; 8, 9, 2.

κατοικητήριον, ου, τό (s. two prec. and two next entries; the termination -τηριον freq. indicates a 'place where someth. happens' [B-D-F §109, 9]) (LXX; Cat. Cod. Astr. VIII/1 p. 189,

10; Christian ins CIA III 3508.—The adj. κατοικητήριος Soranus p. 37, 16) ***dwelling(-place)*** ἐγένετο κ. δαιμονίων *it has become a dwelling-place of evil spirits* i.e. they have taken possession of it **Rv 18:2** (cp. Jer 9:10 κ. δρακόντων). Of the Christians συνοικοδομεῖσθε εἰς κ. τοῦ θεοῦ *you are built up together for a dwelling-place of God* **Eph 2:22.** τὸ κ. τῆς καρδίας *the habitation of the heart* a temple of God B 6:15; cp. 16:7f.—TW.

κατοικία, ας, ἡ ***dwelling(-place), habitation*** (s. three prec. entries and next; Polyb. 2, 32, 4; Diod. S. 18, 7, 7; Strabo 5, 4, 8; Mitt-Wilck. II/2, 31 I, 23 [116 BC]; Sb 5620, 3; ins [s. New Docs 4, 142]; 1 Esdr 9:12, 37; 1 Macc 1:38; 2 Macc 3:39; Jos., Ant. 10, 223; 18, 37) **Ac 17:26.** εἰς τὸν πύργον *in the tower* Hs 8, 7, 3; 8, 8, 2f; 8, 9, 4; 8, 10, 1; 4; 9, 13, 5; cp. 8, 3, 4; 8, 6, 3; 6.—M-M.

κατοικίζω (s. four prec. entries) fut. κατοικιῶ; 1 aor. κατῴκισα. Pass.: fut. κατοικισθήσομαι; aor. κατῳκίσθην; pf. κατῴκισται (all LXX) ***cause to dwell, establish, settle*** (so Hdt. et al.; POxy 705, 24; LXX; EpArist; Jos., Ant. 1, 110 εἰς; 11, 19 ἐν) of the Spirit τὸ πνεῦμα ὃ κατῴκισεν ἐν ἡμῖν *the Spirit which (God) has caused to live in us* **Js 4:5.** τὸ πνεῦμα ὃ ὁ θεὸς κ. ἐν τῇ σαρκὶ ταύτῃ Hm 3:1. τὸ πνεῦμα κατῴκισεν ὁ θεὸς εἰς σάρκα *God caused the Spirit to dwell in flesh* s 5, 6, 5.—M-M. TW.

κατοικτίρω 1 aor. subj. 1 pl. κατοικτίρωμεν 4 Macc 8:20, ptc. κατοικτίρας 4 Macc 12:2, inf. κατοικτίραι or κατοικτεῖραι (s. οἰκτίρω; Soph., Hdt.+; 4 Macc) ***have pity*** τὶ *on someth.* (Alciphron 3, 39, 3) τὴν ἡλικίαν (cp. 4 Macc 8:20 τὸ τ. μητρὸς γῆρας) MPol 3, 1.—DELG s.v. οἶκτος.

κατοπτρίζω (the noun κάτοπτρον is the most common term in the pap for mirror [New Docs 4, 150]; act.='produce a reflection' in Plut., Mor. 894f; mid.='look at oneself in a mirror' in Diog. L. 2, 33; 3, 39; 7, 17; Artem. 2, 7; Athen. 15 p. 687c. In the same mng. ἐγκατοπτρίξασθαι εἰς τὸ ὕδωρ SIG 1168, 64 [III BC]. Pass. τὰ κατοπτριζόμενα='what is seen in a mirror' POxy 1609, 19) occurs once in our lit., in the middle, prob. w. the mng. **look at someth. as in a mirror, *contemplate someth.*** (cp. Philo, Leg. All. 3, 101. The Itala and Vulg. transl. 'speculantes'; Tert., Adv. Marc. 5, 11 'contemplantes'. Likew. the Peshitto, Bohairic, and Sahidic versions) τὴν δόξαν κυρίου *the glory of the Lord* **2 Cor 3:18** (cp. 1 Cor 13:12, s. Straub 24).—Rtzst., NGG 1916, 411, Hist. Mon. 242ff, Mysterienrel.[3] 357; PCorssen, ZNW 19, 1919/20, 2–10; ABrooke, JTS 24, 1923, 98; NHugedé, La Métaphore du Miroir dans 1 et 2 Cor '57; JLambrecht, Biblica 64, '83, 243–54.—Schlatter, Allo, WKnox, St. Paul and the Church of the Gentiles '39, 132; JDupont, RB 56, '49, 392–411; KPrümm, Diakonia Pneumatos I, '67, 166–202; WvanUnnik, NovT 6, '63, 163–69, et al. prefer the mng. *reflect.* See s.v. ἔσοπτρον.—DELG s.v. ὄπωπα B. M-M. TW.

κατορθόω fut. κατορθώσω; 1 aor. κατώρθωσα (LXX, TestSol); aor. mid. κατωρθωσάμην; aor. pass. 3 sg. κατωρθώθη (2 Ch 29:35; 35:10, 16) (s. ὀρθός and next entry; trag., Thu.+) **to cause someth. to be correct or to come out right, *set straight, complete, bring to a successful conclusion*** of God (Menand., Epitr. 556 S. [380 Kö.]; Alex. Aphr., Fat. 34, II 2 p. 206, 31; cp. Jos., Ant. 12, 312) τὰς μερίμνας *he will set your cares straight* Hv 4, 2, 5 (Polyaenus 8, 23, 30 of τοὺς πολέμους to bring them to a fortunate end). Mid. κ. τὰς ἐντολάς *carry out the commands* v 3, 5, 3. τὰς ὁδούς (cp. Ps 118:9) 2, 2, 6.—Pass. 1, 1, 8.—DELG s.v. ὀρθός. M-M s.v. κατόρθωμα. TW.

κατόρθωμα, ατος, τό (s. prec. entry and διόρθωμα; Aristot., Polyb. et al.; Philo; Jos., Bell. 1, 55; 7, 5) **the condition of coming out right, *success, prosperity, good order,*** pl. (as Chariton 7, 6, 5; X. Eph. 1, 1, 4; SIG 783, 15; PHermWess (=StudPal V) 125 II, 4 τ. μέγιστα κατορθώματα τῇ πατρίδι; Ath., R. 21 p. 73, 25) **Ac 24:2 v.l.** (for διόρθωμα).—DELG s.v. ὀρθός. M-M. TW.

κάτω adv. of place (s. three next entries; Hom.+).—**❶ to be relatively lower in positional orientation (location), *below*** συμφθαρέντα κάτω of seeds that *perish in the earth* AcPlCor 2:26. κ. ἐν τῇ αὐλῇ, *below in the courtyard* **Mk 14:66.** ἐπὶ τῆς γῆς κ. (Dt 4:39; Josh 2:11; 3 Km 8:23) **Ac 2:19.** κ. τοῦ βυθοῦ *at the bottom of the sea* B 10:5. Subst. τὰ κάτω (opp. τὰ ἄνω) *this world* (in contrast to 'that' world as Maximus Tyr. 11, 10c) **J 8:23** (for the opp. τὰ ἄνω . . . τὰ κάτω cp. Ael. Aristid. 36, 32 K.=48 p. 449 D.; Herm. Wr. 11, 5; 14, 5; SIG 610, 52f [190 BC]). For **Mt 2:16** D s. 2.

❷ extension toward a point that is the opposite of up (direction), *downwards, down* (Herodian 3, 11, 3; En 14:25; TestSol 4:13 D; TestAbr B 12 p. 116, 13 [Stone p. 80]; ApcEsdr; Jos., Ant. 19, 349; Tat. 16, 1 γνώμας . . . κ. νενευκυίας) βάλλειν κάτω **J 12:31 v.l.;** κεκυφὼς κ. AcPl Ha 4, 12; βάλλειν σεαυτὸν κ. *throw yourself down* **Mt 4:6; Lk 4:9.** κ. κύπτειν **J 8:6, 8 v.l.;** πίπτειν κ. **Ac 20:9;** ἀπενεχθῆναι κ. *be brought down* Hs 9, 4, 7. ἔτι κ. χώρει *go down farther* **Mt 20:28** D=Agr 22. ἀπ' ἄνωθεν ἕως κ. *from top to bottom* (cp. Aëtius 86, 5 ἄνωθεν κάτω) **Mt 27:51** (ἐπάνωθεν ἕως κ. v.l.); **Mk 15:38** (ἕως κ. as Ezk 1:27; 8:2). ἐπάνωθεν ἕως κ. GJs 24:3. Of time ἀπὸ διετίας καὶ κάτω **Mt 2:16** D; GJs 22:1 (s. deStrycker 433).—DELG s.v. κάτα, κατά. M-M. TW.

κατώτατος, η, ον (s. prec. and two next entries; Hdt. [n. pl. as adv.], X. et al.; LXX adv. κατωτάτω Tob 4:19 S; 13:2 S; Philo, Spec. Leg. 1, 94; Just., D. 40, 3) superl. of κάτω ***deepest*** ἐκ τοῦ κατωτάτου [ʻΑ]δου *from the depths of the nether world* AcPlCor 2:30.—M-M.

κατώτερος, α, ον comp. of κάτω (s. two prec. entries and next entry; Hippocr. et al.; Vett. Val. 34, 21; IG XIV, 2476; Gen 35:8; TestLevi 3:1; ApcEsdr 4:5 p. 28, 4 Tdf. al.; Tat.) ***lower*** κατέβη εἰς τὰ κατώτερα μέρη τῆς γῆς *he went down into the lower regions of the earth* **Eph 4:9** (on the expr. cp. Galen VIII 894 K. μέρη τῆς καρδίας κατωτέρω; Ps 138:15 ἐν τοῖς κατωτάτοις τῆς γῆς; Tob 13:2 S). Some think the pass. refers to Jesus' burial. Many (e.g. Tert., Chrysostom, Bengel; Clemen[2] 90; JRobinson, Eph.) take τὰ κατ. μέρη τ. γῆς to be Hades (cp. Ael. Aristid. 26, 103 K.=14 p. 367 D. of the Titans: εἰς τ. κατωτάτους μυχοὺς τῆς γῆς ἀπελθεῖν; ApcEsdr 4:5). Others hold that Jesus' coming on earth, the incarnation, is meant (s. lit. cited by MBarth, Eph [AB] '74, 434 n. 49).—ALindroth, Descendit ad inferna: SvTK 8, '32, 121–40. B-D-F §167. S. on πνεῦμα 2 and 4c.—M-M. TW.

κατωτέρω adv. of κατώτερος (s. three prec. entries; Aristoph. et al.; Jos., Bell. 4, 505, Ant. 8, 154; Just., D. 58, 8 [for κατώτερος Gen 35:8]; Ath. 25, 2) ***lower, below*** w. numbers ἀπὸ διετοῦς καὶ κατωτέρω *two years old and under* **Mt 2:16** (κάτω D; s. the entry; cp. 1 Ch 27:23 ἀπὸ εἰκοσαετοῦς καὶ κάτω.—B-D-F §62; Rob. 297f).—TW.

Καῦδα *Cauda (Clauda),* a small island 9 km. by 5 km. south of Crete (mod. Gaudos; Pliny, NH 4, 12 [61] and Pomponius Mela 2, 7: Gaudus) **Ac 27:16.** The mss. and edd.vary: also Κλαῦδα, -αν, -ην (Ptolemy 3, 15, 8: Κλαῦδος); Γαῦδην. The reason for this is prob. not a confusion betw. two different islands (W-S. §5, 31, p. 68 note 72); rather, the name of the same island is variously written (RHarris, ET 21, 1910, 17ff; Haenchen ad loc.; Warnecke, Romfahrt 35, 1; Pauly-W. VII 861; IX 57; BHHW II 961).

καῦμα, ατος, τό (s. καίω and six next entries; Hom.+; Kaibel 649, 5; PLond III, 1166, 6 p. 104 [42 AD]; PSI 184, 6; LXX; JosAs 3:3 codd. DFH [s. καύσων]; ParJer; ApcMos 24; Jos., Bell. 3, 312, Ant. 18, 192; Just.) ***burning, heat*** **Rv 7:16** (Crinagoras no. 14, 4 ἡελίου καῦμα τὸ θερμότατον). καυματίζεσθαι κ. μέγα *be burned with a scorching heat* **16:9.**—DELG s.v. καίω 1. M-M. TW.

καυματίζω (s. prec. and next entry) 1 aor. ἐκαυμάτισα, pass. ἐκαυματίσθην (Epict. 1, 6, 26; 3, 22, 52; M. Ant. 7, 64, 3; of fever Plut., Mor. 100d; 691e) ***burn up*** *someone* τινὰ ἐν πυρί **Rv 16:8.** Pass. *be burned, be scorched* of plants withering in the heat **Mt 13:6; Mk 4:6.** κ. καῦμα μέγα **Rv 16:9** (s. καῦμα).—DELG s.v. καίω 1. TW.

καυματόω (s. καῦμα; only in Eustathius Macrembolita 8, 4 p. 18 ἀνδρὶ διψῶντι καὶ καυματουμένῳ) pass. ***be scorched by the heat*** **Mt 13:6 v.l.**

καῦσις, εως, ἡ (s. καίω; Hdt.+; IMagnMai 179, 11; Mitt-Wilck. I/2, 70, 10 [57/56 BC]; PLond III, 1166, 14 p. 105 [42 AD]; 1177, 74; LXX; En 102:1; TestSol 18:29 P; JosAs 17:3; GrBar 8:6; Philo, Decal. 150) ***burning*** ἧς τὸ τέλος εἰς καῦσιν *its* (the land's) *end is to be burned over* **Hb 6:8.**—τῇ καύσει τῶν εἰδωλομανῶν *with the burning of the idol-crazed* (probable restoration by JBartlet) ApcPt Bodl. verso 5–8 p. 369 J. S. εἰδωλομανής.—DELG s.v. καίω 2. M-M. TW.

καυσόω ('to suffer from καῦσος [burning heat]'; Ptolem., Apotelesm. 1, 4, 4 Boll-B.; PHolm 25, 27) pass. ***be consumed by heat, burn up*** (Diosc. 2, 134 W.; Antyllus in Oribas. 9, 13, 1; Galen, CMG V 9, 1 p. 264, 13; Philumen. p. 26, 21 of fever) στοιχεῖα καυσούμενα λυθήσεται *the elements will be destroyed by burning* **2 Pt 3:10;** cp. vs. **12.**—On the destruction of the world by fire s. Rtzst., Weltuntergangsvorstellungen 1924; s. also FOlivier, 2 Pt 3:10: Religio 11, '35, 481–89; Hengel, Judaism II 128 n. 552.—DELG s.v. καίω 4. TW.

καυστηριάζω (καυτήρ 'burner' Pind., P. 1, 95, also καυστήρ) pf. pass. ptc. κεκαυστηριασμένος (Strabo 5, 1, 9 ed. GKramer [1844] v.l.; Leontius 40 p. 79, 9; perh. BGU 952, 4.—καυτηριάζω in Hippiatr. 1, 28 vol. I p. 12, 4) 'brand with a red-hot iron' (Strabo), ***sear*** fig., pass. κεκαυστηριασμένων τὴν ἰδίαν συνείδησιν *seared in their own consciences* **1 Ti 4:2** (v.l. κεκαυτηριασμένων; schol. on Lucian 137, 11 Rabe is dependent on this; the imagery suggests crime published w. a branding mark on the perpetrator: Straub 20f).—DELG s.v. καίω 5. M-M. TW.

καύσων, ωνος, ὁ (s. καίω and cp. καῦμα) ***heat, burning (sun)*** (so Diphilus [c. 300 BC] in Athen. 3, 2, 73a; Leo 9, 5; Syntipas collection of Aesop's fables 54 p. 547 P.; Cyrill. Scyth. p. 94, 23 and 25; 109, 21; Gen 31:40 A; Sir 18:16; TestGad 1:4; JosAs 3:3 codd. AB [s. καῦμα]) **Mt 20:12.** κ. ἔσται *it will be a hot day* **Lk 12:55.** ἀνέτειλεν ὁ ἥλιος σὺν τῷ κ. *the sun came up with its scorching heat* **Js 1:11** (since the sun brings w. it burning heat, but not the scorching east wind, which is usu. meant by καύσων in the LXX, it is not likely that a hot wind is meant in the Js passage. On the combination of κ. with ἥλιος cp. Is 49:10).—DELG s.v. καίω 4. M-M. TW.

καυτηριάζω **1 Ti 4:2 v.l.,** s. καυστηριάζω.—DELG s.v. καίω 5.

καυχάομαι (s. two next entries; Pind., Hdt.+) mid. dep.; 2 sing. καυχᾶσαι **Ro 2:17, 23; 1 Cor 4:7** (s. Mayser 328; JWackernagel, TLZ 33, 1908, 639; Thackeray 218; Mlt-H. 198); fut. καυχήσομαι; 1 aor. ἐκαυχησάμην; pf. κεκαύχημαι. In our lit. restricted to Paul, except for two pass. each in Js and Ign., and one in 1 Cl (a quot. fr. the OT).

❶ to take pride in someth., ***boast, glory, pride oneself, brag,*** intr. (Sappho, fgm. 26, 10 D.[2]) ἔν τινι *in* or *about a person* or *thing* (schol. on Apollon. Rhod. 3, 976 οἱ καυχώμενοι ἐν ἑτέρων διαβολαῖς; LXX; TestJud 13:2; ἐν τοῖς θεοῖς Theoph. Ant. 1, 1 [p. 58, 6].—B-D-F §196; s. Rob. 532) ἐν θεῷ **Ro 2:17.** ἐν τῷ θεῷ **5:11.** ἐν κυρίῳ **1 Cor 1:31b; 2 Cor 10:17b;** 1 Cl 13:1 (cp. on the three Jer 9:23). ἐν Χριστῷ Ἰησοῦ **Phil 3:3.** ἐν ἀνθρώποις **1 Cor 3:21.**—ἐν νόμῳ (cp. Sir 39:8) **Ro 2:23;** in afflictions **5:3;** in the work of others **2 Cor 10:15;** in weaknesses **12:9;** in high position **Js 1:9;** in wisdom, etc. 1 Cl 13:1 (Jer 9:22f). ἐν τῇ ὑμετέρᾳ σαρκί **Gal 6:13.** ἐν τῷ σταυρῷ vs. **14.** ἐν τῷ προσώπῳ κ., opp. ἐν τῇ καρδίᾳ *pride oneself on externals . . . on the heart* **2 Cor 5:12.** ἐν ᾧ καυχῶνται **11:12.** On **2 Th 1:4 v.l.** see ἐγκαυχάομαι.—The ἐν is to be taken somewhat differently **Js 4:16** (s. ἀλαζονεία).—εἴς τι *boast with regard to someth.* **2 Cor 10:16.** Differently εἰς τὰ ἄμετρα κ. *boast beyond limit* (s. ἄμετρος) vss. **13, 15.**—ἐπί τινι *based on someth., in someth.* (Cratinus Com. [V BC] 95; Diod. S. 15, 6, 2 ἐπὶ τοῖς ποιήμασιν; 16, 70, 2; iambic poet in Ps.-Callisth. 2, 20, 11 ἐπὶ τέκνοισι; SIG 1268, 23 ἐπὶ ῥώμῃ; Ps 48:7) **Ro 5:2** (JBover, Biblica 22, '41, 41–45). ὑπέρ τινος *on behalf of someone* **2 Cor 12:5ab.** κατά τι *in accordance with someth.* **2 Cor 11:18a.**—ἐνώπιον τ. θεοῦ *before God* **1 Cor 1:29.**—W. ὅτι foll. (Strabo 13, 1, 27) IPhld 6:3. (W. inf. TestJob 41:3; Just., D. 101, 1.)—Abs. (TestReub 3:5) **1 Cor 1:31a; 4:7; 2 Cor 10:17a; 11:18b, 30a; 12:1, 6, 11 v.l.; Eph 2:9;** IPol 5:2.—**1 Cor 13:3,** a variety of witnesses have καυχήσωμαι (read by N. and defended e.g. by Harnack, SBBerlAk 1911, 139ff; Goodsp., Probs. 162–65; KClark, Studia Paulina [deZwaan Festschr.] '53, 61f) instead of the v.l. καυθήσομαι, which is preferred by others (e.g., EPreuschen, ZNW 16, 1915, 127ff; JKElliott, ZNW 62, '71, 297f; et al.).—S. καίω 2.

❷ to make a boast about someth., ***boast about, mention in order to boast of, be proud of,*** trans. τὶ *someth.* (Philemon Com. [IV–III BC], fgm. 141 p. 521; Diod. S. 20, 63, 4) τὰ τῆς ἀσθενείας μου *boast about my weaknesses* **2 Cor 11:30b** (cp. Pr 27:1 κ. τὰ εἰς αὔριον).τὶ περί τινος **10:8.** τί τινι ὑπέρ τινος *say someth. boastingly* (or *in pride*) *to someone concerning someone* **7:14; 9:2** (here a ὅτι-clause defines τὶ more closely). μικρόν τι **11:16.**—For Gr-Rom. cultural background on Paul's theme of boasting in 2 Cor s. Plut., Mor. 539–547 'On Inoffensive Self-Praise'; FDanker, Augsburg Comm. on the NT: II Cor '89, esp. 147–214; idem, Paul's Debt to Demosthenes' 'De Corona', in Persuasive Artistry [GKennedy Festschr.], ed. DWatson, '91, 262–80; JLambrecht, Dangerous Boasting, Paul's Self-Commendation in 2 Cor 10–13, in RBieringer, ed., The Corinthian Correspondence '96, 325–46.—JBosch, 'Gloriarse' según San Pablo, Sentido y teologia de καυχάομαι, '70. BDowdy, The Meaning of καυχᾶσθαι in the NT, diss. Vanderbilt '55.—B. 1281. DELG. M-M. EDNT. TW. Spicq.

καύχημα, ατος, τό (s. prec. and next entry; Pind., I. 5, 51 [65]; LXX; TestJob; Tat. 2, 1). On Gr-Rom. perspectives s. καυχάομαι 2.

❶ **act of taking pride in someth. or that which constitutes a source of pride,** ***boast*** (Ael. Aristid. 32, 5 K.=12 p. 135 D.), then also used when the boast is not made in words, to denote *the thing of which one is proud,* in this sense *pride* (Dt 33:29; Pr 17:6) κ. ἔχει *he has someth. to boast about* **Ro 4:2.** οὐκ ἔστιν μοι κ. *I have no right to boast* **1 Cor 9:16.** εἰς ἑαυτὸν τὸ κ. ἔχειν *have a reason for boasting on one's own account* **Gal 6:4** (PHaeuser, BZ 12, 1914, 45–56). With gen. (Ps.-Callisth. 2, 22, 7 and 11 Περσῶν κ.) τὸ κ. μου οὐδεὶς κενώσει **1 Cor 9:15.** κ. τινος εἶναι *be someone's pride* **2 Cor 1:14.** εἰς κ. ἐμοὶ εἰς ἡμέραν Χριστοῦ *as my pride* (and joy) *in the day of Christ* **Phil 2:16.** τὸ κ. ἡμῶν *what we are proud of* 1 Cl 34:5. τὸ κ. ὑμῶν *what you can be proud of* **Phil 1:26.** οὐ καλὸν τὸ κ. ὑμῶν *what you are* (so) *proud of* **1 Cor 5:6.** τὸ κ. τῆς ἐλπίδος *that for which we are proud to hope* (cp. Ro 5:2) **Hb 3:6.**

❷ **expression of pride,** ***boast, what is said in boasting*** ἵνα μὴ τὸ κ. ἡμῶν τὸ ὑπὲρ ὑμῶν κενωθῇ *so that what we say in praise of you may not prove to be empty words* **2 Cor 9:3.**—In effect=*boasting* (cp. Pind., I. 5, 51 καύχημα=act. 'boasting') ἀφορμὴν διδόναι τινὶ καυχήματος ὑπέρ τινος *give someone an occasion to be proud of someone* **5:12.**—PGenths, D. Begriff des καύχημα b. Pls: NKZ 38, 1927, 501–21.—DELG s.v. καυχάομαι. TW. Spicq.

καύχησις, εως, ἡ (Epicurus fgm. 93; Philod., περὶ κακιῶν p. 27 J.; Philo, Congr. Erud. Gr. 107; LXX; Just., D. 141, 3). On Gr-Rom. perspectives s. καυχάομαι 2.

❶ **act of taking pride in someth.,** ***boasting*** (Jer 12:13) **Ro 3:27; 2 Cor 9:4 v.l.; 11:10, 17; Js 4:16;** IEph 18:1. In a list of vices Hm 8:3. στέφανος καυχήσεως *crown of pride,* i.e. to be proud of (Ezk 16:12; Pr 16:31) **1 Th 2:19.** κ. ὑπέρ τινος *pride that one has in someone* **2 Cor 7:4; 8:24.** ἡ καύχησις ἡμῶν ἡ ἐπὶ Τίτου *our boasting in the presence of Titus* **7:14.** ἐν κ. ἀπολέσθαι *be lost because of bragging* ITr 4:1. ἔχω τὴν κ. ἐν Χριστῷ Ἰησοῦ τὰ πρὸς τὸν θεόν *I may boast in Christ of my relation to God* **Ro 15:17;** νὴ τὴν ὑμετέραν κ. *as surely as I may boast of you* **1 Cor 15:31.**

❷ **that which constitutes a source of pride,** ***object of boasting, reason for boasting*** **2 Cor 1:12.**—RAsting, Kauchesis: NorTT 26, 1925, 129–203; AFridrichsen, SymbOsl 7, 1928, 25–29; 8, 1929, 78–82.—DELG s.v. καυχάομαι. TW. Spicq. Sv.

Καφαρναούμ, ἡ indecl. (כְּפַר נַחוּם; Καφαρν. also P[45] **Lk 10:15** and in the two gosp. fgm. [V AD] Ox 847 [**J 2:12**]; 1596 [**J 6:17**]. In the later tradition the form Καπερναούμ predominates; on the spelling s. B-D-F §39, 2; Rob. 184; 219; FBurkitt, The Syriac Forms of NT Proper Names 1912, 27f, JTS 34, '33, 388–90; F-MAbel, Le nom de C.: JPOS 8, 1928, 24–34) ***Capernaum*** (Ptolem. 5, 16, 4 Καπαρναούμ; cp. Jos., Bell. 3, 519 Καφαρναούμ, Vi. 403 εἰς κώμην Κεφαρνωκόν. Not in OT.), a city on Lake Gennesaret, whose location is still uncertain. Acc. to some (so the Onomastica), its ruins are to be found at Tell Ḥûm (or Telḥûm); this view has the best support at present. Acc. to others the site was at Khan Minyeh (so perh. Jos., Bell. 3, 519). **Mt 4:13; 8:5; 11:23; 17:24; Mk 1:21; 2:1; 9:33; Lk 4:23, 31; 7:1; 10:15; J 2:12; 4:46; 6:17, 24, 59;** GEb 34, 59.—HGuthe, RE X 27ff (lit.); BMeistermann, C. et Bethsaïde 1921; Dalman, Orte[3] 149ff [Eng. tr. 133–59]; HBörge, Kapernaum '40; BHjerl-Hansen, Kapernaum '41; JKennard, Jr., Was C. the Home of Jesus?: JBL 65, '46, 131–41; EBishop, Jesus and C.: CBQ 15, '53, 427–37; CKopp, The Holy Places of the Gospels, tr. RWalls, '63, 171–79; DNélman, Capernaum '67; BHHW II 931; Kl. Pauly III, 112; JLaughlin, BAR 19, '93, 55–61, 90; OEANE I 416–20. Further lit. s.v. συναγωγή 2a.

κε´ numeral ***twenty-five*** Hs 9, 4, 3; 9, 5, 4; 9, 15, 4.

Κεγχρεαί, ῶν, αἱ (Thu. [Κεγχρειαί], X.+; edd. also Κενχρ-) ***Cenchreae,*** the seaport of Corinth (Philo, In Flacc. 155: K., τὸ Κορίνθιον ἐπίνειον) on the eastern side of the isthmus (Strabo 8, 6, 22) **Ac 18:18; Ro 16:1; subscr.** The port on the western side was Lechaeum (Diod. S. 11, 16, 3 ἀπὸ Λεχαίου μέχρι Κεγχρεῶν; 15, 68, 3).—WMichaelis, ZNW 25, 1926, 144–54; New Docs 3, 60 (coins); 4, 139f; BHHW II 939; Kl. Pauly III, 182.

κέδρος, ου, ἡ (Hom. et al.; LXX; TestSim 6:2; JosAs ch. 16 cod. A [p. 64, 17 Bat.]; Philo, Aet. M. 64; Jos., Ant. 8, 44) ***cedar tree*** **J 18:1 v.l.** (s. the next entry); 1 Cl 14:5 (Ps 36:35).—DELG. M-M.

Κεδρών, ὁ (also Κέδρων, קִדְרוֹן) indecl. (Jos., Bell. 5, 70; 252 Κεδρών, ῶνος, Ant. 8, 17 τὸν χειμάρρουν Κεδρῶνα) ***Kidron*** ὁ χειμάρρους τοῦ K. (the Rahlfs LXX does not have the article before K. anywhere; this is in accord w. the good text tradition: 2 Km 15:23; 3 Km 2:37; 15:13; 4 Km 23:6, 12) *the Kidron valley,* a wadi or watercourse (dry except in the rainy season), adjoining Jerusalem on the east and emptying into the Dead Sea **J 18:1** (vv.ll. τοῦ κέδρου, τῶν κεδρῶν, s. κέδρος).—GDalman, Jerusalem u. s. Gelände 1930, 182ff; BHHW II 946f; Kl. Pauly III 174. M-M. s.v. κέδρος.

κεῖμαι impf. 3 sg. ἔκειτο; fut. 3 pl. κείσονται (Tat. 31, 1) (Hom.+)

❶ **to be in a recumbent position,** ***lie, recline;*** can serve as passive of τίθημι, of pers.: w. indication of place ἔν τινι *in someth.,* of a child ἐν φάτνῃ **Lk 2:12, 16;** of a dead person (Hom. et al.; also in Palest. [PhilolWoch 49, 1929, 247] and Alexandrian [Sb 1397] grave ins; PRyl 114, 17 τοῦ σώματος κειμένου) w. οὗ or ὅπου (ApcMos 33; PGM 4, 2038) **Mt 28:6; Lk 23:53; J 20:12.**

❷ **to be in a place so as to be on someth.,** ***lie,*** of things ἐπί τι *on someth.* **2 Cor 3:15.** Also ἐπάνω τινός (TestAbr A 12 p. 91, 1 [Stone p. 30] ἐπάνω τῆς πραπέζης) **Mt 5:14** (κ. of location of a place since Hdt., Thu.; SIG 685, 46 [139 BC]; Tob 5:6 S ἐν τῷ ὄρει; Jos., Ant. 9, 7).—Abs. (as Hom. et al.; Josh 4:6) of a throne, a bench *stand* (Hdt. 1, 181, 5 κλίνη κ.; Arrian, Anab. 6, 29, 6 τράπεζα κ.; Chariton 5, 4, 5; Polyaenus 4, 3, 24 and Paus. 2, 31, 3 θρόνος κ.) **Rv 4:2;** Hv 3, 1, 4. Of cloths *lie (there)* **Lk 24:12 v.l.; J 20:5, 6, 7.—21:9.** Of vessels *stand (there)*(X., Oec. 8, 19; Paus. 9, 31, 3 τρίποδες; cp. 1 Esdr 6:25; Jer 24:1) **2:6; 19:29.** σκάφην GJs 18:2 (codd.). Of goods *be laid* up, *be stored* up **Lk 12:19** (Hom. et al.; cp. PSI 365, 20 [251/250 BC] ὁ σῖτος ἐπὶ τῆς ἅλω κείμενος).—Of a foundation *be laid* **1 Cor 3:11.** ἡ πόλις τετράγωνος κεῖται *is laid out as a square* **Rv 21:16.** κ. πρός τι *be laid at someth.* the ax at the roots (ready for felling of the tree) **Mt 3:10; Lk 3:9.** κ. πρός w. acc. also means *be very close to someone* in ὁ ἄγγελος τ. πνεύματος τοῦ προφητικοῦ ὁ κείμενος πρὸς αὐτόν (i.e. τ. ἄνθρωπον) Hm 11:9 (Ox 5 recto, 3 reads: ἐπ᾽ αὐτῷ).

❸ In a variety of transferred senses involving esp. abstractions **to exist, have place, or be there (for someth.)**—ⓐ ***be appointed, set, destined*** εἴς τι *for someth.* εἰς πτῶσιν καὶ ἀνάστασιν *for the fall and rising* **Lk 2:34.** εἰς ἀπολογίαν τοῦ εὐαγγελίου **Phil 1:16.** εἰς τοῦτο **1 Th 3:3.**—κ. ἐπί τινος *be put in charge of someth.* of the angel of punishment ἐπὶ τῆς τιμωρίας *in charge of the punishment* Hs 6, 3, 2.

ⓑ ***be given, exist, be valid*** of legal matters (legal t.t. since Eur.; Thu. et al.; s. also BGU 1002, 14 [55 BC] πᾶσαι αἱ κατ᾽ αὐτῶν κείμεναι συγγραφαί; PTebt 334, 7 of a marriage contract κατὰ τ. κειμένην ἡμῖν συγγραφήν; 2 Macc 4:11; κειμένου νόμου

Just., D. 123, 1) τινί *for someone* of law (Menand., PDidot I, 14 p. 329 S. ἔστ' ἀνδρὶ κ. γυναικὶ κείμενος νόμος; Dio Chrys. 64 [14], 13; OGI 111, 30 [II BC] ὁ κείμενος νόμος; pap; EpArist 15; Philo, Det. Pot. Ins. 18 νόμος κεῖται; Jos., Ant. 4, 182 ὑμῖν κεῖται=are there for you) **1 Ti 1:9.** Of powers κ. ἐπί τινι *exist for someth., relate* or *apply to someth.* Hm 6, 1, 1.

ⓒ ***occur, appear, be found*** (Hellanicus [V BC] 4 fgm. 93 Jac. αὕτη [i.e. Πιτάνη] παρ' Ἀλκαίῳ κεῖται=is found in Alcaeus) ἐν παραβολαῖς B 17:2. διὰ τί ὁ υἱὸς τοῦ θεοῦ εἰς δούλου τρόπον κεῖται ἐν τῇ παραβολῇ; *why does the Son of God appear in the parable as a slave?* Hs 5, 5, 5; cp. 5, 6, 1.

ⓓ ***find oneself, be,*** in a certain state or condition (Hdt. 8, 102 al.; Menand., fgm. 576, 2 Kö. τὴν ἐν ἑτέρῳ κειμένην ἁμαρτίαν; PTebt 27 I, 7 [113 BC] ἐν περιστάσει κειμένων; 2 Macc 3:11; 4:31, 34; 3 Macc 5:26) ὁ κόσμος ἐν τῷ πονηρῷ κ. *the world lies in (the power of) the evil one* **1J 5:19** (also probable is the mng. κ. ἔν τινι *be dependent on someone* [Soph., Oed. R. 247f; Polyb. 6, 15, 6]).—B. 834. DELG. M-M. TW.

κειμήλιον, ου, τό (Hom. et al.; ApcEsdr 1:20 p. 25, 14 Tdf.; Philo, Joseph.) ***store, treasure, investment*** **1 Ti 6:19** cj.—DELG s.v. κεῖμαι.

κειρία, ας, ἡ (Aristoph.; Plut., Alcib. 16, 1: Alc. has some planking cut away on his ship's deck so that he can sleep in suspension supported by webbing rather than on hard planks; Pr 7:16 sim. refers to material for a comfortable bed; cp. κιρία PEdgar 69 [=Sb 6775], 9; PSI 341, 7; 387, 4. On the spelling B-D-F §24; s. Mlt-H. 71f) in ref. to the preparation of bodies for burial ***binding material*** (schol. on Aristoph., Av. 816 κειρία· εἶδος ζώνης ἐκ σχοινίων, παρεοικὸς ἱμάντι, ᾗ δεσμοῦσι τὰς κλίνας = 'κειρία: a kind of belt made of cords, someth. like the strapping material used to web couches') **J 11:44.**—DELG. M-M.

κείρω fut. 2 sg. κερεῖς Pr 27:25; 1 aor. ἔκειρα; aor. mid. ἐκειράμην. Pass.: 2 aor. inf. καρῆναι (TestJob 9:3); pf. ptc. κεκαρμένος LXX (Hom. et al.; ins, pap, LXX; Jos., Bell. 6, 5; SibOr 3, 359) ***shear*** a sheep (Artem. 4, 51 πρόβατον; Babrius 51, 3; Jos., Ant. 6, 297 after 1 Km 25:2; TestJud 12:1) ὁ κείρας (v.l. ὁ κείρων [Aesop, Fab. 212 P.=382 H.]) **Ac 8:32;** 1 Cl 16:7; B 5:2 (all three after Is 53:7, where both readings are found) *the shearer.* Mid. *cut one's hair* or *have one's hair cut* (B-D-F §317; Rob. 809.—X., Hell. 1, 7, 8.) τὴν κεφαλήν *have one's hair cut* (as the result of a vow; s. εὐχή 2) **Ac 18:18.** Abs. (Quint. Smyrn. 3, 686 and 688) **1 Cor 11:6ab.**—DELG. M-M.

κέκμηκα s. κάμνω.

κέλευσις, εως, ἡ (s. κελεύω; OGI 455, 3 [I BC]; Plut., Mor. 32c; freq. ins and pap fr. [III AD]; also TestAbr A 16 p. 96, 23 [Stone p. 40]; Jos, Ant. 17, 65; Just., D. 42, 3; 102, 2) ***directive*** or ***order.*** Of an imperial decree (s. δόγμα 1b) GJs 17:1.—DELG s.v. κελεύω. TW.

κέλευσμα, ατος, τό (s. κελεύω; a summons to carry out a procedure, e.g. battle engagement, rowing, hunting: Aeschyl., Hdt. et al.; Sb 4279, 3 [I AD]; Pr 30:27; TestSol 6:6 P; GrBar ins [κελεύματι]; Philo, Abr. 116; Jos., Ant. 17, 140; 199; on the spelling s. B-D-F §70, 3) ***signal, (cry of) command*** (Hdt. 4, 141 of a signal for engagement in battle) ὁ κύριος ἐν κ. καταβήσεται *the Lord will come down with a cry of command = when the command is given* **1 Th 4:16** (cp. on the κέλευσμα of God, Galen XIX 179 K. τοῦ δημιουργοῦ; Philo, Praem. 117 and Descensus Mariae in Rtzst., Poim. 5, 3).—DELG s.v. κελεύω. TW.

κελεύω (Hom.+) impf. ἐκέλευον; fut. κελεύσω (TestAbr B); 1 aor. ἐκέλευσα; plpf. 3 sg. ἐκεκελεύκει (Just., D. 103, 3). Pass.: aor. ἐκελεύσθην (TestAbr A, Just.); ptc. pl. κελευσθέντες 4 Macc 9:11; pf. pass. 1 pl. κεκελεύσμεθα (Just., D. 48, 4) **to give a command, ordinarily of an official nature, *command, order, urge*** foll. by the aor. inf. (B-D-F §338, 2; Rob. 857), which indicates the action to be carried out; the pers. who receives the order is in the acc. (SibOr 3, 298; w. acc. and ἵνα TestAbr B 11 p. 116, 6 [Stone p. 80]) not in Mk, J, Paul, B, IPol. κέλευσόν με ἐλθεῖν πρός σε *command me to come to you* **Mt 14:28,** cp. vs. **19; Ac 4:15; 22:30; 23:10; 24:8 v.l.;** 1 Cl 43:2. This constr. can also be understood simply as acc. w. inf. as such, as plainly **Ac 8:38;** MPol 16:1.—The constr. in which κ. is followed by the acc. and the pass. inf., indicating that something is to happen to someone or something without giving the person who is to carry out the command, is more in accord w. Lat. usage than w. older Gk. (TestJob 5:3 ἀσφαλισθῆναι τὰς θύρας; s. B-D-F §5, 3b; 392, 4; Rob. 111) ἐκέλευσεν αὐτὸν ὁ κύριος πραθῆναι **Mt 18:25.** Cp. **27:64; Lk 18:40; Ac 12:19; 25:6, 17;** so esp. Hs 9, 8, 5 (λίθους) ἐκέλευσεν εἰς τὴν οἰκοδομὴν τεθῆναι al.; ἐκέλευσεν αὐτῷ (against Paul) ἀφεθῆναι λέοντα AcPl Ha 4, 19; λυθῆναι τοὺς δεσμίους 11, 9.—W. inf. alone, so that everything else must be supplied fr. context **Mt 8:18; 14:9; 27:58; Ac 5:34; 21:33;** MPol 7:2.—The pres. inf. occurs more rarely (B-D-F §338, 2): w. acc. (X., An. 2, 1, 8; Chariton 7, 6, 2; TestJob 9:6; TestJos 13:9) **Ac 21:34; 22:24; 23:3, 35; 25:21; 27:43;** 1 Cl 33:3; 40:1f; Hs 8, 1, 6f; 9, 3, 1 and 3f. Without acc. (X., Cyr. 2, 2, 2; Appian, Liby. 55 §241; Herodian 2, 3, 3) **Ac 16:22;** Dg 7:2.—Abs. κελεύσαντος τοῦ Φήστου *at Festus' command* **Ac 25:23** (cp. Michel 594, 53 [279 BC] ἐπιμελητῶν κελευόντων; Jos., Ant. 11, 78 Δαρείου κελεύσαντος). θελήματι τοῦ κελεύοντος λόγου Dg 11:8.—W. dat. of pers. and inf. (Longus 3, 8, 2; Polyaenus 3, 10, 11; Tob 8:18 BA; ApcMos 27:29 [aor.].—Thu. 1, 44, 1; Diod. S. 19, 17, 3; Herm. Wr. 1, 29; 2 Macc 5:12; EpArist 184; TestJob 9:8; Jos., Ant. 20, 132 [pres.]; w. dat. and ἵνα TestJob 39:8) **Mt 15:35 v.l.** for παραγγείλας (κ. is also toned down to *urgently request, invite:* Nicol. Dam.: 90 fgm. 4 p. 332, 9ff Jac.; Epict., fgm. 17 in an invitation; Arrian, Anab. 2, 6, 1 his friends do this to Alex. the Great; 3, 9, 3; 7, 2, 1; 7, 8, 3) AcPl Ha 4, 10.—Pass. in personal construction (TestAbr B 7 p. 112, 12 [Stone p. 72]) καθὼς ἐκελεύσθησαν Hs 9, 4, 1.—B. 1337. DELG. M-M. TW. Sv.

κενεμβατεύω a form supplied purely by conjecture (W-H. and FHitzig; s. N.[25]; cp. TAbbott [ICC] 269f) for ἐμβατεύω (q.v.) **Col 2:18 *misstep.*** The closely related κενεμβατέω 'step on emptiness, make a misstep' in rope-walking is found Plut., Lucian et al. Mlt-H. 273f; B-D-F §154.—Cp. DELG s.v. κενός.

κενοδοξέω to hold a vain or useless opinion, *vainly imagine* (s. next entry; Polyb. 12, 26c, 4; Dio Chrys. 21 [38], 29; 4 Macc 5:10; 8:24 κενοδοξήσωμεν; Philo, Mut. Nom. 226; Tat. 12, 1) MPol 10:1.

κενοδοξία, ας, ἡ (s. next entry)—**❶ a vain or exaggerated self-evaluation, *vanity, conceit, excessive ambition*** (Polyb. 3, 81, 9; Plut., Mor. 57d; Lucian, Dial. Mort. 20, 4; Vett. Val. 358, 31; 4 Macc 2:15; 8:19; AscIs 3, 26 and 28; Philo, De Jos. 36; Tat. 32, 1) κατὰ κενοδοξίαν *from empty conceit* **Phil 2:3;** IPhld 1:1. In a catalogue of vices (as Cebes 24, 2) 1 Cl 35:5; Hm 8:5.

❷ vain or worthless opinion, *illusion, delusion, error* (since Epicurus p. 78, 7 Us.; Wsd 14:14; Philo, Mut. Nom. 96, Leg. ad Gai. 114) ἐμπίπτειν εἰς τὰ ἄγκιστρα τῆς κ. *be caught on the fishhooks of error* IMg 11. φέρεσθαι ταῖς κ. τινός *let oneself be* *misled by someone's delusions* Hs 8, 9, 3.—FWilhelm, RhM 70, 1915, 188; 72, 1917/18, 383f w. many exx.—M-M. TW. Sv.

κενόδοξος, ον pert. to having exaggerated self-conceptions, *conceited, boastful* (s. κενός, δόξα Polyb. 27, 7, 12; 38, 7, 1; Epict. 3, 24, 43; M. Ant. 5, 1, 6; Vett. Val. 271, 2; PLond 1927, 33 [IV AD]; EpArist 8; Philo, Somn. 2, 105; adv. κενοδόξως Tat. 12, 3) D 3:5. μὴ γινώμεθα κενόδοξοι *let us not become conceited* **Gal 5:26.**—DELG s.v. κενός. M-M. TW.

κενός, ή, όν (Hom.+) gener. 'empty'—**❶ pert. to being without someth. material, *empty*** (TestJob 10:4; GrBar 12:6; Jos., Vi. 167) κεράμιον *empty jar* Hm 11:15. σκεῦος (4 Km 4:3) m 11:13. κ. ἀποστέλλειν τινά *send someone away empty-handed* (cp. PRein 55, 9 [III AD] μὴ ἀναπέμψῃς αὐτὸν κενόν; Gen 31:42; Dt 15:13; Job 22:9) **Mk 12:3;** cp. **Lk 1:53; 20:10f.**

❷ pert. to being devoid of intellectual, moral, or spiritual value, *empty* fig. extension of mng. 1—ⓐ of things: *without content, without any basis, without truth, without power* κ. λόγοι *empty words* (Pla., Laches 196b; Menand., Mon. 512 [752 J.] Mei.; Herm. Wr. 16, 2; Ex 5:9; Dt 32:47; Jos., C. Ap. 2, 225; TestNapht 3:1.—PParis 15, 68 [120 BC] φάσει κενῇ) **1 Cor 3:18** D; **Eph 5:6;** Dg 8:2; AcPl Ox 6, 13 (cp. Aa I 241, 14); cp. D 2:5. πνεῦμα Hm 11:11, 17. κ. ἀπάτη *empty deceit* **Col 2:8** (cp. Arrian, Anab. 5, 10, 4 κενὸς φόβος=false alarm). Of the things of everyday life *vain* Hm 5, 2, 2. τρυφή 12, 2, 1. πεποίθησις s 9, 22, 3. Of preaching and faith **1 Cor 15:14ab** (cp. the theme of 'empty hope' Reader, Polemo p. 313); **Js 2:20** P^{74} (cp. Demosth. 18, 150 κ. πρόφασις; Aeschyl., Pers. 804 κ. ἐλπίς; cp. Wsd 3:11; Sir 34:1). As κ. =μάταιος (**1 Cor 15:17**), the two words are found together in the same sense (cp. Demosth. 2, 12; Plut., Artox. 1018 [15, 6], Mor. 1117a; Oenomaus in Eus., PE 5, 21, 5 κενὰ καὶ μάταια of oracles; Hos 12:2; Job 20:18; EpArist 205) 1 Cl 7:2; cp. κενὴ ματαιολογία Pol 2:1.

ⓑ of pers. (Pind. et al.; Soph., Ant. 709; Plut., Mor. 541a ἀνόητοι καὶ κενοί; Epict. 2, 19, 8; 4, 4, 35; Judg 9:4; 11:3 B; Philo, Spec. Leg. 1, 311; Just., D. 64, 2 οἱ προφῆται οἱ κενοί): *foolish, senseless, empty* Hm 12, 4, 5. οἱ προφῆται οἱ κενοί 11:15. ἄνθρωπος κ. **Js 2:20;** Pol 6:3; τῶν δούλων τοῦ θεοῦ τῶν κ. Hs 6, 2, 1. ἄνθρωπος κενὸς ἀπὸ τοῦ πνεύματος τοῦ δικαίου *empty of the upright spirit* Hm 5, 2, 7. κ. ἀπὸ τῆς ἀληθείας 11:4; ἀπὸ τῆς πίστεως κ. s 9, 19, 2 (cp. κενοὶ τῆς τοῦ θεοῦ ἀγάπης Iren. 4, 33, 7 [Harv. II 261, 2]). In paronomasia (cp. Job 27:12) αὐτὸς κ. ὢν κενὰς καὶ ἀποκρίνεται κενοῖς *he himself, empty* (of God's Spirit) *as he is, gives empty answers to empty people* m 11:3.—Vs. 13.

❸ pert. to being without purpose or result, *in vain* κενὰ μελετᾶν *imagine vain things* **Ac 4:25** (Ps 2:1). κενὸν γενέσθαι *be in vain:* ἡ χάρις αὐτοῦ οὐ κενὴ ἐγενήθη **1 Cor 15:10.** ἡ εἴσοδος ἡμῶν ἡ πρὸς ὑμᾶς οὐ κ. γέγονεν **1 Th 2:1.** κόπος **1 Cor 15:58.**—εἰς κενόν *in vain, to no purpose* (Diod. S. 19, 9, 5; Heliod. 10, 30; PPetr II, 37, 1b recto, 12 [III BC]; Kaibel 646, 10; Lev 26:20; Is 29:8; 65:23; Jer 6:29; TestJob 24:2 [εἰς τὸ κ. codd., S. and V. with Job 2:9f]; Jos., Ant. 19, 27; 96) **2 Cor 6:1.** εἰς κ. τρέχειν *run in vain* (cp. Menand., Mon. 51 Mei. ἀνὴρ ἄβουλος εἰς κ. μοχθεῖ τρέχων) **Gal 2:2; Phil 2:16a,** echoed in Pol 9:2; cp. **Phil 2:16b; 1 Th 3:5.**—B. 932. DELG. M-M. EDNT. TW. Spicq. Sv.

κενόσπουδος, ον *concerning oneself about worthless things* (Plut., Mor., 560b; 1061c; 1069b; Diog. L. 9, 68) ἐὰν κ. μὴ εὑρεθῇς *if it is not found that you concern yourself about worthless things* Hs 9, 5, 5.—DELG s.v. κενός.

κενοφωνία, ας, ἡ (s. κενός, φωνέω; Diosc., Mat. Med. Praef. 2 W.; Porphyr., Adv. Christ. 58, 15 Harnack; Hesychius and Suda=ματαιολογία) **talk that has no value, *chatter, empty talk*** βέβηλοι κενοφωνίαι *profane chatter* i.e. devoid of Christian content **1 Ti 6:20; 2 Ti 2:16** (as v.l. in both pass. καινοφωνίαι *contemporary jargon,* unless this is simply a phonetic variant or itacism, since in this period αι was pronounced as ε).—M-M. TW.

κενόω fut. κενώσω; 1 aor. ἐκένωσα. Pass. aor. ἐκενώθην; pf. pass. κεκένωμαι (s. κενός; trag., Hdt. et al.; pap; Jer 14:2; 15:9; Philo; Jos., Ant. 8, 258 v.l.)

❶ to make empty, *to empty*—ⓐ of desertion by an earthly spirit, pass. κενοῦται ὁ ἄνθρωπος *the man is emptied* Hm 11:14.

ⓑ of divestiture of position or prestige: of Christ, who gave up the appearance of his divinity and took on the form of a slave, ἑαυτὸν ἐκένωσεν *he emptied himself, divested himself of his prestige* or *privileges* **Phil 2:7** (s. ἁρπαγμός 2 and JRoss, JTS 10, 1909, 573f, supported by WWarren, On ἑαυτὸν ἐκένωσεν: JTS 12, 1911, 461–63; KPetersen, ἑαυτ. ἐκέν.: SymbOsl 12, '33, 96–101; WWilson, ET 56, '45, 280; ELewis, Interpretation 1, '47, 20–32; ESchweizer, Erniedrigung u. Erhöhung bei Jesus u. seinen Nachfolgern '62; HRobinson, The Cross in the OT '55, 103–5; RMartin, An Early Christian Confession '60; JJeremias, TW V 708, holds that the kenosis is not the incarnation but the cross [Is 53:12], and defends his position NovT 6, '63, 182–88; D Georgi, Der Vorpaulinische Hymnus Phil 2:6–11 in Bultmann Festschr., '64, 263–93; JHarvey, ET 76, '65, 337–39 [Adam typology]; the counter-cultural perspective in this vs. contrasts w. the view of Eteocles in Eur., Phoen. 504–9).—Cp. πολλοὶ ἐκενώθησαν *many have been turned into fools* Hs 9, 22, 3.

❷ to cause to be without result or effect, *destroy, render void* or ***of no effect*** (Vett. Val. 90, 7) τὸ καύχημά μου οὐδεὶς κενώσει *no one will deprive me of my reason for boasting* **1 Cor 9:15.** Pass. κεκένωται ἡ πίστις *faith is made invalid* **Ro 4:14.** ἵνα μὴ κενωθῇ ὁ σταυρὸς τοῦ Χριστοῦ **1 Cor 1:17.** ἵνα μὴ τὸ καύχημα ἡμῶν … κενωθῇ *so that our boast about you might not prove empty* **2 Cor 9:3** (cp. καύχημα 2).—DELG s.v. κενός. M-M. EDNT. TW. Spicq.

κέντρον, ου, τό (κεντέω 'prick, spur on'; Hom. et al.; BGU 544, 12; LXX; PsSol 16:4; JosAs 16:13; Philo; Jos., Bell. 2, 385, Ant. 7, 169; Ath. 13:1) gener. 'sharp point'.

❶ *the sting* of an animal (Aristot. et al.; Aelian, NA 16, 27 σκορπίου) **Rv 9:10** (s. Ctesias: 688 fgm. 45 p. 490, 1 Jac. [Indica 7], a strange beast of India τὸ πρόσωπον ἐοικὸς ἀνθρώπῳ … ὥσπερ λέων … horrible teeth … σκορπίος … τὸ κέντρον in its tail, whose sting is deadly). In imagery (Aesop, Fab. 276 P. [also H-H. 273 app.]=Babr. no. 185 Cr. κ. τῆς λύπης) of death **1 Cor 15:55f** after Hos 13:14 (s. ESellin, RSeeberg Festschr. I 1929, 307–14, cp. Straub 35; the imagery is transcultural: a friend of a teacher named Theodoros records in an epitaph that he felt a κέντρον ἄπαυστον, 'unceasing sting' because of his death [Kaibel 534, 8=Peek, GVI 1479, 8, s. New Docs 4, 157 no. 64]).

❷ a pointed stick that serves the same purpose as a whip, *a goad* (Hom. et al.; Pr 26:3), in a proverbial expr. (Pind., P. 2, 94 [173] [s. Ael. Aristid. 45 p. 70 D.]; Aeschyl., Ag. 1624, Prom. 323; Eur., Bacch. 795 [WNestle, Anklänge an Eur. in AG: Philol. 59, 1900, 46–57]; Fgm. Iamb. Adesp. 13 in AnthLG [D-B.] III 75: ἵππος ὄνῳ· 'πρὸς κέντρα μὴ λακτιζέτω' 'a horse to an ass: "No kicking against the goads!"' [The cj. λάκτιζέ πω proposed by Crusius—s. JEdmonds, ed., Greek Elegy and Iambus

II, '31, repr. '79, p. 310 no. 64—is unnecessary]; ins fr. Asia Minor [JHS 8, 1887, 261]: λακτίζεις πρὸς κέντρα; AOtto, D. Sprichwörter d. Römer 1890, 331f) πρὸς κέντρα λακτίζειν *kick against the goads* of a balking animal, fig. of one who resists a divine call **Ac 9:4 v.l.; 26:14** (on the pl. cp. Eur., loc. cit., the iambic fragment, the ins, and PGM 4, 2911 κέντροισι βιαίοις of the stings of passion; Herm. Wr. p. 482, 26 Sc.; Philo, Det. Pot. Ins. 46 πάθους κέντροις).—FSmend, Αγγελος I 1925, 34–45, esp. 41ff, but s. WKümmel, Rö 7 u. die Bekehrung des Paulus 1929, 155–57; HWindisch, ZNW 31, '32, 10–14; further lit. in Haenchen ad loc.—B. 864. DELG s.v. κεντέω. M-M. TW.

κεντυρίων, ωνος, ὁ (Lat. loanw.; since Polyb. 6, 24, 5; ins, pap [exx. in Hahn 122, 7; 227, 8; 233, 3]; loanw. in rabb.) ***centurion*** (=ἑκατοντάρχης) **Mk 15:39, 44f;** GPt 8:31; 10:38; 11:45, 47, 49; MPol 18:1; AcPl Ha 11, 4f and 12.—S. on ἑκατοντάρχης and CSchneider, D. Hauptmann am Kreuz: ZNW 33, '34, 1–17; JMichaels, The Centurion's Confession and the Spear Thrust: CBQ 29, '67, 102–9.—Mason 60; M-M.

Κενχρεαί s. Κεγχρεαί.

κένωμα, ατος, τό (s. κενός; Philo Mech. 57, 17; 21; Polyb. 6, 31, 9; 11; Hero Alex. I 432, 5; Plut., Aemil. 266 [20, 8], Mor. 655b al.; PAmh 48, 8 [106 BC]; POxy 1292, 4 [c. 30 AD]; Aq.) ***empty space, emptiness*** τοῦ ἀνθρώπου of a person who does not possess the divine Spirit Hm 11:3.—DELG s.v. κενός.

κενῶς adv. of κενός (Aristot. et al.) **pert. to being without effect or to no purpose,** ***in an empty manner, idly, in vain*** (Epict. 2, 17, 8; Plut., Mor. 35e; 40c; PLond III, 908, 28 p. 133 [139 AD] κενῶς κ. ἀνωφελῶς; Is 49:4) λαλεῖν (κ. καὶ τολμηρῶς Iren. 1, 13, 3 [Harv. I 119, 4]) Hm 11:13 of speech that has nothing to it. λέγειν **Js 4:5.**

κεραία, ας, ἡ (some edd. κερέα; s. κέρας; Aeschyl., Thu. et al.; SIG 374, 14; PMagd 11, 4 of a sailyard; Jos., Bell. 3, 419) lit. 'horn', then **anything that projects like a horn,** ***projection, hook*** as part of a letter, a *serif* (of letters, SibOr 5, 21; 24; 25 al.; of accents and breathings in IG II, 4321, 10; Apollon. Dysc.; Plut., Numa 13, 9, Mor. 1100a. In the last-named pass. in the sense of someth. quite insignificant: ζυγομαχεῖν περὶ συλλαβῶν καὶ κεραιῶν. Likew. Dio Chrys. 14 [31], 86 κεραίαν νόμου τινός ἢ ψηφίσματος μίαν μόνην συλλαβὴν ἐξαλείφειν; Philo, In Flacc. 131 τὰ γράμματα κατὰ συλλαβήν, μᾶλλον δὲ καὶ κεραίαν ἑκάστην) **Mt 5:18; Lk 16:17** (s. on ἰῶτα).—DELG s.v. κέρας A. M-M s.v. κερέα. TW.

κεραμεύς, έως, ὁ (s. κέραμος; Hom. et al.; ins, pap, LXX; PsSol 17:23; TestNapht 2:2; 4; Ath. 15, 2, R. 9 p. 57, 23) ***potter*** Dg 2:3, and his clay (cp. Is 45:9; 29:16; Jer 18:6; Sir 33:13; Wsd 15:7; 1QS 11, 21f) **Ro 9:21;** 2 Cl 8:2. ὁ ἀγρὸς τοῦ κ. *the potter's field* **Mt 27:7, 10.**—DELG s.v. κέραμος. M-M.

κεραμικός, ή, όν (Aristoph., Hippocr. et al.; ins; PGM 7, 867; Da 2:41) ***belonging to the potter*** (if κεραμεικός fr. κεραμεύς) or ***made of clay*** (if fr. κέραμος B-D-F §113, 2; Mlt-H. 379) τὰ σκεύη τὰ κ. **Rv 2:27.**—DELG s.v. κέραμος. M-M.

κεράμιον, ου, τό (Hdt. et al.; ins, pap, LXX) ***an earthenware vessel, jar*** ὕδατος *(water) jar* (Theophr., Caus. Plant. 3, 4, 3) **Mk 14:13; Lk 22:10.** οἴνου (X., An. 6, 1, 17; Polyb. 4, 56, 3; SIG 1109, 162; POxy 1211, 5; O. Wilck II, 757, 3; Jer 42:5), ἐλαίου (Jos., Ant. 8, 322; cp. 9, 48) *(wine, oil) jar* D 13:6. κ. κενόν *an empty jar* Hm 11:15. κεράμια ἱκανώτατα *very many jars* 12, 5, 3. κ. μέλιτος *(honey) jar* 5, 1, 5.—Hv 4, 1, 6 v.l. for κέραμος, q.v.—DELG s.v. κέραμος. M-M.

κέραμος, ου, ὁ (of uncertain derivation. s. three prec. entries; Hom. et al.; ins, pap; 2 Km 17:28; Jos., Bell. 4, 462; Ath.).

❶ ***clay,*** also ***earthenware vessel*** (Hom. et al.; PHib 54, 26; 2 Km loc. cit.) κεφαλὴν εἶχεν ὡς κεράμου *it had a head as if made of clay* Hv 4, 1, 6 (the text is uncertain; as v.l., supported by Lat. versions, καιραμίου [=κεραμίου adopted as conj. rdg. by Joly], which would be identical w. the second mng. of κέραμος given above: *like a* [large] *jar* [?]).

❷ ***a roof tile*** (Herodas 3, 44; Paus. 1, 13, 8; schol. on Apollon. Rhod. 2, 1075a) **Lk 5:19** (LFonck, Biblica 2, 1921, 30–44; KJäger, D. Bauernhaus in Palästina 1912, 11ff; 22ff; HThiersch, ZDPV 37, 1914, 81f; CMcCown, JBL 58, '39, 213–16). Then collectively *tile roof* (so Aristoph. et al.; Appian, Bell. Civ. 1, 32 §145; SIG 1200, 6f; Michel 594, 52; 1387, 123) ἀπὸ τοῦ κεράμου a drop *from the roof* hollows out the stone Hm 11:20.—B. 618f. DELG. M-M.

κεράννυμι 1 aor. ἐκέρασα. Pass.: aor. ἐκράθην, ptc. κερασθείς; pf. ptc. κεκερασμένος (Bel 11 LXX) (Hom. et al.; ins, pap, LXX, PsSol 8:14; Philo; SibOr 11, 126) gener. 'mix'.

❶ **to mix liquid components, mostly of water with wine (to dilute high alcoholic strength),** ***mix,*** χολὴν μετὰ ὄξους=*gall (mixed) with vinegar,* supplied fr. the context containing the abs. κεράσαντες, GPt 5:16.—Fig. ἐν τῷ ποτηρίῳ ᾧ ἐκέρασεν κεράσατε αὐτῇ διπλοῦν *in the cup in which she has mixed, mix her a double portion!* **Rv 18:6.** But perh. κ. means *pour (in),* w. focus on the preparation of the drink, as **14:10** ἐκ τ. οἴνου τ. θυμοῦ τ. θεοῦ τ. κεκερασμένου ἀκράτου ἐν τῷ ποτηρίῳ τ. ὀργῆς αὐτοῦ (some) *of the wine of God's wrath, poured out unmixed* (=*full-strength* [lit., in an oxymoron: 'mixed unmixed']; s. Jer 32:15) *into the cup of God's anger* (cp. Anth. Pal. 11, 137, 12; Is 19:14; PsSol 8:14). See Charles, Comm. Rev. (ICC), ad loc.

❷ **to make a mixture of various ingredients,** ***make a mixture,*** fig. extension of mng. 1 (Oenomaus, fgm. 6, in Eus., PE 5, 24, 7 ἐκέρασε τὸ λόγιον=he made the oracle a mixture [of favorable and unfavorable things]) κραθέντες τῇ σαρκὶ αὐτοῦ καὶ τῷ πνεύματι *closely united w. his flesh and spirit* ISm 3:2.—B. 335. DELG. M-M. TW.

κέρας, ατος, τό (Hom.+) gener. 'horn'.—❶ **bony projection from the head of an animal,** ***horn*** lit., in the description of the apocal. beasts (Achmes 189, 16ff, interpretation of three, four, and more horns of an ox seen in a dream, as referring to the corresponding number of the χρόνοι of a ruler) **Rv 5:6; 12:3; 13:1, 11; 17:3, 7, 12, 16;** B 4:5 (Da 7:7f). Of a calf κέρατα ἐκφέρειν *grow horns* 1 Cl 52:2 (Ps 68:32).

❷ **horn-shaped projections,** ***corners*** or simply ***ends, extensions*** transf. sense of 1 (Apollon. Rhod. 4, 282 κ. Ὠκεανοῖο of a river at the end of the Ocean) of the altar (cp. Ex 27:2; 29:12; Lev 4:7 al.; Philo) **Rv 9:13.**

❸ **exceptional kind of might or power,** ***horn (of power)*** fig. extension of mng. 1 (cp. Ps 88:18; 131:17; 148:14; 1 Km 2:1, 10; Sir 47:7, 11; 1 Macc 2:48. But also Cephalion [c. 120 AD]: 93 fgm. 7 p. 445, 29 Jac. as a poetic expr. κέρας . . ., ὅπερ ἐστὶ . . . δύναμις), hence κ. σωτηρίας *horn of salvation* (of God Ps 17:3; 2 Km 22:3) of the Messiah ἤγειρεν κ. σωτ. ἡμῖν **Lk 1:69** (Goodsp., Probs. 70f *a mighty Savior*).—IScheftelowitz, D. Hörnermotiv in den Religionen: ARW 15, 1912, 451–87.—B. 209. DELG. M-M. TW. Sv.

κεράτιον, ου, τό (Aristot.; Polyb. 26, 1, 4) dim. of κέρας, 'little horn'; in pl. of the fruits of the carob tree, ***carob pods***

(Diosc. 1, 114; Aëtius 160, 3; PLond I, 131, 7 p. 170 [78/79 AD]) **Lk 15:16** (as fodder for swine Lycophron from 675 to 678).—ESchmitz, D. Johannisbrotbaum im Hl. Land: Das Hl. Land 50, 1917, 171–73; Zohary, Plants 63. BHHW II 875f.—DELG s.v. κέρας B. M-M. TW. Spicq.

κερβικάριον, ου, τό (Lat. loanw., cervical; exx. in CWessely, Wiener Studien 24, 1902, 99ff; cp. e.g. PFay 347; BGU 814, 11; Sb 7994, 15; Herodian Gramm. [II AD] in the Lex. Vind. p. 312, 2 states that the use of the foreign word κερβ. for ὑπαυχένιον='a pillow under the neck' is a barbarism; loanw. in rabb.) ***pillow*** κ. λινοῦν *a linen p.* Hv 3, 1, 4.

κερδαίνω (s. κέρδος; Hes., Hdt. et al.; pap; not LXX and Test12Patr, but occasionally EpArist, Philo, Joseph.; Just., A I, 44, 13) 3 sg. κερδανεῖ Job 22:3 Sym; fut. κερδήσω (Jos., Bell. 2, 324; 5, 74); 1 aor. ἐκέρδησα (Jos., Ant. 8, 210) and ἐκέρδανα (Jos., Ant. 4, 129 κερδᾶναι.—Subj. κερδήσω, but κερδάνω **1 Cor 9:21,** where W-H. accent κερδανῶ and read it as a future); 1 fut. pass. κερδηθήσομαι (B-D-F §101; W-S. §13, 12; Mlt-H. 243).

❶ **to acquire by effort or investment, *to gain.*—ⓐ** lit. τὶ *someth.* πέντε τάλαντα **Mt 25:16f;** cp. vss. **20, 22.** τὸν κόσμον ὅλον *the whole world,* i.e. the sum total of earthly riches **Mt 16:26; Mk 8:36; Lk 9:25;** 2 Cl 6:2. Abs. (POxy 1477, 10; EpArist 270) *make a profit* **Js 4:13.**

ⓑ fig. τινά *someone* for the Reign of God **Mt 18:15; 1 Cor 9:19–22.** Pass. **1 Pt 3:1.**—Χριστὸν κ. *gain Christ, make him one's own* **Phil 3:8** (AcPlCor 2:35).—DDaube, κερδαίνω as a Missionary Term: HTR 40, '47, 109–20.

❷ Since the avoidance of loss is a gain, κ. can also mean ***spare oneself someth., avoid someth.*** (Eur., Cycl. 312 ζημίαν; Philemon Com. [IV–III BC] fgm. 92, 10; Diog. L. 7, 14; Himerius, Ecl. 3, 8 W. τ. δίκην; Jos., Ant. 2, 31; 10, 39) ὕβριν καὶ ζημίαν *injury and loss* **Ac 27:21** (Field, Notes 145).—DELG s.v. κέρδος. M-M. TW. Spicq.

κερδαλέος, α, ον (s. κέρδος; Hom. et al.; Artem. 4, 62) ***profitable, gainful*** τὸ κ. διώκειν *pursue gain* 2 Cl 20:4.—DELG s.v. κέρδος.

κέρδος, ους, τό (Hom. et al.; rare in ins, pap; not at all in LXX, EpArist, and Test12Patr, but in Aq., Sym., Theod.; Philo; Jos., Bell. 4, 102, Ant. 15, 158, Vi. 325; Ath. 31, 2) **that which is gained or earned, *a gain, profit*** (AnthLG: fgm. Mel. Chor. Adesp. no. 11 Diehl[2] ['42]=961 Campbell ['93] ἄδικον κ.) **Tit 1:11;** IPol 1:3.—Of someth. advantageous (Chion, Ep. 8; Philo, Spec. Leg. 3, 154) ἐμοὶ τὸ ἀποθανεῖν κέρδος **Phil 1:21** (Aeschyl., Prom. 747; Soph., Ant. 461–64; Aelian, VH 4, 7 τ. κακοῖς οὐδὲ τὸ ἀποθανεῖν κέρδος; Pla., Ap. 32, 40d θαυμάσιον κέρδος ἂν εἴη ὁ θάνατος; on the topic: MEnders FZPhT 42, '95, 237–66). Pl. **Phil 3:7.**—B. 807. DELG. M-M. TW. Spicq.

κερέα s. κεραία.

κέρμα, ατος, τό (κείρω 'cut short, clip', s. next entry; Aristoph., Demosth. et al.) ***piece of money, coin, (small) change*** (usu. copper) collective sing. τὸ κέρμα (Eubul. Com. [IV BC] 84; PSI 512, 13 [253/252 BC]; POxy 114, 14; PGen 77, 5; PTebt 418, 12 ἐὰν χρείαν ἔχῃ κέρματος) ἐκχέειν τ. κ. *pour out the coins* (Diog. L. 6, 82 τὸ κέρμα διερρίπτει=throw the coins of a money-changer into confusion) **J 2:15,** where numerous mss. have the pl. τὰ κέρματα (Attic [Pollux 9, 87], also UPZ 81 IV, 20 [II BC]; Jos., Bell. 2, 295).—DELG s.v. κείρω. M-M.

κερματιστής, οῦ, ὁ (s. κέρμα; exc. for PGissUniv 30, 14 [III/IV AD], cited in L-S-J-M Suppl., not found outside our lit., but κερματίζω is used freq. in papyri in the sense 'change money'; the rdg. κερμ. [for χρηματιστής] in Maximus Tyr. 31, 2b and d has no support in the ms. tradition) ***money-changer.*** In the outer court of the temple (s. Jos., Ant. 15, 410–17) **J 2:14.**—On coinage in use s. Schürer II 66f; and esp. 272 n. 54 (lit.).—DELG s.v. κείρω. M-M. Spicq.

Κέσκος s. Κέστος.

Κέστος, ου Rom. name, Thesaurus-Onomasticon II 356, 3ff ***Cestus,*** a centurion AcPl Ha 9, 18 (name after Aa I 112, 5, [Κε]σκῳ in the pap; CSchmidt reads Κέσκος also in the lacuna of AcPl Ha 9, 30=Aa I 114, 1).

κεφάλαιον, ου, τό (s. κεφαλή; Pind.+; ins, pap, LXX; TestSol 12:3 P) in our lit. the adj. κεφάλαιος, -α, -ον is used only as subst.

❶ **a brief statement concerning some topic or subject, *main thing, main point*** (Thu. 4, 50, 2; Isocr. 4, 149 κ. δὲ τῶν εἰρημένων; Pla., Phd. 44, 95b; Demosth. 13, 36; Epict. 1, 24, 20; POxy 67, 18; Philo, Leg. All. 2, 102; Jos., C. Ap. 1, 219, Ant. 17, 93; Just.; Tat. 51, 4; Ath., R. 20 p. 73, 16) Hv 5:5. κ. ἐπὶ τοῖς λεγομένοις *the main point in what has been said* (is this) **Hb 8:1** (Menand., Georg. 75 κ. . . . τοῦ παντὸς λόγου; Menand. in Plut., Mor. 103d τὸ δὲ κ. τῶν λόγων; PKöln II, 114, 2–3=ZPE 4, '69, 192; cp. pl. Pind., P. 4, 116).—*Summary, synopsis* (limited to the main points) ἐπὶ κεφαλαίῳ *in summary, in brief* (uncertain in Aristot., EN 1107b, 14, otherw. either ἐν κεφαλαίῳ X., Cyr. 6, 3, 18; Appian, Bell. Civ. 4, 93 §388 ἐν κ. εἰπεῖν; PLips 105, 35; POxy 515, 6 al. pap; or ἐπὶ κεφαλαίου Polyb 1, 65, 5; PTebt 24, 52; ἐπὶ κεφαλαίων Just., D. 85, 4; Tat. 31, 4) MPol 20:1.

❷ accumulated goods, oppos. of interest or income, 'capital' (Pla., Demosth., ins, pap), then a ***sum of money*** gener. (Artem. 1, 17 p. 21, 19; 1, 35 p. 36, 17 and 37, 16; GDI 2503, 14 [Delphi]; Cyr.-Ins. 132; BGU 1200, 17 [I BC] οὐ μικρῷ κεφαλαίῳ; POxy 268, 7; other exx. New Docs 3 no. 43; Lev 5:24; Num 5:7; 31:26; EpArist 24; Jos., Ant. 12, 30; 155) πολλοῦ κ. τὴν πολιτείαν ταύτην ἐκτησάμην *I acquired this citizenship for a large sum of money* **Ac 22:28.**—DELG s.v. κεφαλή. M-M. TW.

κεφαλαιόω (s. κεφάλαιον; Thu. et al.; Philod., Οἰκ. col. 7, 40 Jensen; Diog. L. 7, 126; 'sum up', etc.)

❶ ***sum up*** the full measure of sins B 5:11 v.l.

❷ of physical mistreatment, lit. 'strike on the head', ***treat brutally,*** an unparalleled use, perh. colloq. imagery in ref. to some kind of thorough beating (cp., e.g., our 'total' in sense of demolish) **Mk 12:4 v.l.;** or perh. better (B-D-F §108, 1; Mlt-H. 395) κεφαλιόω, q.v., except that the latter is otherwise unknown. S. VTaylor, Comm. '66, ad loc.—DELG s.v. κεφαλή. M-M. TW.

κεφαλή, ῆς, ἡ (Hom.+) gener. 'head'.—❶ **the part of the body that contains the brain, *head*—ⓐ** of humans, animals, and transcendent beings. Humans: **Mt 5:36** (on swearing by the head s. Athen. 2, 72, 66c; Test12Patr; PGM 4, 1917; cp. Juvenal, Satires 6, 16f); **6:17; 14:8, 11; 26:7; 27:29f; Mk 6:24f, 27f; 14:3; 15:19; Lk 7:46; J 13:9; 19:2; 20:7; 1 Cor 11:4b** (JMurphy-O'Connor, CBQ 42, '80, 485 [lit.] 'his head'='himself'), **5ab, 7, 10; 12:21; Rv 18:19** (cp. Josh 7:6; La 2:10); 1 Cl 37:5; 56:5 (Ps 140:5); B 13:5 (Gen 48:14); Hm 11:20; Papias (3:2 [not g and h]); GJs 2:4; 9:1; AcPl Ha 11, 1.—Animals: B 7:8 (of the scapegoat Lev 16; cp. vs. 21).—In apocal. presentations in connection w. human figures: **Rv 1:14; 4:4; 9:7 12:1; 14:14; 19:12;** w. animals: **9:7, 17, 19; 12:3** (s.

δράκων); **13:1, 3; 17:3, 7, 9** (cp. Ael. Aristid. 50, 50 K.=26 p. 517 D.: ὤφθη τὸ ἕδος [of Asclepius] τρεῖς κεφαλὰς ἔχον. A person sees himself in a dream provided with a plurality of heads Artem. 1, 35 p. 37, 14: δύο ἔχειν κεφαλὰς ἢ τρεῖς. Also the many-headed dog Cerberus of the underworld in Hesiod, Theog. 311 al. as well as Heraclit. Sto. 33 p. 49, 14); Hv 4, 1, 6;10; of angels **Rv 10:1.**—The hair(s) of the *head* (Philo, Leg. ad Gai. 223) **Mt 10:30; Lk 7:38, 44 v.l.; 12:7; 21:18; Ac 27:34.** τὴν κ. κλίνειν *lay down the head* to sleep **Mt 8:20; Lk 9:58.** Sim. **J 19:30** (s. Hdb. ad loc.). κινεῖν τὴν κ. (s. κινέω 2a) **Mt 27:39; Mk 15:29;** 1 Cl 16:16 (Ps 21:8); ἐπαίρειν τὴν κ. (s. ἐπαίρω 1) **Lk 21:28;** *shear the head,* i.e. *cut the hair* as a form of a vow **Ac 21:24;** cp. **18:18.** Of baptism ἔκχεον εἰς τὴν κεφαλὴν τρὶς ὕδωρ D 7:3. Of the anointing of Jesus' head IEph 17:1. κατὰ κεφαλῆς ἔχειν *have (someth.) on the head* (s. κατά A 1a) **1 Cor 11:4a;** also w. specification of object ἐπί w. gen. **Rv 14:14;** Hv 4, 1, 10; or εἰς 4, 3, 1. ἐπάνω τῆς κ. *above his head* **Mt 27:37.** Also πρὸς τῇ κ. **J 20:12.** (ἀστὴρ) ἔστη ἐπὶ τὴν κ. τοῦ παιδίου GJs 21:3 (cp. Mt 2:9).—Well-known expr. fr. the OT: ἄνθρακας πυρὸς σωρεύειν ἐπὶ τὴν κ. τινος **Ro 12:20** (s. ἄνθραξ). A curse-formula: τὸ αἷμα ὑμῶν ἐπὶ τὴν κ. ὑμῶν *your blood be on your own heads* (s. αἷμα 2a and cp. Demosth., Ep. 4, 10 τ. ἄδικον βλασφημίαν εἰς κεφαλὴν τῷ λέγοντι τρέπουσι; 6, 1; Maximus Tyr. 5, 1d; Aesop, Fab. 206 P.=372 H.//313 Ch.//222 H-H. ὃ θέλεις σὺ τούτοις ἐπὶ τῇ σῇ κεφαλῇ γένοιτο; Phalaris, Ep. 102 εἰς κεφαλὴν σοί τε καὶ τῷ σῷ γένει)=you are responsible for your own destruction **Ac 18:6;** cp. GPt 5:17.

ⓑ in imagery οὐκ ἔκλινας τὴν κ. σου ὑπὸ τὴν κραταιὰν χεῖραν *you have not bowed your head under the mighty hand* (of God) GJs 15:4. Of pers. (Plut., Galba 1054 [4, 3] G. as κ. ἰσχυρῷ σώματι, namely of the Galatian territories) Christ the κ. of the ἐκκλησία thought of as a σῶμα **Col 1:18;** cp. **2:19** (Artem. 2, 9 p. 92, 25 ἡ κεφαλὴ ὑπερέχει τοῦ παντὸς σώματος; schol. on Nicander, Alexiph. 215 ἡ κεφαλὴ συνέχει πᾶν τὸ σῶμα); Christ and Christians as head and members ITr 11:2. (SBedale, JTS 5, '54, 211–15; New Docs 3, 45f [lit.]; not 'source': JFitzmyer, NTS 35, '89, 503–11.) S. mng. 2a.

❷ **a being of high status, *head,*** fig. (of Asclepius IG II², 4514, 6; in gnostic speculation: Iren. 1, 5, 3 [Harv. I 45, 13]. ὁ μέγας ἄρχων, ἡ κ. τοῦ κόσμου Hippol., Ref. 7, 23, 3).

ⓐ in the case of living beings, to denote superior rank (cp. Artem. 4, 24 p. 218, 8 ἡ κ. is the symbol of the father; Judg 11:11; 2 Km 22:44) *head* (Zosimus of Ashkelon [500 AD] hails Demosth. as his master: ὦ θεία κεφαλή [Biogr. p. 297]) of the father as head of the family Hs 7, 3; of the husband in relation to his wife **1 Cor 11:3b; Eph 5:23a.** Of Christ in relation to the Christian community **Eph 4:15; 5:23b.** But Christ is the head not only of the body of Christians, but of the universe as a whole: κ. ὑπὲρ πάντα **Eph 1:22,** and of every cosmic power κ. πάσης ἀρχῆς καὶ ἐξουσίας *the head of all might and power* **Col 2:10.** The divine influence on the world results in the series (for the growing distance from God with corresponding results cp. Ps.-Aristot. De Mundo 6, 4): God the κ. of Christ, Christ the κ. of man, the man the κ. of the woman **1 Cor 11:3cab** (s. on γυνή 1). JFitzmyer, Int 47, '93, 52–59.

ⓑ of things *the uppermost part, extremity, end, point* (Pappus of Alex., mathematician [IV AD] in the 8th book [ed. CGerhardt 1871 p. 379 τῇ κεφαλῇ τοῦ κοχλίου=at the point of the screw; Judg 9:25; En 17:2; Jos., Bell. 2, 48, Ant. 3, 146; oft. pap of plots of ground) κ. γωνίας the *cornerstone* (so M'Neile, Mt ad loc.; REB (*main*) *corner-stone,* and w. proper omission of the alternative rendering at 1 Pt 2:7 in NEB mg.; the cornerstone thus forms the farthest extension [cp. PFlor 50, 83] of the corner, though JJeremias, Αγγελος I 1925, 65–70, ZNW 29, 1930, 264–80, TW IV 277–79 thinks of it as the *capstone* above the door; so also OMichel, TW IV 892, V 129 [diff. 151]; KSchelkle, RAC I 233f; RMcKelvey, NTS 8, '62, 352–59 [lit. 353 n. 1–3]. S. HGressmann, Pj 6, 1910, 38–45; GWhitaker, Exp. 8th ser., 22, 1921, 470ff. For another view s. lit. s.v. ἀκρογωνιαῖος) **Mt 21:42; Mk 12:10; Lk 20:17** (on these three pass. s. JDerrett, TU 102, '68, 180–86); **Ac 4:11; 1 Pt 2:7** (Selwyn ad loc.: "extremity and not height is the point connoted"); B 6:4 (all Ps 117:22).—κ.=*capital* (city) (Appian, Illyr. 19 §54) **Ac 16:12** D (but 'frontier city' AClark, Acts of the Apostles '33, 362–65 and JLarsen, CTM 17, '46, 123–25).—B. 212. Schmidt, Syn. I 361–69. DELG. M-M. EDNT. TW. Sv.

κεφαλιόω 1 aor. ἐκεφαλίωσα (Phryn. 95 Lob.; B-D-F §108, 1; Mlt-H. 395) ***strike on the head*** **Mk 12:4** (v.l. κεφαλαιόω [q.v.]).—GBjörck, ConNeot 1, '36, 1–4: 'ruin, kill outright'.—Field, Notes 36f.—DELG s.v. κεφαλή.

κεφαλίς, ίδος, ἡ (in var. mngs. Aristot. et al.; PCol IV, 108, 1 [III BC]; PLond III, verso 755, 6 p. 222 [IV AD]; LXX; EpArist 68; Philo, Mos. 2, 77; Jos., Ant. 12, 73 [after EpArist]) dim. of κεφαλή, lit. 'little head', in our lit. only once, modelled after the OT (Ezk 2:9) and in a quot. fr. Ps 39:8 κ. βιβλίου ***roll of a book*** (s. TBirt, RhM n.s. 62, 1907, 488; VGardthausen, Griech. Paläographie² I 1911, 141) **Hb 10:7.**—DELG s.v. κεφαλή. M-M.—OMichel, KEK '75, 337.

κεφαλοδέσμιον, ου, το (otherwise only since IV AD) ***headband*** GJs 2:2.

κέχρημαι s. χράομαι.

κηδεύω 1 aor. inf. κηδεῦσαι (trag. et al.; ins, pap) **to attend to a corpse, *take care of, bury*** (Soph., El. 1141; Polyb. 5, 10, 4; IG XIV, 1860; ISmyrna McCabe 421, 6; Boffo, Iscrizioni no. 39, 8 p. 320, 8 [SEG VIII, 13] PParis 18b, 4; PLond III, 932, 10 p. 149 [211 AD]; TestAbr A 20 p. 103, 22 [Stone p. 54] ἐκήδευσαν; TestJob 39:10 κεκήδευκα; ParJer; ApcEsdr 7:15 p. 33, 1 Tdf.; ApcMos; Philo, Migr. Abr. 159; Jos., Ant. 3, 262; 9, 227) **Mk 6:29 v.l.**—DELG s.v. κήδω.

κημόω fut. κημώσω ***to muzzle*** (X., R. Equ. 5, 3) βοῦν ἀλοῶντα *an ox that is treading out the grain* **1 Cor 9:9** (v.l. φιμόω, q.v.); **1 Ti 5:18** D.—DELG s.v. κημός.

κῆνσος, ου, ὁ (Lat. loanw., census, also in rabb., quotable in Gk. since I BC [ins: AnnBSA 12, 1905/6, p. 178]. Cp. BGU 917, 6; PAmh 83, 2; other ins and pap New Docs 3, 70f) a capitation-tax (opp. 'toll-tax' s. τέλος 5) ***tax, poll-tax*** κῆνσον διδόναι *pay a tax* **Mt 22:17; Mk 12:14.** λαμβάνειν *collect taxes* **Mt 17:25.** τὸ νόμισμα τοῦ κ. *the coin with which the tax is paid* **22:19** (cp. Hesychius κῆνσος: εἶδος νομίσματος, ἐπικεφάλαιον).—Pauly-W. III 1899, 1914ff; RAC II 961ff. S. φόρος.—M-M. EDNT. TW.

κῆπος, ου, ὁ (Hom. et al.; ins, pap, LXX; Jos., Bell. 5, 410, Ant. 9, 227) ***garden*** **Lk 13:19; J 18:1, 26; 19:41;** GPt 6:24.—B. 490. DELG. M-M.

κηπουρός, οῦ, ὁ (s. prec. entry, also οὖρος 'one who watches'; Pla. et al.; Polyb. 18, 6, 4; Epict. 3, 5, 17; 24, 44f; Plut., Mor. 927b, Aratus 5, 5; 6, 3; 7, 3; SIG 120B, 6 [c. 400 BC κηπορός]; MAMA III, 13; PSI 336, 6; 13 [257/256 BC]; BGU 111 I, 21; PLips 97 XIV, 3) ***gardener*** **J 20:15** (NWyatt, ZNW 81, '90, 21–38, Paradise motif).—DELG s.v. κῆπος. M-M.

κηρίον, ου, τό (Hes.+; ins, pap, LXX; JosAs; Jos., Ant. 6, 118; 126) ***wax, honey-comb*** B 6:6 (Ps 117:12); **Lk 24:42 v.l.** (cp. JosAs 16:1ff; s. μελίσσιος)—DELG s.v. κηρός. M-M.

κήρυγμα, ατος, τό (s. κηρύσσω and next entry)—**❶ an official announcement, *proclamation,*** of the content of a herald's proclamation (so Soph., Hdt.+; ins, PPetr III, 125, 9; PHamb 29, 10; LXX; Philo, Agr. 117 al.; Jos., Ant. 10, 236) of a call to assemble κηρύγματι καλεῖν *call together by a proclamation* B 12:6. Elsewh. in our lit.:

❷ a public declaration, *someth. proclaimed aloud, proclamation,* by a herald sent by God (cp. Herm. Wr. 4, 4; Himerius, Or. 69 [=Or. 22], 7 and 8 the speaker makes the κήρυγμα known to the μύσται and ἐπόπται; ParJer 7:16 [cod. C] τοῦ καλοῦ κηρύγματος; ApcEsdr 5:17 p. 30, 17 Tdf. εἶπεν ὁ θεὸς ὑψηλῷ τῷ κηρύγματι 'in majestic tones'; also Jon 3:2; Philo, Mos. 2, 167; 170; Jos., Bell. 6, 288 τὰ τοῦ θεοῦ κ.; Ar. 15:2; Just.): of prophetic proclamation τὸ κ. Ἰωνᾶ **Mt 12:41; Lk 11:32** (κατὰ τὸν Ἰωνᾶν Did., Gen. 185, 8). τὸ κ. Ἰησοῦ Χριστοῦ *proclamation about Jesus Christ* **Ro 16:25.** Abs. of apostolic proclamation **1 Cor 1:21; 2 Ti 4:17;** Hs 8, 3, 2 (Did., Gen. 151, 14). τὸ κ. μου *my (gospel) proclamation* **1 Cor 2:4;** cp. **15:14** (cp. τῶν ἀποστόλων Iren. 3, 3, 3 [Harv. II 10, 8]; τῶν δώδεκα μαθητῶν Hippol., Ref. 5, 8, 12; Χριστιανῶν Orig., C. Cels. 1, 7, 3). διδάσκαλοι τοῦ κ. τοῦ υἱοῦ τοῦ θεοῦ *teachers of the proclamation about the Son of God* Hs 9, 15, 4. κ. τῆς σωτηρίας **short ending of Mk** (Polyaenus 4, 7, 6 τὸ κ. τῆς ἐλευθερίας; τῆς ἀληθείας Hippol., Ref. 7, 32, 6); σφραγὶς τοῦ κ. *the seal on the (gospel) proclamation* i.e. baptism Hs 9, 16, 5. κήρυγμα ὃ ἐπιστεύθην ἐγώ *the proclamation w. which I have been entrusted* **Tit 1:3.**—CDodd, The Apostolic Preaching and Its Developments '36. KGoldammer, ZNW 48, '57, 77–101; WBaird, JBL 76, '57, 181–91.—DELG s.v. κῆρυξ. M-M. EDNT. TW. Sv.

κῆρυξ, υκος, ὁ (also κήρυξ; on the accent according to Herodian Gr. s. B-D-F §13; Mlt-H. 57; PKatz, TLZ 83, '58, 316 n. 6. S. κηρύσσω and prec. entry.).

❶ an official entrusted with a proclamation, *herald* (Hom.+; ins, pap, LXX; Philo, Agr. 112; Jos., Bell. 2, 624, Ant. 10, 75) MPol 12:1f; GJs 8:3.

❷ one who makes public declarations, esp. of a transcendent nature, *herald, proclaimer* (in the usage of the mystery cults: X., Hell. 2, 4, 20 ὁ τῶν μυστῶν κῆρυξ; Philostrat., Vi. Soph. 2, 33, 4 τοῦ Ἐλευσινίου ἱεροῦ κῆρυξ; SIG 728B, 9 κῆρυξ τοῦ θεοῦ, 773, 5 κ. τοῦ Ἀπόλλωνος, 845, 2 ὁ τῶν ἱερῶν κ.; Just. [of John the Baptist]; τῆς ἀληθείας Tat. 17, 1 and Iren. 1, 15, 6 [Harv. I 155, 14]. S. Poland, 395.—The Cynic, as a messenger fr. God, calls himself a κ.: Epict. 3, 22, 69; 3, 21, 13.—Herm. Wr. 4, 4. Cp. JosAs 14:2 ἄγγελος καὶ κ. ἐστὶ φωτὸς τῆς μεγάλης ἡμέρας [of the morning star]; sun, moon, and the stars as κ.and ἄγγελοι of God Orig., C. Cels. 5, 12, 38ff.) (God's) herald, one who proclaims, of Noah δικαιοσύνης κ. **2 Pt 2:5.** Of the ap. Paul (w. ἀπόστολος) **1 Ti 2:7;** (w. ἀπόστολος and διδάσκαλος) **2 Ti 1:11.** Likew. of Paul 1 Cl 5:6.

❸ *trumpet-shell* (Aristot., HA 5, 544, 546, 547 al.; Machon 133 in Athen. 8, 349c), a large, sharp seashell, used in torturing MPol 2:4.—DELG. M-M. TW.

κηρύσσω impf. ἐκήρυσσον; fut. κηρύξω; 1 aor. ἐκήρυξα, inf. κηρύξαι (also κηρῦξαι, so Tdf.); on the accent s. B-D-F §13; PKatz-Walters, The Text of the Septuagint, Cambridge '73, 97); pf. inf. κεκηρυχέναι (Just., D. 49, 2). Pass.: 1 fut. κηρυχθήσομαι; 1 aor. ἐκηρύχθην; pf. κεκήρυγμαι (Just.) (s. two prec. entries; Hom.+; ins, pap, LXX; PsSol 11:1; TestLevi 2:10; GrBar 16:4 [-ττ-]; Philo, Joseph.; loanw. in rabb.; apolog. exc. Ar.).

❶ to make an official announcement, *announce, make known,* by an official herald or one who functions as such (Maximus Tyr. 1, 6c κηρύττομαι=I am being announced by the herald) MPol 12:1 of the pro-consul, who announced three times that Pol. had confessed to being a Christian.—**Rv 5:2.**

❷ to make public declarations, *proclaim aloud*—ⓐ gener. *speak of, mention publicly* w. acc. κ. πολλὰ τὸν λόγον *spread the story widely* **Mk 1:45.** The hospitality of the Cor. church 1 Cl 1:2. W. indir. discourse foll. **Mk 5:20; Lk 8:39.** Abs. **Mk 7:36.**—S. below 2bβ.

ⓑ of proclamation that is divine in origin or relates to divinity (Epict. 3, 13, 12 of the peace of wise men, which does not originate w. the emperor, but is ὑπὸ τοῦ θεοῦ κεκηρυγμένη διὰ τ. λόγου. Of the [objectionable] myths of the Greeks ταῦτα … οἱ … συγγραφεῖς καὶ ποιηταὶ κ. Theoph. Ant. 1, 9 [p. 78, 13]).

α. of the proclamation or oracles of the older prophets (Jo 2:1; 4:9; Jon 1:2; 3:2; Jos., Ant. 10, 117; Just., A I, 54, 2) Ἰωνᾶς Νινευΐταις καταστροφὴν ἐκήρυξεν 1 Cl 7:7 (Jonah as Jos., Ant. 9, 214; Just., D. 107, 2f; Orig., C. Cels. 7, 57, 3); cp. vs. 6; 9:4 (Noah as SibOr 1, 128); 17:1 (Elijah and Elisha, also Ezekiel); B 6:13 (ὁ προφήτης). προφήτας [ἐξ]έπεμψεν κ. … χριστὸν Ἰησοῦν AcPl Ha 8, 17//Ox 1602, 19–21//BMM recto 21f. Ἰωνᾶς … [ἵνα] εἰς Νεινεύη μὴ κηρύξῃ AcPl Cor 2:29. οἵτινες τὴν ἀπλανῆ θεοσέβειαν ἐκήρυσσον *who proclaimed the inerrant way of revering God* 2:10.

β. of contemporary proclaimers (POxy 1381, 35; 144 [II AD]: of the great deeds of the gods; Herm. Wr. 1, 27; 4, 4.—Philo, Agr. 112 κήρυξον κήρυγμα τοιοῦτον. S. κῆρυξ 2.—Also of false prophets: Jos., Bell. 6, 285), of Mosaic tradition and its publication, the preaching of John the Baptist, and propagation of the Christian message in the widest sense: Μωϋσῆν *preach (=advance the cause of) Moses* i.e. the keeping of the law **Ac 15:21.** περιτομὴν *proclaim circumcision* i.e. the necessity of it **Gal 5:11** (here and 2a the mng. *praise publicly* is also prob.: X., Cyr. 8, 4, 4; Polyb. 30, 29, 6). κ. μὴ κλέπτειν *inveigh against stealing (=preach: No stealing!)* **Ro 2:21.**—κ. τι *proclaim,* someth. (ἕνα θεὸν παντοκράτορα καὶ ἕνα μονογενῆ Χριστὸν Ἰησοῦν κ. Iren. 1, 9, 2 [Harv. I 82, 5]; τὸν ἄγνωστον πατέρα 1, 26, 1 [Harv. I 211, 11]; Hippol., Ref. 1, Prol. 7; Did., Gen. 183, 6; 209, 13) **Mt 10:27;** pass. **Lk 12:3.** ἐνιαυτὸν κυρίου δεκτόν **4:19** (cp. Is 61:1f). τὸν λόγον **2 Ti 4:2.** τὸ ῥῆμα τῆς πίστεως *the message of faith* **Ro 10:8.** τὴν βασιλείαν τοῦ θεοῦ **Lk 8:1; 9:2;** cp. **Ac 20:25; 28:31.** τὸ εὐαγγέλιον **Mk 16:15; Ac 1:2** D; **Gal 2:2;** B 5:9; GMary Ox 3525, 28; 32. τὸ εὐ. τ. βασιλείας **Mt 4:23; 9:35** (cp. τὸν περὶ τοῦ θεοῦ καὶ τῆς βασιλείας αὐτοῦ λόγον Orig., C. Cels. 3, 40, 20); τὸ ὄνομα τοῦ υἱοῦ τοῦ θεοῦ Hs 9, 16, 5. W. dat. of pers. (Hippol., Ref. 5, 26, 30) **1 Cor 9:27** (on the topic of dreaded failure s. APapathomas, NTS 43, '97, 240); **1 Pt 3:19** (CCranfield, ET 69, '57/58, 369–72; see lit. s.v. πνεῦμα 4c); GPt 10:41. εἰς τὰς συναγωγάς *in the synagogues* **Mk 1:39; Lk 4:44.** τινί τι *someth. to someone* (of Jesus κ. μετάνοιαν ὅλῳ τῷ κόσμῳ Orig., C. Cels. 7, 57, 4; τὸ κηρῦξαι αὐτοῖς τὸ εὐαγγέλιον Did., Gen. 53, 13) 4:18; B 14:9 (both Is 61:1). τὶ εἴς τινα *someth. to someone* τὸ εὐαγγέλιον εἰς ὑμᾶς **1 Th 2:9.** εἰς ὅλον τὸν κόσμον Hs 9, 25, 2. Pass. εἰς τὰ ἔθνη **Mk 13:10** (DBosch, Die Heidenmission in der Zukunftsschau Jesu '59, 159–71); κ. τὸ εὐ. **Mt 24:14; 26:13; Mk 14:9; Col 1:23.**—βάπτισμα *proclaim baptism* i.e. the necessity of it **Mk 1:4; Lk 3:3; Ac 10:37.** ἐκηρύχθη ἡ σφραγὶς αὕτη H 9, 16, 4. κηρυχθῆναι … μετάνοιαν εἰς ἄφεσιν ἁμαρτιῶν *repentance for the forgiveness of sins* **Lk 24:47.** ἵνα μετανοῶσιν **Mk 6:12.** [ἀνδρῶν τῶν] κηρυσσόντων, ἵνα μετανοῆται (read:

-ῆτε) AcPl Ha 1, 17.—τινά (τινι) *someone (to someone)* Χριστόν **Ac 8:5;** cp. **1 Cor 1:23; Phil 1:15.** Ἰησοῦν **Ac 19:13; 2 Cor 11:4.** οὐχ ἑαυτοὺς κηρύσσομεν ἀλλὰ Χριστὸν Ἰησοῦν κύριον *we do not publicize ourselves, but Christ Jesus as Lord* **4:5.** Pass. ὃς (Χριστός) . . . ἐκηρύχθη **1 Ti 3:16;** cp. Hs 8, 3, 2; 9, 17, 1; Dg 11:3. διά τινος *through someone* (cp. Epict. 3, 13, 12) Χρ. Ἰ. ὁ ἐν ὑμῖν δι' ἡμῶν κηρυχθείς **2 Cor 1:19.** W. an addition that indicates the content of the proclamation, introduced by ὅτι (cp. Epict. 4, 5, 24): κ. w. acc. and ὅτι foll. **Mk 1:14 v.l.; Ac 9:20;** pass. Χρ. κηρύσσεται ὅτι ἐκ νεκρῶν ἐγήγερται *Christ is proclaimed as having risen fr. the dead* **1 Cor 15:12.** κ. τινί, ὅτι **Ac 10:42;** οὕτως κ. **1 Cor 15:11.** The content of the proclamation is introduced by λέγων **Mt 3:1f; 10:7; Mk 1:7;** cp. vs. **14;** IPhld 7:2. Beside λέγειν w. direct discourse (Epict. 4, 6, 23) **Mt 4:17.** Abs. **Mt 11:1; Mk 1:38; 3:14; 16:20; Ro 10:15;** 1 Cl 42:4; B 5:8 (Jesus' proclamation defined as teaching and the performance of wonders and signs); 8:3. κηρύσσων *a proclaimer* **Ro 10:14.**—S. lit. under κήρυγμα; also MGrumm, translating *kērussō* and Related Verbs: BT 21, '70, 176–79.—B. 1478. DELG s.v. κῆρυξ. M-M. EDNT. TW. Sv.

κῆτος, ους, τό (Hom. et al.; Diod. S. 17, 41, 5 κῆτος ἄπιστον τὸ μέγεθος; LXX; TestJud 21:7; TestSol 2:8; JosAs 12:10) ***sea-monster*** (such as tried to swallow Andromeda: Eur., Andr. fgm. 121; 145 TGF) of Jonah's fish (דָּג גָּדוֹל) ἐν τῇ κοιλίᾳ τ. κήτους (Jon 2:1; cp. 3 Macc 6:8; Jos., Ant. 9, 213) **Mt 12:40;** AcPlCor 2:29 (all the details are from Jon 2:1. But Tzetzes on Lycophron 34 has Heracles staying in the belly of the κῆτος for three days when he rescues Hesione). Of an apocalyptic animal Hv 4, 1, 6; 9.—DELG. TW.

Κηφᾶς, ᾶ, ὁ (כֵּיפָא 'rock') ***Cephas,*** Aram. surname of Simon; the Gk. form of the surname is Πέτρος (s. the lit. on πέτρα 1b and Πέτρος) **1 Cor 1:12; 3:22; 9:5; 15:5; Gal 1:18; 2:9, 11, 14;** 1 Cl 47:3. Κ=Πέτρος **J 1:42** (s. JFitzmyer, To Advance the Gospel, '81, 112–24).—M-M. EDNT. TW.

κιβώριον, ου, τό the seed vessel of the Egyptian bean, *ciborium* (WWeber, Ägypt.-griech. Terrakotten 1914, 63f), also a *vessel* of similar shape (Diod. S. 1, 34, 6; Nicander, fgm. 81; Strabo; Didymus Gramm. in Athen. 11, 477e; POxy 105, 18 [II AD]; Am 9:1 Sym., Theod.; cp. TestSol PVindob at 18:35 [κι]βωρ[ιον]) **Ac 19:24 v.l.** (s. N.[26] and earlier edd.) as gloss on ναοὺς ἀργυροῦς: ἴσως ὡς κιβώρια μικρά=*silver shrines, someth. like receptacles resembling small seed-vessels.*—DELG.

κιβωτός, οῦ, ἡ (Aristoph., Lysias et al.; ins, pap, LXX; JosAs 10:9 cod. A and 18:3 codd. A D G for κιβώτιον [cod. B]; ParJer 7:8; GrBar 4:11; Just., D. 127, 3) gener.'box, chest', in our lit. in specialized senses.

❶ **sea-faring vessel,** ***boat, ark*** (someth. like a 'barge' [Moffatt]; the Lat. arca [hence 'ark'] 'chest, box'=תֵּבָה) of Noah (Gen 6:14ff; 4 Macc 15:31; SibOr 1, 266; Theoph. Ant. 3, 19 [p. 240, 23]) **Mt 24:38; Lk 17:27** (both Gen 7:7); **Hb 11:7; 1 Pt 3:20;** 1 Cl 9:4.

❷ **sacred repository,** ***covenant chest, ark*** (אָרוֹן) in the Holy of Holies ἡ κ. τῆς διαθήκης *the ark of the covenant* (Ex 39:14 al.; Philo; Jos., Ant. 3, 134 al.) **Hb 9:4;** also found in the temple in heaven **Rv 11:19.**—DELG. M-M. TW.

κιθάρα, ας, ἡ (Hom. Hymns, Hdt. et al.; LXX, TestJob, Philo; Jos., Ant. 1, 64; SibOr 8, 119; Ar. 11, 11; Ath. 16, 2) ***lyre, harp*** **Rv 5:8; 14:2.** κ. τοῦ θεοῦ lit. *harps of God* **Rv 15:2,** i.e. *belonging to* or *given by God* (cp. ἐν σάλπιγγι θεοῦ **1 Th 4:16**), or *harps used in the praise of God.* Perh. the expression is a Semitic superlative formation, *great harps,* analogous to ὄρη θεοῦ=mighty mountains Ps 35:7; cp. 79:11; cp. also ἀστεῖος τῷ θεῷ **Ac 7:20** and s. θεός 3gβ. W. the flute (s. αὐλός; Philo, Leg. All. 2, 75; 3, 221) **1 Cor 14:7.** The strings of the harp IEph 4:1; IPhld 1:2.—Kl. Pauly III 1581f; OEANE IV 70–79; s. lit. on κύμβαλον.—DELG.

κιθαρίζω (κίθαρις 'lyre'; Hom. et al.; SIG 578, 18 [II BC] κιθαρίζειν ἢ ψάλλειν; Is 23:16; TestAbr A 10 p. 87, 24 [Stone p. 22]; Jos., C. Ap. 2, 242) ***play the lyre*** or ***harp,*** w. blowing the flute (Dio Chrys. 2, 55; 52 [69], 3; Polyaenus 5, 3, 3; Achmes 207, 16) **1 Cor 14:7.** κ. ἐν κιθάρᾳ **Rv 14:2.**—Haifa Museum, Music in Ancient Israel, '72; SMichaelides, The Music of Ancient Greece, '78.—DELG s.v. κιθάρα. M-M.

κιθαρῳδός, οῦ, ὁ (κιθάρα [above], ἀοιδός 'singer'; Hdt., Pla.; Diphil. Com. fgm. 75 Kock [Athen. 6, 247d]; Plut., Mor. 166a; Aelian, VH 4, 2; SIG [index]; OGI 51, 41 [III BC]; 352, 67; IPriene 113, 80; PEdgar 77 [=Sb 6783], 17 [257 BC]; Philo; Ar. 11, 1) ***lyre-player, harpist*** who plays an accompaniment to his own singing (the κιθαριστής plays the instrument without singing; both words together Philo, Agr. 35; differentiated Diog. L. 3, 88; Aristoxenus, fgm. 102 carries the contrast back to two different instruments: κίθαρις [=λύρα] and κιθάρα) **Rv 14:2; 18:22.**—DELG s.v. κιθάρα. M-M.

Κιλικία, ας, ἡ (Hdt. et al.; ins, LXX; Philo, Leg. ad Gai. 281; Joseph.) ***Cilicia,*** a province in the southeast corner of Asia Minor, whose capital is Tarsus; home of Paul **Ac 6:9; 15:23, 41; 21:39; 22:3; 23:34; 27:5; Gal 1:21** (on the connection with Συρία s. that entry); IPhld 11:1.—Ramsay, Hist. Geogr. 361ff; RHeberdey-AWilhelm, Reisen in Kilikien 1896; FSchaffer, Cilicia 1903; VSchultze, Altchristl. Städte u. Landschaften II 2, 1926; AJones, Cities of the East. Rom. Provinces, '37, 197ff; Pauly-W. XI 385ff; Kl. Pauly III 208f.—M-M.

Κίλιξ, ικος, ὁ (Hom. et al.; ins [incl. IGUR 1286, 1; 1361; s. New Docs 4, 173], Joseph., SibOr; Ath. 14, 1) ***a Cilician*** **Ac 23:34 v.l.**

κινδυνεύω impf. ἐκινδύνευον (s. next entry; Pind., Hdt. et al.; ins, pap, LXX, TestJud 21:6; Joseph.) ***be in danger, run a risk*** abs. (SIG 708, 8; BGU 423, 7; Is 28:13) **Lk 8:23** (cp. Jos., Vi. 14). οἱ κινδυνεύοντες *those who are in danger* (SIG 570, 4) 1 Cl 59:3. κ. πᾶσαν ὥραν *be in peril every hour* (indeed, in danger of one's life; cp. κινδυνεύω used abs. Diog. L. 9, 57) **1 Cor 15:30.** κινδυνεύειν τινὸς χάριν *face danger for the sake of someone* 1 Cl 55:6.—W. inf. foll. (X., Mem. 2, 3, 16; Diod. S. 12, 51, 1; SIG 852, 32f; 888, 68f; UPZ 161, 10 [119 BC]; BGU 530, 12; 30; POxy 44, 9; 3 Macc 5:41; Jos., Ant. 4, 188; Theoph. Ant. 3, 26 [p. 258, 23]; s. B-D-F §392, 2) κινδυνεύομεν ἐγκαλεῖσθαι στάσεως *we run the risk of being charged w. rioting* **Ac 19:40.** τοῦτο κινδυνεύει ἡμῖν τὸ μέρος εἰς ἀπελεγμὸν ἐλθεῖν *there is danger that this trade of ours may come into disrepute* vs. **27.**—DELG s.v. κίνδυνος. M-M.

κίνδυνος, ου, ὁ (s. prec. entry; Pind., Hdt.+; ins, pap, LXX; TestJob 15:5; JosAs 26:7; EpArist 199; Jos., Vi. 272; Ath. 21, 2, R. 6 p. 54, 19) ***danger, risk*** **Ro 8:35** (s. New Docs 3, 58f). That which brings the danger is expressed with the gen. alone (Pla., Euthyd. 279e τῆς θαλάσσης, Rep. 1, 332e; Heliod. 2, 4, 1; Hippiatr. II 234, 13 ποταμῶν; Ps 114:3; Sir 43:24) **2 Cor 11:26a,** or by ἐκ vs. **26b.** The words ἐν πόλει, ἐν ἐρημίᾳ, ἐν θαλάσσῃ (Plut., Mor. 603e κινδύνους ἐν θαλ.), ἐν ψευδαδέλφοις ibid. **c** have a somewhat different sense, and indicate the place where the danger lurks (cp. Ps.-Ael. Aristid. 25, 20 K.=43 p. 804 D.: θάνατοι κατ' οἰκίας, ἐν ἱεροῖς, ἐν θύραις, ἐν πύλαις; Ps.-Pla., 11th Letter 358e κινδυνεύειν κατά τε γῆν καὶ κατὰ θάλατταν, καὶ νῦν πάντα κινδύνων ἐν ταῖς πορείαις ἐστὶ μεστά 'to face hazard on land and sea; and now on trips everything is full of hazards'). ὑπὸ κίνδυνον *in danger* IEph 12:1; ITr 13:3. κ. ὑποφέρειν *incur danger* 1 Cl 14:2. κινδύνῳ ὑποκεῖσθαι *incur a risk* 41:4. κ. ἑαυτῷ ἐπεξεργάζεσθαι *bring danger upon oneself* 47:7. παραδοῦναι ἑαυτὸν τῷ κ. *expose oneself to danger* 55:5; also παραβαλεῖν vs. 6. κινδύνῳ ἑαυτὸν ἐνδῆσαι *involve oneself in danger* 59:1. Of critical illness εἰς νόσον καὶ ἔσχατον κ. AcPl Ha 4, 16.—B. 1155. DELG. M-M. Sv.

κινέω fut. κινήσω; 1 aor. ἐκίνησα; pf. ptc. κεκινηκώς (Ath.). Pass.: fut. κινηθήσομαι LXX; aor. ἐκινήθην (s. next entry; Hom.+) 'move'.

❶ **to cause someth. to be moved from its customary or established place, *move away, remove*** τὶ *someth.* (Lysimachus [200 BC]: 382 fgm. 2 Jac.; Diod. S. 20, 110, 1 κινῆσαι τὸ ἔθος=put an end to the custom; Jos., C. Ap. 2, 272 τὰ νόμιμα κ.='remove the law fr. its proper place') τῷ δακτύλῳ φορτία *move burdens w. so much as a finger* **Mt 23:4** (Artem. 1, 31 p. 32, 18f φορτία κινούμενα). κ. τι ἔκ τινος *remove someth. from someth.* κ. τὴν λυχνίαν ἐκ τοῦ τόπου αὐτῆς **Rv 2:5.** Pass. **6:14** (cp. Astrampsychus p. 5 ln. 12 εἰ κινηθήσομαι τοῦ τόπου μου=whether I lose my place).

❷ **to cause someth. to go into motion, *move, set in motion*** ⓐ *shake* the head (Hom. et al.; Job 16:4; Da 4:19; Sir 12:18; 13:7; TestJob 30:1) κ. τὴν κεφαλήν *shake the head to and fro* as a sign of scorn and derision (Nicol. Dam.: 90 fgm. 4 p. 335, 18 Jac.) **Mt 27:39; Mk 15:29;** 1 Cl 16:16 (Ps 21:8).

ⓑ to cause to be in turmoil *arouse* pass. (Jos., Ant. 3, 13) of a riotous situation ἐκινήθη ἡ πόλις ὅλη *the whole city was aroused* **Ac 21:30.** ἐπὶ τῇ διδαχῇ **14:7** D.

❸ **to be in motion, *move, move around,*** pass., intr. sense (Hom. et al.; Gen 7:14, 21 al.; En 101:8; TestSol 4:17 D; ApcSed 11:10; Philo; Just., D. 127, 2; Tat. 22:2) Hv 4, 1, 9. As an expression of being a living being ἐν αὐτῷ ζῶμεν καὶ κινούμεθα καὶ ἐσμέν *in him we live and move and have our being* **Ac 17:28** (on the mng. and origin of this saying, specif. of ἐν αὐτῷ κινεῖσθαι s. Norden, Agn. Th. 19ff; MDibelius, Pls auf. d. Areop. '39, 26; MPohlenz, Pls u. d. Stoa: ZNW 42, '49, 69–104, esp. 88ff.—Perh. κ. in this passage, coming as it does betw. 'living' and 'being', emphasizes 'moving' less than 'existence'; cp. Achilles Tat. 2, 37, 1 τὸ κινούμενον ἐν φθορᾷ='that which exists amid corruptibility').

❹ **to cause someth. to happen**—ⓐ of external circumstances ***cause, bring about*** (Pla., Rep. 8, 566e πολέμους; Jos., Bell. 2, 175 ταραχήν; PParis 68a, 6 θόρυβος ἐκινήθη) στάσεις **Ac 24:5.**

ⓑ of inward condition ***move, cause*** (Plut., Cim. 489 [16, 10]; Ael. Aristid. 19, 6 K.=41 p. 764 D.: ἐκίνησέν με ὁ θεός; POxy 1121, 16 τίνι λόγῳ ἢ πόθεν κεινηθέντες; TestAbr; Just., A I, 36, 1; Ath. 9, 1) pass. w. inf. foll. (PFlor 58, 15) Dg 11:8 (cp. Ath., R. 12 p. 61, 5 πρὸς τὸ ποιεῖν τι κινουμένους).—B. 662. Schmidt, Syn. III 128–49. DELG. M-M. TW.

κίνησις, εως, ἡ (s. prec. entry; Pla.+; OGI 543, 15 [II AD]; pap, LXX; TestReub 2:4 v.l.; ApcSed 11:3 p. 134, 14 Ja.; EpArist; oft. Philo; Jos., Ant. 1, 31; 17, 251; Just., D. 6, 1; Tat. 22, 2; Ath.; Mel., fgm. 8b [ln. 37 Perler]) ***motion*** τοῦ ὕδατος **J 5:3 v.l.** (Diod. S. 11, 89, 4 κίνησις of a movement in water caused by a god; Epict. 3, 3, 21 ὅταν τὸ ὕδωρ κινηθῇ). ἄστρων Hm 12, 4, 1 (addition by cod. Athous).—DELG s.v. κινέω. M-M. TW. Sv.

κιννάμωμον, ου, τό (Semitic loanw., cp. קִנָּמוֹן; s. Hdt. 3, 111; Aristot.; Diod. S. 2, 49, 3; OGI 214, 59 [III BC]; PTebt 190; 250; PSI 628, 8; PGM 13, 100; 358; LXX, En; Jos., Bell. 6, 390; a member of the tropical laurel family: Zohary 202) ***cinnamon*** **Rv 18:13** (v.l. κινάμ.).—DELG. M-M.

Κίς, ὁ indecl. (also Κείσ, קִישׁ) ***Kish,*** father of Saul (1 Km 9:1 al.; Jos., Ant. 6, 45f; 130 [Κείς]; 56; 62 [Κείσαιος]; 268 [Κεῖσος]) **Ac 13:21.**

κισσάω 1 aor. ἐκίσσησα ***crave*** (Aristoph. et al.; also Just., D. 58, 4 [for ἐγκισσάω Gen 31:10]; of the cravings of pregnant women for strange food Aristot. et al.); *become pregnant with* τινά *someone* 1 Cl 18:5 (Ps 50:7).—DELG s.v. 2 κίσσα.

κίχρημι 1 aor. ἔχρησα (Hdt. et al.; ins, pap, LXX) ***lend*** τινί τι (Hdt. 3, 58; Plut., Pomp. 634[29, 4]; SIG 241 B, 87; 1 Km 1:28; Jos., Bell. 3, 359) **Lk 11:5.**—DELG s.v. χρή. M-M.

κλάδος, ου, ὁ (trag.; Hdt. 7, 19 [τῆς ἐλαίης τ. κλάδους] +) ***branch*** **Mt 13:32; 24:32; Mk 13:28; Lk 13:19;** Hs 8, 1, 4; 8, 2, 9; 8, 3, 1. ποιεῖν κλάδους *produce branches* **Mk 4:32** (birds on the branches as Da 4:12, 14 Theod.). κόπτειν κλάδους ἀπό τινος *cut branches from someth.* **Mt 21:8;** Hs 8, 1, 2.—Paul speaks fig. (cp. Comp. II 155f [Menand., fgm. 716 Kock]; Sir 23:25; 40:15; SibOr 5, 50) of root and branches of the olive tree (Kaibel 368, 7 a young woman who has died is called κλάδος ἐλέας) **Ro 11:16ff, 21.** Also fig., orthodox Christians are called κλάδοι τοῦ σταυροῦ *branches of the cross* ITr 11:2.—B. 523. DELG. M-M. TW.

κλαίω (Hom.+) impf. ἔκλαιον; fut. (B-D-F §77; Mlt-H. 244) κλαύσω (TestJob, ApcMos, Just., Tat.) and κλαύσομαι (LXX; **Rv 18:9 v.l.;** Hv 3, 3, 2; Jos., Bell. 1, 628; SibOr 5, 170); 1 aor. ἔκλαυσα; mid.-pass. ἐκλαύσθην; fut. κλαυσθήσομαι LXX.

❶ ***weep, cry*** **Mk 14:72; Lk 7:38; J 11:31, 33; 20:11, 13, 15; Ac 9:39; 21:13;** 1 Cl 48:1; Hv 4, 1, 7; GJs 3:1 v.l.; AcPl Ha 1, 31; 6, 4. πικρῶς (q.v.) **Mt 26:75; Lk 22:62;** GJs 13:1; 15:3. πολύ *vehemently* **Rv 5:4.** πολλά **Ac 8:24** D; λίαν κ. *weep bitterly* Hm 3:3. μὴ κλαῖε, μὴ κλαίετε *do not weep* **Lk 7:13; 8:52b; 23:28a; Rv 5:5.** Of mourning for the dead (s. on ἀλαλάζω 1) **Mk 5:38f; Lk 7:32; 8:52.** ἐπί w. acc. *over* (Judg 14:17 A; TestJob 40:11 al.; s. B-D-F §233, 2) **Lk 19:41; 23:28ab.** Also ἐπί τινι (Plut., Mor. 216d; Synes., Ep. 140 p. 277a; Sir 22:11) **Lk 19:41 v.l.** (on weeping and lamenting over the imminent destruction of Jerusalem cp. τὸν ἐπὶ τῇ πόλει θρῆνον by Jesus, son of Ananias: Jos., Bell. 6, 304–9). W. κόπτεσθαι (Jos., Ant. 13, 399; on lamentation for one yet living cp. Thetis for Achilles Il. 18, 52–64; Andromache for Hector 6, 407–39.) **Lk 8:52; Rv 18:9;** GPt 12:52, 54. W. λυπεῖσθαι (TestZeb 4:8; ParJer 7:26; Iren. 1, 4, 2 [Harv. I 36, 1]) GPt 14:59. W. πενθεῖν (POxy 528, 8 νυκτὸς κλαίων ἡμέρας δὲ πενθῶν) **Mk 16:10; Lk 6:25; Js 4:9; Rv 18:11, 15, 19;** GPt 7:27.—As an expression of any feeling of sadness, care, or anxiety **J 16:20** (w. θρηνεῖν, as Iren. 1, 14, 8 [Harv. I 143, 4]); **1 Cor 7:30; Js 5:1.** (Opp. γελᾶν) **Lk 6:21, 25;** GJs 17:2. (Opp. χαίρειν as Hippocr., Ep. 17, 49) **J 16:20; Ro 12:15** (cp. Diod. S. 13, 22, 5); Hv 3, 3, 2. κλαίων λέγω *I say with tears* **Phil 3:18;** Hv 1, 2, 2. κλαίουσα προσεύξομαι GJs 2:4 (sc. cod. A).

❷ ***weep for, bewail*** τινά *someone* trans. (as early as Hom.; Sb 4313, 15; Jer 8:23; 22:10; 1 Macc 9:20; TestSim 9; ParJer 4:5; ApcEsdr 6:25 p. 32, 4 Tdf.; Ar. 11:3; Just., D. 78, 8; Tat. 8:4) **Mt 2:18; Rv 18:9 v.l.** (B-D-F §148, 2; Rob. 475).—MGolden, Did the Ancients Care When Their Children Died?: Greece and Rome 35, '88, 152–63; IMorris, Death, Ritual and Social Structure in Classical Antiquity '92.—B. 1129. DELG. M-M. EDNT. TW.

κλάσις, εως, ἡ (s. κλάω; Pla. et al.; Philo)—❶ ***breaking/fracturing***—ⓐ ἐν τῇ κ. τοῦ ἄρτου *in the breaking of the bread = when he broke the bread,* **Lk 24:35** w. spec. ref. to the action of Jesus vs. 30. But s. 2 below.

ⓑ ἡ τῶν σκελῶν κ. *breaking of the legs* (s. σκέλος) Phlm subscr. v.l.

❷ **cultic action of breaking bread, *breaking*** ἡ κ. τοῦ ἄρτου *the breaking of bread* **Ac 2:42.** Whether there is a ref. to Eucharistic observance cannot be determined with certainty. Some would also put **Lk 24:35** here.—TSchermann, D. 'Brotbrechen' im Urchristentum: BZ 8, 1910, 33–52; 162–83; JWeiss, D. Urchristentum 1917, 41ff; JGewiess, D. urapostol. Heilsverkünd. nach d. AG '39, 146–57; JWanke. BZ 18, '74, 180–92. S. ἀγάπη 2 and εὐχαριστία 3 end.—DELG s.v. κλάω 1. EDNT. TW.

κλάσμα, ατος, τό (s. κλάω; Ps.-X., Cyn. 10, 5; Diod. S. 17, 13, 4; Plut., Tib. Gr. 19, 1; Vett. Val. 110, 31; 34; SIG[2] 588, 192; 196; Michel 833; PLond IV, 1431, 26; 36; 1435, 158; LXX; TestSol 5:13; ApcrEzk [Epiph 70, 8]; Jos., Ant. 10, 244) ***fragment, piece, crumb*** (cp. Artem. 4, 33 p. 224, 7 and Ezk 13:19 v.l. κλάσματα ἄρτων) of surplus pieces of bread **Mt 14:20; 15:37; Mk 6:43; 8:8, 19f; Lk 9:17; J 6:12f.** Of the pieces of bread at the Lord's Supper D 9:3f (CMoule, JTS 6, '55, 240–43).—DELG s.v. κλάω 1. M-M. TW.

Κλαῦδα s. Καῦδα.

Κλαυδία, ας, ἡ (s. e.g., Sb index) ***Claudia,*** a Christian mentioned in **2 Ti 4:21.**—LGPN I. M-M.

Κλαύδιος, ου, ὁ (freq. found) ***Claudius.***—❶ Tiberius ***Claudius*** Drusus Nero Germanicus, Roman emperor (41–54 AD); his measures taken against Jews in Rome (Sueton., Claudius 25; Cass. Dio 60, 6; s. Schürer III 77f ; Zahn on Ac 18:2; ABludau, Der Katholik 83, 1903, 113ff; 193ff; Harnack, SBBerlAk 1912, 674ff; JJuster, Les Juifs dans l'empire romain 1914, II 171; 199; AWikenhauser, Die AG 1921, 323f), **Ac 18:2.** A famine during his reign (Schürer I 457, 8; VWeber, D. antiochen. Kollekte 1917, 38f; Wikenhauser, op. cit. 407ff; KGapp, The Universal Famine under Claudius: HTR 28, '35, 258–65; Haenchen ad loc.) **Ac 11:28.**—HDessau, Gesch. d. röm. Kaiserzeit II 1, 1926; AMomigliano, Claudius[2] '61; Pauly-W. III 2778ff; Kl. Pauly I 1215–18.

❷ ***Claudius Lysias,*** Rom. official in Jerusalem (χιλίαρχος τ. σπείρης Ac 21:31; s. Schürer I 378) at the time Paul was arrested **Ac 23:26.**

❸ ***Claudius Ephebus,*** Rom. Christian, sent to Corinth as representative of the Rom. church 1 Cl 65:1.

❹ Christian in Puteoli, who showed hospitality to Paul AcPl Ha 8, 1; 3; 7.

κλαυθμός, οῦ, ὁ (s. κλαίω; Hom. et al.; ins [Sb 7541, 15: II AD]; LXX; pseudepigr., Philo, Joseph., Just.) ***weeping, crying*** (w. ὀδυρμός) **Mt 2:18** (Jer 38:15; θρῆνος, which is found w. both of them here as well as **Mt 2:18 v.l.,** occurs also TestJob 31:7; Philo, Vi. Cont. 73 and Jos., Ant. 20, 112 w. κλαυθμός). ἱκανὸς κ. ἐγένετο πάντων *they all began to weep loudly* **Ac 20:37.** ὁ κ. with ὁ (the art. indicates the unique and extreme character of the action) βρυγμὸς τ. ὀδόντων **Mt 8:12; 13:42, 50; 22:13; 24:51; 25:30; Lk 13:28** (on these passages s. BSchwanke, BZ 16, '72, 121f).—DELG. s.v. κλαίω. M-M. TW.

κλάω 1 aor. ἔκλασα (Hom.+; ins of Gaza: SEG VIII, 269, 6 [III/II BC]; PLips 39, 12; LXX, Philo; Jos., Bell. 5, 407, Vi. 212 al.) ***break*** in our lit. only of the breaking of bread (cp. Jer 16:7; PGM 4, 1392f. But as early as Anacr., fgm. 69 Diehl[2] ἰτρίου λεπτοῦ μικρὸν ἀποκλάς. Also Diod. S. 17, 41, 7 οἱ διακλώμενοι τῶν ἄρτων=those of the loaves that were broken through.—LXX also has διαθρύπτειν τ. ἄρτον: Is 58:7) by which the father of the household gave the signal to begin the meal (פָּרַס, פָּתַח לֶחֶם). This was the practice of Jesus **Mt 14:19; 15:36; 26:26; Mk 8:6, 19; 14:22; Lk 22:19; 24:30; 1 Cor 11:24.** Likew. of the cultic meals of the early Christians **Ac 2:46; 20:7, 11; 27:35; 1 Cor 10:16;** D 14:1; IEph 20:2; AcPl Ha 4, 4.—Lit. on κλάσις.—B. 563. DELG. M-M. TW.

κλεῖθρον, ου, τό (s. κλείω and next entry; X., Pla. et al.; Sb 6253, 9 [137 BC]; PGM 4, 2261; 2294; LXX; ApcEsdr 5:13 p. 30, 12 Tdf. τὰ κλ. τοῦ πυλῶνος τῆς γυναικός; SibOr 2, 228) lit. a *bar* or *bolt* for closing a door; fig., a ***barrier,*** of the coast as a barrier for the sea 1 Cl 20:6 (Appian, Mithr. 24 §96 of the 'bars' with which an endangered seaport was closed).—B. 467. DELG s.v. κλείς.

κλείς, κλειδός, ἡ (cp. Lat. 'clavis'=key; Hom. et al.; ins, pap, LXX; ParJer 4:4 κλεῖδας [κλεῖς cod. C]; loanw. in rabb.; Just., D. 17, 4 [ref. Mt 24:13]) acc. κλεῖδα **Lk 11:52** (POxy 113, 3; LXX [Thackeray 150]) and κλεῖν **Rv 3:7; 20:1** (both κλεῖδα v.l.; SIG 996, 24; POxy 1127, 25), pl. κλεῖδας **Mt 16:19;** 1 Cl 43:3 (OGI 229, 96 and 98; PHerm 8 II, 5; BGU 253, 18) and κλεῖς **Mt 16:19 v.l.; Rv 1:18** (Ctesias [IV BC]: 688 fgm. 13, 16 Jac.=Persians 14 ὃς τὰς κλεῖς πάσας τῶν βασιλείων εἶχε; POxy 729, 23 [137 AD]; BGU 75, 13; Just., D. 17, 4.—B-D-F §47, 3; W-S. §9, 7; Mlt-H. 131f; Mayser 272 [lit.]; Reinhold 51).

❶ **someth. used for locking, *key*** lit. σφραγίζειν τὰς κ. 1 Cl 43:3 (ins [218 BC]: ΕΛΛΗΝΙΚΑ 7, '34 p. 179, 9f κλεῖδας ἐχέτωσαν, . . . σφραγιζέσθωσαν).—The foll. exprs. come close to the fig. mng.: κ. τοῦ θανάτου καὶ τοῦ ᾅδου (ᾅδης 1) **Rv 1:18** (cp. IKourion 127, 53=IDefixAudollent 22). κ. τῆς ἀβύσσου **20:1** or κ. τοῦ φρέατος τῆς ἀβύσσου **9:1** (ἄβυσσος 2; on key to the netherworld s. Paus. 5, 20, 3; PGM 4, 341–42; New Docs 1, no. 8 ln. 3 and p. 5: "the notion of Anoubis as the custodian of the keys of Hades [no. 8, 3] is a standard element in magical charms"). Likew. the portrayal of Peter as the keeper of heaven's gate δώσω σοι τὰς κλεῖδας τῆς βασιλείας τῶν οὐρανῶν **Mt 16:19** (cp. Ctesias above; s. JGrill, D. Primat des Petrus 1904; WKöhler, ARW 8, 1905, 214ff [lit.]; ADell, ZNW 15, 1914, 27ff, esp. 33ff; VBurch, JBL 52, '33, 147–52; HvCampenhausen, D. Schlüsselgewalt der Kirche: EvTh 4, '37, 143–69. S. also on πέτρα 1b and Πέτρος end). ἔχειν τὴν κ. Δαυίδ (cp. Is 22:22 v.l. τὴν κ. οἴκου Δ.) *hold the key of David* **Rv 3:7** (GMinestrina, Bibbia e oriente 20, '78, 182; on authority over the keys cp. Parmenides 1, 14 Δίκη ἔχει κληῖδας, i.e., of the gate that leads to the realm of light and knowledge; OGI 229, 56 [III BC] κυριεύσοντα τῶν κλειδῶν; likewise Polyb. 4, 18, 2. The phrase ἔχειν τὰς κλεῖς=*hold the keys* **Rv 1:18;** cp. 3:7; 20:1 is as early as Pind., P. 8, 4).

❷ **a means of acquiring access to someth., *key*** fig. (for other types of fig. use s. Diod. S. 2, 8, 3 καθαπερεὶ τὰς κλεῖς ἔχειν=hold the keys as it were; Artem. 3, 54 κλείς is a symbol of πίστις=trust) αἴρειν τὴν κλεῖδα τῆς γνώσεως *take away the key* (to the door) *of knowledge* **Lk 11:52;** cp. here the badly damaged apocryphal gospel fragment POxy 655, 41–46 (A Syn. 194, 135) and the restoration [τὴν κλεῖδα] τῆς [γνώσεως]. AHultgren, Forum 7, 91, 165–82.—B. 468f. DELG. M-M. EDNT. TW.

κλείω fut. κλείσω **Rv 3:7;** 1 aor. ἔκλεισα; pf. 3 pl. κεκλείκασιν 1 Km 23:20; aor. mid. impv. κλεῖσαι (ApcMos 12). Pass.: 1 aor. ἐκλείσθην; pf. κέκλεισμαι, 3 pl. κέκλεινται Sus 20 Theod., ptc. κεκλεισμένος (s. κλεῖς; Hom. et al.; ins, pap, LXX, JosAs, GrBar, Joseph.)

❶ **to prevent passage at an opening, *shut, lock, bar***

ⓐ lit. τὴν θύραν (Aristophon Com. [IV BC] 7 ed. Kock II p. 278; Herodas 6, 98; Epict. 3, 22, 14; 2 Ch 28:24; JosAs 5:9) **Mt 6:6; Rv 3:8.** Pass. (Menand., Epitr. 1076 S. [718 Kö.]; Jos., Ant. 18, 74; cp. X., Cyr. 7, 5, 27; JosAs 10:6; 14:5; GrBar 17:1; Did., Gen. 192, 4) **Mt 25:10; Lk 11:7; J 20:19, 26; Ac 21:30.** οἱ πυλῶνες *the gates* (of the heavenly Jerusalem; cp. Is 60:11) **Rv 21:25.**—Of structures *close, lock* (BGU 1116, 15 [13 BC]; Is 24:10) κ. τὴν σκηνήν *close the tabernacle* 1 Cl 43:3. Pass. δεσμωτήριον ... κεκλεισμένον **Ac 5:23.** *Shut* (someone) *in* [Παῦλος ἐ]κ[έ]κλιστο AcPl Ha 2, 6; [οἱ κ]εκλισμένοι 3, 19.—Abs. *shut* (Jos., Vi. 153) **Rv 3:7ab** (cp. Is 22:22 v.l.); **20:3.**

ⓑ fig. κ. τὸν οὐρανόν *shut the heavens,* so that it does not rain **Rv 11:6;** pass. **Lk 4:25.** In a vision ἐκλείσθησαν οἱ οὐρανοί *the heavens were closed* Hv 1, 2, 1. κ. τὴν βασιλείαν τῶν οὐρανῶν *shut the kingdom of heaven* i.e. prevent people fr. entering it **Mt 23:13** (MBlack, An Aramaic Approach[3], '67, 259–61 [Sin. Syriac]).

❷ κ. τὰ σπλάγχνα ἀπό τινος ***close one's heart against someone,*** an idiom **1J 3:17** (cp. a sim. figure στόμα κεκλεισμένον Sir 30:18).—B. 847f. DELG s.v. κλείς. M-M.

κλέμμα, ατος, τό (s. κλέπτω) ***stealing, theft*** (so, denoting an action, Eur. et al.—LXX only='stolen goods') μετανοεῖν ἐκ τῶν κλεμμάτων *repent of the thefts* **Rv 9:21.** In a list of vices Hm 8:5; cp. **Mk 7:22** D.—DELG s.v. κλέπτω. M-M.

Κλεόβιος, ου (Suda K 1717 [ὄνομα ἱερέως εἰδώλων], s. also AcPt 3 [Aa I 48, 6]) ***Cleobius,*** a gnostic in Corinth AcPlCor 1:2 (perh. the same mentioned Eus., HE 4, 22, 5). AcPl Ha 6, 28.

Κλεοπᾶς, ᾶ, ὁ (also Κλεόπας edd.) *Cleopas* (O. Wilck II, 1438; 1442; 1448 [all II AD]; short form of Κλεόπατρος). This genuinely Gk. name, which evidently takes the place of the Semitic Κλωπᾶς (q.v.), without necessarily denoting the identity of the two persons w. these names in the gospels, is borne by an otherwise unknown disciple in Jerusalem **Lk 24:18.** (S. B-D-F §53, 2d; 125, 2; Dssm., B 184, 6 [BS 315, 2]; Dalman, Gramm.[2] 179, 4; Mlt-H. p. 88.)—M-M.

κλέος, ους, τό (Hom. et al.; pap; Job 28:22; 30:8; Philo; Jos., Ant. 4, 105; 115; 19, 223; SibOr 3, 431; 5, 428) ***fame, glory*** τὸ γενναῖον τῆς πίστεως κ. 1 Cl 5:6. κ. περιποιεῖσθαι ἑαυτῷ *win fame for oneself* 54:3. ποῖον κ. w. εἰ foll. *what credit is it, if* **1 Pt 2:20.**—DELG. M-M. TW. SV.

κλέπτης, ου, ὁ (s. next entry; Hom. et al.; pap, LXX; TestSol 10:38 C; TestAbr A 10 p. 88, 2 [Stone p. 24]; JosAs ch. 13 cod. A [p. 57, 24 Bat.]; Philo; Jos., Ant. 16, 3; Ar.; Just., D. 12, 3) ***thief*** **Mt 6:19f; 24:43; Lk 12:33, 39; J 10:1** (w. λῃστής as vs. **8** and EpJer 57. Opp. ποιμήν as Il. 3, 11; Maximus Tyr. 19, 4e), **10; 1 Pt 4:15;** 1 Cl 35:8 (Ps 49:18). Excluded fr. the kgdm. of God **1 Cor 6:10.** Of Judas the informer **J 12:6.** The breaking in of a thief as a figure for someth. sudden, surprising, unexpected; used of the Parousia (as in **Mt 24:43; Lk 12:39** above) ὡς κ. ἐν νυκτὶ ἔρχεσθαι *come as a thief in the night* **1 Th 5:2** (the thief in the night: Dio Chrys. 52 [69], 8; Job 24:14; Philo, Spec. Leg. 4, 10); cp. vs. **4; 2 Pt 3:10; Rv 3:3; 16:15.**—GFörster, ZNW 17, 1916, 169–77; WHarnisch, Eschatologische Existenz, '73: Exkurs II, 84–116.—In the saying concerning the shepherds, the relig. leaders who came before Jesus are fig. called thieves **J 10:8.**—M-M. TW.

κλέπτω fut. κλέψω; 1 aor. ἔκλεψα. Pass: 2 aor. ἐκλάπην; pf. ptc. κεκλεμμένον Gen. 30:33; Dg 2:2 (s. prec. entry; Hom.+) ***steal*** τὶ *someth.* τοὺς γάμους *consummate marriage secretly* i.e. without the blessing of the community GJs 15:2, 4. Pass. Dg 2:2, 7 (on sacrilege through theft s. Juvenal, Satires 13, 147–52; other reff. EBlakeney, The Epistle to Diognetus '43, 36f). τινά *someone* of a dead pers. (Chariton 3, 2, 7; 2 Km 21:12; Tob 1:18 BA); of Jesus **Mt 27:64; 28:13;** GPt 8:30. Abs. **Mt 6:19f; 19:18; Mk 10:19; Lk 18:20; Ro 13:9;** D 2:2 (the last five Ex 20:14.—In Epict. 3, 7, 12 the command takes the form: μὴ κλέπτετε); **J 10:10; Ro 2:21; Eph 4:28.**—B. 789. DELG. M-M. TW.

κλῆμα, ατος, τό ***branch,*** esp. of a vine (Aristoph. et al.; Pla., Rep. 1, 353a ἀμπέλου κλῆμα; Theophr., HP 4, 13, 5; Pollux 1, 237 ὁ τῆς ἀμπέλου [sc. κλάδος] κλῆμα; PFlor 148, 9; LXX; GrBar; ApcSed 8:3 p. 132, 38 Ja; Jos., Ant. 2, 64; 12, 75 κ. ἀμπέλων; SibOr 7, 148) in the saying about the vine and branches **J 15:2, 4–6** (ESchweitzer, in TWManson mem. vol. '59, 230–45).—DELG. M-M. TW.

Κλήμης, εντος, ὁ ***Clement*** (the Gk. form of this Lat. name [Clemens] is found e.g. Philostrat., Vi. Soph. 2, 27, 2; Jos., Ant. 19, 37–47; OGI 207, 1; 574, 9; POxy 241, 1; 340; Sb 4613; 8089, 1 [beg. II AD]).

❶ a member of the church at Philippi, honored by Paul w. the title 'co-worker' (a Clement of Philippi is mentioned CIL III 633) **Phil 4:3.**

❷ a member of the church at Rome, in charge of relations w. other churches Hv 2, 4, 3, sometimes Identified w. 1, though without sufficient reason. The pers. meant is certainly the author of 1 Cl; he is named in the subscr. of that letter; also subscr. of 2 Cl., and tradition from the middle of the second cent. recognizes him as the third bishop of Rome.—M-M.

κληρονομέω fut. κληρονομήσω; 1 aor. ἐκληρονόμησα; pf. κεκληρονόμηκα (s. four next entries; Demosth. et al.; ins, pap, LXX, En; TestSol 9:5; TestJob; TestNapht 5:8; Philo, Joseph.; Just.).

❶ **to be an inheritor, *inherit*—**ⓐ abs. *inherit, be an heir* (Epict. 3, 2, 8; SIG 833, 8; Sb 4638, 12 [II BC]) **Gal 4:30** (Gen 21:10); B 13:1. Jesus as ὁ κληρονομῶν *the heir* 14:5.

ⓑ used with pers. obj. the verb signifies *succeed someone as heir, be someone's heir* (Posidon.: 87 fgm. 36 p. 243, 32f Jac.; POxy 1067, 8; PRyl 28, 226 δοῦλος αὐτὸν κληρονομήσει; Gen 15:3 of Eliezer as Abraham's heir; Pr 13:22; Tob 3:15; Jos., Ant. 20, 241; in sardonic vein Sir 19:3) 1 Cl 16:13 (Is 53:12).

❷ ***acquire, obtain, come into possession of*** τὶ *someth.* (H. Gk. [Phryn. 129 Lob.; Moeris 149]; cp. Polyb. 18, 38, 8 φήμην; 15, 22, 3; Lucian, Dial. Mort. 11, 3; BGU 19 II, 1; 1024 VIII 16; PRyl 117, 13; LXX; TestSol 9:5; TestJob 18:6; Philo, Rer. Div. Her. 98 σοφίαν) esp. of participation in Messianic salvation: τὴν γῆν (Ps 24:13; 36:9, 11, 22; En 5:6; 7; cp. Iren. 5, 9, 4 [Harv. II 344]) **Mt 5:5;** D 3:7. βασιλείαν θεοῦ *the kgdm. of God* (cp. 1 Macc 2:57) **1 Cor 6:9f** (=Pol 5:3); **15:50a; Gal 5:21;** IEph 16:1; IPhld 3:3; cp. **Mt 25:34.** ζωὴν αἰώνιον *receive, share in eternal life* (cp. SibOr fgm. 3, 47) **19:29; Mk 10:17; Lk 10:25; 18:18;** Hv 3, 8, 4. δόξαν καὶ τιμήν 1 Cl 45:8. τὴν ἐν τ. οὐρανῷ πνευματικὴν καὶ ἄφθαρτον τῆς δικαιοσύνης δόξαν κ. **ending of Mk** in the Freer ms. 10ff. σωτηρίαν **Hb 1:14.** τὰς ἐπαγγελίας (PsSol 12:6) *what is promised* **Hb 6:12;** 1 Cl 10:2. τὴν ἀφθαρσίαν **1 Cor 15:50b** (cp. Just., D. 139, 5). (τὴν) εὐλογίαν **Hb 12:17; 1 Pt 3:9.** διαφορώτερον ὄνομα **Hb 1:4** (=1 Cl 36:2.—κλ. ὄνομα as Dionys. Byz. §7; Themist., Paraphrases Aristot. II p. 172, 13 Spengel [1866]). ταῦτα *all this* **Rv 21:7** (s. New Docs 5, 35).—DELG s.v. κλῆρος and νέμω. M-M. TW.

κληρονομία, ας, ἡ (s. prec. entry; Isocr., Demosth. et al.; ins, pap, LXX; En 99:14; TestJob, TestBenj, JosAs, Philo; Jos., Bell. 2, 249; Just.; Tat. 3, 3; Mel.).

❶ ***inheritance*** (so almost always in gener. lit., also Num 26:54, 56.—Fig. ἵνα ἐκβάλωσι τὴν τῆς σαρκὸς κ. [of those who deny Christ's human nature] Iren. 3, 22, 1 [Harv. II 121, 7]) **Mt 21:38; Mk 12:7; Lk 20:14;** Hv 3, 12, 2; s 5, 6, 4. μερίσασθαι μετά τινος τὴν κ. *divide the inheritance w. someone* **Lk 12:13.** λαὸς κληρονομίας *people of the inheritance* B 14:4. At his coming again the Beloved shall come to his inheritance 4:3.

❷ ***possession, property*** (Sir 22:23; 24:20; Jdth 16:21; 1 Macc 2:56; 6:24) διδόναι τινὶ κληρονομίαν *give someone property* **Ac 7:5; 13:33** D; 1 Cl 36:4 (the two last Ps 2:8). λαμβάνειν τι εἰς κ. *receive someth. as a possession* (cp. Aristot., EN 7, 14 p. 1153b, 33; TestBenj 10:4f) **Hb 11:8.** σχοίνισμα κληρονομίας αὐτοῦ Jahweh's *inherited portion* viz. Israel 1 Cl 29:2 (Dt 32:9).

❸ common in Christian usage (corresp. to the LXX) (the possession of) ***transcendent salvation*** (as the inheritance of God's children) **Gal 3:18.** ἀπολαμβάνειν τὴν ἀνταπόδοσιν τῆς κ. *receive the inheritance as reward* **Col 3:24.** ἡ ἐπαγγελία τῆς αἰωνίου κ. *the promise of the eternal inheritance* **Hb 9:15.** ἐσφάλησαν τῆς κ. τῆς αἰωνίας (αἰωνίου Ox 1602, 27–29=AcPl BMM recto, 26–27) AcPl Ha 8, 21 (of the Jews as God's people). κ. ἄφθαρτος *an imperishable* possession **1 Pt 1:4.** ἡ κ. ἡμῶν *our salvation* **Eph 1:14;** granted by God vs. **18.** δοῦναι τὴν κ. ἐν τοῖς ἡγιασμένοις *grant salvation among those who are consecrated* **Ac 20:32.** κ. ἔχειν ἐν τῇ βασιλείᾳ τοῦ Χριστοῦ *have a share in the kgdm. of Christ* **Eph 5:5** (cp. Just., D. 122, 6 and s. PHammer, JBL 79, '60, 267–72).

❹ abstr. for concr.=***the heirs*** (cp. ἀκροβυστία 3) **Ro 11:1 v.l.**—M-M. EDNT. TW.

κληρονόμος, ου, ὁ (s. two prec. entries; Pla.+; ins, pap, LXX; PsSol 8:11; Philo; Jos., Ant. 13, 322; Tat. 25, 2) gener. 'heir'.

❶ **one who is designated as heir, *heir*** (Appian, Bell. Civ. 3, 11 §36 υἱὸς καὶ κ.) **Mt 21:38; Mk 12:7; Lk 20:14; Gal 4:1;** Hs 5, 2, 6.

❷ **one who receives someth. as a possession, *beneficiary,*** fig. extension of mng. 1: in our lit. of God as the one who bestows (cp. Hs 5, 2, 6; ApcSed 6:2).

ⓐ of Christ ὃν ἔθηκεν κ. πάντων *whom God has appointed heir of all things* **Hb 1:2** (cp. Did., Gen. 41, 23 οὐ γὰρ ὕστερον πεποίηκεν αὐτὸν κληρονόμον, ἀλλ' ὄντα ἐφανέρωσεν=for [the Father] did not subsequently make him [the Savior] an heir, but revealed him as one who was such).

ⓑ of believers; as τέκνα they are: κληρονόμοι, κληρονόμοι θεοῦ **Ro 8:17;** cp. **Gal 4:7.** More definitely κ. τῆς διαθήκης τοῦ κυρίου, where διαθήκη (q.v. 2) fluctuates betw. 'last will and testament' and 'decree' B 6:19; 13:6. κατ' ἐπαγγελίαν κληρονόμοι *heirs according to the promise* **Gal 3:29** (on the imagery s. Straub 96f); cp. **Hb 6:17.** κ. τῆς βασιλείας *heirs of the kingdom* **Js 2:5.** ἵνα κληρονόμοι γενηθῶμεν κατ' ἐλπίδα ζωῆς αἰωνίου *that we might become heirs in accordance w. the hope of eternal life* **Tit 3:7.** τῆς κατὰ πίστιν δικαιοσύνης ἐγένετο κ. *he* (Noah) *became an heir of the righteousness that comes by faith* **Hb 11:7** (on the gen. of the abstract noun cp. Demosth. 22, 34 κ. τῆς ἀτιμίας). Abraham and all those who are expecting the 'righteousness of faith' as he did, are κ. κόσμου, in contrast to those who depend on the law **Ro 4:13f** (cp. Philo, Somn. 1, 175 τῶν τοῦ κόσμου κληρονόμον μερῶν).—On inheritance in Paul, esp. in Gal, s. MConrat, ZNW 5, 1904, 204–27; OEger, ibid. 18, 1918, 84–108; WCalder, JTS 31, 1930, 372–74.—B. 779. DELG s.v. κλῆρος and νέμω. M-M. TW.

κλῆρος, ου, ὁ (Hom.+; loanw. in rabb.)—❶ **a specially marked object, such as a pebble, a piece of pottery, or a stick, used to decide someth., *lot*** (Diod. S. 13, 34, 6 κλήρῳ=by lot) βάλλειν κ. (ἐπί τι) *cast lots (for someth.)* **Mt 27:35; Mk 15:24; Lk 23:34; J 19:24;** B 6:6 (Ps 21:19. The expr. as such is oft. found in LXX, also Jos., Ant. 6, 61; schol. on Soph., Antig. 275 p. 232 Papag.; cp. 1QS 6, 16–22). ἔπεσεν ὁ κ. ἐπί τινα *the lot fell upon someone* (Jon 1:7) **Ac 1:26b.** ἀνέβη ὁ κ. ἐπὶ Συμεών GJs 24:4. ἔδωκαν κλήρους αὐτοῖς *they gave them* (the candidates) *lots* vs. **26a.** On this LThornton, JTS 46, '45, 51–59. JLindblom, VetusT 12, '62, 164–78 (OT background); WBeardslee, NovT 4, '60, 245–52 (Qumran).

❷ **that which is assigned by lot or simply given as a portion or share, *portion, share*** (Pla.; Diod. S. 40, 3, 7 in connection with the distribution of the country conquered by the Jews; JosAs 10:1 Potiphar and his family go to their estate; ApcMos 22 τὰ φυτὰ . . . τοῦ κλήρου; Mitt-Wilck. I/1, pp. 280–83; Jos., Bell. 2, 83) esp. what comes to someone by divine grace (Ael. Aristid. 30, 23 K.=10 p. 123 D.; Hierocles 4, 426 ἀθάνατος κ.=the eternal portion bestowed by the gods; LXX) λαγχάνειν τὸν κ. τῆς διακονίας ταύτης **Ac 1:17** (cp. κλῆρον τῆς ἐπισκοπῆς ἔχειν Iren. 1, 27, 1 [Harv. I 215, 1]); cp. vs. **25 v.l.** λαβεῖν κ. ἐν τοῖς ἡγιασμένοις *receive a place among God's holy people* **26:18** (cp. Wsd 5:5 ἐν ἁγίοις ὁ κ. αὐτοῦ). μερίς and κλῆρος together (schol. on Apollon. Rhod. 1, 1082a; Dt 10:9; 12:12 al.; Is 57:6) οὐκ ἔστιν σοι μερὶς οὐδὲ κ. ἐν τῷ λόγῳ τούτῳ *you have neither part nor share in this matter* **8:21.** μερὶς τοῦ κ. τῶν ἁγίων ἐν τῷ φωτί *a share in the inheritance of God's people in (the realm of) light* **Col 1:12** (cp. 1QH 11, 11f). καὶ κλῆρον καὶ μερισμὸν λαμβάνοντες ὑπὸ πνεύματος τοῦ Χριστοῦ *receiving a portion and share through the spirit of Christ* AcPl Ha 8, 18//Ox 1602, 22f=BMM recto 23f (of prophets). κ. Ἐφεσίων *the class of the Ephesians* IEph 11:2.—**1 Pt 5:3** the κλῆροι seem to denote the 'flock' as a whole, i.e. the various parts of the people of God which have been assigned as 'portions' to individual elders or shepherds (of the various portions that combine to form a whole: Simplicius in Epict. p. 71, 10, where the κλῆροι of good and evil [acc. to the teaching of those who assume two original principles] are differentiated ἐξ ἀϊδίου [eternally]). Cp. Goppelt, KEK ad loc.

❸ **someth. that inevitably happens, *lot, destiny*** esp. of martyrs τὸν ἴδιον κ. ἀπαρτίζειν *fulfill one's own destiny* MPol 6:2; cp. ITr 12:3; IRo 1:2; IPhld 5:1.—Pauly-W., XI 810ff; XIII 1451–1504; Kl. Pauly III 252.—DELG. M-M. TW.

κληρόω aor. mid. ἐκληρωσάμην (GJs 19:1 codd.); pf. mid. 2 sg. κεκλήρωσαι (GJs 9:1); pf. ptc. κεκληρωμένος (MPol 6:2); 1 aor. pass. ἐκληρώθην (s. κλῆρος and the three entries preceding it; Pind., Hdt.+; ins, pap, LXX; TestIss 5:7; Philo; SibOr 5, 322).

❶ ***appoint by lot*** (act. Diod. S. 15, 18, 3 κληρώσαντες) pass. *be appointed by lot* (Appian, Mithrid. 102 §471 τοὺς κληρουμένους=those chosen by lot) gener. ὡς ἕκαστος ἐκληρώθη *as each one's lot is cast* Dg 5:4. If εἰς τὸ εἶναι . . . Eph 1:12 is dependent on ἐκληρώθημεν vs. **11,** the mng. of κ. in vs. **11** could be *chosen* (cp. PIand 27, 4 ἐκληρώθημεν εἰς γεωργίαν; BGU 625, 5 ἐκληρώθην εἰς τὰ βουκόλια). But some render ἐν ᾧ ἐκληρώθημεν *in whom our lot is cast = in whom we have our destiny,* suggesting a total involvement in the fortunes of Christ. S. 2 below.

❷ ***obtain by lot,*** mid., also simply *receive, have* τὶ *someth.* (since Eur., Tro. 29; Herm. Wr. 16, 14; Philo, Mos. 2, 101 al.; Sb 7031, 23 [72 AD]; 7032, 22) ὁ κεκληρωμένος τὸ αὐτὸ ὄνομα *who bore the same name* MPol 6:2. τινά someone κεκλήρωσαι τὴν παρθένον *you received the young woman by lot* (so that you might protect her) GJs 9:1. W. double acc. ἐκληρωσάμην αὐτὴν γυναῖκα 19:1 (codd.). Pass. ἐν ᾧ ἐκληρώθημεν *in whom we have obtained an inheritance* **Eph 1:11** appears to be the most probable rendering for this pass., the point being that the nations are also included, but s. 1 above.—DELG s.v. κλῆρος. M-M. TW.

κλῆσις, εως, ἡ (s. καλέω; Aristoph., X., Pla.; pap, LXX, TestSol, Philo, Just.; Tat. 15, 4).

❶ **invitation to experience of special privilege and responsibility, *call, calling, invitation.*** In our lit. almost exclusively of divine initiative (cp. κλῆσις, ἣν κέκληκεν [ὁ θεός] Epict. 1, 29, 49; s. also Maximus Tyr. 11, 11a) of the divine call, of the invitation to enter the kgdm. of God κ. ἐπουράνιος *a heavenly* (=divine) *call* **Hb 3:1.** ἡ κ. τοῦ θεοῦ *the call that comes fr. God* **Ro 11:29; Lk 11:42 v.l.** (Marcion's rdg., accord. to Epiph.; the latter has κρίσις). ἵνα ἐνμίνωσι (=ἐμμείνωσι) τῇ πρὸς τὸν πατέρα κλήσι *so that they might remain steadfast in their calling to the Father* AcPl Ha 7, 33. ἡ ἐλπὶς τῆς κλήσεως αὐτοῦ (=τοῦ θεοῦ) *the hope to which God calls* **Eph 1:18.** ἐλπὶς τῆς κ. ὑμῶν *the hope that your calling brings you* **4:4.** ἡ ἄνω κ. τοῦ θεοῦ ἐν Χριστῷ *the upward call of God in Christ* **Phil 3:14;** cp. 1 Cl 46:6. καλεῖν κλήσει ἁγίᾳ *call with a holy calling* **2 Ti 1:9;** cp. **Eph 4:1, 4** (cp. Orig., C. Cels. 3, 61, 21); ἀξιοῦν τινα τῆς κ. **2 Th 1:11** (s. ἀξιόω 1). ἡ κ. τινος *the call that has come to someone* (Orig., C. Cels. 2, 78, 5) **2 Pt 1:10.** βλέπετε τὴν κ. ὑμῶν *consider your call* i.e., what happened when it occurred **1 Cor 1:26.** κ. τῆς ἐπαγγελίας *the calling of* (i.e. that consists in) *God's promise* B 16:9. Of baptism (s. HKoch, Die Bussfrist des Pastor Hermae: Festgabe für AvHarnack 1921, 175f) μετὰ τὴν κ. ἐκείνην τὴν μεγάλην καὶ σεμνήν *after that great and sacred call* Hm 4, 3, 6; ὁ κύριος θέλει τὴν κ. τὴν γενομένην διὰ τοῦ υἱοῦ αὐτοῦ σωθῆναι *the Lord desires the salvation of those who are called through his Son* s 8, 11, 1.—Cp. AcThom 50 (Aa II/2, 166, 17); ὑπὸ πάντων τῶν τῆς κλήσεως 'by all those who are called' Iren. 1, 4, 4 (Harv. I 136, 13); also Hippol., Ref. 6, 45, 3.

❷ **position that one holds, *position, condition*** (Libanius, Argumenta Orationum Demosth. 2: VIII 601, 6 F. τὴν τοῦ μαχαιροποιοῦ κλῆσιν ἔλαβεν=took up the occupation; idem Progymn. 9, 2, 1: VIII 290, 14 ἐν τῇ κλήσει ταύτῃ=in this characteristic, i.e. as Phrygians; Philo, Leg. ad Gai. 163 θεοῦ κλῆσις=the position of a god [is a thing so sacred to the Alexandrians that they even give animals a share in it]) ἕκαστος ἐν τῇ κ. ᾗ ἐκλήθη, ἐν ταύτῃ μενέτω *everyone is to remain in the (same) condition/position in which the person was when called (to salvation)* **1 Cor 7:20.**—For other perspectives s. KHoll, D. Gesch. des Wortes Beruf: SBBerlAk 1924, xxixff; ENorden, Antike Menschen im Ringen um ihre Berufsbestimmung: SBBerlAk '32, p. xxxviiiff; WBieder, D. Berufung im NT '61.—DELG s.v. καλέω. M-M. TW. Sv.

κλητός, ή, όν (s. καλέω; Hom.; Aeschin. 2, 162; Aelian, NA 11, 12; PAmh 79, 5; LXX; Hippol., Ref. 5, 6, 7) **pert. to being invited, *called, invited*** to a meal (3 Km 1:41, 49; 3 Macc 5:14) in imagery of invitation to the kgdm. of God **Mt 22:14** (=B 4:14); cp. **20:16 v.l.**—Also without the figure consciously in the background *called* to God's kgdm. κ. ἅγιοι *saints who are called* (by God) **Ro 1:7; 1 Cor 1:2;** cp. B 4:13 ὡς κλητοί.—Subst. (SibOr 8, 92) κλητοὶ Ἰησοῦ Χριστοῦ *called by Jesus Christ* **Ro 1:6** (for the gen. cp. 3 Km 1:49 οἱ κλητοὶ τοῦ Αδωνιου). τοῖς κλητοῖς μου ApcPtRainer 1. κατὰ πρόθεσιν κ. ὄντες *called in accordance w.* (God's) *purpose* **8:28.** οἱ κλητοί *those who are called* **1 Cor 1:24; Jd 1.** οἱ μετ' αὐτοῦ κλητοὶ κ. ἐκλεκτοὶ κ. πιστοί **Rv 17:14.** κ. ἡγιασμένοι ἐν θελήματι θεοῦ διὰ τοῦ κυρίου ἡμῶν Ἰ. Χρ. *those who are called and consecrated acc. to God's will through our Lord Jesus Christ* 1 Cl ins.—Of calling to an office: κ. ἀπόστολος *called* (by God) *as an apostle* **Ro 1:1; 1 Cor 1:1.**—DELG s.v. καλέω. M-M. TW.

κλίβανος, ου, ὁ (Doric form Etym. Mag. 538, 19 [Hdt. 2, 92, also PPetr III, 140a, 3; BGU 1117, 10; 28; LXX; Philo, Rer. Div. Her. 311] for the Att. κρίβανος [Schwyzer I 39]; cp. Phryn. 179 Lob.; Crönert 77, 4) ***an oven*** (made of pottery) εἰς κ. βάλλειν *put into the furnace* **Mt 6:30; Lk 12:28.** The Day of Judgment ὡς κ. καιόμενος *like a burning oven* (cp. Hos 7:4) 2 Cl 16:3.—B. 340. DELG s.v. κρίβανος. M-M.

κλίμα, ατος, τό (s. κλίνω; Aristot. et al.; BGU 1549, 7; 1550, 5 [III BC]; Judg 20:2 A; EpArist. On the accent s. B-D-F §13; 109, 3; Mlt-H. 57; 354) ***district*** (Polyb. 5, 44, 6; 7, 6, 1; OGI 519, 18; Philo; Jos., Bell. 5, 506, Ant. 14, 401; SibOr 5, 339) τὰ κ. τῆς Ἀχαίας *the region of Achaia,* the province in its entirety **2 Cor 11:10.** τὰ κ. τῆς Συρίας καὶ τῆς Κιλικίας **Gal 1:21.** ἐν τοῖς κ. τούτοις *in these regions* **Ro 15:23.**—On νερτέρων ἀνεκδιήγητα κλίματα 1 Cl 20:5, s. ἀνεκδιήγητος.—DELG s.v. κλίνω. M-M.

κλῖμαξ, ακος, ἡ (s. κλίνω; Hom.+) ***ladder, flight of stairs*** Ox 840, 26.—DELG s.v. κλίνω.

κλινάριον, ου, τό (Aristoph., fgm. 239; Epict. 3, 5, 13; M. Ant. 11, 18, 3; Artem. 2, 57 v.l.; PSI 616, 14; POxy 1645, 9; TestAbr A 4 p. 80, 17 and 31 [Stone p. 8]—B-D-F §111, 3) dim. of κλίνη ***bed*** (w. κράβαττος) **Ac 5:15.**—DELG s.v. κλίνω II. M-M.

κλίνη, ης, ἡ (Eur., Hdt. et al.; ins, pap, LXX, TestSol, TestAbr, TestJob; TestLevi 19:4; JosAs; AscIs 2:14; EpArist 320) a place for those who are resting (2 Km 4:7; Ps 6:7), suffering (Gen 48:2; 49:33), or dining (Xenophanes 18, 2 Diehl[2]; Ezk 23:41).

❶ ***bed, couch*** **Mk 4:21; 7:30; Lk 8:16; 17:34;** καθίσαι εἰς τὴν κ. *sit on the bed* Hv 5:1.—*Pallet, stretcher* on which a sick man was carried (Appian, Bell. Civ. 1, 45 §199 ἔφυγεν ἐπὶ κλίνης διὰ νόσον; as a bier for the dead Pla., Leg. 12, 947b; Jos., Ant. 7, 40=2 Km 3:31.—2 Ch 16:14), prob. not differentiated fr. 'bed' **Mt 9:2, 6; Lk 5:18** (φέρειν ἐπὶ κλίνης as SIG 1169, 31; Jos., Ant. 17, 197). **Ac 5:15 v.l.** (for κλινάριον); βάλλειν τινὰ εἰς κ. *lay someone on a sickbed* i.e. strike her w. an illness **Rv 2:22** (a lingering illness as a divine punishment: Diod. S. 16, 61, 3; cp. also PUps 8, 4 s.v. ξηραίνω 2). GDalman, Arbeit 7, 189; Kl. Pauly III 255f (lit.)

❷ ***dining couch*** **Mk 7:4** as suggested by the context; the only NT pass. that qualifies for this mng. S. New Docs 1, 6–9, but without ref. to this pass.—B. 480. DELG s.v. κλίνω. M-M. TW.

κλινίδιον, ου, τό (s. κλινή; Dionys. Hal. 7, 68; Artem. 1, 2 p. 7, 22; M. Ant. 10, 28, 2; Plut., Mor. 466c, Coriol. 225 [24, 5]; Pollux 10, 7; Jos., Ant. 17, 161.—B-D-F §111, 3; Mlt-H. 346) dim. of κλίνη (q.v.) ***small bed = pallet, stretcher*** **Lk 5:19, 24.**—DELG s.v. κλίνω. M-M.

κλίνω 1 aor. ἔκλινα; pf. κέκλικα; 1 aor. pass. ἐκλίθην (B-D-F §76, 1; W-S. §13, 9f) (Hom.+).

❶ **to cause someth. to incline or bend, *incline, bow,*** trans. τὴν κεφαλήν *the head* of Jesus as he was dying **J 19:30** (but since the bowing of the head came before the giving up of his spirit, and since esp. in John's Gosp. the Passion is a voluntary act of Jesus to the very last, the bowing is not to be regarded as a sign of weakness; the Crucified One acted of his own accord; cp. BGU

954, 5 κλίνω τ. κεφαλήν μου κατενώπιόν σου); GJs 15:4 (s. κεφαλή 1b). τὸ πρόσωπον εἰς τὴν γῆν *bow one's face to the ground* **Lk 24:5.** τὰ γόνατα πρὸς τὸν δεσπότην (in prayer) GJs 20:2 (codd.). In uncertain context οὐδὲ γό[νατα ἔκλι]|ναν, ἀλλὰ … προσηύχοντο [ἑστῶτες] *nor did they kneel, but they prayed (standing)* AcPl Ha 1, 31.

❷ *lay (down)* trans. τὴν κεφαλήν (to sleep) **Mt 8:20; Lk 9:58.**

❸ *cause to lean,* trans., pass. in act. sense *lean, fall (over)* λέγει κύριος· ὅταν ξύλον κλιθῇ καὶ ἀναστῇ *when a tree falls over and rises again* B 12:1 (quot. of uncertain origin).

❹ *cause to fall, turn to flight,* trans. and fig. (as early as Hom.; Jos., Ant. 14, 416) παρεμβολὰς κ. ἀλλοτρίων **Hb 11:34.**

❺ intr. (B-D-F §308; Rob. 800) ('turn, change course'; X. et al.; PHib 38, 8 [252/251 BC]; TestJob 34:5 ἔκλινεν ἀπ' αὐτῶν=he turned away from them) ***decline, be far spent*** of the day, at dusk **Lk 9:12; 24:29** (cp. Apollon. Rhod. 1, 452 κλίνοντος ἠελίοιο; Polyb. 3, 93, 7; Arrian, Anab. 3, 4, 2; Jer 6:4 κέκλικεν ἡ ἡμέρα).—DELG. M-M.

κλισία, ας, ἡ (κλίνω; Hom. et al.; Lucian, Dial. Deor. 24, 1; Plut., Sert. 582 [26, 9] Ziegler v.l.; SIG 1109, 74; 3 Macc 6:31; EpArist 183; Jos., Ant. 12, 96) ***a group of people eating together*** κατακλίνατε αὐτοὺς κλισίας *have them sit down in groups (to eat)* **Lk 9:14** (cp. New Docs 4, 184).—DELG s.v. κλίνω. M-M. TW.

κλοπή, ῆς, ἡ (s. κλέπτω; Aeschyl.+) ***theft, stealing*** in list of vices (Jos., Bell. 2, 581) D 3:5a. Plural (TestReub 3:6; GrBar; Jos., Bell. 5, 402; Ar., Ath.) **Mt 15:19; Mk 7:21;** D 3:5b; 5:1.—M-M.

κλύδων, ωνος, ὁ (s. next entry; Hom. et al; Sb 8026, 19; LXX; En; TestSol 10:37 C; Jos., Bell. 3, 423, rarely in pl. [as Polyb. 10, 3, 3; Vett. Val. 344, 15; 4 Macc 15:31]) **a succession of waves, *rough water*** κ. τοῦ ὕδατος **Lk 8:24;** *surf* κ. θαλάσσης (Philo, Op. M. 58, Gig. 51; cp. Jon 1:4, 11; Jos., Ant. 9, 210) **Js 1:6.**—DELG s.v. κλύζω. M-M. Sv.

κλυδωνίζομαι (s. κλύδων; Vett. Val. 354, 26; Aristaen., Ep. 1, 27 H.; Is 57:20; Jos., Ant. 9, 239 ὁ δῆμος ἅπας ταρασσόμενος κ. κλυδωνιζόμενος; SibOr 1, 289) ***be tossed here and there by waves*** fig. κλυδωνιζόμενοι καὶ περιφερόμενοι παντὶ ἀνέμῳ τ. διδασκαλίας *tossed about by the waves and blown about by every wind of teaching* **Eph 4:14.**—DELG s.v. κλύζω. M-M.

κλώθω pf. pass. 3 sg. κέκλωσται (Joseph.) (Hdt. et al., ins [New Docs 4, 29], pap, LXX; Jos. Bell. 6, 49) ***spin*** by twisting of fibers Μαρία … ἔκλωθεν GJs 10:2.—DELG.

Κλωπᾶς, ᾶ, ὁ ***Clopas.*** Among the women who were standing at the cross of Jesus acc. to **J 19:25** there was a Μαρία ἡ τοῦ Κλωπᾶ *Mary, the wife of Clopas.* This woman can scarcely be identical w. the sister of Jesus' mother who has just been mentioned (without being named), since then we should have to postulate two sisters w. the same name, Mary (but s. Artem. 4, 30 p. 222, 3f, where we find a woman with her ἀδελφὴ ὁμώνυμος). Hegesippus mentions a Clopas as a brother of Joseph (in Eus. HE 3, 11; 32, 1–4; 6; 4, 22, 4).—The name cannot be explained w. certainty, but is prob. Semit. (Palmyr. קלופא; Journal Asiatique 10, 1897, 327). S. Κλεοπᾶς.—M-M.

κνήθω (Aristot.; Herodas 4, 51 et al.='scratch'; acc. to Moeris p. 234 H. Gk., not Att. There is an older form κνάω which, as ἐπικνάω, is found as early as Il. 11, 639. The aor. mid. is found in Lucian, Bis Accusatus 1 οὐδ' ὅσον κνήσασθαι τὸ οὖς σχολὴν διάγων=he does not even have enough time to scratch his ear) ***itch*** pass. w. act. sense *feel an itching* κνηθόμενοι τὴν ἀκοήν (s. ἀκοή 3). Fig. of curiosity, that looks for interesting and juicy bits of information. This itching is relieved by the messages of the new teachers. W. the same components as a background, one might transl.: *to have one's ear tickled* (a κνῆσις ὤτων takes place τρυφῆς ἕνεκα: Plut., Mor. 167b) **2 Ti 4:3** (s. Clem. Al., Strom. I 3, 22, 5 p. 15 Stähl.).—DELG s.v. -κναίω. M-M.

Κνίδος, ου, ἡ (Hom. Hymns, Hdt. et al.; Jos., Ant. 13, 370; 1 Macc 15:23; Ath. 17:3 ἡ Ἀφροδίτη ἐν Κ.) ***Cnidus,*** a peninsula w. a city of the same name on the coast of Caria in Asia Minor, touched by Paul on his journey to Crete **Ac 27:7.**—Pauly-W. XI 914ff; Kl. Pauly III 260 (lit.).

κνῖσα, ης, ἡ (Hom. [κνίση] et al.; Philo, Somn. 1, 49 v.l. [for κνίσσα]; Just., Ath.) ***the odor of burning fat*** on a sacrifice Dg 2:8; 3:5 (used both times w. αἷμα). εἰδώλοις … καὶ κνείσαις AcPl Ha 2, 32.—DELG.

κοδράντης, ου, ὁ (Lat. loanw., 'quadrans'; also in rabb.; actually one quarter of an 'as'. Cp. Plut., Cic. 875 [29, 5] τὸ λεπτότατον τοῦ χαλκοῦ νομίσματος κουαδράντην ἐκάλουν [the Romans]. For the spelling s. B-D-F §41, 2) ***quadrans, penny***=two λεπτά **Mk 12:42** (DSperber, Mk 12:42 and Its Metrological Background, NovT 9, '67, 178–90), 1/64 of a denarius (s. δηνάριον). It was the smallest Roman coin. ἕως ἂν ἀποδῷς τὸν ἔσχατον κ. *until you have repaid the last cent* **Mt 5:26; Lk 12:59** D; D 1:5 (Sextus 39 μέχρις οὗ καὶ τ. ἔσχατον κοδράντην ἀπολάβῃ [the punishing demon]).—Lit. under ἀργύριον 2c.—Schürer II 66. M-M.

Κοδρᾶτος, ου, ὁ ***Quadratus*** (Epict. 3, 23, 23; Ael. Aristid. 47, 22 K.=23 p. 451 D.; Herodian; OGI 683, 5; Jos., Bell. 2, 241) a proconsul MPol 21; s. Στάτιος. Name of the apologist, abbr. Qua in this lexicon (cp. Eus., HE 4, 3, 1f).

κοιλία, ας, ἡ (κοῖλος 'hollow'; Hdt., Aristoph.+; loanw. in rabb.) in its broadest sense the 'cavity' of the body (Gen 3:14 w. στῆθος) that stores such organs as the stomach, intestines, and womb, then in ref. to such parts.

❶ **the organ of nourishment**—ⓐ the digestive tract in its fullest extent, ***belly, stomach*** (Jer 28:34; Ezk 3:3; Sir 36:18 al.) εἰς τὴν κ. χωρεῖν (cp. Plut., Mor. 699f εἴπερ εἰς κοιλίαν ἐχώρει διὰ στομάχου πᾶν τὸ πινόμενον. Even the last part of the alimentary canal is κ.: Herodian 1, 17, 10) **Mt 15:17;** cp. **Mk 7:19.**

ⓑ esp., the body's receptacle for aliments, ***belly, stomach*** (so Diod. S. 2, 58, 3 between φάρυγξ [gullet] and σπλάγχνα [intestines]; Aelian, VH 1, 1 al.) of Jonah's fish (Jon 2:1f; Just., D. 107, 2) **Mt 12:40.** Of the human *stomach* **1 Cor 6:13.** γεμίσαι τὴν κ. ἔκ τινος *fill the stomach w. someth.* i.e. eat one's fill of someth. **Lk 15:16 v.l.** Of the working of a scroll eaten by the writer of the Apc. (cp. Ezk 3:3) πικρανεῖ σου τὴν κ. **Rv 10:9;** cp. vs. **10;** δουλεύειν τῇ κ. *be a slave to one's stomach* **Ro 16:18;** ὧν ὁ θεὸς ἡ κ. *whose god is their stomach* **Phil 3:19.**

❷ ***womb, uterus*** (Epict. 2, 16, 43; 3, 22, 74; Dt 28:4, 11; Job 1:21; Ruth 1:11; TestJob 24:2) **Lk 1:41, 44; 2:21; 11:27; 23:29; J 3:4;** B 13:2 (Gen 25:23). ἐκ κοιλίας *from birth* i.e. from earliest youth (Judg 16:17 A; Is 49:1) **Mt 19:12; Lk 1:15; Ac 3:2; 14:8; Gal 1:15;** καρπὸς τῆς κ. *fruit of the womb* (cp. Mi 6:7; La 2:20) **Lk 1:42.**

❸ **seat of inward life, of feelings and desires, *belly*** (but Eng. prefers the functional equivalent ***heart***): κ. denotes the hidden, innermost recesses of the human body (=בֶּטֶן Job 15:35; Pr 18:20; 20:27, 30; Sir 19:12; 51:21), so that a variation betw. κοιλία and καρδία becomes poss.: **Ac 2:30 v.l.** (κοιλία and καρδία for ὀσφῦς); **Rv 10:9** (v.l. καρδία) (Hab 3:16; Ps 39:9; cp. schol. on Nicander, Alexipharmaca 21 τοῦ στόματος τῆς κοιλίας, ἣν οἱ μὲν καρδίαν καλοῦσιν, οἱ δὲ δοχεῖον τῶν ἐντέρων τῆς βρώσεως [καρδία of the upper opening of the stomach: Theocr. 2, 49]; PGM 4, 3141: the κοιλία is the place where the καρδία is found). ποταμοὶ ἐκ τῆς κ. αὐτοῦ ῥεύσουσιν ὕδατος ζῶντος *rivers of living water shall flow from the person's heart* **J 7:38** (thought of as a scripture quot., though its source can no longer be determined w. certainty. The expr. may be proverbial; cp. Cicero, De Orat. 2, 39 [162]. The κ. has often been taken to be that of the believer, but there is an increasing tendency to punctuate w. a period after ἐμέ in vs. **38** rather than after πινέτω at the end of vs. 37 [s. RSV mg. and NRSV text] and understand κ. of Jesus; s. Hdb. ad loc.; JJeremias, Golgotha 1926, 80–84; HBornhäuser, Sukka '35, 34–39; Bultmann, Ev. d. Joh. '41, 228–30. For patristic interpr., HRahner, Biblica 22, '41, 269–302; 367–403. Differently, A-MDubarle, Vivre et Penser 3, '43/44, 238–41). JBlenkinsopp, NTS 6, '59, 95–99.—B. 253. DELG s.v. κοῖλος. M-M. TW.

κοιμάω (s. two next entries) aor. mid. impv. 2 sg. κοιμῆσαι (TestAbr B 4, 109, 11 [Stone p. 66]). Pass.: 1 fut. κοιμηθήσομαι; 1 aor. ἐκοιμήθην; pf. κεκοίμημαι (Hom.+) in our lit. only in pass. and w. act. sense.

❶ **to be asleep,** ***sleep, fall asleep*** (Hom.+ usu.; Diod. S. 15, 25, 2; PGM 36, 151; 305; Jos., Bell. 4, 306, Ant. 8, 28, Vi. 132; Test12Patr, SibOr 3, 794) **Mt 28:13; Lk 22:45; J 11:12; Ac 12:6;** Hv 2, 4, 1; s 9, 11, 3; 6; φυλάκων κοιμωμένων AcPl Ha 4, 4. Fig. of the night (as of the sun: Pythagoras in Geminus, Elementa Astronomiae p. 22e) κοιμᾶται ἡ νύξ *the night falls asleep* 1 Cl 24:3.

❷ **to be dead,** ***sleep,*** fig. extension of mng. 1, of the sleep of death, in which case additional words often emphasize the figurative nature of the expression (as early as Il. 11, 241; OGI 383, 43 [I BC]; IG XIV, 549, 1; 929, 13 κοιμᾶται τ. αἰώνιον ὕπνον). Yet the verb without these additions can have this mng. (Soph., Electra 509 Μυρτίλος ἐκοιμάθη; Aeschrion Lyr. [IV BC] 6, 2 Diehl[2], grave-epigram, ἐνταῦθα κεκοίμημαι; PFay 22, 28 [I BC] ἐὰν τὸ παιδίον κοιμήσηται; Gen 47:30; Dt 31:16; 3 Km 11:43; Is 14:8; 43:17; 2 Macc 12:45.—OMerlier, BCH 54, 1930, 228–40; MOgle, The Sleep of Death: Memoirs of the Amer. Acad. in Rome 11, '33, 81–117; JBowmer, ET 53, '42, 355f [on **1 Cor 15:20,** 22]; JKazakis, Hellenika 40, '89, 21–33, funerary motifs. S. ἐξυπνίζω. New Docs 4, 37).

ⓐ *fall asleep, die, pass away* (Did., Gen. 215, 20) **J 11:11; Ac 7:60; 13:36; 1 Cor 7:39; 11:30; 15:6, 51; 2 Pt 3:4;** 1 Cl 44:2; Hm 4, 4, 1. ἐκοιμήθην καὶ ὕπνωσα (Ps 3:6) is interpr. to mean 'die' in 1 Cl 26:2. ἐν δικαιοσύνῃ ἐκοιμήθησαν *they fell asleep as righteous people* Hs 9, 16, 7. κοιμηθείς *after my death* IRo 4:2. οἱ διδάσκαλοι … κοιμηθέντες ἐν δυνάμει καὶ πίστει τ. υἱοῦ τ. θεοῦ *teachers who died in the power of the Son of God, and in faith in him* Hs 9, 16, 5. οἱ κοιμηθέντες *those who have already died* **1 Th 4:14f.** οἱ κ. ἐν Χριστῷ *those who died in communion w. Christ* **1 Cor 15:18** (contrast Catullus 5, 6 nox est perpetua una dormienda = one everlasting night awaits our sleeping).

ⓑ the pres. ptc. and perf. ptc. denoting a state of being, w. art., subst. *the one who has fallen asleep* οἱ κοιμώμενοι (2 Macc 12:45) **1 Th 4:13;** GPt 10:41.—οἱ κεκοιμημένοι **1 Cor 15:20;** Hs 9, 16, 3.—Not subst. οἱ κεκοιμημένοι ἅγιοι **Mt 27:52;** οἱ μὲν κεκοιμημένοι, οἱ δὲ ἔτι ὄντες *some are dead, the others are still living* Hv 3, 5, 1.—B. 269. DELG s.v. κεῖμαι. M-M s.v. κοιμάομαι. TW.

κοίμησις, εως, ἡ (s. prec. entry; Pla., ins, LXX)—❶ **state of sleep,** ***lying down to sleep, sleep*** (Pla., Symp. 10 p. 183a) ἡ κ. τοῦ ὕπνου (epexeg. gen.) *the sleep of slumber* **J 11:13.** S. New Docs 3, 93.

❷ **state of death,** ***sleep,*** fig. extension of 1 (Sir 46:19; 48:13; inscriptions on Jewish graves in Rome [ABerliner, Gesch. d. Juden in Rom I 1893, 72f; Schürer II 438, 45 ἐν εἰρήνῃ ἡ κοίμησις αὐτοῦ; s. also CIJ]; Sb 1540, 5; IDefixWünsch 4, 30; Pel.-Leg. p. 15, 16; JosAs ch. 29 cod. A end; ApcMos 42) Hv 3, 11, 3; s 9, 15, 6.—FCumont, Le symbolisme funéraire des Romains '42, 360–79.—DELG s.v. κεῖμαι. M-M.

κοιμητήριον, ου, τό (s. two prec. entries) (IG VII, 235, 43 [IV BC] Dosiadas Epigrammatist [III BC] in Athen. 4, 143c) ***bedroom, place of rest,*** in Christian usage (s. ins New Docs 3, 138; 4, 234, incl. Jewish) also ***graveyard, cemetery*** AcPl BMM verso 22 κο[ι]μητηρίων (fragmentary text, hence mng. is uncertain; but if persecution is suggested, 'cemetery' is probably meant).—DELG s.v. κεῖμαι.

κοινῇ s. κοινός 1c.

κοινός, ή, όν (s. the numerous cognates that follow this entry; Hes.+) prim. 'common' (opp. ἴδιος)

❶ **pert. to being of mutual interest or shared collectively,** ***communal, common*** (so gener. Gk. lit., also LXX; EpArist, Philo, Joseph., SibOr).

ⓐ adj. (ὁ κ. πάντων πατήρ Orig., C. Cels. 8, 53, 27) τράπεζα (Diod. S. 4, 74, 2) Dg 5:7a. πίστις **Tit 1:4.** σωτηρία (cp. SIG 409, 33f [ca. 275 BC]; X., An. 3, 2, 32; Diod. S. 37, 2, 5; Polyaenus 5, 31) **Jd 3.** κ. ἐλπίς IEph 21:2; IPhld 5:2; 11:2. κ. ὄνομα (Philo, Abr. 7, Leg. ad Gai. 194) IEph 1:2; εἶχον ἅπαντα κ. *they had everything in common* (κοινὰ πάντα ἔχειν: Strabo 7, 3, 9.—Diod. S. 5, 9, 4: the inhabitants of Lipara τὰς οὐσίας κοινὰς ποιησάμενοι καὶ ζῶντες κατὰ συσσίτια=they made their possessions common property and lived acc. to the custom of common meals; Iambl., Vi. Pyth. 30, 168 of the Pythagoreans: κοινὰ πᾶσι πάντα … ἦν, ἴδιον δὲ οὐδεὶς οὐδὲν ἐκέκτητο. Porphyr., Vi. Pyth. 20. The word occurs in a sim. context w. ref. to the Essenes: Philo, Prob. Lib. 85; 86; Jos., Ant. 18, 20, and the Therapeutae: Philo, Vi. Cont. 32; 40; HBraun, Qumran u. d. NT, I, '66, 43–50. Even Pla., Phdr. 279c κοινὰ τὰ τῶν φίλων) **Ac 2:44;** cp. **4:32** (cp. 1QS 6:2; for the recurring idea of the "other self" in antiquity s. also Persius, Satires 5, 22f; Horace, Odes 1, 3, 8; 2, 17, 5).—PSchmiedel, Die Gütergemeinschaft der ältesten Christenheit: PM 2, 1898, 367–78; EvDobschütz, Probleme des apost. Zeitalters 1904, 39ff; JBehm, Kommunismus im Urchristentum: NKZ 31, 1920, 275–97; KLake: Beginn. I/5, '33, 140–51; Haenchen ad loc. (lit.). κοινῆς εἰκαιότητος καὶ ἀπάτης *of general silliness and deceit* Dg 4:6—Of body and spirit ἀμφότερα κ. ἐστιν *both are in communion = belong together, cannot be separated* Hs 5, 7, 4.

ⓑ subst. τὸ κοινόν *what is (in) common* τὸ κ. τῆς ἐλπίδος *the common ground of hope* 1 Cl 51:1.—τὸ κ. *the society, the community* (to designate all those who belong to a given group: POxy 53, 2 τὸ κ. τῶν τεκτόνων; 84, 3; Jos., Vi. 65; Orig., C. Cels. 1, 31, 26; Hippol., Ref. 9, 19, 1) διακονία εἰς τὸ κ. *service for the (Christian) community* IPhld 1:1. Also the *common treasury* (Appian, Iber. 8, §31 τὸ κ.=the state treasury) of slaves ἐλευθεροῦσθαι ἀπὸ τοῦ κ. *to be freed at the expense of the common treasury* (i.e. of the Christian community) IPol 4:3 (cp. X., An. 4, 7, 27; 5, 1, 12 ἀπὸ κοινοῦ=at state expense; Jos., Vi. 297 ἐκ τοῦ κ.; 298).

ⓒ adv. κοινῇ *together, collectively* (Soph., Thu.+; ins; PMagd 29, 2; LXX; Jos., C. Ap. 1, 70; 2, 166; Just., A I, 67, 5 and 7) IEph 20:2; ISm 12:2 (both in contrast to κατ' ἄνδρα ['man for man', 'individually'], as SIG 1073, 18); 7:2 (opp. κατ' ἰδίαν, as Diod. S. 11, 24, 4; Dio Chrys. 34 [51], 9; SIG 630, 15 (restored rdg.); 2 Macc 9:26). τὸ κοινῇ συμφέρον *the common good* B 4:10.

❷ **pert. to being of little value because of being common, *common, ordinary, profane*—ⓐ** in a general sense (cp. Alcman [VII BC], fgm. 49 D.[2] τὰ κοινά of that which ordinary people eat, in contrast to those of more refined tastes; Plut., Mor. 751b καλὸν γὰρ ἡ φιλία καὶ ἀστεῖον, ἡ δὲ ἡδονὴ κοινὸν καὶ ἀνελεύθερον [Ltzm., Hdb. on Ro 14:14]; cp. 1 Macc 1:47, 62; EpArist 315=Jos., Ant. 12, 112 κοινοὶ ἄνθρωποι; 13, 4; Iren. 4, 18, 5 [Harv. II 206, 11]). κ. ἡγεῖσθαί τι *consider someth. ordinary* **Hb 10:29,** unless this belongs in 2b.

ⓑ specifically, of that which is ceremonially impure: **Rv 21:27.** χεῖρες (ceremon.) *impure* **Mk 7:2, 5** (MSmith, Tannaitic Parall. to the Gosp. '51, 31f); οὐδὲν κ. δι' ἑαυτοῦ *nothing is unclean of itself* **Ro 14:14a;** cp. **bc** of this same vs. οὐδέποτε ἔφαγον πᾶν κ. καὶ ἀκάθαρτον *I have never eaten anything common or unclean* (1 Macc 1:62) **Ac 10:14;** cp. vs. **28; 11:8** (CHouse, Andrews University Seminary Studies 21, '83, 143–53); GJs 6:1 (s. deStrycker). **Hb 10:29,** s. 2a.—Dg 5:7b (see κοίτη 1b).—B. 1365. DELG. M-M. EDNT. TW. Sv.

κοινόω 1 aor. ἐκοίνωσα; pf. κεκοίνωκα, pass. ptc. κεκοινωμένος (Pind., Thu. et al. in the sense of κοινός 1 'make one a participant in someth.', 'share'; Jos., Ant. 5, 267; 18, 231; Iren. 1, 2, 2 [Harv. I 15, 1]; for ins s. 1 below).

❶ ***share*** (Aeschyl., Suppl. 369; Thu. 2, 73, 1; Alciphron 3, 36, 4) mid. *Paul shared the (Christian) message with them and said* AcPl Ha 9, 32 [Παῦλος] κοινω[σά|μενος αὐτοῖς τὸν λόγον εἶπεν] (restored after Aa I 114, 4; cp. I 112, 4; cp. IEph Ia, 25, 8 of information that was communicated [New Docs 4, 9]).

❷ most freq. in the sense of κοινός 2 ***make common*** or ***impure, defile*** in the cultic sense (4 Macc 7:6; cp. John Malalas [VI AD], Chronographia 277, 2 LDind. [1831] κοινώσας τὰ ὕδατα).

ⓐ τινά *someone* **Mt 15:11, 18, 20; Mk 7:15, 18, 20, 23.** Aor. pass. 3 pl. ἐκοινώθησαν (AssMos fgm. g); pf. pass. ptc. w. the art., subst. οἱ κεκοινωμένοι *those who are defiled* i.e. according to Levitic ordinance **Hb 9:13.**

ⓑ τὶ *someth.* the temple *profane, desecrate* **Ac 21:28.** Pass., of a sacrifice *become defiled* D 14:2.

ⓒ abs. **Rv 21:27 v.l.** (for κοινόν).

❸ ***consider/declare (ritually) unclean*** **Ac 10:15; 11:9.**—On Judean perspective s. WPascher, Rein u. Unrein '70, 165–68; cp. Jos., Ant. 11, 8, 7.—DELG s.v. κοινός. M-M. TW.

Κόϊντος, ου, ὁ (Diod. S. 11, 27, 1 of a contemporary of the battle of Salamis [480 BC]; Plut. et al.; SIG[2] 588, 34; SIG 1127, 3; OGI 684, 1; pap [Preisigke, Namenbuch]; 2 Macc 11:34; Jos., Ant. 14, 219) ***Quintus,*** a Christian in Smyrna MPol 4.

κοινωνέω (s. κοινός and cognates) fut. κοινωνήσω; 1 aor. ἐκοινώνησα; pf. κεκοινώνηκα (Aeschyl.+).

❶ ***share, have a share*—ⓐ** τινός *in someth.* (X., Rep. Lac. 1, 9, Mem. 2, 6, 23; Pla., Leg. 12 p. 947a; Diod. S. 5, 49, 6 τοὺς τῶν μυστηρίων κοινωνήσαντας=those who participated in, i.e. were initiated into, the mysteries; 5, 68, 3 τῆς τροφῆς ταύτης; 15, 68, 1; 19, 4, 3; Herodian 3, 10, 8; ins [Kl. T. 121 no. 32, 41]; pap; Pr 1:11; 3 Macc 2:31; Philo, Post. Cai. 160 al.; Jos., Ant. 4, 75, C. Ap. 2, 174; ὁ μιλίας ἢ ἑστίας Just., D. 47, 2; τραπέζης Orig., C. Cels. 2, 21, 6 and 17; αἰσθήσεως Did., Gen. 149, 2.—B-D-F §169, 1; Rob. 509f) of human beings αἵματος καὶ σαρκός *share in flesh and blood* **Hb 2:14** (ins fr. Commagene in IReisenKN, Humann-Puchstein p. 371, 46–47 [I BC] πᾶσιν ὅσοι φύσεως κοινωνοῦντες ἀνθρωπίνης).

ⓑ τινί *in someth.* (Demosth., Prooem. 25, 2 [bracketed by Blass]; Plut., 1030 [Arat. 8, 3]; Just., D. 35, 6; Tat. 19, 2; τῷ θανάτῳ Did., Gen. 148, 25; but Wsd 6:23 [s. JCampbell, JBL 51, '32, 359] 'associate with' so NRSV; difft. REB).

α. τοῖς πνευματικοῖς *in spiritual blessings* **Ro 15:27.** τοῖς τοῦ Χριστοῦ παθήμασιν **1 Pt 4:13** (cp. Achilles Tat. 7, 2, 3 εἰς τὸ παθεῖν κοινωνία=fellowship in suffering). Of a martyr's body: *receive a part of,* i.e. a part of the body as a 'relic' κ. τῷ ἁγίῳ σαρκίῳ MPol 17:1.

β. To *share, participate* in the deeds of others means to be equally responsible for them ἁμαρτίαις ἀλλοτρίαις **1 Ti 5:22** (Artem. 3, 51 κ. τῶν ἁμαρτημάτων ἐκείνῳ; Ath., R. 21 p. 73, 27 [of the body] κ. τῇ ψυχῇ τῶν . . . πόνων). τοῖς ἔργοις αὐτοῦ τ. πονηροῖς **2J 11.**

γ. Participation in someth. can reach such a degree that one claims a part in it for oneself: *take an interest in, share* (Philostrat., Vi. Apoll. 5, 25; Pr 1:11) ταῖς χρείαις τῶν ἁγίων **Ro 12:13.** W. dat. of pers. and inf. foll. ἐκοινώνησεν ὁ Ἀρτέμων . . . Παύλῳ . . . ἐν χά[ριτι θεοῦ] δόξαι (error for δοξάσαι) τὸν κύριον *A. joined Paul . . . in praising the Lord in God's grace* AcPl Ha 7, 22. The transition to the next mng. is easy.

❷ ***give/contribute a share*** (Philo, Spec. Leg. 2, 107) w. dat. of pers. (cp. Demosth. 25, 61; Appian, Bell. Civ. 1, 31 §139; Artem. 5 p. 252, 14; Sextus 350; Jos., C. Ap. 2, 258; Just. A I, 14, 2) foll. by ἔν τινι *give someone a share of someth.* **Gal 6:6.** κοινωνήσεις ἐν πᾶσιν τῷ πλησίον σου B 19:8. Also τινὶ εἴς τι (cp. Pla., Rep. 453a; PLond V, 1794, 7; TestZeb 3:1) οὐδεμία μοι ἐκκλησία ἐκοινώνησεν εἰς *no congregation made me its partner in* **Phil 4:15.** W. acc. of the pers. κοινωνῆσαί με τῇ ἁμαρτίᾳ σου *make me an accomplice in your sin* GJs 2:3 (s. deStrycker p. 306f).

❸ ***make (ritually) unclean, defile.*** Ms. D uses κ. **Mt 15:11** (twice), **18, 20** in the sense of κοινόω 2 (cp. Diod. S. 5, 33, 5 κ.=partake [in unsanitary practice]).—DELG s.v. κοινός. M-M. TW.

κοινωνία, ας, ἡ (s. prec. entry; Pind.+; ins, pap, LXX; JosAs 7:6 cod. A; Philo [Mos. 1, 158 of communion w. God]; Joseph.; loanw. in rabb.; Just.; Tat. 18, 2; Ath.; Iren. 4, 18, 5 [Harv. II 205, 4] w. ἕνωσις).

❶ **close association involving mutual interests and sharing, *association, communion, fellowship, close relationship*** (hence a favorite expr. for the marital relationship as the most intimate betw. human beings Isocr. 3, 40; BGU 1051, 9 [I AD]; 1052, 7; POxy 1473, 33; 3 Macc 4:6; Jos., Ant. 1, 304; Did., Gen 235, 18. But s. also Diod. S. 10, 8, 2 ἡ τοῦ βίου κ.=the common type or bond of life that unites the Pythagoreans) τινός *with* or *to someone* (Amphis Com. [IV BC] 20, 3; Herodian 1, 10, 1; τοῦ θεοῦ Orig., C. Cels. 3, 56, 6); hence there is linguistic warrant to transl.: κ. τοῦ υἱοῦ αὐτοῦ *fellowship with God's Son* **1 Cor 1:9** (s. 4 below) and κ. τοῦ ἁγίου πνεύματος *fellowship w. the Holy Spirit* **2 Cor 13:13** (so JSickenberger comm. [Bonnerbibel 1919; 4th ed. '32] ad loc. in the Trinitarian sense but s. WKümmel, appendix to HLtzm. comm. [Hdb]). Others take the latter gen. as a subjective gen. or gen. of quality *fellowship brought about by the* Holy Spirit (APlummer, w. reservations, comm. 2 Cor [ICC] et al.; TSchmidt, D. Leib Christi 1919, 135; s. 4 below). Corresp. κ. πνεύματος *fellowship w. the Spirit* **Phil 2:1** (Synes., Prov. 1, 15 p. 108c κ. γνώμης=community of will and s. 2 below).—κοινωνία(ν ἔχειν) μετά τινος *(have) fellowship w. someone* (cp. Job 34:8) w. God **1J 1:3b, 6** (cp. Epict.

2, 19, 27 περὶ τῆς πρὸς τὸν Δία κοινωνίας βουλευόμενον; Jos., Bell. 7, 264, C. Ap. 1, 35 [both πρός w. acc.]); w. fellow Christians vss. **3a, 7.** εἴς τι (POxf 5f) ἡ κ. εἰς τὸ εὐαγγέλιον *close relationship w. the gospel* **Phil 1:5.** ηὐδόκησαν κ. τινὰ ποιήσασθαι εἰς τοὺς πτωχούς *they have undertaken to establish a rather close relation w. the poor* **Ro 15:26** (sim. GPeterman, Make a Contribution or Establish Fellowship: NTS 40, '94, 457–63; but some prefer 3 below).—κ. πρός w. acc. *connection with, relation to* (Pla., Symp. 188c; Galen, Protr. 9 p. 28, 7 J.; SIG 646, 54 [170 BC]; Philo, Leg. ad Gai. 110 τίς οὖν κοινωνία πρὸς Ἀπόλλωνα τῷ μηδὲν οἰκεῖον ἐπιτετηδευκότι; cp. Jos., C. Ap. 2, 208; τοῦ πατρὸς πρὸς τὸν υἱὸν κ. Ath. 12, 2; πρὸς τὸ θειότερον κ. Orig., C. Cels. 3, 28, 47) τίς κ. φωτὶ πρὸς σκότος; *what does darkness have in common with light?* **2 Cor 6:14** (cp. Sir 13:2, 17f; Aristoph., Thes. 140 τίς κατόπτρου καὶ ξίφους κοινωνία;).—Abs. *fellowship,* (harmonious) *unity* (Hippol., Ref. 9, 12, 26) **Ac 2:42** (s. JFitzmyer, PSchubert Festschr. '66, 242–44 [Acts-Qumran] suggests that 'community of goods' [יחד] may be meant here, as 1QS 1, 11–13; 6, 17. On the problem of this term s. HBraun, Qumran u. d. NT, I, '66; 143–50; s. also ACarr, The Fellowship of Ac 2:42 and Cognate Words: Exp. 8th ser., 5, 1913, 458ff). δεξιὰς κοινωνίας διδόναι τινί *give someone the right hand of fellowship* **Gal 2:9** (JSampley, Pauline Partnership in Christ '80, argues for a legal notion of 'consensual societas' but s. New Docs 3, 19).—κ. also has the concrete mng. *society, brotherhood* as a closely knit majority, naturally belonging together: Maximus Tyr. 15, 4b τί ἐστιν τὸ τῆς κοινωνίας συμβόλαιον; what is the contribution (i.e., of the philosopher) to the community or (human) society? 16, 2m δημώδεις κοινωνίαι=meetings of the common people.—On ancient clubs and associations s. Poland; also JWaltzing, Étude historique sur les corporations professionnelles chez les Romaine, 4 vols. 1895–1900; EZiebarth, Das griechische Vereinswesen 1896.

❷ **attitude of good will that manifests an interest in a close relationship, *generosity, fellow-feeling, altruism*** (Epict. in Stob. 43 Sch. χρηστότητι κοινωνίας; Arrian, Anab. 7, 11, 9 κ. beside ὁμόνοια; Herm. Wr. 13, 9 [opp. πλεονεξία]) ἁπλότης τῆς κ. εἴς τινα **2 Cor 9:13.** W. εὐποιΐα **Hb 13:16.** The context permits this mng. also **Phil 2:1** (s. 1 above). The transition to the next mng. is easy.

❸ abstr. for concr. ***sign of fellowship, proof of brotherly unity,*** even ***gift, contribution*** (Lev 5:21; ins of Asia Minor: κ.='subsidy' [Rdm.[2] 10]) **Ro 15:26** (s. 1 above). Under this head we may perh. classify κοινωνία τ. αἵματος (σώματος) τοῦ Χριστοῦ *a means for attaining a close relationship with the blood (body) of Christ* **1 Cor 10:16ab** (s. 4 below).

❹ ***participation, sharing*** τινός *in someth.* (Appian, Bell. Civ. 1, 67 §306 κ. τῶν παρόντων=in the present undertakings; 5, 71 §299 κ. τῆς ἀρχῆς in the rule; Polyaenus 6, 7, 2 κ. τοῦ μιάσματος in the foul deed; Maximus Tyr. 19, 3b τῆς ἀρετῆς; Synes., Kgdm. 13 p. 12c. κ. τῶν ἔργων=in the deeds of others; Wsd 8:18; Jos., Ant. 2, 62) ὅπως ἡ κ. τῆς πίστεώς σου ἐνεργὴς γένηται *that your participation in the faith may be made known through your deeds* **Phlm 6.** γνῶναι κοινωνίαν παθημάτων αὐτοῦ *become aware of sharing his sufferings* **Phil 3:10.** ἡ κ. τῆς διακονίας τῆς εἰς τοὺς ἁγίους *taking part in the relief of God's people* **2 Cor 8:4.** Perh. this is the place for **1 Cor 1:9** (s. 1 above); **2 Cor 13:13** (*participation in the Holy Spirit:* Ltzm., Kümmel in appendix to Ltzm. comm., Windisch, Seesemann [s. below] 70; Goodsp., Probs. 169f; s. 1 above.—Cp. τοῦ ἁγίου πνεύματος κ. of ecstasy Did., Gen. 230, 16); **1 Cor 10:16** (*participation in the blood [body] of Christ.* So ASchlatter, Pls der Bote Jesu '34, 295f et al.; s. 3 above. But perh. here κοινωνία w. gen. means *the common possession* or *enjoyment of someth.* [Diod. S. 8, 5, 1 ἀγελῶν κ.= of the flocks; Maximus Tyr. 19, 3b ἐπὶ κοινωνίᾳ τῆς ἀρετῆς=for the common possession of excellence; Diog. L. 7, 124; Synes., Kgdm. 20 p. 24b; Hierocles 6, 428: we are to choose the best man as friend and unite ourselves with him πρὸς τὴν τῶν ἀρετῶν κοινωνίαν=for the common possession or enjoyment of virtues; 7, 429 τῶν καλῶν τὴν κ.]. Then **1 Cor 10:16** would be: Do not the cup and the bread mean the common partaking of the body and blood of Christ? After all, we all partake of one and the same bread). **Eph 3:9 v.l.** (for οἰκονομία)—JCampbell, Κοινωνία and Its Cognates in the NT: JBL 51, '32, 352–80; EGroenewald, Κοινωνία (gemeenskap) bij Pls, diss. Amst. '32; HSeesemann, D. Begriff Κοινωνία im NT '33; PEndenburg, Koinoonia . . . bij de Grieken in den klass. tijd '37; HFord, The NT Conception of Fellowship: Shane Quarterly 6, '45, 188–215; GJourdan, Κοινωνία in 1 Cor 10:16: JBL 67, '48, 111–24; KNickle, The Collection, A Study in Paul's Strategy, '66.—EDNT additional bibl. S. also RAC IX 1100–1145.—DELG s.v. κοινός. M-M. TW. Sv.

κοινωνικός, ή, όν (s. κοινωνία and cognates; since Ps.-Pla., Def., and Aristot.; Vett. Val., pap, Philo; Jos., Bell. 2, 122) **pert. to giving or sharing what is one's own, *liberal, generous*** (Aristot., Rhet. 2, 24, 2: 1401a, 20; Polyb. 2, 44, 1; Lucian, Tim. 56 ἀνὴρ τῶν ὄντων κοινωνικός; Iambl., Protr. 21, 19 [p. 117, 8]; 30 [123, 6]) w. εὐμετάδοτος **1 Ti 6:18.**—DELG s.v. κοινός. M-M. TW.

κοινωνός, οῦ, ὁ and **ἡ** (s. κοινός and cognates; trag. et al.; ins, pap, LXX, Philo, Joseph., Just.)

❶ **one who takes part in someth. with someone, *companion, partner, sharer.*—ⓐ** *with someone,* expressed—**α.** by the dat. (Philo, Spec. Leg. 1, 131 θεῷ τινος ['in someth.']; Jos., Ant. 8, 239 σοί τινος; Himerius, Or. 48 [=Or. 14], 15 κ. ἐκείνοις τῆς γνώμης=with those men [the seven wise men] in knowledge) ἦσαν κοινωνοὶ τῷ Σίμωνι (who) *were partners* (in business) *with Simon* **Lk 5:10** (not a t.t. here, but cp. PAmh 100, 4: Hermes the fisherman takes Cornelius as his κ.=partner; sim. Diod. S. 8, 5, 3 ὁ κ.=partner; BGU 1123, 4; s. New Docs 1, 85; 3, 19).

β. by the gen. (Pr 28:24; Is 1:23; Mal 2:14; Orig., C. Cels. 3, 69, 33) κ. τῶν οὕτως ἀναστρεφομένων γενηθέντες **Hb 10:33.** Of a martyr (who shares a bloody death w. Christ) Χριστοῦ MPol 6:2; cp. 17:3. κ. τῶν δαιμονίων *be a partner w. the divinities (of polytheists)* (in the sacrifices offered to them) **1 Cor 10:20** (κ. τραπέζης τῶν δαιμονίων Orig., C. Cels. 8, 24, 32.—HGressmann, Ἡ κοινωνία τῶν δαιμονίων: ZNW 20, 1921, 224–30; Clemen[2] 182–88).

γ. by μετά and gen. μετὰ τοῦ πνεύματος κ. Hs 5, 6, 6.

ⓑ *in someth.,* expressed—**α.** by the gen. of thing (Diod. S. 14, 61, 5; Epict. 3, 22, 63 κ. τῆς βασιλείας [of the Cynic]; Plut., Mor. 45e; 819c, Brut. 13, 5; Aelian, VH 2, 24; Appian, Samn. 10 §12 τ. ἀγαθῶν; Maximus Tyr. 31, 5c; Sir 6:10; Esth 8:12n; Jos., Vi. 142, Ant. 4, 177 κ. τῆς ταλαιπωρίας; Just., A II, 2, 6 κ. τῶν ἀδικημάτων). κ. τοῦ θυσιαστηρίου **1 Cor 10:18** (Pla., Ep. 7, 350c κοινωνὸς ἱερῶν; Philo, Spec. Leg. 1, 221 κοινωνὸν τοῦ βωμοῦ). τῶν παθημάτων (Diod. S. 4, 20, 2 τῶν κακοπαθειῶν κ.), τῆς παρακλήσεως **2 Cor 1:7.** ὁ τῆς μελλούσης ἀποκαλύπτεσθαι δόξης κ. **1 Pt 5:1.** θείας φύσεως **2 Pt 1:4** (cp. the ins fr. Commagene under κοινωνέω 1a; on the subj. s. also Plut., Mor. 781a). τῆς μοιχείας *a partner in adultery* Hm 4, 1, 5 (Socrat., Ep. 7, 1 κοι. τ. ἀδικήματος; Polyaenus 2, 14, 1 κ. τῆς ἐπαναστάσεως in the uprising). ἀμφότεροι κοινωνοὶ τοῦ ἔργου τ. δικαίου Hs 2:9 (Pla., Ep. 7, 325a ἀνοσίων αὐτοῖς ἔργων κοι.).

β. by ἐν: D 4:8. ἐν τῷ ἀφθάρτῳ κ. *in what is imperishable* B 19:8.

ⓒ *with someone in someth.* αὐτῶν κ. ἐν τῷ αἵματι τῶν προφητῶν **Mt 23:30.**

ⓓ abs. (4 Km 17:11) κ. ἐμὸς καὶ συνεργός **2 Cor 8:23** (for the combination of κ. and συνεργός cp. the first two Plut.-pass. given under bα; also X., Mem. 2, 6, 26). ἔχειν τινὰ κοινωνόν *consider someone a partner* **Phlm 17** (of Eve: κοινωνὸν δὲ καὶ τὸν ἄνδρα δέχεται Did., Gen. 82, 28; cp. Diod. S. 18, 53, 6 ἔσχε κοινωνοὺς τ. αὐτῶν ἐλπίδων).

❷ **one who permits someone else to share in someth.,** ***sharer*** τινί τινος: τῶν ἀποκαλυφθέντων ἡμῖν γινόμεθα ὑμῖν κοινωνοί *we let you share in what has been revealed to us* Dg 11:8.—The concrete mng. 'member' (Idomeneus Hist. [III BC]: 338 fgm. 8 Jac. κ. τῆς προαιρέσεως='member of the party') does not seem to be found in our lit.—DELG s.v. κοινός. M-M. TW. Sv.

κοινῶς adv. of κοινός (Eur. et al.) ***in the common language/dialect*** (Apollon. Dysc., Pron. 82, 27 al.) **Mk 3:17 v.l.**

κοινωφελής, ές (s. κοινός, ὠφέλεια; Epict. 4, 10, 12; M. Ant. 1, 16, 4; 3, 4, 1; 4, 12, 2; POxy 1409, 19 [III AD]; Philo, De Jos. 34; 73, Mos. 2, 9; 28, Spec. Leg. 4, 157; 170 al.) ***generally useful*** ζητεῖν τὸ κ. πᾶσιν *seek the common good of all* 1 Cl 48:6.—DELG 2 ὀφέλλω.

κοίτη, ης, ἡ (s. κεῖμαι and next entry; Hom.+; ins, pap, LXX; PsSol 17:16; TestSol 2:11 D; TestReub 1:6; Joseph., SibOr; loanw. in rabb.).

❶ **a structure for lying down—ⓐ** gener. ***bed*** (Cass. Dio 61, 13, 5; Herm. Wr. 1, 29; 2 Km 4:5; Jos., Ant. 6, 52 κοίτης ὥρα) εἰς τὴν κ. εἶναι *be in bed* **Lk 11:7** (Jos., Ant. 1, 177 τ. ἐν ταῖς κοίταις ὄντας).

ⓑ esp. (trag. et al.; SibOr 4, 33) ***marriage-bed*** (w. γάμος) **Hb 13:4** (s. 2a, below; on the 'defiling' of the marriage-bed by adultery cp. Ps.-Plut., Fluv. 8, 3 and Jos., Ant. 2, 55 τ. κοίτην μιαίνειν; Artem. 2, 26; Synes., Dreams 11 p. 143b κοίτην ἀμόλυντον; Gen 49:4; TestReub 1:6).—τράπεζαν κοινὴν παρατίθενται, ἀλλ' οὐ κοιτήν *they furnish a common table, but not a bed (for sex)* Dg 5:7 (cj. for κοινήν, s. Bihlmeyer, mg.)

❷ **engagement in sexual relations,** fig. extension of mng. 1

ⓐ ***sexual intercourse*** (Eur., Med. 152, Alc. 249; Lev 15:21–26; Wsd 3:13, 16) pl. (w. ἀσέλγειαι) *sexual excesses* **Ro 13:13.** Perh. **Hb 13:4.**

ⓑ ***seminal emission*** (Num 5:20 ἔδωκέν τις τὴν κοίτην αὐτοῦ ἐν σοί. In full κοίτη σπέρματος: Lev 15:16f, 32; 18:20; 22:4) κοίτην ἔχειν ἐξ ἑνός *conceive children by one man* **Ro 9:10.** κοίτη κοινή *sexual promiscuity* Dg 5:7 cj.—B. 480. DELG s.v. κεῖμαι. M-M.

κοιτών, ῶνος, ὁ (s. prec. entry; this word, rejected by Atticists [Phryn. p. 252 Lob.], in Diod. S. 11, 69, 2; Epict. et al.; ins, pap, LXX; TestAbr B 6 p. 110, 4 [Stone p. 68]; JosAs 25:1 cod. A for θάλαμος; Jos., Vi. 382; TestReub 3:13; loanw. in rabb.) ***bedroom;*** used as part of a title: ὁ ἐπὶ τοῦ κοιτῶνος *the one in charge of the bed-chamber, the chamberlain* (Epict. 4, 7, 1; OGI 256, 5 [c. 130 BC] ἐπὶ τ. κοιτῶνος τῆς βασιλίσσης. Other exx. in Magie 73) **Ac 12:20;** AcPl Ha 5, 21; 32; GJs 6:1. ἐν τῷ ἁγιάσματι τοῦ κ. and ἐν τῷ κ. τοῦ ἁγιάσματος 6:3 (s. ἁγίασμα).—DELG s.v. κεῖμαι. M-M.

κοκκάριον, ου, τό (Rufus [II AD] in Oribasius 8, 47, 11) dim. of κόκκος, ***little grain*** of a hailstone Hm 11:20.

κόκκινος, η, ον (s. next entry; Herodas 6, 19; Martial 2, 39; Plut., Fab. 15, 1; Epict.; PHamb 10, 24; PLond II, 191, 5 p. 264 [103–17 AD]; 193 verso, 22 p. 246 [II AD]; LXX [for underlying Hebr. terminology s. Gradwohl, below, 73]; ParJer 9:18; Philo; Jos., Ant. 8, 72 v.l.; Just., D. 46, 5) ***red, scarlet*** χλαμὺς κ. *a red cloak* of the 'sagum purpureum (paludamentum)' of Roman soldiers, a cheaply dyed garment in contrast to the expensive 'purple' garments (cp. Gradwohl 73–75; WBorn, Scarlet: CIBA Review 7, '38, 206–27; GFaber, Dyeing in Greece, ibid. 284; LJensen, JNES 22, '63, 111) whose hues were derived from shellfish and worn in the upper classes (s. πορφυροῦς) **Mt 27:28;** ἔριον κ. **Hb 9:19;** B 7:8ff, 11; 8:1. As the color of an apocalyptic beast or its covering **Rv 17:3.**—τὸ κ. *scarlet cloth, a scarlet garment* (Epict. 3, 22, 10 ἐν κοκκίνοις περιπατεῖν; 4, 11, 34; 2 Km 1:24.—Gen 38:28; Ex 25:4; Josh 2:18; 2 Ch 2:13) ἡ γυνὴ ἦν περιβεβλημένη πορφυροῦν κ. κόκκινον **Rv 17:4;** cp. **18:16** (the fabrics were variously dyed; πορφ. κ. κόκκ.; cp. PTebt 405, 5; Ex 39:12; 2 Ch 2:6), vs. **12;** GJs 10:1 (three times); 12:1f; (opp. ἔριον 'white wool') 1 Cl 8:4 (Is 1:18); *scarlet cord* 12:7. —EWunderlich, Die Bed. der roten Farbe im Kultus der Griechen u. Römer 1925; RGradwohl, D. Farben im AT, Beih. ZAW 83, '63, 73–78. ABD, article 'Purple' (lit.).—DELG s.v. κόκκος. M-M. TW.

κόκκος, ου, ὁ (s. prec. entry; Hom. Hymns, Hdt. et al.; Lam 4:5 'purple (garments)'; TestSol 18:33; JosAs 16:13 cod. A; SIG 1173, 12; PGM 7, 638) gener. 'grain, seed'.

❶ **the kernel of various plants,** ***seed, grain:*** mustard **Mt 13:31; 17:20; Mk 4:31; Lk 13:19; 17:6;** of wheat, etc. (Favorinus [beg. II AD] in Diog. L. 6, 88) **J 12:24** (Ocellus [II BC] c. 16 H.: the ἀνάλυσις of the fruit makes the seed free; cp. Philo, Aet. M. 94ff); **1 Cor 15:37** (HRiesenfeld, TU 77, '61, 43–55; on the imagery s. Straub 70–72).

❷ Formerly thought to be a berry, the kermes, a female scale insect (similar to the cochineal), clings to the leaves of an oak tree. The dried bodies of these insects were used by the ancients to prepare a purplish-red dye (s. Theophr., HP 3, 7, 3; 3, 16, 1; Gradwohl [s. κόκκινος end] 73–78; WBorn, Scarlet: CIBA Review 7, '38, 206–14). By metonymy κ. was applied to the color ('scarlet') as well as to fabric treated with the dye (Dromo Com. [IV BC] fgm. 1, 4 Kock [in Athen. 6, 240d]; PHolm 22, 1; Sir 45:10; Jos., Bell. 6, 390) ***scarlet (color)*** 1 Cl 8:3 (quot. of unknown orig.; here prob. of purple-dyed fabric [cp. Lam 4:5] because of the corresponding σάκκος).—DELG. M-M. TW.

κοκκύζω (κόκκυ 'the cry of a cock'; Hes. et al.; TestSol 9:3 C) ***to crow*** of a cock (Cratinus et al.; Plato Com. [V/IV BC] 209 p. 659 K.; Hyperid., fgm. 239) gospel fragment fr. Fayum, restored (Kl. T. 8[3], p. 23, 10=Otero [after Harnack] I 85 fgm. ln. 7 [lit.]=ASyn. 315, 53; cp. Mk 14:30).—DELG s.v. κόκκυ.

κολαβρίζω 1 aor. pass. ἐκολαβρίσθην (Hesychius) ***mock, ridicule*** (Suda) 1 Cl 39:9 (Job 5:4).—DELG s.v. κόλαβρος.

κολάζω fut. κολάσω; 1 aor. mid. ἐκολασάμην. Pass.: 1 fut. κολασθήσομαι; aor. 3 pl. ἐκολάσθησαν LXX; pf. inf. κεκολάσθαι (s. three next entries) ***penalize, punish*** (so trag., Pla.+; also OGI 90, 28; PSI 446, 14; PRyl 62, 9) act. τινά *someone* lit., of the punishment of slaves Hs 9, 28, 8. In imagery *do someone an injury,* of polytheists who penalize their cult images by locking them up Dg 2:8. In an apocalyptic place of punishment are οἱ κολάζοντες ἄγγελοι ApcPt 6:21b (Chariton 4, 2, 7 οἱ κολάζοντες='constables, police'; Sallust. 19 p. 34, 15 δαίμονες κολάζοντες).—Mid. (Aristoph., Vesp. 405; Pla., Protag. 324c; 3 Macc 7:3; ApcEsdr 1:11 p. 25, 4 Tdf.; Just., A

II, 2, 9; 11; 16) **Ac 4:21.**—Mostly pass. of the punishment of Christians **1 Pt 2:20 v.l.;** Dg 5:16; 6:9; 7:8; 10:7; MPol 2:4. Of the Last Judgment **2 Pt 2:9.** βασάνοις 2 Cl 17:7 (on the dat., cp. Appian, Bell. Civ. 2, 90 §377 κ. θανάτῳ; Polyaenus 3, 9, 56; Lucian, Dial. Mort. 17, 2; Jos., Ant. 18, 314 κ. πληγαῖς.—Just., A II, 1, 2 ἐν πυρί). διssῶς *be punished doubly* Hs 9, 18, 2. Of hell οἱ κολαζόμενοι ἐκεῖ ApcPt 6:21a. (Of punishment by God: TestAsh 6:2; ApcEsdr 1:11; Just., D. 88, 5; Diod. S. 16, 32, 1; Epict. 3, 11, 3; Dio Chrys. 59 [76], 5; Aesop, Fab. 77 P.=127 H. ὑπὸ θεῶν κολάζονται; oft. in ins in FSteinleitner, D. Beicht 1913, p. 10ff; LRobert, Nouvelles Inscriptions de Sardes '64, 24ff; LXX; Jos., Bell. 2, 163; cp. Theoph. Ant., 2, 36 [p. 196, 24]). Aristotle's limitation of the term κόλασις to disciplinary action Rhet. 1, 10, 17 is not reflected in gener. usage.—DELG s.v. κόλος 3. M-M. TW.

κολακεία, ας, ἡ (s. next entry; edd. also -ία; Pla.+; Philod. [Περὶ κολακείας: RhM n.F. 56, 1901, 623]; SIG 889, 30 κολακείᾳ; PLond V, 1727, 24; TestAbr A [-ία]; Philo; Jos., Bell. 4, 231, Ant. 16, 301. On the spelling s. B-D-F §23; W-S. §5, 13c; Mlt-H. 339) ***flattery*** λόγος κολακείας *flattering words* **1 Th 2:5.**—JLofberg, The Sycophant-Parasite: ClPh 15, 1920, 71.—DELG s.v. κόλαξ. M-M. TW. Spicq.

κολακεύω fut. κολακεύσω; 1 aor. ἐκολάκευσα (s. prec. entry; Aristoph., Pla.+; PSI 586, 4; LXX; TestJos 4:1; Philo; Jos., Bell. 2, 213, Vi. 367; Just., A I, 2, 3; Tat.). Ordinarily, 'flatter'. In our lit. only in Ign., and here in a good sense, someth. like ***entice, deal graciously with,*** w. acc. (Philo, Spec. Leg. 1, 60) τὰ θηρία (Vi. Aesopi W c. 49 κολακεύω τὴν κύνα=stroke the dog) IRo 4:2; 5:2. τὰ φαινόμενά σου εἰς πρόσωπον *the things that appear before your face* IPol 2:2. On IRo 6:2 s. Bihlmeyer, mg.—DELG s.v. κόλαξ.

κόλασις, εως, ἡ (s. prec. three entries; 'punishment, chastisement' so Hippocr.+; Diod. S. 1, 77, 9; 4, 44, 3; Aelian, VH 7, 15; SIG[2] 680, 13; LXX; TestAbr, Test12Patr, ApcEsdr, ApcSed; AscIs 3:13; Philo, Leg. ad Gai. 7, Mos. 1, 96; Jos., Ant. 17, 164; SibOr 5, 388; Ar. [Milne 76, 43]; Just.)

❶ **infliction of suffering or pain in chastisement, *punishment*** so lit. κ. ὑπομένειν *undergo punishment* Ox 840, 6; δειναὶ κ. (4 Macc 8:9) MPol 2:4; ἡ ἐπίμονος κ. *long-continued torture* ibid. Of the martyrdom of Jesus (Orig., C. Cels. 1, 48, 95; 8, 43, 12) PtK 4 p. 15, 34. The smelling of the odor arising fr. sacrifices by polytheists ironically described as *punishment, injury* (s. κολάζω) Dg 2:9.

❷ **transcendent retribution, *punishment*** (ApcSed 4:1 κόλασις καὶ πῦρ ἐστιν ἡ παίδευσίς σου.—Diod. S. 3, 61, 5; 16, 61, 1; Epict. 3, 11, 1; Dio Chrys. 80 [30], 12; 2 Macc 4:38 al. in LXX; Philo, Spec. Leg. 1, 55; 2, 196; Jos., Ant. 1, 60 al.; Just.; Did., Gen., 115, 28; 158, 10) ApcPt 17:32; w. αἰκισμός 1 Cl 11:1. Of eternal punishment (w. θάνατος) Dg 9:2 (Diod. S. 8, 15, 1 κ. ἀθάνατος). Of hell: τόπος κολάσεως ApcPt 6:21 (Simplicius in Epict. p. 13, 1 εἰς ἐκεῖνον τὸν τόπον αἱ κολάσεως δεόμεναι ψυχαὶ καταπέμπονται); ἐν τῇ κ. ἐκείνῃ 10:25; ibid. ἐφορῶσαι τὴν κ. ἐκείνων (cp. ApcEsdr 5:10 p. 30, 2 Tdf. ἐν τῇ κ.). ἐκ τῆς κ. ApcPt Rainer (cp. ἐκ τὴν κ. ApcSed 8:12a; εἰς τὴν κ. 12b and TestAbr B 11 p. 116, 10 [Stone p. 80]). ἀπέρχεσθαι εἰς κ. αἰώνιον *go away into eternal punishment* **Mt 25:46** (οἱ τῆς κ. ἄξιοι ἀπελεύσονται εἰς αὐτήν Iren. 2, 33, 5 [Harv. I 380, 8]; κ. αἰώνιον as TestAbr A 11 p. 90, 7f [Stone p. 28]; TestReub 5:5; TestGad 7:5; Just., A I, 8, 4; D. 117, 3; Celsus 8, 48; pl. Theoph. Ant. 1, 14 [p. 90, 13]). ῥύεσθαι ἐκ τῆς αἰωνίου κ. *rescue fr. eternal punishment* 2 Cl 6:7. τὴν αἰώνιον κ. ἐξαγοράζεσθαι *buy one's freedom fr. eternal pun.* MPol 2:3 v.l. κακαὶ κ. τοῦ διαβόλου IRo 5:3. κ. τινος *punishment for someth.* (Ezk 14:3, 4, 7; 18:30; Philo, Fuga 65 ἁμαρτημάτων κ.) ἔχειν κόλασίν τινα τῆς πονηρίας αὐτοῦ Hs 9, 18, 1. ἀναπαύστως ἕξουσιν τὴν κ. *they will suffer unending punishment* ApcPt Bodl. 9–12. ὁ φόβος κόλασιν ἔχει *fear has to do with punishment* **1J 4:18** (cp. Philo, In Flacc. 96 φόβος κολάσεως).—M-M. TW.

Κολασσαεύς (Κολοσσαεύς, Κολοσαεύς, Κολασαεύς), **έως, ὁ** ***a Colossian*** (s. Κολοσσαί). Only as v.l. (but as early as P^{46}) in the title of Col.—B-D-F §42, 3; Mlt-H. 73; 350.

Κολασσαί s. Κολοσσαί.

κολαφίζω 1 aor. ἐκολάφισα (non-Attic, vernacular word fr. κόλαφις; s. Lobeck, Phryn. 175 [cp. Terence, Adelphi. 245 colaphis tuber est totum caput=(my) head is lumpy from (his) blows]; Mlt-H. 364; 407. Found almost exclusively in Christian lit.; also in Paus. Attic. κ, 38; a Gr-Rom. letter: Sb 6263, 23 [Rom. times]; TestJos 7:5 v.l.—Hesychius: κολαφιζόμενος· ῥαπιζόμενος; Etym. Mag. 525, 4)

❶ **to strike sharply, esp. with the hand, *strike with the fist, beat, cuff*** τινά *someone.* Lit. **Mt 26:67; Mk 14:65** (KSchmidt, MGoguel Festschr. '50, 218–27); MPol 2:4 (v.l.). Of mistreatment in general: *we are roughly treated* **1 Cor 4:11.** εἰ κολαφιζόμενοι ὑπομενεῖτε *if you endure being beaten* **1 Pt 2:20** (κολαζόμενοι v.l.).

❷ **to cause physical impairment, *torment,*** fig. extension of 1, of painful attacks of an illness, described as a physical beating by a messenger of Satan **2 Cor 12:7.** The data for a scientific diagnosis are few, and it is not surprising that a variety of views, characterized by much guesswork, have been held:

ⓐ epilepsy: MKrenkel, Beiträge 1890, 47ff; Schmiedel and Bousset ad loc.; WWrede, Paulus[2] 1907, 17; HFischer (physician), D. Krankheit d. Ap. Pls. 1911; s. also WWeber (psychiatrist), TLZ 37, 1912, 623; FConybeare in WBundy, The Psychic Health of Jesus 1922, 226f; ASchweitzer, D. Mystik des Ap. Pls. 1930, 152; JKlausner, From Jesus to Paul '43, 325–30.

ⓑ hysteria: ELombard, Les extases et les souffrances de l'apôtre Paul: RTP 36, 1903, 450–500; Windisch ad loc.; FFenner, D. Krankheit im NT 1930, 30–40.

ⓒ periodic depression, s. KBonhoeffer (physician) in Ltzm., Hdb. ad loc.

ⓓ headaches, severe eye-trouble: Seeligmüller (physician), War Paulus Epileptiker? 1910; cp. WWeber, TLZ 36, 1911, 235; Uhle-Wettler, Evang. Kirchenztg. 87, 1913, 130ff; 145ff.

ⓔ malaria: Ramsay, Church[2] 63ff; Sickenberger, comm. ad loc.

ⓕ leprosy: EPreuschen, ZNW 2, 1901, 193f; REisler, Ιησους βασιλευς II 1930, 426ff; 794.

ⓖ an impediment in speech (stammering): WClarke, ET 39, 1928, 458–60. S. also on σκόλοψ.—On interpretations (formerly favored by many) in the direction of inward temptations, brought about by opponents, or pangs of conscience, or distressed states of mind, s. GHeinrici in KEK[8] 1900 ad loc.; PMenoud: JdeZwaan Festschr. '53 thinks of the anxieties of a missionary's life.—B. 553 s.v. κόλαφος. DELG s.v. κόλαφος. M-M. TW.

κολλάω aor. ἐκόλλησα LXX; pf. κεκόλληκα Job 38:38. Pass.: 1 fut. κολληθήσομαι **Mt 19:5;** 1 aor. ἐκολλήθην; pf. pass. κεκόλλημαι LXX (κόλλα 'glue'; Aeschyl. et al.; Pla., Diod. S., Plut., ins, pap, LXX; TestAbr A 20 p. 103, 18 [Stone p. 54]; Test12Patr; AscIs 97; EpArist 97; Philo) gener. 'join together.'

❶ **to join closely together, *bind closely, unite*** τινά τινι *someone with* or *to someone;* fig. extension of the lit. mng. 'to glue' or 'join' substances, act. ἡ ἀγάπη κολλᾷ ἡμᾶς τῷ θεῷ *love* *unites us w. God* 1 Cl 49:5. ἡ νουθέτησις ... κολλᾷ ἡμᾶς τῷ θελήματι τοῦ θεοῦ *admonition unites us w. God's will* 56:2.

❷ **to be closely associated,** ***cling to, attach to,*** pass. most freq. in act. sense

ⓐ *cling (closely) to someth.*—**α.** lit. τινί (Job 29:10) of stones ἐκολλῶντο ἀλλήλοις *they were joined* Hv 3, 2, 6. Of dust: τὸν κονιορτὸν τὸν κολληθέντα ἡμῖν ἐκ τῆς πόλεως ὑμῶν *the dust of your city that clings to us* **Lk 10:11.**

β. fig. *cling to = come in close contact with* (cp. Ps 21:16; 43:26 ἐκολλήθη εἰς γῆν ἡ γαστὴρ ἡμῶν. The act.='bring into contact' PGM 5, 457 κολλήσας τ. λίθον τῷ ὠτίῳ) ἐκολλήθησαν αἱ ἁμαρτίαι ἄχρι τ. οὐρανοῦ *the sins have touched the heaven = reached the sky* (two exprs. are telescoped) **Rv 18:5.**

γ. fig. of the Spirit, which is *(closely) joined* to the flesh 2 Cl 14:5.

ⓑ *join oneself to, join, cling to, associate with*—**α.** of a pers., w. dat. of thing κολλήθητι τῷ ἅρματι τούτῳ **Ac 8:29** (a rendering like *stick to this chariot* suggests the imagery).—W. dat. of pers. (which may very rarely be replaced w. a prepositional constr. [AscIs 3:1 πρὸς αὐτόν but τῷ Μανασσῇ, cp. Tob 6:19 εἰς αὐτήν S, αὐτῇ BA]) 1 Cl 30:3; cp. 46:1. τοῖς εἰρηνεύουσι 15:1. τοῖς ἁγίοις 46:2 (quot. of unknown orig.); Hv 3, 6, 2; s 8, 8, 1. τοῖς δούλοις τοῦ θεοῦ 9, 20, 2; 9, 26, 3. τοῖς δικαίοις 8, 9, 1. τοῖς ἀθῴοις κ. δικαίοις 1 Cl 46:4. τοῖς διψύχοις καὶ κενοῖς *the doubters and the senseless* Hm 11:13. τοῖς ἀκαθάρτοις B 10:8; cp. 10:3ff. Also μετά τινος (cp. Ruth 2:8) 10:11; 19:2, 6; D 3:9. τῷ κυρίῳ *join oneself to the Lord* (cp. 4 Km 18:6; Sir 2:3; on this vs. and 6:16 below s. SPorter, ETL 67, '91, 104f: economic connotation; cp. **Lk 15:15** below) **1 Cor 6:17;** Hm 10, 1, 6. τῇ γυναικὶ αὐτοῦ *be joined to his wife* **Mt 19:5** (cp. Vi. Aesopi G 30 P. p. 46, 14, where a woman says to Aesop: μή μοι κολλῶ=don't come too near me; 1 Esdr 4:20; Philo, Leg. All. 2, 50). τῇ πόρνῃ *join oneself to a prostitute* **1 Cor 6:16** (cp. Sir 19:2). *Associate with* on intimate terms, *join* **Ac 5:13; 9:26; 10:28** (CBurchard, ZNW 61, '70, 159f). *Become a follower* or *disciple of someone* (cp. 2 Km 20:2; 1 Macc 3:2; 6:21) **17:34.** *Hire oneself out to someone* **Lk 15:15** (JHarrill, JBL 115, '96, 714–17, "he was indentured"). *Have someth. to do with:* lying spirits Hm 11:4.

β. of impers. things: of anger ὅταν κολληθῇ τῷ ἀνθρώπῳ *when it attaches itself to a pers.* Hm 10, 2, 3. Also of punishment s 6, 5, 3.

ⓒ w. dat. of thing *cling to, enter into a close relation w.* (Ps 118:31; TestIss 6:1, Dan 6:10 τ. δικαιοσύνῃ, Gad 5:2) ταῖς δωρεαῖς *cling to the gifts* 1 Cl 19:2. τῷ ἀγαθῷ *be attached* or *devoted to what is good* **Ro 12:9;** B 20:2; D 5:2 (cp. TestAsh 3:1 τῇ ἀγαθότητι). τῇ εὐλογίᾳ *cling to the blessing* 1 Cl 31:1. κρίσει δικαίᾳ B 20:2.—DELG s.v. κόλλα. M-M. TW.

κολλούριον, ου, τό (this is the later spelling, attested **Rv 3:18** by mss. A P et al.; Philumen. p. 9, 16; PHolm 1, 16; PFlor 177, 20 [257 AD]; PGM 4, 1316; 2691; 2893. On the other hand some mss. and edd. have κολλύριον, as do Epict. 2, 21, 20; 3, 21, 21; Galen: CMG V 4, 2 p. 192, 30; Philumen. p. 33, 18; 22; Aëtius very oft.; SIG 1173, 16 [138 AD]; POxy 1088, 1 and 42 [I AD]; PGM 4, 2682; LXX [Thackeray 92].—S. B-D-F §42, 4; Mlt-H. 78f; Crönert 130; KDieterich, Untersuchungen z. griech. Sprache 1898, 23) a medical compound applied to the eyes ***eye-salve*** (so Epict., SIG, PFlor, loc. cit. ; loanw. in rabb.; dim. of κολλύρα 'roll' or 'loaf of bread', perh. because of the shape of the compound; Mussies 25) **Rv 3:18.**—S. Wetstein for Gr-Rom. par.; FBayer, RAC 7, '44, 973ff; HNielsen, Ancient Ophthalmological Agents, 1974; CHemer in New Docs 3, 56f; idem The Letters to the Seven Churches of Asia Minor in Their Local Setting '89 ('86), 196–99; Kl. Pauly III 272; RJackson, Eye Medicine in the Rom. Empire: ANRW II Principat 37/3, '96, 2228–51, esp. 2238–43.—DELG s.v. κολλύρα. M-M.

κολλυβιστής, οῦ, ὁ (κόλλυβος 'small coin'; Lysias in Pollux 7, 33; 170; Menand., fgm. 861 Kö. [in Phryn. 440 Lob.; but the Atticists reject the word, ibid.]; PPetr III, 59a I, 7 [III BC]) ***money-changer*** **Mt 21:12; Mk 11:15; Lk 19:45 v.l.; J 2:15.**—DELG s.v. κόλλυβος. M-M. Spicq.

κολλύριον s. κολλούριον.

κολοβός, όν (s. next entry; X. et al.; PGen 23, 5 [70 AD]; PPetr III, 19g, 2; POxy 43 verso V, 9; Aq. and Sym. Is 37:27) gener. of someth. without a projection (κόλος): of oxen or goats without horns, then 'stunted'.

❶ **pert. to being deficient in some respect,** ***mutilated,*** in imagery of hewn stones: *with some part broken off* (opp. ὁλοτελής; cp. our 'does not measure up' or 'fall short') Hv 3, 6, 4; s 9, 6, 4; 9, 8, 4; 9, 26, 7. κ. ἀπὸ τῆς πίστεως *damaged in the faith* 9, 26, 8.

❷ **pert. to not being tall,** ***short, stocky*** (Peripl. Eryth. c. 65; Galen, De Usu Part. I p. 58, 19 Helmr.; Procopius of Caesarea, Anecdota 8, 12 [opp. μακρός]; 10, 11) ἄνθρωπος (opp. μακρός) Gospel of Eve: Kl. T. 8^3, p. 18.—DELG s.v. κόλος. M-M s.v. κολοβόω.

κολοβόω 1 aor. ἐκολόβωσα. Pass.: 1 fut. κολοβωθήσομαι; 1 aor. ἐκολοβώθην; pf. ptc. κεκολοβωμένος (s. prec. entry; Aristot., HA 1, 1, 487b, 24; Diod. S. 1, 78, 5; 2 Km 4:12 'cut off, cut short'; GrBar 9:7; Ar.13, 2) 'mutilate, curtail' (so Polyb. 1, 80, 13; Epict. 2, 10, 20).

❶ **to cause someth. not to be full length,** ***to shorten,*** lit., of stones κεκολοβωμένοι *short* Hv 3, 2, 8; 3, 6, 4 (s. NBrox, Der Hirt des Hermas '91, 135). ὅλως ἐξ αὐτῶν οὐδὲν ἐκολοβώθη *nothing at all was too short about them* s 9, 8, 5.

❷ **to reduce the duration of someth.,** ***shorten,*** fig. extension of 1: the last days **Mt 24:22ab; Mk 13:20ab** (cp. GrBar 9:7 θεὸς ... ἐκολόβωσεν τὰς ἡμέρας αὐτῆς [i.e. τῆς σελήνης]).—DELG s.v. κόλος. M-M. TW.

Κολοσσαεύς, έως (Suda on Ῥόδος: IV p. 297, 15) ***Colossian,*** subst. ὁ Κ. *the Colossian* **Col ins**—some mss. and edd. write Κολασσ. (q.v.), which is also found in Suda, loc. cit., as v.l. (Strabo 12, 8, 16 uses the form Κολοσσηνός).

Κολοσσαί, ῶν, αἱ ***Colossae,*** once a flourishing city (Hdt. 7, 30; X., An. 1, 2, 6), later less important (Strabo 12, 8, 13 πόλισμα), in Phrygia in Asia Minor. The congregation there was prob. founded by Epaphras (Col 1:7), who was from Colossae (4:12). **Col 1:2; Phlm subscr. v.l.**—Lghtf., Col and Phlm p. 1ff; Ramsay, Church 465ff, Phrygia I/1, 208ff; VSchultze, Altchr. Städte u. Landschaften II 1, 1922, 445ff; Zahn, Einl. I^3 318, who, like Lghtf. 16, 4, deals w. the var. forms of the name (Κολασσαί, Κολασαί). BHHW II 975f.

κόλπος, ου, ὁ (Hom.+; ins, pap, LXX; TestSol 2:3 W; TestAbr; TestJob 10:4; JosAs ch. 11 cod. A [p. 52, 11 Bat.]; ApcSed 14:6; Philo, Joseph.) var. mngs. in gener. lit. usage, freq. w. suggestion of curvature and the hollow so formed, as of a person's chest, folds in a garment or a bay of the sea; our lit. contains no application of the term to anatomical parts uniquely female.

❶ ***bosom, breast, chest*** ἀνακεῖσθαι ἐν τῷ κόλπῳ τινός *lie* (at a meal) w. one's head *on someone's breast* (a position dictated by ancient banqueting practice: s. ἀνάκειμαι 2) **J 13:23.** ἐν τοῖς κόλποις αὐτοῦ (=τοῦ Ἀβραάμ. In this case ἀνακείμενον is to be supplied) *lying in Abraham's bosom* (in the place of honor at the banquet in the next world. On the pl. s. B-D-F §141, 5; Rob. 408; Theocr. 2, 120 and below; Plut., Cato Min. 775 [33, 4], cp. also Sb 2034, 11 ἐν κόλποις Ἀβρὰμ κ. Ἰσὰκ κ. Ἰακώβ) **Lk 16:23.** ἀπενεχθῆναι εἰς τὸν κ. Ἀβραάμ *be carried to Abraham's bosom* vs. **22** (New Docs 3, 106f). The mng. *lap* is also poss. for κόλποι (Ael. Aristid. 13 p. 163 D.: ἐκ τῶν κόλπων τ. γῆς; Diog. L. 3, 44; Meleager, Anth. Pal. 5, 165 ἐν κόλποισιν ἐκείνης=lying on her lap; Anonymous Vita Pla. ed. Westerm. 1850 p. 5, 31 ἐντὸς κόλπων for 2, 44 ἐν τοῖς γόνασιν); the sing. in this sense: ἦλθεν εἰς τὸν κ. τῆς μητρός GJs 6:1 (Epict. 2, 5, 16; 4, 7, 24; Vi. Aesopi G 82; 137 P.; Ps.-Clem., Hom. 8, 12 [cp. Piers Plowman, version C 9, 283 'in Abrahammes lap'; PHaupt, AJP 42, 1921, 162–67; ESchwyzer, Der Götter Knie—Abrahams Schoss: JWackernagel Festschr. 1923, 283–93; MMieses, Im Schosse Abrahams: OLZ 34, '31, 1018–21. Opposing him BHeller, ibid. 36, '33, 146–49.—Rabb. in RMeyer, TW III 825]). ἐὰν ἦτε συνηγμένοι ἐν τῷ κ. μου *if you are gathered in my bosom* 2 Cl 4:5 (a saying of Jesus; cp. Judaicon 68, 41f twice). Furthermore, apart fr. the idea of dining together on the same couch, 'being in someone's bosom' denotes the closest association (cp. Plut., Pericl. 1, 1, Demosth. 31, 6, Cato Min. 33, 7 Ziegler v.l.: Gabinius, an ἄνθρωπος ἐκ τῶν Πομπηΐου κόλπων; Longus, Past. 4, 36, 3; Num 11:12; Dt 13:7; 28:54, 56; 2 Km 12:3; 3 Km 17:19; Ruth 4:16): ὁ ὢν εἰς τὸν κ. τοῦ πατρός *who rests in the bosom of the Father* **J 1:18** (M-EBoismard, RB 59, '52, 23–39; OHofius, ZNW 80, '89, 163–71).

❷ **the fold of a garment,** ***fold,*** formed as it falls from the chest over the girdle (Hom. et al.; Jos., Ant. 2, 273). Fr. early times (e.g. Od. 15, 468; Herodas 6, 102; Diod. S. 25, 16; Appian, Iber. 13 §49; Polyaenus 7, 48; 8, 64; Dio Chrys. 67 [17], 22; Ex 4:6f; Jos., Bell. 6, 195) this fold was used as a pocket. διδόναι τι εἰς τὸν κ. τινός *put someth. into the fold of someone's garment* (cp. Polyb. 3, 33, 2; Ps 78:12; Is 65:6; Jer 39:18; TestJob 10:4 κόλπῳ κενῷ) **Lk 6:38.**

❸ **a part of the sea that indents a shoreline,** ***bay*** (Hom. et al.; OGI 441, 218; Philo, Op. M. 113; Jos., Ant. 3, 25) **Ac 27:39.**—B. 39. DELG. M-M. TW.

κολυμβάω (s. next entry; Pla. et al.)—❶ ***swim up and down,*** lit. 'dive' B 10:5.

❷ ***swim*** (Paradoxogr. Flor. 10; Palaeph. p. 36, 5; Babrius 165, 1; 3 C.; Is 25:11 Aq.; Jos., Ant. 20, 248) τοὺς δυναμένους κ. *those who could swim* **Ac 27:43.**—M-M.

κολυμβήθρα, ας, ἡ (s. κολυμβάω; Pla. et al.; Diod. S. 4, 78, 1; 11, 25, 4; Jos., Ant. 9, 239; 15, 54; POxy 147, 2; LXX) ***pool, swimming-pool*** (used for bathing: Ael. Aristid. 48, 21 K.=24 p. 470 D.). Of Bethzatha (s. Βηθζαθά and s. JJeremias, D. Wiederentdeckung von Bethesda '49) **J 5:2, 3 (4) v.l., 7;** Siloam **9:7, 11 v.l.** (2 Esdr 13:15 S κολυμβήθρα τοῦ Σιλωάμ).—DELG s.v. κόλυμβος. M-M.

κολωνία, ας, ἡ (Lat. loanw., colonia; found also in rabb. Exx. in Hahn 271 Lat. word-index; edict of Claudius in Jos., Ant. 19, 291) a city or town outside Italy whose inhabitants enjoyed special political privileges: ***colony,*** of Philippi in Macedonia, settled by Augustus (s. Φίλιπποι) **Ac 16:12.**—M-M.

κομάω (s. κόμη, cp. Lat. comans; Hom. et al.; BGU 16, 11; Philo, Deus Imm. 88, Spec. Leg. 3, 37; Jos., Ant. 4, 72) ***wear long hair, let one's hair grow long*** (Diod. S. 20, 63, 3) **1 Cor 11:14, 15** (Paul argues from nature, but has Roman custom on his side; ancient authors are not unanimous about Greek custom: s. Il. 2, 11 al. 'long-haired Achaeans'; Hdt. 1, 82, 7 in ref. to a vow; Aristot. Rhet. 1367a, 26 long hair a sign of nobility in Lacedemonia; Plut., Mor. 267b Greeks do not ordinarily wear their hair long; Ps.-Phoc. 212 ἄρσεσιν οὐκ ἐπέοικε κομᾶν; JMurphy-OConnor, CBQ 42, '80, 484–87: to some an indication of effeminacy, cp. Juvenal 2, 96. For an Israelite perspective s. Judg 16:19; cp. Philo, Spec. Leg. 3, 37; Billerb. III 441f; CGordon, Homer and Bible: HUCA 26, '55, 84f. Other reff. PvanderHorst, The Sentences of Pseudo-Phocylides '78, 249f. Perh. Paul refers to the effeminate manner in which some males coiffured their long hair, rather than to the mere wearing of hair in full length.)—MAndronicos et al., The Gk. Museum '75 (illustr.); RAC IV 629f. DELG s.v. κόμη. M-M.

κόμη, ης, ἡ (s. prec. entry; Hom. et al.; WSchubart, Der Gnomon des Idios Logos1919 [=BGU V], 71; 76 [II AD]: ἱερεῦσι οὐκ ἐξὸν κόμην φορεῖν; LXX; Philo, Sacr. Abel. 25; Jos., Bell. 4, 561, Ant. 14, 45; Tat. 25, 1; loanw. in rabb.) hair of a person's head, ***(long) hair*** of women (Xenophon Eph. 1, 2, 6; Achilles Tat. 8, 6, 8; the contexts of these reff. suggest that the hair of the female characters was long) **1 Cor 11:15,** of hair without spec. ref. to length, a matter that is treated in the clause that precedes. Well-bred women would wear their tresses gathered up on their heads. κ. οὔλη *curly hair* ApcPt 3:10.—DELG. M-M.

κομίζω 1 aor. ἐκόμισα. Mid.: fut. κομίσομαι and κομιοῦμαι **Col 3:25 v.l.;** 1 aor. ἐκομισάμην; pf. κεκόμισμαι. Pass.: aor. 3 sg. ἐκομίσθη 1 Esdr 2:14 (κομέω 'take care of'; Hom.+).

❶ **to convey someth. to a specific destination,** ***bring*** act. (SIG 409, 29; 434, 42; 559, 28; PPetr III, 53k, 5; PTebt 55, 4; 1 Esdr 4:5; 3 Macc 1:8) τὶ *someth.* (Jos., Vi. 50 ἐπιστολάς; TestJos 6:2) a jar of ointment **Lk 7:37.**

❷ **to get back someth. that is one's own or owed to one,** ***get back, recover*** mid. (Eur., Thu. et al.; Isaeus 8, 8; Polyb. 1, 83, 8; 3, 40, 10; 10, 34, 3; Sir 29:6; Philo, De Jos. 210; 231; Jos., Ant. 13, 80) τὸ ἐμὸν σὺν τόκῳ *what is mine with interest* (for commercial usage cp. Lys. 32, 14; Andoc. 1, 38) **Mt 25:27.** Of Abraham: *receive* (his son) *back* (cp. Jos., Ant. 1, 236; Isaeus 8:8 of a daughter) **Hb 11:19** (Himerius, Or. 6 [2], Demeter τὴν ζητουμένην κομίζεται=receives the woman whom she sought [her daughter]).

❸ **to come into possession of someth. or experience someth.,** ***carry off, get (for oneself), receive*** freq. as recompense, mid. (Diod. S. 17, 69, 1; 20, 28, 3; Appian, Bell. Civ. 5, 60, §252 γράμματα) τὰ ὀψώνια *pay, wages* IPol 6:2. μισθόν (Polystrat. p. 22; Lucian, Phal. 2, 5; SIG 193, 9; 11; 1077, 4; 2 Macc 8:33; Ath., R. 18 p. 70, 30 κομίσασθαι τὰ ἐπίχειρα) 2 Cl 11:5; cp. B 4:12, where μισθόν is to be supplied (as En 100:7). μισθὸν ἀδικίας *reward for wrongdoing* **2 Pt 2:13 v.l.** (ἀδικέω 2 end). Of special divine favor in recognition of piety (Diod. S. 3, 2, 4) τῆς δόξης στέφανον **1 Pt 5:4** (cp. Eur., Hipp. 432 codd. κ. δόξαν; 1 Macc 13:37). κ. τὰ διὰ τοῦ σώματος πρὸς ἃ ἔπραξεν *receive a recompense for what (each one) has done during life in the body* **2 Cor 5:10** (cp. the judgment scenes Pla., Phd. 113 and 114; s. also Diod. S. 8, 15); cp. **Col 3:25.** τοῦτο κομίσεται παρὰ κυρίου **Eph 6:8** (PSI 438, 11 [III BC] κεκόμισμαι παρὰ Φανίου ἐπιστολήν). τὴν ἐπαγγελίαν *the promise* (i.e. what is promised) **Hb 10:36; 11:13 v.l., 39.** τὸ τέλος τῆς πίστεως σωτηρίαν ψυχῶν *obtain as an outcome of faith the salvation of souls* **1 Pt 1:9** (contrast **4:17**).—DELG s.v. κομέω. M-M.

κόμπος, ου, ὁ (Hom. et al.) **ostentatious self-promotion,** ***boasting, brassiness*** (so trag., Hdt.; Esth 8:12d; 3 Macc 6:5;

Philo, Congr. Erud. Gr. 61; Jos., Bell. 6, 260; Just., A II, 9, 1) 1 Cl 16:2.—Adj. κομπός *boastful* AcPl Ha 2, 22.—DELG.

κομφέκτωρ, ορος, ὁ (Lat. loanw., confector, Suetonius, Octav. 43, Nero 12. The Gk. form: Acta S. Meletii 39) an ***executioner,*** who gave the coup de grâce to wounded gladiators MPol 16:1 (s. Lghtf. ad loc.).

κομψότερον adv. of the comp. of κομψός (the word Eur. et al.; the comp. in Pla., Crat. 429d; POxy 935, 5 [III AD]) ***better*** of sick persons: κ. ἔχειν *begin to improve* **J 4:52** (κομψῶς ἔχειν in this sense in Epict. 3, 10, 13; PParis 18, 3; PTebt 414, 10. This use develops as a transferred sense of κομψός 'nice' [cp. our 'N.N. is doing nicely']. On the comp. cp. POxy 935, 5 θεῶν συνλαμβανόντων ἡ ἀδελφὴ ἐπὶ τὸ κομψότερον ἐτράπη; FBilabel, Badische Papyri 1923 no. 34, 4 [I AD] κομψότερον ἔσχεν).—DELG s.v. κομψός. M-M. s.v. κομψῶς.

κονιάω pf. pass. ptc. κεκονιαμένος (Aesop, Fab. 121 P.=193 H. ἐν κεκονιαμένῳ οἴκῳ) (κόνις 'dust, plaster'; Demosth. et al.; Michel 594, 96; SIG 695, 88. Pass. CIG I 1625, 16; Dt 27:2, 4; Pr 21:9) ***whitewash*** τοῖχος κ. *a whitewashed wall* **Ac 23:3** (s. τοῖχος). τάφοι κ. *whitewashed tombs* **Mt 23:27** (BMcCane, Is a Corpse Contagious? Early Jewish and Christian Attitudes toward the Dead: SBLSP '92, 378–88) w. implicit satire: the Pharisees are unwittingly a source of defilement. GNaass 284, 153 (cp. Aesop, above).—KRengstorf, Rabb. Texte, 1. Reihe III '33ff, p. 34f.—DELG s.v. κόνις. M-M. TW.

κονιορτός, οῦ, ὁ (κόνις 'dust' + ὄρνυμι 'stir up'; Hdt. et al.; Mitt-Wilck. I/2, 198, 16 [III BC]; LXX; TestSol 7:2f; Philo, Exs. 133; Jos., Ant. 3, 193; Tat. 30, 1) ***dust*** ἐκτινάσσειν τὸν κ. τῶν ποδῶν (cp. Heraclit. Sto. 10 p. 17, 8 after Il. 2, 150 ποδῶν . . . κονίη; Na 1:3 κ. ποδῶν αὐτοῦ) *shake the dust from one's feet* **Mt 10:14;** cp. **Lk 9:5; 10:11; Ac 13:51** (s. on ἐκτινάσσω 1). Of an unruly mob κονιορτὸν βάλλειν εἰς τὸν ἀέρα *throw dust into the air* **Ac 22:23.** κ. ἐγείρειν *raise dust* (cp. Appian, Mithrid. 87 §396 κονιορτὸς ἠγείρετο; Jos., Bell. 5, 471; also s. ἐγείρω 10) Hv 4, 1, 5b.—*A cloud of dust* (Aristodem. [IV AD]: 104 fgm. 1, 8 Jac.) κ. ὡς εἰς τ. οὐρανόν *a cloud of dust reaching, as it were, to heaven* 4, 1, 5a (Quint. Smyrn. 2, 469f κόνις ἄχρις ἐς οὐρανόν). γινομένου μείζονος καὶ μείζονος κονιορτοῦ *when the dust-cloud became greater and greater* 4, 1, 6.—B. 19. DELG s.v. κόνις. M-M.

κοπάζω (s. κόπος) 1 aor. ἐκόπασα; pf. κεκόπακα LXX (Hdt. et al.; LXX and fr. Num 17:13 in Philo, Somn. 2, 235, fr. Gen 8:8 in SibOr 1, 246; AWilhelm, SymbOsl, Suppl. 13, '50, 32, a Gk. epigram: ἡ μακρὴ κατ' ἐμοῦ δυσπλοΐη κοπάσει=the long hard sailing that I've faced will soon abate) ***abate, stop, rest, cease*** ὁ ἄνεμος ἐκόπασεν *the wind fell* (so Hdt. 7, 191; cp. Aelian in Suda [Anz 316]) **Mt 14:32; Mk 4:39; 6:51.**—DELG s.v. κόπτω. M-M. TW.

κοπετός, οῦ, ὁ (Eupolis Com. [V BC], fgm. 347; Dionys. Hal. 11, 31; Plut., Fab. 17, 7; Kaibel 345, 4; LXX; TestJob 40:13; 52:1 [cod. V]; SibOr 5, 193; Joseph.; Mel., P. 18, 121; 28, 194; Ath. 14, 2) ***mourning, lamentation*** acc. to custom in many parts of the Mediterranean world this was accompanied by breast-beating (frowned on by Plut., Mor. 609b; s. κόπτω 2) ἐποίησαν κ. μέγαν ἐπ' αὐτῷ *they made loud lamentation over him* **Ac 8:2** (Mi 1:8 κ. ποιεῖσθαι [MWilcox, The Semitisms of Ac, '65, 136f]; Zech 12:10 κ. ἐπί τινα; cp. Jer 9:9; Jos., Bell. 2, 6). δύο κοπετοὺς ἐκόπτετο (Anna) *mourned twofold* (viz. her widowhood and childlessness) GJs 2:1.—DELG s.v. κόπτω A6. Frisk s.v. κόπτω 8 (via κόπος?). M-M. TW.

κοπή, ῆς, ἡ (s. κόπτω; Strabo et al.; pap; JosAs 23:7 cod A [κ. τῆς ῥομφαίας 'hilt']) ***cutting down, slaughter*** (Josh 10:20; Jdth 15:7) ὑποστρέφειν ἀπὸ τῆς κ. τῶν βασιλέων *return fr. the defeat of* (i.e., fr. defeating) *the kings* **Hb 7:1** (Gen 14:17).—DELG s.v. κόπτω A2. M-M.

κοπιάω fut. κοπιάσω LXX; 1 aor. ἐκοπίασα; pf. κεκοπίακα; 2 sg. κεκοπίακες or -κας (v.l.; s. B-D-F §83, 2; Mlt-H. 221); aor. pass. 3 sg. ἐκοπιάθη (fr. κόπτω via κόπος; TestAbr B 2 p. 107, 1 [Stone p. 62]) (Aristoph. et al.; Hippocr.; Epicurus 59, 3 Us.; ins, pap, LXX, En; TestJob 24:2; ApcSed 4:3; ApcMos 24; Philo, Joseph.).

❶ ***become weary/tired*** (Aristoph. et al.; Sir 16:27; 1 Macc 10:81; 4 Macc 9:12; Jos., Bell. 6, 142) **Rv 2:3** (the pf. here expresses the thought that the Ephesian congregation has not become tired to the extent of 'giving up'). ἔκ τινος *from someth.* ἐκ τῆς ὁδοιπορίας *from the journey* **J 4:6** (cp. Jos., Ant. 2, 321 ὑπὸ τῆς ὁδοιπορίας κεκοπωμένοι; Is 40:31). οἱ κοπιῶντες *those who are weary* (Diocles 142 p. 186, 28; cp. 1QH 8:36) **Mt 11:28** (s. φορτίζω).

❷ **to exert oneself physically, mentally, or spiritually,** ***work hard, toil, strive, struggle*** (Vett. Val. 266, 6; Syntipas p. 107, 15; POslo 160, 1; Philo, Mut. Nom. 254, Cher. 41), abs. (Aesop, Fab. 391 P.) **Mt 6:28; Lk 5:5; 12:27; J 4:38b; 21:6 v.l.; Ac 20:35; 1 Cor 4:12; 16:16; Eph 4:28; 2 Ti 2:6.** τὶ *labor for someth.* (En 103:9 κόπους κ.) **J 4:38a.** πολλά *work hard* **Ro 16:6, 12b;** Hs 5, 6, 2; 2 Cl 7:1. περισσότερον **1 Cor 15:10.** κ. ἔν τινι *work at something* (Sir 6:19) ἐν λόγῳ καὶ διδασκαλίᾳ *work hard at preaching and teaching* **1 Ti 5:17.** διὰ λόγου *labor by word of mouth* B 19:10. The sphere in which the work is done: ἐν ὑμῖν *among you* **1 Th 5:12.** The manner: ἐν κυρίῳ **Ro 16:12ab;** εἴς τινα κ. *work hard for someone* vs. **6; Gal 4:11.** εἰς τοῦτο *for this* **1 Ti 4:10.** εἰς ὅ κοπιῶ *this is what I am toiling for* **Col 1:29.** εἰς κενόν *toil in vain* (cp. Is 49:4 κενῶς ἐκοπίασα; 65:23 κοπιάσουσιν εἰς κενόν; TestJob 24:2) **Phil 2:16.** Also εἰς μάτην (Ps 126:1) Hs 9, 4, 8.—B. 312. DELG s.v. κόπτω A1. M-M. TW. Spicq.

κόπος, ου, ὁ—❶ a state of discomfort or distress, ***trouble, difficulty,*** a transferred sense of κόπος='beating' (s. κόπτω; trag.; pap; Ps 106:12; Sir 22:13; 1 Macc 10:15; ParJer 5:6; Jos., Ant. 2, 257; Just., D. 68, 2) κόπους (κόπον) παρέχειν τινί *(cause) trouble (for) someone, bother someone* (κόπους παρέχειν τινί PTebt 21, 10 [115 BC]; BGU 844, 12; PGissUniv 27, 13f [IIIAD]; PGM 14b, 4f; κόπον παρ. τινί Sir 29:4) **Mt 26:10; Mk 14:6; Lk 11:7; 18:5; Gal 6:17;** Hv 3, 3, 2; AcPlCor 2:34. πολλοὺς κόπους ἠντληκώς *after he had endured many hardships* Hs 5, 6, 2a (cp. Did.. Gen. 105, 9). W. other terms relating to a peristasis (FDanker, 2 Cor [Augsburg Comm.], '89, 85–91; 180–86) **2 Cor 6:5** and **11:23;** on **10:15** s. 2 below.

❷ **to engage in activity that is burdensome,** ***work, labor, toil*** (Eur., Aristoph.; SIG 761, 6 [I BC]; PAmh 133, 11; POxy 1482, 6; LXX; En; TestIss 3:5; Apc4Esdr fgm. a; ApcSed 14:2; Jos., Ant. 3, 25; 8, 244; Iren.1, 13, 5 [Harv I 122, 3]; Did., Gen. 104, 7.) sing. κ. τῆς ἀγάπης *labor of love,* i.e. *loving service* **1 Th 1:3.** W. ἔργα **Rv 2:2.** W. ἱδρώς B 10:4. W. μόχθος (q.v.) **2 Cor 11:27; 1 Th 2:9; 2 Th 3:8;** Hs 5, 6, 2b. ὁ κ. ὑμῶν οὐκ ἔστιν κενός *your labor is not in vain* **1 Cor 15:58.** μήπως εἰς κενὸν γένηται ὁ κ. ἡμῶν *that our work may not be fruitless* **1 Th 3:5.** Fig. of work at harvest time εἰς τὸν κ. τινὸς εἰσέρχεσθαι *enter into someone's labor* i.e. reap the rewards of another person's work **J 4:38;** τὸν μισθὸν λαμβάνειν κατὰ τὸν κ. *receive pay in accordance w. the work done* **1 Cor 3:8.** ὅπου πλείων κ., πολὺ κέρδος *the greater the toil, the richer the gain* IPol 1:3.—Pl., of individual acts (En 7:3) **2 Cor 10:15** (**6:5** and **11:23** appear to fit best under 1 above); **Rv 14:13.** Also abstr. for concr. *reward for labor* (Sir 14:15) Hm 2:4; s 9, 24, 2f.—AvHarnack, Κόπος (κοπιᾶν, οἱ κοπιῶντες) im frühchristl. Sprachgebr.: ZNW 27, 1928, 1–10; HKuist, Bibl. Review 16, '31, 245–49. B. 540.—DELG s.v. κόπτω. M-M. TW. Spicq. Sv.

κοπρία, ας, ἡ (s. three next entries; Strattis Com. [V BC], fgm. 43; Strabo 7, 5, 7; 16, 4, 26; Epict. 2, 4, 5; M. Ant. 8, 51, 2; POxy 37 I, 6 [49 AD]; PRyl 162, 17; LXX, TestJob.—UWilcken, APF 2, 1903, 311f) ***manure pile* Lk 13:8 v.l.; 14:35.**—DELG s.v. κόπρος. M-M.

κόπριον, ου, τό (s. prec. and two next entries; Heraclitus 96; Epict. 2, 4, 5; Plut., Pomp. 48, 2; OGI 483, 81 [II BC]; PFay 110, 5; 10; POxy 502, 32 καθαρὰ ἀπὸ κοπρίων; Jer 32:33; Sir 22:2)

❶ ***dung, manure*** κόπρια βάλλειν *put manure on* **Lk 13:8** (Theophr., Caus. Pl. 3, 9, 5 παραβάλλειν κόπρον).

❷ ***filth, dirt,*** transf. sense of 1 (BGU I, 15, 50 [I BC]) τὰ κ. αἴρειν (PGM 4, 1441) *take away the dirt* Hs 9, 10, 3.—DELG s.v. κόπρος. M-M.

κόπρον, ου, τό (s. two prec. entries and next entry; Galen XII 290 K.—For the LXX ἡ κόπρος [s. the foll. entry] is surely correct wherever the gender can be established. But there is also the acc. κόπρον which, without the article, may be fem. or neut. [Is 30:22; 36:12, which latter form has τήν w. it as a v.l.]; TestBenj 8:3; ApcMos 6; and likew. the gen. κόπρου [4 Km 6:25; Ezk 4:12; Jos., Ant. 9, 62; PGM 7, 485]) Hs 9, 10, 3 if the restoration τὰ κό[πρα] in FXFunk[2] 1901 is correct, and perh. κόπρον **Lk 13:8 v.l.** But the latter form more likely belongs under the next entry.

κόπρος, ου, ἡ (s. three prec. entries; Hom. et al.; Diod. S. 4, 13, 3; Dio Chrys. 13 [7], 16; 15 [32], 87; ins, pap, LXX; Tat. 3, 1 [s. κόπρον]) ***dung, manure.*** Since this form is so incomparably better attested than the neut. in the entry above, it is almost certain that the doubtful cases mentioned there belong under this word.—DELG.

κόπτω impf. ἔκοπτον; 1 aor. ἔκοψα, mid. ἐκοψάμην; fut. mid. κόψομαι. Pass.: 2 aor. ἐκόπην (Hs 8, 1, 4); pf. ptc. κεκομμένος (Hs 8, 1, 4) (Hom.+; ins, pap, LXX; TestSol; ApcSed 7:10; Ar. 8, 2; Just.; Mel., P. 19, 128; 29, 201)

❶ ***cut (off)*** act. (Jos., Vi. 171; Just., D. 86, 6) τὶ ἀπό (or ἔκ) τινος *someth. fr. someth.* (Quint. Smyrn. 11, 71 κ. τι ἀπό τινος) κλάδους ἀπὸ τ. δένδρων **Mt 21:8.** κλάδους ἀπὸ τῆς ἰτέας Hs 8, 1, 2; cp. 4; 8, 3, 1; 8, 4, 4f. στιβάδας ἐκ τῶν ἀγρῶν *leafy branches from the fields* **Mk 11:8** (cp. X., Hell. 5, 2, 43; POslo 17, 7 [136 AD]; Is 44:14 ξύλον ἐκ τοῦ δρυμοῦ; 2 Ch 2:15; SibOr 3, 651).—Fig. πολὺ κόψετε τῶν προτέρων ὑμῶν ἁμαρτιῶν *you will cut off many of your former sins* Hs 6, 1, 4.

❷ ***beat*** one's breast as an act of mourning, mid. (Aeschyl., Pers. 683, cp. Cho. 22–31; Pla., Phd. 60b; LXX; Jos., Ant. 7, 41; s. κοπετός) κ. τὰ στήθη *beat their breasts* (PGM 36, 139) GPt 8:28. Then abs. *mourn (greatly)* (Lucian, De Sacrific. 15; 3 Km 13:29 v.l.; Zech 7:5) **Mt 24:30;** GPt 7:25; (w. θρηνεῖν, q.v. 2 and 3 and Jos., Ant. 8, 273) **Mt 11:17; Lk 23:27;** (w. κλαίειν, q.v. 1) GPt 12:52, 54; GJs 17:2. W. cognate acc. δύο κοπετοὺς ἐκόπτετο GJs 2:1. κ. ἐπὶ σάκκου καὶ σποδοῦ *mourn in sackcloth and ashes* B 7:5 (the unusual use of ἐπί is prob. to be explained by the fact that the mourner sat on ashes; cp. 3:2). W. acc. foll. *mourn someone* (Aristoph., Lys. 396; Pla., Rep. 10, 619c; Anth. Pal. 11, 135, 1; Gen 23:2; 1 Km 25:1 al.; Jos., Ant. 13, 399) **Lk 8:52;** cp. **23:27;** GJs 24:3. τὴν χηροσύνην . . . τὴν ἀτεκνίαν 2:1. Also ἐπί τινα *mourn for someone* (2 Km 1:12; 11:26 v.l.) **Rv 1:7; 18:9.**—EMartino, Morte e pianto rituale nel mondo antico, '58, 217–20 (lit.). The principal themes of lamentation Hom., Il. 18, 22–64.—B. 553; 557. DELG. M-M. TW.

κόραξ, ακος, ὁ (Hom. et al.; PMagd 21, 5; LXX; PsSol 4:20; TestJud 21:8; ParJer 7:8; Jos., Ant. 1, 91 al.; Tat. 1, 3) ***crow, raven* Lk 12:24.** Jews were forbidden to eat it B 10:1, 4 (Lev 11:15; Dt 14:14).—DELG. M-M.

κοράσιον, ου, τό (Pla. in Diog. L. 3, 33; Philippides Com. [IV/III BC] 36; Epict. 2, 1, 28; 3, 2, 8; 4, 10, 33; Anth. Pal. 9, 39, 1; IG VII, 3325; PStras 79, 2 [16/15 BC]; BGU 887, 9; 913, 7; LXX. See Lob. on Phryn. 73–75; PKretschmer, D. Entstehung der Κοινή 1900, 17; FSolmsen, RhM 59, 1904, 503f) dim. of κόρη ***girl*** (acc. to Wellhausen transl. of the Aramaic רְבִיתָא for which the more elegant טְלִיתָא was inserted as a correction: s. Wlh., EKlostermann ad loc.) **Mk 5:41** (on τὸ κ. as a voc., s. B-D-F §147, 3; Rob. 461).—**Mt 9:24f; 14:11; Mk 5:42; 6:22, 28.**—DELG s.v. 2 κόρος. M-M.

κορβᾶν indecl. (edd. also -άν; קָרְבָּן) Hebr. word, explained by the notation ὅ ἐστι δῶρον (transl. corresp. to the LXX Lev 2:1, 4, 12, 13) **someth. consecrated as a gift for God and closed to ordinary human use, *gift to God, corban*** (cp. Jos., Ant. 4, 73 of the Nazirites οἱ κορβᾶν αὑτοὺς ὀνομάσαντες τῷ θεῷ, δῶρον δὲ τοῦτο σημαίνει κατὰ Ἑλλήνων γλῶτταν, C. Ap. 1, 167; for Heb. ins s. Fitzmyer, below) **Mk 7:11** (cp. κορβανᾶς). On this subject cp. Philo, Spec. Leg. 2, 16f; Billerb. I 711ff; Dalman, Gramm.[2] 174, 3; HOrt, De verbintenissen met 'Korban': TT 37, 1903, 284–314; JHart, Corban: JQR 19, 1907, 615–50; HLaible, Korban: Allg. Ev.-Luth. Kirchenzeitung 54, 1921, 597ff; 613ff; MBlack, Aramaic Approach[3], '67, 139; HHommel, D. Wort Korban u. seine Verwandten: Philologus 98, '54, 132–49; JFitzmyer, JBL 78, '59, 60–65=Essays on the Semitic Background of the NT '71, 93–100; SZeitlin, JQR 53, '62, 160–63.—TW.

κορβανᾶς, ᾶ, ὁ (קָרְבָּן; Aram. קָרְבָּנָא; s. B-D-F §58;= γαζοφυλακεῖον) ***temple treasury*** (Jos., Bell. 2, 175 ἱερὸς θησαυρός, καλεῖται δὲ κορβωνᾶς.—Dalman, Gramm.[2] 174, 3) εἰς τὸν κ. βάλλειν *put into the temple treasury* **Mt 27:6** (vv.ll. κορβάν, κορβονᾶν; on the legal fiction cp. Mishnah: Erubin).—TW.

Κόρε, ὁ indecl. (edd. also Κορέ; קֹרַח) ***Korah,*** head of a rebellion against Moses (Num 16; Sir 45:18; Philo, Fuga 145.—Jos., Ant. 4, 14ff: Κορῆς, έου) **Jd 11;** GJs 9:2.

κορέννυμι 1 aor. ἐκορέσθην; pf. pass. ptc. κεκορεσμένος (Hom. et al.; Kaibel 314, 21f; ParJer; Jos., Ant. 2, 86; 10, 261) ***satiate, fill*** pass. *be satiated, have enough* w. gen. of that with which one is satiated or satisfied (Hom. et al.; SibOr 3, 697).

ⓐ lit. κορεσθέντες τροφῆς *when they had eaten enough* **Ac 27:38.**

ⓑ fig. (Kaibel, s. above; Appian, Hann. 27 §115, Bell. Civ. 1, 3, §10; Philo; Jos., Bell. 4, 314) ironically (Straub 24) ἤδη κεκορεσμένοι ἐστέ *you already have eaten your fill,* i.e., you think you already have all the spiritual food you need **1 Cor 4:8.**—DELG s.v. κορε-; Frisk s.v. κορρέννυμι. M-M.

κόρη, ης, ἡ (primary mng. 'girl, young woman' Hom. et al.; TestSol 26:5; Just., A I, 27, 1; Tat. 19, 2; Ath.; on a smaller scale 'doll' Dio Chrys. 31, 153). The tiny image reflected in the iris of the eye gave rise to the use of the term κ. (=Lat. pupilla) to denote the 'pupil' of the eye (trag., Hippocr. et al.; SIG 1169,

67 restored; LXX; Philo; Ps-Orph. [Denis 165, 22; Theosophien 181 §56]) ***pupil,*** in our lit. used in imagery of something held dear: ἀγαπᾶν ὡς κ. τοῦ ὀφθαλμοῦ *love as the pupil of one's eye = love as the darling, favorite,* or *'apple' of the eye* B 19:9 (cp. Dt 32:10; Ps 16:8; Pr 7:2, all w. trans. of the term אִישׁוֹן, 'little human'; JosAs 25:5; 26:2.).—The Eng. rendering 'apple of the eye' in the OT pass. cited above confounds the imagery, but conveys the sense of something cherished (cp. Coverdale's rendering of Zech 2:8: 'who so toucheth you, shal touche the aple of his owne eye' [OED s.v. 'apple']).—Betz, SM 442 n. 141 (lit.). DELG s.v. 2 κόρος.

Κορίνθιος, ου, ὁ ***the Corinthian*** (trag., Hdt. et al.; ins; Ath. 17, 2) **Ac 18:8, 27** D; **2 Cor 6:11;** 1 Cl 47:6. Also in the title of 1 and 2 Cor and 1 and 2 Cl and the subscr. of Ro v.l. and 1 Cl; 2 Cl 20:5 (subscr.) Funk; AcPlCor as appellation ἡ Κορινθίων ἐκκλησία 1:16.

Κόρινθος, ου, ἡ (Hom. et al.; ins, Philo, SibOr 3, 487 al.; Just., D. 1, 3; Ath. 17, 2) ***Corinth*** a city in Greece on the isthmus of the same name. From 27 BC capital of the senatorial province of Achaia, and seat of the proconsul. The Christian congregation there was founded by Paul on his so-called second missionary journey, **Ac 18:1, 27** D; **19:1; 1 Cor 1:2; 2 Cor 1:1, 23; 2 Ti 4:20;** 1 Cl ins; MPol 22:2; EpilMosq 5; AcPl Ha 6, 1f; AcPlCor 1:2; 2:1; ἄνδρες Κ. 2:26. Also **subscr.** of **Ro v.l.** and **1 Th.**—ECurtius, Peloponnesos II 1852, 514ff; JCladder, Korinth 1923; OBroneer, BA 14, '51, 78–96; Pauly-W. Suppl. IV 991–1036; VI 182ff, 1350f; Kl. Pauly III 301ff; BHHW II 988ff; Corinth, Results of Excavations Conducted by the American School of Classical Studies at Athens 1929ff; RCarpenter, Korinthos[6] '60; FJdeWaele, Corinth and St. Paul '61; DESmith, The Egyptian Cults at Corinth: HTR 70, '77, 201–31; GTheissen, The Social Setting of Pauline Christianity '82 (Eng. tr.); JMurphy-O'Connor, St. Paul's Corinth '83 (reff.), Corinth: ABD I 1134–39 (add. lit.); PECS 240–43.—S. the Corinthian ins (Dssm., LO 12, 8 [LAE 16, 7]): [συνα]γωγὴ Ἑβρ[αίων]=Boffo, Iscrizioni no. 45 and lit. p. 361f. Strabo 8, 6, 20 suggests the problems of immorality associated with a major port city, but his references to cult prostitution, as in his quotation of the proverb οὐ παντὸς ἀνδρὸς ἐς Κόρινθον ἔσθ' ὁ πλοῦς ibid. (=Aristoph. fgm. 902a; cp. Ael. Aristid. 29, 17 K.=40 p. 755 D.) concern pre-Roman times and have been used without adequate caution for inferences about Paul's Corinth.

Κορνήλιος, ου, ὁ (found frequently: s. Diod. S. 11, 27, 1 [of a man contemporary with the battle of Salamis, 480 BC]; 11, 86, 1; 14, 110, 1; SIG and OGI indices; Preisigke, Namenbuch; Joseph.) ***Cornelius,*** a Roman centurion (ἑκατοντάρχης) in Caesarea by the sea **Ac 10:1, 3, 7 v.l., 17, 22, 24f, 30f.**—CBurchard, D. dreizehnte Zeuge '70, 54 n. 11.

κόρος, ου, ὁ (PSI 554, 14 [259 BC]; LXX; TestJud 9:8; Eupolemus the Jewish historian [II BC]: 723 fgm. 2, 33 Jac. [in Eus., PE 9, 33]; Joseph.) a Heb. dry measure (כֹּר 'cor, kor'; HLewy, D. Semit. Fremdwörter im Griech. 1895, 116), a measure of capacity for grain, flour, etc.; acc. to Jos., Ant. 15, 314=ten Attic medimni, hence about 393 liters=about 4 hectoliters, or betw. ten and twelve bushels; ***measure*** **Lk 16:7.**—Lit. under II βάτος.—DELG s.v. 3 κόρος. M-M. TW. Sv.

κοσμέω impf. ἐκόσμουν; fut. κοσμήσω LXX; 1 aor. ἐκόσμησα. Pass.: aor. ἐκοσμήθην LXX; pf. 3 sg. κεκόσμηται, ptc. κεκοσμημένος; plpf. 3 sg. ἐκεκόσμητο (s. κόσμος; Hom.+).

❶ to put in order so as to appear neat or well organized, ***make neat/tidy*** (Od. 7, 13; X., Cyr. 8, 2, 6; 6, 11; SIG 1038, 11 τράπεζαν; PThéad 14, 18; Sir 29:26; 50:14; Just., A II, 5, 2 al; Tat. 12, 1; τὸν κόσμον Mel., P. 82, 616) ***trim,*** of lamps **Mt 25:7.** In imagery of a person as a house from which a possessive spirit has departed *tidied, fixed up, put in order* **Mt 12:44; Lk 11:25** (for another nuance s. 2aβ below).

❷ to cause someth. to have an attractive appearance through decoration, ***adorn, decorate*** (Hes. et al.; LXX; SibOr 3, 426)

ⓐ lit.—**α.** of pers. τινὰ ἔν τινι *someone w. someth.* (Diod. S. 17, 53, 3 ἐν ὅπλοις=with [splendid] weapons; TestJud 13:5 ἐν χρυσίῳ καὶ μαργαρίταις) **1 Ti 2:9.** Pass. (Xenophon Eph. 1, 2, 2 παρθένοι κεκοσμημέναι; TestSol 7:4 D; JosAs 4:2; Jos., Bell. 2, 444) νύμφη κεκοσμημένη *a bride adorned* for her husband (Achilles Tat. 3, 7, 5; s. TestJud 12:1) **Rv 21:2;** cp. Hv 4, 2, 1. Of women (POxy 1467, 5 γυναῖκες κεκοσμημέναι) κοσμηθεῖσαι πρὸς μοιχείαν *beautified for adultery* ApcPt 9:24 (cp. TestReub 5:5 κ. πρὸς ἀπάτην διανοίας; TestJos 9:5).

β. of things τί *someth.* pass. the temple in Jerusalem λίθοις καλοῖς καὶ ἀναθήμασιν κεκόσμηται *is adorned w. beautiful stones and votive offerings* (SIG 725, 2f τὸ ἱερὸν ἀναθέμασι κεκόσμηται; 1100, 21f; 1050, 6; 2 Macc 9:16; TestSol 10:5; 25:9; Philo, Det. Pot. Ins. 20) **Lk 21:5;** cp. **Rv 21:19.** κ. τὰ μνημεῖα (cp. X., Mem. 2, 2, 13; Jos., Ant. 14, 284 κ. τάφον) **Mt 23:29.** δένδρα καρποῖς κεκοσμημένα *trees adorned w. fruit* Hs 9, 1, 10; 9, 28, 1. This interpretation has also been assigned by some to οἶκος κεκοσμημένος *a decorated house* **Mt 12:44; Lk 11:25** (ins ZPE 29, '78, 213–28, ln. 67 [I AD]; Philo, Deus Imm. 150; SIG 326, 15 κεκοσμημένην τὴν πόλιν; Ath. 26, 2).

ⓑ fig.—**α.** *make beautiful* or *attractive* inwardly, morally (of exceptional persons Pind., N. 6, 46 [78]; Thu. 2, 42, 2 αἱ ἀρεταὶ ἐκόσμησαν; X., Cyr. 8, 1, 21; IGR IV, 288, 9 κεκόσμηκε τὸν αὐτοῦ βίον τῇ καλλίστῃ παρρησίᾳ; IPriene 105, 36; TestAbr B 13 p. 117, 14 [Stone p. 82] ἐν πολλῇ ὡραιότητι) κ. ἑαυτόν *adorn oneself* **1 Pt 3:5** (cp. Epict. 3, 1, 26; Just., A I, 12, 2); **1 Ti 2:9.**—Pass., w. dat. of the thing that adorns (Diod. S. 16, 65, 2 ἀρεταῖς κεκοσμημένος; IK 30, 14, 4f; 3 Macc 6:1; Philo, Op. M. 139; Just., A II, 11, 4 κεκοσμημένον τῷ . . . κόσμῳ) παντὶ καλῷ ἐκεκόσμητο *he was adorned w. every good thing* MPol 13:2. καρποῖς Dg 12:1. τ. παναρέτῳ πολιτείᾳ 1 Cl 2:8. τῷ ἐνδόξῳ ὀνόματι 43:2. Also ἔν τινι (Sir 48:11 B, S, A οἱ ἐν ἀγαπήσει κεκοσμημένοι; TestAbr A 11 p. 89, 19f [Stone p. 26] ὁ ἐν τοιαύτῃ δόξῃ κοσμούμενος) ἐν ἔργοις ἀγαθοῖς 1 Cl 33:7. ἐν τ. ἐντολαῖς Ἰησοῦ Χριστοῦ *with the commandments of Jesus Christ* IEph 9:2.

β. *adorn, do credit to* (Theognis 947 Diehl πατρίδα κοσμήσω) ἵνα τὴν διδασκαλίαν κοσμῶσιν ἐν πᾶσιν *that they may do credit to the teaching in all respects* **Tit 2:10.**—DELG s.v. κόσμος. M-M. TW. Spicq. Sv.

κοσμικός, ή, όν (s. κόσμος; Aristot., Phys. 2, 4 p. 196a, 25 τοὐρανοῦ τοῦδε καὶ τῶν κοσμικῶν πάντων; Vett. Val. Index II; Lucian, Paras. 11 [opp. ἀνθρώπινος]; Ps.-Plutarch, Consol. ad Apoll. 34, Mor. 119e κοσμικὴ διάταξις; ins; PGM 4, 2533 τὰ κοσμικὰ πάντα; TestAbr A 7 p. 84, 25 [Stone p. 16] τὸν κοσμικὸν βίον; TestJos 17:8 κ. . . . δόξαν; Philo, Aet. M. 53; Jos., Bell. 4, 324; Tat. 12, 5 κ. καταλήψεως; Ath. 24, 5 κ. σοφίας; loanw. in rabb.).

❶ pert. to the earth as a physical phenomenon, ***earthly*** (TestJos. 17:8) τὸ ἅγιον κ. *the earthly sanctuary* (opp. heavenly) **Hb 9:1.** τὸ κ. μυστήριον ἐκκλησίας *the earthly mystery of the church* D 11:11. κοσμικαὶ βάσανοι *earthly tortures* MPol

2:3.—Subst. τὰ κ. ταῦτα *these earthly things* 2 Cl 5:6 (cp. Did., Gen. 149, 11).

❷ **pert. to interests prevailing on earth, *worldly,*** w. the implication of that which is at enmity w. God or morally reprehensible: αἱ κοσμικαὶ ἐπιθυμίαι *worldly desires* **Tit 2:12;** 2 Cl 17:3 (cp. Iren.1, 16, 3 [Harv. I 164, 5]).—DELG s.v. κόσμος. TW. Sv.

κόσμιος, (ία), ον (s. κόσμος; Aristoph., Pla. et al.; ins, pap; Eccl 12:9, Just., 12, 5)

❶ **pert. to having characteristics or qualities that evoke admiration or delight, an expression of high regard for pers., *respectable, honorable*** pers. (Nicophon Com. [V/IV BC] 16; OGI 485, 3 ἄνδρα κόσμιον; Philo, Spec. Leg. 3, 89; Just.) w. σώφρων (IG IV^2/1, 82, 27 [40/42 AD] honorary ins for a man) **1 Ti 3:2.**

❷ **pert. to being appropriate for winning approval, *appropriate,*** used w. an impers. noun, yet w. ref. to a pers., whose special status is prob. signalled thereby (cp. IMagnMai 165, 6 κ. ἀναστροφή; 179, 4) ἐν καταστολῇ κ. *in modest apparel* (of women, as Epict., Ench. 40; Dio Chrys. 5, 14; PSI 97, 1) **1 Ti 2:9.**—Subst. pl. τὰ κόσμια *adornment* AcPl Ha 2, 21: κοσμί[ων]; s. ed. CSchmidt's remarks p. 125.—DELG s.v. κόσμος. M-M. TW. Spicq. Sv.

κοσμίως adv. of κόσμιος (Aristoph., Pla.+; ins e.g. IGR IV, 255, 9; Philo, Spec. Leg. 1, 153) **pert. to being in accord with accepted standards of propriety, *modestly, decorously, observing decorum,*** of self-adornment **1 Ti 2:9 v.l.** (in wordplay: κοσμίως-κοσμεῖν 'to decorate' themselves 'decorously', oppos. of conspicuous consumption).—DELG s.v. κόσμος. M-M.

κοσμοκράτωρ, ορος, ὁ (s. κόσμος, κρατέω) ***world-ruler*** (used of world-ruling gods [Orphica: Hymns 8, 11 Helios; 11, 11 Pan; Vett. Val. 170, 36 κ. Ζεύς; 171, 6; 314, 16 κ. Ἥλιος; PGM 4, 1599; 2198; 5, 400 and 17b, 1 Ἑρμῆς; 13, 619 Σάραπις] and of the emperor Caracalla [Egypt. ins APF 2, 1903, 449 no. 83]. Then gener. of spirit beings, who have parts of the cosmos under their control: Vett. Val. 278, 2; 360, 7; Iambl., Myst. 2, 9; 3, 10; TestSol; Iren. 1, 5, 4 [Harv. I 48, 2]; τὸν διάβολον . . . , ὃν καὶ κοσμοκράτωρα καλοῦσι 1, 5, 4 [Harv. I 47, 4].—FCumont, Compt. rend. Acad. des ins 1919, 313f; EPeterson, Εἷς θεός 1926, 238, 3. Also loanw. in rabb., e.g. of the angel of death) of evil spirits (w. ἀρχαί and ἐξουσίαι) οἱ κ. τοῦ σκότους τούτου *the world-rulers of this darkness* i.e. the rulers of this sinful world **Eph 6:12** (s. TestSol [18, 2] in Dibelius, Geisterwelt 230: spirits come to Sol. and call themselves οἱ κοσμοκράτορες τ. σκότους τούτου. On the subject s. Hdb. on J 12:31 and FDölger, D. Sonne d. Gerechtigkeit 1918, 49ff; GMacgregor, Principalities and Powers: ACPurdy Festschr. '60, 88–104).—DELG s.v. κόσμος. M-M. TW.

κοσμοπλανής, ῆτος, ὁ (s. κόσμος, πλανάω) ***deceiver of the world,*** of an apocalyptic apotheosis of evil D 16:4 (Harnack and Knopf read κοσμοπλάνος).

κοσμοπλάνος s. κοσμοπλανής.

κόσμος, ου, ὁ (Hom.+)—❶ **that which serves to beautify through decoration, *adornment, adorning*** (Hom.+; Diod. S. 20, 4, 5 τῶν γυναικῶν τὸν κόσμον; OGI 531, 13; SIG 850, 10; IMaronIsis 41; PEleph 1, 4; PSI 240, 12 γυναικεῖον κόσμον; LXX; TestJud 12:1; JosAs 2:6 al.; Philo, Migr. Abr. 97 γυναικῶν κ.; Jos., Ant. 1, 250; 15, 5; Just., A II, 11, 4f) of women's attire, etc. ὁ ἔξωθεν . . . κόσμος *external adorning* **1 Pt 3:3** (Vi. Hom. 4 of the inward adornment of a woman, beside σωφροσύνη; Crates, Ep. 9; Pythag., Ep. 11, 1; Plut., Mor. 141e; on the topic of external adornment cp. SIG 736, 15–26).

❷ **condition of orderliness, *orderly arrangement, order*** (Hom. et al.; s. HDiller, Die vorphilosophische Gebrauch von κ. und κοσμεῖν: BSnell Festschr., '56, 47–60) μετὰ κόσμου *in order* Dg 12:9 (text uncertain; s. μετακόσμιος).

❸ **the sum total of everything here and now, *the world, the (orderly) universe,*** in philosophical usage (so, acc. to Plut., Mor. 886b, as early as Pythagoras; certainly Heraclitus, fgm. 66; Pla., Gorg. 508a, Phdr. 246c; Chrysipp., fgm. 527 v. Arnim κόσμος σύστημα ἐξ οὐρανοῦ καὶ γῆς καὶ τῶν ἐν τούτοις περιεχομένων φύσεων. Likew. Posidonius in Diog. L. 7, 138; Ps.-Aristot., De Mundo 2 p. 391b, 9ff; 2 and 4 Macc; Wsd; EpArist 254; Philo, Aet. M. 4; Jos., Ant. 1, 21; Test12Patr; SibOr 7, 123; AssMos fgm. b Denis [=Tromp p. 272]; Just., A I, 20, 2 al.; Ath. 19, 2 al.; Orig., C. Cels. 4, 68, 14; Did., Gen. 36, 7; 137, 13.—The other philosoph. usage, in which κ. denotes the heaven in contrast to the earth, is prob. without mng. for our lit. [unless perh. **Phil 2:15** κ.='sky'?]). ἡ ἀέναος τοῦ κ. σύστασις *the everlasting constitution of the universe* 1 Cl 60:1 (cp. OGI 56, 48 εἰς τὸν ἀέναον κ.). Sustained by four elements Hv 3, 13, 3. πρὸ τοῦ τὸν κ. εἶναι *before the world existed* **J 17:5.** ἀπὸ καταβολῆς [κόσμου] *from the beginning of the world* **Mt 13:35; 25:34; Lk 11:50; Hb 4:3; 9:26; Rv 13:8; 17:8.** Also ἀπ' ἀρχῆς κ. **Mt 24:21** or ἀπὸ κτίσεως κ. **Ro 1:20.**—B 5:5 ἀπὸ καταβ. κ. evidently means *at the foundation of the world* (s. Windisch, Hdb. ad loc.). πρὸ καταβολῆς κ. *before the foundation of the world* **J 17:24; Eph 1:4; 1 Pt 1:20** (on the uses w. καταβολή s. that word, 1). οὐδὲν εἴδωλον ἐν κ. *no idol has any real existence in the universe* (Twentieth Century NT) **1 Cor 8:4.** Of the creation in its entirety **3:22.** ὁ κόσμος ὅλος = πᾶσα ἡ κτίσις (Sallust. 21 p. 36, 13; TestSol 5:7; TestJob 33:4) Hs 9, 2, 1; 9, 14, 5. φωστῆρες ἐν κόσμῳ *stars in the universe* **Phil 2:15** (s. above). Esp. of the universe as created by God (Epict 4, 7, 6 ὁ θεὸς πάντα πεποίηκεν, τὰ ἐν τῷ κόσμῳ καὶ αὐτὸν τὸν κόσμον ὅλον; Wsd 9:9; 2 Macc 7:23 ὁ τοῦ κ. κτίστης; 4 Macc 5:25; Just., A I, 59, 1 al.; Ath. 8, 2 al.) ὁ ποιήσας τὸν κ. *who has made the world* **Ac 17:24.** ὁ κτίστης τοῦ σύμπαντος κ. 1 Cl 19:2; ὁ κτίσας τὸν κ. Hv 1, 3, 4; cp. m 12, 4, 2. ὁ τοῦ παντὸς κ. κυριεύων B 21:5. οὐδ' εἶναι τὸν κόσμον θεοῦ ἀλλὰ ἀγγέλων AcPlCor 1:15. Christ is called παντὸς τοῦ κ. κύριος 5:5; and the κ. owes its origin to his agency **J 1:10b.** The world was created for the sake of the church Hv 2, 4, 1.—The universe, as the greatest space conceivable, is not able to contain someth. (Philo, Ebr. 32) **J 21:25.**

❹ **the sum total of all beings above the level of the animals, *the world,*** as θέατρον ἐγενήθημεν (i.e. οἱ ἀπόστολοι) τῷ κόσμῳ καὶ ἀγγέλοις καὶ ἀνθρώποις **1 Cor 4:9.** Here *the world* is divided into *angels and humans* (cp. the Stoic definition of the κόσμος in Stob., Ecl. I p. 184, 8 τὸ ἐκ θεῶν καὶ ἀνθρώπων σύστημα; likew. Epict 1, 9, 4.—Acc. to Ocellus Luc. 37, end, the κ. consists of the sphere of the divine beyond the moon and the sphere of the earthly on this side of the moon).

❺ **planet earth as a place of inhabitation, *the world*** (SIG 814, 31 [67 AD] Nero, ὁ τοῦ παντὸς κόσμου κύριος; the meaning of the birthday of Augustus for the world OGI 458, 40 [=IPriene 105]; 2 Macc 3:12; Jos., Ant. 9, 241; 10, 205; Orig., C. Cels. 4, 68)

ⓐ gener. **Mk 16:15.** τὰς βασιλείας τοῦ κ. **Mt 4:8;** ἐν ὅλῳ τῷ κ. **26:13.** Cp. **13:38** (cp. Hs 5, 5, 2); **Mk 14:9;** Hs 9, 25, 2. τὸ φῶς τοῦ κ. τούτου *the light of this world* (the sun) **J 11:9.** In rhetorical exaggeration ἡ πίστις ὑμῶν καταγγέλλεται ἐν ὅλῳ τ. κόσμῳ **Ro 1:8** (cp. the Egypt. grave ins APF 5, 1913, 169 no. 24, 8 ὧν ἡ σωφροσύνη κατὰ τὸν κ. λελάληται).

Abraham as κληρονόμος κόσμου *heir of the world* **4:13.**—Cp. **1 Cor 14:10; Col 1:6.** ἡ ἐν τῷ κ. ἀδελφότης *the brotherhood in the* (whole) *world* **1 Pt 5:9.** ἐγένετο ἡ βασιλεία τοῦ κ. τοῦ κυρίου ἡμῶν *our Lord has assumed the sovereignty of the world* **Rv 11:15.** τὰ ἔθνη τοῦ κ. (not LXX, but prob. rabbinic אֻמּוֹת הָעוֹלָם=humankind apart fr. Israel; Billerb. II 191; Dalman, Worte 144f) *the unconverted in the world* **Lk 12:30.** In this line of development, κόσμος alone serves to designate the polytheistic *unconverted world* **Ro 11:12, 15.**—Other worlds (lands) beyond the ocean 1 Cl 20:8.—Many of these pass. bear the connotation of

ⓑ *the world* as the habitation of humanity (as SibOr 1, 160). So also Hs 9, 17, 1f. εἰσέρχεσθαι εἰς τὸν κ. of entrance into the world by being born 1 Cl 38:3. ἐκ τοῦ κ. ἐξελθεῖν *leave this present world* (Philo, Leg. All. 3, 5 ἔξω τ. κόσμου φεύγειν; s. ἐξέρχομαι 5; cp. Hippol., Ref. 5, 16, 7) **1 Cor 5:10b;** 2 Cl 8:3. γεννηθῆναι εἰς τὸν κ. *be born into the world* **J 16:21.** ἕως ἐσμὲν ἐν τούτῳ τῷ κ. 2 Cl 8:2. οὐδὲν εἰσφέρειν εἰς τὸν κ. (Philo, Spec. Leg. 1, 294 τὸν μηδὲν εἰς τὸν κόσμον εἰσενηνοχότα) **1 Ti 6:7** (Pol 4:1). πολλοὶ πλάνοι ἐξῆλθον εἰς τὸν κ. **2J 7.**—ἐν τῷ κόσμῳ τούτῳ **J 12:25** (κ. need not here be understood as an entity hostile to God, but the transition to the nuance in 7b, below, is signalled by the term that follows: ζωὴν αἰώνιον). ἵνα εἰς κόσμον προέλθῃ AcPlCor 2:6.

ⓒ *earth, world* in contrast to heaven (Dio Chrys. 19 [36], 59; Iren., 1, 4, 2 [Harv. I 35, 5]; Orig., C. Cels. 8, 15, 24) ἐν τῷ κόσμῳ τούτῳ 2 Cl 19:3.—Esp. when mention is made of the preexistent Christ, who came fr. another world into the κόσμος. So, above all, in John (Bultmann, index I κόσμος) ἔρχεσθαι εἰς τὸν κ. (τοῦτον) **J 6:14; 9:39; 11:27; 16:28a; 18:37;** specif. also *come into the world as light* **12:46;** cp. **1:9; 3:19.** Sending of Jesus into the world **3:17a; 10:36; 17:18; 1J 4:9.** His εἶναι ἐν τῷ κόσμῳ **J 1:10a; 9:5a; 17:12 v.l.** Leaving the world and returning to the Father **13:1a; 16:28b.** Cp. **14:19; 17:11a.** His kingship is not ἐκ τοῦ κ. τούτου *of this world* i.e. not derived from the world or conditioned by its terms and evaluations **18:36ab.**—Also Χρ. Ἰησοῦς ἦλθεν εἰς τ. κόσμον **1 Ti 1:15;** cp. ἐπιστεύθη ἐν κόσμῳ (opp. ἀνελήμφθη ἐν δόξῃ) **3:16.**—εἰσερχόμενος εἰς τὸν κ. **Hb 10:5.**

ⓓ *the world* outside in contrast to one's home PtK 3 p. 15, 13; 19.

❻ **humanity in general,** ***the world*** (TestAbr B 8 p. 113, 11 [Stone p. 74]; ApcEsdr 3:6 p. 27, 14; SibOr 1, 189; Just., A I, 39, 3 al.)

ⓐ gener. οὐαὶ τῷ κ. ἀπὸ τῶν σκανδάλων *woe to humankind because of the things that cause people to sin* **Mt 18:7;** τὸ φῶς τοῦ κ. *the light for humanity* **5:14;** cp. **J 8:12; 9:5.** ὁ σωτὴρ τοῦ κ. **4:42; 1J 4:14** (this designation is found in inscriptions, esp. oft. of Hadrian [WWeber, Untersuchungen z. Geschichte des Kaisers Hadrianus 1907, 225; 226; 229]).—**J 1:29; 3:17b; 17:6.**—κρίνειν τὸν κ. (SibOr 4, 184; TestAbr A 13 p. 92, 11 [Stone p. 32]; ApcMos 37) of God, Christ **J 12:47a; Ro 3:6;** B 4:12; cp. **Ro 3:19.** Of believers 1 Cor 6:2ab (cp. Sallust. 21 p. 36, 13 the souls of the virtuous, together w. the gods, will rule the whole κόσμος). Of Noah δι' ἧς (sc. πίστεως) κατέκρινεν τὸν κ. **Hb 11:7.** ἡ ἁμαρτία εἰς τὸν κ. εἰσῆλθεν **Ro 5:12;** likew. θάνατος εἰσῆλθεν εἰς τὸν κ. 1 Cl 3:4 (Wsd 2:24; 14:14). Cp. **Ro 5:13; 1 Cor 1:27f.** περικαθάρματα τοῦ κ. *the refuse of humanity* **4:13.** Of persons before conversion ἄθεοι ἐν τῷ κ. **Eph 2:12.**—**2 Cor 1:12; 5:19; Js 2:5; 1J 2:2; 4:1, 3.** ἀρχαῖος κόσμος *the people of the ancient world* **2 Pt 2:5a;** cp. vs. **5b; 3:6.** Of pers. of exceptional merit: ὧν οὐκ ἦν ἄξιος ὁ κ. *of whom the world was not worthy* **Hb 11:38.**—ὅλος ὁ κ. *all the world, everybody* **Ac 2:47** D; 1 Cl 5:7; cp. ἐν ὅλῳ τῷ κ. 59:2; εἰς ὅλον τὸν κ. Hs 8, 3, 2. Likew. ὁ κόσμος (cp. Philo, De Prov. in Eus., PE 8, 14, 58) ὁ κ. ὀπίσω αὐτοῦ ἀπῆλθεν **J 12:19.** ταῦτα λαλῶ εἰς τὸν κ. **8:26;** ἐν τῷ κ. **17:13;** ἐγὼ παρρησίᾳ λελάληκα τῷ κ. **18:20;** cp. **7:4; 14:22.** ἵνα γνῷ ὁ κ. **14:31;** cp. **17:23;** ἵνα ὁ κ. πιστεύῃ **17:21.**

ⓑ of all humanity, but especially of believers, as the object of God's love **J 3:16, 17c; 6:33, 51; 12:47b.**

❼ **the system of human existence in its many aspects,** ***the world***—ⓐ as scene of earthly joys, possessions, cares, sufferings (cp. 4 Macc 8:23) τὸν κ. ὅλον κερδῆσαι *gain the whole world* **Mt 16:26; Mk 8:36; Lk 9:25;** 2 Cl 6:2 (cp. Procop. Soph., Ep. 137 the whole οἰκουμένη is an unimportant possession compared to ἀρετή). τὰ τερπνὰ τοῦ κ. *the delightful things in the world* IRo 6:1. οἱ χρώμενοι τὸν κ. ὡς μὴ καταχρώμενοι *those who use the world as though they had no use of it* or *those who deal with the world as having made no deals with it* **1 Cor 7:31a.** ἔχειν τὸν βίον τοῦ κ. *possess worldly goods* **1J 3:17.** τὰ τοῦ κόσμου *the affairs of the world* **1 Cor 7:33f;** cp. **1J 2:15f.** The latter pass. forms an easy transition to the large number of exprs. (esp. in Paul and John) in which

ⓑ *the world,* and everything that belongs to it, appears as that which is hostile to God, i.e. lost in sin, wholly at odds w. anything divine, ruined and depraved (Herm. Wr. 6, 4 [the κόσμος is τὸ πλήρωμα τῆς κακίας]; 13, 1 [ἡ τοῦ κ. ἀπάτη], in Stob. p. 428, 24 Sc.; En 48:7; TestIss 4:6; AscIs 3:25; Hdb., exc. on **J 1:10;** Bultmann ad loc.—cp. Sotades Maronita [III BC] 11 Diehl: the κόσμος is unjust and hostile to great men) IMg 5:2; IRo 2:2. ὁ κόσμος οὗτος *this world* (in contrast to the heavenly realm) **J 8:23; 12:25, 31a; 13:1; 16:11; 18:36; 1J 4:17; 1 Cor 3:19; 5:10a; 7:31b;** Hv 4, 3, 2ff; D 10:6; 2 Cl 5:1, 5; (opp. ὁ ἅγιος αἰών) B 10:11. 'This world' is ruled by the ἄρχων τοῦ κ. τούτου *the prince of this world,* the devil **J 12:31b; 16:11;** without τούτου **14:30.** Cp. ὁ κ. ὅλος ἐν τῷ πονηρῷ κεῖται *the whole world lies in the power of the evil one* **1J 5:19;** cp. **4:4;** also ὁ αἰὼν τοῦ κ. τούτου **Eph 2:2** (s. αἰών 4).—Christians must have nothing to do with this world of sin and separation fr. God: instead of desiring it IRo 7:1, one is to ἄσπιλον ἑαυτὸν τηρεῖν ἀπὸ τοῦ κ. *keep oneself untainted by the world* **Js 1:27.** ἀποφεύγειν τὰ μιάσματα τοῦ κ. **2 Pt 2:20;** cp. **1:4** (s. ἀποφεύγω 1).—Pol 5:3. ἡ φιλία τοῦ κ. ἔχθρα τ. θεοῦ ἐστιν **Js 4:4a;** cp. vs. **4b.** When such an attitude is taken Christians are naturally hated by the world IRo 3:3; **J 15:18, 19ad; 17:14a; 1J 3:13,** as their Lord was hated **J 7:7; 15:18;** cp. **1:10c; 14:17; 16:20.**—Also in Paul: God and world in opposition τὸ πνεῦμα τοῦ κ. and τὸ πνεῦμα τὸ ἐκ θεοῦ *the spirit of the world* and *the spirit that comes fr. God* **1 Cor 2:12;** σοφία τοῦ κ. and σοφία τοῦ θεοῦ **1:20f.** ἡ κατὰ θεὸν λύπη and ἡ τοῦ κ. λύπη *godly grief* and *worldly grief* **2 Cor 7:10.** The world is condemned by God **1 Cor 11:32;** yet also the object of the divine plan of salvation **2 Cor 5:19;** cp. 1 Cl 7:4; 9:4. A Christian is dead as far as this world is concerned: δι' οὗ (i.e. Ἰ. Χρ.) ἐμοὶ κ. ἐσταύρωται κἀγὼ κόσμῳ *through Christ the world has been crucified for me, and I have been* (crucified) *to the world* **Gal 6:14;** cp. the question τί ὡς ζῶντες ἐν κ. δογματίζεσθε; **Col 2:20b.** For στοιχεῖα τοῦ κ. **Gal 4:3; Col 2:8, 20a** s. στοιχεῖον.—The use of κ. in this sense is even further developed in John. The κ. stands in opposition to God **1J 2:15f** and hence is incapable of knowing God **J 17:25;** cp. **1J 4:5,** and excluded fr. Christ's intercession **J 17:9;** its views refuted by the Paraclete **16:8.** Neither Christ himself **17:14c, 16b; 14:27,** nor his own **15:19b; 17:14b, 16a; 1J 3:1** belong in any way to the 'world'. Rather Christ has chosen them 'out of the world' **J 15:19c,** even though for the present they must still live 'in the world' **17:11b;** cp. **13:1b; 17:15, 18b.** All the trouble that they must undergo because of this, **16:33a,** means nothing compared w. the victorious conviction that Christ (and the believers w. him) has overcome 'the world' vs. **33b; 1J 5:4f,** and that it is doomed to pass away **2:17** (TestJob 33:4; Kephal. I 154, 21: the κόσμος τῆς σαρκός will pass away).

❽ collective aspect of an entity, *totality, sum total* (SIG 850, 10 τὸν κόσμον τῶν ἔργων (but s. 1 above); Pr 17:6a) ὁ κ. τῆς ἀδικίας ἡ γλῶσσα καθίσταται *the tongue becomes* (or *proves to be*) *the sum total of iniquity* **Js 3:6** (so, approx., Meinertz; FHauck.—MDibelius, Windisch and ASchlatter find mng. 7b here, whereas ACarr, Exp. 7th ser., 8, 1909, 318ff thinks of mng. 1). Χρ. τὸν ὑπὲρ τῆς τοῦ παντὸς κόσμου τῶν σῳζομένων σωτηρίας παθόντα *Christ, who suffered* or *died* (s. πάσχω 3αα) *for the salvation of the sum total of those who are saved* MPol 17:2.—FBytomski, D. genet. Entwicklung des Begriffes κόσμος in d. Hl. Schrift: Jahrb. für Philos. und spekul. Theol. 25, 1911, 180–201; 389–413 (only the OT); CSchneider, Pls u. d. Welt: Αγγελος IV '32, 11–47; EvSchrenck, Der Kosmos-Begriff bei Joh.: Mitteilungen u. Nachrichten f. d. evang. Kirche in Russland 51, 1895, 1–29; RLöwe, Kosmos u. Aion '35; RBultmann, D. Verständnis v. Welt u. Mensch im NT u. im Griechentum: ThBl 19, '40, 1–14; GBornkamm, Christus u. die Welt in der urchr. Botschaft: ZTK 47, '50, 212–26; ALesky, Kosmos '63; RVölkl, Christ u. Welt nach dem NT '61; GJohnston, οἰκουμένη and κ. in the NT: NTS 10, '64, 352–60; NCassem, ibid. 19, '72/73, 81–91; RBratcher, BT 31, '80, 430–34.—B. 13; 440. DELG. M-M. EDNT. TW.

Κούαρτος, ου, ὁ (edd. also Κουᾶρτος; on the accent s. B-D-F §41, 2; 3; Rob. 235f) ***Quartus,*** an otherw. unknown Christian **Ro 16:23; 1 Cor subscr. v.l.**—LGPN I.

κουμ (mss. and edd. also κούμ, κοῦμ, κουμί) Mesopotamian form of the impv. קוּם, for which Palestinian Aramaic has קוּמִי ***stand up*** **Mk 5:41** (Wlh. ad loc.).—TRE III 609.

Κοῦμαι, ῶν, αἱ (the Gk. form: Paradoxogr. Flor. 28; Ptolem. 3, 1, 6) ***Cumae,*** a city in Campania, Italy, not far fr. Naples; an old Gk. colony, famed for its Sibyl (on Cumae as the residence of the Sibyl s. MDibelius, Hdb. exc. on Hv 2, 4, 1). Hv 1, 1, 3; 2, 1, 1.—PECS 251–52.

κουμι s. κουμ.

κουστωδία, ας, ἡ (POxy 294, 20 [22 AD]; PRyl 189, 2; BGU 341, 3; s. Hahn 233, 6; 234, 7 w. lit.—Lat. loanw., custodia, also in rabb.) **a group of soldiers doing guard duty, *a guard*** composed of soldiers **Mt 27:66; 28:11.** ἔχειν κουστωδίαν *take a guard* **27:65.**—M-M.

κουφίζω (κοῦφος 'light', s. also next entry) impf. ἐκούφιζον; fut. κουφιῶ; aor. ἐκούφισα; aor. pass. inf. κουφισθῆναι (all LXX) (Hes. et al.) **to make someth. less heavy, *make light, lighten*** (so trag.; Dio Chrys. 80 [30], 40; ins, pap, LXX; Jos., Bell. 2, 96, Ant. 18, 149) τὶ *someth.* (1 Km 6:5) τὸ πλοῖον *lighten the ship* by throwing out the cargo **Ac 27:38** (Polyb. 20, 5, 11; Jon 1:5; GMiles/GTrompf, HTR 69, '76, 259–67, w. ref. to the shipwreck description Antiphon [the Orator], The Murder of Herodes).—New Docs 2, 74. DELG s.v. κοῦφος. M-M.

κούφισμα, ατος, τό (s. prec. entry; Eur., Phoen. 860; Plut., Mor. 114c) **the cause of someth. being less burdensome, *lightening, alleviation*** of almsgiving κ. ἁμαρτίας γίνεται *lightens the load of sin* 2 Cl 16:4 (after 1 Esdr 8:84 σύ, κύριε, ἐκούφισας τὰς ἁμαρτίας ἡμῶν; cp. 2 Esdr 9:13).—DELG s.v. κοῦφος.

κόφινος, ου, ὁ (Aristoph., X.+; ins, pap; Judg 6:19 B; Ps 80:7; ParJer; loanw. in Lat. s. Juvenal below) ***basket,*** in the NT prob. a large, heavy basket, probably of var. sizes, for carrying things (s. Juvenal 3, 14; 6, 542; RHorn, Lutheran Quarterly 1, '49, 301; FHort, JTS 10, 1909, 567ff; Artem. 2, 24; Jos., Bell. 3, 95) **Mt 14:20; Mk 6:43; Lk 9:17; J 6:13.** W. σφυρίς (Mt 16:10; Mk 8:20; cp. on this APF 6, 1920, 220 no. 8, 4f [III BC] Φίλωνι κόφινοι β', Πτολεμαίῳ σφυρίδιον) **Mt 16:9; Mk 8:19.** κ. κοπρίων *a basket of manure* **Lk 13:8** D (Nicol. Dam.: 90 fgm. 66, 13 Jac. κόπρον ἐν κοφίνῳ).—B. 623. DELG. M-M.

κράβαττος, ου, ὁ (mss. and edd. also κράβατος, κράββατος, κρέβαττος [**Mk 2:3 v.l.**]; a loanw., found also in rabb., but of uncertain origin and late in appearing [Phryn. 62 Lob.]. Acc. to Pollux 10, 35 in the form κράββατος in the comic poets Rhinto [III BC] and Crito [II BC]; so also TestJob [ms. P, κράβαττ- SV]; also Epict 1, 24, 14; Aesop, Fab. 413 H.; PLond II, 191, 16 p. 265 [II AD] κράββατος. Ostracon in Mélanges Nicole 1905 p. 184=Sb 4292, 9 and Moeris p. 58; 354 κράβατος. The form κράβακτος also occurs: PTebt 406, 19.—Am 3:12 Aq. On the form of the word s. B-D-F §42, 4; W-S. §5, 26a n.; Mlt. 244; Mlt-H. 102 [§41d]; Rob. 119; 213) ***mattress, pallet,*** the poor man's *bed* **Mk 2:4; 6:55.** W. κλινάριον **Ac 5:15.** αἴρειν τὸν κ. **Mk 2:9, 11f; J 5:8–11, 12 v.l.** (cp. Lucian, Philopseud. 11 ὁ Μίδας αὐτὸς ἀράμενος τὸν σκίμποδα, ἐφ' οὗ ἐκεκόμιστο, ᾤχετο ἐς τὸν ἀγρὸν ἀπιών 'Midas himself took up the pallet on which he had been carried, made his departure, and went back to the field [i.e. to his task of viticulture]'). κατακεῖσθαι ἐπὶ κραβάττου *lie in bed* **Ac 9:33.** JKramer, APF 41/2, '95.—DELG. M-M.

κράζω (Aeschyl.+; also Aesop, Fab. 252 P. a rooster) neut. ptc. κρᾶζον (B-D-F §13; W-S. §6, 2; Rob. 231); impf. ἔκραζον; fut. κράξω and κεκράξομαι (B-D-F §77; W-S. §13, 2; Mlt. 154; Rob. 361); 1 aor. ἔκραξα and ἐκέκραξα (**Ac 24:21,** s. B-D-F §75; W-S. §13, 2; 10 note 10; Mlt. 147; cp. Mlt-H. 244); pf. κέκραγα; plpf. 3 sg. ἐκεκράγει (3 Macc 5:23 v.l.).

❶ to make a vehement outcry, *cry out, scream, shriek,* when one utters loud cries, without words capable of being understood (cp. Hippol., Ref. 4, 28, 3 and 6): of mentally disturbed persons, epileptics, or the evil spirits living in them **Mk 5:5; 9:26; Lk 4:41 v.l.; 9:39.** Of the death-cry of Jesus on the cross **Mk 15:39 v.l.** Of the cry of a woman in childbirth **Rv 12:2.** ἀπὸ τοῦ φόβου *cry out in fear* **Mt 14:26.** φωνῇ μεγάλῃ *cry out in a loud voice* **27:50; Mk 1:26 v.l.** (for φωνῆσαν); **Ac 7:57; Rv 10:3a,** cp. **3b.**

❷ to communicate someth. in a loud voice, *call, call out, cry*—ⓐ lit. κράζει ὄπισθεν ἡμῶν *she is calling out after us* **Mt 15:23.** τὶ *someth.* of a crowd **Ac 19:32.** φωνὴν κ. *call out a thing loudly* **24:21.** W. direct discourse foll. (B-D-F §397, 3) **Mk 10:48; 11:9; 15:13f; Lk 18:39; J 12:13 v.l.** (s. κραυγάζω); **Ac 19:34; 21:28, 36; 23:6.** W. φωνῇ μεγάλῃ and direct discourse foll. **Mk 5:7; Ac 7:60.** Also ἐν φωνῇ μεγάλῃ **Rv 14:15.** Used w. λέγειν (B-D-F §420, 2 app.) of loud speaking κράζω λέγων *I say loudly* (Ex 5:8; TestAbr B 6 p. 110, 5 [Stone p. 68]) **Mt 8:29; 14:30; 15:22** (s. κραυγάζω); **20:30f; 21:9; 27:23; Mk 3:11; J 7:37; 19:12 v.l.** (for ἐκραύγασαν); **Ac 16:17; Rv 18:18f.** Also pleonast. κ. φωνῇ μεγάλῃ λέγων *I call out w. a loud voice and say* **6:10; 7:10.** κ. ἐν φωνῇ μεγάλῃ λέγων **19:17;** cp. **18:2.** κράξας ἔλεγε **Mk 9:24.** κ. καὶ λέγειν **Mt 9:27; 21:15; Mk 10:47; Lk 4:41 v.l.; Ac 14:14f.** ἔκραξεν καὶ εἶπεν **J 12:44.** ἔκραξεν διδάσκων καὶ λέγων *he cried out as he was teaching, and said* **7:28.** The pf. κέκραγα has present mng. (Hippocr., Περὶ ἱερ. νούσ. 15 vol. VI 388 Littré βοᾷ καὶ κέκραγεν; Menand., Sam. 226; 239 S. [11; 24 Kö.]; Plut., Cato Min. 58, 1 μαρτυρόμενος καὶ κεκραγώς; Lucian, Demon. 48 κεκραγότα κ. λέγοντα; Ex 5:8; 2 Km 19:29; Is 15:4; Job 30:20, 28; 34:20;

Ps 4:4; 140:1) Ἰωάννης μαρτυρεῖ περὶ αὐτοῦ καὶ κέκραγεν λέγων **J 1:15.** κ. τινὶ (ἐν) φωνῇ μεγάλῃ (λέγων) *call out to someone in a loud voice* **Rv 7:2; 14:15.**—Of angel choirs 1 Cl 34:6 (Is 6:3).

ⓑ fig.—**α.** of the urgent speech of the prophet (Jos., Ant. 10, 117: Jeremiah) or what his book says (Ammonius Herm. in Aristot. Lib. De Interpret. p. 183, 30 Busse: ἀκουέτω τοῦ Ἀριστοτέλους κεκραγότος ὅτι . . . ; Just., D. 70, 5 αἱ γραφαὶ κεκράγασιν) Ἠσαΐας κράζει ὑπὲρ τοῦ Ἰσραήλ **Ro 9:27.** Of prayer, rather fervent than loud **8:15.** ἐκέκραξεν ὁ δίκαιος 1 Cl 22:7 (Ps 33:18). Of the divine Spirit in the heart **Gal 4:6.**

β. of things (Epict 1, 16, 11 κέκραγεν ἡ φύσις; Achilles Tat. 5, 17, 4 κέκραγέ σου ἡ μορφὴ τ. εὐγένειαν): stones, that *cry out* if the disciples were to hold back with their confession of Jesus' messiahship **Lk 19:40.** The laborers' wages, held back, κράζει **Js 5:4** (cp. Gen 4:10; 18:20; Philo, Ebr. 98 κ. ἐν ἡμῖν αἱ ἄλογοι ὁρμαί; Jos., Bell. 1, 197. On the topic s. KBerger, Die Gesetzesauslegung Jesu I, '72, 382–84; other reff. PvanderHorst, The Sentences of Pseudo-Phocylides '78, 126.).—B. 1250. DELG. M-M. TW.

κραιπάλη, ης, ἡ (also κρεπάλη, q.v.; both 'carousing, intoxication' and its result 'drunken headache, hangover' are associated in the use of the term, since it means 'dizziness, staggering' when the head refuses to function [Aristoph.; Plut., Mor. 127f; Lucian, Bis Accus. 16; Soranus p. 16, 26; Aretaeus p. 110, 2]) **unbridled indulgence in a drinking party,** ***drinking bout*** (Aristoph., Ach. 277; Vesp. 1255) ἐν κ. καὶ μέθῃ *w. dissipation and drunkenness* **Lk 21:34** (cp. Herodian 2, 6, 6 παρὰ μέθην κ. κρ.; Is 24:20). πολυτέλεια μεθυσμάτων καὶ κραιπαλῶν *extravagance in drunkenness and carousing* Hm 6, 2, 5.—HCadbury, Style 54.—DELG. M-M.

κρανίον, ου, τό (Hom. et al.; pap, LXX; ApcEsdr 5:24 p. 30, 28 Tdf.; Jos., Bell. 3, 245, Ant. 8, 390) ***skull*** κρανίου (epexegetic gen.) τόπος *the place that is called (a) Skull* as a transl. of Γολγοθᾶ (q.v.) **Mt 27:33; Mk 15:22; J 19:17.** Cp. **Lk 23:33,** where 'Calvary' of the KJV is not a NT place name, but the Lat. transl. of κ. (s. Goodsp., Probs. 89f). Schol. on Lucian 251, 20f Κρανίον· ἔστι τόπος ἐν Κορίνθῳ; Diog. L. 6, 77 ἐν τῷ Κρανείῳ τῷ πρὸ τῆς Κορίνθου γυμνασίῳ.—For other lit. s. on Γολγοθᾶ.—B. 213f. DELG. M-M.

κράσπεδον, ου, τό (trag., X. et al.; LXX; loanw. in rabb.)

❶ ***edge, border, hem*** of a garment (Theocr. 2, 53; Appian, Bell. Civ. 1, 16 §68 τὸ κ. τοῦ ἱματίου of the Pontifex Maximus; Ael. Aristid. 47 p. 416 D.; Athen. 4, 49, 159d; 9, 16, 374a; PGM 7, 371 ἐξάψας κράσπεδον τοῦ ἱματίου σου; Zech 8:23) ἥψατο τοῦ κ. τοῦ ἱματίου αὐτοῦ **Mt 9:20; Lk 8:44** (s. Acta Pilati 7=ASyn. 95, 90) cp. **Mt 14:36; Mk 6:56.**—But mng. 2 is also prob. for these passages, depending on how strictly Jesus followed the Mosaic law, and also upon the way in which κ. was understood by the authors and first readers of the gospels.

❷ ***tassel*** (צִיצִת), which an Israelite was obligated to wear on the four corners of his outer garment, acc. to Num 15:38f; Dt 22:12 (Schürer II 479 [sources and lit.]; Billerb. IV 276–92). Of the Pharisees μεγαλύνειν τὰ κ. *make the tassels on their garments long* **Mt 23:5.**—B. 859f. DELG. M-M. TW.

κραταιός, ά, όν (s. next entry; in Hom. and other poets; in prose it appears late: Philo Mech. 80, 22; Polyb. 2, 69, 8; Cornutus 31 p. 63, 1; Plut., Crass. 24, 4, Mor. p. 967c; Lucian, Anach. 28; Vett. Val. index; Mitt-Wilck. I/2, 122, 1 [6 AD] τῷ μεγίστῳ κραταιῷ θεῷ Σοκνοπαίῳ; PGM 7, 422 θεοὶ κραταιοί; 563; 789; LXX; TestJud 5:1; 6:3; JosAs ch. 11 [cod. A 54, 4 Bat. and Pal. 364]; Philo, Spec. Leg. 1, 307 θεὸς μέγας κ. ἰσχυρὸς κ. κραταιός) ***powerful, mighty*** of God's hand (oft. LXX; TestJos 1:5; PGM 4, 1279; 1307) **1 Pt 5:6;** 1 Cl 28:2; 60:3; GJs 15:4; δύναμις *mighty power* (cp. Philo, Conf. Lingu. 51) Hv 1, 3, 4.—DELG s.v. κράτος. M-M. TW.

κραταιόω ('to strengthen'; derived fr. κραταιός; a later form of κρατύνω. Hippocr.: CMG I 1 p. 88, 12; LXX.—Philo has the mid. in act. sense: Conf. Lingu. 101; 103) impf. pass. ἐκραταιούμην; 1 aor. pass. inf. κραταιωθῆναι. In our lit. only pass.: ***become strong.*** In the physical sense (Philo, Agr. 160, Omn. Prob. Lib. 27; TestNapht 1:4): w. αὐξάνειν **Lk 2:40,** as also GJs 6:1. In the psychological sense of encouragement to remain firm: **1 Cor 16:13** (w. ἀνδρίζεσθαι, as Ps 30:25; 2 Km 10:12); κ. πνεύματι *grow strong in spirit* **Lk 1:80;** δυνάμει κ. διὰ τοῦ πνεύματος *be mightily strengthened through the Spirit* **Eph 3:16.**—DELG s.v. κράτος. TW.

κρατέω impf. ἐκράτουν; fut. κρατήσω; 1 aor. ἐκράτησα; pf. 1 pl. κεκρατήκαμεν 1 Macc 15:33, inf. κεκρατηκέναι; plpf. 3 sg. κεκρατήκει 4 Macc 6:32. Pass.: impf. ἐκρατούμην; fut. 3 pl. κρατηθήσονται; aor. ἐκρατήθην Eccl 9:12 v.l.; pf. κεκράτημαι, 3 pl. κεκράτηνται (Hom.+). The primary signification is exercise of power, then by transference

❶ **to accomplish someth. by overcoming obstacles,** ***attain*** (Diod. S. 3, 54, 7 κ. τῆς ἐπιβολῆς=attain the purpose; likew. 17, 77, 4 and 20, 25, 3; Appian, Bell. Civ. 3, 61 §249 οὐ . . . ἐκράτησε) τῆς προθέσεως *the purpose* **Ac 27:13** (s. Field, Notes 144).

❷ **to use one's hands to establish a close contact,** ***hold***

ⓐ *hold* τινά *someone (fast)* w. the hand (TestAbr A 12 p. 91, 19 [Stone p. 30]), so that the pers. cannot go away **Ac 3:11.**

ⓑ *hold* in the hand (SibOr 3, 49; TestAbr A 10 p. 87, 29 [Stone p. 22]; A 12 p. 91, 5 [Stone p. 30] al.; GrBar 11:8) τὶ ἐν τῇ δεξιᾷ **Rv 2:1** (Polemo Perieg. [c. 200 BC] in Athen. 11, 67, 484c ἐν τῇ δεξιᾷ κώθωνα κ.; cp. Plut., Mor. 99d).

❸ **to take control of someone or someth.,** ***seize, control***

ⓐ of taking into custody *arrest, apprehend* τινά *someone* (cp. Ps 136:9; AscIs 3:12) **Mt 14:3; 21:46; 26:4, 48, 50, 55, 57** (on the arrest of Jesus s. Feigel, Weidel, Finegan s.v. Ἰούδας 6); **Mk 6:17; 12:12; 14:1, 44, 46, 49, 51; Ac 24:6; Rv 20:2.**

ⓑ of taking hold of forcibly and also without the use of force *take hold of, grasp, seize* (cp. 2 Km 6:6; SSol 3:4; TestSol 22:10); w. acc. of pers. or thing **Mt 12:11; 18:28; 22:6; 28:9;** κρατῆσαι αὐτόν *take control of (Jesus)* **Mk 3:21.** κ. ῥάβδον τῇ χειρί *take hold of a staff w. the hand* Hs 9, 6, 3 (cp. PGM 5, 451 κράτει τῇ ἀριστερᾷ σου τὸν δακτύλιον; Synes., Ep. 58 p. 202 πόδα). τῆς χειρός (τινος) *take hold of (someone's) hand* (B-D-F §170, 2; Rob. 475; 1391; Ps 72:23; Gen 19:16; JosAs 29:3; ParJer 6:2; Jos., Bell. 1, 352) **Mt 9:25; Mk 1:31; 5:41; 9:27; Lk 8:54;** B 14:7 (Is 42:6). τινὰ τῆς χειρός *take someone by the hand* **Mk 9:27 v.l.;** cp. B 12:11 (Is 45:1).

❹ **to hold up or serve as a foundation for someth.,** ***hold upright, support*** τὶ *someth.* Hs 9, 8, 5. τὰς χεῖρας v 3, 8, 3 (s. MDibelius, Hdb. ad loc.). Pass. *be supported* ὑπό τινος *by someth.* Hv 3, 3, 5. W. ἀπό instead of ὑπό: κρατοῦνται ἀπ' ἀλλήλων *receive support fr. one another* (here w. focus on mutuality) 3, 8, 7. W. διά: ὁ κόσμος διὰ τεσσάρων στοιχείων κρατεῖται *the world is supported by four elements* 3, 13, 3.

❺ **to control in such a way that someth. does not happen,** ***hold back*** **or** ***restrain from, hinder in*** an action: w. acc. (so TestJob 35:1), foll. by ἵνα μή **Rv 7:1.** Pass. *be prevented* foll.

by τοῦ μή and inf. (TestSol 10:43 C; B-D-F §400, 4; Rob. 1061; 1425) their eyes ἐκρατοῦντο τοῦ μὴ ἐπιγνῶναι **Lk 24:16,** prob. w. a suggestion of both physical and inward sight (cp. 4 Km 6:15–23; s. διανοίγω 1b).—*Hold in one's power* (PTebt 61b, 229; POxy 237 VIII, 34; TestSol 6:3; Jos., C. Ap. 1, 84; Mel., P. 100, 769) pass. οὐκ ἦν δυνατὸν κρατεῖσθαι αὐτὸν ὑπ᾽ αὐτοῦ *it was impossible for him* (Christ) *to be held in its* (death's) *power* **Ac 2:24.**

❻ **to adhere strongly to, *hold*—ⓐ** of commitment to someone or someth. *hold fast (to)* someone or someth., and hence remain closely united. W. acc. τὴν κεφαλήν *hold fast to the Head* (i.e. to Christ) **Col 2:19** (cp. SSol 3:4 ἐκράτησα αὐτὸν καὶ οὐκ ἀφήσω [ἀφῆκα BS] αὐτόν). τί *to someth.* (TestNapht 3:1 τὸ θέλημα τ. θεοῦ) τὴν παράδοσιν **Mk 7:3;** cp. vss. **4, 8; 2 Th 2:15.** τὴν διδαχήν **Rv 2:14f.** τὸ ὄνομά μου vs. **13.**—W. gen. of thing (Stephan. Byz. s.v. Γυναικόπολις: in the absence of the men τὰς γυναῖκας κρατῆσαι τοῦ πολέμου=the women kept the war going; Pr 14:18; Jos., Ant. 6, 116 τοῦ λογισμοῦ) τῆς ὁμολογίας *hold fast to our confession* **Hb 4:14.** τῆς ἐλπίδος **6:18.** τῶν ἔργων τινός Hv 3, 8, 8.

ⓑ *hold fast, keep hold of* someth. that belongs to oneself, so that it cannot be taken away **Rv 2:25; 3:11.**

ⓒ *keep* to oneself a saying, in order to occupy oneself w. it later **Mk 9:10.**

❼ **to cause a condition to continue, *hold in place*** κ. τὰς ἁμαρτίας *pronounce the sins unforgiven* (opp. ἀφιέναι) **J 20:23.**—B. 746. DELG s.v. κράτος. M-M. TW.

κράτιστος, η, ον (Hom. et al.; IBM III/2, 482A, 6 et al.; pap, LXX, EpArist, Philo, Joseph. Isolated superl. of κρατύς 'strong, mighty') **strongly affirmative honorary form of address, *most noble, most excellent,*** used in address of pers. of varied social status. Of the governor of Judea (on formula of address to officials, s. Magie 31; 112; Hahn 259; OSeeck in Pauly-W. V 2006f; OHirschfeld, Kleine Schriften 1913, 651, 5; 654; Wilcken, Her. 20, 1885, 469ff; WSchubart, Einf. in d. Papyruskunde 1918, 259. Cp. PHerrmann, Inschriften von Sardeis: Chiron 23, '93, 236 n. 13.—Jos., Ant. 20, 12; whether the Lat. rendering 'vir egregius' was applied in the first cent. to highly placed officials cannot be determined with certainty) **Ac 23:26; 24:3; 26:25.** In a form of polite address with no official connotation (Theophr., Char. 5; Dionys. Hal., De Orat. Ant. 1 ὦ κράτιστε Ἀμμαῖε; Jos., Vi. 430 κράτιστε ἀνδρῶν Ἐπαφρόδιτε [a freedman of Domitian, to whom Joseph. dedicated his Antiquities and his books against Apion]; likew. C. Ap. 1, 1 [but 2, 1 τιμιώτατέ μοι Ἐ.; 2, 296 simply his name]. κ. is also found in dedications Diosc., Mat. Med. I 3, 1f; Hermog., Inv. 3 p. 126, 2f; Artem. 236, 2f P.; Galen X 78; XIV 295; XIX 8 Kühn.—B-D-F §60, 2) **Lk 1:3;** Dg 1:1. S. Zahn, Einl. II[3] 340; 365; 390, Ev. des Lk.[3, 4] 1920, 56f; Cadbury, Making of Luke-Acts 314f; LAlexander, The Preface to Luke's Gospel '93 132f; 188–90 (the social status of Luke's addressee remains undetermined).—M-M.

κράτος, ους, τό (Hom.+)—❶ **ability to exhibit or express resident strength, *might*—ⓐ** of God's power (Theognis 376 al.; Ael. Aristid. 37, 8 K.=2 p. 15D.; 2 Macc 3:34; 7:17; 11:4; s. also 3 below) 1 Cl 33:3; 61:1; 64; AcPl Ha 5, 26. Of the power of Jesus 2 Cl 17:5.—τὸ κ. τῆς δόξης αὐτοῦ *his glorious* (divine) *might* **Col 1:11.** κατὰ κράτος αὐξάνειν *grow mightily, wonderfully* **Ac 19:20** (κατὰ κράτος like Menand., Per. 407; Dio Chrys. 26 [43], 11; IG XII/5, 444, 103 [264/263 BC]; PTebt 27, 83 [113 BC]; AArgyle, ET 75, '64, 151 connects κατὰ κ. with τ. κυρίου, *by the might of the Lord*).

ⓑ of intensity in might (cp. Appian, Bell. Civ. 2, 35 §141 κατὰ κράτος=with all his might; Ps.-Callisth. 1, 8, 2 ἡλίου κ.; Ps 89:11) τὸ κ. τῆς ἰσχύος αὐτοῦ *the working of his strength = mighty strength* **Eph 1:19; 6:10;** 1 Cl 27:5 (cp. Is 40:26; Da 4:30 Theod.; s. 1QS 11, 19f; 1QH 4, 32).

❷ **a specific product of resident strength, *mighty deed*** ποιεῖν κ. (cp. עָשָׂה חָיִל Ps 118:15) *do mighty deeds* **Lk 1:51.**

❸ **exercise of ruling ability, *power, rule, sovereignty*** (Arrian, Anab. 4, 20, 3 the ruling might of the great king; POxy 41 I, 2 εἰς αἰῶνα τὸ κράτος τῶν Ῥωμαίων; Mel., HE 4, 26, 7 τὸ Ῥωμαίων … κράτος. Of deities: Apollon. Rhod. 4, 804 Zeus; UPZ 81 II, 17 [II BC] Isis: ἐλθέ μοι θεὰ θεῶν, κράτος ἔχουσα μέγιστον; PSI 29, 21 τὸ κ. τοῦ Ἀδωναΐ; POxy 1380, 238 ἀστραπῶν τὸ κ. ἔχεις; Philo, Spec. Leg. 1, 307 τ. ὅλων τὸ κ.; Jos., Ant. 10, 263 τὸ πάντων κ. ἔχων) τὸν τὸ κ. ἔχοντα τοῦ θανάτου *the one who has power over death* **Hb 2:14** (τὸ κ. ἔχειν τινός since Hdt. 3, 69).—In a doxology (Mel., P. 105, 823): **1 Ti 6:16; 1 Pt 4:11; 5:11; Jd 25; Rv 1:6; 5:13;** 1 Cl 65:2; MPol 20:2.—DELG. M-M. TW.

κραυγάζω (s. next entry) impf. ἐκραύγαζον; fut. κραυγάσω; 1 aor. ἐκραύγασα (poet. fgm. in Pla., Rep. 10 p. 607b [of a dog]; Demosth. 54, 7; Epict 3, 1, 37 [of a raven]; 3, 4, 4; 2 Esdr 3:13 λαὸς ἐκραύγασεν φωνῇ μεγάλῃ; TestSol) **to utter a loud sound, ordinarily of harsh texture, *cry (out),*** with context indicating kind of articulation. Of animal sounds, as the grunting of hungry swine B 10:3.—Of the human voice, *cry out, cry for help, scream* excitedly (Epict 1, 18, 19; Polemo, Decl. 1, 40 p. 14, 16) **Mt 12:19; Ac 22:23.** Also w. λέγοντες foll., which introduces direct discourse **Mt 15:22 v.l.; J 18:40; 19:6, 12** (s. κράζω 2a). Without λέγ. w. direct discourse foll. vs. **15.** Of a loud cry in a moment of exaltation κ. ὡσαννά **J 12:13** (v.l. ἔκραζον + λέγοντες). κ. φωνῇ μεγάλῃ w. direct discourse foll. **J 11:43;** IPhld 7:1.—Of possessive spirits coming out of persons, and speaking in human languages δαιμόνια κραυγάζοντα καὶ λέγοντα ὅτι w. direct discourse foll. **Lk 4:41** (to N. app. add P[75]; for the expression cp. TestSol 1:12 ἐκραύγασε λέγων).—B 1250. DELG s.v. κραυγή. TW.

κραυγή, ῆς, ἡ (s. prec. entry; Eur., X. et al.; Vett. Val. 2, 35; PPetr II, 45 III, 25 [246 BC]; POxy 1242 III, 54; PTebt 15, 3; LXX; En 104:3; PsSol 1:2; TestJob 33:2; EpArist; Joseph.; Ath. 11:1).

❶ **a loud cry or call, shout** lit.—**ⓐ *shout(ing), clamor*** of excited persons **Eph 4:31.** Of people shouting back and forth in a quarrel: ἐγένετο κ. μεγάλη *there arose a loud outcry* **Ac 23:9** (cp. Ex 12:30; without μεγ. X., Cyr. 7, 5, 28). Of people who incite one another to enjoy a spectacle AcPl Ha 4, 6.

ⓑ ***a loud (articulate) cry*** κ. γέγονεν w. direct discourse foll. *there arose a shout* **Mt 25:6** (EGrässer, D. Problem der Parousieverzögerung, ZNW Beih. 22, '57, 124f). ἀνεφώνησεν κραυγῇ μεγάλῃ καὶ εἶπεν w. direct discourse foll. **Lk 1:42;** cp. **Rv 14:18 v.l.** Of fervent prayer (Ps 17:7; 101:2; Jon 2:3) μετὰ κ. ἰσχυρᾶς *with loud crying* **Hb 5:7** (cp. Diod. S. 19, 83, 3 and Ath. 11:1 μετὰ πολλῆς κραυγῆς—μετὰ κ. as Diod. S. 11, 36, 1; Nicol. Dam.: 90, fgm. 130, 25 p. 409, 20 Jac.; UPZ 8, 17 [161 BC]; EpArist 186; Jos., Bell. 2, 517). ἀκουσθῆναι ἐν κ. τὴν φωνὴν ὑμῶν *so that your voice is heard in loud cries* B 3:1 (Is 58:4).—τρία μυστήρια κραυγῆς, ἅτινα ἐν ἡσυχίᾳ θεοῦ ἐπράχθη *three mysteries (to be) loudly acclaimed, which were quietly accomplished by God* IEph 19:1. The three 'mysteries' are the virginity of Mary, her childbearing, and the death of Jesus. In contrast to God's quiet performance, Ign appears to have in mind their public proclamation in a cultic setting as part of the divine design, with a responsory cry of acclamation. Others interpret κ. here as the proclamation itself.

❷ **outcry in grief or anxiety,** ***wailing, crying*** (cp. Ex 3:7; 11:6; Esth 4:3; Is 65:19; TestJob 33:2) **Rv 21:4.**—DELG. M-M. TW.

κρέας, κρέως and later **κρέατος** (s. Thumb 96; Meisterhans[3]-Schw. p. 143 [an Attic ins of 338 BC w. κρέατος]; Thackeray 149, 3; Soph., Lex. s.v. κρέας), **τό** *meat* (Hom.+) pl. τὰ κρέα (B-D-F §47, 1; PsSol 8:12; JosAs 10:14; Jos., Ant. 10, 261) φαγεῖν κρέα (LXX; TestJud 15:4) **Ro 14:21; 1 Cor 8:13;** κρέας (Gen 9:4; Just., D. 126, 6) GEb 308, 32; 34f.—B. 202. DELG. M-M. TW.

κρείσσων s. κρείττων.

κρείττων, ον, gen. **ονος,** and **κρείσσων** (B-D-F §34, 1; W-S. §5, 27c; Mlt-H. 107; JWackernagel, Hellenistica 1907, 12–25; Reinhold 43f; Thackeray 121, 2. The ms. tradition fluctuates in most places betw. ττ and σσ. The word occurs Hom.+) in our lit. always a real comp. (cp. κρατύς, but functions as comp. of ἀγαθός).

❶ **pert. to being of high status,** ***more prominent, higher in rank, preferable, better*** (Pind., Hdt. et al.) of pers. IPhld 9:1; **Hb 7:7** (opp. ἐλάττων). τοσούτῳ κ. γενόμενος τῶν ἀγγέλων *as much superior to the angels* **1:4** (Jos., Ant. 8, 111 τ. ἄλλων . . . κρείττονες γεγόναμεν).—Of things **7:19, 22; 8:6; 9:23; 10:34; 11:16, 35;** IRo 2:1; IPol 4:3. χαρίσματα **1 Cor 12:31a v.l.** (for the continuation of vs. 31b here cp. Appian, Mithrid. 60 §247 ἑτέραν ὁδὸν ἔχειν κρείττονα=know another way, a better one). W. gen. foll. *better than* (LXX; TestJob 27:7; Jos., C. Ap. 1, 273; Tat. 20, 1) Dg 2:2. κρεῖττόν τι *someth. better* **Hb 11:40.** ἐν ᾧ κρείσσων ἐστίν *in the respect in which he is better off* (than the other man) Dg 10:6. ἡ ἀπὸ τῶν κρειττόνων ἐπὶ τὰ χείρω μετάνοια *a change of mind from better to worse* MPol 11:1.

❷ **pert. to having a relative advantage in value—ⓐ** adj., ***more useful, more advantageous, better*** πεπείσμεθα περὶ ὑμῶν τὰ κ. *we are sure of better things concerning you* **Hb 6:9.** εἰς τὸ κ. συνέρχεσθαι (opp. εἰς τὸ ἧσσον; s. ἥσσων) **1 Cor 11:17.** W. gen. *better, more advantageous than* (Artem. 2, 11 p. 98, 24 κρεῖττον τὸ κακοῦν τοῦ ὑπό τινος κακοῦσθαι) 2 Cl 16:4. κρεῖσσόν ἐστιν (w. inf. foll. *it is better* [Sir 33:22 =30:30 Ziegler]; Diod. S. 12, 16, 2 κρεῖττον [v.l. -σσ-] γάρ ἐστιν ἀποθανεῖν ἢ . . . πειρασθῆναι; Demosth., Ep. 2, 21 εἰ . . . , τεθνάναι με κρεῖττον ἦν) **1 Cor 7:9;** cp. **1 Pt 3:17.** κρεῖττον ἦν αὐτοῖς w. inf. foll. *it would be better for them* **2 Pt 2:21** (s. B-D-F §410; Rob. 1084); cp. 1 Cl 46:8. Pleonast. πολλῷ μᾶλλον κ. *much better indeed* **Phil 1:23.**

ⓑ adv., ***better*** κρεῖσσον ποιεῖν **1 Cor 7:38.** κρεῖττον λαλεῖν **Hb 12:24** (παρά w. acc. *than*). —DELG s.v. κράτος 4. M-M. TW.

κρέμαμαι s. κρεμάννυμι 2.

κρεμάννυμι (this form of the present not in the Gk. Bible, but Job 26:7 has κρεμάζω. The word, in mngs. 1 and 2, Hom. et al.; ins, pap, LXX, TestSol, TestAbr; TestLevi 2:7; JosAs 22:5; ParJer; GrBar 9:8; ApcMos 17; ApcrEzk P 2 verso 10; Philo; Jos., Vi. 147 al.) fut. κρεμάσω LXX; 1 aor. ἐκρέμασα, pass. ἐκρεμάσθην.

❶ **to cause to hang,** trans. ***hang (up)*** ἐπὶ ξύλου *on the tree* i.e. *cross* (cp. Gen 40:19; Dt 21:22; Esth 8:7) **Ac 5:30; 10:39.** The verb κ. by itself can also mean *crucify* (Diod. S. 17, 46, 4; Appian, Mithrid. 8 §25; 29 §114 δούλους ἐκρέμασε, Bell. Civ. 2, 90 §377; Arrian, Anab. 6, 17, 2; 6, 30, 2; 7, 14, 4). Pass. **Lk 23:39** (cp. Appian, Bell. Civ. 3, 3 §9; Sb 6739 [255 BC], 9).—ἵνα κρεμασθῇ μύλος ὀνικὸς περὶ (vv.ll. εἰς, ἐπί, ἐν [τῷ -λῷ]) τὸν τράχηλον αὐτοῦ *that a millstone were hung around that person's neck* **Mt 18:6.** Reflex. ἐκρέμασεν ἀτὴν (=αὐτὴν) εἰς τὸν τράχηλον αὐτοῦ Ἄννα *Hannah (Anna) hung on his neck* GJs 4:4 (cp. TestAbr A 5 p. 82, 19 [Stone p. 12] ἐκρεμάσθη ἐπὶ τὸν τράχηλον αὐτοῦ; likew. JosAs 22:5).—1 Cl 12:7 v.l. Funk.

❷ dep. κρέμαμαι (s. B-D-F §93; Rob. 316f) **to hang down from some point,** intrans., ***hang*—ⓐ** lit. (TestSol 24:4; recension D 6:14; TestLevi 2:7; GrBar 9:8; ApcEsdr 4:22 p. 28, 25 Tdf. al.; Jos., Ant. 7, 241) ἐπί τινος *on a thing* (X., An. 3, 2, 19) ἐπὶ ξύλου (s. 1 above) **Gal 3:13** (Dt 21:23). Of the branch of a vine μὴ κρεμαμένη ἐπὶ τῆς πτελέας *if it does not hang on the elm tree* Hs 2:3; cp. vs. 4. ἔκ τινος *on someth.* (Pla., Leg. 8, 831c; SIG[2] 588, 201; cp. Jdth 8:24) of a snake κ. ἐκ τῆς χειρός *hung on the hand* **Ac 28:4.** Of those being punished in hell ἐκ τῆς γλώσσης κρεμάμενοι ApcPt 7:22 (cp. ApcEsdr 4:22 p. 28, 25 Tdf. ἐκ τῶν βλεφάρων).

ⓑ fig. (Philo, Post. Cai. 24; 25; SibOr 7, 55) ἐν ταύταις τ. δυσὶν ἐντολαῖς ὅλος ὁ νόμος κρέμαται καὶ οἱ προφῆται *all the law and the prophets hang (depend) on these two commandments* **Mt 22:40** (as a door hangs on its hinges, so the whole OT hangs on these two comm. For the thought cp. Plut., Mor. 116d.—On κ. ἐν cp. 2 Km 18:9; Billerb. I 775ff; 967f).—DELG. M-M. TW.

κρεπάλη (s. Mlt-H. 81) for κραιπάλη (q.v.). But Aristoph., Ach. 277, Wasps 1255 prove the length of the first syllable.

κρημνός, οῦ, ὁ (s. next entry; Hom. et al.; Kaibel 225, 2; PPetr III, 39 II, 8; 2 Ch 25:12; TestSol, TestAbr, Test12Patr; EpArist 118; Jos., Ant. 3, 76) ***steep slope*** or ***bank, cliff*** κατὰ τοῦ κ. *down the steep bank* (Dio Chrys. 7, 3; Philo, Agr. 76; Jos., Bell. 1, 313) **Mt 8:32; Mk 5:13; Lk 8:33.** ἀπὸ κ. μεγάλου *down from a high cliff* ApcPt 17:32 (ἀπὸ κ. as Celsus 6, 34).—DELG. M-M.

κρημνώδης, ες (κρημνός + -ώδης; s. prec. entry; since Thu. 7, 84, 4; Jos., Bell. 7, 280) ***steep, precipitous*** ἦν ὁ τόπος κ. *the place was precipitous* (Stephan. Byz. s.v. Ὄαξος: τὸν τόπον κρημνώδη ὑπάρχειν) Hv 1, 1, 3; cp. s 6, 2, 6.—DELG s.v. κρημνός.

Κρής, ητός, ὁ pl. Κρῆτες (Hom.+; ins; UPZ 20, 32 [163 BC]; 29, 2; Jos., Ant. 13, 86, C. Ap. 2, 172; Tat.; SibOr 3, 140) ***a Cretan,*** inhabitant of the island of Crete **Ac 2:11** (OEissfeldt, Kreter u. Araber: TLZ 72, '47, 207–12); **subscr. Tit v.l.** An unfavorable generalization about Cretan character (s. on this ἀργός 2) **Tit 1:12.**—RHarris, Exp. 2, 1906, 305–17; 3, 1907, 332–37; 4, 1912, 348–53; 1, 1915, 29–35; MGöbel, Ethnica, diss. Breslau 1915, 77ff; RCharles, Anthropologie arch. de la Crète, '65.

Κρήσκης, εντος, ὁ (Lat. Crescens; the Gk. form is quite rare [Κρί- Just., A II, 3, 1; Tat. 19, 1], the Lat. form common, incl. Pol 14, which is preserved only in Lat.) ***Crescens,*** a companion of Paul **2 Ti 4:10.** S. Κρίσπος. New Docs 3, 91.—LGPN I.

Κρήτη, ης, ἡ (Hom. et al.; ins; 1 Macc 10:67; Philo, Spec. Leg. 3, 43; Joseph.; Tat. 39, 3; SibOr) ***Crete*** **Ac 27:7, 12**f, **21; Tit 1:5; subscr. v.l.** (as early as Il. 2, 649 Crete was famous for its many cities; Ps.-Scylax [ed. BFabricius 1878] has the names of many cities).—LCottrell, The Bull of Minos '53; RWilletts, Everday Life in Ancient Crete '69; Warnecke, Romfahrt 21–28.—OEANE II 70–72. M-M.

κριθή, ῆς, ἡ (s. next entry; Hom.+, but in earlier Gk. only in pl. On the other hand, in later wr. [Dionys. Hal. 2, 25; Cornutus

28 p. 54, 4; Libanius, De Vita Sua 8 Förster v.l.; Herm. Wr. 14, 10; Philo, Spec. Leg. 2, 175; 3, 57; Jos., Bell. 5, 427], in ins, pap, LXX also in sing.) ***barley,*** used in the preparation of cheap kinds of bread (s. Hdb. on J 6:9; Appian, Illyr. 26 §76 κριθὴ ἀντὶ σίτου for inferior soldiers). τρεῖς χοίνικες κριθῶν *three liters/quarts of barley* (t.r. κριθῆς) **Rv 6:6** (s. χοῖνιξ); GDalman, Arbeit II '32, 252f; III '33, 300ff.—B. 516. DELG. M-M.

κρίθινος, η, ον (s. prec. entry; since Hipponax [VI BC] 39, 6 Diehl; PEleph 5, 25 [284/283 BC]; BGU 1092, 28; LXX; Philo, Spec. Leg. 2, 175; Jos., Ant. 5, 219) ***made of barley flour*** ἄρτος κ. *barley bread* (Plut., Anton. 45, 8; Artem. 1, 69; above all 4 Km 4:42) **J 6:9, 13.**—M-M.

κρίκος, ου, ὁ (Hom.+; ins, pap, LXX; Jos., Ant. 3, 109f; 136) ***ring*** κάμπτειν ὡς κρίκον τὸν τράχηλον *bend the neck as a ring,* i.e. so it is as round as a ring B 3:2 (Is 58:5).—DELG.

κρίμα, ατος, τό (s. κρίνω; Aeschyl.+—On the accent s. B-D-F §13; 109, 3; W-S. §6, 3; Mlt-H. 57; κρίσμα GJs 14:1).

❶ legal action taken against someone, *dispute, lawsuit* (Ex 18:22) κρίματα ἔχετε μεθ' ἑαυτῶν *you have lawsuits with one another* **1 Cor 6:7.**

❷ content of a deliberative process, *decision, decree* (IGal 25, 2 [II AD] κατὰ τὸ κ. τῆς βουλῆς; Ps 18:10; 118:75; Jos., Ant. 14, 318; 321; ParJer 7:32 [28]; Did., Gen. 116, 24), also of the fixed purposes of divine grace **Ro 11:33.**

❸ action or function of a judge, *judging, judgment,* the κρίμα ἐδόθη αὐτοῖς *authority to judge was given them* **Rv 20:4.**—Of God's judgment: τὸ κρίμα τὸ μέλλον **Ac 24:25.** κ. αἰώνιον *judgment* whose decision is valid *eternally* **Hb 6:2.** God's judgment begins with God's people **1 Pt 4:17.** Pl.: God is δίκαιος ἐν τοῖς κρίμασιν *righteous in judgments* 1 Cl 27:1; 60:1.—Unauthorized use of judicial authority is subject to critique in **Mt 7:2; Ro 2:1 v.l.**

❹ legal decision rendered by a judge, *judicial verdict*

ⓐ gener. (Polyb. 23, 1, 12) τὸ κ. ἐξ ἑνὸς εἰς κατάκριμα *the verdict came as the result of one violation, and led to punishment* **Ro 5:16.**

ⓑ mostly in an unfavorable sense, of the *condemnatory verdict* and sometimes the subsequent *punishment* itself **2 Pt 2:3; Jd 4.** τὸ κ. τοῦ θεοῦ *the condemnation of God* (i.e. pronounced by God) **Ro 2:2f.** ὧν τὸ κ. ἔνδικόν ἐστιν *their condemnation is just* **3:8** (but WFitch, ET 59, '47/48, 26 'verdict'). πρόδηλον ἐγενήθη *their condemnation has been made plain* 1 Cl 51:3. τὸ κ. τῆς πόρνης *the condemnation and punishment of the prostitute* **Rv 17:1.** εἰς κ. συνέρχεσθαι **1 Cor 11:34.** κ. ἑαυτῷ ἐσθίειν *eat condemnation upon oneself* vs. **29;** λαμβάνεσθαι κ. *be condemned* **Mt 23:13 v.l.; Mk 12:40; Lk 20:47; Ro 13:2; Js 3:1.** ἔχουσαι κ., ὅτι *they are subject to condemnation because* **1 Ti 5:12;** βαστάζειν τὸ κ. **Gal 5:10.** εἰς κ. γίνεσθαι *incur condemnation* 1 Cl 11:2. εἰς κ. γίνεσθαί τινι *turn out to be condemnation for someone* 21:1; IEph 11:1 (cp. TestJob 43:6 ἀποβήσετα εἰς κ.). ἐν τῷ αὐτῷ κ. εἶναι *be under the same condemnation* **Lk 23:40.** εἰς κ. ἐμπίπτειν τοῦ διαβόλου **1 Ti 3:6.** κ. θανάτου (cp. Dt 21:22; Sir 41:3) *death sentence* **Lk 24:20;** GJs 14:1 (τοῦ θανάτου pap [?], s. deStrycker p. 236).—Pl. (cp. BGU 471, 9 [II AD]) τὰ μέλλοντα κρίματα *the impending punishments* 1 Cl 28:1. On 1 Cl 20:5 s. ἀνεκδιήγητος.—GWetter, Der Vergeltungsgedanke bei Pls 1912, 1ff.—The OT is the source of the expr. κρίνειν τὸ κ. (cp. Zech 7:9; 8:16; Ezk 44:24) ἔκρινεν ὁ θεὸς τὸ κρίμα ὑμῶν ἐξ αὐτῆς *God has pronounced judgment for you against her* or *God has pronounced on her the judgment she wished to impose on you* (HHoltzmann, Hdb. 1893 ad loc.) **Rv 18:20.**

❺ proper recognition of someone's rights, *justice.* The OT is the source of the close relation betw. κ. and δικαιοσύνη, and the expr. ποιεῖν κ. καὶ δικαιοσύνην (Jer 23:5; Ezk 33:14) *do justice and righteousness* 1 Cl 13:1.

❻ In J κ. shows the same two-sidedness as the other members of the κρίνω family ('judgment' and 'separation'; s. Hdb. on J 3:17), and means the judicial decision which consists in the separation of those who are willing to believe fr. those who are unwilling to do so **J 9:39.**—B. 1422. DELG s.v. κρίνω. M-M. EDNT. TW.

κρίνον, ου, τό (Aristoph., Hdt. et al.; Longus 2, 3, 4 [ῥόδα, κρίνα, ὑάκινθος as spring flowers]; Kaibel 547, 1 [I AD]; PSI 297, 8; Stephan. Byz. s.v. Σοῦσα [the land around Susa is full of κρίνα]; LXX; EpArist 68; 75; cp. Jos., Ant. 8, 77; TestSim 6:2; loanw. in rabb.) ***lily.*** In this connection the principal opinions include the autumn crocus, Turk's cap lily, anemone, or gladiolus, but the data do not permit certainty. Perh. Jesus had no definite flower in mind, but was thinking of all the wonderful blooms that adorn the fields of Galilee. As an extremely beautiful flower (as Theodor. Prodr. 6, 296 H.) it is mentioned **Mt 6:28; Lk 12:27.**—LFonck, Streifzüge durch die biblische Flora 1900, 53ff; JBoehmer, Die Lilien auf dem Felde: Studierstube 6, 1908, 223ff; FLundgreen, Die Pflanzen im NT: NKZ 28, 1917, 828ff; GDalman, Die Lilie der Bibel: Pj 21, 1925, 98ff, Arbeit I, 1928, 357ff al.; ILöw, D. Flora d. Juden II 1924, 160ff, also IV '34, 669 (indices); GKing, Consider the Lilies: Crozer Quarterly 10, '33, 28–36; TSkeat, The Lilies of the Field: ZNW 37, '39, 211–14; M. et Mme. EHa-Reubeni, RB 54, '47, 362–64 (anthemis or Easter daisy, Fr. pâquerette); Zohary, Plants 169–71.—Pauly-W. VII 792ff; Kl. Pauly III 650f; BHHW II 1093.—DELG. M-M.

κρίνω (s. κρίμα; Hom.+) fut. κρινῶ; 1 aor. ἔκρινα; pf. κέκρικα; plpf. 3 sg. κεκρίκει (on the lack of augment s. B-D-F §66, 1; W-S. §12, 4; Mlt-H. 190; ἐκεκρίκει Just., D. 102, 2). Pass.: impf. ἐκρινόμην; 1 fut. κριθήσομαι; 1 aor. ἐκρίθην; pf. κέκριμαι. Primary mng.: 'to set apart so as to distinguish, separate', then by transference

❶ to make a selection, *select, prefer* (Aeschyl., Suppl. 39 τὶ; Pla., Rep. 3, 399e κρίνειν τινὰ πρό τινος 'prefer someone to someone', cp. Phlb. 57e; Himerius, Or. 40 [=Or. 6], 3 κ. τί τινι=select someth. because of someth. [a place because of its size]; κ. τὸ πρακτέον καὶ μὴ πρακτέον Did., Gen. 27, 3) ὃς μὲν γὰρ κρίνει ἡμέραν παρ' ἡμέραν *the one prefers one day to another* **Ro 14:5a.** In the other half of the sentence ὃς δὲ κρίνει πᾶσαν ἡμέραν, κ. prob. has the sense *recognize, approve* (X., Hell. 1, 7, 34 ἔκριναν τὴν τῆς βουλῆς γνώμην) *the other holds every day in esteem* vs. **5b.** Closely associated is mng.

❷ to pass judgment upon (and thereby seek to influence) the lives and actions of other people—ⓐ *judge, pass judgment upon, express an opinion about* Mt 7:1a, 2a; Lk 6:37a; 1 Cl 13:2; Pol 2:3 (Sextus 183 ὁ κρίνων ἄνθρωπον κρίνεται ὑπὸ τ. θεοῦ). κ. δικαίως D 4:3; B 19:11. κ. κατ' ὄψιν *by the outward appearance* **J 7:24a.** κατὰ τὴν σάρκα **8:15.** τὴν δικαίαν κρίσιν κ. *pass a right judgment* **7:24b** (on the expr. cp. Dt 16:18). This is perh. the place for **1 Pt 4:6** ἵνα κριθῶσιν κατὰ ἀνθρ. (s. ESelwyn, comm. ad loc. ref. to Lghtf.; cp. Wsd 3:4).

ⓑ esp. ***pass an unfavorable judgment upon, criticize, find fault with, condemn*** (Epict. 2, 21, 11) **Ro 2:1abc, 3; 14:3f, 10, 13a** (a play on words, w. κρίνειν used in two different mngs. in the same vs.; s. 4 below on vs. **13b**); **Col 2:16; Js 4:11, 12;** D 11:12. μή τι κρίνετε *do not pronounce judgment on anything* **1 Cor 4:5.** ἱνατί γὰρ ἡ ἐλευθερία μου κρίνεται ὑπὸ ἄλλης συνειδήσεως; *why is my freedom* (of action) *to be unfavorably* *judged by another person's scruples?* **1 Cor 10:29.** μακάριος ὁ μὴ κρίνων ἑαυτόν *happy is the one who finds no fault w. himself* **Ro 14:22.**—Also of a human judgment directed against God ὅπως ἂν νικήσεις ἐν τῷ κρίνεσθαί σε *that you may win when you are judged* **Ro 3:4** (OMichel in KEK prefers active sense); 1 Cl 18:4 (both Ps 50:6).

❸ **to make a judgment based on taking various factors into account,** ***judge, think, consider, look upon*** w. double acc. of the obj. and the predicate (Soph., Oed. R. 34; Pla., Rep. 9, 578b and s. Cebes 39, 4; 3 Macc 2:33; Just., D. 112, 1) οὐκ ἀξίους κρίνετε ἑαυτούς *you do not consider yourselves worthy* **Ac 13:46** (Jos., Ant. 6, 159 ὃν αὐτὸς τ. βασιλείας ἄξιον ἔκρινεν; EpArist 98); cp. PtK 3 p. 15, 17. τὰ ὑστερήματα αὐτῶν ἴδια ἐκρίνετε *you considered their shortcomings as your own* 1 Cl 2:6. Pass. (Thu. 2, 40, 3; Jos., Ant. 4, 193) τί ἄπιστον κρίνεται παρ' ὑμῖν; *why do you think it is incredible?* **Ac 26:8** (Jos., Ant. 18, 76 ἄπιστα αὐτὰ κρίνειν).—Foll. by acc. w. inf. (Pla., Gorg., 452c, Rep. 9, 578b; X., An. 1, 9, 5; 28) κεκρίκατέ με πιστὴν ... εἶναι **Ac 16:15.**—W. inf. foll. κρίνω μὴ παρενοχλεῖν τοῖς κτλ. **15:19.**—Foll. by τοῦτο ὅτι **2 Cor 5:14.**—W. direct quest. foll. ἐν ὑμῖν αὐτοῖς κρίνατε *judge, decide for yourselves* **1 Cor 11:13.**—W. indirect quest. foll. (Thu. 4, 130, 7 κρίναντες ἐν σφίσιν αὐτοῖς, εἰ ... ; X., Cyr. 4, 1, 5) εἰ δίκαιόν ἐστιν, ὑμῶν ἀκούειν μᾶλλον ἢ τοῦ θεοῦ, κρίνατε *decide whether it is right to obey you rather than God* **Ac 4:19.**—κρίνατε ὑμεῖς ὅ φημι *pass your own judgment on what I say* **1 Cor 10:15.**—ὀρθῶς ἔκρινας *you have judged rightly* **Lk 7:43.**

❹ **to come to a conclusion after a cognitive process,** ***reach a decision, decide, propose, intend*** (Isocr. 4, 46; Polyb. 3, 6, 7; 5, 52, 6; 9, 13, 7; Epict. 2, 15, 7; Appian, Bell. Civ. 14, 118 §497 ὅταν οἱ θεοὶ κρίνωσιν; LXX) τί οὖν θέλετε, κρίνατε (restored) *so decide now what you wish (to be done);* w. inf. (Diod. S. 4, 33, 10; 17, 95, 1; UPZ 42, 37 [162 BC]; PTebt 55, 4 [II BC] ἔκρινα γράψαι; PLond III, 897, 11 p. 207 [84 AD]; 1 Macc 11:33; 3 Macc 1:6; Jdth 11:13; Wsd 8:9; Jos., Ant.7, 33; 12, 403; 13, 188; Did., Gen. 179, 7) **Ac 3:13; 20:16; 25:25; 1 Cor 2:2; 5:3; Tit 3:12.** W. τοῦ and inf. (B-D-F §397, 2) ἐκρίθη τοῦ ἀποπλεῖν ἡμᾶς **Ac 27:1.** ἐπεὶ ἤδη σεαυτῷ κέκρικας τοῦ μὴ δύνασθαι τὰς ἐντολὰς ταύτας ὑπὸ ἀνθρώπου φυλαχθῆναι *since you have already decided in your own mind that these commandments cannot be kept by anyone* Hm 12, 3, 6.—W. acc. and inf. (2 Macc 11:25, 36; 3 Macc 6:30; TestSol 10:8; SibOr 3, 127; Just., D. 102, 2) **Ac 21:25** (even in the substantially different rdgs.). τοῦτο κέκρικεν ..., τηρεῖν τὴν ἑαυτοῦ παρθένον *he has determined this, namely to keep his fiancée* (pure and undefiled) **1 Cor 7:37** (s. s.v. γαμίζω 2; Diod. S. 4, 73, 2 of a father: κρίναι ταύτην [i.e. his daughter] παρθένον διαφυλάττειν). τοῦτο κρίνατε μᾶλλον, τὸ μὴ τιθέναι πρόσκομμα *but rather decide this,* (namely) *to give no offense* **Ro 14:13b.** ἔκρινα ἐμαυτῷ τοῦτο, τὸ ... ἐλθεῖν **2 Cor 2:1.** τὰ δόγματα τὰ κεκριμένα ὑπὸ τ. ἀποστόλων **Ac 16:4** (cp. Polyb. 5, 52, 6 πράξας τὸ κριθέν; Epict. 2, 15, 7 τοῖς κριθεῖσιν ἐμμένειν δεῖ).

❺ **to engage in a judicial process,** ***judge, decide, hale before a court, condemn,*** **also** ***hand over for judicial punishment,*** freq. as a legal t.t. (in a forensic sense Hom. et al.; ins, pap, LXX).

ⓐ of a human court—**α.** act. and pass. abs. **Ac 13:27.** W. adv. GPt 3:7. κ. τινά: κατὰ τὸν νόμον **J 18:31; Ac 23:3; 24:6 v.l.** οὐδὲ ἐγὼ κρίνω ὑμᾶς GJs 16:3. Of the right of the apostle and the church to judge believers **1 Cor 5:12ab.** μὴ ὁ νόμος ἡμῶν κρίνει τὸν ἄνθρωπον; *does our law* (personified) *judge a person?* **J 7:51** (Appian, Bell. Civ. 3, 50 §205 certain senators desire that before Mark Antony is declared a public enemy he should be brought to trial, ὡς οὐ πάτριον σφίσιν ἀκρίτου καταδικάζειν 'on the ground that it was not their ancestral custom to condemn someone without a hearing'). ἐκ τ. στόματός σου κρινῶ σε *I will punish you on the basis of your own statement* **Lk 19:22.** Pass. **Ac 25:10.** κρίνεσθαι ἐπί τινι *be on trial because of a thing* **26:6** (Appian, Basil. 12 κρινόμενος ἐπὶ τῷδε=be brought to trial because of this thing; likew. Iber. 55 §233; Ath. 2, 3; of God ApcrEzk fgm. d). Also περί τινος (Diod. S. 12, 30, 5) **23:6; 25:20;** w. addition of ἐπί w. gen. of the court of judicature *before someone* (schol. on Hes., Op. 9) **24:21; 25:9;** D 11:11.—τί δὲ καὶ ἀφ' ἑαυτῶν οὐ κρίνετε τὸ δίκαιον; **Lk 12:57,** which leads over into the sphere of jurisprudence (vs. 58), means: *why cannot you yourselves decide what is right?* (cp. the prayer for vengeance fr. Amorgos [BCH 25, 1901 p. 416; Dssm., LO 94=LAE 118] ἐπάκουσον, θεά, καὶ κρῖναι τὸ δίκαιον; cp. Appian, Mithrid. 89 §403 κρίνειν τὴν μάχην=decide the battle; Just., A II, 15, 5).

β. mid. and pass.: 'dispute, quarrel, debate', also *go to law* (so Thu. 4, 122, 4 δίκῃ κρίνεσθαι; Hos 2:4 al. in LXX; TestSol 4:4ff D; Mel., P. 101, 773) τινί *with someone* (Job 9:3; 13:19) **Mt 5:40;** B 6:1 (Is 50:8); μετά τινος (Vi. Aesopi W 76 κριθῆναί με μετὰ τῆς κυρίας μου ἐπὶ σοί=I am pleading my case with my mistress before you; Eccl 6:10) **1 Cor 6:6.** ἐπί τινος *before someone* (as judge) vs. **1** (on the beginning of 1 Cor 6 cp. the decree of Alexander to the Greeks in Ps.-Callisth. 2, 21, 21: βούλομαι δὲ μὴ ἐν ἑαυτοῖς κρίνειν ὅσον τις ὑμῶν ἔχει πρὸς ἕτερον, οὐδὲ ἐφ' οὗ βούλεσθε=it is my wish [will] that you are not to go to law among yourselves, no matter what any of you may have against another, nor before anyone you wish).

ⓑ of the divine tribunal—**α.** occupied by God or Christ: abs. *administer justice, judge* **J 5:30; 8:16, 50;** cp. vs. **26; Rv 6:10;** B 5:7. Pass. *be judged* **Mt 7:1b, 2b; Lk 6:37b; Rv 11:18.**—W. acc. foll. (PGM 4, 1013 of Horus ὁ κρίνων τὰ πάντα) **J 5:22; 8:15b.** τοὺς ἔξω **1 Cor 5:13.** ζῶντας καὶ νεκροὺς *judge the living and the dead* **2 Ti 4:1; 1 Pt 4:5;** B 7:2. τὰ κρυπτὰ τῶν ἀνθρώπων **Ro 2:16.** τὸν κόσμον B 4:12 (TestAbr A 13 p. 92, 10 [Stone p. 32]; ApcEsdr 3:3 p. 27, 8 Tdf.). τὴν οἰκουμένην **Ac 17:31;** AcPl Ha 9, 29. κ. κατὰ τὸ ἑκάστου ἔργον *judge each one by what that person does* **1 Pt 1:17;** cp. **Rv 20:13.** ἐκρίθησαν οἱ νεκροὶ ἐκ τῶν γεγραμμένων ἐν τοῖς βιβλίοις κατὰ τὰ ἔργα αὐτῶν *the dead were judged by what was written in the books* (of life and of death), *in accordance w. their deeds* vs. **12;** δικαίως κ. *judge uprightly* (Sotades [280 BC] fgm. 11, 2 Diehl[2] II 6 p. 191 [in Stob. 4, 34, 8 vol. V p. 826, 5=Coll. Alex. p. 243] ὁ παντογενὴς ... οὐ κρίνει δικαίως) **1 Pt 2:23;** B 19:11. Also ἐν δικαιοσύνῃ **Rv 19:11.** διὰ νόμου κρίνεσθαι *be judged on the basis of the law* **Js 2:12.**—Oft. the emphasis is unmistakably laid upon that which follows the Divine Judge's verdict, upon the condemnation or punishment: *condemn, punish* (opp. σῴζειν as TestJud 24:6; Mel., P. 104, 810; cp. ApcEsdr 1, 11 p. 25, 3 Tdf. ἐμὲ κρῖνον ὑπὲρ τῶν ψυχῶν τῶν ἁμαρτωλῶν) **J 3:17;** cp. **18ab; 12:47ab, 48a;** cp. **48b; Ac 7:7** (Gen 15:14); Dg 7:5f (opp. ἀγαπᾶν). διὰ νόμου κ. *punish on the basis of the law* **Ro 2:12.—3:6f; 1 Cor 11:31f** (here of the temporal punishment which God brings upon sinners); **2 Th 2:12; Hb 10:30** (κρινεῖ κύριος τὸν λαὸν αὐτοῦ *the Lord will judge = punish his people* is derived fr. Dt 32:36=Ps 134:14, where the judgment of God is spoken of, resulting in the vindication of the innocent [the thought prominent in the two OT pass.] and the punishment of the guilty [the thought prominent in the Hb pass.]); **13:4; Js 5:9;** for **1 Pt 4:6** s. 2a above; **Rv 18:8; 19:2;** B 15:5.—W. the punishment given κ. διὰ πυρός 1 Cl 11:1; διὰ τῶν μαστίγων 17:5. κεκριμένοι ἤδη τῷ θανάτῳ *already condemned to death* B 10:5. Also εἰς θάνατον *condemned to death* Hs 9, 18, 2. οἱ κρινόμενοι ἀσεβεῖς *the godless, who are condemned* 2 Cl 18:1. Of the devil ὁ ἄρχων τοῦ κόσμου τούτου κέκριται **J 16:11.**—

ταῦτα ἔκρινας *you have imposed these punishments* **Rv 16:5.**—On κρίνειν τὸ κρίμα **18:20** s. κρίμα 4.

β. occupied by those who have been divinely commissioned to judge: the 12 apostles judge the 12 tribes **Mt 19:28; Lk 22:30** (PBatiffol, RB n.s. 9, 1912, 541–43. But here κ. could have the broader sense *rule;* cp. 4 Km 15:5; Ps 2:10; 1 Macc 9:73; PsSol 17:29). κρινεῖ ἡ ἐκ φύσεως ἀκροβυστία ... σέ *the one who is physically uncircumcised will sit in judgment upon you* **Ro 2:27.** οἱ ἅγιοι as judges of the cosmos **1 Cor 6:2ab** (κρίνεσθαι ἐν: Diod. S. 19, 51, 4.—On the saints as co-rulers with God cp. Epict., Ench. 15; Sallust. 21 p. 36, 14) as well as of the angels vs. **3** (cp. Da 7:22).

❻ to ensure justice for someone, ***see to it that justice is done*** (LXX) τινί *to someone* 1 Cl 8:4 (Is 1:17).—B. 1428. DELG. M-M. EDNT. TW.

κριός, οῦ, ὁ (Hom.+) ***male sheep, ram*** MPol 14:1 (ἐπίσημος 1); B 2:4 v.l. (cp. Is 1:11).—DELG.

κρίσις, εως, ἡ (s. κρίνω; Aeschyl., Hdt.+).**—❶ legal process of judgment,** ***judging, judgment*****—ⓐ** of the activity of God or the Messiah as judge, esp. on the Last Day (Bacchylides 3, 26 of judgment by Zeus).

α. ἡ δικαία κ. τοῦ θεοῦ *God's righteous judgment* **2 Th 1:5.** ἡ κρίσις ἡ ἐμὴ δικαία ἐστίν **J 5:30** (cp. δικαία περὶ πάντων κ. Orig., C. Cels. 4, 9, 10). θεία κ. 2 Cl 20:4. κρίσιν ποιεῖν *execute judgment, act as judge* (Aristoph., Ran. 778; 785; X., Hell. 4, 2, 6; 8; Dt 10:18.—Likew. κ. ποιεῖσθαι: 1 Macc 6:22; Jos., Ant. 6, 34; Just., A I, 2, 3; D. 124, 1; Iren. 1, 10, 1 [Harv. I 91, 10]) **J 5:27.** τ. κρίσιν διδόναι τινί *commit judgment* or *judging to someone* vs. **22** (TestAbr A 13 p. 92, 10 [Stone p. 32]). ἡ ἡμέρα (τῆς) κρίσεως *the Day of Judgment* (Jdth 16:17; Is 34:8; Pr 6:34; PsSol 15:12; GrBar 1:7; ApcEsdr 2:27 p. 26, 21 Tdf. al.; ApcMos 12:26; Just.) **Mt 10:15; 11:22, 24; 12:36; Mk 6:11 v.l.; 2 Pt 2:9; 3:7; 1J 4:17;** 2 Cl 16:3; 17:6; B 19:10; 21:6.—ἡ κ. ἡ μέλλουσα *the judgment to come* 2 Cl 18:2; MPol 11:2. ἡ κ. ἡ ἐπερχομένη *the approaching judgment* Hv 3, 9, 5 (περὶ τῆς ἐσομένης κ. Orig., C. Cels. 1, 56, 7; cp. μετὰ τὴν ἀνάστασιν καὶ κ. Theoph. Ant. 2, 26 [p. 164, 1]). Denial of the Last Judgment Pol 7:1. κ. μεγάλης ἡμέρας *the judgment of the Great Day* **Jd 6.** ἡ ὥρα τῆς κ. αὐτοῦ *the hour when (God) is to judge* **Rv 14:7.** οὐκ ἀναστήσονται οἱ ἀσεβεῖς ἐν κ. *the wicked will not rise in the judgment* (or *on the J. Day*) B 11:7 (Ps 1:5); cp. **Mt 12:41f; Lk 10:14; 11:31f.** δικαιοσύνη κρίσεως ἀρχὴ καὶ τέλος *righteousness* (on the part of the judge) *is the beginning and end of judging* B 1:6. Divine judgment (cp. Iambl., Vi. Pyth. 8, 40 τῶν ἀθανάτων κ.; Hierocles 11, 441 and 442 al. θεία κρίσις) is also mentioned **1 Ti 5:24; Hb 9:27** (cp. Diog. L. 3, 79 after Plato: one must fulfill the δικαιοσύνη θεοῦ, ἵνα μὴ καὶ μετὰ τὸν θάνατον δίκας ὑπόσχοιεν οἱ κακοῦργοι=so that after death they might not as evil-doers be subject to penalties); **2 Pt 2:4, 9;** 2 Cl 20:4; D 11:11.

β. The word oft. means *judgment* that goes against a person, *condemnation,* and the *sentence* that follows (TestAbr A 14 p. 93, 24 [Stone p. 34]; ApcEsdr 1:24 p. 25, 19 Tdf.; SibOr 3, 670; Just., D. 56, 1; 60, 2 κ. τῶν Σοδόμων) GPt 7:25. δισσὴν ἕξουσιν τὴν κ. *they will receive double punishment* 2 Cl 10:5. ἡ κ. σου *your judgment* **Rv 18:10.** κἀκείνοις κ. ἐστίν *judgment comes upon them, too* ISm 6:1. φοβερά τις ἐκδοχὴ κρίσεως *a fearful prospect of judgment* **Hb 10:27** (Iambl., Vi. Pyth. 30, 179 a reference to the κ. τῶν ψυχῶν serves to arouse φόβος τ. ἀδικίας). ἡ κ. αὐτοῦ ἤρθη *his punishment was taken away* **Ac 8:33;** 1 Cl 16:7 (both Is 53:8). ὑπὸ κρίσιν πίπτειν *come under judgment* **Js 5:12;** cp. **2:13ab.** ἡ κ. τῆς γεέννης *being punished in hell* **Mt 23:33** (gen. as Diod. S. 1, 82, 3 θανάτου κ.=punishment by death; πυρὸς κ. Hippol. Ref. 10, 34, 2; cp. 9, 10, 7). ἔνοχός ἐστιν αἰωνίου κ. *liable for eternal punishment* **Mk 3:29 v.l.** κ. κατά τινος *upon, against someone* (Aelian, VH 2, 6) ποιῆσαι κρίσιν κατὰ πάντων *execute judgment upon all* **Jd 15** (En 1:9).—(Opp. ζωή) ἔχει ζωὴν αἰώνιον καὶ εἰς κ. οὐκ ἔρχεται **J 5:24** (cp. Philip [=Demosth. 12, 16] εἰς κ. ἐλθεῖν; ApcSed 11:16 [134, 36 Ja.]τὸ σῶμα ... ἀπέρχεται εἰς κρίσιν). ἀνάστασις ζωῆς ... ἀνάστασις κρίσεως vs. **29.** κρίσις τοῦ κόσμου τούτου *judgment of* (or *upon*) *this world* **12:31;** cp. **16:8,** interpreted as a judgment on the prince of this world **16:11** (cp. 12:31b; 1QM 1, 5; but s. also LLutkemeyer, CBQ 8, '46, 225f 'good judgment', and BNoack, Satanas u. Soteria '48, 79; also s. δικαιοσύνη 3a end).—Some interpreters see in **3:19** a double sense for κ., containing in addition to the senses 'judgment' and 'condemnation' the clear connotation of 'separation, division' (Hecataeus [320 BC]: 264 fgm. 6, 1 Jac. [in Diod. S. 40, 3, 2 Dind. w. the ms. trad.] κρίσις τῶν κακῶν='separation fr. the evils'. A double sense as in J is found in Artem. 5, 5 κριτής='judge' and 'divider'). The 'judgment', which is operative here and now, is said to consist in the fact that people divide themselves into two groups, those who accept Christ and those who reject him (Hdb.; Bultmann). But it is also prob. that κ. in this vs. simply refers to the judicial process, which includes a statement of rationale or basis for the adverse verdict, here expressed in the clause ὅτι ... τὰ ἔργα.—Pl. *judgments, punishments* (Diod. S. 1, 75, 2; Appian, Bell. Civ. 1, 96 §446 κρίσεις πικραί=severe punishments) ἀληθιναὶ καὶ δίκαιαι αἱ κρίσεις σου **Rv 16:7; 19:2.**—Bousset, Rel.[3] 257ff; LRuhl, De Mortuorum Judicio 1903; JBlank, Krisis (J), diss. Freiburg, '64.

ⓑ of the *judgment* of one person upon or against another, in the nature of an *evaluation*

α. of one human being toward another κ. δικαία B 20:2; D 5:2. κ. ἄδικος *unjust judgment* Pol 6:1; ἀπότομος ἐν κ. *relentless in judgment* ibid. τὴν δικαίαν κρίσιν κρίνετε **J 7:24** (κρίνω 2a). Cp. ἡ κ. ἡ ἐμὴ ἀληθινή ἐστιν **8:16.**

β. of archangel against the devil οὐκ ἐτόλμησεν κρίσιν ἐπενεγκεῖν βλασφημίας *he did not presume to pronounce a reviling judgment* **Jd 9.** Cp. the corresp. pass. in **2 Pt 2:11** ἄγγελοι οὐ φέρουσιν κατ' αὐτῶν παρὰ κυρίου βλάσφημον κρίσιν *angels do not pronounce a reviling judgment against them from the Lord.*

❷ a board of judges, ***court,*** specif. *a local court* (s. Schürer II 187f; Diod. S. 17, 80, 2; Aesop, Fab. 190 H.=459 P.; Theod. Prodr. 1, 402 H.) ἔνοχος ἔσται τῇ κ. *he will have to answer to a (local) court* **Mt 5:21f.**—RGuelich, ZNW 64, '73, 44ff.

❸ administration of what is right and fair, ***right*** in the sense of *justice/righteousness* (Michel 542, 6 [II BC] πίστιν ἔχοντα καὶ κρίσιν ὑγιῆ; OGI 383, 207 [I BC]; LXX; cp. מִשְׁפָּט) ἀφήκατε τὴν κρίσιν καὶ τὸ ἔλεος καὶ τὴν πίστιν **Mt 23:23;** cp. **Lk 11:42.** ἐκζητεῖν κ. *seek out justice* 1 Cl 8:4 (Is 1:17). κρίσιν τ. ἔθνεσιν ἀπαγγελεῖ *he will proclaim justice for the gentiles* **Mt 12:18** (Is 42:1). ἕως ἂν ἐκβάλῃ εἰς νῖκος τ. κρίσιν *until he leads justice to victory* vs. **20** (cp. Is 42:3.—Other prob. renderings are *legal action, trial, case* [X., An. 1, 6, 5; Diod. S. 2, 42, 4 αἱ κρίσεις=legal suits, transactions; En 9:3 εἰσαγάγετε τὴν κρίσιν ἡμῶν πρὸς τὸν ὕψιστον], and, influenced by νῖκος, a [military] *decision* [Dionys. Hal. 9, 35; 2 Macc 14:18]). The rendering *right, justice* may also be valid for such passages as **J 7:24; 12:31; 16:8, 11; Ac 8:33** [so NRSV] and perh. others.—GWetter, s.v. κρίμα 4b near end; HBraun, Gerichtsgedanke u. Rechtfertigungslehre b. Pls 1930; FFilson, St. Paul's Conception of Recompense '31.—For add. reff. to the theme of justice in antiquity s. PvanderHorst, The Sentences of Pseudo-Phocylides 78, 117–28.—DELG s.v. κρίνω. M-M. TW.

κρίσμα s. κρίμα.

Κρίσπος, ου, ὁ (also Κρῖσπος; Diod. S. 15, 38, 1; Crinagoras no. 48, 2; ins, pap; Jos., Vi. 33; on the accent s. B-D-F §41, 3; Rob. 235) ***Crispus,*** leader of the synagogue in Corinth **Ac 18:8;** baptized by Paul **1 Cor 1:14.** As v.l. (Syr., Goth.) 2 Ti 4:10. BHHW II, 1014; Haenchen ad loc.—LGPN I. M-M.

κριτήριον, ου, τό (s. κρίνω; Pla.+) prim. 'means for judging/trying, a standard.' Neither this nor the mng. 'judgment' (as SEG XXXVIII, 1224, 16) is found in the NT.

❶ **a forum for justice,** ***lawcourt, tribunal*** (so since Pla., Leg. 6, 767b, also Polyb.; Diod. S.; SIG 683, 48; 807, 9; UPZ 118, 15; PHib 29=Mitt-Wilck. I/2, 259, 5; BGU 1054, 1; LXX; TestAbr; ApcEsdr 2:30 p. 26, 24 Tdf. al.; cp. Philo, Virt. 66) ἕλκειν τινὰ εἰς κριτήρια *drag someone into court* **Js 2:6** (cp. PTurin I, 1 VI, 11 [117 BC] ἑλκυσθέντων ἁπάντων εἰς τὸ κριτήριον). ἔστη εἰς τὸ κ. (Mary) *appeared before the tribunal* (of the priests) GJs 15:2; [ἀπ] ἤγαγον αὐτὴν εἰς τὸ κ. 15:2 v.l. This mng. may underlie two other pass. in our lit. where κ. is found: ἀνάξιοί ἐστε κριτηρίων ἐλαχίστων; could perh. mean: *are you unfit to form even the most insignificant courts* (i.e. those that have jurisdiction over the petty details of everyday life)? **1 Cor 6:2.** Likew. βιωτικὰ κριτήρια ἐὰν ἔχητε, τοὺς ἐξουθενημένους καθίζετε; *if you have* (need for) *courts for the matters of everyday life, do you appoint insignificant people* (as judges)? vs. **4** (καθίζειν κριτήριον as Polyb. 9, 33, 12). But in both cases the trend is to prefer for κ. the sense

❷ **case before a court,** ***lawsuit, legal action*** (e.g., JWeiss, Ltzm., Sickenberger, H-DWendland). Cp. Cyr. Ins. ln. 21 θανατηφόρα κριτήρια=lawsuits involving capital punishment (corresp. to Lat. judicia capitis); SEG VIII, 13 (=Διάταγμα Καίσαρος [I AD]; Boffo, Iscrizioni no. 39 [lit.]) ln. 14 κριτήριον γενέσθαι=the lawsuit is to be tried. Sim. Diod. S. 1, 72, 4; 36, 3, 3.—New Docs 4, 157 (Pfuhl-Möbius ref.=SEG above). DELG s.v. κρίνω. M-M. TW. Sv.

κριτής, οῦ, ὁ (s. κρίνω; trag., Hdt.+; loanw. in rabb.) 'one who reaches a decision, passes judgment'.

❶ **one who has the right to render a decision in legal matters,** ***a judge***—ⓐ lit., in jurisprudence (not older Gk. in this sense, but Diod. S. 1, 92, 4; Epict. 3, 7, 30; ins; POxy 97, 5; 726, 20; 1195, 1; PTebt 317, 20; LXX).

α. of human beings **Mt 5:25; Lk 12:14, 58; 18:2.** ὁ κ. τῆς ἀδικίας *the unjust judge* **18:6** (for the gen. s. ἀδικία 2 end; W-S. §30, 8; Mlt-H. 440; JDerrett, NTS 18, '71/72, 178–91). πενήτων ἄνομοι κ. *lawless judges of the poor* B 20:2; D 5:2. Of Herod Antipas' judges GPt 1:1. Of the procurator **Ac 24:10** (v.l. κ. δίκαιος; so of a human judge Epict., Gnomolog. 48; ApcrEzk [Denis p. 122 ln. 4 =Epiph., Haer. 70, 15]). Of the proconsul κ. τούτων οὐ βούλομαι εἶναι *I do not wish to render a decision on these matters* **18:15.**

β. of God (LXX; Philo; Jos., Bell. 5, 390; TestJud 20:5; PsSol 4:24 al.; Did., Gen. 233, 5; cp. Iren. 1, 13, 6 [Harv. I 124, 1]. Cp. Ael. Aristid. 13 p. 230 D.: τὶς τῶν ἐξ οὐρανοῦ κριτής) and Christ (Iren. 3, 12, 9 [Harv. II 63, 8]) **Hb 12:23; Js 4:12;** δίκαιος κ. **2 Ti 4:8;** Hs 6, 3, 6 (PsSol 2:18 al.). Of God or Christ κ. ζώντων καὶ νεκρῶν *judge of the living and the dead* 2 Cl 1:1.—**Ac 10:42;** Pol 2:1. ὁ κ. πρὸ τῶν θυρῶν ἕστηκεν *the judge stands at the door* **Js 5:9.**

ⓑ in a more general sense (Appian, Liby. 52 §227 κριτής τινος judge, critic of someth.) κριταὶ διαλογισμῶν πονηρῶν **Js 2:4;** Tat. 23, 2 of spectators at gladiatorial combats. κριτὴς (νόμου) *a judge of the law* **4:11.** Of the 'sons' of the Pharisees κριταὶ ἔσονται ὑμῶν *they will be your judges* i.e. they will convict you of wrongdoing **Mt 12:27; Lk 11:19.** Of Moses 1 Cl 4:10 v.l. (cp. Ex 2:14).

❷ **one who rules in a special sense in the accounts of Israel's theocratic period,** ***ruler,*** traditionally rendered *judge,* a leader of the people in the period before the rise of the Hebrew kgdm. (cp. Judg 2:16, 18f; Ruth 1:1; Jos., Ant. 6, 85; 11, 112) **Ac 13:20.**—DELG s.v. κρίνω. M-M. TW.

κριτικός, ή, όν (s. κρίνω; Pla. et al.; Strabo, Plut., Lucian et al.; Philo, Mut. Nom. 110) ***able to discern/judge*** foll. by obj. gen. κ. ἐνθυμήσεων καὶ ἐννοιῶν καρδίας *able to judge the thoughts and deliberations of the heart* **Hb 4:12.**—DELG s.v. κρίνω. TW.

Κρόκος, ου, ὁ (not a very common name; in the Gk. form e.g. OGI 140; CIG add. 4716d, 44; Κυπρ. I p. 100 no. 74; PLond II, 257, 221; 223 p. 26 [94 AD]; BGU 90, 1; 537, 1) ***Crocus,*** an Ephesian Christian: θεοῦ ἄξιος καὶ ὑμῶν IEph 2:1. τὸ ποθητόν μοι ὄνομα *a person dear to me* IRo 10:1.

κροκώδης, ες (κρόκος 'saffron'+ -ώδης q.v. [s. Schwyzer I 418]; Diod. S. 2, 52, 5; Diosc. 1, 27; Heraclides [KDeichgräber, D. griech. Empirikerschule 1930, 195, 22]; Aretaeus p. 58, 24) ***saffron-yellow*** Hs 6, 1, 5.—DELG s.v. κρόκος.

κρούω 1 aor. ἔκρουσα (since Soph. and X., De Re Equ. 11, 4; PGM 5, 75; 92 al.; LXX; TestSol; TestJob 6:4; TestJud 3:1 [αὐτόν]; Philo, Mut. Nom. 139; Jos., Ant. 7, 306) **to deliver a blow against someth.,** ***strike, knock,*** in our lit. only of knocking at a door; abs. (on the contrast κρ. . . . ἀνοίγω cp. SSol 5:2 κρούει ἐπὶ τὴν θύραν Ἄνοιξόν μοι and UPZ 79, 7 [159 BC] κρούει θύραν κ. ἀνοίγεται; Eunap., Vi. Soph. p. 94, where it is said fig. of a sophist: ἔκρουε μὲν τὴν θύραν ἱκανῶς, ἠνοίγετο δὲ οὐ πολλάκις) **Mt 7:7f; Lk 11:9f; 12:36; Ac 12:16; Rv 3:20.** W. acc. τὴν θύραν *knock at the door* (Aristoph., Eccles. 317; 990; X., Symp. 1, 11; Pla., Prot. 310a; 314d, Symp. 212c; PGM 4, 1854; TestJob 6:4. Further exx. fr. later Gk. in Field, Notes 120. The Atticists reject this expr. in favor of κόπτειν τ. θύραν [Phryn. p. 177 Lob.]. κρ. τὴν θύραν Judg 19:22 A) **Lk 13:25; Ac 12:13.** ἔκρουσεν πρὸς τὴν θύραν GJs 12:2 (ἔ. τὴν θύραν v.l.; cp. w. ἐπί Judg 19:22 B; SSol 5:2).—B. 553. DELG. M-M. TW.

κρύβω s. κρύπτω.

κρύπτη, ης, ἡ (s. κρυπτός, κρύπτω; cp. Lat. crypta; Callixenus: 627, fgm. 1, 38 p. 163 ln. 22 Jac.; Strabo 17, 1, 37; Athen. 5, 205a; TestJob 46:5 κρυπτήν; Jos., Bell. 5, 330 [Niese accents κρυπτῄ]; PSI 547, 18 [III BC]) **a place for hiding or storing someth.,** ***a dark and hidden place, a cellar*** λύχνον εἰς κ. τιθέναι *put a lamp in a cellar* **Lk 11:33** (v.l. κρυπτόν).—Renehan '75, 127. DELG s.v. κρύπτω. M-M. TW. Spicq.

κρυπτός, ή, όν (s. κρύπτω; Hom. et al.; pap, LXX; TestReub 1:4; TestJud 12:5; JosAs 6:3 [also cod. A 24:5 p. 76, 14 λόγος])

❶ **pert. to being unknown because of being kept secret,** ***hidden, secret,*** adj. (Herodian 5, 6, 3 κ. καὶ ἀόρατος; SIG 973, 5f; BGU 316, 28; 3 Km 6:4; Ezk 40:16; 2 Macc 1:16; Jos., Ant. 15, 424; τὰ κρυπτὰ τῆς φύσεως μυστήρια Hippol., Ref. 1, 24, 2) ὁ κρυπτὸς τῆς καρδίας ἄνθρωπος *the heart's inner self* **1 Pt 3:4** (s. ἄνθρωπος 5a; cp. Epict. 4, 11, 33). οὐδὲν . . . κ. ὃ οὐ γνωσθήσεται *there is nothing secret that shall not be made known* **Mt 10:26; Lk 12:2;** cp. **Mk 4:22** (Philemon Com. 192

χρόνος τὰ κρυπτὰ πάντα εἰς φάος ἄγει; JosAs 6:3 οὐδὲν κρυπτὸν λέληθεν αὐτῷ).

❷ **a hidden entity, *something hidden*,** subst. τὸ κρυπτόν

ⓐ *a hidden thing* (Menand., Mon. 225 Mei. [316 J.]; Did., Gen. 171, 1) **Lk 8:17.** Esp. in pl. τὰ κρυπτά (Dt 29:28; Is 29:10; Sus 42 Theod.; Jos., Bell. 5, 402; 413 ὁ θεὸς τὰ κ. πάντα ἐφορᾷ) τὰ κ. ἐλέγχει *it exposes the secret things* (so, word for word, Artem. 1, 14 p. 19, 4 and 1, 44 p. 42, 8) IPhld 7:1. τὰ κ. τινος *someone's secret thoughts, plans, purposes* (Philemon Com. 233 φίλου; Iambl., Myst. 6, 5 Partey; PGM 57, 13 τὰ κ. τ. θεᾶς Ἴσιδος; Sir 1:30; Jer 30:4) **Ro 2:16;** IEph 15:3; IPhld 9:1. τὰ κ. τῆς καρδίας αὐτοῦ (TestReub 1:4 ἐν τῇ καρδίᾳ μου τὰ κ.; cp. Is 22:9 τὰ κ. τῶν οἴκων τῆς ἄκρας) *the secret thoughts of the person's* (unbeliever's) *heart* **1 Cor 14:25;** cp. Pol 4:3. τὰ κ. τοῦ σκότους *what is hidden in darkness* **1 Cor 4:5.** τὰ κ. τῆς αἰσχύνης *the things that are hidden out of a sense of shame* **2 Cor 4:2** (on the topic s. RKaster, The Shame of the Romans: TAPA 127, '97, 1–19 [lit.]).

ⓑ *a hidden place* ἐν τῷ κ. *in secret* (Vi. Aesopi W 104 P.; Orig., C. Cels. 8, 74, 4) **Mt 6:4ab, 6ab, 18 v.l.;** ἐν κ. *in a secret place* **J 7:4; 18:20;** *in secret, secretly* (TestJud 12:5; Orig., C. Cels. 7, 22, 31) ὁ ἐν τῷ κ. Ἰουδαῖος *the Judean who is one inwardly,* not only by the outward sign of circumcision **Ro 2:29;** ἀνέβη ὡς ἐν κ. *he went up privately, as it were* **J 7:10.**—On **Lk 11:33 v.l.** s. κρύπτη.—DELG s.v. κρύπτω. M-M. EDNT. TW.

κρύπτω (s. κρυπτός; Hom.+, w. broad range of mng. 'hide, conceal, cover'; also **κρύβω** [PGM 12, 322; ApcMos; Mel., P. 23, 155; Jos., Ant. 8, 410, C. Ap. 1, 292], whence the impf. act. ἔκρυβεν GJs 12:3 and the mid. ἐκρυβόμην GPt 7:26, is a new formation in H. Gk. fr. the aor. ἐκρύβην [B-D-F §73; Mlt-H. 214; 245; Reinhold 72. On the LXX s. Helbing 83f]) fut. κρύψω (LXX; GJs 14:1); 1 aor. ἔκρυψα. Pass.: 2 fut. κρυβήσομαι (PsSol 9:3; JosAs 6:3; ApcEsdr; Plut., Mor. 576d); 2 aor. ἐκρύβην (Hellenistic: Lob., Phryn. p. 317; LXX; JosAs 24:21; ApcMos 22 al.; Jos., Ant. 8, 384); pf. 3 sg. κέκρυπται, ptc. κεκρυμμένος.

❶ **to keep from being seen, *hide*—**ⓐ of things and persons, money **Mt 25:18** (cp. vs. **25** in 2 below); a treasure that has been found **13:44b** (cp. vs. **44a** in 2 below). κ. τινὰ ἀπὸ προσώπου τινός **Rv 6:16.** Fig. of the key of knowledge **Lk 11:52 v.l.** Pass. (Philo, Det. Pot. Ins. 128 τὰ ἀποκείμενα ἐν σκότῳ κέκρυπται; Iren. 1, 18, 1 [Harv. I 171, 12]) of a city on an eminence οὐ δύναται κρυβῆναι **Mt 5:14;** Ox 1 recto, 19f ([Logion 7]=ASyn. 53, ln. 22; s. GTh 32). Of Moses, who escaped detection **Hb 11:23.** τὸ μάννα τὸ κεκρυμμένον *the hidden manna,* kept fr. human eyes because it is laid up in heaven **Rv 2:17.** This is also the place for the pass. κρυβῆναι used in an act. sense *hide* (Gen 3:8, 10; Judg 9:5; 1 Km 13:6; 14:11; Job 24:4; 29:8; JosAs 6:3 al.; ApcEsdr; ApcMos) Ἰησοῦς ἐκρύβη **J 8:59.** ἐκρύβη ἀπ' αὐτῶν **12:36.**—ποῦ κρυβήσομαι ἀπὸ τοῦ προσώπου σου; 1 Cl 28:3.

ⓑ of states or conditions *withdraw from sight* or *knowledge, hide, keep secret* (Delphic commandments: SIG 1268 II, 16 [III BC] ἀπόρρητα κρύπτε; Just., D. 90, 2 τύποις τὴν . . . ἀλήθειαν; Orig., C. Cels. 4, 39, 49) ἐὰν αὐτῆς κρύψω τὸ ἁμάρτημα *if I were to conceal (Mary's) sin* GJs 14:1. τὶ ἀπό τινος *someth. fr. someone* (Synes., Ep. 57 p. 195d; Gen 18:17; TestSol 5:10; TestBenj 2:6) **Mt 11:25.** Pass. **Lk 18:34.** Fig. ἐκρύβη ἀπὸ ὀφθαλμῶν σου *it is hidden from your eyes = from you* **19:42** (cp. [τὰ] βαθύτερα τῶν κεκρυμμένων νοημάτων ἐν ταῖς γραφαῖς Orig., C. Cels. 7, 60, 34). Of the moral conduct of a person κρυβῆναι οὐ δύνανται **1 Ti 5:25** (Diod. S. 14, 1, 3 ἀδυνατεῖ κρύπτειν τὴν ἄγνοιαν; cp. Ath., R. 19 p. 71, 30).—κεκρυμμένα *hidden, unknown things* (Philo, Spec. Leg. 3, 61; Tat. 13, 3 τὸ κεκρυμμένον) **Mt 13:35.** μαθητὴς κεκρυμμένος *a secret disciple* **J 19:38** (τὸ κεκρυμμένον μυστήριον Hippol., Ref. 5, 8, 7).—W. the result of hiding someth. fr. view (Hipponax [VI BC] 25 D. ἀσκέρῃσι τοὺς πόδας δασείῃσιν ἔκρυψας=you have put my feet in furlined shoes) *put (in), mix (in)* τὶ εἴς τι *someth. in someth.* (ζύμην) γυνὴ ἔκρυψεν εἰς ἀλεύρου σάτα τρία **Lk 13:21 v.l.** (s. ἐγκρύπτω).

ⓒ *cause to disappear,* pass. ἵνα ἀνομία πολλῶν ἐν δικαίῳ ἑνὶ κρυβῇ *that the lawlessness of so many should be made to disappear in one who is righteous* Dg 9:5.

ⓓ *hide* in a safe place ἀπὸ μάστιγος γλώσσης σε κρύψει *he will hide you from the scourge of a tongue* 1 Cl 56:10 (Job 5:21). Pass. (ParJer 9:6 ᾧ πᾶσα κτίσις κέκρυπται ἐν αὐτῷ) ἡ ζωὴ ὑμῶν κέκρυπται σὺν τῷ Χριστῷ ἐν τῷ θεῷ **Col 3:3.**—If mention is made of the place to which persons or things are brought to hide them fr. view, the word usually means

❷ **to keep something from being divulged or discovered, *conceal, hide*** of someth. put in a specific place κ. τι ἐν τῇ γῇ *hide someth. in the earth* (Apollon. Rhod. 4, 480 κρ. τι ἐν γαίῃ) **Mt 25:25** (cp. vs. **18** in 1a above); likew. in pass. θησαυρὸς κεκρυμμένος ἐν τῷ ἀγρῷ *a treasure hidden in a field* **13:44a** (cp. vs. **44b** in 1a above). Cp. **Ac 7:24** D (cp. ἡ γῆ οὖν κεκρυμμένη ὑπὸ τῶν ὑδάτων='totally inundated' Did., Gen. 31, 2). Of living persons (Paus. 9, 19, 1) Ῥαὰβ αὐτοὺς ἔκρυψεν εἰς τὸ ὑπερῷον ὑπὸ τὴν λινοκαλάμην *Rahab concealed them in the upper room under the flax* 1 Cl 12:3 (Diod. S. 4, 33, 9 κ. εἰς; Ps.-Apollod. 1, 4, 1, 4 [=p. 12 ln. 1] and schol. on Apollon. Rhod. 4, 532, 33 ὑπὸ γῆν ἔκρυψε).—κρύπτειν ἑαυτόν *hide oneself* (En 10:2 κρύψον σεαυτόν; Nicander in Anton. Lib. 28, 3) ἀπό τινος *fr. someone* (Mary) ἔκρυβεν αὑτὴν ἀπὸ τῶν υἱῶν Ἰσραήλ (M.) *went into hinding from the people of Israel* i.e. she did not go out in public GJs 12:3 (cp. Lk 1:24). εἴς τι in *someth.* ἔκρυψαν ἑαυτοὺς εἰς τὰ σπήλαια *they hid themselves in the caves* (Diod, S. 4, 12, 2 ἔκρυψεν ἑαυτὸν εἰς πίθον) **Rv 6:15.**—ἐκρυβόμεθα *we remained in hiding* GPt 7:26 (Δαυίδ . . . ἐκρύβετο ἐν τῷ ἀγρῷ Iren. 1, 18, 4 [Harv. I 175, 1]; Did., Gen. 92, 20).—B. 850. DELG. M-M. EDNT. TW.

κρυσταλλίζω (s. next entry; hapax leg.) ***shine like crystal, be as transparent as crystal*** of jasper **Rv 21:11.**

κρύσταλλος, ου, ὁ (κρύος 'frost') ***rock-crystal*** (so Diod. S. 2, 52, 2; Strabo 15, 1, 67; Dio Chrys. 12 [13], 34; Aelian, NA 15, 8; Arrian, Anab. 3, 4, 4 of a kind of salt: καθαρὸς ὥσπερ κρύσταλλος; Is 54:12; TestAbr A 12 p. 90, 22 [Stone p. 28]; ApcEsdr 5:23 p. 30, 27 Tdf.; EpArist 67; Philo, Somn. 1, 21) **Rv 4:6** (cp. PLond I, 130, 150 p. 137 [I/II AD] ὁμοία κρυστάλλῳ; Aëtius p. 4, 2 προσέοικε κρυστάλλῳ); **22:1.** Or is it prob. that, since κ. is compared w. θάλασσα and ποταμὸς ὕδατος in the two pass., the older mng. *ice* (Hom.; Hdt.; Antig. Car. 144; Diod. S. 3, 34, 2; 17, 82, 5; Longus 3, 3, 2; Job 6:16; Wsd 16:22; Jos., Ant. 1, 30; TestLevi 3:2; SibOr 14, 151, fgm. 1, 34) is to be preferred?—B. 69. DELG s.v. κρύος. M-M.

κρυφαῖος, αία, αῖον (s. two next entries and κρύπτω; Pind., Pla. et al.; LXX; TestAbr A 3 p. 80, 13 [Stone p. 8] [adv. -αίως]; JosAs 8:11 cj. MPhilonenko) **pert. to being kept from general knowledge, *hidden, private*** as description of God ἐν τῷ κ. *unseen* **Mt 6:18a;** of God's ability to see what goes on in private ὁ βλέπων ἐν τῷ κρυφαίῳ ἀποδώσει σοι *who sees what is done privately, will reward you* vs. **18b** (cp. ἐν κρυφαίοις Jer 23:24; La 3:10).—DELG s.v. κρύπτω 6. TW.

κρυφῇ (s. prec. entry) adv. (κρυφῆ Tdf.; s. W-S. §5, 11c; B-D-F §26 and 73; Mlt-H. 84.—Soph., X. et al.; ostracon: APF 6, 1920, 220 no. 8, 3 κρυφῆι [III BC]; POxy 83, 14; LXX, Test12Patr, JosAs, ParJer) ***in secret*** τὰ κ. γινόμενα ὑπ' αὐτῶν *the things they do in secret* **Eph 5:12** (cp. Lucian, Am. 21).—DELG s.v. κρύπτω 5. M-M. TW.

κρύφιος, ία, ιον (s. two prec. entries; Hes. et al.; LXX; PsSol 8:9) ***hidden, secret*** τὰ κρύφια ἔργα 2 Cl 16:3. Subst. τὰ κ. *hidden* or *secret things* (LXX) 1 Cl 18:6 (Ps 50:8); B 6:10; IMg 3:2.—ἐν κρυφίᾳ *in secret* **Mt 6:18** D.—DELG s.v. κρύπτω 5.

κτάομαι fut. κτήσομαι; 1 aor. ἐκτησάμην; pf. κέκτημαι; fut. pf. 3 sg. κεκτήσεται (Tat. 20, 3 as Aeschyl., Th. 1022 et al.). Pass.: fut. 3 pl. κτηθήσονται Jer 39:45 (s. next entry; Hom.+)

❶ **to gain possession of,** ***procure for oneself, acquire, get*** τὶ *someth.* 2 Cl 5:7. πάντα ὅσα κτῶμαι *my whole income* **Lk 18:12.** W. acc. and εἴς τι foll.: χρυσὸν . . . εἰς τὰς ζώνας *acquire gold* (in order to put it) *into your (money-) belts* **Mt 10:9.** *Procure* τὶ *someth.* (Plut., Mor. 189d βιβλία κτᾶσθαι) τὴν δωρεὰν τ. θεοῦ διὰ χρημάτων κτᾶσθαι *secure the gift of God with money* **Ac 8:20** (Herodian 2, 6, 5 χρήμασι κ. τι). Also ἐκ: χωρίον ἐκ μισθοῦ τ. ἀδικίας *acquire a field w. the reward of his wickedness* **1:18** (JSickenberger, BZ 18, '29, 69–71). Also w. gen. of price πολλοῦ κεφαλαίου *for a large sum* **Ac 22:28.** τὸ ἑαυτοῦ σκεῦος κτᾶσθαι ἐν ἁγιασμῷ καὶ τιμῇ *take a wife for himself* (or: *gain control over his own body;* s. σκεῦος 3) *in consecration and honor* **1 Th 4:4** (cp. κτᾶσθαι γυναῖκα X., Symp. 2, 10; Sir 36:24). ἐν τῇ ὑπομονῇ ὑμῶν κτήσεσθε τὰς ψυχὰς ὑμῶν *you will win your lives by your endurance* **Lk 21:19.**

❷ ***bring upon oneself,*** of misfortunes, etc. (Soph.; Eur.; Thu. 1, 42, 2 ἔχθραν; Pr 3:31; ApcEsdr 2:12 p. 26, 5 Tdf. παρακοήν) εὔχομαι, ἵνα μὴ εἰς μαρτύριον αὐτὸ κτήσωνται *I pray that they may not bring it* (my message) *upon themselves as a witness* (against them) IPhld 6:3.

❸ ***possess,*** the pf. (only in Ign. in our lit.) has this present mng. (Appian, Bell. Civ. 5, 67 §282 οἱ κεκτημένοι=those who possessed [slaves]; En 97:10; TestSol 1:10 D; TestJob 11:2; JosAs 2:10 cod. A; EpArist 229; Philo, Cher. 119, Mos. 1, 157 al.; Jos., C. Ap. 1, 66; Just., D. 29, 2; Tat. 1:2 al.) τινά *someone* ἐπίσκοπον IEph 1:3. τὶ *someth.* ὄνομα 1:1. ἀγάπην 14:2. λόγον Ἰησοῦ 15:2. πνεῦμα IMg 15; IPol 1:3. διακονίαν IPhld 1:1. γνώμην IPol 8:1.—M-M. DELG. TW.

κτῆμα, ατος, τό (s. prec. entry; Hom.+)—❶ **that which is acquired or possessed,** gener. of any kind (Menand., Dyscolus 156). πᾶν κ. D 13:7. Pl. *possessions* (PRyl 28, 182; 76, 11; Jos., Ant. 14, 157) τὰ κτήματα καὶ αἱ ὑπάρξεις **Ac 2:45.** Beside fields and houses of movable property, furniture Hs 1:9. ἔχειν κτ. πολλά **Mt 19:22; Mk 10:22** (cp. Diog., Ep. 38, 5, a rich youth follows Diogenes διανείμας τὴν οὐσίαν. Porphyr., Vi. Plotini 7: Rogatianus the senator gives away πᾶσα κτῆσις and becomes a Cynic).

❷ ***landed property, field, piece of ground,*** in later usage κ. came to be restricted to this mng. (since Demosth. 18, 41; Menand., Dyscolus 40, 328, 737; Plut., Crass. 543 [1, 5]; Herodian 2, 6, 3; PTebt 5, 52; 120, 9; BGU 530, 21; Pr 23:10; 31:16; Philo, Spec. Leg. 2, 116; Jos., Bell. 4, 574) **Ac 5:1** (=χωρίον vs. 3).—B. 769. Renehan 75, 127. DELG s.v. κτάομαι 4. M-M. TW.

κτῆνος, ους, τό a domestic animal capable of carrying loads, *domesticated animal, pet, pack-animal, animal used for riding* (mostly in pl. as collective, 'flocks, herds': since Hom. Hymns and Hdt.: ins, pap, LXX, TestSol, TestAbr, TestJob, Test12Patr, ApcMos; SibOr, fgm. 3:12; EpArist, Philo, Mel.; Ath. 20, 4, R. 24 p. 78, 5; infreq. in sing.: X., An. 5, 2, 3; SIG 986, 8; Ex 22:4; TestAbr B 2 p. 106, 25 [Stone p. 60]; TestReub 2:9; Mel., P. 11, 93 παντὸς κτήνους Theoph. Ant. 3, 9 [p. 224, 3]) of livestock (PTebt 56, 8; LXX) Hv 4, 1, 5; s 9, 1, 8 (in contrast to wild and dangerous animals 9, 1, 9; cp. M. Ant. 5, 11 and Philo, Op. M. 64: κτ. . . . θηρίον); 9, 24, 1. Also **1 Cor 15:39;** PtK 2 p. 14, 18 refer to domesticated animals. *Cattle* alone seem to be meant in the combination κτήνη καὶ πρόβατα **Rv 18:13** (cp. PRyl 126, 15 τὰ ἑατοῦ πρόβατα καὶ βοικὰ κτήνη).—Of animals used for riding (POxy 2153, 20 [III AD]; TestAbr s. above; Jos., Ant. 8, 241) **Lk 10:34; Ac 23:24.**—DELG s.v. κτάομαι 5. M-M. Sv.

κτήτωρ, ορος, ὁ (Diod. S. 34 + 35, 2, 31; POxy 237 VIII, 31; 718, 13; PTebt 378, 24; et al. [New Docs 2, 89] Jo 1:11 Sym.) ***owner*** of houses and lands χωρίων ἢ οἰκιῶν **Ac 4:34** (cp. 1QS 1:11f).—DELG s.v. κτάομαι 7. M-M.

κτίζω (s. three next entries) 1 aor. ἔκτισα; pf. inf. ἐκτικέναι (Just., D. 41, 1). Pass.: fut. κτισθήσομαι LXX; 1 aor. ἐκτίσθην; pf. ἔκτισμαι (Hom.+) **to bring someth. into existence, *create,*** in our lit. of God's creative activity (LXX, pseudepigr.; Eupolem. Hist. [II BC]: 723 fgm. 2, 31 Jac. [in Eus., PE 9, 31]; Philo, Decal. 97; Jos., Bell. 3, 369; 379, Ant. 1, 27; Just.; SibOr 3, 20; IDefixWünsch 4, 1; PGM 5, 98ff) τὶ *someth.* **1 Ti 4:3.** κτίσιν **Mk 13:19.** τὸν οὐρανὸν καὶ τὰ ἐν αὐτῷ *the heaven and what is in it* **Rv 10:6.** δημιουργὸν . . . ᾧ τοὺς οὐρανοὺς ἔκτισεν *through whom (God) created the heavens* Dg 7:2 (on the dat. s. Kühner-G. §425, 7; cp. Menand., Dyscolus 156). τὰ πάντα (Herm. Wr. 13, 17) **4:11a;** D 10:3; cp. **Rv 4:11b.** ὁ θεὸς ὁ τὰ πάντα κτίσας **Eph 3:9;** Hm 1:1; cp. s 5, 5, 2. Pass. **Col 1:16ab** (cp. ἐν 4a). ὁ θεὸς κτίσας ἐκ τοῦ μὴ ὄντος τὰ ὄντα *what is from what is not* Hv 1, 1, 6 (cp. Iren. 4, 38, 3 [Harv. II 295, 9]). τὸν κόσμον Hv 1, 3, 4. τὸν κόσμον ἕνεκα τοῦ ἀνθρώπου m 12, 4, 2. τὰ ἔθνη s 4:4. τὸν λαόν s 5, 6, 2. τὴν οἰκουμένην 1 Cl 60:1 (cp. Ps 88:12). Pass. ἐκτίσθη ἀνήρ **1 Cor 11:9.** τῶν ὑπὸ τοῦ θεοῦ κτισθέντων . . . καλῶς κτισθέντα Dg 4:2. στοιχείων . . . ἐκτισμένων 8:2. Of the Christian community imaged as transcending time πάντων πρώτη ἐκτίσθη Hv 2, 4, 1; πρὸ ἡλίου καὶ σελήνης ἐκτισμένης 2 Cl 14:1 (cp. Ps 71:5). Of the angels οἱ πρῶτοι κτισθέντες v 3, 4, 1; s 5, 5, 3. Abs. ὁ κτίσας *the Creator* (Jos., Bell. 3, 354) **Ro 1:25; Mt 19:4** (v.l. ποιήσας). ὁ τὰ πάντα κτίσας *the Creator of the universe* Hs 7:4 (PGM 13, 62 τὸν πάντα κτίσαντα; 983).—Also of the Spirit τὸ πνεῦμα τὸ κτίσαν πᾶσαν τὴν κτίσιν Hs 5, 6, 5.—Of the divine creative activity w. regard to the inner life: of pers. who were κτισθέντες ἐν Χριστῷ Ἰησοῦ ἐπὶ ἔργοις ἀγαθοῖς *created* (by God) *in Christ Jesus for good deeds* **Eph 2:10.** In ref. to Gen 1:26f: ἵνα τοὺς δύο κτίσῃ ἐν αὐτῷ εἰς ἕνα καινὸν ἄνθρωπον *in order that he* (Christ) *might make them both* (Israelites and non-Israelites) *one new being* (or *humanity*) *in him* vs. **15;** τὸν καινὸν ἄνθρωπον τὸν κατὰ θεὸν κτισθέντα ἐν δικαιοσύνῃ *the new being, created in the likeness of God in righteousness* **4:24.** Corresp. τὸν νέον (ἄνθρωπον) τὸν ἀνακαινούμενον εἰς ἐπίγνωσιν κατ' εἰκόνα τοῦ κτίσαντος αὐτόν *the new being, renewed in knowledge according to the image of its Creator* **Col 3:10.** ἐγενόμεθα καινοί, πάλιν ἐξ ἀρχῆς κτιζόμενοι *we became new, created again from the beginning* B 16:8. καρδίαν καθαρὰν κτίσον ἐν ἐμοί 1 Cl 18:10 (Ps 50:12). τῷ θεῷ τῷ κτίσαντι ἡμᾶς 2 Cl 15:2. Fig. ὁ . . . κτίσας τὸ δένδρον τοῦτο Hs 8, 2, 9 (cp. 8, 3, 2). S. on ἐκλογή, end, and Teschendorf under γίνομαι 2a.—PKatz, The mng. of the root קנה: JJS 5, '54, 126–31.—DELG. M-M. TW. Sv.

κτίσις, εως, ἡ (s. prec. and two next entries; Pind.+).—❶ **act of creation, *creation*** (Iren. 1, 17, 1 [Harv. I 164, 11]; Hippol.,

Ref. 6, 33 κ. τοῦ κόσμου; 6, 55, 1; Did., Gen. 24, 4): ἀπὸ κτίσεως κόσμου *since the creation of the world* **Ro 1:20** (cp. PsSol 8, 7; ApcSed 8:10; Jos., Bell. 4, 533). The Son of God was σύμβουλος τῷ πατρὶ τῆς κτίσεως αὐτοῦ *counselor to the Father in his creative work* Hs 9, 12, 2.

❷ **the result of a creative act, *that which is created*** (EpArist 136; 139; TestReub 2:9).—ⓐ of individual things or beings created, *creature* (Tob 8:5, 15) *created thing* τὶς κ. ἑτέρα *any other creature* **Ro 8:39.** οὐκ ἔστιν κ. ἀφανὴς ἐνώπιον αὐτοῦ *no creature is hidden from (God's) sight* **Hb 4:13.** πᾶν γένος τῆς κ. τοῦ κυρίου *every kind of creature that the Lord made* Hs 9, 1, 8; πᾶσα κ. *every created thing* (cp. Jdth 9:12) MPol 14:1. Of Christ πρωτότοκος πάσης κ. **Col 1:15.** Of the name of God ἀρχέγονον πάσης κ. 1 Cl 59:3. τὸ εὐαγγέλιον ... τὸ κηρυχθὲν ἐν πάσῃ κτίσει *the gospel ... which has been preached to every creature* (here limited to human beings) **Col 1:23.**—Pl. (En 18:1) δοξάζειν τὰς κτίσεις τοῦ θεοῦ *praise the created works of God* Hv 1, 1, 3.—The Christian is described by Paul as καινὴ κ. *a new creature* **2 Cor 5:17,** and the state of being in the new faith by the same words as *a new creation* **Gal 6:15** (cp. Jos., Ant. 18, 373 καιναὶ κτίσεις). S. on ἐκλογή end.

ⓑ the sum total of everything created, *creation, world* (ApcMos 32; SibOr 5, 152; ὁρωμένη κ. Did., Gen. 1 B, 6; 13 A, 2) ἡ κ. αὐτοῦ Hv 1, 3, 4. ἐν ἀρχῇ τῆς κ. *at the beginning of the world* B 15:3; ἀπʼ ἀρχῆς κ. *from the beginning of the world* **Mk 13:19; 2 Pt 3:4.** Likew. **Mk 10:6;** πᾶσα ἡ κ. *the whole creation* (Jdth 16:14; Ps 104:21 v.l.; TestAbr A 13 p. 92, 7 [Stone p. 32], B 12 p. 116, 31 [St. p. 80]; TestLevi 4:1; TestNapht 2:3; ParJer 9:6; PGM 12, 85) Hv 3, 4, 1; m 12, 4, 2; s 5, 6, 5; 9, 14, 5; 9, 23, 4; 9, 25, 1. The whole world is full of God's glory 1 Cl 34:6. ἀόργητος ὑπάρχει πρὸς πᾶσαν τὴν κτίσιν αὐτοῦ 19:3. ὁ υἱὸς τ. θεοῦ πάσης τ. κτίσεως αὐτοῦ προγενέστερός ἐστιν *the Son of God is older than all his creation* Hs 9, 12, 2. πᾶσα ἡ κ. limited to humankind **Mk 16:15;** Hm 7:5. Also ἡ κτίσις τῶν ἀνθρώπων D 16:5.—αὕτη ἡ κ. *this world* (earthly in contrast to heavenly) **Hb 9:11.**—κ. *the creation, what was created* in contrast to the Creator (Wsd 16:24) **Ro 1:25** (EpArist 139 θεὸν σεβόμενοι παρʼ ὅλην τὴν κτίσιν).—Of Christ ἡ ἀρχὴ τῆς κτίσεως τοῦ θεοῦ **Rv 3:14** (s. ἀρχή 3).—The mng. of κτ. is in dispute in **Ro 8:19–22,** though the pass. is usu. taken to mean the waiting of the whole creation below the human level (animate and inanimate—so, e.g., OCullmann, Christ and Time [tr. FFilson] '50, 103).—HBiedermann, D. Erlösg. der Schöpfung beim Ap. Pls. '40.

❸ **system of established authority that is the result of some founding action, *governance system, authority system.*** Corresponding to 1, κτίσις is also the act by which an authoritative or governmental body is created (ins in Ramsay, CB I/2, 468 no. 305 [I AD]: founding of the Gerousia [Senate]. Somewhat comparable, of the founding of a city: Scymnus Chius vs. 89 κτίσεις πόλεων). But then, in accordance with 2, it is prob. also the result of the act, *the institution* or *authority* itself **1 Pt 2:13** (Diod. S. 11, 60, 2 has κτίστης as the title of a high official. Cp. νομοθεσία in both meanings: 1. lawgiving, legislation; 2. the result of an action, i.e. law.) To a Hellene a well-ordered society was primary (s. Aristot., Pol. 1, 1, 1, 1252). It was understood that the function of government was to maintain such a society, and the moral objective described in vs. 14 is in keeping with this goal.—BBrinkman, 'Creation' and 'Creature' I, Bijdragen (Nijmegen) 18, '57, 129–39, also 359–74; GLampe, The NT Doctrine of κτίσις, SJT 17, '64, 449–62.—DELG s.v. κτίζω. M-M. TW. Sv.

κτίσμα, ατος, τό (s. two prec. entries and next entry; Polyb. 4, 70, 3; Dionys. Hal. 1, 59; Strabo 7, 5, 5; Vett. Val. 213, 6; SIG 799, 7 [38 AD]; PGM 7, 483; BGU 3, 19; LXX, pseudepigr.; Just.; Iren. 1, 5, 4 [Harv. I 48, 2] in gnostic speculation; loanw. in rabb.) in our lit. always (as Wsd 9:2; 13:5; 14:11; Sir 36:14; 38:34; 3 Macc 5:11; EpArist 17; Iren. 1, 10, 2 [Harv. I 93, 3]; Did., Gen. 220, 28) **product of creative action, *that which is created*** (by God), ***creature*** (created by God) πᾶν κ. θεοῦ καλόν *everything created by God is good* **1 Ti 4:4.** πᾶν κ. ὃ ἐν τῷ οὐρανῷ *every creature in heaven* **Rv 5:13.**—Pl., of the components of creation (TestAbr B 7 p. 12, 8 [Stone p. 72] τὰ κτίσματα ἃ ἐκτίσατο ... ὁ θεός; TestJob 47:11; Herm. Wr. 1, 18 πάντα τὰ κ.; Sextus 439; Orig., C. Cels. 7, 46, 39; Did., Gen. 109, 25) Dg 8:3.—τὰ κ. τὰ ἐν τῇ θαλάσσῃ **Rv 8:9.**—τὰ κ. τοῦ θεοῦ *what God has created* Hv 3, 9, 2; m 8:1; humankind is lord of it 12, 4, 3. The Christians are ἀπαρχή τις τῶν αὐτοῦ κ. *a kind of first-fruits of (God's) creatures* (here κ. is to be thought of as referring chiefly to human beings; for a similar restriction in the use of κτίσις s. that entry 2) **Js 1:18.**—DELG s.v. κτίζω. M-M. TW. Sv.

κτίστης, ου, ὁ (s. three prec. entries; on the accent s. Kühner-Bl. I §107, 4eβ p. 392; Rob. 231; the word Aristot.+.—As designation of rulers and others of high rank: SIG 751, 2; 839, 8 [both κ., sc. τῆς πόλεως, w. σωτήρ]; IPriene 229, 4; CIG II 2572 the Rom. emperor as τῆς οἰκουμένης κ.; ins [Caracella and Geta period] in ÖJh 64, '95, 72; of Androclus, K. of Ephesus Jos., C. Ap. 2, 39.—Also w. ref. to a deity: Diod. S. 5, 74, 6 Apollo κ. of the medical art; PGM 4, 591 φωτὸς κτίστα; 5, 248; 7, 963) in our lit. only of God as ***the Creator*** (hymn to Isis: SEG VIII, 549, 11 [I BC] the god Σοκονῶπις as κ. καὶ γαίης τε καὶ οὐρανοῦ; Herm. Wr. 13, 17; Sir 24:8 ὁ κ. ἁπάντων; 2 Macc 1:24; 4 Macc 11:5; EpArist 16; Philo, Spec. Leg. 1, 30 al.; SibOr, fgm. 3, 17 al.; Ar. 15:3; Just., A II, 6, 2) **1 Pt 4:19;** 1 Cl 62:2. κ. τοῦ σύμπαντος κόσμου *Creator of the whole universe* 19:2 (cp. ὁ τοῦ κόσμου κ. 2 Macc 7:23; 4 Macc 5:25; PGM 4, 1200; τὸν τῶν πάντων κ. καὶ δημιουργὸν καὶ ποιητὴν λόγον τοῦ θεοῦ Iren. 1, 15, 5 [Harv. I 154, 11]; τὸν κ. καὶ ποιητὴν καὶ δημιουργὸν τοῦδε τοῦ παντὸς κόσμου Theoph. Ant. 3, 9 [p. 222, 14]). κ. παντὸς πνεύματος *Creator of every spirit* 59:3.—HWeiss, TU 97, '66, 55–58 (cosmology); SEG XLII, 1846 (reff.).—DELG s.v. κτίζω. M-M. EDNT. TW.

κυβεία, ας, ἡ (also -ία edd.) lit. 'dice-playing' (Pla., Phdr. 274d; X., Mem. 1, 3, 2, Oec. 1, 20; Dio Chrys. 53 [70], 4. As a loanw. קוּבְיָא in the Bab. Talmud, Sabb. 149b) ἡ κυβεία τῶν ἀνθρώπων is shown by the succeeding phrase, ἐν πανουργίᾳ κτλ., to be used metaph. (as in our 'play with loaded dice') in the sense ***craftiness, trickery*** **Eph 4:14** (κυβεύω='deceive' Epict. 2, 19, 28; 3, 21, 22).—Straub 34f. DELG s.v. κύβος. M-M.

κυβερνάω (s. two next entries; since Hom., Od. 3, 283, also ins, pap, LXX, EpArist, Philo, Joseph.) aor. ptc., fem. κυβερνήσασα Wsd 10:4, pass. κυβερνηθεῖσα Wsd 14:6. 'Steer, pilot' a vessel, then metaph. ***guide*** ὅτι οὕτως ἰσοψύχως τὰ περὶ αὐτοῦ ἑκάστης ἡμέρας κυβερνῶσει ἐν τῇ πρὸς τὸν κύριον προσευχῇ (Paul counted himself blessed) *that with such unanimous spirit they directed his needs each day to the Lord in prayer* AcPl Ha 6, 7–9.—DELG.

κυβέρνησις, εως, ἡ (s. prec. and next entry; Pind. et al.; Plut., Mor. 162a [θεοῦ κ.]; PLond IV, 1349, 20; Pr 1:5; 11:14; 24:6) ***administration,*** the pl. indicates varieties of such leading positions in the ecclesial body of Christ **1 Cor 12:28.**—DELG s.v. κυβερνάω. M-M.

κυβερνήτης, ου, ὁ (s. two prec. entries; Hom. et al.; ins, pap, LXX, Philo; Jos., Vi. 163; TestNapht 6:2; loanw. in rabb.; variously, 'shipmaster, steersman').

❶ **one who is responsible for the management of a ship,** ***shipmaster,*** lit. **Rv 18:17;** IPol 2:3; AcPl Ha 7, 19; 38. W. ναύκληρος, the 'shipowner' (Plut., Mor. 807b ναύτας μὲν ἐκλέγεται κυβερνήτης καὶ κυβερνήτην ναύκληρος=a shipmaster selects a crew, and a shipowner a shipmaster; Jos., Ant. 9, 209) **Ac 27:11** (LCasson, Ships and Seamanship in the Ancient World '71, 316–18).

❷ **one who directs the destiny of humans,** ***pilot,*** fig. extension of 1 (Pla., Polit. 272e of God; Vett. Val. 340 κυβερνήτης βίου. Oft. Philo, somet. of God, and Migr. Abr. 67 of the λόγος θεῖος; Herm. Wr. 12, 4 of the νοῦς) of Christ κ. τῶν σωμάτων ἡμῶν *the Pilot of our bodies* MPol 19:2 (the figure of the κυβερνήτης is also used in the martyr-narrative in 4 Macc 7:1).—DELG s.v. κυβερνάω. M-M. TW.

κυβία s. κυβεία.

κυέω (Att.) s. κύω.

κύθρα, ας, ἡ (Ionic and later Gk. for χύτρος [χέω]; Herodas 7, 76; Etym. Mag. p. 454, 43; PTebt 112, 42; 47, 75 [112 BC]; PAmh 125, 5; s. Mayser p. 184. For the LXX s. Thackeray p. 103) ***a pot*** 1 Cl 17:6 (quot. of unknown origin; s. RHarris, JBL 29, 1910, 190f).—DELG s.v. χέω III.

κυκλεύω (κύκλος, 'ring, circle', also s. three next entries) 1 aor. ἐκύκλευσα (Strabo 6, 3, 7; PLond I, 131 recto, 508 p. 185 [78/79 AD]; PGrenf I 58, 7; 4 Km 3:25; JosAs 1:1 'make a circuit of the entire country')

❶ **to move so as to encircle an object,** ***surround*** τὴν παρεμβολὴν τῶν ἁγίων **Rv 20:9.** τινά *someone* **J 10:24 v.l.**

❷ **to make a complete movement around an object,** ***go around*** abs. ἐκύκλευον ἐγὼ μετ' αὐτοῦ *I went with him* (around the tower) Hs 9, 9, 6. S. κυκλόω 2.—DELG s.v. κύκλος. M-M.

κυκλόθεν (s. prec. and two next entries; Lysias 7, 28; Kaibel 546, 7f; LXX) adv. of place 'all around, from all sides'.

❶ as adv., **over all the area of an outside surface,** ***around*** (BGU 1117, 25 [13 BC]; TestJob 31:3; JosAs 2:17; SibOr 3, 706) κυκλόθεν κ. ἔσωθεν **Rv 4:8.**

❷ funct. as prep. w. gen. (Sb 6152, 20 [93 BC]; Sir 50:12; 4 Macc 14:17; Aristob. in Eus., PE 8, 10, 14) **in a circle,** ***around*** κ. τοῦ θρόνου *around the throne* **Rv 4:3f; 5:11 v.l.**—DELG s.v. κύκλος. M-M.

κυκλόω fut. κυκλώσω; 1 aor. ἐκύκλωσα, pass. ἐκυκλώθην (s. two prec. entries; Pind.+; LXX; PsSol 10:1; TestAbr; TestJob 44:1; JosAs 9:3; ParJer; Philo, Leg. All. 1, 85; 86; Jos., Bell. 4, 557, Ant. 10, 137; SibOr 5, 251; Just., D. 103, 1).

❶ **to move so as to encircle an object,** ***surround, encircle***

ⓐ w. hostile intent (Eur., Thu. et al.; LXX) τινά *someone* **J 10:24; Ac 14:20;** B 6:6 (cp. Ps 21:17; 117:12). A place (cp. Jos., Vi. 114): pass. κυκλουμένην ὑπὸ στρατοπέδων Ἰερουσαλήμ **Lk 21:20; Rv 20:9 v.l.** (s. κυκλεύω 1).

ⓑ to provide protection: fig., of mercy ἔλεος κυκλώσει *mercy will encompass (them)* 1 Cl 22:8 (Ps 31:10).

❷ **to move full circle around an object,** ***go around, circle round*** τὸν πύργον Hs 9, 9, 6 (cp. Gen 2:11; Dt 2:1, 3; TestAbr B 12 p. 116, 30 [Stone p. 80]). Pass., of Jericho's walls ἔπεσαν κυκλωθέντα ἐπὶ ἑπτὰ ἡμέρας *they fell after the Israelites had marched around them seven days* **Hb 11:30** (cp. Josh 6:20). DELG s.v. κύκλος.

κύκλῳ dat. (of κύκλος) of place, fixed as an adv. (B-D-F §199; Rob. 295f; 644) 'around, all around', lit. 'in a circle' (Hom.+).

❶ **pert. to encirclement,** ***around*** as adv. (Jos., Ant. 14, 418; 15, 337) κ. περιτειχίζειν MPol 15:2. πόλις περιτετειχισμένη κύκλῳ Hs 12, 9, 5. οἱ περὶ αὐτὸν κύκλῳ καθήμενοι **Mk 3:34** (cp. 1 Esdr 4:11 and κύκλῳ περί τι Hdt. 1, 185; Pla., Phd. 111c; EpArist 63).—Sim. used as prep. w. gen. (X., Cyr. 4, 5, 5; Polyb. 4, 21, 9; OGI 455, 12; CPR I, 42, 10; PFay 110, 7; PTebt 342, 26; Gen 35:5; Ex 7:24; 16:13 al.; En 14:11; OdeSol 11:16; TestAbr A 15 p. 95, 22 [Stone p. 38] and B 8 p. 112, 23 [St. p. 72]) κ. τοῦ θρόνου *around the throne* **Rv 4:6; 5:11** (s. κυκλόθεν 2 end); **7:11.** κ. τοῦ πύργου *around the tower* Hv 3, 2, 8; 3, 4, 2; 3, 8, 2; s 9, 7, 3; 9, 9, 6; 9, 11, 4; κ. τοῦ πεδίου *around the plain* 9, 1, 4; cp. τὰ κ. τοῦ πύργου 9, 7, 6; 9, 10, 1f; κ. τῆς πύλης *around the gate* 9, 2, 3; 9, 3, 1; 9, 4, 1; around Christ 9, 6, 2.

❷ **pert. to all directions from a point of reference,** ***around,*** as adv. περιῆγεν τ. κώμας κ. *he went around among the villages* **Mk 6:6.**—Sim. preceded by the art., and used as an adj. *around, nearby* (X., Cyr. 7, 2, 23; Arrian, Anab. 6, 15, 7 τὰ κύκλῳ ἔθνη; Bar 2:4b; 2 Macc 4:32 αἱ κ. πόλεις TestJob 30:5) εἰς τοὺς κ. ἀγροὺς *into the farms nearby* **Mk 6:36.** εἰς τὰς κ. κώμας *into the villages around here* **Lk 9:12.**

❸ **pert. to completion of a circuit,** ***around,*** as adv. ἀπὸ Ἰερουσαλὴμ καὶ κύκλῳ **Ro 15:19** (AGeyser, Un Essai d'Explication de Ro 15:19, NTS 6, '60, 156–59) is either *(beginning) from Jerusalem and its environs* (BWeiss) or prob. better *beginning from Jerus. and traveling around (describing a circle)* (Zahn, Ltzm., Sickenberger, Althaus). This avoids giving the impression that Paul traveled in a straight line, and agrees better w. the comprehensive nature of his activity (cp. PLond III, 981, 8–11 p. 242 [IV AD] ἡ εὐφημία σου περιεκύκλωσεν τ. κόσμον ὅλον='travel about in'. Maximus Tyr. 25, 1c Ἀνάχαρσις περιῄει τὴν Ἑλλάδα ἐν κύκλῳ). Perhaps it would be better to render κύκλῳ with *in an arc* or *curve* (Appian, Mithrid. 101 §467: Mithridates, on his march from Dioscurias on the east shore of the Black Sea wishes to go around τὸν Πόντον ὅλον ἐν κύκλῳ=the whole Black Sea in a curved path, as far as Lake Maeotis=the Sea of Azov).—περιάγειν κύκλῳ τοῦ πύργου Hs 9, 11, 4f.—See B. 905. DELG s.v. κύκλος. M-M.

κύλισμα, ματος, τό s. κυλισμός.

κυλισμός, οῦ, ὁ (s. next entry; Hippiatr. 75, 12 [=I p. 291, 23]; Pr 2:18 Theod.) ***rolling, wallowing,*** of a swine λουσαμένη εἰς κ. βορβόρου (s. on βόρβορος) **2 Pt 2:22** (κύλισμα v.l. is prob. on the analogy of ἐξέραμα. κύλισμα is found Ezk 10:13 Sym.; JZiegler, Ezk p. 126).—DELG s.v. κυλίνδω. M-M.

κυλίω (s. prec. entry) 1 aor. ἐκύλισα. Pass.: impf. ἐκυλιόμην; aor. ἐκυλίσθην; fut. 3 sg. κυλισθήσεται LXX (perh. also earlier Gk. [Kühner-Bl. II 453]; Polyb. 26, 10, 16; Hero Alex. I p. 342, 19; LXX; En 18:15; TestJud 6:4; Joseph.)

❶ **to move an object by rolling it,** ***roll (up)*** τί *someth.* act. λίθον (BGU 1290, 10; 19 [II BC]; 1 Km 14:33; Pr 26:27; Jos., Ant. 6, 121 [pass.]; TestJud 6:4) GPt 8:32; **Lk 23:53 v.l.**

❷ **to move on a surface by turning over and over,** ***roll (oneself)*** pass. in act. sense (Aristot., HA 5, 19, 18; Polyb. 26, 1, 14; Dionys. Hal. 8, 39; Aelian, NA 7, 33; Epict. 4, 11, 29; LXX; En 18:15) of one possessed by a hostile spirit **Mk 9:20.** Of sinners in the place of punishment ApcPt 15, 30. Of stones: *roll* (Alex. Aphr., Fat. 36 II 2 p. 208, 24 κυλίεσθαι=roll [of a ball on an inclined plane]; Quint. Smyrn. 2, 384 κυλίνδεσθαι=roll [of a stone]; cp. Zech 9:16; Jos., Ant. 5, 219) ἐκ τῆς ὁδοῦ εἰς τὴν ἀνοδίαν or εἰς τὸ ὕδωρ *from the road into the pathless ground* or *into the water* Hv 3, 2, 9; 3, 7, 1; cp. 3; GPt 9:37.—DELG s.v. κυλίνδω. M-M.

κυλλός, ή, όν (Aristoph., Hippocr. et al.; in description of a wanted felon PMich IV/1, 223, 1642; 224, 1441 [both II AD]) of a limb of the human body that is in any way abnormal or incapable of being used; also of persons who have such limbs (Ar. 8:2) ***crippled, deformed:*** w. ref. to the hand (Anth. Pal. 11, 84; Galen II 394, 1 K.=ἄχρηστον ἔχων τ. χεῖρα) **Mt 18:8; Mk 9:43.** The subst. (ὁ) κυλλός also has the special sense *(the) cripple, injured person* **Mt 15:30f** (acc. to Ael. Dion. χ, 23 the Attic writers used the word of hands and feet; κ, 43). κυλλοὺς ἰώμενος AcPl BMM verso 11.—DELG. M-M.

κῦμα, ατος, τό (Hom. et al.; PChicaginiensis col. 6, 15 p. 85 Coll. Alex. [II AD] κῦμα θαλάττης; PGM 5, 276 τὰ τ. θαλάσσης κύματα; LXX; PsSol 2:27; TestSol 16:2, 4; TestJob 33:6; ApcSed 8:9; EpArist, Philo; Jos., C. Ap. 2, 33) ***wave*** pl. **Mt 8:24; 14:24; Mk 4:37; Ac 27:41;** 1 Cl 20:7 (Job 38:11). As a figure of the inconstancy and stormy confusion (Appian, Bell. Civ. 3, 20 §76 ὁ δῆμός ἐστιν ἀστάθμητος ὥσπερ ἐν θαλάσσῃ κῦμα κινούμενον) of dissident teachers κύματα ἄγρια θαλάσσης *wild waves of the sea* **Jd 13** (ἄγρια κύματα as Wsd 14:1); GJs 3:3 (codd.).—B. 40. M-M.

κυμαίνω (Hom. et al.; LXX, Philo) **rise in waves, *surge, swell, billow*** ὥστε τὴν θ[άλασσαν σφόδρα κυμαί]νεσθαι *so that the sea surged exceedingly* AcPl Ha 3, 33.—DELG s.v. κυέω II.

κύμβαλον, ου, τό (κύμβος 'cup'; Pind. et al.; PHib 54, 13 [c. 245 BC]; PGM 4, 2296; 36, 158; LXX; Jos., Bell. 5, 385, Ant. 7, 80; 306; 11, 67; SibOr 8, 114) ***cymbal,*** a metal basin, also used in ritual observances; when two of them were struck against each other, a shrill sound resulted. κ. ἀλαλάζον *a clashing cymbal* **1 Cor 13:1** (s. ἀλαλάζω 2).—JQuasten, Musik u. Gesang in den Kulten d. hdn. Antike u. christl. Frühzeit 1930. FDölger, Antike u. Christent. I 1929, 184f: 'D. gellende Klingel' b. Pls 1 Cor 13:1; HRiesenfeld, Con. Neot. 12, '48, 50–53.—DELG s.v. κύμβη. M-M. TW.

κύμινον, ου, τό (a word of Phoenician origin, cp. Hb. כַּמֹּן; Hippocr., Theophr. et al.; PTebt 112, 13; 314, 19; PFay 101 I, 9; Is 28:25, 27) ***cuminum cyminum*** (Zohary, Plants 88), ***cum(m)in.*** The tiny fruits ('seeds') of the cumin, an annual herb, were tithed despite their slight value **Mt 23:23** (to show how relative this slightness of value was cp. Sb. 7667 [320 AD], a contract for the delivery of cumin to be paid for in advance).—Schürer II 263; Billerb. I 933.—M-M.

κυνάριον, ου, τό (Theopomp. Com. [V BC] 90; Pla., Euthyd. 298d; X., Cyr. 8, 4, 20; Epict. 4, 1, 111; IEph II, 506, 4; PGM 4, 2945; 2947; 2951. Rejected by Phryn. p. 180 Lob. in favor of κυνίδιον) dim. of κύων; a house-dog or lap-dog in contrast to a dog of the street or farm (s. B-D-F §111, 3; Mlt-H. 346f), but also used with no diminutive force at all (Plut., Arat. 7, 3) ***little dog, dog*** **Mt 15:26f; Mk 7:27f** (Eutecnius 1 p. 17, 11f, house-dogs that eat the scraps fr. the τράπεζα; cp. Ael. Dion., α, 159: ψωμὸς εἰς ὃν ἐκματτόμενοι τὰς χεῖρας μετὰ τὸ δεῖπνον ἐρρίπτουν τοῖς κυσίν. Similarly Paus. Attic., α, 134). AConnolly in New Docs 4, 157–59.—DELG s.v. κύων. M-M. TW.

κυνηγέσιον, ου, τό (s. two next entries; Eur., Hdt.+) ***animal hunt*** (usu. in pl., as e.g. OGI 529, 14; CIG 2511), instituted on some festival days by certain officials, e.g. in Smyrna by the Asiarchs. MPol 12:2. B. 190.

κυνηγέω (s. prec. and two next entries; later form of κυνηγετέω) 1 aor. ptc. pl. κυνηγήσαντες Just.; aor. pass. ἐκυνηγήθην ***to hunt*** (Pla., Aristot.; Gen 25:27; Jos., Bell. 1, 496; Just., D. 104, 1; Sb 6319, 47 [I BC]; pap, e.g., PSI 901, 13; 22 [46 AD]) πῶς ἐκυνηγήθης; *how were you captured?* AcPl Ha 5, 3.—DELG s.v. ἄγω.

κυνηγία (s. prec. and also next entry; trag., Aristot., Polyb. et al.; PTebt 339, 9) ***hunt,*** perh. in a transf. sense *display of animals, procession of animals* ἐποίε̣ι ὁ̣ Ἱερώνυμος κυν[ηγίαν] AcPl Ha 1, 33 (the mng. 'parade of animals' for this restoration can be derived from the context, but an alternate restoration κυν[ήγιον] (s. next entry) 'beast-hunt' (Lat. venatio) is also prob. The author had at disposal the term πόμπη, ordinarily used of solemn processions, had it been the intention to highlight that aspect (for the terms πόμπη and πομπεύω s. AcPlTh: Aa I 255, 5 and 11; 256, 5).

κυνήγιον, ου, τό (s. prec. entry; later form for κυνηγέσιον 'beast-hunt'; in var. mngs. since Polyb.; also Sir 13:19 ['booty']) pl. τὰ κ. ***beast-hunt*** involving humans fighting for their lives with animals AcPl Ha 3, 5.

κυοφορέω (κύος [=κύημα] 'embryo, fetus' + φορέω 'carry [for an extended time]', s. also κύω; Hippocr. et al.; M. Ant. 9, 3, 2; Eccl 11:5; Philo, Sacr. Abel. 102 and oft.; Just., D. 33, 4) ***be pregnant,*** metaph. ***be fruitful*** γῆ κυοφοροῦσα *the fruitful earth* 1 Cl 20:4 (cp. Philo, Opif. Mundi 43). Pass. *be conceived* (Artem. 4, 84; Galen XIX p. 174 K.) of Jesus ἐκυοφορήθη ὑπὸ Μαρίας *he was conceived by Mary* IEph 18:2. τὸν προφητικὸν λόγον ὃς ἐ[κ]υοφορήθη . . . ὑπ' αὐτῆς AcPl Ha 8, 27f=BMM recto 36.—DELG s.v. κυέω.

Κύπριος, ου, ὁ (Pind., Hdt. et al.; ins; 2 Macc 4:29; Joseph.; Tat. 41, 1) ***a Cypriot, an inhabitant of Cyprus*** Μνάσων τις Κ. **Ac 21:16;** ἄνδρες Κ. **11:20;** Κ. τῷ γένει **4:36.**

Κύπρος, ου, ἡ (Hom. et al.; ins; 1 Macc 15:23; 2 Macc 10:13; Philo, Leg. ad Gai. 282; Joseph., SibOr; Tat. 9:3) ***Cyprus,*** an island in the bay formed by the south coast of Asia Minor and the Syrian coast. From 22 BC it was a senatorial province governed by a proconsul (ἀνθύπατος, q.v.) Visited by Paul on his so-called first missionary journey **Ac 13:4.** But Christianity had already been brought there by fugitives fr. Jerusalem **11:19.** Cp. also **15:39; 21:3; 27:4.**—WEngel, Kypros 1841; AMurray-ASmith-HWalters, Excavations in Cyprus 1900; EOberhummer, D. Insel Cypren 1903; Pauly-W. XII 1924, 59–117; Baedeker 363ff; Ramsay, Bearing 150ff; EPower, Dict. de la Bible, Suppl. II '34, 1–23; Kl.-Pauly III 404ff; RGunnis, Historic Cyprus '36–'56; GHill, A History of Cyprus, 4 vols. '48–'52; TMitford, in ANRW II/7/2 '80, 1298–1308.—OEANE II 89–96. ABD I 1228–30.

κύπτω 1 aor. ἔκυψα ***bend (oneself) down*** (so Hom. et al.; LXX; En 14:25; JosAs 18:7) **Mk 1:7.** κάτω κ. *bend down to the ground* (Aristoph., Vesp. 279; Theophr., Char. 24, 8; Chariton 2, 3, 6; 2, 5, 5; Pel.-Leg. 23, 18) **J 8:6, 8 v.l.;** AcPl Ha 4, 12.—M-M. TW.

Κυρεῖνος Lk 2:2 v.l. see Κυρήνιος.

Κυρηναῖος, ου, ὁ (s. next entry; Hdt. et al.; OGI 767, 31; Michel 897, 26; PPetr I, 16 [1], 3; 22 [1], 3; 2 Macc 2:23; Joseph.) ***a Cyrenian*** (s. Κυρήνη) with the article **Ac 13:1** (Socrates, Ep. 28, 1 Θεόδωρος ὁ Κ.; Athen. 7, 14 p. 281c). Without the article **Mk 15:21; Lk 23:26** (Diod. S. 11, 84, 1 Πολύμναστος Κυρηναῖος).—Adj. ἄνθρωπος Κ. **Mt 27:32.** ἄνδρες Κ. **Ac 11:20.** In Jerusalem the Cyrenian Jews had a synagogue, either for themselves alone, or together w. other Jews of the Diaspora

6:9 (Schürer II 428; III 60f).—BZimolong, BZ 21, '33, 184–88; EBishop, ET 51, '39/40, 148–53; WBarclay, ET 72, '60, 28–31.

Κυρήνη, ης, ἡ (s. next entry; Pind., Hdt. et al.; ins; 1 Macc 15:23; Jos., Bell. 7, 437–46, Ant. 14, 114–18; SibOr 5, 198) ***Cyrene,*** capital city of the N. African district of Cyrenaica (Pentapolis); from 27 BC Cyrenaica was combined w. Crete as a senatorial province, and ruled by a proconsul. Cyrene was an old Greek colony, and many Jews settled there (Schürer III 60f). τὰ μέρη τῆς Λιβύης τῆς κατὰ Κυρήνην *the parts of Libya near Cyrene,* i.e. Libya Cyrenaica **Ac 2:10.**—LMalten, Kyrene 1911; Italian researches: RivFil, n.s. 6, fasc. 2; 3, 1928; UvWilamowitz, Kyrene 1928; PRomanellis, La Cirenaica Romana '43; EKirsten, Nordafrikanische Stadtbilder '61, 39ff; Pauly-W. XII, 156ff; Kl.-Pauly III 410ff; BHHW II, 1034; PECS 253–55; OEANE II 97f.—M-M.

Κυρήνιος (s. prec. entry; IG III/1, 599 [=IG II^2, 4143] Μᾶρκον Κυρήνιον; ARoos, Mnemos. 9, '41, 306–18), more correctly **Κυρίνιος** (B-D-F §41; Mlt-H. 72), **ου, ὁ** which is also found in some mss.***Quirinius*** (*P. Sulpicius.* Cp. Jos., Bell. 2, 433; 7, 253, Ant. 17, 355; 18, 1; 26; 29; 20, 102; Just.), imperial governor of Syria, mentioned in the NT in connection w. the census **Lk 2:2.**—Concerning him s. the lit. on ἀπογραφή and ἡγεμονεύω, also FSpitta, ZNW 7, 1906, 290–303; WWeber, ibid. 10, 1909, 307–19; Ramsay, Bearing 275–300, JRS 7, 1917, 273ff; WLodder, D. Schätzung des Qu. bei Fl. Josephus 1930; GOgg, ET 79, '68, 231–36; Schürer I 399–427; Boffo, Iscrizioni no. 23 (lit.: p. 182f); Pauly-W. IV A 1, 822ff; BHHW III 1536ff.—M-M.

κυρία, ας, ἡ (fem. form of the subst. adj. κύριος [q.v. I]. Rare and late as a proper name: Preisigke, Namenbuch 188; HBeyer-HLietzmann, D. jüd. Katakombe der Villa Torlonia '31, ins 41)

❶ **a woman of special status, *lady, mistress*** ἡ κ. τοῦ ἔργου *the housekeeper* prob. the one in charge of the household work assignments (cp. Tob. 2:12, w. ref. to 'employers') GJs 2:2. Used in addressing a definite person (Plut., Mor. 271d; Epict., Ench. 40; Cass. Dio 48, 44; POxy 112, 1; 3; 7; 744, 2=Ltzm., Griech. Papyri^2 1910, 7; letter in Dssm., LO 160 [LAE^2 193, n. 6]; κ. μου μήτηρ TestAbr A 3 p. 79, 25 [Stone p. 6].—LXX uses κ. to designate the mistress as opposed to the slave; so also JosAs; Philo, Congr. Erud. Gr. 154; Jos., Ant. 17, 137; 139; PTebt 413, 1; 6; 20) Hv 1, 1, 5; 1, 2, 2; 1, 3, 3; 1, 4, 2; 2, 1, 3; 3, 1, 3; 8; 3, 2, 4; 3, 3, 1; 4f; 3, 4, 1; 3; 3, 5, 3; 3, 6, 5f; 3, 8, 2; 5f; 4, 2, 2f; 4, 3, 1. Many take **2J 1; 5** in this lit. sense (e.g. BWestcott, The Epistles of St. John 1886, 214; HPoggel, D. 2. u. 3. Brief d. Apostels Joh. 1896, 127ff). For the less formal sense *dear* found in pap s. M-M. s.v.—Other scholars consider it more probable that

❷ κ. is fig. here and refers to Christians as a group: ***congregation*** (s. ἀδελφή 2b), and ἐκλεκτὴ κυρία is usually translated the *chosen* (or *elect*) *lady* (so BWeiss et al.; s. BBresky, Das Verhältnis des zweiten Johannesbriefs zum dritten 1906, 2ff; FDölger, AC V/3, '36, 211–17, Domina mater ecclesia u. d. 'Herrin' im 2 J; ABrooke, ICC; RBultmann, Hermeneia comm. On the precarious nature of ref. to Lex. Cantabr. [p. 79f, w. note p. 119f, Houtsma; also Demetr. of Phaleron: 228 fgm. 4 p. 961] s. H-JKlauck, ZNW 81, '90, 135–42). For the imagery of God's people as a woman s. Jer 4:31; 38:21; Zeph 3:14; Gal 4:25f; 1 Pt 5:13. The proposal (HGibbins, Exp. 6th ser., 6, 1902, 228f) to make ἐκλεκτή a proper noun and κυρία an adj. has little to recommend it.—DELG s.v. κύριος. M-M. TW.

κυριακός, ή, όν (s. κύριος) **pert. to belonging to the Lord, *the Lord's*** (oft. in ins [since 68 AD: OGI 669, 13; 18] and pap.='imperial' in certain exprs.: imperial treasury, service, etc. See Dssm., NB 44ff [BS 217ff], LO 304ff [LAE^2 362ff]; Hatch 138f; and πρῶτος 1aα end; Iren. 1, 8, 1 [Harv. I 67, 1; 6f]) κ. δεῖπνον *the Lord's Supper* **1 Cor 11:20.** κ. ἡμέρα *the Lord's day* (Kephal. I 192, 1; 193, 31; ὁ μὲν τέλειος . . . ἀεὶ ἄγει κ. ἡμέρας Orig, C. Cels. 8, 22, 6) i.e. certainly Sunday (so in Mod. Gk., and cp. POxy 3407 [IV AD]) **Rv 1:10** (WStott, NTS 12, '65, 70–75). For this κυριακὴ κυρίου D 14:1. Without κυρίου (Kephal. I 194, 9; 195, 6; Did., Gen. 190, 2) GPt 9:35; 12:50. τῷ σαββάτῳ ἐπερχομένης τῆς κ. AcPl Ha 3, 9. κατὰ κυριακὴν ζῆν *observe the Lord's day* (opp. σαββατίζειν) IMg 9:1 (on the omission of ἡμέρα cp. Jer 52:12 δεκάτῃ τοῦ μηνός and s. ἀγοραῖος 2). σύνταξιν τῶν κυριακῶν ποιούμενος λογίων *making an orderly presentation of the dominical words* Papias (2:15) (s. also ἐξήγησις end); κ. λογίων (11:1; 12:2); κ. λόγων (3:1); κ. ἐξηγήσεων (8:9).—SMcCasland, The Origin of the Lord's Day: JBL 49, 1930, 65–82; JBoehmer, D. christl. Sonntag nach Urspr. u. Gesch. '31; PCotton, From Sabbath to Sunday '33; WRordorf, Der Sonntag . . . im ältesten Christentum '62 (Eng. tr. AGraham '68); HRiesenfeld, Sabbat et Jour du Seigneur: TWManson memorial vol. '59, 210–17.—B. 1008. DELG s.v. κύριος. M-M. TW. Spicq. Sv.

κυριεύω (s. κύριος) fut. κυριεύσω; 1 aor. ἐκυρίευσα; pf. 1 pl. κεκυριεύκαμεν; aor. pass. subj. κυριευθῇ TestJud 21:4, ptc. κυριευθείς TestAsh 1:8 (X.+) gener. 'to be lord/master of'

❶ **to exercise authority or have control, *rule,*** of persons, w. gen. of that over which rule or control is exercised (X., Mem. 2, 6, 22; Polyb. 4, 18, 2; OGI 229, 56 [III BC]; Gen 3:16; 37:8; En 22:14; TestJos 3:2; ApcMos 24:25; Iren. 1, 25, 3 [Harv. I 206, 11]; Jos., Bell. 1, 39; Just.) οἱ βασιλεῖς τ. ἐθνῶν κυριεύουσιν αὐτῶν **Lk 22:25.**—**Ac 19:16 v.l.** θλιβέντα κυριεῦσαι αὐτοῦ *gain it through suffering* B 7:11. ἐντολῆς κ. *master a commandment,* i.e. make it one's own Hm 5, 2, 8. κ. τῆς πίστεώς τινος *lord it over someone's faith* **2 Cor 1:24.**—Of God (Theod. Da 4:25, 32; 5:21; En 22:14; EpArist 45; 269 δόξης πάσης; PGM 1, 214 ὁ κυριεύων πάντων ἀγγέλων; 12, 115 ὁ κυριεύων τοῦ παντὸς κόσμου) ὁ πάντων κυριεύων Hs 9, 23, 4. ὁ τοῦ παντὸς κόσμου κυριεύων B 21:5. Of Christ νεκρῶν καὶ ζώντων κ. **Ro 14:9.**—Abs. (En 103:12 οἱ κυριεύουσιν; Orig., C. Cels. 8, 4, 16; τὸ κυριεύειν Did., Gen. 113, 15) B 6:18. οἱ κυριεύοντες *lords* **1 Ti 6:15.**

❷ ***be master of, dominate,*** of things that take control of a pers., transf. sense of 1 and likew. w. the gen. (Sextus 41; 363a; Philo, Leg. All. 3, 187 πάθος; TestSim 3:2, Iss 7:7): of the law κυριεύει τοῦ ἀνθρώπου **Ro 7:1** (JDerrett, Law in the NT, '70, 461–71). Of sin **6:14.** Of death vs. **9.**—B. 1319. DELG s.v. κύριος. M-M. TW. Spicq.

I. κύριος, ία, ιον (Pind. et al.; ins, pap) comp. κυριώτερος (Just., A II, 13, 3); superl. κυριώτατος (Just., D. 11, 2); adv. κυρίως. The primary mng. relates to possession of power or authority, in various senses: 'strong, authoritative, valid, ruling'; then to that which is preeminently important ***principal, essential*** (Aeschyl. et al.; 4 Macc 1:19; Jos., Ant. 20, 41, C. Ap. 1, 19; 2, 177; Just.; Ath. 22:2) τὸ δὲ κυριώτερον *but what is more important* IMg 1:2 (cp. Diog. L. 4, 26 ἐν τῷ κυρίῳ=quite definitely).—DELG.

II. κύριος, ου, ὁ (the masc. form of the subst. adj. κύριος [s. I], Aeschyl.+; Appian, Bell. Civ. 4, 92 §385 [=ὁ τὸ κῦρος ἔχων]; ins, pap, LXX, pseudepigr.; Philo, Joseph., apolog.;

loanw. in rabb. For the corresp. fem. s. κυρία.) gener. 'lord, master'.

❶ **one who is in charge by virtue of possession,** *owner* (X., Symp. 6, 1; Diod. S. 4, 15, 3; 14, 7, 6; ins, pap, LXX) κ. πάντων **Gal 4:1** (Diod. S. 33, 7, 1; Philostrat., Vi. Apoll. 1, 13 p. 12, 10 of one who has come of age and controls his own property).

ⓐ of things w. impers. obj. κ. τοῦ ἀμπελῶνος *owner of the vineyard* (cp. SIG 742, 6 κ. τῆς χώρας) **Mt 20:8; 21:40; Mk 12:9; Lk 20:13, 15;** ὁ κ. τῆς οἰκίας *the master of the house* (Ex 22:7; SIG 1215, 28; PTebt 5, 147 [118 BC] τοὺς κ. τῶν οἰκιῶν) **Mk 13:35.** Of a πῶλος: οἱ κ. αὐτοῦ *its owners* (PHib 34, 3 a span of oxen; Ex 21:29 [αὐτοῦ=τοῦ ταύρου]) **Lk 19:33** (ASouter, Exp. 8th ser., 8, 1914, 94f, in connection w. the pl. here and Ac 16:16, 19 thinks of the owners as man and wife; the pl. οἱ κύριοι has this mng. Diod. S. 34 + 35, fgm. 2, 10 and 2, 37: a married couple who are slave-owners. On the other hand in the Syntipas collection of Aesop's Fables 16 p. 534 P. οἱ κύριοι of a dog are a number of metalworkers. On Hebr. background for possible understanding of the pl. in the sing. sense 'owner', s. RButh, JBL 104, '86, 680–85.). The mng. *owner* easily passes into that of *lord, master,* one who has full control of someth. (Diod. S. 5, 42, 5 θανάτου κύριοι=lords over [life and] death; 10, 17, 1 and 2 κ. τοῦ σώματος=master of one's own body; Ptolem., Apotel. 3, 11, 10 ὁ κ. τῆς ζωῆς; PsSol 2:29 κ. γῆς καὶ θαλάσσης; Philo, Spec. Leg. 3, 67; Jos., C. Ap. 2, 200) ὁ κ. τοῦ θερισμοῦ *the Lord of the harvest* (Jos., Ant.4, 227 κύριος ἔστω τὰ φυτὰ καρποῦσθαι) **Mt 9:38; Lk 10:2.** κ. τοῦ σαββάτου *Lord of the Sabbath* **Mt 12:8; Mk 2:28; Lk 6:5.**

ⓑ w. a personal obj.: opp. δοῦλος **J 13:16;** foll. by gen. of pers. (cp. Judg 19:11; Gen 24:36; TestSol 22:5; TestJob 7:9; TestGad 4:4; JosAs 4:14) **Mt 10:24f; 18:31f; 24:48; Lk 12:36.** ὁ κ. τοῦ δούλου **Lk 12:46.** Abs., though the sense is unmistakable (Diod. S. 8, 5, 3; ApcEsdr 3:14 p. 27, 27f Tdf.) **12:37, 42b; 14:23; J 15:15;** cp. **Ro 14:4a; Eph 6:9a; Col 4:1.** Several masters of the same slave (Billerb. I 430.—TestJos 14:2): δυσὶν κυρίοις δουλεύειν **Mt 6:24; Ac 16:16, 19** (s. Souter under a above). κατὰ σάρκα designates more definitely the sphere in which the service-relation holds true οἱ κατὰ σάρκα κ. **Eph 6:5; Col 3:22.** As a form of address used by slaves κύριε **Mt 13:27; 25:20, 22, 24; Lk 13:8; 14:22; 19:16, 18, 20, 25.**

❷ **one who is in a position of authority,** ***lord, master***—ⓐ of earthly beings, as a designation of any pers. of high position: of husband in contrast to wife **1 Pt 3:6** (Gen 18:12; TestAbr A 15 p. 95, 15 [Stone p. 38]; ApcMos 2. cp. Plut., De Virt. Mul. 15 p. 252b; SIG 1189, 7; 1190, 5; 1234, 1); of a father by his son **Mt 21:29** (cp. BGU 423, 2 Ἀπίων Ἐπιμάχῳ τῷ πατρὶ καὶ κυρίῳ; 818, 1; 28; Gen 31:35; by his daughter TestJob 46:2; JosAs 4:5); of an official in high position, by those who have dealings with him (cp. PFay 106, 15; 129, 1; 134, 2; BGU 648, 16) **Mt 27:63.** As a form of address to respected pers. gener.; here, as elsewhere, = our *sir* (as Mod. Gk.) **Mt 25:11; J 12:21; 20:15** (but s. NWyatt, ZNW 81, '90, 38); **Ac 16:30; Rv 7:14** (cp. Epict. 3, 23, 11; 19; Gen 23:6; 44:18; TestAbr A 2 p. 78, 33 [Stone p. 4]; JosAs 7:8 al.). The distinctive Gr-Rom. view of 'deified' rulers requires treatment under 2bβ.

ⓑ of transcendent beings—**α.** as a designation of God (for this custom, which has its roots in the Orient, s. the references in Ltzm., Hdb. exc. on Ro 10:9; Bousset, Kyrios Christos[2] 1921, 95–98; Dssm., LO 298f [LAE 353ff]; s. also SEG XXXVI, 350 and add. ins cited by DZeller, DDD 918f; LXX (where it freq. replaces the name Yahweh in the MT); pseudepigr.; Philo, Just.; Hippol. Ref. 8, 17, 1; Orig., C. Cels. 1, 35, 6.—FDoppler, D. Wort 'Herr' als Göttername im Griech.: Opusc. philol. v. kath. akad. Philologenverein in Wien I 1926, 42–47; MParca, ASP 31, '91, 51 [lit.]) ὁ κ. **Mt 5:33; Mk 5:19; Lk 1:6, 9, 28, 46; 2:15, 22; Ac 4:26** (Ps 2:2); **7:33; 8:24; Eph 6:7** (perh. w. ref. to Christ); **2 Th 3:3; 2 Ti 1:16, 18; Hb 8:2; Js 1:7; 4:15.** Without the art. (on the inclusion or omission of the art. s. BWeiss [θεός, beg.]; B-D-F §254, 1; Mlt-Turner 174), like a personal name (οὐδένα κύριον ὀνομάζουσι πλὴν τὸν θεόν Hippol. Ref. 9, 26, 2) **Mt 27:10; Mk 13:20; Lk 1:17, 58; Ac 7:49; Hb 7:21** (Ps 109:4); **12:6** (Pr 3:12); **2 Pt 2:9; Jd 5** (θεὸς Χριστός P[72]); **9.** ἄγγελος κυρίου (LXX, TestSol, GrBar et al.) **Mt 1:20, 24; 2:13, 19; 28:2; Lk 1:11; 2:9a; J 5:3 v.l.; Ac 5:19; 7:30 v.l.; 8:26; 12:7, 23.** δόξα κυρίου (Is 40:5; PsSol 5:19; 7:31; TestLevi 8:11; ApcMos 37) **Lk 2:9b;** δούλη κ. **1:38;** ἡμέρα κ. **Ac 2:20** (Jo 3:4); νόμος κ. **Lk 2:23f, 39;** τὸ ὄνομα κ. **Mt 21:9** (Ps 117:26; PsSol 6:1 al.); **Ac 2:21** (Jo 3:5); πνεῦμα κ. **Lk 4:18** (Is 61:1); **Ac 8:39;** τὸ ῥῆμα κ. **1 Pt 1:25** (Gen 15:1 al.); φωνὴ κ. (Gen 3:8 al.); **Ac 7:31;** χεὶρ κ. (Ex 9:3 al.; TestJob 26:4; ApcMos prol.) **Lk 1:66.** ὁ Χριστὸς κυρίου **2:26** (PsSol 17:32 [Χριστὸς κύριος, s. app.]).—W. the sphere of his lordship more definitely expressed (Diod. S. 3, 61, 5 Zeus is κ. τοῦ σύμπαντος κόσμου; 6 θεὸς καὶ κ. εἰς τὸν αἰῶνα τοῦ σύμπαντος κόσμου; Jos., Ant. 20, 90 τῶν πάντων κ.; Just., D. 127, 2 κ. τῶν πάντων) κ. τοῦ οὐρανοῦ καὶ τῆς γῆς (PGM 4, 640f; ParJer 5:32 [Harris]) **Mt 11:25; Lk 10:21;** cp. **Ac 17:24.** κ. τῶν κυριευόντων *Lord of lords* **1 Ti 6:15.** ὁ κ. ἡμῶν **1:14; 2 Pt 3:15; Rv 11:15** (LXX; PsSol 10:5). Cp. **22:6** (s. Num 16:22; 27:16). κ. ὁ θεός **Lk 1:32; Rv 1:8;** with μου (σου, etc.) **Mt 4:7** (Dt 6:16), 10 (Dt 6:13); **22:37** (Dt 6:5); **Mk 12:29f** (Dt 6:4f); **Lk 1:16** al. κ. ὁ θεὸς τοῦ Ἰσραήλ **1:68** (PsSol 16:3; TestSol 1:13). κ. ὁ θεὸς (ἡμῶν) ὁ παντοκράτωρ *God, the (our) Lord, the Almighty* **Rv 4:8; 15:3; 16:7; 19:6; 21:22** (TestSol D 4:7; cp. ParJer 9:6). κ. Σαβαώθ **Ro 9:29** (Is 1:9; TestSol 1:6 al.; Just., D. 64, 2); **Js 5:4.**—W. prep. ἐνώπιον τοῦ κυρίου **Lk 1:15** (Ex 23:17; 1 Km 1:25 al.; TestJob 15:6 al.; TestReub 1:9 al.). παρὰ κυρίου **Mt 21:42; Mk 12:11** (both Ps 117:23). παρὰ κυρίῳ **2 Pt 3:8.** πρὸς τὸν κύριον Hs 9, 12, 6 (LXX; PsSol 1:1 al.).

β. Closely connected w. the custom of applying the term κ. to deities is that of honoring (deified) rulers with the same title (exx. [2bα beg.] in Ltzm., op. cit.; Bousset 93; Dssm., 299ff [LAE 356]; FKattenbusch, Das apostol. Symbol II 1900, 605ff; KPrümm, Herrscherkult u. NT: Biblica 9, 1928, 3–25; 119–40; 289–301; JFears, RAC XIV, 1047–93; JvanHenten, DDD 1341–52 [lit.]; cp. the attitude of the Lacedaemonians: φοβούμενοι τὸν ἕνα κ. αὐτῶν τὸν Λυκούργου νόμον='respecting their one and only lord, the law of Lycurgus' Orig., C. Cels. 8, 6, 12). Fr. the time of Claudius (POxy. 37, 6; O. Wilck II 1038, 6) we find the Rom. emperors so designated in increasing measure; in isolated cases, even earlier (OGI 606, 1; on Augustus' attitude s. DioCass. 51, 7f). **Ac 25:26.**—On deified rulers in gener. s. LCerfaux-JTondriau, Un concurrent du Christianisme: le culte des souverains dans la civilisation gréco-romaine '57; FTaeger, Charisma, 2 vols. '57–60; DRoloff, Göttlichkeit, Vergöttlichung und Erhöhung zu seligem Leben, '70. S. esp. the collection of articles and reviews by various scholars, in Römischer Kaiserkult, ed. AWlosok '78.

γ. κύριος is also used in ref. to Jesus:

ℵ. in OT quotations, where it is understood of the Lord of the new community ἡ ὁδὸς κ. (Is 40:3) **Mt 3:3; Mk 1:3; Lk 3:4; J 1:23.** εἶπεν κύριος τ. κυρίῳ μου (Ps 109:1: the first κ. is God, the second Christ; s. Billerb. IV 452–65: Der 110. Ps. in d. altrabb. Lit.; βασιλεὺς αὐτῶν χριστὸς κ. [or κυρίου; s. 2bα] PsSol 17:32) **Mt 22:44** (cp. vss. **43, 45**); **Mk 12:36** (cp. vs. **37**); **Lk 20:42** (cp. vs. **44**); **Ac 2:34.** ὁ καυχώμενος ἐν κυρίῳ καυχάσθω **1 Cor 1:31** (cp. Jer 9:22f). τὸ ὄνομα κυρίου **Ro**

10:13 (cp. Jo 3:5). σὺ κατ' ἀρχάς, κύριε, τὴν γῆν ἐθεμελίωσας **Hb 1:10** (cp. Ps 101:26). εἰ ἐγεύσασθε ὅτι χρηστὸς ὁ κύριος **1 Pt 2:3** (cp. Ps 33:9). **1 Pt 3:15** adds Χριστόν to κύριον ἁγιάσατε Is 8:13.

ב. Apart from OT quots., Mt and Mk speak of Jesus as κύριος only in one pass. (words of Jesus himself) **Mk 11:3=Mt 21:3** (but s. RBratcher, ET 64, '52/53, 93; New Docs 1, 43; JDerrett, NovT 13, '71, 241–58 on the public transport system; cp. **Lk 19:31, 34**), but they record that he was addressed as 'Lord' (κύριε), once in **Mk (7:28)** and more oft. in **Mt**, e.g. **8:2, 6, 8, 21, 25; 9:28; 14:28, 30; 15:22, 25, 27; 16:22** (also ApcSed 12:2).—**Lk** refers to Jesus much more frequently as ὁ κ. (Iren. 1, prol. 2 [Harv. I 4, 5] and 5, 26, 2 [Harv. II 396, 2]): **7:13; 10:1, 39** ('Ιησοῦ P[75]; τοῦ 'Ιησοῦ P[45] et al.), **41; 11:39; 12:42a; 13:15; 17:5f; 18:6; 19:8** al. The voc. κύριε is also found oft.: **5:8, 12; 9:54, 61; 10:17, 40; 11:1; 12:41** al.—In **J** the designation ὁ κ. occurs rarely, in the first 19 chapters only in passages that are text-critically uncertain (**4:1 v.l.; 6:23,** with omission in some mss.) or that have been suspected on other grounds (**11:2**); then **20:2, 18, 20, 25;** cp. vss. **13, 28; 21:7ab, 12.** On the other hand, κύριε in address is extraordinarily common throughout the whole book: **4:11, 15, 19, 49; 5:7; 6:34, 68** al. (more than 30 times).—In the **long ending of Mk** we have the designation ὁ κ. twice, **16:19, 20.** In GPt ὁ κ. occurs 1:2; 2:3ab; 3:6, 8; 4:10; 5:19; 6:21, 24; 12:50ab; 14:59, 60 (in the last pass. without the art.); the fragment that has been preserved hardly affords any opportunity for the use of the voc. 2 Cl introduces apocryphal sayings of Jesus with λέγει ὁ κ. 5:2; λ. ὁ κ. ἐν τ. εὐαγγελίῳ 8:5.—Repeated κύριε, κύριε **Mt 7:21f; Lk 6:46;** 2 Cl 4:2 (TestAbr A 9 p. 86, 26 [Stone p. 20]; ApcMos 25 p. 14, 1 Tdf.; s. KKöhler, StKr 88, 1915, 471–90).

ג. Even in the passages already mentioned the use of the word κ. raises Jesus above the human level (Mani is also κ. for his people: Kephal. I 183, 11; 13; 16); this tendency becomes even clearer in the following places: ὁ κύριος **Ac 5:14; 9:10f, 42; 11:23f; 22:10b; Ro 12:11; 14:8; 1 Cor 6:13f, 17; 7:10, 12; 2 Cor 5:6, 8; Gal 1:19; Col 1:10; 1 Th 4:15b; 2 Th 3:1; Hb 2:3; Js 5:7f;** B 5:5; IEph 10:3; AcPl Ha 6, 21; 7, 5; 27; 8, 2; AcPlCor 1:6, 14.—Without the art. **1 Cor 4:4; 7:22b; 10:21ab; 2 Cor 12:1; 1 Th 4:15a; 2 Ti 2:24;** AcPlCor 1:8. So esp. in combinations w. preps.: ἀπὸ κυρίου **Col 3:24.** κατὰ κύριον **2 Cor 11:17.** παρὰ κυρίου **Eph 6:8.** πρὸς κύριον **2 Cor 3:16;** AcPl Ha 6, 9. πρὸς τὸν κ. 8, 23. σὺν κυρίῳ **1 Th 4:17b.** ὑπὸ κυρίου **1 Cor 7:25b; 2 Th 2:13.** Esp. freq. is the Pauline formula ἐν κυρίῳ (lit. on ἐν 4c), which appears outside Paul's letters only **Rv 14:13;** IPol 8:3; AcPl Ha 3, 23; AcPlCor 1:1, 16 (cp. Pol 1:1 ἐν κυρίῳ ἡμῶν 'Ι. Χριστῷ): **1 Cor 11:11; Phlm 16;** πιστὸς ἐν κ. **1 Cor 4:17;** cp. **Eph 6:21;** Hm 4, 1, 4; φῶς ἐν κ. **Eph 5:8.** ἡ σφραγίς μου τ. ἀποστολῆς ὑμεῖς ἐστε ἐν κ. **1 Cor 9:2.** W. verbs: ἀσπάζεσθαι **Ro 16:22** (GBahr, CBQ 28, '66, 465f renders: in the service of my master, i.e. Paul); **1 Cor 16:19.** ἐνδυναμοῦσθαι **Eph 6:10.** καλεῖσθαι **1 Cor 7:22a.** καυχᾶσθαι **1:31.** κοπιᾶν **Ro 16:12ab;** μαρτύρεσθαι **Eph 4:17.** παραλαμβάνειν διακονίαν **Col 4:17.** πεποιθέναι εἴς τινα **Gal 5:10.** ἐπί τινα **2 Th 3:4;** cp. **Phil 1:14; 2:24.** προΐστασθαι **1 Th 5:12.** προσδέχεσθαι **Ro 16:2; Phil 2:29.** στήκειν **4:1; 1 Th 3:8.** ὑπακούειν **Eph 6:1.** τὸ αὐτὸ φρονεῖν **Phil 4:2.** θύρας μοι ἀνεῳγμένης ἐν κ. **2 Cor 2:12.**—W. διδάσκαλος **J 13:13f.** W. σωτήρ **2 Pt 3:2;** cp. **1:11; 2:20** (Just., D. 39, 2). W. Χριστός **Ac 2:36;** cp. Χριστὸς κύριος (La 4:20; PsSol 17, 32 v.l. [GBeale, Christos Kyrios in PsSol 17:32—'The Lord's Anointed' Reconsidered: NTS 31, '85, 620–27]; PsSol 18 ins) **Lk 2:11.** ὁ κ. Χριστός AcPlCor 2:3. Esp. freq. are the formulas ὁ κ. 'Ιησοῦς **Ac 1:21; 4:33; 8:16; 11:20; 15:11; 16:31; 19:5, 13, 17; 20:24, 35; 21:13; 1 Cor 11:23; 16:23; 2 Cor 4:14; 11:31; Gal 6:17 v.l.; Eph 1:15; 1 Th 2:15; 4:2; 2 Th 1:7; 2:8; Phlm 5.**—ὁ κ. 'Ιησοῦς Χριστός **Ac 11:17; 28:31; Ro 13:14; 2 Cor 13:13; Phil 4:23; 2 Th 3:6; Phlm 25;** 1 Cl 21:6 (Ar. 15, 1). Without the art. mostly in introductions to letters **Ro 1:7; 1 Cor 1:3; 2 Cor 1:2; Gal 1:3; Eph 1:2; 6:23; Phil 1:2; 3:20; 1 Th 1:1; 2 Th 1:2, 12b; 1 Ti 5:21 v.l.; Js 1:1;** Χριστὸς 'Ιησοῦς κ. **2 Cor 4:5;** Χριστὸς 'Ιησοῦς ὁ κ. **Col 2:6.** Χριστὸς ὁ κ. 2 Cl 9:5. In an appeal κύριε 'Ιησοῦ (cp. Sb 8316, 5f κύριε Σάραπι; PGM 7, 331 κύριε Ἄνουβι) **Ac 7:59; Rv 22:20.** κύριε AcPl Ha 7:30f, 40.—W. gen. of pers. (in many places the mss. vary considerably in adding or omitting this gen.) ὁ κ. μου ISm 5:2. ὁ κ. ἡμῶν **2 Ti 1:8; Hb 7:14;** IPhld ins; ὁ κ. ἡμῶν 'Ιησοῦς **Ac 20:21; 1 Cor 5:4; 2 Cor 1:14; 1 Th 2:19; 3:11, 13; 2 Th 1:8; Hb 13:20.** 'Ιησοῦς ὁ κ. ἡμῶν **1 Cor 9:1.** ὁ κ. ἡμῶν Χριστός **Ro 16:18** (the only pass. in Paul without 'Ιησοῦς). ὁ κ. ἡμῶν 'Ιησοῦς Χριστός **Ac 15:26; Ro 5:1, 11; 15:6, 30; 1 Cor 1:2, 7f, 10; 6:11 v.l.; 15:57; 2 Cor 1:3; 8:9; Gal 6:14, 18; Eph 1:3; 5:20; 6:24; Col 1:3; 1 Th 1:3; 5:9, 23, 28; 2 Th 2:1, 14, 16; 3:18; 1 Ti 6:3, 14; Js 2:1; 1 Pt 1:3; 2 Pt 1:8, 14, 16; Jd 4, 17, 21** (also TestSol 1:12 D). ὁ κ. ἡμῶν Χριστὸς 'Ιησοῦς AcPlCor 2:5; cp. AcPl Ha 8, 17=Ox 1602, 20f//BMM recto 22. 'Ιησοῦς Χριστὸς ὁ κ. ἡμῶν **Ro 1:4; 5:21; 7:25; 1 Cor 1:9; Jd 25** (Just., D. 41, 4). (ὁ) Χριστὸς 'Ιησοῦς ὁ κ. ἡμῶν **Ro 6:11 v.l., 23; 8:39; 1 Cor 15:31; Eph 3:11; 1 Ti 1:2, 12; 2 Ti 1:2** (ὁ ἡμέτερος κ. Χριστὸς 'Ιησοῦς Just., D. 32, 3 and 47, 5 al.). Χριστὸς 'Ιησοῦς ὁ κ. μου **Phil 3:8.** ὁ κ. μου Χριστὸς 'Ιησοῦς AcPl Ha 7, 29. ὁ κ. αὐτῶν **Rv 11:8.**—W. other genitives: πάντων κ. *Lord over all* (cp. Pind., I. 5, 53 Ζεὺς ὁ πάντων κ.; Plut., Mor. 355e Osiris; PGM 13, 202) **Ac 10:36; Ro 10:12.** κ. κυρίων (cp. En 9:4) **Rv 17:14; 19:16.**—That 'Jesus is κύριος' (perh. 'our κύριος is Jesus') is the confession of the (Pauline) Christian church: **Ro 10:9; 1 Cor 12:3;** cp. **8:6; Phil 2:11** (on the latter pass. s. under ἁρπαγμός and κενόω 1. Cp. also Diod. S. 5, 72, 1: after Zeus was raised ἐκ γῆς εἰς τὸν οὐρανόν, there arose in the ψυχαῖς of all those who had experienced his benefactions, the belief ὡς ἁπάντων τῶν γινομένων κατὰ οὐρανὸν οὗτος εἴη κύριος; s. also 3, 61, 6 Zeus acclaimed 'God and Lord').—In J the confession takes the form ὁ κύριός μου καὶ ὁ θεός μου **J 20:28** (on the combination of κύριος and θεός s. θεός, beg., and 3c).—JFitzmyer, The Semitic Background of the NT Kyrios-Title: A Wandering Aramaean—Collected Aramaic Essays '79, 115–42; s. also 87–90.

δ. In some places it is not clear whether God or Christ is meant, cp. **Ac 9:31; 1 Cor 4:19; 7:17; 2 Cor 8:21; Col 3:22b; 1 Th 4:6; 2 Th 3:16** al.

ε. of other transcendent beings

א. an angel **Ac 10:4** (JosAs 14:6 al.; GrBar 4:1 al.; ApcZeph). p. 129 Denis.

ב. in contrast to the one κύριος of the Christians there are θεοὶ πολλοὶ καὶ κύριοι πολλοί *many gods and many lords* **1 Cor 8:5** (cp. Dt 10:17); we cannot say just what difference, if any, Paul makes betw. these θεοί and κύριοι; unless we have here an hendiadys, the apostle may imply that the κ. are of lower rank than the θ. (sim. Did., Gen. 248, 5. On the many θεοί and lesser divinities cp. Maximus Tyr. 11, 5ab θεὸς εἷς πάντων βασιλεὺς κ. πατήρ, κ. θεοὶ πολλοί, θεοῦ παῖδες [= δαίμονες 11, 12a], συνάρχοντες θεοῦ. Ταῦτα κ. ὁ Ἕλλην λέγει, κ. ὁ βάρβαρος; 8, 8ef. Also Diog. L. 8, 23 the saying of Pythagoras, that humankind must τοὺς θεοὺς δαιμόνων προτιμᾶν=honor the deities more than the divinities or demi-gods δαίμονες; Heraclitus, fgm. 5 divides the celestial realm into θεοὶ καὶ ἥρωες. S. also κυριότης 3 and, in a way, PGM 36, 246 κύριοι ἄγγελοι; s. also θεός 1).—On the whole word s. WGraf Baudissin, Kyrios als Gottesname im

Judentum u. s. Stelle in d. Religionsgesch., 4 vols. 1926–29; SvenHerner, Die Anwendung d. Wortes κ. im NT 1903; Dssm., LO 298ff [LAE 353ff]; BBacon, Jesus as Lord: HTR 4, 1911, 204–28; WHeitmüller, ZNW 13, 1912, 333ff; HBöhlig, D. Geisteskultur v. Tarsos 1913, 53ff, Zum Begriff κύριος bei Pls: ZNW 14, 1913, 23ff, Ἐν κυρίῳ: Heinrici Festschr. 1914, 170ff; WBousset, Kyrios Christos[2] 1921 [Engl. tr. JSteely '70]; PWernle, ZTK 25, 1915, 1–92; PAlthaus, NKZ 26, 1915, 439ff; 513ff; Heitmüller, ZTK 25, 1915, 156ff; Bousset, Jesus der Herr 1916; GVos, The Continuity of the Kyrios Title in the NT: PTR 13, 1915, 161–89, The Kyrios Christos Controversy: ibid. 15, 1917, 21–89; EWeber, Zum Gebrauch der κύριος-Bez.: NKZ 31, 1920, 254ff; ERohde, Gottesglaube u. Kyriosglaube bei Paulus: ZNW 22, 1923, 43ff; RSeeberg, D. Ursprung des Christenglaubens 1914; JWeiss, D. Urchristentum 1917, 351ff; Ltzm., Hdb. exc. on Ro 10:9; Burton, ICC Gal 1921, 399–404; WFoerster, Herr ist Jesus 1924; AFrövig, D. Kyriosglaube des NTs 1928; ELohmeyer, Kyr. Jesus 1928; EvDobschütz, Κύριος Ἰησοῦς: ZNW 30, '31, 97–123 (lit.); OMichel, D. Christus des Pls: ZNW 32, '33, 6–31; also 28, 1929, 324–33; Dodd 9–11; LCerfaux, 'Kyrios' dans les citations paul. de l'AT: ETL 20, '43, 5–17; FGrant, An Introd. to NT Thought '50, 130–37; PÉLangevin, Jésus Seigneur '67; IPotterie, BRigaux Festschr. '70, 117–46 (Luke); JKingsbury, JBL 94, '75, 246–55 (Mt); FDanker, Luke '87, 60–81; DZeller, DDD 925–28 (lit.).—B. 1330. Schürer II 326. DELG. M-M. EDNT. TW. Spicq. Sv.

κυριότης, ητος, ἡ (Memnon Hist. [I BC/I AD]: 434 fgm. 1, 4, 6 Jac. κ. πολλῶν='rule over many'; Achmes 229, 17 κ. λαοῦ; Soranus p. 10, 23 κ. πρὸς τὸ ζῆν='mng. for life'; Dositheus 1, 1, of the special mng. of a thing [w. δύναμις]; schol. on Pla. 111a κ. τῶν ὀνομάτων=meaning of the words. Elsewh. in eccl. writers and Byz. authors, as well as late pap: PCairMasp 151, 199 [VI AD] παρακαλῶ πάντα κριτὴν κ. δικαστὴν κ. ἐξουσίαν κ. κυριότητα; 132 ἐπὶ πάσης ἀρχῆς κ. ἐξουσίας κ. θρόνου κ. κυριότητος ὑφ' ἡλίῳ).

❶ **the essential nature of the κύριος,** ***the Lord's nature,*** w. ref. to God D 4:1.

❷ esp. **the majestic power that the κύριος wields,** ***ruling power, lordship, dominion*** (cp. θειότης as the essential aspect of θεός), ὁ υἱὸς τοῦ θεοῦ εἰς ἐξουσίαν μεγάλην κεῖται καὶ κυριότητα *the Son of God appears in great authority and ruling power* Hs 5, 6, 1 (κεῖμαι 3c). κυριότητα ἀθετεῖν **Jd 8** and κυριότητος καταφρονεῖν **2 Pt 2:10,** which is usu. considered dependent on it, is oft. (Ritschl, Spitta, HvSoden, BWeiss, Kühl, Mayor, Windisch, Knopf, Vrede et al.—FHauck leaves the choice open betw. 2 and 3) taken to mean the *glory of the Lord* which is rejected or despised by the dissident teachers. Perh. it is abstr. for concr., κυριότης for κύριος; s. the foll.

❸ **a special class of angelic powers,** ***bearers of the ruling power, dominions*** (cp. En 61:10; Slav. En 20; TestSol 8:6 D and s. κύριος II 2bεℶ) **Col 1:16; Eph 1:21;** AcPl Ha 1, 7 [restored].—GMacGregor, Principalities and Powers; the Cosmic Background of Paul's Thought: NTS 1, '54, 17–28. ADupont-Sommer, Jahrb. f. kleinasiat. Forschung 1, '50, 210–18.—DELG s.v. κύριος. EDNT. TW.

κυρόω (cp. κῦρος, τό 'supreme power') 1 aor. ἐκύρωσα. Pass.: fut. 3 sg. κυρωθήσεται Lev 25:30; aor. 3 sg. ἐκυρώθη Gen 23:20; pf. ptc. κεκυρωμένος (Aeschyl., Hdt. et al.; ins, pap, LXX, EpArist, Joseph.).

❶ **to give sanction to someth.,** ***confirm, ratify, validate, make legally binding*** (Dio Chrys. 59 [76], 1; SIG 368, 25; 695, 68f τὸ κεκυρωμένον ψήφισμα; OGI 383, 122; Michel 478, 6; other ins New Docs 4, 171; PAmh 97, 14; 17; PTebt 294, 16; EpArist 26; s. OEger, ZNW 18, 1918, 88ff) κεκυρωμένην διαθήκην ἀθετεῖν *set aside a will that has been ratified* **Gal 3:15.**

❷ **to come to a decision in a cognitive process,** ***conclude, decide in favor of*** (Hdt. 6, 86, 8; 6, 126; Thu. 8, 69, 1; Jos., Bell. 4, 362, Ant. 2, 18) κ. εἴς τινα ἀγάπην *decide in favor of love for someone* **2 Cor 2:8** (though perh. the act. may have the same mng. as the middle in Pla., Gorg. 451b=*make valid, affirm;* in the 2 Cor passage also *reaffirm* [as NRSV] deserves consideration).—DELG s.v. κύριος. M-M. TW.

κυσί see κύων.

κύτος, ους, τό (since Alcman [VII BC] 49 Diehl; Galen XIX 168 K.; Herm. Wr. 16, 8; LXX; Jos., Ant. 8, 79) ***hollow (place)*** τὸ κύτος τῆς ἀπείρου θαλάσσης *the hollow of the boundless sea* 1 Cl 20:6 (κύτος τ. θαλάσσης as Ps 64:8).—DELG.

κύω impf. 1 pl. ἐκύομεν Is 59:13; fut. 2 pl. κυήσεσθε Is 33:11 Sym.; aor. 3 sg. (Att.) ἐκύησεν (Mel., P. 52, 386); aor. pass. ptc. n. pl. κυηθέντων (Ath., R. 17 p. 69, 8) (later form of κυέω; Hom. Hymns et al.; PSI 167, 19 [II BC]; Is 59:4, 13; Philo; Joseph.) ***conceive, become pregnant*** (Jos., Ant. 1, 257) τῷ στόματι *through the mouth,* of the weasel B 10:8 (for the idea s. Windisch, Hdb. ad loc., and the passages given under γαλῆ; also TDuncan, The Weasel in Myths, Superstition and Religion: Washington Univ. Studies, Humanistic Ser. XII 1925, 33ff).—DELG s.v. κυέω I.

κύων, κυνός, ὁ (Hom. et al. in lit. and transf. sense, and either masculine or feminine)

❶ *dog* **Lk 16:21** (licking sores: SIG 1169, 37; IG IV, 951; cp. Aelian, NA 8, 9) **2 Pt 2:22** (Pr 26:11; cp. Paroem. Gr.: Gregor. Cypr. 2, 83 κ. ἐπὶ τὸν ἴδιον ἔμετον); PtK 2 p. 14, 20. As an unclean animal w. χοῖρος Ox 840, 33 (cp. Ps.-Aristot., Mirabilia 116 κύνες and ὕες as unclean animals that eat human filth; s. KRengstorf, Rabb. Texte, ser. 1, vol. III '33ff, p. 35f; but s. SLonsdale, Attitudes towards Animals in Ancient Greece: Greece and Rome 26, '79, 146–59 [lit. p. 158, n. 1]); this pass. is taken fig. of unclean persons (s. 2 below) by JJeremias, ConNeot XI, '47, 104f. μὴ δῶτε τὸ ἅγιον τ. κυσίν **Mt 7:6** (s. χοῖρος) must be a proverbial saying, and in its present context appears to be a warning against untimely or imprudent approaches to those in need of counsel or correction. Differently D 9:5 in the citation of this pass., s. 2.

❷ **a cultically impure person,** ***unqualified,*** the mng. assigned in D 9:5 to κ. **Mt 7:6,** a pass. that readily adapts itself to a variety of applications. Thus as early as the Didache the 'dogs' and 'swine' of the pass. were taken as specific referents to those who were unbaptized and therefore impure.

❸ **an infamous pers.,** ***dog,*** fig. extension of 1: in invective (as early as Homer; s. also Dio Chrys. 8 [9], 3; BGU 814, 19; Ps 21:17; Just., D. 104, 1) **Phil 3:2** (Straub 58); **Rv 22:15.** Dissidents are compared to mad dogs IEph 7:1 (s. Philo, Omn. Prob. Lib. 90. Μαρκίων ἢ τῶν ἐκείνου κυνῶν τις Hippol., Ref. 7, 30, 1).—Billerbeck I 477, 722f; III 621f, 773; Kl.-Pauly II 1245ff.—B. 179. DELG (read κύων). M-M. EDNT. TW.

κῶλον, ου, τό (Aeschyl. et al.='limb') in LXX and NT only pl., and in the sense ***dead body, corpse*** (1 Km 17:46; Lev 26:30; Is 66:24), esp. still unburied ὧν τὰ κῶλα ἔπεσεν ἐν τῇ ἐρήμῳ *whose bodies fell in the desert* **Hb 3:17** (cp. Num 14:29, 32).—DELG.

κωλύω impf. ἐκώλυον; fut. κωλύσω LXX; 1 aor. ἐκώλυσα. Pass.: fut. 3 sg. κωλυθήσεται Sir 20:3; 1 aor. ἐκωλύθην (Pind.+).

❶ **to keep someth. from happening, *hinder, prevent, forbid***

ⓐ in relation to persons abs. (X., An. 4, 2, 25b) **Lk 9:50; Ac 19:30** D. ἐάνπερ ὑμεῖς μὴ κωλύσητε *if you do not stand in the way* IRo 4:1. τινά *someone* **Mk 9:38f; 10:14; Lk 9:49; 11:52; 18:16; Ac 11:17; 3J 10.** W. λέγων and direct discourse foll. GEb 18, 39. Pass. ἐκωλύθην **Ro 1:13.**—τινά τινος *prevent someone fr. (doing) someth.* (X., Cyr. 2, 4, 23, An. 1, 6, 2, Hell. 3, 2, 21; PPetr II, 11 [1], 3 [III BC] μηθέν σε τῶν ἔργων κωλύει; SIG 1109, 100; cp. 1 Esdr 6:6.—Pass.: Iren. 1, 8, 2 [Harv. I 70, 7]) ἐκώλυσεν αὐτοὺς τοῦ βουλήματος *he kept them fr. carrying out their plan* **Ac 27:43.**—τινά *forbid* or *prevent someone* w. inf. foll. *to do* or *from doing someth.* (X., Cyr. 6, 2, 18; Herodian 1, 2, 4; Jos., Ant. 11, 61; Did., Gen. 110, 26.—B-D-F §392, 1f; Rob. 1089. On the omission of μή w. the inf., contrary to the usage of Attic Gk., cp. PMagd 2, 5 [222 BC] κεκώλυκεν οἰκοδομεῖν; PEleph 11, 6.—B-D-F §400, 4; 429; s. Kühner-G. II 214f; Rob. 1171) **Mt 19:14; Ac 24:23; 1 Th 2:16.** τινὰ τοῦ μή w. inf. *someone fr. doing someth.* **Ac 11:17** D. τί κωλύει με βαπτισθῆναι; *what is there to prevent me from being baptized?* **Ac 8:36** (cp. Ael. Aristid. 46 p. 240 D.: τί κωλύει ἡμᾶς ἐξετάσαι; Jos., Bell. 2, 395, Ant. 16, 51; Plut., Mor. 489b; Just., A I, 30, 1 s. OCullmann, D. Tauflehre des NTs '48, 65–73 [Eng. tr. JReid, '70, 71–80]). Pass. (X., Mem. 4, 5, 4; TestJob 39:2; Tat. 29:2) **16:6** (on the aor. s. Hemer, Acts 281f); **17:15** D; **Hb 7:23.** Of the flesh or old self τ. ἡδοναῖς κωλύεται χρῆσθαι Dg 6:5.

ⓑ in relation to things *hinder, prevent, forbid* τὶ *someth.* (X., An. 4, 2, 24; Diod. S. 17, 26, 5 τὸ πῦρ κωλύειν; Herodian 3, 1, 6; 1 Macc 1:45) τὴν τοῦ προφήτου παραφρονίαν *restrain the prophet's madness* **2 Pt 2:16.** τὸ λαλεῖν (v.l. + ἐν) γλώσσαις *speaking in tongues* **1 Cor 14:39.** W. inf. without the art. (Herodian 2, 4, 7; pap; Is 28:6; Jos., C. Ap. 1, 167) κ. γαμεῖν *forbid marriage* **1 Ti 4:3;** cp. **Lk 23:2;** Dg 4:3 (the specific mng. *forbid* in Philochorus [IV/III BC]: 328 fgm. 169a Jac.).

❷ **keep someth. back, *refuse, deny, withhold, keep back*** τὶ *someth.* τὸ ὕδωρ **Ac 10:47.** τὶ ἀπό τινος *someth. fr. someone* (Gen 23:6; TestSim 2:12; s. B-D-F §180, 1) **Lk 6:29.**—B. 1275; 1355. DELG. M-M. TW.

κώμη, ης, ἡ (Hes., Hdt.+; ins, pap, LXX; TestSol 5:12 H; TestJob; TestNapht 1:11; Philo, Joseph., Apolog.)

❶ **a relatively small community with a group of houses, *village, small town,*** with (and in contrast to [cp. Manetho: 609 fgm. 10, 247 Jac.; Diod. S. 1, 31, 7; Dio Chrys. 3, 38; 23 (40), 22; Herodian 3, 6, 9; EpArist 113; Jos., Bell. 4, 241, Vi. 235; 237]) πόλις (TestJob 9:5) **Mt 9:35; 10:11; Lk 8:1; 13:22.** (A πόλις ordinarily is walled, whereas a κ. is an open settlement, Schürer II 188.) W. ἀγρός **Mk 6:36; Lk 9:12.** W. πόλις and ἀγρός **Mk 6:56.** In the pl., used w. the gen. of a larger district, to denote the villages located within it (s. Num 21:32; 32:42 and oft. in LXX) **Mk 8:27.** Mentioned by name: Bethany (near the Mt. of Olives) **J 11:1, 30.** Bethsaida **Mk 8:23, 26;** Bethlehem **J 7:42.** Emmaus **Lk 24:13, 28.**—Also **Mt 14:15; 21:2; Mk 6:6; 11:2; Lk 5:17; 9:6, 52, 56; 10:38; 17:12; 19:30; Ac 21:16** D.

❷ ***the inhabitants of a village,*** fig. **Ac 8:25.**—B. 1310. DELG. M-M. TW.

κωμόπολις, εως, ἡ (s. κώμη, πόλις; Strabo 12, 2, 6 al. Freq. in Byz. authors) lit. a city that 'has only the position of a κώμη as far as its constitution is concerned' (Schürer II 188), in **Mk 1:38** someth. like ***market-town.***—DELG s.v. κώμη. TW.

κῶμος, ου, ὁ (Hom. Hymns, Hdt. et al.; SIG 1078 κῶμοι τῷ Διονύσῳ; APF 5, 1913, 180 no. 38, 5; LXX) orig. a festal procession in honor of Dionysus (cp. our festival of Mardi Gras), then a joyous meal or banquet, in the NT (as Polyb. 10, 26, 3; in the only two LXX pass. [Wsd 14:23; 2 Macc 6:4] and in Philo; Jos., Ant. 17, 65; SibOr 8, 118) only in a bad sense ***excessive feasting,*** w. μέθαι (cp. Philo, Cher. 92; Polyaenus 2, 2, 7 μεθύειν καὶ κωμάζειν) *carousing, revelry* **Ro 13:13; Gal 5:21.** Likew. w. πότοι (Epicurus in Diog. L. 10, 132; Plut., Mor. 12b; Appian, Bell. Civ. 1, 113 §526) **1 Pt 4:3.**—DELG. M-M. Spicq.

κώνωψ, ωπος, ὁ (Aeschyl., Hdt.) ***gnat, mosquito*** in a proverb διυλίζειν τὸν κ. *strain out a gnat* (s. διυλίζω) **Mt 23:24** (or is this a ref. to a certain worm found in wine, which Aristot., HA 5, 19, 552b describes as a κώνωψ?).—CTorrey, HTR 14,'21, 195f.—DELG.

Κῶς, Κῶ, ἡ acc. Κῶ (Meisterhans[3]-Schw. 128f.—The t.r. has Κῶν.) ***Cos*** (Hom. et al.; ins; 1 Macc 15:23 εἰς Κῶ; Joseph.), an island in the Aegean Sea **Ac 21:1.**—IKosPH; RHerzog, Koische Forschungen u. Funde 1899; ANeppi Modona, L'isola di Coo nell' antichita class. '33; KSudhoff, Kos u. Knidos '27; Pauly-W. XI 1467ff; Kl.-Pauly III 312ff; PECS 465–67 (lit.).—M-M.

Κωσάμ, ὁ (קֹסָם) indecl. ***Cosam,*** in the genealogy of Jesus **Lk 3:28.**

κωφός, ή, όν (s. next entry; Hom.+; ins, pap, LXX, TestSol, JosAs; Ar. 13, 1; Tat. 26, 3) prim. mng. 'blunt, dull'

❶ **pert. to lack of speech capability, *mute*** (Hdt. 1, 47, 3; Wsd 10:21; Philo, In Flacc. 20; Jos., Ant. 18, 135) ἐλάλησεν ὁ κωφός **Mt 9:33;** cp. vs. **32; 12:22ab; 15:30f; Lk 1:22; 11:14ab.**

❷ **pert. to lack of hearing capability, *deaf*** (Hom. Hymns; X., Cyr. 3, 1, 19 al.; fgm. of Ostanes A 15 [JBidez-FCumont, Les mages hellénisés '38 II p. 334]: it praises a θεῖον ὕδωρ, which heals all infirmities: ὀφθαλμοὶ βλέπουσι τυφλῶν, ὦτα ἀκούουσι κωφῶν, μογιλάλοι τρανῶς λαλοῦσιν; Ex 4:11; Is 43:8; Ps 37:14; Philo, Mut. Nom. 143 οὐδὲ κωφὸς ἀκούειν) κωφοὶ ἀκούουσιν **Mt 11:5; Mk 7:32, 37; 9:25; Lk 7:22** (**Mt 11:5; Lk 7:22** have also been taken fig. [so Parmenides 6, 7 κωφοὶ κ. τυφλοί of those without knowledge; Heraclitus B, 34; Epict. 2, 23, 22; 2, 24, 19; Tat. 26, 3 τυφλὸς κωφῷ debate in the manner of the *blind with the deaf;* Dio Chrys. 80 (30), 42 τυφλοὶ κ. κωφοί]: HHoltzmann; Wlh.; JMoffatt, ET 18, 1907, 286f; OHoltzmann; EKlostermann).

❸ ***deaf and mute*** (Philo, Spec. Leg. 4, 197; SibOr 4, 28) fig. of cult images, that neither hear nor answer (Hab 2:18; 3 Macc 4:16; JosAs; Ar. 13:1) Dg 2:4; 3:3, 5.—B. 320f. DELG. M-M. TW.

κωφόω (s. prec. entry; 'make blunt' or 'dull': ὀδύνας κωφοῖ='deadens pain' Hippocr., Liqu. 1, 1) in our lit. only pass.

❶ ***become deaf*** (Hippocr., Aphor. 4, 90 ed. Littré IV 524; Philo, Det. Pot. Ins. 175) ITr 9:1.

❷ ***be rendered speechless*** (Ps 38:3, 10; Philo, Conf. Lingu. 9) Hm 11:14.—DELG s.v. κωφός.

λʹ numerical sign = ***30*** (τριάκοντα) **Lk 3:23** D; Hv 4, 2, 1.

λαβ- s. λαμβάνω.

Λαβάν, ὁ indecl. (לָבָן; LXX, Philo, Test12Patr; Just., D. 134, 3 and 5.—In Joseph. Λάβανος, ου [Ant. 1, 278]) ***Laban,*** Jacob's uncle and father-in-law. Jacob's flight to him (Gen 28ff) as an example of his humility 1 Cl 31:4.

λαγχάνω 2 aor. ἔλαχον, subj. λάχω, ptc. λαχών; pf. 3 sg. εἴληχεν (Ath., R. 13 p. 63, 27; LMelazzo, Glotta 71, '93, 30–33), ptc. λελογχώς 3 Macc 6:1 (Hom.+) for its constr. s. B-D-F §171, 2; Rob. 509. Pass. of κληρόω.

❶ **to obtain someth. as a portion, *receive, obtain*** (by lot, or by divine will; Hom.+; IPriene 205, 2; PTebt II, 382, 5; 383, 14) τὶ *someth.* ἔλαχεν τὸν κλῆρον τῆς διακονίας ταύτης **Ac 1:17.** πίστιν **2 Pt 1:1.**

❷ **to be selected through casting of lots, *be appointed/ chosen by lot*** (Hom. et al.; Pla., Pol. 290e ὁ λαχὼν βασιλεύς; SIG 486, 9; 762, 12 λαχὼν ἱερεύς. Oft. used sim. in ins; Jos., Bell. 3, 390. In the broader sense 'befall': ApcMos 15 τὸ λαχὸν αὐτοῦ μέρος ἀπὸ τοῦ θεοῦ.) ἔλαχεν τοῦ θυμιᾶσαι *he was chosen by lot to burn incense* **Lk 1:9** (on the constr. s. B-D-F §400, 3; Rob. 1060; 1 Km 14:47 v.l. Σαοὺλ ἔλαχεν τοῦ βασιλεύειν).

❸ **to allot a portion or make an assignment by casting lots, *cast lots*** (Isocr. 7, 23; Diod. S. 4, 63, 3b) περί τινος *for someth.* (Ps.-Demosth. 21 Hyp. 2 §3.—B-D-F §229, 2; s. Rob. 509) **J 19:24.** λάχετέ μοι ὧδε, τίς νήσει τὸν χρυσόν *cast lots, now, for the one who will weave the gold* (for the temple curtain) GJs 10:2, w. some mss. adding καὶ ἔλαχεν τὴν Μαρίαν ἡ ἀληθινὴ πορφύρα *and to Mary fell the lot of* (weaving) *real purple* (i.e. high-quality fabric colored with the dye of shellfish rather than cheap imitations made w. vegetable or other dyes).—DELG. M-M. TW. Spicq. Sv.

λαγωός, οῦ, ὁ (epic and late for Attic λαγώς [λαγῶς]; Ps.-X., Cyn. 10, 2 and not infreq. in later writers [Phryn. p. 179 Lob.]; Ps 103:18 v.l.; Herm. Wr. p. 510, 2 Sc.) ***hare*** B 10:6 (s. ἀφόδευσις).—DELG s.v. λαγώς.

Λάζαρος, ου, ὁ ***Lazarus*** (לְעָזָר, rabbinic abbreviation of אֶלְעָזָר; s. Schürer II 375, 102.—Jos., Bell. 5, 567 Μανναῖος ὁ Λαζάρου; Thomsen, Ins. [s. Ἰάϊρος] no. 199).

❶ in J, brother of Mary and Martha, resident in Bethany in Judaea **J 11:1f, 5, 11, 14, 43; 12:1f, 9f, 17.** Following others, FFilson, JBL 68, '49, 83–88, identifies L. as the disciple whom Jesus loved. Likew. JNSanders, NTS 1, '54, 29–41.

❷ name of a beggar in a parable **Lk 16:20, 23ff.**—Jülicher, Gleichn. 621; HOort, Lazarus: TT 53, 1919, 1–5; HGressmann, Vom reichen Mann u. armen L.: ABA 1918; MvRhijn, Een blik in het onderwijs van Jezus (attempt at a new interpr. of Lk 16:19–31) 1924; HWindisch, NThT 14, 1925, 343–60; HÅkerhielm, Svensk exegetisk Årsbok 1, '37, 63–83; LLefort, Le nom du mauvais riche: ZNW 37, '38, 65–72 (s. Νινευής); on the relation betw. the reff. in J and Lk s. RDunkerley, NTS 5, '59, 321–27.—JDerrett, Law in the NT, '70, 78–99; RJensen, The Raising of Lazarus: BRev 11/2, '95, 20–28 and 45 (lit. n. 2).—BHHW II 1054. M-M.

λαθ- s. λανθάνω.

λάθρᾳ adv. (on the spelling with or without ι s. B-D-F §26; W-S. §5, 11c; Mlt-H. 84; Boisacq 549) (s. λανθάνω; Hom. [λάθρῃ] et al.; SIG 609, 6 [?]; UPZ 19, 28 [163 BC]; BGU 1141, 48; TestSol; TestJud 5:4).

❶ **(to do someth.) without others being aware, *secretly,*** used as adv. (Diod. S. 11, 88, 4; 11, 91, 2; Dt 13:7 λ. λέγειν; 1 Macc 9:60; Jos., Bell. 2, 408) opp. φανερῶς (TestSol 4:6; Diod. S. 16, 24, 2; Appian, Bell. Civ. 3, 91 §376; Cass. Dio 69, 13, 1) IPhld 6:3; cp. GMary 463, 13; ἀπολύειν **Mt 1:19** (so also GJs 14:1). ἐκβάλλειν **Ac 16:37.** καλεῖν (Jos., Vi. 388) **Mt 2:7.** ποιεῖν **Mk 5:33 v.l.** φωνεῖν **J 11:28.** λαλεῖν GMary 463, 13.

❷ **(to do someth.) without going through proper channels, *without the knowledge of, behind the back of,*** as prep. w. gen. (Hom.+; Diod. S. 5, 65, 4 λ. τοῦ πατρός; Sb 6222, 17; Ps 100:5 λ. τοῦ πλησίον αὐτοῦ) λ. ἐπισκόπου ISm 9:1.—DELG s.v. λανθάνω. M-M. Spicq.

λαθροδήκτης, ου, ὁ (s. λάθρᾳ, δάκνω; Phryn. in Bekker, Anecdot. p. 50; Chrysostom, Hom. 15, 4 on Eph 4:31 in MPG LXII 111 οἱ λαθροδῆκται τῶν κυνῶν.—Aesop, Fab. 332 P.=224 H.=Babr. 104 Cr. λάθρη κύων ἔδακνε; Paroem. Gr.: Zenob. 4, 90 κύων λάθρᾳ δάκνων) ***one who bites in secret, stealthily*** of dogs IEph 7:1.

λαϊκός, ή, όν (lit. 'belonging to the people, common'; a status term; PLille 10, 4; 7 [III BC]; PStras 93, 4 [II BC]; BGU 1053 II, 10 [I BC]; not LXX, but 1 Km 21:4 Aq., Sym., Theod.; Ezk 48:15 Sym., Theod., 22:26 Sym.; Ps.-Clem., Hom. p. 7, 38 Lagarde; Clem. Al., Strom. 3, 90, 1; 5, 33, 3 and in later Christian wrs.) **pert. to being unofficial, *lay*** as opposed to appointed officiants, ὁ λ. ἄνθρωπος *the layperson* 1 Cl 40:5. τὰ λ. προστάγματα *ordinances for the layperson* ibid. Here λ. is contrasted w. the OT priesthood, but clearly w. ref. to the situation within the Christian community.—Lampe s.v. 2. DELG s.v. λαός. TW. Sv.

λαῖλαψ, απος, ἡ (Hom. et al.; Plut., Tim. 28, 3; Sb 4324, 15; LXX; TestJob 42:1; Philo, Mut. Nom. 214; SibOr 8, 204) ***whirlwind, hurricane*** (Ps.-Aristot., De Mundo 4 p. 395a, 7 defines it as πνεῦμα εἰλούμενον κάτωθεν ἄνω) **2 Pt 2:17.** λ. ἀνέμου (TestNapht 6:4) *a fierce gust of wind* **Mk 4:37; Lk 8:23** (Semonides 1, 15ff Diehl³ ἐν θαλάσσῃ λαίλαπι κλονεύμενοι . . . κ. κύμασιν πολλοῖσι . . . θνήσκουσιν).—DELG. M-M.

λακάω (PGM 4, 3074 σίδηρος λακᾷ='iron breaks apart, bursts'; Hippiatr. I 423, 16f φλύκταιναι . . . διαλακῶσιν [as pres. ind.]='blisters burst'. Hence the ambiguous forms [Aristoph., Nub. διαλακήσασα 410; AcThom 33: Aa II 2 p. 150, 18b ἐλάκησεν; PGM 12, 197 λακηθῇ] are also to be referred to a pres. λακάω rather than λακέω [as B-D-F §101 p. 46; Mlt-H. 246]) ***burst apart, burst open*** ἐλάκησεν μέσος *he burst open in the middle* **Ac 1:18** (cp. Papias [3:1]).—See Beginn. V 22–30 for patristic material on the death of Judas.—DELG s.v. λάσκω. M-M s.v. λακέω.

λάκκος, ου, ὁ (Hdt., Aristoph.+; GDI 5056, 4; 5060, 60; 64 [Crete]; Sb 7167, 7; LXX, Test12Patr; ParJer 3:13; Philo; Jos., Bell. 5, 164; 7, 291 al.; Just., D. 19, 2) ***pit, den*** λ. λεόντων 1 Cl 45:6 (cp. Da 6:6ff; Jos., Ant. 10, 253).—DELG s.v. 1 λάκκος. TW.

λακτίζω (λάξ adv.: 'with the foot'; Hom. et al.; Herodas 7, 118; BGU 1007, 7 [III BC]; PTebt 798, 15 [II BC]; Jos., Ant. 4, 278) ***kick*** of draft animals, as a figure for unreasoning resistance: πρὸς κέντρα *against the goad* of the driver **Ac 9:6 v.l.; 26:14** (s. κέντρον 2).—DELG s.v. λάξ. M-M. TW. Spicq.

λαλέω impf. ἐλάλουν; fut. λαλήσω; 1 aor. ἐλάλησα; pf. λελάληκα. Pass.: 1 fut. λαληθήσομαι; 1 aor. ἐλαλήθην; pf. λελάλημαι (Soph.+). In older Gk. usu. of informal communication ranging from engagement in small talk to chattering and babbling, hence opp. of λέγω; in later Gk the trend, expressed esp. in the pseudepigr. and our lit., is toward equation with λέγω and broadening of the earlier usage.

❶ **to make a sound,** ***sound, give forth sounds/tones*** (Aesop fab. 248b H.//146 H-H.//202 Ch.//v.l. 141 P.) that form a kind of speech, esp. of inanimate things (e.g. of the echo, Cass. Dio 74, 21, 14; of streams of water Achilles Tat. 2, 14, 8; OdeSol 11:6 τὸ ὕδωρ τὸ λαλοῦν), of thunder ἐλάλησαν αἱ βρονταί **Rv 10:4ab.** ἐλάλησαν αἱ βρονταὶ τὰς ἑαυτῶν φωνάς vs. **3.** Of a trumpet **4:1** (cp. Aristot., De Aud. p. 801a, 29 διὰ τούτων=flutes, etc.; Achilles Tat. 2, 14, 8 of the κιθάρα). Of the blood of Christ, that *speaks more effectively than that of Abel* (Gen 4:10) **Hb 12:24;** s. **11:4** (Goodsp., Probs. 188). Cp. **J 12:29.**

❷ **to utter words,** ***talk, speak,*** of pers.—ⓐ of the act of speaking, intr.

α. *(be able to) speak;* to have and use the faculty of speech, in contrast to one who is incapable of speaking (cp. Ps 113:13; 134:16; 3 Macc 4:16; TestSol 10:3 C λ. ἀνθρωπίνως) **Mt 9:33; 12:22; 15:31; Mk 7:37; Lk 1:20, 64; 11:14.** ἐλάλει ὀρθῶς *he could speak plainly* (in contrast to the unintelligible utterances of a deaf-mute) **Mk 7:35.**

β. *speak, express oneself* (Aesop, Fab. 146 H-H. et al.) οὐ γὰρ ὑμεῖς ἐστε οἱ λαλοῦντες *it is not you who (will) speak* **Mt 10:20** (cp. TestAbr A 6 p. 83, 5 [Stone p. 14] ἄγγελος κυρίου ἐστὶν ὁ λαλῶν; AscIs 1, 7, τὸ πνεῦμα … τὸ λαλοῦν ἐν ἐμοί). προφῆται δύο ἢ τρεῖς λαλείτωσαν *two or three prophets are to express themselves* **1 Cor 14:29.** ἔτι αὐτοῦ λαλοῦντος *while he was still speaking* **Mt 17:5; 26:47; Mk 5:35; 14:43; Lk 8:49; 22:47, 60.** μηκέτι αὐτοῦ λαλοῦντος AcPl Ha 5, 14 of a lion (?); μηκέτι λαλήσας 10, 25=MartPl Aa I 115, 16.—**Lk 5:4; 1 Cor 14:11ab,** al.—In contrast to listening (Plut., Mor. 502c λαλοῦντι μὲν πρὸς τ. ἀκούοντας μὴ ἀκούοντι δὲ τ. λαλούντων) **Js 1:19;** cp. **1 Cor 14:35.**—In contrast to keeping silent (Lucian, Vit. Auct. 3) οὐκ ἤφιεν λαλεῖν τ. δαιμόνια **Mk 1:34; Lk 4:41** (λέγειν v.l.). λάλει καὶ μὴ σιωπήσῃς **Ac 18:9.** οὐ γὰρ ἐπιτρέπεται λαλεῖν (women) *are not permitted to express themselves* **1 Cor 14:34f** (cp. Plut., Mor. 142d: a woman ought to take care of her home and be quiet; for she should either converse with her husband or through him). This pass. refers to expression in a congregational assembly, which would engage not only in worship but in discussion of congregational affairs; the latter appears to be implied here, for it was contrary to custom for Hellenic women, in contrast to their privileges in certain cultic rites (cp. 1 Cor 11:5), to participate in public deliberations (s. Danker, Benefactor 164, w. ref. to IG II, 1369, 107–9; for other views s. comm.).—In contrast to acting **Js 2:12.**

γ. The pers. to whom or with whom one is speaking is mentioned in various ways: in the dat. λ. τινί *speak to* or *with someone* (Aristoph., Equ. 348; Philemon Com. 11 Kock; Menander, Periciromene 220 σοί; Aelian, Ep. 14 p. 181, 1; Diog. L. 9, 64; pseudepigr.; Just., A I, 63, 14. λ. ἑαυτῷ=with oneself; Lev 1:1f; Ezk 33:30b) **Mt 12:46ab, 47; 13:10; Mk 16:19; Lk 1:22; 24:6, 32; J 4:26** (cp. Ramsay, CB I/2, 566f no. 467–69 Ἀθάνατος Ἐπιτύνχανος says of himself: ἐγὼ εἶμαι ὁ λαλῶν πάντα); **9:29; 12:29; 15:22; Ac 9:27; Ro 7:1; 1 Cor 3:1; 1 Th 2:16; Hb 1:1f;** by πρός and the acc. (Plut. Mor. 502c [s. β above]; Ps.-Lucian, Asin. 44; Gen 27:6; Ex 30:11, 17, 22; JosAs 14:7 al.; ParJer 3:5; ApcMos 28; SibOr 3, 669; Just., D. 27, 3) **Lk 1:19, 55; Ac 4:1; 8:26; 11:20; 26:31** (cp. Lat. ire in consilium; Taubenschlag, OpMin. II 725 [the pap ref. is unsatisfactory]); by μετά and the gen. (Gen 35:13) **Mk 6:50; J 4:27; 9:37; 14:30; Rv 1:12; 10:8; 17:1; 21:9, 15.** μὴ διαλίπῃς λαλῶν εἰς τὰ ὦτα τῶν ἁγίων Hv 4, 3, 6.—The pers. or thing spoken about is expressed by περί w. the gen. (PSI 361, 5 [251 BC] λαλήσας περί μου; PFay 126, 4 [c. 200 AD]; Gen 19:21; Ezk 33:30a; TestAbr B 8 p. 112 14 [Stone p. 72]; TestJob 46:7; JosAs 6:2 al.; Philo, Fuga 33, 30a) **J 8:26; 12:41; Ac 2:31; Hb 2:5; 4:8.**—τινὶ περί τινος (PPetr II, 13 (6), 9 [III BC]) **Lk 2:38; 9:11;** pass. **Ac 22:10.**

δ. The speaking or uttering can be more closely defined: κακῶς, καλῶς **J 18:23.** ὡς νήπιος **1 Cor 13:11.** ὡς δράκων *(hissed?)* **Rv 13:11.** στόμα πρὸς στόμα *face to face* (cp. Num 12:8; ApcEsdr 6:6 p. 31, 10 Tdf.) **2J 12; 3J 14.** εἰς ἀέρα **1 Cor 14:9.** κατὰ κύριον **2 Cor 11:17.** ἐκ τοῦ περισσεύματος τ. καρδίας τὸ στόμα λαλεῖ **Mt 12:34; Lk 6:45.** ἐκ τῆς γῆς **J 3:31** (cp. Lev 1:1 λ. ἐκ τῆς σκηνῆς). ἐκ τῶν ἰδίων **J 8:44.** παρρησίᾳ **7:13, 26.** ἐν παρρησίᾳ **16:29.** ἐν παραβολαῖς **Mt 13:10, 13.** χωρὶς παραβολῆς **Mk 4:34.** λ. (ἐν) ψαλμοῖς *speak in psalms* **Eph 5:19.** Of prophets λ. ἐν πνεύματι D 11:7 (Just., D. 7, 1). Of God λ. διὰ στόματος τ. προφητῶν **Lk 1:70;** cp. **Ac 28:25.**

ε. as subst. ptc. τὰ λαλούμενα (Paradox. Vat. 2 Keller; Jos., Ant. 16, 321; Just., D. 7, 2) ὑπό τινος **Ac 13:45; 16:14.** τὰ λελαλημένα (EpArist 299; cp. TestSol 20:21 τὰ … λαληθέντα μοι) αὐτῇ παρὰ κυρίου **Lk 1:45.**—For λαλεῖν γλώσσῃ and λ. γλώσσαις s. γλῶσσα 3.

ⓑ of speech with ref. to what is expressed (the ability to λ. can generate λόγοι Aesop, Vi. G 7f P.), trans. *speak* and thereby *assert, proclaim, say* τὶ *someth.* (X., Cyr. 1, 4, 1 πολλά; Demosth. 45, 77 μέγα; Paradox. Vat. 2 τὰ ὀνόματα) τὰ ῥήματα τ. θεοῦ **J 3:34.** ῥῆμα **Mt 12:36;** cp. **J 8:20** (JosAs 14:14 al.; ParJer 3:4.). τὸν λόγον **Mk 8:32; J 12:48; Ac 4:29, 31** (λαλ. τι μετὰ παρρησίας as Jos., Ant. 16, 113); **8:25; 14:25; 16:6, 32.** τὰ μεγαλεῖα τ. θεοῦ **Ac 2:11** (TestJob 38:1). βλασφημίας **Lk 5:21;** cp. **Ac 6:11** (JosAs 13:9; Just., D. 32, 3). σοφίαν **1 Cor 2:6f.** μυστήρια **14:2;** cp. **Col 4:3.** τὰ μὴ δέοντα **1 Ti 5:13.** τὸ στόμα λαλεῖ ὑπέρογκα **Jd 16;** μεγάλα **Rv 13:5.** τί **Mt 10:19; Mk 13:11; J 12:49.** ὃ λαλεῖ **Mk 11:23;** cp. **J 10:6; 12:50.** ταῦτα **Lk 24:36; J 8:28, 30; 12:36; 17:1;** AcPl Ha 10, 11. ἐλάλησέν τι περὶ σοῦ πονηρόν **Ac 28:21** (cp. 3 Km 22:8, 13b; JosAs 12:5). ἐσύρετο μηδὲν λαλῶν (Paul) *let himself be dragged in without saying a word* AcPl Ha 4, 11.—Pass. λαλεῖταί τι *someth. is said, proclaimed, reported* (cp. the ins for mother and brother [APF 5, 1913, 169 no. 24, 8] ὧν καὶ ἡ σωφροσύνη κατὰ τ. κόσμον λελάληται, also Ps 86:3) **Mt 26:13; Mk 14:9;** cp. **Hb 2:3; 9:19** ἡ λαλουμένη διδαχή **Ac 17:19.** ὁ λαληθεὶς λόγος **Hb 2:2.** ἐλαλήθη ὅτι **11:18** (B-D-F §397, 3).—Oft., in addition, the pers. spoken to is mentioned, in the dat. ἄλλην παραβολὴν ἐλάλησεν αὐτοῖς **Mt 13:33.** ἐλάλει αὐτοῖς τὸν λόγον *he proclaimed the word to them* **Mk 2:2; 4:33; J 15:3; Ac 11:19.** ἐλάλησεν αὐτοῖς πολλὰ ἐν παραβολαῖς **Mt 13:3;** cp. vs. **34.** τὸ ῥῆμα … αὐτοῖς **Lk 2:50;** cp. **J 6:63.—8:40** (ἀλήθειαν λ. as **Eph 4:25** below); **14:25; 15:11; 16:1, 4, 6.** ἀνθρώποις λαλεῖ οἰκοδομήν **1 Cor 14:3;** w. πρός and acc. (Gen 18:19; Zech 8:16) λόγους … ἐλάλησα πρὸς ὑμᾶς **Lk 24:44** (cp. Dt 10:4).—**Ac 3:22; 11:14; 1 Th 2:2;** w. ἐν and the dat. σοφίαν λαλοῦμεν ἐν τ. τελείοις *we discourse of wisdom among those who are mature*

1 Cor 2:6; w. μετά and the gen. λαλεῖτε ἀλήθειαν ἕκαστος μετὰ τοῦ πλησίον αὐτοῦ **Eph 4:25** (cp. Zech 8:16). ὅσα ἂν λαλήσω μετὰ σοῦ Hs 5, 3, 2; cp. Hs ins.—W. the speaking definitely characterized ταῦτα ἐν παροιμίαις λελάληκα ὑμῖν **J 16:25a.** κατὰ ἄνθρωπον ταῦτα λαλῶ **1 Cor 9:8.** ἐν ἐκκλησίᾳ θέλω πέντε λόγους τῷ νοΐ μου λαλῆσαι **14:19.** πάντα ἐν ἀληθείᾳ ἐλαλήσαμεν ὑμῖν **2 Cor 7:14.** ἀφόβως τὸν λόγον τ. θεοῦ λαλεῖν **Phil 1:14.** λ. τι εἰς τὰ ὦτά τινος *communicate someth. to someone personally* (cp. Dt 5:1) Hv 3, 8, 11 (for 4, 3, 6 s. 2aγ above). λ. τι πρὸς τὸ οὖς *whisper someth. in someone's ear* (so that no one else hears it; cp. Jos., Ant. 6, 165) **Lk 12:3.**

❸ In a number of passages the content of the speaking is introduced by λέγων (s. λέγω 1bθℵ), just as in the OT (Gen 34:8; 41:9; 42:22; Ex 31:12; Lev 20:1; TestAbr B 12 p. 116, 28 [Stone p. 80]; TestJob 7:1 al.; ParJer 1:1; 1:6 al.; ApcMos 16) **Mt 13:3; 14:27; 23:1; 28:18; J 8:12; Ac 8:26; Rv 4:1; 17:1** al. Optional: εἶπον, q.v., end.—B. 1254. DELG. M-M. EDNT. TW.

λαλιά, ᾶς, ἡ (Aristoph.+, mostly in an unfavorable sense= 'gossip, common talk'; so also Sb 2266, 13) in our lit. always in a good sense.

❶ **content of speech,** ***speech, speaking*** (Epict. 3, 16, 1; Himerius, Or. 64 [=Or. 18] superscription [of a speech by Himerius]; Ps.-Callisth. 1, 17, 3; Is 11:3; SSol 4:3; Job 33:1; 2 Macc 8:7; TestReub 2:6; GrBar 6:16; Jos., Bell. 2, 132) οὐκ εἰσὶν λόγοι οὐδὲ λαλιαί *there is neither word nor speech* 1 Cl 27:7 (Ps 18:4). διὰ τ. σὴν λ. *because of what you said* **J 4:42.**

❷ **manner of expressing oneself,** ***form of speech, way of speaking*** (Hellen. acc. to Moeris 203 P.).—ⓐ lit., of dialectal peculiarities **Mt 26:73; Mk 14:70 v.l.** (s. Zahn, Einl. I[3] 19.—Similarly Ps.-Callisth. 2, 15, 7 of Alexander at the Persian court: ἡ φωνὴ αὐτὸν ἤλεγξε; cp. γλῶ[ττα] in this sense Acta Alex. III, col. 3, 12).

ⓑ of the characteristic way in which Jesus spoke **J 8:43.**—DELG s.v. λαλέω. M-M.

λαμά (לָמָה, Aram. לְמָא) *why?* **Mt 27:46 v.l.; Mk 15:34 v.l.** (s. λεμά).—M-M.

λαμβάνω (Hom.+) impf. ἐλάμβανον; fut. λήμψομαι (PTurin II, 3, 48; POxy 1664, 12; on the μ s. Mayser 194f; Thackeray 108ff; B-D-F §101; W-S. §5, 30; Mlt-H. 106; 246f; Reinhold 46f; WSchulze, Orthographica 1894.—On the middle s. B-D-F §77); 2 aor. ἔλαβον, impv. λάβε (B-D-F §101 p. 53 s.v. λαμβάνειν; W-S. §6, 7d; Mlt-H. 209 n. 1), impv. 3 pl. λαβέτωσαν (LXX; GJs 4:2); pf. εἴληφα (DRinge, Glotta 62, '84, 125–28), 2 sing. εἴληφας and εἴληφες **Rv 11:17 v.l.** (W-S. §13, 16 note; Mlt-H. 221), ptc. εἰληφώς. Pass.: fut. 3 pl. λημφθήσονται Jdth 6:9; aor. εἰλήφθην LXX; pf. 3 sing. εἴληπται; plpf. 3 sg. εἴληπτο (Just., D. 132, 3). For Attic inscriptional forms s. Threatte II 645. In the following divisions, nos. 1–9 focus on an active role, whereas 10 suggests passivity.

❶ **to get hold of someth. by laying hands on or grasping someth., directly or indirectly,** ***take, take hold of, grasp, take in hand*** ἄρτον (Diod. S. 14, 105, 3 ῥάβδον; TestSol 2:8 D τὴν σφραγῖδα; TestJob 23:10 ψαλίδα) **Mt 26:26a; Mk 14:22a; Ac 27:35.** τ. βιβλίον (Tob 7:14) **Rv 5:8f.** τ. κάλαμον **Mt 27:30.** λαμπάδας *take (in hand)* (Strattis Com. [V BC], fgm. 37 K. λαβόντες λαμπάδας) **25:1, 3.** λαβέτωσαν ἀνὰ λαμπάδα GJs 7:2. μάχαιραν *draw the sword* (Gen 34:25; Jos., Vi. 173 [cp. JosAs 23:2 τὴν ῥομφαίαν]) **Mt 26:52.** Abs. λάβετε *take* (this) **Mt 26:26b; Mk 14:22b.**—*Take hold of* (me) GHb 356, 39=ISm 3:2.—ἔλαβέ με ἡ μήτηρ μου τὸ ἅγιον πνεῦμα ἐν μιᾷ τῶν τριχῶν μου *my mother, the Holy Spirit, took me by one of my hairs* GHb 20, 63. Ἐλισάβεδ . . . λαβουμένη (λαβοῦσα codd.) αὐτὸν ἀνέβη ἐν τῇ ὀρεινῇ *E. took (John) and went up into the hill-country* GJs 22:3. λαβών is somet. used somewhat pleonastically to enliven the narrative, as in Hom. (Od. 24, 398) and dramatists (Soph., Oed. R. 1391 et al.), but also in accord w. Hebr. usage (JViteau, Étude sur le Grec du NT 1893, 191; Dalman, Worte 16ff; Wlh., Einleitung[2] 1911, 14; B-D-F §419, 1 and 2; s. Rob. 1127; s., e.g., ApcBar 2:1 λαβών με ἤγαγε; Josh 2:4; Horapollo 2, 88 τούτους λαβὼν κατορύττει) **Mt 13:31, 33; Mk 9:36; Lk 13:19, 21; J 12:3; Ac 9:25; 16:3;** Hs 5, 2, 4. The ptc. can here be rendered by the prep. *with* (B-D-F §418, 5; Rob. 1127) λαβὼν τὴν σπεῖραν ἔρχεται *he came with a detachment* **J 18:3** (cp. Soph., Trach. 259 στρατὸν λαβὼν ἔρχεται; ApcrEsd 6, 17 p. 31, 24 Tdf. λαβὼν . . . στρατιὰν ἀγγέλων). λαβὼν τὸ αἷμα . . . τὸν λαὸν ἐρράντισε *with the blood he sprinkled the people* **Hb 9:19** (cp. ParJer 9:32 λαβόντες τὸν λίθον ἔθηκαν ἐπὶ τὸ μνῆμα αὐτοῦ 'they crowned his tomb with a stone'; Mel., P. 14, 88 λαβόντες δὲ τὸ . . . αἷμα). Different is the periphrastic aor. ptc. use of λ. w. ἔχει: Dg 10:6 ἃ παρὰ τοῦ θεοῦ λαβὼν ἔχει *what the pers. has received fr. God* (cp. Eur., Bacchae 302 μεταλαβὼν ἔχει; Goodwin §47; Gildersleeve, Syntax §295; Schwyzer I, 812). Freq. parataxis takes the place of the ptc. constr. (B-D-F §419, 5) ἔλαβε τὸν Ἰησοῦν καὶ ἐμαστίγωσεν (instead of λαβὼν τ. Ἰ. ἐ.) *he had Jesus scourged* **J 19:1.** λαβεῖν τὸν ἄρτον . . . καὶ βαλεῖν *throw the bread* **Mt 15:26; Mk 7:27.** ἔλαβον τὰ ἱμάτια αὐτοῦ καὶ ἐποίησαν τέσσερα μέρη *they divided his garments into four parts* **J 19:23.**—In transf. sense ἀφορμὴν λ. *find opportunity* **Ro 7:8, 11** (s. ἀφορμή); ὑπόδειγμα λ. *take as an example* **Js 5:10;** so also λ. alone, λάβωμεν Ἐνώχ 1 Cl 9:3.—Of the cross as a symbol of the martyr's death *take upon oneself* **Mt 10:38** (cp. Pind., P. 2, 93 [171] λ. ζυγόν). We may class here ἔλαβεν τὰ ἱμάτια αὐτοῦ *he put his clothes on* **J 13:12** (cp. Hdt. 2, 37; 4, 78; GrBar 9:7 τὸν ὄφιν ἔλαβεν ἔνδυμα). Prob. sim. μορφὴν δούλου λ. *put on the form of a slave* **Phil 2:7.**—Of food and drink *take* (cp. Bel 37 Theod.) **Mk 15:23.** ὅτε ἔλαβεν τὸ ὄξος **J 19:30;** λαβὼν τροφὴν ἐνίσχυσεν **Ac 9:19;** τροφὴν . . . λα[βεῖν] AcPl Ha 1, 19. (βρέφος) ἔλαβε μασθὸν ἐκ τῆς μητρὸς αὐτοῦ Μαρίας (the infant) *took the breast of his mother Mary* GJs 19:2.—**1 Ti 4:4** (s. 10b below) could also belong here.

❷ **to take away,** ***remove*** (τὴν ψυχήν ApcEsdr 6:16 p. 31, 23 Tdf.) with or without the use of force τὰ ἀργύρια *take away the silver coins* (fr. the temple) **Mt 27:6.** τὰς ἀσθενείας *diseases* **8:17.** τὸν στέφανον **Rv 3:11.** τὴν εἰρήνην ἐκ τῆς γῆς *remove peace from the earth* **6:4** (λ. τι ἐκ as UPZ 125, 13 ὃ εἴληφεν ἐξ οἴκου; 2 Ch 16:2; TestSol 4:15 D; TestAbr B 7 p. 111, 12 [Stone p. 70]; Mel., P. 55, 403).

❸ **to take into one's possession,** ***take, acquire*** τί *someth.* τὸν χιτῶνα **Mt 5:40.** οὐδὲ ἕν **J 3:27.** ἑαυτῷ βασιλείαν *obtain kingly power for himself* **Lk 19:12** (cp. Jos., Ant. 13, 220). λ. γυναῖκα *take a wife* (Eur., Alc. 324; X., Cyr. 8, 4, 16; Gen 4:19; 6:2; Tob 1:9; TestSol 26:1; TestJob 45:3; ParJer 8:3; Jos., Ant. 1, 253; Just., D. 116, 3; 141, 4) **Mk 12:19–21; 22 v.l.; Lk 20:28–31** (s. also the vv.ll. in **14:20** and **1 Cor 7:28**). Of his life, that Jesus voluntarily gives up, in order to *take possession of* it again on his own authority **J 10:18a.** [ἀπολείπ]ετε τὸ σκότος, λάβεται τὸ φῶς *[abandon] the darkness, seize the light* AcPl Ha 8, 32. ἑαυτῷ τ. τιμὴν λ. *take the honor upon oneself* **Hb 5:4.**—*Lay hands on, seize* w. acc. of the pers. who is seized by force (Hom. et al.; LXX; mid. w. gen. Just., A II, 2, 10, D. 105, 3) **Mt 21:35, 39; Mk 12:3, 8.** Of an evil spirit that seizes the sick man **Lk 9:39** (cp. PGM 7, 613 εἴλημπται ὑπὸ τοῦ δαίμονος; TestSol 17:2 εἰ λήμψομαί τινα, εὐθέως ἀναιρῶ αὐτὸν τῷ ξίφει; Jos.,

Ant. 4, 119 ὅταν ἡμᾶς τὸ τοῦ θεοῦ λάβῃ πνεῦμα; Just., A I, 18, 4 ψυχαῖς ἀποθανόντων λαμβανόμενοι).—Esp. of feelings, emotions *seize, come upon* τινά *someone* (Hom. et al.; Ex 15:15; Wsd 11:12; Jos., Ant. 2, 139; 14, 57) ἔκστασις ἔλαβεν ἅπαντας *amazement seized (them) all* **Lk 5:26.** φόβος **7:16.** Sim. πειρασμὸς ὑμᾶς οὐκ εἴληφεν εἰ μὴ ἀνθρώπινος **1 Cor 10:13.**—Of hunting and fishing: *catch* (X., Cyr. 1, 4, 9; Aelian, VH 4, 14) οὐδέν **Lk 5:5=J 21:6 v.l.** Fig. εἴ τις λαμβάνει (ὑμᾶς) *if someone puts something over on you, takes advantage of you* **2 Cor 11:20** (the exx. cited in Field, Notes, 184f refer to material plunder, whereas Paul appears to point to efforts of his opposition to control the Corinthians' thinking for their own political purposes; also s. CLattey, JTS 44, '43, 148); in related vein δόλῳ τινὰ λ. *catch someone by a trick* **12:16.**

❹ **to take payment,** ***receive, accept,*** of taxes, etc. *collect* the two-drachma tax **Mt 17:24;** *tithes* **Hb 7:8f;** portion of the fruit as rent **Mt 21:34.** τὶ ἀπό τινος *someth. fr. someone* (Plut., Mor. 209d, Aem. Paul. 5, 9) **17:25.** παρὰ τῶν γεωργῶν λ. ἀπὸ τῶν καρπῶν *collect a share of the fruit fr. the vinedressers* **Mk 12:2.**—τὶ παρά τινος *someth. fr. someone* (Aristarch. Sam. p. 352, 4; Jos., Ant. 5, 275; Just., D. 22, 11; Tat. 19, 1) οὐ παρὰ ἀνθρώπου τὴν μαρτυρίαν λ. *the testimony which I receive is not from a human being* or *I will not accept mere human testimony* (PSI 395, 6 [241 BC] σύμβολον λαβὲ παρ' αὐτῶν=have them give you a receipt) **J 5:34;** cp. vs. **44; 3:11, 32f.**

❺ **to include in an experience,** ***take up, receive*** τινὰ *someone* εἰς *into* (Wsd 8:18) lit. εἰς τὸ πλοῖον *take someone (up) into the boat* **J 6:21.** εἰς οἰκίαν *receive someone into one's house* **2J 10.** εἰς τὰ ἴδια *into his own home* **J 19:27.** *Receive someone* in the sense of recognizing the other's authority **J 1:12; 5:43ab; 13:20abcd.**—οἱ ὑπηρέται ῥαπίσμασιν αὐτὸν ἔλαβον **Mk 14:65** does not mean 'the servants took him into custody with blows' (BWeiss, al.), but is a colloquialism (s. B-D-F §198, 3, w. citation of AcJo 90 [Aa II 196, 1] τί εἰ ῥαπίσμασίν μοι ἔλαβες; 'what if you had laid blows on me?') *the servants treated him to blows* (Moffatt: 'treated him to cuffs and slaps'), or even *'got' him w. blows, 'worked him over'* (perh. a Latinism; Cicero, Tusc. 2, 14, 34 verberibus accipere. B-D-F §5, 3b; s. Rob. 530f); the v.l. ἔβαλον is the result of failure to recognize this rare usage. καλῶς ἔλαβόν σε; *have* (the young women) *treated you well?* Hs 9, 11, 8.

❻ **to make a choice,** ***choose, select*** πᾶς ἀρχιερεὺς ἐξ ἀνθρώπων λαμβανόμενος *who is chosen fr. among human beings* **Hb 5:1** (cp. Num 8:6; Am 2:11; Just., D. 130, 3). The emphasis is not on gender but the human status of the chief priest in contrast to that of the unique Messiah vs. 5.

❼ **to accept as true,** ***receive*** τὶ *someth.* fig. τὰ ῥήματά τινος *receive someone's words* (and use them as a guide) **J 12:48; 17:8;** AcPl Ha 1, 6 (s. καρδία 1bβ). τὸν λόγον *receive the teaching* **Mt 13:20; Mk 4:16** (for μετὰ χαρᾶς λ. cp. PIand 13, 18 ἵνα μετὰ χαρᾶς σε ἀπολάβωμεν).

❽ **to enter into a close relationship,** ***receive, make one's own, apprehend/comprehend*** mentally or spiritually (Soph., Pla. et al.) of the mystical apprehension of Christ (opp. κατελήμφθην ὑπὸ Χριστοῦ) ἔλαβον (i.e. Χριστόν) *I have made (him) my own* **Phil 3:12.**

❾ Special uses: the OT is the source of λαμβάνειν πρόσωπον *show partiality/favoritism* (s. πρόσωπον 1bα end) **Lk 20:21; Gal 2:6;** B 19:4; D 4:3.—θάρσος λ. *take courage* s. θάρσος; πεῖράν τινος λ. *try someth.* (Pla., Prot. 342a; 348a, Gorg. 448a; X., Cyr. 6, 1, 28; Polyb. 1, 75, 7; 2, 32, 5; 5, 100, 10; Aelian, VH 12, 22; Dt 28:56; Jos., Ant. 8, 166; diff. Dio Chrys. 50, 6) **Hb 11:29** (this expr. has a different mng. in vs. **36;** s. 10b below).—συμβούλιον λαμβάνειν *consult (with someone),* lit. 'take counsel', is a Latinism (consilium capere; s. B-D-F §5, 3b; Rob. 109) **Mt 27:7; 28:12;** w. ὅπως foll. **22:15;** foll. by κατά τινος *against someone* and ὅπως **12:14;** foll. by κατά τινος and ὥστε **27:1.** οὐ λήψῃ βουλὴν πονηρὰν κατὰ τοῦ πλησίον σου D 2:6.

❿ **to be a receiver,** ***receive, get, obtain***—ⓐ abs. λαβών (of a hungry hog) *when it has received someth.* B 10:3. (Opp. αἰτεῖν, as Appian, fgm. [I p. 532–36 Viereck-R.] 23 αἰτεῖτε καὶ λαμβάνετε; PGM 4, 2172) **Mt 7:8; Lk 11:10; J 16:24.** (Opp. διδόναι as Thu. 2, 97, 4 λαμβάνειν μᾶλλον ἢ διδόναι; Ael. Aristid. 34 p. 645 D.; Herm. Wr. 5, 10b; Philo, Deus Imm. 57; SibOr 3, 511) **Mt 10:8; Ac 20:35;** B 14:1; but in D 1:5 λ. rather has the 'active' sense *accept a donation* (as ἵνα λάβῃ ἐξουσίαν TestJob 8:2).

ⓑ w. acc. of thing τὶ *someth.* (Da 2:6; OdeSol 11:4 σύνεσιν; TestJob 24:9 τρεῖς ἄρτους al.; ApcEsdr 5:13 p. 30, 11 Tdf. τὴν ψυχήν) τὸ ψωμίον *receive the piece of bread* **J 13:30.** ὕδωρ ζωῆς δωρεάν *water of life without cost* **Rv 22:17.** μισθόν (q.v. 1 and 2a) **Mt 10:41ab; J 4:36; 1 Cor 3:8, 14;** AcPlCor 2:36 (TestSol 1:2, 10). Money: ἀργύρια **Mt 28:15;** ἀνὰ δηνάριον *a denarius each* **Mt 20:9f.** ἐλεημοσύνην **Ac 3:3.** βραχύ τι *a little* or *a bite* **J 6:7;** eternal life **Mk 10:30** (Jos., C. Ap. 2, 218 βίον ἀμείνω λαβεῖν); the Spirit (schol. on Plato 856e ἄνωθεν λαμβάνειν τὸ πνεῦμα) **J 7:39; Ac 2:38;** cp. **Gal 3:14; 1 Cor 2:12; 2 Cor 11:4;** forgiveness of sin **Ac 10:43** (Just., D. 54, 1); grace **Ro 1:5;** cp. **5:17;** the victor's prize **1 Cor 9:24f;** the crown of life **Js 1:12** (cp. Wsd 5:16 λ. τὸ διάδημα). συμφύγιον/σύμφυτον καὶ ὅπλον εὐδοκίας λάβωμεν Ἰησοῦν χριστόν the sense of this clause, restored from AcPl Ha 8, 23–24 and AcPl Ox 1602, 33–35 (=BMM recto 29–31) emerges as follows: *and let us take Jesus Christ as our refuge/ally and shield, the assurance of God's goodwill toward us.* The early and late rain **Js 5:7.** ἔλεος *receive mercy* **Hb 4:16** (Just., D. 133, 1). λ. τὸ ὄνομα τοῦ υἱοῦ (θεοῦ) *receive the name of the Son of God* (in baptism) Hs 9, 12, 4. διάδοχον *receive a successor* **Ac 24:27** (cp. Pliny the Younger, Ep. 9, 13 successorem accipio). τὴν ἐπισκοπὴν αὐτοῦ λαβέτω ἕτερος *let another man receive his position* **1:20** (Ps 108:8). τόπον ἀπολογίας λ. (τόπος 4) **25:16.** λ. τι μετὰ εὐχαριστίας *receive someth. w. thankfulness* **1 Ti 4:4** (but s. 1 above, end.—On the construction with μετά cp. Libanius, Or. 63 p. 392, 3 F. μετὰ ψόγου λ.). τί ἔχεις ὃ οὐκ ἔλαβες; *what have you that you did not receive?* **1 Cor 4:7** (Alciphron 2, 6, 1 τί οὐ τῶν ἐμῶν λαβοῦσα ἔχεις;). Of punishments (cp. δίκην λ. Hdt. 1, 115; Eur., Bacch. 1312. ποινάς Eur., Tro. 360. πληγάς Phillyllius Com. [V BC] 11 K.; GrBar 4:15 καταδίκην; Jos., Ant. 14, 336 τιμωρίαν) λ. περισσότερον κρίμα *receive a punishment that is just so much more severe* **Mt 23:13 [14] v.l.** (cp. κρίμα 4b); **Mk 12:40; Lk 20:47;** cp. **Js 3:1.** οἱ ἀνθεστηκότες ἑαυτοῖς κρίμα λήμψονται *those who oppose will bring punishment upon themselves* **Ro 13:2.** πεῖράν τινος λ. *become acquainted with, experience, suffer someth.* (X., An. 5, 8, 15; Polyb. 6, 3, 1; 28, 9, 7; 29, 3, 10; Diod. S. 12, 24, 4 τὴν θυγατέρα ἀπέκτεινεν, ἵνα μὴ τῆς ὕβρεως λάβῃ πεῖραν; 15, 88, 4; Jos., Ant. 2, 60; Preisigke, Griech. Urkunden des ägypt. Museums zu Kairo [1911] 2, 11; 3, 11 πεῖραν λ. δαίμονος) μαστίγων πεῖραν λ. **Hb 11:36** (the phrase in a diff. mng. vs. **29;** s. 9b above).

ⓒ Also used as a periphrasis for the passive: οἰκοδομὴν λ. *be edified* **1 Cor 14:5.** περιτομὴν *be circumcised* **J 7:23** (Just., D. 23, 5 al.). τὸ χάραγμα *receive a mark = be marked* **Rv 14:9, 11; 19:20; 20:4.** καταλλαγήν *be reconciled* **Ro 5:11.** ὑπόμνησίν τινος *be reminded of = remember someth.* **2 Ti 1:5** (Just., D 19, 6 μνήμην λαμβάνητε); λήθην τινὸς λ. *forget someth.* (Timocles Com. [IV BC], fgm. 6, 5 K.; Aelian, VH 3, 18 end, HA 4, 35;

Jos., Ant. 2, 163; 202; 4, 304; Just., D. 46, 5 ἵνα μὴ λήθη ὑμᾶς λαμβάνῃ τοῦ θεοῦ) **2 Pt 1:9;** χαρὰν λ. *experience joy, rejoice* Hv 3, 13, 2 ; GJs 12:2; ἀρχὴν λ. *be begun, have its beginning* (Pla et al.; Polyb. 1, 12, 9; Sext. Emp., Phys. 1, 366; Aelian, VH 2, 28; 12, 53; Dio Chrys. 40, 7; Philo, Mos. 1, 81 τρίτον [σημεῖον] . . . τὴν ἀρχὴν τοῦ γίνεσθαι λαβὸν ἐν Αἰγύπτῳ; Just., D. 46, 4 τὴν ἀρχὴν λαβούσης ἀπὸ Ἀβραὰμ τῆς περιτομῆς; Ath. 19, 2 ἑτέραν ἀρχὴν τοῦ κόσμου λαβόντος) **Hb 2:3;** ApcPt Rainer ln. 19.—λ. τι ἀπό τινος *receive someth. from someone* (Epict. 4, 11, 3 λ. τι ἀπὸ τῶν θεῶν; Herm. Wr. 1, 30; ApcMos 19 ὅτε δὲ ἔλαβεν ἀπʼ ἐμοῦ τὸν ὅρκον; Just., D. 78, 10 τῶν λαβόντων χάριν ἀπὸ τοῦ θεοῦ) **1J 2:27; 3:22.** Also τὶ παρά τινος (Pisander Epicus [VI BC] fgm. 5 [in Athen. 11, 469d]; Diod. S. 5, 3, 4 λαβεῖν τι παρὰ τῶν θεῶν; TestAbr A 5 p. 82, 8 [Stone p. 12] λαβὼν τὴν εὐχὴν παρʼ αὐτῶν; Just., A I, 60, 3 ἐνέργειαν τὴν παρὰ τοῦ θεοῦ λεγομένην λαβεῖν τὸν Μωυσέα.—παρά A3aβ) **J 10:18b; Ac 2:33; 3:5; 20:24; Js 1:7; 2J 4; Rv 2:28.** λ. τὸ ἱκανὸν παρὰ τοῦ Ἰάσονος *receive bail from Jason* **Ac 17:9** (s. ἱκανός 1). λ. τι ὑπό τινος *be given someth. by someone* **2 Cor 11:24.** κλῆρον καὶ μερισμὸν λαμβάνοντες AcPl Ha 8, 18//Ox 1602, 22f [λαβόντες]=BMM recto 23f (s. κλῆρος 2). λ. τι ἔκ τινος *receive someth. fr. a quantity of someth.:* ἐκ τοῦ πληρώματος αὐτοῦ ἐλάβομεν χάριν *from his fullness we have received favor* **J 1:16.** ἐκ τοῦ πνεύματος αὐτοῦ ἐλάβετε Hs 9, 24, 4.—λ. ἐξ ἀναστάσεως τοὺς νεκροὺς αὐτῶν (s. ἀνάστασις 2a) **Hb 11:35.** On ἐν γαστρὶ εἴληφα (LXX) GJs 4:2 and 4 s. γαστήρ 2 and συλλαμβάνω 3.—B. 743. Schmidt, Syn. III 203–33. DELG. M-M. EDNT. TW. Sv.

Λάμεχ, ὁ indecl. (לֶמֶךְ, in pause לָמֶךְ) ***Lamech*** (Gen 4:18ff; 5:25ff; Philo; TestBenj 7:4.—En 10:1 Raderm. has Λέμεχ, but 106:1, 4 al. Bonner Λάμεχ; Joseph. Λάμεχος, ου [Ant. 1, 79]), father of Noah; in the genealogy of Jesus **Lk 3:36** (cp. 1 Ch 1:3).

λαμπάς, άδος, ἡ (s. λάμπω; Aeschyl., Hdt.+; ins, pap, LXX, TestSol 10:8; TestJob; ParJer 3:2; Philo, Joseph., SibOr; Mel., fgm. 8b [περὶ λουτροῦ] 3; loanw. in rabb.).

❶ ***torch*** (in this mng. in trag.; Thu. 3, 24, 1; Polyb. 3, 93, 4; Herodian 4, 2, 10; OGI 764, 43; 50; 54; Sir 48:1; Jos., Bell. 6, 16, Ant. 5, 223; SibOr fgm. 3, 44), so prob. **J 18:3** w. φανοί (=lanterns; both articles together Dionys. Hal. 11, 40, 2; PLond II, 1159, 59 p. 113 [II AD]=Mitt-Wilck. I/2, p. 493).—Celestial phenomena that resemble burning torches (Diod. S. 16, 66; Ps.-Aristot., De Mundo 4; Erot. Gr. fgm. pap ed. BLavagnini 1922, Herp. 47; PGM 4, 2939ff ἀστέρα ὡς λαμπάδα) ἀστὴρ μέγας καιόμενος ὡς λαμπάς **Rv 8:10** (Diod. S. 15, 50, 2 ὤφθη κατὰ τὸν οὐρανὸν ἐπὶ πολλὰς νύκτας λαμπὰς μεγάλη καομένη; Artem. 2, 9 p. 92, 22 λαμπάδες ἐν οὐρανῷ καιόμεναι). Cp. ἑπτὰ λαμπάδες πυρὸς καιόμεναι ἐνώπιον τ. θρόνου **4:5** (λαμπάδες πυρός as Eutecnius 4 p. 39, 6; Gen 15:17; Na 2:5; Da 10:6; Philo, Rer. Div. Her. 311.—λαμπάδες καιόμεναι as Artem. [see above]; Job 41:11).

❷ ***lamp*** (so POxy 1449 [III AD]; Jdth 10:22; Da 5:5 Theod.) w. a wick and space for oil **Mt 25:1, 3f, 7f** (acc. to FZorell, Verbum Domini 10, 1930, 176–82; HAlmqvist, Plut. u. d. NT '46, 46 [Mor. 263f] the wedding torch [s. 1] is meant here); **Ac 20:8.** It is uncertain whether λαβέτωσαν ἀνὰ λαμπάδα *let each* (daughter) *take a lamp* (or *torch*) GJs 7:2 ('lampe' deStrycker; 'flambeau' EAmann, Le Protévangile de Jacques et ses remaniements latins 1910) belongs under 1 or 2 (cp. **Mt 25:1** and Lk 12:35).—RAC VII 154–217. B. 484. DELG s.v. λάμπω. M-M. TW.

λαμπηδών, όνος, ἡ (λάμπη + suff. -δών [Schwyzer I 529]; Hippocr. V 632 L.; Epicurus 45, 8 Us.; Diod. S. 3, 37, 9; Plut.; Aelian, NA 2, 8 p. 36, 16; Artem. 5, 90; Herm. Wr. 10, 4b; PGM 4, 531; Is 58:11 Aq.; Jos., Ant. 3, 207) ***brightness, brilliance*** Hs 9, 2, 2.—DELG s.v. λάμπω.

λαμπρός, ά, όν (s. λάμπω; Hom.+; ins, pap, LXX, TestSol, TestAbr, Test12Patr, JosAs; ApcMos 33; Philo, Joseph., Just., Mel.)

❶ **pert. to radiating light, *bright*** of heavenly bodies (Hom. et al.; X., Mem. 4, 7, 7; EpJer 59; TestNapht 5:4; Cat. Cod. Astr. IX/1, 174, 30) the sun (Philo, Somn. 2, 282) Hs 9, 17, 4. The morning star **Rv 22:16.**

❷ **pert. to being free of anything that impedes clear perception, *clear, transparent*** (Aeschyl., Eum. 695; X., Hell. 5, 3, 19) ποταμὸν ὕδατος ζωῆς λαμπρὸν ὡς κρύσταλλον **Rv 22:1.**

❸ **pert. to having a glistening quality**—ⓐ of garments, esp. white ones: ***bright, shining*** (Od. 19, 234; Polyb. 10, 4, 8; 10, 5, 1; SIG 1157, 39f ἐν ἐσθῆσιν λαμπραῖς; Philo, De Jos. 105 λ. ἐσθής) ἱματισμὸς λαμπρότατος *a brightly shining garment* Hv 1, 2, 2. ἐσθής **Lk 23:11** (PJoüon, RSR 26, '36, 80–85); **Ac 10:30; Js 2:2f.** στολή (Jos., Vi. 334; TestSol 10:28 C στολὰς λαμπράς; TestAbr A 16 p. 97, 8f [Stone p. 42] στολὴν λαμπροτάτην; JosAs 14:15) GPt 13:55. βύσσινον λ. καθαρόν **Rv 19:8** (cp. Jos., Ant. 8, 72). λίνον καθαρὸν λ. **15:6.**

ⓑ of other objects: ***gleaming, bright,*** stones Hv 3, 2, 4b; s 9, 3, 3; 9, 4, 6; 9, 6, 7f; 9, 8, 7; 9, 9, 3f; 9, 17, 3; 9, 30, 2 and 4; cp. οἰκοδομὴ τοῦ πύργου 9, 30, 1. ἐπάρασα ῥάβδον τινὰ λαμπράν *as she lifted up a sort of glittering staff* Hv 3, 2, 4a.

❹ as subst. τὰ λαμπρά ***splendor*** (Philo, In Flacc. 165, Leg. ad Gai. 327; Mel., HE 26, 8), in which a rich man takes delight (cp. Jos., Ant. 12, 220 δωρεὰς δοὺς λαμπράς) **Rv 18:14.**—DELG s.v. λάμπω. M-M. TW. Spicq.

λαμπρότης, ητος, ἡ (s. λαμπρός; Hdt.+; ins, pap, LXX, EpArist, Philo, Joseph.) gener. 'brilliance, splendor'.

❶ **the state of being splendid, *shining*** (X., An. 1, 2, 18 of the splendor of weapons; Jos., Bell. 5, 271, Ant. 12, 81) *brightness* of the sun (Vi. Aesopi W 115. Of a constellation Diod. S. 15, 50, 3) **Ac 26:13.**

❷ **exceptional personal quality, *distinction, brilliance*** transf. sense of 1: used esp. of those who are outstanding in intelligence and enterprising spirit (Polyb. 32, 8, 1 of personal brilliance in contrast to loss of bodily vigor; Diod. S. 2, 22, 3; 4, 10, 2; 4, 40, 1 ψυχῆς λαμπρότητι; EpArist 16; Jos., Ant. 11, 342 of a greeting party that extends 'VIP' treatment) λ. ἐν δικαιοσύνῃ *brilliance in uprightness,* i.e. above and beyond the ordinary, 1 Cl 35:2.—DELG s.v. λάμπω. M-M. Spicq.

λαμπρῶς adv. fr. λαμπρός (Aeschyl.+; SIG 545, 12; 1045, 15; PSI 406, 30; Jos., Ant. 6, 15 al.) ***splendidly*** εὐφραίνεσθαι καθʼ ἡμέραν λαμπρῶς *fare sumptuously every day* **Lk 16:19** (PYadin 15, 10; 26 of opulent lifestyle; PGM 1, 111 ἐξαρτίσαι τὸ δεῖπνον λαμπρῶς; s. δαπανάω 1).—M-M. Spicq.

λάμπω fut. λάμψω; 1 aor. ἔλαμψα (Hom.+; LXX, En, TestSol; TestAbr B 7 p. 111, 10f [Stone p. 70]; Test12Patr; SyrBar 12:2 [?]; GrBar, Joseph., SibOr; Christian ins in OGI 610, 1f [VI AD] φῶς σωτήριον ἔλαμψεν ὅπου σκότος ἐκάλυπτεν; Just.) **to emit rays of light, *shine*** (Jos., Ant. 3, 218 of precious stones) of a lamp **Mt 5:15;** of lightning *flash* **Lk 17:24.**—*Shine out, shine forth, gleam* (Chariton 1, 9, 5 of a gleaming sword; Jos., Ant. 5, 284) light **Ac 12:7;** a star (cp. IAndrosIsis [I BC] 23; Bar 3:34; SibOr 3, 334 ἀστὴρ λάμψει) IEph 19:2; sun (Archilochus [VII BC] 74, 4 Diehl[2]; SyrBar 12:2 ἀκτίνες τοῦ ἡλίου λάμπουσιν; GrBar 7:5 λάμψαι τὸν ἥλιον; 9:8) GPt 6:22. Of the face of the transfigured Jesus ὡς ὁ ἥλιος (cp. EpJer 66; En 14:18; 106:2;

TestLevi 18:4; difft., but of a pers. SEG XXVIII, 1251, 2 [III or IV AD]) **Mt 17:2.** Of the light that shone forth at creation by God's command **2 Cor 4:6a.** Of an angel ὁ λάμπων καὶ φαίνων AcPl Ha 3, 36.—In transf. sense w. φῶς (cp. Pr 4:18; Tob 13:13 S; Is 9:1) *shine* λαμψάτω τ. φῶς ὑμῶν ἔμπροσθεν τ. ἀνθρώπων **Mt 5:16** (cp. SEG above). Of God, prob. *shine forth* θεὸς . . . ὃς ἔλαμψεν ἐν ταῖς καρδίαις ἡμῶν *God, who has shone in our hearts* **2 Cor 4:6b** (perh. *reflect,* as PGM 13, 770 of the heavenly eyes of a divinity λάμποντες ἐν ταῖς κόραις τ. ἀνθρώπων. GMacRae, Anti-Dualist Polemic in 2 Cor 4:6? TU 102, '68, 420–31).—DELG. New Docs 3, 49f. M-M. TW.

λανθάνω (Hom.+) fut. λήσω (Just., A I, 35, 1; Ath. 22:2) or λήσομαι (2 Km 18:13; Ath., R. 10 p. 59, 2); 2 aor. ἔλαθον; pf. 3 sg. λέληθεν **to succeed in avoiding attention or awareness, *escape notice, be hidden*** abs. (Jos., Bell. 3, 343; Just., A I, 11, 2) **Mk 7:24; Lk 8:47;** MPol 6:2.—λανθάνει τί τινα *someth. is hidden from someone, escapes someone's notice* (Hom. et al.; BGU 531 II, 13; POxy 34 verso III, 3; 1253, 22; Job 34:21 λέληθεν αὐτὸν οὐδέν; EpArist 132; Jos., Ant. 17, 38, Vi. 83; JosAs 6:3 οὐδὲν κρυπτὸν λέληθεν αὐτῷ [-όν v.l.]; Just., A I, 12, 3) IEph 19:1; **2 Pt 3:8.** οὐδὲν λέληθεν αὐτόν 1 Cl 21:3; cp. 27:6; IEph 14:1; 15:3; Pol 4:3. λανθάνειν αὐτὸν τούτων οὐ πείθομαι οὐθέν *I cannot bring myself to believe that any of these things has escaped his notice* **Ac 26:26.** [ὅσα] ὑμᾶς λανθάνει καὶ ἀπομνημονεύω, ἀπα[γγέλω ὑμῖν]*whatever has escaped your notice and I* (Mary) *recall, I [declare to you.]* Ox 3525, 18.—That which escapes notice can also be expressed by a ὅτι- clause (X., Mem. 3, 5, 24; Isocr., Ep. 6, 12; Dio Chrys. 16 [33], 37) λανθάνει αὐτοὺς τοῦτο θέλοντας ὅτι *when they maintain this, it escapes their notice* (i.e. they forget or ignore) *that* **2 Pt 3:5** (s. θέλω 4). Likew. by the ptc. (Maximus Tyr. 4, 6b; Jos., Vi. 425; Just., A I, 12, 3; Ath. 22, 2; B-D-F §414, 3; Rob. 1120) ἔλαθόν τινες (sc. ἑαυτούς) ξενίσαντες ἀγγέλους *some, without knowing it, have entertained angels* **Hb 13:2** (cp. Hdt. 1, 44 φονέα τοῦ παιδὸς ἐλάνθανε βόσκων=he fed the murderer of his son without knowing it; X., Mem. 4, 3, 9 al.; Lucian, De Merc. Cond. 7 ἔλαθον γηράσαντες=they had grown old without noticing it).—DELG. M-M. Spicq.

λαξευτός, ή, όν (λᾶας 'stone' and ξέω 'make smooth' Dt 4:49; four times in Aq.: Num 21:20; 23:14; Dt 34:1; and Josh 13:20; Judg 7:11 Theod.; s. B-D-F §2) **pert. to being hewn in rock, *hewn*** μνῆμα *a tomb* **Lk 23:53.**—DELG s.v. λᾶας. M-M. (cognates only).

Λαοδίκεια, ας, ἡ edd. also Λαοδικεία, -δικία (s. next entry; Strabo 12, 8, 16; ins; SibOr; Mel., HE 4, 26, 3) ***Laodicea*** a city in Phrygia (in Asia Minor) on the Lycus R. A large colony of Jews resided there (Jos., Ant. 14, 241ff; Schürer III 27; 116, 37), and Christianity took root at an early date. **Col 2:1; 4:13, 15f. Subscr.** of **1** and **2 Ti v.l.; Rv 1:11; 3:14.**—Ramsay, CB I/1, 32ff; 341f; I/2, 512; 542ff; Lghtf., Col 1ff; VSchultze, Altchristliche Städte II/1, 1922, 384ff, 435ff.—Paul wrote a letter to the congregation at Laodicea, **Col 4:16.** S. Harnack, D. Adresse des Eph des Pls: SBBerlAk 1910, 696–709; Goodsp., Introd. to the NT, '37, 114–24; CAnderson, JBL 85, '66, 436–40; CHemer, The Letters to the Seven Churches in Their Local Settings '89 ('86), 178–209; also in New Docs 3, '83, 56–58; Pauly-W. XII 713ff; DACL VIII 1321ff. BHHW II 1049; PECS 481–82.

Λαοδικεύς, έως, ὁ (s. prec. entry; ins; Appian, Mithrid. 20 §78; 117 §573; Artem. 4, 1 p. 202, 8; Jos., Ant. 14, 241) ***a Laodicean,*** inhabitant of Laodicea in Phrygia **Col 4:16; Rv 3:14 v.l.** Cp. also the superscr. of Eph in Marcion (N. app.).—M-M.

λαός, οῦ, ὁ (Hom.+; ins; pap [here the pl. λαοί, Mayser 27; 29]; LXX, pseudepigr, Philo, Joseph., apolog.)

❶ ***people,*** in a general sense—ⓐ distributively, *populace* **Mt 27:64.** ἐν τῷ λαῷ *among the people* **Mt 4:23; Ac 6:8.**

ⓑ a close gathering of people *crowd* **Lk 1:21; 3:15, 18; 7:1; 20:1; Ac 3:12; 4:1f; 13:15; 21:30.** πᾶς ὁ λ. *the whole crowd, all the people* (TestSim 6:4; Jos., Ant. 13, 201) **Mt 27:25; Lk 8:47; 9:13; 18:43; 21:38; J 8:2; Ac 3:9, 11.** Also ἅπας ὁ λ. (Jos., Ant. 7, 63; 211) **Lk 3:21.** ὁ λ. ἅπας (Jos., Ant. 6, 199; 8, 101) **19:48;** GPt 8:28. λ. ἱκανός **Ac 5:37 v.l.** πᾶν τὸ πλῆθος τ. λαοῦ **Lk 1:10;** cp. **Ac 21:36.** πλῆθος πολὺ τοῦ λαοῦ *a large crowd of people* **Lk 6:17; 23:27** (PsSol. 8:2 λαοῦ πολλοῦ; TestJud 3:1 λ. πολύς).

❷ the mass of a community as distinguished from special interest groups (OGI 90, 12 [II BC priests, civil officials, and soldiers]) ***people***

ⓐ in contrast to their leaders **Mt 26:5; Mk 11:18 v.l., 32 v.l.; 14:2; Lk 19:48; 20:6, 19, 26; 23:13; Ac 2:47; 4:17, 21; 5:26; 6:12; 12:4.**

ⓑ in contrast to Pharisees and legal experts **Lk 7:29.**

ⓒ in contrast to priests **Hb 2:17; 5:3; 7:5, 27** (a Christian congregation in liturgical response Just., A I, 65, 3 al.).—RMeyer, Der ʿAm hā- ʾAreṣ, Judaica 3, '47, 169–99.

❸ a body of people with common cultural bonds and ties to a specific territory, *people-group, people* as nation (w. φυλή, ἔθνος, γλῶσσα; cp. Da 3:4) **Rv 5:9; 13:7; 14:6.** Pl. (a Sibylline oracle in Appian, Maced. 2; En 10:21; PsSol 5:11; 17:30 λαοὶ τῶν ἐθνῶν; Just., A I, 49, 1) **7:9; 10:11; 11:9; 17:15.—Lk 2:31.** Of a monstrous animal θηρίον δυνάμενον λαοὺς διαφθεῖραι *a beast capable of destroying (whole) peoples* Hv 4, 2, 3.

❹ people of God, *people*—ⓐ of the people of Israel ὁ λαός (s. also Jewish inscriptions in SIG 1247; GKittel, TLZ 69, '44, 13; En 20:5; PsSol 17:20; ParJer 2:2 [throughout w. art.]; Just.; Mel., P.; Iren., Orig., Did.—λαός of the native Egyptian population since III BC at least: UWilcken on UPZ 110, 100f) **Ac 3:23; 7:17; 28:17; 2 Pt 2:1;** AcPl Ha 8, 19. Without the art. (Sir 46:7; Wsd 18:13; PsSol [throughout, exc. 17:20]) **Jd 5;** οὗτος ὁ λ. **Mt 15:8; Mk 7:6** (both Is 29:13); **Lk 21:23;** B 9:3; 10:2; πᾶς ὁ λ. (ParJer 5:17) **Lk 2:10** *all the people* (prob., as the involvement of the shepherds suggests, without cultic restrictions, namely to 'everyone'); B 12:8. πᾶς ὁ λ. Ἰσραήλ **Ac 4:10.** οἱ ἀρχιερεῖς τοῦ λ. **Mt 2:4; 26:47; 27:1;** οἱ πρεσβύτεροι τοῦ λ. **21:23;** τὸ πρεσβυτέριον τοῦ λ. **Lk 22:66;** οἱ ἄρχοντες τοῦ λ. **Ac 4:8;** B 9:3; PEg[2], 6; οἱ πρῶτοι τοῦ λ. **Lk 19:47.** Opp. τὰ ἔθνη *the nations, non-Israelites (gentiles)* (s. ἔθνος 2 and cp. Appian, Bell. Civ. 5, 67 §283 the contrast τὰ ἔθνη . . . τὴν Ἰταλίαν) **Ac 26:17, 23; Ro 15:10** (Dt 32:43).—W. a gen. that denotes the possessor ([τοῦ] θεοῦ, αὐτοῦ, μοῦ etc.; cp. TestJud 25:3; ParJer 3:15; ApcrEzk P 1 verso 3; Jos., Ant. 10, 12; Just., D. 110, 4): λ. τοῦ θεοῦ **Lk 1:68; Hb 11:25.** ὁ λαός μου **Ac 7:34** (Ex 3:7). **Rv 18:4** (pl. verb with λαός in sing. as Περὶ ὕψους 23, 2 after a poet λαὸς . . . κελάδησαν).—**Lk 7:16.** λ. σου Ἰσραήλ **Lk 2:32.** ὁ λ. μου ὁ Ἰσραήλ **Mt 2:6.** ὁ λ. Ἰσραήλ B 16:5 (cp. ὁ λ. τῶν Ἰουδαίων Orig., C. Cels. 2, 1, 6). Pl. of the tribes of Israel (Jos., C. Ap. 2, 159, unless the pl. here means 'the people', as Hes., Op. 763f πολλοὶ λαοί; Aristoph., Equ. 163, Ran. 216; 677 πολὺν λαῶν ὄχλον; Callim., Epigr. 47; Isyllus E 1 [IG IV, 950=Coll. Alex. p. 133, 37=D 1 in Diehl[2] II, 6 p. 115, s. Anth LG] θεὸν ἀείσατε, λαοί = ἐνναέται Ἐπιδαύρου [inhabitants of Epidaurus]; Diod. S. 1, 45, 1; 3, 45, 6 διὰ τὴν τῶν λαῶν ἀπειρίαν=because of the inexperience of the people; 4, 67, 6; 5, 7, 6; 5, 48, 1 συναγαγεῖν τ. λαοὺς σποράδην οἰκοῦντας=gather the people who live in scattered places; 5, 59, 5 al.; Orphica 34, 10 Q.; Herm. Wr. 1, 27;

PRev 42, 17 [258 BC] γραφέτωσαν οἱ λαοί=the people are to submit a written statement; Jos., Ant. 18, 352; Just., A I, 47, 1 al; Ath.; Basilius, epistle 92, 2 ln. 44 [=MPG XXXII 481a] οἱ λαοί; Theophanes, Chron. 172, 7 de Boor ἀπέθανον λαοὶ πολλοί) **Ac 4:25** (Ps 2:1), **27; Ro 15:11** (Ps 116:1).

ⓑ of Christians **Ac 15:14; 18:10; Ro 9:25** (Hos 2:25); **Hb 4:9; 1 Pt 2:10; Rv 18:4** (Jer 28:45 SAQ); 1 Cl 59:4; 2 Cl 2:3; B 13:1ff. Prepared by Christ B 3:6; cp. Hs 5, 5, 2. Protected by angels 5, 5, 3; specif. entrusted to Michael 8, 3, 3; cp. 8, 1, 2.—Also in pl. (s. 3 end) λαοὶ αὐτοῦ **Rv 21:3;** cp. Hs 8, 3, 2.—λ. εἰς περιποίησιν *a people (made God's) own possession* **1 Pt 2:9.** Also λ. περιούσιος (Ex 19:5) **Tit 2:14;** 1 Cl 64. λ. κατεσκευασμένος *a people made ready* **Lk 1:17.** λ. καινός B 5:7; 7:5.—OKern, ARW 30, '33, 205–17; EKäsemann, D. wandernde Gottesvolk '39; N Dahl, D. Volk Gottes: E. Untersuchg. z. Kirchenbewusstsein des Urchristent. '41; HSahlin, D. Messias u. d. Gottesvolk '45; AOepke, D. neue Gottesvolk '50; CVandersleyen, Le mot λαός dans la langue des papyrus: Chronique d' Égypte 48, '73, 339–49; OMontevecchi, PapBrux XIX (in Actes du XVe Congrès International de Papyrologie '78–79), pp. 51–67.—B. 1313; 1315. Schmidt, Syn. IV 570–75. DELG. M-M. EDNT. TW. Spicq. Sv. S. also LfgrE s.v. col. 1634 (lit.).

λάρυγξ, γγος, ὁ (Eur. et al.; LXX; TestSol 10:3; ApcSed 10:3 p. 133, 37 Ja.; s. B-D-F §46, 4; Mlt-H. 108) ***throat, gullet*** (orig. 'larynx'), fig. τάφος ἀνεῳγμένος ὁ λάρυγξ αὐτῶν (ἀνοίγω 2) **Ro 3:13** (Ps 5:10; 13:3).—DELG. TW.

Λασαία, ας or **Λασέα , ας** (W-H.), **ἡ** ***Lasaea,*** a city on the south coast of the island of Crete. **Ac 27:8.**—PECS 486. M-M.

λάσκω 1 aor. ἐλάκησα, ***crash*** etc., erroneously thought to be the source of ἐλάκησεν **Ac 1:18;** s. λακάω.—DELG. M-M.

λατομέω (λατόμος 'stonecutter', fr. λᾶας 'stone' and τέμνω) fut. 2 sg. λατομήσεις Dt 8:9 Aq.; 1 aor. ἐλατόμησα. Pass.: aor. 2 pl. ἐλατομήθητε Is 51:1 Sym., Theod.; pf. ptc. λελατομημένος (Antig. Car. 161; Posidonius: 87 fgm. 57 Jac.; Diod. S. et al.; SIG 1169, 25 [III BC] λατομήσας τ. πέτραν; PPetr II, 4 (9), 3 [255 BC]; PCairZen 296, 34 [III BC]; LXX; Artapanus: 726 fgm. 3:11 Jac. [in Eus., PE 9, 27, 11]; Jos., Ant. 8, 59; Just., D. 135, 3).

➊ **to form a cavity or chamber by cutting away rock, *hew out of a rock*** (2 Ch 26:10; 2 Esdr 19:25) a grave (Is 22:16 μνημεῖον) **Lk 23:53** D; λελατομημένον ἐκ πέτρας **Mk 15:46.** λ. ἐν τῇ πέτρᾳ *cut in the rock* **Mt 27:60.**

➋ **to shape stones by cutting, *hew, shape*** stones (1 Ch 22:2; Is 51:1) Hv 3, 5, 3; s 9, 3, 3; 9, 4, 5; 9, 5, 3; 9, 6, 8; 9, 7, 4; 9, 8, 2ff; 6; 9, 9, 3.—DELG s.v. λᾶας. M-M.

λατόμος, ου, ὁ (s. prec. entry; Ptolem., Apotel. 4, 4, 5; Pollux 7, 118; OGI 660, 3 [I AD]; PSI 423, 1; 37 [III BC]; PPetr III, 47 [a], 2 al.; LXX; Jos., Ant. 11, 78) ***stonecutter, stonemason*** Hs 9, 9, 2.—DELG s.v. λᾶας.

λατρεία, ας, ἡ (cp. λάτρον 'payment' and s. next entry; Pind. et al.; LXX. On the cultic t.t. עֲבוֹדָה s. Elbogen 4) in cultic usage ***service/worship (of God)*** (Pla., Apol. 23b τοῦ θεοῦ, Phdr. 244e; Sb 1934, 3 [?]; LXX; Philo, Ebr. 144 al.; Jos., Bell. 2, 409; Ar. 2, 1; Mel., P. 67, 475; Ath. 13, 2; Orig., C. Cels. 2, 78, 16; 4, 22, 13; Did., Gen. 135, 18) **Ro 9:4;** λογικὴ λ. **12:1** (s. λογικός).δικαιώματα λατρείας *regulations for worship* **Hb 9:1.** τὰς λ. ἐπιτελεῖν *perform the rites* vs. **6.** λ. προσφέρειν τῷ θεῷ *offer a service to God* **J 16:2.** Of image-worship λ. θεῶν νεκρῶν D 6:3; cp. Dg 3:2.—DELG s.v. λάτρον. M-M. TW.

λατρεύω fut. λατρεύσω; 1 aor. ἐλάτρευσα (trag. et al. in var. senses, 'work for pay, be in servitude, render cultic service'; ins, LXX; ApcMos 13; En, Philo, SibOr 4, 104; Just.) ***serve,*** in our lit. only of the carrying out of religious duties, esp. of a cultic nature, by human beings: λ. θεῷ (Eur., Ion 152; Plut., Mor. 405c; 407e; Philo, Spec. Leg. 1, 300 ὅλῃ τ. ψυχῇ; cp. En 10:21; Orig., C. Cels. 5, 11, 39 [w. προσκυνέω]) **Mt 4:10; Lk 4:8** (both Dt 6:13); **1:74; Ac 7:7** (cp. Ex 3:12); **24:14; 27:23; Hb 9:14; Rv 7:15; 22:3;** Pol 2:1. τῷ ὀνόματι (θεοῦ) 1 Cl 45:7; τῷ διαβόλῳ λ. *serve the devil* (in reality) ISm 9:1. Of the Jews λ. ἀγγέλοις PtK 2 p. 14, 26. Of image-worship (Ex 20:5; 23:24; Ezk 20:32; En 99: 7; Just., A I, 53, 6; Theoph. Ant. 2, 34 p. 184, 26; 3, 9 p. 222, 23) **Ac 7:42; Ro 1:25;** εἰδώλοις AcPl Ha 2, 32.—W. indication of the manner in which the service (τῷ θεῷ) is performed (cp. τὴν ἀληθῆ λαθρείαν λ. τῷ θεῷ Orig., C. Cels. 2, 2, 42) (τῷ θεῷ) ἐν καθαρᾷ συνειδήσει *serve (God) w. a clear conscience* **2 Ti 1:3.** (διὰ χάριτος) λ. εὐαρέστως τῷ θεῷ μετὰ εὐλαβείας καὶ δέους *(in thankfulness) serve God acceptably with reverence and awe* **Hb 12:28.** (τῷ θεῷ) λ. ἐν τῷ πνεύματί μου ἐν τῷ εὐαγγελίῳ *I serve (God) with my spirit in the gospel* **Ro 1:9** (cp. **Phil 3:3 v.l.**).—Without the dat. of the one to whom service is given: ἐν ἐκτενείᾳ νύκτα κ. ἡμέραν λ. *serve (God) earnestly night and day* **Ac 26:7.** νηστείαις κ. δεήσεσιν λ. νύκτα κ. ἡμέραν *serve (God) night and day w. fasting and prayer* **Lk 2:37.** οἱ πνεύματι θεοῦ λατρεύοντες *those who worship by the Spirit of God* **Phil 3:3** (HKoester, NTS 8, '62, 320f: *work as a missionary in the Spirit of God*). ὁ λατρεύων *the worshiper* (who is concerned w. the rituals prescribed by Mosaic ordinance) **Hb 9:9; 10:2.**—Hb also adds to λ. in the dat. the holy objects by means of which the priest renders service **8:5; 13:10.**—WBrandt, Dienst u. Dienen im NT '31; CCranfield, Interpretation 12, '58, 387–98; BReicke, NT Studies: TManson memorial vol., '59, 194–209.—DELG s.v. λάτρον. M-M. EDNT. TW.

λαχ- s. λαγχάνω.

λάχανον, ου, τό (Cratinus et al.; pap, LXX; Jos., Bell. 5, 437; Just., D. 20, 3) ***edible garden herb, vegetable*** **Mt 13:32; Mk 4:32.** πᾶν λάχανον *every kind of garden herb* **Lk 11:42.**—Of one who is a vegetarian for religious reasons ὁ ἀσθενῶν λάχανα ἐσθίει *the one who is weak* (in convictions) *eats* (only) *vegetables* **Ro 14:2** (cp. the Neopythagoreans in Diog. L. 8, 38 ἐσθίουσι λάχανα; Philostrat., Vi. Apoll. 1, 8 λάχανα ἐσιτεῖτο.—JHaussleiter, D. Vegetarismus in der Antike '35; DTsekourakis, ANRW II/36/1, '87, 366–93). B. 369.—DELG s.v. λαχαίνω. M-M. TW.

λαχμός, οῦ, ὁ (s. λαγχάνω) **an object used as a device for making a decision through sortilege, *lot*** (schol. on Soph., Aj. 1281; schol. on Eur., Hippol. 1057; schol. on Theocr. 8, 30; Etym. Mag. p. 519, 10; Eustath.) λαχμὸν βάλλειν ἐπί τινι *cast lots for someth.* GPt 4:12 (cp. Just., D. 97, 3).—DELG s.v. λαγχάνω.

λε´ numeral=*35,* Hs 9, 4, 3; 9, 5, 4; 9, 15, 4.

Λεββαῖος, ου, ὁ (לִבַּי) ***Lebbaeus,*** in the list of apostles **Mt 10:3** and **Mk 3:18** as v.l. for Θαδδαῖος (q.v.).—Dalman, Worte 40; MLidzbarski, Handbuch der nordsem. Epigr. 1898, 301; BHHW II 1055.

λεγιών, ῶνος, ἡ (Lat. loanw.: legio, also in rabb. In Gk. since Diod. S. 26, 5; Nicol. Dam.: 90 fgm. 130 §132 Jac.; ins fr. the time of the triumvirs [fr. Ephesus, JÖAI 2, 1899, Beiblatt, col. 83/84]; pap, fr. about the beginning of our era [BGU 1108, 3: 5 BC; PLond II, 256 recto (a), 3 p. 99: 15 AD]; SibOr 8, 78. The spellings λεγεών [also TestSol 11:3; 5:6f] and λεγιών [crit. editions] are about equally attested [s. the reff. in Hahn, index; OGI index]; s. on this TEckinger, D. Orthographie latein. Wörter in griech. Inschriften, diss. Zürich 1892, 30; AMeuwese, De rerum gestarum D. Augusti versione graeca, diss. Amsterdam 1920, 15; B-D-F §41, 1; W-S. §5, 20a; Mlt-H. 76) a ***legion,*** numbering in the time of Augustus about 6,000 soldiers, usu. w. approx. an equal number of auxiliary troops. The angels divided into legions **Mt 26:53** (for this concept cp. Maximus Tyr. 4, 4c after Pla., Phdr. 26, 246e: Zeus with the heavenly στρατιά made up of eleven hosts [Maximus Tyr. 10, 9c the souls of good men are counted as members of the στρατιὰ θεῶν]; Aristodem. [IV AD]: 104 fgm. 1, 8 Jac.: at Salamis οἱ θεοὶ συνεμάχησαν τ. Ἕλλησιν . . . κονιορτὸν ὡς δισμυρίων ἀνδρῶν=the gods fought on the side of the Hellenes, [according to report] a dust-cloud as of twenty-thousand warriors). As the name of a hostile spirit **Mk 5:9, 15** (ὁ λ., here and TestSol, where it expresses the totality of lesser spirits subjects to one spirit, is explained by the fact that the spirit was masculine: cp. correspondingly Dio Chrys. 46 [63], 1 ἡ δαίμων of τύχη as a divinity; cp. Is 65:35, s. JMateos, Filología Neotestamentaria 1, '88, 211–16); **Lk 8:30.**—M-M. TW.

λέγω (Hom.+; on the mng. of the word ADebrunner, TW IV 71–73) impf. ἔλεγον (3 pl. ἔλεγαν s. B-D-F §82 app.; Mlt-H. 194; KBuresch, RhM 46, 1891, 224). Only pres. and impf. are in use; the other tenses are supplied by εἶπον (q.v., also B-D-F §101 p. 46; Mlt-H. 247), but the foll. pass. forms occur: fut. 3 sg. λεχθήσεται; aor. ptc. fem. sg. λεχθεῖσα (SyrBar 14:1), neut. pl. τὰ λεχθέντα (Jos. 24, 27; Esth 1:18; Papias, Just.), 3 sg. ἐλέχθη and pl. ἐλέχθησαν; pf. 3 sg. λέλεκται; plupf. ἐλέλεκτο; pf. ptc. λελεγμένος (all Just.; B-D-F §101) 'say' (beginning w. Hes. [Hom. uses the word in the senses 'gather, collect', as Il. 11, 755 al., and mid. 'select', as Il. 21, 27, and esp. of stories that one elects to 'tell over' or 'recount', as Od. 14, 197] and more freq. in Pind.; the usual word since the Attic writers; ins, pap, LXX, pseudepigr., Philo, Joseph., apolog.).

❶ to express oneself orally or in written form, *utter in words, say, tell, give expression to,* the gener. sense (not in Hom., for this εἶπον, ἐν[ν]έπω, et al.)

ⓐ w. an indication of what is said—**α.** in the acc. ταύτην τ. παραβολήν **Lk 13:6.** (τὴν) ἀλήθειαν (Teles p. 4, 14; TestAbr A 16 p. 97, 27 [Stone p. 42]) **J 8:45f; Ro 9:1; 1 Ti 2:7.** ἀληθῆ (cp. Herodian 4, 14, 4) **J 19:35.** παροιμίαν οὐδεμίαν **16:29.** τὶ καινότερον **Ac 17:21** (w. ἀκούω as Pla., Prot. 310a; Dio Chrys. 3, 28; 4, 37). τί λέγουσιν *what they say* **Mt 21:16;** cp. **Lk 18:6; 1 Cor 14:16.** τί λέγω; *what shall I say?* **Hb 11:32.** ὃ λέγει **Lk 9:33;** cp. **2 Ti 2:7; Phlm 21.** ἃ λέγουσιν **1 Ti 1:7;** AcPlCor 1:9. ταῦτα (τοῦτο) λ. (Jos., Vi. 291) **Lk 9:34; 11:45b; 13:17; J 2:22;** τοιαῦτα λ. **Hb 11:14.** τὸ αὐτὸ λέγειν *be in agreement* (not only in words: Thu. 4, 20, 4; 5, 31, 6; Polyb. 2, 62, 4; 5, 104, 1; Jos., Ant. 18, 375; 378) **1 Cor 1:10.**—Also τινί τι *tell someone someth.* παραβολὴν αὐτοῖς **Lk 18:1.** μυστήριον ὑμῖν **1 Cor 15:51.** τ. ἀλήθειαν ὑμῖν **J 16:7.** ὃ λέγω ὑμῖν **Mt 10:27.** μηδενὶ λ. τοῦτο **Lk 9:21.** οὐδὲν αὐτῷ λέγουσιν *they say nothing to him* **J 7:26.** ταῦτα ἔλεγον ὑμῖν **2 Th 2:5.**—τὶ πρός τινα (Pla, Gorg. 465a) παραβολὴν πρὸς αὐτούς **Lk 5:36;** cp. **14:7; 20:9.—24:10; 11:53 v.l.** W. double acc. ἀδύνατα ταῦτα εἴρηκας Hm 11:19.

β. by direct discourse or direct question foll., mostly abs. (extremely freq.) **Mt 9:34; 12:44; Mk 3:30; Lk 5:39; J 1:29, 36; 1 Cor 12:3; Js 4:13.** Also oft. introduced by recitative ὅτι **Mt 9:18; Mk 1:15; 2:12; 3:21f; 5:28; 6:14f** (on the textual problem s. FNeirynck, ETL 65, '89, 110–18), **35; 7:20; Lk 1:24; 4:41; 17:10; 21:8 v.l.; J 6:14; 7:12; 8:33; Ac 2:13; 11:3** and oft.—καὶ ἔλεγεν **Mk 4:21, 24, 26, 30** may *=he used to say* (so that they might memorize): WEssame, ET 77, '66, 121.

γ. by indirect discourse or indirect question foll.; abs. **Mt 21:27; Mk 11:33c; Lk 20:8.**—Introduced by ὅτι (Diod. S. 11, 4, 3; 11, 6, 2; 14, 4, 3; Petosiris, fgm. 14c; Jos., Bell. 4, 543) **Lk 22:70; Ac 20:23.**—In acc. w. inf. τίνα λέγουσιν οἱ ἄνθρωποι εἶναι τ. υἱὸν τ. ἀνθρώπου; **Mt 16:13;** cp. vs. **15; Lk 9:20; 11:18; 23:2b; 24:23b; J 12:29a; Ac 4:32; 8:9; 17:7.**—W. the inf. only **Lk 24:23a; Js 2:14; 1J 2:6, 9.**

ⓑ w. indication of the pers. or thing about which someth. is said, or that is meant by someth.

α. by a prep. περί τινος (Soph., Thu. et al.) οἱ Φαρισαῖοι ἔγνωσαν ὅτι περὶ αὐτῶν λέγει *the Pharisees perceived that he was talking about them* **Mt 21:45.** λέγει περὶ αὐτοῦ *he said concerning him* **J 1:47;** cp. **2:21; 11:13; 13:18, 22.** εἴς τινα (Eur., Med. 453; X., Mem. 1, 5, 1) **Ac 2:25; Eph 5:32.** ἐπί τινα **Hb 7:13.** πρός τινα **Lk 12:41; Hb 1:7.**

β. by the acc. alone *mean someone* or *someth.* (Demosth. 18, 88; Diod. S. 15, 23, 5; Phalaris, Ep. 142, 1 ἣν λέγω; Ael. Aristid. 48, 35 K.=24 p. 474 D.: τὸν Φιλάδελφον λέγων; Aelian, NA 8, 3 ὃ δὲ λέγω, τοιοῦτόν ἐστιν, VH 3, 36; Lucian, Dial. Deor. 3; 10, 2; 2 Macc 14:7; Jos., Ant. 6, 86; TestSol 4:6 D τὸν δύστηνον λέγω γέροντα; Just., D. 130, 2 μετὰ τοῦ λαοῦ αὐτοῦ, λέγω Ἀβραὰμ καὶ Ἰσαὰκ . . .) τ. ἄνθρωπον τοῦτον ὃν λέγετε *this man whom you mean* **Mk 14:71.** ἔλεγεν τὸν Ἰούδαν **J 6:71.** συνείδησιν λέγω οὐχὶ τὴν ἑαυτοῦ *I mean not your own conscience* **1 Cor 10:29.** τοῦτο δὲ λέγω *but this is what I mean* **Gal 3:17;** cp. **1 Cor 1:12a** (Ptolem., Apotel. 2, 3, 12; 2, 11, 1 λέγω δέ . . . but I mean).—**Mt 26:70; Mk 14:68; Lk 22:60.** Cp. 4 end.

γ. w. an indication of the one to whom someth. is said (on the synoptics and Ac s. WLarfeld, Die ntl. Ev. 1925, 237f); mostly in dat. (Aeschyl., Ag. 103; Herodas 4, 42 σοί; POxy 413, 99; s. also 1aα above) **Mt 8:7; Mk 2:8, 17f; Lk 3:7; 5:24; J 1:39, 41, 43** and oft.—πρός τινα (Epict. 2, 17, 34 πρὸς ἄλλους ἐρεῖς; TestSol 1:6 D λέγει Νάθαν πρὸς τὸν ἄγγελον; ApcEsdr 6:16; s. also 1aα above) **Mk 4:41; 16:3; Lk 4:21; 8:25** (λ. πρὸς ἀλλήλους as Jos., Ant. 2, 108; 9, 239); **9:23; 12:1; 16:1; J 2:3; 3:4; Ac 2:12; 28:4.** μετά τινος: ἔλεγον μετ' ἀλλήλων *they said to each other* **J 11:56.**

δ. in other (s. 1aα, 1bα, 1bγ) prep. uses ἀφ' ἑαυτοῦ (=ἀπὸ σεαυτοῦ v.l.) σὺ τοῦτο λέγεις; *do you say this of your own accord?* **J 18:34** (TestAbr A 15 p. 95, 26 [Stone p. 38] al.). εἴς τινα *against someone* **Lk 22:65.** τὶ περί τινος *say someth. about* or *concerning someone* **J 1:22; Ac 8:34; Tit 2:8.** λ. περὶ τοῦ ἱεροῦ, ὅτι *say, with reference to the temple, that* **Lk 21:5.** τί σὺ λέγεις περὶ αὐτοῦ, ὅτι; *what have you to say about him, since?* **J 9:17b** (λ. τι περί τινος, ὅτι as Jos., Bell. 7, 215). τινὶ περί τινος *say to someone about someone* w. direct discourse foll. **Mt 11:7.** Also πρός τινα περί τινος (Jos., C. Ap. 1, 279 πρὸς αὐτὸν περὶ Μωϋσέως) **Lk 7:24.** πρός τινα ἐπί τινος *bring charges against someone before someone* **Ac 23:30** (λ. ἐπί τινος as Jos., Vi. 258). λ. περί (v.l. ὑπέρ) τινος *say* (someth.), *speak in someone's defense* **26:1.**

ε. in connection w. adverbs and adv. exprs.: Λυκαονιστὶ λ. *say in (the) Lycaonian (language)* **Ac 14:11.** καλῶς *correctly* (X., Mem. 2, 7, 11; 3, 3, 4; TestJob 7:8; EpArist 125; 196) **J 8:48; 13:13.** ὡσαύτως *in the same way* **Mk 14:31.** ἀληθῶς λέγω ὑμῖν *truly, I tell you* **Lk 12:44; 21:3.** κατὰ ἄνθρωπον (s. ἄνθρωπος 2b) **Ro 3:5; Gal 3:15.** κατὰ συγγνώμην, οὐ κατ' ἐπιταγήν (s. ἐπιταγή) **1 Cor 7:6;** cp. **2 Cor 8:8.** καθ' ὑστέρησιν **Phil 4:11.**

ζ. w. emphasis on a certain kind of saying: φωνῇ μεγάλῃ *in a loud voice* **Rv 5:12; 8:13** (cp. TestSol 16:1). Also ἐν φωνῇ μεγάλῃ **14:7; 9.** ἄγγελος ἐν φωνῇ λέγων GJs 20:4 (pap, s. deStrycker p. 387f). Opp. ἐν τῇ καρδίᾳ (cp. Ps 13:1) **18:7.** Also ἐν ἑαυτῷ (TestAbr B 3 p. 107, 11 [Stone p. 62]; TestJob 23:8) **Mt 3:9; 9:21; Lk 3:8; 7:39, 49;** GJs 1:1,4; 3:1; 5:1; cp. 1:3 (codd.); 2:1 v.l.; 14:1 v.l.

η. in quotations fr. scripture (but s. also Epict. 1, 28, 4 ὡς λέγει Πλάτων with a quotation) Ἠσαΐας λέγει *Isaiah says* **Ro 10:16, 20; 15:12.** Μωϋσῆς λέγει **10:19.** Δαυὶδ λέγει **11:9.** ἡ γραφὴ λέγει (Just., D. 56, 17; cp. Paus. 2, 16, 4 τὰ ἔπη λέγει=the epic poets say) **4:3; 10:11; Gal 4:30; 1 Ti 5:18; Js 4:5;** cp. **2:23; J 19:24;** 2 Cl 14:2. In the case of the quot. formula λέγει without the subj. expressed, ἡ γραφή or ὁ θεός is easily understood (B-D-F §130, 3; Rob. 392.—On the omission of the subj. [Just., D. 101, 1 al.] cp. Epict. 1, 24, 12 λέγει σοι 'θὲς κτλ.'=someone says to you 'lay aside [this and that sign of prestige]'). It could prob. be translated indefinitely *it says:* **Ro 15:10; 2 Cor 6:2; Gal 3:16; Eph 4:8; 5:14.** ὁ θεός is obviously the subj. (Clearch., fgm. 69c; Epict. 1, 1, 10 λέγει ὁ Ζεύς, followed by a divine revelation to Epictetus) **Hb 5:6.** λέγει ὁ κύριος 2 Cl 13:2; cp. **Hb 8:8–10** (λέγει κύριος Am 5:27; Is 1:18; Jer 9:24; ParJer 6:16 al.). W. the passage more definitely indicated (schol. on Pind., O. 7, 66 ἐν τοῖς Μουσαίου λέγεται; schol. on Apollon. Rhod. 3, 1179 Wendel v.l. ἐν τῇ γ' τῆς Μουσαίου Τιτανογραφίας λέγεται ὡς) ἐν Ἠλίᾳ τί λέγει ἡ γραφή **Ro 11:2** (Epict. 2, 17, 34 τί λέγει Χρύσιππος ἐν τοῖς περὶ τοῦ ψευδομένου). Δαυὶδ λέγει ἐν βίβλῳ ψαλμῶν **Lk 20:42** (Epict. 2, 19, 14 Ἑλλάνικος λέγει ἐν τοῖς Αἰγυπτιακοῖς with quot.). ἐν τ. Ὡσηὲ λέγει **Ro 9:25.** λέγει ἐν τῷ Ἠσαΐᾳ 2 Cl 3:5 (Just., D. 123, 8); cp. ἐν Δαυίδ **Hb 4:7.** ὁ νόμος λέγει (cp. Pla., Crito 12, 50c; Epict. 3, 24, 43 τί γὰρ λέγει; [i.e. ὁ νόμος θεῖος]) **1 Cor 14:34.** λέγει τὸ πνεῦμα τὸ ἅγιον **Hb 3:7** (Just., D. 124, 1). Of words of Jesus: λέγει ὁ κύριος ἐν τῷ εὐαγγελίῳ 2 Cl 8:5. λέγει ὁ κύριος 5:2; 6:1. λέγει αὐτός (i.e. ὁ Χριστός 2:7) 3:2. λέγει 4:2.

θ. Hebraistic, though by no means limited to the OT (s. EKieckers, IndogF 35, 1915, 34ff; B-D-F §420; Mlt-H. 454), is the freq. use of λ. to introduce

א. direct discourse (like לֵאמֹר), even though it is preceded by a verb of saying, or one that includes the idea of saying. Esp. λέγων is so used, as in the LXX, e.g. after ἀναβοᾶν, ἀνακράζειν **Mk 1:23** (cp. Phlegon: 257 fgm. 36, 3, 9 Jac. ἀνεκεκράγει λέγων), ἀπαγγέλλειν, ἀποκρίνεσθαι, ἀρνεῖσθαι, βοᾶν, γογγύζειν, διαγογγύζειν, διαλογίζεσθαι, διαμαρτύρεσθαι, διαστέλλεσθαι, διδάσκειν, δοξάζειν, εἰπεῖν **Mt 22:1; Lk 12:16; 20:2** (s. B-D-F §101, p. 46; s. Rob. 882f; Kieckers, loc. cit. 36f), ἐμβριμᾶσθαι, ἐντέλλεσθαι, ἐπερωτᾶν, ἐπιτιμᾶν, ἐπιφωνεῖν, ἐρωτᾶν, κατηγορεῖν, κηρύσσειν, κράζειν, κραυγάζειν, λαλεῖν, μαρτυρεῖν, μεριμνᾶν, παραινεῖν, παρακαλεῖν, παρατιθέναι παραβολήν, προσεύχεσθαι, προσφωνεῖν, προφητεύειν, συζητεῖν, συλλαλεῖν, φωνεῖν, ψευδομαρτυρεῖν; s. these entries. Also after such verbs as denote an action accompanied by a statement of some kind: ἄγγελος κυρίου . . . ἐφάνη αὐτῷ λέγων *appeared to him and said* **Mt 1:20;** cp. **2:13;** προσεκύνει αὐτῷ λ. *fell before him and said* **8:2; 9:18;** cp. **14:33.** ἅπτεσθαι **8:3; 9:29.** ἔρχεσθαι **Mk 5:35; Lk 18:3; 19:18** al.; cp. **Lk 1:66; 5:8; 8:38; 15:9; Ac 8:10, 19; 12:7; 27:23f; 1 Cor 11:25** al.

ב. the content of a written document (2 Km 11:15; 4 Km 10:6.—1 Macc 8:31; 11:57; Jos., Ant. 11, 26) ἔγραψεν λέγων (=יִכְתֹּב לֵאמֹר) *he wrote as follows* **Lk 1:63.**

ג. orders or instructions to be carried out by other persons: ἔπεμψεν λέγων *he sent and had them say* **Lk 7:19.** ἀπέστειλεν λ. (Judg 11:14f; Jdth 3:1; JosAs 3:2; ParJer 3:21 al.) **Mt 22:16; 27:19; Lk 7:20; 19:14; J 11:3.** If the persons carrying out the orders are named, the ptc. can refer to them **Mt 22:16 v.l.**

ד. When it is used w. the ptc. λ. appears in its finite forms ἐμπαίζοντες ἔλεγον *they mocked and said* **Mt 27:41.** προσελθὼν αὐτῷ λέγει *he approached him and said* **Mk 14:45.** διαρρήξας . . . λέγει *he tore his clothes as he said* vs. **63;** cp. vs. **67; 15:35; Lk 6:20; J 1:36; Hb 8:8a** al.—Also pleonastically (TestSol 2:2; TestJob 23:4; cp. Homeric ἀμειβόμενος προσέειπε Il. 3, 437 al., προσηύδα 14, 270 al.) ἀποκριθεὶς λέγει *he answered* **Mk 8:29b; 9:5, 19; 10:24; 11:22; Lk 3:11; 11:45; 13:8.** κράξας λέγει *he cried out* **Mk 5:7; 9:24** (cp. TestAbr B 6 p. 109, 29 [Stone p. 66] κράζων καὶ λέγων; ApcEsdr 1:2 κράξας λέγων).

ι. Now and then short exprs. with λ. are inserted as parentheses (B-D-F §465, 2; Rob. 434): πολλοί, λέγω ὑμῖν, ζητήσουσιν *many, I tell you, will seek* **Lk 13:24.** ἐν ἀφροσύνῃ λέγω **2 Cor 11:21b.** ὡς τέκνοις λέγω **6:13.**

κ. ptc. w. the article τὰ λεγόμενα *what was said* (EpArist 215, 298; TestSol 15:13; ApcEsdr 2:15; Jos., Ant. 3, 85; 207; Just., D. 46, 4; 115, 1) **Lk 18:34.** προσεῖχον τ. λεγομένοις ὑπὸ τ. Φιλίππου (προσέχω 2b) **Ac 8:6** (προσέχ. τοῖς λεγ. as Jos., Ant. 13, 303; τὰ λ. ὑπό τινος as Bell. 7, 56; 423; Esth 3:3, also Nicol. Dam.: 90 fgm. 24, p. 408, 19 ὑπὸ τῶν μάντεων; fgm. 30 p. 417, 23 Jac.; Epict. 1, 18, 1; SIG 679, 87). τὰ ἢ λεχθέντα ἢ πραχθέντα (Ps.-Libanius, Charact. Ep. p. 48, 18; 64, 18; Jos., C. Ap. 1, 55) Papias (2:15) in Eus., HE 3, 39, 15 (=Geb., Harn., Zahn 15, p. 72, 17).

❷ **to express oneself in a specific way, *say*—ⓐ** *ask* w. direct question foll: **Mt 9:14; 15:1; 18:1; Mk 5:30f.** ὁ διδάσκαλος λέγει *the Master asks* **14:14.** W. dat. of pers. and a direct question foll.: **Mt 9:28a; 15:34; 16:15; 20:6.**

ⓑ *answer* (Lucian, Syr. Dea 18; TestSol 5:8 al.; ApcMos 5) **Mt 17:25; Mk 8:24; J 1:21; 18:17b.** W. dat. of pers. and direct discourse: **Mt 4:10; 8:26; 9:28b; 14:17; 15:33; 18:22; 19:7, 20** al. W. dat of pers. and direct discourse introduced by ὅτι **Mt 19:8.**

ⓒ *order, command, direct, enjoin, recommend* more or less emphatically (Syntipas p. 9, 4; Num 32:27; TestSol 4:7 D; TestAbr A 17 p. 98, 21 [Stone p. 44]) τὶ *someth.* 2 Cl 6:4. ἃ λέγω **Lk 6:46.** τί τινι *command someone* (to do) *someth.* ὅ τι ἂν λέγῃ ὑμῖν **J 2:5b** (TestAbr A 4 p. 81, 8 [Stone p. 10]); cp. **Ac 21:23** (s. Num 32:31). ὃ ὑμῖν λέγω, πᾶσιν λέγω, γρηγορεῖτε *the order I give to you I give to everyone: be on your guard!* **Mk 13:37** (for the formal nuance cp. reff. at end of this parag.). Gener. w. dat. of pers. and direct discourse foll.: **Mt 5:44; 6:25; 8:4, 9; 26:52; Mk 3:3, 5; 5:8; 6:10; Lk 6:27; 7:8; J 2:7f.** W. dat. of pers. and inf. foll.: **Rv 10:9; 13:14;** w. an inf. and a negative *forbid* (X., An. 7, 1, 40) **Mt 5:34, 39.**—Here belongs χαίρειν τινὶ λέγειν (Epict. 3, 22, 64) *extend a greeting to someone,* since the greeting consists in saying χαῖρε='may you prosper' **2J 10f.** W. ἵνα foll. *recommend that, tell to* τῷ λαῷ λέγων . . . ἵνα πιστεύσωσιν **Ac 19:4.** οὐ περὶ ἐκείνης λέγω ἵνα ἐρωτήσῃ *I do not recommend that anyone should pray about that* (sin) **1J 5:16.** W. inf. foll.: **Ro 2:22.**—τάδε λέγει is the formal style of one who is giving an order (introductory formula for the edicts of the Persian kings [IMagnMai 115, 4]; in the OT a favorite method of introducing a prophetic statement [Thackeray p. 11]) **Ac 21:11, 8, 12, 18; 3:1, 7, 14** (s. Gerhard, Philol. 64, 1905, 27ff; Thieme 23; GRudberg, Eranos 11, 1911, 177f; LLafoscade, De epistulis imperatorum 1902, 63 and 77. Roman edicts gener. use the simple λέγει as in the praescriptio of SEG IX, 8 I, 1–3 αὐτοκράτωρ Καῖσαρ Σεβαστὸς . . . λέγει; also by Augustus: Jos., Ant., 16, 162; s. MBenner, The Emperor Says '75).

ⓓ *assure, assert;* w. direct discourse foll. Esp. in the formulas λέγω σοι, λ. ὑμῖν, ἀμὴν (ἀμὴν) λ. ὑμῖν (TestAbr A 8 p. 85, 19f [Stone p. 18]) **Mt 11:22; 12:31; 19:24; 23:39; Mk 11:24; Lk 4:25; 7:9, 28; 9:27.—Mt 5:26; 6:2, 5; 8:10; Mk 3:28; 9:41; 10:15; Lk 4:24; 18:17, 29; 23:43; J 1:51; 3:3, 5, 11; 5:19, 24f; 6:26, 32** al.

ⓔ *maintain, declare, proclaim* as teaching, w. direct discourse foll.: **Gal 4:1; 1J 2:4.** Foll. by acc. and inf. (X., Symp. 5, 5) **Mt 22:23; Mk 12:18; Lk 20:41; 23:2b; Ro 15:8; 2 Ti 2:18.** Foll. by ὅτι and direct discourse **Mk 12:35b; 1 Cor 15:12.** W. dat. of pers. and direct discourse after ὅτι **Mt 5:20, 22, 28, 32; 8:11** al. Someth. like *interpret* εἰς *w. ref. to* **Eph 5:32.**—σὺ λέγεις (that is what) *you maintain* **Mt 27:11; Mk 15:2; Lk 23:3** (cp. σὺ εἶπας Mt 26:25 and s. εἶπον 1a). Cp. also **Lk 22:70; J 18:37** (s. OMerlier, RevÉtGr 46, '33, 204–19; Goodsp., Probs. 64–68 [strong affirmative, *yes*]; MSmith, JBL 64, '45, 506–10 [intentionally ambiguous, *so you say,* Tannaitic Parallels to the Gospels, '51, 27–30]; DCatchpole, NTS 17, '70/71, 213–26). τί λέγει ἡ γνῶσις; *what does Gnosis teach* about this? With the answer in direct discourse B 6:9 (cp. Epict. 3, 13, 11 καὶ τί λέγει [i.e., ὁ λόγος ὁ τῶν φιλοσόφων=philosophy]; direct discourse follows).

ⓕ of written communications (Hdt. 3, 40; 122; 8, 140; UPZ 68, 5 [152 BC]; Jos., Ant. 13, 80) **1 Cor 6:5; 7:6; 15:51; 2 Cor 6:13; 8:8; Gal 5:2; Phil 4:11; Col 2:4; Phlm 21,** al. in Paul.

❸ **to inform about / tell of someth.,** ***speak, report*** (Diog. L. 1, 31) τινί *to someone* **Mk 7:36.** τὶ *about someth.* (X., Cyr. 1, 2, 16 νῦν λέξομεν τὰς Κύρου πράξεις)τὴν ἔξοδον αὐτοῦ *of his death (lit., departure)* **Lk 9:31.** τὰ περὶ τ. βασιλείας **Ac 1:3.** τὰ γινόμενα ὑπ' αὐτῶν αἰσχρόν ἐστιν καὶ λέγειν *it is a disgrace even to speak of the things they do* **Eph 5:12** (Demosth. 10, 27 ὃ . . . οὔτε λέγειν ἄξιον). τινὶ περί τινος *bring a report about someone to someone* **Mk 1:30; 8:30.** Likew. τινί τινα **Phil 3:18.**

❹ **to identify in a specific manner,** ***call, name*** (Aeschyl. et al.) w. double acc. (Epict. 2, 19, 19 τί Στωικὸν ἔλεγες σεαυτόν; Diog. L. 8, 88 τὴν ἡδονὴν λέγειν τὸ ἀγαθόν=call pleasure the [real] good; 2 Macc 4:2; Just., D. 61, 1 ἀρχηστρατηγὸν ἑαυτὸν λέγει) τινά τι *describe someone as someth.* τί με λέγεις ἀγαθόν; *why do you call me good?* **Mk 10:18; Lk 18:19.** Δαυὶδ λέγει αὐτὸν κύριον *David calls him Lord* **Mk 12:37.** πατέρα ἴδιον ἔλεγεν τὸν θεόν *he called God his Father* **J 5:18.** οὐκέτι λέγω ὑμᾶς δούλους *I no longer call you slaves* **15:15;** cp. **Ac 10:28; Rv 2:20.** Pass. *be called, named* **Mt 13:55; Hb 11:24.** ὁ λεγόμενος *the so-called* (Epict. 4, 1, 51 οἱ βασιλεῖς λεγόμενοι; Socrat., Ep. 14, 7 ὁ λ. θάνατος) λεγόμενοι θεοί *so-called gods* **1 Cor 8:5** (Herm. Wr. 2, 14 the λεγόμενοι θεοί in contrast to μόνος ὁ θεός. Somewhat differently Jos., Ant. 12, 125 Ἀντίοχος ὁ παρὰ τοῖς Ἕλλησιν θεὸς λεγόμενος). οἱ λεγόμενοι ἀκροβυστία ὑπὸ τῆς λ. περιτομῆς *those who are called 'the uncircumcised'* (i.e. gentiles) *by the so-called circumcision* (i.e. Jews) **Eph 2:11.** ὁ λεγόμενος (B-D-F §412, 2; Rob. 1107; cp. BGU 1117, 9 [13 BC]; PRyl 133, 11; 137, 19; 2 Macc 12:17; 14:6; 3 Macc 1:3; TestAbr B 13 p. 118, 14 [Stone p. 84]; TestJob 46:5; 47:1; Just., A I, 22, 1, D. 32, 1) *who is called . . .* **Mt 1:16; 27:17;** *whose surname is* (Appian, Liby. 49 §213 Ἄννων ὁ μέγας λεγόμενος; Jos., Ant. 13, 370, Vi. 4) **10:2; Col 4:11;** *by name* **Mt 9:9; 26:3, 14; 27:16; Mk 15:7; Lk 22:47; J 9:11.**—Of things: of the name of a star **Rv 8:11.** Of place-names (BGU 326, 19 [II AD]; 2 Macc 9:2; 12:21) **Mt 2:23; 26:36; J 4:5; 11:54; 19:13; Ac 3:2; 6:9; Hb 9:3.** Of the local, vernacular name λ. Ἑβραϊστί **J 5:2 v.l.; 19:17b.**—In the transl. of foreign words *(which) means:* ὅ ἐστιν κρανίου τόπος λεγόμενος *which means 'Place of a Skull'* **Mt 27:33b.** Cp. also **J 4:25; 11:16; 20:24; 21:2.** Also ὃ λέγεται **20:16.** ὃ λ. μεθερμηνευόμενον *which, when translated, means* **1:38.** ἣ διερμηνευομένη λέγεται **Ac 9:36.**—Other exx. of the significance *mean* (Aeschyl. et al.) are **Gal 4:1;** 2 Cl 6:4; 8:6 Cp. 1bβ.—B. 1253f; 1257; 1277. DELG. M-M. EDNT. TW. Sv. S. λόγος, ῥῆμα, λαλέω.

λεῖμμα, ατος, τό (s. λείπω; edd. also λείμμα, λίμμα; Hdt. 1, 119 et al.; Plut., Mor. 78a.—PTebt 115, 2 [115/113 BC] τὸ γεγονὼς [=-ὸς] λίμμα [Mayser p. 843]; 4 Km 19:4 A λίμματος [Thackeray p. 84]; W-S. §5; 13e; New Docs 4, 186) ***remnant*** λ. κατ' ἐκλογὴν χάριτος γέγονεν *there is a remnant chosen by grace* **Ro 11:5** (cp. CD 1, 4).—JJeremias, D. Gedanke des 'Heiligen Restes' usw., ZNW 42, '49, 154–94.—DELG s.v. λείπω. M-M. TW.

λεῖος, α, ον (cp. Lat. levis; Hom. et al.; SIG 972, 119; BGU 162, 5; 781 II, 15; LXX; En 22:2; EpArist 76; Philo; Jos., Ant. 15, 400) ***smooth, level*** of a road (opp. τραχύς *rough,* as X., Mem. 3, 10, 1; Philo, Abr. 239) **Lk 3:5** (Is 40:4 v.l.).—B. 1068. DELG. M-M. TW.

λειποτακτέω or λιποτακτέω (s. λείπω, τάξις; milit. t.t. 'leave the ranks, desert'; Plut., Mor. 241a; Polemo, Decl. 2, 44 p. 31, 17; PLips 45, 18; 46, 15; PLond III, 1247, 14 p. 225 [IV AD]; 4 Macc 9:23) transf. sense ***turn away*** ἀπό τινος *from someth.* ἀπὸ τοῦ θελήματος (θεοῦ) 1 Cl 21:4 (cp. Philo, Gig. 43 [268] καλὸν δὲ μὴ λιποτακτῆσαι τῆς τοῦ θεοῦ τάξεως).—DELG s.v. τάσσω.

λείπω fut. 3 sg. λείψει ApcEsdr; 2 aor. ἔλιπον, subj. 3 sg. λίπῃ **Tit 3:13 v.l.;** pf. pass. ptc. λελειμμένος 2 Macc 4:45 (Hom.+, 'leave [behind]' and other senses).

❶ **to leave behind,** trans., mid. and pass.—ⓐ ***fall short, be inferior, lack*** (Hdt. 7, 8, 1; Diod. S. 17, 46, 1; Jos., Bell. 3, 482, Ant. 14, 474; Just., A I, 67, 1 and 6) ἔν τινι *in someth.* (Sb 620, 6 [97/96 BC] of a temple λείπεσθαι ἐν τῷ μὴ εἶναι ἄσυλον; SIG 618, 15; 800, 29; PGM 4, 2347) ἐν μηδενί *fall short in no respect* **Js 1:4.**

ⓑ ***be/do without, lack, be in need or want (of)*** w. gen. (B-D-F §180, 4; cp. Soph., El. 474; Ps.-Pla., Axioch. 366d; later, e.g. Libanius, Progym.: Confirm. 1, 1 vol. VIII p. 138f. τῆς ἐνθέου μανίας) σοφίας *be deficient in wisdom* **Js 1:5.** τῆς ἐφημέρου τροφῆς *be in need of daily food* **2:15.** θεοῦ *lack God* ITr 5:2b. μηδενός *lack nothing* IPol 2:2.

❷ **to be deficient in someth. that ought to be present for whatever reason,** ***lack,*** intr., act. (λείπει τί τινι: Polyb. 10, 18, 8; Epict. 2, 14, 19; Jos., Ant. 12, 36; λείπει τίς τινι ApcEsdr 6:18 p. 31, 27 Tdf.) σοὶ πολλὰ λείπει *you fall far short* Hv 3, 1, 9. πολλὰ ἡμῖν λείπει *we lack much* ITr 5:2a. ἔτι ἕν σοι λείπει *there is one thing that you still lack* **Lk 18:22** (cp. Jos., Bell. 4, 257 τοῖς τολμήμασιν ἓν μόνον λείπει; TestAbr A 14 p. 93, 26f [Stone p. 34] τί ἔτι λείπεται τῇ ψυχῇ εἰς τὸ σώζεσθαι;) ἵνα μηδὲν αὐτοῖς λείπῃ *that they may lack nothing* **Tit 3:13.** τὰ λείποντα (Just., A I, 52, 2; τὰ λ. τοῦ ψαλμοῦ Just., D 106, 1; Lucian, Syr. Dea 26) *what is lacking, the defects* **1:5.** W. inf. foll. (cp. B-D-F §393, 4) λείπει τῷ πύργῳ ἔτι μικρὸν οἰκοδομηθῆναι *the tower still lacks a little of being finished, is still not quite finished* Hs 9, 9, 4.—B. 839. DELG. M-M. Spicq.

λειτουργέω impf. ἐλειτούργουν; fut. λειτουργήσω LXX; 1 aor. ἐλειτούργησα (cp. Att. λεώς = λαός, q.v. + ἔργον; X.+; ins, pap, LXX; TestSol 12:6 v.l.; TestLevi 3:5, TestAsh 2:2; EpArist, Philo, Joseph.; on the spelling s. Mayser 127; Mlt-H. 76f) gener. 'perform a public service, serve in a public office' (in the Gr-Rom. world distinguished citizens were expected to serve in a variety of offices, including esp. as high priests, with all costs that such service involved, or to assume the costs of construction or maintenance of public buildings and production of dramas and games; for their services they would be recognized as people of exceptional merit [s. ἀρετή] or benefactors [s. εὐεργέτης]; but the word is also used of less prestigious activity SEG XXVI, 1392, 31 supply carts and mules; New Docs 1, 42–44) in our lit. almost exclusively of religious and ritual services both in a wider and a more restricted sense (SIG 717, 23f [100 BC] ἐλειτούργησαν ἐν τῷ ἱερῷ εὐτάκτως; 736, 73; 74f λειτουργούντω τοῖς θεοῖς; 97f [92 BC]; PLond I, 33a, 3 p. 19 [II BC]; 41 B, 1; UPZ 42, 2 [162 BC]; 47, 3; BGU 1006, 10; LXX; EpArist 87; Dssm., B 137 [BS 140f]; Anz 346f; Danker, Benefactor [lit.]). Through the use of this term NT writers suggest an aura of high status for those who render any type of service.

❶ **to render special formal service, *serve, render service,*** of cultic or ritual responsibilities—ⓐ of priests and Levites in God's temple (cp. Ex 28:35, 43; 29:30; Num 18:2; Sir 4:14; 45:15; Jdth 4:14; 1 Macc 10:42; Philo, Mos. 2, 152; Jos., Bell. 2, 409, Ant. 20, 218) abs. **Hb 10:11.** λ. τῷ θυσιαστηρίῳ τοῦ θεοῦ *perform services at the altar of God* 1 Cl 32:2 (cp. Jo 1:9, 13); (w. ἱερατεύειν as Sir 45:15) λ. τῷ θεῷ 43:4; GJs 4:1 (1 Km 3:1).—Of Christian services ἐν τ. θυσιαστηρίῳ λ. τὸ θεῖον *perform service to God at the altar* **Tit 1:9 v.l.**—Of officials of Christian congregations: λ. ἀμέμπτως τῷ ποιμνίῳ τοῦ Χριστοῦ *serve Christ's flock blamelessly* 1 Cl 44:3. Of supervisors Hs 9, 27, 3. Of supervisors and servers λ. τὴν λειτουργίαν τῶν προφητῶν καὶ διδασκάλων *perform the service of prophets and teachers* D 15:1 (s. b, below on **Ac 13:2.**—λειτ. λ. Demosth. 21, 154; oft. in LXX; also Philo, Spec. Leg. 1, 82; SIG 409, 61).—Of angels (TestLevi 3:5) τῷ θελήματι αὐτοῦ (sc. θεοῦ) λειτουργοῦσιν παρεστῶτες *they stand at (God's) side and serve (God's) will* 1 Cl 34:5; cp. vs. 6 (Da 7:10 Theod.).

ⓑ of other expression of religious devotion (Dionys. Hal. 2, 22, 2 ἐπὶ τῶν ἱερῶν of the wives of priests and their children who perform certain rites that would not be approved for males) including *prayer* (w. νηστεύειν, and of the prophets and teachers) τ. κυρίῳ **Ac 13:2.** λ. τῷ θεῷ (cp. Jo 1:13b) Hm 5, 1, 2; cp. 3; s 7:6. Of OT worthies οἱ τελείως λειτουργήσαντες *those who have rendered superb service* to God 1 Cl 9:2.

❷ **to confer a special material benefit,** ***serve*** (X., Mem. 2, 7, 6; Chares Hist.: 125 fgm. 4 p. 659, 28 Jac. [in Athen. 12, 54, 538e]; τῷ βίῳ λ. Orig., C. Cels. 8, 57, 1 and 6) ἐν τοῖς σαρκικοῖς λ. *do a service in material things* **Ro 15:27**—On this entry and the foll. one s. Elbogen 5; 511; FOertel, D. Liturgie, 1917; NLewis, Inventory of Compulsory Services in Ptolemaic and Roman Egypt '68; WBrandt, D. Wortgruppe λειτουργεῖν im Hb u. 1 Kl: Jahrb. d. Theol. Schule Bethel 1, 1930, 145–76; OCasel, λειτουργία—munus: Oriens Christ. III 7, '32, 289–302; EPeterson, Nuntius 2, '49, 10f; ARomeo, Miscellanea Liturgica (LMohlberg Festschr.), vol. 2, '49, 467–519; FDanker, Gingrich Festschr. '72, 108ff.—S. λειτουργία, λειτουργικός, λειτουργός.—DELG s.v. λαός. M-M. TW. Spicq. Sv.

λειτουργία, ας, ἡ (s. prec. entry; Pla.+; ins, pap, LXX, ParJer 3; ApcSed 14, 3 and 11; EpArist, Philo, Joseph., loanw. in rabb.) prim. 'public service', the usual designation for a service performed by an individual for the state or public cult (oft. free of charge, s. lit. under λειτουργέω 2), in our lit. almost always used w. some sort of relig. connotation. As with the use of the verb λειτουργέω NT writers suggest an aura of high status for those who render any type of service.

❶ **service of a formal or public type, *service***—ⓐ of ritual and cultic services (Diod. S. 1, 21, 7; SIG 1109, 111; UPZ 17, 17 [163 BC] λ. τῷ θεῷ; 40, 19 [161 BC]; PTebt 302, 30 [s. Dssm. B 138=BS 141]; Ex 37:19; Num 8:22; 16:9; 18:4; 2 Ch 31:2; EpArist; Philo, Virt. 54 al.; Jos., Bell. 1, 26, Ant. 3, 107 al.; Hippol., Ref. 9, 30, 4) *service as priest* **Lk 1:23.** τὰς προσφορὰς καὶ λειτουργίας ἐπιτελεῖσθαι *bring offerings and perform (other) ceremonial services* 1 Cl 40:2. τὰ σκεύη τῆς λ. *the vessels used in priestly service* **Hb 9:21** (ParJer 3:9, 11, 18). Of the high priest's service 1 Cl 40:5. Fig., of the high-priestly office of Christ **Hb 8:6.**

ⓑ of other kinds of service to God 1 Cl 20:10. Of Noah 1 Cl 9:4. Of Paul (w. θυσία, q.v. 1; cp. BGU 1201, 7 [2 AD] πρὸς τὰς λιτουργείας καὶ θυσείας τῶν θεῶν) *sacrificial service* **Phil 2:17.**—Of officials in Christian congregations (ἡ τῆς ἐπισκοπῆς λ. Iren. 3, 3, 3 [Harv. II 10, 3]) διαδέχεσθαι τὴν λ. αὐτῶν *succeed to their office* 1 Cl 44:2; ἡ αὐτοῖς τετιμημένη λ. *the office held in honor by them* 44:6; ἀποβάλλεσθαι τῆς λ. *be removed from office* 44:3. On D 15:1 cp. λειτουργέω 1a.—Also of the activities of a nonofficial pers. in the church service μὴ παρεκβαίνειν τὸν ὡρισμένον τῆς λ. αὐτοῦ κανόνα *not overstepping the fixed boundaries of his service* 1 Cl 41:1. Of acts that show forth Christian charity and other virtues that are beyond the call of ordinary duty and are therefore more like those rendered by public-spirited citizens and thus evoke God's special approval: αἱ λ. αὗται *these services* Hs 5, 3, 3; cp. 5, 3, 8 (λ. ἐκκλησίας θεοῦ ἐπὶ σωτηρίᾳ ἀνθρώπων Orig., C. Cels. 8, 75, 18).—Of angels: λ. τῆς κτίσεως 'service to the creation' Hippol., Ref. 9, 30, 2.

❷ **service of a personal nature, *help, assistance, service*** transf. sense of the primary mng. and mng. 1: of Epaphroditus' services to Paul ἵνα ἀναπληρώσῃ τὸ ὑμῶν ὑστέρημα τῆς πρός με λειτουργίας *in order that he might supply what was lacking in your service to me* **Phil 2:30.** W. ref. to the collection ἡ διακονία τῆς λ. ταύτης **2 Cor 9:12.**—ESchweizer, D. Leben d. Herrn in d. Gemeinde u. ihren Diensten, '46, 19–23; AHillorst, Filología Neotestamentaria 1, '88, 27–34.—DELG s.v. λαός. M-M. EDNT. TW. Spicq. Sv.

λειτουργικός, ή, όν (PPetr II, 39 [e] [6 times]; s. Dssm., B 138=BS 141]; PTebt 5, 49 [118 BC]; 102, 3. But also in a ritual sense PTebt 88, 3 [115/114 BC] ἡμέραι λειτουργικαί=the days when the prophets of the temple are permitted to perform certain holy acts [Mitt-Wilck. I/2, p. 94; WOtto, Priester u. Tempel im hellenist. Ägypt. II 1908 p. 33, 2; 39, 2]; likew. Mitt-Wilck. I /2, 115, 15; 146; Ex 31:10; 39:12; Num 4:12, 26; 2 Ch 24:14) ***engaged in special service,*** of angels λ. πνεύματα *spirits in special service (to God)* **Hb 1:14** (cp. Philo, Virt. 74 ἄγγελοι λειτουργοί).—S. λειτουργέω, λειτουργία, λειτουργός.—DELG s.v. λαός. M-M. TW. Spicq.

λειτουργός, οῦ, ὁ (s. λειτουργέω; Polyb. et al.; pap, LXX; pseudepigr.; Ath. 10:3) prim. 'one who performs public service', in our lit. (exc. TestAsh 2:2) always w. sacred connotations (λ. τῶν θεῶν Dionys. Hal. 2, 2, 3; 2, 73, 2; Plut., Mor. 417a; ins [I BC: REA 32, 1930, p. 5] θεοῖς λιτουργοί; ins fr. Miletus: GKawerau and ARehm, D. Delphinion in M. 1914, 396; LXX; TestSol 4:13 D; TestAbr A 15 p. 95, 5 [Stone p. 38]; TestLevi; EpArist 95; Philo; Hippol., Ref. 10, 9, 1 τοῦ ὄφεως λ.).

❶ **one engaged in administrative or cultic service, *servant, minister,*** the formal sense—ⓐ of Gr-Rom officials λ. θεοῦ *servants of God* **Ro 13:6** (s. AvanVeldhuizen, Wie zijn λειτουργοὶ θεοῦ in Ro 13:6: TSt 32, 1914, 302–11). Of heavenly beings as *servants* of God **Hb 1:7;** 1 Cl 36:3 (both Ps 103:4; cp. 102:21; Philo, Virt. 74 ἄγγελοι λειτουργοί).

ⓑ of priests 1 Cl 41:2; GJs 23:1. Of Christ, the true High Priest τῶν ἁγίων λ. καὶ τῆς σκηνῆς τῆς ἀληθινῆς *a minister in the sanctuary and in the true tabernacle* **Hb 8:2** (Philo, Leg. All. 3, 135 λειτουργὸς τῶν ἁγίων).—Also of the prophets οἱ λειτουργοὶ τῆς χάριτος τοῦ θεοῦ 1 Cl 8:1. Of Paul, apostle to the nations/gentiles, λ. Χριστοῦ Ἰησοῦ εἰς τὰ ἔθνη *a servant of Christ Jesus for the gentiles* **Ro 15:16.** The term φιλοτιμέομαι in the immediate context (vs. 20) is freq. used in connection w. service rendered by public-spirited citizens (s. s.v.).

❷ **one engaged in personal service, *aide, assistant,*** a transf., sense of 1, thus heightening the status of the referent: of Epaphroditus λειτουργὸς τῆς χρείας μου *the one who has served my needs* (=*my aide*) **Phil 2:25.**—DELG s.v. λαός. M-M. TW. Spicq. S. lit. s.v. λειτουργέω 2.

λείχω fut. 3 pl. λείξουσιν; aor. ἔλειξαν LXX (Aeschyl., Hdt.+; LXX) ***lick*** τὶ *someth.*, of dogs (3 Km 20:19) **Lk 16:21 v.l.** B. 267.—DELG.

Λέκτρα, ας, ἡ ***Lectra*** wife of Onesiphorus AcPl Ant 13, 7f (cp. Aa 1, 236, 7) **2 Ti 4:19 v.l.** as wife of Aquila (s. Dibelius, Hdb. ad loc.).

λεμά (Aram. לְמָא) ***why?*** **Mt 27:46; Mk 15:34** (Ps 22:2); (vv.ll. λαμά, λιμά) s. λαμά.

λέντιον, ου, τό (Lat. loanw.: linteum, also in rabb.; Peripl. Eryth. c. 6; Arrian, Peripl. 4; IMagnMai 116, 34; POxy 929, 10 λίνον καὶ λέντιον; Ostraka II 1611, 1; Hahn 235; 262; 266; GrBar 3:5) ***linen cloth*** Hv 3, 1, 4; ***towel*** **J 13:4f** (Vi. Aesopi I c. 61 of a woman who is preparing to wash another person's feet: περιζωσαμένη λέντιον).

λεόπαρδος, ου, ὁ (Galen: CMG V 4, 1, 1 p. 86, 15; Anecdota Astrol. [ALudwich, Maximi et Ammonis carmina 1877] p. 122, 2; Theognost.: Anecd. Gr. p. 1394; AcPh 94–101 [Aa II/2, 36–39]; 121 [Aa II/2, 50]; Athanasius, Vi. Anton. 9 vol. I 640) ***leopard,*** metaph. for rough soldiers ἐνδεδεμένος (v.l. δεδεμένος) δέκα λεοπάρδοις *bound to ten 'leopards'* IRo 5:1 (the addition of ὅ ἐστι στρατιωτικὸν τάγμα suggests that the language is metaph. here; it is all the more appropriate because Ignatius is being taken as a prisoner to Rome to fight w. wild beasts; but s. DSaddington, JTS 38, '87, 411f [a 'cohors' named Lepidiana]).—DELG.

λεπίς, ίδος, ἡ (λέπω 'to peel'; a thin layer that covers someth., such as 'scales' of fish, Hdt. et al.; Michel 833, 11 [279 BC]; BGU 544, 8; PGM 4, 258 al.; LXX; TestJob 43:8; Philo; Jos., Ant. 3, 149) 'scale'.

❶ **flattened plate covering the skin of marine creatures, *scales,*** a collective B 10:1 (cp. Lev 11:9ff; Dt 14:9f; TestJob 43:8 λεπίδας τοῦ δράκοντος).

❷ **a thin flaky piece, *scale*** in a simile ἀπέπεσαν αὐτοῦ ἀπὸ τῶν ὀφθαλμῶν ὡς λεπίδες *someth. like scales fell fr. his eyes,* i.e. he suddenly regained his sight **Ac 9:18.** For the expr. cp. Galen: CMG V 4, 1, 1 p. 77, 3 οἷον λεπὶς ἀπέπιπτε='someth. like a scale fell off' (other exx. in Hobart 39). On the figure cp. Tob 11:12.—DELG s.v. λέπω A 1. M-M. TW. Spicq.

λέπρα, ας, ἡ (s. λεπρός; Hdt. et al.; Galen: CMG V 4, 2 p. 333, 5; 429, 11; PSI X, 1180, 36 [II AD]; LXX, Philo; Jos., Ant. 3, 265, C. Ap. 1, 235; Theoph. Ant. 3, 21 [p. 244, 19]) a serious skin disease, poss. including leprosy. Gk. medical writers include a variety of skin disorders under the term λ. There is abundant evidence that not all the צָרַעַת (cp. Lev 13f) and λέπρα of the Bible is true 'leprosy' caused by Hansen's bacillus as known in modern times; indeed, there are many (see Gramberg and Cochrane below) who hold that Hansen's disease was unknown in biblical times, or known by a different name than leprosy. λέπρα in LXX and NT may at times refer to what is generally termed leprosy, but probability extends to such skin diseases as psoriasis, lupus, ringworm, and favus, and in the absence of more precise data it is best to use the more general term ***serious skin disease*** **Mt 8:3; Mk 1:42; Lk 5:12f;** PEg[2] 39 [ἀ]π̣έστη ἀπ' αὐτοῦ ἡ λέπ[ρα]=ASyn. 42, 32.—GMünch, Die Zaraath (Lepra) der hebr. Bibel 1893; EMcEwen, Biblical World 38, 1911, 194–202; 255–61; LHuizinga, Leprosy: BiblSacra 83, 1926, 29–46; 202–12; Billerb. IV 1928, 745–63; Handb. d. Haut-u. Geschlechtskrankheiten, ed. JJadassohn, vol. X: Die Lepra 1930; FLendrum, The Name 'Leprosy': Amer. Journ. of Tropical Medicine and Hygiene 1, '52, 999–1008. Series of articles in BT: KGramberg, 11, '60, 10–20; JSwellengrebel, 11, '60, 69–80, with note by ENida; RCochrane, Biblical Leprosy, 12 '61, 202f, w. mention of a separate publ. of the same title, '61; DWallington, 12, '61, 75–79; SBrowne, Leprosy in the Bible, in Medicine and the Bible, ed. BPalmer, '86, 101–25; MGrmek, Diseases in the Ancient Greek World '89, 160–61.—ABD IV 277–82 (lit.). TW.

λεπράω 1 aor. ἐλέπρησα (Hdt., Hippocr. et al.; Num 12:10) ***suffer from a skin disorder*** (the etymological association with λεπίς 'scale' is not to be pressed) ἐλ[έπρησα] PEg[2] 35=ASyn. 42, 31 and 84, 31.—DELG s.v. λέπω.

λεπρός, ά, όν (s. λεπίς and λέπρα; Aristoph., fgm. 723 K.; Theophr.; Herodas 6, 36 et al.; in description of a wanted felon PMich IV/1, 223; 1189; 224, 2024; 225, 1751 [all III AD and in ref. to the same pers.]; LXX; Mel., P. 72, 526; Theoph. Ant. 3, 21 [p. 244, 24]; 'scaly') **pert. to having a serious skin disorder, *with a bad skin disease*** (so Theophr., CP 2, 6, 4 of pers. becoming 'scaly', w. similar condition in plants; LXX) λεπροὶ ἄνδρες **Lk 17:12.**—Subst. ὁ λ. *a person with a bad skin disease* (Philo, Leg. All. 3, 7; Jos., Ant. 3, 264, C. Ap. 1, 278) **Mt 8:2; 10:8; 11:5; Mk 1:40** (CMasson, La péricope du lépreux [Mk 1:40–45]: RTP n.s. 23, '39, 287–95); **Lk 4:27; 7:22** (on **Mt 11:5** and **Lk 7:22** s. κωφός 2); PEg[2] 32=ASyn. 42, 30. As surname of Simon of Bethany (cp. Sb 7638, 4f [257 BC] τὴν Νικάνορος τοῦ ποδαγρικοῦ οἰκίαν) **Mt 26:6** (λεπρωσοῦ; D after Lat.: leprosi) **Mk 14:3.**—DELG s.v. λέπω. TW.

λεπτός, ή, όν (Hom.+; SIG 567, 6; pap, LXX, TestSol 11:7; JosAs 10:13; Philo; Jos., Bell. 2, 154; SibOr 1, 361; superl. λεπτότατος Just., D. 46, 5).

❶ **pert. to being relatively small in bulk, *small, thin, light*** ὄστρακον λ. Hs 9, 10, 1; θηρία λ. *tiny animals* ApcPt fgm. 2 p. 12, 27.

❷ τὸ λ. (sc. νόμισμα with Artem. 2, 58; Pollux 9, 92 or κέρμα w. Alciphron 1, 9, 1) ***small copper coin,*** 1/128 of a denarius, something between a penny and a mill, **Mk 12:42; Lk 12:59; 21:2.** (cp. OGI 484, 35; SIG 1109, 80; 98f)—S. ἀργύριον 2c.—Schürer II 66; Kl. Pauly III 582; B. 889. DELG s.v. λέπω. M-M.

Λευί, ὁ (לֵוִי) indecl. (B-D-F §53, 1) and Λευίς, gen. Λευί, acc. Λευίν (B-D-F §55, 1e; W-S. §10, 5; Wuthnow 67; Mlt-H. 146 Λευείς; the mss. and edd. form and sp. fluctuate: Λευΐ-, Λευεί-) ***Levi*** (LXX; Test12Patr [Λευί; vv.ll. Λευίς, Λευίν]; JosAs [Λευίς; v.l. Λευί]; EpArist 48; Philo, Joseph.).

❶ son of Jacob **Hb 7:9.** οἱ υἱοὶ Λευί vs. **5;** φυλὴ Λ. **Rv 7:7.**

❷ son of Melchi; in the genealogy of Jesus **Lk 3:24.**

❸ son of Symeon; in the genealogy of Jesus vs. **29.**

❹ a disciple of Jesus, called by him fr. the tax-collector's office **Lk 5:27, 29.** Acc. to **Mk 2:14** this disciple was a son of Alphaeus (s. Ἁλφαῖος 1). GPt 14:60 also speaks of a Λευὶς ὁ τοῦ ῾Αλφαίου as a disciple of Jesus. GMary 463, 18; 31. On **Mt 9:9** s. Μαθθαῖος.

❺ name of a high priest, partly restored Λευ[είς?] Ox 840, 10.—Pauly-W. XII 2207f; BHHW III 1076. TW.

Λευίτης, ου, ὁ (mss. and edd. also Λευΐ-, Λευειτ-. LXX, Philo, Joseph.; Plut., Mor. 671e) ***a Levite,*** member of the tribe of Levi, esp. one who did not belong to the family of Aaron, and whose duty it was to perform the lowlier services connected w. the temple ritual. W. ἱερεύς **Lk 10:32; J 1:19;** 1 Cl 32:2; 40:5. Of Joseph Barnabas **Ac 4:36.**—JEmerton, VetusT 12, '62, 129–38 (Deut.); AGunneweg, Leviten u. Priester, '65.—TW.

Λευιτικός, ή, όν (for the sp. s. Λευίτης. Lev, title; Philo; Just., D. 16, 1 ἐν τῷ Λ.; Mel., HE 4, 26, 14 Λευιτικόν) ***Levitical*** Λ. ἱερωσύνη *the Levitical* (i.e. OT) *priesthood* **Hb 7:11.**

λευκαίνω fut. λευκανῶ Is 1:18; 1 aor. ἐλεύκανα (B-D-F §72; Mlt-H. 214f), inf. λευκᾶναι. Pass.: fut. λευκανθήσομαι Ps 50:9; pf. ptc. fem. acc. λελευκασμένην TestSol (s. λευκός; Hom. et al.; Apollod. [II BC]: 244 fgm. 107c Jac.; Sb 6754, 18; LXX; TestSol C prol. 1; Philo, Leg. All. 2, 43) ***make white*** of clothes whitened by a fuller (Aesop, Fab. 29 P.=59 H.) **Mk 9:3.** In imagery, *make* blood-red sins *white* 1 Cl 8:4 (Is 1:18); cp. 18:7 (Ps 50:9). In apocal. figure, of martyrs: ἐλεύκαναν τὰς στολὰς αὐτῶν ἐν τῷ αἵματι τοῦ ἀρνίου *they have made their robes white in the blood of the Lamb* **Rv 7:14.**—DELG s.v. 1 λευκός. TW.

λευκοβύσσινος s. λευκός 2 end.

λευκός, ή, όν (s. λευκαίνω; Hom.+; ins, pap, LXX, En; TestSol 5:13; Test12Patr; JosAs; ParJer 9:18; Philo, Joseph.; SibOr 3, 617; 622; loanw. in rabb. Fig. [w. οἱ συνιέντες]: οἱ λευκοί Iren.1, 19, 2 [Harv. I 177, 1])

❶ ***bright, shining, gleaming*** (Hom. et al.) λ. ὡς τὸ φῶς (Il. 14, 185 λ. ἠέλιος ὥς) *brilliant as light* **Mt 17:2.** λ. ἐξαστράπτων **Lk 9:29.** This mng. is also poss. for some of the foll. pass.

❷ ***white*** (including, for the Greeks, many shades of that color, and always opp. of μέλας; cp. our 'white' wine) of hair (Tyrtaeus [VII BC] 7, 23 of an elderly man's hair; Soph., Ant. 1092; Lev 13:3ff) **Mt 5:36** (opp. μέλας as Menand., Samian 262 [Bodmer p. 61 app.=OxfT p. 259] of Androcles, who dyes his white hair); **Rv 1:14a.** Of a goatskin Hv 5:1; s 6, 2, 5. Of a pebble, used for voting etc. (Lucian, Harmonides 3 p. 855f ψῆφον . . . τὴν λευκὴν καὶ σῴζουσαν) **Rv 2:17.** Of wool (PRyl 146, 15 [39 AD]; Da 7:9 ὡσεὶ ἔριον λ.; En 106:2; ParJer 9:18) **1:14b.** Of apocal. horses (cp. JosAs 5:5; Zech 1:8. S. πυρρός) **6:2; 19:11, 14a.** Of an apocal. monster w. the colors black, red, gold and white Hv 4, 1, 10; cp. 4, 3, 5. Of a cloud **Rv 14:14.** Of stones (Michel 509, 17 [241 BC]; OGI 219, 36; 268, 17; 339, 34; 105; et al. in ins) Hv 3, 2, 8; 3, 5, 1; 3, 6, 5; s 9, 4, 5; 9, 6, 4; 9, 8, 5; 9, 9, 1. Of a chair v 1, 2, 2. Of fields of ripe grain λ. πρὸς θερισμόν *white for the harvest* **J 4:35.** Of a mountain Hs 9, 1, 10; 9, 29, 1; 9, 30, 1f; 4. Of a rock 9, 2, 1. Of a throne **Rv 20:11.** Of garments (Plut., Aristid. 21, 4 festive garment; IPriene 205 εἰσίναι εἰς τὸ ἱερὸν ἁγνὸν ἐν ἐσθῆτι λευκῇ; POxy 471, 95ff; 531, 13; PGM 4, 636; Eccl 9:8; 2 Macc 11:8; Jos., Bell. 2, 1, Ant. 11, 327; TestLevi 8:2; JosAs 5:6 χιτῶνα λευκόν) **Mk 9:3; 16:5** (Lucian, Philops. 25 of a heavenly messenger: νεανίας πάγκαλος λευκὸν ἱμάτιον περιβεβλημένος); **Ac 1:10; Rv 3:5, 18; 4:4; 6:11; 7:9, 13.** A garment is λ. ὡς χιών (Da 7:9 Theod.) **Mt 28:3** (opp. of garments appropriate for mourning: Aeschines, Against Ctesiphon 77); **Mk 9:3 v.l.;** Hs 8, 2, 3f. ἐν λευκοῖς (sc. ἱματίοις) *in white* (Artem. 2, 3 p. 86, 17; 4, 2 p. 205, 9) **J 20:12; Rv 3:4;** Hv 4, 2, 1; s 8, 2, 4; βύσσινον λ. *a white linen garment* **Rv 19:14b** (v.l. λευκοβύσσινον). Of a priest's clothing made of white linen (s. Schürer II 293) Ox 840, 27. Of shoes Hv 4, 2, 1.—GRadke, D. Bedeutg. d. weissen u. schwarzen Farbe in Kult u. Brauch d. Griech. u. Römer, diss. Berlin '36; RGradwohl, D. Farben im AT, '63, 34–50.—On special clothing in some mystery celebrations s. SCole, Theoi Megaloi '84, 114 n. 125.—B. 1052; 1054. DELG. EDNT. M-M. TW. Sv.

λέων, οντος, ὁ (Hom.+; also BGU 957, 4 [10 BC]; PGrenf II, 84, 7) ***lion*** **Hb 11:33;** MPol 12:2; Philo; AcPl Ha 2, 7; 4, 19; 34; 38; 5, 2; 4f; 9; 13; 18. Symbol of rapacity 1 Cl 35:11 (Ps 49:22 v.l. [ARahlfs, Psalmi cum Odis '31]). λάκκος λεόντων (s. λάκκος) 45:6. Of the devil ὡς λ. ὠρυόμενος περιπατεῖ *he goes about like a roaring lion* **1 Pt 5:8** (Ps 21:14; TestSol 11:1 βρυχώμενος ὡς λεών; cp. JosAs 12:9 ὁ λέων ὁ ἄγριος ὁ παλαιὸς καταδιώκει με). Apocalyptic usage also makes comparisons w. the lion, or parts of his body, or his actions (Il. 6, 181; Strabo 16, 4, 16 fabulous beings: σφίγγες κ. κυνοκέφαλοι κ. κῆβοι [monkeys] λέοντος μὲν πρόσωπον ἔχοντες τὸ δὲ λοιπὸν σῶμα πάνθηρος κτλ.; quite similarly Diod. S. 3, 35, 6; TestAbr A 17 p. 99, 21 [Stone p. 46]; Ath. 18, 3) **Rv 4:7; 9:8** (cp. Jo 1:6), **17; 10:3; 13:2.** Metaphorically (cp. Il. 21, 483, of Artemis) of a lion-hearted hero (cp. Lycophron 33 [Heracles]; Ael. Aristid. 46 p. 191f D. [Pericles]; Esth 4:17s; Jos., Ant. 18, 228), the Messiah ὁ λ. ὁ ἐκ τῆς φυλῆς Ἰούδα *the lion fr. the tribe of Judah* **Rv 5:5** (cp. Gen 49:9).—ῥυσθῆναι ἐκ στόματος λ. *be rescued from the jaws of the lion,* i.e. fr. great danger **2 Ti 4:17** (cp. Ps 21:22). The rapacious lion is found as funerary motif, and both **1 Pt 5:8** (above) and **2 Ti 4:17** may refer to death (the former to physical death, the latter to spiritual death or apostasy: New Docs 3, 50f).—OKeller, Die Antike Tierwelt, 2 vols. 1909–13: II 24–61. EGoodenough, Jewish Symbols VII, '58, 29–86. Pauly-W. XIII/1 968–90.—B. 185. DELG. M-M. TW.

λήθη, ης, ἡ (s. λανθάνω of which λήθω is a collateral form; Hom. et al.; Vett. Val. 242, 4; PCairMasp 4, 4; LXX; En 5:8 [Rademacher for ἀλήθειαν]; TestJob 47:8; Philo; Jos., Ant. 15, 376; Just., D. 46, 5; Ath. 12:2) ***forgetfulness*** λήθην λαμβάνειν τινός *forget someth.* (s. λαμβάνω 10c) **2 Pt 1:9.**—DELG s.v. λανθάνω. M-M. TW. Sv.

λῆμμα, ατος, τό (s. λαμβάνω and next entry; Soph., Pla. et al.; pap, LXX, Philo; Jos., Bell. 1, 289, Ant. 14, 393) someth. received ***gain*** διὰ τ. ἐπιθυμίαν τοῦ λ. *because of the desire for gain* Hs 9, 19, 3.—DELG s.v. λαμβάνω B.

λῆμψις, εως, ἡ (edd. also λῆψις; Soph., Thu. et al.; PTebt 238 [II BC]; POxy 71 I, 18. On the spelling s. the lit. given s.v. λαμβάνω, beg., on λήμψομαι) **a condition of being in receipt of someth., *receiving,*** as a commercial term ἐν πικρίᾳ γίνεσθαι . . . περὶ δόσεως καὶ λ. *become bitter . . . about giving and receiving, 'debit and credit'* Hm 5, 2, 2. In commercial imagery κοινωνεῖν εἰς λόγον δόσεως καὶ λ. **Phil 4:15** (s. δόσις 2; GPeterman, Paul's Gift from Philippi '97). On the commercial aspect s. λόγος.—DELG s.v. λαμβάνω B. M-M.

ληνός, οῦ, ἡ a term for someth. hollow, such as a vat or trough, hence also ***wine-press*** (so Theocr.; Diod. S. 3, 63, 4; ins: Sb 7541, 11 [II AD]; PAmh 48, 7 [106 BC]; POxy 729, 19; LXX; JosAs 2:20 'trough'; Jos., Ant. 5, 213 al.; Just., D. 86, 2) γεννήματα λ. *produce of the wine-press* (cp. Num 18:30) D 13:3 (s. γέννημα). Hewn in the rock (cp. POxy 502, 36 [164 AD] τὰς ληνοὺς λιθίνας) **Mt 21:33.**—In Rv fig. πατεῖν τὴν λ. *tread* *the wine-press* (i.e. the grapes in it; Diod. S. 4, 5, 1 πατῆσαι τ. σταφυλὰς ἐν ληνῷ; s. also 2 Esdr 23:15; La 1:15; cp. Jer 31:33) **Rv 19:15;** pass. **14:20a.** βάλλειν εἰς τὴν ληνόν *pour into the wine-press* (cp. Anacreontea 59, 4 Pr. κατὰ ληνὸν βάλλειν . . . πατεῖν) **14:19.** Blood (cp. the 'blood of the grape') flows fr. the wine-press vs. **20b.**—DELG. M-M. TW.

λῆρος, ου, ὁ (Aristoph. et al.; X., An. 7, 7, 41; PSI 534, 16; 4 Macc 5:11; TestSol 26:6; Philo, Post. Cai. 165; Jos., Bell. 3, 405; Just., A I, 68, 1; Tat., Ath.) **that which is totally devoid of anything worthwhile,** ***idle talk, nonsense, humbug*** ἐφάνησαν ἐνώπιον αὐτῶν ὡσεὶ λῆρος τὰ ῥήματα ταῦτα *these words seemed to them to be nonsense* **Lk 24:11.** S. ληρώδης.—DELG 1. M-M. Spicq.

ληρώδης, ες (s. λῆρος + -ώδης; Pla. et al.; BGU 1011 II, 15 [II BC]; 2 Macc 12:44; Philo, Leg. ad Gai. 168; Just., A I, 68, 1) ***foolish, silly, frivolous*** οἱ λ. λόγοι *the foolish pronouncements* Dg 8:2.—DELG s.v. 1 λῆρος. M-M. s.v. λῆρος.

λῃστής, οῦ, ὁ (ληΐς, epic form of λεία 'booty, spoils'; Soph., Hdt.+; ins, pap, LXX; ApcSed 15:3; Joseph.; loanw. in rabb.; Ar. 3, 2; Just., Tat., Ath., R. 19 p. 72, 25; Theoph. Ant. 3, 14 [p. 232, 13]).

❶ ***robber, highwayman, bandit*** (in Palestine: Jos., Bell. 2, 125; 228 al.) **Lk 10:30, 36; 2 Cor 11:26** (Chariton 6, 4, 6 λῃσταῖς θαλάττῃ); **Mt 26:55; Mk 14:48; Lk 22:52;** so also MPol 7:1. Crucified w. Christ **Mt 27:38, 44; Mk 15:27.** W. κλέπτης (Pla., Rep. 351c; Ep. 63 of Apollonius of Tyana [Philostrat. I 363, 21]) **J 10:1, 8.** σπήλαιον λῃστῶν *a bandits' cave* or *hideout* (Jer 7:11) **Mt 21:13; Mk 11:17; Lk 19:46;** 2 Cl 14:1 (GBuchanan, HUCA 30, '59, 169–77: 'cave of brigands'; s. ἱερόν b, end; Schürer II 600).—This mng. was extended to signify

❷ ***revolutionary, insurrectionist, guerrilla*** (Jos., Bell. 2, 254=σικάριος; 253; 4, 504, Ant. 14, 159f; 20, 160f; 167) of Barabbas (cp. μετὰ τ. στασιαστῶν Mk 15:7) **J 18:40** (HRigg, Jr., JBL 64, '45, 444 n. 95; HWood, NTS 2, '55/56, 262–66 and JTwomey, Scripture (Edinburgh) 8, '56, 115–19 support this, but see MHengel, Die Zeloten, '61, 25–47; 344–48); prob. also in the words of Jesus **Mt 26:55; Mk 14:48; Lk 22:52;** MPol 7:1 (cp. **Mt 26:55**). —More precise def. depends on assessment of 'social banditry', s. RHorsley, Josephus and the Bandits: Journal for the Study of Judaism 10, '79, 37–63; RHorsley/JHanson, Bandits, Prophets, and Messiahs '85.—B. 791. DELG s.v. λεία. M-M. TW. Spicq.

λῆψις s. λῆμψις.

λίαν adv. (Hom. et al. as λίην; as λίαν Pind.+) **to a high degree,** ***very (much), exceedingly.***—ⓐ used w. verbs: preceding them (EpArist 312; Jos., Vi. 404) λ. ἀντέστη *he vehemently opposed* **2 Ti 4:15.** λ. πρόσεχε *be scrupulously on your guard* D 6:3. λ. ἐκκέχυμαι ἀγαπῶν ὑμᾶς *I pour out my love over you* IPhld 5:1. ὅταν . . . λ. πικρανθῇ *when the person becomes very bitter* Hm 10, 2, 3; cp. 9:9b; 12, 1, 2; 12, 4, 1; s 5, 2, 7; 6, 2, 7; 7:1; 8, 3, 8; 9, 11, 3. Following the verb (Gen 4:5) ἐθυμώθη λ. *he became very angry* **Mt 2:16.** θαυμάζειν . . . λ. **27:14;** ἔκλαυσα λ. *I wept bitterly* Hm 3:3; ἐχάρη λ. *he was very glad* **Lk 23:8;** Hs 5, 2, 5; 8, 1, 16; also λ. ἐχάρη 5, 2, 11. In a letter ἐχάρην λ. *I was very glad* (BGU 632, 10; PGiss 21, 3) **2J 4; 3J 3.** ἐλυπήθη λ. (Cain) *was filled with grief* 1 Cl 4:3 (cp. Gen. 4:5). Strengthened λίαν ἐκ περισσοῦ *altogether* **Mk 6:51.**

ⓑ used w. adjs., which—α. serve as attribute (SIG 1102, 12 αἱ λίαν ἄκαιροι δαπάναι): preceding the adj(s).: καί γε λ. πιστοὺς κ. ἰσχυρούς *also very committed and steadfast* Hm 9, 9, 9a; λ. ὑψηλός *grown very high* s 8, 1, 2; λ. εὐειδής *very charming* AcPl Ha 3, 13. Following the adj.: ὄρος ὑψηλὸν λ. *very high* **Mt 4:8;** χαλεποὶ λ. *very dangerous* **8:28.** ἀψινθίου μικρὸν λ. *only a little bit* Hm 5, 1, 5. πρόβατα πολλὰ λ. *very many sheep* s 6, 1, 6a. ῥάβδον σκληρὰν λ. *a very sturdy stick* 6, 2, 5. πικρὸν λ. AcPl Ha 4, 20 *very fierce.*

β. serve as predicate: preceding (Diod. S. 14, 58, 2 λίαν ὀχυρός; PTebt 315, 18 ὁ ἄνθρωπος λείαν ἐστὶν αὐστηρός; TestJob 13:6 λ. μου χρηστοῦ ὄντος) αἰσχρὰ καὶ λ. αἰσχρά *shameful, very shameful* 1 Cl 47:6. λ. ἄφρων εἰμί Hm 4, 2, 1; cp. κἂν λ. σύνετος ἦν τις s 5, 5, 4. ὤφθη . . . μοι . . . λ. πρεσβυτέρα *a very elderly woman* v 3, 10, 3; cp. m 8, 6; s 2:5; 5, 3, 5; 6, 1, 6bc; 6, 2, 3; 8, 1, 17f; 9, 1, 7b; 10a; 9, 2, 4; 9, 3, 1; 9, 6, 8; 9, 9, 2; 7. Following (Gen 1:31; Tob 6:12 S) ἐγένετο λευκὰ λ. **Mk 9:3.** ὃν ἀγαπητὸν λ. ἔχετε *for whom you have a special affection* 1 Pol 7:2. περίλυπος ἤμην λ. *I was extremely unhappy* Hv 3, 10, 6. ἐντολαὶ . . . σκληραὶ . . . σκληραί εἰσι *very demanding* or *severe* m 12, 3, 4; (λίθοι) σκληροὶ . . . λ. εὑρέθησαν *turned out to be too hard* to dress/shape s 9, 8, 6. αὐθάδης εἶ λ. *you are very stubborn* 5, 4, 2. Cp. 9, 1, 7a; 10b; 9, 9, 4.

ⓒ used w. an adv., following it (Da 11:25) πρωῒ ἔννυχα λ. *early in the morning, when it was still quite dark* **Mk 1:35.** Preceding it (2 Macc 11:1; EpArist 230; Jos., C. Ap. 1, 286; 2, 3; Tat. 2, 1; 21, 3; PMich 154, 17 λ. νυκτός) λ. πρωῒ *very early in the morning* **16:2.** λ. ὀργίλως ἐλάλησεν *with vehement anger* Hm 12, 4, 1. S. ὑπερλίαν.—DELG. M-M.

λίβα s. λίψ.

Λίβανος, ου, ὁ (Theophr., On Plants 9, 7, 1; Diod. S. 19, 58, 2f) ***(the) Lebanon,*** a mountain range in Syria following the coast of the Mediterranean, famous for its cedars 1 Cl 14:5 (Ps 36:35).—Pauly-W. XIII, 1, 1–11. ABD IV 269f.

λίβανος, ου, ὁ (=the frankincense tree Hdt. et al.; = the resinous gum Pind.+; cp. Phryn. 187 Lob.) ***frankincense,*** a white resinous gum, obtained fr. several kinds of a certain tree in Arabia, used both medicinally and for sacral purposes (EMaehler, ZPE 4, '69, 99; Zohary, Plants 197). 1 Cl 25:2; **Rv 18:13.** W. gold and myrrh as a precious gift (highest grade of fr. six denarii for about .4 kg. Pliny, HN 12, 65) **Mt 2:11;** GJs 21:3 (cp. Diod. S. 19, 94, 5; Is 60:6; for fr. and myrrh together s. Diod. S. 3, 46, 3; Strabo 16, 4, 14 p. 774; Polyaenus 8, 26; En 29:2; PGM 13, 354.—As early as Empedocles 128, 6 [Vorsokr. 31] σμύρνη and λίβανος are appropriate sacrificial gifts to gods. SibOr 3, 772: a messianic gift).—ILöw, D. Flora d. Juden I 1928, 312–14; GvanBeek, BA 23, '60, 70–95; WMüller, Glotta 52, '74, 53–59; JBrown, JSS 25, '80, 16–21; New Docs 4, 129–31 (Connolly).—DELG. M-M. TW. Sv.

λιβανωτός, οῦ, ὁ—❶ ***(frank)incense*** (so Hdt. et al.; Diod. S. 2, 49, 2 [offered to gods throughout the world]; OGI 383, 142 [I BC] λιβανωτοῦ κ. ἀρωμάτων; et al. in ins; PHib 121, 54 [III BC]; POxy 118, 20; 234 II, 38; Mayser 40; 1 Ch 9:29 λ. κ. τῶν ἀρωμάτων; 3 Macc 5:2; Philo, Spec. Leg. 1, 275; Jos., Ant. 3, 256) ὡς λιβανωτοῦ πνέοντος ἢ ἄλλου τινὸς τῶν ἀρωμάτων MPol 15:2.

❷ ***censer,*** in which incense is burned **Rv 8:3, 5.**—New Docs 4, 129–31 (Connolly). DELG s.v. λίβανος. M-M. TW. Sv.

Λιβερτῖνος, ου, ὁ (Lat. loanw.: libertinus, meaning a person who was manumitted; IG XIV, 1781) ***Freedperson*** **Ac 6:9,** a designation for certain Israelites in Jerusalem who had their own synagogue (Schürer II 76; 428, 8; III 133, 26; Ltzm., ZNW 20, 1921, 172; GdeRossi's attempt, Bull. di arch. christ. 1864, 70;

92f, to interpret CIL, IV 117 as a ref. to an alleged synagogue of freedpersons in Pompeii is rejected Beginn. IV 67). The name describes these people as former slaves or their descendants. The change to Λιβυστίνων, conjectured by Beza in the 16th century (RHarris, ET 6, 1895, 378–90) and listed in Stephan. Byz. (s.v. Λίβυς)='Libyans' (so the Armen. version) is favored by FBlass, Philol. of the Gospels 1898, 69f; Moffatt; Goodsp., Probs. 127–30, but is declared 'attractive but unnecessary' by Jackson and Lake, Beginn. III 58; on the relation of Luke's diction and syntax to decoding of the term s. ISBE II, '82, 360.—M-M. TW.

Λιβύη, ης, ἡ (Hom. et al.; OGI 54, 5 [III BC]; Sb 4456 gravestone [II BC] al. in ins, pap [Mayser 101]; Philo, Joseph., SibOr) ***Libya,*** a district in N. Africa betw. Egypt and Cyrene; the western part, Libya Cyrenaica, is meant by τὰ μέρη τῆς Λ. τῆς κατὰ Κυρήνην *the parts of Libya near Cyrene* **Ac 2:10** (Jos., Ant. 16, 160 ἡ πρὸς Κυρήνῃ Λιβύη).

Λιβυστῖνος s. Λιβερτῖνος.

λιθάζω 1 aor. ἐλίθασα, pass. ἐλιθάσθην (λιθάς [=λίθος] Mlt-H. 404; since Anaxandrides Com. [IV BC], fgm. 16; Aristot., mostly abs. 'throw stones'; 2 Km 16:6, 13; Jos., C. Ap. 2, 206 cod.) ***stone*** τινά *someone.* In the OT and the Mishnah (Sanhedrin 6; 7, 4–8, 5) a means of capital punishment for certain crimes: adultery **J 8:5** (v.l. λιθοβολεῖσθαι; s. the entry); esp. defamation of God; somet. the populace became aroused and took upon itself the task of pronouncing and carrying out such a sentence: **10:31ff** (on λιθάζετε vs. **32** *you are trying to stone* cp. Rob. 880); **11:8; Ac 5:26; 14:19; 2 Cor 11:25;** 1 Cl 5:6; GPt 11:48. W. other forms of death **Hb 11:37;** cp. 1 Cl 45:4.—RHirzel, Die Strafe der Steinigung: Abh. d. Sächs. Ges. d. Wiss. 27, 1909, 223–66; JBlinzler, Moule Festschr. '70, 147–61.—DELG s.v. λίθος. M-M. TW.

λίθινος, ίνη, ον (Pind., Hdt.+; ins, pap, LXX; En 99:7 [cj.]; TestSol 11:8 C; Jos., Ant. 14, 57; 15, 401; Just., D. 9, 3) ***(made of) stone.*** εἴδωλα **Rv 9:20;** θεοί AcPl Ha 1, 19; cp. Dg 2:7 (s. Da 5:4, 23 Theod.; Hermocles [IV/III BC] p. 174, 19 Coll. Alex. [=Athen. 6, 63, 253e] in contrast to a ξύλινος or λίθινος θεός, Demetrius Poliorcetes is an ἀληθινός.—Diod. S. 22, 9, 4 ἀγάλματα [= θεοί] λίθινα κ. ξύλινα). ὑδρίαι *water-jars* **J 2:6** (Athen. 13 p. 589 B ὑδρία λιθίνη; cp. POxy 937, 13 τῆς φιάλης τῆς λιθίνης). Of the tables of the law πλάκες λ. (LXX) **2 Cor 3:3;** B 4:7 (Ex 31:18).—Fig. (Herodas 7, 109; Dio Chrys. 71 [21], 13; Ps.-Aeschin., Ep. 10, 10; Alciphron 4, 16, 7; Libanius, Or. 25, 47 vol. II 559, 12f.; Philo, Mos. 2, 202 λ. ψυχή) of the heart καρδία λ. *a stony heart,* i.e. one without feeling B 6:14 (Ezk 11:19; 36:26).—DELG s.v. λίθος. M-M. TW.

λιθοβολέω (s. λίθος, βάλλω) impf. ἐλιθοβόλουν; fut. pl. λιθοβολήσουσιν LXX; 1 aor. ἐλιθοβόλησα. Pass.: 1 fut. λιθοβοληθήσομαι; pf. 3 sg. λελιθοβόληται 3 Km 20:14.

❶ ***throw stones at*** someone (Diod. S. 13, 10, 6; 17, 41, 8; Plut., Mor. 1011e) **Mt 21:35; Mk 12:4 v.l.; Ac 14:5** (for the acc. to denote the goal, *at somebody* or *someth.* cp. Ps.-Demetr. c. 115).

❷ ***stone (to death)*** (LXX) τινά *someone* God's messengers (ParJer 9:22; 28:30) **Mt 23:37; Lk 13:34.** Stephen **Ac 7:58f.** (Arrian, Anab. 4, 14, 3: the conspirators against Alexander are stoned after the trial by those present [πρὸς τῶν παρόντων]). Pass. (Aristodemus [II BC]: 383 fgm. 6 Jac.) **J 8:5 v.l.** (for λιθάζειν). An animal **Hb 12:20** (cp. Ex 19:13).—M-M. TW.

λιθοξόος, ου, ὁ (λίθος + ξέω 'carve'; Timon fgm. 25 D. [in Diog. L. 2, 19]) ***sculptor*** (so Plut., Mor. 74d; Ptolem., Apotel. 4, 4, 5; IG III, 1372) Dg 2:3.

λίθος, ου, ὁ (Hom.+; in our lit. always masc.)—**❶** ***stone,*** in general: **Mt 3:9** (ZNW 9, 1908, 77f; 341f); **4:3, 6** (Ps 90:12); **7:9; Mk 5:5; Lk 3:8; 4:3, 11** (Ps 90:12); **11:11 v.l.; 19:40** (cp. 4 Esdr 5:5 and the 'hearing' πέτραι PGM 36, 263); **22:41; J 8:7, 59; 10:31;** Ox 1 recto, 6 (ASyn. 171, 5)=GTh 77 (s. AWalls, VigChr 16, '62, 71–78; cp. Lucian, Hermotim. 81 p. 826 ὁ θεὸς οὐκ ἐν οὐρανῷ ἐστιν, ἀλλὰ διὰ πάντων πεφοίτηκεν, οἷον ξύλων κ. λίθων κ. ζῴων). Of blood (but πτῶμα pap) of Zachariah, which turned to stone GJs 24:3.

❷ ***stone,*** of a special kind—ⓐ of stones used in building (Dio Chrys. 57 [74], 26; Oenomaus in Eus., PE 5, 24, 4 λίθοι καὶ ξύλοι; Palaeph. p. 62, 7; PPetr II, 13 [18a], 7 [258 BC]; Dt 27:5f; 3 Km 6:7; TestSol 2:5 al.; JosAs 2:17) **Mt 24:2; Mk 13:1f** (LGaston, No Stone on Another, '70 [fall of Jerus.]); **Lk 19:44; 21:6** (λίθος ἐπὶ λίθῳ as Aristippus fgm. 20 FPhGr [in Diog. L. 2, 72]); Hv 3, 2, 4–9; 3, 4, 2f; 3, 5, 1–3; 3, 6, 3; 6f; 3, 7, 1; 5; s 9, 3, 3ff al.; λ. καλοί *costly stone(s)* (prob. kinds of marble; cp. Diod. S. 1, 66, 3 κάλλιστοι λίθοι; Jos., Ant. 15, 392) **Lk 21:5.—1 Cor 3:12** is also classed here by Blass and Dssm., Pls[2] 1925, 245f (Paul, 1926, 212ff); s. b below.

ⓑ of precious stones, jewels (TestSol 1:3 al.; TestAbr, JosAs, Joseph.; Ant. 17, 197; Synes., Ep. 3 p. 158b) λίθος καθαρός **Rv 15:6 v.l.** Mostly in the combination λίθος τίμιος (τιμιώτατος) and mentioned beside gold, silver, or even pearls (Appian, Liby. 66 §297; Herodian 5, 2, 4; Da 11:38 Theod.; 2 Km 12:30; TestSol 1:6; TestAbr A 6 p. 83, 23 [Stone p. 14]; JosAs 2:3; 18:4; cp. TestAbr A 3 p. 80, 12 [Stone p. 8] πολύτιμοι; TestJob 28:5 πολυτελεῖς, ἔνδοξοι; JosAs 2:7 al. πολυτελεῖς); **Rv 17:4; 18:12, 16; 21:11, 19** (s. the lit. s.v. ἀμέθυστος. Also FCumont[3] 246, 87). Likewise in **1 Cor 3:12** the way in which the word is used scarcely permits another mng., and hence we must assume (unless it is enough to think of the edifice as adorned w. precious stones [Diod. S. 3, 47, 6f: the use of gold, silver, and precious stones in the building of palaces in Sabae; Lucian, Imag. 11 ὁ νεὼς λίθοις τ. πολυτελέσιν ἠσκημένος κ. χρυσῷ]) that Paul either had in mind imaginary buildings (Ps.-Callisth. 3, 28, 4: in the city of Helios on the Red Sea there are 12 πύργοι χρυσῷ καὶ σμαράγδῳ ᾠκοδομημένοι· τὸ δὲ τεῖχος ἐκ λίθου Ἰνδικοῦ κτλ.) as **Rv 21:18ff;** Is 54:11f; Tob 13:17, or simply mentioned the costliest materials, without considering whether they could actually be used in erecting a building (in Phoenix of Colophon [III BC] 1, 9: AnthLG I/3[3] '54 Diehl the rich snob thinks of houses ἐγ [=ἐκ] λίθου σμαραγδίτου. S. χρυσίον.—S. a above).—λ. ἴασπις (q.v.) **Rv 4:3.**

ⓒ of millstones λ. μυλικός **Lk 17:2.** Two times as v.l. for μύλος ὀνικός: **Mt 18:6; Mk 9:42. v.l.** λ. ὡς μύλινος **Rv 18:21.**

ⓓ of large stones used to seal graves (Chariton 3, 3, 1 παραγενόμενος εὗρε τ. λίθους κεκινημένους κ. φανερὰν τὴν εἴσοδον) **Mt 27:60, 66; 28:2; Mk 15:46; 16:3f; Lk 24:2; J 11:38f, 41; 20:1;** GPt 8:32 al. Also of the tables of the Mosaic law **2 Cor 3:7.**

ⓔ of stone images of the gods (Dt 4:28; Ezk 20:32; Just., D. 113, 6) **Ac 17:29;** 2 Cl 1:6; cp. PtK 2 p. 14, 14; Dg 2:2.

ⓕ in imagery relating to God's people and the transcendent (in the pass. fr. Hv 3 and s 9 mentioned in 2a above, the tower and its stones are symbolic): of Christ (cp. Just., D. 86, 3) λ. ζῶν **1 Pt 2:4.** Likew. of the Christians λίθοι ζῶντες *living stones* (in the spiritual temple) vs. **5** (JPlumpe, Vivum saxum, vivi lapides: Traditio 1, '43, 1–14). ὡς ὄντες λίθοι ναοῦ πατρός *as building-stones of the Father's temple* IEph 9:1. 1 Pt and B 6:2c,

3 (s. LBarnard, Studia Evangelica, ed. FCross, '64, III, 306–13: NT and B) also refer to Christ as the λ. ἐκλεκτὸς ἀκρογωνιαῖος **1 Pt 2:6** (cp. Is 28:16; ESiegman, CBQ 18, '56, 364–79; JElliott, The Elect and the Holy '66, esp. 16–38; s. ἀκρογωνιαῖος), the λ., ὃν ἀπεδοκίμασαν οἱ οἰκοδομοῦντες vs. **7** (Ps 117:22)—likew. **Mt 21:42; Mk 12:10; Lk 20:17;** cp. **Ac 4:11; Eph 2:20 v.l.** (for lit. s. on κεφαλή 2b)—and finally the λ. προσκόμματος **1 Pt 2:8** (Is 8:14)—likew. **Ro 9:32f.** The same OT (Is 8:14f) infl. is felt in **Mt 21:44; Lk 20:18** (Daimachus [IV BC]: 65 fgm. 8 Jac. speaks in his work περὶ εὐσεβείας of the fall of a holy stone fr. heaven πεσεῖν τὸν λίθον).—SKottek, Names, Roots and Stones in Jewish Lore: Proceedings XXXII Intern. Congr. of History of Medicine, Antwerp n.d. ['91] 63–74; also idem: ANRW II/37/3 p. 2855 n. 53 on use of stones in antiquity. B. 51; 442. DELG. M-M. TW. Spicq.

λιθόστρωτος, ον (s. λίθος, στρώννυμι; Soph. et al.; Epict. 4, 7, 37 v.l.; POxy 2138, 15; PFlor 50, 97 [268 AD] ἐπὶ τοῦ λιθοστρώτου δρόμου Ἕρμου; 2 Ch 7:3; Esth 1:6; SSol 3:10; EpArist 88; Jos., Bell. 6, 85; 189) 'paved w. blocks of stone', also subst. τὸ λιθόστρωτον (IG IV^2/1, 110, 19 [IV/III BC]; Κυπρ. I p. 58 no. 1 ἀπὸ τοῦ Ἡραίου ἕως τοῦ λιθοστρώτου; 2 Ch 7:3) ***stone pavement*** or ***mosaic.*** In **J 19:13** either *pavement* or *mosaic* is poss.; the place meant is the one called 'in Hebrew Gabbatha' (s. Γαβ.), where Pilate pronounced judgment on Jesus.—REngelmann, BPhW 27, 1907, 341; 1652ff; Vincent-Abel, Jérusalem II 1926, 570; LVincent, RB 42, '33, 83–113; 46, '37, 563–70; 59, '50, 513–30; ECerny, CBQ 4, '42, 159f; PBenoit, RB 59, '50, 531–50.—DELG s.v. στόρνυμι. M-M. Spicq.

λικμάω fut. λικμήσω; aor. ἐλίκμησα LXX. Pass.: aor. ptc. n. λικμηθέντες Wsd 11:20; pf. ptc. n. λελικμημένα Is 30:24 (in the sense 'winnow' Hom. et al.; PSI 522, 2 [248/247 BC]; BGU 1040, 11; LXX; Philo, De Jos. 112; Jos., Ant. 5, 328); in our lit. only **Mt 21:44=Lk 20:18** ἐφ' ὃν δ' ἂν πέσῃ (i.e. ὁ λίθος, q.v., end), λικμήσει αὐτόν, where the Sin. and Cur. Syriac and Vulgate take it to mean ***crush*** (for this mng. cp. schol. on Nicander, Ther. 114 [beside τοὺς στάχυας τρίβω]; Da 2:44 Theod. and BGU 146, 8, the latter a complaint against those who ἐλίκμησάν μου τὸ λάχανον 'stamped on, destroyed my vegetables' [Dssm., NB 52f; BS 225f], and s. Boll 130, 1).—DELG. M-M. TW. Spicq.

λιμά, s. λαμά, λεμά.

λιμήν, ένος, ὁ (Hom. et al.; ins, pap, LXX; EpArist 115; Philo; Jos., Ant. 17, 87 al.; loanw. in rabb., but on this s. MLubetski, JQR 69, '79, 158–80) ***harbor*** **Ac 27:12a;** λιμὴν τῆς κρήτης *a harbor to/for Crete* (='a harbor for sailing from and to Crete' Warnecke, Romfahrt 28f) **b;** AcPl Ha 5, 15 (?); 7, 37. Fig. (trag.+; Περὶ ὕψους p. 15, 6 V.; Herm. Wr. 7, 1b; Philo, Decal. 67 and oft.) λιμένος τυγχάνειν *reach the harbor* ISm 11:3. The storm-tossed sailor longs for it IPol 2:3.—As a place name: Καλοὶ λιμένες (q.v. as a separate entry. On the pl. cp. Jos., Ant. 13, 261; 14, 76) **Ac 27:8.**—B. 738. DELG s.v. λειμών B. M-M. Sv.

λίμμα s. λεῖμμα.

λίμνη, ης, ἡ (Hom. et al.; ins, pap, LXX; GrBar; ApocMos 37; Philo, Aet. M. 147; 148; Jos., Ant. 5, 81) a body of water, smaller than, e.g., the Mediterranean Sea, but not limited to what is ordinarily termed a lake.

❶ **a body of inland water as natural phenomenon,** varying in size from ***lake*** to ***pool***—ⓐ *lake* of the Lake of Gennesaret (except in Luke, usu. called θάλασσα; s. that entry 2 and cp. יָם) ἡ λ. Γεννησαρέτ **Lk 5:1.** The abs. ἡ λ. also has this sense (Jos., Vi. 96; 165; 304, Ant. 14, 450) vs. **2; 8:22f, 33.**

ⓑ *pool* ἡ λ. τοῦ Δαυίδ *the pool of David,* acc. to Ox 840, 25 a basin in the temple enclosure used by the priests for bathing (ZNW 9, 1908, 6f; 15, 1914, 338; Unknown Sayings 36–49).

❷ **a transcendent lake-like phenomenon, *lake*** (in apocalyptic scenario)—ⓐ *lake of fire* **Rv 20:14ab, 15** (cp. JosAs 12:10 ἄβυσσος τ. πυρός) or *of fire and brimstone* vs. **10;** cp. **19:20; 21:8,** in which the enemies of God are punished. ApcPt 8:23 sinners are punished in a λίμνη μεγάλη πεπληρωμένη βορβόρου φλεγομένου. On 11:26 s. ἰχώρ. λ. μεγάλη πεπληρωμένη πύρου καὶ αἵματος 16:31.

ⓑ *lake of salvation* βάπτισμα ἐν σωτηρίᾳ Ἀχερουσίας λίμνης, ἣν καλοῦσιν ἐν τῷ Ἠλυσίῳ πεδίῳ *in the cleansing of the saving (waters) of the Acherusian Lake, as they call the place (alleged to be) in the Elysian Plain* ApcPt Rainer 4–6 (ApcMos 37; cp. GrBar 10:2ff).—B. 38. DELG s.v. λειμών C. M-M.

λιμός, οῦ, ὁ and **ἡ** (for the fem. s. **Lk 4:25 v.l.; 15:14; Ac 11:28;** B-D-F §2 end; 49, 1; Mlt-H. 123f; W-S §8, 10; Phryn. 188 Lob.; Ael. Dion. λ, 16; Thumb 67.—The word Hom.+; UPZ 11, 27 and 19, 21 τῷ λ.; 42, 9 τῆς λ.; PSI 399, 10 [III BC] τῇ λ.; LXX [Thackeray 146]; TestSol 18:8 H; Test12Patr; JosAs; 4 [6] Esdr [POxy 1010, 13 and 19]; Ath., R. 4 p. 52, 19; 21 p. 75, 2).

❶ ***hunger*** **Ro 8:35.** λιμῷ ἀπόλλυμαι *I am dying of hunger = I'm starving to death* (Ael. Aristid. 46 p. 271 D.) **Lk 15:17;** (w. δίψος; cp. Aeschyl., Pers. 483; X., Mem. 1, 4, 13; Is 5:13; TestJos 1:5; Jos., Bell. 3, 189) **2 Cor 11:27.**

❷ ***famine*** (schol. on Aristoph., Plut. 31 λιμοῦ γενομένου ἐν τῇ Ἀττικῇ; Gen 12:10; JosAs; Philo, Rer. Div. Her. 287) **Lk 4:25** (4 Km 6:25 ἐγέν. λ. μέγας); **15:14; Ac 7:11** (cp. Gen 41:54); **11:28** (Jos., Ant. 3, 320; 20, 101 μέγας λ.—KGapp, The Universal Famine under Claudius: HTR 28, '35, 258–65; RFunk, JBL 75, '56, 130–36; Haenchen, on Acts 11:29f); **Rv 6:8; 18:8.** ἐν λιμῷ *in famine* 1 Cl 56:9 (Job 5:20; 4 [6] Esdr [POxy 1010, 13f] ἐν λειμῷ διαφθαρήσονται). λιμοί *famines* among the tribulations of the last days **Mt 24:7; Mk 13:8; Lk 21:11;** in the last pass. and **Mt 24:7 v.l.** λοιμοί ('plagues, pestilences') are connected w. them (for this combination cp. Hes., Op. 243; Hdt. 7, 171; Thu. 2, 54, 3; Plut., Mor. 370b; Delph. Orac. 487, 13 [II 198 W.]; Cat. Cod. Astr. VII 166, 13; VIII 3, 186, 1; Herm. Wr. 414, 9 Sc.; Philo, Mos. 1, 110; 2, 16; Jos., Bell. 1, 377; 4, 361; TestJud 23:3; SibOr 2, 23; 8, 175.—For an enumeration of περιστάσεις [crises, troubles] see Ptolem., Apotel. 2, 1, 4 πολέμων ἢ λιμῶν ἢ λοιμῶν ἢ σεισμῶν ἢ κατακλυσμῶν καὶ τῶν τοιούτων; on περίστασις s. Danker, Benefactor p. 363–66, and 390, n. 216 for lit.).—PGarnsly, Famine and Food Supply in the Graeco-Roman World '88.—B. 332. DELG. M-M. TW.

λινοκαλάμη, ης, ἡ (s. λίνον, καλάμη; schol. on Pla., Ep. 13 p. 363a; oft. in pap fr. III BC) ***a stalk of flax*** 1 Cl 12:3 (Josh 2:6; the sing. is collective).

λίνον, ου, τό (Hom. et al.; pap, LXX; PsSol 8:5; Jos., Bell. 5, 275, Ant. 5, 9) variously of the flax plant and products made from its fibers. In the latter sense in our lit.

❶ ***lamp-wick*** λ. τυφόμενον *a smoldering wick* **Mt 12:20** (cp. Is 42:3).—S. on κάλαμος 1.

❷ ***linen garment*** (since Aeschyl., Suppl. 120; 132; IG IV^2/1, 118, 71 [III BC]; POxy 1281, 6 [21 AD]; PTebt 314, 16; 406, 18 λίνα λευκά; PGM 13, 313 στόλισον αὐτὸν λίνῳ καθαρῷ; cp. 650) **Rv 15:6.**

❸ ***fish-net*** (Il. 5, 487; Antig. Car. 27; Philo, Agr. 24, Poster. Cai. 116) **Mk 1:18 v.l.** (for δίκτυα) GPt 14:60.—B. 401. DELG. M-M.

Λίνος, ου, ὁ (Tat. 41, 1; Diog. L. 1, 3f; Biogr. p. 78; Sb 1283; 3169; 3625 a potter's stamp Λίνου) ***Linus,*** otherw. unknown Christian, acc. to tradition (e.g. Iren. 3, 3, 3 [Harv. II 10, 2]) the first bishop of Rome, **2 Ti 4:21.**—LGPN I.

λινοῦς, ῆ, οῦν (Hdt., Aristoph. et al.; ins, pap, LXX; Jos., Ant. 20, 216) ***(made of) linen*** κερβικάριον λ. *a linen pillow* Hv 3, 1, 4a. λ. χιτών (Paus. 9, 39, 8; Philostrat., Ep. 60; SIG 736, 17 [92 BC]; POxy 285, 11 [c. 50 AD]; BGU 816, 19; Lev 6:3; 16:4) *linen garment, linen shirt* s 9, 2, 4; 9, 11, 7. λέντιον λινοῦν καρπάσινον *a fine linen cloth* v 3, 1, 4b.—DELG s.v. λίνον.

λιπαίνω 1 aor. ἐλίπανα, impv. λιπανάτω. Pass.: fut. 3 sg. λιπανθήσεται Is 34:7 Theod.; aor. 3 sg. ἐλιπάνθη LXX. ***anoint*** τὶ *someth.* (Philo Mech. 61, 37; Philostrat., Imag. 1, 18 p. 320, 18; PGM 36, 212) 1 Cl 56:5 (Ps 140:5).—DELG s.v. λίπα.

λιπαρός, ά, όν (Hom. et al.; pap, LXX) prim. mng. 'oily, fat', then **pert. to being bright or radiant, with implication of being luxurious, *bright, costly, rich*** (Jos., C. Ap. 2, 229; SibOr 7, 18) subst. τὰ λιπαρά (w. τὰ λαμπρά; cp. SEG VIII, 550, 10 [I BC]) *luxury* **Rv 18:14.** In imagery (Jos., Ant. 4, 107 δέησις λ.; 8, 2 γῆρας λ.; sim. Cat. Cod. Astr. XII 176, 20 λ.γ.) εἰρήνη *rich, fruitful peace* 1 Cl 2:2.—DELG s.v. λίπα.

λιποτακτέω s. λειποτακτέω.

λιτανεύω fut. 3 pl. λιτανεύσουσιν (Ps 44:13); 1 aor. ἐλιτάνευσα (Hom. et al.; Ps 44:13) **to make an entreaty, *pray to, petition*** Ἄννα ἐλιτάνευσα τὸν δεσπότην GJs 2:4; τινὰ ὑπέρ τινος *someone on someone's behalf* τὸν Χριστὸν ὑπὲρ ἐμοῦ IRo 4:2 (of praying to a divinity: Strabo 15, 1, 60; Dionys. Hal. 4, 76; Theosophien 39; 2 Macc 14:15; EpArist 227).—DELG s.v. λίσσομαι. M-M. s.v. -εία.

λίτρα, ας, ἡ (cp. Lat. libra; Polyb. 22, 26, 19; Diod. S. 14, 116, 7; Plut., Tib. et C. Gracch. 825 [2, 3]; Jos., Ant. 14, 106; TestJud 3:3; TestSol 21:1 Q; SIG 890: 13, 23, 24 [251 AD]; 954: 7, 11, 13f al.; OGI 521, 4; POxy 1454, 5; 1513, 7; 1543, 6) ***a (Roman) pound*** (327.45 grams) **J 12:3; 19:39** (does the quantity suggest a royal burial?).—DELG. M-M.

λίψ, λιβός, ὁ acc. λίβα (λείβω 'pour, drip'; Hdt. et al.; ins, pap, LXX; Jos., Bell. 1, 409, Ant. 3, 294; cp. Dssm., B 139 [BS 141f]) ***the southwest,*** of a harbor: βλέπειν κατά *be open toward the southwest* **Ac 27:12** (s. EGoodspeed, Exp. 6th ser., 8, 1903, 130f, APF, 3, 1906, 406f; Haenchen ad loc.). In the OT it almost always means *south* (s. Dssm., loc. cit.) 1 Cl 10:4 (Gen 13:14).—DELG s.v. λείβω C. M-M.

Λογγῖνος, ου, ὁ (Lat. cognomen; s. Groag-Stein, Prosopographia J 384 [I AD]; IGLSyria 359, 3; pap; also s. Aa index 1, 301 and Acta Pilati Ea p. 283, 3 Tdf.) ***Longinus,*** a prefect, read by CSchmidt AcPl Ha 9, 17f: τῷ] προφέκτῳ Λογ[γίνῳ . . .] after the Coptic (for this τῷ πραιφέκτῳ Λόγγῳ Aa I 112, 4. Sim. restoration by Schmidt 9, 30; 10, 7; 17 etc.). S. next entry.

Λόγγος, ου, ὁ (Lat. cognomen; pap; Jos., Bell. 6, 186) ***Longus*** Aa I 112, 4 (par. AcPl Ha 9, 17f). S. prec. entry.

λογεία, ας, ἡ (λογεύω 'collect' contributions, taxes, etc., s. Dssm. BS 142–44; ins, pap: many exx. in the works named below) ***collection*** of money (λογεία is etymologically correct; λογία predominates in the mss. and edd.; s. B-D-F. §23; Mlt-H. 339), esp. a collection for sacred purposes (PSI 262, 3 [I AD] λ. τοῦ θεοῦ; O. Wilck no. 412, 5; 414, 5; s. ibid. I 253–56 on the term) **1 Cor 16:1.** λογεῖαι γίνονται *collections are made* vs. **2.**—Dssm., B 139ff, NB 46f (BS 142–44; 219f)], LO 83f (LAE 104); Mayser 417; WOtto, Priester u. Tempel I 1905, 359ff; KHoll, SBBerlAk 1921, 939f; WFranklin, D. Koll. des Pls, diss. Hdlbg. '38; DGeorgi, D. Kollekte d. Paulus für Jerusalem '65.—DELG s.v. λέγω B 2. M-M. TW.

λογίζομαι (λόγος) impf. ἐλογιζόμην; fut. λογιοῦμαι LXX; 1 aor. ἐλογισάμην; pf. λελόγιμαι LXX. Pass.: 1 aor. ἐλογίσθην; 1 fut. λογισθήσομαι. Mid. dep. (B-D-F §311; Rob. 816; 819) (Soph., Hdt.+) prim. a mathematical and accounting term, then of cognitive processes. In our lit. esp. used by Paul.; s. GThomas, ET 17, 1906, 211ff.

❶ **to determine by mathematical process, *reckon, calculate,*** freq. in a transf. sense—ⓐ *count, take into account* τὶ *someth.* ἡ ἀγάπη οὐ λογίζεται τὸ κακόν *love keeps no score of wrongs* (REB) **1 Cor 13:5** (cp. Zech 8:17). λ. τί τινι *count someth. against someone,* to punish the person for it (Simplicius in Epict. p. 79, 15 τὴν ἁμαρτίαν οὐ τῷ πράττοντι λογίζονται; TestZeb 9:7; Just., D. 141, 2f) μὴ λογιζόμενος αὐτοῖς τὰ παραπτώματα **2 Cor 5:19.**—οὗ (v.l. ᾧ) οὐ μὴ λογίσηται κύριος ἁμαρτίαν **Ro 4:8;** 1 Cl 50:6 (both Ps 31:2; cp. 1 Cl 60:2). Pass. (Lev 17:4) μὴ αὐτοῖς λογισθείη (on the form s. Mlt-H. 217) **2 Ti 4:16.**—But 'place to one's account' can also mean *credit* τῷ ἐργαζομένῳ ὁ μισθὸς οὐ λογίζεται κατὰ χάριν *a worker's wages are not credited as a favor* (but as a claim) **Ro 4:4.** ᾧ ὁ θεὸς λογίζεται δικαιοσύνην vs. **6.** Pass. εἰς τὸ λογισθῆναι αὐτοῖς τ. δικαιοσύνην vs. **11.**—λ. τινί τι εἴς τι *credit someth. to someone as someth.* pass. ἐλογίσθη αὐτῷ εἰς δικαιοσύνην (after Gen 15:6; cp. Ps 105:31; 1 Macc 2:52) **Ro 4:3, 5, 9, 22** (WDiezinger, NovT 5, '62, 288–98 [rabbinic use of λογ.]); **Gal 3:6; Js 2:23;** 1 Cl 10:6.—Cp. also **Ro 4:10, 23f.**—H-WHeidland, D. Anrechnung des Glaubens zur Gerechtigkeit '36; FDanker, in Gingrich Festschr. '72, 104.—λ. εἴς τινα *put on someone's account, charge to someone* (cp. the commercial terminology OGI 595, 15 τὰ ἕτερα ἀναλώματα ἑαυτοῖς ἐλογισάμεθα, ἵνα μὴ τὴν πόλιν βαρῶμεν; PFay 21, 9) μή τις εἰς ἐμὲ λογίσηται *so that no one may credit me* **2 Cor 12:6.**

ⓑ as a result of a calculation *evaluate, estimate, look upon as, consider* (Hyperid. 2, 20; TestSol 4:11) εἰς οὐθὲν λογισθῆναι *be looked upon as nothing* (Is 40:17; Wsd 3:17; 9:6) **Ac 19:27.** τὰ τέκνα τ. ἐπαγγελίας λογίζεται εἰς σπέρμα *the children of the promise are looked upon as seed* **Ro 9:8** (cp. La 4:2). οὐχ ἡ ἀκροβυστία αὐτοῦ εἰς περιτομὴν λογισθήσεται; *will not his uncircumcision be regarded as circumcision?* **2:26.** οὔτε τοὺς νομιζομένους ὑπὸ τῶν Ἑλλήνων θεοὺς λογίζονται *they do not recognize the deities honored by the Greeks* Dg 1:1.—*Count, class* (PLond II, 328, 8 p. 75 [II AD] of a camel's colt: λογιζομένου νυνὶ ἐν τελείοις='which is now classed among the full-grown') μετὰ ἀνόμων ἐλογίσθη *he was classed among the criminals* (Is 53:12) **Mk 15:27 [28] v.l.; Lk 22:37.** Also (exactly like the LXX) ἐν τοῖς ἀνόμοις ἐλογίσθη 1 Cl 16:13. μετὰ τῶν ἐθνῶν ἐλογίσθησαν *they were counted with the nations* Hs 8, 9, 3.—οὐκ ἐλογίσθη *he was held in disrespect* 1 Cl 16:3 (Is 53:3).—λ. τινα ὡς w. acc. *consider, look upon someone as:* ἡμᾶς λογιζέσθω ἄνθρωπος ὡς ὑπηρέτας Χριστοῦ **1 Cor 4:1.** λ. ἡμᾶς ὡς κατὰ σάρκα περιπατοῦντας **2 Cor 10:2b.** Pass. ἐλογίσθημεν ὡς πρόβατα σφαγῆς **Ro 8:36** (Ps 43:23). πιστοὶ λογισθέντες *regarded as believers* Dg 11:2. ὁ σήμερον υἱὸς λογισθείς *who today is celebrated as a Son* 11:5 (Ps 2:7). λ. τινα foll. by acc. and inf. (Is 53:4) λογίζεσθε ἑαυτοὺς εἶναι νεκρούς *consider yourselves dead* **Ro 6:11.** ἡμεῖς ἐλογισάμεθα αὐτὸν εἶναι ἐν πόνῳ *we deemed him to be in pain* (as punishment) 1 Cl 16:4.

❷ to give careful thought to a matter, ***think (about), consider, ponder, let one's mind dwell on*** τὶ *someth.*(PsSol 2, 28b; ApcEsdr 3:9; Philo, Leg. All. 3, 227 ταῦτα; Jos., Ant. 6, 211) **Phil 4:8.** Foll. by ὅτι (PsSol 2, 28a; Philo, Somn. 2, 169; Jos., Ant. 11, 142; Ath., R. 9 p. 57, 30) **J 11:50; Hb 11:19.** τοῦτο λ. ὅτι **2 Cor 10:11, 7** (here ἐφ' [v.l. ἀφ'] ἑαυτοῦ *in his own mind* is added); B 1:5. W. ἐν ἑαυτῷ and direct speech Hs 5, 2, 4 (cp. GrBar 4:12); w. ἐν ἑαυταῖς and direct question foll. **Lk 24:1** D; also ἐν ταῖς καρδίαις αὐτῶν πότερον . . . ἢ Hs 9, 28, 4.—*Have in mind, propose, purpose* Dg 7:3 (Mel., P. 63, 455); w. inf. foll. (X., An. 2, 2, 13; 1 Macc 6:19) **2 Cor 10:2a.** *Think out* τὶ *someth.* (Ps 51:4) ὡς ἐξ ἑαυτῶν *as (if) of ourselves* **3:5.** *Reason* or *make plans* (Wsd 2:1) ὡς νήπιος *like a child* **1 Cor 13:11.**

❸ to hold a view about someth., ***think, believe, be of the opinion*** w. ὅτι foll. (Just., A I, 8, 1 al.) **Ro 8:18.** W. acc. and ὅτι foll.: λογίζῃ τοῦτο . . . , ὅτι; *do you imagine that?* **2:3.** Foll. by acc. and inf. (Wsd 15:12; Just., A I, 53, 1; Tat., Ath.) λογιζόμεθα δικαιοῦσθαι ἄνθρωπον *we hold a person to be justified* **3:28.** λ. τι κοινὸν εἶναι **14:14.** ἐμαυτὸν οὐ (v.l. οὔπω) λ. κατειληφέναι *I consider that I have not yet attained* **Phil 3:13.** ὃν λογίζομαι καὶ τοὺς ἀθέους ἐντρέπεσθαι *whom, I think, even the godless respect* ITr 3:2. Foll. by the inf. alone **2 Cor 11:5;** Dg 3:3 (Just., D. 102, 7 al.).—ὡς λογίζομαι *as I think* **1 Pt 5:12; Mk 11:31 v.l.**—DELG s.v. λέγω 2. M-M. EDNT. TW.

λογικός, ή, όν ([adv. λογικῶς Ath. 27, 2] a favorite expr. of philosphers since Aristot.; SIG 803, 5. Not LXX, but oft. Philo, Just., Tat., Ath.) **pert. to being carefully thought through,** ***thoughtful*** λογικὴ λατρεία *a thoughtful service* (in a dedicated spiritual sense) **Ro 12:1** (the cognitive aspect anticipates the phrase εἰς τὸ δοκιμάζειν ὑμᾶς τί τὸ θέλημα τοῦ θεοῦ; cp. Herm. Wr. 1, 31 λογικὴ θυσία; 13, 18; 21; Epict. 1, 16, 20f the singing of hymns is the sacred service of a human being, as a λογικός=one endowed with reason; 3, 1, 26 τὸ λογικὸν ἔχεις ἐξαίρετον· τοῦτο κόσμει καὶ καλλώπιζε. Philo, Spec. Leg. 1, 277 God places no value on sacrificial animals, but on τοῦ θύοντος πνεῦμα λογικόν. TestLevi 3:6 λ. καὶ ἀναίμακτος προσφορά [v.l. θυσία]; Ath., 13, 2; Eus., HE 4, 23, 13; cp. the exhortative pattern of Plut., Mor. 478de.—Rtzst., Mysterienrel.[3] 328f; Ltzm., Hdb. exc. on Ro 12:1; BSchmidt, D. geistige Gebet, diss. Bresl. 1916; OCasel, Jahrb. f. Liturgiewissensch. 4, 1924, 38ff; CMoule, JTS n.s. 1, '50, 34f). Most likely τὸ λογικὸν ἄδολον γάλα **1 Pt 2:2** is to be taken in a related way *pure spiritual milk;* it is to be borne in mind that λ. means *spiritual* not only in the sense of πνευματικός, but also in contrast to 'literal', w. the mng. 'metaphorical' (cp. Pel-Leg. p. 20: the bishop is the shepherd τῶν λογικῶν προβάτων τοῦ Χριστοῦ; Eus., HE 1, 1, 4 ἐκ λογικῶν λειμώνων; s. DMcCartney, ZNW 82, '91, 128–32, w. emphasis on Hellenic connection of reason and verbal communication).—DELG s.v. λέγω B 2. M-M. TW.

λόγιον, ου, τό (Eur., Hdt.+, mostly of short divine sayings: Hdt. 8, 60, 3; Thu. 2, 8, 2; Polyb. 3, 112, 8; 8, 30, 6; Diod. S. 2, 14, 3; 2, 26, 9; 4, 65, 3 al.; Aelian, VH 2, 41. Likew. LXX [TManson, Goguel Festschr. '50, 142f]; TestLevi 8:2; TestBenj 9:1 v.l.; EpArist 177; Philo, Congr. Erud. Grat. 134, Fuga 60, Mos. 2, 262, Praem. 1, Vi. Cont. 25; Jos., Bell. 6, 311; Just.) ***a saying,*** in our lit. only pl. (as also predom. in other wr.); of the revelations received by Moses λόγια ζῶντα **Ac 7:38.** Of God's promises to the Jews **Ro 3:2** (JDoeve, Studia Paulina [JdeZwaan Festschr.] '53, 111–23). Of words fr. Scripture gener. (as Plut., Fab. 4, 5 of words fr. the Sibylline books; contrast the sg. of a biblical statement: Just., A I, 32, 14 κατὰ τὸ λόγιον [Is 11:1]; Did., Gen. 122, 24 [Eccl 8:1]); τὰ λόγια τοῦ θεοῦ (LXX; Iren. 1, 8, 1 [Harv. I 68, 11]; cp. τὰ θεῖα λ. Did., Gen. 174, 16) **Hb 5:12.**—1 Cl 13:4; 19:1; 53:1. τὰ λ. τῆς παιδείας τοῦ θεοῦ *the oracles of God's teaching* 62:3 (cp. τὰ τῆς τοῦ θεοῦ σοφίας λ. Orig., C. Cels. 5, 29, 50). Also of NT sayings 2 Cl 13:3 (cp. vs. 4). Likew. τὰ λόγια τοῦ κυρίου *the sayings of the Lord* (Jesus; Marinus, Vi. Procli 26 p. 163, 50 Boiss. τὰ 'Ορφέως λόγια; TestBenj 9:1 v.l. ἀπὸ λογίων 'Ενώχ) Pol 7:1; cp. Papias (2:15f; in Eus., HE 3, 39, 1); AcPlCor 2:3 (Clem. Al., Quis Div. Salv. 3, 1; Iren. 1, Praef. 1 [Harv. I 2, 4]; cp. Just., D. 18, 1). Of the sayings of Christians who have been endowed with the gift of ministry through spoken words **1 Pt 4:11.** For Papias s. also ἐξήγησις and κυριακός.—PNepper-Christensen, Mt ein Judenchristliches Evangelium? '58, 37–56.—DELG s.v. λέγω B 2. M-M. TW.

λόγιος, ία, ιον (s. λόγος; [superl. λογιώτατος Ath. 28, 4] Pind. et al.; ins, pap)

❶ ***eloquent*** (Plut., Pomp. 51, 8; Lucian, Pseudolog. 24, Pro Merc. Cond. 2 Hermes as ὁ λόγιος; Philo, Mut. Nom. 220, Cher. 116. This mng. rejected by Phryn. [p. 198 Lob.]; defended by Field [Notes 129]).

❷ ***learned, cultured*** (Hdt. 1, 1; 2, 3; Aristot., Pol. 2, 8; Heliod. 4, 7, 4 of an ἰατρός; EpArist 6; Philo, Mos. 1, 23 al.; Jos., Bell. 1, 13, Ant. 17, 149; Ar. 13, 7; Tat. 40, 1.—Subst. Orig., C. Cels. 1, 12, 34; 5, 21, 13). In **Ac 18:24,** where Apollos is called ἀνὴρ λ. (as Ps.-Libanius, Charact. Ep. p. 20, 12; PLond 2710 recto, 6, cited in HTR 29, '36, 40f; 45; Philo, Poster. Cai. 53), either mng. is prob, even though the ancient versions (Lat., Syr., Armen.) prefer the first.—EOrth, Logios 1926.—DELG s.v. λέγω B 2. M-M. TW. Spicq.

λογισμός, οῦ, ὁ (Thu. +).—**❶ the product of a cognitive process,** ***calculation, reasoning, reflection, thought*** in our lit. in pl. W. ἔννοιαι *thoughts and sentiments* Pol 4:3 (Ath. 9, 1). μεταξὺ ἀλλήλων τῶν λ. κατηγορούντων *as their thoughts accuse one another* **Ro 2:15** (here the thoughts are personified as prosecution and defense; Straub 30; cp Pr 19:21). Not infreq. in an unfavorable sense (as e.g. Vett. Val. 49, 8; 173, 11; λ. κακοί Pr 6:18; cp. Wsd 1:3, 5; 11:15) οἱ προκατέχοντές σου τὴν διάνοιαν λογισμοί *the* (prejudiced) *thoughts that preoccupy your mind* Dg 2:1. λογισμοὶ ἐθνῶν *the designs of nations* 1 Cl 59:3. λογισμοὺς καθαιροῦντες *we demolish sophistries* **2 Cor 10:4.**

❷ the capability of reasoning, ***reasoning power, wisdom*** (Epicurus in Diog. L. 10, 132 νήφων λογισμός=sober reasoning; TestGad 6:2 τὸ πνεῦμα τοῦ μίσους ἐτάρασσέ μου τὸν λογισμὸν πρὸς τὸ ἀνελεῖν αὐτόν; TestJob 21:4 ἀνελάμβανον λογισμὸν μακρόθυμον; Jos., Bell. 2, 31; Just., A I, 17, 3 al.) ἄνθρωπος αἴσθησιν ἔχει κ. λογισμόν *a pers. has the power to feel and think* Dg 2:9 (λ. w. αἴσθησις as Philo, Praem. 28).—DELG s.v. λέγω B 2. M-M. TW. Sv.

λογομαχέω (Eustath., Opusc. p. 47, 96) ***to dispute about words, split hairs*** **2 Ti 2:14.**—TW.

λογομαχία, ας, ἡ (λόγος + μάχομαι; Conon [I BC/I AD: 26 fgm. 1, 38 p. 204, 1 Jac. [Narrat. 38 in Photius, Bibl. Cod. 186]; Porphyr., Ep. ad Anebonem 2; 19 p. 29, 19; Eus., PE 14, 10, 2; Cat. Cod. Astr. VIII/1 p. 167, 21) ***word-battle, dispute about words*** **1 Ti 6:4; Tit 3:9 v.l.**—TW.

λόγος, ου, ὁ (verbal noun of λέγω in the sense 'pick'; Hom.+).

❶ a communication whereby the mind finds expression, *word*—ⓐ of utterance, chiefly oral.—**α.** as expression, *word* (oratorical ability plus exceptional performance were distinguishing marks in Hellenic society, hence the frequent association of λ. and ἔργον 'deed'; a sim. formulation as early as Il. 9, 443 μύθων τε ῥητῆρ' ἔμεναι πρηκτῆρά τε ἔργων; Polystrat. p. 33 μὴ λόγῳ μόνον ἀλλ' ἔργῳ; Just., A II, 4, 2 ἢ λόγῳ ἢ ἔργῳ and D. 35, 7 λόγον ἢ πρᾶξιν) δυνατὸς ἐν ἔργῳ κ. λόγῳ, i.e. an exceptional personage **Lk 24:19;** pl. of Moses **Ac 7:22** (the contrast expressed w. a verb Choix 20, 6–8 ποιεῖ ἀγαθὸν ὅτι δύναται καὶ λόγῳ καὶ ἔργῳ of Apollordorus, a benefactor in Cyzicus, a flourishing city in Phrygia; sim. New Docs 7, 233, no. 10, 8f πολιτευόμενος … λόγῳ καὶ ἔργῳ; cp. IKourion 32, 8; without contrast Diod. S. 13, 101, 3 ἄνδρας λόγῳ δυνατούς; for sim. constructions using λέγω and πράσσω s. Danker, Benefactor 339–43). Cp. **Ro 15:18; 2 Cor 10:11; Col 3:17; 2 Th 2:17; Hb 13:21 v.l.; 1J 3:18** (cp. Theognis 1, 87f Diehl[3] μή μ' ἔπεσιν μὲν στέργε κτλ.—For the contrast λόγῳ … ἀληθείᾳ cp. Diod. S. 13, 4, 1). In contrast to a sinful deed we also have the λόγος ἁμαρτίας *sinful word* Judaicon 172, 9. W. γνῶσις: ἐν παντὶ λόγῳ κ. πάσῃ γνώσει **1 Cor 1:5.** ἰδιώτης τῷ λόγῳ, ἀλλ' οὐ τῇ γνώσει **2 Cor 11:6.** (Opp. δύναμις 'revelation of power') **1 Cor 4:19, 20.** τὸ εὐαγγέλιον οὐκ ἐγενήθη ἐν λόγῳ μόνον, ἀλλὰ καὶ ἐν δυνάμει **1 Th 1:5** (cp. Ar. 13, 7 of mythical accounts οὐδέν εἰσιν εἰ μὴ μόνον λόγοι 'they're nothing but words'). W. ἐπιστολή: **2 Th 2:2, 15.** W. ἀναστροφή: **1 Ti 4:12; 1 Pt 3:1b.** Opp. 'be silent': IRo 2:1.—μόνον εἰπὲ λόγῳ *just say the word* **Mt 8:8;** cp. **Lk 7:7** (Ath. 17, 1 ὡς λόγῳ εἰπεῖν; 29, 2; Phalaris, Ep. 121, 1 λόγῳ λέγειν; cp. schol. on Pla. 341a ἐν λόγῳ μόνον εἰπεῖν). οὐδεὶς ἐδύνατο ἀποκριθῆναι αὐτῷ λόγον *no one was able to answer him a (single) word* **Mt 22:46;** cp. **15:23** (cp. TestAbr A 16 p. 98, 11 [Stone p. 44] οὐκ ἀπεκρίθη αὐτῷ λόγον).—*The* (mighty) *word* (of one who performs miracles) ἐξέβαλεν τὰ πνεύματα λόγῳ **Mt 8:16** (a rare use of λ. as 'single utterance', s. L-S-J-M s.v. VII).—διὰ λόγου *by word of mouth* (opp. 'by letter') **Ac 15:27.**—In the textually uncertain pass. **Ac 20:24** the text as it stands in N., οὐδενὸς λόγου (v.l. λόγον) ποιοῦμαι τὴν ψυχὴν τιμίαν, may well mean: *I do not consider my life worth a single word* (cp. λόγου ἄξιον [ἄξιος 1a] and our 'worth mention'; s. Conzelmann ad loc.).

β. The expression may take on a variety of formulations or topical nuances: *what you say* **Mt 5:37;** *statement* (PGM 4, 334) **Lk 20:20;** *question* (Sext. Emp., Math. 8, 295; 9, 133; Diog. L. 2, 116) ἐρωτήσω ὑμᾶς λόγον *I will ask you a question* (cp. TestJob 36:5; GrBar 5:1; ApcSed 13:6; Jos., Ant. 12, 99) **Mt 21:24;** cp. **Mk 11:29; Lk 20:3;** *prayer* (PGM 1, 25; 4, 90; 179; 230 al.; 5, 180; 196 al.) **Mt 26:44; Mk 14:39.** ἡγούμενος τοῦ λ. *principal speaker* **Ac 14:12.** W. epexeget. gen. λ. παρακλήσεως **13:15.** W. κήρυγμα *our manner of presentation and our proclamation* **1 Cor 2:4a** (but s. comm.). (W. διδασκαλία) *preaching* **1 Ti 5:17;** *prophecy* (Biogr. p. 364 [Pythia]) **J 2:22; 18:32.** *Command* (Aeschyl., Pers. 363) **Lk 4:36; 2 Pt 3:5, 7;** via a letter **2 Th 3:14.** *Report, story* (X., An. 1, 4, 7; Diod. S. 3, 40, 9; 19, 110, 1 λ. διαδιδόναι=spread a report; Appian, Iber. 80 §346, Maced. 4 §1 [both=rumor]; Diod. S. 32, 15, 3 ἦλθεν ὁ λ. ἐπί τινα=the report came to someone; Arrian, Anab. 7, 22, 1 λόγος λέγεται τοιόσδε=a story is told like this, Ind. 9, 2; Diod. S. 3, 18, 3 λ.=story, account; Jos., Ant. 19, 132; Tat. 27, 2 τοῦ καθ' Ἡρακλέα λόγου) **Mt 28:15; Mk 1:45; Lk 5:15** (λ. περί τινος as X., An. 6, 6, 13; Jos., Ant. 19, 127) **7:17; J 21:23.** ἠκούσθη ὁ λόγος εἰς τὰ ὦτα τ. ἐκκλησίας *the report came to the ears of the assembly* in Jerusalem **Ac 11:22.** λόγον ἔχειν σοφίας *have the appearance of wisdom, pass for wisdom* **Col 2:23** (cp. Pla., Epinomis 987b ἔχει λόγον; Demosth., C. Lept. 462 [20, 18] λόγον τιν' ἔχον; but mng. 2f is possible). *Proverb* (Pla., Phdr. 17, 240c, Symp. 18, 195b, Gorg. 54, 499c, Leg. 6, 5, 757a; Socrat., Ep. 22, 1) **J 4:37** (Ps.-Callisth. 1, 13, 7 ἀληθῶς ἐν τούτῳ ὁ λ. foll. by a proverb). *Proclamation, instruction, teaching, message* **Lk 4:32; 10:39; J 4:41; 17:20; Ac 2:41; 4:4; 10:44; 20:7; 1 Cor 1:17; 2:1.** In **Ac 18:15** ζητήματα περὶ λόγου καὶ ὀνομάτων καὶ νόμου the sense appears to be someth. like this: *controversial issues involving disputes about words and your way of life* with λ. prob. referring to the presentation of controversial subjects, which in turn arouses heated ζητήματα debates. λόγος σοφίας *proclamation of wisdom, speaking wisely* **1 Cor 12:8a** (Ps.-Phoc. 129 τῆς θεοπνεύστου σοφίης λ.); corresp. λ. γνώσεως vs. **8b.** Cp. **14:9; 15:2; 2 Cor 1:18; 6:7; 10:10.** λ. μαρτυρίας *word of witness* **Rv 12:11.** ὁ κατὰ τ. διδαχὴν πιστὸς λ. *the message of faith, corresponding to the teaching* **Tit 1:9;** the opp. **2 Ti 2:17.** *A speech* (Aristot. p. 14b, 2; Diod. S. 40, 5a) διὰ λόγου πολλοῦ *in a long speech* **Ac 15:32;** cp. **20:2.** λ. κολακείας *flattering speech* **1 Th 2:5.** *Speaking* gener. **2 Cor 8:7; Eph 6:19; Col 4:6;** D 2:5. ἐν λόγῳ πταίειν *make a mistake in what one says* **Js 3:2.**—Of God's word, command, commission (LXX; ParJer 5:19 κατηχῆσαι αὐτοὺς τὸν λόγον; SyrBar 13:2; ApcSed 14:10; Just., D. 84, 2; Ael. Aristid. hears a ἱερὸς λ. at night fr. a god: 28, 116 K.=49, p. 529 D.; Sextus 24) ἠκυρώσατε τ. λόγον τοῦ θεοῦ **Mt 15:6** (v.l. νόμον, ἐντολήν); cp. **Mk 7:13.**—**J 5:38; 8:55; 10:35; Ro 3:4** (Ps 50:6). Of God's promise **Ro 9:6, 9** (but these two vss., and **Gal 5:14** below, prob. fit better under 2a), **28** (Is 10:22f). Cp. **Hb 2:2; 4:2** (s. ἀκοή 4b); **7:28; 12:19.** For B 15:1 see 1aδ. The whole law (as the expr. εἴ τι ἑτέρα ἐντολή indicates not limited to a narrow list of commandments), acc. to **Ro 13:9.** In what is prob. a play on words (s. 2a and b), **Gal 5:14** (s. 2a below) is summed up in the λόγος as expressed in Lev 19:18.—That which God has created ἁγιάζεται διὰ λόγου θεοῦ **1 Ti 4:5;** in line w. the context, this hardly refers to God's creative word (so SibOr 3, 20; PtK 2; πάντα γὰρ λόγῳ ποιήσας ὁ θεός Theoph. Ant. 2, 18 [144, 8]), but to table prayers which use biblical expressions. The divine word as judge of thoughts **Hb 4:12.** τελεσθήσονται οἱ λ. τοῦ θεοῦ **Ac 17:17;** cp. **19:9.**—Of the divine revelation through Christ and his messengers (Just., A I, 61, 9 λόγον … παρὰ τῶν ἀποστόλων ἐμάθομεν τοῦτον) θεὸς ἐφανέρωσεν τὸν λ. αὐτοῦ ἐν κηρύγματι **Tit 1:3.** δέδωκα αὐτοῖς τὸν λ. σου **J 17:14;** cp. vss. **6, 17; 1J 1:10; 2:14.** ἵνα μὴ ὁ λ. τοῦ θεοῦ βλασφημῆται **Tit 2:5.** The apostles and other preachers, w. ref. to the λόγος of God, are said to: λαλεῖν **Ac 4:29, 31; 13:46; Phil 1:14; Hb 13:7;** καταγγέλλειν **Ac 13:5; 17:13;** διδάσκειν **18:11;** μαρτυρεῖν **Rv 1:2.** Of their hearers it is said: τὸν λ. τοῦ θεοῦ ἀκούειν **Ac 13:7;** δέχεσθαι **8:14; 11:1.** Of the λ. τοῦ θεοῦ itself we read: ηὔξανεν **Ac 6:7; 12:24; 19:20;** οὐ δέδεται **2 Ti 2:9.** In these places and many others ὁ λόγος τοῦ θεοῦ is simply *the Christian message, the gospel:* **Lk 5:1; 8:11, 21; 11:28** (Simplicius in Epict. p. 1, 20 μὴ μόνον ἀκουόντων ἀλλὰ πασχόντων καὶ ὑπὸ τῶν λόγων=let the message have its effect on oneself); **Ac 6:2** (s. καταλείπω 7c; for prob. commercial metaph. s. 2a below); **13:44 v.l.** (for κυρίου); **16:32 v.l.; 1 Cor 14:36; 2 Cor 2:17; 4:2; Col 1:25; 1 Pt 1:23; Rv 1:9; 6:9; 20:4;** IPhld 11:1. Cp. **1 Th 2:13ab; 1J 2:5.**—Since this 'divine word' is brought to humanity through Christ, his word can be used in the same sense: ὁ λόγος μου **J 5:24;** cp. **8:31, 37, 43, 51f; 12:48; 14:23f; 15:3, 20b; Rv 3:8.** ὁ λόγος τοῦ Χριστοῦ **Col 3:16;** cp. **Hb 6:1.** ὁ λ. τοῦ κυρίου **Ac 8:25; 12:24 v.l.; 13:44, 48f; 14:25 v.l.; 15:35, 36; 16:32** (cp. λ. θεοῦ); **19:10; 1 Th 1:8; 2 Th 3:1.** Pl. **Mk 8:38 (Lk 9:26); 1 Ti 6:3;** cp. **Lk 24:44;**

s. also 1aδ.—Or it is called simply ὁ λόγος=*the 'Word'*, for no misunderstanding would be possible among Christians: **Mt 13:20–23; Mk 2:2; 4:14–20, 33; 8:32** (s. 1aε below); **16:20; Lk 1:2; 8:12f, 15; Ac 6:4; 8:4; 10:36** (on the syntax s. FNeirynck, ETL 60, '84, 118–23); **11:19; 14:25** (cp. λ. κυρίου above); **16:6; 17:11; 18:5; Gal 6:6; Phil 1:14; Col 4:3; 1 Th 1:6; 2 Ti 4:2; Js 1:21ff; 1 Pt 2:8; 3:1; 1J 2:7;** AcPl Ha 7, 6 (so also Mel., HE 4, 26, 13; Ath. 2, 3).—Somet. the 'Word' is more closely defined by a gen.: ὁ λ. τῆς βασιλείας *the word of the reign/rule* (of God) **Mt 13:19.** τῆς σωτηρίας **Ac 13:26.** τῆς καταλλαγῆς **2 Cor 5:19.** τοῦ σταυροῦ **1 Cor 1:18.** δικαιοσύνης (q.v. 3a) **Hb 5:13.** ζωῆς **Phil 2:16.** (τῆς) ἀληθείας (Theoph. Ant. 3, 4 [p. 212, 2]; cp. περὶ ἀληθείας Hippol., Ref. 10, 6, 1) **Eph 1:13; Col 1:5; 2 Ti 2:15; Js 1:18;** AcPl Ha 8, 8 (Just., D. 121, 2). τῆς χάριτος αὐτοῦ (=τοῦ κυρίου) **Ac 14:3; 20:32.** (Differently the pl. οἱ λόγοι τ. χάριτος *gracious words* **Lk 4:22;** cp. Marcellinus, Vi. Thu. 57 Hude λόγοι εἰρωνείας.) ὁ λ. τοῦ εὐαγγελίου **Ac 15:7;** ὁ τοῦ Χριστιανισμοῦ λ. MPol 10:1. In **Rv 3:10** the gospel is described by the 'One who has the key of David' as ὁ λ. τῆς ὑπομονῆς μου *my word of endurance* (W-S. §30, 12c). λ. τῶν ὑ[πο]μονῶν AcPl Ha 6, 11. παρελάβετε τὸν λ. ὅτι AcPl Ha 8, 25.—The pastoral letters favor the expr. πιστὸς ὁ λόγος (sc. ἐστίν, and s. πιστός 1b) **1 Ti 1:15; 3:1; 4:9; 2 Ti 2:11; Tit 3:8;** cp. **Rv 21:5; 22:6.** λ. ὑγιής *sound preaching* **Tit 2:8;** cp. the pl. ὑγιαίνοντες λόγοι **2 Ti 1:13** (on medicinal use of words for the mind or soul s. VLeinieks, The City of Dionysos '96, 115–22, on Eur.).—The pl. is also used gener. of Christian teachings, the words of the gospel **Lk 1:4** (s. κατηχέω 2a); **1 Th 4:18.** οἱ λ. τῆς πίστεως **1 Ti 4:6.** On λόγοι κυριακοί for λόγια κυριακά in the title of the Papias document s. ἐξήγησις 2.—JSchniewind, Die Begriffe Wort und Evangelium bei Pls, diss. Bonn 1910; RAsting (εὐαγγέλιον, end).

γ. of an individual declaration or remark: *assertion, declaration, speech* ἀκούσαντες τὸν λ. *when they heard the statement* **Mt 15:12;** cp. **19:11, 22; 22:15; Mk 5:36.** διὰ τοῦτον τὸν λ. *because of this statement of yours* **7:29** (TestAbr A 15 p. 95, 29 [Stone p. 38] τὸν λ. τοῦτον; ApcMos 25 εἰς τὸν λόγον σου κρινῶ σε). Cp. **10:22; 12:13; Lk 1:29; 22:61 v.l.** (for ῥήματος); **J 4:39, 50; 6:60; 7:36, 40 v.l.; 15:20a; 18:9; 19:8; Ac 6:5; 7:29; 20:38; 22:22; 1 Th 4:15.** ὃς ἐὰν εἴπῃ λόγον κατὰ τοῦ υἱοῦ τοῦ ἀνθρώπου *whoever utters a* (defamatory) *word against the Son of Humanity* **Mt 12:32** (λ. εἰπεῖν κατά τινος as Jos., Ant. 15, 81); cp. **Lk 12:10.** λόγος σαπρός *unwholesome talk* **Eph 4:29.** λόγον ποιεῖσθαι *make a speech* **Ac 11:2** D (cp. Hyperid. 3, 20; Jos., Ant. 11, 86).

δ. the pl. (οἱ) λόγοι is used, on the one hand, of words uttered on various occasions, of speeches or instruction given here and there by humans or transcendent beings (TestAbr A 14 p. 94, 19 [Stone p. 36]; Jos., Ant. 4, 264; Just., D. 100, 3) ἐκ τῶν λόγων σου δικαιωθήσῃ (καταδικασθήσῃ) **Mt 12:37ab; 24:35; Mk 13:31; Lk 21:33; Ac 2:40; 7:22** (ἐν λόγοις καὶ ἔργοις αὐτοῦ. On the word-deed pair cp. Dio Chrys. 4, 6 the λόγοι and ἔργα of Diogenes; s. α above). οἱ δέκα λόγοι *the ten commandments* (Ex 34:28; Dt 10:4; Philo, Rer. Div. Her. 168, Decal. 32; Jos., Ant. 3, 138; cp. 91f; Did., Gen. 36, 10) B 15:1. **Ac 15:24; 20:35; 1 Cor 2:4b, 13; 14:19ab;** κενοὶ λ. **Eph 5:6;** AcPl Ox 6, 13 (cp. Aa 1, 241, 14); Dg 8:2; πλαστοὶ λ. **2 Pt 2:3.** λ. πονηροί **3J 10.**—Also of words and exprs. that form a unity, whether it be connected discourse (Jos., Ant. 15, 126; Just., A II, 12, 6, D. 11, 5; 81, 3 al.), a conversation, or parts of one and the same teaching, or expositions on the same subject (Diod. S. 16, 2, 3 μετέσχε τῶν Πυθαγορίων λόγων; Dio Chrys. 37 [54], 1; Ael. Aristid. 50, 55 K.=26 p. 519 D.: οἱ Πλάτωνος λόγοι; PsSol 17:43 [words of the Messiah]; AscIs 3:12 οἱ λόγοι τοῦ Βελχειρά) πᾶς ὅστις ἀκούει μου τοὺς λόγους τούτους **Mt 7:24;** cp. vss. **26, 28; 10:14; 19:1; 26:1; Mk 10:24; Lk 1:20; 6:47; 9:28, 44.** ἐπηρώτα αὐτὸν ἐν λόγοις ἱκανοῖς *he questioned him at some length* **23:9.** τίνες οἱ λ. οὗτοι οὓς ἀντιβάλλετε; *what is this conversation that you are holding?* **24:17; J 7:40** (s. γ); **10:19; J 14:24a; 19:13; Ac 2:22; 5:5, 24; 16:36; 2 Ti 4:15;** 1 Cl 13:1; 46:7. λόγοις φθοριμαίοις AcPlCor 1:2.

ε. *the subject* under discussion, *matter, thing* gener. (Theognis 1055 Diehl; Hdt. 8, 65 μηδενὶ ἄλλῳ τὸν λόγον τοῦτον εἴπῃς. Cp. Hebr. דָּבָר) τὸν λ. ἐκράτησαν *they took up the subject* **Mk 9:10;** cp. **Mt. 21:24** (s. 1aβ beg.). οὐκ ἔστιν σοι μερὶς ἐν τῷ λόγῳ τούτῳ *you have no share in this matter* **Ac 8:21.** ἰδεῖν περὶ τ. λόγου τούτου *look into this matter* **15:6.** ἔχειν πρός τινα λόγον *have a complaint against someone* (cp. Demosth. 35, 55 ἐμοὶ πρὸς τούτους ὁ λόγος; PIand 16, 3 δίκαιον λόγον ἔχει πρὸς σέ) **19:38.** παρεκτὸς λόγου πορνείας **Mt 5:32; 19:9 v.l.** (2d is also prob.).—Perh. also **Mk 8:32** *he discussed the subject quite freely* (but s. 1aβ above).

ⓑ of literary or oratorical productions: of the separate books of a work (Hdt. 5, 36 ἐν τῷ πρώτῳ τ. λόγων; Pla., Parmen. 2, 127d ὁ πρῶτος λόγος; Philo, Omn. Prob. Lib. 1 ὁ μὲν πρότερος λόγος ἦν ἡμῖν, ὦ Θεόδοτε, περὶ τοῦ ...) *treatise* **Ac 1:1** (s. on the prologue to Ac: AHilgenfeld, ZWT 41, 1898, 619ff; AGercke, Her 29, 1894, 373ff; RLaqueur, Her 46, 1911, 161ff; Norden, Agn. Th. 311ff; JCreed, JTS 35, '34, 176–82; Goodsp., Probs. 119–21). Παπίας ... πέντε λόγους κυριακῶν λογίων ἔγραψεν Papias (11:1; cp. 3:1 e; 11:2; 12:2).—περὶ οὗ πολὺς ἡμῖν ὁ λόγος *about this we have much to say* **Hb 5:11.** Hb is described as ὁ λ. τῆς παρακλήσεως *a word of exhortation* (in literary form) **13:22.** Of writings that are part of Holy Scripture ὁ λ. Ἠσαΐου **J 12:38.** ὁ λ. ὁ ἐν τῷ νόμῳ γεγραμμένος **15:25;** ὁ προφητικὸς λ. **2 Pt 1:19;** 2 Cl 11:2 (quot. of unknown orig.); AcPl Ha 8, 27//BMM recto 35 (Just., D. 77, 2 al.). ὁ ἅγιος λ. *the holy word* 1 Cl 56:3. ὁ λ. ὁ γεγραμμένος **1 Cor 15:54** (Is 25:8 and Hos 13:14 follow). Pl. οἱ λόγοι τ. προφητῶν **Ac 15:15.** ὡς γέγραπται ἐν βίβλῳ λόγων Ἠσαΐου **Lk 3:4** (Pla., 7th Epistle 335a πείθεσθαι ἀεὶ χρὴ τοῖς παλαιοῖς καὶ ἱεροῖς λόγοις; TestJob 1:1 βίβλος λόγων Ἰώβ; ParJer 9:32 v.l. τὰ λοιπὰ τῶν λόγων Ἱερεμίου; ApcEsdr 1:1 καὶ ἀποκάλυψις τοῦ ... Ἐσδράμ; ApcSed prol.; Just., D. 72, 3f).—Of the content of Rv: ὁ ἀναγινώσκων τ. λόγους τῆς προφητείας **1:3.** οἱ λόγοι (τ. προφητείας) τ. βιβλίου τούτου **22:7, 9f, 18f.**

❷ ***computation, reckoning***—ⓐ a formal accounting, esp. of one's actions, and freq. with fig. extension of commercial terminology *account, accounts, reckoning* λόγον δοῦναι (Hdt. 8, 100; X., Cyr. 1, 4, 3; Diod. S. 3, 46, 4; SIG 1099, 16; BGU 164, 21; Jos., Ant. 16, 120; Just., D. 115, 6) *give account, make an accounting* ἕκαστος περὶ ἑαυτοῦ λόγον δώσει τ. θεῷ **Ro 14:12.** Also λ. ἀποδοῦναι abs. (Just., D. 116, 1 al.; Diod. S. 16, 56, 4; 19, 9, 4) **Hb 13:17.** τινί *to someone* (Diod. S. 16, 27, 4; Plut., Alcib. 7, 3; Chariton 7, 6, 2; SIG 631, 13 τᾷ πόλει; 2 Ch 34:28; Da 6:3 Theod.; Jos., Bell. 1, 209) τῷ ἑτοίμως ἔχοντι κρῖναι **1 Pt 4:5.** τινός of someth. (SIG 1044, 46; 1105, 10 τοῦ ἀναλώματος; Jos., Ant. 19, 307) **Lk 16:2** (here λ. w. the art.; on the subject of undergoing an audit cp. Aeschin. 3, 22). Likew. περί τινος (Diod. S. 18, 60, 2 δοὺς αὑτῷ περὶ τούτων λόγον=taking account [considering] with himself; BGU 98, 25 περὶ τούτου) **Mt 12:36; Ac 19:40.** ὑπέρ τινος *concerning someone* Hv 3, 9, 10.—αἰτεῖν τινα λόγον περί τινος *call someone to account for someth.* **1 Pt 3:15** (cp. Pla., Pol. 285e; Dio Chrys. 20 [37], 30; Apc4Esdr fgm. b ἕκαστος ὑπὸ τοῦ οἰκείου ἔργου τὸν λόγον ἀπαιτηθήσεται; Just., A I, 17, 4. For another perspective s. d below.).—Of banking responsibility ὁ λόγος τοῦ θεοῦ (PStras 72, 10 [III AD] ὁ τῶν θεῶν λ.; PHerm 108 [III AD] λ. τοῦ Σαραπείου) in wordplay **Ac 6:2** (w. τράπεζα q.v. 1c); s. also 1aβ.—Of a *ledger heading* (POxy 1333 [II/III AD] δὸς αὐτῷ λόγῳ θεωρικῶν=credit him under 'festivals'; for others s. Preisig., Wörterbuch s.v. λ. 14; s. also Fachwörter 119) **Ro 9:6** (the point is that God's 'list' of Israelites is accurate; on ἐκπίπτω in the sense 'is not deficient' s. s.v. 4); vs. **9** (the 'count' is subsumed by metonymy in divine promise); **Gal 5:14** (all moral obligations come under one 'entry': 'you shall love your neighbor as yourself'; for commercial association of ἀναλίσκω vs. 15, which rounds out the wordplay, s. s.v.). The contexts of these three passages suggest strong probability for commercial associations; for another view s. 1aβ.

ⓑ *settlement (of an account)* (εἰς λόγον commercial t.t. 'in settlement of an account' POxy 275, 19; 21) εἰς λόγον δόσεως κ. λήμψεως *in settlement of a mutual account* (lit., 'of giving and receiving', 'of debit and credit') **Phil 4:15** (cp. Plut., Mor. 11b λόγον δοῦναι καὶ λαβεῖν; a parallel formulation POxy 1134,10 [421 AD] λ. λήμματος καὶ ἐξοδιασμοῦ=ledger of income and expenditures); for the linked accounting terms δόσις and λῆμψις s. PCairMasp 151, 208 [VI AD]. The same ideas are in the background of εἰς λόγον ὑμῶν *credited to your account* vs **17.**—συναίρειν λόγον *settle accounts* (BGU 775, 18f. The mid. in the same mng. PFay109, 6 [I AD]; POxy 113, 27f.—Dssm., LO 94 [LAE 118f]) μετά τινος **Mt 18:23; 25:19.**

ⓒ *reflection, respect, regard* εἰς λόγον τινός *with regard to, for the sake of* (Thu. 3, 46, 4; Demosth. 19, 142 εἰς ἀρετῆς λόγον; Polyb. 11, 28, 8; Ath. 31, 1; Ael. Aristid. 39 p. 743 D.: εἰς δεινότητος λ.) εἰς λ. τιμῆς IPhld 11:2. εἰς λ. θεοῦ ISm 10:1.

ⓓ reason for or cause of someth., *reason, ground, motive* (Just., D. 94, 3 δότε μοι λόγον, ὅτου χάριν . . . ; Ath. 30, 3 τὶς γὰρ . . . λόγος; Dio Chrys. 64 [14], 18 ἐκ τούτου τ. λόγου; Appian, Hann. 29 §126 τῷ αὐτῷ λόγῳ; Iambl., Vi. Pyth. 28, 155) τίνι λόγῳ; *for what reason?* **Ac 10:29** (cp. Pla., Gorg. 512c τίνι δικαίῳ λ.; Appian, Mithrid. 57 §232 τίνι λόγῳ;). λόγον περὶ τῆς ἐν ὑμῖν ἐλπίδος **1 Pt 3:15** (but s. a above); κατὰ λόγον **Ac 18:14** (s. κατά B 5bβ). παρεκτὸς λόγου πορνείας **Mt 5:32; 19:9 v.l.** (though 1aε is also poss.).

ⓔ πρὸς ὃν ἡμῖν ὁ λόγος (ἐστίν) *with whom we have to do* (i.e. *to reckon*) (Dio Chrys. 31, 123; other exx. in FBleek, Hb II/1, 1836, 590ff), in his capacity as judge (Libanius, Legat. Ulixis [=Declamatio IV] 2 F. τοῖς δὲ ἀδίκως ἀποκτενοῦσι καὶ πρὸς θεοὺς καὶ πρὸς ἀνθρώπους ὁ λόγος γίγνεται) **Hb 4:13.** οὐ πρὸς σάρκα ὁ λόγος, ἀλλὰ πρὸς θεόν *he has to do not with flesh, but with God* IMg 3:2.

ⓕ In **Col 2:23** (s. 1aβ) λόγον μὲν ἔχοντα σοφίας may=*make a case for wisdom* (cp. λόγος ἡμῖν οὐδείς Plut., Mor. 870b).

❸ **the independent personified expression of God, *the Logos.*** Our lit. shows traces of a way of thinking that was widespread in contemporary syncretism, as well as in Jewish wisdom lit. and Philo, the most prominent feature of which is the concept of the Logos, the independent, personified 'Word' (of God): GJs 11:2 (word of the angel to Mary) συνλήμψῃ ἐκ Λόγου αὐτοῦ (sc. τοῦ πάντων Δεσπότου). **J 1:1abc, 14** (cp. Just., A I, 23, 2; Mel., P. 9, 61 and oft. by all apolog., exc.. Ar.). It is the distinctive teaching of the Fourth Gospel that this divine 'Word' took on human form in a historical person, that is, in Jesus (s. RSeeberg, Festgabe für AvHarnack '21, 263–81.—Λόγος w. ζωή in gnostic speculation: Iren.1, 1, 1 [Harv. 1, 10, 4]; Aelian, VH 4, 20 ἐκάλουν τὸν Πρωταγόραν Λόγον. Similarly Favorinus [II AD]: Vorsokr. 80 A 1 ln. 22 [in Diog. L. 9, 50] of Democritus: ἐκαλεῖτο Σοφία. Equating a divinity with an abstraction that she personifies: Artem. 5, 18 φρόνησις εἶναι νομίζεται ἡ θεός [Athena]). Cp. **1J 1:1; Rv 19:13.** εἷς θεός ἐστιν, ὁ φανερώσας ἑαυτὸν διὰ Ἰ. Χριστοῦ τοῦ υἱοῦ αὐτοῦ, ὅς ἐστιν αὐτοῦ λόγος, ἀπὸ σιγῆς προελθών *there is one God, who has revealed himself through Jesus Christ his Son, who is his 'Word' proceeding from silence* (i.e., without an oral pronouncement: in a transcendent manner) IMg 8:2 (s. σιγή). The Lord as νόμος κ. λόγος PtK 1. Cp. Dg 11:2, 3, 7, 8; 12:9.—HClavier, TManson memorial vol., '59, 81–93: the Alexandrian eternal λόγος is also implied in **Hb 4:12; 13:7.**—S. also the 'Comma Johanneum' (to the bibliography in RGG[3] I, '54 [HGreeven] add AJülicher, GGA 1905, 930–35; AvHarnack, SBBerlAk 1915, 572f [=Studien I '31, 151f]; MMeinertz, Einl. in d. NT[4] '33, 309–11; AGreiff, TQ 114, '33, 465–80; CDodd, The Joh. Epistles '46; WThiele, ZNW 50, '59, 61–73) ὁ πατήρ, ὁ λόγος καὶ τὸ ἅγιον πνεῦμα **1J 5:7 v.l.** (s. N. app.; Borger, TRu 52, '87, 57f). (Such interpolations were not unheard of. According to Diog. L. 1, 48 some people maintain that Solon inserted the verse mentioning the Athenians after Il. 2, 557.—τῆς τριάδος, τοῦ θεοῦ καὶ τοῦ λόγου αὐτοῦ καὶ τῆς σοφίας αὐτοῦ Theoph. Ant. 2, 15 [p. 138, 19].)—On the Logos: EZeller, D. Philosophie der Griechen III 2[4] 1903, 417–34; MHeinze, D. Lehre v. Logos in d. griech. Philosophie 1872; PWendland, Philo u. d. kynisch-stoische Diatribe (Beiträge z. Gesch. der griech. Philosophie u. Religion by Wendl. and OKern 1895, 1–75); AAall, Gesch. d. Logosidee 1896, 1899; MPohlenz, D. Stoa '48f, I 482; 490 (index); LDürr, D. Wertung des göttl. Wortes im AT u. im ant. Orient '38 (§9 of the Joh. Logos); EBréhier, Les idées philosophiques et religieuses de Philon d'Alexandrie 1907, 83–111; ([2] '25); JLebreton, Les théories du Logos au début de l'ère chrétienne 1907; ESchwartz, NGG 1908, 537–56; GVos, The Range of the Logos-Title in the Prologue of the Fourth Gospel: PTR 11, 1913, 365–419; 557–602; RHarris, The Origin of the Prologue to St. John's Gospel 1917, Athena, Sophia and the Logos: BJRL 7, 1, 1922 p. 56–72; M-JLagrange, Vers le Logos de S. Jean: RB 32, 1923, 161–84, Le Logos de Philon: ibid. 321–71; HLeisegang, Logos: Pauly-W. XIII 1926, 1035–81; TGlasson, Heraclitus' Alleged Logos Doctr., JTS 3, '52, 231–38.—NWeinstein, Z. Genesis d. Agada 1901, 29–90; Billerb. II 302–33.—Rtzst., Zwei religionsgeschichtl. Fragen 1901, 47–132, Mysterienrel.[3] 1927, 428 index; WBousset, Kyrios Christos[2] 1921, 304ff; 316f; JKroll, D. Lehren d. Hermes Trismegistos1914, 418 index.—RBultmann, D. religionsgesch. Hintergrund des Prol. z. Joh.: HGunkel Festschr., 1923, II 1–26, Comm. '41, 5ff; AAlexander, The Johannine Doctrine of the Logos: ET 36, 1925, 394–99; 467–72; (Rtzst. and) HSchaeder, Studien z. antiken Synkretismus 1926, 306–37; 350; GAvdBergh-vanEysinga, In den beginne was de Logos: NThT 23, '34, 105–23; JDillersberger, Das Wort von Logos '35; RBury, The 4th Gosp. and the Logos-Doctrine '40; EMay, CBQ 8, '46, 438–47; GKnight, From Moses to Paul '49, 120–29. TW IV 76–89; 126–40 (on this s. SLyonnet, Biblica 26, '45, 126–31); CStange, ZST 21, '50, 120–41; MBoismard, Le Prologue de St. Jean '53; HLangkammer, BZ 9, '65, 91–94; HRinggren, Word and Wisdom [hypostatization in Near East] '47; WEltester, Haenchen Festschr., '64, 109–34; HWeiss, Untersuchungen zur Kosmologie etc., TU 97, '66, 216–82; MRissi, Die Logoslieder im Prolog des vierten Evangeliums, TZ 31, '75, 321–36; HLausberg, NAWG, Ph. '87, 1 pp. 1–7.—B. 1262. DELG s.v. λέγω B 1. M-M. EDNT. TW.

λόγχη, ης, ἡ (Pind., Hdt. et al.; ins, pap, LXX; Jos., Bell. 3, 95, Ant. 16, 315; SibOr 3, 688; loanw. in rabb.) ***spear, lance*** **Mt 27:49 v.l.** (HVogels, BZ 10, 1912, 396–405); **J 19:34.** In the latter pass. the mng. *spear-point* (Hdt. 1, 52; X., An. 4, 7, 16;

SIG 1168, 95; 1169, 65) is also prob.—B. 1390. DELG. M-M. TW.

λοιδορέω 1 aor. ἐλοιδόρησα; mid.-pass. 3 pl. ἐλοιδορήθησαν (s. two next entries; since Pind, O. 9, 56 λ. θεούς; Dio Chrys. 15 [32], 89 θεούς; Epict. 3, 4, 7 τὸν Δία; SIG 1109, 75ff; PPetr III, 21 [g], 19 [III BC]; BGU 1007, 6; LXX; Just., Tat.; Ath. 34, 1) ***revile, abuse*** τινά *someone* (X., An. 7, 5, 11; Theophr., Char. 28, 5; Dt 33:8; Jos., Bell. 2, 302, C. Ap. 2, 148) **J 9:28; Ac 23:4.** τὸν Χριστόν MPol 9:3. Pass. λοιδορούμενοι εὐλογοῦμεν *when we are reviled, we bless* **1 Cor 4:12;** cp. Dg 5:15. Of Christ λοιδορούμενος οὐκ ἀντελοιδόρει *when he was reviled he did not revile in return* **1 Pt 2:23** (cp. the advice Plut., Mor. 88–89).—Schmidt, Syn. I 136–49. DELG. M-M. TW. Spicq.

λοιδορία, ας, ἡ (s. prec. and next entry; Aristoph., Thu.+; PPetr II, 18 [1], 8; PSI 222, 14 μεθ᾽ ὕβρεως κ. λοιδοριῶν; LXX; TestBenj 6:4 λοιδορίαν; Philo; Jos., Ant. 17, 37, C. Ap. 2, 4; Tat. 27, 1; Ath. 11, 2) **speech that is highly insulting, *abuse, reproach, reviling*** ἀποδιδόναι λοιδορίαν ἀντὶ λοιδορίας *return abuse for abuse* **1 Pt 3:9** (=Pol 2:2; cp. Philo, Agr. 110). μηδεμίαν ἀφορμὴν διδόναι τῷ ἀντικειμένῳ λοιδορίας χάριν *give the opponent no occasion* (for criticism) *because of the abuse* (which it might produce); perh. also simply: *for abuse, abusing us* (if the opponent is human; s. ἀντίκειμαι) **1 Ti 5:14.**—DELG s.v. λοιδορέω. M-M. TW. Spicq.

λοίδορος, ου, ὁ (s. two prec. entries; Eur.+; Plut.; IGR I, 307, 3) ***reviler, abusive person*** (so Plut., Mor. 177d; Sir 23:8; TestBenj 5:4) **1 Cor 5:11; 6:10.**—DELG s.v. λοιδορέω. M-M. TW.

λοιμικός, ή, όν (s. λοιμός I; Hippocr. et al.; Lycophron, vs. 1205; IG XII/1, 1032, 7; SIG 731, 7 [I BC]; PMich 149, 5, 8; 10 [II AD]; Philo, Gig. 10) ***pestilential*** λ. καιρός *a time of pestilence* 1 Cl 55:1 (unless metaphor of sedition).

I. λοιμός, οῦ, ὁ ***pestilence*** (Hom.+; SIG 620, 15; 921, 58 λ. ἢ πόλεμος; POxy 1666, 20; 4 Macc 15:32 v.l.; TestJud 23:3; Philo; Jos., Ant. 9, 289f al.) λοιμοί *plagues, diseases* (pl. as Pla., Leg. 4, 709a; Hymn to Isis [I BC] 24 P.) among the signs of the last time (w. λιμός, q.v. 2) **Mt 24:7 v.l.; Lk 21:11.**—DELG. M-M.

II. λοιμός, ή, όν (LXX) comp. λοιμότερος—❶ **pert. to being diseased, *pestilential, diseased,*** of birds of prey ὄρνεα . . . ὄντα λοιμὰ τῇ πονηρίᾳ αὐτῶν B 10:4. For the names of the birds in this pass. s. Lev. 11:13–16. B views them as typical of certain persons.

❷ subst., of humans ***public menace/enemy*** (1 Macc 15:21 of wanted criminals) B 10:10 (Ps 1:1 'pestilent pers.'). οἱ λοιμότεροι *the more troublesome ones* IPol 2:1. εὑρόντες τὸν ἄνδρα τοῦτον λοιμόν *we have found this man to be a public enemy* **Ac 24:5** (the noun λοιμός as designation of a person dangerous to the public weal [cp. Lat. pestis] in Demosth. 25, 80; Aelian, VH 14, 11. The adj. in Libanius, Or. 1, 186 F. τὸν λοιμὸν Γερόντιον. S. Ἐλύμας and OHoltzmann, ZKG 14, 1894, 495–502).—DELG. M-M.

λοιπός, ή, όν (Pind., Hdt.+) gener. 'remaining'.—❶ **pert. to that which remains over, esp. after action has been taken, *left***

ⓐ adj. αἱ λοιπαὶ φωναί *the remaining blasts* **Rv 8:13.**

ⓑ subst. οἱ λοιποί *those who were left* **Rv 11:13.** W. gen. (Iambl., Vi. Pyth. 35, 251) οἱ λ. τῶν ἀνθρώπων **9:20.**

❷ **pert. to being one not previously cited or included, *other, rest of***—ⓐ adj. (LXX; JosAs 2:10; ApcMos 29; Jos., Ant. 5, 129 αἱ λ. φυλαί; Ar. 3:2) οἱ λ. ἀπόστολοι *the other apostles* **Ac 2:37; 1 Cor 9:5;** Pol 9:1. αἱ λ. παρθένοι **Mt 25:11.** τὰ λ. ἔθνη *the rest of the nations* (gentiles) **Ro 1:13; Eph 4:17 v.l.** οἱ λ. Ἰουδαῖοι **Gal 2:13.** αἱ λ. ἐκκλησίαι **2 Cor 12:13;** IMg 15:1. οἱ λ. συνεργοί *the other coworkers* **Phil 4:3.** αἱ λ. γραφαί *the rest of the scriptures* **2 Pt 3:16.** ὡς τὰ λοιπὰ (ἰχθύδια) B 10:5. καὶ τῶν λ. ἀρωμάτων *and* (of) *other spices* 1 Cl 25:2. τὰ δὲ λ. σκῆπτρα αὐτοῦ *the rest of his tribes* 32:2. προφῆται 43:1. τὰ δὲ λ. πάντα ἄστρα *all the other stars* IEph 19:2. τὰς λ. τῆς ζωῆς ἡμέρας *the remaining days of (your) lives* Hv 4, 2, 5; cp. 5:2; m 12, 3, 2; 12, 6, 2; s 6, 3, 6. ἐντολάς m 5, 2, 8; μέρη s 8, 1, 15; 8, 5, 6; λίθοι 9, 7, 2; 4; 9, 8, 2f; 5–7; 9, 9, 4. Cp. 5, 2, 9 τὰ δὲ λ. (ἐδέσματα; opp. τὰ ἀρκοῦντα αὐτῷ). σκεύη Dg 2:4; ἄνθρωποι 5:1; κτίσματα 8:3; δοῦλοι AcPl Ha 4, 10.—Sg. τῆς λ. ὑπάρξεως *and other property* Hs1:5. ἐν . . . τῷ λ. βίῳ *in the rest of (their) style of life* Dg 5:4

ⓑ subst.—α. οἱ λοιποί, αἱ λοιπαί *the others* (LXX, En; TestJob 41:1; Plut., Mor. 285d; Herodian 4, 2, 10; Jos., Bell. 3, 497; Ath. 8:2) **Mt 22:6; 27:49; Mk 16:13; Lk 8:10; 18:9; 24:10; Ac 5:13** (difft. CTorrey, ET 46, '35, 428f); **16:30** D; **17:9; 27:44; Ro 11:7; 1 Cor 7:12; 2 Cor 2:17 v.l.; Eph 2:3; 1 Th 5:6; 1 Ti 5:20; Rv 19:21;** Hv 3, 2, 1; s 9, 22, 4; 9, 23, 2; 9, 26, 8; MPol 15:1. οἱ λ. πάντες *all the others* **2 Cor 13:2; Phil 1:13;** AcPl Ha 5, 8 (SIG 593, 2f καὶ ἐν τοῖς λοιποῖς πᾶσιν φανερὰν πεποιήκαμεν τὴν προαίρεσιν). πάντες οἱ λ. *all the rest* **Lk 24:9.** οἱ λ. ἔχοντες ἀσθενείας *the others who were sick* **Ac 28:9.** οἱ λ. οἱ μὴ ἔχοντες ἐλπίδα *the rest who have no hope* **1 Th 4:13.** οἱ λ. οἱ ἐν Θυατίροις **Rv 2:24.** W. gen. foll. (TestJob 16:5 τὰ λ. τῶν κτηνῶν μου; Lucian, Tox. 28 οἱ λ. τῶν οἰκετῶν) οἱ λ. τῶν ἀνθρώπων *other people* **Lk 18:11** (Just., D. 102, 6). οἱ λ. τῶν νεκρῶν *the rest of the dead* **Rv 20:5.** οἱ λ. τοῦ σπέρματος αὐτῆς *the rest of her offspring* **12:17.**

β. τὰ λοιπά *the other things, the rest* (Appian, Bell. Civ. 5, 67 §284; TestSol 23:4; TestJob 16:5; Jos., Ant. 2, 312; Ar. 1, 1; Just., D. 56, 2) **Lk 12:26; 1 Cor 11:34; 15:37; Rv 3:2** (but s. Mussies 124, of pers.; cp. B-D-F §138, 1); Hs 1:4; 8, 3, 8; 8, 11, 5; 9, 2, 7ab; 9, 5, 5. τῶν λ. τῶν ἀκολουθούντων πάντων *all the rest that follow* 5, 5, 1; αἱ περὶ τὰ λοιπὰ ἐπιθυμίαι *desires for other things* **Mk 4:19.**

❸ adverbial uses (B-D-F §160; 451, 6)—ⓐ of time—α. (τὸ) λοιπόν ***from now on, in the future, henceforth*** (Pind. et al.) **1 Cor 7:29** (but see 3b below); Dg 9:2; ISm 9:1; Hv 3, 13, 2; m 5, 2, 7; s 5, 7, 4; AcPl Ha 6, 6. λοιπὸν ἀπόκειταί μοι *for the future there is reserved for me* **2 Ti 4:8** (but see 3b below). τὸ λοιπὸν ἐκδεχόμενος *then waiting* **Hb 10:13.** καθεύδετε τὸ λοιπόν, which is variously interpreted, conveys a mild rebuke: *you are still sleeping!* or: *do you intend to sleep on and on?*; the expression is prob. colloquial and is succinctly rendered by numerous versions: *Still asleep?* **Mt 26:45; Mk 14:41.** Also poss. for this pass.: *meanwhile, you are sleeping! you are sleeping in the meantime?* (so τὸ λ. Jos., Ant. 18, 272) w. the sense: 'A fine time you've chosen to sleep!'—λοιπόν *finally* (τότε λοιπόν TestJob 16:20 and TestAbr A 13 p. 92, 19 [Stone p. 32]. καὶ λοιπόν 'and then' TestAbr B 7 p. 111, 12 [Stone p. 70]; TestJob 17:5. TestJud 16:2 ἐὰν . . . λοιπὸν γίνεται μέθη. Jos., Ant. 6, 46; Tat. 42, 1) **Ac 27:20;** MPol 9:1. τὰ λοιπά *in the future* Hs 6, 3, 6.

β. τοῦ λοιποῦ ***from now on, in the future*** (Hdt. 2, 109; Aristoph., Pax 1084; X., Cyr. 4, 4, 10, Oec. 10, 9; SIG 611, 17; 849, 12; PHal 1, 171 [III BC]; POxy 1293, 14; GrBar 1:7; 16:10; Jos., Ant. 4, 187.—B-D-F §186, 2; Rob. 295) **Gal 6:17;** Hs 9, 11, 3.—In **Eph 6:10** the mng. is prob. rather *finally,* bringing the matter to a conclusion (s. b, below; a v.l. has τὸ λοιπόν).

ⓑ (τὸ) λοιπόν (Herodas 2, 92; Longus 2, 22, 2) ***as far as the rest is concerned, beyond that, in addition, finally*** λοιπὸν οὐκ οἶδα *beyond that I do not know* **1 Cor 1:16** (POxy 120, 1 [IV AD] λοιπὸν . . . οὐκ οἶδα). σκάψω λοιπὸν τ. ἀμπελῶνα *in addition I will dig the vineyard* Hs 5, 2, 4. As a transition to someth. new (**Phil 3:1**), esp. when it comes near the end of a literary work *finally* (UPZ 78, 43 [159 BC]; POxy 119, 13) **2 Cor 13:11; Phil 4:8; 1 Th 4:1** (λ. οὖν as BGU 1079, 6 [41 AD]); **2 Th 3:1;** 1 Cl 64:1.—ὧδε λοιπόν (Epict. 2, 12, 24) *in this connection, then; furthermore* **1 Cor 4:2.**—Inferentially *therefore* (Epict. 1, 24, 1; 1, 27, 2 al.; POxy 1480, 13 [32 AD]; TestAbr A 7 p. 84, 27 [Stone p. 16]; TestJob 53:4) IEph 11:1; perh. also **1 Cor 7:29; 2 Ti 4:8.**—ACavallin, Eranos 39, '41, 121–44; AFridrichsen, K. Human. Vetenskaps-Samfundet i Upps. Årsbok '43, 24–28.—DELG s.v. λείπω. M-M. Sv.

Λουκᾶς, ᾶ, ὁ (as a Gr-Rom. name CIG III, 4759; III, add. 4700k; 4790; ins in Pisidian Antioch: Ramsay, Bearing 370–84; CIL VI, 17685; Ephem. Epigr. VIII/3 no. 477; Sb 224) ***Luke*** (an affectionate or pet name for Lucius [another ins fr. Pisidian Antioch closely connected w. the one mentioned above—Ramsay, loc. cit.—calls the man Λούκιος who is named Λουκᾶς in the former one]: WSchulze, Graeca Latina 1901, 12; B-D-F §125, 2; Mlt-H. 88 [favors Lucanus]; Dssm., Festgabe für AvHarnack 1921, 117–20=LO 372–77 [LAE[2] 435ff] w. ins; EKlostermann, Hdb. on Lk 1:1 [considers still other possibilities]), companion and co-worker of Paul **Phlm 24; 2 Ti 4:11; 2 Cor subscr.;** cp. the restoration AcPl Ha 11, 16, based on Aa I 116, 17; 117, 5; acc. to **Col 4:14** a physician (cp. Lucian, Pereg. 44 Ἀλέξ. ὁ ἰατρός), and in line w. tradition (Iren. 3, 1, 1 [Harv. II 6, 1]; Murat. Canon 2–8; 34–39) author of the third gospel, **Lk title** κατὰ Λουκᾶν, and **Ac title v.l.** (ApcEsdr 5:22 Πέτρον καὶ Παῦλον καὶ Λουκᾶν καὶ Ματθείαν). The proposition that the language of these books shows that their author was a physician (so Hobart; Harnack [s. below] 122ff; Zahn, Einl.[3] II 433ff et al.) is disputed by GAvdBerghvanEysinga, De geneesher L.: NThT 5, 1916, 228–50; Cadbury, Style, 39ff, JBL 45, 1926, 190–209 et al. The idea, known since Origen, In Rom. Comm. 10, 39, that Luke is to be identified w. the Lucius of Ro 16:21 (Λούκιος 2) was revived by Dssm., loc. cit. Ephraem Syrus identified L. with Lucius of Cyrene (Λούκιος 1) Ac 13:1 (AMerk, D. neuentdeckte Komm. d. hl. E. zur AG: ZKT 48, 1924, 54).—Harnack, Lukas d. Arzt 1906; Ramsay, Luke the Physician 1908; AvanVeldhuizen, Lukas de medicijnmeester 1926; HCadbury, The Making of Luke-Acts 1927; EMeyer I 1ff; 46ff; 100ff; 304ff. WReilly, CBQ 1, '39, 314–24.—TRE III 483–528. ABD IV 401f (lit.). LGPN I. M-M.

Λούκιος, ου, ὁ (Diod. S. 11, 81, 1; 12, 43, 1; 14, 38, 1; SIG 1173, 7; Sb II 258f; PFay 110, 1 [94 AD]; PWarr 1, 1; PVindob-Bosw 2, 11; Jos., Bell. 6, 188; Just., A I, 1, 1 [Verus, adopted son of Antonius]; A II 2, 15 Λούκιός τις al.; Ath. ins [Commodus]; B-D-F §41, 1; Mlt-H. 88) ***Lucius.***

❶ of Cyrene, a teacher or prophet at Antioch **Ac 13:1.**—HCadbury, Beginn. I 5, '33, 489–95.

❷ an otherw. unknown Christian, sender of a greeting **Ro 16:21.**—On both s. Λουκάς.—M-M.

λουτρόν, οῦ, τό (λούω; since Hom. [λοετρόν], contracted since Hes.; ins, pap; SSol 4:2; 6:6; Sir 34:25; Jos., Ant. 8, 356; Just.; Mel.) ***bath, washing*** of baptism (for the ceremonial usage cp. Ael. Aristid. 48, 71 K.=24 p. 483 D.: λουτρὰ θεῖα; Arrian, Tact. 33, 4; Philostrat. Junior [III AD] at the end of his Εἰκόνες [APF 14, '41] ln. 77, p. 8; 19 λουτρὰ σεμνά; mystery ins fr. Andania: SIG 736, 106 [92 BC]; Philo, Cher. 95 al.; s. also λούω 2; Hippol., Ref. 5, 27, 2) τὸ λ. τοῦ ὕδατος *the washing in water* **Eph 5:26** (Jos., C. Ap. 1, 282 ὑδάτων λουτροῖς; Just., A I, 61, 3 τὸ ἐν τῷ ὕδατι . . . λουτρόν). λ. παλιγγενεσίας *the bath that brings about regeneration* **Tit 3:5** (cp. Philo, Mut. Nom. 124 τοῖς φρονήσεως λουτροῖς χρησαμένη [ἡ ψυχή]; Just., A I, 66, 1 τὸ . . . εἰς ἀναγέννησιν λουτρόν).—DELG s.v. λούω. M-M. TW. Spicq.

λούω (s. prec. entry; Hom.+) fut. λούσω LXX; 1 aor. ἔλουσα. Pass. 1 aor. 2 sg. ἐλούσθης Ezk 16:4; pf. ptc. λελουμένος **J 13:10** and λελουσμένος **Hb 10:22** (B-D-F §70, 3; W-S. §13, 1; Mlt-H. 248; Helbing 100f)

❶ **to use water to cleanse a body of physical impurity, *wash,*** as a rule of the whole body, ***bathe***—ⓐ act., abs. of the washing of a corpse (Hom. et al.) **Ac 9:37;** GPt 6:24. Of persons who have been scourged ἔλουσεν ἀπὸ τῶν πληγῶν *he washed their wounds* (lit., 'by washing he freed them from the effects of the blows') **Ac 16:33** (on the constr. w. ἀπό s. 3 below. Also Antig. Car. 163 of Europa: λούσασθαι ἀπὸ τῆς τοῦ Διὸς μίξεως=wash off the traces of intercourse with Zeus). For **Rv 1:5 v.l.** s. 3.

ⓑ mid. *I wash myself, I bathe myself* (Hom. et al.) lit., of man or beast: of a woman λουομένη εἰς τὸν ποταμόν *bathing in the river* Hv 1, 1, 2 (λ. εἰς also Ptolem. Euerg. II [II BC]: 234 fgm. 3 Jac.; Alciphron 3, 7, 1 λουσάμενοι εἰς τὸ βαλανεῖον; Cyranides p. 57, 6; Iren. 3, 3, 4 [Harv. II 13, 11 and 12]). ὗς λουσαμένη **2 Pt 2:22** (s. βόρβορος 2).

❷ **to use water in a cultic manner for purification, *wash oneself, bathe oneself, cleanse, bathe,*** mid., of cultic washings

ⓐ (Soph., Ant. 1201 τὸν μὲν λούσαντες ἁγνὸν λουτρόν; Apollon. Rhod. 3, 1203 λοέσσατο ποταμοῖο . . . θείοιο . . . before the sacrifice Jason washed himself clean of pollution, in the divine river; Plut., Mor. 264d λούσασθαι πρὸ τῆς θυσίας; Ael. Aristid. 33, 32 K.=51 p. 582 D.: πρὸς θεῶν λούσασθαι κέρδος ἐστὶ ζῶντα, ὃ καὶ τελευτήσαντι μένει; Dssm., NB 54 [BS 226f] cites for this usage three ins, all of which have the mid., two in combination w. ἀπό τινος; Sb 4127, 14 ἐν ᾧ καὶ ἁγίῳ τῷ τῆς ἀθανασίας ὕδατι λουσάμενος; Ramsay, Exp. 7th ser., 8, 1909, p. 280, 1; LXX; Jos., Vi. 11 λ. πρὸς ἁγνείαν) of the act of purification necessary before entering the temple Ox 840, 14; 19; 24f (ἐν τῇ λίμνῃ τοῦ Δαυίδ); 32 (ὕδασιν). ὁ λελουμένος *the one who has bathed* (in contrast to the one who has his feet washed, and with allusion to the cleansing of the whole body in baptism [λελουμένος 'newly bathed, after the bath' Hdt. 1, 126; Aristoph., Lysist. 1064; Plut., Mor. 958b λουσαμένοις ἢ νιψαμένοις; Lev 15:11 τ. χεῖρας νίπτεσθαι, λούεσθαι τὸ σῶμα]; difft. HWindisch, Johannes u. d. Synoptiker 1926, 77. On foot-washing s. also GKnight, Feetwashing: Enc. of Rel. and Ethics V 814–23; PFiebig, Αγγελος III 1930, 121–28; BBacon, ET 43, '32, 218–21; HvCampenhausen, ZNW 33, '34, 259–71; FBraun, RB 44, '35, 22–33; ELohmeyer, ZNW 38, '39, 74–94; AFridrichsen, ibid. 94–96; Bultmann, comm. J ad loc., 355–65; JDunn, ZNW 61, '70, 247–52) **J 13:10** (λού. beside νίπτ. in eating Tob 7:9 S; λού. before eating AcThom 89=Aa p. 204 l. 7f). λούσασθε *wash yourselves* 1 Cl 8:4 (Is 1:16). Always of baptism (Hippol., Ref. 5, 7, 19) AcPl Ha 2, 35; 3, 6; 5, 1f; 7, 20.—The sense is in doubt in εἴ τις μεταλάβῃ τὸ σῶμα τοῦ κυρίου καὶ λούσεται *if anyone receives the body of the Lord* (in the Eucharist) *and then mouth-rinses* or *bathes* Agr 19.

ⓑ *I wash for myself* w. obj. in acc. (Hes.+) τὸ σῶμα ὕδατι καθαρῷ (cp. Dt 23:12) **Hb 10:22** (of baptism).

❸ **to cause to be purified, *cleanse,*** act. (in imagery, via liquid other than water) τῷ λούσαντι ἡμᾶς ἀπὸ τῶν ἁμαρτιῶν ἡμῶν ἐν τῷ αἵματι αὐτοῦ **Rv 1:5 v.l.** (For the use of an agent other than water in connection with λ., but in a difft. sense, s. Simonid. 144 a bow bathed in blood [Diehl[2] II p. 113=Bergk

143]; Lucian, Dial. Meretr. 13, 3 pers. bathed in blood.) On this rdg. s. PvonderOsten-Sacken, ZNW 58, '67, 258 n. 17.—B. 579. DELG. M-M. TW.

Λύδδα (לוֹד.—1 Macc 11:34; Joseph. index), gen. Λύδδας **Ac 9:38** (s. Thackeray 161), where Λύδδης is also attested. The acc. Λύδδα (Jos., Bell. 2, 242; 515 beside Λύδδαν Ant. 20, 130) vss. **32, 35** (both v.l. -αν) functions as an indecl. form or a neut. pl. (Jos., Bell. 1, 302 ἐν Λύδδοις; 2, 244; 4, 444; s. B-D-F §56, 2), **ἡ,** ***Lydda,*** a city about 17 km. southeast of Joppa on the road to Jerusalem. **Ac 9:32, 35, 38.** Schürer index, esp. II 193, 34; BHHW II 1101; Kl. Pauly III 797.—M-M.

Λυδία, ας, ἡ (as a woman's name Horace, Odes 1, 8, 1; 1, 13, 1; 1, 25, 8; 3, 9, 6f; Martial, Epigr. 11, 21. In Gk. preserved in the form Λύδη: CIG 653; 6975; CIA III, 3261f) ***Lydia,*** a merchant fr. Thyatira in Lydia, who dealt in purple cloth; she was converted by Paul in Philippi, after having been σεβομένη τ. θεόν (s. σέβω 1b) **Ac 16:14, 40** (on her social status s. New Docs 2, 27f). BHHW II 1115; CHemer in New Docs 3, 53–55; LSchottroff, Let the Oppressed Go Free, tr. AKidder '93 ['91], 131–37.—M-M.

Λυκαονία, ας, ἡ (X. et al.; ins) ***Lycaonia,*** a province in the interior of Asia Minor, bounded by Cappadocia, Galatia (s. Γαλατία), Phrygia, Pisidia and Cilicia. Its main cities were those visited by Paul: Lystra, Iconium, and Derbe. **Ac 14:6.**—Ramsay, Histor. Comm. on Gal 1899, 19ff.; Pauly-W. XIII 2253ff; Kl. Pauly III 807f; BHHW II 1115f; Haenchen ad loc.

Λυκαονιστί adv. ***in (the) Lycaonian (language),*** a dialect spoken in Lycaonia, no longer known **Ac 14:11.**—PKretschmer, Einleitung in die Geschichte der griech. Sprache 1896, 396; KHoll, Her. 43, 1908, 240ff.; Haenchen ad loc.—M-M.

Λυκία, ας, ἡ (Hdt. et al.; ins; 1 Macc 15:23; SibOr) ***Lycia,*** a projection on the south coast of Asia Minor between Caria and Pamphylia **Ac 27:5.**—IAsMinLyk; EKalinka, Zur histor. Topographie Lykiens: HKiepert Festschr., 1898, 161f; Kl. Pauly III 809f; BHHW II 1118.

λύκος, ου, ὁ (Hom. et al.; ins, pap, LXX, Test12Patr; JosAs 12:10; SibOr 8, 41; 13, 28; Philo; Just., A I, 58, 2; loanw. in rabb., but s. KRengstorf, ELittmann Festschr., '35, 55–62)

❶ ***wolf,*** lit., as a symbol **Mt 10:16; Lk 10:3; J 10:12ab;** D 16:3 (in all these pass. in contrast to sheep; cp. Dio Chrys. 64 [14], 2; Philostrat., Vi. Apoll. 8, 22; Philo, Praem. 86; Just., A I, 58, 2; Iren. 1, Prologue 2 [Harv. I 4, 3]; Did., Gen. 86, 18).

❷ a fierce or vicious pers., *wolf* metaph., ext. of mng. 1 (in imagery as early as Il. 4, 471; 16, 156; Epict. 1, 3, 7 al.; cp. Zeph 3:3; Jer 5:6; Ez 22:27; Rhodon [in Eus., HE 5, 13, 4] refers to Marcion as ὁ Ποντικὸς λύκος), of evil people IPhld 2:2; 2 Cl 5:2–4 (fr. a noncanonical gospel). λ. ἅρπαγες *ravenous wolves* **Mt 7:15.** λ. βαρεῖς *fierce wolves* **Ac 20:29.**—B. 185. DELG. M-M. TW. Spicq.

λυμαίνω 1 aor. inf. λυμᾶναι; impf. mid. ἐλυμαινόμην; fut. 3 sg. λυμανεῖται LXX; quite predom., in earlier times exclusively, used as a mid. dep. (cp. λῦμα 'filth left from washing'; Aeschyl., Hdt.+; ins, pap, LXX; En 19:1; EpArist 164; Philo; Jos., Bell. 2, 271; 4, 534 al.; Ath., R. 1 p. 49, 8 [w. dat.]) ***to cause harm to, injure, damage, spoil, ruin, destroy*** (so Thu. et al.) τὶ *someth.* Σαῦλος ἐλυμαίνετο τὴν ἐκκλησίαν *Saul was making it hard for the (Christian) community* **Ac 8:3.** Of gluttons who, by their intemperance, damage τὴν σάρκα αὐτῶν their bodies Hv 3, 9, 3a (Epict. 3, 22, 87 τὸ σῶμα λυμαίνεται=he injures his body).—Also used as a passive (UPZ 187, 20 [127/126 BC]; M-M s.v. λυμαίνομαι) λυμαίνεται ἡ σὰρξ αὐτῶν *their bodies become injured* Hv 3, 9, 3b (cp. Jos., Ant. 12, 256 λ. τὰ σώματα).—The act. λυμαίνω appears quite late (Libanius, Decl. 13, 6 vol. VI p. 10, 13 F.; PGM 13, 302 πῦρ, οὐ μή μου λυμάνῃς σάρκα; Herm. Wr. 10, 20; TestAbr A). It has the same mng. πόλιν λυμᾶναι *destroy a city* Hv 4, 1, 8. τινά *hurt someone* 4, 2, 4.—B. 760. DELG s.v. λῦμα. TW.

λυπέω 1 aor. ἐλύπησα; pf. λελύπηκα. Pass.: 1 fut. λυπηθήσομαι; 1 aor. ἐλυπήθην; pf. λελύπημαι (fr. λύπη 'pain, grief'; Hes.+) gener. 'grieve, pain'.

❶ to cause severe mental or emotional distress, *vex, irritate, offend, insult,* act. τινά *someone* (Test Abr A 8 p. 86, 9 [Stone p. 20]; Dio Chrys. 28 [45], 3; BGU 531 II, 18 [I AD], freq. in the sense *vex, irritate, offend* TestSol 2:3 D; Herodas 5, 7, 3; Ar. 15:7) **2 Cor 2:2a; 7:8ab.** The object of λυπεῖν can also be a deity (Diod. S. 1, 65, 7; 8 τὸν θεόν; schol. on Apollon. Rhod. 2, 313 λ. τὸν Δία; cp. τοὺς ἀγγέλους μου ApcSed 14:10) μὴ λυπεῖτε τὸ πνεῦμα τὸ ἅγιον τοῦ θεοῦ **Eph 4:30;** Hm 10, 2, 2; 10, 3, 2ab; cp. 10, 2, 4. χάριν Dg 11:7. In εἴ τις λελύπηκεν **2 Cor 2:5** λ. used abs. is certainly more than *cause pain* or *vexation.* In Polyaenus 8, 47 it is used of the severe *humiliation* or *outrage* experienced by a king who has been deposed by his subjects.

❷ to experience sadness or distress, pass.—ⓐ aor. λυπηθῆναι ***become sad, sorrowful, distressed*** (BGU 1079, 9 [41 AD]; Esth 2:21; Ps 54:3; 2 Esdr 15:6; TestJob, Test12Patr, GrBar; Jos., Ant. 8, 356) **Mt 14:9;** AcPl Ha 7, 17; **J 16:20; 2 Cor 2:4; 7:9a; 1 Pt 1:6;** Dg 1. W. σφόδρα (Da 6:15 LXX; 1 Macc 10:68; JosAs 8:8 al.) **Mt 17:23; 18:31;** GJs 1:3; 2:4; AcPl Ha 7, 15; w. λίαν 1 Cl 4:3 (Gen 4:5 Cain took offense). W. ὅτι foll. *become distressed because* (cp. En 102:5) **J 21:17.** λυπηθῆναι εἰς μετάνοιαν *become sorry enough to repent* **2 Cor 7:9b.** λ. κατὰ θεόν *as God would have it* vss. **9c, 11.**

ⓑ pres. λυπεῖσθαι ***be sad, be distressed, grieve*** (La 1:22) **1 Th 4:13.** λυπῇ; *are you grieved* or *hurt?* Hv 3, 1, 9b. λυπούμενος (being) *sad, sorrowful* **Mt 19:22; 26:22; Mk 10:22;** Hv 1, 2, 2; 3, 13, 2 (TestAbr A 7 p. 84, 9 [Stone p. 16]; Jos., Vi. 208). (Opp. χαίρων as Dio Chrys. 50 [67], 5; Philo, Virt. 103) **2 Cor 6:10.** λυπουμένου (μου) ὅτι *because* Hv 3, 1, 9a. ἤμην λυπούμενος 1, 2, 1. ὁ λυπούμενος *the mournful man* (Ael. Aristid. 46 p. 404 D.) m 10, 3, 3. ὁ λ. ἐξ ἐμοῦ **2 Cor 2:2b** gives the source of the pain or sadness. ἤρξατο λυπεῖσθαι *he began to be sorrowful* **Mt 26:37;** cp. **Mk 14:19.** λ. διά τι *because of someth.* (schol. on Apollon. Rhod. 4, 1090; JosAs 24:19 δι' Ἀσενέθ; ParJer 4:11 διὰ σέ): εἰ διὰ βρῶμα ὁ ἀδελφὸς λυπεῖται *if a member's feelings are hurt because of food* **Ro 14:15** (but λ. can also mean *injure, damage:* X., Mem. 1, 6, 6, Cyr. 6, 3, 13). μὴ λυπείσθω ὁ εὐσεβὴς ἐάν *the godly man is not to grieve if* 2 Cl 19:4. λ. ἐπί τινι *at someth.* (X., Mem. 3, 9, 8; Lucian, Dial. Mort. 13, 5, Tox. 24; Artem. 2, 60; PGrenf II, 36, 9 [95 BC]; Jon 4:9; ApcMos 39 p. 21, 1 Tdf.; Philo, Abr. 22; Just., D. 107, 3) Hm 10, 2, 3; cp. s 6, 3, 1. ἐλυπεῖτο περὶ τῆς γυναικὸς οὐ μικρῶς *(Hieronymus) was quite upset with his wife,* who had displayed interest in Paul's message AcPl Ha 4, 16f (w. περί as Da 6:18 LXX; ApcMos 18 p. 9, 13 Tdf.).—Impf. ἐλυπούμην *I was sad* GPt 7:26; cp. 14:59 (TestSol 2:2 D; TestSim 4:3; ParJer 7:30); w. σφόδρα (JosAs 24:1) GJs 1:4 (aor. v.l.).—DELG s.v. λύπη. M-M. TW. Spicq.

λύπη, ης, ἡ (s. λυπέω; Aeschyl., Hdt.+) **pain of mind or spirit, *grief, sorrow, affliction*** **J 16:6;** Hm 10, 1, 2; 10, 2, 1–6; 10, 3, 1; 3f; AcPl Ha 6, 16. περισσοτέρα λ. *excessive sorrow* **2 Cor 2:7.** Opp. χαρά (X., Hell. 7, 1, 32; Eth. Epic. col. 3, 16;

Philo, Abr. 151, Leg. ad Gai. 15; JosAs 9:1; ApcMos 39) **J 16:20; Hb 12:11.** λύπην ἔχειν *have pain, be sorrowful* (Dio Chrys. 46 [63], 1; ApcMos 3) in childbirth **J 16:21;** cp. vs. **22.** λ. ἔχειν ἀπό τινος *be pained by someone* **2 Cor 2:3.** λύπην ἐπὶ λύπην ἔχειν *sorrow upon sorrow* **Phil 2:27;** opp. πολυτέλεια λύπην μὴ ἔχουσα *wealth without pain* Hs 1:10. λ. μοί ἐστιν μεγάλη *I am greatly pained* **Ro 9:2** (cp. Tobit 3:6; TestJud 23:1 πολλὴ λύπη μοί ἐστι.—λ. μεγάλη as Jon 4:1; TestJob 34:5; ApcMos 9). βαλεῖν τινα εἰς λύπην *plunge someone into grief* 1 Cl 46:9. τὸ μὴ πάλιν ἐν λ. πρὸς ὑμᾶς ἐλθεῖν *not to come to you again in sorrow* **2 Cor 2:1.** τί . . . σεαυτῷ λύπην ἐπισπᾶσαι *why are you bringing sorrow on yourself* Hs 9, 2, 6. ἀποβαλεῖν πᾶσαν λ. *lay aside all sorrow* Hv 4, 3, 4; ἀποθέμενον τὸ τῆς λ. AcPl BMM recto 7 (for this AcPl Ha 8, 8: το]|[κατηφ]ὲς ἀποθέμενον, as restored by Schmidt, but on this s. κατηφής). Also αἴρειν ἀφ' ἑαυτοῦ τὴν λ. Hm 10, 1, 1 (opp. ἱλαρότης 10, 3, 1). ἐξέπτη ἡ λ. αὐτοῦ *his anxiety* (over the combat with beasts) *took wings* AcPl Ha 3, 17. συγκόπτεσθαι ἀπὸ τῆς λύπης *be crushed with sorrow* Hv 5:4. ἀπὸ τῆς λ. *from sorrow* **Lk 22:45** (TestJos 8:5 συνείχετο ἀπὸ τῆς λύπης; ParJer 7:26 ἵνα μὴ διαφθαρῇ ἀπὸ τῆς λ.; cp. UPZ 18, 13 [163 BC] ἀποθνήσκει ὑπὸ τῆς λ.; Jos., Ant. 6, 337). ἐκ λύπης *reluctantly* **2 Cor 9:7** (cp. Soph., O.C. 1636f of Theseus's generous acceptance, οὐκ οἴκτου μέτα, of Oedipus's last mandate; cp. 1 Pt 4:9; on the grammar cp. ἐκ τῆς λύπης Aesop, Fab. 275 P.; JosAs 29:9). διὰ τὴν λ. *in sorrow* AcPl Ha 5, 24. ἡ κατὰ θεὸν λ. *sorrow that God approves* **2 Cor 7:10a** (leading to μετάνοια as Plut., Mor. 961d). In contrast to this ἡ τοῦ κόσμου λύπη *the sorrow of the world* vs. **10b.** λύπην ἐπάγειν τῷ πνεύματι *bring grief to the spirit* Hm 3:4. λύπη personified Hs 9, 15, 3.—Pl. (Demosth., Ep. 2, 25; Dio Chrys. 80 [30], 14; Gen 3:16f; 5:29; Pr 15:13; 31:6; PsSol 4:15; ParJer 7:36 διὰ τὰς λ.) αἱ πρότεραι λῦπαι *the former sorrows* Hv 3, 13, 2. ὑποφέρειν λύπας **1 Pt 2:19.** παλαιοῦσθαι ταῖς λύπαις *be aged by sorrows* Hv 3, 11, 3.—B. 1118. BHHW III 2021ff. Schmidt, Syn. II 574–95; DELG. M-M. EDNT. TW. Spicq. Sv.

λυπηρός, ά, όν (s. λύπη; trag., Hdt. et al.; pap, LXX, Philo; Jos., Ant. 15, 61)

➊ ***painful, distressing,*** act. τινί *to someone* (PPetr II, 13 [19], 13 [III BC] οὐθέν σοι μὴ γενηθῇ λυπηρόν; Gen 34:7; Jos., Ant. 17, 175; Tat. 14, 2) ἀμφότερα λυπηρά ἐστι τῷ πνεύματι Hm 10, 2, 4.

➋ ***sad, mournful, downcast,*** pass. ἀνήρ (Pr 17:22) opp. ἱλαρός 10, 3, 2.—DELG s.v. λύπη. Spicq.

Λυσανίας, ου, ὁ (on the gen. s. Mlt-H. 119) ***Lysanias,*** tetrarch of Abilene **Lk 3:1.** There was a Lysanias, son of the dynast Ptolemaeus of Chalcis, who ruled 40–36 BC and was executed by Mark Antony. If Luke had meant this Lysanias (so HHoltzmann and Wlh. ad loc. and E Schwartz, NGG 1906, 370f), he would have committed a grave chronological error. But there was a younger Lysanias in the period 25–30 AD, to whom Josephus' expressions Ἄβιλαν τὴν Λυσανίου (Ant. 19, 275) and Ἀβέλλα (=Ἄβιλα) as Λυσανία τετραρχία (20, 138) are best referred, and to whom the ins CIG 4521=OGI 606 and IGR III, 1086; CIG 4523 refer.—Schürer I 568–70; EKlostermann and Zahn ad loc.; RSavignac, Texte complet de l'inscription d'Abila relative à Lysanias: RB n.s. 9, 1912, 533–40; Ramsay, Bearing 297–300; EMeyer I 47ff; Boffo, Iscrizioni 171–76 (sources and lit. p. 171); Hemer, Acts 159f; Schürer I 567–69; DACL X '31, 405–11; Kl. Pauly III 831.—M-M.

Λυσίας, ου, ὁ (lit., ins, pap, LXX, Joseph.) ***(Claudius) Lysias*** (s. Κλαύδιος 2) **Ac 23:26; 24:7, 22;** Haenchen ad loc.

λύσις, εως, ἡ (s. λύω; Hom.+; Diod. S. 18, 25, 2 [λύσις τῶν κακῶν=resolution, removal of difficulties]; ins, pap, LXX; En 5:6; TestSim 3:4; Philo; Jos., Ant. 9, 70; Mel., P. 55, 405; Ath. 16, 4) ***release, separation,*** (in marriage) *a divorce* **1 Cor 7:27.**—DELG s.v. λύω. M-M. Sv.

λυσιτελέω (λυσιτελής adj. [s. λύω, τέλος 5]='paying for expenses incurred' [on the commercial aspect s. Schmidt, Syn. IV 162f], hence 'useful, profitable'; Hdt., Aristoph. et al.; LXX; Jos., Ant. 15, 110 al.) ***be advantageous, be better*** impers. λυσιτελεῖ (fut. λυσιτελήσει LXX) *it is better, it profits* (Pla. [Crat. 417 b] et al.) w. dat. (Dio Chrys. 48 [65], 3; SIG 344, 96 [c. 303 BC]; PHamb 27, 17 [250 BC]; Tob 3:6; Philo, Det. Pot. Ins. 68) λυσιτελεῖ αὐτῷ εἰ περίκειται . . . ἢ ἵνα *it would be better for that person if . . . , than that* **Lk 17:2** (Andoc. 1, 125 τεθνάναι λυσιτελεῖ ἢ ζῆν).—M-M.

λυσσάω (Soph. et al.; SibOr 5, 96) ***be raving, be mad*** of dogs (Aristoph. et al.) κύνες λυσσῶντες *mad dogs* (fig. as Jos., Bell. 6, 196) IEph 7:1.—DELG s.v. λύσσα.

Λύστρα (Ptolem. 5, 4, 12; OGI 536; cp. Pliny, Nat. Hist. 5, 147; CIL III Suppl. 6786; 6974) acc. Λύστραν (but in **Ac 27:5** cod. A reads Λύστρα); dat. Λύστροις (on its declension s. B-D-F §57; Mlt. 48; Mlt-H. 147; Thackeray 167f) **ἡ** or **τά** ***Lystra,*** a city in Lycaonia in Asia Minor, where a church was founded by Paul. **Ac 14:6, 8, 21; 16:1f; 27:5 v.l.; 2 Ti 3:11;** AcPl Ant 13, 21 (ἐπὶ Λύστραν Aa I 237, 4).—ABludau, Pls in L., Ac 14:7–21: Der Katholik 87, 1907, 91–113; 161–83; WCalder, Zeus and Hermes at Lystra: Exp. 7th ser., 10, 1910, 1–6, also The 'Priest' of Zeus at Lystra: ibid. 148–55; AWikenhauser, D. AG 1921, 362f; LCurtius, Zeus u. Hermes '31; ACook, Zeus III/2, '40, 1071; MMeunier, Apoll. de Ty. ou le séjour d'un dieu parmi les hommes '36; SEitrem, ConNeot 3, '39, 9–12; Pauly-W. XIV 71f; Kl. Pauly III 846; Haenchen ad loc.; BAFCS II 81–85.— M-M.

λύτρον, ου, τό (s. λύω and next entry; Pind., Hdt. et al.; ins, pap, LXX, Philo, Joseph.; Mel., P. 91, 684; 103, 792) ***price of release, ransom*** (esp. also the ransom money for the manumission of slaves, mostly in pl.: Diod. S. 19, 85, 3; Polyaenus 4, 10, 1; POxy 48, 6 [86 AD]; 49, 8; 722, 30; 40; Mitt-Wilck. II/2, 362, 19; Jos., Ant. 12, 46, but also in sing.: Diod. S. 20, 84, 6 δοῦναι λύτρον; ins in KBuresch, Aus Lydien 1898 p. 197 [on this ins. and Dssm's ref. to it, s. New Docs 2, 90]; Jos., Ant. 14, 371.—LMitteis, Reichsrecht und Volksrecht 1891, 388; FSteinleitner, Die Beicht 1913, 36ff; 59; 111) give up one's life λ. ἀντὶ πολλῶν *as a ransom for many* (s. πολύς 1aβℵ) **Mt 20:28; Mk 10:45** (BBlake, ET 45, '34, 142; WHoward, ET 50, '38, 107–10; JJeremias, Judaica 3, '48, 249–64; ELohse, Märtyrer u. Gottesknecht, '55, 116–22; CBarrett, NT Essays: TManson mem. vol. '59, 1–18 [refers to 2 Macc 7:37].—Cp. Diod. S. 12, 57, 2; Dio Chrys. 64 [14], 11 λύτρα διδόναι; Jos., Ant. 14, 107 λ. ἀντὶ πάντων; Philo Bybl. [I/II AD]: 790 fgm. 3b p. 814, 9 Jac. [in Eus., PE 1, 16, 44] ἀντὶ τῆς πάντων φθορᾶς . . . λ.). God gave his Son λ. ὑπὲρ ἡμῶν *as a ransom for us* Dg 9:2 (Mel., P. 103, 792 ἐγὼ τὸ λύτρον ὑμῶν [λουτρόν Bodmer]; Lucian, Dial. Deor. 4, 2 κριὸν λύτρον ὑπὲρ ἐμοῦ; schol. on Nicander, Alexiph. 560 λύτρα ὑπὲρ τῶν βοῶν; Philo, Spec. Leg. 2, 122; Jos., Ant. 14, 371 λ. ὑπὲρ αὐτοῦ). ἐπὶ σοὶ φανερώσει κύριος τὸ λ. τοῖς υἱοῖς Ἰσραήλ *because of you the Lord will reveal the (promised) salvation to the people of Israel* GJs 7:2. λ. τῶν ἁμαρτιῶν*a ransom for sins* B 19:10 v.l.—S. lit. on ἀπολύτρωσις, 2 end; also NLevinson, SJT 12, '59, 277–78; DHill, Gk. Words and Heb. Mngs. '67, 49–81, with correction of perspective in light of new discoveries New Docs 3, 72–75. S. SEG XXXIX, '89, 1863 for list of ins.—DELG s.v. λύω. M-M. EDNT. TW. Spicq (in citation of SB III, 6293, 10 ὑπὲρ λυτρῶν is restored). Sv.

λυτρόω (s. prec. entry; Pla.+) in our lit. only mid. (and pass.) **λυτρόομαι** (Demosth.+) fut. mid. λυτρώσομαι LXX; 1 aor. mid. ἐλυτρωσάμην, impv. λύτρωσαι. Pass.: 1fut. λυτρωθήσομαι (LXX); 1 aor. ἐλυτρώθην; pf. 3 sg. λελύτρωται, ptc. λελυτρωμένος LXX.—DELG s.v. λύω.

❶ **to free by paying a ransom,** ***redeem***—ⓐ lit. (Demosth. 19, 170) of prisoners (Diod. S. 5, 17, 3; Jos., Ant. 14, 371) 1 Cl 55:2.

ⓑ fig. λύτρωσαι τ. δεσμίους ἡμῶν (in a prayer) 1 Cl 59:4.—Pass. ἀργυρίῳ ἢ χρυσίῳ λυτρωθῆναι ἐκ τῆς ματαίας ὑμῶν ἀναστροφῆς *be ransomed with silver or gold from your futile way of life* **1 Pt 1:18** (on λ. ἔκ τινος s. 2 below.—WvanUnnik, De verlossing 1 Pt 1:18, 19 en het problem van den 1 Pt '42).

❷ **to liberate from an oppressive situation,** ***set free, rescue, redeem,*** fig. ext. of mng. 1 (Ps.-Callisth. 2, 7, 4 τὴν Ἑλλάδα λυτρώσασθαι; 3, 19, 10; LXX; Philo) τινά *someone* (Iren. 5, 1, 1 [Harv. II 315, 1]) B 14:8. Of Christ in his coming again λυτρώσεται ἡμᾶς *he will redeem us* 2 Cl 17:4. Of the Messiah ὁ μέλλων λυτροῦσθαι τὸν Ἰσραήλ **Lk 24:21** (cp. Is 44:22–4; 1 Macc 4:11; PsSol 8:30; 9:1). τινὰ ἀπό τινος *someone fr. someth.* (Ps 118:134; cp. the ancient Christian prayer: CSchmidt, Heinrici Festschr. 1914, p. 69, 32f) λ. ἡμᾶς ἀπὸ πάσης ἀνομίας **Tit 2:14** (TestJos 18:2 ἀπὸ παντὸς κακοῦ). Also τινὰ ἔκ τινος (non-bibl. ins in Ramsay, CB I/2 566f ἐλυτρώσατο πολλοὺς ἐκ κακῶν βασάνων; Dt 13:6; Ps 106:2; Sir 51:2; Mel., P. 67, 475 ἐκ τῆς τοῦ κόσμου λατρείας) someone fr. a monster Hv 4, 1, 7. ἐξ ἀναγκῶν m 8:10. ἐκ τοῦ σκότους B 14:5f; cp. vs. 7. ἐκ θανάτου (Hos 13:14) 19:2. τ. ψυχὴν ἐκ θανάτου **Ac 28:19 v.l.** ἐκ τοσούτων κακῶν AcPl Ha 3, 10.—Pass. (Aristot., EN 10, 2 [1164b, 34]; LXX; TestJos 18:2; Just., D. 131, 3; Iren. 1, 21, 4 [Harv. I 186, 12]) *be redeemed* ἐν τῇ χάριτι *by grace* IPhld 11:1 (on λ. ἐν cp. 2 Esdr 11:10 ἐν τ. δυνάμει; Ps 76:16; Sir 48:20). γινώσκομεν οὖν πόθεν ἐλυτρώθημεν *we know, then, the source of our redemption* B 14:7.—New Docs 3, 72–75. DELG s.v. λύω. M-M. TW. Spicq. Sv.

λύτρωσις, εως, ἡ (s. λυτρόω; as legal and commercial t.t. in pap)

❶ **experience of being liberated from an oppressive situation,** transf. sense of commercial usage 'redemption of someth. for a price': ***ransoming, releasing, redemption*** (Plut., Arat. 11, 2 λ. αἰχμαλώτων; Palaeph. exc. Vat. p. 99, 10; LXX; TestJos 8:1) ποιεῖν λύτρωσιν τῷ λαῷ *bring about a deliverance for the people* **Lk 1:68** (cp. TestLevi 2:10 Armenian vers.: s. Charles). προσδέχεσθαι λύτρωσιν Ἰερουσαλήμ *wait for the redemption of Jerusalem* **2:38;** αἰωνία λ. **Hb 9:12.** διὰ τοῦ αἵματος τοῦ κυρίου λ. ἔσται πᾶσιν τοῖς πιστεύουσιν *redemption will come* 1 Cl 12:7.

❷ abstr. for concr. *ransom(-money)* δώσεις λ. ἁμαρτιῶν σου *you must give a ransom for your* sins D 4:6; cp. B 19:10.—M-M. TW. Spicq.

λυτρωτής, οῦ, ὁ (s. λυτρόω) *redeemer* (not in non-bibl. wr.; of Horus: Iren. 1, 2, 4 [Harv. I 18,4]; LXX of God: Ps 18:15; 77:35; AcThom 60 [Aa II/2 p. 177, 11]) of Moses **Ac 7:35.**—M-M. TW.

λυχνία, ας, ἡ (Hero Alex. I p. 264, 20; Plut., Dio 961 [9, 2]; Ps.-Lucian, Asin. 40; Artem. 1, 74; ins; pap since PEleph 5, 7 [284/283 BC]; LXX, TestAbr; TestJob 32:9; Philo; Joseph. [s. λύχνος, beg.]; Just., A I, 26, 7 λυχνίας … ἀνατροπήν; s. Phryn. p. 313f Lob.) ***lampstand*** upon which lamps were placed or hung (s. λύχνος, beg.); not a candlestick. τιθέναι ἐπὶ τὴν λ. (ἐπὶ λυχνίας) *put on the (lamp)stand* (TestAbr B 5 p. 109, 19 [Stone p. 66]) **Mt 5:15; Mk 4:21; Lk 8:16; 11:33.** Of the seven-branched lampstand (Ex 25:31ff; Jos., Ant. 14, 72) **Hb 9:2.** In Rv the seven churches of Asia appear as seven lampstands **Rv 1:12f, 20ab; 2:1.** Cp. κινήσω τὴν λ. σου ἐκ τοῦ τόπου αὐτῆς *I will remove your lampstand from its place,* i.e. remove you fr. the circle of the churches **2:5.** Rv also likens the two witnesses of Christ to two lampstands **11:4** (cp. Zech 4:11).—DELG s.v. λύω. M-M. TW.

λύχνος, ου, ὁ (Hom.+; ins, pap, LXX, TestSol, TestAbr, TestJob; TestSim 8:4; ParJer 9:14 [Christ.]; Just., D. 10, 1) ***lamp*** (of metal or clay [Artem. 2, 9 p. 96, 20f λύχνος χαλκοῦς, ὀστράκινος].—Oil-burning: Posidonius: 87 fgm. 94 Jac.; Diod. S. 1, 34, 11; Chariton 1, 1, 15; PGM 7, 359–64. S. λυχνία.—λυχνία beside λύχνος: Artem. 1, 74 p. 67, 12; IKos 36d, 7; 8; TestAbr B p. 109, 19 [Stone p. 66]; TestJob 32:9; Philo, Spec. Leg. 1, 296 καίεσθαι λύχνους ἐπὶ τῆς λυχνίας; Jos., Bell. 7, 429, Ant. 3, 182; 199)

ⓐ lit. **Lk 11:36;** GPt 5:18. φῶς λύχνου (Chariton 1, 1, 15; M. Ant. 12, 15) *light of a lamp* **Rv 22:5;** cp. **18:23;** ἔρχεται ὁ λ. *a lamp is brought in* **Mk 4:21;** καίειν λ. **Mt 5:15** (Paus. 3, 17, 8 τὸν καιόμενον λύχνον). λ. ἅπτειν *light a lamp* (ἅπτω 1.—As a symbol of someth. out of place Paroem. Gr.: Diogenian 6, 27 λ. ἐν μεσημβρίᾳ ἅπτειν. Likew. an unknown comic poet: fgm. 721 K.) **Lk 8:16; 11:33; 15:8.** φαίν[ων] οὐ λύχνῳ *illumined without a lamp* AcPl Ha 3, 28f.—Use of the lamp as a symbol: ἔστωσαν ὑμῶν … οἱ λύχνοι καιόμενοι **Lk 12:35** (Artem. 2, 9 λ. καιόμενος); cp. D 16:1. The Baptist as ὁ λύχνος ὁ καιόμενος κ. φαίνων **J 5:35** (of Christ ὁ ἄσβεστος λ. ParJer 9:14). The believers are to pay attention to the prophetic word ὡς λύχνῳ φαίνοντι **2 Pt 1:19** (cp. Ps 118:105 λύχνος … ὁ λόγος σοῦ).

ⓑ as metaph. (Lycophron vs. 422 λύχνοι are the eyes as vs. 846 λαμπτήρ an eye) ὁ λ. τοῦ σώματός ἐστιν ὁ ὀφθαλμός *the lamp of the body is the eye* **Mt 6:22; Lk 11:34** (FSchwencke, ZWT 55, 1913, 251–60; WBrandt, ZNW 14, 1913, 97–116; 177–201; BBacon, Exp. 8th ser., 7, 1913, 275–88; JDerrett, Law in the NT, '70, 189–207; GSchneider, Das Bildwort von der Lampe etc., ZNW 61, '70, 183–209.—Further lit. s.v. ἁπλοῦς). Of the Spirit of God λ. ἐρευνῶν τὰ ταμιεῖα τῆς γαστρός 1 Cl 21:2 (Pr 20:27 A). Of the heavenly Jerusalem ὁ λ. αὐτῆς τὸ ἀρνίον **Rv 21:23.**—KGalling, D. Beleuchtungsgeräte im isr.-jüd. Kulturgebiet: ZDPV 46, 1923, 1–50; RSmith, BA 27, '64, 1–31, 101–24; 29, '66, 2–27.—B. 484; Pauly-W. XIII 1566ff; Kl. Pauly III 478ff. OEANE III 326–30. DELG. M-M. EDNT. TW.

λύω impf. ἔλυον; fut. λύσω LXX; 1 aor. ἔλυσα. Pass.: impf. ἐλυόμην; 1 fut. λυθήσομαι; 1 aor. ἐλύθην; pf. λέλυμαι, 2 sg. λέλυσαι, ptc. λελυμένος (Hom.+).

❶ **to undo someth. that is used to tie up or constrain someth.,** ***loose, untie*** bonds (Da 5:12 Theod.), fetters (Lucian, Dial. Mar. 14, 3; Job 39:5 δεσμούς; Philo, Somn. 1, 181; Hippol., Ref. 5, 19, 20) or someth. similar.

ⓐ lit. τὰ δεσμά AcPl Ha 3, 14; τὸν ἱμάντα **Mk 1:7; Lk 3:16; J 1:27.** τὴν ζώνην MPol 13, 2 (JosAs 10:11; 13:3); σφραγῖδας *break* (Polyaenus 5, 2, 12) **Rv 5:2, 5 v.l.** (of the broken seals of a will: BGU 326 II, 21 ἡ διαθήκη ἐλύθη; POxy 715, 19.—λύω of the opening of a document: ParJer 7:21 λῦσον τὴν ἐπιστολὴν ταύτην; 7:36; Plut., Dio 31, 4 [a letter]; Vi. Aesopi W 92 P.)

ⓑ fig. ἐλύθη ὁ δεσμὸς τ. γλώσσης αὐτοῦ **Mk 7:35;** cp. **Lk 1:63** D. λύε πάντα σύνδεσμον ἀδικίας *loose every unjust fetter* B 3:3 (Is 58:6).

❷ **to set free someth. tied or similarly constrained,** ***set free, loose, untie***—ⓐ lit. a pers., animal, or thing that is bound or tied:

a prisoner (Jos., Bell. 2, 28, Ant. 13, 409; Ps 145:7) **Ac 22:30;** cp. vs. **29 v.l.;** ISm 6:2 (cp. b below); AcPl Ha 3, 6. Angels that are bound **Rv 9:14f.** Also more gener. (IAndrosIsis, Kyme 48 ἐγὼ τοὺς ἐν δεσμοῖς λύω) *release, set free* prisoners **Ac 24:26 v.l.;** τοὺς δεσμίους AcPl Ha 11, 9. Of Satan, bound and imprisoned in an abyss **Rv 20:3.** λυθήσεται ὁ σατανᾶς ἐκ τῆς φυλακῆς αὐτοῦ vs. **7.**—Of Lazarus, bound in grave-clothes λύσατε αὐτόν *unbind him* **J 11:44** (Vi. Aesopi I 83 λύσατε αὐτόν=take off his fetters).—Of animals (X., An. 3, 4, 35) a colt that is tied up **Mt 21:2; Mk 11:2, 4f; Lk 19:30f, 33ab** (perh. these passages suggest a kind of commandeering of transport indicated by the term ἀγγαρεύω JDerrett, NovT 13, '71, 241–58), τὸν βοῦν ἀπὸ τῆς φάτνης *untie the ox from the manger* **Lk 13:15** (λ. ἀπό as Quint. Smyrn. 4, 373; Is 5:27; Jer 47:4).—λ. τὸ ὑπόδημα *untie the sandal* **Ac 7:33** (Ex 3:5; Josh 5:15); **13:25.**—Pass. τὰς τρίχας λελυμέναι *with unbound hair* Hs 9, 9, 5; cp. τὰς τρίχας λελυμένας Hs 9, 13, 8.

ⓑ fig. *free, set free, release* ἀπό τινος (TestJos 15:6; Cyranides p. 97, 12) λυθῆναι ἀπὸ τ. δεσμοῦ τούτου *be set free from this bond* **Lk 13:16.** λέλυσαι ἀπὸ γυναικός; *are you free from a wife,* i.e. not bound to a wife? **1 Cor 7:27** (a previous state of being 'bound' need not be assumed; cp. Chion, Ep. 7, 3 λελυμένως=[speak] in an unrestrained manner. See also Simplicius in Epict. p. 129, 3: 'one who does not found a family is εὔλυτος', i.e. free). The pf. pass. ptc. IMg 12:1 is the negation of δέδεμαι i.e. unbound. On ISm 6:2 s. comm. by WBauer. ἐκ instead of ἀπό: λ. τινὰ ἐκ τῶν ἁμαρτιῶν *free someone from sins* **Rv 1:5.** τινὰ ἐκ χειρὸς σιδήρου 1 Cl 56:9 (Job 5:20). Bonds from pers. *loose, remove* (Χριστὸς) λύσει ἀφ' ὑμῶν πάντα δεσμόν IPhld 8:1.

❸ **to reduce someth. by violence into its components,** ***destroy*** (Iren. 1, 8, 1 [Harv. I 67, 9]), of a building *tear down* (Il. 16, 10; X., An. 2, 4, 17f; Herodian 7, 1, 7; 1 Esdr 1:52; Jos., Bell. 6, 32; SibOr 3, 409) τ. ναὸν τοῦτον **J 2:19.** τὸ μεσότοιχον **Eph 2:14** (in imagery).—ἡ πρύμνα ἐλύετο *the stern began to break up* **Ac 27:41** (PLond III 1164h, 19 p. 164 [III AD] uses λ. of the dismantling of a ship). Of the parts of the universe, as it is broken up and destroyed in the final conflagration **2 Pt 3:10–12** (cp. Just., D. 5, 4; Tat. 25, 2).—Of a meeting (Il. 1, 305; Od. 2, 257; Apollon. Rhod. 1, 708; X., Cyr. 6, 1, 2; Diod. S. 19, 25, 7; EpArist 202; Jos., Ant. 14, 388 λυθείσης τ. βουλῆς) λυθείσης τ. συναγωγῆς *when the meeting of the synagogue had broken up* **Ac 13:43.**—λυθεῖσα Ox 1081, 3 as edited (so also Otero I 82, no. 3) is incorrectly read instead of ἐ]ληλύθεισαν, s. s.v. ἔρχομαι 1aζ.

❹ **to do away with,** ***destroy, bring to an end, abolish*** (Socrat., Ep. 28, 2 and 4 'dispel' slanders; Tat. 13, 1 ψυχὴ . . . λύεται μετὰ τοῦ σώματος; Mel., P. 43, 301 ὁ τύπος ἐλύθη=the type was abolished [when the antitype made its appearance]) λ. τὰ ἔργα τ. διαβόλου *destroy the works of the devil* **1J 3:8.** Pass. ἐλύετο πᾶσα μαγεία *all magic began to be dissolved* IEph 19:3. λύεται ὁ ὄλεθρος ἐν τ. ὁμονοίᾳ *his destructiveness comes to an end through the unity* 13:1.—λ. τ. ὠδῖνας τ. θανάτου must mean in its context: *(God) brought the pangs to an end* (IG IV^2, 128, 49 [280 BC] ἔλυσεν ὠδῖνα; Lycophron vs. 1198 ὠδῖνας ἐξέλυσε γονῆς; Himerius, Or. 64 [=Or. 18], 1 λυθῆναι τὰς ὠδῖνας of the cessation of labor pains; Job 39:2; Aelian, HA 12, 5 τοὺς τῶν ὠδίνων λῦσαι δεσμούς; Eutecnius 3 p. 30, 26), so that the 'birth' which is to bring Christ to light may attain its goal (Haenchen ad loc.) **Ac 2:24** (but s. θάνατος 1bβ; originally it is probable that 'the bonds of death' went with 'loose'); Pol 1:2—Of commandments, laws, statements *repeal, annul, abolish* (Hdt. 1, 29, 1 νόμον. Text fr. Nysa in Diod. S. 1, 27, 4 ὅσα ἐγὼ ἐνομοθέτησα, οὐδεὶς αὐτὰ δύναται λῦσαι; Ael. Aristid. 30 p. 573 D.: νόμους; Achilles Tat. 3, 3, 5; SIG 355, 21; 1219, 12; Jos., Ant. 11, 140) ἐντολήν **Mt 5:19.** τὸ σάββατον *abolish the Sabbath* **J 5:18** (in John, Jesus is accused not of breaking the Sabbath, but of doing away w. it as an ordinance). Pass. (Dio Chrys. 58 [75], 10 τ. νόμου λυθέντος) **7:23; 10:35** (RJungkuntz, CTM 35, '64, 556–65 [J 10:34–6]).—λύειν τὸν Ἰησοῦν *annul* (the true teaching about) *Jesus* (by spurning it); (cp. Alex. Aphr., Fat. 26, II 2 p. 196, 18 λ. τινὰ τῶν Ζήνωνος λόγων=certain teachings of Zeno; opp. ὁμολογεῖν: s. Iren. 1, 9, 3 [Harv. I 85, 10]) **1J 4:3 v.l.** (for the rdg. λύει s. Iren. 3, 16, 8 [Harv. II 90, 3]; Cl. Al., fgm. 35 p. 218, 10ff Stählin; Orig. XI [GCS] 152, 28; Socrates, HE 7, 32; EHarnack, SBBerlAk 1915, 556–61=Studien I '31, 132–37; A Rahlfs, TLZ 40, 1915, 525; OPiper, JBL 66, '47, 440–44 [exorcistic, *break a spell*]).

❺ On the combination and contrast of δέειν and λύειν **Mt 16:19; 18:18** s. δέω 4; also GLambert, Vivre et Penser, IIIe s., '43/44, 91–103.—B. 1239f. M-M. EDNT. TW. Sv.

Λωΐς, ΐδος, ἡ (PPetr II, 39b, 15 [III BC] has the genitive Λωΐτος from a nominative Λωΐς. Or does the name—which is found nowhere else—belong to a positive degree of comparison λῷϊς [claimed by Buttmann for the not uncommon λωΐων, a nom. sing.=more pleasant, more desirable]? Cp. Semonides 7, 30 D.[3] [=West p. 102] οὐκ ἔστιν ἄλλη τῆσδε λωΐων γυνή=no other woman is more worthy of being desired than this one.) ***Lois,*** grandmother of Timothy **2 Ti 1:5.**—BHHW II 1103.

Λώτ, ὁ indecl. (לוֹט.—LXX, TestAbr, Philo.—In Joseph. Λῶτος, ου [Ant. 1, 201]) ***Lot,*** son of Haran, nephew of Abraham (Gen 11:27); he lived in Sodom **Lk 17:28f;** was rescued fr. that doomed city, having led a virtuous life **2 Pt 2:7;** 1 Cl 11:1 (SRappaport, D. gerechte Lot: ZNW 29, 1930, 299–304). His wife perished because, upon leaving the city, she looked back, contrary to God's command **Lk 17:32** (on the whole s. Gen 19). His separation fr. Abraham 1 Cl 10:4 (s. Gen 13, esp. vss. 14–16).—(On the spelling s. JWordsworth-HWhite on **Mt 1:17.**)—BHHW II 1105f. DELG.

M

μ΄ numerical sign = ***40*** (τεσσε[α]ράκοντα; Diod. S. 22, 13, 2) **Ac 10:41** D; Hs 9, 4, 3; 9, 5, 4; 9, 15, 4; 9, 16, 5; GJs 1:4 Bodmer.—Pauly-W. XVI 1661.

Μάαθ, ὁ indecl. (cp. the name מַחַת 1 Ch 6:20 [Μεθ]; 2 Ch 29:12 [Μααθ]; 31:13) *Maath,* in the genealogy of Jesus **Lk 3:26.**

Μαγαδάν, ἡ indecl. ***Magadan,*** place of uncertain location on Lake Gennesaret **Mt 15:39; Mk 8:10 v.l.** the parallel pass., has Δαλμανουθά (q.v.), whose location is similarly uncertain. Other vv.ll. for both pass.: Μαγαδά, Μαγεδά (-άν), Μαγδαλά (-άν); for Mk: (Μελεγαδά [D]).—JBoehmer, ZNW 9, 1908, 227–29; CKopp, Dominican Studies 4, '50, 344–50; BHHW II 1121; OEANE III 399f.

Μαγδαλά(ν) s. Μαγαδάν.

Μαγδαληνή, ῆς, ἡ (subst. fem. of Μαγδαληνός, ή, όν) **woman from Magdala, *Magdalene,*** surname of a certain Mary (s. Μαρία 2), prob. fr. the town of Magdala which, acc. to the Talmud, lay about a twenty minutes' walk fr. Tiberias on the west side of the Lake of Gennesaret (s. Μαγαδάν; Buhl 225f; CKopp, The Holy Places of the Gospels, tr. RWalls, '63, 190–97) **Mt 27:56, 61; 28:1; Mk 15:40, 47; 16:1, 9; Lk 8:2; 24:10; J 19:25; 20:1, 18;** GPt 12:50.

Μαγεδών s. Ἁρμαγεδ(δ)ών.

μαγεία, ας, ἡ (s. next entry and μάγος; Pla. et al.; on the spelling s. B-D-F §23; s. Mlt-H. 339) **a rite or rites ordinarily using incantations designed to influence/control transcendent powers, *magic*** (Theophr., HP 9, 15, 7; Vett. Val. 210, 4; IDefixWünsch 4, 15; PGM 1, 127; Zosimus 7: Herm. Wr. IV p. 105 Sc.; the Herm. document Κόρη κόσμου in Stob. I 407, 4 W.=p. 494, 7 Sc.; Jos., Ant. 2, 286) in a list of vices B 20:1 (AscIs 2:5 μαγεία w. φαρμακεία and other vices). ἐλύετο πᾶσα μαγεία IEph 19:3 (λύω 4). Pl. *magic arts* (Jos., Ant. 2, 284) in a list of vices D 5:1. Of Simon **Ac 8:11** (cp. PGM 4, 2447ff: Παχράτης, ὁ προφήτης Ἡλιουπόλεως, Ἁδριανῷ βασιλεῖ ἐπιδεικνύμενος τ. δύναμιν τῆς θείας αὐτοῦ μαγείας 'Pachrates, prophet of Heliopolis, demonstrating the force of his divine magic').—R. Kotansky, Israel Exploration Journal 41, '91, 267–81, amulets used in prayers to angels; Kl. Pauly III 873f. Lit. s.v. Σίμων 9.—B. 1494. DELG s.v. μάγος. M-M. TW.

μαγεύω fut. μαγεύσω ***practice magic*** (s. prec. entry and μάγος; Eur., Iph. 1338; TestSol 15:5 [pass.]; Tat. 1, 1; Plut., Artax. 3, 6, Numa 15, 8; Gk.-Aram. ins in CClemen, D. Einfluss d. Mysterienreligionen auf d. älteste Christentum 1913 p. 10, 3 στρατηγὸς . . . ἐμάγευσε Μίθρῃ) **Ac 8:9** (JFossum, Simon Magus: DDD 1473–77). In a list of vices D 2:2.—DELG s.v. μάγος. M-M. TW.

μαγία s. μαγεία.

Μαγνησία, ας, ἡ (Hdt. et al.; ins) ***Magnesia,*** a city in Asia Minor a short distance southeast of Ephesus, IMg ins. A temple of Artemis was one of its adornments. In order to differentiate this city from Magnesia in Thessaly, which was considered its mother (OGI 503 Μάγνητες οἱ πρὸς τῷ Μαιάνδρῳ ποταμῷ, ἄποικοι ὄντες Μαγνήτων τῶν ἐν Θεσσαλίᾳ, also the notes; SIG 636 and1157), and fr. another Magnesia in Asia Minor near Mt. Sipylus (OGI 501, 13; 229 s. note 12; for the ins s. IMagnSip), it is called Magnesia on the Maeander, despite the fact that it lies on the Lethaeus, about $6^1/_2$ km. distant fr. the Maeander. The name of the river is usu. added w. a prep., in our passage πρός w. dat., as also in OGI 229, 84; 503 (s. above); IMagnMai 40, 11 and 16; 44, 4; 101, 8. An inhabitant of the city is called Μάγνης, ητος (Hdt. et al. in lit.; also on ins and coins [cp. the material in Lghtf. on IMg ins, also OGI 12; 231; 232; 234; 319; 501. For reff. to the name s. IMagnMai index III p. 206]); not Μαγνησιεύς (v.l.) or Μαγνήσιος (the longer form in Ignatius).—Pauly-W. XIV 471f; Kl. Pauly III 885f. PECS 544.

μάγος, ου, ὁ (s. μαγεία, μαγεύω)—**❶** ***a Magus,*** a (Persian [SNyberg, D. Rel. d. alten Iran '38], then also Babylonian) wise man and priest, who was expert in astrology, interpretation of dreams and various other occult arts (so Hdt.+; Jos., Ant. 20, 142; s. Da 2:2, 10; in still other pass. in Da, Theod.; Tat. 28, 1. Beside φιλόσοφος of Apollonius of Tyana: Orig., C. Cels. 6, 41, 13). After Jesus' birth μάγοι *Magi* **Mt 2:7** (cp. Jos., Ant. 10, 216), **16a** (=GJs 22:1); vs. **16b;** GJs 21:1, 3 (apart fr. the pap text, μάγοι appears in codd. of GJs twice in 21:2; once in vs. 3), or more definitely μάγοι ἀπὸ ἀνατολῶν (ἀπὸ Ἀρραβίας Just., D. 77, 4; ἀπὸ ἀνάτολῆς Orig., C. Cels. 1, 40, 20) *Magi from the east* **Mt 2:1** came to Palestine and declared that they had read in the stars of the birth of the Messianic King. Diog. L. 2, 45 φησὶ δ' Ἀριστοτέλης μάγον τινὰ ἐλθόντα ἐκ Συρίας εἰς Ἀθήνας in order to announce to Socrates that he would come to a violent end.—ADieterich, ZNW 3, 1902, 1–14; FSteinmetzer, D. Gesch. der Geburt u. Kindheit Christi 1910; GFrenken, Wunder u. Taten der Heiligen 1929, 186–93; KBornhäuser, D. Geburts- u. Kindheitsgesch. Jesu 1930. FCumont, L'Adoration des Mages: Memorie della Pontif. Acc. Rom. di Archeol. 3, '32, 81–105. EHodous, CBQ 6, '44, 71–74; 77–83.—On the Magi HMeyboom, Magiërs: TT '39, 1905, 40–70; GMessina, D. Ursprung der Magier u. d. zarath. Rel., diss. Berl. 1930, I Magi a Betlemme e una predizione di Zoroastro '33 (against him GHartmann, Scholastik 7, '32, 403–14); RPettazzoni, RHR 103, '31, 144–50; Goodsp., Probs. 14f.—On the star of the Magi HKritzinger, Der Stern der Weisen 1911; HGVoigt, Die Geschichte Jesu u. d. Astrologie 1911; OGerhardt, Der Stern des Messias 1922; DFrövig, D. Stern Bethlehems in der theol. Forschung: TK 2, '31, 127–62; CSSmith, CQR 114, '32, 212–27; WVischer, D. Ev. von den Weisen aus dem Morgenlande: EVischer Festschr. '35, 7–20; ELohmeyer, D. Stern d. Weisen: ThBl 17, '38, 288–99; GHartmann, Stimmen d. Zeit 138, '41, 234–38; JSchaumberger, Ein neues Keilschriftfragment über d. angebl. Stern der Weisen: Biblica 24, '43, 162–69, but s. ASachs and CWalker, Kepler's View of the Star of Bethlehem and the Babylonian Almanac for 7/6 BC: Iraq 46/1, '84, 43–55. Cp. ποιμήν 1.

❷ ***magician*** (trag. et al.; Aeschin. 3, 137 [μάγος=πονηρός]; Diod. S. 5, 55, 3; 34 + 35 fgm. 2, 5 τὶς . . . ἄνθρωπος μάγος, a false prophet, who πολλοὺς ἐξηπάτα; Vett. Val. 74, 17; Philo, Spec. Leg. 3, 93; TestReub 4:9) of Barjesus=Elymas on Cyprus **Ac 13:6, 8.** Cp. Hm 11:2 v.l.—On the history of the word ANock, Beginn. I 5, '33, 164–88=Essays I 308–30; HKippenberg, Garizim u. Synagoge '71, 122–24 on Ac 8:10; MMeyer/PMirecki, edd., Ancient Magic and Ritual Power '95. M-LThomsen,

Zauberdiagnose und Schwarze Magie in Mesopotamien (CNI Publikations 2) n.d.: ancient Mesopotamian background. S. also MSmith, Clement of Alexandria and a Secret Gospel of Mark '73, esp. 220–78 for ancient sources and 423–44 for bibl. (for caution about media hype and fantastic hypotheses relating to this work s. JFitzmyer, How to Exploit a Secret Gospel: America, June 23, '73, 570–72). FGraf, La magie dans l' antiquité Gréco-Romaine, '95.—B. 1494f. Renehan '82 s.v. DELG. M-M. TW.

Μαγώγ, ὁ indecl. (מָגוֹג) ***Magog,*** mentioned w. Gog (s. Γώγ) among the enemies of God in the last days **Rv 20:8.** The idea and the names are fr. Ezk 38:2–39:16; but there Gog is prince of Magog, and in Rv G. and M. are two peoples (cp. SibOr 3, 319 χώρα Γὼγ ἠδὲ Μαγώγ; 512).—Lit. s.v. Γώγ; also RdeVaux, Magog-Hierapolis: RB 43, '34, 568–71.

Μαδιάμ, ὁ (also Μάδιαμ) indecl. (מִדְיָן; also Philo, Mut. Nom. 110.—Jos., Ant. 2, 257 Μαδιανή, ῆς) ***Midian,*** a people in Arabia. γῆ *M.* is (after Ex 2:15) the place where Moses stayed for a while **Ac 7:29.**—BHHW II 1214; Kl. Pauly III 1290.

μαζός, οῦ, ὁ (Hom. et al.; Kaibel 644, 4; 690, 2; PSI 253, 134; s. Schwyzer I 472; collateral forms μασθός and μαστός [q.v.]) 'one of the breasts' (distinguished from the στῆθος 'chest', the area of the torso where the μαζοί are located; the distinction noted Il. 4, 480f βάλε στῆθος παρὰ μαζὸν δεξίον=he smote him in the chest near his right nipple).

❶ **one of the mammillae of a male, *nipple*** (oft. Hom.; Apollon. Rhod. 3, 119; Achilles Tat. 3, 8, 6; Etym. Mag. *574, 220) of the triumphant Christ **Rv 1:13 v.l.**

❷ **mammary gland of a female, *mamma, breast*** (Hom. et al.; Artem. 1, 16; TestNapht 1:12 v.l.; also of an animal's udder: Callim. 1, 48; Aratus, Phaen. 163; Crinagoras no. 26, 6). Fig. (Philo, Aet. M. 66) of springs (Pampretius of Panopolis [V AD] 1, 90 [ed. HGerstinger: SBWienAk 208, 3, 1928]) which offer to humans τοὺς πρὸς ζωῆς μαζούς *their life-giving breasts* 1 Cl 20:10.—DELG s.v. μαστός. M-M.

Μαθαῖος s. Μαθθαῖος.

μαθεῖν s. μανθάνω.

μάθημα, ατος, τό (s. μανθάνω; Soph., Hdt. et al.; ins, pap; Jer 13:21; Philo; Just.) **someth. that is learned, *knowledge, teaching*** Dg 5:3.—DELG s.v. μανθάνω. TW. Sv.

μαθηματικός, ή, όν (s. prec. entry; the adj. in various senses: 'fond of learning, mathematical, astronomical': Pla. et al.; SibOr 13, 67), subst. μαθηματικός, οῦ, ὁ (Aristot. et al). The study of mathematics was a core feature of ancient learning and was closely associated with study of celestial phenomena. The latter emphasis in our lit. and in the sense ***astrologer*** (M. Ant. 4, 48; Sext. Emp., Adv. Math.; Philo, Mut. Nom. 71) D 3:4.—DELG s.v. μανθάνω.

μαθητεία, ας, ἡ (s. μαθητής) ***lesson, instruction*** (Timo [III BC] 54 in Poet. Philos.; Dio Chrys. 4, 41; AscIs 3:13; Just., D. 53, 6; Suda) οὗ τὸ κατάστημα μεγάλη μ. *whose demeanor is a great lesson* ITr 3:2.—DELG s.v. μανθάνω.

μαθητεύω (s. μαθητής) 1 aor. ἐμαθήτευσα, pass. ἐμαθητεύθην.

❶ ***to be a pupil,*** with implication of being an adherent of the teacher—ⓐ intr., *be* or *become a pupil* or *disciple* (Plut., Mor. 832b; 837c; Ps.-Callisth. 2, 4, 4 τινί; Iambl., Vi. Pyth. 23, 104 μ. τῷ Πυθαγόρᾳ; schol. on Apollon. Rhod. Proleg. A a) τινί (Orig., C. Cels. 2, 9, 60) *of someone* (Ἰωσήφ) ἐμαθήτευσεν τῷ Ἰησοῦ *Joseph had become a disciple of Jesus* **Mt 27:57 v.l.** Likew. as

ⓑ pass. dep. (Just., A I, 15, 6; Hippol., Ref. 1, 2, 16) μαθητεύομαι *become a disciple* τινί: (Ἰ.) ἐμαθητεύθη τῷ Ἰησοῦ **Mt 27:57.** γραμματεὺς μαθητευθεὶς τῇ βασιλείᾳ τ. οὐρανῶν *a scribe who has become a disciple of the kgdm. of heaven* or *who has been trained for the kgdm.* **Mt 13:52** (γραμματεύς 2b). Abs. IEph 3:1. μᾶλλον μαθητεύομαι *I am becoming a disciple more and more* IRo 5:1. This gave rise to a new active form (B-D-F §148, 3; Rob. 800)

❷ **to cause one to be a pupil, *teach,*** trans. (AscIs 3:18 καὶ μαθητεύσουσιν πάντα τὰ ἔθνη καὶ πᾶσαν γλῶσσαν εἰς τὴν ἀν[ά]στασιν τοῦ ἀγαπ[η]τοῦ; Just., D. 53, 1 Χριστὸς . . . ἐμαθήτευσεν αὐτούς) *make a disciple of, teach* τινά *someone* **Mt 28:19.** ἱκανούς *make a number of disciples* **Ac 14:21.** Abs. ἃ μαθητεύοντες ἐντέλλεσθε *what you command when you are instructing* or *winning disciples* IRo 3:1.—ὑμῖν μαθητευθῆναι *become your disciples, be instructed by you* IEph 10:1 (cp. pres. subst. ptc. οἱ μαθητευόμενοι = οἱ μαθηταί Did., Gen. 69, 24; 245, 17; aor. ptc. αἱ δὲ τοῦ θεοῦ Χριστῷ μαθητευθεῖσαι ἐκκλησίαι Orig., C. Cels. 3, 29, 24; Πολύκαρπος . . . ὑπὸ ἀποστόλων μαθητευθείς Iren. 3, 3, 4 [Harv. II 12, 4]).—DELG s.v. μανθάνω. M-M. EDNT. TW. Sv.

μαθητής, οῦ, ὁ (s. μανθάνω; Hdt.+; ins; BGU 1125, 9 [I BC]; POxy 1029, 25. In LXX only in two places in Jer [13:21; 20:11], and then as v.l. of codex A; AscIs 3:17, 21; Philo, Joseph., apolog. exc. Ar.) gener. 'learner, pupil, disciple'

❶ **one who engages in learning through instruction from another, *pupil, apprentice*** (in contrast to the teacher [Ath. 17, 3 μ. Δαιδάλου]; Did., Gen. 66, 25) **Mt 10:24f; Lk 6:40** (TManson, The Teaching of Jesus, '55, 237–40).

❷ **one who is rather constantly associated with someone who has a pedagogical reputation or a particular set of views, *disciple, adherent*** (Pla., Apol. 33a; X., Mem. 1, 6, 3; Dio Chrys. 11 [12], 5; Lucian, M. Peregr. 28 al.; Diog. L. 7, 7, 179; 8, 1, 3; 10, 11, 22; Iambl., Vi. Pyth. 35, 254 οἱ μ.; SIG 1094, 5f αὐτὸς καὶ οἱ μαθηταὶ αὐτοῦ; Jos., Ant. 9, 68; 13, 289), oft. w. an indication of the pers. whose disciple one is, mostly in the gen. (Jos., C. Ap. 1, 176 Ἀριστοτέλους μ., Ant. 9, 33; 15, 3; Just., A I, 26, 4 τοῦ Σίμωνος; Tat. 39, 3 Ὀρφέως; Iren. 1, prologue 2 [Harv. I 4, 7] Οὐαλεντίνου; Theosophien 66 Φορφυρίου μ.).

ⓐ μ. Ἰωάννου **Mt 9:14a; 11:2; 14:12; Mk 2:18ab; 6:29; Lk 5:33; 7:18f; 11:1; J 1:35, 37; 3:25.** τ. Μωϋσέως **9:28b** τῶν Φαρισαίων **Mt 22:16; Mk 2:18c** τοῦ Πολυκάρπου MPol 22:2; EpilMosq 1.

ⓑ esp. of the disciples of Jesus (of Paul: Orig., C. Cels. 1, 48, 70)

α. of the Twelve οἱ δώδεκα μ. αὐτοῦ *his twelve disciples* **Mt 10:1; 11:1;** οἱ ἕνδεκα μ. **28:16.** οἱ μαθηταὶ αὐτοῦ (or w. another gen. of similar mng.; cp. Just., A I, 67, 7 τοῖς ἀποστόλοις αὐτοῦ καὶ μαθηταῖς; Just., D. 53, 1 al.; Did., Gen. 38, 21; Orig., C. Cels. 2, 2, 10.—Yet it is somet. doubtful whether a particular pass. really means the Twelve and not a larger [s. β below] or smaller circle; EMartinez, CBQ 23, '61, 281–92 [restricted to the 12, even in Mt 18]) **Mt 8:21; 12:1; 15:2; Mk 5:31; 6:1, 35, 45; 8:27; Lk 8:9; J 2:2; 3:22** and oft. Also without a gen. (but freq. vv.ll. + αὐτοῦ) οἱ μ. **Mt 13:10; 14:19; 16:5; Mk 8:1; 9:14; 10:24; Lk 9:16; J 4:31; 11:7f** and oft.—LBrun, D. Berufung der ersten Jünger Jesu: SymbOsl 11, '32, 35–54; SvanTilborg, The Jewish Leaders in Mt, '72, 99–141; ULuz, Die Jünger im Mt, ZNW 62, '71, 141–47; on the 'beloved disciple' of **J 13:23** al. s. FFilson, JBL 68, '49, 83–88; ETitus, ibid. '50, 323–28;

M

FNeirynck, The Anonymous Disciple in John 1: ETL 66, '90, 5–37.

β. of Jesus' disciples, male and female, gener. ὄχλος πολὺς μ. αὐτοῦ *a large crowd of his adherents* **Lk 6:17;** ἅπαν τὸ πλῆθος τῶν μ. the whole *crowd of the disciples* **19:37.** οἱ μ. αὐτοῦ ἱκανοί *a large number of his disciples* **7:11 v.l.** πολλοὶ ἐκ (v.l. om.) τῶν μ. αὐτοῦ **J 6:66.**—Papias (2:4).

γ. Even after Jesus' resurrection those who followed him were called μ. (generations later, as Socrates is called the μ. of Homer: Dio Chrys. 38 [55], 3ff) οἱ μ. τοῦ κυρίου **Ac 9:1;** μ. Ἰησοῦ Χριστοῦ IMg 9:2 (opp. ὁ μόνος διδάσκαλος, who also had the prophets as his μαθηταί vs. 3; 10:1). Ac uses μ. almost exclusively to denote the members of the new community of believers (Just., D. 35, 2; s. Rtzst., Erlösungsmyst. 127f), so that it almost=*Christian* (cp. **11:26**) **6:1f, 7; 9:19; 11:26, 29; 13:52; 15:10** al. τῶν μαθητῶν (without τινές) *some Christians* **21:16** (cp. X., Cyr. 1, 4, 20, An. 3, 5, 16; Herodas 2, 36 τῶν πορνέων; Polyaenus 5, 17, 2 καὶ ἦσαν τῶν Μακεδόνων).—καλοὶ μαθηταί IPol 2:1. Individuals (Aberciusins. 3: Ἀ., ὁ μ. ποιμένος ἁγνοῦ): Ananias **Ac 9:10;** Mnason **21:16b;** Timothy **16:1.**

δ. The martyrs (s. on μάρτυς 3) are specif. called μ. κυρίου MPol 17:3. Also absol. μ. IEph 1:2; ITr 5:2; IRo 5:3; IPol 7:1. As long as a Christian's blood has not been shed, the person is only a beginner in discipleship (IRo 5:3), not a μαθητὴς ἀληθῶς Ἰησοῦ Χριστοῦ IRo 4:2.—For lit. s. on ἀπόστολος and s. also JWach, Meister and Jünger 1925; ESchweizer, Lordship and Discipleship, '60, 464–66; GBornkamm, Bultmann Festschr., '64, 171–91 (Mt 28:16–20)—B. 1225. DELG s.v. μανθάνω. M-M. TW. Sv.

μαθήτρια, ας, ἡ (Diod. S. 2, 52, 7; Diog. L. 4, 2; 8, 42) ***(female) disciple:*** Mary Magdalene μ. τοῦ κυρίου GPt 12:50; Eubula, one of Paul's disciples AcPl Ha 2, 9.—Also abs. ***disciple*** (s. μαθητής 2bγ) of Tabitha in Joppa **Ac 9:36.**—DELG s.v. μανθάνω. M-M. TW.

Μαθθάθ s. Μαθθάτ.

Μαθθαῖος, ου, ὁ (edd. mostly Ματθαῖος; so also GEb 19, 83; Papias [2:4, 16]). Cp. FBurkitt, JTS 34, '33, 387–90. Also Μαθαῖος; Preisigke, Namenb.; HMilne, Catal. of the Lit. in the Brit. Mus. 1927, no. 99, 2 ***Matthew.*** His name is included in all the lists of the 12 apostles: **Mk 3:18; Lk 6:15; Ac 1:13.** The first gospel (title κατὰ M-ον) describes him in its list as ὁ τελώνης **Mt 10:3,** thereby identifying him w. the tax-collector of **9:9;** sim. GEb 19, 83.—AJülicher, RE XII 1903, 428ff; Zahn, Einl. II[3] 258ff; EvDobschütz, Matth. als Rabbi u. Katechet: ZNW 27, 1928, 338–48; Kl. Pauly III 1085f; BHHW II 1171ff. EDNT.

Μαθθάν s. Ματθάν.

Μαθθάτ (edds. and mss. also Ματθάτ, Μαθθαθ; מַתָּת) indecl. ***Matthat,*** in the genealogy of Jesus.

➊ son of Levi, father of Eli and grandfather of Joseph **Lk 3:24.**—➋ son of Levi, father of Jorim vs. **29.**

Μαθθίας, ου, ὁ (Joseph.—Edd. and mss. also Ματθίας. Prob. a short form of Ματταθίας) ***Matthias,*** the successful candidate in the election to replace the traitor Judas **Ac 1:23, 26.**—PGaechter, Petrus u. seine Zeit, '58, 31–66; KRengstorf, OPiper Festschr. '62, 178–92; Kl. Pauly III 1086; BHHW II 1174.

Μαθουσαλά, ὁ indecl. (מְתוּשֶׁלַח.—So also Philo and En 106:1; 107:3, the latter in the form Μεθουσάλεκ.—Joseph. has Μαθουσάλας, but only in nom.) ***Methuselah,*** son of Enoch and grandfather of Noah (Gen 5:21ff); in the genealogy of Jesus **Lk 3:37.**—BHHW II 1208.

μαῖα, ας, ἡ (Hom. et al.; LXX; En 106:3, 11; Philo; APF 370 II 3 [II AD]); lit. 'mama', also ***midwife*** GJs 5:2 (twice); 18:1; 19:1 (Bodmer once; codd. twice); 19:2 (twice); 20:1 (codd.).

Μαίανδρος, ου, ὁ (Hom.+; ins; SibOr 4, 149; 151) ***Maeander,*** a river in Caria in Asia Minor IMg ins; s. Μαγνησία.

Μαϊνάν s. Μεννά.

μαίνομαι (Hom. et al.; POxy 33 IV, 9ff; PHerm 7 I, 18; LXX; TestJob; TestJos 8:3; ParJer 5:20; SibOr 4, 83; Philo; Jos., Bell. 1, 352, C. Ap. 1, 204; apolog. exc. Mel.) ***be mad, be out of one's mind*** beside δαιμόνιον ἔχειν and as a result of it: *have no control over oneself* **J 10:20** (cp. Eur., Bacch. 291ff; Hdt. 4, 79 ὁ δαίμων τὸν βασιλέα λελάβηκε καὶ ὑπὸ τ. θεοῦ μαίνεται; Dio Chrys. 11 [12], 8: the owl warns the other birds about humans, but the birds ἀνόητον αὐτὴν ἡγοῦντο καὶ μαίνεσθαι ἔφασκον; the same Aesop, Fab. 437 P.=105 H.; Diog. L. 1, 49 the members of the Athenian council concerning Solon: μαίνεσθαι ἔλεγον αὐτόν; Orig., C. Cels. 4, 19, 23). Opp. ἀληθείας καὶ σωφροσύνης ῥήματα ἀποφθέγγεσθαι **Ac 26:25.** μαίνῃ *you're crazy,* said to one who has brought incredible news **12:15;** *you're out of your mind, you're raving,* said to one whose enthusiasm seems to have outrun better judgment **26:24** (Ath. 31, 1 and Sallust. 4 p. 6, 8 μ. as a judgment on a man proclaiming certain teachings; Porphyr., Vi. Plotini c. 15 μαίνεσθαι τὸν Πορφύριον as a judgment on a poem that has been recited). Of the impression made on strangers by speakers in 'tongues' **1 Cor 14:23** (Herm. Wr. 9, 4 those who were filled w. divine Gnosis made a similar impression on outsiders: μεμηνέναι δοκοῦσι; cp. Hippol., Ref. 5, 8, 6; Did., Gen. 230, 11).—DELG. M-M. TW. Spicq.

μακαρίζω Att. fut. μακαριῶ; 1 aor. ἐμακάρισα; fut. pass. μακαρισθήσομαι 4 Macc 16:9 (μάκαρ 'blest', s. two next entries; Hom. et al.; Vett. Val. 88, 25; LXX; Philo, Exs. 152; Joseph.) **to call or consider someone especially favored, *call/consider blessed, happy, fortunate*** τινά *someone* (Hippocr., Ep. 17; IEph Ia, 11, 17f; Diod. S. 13, 58, 2; Chariton 5, 8, 3; Appian, Bell. Civ. 4, 114 §476; Gen 30:13; Sir 11:28; Jos., Bell. 7, 356; τὸ μακαρίζεσθαι μὲν τοὺς πτωχοὺς ὑπὸ τοῦ Ἰησοῦ Orig., C. Cels. 6, 16, 30, w. εὐφημέω 8, 57, 27; Did., Gen 72, 1; 149, 27) or τὶ *someth.* (Herodian 5, 1, 5; Jos., C. Ap. 2, 135) **Lk 1:48** (cp. 4Q434 II–III); IEph 5:1; GJs 12:2. τοὺς ὑπομείναντας *those who showed endurance* **Js 5:11.** ἑαυτόν *oneself* Hs 9, 28, 6; AcPl Ha 6, 7. τὴν τελείαν γνῶσιν 1 Cl 1:2. τὴν εἰς θεὸν αὐτοῦ γνώμην *his* (the bishop's) *attitude toward God* IPhld 1:2. Perh. abs. (X., Mem. 1, 6, 9) Dg 10:8.—New Docs 4, 39. DELG s.v. μάκαρ. M-M. TW.

μακάριος, ία, ιον (s. prec. and next entry; Pind., Pla., X.+)

➊ **pert. to being fortunate or happy because of circumstances, *fortunate, happy.***—ⓐ of humans, with less focus on the transcendent dimension compared to usage in 2 below (Chrysippus in Diog. L. 7, 179 calls himself a μακάριος ἀνήρ; Epict. 2, 18, 15; Jos., Ant. 16, 108; 20, 27) ἥγημαι ἐμαυτὸν μακάριον **Ac 26:2.** Of the widow who remains unmarried μακαριωτέρα ἐστίν *she is happier* **1 Cor 7:40.** μ. ἤμην εἰ τοιαύτην γυναῖκα εἶχον Hv 1, 1, 2 (Chariton 6, 2, 9 μ. ἦν εἰ). Cp. **Lk 23:29.**

ⓑ of transcendent beings, viewed as ***privileged, blessed*** (Aristot., EN 10, 8:1178b, 25f τοῖς θεοῖς ἅπας ὁ βίος μακάριος; Epicurus in Diog. L. 10, 123 τ. θεὸν ζῷον ἄφθαρτον κ.

μακάριον νομίζων; Herm. Wr. 12, 13b; Sextus 560; Philo, Cher. 86, Deus Imm. 26 ὁ ἄφθαρτος κ. μακάριος, Leg. ad Gai. 5 [other pass. in MDibelius, Hdb./Hermeneia on 1 Ti 1:11]; Jos., C. Ap. 2, 190, cp. Ant. 10, 278; cp. Ἰησοῦς ὁ μ. Hippol., Ref. 5, 9, 21) **1 Ti 1:11; 6:15** (BEaston, Pastoral Epistles '47, 179).

❷ **pert. to being esp. favored, *blessed, fortunate, happy, privileged,*** fr. a transcendent perspective, the more usual sense (the general Gr-Rom. perspective: one on whom fortune smiles)

ⓐ of humans *privileged recipient of divine favor* (Jos., Ant. 9, 264), of Biblical persons (Ἰωβ Did., Gen. 101, 14; cp. ἄγγελοι Orig., C. Cels. 8, 25, 12): Moses 1 Cl 43:1; Judith 55:4; prophets AcPlCor 2:36 (Just., D. 48, 4); Paul (Hippol., Ref. 8, 20, 3; ὁ μ. ἀπόστολος Iren. 5, 2, 3 [Harv. II 321, 4] of Paul; cp. Orig., C. Cels. 5, 65, 7) 1 Cl 47:1; Pol 3:2 (11:3); AcPl Ha 3, 27. Of other prominent Christians, esp. martyrs: Ignatius, Zosimus, Rufus Pol 9:1. Polycarp MPol 1:1; 19:1, 21; 22:1, 3. Of presbyters who have died 1 Cl 44:5. μ. εἶναι ἐν τῇ ποιήσει αὐτοῦ *be blessed in what the person does* **Js 1:25.**—In various sentence combinations, in which the copula belonging with μ. is often omitted (B-D-F §127, 4; Rob. 395; Maximus Tyr. 14, 6f; μ. [opp. δυστυχής] εὐσεβὴς φίλος θεοῦ; but Did., Gen. 103, 2: μ. γάρ ἐστιν ἡ ἐκκλησία, ὅτε): as the apodosis of a conditional sentence **Lk 6:4** D (Unknown Sayings 49–54); **1 Pt 3:14; 4:14;** Hm 8:9. The conditional sentence follows **J 13:17;** 1 Cl 50:5; Hs 6, 1, 1a. W. relative clause foll. **Mt 11:6; Lk 7:23; 14:15** (μ. ὅστις Menand., fgm. 101 Kö., Mon. 340 Mei. al.); **Ro 4:7f;** 1 Cl 50:6 (both Ps 31:1f); **Js 1:12** (PsSol 6:1; 10:1; Sext. 40 μ. ἀνήρ w. rel.); 1 Cl 56:6 (Job 5:17); B 10:10 (Ps 1:1.—Maximus Tyr. 33, 5e ὁ μ. ἀνήρ, ὅν); 11:8; Hv 2, 2, 7; s 9, 29, 3. μ. ἐν Ἰησοῦ Χριστῷ, ὅς IPhld 10:2. The relative clause precedes Hv 3, 8, 4; s 5, 3, 9b; 6, 1, 1b. As a predicate w. a subst. or subst. adj. or ptc. μ. ὁ *blessed is the one who* . . . (2 Ch 9:7; Da 12:12; PsSol 4:23; ApcEsdr 5:11) **Mt 5:3ff** (the transl. *0, the happiness of* or *hail to those,* favored by some [Zahn, Wlh., EKlostermann, JWeiss; KBornhäuser, Die Bergpredigt 1923, 24 al.] appears to be exactly right for the Aramaic original [=Hebr. אַשְׁרֵי], but scholars have disputed whether it exhausts the content that μακάριος had in the mouths of Gk.-speaking Christians [s. e.g. Maximus Tyr. 14, 6f μακάριος εὐσεβὴς φίλος θεοῦ, δυστυχὴς δὲ ὁ δεισιδαίμων; Artem. 4, 72 the state of μ. εἶναι is brought about by ascension into heaven and the ὑπερβάλλουσα εὐδαιμονία enjoyed there; other reff. in Betz, SM 97–99].—CMcCown, The Beatitudes in the Light of Ancient Ideals: JBL 46, 1927, 50–61; JRezevskis [Resewski], D. Makarismen bei Mt u. Lk, ihr Verhältnis zu einander u. ihr histor. Hintergrund: StThR I [=IBenzinger Festschr.] '35, 157–70; JDupont, Les Béatitudes '54; GStrecker, Die Makarismen der Bergpredigt, NTS 17, '70/71, 255–75; see lit. s.v. ὄρος); **24:46; Lk 1:45; 6:20ff; 11:28; 12:37;** cp. vs. **38, 43; J 20:29; Ro 14:22; Rv 1:3; 14:13; 16:15; 19:9; 20:6; 22:7, 14;** 1 Cl 40:4; 48:4; 2 Cl 16:4; 19:3; D 1:5; Pol 2:3 (=**Lk 6:20;** Hv 2, 3, 3). W. ὅτι foll. (JosAs 16:7) **Mt 16:17; Lk 14:14; Hs 2:10; 9, 30, 3.** W. ὅταν **Mt 5:11.** Acc. to the reading of Michigan Pap. (ed. CBonner '34, p. 46, 11f) and of a parchment leaf at Hamburg (SBBerlAk 1909, 1081) Hs 5, 1, 3 contains the words μακάριόν με ποιήσεις ἐάν (so Whittaker and Joly) *you will make me happy, if.* W. γίνεσθαι 9, 24, 2.

ⓑ of things or experiences *blessed* (Eur.+; Eccl 10:17)

α. of parts of the body of persons who are the objects of special grace, which are themselves termed blessed: μ. οἱ ὀφθαλμοί **Mt 13:16; Lk 10:23.** μ. ἡ κοιλία **11:27** (Cleopatra ln. 168f; prob. Christian despite the ref. to Cleop. Of parallels in non-bibl. wr., the next closest is Musaeus, Hero 137 . . . γαστήρ, ἥ σ' ἐλόχευσε μακαρτάτη).

β. of things that stand in a very close relationship to the divinity: τὰ δῶρα τ. θεοῦ 1 Cl 35:1. Of the πνεύματα implanted in Christians B 1:2 (cp. Maximus Tyr. 41, 51 the εὐδαίμων κ. μακαρία ψυχή). Of the age to come 2 Cl 19:4 (cp. OGI 519, 9 ἐν τοῖς μακαριοτάτοις ὑμῶν καιροῖς; 17).

γ. of martyrdoms MPol 2:1. Of the object of the Christian hope προσδεχόμενοι τὴν μ. ἐλπίδα **Tit 2:13** (cp. OGI 383, 108 μακαριστὰς ἐλπίδας). μακάριόν ἐστιν μᾶλλον διδόναι ἢ λαμβάνειν **Ac 20:35** (cp. Pla., Rep. 496c ὡς μακάριον τὸ κτῆμα; 1 Cl 2:1; Beginn. IV 264; Unknown Sayings, 78–81; EHaenchen, Ac ad loc. On Thu. 2, 97, 4 λαμβάνειν μᾶλλον ἢ διδόναι s. JKilgallen, JBL 112, '93, 312–14.).—HSanders, HTR 36, '43, 165–67. S. the lit. s.v. ὄρος and cp. εὐδαιμονέω.—B. 1105. DELG s.v. μάκαρ. Schmidt, Syn. IV 402–6. M-M. EDNT. TW. Spicq. Sv.

μακαρισμός, οῦ, ὁ (s. two prec. entries; Pla., Rep. 9, 591d; Aristot., Rhet. 1, 9, 34 [1367b, 25–36]; Plut., Sol. 27, 7, Mor. 471c; Stob., Ecl. III 57, 14 H.; Philo, Somn. 2, 35; Jos., Bell. 6, 213; SibOr 13, 117; Orig., C. Cels. 2, 64, 16; Did., Gen. 26, 19f) **pronouncement of being in receipt of special favor, *blessing,*** of a quot. fr. the Psalms beginning w. אַשְׁרֵי=μακάριος **Ro 4:6, 9;** 1 Cl 50:7 (both Ps 31:1f). ποῦ οὖν ὁ μ. ὑμῶν; *where, then, is your blessing?* i.e. the frame of mind in which you blessed yourselves **Gal 4:15** (cp. Betz, Gal. 226f).—GDirichlet, De veterum macarismis 1914; CClassen, WienerStud 107/108, '94/95, 328f. Also εὐλογέω, end.—DELG s.v. μάκαρ. M-M. TW.

Μακεδονία, ας, ἡ (Hdt. et al.; ins [esp. IMakedD], Philo, Joseph., SibOr [-ίη]) ***Macedonia,*** a Roman province since 146 BC, in Paul's day a senatorial province. Visited by Paul several times **Ac 16:9f, 12; 18:5; 19:21f; 20:1, 3; 2 Cor 2:13; 7:5; Phil 4:15; 1 Th 1:7f; 4:10;** AcPl Ha 5, 16; 27. Travel plan w. ref. to Mac. **1 Cor 16:5ab; 2 Cor 1:16ab; 1 Ti 1:3.** Support for Paul fr. the Macedonian congregation **2 Cor 11:9.** They were also active in the collection for Jerusalem **Ro 15:26; 2 Cor 8:1.**—Pauly-W. XIV 638ff; Kl. Pauly III 910ff; BHHW II 1178f.

Μακεδών, όνος, ὁ (Hdt. et al.; Περὶ ὕψους 18, 1; Arrian: 156 fgm. 9, 17 Jac.; Polyaenus 1, prooem., 1 [all three M. ἀνήρ]; ins, pap; Esth 8:12k; Philo, Omn. Prob. Lib. 94; Joseph., SibOr) ***a Macedonian*** **Ac 16:9** (AWikenhauser, Religionsgesch. Parallelen zu Ac 16:9; BZ 23, '35, 180–86). Of Gaius and Aristarchus **19:29.** Of Aristarchus **27:2.** Pl. of the Maced. Christians or their representatives **2 Cor 9:2, 4.**—Haenchen ad loc.

μάκελλον, ου, τό (not originally a Lat. word taken into Gk. [as Rob. 109], since it is quotable in Gk. fr. c. 400 BC in an ins fr. Epidaurus [GDI III/1, 3325=IG IV^2/1, 102, 107; 296; 298; 301 in the form μάκελλον w. the mng. 'enclosure, grating']. The sense 'meat market' is found for the Lat. macellum Plautus and Terence+ [III/II BC]; the earliest Gk. ex. of μ. in this sense is SIG 783 [IG V/2, 268], 45 [I BC] where it is masc., μάκελλος, as also schol. on Aristoph., Eq. 137; Vi. Aesopi G 51 P.; cp. macellus in Martial, and Sahidic and Bohairic versions of **1 Cor 10:25.** S. Cadbury below 134 n. 2. Elsewh. the word is neut. [so also Peshîttâ and Harclean Syriac] or the gender cannot be determined. μ. may have reëntered H. Gk. in this new sense; so Hahn 249 n. 6. For the view that μ. may be of Semitic origin [AWalde, IndogF 39, 1921, 82; B-D-F §5, 1 app.], though Doric-Ionic acc. to Varro, De Lingua Lat. 5, 146 Goetz-Schoell, s. JSchneider, TW IV 373f.—Plut., Mor. 277d; Cass. Dio 61, 18, 3 τ. ἀγορὰν τῶν ὀψῶν, τὸ μάκελλον; Vita Aesopi G 51 ὁ μάκελλος where pork is for sale; IG V/1, 149; 150; SIG 783, 45 [μάκελλος]; BCH 17, 1893, 261; 20, 1896, 126; PHerm127 [3] verso, 5) ***meat market, food market***

(s. the plan of one at Pompeii in AMau, Pompeji[2] 1908, 90–97, fr. here in Ltzm., Hdb. on **1 Cor 10:25.** Also HCadbury, The Macellum of Corinth: JBL 53, '34, 134–41 w. a Lat. ins found at Corinth containing the word 'macellum': Corinth, Results of Excavations VIII/2, '31, no. 124; 125) τὸ ἐν μ. πωλούμενον ἐσθίειν *eat what is sold in the meat market* **1 Cor 10:25.**—B. 365. DELG. M-M. TW.

μακράν (a fixed fem. form, orig. an acc. of extent of space, w. ὁδόν to be supplied.—Aeschyl. et al., also pap, LXX, En; TestSim 6:2; TestNaphth 4:5; GrBar 4:16; Philo, Joseph., Tat.)

❶ **pert. to being at a relatively great distance from some position,** ***far (away)***—ⓐ adv. of place—**α.** of extension in space (Sir 24:32) μ. ἀπέχειν *be far away* **Lk 15:20** (PCairZen 605, 3 οὐ μακράν σου ἀπέχομεν). εἰς ἔθνη μακρὰν ἐξαποστελῶ σε *I will send you far away to the gentiles* **Ac 22:21.** μ. ἀπό τινος (Polyb. 3, 45, 2; LXX; Jos., C. Ap. 1, 60; SibOr 8, 33f): ῥίπτειν μ. ἀπὸ τοῦ πύργου *throw far away from the tower* Hv 3, 2, 7 and 9; 3, 6, 1; 3, 7, 1; s 9, 7, 2; cp. μακρὰν οὐκ ἀπερίφησαν ἔξω τοῦ πύργου v 3, 5, 5. μ. εἶναι ἀπό τινος *be far away fr. someone* or *someth.* **Mt 8:30; J 21:8;** Hs 1:1 (s. β below). μ. ἀπέχειν ἀπό τινος (Pr 15:29; 1 Macc 8:4) **Lk 7:6;** MPol 5:1. Of God οὐ μ. ἀπὸ ἑνὸς ἑκάστου ἡμῶν ὑπάρχοντα *not far from each one of us* **Ac 17:27** (cp. Dio Chrys. 11 [12], 28 οὐ μακρὰν οὐδ' ἔξω τοῦ θείου . . . , ἀλλὰ ἐν αὐτῷ μέσῳ [s. σύμφυτος]; Jos., Ant. 8, 108). The spatial sense, as **Ac 22:21,** is prob. expressed τοῖς τέκνοις ὑμῶν κ. πᾶσιν τοῖς εἰς μ. *to your children and to all who far away* **Ac 2:39** (cp. REB; NRSV), but s. 2 below.

β. transf. sense (Epict. 3, 22, 11 μ. ἀπ' αὐτοῦ=far from a true Cynic) μ. ὄντες ἀπὸ τοῦ κυρίου Hm 12, 4, 4. οὐ μ. εἶ ἀπὸ τῆς βασιλείας τοῦ θεοῦ *you are not far from the kgdm. of God* i.e. you are almost ready to enter it **Mk 12:34** (cp. Ps 21:2 μ. ἀπὸ τ. σωτηρίας μου). ἡ πόλις ὑμῶν μακράν ἐστιν ἀπὸ τῆς πόλεως ταύτης Hs 1:1 (s. α above; cp. Hb 13:14). οἱ μ. (opp. οἱ ἐγγύς; cp. Is 57:19; Da 9:7 Theod.; Esth 9:20) *those who are far away* of gentiles (in contrast to Israelites, cp. vs. 12) **Eph 2:17.** οἵ ποτε ὄντες μ. *who once were far away* vs. **13.** ἡ ἐπιθυμία ἡ πονηρά . . . φεύξεται ἀπό σου μ. *the base desire . . . will flee far from you* Hm 12, 2, 4.

ⓑ used as a prep. μ. τινος *far away fr. someone* or *someth.* (Herodas 7, 111 θεῶν ἐκεῖνος οὐ μακρὴν ἀπῴκισται; Polyb. 3, 50, 8; Polyaenus 5, 2, 10; GrBar 4:16 τῆς τοῦ θεοῦ δόξης μ. γίνονται; Just., D. 3, 1 οὐ μ. θαλάσσης; Tat. 12, 4 μ. δὲ τῆς εὐταξίας; PCairZen 605, 3 [s. 1aα above, beginning]; POxy 113, 18; Sir 15:8) **Lk 7:6 v.l.** μ. πάσης ἁμαρτίας Pol 3:3; cp. 4:3; 6:1. ὧν μ. πραΰτης D 5:2. ὧν μ. καὶ πόρρω πραΰτης B 20:2.

❷ **pert. to a position in time relatively far removed from the present,** ***in time to come*** τοῖς τέκνοις ὑμῶν κ. πᾶσιν τοῖς εἰς μ. **Ac 2:39** (cp. 2 Km 7:19 εἰς μ.=vs. 16 εἰς τὸν αἰῶνα; Sir 24:32 ἐκφανῶ αὐτὰ ἕως εἰς μ.—εἰς μ. also Demosth. 18, 36; Polyaenus 6, 7, 1; Jos., Ant. 6, 278; 20, 153; TestSim 6:2; Just., D. 2, 5; PMeyer 66, 2 [ostracon]), but s. 1 aα above.—DELG s.v. μακρός. M-M. TW.

μακρόβιος, ον (s. μακρός, βίος; Hippocr.+; LXX; Philo; Jos., Bell. 2, 151) ***long-lived*** σπέρμα μ. *a long-lived posterity* 1 Cl 16:11 (after Is 53:10).

μακρόθεν adv. of μακρός (H. Gk.: Chrysippus in Athen. 4, 137f; Polyb. 29, 8, 4; Strabo 3, 3, 4; Epict. 1, 16, 11; Dio Chrys.1, 68 al.; Aelian, NA 2, 15; 15, 12; PTebt 230 [II BC]; LXX; En 32:3; PsSol 11:3; TestJob 28:3; JosAs 24:17; ParJer 8:11; Philo; s. Phryn. 93 Lob.) ***from far away, from a distance*** (Ezk 23:40 ἔρχεσθαι μ.; Tob 13:13) μ. ἀκολουθεῖν *follow at a distance* **Mt 26:58 v.l.; Lk 22:54.** ἑστὼς μ. *stood some distance away* **18:13** (Syntipas collection of Aesop's Fables 37 p. 541 P. μ. ἑστῶσα).—Mostly ἀπὸ μ. (Ps.-Polemo Physiogn. 15 p. 319, 9 F.; Ps 137:6; 2 Esdr 3:13), since the suffix -θεν has lost its orig. separative force (B-D-F §104, 3; Rob. 300; KDieterich, Untersuchungen z. Geschichte d. griech. Sprache 1898, 183f.—Cp. ἀπ' οὐρανόθεν: Eratosthenes [III BC] 16, 11 Coll.; PGM 2, 83; SibOr 3, 691.—ἀπὸ μικρόθεν: POxy 1216, 6 [II/III AD]). ἀκολουθεῖν ἀπὸ μ. *follow at a distance* **Mt 26:58** (the rdg. varies; v.l. omits ἀπό); **Mk 14:54.** ἀπὸ μ. θεωρεῖν *look on from a distance* **Mt 27:55; Mk 15:40.** ὁρᾶν ἀπὸ μ. **5:6; 11:13; Lk 16:23.** ἀπὸ μ. ἑστηκέναι *stand at a distance* (Ps 37:12) **Lk 23:49** (for the whole situation as well as details in expression cp. Appian, Bell. Civ. 2, 85 §360 τὸ γύναιον τοῦ Πομπηίου καὶ οἱ φίλοι ταῦτα [i.e. the murder of Pompey] μακρόθεν ὁρῶντες); **Rv 18:10, 15, 17.** ἀπὸ μ. ἥκειν *live far away* **Mk 8:3** (FDanker, JBL 82, '63, 215; BvanIersel, NovT 7, '64, 184f).—DELG s.v. μακρός. M-M. TW.

μακροθυμέω (s. μακρόθυμος) 1 aor. ἐμακροθύμησα

❶ **to remain tranquil while waiting,** ***have patience, wait*** (Plut., Mor. 59f; Job 7:16; Sir 2:4; Bar 4:25; TestJob 22:5 al.; TestJos 2:7) abs. **Hb 6:15; Js 5:8.** μ. ἐπί τινι *wait patiently for someth.* **Js 5:7b.** μ. ἕως τ. παρουσίας τ. κυρίου *have patience until the coming of the Lord* vs. **7a.**

❷ **to bear up under provocation without complaint,** ***be patient, forbearing*** (LXX; ApcEsdr 3:6 p. 27, 11 Tdf.) abs. (Pr 19:11) of God (Iren. 1, 10, 3 [Harv. I 95, 5]; Hippol., Ref. 1 pref.) Dg 9:2. Of love **1 Cor 13:4.** ἀγάπη πάντα μακροθυμεῖ *love is patient about everything* 1 Cl 49:5. πρός τινα *toward someone* **1 Th 5:14.** μετά τινος *w. someone* IPol 6:2. εἴς τινα *toward someone* **2 Pt 3:9.** ἐπί τινι *w. someone* (Sir 18:11; 29:8; cp. ἐφ' ἡμᾶς TestJob 11:10; ἐπ' αὐτούς ApcEsdr 3:6) **Mt 18:26, 29; Lk 18:7** (s. FDanker, Jesus and the New Age, '88 ad loc. on the sequence of thought; for an alternate view s. 3 below).

❸ ***delay*** **Lk 18:7** μακροθυμεῖ (textually uncertain [v.l. -θυμῶν ἐπ' αὐτοῖς] and difficult to interpret, but cp. Mt 18:12 for the mixture of tenses in a question) may be transl.: *will (God) delay long in helping them?* (NRSV; s. Weizsäcker[3–8]; Fitzmyer, Luke ad loc., w. emphasis on Sir 35:19; μ.=delay: Artem. 4, 11).—Jülicher, Gleichn. 286ff; HSahlin, Zwei Lk-Stellen: Lk 6:43–45; 18:7: SymbBUps 4, '45, 9–20; HRiesenfeld, NT Aufsätze (JSchmid Festschr.), '63, 214–17 (Lk 18:7); but see KBeyer, Semit. Syntax im NT, '62, 268 n. 1.—DELG s.v. θυμός. M-M. TW.

μακροθυμία, ας, ἡ (s. two next entries; Menand.; Strabo 5, 4, 10; Comp. I, 282ff; LXX; TestJob, Test12Patr; SyrBar 12:4 [?]; ApcEsdr 2:8 p. 25, 30 Tdf.)

❶ **state of remaining tranquil while awaiting an outcome,** ***patience, steadfastness, endurance*** (Menand., fgm. 19; Plut., Lucull. 514 [32, 3; 33, 1]; Comp. I, 282ff; Is 57:15; PLond VI, 1917, 5 [IV AD]; 1 Macc 8:4; TestJob 27:7; TestDan 2:1; Jos., Bell. 6, 37; Orig., C. Cels. 2, 34, 41 [w. ἀνεξικακία]) w. ὑπομονή (TestJos 2:7) **Col 1:11;** 1 Cl 64; IEph 3:1; cp. **2 Ti 3:10.** διὰ πίστεως καὶ μακροθυμίας *through faith and steadfastness* **Hb 6:12.** ὑπόδειγμα τ. κακοπαθίας κ. τ. μακροθυμίας **Js 5:10.** W. ταπεινοφροσύνη Hs 8, 7, 6; cp. 9, 15, 2.

❷ **state of being able to bear up under provocation,** ***forbearance, patience*** toward others (Artem. 2, 25 p. 119, 10)

ⓐ of human beings (Pr 25:15; Sir 5:11; TestJos 17:2) w. other virtues **2 Cor 6:6; Gal 5:22;** 1 Cl 62:2. W. ἐπιείκεια (cp. EpArist 188) 1 Cl 13:1. W. πραΰτης **Col 3:12.** W. ἐγκράτεια B 2:2. ἐν πάσῃ μακροθυμίᾳ **2 Ti 4:2.** In contrast to ὀξυχολία: Hm 5, 1, 3 and 6; 5, 2, 3 and 8. μετὰ μακροθυμίας ἀνεχόμενοι ἀλλήλων **Eph 4:2.**

ⓑ of transcendent beings—**α.** of God (ApcEsdr 2:8; Did., Gen. 186, 10 [restored]) **Ro 2:4; 9:22; 1 Pt 3:20;** IEph 11:1.

β. of Christ **1 Ti 1:16; 2 Pt 3:15.**—S. ὑπομονή 1, end.—DELG s.v. θυμός. M-M. EDNT. TW.

μακρόθυμος, ον (s. two prec. entries and next; M. Ant. 6, 30, 10; Anth. Pal. 11, 317, 1; LXX; TestJob 21:4; TestDan 6:9; JosAs 11 cod. A [p. 54, 7 Bat.] and Pal 364) **pert. to being self-controlled in the face of provocation, *patient, forbearing, tolerant, even-tempered.***

ⓐ of human beings (Pr 14:29; 15:18; 16:32 al.) Hv 1, 2, 3; m 5, 1, 1; cp. 2; D 3:8. μακρόθυμον εἶναι Hm 8:10.

ⓑ of God (PLond VI 1917, 25 [IV AD, Christ.]; Ex 34:6; Num 14:18; 2 Esdr 19:17 al.) Hs 8, 11, 1. W. φιλάνθρωπος Dg 8:7; ὁ μ. *the one who is patient* i.e. God B 3:6. τὸ μ. αὐτοῦ βούλημα 1 Cl 19:3.—TW.

μακροθύμως (adv. of μακρόθυμος) ***patiently*** ἀκούειν τινός *listen to someone with patience* **Ac 26:3.**—TW.

μακρός, ά, όν (Hom.+; loanw. in rabb.).—❶ **pert. to taking a relatively long time, *long;*** the neut. as adv. (such use of the neut. either of space or time: since Hom., of space e.g. Il. 2, 224 μακρὰ βοᾶν=to shout so as to be heard at a great distance; TestJob 31:2 οἱ δὲ μακρά μου ὄντες [funct. as prep.]; of time ViZech 6 ἐν γήρει μακρῷ; Jos.Jos., Ant. 6, 241) μακρὰ προσεύχεσθαι *make long prayers* **Mt 23:13 [14] v.l.; Mk 12:40; Lk 20:47.**

❷ **pert. to being relatively distant, *far away, distant*** (Aeschyl., Prom. 814 μ. ἀποικία; Mi 4:3=ViHab 6 [p. 86, 8 Schermann] εἰς γῆν μακράν) εἰς χώραν μ. **Lk 15:13; 19:12.**—B. 882. DELG. M-M.

μακροχρόνιος, ον (s. μακρός, χρόνος; Hippocr.+; Philo, Rer. Div. Her. 34; TestSol PVindobBosw 18, 34) ***long-lived*** (Porphyr., Vi. Pyth. 24 N.) ἵνα … ἔσῃ μ. ἐπὶ τῆς γῆς *that you may have a long life on the earth* **Eph 6:3** (Ex 20:12; Dt 5:16; cp. CPR V, 19, 5 ἰς μακροὺς χρόνους 'for long years to come').—M-M. TW.

μάλα 'very, exceedingly' s. the comparative form μᾶλλον.

μαλακία, ας, ἡ (s. two next entries; variously 'softness, weakness, weakliness, ailment' Hdt. et al.; pap, LXX, Philo; Jos., Ant. 4, 169; 17, 109; TestJos 17:7; loanw. in rabb.)

❶ **condition of bodily weakness, *debility, weakness, sickness*** (Menand., fgm. 177, 5 Kö.; Vit. Hom. 36; Dt 7:15; 28:61; Is 38:9) w. νόσος (as in Christian amulets, which are obviously dependent upon NT language: POxy 1151, 27; BGU 954, 12) **Mt 4:23; 9:35; 10:1.** εἰδὼς φέρειν μαλακίαν *who knows how to endure weakness* 1 Cl 16:3 (Is 53:3).

❷ **condition of inner weakness, *faint-heartedness, despondency, lack of energy*** (Thu. 1, 122, 4; Demosth. 11, 22) pl. (w. διψυχία) Hv 3, 11, 2; 3, 12, 3.—DELG s.v. μαλακός. M-M. TW.

μαλακίζομαι (s. μαλακός) perf. mid.-pass. 3 sing. μεμαλάκισται; 1 aor. pass. ἐμαλακίσθην (usually w. a neg. connotation 'be softened, be made effeminate, show cowardice' Thu.+; SIG[2] 850, 24; PSI 420, 16 [III BC]; PPetr II, 19, 2, 6 [III BC]; Sb 158; LXX, Test12Patr; JosAs 29:9; Philo; Jos., Bell. 4, 43, Ant. 6, 365; 18, 205) **to be in a weakened condition, *be/become weak, discouraged, sick*** μαλακισθέντες ἀπὸ τῶν βιωτικῶν πραγμάτων *weakened by the duties of everyday life* Hv 3, 11, 3 (μαλακίζεσθαι ἀπό as TestGad 1:4 v.l.).—μεμαλάκισται διὰ τὰς ἀνομίας ἡμῶν *he was made to suffer for our misdeeds* 1 Cl 16:5; cp. B 5:2 (both Is 53:5).—DELG s.v. μαλακός. M-M. s.v. μαλακία.

μαλακός, ή, όν (s. two prec. entries; 'soft': Hom. et al.; ins, pap, LXX, Philo; Jos., Ant. 8, 72 βύσσος μ.; Mel., P. 80, 594 στρωμνῆς μ.)

❶ **pert. to being yielding to touch, *soft,*** of things: clothes (Hom. et al.; Artem. 1, 78 p. 73, 10 ἱματίων πολυτελῶν κ. μαλακῶν; PSI 364, 5 ἱμάτιον μαλ.) μ. ἱμάτια *soft garments,* such as fastidious people wear **Lk 7:25.** (τὰ) μ. *soft clothes* (Sb 6779, 57; s. λευκός 2, end) **Mt 11:8ab.**

❷ **pert. to being passive in a same-sex relationship, *effeminate*** esp. of *catamites,* of men and boys who are sodomized by other males in such a relationship, opp. ἀρσενοκοίτης (Dionys. Hal. 7, 2, 4; Dio Chrys. 49 [66], 25; Ptolem., Apotel. 3, 15, 10; Vett. Val. 113, 22; Diog. L. 7, 173; PHib 54, 11 [c. 245 BC] may have this mng.: a musician called Zenobius ὁ μαλακός [prob. with a sideline, according to Dssm., LO 131, 4—LAE 164, 4]. S. also a Macedon. ins in LDuchesne and CBayet, Mémoire sur une Mission au Mont Athos 1876 no. 66 p. 46; Plautus, Miles 668 cinaedus [Gk. κίναιδος] malacus; cp. the atttack on the morality of submissive homoeroticism Aeschin. 1, 188; DCohen, Greece and Rome 23, '76, 181f) **1 Cor 6:9** ('male prostitutes' NRSV is too narrow a rendering; 'sexual pervert' REB is too broad)=Pol 5:3.—S. lit. s.v. ἀρσενοκοίτης. B. 1065. DELG. M-M.

Μαλελεήλ, ὁ indecl. (מַהֲלַלְאֵל; in Jos., Ant. 1, 79; 84 Μαλάηλος, ου) ***Maleleel*** (Gen 5:12), in the genealogy of Jesus **Lk 3:37.**

μαλία s. τρυμαλιά.

μάλιστα (superl. of the adv. μάλα; Hom.+).—❶ **to an unusual degree, *most of all, above all, especially, particularly, (very) greatly*** **Ac 20:38; 1 Ti 4:10; 5:17; 2 Ti 4:13; Tit 1:10; Phlm 16;** 1 Cl 13:1; Dg 1; 3:1; IEph 20:2; IPhld ins; MPol 13:1; Hv 1, 1, 8. καὶ μ. *and above all, particularly* (Plut., Mor. 835e; Jos., C. Ap. 1, 27; Just., D. 84, 4) **Ac 25:26; 1 Ti 5:8;** Hv 1, 2, 4. μ. δέ *but especially* (Il. 1, 16; Lesbonax Gramm. [II AD] p. 8 [ed. RMüller 1900]; TestAbr B 4 p. 109, 6 [Stone p. 66]; Jos., Vi. 14; Just., D. 4, 5; 48, 2) **Gal 6:10; Phil 4:22; 2 Pt 2:10;** IPol 3:1; Hm 12, 1, 2; s 8, 6, 5; 9, 10, 7. μ. γνώστην ὄντα σε *since you are outstandingly familiar* **Ac 26:3** (cp. Appian, Bell. Civ. 2, 26 §100 ὁ μάλιστα ἐχθρός=the bitterest enemy).

❷ **marker of high level of certitude, in answer to a question, *most assuredly, certainly*** 1 Cl 43:6 (Just., A II, 2, 18; D. 49, 2 al.).—DELG s.v. μάλα. M-M.

μᾶλλον (comp. of the adv. μάλα; Hom.+) 'more, rather'

❶ **to a greater or higher degree, *more*** **Phil 1:12.** πολλῷ μᾶλλον ἔκραζεν *he cried out even more loudly* **Mk 10:48; Lk 18:39.** ἔτι μᾶλλον καὶ μᾶλλον *more and more* (cp. Diog. L. 9, 10, 2) **Phil 1:9;** Hs 9, 1, 8. ἐγὼ μᾶλλον *I can do so even more* **Phil 3:4.** The thing compared is introduced by ἤ (Apollon. Paradox. 9; Appian, Iber. 90 §392; Lucian, Adv. Ind. 2) **Mt 18:13** or stands in the gen. of comparison (X., Mem. 4, 3, 8, Cyr. 3, 3, 45) πάντων ὑμῶν μ. γλώσσαις λαλῶ *I (can) speak in tongues more than you all* **1 Cor 14:18** (Just., A I, 12, 1 πάντων μᾶλλον ἀνθρώπων).—Abs. μ. can mean *to a greater degree (than before), even more, now more than ever* **Lk 5:15; J 5:18; 19:8; Ac 5:14; 22:2; 2 Cor 7:7.** Somet. it is also added to verbs: Σαῦλος μ. ἐνεδυναμοῦτο **Ac 9:22.**—In combination w. an adj. it takes the place of the comparative (Hom. et al.; Just., D. 107,

2 γενεὰν . . . μοιχαλίδα μ.; Synes., Ep. 123 p. 259d μ. ἄξιος) μακάριόν ἐστιν μᾶλλον **Ac 20:35** (s. 3c below). καλόν ἐστιν αὐτῷ μᾶλλον **Mk 9:42;** cp. **1 Cor 9:15.** πολλῷ μ. ἀναγκαῖά ἐστιν *they are even more necessary* **1 Cor 12:22.** πολλὰ τ. τέκνα τῆς ἐρήμου μᾶλλον ἢ τῆς ἐχούσης τ. ἄνδρα *the children of the desolate woman are numerous to a higher degree than* (the children) *of the woman who has a husband = the children are more numerous* **Gal 4:27** (Is 54:1).—Pleonastically w. words and expressions that already contain the idea 'more' (Kühner-G. I 26; OSchwab, Histor. Syntax der griech. Komparation III 1895, 59ff; B-D-F §246; Rob. 278) μ. διαφέρειν τινός **Mt 6:26; Lk 12:24.** περισσεύειν μᾶλλον **1 Th 4:1, 10;** w. a comp. (trag.; Hdt. 1, 32; X., Cyr. 2, 2, 12; Dio Chrys. 23 [40], 17; 32 [49], 14; Lucian, Gall. 13; Ps.-Lucian, Charid. 6; Just., A I, 19, 1 and D. 121, 2; Synes., Ep. 79 p. 227c; 103 p. 241d) πολλῷ μᾶλλον κρεῖσσον **Phil 1:23.** μᾶλλον περισσότερον ἐκήρυσσον **Mk 7:36.** περισσοτέρως μᾶλλον ἐχάρημεν *we rejoiced still more* **2 Cor 7:13.** μ. ἐνδοξότεροι Hs 9, 28, 4. ὅσῳ δοκεῖ μ. μείζων εἶναι *the more he seems to be great* 1 Cl 48:6b.

❷ **for a better reason, *rather, all the more*—ⓐ** *rather, sooner* (ApcMos 31 ἀνάστα μ., εὖξαι τῷ θεῷ) μ. χρῆσαι (X., Mem. 1, 2, 24) *rather take advantage of it* (i.e. either freedom or slavery) **1 Cor 7:21** (lit. on χράομαι 1a). The slaves who have Christian masters μᾶλλον δουλευέτωσαν *should render them all the better service* (so REB, NRSV) **1 Ti 6:2.** νῦν πολλῷ μ. ἐν τ. ἀπουσίᾳ μου *much more in my absence* **Phil 2:12.** οὐ πολὺ μ. ὑποταγησόμεθα τ. πατρί; *should we not much rather submit to the Father?* **Hb 12:9.** τοσούτῳ μ. ὅσῳ *all the more, since* **10:25.**

ⓑ *more (surely), more (certainly)* πόσῳ μ. σοί *how much more surely to you* **Phlm 16.** πόσῳ μ. ὑμᾶς . . . ἐξεγείρει *how much more will he raise you up* (vivid use of the pres.) AcPlCor 2:31. πολλῷ μ. **Ro 5:9** (s. HMüller, Der rabb. Qal-Wachomer Schluss. in paul. Theol., ZNW 58, '67, 73–92). Very oft. a conditional clause (εἰ) precedes it (Epicurus in Diog. L. 10, 91 εἰ γὰρ . . . , πολλῷ μᾶλλον ἄν=if . . . , how much more surely) εἰ τὸν χόρτον ὁ θεὸς οὕτως ἀμφιέννυσιν, οὐ πολλῷ μ. ὑμᾶς; *if God so clothes the grass,* (will God) *not much more surely* (clothe) *you?* **Mt 6:30.** Likew. εἰ . . . πολλῷ μ. **Ro 5:10, 15, 17; 2 Cor 3:9, 11;** εἰ . . . πόσῳ μ. *if . . . how much more surely* **Mt 7:11; 10:25; Lk 11:13; 12:28; Ro 11:12, 24; Hb 9:14.** εἰ . . . πῶς οὐχὶ μ.; *if . . . why should not more surely?* **2 Cor 3:8.** εἰ . . . πολὺ μ. ἡμεῖς *if . . . then much more surely we* **Hb 12:25.** εἰ ἄλλοι . . . οὐ μᾶλλον ἡμεῖς; *if others* (have a claim), *do we not more surely* (have one)*?* **1 Cor 9:12** (μ. can also mean *above all, especially,* e.g. Himerius, Or. 40 [Or. 6], 2).—CMaurer, Der Schluss 'a minore ad majus' als Element paul. Theol., TLZ 85, '60, 149–52.

❸ **marker of an alternative to someth., *rather*** in the sense *instead* (of someth.)**—ⓐ** following a negative that—**α.** is expressed: μὴ εἰσέλθητε. πορεύεσθε δὲ μ. *do not enter (into); go instead* **Mt 10:6.** μὴ φοβεῖσθε . . . φοβεῖσθε δὲ μ. vs. **28;** ἵνα μὴ τὸ χωλὸν ἐκτραπῇ, ἰαθῇ δὲ μ. **Hb 12:13.** μὴ . . . , μᾶλλον δέ **Eph 4:28; 5:11.** μὴ or οὐ . . . , ἀλλὰ μ. (TestBenj 8:3; JosAs 26:2 A [p. 80, 2 Bat.]; ParJer 2:5; Just., A I, 27, 5; Syntipas p. 17, 3; 43, 17) **Mt 27:24; Mk 5:26; Ro 14:13; Eph 5:4;** AcPt Ox 849, 20.

β. is unexpressed, though easily supplied fr. the context: πορεύεσθε μ. (do not turn to us), *rather go* **Mt 25:9.** ἵνα μ. τὸν Βαραββᾶν *that he should (release) Barabbas instead* (of Jesus) **Mk 15:11.** ἥδιστα μᾶλλον καυχήσομαι (I will not pray for release), *rather I will gladly boast* **2 Cor 12:9.** μᾶλλον παρακαλῶ (I do not order), *rather I request* **Phlm 9;** τοὐναντίον μ. *on the other hand rather* **2 Cor 2:7.** μᾶλλον αἰσχυνθῶμεν *we should be ashamed of ourselves* (rather than mistrust Mary of Magdala) GMary Ox 463, 25.

ⓑ οὐχὶ μᾶλλον *not rather* follows a positive statement: ὑμεῖς πεφυσιωμένοι ἐστέ, καὶ οὐχὶ μᾶλλον ἐπενθήσατε; *you are puffed up; should you not rather be sad?* **1 Cor 5:2.** διὰ τί οὐχὶ μ. ἀδικεῖσθε; *why do you not rather suffer wrong* (instead of doing wrong to others)*?* **6:7a;** cp. **7b.**

ⓒ μᾶλλον ἤ(περ) usually (exceptions: **Ac 20:35** [Unknown Sayings, 77–81: this is not an exception, and renders 'giving is blessed, not receiving']; **1 Cor 9:15** [but see s.v. ἤ]; **Gal 4:27**) excludes fr. consideration the content of the phrase introduced by ἤ (Tat. 13, 3 θεομάχοι μ. ἤπερ θεοσεβεῖς; Appian, Iber. 26 §101 θαρρεῖν θεῷ μᾶλλον ἢ πλήθει στρατοῦ=put his trust in God, not in . . .) ἠγάπησαν οἱ ἄνθρωποι μ. τὸ σκότος ἢ τὸ φῶς *people loved not light, but darkness* **J 3:19;** cp. **12:43.** ὑμῶν ἀκούειν μ. ἢ τοῦ θεοῦ, *not obey God, but you instead* **Ac 4:19;** cp. **5:29.—1 Ti 1:4; 2 Ti 3:4.** τῷ ναυκλήρῳ μ. ἐπείθετο ἢ τοῖς ὑπὸ Παύλου λεγομένοις *he did not pay attention to what Paul said, but to the captain of the ship* **Ac 27:11.** Likew. μᾶλλον ἑλόμενος ἤ *he chose the one rather than the other* **Hb 11:25.**

ⓓ μᾶλλον δέ *but rather, or rather,* or simply *rather,* introduces an expr. or thought that supplements and thereby corrects what has preceded (Aristoph., Plut. 634; X., Cyr. 5, 4, 49; Demosth. 18, 65; Philo, Aet. M. 23; Just., D. 27, 4; 29, 2; Ath. 17, 3 μ. δέ; cp. Ar.; Just., A I, 17, 4 and D. 79, 1 μ. δὲ καί) Χρ. Ἰ. ὁ ἀποθανών, μᾶλλον δὲ ἐγερθείς *Chr. J. who died, yes rather was raised* **Ro 8:34.** γνόντες θεόν, μᾶλλον δὲ γνωσθέντες ὑπὸ θεοῦ *since you have known God, or rather have been known by God* **Gal 4:9;** cp. **1 Cor 14:1, 5.**—Rydbeck 80ff. DELG s.v. μάλα. M-M. EDNT.

Μάλχος, ου, ὁ (Porphyr., Pyth. Vi. ins Πορφύριος ὁ καὶ Μ. [fr. Tyre] and Porphyr., Vi. Plot. 17 p. 111, 3ff Westerm.; Joseph. index, almost entirely of Gentiles, in fact of Nabataean Arabs; OGI 640, 3 [Palmyra]; ins in RDussaud, Mission dans les régions désertiques de la Syrie moyenne 1902, p. 644 no. 9; ins from the Hauran: RB 41, '32, p. 403 no. 12; p. 578 no. 130; 131; PBrem 5, 3 [117/19 AD]; 6, 3; HWuthnow, E. palmyren. Büste: ELittmann Festschr. '35, 63–69.—Zahn ad loc. [w. lit.]) ***Malchus,*** slave of the high priest, whom Peter wounded when Jesus was arrested **J 18:10.**—BHHW II 1130. M-M.

μάμμη, ης, ἡ (orig. 'mother', later) ***grandmother*** (so Menand., Sam. 28; Herodas 3, 34; 38; Plut., Mor. 704b al.; SIG 844b, 5; POxy 1644, 12 [63/62 BC]; PRein 49, 14; BGU 19 II, 7 al.; 4 Macc 16:9; Philo, Spec. Leg. 3, 14; Jos., Ant. 10, 237.—Lob. on Phryn. 133–35) **2 Ti 1:5** (μάμμη and μήτηρ mentioned together by name as Plut., Agis 4, 1.—Cp. also the influence of his grandmother Macrina and his mother Emmelia on the religious life of the fourth-century church father Basilius as he was growing up [Basilius, Ep. 223, 3 ἐκ παιδὸς ἔλαβον ἔννοιαν περὶ θεοῦ παρὰ τῆς μακαρίας μητρός μου καὶ τῆς μάμμης Μακρίνης]).—B. 109. DELG s.v. μάμμη. M-M.

μαμωνᾶς, ᾶ, ὁ (Aram. מָמוֹן, emphat. state מָמוֹנָא) *wealth, property* **Lk 16:9, 11** (SColella: ZNW 64, '73, 124–26). Personified, 'Mammon' **Mt 6:24; Lk 16:13;** 2 Cl 6:1.—EbNestle, EncBibl 2912ff; here (2914f) the etymology of the word is also treated in detail. S. also EKautzsch, Gramm. des Bibl.-Aram. 1884, 10; Dalman, Gramm.[2] 170f, RE[3] XII 1903, 153f; HZimmern, Akkadische Fremdwörter[2] 1917, 20; ERiggenbach, ASchlatter Festschr. 1922, 21ff; MBlack, An Aramaic Approach, 102.—The word is also found Mishnah Aboth 2, 17 and in the Damascus document p. 14, 20 Schechter 1910=LRost

(Kl. T. 167) ’33, p. 26, which cannot be dated w. certainty (s. Bousset, Rel. 15f); EMeyer, ABA 1919, 9, Abhdlg. p. 50; HRüger: ZNW 64, ’73, 127–31 (Canaanite loanword w. orig. mng. ‘food, maintenance, provisions’ fr. the root מון).—M-M. TW.

Μαναήν, ὁ indecl. (מְנַחֵם; 4 Km 15:14 Μαναήμ; Jos., Ant. 9, 229; 232 Μανάημος, ου [15, 374]. Other Jews w. this name in Schürer index) ***Manaen,*** one of the prophets and teachers in the Antioch church, described as Ἡρῴδου τοῦ τετραάρχου σύντροφος **Ac 13:1.**—On the name TNöldeke, Beiträge z. semit. Sprachwissensch. 1904, 99; Haenchen ad loc.; BHHW II 1136.—M-M.

Μαναΐμος, ου (Μανάημος Joseph.) ***Manaimos,*** name of a Christian man τὴν μητέρα Μαναΐμου τὴν ἐκ νεκρῶν ἀναστᾶσαν Papias (11:2); cp. Μαναήν.

Μανασσῆς, ῆ, acc. ῆ (-ῆν **Mt 1:10 v.l.;** Demetr.: 722 fgm. 1, 12 Jac.; מְנַשֶּׁה) ***Manasseh*** (predominantly a Jewish name. But a Cyprian ins [OHoffmann, D. griech. Dialekte I 1891 p. 75 no. 140] gives it as the name of a Gr-Rom. as well. See ἀββᾶ, end.)

❶ firstborn son of Joseph (Gen 41:51; JosAs 21:8; Philo, Joseph.), father of a tribe B 13:5 (cp. Gen 48:14). Of the tribe **Rv 7:6.**

❷ son of Hezekiah, Hebrew king (4 Km 21:1ff; 2 Ch 33:1ff; AscIs; Joseph.); in the genealogy of Jesus **Mt 1:10; Lk 3:23ff** D.—BHHW II 1136f (lit.).

μάνδρα, ας, ἡ (etym. uncertain; Soph. et al.; pap, LXX) ***sheep-fold*** B 16:5 (quotation of uncertain origin; cp. En 89:56; 66f).—DELG.

μανθάνω fut. μαθήσομαι LXX; 2 aor. ἔμαθον; impv. pl. μάθετε, ptc. μαθών; perf. 3 sg. μεμάθηκεν Jer 9:4, ptc. pl. μεμαθηκότες Jer 13:23; inf. μεμαθηκέναι Ps 118:7 (Hom.+)

❶ **to gain knowledge or skill by instruction, *learn*** abs. **1 Cor 14:31; 1 Ti 2:11; 2 Ti 3:7.** παρά τινος *learn from someone* as teacher (X., Cyr. 2, 2, 6; Appian, Iber. 23 §89 παρὰ τοῦ θεοῦ μ.; Sextus 353 μ. παρὰ θεοῦ; Philo, Deus Imm. 4; Just., D. 32, 5; 78, 1; Ath. 7:2) vs. **14b;** *be someone’s disciple* (μαθητής) EpilMosq 2. ἀπό τινος *from someone* (Theognis 1, 28f: Theognis teaches what ‘I myself as a παῖς ἔμαθον ἀπὸ τῶν ἀγαθῶν’; 1, 35; Jos., Ant. 8, 317) **Mt 11:29; Col 1:7.** W. acc. of the thing learned τὶ *someth.* **1 Cor 14:35.** ταῦτα AcPl Ha 1, 26. πάντα Hs 9, 1, 3 v.l. Teaching **Ro 16:17.** τὴν θεοσέβειαν τ. Χριστιανῶν Dg 1; cp. 11:2. τὰ δικαιώματα τ. κυρίου *the ordinances of the Lord* B 21:1. τὸν Χριστόν=Christian teaching **Eph 4:20** (Chion, Ep. 16, 8 θεὸν ἔμαθες=you have learned to know God; Tat. 2:2 ἕνα τὸν ἀπλανῆ δεσπότην μεμαθήκαμεν). W. attraction of a relative μένε ἐν οἷς (=ἐν τούτοις ἃ) ἔμαθες *stick to what you have learned* **2 Ti 3:14a.** W. obj. to be supplied fr. the context (γράμματα) **J 7:15** (Goodsp., Probs. 102–4). μ. τι ἀπό τινος *learn someth. from someone* B 9:9. μ. περὶ πάντων *receive instruction concerning all things* vs. 7 (περί τινος as Philo, Spec. Leg. 1, 42; Just., D. 87, 1; Ath. 7, 2). μ. τι ἔν τινι *learn fr. someone’s example* **1 Cor 4:6** (B-D-F §220, 2; Rob. 587).—μ. τι ἀπό τινος *learn someth. fr. someth.*: ἀπὸ τ. συκῆς μάθετε τ. παραβολήν **Mt 24:32; Mk 13:28.**—W. ὅτι foll. (Philo, Leg. All. 3, 51) B 9:8. W. inf. foll. (Aristoxenus, fgm. 96 αὐλεῖν) 1 Cl 8:4 (Is 1:17); 57:2. W. indirect question foll. (Just., A I, 40, 5 and D. 32, 2 al.; Mel., P. 46, 328) 1 Cl 21:8. τί ἐστιν *what this means* **Mt 9:13.** W. the question preceding (Just., A I, 56, 1) B 5:5; 6:9; 14:4; 16:2, 7; Dg 4:6. Used w. other verbs: ἀκούειν κ. μ. (Pla., Ap. 33b, 7, Ep. 344d; Theocr. 5, 39; Ael. Aristid. 45 p. 33 D. p. 40; cp. Polyb. 3, 32, 9 ὅσῳ διαφέρει τὸ μαθεῖν τοῦ μόνον ἀκούειν, τοσούτῳ . . .) **J 6:45.** μ. καὶ παραλαμβάνειν **Phil 4:9.** οὐδεὶς ἐδύνατο μαθεῖν τ. ᾠδήν *no one was able to learn the song* (so e.g. Bousset; Allo; REB; NRSV) **Rv 14:3;** others prefer the related sense *understand* (as Lysias 10, 15; Pla., Meno 84d, Tht. 174b, Euthyd. 277e); for mng. *hear,* s. 4 below.

❷ **make the acquaintance of someth.,** ***learn***—ⓐ *learn about, come to know* τὸν τοῦ Χριστιανισμοῦ λόγον *Christian teaching* MPol 10:1. τὶ παρά τινος *someth. fr. someone* (Sir 8:8f; EpArist 198; Philo, Fuga 8, Leg. All. 3, 194; Jos., Vi. 62; Just., D. 2, 2; 78, 10; Tat. 36, 2) Dg 4:1; Papias (2:3). *Take note* τὶ *of someth.* MPol 20:1.

ⓑ *find out, ascertain* (trag., X.; PRyl 77, 42; POxy 1067, 6; 1671, 20; LXX) τὶ ἀπό τινος *find someth. out fr. someone* **Gal 3:2.** W. ὅτι foll. (Arrian, Anab. 2, 5, 7; Esth 1:1n; Jos., Ant. 12, 208) **Ac 23:27.** Abs. B 16:8.

❸ **to come to a realization, with implication of taking place less through instruction than through experience or practice, *learn, appropriate to oneself:*** ἔμαθεν ἀφ’ ὧν ἔπαθεν τὴν ὑπακοήν *he learned obedience through what he suffered = he realized obedience through suffering* **Hb 5:8** (for the consonance cp. Aeschyl., Agam. 177 τῷ πάθει μάθος; Hdt. 1, 207, 1 τὰ δέ μοι παθήματα . . . μαθήματα; schol. on Pla. 222b ἐὰν μὴ πάθῃς, οὐ μὴ μάθῃς; Philo, Fuga 138 ἔμαθον μὲν ὃ ἔπαθον. Further exx. in HWindisch ad loc. and CSpicq, RB 56, ’49, 551.—A similar play on words in Theognis 369f μωμεῖσθαι . . . μιμεῖσθαι=[they can] find fault [with me, but not] do as I do]).—W. inf. foll. (X., Cyr. 1, 6, 6; Lucian, Dial. Deor. 14, 2; Dt 14:23; Is 2:4; Just., D 15, 1; Ath. 1, 4) τ. ἴδιον οἶκον εὐσεβεῖν **1 Ti 5:4;** cp. **Tit 3:14.** μ. κατὰ Χριστιανισμὸν ζῆν IMg 10:1, cp. IRo 4:3. ἔμαθον ἐν οἷς εἰμι αὐτάρκης εἶναι *I have learned, in whatever state I am, to be content* (s. αὐτάρκης) **Phil 4:11.** ἀργαὶ μανθάνουσιν περιερχόμεναι τὰς οἰκίας **1 Ti 5:13** presents many difficulties fr. a linguistic point of view. Perh. εἶναι or ζῆν is to be inserted after ἀργαί (X., An. 3, 2, 25 ἂν ἅπαξ μάθωμεν ἀργοὶ ζῆν; so B-D-F §416, 2; Mlt. 229; Dibelius, Hdb./Hermeneia ad loc.). Others substitute λανθάνουσιν by conjecture (e.g. PSchmiedel, ThBl 1, 1922, 222, Zürcher Bibelübers. ’31, appendix to NT, note 12).

❹ ***hear*** οὐδεὶς ἐδύνατο μαθεῖν τ. ᾠδήν **Rv 14:3** according to some this means *no one was able to hear the song* (Boll 18ff; Lohmeyer; Behm). But s. 1 end.—B. 1222. M-M. TW. Sv.

μανία, ας, ἡ (Pind. et al.; pap, LXX, Philo; Jos., Bell. 1, 506, Ant. 2, 330; apolog. exc. Mel.) ***madness, frenzy, delirium.*** Freq. in a non-diagnostic sense of eccentric or bizarre behavior in word or action (cp. the passage [II BC] fr. an unedited Tebtunis papyrus in M-M s.v. φαίνῃ εἰς μανίαν ἐμπεπτωκέναι, διὸ λόγον σαυτοῦ οὐ ποιεῖς καὶ ὑπομεμένηκας=you appear to have lost your mind, for you show little respect for yourself, and your behavior is quite bizarre. So Solon is reproached with μανία by his opponents: Solon 9, 1 D.[3] s. μαίνομαι) τὰ πολλά σε γράμματα εἰς μανίαν περιτρέπει *too much study is driving you mad* (i.e. *turning you into a fanatic*) **Ac 26:24.**—DELG. M-M. EDNT. TW. Sv.

μάννα, τό indecl. (מָן. The Gk. form μάννα [LXX—only Ex 16 μάν; GrBar 6:11; Philo, Leg. Alleg. 2, 84, Det. Pot. Insid. 118; Jos., Ant. 3, 32; Just.] is prob. explained by the influence of the Gk. word ἡ μάννα=‘little grain, granule’ [Hippocr. et al.; POxy 1088, 21; PGM 4, 1874]. The fem. inflection also Jos., Ant. 3, 296; 5, 21; SibOr 7, 149.) ‘manna’, often identified with the sweetish exudate of the manna tamarisk and related trees, produced by the sting of an insect; it dries and falls down in the form of small grains. S. AKaiser, Der heutige Stand der Mannafrage: Mitteilungen d. Thurgauischen Naturforsch. Gesellschaft, Heft 25, 1924, Wanderungen u. Wandlungen in d. Sinaiwüste 1886–1927: ibid. 1928, 21ff; HDarlington, Open Court 42, 1928, 372–81; FBodenheimer and OTheodor, Ergebnisse d. Sinai-Exped. 1927 der hebr. Univers. Jerus. 1930; BMalina, The Palestinian Manna Tradition, '68.

❶ **a food esp. associated with Israel's experience,** ***manna***

ⓐ supplied to the Israelites during their wanderings **J 6:31, 49.**

ⓑ kept, acc. to Ex 16:32ff, in the tabernacle **Hb 9:4.**

ⓒ in imagery of honey eaten by John the Baptist: οὗ ἡ γεῦσις ἡ τοῦ μ. *that tasted like manna* GEb 13, 79.

❷ **a heavenly food, linked by name with the foregoing,** ***manna*** τὸ μ. τὸ κεκρυμμένον *the hidden manna,* **Rv 2:17.**—W-S. 10a 2 p. 92; BHHW II 1141ff.—M-M. TW.

μαντεύομαι (s. next entry; Hom. et al.; ins, LXX, Philo, Joseph.) mid. dep. aor.: impv. 2 sg. μάντευσαι 1 Km 28:8; inf. μαντεύσασθαι Ez 21:26; also w. pass. mng. for pass. forms; in our lit., as well as LXX, always in a context critical of the practitioner.

❶ **to practice divination,** ***prophesy, divine, give an oracle*** (Hom. et al.; 1 Km 28:8=Jos., Ant. 6, 330; SibOr 4, 3; Ar., Tat., Ath., Iren.; Orig., C. Cels. 7, 4, 15 [of the Pythia]; Hippol., Ref. 4, 13, 2) of a soothsayer possessed by a ventriloquistic spirit **Ac 16:16.**

❷ **to consult a diviner,** ***consult an oracle*** (Pind. et al.; Artem. 3, 20; Jos., C. Ap. 1, 306) of doubting Christians Hm 11:4.—M-M.

μάντις, εως, ὁ (Hom. et al.; ins, LXX, Philo; Jos., Bell. 1, 80, C. Ap. 1, 257 al.; Ath. 21, 5; Theoph. Ant. 3, 17 [p. 283, 6] w. προγνώστης) **one who practices divination,** ***soothsayer, diviner, prophet,*** of dissident Christian prophets, to whom poorly grounded believers go, as to soothsayers Hm 11:2.—DELG. TW. Sv.

Μάξιμος, ου, ὁ a name freq. (Polyb. 3, 87, 6 al.; ins, pap, Joseph.) found, ***Maximus,*** a Christian Hv 2, 3, 4.

μαραίνω aor. 3 pl. ptc. ἐμάραναν Wsd 19:21, opt. 3 sg. μαράναι Job 15:30. Pass.: 1fut. μαρανθήσομαι; 1 aor. ἐμαράνθην; pf. ptc. μεμαραμμένος (B-D-F §72) (Hom. et al.; ins, pap, LXX; gener. 'quench, destroy') in our lit. only pass. in act. sense: **to disappear gradually,** ***die out, fade, disappear, wither*** of plants (schol. on Nicander, Ther. 677; Job 15:30; Wsd 2:8) ὡς μεμαραμμέναι *as if withered* Hs 9, 1, 7; cp. 9, 23, 1f. Of one's spirit v 3, 11, 2 (cp. Appian, Bell. Civ. 5, 90 §379 μαραίνεσθαι of the πνεῦμα, wind=abate fully, die down; Jos., Ant. 11, 56; ApcSed 7:6 of beauty). Of Mary's name τὸ ὄνομα αὐτῆς οὐ μαρανθήσεται εἰς τὸν αἰῶνα GJs 6:3 (codd. not Bodmer). Of pers. (Aristaen., Ep. 1, 10 μαραινόμενος τ. νοῦν), in gnomic statement: ὁ πλούσιος ἐν ταῖς πορείαις … μαρανθήσεται *a rich person will wither away while trafficking* **Js 1:11** (s. the grave-inscription Sb 5199, 2 ἐμαράνθη; Jos., Bell. 6, 274 λιμῷ μαραινόμενοι; TestSim 3:3).—**Mt 5:13 v.l.; Lk 14:34 v.l.** (both for μωρανθῇ).—BHHW II 1144. DELG. M-M. TW. Spicq.

μαράνα θά=מָרַנָא תָא (our) ***Lord, come!*** (μαρὰν ἀθά [some mss. and edd.] renders מָרַן אֲתָא [our] *Lord has come*) an Aramaic formula which D 10:6 associates with what appears to be the early Christian liturgy of the Lord's Supper. Used without explanation by Paul **1 Cor 16:22.** (On D 10:6 s. JEmerton, Maranatha and Ephphatha, JTS 18, '67, 427–31 and Moule below. On both passages P-ÉLangevin, Jésus Seigneur, '67, 168–208; 236–98.)—EKautzsch, Gramm. d. Bibl.-Aram. 1884, 12; 174, StKr. 74, 1901, 296; EbNestle, Theol. Studien aus Württemb. 5, 1884, 186ff; TNöldeke, GGA 1884, 1023; Dalman, Gramm.[2] 152, 3; 357, 1, Worte 269; FSchulthess, D. Problem d. Sprache Jesu 1917, p. 28, 50; Dssm., D. Urgeschichte d. Christentums im Lichte der Sprachforschung 1910, 26ff; Zahn, Einl. I[3] 216f; WBousset, Jesus der Herr 1916, 22ff; EHommel, ZNW 15, 1914, 317–22ff (מָרַן אָתָא='our Lord is the sign'='the א and the ת'. So earlier CBruston, Rev. de Théol. et des Quest. Rel. 22, 1913, 402–8); FDölger, Sol Salutis 1920, 153ff; CFabricius, Urbekenntnisse d. Christenheit: RSeeberg Festschr. 1929 I 21–41; Field, Notes, 180; HCadbury, JBL 58, '39, p. x; Goodsp., Probs. 166–68; CMoule, NTS 6, '60, 307–10; SSchulz, ZNW 53, '62, 125–44; JFitzmyer, To Advance the Gospel '81, 218–35.—TW.

μαργαρίτης, ου, ὁ (Theophr.; Strabo; Aelian, NA 10, 13; pap; En 18:7; TestJud 13:5; loanw. in rabb.) ***pearl***—ⓐ w. gold **1 Ti 2:9.** W. gold and precious stones **Rv 17:4; 18:12, 16.** Of the pearls that serve as gates for the heavenly city **21:21** (each gate a single pearl: EBurrows, JTS 43, '42, 177–79). καλοὶ μ. **Mt 13:45;** πολύτιμος μ. *a very valuable pearl* vs. **46** (μ. more in demand than gold, Chares of Mitylene [IV BC]: 125 fgm. 3 Jac. Among the Indians worth 3 times as much as pure gold: Arrian, Ind. 8, 13 and always in great demand: ibid. 8, 9)

ⓑ in imagery, in a proverb (s. χοῖρος) βάλλειν τοὺς μ. ἔμπροσθεν τ. χοίρων *throw pearls to swine* i.e. entrust someth. precious (cp. the reff. cited in Betz, SM 499 n. 590; s. also Eur., Bacch. 480; on the value placed on pearls in antiquity s. also HUsener, Die Perle: Weizsäcker Festschr. 1892, 203–13) to people who cannot or will not appreciate it **Mt 7:6** (difft. GSchwartz, NovT 14, '72, 18–25). πνευματικοὶ μ. *spiritual pearls* of a martyr's bonds IEph 11:2.—HKahane, Traditio 13, '57, 421–24; RAC 505–52; Kl. Pauly 3, 1020f; BHHW III 1422f.—DELG. EDNT. TW. Sv.

Μάρθα, ας, ἡ (מָרְתָא 'mistress'; s. B-D-F §53, 3. Plut., Mar. 414 [17, 2] Σύραν γυναῖκα, Μάρθαν ὄνομα; BGU 1153 I, 3 [14 BC]; 1155, 4 [10 BC]) ***Martha,*** acc. to **Lk 10:38, 40f** sister of Mary (JBrutscheck, Die Maria-Marta-Erzählung '86; WCarter, CBQ 58, '96, 264–80), acc. to **J 11:1, 5, 19ff, 24, 30, 39** also sister of Lazarus of Bethany.—**12:2.**—BHHW II 1156. M-M.

Μαρία, ας, ἡ (vase ins fr. Samaria-Sebaste: SEG VIII, 110 [I BC/I AD]; two ostraca: PMeyer, nos. 33 and 56 [both II AD]; s. Dssm., LO 97f; 302; a third ostracon in Dssm., LO 260 [s. LAE[2] 121, n. 11; 122; 306, n. 6: the addition of the mother's name is regular in magical texts]; Jos., Bell. 6, 201; Just., Mel.) and Μαριάμ indecl. (מִרְיָם, Miriam [prophet and sister of Moses Ex 15:20f; Demetr.: 722 fgm. 2, 3 Jac.; Ezech. Trag. 5, 18 and 23 in Clem. of Al., Strom. 1, 23, 155, 4; Philo; Just., D. 78, 3] 1 Cl 4:11) and Μαριάμμη (GMary 463, 3; GJs 16:3; 17:2f.—Joseph. writes the name Μαριά[μ]μη, ης [Ant. 3, 54].—On the name and its various forms s. B-D-F §53, 3; Mlt-H. 144f; OBardenhewer, Der Name Maria 1895; HvSoden, Die Schriften des NTs I 1906, 1373f; FZorell, ZKT 30, 1906, 356ff; EKönig, ZNW 17, 1916, 257–63; MNoth, D. isr. Personennamen 1929; WvonSoden, Bibel u. Alter Orient: ZAW Beih. 162, 129–33; MGörg, BZ '79, 285–89) ***Mary.***

❶ the mother of Jesus. The foll. forms of the name are attested in the var. cases: Μαρία as nom. **Lk 2:19,** otherw. only occasionally as v.l. (D **Lk 1:30, 39, 56;** cp. vss. **34, 38, 46**). Gen. Μαρίας **Mt 1:16, 18; 2:11; Mk 6:3; Lk 1:41;** IEph 7:2; 18:2; 19:1; ITr 9:1; AcPlCor 1:14; 2:5. Acc. Μαρίαν **Mt 1:20** (v.l. -άμ); AcPl

Ha 8, 26; M. τὴν Γαλιλαίαν AcPlCor 2:14.—Μαριάμ as nom. **Mt 1:16 v.l.; 13:55; Lk 1:27, 34, 38f, 46, 56; 2:19** (v.l. -ρία); as acc. **Mt 1:20 v.l.; Lk 2:16;** GJs 6:3 (not Bodmer); as voc. **Lk 1:30;** σὺν Μαριάμ **Lk 2:5; Ac 1:14;** πρὸς Μαριάμ **Lk 2:34.** Little is known about the life of this Mary; in the infancy narratives **Mt 1f; Lk 1f** and esp. in the apocryphal gospels (29 times GJs; s. AFuchs, Konkordanz) she plays a great role; s. WBauer, D. Leben Jesu im Zeitalter d. ntl. Apokryphen 1909; HUsener, ZNW 4, 1903, 1ff. In **Mk 3:31f** and parallels, where she and the brothers and sisters of Jesus are prominently mentioned, no indication of any interest in his movement is given. But **Ac 1:14** mentions Mary and his brothers (brothers and sisters? s. ἀδελφός 1) among the members of the early church. The mother of Jesus is also mentioned in the Fourth Gospel, though not by name.—RSeeberg, Die Herkunft der Mutter Jesu: Bonwetsch Festschr. 1918, 13ff; JBlinzler, Jes. u. s. Mutter nach dem Zeugn. der Evv.: Klerusblatt 23, '42; 24, '43; UHolzmeister, De anno mortis Deip. Virg.: Marianum 4, '42, 167–82; FWillam, D. Leb. Marias[3] '42; HRäisänen, D. Mutter Jesu im NT, '69; JMcHugh, The Mother of Jesus in the NT '75; RBrown, KDornfried et al., Mary in the NT '78; RBrown, The Birth of the Messiah '77.—ABD IV 586 (lit.). LexThK VII 25–28. TRE XXII 115–19. EDNT. II 386f.

❷ *Mary Magdalene* (s. Μαγδαληνή). Forms of her name: Μαρία **Mt 27:56; 61 v.l.; 28:1 v.l.; Mk 15:40, 47; 16:1, 9** (Μαρίᾳ); **Lk 8:2; 24:10; J 19:25; 20:1, 11, 16 v.l., 18 v.l.** Μαριάμ **Mt 27:56 v.l., 61; 28:1; Mk 15:40 v.l.; J 19:25 v.l.; 20:1 v.l., 11 v.l., 16** (voc.), **18;** GPt 12:50. Acc. to the gospels this woman, one of Jesus' most faithful followers, was cured by Jesus of possession by seven hostile spirits (**Mk 16:9; Lk 8:2**). She appears in the Passion Narrative w. women companions; also in the synoptic account of Easter morning. In J she is the only one mentioned at the grave, and sees the resurrected Lord (likew. in the long ending of Mk). Later ecclesiastical gossip identified her without warrant w. the sinful woman who anointed Jesus in the house of the Pharisee (Lk 7:37, 39). CLattey: Exp 7th ser., 8, 1909, 55–63; UHolzmeister, Die Magdalenenfrage in der kirchl. Überl.: ZKT 46, 1922, 402ff; JSickenberger, Ist die Magdalenenfrage wirklich unlösbar? BZ 17, 1926, 63ff; PKetter, D. Magdalenenfrage 1929; RBruckberger, M. Magdalena, '54; MHengel, M. Magdalena u. d. Frauen als Zeugen: FMichel, '63, 243–56; AMarjanen, The Woman Jesus Loved '96 (Nag Hammadi); HMelzer-Keller, Geist und Leben 72, '99, 97–111. LexThK VII 39f; BHHW II 1151. S. Simpson and Burkitt under 5 below.

❸ the 'other' *Mary,* mother of James (s. Ἰάκωβος 3) and Joses (s. Ἰωσῆς 2). Form of the name Μαρία **Mt 27:56, 61** (ἡ ἄλλη Μαρία; cp. PPetr III, 59[c]); **28:1** (ἡ ἄλλ. M.—JMackay, The Other M.: ET 40, 1929, 319–21); **Mk 15:40, 47; 16:1; Lk 24:10.** She was one of the followers of Jesus present as a spectator at the events on Golgotha. Hence she could be identical with

❹ Μαρία (v.l. Μαριάμ) ἡ τοῦ Κλωπᾶ M., *the wife of Clopas* **J 19:25.**

❺ *Mary,* acc. to **Lk 10:39, 42** sister of Martha, acc. to **J 11:1f, 19f, 28, 31f, 45; 12:3** also sister of Lazarus, resident in Bethany. Forms of the name: Μαρία **Lk 10:39 v.l., 42 v.l.; J 11:2 v.l., 20 v.l., 32 v.l.; 12:3 v.l.;** Μαρίας **J 11:1;** Μαρίαν **J 11:19 v.l., 28 v.l., 31 v.l., 45 v.l.** Μαριάμ **Lk 10:39, 42; J 11:2, 20, 32; 12:3;** as acc. **J 11:19, 28, 31, 45.**—ASimpson, M. of Bethany, M. of Magdala, and Anonyma: ET 20, 1909, 307–18; FBurkitt, M. Magd. and M., Sister of Martha: ET 42, '31, 157–59.

❻ the mother of John Mark, owner of a house in Jerusalem (οἰκία τῆς Μαρίας), who placed it at the disposal of Christians for meetings **Ac 12:12.**

❼ an otherw. unknown Christian, probably of Jewish descent (yet Μαρία appears in Ramsay, CB I/2, 557f nos. 439 and 440 as the fem. form of the Roman name Marius), who is greeted **Ro 16:6** (ἀσπάσασθε Μαρίαν; v.l. Μαριάμ [as early as P[46]]), w. the additional note that she rendered outstanding service to the receivers of the letter.—EDNT. M-M.

Μαριάμ, ἡ indecl. (on the form of the name see the beginning of the preceding entry) ***Miriam,*** a prophet and sister of Aaron and Moses (Ex 15:20f; Num 12) 1 Cl 4:11.

Μαρκίων, ωνος, ὁ ***Marcion,*** a rare name (Sb 4604, 3).

❶ a Christian of Smyrna MPol 20:1 (Μάρκου is also attested, as well as the form Μαρκιανοῦ, which is in the Lat. version and is preferred by Lghtf.; s. on this OvGebhardt, ZWT18, 1875, 370ff).

❷ the famous heretic EpilMosq 3 (Just., A I, 26, 5; 58, 1).—AvHarnack, Marcion[2] 1924; MEnslin, The Pontic Mouse: ATR 27, '45, 1–16.—ABD IV 514–20.

Μαρκιωνιστής, οῦ, ὁ ***Marcionite,*** *follower of Marcion* EpilMosq 3 (s. Μαρκίων 2).

Μᾶρκος, ου, ὁ (on the accent s. B-D-F §41, 3; Rob. 235) ***Mark,*** a name found rather freq. (Diod. S. 11, 63, 1; Plut., ins, pap; Philo, Leg. ad Gai. 62; 294; Joseph.; Just., D. 141, 5; Ath. [ins]); surname of John (s. Ἰωάν[ν]ης 6), son of Mary of Jerusalem (s. Μαρία 6). Perh. introduced to Paul by Barnabas, his cousin (**Col 4:10**); he accompanied Paul and Barnabas on the so-called first missionary journey, but left them before it was completed, and later became the cause of an open break betw. them. **Ac 12:12, 25; 15:37, 39.** The same pers. is certainly referred to **Phlm 24; 2 Ti 4:11; 1 Pt 5:13. Title of the second gosp.** κατὰ Μᾶρκον; cp. Papias (2:14) (on the two names of a man who was active and well known, among Semites and Greeks, we may compare the circumstance that the Carthaginian Ἀσδρούβας [Hasdrubal, II BC] was known as Κλειτόμαχος among the Greeks [Diog. L. 4, 67]). M. . . . ἑρμηνευτὴς Πέτρου γενόμενος Papias (2:15).—Zahn, Einl. II[3] 204ff; Jülicher, RE XII 288ff; EBarnikol, Personenprobleme d. AG, Joh. Markus, Silas u. Titus '31; WReilly, CBQ 1, '39, 223–31; RTaylor, ET 54, '43, 136–38; KNiederwimmer, ZNW 58, '67, 172–87.—M-M.

μάρμαρος, ου, ὁ (Hom. et al. in the sense 'stone, block of rock') ***marble*** (so since Theophr., Lap. 9; Strabo 9, 1, 23; IG IV[2]/1, 109 III, 103 [III BC]; PLeid X, 10, 12; BGU 952, 10; EpJer 71; Jos., Bell. 4, 532; both masc. and fem.; neut. TestSol) as precious material **Rv 18:12.**—M-M.

Μάρτιος, ίου, ὁ (Lat. loanw.: Martius) ***March*** πρὸ ἑπτὰ καλανδῶν Μαρτίων=February 23, MPol 21.

μαρτυρέω impf. ἐμαρτύρουν; fut. μαρτυρήσω; 1 aor. ἐμαρτύρησα; pf. μεμαρτύρηκα. Pass.: impf. ἐμαρτυρούμην; 1 aor. ἐμαρτυρήθην **Hb 11:2, 4, 39;** pf. μεμαρτύρημαι (s. four next entries; Semonides, Hdt.+)

❶ **to confirm or attest someth. on the basis of personal knowledge or belief,** ***bear witness, be a witness.***—ⓐ to offer testimony—α. act. ὑμεῖς μαρτυρεῖτε *you are witnesses* **J 15:27.** ἐὰν θέλωσιν μαρτυρεῖν *if they are willing to appear as witnesses* **Ac 26:5.**—**J 12:17; 1J 5:6f.** Parenthetically, emphasizing the correctness of a statement, μαρτυρῶ *I can testify* (POxy 105, 13 Σαραπίων μαρτυρῶ='I, S., am witness'; PLond III, 1164 [f], 35 al. p. 162.—B-D-F §465, 2; Rob. 434) **2 Cor 8:3.** περί τινος *bear witness, testify concerning someone* or *someth.* (PGrenf II, 73, 16 ὅταν ἔλθῃ σὺν θεῷ, μαρτυρήσει σοι περὶ ὧν αὐτὴν πεποιήκασιν; Jos., C. Ap. 1, 217, Vi. 259) **J 1:7f, 15** (in the very likely case that μαρτυρεῖ refers to the past, cp. Caecil. Calact., fgm. 75 p. 58, 2ff, where examples are given of the interchange of tenses: Demosth. 59, 34 τοὺς ὁρῶντας for τ. ἑωρακότας; Eur., Androm. fgm. 145 Nauck[2] ὁρῶ ἀντὶ τοῦ εἶδον; Thu. 2, 35, 1 ἐπαινοῦσι ἀντὶ τοῦ ἐπῄνεσαν); **2:25; 5:31, 32a, 36f, 39; 7:7; 8:13f, 18ab; 10:25; 15:26; 21:24; 1J 5:9.** μαρτύρησον περὶ τοῦ κακοῦ *testify to the wrong* **J 18:23** (μ.=furnish proof X., Symp. 8, 12). Also ἐπί τινι **Hb 11:4b** (on ἐπί w. dat. in this pass. s. Gen 4:4). W. dat. of thing (Jos., Ant. 12, 135; Ath. 16, 3 τῷ λόγῳ. Πλάτων) μ. τῇ ἀληθείᾳ *bear witness to the truth* **J 5:33; 18:37.** μ. σου τῇ ἀληθείᾳ *testify to the truth of your (way of life)* **3J 3;** σου τῇ ἀγάπῃ vs. **6.** W. dat. of pers. about whom testimony is given (Appian, Bell. Civ. 3, 73 §298; Just., D. 122, 2.—It is dat. of advantage or disadv.) **Ac 10:43; 22:5;** GJs 15:2; w. ptc. foll. (μ. Ἰακὼβ λέγων Did., Gen. 221, 2) θεὸς ἐμαρτύρησεν αὐτοῖς δοὺς κτλ. *God testified for them by giving* **Ac 15:8** (though αὐτοῖς can also be taken w. δούς); w. ὅτι foll. *bear someone witness that* **J 3:28; Ro 10:2; Gal 4:15; Col 4:13.** μ. ἑαυτῷ, ὅτι *bear witness to oneself that* **Mt 23:31.** The dat. can also designate the pers. who is informed or instructed by the testimony: *bear witness to someone* **Hb 10:15; Rv 22:18.**—μ. ὅτι *testify that* (Aelian, VH 9, 11; Did., Gen. 156, 28) **J 1:34; 4:44; 12:17 v.l.; 1J 4:14.** ὅτι introducing direct discourse **J 4:39.** μ. κατὰ τ. θεοῦ ὅτι *bear witness against God by declaring that* **1 Cor 15:15** (PPetr II, 21 [d], 12 [III BC] καθ᾽ οὗ μαρτυρῶ). ἐμαρτύρησεν καὶ εἶπεν w. direct discourse foll. **J 13:21.** μ. λέγων w. direct disc. foll. **J 1:32.** Of God μοι μαρτυρεῖ λέγων (Ps 89:4 follows) *he testifies (of it) to me by saying* B 15:4. For **1 Ti 6:13** s. c below.

β. pass., *be witnessed, have witness borne* ὑπό τινος *by someone* (Philo, Leg. All. 3, 46 σοφία μαρτυρουμένη ὑπὸ θεοῦ; Just., D. 63, 5 Χριστὸς ὑπὸ τοῦ ταῦτα ποιήσαντος μαρτυρούμενος. Of Jesus: ὑπὸ τῶν προφητῶν πολλαχοῦ μεμαρτ. Orig., C. Cels. 2, 9, 30) **Ro 3:21** (the witness of the law and prophets points to God's righteousness). Foll. by ὅτι and a quot. in direct discourse **Hb 7:17.** μαρτυρούμενος ὅτι ζῇ *one of whom it is testified that he lives* vs. **8.**

ⓑ to confirm *bear witness to, declare, confirm*, act. (Eunap., Vi. Soph. p. 76 ὁ θεὸς ἐμαρτύρησε; Iren. 2, 22, 5 [Harv I 331, 1]) τὶ *someth.* (Demosth. 57, 4 ἀκοήν; Aeschin. 1, 46 τἀληθῆ). ὃ ἑωράκαμεν μαρτυροῦμεν **J 3:11;** cp. vs. **32.** τὸν λόγον τ. θεοῦ **Rv 1:2.** ταῦτα **22:20.** τινί τι *someth. to* or *for someone* (Dionys. Hal. 3, 67, 1; Jos., Ant. 6, 355) vs. **16.** ὑμῖν τ. ζωήν **1J 1:2.** The acc. is to be supplied fr. the context **J 19:35; Ac 23:11.** W. ptc. ἀκούσαντες μαρτυρήσωσιν *they must admit that they have heard* PtK 3 p. 15, 23.—μαρτυρίαν μ. *bear witness, confirm, attest* (Ps.-Pla., Eryx. 399b; Epict. 4, 8, 32) περί τινος *concerning someone* **J 5:32b; 1J 5:10** (POxy 3313, 25f μαρτυρήσει σοι Σαραπᾶς περὶ τῶν ῥόδων S. will confirm to you about the roses).

ⓒ to support one's testimony with total selfgiving, eccl. usage w. regard to martyrdom *bear witness, testify, be a witness (unto death), be martyred*, act. (TestAbr B 11 p. 115, 16 [Stone p. 787] Ἄβελ ὁ ἐν πρώτοις μαρτυρήσας; Mel., HE 4, 26, 3; τοῖς μαρτυροῦσι τῷ χριστιανισμῷ μέχρι θανάτου Orig., C. Cels. 1, 8, 2): of Paul μαρτυρήσας ἐπὶ τῶν ἡγουμένων ... εἰς τὸν ἅγιον τόπον ἐπορεύθη 1 Cl 5:7; cp. vs. 4; MPol 1:1; 19:1; 21f (Iren. 3, 3, 4 [Harv. II 12, 8]); EpilMosq 4. Prob. **1 Ti 6:13** also belongs here: Χριστοῦ Ἰησοῦ τοῦ μαρτυρήσαντος ἐπὶ Ποντίου Πιλάτου τ. καλὴν ὁμολογίαν *Christ Jesus, who made the good confession before Pontius Pilate* (s. GBaldensperger, RHPR 2, 1922, 1–25; 95–117); otherwise the passage may be classed under a above.

❷ **to affirm in a supportive manner,** ***testify favorably, speak well (of), approve*****—ⓐ** act. (Dio Chrys. 23 [40], 19; SIG 374, 37 [III BC]; POxy 930, 16) w. dat. of the pers. (Appian, Samn. 11, §2 τοῖς ὑπάτοις, Liby. 105 §495, Bell. Civ. 4, 92 §387; Aelian, VH 1, 30; Jos., Ant. 12, 134) or of the thing approved **Lk 4:22** (OFearghus, ZNW 75, '84, 60–72 [pap and ins]; JNolland, JBL 98, '79, 219–29); **J 3:26.** Of God toward David **Ac 13:22.** μὴ ἑαυτῷ μαρτυρείτω *he must not testify (favorably) concerning himself* 1 Cl 38:2. W. dat. to be supplied **3J 12b.** μαρτυρίᾳ, ᾗ ἐμαρτύρησεν αὐτῷ ὁ δεσπότης Hs 5, 2, 6. Of the flesh ἵνα τὸ πνεῦμα ... μαρτυρήσῃ αὐτῇ Hs 5, 7, 1.—ὁ κύριος ὁ μαρτυρῶν ἐπὶ (which a v.l. omits; μ. ἐπί τινι as Jos., Ant. 3, 189) τῷ λόγῳ τ. χάριτος αὐτοῦ *the Lord, who attested the word of his grace* **Ac 14:3.** With συνευδοκέω **Lk 11:48 v.l.**

ⓑ pass., *be well spoken of, be approved* (Ep. 12 of Apollonius of Tyana: Philostrat. I 348, 26; Just., D. 29, 1. Exx. fr. ins in Dssm., NB 93 [BS 265], LO 69, 2 [LAE 84, 5]) ἀνὴρ μαρτυρούμενος or μεμαρτυρημένος *a man of good reputation* **Ac 6:3;** IPhld 11:1. Of OT worthies *people of attested merit* 1 Cl 17:1; 19:1. Of David 18:1. Of Abraham μεγάλως ἐμαρτυρήθη *his merit was gloriously attested* 17:2 (cp. Just., D. 11, 5 ἐπὶ τῇ πίστει μαρτυηθέντος ὑπὸ τοῦ θεοῦ). Of the apostles 47:4. Of Paul IEph 12:2. Of church leaders 1 Cl 44:3.—Foll. by nom. and inf. **Hb 11:4a;** cp. vs. **5.** διά τινος *be praised for someth.* **11:4a, 39.** ἐν ἔργοις καλοῖς μαρτυρούμενος *well attested in good deeds* **1 Ti 5:10;** cp. **Hb 11:2.** ὑπό τινος *be well spoken of by someone* (M. Ant. 7, 62; SIG 799, 28; Jos., Ant. 3, 59; Just., D. 29, 3; 92, 4; New Docs 7, 233, no. 10, 10 of a benefactor) **Ac 10:22; 16:2; 22:12;** IPhld 5:2.—Impersonally μαρτυρεῖταί τινι ὑπό τινος *a good testimony is given by someone to someone* (Dionys. Hal., Thu. 8 μαρτυρεῖται τῷ ἀνδρὶ τάχα μὲν ὑπὸ πάντων φιλοσόφων; BGU 1141, 15 [14 BC] ὡς καὶ μαρτυρηθήσεταί σοι ὑπὸ τῶν φίλων) Δημητρίῳ μεμαρτύρηται ὑπὸ πάντων καὶ ὑπὸ αὐτῆς τῆς ἀληθείας *Demetrius has received a good testimony from everyone and from the truth itself* **3J 12a.**—Dg 12:6.—OMichel, Bibl. Bekennen u. Bezeugen, Ὁμολογεῖν und μαρτυρεῖν im bibl. Sprachgebr.: Evang. Theologie 2, '35, 231–45; EBurnier, La notion de témoignage dans le NT '39.—DELG s.v. μάρτυς. M-M. EDNT. TRE XXII 196–212. TW.

μαρτυρία, ας, ἡ (s. μαρτυρέω; Hom.+—KLatte, Martyria: Pauly-W. XIV 2, 2032–39; Kl. Pauly III 1058).

❶ **confirmation or attestation on the basis of personal knowledge or belief,** ***testimony*****—ⓐ** act of testifying *testimony, testifying* (Pla., Leg. 11 p. 937a εἰς μαρτυρίαν κληθείς; Epict. 3, 22, 86 the μ. of the Cynic; PHal 1, 222 εἰς μαρτυρίαν κλῆσις; Iren. 5, 28, 4 [Harv. II 403, 5] διὰ τὴν πρὸς τὸν θεὸν μ. κατακριθεὶς πρὸς θηρία) οὗτος ἦλθεν εἰς μαρτυρίαν **J 1:7.** Of the two witnesses: ὅταν τελέσωσιν τ. μαρτυρίαν αὐτῶν **Rv 11:7.**

ⓑ content of testimony—**α.** of historical *attestation* or *testimony* (Diod. S. 11, 38, 6 τῆς ἱστορίας δικαία μαρτυρία; Just., D. 79, 2 ἀπ᾽ αὐτοῦ τοῦ Ἠσαίου) **J 19:35; 21:24** (JChapman, JTS 31, 1930, 379–87); Papias (2:17).

β. esp. w. ref. to Jesus

ℵ. of human testimony concerning Jesus: by the Baptist **J 1:19.** By Paul **Ac 22:18** (s. TRE XXIII 23–31). By believers **Rv 12:11.** Human testimony rejected **J 5:34.**

ב. of transcendent testimony concerning Jesus: he bears witness to himself as the central point of the Christian message: **J 3:11, 32f; 8:14.** His self-attestation is rejected vs. **13;** cp. **5:31.** Jesus also testifies concerning himself in **Rv 1:2, 9.**—God attests him (cp. Ael. Aristid. 45 p. 12 D.: μ. παρὰ Ἀπόλλωνος, p. 13 ἐκ Διός; Dexippus Athen. [III AD]:100 fgm. 1, 7 Jac. ἡ τοῦ θεοῦ μ. for the 'god' Lycurgus) **J 5:32, 36** (μαρτυρία μείζων as Dionys. Soph., Ep. 77.—Cp. Orig., C. Cels. 8, 9, 25 τὰ ὑπ' αὐτοῦ γενόμενα παράδοξα … τὴν ἀπὸ θεοῦ εἶχε μ.). **1J 5:9bc, 10ab, 11.**—RAsting (s. εὐαγγέλιον, end).—On John s. EHoskyns, The Fourth Gosp., ed. FDavey '47 p. 58–95.

ℶ. **Rv** speaks of the μαρτυρία or the μ. Ἰησοῦ which the Christians, or certain Christians (martyrs, prophets), possess: **6:9; 12:17; 19:10ab; 20:4.**—FMazzaferri, Bible Translator 39, '88, 114–22: John's book is the personal testimony of Jesus.

❷ **testimony in court, *testimony*** (Demosth. 29, 7 al.; Jos., Ant. 4, 219) **Mk 14:56, 59; Lk 22:71.** κατά τινος *against someone* **Mk 14:55;** δύο ἀνθρώπων ἡ μ. *the testimony of two persons* **J 8:17.**

❸ **attestation of character or behavior, *testimony, statement of approval*** (Jos., Ant. 6, 346; cp. Did., Gen. 212, 1) **1J 5:9a; 3J 12; Tit 1:13.** ἡ μ. τῆς ἀγαθῆς πράξεως *testimony concerning good deeds* 1 Cl 30:7. μαρτυρίαν καλὴν ἔχειν ἀπὸ τῶν ἔξωθεν *have a good standing with outsiders* **1 Ti 3:7** (μ.=recommendation: Dio Chrys. 28 [45], 9; Chion, Ep. 2; SIG1073, 17 [II AD]).—In the obscure concatenation of clauses B 1:6, love seems to be ἔργων δικαιοσύνης μαρτυρία *a testimony of upright deeds.*—Of a good testimony fr. God (Dio Chrys. 16 [33], 12 τῆς μεγίστης ἔτυχε μαρτυρίας παρὰ τοῦ δαιμονίου) Hs 5, 2, 6.

❹ **testimony that invites death, *a martyr's death, martyrdom*** (Iren. 1, 28, 1 [Harv. I 220, 10]) MPol 1:1; 13:2; 17:1.—DELG s.v. μάρτυς. M-M. TW. Sv.

μαρτύριον, ου, τό (s. μάρτυς; Pind., Hdt.+; ins, pap, LXX oft.; EpArist 306; Philo, Joseph., Just.).

❶ **that which serves as testimony or proof, *testimony, proof***

ⓐ consisting of an action, a circumstance, or a thing that serves as a testimony (Pla., Leg. 12, 943c [τ. στέφανον] ἀναθεῖναι μαρτύριον εἰς … κρίσιν; Jos., Ant. 6, 66; Just., D. 141, 3; Did., Gen. 63, 24) προσένεγκον τὸ δῶρον εἰς μαρτύριον αὐτοῖς **Mt 8:4** (JZoller, 'Z. Zeugnis für sie': Ricerche Relig. 5, 1929, 385–91 against SZeitlin: Rev. des Études juives 87, 1929, 79–82); cp. **Mk 1:44; Lk 5:14.** ἐκτινάξατε τὸν χοῦν εἰς μ. αὐτοῖς **Mk 6:11;** cp. **Lk 9:5** (ἐπ' αὐτούς). ἐπὶ ἡγεμόνας ἀχθήσεσθε ἕνεκεν ἐμοῦ εἰς μαρτύριον αὐτοῖς **Mt 10:18;** cp. **Mk 13:9;** ἀποβήσεται ὑμῖν εἰς μ. **Lk 21:13** (s. ἀποβαίνω 2). κηρυχθήσεται ἐν ὅλῃ τ. οἰκουμένῃ εἰς μ. **Mt 24:14.** ἐδίδου τὸ μ. (Paul) *bore witness* (through his fearless facing of the lion) AcPl Ha 4, 28 (cp. Kaibel 397, 1 μαρτύριον ὀρθοῦ βίου, 'the witness of an upright life').—A spoken statement serves εἰς μ. *as a testimony* B 9:3; IPhld 6:3; a written statement εἰς μ. ἐν ὑμῖν (cp. Dt 31:26) ITr 12:3. The fact that certain numbers occur in the OT serves as an indication, amounting to a testimony, of certain details in the plan of salvation B 8:3f; cp. GEb 34, 62. The redeeming death of Jesus was a testimony (of God) **1 Ti 2:6** (others find the referent in vs. 5). The rust on the money of the wealthy will turn out εἰς μ. for them **Js 5:3.** Moses as a servant (whose service is directed) εἰς μ. τῶν λαληθησομένων, toward testifying about revelations still to come **Hb 3:5.** The μείωσις τῆς σαρκός as μ. ἐκλογῆς *testimony* or *proof of (s)election* Dg 4:4.

ⓑ consisting of a statement that is brought out as testimony: w. subj. gen. τὸ μ. τῆς συνειδήσεως *the testimony that our conscience gives* **2 Cor 1:12.** W. obj. gen. ἀπεδίδουν τὸ μ. … τῆς ἀναστάσεως *they gave testimony to the resurrection* **Ac 4:33.** τὸ μ. τοῦ σταυροῦ *the testimony of the cross* Pol 7:1. Of Christian preaching and the gospel gener. τὸ μ. τοῦ Χριστοῦ *the testimony to Christ* **1 Cor 1:6;** cp. **2 Ti 1:8.** τὸ μ. τοῦ θεοῦ *the testimony of God* **1 Cor 2:1.** ἐπιστεύθη τὸ μ. ἡμῶν ἐφ' ὑμᾶς *our testimony to you was believed* **2 Th 1:10.**

❷ used in the LXX as the transl. of מוֹעֵד in the expr. ἡ σκηνὴ τοῦ μ.=אֹהֶל מוֹעֵד ***tent of meeting, tent/tabernacle of testimony*** (Ex 28:43 al.; Just.) **Ac 7:44; Rv 15:5;** 1 Cl 43:2, 5.

❸ ***martyrdom*** Papias (12:1); MPol 1:1; 2:1; 18:3; 19:1; Epil-Mosq 2; Phlm subscr. v.l.—On absence in John, s. M-EBoismard, Le Chapitre 21 de St Jean: RB '54 ('47), 482.—DELG s.v. μάρτυς. M-M. EDNT. TW. Sv.

μαρτύρομαι aor. inf. μαρτύρασθαι 1 Macc 2:56 (trag., Thu. et al.; pap, LXX, Did.)

❶ **to affirm someth. with solemnity, *testify, bear witness*** (Pla., Phileb. 47d; Jos., Bell. 3, 354; POxy 1120, 11; PAmh II, 141, 17; PStras I, 5, 14; 1 Macc 2:56 τῇ ἐκκλησίᾳ) τινί *to someone* μικρῷ τε καὶ μεγάλῳ *to great and small* **Ac 26:22.** τινί w. ὅτι foll. **20:26; Gal 5:3.**

❷ **to urge someth. as a matter of great importance, *affirm, insist, implore*** (someone Polyb. 13, 8, 6; Jdth 7:28; Jos., Ant. 10, 104) w. λέγειν and acc. w. inf. foll. **Eph 4:17.** τινά foll. by εἰς and subst. inf. w. acc. παρακαλοῦντες ὑμᾶς καὶ παραμυθούμενοι καὶ μαρτυρόμενοι εἰς τὸ περιπατεῖν ὑμᾶς ἀξίως **1 Th 2:12.**—DELG s.v. μάρτυς. M-M. TW.

μάρτυς, μάρτυρος, ὁ dat. pl. μάρτυσιν (Pind., Hdt.+; ins, pap, LXX; TestAbr A 13 p. 92, 22 [Stone p. 32]; TestLevi 19:3; Philo, Joseph.; apolog. exc. Ar.)

❶ **one who testifies in legal matters, *witness*** (Just., A I, 23, 3; Ath. 3, 2) **Ac 7:58; Mt 18:16; 2 Cor 13:1; 1 Ti 5:19** (the last 3 after Dt 19:15; cp. Jos., Vi. 256 and Hipponax [VI BC] 47 D.[3] ἐλθὼν σὺν τριοῖσι μάρτυσιν); **Hb 10:28** (Dt 17:6.—ἐπὶ μάρτυσι also Appian, Bell. Civ. 3, 14 §49). τί ἔτι χρείαν ἔχομεν μαρτύρων; *what further need have we of witnesses?* (Pla., Rep. 1, 340a τί δεῖται μάρτυρος; αὐτὸς γὰρ ὁ Θρασύμαχος ὁμολογεῖ) **Mt 26:65; Mk 14:63.** μάρτυρες ψευδεῖς *false witnesses* (Demosth. 29, 28) **Ac 6:13** (Mel., P. 79, 572). There is a suggestion of bureaucratic protocol relating to the account of the prudent and blameless men whom the Roman church sent to Corinth and who μάρτυρες ἔσονται μεταξὺ ὑμῶν κ. ἡμῶν 1 Cl 63:3.

❷ **one who affirms or attests, *testifier, witness*** transf. sense of mng. 1, of anyone who can or should testify to anything.

ⓐ of God (or the exalted Christ) as witness (deities as witnesses oft. Pind. et al.; Philo; Jos., Bell. 1, 595, Ant. 1, 209; TestLevi 19:3; SibOr, fgm. 1, 4; Just., A II, 12, 4 θεὸν … μάρτυρα ἔχοντες. Orig., C. Cels. 1, 46, 26 θεὸς [sc. ἐστιν] μ. τοῦ ἡμετέρου συνειδότος); as a formula *God is my witness* (that I am telling the truth) **Ro 1:9; Phil 1:8;** shortened θεὸς μ. **1 Th 2:5;** cp. vs. **10** (here also Jos., Ant. 15, 130 μ. ὑμᾶς ποιούμενος). μ. μοι ἐν ᾧ δέδεμαι IPhld 7:2. μάρτυρα τὸν θεὸν ἐπικαλεῖσθαι *call upon God as witness* **2 Cor 1:23** (cp. 1 Km 12:5f; 20:23; Polyb. 11, 6, 4 τ. θεοὺς ἐπικαλέσεσθε μάρτυρας; Heliod. 1, 25, 1; Galen VI 775 Kühn; likewise of calling upon deities, Hippol., Ref. 9, 15, 6: τοὺς ἑπτὰ μάρτυρας μαρτύρομαι).

ⓑ of humans (cp. Pind. O. 4, 5): witnessing by eye and ear (X., Ages. 4, 5; Pla., Ep. 1 p. 309a; Aelian, VH 10, 6; Jos., Ant. 18, 299; Tat. 31, 1; 36, 1) **1 Th 2:10; 1 Ti 6:12; 2 Ti 2:2.**—Also of those witnesses whose faith is tried and true τοσοῦτον νέφος μαρτύρων **Hb 12:1.**—Of witnesses of events which they know about, without having experienced them personally (acc. to Strabo 7, 3, 7 p. 300 Hesiod is μάρτυς with regard to the Scythians): the teachers of the law bear witness to the murder of the prophets by their ancestors, by erecting tombs for the prophets **Lk 11:48** (μαρτυρεῖτε v.l.).

ⓒ of witnesses who bear a divine message (Epict. 3, 26, 28 God uses the wise men as his μάρτυρες) **Rv 11:3** (though the mng. approaches *martyr* [s. 3 below] here; cp. vs. 7. S. DHaugg, D. zwei Zeugen-Apk 11:1–13, '36; JConsidine, CBQ 8, '46. 377–92). In this sense, above all, of Jesus' disciples as the witnesses of his life, death, and resurrection: ἔσεσθέ μου μάρτυρες *you will be my witnesses* **Ac 1:8;** cp. **13:31** (Ps.-Demetr. 222 μάρτυς σου γίνεται). W. obj. gen. of the thing witnessed: *witness for/of* (Jos., C. Ap. 1, 4 τῶν ὑπ' ἐμοῦ λεγομένων μ., Ant. 4, 40; ἀληθείας μ. of Polycarp Iren. 3, 3, 4 [Harv. II 13, 4]; παραδόσεως of the Ephesian congregation 3, 3, 4 [Harv. II 15, 6]; Orig., C. Cels. 1, 47, 24) **Lk 24:48; Ac 1:22; 3:15; 5:32; 10:39; 26:16.** μ. τῶν τοῦ Χριστοῦ παθημάτων *a witness of the sufferings of Christ* **1 Pt 5:1.** ἔσῃ μ. αὐτῷ πρὸς πάντας ἀνθρώπους *you will be a witness for him to all people* **Ac 22:15** (Epict. 3, 24, 113 μ. πρὸς τοὺς ἄλλους).—**10:41.** Danker, Benefactor 442–47.

❸ **one who witnesses at cost of life,** ***martyr,*** in the usage of the persecuted church τὸ αἷμα Στεφάνου τοῦ μάρτυρός σου **Ac 22:20.** Of Antipas ὁ μ. μου ὁ πιστός μου **Rv 2:13** (cp. Pind., P. 1, 88 μάρτυρες πιστοί=dependable witnesses; on the textual problems of **Rv 2:13** s. RBorger, TRu 52, '87, 45–47). Onesimus μ. Χριστοῦ γεγένηται **Phlm subscr. v.l.** Gener. μάρτυρες Ἰησοῦ **Rv 17:6;** cp. MPol 2:2; 14:2; 15:2; 16:2 v.l.; 17:3; 19:1. Of Zacharias μ. εἰμι τοῦ θεοῦ GJs 25:3 (s. de Strycker ad loc.). Since Rv also calls Jesus (as well as Antipas) ὁ μάρτυς ὁ πιστός **1:5; 3:14,** these pass. are prob. to be classed here (cp. Ps 88:38), but with awareness of strong focus in all the NT passages in this classification on the fact of witness. The death of Jesus was early regarded as the first martyrdom.—For an analysis of the question how μάρτυς='witness' came to mean 'martyr', s. FKattenbusch, ZNW 4, 1903, 111ff; KHoll, variously, then Gesamm. Aufsätze II 1928, 103ff; ASchlatter, BFChTh 19, 3, 1915; PCorssen, NJklA 35, 1915, 481ff, 37, 1916, 424ff, ZNW 15, 1914, 221ff w. several continuations until 18, 1917, 249ff, Sokrates 6, 1918, 106ff; Rtzst., Hist. Mon. 1916, 85; 257, NGG 1916, 417ff, Her 52, 1917, 442ff; FDornseiff, ARW 22, 1923/24, 133ff; HDelehaye, Analecta Bollandiana 39, 1921, 20ff, Sanctus 1927 ([2]'33), 74ff (75, 1 lit.). ELohmeyer, D. Idee des Martyriums im Judent. u. Urchristent.: ZST 5, 1927/28, 232–49; GFitzer, D. Begriff des μ. im Judent. u. Urchristent., diss. Bresl. 1929; HLietzmann, Martys: Pauly-W. XIV 2, 1930, 2044–52; OMichel, Prophet u. Märt. '32; RCasey, Μάρτυς: Beginn. I 5, '33, 30–37; EStauffer, Märtyrertheologie u. Täuferbewegg.: ZKG 52, '33, 545–98; DRiddle, The Martyr Motif in Mk: JR 4, 1924, 174–91, Hb, 1 Cl and the Persecution of Domitian: JBL 43, 1924, 329–48, From Apocalypse to Martyrology: ATR 9, 1927, 260–80, The Martyrs: A Study in Social Control '31, Die Verfolgungslogien im formgesch. u. soziol. Bed.: ZNW 33, '34, 271–89; HvCampenhausen, D. Idee des Martyriums in d. alten Kirche[2] '64; EPeterson, Zeuge d. Wahrh. '37; EBurnier, Le notion de témoignage dans le NT '37; HSurkau, Martyrien in jüd. u. frühchristl. Zt. '38; HFischel, Martyr and Prophet (in Jewish lit.), JQR 37, '46/47, 265–80; 363–86; EGünther, Μάρτυς, D. Gesch. eines Wortes '41, Zeuge u. Märtyrer, ZNW 47, '56, 145–61. ELohse, Märtyrer u. Gottesknecht '55; HvanVliet, No Single Testimony (Dt 19:15) '58; NBrox, Zeuge u. Märtyrer '61.—B. 1436; ATrites, Μάρτυς and Martyrdom in the Apocalypse, A Semantic Study: NovT 15, '73, 72–80, The NT Concept of Witness '77; GDragas, Martyrdom and Orthodoxy in the NT Era: Greek Orthodox Theological Review 30, '85, 287–96; PVassiliadis, The Translation of μαρτυρία Ιησοῦ in Rv: BT 36, '85, 129–34; M-ERosenblatt, Paul the Accused '95, 1–21; Kl. Pauly III 1059f; BHHW II 1156f.—DELG. M-M. EDNT. TW. Spicq. Sv.

μαρυκάομαι (a colloquialized Doric form [Aelian, NA 2, 54; Hesych. s.v. ἐμαρυκᾶτο and ἤνυστρον; Lev 11:26=Dt 14:8; s. Thackeray 76]) ***ruminate, chew the cud*** Hs 9, 1, 9. πᾶν μαρυκώμενον *any ruminant* B 10:11.—PKatz, Philo's Bible '50, 157–59.

μασάομαι (μασσ-, a less correct form, v.l.) impf. ἐμασώμην (Aristoph., Hippocr. et al.; Artem. 4, 33; Philostrat., Vi. Apoll. 7, 21 p. 276, 2; PGM 5, 280; Job 30:4; Jos., Bell. 6, 197; Just., D. 57, 2) ***bite*** w. acc. τὰς γλώσσας *bite their tongues* **Rv 16:10;** ApcPt 14:29. τὰ χείλη *bite their lips* 13:28. In Joseph's vision οἱ μασώμενοι οὐκ ἐμασῶντο GJs 18:2 (codd., not Bodmer).—M-M. TW.

μασθός s. μαστός.

μαστιγόω fut. μαστιγώσω; 1 aor. ἐμαστίγωσα. Pass.: fut. 3 pl. μαστιγωθήσονται Ps 72:5; 1 aor. ἐμαστιγώθην; pf. μεμαστίγωμαι LXX ('whip, flog' Hdt. et al.; ins, pap, LXX; Philo, In Flacc. 85; Joseph.; TestJos 8:4 v.l.)

❶ **to beat with a whip or lash,** ***whip, flog, scourge***—ⓐ of flogging as a punishment decreed by the synagogue (Dt 25:2f; s. the Mishna Tractate Sanhedrin-Makkoth, edited w. notes by SKrauss '33) w. acc. of pers. **Mt 10:17; 23:34.** Of the beating administered to Jesus **J 19:1.** If J refers to the 'verberatio' given those condemned to death (TMommsen, Röm. Strafrecht 1899, 938f; Jos., Bell. 2, 308; 5, 449), it is odd that Pilate subsequently claims no cause for action (vs. 6); but if the latter statement refers only to the penalty of crucifixion, μ. vs. **1** may be equivalent to παιδεύω (q.v. 2bγ) in **Lk 23:16, 22** (for μ.of a non-capital offense PFlor I, 61, 61 [85 AD]=Mitt-Wilck. II/2, 80 II, 61). The 'verberatio' is denoted in the passion predictions and explicitly as action by non-Israelites **Mt 20:19; Mk 10:34; Lk 18:33.**—As a punishment for cheating in athletic contests (Ps.-Dionys. Hal., Ars Rhet. 7, 6 p. 292, 5 R. μάστιγες . . . κ. τὸ ἐκβάλλεσθαι ἐκ τ. σταδίων κ. ἀγώνων) 2 Cl 7:4. Of a whipping as netherworld punishment ApcPt Bodl at vs. 34 (for τύπτοντες Akhmim text ln. 107 Dieterich).

ⓑ gener., in a transf. sense, *afflict, torment, mistreat* (Artem. 1, 24 p. 25, 16 μ. τὰ ὦτα=pulling the ears; UPZ 119, 29; 44 [156 BC]; Sir 30:14) ITr 4:1; Hs 6, 3, 1.

❷ **to punish with discipline in mind,** ***punish, chastise,*** metaph. ext. of 1: of God (Jer 5:3; Jdth 8:27) for discipline (Maximus Tyr. 19, 5e of the soul) **Hb 12:6;** 1 Cl 56:4 both Pr 3:12.—DELG s.v. μάστιξ. M-M. TW. Spicq.

μαστίζω aor. ἐμάστιξα LXX; TestJos 8:4 (Hom.+; Diod. S. 14, 112, 2; Plut., Mor. 165e; Lucian, Pro Imag. 24; Palestin. ins: SEG VIII, 246, 17 [II AD]; LXX, TestSol, Test12Patr, ApcEsdr 4:22 p. 28, 26 Tdf.) ***strike with a whip*** GPt 3:9. Specif. of interrogation under torture *scourge* **Ac 22:25** (it was prohibited to expose a Roman citizen to flogging: Cicero, Verr. 2, 5, 66; Appian, Bell. Civ. 2, 26 §98. Further, s. HCadbury, Beginn. V '33, 297–338, esp. 319; Haenchen, ad loc.)—DELG s.v. μάστιξ. M-M. TW. Spicq.

μάστιξ, ιγος, ἡ ('whip, lash', used esp. to urge on horses or laborers: Hom.+; ins, pap, LXX, En; ApcrEzk [Epiph 70, 15]; Just., A I, 5, 1; Mel.)

❶ **a flexible instrument used for lashing,** ***whip, lash*** Hs 6, 2, 5. Mostly pl. *lashing* or *lashes* (Jos., Bell. 2, 306, Vi. 147; Mel., P. 79, 573 al.) B 5:14 (Is 50:6); MPol 2:2; Hv 3, 2, 1. μάστιξιν ἀνετάζειν τινά *examine someone by scourging* **Ac 22:24** (cp. PAmh 31 I, 10f; s. Taubenschlag, OpMin II 723 on the interrogation process). W. ἐμπαιγμός **Hb 11:36.**

❷ **a condition of great distress,** ***torment, suffering,*** fig. ext. of mng. 1 (sent by God to human beings: Il. 12, 37 Διὸς μ.; Proverbia Aesopi 105 P.; Ps 38:11; 2 Macc 7:37; 9:11; En 25:6;

100, 13; ins in Ramsay, CB I/2, 520 no. 361 λήψεται παρὰ τοῦ θεοῦ μάστειγα αἰώνιον; also in ref. to harmful divinities Just., A I, 5, 1) of bodily illness **Mk 3:10; 5:29, 34; Lk 7:21.** Of a sinner's afflictions 1 Cl 22:8 (Ps 31:10); Hv 4, 2, 6. W. αἰκίσματα of the Egyptian plagues 1 Cl 17:5 (Mel., P. 11, 75f). μ. γλώσσης *scourge of the tongue* 1 Cl 56:10 (Job 5:21).—Eitrem (s. πειράζω 4, end) 12f.—DELG. M-M. TW. Spicq.

μαστός, οῦ, ὁ (collateral forms μασθός GJs Bodmer [Heraclid. Miles., fgm. 25 LCohn 1884; IG III, 238b; POslo 95, 19: 96 AD; PGM 7, 208; TestSol 9:4 H; JosAs 8:4 cod. A; 29:11 cod. A; Thackeray 104] and μαζός [q.v.] are found as vv.ll., but most freq. μασθός; s. Kühner-Bl. I 157; B-D-F §34, 5; W-S. §5, 27d; Mlt-H. 110) 'one of the breasts' (pl. in imagery Jos., Bell. 7, 189; Mel.), distinguished from the στῆθος 'chest'; s. citation of Hom. s.v. μαζός.

❶ **one of the mammillae, of a male, *nipple*** (X., An. 4, 3, 6 of water ὑπὲρ τῶν μαστῶν; Eratosth. p. 33, 2; SIG 1170, 24; TestSol 9:4 LC, opp. στῆθος: a hostile spirit (δαίμων) is asked by Solomon, who has put a seal on the spirit's chest, how it sees. Answer: 'through my breasts' = his nipples which function as eyes) περιεζωσμένος πρὸς τοῖς μ. ζώνην χρυσᾶν *with a golden belt around his breast* **Rv 1:13** (μασθοῖς Tdf. in text; Diod. S. 1, 72, 2 περιεζωσμένοι ὑποκάτω τῶν μαστῶν).

❷ **mammary gland or mamma of a female, *breast*** (Hdt. et al.; Sb 6706, 9; LXX; ApcEsdr 5:2 p. 29, 26 Tdf.; Philo, Op. M. 38; Mel., P. 52, 384) **Lk 11:27; 23:29;** GJs 5:2; 6:3; 19:2; ApcPt fgm. 2 p.12, 25.—DELG. M-M.

μαστώδης, ες (s. μαστός, -ώδης); **pert. to having the appearance of a woman's breast, *breast-shaped, rounded*** of a mountain Hs 9, 1, 4 (Strabo 14, 6, 3 ὄρος μαστοειδὲς Ὄλυμπος; Diod. S. 17, 75, 2 πέτρα μαστοειδής; Jos., Bell. 1, 419, Ant. 15, 324).—DELG s.v. μαστός.

ματαιολογία, ας, ἡ (s. μάταιος, λόγος and next entry; Plut., Mor. 6f; Vett. Val. 150, 24; 257, 23; 360, 4; Diogenianus Epicureus [II AD], fgm. II, 16 Gercke, in Eus., PE 6, 8, 11; Porphyr., Abst. 4, 16; Herm. Wr. 14, 5) ***empty, fruitless talk*** ἐκτρέπεσθαι εἰς μ. *turn to fruitless discussion* **1 Ti 1:6.** Tautologically(?) κενὴ μ. Pol 2:1.—DELG s.v. μάτη. M-M. TW.

ματαιολόγος, ον (s. prec. entry; Telestes Lyr. [IV BC] 1, 9 Diehl; Vett. Val. 301, 11; Physiogn. I 379, 10; II 231, 5) ***talking idly,*** subst. ὁ μ. *an idle talker, windbag* **Tit 1:10.**—TW.

ματαιοπονία, ας, ἡ (s. μάταιος, πόνος; Strabo 17, 1, 28; Plut., Mor. 119e; Lucian, Dial. Mort. 10, 8) ***fruitless toil*** 1 Cl 9:1.—DELG s.v. μάτη.

μάταιος, αία, αιον (Pind., Hdt. et al.; PEdg 11, 3 [=Sb 6717], 3 [257 BC]; POxy 58, 20; LXX, En; OdeSol 11:9; TestAbr A 1 p. 78, 9 [Stone p. 4] [κόσμος]; Test12Patr; ApcMos 25; EpArist, Philo; Jos., C. Ap. 1, 6; Just.; Ath., R. 9 p. 58, 4 al.) also, as somet. in Attic wr., varying betw. two and three endings (B-D-F §59, 2; Mlt-H. 157) **pert. to being of no use, *idle, empty, fruitless, useless, powerless, lacking truth*** (Hippol., Ref. 4, 2) τούτου μ. ἡ θρησκεία *this person's worship is worthless* **Js 1:26;** νηστεία μ. *useless fasting* Hs 5, 1, 4; ἀνωφελὴς καὶ μ. *useless and fruitless* **Tit 3:9.** ἐλπίς *vain, empty* (Artem. 1, 67 p. 62, 5; Lucian, Alex. 47; Is 31:2) B 16:2. διαλογισμοί *foolish thoughts* **1 Cor 3:20** (Ps 93:11). φροντίδες 1 Cl 7:2. ἐπιθυμία *futile desire,* directed toward worthless things Hm 11:8; pl. 2 Cl 19:2; Hm 12, 6, 5. πίστις μ. *empty* **1 Cor 15:17.** τρυφαί *idle luxury* Hs 6, 2, 2. ἐπιθυμία ἐδεσμάτων πολλῶν ματαίων *a desire for many needless things to eat* m 12, 2, 1. οἰκήματα *dwellings that will pass away* s 1:1. ἡ μ. στάσις *futile dissension* 1 Cl 63:1. ἡ μ. ἀναστροφή *futile way of living* **1 Pt 1:18.**—μάταιον (sc. ἐστίν) *it is useless* B 2:5 (Is 1:13; δοκεῖ μοι εἶναι μ. Orig., C. Cels. 2, 32, 19). οὐ μὴ λάβῃς ἐπὶ ματαίῳ τὸ ὄνομα κυρίου *you must never use the Lord's name for an unworthy purpose* 19:5 (Ex 20:7; Dt 5:11).—(μάταιοι οὖν οἱ ἀπὸ Οὐαλεντίνοι, τοῦτο δογματίζοντες Iren. 5, 1, 2 [Harv. II 316, 9] cp. 3, 11, 9 [Harv. II 50, 12]).—Subst. μάταια *what is worthless, empty* (Vett. Val. 356, 16; Zech 10:2; Pr 12:11; OdesSol 16:9; Jos., Bell. 7, 330) ἀγαπᾶν B 20:2; D 5:2; λαλεῖν IPhld 1:1. τὰ μάταια (or οἱ μάταιοι, i.e. θεοί) *idols* (Esth 4:17p; Jer 2:5; 8:19; 3 Macc 6:11) **Ac 14:15.**—DELG s.v. μάτη. M-M. TW.

ματαιότης, ητος, ἡ (s. prec. entry; Philod., Rhet. II p. 26, 6 Sudh. μ. ἀνθρώπων; Sext. Emp., Adv. Math. 1, 278; Pollux 6, 134; LXX; TestSol 8:2 D; Philo, Conf. Lingu. 141. Perh. also CIG IV, 8743, 6) **state of being without use or value, *emptiness, futility, purposelessness, transitoriness*** τῇ μ. ἡ κτίσις ὑπετάγη *the creation was subjected to frustration* **Ro 8:20.** Of the heathen περιπατεῖν ἐν μ. τοῦ νοός *walk with their minds fixed on futile things* **Eph 4:17.** φεύγειν ἀπὸ πάσης μ. *flee from all idle speculations* B 4:10; cp. Pol 7:2 (καθαρεύειν ἀπὸ πάσης μ. νοημάτων καὶ λέξεων Orig., C. Cels. 5, 46, 5). ὑπέρογκα ματαιότητος φθέγγεσθαι *utter highsounding but empty words* **2 Pt 2:18** (cp. Ps 37:13). ἐπὶ ματαιότητι *out of folly* (Arrian, Ind. 36, 1 ἐπὶ τῆς ἀγγελίης τῇ ματαιότητι) ITr 8:2.—DELG s.v. μάτη. M-M. TW.

ματαιόω (s. μάταιος) pres. 3 pl. ματαιοῦσιν Jer 23:16. Pass.: fut. 3 sg. ματαιωθήσεται; 1 aor. ἐματαιώθην; pf. μεματαίωμαι (Herodian, Gramm. I 453, 13; schol. on Soph., Trach. 258 Papag.; Dositheus 71, 17; otherw. in bibl. and eccl. usage; LXX) ***render futile/worthless*** pass. *be given over to worthlessness, think about idle, worthless things, be foolish* (1 Ch 21:8) ἐματαιώθησαν ἐν τοῖς διαλογισμοῖς αὐτῶν *their thoughts became directed to worthless things* **Ro 1:21** (w. ref. to idolatry; s. μάταιος and cp. Jer 2:5 ἐπορεύθησαν ὀπίσω τῶν ματαίων καὶ ἐματαιώθησαν).—DELG s.v. μάτη.

ματαίωμα, ατος, τό (s. μάταιος) ***emptiness, worthlessness*** τὰ μ. τοῦ αἰῶνος τούτου *the worthless things of this age* Hm 9:4; s 5, 3, 6.—DELG s.v. μάτη.

μάτην adv. acc. of μάτη 'fault'; B-D-F §136 (Hom. Hymns, Hdt. et al.; ins, pap, LXX; Jos., Bell. 7, 135, C. Ap. 1, 142; Just.; Ath., R. 12 p. 60, 32) ***in vain, to no end*** **Mt 15:9; Mk 7:7** (both Is 29:13); Hs 5, 4, 2a. Also εἰς μ. (Ael. Aristid. 33, 3 K.=51 p. 572 D.; Ps.-Lucian, Trag. 28; Tetrast. Iamb. 1, 14, 4 p. 269; Ps 62:10; 126:1ab, 2; Theoph. Ant. 2, 35 [p. 188, 25]) Hs 5, 4, 2b; 6, 1, 3; 9, 4, 8; 9, 13, 2.—DELG s.v. μάτη. M-M. TW.

Ματθαῖος, ου s. Μαθθαῖος.

Ματθάν, ὁ indecl. (מַתָּן; the name is found 2 Ch 23:17; Jer 45:1—mss. also Μαθθαν; s. Μαθθαῖος) ***Matthan,*** in the genealogy of Jesus **Mt 1:15; Lk 3:23ff** D (Μαθθαν).

Ματθάτ s. Μαθθάτ.

Ματθίας s. Μαθθίας.

ματρῶνα, ης, ἡ (since I AD, s. Preis. II 55; Lat. matrona) ***married woman*** AcPl Ha 3, 26; 4, 2 (of Artemilla).

Ματταθά, ὁ indecl. (מַתָּתָה; 2 Esdr 10:33 Μαθαθα and v.l. Μαθθαθα) ***Mattatha,*** son of Nathan, grandson of David; in the genealogy of Jesus **Lk 3:31.**

Ματταθίας, ου, ὁ (מַתִּתְיָה; 2 Esdr 10:43 Μαθαθία, v.l. Μαθθαθίας; 18:4 v.l. Ματθαθίας, in the text Ματταθίας, as 1 Ch 9:31; 16:5; 1 Macc 2:1, 14 al.; EpArist 47; Joseph.) *Mattathias,* in the genealogy of Jesus

❶ son of Amos **Lk 3:25.—❷** son of Semeïn vs. **26.**

μάχαιρα, ης, ἡ (Hom.+. The Ptolemaic pap as a rule decline it [Mayser p. 12] μαχαίρας, -χαίρᾳ; likew. LXX [Thackeray p. 141f; Helbing p. 31ff]; ISm 4:2b; also mss. and some edd. of the NT. The pap fr. Roman times prefer -ρης, -ρῃ [isolated exx. fr. earlier times, e.g. PTebt 16, 14: 114 BC; 112, 45: 112 BC]; sim. 4 [6] Esdr [POxy 1010]; likew. the NT)

❶ **a relatively short sword or other sharp instrument, *sword, dagger*** **Mt 26:47, 55; Mk 14:43, 48; Lk 22:36, 38** (ASchlatter, Die beiden Schwerter: BFCT 20, 6, 1916; TNapier, ET 49, '38, 467–70; IZolli, Studi e Mat. di Storia delle Rel. 13, '38, 227–43; RHeiligenthal, NTS 41, '95, 39–58. Field, Notes 76f suggests 'knives' here), **52; Rv 6:4; 13:10.** ἐν φόνῳ μαχαίρης ἀποθανεῖν *be killed with the sword* **Hb 11:37** (Ex 17:13; Dt 13:16). ἀποσπᾶν τὴν μ. *draw the sword* **Mt 26:51.** Also σπάσασθαι τὴν μ. (1 Ch 21:5; 1 Esdr 3:22; Jos., Vi. 303) **Mk 14:47; Ac 16:27.** λαμβάνειν μάχαιραν *take, grasp the sword* (Jos., Vi. 173) **Mt 26:52b** (HKosmala, NovT 4, '60, 3–5: Targum Is 50:11 as parallel); ἑλκύειν μ. **J 18:10;** πατάσσειν ἐν μ. *strike w. the sword* **Lk 22:49.** βάλλειν τὴν μ. εἰς τὴν θήκην *put the sword into its sheath* **J 18:11;** cp. **Mt 26:52a.** Of execution by the sword ISm 4:2ab. ἀναιρεῖν μαχαίρῃ *have someone put to death w. the sword* **Ac 12:2;** ἔχειν πληγὴν τῆς μ. *have a sword-wound* **Rv 13:14.** στόμα μαχαίρης *the edge of the sword* (cp. Gen 34:26; 2 Km 15:14; TestJud 5:5; Theod. Prodr. 1, 19 Hercher; 2, 264; 6, 101) **Lk 21:24; Hb 11:34** (OHofius, ZNW 62, '71, 129f); the corresponding figure μ. κατέδεται (cp. 2 Km 11:25; Theod. Prodr. 6, 122 H. ἔτρωγεν . . . τὸ ξίφος κρέα, ἔπινεν ἡ μ. πηγὰς αἱμάτων) 1 Cl 8:4 (Is 1:20). (S. also πίπτω 1bα**ℵ**.) μ. δίστομος *a double-edged sword* (Judg 3:16; Pr 5:4) **Hb 4:12** (for the interpretation 'scalpel' or 'bistoury' s. CSpicq, RB 58, '51, 482–84 [difft. idem, Lexique s.v. δίστομος], but the chief objections to such renderings are the absence of references in ancient medical writers to a double-edged surgical instrument and their preference for the diminutive μαχαίριον in connection w. such instruments).

❷ in various images μ. ***sword*** stands for—ⓐ violent death **Ro 8:35**—ⓑ for war (Gen 31:26; SibOr 8, 120.—Opp. εἰρήνη.) **Mt 10:34** (Harnack, ZTK 22, 1912, 4–6).

ⓒ the powerful function of the divine word ἡ μ. τοῦ πνεύματος*the sword of the Spirit,* explained as the Word of God **Eph 6:17** (cp. **Hb 4:12** in 1 above).

ⓓ the power of authorities to punish evildoers τὴν μάχαιραν φορεῖν *carry the sword* **Ro 13:4** (cp. Philostrat., Vi. Soph. 1, 25, 3 δικαστοῦ ξίφος ἔχοντος; Ulpian in Digest of Justinian 2, 1, 3).—B. 559; 1392. DELG. M-M. EDNT. TW.

μάχη, ης, ἡ (s. μάχομαι; Hom.+) 'battle' (one fighter on each side is enough: Maximus Tyr. 22, 4b), in our lit. only in pl. and only of battles fought without actual weapons ***fighting, quarrels, strife, disputes*** (Pythag., Ep. 5, 7; SIG 1109, 72; Kaibel 522, 5; PRyl 28, 203 μάχας ἕξει διὰ θῆλυ; Cat. Cod. Astr. XII 160, 1 of marital discord; LXX, Philo; Ar. 13, 5 μ. καὶ διαφωνία) w. πόλεμοι (Il. 5, 891 πόλεμοί τε μάχαι τε; Dio Chrys. 21 [38], 11; Plut., Mor. 108a) **Js 4:1.** ἔξωθεν μάχαι ἔσωθεν φόβοι **2 Cor 7:5.** γεννᾶν μάχας *breed quarrels* **2 Ti 2:23.** μάχαι νομικαί *strife about the law* **Tit 3:9** (cp. Pla., Tim. p. 88a μάχας ἐν λόγοις ποιεῖσθαι).—DELG s.v. μάχομαι. M-M.

μάχομαι (s. μάχη) impf. ἐμαχόμην; aor. ἐμαχησάμην. Mid. dep. (Hom.+).

❶ **to engage in physical combat, *fight*** (betw. two persons Ex 21:22) **Ac 7:26.**

❷ **to engage in heated dispute, without use of weapons, *fight, quarrel, dispute*** (Hom. et al.; SIG 1109, 95 ἐκβάλλειν τοὺς μαχομένους; POxy 120, 6; Gen 26:20; 31:36; TestSol 25:4; TestJos 11:4; Jos., C. Apion 1:38; Just.) abs. *be quarrelsome* **2 Ti 2:24.** W. πολεμεῖν **Js 4:2.** μαχομένους συναγαγεῖν *bring together those who are at enmity* B 19:12; cp. D 4:3. πρός τινα (EpArist 13; Philo, Leg. All. 2, 106; Just., D. 120, 4 μ. πρὸς ὑμᾶς περὶ τῆς λέξεως) *dispute with someone* πρὸς ἀλλήλους *among themselves* **J 6:52** (πρ. ἀλλ. fig. as Lucian, Tim. 9; Aesop, Fab. 62 P.=116 H.//Ch. 95//H-H. 73). τινὶ *against someone* μ. τῷ νόμῳ κυρίου *go contrary to the law of the Lord* GJs 14:1.—B. 1370. DELG. M-M.

μεγαλαυχέω (Aeschyl. et al.; Polyb. 12, 13, 10; 8, 23, 11; Diod. S. 15, 16, 3; Vett. Val. 257, 19; 262, 4; 358, 29; LXX; ParJer 9:17; Philo) ***become proud, boast*** **Js 3:5 v.l.** (for μεγάλα αὐχεῖ, s. αὐχέω).—DELG s.v. αὐχέω. M-M.

μεγαλεῖος, α, ον (s. next entry; X. et al.; ins, pap, LXX; comp. μεγαλειότερος Just., A II, 10, 1) 'magnificent, splendid, grand' in our lit. only subst. of what impresses mind or spirit: τὸ μ. ***greatness, sublimity*** (Polyb. 3, 87, 5; 8, 1, 1; Artem. 3 p. 169, 1 τὸ μ. τῆς σοφίας; SIG 798, 4 [37 AD]; Sir 17:8; TestJob; TestLevi 11:6; Philo; Jos., Ant. 8, 49; 15, 187; Just., A II, 3, 3) τῆς ἐπαγγελίας 1 Cl 26:1. τὸ μ. τῆς καλλονῆς αὐτοῦ *its* (or *God's*) *sublime beauty* 49:3.—Pl. τὰ μ. *the mighty deeds* (Dt 11:2; Ps 70:19; Sir 36:7; 42:21) τὰ μ. τοῦ θεοῦ **Ac 2:11;** cp. Hv 4, 2, 5; s 9, 18, 2. Abs. v 4, 1, 8. Of the *great and good deeds* of God (TestJob 51:4) **Lk 1:49 v.l.** (cp. Ps 70:19). πηλίκα μεγαλεῖα ἐδόθη αὐτῷ *what great deeds he was granted to perform (by God's grace)* AcPl Ha 6, 13. μ. τῶν δωρεῶν *the greatness of (God's) gifts* 1 Cl 32:1.—DELG s.v. μέγας. M-M. TW. Spicq. Sv.

μεγαλειότης, ητος, ἡ (s. prec. entry; Athen. 4, 6, 130f; Vett. Val. 70, 4; OGI 666, 26 [I AD] the pyramids as an awesome sight; 669, 9 [I AD]; PGiss 40 I, 5; 11; LXX) in our lit. only of a divine figure or of divine attributes.

❶ **quality or state of being foremost in esteem, *grandeur, sublimity, majesty*** (of God: Aristob. in Eus., PE 8, 10, 17; Jos., Ant. 1, 24; 8, 111, C. Ap. 2, 168), of Artemis **Ac 19:27.** Of Christ **2 Pt 1:16,** who was endorsed by a heavenly voice.

❷ **quality or state of experiencing high esteem because of awesome performance, *impressiveness*** (cp. the use of θειότης q.v.), **Lk 9:43** in ref. to a healing; Dg 10:5 in ref. to actions that would be out of character for God; IRo ins, in ref. to expression of divine mercy. ἡ μ. τῆς προνοίας τοῦ δεσπότου *the Master's wondrous providence* 1 Cl 24:5.—DELG s.v. μέγας. M-M. TW. Spicq.

μεγαλοπρέπεια, ας, ἡ (s. μέγας, πρέπω and next entry; Hom. et al.; SIG 695, 14; pap [as honorary title]; LXX [only Ps, but not rare there]) ***majesty, sublimity,*** of God, with implication that the awesome regard in which God is held derives from awesome performance, w. ἰσχύς 1 Cl 60:1.

μεγαλοπρεπής, ές (s. prec. entry; Hdt., Aristoph.+; ins, pap, LXX; En 32:3; Philo; Jos., Ant. 9, 182; 13, 242) ***magnificent, sublime, majestic, impressive*** δόξα **2 Pt 1:17;** 1 Cl 9:2. κράτος θεοῦ 61:1. βούλησις θεοῦ 9:1. δωρεαὶ θεοῦ 19:2 (Diod. S. 3, 54, 6 δῶρα μεγαλοπρεπῆ). ἡ μ. θρησκεία τοῦ ὑψίστου *the exalted/impressive worship of the Most High* 45:7 (Appian, Bell. Civ. 5, 4 §15 τῇ θεῷ μεγαλοπρεπῶς ἔθυε; cp. the adj. Theopomp. 115: fgm. 344, Jac. p. 607, 16). τὸ μ. καὶ ἅγιον ὄνομα Χριστοῦ 1 Cl 64 (cp. 2 Macc 8:15).—τὸ μ. τῆς φιλοξενίας ὑμῶν ἦθος *the impressive character of your hospitality* 1:2.—New Docs 2, 108f. DELG s.v. πρέπω. M-M. TW. Spicq.

μεγαλο(ρ)ρημονέω (s. μέγας, ῥῆμα and two next entries) 1 aor. ἐμεγαλορημόνησα (Strabo 13, 1, 40; LXX; TestJob 41:1; ApcSed 14:12 p. 136, 22 Ja.) ***use great words, boast*** 1 Cl 17:5.

μεγαλο(ρ)ρημοσύνη, ης, ἡ (s. prec. and next entry) ***proud/boastful talking*** (Anonymus in Suda s.v. σεμνομυθοῦσιν=Polyb. 38, 19 v.l.; Philostrat., Her. 2, 19 p. 161, 19; Alex. Ep. 15, 12 p. 205 M.=PSI 1285 IV, 33; 1 Km 2:3; Alex. Ep. 15, 12 p. 205; TestJob 42:1) pl. *arrogant rhetoric* IEph 10:2.

μεγαλο(ρ)ρήμων, ονος (s. two prec. entries; Philostrat., Vi. Apoll. 6, 11 p. 222, 21) ***boastful*** γλῶσσα (Ps 11:4; 3 Macc 6:4; Jos., Ant. 20, 90 v.l.) 1 Cl 15:5.

μεγαλύνω (s. μέγας) impf. ἐμεγάλυνον, mid. ἐμεγαλυνόμην; fut. μεγαλυνῶ; 1 aor. ἐμεγάλυνα LXX. Pass.: fut. μεγαλυνθήσομαι; 1 aor. ἐμεγαλύνθην; pf. 3 sg. μεμεγάλυνται Ezk 9:9 ('make large/long, magnify' Aeschyl. et al.; Thu. 5, 98; POxy 1592, 3; LXX; TestLevi 18:3; JosAs 21:4 cod. A [p. 71, 21 Bat.])

❶ **to cause to be large, of either physical or nonphysical entities, *make large/long, make great*** τὶ *someth.* τὰ κράσπεδα (τῶν ἱματίων: v.l. addition, correct as to subject matter) *the tassels (on their garments)* **Mt 23:5.** μ. τὸ ἔλεος μετά τινος *show someone great mercy* **Lk 1:58** (cp. Gen 19:19 ἐμεγάλυνας τ. δικαιοσύνην σου). μ. τὸ ὄνομά τινος *make great someone's name* 1 Cl 10:3 (Gen 12:2; so also Eur., Bacch. 320); GJs 7:2; 12:1.—Pass. *increase, grow* (1 Km 2:21; 3 Km 10:26) **2 Cor 10:15.** ἐμεγαλύνθη ἡ ψυχή μου *my spirit is magnified* i.e. 'I am lost in wonder' GJs 5:2; 19:2 (cp. 1 Km 26:24).

❷ **to cause to be held in greater esteem through praise or deeds, *exalt, glorify, magnify, speak highly of*** (Eur., Thu. et al.; LXX) w. the acc. of the one praised τὸν κύριον (Sir 43:31) **Lk 1:46** (UMittman-Richert, Magnifikat und Benediktus '96). τὸν θεόν (Ps 68:31.—Cp. Diod. S. 1, 20, 6 μ. τοῦ θεοῦ τὴν δύναμιν) **Ac 10:46.** Of the apostles ἐμεγάλυνεν αὐτοὺς ὁ λαός *the people spoke highly of them* **5:13** (difft. NRSV). Boasters say: τ. γλῶσσαν ἡμῶν μεγαλυνοῦμεν *we will glorify our tongue* i.e. our speech will display our mastery 1 Cl 15:5 (Ps 11:5).—Pass. *be glorified, aggrandized* (2 Km 7:26) τὸ ὄνομα τοῦ κυρίου **Ac 19:17** (μ. τὸ ὄνομά τινος as Gen 12:2; Eur., Bacch. 320 ὅταν . . . τὸ Πενθέως δ' ὄνομα μεγαλύνῃ πόλις). μεγαλυνθήσεται Χριστὸς ἐν τῷ σώματί μου *Christ will be glorified in my person* (i.e. the prestige of Christ will be advanced in connection with me) **Phil 1:20.** W. δοξασθῆναι 1 Cl 32:3.—DELG s.v. μέγας. M-M. TW. Spicq.

μεγάλως adv. of μέγας (Hom. et al.) ***greatly*** μ. εἶναι (w. θαυμαστῶς) *be great* Hv 3, 4, 1; Hs 5, 5, 4 (s. HLjungvik, Eranos 62, '64, 28); on v 1, 3, 3 s. Dibelius, Hdb. W. εὐδόξως 9, 18, 4. Used to strengthen a verb *very (much), greatly* (Polyb. 1, 52, 2; Herodian 4, 15, 2; Jos., Vi. 154; SibOr 5, 61) ἐβόησεν μ. *let out a tremendous roar* AcPl Ha 2, 6; ἐμαρτυρήθη μ. Ἀβραάμ *Abraham had received a glorious witness* 1 Cl 17:2; χαρῆναι μ. *be very glad* (PAmh 39, 8 [II BC] μεγάλως ἐχάρημεν; EpArist 42; 312) **Phil 4:10;** Hs 8, 6. ἠγαλλιάσαντο μ. AcPl Ha 8, 5. συνεχάρην . . . μ. Pol. 1:1. παραδέχεσθαι μ. *be welcomed heartily* **Ac 15:4 v.l.** δοξασθεὶς μ. 1 Cl 17:5; cp. μ. ἡ δόξα κυρίου . . . ἐπ' αὐτόν AcPl Ha 7, 7.—GPt 11:45 (s. ἀγωνιάω). It is textually uncertain whether the verb w. μ. in 1 Cl 1:1 is βλασφημηθῆναι or βλαφθῆναι. In a fragmentary context AcPl BMM verso 23.—DELG s.v. μέγας. M-M.

μεγαλωσύνη, ης, ἡ (s. prec. and next entry; Herodian, Gramm. I 335, 18; LXX; En 98:2; 101:3; the Gizeh text [5:4] has μεγαλοσύνη; EpArist 192; TestLevi 3:9; 18:8; Ar. 15, 2; Suda; Etym. Mag. p. 275, 44; Byz. Chron. in Psaltes p. 267) **a state of greatness or preeminence, *majesty,*** used only of God; in a doxology w. δόξα (and other sim. ideas; En 14:16) **Jd 25;** 1 Cl 20:12; 61:3; 64; 65:2; MPol 20:2; 21:1 (here, as Ar. 15, 2, referred to Christ). τὸ σκῆπτρον τῆς μ. τοῦ θεοῦ *the scepter of the majesty of God* 1 Cl 16:2; ἐν λόγῳ τῆς μ. *by God's majestic word* 27:4. ἀπαύγασμα τῆς μ. *a reflection of God's majesty* 36:2 (cp. **Hb 1:3**). τὸ τῆς μ. ὄνομα αὐτοῦ *God's glorious name* **58:1.**—As a periphrasis for God himself ἐν δεξιᾷ τῆς μ. *at the right hand of God's Majesty* **Hb 1:3.** ὁ θρόνος τῆς μ. **8:1.**—DELG s.v. μέγας. M-M. TW. Spicq.

μέγας, μεγάλη, μέγα (Hom.+) comp. μείζων and beside it, because of the gradual disappearance of feeling for its comp. sense, μειζότερος **3J 4** (APF 3, 1906, 173; POxy 131, 25; BGU 368, 9; ApcSed 1:5 [cp. **J 15:13**]; s. B-D-F § 61, 2; W-S. §11, 4; Mlt-H. 166; Gignac II 158). Superl. μέγιστος (**2 Pt 1:4**).

❶ **pert. to exceeding a standard involving related objects, *large, great***—ⓐ of any extension in space in all directions λίθος **Mt 27:60; Mk 16:4.** δένδρον **Lk 13:19 v.l.** (TestAbr B 3 p. 107, 6 [Stone p. 62]). κλάδοι **Mk 4:32.** Buildings **13:2.** Fish **J 21:11.** A mountain (Tyrtaeus [VII BC], fgm. 4, 8 D.[2]; Ps.-Aristot., Mirabilia 138; Theopomp. [IV BC]: 115 fgm. 78 Jac.) **Rv 8:8.** A star vs. **10.** A furnace **9:2** (ParJer 6:23). A dragon (Esth 1:1e; Bel 23 Theod.) **12:3, 9.** ἀετός (Ezk 17:3; ParJer 7:18 [RHarris; om. Kraft-Purintun]) vs. **14.** μάχαιρα *a long sword* **6:4.** ἅλυσις *a long chain* **20:1.** πέλαγος AcPl Ha 7, 23 (first hand).

ⓑ with suggestion of spaciousness ἀνάγαιον *a spacious room upstairs* **Mk 14:15; Lk 22:12.** θύρα *a wide door* **1 Cor 16:9.** A winepress **Rv 14:19** (ληνός μ. 'trough' JosAs 2:20); χάσμα *a broad chasm* (2 Km 18:17) **Lk 16:26.** οἰκία (Jer 52:13) **2 Ti 2:20.**

ⓒ with words that include the idea of number ἀγέλη μ. *a large herd* **Mk 5:11.** δεῖπνον *a great banquet,* w. many invited guests (Da 5:1 Theod.; JosAs 3:6) **Lk 14:16.** Also δοχὴ μ. (Gen 21:8) **Lk 5:29;** GJs 6:2.

ⓓ of age (Jos., Ant. 12, 207 μικρὸς ἢ μέγας='young or old'); to include all concerned μικροὶ καὶ μεγάλοι *small and great* (PGM 15, 18) **Rv 11:18; 13:16; 19:5, 18; 20:12.** μικρῷ τε καὶ μεγάλῳ **Ac 26:22.** ἀπὸ μικροῦ ἕως μεγάλου (Gen 19:11; 4 Km 23:2; 2 Ch 34:30; POxy 1350) **8:10; Hb 8:11** (Jer 38:34). μέγας γενόμενος *when he was grown up* **11:24** (Ex 2:11). ὁ μείζων *the older* (O. Wilck II, 144, 3 [128 AD]; 213, 3; 1199, 2; LXX; cp. Polyb. 18, 18, 9 Σκιπίων ὁ μέγας; 32, 12, 1) **Ro 9:12;** B 13:2 (both Gen 25:23).

❷ **pert. to being above average in quantity, *great*** πορισμός *a great means of gain* **1 Ti 6:6.** μισθαποδοσία *rich reward* **Hb 10:35.**

❸ **pert. to being above standard in intensity, *great*** δύναμις **Ac 4:33; 19:8** D. Esp. of sound: *loud* φωνή **Mk 15:37; Lk 17:15; Rv 1:10;** φωνῇ μεγάλῃ (LXX; TestAbr A 5 p. 82, 20f [Stone p. 12]; ParJer 2:2; ApcMos 5:21) **Mt 27:46, 50; Mk 1:26; 5:7; 15:34; Lk 4:33; 8:28; 19:37; 23:23** (Φωναῖς μεγάλαις), **46; J 11:43; Ac 7:57, 60; 8:7; Rv 5:12; 6:10** al.; μεγ. φωνῇ (ParJer

5:32); **Ac 14:10; 16:28;** μεγ. τῇ φωνῇ (ParJer 9:8; Jos., Bell. 6, 188) **14:10 v.l.; 26:24;** ἐν φωνῇ μ. **Rv 5:2.** μετὰ σάλπιγγος μεγάλης *with a loud trumpet call* **Mt 24:31.** κραυγή (Ex 11:6; 12:30) **Lk 1:42; Ac 23:9;** cp. μεῖζον κράζειν *cry out all the more* **Mt 20:31.** κοπετός (Gen 50:10) **Ac 8:2.**—Of natural phenomena: ἄνεμος μ. *a strong wind* **J 6:18; Rv 6:13.** λαῖλαψ μ. (Jer 32:32) **Mk 4:37.** βροντή (Sir 40:13) **Rv 14:2.** χάλαζα **Rv 11:19; 16:21a.** χάλαζα λίαν μ. σφόδρα AcPl Ha 5, 7. σεισμὸς μ. (Jer 10:22; Ezk 3:12; 38:19; Jos., Ant. 9, 225) **Mt 8:24; 28:2; Lk 21:11a; Ac 16:26.** γαλήνη μ. *a deep calm* **Mt 8:26; Mk 4:39;** φῶς μ. *a bright light* (JosAs 6:3; ParJer 9:18 [16]; Plut., Mor. 567f: a divine voice sounds forth from this light; Petosiris, fgm. 7, ln. 39 τὸ ἱερὸν ἄστρον μέγα ποιοῦν φῶς) **Mt 4:16a;** GJs 19:2 (Is 9:1). καῦμα μ. *intense heat* **Rv 16:9** (JosAs 3:3).—Of surprising or unpleasant events or phenomena of the most diverse kinds (ἀπώλεια Dt 7:23; θάνατος Ex 9:3; Jer 21:6; κακόν Philo, Agr. 47) σημεῖα (Dt 6:22; 29:2) **Mt 24:24; Lk 21:11b; Ac 6:8.** δυνάμεις **8:13.** ἔργα μ. *mighty deeds* (cp. Judg 2:7) **Rv 15:3.** μείζω τούτων *greater things than these* **J 1:50** (μείζονα v.l.); cp. **5:20; 14:12.** διωγμὸς μ. *a severe persecution* **Ac 8:1;** θλῖψις μ. *(a time of) great suffering* (1 Macc 9:27) **Mt 24:21; Ac 7:11; Rv 2:22; 7:14.** πειρασμός AcPl Ha 8, 22. πληγή (Judg 15:8; 1 Km 4:10, 17 al.; TestReub 1:7; TestSim 8:4; Philo, Sacr. Abel. 134) **16:21b.** θόρυβος GJs 21:1; AcPl Ha 1, 28f (restored, s. AcPlTh [Aa I 258, 6]) λιμὸς μ. (4 Km 6:25; 1 Macc 9:24) **Lk 4:25; Ac 11:28;** ἀνάγκη μ. **Lk 21:23;** πυρετὸς μ. *a high fever* (s. πυρετός) **4:38.**—Of emotions: χαρά *great joy* (Jon 4:6; JosAs 3:4; 4:2 al.; Jos., Ant. 12, 91) **Mt 2:10; 28:8; Lk 2:10; 24:52.** φόβος *great fear*(X., Cyr. 4, 2, 10; Menand., fgm. 388 Kö.; Jon 1:10, 16; 1 Macc 10:8; TestAbr B 13 p. 117, 18 [Stone p. 82]; JosAs 6:1; GrBar 7:5) **Mk 4:41; Lk 2:9; 8:37; Ac 5:5, 11;** AcPl Ha 3, 33. θυμὸς μ. *fierce anger* (1 Macc 7:35) **Rv 12:12.** μείζων ἀγάπη *greater love* **J 15:13.** λύπη *profound* (Jon 4:1; 1 Macc 6:4, 9, 13; TestJob 7:8) **Ro 9:2.** σκυθρωπία AcPl Ha 7, 36. πίστις *firm* **Mt 15:28.** ἔκστασις (cp. Gen 27:33; ParJer 5:8, 12) **Mk 5:42.**

❹ **pert. to being relatively superior in importance, *great***

ⓐ of rational entities: of God and other deities θεός (SIG 985, 34 θεοὶ μεγάλοι [LBlock, Megaloi Theoi: Roscher II 2523–28, 2536–40; SCole, Theoi Megaloi, The Cult of the Great Gods at Samothrace '84]; 1237, 5 ὀργὴ μεγάλη τ. μεγάλου Διός; OGI 50, 7; 168, 6; 716, 1; PStras 81, 14 [115 BC] Ἴσιδος μεγάλης μητρὸς θεῶν; POxy 886, 1; PTebt 409, 11; 22 ὁ θεὸς μ. Σάραπις, al.; PGM 4, 155; 482; 778 and oft.; 3052 μέγ. θεὸς Σαβαώθ; 5, 474; Dt 10:17 al. in LXX; En 103:4; 104:1; Philo, Cher. 29 al.; Jos., Ant. 8, 319; SibOr 3, 19; 71 al.—Thieme 36f) **Tit 2:13** (Christ is meant). Ἄρτεμις (q.v.) **Ac 19:27f, 34f** (cp. Ael. Aristid. 48, 21 K.=24 p. 471 D. the outcry: μέγας ὁ Ἀσκληπιός); s. New Docs 1, 106 on this epithet in ref. to deities. Simon the magician is called ἡ δύναμις τ. θεοῦ ἡ καλουμένη μεγάλη **Ac 8:10b** (s. δύναμις 5). The angel Michael Hs 8, 3, 3; cp. 8, 4, 1.—Of people who stand in relation to the Divinity or are otherw. in high position: ἀρχιερεύς (s. ἀρχιερεύς 2a and ἱερεύς aβ.—ἀρχ. μέγ. is also the appellation of the priest-prince of Olba [s. PECS 641f] in Cilicia: MAMA III '31 p. 67, ins 63; 64 [I BC]) **Hb 4:14.** προφήτης (Sir 48:22) **Lk 7:16.** ποιμήν **Hb 13:20.** Gener. of rulers: οἱ μεγάλοι *the great ones, those in high position* **Mt 20:25; Mk 10:42.** Of people prominent for any reason **Mt 5:19; 20:26; Mk 10:43; Lk 1:15, 32; Ac 5:36** D; **8:9** (MSmith, HWolfson Festschr., '65, 741: μ. here and **Lk 1:32** may imply a messianic claim).—μέγας in the superl. sense (2 Km 7:9.—The positive also stands for the superl., e.g. Sallust. 4 p. 6, 14, where Paris calls Aphrodite καλή=the most beautiful. Diod. S. 17, 70, 1 πολεμία τῶν πόλεων=the most hostile [or especially hostile] among the cities) **Lk 9:48** (opp. ὁ μικρότερος).—Comp. μείζων *greater* of God (Ael. Aristid. 27, 3 K.=16 p. 382 D.; PGM 13, 689 ἐπικαλοῦμαί σε, τὸν πάντων μείζονα) **J 14:28; Hb 6:13; 1J 3:20; 4:4.** *More prominent* or *outstanding* because of certain advantages **Mt 11:11; Lk 7:28; 22:26f; J 4:12; 8:53; 13:16ab; 1 Cor 14:5.** More closely defined: ἰσχύϊ καὶ δυνάμει μείζων *greater in power and might* **2 Pt 2:11.** μεῖζον τοῦ ἱεροῦ *someth. greater than the temple* **Mt 12:6.** μείζων with superl. mng. (Ps.-Apollod., Epit. 7, 8 Wagner: Ὀδυσσεὺς τρεῖς κριοὺς ὁμοῦ συνδέων . . . καὶ αὐτὸς τῷ μείζονι ὑποδύς; Appian, Bell. Civ. 2, 87 §366 ἐν παρασκευῇ μείζονι= in the greatest preparation; Vett. Val. 62, 24; TestJob 3:1 ἐν μείζονι φωτί) **Mt 18:1, 4; 23:11; Mk 9:34; Lk 9:46; 22:24, 26.**

ⓑ of things: *great, sublime, important* μυστήριον (GrBar 1:6; 2;6; ApcMos 34; Philo, Leg. All. 3, 100 al.; Just., A I, 27, 4) **Eph 5:32; 1 Ti 3:16.** Of the sabbath day that begins a festival period **J 19:31;** MPol 8:1b. Esp. of the day of the divine judgment (LXX; En 22:4; ApcEsdr 3:3 p. 27, 7 Tdf.; Just., D. 49, 2 al.; cp. TestAbr A 13 p. 92, 11 [Stone p. 32]) **Ac 2:20** (Jo 3:4); **Jd 6; Rv 6:17; 16:14.** Of Paul's superb instructional ability μεγάλῃ καθ[ηγήσει] AcPl Ha 6, 30f.—μέγας in the superl. sense (Plut., Mor. 35a w. πρῶτος; Himerius, Or. 14 [Ecl. 15], 3 μέγας=greatest, really great; B-D-F §245, 2; s. Rob. 669) ἐντολή **Mt 22:36, 38.** ἡμέρα ἡ μ. τῆς ἑορτῆς *the great day of the festival* **J 7:37** (cp. Lucian, Pseudolog. 8 ἡ μεγάλη νουμηνία [at the beginning of the year]); Mel., P. 79, 579; 92, 694 ἐν τῇ μ. ἑορτῇ; GJs 1:2; 2:2 (s. deStrycker on 1:2). Of Mary's day of parturition ὡς μεγάλη ἡ σήμερον ἡμέρα *what a great day this is* GJs 19:2. μείζων as comp. (Chion, Ep. 16, 8 philosophy as νόμος μείζων=higher law; Sir 10:24) **J 5:36; 1J 5:9.** μ. ἁμαρτία **J 19:11** (cp. schol. on Pla. 189d ἁμαρτήματα μεγάλα; Ex 32:30f). τὰ χαρίσματα τὰ μείζονα *the more important spiritual gifts* (in the sense Paul gave the word) **1 Cor 12:31.** As a superl. (Epict. 3, 24, 93; Stephan. Byz. s.v. Ὕβλαι: the largest of three cities is ἡ μείζων [followed by ἡ ἐλάττων, and finally ἡ μικρά=the smallest]. The comparative also performs the function of the superlative, e.g. Diod. S. 20, 22, 2, where πρεσβύτερος is the oldest of 3 men) **Mt 13:32; 1 Cor 13:13** (by means of the superl. μ. Paul singles out from the triad the one quality that interests him most in this connection, just as Ael. Aristid. 45, 16 K. by means of αὐτός at the end of the θεοί singles out Sarapis, the only one that affects him).—The superl. μέγιστος, at times used by contemporary authors, occurs only once in the NT, where it is used in the elative sense *very great, extraordinary* (Diod. S. 2, 32, 1) ἐπαγγέλματα **2 Pt 1:4.**—On the adv. usage **Ac 26:29** s. ὀλίγος 2bβ.—Neut. pl. μεγάλα ποιεῖν τινι *do great things for someone* **Lk 1:49** (cp. Dt 10:21). λαλεῖν μεγάλα καὶ βλασφημίας *utter proud words and blasphemies* **Rv 13:5** (Da 7:8; cp. En 101:3). ἐποίει μεγ[ά]λα καὶ [θα]υ[μά]σια (Just., A I, 62, 4) *(Christ) proceeded to perform great and marvelous deeds* AcPl Ha 8, 33//BMM verso 6.

❺ **pert. to being unusual, *surprising,*** neut. μέγα εἰ . . . θερίσομεν; *is it an extraordinary thing* (i.e. are we expecting too much = our colloquial 'is it a big deal') *if we wish to reap?* **1 Cor 9:11.** οὐ μέγα οὖν, εἰ *it is not surprising, then, if* **2 Cor 11:15** (on this constr. cp. Pla., Menex. 235d; Plut., Mor. 215f; Gen 45:28; s. AFridrichsen, ConNeot 2, '36, 46).—B. 878f; 1309. DELG. M-M. TW. Sv.

μέγεθος, ους, τό (s. μέγας; Hom.+)—❶ **quality of exceeding a standard involving physical magnitude, *size,*** lit. (Appian, Bell. Civ. 1, 50 §219 ἀνὴρ μεγέθει μέγας; Heraclid. Crit. 23 [p. 82, 14 Pfister]; μεγάλη τῷ μεγέθει: Ps.-Dicaearch.

p. 145 ln. 5 F.; Did., Gen. 35, 10) ὑψηλὸς τῷ μεγέθει *very tall indeed* Hs 9, 6, 1. τὰ μεγέθη [τῶν θηρίων] *the enormous size of* the beasts AcPl Ha 1, 34.

❷ **quality of exceeding a standard of excellence, *greatness:*** τὸ τῆς χαρᾶς μ.=*the great joy* AcPl Ha 6, 9f. Of God (ins in Ramsay, CB I/2, 700 no. 635, 4 τὸ μέγεθος τ. θεοῦ; Philo, Spec. Leg. 1, 293 τὸ τ. θεοῦ μ.; Ath. 22, 7 τοῦ μ. τοῦ θεοῦ. Divine hypostases Hippol., Ref. 5, 8, 3; 10, 10, 2) τί τὸ ὑπερβάλλον μέγεθος τ. δυνάμεως αὐτοῦ *how surpassingly great (God's) power* **Eph 1:19** (cp. Philo, Op. M. 23, end τὸ μ. [τῶν δυνάμεων θεοῦ]; see also New Docs 4, 107). ἐν μεγέθει IEph ins, to be sure, does not belong grammatically w. θεοῦ, which rather goes w. πληρώματι foll.; nevertheless it describes the nature of God. τὸ μ. τῆς μαρτυρίας *the greatness of his martyrdom* MPol 17:1 (cp. τῆς γνώσεως Iren. 1, 13, 6 [Harv. I, 123, 3]; Did., Gen. 115, 2). ἀπολαμβάνειν τὸ ἴδιον μ. *recover their proper greatness,* of a congregation ISm 11:2. μεγέθους ἐστὶν ὁ Χριστιανισμός *Christianity is (truly) great* IRo 3:3.—DELG s.v. μέγας. M-M. TW. Spicq.

μεγιστάν, ᾶνος, ὁ (fr. μέγας via μέγιστος); almost exclusively, in our lit. always, in pl. μεγιστᾶνες, ων (LXX; PsSol 2:32; TestSol 10:28 C [acc. -ους]; JosAs; Manetho, Apot. 4, 41; Artem. 1, 2 p. 8, 16; 3, 9; Jos., Ant. 11, 37; 20, 26, Vi. 112; 149; Just., D. 107, 2; Tat. 3, 4;; PGM 13, 251 [sing.]; Phryn. 196f Lob.—B-D-F §2: Dorism) **a person of high rank, *great man, courtier, magnate*** at Herod's court **Mk 6:21.** Gener. οἱ μ. τῆς γῆς **Rv 18:23;** (w. βασιλεῖς) **6:15.** C-HHunzinger, ZNW Beih. 26, '60, 209–20: Gospel of Thomas.—DELG s.v. μέγας. M-M.

μέγιστος s. μέγας 4.—M-M.

μεθερμηνεύω (s. ἑρμηνεύω) aor. inf. μεθερμηνεῦσαι Sir prol. ln. 30 (Polyb. 6, 26, 6; Diod. S. 1, 11, 2; Plut., Cato Maj. 2, 6; Herm. Wr. 12, 13a; PTebt 164 I, 1 [II BC]; BGU 1002 II, 1 al.; Sir prol., s. above; EpArist 38; Jos., Ant. 8, 142, C. Ap. 1, 54) ***translate*** **Ac 13:8** (here 'Elymas' either explains Bar-Jesus or translates μάγος, s. Ἐλύμας). Mostly in the formula ὅ ἐστιν μεθερμηνευόμενον *which means (when translated)* (Theophilus: 296 fgm. 3 Jac.)**Mt 1:23; Mk 5:41; 15:22, 34; J 1:41; Ac 4:36.** Also ὃ λέγεται μ. (v.l. ἑρμηνευόμενον) **J 1:38.**—DELG s.v. ἑρμηνεύς. M-M.

μέθη, ης, ἡ (s. μεθύω; Antiphon+; Epict. 3, 26, 5; Herm. Wr. 1, 27; pap, LXX; PsSol 8:14; OdeSol 11:8; TestSol 18:16 P; Test12Patr; GrBar; Philo; Jos., Ant. 1, 301; 11, 42; Ar. 10, 8; Just., A II, 2, 7) ***drunkenness*** ἐν κραιπάλῃ καὶ μ. *with dissipation and drunkenness* **Lk 21:34.** Also pl. w. the same mng. (Pla. et al.; also Vett. Val. 90, 13; PGiss 3, 8; Jdth 13:15; GrBar) 1 Cl 30:1; AcPl Ha 1, 12; w. κῶμοι **Ro 13:13.** In a list of vices **Gal 5:21** (yet it seems that in the last two passages the proximity of κῶμοι='unrestrained revelry' may influence μέθαι in the direction of *drinking-bout;* on this cp. Diod. S. 16, 19, 2, where all mss. agree in the reading οἱ στρατηγοὶ ἐκ τῆς μέθης μεθύοντες = the generals who were drunken from the revelry).—DELG s.v. μέθυ. M-M. TW.

μεθιστάνω s. next entry.

μεθίστημι (s. ἵστημι) by-form μεθιστάνω (Hv 1, 3, 4; **1 Cor 13:2 v.l.**) fut. μεταστήσω LXX; 1 aor. μετέστησα; 2 aor. μετέστην LXX. Pass.: aor. μετεστάθην; subj. μετασταθῶ (Hom.+; ins, pap, LXX, TestSol; TestAbr A 20 p. 103, 8 [Stone p. 54]; TestIss 1:13; Joseph.)

❶ **transfer from one place to another, *remove*—ⓐ** of things τὶ *someth.* ὄρη **1 Cor 13:2** (Is 54:10). Heavens, mountains, hills, seas Hv 1, 3, 4. (ἡμᾶς) μετέστησεν εἰς τὴν βασιλείαν *(God) transferred us to the kingdom* **Col 1:13** (cp. Jos., Ant. 9, 235 μ. εἰς τ. αὐτοῦ βασιλείαν.—μ. εἰς='transplant into' also Alex. Aphr., Mixt. II 2 p. 219, 28; 230, 29; cp. τὸ μεταστῆναι ἀπὸ τῶν ὁρατῶν ἐπὶ τὰ ἀόρατα as a description of ἔκστασις Did., Gen. 230, 9).

ⓑ of persons *remove, depose* (3 Km 15:13; 1 Macc 11:63; Jos., Ant. 19, 297; 20, 16) τινὰ ἀπὸ τοῦ τόπου *remove someone from his place* 1 Cl 44:5. Pass. *be removed* ὅταν μετασταθῶ ἐκ τ. οἰκονομίας *when I am discharged fr. my position as manager* **Lk 16:4** (Vi. Aesopi G 9 μεταστήσω σε τῆς οἰκονομίας=I will remove you from your position as steward.—μ. ἐκ as Jos., Vi. 195).—This is prob. also the place for **Ac 13:22** μεταστήσας αὐτόν *after he had removed him* (fr. the throne; cp. Da 2:21). The expr. in its fullest form, μ. τινὰ ἐκ τοῦ ζῆν 'put someone to death' (Diod. S. 2, 57, 5; 4, 55, 1; cp. 3 Macc 6:12), scarcely seems applicable here.

❷ **to bring to a different point of view, *turn away, mislead,*** also in an unfavorable sense, fig. ext. of 1 (X., Hell. 2, 2, 5; Plut., Galba 1059 [14, 3] τοὺς πλείους μετέστησαν; Josh 14:8) ἱκανὸν ὄχλον **Ac 19:26.**—DELG s.v. ἵστημι. M-M.

μεθοδεία, ας, ἡ also -δία (POxy 136, 18; 24; 1134, 9 al., though only in late pap [421 AD and later], and in the sense 'method', etc.; Hesychius; Suda) in our lit. (only Eph) only in an unfavorable sense (s. μεθοδεύω) ***scheming, craftiness*** πρὸς τὴν μ. τῆς πλάνης *in deceitful scheming* **Eph 4:14.** Pl. *wiles, stratagems* (Suda: μεθοδείας: τέχνας ἢ δόλους; Iren. 1, 9, 1 [Harv. I 82, 1]: ἵνα … κατανοήσῃς τὴν πανουργίαν τῆς μ. καὶ τὴν πονηρίαν τῆς πλάνης) αἱ μ. τοῦ διαβόλου (Cyrill. of Scyth. p. 30, 21 μ. τῶν δαιμόνων) **6:11, 12** P[46].—DELG s.v. ὁδός. M-M. TW. Spicq.

μεθοδεύω (s. prec. entry) aor. 3 sg. μεθώδευσεί 2 Km 19:28 (found not infreq. in later wr., incl. PGM 13, 713; LXX, Philo) in an unfavorable sense ***defraud, deceive, pervert*** (Chariton 7, 6, 10 μεθοδεύεται γυνὴ ἐπαγγελίαις=is deceived by promises; POxy 2342, 27 [102 AD]; Philo, Mos. 2, 212 ὅπερ μεθοδεύουσιν οἱ λογοθῆραι καὶ σοφισταί; 2 Km 19:28) τὰ λόγια τοῦ κυρίου πρὸς τὰς ἰδίας ἐπιθυμίας *pervert the words of the Lord to suit one's own desires* Pol 7:1.—DELG s.v. ὁδός. M-M. TW.

μεθόριον, ου, τό (subst. neut. of μεθόριος [w. two or three endings]; the subst. in Thu. et al.; Josh 19:27 A; Philo; Jos., Ant. 18, 111; loanw. in rabb.) ***boundary;*** pl. (Thu. 4, 99; X., Cyr. 1, 4, 16; 17) also the *region* included by the boundaries (Ael. Aristid. 38 p. 721 D.: ἐν μεθορίοις τῆς Ἀττικῆς) **Mk 7:24 v.l.** (for ὅρια, q.v.).—DELG s.v. ὅρος. M-M. Sv.

μεθύσκω fut. μεθύσω; 1 aor. ἐμέθυσα LXX (causal of μεθύω; Pla. et al.; LXX; OdeSol 11:7) ***cause to become intoxicated;*** in our lit. only pass. μεθύσκομαι (Eur., Hdt. et al.; Pr 4:17; 23:31; Jos., Bell. 2, 29; TestJud 14:1) 1 aor. ἐμεθύσθην; fut. μεθυσθήσομαι, in act. sense *get drunk, become intoxicated* οἴνῳ *with wine* **Eph 5:18** (as Pr 4:17; s. B-D-F §195, 2; Rob. 533). οἱ μεθυσκόμενοι (Cornutus 30 p. 59, 21; Dio Chrys. 80 [30], 36) **1 Th 5:7** (s. μεθύω). W. πίνειν (X., Cyr. 1, 3, 11) **Lk 12:45.** μεθυσθῆναι *be drunk* (Diod. S. 23, 21 μεθυσθέντες=those who had become drunk. Likewise 5, 26, 3; 17, 25, 5; Jos., Vi. 225 of one who revealed secrets in an intoxicated state) **J 2:10.** ἐκ τοῦ οἴνου (like שָׁכַר מִיַּיִן) **Rv 17:2.** S. μέθη.—M-M. DELG s.v. μέθυ. TW.

μέθυσμα, ατος, τό (s. prec. and two next entries; LXX; Philo, Agr. 157, Deus Imm. 158 al.) ***intoxicating drink*** μ.

ἀνομίας *intox. drink that leads to lawlessness* Hm 8:3. Pl. (w. ἐδέσματα) 6, 2, 5; 12, 2, 1.—DELG s.v. μέθυ.

μέθυσος, ου, ὁ (s. two prec. and next entry; masc. subst. of the adj., which is found Aristoph. et al.; POxy 1828, 3; LXX; TestJud 14:8. From Menand. [fgm. 67 Kö.] on, it is used of both sexes [Lucian, Tim. 55; Plut., Brut. 5, 4; Sext. Emp., Hyp. 3, 24; Pr 23:21; 26:9], though the older writers used it only of women: Phryn. 151f Lob.) ***drunkard*** w. those addicted to other vices (as Cebes 34, 3 and in the pap above) Hs 6, 5, 5. Likew., but closely connected w. λοίδορος, **1 Cor 5:11; 6:10.**—DELG s.v. μέθυ. M-M.

μεθύω (μέθυ 'wine'; Hom. et al.; PHal 1, 193f; PGM 7, 180 πολλὰ πίνειν καὶ μὴ μεθύειν, al. in pap; LXX, Test12Patr; Philo; Jos., Bell. 6, 196, Vi. 225; 388; Just., D. 14, 6) **to drink to a point of intoxication, *be drunk*** **Ac 2:15;** Ox 1 verso, 15 (ASyn. 240, 40; cp. GTh 28; Unknown Sayings 69–74). Opp. πεινᾶν **1 Cor 11:21.** οἱ μεθυσκόμενοι νυκτὸς μεθύουσιν *those who get drunk are drunk at night* **1 Th 5:7.** οἱ μεθύοντες *those who are drunken* (Diod. S. 4, 5, 3; Cornutus 30 p. 61, 6; Job 12:25) **Mt 24:49.**—In imagery (X., Symp. 8, 21; Pla., Lysias 222c; Philostrat., Vi. Soph. 2, 1, 2 πλούτῳ μ.; Achilles Tat. 1, 6, 1 ἔρωτι; OdeSol 11:6 ὕδωρ τὸ ἀθάνατον; Philo) of the apocal. woman who has sated her thirst for blood (sim. in hue to wine) εἶδον τὴν γυναῖκα μεθύουσαν ἐκ τ. αἵματος τ. ἁγίων **Rv 17:6.**—DELG s.v. μέθυ. M-M. TW.

μείγνυμι, μειγνύω s. μίγνυμι.

μειδιάω fut. 3 sg. μειδιάσει Sir 21:20; aor. ptc. μειδιάσας (Hom. et al.; Philo, Joseph.) ***smile*** μειδιάσαντος τοῦ παιδός AcPl Ha 3, 14; 4, 2 (of a celestial being).—DELG.

μειζότερος s. μέγας.

μείζων s. μέγας.—M-M.

μειλίσσω (in various senses: Hom., trag., Aristoph. et al.; Jos., Bell. 1, 161; Just., D. 90, 5) ***treat kindly, be appealing/winning in manner/words,*** *speak winsomely* τὴν παρα[θαλασσίαν γὴν ἀ]νῆλθε[ν δια]|κονῶν καὶ μ̣ε̣ιλει[σσόμενος] *(Jesus) traveled through the land along the sea, rendering service and being winsome in his words* AcPl BMM verso 14 (restoration as suggested by HSanders, HTR 31, '38, 89).—DELG s.v. μείλια.

μειόω 1 aor. ἐμείωσα (s. μείωσις; X., Pla. et al.; Strabo: 91 fgm. 18 Jac. [Jos., Ant. 15, 10]; PFay 26, 15 [II AD] al. in pap; Sir 43:7; Philo, Rer. Div. Her. 140; SibOr 12, 134; Ar. 6, 2; Ath., R. 7 p. 56, 7) ***lessen*** τὶ *someth.* τὸ σεμνὸν τῆς φιλαδελφίας ὑμῶν *the respect that is due your brotherly love* 1 Cl 47:5 (cp. SIG 783, 8f οὐκ ἐμίωσέν τι τῆς πατρῴας ἀρετῆς).—DELG s.v. μείων.

μείωσις, εως, ἡ (s. μειόω; Hippocr. et al.; Polyb. 9, 43, 5; Sext. Emp., Math. 9, 400; Vett. Val. index; PMich XIII, 659, 227 [VI AD] taxes; Philo) ***lessening, diminution*** τῆς σαρκός *mutilation of the flesh* Dg 4:4.—DELG s.v. μείων. New Docs 2, 78.

μέλαν, τό s. μέλας, end.

μελανέω fut. μελανήσω; 1 aor. ἐμελάνησα (s. μέλας; Theophr. et al.; PLond III, 897, 22f p. 207 [84 AD]) ***turn black*** of stones Hs 9, 30, 2.—In 9, 8, 7 the ἐμελάνωσαν of the mss. was corrected by Gebhardt to ἐμελάνησαν (otherwise only mid. pf. μεμελάνωμαι LXX; JosAs 10:9 cod. A [p. 51, 21 Bat.]; GrBar 13:1).—Reinhold §14, 3. DELG s.v. μέλας.

μέλας, μέλαινα, μέλαν gen. ανος, αίνης, ανος (s. prec. entry; Hom.+; ins, pap, LXX, JosAs 10:1; 14:15; Sib. Or. 4, 75; Philo, Joseph.; Tat. 33, 3) by-form μελανός (acc. sg. -όν JosAs 10:9; 13:2; 14:12 [each μέλαν cod. B]; pl. -ούς TestSol 9:9 C) comp. μελανώτερος (Strabo 16, 4, 12) 1 Cl 8:3.

❶ ***black***—ⓐ hair (Lev 13:37) **Mt 5:36** (opp. λευκός as Artem. 1, 32 p. 34, 5; 9f). Of clothing used in mourning (Polyaenus 6, 7, 1 ἐν μελαίνῃ ἐσθῆτι; Jos., Vi. 138) μ. ὡς σάκκος τρίχινος **Rv 6:12;** cp. 1 Cl 8:3.

ⓑ apocal. color: w. others **Rv 6:5** (cp. Zech 6:2, 6 and s. πυρρός); Hv 4, 1, 10; 4, 3, 2; named alone, and as the color of evil, forming a contrast to the world of light (*evil, malignant* in the moral realm Solon, Pind. et al.; Diphilus Com. [IV/III BC] 91e of a woman; Plut., Mor. 12d μ. ἄνθρωποι; M. Ant. 4, 28 μ. ἦθος; Philostrat., Vi. Apoll. 5, 36 p. 196, 19 of misused gold) Hs 9, 1, 5; 9, 6, 4; 9, 8, 1f; 4f; 9, 9, 5; 9, 13, 8; 9, 15, 1; 3; 9, 19, 1. Hence ὁ μ. *the Black One* of the devil B 4:9; 20:1 (Lucian, Philops. 31 ὁ δαίμων μελάντερος τοῦ ζόφου).—FDölger, D. Sonne der Gerechtigkeit u. der Schwarze 1918; LZiehen, ARW 24, 1926, 48ff; RGradwohl, Die Farben im AT Beih. ZAW 83, '63, 50–53. S. also AcThom 55 [Aa II/2, 171, 15]; 64 [180, 16].

❷ neut. τὸ μέλαν, ανος ***ink*** (Pla., Phdr. 276c; Demosth. 18, 258; Plut., Mor. 841e, Solon 17, 3; Synes., Ep. 157 p. 294b κάλαμον κ. χάρτην κ. μέλαν; PGrenf II, 38, 8 [81 BC]; POxy 326; PLeid X, 10, 1ff; ParJer 6:19 χάρτην καὶ μέλανα; TestAbr A 12 p. 91, 3f [Stone p. 30] χάρτην καὶ μέλανα καὶ κάλαμον; loanw. in rabb.) ἐπιστολὴ ἐγγεγραμμένη μέλανι **2 Cor 3:3.** διὰ μέλανος καὶ καλάμου γράφειν *write with pen and ink* **3J 13.** διὰ χάρτου καὶ μέλανος **2J 12.**—Pauly-W. Suppl. VII 1574ff; Kl. Pauly V 856; BHHW III 1991. B. 1052; 1055; 1291. DELG. M-M. TW.

Μελεά, ὁ indecl. (מְלֵאָה?; in a list of indecl. names scarcely Μελεᾶ as gen. of Μελεᾶς) ***Melea,*** in the genealogy of Jesus **Lk 3:31.**

μέλει third pers. sing. of μέλω, used impersonally and personally; impf. ἔμελεν; 1 aor. ἐμέλησεν, subj. μελήσῃ (B 1:5) (Hom. et al.; pap, LXX; TestAbr A 4 p. 81, 21 [Stone p. 10]; Just.; Tat. [μέλον ἐστίν]) w. dat. of pers.

❶ ***it is a care/concern, is of interest to someone***—ⓐ w. gen. of the thing about which concern is felt (trag., Pla. et al.; Ael. Aristid. 51, 34 K.=27 p. 542 D.: τούτων ἐμέλησε τῷ θεῷ; Oenomaus fgm. 12 [in Eus., PE 5, 34, 14] satirical statement by a Cynic: τί μέλει τοῖς φιλανθρώποις θεοῖς ἀνθρώπων; Jos., Ant. 7, 45 θεός, ᾧ μέλει πάντων; Just., A I, 28, 4; D. 6, 1: Ath. 35, 2) μὴ τῶν βοῶν μ. τῷ θεῷ; *is it about oxen that God is concerned?* **1 Cor 9:9** (Ael. Dion. τ, 35; Paroem. Gr.: Apostol. 17, 43 τῶν δ' ὄνων οὔμοι μέλει. For the idea cp. Aeschin. 1, 17; EpArist 144; Philo, Spec. Leg. 1, 260 οὐ γὰρ ὑπὲρ ἀλόγων ὁ νόμος).

ⓑ foll. by περί τινος *about someone* or *someth.* (Aeschyl., Hdt. et al.; Diod. S. 4, 38, 3 περὶ τῶν λοιπῶν Διΐ μελήσειν = Zeus will care for the rest; Alciphron 4, 6, 5; PLond III, 897, 27 p. 207 [84 AD]; POxy 1155, 5; 1 Macc 14:42, 43; Wsd 12:13; Jos., Ant. 6, 253; Just., D. 8, 2 περὶ σεαυτοῦ) οὐ μ. σοι περὶ οὐδενός *you care for no one,* i.e. *you court no one's favor* or *you don't care what anybody thinks or says about you* **Mt 22:16; Mk 12:14.** περὶ τῶν προβάτων *care for the sheep* **J 10:13.** περὶ τῶν πτωχῶν **12:6;** cp. **1 Pt 5:7;** Hv 2, 3, 1. περὶ ἀγάπης οὐ μ. αὐτοῖς *they are not concerned about love* ISm 6:2.

ⓒ foll. by ὅτι (Hdt. 9, 72; PSI 445; Tob 10:5 BA) *someone is concerned that* **Mk 4:38; Lk 10:40.** W. inf. foll. (POxy 930, 11) *someone takes care* or *is pleased to do someth.* B 11:1. W. περί τινος and a subst. inf. foll. τοῦ μεταδοῦναι 1:5.

ⓓ a rather clear case of the personal constr. (Hom. et al.; EpArist 92) οὐδὲν (subj.) τούτων (partitive gen.) τῷ Γαλλίωνι ἔμελεν *none of these things concerned Gallio = he paid no attention to this* **Ac 18:17** (s. B-D-F §176, 3; Rob. 508f. But s. οὐδείς 2bγ). Sim. πάντα σοι μ. *you are concerned about everything,* lit. 'everything is a care to you'=*you want to know about everything* Hs 9, 13, 6. —S. also μέλομαι.

❷ ***be a source of concern*** abs. (X., Cyr. 4, 3, 7; IG IX, 1, 654 τῇ θεῷ μελήσει) μή σοι μελέτω *never mind* **1 Cor 7:21.**—DELG s.v. μέλω. M-M.

Μελελεήλ s. Μαλελεήλ.

μελετάω (s. μελέτη) fut. μελετήσω LXX; 1 aor. ἐμελέτησα (Hom. Hymns, Thu.; Vett. Val. 330, 22; pap, LXX; TestAbr B 2 p. 106, 19 [Stone p. 60]; Philo; Just., D. 86, 6; Tat. 21, 1).

❶ **to work with someth. definite in mind,** ***take care, endeavor*** (Hes. et al.; PSI 94, 18) εἰς τὸ σῶσαι ψυχήν *to save a soul* B 19:10.

❷ **to improve by care or study,** ***practice, cultivate, take pains with*** w. acc. (Aristoph., Plut. 511; Hdt. 6, 105; Philo; Jos., Bell. 6, 306 al.) ταῦτα (Epict. 2, 1, 29 ταῦτα μελετᾶτε; 1, 1, 25;ταῦτα μελ. . . . ἐν τούτοις . . . ; Tat. 21, 1) **1 Ti 4:15;** B 21:7. μ. τὸν φόβον τοῦ θεοῦ *cultivate the fear of God* B 4:11; cp. 11:5 (=Is 33:18). Pass. διὰ τὸ μελετᾶσθαι θανάτου κατάλυσιν *because the destruction of death was being carried out* IEph 19:3.

❸ **to fix one's mind on someth.,** ***think about, meditate upon*** (Ps.-Demosth. 61, 43; Just., D. 86, 6) τὶ *someth.* (Epict. 1, 25, 6; Job 27:4; Pr 15:28; EpArist 160; Jos., Ant. 4, 183) κενά *think vain thoughts, conspire in vain* (הָגָה רִיק) **Ac 4:25** (Ps 2:1). διάσταλμα ῥήματος B 10:11.—Abs. μηδὲ μελετᾶτε *and do not rack your brains* **Mk 13:11 v.l.**—DELG s.v. μέλω. M-M. TW. Sv.

μελέτη, ης, ἡ (cp. prec. entry; Hes. et al.; IG II², 1028, 19 al.; BGU 1125, 7 [13 BC]; LXX; ParJer 9:5; Jos.Philo; Jos., C. Ap. 2, 276, Ant. 16, 43; Ath. 33, 2 μ. λόγων) ***meditation, study*** B 10:11.—B. 1092. DELG s.v. μέλω. Sv.

μέλι, ιτος, τό (Hom.+) ***honey;*** sweet **Rv 10:9f** (Ezk 3:3); Hm 5, 1, 5f. W. milk as food for children (Diod. S. 5, 70, 3; Philostrat., Her. 19, 19; Is 7:15, 22) B 6:17; sign of fertility (schol. on Pind., O. 1, 157c [98] γῆ μέλι ῥέουσα) 6:8, 10, 13 (Ex 33:3; on the formula s. HUsener [s. γάλα b]; NDahl, MGoguel Festschr. '50, 62–70). μ. ἄγριον (s. ἄγριος 1) **Mt 3:4; Mk 1:6;** GEb13, 79 (in antiquity μ. freq. associated w. divine inspiration and oracular expression, cp. Pind., P. 4, 60 and schol. on the same).—As healing remedy μέλιτι θεράπευε σεαυτόν AcPl Ha 5, 36. SKrauss, Honig in Palästina: ZDPV 32, 1909, 151–64; Dalman, Arbeit VII (s. οἰκία 1a).—AMayor, Mad Honey!: Archaeology 48/6, 32–40 (informative, but without detailed documentation of ancient sources); BHHW II 747.—B. 384. DELG. M-M. TW.

μέλισσα, ης, ἡ (cp. μέλι; Hom. et al.; PSI 426, 13; Ps.-Phoc. 127; JosAs; Philo in Eus., PE. 8, 11, 8; Jos., Ant. 5, 288; 6, 118) ***bee*** B 6:6 (Ps 117:12).—B. 192. DELG s.v. μέλι.

μελίσσιος, ιον (s. prec. entry) ***pert. to the bee*** (Syntipas p. 28, 9; 29, 3) μελίσσιον κηρίον *(bee-)honeycomb* (Biogr. p. 93; Syntipas 28, 7) ἀπὸ μελισσίου κηρίου *some honeycomb* **Lk 24:42 v.l.** As subst. **τὸ μελίσσ(ε)ιον** *bee-hive* (ApcSed 8, 5 p. 132, 38 Ja. ['bee']; PCairZen 467 [III BC]; schol. on Nicander, Alexiph. 547; Hesych.) ἀπὸ μελισσίου κήριον *a honeycomb from a bee-hive* vs. **42 v.l.**—EbNestle, ZDPV 30, 1907, 209f; EGrafvMülinen, ibid. 35, 1912, 105ff; LKöhler, ibid. 54, '31, 289ff; GDalman, ibid. 55, '32, 80f; PKatz, TLZ 83, '58, 315. DELG s.v. μέλι.

Μελίτη, ης, ἡ ***Malta,*** an island located south of Sicily (M. is attested as the name of this island in Diod. S. 15, 12, 2; Strabo 6, 2, 11; 17, 3, 16; Ps.-Scylax 94 [p. 37 BFabricius 1878]; ins) **Ac 28:1.**—On debate respecting identification w. Mijet, off the Dalmatian coast (among the first in modern times AAcworth, JTS 24, '73, 190–93) and Cephallenia (Warnecke, Romfahrt 59–69; 145–56) s. BRapske, BAFCS II 36–43.—AMayr, D. Insel Malta im Altertum 1909; Zahn, AG 841–44; JvonFreeden, Malta u. die Baukunst seiner Megalith-Tempel '93; Pauly-W. XV 543ff; Kl. Pauly III 1179; DAC X 1320ff; BHHW II 1132f; OEANE III 402–5.—Boffo, Iscrizioni no. 22. M-M.

Μελιτήνη v.l. for Μελίτη.

μέλλω (Hom.+) fut. μελλήσω; impf. ἔμελλον (all edd. **J 6:6; Ac 21:27**) and ἤμελλον (all edd. **Lk 7:2; 19:4; J 4:47; 12:33; 18:32; Hb 11:8;** s. B-D-F §66, 3; W.-S. §12, 3; Mlt-H. 188. In Att. ins the ἠ- appears after 300 BC [Meisterhans³-Schw. 169]. In IPriene ἐ- occurs only once: 11, 5 [c. 297 BC]).

❶ **to take place at a future point of time and so to be subsequent to another event,** ***be about to,*** used w. an inf. foll.

ⓐ only rarely w. the fut. inf., w. which it is regularly used in ancient Gk. (Hom. et al.), since in colloquial usage the fut. inf. and ptc. were gradually disappearing and being replaced by combinations with μέλλω (B-D-F §338, 3; 350; s. Rob. 882; 889). W. the fut. inf. μ. denotes certainty that an event will occur in the future μ. ἔσεσθαι (SIG 914, 10 μέλλει ἔσεσθαι; 247 I, 74 ἔμελλε . . . [δώσε]ιν; Jos., Ant. 13, 322; Mel., P. 57, 415) *will certainly take place* or *be* **Ac 11:28; 24:15; 27:10;** 1 Cl 43:6; cp. Dg 8:2.

ⓑ w. the aor. inf. (rarely in ancient Gk. [but as early as Hom., and e.g. X., Cyr. 1, 4, 16]; Herodas 3, 78 and 91; UPZ 70, 12 [152/1 BC]; PGiss 12, 5; POxy 1067, 17; 1488, 20; Ex 4:12; Job 3:8; 2 Macc 14:41; JosAs 29:3; ParJer 9:13; GrBar 4:15 [Christ.]; ApcMos13; s. Phryn. p. 336; 745ff Lob.; WRutherford, New Phryn. 1881, 420ff) *be on the point of, be about to,* μ. ἀποκαλυφθῆναι *be about to be revealed* **Ro 8:18.** τὸ δωδεκάφυλον τοῦ Ἰσραὴλ μέλλον ἀπολέσθαι *the twelve tribes of Israel that were about to be destroyed* 1 Cl 55:6. ἤμελλεν προαγαγεῖν **Ac 12:6.** ἀποθανεῖν **Rv 3:2.** ἐμέσαι vs. **16.** τεκεῖν **12:4.**

ⓒ w. the pres. inf. So mostly (ca. 80 times in the NT.; oft. in lit., ins, pap, LXX; TestAbr B 4 p. 108, 14 [Stone p. 64]; ApcEsdr 6:23f p. 32, 2f Tdf.; EpArist; Demetr.: 722 fgm. 7 Jac.; Just., A I, 51, 8; D. 32, 4 al.; Tat. 14, 1; Mel., P. 38, 263; Ath. 32, 1).

α. *be about to, be on the point of* ἤμελλεν τελευτᾶν *he was at the point of death* (Aristot. fgm. 277 [in Apollon. Paradox. 27] and Diod. S. 6, 4, 3 μέλλων τελευτᾶν; cp. Jos., Ant. 4, 83; 12, 357) **Lk 7:2.** Also ἤμελλεν ἀποθνήσκειν (Artem. 4, 24 p. 217, 5 γραῦς μέλλουσα ἀποθνήσκειν; Aesop, Fab. 131 P.=202 H.; 233 P.=216 H.; 2 Macc 7:18; 4 Macc 10:9) **J 4:47.** ἤμελλεν ἑαυτὸν ἀναιρεῖν *he was about to kill himself* **Ac 16:27.** Of God's eschat. reign μέλλειν ἔρχεσθαι 1 Cl 42:3. Of heavenly glory ἡ μέλλουσα ἀποκαλύπτεσθαι **1 Pt 5:1.** Cp. **Lk 19:4; J 6:6; Ac 3:3; 5:35; 18:14; 21:27; 22:26; 23:27.**—Occasionally almost = *begin* ἤμελλον γράφειν **Rv 10:4.** ὅταν μέλλῃ ταῦτα συντελεῖσθαι πάντα *when all these things are* (or *begin*) *to be accomplished* **Mk 13:4;** cp. **Lk 21:7; Rv 10:7.**

β. in a weakened sense it serves simply as a periphrasis for the fut. (PMich III, 202, 8ff; 13ff [105 AD].—Mayser II/1, 226) ὅσα λαλῶ ἢ καὶ μ. λαλεῖν (=ἢ καὶ λαλήσω) *what I tell or* *shall tell* Hm 4, 4, 3. So esp. oft. in Hermas: μ. λέγειν v 1, 1, 6; 3, 8, 11; m 11:7, 17; s 5, 2, 1. μ. ἐντέλλεσθαι v 5:5; m 5, 2, 8. μ. κατοικεῖν s 1:1; 4:2. μ. χωρεῖν (=χωρήσω) IMg 5:1. μ. βασιλεύειν GJs 23:2.—Substitute for the disappearing fut. forms (inf. and ptc. B-D-F §356); for the fut. inf.: προσεδόκων αὐτὸν μέλλειν πίμπρασθαι **Ac 28:6;** for the fut. ptc.: ὁ μέλλων ἔρχεσθαι **Mt 11:14.** ὁ τοῦτο μέλλων πράσσειν *the one who was going to do this* **Lk 22:23;** cp. **24:21; Ac 13:34.** οἱ μέλλοντες πιστεύειν *those who were to believe* (in him) *in the future* **1 Ti 1:16;** 1 Cl 42:4; Hm 4, 3, 3. μέλλοντες ἀσεβεῖν *those who were to be ungodly in the future* **2 Pt 2:6 v.l.** (s. 3, end). Of Christ ὁ μέλλων κρίνειν **2 Ti 4:1;** B 7:2. οἱ μέλλοντες ἀρνεῖσθαι = οἱ ἀρνησόμενοι Hv 2, 2, 8. πυρὸς ζῆλος ἐσθίειν μέλλοντος τοὺς ὑπεναντίους *raging fire that will devour the opponents* **Hb 10:27.**

γ. denoting an intended action: *intend, propose, have in mind* μέλλει Ἡρῴδης ζητεῖν τὸ παιδίον *Herod intends to search for the child* **Mt 2:13.** οὗ ἤμελλεν αὐτὸς ἔρχεσθαι *where he himself intended to come* **Lk 10:1.** μέλλουσιν ἔρχεσθαι *they intended to come* **J 6:15.** Cp. vs. **71; 7:35; 12:4; 14:22; Ac 17:31; 20:3, 7, 13ab; 23:15; 26:2; 27:30; Hb 8:5; 2 Pt 1:12.** τί μέλλεις ποιεῖν; *what do you intend to do?* Hs 1:5. οὐ μ. ποιεῖν *I have no intention of doing* MPol 8:2. μ. προσηλοῦν *they wanted to nail him fast* 13:3. μ. λαμβάνειν *we wanted to take him out* 17:2.

❷ **to be inevitable, *be destined, inevitable*—ⓐ** w. pres. inf. to denote an action that necessarily follows a divine decree *is destined, must, will certainly* . . . μ. πάσχειν *he is destined to suffer* **Mt 17:12;** B 7:10; 12:2; cp. 6:7. μ. σταυροῦσθαι *must be crucified* 12:1. μ. παραδίδοσθαι **Mt 17:22; Lk 9:44;** B 16:5. ἔμελλεν ἀποθνήσκειν **J 11:51; 12:33; 18:32.** ἐν σαρκὶ μ. φανεροῦσθαι B 6:7, 9, 14. Cp. **Mt 16:27; 20:22; Ro 4:24; 8:13; Rv 12:5.** οὐκέτι μέλλουσιν . . . θεωρεῖν *they should no more see* . . . **Ac 20:38.** τὰ μ. γίνεσθαι *what must come to pass* **26:22;** cp. **Rv 1:19.** διὰ τοὺς μέλλοντας κληρονομεῖν σωτηρίαν *those who are to inherit salvation* **Hb 1:14.** μέλλομεν θλίβεσθαι *that we were to be afflicted* **1 Th 3:4.—Mk 10:32; Lk 9:31; J 7:39; Hb 11:8.** ἐν ἡμέρᾳ ᾗ ἔμελλε θηριομαχεῖν *on the day on which Paul was to fight the wild animals* AcPl Ha 3, 9. ὡς μελλούσης τῆς πόλεως αἵρεσθαι *in expectation of the city's destruction* 5, 16. ἄνωθεν μέλλω σταυροῦσθαι *I (Jesus) am about to be crucified once more* 7, 39.

ⓑ w. aor. inf. ἀποκαλυφθῆναι *that is destined (acc. to God's will) to be revealed* **Gal 3:23.**

❸ The ptc. is used abs. in the mng. ***(in the) future, to come*** (Pind., O. 10, 7 ὁ μέλλων χρόνος 'the due date') ὁ αἰὼν μέλλων *the age to come* (s. αἰών 2b), which brings the reign of God (opp. ὁ αἰὼν οὗτος or ὁ νῦν αἰών) **Mt 12:32; Eph 1:21;** 2 Cl 6:3; Pol 5:2; cp. **Hb 6:5.** Also ὁ μ. καιρός (opp. ὁ νῦν κ.) B 4:1. ἡ μ. ζωή (opp. ἡ νῦν ζ.) **1 Ti 4:8.** ὁ μ. βίος (opp. ὁ νῦν β.) 2 Cl 20:2. ἡ μ. βασιλεία 5:5; ἡ οἰκουμένη ἡ μ. *the world to come* **Hb 2:5.** ἡ μέλλουσα πόλις (as wordplay, opp. [οὐ . . .] μένουσα π.) **13:14.** ἡ μ. ἐπαγγελία *the promise for the future* 2 Cl 10:3f. τὰ μ. ἀγαθά **Hb 9:11 v.l.;** Hv 1, 1, 8. ἡ μ. ἀνάστασις 1 Cl 24:1; τὸ κρίμα τὸ μ. *the judgment to come* **Ac 24:25;** cp. 1 Cl 28:1; 2 Cl 18:2; MPol 11:2. ἡ μ. ὀργή **Mt 3:7;** IEph 11:1. ἡ μ. θλῖψις Hv 4, 2, 5. τὰ μ. σκάνδαλα B 4:9.—ἡ μέλλουσά σου ἀδελφή *your future sister*=the one who in the future will be your sister, no longer your wife Hv 2, 2, 3. Several times the noun can be supplied fr. the context: τύπος τοῦ μέλλοντος, i.e. 'Αδάμ **Ro 5:14.**—Subst. τὸ μέλλον *the future* (Aeneas Tact. 422; 431 al.; Antiphanes Com. [IV BC] 227 K.; Menand., Monostich. 412 [608 Jaekel] Mei.; Anacreont. 36; Plut., Caes. 14, 4; Herodian 1, 14, 2; SIG 609, 5; ViEzk 13 [p. 75, 12 Sch.]; Philo, Mel.) 1 Cl 31:3. εἰς τὸ μ. *for the future* (Jos., Ant. 9, 162) **1 Ti 6:19;** specif. *(in the) next year* (PLond III, 1231, 4 p. 108 [144 AD] τὴν εἰς τὸ μέλλον γεωργείαν; s. Field, Notes 65) **Lk 13:9.** τὰ μ. *the things to come* (X., Symp. 4, 47; Aeneas Tact. 1050; Artem. 1, 36; Wsd 19:1; TestJob 47:9; JosAs 23:8; Philo; Just., D. 7, 1; Ath. 27, 2) **Col 2:17;** PtK 3 p. 15, 21. (Opp. τὰ ἐνεστῶτα *the present* as PGM 5, 295) **Ro 8:38; 1 Cor 3:22;** B 1:7; 5:3; 17:2. Ox 1081 39f (SJCh 91, 2) (s. ἀρχή 2). Uncertain **2 Pt 2:6** (if ἀσεβέσιν is to be retained, the ref. is to impending judgment for the impious).

❹ ***delay*** τί μέλλεις; *why are you delaying?* (cp. Aeschyl., Prom. 36; Eur., Hec. 1094; Thu. 8, 78; Lucian, Dial. Mort. 10, 13; Jos., Bell. 3, 494 τί μέλλομεν; 4 Macc 6:23; 9:1) **Ac 22:16.** οὐ μελλήσας *without delay* AcPl Ha 8, 4. The connection in AcPt Ox 849, 1 is uncertain.—B. 974. DELG. M-M. TW.

μέλομαι (cp. μέλει; mid. Hom., Od. 10, 505, also pap) ***be an object of care, be a cause of concern*** μεμελημένη θεῷ *you (Mary), for whom God shows care and concern* GJs 13:2 (γενέθλη χρυσείη . . . θεῷ μεμελημένη ἔσται SibOr 1, 286.—For the sense cp. ἄνθρωπε τοῦ θεοῦ μεμελετημένε TestAbr B 2 p. 106, 19 [Stone p. 60]). See deStrycker p. 307.—DELG s.v. μέλι.

μέλος, ους, τό (Hom.+)—❶ **a part of the human body, *member, part, limb*** lit., of parts of the human body (cp. Did., Gen. 8 A, 7) καθάπερ ἐν ἑνὶ σώματι πολλὰ μ. ἔχομεν *as we have many parts/members in one body* **Ro 12:4ab;** cp. **1 Cor 12:12a, 14, 18–20, 25f; Js 3:5** (Apollod. [II BC]: 244 fgm. 307 Jac. κράτιστον τῶν μελῶν ἡ γλῶσσα). τὰ μ. τοῦ σώματος *the parts of the body* (Diod. S. 5, 18, 12; Philo, In Flacc. 176; Orig., C. Cels. 7, 38, 13) **1 Cor 12:12b, 22;** 1 Cl 37:5; Dg 6:2. W. σάρξ 6:6. μ. σκοτεινόν **Lk 11:36 v.l.** W. gen. of pers. **Mt 5:29f** (cp. Sextus 13); **Ro 6:13ab; 19ab; 7:5, 23ab; Js 3:6; 4:1** (the pl. in these pass. may also refer to the 'body' as the sum of its parts, but the pl. τὰ μέλη Pind., N. 11, 15 which has been used in support does not mean the body as such, but is used with pathos in reference to the athlete's limbs, so vital to his profession, as θνατά, i.e. while enjoying vigor the athlete must recognize his mortality). συγκοπὴ μελῶν *mangling of limbs* (leading to martyrdom; Diod. S. 17, 83, 9 describes a procedure of this kind) IRo 5:3.—Metaph. of sinful characteristics or behavior νεκρώσατε τὰ μέλη τὰ ἐπὶ τῆς γῆς *put to death your worldly parts = put to death whatever in you is worldly* **Col 3:5.**

❷ **a part as member of a whole, *member*** fig. extension of 1: of the many-sided organism of the Christian community (on the figure of the body and its members, a favorite one in ancient lit., e.g. Aristot., Pol. 1253a 20–29; cp. Ar. 13, 5; Ath. 8, 1; s. Ltzm., Hdb. on 1 Cor 12:12; WNestle, D. Fabel des Menenius Agrippa: Klio 21, 1927, 350–60): the individual Christians are members of Christ, and together they form his body (for this idea cp. Simplicius in Epict. p. 70, 51: souls are μέρη τοῦ θεοῦ; 71, 5.—At p. 80, 54 the soul is called μέρος ἢ μέλος τοῦ θεοῦ; Iren. 5, 2, 2 [Harv. II 319, 2, 1]) **1 Cor 12:27; Eph 5:30;** 1 Cl 46:7; IEph 4:2; ITr 11:2; cp. **Eph 4:16 v.l.** ἀλλήλων μέλη *members of each other* **Ro 12:5; Eph 4:25;** 1 Cl 46:7b. In **1 Cor 6:15a** for a special reason the σώματα of the Christians are called μέλη Χριστοῦ. Since acc. to Paul's understanding of Gen 2:24 sexual intercourse means fusion of bodies (1 Cor 6:16), relations w. a prostitute fr. this point of view become particularly abhorrent vs. **15b.**—DELG. M-M. TW. Sv.

Μελχί, ὁ indecl. (מַלְכִּי) ***Melchi,*** in the genealogy of Jesus (AssMos fgm. c)

❶ son of Jannai, father of Levi **Lk 3:24.—❷** son of Addi, father of Neri vs. **28.**

Μελχισέδεκ, ὁ also -σεδέκ; indecl. (מַלְכִּי־צֶדֶק; Gen 14:18; Philo, Leg. All. 3, 79; Jos., Ant. 1, 180f.—FBurkitt, The Syriac Forms of NT Proper Names 1912, 82; Billerbeck IV 252f, 452ff) ***Melchizedek*** king of Salem and priest of God Most High in the time of Abraham (both after Gen 14:18). In the typology of Hb, a type of Christ as High Priest (Mel. is not called ἀρχιερεύς in LXX, Philo, or Joseph., but ὁ μέγας ἱερεύς Philo, Abr. 235) **5:6, 10; 6:20; 7:1, 10f, 15, 17** (nearly always Ps 109:4b has influenced these passages, if it is not quoted in full: σὺ εἶ ἱερεὺς εἰς τὸν αἰῶνα κατὰ τὴν τάξιν Μελχισέδεκ).—On Mel. in the NT: FrJJérome, D. gesch. M-Bild u. s. Bed. im Hb., diss. Freib. 1920; GWuttke, M., der Priesterkönig von Salem: E. Studie zur Gesch. der Exegese 1927; RGyllenberg, Kristusbilden i Hebréer brevet 1928; GBardy, M. dans la trad. patrist.: RB 35, 1926, 496–509; 36, 1927, 25–45; HStork, D. sog. Melchisedekianer 1928; HWindisch, Hdb., exc. on Hb 7:4 ([2]'31); EKäsemann, D. wandernde Gsvolk '39; HdelMedico, ZAW 69, '57, 160–70; JPetuchowski, HUCA 28, '57, 127–36; JFitzmyer, CBQ 25, '63, 305–21; MdeJonge and ASvd Woude, 11 Q Melch. and the NT, NTS 12, '66, 301–26 (on this Qumran pass. s. also AAschim, TTK 66, '95, 85–103); SLyonnet, Sin, Redemption and Sacrifice, '70, 310–12 (lit.).—M-M. EDNT. TW.

μέλω s. μέλομαι.

μεμβράνα, ης, ἡ (Lat. loanw.: membrana; s. B-D-F §5, 1 [μεμβράνη]; Rob. 109; GMeyer, D. lat. Lehnworte im Neugriech.: SBWienAk 132, 1895, 44 [μεμβρᾶνα];—Charax of Pergamum [II/III AD]: 103 fgm. 37 Jac.; Acta Barn. 6 p. 66 Tisch. τὰς μεμβράνας; POxy 2156, 9 [c. 400 AD]) ***parchment,*** used for making of books or for sundry writing purposes. τὰ βιβλία, μάλιστα τὰς μ. *the books* (better: 'the written works', i.e. scrolls, whether Jewish or others, made of papyrus or animal skins), *especially the parchments* **2 Ti 4:13** (in favor of 'scrolls' cp. Theodoret 3, 695 Sch. μεμβράνας τὰ εἰλητὰ κέκληκεν· οὕτω γὰρ Ῥωμαῖοι καλοῦσι τὰ δέρματα. ἐν εἰλητοῖς δὲ εἶχον πάλαι τὰς θείας γραφάς. οὕτω δὲ καὶ μέχρι τοῦ παρόντος ἔχουσιν οἱ Ἰουδαῖοι 'he calls the scrolls μεμβράνας, for the Romans apply this term to skins. Of old they had the sacred scriptures in rolls and so the Jews do up to the present time'. But WHatch [letter of Sept. 12, '53] concluded that the μεμβράνα of 2 Ti were parchment *codices,* pointing to Martial, Ep. 14, 7; 184: pugillares membranei = 'parchments of a size to be held in one's fist'; cp. Ep. 14, 186; 188; 190; 192; MJames, Companion to Latin Studies[3] '43, 238. So also CMcCown, HTR 34, '41, 234f.—RAC 2, 664ff (lit.); Kl. Pauly III 1185f (lit.).—B. 1289. M-M.

μεμενήκεισαν s. μένω.

μέμιγμαι s. μίγνυμι.

μεμμίαμαι s. μιαίνω.

μέμνημαι s. μιμνήσκομαι.

μέμφομαι fut. 3 sg. μέμψεται Sir 41, 7; 1 aor. ἐμεμψάμην (cp. next entry; Hes. et al.; ins, pap, LXX; TestJob 42:2; Just.) ***find fault with, blame*** w. acc. τινά *someone* (Hes. et al.; PFay 111, 3 [95/96 AD]; POxy 1481, 5; PRyl 239, 13; TestJob, Philo; Jos., Ant. 13, 109; SibOr 5, 237) and τὶ *someth.* (Pind. et al.), or w. dat. τινί *someone* (Aeschyl. et al.; Alex. Polyhistor [I BC]: 273 fgm. 46 Jac.; Jos., C. Ap. 1, 142; Sir 41:7; 2 Macc 2:7.—B-D-F §152, 1; Rob. 473; RSchekira, De imperatoris Marci Aurelii Ant. librorum τὰ εἰς ἑαυτόν sermone, diss. Greifswald 1919, 147) μεμφόμενος αὐτοὺς λέγει *he finds fault with them when he says* **Hb 8:8** (v.l. αὐτοῖς; JWolmarans, ZNW 75, '84, 139–44). οὐκ ἔχει ἡμῶν οὐδὲν μέμψασθαι *he will have nothing to blame us for* Hs 9, 10, 4, γνῶσιν Dg 12:5. Abs. (Sir 11:7) **Mk 7:2 v.l.;** Hs 10, 3, 3 Lat. (=Ox 404 recto, fgm. c, 13–15 twice).—τί ἔτι μέμφεται; (Aristippus in Diog. L. 2, 77: τί οὖν ἐμέμφου; Ael. Aristid. 32 p. 604 D.: τί μέμφονται;) *why does he still find fault?* or *what fault can he still find?* **Ro 9:19** (Appian, Maced. 11 §5 εἴ τι μέμφονται=if they have any fault to find.—*Complain* is also poss., as Jos., Ant. 2, 63; Ps.-Pla., Axioch. 7, 368a. For the subject matter cp. Oenomaus in Eus., PE 6, 7, 36: ὁ Ζεὺς οὗτος, under whose control everything is found, τί ἡμᾶς τίνυται [punish]; ... τί δὲ καὶ ἀπειλεῖ ἡμῖν;).—DELG. M-M. TW. Sv.

μεμψίμοιρος, ον (Isocr. 12, 8; Aristot., HA 608b, 10 [spurious]; cp. Theophr., Char. 17 [22], 1 ἔστι δὲ ἡ μεμψιμοιρία ἐπιτίμησίς τις παρὰ τὸ προσῆκον τῶν δεδομένων grumbling is a species of immoderate complaint about one's allotted circumstances; Lucian, Cynic. 17, Tim. 55; Plut., De Ira Cohib. 13 p. 461b; Ptolem., Apotel. 3, 14, 23; Vett. Val. 17, 12) the compound μέμφομαι 'blame' + μοῖρα 'lot in life, fate'=***complaining about one's lot, discontented*** (w. γογγυστής) **Jd 16** in a satirical comment about people who choose a deviant life style and then complain (with tongue in cheek?) that this is their 'unfortunate fate'. Cp. Edmund's speech in WShakespeare, King Lear Act 1, sc. 2: "This is the excellent foppery of the world ... we make guilty of our disasters the sun, the moon and the stars: as if we were villains on necessity; fools by heavenly compulsion ... and all that we are evil in, by a divine thrusting on."—DELG s.v. μέμφομαι. TW.

μέμψις, εως, ἡ (s. μέμφομαι; Aeschyl.+; BGU 926, 6; POxy 140, 16; 1255, 19; LXX; Philo; Jos., C. Ap. 2, 242, Vi. 266) ***reason for complaint*** **Col 3:13** D.—DELG s.v. μέμφομαι.

μέν affirmative particle, a weakened form of μήν (Hom.+). One of the commonest particles in Hom., Hdt. et al., but its usage declines sharply in later times. Found only 180 times in the NT. In seven of these places the editions vary (Mk 9:12; Ac 23:8; Ro 7:25; 16:19; 1 Cor 2:15; 12:20: in Ro 16:19; Gal 4:23 W-H. bracket the word). The mss. show an even greater variation. In Rv, 2 Th, 1 Ti, Tit, Phlm, 2 Pt, 1, 2, 3J it does not occur at all; Eph, Col, 1 Th, Js have only one occurrence each. It is also quite rare in 1, 2 Cl, Ign, GPt, but is common in Ac, Hb, B and esp. in Dg. It never begins a clause. Cp. Kühner-G. II p. 264ff; Schwyzer II 569f; Denniston 359–97; B-D-F §447; Rob. 1150–53; Mlt-Turner 331f.

❶ marker of correlation, w. other particles—**ⓐ** introducing a concessive clause, followed by another clause w. an adversative particle: *to be sure ... but, on the one hand ... on the other hand,* though in many cases an equivalence translation will not fit this scheme; rather, the contrast is to be emphasized in the second clause, often with *but.*

α. μὲν ... δέ: ἐγὼ μὲν ὑμᾶς βαπτίζω ... ὁ δὲ ὀπίσω μου ἐρχόμενος **Mt 3:11.** ὁ μὲν θερισμὸς ... οἱ δὲ ἐργάται **9:37.** τὸ μὲν ποτήριόν μου πίεσθε ... τὸ δὲ καθίσαι **20:23.** ὁ μὲν υἱὸς τοῦ ἀνθρώπου ... οὐαὶ δὲ τῷ ἀνθρώπῳ ἐκείνῳ **Mk 14:21.** τοῦ μὲν πρώτου κατέαξαν τὰ σκέλη ... ἐπὶ δὲ τὸν Ἰησοῦν ἐλθόντες **J 19:32** and oft. Cp. **Mt 22:8; Ac 21:39; Ro 6:11; 1 Cor 9:24; 11:14; 12:20; 2 Cor 10:10; Hb 3:5; 1 Pt 1:20.**—In combination w. conjunctions: εἰ μὲν ... εἰ δέ *if ... but if* Dg 3:2 (TestJob 23:5; Ar. 13:7). εἰ μὲν οὖν ... εἰ δέ *if then ... but if* **Ac 19:38;** cp. **25:11.** εἰ μὲν ... νῦν δέ *if ... but now* **Hb 11:15.** μὲν οὖν ... δέ *(now) indeed ... but* **J 19:24; 20:30; Ac 8:4; 12:5; 1 Cor 9:25.** μὲν γὰρ ... δέ/ἀλλά *for indeed ... but* (Wsd

7:30; Job 28:2; 2 Macc 6:4; 7:36; 4 Macc 9:8f, 31f) **Ac 13:36f; 23:8; 28:22; Ro 2:25; 1 Cor 5:3; 11:7; 2 Cor 9:1–3; 11:4; Hb 7:18, 20f; 12:10; Ac 28:22** (in reverse order): also ἀλλά for δέ in apodosis **4:16f** (as 3 Macc 2:15f), s. β. κἂν μὲν . . . , εἰ δὲ μήγε *if . . . but if not* **Lk 13:9.** ἐὰν μὲν . . . , ἐὰν δὲ μή **Mt 10:13.** W. prep. εἰς μὲν . . . εἰς δέ **Hb 9:6.**

β. μὲν . . . ἀλλά *to be sure . . . but* (Thu. 3, 2, 1; X., Oec. 3, 6; Tetr. Iamb. 1, 2, 3; TestJob 4:1; Ath. 16, 1) **Mk 9:12** (v.l. without μέν). πάντα μὲν καθαρὰ ἀλλὰ κακὸν τῷ ἀνθρώπῳ *to be sure everything is clean, but . . .* **Ro 14:20.** σὺ μὲν γὰρ καλῶς . . . ἀλλ' ὁ ἕτερος **1 Cor 14:17.** Cp. **Ac 4:16** (s. α).

γ. μὲν . . . πλήν *indeed . . . but* (Galen, Inst. Log. c. 8, 2 Kalbfl. [1896]) **Lk 22:22.**

ⓑ without any real concessive sense on the part of μέν, but adversative force in δέ, so that μέν need not be translated at all: αὐτοὶ μὲν . . . ὑμεῖς δέ **Lk 11:48;** cp. **Ac 13:36.** ἐγὼ μὲν . . . ἐγὼ δέ **1 Cor 1:12.** τοῖς μὲν ἀπολλυμένοις . . . τοῖς δὲ σῳζομένοις vs. **18.** Ἰουδαίοις μὲν . . . ἔθνεσι δέ vs. **23.** ἐμοὶ μὲν . . . ὑμῖν δέ **Phil 3:1.** εἰ μὲν . . . εἰ δέ **Ac 18:14;** Dg 2:8.

ⓒ Somet. the combination μὲν . . . δέ does not emphasize a contrast, but separates one thought from another in a series, so that they may be easily distinguished: πρῶτον μὲν . . . ἔπειτα δέ *in the first place . . . then* **Hb 7:2.** ὃ μὲν . . . ὃ δέ *the one . . . the other* **Mt 13:8, 23** (cp. Lucian, Hermot. 66 ὁ μὲν ἑπτά, ὁ δὲ πέντε, ὁ δὲ τριάκοντα; Just., D. 35, 6; 39, 2; cp. TestAbr A 10 p. 87, 21 [Stone p. 22] ἄλλους μὲν . . . ἑτέρους); **Ro 9:21.** ὃς μὲν . . . ὃς δέ *the one . . . the other* **Mt 21:35; 25:15; Lk 23:33; Ac 27:44; Ro 14:5; 1 Cor 11:21; Jd 22.** ἃ μὲν . . . ἃ δέ *some . . . others* **2 Ti 2:20.** ὁ μὲν . . . ὁ δέ *the one . . . the other,* but pl. *some . . . others* **Ac 14:4; 17:32; Gal 4:23; Eph 4:11; Phil 1:16;** Dg 2:2f. ἕκαστος . . . , ὁ μὲν οὕτως ὁ δὲ οὕτως *each one . . . , one in one way, one in another* **1 Cor 7:7.** ὃς μὲν πιστεύει φαγεῖν πάντα, ὁ δὲ ἀσθενῶν *the one is confident about eating anything, but the weak person* **Ro 14:2.** τινὲς μὲν . . . τινὲς δέ *some . . . but still others* **Phil 1:15.** ἄλλη μὲν . . . , ἄλλη δὲ . . . , ἄλλη δέ . . . **1 Cor 15:39.** ἑτέρα μὲν . . . , ἑτέρα δέ vs. **40.** οἱ μὲν . . . , ἄλλοι δὲ . . . , ἕτεροι δέ **Mt 16:14.** ᾧ μὲν γὰρ . . . , ἄλλῳ δὲ . . . , ἑτέρῳ **1 Cor 12:8ff.** ἃ μὲν . . . , ἄλλα δὲ . . . , ἄλλα δέ **Mt 13:4ff.** τοῦτο μὲν . . . , τοῦτο δέ *in part . . . in part* (Hdt. 3, 106; Isocr. 4, 21; 22) **Hb 10:33** (μέν followed by more than one δέ: two, Libanius, Or. 18, p. 251, 3f; Or. 59 p. 240, 13; four, Or. 64 p. 469, 14).

❷ **marker of contrast or continuation without express correlation and frequently in anacolutha—**ⓐ when the contrast can be supplied fr. the context, and therefore can be omitted as obvious: λόγον μὲν ἔχοντα σοφίας (sc. ὄντα δὲ ἄλογα or someth. sim.) *they have the reputation of being wise* (but are foolish) **Col 2:23** (difft. BHollenbach, NTS 25, '79, 254–61: a subordinate clause embedded in its main clause). τὰ μὲν σημεῖα τοῦ ἀποστόλου κατειργάσθη ἐν ὑμῖν *the signs that mark a true apostle were performed among you* (but you paid no attention) **2 Cor 12:12.** ἤδη μὲν οὖν ἥττημα *indeed it is already a defeat for you* (but you make it still worse) **1 Cor 6:7.**—μέν serves to emphasize the subject in clauses which contain a report made by the speaker's personal state of being, esp. intellectual or emotional; so ἐγὼ μ. Παῦλος **1 Th 2:18.** ἡ μ. εὐδοκία τῆς ἐμῆς καρδίας **Ro 10:1.**

ⓑ Somet. the contrast is actually expressed, but not in adversative form (Diod. S. 12, 70, 6 Ἀθηναῖοι μὲν οὖν ἐπιβουλεύσαντες τοῖς Βοιωτοῖς τοιαύτῃ συμφορᾷ περιέπεσον=so the Ath., one can see, after plotting against the B., had their fortunes reversed in such a disaster; Polyaenus with dramatic effect: 4, 3, 20 οἱ μὲν . . . , Ἀλέξανδρος . . . ; 2, 3, 2) τότε μὲν . . . ἔπειτα (here we expect δέ) **J 11:6f.** ἐφ' ὅσον μὲν οὖν εἰμι ἐγὼ ἐθνῶν ἀπόστολος *in so far, then, as I am an apostle to the nations* **Ro 11:13** (the contrast follows in vs. **14**); cp. **7:12** and **13ff.**

ⓒ We notice anacoluthon in enumerations, either if they are broken off or if they are continued in some manner that is irregular in form: πρῶτον μέν *in the first place* **Ro 1:8; 3:2; 1 Cor 11:18.** πρῶτον μὲν . . . ἔπειτα (X., Cyr. 7, 5, 1) **Js 3:17.** In the prologue to **Ac** (s. λόγος 1b) the clause w. δέ corresponding to τὸν μὲν πρῶτον λόγον **1:1** (Diod. S. 11, 1, 1 Ἡ μὲν οὖν πρὸ ταύτης βίβλος . . . τὸ τέλος ἔσχε τῶν πράξεων . . . ἐν ταύτῃ δέ . . . The preceding book . . . contained . . . ; in this one, on the other hand . . .) may have been omitted through editorial activity acc. to Norden, Agn. Th. 311ff; 397.

ⓓ μέν followed by καί is not customary (Ael. Aristid. 31, 19 K.=11 p. 133 D.; IAsMinSW 325, 10ff μὲν . . . καί; POxy 1153, 14 [I AD] two armbands ἓν μὲν σανδύκινον καὶ ἓν πορφυροῦν; TestJob 40:7f; ApcMos 15) **Mk 4:4ff; Lk 8:5ff;** MPol 2:4.

ⓔ μὲν οὖν denotes continuation (TestJob 40:14; Just., A I, 7, 3; s. B-D-F §451, 1; Kühner-G. II 157f, but note Denniston's caution, p. 473, n. 1; Mayser II/3, 152f; Rob. 1151; 1191) *so, then* **Lk 3:18.** Esp. in Ac: **1:6, 18; 2:41; 5:41; 8:25; 9:31; 11:19; 13:4; 14:3** (DSharp, ET 44, '33, 528); **15:3, 30; 16:5; 17:12, 17, 30; 19:32; 23:18, 22, 31; 25:4; 26:4, 9; 28:5.** Also **1 Cor 6:4** (B-D-F §450, 4); **Hb 9:1;** Papias (2:16). εἰ μὲν οὖν *now if* **Hb 7:11; 8:4.**

ⓕ μενοῦν, οὐμενοῦν, and μενοῦνγε s. under these entries.—JLee, Some Features of the Speech of Jesus in Mark's Gospel: NovT 27, '85, 1–26.—DELG s.v. 1 μήν. M-M.

Μεννά, ὁ indecl. (in a series of indecl. names, hardly Μεννᾶ as gen. of Μεννᾶς) ***Menna*** in the genealogy of Jesus **Lk 3:31** (Μαινάν v.l.).

μενοῦν (also μὲν οὖν) **Lk 11:28** (for negative s. οὐ μὲν οὖν) and **μενοῦνγε** (also μενοῦν γε), particles used esp. in answers, to emphasize or correct (B-D-F §450, 4; Rob. 1151f), even—contrary to earlier Gk. usage—at the beginning of a clause (Phryn. 342 Lob. [322 R.]) ***rather, on the contrary*** (Soph., Aj. 1363; Pla., Crito 44b; X., Cyr. 8, 3, 37) **Lk 11:28 v.l.** *Indeed* **Ro 10:18.** ἀλλὰ μενοῦνγε *more than that* **Phil 3:8.** μενοῦνγε σὺ τίς εἶ . . . ; *on the contrary, who are you . . . ?* (or, *who in the world are you to [take issue with God]?*) **Ro 9:20.**—M-M.

μέντοι particle (trag., Hdt.+; ins, pap, LXX; TestSol 11:9 C; TestJob; Jos., Ant. 14, 162, C. Ap. 1, 8; 13 al.—Denniston 397–412).

❶ ***really, actually*** **Js 2:8.**

❷ mostly adversative (cp. οὐ μέντοι γε 'though not' Just., D. 5, 1) ***though, to be sure, indeed*** οὐδεὶς μ. εἶπεν *though no one said* **J 4:27;** cp. **7:13.** οὐ μ. *though not, indeed not* **20:5; 21:4;** Hs 6, 1, 6 v.l.; Papias (2:15). ὁ μ. θεμέλιος ἕστηκεν *nevertheless the firm foundation stands* **2 Ti 2:19.** ὅμως μ. *yet, despite that* (Kühner-G. II 280) **J 12:42.**—Weakened to *but* **Jd 8** (B-D-F §450, 1; Rob. 1154; 1188).—M-M.

μένω (Hom.+) impf. ἔμενον; fut. μενῶ; 1 aor. ἔμεινα, impv. μεῖνον (Hv 3, 1, 9); pf. ptc. pl. μεμενηκότας 2 Macc 8:1; plpf. μεμενήκειν **1J 2:19** (on the lack of augment s. B-D-F §66, 1; W-S. §12, 4; Mlt-H. 190).

❶ ***remain, stay,*** intr.—ⓐ a pers. or thing remains where he, she, or it is.—**α.** of a location *stay,* oft. in the special sense *live, dwell, lodge* (Horapollo 2, 49 μ. alternating w. οἰκέω) w. ἐν and the dat. (Ps.-Demosth. 43, 75 μ. ἐν τοῖς οἴκοις; Vi. Aesopi G 12 p. 259, 6 P.) ἐν οἰκίᾳ **Lk 8:27;** ἐν αὐτῇ τῇ οἰκίᾳ **Lk 10:7; J 8:35a;** ἐν τ. οἴκῳ σου **Lk 19:5.** ἐν τῷ πλοίῳ *remain in the ship*

Ac 27:31. μ. ἐν τῇ Γαλιλαίᾳ **J 7:9.**—**Ac 9:43; 20:15 v.l.; 2 Ti 4:20.** κατὰ πόλιν *remain in the city* MPol 5:1 (Just., A I, 67, 3). W. an adv. of place ἐκεῖ **Mt 10:11; Mk 6:10; Lk 9:4; J 2:12; 10:40; 11:54** (s. διατρίβω); Hs 9, 11, 7. ὧδε **Mt 26:38; Mk 14:34;** Hs 9, 11, 1. ποῦ μένεις; *where do you live?* **J 1:38;** cp. vs. **39** (Sb 2639 ποῦ μένι Θερμοῦθις; Pel.-Leg. 7, 27; Nicetas Eugen. 1, 230 H. ποῦ μένεις;). W. acc. of time (Demetr.: 722 fgm. 1, 11 Jac.; JosAs 20:8; Jos., Ant. 1, 299) **J 1:39b; 4:40b; 11:6; Ac 21:7;** D 11:5; 12:2. W. time-indications of a different kind ἕως ἂν ἐξέλθητε **Mt 10:11.** ὡς μῆνας τρεῖς **Lk 1:56.** εἰς τὸν αἰῶνα **J 8:35b.** ἐπὶ πλείονα χρόνον **Ac 18:20.** W. prep. παρά τινι μ. *stay with someone* (Cebes 9, 2; Jos., Ant. 20, 54) **J 1:39b; 4:40a; Ac 18:3** (*live with* is also prob.: Lucian, Timon 10); **21:7, 8.** παρ᾽ ὑμῖν μένων *when I was (staying) with you* **J 14:25.** πρός τινα *with someone* **Ac 18:3** D; D 12:2. ἐπί τινα *remain on someone* **J 1:32f.** σύν τινι *with someone* (4 Macc 18:9) **Lk 1:56; 24:29b.** Also μ. μετά τινος (Gen 24:55) **Lk 24:29a;** Hs 9, 11, 1; 3; 6; 7. καθ᾽ ἑαυτόν *live by oneself, in one's own quarters* **Ac 28:16** (of what is called in Lat. custodia libera; s. BAFCS III 276, 364f; 384f). Of a corpse μ. ἐπὶ τοῦ σταυροῦ *stay (hanging) on the cross* **J 19:31.** Of a branch: ἐν τῇ ἀμπέλῳ *remain on the vine,* i.e. not be cut off **15:4b.** Of stones μ. ἐν τῇ ὁδῷ *stay on the road* Hv 3, 2, 9. Of stones that *remain* in the divine structure, and are not removed Hs 9, 13, 4; 9. Also in imagery τὸ κάλυμμα ἐπὶ τῇ ἀναγνώσει τῆς παλαιᾶς διαθήκης μένει *the veil remains unlifted at the reading of the OT* (and hinders the right understanding of it) **2 Cor 3:14.** Abs. **Ac 16:15.**

β. in transf. sense, of someone who does not leave a certain realm or sphere: *remain, continue, abide* (Pla., Ep. 10, 358c μένε ἐν τοῖς ἤθεσιν, οἷσπερ καὶ νῦν μένεις; Alex. Aphr., An. II 1 p. 2, 15 μ. ἐν ταῖς ἀπορίαις=remain overcome by doubts; Jos., Ant. 4, 185; TestJos. 1:3 ἐν τ. ἀληθείᾳ; Just., D. 8, 3 ἐν … τῷ τῆς φιλοσωφίας τρόπῳ) ἐν ἁγνείᾳ IPol 5:2; cp. IEph 10:3. ἐν τῇ διδαχῇ τοῦ Χριστοῦ *remain in the teaching of Christ* **2J 9a;** cp. vs. **9b** (2 Macc 8:1 μ. ἐν τῷ Ἰουδαϊσμῷ). ἐν πίστει καὶ ἀγάπῃ **1 Ti 2:15.** μένε ἐν οἷς ἔμαθες *continue in what you have learned* **2 Ti 3:14.** ἐν τῷ λόγῳ τῷ ἐμῷ **J 8:31.** μείνατε ἐν τῇ ἀγάπῃ τῇ ἐμῇ *continue in my love* **15:9f;** cp. **1J 4:16.** ἐν τῷ φωτί **2:10.** ἐν τῷ θανάτῳ **3:14.** ἐν τῇ σκοτίᾳ **J 12:46.** Without ἐν AcPlCor 2:36. The phrase μ. ἔν τινι is a favorite of J to denote an inward, enduring personal communion. So of God in his relation to Christ ὁ πατὴρ ἐν ἐμοὶ μένων *the Father, who abides in me* **J 14:10.** Of Christians in their relation to Christ **J 6:56; 15:4ac, 5–7; 1J 2:6, 24c.** Of Christ relating to Christians **J 15:4a, 5** (Goodsp., Probs. 112–15). Of Christians relating to God **1J 2:24c, 27f; 3:6, 24a; 4:13.** Of God relating to Christians **1J 3:24; 4:12f, 15.**—Vice versa, of someth. that remains in someone; likew. in Johannine usage: of the word of God **1J 2:14.** Of the words of Christ **J 15:7b;** cp. **1J 2:24ab.** Of the anointing fr. heaven vs. **27.** Of the love of God **1J 3:17.** Of the seed of God **3:9.** Of truth **2J 2.** The possession is shown to be permanent by the expr. ἔχειν τι μένον ἐν ἑαυτῷ *have someth. continually, permanently* **1J 3:15;** the word of God **J 5:38.** Instead of μ. ἔν τινι also μ. παρά τινι *remain with someone:* of the Spirit of truth **J 14:17.** Also of the wrath of God, μένει ἐπ᾽ αὐτόν *it remains upon him* **3:36.**—GPercorara, De verbo 'manere' ap. Jo.: Div. Thomas Piac. 40, '37, 159–71.

ⓑ a pers. or thing continues in the same state (ParJer 7:37 ἔμεινε διδάσκων; ApcSed 11:13 ἀκίνητοι μένετε; Just., D. 90, and Lucian, Laps. 16 ἐν τῇ τάξει μ.) **1 Cor 7:20, 24.** μένει ἱερεὺς εἰς τὸ διηνεκές *he remains a priest forever* **Hb 7:3.** αὐτὸς μόνος μένει *it remains alone* **J 12:24.** μενέτω ἄγαμος **1 Cor 7:11.** ἀσάλευτος **Ac 27:41.** πιστός **2 Ti 2:13.** ἀόρατος Dg 6:4. (μ̣ε̣ί̣νατε νικηταί: μείν̣[α]τε Ox 1602, 30f is a misreading; difft. AcPl Ha 8, 22//BMM recto 28=HTR 31, 79 n. 2, ln. 10; s. CSchmidt mg. on AcPl Ha 8, 22 [μ]ε̣γα̣ς ἐπίκειται πιρασμός; Borger GGA 137). ἀσκανδάλιστος μείνῃ ἡ … ἐκκλησία AcPlCor 1:16. μ. μετά τινος *remain in fellowship w. someone* **1J 2:19.** Of one who has divorced his wife *remain by himself, remain unmarried* Hm 4, 1, 6; 10; 4, 4, 2. οὐχὶ μένον σοὶ ἔμενεν; *was it* (the piece of ground) *not yours, as long as it remained (unsold)?* **Ac 5:4** (cp. 1 Macc 15:7 and s. OHoltzmann, ZKG 14, 1893, 327–36).—W. adv. (Just., A I, 29, 3, D. 58, 3 βεβαίως) οὕτως μ. *remain as one is* (i.e., unmarried) **1 Cor 7:40.** ἁγνῶς B 2:3. μ. ὡς ἐγώ *remain as I am* **1 Cor 7:8.**

❷ **to continue to exist, *remain, last, persist, continue to live,*** intr.—ⓐ of pers. (Ps 9:8 ὁ κύριος εἰς τ. αἰῶνα μ.; 101:13; Da 6:27; Just., D. 128, 4 ἄγγελοι … ἀεὶ μένοντες) ὁ Χριστὸς μ. εἰς τὸν αἰῶνα *Christ remains (here) forever* **J 12:34;** cp. **Hb 7:24; 1J 2:17.** Of God AcPl Ha 2, 28; 9, 11. Pregnant *remain (alive), be alive* (Epict. 3, 24, 97; Diog. L. 7, 174; Achilles Tat. 8, 10. μένειν ἐν τῷ ζῆν Plut., Mor. 1042d; Eccl 7:15; Just., A I, 63, 17) **J 21:22f; 1 Cor 15:6; Phil 1:25; Rv 17:10.**

ⓑ of things (Maximus Tyr. 4, 8b and Polyaenus 7, 34: γῆ μένει; Socrat., Ep. 31 [=33]; Hierocles 15, 454 ὁ πόνος παρῆλθεν, τὸ καλὸν μένει; Just., A I, 18, 2 αἴσθησις … μένει; Ath. 19, 2 μένει σύστασις) of a city ἔμεινεν ἂν μέχρι τῆς σήμερον *it would have lasted until today* **Mt 11:23.** μένουσα πόλις *a permanent city* **Hb 13:14.**—ἡ φιλαδελφία μενέτω *continue* **13:1** (JCambier, Salesianum 11, '49, 62–96).—**J 9:41; 15:16.** εἰ τὸ ἔργον μενεῖ *if the work survives* **1 Cor 3:14.** ὕπαρξις **Hb 10:34.** δικαιοσύνη **2 Cor 9:9** (Ps 111:9). ἡ κατ᾽ ἐκλογὴν πρόθεσις τοῦ θεοῦ **Ro 9:11** (of God's counsel Ps 32:11). λόγος θεοῦ *endure* **1 Pt 1:23** (Just., D. 61, 2; cp. 1 Esdr 4:38 ἡ ἀλήθεια μένει). τ. ῥῆμα κυρίου μένει εἰς τ. αἰῶνα vs. **25** (Is 40:8). ἡ βρῶσις ἡ μένουσα εἰς ζωὴν αἰώνιον **J 6:27.** τὴν δύναμιν σου τὴν μένουσαν **Rv 11:7 v.l.** ζώσης φωνῆς καὶ μενούσης Papias (2:4). τὸ μένον *what is permanent* (Philo, Leg. All. 3, 100.—Opp. τὸ καταργούμενον) **2 Cor 3:11.** μένει πίστις, ἐλπίς, ἀγάπη **1 Cor 13:13** (WMarxsen, D. 'Bleiben' im 1 Cor 13:13, OCullmann Festschr., '72, 223–29; on the eschatology cp. En 97:6–10 and s. the lit. on ἀγάπη 1a.—For the contrast πίπτει [vs. **8**]—μένει cp. Pla., Crat. 44, 440a εἰ μεταπίπτει πάντα χρήματα καὶ μηδὲν μένει). Opp. σαλευόμενα **Hb 12:27.**

❸ ***wait for, await,*** trans.—ⓐ of pers.: *wait for* someone who is arriving (Hom.; Thu. 4, 124, 4; X., An. 4, 4, 20; Pla., Leg. 8, 833c; Polyb. 4, 8, 4; Tob 2:2 BA; 2 Macc 7:30; TestJob 11:1; Jos., Ant. 13, 19) τινά w. the place indicated ἔμενον ἡμᾶς ἐν Τρῳάδι *they were waiting for us in Troas* **Ac 20:5.**

ⓑ of things, such as dangers or misfortunes that *await* or *threaten someone* (trag.; Kaibel 654, 9 κἀμὲ μένει τὸ θανεῖν; SibOr 4, 114 v.l. σὲ) θλίψεις με μένουσιν **Ac 20:23.**—Of the 118 passages in which μένω occurs in the NT, 67 are found in the Johannine writings (40 in the gosp.; 24 in 1J; 3 in 2J).—JHeise, Bleiben: Menein in d. Johan. Schr., '67; FHauck, TW IV 578–93: μένω and related words.—B. 836. DELG. M-M. TW.

μερίζω (μέρος) Att. fut. μεριῶ 1 Cl 16:13; LXX; 1 aor. ἐμέρισα; pf. μεμέρικα; 1 aor. mid. inf. μερίσασθαι. Pass.: 1 fut. μερισθήσομαι LXX; 1 aor. ἐμερίσθην; pf. μεμέρισμαι ('divide, separate' X.+)

❶ **to separate into parts, *divide***—ⓐ of an amount of money, mid. μερίζεσθαί τι μετά τινος *share someth. with someone* (Demosth. 34, 18; cp. Jos., Ant. 1, 169 τὶ πρός τινα) **Lk 12:13.**

ⓑ of pers. or states, act. and pass., transf. sense—**α.** *divide* (Mel., P. 56, 407 ἄνθρωπος ὑπὸ τοῦ θανάτου μεριζόμενος;

Tat. 26, 2 μερίζοντες τὴν σοφίαν; Procop. Soph., Ep. 17 ψυχὴ μεριζομένη) μεμέρισται ὁ Χριστός; *has Christ been divided?* **1 Cor 1:13** (GWhitaker, Chrysostom on 1 Cor 1:13: JTS 15, 1914, 254–57). *Divide* ὑμᾶς IMg 6:2. βασιλεία, πόλις, οἰκία μερισθεῖσα καθ' ἑαυτῆς *a kingdom, city, family divided against itself, disunited* **Mt 12:25.** ἐφ' ἑαυτὸν ἐμερίσθη *he is disunited* vs. **26;** cp. **Mk 3:24–26.** Abs. ὁ γαμήσας μεμέρισται *the married man* (i.e., his attention) *is divided,* since he tries to please the Lord and his wife at the same time **1 Cor 7:34.**

β. *take a part* (from a whole), *separate* μερίσας . . . ἀπὸ τοῦ πνεύματος τοῦ χριστοῦ ἔπεμψεν εἰς τοὺς προφήτας *(God) took a portion of the spirit of Christ and dispatched it into the prophets* AcPlCor 2:10.

❷ **to make an allotment**—ⓐ ***distribute*** τί τισιν *someth. to some people* (PTebt 302, 12; POxy 713, 29; Pr 19:14; Just., D. 104, 2 ἐμέρισαν ἑαυτοῖς . . . τὰ ἱμάτια; cp. A I, 35, 8 ἐμερίσαντο ἑαυτοῖς [διεμερίσαντο Mt 27:35]) τοὺς δύο ἰχθύας πᾶσιν **Mk 6:41.** Without dat. τῶν ἰσχυρῶν μεριεῖ σκῦλα *he will distribute the spoils of the strong* 1 Cl 16:13 (Is 53:12).

ⓑ ***deal out, assign, apportion*** τί τινι *someth. to someone* (Polyb. 11, 28, 9; Diod. S. 13, 22, 8 μ. τινὶ τὸν ἔλεον; UPZ 19, 20 [163 BC]; 146, 38; Sb 8139, 19f [ins I BC, of Isis] πᾶσι μερίζεις, οἷσι θέλεις, ζωὴν παντοδαπῶν ἀγαθῶν; PGM 13, 635 μέρισόν μοι ἀγαθά; Sir 45:20; ApcMos 15; EpArist 224 [θεός]) ἑκάστῳ μέτρον πίστεως **Ro 12:3.** κατὰ τὸ μέτρον τοῦ κανόνος οὗ ἐμέρισεν ἡμῖν ὁ θεὸς μέτρου *according to the measure of the limit* (or *area*) *that God has assigned us* **2 Cor 10:13.** ᾧ δεκάτην ἀπὸ πάντων ἐμέρισεν Ἀβραάμ *to whom Abraham apportioned a tenth of everything* **Hb 7:2.** W. dat. of the pers. alone (En 27:4) ἑκάστῳ ὡς ἐμέρισεν (v.l. μεμέρικεν) ὁ κύριος **1 Cor 7:17.**—DELG s.v. μείρομαι. M-M.

μέριμνα, ης, ἡ (Hes.; Vett. Val. 131, 3; 6; 271, 3; PGiss 19, 8; 22, 11; EpArist 271; LXX.—In LXX the pl. only Da 11:26, as Hes., Op. 178 al.; PRyl 28, 219) ***anxiety, worry, care*** πᾶσα ἡ μ. ὑμῶν *all your anxiety* **1 Pt 5:7** (Ps 54:23); cp. Hv 3, 11, 3; 4, 2, 4f. W. obj. gen. μ. πασῶν τῶν ἐκκλησιῶν *anxiety about all the churches* **2 Cor 11:28.** μ. τοῦ βίου *the worries of life* (in case τοῦ β. belongs w. μ.—UPZ 20, 29 [163 BC] τὴν τ. βίου μέριμναν) **Lk 8:14.** Also μ. βιωτικαί **21:34.** ἡ μ. τοῦ αἰῶνος *the worry of the world* i.e. of the present age **Mt 13:22** (s. αἰών 2a); pl. **Mk 4:19.** S. next entry.—B. 1092. DELG. M-M. TW.

μεριμνάω fut. μεριμνήσω; 1 aor. ἐμερίμνησα (μέριμνα; since Soph., Oed. Rex 1124; X., Pla. et al.; pap, LXX; ParJer 6:15; EpArist 296; SibOr 3, 222; 234; Just., A I, 25, 2).

❶ **to be apprehensive, *have anxiety, be anxious, be (unduly) concerned*** (PTebt 315, 9 [II AD] γράφω ὅπως μὴ μεριμνῇς; Ps 37:19) μηδέν *have no anxiety* **Phil 4:6** (WWeeda, Filipp. 4:6 en 7: TSt 34, 1916, 326–35). περί τινος **Mt 6:28; Lk 12:26;** Dg 9:6. W. indir. question foll.: πῶς ἢ τί λαλήσητε *about how you are to speak or what you are to say* **Mt 10:19;** cp. **Lk 12:11** (cp. ParJer 6:15 τὸ πῶς ἀποστείλῃς πρὸς Ἰερεμίαν). W. dat. and a question foll. μὴ μεριμνᾶτε τῇ ψυχῇ (dat. of advantage: *for your life,* B-D-F §188, 1; Rob. 539) ὑμῶν τί φάγητε **Mt 6:25; Lk 12:22.** Abs. **Mt 6:31;** in ptc. (s. Mlt. 230) **Mt 6:27; Lk 12:25.** Beside θορυβάζεσθαι περὶ πολλά of the distracting cares of housekeeping **10:41** (the text is uncertain; s. Zahn and EKlostermann, also FSträhl, Krit. u. exeget. Beleuchtung von Lk 10:41f: SchTZ 4, 1887, 116–23). εἰς τὴν αὔριον *do not worry about tomorrow* **Mt 6:34a.**

❷ **to attend to, *care for, be concerned about*** τί *someth.* (Soph., loc. cit.; cp. Bar 3:18) τὰ τοῦ κυρίου *the Lord's work* **1 Cor 7:32; 34a.** τὰ τοῦ κόσμου vss. **33, 34b.** τὰ περί τινος *someone's welfare* **Phil 2:20.** ἡ αὔριον μεριμνήσει ἑαυτῆς *will look after itself* (Itala 'sibi'.—B-D-F §176, 2; Rob. 509) **Mt 6:34b** (v.l. τὰ ἑαυτῆς care about its own concerns). τὶ ὑπέρ τινος: ἵνα τὸ αὐτὸ ὑπὲρ ἀλλήλων μεριμνῶσιν τὰ μέλη *that the parts may have the same concern for one another* **1 Cor 12:25.**—DELG s.v. μέριμνα. M-M. TW.

μερίς, ίδος, ἡ (s. μερίζω and three next entries; Antiphon, Thu.+; ins, pap, LXX, TestSol; TestJob 38:2; 41:5; Test12Patr; Philo; Jos., Ant. 11, 292, Vi. 36; Just.).

❶ **a portion of a whole that has been divided, *part*** (Pla., Soph. p. 266a; Demetr.: 722 fgm. 1, 14 Jac.; Diod. S. 15, 31, 2; 15, 64, 1 [where comparison with 15, 63, 4 τέτταρα μέρη . . . ἡ πρώτη μερίς shows that it is not necessary to assume that there is a difference in the meanings of these word-forms]. In ins and pap oft.=*district:* OGI 177, 9; 179, 8; PPetr III, 32 recto, 3 τῆς Θεμίστου μερίδος; BGU 975, 6 [45 AD]; PTebt 302, 4; 315, 13; Diod. S. 1, 54, 3; Josh 18:6). The wording of **Ac 16:12 v.l** in describing Philippi ἥτις ἐστὶν πρώτη τῆς μερίδος Μακεδονίας πόλις (vv.ll., among others, πρ. τῆς μερ. τῆς Μακ.; πρ. τῆς Μακ.) is difficult because of τῆς μερίδος.The transl. *leading city of the district of Macedonia* (e.g. Beyer, Steinmann, Bauernfeind, NRSV) is tolerable only through lack of a better one. As far as the form is concerned, the article is lacking w. πρώτη, and as far as subject matter goes, Philippi was not the capital city (which πρώτη means in such a context: Ps.-Scylax, Peripl. 35 [BFabricius 1878]; schol. on Pind., O. 8, 1h; cp. 6, 144g; Eunap. 7; 96; Procop., Aedif. 5, 4, 18 μητρόπολις . . . οὕτω πόλιν τ. πρώτην τοῦ ἔθνους καλοῦσι Ῥωμαῖοι) either of the province of Macedonia or of any of its districts. The Nestle text follows Blass, who favored the conjecture of Johannes Clericus (LeClerc), and reads πρώτη[ς] μερίδος τῆς Μακεδονίας *of the first district of Macedonia,* w. ref. to the fact that the Romans (Livy 45, 29) divided Macedonia into four μερίδες=districts in 167 BC (so also Hoennicke, Preuschen, Wlh., Zahn; Field, Notes 124; EHaupt, Gefangenschaftsbriefe[7] 1902, 83f; Belser; Zürcher Bibel '31; Haenchen ad loc; RBorger, TRu 52, '87, 37f. On the textual variants, s. Metzger, Textual Commentary ad loc. S. also AClark and JLarsen s.v. κεφαλή 2b, end.—If the restoration of the apparently damaged text should result in a wording that would make it possible for πρώτη to refer to the progress of a journey, we might compare Arrian, Anab. 4, 23, 3 ἡ πρώτη καθ' ὁδὸν πόλις; Appian, Bell. Civ. 2, 35 §137 Ariminum ἐστὶν Ἰταλίας πρώτη [i.e., πόλις] μετὰ τὴν Γαλατίαν=the first city in Italy after [leaving] Gaul; Ps.-Scylax §67: from Thessaly the πρώτη πόλις Μακεδονίας is Ἡράκλειον.—Linguistically πρ. πόλ. can, of course, be understood of time as well, and can mean the first city in connection with which someth. happens [Diod. S. 12, 67, 2 Acanthus was the first city, πρ. πόλ., to revolt from Athens]).

❷ ***share, portion*** (Demosth. 43, 82; Plut., Ages. 17, 5; Lucian, De Merc. Cond. 26; Vett. Val. 345, 16; SIG 1013, 4; BGU 996 III, 1; PLond III, 880, 18ff p. 9 [113 BC]; POxy 1482, 21; LXX) τὴν ἀγαθὴν μ. ἐκλέγεσθαι *choose the better portion* **Lk 10:42** (fig., of food? Cp. Mft., transl., 'Mary has chosen the best dish', and s. Gen 43:34; 1 Km 9:23, but against him TGillieson, ET 59, '47/48, 111f. For other reff. Field, Notes 63f; HAlmqvist, Plutarch u. d. NT '46, 65). μ. κυρίου *the Lord's portion* 1 Cl 29:2 (Dt 32:9); cp. 30:1. τίς μερὶς πιστῷ μετὰ ἀπίστου; *what has a believer in common with an unbeliever?* (i.e., with ref. to the same thing; on μετά s. below) **2 Cor 6:15.** Sim. μετὰ μοιχῶν τὴν μερίδα σου ἐτίθεις *you cast your lot w. adulterers* 1 Cl 35:8 (Ps 49:18). οὐκ ἔστιν σοι μ. οὐδὲ κλῆρος ἐν τῷ λόγῳ τούτῳ *you have neither share nor lot in this matter* **Ac 8:21** (cp. Dt 12:12 οὐκ ἔστιν αὐτῷ μ. οὐδὲ κλῆρος μεθ' ὑμῶν.—μ. καὶ κλῆρος also TestSol 14:5 and Philo, Plant. 60.—μ. ἐν as 2 Km 20:1; TestJob 38:2 ἐν γῇ καὶ σποδῷ). ἡ μερὶς τοῦ κλήρου τῶν ἁγίων *a share in the inheritance of the saints / holy ones* (cp. 1QS 11:7f) **Col 1:12.**—DELG s.v. μείρομαι II p. 679. M-M. TW.

μερισμός, οῦ, ὁ (μερίζω; Pla. +; ins, pap, LXX, TestJob 46:1; Philo; Jos., C. Ap. 2, 203; Ar. 6, 1; Tat. 5, 1).

❶ ***division, separation*—ⓐ** ἄχρι μερισμοῦ ψυχῆς καὶ πνεύματος *to the separation of soul and spirit,* i.e. *so as to separate soul and spirit* **Hb 4:12.**

ⓑ in Ign. w. ref. to dissidents, who have separated themselves: *(the) division* partly as action, partly as result IPhld 2:1; 3:1; 8:1; pl. ISm 7:2. ὥς προειδότα τὸν μ. τινων *as one who knew of the division caused by certain people* IPhld 7:2.

❷ ***distribution, apportionment*** (Aeneas Tact. ln. 27; Polyb. 31, 10, 1; SIG 1017, 16 [III BC]; TestJob 46:1; Josh 11:23; Philo, Poster. Cai. 90) ἁγίου πνεύματος μερισμοί *distributions of the Holy Spirit,* i.e. of the various gifts proceeding from the Holy Spirit **Hb 2:4.** AcPl Ha 8, 18 κατὰ … μ. λαμβάνοντες//Ox 1602, 22 κατὰ μ. λαβόντες//BMM recto 22–24.—DELG s.v. μείρομαι II. M-M.

μεριστής, οῦ, ὁ (μερίζω; SEG VIII, 551, 25 [I BC]; Pollux 4, 176; Vett. Val. 62, 4; PGM 13, 638 epithet of Sarapis) ***divider, arbitrator*** **Lk 12:14** (omitted in v.l.).—DELG s.v. μείρομαι II. M-M. Spicq.

μέρος, ους, τό (Pind., Hdt.+).—❶ ***part,*** in contrast to the whole—ⓐ gener. (Ocellus Luc. c. 12 τὸ πᾶν ἢ μέρος τι τοῦ παντός; Alex. Aphr., An. II 1 p. 13, 16 μ. ἐν ὅλῳ; Gen 47:24; Philo, Spec. Leg. 3, 189 τ. ὅλου κ. τῶν μερῶν al.; Ath. 12, 3 μικρῷ μέρει τοῦ παντὸς τὸ πᾶν … δοκιμάζουσιν) w. the gen. of the whole τὸ ἐπιβάλλον μ. τῆς οὐσίας *the part of the property that falls to me* **Lk 15:12** (SIG 346, 36 τὸ μέρος τὸ ἐπιβάλλον; 1106, 80). μ. τι τοῦ ἀγροῦ *a part of the field* Hs 5, 2, 2. δύο μέρη τῆς ῥάβδου *two thirds of the stick* (Thu. 1, 104, 2 τῆς Μέμφιδος τῶν δύο μερῶν πρὸς τὸ τρίτον μέρος; SIG 975, 24f) Hs 8, 1, 12f; cp. 8, 5, 3ff; 8, 8, 4; 8, 9, 1. τὸ πλεῖστον μ. αὐτῶν 8, 2, 9; cp. 9, 7, 4 and 8, 1, 16. τὰ λοιπὰ μ. 8, 1, 15. Also without gen., when it is plain fr. the context how much of a contrast betw. part and whole is involved μὴ ἔχον μέρος τι σκοτεινόν *with no dark part* **Lk 11:36;** cp. **J 19:23** (Jos., Ant. 1, 172 μέρη τέσσαρα ποιήσαντες); **Ac 5:2; Rv 16:19;** Hv 4, 3, 4f. Of the Christians ἐκλογῆς μ. *a chosen portion* fr. among all humankind 1 Cl 29:1.

ⓑ specialized uses—**α.** *component, element* τινὰ μέρη ἔχουσιν τ. ἀνομίας *they still have certain elements of lawlessness* Hv 3, 6, 4b.

β. of parts of the body (Diod. S. 32, 12, 1 τὰ τοῦ σώματος μέρη; Dio Chrys. 16 [33], 62; Plut., Mor. 38a μ. τ. σώματος; Artem. 3, 51 al.; Herodian 8, 4, 10; PRyl 145, 14 [38 AD]; PGM 4, 2390; 2392; Tat. 16, 1) fig., of the body whose head is Christ **Eph 4:16** (on the text s. μέλος 2; for the idea σῶμα, end).

γ. τὰ μέρη *the parts* (of a geographical area), *region, district* (Herodian 6, 5, 7; Jos., Ant. 12, 234; B-D-F §141, 2; s. Rob. 408) τῆς Γαλιλαίας **Mt 2:22.** τὰ μ. τῆς Λιβύης τῆς κατὰ Κυρήνην **Ac 2:10;** cp. **20:2.** Also of a district in or around a city (cp. UPZ 180b, 8 [113 BC] οἰκίας τῆς οὔσης ἐν τῷ ἀπὸ νότου μέρει Διὸς πόλεως) τὰ μ. Τύρου καὶ Σιδῶνος *the district of Tyre and Sidon* **Mt 15:21;** cp. **16:13; Mk 8:10; J 6:1** D; **Ac 7:43** D. τὰ ἀνωτερικὰ μέρη *the upper (=inland) regions, interior* (cp. PHamb 54 I, 14 τὰ ἄνω μέρη of the upper Nile valley) **Ac 19:1.—Eph 4:9** (s. κατώτερος).

δ. *side* (Diod. S. 2, 9, 3 ἐφ' ἑκάτερον μέρος=on both sides; Ex 32:15; 1 Macc 9:12; TestJud 5:4; Ath. 1, 4 τὸ ἕτερον … τῆς κεφαλῆς μέρος) Hs 9, 2, 3. τὰ δεξιὰ μ. *on the right side,* τὰ ἀριστερὰ μ. *on the left side* v 3, 1, 9; 3, 2, 1. Of a vessel τὰ δεξιὰ μ. τοῦ πλοίου *the right side of the boat* (as the lucky side? cp. Il. 12, 239; 13, 821 of a bird of omen) **J 21:6** (of a body part POxy 3195, II 40, 43 [331 AD]). τὰ ἐξώτερα μ. τῆς οἰκοδομῆς *the outside of the building* Hs 9, 9, 3.—New Docs 3, 75.

ε. *piece* ἰχθύος ὀπτοῦ μέρος *a piece of broiled fish* **Lk 24:42.**—μ. τι λαμβάνειν *take a portion* Hv 3, 1, 6.

ζ. *party* (Jos., Bell. 1, 143; POxy 1278, 24; PFlor 47, 17; PLond III, 1028, 18 p. 277 [VII AD] τοῦ πρασίνου μέρους='of the green party') **Ac 23:6.** τινὲς τ. γραμματέων τ. μέρους τ. Φαρισαίων vs. **9.**

η. *branch* or *line of business* (cp. PFlor 89, 2 after Preisigke, Berichtigungsliste 1922, 147 τὰ μέρη τῆς διοικήσεως='the branches of the administration') **Ac 19:27.**

θ. *matter, affair* (Menand., Epitr. 234 S. [58 Kö.], Per. 297 S. [107 Kö.]; Diod. S. 2, 27, 1; Περὶ ὕψους 12, 5 [μέρη=objects]; Jos., Ant. 15, 61 τούτῳ τῷ μέρει; PRyl 127, 12 [29 AD] ἀναζητῆσαι ὑπὲρ τοῦ μέρους='begin an investigation concerning the matter') ἐν τούτῳ τῷ μέρει *in this case, in this matter* (cp. Polyb. 18, 18, 2 τ. πίστιν ἐν τούτῳ τῷ μέρει διαφυλάττειν) **2 Cor 3:10; 9:3** (s. also ἐν μέρει in c below). Cp. **1 Pt 4:16 v.l.**

ⓒ used w. prepositions: ἀνὰ μέρος *one after the other, in succession* (s. ἀνά 2) **1 Cor 14:27.**—ἀπὸ μέρους *in part* (Dio Chrys. 28 [45], 3; Ael. Aristid. 32, 4 K.=12 p. 135 D.; Ptolem., Apotel. 2, 10, 2; Epict. 1, 27, 17 δι' ὅλων ἢ ἀ. μ.; PRyl 133, 17; BGU 1201, 15 [2 AD]; PTebt 402, 2; POxy 1681, 9; Just., A II, 10, 8 Χριστῷ … τῷ … ἀ. μ. γνωσθέντι) πώρωσις ἀ. μ. *a partial hardening* **Ro 11:25.** τολμηρότερον … ἀ. μ. *very boldly on some points* **15:15.** καθὼς ἐπέγνωτε ἡμᾶς ἀ. μ. *as you have understood us in part* **2 Cor 1:14.** Also *for a while:* ἀ. μ. ἐμπλησθῆναί τινος *enjoy someone's company for a while* **Ro 15:24;** cp. **2 Cor 2:5** *in some degree.*—ἐκ μέρους *in part, individually* (Ael. Aristid. 54 p. 695 D.; 698; SIG 852, 30 … ὅλη, ἐκ μέρους δέ … ; PLond III, 1166, 14 p. 105 [42 AD]; BGU 538, 33; PRyl 233, 6; Philo, Mos. 2, 1 al.) *individually* **1 Cor 12:27.** ἐκ μ. γινώσκειν *know in part* **13:9a, 12;** cp. vs. **9b.** τὸ ἐκ μ. *what is 'in part' = imperfect* vs. **10.**—ἐν μέρει *in the matter of, with regard to* (Antig. Car. 24; Diod. S. 20, 58, 5; Plut., Mor. 102e; Horapollo 1, 57 ἐν τροφῆς μέρει='as food'; GDI 5185, 30 [Crete] ἐν χάριτος μέρει; Philo, Det. Pot. Ins. 5 ἐν μέρει λόγου al.) ἐν μέρει ἑορτῆς *with regard to a festival* **Col 2:16** (cp. ApcrEzk [Epiph. 70, 14] ἐν τῷ μέρει τῆς ἀδυναμίας 'in connection with my disability'. See bθ above).—κατὰ μέρος *part by part, in detail* (ins [s. SIG ind. IV p. 444a]; PTebt 6, 24) περὶ ὧν οὐκ ἔστιν νῦν λέγειν κατὰ μέρος (κ. μ. of the detailed treatment of a subj. as Pla., Theaet. 157b, Soph. 246c; Polyb. 1, 4, 6; 3, 19, 11; 3, 28, 4; 10, 27, 7 λέγειν κ. μ.; Ptolem., Apotel. 2, 11, 7; 2 Macc 2:30; Jos., Ant. 12, 245) *point by point* **Hb 9:5.**—παρὰ μέρος *to one side* (Appian, Liby. 14 §55 γιγνόμενος παρὰ μ.=going to one side, Bell. Civ. 5, 81 §345; PGM 13, 438 βάλε παρὰ μέρος='put to one side') ὁ λίθος ὑπεχώρησε παρὰ μ. *the stone went back to one side* GPt 9:37.

ⓓ as adv. acc. μέρος τι *in part, partly* (Thu. 2, 64; 4, 30, 1; X., Eq. 1, 12; SIG 976, 65; 1240, 8 ἤτι μέρος ἢ σύμπαν; 3 Km 12:31) **1 Cor 11:18;** τὸ πλεῖστον μ. *for the most part* (Menand., fgm. 789 Kö.; Diod. S. 22, 10, 5) Hs 8, 5, 6; 8, 10, 1. τὸ πλεῖον μ. *for the greater part* v 3, 6, 4a.

❷ ***share*** (trag. et al.) μ. τι μεταδοῦναι ἀπό τινος *give a share of someth.* B 1:5 (on μέρος ἀπό τινος cp. PStras 19, 5 [105

AD] τοῦ ὑπάρχοντος αὐτῷ μέρους ἑνὸς ἀπὸ μερῶν ἐννέα) δώσω αὐτοῖς … μέρος δικαιοσύνης μετὰ τῶν ἁγίων μου *I will give them … a share of uprightness with my holy ones* i.e. those rescued from perdition will enjoy the same redeemed status as those who are already in the divine presence ApcPt Rainer 6. ἔχειν μ. ἔν τινι *have a share in someth.* (cp. Synes., Ep. 58 p. 203a οὐκ ἔστι τῷ διαβόλῳ μέρος ἐν παραδείσῳ) **Rv 20:6** (Dalman, Worte 103f). ἀφελεῖ ὁ θεὸς τὸ μέρος αὐτοῦ ἀπὸ τοῦ ξύλου τῆς ζωῆς **22:19.**—*Place* (Appian, Bell. Civ. 1, 34 §154 ἐν ὑπηκόων ἀντὶ κοινωνῶν εἶναι μέρει=to be in the place of subjects instead of partners) τὸ μ. αὐτῶν ἐν τ. λίμνῃ *their place is in the lake* **Rv 21:8.** ἔχειν μ. μετά τινος *have a place with someone* **J 13:8.** τὸ μ. τινὸς μετὰ τῶν ὑποκριτῶν τιθέναι *assign someone a place among the dissemblers (hypocrites)* **Mt 24:51;** cp. **Lk 12:46.** μετ' αὐτῶν μοι τὸ μ. γένοιτο σχεῖν ἐν (v.l. παρὰ) θεῷ *may I have my place with them in* (or *with*) *God* IPol 6:1. τοῦ λαβεῖν μ. ἐν ἀριθμῷ τῶν μαρτύρων MPol 14:2.—B. 934. DELG s.v. μείρομαι II. M-M. EDNT. TW. Sv.

μεσάζω (s. μεσόω; Hippocr. et al.; Diod. S. 1, 32, 9; PSI 151, 6; Wsd 18:14) ***be in*** or ***at the middle*** **J 7:14 v.l.** (Ps.-Callisth. 3, 26, 7 p. 127, 2 θέρους μεσάζοντος); s. μεσόω.—DELG s.v. μέσος.

μεσημβρία, ας, ἡ (μέσος, ἡμέρα; s. Schwyzer I 277 on the shift μβρ; 'midday, noon' Aeschyl., Hdt.+; ins, pap, LXX, JosAs; SyBar 12:2; ApcEsdr 4:22 p. 28, 25 Tdf.; Philo, Joseph.).

❶ of time ***midday, noon*** (Aeschyl., Hdt. et al.; PRyl 27, 66; PGM 7, 157. So as a rule in LXX; Jos., Ant. 11, 155) **Ac 22:6;** GPt 5:15. κατὰ μεσημβρίαν **Ac 8:26** *about noon* (Philo, Somn. 1, 202; so EbNestle, StKr 65, 1892, 335–37; Wendt et al.).

❷ of place ***the south*** (Hdt. 1, 6; 142; 2, 8 al.; SIG 972, 96; 1112, 26; Da 8:4, 9; Philo; JosAs 2:13; ApcEsdr 4:22 p. 28, 25 Tdf.; Jos., Bell. 5, 505; SibOr 3, 26) as the position of the sun at midday κατὰ μεσημβρίαν **Ac 8:26** *toward the south* (s. B-D-F §253, 5; Preuschen, Zahn, Bauernfeind, Haenchen ad loc.—Conzelmann [Hermeneia] is undecided betw. 1 and 2).—B. 873; 996. DELG s.v. μέσος. M-M.

μεσιτεύω (fr. μεσίτης) 1 aor. ἐμεσίτευσα. Fr. the sense 'mediate, act as surety' (Aristot. et al.; OGI 437, 76 [I BC]; 79; BGU 906, 7; CPR I, 1, 19; 206, 13; Philo) intr. (Jos., Ant. 7, 193; 16, 118 'act as mediator, peacemaker') is readily derived ***guarantee,*** in the sense of settling a matter, ὅρκῳ *by means of an oath* **Hb 6:17.**—DELG s.v. μέσος B. M-M. TW.

μεσίτης, ου, ὁ (s. μεσιτεύω; since Polyb. 28, 17, 8; Ps.-Lucian, Amor. 47 θεὸν μεσίτην λαβόντες; pap; Job 9:33; TestDan 6:2; AssMos fgm. a; Philo; Jos., Ant. 4, 133; 16, 24. On this many-sided t.t. of Hellenistic legal language s. LMitteis, Her 30, 1895, 616ff; JBehm, D. Begriff Διαθήκη im NT 1912, 77ff w. numerous exx.; s. lit. in JModrzejewski, Private Arbitration in Greco-Roman Egypt, JJP 6, '52, 247 n. 79) **one who mediates betw. two parties to remove a disagreement or reach a common goal, *mediator, arbitrator,*** of Christ (Mithras as μεσίτης: Plut., Mor. 369e) w. gen. of the pers. betw. whom he mediates μ. θεοῦ καὶ ἀνθρώπων *mediator between God and humans* (Iren. 3, 18, 7 [Harv. II 100, 7]; cp. TestDan 6:2) **1 Ti 2:5;** w. gen. of the thing that Jesus mediates: κρείττονος **Hb 8:6,** καινῆς **9:15,** νέας διαθήκης **12:24** (s. διαθήκη 2. AssMos. fgm. a, Denis 63, 10=Tromp p. 272], Moses calls himself τῆς διαθήκης μεσίτης). Of the law διαταγεὶς δι' ἀγγέλων ἐν χειρὶ μεσίτου *ordered through the angels, by the hand of a mediator* **Gal 3:19** (Moses, as mediator betw. God and the people, called μεσίτης e.g. Philo, Mos. 2, 166, Somn. 1, 143; Betz, Gal [Hermeneia] ad loc.). The sense of vs. **20,** ὁ δὲ μ. ἑνὸς οὐκ ἔστιν *an intermediary does not exist for one party alone,* is disputed. It prob. means that the activity of an intermediary implies the existence of more than one party, and hence may be unsatisfactory because it must result in a compromise. The presence of an intermediary would prevent attainment, without any impediment, of the purpose of the εἷς θεός in giving the law.—NKZ 39, 1928, 21–24; 549–52; 552f; HStegmann, BZ 22, '34, 30–42; Straub 67.—DELG s.v. μέσος B. M-M. EDNT. TW. Spicq.

μεσονύκτιον, ου, τό (μέσος, νύξ; subst. neut. of μεσονύκτιος [Pind. et al.]; as a noun Hippocr. et al.; Diod. S. 20, 48, 6; Chariton 1, 9, 1; POxy 1768, 6; LXX; TestJob 31:5 ἐν τῷ μ. The spelling μεσανύκτιον is not well attested [POxy 1768, 6 of III AD. Cp. B-D-F §35, 2; W-S. §5, 20b; Mlt-H. 73]. On its formation s. B-D-F §123, 1; W-S. §16, 5; Mlt-H. 341; Phryn. p. 53 Lob.) ***midnight*** μεσονύκτιον acc. of time *at midnight* **Mk 13:35** (Hippocr. VII p. 72 Littré; Ps 118:62.—PGM 13, 680 τὸ μεσονύκτιον). Also the gen. (which is read in the Hippocr. pass. just quoted, by the edition of Kühn II p. 260; s. B-D-F §186, 2) μεσονυκτίου **Lk 11:5.** κατὰ τὸ μ. *about midnight* (Strabo 2, 5, 42) **Ac 16:25.** μέχρι μεσονυκτίου *until midnight* **20:7** (on the omission of the article s. B-D-F §255, 3; Rob. 792).—DELG s.v. μέσος. M-M.

Μεσοποταμία, ας, ἡ (subst. fem. of μεσοποτάμιος, α, ον='located betw. rivers'. ἡ μεσοποταμία, sc. χώρα='the land betw. rivers' [Polyb. 5, 44, 6; Strabo 11, 12, 2], esp. that betw. the Euphrates and Tigris) ***Mesopotamia*** (Diod. S. 2, 11, 2; 18, 6, 3; Appian, Syr. 48 §246; 53 §269; Arrian, Anab. 3, 7, 3; 7, 7, 3; Polyaenus, Exc. 9, 2; Ptolem., Apotel. 2, 3, 22; 28; OGI 54, 18; LXX; Demetr.: 722 fgm. 1, 1f Jac.; Philo, Joseph.; TestJud 9:1; 10:1) **Ac 2:9.** In the narrative about Abraham (cp. Gen 24:10) **7:2.**—LDillemann, Haute Mésopotamie orient. et pays adjacents, '62; Pauly-W. XV 1105–63; Kl. Pauly III 1237–41.

μέσος, η, ον (Hom.+). The distinction between 'middle' and 'among' for μ. is sometimes rather fluid, and some of the passages here cited may fit equally well under 1 or 2.

❶ **pert. to a middle position spatially or temporally, *middle, in the middle.*—ⓐ** as adj. (of intermediate terms: Pla., Rep. 330b, Pol. 303a) ὁ μέσος αὐτῶν ἀνήρ *the man in their midst,* apparently surrounded by them Hs 9, 12, 7. μέσης νυκτός *at midnight* (3 Km 3:20.—B-D-F §270, 2; Rob. 495; Lobeck, Phryn. p. 53; 54; 465) **Mt 25:6.** ἡμέρας μέσης *at midday* (Jos., Bell. 1, 651, Ant. 17, 155) **Ac 26:13.** εἰς μέσην τὴν οἰκοδομήν *into the middle of the building* Hs 9, 7, 5; cp. 9, 8, 2; 4; 6 (cp. Philo, Fuga 49 εἰς μέσον τὸν ποταμόν; Jos., Ant. 4, 80 εἰς μέσον τὸ πῦρ). ἐσταύρωσαν … μέσον τὸν Ἰησοῦν *they crucified Jesus between (them)* **J 19:18.** ἐσχίσθη τὸ καταπέτασμα μέσον *the curtain was torn in two* **Lk 23:45** (cp. Artem. 4, 30 τὸ ἱμάτιον μέσον ἐρρωγέναι). ἐλάκησεν μέσος **Ac 1:18** (cp. Aristoph., Ran. 955). ἐν μέσοις τοῖς ὀργάνοις τοῦ διαβόλου *in the midst of the tools of the devil* 2 Cl 18:2 (for the syntax cp. Gen 2:9 ἐν μέσῳ τῷ παραδείσῳ).

ⓑ as subst. neut. τὸ μ. *the middle* (on the absence of the art. s. B-D-F §264, 4; cp. Rob. 792) ἀνὰ μέσον τινός (s. ἀνά 1) ἀνὰ μέσον τῶν ὁρίων *within* or *through the region* **Mk 7:31.** ἀνὰ μ. αὐτῶν *between them* GPt 4:10; Hs 9, 2, 3; 9, 15, 2. ἀνὰ μ. ἐκκλησίας ἁγίων B 6:16; 4:10; διακρῖναι ἀνὰ μ. τοῦ ἀδελφοῦ *between one (congregation) member and another* **1 Cor 6:5** (s. ἀνά 1b. Perh. μέσος prompted a shortening of the sentence tending to obscurity; cp. the Stoic expr. μέσα καθήκοντα = καθήκοντα ἃ ἐν μέσῳ ἐστὶ κατορθωμάτων κ. ἁμαρτημάτων: MPohlenz, D. Stoa II '49, 73f). τὸ ἀρνίον τὸ ἀ. μ. τοῦ θρόνου *the lamb who is (seated) on the center of the throne* **Rv 7:17.** ἀνὰ μ. τῆς ὁδοῦ *(they made) half their journey* GJs 17:3.—διὰ μέσου αὐτῶν *through the midst of them* (X., An. 1, 4, 4; Aesop. Fab. 147 P.=247 H.//201a Ch.//152 [I, II] H-H.; Am 5:17; Jer 44:4; Jdth 11:19; 1 Macc 5:46; Ath. 18, 3 'between') **Lk 4:30; J 8:59 v.l.** διὰ μέσον Σαμαρείας καὶ Γαλιλαίας **Lk 17:11** prob. can only mean *through Samaria and Galilee;* but this raises a practical difficulty, since we should expect to find the provinces mentioned in the opposite order. Perh. the text is damaged (cp. the vv.ll. διὰ μέσου and μέσον; s. B-D-F §222; Rob. 648; JBlinzler, AWikenhauser Festschr. '54, 46ff. If the v.l. διὰ μέσου Σ. καὶ Γ. should be correct, we could compare Maximus Tyr. 28, 4a διὰ μέσου πίστεως κ. ἀπιστίας=throughout between). For the view that μέσον signifies the area betw. S. and G. s. the comm. Cp. δια B1.—εἰς τὸ μέσον *into the middle* or *center* (X., Cyr. 3, 1, 6; Dio Chrys. 19 [36], 24; 3 Km 6:8; Jos., Ant. 9, 149) **Mk 3:3; Lk 4:35; 5:19; 6:8; J 20:19, 26** (ἔστη εἰς τὸ μέσον as Vi. Aesopi G 82 P.); Hs 9, 8, 5; also *in the middle* 9, 6, 1. W. gen. (X., An. 1, 5; 14a; Jer 21:4; 48:7; Sb 6270, 13) εἰς τὸ μ. αὐτῶν *in the midst of them* 9, 11, 7. Without the art. (LXX; Jos., Vi. 334; SibOr 3, 674) εἰς μ. τοῦ πεδίου *in the middle of the plain* s 9, 2, 1 (εἰς μ.='in the middle', as Ps.-Clem., Hom. 3, 30 p. 44, 21 Lag.). τί . . . τὸ ἔριον εἰς μ. τῶν ἀκανθῶν τιθέασιν; *Why do they place the wool in the middle of the thorns?* B 7:11. ἀναστὰς εἰς μ. *he arose (and came) forward* **Mk 14:60** (cp. Theocr. 22, 82 ἐς μέσον=into the middle; Himerius, Or. 63 [=Or. 17], 2 εἰς μέσον ἔρχεσθαι=come into the open; X., Cyr. 4, 1, 1 στὰς εἰς τὸ μ.).—ἐν τῷ μ. *among, before* (more closely defined by the context, or = *in public* [so Clearch., fgm. 45 οἴκοι καὶ μὴ ἐν τῷ μέσῳ; Appian, Liby. 15 §63]) **Mt 14:6** (Dio Chrys. 30 [79], 39 ὀρχεῖσθαι ἐν τῷ μέσῳ; Lucian, Pereg. 8) and *into the middle, before (them)* (Vi. Aesopi W c. 86 στὰς ἐν τῷ μέσῳ ἔφη) **Ac 4:7.** Without the art. (LXX) ἐν μέσῳ (on the spelling ἐμ μέσῳ, which occurs several times as v.l., s. B-D-F §19, 1; Mlt-H. 105) abs. *into the middle, before (someone)* (Appian, Hann. 16 §67, Liby. 14 §59; Jos., Ant. 7, 278) **J 8:3;** MPol 18:1 and *in the middle* (Pla., Rep. 558a; Herm. Wr. 4, 3; PLille 1 recto, 5 [259 BC]; GrBar 13:4) **J 8:9.** W. gen. of place (Aeneas Tact. 1529; 1532; TestAbr A 12 p. 90, 21 [Stone p. 28], B 8 p. 113, 3 [St. p. 74]; ParJer 1:2; GrBar 10:2) τῆς θαλάσσης (En 97:7) *in the middle of the lake* **Mk 6:47.** τῆς πλατείας *through the middle of the street* **Rv 22:2.** ἐν μ. τῆς αὐλῆς *in the middle of the courtyard* **Lk 22:55a;** τοῦ τάφου GPt 13:55. ἐν μ. αὐτῆς *within it* (the city of Jerusalem) **Lk 21:21;** cp. Dg 12:3; MPol 12:1; B 12:2(?). ἐν μ. τοῦ θρόνου καὶ τῶν τεσσάρων ζῴων *on the center of the throne and among the four living creatures* **Rv 5:6a** (w. double gen. also *between:* Appian, Hann. 14 §60, Bell. Civ. 5, 23 §92; Arrian, Anab. 1, 20, 2; 3, 28, 8 al.; Lucian, Fugit. 10 ἐν μ. ἀλαζονείας κ. φιλοσοφίας). ἐν μέσῳ τ. θρόνου *around* (on every side of) *the throne* **4:6** (but *between* the throne and a more remote point: RBrewer, JBL 71, '52, 227—31).—ἐν μέσῳ ἐκκλησίας **Hb 2:12** (Ps 21:23); cp. **Ac 17:22.** κατὰ μέσον (Jos., Bell. 5, 207; SibOr 3, 802 κατὰ μέσσον='in the middle' [of the day]) κατὰ μ. τῆς νυκτός *about midnight* **Ac 16:25** D; **27:27.**

ⓒ The neut. μέσον serves as adv. (e.g., Appian, Bell. Civ. 3, 43 §175 μ.=meanwhile) ἦν μέσον ὡς *he was in the center of it as* MPol 15:2; and is used as prep. w. gen. (B-D-F §215, 3; Rob. 644. Cp. Hdt. 9, 107, 2; Polyb. 8, 25, 1; Epict. 2, 22, 10; LXX, TestSol; TestAbr A 4 p. 80, 31 [Stone p. 8]; JosAs 24:21; Jos., Ant. 6, 65; SibOr 3, 319) μ. τῆς θαλάσσης *in the middle of the lake* **Mt 14:24 v.l.;** μ. γενεᾶς σκολιᾶς *in the midst of a crooked generation* **Phil 2:15** (cp. Maximus Tyr. 36, 5a ἐν μέσῳ τῷ σιδηρῷ τούτῳ γένει).

❷ **pert. to a position within a group, without focus on mediate position, *among.*—ⓐ** as adj. ἐκάθητο ὁ Πέτρος μέσος αὐτῶν *Peter was sitting among them* **Lk 22:55** (the point being not as center of attention but inconspicuously in the group; cp. Jos., Ant. 9, 107). μέσος ὑμῶν ἕστηκεν **J 1:26** (Jos., Ant. 14, 23). τοῦ πύργου μέσου Hs 9, 8, 2. εἶδον . . . μέσον αὐτῶν τὸν Παῦλον AcPl Ha 11, 14.

ⓑ as subst. neuter ἀνὰ μέσον τινός (s. ἀνά 1) *among someth.* **Mt 13:25.** W. gen. pl. (TestJob 32:6 ἐν μέσῳ τῶν τέκνων σου) *in the midst of, among* in answer to the questions where and whither (B-D-F §215, 3 app.) **Mt 18:2, 20; Mk 9:36; Lk 2:46; 24:36; Ac 1:15; 2:22; 6:15** D; **27:21; Rv 5:6b;** cp. **6:6.** Of close personal relationship ἐν μέσῳ ὑμῶν *among you = in communion with you* **Lk 22:27; 1 Th 2:7.**—ἐν μ. λύκων *among wolves* **Mt 10:16; Lk 10:3;** 2 Cl 5:2.—W. gen. pl. of things (Alciphron 3, 24, 3) **Lk 8:7; Rv 1:13; 2:1.** ἐκ (τοῦ) μ. *from among* (X., An. 1, 5, 14b; oracular response in Diod. S. 9, 3, 2; LXX=מִתּוֹךְ): αἴρειν τι (or τινά) ἐκ (τοῦ) μέσου (τινῶν) **Col 2:14; 1 Cor 5:2** (s. αἴρω 3). ἁρπάσαι αὐτὸν ἐκ μ. αὐτῶν **Ac 23:10** (s. ἁρπάζω 2a). ἀφορίζειν τοὺς πονηροὺς ἐκ μ. τῶν δικαίων **Mt 13:49** (s. ἀφορίζω 1). γίνεσθαι ἐκ μ. **2 Th 2:7** (s. γίνομαι 6b). ἐξέρχεσθαι ἐκ μ. αὐτῶν *from among them* **Ac 17:33;** cp. **2 Cor 6:17** (cp. Is 52:11). κύριος λαμβάνει ἑαυτῷ ἔθνος ἐκ μ. ἐθνῶν 1 Cl 29:3 (cp. Dt 4:34).—B. 864. DELG. M-M. EDNT. TW. Sv.

μεσότοιχον, ου, τό (the noun ὁ μεσότοιχος [μέσος, τοῖχος]=*dividing wall* in Eratosthenes: Athen. 7, 14, 281d; ins fr. Argos: BCH 33, 1909, 452 no. 22, 16.—But cp. an ins fr. Didyma: ABA 1911, 56 ln. 13 ἐπὶ τοῦ μεσοτοίχου, where μ. can just as well come fr. τὸ μεσότοιχον; this occurs in Vi. Aesopi W 75 P.; cp. Jos., Ant. 8, 71 ὁ μέσος τοῖχος; in PAmh II, 98, 9 μέρος μεσοτύχ(ων) οἰκιῶν, the ed. suggests the adj. form μεσοτοίχων) *dividing wall* τὸ μ. τοῦ φραγμοῦ *the barrier formed by the dividing wall* between us **Eph 2:14.**—M-M. TW.

μεσουράνημα, ατος, τό (Posidon.: 87 fgm. 85 p. 273, 15 Jac.; Manetho, Plut.; Sext. Emp., POxy 235, 13 [I AD]) lit., in astronomy the 'meridian' ('culmination'; μεσουρανεῖν means 'be at the zenith', of the sun [Aristot., Plut.; schol. on Apollon. Rhod. 1, 450; PGM 4, 2992]) ***zenith*** ἐν μεσουρανήματι *in midheaven* **Rv 8:13; 14:6; 19:17.**—M-M.

μεσόω (μέσος; Aeschyl., Hdt. et al.; LXX) ***be in/at the middle*** in gen. abs. (Thu. 6, 30, 1 θέρους μεσοῦντος; Ael. Aristid. 13 p. 274 D.: πολέμου μεσοῦντος; Sb 7464, 10 [III AD]; Ex 12:29; 34:22; 3 Macc 5:14; Philo, Spec. Leg. 1, 183 μεσοῦντος ἔαρος; Jos., Ant. 5, 190) τῆς ἑορτῆς μεσούσης *when the festival was half over* **J 7:14** (v.l. μεσαζούσης; s. μεσάζω).—DELG s.v. μέσος D.

Μεσσίας, ου, ὁ Hellenized transliteration of מָשִׁיחַ, Aram. מְשִׁיחָא (s. Schürer II 517, and n. 16 w. ref. to Dalman, Gramm.^{2} 157, 3) ***the Messiah = the Anointed One*** (ThNöldeke, ZDMG 32, 1878, 403; W-S. §5, 26c p. 57 note 54) in our lit. only twice, and in J: in the mouth of a disciple **J 1:41** and of a Samaritan woman **4:25,** in both cases translated by Χριστός, q.v.—BHHW II 1197–1204; ABD IV 777–88; Schürer II 488–54; HKippenberg, Garizim u. Synagoge '71, on Messianic expectation 115f; JCharlesworth, ed., The Messiah, Developments in Earliest Judaism and Christianity '92; IGrünewald et al., edd., Messiah and Christos, DFlusser Festschr. '92.—M-M. TW.

μεστός, ή, όν (s. μεστόω; trag., X., Pla.+) prim. 'full'.

❶ **pert. to filling up a space, *full,*** lit., w. gen. of thing (X., An. 1, 4, 19; Alciphron 2, 11; Jos., Ant. 4, 93; PGrenf I, 14,

9; POxy 1070, 31f [III AD]) σκεῦος ὄξους μ. *full of vinegar* **J 19:29a.** Likew. of a sponge μ. τοῦ ὄξους vs. **29b.** τὸ δίκτυον μ. ἰχθύων μεγάλων *the net full of large fish* **21:11.** In imagery of the tongue μ. ἰοῦ *full of poison* **Js 3:8.**

❷ **pert. to being thoroughly characterized by someth., *filled w. somet.,*** fig. ext. of 1, w. gen.—ⓐ of pers. (Dio Chrys. 51 [68], 4; Ael. Aristid. 46 p. 267 D.: ὕβρεων κ. κακῶν μ.; 47 p. 435 εὐλαβείας; CPR I, 19, 15 μ. ψευδολογίας; POxy 130, 6 μ. ἐλεημοσύνης; Pr 6:34; Jos., Ant. 16, 351) μ. ὑποκρίσεως καὶ ἀνομίας *full of pretense and lawlessness* **Mt 23:28.** μ. φθόνου (Maximus Tyr. 35, 4e; Tetrast. Iamb. 1, 31, 2 p. 276) **Ro 1:29.** μ. πολλῆς ἀνοίας καὶ πονηρίας 2 Cl 13:1 (Isocr. 5, 45 πολλῆς ἀνοίας μ.; Dio Chrys. 15 [32], 15 μ. πονηρίας). μ. ἀγαθωσύνης **Ro 15:14.** μ. ἐλέους **Js 3:17** (plus μεστὴ καρπῶν ἀγαθῶν P[74]). μ. ὁσίας βουλῆς 1 Cl 2:3.

ⓑ of things (Epicurus in Diog. L. 10, 146 πάντα ταραχῆς μεστά; Menand., fgm. 386 Kö.; μεστόν ἐστι τὸ ζῆν φροντίδων; Philo, Op. M. 2; 22 al.; Just., D. 131 ὀνείδους μεστοῦ μυστηρίου τοῦ σταυροῦ; Tat. 32, 3 φθόνου μεστά) ὀφθαλμοὶ μ. μοιχαλίδος (s. μοιχαλίς a; μ. w. an abstr. noun Sb VI, 9622, 16 [343 AD] ἦθος … ἀπονοίας μεστὸν ἀναλαβόμενοι=displaying a manner fraught with rebellion) **2 Pt 2:14.** The way of death is κατάρας μ. B 20:1; D 5:1.—B. 931. DELG. M-M. TW.

μεστόω pf. pass. ptc. μεμεστωμένος (fr. μεστός; Soph. et al.) ***fill*** w. gen. of the thing w. which an entity becomes full (so mostly, e.g. 3 Macc 5:10; TestAbr 17 p. 99, 28 [Stone p. 46; but elsewhere in TestAbr w. acc. of thing]; Just.) γλεύκους μεμεστωμένοι *full of new wine* **Ac 2:13.** W. dat. of thing (3 Macc 5:1) λόγος μεμεστωμένος πράξει *speech filled with (=fulfilled in) action* D 2:5.—DELG s.v. μεστός. M-M. TW.

μετά (Hom.+) prep. w. gen. and acc., in the NT not (B-D-F §203; Rob. 610) w. dat.—For lit. s. ἀνά, beg.; also for μετά (and σύν) Tycho Mommsen, Beiträge zu d. Lehre v. den griech. Präp. 1895. Basic idea: 'in the vicinity of'.

A. w. gen. **with—❶ marker of placement, *with, among, in company with someone*** (Gen 42:5; EpArist 180; En 22:13; 99:10; PsSol 4:6; JosAs 10:3 al.) or *someth.* ἦν μετὰ τῶν θηρίων *he was among the wild animals* **Mk 1:13** (Diog. L. 6, 92 μόσχοι μετὰ λύκων). ἦν συγκαθήμενος μ. τῶν ὑπηρετῶν *he sat down among the servants* **14:54.** μετὰ ἀνόμων ἐλογίσθη *he was classed among the criminals* **Mk 15:28; Lk 22:37.** τὸ μέρος αὐτοῦ μ. τῶν ἀπίστων θήσει *he will assign him his lot among the faithless* (unbelievers?) **Lk 12:46;** cp. **Mt 24:51.** ζητεῖν τὸν ζῶντα μ. τῶν νεκρῶν *seek the living among the dead* **Lk 24:5.** μὴ γογγύζετε μετ' ἀλλήλων *do not grumble among yourselves* **J 6:43.** εἱστήκει Ἰούδας μετ' αὐτῶν **18:5.** ἡ σκηνὴ τ. θεοῦ μετὰ τ. ἀνθρώπων **Rv 21:3a.** μετὰ τῶν νεφελῶν *in the midst of the clouds* **1:7.**

❷ **marker of assoc. in gener. sense denoting the company within which someth. takes place, *with*—ⓐ** w. gen. of pers. in company w. whom someth. takes place

α. w. verbs of going, remaining, etc. προσέρχεσθαι μ. τινος *come (in company) with someone* **Mt 20:20;** cp. **5:41; Mk 1:29; 3:7; 5:24, 37; 11:11; 14:17; Lk 2:51; 6:17; 9:49; 14:31; J 3:22b; 11:54; Ac 24:1; Gal 2:1.** Angels accompanying the Messiah **Mt 25:31;** cp. **16:27; Mk 8:38; 1 Th 3:13; 2 Th 1:7.** περιπατεῖν μ. τινος (Menand., fgm. 178 Kö., Sam. 587f S. [242f Kö.]; ApcEsdr 6:12) **J 6:66.** γίνεσθαι μ. τινος *be, remain with someone* **Ac 7:38; 9:19; 20:18;** AcPlCor 2:4 (ApcMos 2 ἐγένοντο μ. ἀλλήλων). οἱ μ. αὐτοῦ γενόμενοι *his companions* **Mk 16:10.** μένειν μ. τινος *stay with someone* **1J 2:19** (ParJer 3:15). ζήσασα μ. ἀνδρός **Lk 2:36.** ἀκολουθεῖν μ. τινος *follow* (after) *someone* **Rv 6:8; 14:13** (s. ἀκολουθέω 2).

β. used w. trans. verbs ἄγειν τινὰ μ. ἑαυτοῦ *bring someone along* (s. ἄγω 1b) **2 Ti 4:11.** παραλαμβάνειν τινὰ μεθ' ἑαυτοῦ *take* or *bring someone along (as a companion)* (Gen 22:3) **Mt 12:45; 18:16; Mk 14:33.** ἔχειν τι μ. ἑαυτοῦ *have someth. with oneself:* bread **8:14;** τινά *someone* (PGM 4, 1952): the lame **Mt 15:30;** the poor **Mk 14:7; Mt 26:11; J 12:8;** the bridegroom **Mk 2:19b.** Pass. συγκατεψηφίσθη μετὰ τ. ἕνδεκα ἀποστόλων *he was chosen (to serve) with the eleven apostles* **Ac 1:26** (cp. Himerius, Or. 44 [=Or. 8], 3 μετὰ τῶν θεῶν ἀριθμούμενος=numbered with the gods).

γ. esp. εἶναι μ. τινος *be with someone, in someone's company.*

א. lit. of close association: the disciples w. Jesus **Mt 26:69, 71; Mk 3:14; 14:67; Lk 22:59; J 15:27; 17:24.** Also of accompaniment for a short time **Mt 5:25; J 3:26; 9:40; 12:17; 20:24, 26.** Of Jesus' association w. his disciples **13:33; 14:9; 16:4; 17:12.** Of relations between the superintendent and the congregation μετὰ τ. ἐπισκόπου εἶναι *be with, on the side of, the supervisor/bishop* IPhld 3:2. οἱ μ. τινος (sc. ὄντες) *someone's friends, companions,* etc. (Diod. S. 17, 96, 2 οἱ μεθ' Ἡρακλέους; SIG 175, 5; 659, 5; 826e II, 30; Am 4:2; 8:10; Gen 24:59; 1 Macc 7:23; JosAs 27:7; AscIs 2:15; 3:6, 14; Jos., Vi. 397, Ant. 7, 20; Just., D. 8, 3 al.) **Mt 12:3f; 26:51; Mk 1:36; 2:25; Lk 6:3f.** Of things ἄλλα πλοῖα ἦν μ. αὐτοῦ *other boats were with him, accompanied him* **Mk 4:36.** ὁ μισθός μου μετ' ἐμοῦ (sc. ἐστιν) **Rv 22:12.** τὸ πῦρ ἐστι μετ' αὐτοῦ *the fire (of judgment) awaits him* (the interpretation of the Armenian text; sim. the Lat.) AcPlCor 2:37.

ב. in ref. to supportiveness *be with someone, stand by, help someone* of God's help (Gen 21:20; 26:3; 28:20 al.; Jos., Ant. 15, 138) **J 3:2; 8:29; 16:32; Ac 7:9** (cp. Gen 39:2, 21); **10:38;** cp. **Mt 1:23** (Is 8:8); **Lk 1:28; Ro 15:33.** Of God's hand (1 Ch 4:10) **Lk 1:66; Ac 11:21.** Of Christ: **Mt 28:20; Ac 18:10.**

ג. a favorite expr. in conclusions of letters ὁ θεὸς τῆς ἀγάπης καὶ εἰρήνης ἔσται μ. ὑμῶν *will be with you* **2 Cor 13:11;** cp. **Phil 4:9;** ὁ κύριος κτλ. **2 Th 3:16** (cp. Ruth 2:4); **2 Ti 4:22.** ἡ χάρις τοῦ κυρίου Ἰησοῦ μ. ὑμῶν (sc. ἔσται) **1 Cor 16:23;** cp. **1 Th 5:28;** 1 Cl 65:2. μ. τοῦ πνεύματος ὑμῶν **Gal 6:18; Phil 4:23; Phlm 25;** B 21:9. μ. πάντων ὑμῶν **2 Th 3:18;** cp. **Eph 6:24.** Short and to the point: ἡ χάρις μ. ὑμῶν **Col 4:18; 1 Ti 6:21;** cp. **Tit 3:15; Hb 13:25.** ἔσται μεθ' ἡμῶν χάρις ἔλεος εἰρήνη **2J 3.**—ἡ ἀγάπη μου μ. πάντων ὑμῶν ἐν Χριστῷ Ἰησοῦ *my love is with you all in Christ Jesus* **1 Cor 16:24.** ἡ χάρις τοῦ κυρίου Ἰ. Χρ. καὶ ἡ ἀγάπη τ. θεοῦ καὶ ἡ κοινωνία τοῦ ἁγίου πνεύματος μετὰ πάντων ὑμῶν **2 Cor 13:13** (WvanUnnik, Dominus Vobiscum: liturg. formula, TManson memorial vol., '59, 270–305; on the Trinitarian formula s. the lit. on πνεῦμα 8).—In the expr. ὅσα ἐποίησεν ὁ θεὸς μ. αὐτῶν **Ac 14:27; 15:4** (cp. Hs 5, 1, 1) ὧν could be supplied *what God has done in helping them;* but ποιεῖν can just as well go w. μ. αὐτῶν *has done for them,* after the analogy of עָשָׂה עִם פּ (Tob 12:6; 13:7 ἃ ποιήσει μεθ' ὑμῶν; Jdth 8:26 ὅσα ἐποίησεν μετὰ Ἀβραάμ; 15:10; 1 Macc 10:27. In addition, cp. BGU 798, 8 εὐχαριστοῦμεν τῇ ἡμῶν δεσποίνῃ εἰς πάντα τὰ καλὰ ἃ ἐποίησεν μετὰ τ. δούλων αὐτῆς. But s. also LMaloney, 'All That God Had Done with Them' '91, 118–21: God works 'with' the apostles and 'through' them). Here also belongs ποιεῖν ἔλεος μ. τινος *have mercy on someone, show mercy to someone* (Gen 24:12; 2 Km 3:8; JosAs 23:4) **Lk 1:72; 10:37** (MWilcox, The Semitisms in Ac, '65, 84f). ἐμεγάλυνεν κύριος τὸ ἔλεος αὐτοῦ μετ' αὐτῆς *the Lord has shown great mercy to her* **1:58** (cp. 1 Km 12:24; Ps 125:2f).—In πληρώσεις με εὐφροσύνης μ. τοῦ προσώπου σου **Ac 2:28**=Ps 15:11 the LXX has literally translated אֶת־פָּנֶיךָ; it means *in your presence.*

ד. in ref. to taking sides or being allied in some way with someone: in contrast to εἶναι κατά τινος *be against someone* is εἶναι μ. τινος *be with someone, on someone's side* **Mt 12:30a; Lk 11:23a** (AFridrichsen, ZNW 13, 1912, 273–80).

ⓑ to denote the company in which an activity or experience takes place: ἀνακεῖσθαι μ. τινος *recline at table with someone* (for a meal) **Mt 26:20.** ἀνακλιθῆναι **8:11**; cp. **Lk 24:30.** βασιλεύειν **Rv 20:4, 6.** γρηγορεῖν **Mt 26:38, 40.** δειπνεῖν **Rv 3:20** (TestJob 15:2). δουλεύειν **Gal 4:25.** ἐμπαίζειν **Mt 27:41.** ἐσθίειν **9:11; 24:49; Mk 2:16ab; 14:14, 18; Lk 5:30** (TestAbr A 4 p. 81, 9 [Stone p. 10]). ἠρώτα … ἵνα φάγῃ μ. αὐτοῦ *he asked (him) to eat with him* **7:36** (cp. TestAbr B 6 p. 110, 21 [Stone p. 68]; JosAs 7:1). εὐφραίνεσθαι **15:29; Ro 15:10** (Dt 32:43). κλαίειν **12:15b.** κληρονομεῖν **Gal 4:30** (Gen 21:10; Just., D. 26, 1; cp. συγκληρονομεῖν JosAs 24:9). πίνειν **Mt 26:29.** ποιεῖν τὸ πάσχα *celebrate the Passover (with someone)* **26:18.** συνάγειν **12:30b; Lk 11:23b.** συνεσθίειν **Gal 2:12.** ταράττεσθαι **Mt 2:3.** τρώγειν **J 13:1 v.l.** χαίρειν **Ro 12:15a.**

ⓒ The associative aspect can also derive expression from the fact that two opposite parties exert influence upon one another or that one party brings the other to adopt a corresponding, and therefore common, attitude

α. in friendly, or at least not in hostile, fashion: εἰρηνεύειν (3 Km 22:45) **Ro 12:18**; cp. **2 Ti 2:22; Hb 12:14.** εὐθηνίαν ἔχειν Hm 2:3. κοινωνίαν ἔχειν **1J 1:3a, 7.** λαλεῖν μετά τινος (cp. Gen 31:24, 29; 1 Macc 7:15) **Mk 6:50; J 4:27ab.** συλλαλεῖν μ. τινος **Mt 17:3; Ac 25:12.** συμβούλιον διδόναι **Mk 3:6.** συνάγεσθαι **Mt 28:12; J 18:2.** συνᾶραι λόγον **Mt 18:23; 25:19.** ἐγένοντο φίλοι ὅ τε Ἡρῴδης καὶ ὁ Πιλᾶτος μετ᾽ ἀλλήλων **Lk 23:12.** οἱ μοιχεύοντες μετ᾽ αὐτῆς *those who commit adultery with her* **Rv 2:22.** πορνεύειν (cp. Ezk 16:34; TestAbr A 10 p. 88, 7 [Stone p. 24]) **17:2; 18:3, 9.** μολύνεσθαι **14:4** (cp. En 12:4 τῶν γυναικῶν ἐμιάνθησαν).

β. in hostile fashion; after verbs of fighting, quarreling, etc. to denote the pers. w. whom the strife is being carried on πολεμεῖν μ. τινος *carry on war with = against someone* (נלחם עם פּ 1 Km 17:33; 3 Km 12:24; ParJer 7:10. But s. also OGI 201, 3 ἐπολέμησα μετὰ τῶν Βλεμύων; BGU 1035, 9; 11. Also in Mod. Gk. [AThumb, Hdb. der neugriech. Volkssprache[2] 1910 §162, 1 note]) **Rv 2:16; 12:7; 13:4; 17:14** (B-D-F §193, 4; Rob. 610). Also πόλεμον ποιεῖν (Gen 14:2; 1 Ch 5:19) **11:7; 12:17; 13:7** (Da 7:21 Theod.); **19:19.** ζητεῖν μ. τινος *deliberate* or *dispute w. someone* **J 16:19**; cp. **3:25** (cp. ApcEsdr 2:6 δικάζου μεθ᾽ ἡμῶν). κρίνεσθαι *go to law w. someone* **1 Cor 6:6.** κρίματα ἔχειν μ. τινος *have lawsuits w. someone* vs. **7.**

ⓓ of any other relation betw. persons, whether already existing or brought about in some manner εἶδον τὸ παιδίον μ. Μαρίας **Mt 2:11.** ἀνταποδοῦναι ὑμῖν ἄνεσιν μ. ἡμῶν **2 Th 1:7.** ἐκδέχομαι αὐτὸν μ. τῶν ἀδελφῶν **1 Cor 16:11.** Of delegations, composed of several units **Mt 22:16; 2 Cor 8:18.** συμφωνεῖν **Mt 20:2.**

ⓔ of things ὧν τὸ αἷμα ἔμιξεν μ. τῶν θυσιῶν αὐτῶν **Lk 13:1.** Pass. πιεῖν οἶνον μ. χολῆς μεμιγμένον **Mt 27:34.**

ⓕ to show a close connection betw. two nouns, upon the first of which the main emphasis lies (Thu. 7, 75, 3 λύπη μ. φόβου; Pla., Rep. 9, 591b ἰσχύν τε καὶ κάλλος μετὰ ὑγιείας λαμβάνειν; Ar. 11:2 τόξον ἔχειν μ. φαρέτρας) ἀγάπη μ. πίστεως **Eph 6:23.** πίστις μ. σωφροσύνης **1 Ti 2:15.** εὐσέβεια μ. αὐταρκείας **6:6.** Cp. **Eph 4:2b; Col 1:11; 1 Ti 1:14.** φάρμακον μ. οἰνομέλιτος ITr 6:2.

❸ **marker of attendant circumstances of someth. that takes place, *with*—ⓐ** of moods, emotions, wishes, feelings, excitement, states of mind or body (Xenophon Eph. 1, 15, 5 μ. ἀδείας; 2, 10, 4 μ. ἐπιμελείας; PAmh II, 133, 11 μετὰ πολλῶν κόπων; PLond II, 358, 8 p. 172 [II AD]; SIG index IV p. 445f; LXX [Johannessohn, Präp. 209ff]; En et al.) μ. αἰδοῦς *with modesty* **1 Ti 2:9.** μ. αἰσχύνης *with shame* (s. αἰσχύνη 2) **Lk 14:9.** μ. εὐνοίας **Eph 6:7.** μ. εὐχαριστίας **Phil 4:6; 1 Ti 4:3f**; cp. **Ac 24:3.** μετὰ χαρᾶς (2 Macc 15:28; 3 Macc 5:21; 6:34; En 10:16; PsSol 8:16 al.; s. χαρά 1a) **1 Th 1:6; Hb 10:34; 13:17**; cp. **Phil 2:29.** μ. φόβου καὶ τρόμου **2 Cor 7:15; Eph 6:5; Phil 2:12.** μ. φόβου καὶ χαρᾶς **Mt 28:8.** μ. πραΰτητος καὶ φόβου **1 Pt 3:16.** μ. παρρησίας (Lev 26:13; 1 Macc 4:18; s. παρρησία 3a) **Ac 2:29; 4:29, 31; 28:31; Hb 4:16.** μ. πεποιθήσεως 1 Cl 31:3. μ. σπουδῆς (3 Macc 5:24, 27; Mel., P. 12, 80) **Mk 6:25; Lk 1:39.** μ. ταπεινοφροσύνης **Eph 4:2a**; cp. **Ac 20:19.** μ. ὀργῆς (3 Macc 6:23; TestJob 4:4) **Mk 3:5.** μ. δακρύων *in tears* (3 Macc 1:16; 4:2; 5:7; TestAbr A 9 p. 86, 19 [Stone p. 20]; 14 p. 94, 21 [St. p. 36]; JosAs 28:8; ApcEsdr 6:23; s. δάκρυον) **Mk 9:24 v.l.; Hb 5:7; 12:17.** μ. εἰρήνης (s. εἰρήνη 1b) **Ac 15:33; Hb 11:31.**

ⓑ of other accompanying phenomena (Antig. Car. 148 μετὰ φλογὸς καίεσθαι) μ. διωγμῶν *though with persecutions* **Mk 10:30.** μ. ἐπιθέσεως τῶν χειρῶν **1 Ti 4:14.** μ. νηστειῶν **Ac 14:23.** μ. θορύβου (Jos., Ant. 5, 216) 24:18. μ. παρακλήσεως **2 Cor 8:4.** μ. παρατηρήσεως **Lk 17:20.** μ. ὕβρεως καὶ πολλῆς ζημίας **Ac 27:10** (s. ὕβρις 3). μ. φαντασίας **25:23.** μ. δυνάμεως καὶ δόξης **Mt 24:30; Mk 13:26; Lk 21:27** (Just., A I, 50, 1 al. μ. δόξης, D. 132, 1 w. δυνάμεως). μ. ἐξουσίας καὶ ἐπιτροπῆς **Ac 26:12** (Jos., Ant. 20, 180 μετ᾽ ἐξουσίας). μ. βραχίονος ὑψηλοῦ ἐξάγειν τινά (s. βραχίων) **Ac 13:17.** μ. φωνῆς μεγάλης *w. a loud voice* **Lk 17:15** (cp. EpArist 235; 281; JosAs 28:9). μ. σάλπιγγος *with a trumpet call* **Mt 24:31** (Plut., Mor. 1135f μετ᾽ αὐλῶν=with the sound of flutes). σφραγίσαντες τ. λίθον μετὰ τ. κουστωδίας makes the stationing of the guard an accompaniment to the sealing of the stone **Mt 27:66** (another possibility here is the instrumental use of μετά [Lycurgus the orator 124 μ. παραδειγμάτων διδάσκειν; SEG VIII, 246, 8 μετὰ κυνῶν—an instrument of torture—βασανίσαι; CWessely, Neue griech. Zauberpap. 1893, 234 γράφε μ. μέλανος; 2 Macc 6:16]: *secure the stone by means of a guard;* s. σφραγίζω 1).

ⓒ of concrete objects, which serve as equipment (Appian, Maced. 9 §4 μετὰ χρυσῶν στεφάνων; POxy 123, 15; 19 μετὰ τῶν χλαμύδων εἰσβῆναι; 1 Esdr 5:57; Jdth 15:13; TestJob 24:10 μ. ψαλίδος; JosAs 7:4 μ. χρυσίου καὶ ἀργυρίου; ParJer 9:31 μ. πολλῶν λίθων; ApcSed 7:10 μ. χαλιναρίου; ApcMos 40 μ. τῶν σινδόνων) μ. μαχαιρῶν καὶ ξύλων **Mt 26:47; 55; Mk 14:43, 48; Lk 22:52.** μ. φανῶν καὶ λαμπάδων καὶ ὅπλων (Xenophon Eph. p. 336, 20 μ. λαμπάδων) **J 18:3.**

B. w. acc. In our lit. only in the mng. **after, behind—❶ marker of position that is behind someth., *behind*** (Hom.+; Polyb.; Just., A I, 13, 4; Tat. 2, 2; not LXX) μ. τὸ δεύτερον καταπέτασμα *behind the second curtain* **Hb 9:3.**

❷ **marker of time after another point of time, *after*** (Hom.+; ins, pap, LXX)**—ⓐ** with the time expressly given μ. πολὺν χρόνον (2 Macc 6:1.—μετ᾽ οὐ πολὺν χρ.: Hero Alex. I p. 340, 6; SIG 1169, 54; Jos., Vi. 407) **Mt 25:19.** μ. τοσοῦτον χρόνον (4 Macc 5:7; ParJer 5:18) **Hb 4:7.** μ. χρόνον τινά (Diod. S. 9, 10, 2; Witkowski 26, 9 [III BC]; Jos., Ant. 8, 398; cp. En 106:1 μ. δὲ χρόνον; ApcSed 13:3 μ. χρόνον) Hv 1, 1, 2f; s 5, 2, 5; 9, 13, 8. μ. ἡμέρας ἕξ *after six days* **Mt 17:1; Mk 9:2** (ApcMos 42 μ. τὰς ἓξ ἡμέρας). μ. τρεῖς ἡμέρας (Artem. 4, 33 p. 224, 5; Polyaenus 6, 53; 8, 62; EpArist 301; TestJob 52:1f; 53:7; ParJer 9:14; Jos., Ant 7, 280) **Mt 27:63; Mk 8:31; 10:34; Lk 2:46**; cp. μ. τρεῖς ἡμέρας καὶ τρεῖς νύκτας AcPlCor 2:30. μ. δύο ἡμέρας **Mt 26:2; Mk 14:1** (cp. Caesar, Bell. Gall. 4, 9, 1 post tertiam diem=on the third day). μ. τινας ἡμέρας **Ac**

15:36; 24:24. μετ' οὐ πολλὰς ἡμέρας (Artem. 1, 78 p. 72, 30; Jos., Ant. 5, 328, Vi. 309) **Lk 15:13.** οὐ μ. πολλὰς ταύτας ἡμέρας *not long after these days= within a few days* **Ac 1:5** (B-D-F §226; 433, 3; Rob. 612; 1158; Dssm., ZVS 45, 1913, 60). W. gen. foll. μ. ἡμέρας εἴκοσι τῆς προτέρας ὁράσεως *twenty days after the former vision* Hv 4, 1, 1 (cp. Biogr. p. 31 μετὰ ξ' ἔτη τοῦ Ἰλιακοῦ πολέμου; Gen 16:3). μ. τρεῖς μῆνας **Ac 28:11.** μ. τρία ἔτη **Gal 1:18.** ὁ μ. τετρακόσια καὶ τριάκοντα ἔτη γεγονὼς νόμος **3:17.**

ⓑ w. designations that are general, but include the idea of time: μ. τὴν ἄφιξίν μου **Ac 20:29.** μ. τὸ πάσχα *after the Passover* **12:4.** μ. τὴν μετοικεσίαν Βαβυλῶνος **Mt 1:12.**

ⓒ gener. μ. τὴν θλῖψιν *after the (time of) tribulation* **Mk 13:24;** cp. μ. τὴν θλῖψιν τῶν ἡμερῶν ἐκείνων **Mt 24:29.** μ. τὴν ἔγερσιν **27:53.** μ. τὴν ἀνάγνωσιν **Ac 13:15.** μ. τὸ βάπτισμα **10:37.** μ. μίαν καὶ δευτέραν νουθεσίαν **Tit 3:10.** μ. τὸ ψωμίον *after he had eaten the piece of bread* **J 13:27.**—Quite gener. μ. τοῦτο *after this, afterward* (Lucian, Hermot. 31; Gen 18:5; Lev 14:19; EpArist 258; TestJob 11:4; TestReub 1:9; TestLevi 6:3; Just., D. 57, 4) **J 2:12; 11:7, 11; 19:28; Hb 9:27; Rv 7:1.** μ. ταῦτα *after this* (Aeneas Tact. 240; 350; Diod. S. 1, 7, 1; Ex 3:20; 11:8 and oft.; TestJob 21:4; TestLevi 6:5; TestJos 19:5; JosAs 10:15; ParJer 3:10; ApcEsdr 4:36; ApcMos 2; Just., A I, 32, 6) **Mk 16:12; Lk 5:27; 10:1** and oft. μ. οὐ πολύ (Dio Chrys. 56 [73], 8; Lucian, Scyth. 1; Herodian 1, 9, 7; BGU 614, 14; Mitt-Wilck. II/2, 96 II, 9; 1 Esdr 3:22; Jos., Ant. 12, 132) *not long afterward* **Ac 27:14.** μ. μικρόν *a short while afterward* **Mt 26:73; Mk 14:70** (Just., D. 56, 17). Also μ. βραχύ **Lk 22:58** (cp. μετ' ὀλίγον: Lucian, Dial, Mort. 15, 3; PRyl 77, 41; Wsd 15:8; Jdth 13:9; TestAbrA 7 p. 84, 8 [Stone p. 16]; GrBar 9:3; Jos., Ant. 12, 136; 10:15; Just., D. 56, 18).

ⓓ w. subst. aor. inf. foll.—**α.** w. acc. (SIG 633, 105; 640, 13; 695, 78; 1233, 1; Sir 46:20; Jdth 16:25; Bar 1:9; 1 Macc 1:1, 9; TestAbr B 12 p. 116, 11 [Stone p. 80]; 117, 5 [St. p. 82]; TestJob 5:2; TestLevi 18:1; ApcMos 1; Just., A I, 50, 12.—B-D-F §406, 3; Rob. 979) μ. τὸ ἐγερθῆναί με *after I am raised up* **Mt 26:32; Mk 14:28.** μ. τὸ παραδοθῆναι τὸν Ἰωάννην *after John was arrested* **Mk 1:14.—Ac 1:3; 7:4; 10:41; 15:13; 19:21; 20:1;** Hv 2, 1, 3; m 4, 1, 7; s 8, 1, 3; 8, 2, 5.

β. without acc. (Aelian, VH 12, 1 p. 118, 27; Herodian 2, 9, 5; SIG 976, 39; UPZ 110, 193 [164 BC]; Sir 23:20; 32:18 v.l.; 1 Macc 1:20; ApcMos 26:42f; Just., A I, 14, 1; Tat. 16, 1) μ. τὸ λαλῆσαι αὐτοῖς *after he had spoken to them* **Mk 16:19.—Lk 12:5; 1 Cor 11:25; Hb 10:26.**—W. perf. inf. **10:15.**—M-M. EDNT. TW.

μεταβαίνω (μετά, βαίνω; Hom.+) fut. μεταβήσομαι; 2 aor. μετέβην, impv. μετάβηθι (**J 7:3**) and μετάβα (**Mt 17:20;** s. B-D-F §95, 3; Mlt-H. 209f); pf. μεταβέβηκα.

❶ **to transfer from one place to another,** ***go/pass over***

ⓐ of pers.—**α.** w. indications of the place from which ἀπὸ τῶν ὁρίων αὐτῶν *from their district* **Mt 8:34.** ἐντεῦθεν **J 7:3.** ἐκεῖθεν **Mt 11:1; 12:9; 15:29; Ac 18:7.** ἐκ τοῦ κόσμου τούτου πρὸς τ. πατέρα **J 13:1.**

β. specif. *change one's place of residence, move* (Diog. L. 5, 89 εἰς θεούς=go over or be removed to the gods; PTebt 316, 20; 92; Jos., Bell. 6, 299) w. the goal given εἰς ἕτερον ἀγρίδιον MPol 6:1. W. the place fr. which and place to which given: ἐξ οἰκίας εἰς οἰκίαν *go from one house to another* **Lk 10:7** (μ. ἐξ . . . εἰς as Jos., Ant. 11, 204).

ⓑ of things (Epict. 3, 19, 4 a stone; Jos., Bell. 2, 163; Ar. 6, 1, 3 sun) ἐρεῖτε τῷ ὄρει· μετάβα ἔνθεν ἐκεῖ, καὶ μεταβήσεται **Mt 17:20** (Ps.-Callisth. 1, 33, 10: the transference of a mountain is impossible).

❷ **to change from one state or condition to another state,** ***pass, pass on,*** ext. of mng. 1 (Pla. et al.; Anth. Pal. 9, 378 κοιμῶ μεταβὰς ἀλλαχόθι; OGI 458, 7 [c. 9 BC]; Jos., Vi. 149).

ⓐ ἐκ τοῦ θανάτου εἰς τὴν ζωήν *pass* (or 'move') *from death into life* (s. 1aβ) **J 5:24; 1J 3:14** (Sb 6648, 3 vice versa of one deceased: τὸν μεταβάντα εἰς μυχὸν αἰώνων ἐν σκοτίᾳ διάγειν 'who departed for eternal seclusion, to spend his time in darkness').

ⓑ rhetor. t.t. *pass on* to another subject (Pla., Phdr. 265c, Crat. 438a; Just., D. 47, 4 ἐπὶ τὴν ἔννομον πολιτείαν; Tat. 25, 1 ἐπὶ τὴν ἀλόγων μίμησιν) ἐπὶ ἑτέραν γνῶσιν καὶ διδαχήν *pass on to a different kind of knowledge and teaching* B 18:1 (cp. 2 Macc 6:9).—M-M. TW.

μεταβάλλω fut. 3 sg. and pl. μεταβαλεῖ, -οῦσιν LXX; aor. μετέβαλον LXX; pf. ptc. fem. acc. μεταβεβληκυῖαν Jdth 10:7; 2 aor. mid. μετεβαλόμην. Pass.: fut. 3 sg. μεταβληθήσεται (GrBar); aor. ptc. pl. μεταβληθέντες (OdeSol) (Hom.+; apolog. [only act. and pass.] exc. Tat., Mel.) in our lit. only mid. **to change one's way of thinking,** ***change*** (Thu. et al.) abs. (Pla., Gorg. 481e μεταβαλόμενος λέγεις; X., Hell. 2, 3, 31; IMagnMai 115, 20; 4 Macc 6:18; Philo, Mos. 1, 147; Jos., Bell. 1, 296; Just., A I, 12, 11) **Ac 28:6.** W. εἴς τι *turn to someth.* (Jos., Ant. 5, 256; ἀπὸ σκότους εἰς τὸ φῶς OdeSol 11:19; TestDan 4:3) εἰς νέαν ζύμην *to the new leaven* (=Christ) IMg 10:2 (cp. OdeSol 11:19).—M-M. TW.

μεταγράφω 1 aor. mid. μετεγραψάμην (Eur., Thu. et al.; ins, pap, EpArist; ApcEsdr 7:9 p. 32, 21 Tdf.) in our lit. only mid.: ***copy, transcribe*** τὶ ἔκ τινος *someth. from someth.* (cp. the act. Philo, Spec. Leg. 4, 61) MPol 22:2; EpilMosq 1; 5. βιβλίδιον *copy a little book* Hv 2, 1, 3; cp. 4.

μετάγω 2 aor. μετήγαγον; 1 aor. inf. μετάξαι Esth 8:17; aor. pass. 3 pl. μετήχθησαν LXX (X. et al.; ins, pap, LXX, EpArist, Tat.).

❶ **to direct or bring from one area/direction to another,** ***guide*** (='lead to another place': Polyb.; Diod. S. 20, 3, 3 transfer war; POxy 244, 3 [πρόβαπα]; 259, 19; 1 Esdr 1:43; 3 Km 8:48; 2 Ch 36:3) lit., the bodies of horses **Js 3:3** (Philosoph. Max. p. 486, 18 οἱ ἵπποι τοῖς χαλινοῖς μετάγονται). Pass. of a ship μετάγεται *is steered, guided* vs. **4.** Of corpses *be brought (back)* **Ac 7:16** D.

❷ **to cause to undergo a change in state or condition,** ***move, remove,*** fig. ext. of 1 (Plut., Mor. 225f; EpArist 227; Tat. 21, 3 'conversion of everything to allegory') τινὰ ἔκ τινος *force someone out of someth.,* i.e. *remove someone* from an office 1 Cl 44:6.—M-M.

μεταδίδωμι 2 aor. μετέδωκα LXX, subj. μεταδῶ; impv. μεταδότω, inf. μεταδοῦναι (Theognis, Hdt.+; ins, pap, LXX, EpArist; TestSol 10:53 C; TestJob 4:1; Test12Patr, Philo; Jos., Ant. 4, 237; 6, 255; Just., A I, 66, 3; Mel., P. 47, 334; Ath. 30, 2) ***give (a part of), impart, share*** τινί τι (Hdt. 9, 34; X., An. 4, 5, 5; Tob 7:10 BA; EpArist 43; Mel., P. 47, 334) *someth. to* or *with* someone (B-D-F §169, 1; Rob. 510) ἵνα τι μεταδῶ χάρισμα ὑμῖν πνευματικόν *in order that I might impart some spiritual gift to you* **Ro 1:11.** ὑμῖν τὸ εὐαγγέλιον τοῦ θεοῦ *share God's gospel with you* **1 Th 2:8** (cp. Wsd 7:13 sagacious instruction; TestJob 4:1 divine precepts). W. omission of the acc., which is supplied fr. the context **Lk 3:11;** of alms-giving *to the needy* **Eph 4:28;** cp. Hv 3, 9, 2; 4. Without the dat., which is to be supplied fr. the context B 1:5. Abs. ὁ μεταδιδοὺς ἐν ἁπλότητι *one who gives, (let the pers. do it) with liberality,* or *in all sincerity,* i.e., without grudging **Ro 12:8.**—M-M.—S. εὐεργετέω.

μετάθεσις, εως, ἡ (μετατίθημι; Thu. et al.; pap; 2 Macc 11:24; EpArist, Philo, Joseph.).

❶ ***removal*** to another place (Diod. S. 1, 23, 3) of the *taking up* or *taking away* (to heaven) of Enoch (Philo, Praem. 17) **Hb 11:5.**

❷ ***change, transformation*** (Thu. 5, 29, 3 al.; PSI 546, 3; EpArist 160; Philo, Gig. 66; Jos., C. Ap. 1, 286) νόμου **Hb 7:12;** τῶν σαλευομένων **12:27.**—DELG s.v. τίθημι. M-M. TW.

μεταίρω 1 aor. μετῆρα (Demosth. 19, 174; OGI 573, 16f; PMerton 5, 11 [II BC]; LXX; Jos., Ant. 1, 161) in our lit. (exclusively Mt) only intr. (B-D-F §308; s. Rob. 799) ***go away*** w. indication of the place from which ἀπὸ τῆς Γαλιλαίας **Mt 19:1.** ἐκεῖθεν **13:53** (Gen 12:9 Aq.).—M-M.

μετακαλέω 1 aor. mid. μετεκαλεσάμην; fut. μετακαλέσομαι (Thu. et al.; pap, LXX, TestSol, Philo, Joseph.) in our lit. (exclusively Ac) only mid. ***call to oneself, summon*** (POxy 33 verso II, 2 μετεκαλέσατο αὐτόν; 1252 recto, 26; Jos., Vi. 78) τινά *someone* (Jos., Ant. 2, 226) **Ac 24:25.** Ἰακώβ **7:14.**—**10:32.** τ. πρεσβυτέρους τῆς ἐκκλησίας **20:17.**—M-M. TW.

μετακινέω aor. 3 sg. μετεκίνησεν 4 Macc 14:20; fut. pass. 3 pl. μετακινηθήσονται Is 54:10 (Hdt. et al.; ins, LXX; Jos., Ant. 5, 179, C. Ap. 2, 184; SibOr 3, 209) ***shift, remove*** mid. (cp. Hdt. 9, 51) fig. μὴ μετακινούμενοι ἀπὸ τῆς ἐλπίδος *without shifting from the hope* **Col 1:23.**—M-M. TW.

μετακόσμιος, ον (κόσμος; Diog. L. 10, 89; Plut.; Philo, Somn. 1, 184, Conf. Lingu. 134) ***between/after the world(s);*** elsewh. an Epicurean expr., denoting the space betw. heaven and earth (intermundia: Cicero, Nat. Deor. 1, 8, 18); here prob. *what is to come after this world* (in time) Dg 12:9 (text uncertain; s. ἁρμόζω 2).—DELG s.v. κόσμος.

μεταλαμβάνω impf. μετελάμβανον; fut. inf. μεταλήμψεσθαι Wsd 18:9; 2 aor. μετέλαβον; inf. μεταλαβεῖν; ptc. μεταλαβών; pf. μετείληφα ('have a share, receive'; Pind., Hdt.+)

❶ **to share or participate in someth.,** ***have a share in*** w. gen. of the thing (so as a rule; s. B-D-F §169, 1; Rob. 510; 519) καρπῶν *receive one's share of the crops* **2 Ti 2:6** (Paroem. Gr.: Zenob. [II AD] 5, 71 ἔφη μὴ μεταλήψεσθαι τὸν δεσπότην τοῦ καρποῦ). τῶν ἐπηγγελμένων δωρεῶν 1 Cl 35:4. τῆς τιμῆς Dg 3:5. εὐλογίας **Hb 6:7.** τῆς ἁγιότητος **12:10.** μετειληφότες πράξεων *have a share in the* (blessings of the) *deeds* 1 Cl 19:2. τῆς ἐν Χριστῷ παιδείας 21:8. τοῦ ῥήματος τοῦ δικαίου Hv 3, 7, 6. τοῦ πνεύματος 2 Cl 14:3b, 4 (contrast the use w. acc. 2 below). τοσαύτης χρηστότητος *since we have shared in such great kindness* 15:5. τοῦ ἐλέους Ἰησοῦ *share in the mercy of Jesus* 16:2.—Esp. μ. τροφῆς (Jos., Bell. 2, 143; PRyl 77, 19 τροφῶν μεταλαβεῖν; TestAbr B 13 p. 117, 22 [Stone p. 82] βρώσεως καὶ πόσεως) *take/eat food* **Ac 2:46; 27:33f.** τοῦ ἄρτου AcPl Ha 7, 9 (cp. Just., A I, 65, 5 ἀπὸ ἄρτου).

❷ **to come into possession of someth.,** w. acc. of thing (Eur., Pla. et al.; Diod. S. 5, 75, 1 τὴν εἰρήνην; PTebt 79, 49; PAmh 39, 6; Jos., Bell. 2, 1) ***receive,*** τὸ αὐθεντικόν *receive the original* 2 Cl 14:3a. ζωήν *receive life* 14:5. τὰ κτίσματα τοῦ θεοῦ *take possession of what God has created* Hv 3, 9, 2; καιρὸν μ. *have an opportunity = find time* (Polyb. 2, 16, 15; Diod. S. 19, 69, 2; Jos., Ant. 4, 10) **Ac 24:25.**—M-M. TW.

μετάλημψις (v.l. μετάληψις; on the μ cp. λαμβάνω, beg.), **εως, ἡ** (Pla.+; OGI 764, 15; POxy 1200, 36; 1273, 39; Philo, Plant. 74; Just., A I, 67, 5) **the condition of having a share in someth.,** ***sharing*** ἃ ὁ θεὸς ἔκτισεν εἰς μ. τοῖς πιστοῖς *which God created for the faithful to share in* **1 Ti 4:3** (cp. μεταλαμβάνω 1). Others: *receive* (so NRSV).—DELG s.v. λαμβάνω. M-M. TW.

μεταλλάσσω 1 aor. μετήλλαξα; pf. ptc. gen. μετηλλαχότος 2 Macc 4:37; 5:5 (Hdt. et al.; ins, pap, LXX; OdeSol 11:21; ApcMos 11; SibOr 7, 96; Berosus: 680 fgm. 8a 136 Jac. [in Jos., C. Ap. 1, 136]) ***exchange*** τὶ ἔν τινι *someth. for someth.* τὴν ἀλήθειαν τοῦ θεοῦ ἐν τῷ ψεύδει *the truth of God (=the true God) for a lie (=a false god;* s. ψεῦδος) **Ro 1:25.** Also τὶ εἴς τι (Diod. S. 4, 51, 5; intrans. Hippol., Ref. 1, 3, 3) τὴν φυσικὴν χρῆσιν εἰς τὴν παρὰ φύσιν *exchange natural sex relations for those that are contrary to nature* vs. **26** (of tribadism, the same connection between inversion in religion and in sex TestNapht 3:4 ἐνήλλαξε τάξιν φύσεως). On female homoeroticism s. ALardinois, Subject and Circumstance in Sappho's Poetry: TAPA, '94, 57–84 (lit. 80–84); JMiller, NovT 37, '95, 1–11; s. also HLicht, Sexual Life in Ancient Greece '32.—DELG s.v. ἄλλος. Frisk s.v. ἀλλάσσω. M-M. TW. Spicq.

μεταμέλομαι pass. dep.; impf. μετεμελόμην; 1 fut. μεταμεληθήσομαι; 1 aor. μετεμελήθην; pf. μεταμεμέλημαι 1 Macc 11:10 (Thu. et al.; OGI 458, 11; BGU 1040, 20; LXX; TestJud 23:5; ApcMos 19; Ar. 7:3)

❶ **to have regrets about someth., in the sense that one wishes it could be undone,** ***be very sorry, regret*** (cp. PWisc II, 74, 20 [III/IV AD]; Simplicius in Epict. p. 107, 21 μεταμελομένων τῶν ἁμαρτανόντων; Plut., Artox. 1020 [18]) **Mt 27:3; 2 Cor 7:8ab.**—**Mt 21:29, 32** prob. fit better under 2.

❷ **to change one's mind about someth., without focus on regret,** ***change one's mind, have second thoughts*** (Polyb. 4, 50, 6 about engaging in a conflict) **Mt 21:29, 32; Hb 7:21** (Ps 109:4 Hb. נִחָם.—Of God's mind in change also Jos., Ant. 6, 145; of the deity Apollo Diod. S. 5, 75, 3).—EThompson, Μετανοέω and Μεταμέλει in Gk. Lit. until 100 AD, diss. Chicago, 1908; Windisch, Exc. on **2 Cor 7:8.**—DELG s.v. μέλω. M-M. TW.

μεταμορφόω 1 aor. pass. μετεμορφώθην; pf. pass. ptc. μεταμεμορφωμένος (Diod. S. 4, 81, 5; Castor of Rhodes [50 BC]: 250 fgm. 17 Jac. εἰς ἕτερα μεταμορφοῦσθαι σώματα; Plut., Mor. 52d al.; Athen. 8, 334c; Aelian, VH 1, 1; Ps.-Lucian, Asin. 11; Herm. Wr. 16, 9; PGM 1, 117; 13, 70; Ps 33:1 Sym.; TestSol; AscIs 3:13; Philo, Mos. 1, 57, Leg. ad Gai. 95; Ar.; Tat. 10, 1; Orig., C. Cels. 5, 42, 30; Theoph. Ant. 2, 6 [p. 108, 16]) 'transform, change in form' in our lit. only in pass.

❶ **to change in a manner visible to others,** ***be transfigured*** of Jesus, who took on the form of his heavenly glory **Mt 17:2; Mk 9:2** (Orig., C. Cels. 2, 65, 17. Simon Magus claims that he came to save the world μεταμορφούμενον καὶ ἐξομοιούμενον ταῖς ἀρχαῖς καὶ ταῖς ἐξουσίαις, καὶ τοῖς ἀγγέλοις Iren. 1, 23, 3 [Harv. I 193, 4]; cp. 1QH 7:24).—RHartstock, Visionsberichte in den syn. Evangelien: JKaftan Festschr. 1920, 130–44; AvHarnack, SBBerlAk 1922, 62–80; ELohmeyer, ZNW 21, 1922, 185–215;UvWilamowitz, Red. u. Vorträge[4] II 1926, 280–93: D. Verklärung Christi; JBernardin, The Transfiguration: JBL 52, '33, 181–89; JBlinzler, D. ntl. Berichte üb. d. Verklärg. Jesu '37; JHöller, D. Verkl. Jesu '37; EDabrowski, La transfiguration de Jésus '39; GHBoobyer, St. Mark and the Transfiguration Story '42; HRiesenfeld, Jésus transfiguré '47; HBaltensweiler, Die Verklärung Jesu '59; SHirsch (βαπτίζω 2a). Of the transformation of raw material into a statue Dg 2:3.

❷ **to change inwardly in fundamental character or condition,** ***be changed, be transformed*** τὴν αὐτὴν εἰκόνα μεταμορφοῦσθαι *be changed into the same form* **2 Cor 3:18** (i.e.

Christians progessively take on the perfection of Jesus Christ through the Spirit's operation; on the acc. s. B-D-F §159, 4; Rob. 486; for the idea Rtzst., Mysterienrel.[3] 262–65; cp. Seneca, Ep. 6, 1, esp. 94, 48). μὴ συσχηματίζεσθε τῷ αἰῶνι τούτῳ, ἀλλὰ μεταμορφοῦσθε τῇ ἀνακαινώσει τοῦ νοός *do not model yourselves after this age, but let yourselves be transformed by the renewing of your minds* **Ro 12:2** (in contrast to the process expressed in συσχηματίζω 'model after' and thus superior to what the world displays).—DELG s.v. μορφή. M-M. TW.

μετανοέω fut. μετανοήσω; 1 aor. μετενόησα (ἐμετενόησαν w. double augment ApcEsdr 2:24) (s. next entry; Antiphon+)

❶ ***change one's mind*** Hv 3, 7, 3; m 11:4 (cp. Diod. S. 15, 47, 3 μετενόησεν ὁ δῆμος; 17, 5, 1; Epict. 2, 22, 35; Appian, Hann. 35 §151, Mithrid. 58 §238; Stob., Ecl. II 113, 5ff W.; PSI 495, 9 [258 BC]; Jos., Vi. 110; 262), then

❷ ***feel remorse, repent, be converted*** (in a variety of relationships and in connection w. varied responsibilities, moral, political, social or religious: X., Hell. 1, 7, 19 οὐ μετανοήσαντες ὕστερον εὑρήσετε σφᾶς αὐτοὺς ἡμαρτηκότας τὰ μέγιστα ἐς θεούς τε καὶ ὑμᾶς αὐτούς= instead of realizing too late that you have grossly sinned against the gods; Plut., Vi. Camill. 143 [29, 3], Galba 1055 [6, 4], also Mor. 74c; M. Ant. 8, 2 and 53; Ps.-Lucian, De Salt. 84 μετανοῆσαι ἐφ' οἷς ἐποίησεν; Herm. Wr. 1, 28; OGI 751, 9 [II BC] θεωρῶν οὖν ὑμᾶς μετανενοηκότας τε ἐπὶ τοῖς προημαρτημένοις; SIG 1268, 2, 8 [III BC] ἁμαρτὼν μετανόει; PSI 495, 9 [258/257 BC]; BGU 747 I, 11; 1024 IV, 25; PTebt 424, 5; Is 46:8; Jer 8:6; Sir 17:24; 48:15; oft. Test12 Patr [s. index]; Philo [s. μετάνοια]; Jos., Bell. 5, 415, Ant. 7, 153; 320; Just.) in (religio-)ethical sense ἐν σάκκῳ καὶ σποδῷ μ. *repent in sackcloth and ashes* **Mt 11:21; Lk 10:13.** As a prerequisite for experiencing the Reign of God in the preaching of John the Baptist and Jesus **Mt 3:2; 4:17; Mk 1:15.** As the subject of the disciples' proclamation **6:12; Ac 17:30; 26:20.** Failure to repent leads to destruction **Lk 13:3, 5; Mt 11:20** (ἢ … μετανοήσωσιν ἢ ἐπιμείναντες δικαίως κριθῶσι Hippol., Ref. 1, pref. 2). Repentance saves (cp. Philo, Spec. Leg. 1, 239 ὁ μετανοῶν σῴζεται; 253; Just., D. 141, 2 ἐὰν μετανοήσωσι, πάντες … τυχεῖν τοῦ παρὰ τοῦ θεοῦ ἐλέους δύνανται) **12:41; Lk 11:32;** cp. **15:7, 10; 16:30.** μ. εἰς τὸ κήρυγμά τινος *repent at* or *because of someone's proclamation* **Mt 12:41; Lk 11:32** (B-D-F §207, 1; Rob. 593; s. εἰς 10a). W. ἐπί τινι to denote the reason *repent of, because of someth.* (Chariton 3, 3, 11; Ps.-Lucian, Salt. 84; M. Ant. 8, 2; 10; 53; Jo 2:13; Jon 3:10; 4:2; Am 7:3, 6; Prayer of Manasseh [=Odes 12] 7; TestJud 15:4; Philo, Virt. 180; Jos., Ant. 7, 264; Just., D. 95, 3.—B-D-F §235, 2) ἐπὶ τῇ ἀκαθαρσίᾳ *of their immorality* **2 Cor 12:21.** ἐπὶ τοῖς ἁμαρτήμασιν *of their sins* 1 Cl 7:7 (Just., D. 141, 2; cp. OGI 751, 9f). ἐπί w. subst. inf. foll. MPol 7:3 (Just., D. 123, 6). Also διά τι Hv 3, 7, 2. Since in μ. the negative impulse of turning away is dominant, it is also used w. ἀπό τινος: *repent and turn away from someth.* ἀπὸ τῆς κακίας (Jer 8:6; Just., D. 109, 1) **Ac 8:22** (MWilcox, The Semitisms of Ac, '65, 102–105). ἀπὸ τῆς ἀνομίας 1 Cl 8:3 (quot. of unknown orig.). Also ἔκ τινος **Rv 2:21b, 22; 9:20f; 16:11.** W. ἐπιστρέφειν ἐπὶ τὸν θεόν **Ac 26:20.** μ. εἰς ἑνότητα θεοῦ *turn in repentance to the unity of God* (which precludes all disunity) IPhld 8:1b; cp. ISm 9:1. But μ. εἰς τὸ πάθος *repent of the way they think about the suffering* (of Christ, which the Docetists deny) 5:3. W. inf. foll. **Rv 16:9.** W. ὅτι foll. *repent because* or *that* (Jos., Ant. 2, 315) Hm 10, 2, 3. W. adv. ἀδιστάκτως s 8, 10, 3. βραδύτερον s 8, 7, 3; 8, 8, 3b. πυκνῶς m 11:4. ταχύ Hs 8, 7, 5; 8, 8, 3a; 5b; 8, 10, 1; 9, 19, 2; 9, 21, 4; 9, 23, 2c. μ. ἐξ ὅλης (τῆς) καρδίας *repent w. the whole heart* 2 Cl 8:2; 17:1; 19:1; Hv 1, 3, 2; 2, 2, 4; 3, 13, 4b; 4, 2, 5; m 5, 1, 7; 12, 6, 1; s 7:4; 8, 11, 3. μ. ἐξ εἰλικρινοῦς καρδίας *repent w. a sincere heart* 2 Cl 9:8.—The word is found further, and used abs. (Diod. S. 13, 53, 3; Epict., En 34; Oenomaus [time of Hadrian] in Eus., PE 5, 19, 1 μετανοεῖτε as directive; Philo, Mos. 2, 167 al.; Jos., Ant. 2, 322; Just., D. 12, 2; Theoph. Ant. 3, 24 [p. 254, 17]; εἰ ἤκουσαν μετανοήσαντες, οὐκ ἐπήγετο ὁ κατακλυσμός Did., Gen. 186, 9; ἁμαρτωλὸς … πρὸς τὸ μετανοεῖν πορευόμενος Orig., C. Cels 3, 64, 5) **Lk 17:3f; Ac 2:38; 3:19; Rv 2:5a** (Vi. Aesopi G 85 P. μετανόησον=take counsel with yourself), vs. **5b, 16, 21; 3:3, 19;** 2 Cl 8:1, 2, 3; 13:1; 15:1; 16:1; IPhld 3:2; 8:1a; ISm 4:1; Hv 1, 1, 9; 3, 3, 2; 3, 5, 5; 3, 7, 6; 3, 13, 4a; 5:7; m 4, 1, 5; 7ff; 4, 2, 2; 4, 3, 6; 9:6; 10, 2, 4; 12, 3, 3; s 4:4; 6, 1, 3f; 6, 3, 6; 6, 5, 7; 7:2; 4f; 8, 6, 1ff; 8, 7, 2f; 8, 8, 2; 5a; 8, 9, 2; 4; 8, 11, 1f; 9, 14, 1f; 9, 20, 4; 9, 22, 3f; 9, 23, 2; 5; 9, 26, 6; 8; D 10:6; 15:3; PtK 3 p. 15, 11; 27.—S. also MPol 9:2; 11:1f, in the sense *regret* having become a Christian; AcPl Ha 1, 17.—Windisch, Exc. on 2 Cor 7:10 p. 233f; Norden, Agn. Th. 134ff; FShipham, ET 46, '35, 277–80; EDietrich, D. Umkehr (Bekehrg. u. Busse) im AT u. im Judent. b. bes. Berücksichtigg. der ntl. Zeit '36; HPohlmann, D. Metanoia '38; OMichel, EvTh 5, '38, 403–14; BPoschmann, Paenitentia secunda '40, 1–205 (NT and Apost. Fathers).—On the distinctive character of NT usage s. Thompson 28f, s.v. μεταμέλομαι, end.—B. 1123. DELG s.v. νόος. M-M. TW. Spicq.

μετάνοια, ας, ἡ (μετανοέω) prim. 'a change of mind' (Thu. 3, 36, 4; Polyb. 4, 66, 7; Appian, Mithrid. 16 §57; pap [s. New Docs 4, 160; Spicq II 475, 17]; TestSol 12:3 C; JosAs, ApcSed; ApcMos 32; Jos., C. Ap. 1, 274, Ant. 16, 125; Just., Tat.), also w. the nuance of 'remorse' (as regret for shortcomings and errors: Batr. 69; Lycon the Peripatetic [III BC], fgm. 23 Wehrli [in Diog. L. 5, 66]; Polyb. 18, 33, 7; Stoic. III 147, ln. 21f; Cebes 10, 4; 11, 1; Plut., Mor. 56a; 68f; 961d, Alex. 11, 4, Mar. 10, 4; 39, 3; Chariton 1, 3, 7; Appian, Liby. 52 §225; 102 §482; 116 §553; M. Ant. 8, 10; Ps.-Lucian, Calumn. 5; Jos., Ant. 13, 314. Of the 'remorse' of Sophia Iren. 1, 3, 1 [Harv. I 24, 7]); in our lit. w. focus on the need of change in view of responsibility to deity (cp. Hierocles 14, 451; Sir 44:16; Wsd 12:10, 19; Prayer of Manasseh [=Odes 12] 8; Philo, Det. Pot. Ins. 96, Spec. Leg. 1, 58, Virt. 175ff [περὶ μετανοίας] al.; EpArist 188; Jos., Ant. 9, 176; TestReub 2:1; TestJud 19:2; TestGad 5:7f; JosAs 15:6ff; 16:7; ApcSed prol.: περὶ ἀγάπης καὶ περὶ μ.; 14:3 ἐν μετανοίαις; SibOr 1, 129; 168; Iren. 1, 21, 2 [Harv. 182, 7]; Orig., C. Cels. 7, 57, 3f; Did., Gen. 97, 15) ***repentance, turning about, conversion;*** as a turning away μετάνοια ἀπὸ νεκρῶν ἔργων *turning away from dead works* **Hb 6:1.** Mostly of the positive side of repentance, as the beginning of a new relationship with God: ἡ εἰς θεὸν μ. *repentance that leads to God* **Ac 20:21.** ἄξια τῆς μετανοίας ἔργα *deeds that are consistent with repentance* **26:20.** Also καρπὸν ἄξιον τῆς μ. **Mt 3:8;** cp. **Lk 3:8.** βαπτίζειν εἰς μ. *baptize for repentance* **Mt 3:11** (s. βαπτίζω 2a; also εἰς 10a). βάπτισμα μετανοίας **Mk 1:4; Lk 3:3;** cp. **Ac 13:24; 19:4** (alt. λουτροῦ … τῆς μ. Just., D. 14, 1) χρείαν ἔχειν μετανοίας *need repentance* or *conversion* **Lk 15:7.** κηρύσσειν μ. εἰς ἄφεσιν ἁμαρτιῶν *preach repentance that leads to the forgiveness of sins* **24:47** (μετάνοιαν καὶ ἄφεσιν ἁμαρτιῶν διὰ … λουτροῦ παλλιγγενεσίας Theoph. Ant. 2, 16 [p. 140. 8f]); cp. 1 Cl 7:6. ἔχειν καιρὸν μετανοίας *still have time for repentance* 2 Cl 8:2. τόπον μετανοίας διδόναι *give an opportunity for repentance* (Wsd 12:10; cp. ἵνα μετάνοια δοθῇ Did., Gen. 169, 4; ἀφορμὴν μετανοίας καὶ ἐξομολογήσεως παράσχειν Theoph. Ant. 2, 29 [p. 170, 17]) 1 Cl 7:5. μετανοίας τόπον εὑρίσκειν **Hb 12:17** (cp. μετανοίας τόπον ἔχειν Tat. 15:3). διδόναι τινὶ (τὴν) μ. (cp. Wsd 12:19; M. J. Brutus, Ep. 7) **Ac 5:31; 11:18; 2 Ti 2:25;** B 16:9; cp. Hv 4, 1, 3; s 8, 6, 2; 8,

11, 1. τιθέναι τινὶ μετάνοιαν *prescribe repentance for someone* Hm 4, 3, 4; cp. 5; καλεῖν τινα εἰς μ. **Lk 5:32** (ApcSed 15:2; Just., A I, 15, 7; 90, 7); **Mt 9:13 v.l.; Mk 2:17 v.l.** (cp. καλοῦνται αὐτοὺς ἐπὶ μ. καὶ διόρθωσιν τῆς ψυχῆς αὐτῶν Orig., C. Cels. 3, 62, 3). περὶ μετανοίας λαλεῖν 1 Cl 8:1. ἀκούσαντες ταύτην τὴν μετάνοιαν *when they heard of this repentance* Hs 8, 10, 3; παιδεύεσθαι εἰς μ. *be disciplined so as to repent* 1 Cl 57:1. εἰς μ. ἄγειν τινά (EpArist 188; Jos., Ant. 4, 144; cp. Appian, Bell. Civ. 2, 63 §262 θεοῦ σφᾶς ἐπὶ μετάνοιαν ἄγοντος) **Ro 2:4;** ἀνακαινίζειν εἰς μ. **Hb 6:6;** χωρῆσαι εἰς μ. *come to repentance* **2 Pt 3:9.** μετάνοιαν λαμβάνειν *receive repentance* (after denying Christ) Hs 9, 26, 6a. μετανοίας μετασχεῖν 1 Cl 8:5. μετάνοιαν ἔχειν *have a possibility of repentance* Hm 4, 3, 3; s 8, 8, 2. ἐστί τινι μετάνοιαν *have a possibility of repentance* Hv 2, 2, 5c; 3, 7, 5; s 8, 8, 5; 8, 9, 4a; 9, 19, 1; 9, 20, 4. τινὶ μετάνοιά ἐστι μία *have (only) one possibility of repentance* m 4, 1, 8; cp. 4, 3, 1. μ. κεῖταί τινι *repentance is ready, available for someone* s 9, 19, 2f; 9, 22, 4; 9, 26, 6b. ἐπίκειταί τινι 8, 7, 2a. γίνεταί τινι 9, 26, 5; εἰς μάτην ἐστὶν ἡ μ. *is in vain* 6, 1, 3. ταχινὴ ὀφείλει εἶναι *must follow quickly* 8, 9, 4b. ἡ μ. σύνεσίς ἐστιν μεγάλη *is great understanding* m 4, 2, 2. μ. καθαρά 12, 3, 2; cp. s 7:6. μ. ἁμαρτίας *rep. for sin* 2 Cl 16:4; cp. Hm 4, 3, 3. μ. ζωῆς *rep. that leads to life* s 6, 2, 3; cp. 8, 6, 6. ἐλπὶς μετανοίας *hope of repentance* or *conversion* IEph 10:1; Hs 6, 2, 4; 8, 7, 2b; 8, 10, 2. W. πίστις and other Christian virtues 1 Cl 62:2. The ἄγγελος τῆς μ. appears in Hermas as a proclaimer of repentance: v 5:7; m 12, 4, 7; 12, 6, 1; s 9, 1, 1; 9, 14, 3; 9, 23, 5; 9, 24, 4; λυπεῖσθαι εἰς μ. *feel pain that leads to repentance* **2 Cor 7:9,** λύπη μετάνοιαν ἐργάζεται (cp. Plut., Mor. 476f) vs. **10.**—W. the Christian use of the word in mind Polycarp says ἀμετάθετος ἡμῖν ἡ ἀπὸ τῶν κρειττόνων ἐπὶ τὰ χείρω μετάνοια *for us 'repentance' from the better to the worse is impossible* MPol 11:1.—WHolladay, The Root Šûbh in the OT, '58.—TRE VII 446–51; RAC II 105–18.—DELG s.v. νόος. M-M. EDNT. TW. Spicq. Sv.

μεταξύ (μετά, ξύν [σύν]) adv. (Hom.+; for LXX s. Johannessohn, Präp. 173f)

❶ marker of an interval that separates, *between, in the middle, next*—ⓐ of space—**α.** as adv. (Hom.+) *between, in the middle* τὸ μεταξύ *what lies between* (Aeneas Tact. 1420; Dio Chrys. 18 [35], 1) Dg 7:2 (cp. Philo, Det. Pot. Ins. 80 τὰ μ.); IPhld 7:1 (Lgtft. renders *when I was among you*).

β. used as prep. w. gen. (Hdt. et al.) *in the middle of* (Polyb. 14, 1, 9; Aelian, VH 3, 1; En 14:11; 18:3; ViJer 14 [p. 73, 14 Sch.]; Jos., Ant. 3, 147 μ. αὐτῆς [τ. λυχνίας] καὶ τ. τραπέζης; Just., A I, 26, 2 μ. τῶν δύο γεφυρῶν) μ. τοῦ ναοῦ καὶ τοῦ θυσιαστηρίου *between the sanctuary and the altar* **Mt 23:35;** cp. **Lk 11:51.** μ. ἡμῶν καὶ ὑμῶν **16:26.** μ. δύο στρατιωτῶν *between two soldiers* **Ac 12:6.** μ. θηρίων μ. θεοῦ *(to be) among the wild beasts (is to be) with God* ISm 4:2. μ. is certainly to be restored Ox 1081, 4 (s. διαφορά). W. a relative foll. μ. ὧν ἐλάλουν *between the words of my discourse* IPhld 7:1 v.l. (s. Hdb. ad loc. on the uncertainity of the text).

ⓑ of time—**α.** *between* (Pla., Rep. 5, 450c; Jos., Ant. 2, 169; Just., D. 51, 2) ἐν τῷ μεταξύ *in the meanwhile* (X., Symp. 1, 14; BGU 1139, 8 [5 BC]; PTebt 24, 42; 72, 190; PFlor 36, 5; TestZeb 2:7; Jos., Ant. 14, 434) **J 4:31.**

β. *afterward, next* (Plut., Mor. 58b; 240a; Achilles Tat. 1, 13, 1; Mitt-Wilck. II/2, 57, 11 [40/41 AD]; 64, 5; Jos., Bell. 2, 211, Ant. 10, 45; Theoph. Ant. 1, 8 [p. 76, 6]; Schwyzer I 625, 2) εἰς τὸ μεταξὺ σάββατον *on the next sabbath* **Ac 13:42** (Renehan '75, 137). Cp. **23:25 v.l.;** 1 Cl 44:2f. ὁ λαὸς ὁ μεταξύ *the people yet to come* B 13:5.

❷ marker of a reciprocal relation, a difference, *between* (PRein 44, 16 [104 AD] τῆς συμφωνίας τῆς γενομένης μεταξὺ αὐτοῦ κ. Ἰσιδώρας; POxy 1117, 3 μ. ἡμῶν κ. ἀρχόντων) μ. σοῦ καὶ αὐτοῦ μόνου *between you and him alone* **Mt 18:15.** Witnesses μ. ὑμῶν καὶ ἡμῶν *betw. us and you* 1 Cl 63:3.—διακρίνειν μ. τινος καί τινος *make a distinction between* **Ac 15:9.** τοσαύτη τις διαφορὰ μ. τῶν τε ἀπίστων κ. τῶν ἐκλεκτῶν MPol 16:1. διαφορὰ πολλὴ μ. τῶν δύο ὁδῶν *a great difference between* D 1:1.—μεταξὺ ἀλλήλων (PGen 48, 11 μ. ἡμῶν ἀλλήλων) *among themselves, with one another* **Ro 2:15.**—DELG s.v. μετά. M-M. Sv.

μεταπαραδίδωμι (Vett. Val. 163, 25; Iambl., Vi. Pyth. 32, 226; ins, pap; PGM 4, 501) in our lit. only intr. and only once ***give place to, succeed, follow*** ἀλλήλοις *one another* of the seasons 1 Cl 20:9.

μεταπέμπω (Hdt. et al.; ins, pap, LXX, Joseph.) in our lit. only mid. and pass.; 1 aor. mid. μετεπεμψάμην, impv. μετάπεμψαι; 1 aor. pass. ptc. μεταπεμφθείς. ***Send for, summon*** τινά *someone* (Hippocr., Ep. 6; Appian, Iber. 10 §38; Gen 27:45; Num 23:7; EpArist 179; Jos., Vi. 69) **Ac 10:5, 29b; 11:13; 20:1** (προσκαλεσάμενος v.l.); **24:24, 26;** GJs 21:2. W. acc. of pers. and indication of the place to which: μεταπέμψασθαί σε εἰς τὸν οἶκον αὐτοῦ *to summon you to his house* **10:22.** αὐτὸν εἰς Ἰερουσαλήμ **25:3** (Jos., C. Ap. 1, 92 τ. ἀδελφοὺς εἰς τὴν Αἴγυπτον). Without the acc. (easily supplied fr. the context) w. indication of the place from which ἀπὸ ἀνατολῆς μεταπεμψάμενος *since* (God) *has summoned* (the bishop) *from the east* IRo 2:2.—Pass. μεταπεμφθείς *when I was sent for* **Ac 10:29a** (Jos., Ant. 6, 164 ἧκεν μεταπεμφθείς).—M-M s.v. μεταπέμπομαι. TW.

μεταστρέφω fut. μεταστρέψω; 1 aor. μετέστρεψα. Pass.: 2 fut. μεταστραφήσομαι; 2 aor. μετεστράφην; impv. μεταστραφήτω (Hom. et al.; PGM 4, 2625; LXX) **to cause a change in state or condition, *change, alter*** τὶ εἴς τι *someth. into someth.*, oft. its opposite (Ps 77:44; Sir 11:31 τὰ ἀγαθὰ εἰς κακά. Cp. TestAsh 1:8) sun into darkness **Ac 2:20** (Jo 3:4). Laughter to grief **Js 4:9 v.l.** (cp. Am 8:10; 1 Macc 9:41; ParJer 6:6). W. acc. of thing μ. τὸ εὐαγγέλιον τοῦ Χριστοῦ *change* or *distort the gospel of Christ* **Gal 1:7.**—Of Mary's influence on the disciples μετέστρεψεν τὸν νοῦν αὐτῶν ἐ[π' ἀγαθόν] (Mary) changed their mind [for the better] GMary Ox 3525, 13.—M-M. TW.

μετασχηματίζω fut. μετασχηματίσω; 1 aor. μετεσχημάτισα.

❶ to change the form of someth., *transform, change* (Pla., Leg. 10 p. 903e; 906c; Aristot., De Caelo 3, 1 p. 298b, 31; Plut., Ages. 603 [14, 2], Mor. 426e; 680a; Sext. Emp., Math. 10, 335; LXX; TestSol 20:13; TestJob; TestReub 5:6; Philo, Aet. M. 79; Jos., Ant. 7, 257; Chaeremon, fgm. 20 D p. 34 H.; Theoph. Ant. 2, 6 [p. 108, 16]) μ. τὸ σῶμα τ. ταπεινώσεως ἡμῶν *change our lowly body* to be like the glorious body **Phil 3:21** (cp. Philo, Leg. ad Gai. 80).—DHall, NTS, 40, '94, 143–47, argues for this 'normal' use **1 Cor 4:6** and against the view in 3 below.

❷ to feign to be what one is not, *change/disguise oneself,* mid. (Jos., Ant. 8, 267) abs. **2 Cor 11:15.** W. εἴς τι *into* or *as someth.* (Diod. S. 3, 57, 5 εἰς ἀθανάτους φύσεις; 4 Macc 9:22; TestJob 17:2 εἰς βασιλέα τῶν Περσῶν) ὁ σατανᾶς εἰς ἄγγελον φωτός *Satan disguises himself as an angel* (fr. the realm) *of light* vs. **14** (cp. TestReub 5:6 the guardian angels μετεσχηματίζοντο εἰς ἄνδρα). Of the false apostles μετασχηματιζόμενοι εἰς ἀποστόλους Χριστοῦ *who masquerade* *as apostles* vs. **13** (JColson, JTS 17, 1916, 379ff; cp. Hippol., Ref. 10, 32, 5 οἱ αἱρεσιάρχοι ὁμοίοις λόγοις τὰ ὑπ᾽ ἐκείνων προειρημένα μετασχηματίσαντες).

❸ **to show a connection or bearing of one thing on another,** ***apply to.*** **1 Cor 4:6** is unique (for sim. usage s. σχηματίζειν and σχῆμα in Philostrat., Vi. Soph. 2, 17, 1; 2, 25, 1. In Ps.-Demetr., Eloc. 287; 292–94 σχηματίζειν means 'say someth. with the aid of a figure of speech'; on the rhetorical features s. BFiore, Covert Illusion in 1 Cor 1–4: CBQ 47, '85, 85–102; CClassen, Wiener-Stud 107/8, '94/95, 326f): ταῦτα μετεσχημάτισα εἰς ἐμαυτὸν κ. Ἀπόλλων *I have applied this to Apollos and myself*=I have given this teaching of mine the form of an exposition concerning Apollos and myself (s. Hall, 1 above).—New Docs 3, 76. DELG s.v. ἔχω. M-M. TW. Sv.

μετατίθημι by-form pres. 3 pl. μετατίθονται AcPl Ha 2, 26 (s. B-D-F §94, 1); fut. μεταθήσω Is 29:14; 1 aor. μετέθηκα; 2 aor. ptc. μεταθείς. Pass.: fut. 3 sg. μετατεθήσεται Is 29:17; 1 aor. μετετέθην (Hom.+) gener. 'change (the position of)'.

❶ **to convey from one place to another,** ***put in another place, transfer*** τὴν χεῖρα ἐπί τι *transfer your hand to someth.* B 13:5. W. acc. of pers. and indication of the goal μεταθέντες αὐτὸν ἐπὶ τὴν καροῦχαν *they had him transferred to the carriage* MPol 8:2. Pass.: of corpses μετετέθησαν εἰς Συχέμ *they were brought back to Shechem* **Ac 7:16.** W. indication of the place fr. which ἐκ τῶν βασάνων *be removed from* (the place of) *torment* Hv 3, 7, 6 (μετατίθημι ἐκ as a grave-ins fr. Amastris: JÖAI 28 Beibl. '33, col. 81f no. 39). Of Enoch *be taken up, translated, taken away (to heaven)* **Hb 11:5a;** 1 Cl 9:3 (cp. Sir 44:16; Wsd 4:10); the act. in the same sense and of the same person **Hb 11:5b** (Gen 5:24).

❷ **to effect a change in state or condition,** ***change, alter*** (Hdt. 5, 68 et al.; Jos., Ant. 15, 9; IAndrosIsis, Kyme 4: the νόμοι of Isis are not subject to alteration by humans) τὶ εἴς τι *someth. into someth.* (Esth 4:17s μετάθες τὴν καρδίαν αὐτοῦ εἰς μῖσος) τὴν τοῦ θεοῦ ἡμῶν χάριτα εἰς ἀσέλγειαν *pervert the grace of our God to dissoluteness* **Jd 4.** Pass. μετατιθεμένης τῆς ἱερωσύνης *when the priesthood is changed,* i.e. passed on to another **Hb 7:12** (Jos., Ant. 12, 387 of the transfer of the office of high priest to another person).—Of a severe alteration in condition *collapse* μεγάλαι πόλεις μετατίθονται AcPl Ha 2, 25f.

❸ **to have a change of mind in allegiance,** ***change one's mind, turn away, desert*** mid. (Polyb. 5, 111, 8; 24, 9, 6; Diod. S. 11, 4, 6; 2 Macc 7:24 ἀπὸ τ. πατρίων.—ὁ μεταθέμενος in Diog. L. 7, 166 and Athen. 7, 281d [the latter without the art.] refers to Dionysius the Turncoat, who left the Stoics and adopted Epicureanism) ἀπό τινος εἴς τι *from someth. to someth.* μ. ἀπὸ τοῦ καλέσαντος ὑμᾶς … εἰς ἕτερον εὐαγγέλιον *desert him who called you (and turn) to another gospel* **Gal 1:6** (cp. Hierocles 7 p. 429: there is to be no yielding to μεταβαλλομένοις ἐκ τῆς περὶ φιλοσοφίαν σπουδῆς εἰς ἑτέραν τινὰ τοῦ βίου πρόθεσιν; Just., D. 47, 5 ἀπὸ εὐσεβείας … ἐπὶ … ἀθεότητα; Field, Notes 188). ἀπὸ τῶν χαλεπῶν ἐπὶ τὰ δίκαια *turn away from evil to good* MPol 11:1 (cp. Just., A I, 45, 6 and D. 107, 2 al.).—M-M. TW.

μετατρέπω 1 aor. 3 sg. μετέτρεψε, inf. μετατρέψαι (both LXX). Pass.: 2 aor. μετετράπην, impv. μετατραπήτω (Hom. et al.; 4 Macc; EpArist 99; Philo) ***turn around*** pass. *be turned* (Quint. Smyrn. 11, 270) laughter into grief **Js 4:9.**—M-M.

μεταυτίκα (Hdt. 2, 161; 5, 112) adv. ***directly after*** AcPl Ha 7, 8f: μεταυ[τίκα δὲ οὔτ]ως.—DELG s.v. αὐτός.

μεταφέρω 1 aor. subj. 1 pl. μετενέγκωμεν 1 Ch 13:3; 1 aor. pass. μετηνέχθην (trag., X., Pla.+; ins, pap, LXX, TestSol, EpArist) ***carry away*** pass. (Jos., Ant. 3, 103) of stones ἐκ τοῦ πύργου Hs 9, 6, 5; 9, 8, 1.

μεταφυτεύω 1 aor. pass. impv. μεταφυτεύθητι (cp. φυτόν; Theophr., HP 2, 6, 3; 4; En; Ps 91:14 Aq., Sym., Theod.; Ps 1:3 Aq.) ***transplant*** pass. *be transplanted* **Lk 17:6** D.—DELG s.v. φύομαι C.

μετέβη s. μεταβαίνω.

μετενδύω (Lucian et al.) mid. (since Strabo, also Joseph.) ***change clothes,*** aor. pct. μετενδυσαμένη σκυθρωπότερα ἱμάτια ἀπῆλθεν πρὸς αὐτόν*she* (Armetilla) *changed into darker clothes and came to him* (Paul) AcPl Ha 2, 16.—DELG s.v. δύω.

μετέπειτα adv. (Hom. et al.; OGI 177, 14; SEG XXVII, 406, 5; LXX, EpArist; Jos., Ant. 6, 66; Just.) *afterwards* **Hb 12:17;** Hv 2, 4, 2.—New Docs 2, 91. DELG s.v. εἶτα. M-M.

μετέχω fut. μεθέξω (Just., Tat.); 2 aor. μετέσχον, inf. μετασχεῖν; pf. μετέσχηκα (Pind., Hdt.+)

❶ **to have a part or share in someth.,** ***share, have a share, participate*** w. gen. of thing *in* or *of someth.* (B-D-F §169, 1; Rob. 509) πάντων Dg 5:5. μετανοίας 1 Cl 8:5. φυλῆς ἑτέρας *belong to another tribe* **Hb 7:13** (cp. Thu. 8, 86, 3). τῶν εὐεργεσιῶν *share in the benefits* Dg 8:11; θεοῦ μ. *share in God* IEph 4:2 (cp. Jos., C. Ap. 1, 232 θείας μ. φύσεως). μετέσχεν τῶν αὐτῶν *he shared the same things* (i.e. flesh and blood) **Hb 2:14.** Also of rights: τῆς ὑμῶν ἐξουσίας μ. *enjoy authority over you* **1 Cor 9:12.** Abs. ἐπ᾽ ἐλπίδι τοῦ μετέχειν (sc. τῶν καρπῶν) *in the hope of enjoying the crops* **1 Cor 9:10,** unless this belongs in 2.—W. acc.: the v.l. ἄνδρα μ. **Lk 1:34** means *be involved with a husband,* i.e. *have a husband.*

❷ **to partake of someth. in common with someone,** ***eat, drink, enjoy,*** esp. w. foods (Just., D. 20, 3 τῶν … τροφιμωτάτων … ἐφιέμεθα καὶ μετέχομεν): ὁ μετέχων γάλακτος *whoever lives on milk* **Hb 5:13.** εἰ ἐγὼ χάριτι μετέχω (sc. τῆς τροφῆς) *if I eat with thanks* **1 Cor 10:30.** Also μ. ἔκ τινος: ἐκ τοῦ ἑνὸς ἄρτου *share, eat one and the same loaf* **10:17** (s. Thieme 29f). On **1 Cor 9:10** s. 1 above.—In synecdoche: τραπέζης κυρίου, δαιμονίων *share in, partake of the table of the Lord, of daemons* i.e. in the Lord's Supper and in polytheistic banquets **1 Cor 10:21** (Philostrat., Vi. Soph. 2, 15, 1 μ. τοῦ ἱεροῦ; New Docs 1, no. 3, 9 [I/II AD] μ. μυστηρίων.—μ. τραπέζης as Lucian, Cyn. 7; Philo, De Jos., 196).—M-M. TW. Spicq. Sv.

μετεωρίζομαι (μετέωρος 'in mid-air') fut. 3 sg. μετεωρισθήσεται Mi 4:1; aor. 3 pl. μετεωρίσθησαν LXX; gener. 'be lifted up, be elevated' (Aristoph. et al. in sense 'raise up'; pap, LXX, Philo, Joseph.) in our lit. only once, pass. and fig. μὴ μετεωρίζεσθε **Lk 12:29.** In the context this can hardly mean anything other than ***do not be anxious, worried*** (the verb has this meaning Polyb. 5, 70, 10; POxy 1679, 16 μὴ μετεωρίζου, καλῶς διάγομεν=do not worry, we are getting along well; Jos., Ant. 16, 135.—Like w. the adj. μετέωρος='hovering between hope and fear, in suspense, restless, anxious': Thu. 2, 8, 1; Polyb. 3, 107, 6; BGU 417, 4; 6 [opp. ἀμέριμνος]; cp. our 'be up in the air' about someth.). The alternate transl. *be overbearing, presumptuous,* though possible on purely linguistic grounds (Diod. S. 13, 80, 1; 13, 92, 2; cp. Simplicius in Epict. p. 32, 13 μετεωρισμός=pride), supported by the LXX, and favored by Vulg., Luther (altered since the revision of 1975), Tyndale et al., can no longer be seriously considered.—AHarnack, Sprüche u. Reden Jesu 1907, 10; KKöhler, StKr 86, 1913, 456ff.—DELG s.v. 1 ἀείρω. M-M. TW. Spicq.

μετῆρα s. μεταίρω.

μετοικεσία, ας, ἡ (=μετοικία, fr. μετοικέω 'to change one's abode'; Leonidas of Tarentum [III BC]: Anth. Pal. 7, 731, 6; Psellus p. 222, 5; LXX; ἐν δὲ τῇ μ. Βαβυλῶνος Theoph. Ant. 3, 25 [p. 256, 24]) ***removal to another place of habitation, deportation*** ἐπὶ τῆς μ. Βαβυλῶνος *at the time of the Babylonian captivity* **Mt 1:11.** μετὰ τὴν μ. Βαβυλῶνος vs. **12;** ἕως τῆς μ. B. vs. 17; ἀπὸ τῆς μ. B. ibid. (of the Bab. exile 4 Km 24:16; 1 Ch 5:22; Ezk 12:11).—M-M.

μετοικίζω (μέτοικος 'settler from abroad') Att. fut. μετοικιῶ (B-D-F §74, 1; s. Mlt-H. 218); 1 aor. μετῴκισα, pass. 3 sg. μετῳκίσθη LXX (Aristoph. et al.; ins, LXX, EpArist, Philo, Joseph.; Tat. 20, 1) ***remove to another place of habitation, resettle*** τινὰ εἴς τι *someone to a certain place* (OGI 264, 7 μετῴκισεν αὐτοὺς εἰς τὴν παλαιὰν πόλιν; 1 Ch 8:6; EpArist 4; Jos., C. Ap. 1, 132) αὐτὸν εἰς τὴν γῆν ταύτην *he removed him to this country* **Ac 7:4.** Of forcible deportation μετοικιῶ ὑμᾶς ἐπέκεινα Βαβυλῶνος *I will deport you beyond Babylon* vs. **43** (Am 5:27—cp. Theoph. Ant. 3, 25 [p. 256, 22]).—DELG s.v. οἶκος II C 2. M-M.

μετοπωρινός, όν (μετά + ὀπώρα 'late summer'='after late summer' or 'autumn'; Hes., Thu. et al.; Philostrat., Vi. Apoll. 5, 6 p. 168, 24; Philo) ***autumnal*** καιροὶ μ. *the autumn* 1 Cl 20:9.—DELG s.v. ὀπώρα.

μετοχή, ῆς, ἡ (s. μετέχω and next entry; Hdt.+ et al.; pap; Ps 121:3; PsSol 14:6; Philo, Leg. All. 1, 22) ***sharing, participation*** (BGU 1123, 11 [I BC]; PLond III, 941, 8 p. 119 [AD 227] al.) τίς μ. δικαιοσύνῃ καὶ ἀνομίᾳ; *what have righteousness and lawlessness in common?* **2 Cor 6:14** (there is a purely formal parallel to **2 Cor 6:14–16** in Himerius, Or. [Ecl.] 3, 6 ποῦ δὲ συμβαίνει κ. μίγνυται ἡδονὴ πόνοις, καρτηρία τρυφῇ, ἀκαδημία καὶ πόρναι, φιλοσοφία καὶ πότος, σωφρονούντων βίος καὶ ἀκόλαστα μειράκια;=Is there really anything in common between pleasure and toil, perseverance and luxury, school and prostitutes, study and partying, the prudent life and undisciplined puerility?).—DELG s.v. 1 ἔχω. M-M. TW. Spicq. Sv.

μέτοχος, ον (s. μετέχω and prec. entry; Eur., Hdt. et al.; pap, LXX, En; TestBenj 2:5)

❶ ***sharing/participating in,*** as adj. w. gen. of pers. or thing (Hdt. 3, 52; Pr 29:10; EpArist 207; SibOr 12, 174; Iren. 1, 13, 1 [Harv. I 118, 1]; Theoph. Ant. 3, 30 [p. 268, 21]) κλήσεως ἐπουρανίου *sharing in a heavenly calling* **Hb 3:1.** In the Lord's discipline **12:8.** In the Holy Spirit **6:4.** In the promises 1 Cl 34:7. *Share in* prayer IEph 11:2. μ. εἶ τῆς ἁμαρτίας αὐτοῦ *you share in his sin* Hm 4, 1, 9.—μ. τοῦ Χριστοῦ *sharing in Christ* (cp. Kaibel 654, 5 πρόσθεν μὲν θνητή, νῦν δὲ θεῶν μέτοχος) **Hb 3:14.** But perh. this pass. belongs under 2.

❷ subst. ὁ μ. ***(business) partner, companion*** (Ps.-Demosth. 61, 31; PPetr III, 37a II, 7 [259 BC]; BGU 1123, 4; BASP XXXIII p. 131 ln. 5 of 'associate' census clerks [189 AD]; et al. pap; En 104:6; TestBenj 2:5; Orig., C. Cels. 6, 79, 25; Did., Gen. 213, 20 [perh. at 1 above]) **Lk 5:7** in the business sense common in pap; cp. **Hb 1:9** (Ps 44:8). WWuellner, The Meaning of 'Fishers of Men' '67.—New Docs 1, 84f. DELG s.v. 1 ἔχω. M-M. TW. Spicq.

μετρέω fut. 2 sg. μετρήσεις Num 35:5; 1 aor. ἐμέτρησα. Pass.: 1 fut. μετρηθήσομαι; pf. 3 sg. μεμέτρηται Wsd 4:8 (fr. μέτρον; Hom.+) gener. 'measure'.

❶ **to take the dimensions of, *measure***—ⓐ spatially w. acc. of thing: τὸν ναόν *measure the temple* **Rv 11:1** (PKetter, Past. Bonus 52, '41, 93–99). τὴν πόλιν *measure the city* **21:15.** αὐλήν **11:2.** τὸν οὐρανόν B 16:2 (Is 40:12; ApcEsdr 7:5 p. 32, 16 Tdf.). W. the measuring instrument given in the dat. (Ex 16:18) τῷ καλάμῳ *measure with the rod* **Rv 21:16;** cp. **11:1.** The measure arrived at is expressed by the gen. of quality ἐμέτρησεν τὸ τεῖχος ἑκατὸν τεσσεράκοντα τεσσάρων πηχῶν *he measured the wall (and it was) 144 cubits* **Rv 21:17;** also by ἐπί and the gen. vs. **16,** where a v.l. has ἐπί and acc. (on the latter cp. Da 3:47).

ⓑ non-spatially αὐτοὶ ἐν ἑαυτοῖς ἑαυτοὺς μετροῦντες *they measure* (i.e. evaluate) *themselves by one another* **2 Cor 10:12.** ἐμαυτὸν μετρῶ *I keep myself within bounds* ITr 4:1 (Sotades Mar. [III BC] 10, 8 Diehl=Coll. Alex. no. 9, 8 p. 242 ἡ σωφροσύνη πάρεστιν, ἂν μετρῇς σεαυτόν; TestJos 10:6 ἐμέτρουν ἐμαυτόν).

❷ **to give out in measured amount, *give out, deal out, apportion*** τινί τι *someth. to someone* (Eur.; Ps.-Demosth. 46, 20; PPetr III, 89, 2; PTebt 459, 4 [5 BC] ὃ ἐὰν περισσὸν γένηται μέτρησον αὐτοῖς) in the proverbial expr. ἐν ᾧ μέτρῳ μετρεῖτε, μετρηθήσεται ὑμῖν *the measure you give will be the measure you get* **Mt 7:2; Mk 4:24.** Likew., except without ἐν, **Lk 6:38 v.l.** (Maximus Tyr. 27, 7b has a play on words μετρεῖ . . . μετρεῖται.—Philo, Rer. Div. Her. 229 μέτροις μεμέτρηται.—The pass.='receive as one's portion': Jos., Bell. 3, 185).—1 Cl 13:2 the saying reads ᾧ μέτρῳ μετρεῖτε, ἐν αὐτῷ μετρηθήσεται ὑμῖν. The text of **Lk 6:38** has ᾧ μέτρῳ μετρεῖτε, ἀντιμετρηθήσεται ὑμῖν, which is repeated verbatim in Pol 2:3.—B. 877f. DELG s.v. μέτρον. M-M. TW.

μετρητής, οῦ, ὁ a liquid measure of about 40 liters, *measure,* orig. fr. Attica (Demosth. 42, 20; Aristot. HA 8, 9; Polyb. 2, 15, 1; ins [since IV BC]; pap, LXX; TestSol 16:7 P; EpArist 76; loanw. in rabb.), similar in content to the Hebr. בַּת, containing 72 sextarii (Jos., Ant. 8, 57) or pints=39.39 liters, or about nine gallons (s. FHultsch, Griech. u. röm. Metrologie[2] 1882, 101f; 108f; 703). As measure for wine (SIG 672, 54 [162–160 BC]; OGI 266, 4; Gk. Pap. fr. Gurob [1921] 8, 14; freq. in pap as wine measure; 1 Esdr 8:20; Bel 3 Theod.) **J 2:6.**—DELG s.v. μέτρον. M-M.

μετριοπαθέω (μέτριος, πάσχω via -παθής; Sext. Emp., Pyrrh. Hyp. 3, 235; 236; Dositheus 71, 11; Philo, Abr. 257; Jos., Ant. 12, 128. μετριοπαθής and μετριοπάθεια are more common) ***moderate one's feelings, deal gently*** w. dat. of pers.: τοῖς ἀγνοοῦσιν *deal gently with those who sin in ignorance* (ἀγνοέω 4) **Hb 5:2.**—DELG s.v. πάσχω. M-M. TW. Spicq.

μέτριος, ία, ιον (s. μέτρον and next entry; Hes., Thu.+; also SIG 783, 53; POxy 120, 7; 1117, 19) superl. μετριώτατος (Tat. 11, 2; Ath. 11, 2) ***moderate*** μέτρια νοεῖν *be moderate, practice self-restraint* 1 Cl 1:3 (μέτρια φρονεῖν in the same sense: Diod. S. 23, 15, 4; 8).—DELG s.v. μέτρον. TW.

μετρίως adv. of μέτριος (Eur., Hdt. et al.; Plut., Tit. Flam. 373 [9, 5] οὐ μ.; UPZ 71, 5 [152 BC]; PRyl 150, 9 ὕβρισεν οὐ μετρίως; PGiss 17, 5 οὐ μ.; Sb 4323, 2 οὐ μ.; 2 Macc 15:38; EpArist 197) ***moderately, somewhat*** οὐ μ. *greatly* (Diod. S. 18, 45, 4; 20, 83, 2; Plut., Mor. 838f; Procop. Soph., Ep. 5; Philo; Jos., Ant. 15, 194; 276; s. μέτριος) **Ac 20:12.** The litotes=*they received no small comfort.*—M-M.

μέτρον, ου, τό (Hom.+; ins, pap, LXX, En, TestSol 15:5; TestAbr A; Test12Patr; GrBar 6:7; ApcMos 13; Sib Or 3, 237; EpArist, Philo; Jos., Ant. 13, 294, C. Ap. 2, 216; Just., 112, 4; Tat. 27, 3; Ath.) gener. 'that by which anything is measured'.

❶ **an instrument for measuring, *measure*—ⓐ** of measures of capacity ἐν μέτρῳ μετρεῖν **Mt 7:2; Mk 4:24;** 1 Cl 13:2b. μέτρῳ μετρεῖν (Maximus Tyr. 32, 9c; 35, 2i) **Lk 6:38b;** 1 Cl 13:2a; Pol 2:3. W. heaping up of attributes μ. καλὸν πεπιεσμένον σεσαλευμένον ὑπερεκχυννόμενον *good measure, pressed down, shaken together, running over* **Lk 6:38a.** In imagery: πληροῦν τὸ μ. τινός *fill up a measure* that someone else has partly filled **Mt 23:32.**

ⓑ of linear measure **Rv 21:15.** μέτρον ἀνθρώπου, ὅ ἐστιν ἀγγέλου *a human measure, used also by angels* vs. **17.**

❷ **the result of measuring, *quantity, number*—ⓐ** lit. τὰ μ. τῶν τῆς ἡμέρας δρόμων φυλάσσειν *keep the measure of its daily courses* Dg 7:2.

ⓑ fig. (Maximus Tyr. 40, 3c ὑγείας μ.; Alex. Aphr., Quaest. 3, 12 II/2 p. 102, 2 μ. τῆς ἀληθείας; Ath. 32, 2 δικαιοσύνης μ.; 33, 1 μ. ἐπιθυμίας ἡ παιδοποιία) ὡς ὁ θεὸς ἐμέρισεν μέτρον πίστεως *as God has apportioned the measure of faith* **Ro 12:3** (CCranfield, NTS 8, '62, 345–51: Christ is the measure of faith). ἑνὶ ἑκάστῳ ἐδόθη ἡ χάρις κατὰ τὸ μ. τῆς δωρεᾶς τοῦ Χριστοῦ *grace was given to each one according to the measure (of it) that Christ gave* **Eph 4:7.** κατὰ τὸ μ. τοῦ κανόνος οὗ ἐμέρισεν ἡμῖν ὁ θεὸς μέτρου *according to the measure of the limit (=within the limits) which God has apportioned us (as a measure)* (s. B-D-F §294, 5; Rob. 719) **2 Cor 10:13.** κατ᾽ ἐνέργειαν ἐν μέτρῳ ἑνὸς ἑκάστου μέρους *according to the functioning capacity of each individual part* **Eph 4:16** (ἐν μ. as Synes., Ep. 12 p. 171c). καταντᾶν εἰς μ. ἡλικίας τοῦ πληρώματος τοῦ Χριστοῦ *attain to the measure of mature age* (or *stature of the fullness*) *of Christ* vs. **13** (s. ἡλικία 2a and cp. μ. ἡλικίας Plut., Mor. 113d; μ. ἥβης Il. 11, 225; Od. 11, 317).—οὐκ ἐκ μέτρου **J 3:34,** an expr. not found elsewh. in the Gk. language, must mean in its context *not from a measure, without (using a) measure* (the opp. is ἐν μέτρῳ Ezk 4:11, 16; Jdth 7:21).—DELG. M-M. TW. Sv.

μέτωπον, ου, τό (Hom.+) ***forehead* Lk 23:48** D. Of a young woman: veiled ἕως τοῦ μ. Hv 4, 2, 1. As the place marked w. a sign of some kind (s. BStade, D. Kainszeichen: ZAW 14, 1894, 250ff; PsSol 15:9; Diphilus Com. [IV BC], fgm. 66, 8 K.; Herodas 5, 79; Lucian, Pisc. 46; Porphyr., Vi. Pyth. 15; Liban., Or. 25, 21 vol. II p. 547, 1 F.; of a branded slave, Martial 3, 21) **Rv 7:3; 9:4; 13:16; 14:1, 9; 17:5; 20:4; 22:4** (SIG 1168, 48 and 54 [letters]; PLille 29 II, 36; Ezk 9:4 al.).—B. 218. DELG 1 μ. M-M. TW.

μέχρι even before vowels as in Attic **Lk 16:16;** Job 32:12. In three places in the NT (**Mk 13:30** and **Gal 4:19** μέχρις οὗ, **Hb 12:4** μέχρις αἵματος) as well as Hv 4, 1, 9 (μέχρις ὅτε), s 9, 11, 1 (μέχρις ὀψέ) the form used before vowels is **μέχρις** (Vett. Val. 357, 19; IG XII, 5, 647; SIG 888, 150 [before a conson.]; 958, 16; 1109, 41; Threatte II 669–71; pap [Mayser p. 244]. On the LXX s. Thackeray p. 136.—B-D-F §21; Mlt-H. 113; 331) gener. 'until': in our lit. as prep. w. gen. (Hom. +) and conj. (Thu., Pla., et al.)

❶ **marker of extension up to a point in an area, *as far as,*** w. gen. μ. τοῦ οὐρανοῦ GPt 10:40. μ. τῆς ᾽Ασίας **Ac 20:4** D. ἀπὸ ᾽Ιερουσαλὴμ . . . μ. τοῦ ᾽Ιλλυρικοῦ **Ro 15:19** (ἀπὸ . . . μ. as SIG 973, 6f). μ. τῶν ἔσω φλεβῶν MPol 2:2 (Jos., Bell. 6, 304 μ. ὀστέων).

❷ **marker of continuance in time up to a point, *until***

ⓐ as prep. w. gen. μ. (τῆς) νῦν IMg 8:1; Papias (3:3) (Chion, Ep. 16, 4; Longus 4, 16, 2; Xenophon Eph. 1, 4, 1; Jos., Ant. 7, 386; 17, 114; Just., D. 82, 1 and 3 al.; cp. μ. τοῦ νῦν X., Cyr. 7, 3, 15; PTebt 50, 26 [112/111 BC]; BGU 256, 9; Just., D. 78, 8). μ. ὀψέ Hs 9, 11, 1. μέχρι τίνος; *how long?* (Just., A I, 32, 2; Alciphron 4, 17, 2; Achilles Tat. 2, 5, 1) v 3, 10, 9. μ. τῆς σήμερον *until today* (Jos., Ant. 9, 28) **Mt 11:23;** cp. **28:15;** Hv 2, 2, 4. μ. μεσονυκτίου *until midnight* **Ac 20:7.** μ. ᾽Ιωάννου *until (the time of) John* **Lk 16:16.** μ. τῆς ἐπιφανείας τοῦ κυρίου ἡμῶν ᾽Ιησοῦ Χριστοῦ **1 Ti 6:14** (Just., D. 120, 3 μ. . . . τῆς παρουσίας τοῦ Χριστοῦ). μ. καιροῦ διορθώσεως **Hb 9:10.** μ. τοῦ θερισμοῦ (for ἕως; another v.l. ἄχρι) *until harvest time* **Mt 13:30 v.l.** μ. τέλους **Hb 3:6 v.l., 14** (cp. Ar. [Milne 76, 47f] μ. τελειώσεως χρόνων).—ἀπό . . . μ. (POxy 1647, 20 ἀπὸ ἀνατολῆς ἡλίου μέχρι δύσεως; EpArist 298): ἀπὸ τετάρτης ἡμέρας μ. ταύτης τῆς ὥρας *from the fourth day to this hour* **Ac 10:30.** ἀπὸ ᾽Αδὰμ μ. Μωϋσέως **Ro 5:14** (cp. Just., D. 92, 2 ἀπὸ ᾽Αβραὰμ μ. Μωϋσέως).

ⓑ as a conjunction *until* (B-D-F §383, 2; Rob. 975) μ. καταντήσωμεν **Eph 4:13** (cp. Hdt. 4, 119, 4; SIG 976, 71 μέχρι ποιήσωσιν; PCairPreis 48, 7 μέχρι τὸ πλοιαρίδιον εὕρωμεν; TestSol 9:8 P; SibOr 3, 570. On the omission of ἄν s. Mlt. 168f; Rydbeck, 144–53). μ. οὗ w. subjunctive (Herodas 2, 43; 8, 8 [Cunningham reads μέχρις εὗ in both]; POxy 293, 7 [27 AD] μέχρι οὗ ἀποστείλῃς Da 11:36 Theod.; EpArist 298) **Mk 13:30** (μ. ὅτου v.l.); **Gal 4:19.** μ. ὅτε (ὅτου v.l.) Hv 4, 1, 9; GJs 10:2 (s. B-D-F §455, 3).

❸ marker of degree or measure, ***to the point of,*** w. gen. (Appian, Bell. Civ. 3, 69 §284 μ. τοῦ τέλους=to the end; Jos., Ant. 11, 81 μ. θρήνων; Ath. 12:3 μ. τοσούτου) κακοπαθεῖν μ. δεσμῶν *suffer even to the point of being imprisoned* **2 Ti 2:9.** μ. αἵματος ἀντικαταστῆναι *resist to the point of shedding one's blood* in being wounded or killed **Hb 12:4** (μ. αἵμ. as Herodian 2, 6, 14). μ. θανάτου διωχθῆναι καὶ μ. δουλείας εἰσελθεῖν 1 Cl 4:9 (cp. 2 Macc 13:14; Jos., Bell. 2, 141). Of Christ ὑπήκοος μ. θανάτου *obedient to the point of death* **Phil 2:8** (cp. PTor I, 1 VII, 28 [116 BC] μ. τελευτῆς βιοῦ). Of Epaphroditus διὰ τὸ ἔργον Χριστοῦ μ. θανάτου ἤγγισεν vs. **30** (μέχρι θανάτου to denote degree: Diod. S. 15, 27, 2; Cebes 26, 3; Appian, Bell. Civ. 2, 113 §471; 3, 77 §314; 3, 90 §372; 4, 135 §570 al.; Polyaenus 7, 30; 8, 49; Just., D. 11, 4 al.; schol. on Apollon. Rhod. 3, 427–31a; 2 Macc 13:14).—DELG. M-M.

μή (Hom.+) negative particle, 'not': 'μή is the negative of will, wish, doubt. If οὐ denies the fact, μή denies the idea' (Rob. 1167). For the Koine of the NT the usage is simplified to such a degree that οὐ is generally the neg. used w. the indicative, and μή is used w. the other moods (B-D-F §426; Rob. 1167).

❶ **marker of negation, *not*—ⓐ** in negative clauses—**α.** in conditional clauses after ἐάν **Mt 5:20; 6:15; 10:13; 12:29; 18:3, 16, 35; 26:42; Mk 3:27; 7:3f; 10:30; 12:19; Lk 13:3, 5; J 3:2f, 5, 27** al. After ὃς ἄν (=ἐάν) **Mt 10:14; 11:6; 19:9; Mk 6:11; 10:15; 11:23; Lk 8:18; 18:17.** After ὅσοι ἄν **Lk 9:5; Rv 13:15.** After ὅστις ἄν **Ac 3:23.** After εἰ in a simple condition (B-D-F §428, 1) **Lk 6:4; 1 Ti 6:3.** After εἰ in a contrary to fact condition (B-D-F §428, 2; Rob. 1169) **Mt 24:22; Mk 13:20; J 9:33; 15:22, 24; 18:30; 19:11; Ac 26:32; Ro 7:7.** εἰ μή *if not, except (that),* εἰ δὲ μήγε *otherwise* with verb and elliptically (B-D-F §428, 3; 439, 1; Rob. 1024f; cp. POxy 1185, 30) **Mt 5:13; 6:1; 9:17; 11:27; 12:4, 24** and very oft. (GHarder, 1 Cor 7:17: TLZ 79, '54, 367–72).

β. in purpose clauses ἵνα μή *in order that . . . not* **Mt 5:29f; 7:1; 17:27; Mk 3:9; 4:12; Lk 8:10, 12; 16:28; J 3:20; 7:23; Ac 2:25** (Ps 15:8); **4:17; 24:4; Ro 11:25; 15:20** al. ὅπως μή *in* *order that ... not* **Mt 6:18; Lk 16:26; Ac 20:16; 1 Cor 1:29.** μὴ ἵνα IRo 3:2. On the inf. w. neg. as periphrasis for purpose clauses s. below.

γ. in result clauses ὥστε μή w. inf. foll. (cp. PHib 66, 5) *so that not* **Mt 8:28; Mk 3:20; 1 Cor 1:7; 2 Cor 3:7; 1 Th 1:8;** w. impv. foll. **1 Cor 4:5.**

δ. in interrog. clauses w. an element of doubt: δῶμεν ἢ μὴ δῶμεν; *should we pay (them) or should we not?* **Mk 12:14.**

ε. in a few relative clauses (B-D-F §428, 4; Mlt. 171; 239f) διδάσκοντες ἃ μὴ δεῖ **Tit 1:11** (cp. Lucian, Dial. Deor. 13, 1; PGM 4, 2653 ὃ μὴ θέμις γενέσθαι; CPR I, 19, 17; 2 Macc 12:14; Sir 13:24). The literary language is the source of ᾧ μὴ πάρεστιν ταῦτα τυφλός ἐστιν **2 Pt 1:9,** where the relat. clause has a hypothetical sense. ὅσα μὴ θέλετε **Ac 15:29** D. Cp. **Col 2:18 v.l.** On ὃ μὴ ὁμολογεῖ (v.l. ὃ λύει) **1J 4:3** s. ARahlfs, TLZ 40, 1915, 525.

ζ. in a causal clause contrary to the rule, which calls for οὐ: ὅτι μὴ πεπίστευκεν εἰς τὸ ὄνομα **J 3:18** (cp. Epict. 4, 4, 8; Jos., C. Ap. 1, 217 διήμαρτον, ὅτι μὴ ταῖς ἱεραῖς ἡμῶν βίβλοις ἐνέτυχον; Ps.-Clem., Hom. 8, 4; 11, 8; 32; Ath. 14, 2 ὅτι μὴ κοινῶς ἐκείνοις θεοσεβοῦμεν; Dio Chrys. 31, 94; 110.—B-D-F §428, 5; Mlt. 171; 239; Mlt-Turner 284; Rahlfs, loc. cit.).

ⓑ w. various moods—**α.** w. inf. (B-D-F §399, 3; 400, 4; 5; Mlt-Turner 285f)

א. after verbs expressing a negative concept, usu. omitted in translation ἀντιλέγοντες ἀνάστασιν μὴ εἶναι **Lk 20:27** (v.l. λέγοντες). ἀπαρνεῖσθαι **22:34.** παραιτεῖσθαι **Hb 12:19.** ἐγκόπτειν τινά **Gal 5:7.** προσέχειν **Mt 6:1.** οὐ δύναμαι μὴ *I can do nothing else than* **Ac 4:20.**

ב. gener., after verbs of saying, reporting, ordering, judging, etc.—in declarative clauses: after ἀποκρίνεσθαι **Lk 20:7.** λέγειν **Mt 22:23; Mk 12:18; Lk 20:27 v.l.; Ac 23:8;** AcPlCor 2:19. ὀμνύναι **Hb 3:18.** θέλειν **Ro 13:3.** χρηματίζεσθαι **Lk 2:26.**—In clauses denoting a summons or challenge: after λέγειν **Mt 5:34, 39; Ac 21:4; Ro 2:22; 12:3.** γράφειν **1 Cor 5:9, 11.** κηρύσσειν **Ro 2:21.** παραγγέλλειν **Ac 1:4; 4:18; 5:28, 40; 1 Cor 7:10f** (w. acc.); **1 Ti 1:3; 6:17.** αἰτεῖσθαι **Eph 3:13.** εὔχεσθαι **2 Cor 13:7** (w. acc.). χρηματίζεσθαι **Mt 2:12.** ἀξιοῦν **Ac 15:38.** βοᾶν **25:24.**

ג. after predicates that contain a judgment upon the thing expressed by the inf. (with or without the art.; cp. Just., D. 68, 8 ταῦτα τολμῶσι λέγειν μὴ οὕτως γεγράφθαι): καλόν (sc. ἐστιν) **1 Cor 7:1** (ApcEsdr 1, 6, 21); **Gal 4:18;** cp. **Ro 14:21.** ἄλογον **Ac 25:27** (w. acc.). κρεῖττον ἦν **2 Pt 2:21.** αἱρετώτερον ἦν αὐτοῖς τὸ μὴ γεννηθῆναι Hv 4, 2, 6. Cp. δεῖ **Ac 27:21** (cp. use w. ἔχρῆν TestJob 37:6).

ד. w. gen. of the subst. inf.: τοῦ μή *that not* (Lat. ne): after verbs of hindering κατέχειν **Lk 4:42.** παύειν **1 Pt 3:10** (Ps 33:14). καταπαύειν **Ac 14:18.** κωλύειν **10:47.** κρατεῖσθαι **Lk 24:16;** cp. ἀνένδεκτόν ἐστιν τοῦ ... μὴ ἐλθεῖν **17:1.**—Also after other expressions: ὀφθαλμοὶ τοῦ μὴ βλέπειν, ὦτα τοῦ μὴ ἀκούειν *eyes that should not see, ears that should not hear* **Ro 11:8, 10** (Ps 68:24). In place of a result clause: τοῦ μὴ εἶναι αὐτὴν μοιχαλίδα *so that she commits no adultery, if* ... **7:3.**

ה. w. subst. inf. after prepositions: εἰς τὸ μή *so that ... not; to the end that ... not* **Ac 7:19; 1 Cor 10:6; 2 Cor 4:4.** W. acc. and inf. foll. **2 Th 2:2; 1 Pt 3:7.**—διὰ τὸ μή *because ... not* (PPetr II, 11, 1, 7 [III BC] τοῦτο δὲ γίνεται διὰ τὸ μὴ ἀθροῦν ἡμᾶς; 2 Macc 2:11; ApcMos 42 διὰ τὸ μὴ γινώσκειν; Just., D. 95, 1 διὰ τὸ μὴ πάντα φυλάξαι; Tat. 2, 1 διὰ τὸ μὴ βούλεσθαι) **Mt 13:5f; Mk 4:5f; Lk 8:6; Js 4:2** (w. acc.).—πρὸς τὸ μή *in order that ... not* (Ptolem. Pap. aus Alexandria 4, 3 in Witkowski p. 51 πρὸς τὸ μὴ γίνεσθαι τῷ βασιλεῖ τὸ χρήσιμον; Esth 3:13d, e; Bar 1:19; 2:5) **2 Cor 3:13; 1 Th 2:9; 2 Th 3:8.**

ו. w. dat. of the subst. inf. τῷ μή *because ... not* **2 Cor 2:13.**

ז. w. nom. or acc. of the subst. inf. (2 Esdr 6:8; s. B-D-F §399, 3; s. Rob. 1038) **Ro 14:13; 2 Cor 2:1; 10:2; 1 Th 4:6.**

β. very oft. w. the ptc., in keeping w. the tendency of later Gk. to prefer μή to οὐ; exceptions in B-D-F §430; s. Rob. 1172.

א. μή is regularly used to negative the ptc. used w. the article, when the ptc. has a hypothet. sense or refers to no particular person, and has a general mng. (Artem. 4, 22 p. 215, 14 οἱ μὴ νοσοῦντες; ParJer 6:24 ὁ δὲ μὴ ἀκούων; Just., A I, 4, 2 τοὺς μὴ ἐλεγχομένους): ὁ μὴ ὢν μετ' ἐμοῦ *every one who is not with me* **Mt 12:30ab; Lk 11:23ab;** ὁ μὴ πιστεύων **J 3:18.** πᾶς ὁ μή ... **Mt 7:26; 1J 3:10ab; 2J 9.** πάντες οἱ μή **2 Th 2:12.** μακάριοι οἱ μή **J 20:29;** cp. **Ro 14:22.** τῶν τὴν ψυχὴν μὴ δυναμένων ἀποκτεῖναι **Mt 10:28b** and oft.

ב. w. the ptc. when it has conditional, causal, or concessive sense: πᾶν δένδρον μὴ ποιοῦν **Mt 3:10; 7:19.** Cp. **9:36; 13:19; Lk 11:24.** θερίσομεν μὴ ἐκλυόμενοι *we will reap, if we do not become weary* (before the harvest) **Gal 6:9.** μὴ ὄντος νόμου *when there is no law* **Ro 5:13.** νόμον μὴ ἔχοντες *although they have no law* **2:14.** μὴ ὢν αὐτὸς ὑπὸ νόμον *though I am not under the law* **1 Cor 9:20** (cp. TestAbr B 11 p. 115, 22 [Stone p. 78] μὴ ἰδὼν θάνατον). μὴ μεμαθηκώς *without having learned (them)* **J 7:15** (cp. TestAbr B 2 p. 106, 1 [Stone p. 60] μὴ εἰδὼς τίς ἐστιν; TestJob 11:7 μὴ λαμβάνων ... ἐνέχυρα; Just., A I, 5, 1 μὴ φροντίζοντες, D. 110, 2 μὴ συνιέντες). μὴ ἔχοντος δὲ αὐτοῦ ἀποδοῦναι *but since he could not pay it back* **Mt 18:25.** μὴ βουλόμενος *since (God) did not wish to* AcPlCor 2:12 (cp. TestAbrB 5 p. 109, 24f [Stone p. 66] μὴ θέλων ... παρακοῦσαι).

ג. when it is to be indicated that the statement has subjective validity (Just., D. 115, 3 ὡς μὴ γεγενημένου ἱερέως): ὡς μὴ λαβών *as though you had not received* **1 Cor 4:7.** ὡς μὴ ἐρχομένου μου vs. **18.**

ד. but also very freq. where earlier Gk. would require οὐ (on developments s. Schwyzer II 595f; B-D-F §430, 3; Burton §485 [464 Z.]; cp. οὐ 2b; for μή here, cp. Just., A I, 3, 9, 3 ἄνδρες δεκαδύο ... λαλεῖν μὴ δυνάμενοι; D. 85, 4 διὰ τοὺς μὴ ... συνόντας ἡμῖν; Mel., P. 71, 518f) : τὰ μὴ ὄντα *what does not exist* (in reality, not only in Paul's opinion) **Ro 4:17; 1 Cor 1:28** (Philo, Op. M. 81 τὸ τὰ μὴ ὄντα εἰς τὸ εἶναι παραγαγεῖν; Ath. 4:2 τὸ ὂν οὐ γίνεται ἀλλὰ τὸ μὴ ὄν); Hv 1, 1, 6. τὰ μὴ βλεπόμενα *what is unseen* **2 Cor 4:18ab.** τὰ μὴ δέοντα **1 Ti 5:13.** τὰ μὴ καθήκοντα (3 Macc 4:16) **Ro 1:28.** τὰ μὴ σαλευόμενα **Hb 12:27.** τὸν μὴ γνόντα ἁμαρτίαν **2 Cor 5:21.** τυφλὸς μὴ βλέπων **Ac 13:11.** S. also μὴ ἀσθενήσας τῇ πίστει κατενόησεν **Ro 4:19** where, as oft., the main idea is expressed by the ptc.

ⓒ in a prohibitive sense in independent clauses, to express a negative wish or a warning

α. w. subjunctive *let us not, we should not:* pres. subj. μὴ γινώμεθα κενόδοξοι **Gal 5:26.** μὴ ἐγκακῶμεν **6:9.** μὴ καθεύδωμεν **1 Th 5:6;** cp. **1 Cor 5:8.** W. aor. subj. μὴ σχίσωμεν αὐτόν **J 19:24.**

β. w. optative (B-D-F §427, 4; Rob. 1170) μὴ αὐτοῖς λογισθείη **2 Ti 4:16** (cp. Job 27:5). ἐμοὶ δὲ μὴ γένοιτο καυχᾶσθαι **Gal 6:14** (cp. 1 Macc 9:10; 13:5). Esp. in the formula μὴ γένοιτο (s. γίνομαι 4a) **Lk 20:16; Ro 3:4, 31; 6:2, 15; 7:7, 13; 9:14; 11:1, 11; 1 Cor 6:15; Gal 2:17; 3:21.**

γ. w. pres. impv.

א. to express a command that is generally valid (TestReub 2:10) μὴ γίνεσθε ὡς οἱ ὑποκριταί **Mt 6:16;** cp. vs. **19.** μὴ μεριμνᾶτε τῇ ψυχῇ ὑμῶν vs. **25; Lk 12:22.—Mt 7:1; 10:31; 19:6; Lk 6:30; 10:4, 7; 1 Cor 6:9; 7:5, 12f, 18; Eph 4:26** (Ps 4:5), **29** and oft.

ב. to bring to an end a condition now existing (Aeschyl., Sept. 1036; Chariton 2, 7, 5 μὴ ὀργίζου='be angry no longer'; PHib 56, 7 [249 BC]; PAmh 37, 7; POxy 295, 5; Wsd 1:12 and elsewh. LXX; TestAbr B 9 p. 113, 20 [Stone p. 74]; JosAs 14:11; GrBar 7:6 and ApcMos 16 μὴ φοβοῦ; Just., D. 87, 1 μὴ … λοιπὸν ὑπολάμβανε; Mlt. 122ff) μὴ φοβεῖσθε *do not be afraid (any longer)* **Mt 14:27; 17:7; Lk 2:10;** cp. **1:13, 30.** μὴ κλαῖε *do not weep (any more)* **7:13;** cp. **23:28** (GrBar16:1). μὴ σκύλλου *do not trouble yourself (any further)* **7:6;** cp. **8:49 v.l.** (TestAbr B 2 p. 107, 2 [Stone p. 62] μὴ σκύλλε τὸ παιδάριον).—**9:50; Mk 9:39; J 2:16; 6:43.** μὴ γράφε *do not write (any longer)*=it must no longer stand written **19:21.** μή μου ἅπτου *do not cling to me any longer = let go of me* **20:17.** μὴ γίνου ἄπιστος vs. **27.**—**Ac 10:15; 20:10; Ro 11:18, 20; 1 Th 5:19; Js 2:1** and oft.

δ. w. aor. impv. (Od. 16, 301; Lucian, Paras. μὴ δότε; 1 Km 17:32; TestJob 45:1 μὴ ἐπιλάθεσθε τοῦ κυρίου) μὴ ἐπιστρεψάτω **Mt 24:18; Lk 17:31b.** μὴ καταβάτω **Mt 24:17; Mk 13:15; Lk 17:31a.** μὴ γνώτω **Mt 6:3.**

ε. w. aor. subj.—**א.** almost always to prevent a forbidden action fr. beginning (Plut., Alex. 696 [54, 6] μὴ φιλήσῃς='don't kiss'; PPetr II, 40a, 12 [III BC]; POxy 744, 11; BGU 380, 19; LXX; TestAbr A 2 p. 79, 8 [Stone p. 6] μὴ ἐνέγκωσιν ἵππους; 16 p. 97, 5 [Stone p. 42] μὴ ἐκφοβήσῃς αὐτόν; TestJob 39:11 μὴ κάμητε εἰκῇ; ParJer 3:5 μὴ ἀπολέσητε τὴν πόλιν; ApcEsdr 7:11 μὴ μνησθῇς; Just., D. 137, 1 μὴ κακόν τι εἴπητε.—This is the sense of μὴ θαυμάσῃς Herm. Wr. 11, 17; s. ב below) μὴ φοβηθῇς **Mt 1:20; 10:26** (JosAs 23:15; cp. TestJob 17:6 μὴ φοβηθῆτε ὅλως). μὴ δόξητε **3:9;** cp. **5:17.** μὴ ἅψῃ **Col 2:21.** μὴ ἀποστραφῇς **Mt 5:42.** μὴ κτήσησθε **10:9** and oft. Also w. the third pers. of the aor. subj. μή τις αὐτὸν ἐξουθενήσῃ *no one is to slight him* **1 Cor 16:11.** μή τίς με δόξῃ εἶναι **2 Cor 11:16.** μή τις ὑμᾶς ἐξαπατήσῃ **2 Th 2:3.** μὴ σκληρύνητε **Hb 3:8, 15** (quot. fr. Ps 94:8) is hardly a pres. subj.; it is rather to be regarded as an aor.

ב. only rarely to put an end to a condition already existing (the pres. impv. is regularly used for this; s. above 1 cγב) (TestAbr B 7 p. 111, 19 [Stone p. 70] μὴ κλαύσῃς *weep no more*) μὴ θαυμάσῃς *you need no longer wonder* **J 3:7** ('you needn't be surprised': s. Mlt. 124; 126; and s. א above).

ζ. in abrupt expressions without a verb (ParJer 1:7 μὴ κύριέ μου): μὴ ἐν τῇ ἑορτῇ (we must) *not* (proceed against him) *during the festival* **Mt 26:5; Mk 14:2.** Cp. **J 18:40.** καὶ μὴ (ποιήσωμεν) **Ro 3:8** (B-D-F §427, 4). μὴ ὀκνηροί (γίνεσθε) **12:11.** Cp. **14:1; Gal 5:13; Eph 6:6** al. (B-D-F §481).

❷ **marker of conjunction**—ⓐ after verbs of fearing, etc. *that … (not), lest* B-D-F §370.

α. w. pres. subj. (3 Macc 2:23) ἐπισκοποῦντες … μή τις ῥίζα … ἐνοχλῇ **Hb 12:15**

β. w. aor. subj. (Pla., Apol. 1, 17a) φοβηθεὶς μὴ διασπασθῇ **Ac 23:10.** Also after a pres. **27:17** (cp. Tob 6:15). After βλέπειν in the mng. *take care* (PLond III, 964, 9 p. 212 [II/III AD] βλέπε μὴ ἐπιλάθῃ μηδέν) **Mt 24:4; Mk 13:5; Lk 21:8; Ac 13:40; 1 Cor 10:12; Gal 5:15; Hb 12:25.** σκοπῶν σεαυτόν, μὴ καὶ σὺ πειρασθῇς **Gal 6:1.** στελλόμενοι τοῦτο, μή τις ἡμᾶς μωμήσηται **2 Cor 8:20.** ὁρᾶν **Mt 18:10; 1 Th 5:15.** Elliptically, like an aposiopesis ὅρα μή *take care! you must not do that!* **Rv 19:10; 22:9** (B-D-F §480, 5; Rob. 932; 1203).

γ. w. fut. ind. instead of the subj. following (X., Cyr. 4, 1, 18 ὅρα μὴ πολλῶν ἑκάστῳ ἡμῶν χειρῶν δεήσει) βλέπετε μή τις ἔσται **Col 2:8;** cp. **Hb 3:12**

ⓑ taking the place of a purpose clause=*so that … not:* w. aor. subj. **Mk 13:36; Ac 27:42; 2 Cor 12:6.**

❸ **marker of expectation of a negative anwer to a question** (B-D-F §427, 2; 4; 440; Rob. 1168; 1175; Mlt-Turner 283).

ⓐ in direct questions (X. Eph. 398, 26 H.; Job 1:9; 8:11; TestAbr A 2 p. 79, 9f [Stone p. 6]; B 6 p. 110, 6 [Stone p. 68]; TestJob 15, 6; 27, 1; ApcSed 7:2; ApcMos 8:27) somewhat along the lines ***'it isn't so, is it, that … ?',*** with expectation of a neg. answer; in tr. the negation can in fact be variously expressed in a form suggesting that an inappropriate answer would be met with complete dismay, e.g. μή τινος ὑστερήσατε; *you didn't lack anything, did you?* **Lk 22:35;** μὴ λίθον ἐπιδώσει αὐτῷ; *will one give the person a stone?* **Mt 7:9;** sim. vs. **10; 9:15; Mk 2:19; Lk 5:34; 11:11 v.l.; 17:9; J 3:4; 4:12, 33; 6:67; 7:35, 51f; 21:5** (cp. μήτι); **Ac 7:28** (Ex 2:14), **42** (Am 5:25); **Ro 3:3, 5** (cp. Job 8:3); **9:14, 20** (Is 29:16); **1 Cor 1:13; 9:8f; 10:22** al. μὴ γάρ **J 7:41; 1 Cor 11:22.**—In cases like **Ro 10:18f; 1 Cor 9:4f** μή is an interrog. word and οὐ negatives the verb. The double negative causes one to expect an affirmative answer (B-D-F §427, 2; s. Rob. 1173f; Tetrast. Iamb. 17, 2 p. 266 μὴ οὐκ ἔστι χλόη;='there is grass, is there not?').

ⓑ in indirect questions ***whether … not*** **Lk 11:35** (cp. Epict. 4, 5, 18a; Arrian, Anab. 4, 20, 2 μή τι βίαιον ξυνέβη=whether anything violent has happened [hopefully not]; Jos., Ant. 6, 115).

❹ **marker of reinforced negation,** in combination w. οὐ, μή has the effect of strengthening the negation (Kühner-G. II 221–23; Schwyzer II 317; Mlt. 187–92 [a thorough treatment of NT usage]; B-D-F §365; RLudwig: D. prophet. Wort 31 '37, 272–79; JLee, NovT 27, '85, 18–23; B-D-F §365.—Pla., Hdt. et al. [Kühner-G. loc. cit.]; SIG 1042, 16; POxy 119, 5, 14f; 903, 16; PGM 5, 279; 13, 321; LXX; TestAbr A 8 p. 85, 11 [Stone p. 46]; JosAs 20:3; GrBar 1:7; ApcEsdr 2:7; Just., D. 141, 2). οὐ μή is the most decisive way of negativing someth. in the future.

ⓐ w. the subj.—α. w. aor. subj. (TestAbr A 17 p. 99, 7 [Stone p. 46] οὐ μὴ δυνηθῇς θεάσασθαι; JosAs 20:3; ParJer 2:5; 8:5; ApcSed 12:5; 13:6; Just., D. 141, 2; Ael. Aristid. 50, 107 K.=26 p. 533 D.: οὐ μὴ ἡμῶν καταφρονήσωσι; Diogenes, Ep. 38, 5; UPZ 62, 34; 79, 19) *never, certainly not,* etc. **Mt 5:18, 20, 26; 24:2; Mk 13:2; Lk 1:15; 6:37ab; 10:19; J 8:52; 10:28; 11:26; 13:8; 1 Cor 8:13; Hb 8:12** (Jer 38:34); **13:5; 1 Pt 2:6** (Is 28:16); **Rv 2:11; 3:12; 18:21–23** al.—Also in a rhetorical question, when an affirmative answer is expected οὐ μὴ ποιήσῃ τὴν ἐκδίκησιν; *will he not vindicate?* **Lk 18:7.** οὐ μὴ πίω αὐτό; *shall I not drink it?* **J 18:11.** τίς οὐ μὴ φοβηθῇ; *who shall not fear?* **Rv 15:4.**—In relative clauses **Mt 16:28; Mk 9:1; Ac 13:41** (Hab 1:5); **Ro 4:8** (Ps 31:2); cp. **Lk 18:30.**—In declarative and interrogative sentences after ὅτι **Mt 24:34; Lk 22:16** (οὐκέτι οὐ μή v.l.); **J 11:56;** without ὅτι **Mt 26:29; Lk 13:35.**—Combined w. οὐδέ: οὐδ' οὐ μὴ γένηται (Mitt-Wilck. I/2, 122, 4 [6 AD]) **Mt 24:21** (B-D-F §431, 3).

β. w. pres. subj. **Hb 13:5 v.l.** ἐγκαταλείπω (accepted by Tdf., whereas most edd. read ἐγκαταλίπω)

ⓑ w. fut. ind. (En 98:12; 99:10; TestAbr A 8 p. 85, 11 [Stone p. 20] οὐ μή σοι ἀκολουθήσω; GrBar 1:7 οὐ μὴ προσθήσω; ApcEsdr 2:7 οὐ μὴ παύσομαι) οὐ μὴ ἔσται σοι τοῦτο **Mt 16:22.**—Hm 9:5; s 1:5; 4:7. Cp. **Mt 15:6; 26:35; Lk 10:19 v.l.; 21:33; J 4:14; 6:35b; 10:5** (ἀκολουθήσωσιν v.l.); **Hb 10:17.** οὐκέτι οὐ μὴ εὑρήσουσιν **Rv 18:14.** οὐ γὰρ μὴ κληρονομήσει **Gal 4:30** (Gen 21:10 v.l.); but the tradition wavers mostly betw. the fut. and aor. subj. (s. Mlt. and B-D-F loc. cit.).—DELG. M-M. EDNT.

μήγε in the formula εἰ δὲ μήγε ***otherwise:*** s. γέ bβ and εἰ 6d.

μηδαμῶς (Aeschyl., Hdt. et al.; pap [Mayser 182; also POxy 901, 11; PStras 40, 34]; LXX; JosAs; Jos., Ant. 18, 20; 70); also **μηθαμῶς** (UPZ 79, 8 [159 BC]) 1 Cl 33:1; 45:7; 53:4 (s. B-D-F §33; W-S. §5, 27f; Reinhold §6, 3). ***By no means, certainly not, no*** adv., stating a negative reaction (Chion, Ep. 16, 7; Lucian,

Dial. Deor. 4, 2; Ael. Aristid. 23, 79 K.=42 p. 794 D.) **Ac 10:14; 11:8;** Hv 1, 2, 4; also the pass. fr. 1 Cl cited above.—M-M.

μηδέ negative disjunctive particle (Hom.+)—❶ ***and not, but not, nor*** continuing a preceding negation (almost always w. μή)

ⓐ in such a way that both negatives have one verb in common: in the ptc. **Mt 22:29; Mk 12:24;** in the pres. subj. **1 Cor 5:8; 1J 3:18;** in the impv. **Mt 6:25; Lk 12:22; 1J 2:15.** More than one μηδέ can also follow μή (Diod. S. 18, 56, 5 μὴ κατιέναι is followed by μηδέ used five times with the same verb) **Mt 10:9f; Lk 14:12.**

ⓑ in such a way that μή and μηδέ each has a verb for itself: introduced by ὃς ἄν (ἐάν) **Mt 10:14; Mk 6:11;** by ἵνα **J 4:15;** ὅπως **Lk 16:26.** Both verbs in ptc. **2 Cor 4:2;** in impv. **Mk 13:15; J 14:27; Ro 6:12f; Hb 12:5** (Pr 3:11). The imperatives can also be wholly or partly replaced by equivalent subjunctive forms: **Mt 7:6; 23:9f; Lk 17:23; 1 Pt 3:14.** Both verbs in inf. (depending on παραγγέλλω) **Ac 4:18; 1 Ti 1:4; 6:17;** cp. **Ac 21:21.** More than one μηδέ after μή (Appian, Bell. Civ. 4, 11 §42 μηδεὶς μηδένα followed by μηδέ thrice; Just., D. 112, 4 μηδέποτε and μηδέ thrice) **Col 2:21;** 2 Cl 4:3; cp. **Ro 14:21; 1 Cor 10:7–10.** The first verb can also be connected w. any compound of μή: μηδείς (Jos., Ant. 8, 395; Just., A I, 5, 1 al.) **Lk 3:14; 1 Ti 5:22.** μήπω **Ro 9:11.**

ⓒ in the apodosis of a conditional sentence εἴ τις οὐ θέλει ἐργάζεσθαι, μηδὲ ἐσθιέτω *one who is unwilling to work, is not to be given anything to eat* **2 Th 3:10.**

❷ ***not even*** (X., Mem. 1, 2, 36; PMagd 28, 4 [218 BC]; PTebt 24, 76; Just., A I, 19, 5; Mel., HE 4, 26, 6; Ath 32, 1) preceded by ὥστε μή (or μηκέτι) **Mk 3:20.** μηδὲ τὰ πρὸς τὴν θύραν *not even about the door* **Mk 2:2.** μηδὲ εἰς τὴν κώμην εἰσέλθῃς *do not even go into the village* (before returning home) **Mk 8:26.** τῷ τοιούτῳ μηδὲ συνεσθίειν *not even to eat with such a person* **1 Cor 5:11.** μηδὲ ὀνομαζέσθω ἐν ὑμῖν *should not even be mentioned among you* **Eph 5:3.** μηδὲ αὐτὸν μόνον τῆς κεφαλῆς ὄγκον *not only the bulk of (his swollen) head* Papias (3:2c).—M-M.

μηδείς, μηδεμία, μηδέν (Hom.+.—For μηθέν **Ac 27:33;** IRo 4:2; 5:3; Hm 2:6, which is found freq. since Aristot. in lit., ins [Meisterhans³-Schw. 258f] and pap [Mayser 180–82], s. B-D-F §33; Mlt-H. 111; Thumb 14. The LXX usage in Thackeray 58–62; EpArist 182).

❶ as adj., **pert. to there not being any,** ***no*** μηδεμία αἰτία **Ac 13:28; 28:18.** Cp. **25:17; 1 Cor 1:7; 1 Ti 5:14; Hb 10:2.**—Used w. another neg. (En 98:3 μηδὲ φρόνησιν μηδεμίαν; Just., D. 110, 2 μηδενὸς μηδέπω καρποῦ . . . γενομένου; Ath. R. 19 p. 72, 4 μηδεμία μηδαμοῦ . . . κρίσις) *no . . . at all* **2 Cor 6:3; 13:7; 1 Pt 3:6.** κατὰ μηδένα τρόπον (τρόπος 1) **2 Th 2:3.**

❷ as subst., **a negative ref. to an entity, event, or condition**

ⓐ μηδείς ***nobody*** ἀκούοντες μὲν τ. φωνῆς μηδένα δὲ θεωροῦντες **Ac 9:7.** μηδενὶ εἴπῃς **Mt 8:4;** cp. **9:30; 16:20; 17:9; Mk 5:43; 7:36; Lk 3:14; 5:14; 10:4; J 15:24** P⁶⁶; **Ac 11:19; Ro 12:17; 1 Cor 3:18; 10:24; Gal 6:17; Eph 5:6; 1 Ti 4:12; Tit 2:15; Js 1:13; 1J 3:7; Rv 3:11** and oft.—Used w. another neg. *nobody at all:* **Mk 11:14; Ac 4:17.**

ⓑ μηδέν ***nothing.***—**α.** μηδὲν αἴρειν εἰς (τὴν) ὁδόν **Mk 6:8; Lk 9:3.** Cp. **6:35; Ac 8:24; 1 Cor 10:25, 27.** ἐκ τοῦ μηδενός *out of nothing,* i.e. *for no good reason at all* Hm 5, 2, 2.—Used w. another neg. (Lucian, Dial. Deor. 24, 1 μὴ λέγε τοιοῦτον μηδέν='anything'; X. Eph. 356, 11 H.) ὅρα μηδενὶ μηδὲν εἴπῃς *see to it that you say nothing to anyone* **Mk 1:44** (cp. ApcMos 3 μὴ εἴπῃς αὐτῷ μηδέν; Just., D. 23, 3 μηδὲν μηδένος ἀποκρινομένου) μηδενὶ μηδὲν ὀφείλετε **Ro 13:8.** Cp. **Phil 1:28.**

β. as acc. of the inner obj. μηδέν can be rendered *not . . . at all, in no way* (Aeschyl., Pla.; also Lucian, Dial. Deor. 2, 4, Tim. 43; PHib 43, 6 [III BC]; PAmh 111, 20; 2 Macc 14:28; 3 Macc 3:9; Jos., Ant. 14, 402; Ath. 20, 4 μ. διενηνόχασιν) μηδὲν ὠφεληθεῖσα *she received no benefit at all* **Mk 5:26.** μηδὲν βλάψαν αὐτόν *without harming him in any way* **Lk 4:35** (Just., D. 35, 1 μηδὲν . . . βλάπτεσθαι).—**Ac 4:21; 10:20; 11:12; Js 1:6; Rv 2:10** (v.l. μή). μεριμνᾶν **Phil 4:6.** ὑστερεῖν **2 Cor 11:5.** μ. ἐμποδίζειν 1 Cl 20:2. μ. ἐναντιοῦσθαι 61:1. ὅλως μ. διψυχήσῃς *don't be double-minded at all* Hs 6, 1, 2; ὅλως μ. σπλαγχνιζόμενος *without any compassion at all* Hs 6, 3, 2; μ. ἀδικεῖσθαι *suffer no harm at all* Dg 6:5.

γ. μηδὲν εἶναι *be nothing=amount to nothing, be a nobody* (Soph., Aj. 767, cp. 1231; 1094; Pla., Apol. 41e) **Gal 6:3.**

δ. ἐν μηδενί *in no way* or *respect* (Heron Alex. III p. 214, 2) **2 Cor 7:9; Js 1:4.** Cp. also the pass. mentioned above, **2 Cor 6:3; Phil 1:28.**—M-M.

μηδέποτε (μηδέ, ποτέ) adv. (X.; Pla. et al.; ins, pap, LXX; Jos., Ant. 14, 142, Vi. 259; Just.) ***never*** w. ptc. (Diod. S. 20, 78, 1; Just., A I, 49, 5; Galen, Inst. Log. 14, 7; PTebt 57, 6 [114 BC]) **2 Ti 3:7;** MPol 2:3; Hm 2:3; 10, 1, 4; s 8, 7, 2. W. inf. B 16:10.—M-M.

μηδέπω (μηδέ, πω an enclitic particle 'up to this time, yet') adv. (Aeschyl. et al.; POxy 471, 6; BGU 1210, 63; Just.; Tat. 5, 1) ***not yet*** w. ptc. (BGU 1124, 10; Jos., Ant. 17, 202; 312; Just., D. 110, 2; Tat. 5, 1) μ. βλεπόμενα **Hb 11:7.**—M-M.

Μῆδος, ου, ὁ (Aeschyl. et al.; ins, LXX; TestSol 15:8; TestNapht 5:8; AscIs 3:2; Joseph., SibOr) ***a Mede,*** inhabitant of Media, where there was a Jewish Diaspora (Schürer III 5–9) **Ac 2:9.** BHHW II 1180.

μηθαμῶς s. μηδαμῶς.

μηθέν s. μηδείς, beg.

μηκέτι adv. (Hom.+; ins, pap, LXX, En, TestSol, TestJob; TestReub; Joseph., Just., Tat.) ***no longer, not from now on*** in the same usages as μή.

ⓐ in purpose clauses; after ἵνα (Just., A II, 7, 1; POxy 528, 23) **2 Cor 5:15; Eph 4:14;** AcPl Ha 2, 32.

ⓑ in result clauses; after ὥστε (2 Macc 4:14) **Mk 1:45; 2:2.** W. the inf. of result **1 Pt 4:2.**

ⓒ w. ptc. (Tob 5:10 S; Jos., Ant. 13, 399; TestReub 3:15; Just., D. 24, 3; 45, 4; Tat. 9:3) **Ac 13:34; Ro 15:23; 1 Th 3:1, 5;** B 15:7; IMg 9:1; Hv 3, 11, 3; AcPl Ha 5, 14.

ⓓ w. the inf. (Josh 22:33; 2 Ch 16:5; 2 Macc 10:4; En 103:10; Demetr.: 722 fgm. 1, 9 Jac.; Jos., Ant. 8, 45; 47; Just., D. 6, 2 al.) **Ac 4:17; 25:24; Ro 6:6; Eph 4:17;** Hm 4, 1, 11; 4, 3, 2; s 9, 9, 6.

ⓔ in a relative clause MPol 2:3; Hs 8, 11, 3.

ⓕ in independent clause—**α.** w. the impv. (Ex 36:6; 1 Macc 13:39) **Lk 8:49; J 5:14; 8:11; Eph 4:28; 1 Ti 5:23;** Hv 3, 3, 2; 16, 9; 61, 4.—Instead of this the aor. subj. (Tob 14:9 BA) **Mk 9:25.** μ. ἐκ σοῦ καρπὸς γένηται εἰς τὸν αἰῶνα *no fruit shall ever come from you again* **Mt 21:19;** Hv 2, 3, 1. W. piling up of negatives (cp. β and γ below) οὐ μηκέτι **Mt 21:19 v.l.** μηκέτι μηδὲν αἰτήσεις περὶ ἀποκαλύψεως *don't ask me any more questions about the revelation* Hv 3, 13, 4.

β. w. the opt., in double negation μ. . . . μηδεὶς καρπὸν φάγοι *may no one ever eat fruit from you again* **Mk 11:14** (cp. μηδείς 2a).

γ. w. the hortatory subjunctive (Sir 21:1 μὴ προσθῇς μηκέτι) **Ro 14:13.**—M-M.

μῆκος, ους, τό (Hom. et al.; ins, pap, LXX, TestSol; EpArist, GrBar 2:5; EpArist, Philo; Jos., Bell. 4, 467; 482, Ant. 12, 231; SibOr 3, 649) ***length*** in our lit. only of space: w. breadth, height, depth **Eph 3:18** (cp. βάθος 1). W. breadth **Rv 21:16a,** and w. breadth and height (Diod. S. 13, 82, 2 μῆκος, πλάτος ὕψος of the temple of Zeus at Acragas with exact measurements; 16, 83, 2) vs. **16b.** τῷ μήκει *in length* = *long* w. the measurement given Hv 4, 1, 6 (Da 4:12 οἱ κλάδοι τῷ μήκει ὡς σταδίων τριάκοντα).—M-M.

μηκύνω (Pind., Hdt. et al.; PLond V 1708, 131; LXX; EpArist 8) ***make long*** ('cause to grow large' Is 44:14) mid. *become long, grow (long)* (Philo, Agr. 17 fig. of trees; Jos., Ant. 12, 357) of sprouting grain **Mk 4:27.**—DELG s.v. μακρός. M-M.

μηλωτή, ῆς, ἡ (Philemon Com. [IV/III BC] 25; Pamphilus [I BC/I AD] in Ael. Dion. ω, 1; cp. ο, 5; Apollon. Dysc., Synt. 191, 9; OGI 629, 32; PTebt 38, 22 [II BC]; PMich 421, 24 [I AD]; LXX) ***sheepskin*** of the cloak worn by prophets (3 Km 19:13, 19; 4 Km 2:8, 13f) **Hb 11:37;** 1 Cl 17:1.—DELG s.v. 2 μῆλον. M-M. TW.

μήν particle (Hom.+; UPZ 59, 27 [168 BC]; LXX; JosAs 1:9 cod. A [p. 40, 11 Bat.] οὐ μὴν ἀλλὰ καί; ApcSed 14, 10 p. 136, 18 Tdf. ἦ μήν; Philo, Joseph., Just., Ath.—Denniston 325–58.) used w. other particles for emphasis.

❶ εἰ μήν q.v.

❷ καὶ μήν (Hom., Pind. et al.; BGU 1024, 7; 24; Jos., C. Ap. 2, 257, Vi. 256) ***and indeed.***—ⓐ in contrast to what precedes *and yet* (Just., D. 35, 1; Ath. 8, 4; Kühner-G. II 137; B-D-F §450, 4) B 9:6.

ⓑ ***indeed*** Hm 4, 1, 8; 5, 1, 7. οὐ μήν *to be sure . . . not, of course . . . not* Dg 5:3 (Diod. S. 2, 18, 8; EpArist 158; Jos. Ant. 15, 42; Ath. 23, 1)

❸ ἀλλὰ μήν ***on the other hand*** (Jos., Ant. 19, 146; C. Ap. 1, 286; 2, 289; Just. D. 5, 3) Dg 4:1.

❹ μήτε μήν ***not even*** Ox 840, 15.—DELG 1 μήν. M-M.

μήν, μηνός, ὁ (Hom.+).—❶ ***month*** **Lk 1:36;** PtK 2 p. 14, 27. Acc. of time answering the question: how long? (B-D-F §161, 2; Rob. 469f) *for five months* **Lk 1:24;** cp. vs. **56; 4:25 v.l.; Ac 7:20; 18:11; 20:3; Js 5:17; Rv 9:5, 10; 11:2; 13:5.** τρεῖς μῆνας GJs 12:3. W. prep.: εἰς μ. (w. hour, day, year) **Rv 9:15.** ἐν μ. **Lk 1:26.** ἐπὶ μῆνας τρεῖς *for a period of three months* (s. Jos., Bell. 2, 180) **Ac 19:8;** cp. **Lk 4:25.** κατὰ μῆνα ἕκαστον *every month* **Rv 22:2** (PRev 16, 2 [258 BC] καθ' ἕκαστον μῆνα; X., Oec. 9, 8 κατὰ μῆνα). μετὰ τρεῖς μῆνας *after three months* **Ac 28:11.** Of a woman giving birth GJs 5:2; 7:1; 13:1. In an exact date: μηνὸς Ξανθικοῦ δευτέρᾳ ἱσταμένου=February 22, MPol 21; on this s. ἵστημι, end and ESchwartz, Christl. u. jüd. Ostertafeln: AGG n.s. 8, 1905, 127ff.

❷ ***new moon*** (festival) **Gal 4:10;** Dg 4:5.—B. 1010. Heath, Aristarchus 284–87. DELG 2 μήν. M-M. TW.

μηνιάω (μῆνις) H. Gk. for older μηνίω (Apollon. Rhod. 2, 247; Dionys. Hal., Rhet. 9, 16; Aelian, NA 6, 17; Chariton 1, 2; Sir 10:6; Philo, Abr. 213; Jos., Ant. 8, 112 v.l.—Phryn. p. 82 Lob.) aor. subj. 2 sg. μηνιάσῃς (Sir 10:6) ***cherish anger, rage*** τινί *against someone* ἀλλήλοις Hs 9, 23, 3.—DELG s.v. μῆνις.

μῆνις, ιος (Ionic form of the gen., cp. the Homeric echo Pla., Rep. 390e and δήριος Aeschyl, Ag. 942: EFraenkel, Aeschylus Agamemnon II, '62 ['50], 427) and later **ιδος, ἡ** (Hom. et al.; PRyl 67, 3 [II BC]; BGU 1026, 22, 14; LXX; Jos., Ant. 9, 104; TestDan 5:2; SibOr 4, 135) ***implacable anger, vengefulness*** w. ὀργή described as the source of μ. Hm 5, 2, 4 (on the relationship betw. ὀργή and μῆνις in the Stoa s. Diog. L. 7, 113. Andronicus, περὶ παθῶν 4 [Stoic. III no. 397]; Ps.-Phoc. 64; Sir 27:30). Described as an incurable sin, ibid.—DELG. TW. Sv.

μηνύω 1 aor. ἐμήνυσα; pf. μεμήνυκα; 1 aor. pass. ἐμηνύθη 2 Macc 14:37; ptc. μηνυθείς (Pind., Hdt.+) **to offer information presumed to be of special interest, *inform, make known, reveal*** μηνύοντες τὰ περὶ αὐτοῦ τοῖς ἀδελφοῖς *informing the brothers and sisters about him* (i.e. Paul's arrival) AcPl Ha 8, 5; w. an affirmative clause preceding (ὅτι; cp. Jos., Ant. 1, 198) **Lk 20:37** (of scripture as Philo, Op. M. 15; 77; Just., D. 56, 1). Obj. easily supplied fr. the context ὁ μηνύσας (Demetr.: 722 fgm. 2, 1 Jac.) *the one who informed you* **1 Cor 10:28.** *Report* in a written communication MPol 20:1 (Ath. 1, 3). Esp. also in a forensic sense *report, give information* to authorities (Appian, Bell. Civ. 4, 7 §30; UPZ 121, 15; 25 [156 BC]; PLond III, 1171 verso c, 7 p. 107 [42 AD]; PGiss 61, 7 al.; Jos., Ant. 4, 220; on the role of the מָסוֹר 'informer' in Israelite polity s. WKlassen, Judas '96, 62–66) **J 11:57.** Pass. μηνυθείσης μοι ἐπιβουλῆς *after it became known to me that there was a plot* **Ac 23:30** (the dat. as Diod. S. 2, 28, 4 μηνυθείσης αὐτῷ τῆς πράξεως=after the deed had been reported to him; APF 8 p. 214, 9 [79 BC] τοῖς στρατηγοῖς).—DELG. M-M.

μὴ οὐ s. μή 4.

μήποτε (Hom.+. On separating it μή ποτε s. KLipsius, Gramm. Unters. über die bibl. Gräzität 1863, 129f).

❶ **a marker of indefinite negated point of time, *never*** w. the indicative (freq. in H. Gk.) ἐπεὶ μήποτε ἰσχύει *since it is never in force* **Hb 9:17** (v.l. μὴ τότε; s. B-D-F §428, 5).

❷ **marker of negated purpose, *that . . . not,*** conj. freq. used as an emphatic form of μή—ⓐ after verbs of fearing, being concerned, etc. *that . . . not, lest* (Diod. S. 11, 20, 2 and ApcMos 16:18, 21 φοβεῖσθαι μήποτε)

α. w. aor. subj. προσέχετε ἑαυτοῖς μ. βαρηθῶσιν αἱ καρδίαι ὑμῶν *take care that . . . not . . .* **Lk 21:34** (cp. Sir 11:33). βλέπε μ. ἀναβῇ Hs 5, 7, 2.

β. w. pres. subj. **Hb 4:1** (JosAs 12:10 μ. ἁρπάζῃ με ὡς λύκος).

γ. w. fut. ind. (En 106:6) **Hb 3:12.**

ⓑ denoting purpose, *(in order) that . . . not,* oft. expressing apprehension:—**α.** w. aor. subj. (Diod. S. 15, 20, 1; Gen 38:23; 2 Esdr 4:22; SSol 1:7) **Mt 4:6** (Ps 90:12); **5:25; 13:15** (Is 6:10), **29; 15:32; 27:64; Mk 4:12** (Is 6:10); **Lk 4:11** (Ps 90:12); **14:12; Ac 5:39; 16:39** D; **20:16** D; **28:27** (Is 6:10); **Hb 2:1;** Hm 10, 2, 5; s 9, 28, 7; AcPl Ha 1, 21. After ἵνα **Lk 14:29.**

β. w. pres. subj. **12:58; 14:8.**

γ. w. fut. ind. **Mt 7:6; Mk 14:2;** but the rdg. varies in both pass.; B 19:7.

δ. in a double negation μήποτε οὐ μὴ φοβηθήσονται *lest they cease to fear* D 4:10.

❸ **marker of inquiry, *whether perhaps.***—ⓐ in a direct quest. (Judg 3:24; Tob 10:2; EpArist 15) μήποτε ἀληθῶς ἔγνωσαν οἱ ἄρχοντες; *can it be that the authorities have really come to know?* **J 7:26.**

ⓑ in indirect quest.—**α.** w. opt. (Jos., Bell. 1, 609) μ. αὐτὸς εἴη ὁ Χριστός *whether perhaps he himself was the Messiah* **Lk 3:15.**

β. w. subj. μ. δώῃ (s. δίδωμι, beg.) αὐτοῖς ὁ θεὸς μετάνοιαν (seeing) *whether God may perhaps grant them repentance* **2 Ti 2:25.**

γ. w. the aor. ind., when the content of the question refers to the past (Arrian, Anab. 7, 24, 3 'whether perhaps', with an indirect question referring to the past) GPt 5:15 (s. also ἀγωνιάω).

❹ Somet. the negation is weakened to such a degree that μήποτε introduces someth. conjectured ***probably, perhaps*** (Aristot., EN 10, 1; 10; M. Ant. 4, 24; Job 1:5; Sir 19:13f; Philo, Sacr. Abel. 72, Det. Pot. Ins. 168) μήποτε οὐκ ἀρκέσῃ **Mt 25:9 v.l.** *perhaps there might not be enough* (s. PJoüon, RSR 15, 1925, 438; Mayser II/2, p. 548). The tone is sharper in the wording of **the text** μήποτε οὐ μὴ ἀρκέσῃ *certainly there would never be enough.*—M-M.

μήπου s. πού.

μήπω adv. (Hom. et al.; POxy 1062, 15; Just., A I, 19, 3; Ath. 17, 2) ***not yet*** w. acc. and inf. μ. πεφανερῶσθαι τὴν τῶν ἁγίων ὁδόν **Hb 9:8.** W. ptc. (Pla., Symp. 187d; Sb 5343, 37 [182 AD]; Jos., Ant. 1, 217) μ. γεννηθέντων **Ro 9:11.** μ. φυγών 2 Cl 18:2.—M-M.

μήπως s. πώς.

μηρός, οῦ, ὁ (Hom. et al.; pap [of a camel marked on the thigh: PLond III, 1132b, 5 p. 142 [142 AD]. Likew. Ps.-Callisth. 1, 15, 2 of Bucephalus: ἐν τῷ μηρῷ αὐτοῦ]; LXX; TestSol 1:12 D; TestNapht 1:6, 7; JosAs, ParJer; Jos., Ant. 1, 243) ***thigh*** **Rv 19:16.**—DELG. M-M.

μήτε (Hom. et al.; pap, LXX, En, EpArist, Joseph., Just., Tat., Ath.) negative copula (B-D-F §445; Rob. 1189) ***and not,*** in the ms. tradition not always carefully distinguished fr. μηδέ (B-D-F §445, 1; Rob. 1189); continues μή *not . . . and not, neither . . . nor* **Lk 7:33** (vv.ll. μή . . . μηδέ, and μήτε . . . μήτε); **Mk 3:20 v.l.; Eph 4:27 v.l.** More than one μ. after μή *neither . . . nor . . . nor* **Ac 23:8; Rv 7:1, 3.** μήτε . . . μήτε *neither . . . nor* (Jos., Bell. 5, 533, Ant. 15, 168; Just., D. 1, 5; 7, 1) **Mt 11:18; Ac 23:12, 21; 27:20** (continued w. τέ as X., An. 4, 4, 6); **Hb 7:3;** B 16:10; 19:11; D 4:13; Pol 7:1; MPol 2:2. καὶ μ. . . . μ. *and neither . . . nor* ISm 7:2.—A preceding negatived item is divided into its components by more than one μήτε foll.: μὴ ὀμόσαι ὅλως, μήτε ἐν τ. οὐρανῷ . . . , μήτε ἐν τῇ γῇ . . . , μήτε . . . *not . . . , either . . . , or . . . , or* **Mt 5:34ff.** Cp. **1 Ti 1:7; Js 5:12.** μηδὲν . . . μήτε . . . μήτε *nothing . . . , neither . . . nor* **Lk 9:3.** μὴ . . . μηδὲ . . . , μήτε . . . μήτε . . . μήτε **2 Th 2:2** (the first two members are equivalent; the second is then divided into three parts. On the piling up of negatives cp. Phalaris, Ep. 91 μήτε. . . μήτε . . . μηδεὶς . . . μηδὲν . . . μηδ'; Aelian, VH 14, 22 μηδένα μηδενὶ διαλέγεσθαι μήτε κοινῇ μήτε ἰδίᾳ; Synes., Dreams 19 p. 153c τὰ μηδαμῇ μηδαμῶς μήτε ὄντα μήτε φύσιν ἔχοντα; IG IV^2/1, 68, 60–65 [302 BC] μή . . . μήτε . . . μηδέ; Tat. 17, 4 μηδέν . . . μήτε . . . ἀλλὰ μηδέ).

μήτηρ, τρός, ἡ ('mother' Hom.+)—❶ **female parent, *mother*** **Mt 1:18; 13:55; 14:8, 11; 20:20; Mk 6:24, 28** and oft.; ApcPt Ox 849, 7. W. her child (cp. EpArist 27) **Mt 2:11, 13f, 20f.** W. the father **10:37; 15:4a** (Ex 20:12). Cp. vs. **4b** (Hes., Works 331–34 also knows that one who abuses or speaks harshly to an aged father is punished by Zeus); **19:5** (Gen 2:24), **19** (Ex 20:12), **29; Mk 5:40** al. W. brothers **Mt 12:46; Mk 3:31–33.** W. a grandmother **2 Ti 1:5** (s. μάμμη).—GHb 20, 61 has the extraordinary notion that the Holy Spirit (רוּחָא דְקֻדְשָׁא, fem. gender) was the mother of Christ; s. πνεῦμα 5cα, end.

❷ **an entity that bears the relation of a mother, *mother*** a transference of mng. 1—ⓐ of pers. respected or loved as a mother (Diod. S. 17, 37, 6 ὦ μῆτερ addressed to an aged lady who is well thought of; POxy 1296, 8; 15; 1678; PGiss 78, 1) **Mt 12:49f; Mk 3:34f; J 19:27** (Duris [III BC]: 76 fgm. 63 Jac.: Polycrates introduces the mothers of those slain in battle to rich citizens w. the words μητέρα σοι ταύτην δίδωμι; Lucian, Tox. 22); **Ro 16:13.**

ⓑ of impers. entities—**α.** of cities (like אֵם) in relation to their citizens; so archetypically of the heavenly Jerusalem, i.e. the Messianic community in relation to its members **Gal 4:26;** cp. vs. **22.**—JPlumpe, Mater Ecclesia: An Inquiry into the Concept of Church as Mother in Early Christianity, '43.

β. of a state or quality viewed as point of origin or source (Theognis 1, 385; Hippocr. in Synes., Ep. 115 p. 255b τ. ἔνδειαν ὑγιείας μητέρα; X., Oec. 5, 17 τ. γεωργίαν τ. ἄλλων τεχνῶν μητέρα εἶναι; Tob 4:13; JosAs 15:7 [of μετάνοια]; Ps.-Phoc. 42 μ. κακότητος; Philo; TestSim 5:3) of faith, as the source of Christian virtues (Hierocles 11, 442 ἡ εὐσέβεια μήτηρ τῶν ἀρετῶν) Hv 3, 8, 5; cp. 7. Babylon ἡ μήτηρ τ. πορνῶν κτλ. **Rv 17:5.**—B. 103. DELG. M-M. TW.

μήτι a marker that invites a negative response to the question that it introduces. This marker is somewhat more emphatic than the simple μή (Aeschyl., Prom. 959; Epict. 2, 11, 20; 4, 1, 133; Mal 3:8 v.l.; Just., D. 68, 3f.—B-D-F §427, 2; 440; Rob. 1172; 1176). A variety of resources (including adverbs, auxiliary verbs, and accentuation) can be used to render the force of this particle: e.g. μήτι συλλέγουσιν κτλ. *surely they do not gather . . . , do they?* **Mt 7:16;** cp. **26:22, 25; Mk 4:21; 14:19; Lk 6:39; J 8:22; 18:35** (in J 21:5 the best rdg. is not μήτι but μή τι προσφάγιον ἔχετε; *you probably have no fish, have you?*); **Ac 10:47; 2 Cor 12:18; Js 3:11;** Hv 3, 10, 8; s 9, 12, 5.—Also in questions in which the questioner is in doubt concerning the answer, *perhaps* (Ps.-Callisth. 2, 14, 9 μήτι σὺ ὁ Ἀλέξανδρος;) **Mt 12:23; J 4:29** (Schwyzer II 629, n. 2); Hm 4, 4, 1; GJs 13:1.—Used w. other particles μ. ἄρα *(then) perhaps* **2 Cor 1:17** (TestJob 35:4; B-D-F §440, 2; Rob. 1190). μήτι γε *not to mention, let alone* (Demosth. 2, 23 μή τί γε δὲ θεοῖς; Nicol. Dam.: 90 fgm. 130, 29 Jac.; Plut., Mor. 14a; PLond I, 42, 23 [μὴ ὅτι γε] p. 30 [172 BC]; Just., D., 92, 1; Tat. 14, 2; B-D-F §427, 3.—To introduce a question JosAs 16, 6; Just., D. 92, 1.—Tat. 8, 2) **1 Cor 6:3.** After εἰ s. εἰ 6j.

μήτιγε s. μήτι, end.

μήτρα, ας, ἡ (μήτηρ; Hdt., Pla. et al.; pap [BGU 1026, 22, 20; APF 5, 1913, 393 no. 312, 10ff]; LXX; TestAbr A 8 p. 85, 18 [Stone p. 18]; Apc4Esdr fgm. a; Philo; SibOr, fgm. 3, 2; Just.; Mel., P. 66, 468; Ath. 22, 4; loanw. in rabb.) ***womb*** ἡ νέκρωσις τῆς μ. Σάρρας *the barrenness of Sarah's womb* **Ro 4:19;** GJs 2:4 v.l.; τὴν μ. σου 2:3; ποία . . . μ. 3:1. Of firstborn πᾶν ἄρσεν διανοῖγον μήτραν *every male that opens the womb* **Lk 2:23** (s. διανοίγω 1a).—DELG s.v. μήτηρ C. M-M.

μητρολῴας, ου, ὁ (μήτηρ, ἀλοιάω 'to strike') in the NT the mss. also attest the later form **μητραλῴας** (B-D-F §26; 35, 2; 119, 2; Mlt-H. 68.—Attic μητραλοίας Aeschyl. et al.; Pla., Phd. 113e; 114a πατραλοῖαι καὶ μητραλοῖαι, Leg. 9, 881a μητραλοῖαι . . . ὃς ἂν τολμήσῃ μητέρα τύπτειν.—Lysias 10, 8; Lucian, Deor. Conc. 12; AscIs 4:2) ***one who murders his mother, a matricide*** (w. πατρολῴας. On these very strong words in a catalogue of vices cp. Physiogn. I 327, 15 πατροφόνοι τε καὶ μητροφόνοι παιδοφθόροι τε καὶ φαρμακοὶ κ. τὰ ὅμοια τούτων) **1 Ti 1:9.**—DELG s.v. ἀλωή.

μητρόπολις, εως, ἡ (μήτηρ, πόλις; Pind., Hdt. et al.) ***capital city*** (so X., An. 5, 2, 3; 5, 4, 15; Diod. S. 17, 70, 1; Strabo 16, 2, 44; Dio Chrys. 16 [33], 17; ins, pap, LXX, JosAs ch. 16 cod. A [p. 64, 19 Bat.] in imagery of Aseneth as promise; Philo;

Jos., Ant. 4, 82; 12, 119) **1 Ti subscr.** (s. Πακατιανός).—New Docs 1, no. 12, 13 (198/199 AD). M-M.

μηχανάομαι (μηχανή) impf. 3 sing. ἐμηχανᾶτο; pf. ptc. μεμηχανημένος 3 Macc 5:28 (pass.) ('construct, artfully design' someth. Hom. et al. in both a good and a bad sense; in our lit. only the latter) **to engage in clever scheming,** ***devise, contrive*** (cp. our nominal derivative 'machination') τὶ *someth.* (Hom. et al.; CPR I, 19, 19 ταῦτα πάντα ἐμηχανήσατο=all this he has thought up himself; 3 Macc 6:24; Philo, Virt. 42; Jos., Ant. 17, 17, Vi. 53; SibOr 126; 172) κατά τινος *devise stratagems against someone* (TestReub 5:3; cp. Vi. Aesopi G 3 P. κατὰ ἄλλου μηχανεύεσθαι κακόν) MPol 3.—DELG s.v. μηχανή 5.

μηχανή, ῆς, ἡ (since Hes.) gener. 'machine' (Aeschyl., Hdt.+; ins, pap, LXX; TestSol 26:8 PQ [fig. 'device, strategem']; Philo; Jos., Ant. 14, 423; 17, 4; Tat. 3, 1; 17, 2 [fig.]; loanw. in rabb.), specif. a ***crane*** for hoisting things (Pla., Crat. 425d) fig. μ. Ἰησοῦ Χριστοῦ IEph 9:1. The figure is carried out thus: the parts of the 'crane of Christ' are the cross (Hdt. 2, 125 μηχ. ξύλων='made of wood') and the Holy Spirit, the latter being the rope. The crane brings the stones, symbolizing Christians, to the proper height for the divine structure (cp. Chrysostom, Hom. 3 in Eph ὥσπερ διά τινος ἕλκων μηχανῆς εἰς ὕψος αὐτὴν [sc. ἐκκλησίαν] ἀνήγαγε μέγα; Martyr. Andreae 1, 14 [Aa II/1, 55] ὦ σταυρὲ μηχάνημα σωτηρίας).—DELG.

μιαίνω (Hom.+) fut. μιανῶ (Hs 5, 7, 2); 1 aor. ἐμίανα, ptc. μιάνας. Pass.: fut. 3 sg. μιανθήσεται LXX; 1 aor. ἐμιάνθην; pf. μεμίαμμαι, ptc. μεμιαμμένος (B-D-F §72; W-S. §13, 1; Mlt-H. 223; 249). The primary sense 'to stain' (as of dye [Il. 4, 141]) prepares the way for the transf. sense of causing defilement through socially or cultically unacceptable behavior. It is well to keep in mind in connection with the use of this term and cognates that in the Gr-Rom. world harmonious relations with the transcendent realm were understood to be dependent on careful observance of certain moral and ritual proprieties. Individuals were subordinate to interests of the community and violations of standard moral and ceremonial expectations could jeopardize the delicate balance between an entire populace and its deities. In our lit. only in transf. sense

❶ **to cause someth. to be ritually impure,** ***stain, defile*** (Jos., Bell. 4, 201; 215, Ant. 11, 300 al.; GJs 8:2) pass. ἵνα μὴ μιανθῶσιν **J 18:28** (cp. 1 Macc 1:63 ἵνα μὴ μιανθῶσιν τοῖς βρώμασι). On this subject s. Schürer II 83f; Bousset, Rel.[3] 93f.

❷ **to cause the purity of someth. to be violated by immoral behavior,** ***defile*** (Pind., Aeschyl. et al.; Kaibel 713, 9 οὐ χεῖρα φόνοισι μιάνας. Less freq. in prose, e.g. SIG 1240, 7 ὑβρίσει μιάνας; PFlor 338, 18; LXX; EpArist 166; Philo; Jos., Bell. 4, 323) τὶ *someth.* τὰς χεῖρας **Ac 5:38** D. σάρκα **Jd 8;** Hm 4, 1, 9; s 5, 7, 2–4. τὸ πνεῦμα 5, 6, 5; 5, 7, 2. ἑαυτόν 9, 17, 5. τὴν ἐντολὴν τοῦ κυρίου *defile the commandment of the Lord* m 3:2; cp. s 9, 29, 2. Eve ὁ ὄφις … ἐμίανεν αὐτὴν GJs 13:1. Mary Ἰωσὴφ … ἐμίανεν αὐτήν 15:2 (JosAs 23:13).—Pass. (UPZ 78, 27 [159 BC]; En 12:4; oft. Philo; TestBenj 8:3; Ar. 12:1) ἡ πορεία τῆς σαρκὸς ταύτης … οὐκ ἐμιάνθη Hs 5, 6, 6. The Holy Spirit, dwelling in a person, is contaminated when the pers. becomes angry m 5, 1, 3; likew. patience 5, 1, 6. The mind of the faithless **Tit 1:15b.** Withdrawing fr. the grace of God leads to defilement by sin **Hb 12:15.** Subst. ὁ μεμιαμμένος *he who is defiled* **Tit 1:15a** (JPlumpe, Theol. Studies 6, '45, 509–23).—DELG. M-M. TW.

μιαρός, ά, όν (μιαίνω; Hom. et al.; SIG 218, 86; PCairMasp 97 II, 45; 2 and 4 Macc; Jos., Ant. 18, 38, C. Ap. 1, 236) prim. sense 'defiled, polluted' (s. μιαίνω), then transf. and only so in our lit., **pert. to something that violates cultic or moral canons to such an extent as to invite revulsion,** ***abominable, wretched, foul, depraved, wanton*** (Soph. et al.; Hyperid. 5, 32; 2 and 4 Macc; Philo; SibOr 3, 667; Tat., Ath.) ἐπιθυμίαι 1 Cl 28:1; (w. ἀνόσιος, as Heraclit. Sto. 76 p. 100, 12; PGM 4, 2475) στάσις 1:1; (w. ἄναγνος) συμπλοκαί 30:1; (w. ἄδικος) ζῆλος 45:4.—DELG s.v. μιαίνω.

μίασμα, ατος, τό (μιαίνω; Aeschyl. et al.; LXX) in Gk. lit. of defilement connected with a crime (Antiphon 5, 82 w. 'unclean hands', of some defilement that exposes one's comrades to special perils of the sea; Ps.-Demosth. 59, 86 [w. ἀσεβήματα] caused by adultery; Polyb. 36, 16, 6; Jdth 13:16; En 10:22; Philo; Jos., Bell. 2, 455; Ath. 35, 2), also w. focus on the crime itself ***shameful deed, misdeed, crime*** (so plainly Conon [I BC/I AD]: 26 fgm. 1, 48, 3 Jac.: τὸ μίασμα πρᾶξαι; Polyaenus 6, 7, 2 κοινωνία τοῦ μιάσματος=participation in the crime; Ezk 33:31) ἀποφυγεῖν τὰ μ. τοῦ κόσμου **2 Pt 2:20.** τὸ μ. τῆς μοιχείας ApcPt 9:24.—DELG s.v. μιαίνω. M-M. TW.

μιασμός, οῦ, ὁ (μιαίνω) ('pollution, corruption' Plut., Mor. 393c, Sol. 12, 3; Iambl., Protr. 21, 16 p. 116, 5 Pistelli; LXX; Test12Patr) fig. use only in ref. to the moral realm (Proclus on Pla., Rep. II 354, 20 Kr. μ. ψυχῶν; Wsd 14:26 ψυχῶν μ.; TestLevi 17:8, Benj 8:2f) ***defilement,*** of dissipations παραχρῆσθαι τῇ σαρκὶ ἐν μ. τινι *misuse the flesh in some defilement* Hs 5, 7, 2. ὀπίσω σαρκὸς ἐν ἐπιθυμίᾳ μιασμοῦ πορεύεσθαι *follow after the flesh in corrupting desire* **2 Pt 2:10.**—RParker, Miasma, Pollution and Purification in Early Gk. Religion '83. DELG s.v. μιαίνω. TW.

μίγμα, ατος, τό (μίγ. [perh. μεῖγ.] B-D-F §13; Mlt-H. 57.—Aristot. et al.; Plut., Mor. 997a; Athen. 15, 17, 675bc; PGM 7, 867; Sir 38:7; Philo, Ebr. 191) ***mixture, compound*** of an ointment μ. σμύρνης καὶ ἀλόης *a mixture of myrrh and aloes* **J 19:39** (vv.ll. ἕλιγμα, σμῆγμα, σμίγμα; s. these).—DELG s.v. μείγνυμι. M-M.

μίγνυμι/μιγνύω (the pres. is lacking in our lit. [B-D-F §92; Mlt-H. 249], as well as in the Ptolemaic pap [Mayser I/2[2], '38, 187].—On the spelling [μιγ- all edd. instead of μειγ-] s. B-D-F §23; Kühner-Bl. II 482; Mayser 91; Mlt-H. 249.—The word is found Hom. [μίσγω] et al.; also ins, pap, LXX, TestSol, Joseph., Just., Ath.) 1 aor. ἔμιξα. Pass.: 1 aor. ptc. μιχθείς (Ath. 18, 4); 2 aor. ἐμίγην; pf. ptc. μεμιγμένος ***mix, mingle,*** lit. τί τινι *mingle someth. with someth.* **Rv 15:2** (Chariton 3, 10, 2 αἵματι μεμιγμένον ὕδωρ; Quint. Smyrn. 6, 281 οἴνῳ δ' αἷμα μέμικτο; schol. on Nicander, Alexiph. 353). Also τὶ ἔν τινι (cp. Ps 105:35) **8:7.** τὶ μετά τινος (Pla., Tim. 35b) οἶνον μετὰ χολῆς μεμιγμένον **Mt 27:34.** ὧν τὸ αἷμα Πιλᾶτος ἔμιξεν μετὰ τ. θυσιῶν αὐτῶν *whose blood Pilate mingled with (the blood of) their sacrifices,* i.e. whom P. ordered slain while they were sacrificing **Lk 13:1** (on quest. of connection w. accounts in Jos. s. JFitzmyer, AB Comm. ad loc.). ὄξος καὶ οἶνος μεμιγμένα ἐπὶ τὸ αὐτό *vinegar and wine mixed together* Hm 10, 3, 3b.—In affective imagery *mix, blend* τί τινι *someth. with someth.* (Jos., Bell. 5, 332, Ant. 15, 52) ἡ ὀξυχολία τῇ μακροθυμίᾳ 5, 1, 6. τὶ μετά τινος: ἡ λύπη μετὰ τῆς ἐντεύξεως, … μετὰ του ἁγίου πνεύματος 10, 3, 3ac.—B. 335. DELG s.v. μείγνυμι. M-M. s.v. μίγν-.

μικρολογία, ας, ἡ ('a small matter' Pla. et al.) **someth. of little or no account,** ***trifle*** in a disdainful sense (Pla., Hipp. Maj. 304b of hair-splitting in debate; Lucian, Vit. Auct. 17; Philo, Somn. 1, 94) Hm 5, 2, 2.—DELG s.v. μικρός.

μικρός, ά, όν ('small' Hom.+) comp. μικρότερος, έρα, ον

❶ pert. to a relatively limited size, measure, or quantity, ***small, short***—ⓐ of stature **Lk 19:3.** Perh. also Ἰάκωβος ὁ μικρός (ὁ μ. after a person's name: Aristoph., Ran. 708; X., Mem. 1, 4, 2; Aristot., Pol. 5, 10 p. 1311b, 3; Diog. L. 1, 79 of a 'younger' Pittacus; Sb 7576, 6 [I AD]; 7572, 10 [II AD]) **Mk 15:40** (s. Ἰάκωβος 3). This pass. may possibly belong to

ⓑ of age. Subst.: *the little one, the child* (ὁ μικρός Menand., Sam. 39f; PLond 893, 7 [40 AD]; PFay 113, 14. ἡ μικρά PLond III, 899, 6 p. 208 [II AD]) **Mt 18:6, 10, 14.**—For the designation of all the members of a group as μικροὶ κ. μεγάλοι, etc. cp. μέγας 1d: **Ac 8:10; 26:22; Hb 8:11** (Jer 38:34); **Rv 11:18; 13:16; 19:5, 18; 20:12.**

ⓒ of distance. Adv.: *a short distance, a little way* (X., Cyr. 1, 2, 15; Dionys. Byz. §8 and 13) προελθὼν μικρόν (Ps.-Demetr. 226) **Mt 26:39; Mk 14:35.**

ⓓ of time—**α.** adj. *short,* of time χρόνον μικρόν (Pla., Rep. 6, 498d; Ael. Aristid. 34 p. 661 D.; Is 54:7) **J 7:33;** cp. **12:35; Rv 6:11; 20:3.**

β. adv. *a short time, a little while* (Jos., Ant. 4, 159; 8, 405) **J 13:33** (cp. Job 36:2); Hs 9, 4, 4; 9, 5, 1 (v.l.). μικρόν *for a moment* (Menand., Epitr. 474 J.=538 Kö.; JosAs 15:14; ParJer 2:9; cp. πρὸς μ. μ. 'little by little' GrBar 7:3) Hv 4, 1, 6. μετὰ μικρόν *after a short while* (Just., D. 56, 17; Phlegon: 257 fgm. 36, 1, 2 Jac.; Lucian, Dial. Mort. 15, 3; Synes., Dio 1 p. 234, 5 NTerzaghi ['44]) **Mt 26:73; Mk 14:70.** (ἔτι) μικρὸν καί . . . *in a little while,* lit. 'yet a little while, and'=*soon* (Ex 17:4; Jer 28:33; Hos 1:4; TestJob 24:1) **J 14:19; 16:16–19.** ἔτι μ. ὅσον ὅσον = *soon* **Hb 10:37;** 1 Cl 50:4 (both Is 26:20; s. B-D-F §127, 2; 304; Rob. 733).

ⓔ of mass or compass relative to things—**α.** *small* (X., Mem. 3, 14, 1 μ. ὄψον; TestAbr B 8 p. 112, 20 [Stone p. 72] πύλη; ApcSed 11:3 μ. κτίσμα; Vils 3 [p. 69, 7 Sch.] ὕδωρ; Just., A I, 19, 1 ῥανίς) μικρότερον πάντων τ. σπερμάτων *the smallest of all seeds* **Mt 13:32; Mk 4:31** (s. σίναπι.—Alex. Aphr., An. II 1 p. 20, 14 οὐδὲν κωλυθήσεται τὸ μέγιστον ἐν τῷ μικροτάτῳ γενέσθαι σώματι). μικρὰ ζύμη *a little (bit of) leaven* **1 Cor 5:6; Gal 5:9.** Of the tongue μικρὸν μέλος *a small member* **Js 3:5** (cp. Eur., fgm. TGF 411).

β. subst. neut. (τὸ) μικρόν *what is insignificant, small* τὸ μ. τηρεῖν 2 Cl 8:5 (apocr. saying of Jesus). μικρὰ φρονεῖν περί τινος *think little of someth.* 2 Cl 1:1f (μικρὸν φρονεῖν Soph., Aj. 1120; Plut., Mor. p. 28c).—Pl. *insignificant things, trifles* (Aelian, VH 2, 27) μικρὰ κατ' ἀλλήλων ἔχειν *have trifling complaints against each other* Hs 8, 10, 1b.

γ. subst. neut. *a little* μικρόν τι (Diod. S. 1, 74, 1; Ael. Aristid. 48, 37 K.=24 p. 474 D.; UPZ 70, 3 [152/151 BC]; cp. Just., D. 115, 6 ἓν δὲ μ. ὁτιοῦν) *a little* **2 Cor 11:16.** μ. τι ἀφροσύνης vs. **1** (Procop. Soph., Ep. 80 μοὶ μικρὸν δίδου νεανιεύεσθαι). παρὰ μικρόν (Isocr. 19, 22; Dionys. Byz. §3 and 50; Ps 72:2; Ezk 16:47; PsSol 16:1; Jos., C. Ap. 2, 270) *except for a little, nearly* Hs 8, 1, 14. κατὰ μικρόν *in brief* (Galen XIX p. 176 K.: Lucian, Catapl. 17, De Merc. Cond. 35) B 1:5. μικροῦ δεῖν *early, almost* AcPl Ha 3, 34 (Jos., C. Ap. 2, 168 al.).

ⓕ *small* in number (Gen 30:30; 47:9) τὸ μικρὸν ποίμνιον **Lk 12:32.**

❷ pert. to being of little import, ***unimportant, insignificant***

ⓐ of pers. lacking in importance, influence, power, etc. εἷς τῶν μικρῶν τούτων *one of these humble folk* (disciples? so Goodsp.) **Mt 10:42; Mk 9:42** (Kephal. I 189, 6–19; 201, 30 interprets 'the little ones who believe' as catechumens. But the Gk. word μικρός is not found in the Coptic text); **Lk 17:2.** OMichel, 'Diese Kleinen', e. Jüngerbezeichnung Jesu: StKr 108, '37/38, 401–15. ὁ μικρότερος ἐν τῇ βασιλείᾳ τ. οὐρανῶν *the one of least importance in the Kingdom of Heaven* (but FDibelius, ZNW 11, 1910, 190–92 and OCullmann, ConNeot 11, '47, 30 prefer 'youngest', and refer it to Christ) **Mt 11:11;** cp. **Lk 7:28.** ὁ μικρότερος ἐν πᾶσιν ὑμῖν ὑπάρχων *the one who is least among you all* **9:48.**

ⓑ *small, insignificant* (Ath. 23, 3 δόξαι) δύναμις **Rv 3:8.** μισθός 2 Cl 15:1b (cp. a: μ. συμβουλία). ἐπιθυμίαι Hs 8, 10, 1a.

❸ the state of being small, ***smallness*** subst. neut. ἐκ μικροῦ αὐξῆσαι **Mt 20:28** D.—B. 880. M-M. TW.

μικρῶς (Pla.; 2 Macc 14:8; Jos., Ant. 15, 213 v.l.) adv. from μικρός ***slightly*** οὐ μ. ὠργίζετο AcPl Ha 3, 2; sim. λυπέω 4, 17; πενθέω 5, 19; ἀγωνιάω 7, 31.—DELG. TW.

Μίλητος, ου, ἡ (Hom. et al.; ins; SibOr 5, 325) ***Miletus,*** a seaport city on the west coast of Asia Minor, south of the mouths of the Meander, and ca. 60 km. south of Ephesus. There was a Jewish community in M. (Schürer III 24f; 117, 2; 167f; AvGerkan, E. Synagoge in Milet: ZNW 20, 1921, 177–81; Dssm., LO 391f [LAE 451f]). Paul touched at the city on his last journey to Jerusalem **Ac 20:15, 17** (on Paul's farewell speech s. JLambrecht in: Les Actes des Apôtres '79, 307–37; WKurz, Farewell Addresses in the NT '90). Acc. to **2 Ti 4:20** Trophimus lay ill in Miletus.—TWiegand, ed., Milet. Ergebnisse der Ausgrabungen u. Untersuchungen seit d. Jahre 1899 (1906ff) 18 vols.; PECS s.v. (bibl.); Pauly-W. XV 1586–1655; Kl. Pauly III 1295–98; BHHW II 1216f.

μίλιον, ου, τό (Eratosthenes [in Julian of Ashkelon, Metr. Script. I 201]; Polyb. 34, 12, 3; Strabo 3, 1, 9; 5, 1, 11 al.; Plut., Cic. 32, 1, C. Gracch. 7, 3; IGR III, 1385; SIG 888, 26; BCH 29, 1905, 99f; APF 2, 1903, 566 no. 122; PStras 57, 6. Latin loanw.: mille. Loanw. in rabb.) a Roman ***mile,*** lit. a thousand paces, then a fixed measure = eight stades = 1,478.5 meters **Mt 5:41;** D 1:4; GJs 17:2.—M-M.

μιμέομαι (μῖμος, 'imitator, mimic') mid. dep.; impv. μιμοῦ; impf. ἐμιμούμην; fut. μιμήσομαι; 1 aor. ἐμιμησάμην (Pind.+) **to use as a model, *imitate, emulate, follow,*** w. acc. of pers., and in our lit. only of behavior (Ael. Aristid. 34 p. 669 D.; Wsd 15:9; Philo; Jos., Ant. 6, 347, C. Ap. 2, 257; Tat. 7, 3) ISm 12:1. ἡμᾶς **2 Th 3:7, 9** (PFlor 367, 3 ἐγὼ οὐ μειμήσομαί σε). θεόν Dg 10:5 (Heraclitus, Ep. 5, 1 θεόν; Eunap. 104 of Oribasius the physician: ἐμιμεῖτο θεόν [Asclepius]; EpArist 281; Philo, Spec. Leg. 4, 73, Virt. 168; TestAsh 4:3 κύριον; Did., Gen. 57, 22; 180, 9).—Of Christ ἂν ἡμᾶς μιμήσεται, καθὰ πράσσομεν *if he were to imitate our way of acting* IMg 10:1. W. acc. of thing *imitate someth.* (Appian, Samn. 10 §1 τὴν ἀρετήν; TestAbr 20 p. 104, 6 [Stone p. 56] τὴν φιλοξενίαν; Philo, Congr. Erud. Gr. 69 τὸν ἐκείνων βίον al.; Jos., Ant. 12, 241, C. Ap. 1, 165; Iren. 1, 17, 2 [Harv. I 168, 7;11]) τὴν πίστιν **Hb 13:7.** *Copy* τὶ *someth.* τὸ κακόν, ἀγαθόν (Sotades 7, 2 μιμοῦ τὸ καλόν [Coll. Alex. p. 241]; Kaibel 85, 3 ἐμιμούμην τὸ καλόν; EpArist 188; Just., A I, 10, 1 ἀγαθά) **3J 11.** τὸ μαρτύριον MPol 19:1.—DELG s.v. μῖμος. M-M. EDNT. TW.

μίμημα, ατος, τό (μιμέομαι; Aeschyl. et al.; Musonius 90, 40 a human being is μ. θεοῦ; Polemo, Decl. 2, 32 p. 27, 7; OGI 383, 63; 404, 26; Wsd 9:8. Oft. Philo; Jos., Bell. 7, 142, Ant. 12, 75; Just., A II, 13, 6; SibOr 8, 116) **that which is imitated, *copy, image*** δέχεσθαι τὰ μ. τῆς ἀληθοῦς ἀγάπης *receive the copies of True Love* (i.e. of Christ), perh. w. ref. to Ign. and fellow prisoners (s. JKleist, transl., ad loc.) Pol 1:1 (Herm. Wr. 382, 18 Sc. μ. τ. ἀληθείας).—DELG s.v. μῖμος.

μιμητής, οῦ, ὁ (μιμέομαι; X., Pla. et al.; Philo, Joseph.) *imitator,* in our lit. mostly used w. εἶναι or γίνεσθαι

ⓐ w. gen. of the pers. imitated (X., Mem. 1, 6, 3 οἱ διδάσκαλοι τοὺς μαθητὰς μιμητὰς ἑαυτῶν ἀποδεικνύουσιν; Jos., Ant. 1, 109; 12, 203 μιμ. γίν. τοῦ γεγεννηκότος) μιμηταί μου γίνεσθε *use me as your model* **1 Cor 4:16** (BSanders, HTR 74, '81, 353–63); **11:1** (EEidem, Imitatio Pauli: Festskrift for EStave 1922, 67–85; WPdeBoer, The Imitation of Paul '62; ELarsson, Christus als Vorbild [diss. Uppsala] '62; ASchulz, Nachfolgen u. Nachahmen '62; further lit. EGüttgemanns, D. leidende Apostel, '66, 185–94; CSpicq, BRigaux Festschr., '70, 313–22). Cp. 1 Cl 17:1. μιμηταὶ τῶν κληρονομούντων τὰς ἐπαγγελίας **Hb 6:12.** μ. ἡμῶν κ. τοῦ κυρίου **1 Th 1:6** (TRE XXIII 685f). τ. κυρίου IEph 10:3; MPol 17:3; cp. 1:2. Χριστοῦ IPhld 7:2; cp. **1 Cor 11:1.** (τοῦ) θεοῦ (Did., Gen. 180, 11; Just., A I, 21, 4 θεῶν) **Eph 5:1;** Dg 10:4b, 6; IEph 1:1; ITr 1:2.—EGulin, Die Nachfolge Gottes: Studia Orientalia I, ed. Societas Orientalis Fennica 1925, 34–50; FTillmann, D. Idee der Nachfolge Christi '34; JNielen in Hlg. Überliefg. (ed. OCasel) '38, 59–85.

ⓑ w. an impersonal gen. (Herodian 6, 8, 2 τ. ἀνδρείας; Philo, Virt. 66; Jos., Ant. 1, 68; 8, 251; τῆς ἀρετῆς Did., Gen. 144, 24) τῶν ἐκκλησιῶν τοῦ θεοῦ **1 Th 2:14.** τοῦ ἀγαθοῦ **1 Pt 3:13 v.l.** τῆς χρηστότητος Dg 10:4a. τῆς ὑπομονῆς Pol 8:2. τοῦ πάθους τοῦ θεοῦ IRo 6:3.—DELG s.v. μῖμος. M-M. TW.

μιμνήσκομαι most mss. lack iota subscr., which is secondary; on the spelling s. B-D-F §26; pres. by-form μνήσκομαι (1 Macc 6:12 v.l.; TestJob 35, 4; ParJer 7:31); 1 fut. μνησθήσομαι; 1 aor. ἐμνήσθην; pf. μέμνημαι (used as a pres. [EpArist 168]; cp. B-D-F §341; Rob. 894 f) (reflexive 'remind oneself, recall to mind, remember' Hom.+).

❶ **to recall information from memory,** ***remember, recollect, remind oneself***—ⓐ w. gen. of thing (1 Macc 6:12; TestJob 18:5; ApcMos 23; Just., D. 55, 1) **Mt 26:75; Lk 24:8; 2 Ti 1:4; 2 Pt 3:2; Jd 17;** 1 Cl 13:1; 46:7; 50:4; Hv 3, 1, 5.

ⓑ w. gen. of pers. (PBad 48, 17 [126 BC] μνήσθητι ἡμῶν; ParJer 5:18 μνησθεὶς τοῦ Ἰερεμίου; Just., D. 142, 1 ὡς φιλῶν ἡμῶν μεμνῆσθαι) πάντα μου μέμνησθε *you think of me in every way* **1 Cor 11:2** (prob. in ref. to various instructions). On GJs s. under c.

ⓒ w. ὅτι foll. (X., Cyr. 3, 1, 27; Is 12:4; Dt 5:15; Job 7:7; Jos., Vi. 209) **Mt 5:23; 27:63; Lk 16:25; J 2:17, 22; 12:16;** GJs 1:3; 10:1, 2 (each w. gen. of pers.).—W. ὡς foll. (Ps.-Clem., Hom. 2, 47, 1) **Lk 24:6.** W. gen. and ὡς foll. **Ac 11:16.**

ⓓ w. rel. clause foll. μνησθεὶς ὧς ἐδίδαξέν με μεγαλείων *I remembered the great things which he had taught me* Hv 4, 1, 8. μνήσθητι, ὅσα ἐποίησεν ὁ Θεός GJs 9:2.

❷ **to think of and call attention to someth. or someone,** ***make mention of someone*** τινός (Pardalas Iamb. in Herodes, Cercidas etc. ed. AKnox 1929 p. 276 μεμνήσομαί σου ἐν ἐμῇσι βύβλοισι=I will mention you in my books) EpilMosq 2. Sim. the pass.: *be mentioned* εἰ διὰ τοῦ Ἀβραὰμ ἐμνήσθη (sc. ὁ λαὸς οὗτος) B 13:7. This may also be the place for μνησθῆναι ἐνώπιον τοῦ θεοῦ *be mentioned before God* **Ac 10:31; Rv 16:19.** But these pass. can also be understood w. God as subj., s. 3 c.

❸ **give careful consideration to,** ***remember, think of, care for, be concerned about, keep in mind***—ⓐ w. gen. (Od. 18, 267 al.; Arrian, Ind. 41, 5 δείπνου; Gen 30:22; Jos., Bell. 4, 340; SibOr 3, 595) μνήσθητί μου *remember me* **Lk 23:42** (Epict. 3, 24, 100: O God μοῦ μέμνησο; cp. GDalman, Jesus-Jeshua [tr. PLevertoff] 1929, 197–201; μοῦ μέμνησο; TestAbr B 6 p. 110, 11 [Stone p. 68] ἐμνήσθη ὑμῶν ὁ θεός).—**Hb 2:6** (Ps 8:5); **13:3;** D 4:1. μ. διαθήκης (cp. διαθήκη 2) **Lk 1:72** (Lev 26:42, 45). μ. ἐλέους vs. **54** (Ps 97:3).—W. gen. and inf. of the purposeful result (B-D-F §391, 4) μνήσθητι, κύριε, τῆς ἐκκλησίας σου τοῦ ῥύσασθαι αὐτήν *remember, O Lord, your congregation to save it* D 10:5 (GSchmidt, ΜΝΗΣΘΗΤΙ: Eine liturgiegeschichtliche Skizze, HMeiser Festschr., '51, 259–64).—μὴ μνησθῆναι τῶν ἁμαρτιῶν τινος *not remember someone's sins, let someone's sins go unpunished* (cp. Ps 24:7; 78:8; Sir 23:18; Is 43:25; ApcEsdr 7:11 p. 32, 24 ἀνομιῶν ἀρχαίων) **Hb 8:12; 10:17** (both Jer 38:34).

ⓑ w. acc. of thing (Hom.; Hdt. 7, 18; Dt 8:2; Is 63:7.—B-D-F §175; cp. Rob. 482f) μνησθήσῃ ἡμέραν κρίσεως *give thought to the day of judgment* B 19:10.

ⓒ pass. αἱ ἐλεημοσύναι σου ἐμνήσθησαν ἐνώπιον τ. θεοῦ *your charities have been called to remembrance by God = have God's attention* **Ac 10:31;** cp. **Rv 16:19.** ἐνώπιον τ. θ. in these passages can be viewed as equiv. to ὑπὸ τ. θ. (ἐνώπιον 2b; but s. 2 above).—CKessler, The Memory Motif in the God-man Relationship of the OT, diss. Northwestern Univ. '56; B. 1228f. RAC VI 43–54.—LfgrE III 214. Schmidt, Syn. I 310–20. DELG s.v. μιμνήσκω. M-M. EDNT. TW. Spicq.

Μισαήλ, ὁ indecl. (מִישָׁאֵל; 1 Esdr 9:44. In Jos. [Ant. 10, 188f] Μισάηλος) ***Mishael*** one of three youths in a fiery furnace (Da 3:88; also 1:6f, 11, 19; 2:17; 1 Macc 2:59; 4 Macc 16:3, 21; 18:12) 1 Cl 45:7.

μισέω impf. ἐμίσουν; fut. μισήσω; 1 aor. ἐμίσησα; pf. μεμίσηκα, Pass.: fut. 3 sg. μισηθήσεται LXX; aor. ἐμισήθην (LXX; Joseph.); pf. 3 sg. μεμίσηται (Jos., Bell. 3, 376); ptc. μεμισημένος (Hom.+; ins, pap, though quite rare in both; LXX, Test12Patr, JosAs; ParJer 8:9; ApcSed 14 p. 136, 13 Ja.; AscIs 2:7; Philo, Joseph., Just., Tat., Ath.) depending on the context, this verb ranges in mng. from 'disfavor' to 'detest'. The Eng. term 'hate' generally suggests affective connotations that do not always do justice esp. to some Semitic shame-honor oriented use of μ.=שָׂנֵא (e.g. Dt 21:15, 16) in the sense 'hold in disfavor, be disinclined to, have relatively little regard for'.

❶ **to have a strong aversion to,** ***hate, detest***—ⓐ w. acc. of pers. (opp. ἀγαπάω as Dt 21:15, 16=Philo, Leg. All. 2, 48. Cp. AFridrichsen, SEÅ 5, '40, 152–62) **Mt 5:43** (PJoüon, RSR 20, 1930, 545f; MSmith, HTR 45, '52, 71–73. Cp. the prayer of Solon [fgm. 1, 5 Diehl[3]] γλυκὺν φίλοισ', ἐχθροῖσι πικρόν; Pind., P. 2, 83f; Archilochus Lyr. fgm. 66 Diehl[3]; 1QS 1:9f; μ. τὸν . . . ψευσμάτων κακοσύνθετον ποιητήν Iren. 1, 15, 4 [Harv. I 152, 6] and s. ESutcliffe, Hatred at Qumran, Revue de Qumran 2, '59/60, 345–55; KStendahl, HTR 55, '62, 343–55; OLinton, StTh 18, '64, 66–79; on the fut. as prescriptive form KMcKay, NovT 27, '85, 219f; New Docs 4, 167 w. ref. to ins fr. Telmessos [II BC]: SEG XXIX, 1516, 4–6). 2 Cl 13:4; D 1:3; 2:7.—**Lk 1:71; 6:22, 27; 19:14; J 7:7ab; 15:18f, 23f; 17:14; 1J 2:9, 11; 3:13, 15; 4:20; Rv 17:16;** B 19:11; Dg 2:6. ἀλλήλους **Mt 24:10; Tit 3:3;** D 16:4. μ. τινα δωρεάν (שָׂנֵא חִנָּם) *hate someone without cause, undeservedly* (s. δωρεάν 2) **J 15:25** (Ps 68:5.—34:19). μ. τινα ἀδίκως *hate someone wrongfully* 1 Cl 60:3. Of God 1 Cl 30:6; Dg 9:2;

ⓑ w. acc. of thing (Jos., Ant. 3, 274 τ. ἀδικίαν; Tat. 11, 1 πορνείαν; Did., Gen. 175, 23 τ. κακίαν) τὸ φῶς **J 3:20.** ἀλήθειαν B 20:2; D 5:2. ἀνομίαν **Hb 1:9** (Ps 44:8). τὴν γαλῆν B 10:8. τὰ ἐνθάδε *earthly things* 2 Cl 6:6 (this pass. may also fit under 2). τὴν πονηρὰν ἐπιθυμίαν Hm 12, 1, 1. τὰ ἔργα τῶν Νικολαϊτῶν **Rv 2:6.** τὰ ἔργα τῆς πονηρᾶς ὁδοῦ *the deeds of the evil way* B 4:10. τὰς ἡδυπαθείας 2 Cl 17:7. παιδείαν 1 Cl 35:8 (Ps 49:17). τὴν πλάνην B 4:1. τὸ πονηρόν19:11. σοφίαν 1 Cl 57:5 (Pr 1:29). τὴν ἑαυτοῦ σάρκα **Eph 5:29** (cp.

Herm. Wr. 4, 6 ἐὰν μὴ τὸ σῶμα μισήσῃς, σεαυτὸν φιλῆσαι οὐ δύνασαι). τὴν ψυχήν Dg 6:5f. πᾶσαν ὑπόκρισιν B 19:2b; D 4:12a. χιτῶνα **Jd 23.** πᾶν ὃ οὐκ ἔστιν ἀρεστὸν τῷ θεῷ B 19:2a; D 4:12b (cp. ApcSed 14, 8 ἃ μισεῖ μου ἡ θεότης). ὃ μισῶ τοῦτο ποιῶ *I do what I detest* **Ro 7:15.**

ⓒ abs. IEph 14:2; IRo 8:3; Dg 5:17 (Just., A I, 57, 1; Tat. 17, 2; Ath. 31, 1).—Pass.: of Christianity ὅταν μισῆται ἀπὸ κόσμου *whenever it is hated by the world* IRo 3:3 (cp. Just., A I, 4, 5 τὸ δὲ χρηστὸν μισεῖσθαι οὐ δίκαιον).—The pres. ptc. w. pres. in periphrastic conjugation, to express the long duration of the attitude (Chariton 2, 6, 1 εἰμὶ μισούμενος ὑπὸ τ. Ἔρωτος) ἔσεσθε μισούμενοι **Mt 10:22; 24:9; Mk 13:13; Lk 21:17** (cp. Herm. Wr. 9, 4b). μεμισημένος (Iren. 1, 6, 3 [Harv. I 55, 14]) w. ἀκάθαρτος *unclean and loathsome* (for cultic reasons) of birds **Rv 18:2.**

❷ **to be disinclined to, *disfavor, disregard*** in contrast to preferential treatment (Gn 29:31; Dt 21:15, 16) **Mt 6:24; Lk 16:13.** τὴν ψυχὴν αὐτοῦ **J 12:25** or ἑαυτοῦ **Lk 14:26** (cp. the formulation Plut, Mor. 556d οὐδ᾽ ἐμίσουν ἑαυτούς; on the theme cp. Tyrtaeus [VII BC] 8, 5 D.[3]). **Ro 9:13** (Mal 1:2f). Perh. 2 Cl 6:6 (s. 1b). (JDenney, The Word 'Hate' in Lk 14:26: ET 21, 1910, 41f; WBleibtreu, Paradoxe Aussprüche Jesu: Theol. Arbeiten aus d. wissensch. Prediger-Verein d. Rheinprovinz, new ser. 20, 24, 15–35; RSockman, The Paradoxes of J. '36).—ACarr, The Mng. of 'Hatred' in the NT: Exp. 6th ser., 12, 1905, 153–60.—DELG. M-M. EDNT. TW.

μισθαποδοσία, ας, ἡ (μισθός, ἀποδίδωμι, s. next entry; only Hb and eccl. lit. But ἀποδίδωμι [q.v. 2a] τὸν μισθόν is quite common) ***recompense,*** whether favorable or unfavorable, lit. 'payment of wages'

ⓐ in a favorable sense ἀποβλέπειν εἰς τὴν μ. *look forward to a reward* **Hb 11:26;** of confidence ἥτις ἔχει μεγάλην μ. **10:35.**

ⓑ in an unfavorable sense: *punishment, retribution* λαμβάνειν ἔνδικον μ. *receive a just penalty* **Hb 2:2.**—DELG s.v. δίδωμι. M-M.

μισθαποδότης, ου, ὁ (μισθός + ἀποδότης 'one who pays wages', s. prec. entry; only Hb and eccl. lit.) ***rewarder,*** lit. 'paymaster' of God (AcThom 142 [Aa II/2, 249, 10]; 159 [ibid. 271, 1b]; PGen [Christian] 14:27) τῷ μισθαποδότῃ θεῷ) τοῖς ἐκζητοῦσιν αὐτὸν μ. γίνεται *(God) proves to be a rewarder of those who seek him* **Hb 11:6.**—New Docs 3, 76; DELG s.v. δίδωμι. M-M. TW.

μίσθιος (actually adj. of two or three terminations. In our lit. only subst.: TestSol [neut.]; ApcEsdr 1:14 p. 25, 7 Tdf.; Jos., Bell. 5, 49; Plut., Lyc. 50 [16, 7] al.; Anth. Pal. 6, 283, 3; PAmh 92, 19; Lev 25:50; Job 7:1; Tob 5:12 BA; Sir 7:20), **ου, ὁ *day laborer, hired man* Lk 15:17, 19, 21 v.l.** (Alciphron 2, 32, 3 δέχου με μισθωτὸν κατ᾽ ἀγρόν, πάντα ὑπομένειν ἀνεχόμενον ὑπὲρ τοῦ τὴν ἀπλήρωτον ἐμπλῆσαι γαστέρα=put me on as a field hand, who's ready to put up with anything just to fill my bottomless belly).—Frisk s.v. μισθός. M-M. TW. Spicq.

μισθός, οῦ, ὁ (Hom.+)—❶ **remuneration for work done, *pay, wages* Lk 10:7; 1 Ti 5:18.** Personified ὁ μ. ὁ ἀφυστερημένος κράζει *the wages you have kept back cry out* (to heaven) **Js 5:4** (cp. TestJob 12:4). τὸν μ. ἀποδιδόναι *pay (out) wages* (s. ἀποδίδωμι 2a) **Mt 20:8** (cp. Iren. 4, 36, 7 [Harv. II 284, 3]; 1, 4, 3 [Harv. I, 36, 11) μισθὸν λαμβάνειν *receive one's wages* (Diod. S. 12, 53, 2; Jos., Bell. 2, 296, Ant. 4, 206) **J 4:36.** μισθοὺς λαμβάνειν τινός *accept payment(s) for someth.* Hm 11:12 (μ. λαμβ. τινός as Philo, Spec. Leg. 4, 98; for the pl. cp. Aesop 87d, 12 Ch.; Jos., Ant. 1, 183; BGU 1067, 15 [II AD]; Just., A I, 27, 2). μ. τῆς ἀδικίας *money paid for treachery* **Ac 1:18.** μ. ἀδικίας *dishonest gain* **2 Pt 2:15;** on ἀδικούμενοι μισθὸν ἀδικίας vs. **13** s. ἀδικέω 2.—In τῇ πλάνῃ τοῦ Βαλαὰμ μισθοῦ ἐξεχύθησαν, μισθοῦ is gen. of price (as in the anonymous comic fgm. 218 Kock; Diod. S. 4, 20, 2; 3 μισθοῦ ἐργάζεσθαι; Tat. 1, 3 μισθοῦ πιπράκοντας; 18, 3; μισθοῦ τοῖς οἰκείοις ἀποκαθιστᾶν) *for pay* or *gain* **Jd 11** (s. ἐκχέω 3).

❷ **recognition (mostly by God) for the moral quality of an action, *recompense*** transf. sense of 1 (Pla., Rep. 10, 614a τῷ δικαίῳ παρὰ θεῶν τε καὶ ἀνθρώπων μισθοὶ καὶ δῶρα γίγνεται; cp. 2, 363d ἡγησάμενοι κάλλιστον ἀρετῆς μισθὸν μέθην αἰώνιον 'considering the finest meed for virtue an eternal spree'; Plut., Mor. 183d; Lucian, Vit. Auct. 24; Jos., Ant. 1, 183; 18, 309; LXX; Did., Gen. 20, 6).

ⓐ in affirmation of laudable conduct *reward* 2 Cl 3:3. μισθὸν ἔχειν *have a reward* **1 Cor 9:17; Mt 5:46; 6:1** (cp. habeo pretium: Horace, Ep. 1, 16, 47). τὸν μ. ἀπέχειν *have received one's reward (in full)* **Mt 6:2, 5, 16** (s. ἀπέχω 1). μισθὸν λαμβάνειν *receive one's reward* **1 Cor 3:8, 14;** cp. **Mt 10:41a** (Jos., Ant. 6, 48 μὴ λαμβάνειν τὸν προφήτην μισθόν), vs. **41b;** GJs 20:2 (codd.); AcPlCor 2:36. Also μ. ἀπολαμβάνειν 2 Cl 9:5; Hs 5, 6, 7b (GrBar 15:3; ApcEsdr 1:14 p. 25:9 Tdf.). τὸν μ. κομίσασθαι 2 Cl 11:5 (Theoph. Ant 2, 27 [p. 164, 19]). μισθὸν πλήρη ἀπολαμβάνειν *receive a full reward* **2J 8.** τὸν μ. ἀποδιδόναι *pay (out) the reward* (Wsd 10:17) 2 Cl 20:4; cp. B 11:8. ὁ τοῦ μ. ἀνταποδότης B 19:11; D 4:7 (cp. τὸν μ. τῆς ἀνταποδόσεως TestJob 14:4). τὸν μισθὸν εὑρεῖν παρὰ τῷ θεῷ *find one's reward with God* Hs 2:5 (μ. εὑρ. as Ezk 27:33). μισθὸν αἰτεῖν *ask as a reward* 2 Cl 19:1. ὁ μ. πολὺς ἐν τ. οὐρανοῖς *the reward in heaven is great* **Mt 5:12;** cp. **Lk 6:23, 35.** οὐκ ἔστιν μικρός 2 Cl 15:1. Coming w. the parousia **Rv 11:18;** B 21:3. W. the obj. gen. (μ. ἀρετῆς, Did., Gen. 174, 8) μ. δικαιοσύνης *reward for righteousness* B 20:2; D 5:2. διδόναι μισθὸν ἀντιμισθίας ὧν ἐλάβομεν *give a recompense for what we have received* 2 Cl 1:5 (δίδ. μ. as Ael. Aristid. 28, 10 K.=49 p. 494 D.; Sir 51:30). ἀπολέσαι τὸν μ. *lose one's reward* (Jos., Ant. 1, 183a) **Mt 10:42; Mk 9:41;** Hs 5, 6, 7a; ἔσται μοι εἰς μ. *it will bring me the reward* B 1:5.—τῷ ἐργαζομένῳ ὁ μ. οὐ λογίζεται κατὰ χάριν ἀλλὰ κατὰ ὀφείλημα *wages are not considered a favor when bestowed on one who works, but as something due the person* **Ro 4:4.**

ⓑ in an unfavorable sense, the *requital* that consists in punishment (trag.; Hdt. 8, 116f; Callim., Hymn. in Dian. 263; Dionys. Hal. 10, 51; 2 Macc 8:33) ὁ μισθὸς αὐτῆς (sc. τῆς ἀδικίας) κόλασις κ. θάνατος Dg 9:2. ὁ μ. τῆς πονηρίας ἔμπροσθεν αὐτοῦ *the reward of wickedness is in store for him* B 4:12.

ⓒ *reward or punishment* as the case may be **Rv 22:12;** 1 Cl 34:3 (both Is 40:10); B 21:3.—Billerb. IV 1245f (index); esp. IV 487–500: Altsynagog. Lohnlehre; KWeiss, D. Frohbotsch. Jesu über Lohn u. Vollkommenheit (Mt 20:1–16) 1927; MWagner, D. Lohnged. im Ev.: NKZ 43, '32, 106–12; 129–39; OMichel, D. Lohnged. in d. Verkünd. Jesu: ZST 9, '32, 47–54.—GWetter, D. Vergeltungsged. b. Pls 1912; FFilson, St. Paul's Conception of Recompense '32; HHeidland, D. Anrechng. des Glaubens z. Gerechtigkeit '36; GBornkamm, D. Lohnged. im NT: EvTh '44, 143–66; BReicke, The NT Conception of Reward: MGoguel Festschr. '50, 195–206; MSmith, Tannaitic Par. to the Gosp. '51, 49–73; WPesch, Der Lohngedanke in d. Lehre Jesu usw., diss. Munich '55 (lit.); GdeRu, NovT 8, '66, 202–22.—B. 814. DELG. M-M. EDNT. TW. Spicq. Sv.

μισθόω (μισθός; in our lit. [Mt] and LXX* only mid.) 1 aor. ἐμισθωσάμην; pf. μεμίσθωμαι LXX; the mid. has the mng. ***hire, engage*** for oneself (Hdt. et al.; ins, pap, LXX) w. acc. ἐργάτας

(111, 11; Jos., Bell. 3, 437, Ant. 11, 174) **Mt 20:1** (on μ. εἰς cp. Appian, Mithrid. 23 §90 ἐς τὸ ἔργον ἐμισθώσαντο), **7.**—Diod. S. 4, 20, 3 ὁ μισθωσάμενος ἐλεήσας καὶ τὸν μισθὸν ἀποδοὺς ἀπέλυσε τῶν ἔργων=the employer took pity on a woman who had just given birth, gave her her wages in full, and released her from work early. It is his goodness alone that prompts him to grant this favor; s. also Strabo 3, 4, 17.—New Docs 2, 91. DELG s.v. μισθός. M-M. TW. Spicq.

μίσθωμα, ατος, τό (μισθόω) the customary act. mng. 'contract price, rent' (Hdt. et al.; ins, LXX; Philo, Spec. Leg. 1, 280) is not found in our lit. (Ac) and the pass. ***what is rented, a rented house*** is a mng. not found outside it (even Ammonius Gramm. [100 AD] p. 93 Valck. knows nothing of it. Hence the transl. *at his own expense* [NRSV] merits attention) ἐν ἰδίῳ μισθώματι *in his own rented lodgings* **Ac 28:30** (for the idea cp. Jos., Ant. 18, 235).—HCadbury, JBL 45, 1926, 321f.—On leasing, s. New Docs 2, 91 (μισθόω). DELG s.v. μισθός. M-M. Spicq.

μισθωτός (μισθόω; actually adj. of three terminations. In our lit. only subst.: Aristoph. et al.; ins, pap, LXX; TestJob 12:4; Philo, Spec. Leg. 2, 82; 83; Jos., Bell. 1, 517), **οῦ, ὁ** ***hired man,*** of hired fishers **Mk 1:20.** Of hired shepherds **J 10:12f** (μ. as inferior: Ael. Aristid. 46 p. 206 D.; Hippocr., Ep. 16, 3; Themist. I p. 10f μ. ἀντὶ βουκόλου; Plut., Mor. 37e μ. forms a contrast to the θεῖος ἡγεμών, the λόγος).—DELG s.v. μισθός. M-M. TW. Spicq.

μῖσος, ους, τό (Aeschyl. et al.; Vett. Val. 242, 25; POslo 15, 14 [II AD] mag. text; LXX; Test12Patr; Jos., Bell. 5, 556; Just., D. 14, 2) ***hate*** ἀγάπη στραφήσεται εἰς μ. *affection will be turned into animosity* D 16:3. Personif. Hs 9, 15, 3. S. μισέω.—B. 1132. DELG s.v. μισέω. TW.

μίτρα, ας, ἡ (Hom. et al.) ***snood*** or ***turban*** as a head-covering (Pind., Hdt. et al.; Ex 29:6; Lev 8:9; Jdth 16:8; Bar 5:2; PsSol 2:21; TestLevi 8:2; EpArist 98; Philo, Mos. 2, 116) ἐν μ. ἦν ἡ κατακάλυψις αὐτῆς *her head-covering was a snood* Hv 4, 2, 1.—The μίτρα may also have been a piece of clothing worn from the throat or back of the neck (Parthenius 11, 3 τὴν μίτραν ἐνθεῖναι τὸν τράχηλον). In any case, a woman was not considered to be properly covered without it (Quint. Smyrn. 13, 110).—DELG.

Μιτυλήνη, ης, ἡ (later [SIG 344, 30: 303 BC; OGI 266, 19: III BC; Strabo, Plut.; Jos., Ant. 15, 350; 16, 20] spelling for the older [Hdt., X., ins—Meisterhans[3]-Schw. p. 29] Μυτιλήνη. Cp. B-D-F §42, 3; Mlt-H. 72; 79) ***Mitylene,*** chief city of the island of Lesbos, in the Aegean Sea off the northwest coast of Asia Minor **Ac 20:14.**—M-M.

Μιχαήλ, ὁ indecl. (מִיכָאֵל) ***Michael,*** archangel (Da 12:1; 10:13, 21; pseudepigr.; ISyriaW 2263; 2637b; ins fr. Asia Minor [Ramsay, CB I/2, 541 no. 404, p. 741 no. 678]; PGM 1, 301; 2, 158; 3, 148; 4, 1815 and 2356; 7, 257; 22b, 29 τῷ μεγάλῳ πατρὶ Ὀσίριδι Μιχαήλ) **Jd 9; Rv 12:7** (M. as ἀρχιστρατηγός PGM 13, 928. On his fighting w. the dragon s. PGM 4, 2769ff); Hs 8, 3, 3. In Israelite tradition M. was the special patron and protector of Israel (Da 12:1).—Bousset, Rel.[3] 325ff; Dssm., LO 396ff [LAE 456f]; WLueken, Der Erzengel M. 1898; JRohland, Der Erzengel M. '77; RAC V 243-51; BHHW II 1212f. —M-M.

μνᾶ, μνᾶς, ἡ (Semitic loanw. [cp. Akkadian Manû: A1 in CAD X 219], as early as Attic wr.; ins, pap, LXX; Jos., Ant. 7, 189; 14, 106; TestJos 16:4) ***mina,*** a Gk. monetary unit=100 drachmas (on purchasing power s. δραχμή) **Lk 19:13, 16, 18, 20, 24f** (on the parable s. PJoüon, RSR 29, '40, 489–94).—Kl. Pauly III 1368f; BHHW II 1166–69. Lit. s.v. ἀργύριον 2c.

μνάομαι (fr. μιμνήσκω in the sense 'woo' [so DELG and Frisk s.v. the latter, and LfgrE s.v. μνάομαι] via special development of the primary sense of μνάομαι 'be mindful of', which does not appear in our lit.; for other derivations s. lit. cited in Frisk II 240f and LfgrE III 232; cp. Hom. μνηστήρ 'suitor'; since Hom., also Philo) ***woo, court for one's bride*** pf. ptc. μεμνησμένη of the woman *engaged, betrothed* **Lk 1:27** D.

Μνάσων, ωνος, ὁ (Anth. Pal.; Lucian; GDI 2580, 25 [Delphi]; SIG 585: 43, 47, 77, 81, 85, 90, 94, 234, 238 [197 BC]; PHib 41, 3 [ca. 261 BC]; Sb 3199) ***Mnason,*** a Christian fr. Cyprus **Ac 21:16** (Μνασέας, father of Zeno the Stoic, was also fr. Cyprus; Κυπρ. I p. 190 no. 4 a Gk. ins from Cyprus contains the name Μνασίας. In Just., D. 85, 6 one of the partners in dialogue bears the name Μνασέας).—HCadbury, Amicitiae Corolla (for RHarris) '33, 51–53; Hemer, Acts 237.—LGPN I. M-M.

μνεία, ας, ἡ (μνάομαι in the sense 'be mindful of' [s. L-S-J-M μνάομαι I]; Soph. et al.; ins, pap, LXX, 8:5; OdeSol; Test Abr A 4 p. 81, 6 [Stone p. 10]; TestNapht 8:5; EpArist).

❶ ***remembrance, memory*** w. obj. gen. τινός *of someone* (OdeSol 11:22; SibOr 5, 486) **Ro 12:13 v.l.;** *of someth.* (SIG 577, 3; Wsd 5:14; Bar 4:27) εἴ τίς ἐστιν ἀγαθοῦ μ. *if there is any remembrance of what is good* B 21:7. μνείαν ἔχειν τινός *think of someone* (Soph., El. 384 al.) ἔχετε μνείαν ἡμῶν ἀγαθὴν πάντοτε *you always think kindly of us* **1 Th 3:6.** ἀδιάλειπτον ἔχω τὴν περὶ σοῦ μ. *I remember you constantly* **2 Ti 1:3.** εἰς μ. ἔρχεταί τινι as in Lat. in mentem venit alicui *comes to someone's recollection* Hv 3, 7, 3.

❷ ***mention*** μνείαν ποιεῖσθαί τινος *mention someone* (Pla., Phdr. 254; Diog. L. 8, 2, 66; IPriene 50, 10; PEdg 14 [=Sb 6720], 3 [256 BC]; UPZ 59, 6; cp. Ps 110:4) in our lit. only of mentioning in prayer (BGU 632, 5 μνείαν σου ποιούμενος παρὰ τοῖς ἐνθάδε θεοῖς; Kaibel 983, 2ff [79 BC] Δημήτριος ἥκω πρὸς μεγάλην Ἶσιν θεάν, μνείαν ἐπ' ἀγαθῷ τ. γονέων ποιούμενος; not in prayer Iren. 1, 9, 2 [Harv. I 83, 2]) **Ro 1:9; 1 Th 1:2 v.l.; Phlm 4.** The gen. is supplied fr. the context **Eph 1:16; 1 Th 1:2.** ἐπὶ πάσῃ τῇ μ. ὑμῶν *as often as I make mention of you* (in prayer) **Phil 1:3.** ἡ πρὸς θεὸν μ. *mention* (in prayer) *before God* (though *remembrance* is also prob. here) 1 Cl 56:1.—DELG s.v. μιμνήσκω 10. M-M. TW. Spicq.

μνῆμα, ατος, τό (μνάομαι [in sense of 'be mindful of, remember'], μιμνήσκω) lit. a 'sign of remembrance', esp. for the dead (Hom. et al.), then gener. ***grave, tomb*** (Hdt., Pla. et al.; SIG 1221; 1237, 3; BGU 1024 IV, 23; LXX; TestSim 8:3; ParJer 9:32; Philo; Jos., Ant. 7, 19; 8, 240; Just., D. 10, 82 [Mt 28:13]) **Mk 16:2 v.l.; Lk 24:1** (μνημεῖον v.l.); **Ac 2:29** (David's μ. Jos., Ant. 7, 393); GPt 8:30–32; 11:44; 12:50, 52. κατατιθέναι ἐν μ. *lay in a tomb* **Mk 15:46a v.l.;** cp. **Ac 7:16.** τιθέναι ἐν μ. λαξευτῷ *lay in a rock-hewn tomb* **Lk 23:53.** τιθέναι εἰς μνῆμα **Rv 11:9** (for the idea s. Jos., Bell. 4, 317). Dwelling-place of possessed pers. **Mk 5:3, 5; Lk 8:27.**—On function of the μ. s. SEG XL, no. 1650 w. reff.—M-M. TW.—S. the foll. entry.

μνημεῖον, ου, τό (s. μνῆμα) lit. 'token of remembrance' (Pind. et al.; Philo, Joseph.), esp. for the dead (Eur., Iph. T. 702; 821; Thu. 1, 138, 5; X., Hell. 2, 4, 17; 3, 2, 15; Pla., Rep. 3, 414a).

❶ ***monument, memorial*** (cp. Jos., Ant. 5, 119 μν. καὶ τάφος; HHäusle, Das Denkmal als Garant des Nachruhms [Zetemata 25] 1980 [ins; on the function of a monument s. pp. 29–40]):

οἰκοδομεῖτε τ. μνημεῖα τῶν προφητῶν **Lk 11:47** (JJeremias, Heiligengräber in Jesu Umwelt '58) is prob. to be understood in this sense (for μ. οἰκοδομεῖν cp. Jos., Ant. 13, 211). But μ. in our lit. usu. has the sense

❷ ***grave, tomb*** (SIG 1229, 4; 1232; 1234; 1242; 1244; PFlor 9, 10; Gen 23:6, 9; Is 22:16 al.; TestSol 17:2; ParJer; ApcEsdr 4:36 p. 29, 14 Tdf.; ApcMos 42; AscIs 3:13; Jos., Ant. 1, 237; 18, 108; Mel., P. 78, 569; 90, 673); of tombs in caves, etc. (s. PThomsen, Grab: Reallex. d. Vorgesch. IV 2, 473ff), into which a person can enter (s. ParJer 7:1; **Mk 16:5; J 20:6) Mt 23:29; 27:52f** (JBlinzler, ThGl 35, '43, 91–93.—Diod. S. 13, 86, 3: when the Carthaginians besieging Acragas destroyed some tombs lying outside the walls, 'throughout the night ghosts of the dead appeared' διὰ νυκτὸς εἴδωλα φαίνεσθαι τῶν τετελευτηκότων.—On an earthquake that opens the graves and frees those inside s. Ps.-Ael. Aristid. 25, 20f K.=43 p. 804 D.: μνήματα ἀνερρήγνυτο . . . τὰ μνήματα ἀνερρίπτει τοὺς κειμένους. EFascher, Die Auferweckung der Heiligen Mt 27:51–53, '51), vs. **60b; 28:8; Mk 15:46ab; 16:2, 3, 5, 8; Lk 23:55; 24:1 v.l., 2, 9, 12, 22, 24; J 11:17, 31** (Aesop, Fab. 109 H. [cp. 299 H-H.] γυνὴ ἀπιοῦσα πρὸς τὸ μνημεῖον ἐθρήνει), **38; 12:17; 19:42; 20:1–4, 6, 8, 11ab;** GPt 9:34; 12:51, 53 (lit. on the Holy Sepulcher: RGG[3] II 1816–18; also FBraun, La Sépulture de Jésu '37; RSmith, The Tomb of Jesus, BA 30, '67, 74–90). τιθέναι εἰς μ. *place in the tomb* **Ac 13:29.** Also τιθέναι ἐν τῷ μ. **Mt 27:60a; Mk 6:29; 15:46a.** μ. καινόν **Mt 27:60a; J 19:41;** οἱ ἐν τοῖς μ. *those who are in their tombs* **5:28.** The haunt of possessed persons **Mt 8:28; Mk 5:2** (acc. to Diog. L. 9, 38 Democritus sought solitude among the graves). Graves were somet. not recognizable as such fr. their outward appearance **Lk 11:44;** s. ἄδηλος 1.—DELG s.v. μιμνήσκω 5. M-M. TW.

μνήμη, ης, ἡ (trag.+) prim. 'remembrance, memory'.—❶ **a recollection that one has of events, opp. of ignoring by forgetting, *recollection, memory,*** w. gen. *of someth.* (EpArist 159; Just., D. 19, 6 al.) τ. μνήμην τινὸς ποιεῖσθαι *recall someth. to mind* **2 Pt 1:15** (PFay 19, 10 [11 AD] τῶν πραγμάτων μνήμην ποιεῖσθαι='hold the things in remembrance'. Likew. schol. on Apollon. Rhod. 4, 839–41a.—The mng. of μ. ποιεῖσθαι, quotable Hdt. et al.; Jos., Ant. 18, 65='make mention' is scarcely applicable here). εἰς τὴν τῶν προηθληκότων μ. *in memory of those who have already contested* MPol 18:2.

❷ **the state of commemorating, *remembrance, memorial*** (Diod. S. 5, 73, 1 and 23, 15, 2 αἰώνιον μνήμην παρὰ πᾶσιν ἀνθρώποις; testament of Epicurus in Diog. L. 10, 18: a memorial meal εἰς τὴν ἡμῶν μνήμην; ΕΛΛΗΝΙΚΑ 1, 1928, p. 18, 18 festivals are arranged εἰς μνήμην Εὐρυκλέους εὐεργέτου; Jos., Ant. 13, 63) pl. ἡ τρυφὴ καὶ ἀπάτη μνήμας οὐκ ἔχει=*have no remembrance = are not long remembered* (like Lat. memoriam non habet) Hs 6, 5, 3; μνήμας μεγάλας ἔχειν *have a lasting remembrance = live long in remembrance* ibid. (cp. Proverbia Aesopi 111 P. μνήμην ἔχειν; EpArist 279).—DELG s.v. μιμνήσκω 6. M-M. TW. Spicq. Sv.

μνημονεύω (μνήμων 'mindful') impf. ἐμνημόνευον; fut. μνημονεύσω LXX; 1 aor. ἐμνημόνευσα (Hdt.+).

❶ ***remember, keep in mind, think of,*** also—w. focus on dramatic aspect of remembrance—***mention.***—ⓐ w. gen. (Pla., Theaet. 191d; Philod., De Piet. 94; Diod. S. 1, 21, 8; Lucian, Dial. Deor. 4, 7; SIG 284, 8; 620, 25; PSI 502, 2; 651, 2 [III BC]; Wsd 2:4; Tob 4:5, 19 BA; Sus 9 Theod.; EpArist 157; PsSol 3:3; 5:16), of pers.: **Lk 17:32; Hb 13:7;** B 21:7; MPol 8:1; IEph 12:2; ISm 5:3; Hm 4, 1, 1. Of mention in prayer (Heidelb. Pap.-Sammlung I ed. Deissmann 1905, no. 6, 15 παρακαλῶ οὖν, δέσποτα, ἵνα μνημονεύῃς μοι [μου?] εἰς τ. ἁγίας σου εὐχάς) IEph 21:1; IMg 14:1.—W. the connotation of solicitude (cp. 1 Macc 12:11) μ. τῶν πτωχῶν *remember the poor* **Gal 2:10.**—W. gen. of the thing (Arrian, Peripl. 16, 3 πόλεως ἐμνημόνευσεν; ParJer 7:31; ApcEsdr 7:9; Jos., Ant. 2, 162; 6, 93 al.) τοῦ λόγου **J 15:20;** pl. **Ac 20:35.** ὧν εἶπεν ὁ κύριος Pol 2:3. τῶν τοῦ κυρίου ἐνταλμάτων 2 Cl 17:3. τῶν ἐντολῶν αὐτοῦ Hs 1:7. τῆς τρυφῆς 6, 5, 4.—**J 16:4, 21.**—μ. μου τῶν δεσμῶν *remember my bonds* **Col 4:18.** Perh. mention or remembering in prayer is meant here, as in ὑμῶν τοῦ ἔργου τῆς πίστεως *your work of faith* **1 Th 1:3** (MDibelius, Hdb., exc. ad loc.). τῆς ἐν Συρίᾳ ἐκκλησίας ITr 13:1; IRo 9:1.—εἰ ἐκείνης (i.e. πατρίδος) ἐμνημόνευον *if they were thinking of* i.e. *meant* or *had that* (the earthly one) *in mind* **Hb 11:15.**

ⓑ w. acc. (Hdt. 1, 36; X., An. 4, 3, 2, also Herodian 6, 1, 7; BGU 1024 V, 20; Jdth 13:19; 2 Macc 9:21) of pers.: Ἰησοῦν Χριστὸν ἐγηγερμένον **2 Ti 2:8.** Pass. of Polycarp *he is especially remembered by everyone* MPol 19:1. W. acc. of thing (Philo, Leg. All. 1, 55; Tat. 33, 4) τοὺς πέντε ἄρτους **Mt 16:9.** τὸν κόπον ἡμῶν **1 Th 2:9.** τὰ προγεγραμμένα Hv 4, 3, 6. Of God: ἐμνημόνευσεν τὰ ἀδικήματα αὐτῆς *God has remembered her wicked deeds* to punish them **Rv 18:5.**

ⓒ foll. by περί τινος **Hb 11:22.**—W. ὅτι foll. (Pla., Rep. 480a) **Ac 20:31; Eph 2:11; 2 Th 2:5.** Foll. by indirect quest. (PStras 41, 40 οὐ μνημονεύω δέ, τί ἐν τῇ μεσειτίᾳ ἐγένετο) **Rv 2:5; 3:3.** W. temporal clause foll.: **Mk 8:18.**

❷ ***retain in one's memory*** (PsSol 6:11 τὸ ὄνομα κυρίου; like Lat. memoria tenere aliquid) w. acc. of thing Hv 1, 3, 3a; 2, 1, 3. τὰ ἔσχατα ῥήματα 1, 3, 3b. ὅσα Papias (2:3, 15).—DELG s.v. μιμνήσκω 4. M-M. TW. Spicq.

μνημοσύνη, ης, ἡ (μνήμων 'mindful'; Hom. et al.) ***memory*** εἰς μνημοσύνην αὐτοῦ *in memory of him* GPt 12:54.—DELG s.v. μιμνήσκω 4.

μνημόσυνον, ου, τό (μνήμων 'mindful'; Hdt. et al.; Kaibel 367, 2; pap, LXX, En; TestSol 26:8 H; TestJos 7:5; TestJob)

❶ **the mental faculty of remembering, *memory:*** ἔγγραφοι ἐγένοντο ἐν τῷ μ. αὐτοῦ *they were inscribed in God's memory* 1 Cl 45:8.

❷ **the state of bearing in mind, *memory*** w. obj. gen. (oft. LXX) εἰς μ. τινος *in memory of someone* **Mt 26:13; Mk 14:9** (JJeremias, ZNW 44, '52/53, 103–7: God's 'eschatological remembrance'). ἐξολεθρεῦσαι ἐκ γῆς τὸ μ. αὐτῶν *root out the memory of them from the earth* 1 Cl 22:6; μήποτε . . . τὸ μ. [ὑμῶν] ἀπόληται *lest . . . you be lost to memory* AcPl Ha 1, 22 (Ps 33:17; cp. Sir 10:17; TestJos 7:5).

❸ **an offering that presents a worshiper to God, *a memorial offering*** (=אַזְכָּרָה Lev 2:2, 9, 16; 5:12; cp. Sir 35:6; 38:11; 45:16) fig. αἱ προσευχαί σου ἀνέβησαν εἰς μνημόσυνον ἔμπροσθεν τ. θεοῦ **Ac 10:4** (the receipt thereof is expressed vs. 31 αἱ ἐλεημοσύναι σου ἐμνήσθησαν).—DELG s.v. μιμνήσκω 4. M-M. Spicq.

μνησικακέω (μιμνήσκω, κακός) fut. μνησικακήσω, 1 aor. ἐμνησικάκησα (Hdt.+; ins, LXX; Test12Patr; Jos., Bell. 4, 94 al.) **to remember some injury with resentment, *remember evil, bear malice, bear a grudge*** τινί *against someone* (Thu. 8, 73; Lysias 30, 9; Philo, Virt. 106, De Jos. 17; Jos., Ant. 1, 323) B 19:4; Hv 2, 3, 1; s 9, 23, 4b. τινί τι: τοῖς ἐξομολογουμένοις τὰς ἁμαρτίας αὐτῶν *bear a grudge against those who have confessed their sins,* or perh. *cast up their sins to those who confess them* 9, 23, 4a (cp. Aristoph., Nub. 999 μ. τὴν ἡλικίαν 'cast his age in his teeth'). ἕκαστος ὑμῶν κατὰ τοῦ πλησίον κακίαν μὴ μνησικακείτω *let no one of you hold a grudge against his* *neighbor* B 2:8 (Zech 7:10). Abs., w. pers. obj. to be supplied *bear a grudge, be resentful* (Diod. S. 31, 8, 2; Lucian, Prom. 8) D 2:3; Dg 9:2. οἱ ἄνθρωποι οἱ μνησικακοῦντες *people who hold a grudge* Hm 9:3.—DELG s.v. μιμνήσκω 11.

μνησικακία, ας, ἡ (μνησικακέω; Plut., Mor. 860a; Appian, Ital. fgm. 7; Philo, De Jos. 261; Jos., Ant. 16, 292) ***bearing a grudge, vengefulness*** Hm 8:3 and 10; causing death Hv 2, 3, 1.—DELG s.v. μιμνήσκω 11.

μνησίκακος, ον (μνησικακέω; Aristot. et al.; Pr 12:28; TestZeb 8:6) ***vengeful*** μ. γίνεσθαι Hs 9, 23, 3.—DELG s.v. μιμνήσκω 11.

μνηστεύω fut. mid. μνηστεύσομαι LXX; pf. 3 sg. μεμνήστευται Dt 20:7. Pass.: 1 aor. ptc. fem. μνηστευθεῖσα; pf. ἐμνηστευμένη, or μεμνηστευμένη (B-D-F §68; Mlt-H. 193) (Hom. et al.; Diod. S. 4, 37, 4; 5; LXX; JosAs 1:9 [ἐμνηστεύοντο αὐτήν 'courted her']; Jos., C. Ap. 2, 200; the mid. PFlo 36, 4) ***woo and win, betroth*** pass. *be betrothed, become engaged* (Dt 22:25, 27f) τινί *to someone* (Artem. 2, 12 p. 101, 4 H. v.l.; Dt 22:23; Jos., Bell. 1, 508) Mary **Mt 1:16 v.l.** (JNolland, CBQ 58, '96, 665–73), **18; Lk 1:27; 2:5;** GJs 19:1.—DELG s.v. μιμνήσκω 1. M-M. Spicq.

μογγιλάλος, ον (μογγός 'with a hoarse, hollow voice', λαλέω; Ptolem., Apotel. 3, 13, 3 p. 151, 2 Boll-B.; Georg. Mon. 492, 14 de Boor [1892]; Is 35:6 v.l. Ziegler; s. Thackeray p. 120f.—B-D-F §34, 6; Mlt-H. 106) ***speaking in a hoarse/hollow voice*** **Mk 7:32 v.l.**—DELG s.v. μογγός. M-M.

μογιλάλος, ον (μόγις, λαλέω; on the form s. B-D-F §34, 6; 119, 5; Rob. 169; 210)

❶ ***speaking with difficulty, having an impediment in one's speech*** (Aëtius 8, 38; schol. on Lucian, p. 68, 5 Rabe; Anecd. Gr. I p. 100, 22; s. JBidez et FCumont, Les mages hellénisés II '38 p. 334, 8 μογιλάλοι with v.l. μογγιλάλοι); this mng. for **Mk 7:32** is supported by vs. 35 ἐλάλει ὀρθῶς (s. AWeatherhead, ET 23, 1912, 381).

❷ ***mute, unable to articulate*** (Vett. Val. 73, 12; POxy 465, 228; Is 35:6;—56:10 Aq.; Ex 4:11 Aq., Sym., Theod.); the ancient versions take **Mk 7:32, 33 v.l.** in this sense.—DELG s.v. μόγος. M-M.

μόγις adv. (Hom. et al.; Diod. S.; Epict.; Polemo Soph., Decl. 2, 3; 15; Lucian; PMagd 11, 6 [221 BC]; POxy 298, 19 [I AD]; PLips 105, 10; PSI 49, 2; Wsd 9:16 v.l.; 3 Macc 7:6; Philo, In Flacc. 113 v.l.; Jos., Ant. 8, 130; 16, 345; Tat. 39, 1.—B-D-F §33; Rob. 296) ***scarcely, with difficulty*** **Lk 9:39; Ac 14:18** D; **Ro 5:7 v.l.** (s. also μόλις).—**Lk 23:53** D.—DELG s.v. μόγος. M-M. TW.

μόδιος, ίου, ὁ (Lat. loanw. [modius]: Dinarchus 1, 43 [?]; Dionys. Hal. 12, 1; Epict. 1, 17, 7; 9; Plut., Demetr. 33, 6; ins [OGI index]; PThéad 32, 25; PGen 62, 17; GrBar 6:7; Jos., Ant. 9, 85; 14, 28; 206. Loanw. in rabb.) a grain measure containing 16 sextarii = about 8.75 liters, almost one peck, ***a peck measure*** **Mt 5:15; Mk 4:21; Lk 11:33** (a vessel used to hide a light, as Judg 7:16 [ὑδρίας]; Jos., Ant 5, 223.—On the figure, ADupont-Sommer, Note archéol. sur le prov. évang.: mettre la lampe sous le boisseau = Mél. Syr. à MRDussaud II '39, 789–94; JJeremias, ZNW 39, '41, 237–40 Pauly-W. III 1775f; Hultsch, Metrologie² 121ff).—M-M.

μοῖρα, ας, ἡ (μείρομαι 'receive one's portion'; Hom. et al.; pap, TestSol; SibOr 3, 121 al.; Philo; Jos., Bell. 4, 86, Ant. 17, 303; Just.; Tat. 7:1 ['portion']) ***lot (in life)*** (PLips 40 II, 26) ApcPt fgm. 2 p. 12, 19.—LfgrE s.v. (lit.). DELG s.v. μείρομαι.

μοιχαλίς, ίδος, ἡ (=μοιχάς [Vett. Val. 104, 11], the older fem. of μοιχός; Aëtius [100 AD]: Dox. Gr. 301a, 14; Heliod. 8, 9; Procop., Anecd. 1, 36; Syntipas p. 23, 6 al. [Phryn. 452 Lob.]; Cat. Cod. Astr. VII p. 109, 6; 20; VIII/1 p. 264, 29; VIII/4 p. 146, 26; PCairMasp 97 II, 42; Suda III p. 421, 10; LXX; TestLevi 14:6; ApcSed 6:4 [masc.]; Ar. 11:3; μοιχοὶ καὶ μοιχαλίδες καὶ ψευδοπροφῆται Hippol., Ref. 9, 15, 3) ***adulteress***

ⓐ lit. **Ro 7:3ab** (the same case sim. described in Achilles Tat. 8, 10, 11f). ὀφθαλμοὶ μεστοὶ μοιχαλίδος *eyes that are full of (desire for) an adulteress* i.e. always looking for a woman with whom to commit adultery **2 Pt 2:14** (on the expr. s. μεστός 2b; cp. Timaeus Hist. [IV BC] in Περὶ ὕψους 4, 5 of a moral man ἐν ὀφθαλμοῖς κόρας, μὴ πόρνας ἔχων=having girls, not call-girls, in his eyes; Plut., Mor. 528e).

ⓑ In bold imagery that moves beyond apparent gender specificity μοιχαλίδες *adulteresses* (*unfaithful creatures* REB et al.) **Js 4:4.** The v.l. μοιχοὶ καὶ μοιχαλίδες suggests a failure to take account of the author's reminiscence of usage found in Hosea (3:1), in which God's relation to Israel is depicted as a marriage, and any beclouding of it becomes adultery (cp. Jer 3:9; 9:1; Ezk 16:32ff, esp. vs. 38; μοιχαλίς used of Adam ApcSed 6:4; s. W-S. §28, 2b). As adj. *adulterous, unfaithful*γενεὰ μοιχαλίς **Mt 12:39; 16:4; Mk 8:38.**—DELG s.v. μοιχός. M-M. TW.

μοιχάω (X. et al.: JWackernagel, Hellenistica 1907, 7ff; B-D-F §101 p. 46f) 'cause to commit adultery', in our lit. (as well as LXX; PsSol 8:10) only pass.

❶ ***be caused to commit adultery, be an adulterer/adulteress, commit adultery***—ⓐ of a woman (Ezk 16:32) ποιεῖ αὐτὴν μοιχᾶσθαι (the man who divorces his wife) *causes her to commit adultery* (if she contracts a new marriage) **Mt 5:32a v.l.** αὐτὴ μοιχᾶται *she commits adultery* **Mk 10:12.** But also

ⓑ of a man (PsSol 8, 10), who marries a divorced woman **Mt 5:32b; 19:9 v.l.** or who marries again after divorcing his wife **19:9;** Hm 4, 1, 6. μοιχᾶται ἐπ᾽ αὐτήν *commits adultery against her* (his first wife) **Mk 10:11** (NTurner, Bible Translator 7, '56, 151f: associates w. Jer 5:9); if understood as a Semitism (Rehkopf §233, 2 note 4; s. BSchaller, in Festschr. JJeremias, '70, 239ff: in Aramaic the corresponding verb w. prep. is used in the sense of 'with', not 'against'), this phrase can be rendered *commits adultery with her* (the second wife).

ⓒ of a man or woman 2 Cl 4:3.

❷ **be guilty of infidelity in a transcendent relationship, *be unfaithful,*** ὃς ἂν τὰ ὁμοιώματα ποιῇ τοῖς ἔθνεσιν, μοιχᾶται *whoever acts as the gentiles do* (i.e. polytheists with their image-worship: NBrox, Der Hirt des Hermas '91, 208), *commits adultery* (and it cannot be expected of the other marriage-partner to maintain marital relations) Hm 4, 1, 9.—DELG s.v. μοιχός. M-M. s.v. μοιχάομαι. TW.

μοιχεία, ας, ἡ (μοιχεύω; Andocides et al.; Heraclit. Sto. 69 p. 89, 15; PMich 148 I, 8; LXX; TestSol 1:2 D; GrBar; Philo; Jos., Ant. 16, 340 al.; apolog.; τὴν μ. τῆς παρθένου καὶ τοῦ Πανθήρα Orig., C. Cels. I, 32, 6) ***adultery*** lit. Hm 4, 1, 5 and 9; ApcPt 9:24. W. other sins (Hos 4:2; Theoph. Ant. 2, 34 [p. 186, 9]) **Gal 5:19 v.l.;** 1 Cl 30:1; 2 Cl 6:4; B 20:1; D 5:1; Hm 8:3. Pl. (as in D 5:1 above) denoting separate acts (Pla., Rep. 4, 443a, Leg. 8, 839a; PTebt 276, 16 πορνεῖαι καὶ μοιχεῖαι; GrBar; Philo, Spec. Leg. 2, 13; Jos., Bell. 5, 402; Just., D. 93, 1; Mel., P. 50, 362.—B-D-F §142; W-S. §27, 4d; s. Rob. 408) *adulterous acts* **Mt 15:19=Mk 7:22** (Did., Gen. 226, 21; Theoph. Ant. 1, 14 [p. 92, 6]; in a list of vices also Plut., Mor. 1050d); cp. D 3:3; AcPl Ha

1, 12. Cp. καταλαμβάνειν ἐπὶ μοιχείᾳ *catch in the act of adultery* **J 8:3** (Plut., Mor. 291f; on the 'adulterous woman' s. REisler, ZNW 22, 1923, 305–7; KBornhäuser, NKZ 37, 1926, 353–63; EBishop, JTS 35, '34, 40–45; JJeremias, ZNW 43, '51, 148f: a temptation story, cp. Mk 12:13–17; TManson, ZNW 44, '52/53, 255f; FSchilling, ATR 37, '55, 91–106; UBecker, Jesus u. die Ehebrecherin '63; JDerrett, Law in the NT, '70, 156–87; JMcDonald, NTS 41, '95, 415–27). Also εὑρίσκειν ἐν μ. Hm 4, 1, 4.—B. 1456; RAC IV 666–77. DELG s.v. μοιχός. M-M. TW. Sv.

μοιχεύω fut. μοιχεύσω; 1 aor. ἐμοίχευσα. Pass.: 1 aor. pass. 3 sg. ἐμοιχεύθη Sir 23:23; inf. μοιχευθῆναι (Xenophanes, Hecataeus Mil., Aristoph., X. et al.; pap [s. bβ], LXX; TestSol 1:1f D; TestAbr B; Test12Patr; Philo; Jos., Ant. 16, 296 al.; Ar.; Just.; Tat., Orig.—HBogner, Was heisst μ.?: Her 76, '41, 318–20) ***commit adultery.***

ⓐ of both sexes, w. ref. to the Ten Commandments (Ex 20:13; Dt 5:17): **Mt 5:27; 19:18; Mk 10:19; Lk 18:20; Ro 13:9; Js 2:11ab.** One or more of these pass. may refer to the man alone, as below.

ⓑ of the man only—**α.** abs.: **Lk 16:18ab; Ro 2:22** (μὴ μοιχεύειν as Jos., Ant. 3, 92); B 19:4; D 2:2.

β. w. obj. τινά (γυναῖκα) *commit adultery w. someone* (Aristoph., Av. 558; Pla., Rep. 2, 360b; Lucian, Dial. Deor. 6, 3; Aristaenet., Ep. 1, 20; PSI 158, 45; TestAbr B 12 p. 116, 14 [Stone p. 80]; Ar. 9, 6; Just., A I, 5, 2; Tat. 34, 2; Hippol., Ref. 5, 23, 13. Cp. Lev 20:10) **Mt 5:28** (cp. Epict. 2, 18, 15; Sextus 233). This explains the use of the passive in the case of a woman (Chariton 1, 4, 6 μοιχευομένην τὴν γυναῖκα; Achilles Tat. 6, 9, 7; Sir 23:23; Philo, Decal. 124; Jos., Ant. 7, 131) ποιεῖ αὐτὴν μοιχευθῆναι *he causes her to commit adultery* (if she contracts a subsequent marriage) **Mt 5:32; 19:9 v.l.** ἡ γυνὴ κατείληπται μοιχευομένη **J 8:4** (JMcDonald, NTS 41, '95, 415–27).

γ. οἱ μοιχεύοντες μετ' αὐτῆς **Rv 2:22** is at least on the way to a fig. mng. (cp. Jer 3:9).—RCharles, The Teaching of the NT on Divorce 1921, 91ff; FDölger, Christl. u. hdn, Ächtung des Ehebr. in d. Kultsatzung: AC III 132–48; GDelling, RAC IV, '59, 666–80; JFitzmyer, Theological Studies 37, '76, 197–226 (Mt).—DELG s.v. μοιχός. M-M. EDNT. TW. Sv.

μοιχός, οῦ, ὁ (since Hipponax [VI BC] 67 D.[3]; Soph.; POxy 1160, 24ff [s. M-M s.v.]; BGU 1024 III, 12; LXX; Test12Patr, Philo, apolog. exc. Mel.; Hippol., Did., Theoph. Ant.)

❶ **one who is unfaithful to a spouse, *adulterer,*** in the sing. the referent is male, but in generic contexts females may be included; lit., w. πόρνος (Just., A II, 2, 16) **Hb 13:4.** W. φθορεύς (cp. Philo, Spec. Leg. 4, 89; Ath. 34:1 [w. παιδερασταί]) B 10:7. W. other sinners (TestLevi 17:11; Ar. 8, 2) **Lk 18:11; 1 Cor 6:9;** Hs 6, 5, 5. Parallel w. κλέπτης 1 Cl 35:8 (Ps 49:18).

❷ **one who is unfaithful to God, *adulterer,*** fig. ext. of 1; w. μοιχαλίς (q.v. b) **Js 4:4 v.l.** S. μοιχάω.—DELG. M-M. EDNT. TW.

μόλιβος, ου, ὁ (Hom.+; PTebt 121, 52; 84; LXX; TestAbr A 20 p. 103, 6f [μολύβδου; Stone p. 54]; GrBar 5:3 'leaden missile'; Jos., Bell. 6, 278, Ant. 15, 398. On the var. forms and spellings s. Thackeray 96; 116) ***lead,*** because of its low melting point a symbol of the earth, destroyed in the fire of the last judgment 2 Cl 16:3.—DELG s.v. μόλυβδος.

μόλις (=Hom. μόγις, fr. μόγος 'toil') adv. 'scarcely' trag., Thu.+; PTebt 19, 10 [114 BC]; PRyl 113, 27; POxy 1117, 19; PGiss 4, 15; LXX; TestAbr A 11 p. 90, 12 [Stone p. 28]; TestJob, EpArist, Philo, Joseph.; Tat. 39, 1 v.l.—B-D-F §33; Rob. 296; s. μόγις).

❶ **pert. to being hard to accomplish, *with difficulty*** (Lycophron vs. 757; Appian, Liby. 3 §14, Bell. Civ. 1, 8 §33; 1, 77 §351; Ael. Aristid. 48, 43 K.=24 p. 476 D.; Wsd 9:16=μετὰ πόνου; Sir 29:6; Philo, Op. M. 80; Jos., Bell. 1, 149) **Lk 9:39 v.l.; Ac 14:18; 23:29 v.l.; 27:7f, 16; 1 Pt 4:18** (Pr 11:31; cp. Artem. 1, 2 p. 4, 13 μόλις ἐσώθη).

❷ **pert. to rarity on a scale of occurrences, *not readily, only rarely*** (Nicander, Ther. 281; Synes., Prov. 1, 11 p. 101d: μόλις [seldom, scarcely ever] do virtue and good fortune meet; Sir 21:20; 26:29; 32:7; Jos., C. Ap. 1, 66, Vi. 173) **Ro 5:7;** another probability here is

❸ **pert. to rarity on a scale of expectation, *ordinarily not*** (Phlegon: 257 fgm. 36, 1; 3 Jac.; Achilles Tat. 2, 26, 1) or ***scarcely*** (Appian, Bell. Civ. 3, 53 §218 ὀλίγοι μόλις=scarcely a few).—DELG. M-M. TW.

Μόλοχ, ὁ (Am 5:26 [Swete] and TestSol 26:2, 4f; s. Λάμεχ and s. W-S. §6, 8b; other edd. Μολόχ—מֶלֶךְ, w. the vowels of בֹּשֶׁת) indecl. ***Moloch,*** the Canaanite-Phoenician god of sky and sun (Baudissin, RE XIII 269ff) **Ac 7:43** in a quot. fr. Am 5:26, where the LXX renders the words סִכּוּת מַלְכְּכֶם by τὴν σκηνὴν τοῦ Μολόχ (סֻכַּת מֶלֶךְ).—OEissfeldt, Molk als Opferbegriff im Punischen u. Hebr. u. d. Ende des Gottes Moloch '35 (on this WvSoden, TLZ 61, '36, 45f).

μολύνω fut. μολυνῶ SSol 5:3; 1 aor. ἐμόλυνα. Pass.: aor. ἐμολύνθην; pf. ptc. μεμολυμμένος or μεμολυσμένος LXX ('stain, defile' Aristoph., Pla. et al.; PSI 1160, 6 [30 BC]; LXX; Test12Patr; GrBar).

❶ **to cause someth. to become dirty or soiled, *stain, soil*** (Lucian, Anach. 1; Gen 37:31; SSol 5:3) μεμολυ[μμένος] *unclean, unwashed,* with the result of not being pure, of one who comes without proper cleansing to a holy site that is otherwise pure (καθαρός) Ox 840, 16. Unsoiled garments as symbol of a spotless life ἃ οὐκ ἐμόλυναν τὰ ἱμάτια αὐτῶν **Rv 3:4.**

❷ **to cause someth. to be ritually impure, *defile*** fig. ext. of 1 (Epict. 2, 8, 13; 2, 9, 17; Porphyr., Abst. 1, 42; Synes., Dreams 10 p. 142d ἀθέων τῶν μολυνάντων τὸ ἐν αὐτοῖς θεῖον; Sir 21:28; Jer 23:11; TestAsh 4:4 τὴν ψυχήν; Orig., C. Cels. 7, 64, 27 τὴν περὶ τοῦ θεοῦ τῶν ὅλων ὑπόληψιν; Hippol., Ref. 9, 23, 4 συνείδησιν ἐπὶ ἀνόμῳ κέρδει; Theoph. Ant. 3, 15 [p. 234, 6]) τ. χεῖρας (Jos., Vi. 244) **Ac 5:38 v.l.** ἡ συνείδησις . . . μολύνεται *conscience is defiled* by eating meat sacrificed to idols **1 Cor 8:7** (Iren. 1, 6, 3 [Harv. I 55, 11]; Amm. Marc. 15, 2 conscientiam polluebat). Esp. of immorality (Theocr. 5, 87; EpArist 152) οἳ μετὰ γυναικῶν οὐκ ἐμολύνθησαν *who have not defiled themselves with women* **Rv 14:4** (on problems connected with this pass. s. RCharles, Comm.).—DELG. M-M. TW.

μολυσμός, οῦ, ὁ (μολύνω; Strabo 17, 2, 4; Plut., Mor. 779c; Heliod. 10, 4, 2; 1 Esdr 8:80; 2 Macc 5:27; Jos., C. Ap. 1, 289) ***defilement*** fig., in sacred and moral context (Vett. Val. 242, 16; Jer 23:15; EpArist 166; TestSim 2:13; Hippol., Ref. 9, 19, 2) ἀπὸ παντὸς μ. σαρκὸς καὶ πνεύματος *from all defilement of body and spirit,* i.e. outwardly and inwardly **2 Cor 7:1** (Theoph. Ant. 1, 2 [p. 62, 2]).—DELG s.v. μολύνω. M-M. TW.

μομφή, ῆς, ἡ (Pind. et al.) ***blame, (cause for) complaint*** πρός τινα ἔχειν μ. *have a complaint against anyone* (ἔχειν μομφήν τινι: Pind. et al.) **Col 3:13.**—DELG s.v. μέμφομαι. TW.

μονάζω (μόνος; Cornutus 14 p. 17, 17; Anth. Pal. 5, 66, 1; Iambl., Vi. Pyth. 3, 14; 35, 253; Apollon. Dysc., Synt. 191, 2, Gramm. Gr. II/2 p. 262, 10; 376, 7; schol. on Soph., Aj. 654, Oed. R. 479; Etym. Mag. p. 627, 13; Ps 101:8) ***live alone, separate oneself*** B 4:10; Hs 9, 26, 3.

μονή, ῆς, ἡ (μένω; Eur., Hdt. et al.; ins, pap; 1 Macc 7:38; TestAbr s. below)

❶ **state of remaining in an area, *staying, tarrying*** (Eur. et al.; OGI 527, 5; Philo, Mos. 1, 316) μονὴν ποιεῖσθαι *live, stay* (Thu. 1, 131, 1; BGU 742; Jos., Ant. 8, 350; 13, 41) **J 14:23.**

❷ **a place in which one stays, *dwelling(-place), room, abode*** (Chariton 1, 12, 1 μονὴν ποιεῖν; Paus. 10, 31, 7; OGI 527, 5) of heavenly dwellings μοναὶ τῶν ἁγίων μου (TestAbr A 20 p. 104, 2 [Stone p. 56]) **J 14:2** (OSchaefer, ZNW 32, '33, 210–17; understood in a transcendent sense: RGundry, ZNW 58, '67, 68–72). τῆς ἀμείνονος τυγχάνειν μονῆς *attain a better abode* ApcPt fgm. 2 p. 12, 22.—M-M. TW.

μονογενής, ές (μόνος, γένος; Hes.; LXX; PsSol 18, 4; TestSol 20:2; TestBenj 9:2; ParJer 7:26; ApcEsdr 6:16; ApcSed 9:2; Joseph., Just.; loanw. in rabb.) acc. μονογενῆ (-ῆν **J 3:16 v.l.; Hb 11:17** D; also ApcEsdr 6:16)

❶ **pert. to being the only one of its kind within a specific relationship, *one and only, only*** (so mostly, incl. Judg 11:34; Tob 3:15; 8:17) of children: of Isaac, Abraham's only son (Jos., Ant. 1, 222) **Hb 11:17.** Of an only son (PsSol 18:4; TestSol 20:2; ParJer 7:26; Plut., Lycurgus 59 [31, 8]; Jos., Ant. 20, 20) **Lk 7:12; 9:38.** Of a daughter (Diod. S. 4, 73, 2) of Jairus **8:42.** (On the motif of a child's death before that of a parent s. EpigrAnat 13, '89, 128f, no. 2; 18, '91, 94 no. 4 [244/45 AD]; GVI nos. 1663–69.)

❷ **pert. to being the only one of its kind or class, *unique (in kind)*** of someth. that is the only example of its category (Cornutus 27 p, 49, 13 εἷς κ. μονογενὴς ὁ κόσμος ἐστί. μονογενῆ κ. μόνα ἐστίν='unique and alone'; Pla., Timaeus 92c; Theosophien 181, §56, 27). Of a mysterious bird, the Phoenix 1 Cl 25:2.—In the Johannine lit. (s. also ApcEsdr and ApcSed: ὁ μονογενὴς υἱός; Hippol., Ref. 8, 10, 3; Did., Gen. 89, 18; ὑμνοῦμέν γε θεὸν καὶ τὸν μ. αὐτοῦ Orig., C. Cels. 8, 67, 14; cp. ἡ δύναμις ἐκείνη ἡ μ. Hippol., Ref. 10, 16, 6) μονογενὴς υἱός is used only of Jesus. The renderings *only, unique* may be quite adequate for all its occurrences here (so M-M., NRSV et al.; DMoody, JBL 72, '53, 213–19; FGrant, ATR 36, '54, 284–87; GPendrick, NTS 41, '95, 587–600). τὸν υἱὸν τὸν μ. ἔδωκεν **J 3:16** (Philo Bybl. [100 AD]: 790 fgm. 2 ch. 10, 33 Jac. [in Eus., PE 1, 10, 33]: Cronus offers up his μονογενὴς υἱός). ὁ μ. υἱὸς τοῦ θεοῦ vs. **18;** τὸν υἱὸν τὸν μ. ἀπέσταλκεν ὁ θεός **1J 4:9;** cp. Dg 10:2. On the expr. δόξαν ὡς μονογενοῦς παρὰ πατρός **J 1:14** s. Hdb. ad loc. and PWinter, Zeitschrift für Rel. u. Geistesgeschichte 5, '53, 335–65 (Engl.). See also Hdb. on vs. **18** where, beside the rdg. μονογενὴς θεός (considered by many the orig.) *an only-begotten one, God* (acc. to his real being; i.e. uniquely divine as God's son and transcending all others alleged to be gods) or *a uniquely begotten deity* (for the perspective s. J 10:33–36), another rdg. ὁ μονογενὴς υἱός is found. MPol 20:2 in the doxology διὰ παιδὸς αὐτοῦ τοῦ μονογενοῦς Ἰησοῦ Χριστοῦ. Some (e.g. WBauer, Hdb.; JBulman, Calvin Theological Journal 16, '81, 56–79; JDahms, NTS 29, '83, 222–32) prefer to regard μ. as somewhat heightened in mng. in J and 1J to *only-begotten* or *begotten of the Only One,* in view of the emphasis on γεννᾶσθαι ἐκ θεοῦ (J 1:13 al.); in this case it would be analogous to πρωτότοκος (Ro 8:29; Col 1:15 al.).—On the mng. of μονογενής in history of religion s. the material in Hdb.[3] 25f on J 1:14 (also Plut., Mor. 423a Πλάτων . . . αὐτῷ δή φησι δοκεῖν ἕνα τοῦτον [sc. τὸν κόσμον] εἶναι μονογενῆ τῷ θεῷ καὶ ἀγαπητόν; Wsd 7:22 of σοφία: ἔστι ἐν αὐτῇ πνεῦμα νοερὸν ἅγιον μονογενές.—Vett. Val. 11, 32) as well as the lit. given there, also HLeisegang, Der Bruder des Erlösers: Αγγελος I 1925, 24–33; RBultmann J (comm., KEK) '50, 47 n. 2; 55f.—DELG s.v. μένω. M-M. EDNT. TW. Sv.

μονόλιθος, ον (since Hdt. 2, 175; Diod. S. 1, 46, 1; Strabo 9, 5, 16; pap; Jos., Bell. 7, 290, Ant. 13, 211) ***(made of) a single stone,*** of a tower Hs 9, 9, 7; 9, 13, 5.

μόνον s. μόνος 2.

μονοούσιος, ον (s. Lampe, s.v.) ***unique*** ἔδωκέν μοι καρπόν . . . μονοούσιον πολυπλάσιον *unique and abundant fruit* GJs 6:3 (μονόσιον Bodm.; s. de Strycker p. 226, note 2).

μόνος, η, ον (Pind.+ [as μοῦνος as early as Hom.])

❶ **pert. to being the only entity in a class, *only, alone*** adj.

ⓐ with focus on being the only one—**α.** used w. verbs like εἶναι, εὑρίσκεσθαι, καταλείπειν: μόνος ἦν ἐκεῖ **Mt 14:23;** cp. **J 8:16.** Λουκᾶς ἐστιν μόνος μετ' ἐμοῦ **2 Ti 4:11.** εὑρέθη Ἰησοῦς μόνος **Lk 9:36.** μόνην με κατέλειπεν **10:40** (w. inf. foll.); pass. κατελείφθη μόνος **J 8:9;** cp. **1 Th 3:1.** κἀγὼ ὑπελείφθην μόνος *I am the only one left* (Theseus Hist. [Roman times]: 453 fgm. 2 Jac. μόνος περιλειφθείς of the only survivor of a battle) **Ro 11:3** (cp. 3 Km 19:10, 14; Job 1:15 al.).—**Ac 15:33 [34] v.l.**

β. used w. a noun (TestJob 10:1 τοῖς ξένοις μόνοις; AssMos fgm. d p. 64 λόγῳ μόνῳ) τὰ ὀθόνια μόνα **Lk 24:12.** μόνοι οἱ μαθηταὶ ἀπῆλθον **J 6:22.** μόνος ὁ ἀρχιερεύς **Hb 9:7.**—Cp. **Mt 12:4** (Jos., Ant. 15, 419 τ. ἱερεῦσιν ἐξὸν ἦν μόνοις). οὗτοι μόνοι συνεργοί **Col 4:11.** μόνῳ πνεύματι AcPl Ant 13, 18 (μόνον πνεύματι Aa I 237, 3). Papias (3:2) αὐτὸν μόνον τῆς κεφαλῆς ὄγκον.—Used w. pronouns (μόνος αὐτός: Nicol. Dam.: 90 fgm. 130, 23 p. 407, 21 Jac.; Ps.-Demetr., De Eloc. 97; 2 Macc 7:37; Philo, Agr. 39; Jos., Ant. 8, 405, C. Ap. 1, 49); αὐτῷ μόνῳ λατρεύσεις (Dt 6:13 v.l.; cp. Jos., Ant. 3, 91 τοῦτον μ.) **Mt 4:10; Lk 4:8.—Mt 18:15; Mk 6:47; 9:2; J 6:15.** εἰς ἑαυτὸν μόνον **Gal 6:4.** σὺ μόνος . . . ; (1 Km 21:2; TestZeb 4:12; cp. σὺ μόνος ApcSed 15:1) *are you the only one?* (Field, Notes 82) **Lk 24:18;** ἐγὼ μ. (En 6:3; TestJud 3:1; ApcMos 27) **Ac 26:14 v.l.; 1 Cor 9:6;** GJs 1:3; ὑμεῖς μόνοι **1 Cor 14:36** (cp. Just., D. 19, 2).

γ. w. a negative and w. ἀλλά foll.: οὐκ ἐπ' ἄρτῳ μόνῳ . . . , ἀλλ' . . . (Dt 8:3) **Mt 4:4=Lk 4:4.** οὐ μόνον τὸ σῶμα . . . ἀλλὰ πολλοστόν AcPlCor 2:27 οὐκ ἐγὼ μ. . . . , ἀλλὰ καί . . . **Ro 16:4; 2J 1.** οὐκ ἐγράφη δὲ δι' αὐτὸν μόνον, ἀλλὰ καί **Ro 4:23.** οὐκ αὐτὸν δὲ μόνον, ἀλλὰ καί **Phil 2:27.** Pleonast. w. εἰ μή after a neg. *not . . . except . . . alone* (Lydus, Magist. 1, 18 p. 22, 22) **Mt 12:4; 17:8; 24:36; Mk 9:8 v.l.** (for ἀλλὰ . . . μόνον); **Lk 5:21; 6:4; Phil 4:15; Rv 9:4 v.l.**

δ. μόνος θεός (cp. Simonides, fgm. 4, 7 Diehl θεὸς μόνος; Da 3:45; SibOr 3, 629; PGM 13, 983) *the only God* **1 Ti 1:17; Jd 25** (GDelling, TLZ 77, '52, 469–76). W. article preceding ὁ μόνος θ. (EpArist 139; Philo, Fuga 71; Just., D. 126, 2 τοῦ μόνου καὶ ἀγεννήτου θεοῦ υἱόν; ὁ θεὸς μόνος 4 Km 19:15, 19; Ps 85:10; Is 37:20. Cp. ENorden, Agn. Theos 1913, 245, 1) **J 5:44** (without θεοῦ v.l.). ὁ μ. ἀληθινὸς θεός *the only true God* **17:3** (Demochares [c. 300 BC]: 75 fgm. 2 Jac. τὸν Δημήτριον οἱ Ἀθηναῖοι ἐδέχοντο . . . ἐπᾴδοντες ὡς εἴη μόνος θεὸς ἀληθινός, οἱ δ' ἄλλοι καθεύδουσιν ἢ ἀποδημοῦσιν ἢ οὐκ εἰσίν. γεγονὼς δ' εἴη ἐκ Ποσειδῶνος καὶ Ἀφροδίτης 'the Athenians welcomed Demetrius . . . adulating him with the surmise that he was the only real god, whereas others were slumbering, or taking a trip, or simply did not exist; and that he was probably a descendant of Poseidon and Aphrodite'). τὸ ὄνομα τ. ἀληθινοῦ καὶ μόνου κυρίου 1 Cl 43:6 (cp. Just., D. 55, 2 κύριος μ.). μ. σοφὸς θεός *the only wise God* **Ro 16:27** (Philo, Fuga 47 ὁ μ. σοφός; Heraclitus, fgm. 32 ἓν τὸ σοφὸν μοῦνον). ὁ μ. δεσπότης *the only one who is master* **Jd 4** (cp. Jos., Bell. 7, 323; 410). ὁ μακάριος καὶ μόνος δυνάστης **1 Ti 6:15.**—Vs. **16; Rv 15:4.**

ⓑ with focus on being helplessly alone: *alone, deserted, helpless* (Hom. et al.; BGU 180, 23 [172 AD] ἄνθρωπος πρεσβύτης καὶ μόνος τυγχάνων; 385, 4; Wsd 10:1; TestJos 1:6; La 1:1) οὐκ ἀφῆκέν με μόνον **J 8:29; 16:32ab** (ἀφ. μόν. as Dio Chrys. 46 [63], 2).

ⓒ with focus on isolation: *isolated, by itself* (cp. Bar 4:16; En 28:1; TestJud 5:3; JosAs 2:16; Ar. 11:2) ἐὰν μὴ ὁ κόκκος τ. σίτου . . . ἀποθάνῃ, αὐτὸς μόνος μένει **J 12:24.** In Hv 3, 9, 2 μ. refers to selfish Christians who isolate themselves fr. the needs of the hungry.

❷ **a marker of limitation,** ***only, alone,*** the neut. μόνον being used as an adv. (Aeschyl., Hdt. et al.)**—ⓐ** limiting the action or state to the one designated by the verb (TestAbr A 4 p. 81, 25 [Stone p. 10]; TestJos 16:4; JosAs 24:10) **Mt 9:21; 14:36; Mk 5:36; Lk 8:50; 1 Cor 7:39; 15:19; Gal 1:23; Phil 1:27; 2 Th 2:7;** Hv 3, 2, 1.—οὐκ ἀλλὰ μ. **Mt 8:8.**

ⓑ w. a noun (Just., A I, 22, 1 μ. ἄνθρωπος) or pron., to separate one pers. or thing fr. others: **Mt 5:47; 10:42; Ac 18:25; Ro 3:29; Gal 2:10; Hb 9:10;** Hm 12, 4, 7; τοῦτο μ. **Gal 3:2.**

ⓒ used w. negatives**—α.** μ. μή *only not, not only* (POxy 2153, 22; TestJob 45:1) **Gal 5:13.** οὐ (μὴ) μ. **4:18; Js 1:22; 2:24** (s. β below). οὐ μ. . . . ἀλλά (without καί when the second member includes the first. X., Cyr. 1, 6, 16; Diod. S. 4, 15, 1; Dio Chrys. 1, 22; 62; 64 [14], 7; Just., A I, 2, 1; B-D-F §448, 1) **Ac 19:26** (but some mss. add καί); **1 Th 1:8; 1J 5:6.** οὐ (or μὴ) μ. . . . , ἀλλὰ καί *not only . . . , but also* (PMich 209, 12 [c. 200 AD]; TestJos 10:3; Jos., Bell. 3, 102; Just., A I, 5, 4 al.) **Mt 21:21; J 5:18; Ac 21:13; 26:29; 27:10; Ro 1:32; 9:24; 13:5; 2 Cor 8:10, 21; 9:12; Eph 1:21; Phil 1:29; 1 Th 2:8; 2 Ti 2:20; Hb 12:26; 1 Pt 2:18;** Qua. οὐ (μὴ) . . . μ., ἀλλὰ καί **J 11:52; 12:9; 13:9; 17:20; Ro 4:12, 16; Phil 2:27; 1 Th 1:5** al. οὐ . . . μόνον ἀλλὰ καί **1J 2:2.** οὐδέπω . . . , μ. δέ *not yet . . . , but . . . only* **Ac 8:16.** οὐ μ. δέ, ἀλλὰ καί *not only this, but also* (ellipsis w. supplementation of what immediately precedes; Mitt-Wilck. II/2, 26, 9=27, 9 [108 BC]; cp. Sb 7616 [II AD]; Wsd 19:15; TestJob 35:1; Just., A I, 49, 5; B-D-F §479, 1; s. Rob. 1201ff) **Ro 5:3, 11; 8:23; 9:10; 2 Cor 8:19.** οὐ μόνον δὲ . . . ἀλλὰ καί (TestZeb 3:7) **Ac 19:27; 2 Cor 7:7; 1 Ti 5:13.** μὴ μ., ἀλλὰ πολλῷ μᾶλλον *not only, . . . but much more* **Phil 2:12.** οὐδὲν (μηδὲν) . . . εἰ μὴ . . . μόνον (TestAbr B 11 p. 116, 3 [Stone p. 80]; TestJob 11:7; Ar 13, 7) **Mt 21:9; Mk 6:8.** μηδενὶ . . . εἰ μὴ μ. **Ac 11:19.** On 1–2c s. KBeyer, Semitische Syntax im NT '62, 126–29.

β. *in isolation* οὐκ ἐκ πίστεως μόνον *not by faith viewed in isolation* **Js 2:24** (NEB: 'not by faith in itself'; Goodsp.: 'not simply by having faith'; sim. Moffatt; s. Athanasius Alexandrinus, De Virginitate PGM 28, 260c; cp. Clem., Strom. 3, 15 οὐ γὰρ μόνον ἡ εὐνουχία δικαιοῖ=being a eunuch does not of itself justify. S. also πίστις 2dδ.)

ⓓ ἵνα μόνον *solely in order that* B 12:8; μόνον ἵνα **Gal 6:12.**

❸ κατὰ μόνας (Thu. 1, 32, 5; X., Mem. 3, 7, 4; Menand., Epitr. 988 S. [658 Kö.], fgm. 146 Kö.; Polyb. 4, 15, 11; Diod. S. 4, 51, 16; Gen 32:16; Ps 4:9; Jer 15:17; 1 Macc 12:36; TestJos 4:1; Jos., Vi. 326, Ant. 17, 336 al.—Also written καταμόνας; cp. BGU 813, 15 in APF 2, 1903, 97) ***alone*** γίνεσθαι κ. μ. *be alone* (Syntipas p. 9, 16) **Mk 4:10.**—**Lk 9:18;** Hm 11:8.—B-D-F §241, 6.—B. 937. DELG. Schmidt, Syn. IV 535–39. M-M. EDNT. Sv.

μονόφθαλμος, ον (Hdt. et al.; rejected by the Atticists for 'deprived of one eye' in favor of ἑτερόφθαλμος [Phryn. 136 Lob.], but used in later colloq. speech in this sense: Polyb. 5, 67, 6; Strabo 2, 1, 9; Lucian, Ver. Hist. 1, 3; Ps.-Apollod. 2, 8, 3, 4 al. Perh. BGU 1196, 97 [I BC], s. HBraunert, ZKG 70, '59, 316 w. ref. to PBrux inv. E 7616 X, 21 and PMich 425, 12 [both II AD]) ***one-eyed*** **Mt 18:9; Mk 9:47.**—M-M.

μονόω pf. pass. ptc. μεμονωμένος (μόνος; Hom. et al.; Musonius 73, 1 H.) ***make solitary*** pass. *be left alone* (Thu. 2, 81, 5; 5, 58, 2; Nicol. Dam.: 90 fgm. 130, 30 p. 416, 15 Jac.; JosAs 13 [p.57, 5 Bat.] cod. A; Philo; Jos., Ant. 5, 280, Vi. 95; Tat. 14, 1) of a widow μεμονωμένη *is left alone* (cp. Anacreontea 37, 13 Preis.) **1 Ti 5:5.**—DELG s.v. μόνος 8. M-M.

μορφή, ῆς, ἡ (Hom.+) ***form, outward appearance, shape*** gener. of bodily form 1 Cl 39:3; ApcPt 4:13 (Job 4:16; ApcEsdr 4:14 p. 28, 16 Tdf.; SJCh 78, 13). Of the shape or form of statues (Jos., Vi. 65; Iren. 1, 8, 1 [Harv. I 67, 11]) Dg 2:3. Of appearances in visions, etc., similar to persons (Callisthenes [IV BC]: 124 fgm. 13 p. 644, 32 Jac. [in Athen. 10, 75, 452b] Λιμὸς ἔχων γυναικὸς μορφήν; Diod. S. 3, 31, 4 ἐν μορφαῖς ἀνθρώπων; TestAbr A 16 p. 97, 11 [Stone p. 42] ἀρχαγγέλου μορφὴν περικείμενος; Jos., Ant. 5, 213 a messenger fr. heaven νεανίσκου μορφῇ): of God's assembly, the church Hv 3, 10, 2; 9; 3, 11, 1; 3, 13, 1; s 9, 1, 1; of the angel of repentance ἡ μ. αὐτοῦ ἠλλοιώθη *his appearance had changed* m 12, 4, 1. Of Christ (ἐν μ. ἀνθρώπου TestBenj 10:7; Just., D. 61, 1; Tat. 2, 1; Hippol., Ref. 5, 16, 10. Cp. Did., Gen. 56, 18; of deities ἐν ἀνθρωπίνῃ μορφῇ: Iambl., Vi. Pyth. 6, 30; cp. Philo, Abr. 118) μορφὴν δούλου λαβών *he took on the form of a slave*=expression of servility **Phil 2:7** (w. σχῆμα as Aristot., Cat. 10a, 11f, PA 640b, 30–36). This is in contrast to expression of divinity in the preëxistent Christ: ἐν μ. θεοῦ ὑπάρχων *although he was in the form of God* (cp. OGI 383, 40f: Antiochus' body is the framework for his μ. or essential identity as a descendant of divinities; sim. human fragility [**Phil 2:7**] becomes the supporting framework for Christ's servility and therefore of his κένωσις [on the appearance one projects cp. the epitaph EpigrAnat 17, '91, 156, no. 3, 5–8]; on μορφὴ θεοῦ cp. Orig., C. Cels. 7, 66, 21; Pla., Rep. 2, 380d; 381bc; X., Mem. 4, 3, 13; Diog. L. 1, 10 the Egyptians say μὴ εἰδέναι τοῦ θεοῦ μορφήν; Philo, Leg. ad Gai. 80; 110; Jos., C. Ap. 2, 190; Just., A I, 9, 1; PGM 7, 563; 13, 272; 584.—Rtzst., Mysterienrel.³ 357f) **Phil 2:6.** The risen Christ ἐφανερώθη ἐν ἑτέρᾳ μορφῇ *appeared in a different form* **Mk 16:12** (of the transfiguration of Jesus: ἔδειξεν ἡμῖν τὴν ἔνδοξον μορφὴν ἑαυτοῦ Orig., C. Cels. 6, 68, 23). For lit. s. on ἁρπαγμός and κενόω 1b; RMartin, ET 70, '59, 183f.—DSteenberg, The Case against the Synonymity of μορφή and εἰκών: JSNT 34, '88, 77–86; GStroumsa, HTR 76, '83, 269–88 (Semitic background).—DELG. Schmidt, Syn. IV 345–60. M-M. EDNT. TW. Spicq. Sv.

μορφόω (μορφή) 1 aor. ptc. μορφώσαντες (Just., A I, 9, 1). Pass.: aor. ἐμορφώθην; pf. ptc. μεμορφωμένος (Philo, Joseph.) (Aratus, Phaen. 375; Nilus: Anth. Pal. 1, 33, 1; Is 44:13 Q in margin and Aq.; Philo, Plant. 3; Ps.-Philo, De Mundo 13; SibOr 4, 182; Jos., Ant. 15, 329; Just., A I, 5, 4 τοῦ λόγου μορφωθέντος καὶ ἀνθρώπου γενομένου; Ath., R. 3 p. 51, 16) ***to form, shape*** act. PtK 2 p. 14, 13. Pass. *take on form, be formed* (Theophr., CP 5, 6, 7; Diod. S. 3, 51, 3) in imagery as in the formation of an embryo (Galen XIX p. 181 K. ἔμβρυα μεμορφωμένα; Philo,

Spec. Leg. 3, 117) μέχρις οὗ μορφωθῇ Χριστὸς ἐν ὑμῖν *until Christ is formed in you* **Gal 4:19** (RHermann, TLZ 80, '55, 713–26).—DELG s.v. μορφή. M-M. TW.

μόρφωσις, εως, ἡ (μορφόω; Theophr., CP 3, 7, 4 al.; TestBenj 10:1) **the state of being formally structured, *embodiment, formulation, form,*** of a Judean ἔχοντα τὴν μ. τῆς γνώσεως καὶ τῆς ἀληθείας ἐν τῷ νόμῳ *you who have the embodiment* or *formulation of knowledge and truth in the book of the law* **Ro 2:20** (νόμος='book of the law' as Jos., Bell. 2, 292, Ant, 12, 256). Of teachers of error ἔχοντες μ. εὐσεβείας *who maintain a form of piety* **2 Ti 3:5** (cp. Philo, Plant. 70 ἐπεὶ καὶ νῦν εἰσί τινες τῶν ἐπιμορφαζόντων εὐσέβειαν κτλ.='since also now there are some who put on a semblance of piety'. The prefix ἐπί contributes the semantic component pointing to mere outward form. In **2 Ti 3:5** the idea of mere outward form is derived from the context.).—DELG s.v. μορφή. M-M. TW.

μοσχοποιέω (μόσχος, ποιέω) 1 aor. ἐμοσχοποίησα (only in Christian wr., e.g. Just.; εἰδωλοποιέω Pla.+) ***manufacture a calf*** of the golden calf **Ac 7:41** (for ἐποίησε μόσχον Ex 32:4).—M-M. TW. Sv.

μόσχος, ου, ὁ ***calf, young bull,*** or ***ox*** (so trag., Hdt. +) ὁ μ. ὁ σιτευτός (Judg 6:25 A, 28 A; Jer 26:21) *the fattened calf* **Lk 15:23, 27, 30.** As an apocalyptic animal (cp. Ezk 1:10) **Rv 4:7.** As a sacrificial animal (Mitt-Wilck. I/2, 87–89) 1 Cl 52:2 (Ps 68:32); GJs 4:3. Esp. of the sin-offering on the Day of Atonement αἷμα τράγων καὶ μόσχων *the blood of goats and calves* **Hb 9:12;** cp. vs. **19.** Denotes the 'red heifer' (Num 19), interpreted to mean Christ B 8:2.—B. 155. DELG s.v. 1 μόσχος. M-M. TW.

μουσικός, ή, όν pert. to being musical, *musical, skilled in music* (so Aristoph. et al.; ins, pap, LXX; TestBenj 11:3; Jos., Ant. 16, 137 al. [ἡ μουσική]; Just. [ἡ μ.]); subst. ὁ μ. *the musician* (X., Cyr. 1, 6, 38; Cornutus 32 p. 67, 17 μ. καὶ κιθαριστής; OGI 383, 162; PFlor 74, 6; POxy 1275, 9 συμφωνίας αὐλητῶν κ. μουσικῶν; Ezk 26:13; Philo), w. harpists, flute-players and trumpeters **Rv 18:22.**—EWerner, The Sacred Bridge (Liturgy and Music) '59.—DELG s.v. μοῦσα. M-M.

μόχθος, ου, ὁ (Hes. and X.+; PRyl 28, 117; Kaibel 851, 1; LXX; TestAbr B 9 p. 114, 2 [Stone p. 76]; TestJob 24:2; TestJud 18:4; Apc4Esdr fgm. a [w. κόπος]; SibOr 2, 272; Philo, Mos. 1, 284) ***labor, exertion, hardship*** w. κόπος (Proverb. Aesopi 11 P.; Anth. Pal. 1, 47, 3; 1, 90, 4; Jer 20:18 v.l.; cp. Job 2:9) **2 Cor 11:27; 1 Th 2:9; 2 Th 3:8;** Hs 5, 6, 2.—πόνος 2, end.—DELG. M-M. Spicq.

μοχλός, οῦ, ὁ (since Hom.) ***bar, bolt*** (so Aeschyl., Thu. et al.; ins, LXX; JosAs 10:5; ApcEsdr 4:25 p. 28, 30 Tdf.; Jos., Bell. 6, 293 μ. σιδηρόδετος; loanw. in rabb.) μ. σιδηροῦς συγκλᾶν *break iron bars* B 11:4 (Is 45:2).—DELG.

μυελός, οῦ, ὁ ('marrow' Hom. et al.; Gen 45:18; Job 21:24; 33:24; TestSol 18:11 P; Jos., Bell. 6, 204; Tat. 12:2 μυελῶν τε καὶ ὀστέων; on the spelling s. B-D-F §29, 2) metaph. of the inmost part (Eur., Hipp. 255 πρὸς ἄκρον μυελὸν ψυχῆς) pl. ***marrow*** (Jos., Bell. 6, 205) **Hb 4:12** (Alciphron 3, 40, 2; Heliod. 3, 7, 3 ἄχρις ἐπ' ὀστέα κ. μυελούς).—DELG.

μυέω pf. pass. μεμύημαι; aor. subj. 3 sg. μυηθῇ t.t. of the mystery religions ***initiate (into the mysteries)*** (trag., Hdt. et al.; OGI 530, 15; 764, 12; 3 Macc 2:30; Philo, Cher. 49, Sacr. Abel. 62; Jos., Ap. 2, 267; Just.; Tat. 1, 1. On μύησις in ins s. SCole, Megaloi Theoi '84, 46f; on mysteries at Samothrace 25–56.). Of baptism ἵνα] Ἀρτεμύλλα μυηθῇ [τῆς ἐ]ν κυρίῳ σφραγίδος *so that Artemilla might be initiated by being sealed in the Lord* AcPl Ha 3, 23. Also gener., without the specific sense (Straub 31): pass., w. inf. foll. (Alciphron 4, 19, 21 v.l., but in all mss., κυβερνᾶν μυηθήσομαι) ἐν παντὶ καὶ ἐν πᾶσιν μεμύημαι καὶ χορτάζεσθαι καὶ πεινᾶν *in any and all circumstances I have learned the secret of being well fed and of going hungry* **Phil 4:12.**—DELG s.v. μύω. M-M. TW.

μύθευμα, ατος, τό (μῦθος; Aristot., Poet. 24; Plut., Mar. 411 [11, 10], Mor. p. 28d; Philostrat., Vi. Apoll. 8, 11 p. 327, 29) ***story, fable*** of the kind found, e.g., in etiological accounts, tribal and folk sagas w. ἑτεροδοξίαι: μυθεύματα τὰ παλαιά *the old fables* in reference to some Judean traditions IMg 8:1.

μυθικός, ή, όν (since Pla.) **pert. to narrative of invented character, *fictional*** καί τινα ἄλλα μυθικώτερα *and other rather fictive tales* (Pa 2:11); Eus. on Papias' writings.

μῦθος, ου, ὁ (Hom. et al.; ins; Sir 20:19; TestJud 23:1 v.l.) prim. 'speech, conversation,' also of 'narrative' or 'story' without distinction of fact or fiction, then of fictional narrative (as opposed to λόγος, the truth of history) such as ***tale, story, legend, myth*** (so Pind., Hdt. et al.; Pla., Tim. 26e μὴ πλασθέντα μῦθον, ἀλλ' ἀληθινὸν λόγον 'not some contrived tale, but a true account', Phd. 61b; Epict. 3, 24, 18; SIG 382, 7; Philo, Congr. Erud. Grat. 61 al.; Joseph.; apolog. exc. Mel.) w. πλάνη 2 Cl 13:3. Pl. (cp. Diod. S. 1, 93, 3; 2, 46, 6; 23, 13 [all three μῦθοι πεπλασμένοι]; Philo, Exsecr. 162 τοὺς ἄπλαστον ἀλήθειαν ἀντὶ πεπλασμένων μύθων μεταδιώκοντας; Jos., C. Ap. 2, 256) σεσοφισμένοις μ. ἐξακολουθεῖν *follow cleverly devised tales* **2 Pt 1:16** (Jos., Ant. 1, 22 τ. μύθοις ἐξακολουθεῖν; cp the contrast between the πράξεις ἐναργεῖς ['manifest performance'] of Isis in Egypt and the inferior Hellenic μυθολογία Diod. Sic. 1, 25, 4; New Docs 4, 80; on Gr-Rom. historians' concern for the truth of history as opposed to mythography s. Spicq 2, 532–33). Of erroneous instruction Ἰουδαϊκοὶ μ. **Tit 1:14.** βέβηλοι καὶ γραώδεις μ. *frivolous old wives' tales* **1 Ti 4:7** (cp. Lucian, Philops. 9 γραῶν μῦθοι; Ael. Aristid. 45 p. 133 D. As early as Pla., Gorg. 527a μ. ὥσπερ γραός; Ps-Xenophon, Ep. 7). W. γενεαλογίαι (q.v.) **1:4.** ἐπὶ τοὺς μ. ἐκτρέπεσθαι *turn to legends* **2 Ti 4:4.**—EHoffmann, Qua ratione ἔπος, μῦθος, αἶνος λόγος . . . adhibita sint, diss. Gött. 1922; LMueller, Wort u. Begriff Mythos im kl. Griech., diss. Hamburg, '54; KGoldammer, ZNW 48, '57, 93–100; CBarrett, ET 68, '57, 345–48; 359–62.—DELG. M-M. EDNT. TRE XXIII 597–661. TW. Spicq. Sv.

μυκάομαι fut. 3 sg. μυκήσεται Job 6:5 Sym. (Hom. et al.; Kaibel 1028, 62; PGM 13, 942; 945) ***roar,*** of lions (onomatopoetic; Theocr. 26, 20f) **Rv 10:3.**—DELG. M-M.

μυκτηρίζω (μυκτήρ 'nostril, nose') aor. ἐμυκτήρισα LXX (Hippocr., Epid. 7, 123='have a nose-bleed') ***turn up the nose at, treat with contempt*** (Lysias in Pollux 2, 78; Sext. Emp., Math. 1, 217; LXX; TestJos 2:3; SibOr 1, 171) τινά *someone* (Pr 15:20; Ps 79:7) w. χλευάζειν 1 Cl 39:1. ἐμοὺς ἐλέγχους 57:5 (Pr 1:30); w. ὀνειδίζω GJs 3:1. Abs. **Lk 23:35** D. Pass. (PTebt 758, 11 [II BC]; Jer 20:7) of God οὐ μ. *he is not to be mocked, treated w. contempt,* perh. *outwitted* **Gal 6:7;** Pol 5:1.—DELG. M-M. TW. Spicq.

μυλικός, ή, όν (μύλη 'mill'; schol. on Eur., Hecuba 362; Syntipas p. 108, 11) ***belonging to a mill*** λίθος μ. *millstone* **Mk 9:42 v.l.** (for μῦλος ὀνικός); **Lk 17:2** (on both s. λίθος 2c and ὀνικός); **Rv 18:21 v.l.**—DELG s.v. μύλη C.

μύλινος, η, ον (μύλη 'mill'; CIG 3371, 4; SIG 996, 16) ***belonging to a mill*** λίθος ὡς μ. μέγας *a stone like a great millstone* **Rv 18:21** (v.l. μύλον).—DELG s.v. μύλη B. M-M.

μύλος, ου, ὁ (H. Gk. for ἡ μύλη [so also Joseph.]; B-D-F §50).

❶ ***mill*** (Diod. S. 3, 13, 2; Plut., Mor. 549e; 830d; PSI 530, 2 [III BC]; POxy 278, 17; Ex 11:5; Dt 24:6; Is 47:2; SibOr 8, 14), made of two flat stones, which varied in the course of time and provenance in size and shape; by moving one over the other, whether by hand or by mechanical contrivance, the grain between the two was turned into flour (s. illustrations in Bible dictionaries). ἀλήθειν ἐν τῷ μ. *grind with the (hand-)mill* (cp. Num 11:8) **Mt 24:41.** φωνὴ μ. *the sound of the mill* (as it turns) **Rv 18:22.**

❷ ***millstone*** (Lycophron 233; Strabo 4, 1, 13; Anth. Pal. 11, 246, 2; PRyl 167, 10; BGU 1067, 5; Judg 9:53 A; 2 Km 11:21) **Rv 18:21 v.l.;** μ. ὀνικός *a great* (lit. 'donkey') *millstone,* i.e. not a stone fr. the small handmill, but one fr. the large mill, worked by donkey-power (s. ὀνικός). As a heavy weight: ἵνα κρεμασθῇ μ. ὀνικὸς περὶ τὸν τράχηλον αὐτοῦ *that a great millstone would be hung around his neck* **Mt 18:6.** Also εἰ περίκειται μ. ὀν. περὶ τὸν τράχηλον αὐτοῦ *if a great millstone were hung around his neck* **Mt 9:42.** More briefly περιτεθῆναι μύλον *have a millstone hung* (on him) 1 Cl 46:8.—**Rv 18:21 v.l.** B. 363.—DELG. M-M.

μυλών, ῶνος, ὁ (Eur. et al.; Thu. 6, 22; also Dio Chrys. 65 [15], 19; ins: BCH 27, 1903, 64, 146 [250 BC]; PCairMasp 139 p. 53, 13; Jer 52:11; on the form s. B-D-F §111, 5) ***mill-house*** (Ps.-Lucian, Asin. 42) **Mt 24:41 v.l.**—DELG s.v. μύλη A6.

μυλωνικός, ή, όν (μυλών) ***belonging to the mill-house*** μ. λίθος *millstone* **Mk 9:42 v.l.,** prob. a correction arising from a misread μύλο(ς) ὀνικός (μ. as subst. is found Mitt-Wilck. I/2, 323, 7 [II AD]; BGU 1900, 1; 12 al.).—DELG s.v. μύλη A6.

Μύρα (Strabo et al. The spelling w. one ρ is correct, made certain by CIG III 4288, 3–6; OGI 441, 214. Also, it is to be taken as a neut. pl. Μύρα, ων: CIG III 4288 3–6; Pliny, H. Nat. 32, 17; Athen. 2, 53, 59a; SibOr 4, 109; AcPlTh 40 [Aa I 266, 2 and 4]; Basilius, Ep. 218. The rdg. Μύραν **Ac 27:5** is found in very few mss.; also AcPlTh 40 p. 266, 4 v.l.—W-S. p. 58; Mlt-H. 101) ***Myra,*** a city on the south coast of Lycia in Asia Minor. Visited by Paul on his journey to Rome **Ac 27:5** (v.l. incorrectly Lystra); acc. to **21:1** D also on his last journey to Jerusalem.—M-M.

μυριάς, άδος, ἡ (μυρίος; Hdt.+)—❶ **a group/collective of 10,000,** ***myriad,*** lit. (Archimedes II 220, 8 Heiberg and oft.) ἀργυρίου μ. πέντε *fifty thousand pieces of silver* (i.e. denarii) **Ac 19:19** (Jos., Ant. 17, 189 ἀργυρίου μ. πεντήκοντα).

❷ **a very large number, not precisely defined,** pl. ***myriads*** (Eur., Phoen. 837 al.; Ps 3:7; Philo, Agr. 35; 113; SibOr 4, 139) **Lk 12:1; Ac 21:20** (cp. Appian, Bell. Civ. 4, 10 §39 τοσάσδε πολιτῶν μυριάδας; Jos., Ant. 7, 318 πόσαι μυριάδες εἰσὶ τ. λαοῦ). μ. ἀνδρῶν Hv 3, 2, 5. Of angel hosts (cp. the Christian amulet PIand 6, 10 and the exx. on p. 26 cited by the editor ESchaefer; Dt 33:2; En; PGM 1, 208; 4, 1203) **Hb 12:22; Jd 14** (En 1:9). As an apocalyptic number μυριάδες μυριάδων *countless thousands* (millions upon millions) **Rv 5:11** (JosAs 16:13 cod. A [p. 65, 1 Bat.]; cp. Gen 24:60 χιλιάδες μυριάδων). μύριαι μυριάδες (En 14:2) 1 Cl 34:6 (Da 7:10). On δισμυριάδες μυριάδων **Rv 9:16** s. δισμυριάς.—DELG s.v. μυρίος. M-M.

μυρίζω (μύρον) 1 aor. ἐμύρισα (Hdt., Aristoph. et al.; PGM 7, 180) ***anoint,*** of prostitutes and flute-girls Ox 840, 36. Of corpses (Philosoph. Max. 495, 127 νεκρὸν μυρίζειν) μ. τὸ σῶμα εἰς τὸν ἐνταφιασμόν *anoint a body for burial* **Mk 14:8.**—DELG s.v. μύρον. M-M. TW.

μύριοι, αι, α ***ten thousand*** (on the accent s. Schwyzer I 593; Hes., Hdt. et al.; ins, pap, LXX; En; TestSol 21:1) in our lit. used hyperbolically, as in Engl. informal usage 'zillion', of an extremely large or incalculable number ὀφειλέτης μυρίων ταλάντων *one who owed zillions of talents* **Mt 18:24** (for the term applied to talents s. Esth 3:9; Jos., Ant. 14, 78). μ. μυριάδες 10,000 *myriads* (lit. 100,000,000) 1 Cl 34:6 (Da 7:10).—DELG s.v. μυρίος.

μυρίος, α, ον (on the accent s. Schwyzer I 593; Hom.+; APF 5, 1913, 383 no. 69a, 12; PFlor 33, 14; LXX, Philo; Jos., Ant. 5, 180; SibOr 1, 147; Just., Tat., Ath.—Kühner-Bl. I 629) ***innumerable, countless*** μ. παιδαγωγοί **1 Cor 4:15** (cp. Philo, Leg. ad Gai. 54 μ. διδάσκαλοι). μ. λόγοι **14:19.**—DELG.

μύρον, ου, τό (s. μυρίζω; since Archilochus [VII BC] fgm. 27 in Athen. 15, 688c; Ion of Chios 27 [Leurini]; Hdt.; OGI 629, 35; 45; 149; POxy 234 II, 9; 736, 13; LXX; Jos., Bell. 4, 561, Ant. 14, 54; Just., D. 86, 3.—Semit. loanw.: HLewy, Die semit. Fremdwörter im Griech. 1895, 42; 44) ***ointment, perfume*** (Pla., Polit. 398a μύρον κατὰ τῆς κεφαλῆς [a proverb, according to the schol.]; Ps 132:2 μ. ἐπὶ κεφαλῆς; Jos., Ant. 19, 239 τὴν κεφ.) **Mt 26:12; Lk 7:38, 46; J 11:2;** IEph 17:1; precious **Mk 14:4f; J 12:3a, 5;** strongly aromatic (Philo, Sacr. Abel. 21, end) vs. **3b;** kept in alabaster flasks (cp. OGI 736, 35 [?]) **Mt 26:7; Mk 14:3; Lk 7:37** (JDerrett, Law in the NT, '70, 266–85). W. other articles of trade **Rv 18:13;** D 10:3 v.l., Funk-B. p. xix ln. 5. Pl. (w. ἀρώματα as Plut., Alex. 20, 13; SSol 1:3) **Lk 23:56** (for embalming a body; cp. POxy 736, 13; Artem. 1, 5).—New Docs 4, 131. DELG. M-M. TW.

Μύρρα s. Μύρα.

Μύρτη, ης, η (IG II 856; 2380 [both IV BC]; Aeschyl.) ***Myrta*** a Christian in Corinth AcPl Ha 7, 9.—FBechtel, Die Attischen Frauennamen 1902, 102.

μῦς, μυός, ὁ (Aeschyl. et al.; pap; Lev 11:29) acc. pl. μῦς (Hdt. 2, 141; Plut., Mor. 537a; Just., A I, 24, 1) ***mouse*** PtK 2 p. 14, 19.—DELG.

μυσερός, ά, όν (μύσος 'defilement'; as μυσαρός Eur., Hdt. et al.; Ins. aus d, Asklepieion v. Kos A, 22 [III BC]: RHerzog, ARW 10, 1907, 402; SibOr 3, 500. On the spelling s. B-D-F §29, 1. In LXX only Lev 18:23, where μυσερός is better attested; s. Thackeray 75.—PGM 2, 148 ἁγνὸς ἀπὸ παντὸς μυσεροῦ; Manetho, Apotel. 4, 269 μυσερός is v.l.; Etym. Mag. 535, 32; 566, 43 μυσε. beside μυσα.; Malalas [VI AD] μυσε. [Psaltes p. 2]) ***loathsome, abominable, detestable*** ζῆλος 1 Cl 14:1. μοιχεία 30:1.—DELG s.v. μύσος.

Μυσία, ας, ἡ (Eur., Hdt. et al.; ins; Jos., Bell. 1, 425) ***Mysia*** a province in the northwest of Asia Minor. Paul touched here on his so-called second miss. journey **Ac 16:7f.**

μυστήριον, ου, τό 'secret, secret rite, secret teaching, mystery' a relig. t.t. (predom. pl.) applied in the Gr-Rom. world mostly to the mysteries w. their secret teachings, relig. and political in nature, concealed within many strange customs and ceremonies. The principal rites remain unknown because of a reluctance in antiquity to divulge them (trag.+; Hdt. 2, 51, 2; Diod. S. 1, 29, 3; 3, 63, 2; Socrat., Ep. 27, 3; Cornutus 28 p. 56, 22; 57, 4; Alciphron 3, 26, 1; OGI 331, 54; 528, 13; 721,

2, SIG s. index; Sb 7567, 9 [III AD]; PGM 1, 131; 4, 719ff; 2477 τὰ ἱερὰ μ. ἀνθρώποις εἰς γνῶσιν; 5, 110; 12, 331; 13, 128 τὸ μυστήριον τοῦ θεοῦ. Only the perfected gnostic is τῶν μυστηρίων ἀκροατής Hippol., Ref. 5, 8, 29.—OKern, D. griech. Mysterien d. klass. Zeit 1927; WOtto, D. Sinn der eleusin. Myst. '40; MNilsson, The Dionysiac Mysteries of the Hell. and Rom. Age, '57; Kl. Pauly III 1533–42; WBurkert, Antike Mysterien '90). Also LXX and other versions of the OT use the word, as well as En (of the heavenly secret) and numerous pseudepigr., Philo, Joseph. (C. Ap. 2, 189, 266), apolog. (exc. Ar.); it is a loanw. in rabb. Our lit. uses μ. in ref. to the transcendent activity of God and its impact on God's people.

❶ **the unmanifested or private counsel of God, *(God's) secret,*** the secret thoughts, plans, and dispensations of God (SJCh 78, 9; τὸ μ. τῆς μοναρχίας τῆς κατὰ τὸν θεόν Theoph. Ant. 2, 28 [p. 166, 17]) which are hidden fr. human reason, as well as fr. all other comprehension below the divine level, and await either fulfillment or revelation to those for whom they are intended (the divine Logos as διδάσκαλος θείων μυστηρίων Orig., C. Cels. 3, 62, 9: the constellations as δεῖγμα καὶ τύπον . . . μεγάλου μυστηρίου Hippol. Ant. 2, 15 [p. 138, 7]; Abraham is τῶν θείων . . . μέτοχος μυστηρίων Did., Gen. 213, 20).

ⓐ In the gospels μ. is found only in one context, where Jesus says to the disciples who have asked for an explanation of the parable(s) ὑμῖν τὸ μυστήριον δέδοται τῆς βασιλείας τ. θεοῦ **Mk 4:11;** the synopt. parallels have the pl. **Mt 13:11** (LCerfaux, NTS 2, '55/56, 238–49); **Lk 8:10.**—WWrede, D. Messiasgeh. in den Evv. 1901; HEbeling, D. Messiasgeh. u. d. Botschaft des Mc-Evangelisten '39; NJohansson, SvTK 16, '40, 3–38; OPiper, Interpretation 1, '47, 183–200; RArida, St Vladimar Theol. Qtly 38, '94, 211–34 (patristic exegesis Mk 4:10–12 par.).

ⓑ The Pauline lit. has μ. in 21 places. A *secret* or *mystery,* too profound for human ingenuity, is God's reason for the partial hardening of Israel's heart **Ro 11:25** or the transformation of the surviving Christians at the Parousia **1 Cor 15:51.** Even Christ, who was understood by so few, is *God's secret* or *mystery* **Col 2:2,** hidden ages ago **1:26** (cp. Herm. Wr. 1, 16 τοῦτό ἐστι τὸ κεκρυμμένον μυστήριον μέχρι τῆσδε τῆς ἡμέρας), but now gloriously revealed among the gentiles vs. **27,** to whom the *secret of Christ,* i.e. his relevance for them, is proclaimed, **4:3** (CMitton, ET 60, '48/49, 320f). Cp. **Ro 16:25; 1 Cor 2:1** (cp. Just., D. 91, 1; 131, 2 al. μ. τοῦ σταυροῦ; 74, 3 τὸ σωτήριον τοῦτο μ., τοῦτ' ἔστι τὸ πάθος τοῦ χριστοῦ). The pl. is used to denote Christian preaching by the apostles and teachers in the expr. οἰκονόμοι μυστηρίων θεοῦ **1 Cor 4:1** (Iambl., Vi. Pyth. 23, 104 calls the teachings of Pyth. θεῖα μυστήρια). Not all Christians are capable of understanding all the mysteries. The one who speaks in tongues πνεύματι λαλεῖ μυστήρια *utters secret truths in the Spirit* which the person alone shares w. God, and which others, even Christians, do not understand **1 Cor 14:2.** Therefore the possession of *all mysteries* is a great joy **13:2** (Just., D. 44, 2). And the spirit-filled apostle can say of the highest stage of Christian knowledge, revealed only to the τέλειοι: λαλοῦμεν θεοῦ σοφίαν ἐν μυστηρίῳ *we impart the wisdom of God in the form of a mystery* (ἐν μυστηρίῳ=in a mysterious manner [Laud. Therap. 11] or =secretly, so that no unauthorized person would learn of it [cp. Cyr. of Scyth. p. 90, 14 ἐν μυστηρίῳ λέγει]) **2:7** (AKlöpper, ZWT 47, 1905, 525–45).—**Eph**, for which (as well as for Col) μ. is a predominant concept, sees the μ. τοῦ θελήματος αὐτοῦ (sc. θεοῦ) **1:9** or μ. τ. Χριστοῦ **3:4** or μ. τ. εὐαγγελίου **6:19** in acceptance of the gentiles as Christians **3:3ff, 9ff.** A unique *great mystery* is revealed **5:32,** where the relation betw. Christ and the Christian community or church is spoken of on the basis of Gen 2:24 (cp. the interpretation of the sun as symbol of God, Theoph. Ant. 2, 15 [p. 138, 8], and s. WKnox, St. Paul and the Church of the Gentiles, '39, 183f; 227f; WBieder, TZ 11, '55, 329–43).

ⓒ In **Rv** μ. is used in ref. to the mysterious things portrayed there. The whole content of the book appears as τὸ μ. τοῦ θεοῦ **10:7.** Also τὸ μ. τῶν ἑπτὰ ἀστέρων **1:20;** τὸ μ. τῆς γυναικός **17:7,** cp. vs. **5,** where in each case μ. may mean *allegorical significance* (so BEaston, Pastoral Epistles '47, 215).

❷ **that which transcends normal understanding, *transcendent/ultimate reality, secret,*** with focus on Israelite/Christian experience.

ⓐ 1 Ti uses μ. as a formula: τὸ μ. τῆς πίστεως is simply *faith* **3:9.** τὸ τ. εὐσεβείας μ. *the secret of (our) piety* vs. **16.**—τὸ μ. τῆς ἀνομίας **2 Th 2:7** s. ἀνομία 1 (Jos., Bell. 1, 470 calls the life of Antipater κακίας μυστήριον because of his baseness practiced in secret. Cp. also SibOr 8, 58 τὰ πλάνης μυστήρια; 56).—PFurfey, CBQ 8, '46, 179–91.

ⓑ in Ign.: the death and resurrection of Jesus as μ. IMg 9:1 (τὸ περὶ τῆς ἀναστάσεως μ. Orig., C. Cels. 1, 7, 9). The virginity of Mary, her childbearing, and the Lord's death are called τρία μ. κραυγῆς *three mysteries (to be) loudly proclaimed* IEph 19:1 (they are mysteries because they go so contrary to human expectation). So also of the annunciation to Mary and her conception GJs 12:2f. The deacons are οἱ διάκονοι μυστηρίων Ἰ. Χρ. ITr 2:3.

ⓒ Quite difficult is the saying about the tried and true prophet ποιῶν εἰς μυστήριον κοσμικὸν ἐκκλησίας *who acts in accord with the earthly mystery of (God's) assembly* D 11:11. This may refer to celibacy; the prophet lives in such a way as to correspond to the relation betw. Christ and the people of God; cp. **Eph 5:32** (so Harnack, TU II 1; 2, 1884, 44ff; HWeinel, Die Wirkungen d. Geistes u. der Geister 1899, 131–38; PDrews, Hdb. z. d. ntl. Apokryphen 1904, 274ff; RKnopf, Hdb. ad loc.—Differently CTaylor, The Teaching of the Twelve Apost. 1886, 82–92; RHarris, The Teaching of the Ap. 1887; FFunk, Patr. Apostol.[2] 1901 ad loc.; Zahn, Forschungen III 1884, 301).

ⓓ μ. occurs oft. in Dg: τὸ τῆς θεοσεβείας μ. *the secret of (our) piety* 4:6 (what Dg means by μ. is detailed in ch. 5). Likew. of Christian teaching (cp. Ps.-Phocyl. 229 and comments by Horst 260–61) πατρὸς μυστήρια 11:2; cp. vs. 5. Hence the Christian can μυστήρια θεοῦ λαλεῖν 10:7. In contrast to ἀνθρώπινα μ. 7:1. οὗ (sc. τ. θεοῦ) τὰ μυστήρια *whose secret counsels* 7:2 (the divine will for orderly management of the universe). Of God keeping personal counsel κατεῖχεν ἐν μυστηρίῳ . . . τὴν σοφὴν αὐτοῦ βουλήν 8:10.—Lghtf., St. Paul's Ep. to the Col. and Phlm. p. 167ff; JRobinson, St. Paul's Ep. to the Eph. 1904, 234ff; GWobbermin, Religionsgesch. Studien 1896, 144ff; EHatch, Essays on Bibl. Gk. 1889, 57ff; HvSoden, ZNW 12, 1911, 188ff; TFoster, AJT 19, 1915, 402–15; OCasel, D. Liturgie als Mysterienfeier[5] 1923; JSchneider, 'Mysterion' im NT: StKr 104, '32, 255–78; TArvedson, D. Mysterium Christi '37; KPrümm, 'Mysterion' v. Pls bis Orig.: ZKT 61, '37, 391–425, Biblica 37, '56, 135–61; RBrown, The Semitic Background of 'Mystery' in the NT, '68; cp. KKuhn, NTS 7, 61, 366 for Qumran parallels to various passages in Eph and Ro; ABöhlig, Mysterion u. Wahrheit, '68, 3–40; JFruytier, Het woord M. in de catechesen van Cyrillus van Jerusalem, '50; ANock, Hellenistic Mysteries and Christian Sacraments, Essays on Religion and the Ancient World II, '72, 790–820; AHarvey, The Use of Mystery Language in the Bible: JTS 31, '80, 320–36.—DELG s.v. μύω. M-M. EDNT. TW. Sv.

Μυτιλήνη s. Μιτυλήνη.

μυωπάζω (μύωψ [μύω 'close' the eyes, ὤψ 'eye'] 'closing or contracting the eyes'=squinting, as nearsighted [myopic] people do) only Christian wr.: Basilius 2, 825b [MPG XXX]; Epiph. 59, 11, 1 Holl; Ps.-Dionys., Eccl. Hierarch. 2, 3, 3) ***be near-sighted*** fig. τυφλός ἐστιν μυωπάζων *he is so near-sighted that he is blind* **2 Pt 1:9** (opp. Χριστοῦ ἐπίγνωσις; JMayor, Comm. ad loc.).—DELG s.v. μύω. M-M.

Μωδάτ, ὁ indecl. ***Modad*** Hv 2, 3, 4; s. on Ἐλδάδ.

μώλωψ, ωπος ὁ (Hyperid., fgm. 200; Plut., Mor. 565b; Herodian Gr. I 247, 20; LXX) ***welt, wale, bruise, wound*** caused by blows (Machon vs. 285; Dionys. Hal. 16, 5, 2; Pausanias Attic. ζ, 5 μώλωψ, τὸ ἐκ πληγῆς οἴδημα 'the swelling from a blow'; Artem. 2, 48 p. 150, 4; Lucian, Philops. 20 of welts from whipping; Sir 28:17) οὗ τῷ μώλωπι ἰάθητε *by his welt(s)/wound(s) you have been healed* **1 Pt 2:24;** cp. 1 Cl 16:5; B 5:2 (all Is 53:5; this passage revised Just., D. 17, 1 δἰ οὗ τῶν μωλώπων ἴασις γίνεται; 137, 1 μηδὲ χλευάσητε αὐτοῦ τοὺς μώλωπας).—DELG. M-M. TW.

μωμάομαι (μῶμος) mid. dep.; fut. 3 sg. μωμήσεται Pr 9:7; 1 aor. ἐμωμησάμην. Pass.: aor. ἐμωμήθην; pf. ptc. fem. μεμωμημένη Sir 34:18 (Hom. et al.; Plut., Mor. 346a; LXX; Philo, Leg. All. 3, 180) ***find fault with, criticize, censure, blame*** τινά *someone* **2 Cor 8:20.** Pass. *have fault found with it* **6:3.**—DELG s.v. μῶμος.

μῶμος, ου, ὁ (s. prec. entry; on the etym. s. LfgrE s.v.)

❶ ***blame*** (Hom. et al.; Kaibel 948, 8; Sir 18:15; SibOr 3, 377) δίχα παντὸς μ. *without any blame* 1 Cl 63:1.

❷ ***defect, blemish*** bodily (Lev 21:17f, 21; 24:19f; TestLevi 9:10) and also moral (Sir 11:31, 33; 20:24; Philo, Sobr. 11 μ. ἐν ψυχῇ) of dissident teachers σπίλοι καὶ μῶμοι *blots and blemishes* **2 Pt 2:13.**—DELG. M-M. TW.

μωμοσκοπέομαι (μῶμος, σκοπέω) mid. dep.; 1 aor. pass. ptc. μωμοσκοπηθείς (Const. Apost. 2, 3; the noun μωμοσκόπος in Philo, Agr. 130; Clem. Al., Strom. 4, 18, 117) ***examine for blemishes.***

ⓐ t.t. in sacrificial usage: of a sacrificial animal, etc. 1 Cl 41:2.

ⓑ fig. of God, who πάντα μωμοσκοπεῖται *examines everything (for blemishes)* Pol 4:3.—Cp. DELG s.v. σκέπτομαι.

μωραίνω (μωρός) 1 aor. ἐμώρανα. Pass.: fut. 3 sg. μωρανθήσεται Is 19:11; 1 aor. ἐμωράνθην (Eur. et al., but intr., also Philo, Cher. 116) in our lit. only trans. (Polemo, Decl. 2, 36; LXX; intr. Just., D. 67, 2; Tat. 21, 1).

❶ ***make foolish, show to be foolish*** οὐχὶ ἐμώρανεν ὁ θεὸς τὴν σοφίαν τοῦ κόσμου; *has not God shown that the wisdom of the world is foolish?* **1 Cor 1:20.** Pass. in act. sense *become foolish* (Sir 23:14) φάσκοντες εἶναι σοφοὶ ἐμωράνθησαν *although they claimed to be wise, they became fools* **Ro 1:22** (cp. Jer 10:14; Ar. 8, 2).

❷ ***make tasteless*** pass. *become tasteless, insipid,* of salt (s. ἄναλος and FPerles, REJ 82, 1926, 122f; MBlack, Aramaic Approach[3], '67, 166f) **Mt 5:13; Lk 14:34** (v.l. μαρανθῇ).—S. ἅλας a.—DELG s.v. 1 μωρός. TW. Spicq.

μωρία, ας, ἡ (μωρός; Soph., Hdt. et al.; PBrem 61, 28 [II AD]; PCairMasp 4, 6 Byz.; Sir 20:31; 41:15; Philo; Jos., Ant. 17, 209; Iren. 1, 16, 3 [Harv. I, 162, 2]) ***foolishness*** gener. of worldly wisdom (Orig., C. Cels. 7, 47, 9) μ. παρὰ τῷ θεῷ ἐστιν **1 Cor 3:19.** Conversely, to all those who are lost **1:18** and esp. to the gentiles vs. **23,** the Christian preaching of a Savior who died a slave's death on the cross was μ. (cp. Theoph. Ant. 2, 1 [p. 94, 7]). It has pleased God to save the believers διὰ τ. μωρίας τοῦ κηρύγματος vs. **21.** The ψυχικὸς ἄνθρ. rejects the things of the spirit as μ., **2:14.** The Judean temple cult is evaluated as μ. (opp. θεοσέβεια) Dg 3:3.—WCaspari, Über d. bibl. Begriff der Torheit: NKZ 39, 1928, 668–95.—DELG s.v. 1 μωρός. TW. Spicq.

μωρολογία, ας, ἡ (μωρός, λογ[ε]ία; Aristot., HA 1, 11; Plut., Mor. 504b; Jos., C. Ap. 2, 115) ***foolish/silly talk*** w. αἰσχρότης and εὐτραπελία **Eph 5:4** (cp. 1QS 10:21–24: KKuhn, NTS 7, '61, 339).—DELG s.v. 1 μωρός. M-M. Spicq.

μωρός, ά, όν (trag., X., Pla.+; pap, LXX; TestLevi 7:2; ParJer 9:30; Philo; Ar.; Just.; loanw. in rabb.; on the accent s. B-D-F §13; Mlt-H.) ***foolish, stupid.***

ⓐ of pers. (Simonides of Ceos 48, 6f [Diehl], who uses the word with reference to his opponent, Cleobulus; Diod. S. 10, 22; Epict. 2, 2, 16; 3, 24, 86; w. ἄνους Hippol. Ref. 6, 34, 8; subst.: Orig., C. Cels. 5, 16, 17; Hippol. Ref. 9, 13, 3) **Mt 5:22** (s. c below); (w. τυφλός) **23:17, 19 v.l.;** (opp. φρόνιμος) **7:26; 25:2f, 8.** The same contrast **1 Cor 4:10,** where the apostle ironically compares himself w. the Corinthians. (Opp. σοφός as Lucian, Epigr. 1; Dt 32:6; Sir 21:26) **3:18.** W. ἀσύνετος (Sir 21:18) Hv 3, 6, 5; s 9, 22, 4. W. ἀσύνετος and other similar predicates 1 Cl 39:1. Of the overly ambitious Hs 8, 7, 4. τὰ μ. τοῦ κόσμου *what is considered foolish in the world* **1 Cor 1:27** also refers to persons, and can do so since it pertains not to individuals but to a general attribute (B-D-F §138, 1; 263, 4; Rob. 411; Mussies 124).

ⓑ of things (SibOr 3, 226; περὶ τροπολογουμένων καὶ οὐ μωρῶν συγγραμμάτων Orig., C. Cels. 4, 51, 28; Theoph. Ant 2, 12 [p. 130, 14]) ὀξυχολία Hm 5, 2, 4. παράδοσις **Mk 7:13 v.l.** ζητήσεις **2 Ti 2:23; Tit 3:9.** πράγματα Hm 5, 2, 2. τρυφαί m 12, 2, 1. διδαχαί s 8, 6, 5. ἀφροσύνη 9, 22, 2. Of the πνεῦμα ἐπίγειον m 11:11.—τὸ μ. τοῦ θεοῦ *the foolishness of God* (in the judgment of unbelievers) **1 Cor 1:25** (cp. Eur., Hipp. 966 τὸ μ.='foolishness').

ⓒ The mng. of μωρέ **Mt 5:22** is disputed. Most scholars take it, as the ancient Syrian versions did, to mean *you fool* (Pla., Leg. 9, 857d and Socrat., Ep. 14, 6 ὦ μῶρε [as it is accented in Att.]=you fool! Likew. Biogr. p. 179.—Epict. 2, 16, 13; 3, 13, 17 μωρέ; Philo, Cher. 75 ὦ μωρέ), somet. also w. the connotation of an obstinate, godless person (like נָבָל; cp. Dt 32:6; Is 32:6; Sir 50:26). Fr. the time of HPaulus, Comm.[2] 1804ff I 671 to FSchulthess, ZNW 21, 1922, 241, and SFeigin, JNES 2, '43, 195 it has been held to be a transliteration of מוֹרֶה *rebel* (Dt 21:18, 20); acc. to KKöhler, ZNW 19, 1920, 91–95 it is simply the Gk. translation of the calque ῥακά; acc. to HPernot, Pages choisies des Évang. 1925, 61, who refers to Mod. Gk., a simple exclamation w. humorous coloring.—RGuelich, ZNW 64, '73, 39–52; Field, Notes 3–5; Mlt-H. 152f.—B. 1215. DELG. M-M. EDNT. TW. Spicq.

μωρῶς adv. of μωρός (X., An. 7, 6, 21 al.) ***foolishly*** ἀπόλλυσθαι *perish in one's folly* IEph 17:2.

Μωσῆς s. Μωϋσῆς.

Μωϋσῆς (the Hebr. מֹשֶׁה seems to have been written so in Gk. orig.; Manetho [III BC]: 609 fgm. 72 Jac. [in Jos., C. Ap. 1, 250]; Diod. S. 1, 94, 2; 34+35 fgm. 1, 3; Nicol. Dam. [I BC]: 90 fgm. 72 Jac., in Jos., Ant. 1, 95; Numenius of Apamea [II AD], in Clem. Al., Strom. 1, 150, 4; LXX, s. Thackeray 163, 3; EpArist 144; TestSol 25:3f; Test12Patr; ParJer 7:20; ApcMos prol.; AscIs, Philo, Joseph., Mel.—W. Μωσῆς AssMos, ApcEsdr.—W. v.l. Μωσῆς: Just., Tat., Ath.—PGM 13=8th Book of Moses

3; 21; 343; 383; 730 al. has Μοϋσῆς. The Μωσῆς of the t.r., also of ISm 5:1 v.l. [s. ed. Bihlmeyer p. xxxvi and ad loc.]; ApcEsdr 6:12 p. 31, 17 Tdf.; Theoph. Ant. 3, 18 [p. 240, 14], occurs Diod. S. 40, 3, 3; 6; Strabo 16, 2, 35; 39; LXX; Demetr.: 722 fgm. 2, 1 al.; Ezk. Trag. vs. 30, in Clem. 1, 155, 5; SibOr. On the spelling B-D-F §38; 53, 1; W-S. §5, 21e; Mlt-H. 86f; EbNestle, ZAW 27, 1907, 111–13; Preisigke, Namenbuch; Wuthnow 79f), **έως, ὁ** (also Mel., P. 11, 77; or Μωϋσῆ w. LXX; AscIs 3:8; Μωσῆ ApcEsdr 6:12 p. 31, 17 Tdf.) dat. εῖ and ῆ (the latter all edd. **Ac 7:44,** also t.r. **Mt 17:4; J 5:46; 9:29; Ro 9:15;** Mel., P. 69, 502, with ms. variations), acc. mostly ῆν (Demetr. [s. above]; Ezk. Trag. vs. 30; all edd. **Ac 6:11; 7:35; 1 Cor. 10:2; Hb 3:3**); rarely έα (all edd. **Lk 16:29;** also Mel., P. 59, 433; both forms Just., Tat.); voc. ῆ (Ezk. Trag. vs. 243 Μωσῆ) B 4:8; 1 Cl 53:2 v.l. On the declension s. B-D-F §55, 1d; Mlt-H. 146; W-S. §10, 5 and note 4. ***Moses,*** brother of Miriam (s. Ex 15:20; Mi 6:4), lawgiver of the Hebrews (as such Manetho: 609, fgm. 10, 250 Jac. [in Jos., C. Ap. 1, 250] without being named, but as author of Gen 1:3, 9f; so also Περὶ ὕψους 9, 9) **Mt 8:4; 19:7f; 22:24** (the quite common introductory formula M. εἶπεν, followed by Dt 25:5, as Epict. 1, 28, 4 ὡς λέγει Πλάτων [Sophista 228c]; Just., D. 20, 1; 126, 4 M. φησιν); **Mk 1:44; 7:10; 10:3f; 12:19; Lk 5:14; 20:28; J 1:17; 7:19, 22f; 8:5.** Details of his life story: summary of his life **Ac 7:20ff.; Hb 11:23f.** His flight 1 Cl 4:10. The theophany at the burning bush **Lk 20:37.** The serpent raised up **J 3:14.** The giving of the manna **6:32.** Moses' conversation w. God **9:29,** sojourn on Sinai 1 Cl 53:2; B 4:7; 14:2ff; 15:1, shining face **2 Cor 3:7** (cp. Ex 34:29ff), a cover on it vs. **13** (cp. Ex 34:33). Jannes and Jambres **2 Ti 3:8.** Dathan and Abiram 1 Cl 4:12. The struggle betw. Michael and the devil for M's. corpse **Jd 9.** πιστὸς θεράπων 1 Cl 43:1 (cp. Num 12:7); cp. 17:5; 51:3, 5; **Hb 3:5.** ὁ δοῦλος τοῦ θεοῦ **Rv 15:3.** Designated a προφήτης (Philo; Jos., Ant. 4, 329; Just., A I, 32, 1 al.; PGM 5, 109 ἐγώ εἰμι Μωϋσῆς ὁ προφήτης σου, ᾧ παρέδωκας τὰ μυστήριά σου) B 6:8. ἐν πνεύματι ἐλάλησεν 10:2, 9; cp. 12:2 (Just., D. 49, 7; 91, 4). ποιεῖ τύπον τοῦ Ἰησοῦ 12:5ff. W. Elijah (PDabeck, Biblica 23, '42, 175–89) **Mt 17:3f; Mk 9:4f; Lk 9:30, 33.** *Moses*=the Books of Moses (as Plut., Mor. 379a, Plato=the writings of Pla.) **2 Cor 3:15.** Correspondingly *M. and the prophets* **Lk 16:29, 31; 24:27; Ac 26:22.** Cp. ISm 5:1.—Lit. on Moses in the Haggadah: Monatsschr. f. Gesch. u. Wiss. d. Judent. 77, '33, 390–92.—M-M. EDNT. TW.

N

Ναασσών, ὁ indecl. (נַחְשׁוֹן Ex 6:23 [quoted by Philo, Poster. Cai. 76]; Num 1:7; Ruth 4:20) ***Nahshon,*** in the genealogy of Jesus **Mt 1:4ab; Lk 3:32.**

Νάβαλ, ὁ (נָבָל; Ναβαλ LXX; Νάβαλος Joseph.) ***Nabal*** AcPl Ha 6, 22f (after 1 Kgm 25:3ff).

Ναγγαί, ὁ indecl. *Naggai* in the genealogy of Jesus **Lk 3:25.**

Ναζαρά, ἡ (**Mt 4:13; Lk 4:16**), **Ναζαρέτ, Ναζαρέθ;** in vv.ll. also **Ναζαράτ, Ναζαράθ** indecl. ***Nazareth.*** Also as neut. pl. AcPl BMM verso 38f [ἐν Να]ζαροῖς//AcPl Ha 8, 30 [ἐν N]αζαρά. On the var. forms of the name s. JZenner, ZKT 18, 1894, 744–47; Dalman, Gramm.[2] 152; FBurkitt, The Syriac Forms of NT Proper Names 1912, 16; 28f, JTS 14, 1913, 475f; Zahn on Mt 2:23; B-D-F §39, 2; W-S. §5, 27e and p. xvi on §5 note 58; Mlt-H. 107f. Ναζαρέτ (also Just., D. 78, 4) and Ναζαρέθ seem to have the best attestation.—Home of Jesus' parents; the place is not mentioned in the OT, Talmud, Midrash, or Joseph., but plays a significant role in Christian tradition: **Mt 2:23; 4:13; 21:11; Mk 1:9; Lk 1:26; 2:4, 39, 51; 4:16** (BViolet, Z. recht. Verst. der Naz.-Perikope Lk 4:16–30: ZNW 37, '39, 251–71); **J 1:45f; Ac 10:38;** AcPl Ha 8, 30//BMM verso 38f.—On N. see HGuthe, RE XIII 1903, 676ff, Palästina[2] 1927, 149ff; Dalman, Orte[3] 61–88; GSchumacher, D. jetzige Naz.: ZDPV 13, 1890, 235ff; PViaud, Naz. et ses deux églises 1910; MBrückner, Naz. die Heimat Jesu: Pj 7, 1911, 74–84; TSoiron, D. Ev. u. die. hl. Stätten 1929, 17–37; PWinter, 'Naz.' and 'Jerus.' in Lk 1 and 2, NTS 3, '56/57, 136–42; CKopp, The Holy Places of the Gospels, tr. RWalls, '63, 49–86.—MAvi-Yonah, The Caesarea Inscription of the Twenty-Four Priestly Courses: The Teacher's Yoke, ed. JVardaman et al., '64, 46–57, esp. p. 48 n. 2. BHHW III 1291f; Kl. Pauly IV 27.—OEANE IV 113f. M-M. TW.

Ναζαρηνός, ή, όν ***coming from Nazareth,*** only subst. ὁ N. ***the Nazarene, inhabitant of Nazareth*** applied only to Jesus **Mk 1:24; 10:47** (vv.ll. Ναζωρηνός and Ναζωραῖος); **14:67; 16:6; Lk 4:34; 24:19** (v.l. Ναζωραῖος); **J 18:5** D. JBecker, Jesus of Nazareth, '98—TW.

Ναζωραῖος, ου, ὁ ***Nazoraean, Nazarene,*** predominantly a designation of Jesus, in Mt, J, Ac and **Lk 18:37,** while Mk has Ναζαρηνός (q.v.). Of the two places where the latter form occurs in Lk, the one, Lk 4:34, apparently comes fr. Mk (1:24), the other, 24:19, perh. fr. a special source. Where the author of Lk-Ac writes without influence fr. another source he uses Ναζωραῖος. **Mt** says expressly **2:23** that Jesus was so called because he grew up in Nazareth. In addition, the other NT writers who call Jesus Ναζωραῖος know Nazareth as his home. But linguistically the transition fr. Ναζαρέτ to Ναζωραῖος is difficult (Dalman, Gramm.[2] 178; Wlh. on Mt 26:69; MLidzbarski, Mandäische Liturgien 1920, xviff, Zeitschrift für Semitistik 1, 1922, 230ff, Ginza 1925, ixf; FBurkitt, The Syriac Forms of NT Proper Names 1912; AvGall, Βασιλεία τοῦ θεοῦ 1926 p. 432, 4; cp. 411f; RBultmann, ZNW 24, 1925, 143f, Jesus 1926, 26 [Eng. tr. 24]; HSchaeder in Rtzst. u. Schaeder, Studien zum antiken Synkretismus 1926 p. 308, 2, also TW IV 879–84; Moore below) and it is to be borne in mind that Ναζωραῖος meant someth. different before it was connected w. Nazareth (cp. Orig. Celsus 7, 18, 9f, who calls Jesus ὁ Ναζωραῖος ἄνθρωπος. JSanders, JBL 84, '65, 169–72 [rev. in: The Gospels and the Scriptures of Israel, ed. CEvans/WStegner '94, 116–28] interprets N. in **Mt 2:23** as meaning both 'coming from Nazareth' and 'miraculously born'). The pass. where Jesus is so called are **Mt 2:23; 26:69 v.l., 71; Lk 18:37; J 18:5, 7; 19:19; Ac 2:22; 3:6; 4:10; 6:14; 22:8; 26:9.** Acc. to **Ac 24:5** the Christians were so called; s. Kl. Texte 3[2] p. 3, ln. 32 and 8[3] p. 6, lines 8, 17, 27; p. 7, note on ln. 1ff; p. 8, ln. 5; p. 9, ln.17; 23; p. 10, ln. 5; 15; p. 11, ln. 28 and note on ln. 9ff, all passages in which Jewish Christians are called Nazaraei, Nazareni, Ναζωραῖοι.—Laud. Therap. 27 the monks are called ναζιραῖοι (with the v.l. Ναζαραῖοι).—EbNestle, ET 19, 1908, 523f, PM 14, 1910, 349f; HZimmern, ZDMG 74, 1920, 429ff; GMoore, Nazarene and Nazareth: Beginn. I/1, 1920, 426–32 (s. I/5, '33, 356f); EMeyer II 408f; 423, 2; HGressmann, ZKG 41=n.s. 4, 1922, 166f; WCaspari, ZNW 21, 1922, 122–27; HSmith, Ναζωραῖος κληθήσεται: JTS 28, 1927, 60; ELohmeyer, Joh. d. Täufer '32, p. 115, 2; HSchlier, TRu n.s. 5, '33, 7f; WOesterley, ET 52, '41, 410–12; SLyonnet, Biblica 25, '44, 196–206; MBlack, An Aramaic Approach[3], '67, 197–200; WAlbright, JBL 65, '46, 397–401, also JKennard, Jr., ibid. 66, '47, 79–81; HShires, ATR 29, '47, 19–27; TNicklin, Gospel Gleanings, '50, 257–60; BGärtner, Die rätselhafte Termini Nazoräer u. Iskariot '57, 5–36; ESchweizer, Judentum, Urchrist., Kirche '60, 90–93; RPesch: The Gospels and the Scriptures of Israel '94, 178–211.—B-D-F §39, 4; BHHW II, 1293. M-M. EDNT. TW.

Ναθάμ, ὁ indecl. (נָתָן) ***Nathan,*** son of David (2 Km 5:14; Zech 12:12 Ναθάν, as **Lk 3:31 v.l.;** Just., D. 118, 2.—In Jos., Ant. 7, 70 Νάθας [acc. -αν]); in the genealogy of Jesus **Lk 3:31.**

Ναθαναήλ, ὁ indecl. (נְתַנְאֵל. Cp. Num 1:8; 2 Esdr [Ezra] 10:22; 1 Ch 2:14; 15:24.—In Jos., Ant. 6, 161; 20, 14 Ναθαναῆλος, ου) ***Nathanael,*** a disciple of Jesus, mentioned only in **J** (**1:45–49; 21:2**). He does not appear in the synoptic lists of the twelve apostles; hence, since antiquity, attempts have been made to identify him w. various apostles, esp. Bartholomew, as well as w. other personalities; some have given up the attempt to place him among the twelve. S. Hdb.[3] exc. on J 1, end. Acc. to **J 21:2** he came fr. Cana in Galilee. S. also the apocryphal gospel fragment fr. the Berlin pap 11710 : ZNW 22, 1923, 153f, cited ASyn. 21, 75.—REisler, Das Rätsel des Joh-Ev. '36, 475–85; JJeremias, D. Berufung des N.: Αγγελος III, 1928, 2–5; UHolzmeister, Biblica 21, '40, 28–39; GQuispel, ZNW 47, '56, 281–83; BHHW II. 1289.

ναί particle denoting affirmation, agreement, or emphasis (Hom.+; POxy 1413, 7 al. in pap; LXX, TestSol, TestAbr; JosAs17:1 cod. A; ApcSed 3:2; ApcMos 17:1; EpArist 201 ναί, βασιλεῦ; Jos., Ant. 17, 169; Just.) ***yes, certainly, indeed, it's true that***

ⓐ in answer to a question—**α.** asked by another pers., *yes* (Ael. Aristid. 34 p. 663 D.; Lucian, Dial. Deor. 4, 1 al.; Alexander Numenianus [time of Hadrian]: Rhet. Gr. ed. LSpengel III 1856 p. 24f: the answer to a question should be ναὶ ἢ οὔ; Ammonius Phil., In Int. p. 199, 21 ἀποκρίν. τὸ ναὶ ἢ τὸ οὔ; Sb 7696, 57 [250 AD]) **Mt 9:28; 13:51; 17:25; 21:16; J 11:27; 21:15f; Ac 5:8; 22:27;** GPt 10:42; Hs 9, 11, 8; GJs 19:1 codd.; AcPl Ha 5, 2 (restored).

β. asked by one who answers: *yes, indeed* ναὶ λέγω ὑμῖν **Mt 11:9; Lk 7:26** gives an affirmative answer to the question directed to the crowd, thereby confirming the correctness of the crowd's opinion; the people are 'on the right track', but need further instruction.—If the question is put in negative form, the answer may be *of course* **Ro 3:29** (cp. after negative assertion TestAbr A 17 p. 99, 9 [Stone p. 46]; ApcMos 17).

ⓑ in declarations of agreement to the statements of others: *certainly, indeed, quite so* (Gen 42:21; Epict. 2, 7, 9 ναί, κύριε; Diod. S. 13, 26, 1 ναί, ἀλλά=indeed, but; Lucian, Jupp. Tr. 6 and 9 ναί. ἀλλὰ . . .) ναί, κύριε: καὶ γάρ *certainly, Lord* (or *sir*); *and yet* **Mt 15:27; Mk 7:28 v.l.** (but it may also mean an urgent repetition of the request: B-D-F §441, 1; AFridrichsen, ConNeot 1, '36, 10–13; Athen. Tafel Elderkin 2 [III AD]: Hesperia 6, '37, 383ff, ln. 7 a fervent invocation in prayer: ναὶ κύριε Τυφώς, ἐκδίκησον . . . καὶ βοήθησον αὐτῷ; PGM 1, 216 ναί, κύριε; cp. 36, 227); Hv 3, 3, 1; 4, 3, 1; m 6, 1, 1. Prob. **Rv 14:13; 16:7; 22:20b v.l.** belong here.

ⓒ in emphatic repetition of one's own statement *yes (indeed)* **Mt 11:26; Lk 10:21; 11:51.** ναὶ λέγω ὑμῖν, τοῦτον φοβήθητε *yes, indeed, that's the one to fear, I tell you* **12:5.—Phlm 20;** B 14:1. The repetition can consist in the fact that one request preceded and a similar one follows ναὶ ἐρωτῶ καὶ σέ *yes, and I ask you* **Phil 4:3.**—1 Cl 60:3.

ⓓ in solemn assurance (Herodas 1, 86 ναὶ Δήμητρα = by Demeter) ναὶ ἔρχομαι ταχύ *surely I am coming soon* **Rv 22:20.** ναί, ἀμήν *so it is to be, assuredly so* **1:7.**

ⓔ In wordplay ναί is used w. οὔ: ἤτω ὑμῶν τὸ ναὶ ναί, καὶ τὸ οὒ οὔ *let your 'yes' be yes, and your 'no' no* i.e., the absolute dependability of your statements should make an oath unnecessary **Js 5:12.** But **Mt 5:37** reads ἔστω ὁ λόγος ὑμῶν ναὶ ναί, οὒ οὔ i.e., *a clear 'yes', a clear 'no'* and nothing more (ναί doubled also Archilochus [VII BC] 99 Diehl[3]; Alciphron 4, 13, 8; Theodor. Prodr. 8, 321 Hercher; PGM 1, 90; PMinear, NovT 13, '71, 1–13). Yet many (B-D-F §432, 1; Wlh., EKlostermann, M'Neile on Mt 5:37; CTorrey, The Four Gospels '33, 291; ELittmann, ZNW 34, '35, 23f) assume that **Mt 5:37** has the same sense as **Js 5:12;** the Koridethi gosp. (ms. Θ) assimilates the text of the Mt pass. to the one in Js.—Paul denies that, in forming his plans, he has proceeded in such a way ἵνα ᾖ παρ' ἐμοὶ τὸ ναὶ ναὶ καὶ τὸ οὒ οὔ *that my 'yes' should at the same time be 'no'* **2 Cor 1:17;** cp. vs. **18.** This is just as impossible as that in the gospel ναὶ καὶ οὔ *'yes' and 'no'* are preached at the same time vs. **19a.** Rather, in Jesus Christ there is only *'yes'* vs. **19b** to all the promises of God vs. **20.**—EKutsch, Eure Rede aber sei ja ja, nein nein: EvTh '60, 206–18.—DELG. M-M.

N

Ναιμάν, ὁ indecl. (נַעֲמָן. On the var. ways of writing the name in the tradition s. B-D-F §37; 53, 2; Mlt-H. p. 84) ***Naaman*** a Syrian army commander, healed of leprosy by Elisha (4 Km 5:1ff; s. BHHW III 1279) **Lk 4:27.**—M-M.

Ναΐν, ἡ indecl. (in the Bible only **Lk 7:11.** The name is applied to an Idumaean locality in Jos., Bell. 4, 511 v.l.; 517) ***Nain,*** a city in Galilee **Lk 7:11.**—Dalman, Pj 9, 1913, 45; Abel, Geographie II '38, 394f; CKopp, The Holy Places of the Gospels, tr. RWalls, '63, 236–41; BHHW II 1283f.

ναός, οῦ, ὁ (Hom.+; s. B-D-F §44, 1; Mlt-H. 71; 121) **a place or structure specifically associated with or set apart for a deity, who is frequently perceived to be using it as a dwelling,** ***temple.***

ⓐ of temples gener. (Diod. S. 5, 15, 2 θεῶν ναούς; Ar. 3:2; Just., A I, 9, 1; Hippol., Ref. 5, 26, 33) **Ac 17:24.** Specif. of temples: of replicas of the temple of Artemis at Ephesus **19:24** (Tat. 3:1); but here, near ἱερόν vs. 27 (cp. OGI 90, 34 [196 BC]; Sb 8745, 6 [pap 171/72 AD] ἐν τῷ ἱερῷ Σοκνοβραίσεως ναὸς ξύλινος περικεχρυσωμένος. Likew. 8747, 5; 3 Macc 1:10; Philo, Leg. ad Gai. 139 ἱερὰ κ. ναοί, Decal. 7; Jos., Ant. 16, 106), ναός can be understood in the more restricted sense *shrine,* where the image of the goddess stood (so Hdt. et al.; Diod. S. 1, 97, 9; 20, 14, 3; UPZ 5, 27=6, 22 [163 BC], s. the editor's note; BGU 1210, 191 ἐν παντὶ ἱερῷ, ὅπου ναός ἐστιν; 211; PErlang 21 [II AD]: APF 14, '41, 100f, a shrine w. a ξόανον of Isis).

ⓑ of the temple at Jerusalem (3 Km 6:5, 17 al.; Jos., Ant. 8, 62ff; Just., D. 36, 6 al; SibOr 3, 575; 657; 702; Stephan. Byz. s.v.

Σόλυμα: ὁ ναὸς ὁ ἐν Ἱεροσολύμοις.—ναός [νεώς] of Herod's temple: Philo, In Flacc. 46, Leg. ad Gai. 278 al.; Jos., Bell. 5, 185; 207; 215, Ant. 15, 380; Orig., C. Cels. 1, 47, 11; Did., Gen. 135, 17; 192, 23; also of the entire temple precinct: Jos., Bell. 6, 293, C. Ap. 2, 119) **Mt 23:17, 35; 27:5, 40; Mk 14:58** (on this saying s. RHoffmann, Heinrici Festschr. 1914, 130–39 and MGoguel, Congr. d'Hist. du Christ. I 1928, 117–36. More generally DPlooij, Jes. and the Temple: ET 42, '31, 36–39); **15:29; Lk 1:21f; J 2:20; Ac 7:48 v.l.; Rv 11:2;** 1 Cl 41:2; B 16:1ff; GPt 7:26. ὁ ν. καὶ ὁ λαὸς Ἰσραήλ B 16:5; οἱ ἱερεῖς τ. ναοῦ 7:3. τὸ καταπέτασμα τοῦ ναοῦ *the curtain of the temple* that separated the Holy of Holies fr. the holy place **Mt 27:51; Mk 15:38; Lk 23:45;** τ. κ. τ. ναοῦ τῆς Ἰερουσαλήμ GPt 5:20. τὰ παθνώματα τοῦ ναοῦ *the paneled ceiling of the temple* GJs 24:3. An oath by the temple **Mt 23:16, 21.** More fully ὁ ναὸς τοῦ θεοῦ (as ParJer 4:4; Jos., Ant. 15, 380; cp. Artem. 2, 26 νεὼς θεοῦ) **Mt 26:61; 2 Th 2:4** (on this s. WWrede, Die Echtheit des 2 Th 1903, 96ff); **Rv 11:1** (on the prophecy of the rescue of the temple fr. the general destruction cp. Jos., Bell. 6, 285). ὁ ναὸς τοῦ κυρίου **Lk 1:9;** cp. 1 Cl 23:5 (Mal 3:1). ναὸς κυρίου GJs (16 times), also τῷ ν. αὐτοῦ 23:1.

ⓒ of a heavenly sanctuary (cp. Ps 10:4; 17:7; Wsd 3:14 ν. κυρίου; Philo, Spec. Leg. 1, 66; TestLevi 5:1) of **Rv:** ὁ ναός **14:15; 15:6, 8ab; 16:1, 17.** ὁ ναὸς αὐτοῦ (=τοῦ θεοῦ) **7:15; 11:19b.** ὁ ναὸς ὁ ἐν τ. οὐρανῷ **14:17.** ὁ ναὸς τοῦ θεοῦ ὁ ἐν τ. οὐρανῷ **11:19a.** ὁ ναὸς τῆς σκηνῆς τ. μαρτυρίου ἐν τ. οὐρανῷ **15:5.** S. also **3:12.** Yet there will be no temple in the New Jerusalem **21:22a;** God in person is the sanctuary of the eternal city vs. **22b.**

ⓓ of a human body or part thereof, in imagery (Philo, Op. M. 136f of the σῶμα as the νεὼς ἱερὸς ψυχῆς; Tat. 15, 2).—Of the spirit-filled body of Christians, which is said to be a habitation of God, therefore a temple (Iren. 5, 9, 4 [PJena]; Hippol., Ref. 5, 19, 15; cp. Sextus 35), which is not to be contaminated by sinful indulgence (on Greco-Roman purity regulations for entry into temples, s. for example SIG 983 and note 3): τὸ σῶμα ὑμῶν ν. τοῦ ἐν ὑμῖν ἁγίου πνεύματός ἐστιν *your body is a temple of the Holy Spirit (dwelling) within you* **1 Cor 6:19.** The habitation of the heart is a ν. ἅγιος τῷ κυρίῳ B 6:15; cp. the development of this thought 16:6–10 (Pythagorean saying in HSchenkl, Wiener Stud 8, 1886, 273 no. 66 νεὼς θεοῦ σοφὸς νοῦς, ὃν ἀεὶ χρὴ παρασκευάζειν κ. κατακοσμεῖν εἰς παραδοχὴν θεοῦ. Cp. Sextus 46a; Synes., Dio 9 p. 49c νεὼς οὗτος [i.e., the νοῦς οἰκεῖος θεῷ=the Νοῦς is the real temple of God]). Of spirit-filled Christians γίνεσθαι ν. τέλειον τῷ θεῷ 4:11. φυλάσσειν τὴν σάρκα ὡς ν. θεοῦ 2 Cl 9:3; τηρεῖν τὴν σάρκα ὡς ν. θεοῦ IPhld 7:2. Hence individual Christians are called αὐτοῦ (=θεοῦ) ναοί IEph 15:3. Of a Christian congregation **1 Cor 3:16, 17ab; 2 Cor 6:16ab.** αὔξει εἰς ναὸν ἅγιον ἐν κυρίῳ **Eph 2:21.** The Christians are λίθοι ναοῦ πατρός *stones for the Father's temple* IEph 9:1. To place great emphasis on the oneness of the Christian community (which permits no division) Christians are challenged thus: πάντες ὡς εἰς ἕνα ναὸν συντρέχετε θεοῦ *come together, all of you, as to one temple of God* IMg 7:2.—(Cp.: ναοῦ τοῦ θεοῦ ὄντος τοῦ παντὸς κόσμου 'the entire world is God's temple' Orig., C. Cels. 7, 44, 38).—S. ἱερόν b.—KBaltzer, HTR 58, '65, 263–77 (Luke); BGärtner, The Temple and the Community in Qumran and in the NT '65; RClements, God and Temple '65 (OT).

ⓔ The uses in **J 2:19, 20, 21** call for special attention. Jesus, standing in Jersualem's temple exclaims, λύσατε τὸν ναὸν τοῦτον καὶ ἐν τρισὶν ἡμέραις ἐγερῶ αὐτόν *destroy this temple, and in three days I will raise it* (vs. **19**), which some persons in the narrative understand as a ref. to the physical structure (vs. **20**), but the narrator interprets it as a reference to the ναὸς τοῦ σώματος αὐτοῦ *temple of his body* (vs. **21**) (AMDubarle, Le signe du Temple [J 2:19]: RB 48, '39, 21–44; OCullmann, TZ 4, '48, 367). Cp. the description of Christ's body δικαιοσύνης ν. AcPlCor 2:17.—B. 1465. DELG. M-M. DLNT 1159–66. EDNT. TW. Sv.

Ναούμ, ὁ indecl. (נַחוּם cp. Na 1:1.—In Jos., Ant. 9, 239 Ναοῦμος) ***Nahum*** in the genealogy of Jesus **Lk 3:25.**

ναοφόρος, ον (ναός, φέρω; hapax leg.) **pert. to bearing the image of a temple or shrine** (s. ναός a), subst. ***temple-bearer*** or ***shrine-bearer*** w. other compounds of -φόρος IEph 9:2. Evidently the writer has a polytheistic relig. procession in mind.—DELG s.v. φέρω D 2 p. 1190.

νάρδος, ου, ἡ (prob. a Semit. loanw. [HLewy, Die sem. Fremdwörter im Griech. 1895, 40], but ultimately of Indo-European orig. [Pers. nārdīn; Sanskr. naladâ])

❶ **an aromatic plant from which oil of nard is derived, *(spike)nard*** (En 32:1) a perennial herb of the Valerian family: Zohary 205, native to India (Onesicritus: 134 fgm. 22 Jac.; Arrian, Anab. 6, 22, 5) στέφανος ἐκ νάρδου στάχυος πεπλεγμένος *a wreath woven of nard blossoms* ApcPt 3:10 (cp. Theophr., HP 9, 7, 2ff).

❷ **an aromatic oil of the (spike)nard plant,** extracted fr. the root (Nicander, Ther. 937, Alexiph. 402 νάρδου ῥίζαι), ***oil of nard*** (s. Peripl. Eryth. c. 39; 48; Diosc., Mat. Med. 1, 6, 75; Pliny, NH 12, 26; 13, 2; 4; PSI 628, 7 [III BC]; PEdg 69 [=Sb 6775], 5 [257 BC]; POxy 1088, 49; PGM 13, 19; 353; SSol 1:12; 4:13f) μύρον νάρδου *ointment* or *perfume of nard* **Mk 14:3; J 12:3.** In the latter pass. a pound of it is valued at 300 denarii=an average worker's wages for a period of almost ten months (vss. **3** and 5). ILöw, D. Flora d. Juden III 1924, 482–88; SNaber, Νάρδος πιστική: Mnemosyne 30, 1902, 1–15; WSchoff, Nard: JAOS 43, 1925, 216–28; JBrown, The Mediterranean Vocab. of the Vine, VetusT 19, '69, 160–64; New Docs 1, 85.—DELG. M-M. S. πιστικός 3.

νάρκη, ης, ἡ (in var. mngs. Hippocr., Aristoph. et al.; TestSol 18:19; Philo) ***numbness, deadness.*** This word is incorrectly restored [.... πολ]|λῇ λυθεῖσα ν[άρκη in some editions of Ox 1081, 3 (CWessely, PatrOr 18, 1924, 494; Kleine Texte 8^3 p. 25 app. [Sweete], and Otero I 82) instead of ἐ]λ̣ηλύθεισαν [διαφο]ρά. S. ἔρχομαι 1aζ.—DELG.

Νάρκισσος, ου, ὁ *Narcissus,* a name found rather freq. among slaves and freedmen (Tacitus, Ann. 13, 1; Sueton., Claudius 28; Cass. Dio 64, 3, 4; IMagnMai 122d, 14; IHierap 80; IG XII, 8, 548, 2; CIL VI 4123; 4346; 5206 al.). Paul greets οἱ ἐκ τῶν Ναρκίσσου οἱ ὄντες ἐν κυρίῳ *those belonging to the household of Narcissus who are Christians* **Ro 16:11** (slaves of N. are meant. Cp. Narcissiani CIL III 3973, VI 15640).—LGPN I. M-M.

ναυαγέω (ναῦς, ἄγνυμι 'break'); 1 aor. ἐναυάγησα (Aeschyl., Hdt.+; POxy 839, 6ff; Philo)

❶ **to live through a ship's destruction, *suffer shipwreck, come to ruin.*** τρὶς ἐναυάγησα *I have been shipwrecked three times* **2 Cor 11:25.** On hazards at sea: New Docs 3, 58f.

❷ **to experience a great loss or disaster, *suffer shipwreck*** fig. ext. of 1 (Cebes 24, 2 ὡς κακῶς διατρίβουσι καὶ ἀθλίως ζῶσι καὶ ναυαγοῦσιν ἐν τῷ βίῳ; Philo, Mut. Nom. 215, Somn. 2, 147) περὶ τὴν πίστιν ἐναυάγησαν *they have suffered shipwreck in their faith* **1 Ti 1:19.**—DELG s.v. ναυαγός. M-M. TW.

Ναυή, ὁ indecl. (נוּן. Cp. Ex 33:11; Num 11:28; Josh 1:1 al. In all these pass. LXX renders נוּן with Ναυή; cp. Jos., Bell. 4, 459; Just., Mel.—1 Ch 7:27; Νούμ; PKatz TZ 9, '53, 230) ***Nun,*** Joshua's father 1 Cl 12:2; B 12:8f.

ναύκληρος, ου, ὁ (ναῦς, κλῆρος; Soph., Hdt.+; Plut., Jos. [both w. κυβερνήτης, q.v. 1]; OGI 344, 4 [I BC]; pap [Preisigke, Fachwörter; for others New Docs, below; En 101:4, 9; Philo, Op. M. 147) freq. 'ship-owner' or 'charterer' of a vessel. But it can also mean ***captain,*** since the sailing-master of a ship engaged in state service (esp. for shipment of grain IG 14, 918) was called a ναύκληρος (MRostovtzeff, APF 5, 1913, 298; LCasson, Ships and Seamanship in the Ancient World, '71, 314–16; but WKunkel, APF 8, '27, 185 'freight contractor', not necessarily as pilot or captain) **Ac 27:11.** (For sailing regulations POxy 3250, 22–24 [63 AD], s. New Docs 2, 74 no. 25.)—Nock, Essays 823; Hemer, Acts 138f; JVélissaropoulos, Les nauclères grecs, '80; New Docs 4, 116f (pap, ins and lit.).—DELG. M-M. Spicq.

ναῦς, ἡ (Hom.+; ins, pap, LXX; Philo, Aet. M. 138 al.; Jos., Vi. 165 al.; SibOr 8, 348) acc. **ναῦν** ***ship*** only of larger vessels **Ac 27:41** (w. ἐπικέλλω as Od. 9, 148)—B. 727. DELG. M-M.

ναύτης, ου, ὁ (ναῦς; Hom. et al.; ins, pap; Ezk 27:9 Aq.; 27:29 Sym.; Jos., Vi. 66, Ant. 9, 209; TestNapht 6:2; loanw. in rabb.) ***sailor*** **Ac 27:27, 30; Rv 18:17.** —DELG s.v. ναῦς. M-M.

Ναχώρ, ὁ indecl. (נָחוֹר) ***Nahor*** (Gen 11:22–26; 1 Ch 1:26f; Philo, Congr. Erud. Gr. 43.—In Joseph. Ναχώρης, ου [Ant. 1, 153]), in the genealogy of Jesus **Lk 3:34.**

νεανίας, ου, ὁ (trag., Hdt. et al.; ins; POxy 471, 114 [II AD]; LXX, TestSol; Jos., Bell. 2, 409, Vi. 129; 170; TestJos 12:3; 16:1) ***youth, young man*** (fr. about the 24th to the 40th year; Diog. L. 8, 10; Philo, Cher. 114; Lob. on Phryn. p. 213.—FBoll, D. Lebensalter: NJklA 31, 1913, 89ff) **Ac 7:58; 20:9; 23:17, 18 v.l., 22 v.l**; Hv 1, 4, 1 (here the transf. sense *servant* is also prob., cp. Judg 16:26 B).—VLeinieks, The City of Dionysos '96, 199–209 (on the third and fourth age-class scheme in Gk. vocabulary). Schmidt, Syn. 22–35. DELG s.v. νέος 3. M-M. Sv.

νεᾶνις, ιδος, ἡ (Hom. et al.; LXX [w. παρθένος Dt 22:23–29], JosAs; Just., D. 84, 3) ***young woman*** (includes women in the teens) GJs 9:2.).—AKamesar, The Virgin of Is 7:14, the Philological Argument from the Second to the Fifth Century: JTS 41, '90, 51–75.—DELG s.v. νέος 3.

νεανίσκος, ου, ὁ (Hdt. et al.; ins, pap, LXX; Jos., Ant. 6, 179, Vi. 126; Test12Patr. In later Gk. more common than νεανίας) dim. of νεάν.

➊ **a relatively young man, *youth, young man*** (on the chron. limits of this period of life cp. what is said on νεανίας and s. Philo, Op. M. 105; an ins at Delos, BCH 13, 1889, 420ff, lists a series of age-classes: παῖδες, ἔφηβοι, νεανίσκοι and equates ν. with νεός [Forbes p. 61]) **Mt 19:20, 22;** Mk 14:51 (SJohnson, The Identity and Significance of the Neaniskos in Mark: Forum 8, '92, 123–39); **16:5** (cp. Jos., Ant. 5, 213; on connection w. 14:51 s. BvanIersel, CBQ 58, '96, 261, n. 52 [lit.]); **Lk 7:14; Ac 2:17** (Jo 3:1); **20:12** D; **23:18, 22; 1J 2:13f;** Hv 2, 4, 1; 3, 1, 6ff; 3, 2, 5; 3, 4, 1; 3, 10, 1 and 7; s 6, 1, 5; 6, 2, 6; GPt 9:37; 13:55; AcPl Ha 3, 28; 4, 2 (of a heavenly being).

➋ **a young man functioning as a servant, *servant*** (Lucian, Alex. 53; Gen 14:24, perh. as early as PEdg 4 [=Sb 6710], 6 [259 BC]) **Mk 14:51b v.l.** οἱ νεανίσκοι; **Ac 5:10** (though here the ref. may simply be to young men of the congregation, who would naturally perform this service); AcPt Ox 849 recto, 19–20.—CForbes, NEOI: A Contribution to the Study of Greek Associations '33, 61–63.—DELG s.v. νέος 3. M-M.

Νεάπολις s. νέος 5.

Νεεμάν s. Ναιμάν.

νεῖκος, εος, τό as v.l. in **1 Cor 15:54f** is not the word for 'strife' w. the same spelling (Hom. et al.), but an itacistic form of νῖκος, q.v.—DELG s.v. νίκη.

νεκρός, ά, όν—A. as adj. (perh. as early as Hom., certainly Pind.; in Ath. only R. title)

➊ **pert. to being in a state of loss of life, *dead,*** of pers.: lit. καταπίπτειν νεκρόν *fall dead* **Ac 28:6.** ἤρθη νεκρός *he was taken up dead* **20:9** (another possibility is *as dead, for dead:* Lucian, Ver. Hist. 1, 22; Eunapius, Vi. Soph. 76 συγχωρήσατε τῷ νεκρῷ [the one who is deathly sick] με δοῦναι φάρμακον.—ἤρθη ν. as TestJud 9:3). νεκρὸς κεῖται (Mel., P. 90, 672) *lies dead* AcPt Ox 849 recto, 15.—**Ac 5:10; Js 2:26a.** ἔπεσα πρὸς τοὺς πόδας αὐτοῦ ὡς ν. *I fell at his feet as if I were dead* **Rv 1:17** (ὡς ν. as Diod. S. 36, 8, 4; TestAbr A 9 p. 86, 17 [Stone p. 20]). ἐγενήθησαν ὡς νεκροί **Mt 28:4.** ἐγένετο ὡσεὶ νεκρός **Mk 9:26.** Of Christ ἐγενόμην ν. *I was dead* **Rv 1:18;** cp. **2:8.**

➋ **pert. to being so morally or spirtually deficient as to be in effect dead, *dead,*** fig. ext. of 1—ⓐ of pers. (Soph., Philoct. 1018 ἄφιλον ἔρημον ἄπολιν ἐν ζῶσιν νεκρόν; Menand., Colax 50; Epict. 3, 23, 28; schol. on Aristoph., Ran. 423 διὰ τὴν κακοπραγίαν νεκροὺς τοὺς Ἀθηναίους καλεῖ; Sextus 175 ν. παρὰ θεῷ; Philo, Leg. All. 3, 35, Conf. Lingu. 55, Fuga 56) of the prodigal son either *thought to be dead, missing,* or morally *dead, depraved* **Lk 15:24, 32.** Of a congregation that is inactive, remiss **Rv 3:1.** Of persons before baptism Hs 9, 16, 3f; 6. W. dat. of disadvantage ν. τῇ ἁμαρτίᾳ *dead to sin* **Ro 6:11.**—ἐκ νεκρῶν ζῶντας **Ro 6:13;** sim. on the mng. of baptism ν. τοῖς παραπτώμασιν *dead in sins* **Eph 2:1, 5; Col 2:13.** Of worldly-minded Christians: τὸ ἥμισυ ν. ἐστι Hs 8, 8, 1 v.l.

ⓑ of things ν. ἔργα *dead works* that cannot bring eternal life **Hb 6:1; 9:14;** Hs 9, 21, 2. ἡ πίστις χωρὶς ἔργων ν. ἐστιν *faith apart from deeds* (i.e. without practical application) *is dead, useless* **Js 2:26b** (κενή P^{74}), cp. vss. **17, 20 v.l.** (DVerseput, Reworking the Puzzle of Faith and Deeds in Js 2:14–26: NTS 43, '97, 97–115). Of sin χωρὶς νόμου ἁμαρτία ν. *where there is no law, sin is dead,* i.e. sin is not perceptible **Ro 7:8** (cp. 5:20). Of the believer, in whom Christ lives: τὸ σῶμα νεκρόν *the body* (of σάρξ and sin) *is dead* **8:10** (Herm. Wr. 7, 2 visible corporeality is called ὁ αἰσθητικὸς νεκρός. Sim. Philo, Leg. All. 3, 69ff, Gig. 15).

➌ **pert. to having never been alive and lacking capacity for life, *dead, lifeless*** (Wsd 15:5; Ar. 3:2; Just., A I, 9, 1 ἄψυχα καὶ νεκρά) of the brass serpent B 12:7. Of polytheistic objects of cultic devotion PtK 2 p. 14, 21. νεκροὶ θεοί 2 Cl 3:1; D 6:3. (On the borderline between 1 and 2: τὰ μὲν ὀνόματα … θεῶν ὀνόματά ἐστιν νεκρῶν ἀνθρώπων Theoph. Ant. 1, 9 [p. 76, 8]).

B. as subst. ὁ ν. (so mostly Hom.+; ins, pap, LXX, En 103:5; TestGad 4:6; ApcEsdr 4:36; Philo; Jos., Bell. 4, 331 al.; Ar. 15, 3; Just., Mel., Ath., R. title; Jos.)

➊ **one who is no longer physically alive, *dead person, a dead body, a corpse,*** lit. **Lk 7:15; Hb 9:17; 11:35; Rv 20:5; 12:13.** μακάριοι οἱ ν. οἱ ἐν κυρίῳ ἀποθνήσκοντες **14:13;** cp. **1 Th 4:16.** Without art. νεκροῦ βληθέντος AcPlCor 2:32 (w. ζῶν as Appian, Liby. 129 §617 τ. νεκροὺς κ. τ. ζῶντας; Aesop, Fab. 69 H.=288 P.; EpArist 146) of God οὐκ ἔστιν (ὁ) θεὸς νεκρῶν ἀλλὰ ζώντων **Mt 22:32; Mk 12:27; Lk 20:38.** καὶ ν. καὶ ζώντων κυριεύειν *rule over the living and the dead* i.e. over all humankind past and present **Ro 14:9.** κρίνειν ζῶντας καὶ νεκρούς **2 Ti 4:1; 1 Pt 4:5;** B 7:2; κριτὴς ζώντων καὶ ν. **Ac 10:42;** 2 Cl 1:1; Pol 2:1. In this combination ν. without the article means all the dead, all those who are in the underworld (νεκροί=the dead: Thu. 4, 14, 5; 5, 10, 12; Lucian, Ver. Hist. 1, 39; Polyaenus 4, 2, 5). Of deceased Christians νεκροῖς εὐαγγελίσθη **1 Pt 4:6** (Selwyn, comm. 337–39). The art. can also be used without special significance: ὁ καιρὸς τῶν ν. κριθῆναι **Rv 11:18;** οἱ ν. ἀκούσουσιν τῆς φωνῆς τοῦ υἱοῦ τοῦ θεοῦ **J 5:25.** In prepositional phrases oft. without the art. ἐκ. ν. and ἀπὸ ν. (B-D-F §254, 2; Rob. 791f). ἐγείρειν ἐκ ν., ἐγείρεσθαι ἐκ ν. **Mt 17:9; Mk 6:14; Lk 9:7; 24:46; J 2:22; 12:1, 9, 17; 21:14; Ac 3:15; 4:10; 13:30; Ro 4:24; 6:4, 9; 7:4; 8:11ab, 34 v.l.; 10:9; 1 Cor 15:12a, 20; Gal 1:1; Eph 1:20; Col 2:12; 2 Ti 2:8; Hb 11:19; 1 Pt 1:21;** IMg 9:3; ITr 9:2; Pol 2:1f; 5:2; AcPlCor 2:6; 5:2. ἀναστῆναι ἐκ ν. and ἀναστῆσαί τινα ἐκ ν. (Just.; Mel., P.) **Mk 9:9f; 12:25; Lk 16:31; J 20:9; Ac 10:41; 13:34; 17:3, 31;** 1 Cl 24:1; B 15:9; GPt 8:30 (KKuhn, NTS 7, '61, 343f); Papias (11:3); Qua. ἡ ἐκ ν. ἀνάστασις (Mel., P. 3, 20) B 5:6; **Lk 20:35; Ac 4:2.** Also ἡ ἐξανάστασις ἡ ἐκ ν. **Phil 3:11;** ζωὴ ἐκ ν. **Ro 11:15;** ἀνάγειν ἐκ ν. (Just., A I, 45, 1; 50, 12 al.) *bring up from the realm of the dead* **Ro 10:7; Hb 13:20.** ἀπὸ ν. πορεύεσθαι πρός τινα *come up to someone fr. the realm of the dead* **Lk 16:30.** Somet. the art. is included in these prep. combinations without appreciable difference in mng.: ἐγείρεσθαι ἀπὸ τῶν ν. **Mt 14:2; 27:64; 28:7** (but ἐγείρεσθαι ἐκ ν. **17:9**). ἐγείρειν ἐκ τῶν ν. **1 Th 1:10 v.l.;** πρωτότοκος ἐκ τῶν ν. **Col 1:18** beside ὁ πρωτότοκος τῶν ν. **Rv 1:5.** The art. is often omitted w. the gen.; so as a rule in ἀνάστασις ν. (Did., Gen. 96, 13) *resurrection of the dead,* an expr. that is explained by the locution ἀναστῆναι ἐκ ν. (also Ar. 15, 3; Just., D. 80, 4) **Ac 17:32; 23:6; 24:21; 26:23; Ro 1:4; 1 Cor 15:12b, 13, 21;** D 16:6. νεκροῦ ἀνάστασιν Papias (2:9). ἀνάστασις ἐκ ν. **1 Pt 1:3;** ἐκ ν. ἀνάστασις AcPlCor 2:35. Also ἀνάστασις τῶν ν. **Mt 22:31; 1 Cor 15:42** (Just., D. 45, 2). νεκροὺς ἐγείρειν *raise the dead* **Mt 10:8; Ac 26:8;** AcPl Ha 8, 35=BMM verso 8f. Pass. (Theoph. Ant. 1, 8 [p. 74, 6]) **Mt 11:5; Lk 7:22** (cp. 4Q 521:12; on the fig. understanding s. κωφός 2); **1 Cor 15:15f, 29b, 32.** Also τοὺς ν. ἐγείρειν **J 5:21; 2 Cor 1:9.** Pass. **Mk 12:26; Lk 20:37; 1 Cor 15:35, 52.** Of God ζωοποιεῖν τοὺς ν. **Ro 4:17.** μετὰ τῶν ν. *among the dead* **Lk 24:5.** βαπτίζεσθαι ὑπὲρ τῶν ν. *be baptized for the dead* **1 Cor 15:29a** (s. βαπτίζω 2c; JWhite, JBL 116, 97, 487–99). τάφοι νεκρῶν IPhld 6:1. ὀστέα νεκρῶν *the bones of the dead* **Mt 23:27.** ἄτονος ὥσπερ νεκροῦ νεῦρα *powerless as the sinews of a corpse* Hm 12, 6, 2. αἷμα ὡς νεκροῦ *blood like that of a dead person* **Rv 16:3.**

❷ **one who is so spiritually obtuse as to be in effect dead,** ***dead pers.,*** fig. ext. of 1 (cp. Philo, Fuga 56) ἄφες τοὺς ν. θάψαι τοὺς ἑαυτῶν ν. *let the dead bury their dead* of those who do not give priority to discipleship **Mt 8:22; Lk 9:60** (cp. Theophyl. Sim., Ep. 25 τ. θνητοῖς τὰ θνητὰ καταλείψομεν.—FPerles, ZNW 19, 1920, 96; 25, 1926, 286f; Bleibtreu [s. μισέω 2]. AEhrhardt, Studia Theologica VI, 2, '53, 128–64.—θάπτειν τοὺς ν. lit. Jos., Bell. 5, 518). The words ἀνάστα ἐκ τ. νεκρῶν **Eph 5:14** appear to belong to a hymn (s. Rtzst., Erlösungsmyst. 1921, 136) that may have become part of the baptism ritual (MDibelius, Hdb. ad loc.; FDölger, Sol Salutis[2], 1925, 364ff).—B. 290. DELG. M-M. EDNT. TW.

νεκροφόρος, ον (νεκρός, φέρω) ***bearing a corpse*** subst. ὁ ν. *the corpse-bearer.* It lit. means a man who carries a corpse to its burial-place (Polyb., 35, 6, 2=Plut., Cato Maj. 341 [9, 2]). Ign. uses it in a play on words to reject the views of the Docetists, who deny that Christ was a σαρκοφόρος. Whoever does this, he says, is himself a νεκροφόρος, evidently mng. that he is *clothed in a corpse* rather than in flesh ISm 5:2 (cp. Philo, Agr. 25 [ψυχὴ] νεκροφοροῦσα).—DELG s.v. φέρω D2.

νεκρόω (νεκρός) 1 aor. ἐνέκρωσα; pf. pass. ptc. νενεκρωμένος (Hellenist. word: Hipponax[?, s. below]; Epict. 1, 5, 7; Plut., Mor. 954d; Themist., Paraphr. Aristot. II p. 51, 15 Spengel; ins; Philo, Aet. M. 125; Just., A I, 18, 6; Ath., R. 24 p. 78, 20 al.) **to deaden or cause to cease completely,** ***put to death*** fig. ext. of the primary mng. 'to put an end to the life of someth., to cause to be dead' τὰ μέλη τὰ ἐπὶ τῆς γῆς *what is earthly in you* **Col 3:5.** Pass.: *be as good as dead* (Longus 2, 7, 5): νενεκρωμένος *worn out, impotent* of persons whose physical capabilities have failed in a certain respect (comm. on Hipponax POxy 2176 fgm. 1 II, 7f=Hipponax fgm. 129 C, 7f p. 137 Degani νενε]κρῶσθαι, but ἀπονε‹νε›]κρῶσθαι p. 153 West [for the reconstructed fgm. of Hipponax on the basis of the comm. s. fgm. X Diehl[3]; 129a–e Degani]; Maximus Tyr. 41, 3h; cp. Epict. 4, 5, 21); e.g. of Abraham in his old age ἀφ' ἑνὸς ἐγενήθησαν καὶ ταῦτα νενεκρωμένου *from one man, and him as good as dead, were born* **Hb 11:12.** τὸ σῶμα νενεκρωμένον *his worn-out body* **Ro 4:19** (cp. IG III/2, 1355 ἄνθρωπε μή μου παρέλθῃς σῶμα τὸ νενεκρωμένον.—Dssm., LO 75 [LAE 94]; BHaensler, BZ 12, 1914, 168ff; 14, 1916, 164ff).—DELG s.v. νεκρός. M-M. TW.

νέκρωσις, εως, ἡ (νεκρόω; Aretaeus p. 32, 16; Soranus p. 140, 3; Galen: CMG V/9, 2 p. 87, 10; 313, 16 ν. τοῦ σώματος; Porphyr., Abst. 4, 20 p. 262, 20 Nauck; Proclus on Pla., Rep. 2, 117, 16 Kr. of the trees in spring: ἐκτινάσσειν τὴν ν.; Photius, Bibl. 513, 36 οἱ γὰρ κόκκοι μετὰ τ. νέκρωσιν ἀναζῶσι).

❶ **death as process,** ***death, putting to death,*** (Iren. 3, 18, 3 [Harv. II 97, 4]) lit. πάντοτε τ. νέκρωσιν τοῦ Ἰησοῦ ἐν τῷ σώματι περιφέροντες *we always carry about in our body the putting to death of Jesus* (of the constant danger of death in which the apostle lives because of his commitment to Jesus) **2 Cor 4:10.**

❷ **cessation of a state or activity,** ***deadness, mortification*** fig. ext. of 1 (cp. the definition of νεκρόω):—ⓐ of the state of being unable to bear children because of passage through menopause ἡ ν. τῆς μήτρας Σάρρας *the deadness of Sarah's womb* **Ro 4:19.**

ⓑ of a state of ineffectual or useless living ἀποτίθεσθαι τὴν ν. τῆς ζωῆς τῆς προτέρας *lay aside the deadness of their former life* i.e. *the dead life they formerly led* (before baptism) Hs 9, 16, 2f. νέκρωσις τῆς καρδίας *deadening* **Mk 3:5** D (cp. Epict. 1, 5, 4 ἀπονέκρωσις τῆς ψυχῆς). —DELG s.v. νεκρός. M-M. TW.

νέμω (Hom. et al. in var. senses; Jos., Ant. 17, 193, C. Apion 1, 60 'tend'; ApcEsdr 7:1 p. 33, 2 Tdf. 'apportion') in our lit. only mid.-pass. νέμομαι; impf. ἐνεμόμην; fut. νεμήσομαι LXX; aor. 3 pl. ἐνημήθησαν Wsd 19:9 of animals eating on the move in open spaces ***graze, feed*** (so Hom. et al.; pap, LXX Jos., Bell. 6, 155) of cattle and birds εἰς τὸ ὄρος *feed on the mountain* Hs 9, 1, 8. Of Mary ὡς περιστερὰ νεμομένη *getting her food like a pigeon* GJs 8:1. Trans. ν. τι *feed on someth.* 9, 24, 1.—DELG. Sv.

νεομηνία, ας, ἡ (νέος, μήν; in the contracted form νουμηνία [Col 2:16 Tdf.; PKatz, Kratylos 5, '60, 158] since Aristoph.; X., An. 5, 6, 23; Antig. Car. 126; Appian, Bell. Civ. 5, 97 §404; 98 §406; ins [SIG and OGI index]; PPetr II, 4, col. 2, 6 [III BC]; BGU 1053, 20 [13 BC]; LXX [Thackeray 98]; Philo; Jos., Bell. 5, 230, Ant. 4, 78. The uncontracted [Ionic] form is not found in ins [Nachmanson 69] and pap [PTebt 318, 12: 166 AD; BGU

859, 6: II AD. S. Mayser p. 153] before the second half of the second century AD, also Alciphron 3, 25, 2.—Proclus on Pla., Cratyl. p. 40, 3 P. νουμηνίαν μὲν Ἀττικοί φασιν, νεομηνίαν δὲ Κρῆτες; Lob., Phryn. 148; on the anachronistic reading in N. [which shows no v.l.], s. M-M and New Docs 3, 76f w. other pap) ***new moon, first of the month,*** oft. celebrated as a festival by Jews and gentiles: **Col 2:16;** B 2:5; 15:8 (the two last Is 1:13 νουμηνία); PtK 2 p. 14, 28. τὴν τῆς νουμηνίας εἰρωνείαν *the postured observance of the new moon* Dg 4:1 (Antig. Car. 126 μύρμηκες ταῖς νουμηνίαις ἀναπαύονται=the ants rest at the time of the new moon).—M-M. TW.

νέος, α, ον (Hom.+; ins, pap, LXX, TestSol; TestAbr A 2 p. 78, 27 [Stone p. 4]; Test12Patr; JosAs 29:11 cod. A [p. 85, 15 Bat. comp.]; ApcEsdr 5:5 p. 29, 29 Tdf.; ApcSed 16:2; AscIs 3:3 [comp.]; Philo, Joseph.; apolog. exc. Ar.) comp. νεώτερος.

❶ **pert. to being in existence but a relatively short time,** ***new, fresh***—ⓐ of things ν. φύραμα *fresh dough* w. no leaven in it; symbolically of Christians **1 Cor 5:7** (s. φύραμα, ζύμη). Also ν. ζύμη of Christ IMg 10:2. οἶνος ν. *new wine* (Simonides 49 D.; Diocles 141 p. 184, 14; POxy 729, 19; 92, 2; 3; Sir 9:10), which is still fermenting **Mt 9:17; Mk 2:22; Lk 5:37f;** (opp. παλαιὸς οἶ. *old, aged wine:* schol. on Pind., O. 9, 74f [49]) vs. **39.**—HImmerwahr, New Wine in Ancient Wineskins: Hesperia 61, '92, 121–32.

ⓑ fig., of Christ πάντοτε νέος ἐν ἁγίων καρδίαις γεννώμενος *he is ever born anew in the hearts of God's people* Dg 11:4 (Diod. S. 3, 62, 6 of Dionysus, who was torn to pieces but later joined together again by Demeter: ἐξ ἀρχῆς νέον γεννηθῆναι).

❷ **pert. to being superior in quality or state to what went before,** ***new*** of pers. ἐνδύσασθαι τὸν ν. (ἄνθρωπον) *put on the new person* **Col 3:10.** διαθήκη ν. *the new covenant* (διαθήκη 2; λόγος Mel., P. 6, 44) **Hb 12:24.**

❸ **pert. to being in the early stages of life,** ***young***

ⓐ as adj.—**α.** positive (Appian, Bell. Civ. 5, 136 §566 νέος ἀνήρ; PsSol 2:8; 17:11; Philo, Post. Cai. 109; Jos., Ant. 8, 23; Jerus. ins: SEG VIII, 209 [I AD]) ὁλοτελῶς νέον εἶναι *be completely young* Hv 3, 13, 4. Also of animals μόσχος νέος *a young ox* or *calf* 1 Cl 52:2 (Ps 68:32).

β. mostly comp.: ὁ νεώτερος υἱός *the younger son* (Gen 27:15; cp. Philo, Sacr. Abel. 42; Jos., Ant. 12, 235, in all these pass. in contrast to πρεσβύτερος as Lk 15:25) **Lk 15:13;** cp. vs. **12;** B 13:5 (Gen 48:14). τὴν ὄψιν νεωτέραν ἔχειν *have a more youthful face* Hv 3, 10, 4; 3, 12, 1. ὡσεὶ νεώτερος ἐγεγόνειν *I felt young again* s 9, 11, 5. On the other hand, the comp. sense is scarcely felt any longer 3, 10, 5; 3, 13, 1. Likew. in νεώτεραι χῆραι **1 Ti 5:11;** cp. vs. **14,** where the noun is to be supplied fr. context. Sim. **J 21:18** (cp. Ps 36:25).

ⓑ as subst.—**α.** positive (οἱ) νέοι *the young people* (X., Cyr. 5, 1, 25; Diod. S. 14, 115, 3; 2 Macc 5:13; 6:28; 15:17; Jos., C. Ap. 2, 206; Just., A I, 54, 1; Tat. 32, 2; Ath. 34, 1; on the non-technical sense s. CForbes, NEOI '33, 5 n. 17) w. οἱ πρεσβύτεροι (s. πρεσβύτερος 1a) 1 Cl 1:3; 3:3; 21:6. σκοπὸν πᾶσι τοῖς νέοις τιθέναι *set a goal for all the young people* 2 Cl 19:1 (οἱ νέοι for young people of both sexes: Nicetas Eugen. 8, 187 H.). AcPl Ox 6, 23 (restored=Aa 1, 242, 2)—αἱ νέαι *the young women* **Tit 2:4.**

β. comp., mostly with little comp. force (POxy 298, 29; TestSol 1:2 L, 3 L, 4 L; Jos., Ant. 15, 407): οἱ νεώτεροι *young men* (Diod. S. 14, 113, 3 [alternating with οἱ νέοι, and with no difference in mng. 14, 115, 3, as 18, 46, 3 οἱ πρεσβύτεροι . . . οἱ νεώτεροι beside 4 οἱ πρεσβύτεροι . . . οἱ νέοι]; 2 Macc 5:24; Just., D. 131, 6; MartIs 3:3 [Denis p. 112, Amh.] sg.) **Ac 5:6; 1 Ti 5:1** (s. on πρεσβύτερος 1a); **Tit 2:6;** Pol 5:3. Opp. πρεσβύτεροι **1 Pt 5:5** (X., An. 7, 4, 5; Timaeus Hist.: 566 fgm. 11a Jac. διακονεῖν τοὺς νεωτέρους τοῖς πρεσβυτέροις; Dio Chrys. 78 [29], 21; Demosth., Ep. 2, 10; EpArist 14; Philo, Spec. Leg. 2, 226; Jos., Ant. 3, 47; PParis 66, 24 πρεσβύτεροι καὶ ἀδύνατοι καὶ νεώτεροι; Plut., Mor. 486 F. On the other hand, also the ins of Ptolemais APF 1, 1901, 202 no. 4, 15 οἱ νεώτεροι καὶ οἱ ἄλλοι πολῖται. On νεώτεροι as t.t. s. Forbes, [α above] 60f; Schürer III 103). (αἱ) νεώτεραι *young(er) women* **1 Ti 5:2.**—ὁ νεώτερος beside ὁ μείζων **Lk 22:26** has the force of a superlative (cp. Gen 42:20); this is influenced by the consideration that the youngest was obliged to perform the lowliest service (cp. **Ac 5:6**).

❹ **a person beginning to experience someth.,** ***novice,*** subst. νέοι ἐν τῇ πίστει Hv 3, 5. 4.

❺ The well-known city name (quotable Hdt.et al.) is prob. to be written **Νέα πόλις** (cp. SIG 107, 35 [410/409 BC] ἐν Νέαι πόληι; Meisterhans^3-Schw. p. 137; PWarr 5, 8 [154 AD]; Diod. S. 20, 17, 1 Νέαν πόλιν; 20, 44, 1 ἐν Νέᾳ πόλει; Jos., Bell. 4, 449. Even in 247 AD τῆς Νέας πόλεως is found in pap [PViereck, Her 27, 1892, 516 II, 29f]; W-S. §5, 7i; Mlt-H. 278; Hemer, Acts 113) acc. Νέαν πόλιν **Ac 16:11** (v.l. Νεάπολιν); IPol 8:1 (where, nevertheless, Νεάπολιν is attested and customarily printed). In both places our lit. means by *Neapolis* (New City, mod. Kavala) the harbor of Philippi in Macedonia (Ptolem. 3, 13; Strabo 7, fgm. 36 p. 331; Appian, Bell. Civ. 4, 106 §446; Pliny, NH 4, 42 p. 58 Detl.; s. PECS 614; PCollart, Philippes '37, 102–32, esp. p. 104).—RHarrisville s.v. καινός; Kl. Pauly IV 29f; B. 957f. Schhmidt, Syn. II 94–123 (syn. of καινός). DELG. M-M. EDNT. TW.

νεοσσός s. νοσσός.

νεότης, τητος, ἡ (νέος) Hom. et al.; ins, pap, LXX; TestAbr B 10 p. 115, 8 [Stone p. 78]; Test12Patr; JosAs 17:4 [cod. A more freq.: p. 64:18 and 72:15 Bat.] Philo; Jos., Vi. 325) **state of youthfulness,** ***youth*** τῆς ν. τινος καταφρονεῖν *look down on someone's youth,* i.e. *on someone because the person is young* **1 Ti 4:12** (Appian, Bell. Civ. 1, 94 §435 ἐπιγελάω τῇ νεότητι). ἀπὸ νεότητος *from youth (up)* (M. Ant. 8, 1, 1; PTebt 276, 38; Jos., Bell. 4, 33; 1 Macc 1:6; 16:2, and used w. a gen. Num 22:30; Jer 3:25) 1 Cl 63:3; B 19:5; D 4:9. Also ἐκ ν. (Il. 14, 86; Gen 48:15; Is 47:15; 54:6 and very oft. in LXX w. a gen.) **Mt 19:20** D; **Lk 18:21; Ac 26:4.** ἐκ νεότητός μου **Mt 19:20 v.l.; Mk 10:20; Lk 18:21 v.l.**—Uncertain reading νε̣ότη̣τα̣ (ed. suggests that νηστείαν would be more meaningful but does not fit as well) AcPl Ha 6, 19.—DELG s.v. νέος 6. M-M. EDNT.

νεόφυτος, ον (νέος, φύω) Aristoph., fgm. 828 I p. 581 Kock; PRyl 138, 9 [34 AD]; BGU 563 I, 9 al. [Dssm., NB 47f—BS 220f]; Ps 127:3; 143:12; Is 5:7; Job 14:9; JosAs 25:2) lit. 'newly planted', fig. (only in Christian lit.) **newly planted in the Christian community,** ***newly converted*** (cp. 'neophyte') **1 Ti 3:6.**—DELG s.v. νέος C1. M-M.

νέρτερος, α, ον (cp. ἔνερθε 'from beneath'; trag. et al.) comp. without a positive **pert. to being lower on a scale of extent,** ***lower, nether*** usu. in positive mng. ***belonging to the lower world*** (τὰ) νέρτερα *the underworld* (Orph. Hymns 3, 10; 57, 2; 78, 5 Qu.) νερτέρων ἀνεκδιήγητα κρίματα *the indescribable verdicts of the underworld* 1 Cl 20:5 (on the text s. ἀνεκδιήγητος).—DELG s.v. ἔνερθε(ν).

Νέρων, ωνος, ὁ *Nero,* Roman emperor (54–68 AD) **2 Ti subscr.** (Mel., HE 4, 26, 9).—Kl. Pauly IV 71–73.

Νευης form of the proper name of the rich man **Lk 16:19** only in P[75]; s. Νινευής.

νεῦρον, ου, τό (Hom. et al.; Herm. Wr. 5, 6; PGM 36, 156; LXX; TestSol; Philo, Jos.; Just., A I, 19, 1; Tat.; Ath., R. 17 p. 68, 28) ***sinew*** ὥσπερ νεκροῦ νεῦρα *like the sinews of a corpse* Hm 12, 6, 2 (cp. Philo, In Flacc. 190).—DELG.

νεύω 1 aor. ἔνευσα (Hom. et al.; pap; Pr 4:25; 21:1; Ezech. Trag. vs. 73 [in Eus., PE 9, 29, 5]; Jos., Bell. 1, 629, Ant. 7, 175) ***nod*** ν. τινί *nod to someone as a signal*, perh. by inclination of the head (Lucian, Catapl. 15; BGU 1078, 9 [39 AD]; Field, Notes 100) w. inf. foll. (Eur., Hec. 545; B-D-F §392, 1d) **J 13:24; Ac 24:10.**—DELG. M-M.

νεφέλη, ης, ἡ (Hom.+; Kaibel 375; pap, LXX, En, TestAbr; TestJob 42:3; TestLevi 18:5; ApcEsdr 5:7 p. 29, 32 Tdf.; Philo, Joseph., Just., Mel.) ***cloud*** ν. λευκή **Rv 14:14a.** Clouds fr. the west bringing rain **Lk 12:54.** νεφέλαι σκότους *dark clouds* as a comparison for a swarm of worms ApcPt 10:25. ν. σκοτεινή GJs 19:2, foll. by ἡ ν. ὑπεστέλλετο *the cloud disappeared.* ν. ἄνυδροι *waterless clouds,* that yield no rain **Jd 12;** cp. **2 Pt 2:17 v.l.** Jesus at the Transfiguration was overshadowed by a νεφέλη φωτεινή *bright cloud* (v. as a sign of God's presence: Jos., Ant. 3, 290; 310) **Mt 17:5;** cp. **Mk 9:7; Lk 9:34f** (HRiesenfeld, Jésus Transfiguré '47, 130–45). περιβεβλημένος νεφέλην (Lucian, Jupp. Trag. 16) *clothed in a cloud* **Rv 10:1.** Christ ascending in a cloud **Ac 1:9** (cp. Dosiadis [III BC]: 458 fgm. 5 Jac. of Ganymede: νέφος ἥρπασεν αὐτὸν εἰς οὐρανόν; Ps.-Apollod. 2, 7, 7, 12 of Heracles). Likew. the believers **1 Th 4:17** (cp. PGM 5, 277 τὸν περιεχόμενον . . . ὑπὸ τῆς τοῦ ἀέρος νεφέλης); cp. **Rv 11:12.** Clouds as the vehicle of Christ at his second coming ἐρχόμενον ἐπὶ τῶν ν. τοῦ οὐρανοῦ (cp. Da 7:13) **Mt 24:30; 26:64.** ἐν νεφέλαις **Mk 13:26.** ἐν νεφέλῃ **Lk 21:27.** μετὰ τῶν ν. τοῦ οὐρανοῦ (Da 7:13 Theod.) **Mk 14:62;** cp. **Rv 1:7.** ἐπάνω τῶν ν. τοῦ οὐρανοῦ D 16:8; καθήμενος ἐπὶ τῆς ν. **Rv 14:15f;** ἐπὶ τὴν ν. vs. **14b.** ὑπὸ τὴν ν. εἶναι *be under the cloud* **1 Cor 10:1** (for the idea cp. Ex 14:19ff; Num 14:14; Ps 104:39; Wsd 10:17; 19:7). πάντες ἐβαπτίσθησαν (v.l. ἐβαπτίσαντο; B-D-F §317; Rob. 808) ἐν τῇ νεφέλῃ *they were all baptized in (by) the cloud* vs. **2** is meant to establish a baptism for those who were in the desert, even though neither the OT nor Jewish tradition views the cloud as a source of moisture.—On the function of clouds in apocalyptic scenarios s. JReeves, Heralds of That Good Realm '96, 169f.—DELG s.v. νεφέλη I. M-M. TW.

Νεφθαλίμ, ὁ indecl. (also -είμ; נַפְתָּלִי; Gen 30:8; 49:21; Judg 4:6, 10 al. With μ at the end Is 8:23 and occas. [Gen 49:21; Dt 33:23; Judg 4:6 B] as v.l.; JosAs 22:5; 24:8 cod. A [p. 76, 20 Bat.]; Demetr.: 722 fgm. 1, 3 al. [- είμ]; Philo, Somn. 2, 36. On this s. PKatz, TLZ 61, '36, 281.—In Jos., Ant. 1, 305 Νεφθάλεις and 2, 181 Νεφθάλις) ***Naphtali,*** Hebrew tribe (and its ancestor) φυλὴ Ν. **Rv 7:6.** Its land γῆ Νεφθαλίμ **Mt 4:15** (Is 8:23). (τὰ) ὅρια Ν. vs. **13; Lk 4:31** D.—BHHW II 1287.

νέφος, ους, τό (Hom.+; ins, LXX; TestJob 42:1; GrBar 10:6; Jos., Bell. 6, 298) ***cloud*** as a symbol of darkness (Chariton 3, 9, 11 νέφος ἀνεκάλυψε τῆς ψυχῆς; IAndrosIsis 158; Philo, Mos. 1, 176; Jos., Ant. 16, 376 ν. ἐπάγειν τοῖς πράγμασιν='spread darkness over the events'; SibOr 3, 173) ἀποθέμενοι ἐκεῖνο ὃ περικείμεθα ν. *we laid aside the cloud that surrounded us* 2 Cl 1:6. ν. ἐγένετο *a cloud formed* Hv 4, 3, 7. Fig. of a compact, numberless throng (Il. 4, 274 al.; Hdt. 8, 109 νέφος τοσοῦτον ἀνθρώπων; Timon [III BC] fgm. 39 [Poet. Philos., 1901 Diels], in Diog. L. 7, 16 throngs of serfs; Diod. S. 3, 29, 2 hordes of locusts; Ps.-Callisth. 1, 2, 2 νέφος ἐχθρῶν. Further exx. in Bleek on **Hb 12:1**) *host* τοσοῦτον ἔχοντες περικείμενον ἡμῖν ν. μαρτύρων *since we have so great a host of witnesses about us* **Hb 12:1** (CRose, Die Wolke der Zeugen '94).—DELG s.v. νεφέλη I. M-M. TW.

νεφρός, οῦ, ὁ (Aristoph., Pla. et al.; LXX; OdeSol 11:2; TestSol; ApcrEzk P 1 recto 7 [Denis p. 125]; Philo; Jos., Ant. 3, 228) usu. pl. 'kidneys'; by fig. ext. (cp. the use of σπλάγχνον), of the inner life ***mind*** (LXX). Of the Human One (Son of Man) ἐρευνῶν νεφροὺς καὶ καρδίας *who searches minds and hearts* (Diod. S. 1, 91, 5 νεφροὶ καὶ καρδία are the only things left in the body cavity by the Egyptian embalmers) **Rv 2:23** (in the OT a similar expr., w. different verbs, is used of God: Ps 7:10; Jer 11:20; 17:10; 20:12).—DELG s.v. νεφροί. M-M. TW.

νέω (since Hom.; s. L-S-J-M νέω [β]; νήθω [q.v.] is formed fr. this verb) ***spin,*** fut. νήσω GJs 10:2: τίς νήσει τον χρυσόν; *who shall spin the gold (fibers)?* The various materials were distributed for spinning as prelude to weaving; Mary was allotted 'pure purple' and 'scarlet', which she proceeded to 'spin' (cp. κλώθω 10:2; ἕλκω 11:1 [=κλώθω v.l. cod. A]).—DELG 2 νέω.

νεωκόρος, ου, ὁ lit., one who is responsible for the maintenance and security of a temple: 'temple keeper' (so X., Pla. et al.; Ael. Aristid. 47, 11 K.=1 p. 23 D.; IPriene 231 [IV BC] Μεγάβυζος νεωκόρος τῆς 'Αρτέμιδος τῆς ἐν 'Εφέσῳ; PMagd 35 [217 BC]; Philo, Spec. Leg. 1, 156; Jos., Bell. 1, 153; 5, 383; SibOr 12, 274. Loanw. in rabb.), then, w. the rise of the emperor cult in Asia Minor, a title assumed by cities that built and maintained temples in honor of the emperor: ***honorary temple keeper.*** In rare cases this custom was extended to other deities; so Ephesus is called ν. τῆς μεγάλης 'Αρτέμιδος *honorary guardian of the temple of the great Artemis* (νεωκόρος τῆς 'Αρτέμιδος CIG 2966; 2972; OBenndorf, Forschungen in Ephesos I 1906, 211 νεωκόρος τῆς ἁγιωτάτης 'Αρτέμιδος; OGI 481, 1ff; Rouffiac 64f. Also on coins [JWeiss, RE X 543; AWikenhauser, Die AG 1921, 366]) **Ac 19:35** (ναοκόρον D; cp. B-D-F §96, 1 on ναός).—WBüchner, De Neocoria 1888; Kl. Pauly IV 55. New Docs 1, 22f.—DELG s.v. ναός. M-M.

νεωτερικός, ή, όν ***youthful*** (so Polyb. 10, 21, 7; Plut., Dion 961 [8, 1]; 3 Macc 4:8; Jos., Ant. 16, 399) ἐπιθυμίαι **2 Ti 2:22** (cp. Vett. Val. 118, 3 νεωτερικὰ ἁμαρτήματα). προσλαμβάνειν τὴν φαινομένην νεωτερικὴν τάξιν *take advantage of his seemingly youthful appearance* IMg 3:1.—DELG s.v. νέος. M-M.

νεωτερισμός, οῦ, ὁ (IG IV^2/1, 68, 43 [302 BC]) prim. an attempt to introduce a change: 'innovation', mostly in a bad sense, ***uprising, revolution, rebellion*** (Pla., Demosth., Plut.; EpArist 101; Philo, In Flacc. 93; Jos., Ant. 5, 101; 20, 106; TestReub 2:2; 2:9 v.l.). Plural (Pla., Leg. 6, 758c) *revolutionary outbreaks* (w. μέθαι and other vices) 1 Cl 30:1.—DELG s.v. νέος.

νεώτερος s. νέος.—M-M.

νή (Aristoph. et al.; pap; Gen 42:15f; Jos., C. Ap. 1, 255) **marker pointing to the basis on which someth. is strongly affirmed,** ***yes indeed, by*** w. acc. of pers. or thing by which one swears, affirms, or invokes sanction (B-D-F §149; Rob. 487; 1150; Reader, Polemo p. 282) νὴ τὴν ὑμετέραν καύχησιν (yes, truly) *by my pride in you* **1 Cor 15:31** (cp. Epict. 2, 20, 29 νὴ τ. σὴν τύχην; PGiss 19, 11 νὴ τὴν σὴν σωτηρίαν; POxy 939, 20; Gen 42:15f νὴ τὴν ὑγίειαν Φαραώ). JWerres, D. Beteuerungsformeln in d. att. Komödie, diss. Bonn '36.—DELG s.v. ναί. M-M.

νήθω formed fr. νέω (q.v.) as πλήθω fr. πλη-, πίμπλημι (s. L-S-J-M νήθω); aor. 3 pl. ἔνησαν Ex 35:26; pf. pass. ptc. νενησμένος LXX (Cratinus Com. 96; Pla., Pol 289c; Anth. Pal. 11, 110, 6; 14, 134, 3; Ex 26:31 al. in Ex; TestSol 4:12) ***spin*** w. κοπιάω **Mt 6:28; Lk 12:27.** W. ὑφαίνω **12:27** D. For GJs 10:2 s. νέω.—B. 408.—Dalman, Arbeit V '37.—DELG s.v. 2 νέω. M-M.

νηκτός, ή, όν (νήχω; Plut., Mor. 636e; 776c; Vett. Val. 344, 15; Philo, Op. M. 63; Jos., Ant. 8, 44) **pert. to the act of swimming, *swimming,*** subst. τὸ νηκτόν *that which swims* (Ps.-Aristot., De Mundo 398b, 31; Galen XVIII 1 p. 207 K.) τῆς θαλάσσης τὰ νηκτά *what swims in the sea* PtK 2 p. 14, 18.—DELG s.v. 1 νέω.

νηπιάζω (νήπιος; Hippocr. IX 360 L.; Erinna Lyrica [IV BC]: PSI IX, 1090, 55+15 [p.xii]=AnthLG, Erinna fgm. 1 B, 29 Diehl; Memnon Hist. [I AD], fgm. 22, 1 CMüller; Porphyr., πρὸς Γαῦρον [ABA 1895] 12, 3 p. 50, 27; 12, 4 p. 51, 6; schol. on Eur., Phoen. 713) ***be (as) a child*** fig., w. dat. (Hippocr., Ep. 17, 25 ἐπιβουλῇσι νηπιάζειν) τῇ κακίᾳ *in evil* **1 Cor 14:20.**—DELG s.v. νήπιος. M-M. TW.

νήπιος, ία, ιον (Hom.+; ins, pap, LXX, En; TestSol 18:25 L; Test12Patr; JosAs 12:7 cod. A; ApcEsdr 5:3 p. 29, 27 Tdf.; SibOr; Philo, Joseph.; Ar. 10, 7; Tat. 30, 1; Ath., R. 17 p. 68, 31) in Gk. lit. ν. gener. refers to beings ranging from fetal status to puberty. In our lit.

➊ **a very young child, *infant, child***—ⓐ lit. (ViDa 1 [p. 76, 13 Sch.]; Jos., Ant. 6, 262; Ar. [Milne 76, 40] ἐὰν δὲ νήπιον ἐξέλθῃ; Orig., C. Cels. 3, 48, 26 ἀμαθὴς καὶ ἀνόητος καὶ ἀπαίδευτος καὶ ν.; Theoph. Ant. 2, 25 [p. 160, 6] Ἀδὰμ ἔτη ν. ἦν) ὡς ν. βρέφη *like veritable babes* Hs 9, 29, 1. Usu. subst. *child* sing. **1 Cor 13:11abcd** (for ν. opp. ἀνήρ Orig., C. Cels. 3, 59, 23); τὰ τοῦ ν. *childish ways* vs. **11e.** Pl. τὰ ν. (sc. βρέφη) Hm 2:1; s 9, 29, 1. The gen. pl. of the neut. is prob. to be understood **Mt 21:16** (Ps 8:3; s. JGeorgacas, ClPl 76, '58, 155).

ⓑ fig.; the transition to the fig. sense is found **Hb 5:13** where the νήπιος, who is fed w. the milk of elementary teaching, is contrasted w. the τέλειος='mature person', who can take the solid food of the main teachings (s. also **1 Cor 3:1f**). In this connection the ν. is one who views spiritual things fr. the standpoint of a child. W. this can be contrasted

α. the state of the more advanced Christian, to which the ν. may aspire (Ps 118:130; Philo, Migr. Abr. 46; Iren. 4, 38, 1 [Harv. II 293, 2]) ITr 5:1. ἵνα μηκέτι ὦμεν νήπιοι **Eph 4:14.** A Judean as διδάσκαλος νηπίων **Ro 2:20.** νήπιος ἐν Χριστῷ *immature Christian* **1 Cor 3:1** (cp. ὡς νηπίοις, ὁ ἄρτος ὁ τέλειος τοῦ πατρός, γάλα ἡμῖν ἑαυτὸν παρέσχεν [on the accent s. Schwyzer I 391] 'seeing that we were but infants, the perfect bread [=the Son of God] of the Father gave himself as milk to us' Iren. 4, 38, 1 [Harv. II 293, 8]; JWeiss, Paulin. Probleme: Die Formel ἐν Χριστῷ Ἰησοῦ, StKr 69, 1896, 1–33). Harnack, Die Terminologie d. Wiedergeburt: TU XLII 3, 1918, 97ff.

β. The contrast can also be w. the ideas expressed by σοφός, συνετός, and then the νήπιοι are the *child-like, innocent* ones, unspoiled by learning, with whom God is pleased **Mt 11:25; Lk 10:21** (GKilpatrick, JTS 48, '47, 63f; WGrundmann, NTS 5, '58/'59, 188–205; SLégasse, Jésus et l'enfant [synopt.], '69). Cp. also 1 Cl 57:7 (Pr 1:32).

➋ **one who is not yet of legal age, *minor, not yet of age,*** legal t.t. (UPZ 20, 22 [II BC] ἔτι νηπίας οὔσας ὁ πατὴρ ἀπέδωκεν εἰς σύστασιν Πτολεμαίῳ) ἐφ' ὅσον χρόνον ὁ κληρονόμος ν. ἐστιν *as long as the heir is a minor* **Gal 4:1.** Fig. vs. **3.**—In **1 Th 2:7** νήπιοι is accepted by Lachmann and W-H., as well as by interpreters fr. Origen to Wohlenberg, Frame, et al.; Goodsp., Probs. 177f. S. also SFowl, NTS 36, '90, 469–73: the metaphors of infant and nurse are complementary. Others, incl. Tdf., HermvSoden, BWeiss, Bornemann, vDobschütz, Dibelius, Steinmann, prefer ἤπιοι (v.l.), and regard the ν of νήπιοι as the result of dittography fr. the preceding word ἐγενήθημεν (s. the entry ἤπιος). MLacroix, Ηπιος/Νηπιος: Mélanges Desrousseaux '37, 260–72.; B. 92.—New Docs 1, 116; 4, 40. DELG. M-M. TW. Sv.

νηπιότης, ητος, ἡ (νήπιος; Pla., Leg. 7 p. 808e; Maximus Tyr. 10, 5c; Ps.-Lucian, Halc. 3; LXX; Philo, Conf. Lingu. 21; Jos., Ant. 1, 287; 2, 233) ***childlikeness*** (w. ἁπλότης) *(childlike) innocence* Hs 9, 24, 3. ἐν ν. διαμένειν *remain in one's innocence* 9, 29, 1. Also μετὰ νηπιότητος διαμένειν 9, 29, 2.—DELG s.v. νήπιος.

Νηρεύς, έως, ὁ ***Nereus*** (the old mythological name as a personal name e.g. IG III, 1053, 11; 1160, 62; 1177, 48 also CIL); freq. borne by freedmen and slaves, some of them in the imperial service (Zahn, Einleitung I[3] 299). W. his sister, recipient of a greeting: ἀσπάσασθε Νηρέα (v.l. Βηρέα) καὶ τ. ἀδελφὴν αὐτοῦ **Ro 16:15.** Kl. Pauly IV 69.—DELG. LGPN I. M-M.

Νηρί, ὁ indecl. (נֵרִי), also Νηρεί, ***Neri,*** in the genealogy of Jesus **Lk 3:27.**

νησίον, ου, τό (Strabo 2, 5, 23; 3, 3, 1; Paradoxogr. Flor. 38; Heliod. 1, 7, 2; loanw. in rabb.) dim. of νῆσος: ***little island*** (oft. no longer felt to be a dim.: Peripl. Eryth. c. 38 νησίον μικρόν) of the island of Cauda (s. Καῦδα) **Ac 27:16.**—DELG s.v. νῆσος.

νῆσος, ου, ἡ (Hom.+; ins, pap, LXX; PsSol 11:3; ParJer 9:19; EpArist; Philo, Aet. M. 120; 138; Jos., Ant. 4, 116 al.; loanw. in rabb.) ***island*** **Ac 27:26.** Cyprus (Jos., Ant. 17, 335) **13:6.** Malta **28:1, 7, 9, 11.** Patmos **Rv 1:9.** Removed fr. their places in the last days **6:14; 16:20.** For the sense 'peninsula' s. Warnecke, Romfahrt 67.—B. 29. DELG. M-M.

νηστεία, ας, ἡ (νηστεύω; since Hdt. 4, 186; pap, LXX; PsSol 3:8; Test12Patr, Philo, Joseph., Just.) 'fasting'.

➊ **the experience of being without sufficient food, *going hungry*** gener., of hunger brought about by necessity: pl. (B-D-F §142; W-S. §27, 4d; s. Rob. 408) of oft-recurring situations (cp. Da 9:3; 2 Macc 13:12) ἐν νηστείαις *through hunger* **2 Cor 6:5.** ἐν νηστείαις πολλάκις *often without food* **11:27.**

➋ **the act of going without food for a devotional or cultic purpose, *fast***—ⓐ of public fasts: of the Day of Atonement (יוֹם כִּפּוּר; Strabo 16, 2, 40 τὴν νηστείας ἡμέραν [for the Jews]; Philo, Spec. Leg. 2, 193ff; Jos., Ant. 14, 66; 18, 94; Just., D. 40, 4) **Ac 27:9;** B 7:4.—For D 8:1 s. on νηστεύω, end.

ⓑ of private fasting Hs 5, 1, 3, end; 5, 2, 1; 5, 3, 5. κατὰ τὴν συνή̣θι̣α̣[ν τῆς]| νη[. . . νη]στίας (prob. ditt. and = κατὰ τὴν συνήθειαν τῆς νηστείας) *according to their habit of fasting* AcPl Ha 7, 10f (context uncertain). διὰ [τ]ά̣ς [νησ]τ̣ί̣α̣ς̣ κ̣α̣[ὶ τὰς]| δι[α]νυκτερεύσις . . . βαρηθεὶ̣ς̣ *wearied by the fasts and vigils* (with his friends) AcPl Ha 7, 25f. Of Moses on the mountain (w. ταπείνωσις; cp. Jdth 4:9 v.l.; Ps 34:13; PsSol 3:8) 1 Cl 53:2; likew. of Esther 55:6. (W. προσευχή; cp. Tob 12:8; Da 9:3) **Mt 17:21; Mk 9:29 v.l.** (νηστεία strengthening prayer as 2 Macc 13:12; Test Jos 10:1f); **1 Cor 7:5 v.l.** (W. δεήσεις; cp. Da 9:3 Theod.) **Lk 2:37.** προσεύχεσθαι μετὰ νηστειῶν *pray and fast* **Ac 14:23.** νηστείαν νηστεύειν (צוֹם צוּם 2 Km 12:16; 3 Km 20:9) *keep, observe a fast* Hs 5, 1, 2f; νηστεύειν τὴν ν. *keep the fast (day)*B 7:3 (ἡ νηστεία=fast day, as Jos., Ant. 18, 94). νηστεύειν τῷ θεῷ νηστείαν *keep a fast to God* Hs 5, 1, 4b (Just., D. 15, 1). μεγάλην ν. ποιεῖν 5, 1, 5. φυλάσσειν τὴν νηστείαν 5, 3, 5; τελεῖν τὴν ν. 5, 3, 8. ἡ ν. τελεία 5, 3, 6, acc. to Hermas, includes abstaining fr. all evil as well as fr. food. τιμίαν ταύτην ν. AcPl Ha 6, 25 (cp. Just., D. 15, 1 ἀληθινήν . . . ν.).—προσκαρτερεῖν νηστείαις *persevere in fasting* Pol 7:2. ἀποθέσθαι τὴν νηστείαν *end the fast* AcPl Ha 6, 37. Fasting better than prayer 2 Cl 16:4 (cp. Tob 12:8f). Rejected by God B 3:1ff (Is 58:5f). τῆς νηστείας εἰρωνεία *affected observance of fast days* Dg 4:1.—RArbesmann, D. Fasten b. d. Griech. u. Römern 1929; MFreiberger, D. Fasten im alten Israel 1929; JMontgomery, Ascetic Strains in Early Judaism: JBL 51, '32, 183–213; IAbrahams, Studies in Pharisaism and the Gospels I 1917, 121–28; GMoore, Judaism II 1927, 55ff; 257ff; Billerb. IV 1928, 77–114: V. altjüd. Fasten; MShepherd, ATR 40, '58, 81–94; RAC VII 447–93.—DELG s.v. 1 νῆστις. TW. Sv.

νηστεύω pres. ptc. fem. pl. by-form νηστέουσαι (AcPl Ha 5, 19f); fut. νηστεύσω; 1 aor. ἐνήστευσα, inf. νηστεῦσαι, impv. νηστεύσατε, ptc. νηστεύσας; pf. 2 pl. νενηστεύκατε Zech 7:5 (Aristoph.; Aristot.; Plut., Mor. 626f; Aelian, VH 5, 20; LXX; Test12Patr; ApcEsdr 1:3 p. 24, 9 Tdf. and oft.; Philo, Spec. Leg. 2, 197; Jos., C. Ap. 1, 308; Ar. [Milne 76, verso 1]; Just.) ***to fast*** as a devotional rite, among Jews and Christians: as a sign of grief (2 Km 1:12; 12:22; Zech 7:5; Bar 1:5) **Mt 9:15 v.l.; Mk 2:19f; Lk 5:34f** (cp. ν. ἐν τῇ ἡμέρᾳ ἐκείνῃ Judg 20:26; 1 Km 7:6); B 7:5; AcPl Ha 5, 19f; GPt 7:27. Moses B 4:7; 14:2 (for the idea cp. Ex 34:28) and Jesus (Iren. 3, 22, 2 [Harv. II 122, 6]; Did., Gen. 190, 13) **Mt 4:2** *fast for forty days and forty nights* (cp. 1 Km 31:13; 1 Ch 10:12 ν. ἑπτὰ ἡμέρας; Marinus, Vi. Procli 19 Boiss. τινὰς ν. ἡμέρας). With lamentation B 7:5. Of Joseph GJs 1:4. As preparation for prayer (Jos., Ant. 20, 89) Hv 3, 10, 6; for baptism D 7:4 (on fasting before being received into the Gr.-Rom. mystery cults s. Knopf, Hdb. ad loc.). W. προσεύχεσθαι (cp. Bar 1:5) **Ac 13:3.** W. δέομαι Hv 3, 1, 2. W. εὐχαριστεῖν 5, 1, 1. To increase the power of his prayer, Hermas fasts μίαν ἡμέραν *for one whole day* 3, 10, 7; a fifteen-day fast 2, 2, 1. His fast consists in taking only bread and water Hs 5, 3, 7. W. λειτουργεῖν τῷ κυρίῳ **Ac 13:2** (EPeterson, Nuntius 2, '49, 9f). Jesus and his disciples do not fast **Mt 9:14; Mk 2:18; Lk 5:33** (HEbeling, D. Fastenfrage [Mk 2:18–22]: StKr 108, '37/38, 387–96, but s. KSchäfer, Synopt. Studien [Wikenhauser Festschr.], '53, 124–47; FCremer, D. Fastenansage Jesu, '65). Right and wrong attitudes in fasting **Mt 6:16–18.** ν. νηστείαν *observe a fast* Hs 5, 1, 2f (s. νηστεία 2b). ν. τῷ θεῷ νηστείαν 5, 1, 4b; opp. ὃς ἂν μὴ νηστεύσῃ τὴν νηστείαν, θανάτῳ ἐξολεθρευθήσεται *one who does not observe the fast-day shall pay the penalty of death* B 7:3 (s. νηστεία 2b). ν. τῷ θεῷ Hs 5, 1, 3; 5, 1, 4a; cp. B 3:1 (Is 58:4). As an act pleasing to God (Hs 5, 3, 7), w. the pers. given, who is to profit from it: νηστεύετε ὑπὲρ τῶν διωκόντων ὑμᾶς *fast for those who persecute you* D 1:3 (where Mt 5:44 has προσεύχεσθε.—Knopf, Hdb. ad loc.). Pious Israelites used to fast twice a week **Lk 18:12,** on Monday and Thursday (s. Schürer II 483f; Elbogen 126f; 225f; 533; 551; Billerb. on Lk 18:12), the Christians on Wednesday and Friday D 8:1.—ν. τὸν κόσμον Ox 1, verso 5–6 (ASyn. 54, 22; cp. GTh 27) has not yet been satisfactorily explained. Could it be taken fig. *abstain from the world* (see s.v. νηστεία 2b on Hs 5, 3, 6 and cp. Empedocles in Plut., Mor. 464b [Vorsokrat. I⁵ 369, 17] νηστεῦσαι κακότητος; LWright, JBL 65, '46, 180)?—B. 1483. DELG s.v. 1 νῆστις. M-M. EDNT. TW.

νῆστις, ὁ, ἡ (νη- neg., ἔδω 'eat') gen. in Ion. and Ep. **ιος,** Attic **ιδος,** acc. pl. νήστεις (s. B-D-F §47, 3; Mlt-H. 132 [strictly should be called an adj.]; 287; 374; on the formation of the word Wackernagel, Kl. Schr. 1150) ***not eating, hungry*** (so Hom.+; Da 6:19 [PKatz, TLZ 81, '56, 605]; cp. JosAs 13:8 cod. A [p. 57, 16 Bat.] νήστης ὑπάρχω) **Mt 15:32; Mk 8:3.**—DELG s.v. 1 νῆστις. M-M. TW. Sv.

νηφαλέος s. next entry.

νηφάλιος, ία, ον (νήφω; Aeschyl. et al.; Plut.; SIG 1040, 26), late form **νηφαλέος, α, ον** (v.l.; Herodian Gr. I 114, 17 et al.; Philo, Leg. All. 3, 82; Etym. Mag. p. 261, 52; 262, 2; AcJ 69 [p. 184, 10]. On the accent s. Kühner-Bl. II p. 297, 11; B-D-F §35, 3; Mlt-H. 76; 362) of pers. (cp. Philo, Sobr. 2, Mos. 1, 187; Jos., Ant. 3, 279)

❶ **pert. to being very moderate in the drinking of an alcoholic beverage,** ***temperate, sober*** (so Dibelius/Conzelmann, Hermeneia comm. ad loc. On the topic of moderation in drinking wine s. Theognis 467–510. For prohibition of strong drink to priests when engaging in official duties s. Lev 10:8) **1 Ti 3:2** (opp. πάροινος vs. 3. The latter term is in a series chiefly composed of negatives that contrast with the positive virtues in vs. 2), **11** (cp. **Tit 2:3** and the sterotyped 'anus' ['hag'] who is given to drink in Lat. lit.: Ovid, Fasti 3, 765f et al.; VRoswach, Classical World 88, '94, 113f; Arnott, Alexis p. 504) **Tit 2:2.** Others interpret metaph.

❷ **pert. to being restrained in conduct,** ***self-controlled, level-headed*** fig. ext. of 1 (s. next entry): **1 Ti 3:2, 11; Tit 2:2.**—DELG s.v. νήφω. M-M. TW.

νήφω 1 aor. ἔνηψα (Soph., Pla., X. et al.; ins, pap) prim. 'be sober'; in the NT only fig. = be free fr. every form of mental and spiritual 'drunkenness', fr. excess, passion, rashness, confusion, etc. ***be well-balanced, self-controlled*** (Aristot. et al.; Epicurus in Diog. L. 10, 132 νήφων λογισμός=sober reasonableness; Περὶ ὕψους 16, 4; Lucian, Hermot. 47 νῆφε; Herodian 2, 15, 1; Achilles Tat. 1, 13 ν. ἐκ τοῦ κακοῦ; Herm. Wr. 7, 1; BGU 1011 III, 9 [II BC]; POxy 1062, 13 ἵνα αὐτὴν [sc. τ. ἐπιστολὴν] ἀναγνοῖς νήφων κ. σαυτοῦ καταγνοῖς; EpArist 209; Philo; Jos., Bell. 2, 225; 4, 42; SibOr 1, 154) **1 Th 5:8; 1 Pt 1:13.** [Ἱερώνυμος ἤδ]η νήψας νυκτὸς| ἐν ὀδύνα[ις] *Hieronymus, in pain* (because of an injury to his ear during a violent storm) *now came to his senses* (concerning his animosity toward Paul) *during the night* AcPl Ha 5, 29f. ν. ἐν πᾶσιν *be self-possessed under all circumstances* (M. Ant. 1, 16, 15) **2 Ti 4:5.** W. γρηγορεῖν (cp. Plut., Mor. 800b ἀγρυπνῶν κ. νήφων κ. πεφροντικώς) **1 Th 5:6; 1 Pt 5:8.** W. σωφρονεῖν (Lucian, Nigrin. 5f): ν. εἰς προσευχάς *exercise self-restraint, to help you pray* **1 Pt 4:7;** Pol 7:2 has ν. πρὸς τὰς εὐχάς. ν. ἐπὶ τὸ ἀγαθόν *exercise self-control for (your own) good* 2 Cl 13:1. W. allusion to the self-control practiced by athletes: νῆφε ὡς θεοῦ ἀθλητής IPol 2:3.—HLevy, Sobria ebrietas 1929.—DELG. M-M. TW.

νήχομαι mid. dep. (Hom. et al.; Hero Alex. I 414, 18; 446, 16; Plut.; Lucian; Job 11:12 [?]; Philo Epicus Jud. [II BC] : 729 fgm. 2 vs. 1 Jac. [in Eus., PE 9, 37, 1]; Philo Alex., De Prov. fgm. 2 [in Eus., PE 8, 14, 65]; Jos., Ant. 15, 55, Vi. 15) ***swim*** ἐν τῷ βυθῷ B 10:5.—B. 681. DELG s.v. 1 νέω.

Νίγερ, ὁ (GDI 1555c, 20; e, 24 [Phocis]; ostracon APF 6, 1920, 213, 1 [174/75 AD] Αἰβύτιος Νίγερ; Sb 46; 8808, 3 [imp. period]; O. Wilck II, 266; 296; wood tablet w. the name of the veteran L. Petronius Niger [94 AD] in Dssm., LO 383 [LAE 443]; Jos., Bell. 2, 520) ***Niger*** (cp. Lat. niger=dark-complexioned), surname of Simeon the prophet **Ac 13:1.**—M-M.

Νικάνωρ, ορος, ὁ (Thu. 2, 80, 5 al.; OGI 21, 4; 196, 11f; 599, 1 al. in ins; Sb 1079; 3763; PFrankf 5 recto, 20 [242/241 BC]; 1, 2 and 4 Macc; EpArist 182; Joseph.—B-D-F §29, 3. In rabb.

נִיקָנוֹר) name freq. found, *Nicanor,* one of the seven assistants of the Jerusalem congregation **Ac 6:5.**—M-M.

νικάω (Hom.+; ins, pap, LXX; PsSol 4:10; TestJob 27:5; Test12Patr, Philo, Joseph., Just., Tat.; Ath. 3, 2) ptc. νικῶν, dat. νικῶντι or νικοῦντι (so some edd. Rv 2:17, in part also vs. 7; on this exchange of -άω and -έω forms s. B-D-F §90; W-S. §13, 26; Rob. 203; s. Mlt-H. 195); fut. νικήσω; 1 aor. ἐνίκησα; pf. νενίκηκα. Pass.: 1 fut. inf. νικηθήσεσθαι (Just., D. 78, 9); 1 aor. ἐνικήθην LXX, ptc. νικηθείς; pf. inf. νενικῆσθαι 4 Macc 13:2.

❶ **to win in the face of obstacles,** ***be victor, conquer, overcome, prevail,*** intr.—ⓐ in a battle or contest (EpArist 281); of Israel as victorious in battle B 12:2 (cp. Ex 17:11); of Christ **Rv 3:21b; 5:5** (the foll. inf. ἀνοῖξαι indicates what the victory enables the victor to do). ἐξῆλθεν νικῶν κ. ἵνα νικήσῃ **6:2.** Of the good athlete (Lucian, Tim. 50; POxy 1759, 4 letter to an athlete) IPol 3:1. The Christian as ὁ νικῶν *the one who is victorious* (s. B-D-F §322; Rob. 865) **Rv 2:7, 11, 17, 26; 3:5, 12, 21; 21:7** (s. Boll 49, 1). οἱ νικῶντες ἐκ τοῦ θηρίου (=τηρήσαντες ἑαυτοὺς ἐκ τ. θ.—B-D-F §212; GBonaccorsi, Primi saggi di filologia neotest. I '33 p. clxii) **15:2.**—Hs 8, 3, 6 v.l.

ⓑ in a legal action (Aristoph., Equ. 95, Av. 445; 447; Protagoras in Diog. L. 9, 56 [νικάω and νίκη]; Artem. 1, 35 p. 36, 20; 4, 31 p. 222, 17 al.; PSI 551, 7 [III BC] ἐνίκων τῇ κρίσει; PHal 1, 51; 58 [III BC]; Jos., Bell. 2, 284, Ant. 12, 126) ὅπως . . . και νικήσεις (v.l. νικήσῃς) ἐν τῷ κρίνεσθαί σε *that you may win when you are accused* **Ro 3:4;** 1 Cl 18:4 (both Ps 50:6.—IG XI/4, 1299, 26f [c. 200 BC] Sarapis and his worshipers win in a lawsuit over a new temple [Eng. tr. in Danker, Benefactor, no. 27]).

❷ **to overcome someone,** ***vanquish, overcome,*** trans.

ⓐ act. w. the obj. in the acc. τινά *overcome someone* (Polyb. 6, 58, 13; Diod. S. 4, 57, 6; Jos., Vi. 81) **Lk 11:22; Rv 11:7; 13:7; 17:14.** Of Christ νενίκηκα τὸν κόσμον *I have overcome the world* (i.e. the sum total of everything opposed to God; s. κόσμος 7b) **J 16:33b** (ν. τι='be stronger than': IAndros Isis, Kyme 55 p. 124). Also said of Christians **1J 5:4f;** cp. αὕτη ἐστιν ἡ νίκη ἡ νικήσασα τὸν κόσμον vs. **4b** (s. νίκη). Also ν. τὸν πονηρόν *overcome the evil one, the devil* **2:13f** (on this passage and **J 16:33b** s. JBruns, JBL 86, '67, 451–53); cp. **Rv 12:11.** αὐτόν (=τὸν διάβολον) Hs 8, 3, 6. αὐτούς (=τοὺς ἐκ τοῦ κόσμου) **1J 4:4.** ν. τὴν ψυχήν *win a victory over the soul* (i.e. the earthly-minded part of man; cp. Sextus 71a νίκα τὸ σῶμα) 2 Cl 16:2. The conquering power added in the dat.: by (means of) ἔν τινι (Pla., Symp. 213e; Himerius, Or. [Ecl.] 3, 11 ἐν δόγμασι νικῶν ἐκείνους): ἐν τῷ μὴ ποιεῖν τὰς ἐπιθυμίας αὐτῆς τὰς πονηράς *by not carrying out its base desires* 2 Cl 16:2. ν. ἐν τῷ ἀγαθῷ τὸ κακόν *overcome evil with good* **Ro 12:21b** (TestBenj 4:3 οὗτος τὸ ἀγαθὸν ποιῶν νικᾷ τὸ κακόν).

ⓑ pass. *be conquered, beaten* (Thu. 1, 76, 2 al.; Posidippus [III BC]: 447 fgm. 2 Jac. νικᾶται ὁ Κύπριος τῷ σχήματι=the Cyprian is 'conquered' by the picture [of Aphrodite] et al.; Philo, De Jos. 200 νικώμενος ὑπὸ πάθους; Jos., Ant. 1, 302 by the force of necessity; Tat. 9, 2 ὁ νικώμενος νῦν εἰσαῦτις ἐπικρατεῖν εἴωθεν; Theoph. Ant. 2, 12 [p. 130, 30] θεὸν γὰρ οὐ χρὴ ὑφ' ἡδονῆς νικᾶσθαι) Hm 12, 5, 2. ὁ πονηρὸς . . . νικηθείς AcPlCor 2:15. *Let oneself be overcome* μὴ νικῶ ὑπὸ τ. κακοῦ **Ro 12:21a;** Dg 7:7.

❸ **to surpass in ability,** ***outstrip, excel,*** trans. w. the superior power added in the dat. (cp. Eur., Herc. Fur. 342 ἀρετῇ; Ael. Aristid. 13 p. 272 D.: ἐπιεικείᾳ; Tat. 15:4 θανάτῳ . . . τὸν θάνατον νενικήκασιν) τοῖς ἰδίοις βίοις νικῶσι τ. νόμους *in their way of life they surpass* (or *outdo*) *the laws* (i.e., they live better lives than the laws require) Dg 5:10.—DELG s.v. νίκη. M-M. TW.

νίκη, ης, ἡ (Hom.+; ins, pap, LXX; TestSol 10:9 C; TestJob 1:3 [proper name]; SibOr 13, 38; EpArist 180; Philo, Leg. All. 3, 186 ὅταν νικήσῃ νίκην; Jos., Ant. 6, 145 al.; Tat. 19, 3) ***victory,*** then as abstr. for concr. *the means for winning a victory* (but cp. also the custom of speaking of the emperor's νίκη; 'victoria' as attribute of the emperor on coinage: Coins of the Roman Empire in the British Museum, ed. Mattingly, I 241, no. 214 [Nero]) **1J 5:4.**—B. 1406. DELG. M-M. TW.

Νικήτης, ου a rather common name (SIG 287, 2; 491, 73; 540, 44; 1029, 62) *Nicetes* MPol 8:2; 17:2.

νικητής, ου, ὁ in a misreading of AcPl Ox 1602, verso 30; s. μένω 1b.—DELG s.v. νίκη.

Νικόδημος, ου, ὁ a name common among Jews and gentiles (exx. in Wettstein; Diod. S. 16, 82; 4; Jos., Ant. 14, 37; SIG[2] and Preisigke, Sb in the indices; PHib 110, 60; 75; 105; PFlor 6, 20 Νικόδημος βουλευτής) ***Nicodemus*** (in rabb. נַקְדִּימוֹן), a member of the Sanhedrin who was favorable to Jesus and his cause, mentioned only in J. Little is known about him, and the connection w. the Talmudic Nicodemus, whose real name is said to have been Buni ben Gorion, and who was held to be a disciple of Jesus (Billerb. II 413f), is questionable. **J 3:1, 4, 9; 7:50; 19:39.**—BZimolong, D. Nikod. perikope (J 2:23–3:22) nach d. syrosinait. Text, diss. Bresl. 1919; SMendner, JBL 77, '58, 293–323.—M-M.

Νικολαΐτης, ου, ὁ *Nicolaitan,* an ethnic substantive (on the form s. Mussies 151) a follower of Nicolaus, an otherw. unknown founder of a sect, ἔργα τῶν Νικολαϊτῶν **Rv 2:6.** διδαχὴ τῶν Νικολαϊτῶν vs. **15.** On the sect of the Nicolaitans s. ESchürer, Die Prophetin Isabel: Weizsäcker Festschr. 1892, 39–58; LSeesemann, StKr 66, 1893, 47–82; GWohlenberg, NKZ 6, 1895, 923ff; Zahn, Einl. II[3] 623f; AvHarnack, The Sect of the Nicolaitans and Nicolaus, the Deacon in Jerus.: JR 3, 1923, 413–22; MGoguel, Les Nicolaïtes: RHR 115, '37, 5–36; NBrox, Nikolaos u. Nikolaitan, VigChr 19, '65, 23–30.—Cp. DELG s.v. νίκη.

Νικόλαος, ου, ὁ (Hdt. et al.; Diod. S. 13, 19, 6; 32, 15, 5; IG XIV, 682; 1252; SIG[2] and Preisigke, Sb indices; Joseph.) ***Nicolaus,*** a proselyte of Antioch and one of the seven assistants of the Jerusalem church **Ac 6:5.** It hardly seems prob. that he had anything to do w. the sect of the Nicolaitans, despite the assertions of the ancients (approved by Zahn) that he did.—DELG s.v. νίκη. M-M.

Νικόπολις, εως, ἡ *Nicopolis;* of the many cities bearing this name (Stephan. Byz. names three of them, in Epirus, Bithynia, and Armenia Minor), the one mentioned **Tit 3:12** and in the **subscr.** of **1 Ti** and **Tit** is usu. taken to be the N. in Epirus (mod. Smyrtoula) and founded by Octavian as monument to his victory over Mark Antony 31 BC at Actium. (Cass. Dio 50, 13; 51, 1; Strabo 7, 7, 5; 10, 2, 2).—Pauly-W. XVII 511–39; Kl. Pauly IV 123–26; MDibelius, Hdb. exc. at Tit 3:14; PECS 625f.—DELG s.v. νίκη.

νῖκος, ους, τό (Manetho, Apot. 1, 358; Orph., Argon. 587; Polemo 1, 12 p. 6, 16; Vett. Val. 358, 5; IG XII/5, 764, 2; BGU 1002, 14 [55 BC]; LXX; SibOr 14, 334; 339; Lob. on Phryn. p. 647) late form for ἡ νίκη (JWackernagel, Hellenistica 1907, 26f; EFraenkel, Glotta 4, 1913, 39ff; B-D-F §51, 1; Mlt-H. 126; 381).

❶ ***victory*** ποῦ σου θάνατε τὸ ν.; *where, O Death, is your victory?* **1 Cor 15:55a** (after Hos 13:14, where our LXX mss. read ποῦ ἡ δίκη σου, θ. [s. WDittmar, V.T. in Novo 1903, 217 and s.

on κέντρον 1], but Paul, influenced by vs. **54,** substitutes νῖκος for δίκη; EEllis, Paul's Use of the OT, '57, 140). In κατεπόθη ὁ θάνατος εἰς νῖκος *death is swallowed up in (*or *by) victory* vs. 54, νῖκος agrees w. the improvement which Theod. made in the LXX wording of Is 25:8 (s. ARahlfs, ZNW 20, 1921, 183f; JZiegler, Is. '39 ad loc.). Vss. **54** and **55** have the **v.l.** νεῖκος, q.v. διδόναι τινὶ τὸ ν. *give someone the victory* vs. **57** (cp. 1 Esdr 3:9; 2 Macc 10:38; Jos., Ant. 6, 145). ἕως ἂν ἐκβάλῃ εἰς ν. τὴν κρίσιν *until he leads justice to victory* **Mt 12:20** (cp. 2 Km 2:26 and variants in Field, Hexapla and the Cambridge LXX; s. κρίσις, end).

❷ ***the prize of victory,*** abstr. for concr. (4 Macc 17, 12 τὸ νῖκος ἀφθαρσία) παραδοὺς αὐτῇ τὸ ν. ὃ ἔλαβες *give over to it the prize of victory you have won* Hm 12, 2, 5 (perh. a phrase like νῖκος λαβών is to be supplied earlier in the sentence).—DELG s.v. νίκη. M-M. TW.

Νινευή (inferior Νινευί [B-D-F §39, 1; s. Rob. 191f]), **ἡ,** indecl. (Gen 10:11f; Is 37:37; Jon 1:2 al.; Zeph 2:13 al. LXX; ViJon 2f [p. 83, 29 Sch.]; Hebr. נִינְוֵה) ***Nineveh,*** capital of the later Assyrian Empire **Lk 11:32 v.l.;** AcPlCor 2:29.

Νινευής (Νινευε Copt.; perh. 'nobody') ***Nineves*** alleged name of the rich man Lk 16:19 (s. Tdf. ad loc.; Νευης P^{75}, s. Νευης). HCadbury, JBL 81, '62, 399–402; KGrobel, NTS 10, '63/64, 373–82; GKilpatrick, The Bodmer and Mississippi Collection: Greek Roman Byzantine Studies 4, '63, 39f; PWeigandt, Zum Text v. Joh. 10, 7: NovT 9, '67, 47f. S. also LLefort, Le nom du mauvais riche et la trad. copte, ZNW 37, '38, 65–72. Cp. the fate of a certain Ninos: Phoenix 1 (Coll. Alex. p 231f).

Νινευίτης, ου, ὁ (-είτης) *Ninevite* pl., *people of Nineveh* as examples of penitence, contrasted w. the contemporaries of Jesus **Mt 12:41; Lk 11:32.** τοῖς Νινευίταις vs. **30.** Jonah's preaching of repentance among them 1 Cl 7:7.

νιπτήρ, ῆρος, ὁ (νίπτω; cp. Hdt. 2, 172 ποδανιπτήρ; a Cyprian ins fr. Roman times has the acc. νιπτῆρα: ASakellarios, Τα Κυπριακα I 1890, p. 191 no. 2=GDI 123, 8; Lex. Vindob. p. 128, 16; TestAbr A 3 p. 80, 11 [Stone p. 8; s. NTS 1, '54, 220]; TestJob 25:6) ***(wash) basin*** **J 13:5** (ποδονιπτήρ P^{66}).—DELG s.v. νίζω.

νίπτω 1 aor. ἔνιψα, mid. ἐνιψάμην, impv. νίψαι (B-D-F § 73; W-S. §15; Mlt-H. 250). Pass.: fut. 3 sg. νιφήσεται Lev 15:11f; pf. 3 sg. νένιπται (Hippocr.; Epict. [s. 1a below]; LXX; Jos., Ant. 8, 87).

❶ **to cleanse with use of water, *wash*—ⓐ** act. *wash* w. acc. τὶ *someth.* τοὺς πόδας (Epict. 1, 19, 5 νίπτω τ. πόδας; Vi. Aesopi G 61 P.; Gen 43:24; 1 Km 25:41; TestAbr A 6 p. 83, 19 [Stone p. 14]; JosAs 7:1) **J 13:5f, 8a, 12, 14a** (on 'foot-washing' s. λούω 2a; for **J 13:14b** s. 2 below); **1 Ti 5:10** (as act of hospitality, cp. 2 below). τινά *someone* **J 13:8b.**

ⓑ mid. *wash oneself* or *for oneself* (TestLevi 9:11 λούου . . . νίπτου)—**α.** *I wash myself* **J 9:7b, 11ab, 15; 13:10 v.l.** (if εἰ μὴ τ. πόδας is omitted); Ox 840, 34f. νίπτεσθαι εἰς τὴν κολυμβήθραν *wash, bathe in the pool* (cp. Epict. 3, 22, 71 ἵν' αὐτὸ [sc. τὸ παιδίον] λούσῃ εἰς σκάφην) **J 9:7a.**

β. *I wash (for myself)* w. acc., ν. τὸ πρόσωπον *wash one's face* (Artem. 4, 41; Achmes 143, 11) **Mt 6:17.** τὰς χεῖρας *wash one's hands* (Diod. S. 23, 2, 1; Ex 30:19; Lev 15:11) **15:2; Mk 7:3** (s. FSchulthess, ZNW 21, 1922, 233); GPt 1:1. τοὺς πόδας (Hes., fgm. 122 Rz.; Artem. 5, 55; Gen 19:2; Judg 19:21; JosAs 20:3) **J 13:10.** JHorst, D. Worte Jesu über d. kult. Reinheit: StKr 87, 1914, 429–54. Branscomb (s. νόμος, end) 156–60. WGrossouw, NovT 8, '66, 124–31.

❷ **to provide generous service, *wash feet,*** as the mng. of the unit term νίπτειν τοὺς πόδας **J 13:14b** (s. 1a above). JATRobinson, The Significance of Footwashing, OCullmann Festschr., '62, 144–47.—B. 578f. DELG s.v. νίζω. M-M. TW.

νοέω fut. νοήσω LXX; 1 aor. ἐνόησα; pf. νενόηκα; plpf. ἐνενοήκειν (Just.). Pass.: fut. 3 sg. νοηθήσεται Sir 14:21; aor. inf. νοηθῆναι (Just.) (Hom.+; pap, LXX, En, TestSol 11:1 P.; TestAbr B 6 p. 110, 22 [Stone p. 68]; Test12Patr; ApcMos 18; EpArist, Philo, Joseph., apolog. exc. Ar.).

❶ **to grasp or comprehend someth. on the basis of careful thought, *perceive, apprehend, understand, gain an insight into***

ⓐ w. obj. in the acc. (X., An. 3, 4, 44; Jos., Vi. 298; SibOr 5, 65) τὴν σύνεσίν μου *my insight* **Eph 3:4.** δικαίως ν. τὰς ἐντολάς *understand the commandments rightly* B 10:12b. τὰς παραβολάς *understand the parables* Hm 10, 1, 4; οὐ δύναμαι νοῆσαι *I cannot understand (them)*s 5, 3, 1 (cp. Pr 1:6); (w. συνιέναι, as B 10:12a) πάντα τὰ λεγόμενα m 10, 1, 6a (Just., D. 73, 3 τὸ λεγόμενον); cp. 6b; τῆς βασάνου τὴν δύναμιν *the power of the torment* s 6, 4, 3a. τὴν πρᾶξιν ἣν ποιεῖ *what he is doing* 6, 5, 3. τὰ ἐπουράνια *understand heavenly things* ITr 5:2; τὴν δόξαν τοῦ θεοῦ Hm 12, 4, 2; s 5, 3, 1 (w. γινώσκειν [as Plato, Rep. 6, 508d and e]); τοὺς χρόνους τ. ἀπάτης 6, 5, 1. Relative clause as obj. **1 Ti 1:7;** Dg 8:11; IRo 6:3. ταῦτα B 10:12a; Hs 5, 5, 4. αὐτά 6, 5, 2; 9, 2, 6b; οὐδὲν ν. *comprehend nothing* Hv 3, 6, 5; s 9, 14, 4. ὅλως οὐδὲν ν. *understand nothing at all* m 4, 2, 1. Also οὐδὲν ὅλως ν. 10, 1, 5 (μηδὲν τούτων Just., D. 125, 5). ὅσα οὐ δύνασαι νοῆσαι *whatever you cannot comprehend* s 9, 2, 6a. οὐδὲ δύναμαι νοῆσαι *nor do I understand anything (about it)* 9, 9, 2.—W. acc. of pers. (Mel., P. 82, 605 οὐκ ἐνόησας τὸν κύριον): of the angel of wickedness πῶς νοήσω αὐτὸν οὐκ ἐπίσταμαι *I do not understand how I am to recognize him* Hm 6, 2, 5.—W. περί τινος instead of the obj. ἔτι οὐ νενόηκα ὅλως περὶ τοῦ χρόνου τῆς ἀπάτης *I have not yet fully understood concerning the time of deceptive pleasure* s 6, 5, 1 v.l.—Pass. τὰ ἀόρατα . . . νοούμενα καθορᾶται *what is invisible . . . is clearly perceived* (w. the eye of the understanding) **Ro 1:20** (νοῆσαι τὸν θεόν: Herm. Wr. 11, 20b; 12, 20b and PGM 3, 597; Orphica fgm. 6 Abel [Eus., PE 13, 12, 5; cp. Denis 165, ln. 5f; Holladay p. 128 ln. 16, s. app.] οὐδέ τις αὐτὸν εἰσοράᾳ ψυχῶν θνητῶν, νῷ δ' εἰσοράαται (difft. Theosophien §56, vs. 10 [p. 180]. S. γνωστός 2). Of the λόγος: ὑπὸ ἀπίστων μὴ νοούμενος Dg 11:2 (cp. Ath. 18, 2 λόγῳ υἱῷ νοουμένῳ ἀμερίστῳ).

ⓑ w. ὅτι foll. (BGU 114 I, 9; 2 Km 12:19; EpArist 224; Philo, Virt. 17, Mos. 1, 287; Just. D. 4, 7; 27, 2; B-D-F §397, 2) **Mt 15:17; 16:11; Mk 7:18; Ac 16:10** D; 1 Cl 27:3; B 7:1; Hm 10, 1, 2; s 1:3; (w. οἶδα) 2:8.

ⓒ foll. by acc. and inf. (2 Macc 14:30; Just. D. 46, 5 ἃ πάντως ἅγια νοοῦμεν εἶναι; 49, 22; 60, 3; B-D-F §397, 2; Rob. 1036) **Hb 11:3;** foll. by acc. and ptc. ἐνόησα ὑμᾶς κατηρτισμένους *I have observed that you are equipped* ISm 1:1 (Kaibel 278, 3 τὸν φίλον ὄντα νόει; Just. D. 46, 5 θεὸν . . . ἐντειλάμενον ὑμῖν).

ⓓ foll. by indirect question (IDefixWünsch 4, 56f ἵνα μὴ νοῶσιν τί ποιῶσιν; Wsd 4:17; SibOr 3, 796; Just. D. 12, 3) Hm 6, 1, 1; μὴ νοῶν ὅτι (τί v.l.) ἐστίν s 5, 4, 2; οὐ ν. w. indir. quest. preceding *I do not understand* m 10, 1, 3. Elliptically πῶς, οὐ νοῶ *how* (this can be) *I do not understand* s 5, 6, 1.

ⓔ abs. (Sir 11:7; TestAbr B 6 p. 110, 22 [Stone p. 68] καλῶς ἐνόησας; Just. D. 119, 1 χάριν τοῦ νοῆσαι) B 6:10; 17:2; Hs 6, 4, 3b; 9, 28, 6; νοῆσαί σε δεῖ πρῶτον *you must understand it first* v 3, 8, 11. *Comprehend, perceive* (EpArist 153) **Mt 16:9; Mk 8:17.** More fully ν. τῇ καρδίᾳ (Is 44:18) **J 12:40.**

❷ **to think over with care,** ***consider, take note of*** ὁ ἀναγινώσκων νοείτω *let the reader/lector note (these words);* s. ἀναγινώσκω) **Mt 24:15; Mk 13:14.** νόει ὃ λέγω *consider what I say* **2 Ti 2:7** (Pla., Ep. 8, 352c νοήσατε ἃ λέγω) ἔτι κἀκεῖνο νοεῖτε *consider this, too* B 4:14. W. indir. quest. foll. 1 Cl 19:3; B 8:2.

❸ **to form an idea about something,** ***think, imagine*** (En 100:8 ν. τὸ κακόν) ὑπερεκπερισσοῦ ὧν νοοῦμεν *far beyond what we imagine* **Eph 3:20.**

❹ **to pay heed with intent to act appropriately,** ***be minded*** σεμνὰ ν. *be honorably minded* 1 Cl 1:3.—DELG s.v. νόος. M-M. TW. Sv.

νόημα, ατος, τό (since Hom.; also LXX; En 5:8; Just.; Ath, 27, 2)

❶ **that which one has in mind as product of intellectual process**

ⓐ ***thought,*** gener. (Hom. et al.; Pla., Symp. 197e; SibOr 3, 585) αἰχμαλωτίζοντες πᾶν ν. εἰς τὴν ὑπακοὴν τοῦ Χριστοῦ *we take captive all our thinking to make it obedient to Christ* **2 Cor 10:5.** Mostly in pl. (Cornutus 16 p. 21, 2; oft. Philo; Herm. Wr. 9, 3) τ. καρδίας ὑμῶν καὶ τὰ ν. ὑμῶν *your hearts and thoughts,* **Phil 4:7** (so REB) probably belongs here, and the same may apply to **2 Cor 3:14.; 4:4** (but s. 2 on these three pass.).

ⓑ ***design, purpose, intention*** (Od. 8, 559; Pla., Pol. 260d) of an evil nature (Il. 10, 104; cp. 18, 318; Bar 2:8) Satan's schemes **2 Cor 2:11.**

❷ **the faculty of processing thought,** ***mind, understanding*** (Il. 19, 218 et al.; 3 Macc 5:30) pl. ἐπωρώθη τὰ νοήματα αὐτῶν **2 Cor 3:14.** ὁ θεὸς τ. αἰῶνος τούτου ἐτύφλωσεν τὰ νοήματα τ. ἀπίστων **4:4.** These two pass. 'minds' REB, NRSV. μή πως φθαρῇ τὰ νοήματα ὑμῶν ἀπὸ τ. ἁπλότητος τῆς εἰς Χριστόν *that perhaps your minds will suffer deterioration of your sincere devotion to Christ* **11:3** (REB and NRSV 'thoughts'). Some would also put **Phil 4:7** here (NRSV 'minds'), but on this and the first two pass. s. 1a.—DELG s.v. νόος. M-M. TW.

νόθος, η, ον (Hom. et al.; pap; Wsd 4:3; Philo) **pert. to being born out of wedlock or of servile origin and therefore without legal status or rights,** ***illegitimate, baseborn*** (opp. γνήσιος 1 [q.v.] Menand., fgm. 248 Kö.; Jos., Ant. 5, 233. The ancient perspective is not to be obscured by modern sensitivity.). As a metaph. of persons who reject God's discipline and hence (after Pr 3:11f) cannot be God's sons: ἄρα νόθοι καὶ οὐχ υἱοί ἐστε *then you are illegitimate and not sons* (i.e. without the rights and privileges that adhere to recognized sonship) **Hb 12:8.**—DELG. M-M.

νομή, ῆς, ἡ (Hom. et al.; ins, pap, LXX; PsSol 17:40; TestSol 5:5; ApcEsdr 2:11 p. 26, 5 Tdf.; ApcEl [PSI I, 7 verso, 3] 'flock'; ApcrEzk P1, verso 4; EpArist 112; Philo; Jos., Ant. 2, 18; 17, 249) gener. 'pasturing-place' or 'grazing land' (Soph., Hdt., X., Plut., pap), and freq. in ref. to the fodder or foraging-opportunity (Pla., Aristot.; 1 Ch 4:40) that such land provides.—In our lit. the word is used only in imagery

❶ ***pasturage*** of one who follows Jesus. ν. εὑρίσκειν *find pasture* (lit. of hungry flocks 1 Ch 4:40; fig. of leaders who are like rams who find no forage La 1:6) **J 10:9.** Of the spiritual sustenance provided by God as Shepherd of the people (i.e. the Christians); the latter are called πρόβατα τῆς νομῆς σου *sheep of your pasture* (Ps 73:1; 78:13; cp. 99:3) 1 Cl 59:4; likew. B 16:5 in a quot. fr. an unknown document (perh. En 89:56, 66f), called γραφή.

❷ **someth. rapaciously destructive,** ***spreading*** (after the spreading out of a flock at pasturage; e.g. fire: Polyb. 1, 48, 5; τὸ πῦρ λαμβάνει νομήν 11, 4 [5], 4; Philo, Aet. M. 127 [conjecture of Usener]) in medical simile *spreading,* as of an ulcer (since Hippocr.; Polyb. 1, 81, 6 νομὴν ποιεῖται ἕλκος; Memnon Hist. [I BC/I AD]: 434 fgm. 1, 2, 4 Jac. [ulcer]; cp. Jos., Bell. 6, 164 parts of the temple complex are compared to diseased body parts) ὁ λόγος αὐτῶν ὡς γάγγραινα νομὴν ἕξει *their teaching will spread like a cancer* **2 Ti 2:17.**—DELG s.v. νέμω Ia. M-M.

νομίζω impf. ἐνόμιζον; 1 aor. ἐνόμισα; pf. νενόμικα (Just., D. 8, 4). Pass.: impf. ἐνομιζόμην; aor. ἐνομίσθην (Just.); pf. νενόμισμαι (Ar.); (Aeschyl., Hdt.+; SIG 47, 25 [early V BC]).

❶ **to follow or practice what is customary,** ***have in common use*** (cp. the primary mng. [difft. GShipp, Nomos 'Law' '78: mng. 'law' is earlier than 'custom'] of νόμος, q.v. beg., as that which is established by use or possession). Pass. *be the custom* (Aeschyl., Hdt.; Diod. S. 10, 3, 4 [τὰ νομιζόμενα]; Joseph.; Just., D. 8, 4; ins, pap) οὗ ἐνομίζετο προσευχὴ εἶναι *where, according to the custom, there was a place of prayer* **Ac 16:13 v.l.**

❷ **to form an idea about someth. but with some suggestion of tentativeness or refraining from a definitive statement,** ***think, believe, hold, consider*** (Aeschyl., Hdt.; ins, pap, LXX, EpArist, Philo; Jos., Ant. 1, 196) foll. by acc. and inf. (X., An. 6, 1, 29, Cyr. 1, 4, 5; ins [SIG ind.]; 4 Macc 4:13; 5:16, 18, 19; 9:4; Philo, Congr. Erud. Gr. 139; Ar. 4, 2) **Lk 2:44; Ac 7:25; 14:19; 16:27; 17:29; 1 Cor 7:26; 1 Ti 6:5.** οὗ ἐνομίζομεν προσευχὴν εἶναι *where we supposed there was a place of prayer* **Ac 16:13.** βράδιον νομίζομεν ἐπιστροφὴν πεποιῆσθαι περί *we consider that we have been somewhat slow in paying attention to matters (that are in dispute among you)* 1 Cl 1:1; μέγα καὶ θαυμαστὸν νομίζομεν εἶναι, εἰ 26:1; 44:3; Dg 4:1, 6. With double acc. οὓς . . . νομίζετε θεούς *whom you revere as deities* Dg 2:1. (This passage and those listed below under pass. usage might well be placed in 1 above, for that which is perceived in common with others is reflected in common tradition and practice; cp. WFahr, Θεοὺς νομίζειν '70). W. inf. foll. (ins [SIG ind.]; PTebt 50, 11 [112/111 BC]; PLips 105, 2; 2 Macc 4:32; Just., D. 18, 1) **Ac 8:20; 1 Cor 7:36;** Dg 2:7; 12:6. W. ὅτι foll. (X., Hell. 5, 4, 62; Lucian, Syr. Dea 28 p. 474; PFay 109, 4 [I AD]; BGU 248, 29 [c. 75 AD]; TestJud 5:3; ParJer 5:24; ApcMos 23) **Mt 5:17** μὴ νομίσητε (as 4 Macc 2:14; Jos., Ant. 5, 109; Just., A I, 36, 1 [w. acc. and inf.]; cp. Just. D. 138, 2 μὴ νομίζητε ὅτι); **10:34; 20:10;** GPt 5:18. W. acc. and ὅτι foll. **Ac 21:29** (TestAbr A 14 p. 94, 28 [Stone p. 36]).—Pass. (Appian, Iber. 18 §68; 2 Macc 8:35; EpArist 128; Philo, Spec. Leg. 2, 122; Just., A I, 26, 2 ὅς . . . θεὸς ἐνομίσθη) Dg 1. ὢν υἱός ὡς ἐνομίζετο Ἰωσήφ *he was, as commonly held, the son of Joseph* **Lk 3:23** (ὡς ἐνομίζετο as Appian, Mithrid. 63 §263, of a monetary estimate; cp. also Appian, Liby. 111 §525 of the Macedonian king τὸν νομιζόμενον υἱὸν εἶναι Περσέως, Bell. Civ. 1, 33 §146; 2, 39 §153 νομιζόμενος εἶναι Ποσειδῶνος; Paus. 2, 10, 3 Ἄρατον Ἀσκληπιοῦ παῖδα εἶναι νομίζουσιν; Olympiodorus, Life of Plato, ed. AWestermann 1850 p. 1, 4: λέγεται ὁ Πλάτων υἱὸς γενέσθαι Ἀρίστωνος, though the writer claims he was of transcendent origin).—B. 1204. Schmidt, Syn. I 333–47. DELG s.v. νέμω Ic. M-M. Sv.

νομικός, ή, όν (νόμος; Pla., Aristot. et al.; ins [Hatch 134ff]; pap, e.g. PMich XIII 659, 319; 668, 9 [both VI AD] al.; 4 Macc 5:4; SibOr 8, 112; Mel., P. 94, 713 ἐν πόλει νομικῇ).

❶ **pert. to matters relating to law,** ***about law*** (ἐν ταῖς ν. καὶ προφητικαῖς γραφαῖς Orig., C. Cels. 2, 76, 9) μάχαι ν.

quarrels about the law (i.e. the validity of the [Mosaic?] law) **Tit 3:9** (cp. Philostrat., Vitae Sophist. 1, 22, 1 ἀγῶνες ν.).

❷ **pert. to being well informed about law,** ***learned in the law,*** hence subst. ὁ νομικός *legal expert, jurist, lawyer* (Strabo 12, 2, 9; Epict. 2, 13, 6–8; IMagnMai 191, 4 [s. Thieme 37]; other exx. from inscriptions in LRobert, Hellenica I 62, 9; BGU 326 II, 22; 361 III, 2; POxy 237 VIII, 2; CPR I, 18, 24 al. in pap; 4 Macc 5:4); **Tit 3:13** mentions a certain Zenas the ν., but it is not clear whether he was expert in Mosaic or non-Mosaic (in the latter case most prob. Roman) law.—Elsewh. in the NT only once in Mt and several times in Lk, always of those expert in Mosaic law: **Mt 22:35; Lk 10:25.** Pl. **11:45f, 52; 14:3.** Cp. PEg[2] 2. Mentioned w. Pharisees **7:30; 11:53** D; **14:3.**—Schürer II 320–80, esp. 324 n. 4; GRuderg, ConNeot II '36, 41f; Kilpatrick s.v. γραμματεύς.—B. 1424. New Docs 2, 89. DELG s.v. νέμω Ic. M-M. TW.

νόμιμος, η, ον (cp. νομίζω; Pind., trag., Hdt. et al.; ins, also IBM III/2, 480, 339f [s. p. 141, cp. ἔννομος]; pap, LXX, Just.; Tat. 4, 1) **pert. to being conformable to traditional standards or law,** ***lawful.*** Subst. τὸ νόμιμον, esp. in pl. τὰ νόμιμα (Pind. et al.; Diog. L. 7, 119 [the θεοσεβεῖς are experts in τῶν περὶ θεοὺς νομίμων=the customary rites or ceremonies relating to deities]; ins, pap; Lev 18:26; Pr 3:1 al.; LXX; EpArist 10; 127; Philo, Mos. 2, 12ff al.; Jos., Ant. 8, 129; 18, 344, Vi. 191; Just., D. 29, 3; 42, 3; 67, 5; Tat. 4:1) *statutes, laws, commandments* πορεύεσθαι ἐν τοῖς ν. τῶν προσταγμάτων αὐτοῦ *walk according to the laws of God's commandments* 1 Cl 3:4 (cp. Jer 33:4; Ezk 5:6f). τοῖς ν. τοῦ δεσπότου ἀκολουθεῖν *follow the ordinances of the Lord* 40:4. ἐν τοῖς ν. τοῦ θεοῦ πορεύεσθαι *walk according to the statutes of God* 1:3 (the mss. have ἐν τοῖς νόμοις; the rdg. νομίμοις, which is found Clem. of Al., Strom. 4, 17, 105, has been taken into the more recent editions). τηρεῖν τὰ ν. τοῦ θεοῦ *keep the commandments of God* Hv 1, 3, 4 (Eur., Suppl. 19 ν. θεῶν).—DELG s.v. νέμω Ic. M-M. TW.

νομίμως adv. of νόμιμος (since Thu. 2, 74, 3; OGI 669, 19; 24; freq. pap; 4 Macc 6:18; SibOr 11, 82; Jos., C. Ap. 2. 152; 217; Ath., R. 23 p. 76, 5) **pert. to being in accordance with normal procedure,** *in accordance with rule(s)/law* (cp. Lysias fgm. 53, 4 ν. ἀποθανεῖν=to die as is the normal human experience) of athletes ν. ἀθλεῖν *compete according to the rules* **2 Ti 2:5** (perh. as opposed to being properly qualified, cp. Epict. 3, 10, 8 ὁ θεός σοι λέγει 'δός μοι ἀπόδειξιν, εἰ νομίμως ἤθλησας'). Wordplay καλὸς ὁ νόμος, ἐάν τις αὐτῷ ν. χρῆται *the law is good, if one uses it lawfully* **1 Ti 1:8** (Rob. 1201).—M-M.

νόμισμα, ατος, τό (νομίζω; primary mng. 'anything sanctioned by common usage': Aeschyl. et al.) **money officially introduced into common use,** ***coin*** (so Hdt., Aristoph. et al.; ins; PTebt 485 [II BC]; PGrenf II, 77, 8; 2 Esdr 17: 72 v.l.; 1 Macc 15:6; EpArist 33; Philo, Spec. Leg. 2, 33; Jos., Bell. 2, 592, Ant. 14, 371) τὸ ν. τοῦ κήνσου *the coin for paying the tax* **Mt 22:19** (foll. by Just., A I, 17, 2 τίνος εἰκόνα τὸ ν. ἔχει;). Pl. (Herodian 1, 9, 7), as metaph. (Philo is also fond of such usage) νομίσματα δύο, ὃ μὲν θεοῦ, ὃ δὲ κόσμου *two coinages, one of God and the other of the world* of the believers and the unbelievers IMg 5:2.—B. 775. DELG s.v. νέμω Ic. M-M.

νομοδιδάσκαλος, ου, ὁ (s. SEG XLII, 1813 on the formation and Jewish provenance; cp. PvanderHorst BZ 36, '92, 161–78, esp. 167f; on the problematic restoration in CIJ I, 201 s. GHorsley/JLee, Filología Neotestamentaria 10, '97, 79; νομοδιδάκτης in Plut., Cato Maj. 20, 4; Artem. 2, 29.—Synesius has νομοδιδάσκαλος Ep. 105 p. 248a in the general sense, and Ep. 4 p. 162a in specif. Jewish mng.) ***teacher of the law*** of deviants from correct teaching θέλοντες εἶναι νομοδιδάσκαλοι *they desire to be teachers of the law* **1 Ti 1:7.** The two other pass. in our lit. clearly refer to teachers of the Mosaic law: Gamaliel **Ac 5:34.** W. Pharisees **Lk 5:17.**—Schürer II 324f. M-M. TW.

νομοθεσία, ας, ἡ (νόμος, τίθημι) lit. 'lawgiving' (Pla., Aristot. et al.; ἡ ν. τοῦ θεοῦ Theoph. Ant. 3, 17 [p. 238, 1]), then also its result, ***legislation,*** collect. ***law*** (Diod. S. 1, 95, 6; 12, 11, 4; Dionys. Hal. 10, 57f; 11, 6; Ps.-Lucian, Am. 22; OGI 326; 26 [II BC]; PLips 35, 7; Mitt-Wilck. I/2, 6, 11; Tat., Orig., Hippol. Specif. of the Mosaic law Philo 2 Macc 6:23; 4 Macc 5:35; 17:16; EpArist; Aristob. in Eus., PE 8, 10, 13; Philo, Mos. 2, 25; 31 al.; Jos., Ant. 6, 93 al.; Just., D. 92, 2) w. other great gifts of God to Israel **Ro 9:4.**—TW.

νομοθετέω (νόμος, θέσις [τίθημι]) fut. νομοθετήσω LXX; 1 aor. ἐνομοθέτησα; perf. νενομοθέτηκα (Tat.). Pass.: aor. subj. 3 sg.; νομοθετηθῇ Dt 17:10; pf. νενομοθέτημαι; ptc. νενομοθετημένος (Lysias, X., Pla. et al.; ins, pap, LXX, EpArist; Aristob. in Eus., PE 8, 10, 12 [Denis p. 219, 36]; Philo, Joseph., Just., Tat., Mel.)

❶ **to function as a lawgiver,** ***legislate*** (of God, Orig., C. Cels. 5, 37, 2; of the Logos: Hippol., Ref. 8, 9, 8; of human lawgivers: Theoph. Ant. 3, 23 [p. 250, 11]) of Moses (Philo, Mos. 2, 9; Jos., C. Ap. 1, 284f, Ant. 1, 19) καλῶς ν. B 10:11. Pass. *receive laws* ὁ λαὸς ἐπ᾽ αὐτῆς (i.e. τῆς Λευιτικῆς ἱερωσύνης) νενομοθέτηται *on the basis of it* (i.e. the Levit. priesthood) *the people received the law* **Hb 7:11** (νομοθετεῖν τινα is found only Ps.-Galen [HWagner, Galeni qui fertur libellus Εἰ ζῷον τὸ κατὰ γαστρός, diss. Marburg 1914] p. 17, 8 v.l. ἐνομοθέτησε Ἀθηναίους ἡ Πάλλας and in LXX Ps 24:8; 26:11; 118:33. Elsewh. in Gk. νομοθετεῖν τινι; but this constr. can also yield a personal passive: Kühner-G. I 124).

❷ **to enact on the basis of legal sanction,** ***ordain, found by law*** (IAndrosIsis, Kyme 4 [=New Docs 1 p. 18 ln. 8]; Tat. 8, 2 ἀποτμήσεις αἰδοίων) μηδὲν ὁρίζοντες μηδὲ νομοθετοῦντες GMary 463, 30 (s. ὁρίζω 2aα). Pass. (Appian, Bell. Civ. 4, 2 §6 καινὴν ἀρχὴν νομοθετηθῆναι=a new magistracy is to be established by law; 4, 7 §27; νομοθετούμενον ἦθος Hippol., Ref. 9, 30, 18) διαθήκη ἥτις ἐπὶ κρείττοσιν ἐπαγγελίαις νενομοθέτηται *a covenant which has been (legally) enacted on the basis of better promises* **Hb 8:6** (cp. Philo, Migr. Abr. 91 τὰ ἐπ᾽ αὐτῇ νομοθετηθέντα). τὰ ὑπ᾽ αὐτοῦ νενομοθετημένα *what was legally ordained by him* (OGI 329, 13 [II BC] τὰ νενομοθετημένα ὑπὸ τ. βασιλέων.—τὰ νομοθετηθέντα: Philo, Spec. Leg. 1, 198 al.; Jos., Ant. 3, 317 ὑπ᾽ αὐτοῦ]) 1 Cl 43:1.—On Hb 7:11; 8:6 s. HHollander, BT 30, '79, 244–47.—DELG s.v. τίθημι. M-M. TW.

νομοθέτης, ου, ὁ (νόμος, τίθημι; since Antiphon 5, 15; Thu. 8, 97, 2; Diod. S. 40, 3, 6 [of Μωσῆς]; ins; Nicol. Dam.: [I BC]: 90 fgm. 72 Jac. [in Jos., Ant. 1, 95]; EpArist, Philo; Jos., Ant. 1, 18; 20; 22 al.; Just.; Tat. 9, 2; Iren. 5, 26, 2 [Harv. II 397, 7]; in LXX only Ps 9:21) ***lawgiver*** (of Jesus: ν. χριστιανῶν Orig., C. Cels. 3, 8, 9) of God (Dio Chrys. 19 [36], 32; Maximus Tyr. 35, 8d νομοθέτης ὁ θεός; Philo, Sacr. Abel. 131, Op. M. 61; cp. Orig., C. Cels. 1, 26, 5. In IAndrosIsis, Kyme p. 122, 4 [=New Docs 1, p. 18 ln. 8f], Isis says: ἐγὼ νόμους ἀνθρώποις ἐθέμην| κ. ἐνομοθέτησα. Also s. Theoph. Ant. 3, 9 [p. 222, 17]) **Js 4:12.** ἑαυτῶν γίνεσθε νομοθέται ἀγαθοί *be your own good lawgivers* B 21:4 (cp. Diod. S. 20, 70, 4 ὁ θεὸς ὥσπερ ἀγαθὸς νομοθέτης; Just., D. 18, 3 ὁ καινὸς ν. [Christ]).—DELG s.v. τίθημι. TW.

νόμος, ου, ὁ (νέμω; [Zenodotus reads ν. in Od. 1, 3] Hes.+; loanw. in rabb.—On the history of the word MPohlenz, Nomos: Philol 97, '48, 135–42; GShipp, Nomos 'Law' '78; MOstwald, Nomos and the Beginnings of Athenian Democracy '69). The primary mng. relates to that which is conceived as standard or generally recognized rules of civilized conduct esp. as sanctioned by tradition (Pind., Fgm. 152, 1=169 Schr. νόμος ὁ πάντων βασιλεύς; cp. SEG XVII, 755, 16: Domitian is concerned about oppressive practices hardening into 'custom'; MGigante, ΝΟΜΟΣ ΒΑΣΙΛΕΥΣ [Richerche filologiche 1] '56). The synonym ἔθος (cp. συνήθεια) denotes that which is habitual or customary, especially in reference to personal behavior. In addition to rules that take hold through tradition, the state or other legislating body may enact ordinances that are recognized by all concerned and in turn become legal tradition. A special semantic problem for modern readers encountering the term ν. is the general tendency to confine the usage of the term 'law' to codified statutes. Such limitation has led to much fruitless debate in the history of NT interpretation.—HRemus, Sciences Religieuses/Studies in Religion 13, '84, 5–18; ASegal, Torah and Nomos in Recent Scholarly Discussion, ibid., 19–27.

❶ **a procedure or practice that has taken hold, *a custom, rule, principle, norm*** (Alcman [VII BC], fgm. 93 D² of the tune that the bird sings; Ocellus [II BC] c. 49 Harder [1926] τῆς φύσεως νόμος; Appian, Basil. 1 §2 πολέμου ν., Bell. Civ. 5, 44 §186 ἐκ τοῦδε τοῦ σοῦ νόμου=under this rule of yours that governs action; Polyaenus 5, 5, 3 ν. πόμπης; 7, 11, 6 ν. φιλίας; Sextus 123 τοῦ βίου νόμος; Just., A II, 2, 4 παρὰ τὸν τῆς φύσεως ν.; Ath. 3, 1 νόμῳ φύσεως; 13, 1 θυσιῶν νόμῳ)

ⓐ gener. κατὰ νόμον ἐντολῆς σαρκίνης *in accordance w. the rule of an external commandment* **Hb 7:16.** εὑρίσκω τὸν νόμον *I observe an established procedure* or *principle* or *system* **Ro 7:21** (ν. as 'principle', i.e. an unwritten rightness of things Soph., Ant. 908). According to Bauer, Paul uses the expression νόμος (which dominates this context) in cases in which he prob. would have preferred another word. But it is also prob. that Paul purposely engages in wordplay to heighten the predicament of those who do not rely on the gospel of liberation from legal constraint: the Apostle speaks of a *principle* that obligates one to observe a code of conduct that any sensible pers. would recognize as sound and valid ὁ νόμος τ. νοός μου vs. **23b** (s. νοῦς 1a). Engaged in a bitter struggle w. this νόμος there is a ἕτερος νόμος which, in contrast to the νοῦς, dwells ἐν τοῖς μέλεσίν μου *in my* (physical) *members* vs. **23a,** and hence is a νόμος τῆς ἁμαρτίας vs. **23c** and **25b** or a νόμος τ. ἁμαρτίας καὶ τ. θανάτου **8:2b.** This sense prepares the way for the specific perspective

ⓑ of life under the lordship of Jesus Christ as a 'new law' or 'system' of conduct that constitutes an unwritten tradition ὁ καινὸς ν. τοῦ κυρίου ἡμῶν Ἰησοῦ Χριστοῦ B 2:6; in brief ν. Ἰησοῦ Χριστοῦ IMg 2 (cp. Just., D. 11, 4; 43, 1; Mel., P. 7, 46). Beginnings of this terminology as early as Paul: ὁ ν. τοῦ Χριστοῦ =the standard set by Christ **Gal 6:2** (as vs. 3 intimates, Christ permitted himself to be reduced to nothing, thereby setting the standard for not thinking oneself to be someth.). The gospel is a νόμος πίστεως *a law* or *system requiring faith* **Ro 3:27b** (FGerhard, TZ 10, '54, 401–17) or ὁ ν. τοῦ πνεύματος τῆς ζωῆς ἐν Χρ. Ἰ. *the law of the spirit* (=the *spirit-code*) *of life in Chr. J.* **8:2a.** In the same sense Js speaks of a ν. βασιλικός (s. βασιλικός) **2:8** or ν. ἐλευθερίας vs. **12** (λόγος ἐλ. P[74]), ν. τέλειος ὁ τῆς ἐλευθερίας **1:25** (association w. 1QS 10:6, 8, 11 made by EStauffer, TLZ 77, '52, 527–32, is rejected by SNötscher, Biblica 34, '53, 193f. On the theme of spontaneous moral achievement cp. Pind., Fgm. 152 [169 Schr.] 1f νόμος ὁ πάντων βασιλεὺς | θνατῶν τε καὶ ἀθανάτων | ἄγει δικαιῶν τὸ βιαιότατον| ὑπερτάτᾳ χειρί=custom is lord of all, of mortals and immortals both, and with strong hand directs the utmost power of the just. Plut., Mor. 780c interprets Pindar's use of νόμος: 'not written externally in books or on some wooden tablets, but as lively reason functioning within him' ἔμψυχος ὢν ἐν αὐτῷ λόγῳ; Aristot., EN 4, 8, 10 οἷον ν. ὢν ἑαυτῷ; Diod. S. 1, 94, 1 ν. ἔγγραπτος; cp. also Ovid, Met. 1, 90 sponte sua sine lege fidem rectumque colebat; Mayor, comm. 'Notes' 73.—RHirzel, ΑΓΡΑΦΟΣ ΝΟΜΟΣ 1903.). Some would put ὁ νόμος **Js 2:9** here (s. LAllevi, Scuola Cattol. 67, '39, 529–42), but s. 2b below.—Hermas too, who in part interprets Israel's legal tradition as referring to Christians, sees the gospel, exhibited in Christ's life and words, as the ultimate expression of God's will or 'law'. He says of Christ δοὺς αὐτοῖς (i.e. the believers) τὸν ν., ὃν ἔλαβε παρὰ τοῦ πατρὸς αὐτοῦ s 5, 6, 3, cp. 8, 3, 3. Or he sees in the υἱὸς θεοῦ κηρυχθεὶς εἰς τὰ πέρατα τῆς γῆς, i.e. *the preaching about the Son of God to the ends of the earth,* the νόμος θεοῦ ὁ δοθεὶς εἰς ὅλον. τ. κόσμον 8, 3, 2. Similarly to be understood are τηρεῖν τὸν ν. 8, 3, 4. ὑπὲρ τοῦ ν. παθεῖν 8, 3, 6. ὑπὲρ τοῦ ν. θλίβεσθαι 8, 3, 7. ἀρνησάμενοι τὸν νόμον ibid. βλασφημεῖν τὸν ν. 8, 6, 2.

❷ **constitutional or statutory legal system, *law***

ⓐ gener.: *by what kind of law?* **Ro 3:27.** ν. τῆς πόλεως *the law of the city* enforced by the ruler of the city (ν. ἐν ταῖς πόλεσι γραπτός Orig., C. Cels. 5, 37, 2); the penalty for breaking it is banishment Hs 1:5f. τοῖς ν. χρῆσθαι *observe the laws* 1:3; πείθεσθαι τοῖς ὡρισμένοις ν. *obey the established laws* Dg 5:10; νικᾶν τοὺς ν. ibid. (νικάω 3). **Ro 7:1f,** as well as the gnomic saying **Ro 4:15b** and **5:13b,** have been thought by some (e.g. BWeiss, Jülicher) to refer to Roman law, but more likely the Mosaic law is meant (s. 3 below).

ⓑ specifically: of the law that Moses received from God and is the standard according to which membership in the people of Israel is determined (Diod. S. 1, 94, 1; 2: the lawgiver Mneves receives the law from Hermes, Minos from Zeus, Lycurgus from Apollo, Zarathustra from the ἀγαθὸς δαίμων, Zalmoxis from Hestia; παρὰ δὲ τοῖς Ἰουδαίοις, Μωϋσῆς receives the law from the Ἰαὼ ἐπικαλούμενος θεός) ὁ ν. Μωϋσέως **Lk 2:22; J 7:23; Ac 15:5.** ν. Μωϋσέως **Ac 13:38; Hb 10:28.** Also ὁ ν. κυρίου **Lk 2:23f, 39;** GJs 14:1. ὁ ν. τοῦ θεοῦ (Theoph. Ant. 2, 14 [p. 136, 4]) **Mt 15:6 v.l.; Ro 8:7** (cp. Tat. 7, 2; 32, 1; Ath. 3:2). ὁ ν. ἡμῶν, ὑμῶν, αὐτῶν etc. **J 18:31; 19:7b v.l.; Ac 25:8.** κατὰ τὸν ἡμέτερον ν. **24:6 v.l.** (cp. Jos., Ant. 7, 131). ὁ πατρῷος ν. **22:3.** τὸν ν. τῶν ἐντολῶν **Eph 2:15.** Since the context of **Ac 23:29** ἐγκαλούμενον περὶ ζητημάτων τοῦ νόμου αὐτῶν points to the intimate connection between belief, cult, and communal solidarity in Judean tradition, the term νόμος is best rendered with an hendiadys: *(charged in matters) relating to their belief and custom;* cp. ν. ὁ καθ' ὑμᾶς **18:15. Ro 9:31** (CRhyne, Νόμος Δικαιοσύνης and the meaning of Ro 10:4: CBQ 47, '85, 486–99).—Abs., without further qualification ὁ ν. **Mt 22:36; 23:23; Lk 2:27; J 1:17; Ac 6:13; 7:53; 21:20, 28; Ro 2:15** (τὸ ἔργον τοῦ νόμου *the work of the law* [=the moral product that the Mosaic code requires] *is written in the heart;* diff. Diod. S. 1, 94, 1 ν. ἔγγραπτος, s. 1b, above), **18, 20, 23b, 26; 4:15a, 16; 7:1b, 4–7, 12, 14, 16; 8:3f; 1 Cor 15:56; Gal 3:12f, 17, 19, 21a, 24; 5:3, 14; 1 Ti 1:8** (GRudberg, ConNeot 7, '42, 15); **Hb 7:19** (s. Windisch, Hdb. exc. ad loc.), **28a; 10:1;** cp. **Js 2:9** (s. 1b above); μετὰ τὸν ν. **Hb 7:28b;** οἱ ἐν τῷ ν. **Ro 3:19;** κατὰ τὸν ν. *according to the* (Mosaic) *law* (Jos., Ant. 14, 173; 15, 51 al.; Just., D. 10, 1) **J 19:7b; Ac 22:12; 23:3; Hb 7:5; 9:22.** παρὰ τ. νόμον *contrary to the law* (Jos., Ant. 17, 151,

C. Ap. 2, 219; Ath. 1, 3 παρὰ πάντα ν.) **Ac 18:13.**—νόμος without the art. in the same sense (on the attempt, beginning w. Origen, In Ep. ad Ro 3:7 ed. Lomm. VI 201, to establish a difference in mng. betw. Paul's use of ὁ νόμος and νόμος s. B-D-F §258, 2; Rob. 796; Mlt-Turner 177; Grafe [s. 3b below] 7–11) **Ro 2:13ab, 17, 23a, 25a; 3:31ab; 5:13, 20; 7:1a** (s. above); **Gal 2:19b; 5:23** (JRobb, ET 56, '45, 279f compares κατὰ δὲ τῶν τοιούτων οὐκ ἔστι νόμος Aristot., Pol. 1284a). δικαίῳ νόμος οὐ κεῖται, ἀνόμοις δὲ . . . **1 Ti 1:9.** Cp. ἑαυτοῖς εἰσιν νόμος **Ro 2:14** (in Pla., Pol. and in Stoic thought the wise person needed no commandment [Stoic. III 519], the bad one did; MPohlenz, Stoa '48/49 I 133; II 75). Used w. prepositions: ἐκ ν. **Ro 4:14; Gal 3:18, 21c** (v.l. ἐν ν.); **Phil 3:9** (ἐκ νόμου can also mean *corresponding to* or *in conformity with the law:* PRev 15, 11 ἐκ τῶν νόμων); cp. ἐκ τοῦ νόμου **Ro 10:5.** διὰ νόμου **Ro 2:12b; 3:20b; 4:13; 7:7b; Gal 2:19a, 21;** ἐν ν. (ἐν τῷ ν. Iren. 3, 11, 8 [Harv. II 49, 9]) **Ro 2:12a, 23; Gal 3:11, 21c v.l.; 5:4; Phil 3:6.** κατὰ νόμον **3:5; Hb 8:4; 10:8** (make an offering κατὰ νόμον as Arrian, Anab. 2, 26, 4; 5, 8, 2); χωρὶς ν. **Ro 3:21a; 7:8f;** ἄχρι ν. **5:13a.** ὑπὸ νόμον **6:14f; 1 Cor 9:20; Gal 3:23; 4:4f, 21a; 5:18** (cp. Just., D. 45, 3 οἱ ὑπὸ τὸν ν.).—Dependent on an anarthrous noun παραβάτης νόμου *a law-breaker* **Ro 2:25b** (**27b** w. art.); **Js 2:11.** ποιητὴς ν. *one who keeps the law* **4:11d** (w. art. **Ro 2:13b**). τέλος ν. *the end of the law* **Ro 10:4** (RBultmann and HSchlier, Christus des Ges. Ende '40). πλήρωμα ν. *fulfilment of the law* **13:10.** ν. μετάθεσις *a change in the law* **Hb 7:12.** ἔργα ν. **Ro 3:20a, 28; 9:32 v.l.; Gal 2:16; 3:2, 5, 10a.**—(ὁ) ν. (τοῦ) θεοῦ **Ro 7:22, 25a; 8:7** because it was given by God and accords w. his will. Lasting **Mt 5:18; Lk 16:17** (cp. Bar 4:1; PsSol 10:4; Philo, Mos. 2, 14; Jos., C. Ap. 2, 277).—Used w. verbs, w. or without the art.: ν. ἔχειν **J 19:7a; Ro 2:14** (ApcSed 14:5). πληροῦν ν. *fulfill the law* **Ro 13:8;** pass. **Gal 5:14** (Mel., P. 42, 291). πληροῦν τὸ δικαίωμα τοῦ ν. *fulfill the requirement of the law* **Ro 8:4.** φυλάσσειν τὸν ν. *observe the law* **Ac 21:24; Gal 6:13.** τὰ δικαιώματα τοῦ ν. φυλάσσειν *observe the precepts of the law* **Ro 2:26;** διώκειν ν. δικαιοσύνης **9:31a;** πράσσειν ν. **2:25a.** ποιεῖν τὸν ν. **J 7:19b; Gal 5:3; Ro 2:14b,** s. below; τὸν ν. τηρεῖν **Js 2:10.** τὸν ν. τελεῖν **Ro 2:27.** φθάνειν εἰς ν. **9:31b.** κατὰ ν. Ἰουδαϊσμὸν ζῆν IMg 8:1 v.l. is prob. a textual error (Pearson, Lghtf., Funk, Bihlmeyer, Hilgenfeld; Zahn, Ign. v. Ant. 1873 p. 354, 1 [difft. in Zahn's edition] all omit νόμον as a gloss and are supported by the Latin versions; s. Hdb. ad loc.). τὰ τοῦ ν. ποιεῖν *carry out the requirements of the law* **Ro 2:14b** (ApcSed 14:5; FFlückiger, TZ 8, '52, 17–42). καταλαλεῖν νόμου, κρίνειν ν. **Js 4:11abc.** ἐδόθη ν. **Gal 3:21a.**—Pl. διδοὺς νόμους μου εἰς τὴν διάνοιαν αὐτῶν **Hb 8:10;** cp. **10:16** (both Jer 38:33).—Of an individual stipulation of the law ὁ νόμος τοῦ ἀνδρός *the law insofar as it concerns the husband* (Aristot., fgm. 184 R. νόμοι ἀνδρὸς καὶ γαμετῆς.—SIG 1198, 14 κατὰ τὸν νόμον τῶν ἐρανιστῶν; Num 9:12 ὁ ν. τοῦ πάσχα; Philo, Sobr. 49 ὁ ν. τῆς λέπρας) **Ro 7:2b;** cp. **7:3** and δέδεται νόμῳ vs. **2a** (on the imagery Straub 94f); **1 Cor 7:39 v.l.**—The law is personified, as it were (Demosth. 43, 59; Aeschin. 1, 18; Herm. Wr. 12, 4 [the law of punishment]; IMagnMai 92a, 11 ὁ ν. συντάσσει; b, 16 ὁ ν. ἀγορεύει; Jos., Ant. 3, 274) **J 7:51; Ro 3:19.**

❸ **a collection of holy writings precious to God's people, *sacred ordinance*—ⓐ** in the strict sense *the law*=the Pentateuch, the work of Moses the lawgiver (Diod. S. 40, 3, 6 προσγέγραπται τοῖς νόμοις ἐπὶ τελευτῆς ὅτι Μωσῆς ἀκούσας τοῦ θεοῦ τάδε λέγει τ. Ἰουδαίοις=at the end of the laws this is appended: this is what Moses heard from God and is telling to the Jews. ὁ διὰ τοῦ ν. μεταξὺ καθαρῶν καὶ ἀκαθάρτων διαστείλας θεός Iren. 3, 12, 7 [Harv. II 60, 3]; cp. Hippol., Ref. 7, 34, 1) τὸ βιβλίον τοῦ νόμου **Gal 3:10b** (cp. Dt 27:26). Also simply ὁ νόμος (Jos., Bell. 7, 162 ὁ ν. or 2, 229 ὁ ἱερὸς ν. of the holy book in a concrete sense) **Mt 12:5** (Num 28:9f is meant); **J 8:5; 1 Cor 9:8** (cp. Dt 25:4); **14:34** (cp. Gen 3:16); **Gal 4:21b** (the story of Abraham); **Hb 9:19.** ὁ ν. ὁ ὑμέτερος **J 8:17** (cp. Jos., Bell. 5, 402; Tat. 40, 1 κατὰ τοὺς ἡμετέρους ν.). ἐν Μωϋσέως νόμῳ γέγραπται **1 Cor 9:9.** καθὼς γέγραπται ἐν νόμῳ κυρίου **Lk 2:23** (γέγραπται ἐν νόμῳ as Athen. 6, 27, 23c; IMagnMai 52, 35 [III BC]; Mel., P. 11, 71; cp. Just., D. 8, 4 τὰ ἐν τῷ ν. γεγραμμένα); cp. vs. **24.** ἔγραψεν Μωϋσῆς ἐν τῷ νόμῳ **J 1:45** (cp. Cercidas [III BC], fgm. 1, 18f Diehl[2] [=Coll. Alex. p. 204, 29=Knox p. 196] καὶ τοῦθ' Ὅμηρος εἶπεν ἐν Ἰλιάδι).—The Sacred Scriptures (OT) referred to as a whole in the phrase ὁ ν. καὶ οἱ προφῆται (Orig., C. Cels. 2, 6, 4; cp. Hippol., Ref. 8, 19, 1) *the law* (הַתּוֹרָה) *and the prophets* (הַנְּבִיאִים) **Mt 5:17; 7:12; 11:13; 22:40; Lk 16:16; Ac 13:15; 24:14; 28:23; Ro 3:21b;** cp. Dg 11:6; **J 1:45.** τὰ γεγραμμένα ἐν τῷ ν. Μωϋσέως καὶ τοῖς προφήταις καὶ ψαλμοῖς **Lk 24:44.**

ⓑ In a wider sense=Holy Scripture gener., on the principle that the most authoritative part gives its name to the whole (ὁ ν. ὁ τοῦ θεοῦ Theoph. Ant. 1, 11 [p. 82, 15]): **J 10:34** (Ps 81:6); **12:34** (Ps 109:4; Is 9:6; Da 7:14); **15:25** (Ps 34:19; 68:5); **1 Cor 14:21** (Is 28:11f); **Ro 3:19** (preceded by a cluster of quotations fr. Psalms and prophets).—**Mt 5:18; Lk 10:26; 16:17; J 7:49.**—JHänel, Der Schriftbegriff Jesu 1919; OMichel, Pls u. s. Bibel 1929; SWesterholm, Studies in Religion 15, '86, 327–36.—JMeinhold, Jesus u. das AT 1896; MKähler, Jesus u. das AT[2] 1896; AKlöpper, Z. Stellung Jesu gegenüber d. Mos. Gesetz, Mt 5:17–48: ZWT 39, 1896, 1–23; EKlostermann, Jesu Stellung z. AT 1904; AvHarnack, Hat Jesus das atl. Gesetz abgeschafft?: Aus Wissenschaft u. Leben II 1911, 225–36, SBBerlAk 1912, 184–207; KBenz, D. Stellung Jesu zum atl. Gesetz 1914; MGoguel, RHPR 7, 1927, 160ff; BBacon, Jesus and the Law: JBL 47, 1928, 203–31; BBranscomb, Jes. and the Law of Moses 1930; WKümmel, Jes. u. d. jüd. Traditionsged.: ZNW 33, '34, 105–30; JHempel, D. synopt. Jesus u. d. AT: ZAW 56, '38, 1–34.—Lk-Ac: JJervell, HTR 64, '71, 21–36.—EGrafe, D. paulin. Lehre vom Gesetz[2] 1893; HCremer, D. paulin. Rechtfertigungslehre 1896, 84ff; 363ff; FSieffert, D. Entwicklungslinie d. paul. Gesetzeslehre: BWeiss Festschr. 1897, 332–57; WSlaten, The Qualitative Use of νόμος in the Pauline Ep.: AJT 23, 1919, 213ff; HMosbech, Pls' Laere om Loven: TT 4/3, 1922, 108–37; 177–221; EBurton, ICC, Gal 1921, 443–60; PFeine, Theol. des NT[6] '34, 208–15 (lit.); PBenoit, La Loi et la Croix d'après S. Paul (Ro 7:7–8:4): RB 47, '38, 481–509; CMaurer, D. Gesetzeslehre des Pls '41; PBläser, D. Gesetz b. Pls '41; BReicke, JBL 70, '51, 259–76; GBornkamm, Das Ende d. Gesetzes '63; HRaisänen, Paul and the Law[2] '87; PRichardson/SWesterholm, et al., Law in Religious Communities in the Rom. Period, '91 (Torah and Nomos); MNobile, La Torà al tempo di Paolo, alcune riflessioni: Atti del IV simposio di Tarso su S. Paolo Apostolo, ed. LPadovese '96, 93–106 (lit. 93f, n. 1).—Dodd 25–41.—B. 1358; 1419; 1421. DELG s.v. νέμω Ic. Schmidt, Syn. I 333–47. M-M. EDNT. TW. Sv.

νοσέω (νόσος) aor. ptc. νοσήσας TestJob 1:2; 35:3 (Aeschyl., Hdt. et al.; SIG 943, 5; pap, TestJob; TestZeb 6:5; ParJer, Tat., Ath.) ***be sick, ailing*** in our lit. only fig. (X., Mem. 3, 5, 18 al.; Diod. S. 11, 86, 3; Heraclit. Sto. 69 p. 89, 20; Wsd 17:8; Philo, Leg. All. 3, 211; Jos., Ant. 16, 244; 18, 25) νοσεῖν περί τι be ailing with, have a morbid craving for someth. (Plut., Mor. 54f ν. περὶ δόξαν) περὶ ζητήσεις καὶ λογομαχίας (s. ζήτησις 1) **1 Ti 6:4.**—DELG s.v. νόσος. M-M. TW.

νόσημα, ατος, τό (fr. νόσος via νοσέω; trag., Thu. et al.; Chion, Ep. 14, 2; Artem. 3, 51; PRein II, 92, 12 [IV AD]; PCair-Masp 159, 40 [VI AD]; TestSol 11:2; Philo; Jos., Ant. 8, 45, C. Ap. 1, 282) ***disease*** ᾧ δήποτε κατείχετο νοσήματι *no matter what disease he had* **J 5:3 v.l.**—DELG s.v. νόσος. TW.

νόσος, ου, ἡ (Hom.+)—❶ **physical malady, *disease, illness*** (freq. viewed in Mediterranean society as socially devaluing) lit. **Ac 19:12;** πεσούσης ... εἰς ν. *when (Artemilla) ... became ill* AcPl Ha 4, 15 (cp. ApcMos 5 περιπεσὼν εἰς ν.). W. μαλακία: θεραπεύειν πᾶσαν ν. **Mt 4:23; 9:35; 10:1** (cp. Jos., Bell. 5, 383 πάσῃ ν.). νόσους θεραπεύειν **Lk 9:1** (Just., A I, 48, 1 πάσας ν.). W. βάσανοι **Mt 4:24.** ἐθεράπευσεν πολλοὺς κακῶς ἔχοντας ποικίλαις ν. *he healed many who were sick w. various diseases* **Mk 1:34** (Tat. 20, 2 ποικίλαι ν.). ἀσθενοῦντες νόσοις ποικίλαις **Lk 4:40.** ἐθεράπευσεν πολλοὺς ἀπὸ νόσων *he healed many people of their illnesses* **7:21.** Pass. ἰαθῆναι ἀπὸ τῶν ν. **6:18.** In imagery βαστάζειν τὰς ν. τινός *bear someone's diseases* (after Is 53:4 where, however, LXX does not have νόσος) **Mt 8:17;** IPol 1:3.

❷ **moral malady, *disease*** fig. ext. of 1: *vice* (Bias in Diog. L. 1, 86 νόσος ψυχῆς of a character defect; Just., D. 30, 1 τὸν λαὸν ... ἐν νόσῳ ψυχικῇ ὑπάρχοντα; Herm. Wr. 12, 3 ἀθεότης; oft. Philo) ὁ μοιχὸς ... τῇ ἰδίᾳ ν. τὸ ἱκανὸν ποιεῖ *the adulterer gives satisfaction to his own diseased inclination* Hs 6, 5, 5.—MGrmek, Diseases in the Ancient Greek World, tr. M and LMueller, '89 [orig. French '83].—DELG. M-M. TW.

νοσσιά, ᾶς, ἡ (νόσσος; H.Gk. for νεοσσιά, s. B-D-F §31, 3; Mlt-H. 92; Thackeray p. 98; Lob. on Phryn. p. 207).

❶ ***nest*** (this mng. Hdt., Aristoph. et al.; LXX) νοσσιᾶς ἀφῃρημένοι *after their nest is robbed* B 11:3

❷ ***brood*** (Lycurgus the orator [IV BC] 132; Dt 32:11) **Lk 13:34;** GJs 3:1 v.l.—DELG s.v. νεοσσός. M-M.

νοσσίον, ου, τό (νοσσός; H.Gk. for νεοσσίον; cp. νοσσιά) ***the young*** of a bird **Mt 23:37** (the word, in the form νεοττίον Aristoph. et al., as νοσσίον also Ps 83:4).—B. 175. DELG s.v. νεοσσός.

νοσσός, οῦ, ὁ (H.Gk. by hypheresis for νεοσσός [cp. νοσσιά and Jos., C. Ap. 2, 213 νεοττός] as v.l. in Lk) ***the young*** of a bird (as νεοσσός Hom. et al.) B 11:3 (cp. Is 16:2). δύο νοσσοὺς περιστερῶν *two young pigeons* **Lk 2:24** (Lev 12:8; 14:22.—Soranus p. 72, 15 νεοσσοὺς περιστερῶν.—νοσσοί of the young of pigeons: Sb 7814, 15 [256 AD]).—DELG s.v. νεοσσός. M-M.

νοσφίζω (νόσφι 'apart'; Hom. et al.) in our lit. only mid.; 1 aor. ἐνοσφισάμην **to put aside for oneself, *keep back,*** of engagement in a type of skimming operation (X., Cyr. 4, 2, 42: Cyrus urges restraint in appropriation of treasure; Polyb. 10, 16, 6: Roman soldiers resist temptation to take booty for themselves without equitable distribution; Plut., Lucull. 517 [37, 2], Aristid. 320 [4, 3]; Jos., Ant. 4, 274; SIG 993, 21; PRyl 116, 10; 2 Macc 4:32) ἀπό τινος *some of someth.* (PSI 442, 4 [III BC]; Josh 7:1.—ἔκ τινος Athen. 6, 23a; Philo, Mos. 1, 253) ἐνοσφίσατο ἀπὸ τῆς τιμῆς *(Ananias) kept back some of the proceeds* (not a case of embezzlement) **Ac 5:2f** (cp. Josh 7:1, 19–26. Diod. S. 5, 34, 3: lot-holders who hold back [νοσφίζεσθαι] some of their crops, which have been declared common property [κοινοποιεῖσθαι], are subject to the death penalty among the Vaccaei, a Celtic tribe). μηδὲν ὅλως ν. εἰς ἐπιθυμίαν πονηράν *keep back* or *reserve nothing at all for the satisfaction of one's base desire* Hs 9, 25, 2. Abs. (ins [I AD]: ΕΛΛΗΝΙΚΑ 1, 1928, p. 18 ln. 13; PPetr III, 56 [b], 10; 12) **Tit 2:10.**—DELG s.v. νόσφι. M-M. Spicq.

νότος, ου, ὁ—❶ **a wind blowing from a southerly direction, *south wind, southwest wind*** (Hom. et al.; LXX; Philo, Mos. 1, 120.—Appian, Bell. Civ. 5, 98 §410 it is the southwest wind beyond doubt) ὑποπνεύσαντος νότου **Ac 27:13** (s. ὑποπνέω). ἐπιγενομένου νότου *when the southwest wind came up* **28:13.** Bringing heat **Lk 12:55** (cp. Jos., Bell. 7, 318 νότος πνεύσας).

❷ **direction to the right as one faces east, *south***—ⓐ of the direction in general (Soph.; Hdt. 6, 139 al.; SIG 691, 18; POxy 255, 7; PTebt 342, 8; LXX; En 26:2; TestSol 7:6; TestJud 4:1; GrBar 11:8; VitIs 7 [p. 70, 7 Sch.]; Jos., Bell. 5, 145, Ant. 8, 319) ἀπὸ βορρᾶ καὶ ν. *from north and south* (s. βορρᾶς) **Lk 13:29.** ἀπὸ νότου *on the south* (ἀπό 2a) **Rv 21:13.**

ⓑ of a southern area or country (Ps 125:4 ἐν τῷ νότῳ; ApcMos 15) βασίλισσα νότου *the queen of the south* (Sheba; TestSol 19:3 al.) **Mt 12:42; Lk 11:31.**—B. 873. DELG. M-M. TW. Spicq.

νουθεσία, ας, ἡ (νουθετέω; Aristoph., Ran. 1009; Diod. S. 15, 7, 1; BGU 613, 21; PAmh 84, 21; Wsd 16:6; TestReub 3:8; Philo, Mos. 1, 119 al.; Jos., Ant. 3, 311; Just., A I, 67, 4; Did.; Lob. on Phryn. 512) **counsel about avoidance or cessation of an improper course of conduct, *admonition, instruction.*** In gener., w. παιδεία (as Philo, Deus Imm. 54; cp. De Mut. 135) **Eph 6:4** νουθ. κυρίου (=Christian instruction).—Of historical incidents used as an example or warning to discourage improper conduct γράφειν πρὸς ν. τινός *write as a warning for someone* **1 Cor 10:11** (πρὸς ν. τινός as Philo, De Praem. 133).—Of quiet reproof about repetition of an improper course of conduct *admonition, rebuke* **Tit 3:10.**—Beside πίστις, ὑπομονή, μακροθυμία IEph 3:1.—DELG s.v. νόος. M-M. TW. Spicq.

νουθετέω fut. νουθετήσω; 1 aor. ἐνουθέτησα. Pass.: aor. ptc. νουθετηθέντες Wsd 12:26; pf. 2 sg. νενουθέτησαι Job 38:18 (s. prec. entry; trag. et al.; PGrenf II 93, 3; LXX; pseudepigr.; Philo; Jos., Ant. 4, 260; 20, 162; Did.) **to counsel about avoidance or cessation of an improper course of conduct, *admonish, warn, instruct*** w. acc. of pers. (Dio Chrys. 56 [73], 10; Sb 6263, 26) **Ac 20:31; 1 Cor 4:14** (Wsd 11:10 τούτους ὡς πατὴρ νουθετῶν; PsSol 13:9; Jos., Bell. 1, 481, Ant. 3, 311); **Col 1:28; 3:16** (in the last two pass. w. διδάσκειν, as Pla., Leg. 8, 84b; Philo, Decal.); **1 Th 5:12; 2 Th 3:15; Tit 1:11 v.l.;** 1 Cl 7:1; 2 Cl 19:2. ἀλλήλους **Ro 15:14;** 2 Cl 17:2. τοὺς ἀτάκτους *warn the idle* **1 Th 5:14** (*punish,* as Plut., Sertor. 578 [19, 11] πληγαῖς ν., probably overstates). τὸν οἶκον Hv 1, 3, 1; also τὰ τέκνα 1, 3, 2. τὰς χήρας καὶ τοὺς ὀρφανούς 2, 4, 3. ἁμαρτάνοντας m 8:10. Pass. νουθετεῖσθαι ὑπό τινος (Philo, Deus Imm. 134; Jos., Ant. 20, 162a) 2 Cl 17:3; Hv 3, 5, 4.—DELG s.v. νόος. M-M. TW. Spicq.

νουθέτημα, ατος, τό (νοῦς, τίθημι; Aeschyl. et al.; also Herodas 7, 11) ***admonition, discipline*** 1 Cl 56:6 (Job 5:17).—DELG s.v. νόος.

νουθέτησις, εως, ἡ (νοῦς, τίθημι; since Eupolis Com. [VBC] 66; Pla.; Diod. S. 1, 70, 8; 1, 77, 7; 3, 33, 5; Iambl., Vi. Pyth. 33, 231; Jdth 8:27; Pr 2:2) ***admonition, warning, reproof*** ἡ ν., ἣν ποιούμεθα εἰς ἀλλήλους *the reproof which we address to each other* 1 Cl 56:2.—DELG s.v. νόος.

νουμηνία read by Tdf. **Col 2:16;** s. νεομηνία.—DELG s.v. 2 μήν.

νουνεχῶς (Aristot. 1436b, 33 νουνεχῶς κ. δικαίως; Polyb. 1, 83, 3; 2, 13, 1; 5, 88, 2; SibOr 1, 7; TestJob 36:6) adv.

of νουνεχής (Just.) ***wisely, thoughtfully*** ἀποκρίνεσθαι **Mk 12:34.**—DELG s.v. νόος. M-M. TW.

νοῦς, νοός, νοΐ, νοῦν, ὁ (contracted fr. νόος.—Hom. et al.; pap, LXX, TestSol, Test12Patr; SibOr 3, 574; EpArist 276; Philo [oft.]; Jos., Ant. 3, 65, Vi. 122 al.; apolog. exc. Mel.—On its declension s. B-D-F §52; W-S. §8, 11; Mlt-H. 127; 142) in the NT only in Pauline lit. except for Lk 24:45; Rv 13:18; 17:9.

❶ **the faculty of intellectual perception—ⓐ** ***mind, intellect*** as the side of life contrasted w. physical existence, the higher, mental part of a human being that initiates thoughts and plans (Apollonius of Tyana [I AD] in Eus., PE 4, 13; Orig., C. Cels. 8, 38, 21; 52, 24; Did., Gen. 57, 26): ὁ νόμος τοῦ νοός (μου) *the law of (my) intellect* **Ro 7:22 v.l., 23.** (Opp. σάρξ) τῷ ν. δουλεύειν νόμῳ θεοῦ *serve the law of God w. one's intellect* vs. **25.**

ⓑ ***understanding, mind*** as faculty of thinking (Hippol., Ref. 4, 43, 2; Did., Gen. 44, 11 [w. λογισμός]) διανοίγειν τὸν ν. τινος *open someone's mind* **Lk 24:45.** ὁ ἔχων νοῦν *whoever has understanding* **Rv 13:18** (ν. ἔχειν as Aristoph., Equ. 482; Hyperid. 3, 23; Dio Chrys. 17 [34], 39; 23 [40], 26; Ael. Aristid. 23, 12 K.=42 p. 771 D.; EpArist 276; Philo, Mos. 1, 141; TestReub 3:8; Ar. 9, 5; Just., D. 30, 1; 60, 2; Tat. 1, 2). ὧδε ὁ ν. ὁ ἔχων σοφίαν *here is* (i.e. *this calls for*) *a mind with wisdom* **17:9.** νοῦν διδόναι *grant understanding* Dg 10:2. Also παρέχειν νοῦν 11:5. ὁ σοφίαν καὶ νοῦν θέμενος ἐν ἡμῖν τῶν κρυφίων αὐτοῦ *who has placed in us wisdom and understanding of his secrets* B 6:10. ποικίλος τῇ φρονήσει καὶ τῷ ν. *diverse in thought and understanding* Hs 9, 17, 2a; cp. vs. 2b. Of the peace of God ἡ ὑπερέχουσα πάντα ν. *which surpasses all power of thought* **Phil 4:7.** In contrast to the divine Pneuma which inspires the 'speaker in tongues': ὁ ν. μου ἄκαρπός ἐστιν *my mind is unfruitful,* because it remains inactive during the glossolalia **1 Cor 14:14.** προσεύχεσθαι τῷ ν. (opp. τῷ πνεύματι.—νόῳ as instrumental dat. as Pind., P. 1, 40) *pray w. the understanding* vs. **15a;** ψάλλειν τῷ ν. vs. **15b.** θέλω πέντε λόγους τῷ ν. μου λαλῆσαι *I would rather speak five words w. my understanding* vs. **19** (cp. 1QS 10:9).—As a designation of Christ (cp. SibOr 8, 284) in a long series of expressions (w. φῶς) Dg 9:6 (cp. Epict. 2, 8, 2 τίς οὖν οὐσία θεοῦ; νοῦς, ἐπιστήμη, λόγος ὀρθός. Theoph. Ant. 1, 3 [p. 62, 14] νοῦν ἐὰν εἴπω, φρόνησιν αὐτοῦ [sc. τοῦ θεοῦ] λέγω; Ath. 10, 2 νοῦς καὶ λόγος τοῦ πατρὸς ὁ υἱὸς τοῦ θεοῦ. The god Νοῦς in the Herm. Wr.: Rtzst., Mysterienrel[3] 47 al.; JKroll, D. Lehren des Hermes Trismegistos 1914, 10ff; 60ff al.; PGM 5, 465 ὁ μέγας Νοῦς; Iren. 1, 1, 1 [Harv. I 9, 7], 1, 2, 1 [Harv. I 13, 7]: names of Aeons in gnostic speculation).—Also the state of *sensibleness, composure* in contrast to the disturbances of soul brought about by the expectation of the Parousia, σαλευθῆναι ἀπὸ τοῦ νοός *be shaken, and thereby lose your calmness of mind* **2 Th 2:2.**

❷ **way of thinking,** ***mind, attitude,*** as the sum total of the whole mental and moral state of being (Just., A I, 15, 16)—ⓐ as possessed by every person μεταμορφοῦσθαι τῇ ἀνακαινώσει τοῦ ν. *be transformed by the renewing of the mind,* which comes about when Christians have their natural νοῦς penetrated and transformed by the Spirit which they receive at baptism **Ro 12:2** (s. Ltzm., Hdb. ad loc.). W. the same sense ἀνανεοῦσθαι τῷ πνεύματι τοῦ ν. ὑμῶν *you must adopt a new attitude of mind* **Eph 4:23** (the piling up of synonyms is a distinctive feature of Eph; s. MDibelius, Hdb. exc. on Eph 1:14). Of polytheists παρέδωκεν αὐτοὺς ὁ θεὸς εἰς ἀδόκιμον ν. *God abandoned them to depraved thoughts* **Ro 1:28.** τὰ ἔθνη περιπατεῖ ἐν ματαιότητι τοῦ ν. αὐτῶν *the nations/gentiles live w. their minds fixed on futile things* **Eph 4:17.** Of one who is in error: εἰκῇ φυσιούμενος ὑπὸ τοῦ ν. τῆς σαρκὸς αὐτοῦ *groundlessly conceited* (lit. 'puffed up') *by his mind, fixed on purely physical things* **Col 2:18.** κατεφθαρμένος τὸν ν. *with depraved mind* **2 Ti 3:8;** also διεφθαρμένος τὸν ν. **1 Ti 6:5** (B-D-F §159, 3; Rob. 486). μεμίανται αὐτῶν καὶ ὁ ν. καὶ ἡ συνείδησις *their minds and consciences are unclean* **Tit 1:15.** ὁ ν. αὐτῶν περὶ τὴν πρᾶξιν αὐτῶν καταγίνεται *their mind is fixed on their own business* Hm 10, 1, 5.

ⓑ specif. of the Christian *attitude* or *way of thinking* κατηρτισμένοι ἐν τῷ αὐτῷ νοΐ **1 Cor 1:10.** Through baptism believers receive μίαν φρόνησιν καὶ ἕνα νοῦν Hs 9, 17, 4; cp. 9, 18, 4. εἷς νοῦς, μία ἐλπίς is to rule in the church IMg 7:1.

❸ **result of thinking,** ***mind, thought, opinion, decree*** (Hom. et al. of gods and humans; cp. Hippol., Ref. 9, 10, 8) ἕκαστος ἐν τῷ ἰδίῳ ν. πληροφορείσθω *each pers. is to be fully convinced in his own mind* **Ro 14:5.** τίς γὰρ ἔγνω νοῦν κυρίου; *who has known the Lord's thoughts?* (Is 40:13) **11:34; 1 Cor 2:16a.** When Paul continues in the latter passage vs. **16b** w. ἡμεῖς νοῦν Χριστοῦ ἔχομεν, he is using the scriptural word νοῦς to denote what he usu. calls πνεῦμα (vs. 14f). He can do this because his νοῦς (since he is a 'pneumatic' person) is filled w. the Spirit (s. 2a above), so that in his case the two are interchangeable. Such a νοῦς is impossible for a 'psychic' person.—OMoe, Vernunft u. Geist im NT: ZST 11, '34, 351–91; RJewett, Paul's Anthropological Terms, '71, 358–90; TKrischer, Glotta 62, '84, 141–49. S. καρδία end; νοέω end.—B. 1198. DELG s.v. νόος. Schmidt, Syn. III 621–55. M-M. EDNT. TW. Sv.

Νύμφα, ας, ἡ (Att. Νύμφη, ης; so PHib 94, 8 [III BC]; StudPal 10, 1910, no. 113, 2 [II AD]) ***Nympha*** **Col 4:15.** The form Νυμφαν of the mss. is definitely an accusative, but could equally derive fr. the masc. Νυμφᾶς (cp. the vv.ll. αὐτῶν and αὐτοῦ and s. next entry), unless as in N., αὐτῆς is preferred (Metzger 627) w. the phrase τὴν κατ' οἶκον ἐκκλησίαν. (On the role of women as philanthropists, s. e.g. the ins in honor of Iounia Theodora: BCH 83, '59, 496ff. [=Pleket no. 8].)—B-D-F §125, 1; Mlt. 48. M-M.

Νυμφᾶς, ᾶ, ὁ (CIG I, 269, 15; 1240, 18f; prob. a shortened form Νυμφόδωρος; s. Νύμφα) ***Nymphas*** **Col 4:15 v.l.** (as acc. Νυμφᾶν).

νύμφη, ης, ἡ (Hom.+; ins, pap, LXX, Philo, Joseph.; TestJud 13:3; JosAs, Philo, Joseph., Mel.; PBodm XII νύμφαι καὶ νυμφίοι; loanw. in rabb.; the church as bride of Christ Did., Gen. 69, 14).

❶ ***bride*** (Diod. S. 5, 2, 3; Iren. 5, 9, 4 [Harv. II 344, 11]) **Rv 21:2.** W. νυμφίος (q.v.; Did., Gen. 63, 13) **Mt 25:1 v.l.** (s. FBurkitt, JTS 30, 1929, 267–70); **J 3:29; Rv 18:23** (Jer 7:34; 16:9 al.). Of the bride of the Lamb **Rv 21:9;** cp. **22:17** (CChavasse, The Bride of Christ '40).—It can also be *the newly married woman* (Istros [III BC]: 334 fgm. 55 Jac.; Iren. 4, 20, 12 [Harv. II 224, 2]).

❷ ***daughter-in-law*** (Gen 11:31; 38:11; Ruth 1:6, 22 al.; Philo, Leg. All. 3, 74; Jos., Ant. 5, 321; SibOr 1, 206; 3, 827.—='daughter' in ins fr. Asia Minor: ENachmanson, Eranos 9, 1909, 78) **Mt 10:35; Lk 12:53** (for both cp. Mi 7:6).—RBatey, NT Nuptial Imagery '71.—B. 125. DELG. M-M. TW.

νυμφικός, ή, όν (νύμφη; Aeschy., Pl. et al.; TestJud 12:1; pap) ***bridal*** τὰ ἱμάτια τὰ νυμφικά *the bridal garments* GJs 2:4.—DELG s.v. νύμφη.

νυμφίος, ου, ὁ (νύμφη; Hom. et al.; SIG 1024, 33f [c. 200 BC]; CPR I, 30, 37; Sb 10; LXX, JosAs, Mel., PBodmer XII.—In gnostic speculation: Iren. 1, 7, 1 [Harv. I 58, 9]; Hippol., Ref. 6,

34, 4) ***bridegroom*** **Mt 9:15bc; 25:1, 5f, 10** (on the coming of the bridegroom, who outshines all other mortals, cp. Sappho 123 Diehl[2], 5 [=Campbell 111]: 'than a large man huger by far'); **Mk 2:19f; Lk 5:34f; J 2:9; 3:29ac; Rv 18:23** (w. νύμφη [q.v. 1] as Diod. S. 5, 18, 1; Philo, Spec. Leg. 1, 110; Jos., Bell. 6, 301). ὁ φίλος τοῦ ν. (1 Macc 9:39; cp. Jos., Ant. 13, 20) the friend of the bridegroom (שׁוֹשְׁבִין) was a go-between in arranging the marriage, and then had a prominent place in the wedding festivities **J 3:29b.** οἱ υἱοὶ τοῦ νυμφίου **Mt 9:15a** D is surely not the original rdg. (Jülicher, Gleichn. 180f).—DELG s.v. νύμφη. M-M. TW.

νυμφών, ῶνος, ὁ (νύμφη)—**❶** ***wedding hall*** **Mt 22:10 v.l.**—**❷** ***bridal chamber*** (Paus. 2, 11, 3; Heliod. 7, 8, 3; PLond III, 964, 19 p. 212 [II/III AD]; Tob 6:14, 17; JosAs 15:7 [s. Philonenko 89]; Clem. of Al., Exc. ex Theod. §64f) Hv 4, 2, 1. οἱ υἱοὶ τοῦ νυμφῶνος (gen. as Ps 149:2; 1 Macc 4:2 οἱ υἱοὶ τῆς Ἄκρας) *the bridegroom's attendants,* that group of the wedding guests who stood closest to the groom and played an essential part in the wedding ceremony **Mt 9:15; Mk 2:19; Lk 5:34** (s. FLewis, ET 24, 1913, 285).—Billerb. I 500–518. DELG s.v. νύμφη. M-M. TW.

νῦν adv. of time (Hom.+) 'now'—**❶ temporal marker with focus on the moment as such, *now*—ⓐ** of time coextensive with the event of the narrative *now, at the present time,* w. focus on the immediate present, designating both a point of time as well as its extent.

α. without definite article. The verbs w. which it is used are found

א. in the pres. **Lk 16:25; J 4:18; 9:21; 16:29; Ac 7:4; 2 Cor 13:2; Gal 1:23; 1 Pt 3:21; 1J 3:2** and oft.

ב. in the perf., when it has pres. mng. ἔρχεται ὥρα καὶ ν. ἐλήλυθεν *it is now here* **J 16:32 v.l.;** ν. ἐγνώκαμεν *now we know* **8:52;** cp. **17:7.** ν. οἶδα **Ac 12:11.** ν. ἡ ψυχή μου τετάρακται **J 12:27.** Cp. **1J 2:18.**

ג. in the aor., mostly in contrast to the past, denoting that an action or condition is beginning in the present: νῦν ἐδοξάσθη ὁ υἱὸς τοῦ ἀνθρώπου *now the glorification of the Human One has begun* **J 13:31.** ν. τὴν καταλλαγὴν ἐλάβομεν *we have now entered into the reconciliation* **Ro 5:11.** οὗτοι ν. ἠπείθησαν *they have now become disobedient* **11:31.** ν. ἀπεκαλύφθη τοῖς ἁγίοις ἀποστόλοις *now it has been revealed to the holy apostles* **Eph 3:5;** cp. vs. **10; 2 Ti 1:10.** ἃ ν. ἀνηγγέλη ὑμῖν *that which is now proclaimed to you* **1 Pt 1:12.** Cp. **Ro 5:9; 16:26; 1 Pt 2:10b, 25.**—More rarely in contrast to the future: οὐ δύνασαί μοι νῦν ἀκολουθῆσαι, ἀκολουθήσεις δὲ ὕστερον **J 13:36** (νῦν ... ὕστερον as Jos., Ant. 4, 295). ἵνα ν. ἔλθῃ: ἐλεύσεται δέ **1 Cor 16:12.** ἐὰν μὴ λάβῃ ... ν., explained by ἐν τῷ καιρῷ τούτῳ **Mk 10:30.**

ד. in the impv., to denote that the order or request is to be complied w. at once; ν. comes after the impv. (B-D-F §474, 3; before the impv.: TestAbr A 6 p. 83, 24 [Stone p. 14] νῦν θέασαι): καταβάτω ν. ἀπὸ τοῦ σταυροῦ *now let him come down from the cross* **Mt 27:42; Mk 15:32.** ῥυσάσθω ν. *let (God) deliver him* **Mt 27:43.** ἀντλήσατε ν. *now draw some out* **J 2:8.**

β. with the definite art.—**א.** as an adj. ὁ, ἡ, τὸ νῦν *the present* (X., An. 6, 6, 13 ὁ νῦν χρόνος; Dio Chrys. 19 [36], 55 ὁ νῦν κόσμος; PAmh 68, 66 ὁ νῦν στρατηγός; BGU 19, 5; GrBar 4:16 οἱ νῦν ἄνθρωποι; Just., D. 68, 8 ἡ νῦν ὁμιλία) ὁ νῦν αἰών *the present age* **1 Ti 6:17; 2 Ti 4:10; Tit 2:12.** ὁ ν. καιρός (Ael. Aristid. 13 p. 239 D.) **Ro 3:26; 8:18; 11:5; 2 Cor 8:14;** B 4:1. ἡ ν. Ἰερουσαλήμ *the present Jerus.* **Gal 4:25.** οἱ ν. οὐρανοί **2 Pt 3:7.** ζωὴ ἡ ν. (opp. ἡ μέλλουσα) **1 Ti 4:8.**

ב. subst. τὸ νῦν *the present time* (Aristot.) w. prep. (X. et al.; ins, pap LXX) ἀπὸ τοῦ ν. *from now on, in the future* (SIG 982, 22; BGU 153, 14; 193 II, 11; POxy 479, 6; cp. IXanthos 86 D, ln. 8; s. LRobert, Nouvelles Inscriptions di Sardes '64, 28f [other exx. in Dssm., NB 81=BS 253]; Sir 11:23f; Tob 7:12; 1 Macc 10:41; 11:35; 15:8; ApcMos 28; Jos., Ant. 13, 50) **Lk 1:48; 5:10; 12:52; 22:69; Ac 18:6; 2 Cor 5:16a;** ἄχρι τοῦ ν. *until now* (s. ἄχρι 1aα.—μέχρι τοῦ ν.: Just., D. 78, 8; Diod. S. 1, 22, 2; SIG 742, 35; BGU 256, 9; 667, 8; 3 Macc 6:28; Jos., Ant. 3, 322) **Ro 8:22; Phil 1:5.** ἕως τοῦ ν. *until now* (SIG 705, 44f [112 BC]; PMich 173, 14 [III BC]; Gen 32:5; 46:34; 1 Macc 2:33) **Mt 24:21; Mk 13:19.**

ג. w. other particles: ἀλλὰ νῦν *but now* **Lk 22:36; 2 Cor 5:16b.** ἀλλὰ καὶ ν. (TestAbr A 16 p. 97, 5 [Stone p. 42]) **J 11:22;** ἄρα ν. *so* or *thus now* **Ro 8:1.** ν. γάρ *for now* **13:11.** ν. δέ *but now* **Lk 16:25; 19:42** (νῦν δέ in the reversal theme also Il. 19, 287–90; 22, 477–514 et al.); **J 16:5; 17:13; Col 1:26; Hb 2:8.** οὐδὲ ἔτι ν. *not even now* **1 Cor 3:2** (ἔτι ν.=even now: Plut., Mor. 162e; Ael. Aristid. 13 p. 302 D.; Jos., Ant. 1, 92; 2, 313). καὶ ν. *even now* (cp. Just., A I, 26, 4; 63, 1, D. 7, 2; Dio Chrys. 13 [7], 121) **J 11:22 v.l.** (perh. *assuredly,* but see HRiesenfeld, Nuntius 6, '52, 41–44); **Phil 1:20;** ἔτι καὶ ν. *and even now* Dg 2:3 (Ath. 17, 2; cp. Just., A I, 26, 5 καὶ νῦν ἔτι, A II, 6, 6 καὶ ἔτι νῦν); *and now* (TestLevi 19:1; JosAs 28:3) **J 17:5; Ac 16:37; 23:21; 26:6; Phil 1:30;** AcPl Ha 8, 21. ν. οὖν *so now* (Gen 27:8; 1 Macc 10:71) **Ac 16:36; 23:15.** καὶ ν. ... ἤδη *and now ... already* **1J 4:3.** ν. μέν *now, to be sure* **J 16:22.** ποτὲ ... ν. δέ *once ... but now* (Mel., P. 43, 306) **Ro 11:30; Eph 5:8; 1 Pt 2:10.** πολλάκις ... ν. δέ *often ... but now* **Phil 3:18.** τότε (μὲν) ... ν. δέ *then to be sure ... but now* **Gal 4:9; Hb 12:26.** ὥσπερ τότε ... οὕτως καὶ ν. *just as then ... so also now* **Gal 4:29.**—ALaurentin, וְעַתָּה—καὶ νῦν. Formule, etc. (J 17:5): Biblica 45, '64, 168–95; 413–32; HBronyers, ... adverbiales וְעַתָּה im AT: VetusT 15, '65, 289–99.

ⓑ of time shortly before or shortly after the immediate pres.: ν. ἠκούσατε **Mt 26:65.** ν. ἐζήτουν σε λιθάσαι *they were just now trying to stone you* **J 11:8.** Cp. **21:10; Ac 7:52.**—*(Soon) now* (Epict. 3, 24, 94) ν. ἀπολύεις τὸν δοῦλόν σου **Lk 2:29.** Cp. **J 12:31ab; 16:5; Phil 1:20.**

❷ temporal marker with focus not so much on the present time as the situation pert. at a given moment, *now, as it is*

ⓐ without art. *as things now stand* (Gen 29:32; Ps.-Clem., Hom. 10, 22) νῦν ζῶμεν ἐάν as *the situation now is, we live if* **1 Th 3:8.** So also νῦν δέ, καὶ νῦν, νῦν οὖν: νῦν οὖν τί πειράζετε τ. θεόν; *since this is so, why are you tempting God?* **Ac 15:10;** cp. **10:33** (νῦν οὖν: TestAbr B 7 p. 112, 3 [Stone p. 72]; TestJob 23:7; ApcMos 11:30; Lucian, Dial. Deor. 25, 3; Babrius 6, 9). καὶ ν. τί μέλλεις; **22:16** (cp. TestAbr A 4 p. 81, 18 [Stone p. 10] καὶ ν., κύριε τί ποιήσω;). Cp. **2J 5.**—Somet. in impv. statements (oft. LXX; cp. JJeremias, ZNW 38, '39, 119f; PsSol 2:32; TestAbr A 4 p. 81, 5 [Stone p. 10]; TestSim 7:1; JosAs 6:8; GrBar 4:1; Tat. 21, 2 πείσθητέ μοι νῦν) καὶ ν. πέμψον *now send* **Ac 10:5.** Cp. **16:36; 23:15; 1J 2:28;** GJs 9:2.—On ἄγε νῦν s. ἄγε.—Not infreq. νῦν δέ serves to contrast the real state of affairs with the statement made in an unreal conditional clause: εἰ ἔγνως ... : νῦν δέ *if you had known ... ; but, as a matter of fact* **Lk 19:42.** Cp. **J 8:40; 9:41; 15:22, 24; 18:36; 1 Cor 12:18 v.l., 20; Hb 11:16.—1 Cor 5:11; 7:14; Js 4:16.**

ⓑ with art.: neut. pl. τὰ ν. (also written τανῦν; cp. Tdf., Prol. p. 111) *as far as the present situation is concerned = now* (trag., Pla. et al.; POxy 743, 30 [2 BC]; 811; PTebt 315, 25; Jdth 9:5; 1 Esdr 1:31; Jos., C. Ap. 1, 217) **Ac 4:29; 17:30; 20:32; 27:22.** καὶ τὰ νῦν λέγω ὑμῖν *for now I tell you this* **5:38.** ἀλλὰ τὰ ν.

Hs 5, 7, 4 (TestLevi 10:1 v.l.).—τὸ νῦν ἔχον *for the present* (Dio Chrys. 21 [38], 42; Tob 7:11 BA v.l.; cp. Tat. 15, 2; 41, 1 τὸ δὲ νῦν συνέχον) **Ac 24:25** (B-D-F §160).—The ms. tradition oft. varies betw. ν. and νυνί.—PTachau, 'Einst' u. 'Jetzt' im NT, '72; FDanker, Proclamation Commentaries: Luke[2], '87, 47–57. B. 962f. DELG s.v. νυ. M-M. TW.

νυνί adv. of time (Hdt. 7, 229 al.; SIG 259, 11 [338/337 BC]; PPetr III, 42 H [8] f, 4 [III BC]; POxy 490, 5 [124 AD]; 506, 25; 908, 5; LXX [Thackeray 191]; TestJob; JosAs cod. A 12, 7; 13, 5 [p. 55, 15; 57, 12 Bat.]; Joseph.; Ar. 13, 7; Just., D. 11, 2; Tat. 28, 1) an emphatic form of νῦν made by adding to it the demonstrative suffix ι (Kühner-Bl. I 620; B-D-F §64, 2; Rob. 296; 523) without alteration of mng. (Mayser 456). Except for **Ac 22:1 v.l.; 24:13; Hb 8:6; 9:26; 11:16 v.l.;** ἐπεὶ δὲ νυνί AcPt Ox 849; 1 Cl 47:5; 2 Cl 2:3, only in the Pauline writings and there always ν. δέ (the ms. tradition oft. varies betw. νῦν and νυνί)

❶ **temporal marker with focus on the moment as such, *now***—ⓐ w. the pres. (Job 30:9; Jos., Ant. 14, 404) **Ac 24:13; Ro 15:23, 25; 2 Cor 8:22; Phlm 9**; cp. **11**; perh. also AcPt Ox 849.

ⓑ w. the perf. in pres. sense ν. δὲ . . . πεφανέρωται *but now . . . has been revealed* **Ro 3:21.**

ⓒ w. aor. (Job 30:1; Just., D. 11, 2) **Ro 6:22; 7:6; 11:30 v.l.; Eph 2:13; Col 1:22;** 2 Cl 2:3. Impv.: **2 Cor 8:11; Col 3:8;** 1 Cl 47:5.

ⓓ w. a subst. (PRyl 111, 4 [161 AD] τὴν νυνεὶ γυναῖκά μου) ἡ πρὸς ὑμᾶς ν. ἀπολογία *the defense which I now make before you* **Ac 22:1.**

❷ **temporal marker with focus on a prevailing situation, w. the idea of time weakened or entirely absent, *now, as it is***

ⓐ ν. δέ *but now,* as the situation is **Ro 7:17; 1 Cor 13:13; 14:6 v.l.** (Tat. 28, 1).

ⓑ introducing the real situation after an unreal conditional clause or sentence *but, as a matter of fact* **1 Cor 5:11 v.l.; 12:18; 15:20; Hb 8:6; 9:26; 11:16 v.l.**—DELG s.v. νυ. M-M.

νύξ, νυκτός, ἡ ('night' Hom.+) for the acc. νύκταν (JosAs 10:17; ApcEsdr 5:4 p. 29, 28 Tdf.) s. B-D-F §46, 1.

❶ **period between sunset and sunrise, *night***—ⓐ **Mt 14:25** φυλακὴ τ. νυκτός (as Jos., Bell. 5, 510); **Mk 6:48; J 13:30** (for the short clause cp. εἰμί 5.—For the scene cp. 1 Km 28:25; Musaeus, Heron and Leander [V AD] v. 309 [ALudwich 1929] νὺξ ἦν); **Ac 16:33; 23:23; 27:27a; Rv 21:25; 22:5;** 1 Cl 27:7 (Ps 18:3); GP 5:18; AcPl Ha 5, 21. ἐν ὁράματι τῆς ν. *in a vision at night* Hv 3, 10, 6. κατὰ μέσον τῆς ν. *at midnight* **Ac 16:25** D; **27:27b;** καὶ ἡ ν. ὁμοίως *and likewise the night,* as well as the day (i.e. μὴ φάνῃ τὸ τρίτον αὐτῆς=it is to lose a third of the light fr. moon and stars) **Rv 8:12** (cp. Job 3:9). W. ἡμέρα (as En 104:8; ApcEsdr 2:9 p. 25, 30 Tdf.; ApcSed 8:2; Philo, Aet. M. 19; Ath. 24, 2; Hippol., Ref. 4, 44, 1; cp. Did., Gen. 37:13) also 1 Cl 20:2; 24:3. κοιμᾶται ἡ ν., ν. ἐπέρχεται *the night sleeps, comes on* vs. 3b. κατέλαβεν αὐτὸν νύξ *the night overtook him* GJs 14:1 (cp. GrBar 9:1).

ⓑ gen. νυκτός *at night, in the night-time* (Hom.+; Diod. S. 18, 34, 6; SIG 521, 5 [III BC]; PHib 36, 5 [229 BC]; PAmh 134, 6; 1 Macc 4:1, 5; 5:29; 2 Macc 12:9; 3 Macc 5:19; JosAs 24:3; Jos., Ant. 6, 215.—B-D-F §186, 2; Rob. 495) **Mt 2:14; 28:13; J 3:2; 19:39; Ac 9:25; 1 Th 5:7ab;** AcPl Ha 5, 29; τῆς ν. *on this night* (X., An. 5, 7, 14; Alexis Com. 148 Kock.—B-D-F §186, 2) **Lk 2:8.** νυκτὸς καὶ ἡμέρας *night and day* (X., Symp. 4, 48, Apol. 31; BGU 246, 12; PGiss 19, 7; Jdth 11:17) **1 Th 2:9; 3:10; 2 Th 3:8; 1 Ti 5:5; 2 Ti 1:3;** B 19:10; IRo 5:1; D 4:1; GPt 7:27; Ox 840, 34; AcPl Ha 2, 10; 3, 1. ἡμέρας καὶ ν. (Dt 28:66; Josh 1:8; 2 Ch 6:20; 2 Esdr 14:3; Ps 1:2; Is 60:11 al.) **Lk 18:7; Rv 4:8; 7:15; 12:10; 14:11; 20:10.** ἡμέρας τε καὶ ν. (IMagnMai 163, 8) **Ac 9:24;** 1 Cl 2:4. διὰ παντὸς νυκτὸς καὶ ἡμέρας *continually, night and day* (cp. UPZ 110, 87 [164 BC]; PTebt 48, 10 [113 BC]) **Mk 5:5.**—W. prep. διὰ νυκτός *through the night* (X., An. 4, 6, 22; Athen. 7, 276c; PGM 4, 2052) **Ac 23:31;** δι' ὅλης ν. *all through the night, during the night* (cp. Just., D. 1, 4 δι' ὅλης ν. καὶ ἡμέρας) **Lk 5:5; J 21:6 v.l.** (s. διά A 2a). διὰ νυκτός *at night, during the night* (s. διά A 2b and cp. also IGR IV, 860, 10 στρατηγήσαντα διὰ νυκτός; BGU 597, 20; PTebt 332, 9; Sb 4317, 4; PGM 6, 47; 7, 407) **Ac 5:19; 17:10.** διὰ τῆς ν. (so Achilles Tat. 8, 19, 1) **16:9** (s. B-D-F §255, 3; Rob. 791). μέσης ν. *at midnight* **Mt 25:6** (s. μέσος 1a).

ⓒ dat., answering the question 'when'? (B-D-F §200, 1; Rob. 522): νυκτί *at night* (Hom. et al.; Philo, Aet. M. 88) φαίνειν Dg 7:2. Pl. (Phlegon: 257 fgm. 36, 2, 1 Jac. τρισὶ νυξί) ταῖς νυξί *at night* 2:7; ταύτῃ τῇ ν. (cp. TestAbr A 7 p. 83, 35 [Stone p. 14]; JosAs 24:13; ApcMos 2 τῇ ν. ταύτῃ) *this very night, tonight* **Mk 14:30; Lk 12:20; 17:34; Ac 27:23;** αὐτῇ τῇ ν. *on the night of that same day* Hv 3, 1, 2; 3, 10, 7. τῇ ν. ἐκείνῃ **Ac 12:6;** τῇ ἐπιούσῃ ν. *the following night* **23:11.** Cp. GPt 9:35.—W. prep. ἐν ν. *at night, in the night* (X. et al.; SIG 527, 40 [c. 220 BC]; Veröffentlichungen aus der pap-Sammlung München 6, 43; 3 Macc 5:11; PsSol 4:5, 16; TestJob 24:4; Tat. 22:2) **Ac 18:9; 1 Th 5:2; 2 Pt 3:10 v.l.;** ἐν τῇ ν. (TestJob 3:1; GrBar 9:8) **J 11:10.** ἐν τῇ ν. ταύτῃ (Jdth 11:3, 5; 13:14) **Mt 26:31.** ἐν ταύτῃ τῇ ν. vs. **34;** ἐν ἐκείνῃ τῇ ν. (cp. 1 Macc 13:22) **J 21:3.** ἐν τῇ ν. ᾗ παρεδίδοτο **1 Cor 11:23.**

ⓓ acc., answering the question 'how long?' (Hom. et al.; B-D-F §161, 2; Rob. 469–71) ἡμέρας τεσσεράκοντα καὶ νύκτας τεσσεράκοντα **Mt 4:2;** 1 Cl 53:2; B 4:7; 14:2 (Ex 24:18; 34:28); GJs 1:4. τρεῖς ἡμέρας καὶ τρεῖς νύκτας **Mt 12:40ab** (Jon 2:1); GJs 24:3; AcPl Ox 6 recto, 3f (sg. opp. pl. Aa I 241, 11); AcPlCor 2:30. τριετίαν νύκτα καὶ ἡμέραν οὐκ ἐπαυσάμην *for three years, night and day, I did not stop* **Ac 20:31.** νύκτα καὶ ἡμέραν *night and day* (Hyperid. 5, 13; Aeneas Tact. 380; Palaeph. p. 57, 5; Jos., Ant. 16, 260) **Mk 4:27; Lk 2:37; Ac 26:7;** MPol 5:1. τὰς νύκτας *during the nights, at night* (Biogr. p. 428; PHal 8, 4; Tob 10:7 BA) **Lk 21:37.** τὴν ν. *through the night* Hs 9, 11, 6. ὅλην τὴν ν. *the whole night through* (Amphis Com. [IV BC] 20, 4 Kock; Ex 14:20f; Lev 6:2 al.; JosAs 25:3) Hs 9, 11, 8.

❷ **night as condition, *night*** fig. ext. of 1: as time for rest from work **J 9:4** (as a symbol of death: Kaibel 1095, 4 νὺξ αὐτοὺς καταλύει). As a time contrasting with eschatological fulfillment ἡ ν. προέκοψεν *the night is far gone* **Ro 13:12;** cp. **1 Th 5:5.**—B. 992. Neugebauer/Hoesen index. M-M. EDNT. TW.

νύσσω 1 aor. ἔνυξα (Hom. et al.; Sir 22:19; PsSol 16:4; Philo, Leg. ad Gai. 42; Jos., Bell. 3, 335 δόρατι; 5, 64 κατὰ πλευρὰν ν.) prim. 'prick'

❶ **to penetrate with a pointed instrument, ordinarily not a violent or deep piercing, *prick, stab*** τινά τινι *someone w. someth.* καλάμῳ αὐτόν GPt 3:9 (cp. Diog. L. 2, 109 νυχθῆναι καλάμῳ [Eubulides dies after a sharp reed pierced him while he was swimming]; Hesychius Miles., Viri Ill. c. 5 JFlach [1880]; SibOr 8, 296). τί τινι *someth. w. someth.* λόγχῃ τὴν πλευράν **J 19:34** (to ensure that Jesus was actually dead, with modification of the more intense wounding suggested by ἐκκεντέω [q.v.] in the citation of Zech 12:12 in a reading of uncertain origin; s. Field, Notes 108); cp. **Mt 27:49 v.l.** (Plut., Cleom. 37, 16 : Panteus pricks Cleomenes in the ankle w. a dagger to determine whether he is dead).

❷ **to touch gently, *nudge, poke*** to waken someone fr. sleep (Od. 14, 485; Plut., Mor. 7e; Diog. L. 6, 53; 3 Macc 5:14) νύξας τ. πλευρὰν τ. Πέτρου ἤγειρεν αὐτόν **Ac 12:7** D. ὁ κύριος . . . νύσσει τὸν Παῦλον AcPl Ha 7, 28.—DELG. M-M. TW.

νυστάζω fut. 3 sg. νυστάξει LXX; 1 aor. ἐνύσταξα (s. B-D-F §71) **to be almost asleep, *nod, become drowsy, doze*** (Aristoph., Hippocr. et al.; PCairZen 534, 35 [III BC]; LXX; ApcMos 38) ἐνύσταξαν πᾶσαι *they all became drowsy* **Mt 25:5.**—Fig. *be drowsy, idle* (Pla.; Ps. 118:28 v.l.; PsSol 16:1; Philo, Congr. Erud. Gr. 81) of retribution personified ἡ ἀπώλεια αὐτῶν οὐ ν. *their destruction is not dozing,* i.e. it is on its way **2 Pt 2:3.**—DELG.

νυχθήμερον, ου, τό (νύξ, ἡμέρα; Petosiris, fgm. 7 ln. 58; Herm. Wr. in Stob. 1, 21, 9 W.=414, 2 Sc.; Galen VII 508 K.; Cleomedes Astron. [II AD] 1, 6, 30f; 2, 1, 73 HZiegler; Anecdota Astrologica [ALudwich, Maximi et Ammonis Carmina 1877] p. 125, 7; Cyranides p. 58, 14; Themist., Paraphr. Aristot. I p. 372, 3 Spengel; Proclus, in Tim. Platon. index EDiehl. Cp. Mitt-Wilck II/2, 78, 6 [376/8 AD] ἐπὶ τέσσαρας ὅλας νυχθημέρους [B-D-F §121; s. Mlt-H. 269; 283]; Kühner-Bl. II 318.—As adj. as early as Peripl. Eryth. c. 15) ***a day and a night***=24 hours **2 Cor 11:25.**—EKönig, Kalenderfragen: ZDMG 60, 1906, 605ff, esp. 608–12.—DELG s.v. νύξ. M-M.

Νῶε, ὁ indecl. (נֹחַ) ***Noah*** (Gen 5:29 al.; En 107:3; TestBenj 10:6; ParJer 7:8; GrBar, Philo, Just.; Mel., P. 83, 624f; in Joseph. Νῶχος, ου [Ant. 1, 99]); in the genealogy of Jesus **Lk 3:36.** As a proclaimer of repentance 1 Cl 7:6 (cp. Jos., Ant. 1, 74 [SRappaport, Agada u. Exegese bei Fl. Josephus 1930, 93f]; SibOr 1, 127ff; Jubilees 7:20–39). Sim. as δικαιοσύνης κῆρυξ **2 Pt 2:5** (N. as δίκαιος Gen 6:9; Wsd 10:4; Sir 44:17; Philo, Congr. Erud. Gr. 90, Migr. Abr. 125; cp. SibOr 1, 126 δικαιότατος). πιστὸς εὑρεθείς (cp. SibOr 1, 120 πιστότατος). 1 Cl 9:4; cp. **Hb 11:7.** ἐν ταῖς ἡμέραις N. **Lk 17:26; 1 Pt 3:20** (ESelwyn, 1 Pt '46, 328–33); cp. **Mt 24:37.** N. in the ark **Mt 24:38; Lk 17:27.** W. Job and Daniel 2 Cl 6:8 (Ezk 14:14ff).—JLewis, A Study of the Interpr. of Noah and the Flood in Jewish and Christian Lit. '68.

νωθρός, ά, όν (Hippocr. et al.; Herm. Wr. 10, 24a ν. ψυχή; PSI XIV 1386 verso, 6 [I BC/I AD]; PBrem 61, 15; LXX) ***lazy, sluggish*** ν. καὶ παρειμένος ἐργάτης *a lazy and careless workman* 1 Cl 34:1 (cp. Sir 4:29). ἵνα μὴ νωθροὶ γένησθε **Hb 6:12.** ν. ταῖς ἀκοαῖς *sluggish in hearing = hard of hearing* (s. ἀκοή 3 and Heliod. 5, 1, 5 νωθρότερος ὢν τὴν ἀκοήν) **5:11.**—DELG s.v. νωθής. M-M. TW. Spicq.

νῶτος, ου, ὁ (Hom.+ [but in Att. almost always τὸ νῶτον] also X., Equ. 3, 3; Aristot., HA 3, 3; 12, 5; LXX [Thackeray p. 155]; PsSol 10:2 [acc. νῶτον]; TestSol 14:1 [κατὰ νώτου, but acc. as v.l.]; TestIss 5:3 [τὸν νῶτον]; TestNapht 5:6 [νώτου]; Philo, Aet. M. 128 [νῶτα]; Jos., Ant. 12, 338; 424 [τὰ νῶτα]; Just., D. 53, 1 [τὸν νῶτον]; B-D-F §49, 2; Mlt-H. 124.—PTebt 21, 8 [II BC] the acc. νῶτον) **back part of the body from the neck to the pelvis, *back* Ro 11:10** (Ps 68:24); B 5:1 (Is 50:6).—B. 211. DELG s.v. νῶτον. M-M.

Ξ

ξαίνω (Hom. et al.; Aristoph., Theophr., Anth. Pal.; not LXX; fig. in Jos., Ant. 1, 46, Bell. 6, 304) **to scratch or comb, esp. wool in preparation for the making of wool thread, *comb, card,*** found in the original rdg. of Cod. א in **Mt 6:28,** where it was erased and later revealed by ultraviolet light (TSkeat, ZNW 37, '38, 211–14 [cp. POxy 2221 col. 2, 8 and note]): πῶς οὐ ξένουσιν (ξαίν.) instead of πῶς αὐξάνουσιν of the texts. This may make it possible to restore the logion Ox 655, 1 (*b*), 9f p. 23 (=Kl. T. 8^3 p. 23; ASyn. 67, 33; s. GTh 36) and there read ο]ὐ ξαίνει instead of α]ὐξα[ι]νει (but s. Fitzmyer p. 544 and Betz, SM 477). This could mean that ξαίνω may have stood in the common source of **Mt 6:28=Lk 12:27;** in that case there would be three negations for the lilies of **Mt 6:28** as well as for the birds of vs. **26.**—PKatz, JTS 5, 2, '54, 207–9; TGlasson, Carding and Spinning: POxy 655: JTS 13, '62, 331f.—DELG.

Ξανθικός, ου, ὁ (so Diod. S. 18, 56, 5 in an edict of remission from the Macedonians in the time of the Diadochi τοῦ Ξανθικοῦ μηνός; 2 Macc 11:30; Joseph., index. The correct form is Ξανδικός; s. OGI ind. V; Mayser 180) ***Xanthicus,*** a month in the Macedonian calendar. The date for the martyrdom of Polycarp μηνὸς Ξανθικοῦ δευτέρᾳ ἱσταμένου MPol 21 is equivalent to Feb. 22 or 23.—Lghtf., Apost. Fathers $II^2/1$, 1889, 677ff; ESchwartz, Jüd. u. christl. Ostertafeln: AGG VIII 6, 1905, 125ff.—EBickerman, Chronology of the Ancient World [2] '80, lists p. 20 and 48.

ξενία, ας, ἡ (ξένος; Hom. et al.; ins, pap, Sir 29:27 v.l.; Philo, Joseph., loanw. in rabb.) ***hospitality, entertainment*** shown a guest (so mostly), less frequently the place where the guest is lodged, ***guest room*** (Suda and sim. Hesychius equate ξενία with καταγώγιον, κατάλυμα. Cp. also Sb 3924, 7; 17 [19 AD]; PMich 473, 13 [II AD]; PSI 50, 16 [IV–V AD]; Philo, Mos. 2, 33; Jos., Ant. 1, 200; 5, 147; Ps.-Clem., Hom. 1, 15; 8, 2; 12, 24; 14, 1; 8). In the two places in our lit. where ξ. occurs, both mngs. are possible, though the second is perh. more probable. ἑτοιμάζειν τινὶ ξενίαν *prepare a guest room for someone* **Phlm 22** (Ps.-Clem., Hom. 12, 2 τὰς ξενίας ἑτοιμάζοντες.—ξενία=guest room also schol. on Nicander, Ther. 486. Cp. Lat. hospitium parare). Of Paul's lodgings in Rome **Ac 28:23** (on the question whether ξ. here=μίσθωμα vs. 30, s. Lghtf. on Phlm 22 and in the comm. on Phil p. 9; also s. HCadbury, JBL 45, 1926, 320ff; Haenchen ad loc.).—DELG s.v. ξένος. M-M. TW. Spicq.

ξενίζω (ξένος) 1 aor. ἐξένισα. Pass.: 1 fut. ξενισθήσομαι; 1 aor. ἐξενίσθην (Hom. et al.; ins, pap, LXX; TestAbr B; Philo, Joseph., Ath.).

➊ **to show hospitality, *receive as a guest, entertain*** (Hom. et al.) τινά *someone* (X., Cyr. 8, 3, 35; Diod. S. 14, 31, 3; Aelian, VH 13, 26) **Ac 10:23.** ἀγγέλους (TestAbr B 2 p. 106, 21f [Stone p. 60]; cp. Polyaenus 6, 1, 3 ξ. θεούς) **Hb 13:2** (after Gen 18:3; 19:2f). The obj. is to be supplied fr. the context (Sir 29:25) **Ac 28:7.**—Pass. *be entertained* as a guest, *stay* ἐν οἰκίᾳ τινός **10:32.**

παρά τινι *with someone* (Diod. S. 14, 30, 3; Philo, Abr. 131; Jos., Ant. 12, 171) vs. **6; 21:16** (on the constr. s. B-D-F §294, 5; Rob. 721); **1 Cor 16:19 v.l.** ἐνθάδε **Ac 10:18.**

❷ **to cause a strong psychological reaction through introduction of someth. new or strange, *astonish, surprise*** (Polyb. 3, 114, 4; Diod. S. 12, 53, 3; Jos., Ant. 1, 45) ξενίζοντά τινα *astonishing things* **Ac 17:20.**—Pass. *be surprised, wonder* (Polyb.; M. Ant. 8, 15; PStras 35, 6; PIand 20, 1; Ath., R. 16 p. 67, 9) w. dat. of the thing causing surprise (Polyb. 1, 23, 5; 3, 68, 9) μὴ ξενίζεσθε τῇ ἐν ὑμῖν πυρώσει *do not be surprised* (*upset,* ESelwyn, 1 Pt '46, 212) *at the fiery ordeal among you* **1 Pt 4:12;** v.l. ἐπὶ τῇ κτλ. (corresponding to Polyb. 2, 27, 4; UPZ 146, 4; 6 [II BC]; Jos., Ant. 1, 35). Also ἔν τινι vs. **4** (B-D-F §196; s. Rob. 532). Abs. 2 Cl 17:5.—M-M. TW. Spicq.

ξενισμός, οῦ, ὁ (ξενίζω; Pla. et al.; Polyb. 15, 17, 1; Diod. S. 3, 33, 7; ins; Pr 15:17; TestAbr B 13 p. 117, 20 [Stone p. 82] 'shelter') **a strong psychological reaction caused by someth. strange, *astonishment*** ξενισμὸν παρεῖχεν ἡ καινότης αὐτοῦ *the newness of it caused astonishment* IEph 19:2.

ξενοδοχέω (ξένος, δέχομαι) 1 aor. ἐξενοδόχησα (Maximus Tyr. 26, 9a; Cass. Dio 78, 3; Ps.-Lucian, Amor. 47 p. 450; Graec. Venet. Gen 26, 17. It stands for the older [Eur., Hdt. et al.] ξενοδοκέω, and is rejected by the Atticists; Phryn. 307 Lob.) ***show hospitality*** abs. **1 Ti 5:10.**—TW. Spicq.

ξένος, η, ον (s. prec. four entries; Hom.+; loanw. in rabb.)

❶ adj. **pert. to being unfamiliar because of someth. being unknown, *strange***—ⓐ in ref. to someth. coming from an external source, *strange, foreign*

α. because it comes from an external source ξ. δαιμόνια *foreign divinities* (δαιμόνιον 1 and Achilles Tat. 2, 30, 1; Jos., C. Ap. 2, 251; 267 ξένους θεούς; cp. Plut., Pompey 631 [24, 5] 'strange sacrifices') **Ac 17:18.** ἀνδρὶ ξένῳ AcPl Ox 6, 11 (=Aa I 241, 14). διδαχαί *strange teachings* (coming fr. outside the community; cp. Jos., Bell. 2, 414 θρησκεία ξένη) **Hb 13:9;** Hs 8, 6, 5 v.l.

β. because it is unheard of, fig. ext. of α: *strange* in kind, *surprising, unheard of, foreign* (Aeschyl., Prom. 688; Diod. S. 3, 15, 6; 3, 52, 2; M. Ant. 8, 14; POxy 1772, 3 οὐδὲν ξένον; Wsd 16:2, 16; 19:5; Philo, Mos. 1, 213; Just., A I, 16, 4, cp. D. 2, 2 τὸ ξ. τῶν λόγων; Tat. 33, 2; Mel., P. 53, 387; τὸ ξ. Did., Gen. 186, 7; ξένον θαῦμα Hippol., Ref. 4, 46, 2) PEg[2] 64. ὡς ξένου ὑμῖν συμβαίνοντος *as though something unheard of were happening to you* **1 Pt 4:12.** οὐ ξένα ὁμιλῶ *I have nothing strange to say* Dg 11:1. W. dat. of pers. ἡ ξένη τοῖς ἐκλεκτοῖς τοῦ θεοῦ στάσις *the uprising* (which is) *foreign to God's chosen people* 1 Cl 1:1.—Papias (2:11, Eus. on Papias) ξένας τέ τινας παραβολὰς τοῦ σωτῆρος *some strange parables of the Savior.*

ⓑ in ref. to an entity that is unacquainted with someth., w. gen. τινός *strange to someth.*, estranged fr. it, unacquainted w. it, without interest in it (Soph., Oed. R. 219; Pla., Apol. 17d; Heliod. 10, 14; POxy 1154, 8 [I AD] εἰμὶ ξένος τῶν ἐνθάδε.—B-D-F §182, 3; Rob. 516) ξ. τῶν διαθηκῶν τῆς ἐπαγγελίας **Eph 2:12.**

❷ as subst. **an entity involved in experience of unfamiliarity**—ⓐ one who comes as a stranger. ὁ ξένος ***stranger, alien*** (Orig., C. Cels. 5, 27, 18) **Mt 27:7; 3J 5.** Opp. πολίτης (cp. Ael. Aristid. 13 p. 163 D.; SIG 495, 115; 708, 16f; 729, 4 al.; OGI 764, 18; Philo, Poster. Cai. 109; Jos., Ant. 11, 159, Vi. 372) Dg 5:5. W. πάροικοι (opp. συμπολίτης) **Eph 2:19** (cp. SIG 799, 24f ξ. ἢ μέτοικος). W. παρεπίδημοι (Diod. S. 4, 27, 3 and OGI 268, 9 τ. παρεπιδημοῦντας ξένους; cp. 339, 29; Just., A I, 67, 6 τοῖς παρεπιδήμοις οὖσι ξένοις) **Hb 11:13;** οἱ ἐπιδημοῦντες ξ. *the strangers who lived* (or *visited*) *there* **Ac 17:21** (SIG 1157, 80f τῶν ἐνδημούντων ξένων).—Because of a firmly entrenched code of hospitality in the Mediterranean world (for a Semitic perspective, s. esp. Gen 18:1–8; the Greek world finds its sanction in Homer, s. esp. Od. 6, 198–210 with its description of the Phaeacians in contrast to the inhospitality of Polyphemus Od. 9, 272–80) ξ. freq. implies the status of a suppliant who ought to be treated as a guest: **Mt 25:35, 38, 43f** (on divine protection of a total stranger cp. Od. 6, 207f [=14, 57f]; 9, 270f; 17, 483–87).

ⓑ ἡ ξένη ***a foreign country*** (Soph., Phil. 135; POxy 251, 11; 253, 7; τις ἀπὸ ξένης Hippol., Ref. 9, 20, 1) Dg 5:5. ἐπὶ ξένης (X., Resp. Lac. 14, 4; Epict. 1, 27, 5; Plut., Mor. 576c; BGU 22, 34 [114 AD]; 159, 7; PFay 136, 10; ACalderini, ΟΙ ΕΠΙ ΞΕΝΗΣ, JEA 40, '54, 19–22 (numerous pap cited); 2 Macc 5:9; 9:28; Philo, Leg. ad Gai. 15; Jos., Ant. 18, 344) ἐπὶ ξένης κατοικεῖν *live in a foreign country* Hs 1:1, 6.

ⓒ ὁ ξένος ***the host,*** one who extends hospitality and thus treats the stranger as a guest (since Il. 15, 532; also Mel., P. 51, 375 ξένον ἠδίκησεν) w. gen. (X., An. 2, 4, 15) ὁ ξ. μου καὶ ὅλης τῆς ἐκκλησίας *host to me and to the whole congregation,* prob. because he furnished space for its meetings **Ro 16:23.**—B. 1350–52. DELG. M-M. EDNT. TW. Spicq. Sv.

Ξένων, ωνος (since V BC, JKirchner, Prosopographia Attica II no. 11320ff; Daniele Foraboschi, Onomasticon alterum papyrologicum [Testi e documenti, serie papyrologica 2, XVI], Mailand, p. 211; Preisigke, Namenbuch p. 238) ***Xenon,*** an elder in Corinth AcPlCor 1:1.

ξέστης, ου, ὁ (Diosc.; Epict. 1, 9, 33f; 2, 16, 22; OGI 521, 24; O. Wilck II, 1186, 2; Sb II word-list p. 360; Jos., Ant. 8, 57, Vi. 75. Loanw. in rabb.—Taken by most to be a corruption of Lat. sextarius; Mlt-H. 155, w. note 3, expresses some doubts on this point) a measure, about equal to 1/2 liter (FHultsch, Griech. u. röm. Metrologie[2] 1882, 103ff; APF 3, 1906, 438; O. Wilck I 762f). But then it comes to mean simply ***pitcher, jug,*** without reference to the amount contained (POxy 109, 21 ξέσται χαλκοῦ; 921, 23; Cat. Cod. Astr. VIII/3, 139) w. ποτήριον, χαλκίον **Mk 7:4;** cp. vs. **8 v.l.**—DELG. M-M.

ξηραίνω (ξηρός) fut. ξηρανῶ LXX; 1 aor. ἐξήρανα. Pass.: fut. 3 sg. ξηρανθήσεται LXX; 1 aor. ἐξηράνθην; pf. ἐξήραμμαι, ptc. ἐξηραμμένος (Hom. et al.; pap, LXX, En, TestSol; TestLevi 4:1; ParJer 19:17; 4Esdr 8:23 [fgm. c]; Joseph.)

❶ **to stop a flow (such as sap or other liquid) in someth. and so cause dryness, *to dry, dry up***—ⓐ act. *dry, dry out* τὶ *someth.* (Thu. 1, 109, 4; schol. on Nicander, Ther. 831 ξηραίνει τὸ δένδρον; PGM 13, 27 ξήρανον [viz. τὰ ἄνθη]; Is 42:15; Jer 28:36; Just., D. 107, 3) of the sun τὸν χόρτον **Js 1:11.**

ⓑ pass. in act. sense *become dry, dry up, wither* of trees (POxy 53, 10; Jo 1:12) **Mt 21:19f; Mk 11:20f.** Of plants without good roots **Mt 13:6; Mk 4:6; Lk 8:6.—1 Pt 1:24** (Is 40:7). A vine-branch when cut off **J 15:6.** Gener. of plants Hs 9, 21, 1; 3. Of water (Gen 8:7; 3 Km 17:7; Is 19:5f ποταμός; En 101:7; Jos., Bell. 5, 409 πηγή; TestLevi 4:1) of a river: *dry up* **Rv 16:12.** Of a flow of blood εὐθὺς ἐξηράνθη ἡ πηγὴ τοῦ αἵματος αὐτῆς *her hemorrhage stopped at once* **Mk 5:29.**

❷ **to become dry to the point of being immobilized, *be paralyzed,*** pass. in act. sense, fig. ext. of 1. As plants are killed by drought, so the human body is damaged by certain harmful things (Hippocr., π. τῶν ἐντὸς παθῶν 22 vol. VII 222 L.—PUps 8, 4 καταξηρανθήτω τὸ σῶμα ἐν κλίνοις=may her body dry up on the sickbed) ἄνθρωπος ἐξηραμμένην ἔχων τ. χεῖρα *a man with a withered hand* (i.e., one incapable of motion; cp. 3 Km

13:4) **Mk 3:1, 3 v.l.** Likew. the whole body of a boy who was possessed stiffens ξηραίνεται *he becomes stiff* **9:18** (Theocr. 24, 61 ξηρὸν ὑπαὶ δείους=stiff with fright. Similarly Psellus p. 212, 6).

❸ **to become dry and therefore be ready for harvesting,** ***be ripe,*** pass. of grain **Rv 14:15.**—DELG s.v. ξηρός. M-M.

ξηρός, ά, όν (Hipponax [VI BC]; Hdt.+; ins, pap, LXX, En; TestSol 10:6 C; TestZeb 2:7; JosAs 13:8; Philo; Jos., Bell. 3, 228, Ant. 5, 249; Just., D. 117, 3; 131, 3; Mel.; Hs 8, 4, 6 adj. with two endings?)

❶ **pert. to total loss of moisture,** ***dry, dried up,*** lit., of ξύλον (q.v. 3 and GDI 4689, 108 [Messenia] ξηρὰ ξύλα; PEdg 93 [=Sb 6808], 1 [256 BC]; Is 56:3; Ezk 17:24) **Lk 23:31;** Hs 4:4. Of trees (Lucian, Sat. 9) 3:1ff; 4:1, 4. Of branches (POxy 1188, 4 [13 AD]; Kaibel 1039, 14) 8, 1, 6f and 11f; 8, 2, 6; 8, 4, 4ff; 8, 5, 2ff; 8, 6, 4f; 8, 8, 1 and 4; 8, 9, 1; 8, 10, 1 and 3. Of plants 9, 1, 6; 9, 21, 1; hence also in imagery θεμέλια (corresp. to ῥίζαι) 9, 21, 2 and even of pers.: δίψυχοι ibid.; cp. 4:4. Of seeds 1 Cl 24:5. ἡ ξ. γῆ *dry land* **Hb 11:29.** Also simply ἡ ξηρά *the dry* (land, ground) (X., Oec. 17, 2; 19, 7; Aristot., HA 5, 10; Gen 1:9 al. in LXX) **Hb 11:29 v.l.;** Hv 3, 2, 7; 3, 5, 3. W. θάλασσα (Jon 1:9; Hg 2:21; 1 Macc 8:23, 32; En 97:7) **Mt 23:15.**

❷ **pert. to being shrunken or withered and therefore immobile because of disease,** ***withered, shrunken, paralyzed,*** fig. ext. of 1 (cp. ξηραίνω 2; ξηρότης Galen VII 666, 1 K.=a wasting disease.—ξηρός in this sense on the third stele of Epidaurus ln. 108 as read by RHerzog, D. Wunderheilungen v. Ep. 1931, 32 and 138. ἡμίξηρος=half-stiffened Hippiatr. I 185, 9; χεὶρ ἡμίξηρος TestSim 2, 12. Cp. also Hipponax 10 West [30 Degani; 11 Diehl[3]] λιμῷ γένηται [Diehl accepts opt. γένοιτο against codd.] ξηρός; Hos 9:14 μαστοὶ ξηροί; Psellus p. 27, 17 νηδὺς ξηρά of the womb of an aged woman) χεὶρ ξηρά *a withered hand* **Mt 12:10; Mk 3:3; Lk 6:6, 8** (Mel., P. 78, 562; 90, 668). ξηροί *withered, paralyzed* (Lucian, Tox. 24 of a woman ξηρὰ τὸ ἥμισυ) **J 5:3.**—On the mng. of the word DHesseling, Sertum Nabericum 1908, 145–54; Renehan '75, 145f.—B. 1076. DELG. M-M.

ξιφίδιον, ου, τό (ξίφος; Aristoph., Thu. et al.; POxy 936, 9 [III AD]; Jos., Ant. 20, 164, Vi. 293) ***short sword, dagger*** MPol 16:1.

ξίφος, εος or **ους, τό** (Hom.+) ***sword*** ApcPt 15:30.—B. 1392.

ξόανον, ου, τό (trag. et al.; ins, pap) ***a wooden cult image*** (so Eur.; X., An. 5, 3, 12; ins, pap; Aq. Ezk 6:4; Manetho in Jos., C. Ap. 1, 244; 249; Philo, Mos. 1, 298 al.; Ath. 4, 1; SibOr 3, 723) ApcPt 18:33.—DELG s.v. ξέω.

ξύλινος, η, ον (ξύλον; Pind., Hdt.+) ***wooden*** τὰ εἴδωλα . . . τὰ ξ. *the wooden cult images/idols* (cp. Aesop, Fab. 66 H.=285 P.//61 Ch.//284 H-H. ἄνθρωπός τις ξύλινον ἔχων θεόν; EpJer 3 θεοὶ ξ., 10, 29, 54, 69, 70; Da 5:4 and 23 Theod.; En 99:7) **Rv 9:20.** θεοὶ ξ. AcPl Ha 1, 19. σκεύη *wooden vessels* or *equipment* (cp. SIG 962, 41ff; 316; Lev 15:12; Num 31:20; 35:18) **2 Ti 2:20.**—DELG s.v. ξύλον. M-M.

ξύλον, ου, τό (Hom.+).—❶ **wood as a plant substance in unmanufactured form,** ***wood*** (the wood for the offering of Isaac linked typologically with the cross of Christ: Iren. 4, 5, 4 [Harv. II 157, 2]; Orig., C. Cels. 6, 70, 12) Dg 2:2; Ox 1 recto, 8 (ASyn. 171, 5; cp. GTh 77; s. λίθος 1). πᾶν ξ. θύϊνον *every kind of citron wood* **Rv 18:12a.** ξ. τιμιώτατον *very precious wood* vs. **12b.** Pl. *wood* as building material (Diod. S. 5, 21, 5 κάλαμοι and ξύλα; PFlor 16, 23; Just., D. 86, 6 εἰς οἰκοδομήν; Tat. 37, 1) **1 Cor 3:12;** for making cult images ξύλα κ. λίθους (Sextus 568; Tat.4, 2) together w. other materials 2 Cl 1:6; PtK 2 p. 14, 13 (Ath. 15, 1). As fuel (POxy 1144, 15 ξύλα εἰς θυσίαν; Gen 22:3, 6; Lev 1:7) MPol 13:1; Hs 4:4.

❷ **object made of wood** (of polytheists' reverence for cult images: σέβονται λίθους καὶ ξύλα Theoph. Ant. 1, 10 [p. 80, 5])

ⓐ of a piece of wood designed for a specific purpose—**α.** a relatively long piece that can be set in the ground, ***pole*** (Diod. S. 5, 18, 4; Maximus Tyr. 2, 8b), as of the one on which Moses raised the brass serpent (Num 21:8f) B 12:7.

β. ***club, cudgel*** (Hdt. 2, 63; 4, 180; Polyb. 6, 37, 3; Herodian 7, 7, 4; PHal 1, 187; PTebt 304, 10; Jos., Bell. 2, 176, Vi. 233) pl. (w. μάχαιραι) **Mt 26:47, 55; Mk 14:43, 48; Lk 22:52.**

ⓑ a device for confining the extremeties of a prisoner, ***stocks*** (Hdt. 6, 75; 9, 37; Lysias 10, 16; Aristoph., Eq. 367; 394; 705; also Chariton 4, 2, 6; OGI 483, 181 [s. the note]; Job 33:11) τοὺς πόδας ἠσφαλίσατο αὐτῶν εἰς τὸ ξύλον *he fastened their feet in the stocks* **Ac 16:24.**

ⓒ a wooden structure used for crucifixion, ***cross*** (Alexis Com. [IV BC] 220, 10 ἀναπήγνυμι ἐπὶ τοῦ ξύλου; Philo, Somn. 2, 213; Just., A II, 3, 1 ξύλῳ ἐμπαγῆναι, D. 138, 2 δι' ὕδατος καὶ πίστεως καὶ ξύλου; Iren. 1, 14, 6 [Harv. I 140, 10]; διὰ ξύλου θάνατος καὶ διὰ ξ. ζωή, θ. μὲν κατὰ τὸν Ἀδάμ, ζ. δὲ κατὰ τὸν χριστόν Orig., C. Cels. 6, 36, 28.—Outside the NT also 'gallows': the scholiast on Aristoph., Ran. 736 cites a proverb ἀπὸ καλοῦ ξύλου κἂν ἀπάγξασθαι=if you must hang yourself choose a decent tree; Esth 5:14; 6:4, reproduced Jos., Ant. 11, 246: a ξ. sixty cubits high is to be cut down. Most often OT refers to hanging or impalement of a criminal's corpse on a post ἐπὶ (τοῦ) ξύλου Gen 40:19; Dt 21:22f; Josh 10:26).—ἡ βασιλεία Ἰησοῦ ἐπὶ ξύλῳ *the reign of Jesus is based on the wood (of the cross)* B 8:5, cp. vs. 1; 12:1 (fr. an apocr. prophetic writing, perh. 4 Esdr 5:5. S. UHolzmeister, Verb Dom 21, '41, 69–73). κρεμάσαι ἐπὶ ξύλου *hang on the cross* **Ac 5:30; 10:39.** ὁ κρεμάμενος ἐπὶ ξύλου **Gal 3:13** (Dt 21:23; cp, Mel., P. 70, 507; 104, 805 ἐπὶ ξύλου κρεμασθείς). καθελεῖν ἀπὸ τοῦ ξ. *take down fr. the cross* (cp. Josh 10:27) **Ac 13:29.** πάσχειν ἐπὶ ξύλου B 5:13. τὰς ἁμαρτίας ἀναφέρειν ἐπὶ τὸ ξ. *bear the sins on* (or *to*) *the cross,* to destroy them on the cross **1 Pt 2:24**=Pol 8:1.—WSvLeeuwen, NThSt 24, '41, 68–81.

❸ ***tree*** (this usage is perceptible in Eur., Hdt.; Ctesias [IV BC]: 688 fgm. 45n p. 500 Jac., in Apollon. Paradox. 17 παρ' Ἰνδοῖς ξύλον γίνεσθαι; Theophr., HP 5, 4, 7; Fgm. Iamb. Adesp. 17 Diehl; Plut., Lycurgus 47 [13, 7]; Harpocration s.v. ὀξυθυμία; PTebt 5, 205 [118 BC]; PFlor 152, 4; Gen 1:29; 2:9; 3:1ff; Is 14:8; Eccl 2:5; PsSol 11:5; GrBar 4:8, 16; ApcSed 8:3; Tat. 919, 3 ξύλῳ μαντικῷ) Dg 12:8. ὑγρόν, ξηρὸν ξ. *a green, a dry tree* **Lk 23:31** (s. ξηρός 1 and cp. Polyaenus 3, 9, 7 ξύλα ξηρά [opp. χλωρά].—AHiggins, ET 57, '45/46, 292–94). πάγκαρπον ξ. *a tree bearing all kinds of fruit* Dg 12:1. ξ. ἄκαρπον *a tree without* (edible) *fruit* (of the elm) Hs 2:3. ξύλῳ ἑαυτὸν συμβάλλειν *compare oneself to a tree* 1 Cl 23:4a; 2 Cl 11:3 (both script. quots. of unknown orig.). τὰ φύλλα τοῦ ξ. **Rv 22:2b;** καρπὸς τοῦ ξ. 1 Cl 23:4b. Of trees by watercourses B 11:6 (Ps 1:3). ξ. γνώσεως Dg 12:2a (cp. Gen 2:9, 17; ApcMos 7 al.; Did., Gen. 94, 16); ξ. (τῆς) ζωῆς (Gen 2:9; TestLevi 18:11; ApcEsdr 2:11 p. 26, 5 Tdf.; ApcSed 4:5; ApcMos 19, 22, 28; Did., Gen. 110, 26; τὰ δὲ δύο ξ. τὸ τῆς ζωῆς καὶ τὸ τῆς γνώσεως Theoph. Ant. 2, 24 [p. 156, 19]) **Rv 2:7; 22:2a** (RSchran, BZ 24, '38/39, 191–98), **14, 19;** Dg 12:2b (cp. vs. 3 and PsSol 14:3 ξύλα τῆς ζωῆς; s. ζωή 2bβ; LvSybel, Ξύλον ζωῆς: ZNW 19, 1920, 85–91; UHolmberg, D. Baum d. Lebens 1923; HBergema, De Boom des Levens in Scrift en Historie, diss. Hilversum '38; CHemer, The Letters to the Seven Churches of Asia in Their Local

Setting ’89 [’86] 41–47; RAC II 1–34; VIII 112–41).—B. 50; 1385. DELG. M-M. EDNT. TW. Sv.

ξυν- s. συν-.

ξυράω (ξύω ‘scrape’; Diod. S. 1, 83, 2; 1, 84, 2; 5, 28, 3; Plut., Mor. 180b; Dio Chrys. 16 [33], 63; Longus 4, 10, 1; Ath. 14, 2; PMich 243, 10 and 11 [I AD]), **ξυρέω** (trag., Hdt., Pla. et al.; Lob. on Phryn. p. 205), **ξύρω** (Hippocr.; Plut., Mor. 336e τὴν κεφαλὴν ξυράμενος; Lucian, De Morte Peregr. 17) fut. 3 sg. ξυρήσει LXX; aor. 3 sg. ἐξύρησε LXX. Pass.: fut. ξυρηθήσομαι LXX; aor. inf. ξυρηθῆναι Lev 13:34; ‘to shave’. In our lit. the foll. verbal forms of the stem ξυρ- are found: mid.: ξύρωνται **Ac 21:24** D; fut. ξυρήσονται **21:24;** aor. subj. ξυρήσωνται ibid. v.l. Pass.: perf. ptc. ἐξυρημένος **1 Cor 11:5.** In vs. **6** ξυρασθαι seems to be marked as a verbal form of ξυράω by ἐξυρημένῃ vs. **5,** and in that case it is to be accented as a pres. mid. inf. ξυρᾶσθαι (cp. Diog. L. 7, 166 ξυρᾶσθαι=to have himself shaved; Jos., Ant. 19, 294 ξυρᾶσθαι and Bell. 2, 313 ξυρήσεσθαι; Philo, Spec. Leg. 1, 5 ξυρῶνται). On the other hand, the immediate proximity of κείρασθαι makes it much more likely that it is an aorist, an aor. mid. inf. of ξύρω, to be accented ξύρασθαι (other edd.; s. B-D-F §101 p. 47; Mlt-H. 200; 250; Anz 310f).—Mid. ***have oneself shaved*** (s. Schwyzer II 232; B-D-F §317; Rob. 809) τὴν κεφαλήν *have one’s head shaved* (Ps.-Callisth. 1, 3, 2; Num 6:9; Ezk 44:20) **Ac 21:24** (s. on εὐχή 2 and Jos., Ant. 19, 294). Abs. **1 Cor 11:6.** Pass. ἐξυρημένη *a woman whose head is shaved* vs. **5.**—DELG s.v. ξύω.

ὁ, ἡ, τό pl. **οἱ, αἱ, τά** article, derived fr. a demonstrative pronoun, ‘the’. Since the treatment of the inclusion and omission of the art. belongs to the field of grammar, the lexicon can limit itself to exhibiting the main features of its usage. It is difficult to set hard and fast rules for the employment of the art., since the writer’s style had special freedom of play here—Kühner-G. I p. 589ff; B-D-F §249–76; Mlt. 80–84; Rob. 754–96; W-S. §17ff; Rdm.[2] 112–18; Abel §28–32; HKallenberg, RhM 69, 1914, 642ff; FVölker, Syntax d. griech. Papyri I, Der Artikel, Progr. d. Realgymn. Münster 1903; FEakin, AJP 37, 1916, 333ff; CMiller, ibid. 341ff; EColwell, JBL 52, ’33, 12–21 (for a critique s. Mlt-H.-Turner III 183f); ASvensson, D. Gebr. des bestimmten Art. in d. nachklass. Epik ’37; RFink, The Syntax of the Greek Article ’53; JRoberts, Exegetical Helps, The Greek Noun with and without the Article: Restoration Qtly 14, ’71, 28–44; HTeeple, The Greek Article with Personal Names in the Synoptic Gospels: NTS 19, ’73, 302–17; Mussies 186–97.

❶ ***this one, that one,*** the art. funct. as demonstrative pronoun ⓐ in accordance w. epic usage (Hes., Works 450: ἡ=this [voice]) in the quot. fr. Arat., Phaenom. 5 τοῦ γὰρ καὶ γένος ἐσμέν *for we are also his* (lit. this One’s) *offspring* **Ac 17:28.**

ⓑ ὁ μὲν ... ὁ δέ *the one ... the other* (Polyaenus 6, 2, 1 ὁ μὲν ... ὁ δὲ ... ὁ δε; PSI 512, 21 [253 BC]); pl. οἱ μὲν ... οἱ δέ (PSI 341, 9 [256 BC]; TestJob 29:1) *some ... others* w. ref. to a noun preceding: ἐσχίσθη τὸ πλῆθος ... οἱ μὲν ἦσαν σὺν τοῖς Ἰουδαίοις, οἱ δὲ σὺν τοῖς ἀποστόλοις **Ac 14:4; 17:32; 28:24; 1 Cor 7:7; Gal 4:23; Phil 1:16f.** Also without such a relationship expressed τοὺς μὲν ἀποστόλους, τοὺς δὲ προφήτας, τοὺς δὲ εὐαγγελιστάς **Eph 4:11.** οἱ μὲν ... ὁ δέ **Hb 7:5f, 20f.** οἱ μὲν ... ἄλλοι (δέ) **J 7:12.** οἱ μὲν ... ἄλλοι δὲ ... ἕτεροι δέ **Mt 16:14.** τινὲς ... οἱ δέ **Ac 17:18** (cp. Pla., Leg. 1, 627a; 2, 658 B.; Aelian, VH 2, 34; Palaeph. 6, 5).—**Mt 26:67; 28:17** οἱ δέ introduces a second class; just before this, instead of the first class, the whole group is mentioned (cp. X., Hell. 1, 2, 14, Cyr. 3, 2, 12; KMcKay, JSNT 24, ’85, 71f)=*but some* (as Arrian, Anab. 5, 2, 7; 5, 14, 4; Lucian, Tim. 4 p. 107; Hesych. Miles. [VI AD]: 390 fgm. 1, 35 end Jac.).

ⓒ To indicate the progress of the narrative, ὁ δέ, οἱ δέ *but he, but they* (lit. this one, they) is also used without ὁ μέν preceding (likew. Il. 1, 43; Pla., X.; also Clearchus, fgm. 76b τὸν δὲ εἰπεῖν=but this man said; pap examples in Mayser II/1, 1926, 57f) e.g. **Mt 2:9, 14; 4:4; 9:31; Mk 14:31** (cp. Just., A II, 2, 3). ὁ μὲν οὖν **Ac 23:18; 28:5.** οἱ μὲν οὖν **1:6; 5:41; 15:3, 30.**—JO’Rourke, Paul’s Use of the Art. as a Pronoun, CBQ 34, ’72, 59–65.

❷ ***the,*** funct. to define or limit an entity, event, or state—ⓐ w. nouns—**α.** w. appellatives, or common nouns, where, as in Pla., Thu., Demosth. et al., the art. has double significance, specific or individualizing, and generic.

ℵ. In its individualizing use it focuses attention on a single thing or single concept, as already known or otherwise more definitely limited: things and pers. that are unique in kind: ὁ ἥλιος, ἡ σελήνη, ὁ οὐρανός, ἡ γῆ, ἡ θάλασσα, ὁ κόσμος, ἡ κτίσις, ὁ θεός (BWeiss [s. on θεός, beg.]), ὁ διάβολος, ὁ λόγος (**J 1:1, 14**), τὸ φῶς, ἡ σκοτία, ἡ ζωή, ὁ θάνατος etc. (but somet. the art. is omitted, esp. when nouns are used w. preps.; B-D-F §253, 1–4; Rob. 791f; Mlt-Turner 171). ἐν συναγωγῇ καὶ ἐν τῷ ἱερῷ **J 18:20.**—Virtues, vices, etc. (contrary to Engl. usage): ἡ ἀγάπη, ἡ ἀλήθεια, ἡ ἁμαρτία, ἡ δικαιοσύνη, ἡ σοφία et al.—The individualizing art. stands before a common noun that was previously mentioned (without the art.): τοὺς πέντε ἄρτους **Lk 9:16** (after πέντε ἄρτοι vs. 13). τὸ βιβλίον **4:17b** (after βιβλίον, vs. 17a), τοὺς μάγους **Mt 2:7** (after μάγοι, vs. 1). **J 4:43** (40); **12:6** (5); **20:1** (19:41); **Ac 9:17** (11); **Js 2:3** (2); **Rv 15:6** (1).—The individ. art. also stands before a common noun which, in a given situation, is given special attention as the only or obvious one of its kind (Hipponax [VI BC] 13, 2 West=D.[3] 16 ὁ παῖς the [attending] slave; Diod. S. 18, 29, 2 ὁ ἀδελφός=his brother; Artem. 4, 71 p. 245, 19 ἡ γυνή=your wife; ApcEsdr 6:12 p. 31, 17 μετὰ Μωσῆ ... ἐν τῷ ὄρει [Sinai]; Demetr. (?): 722 fgm 7 Jac. [in Eus., PE 9, 19, 4] ἐπὶ τὸ ὄρος [Moriah]) τῷ ὑπηρέτῃ *to the attendant* (who took care of the synagogue) **Lk 4:20.** εἰς τὸν νιπτῆρα *into the basin* (that was there for the purpose) **J 13:5.** ἰδοὺ ὁ ἄνθρωπος *here is this* (wretched) *man* **19:5.** ἐκ τῆς παιδίσκης or ἐλευθέρας *by the* (well-known) *slave woman* or *the free woman* (Hagar and Sarah) **Gal 4:22f.** τὸν σῖτον **Ac 27:38.** ἐν τῇ ἐπιστολῇ **1 Cor 5:9** (s. ἐπιστολή) τὸ ὄρος *the mountain* (nearby) **Mt 5:1; 8:1; 14:23;**

Mk 3:13; 6:46; Lk 6:12; 9:28 al.; ἡ πεισμονή *this* (kind of) *persuasion* **Gal 5:8.** ἡ μαρτυρία *the* (required) *witness* or *testimony* **J 5:36.**—The art. takes on the idea of κατ᾽ ἐξοχήν 'par excellence' (Porphyr., Abst. 24, 7 ὁ Αἰγύπτιος) ὁ ἐρχόμενος *the one who is (was) to come* or *the coming one par excellence*=The Messiah **Mt 11:3; Lk 7:19.** ὁ προφήτης **J 1:21, 25; 7:40.** ὁ διδάσκαλος τ. Ἰσραήλ **3:10** (Ps.-Clem., Hom. 5, 18 of Socrates: ὁ τῆς Ἑλλάδος διδάσκαλος); cp. MPol 12:2. With things (Stephan. Byz. s.v. Μάρπησσα: οἱ λίθοι=the famous stones [of the Parian Marble]) ἡ κρίσις *the* (last) *judgment* **Mt 12:41.** ἡ ἡμέρα *the day* of decision **1 Cor 3:13;** (cp. Mi 4:6 MT); **Hb 10:25.** ἡ σωτηρία *(our) salvation* at the consummation of the age **Ro 13:11.**

ב. In its generic use it singles out an individual who is typical of a class, rather than the class itself: ὁ ἀγαθὸς ἄνθρωπος **Mt 12:35.** κοινοῖ τὸν ἄνθρωπον **15:11.** ὥσπερ ὁ ἐθνικός **18:17.** ὁ ἐργάτης **Lk 10:7.** ἐγίνωσκεν τί ἦν ἐν τῷ ἀνθρώπῳ **J 2:25.** τὰ σημεῖα τοῦ ἀποστόλου **2 Cor 12:12.** ὁ κληρονόμος **Gal 4:1.** So also in parables and allegories: ὁ οἰκοδεσπότης **Mt 24:43.** Cp. **J 10:11b, 12.** The generic art. in Gk. is often rendered in Engl. by the indef. art. or omitted entirely.

β. The use of the art. w. personal names is varied; as a general rule the presence of the art. w. a personal name indicates that the pers. is known; without the art. focus is on the name as such (s. Dssm., BPhW 22, 1902, 1467f; BWeiss, D. Gebr. des Art. b. d. Eigennamen [im NT]: StKr 86, 1913, 349–89). Nevertheless, there is an unmistakable drift in the direction of Mod. Gk. usage, in which every proper name has the art. (B-D-F §260; Rob. 759–61; Mlt-Turner 165f). The ms. tradition varies considerably. In the gospels the art. is usu. found w. Ἰησοῦς; yet it is commonly absent when Ἰ. is accompanied by an appositive that has the art. Ἰ. ὁ Γαλιλαῖος **Mt 26:69;** Ἰ. ὁ Ναζωραῖος vs. **71;** Ἰ. ὁ λεγόμενος Χριστός **27:17, 22.** Sim. Μαριὰμ ἡ μήτηρ τοῦ Ἰ. **Ac 1:14.** The art. somet. stands before oblique cases of indecl. proper names, apparently to indicate their case (B-D-F §260, 2; Rob. 760). But here, too, there is no hard and fast rule.—HTeeple, NTS 19, '73, 302–17 (synopt.).

γ. The art. is customarily found w. the names of countries (B-D-F §261, 4; W-S. § 18, 5 d; Rob. 759f); less freq. w. names of cities (B-D-F §261, 1; 2; Rob. 760; Mlt-Turner 170–72). W. Ἰερουσαλήμ, Ἱεροσόλυμα it is usu. absent (s. Ἱεροσόλυμα); it is only when this name has modifiers that it must have the art. ἡ νῦν Ἰ. **Gal 4:25;** ἡ ἄνω Ἰ. vs. **26;** ἡ καινὴ Ἰ. **Rv 3:12.** But even in this case it lacks the art. when the modifier follows: **Hb 12:22.**—Names of rivers have the art. ὁ Ἰορδάνης, ὁ Εὐφράτης, ὁ Τίβερις Hv 1, 1, 2 (B-D-F §261, 8; Rob. 760; Mlt-Turner 172). Likew. names of seas ὁ Ἀδρίας **Ac 27:27.**

δ. The art. comes before nouns that are accompanied by the gen. of a pronoun (μοῦ, σοῦ, ἡμῶν, ὑμῶν, αὐτοῦ, ἑαυτοῦ, αὐτῶν) **Mt 1:21, 25; 5:45; 6:10–12; 12:49; Mk 9:17; Lk 6:27; 10:7; 16:6; Ro 4:19; 6:6** and very oft. (only rarely is it absent: Mt 19:28; Lk 1:72; 2:32; 2 Cor 8:23; Js 5:20 al.).

ε. When accompanied by the possessive pronouns ἐμός, σός, ἡμέτερος, ὑμέτερος the noun always has the art., and the pron. stands mostly betw. art. and noun: **Mt 18:20; Mk 8:38; Lk 9:26; Ac 26:5; Ro 3:7** and oft. But only rarely so in John: **J 4:42; 5:47; 7:16.** He prefers to repeat the article w. the possessive following the noun ἡ κρίσις ἡ ἐμή **J 5:30;** cp. **7:6; 17:17; 1J 1:3** al.

ζ. Adjectives (or participles), when they modify nouns that have the art., also come either betw. the art. and noun: ἡ ἀγαθὴ μερίς **Lk 10:42;** τὸ ἅγιον πνεῦμα **12:10; Ac 1:8;** ἡ δικαία κρίσις **J 7:24** and oft., or after the noun w. the art. repeated τὸ πνεῦμα τὸ ἅγιον **Mk 3:29; J 14:26; Ac 1:16; Hb 3:7; 9:8; 10:15.** ἡ ζωὴ ἡ αἰώνιος **1J 1:2; 2:25.** τὴν πύλην τὴν σιδηρᾶν **Ac 12:10.** Only rarely does an adj. without the art. stand before a noun that has an art. (s. B-D-F §270, 1; Rob. 777; Mlt-Turner 185f): ἀκατακαλύπτῳ τῇ κεφαλῇ **1 Cor 11:5.** εἶπεν μεγάλῃ τῇ φωνῇ **Ac 14:10 v.l.;** cp. **26:24.** κοιναῖς ταῖς χερσίν **Mk 7:5** D.—Double modifier τὸ πῦρ τὸ αἰώνιον τὸ ἡτοιμασμένον τῷ διαβόλῳ **Mt 25:41.** τὸ θυσιαστήριον τὸ χρυσοῦν τὸ ἐνώπιον τοῦ θρόνου **Rv 8:3; 9:13.** ἡ πόρνη ἡ μεγάλη ἡ καθημένη **17:1.**—**Mk 5:36** τὸν λόγον λαλούμενον is prob. a wrong rdg. (B has τὸν λαλ., D τοῦτον τὸν λ. without λαλούμενον).—On the art. w. ὅλος, πᾶς, πολύς s. the words in question.

η. As in the case of the poss. pron. (ε) and adj. (ζ), so it is w. other expressions that can modify a noun: ἡ κατ᾽ ἐκλογὴν πρόθεσις **Ro 9:11.** ἡ παρ᾽ ἐμοῦ διαθήκη **11:27.** ὁ λόγος ὁ τοῦ σταυροῦ **1 Cor 1:18.** ἡ ἐντολὴ ἡ εἰς ζωήν **Ro 7:10.** ἡ πίστις ὑμῶν ἡ πρὸς τὸν θεόν **1 Th 1:8.** ἡ διακονία ἡ εἰς τοὺς ἁγίους **2 Cor 8:4.**

θ. The art. precedes the noun when a demonstrative pron. (ὅδε, οὗτος, ἐκεῖνος) belonging with it comes before or after; e.g.: οὗτος ὁ ἄνθρωπος **Lk 14:30; J 9:24.** οὗτος ὁ λαός **Mk 7:6.** οὗτος ὁ υἱός μου **Lk 15:24.** οὗτος ὁ τελώνης **18:11** and oft. ὁ ἄνθρωπος οὗτος **Mk 14:71; Lk 2:25; 23:4, 14, 47.** ὁ λαὸς οὗτος **Mt 15:8.** ὁ υἱός σου οὗτος **Lk 15:30** and oft.—ἐκείνη ἡ ἡμέρα **Mt 7:22; 22:46.** ἐκ. ἡ ὥρα **10:19; 18:1; 26:55.** ἐκ. ὁ καιρός **11:25; 12:1; 14:1.** ἐκ. ὁ πλάνος **27:63** and oft. ἡ οἰκία ἐκείνη **Mt 7:25, 27.** ἡ ὥρα ἐκ. **8:13; 9:22;** ἡ γῆ ἐκ. **9:26, 31;** ἡ ἡμέρα ἐκ. **13:1.** ὁ ἀγρὸς ἐκ. vs. **44** and oft.—ὁ αὐτός s. αὐτός 3b.

ι. An art. before a nom. noun makes it a vocative (as early as Hom.; s. KBrugman[4]-AThumb, Griech. Gramm. 1913, 431; Schwyzer II 63f; B-D-F §147; Rob. 769. On the LXX Johannessohn, Kasus 14f.—ParJer 1:1 Ἰερεμία ὁ ἐκλεκτός μου; 7:2 χαῖρε Βαρούχ ὁ οἰκονόμος τῆς πίστεως) ναί, ὁ πατήρ **Mt 11:26.** τὸ κοράσιον, ἔγειρε **Mk 5:41.** Cp. **Mt 7:23; 27:29 v.l.; Lk 8:54; 11:39; 18:11, 13** (Goodsp, Probs. 85–87); **J 19:3** and oft.

ⓑ Adjectives become substantives by the addition of the art.

α. ὁ πονηρός **Eph 6:16.** οἱ σοφοί **1 Cor 1:27.** οἱ ἅγιοι, οἱ πλούσιοι, οἱ πολλοί al. Likew. the neut. τὸ κρυπτόν **Mt 6:4.** τὸ ἅγιον **7:6.** τὸ μέσον **Mk 3:3.** τὸ θνητόν **2 Cor 5:4.** τὰ ἀδύνατα **Lk 18:27.** τὸ ἔλαττον **Hb 7:7.** Also w. gen. foll. τὰ ἀγαθά σου **Lk 16:25.** τὸ μωρόν, τὸ ἀσθενὲς τοῦ θεοῦ **1 Cor 1:25;** cp. vs. **27f.** τὸ γνωστὸν τοῦ θεοῦ **Ro 1:19.** τὰ ἀόρατα τοῦ θεοῦ vs. **20.** τὸ ἀδύνατον τοῦ νόμου **8:3.** τὰ κρυπτὰ τῆς αἰσχύνης **2 Cor 4:2.**

β. Adj. attributes whose noun is customarily omitted come to have substantive force and therefore receive the art. (B-D-F §241; Rob. 652–54) ἡ περίχωρος **Mt 3:5;** ἡ ξηρά **23:15** (i.e. γῆ). ἡ ἀριστερά, ἡ δεξιά (sc. χείρ) **6:3.** ἡ ἐπιοῦσα (sc. ἡμέρα) **Ac 16:11.** ἡ ἔρημος (sc. χώρα) **Mt 11:7.**

γ. The neut. of the adj. w. the art. can take on the mng. of an abstract noun (Thu. 1, 36, 1 τὸ δεδιός=fear; Herodian 1, 6, 9; 1, 11, 5 τὸ σεμνὸν τῆς παρθένου; M. Ant. 1, 1; Just., D. 27, 2 διὰ τὸ σκληροκάρδιον ὑμῶν καὶ ἀχάριστον εἰς αὐτόν) τὸ χρηστὸν τοῦ θεοῦ *God's kindness* **Ro 2:4.** τὸ δυνατόν *power* **9:22.** τὸ σύμφορον *benefit* **1 Cor 7:35.** τὸ γνήσιον *genuineness* **2 Cor 8:8.** τὸ ἐπιεικές **Phil 4:5** al.

δ. The art. w. numerals indicates, as in Il. 5, 271f; X. et al. (HKallenberg, RhM 69, 1914, 662ff), that a part of a number already known is being mentioned (Diod. S. 18, 10, 2 τρεῖς μὲν φυλὰς ... τὰς δὲ ἑπτά='but the seven others'; Plut., Cleom. 804 [8, 4] οἱ τέσσαρες='the other four'; Polyaenus 6, 5 οἱ τρεῖς='the remaining three'; Diog. L. 1, 82 Βίας προκεκριμένος τῶν ἑπτά=Bias was preferred before the others of the seven [wise men]. B-D-F §265): οἱ ἐννέα *the other nine* **Lk 17:17.** Cp. **15:4;**

Mt 18:12f. οἱ δέκα *the other ten* (disciples) **20:24; Mk 10:41;** lepers **Lk 17:17.** οἱ πέντε . . . ὁ εἷς . . . ὁ ἄλλος *five of them . . . one . . . the last one* **Rv 17:10.**

ⓒ The ptc. w. the art. receives—**α.** the mng. of a subst. ὁ πειράζων *the tempter* **Mt 4:3; 1 Th 3:5.** ὁ βαπτίζων **Mk 6:14.** ὁ σπείρων **Mt 13:3; Lk 8:5.** ὁ ὀλεθρεύων **Hb 11:28.** τὸ ὀφειλόμενον **Mt 18:30, 34.** τὸ αὐλούμενον **1 Cor 14:7.** τὸ λαλούμενον vs. **9** (Just., D. 32, 3 τὸ ζητούμενον). τὰ γινόμενα **Lk 9:7.** τὰ ἐρχόμενα **J 16:13.** τὰ ἐξουθενημένα **1 Cor 1:28.** τὰ ὑπάρχοντα (s. ὑπάρχω 1). In Engl. usage many of these neuters are transl. by a relative clause, as in β below. B-D-F §413; Rob. 1108f.

β. the mng. of a relative clause (Ar. 4, 2 al. οἱ νομίζοντες) ὁ δεχόμενος ὑμᾶς *whoever receives you* **Mt 10:40.** τῷ τύπτοντί σε **Lk 6:29.** ὁ ἐμὲ μισῶν **J 15:23.** οὐδὲ γὰρ ὄνομά ἐστιν ἕτερον τὸ δεδομένον (ὃ δέδοται) **Ac 4:12.** τινές εἰσιν οἱ ταράσσοντες ὑμᾶς **Gal 1:7.** Cp. **Lk 7:32; 18:9; J 12:12; Col 2:8; 1 Pt 1:7; 2J 7; Jd 4** al. So esp. after πᾶς: πᾶς ὁ ὀργιζόμενος *everyone who becomes angry* **Mt 5:22.** πᾶς ὁ κρίνων **Ro 2:1** al. After μακάριος **Mt 5:4, 6, 10.** After οὐαὶ ὑμῖν **Lk 6:25.**

ⓓ The inf. w. neut. art. (B-D-F §398ff; Rob. 1062–68) is used in a number of ways.—**α.** It stands for a noun (B-D-F §399; Rob. 1062–66) τὸ (ἀνίπτοις χερσὶν) φαγεῖν **Mt 15:20.** τὸ (ἐκ νεκρῶν) ἀναστῆναι **Mk 9:10.** τὸ ἀγαπᾶν **12:33;** cp. **Ro 13:8.** τὸ ποιῆσαι, τὸ ἐπιτελέσαι **2 Cor 8:11.** τὸ καθίσαι **Mt 20:23.** τὸ θέλειν **Ro 7:18; 2 Cor 8:10.**—Freq. used w. preps. ἀντὶ τοῦ, διὰ τό, διὰ τοῦ, ἐκ τοῦ, ἐν τῷ, ἕνεκεν τοῦ, ἕως τοῦ, μετὰ τό, πρὸ τοῦ, πρὸς τό etc.; s. the preps. in question (B-D-F §402–4; Rob. 1068–75).

β. The gen. of the inf. w. the art., without a prep., is esp. frequent (B-D-F §400; Mlt. 216–18; Rob. 1066–68; DEvans, ClQ 15, 1921, 26ff). The use of this inf. is esp. common in Lk and Paul, less freq. in Mt and Mk, quite rare in other writers. The gen. stands

א. dependent on words that govern the gen.: ἄξιον **1 Cor 16:4** (s. ἄξιος 1c). ἐξαπορηθῆναι τοῦ ζῆν **2 Cor 1:8.** ἔλαχε τοῦ θυμιᾶσαι **Lk 1:9** (cp. 1 Km 14:47 v.l. Σαοὺλ ἔλαχεν τοῦ βασιλεύειν).

ב. dependent on a noun (B-D-F §400, 1; Rob. 1066f) ὁ χρόνος τοῦ τεκεῖν **Lk 1:57.** ἐπλήσθησαν αἱ ἡμέραι τοῦ τεκεῖν αὐτήν **2:6.** ἐξουσία τοῦ πατεῖν **10:19.** εὐκαιρία τοῦ παραδοῦναι **22:6.** ἐλπὶς τοῦ σῴζεσθαι **Ac 27:20;** τοῦ μετέχειν **1 Cor 9:10.** ἐπιποθία τοῦ ἐλθεῖν **Ro 15:23.** χρείαν ἔχειν τοῦ διδάσκειν **Hb 5:12.** καιρὸς τοῦ ἄρξασθαι **1 Pt 4:17.** τ. ἐνέργειαν τοῦ δύνασθαι *the power that enables him* **Phil 3:21.** ἡ προθυμία τοῦ θέλειν *zeal in desiring* **2 Cor 8:11.**

ג. Somet. the connection w. the noun is very loose, and the transition to the consecutive sense (=result) is unmistakable (B-D-F §400, 2; Rob. 1066f): ἐπλήσθησαν ἡμέραι ὀκτὼ τοῦ περιτεμεῖν αὐτόν **Lk 2:21.** ὀφειλέται . . . τοῦ κατὰ σάρκα ζῆν **Ro 8:12.** εἰς ἀκαθαρσίαν τοῦ ἀτιμάζεσθαι **1:24.** ὀφθαλμοὺς τοῦ μὴ βλέπειν **11:8.** τὴν ἔκβασιν τοῦ δύνασθαι ὑπενεγκεῖν **1 Cor 10:13.**

ד. Verbs of hindering, ceasing take the inf. w. τοῦ μή (s. Schwyzer II 372 for earlier Gk; PGen 16, 23 [207 AD] κωλύοντες τοῦ μὴ σπείρειν; LXX; ParJer 2:5 φύλαξαι τοῦ μὴ σχίσαι τὰ ἱμάτιά σου): καταπαύειν **Ac 14:18.** κατέχειν **Lk 4:42.** κρατεῖσθαι **24:16.** κωλύειν **Ac 10:47.** παύειν **1 Pt 3:10** (Ps 33:14). ὑποστέλλεσθαι **Ac 20:20, 27.** Without μή: ἐγκόπτεσθαι τοῦ ἐλθεῖν **Ro 15:22.**

ה. The gen. of the inf. comes after verbs of deciding, exhorting, commanding, etc. (1 Ch 19:19; ParJer 7:37 διδάσκων αὐτοὺ τοῦ ἀπέχεσθαι) ἐγένετο γνώμης **Ac 20:3.** ἐντέλλεσθαι **Lk 4:10** (Ps 90:11). ἐπιστέλλειν **Ac 15:20.** κατανεύειν **Lk 5:7.** κρίνειν **Ac 27:1.** παρακαλεῖν **21:12.** προσεύχεσθαι **Js 5:17.** τὸ πρόσωπον στηρίζειν **Lk 9:51.** συντίθεσθαι **Ac 23:20.**

ו. The inf. w. τοῦ and τοῦ μή plainly has final (=purpose) sense (ParJer 5:2 ἐκάθισεν . . . τοῦ ἀναπαῆναι ὀλίγον; Soph., Lex. I 45f; B-D-F §400, 5 w. exx. fr. non-bibl. lit. and pap; Rob. 1067): ἐξῆλθεν ὁ σπείρων τοῦ σπείρειν *a sower went out to sow* **Mt 13:3.** ζητεῖν τοῦ ἀπολέσαι = ἵνα ἀπολέσῃ **2:13.** τοῦ δοῦναι γνῶσιν **Lk 1:77.** τοῦ κατευθῦναι τοὺς πόδας vs. **79.** τοῦ σινιάσαι **22:31.** τοῦ μηκέτι δουλεύειν **Ro 6:6.** τοῦ ποιῆσαι αὐτά **Gal 3:10.** τοῦ γνῶναι αὐτόν **Phil 3:10.** Cp. **Mt 3:13; 11:1; 24:45; Lk 2:24, 27; 8:5; 24:29; Ac 3:2; 20:30; 26:18; Hb 10:7** (Ps 39:9); **11:5;** GJs 2:3f; 24:1.—The apparently solecistic τοῦ πολεμῆσαι **Ro 12:7** bears a Semitic tinge, cp. Hos 9:13 et al. (Mussies 96).—The combination can also express

ז. consecutive mng. (result): οὐδὲ μετεμελήθητε τοῦ πιστεῦσαι αὐτῷ *you did not change your minds and believe him* **Mt 21:32.** τοῦ μὴ εἶναι αὐτὴν μοιχαλίδα **Ro 7:3.** τοῦ ποιεῖν τὰ βρέφη ἔκθετα **Ac 7:19.** Cp. **3:12; 10:25.**

ⓔ The art. is used w. prepositional expressions (Artem. 4, 33 p. 224, 7 ὁ ἐν Περγάμῳ; 4, 36 ὁ ἐν Μαγνησίᾳ; 4 [6] Esdr [POxy 1010 recto, 8–12] οἱ ἐν τοῖς πεδίοις . . . οἱ ἐν τοῖς ὄρεσι καὶ μετεώροις; Tat. 31, 2 οἱ μὲν περὶ Κράτητα . . . οἱ δὲ περὶ Ἐρατοσθένη) τῆς ἐκκλησίας τῆς ἐν Κεγχρεαῖς **Ro 16:1.** ταῖς ἐκκλησίαις ταῖς ἐν τῇ Ἀσίᾳ **Rv 1:4.** τῷ ἀγγέλῳ τῆς ἐν (w. place name) ἐκκλησίας **2:1, 8, 12, 18; 3:1, 7, 14** (on these pass. RBorger, TRu 52, '87, 42–45). τοῖς ἐν τῇ οἰκίᾳ *to those in the house* **Mt 5:15.** πάτερ ἡμῶν ὁ ἐν τ. οὐρανοῖς **6:9.** οἱ ἀπὸ τῆς Ἰταλίας **Hb 13:24.** οἱ ἐν Χριστῷ Ἰησοῦ **Ro 8:1.** οἱ ἐξ ἐριθείας **2:8.** οἱ ἐκ νόμου **4:14;** cp. vs. **16.** οἱ ἐκ τῆς Καίσαρος οἰκίας **Phil 4:22.** οἱ ἐξ εὐωνύμων **Mt 25:41.** τὸ θυσιαστήριον . . . τὸ ἐνώπιον τοῦ θρόνου **Rv 8:3;** cp. **9:13.** On **1:4** s. ref in B-D-F §136, 1 to restoration by Nestle. οἱ παρ᾽ αὐτοῦ **Mk 3:21.** οἱ μετ᾽ αὐτοῦ **Mt 12:3.** οἱ περὶ αὐτόν **Mk 4:10; Lk 22:49** al.—Neut. τὰ ἀπὸ τοῦ πλοίου *pieces of wreckage fr. the ship* **Ac 27:44** (difft. FZorell, BZ 9, 1911, 159f). τὰ περί τινος **Lk 24:19, 27; Ac 24:10; Phil 1:27** (Tat. 32, 2 τὰ περὶ θεοῦ). τὰ περί τινα **2:23.** τὰ κατ᾽ ἐμέ *my circumstances* **Eph 6:21; Phil 1:12; Col 4:7.** τὰ κατὰ τὸν νόμον *what (was to be done) according to the law* **Lk 2:39.** τὸ ἐξ ὑμῶν **Ro 12:18.** τὰ πρὸς τὸν θεόν **15:17; Hb 2:17; 5:1** (X., Resp. Lac. 13, 11 ἱερεῖ τὰ πρὸς τοὺς θεούς, στρατηγῷ δὲ τὰ πρὸς τοὺς ἀνθρώπους). τὰ παρ᾽ αὐτῶν **Lk 10:7.** τὸ ἐν ἐμοί *the (child) in me* GJs 12:2 al.

ⓕ w. an adv. or adverbial expr. (1 Macc 8:3) τὸ ἔμπροσθεν **Lk 19:4.** τὸ ἔξωθεν **Mt 23:25.** τὸ πέραν **Mt 8:18, 28.** τὰ ἄνω **J 8:23; Col 3:1f.** τὰ κάτω **J 8:23.** τὰ ὀπίσω **Mk 13:16.** τὰ ὧδε *matters here* **Col 4:9.** ὁ πλησίον *the neighbor* **Mt 5:43.** οἱ καθεξῆς **Ac 3:24.** τὸ κατὰ σάρκα **Ro 9:5.** τὸ ἐκ μέρους **1 Cor 13:10.**—Esp. w. indications of time τό, τὰ νῦν s. νῦν 2b. τὸ πάλιν **2 Cor 13:2.** τὸ λοιπόν **1 Cor 7:29; Phil 3:1.** τὸ πρῶτον **J 10:40; 12:16; 19:39.** τὸ πρότερον **6:62; Gal 4:13.** τὸ καθ᾽ ἡμέραν *daily* **Lk 11:3.**—τὸ πλεῖστον *at the most* **1 Cor 14:27.**

ⓖ The art. w. the gen. foll. denotes a relation of kinship, ownership, or dependence: Ἰάκωβος ὁ τοῦ Ζεβεδαίου **Mt 10:2** (Thu. 4, 104 Θουκυδίδης ὁ Ὀλόρου [sc. υἱός]; Plut., Timol. 3, 2; Appian, Syr. 26 §123 Σέλευκος ὁ Ἀντιόχου; Jos., Bell. 5, 5; 11). Μαρία ἡ Ἰακώβου **Lk 24:10.** ἡ τοῦ Οὐρίου *the wife of Uriah* **Mt 1:6.** οἱ Χλόης *Chloë's people* **1 Cor 1:11.** οἱ Ἀριστοβούλου, οἱ Ναρκίσσου **Ro 16:10f.** οἱ αὐτοῦ **Ac 16:33.** οἱ τοῦ Χριστοῦ **1 Cor 15:23; Gal 5:24.** Καισάρεια ἡ Φιλίππου *Caesarea Philippi* i.e. the city of Philip **Mk 8:27.**—τό, τά τινος *someone's things, affairs, circumstances* (Thu. 4, 83 τὰ τοῦ Ἀρριβαίου; Parthenius 1, 6; Appian, Syr. 16 §67 τὰ Ῥωμαίων) τὰ τοῦ θεοῦ, τῶν ἀνθρώπων **Mt 16:23; 22:21;**

Mk 8:33; cp. **1 Cor 2:11.** τὰ τῆς σαρκός, τοῦ πνεύματος **Ro 8:5;** cp. **14:19; 1 Cor 7:33f; 13:11.** τὰ ὑμῶν **2 Cor 12:14.** τὰ τῆς ἀσθενείας μου **11:30.** τὰ τοῦ νόμου *what the law requires* **Ro 2:14.** τὸ τῆς συκῆς *what has been done to the fig tree* **Mt 21:21;** cp. **8:33.** τὰ ἑαυτῆς *its own advantage* **1 Cor 13:5;** cp. **Phil 2:4, 21.** τὸ τῆς παροιμίας *what the proverb says* **2 Pt 2:22** (Pla., Theaet. 183e τὸ τοῦ Ὁμήρου; Menand., Dyscolus 633 τὸ τοῦ λόγου). ἐν τοῖς τοῦ πατρός μου *in my Father's house* (so Field, Notes 50–56; Goodsp. Probs. 81–83; difft., 'interests', PTemple, CBQ 1, '39, 342–52.—In contrast to the other synoptists, Luke does not elsewhere show Jesus 'at home'.) **Lk 2:49** (Lysias 12, 12 εἰς τὰ τοῦ ἀδελφοῦ; Theocr. 2, 76 τὰ Λύκωνος; pap in Mayser II [1926] p. 8; POxy 523, 3 [II AD] an invitation to a dinner ἐν τοῖς Κλαυδίου Σαραπίωνος; PTebt 316 II, 23 [99 AD] ἐν τοῖς Ποτάμωνος; Esth 7:9; Job 18:19; Jos., Ant. 16, 302. Of the temple of a god Jos., C. Ap. 1, 118 ἐν τοῖς τοῦ Διός). **Mt 20:15** is classified here by WHatch, ATR 26, '44, 250–53; s. also ἐμός b.

ⓗ The neut. of the art. stands—**α.** before whole sentences or clauses (Epict. 4, 1, 45 τὸ Καίσαρος μὴ εἶναι φίλον; Prov. Aesopi 100 P. τὸ Οὐκ οἶδα; Jos., Ant. 10, 205; Just., D. 33, 2 τὸ γὰρ ... [Ps 109:4]) τὸ Οὐ φονεύσεις, οὐ μοιχεύσεις κτλ. (quot. fr. the Decalogue) **Mt 19:18; Ro 13:9.** τὸ Καὶ μετὰ ἀνόμων ἐλογίσθη (quot. fr. Is 53:12) **Lk 22:37.** Cp. **Gal 5:14.** τὸ Εἰ δύνῃ *as far as your words 'If you can' are concerned* **Mk 9:23.** Likew. before indirect questions (Vett. Val. 291, 14 τὸ πῶς τέτακται; Ael. Aristid. 45, 15 K. τὸ ὅστις ἐστίν; ParJer 6:15 τὸ πῶς ἀποστείλῃς; GrBar 8:6 τὸ πῶς ἐταπεινώθη; Jos., Ant. 20, 28 ἐπὶ πείρᾳ τοῦ τί φρονοῖεν; Pel.-Leg. p. 20, 32 τὸ τί γένηται; Mel., fgm. 8, 2 [Goodsp. p. 311] τὸ δὲ πῶς λούονται) τὸ τί ἂν θέλοι καλεῖσθαι αὐτό **Lk 1:62.** τὸ τίς ἂν εἴη μείζων αὐτῶν **9:46.** τὸ πῶς δεῖ ὑμᾶς περιπατεῖν **1 Th 4:1.** Cp. **Lk 19:48; 22:2, 4, 23f; Ac 4:21; 22:30; Ro 8:26;** Hs 8, 1, 4.

β. before single words which are taken fr. what precedes and hence are quoted, as it were (Epict. 1, 29, 16 τὸ Σωκράτης; 3, 23, 24; Hierocles 13 p. 448 ἐν τῷ μηδείς) τὸ 'ἀνέβη' **Eph 4:9.** τὸ 'ἔτι ἅπαξ' **Hb 12:27.** τὸ ''Αγάρ' **Gal 4:25.**

ⓘ Other notable uses of the art. are—**α.** the elliptic use, which leaves a part of a sentence accompanied by the art. to be completed fr. the context: ὁ τὰ δύο *the man with the two* (talents), i.e. ὁ τὰ δύο τάλαντα λαβών **Mt 25:17;** cp. vs. **22.** τῷ τὸν φόρον **Ro 13:7.** ὁ τὸ πολύ, ὀλίγον *the man who had much, little* **2 Cor 8:15** after Ex 16:18 (cp. Lucian, Bis Accus. 9 ὁ τὴν σύριγγα [sc. ἔχων]; Arrian, Anab. 7, 8, 3 τὴν ἐπὶ θανάτῳ [sc. ὁδόν]).

β. Σαῦλος, ὁ καὶ Παῦλος **Ac 13:9;** s. καί 2h.

γ. the fem. art. is found in a quite singular usage ἡ οὐαί (ἡ θλῖψις or ἡ πληγή) **Rv 9:12; 11:14.** Sim. ὁ 'Αμήν **3:14** (here the masc. art. is evidently chosen because of the alternate name for Jesus).

ⓙ One art. can refer to several nouns connected by καί

α. when various words, sing. or pl., are brought close together by a common art.: τοὺς ἀρχιερεῖς καὶ γραμματεῖς **Mt 2:4;** cp. **16:21; Mk 15:1.** ἐν τοῖς προφήταις κ. ψαλμοῖς **Lk 24:44.** τῇ 'Ιουδαίᾳ καὶ Σαμαρείᾳ **Ac 1:8;** cp. **8:1; Lk 5:17** al.—Even nouns of different gender can be united in this way (Aristoph., Eccl. 750; Ps.-Pla., Axioch. 12 p. 37a οἱ δύο θεοί, of Apollo and Artemis; Ps.-Demetr., Eloc. c. 292; PTebt 14, 10 [114 BC]; En 18:14; EpArist 109) κατὰ τὰ ἐντάλματα καὶ διδασκαλίας **Col 2:22.** Cp. **Lk 1:6.** εἰς τὰς ὁδοὺς καὶ φραγμούς **14:23.**

β. when one and the same person has more than one attribute applied to him: πρὸς τὸν πατέρα μου καὶ πατέρα ὑμῶν **J 20:17.** ὁ θεὸς καὶ πατὴρ τοῦ κυρίου 'I. **Ro 15:6; 2 Cor 1:3; 11:31; Eph 1:3; 1 Pt 1:3.** ὁ θεὸς καὶ πατὴρ (ἡμῶν) **Eph 5:20; Phil 4:20; 1 Th 1:3; 3:11, 13.** Of Christ: τοῦ κυρίου ἡμῶν καὶ σωτῆρος **2 Pt 1:11;** cp. **2:20; 3:18.** τοῦ μεγάλου θεοῦ καὶ σωτῆρος ἡμῶν **Tit 2:13** (PGrenf II, 15 I, 6 [139 BC] of the deified King Ptolemy τοῦ μεγάλου θεοῦ εὐεργέτου καὶ σωτῆρος [ἐπιφανοῦς] εὐχαρίστου).

γ. On the other hand, the art. is repeated when two different persons are named: ὁ φυτεύων καὶ ὁ ποτίζων **1 Cor 3:8.** ὁ βασιλεὺς καὶ ὁ ἡγεμών **Ac 26:30.**

ⓚ In a fixed expression, when a noun in the gen. is dependent on another noun, the art. customarily appears twice or not at all: τὸ πνεῦμα τοῦ θεοῦ **1 Cor 3:16;** πνεῦμα θεοῦ **Ro 8:9.** ὁ λόγος τοῦ θεοῦ **2 Cor 2:17;** λόγος θεοῦ **1 Th 2:13.** ἡ ἡμέρα τοῦ κυρίου **2 Th 2:2;** ἡμ. κ. **1 Th 5:2.** ὁ υἱὸς τοῦ ἀνθρώπου **Mt 8:20;** υἱ. ἀ. **Hb 2:6.** ἡ ἀνάστασις τῶν νεκρῶν **Mt 22:31;** ἀ. ν. **Ac 23:6.** ἡ κοιλία τῆς μητρός **J 3:4;** κ. μ. **Mt 19:12.**—APerry, JBL 68, '49, 329–34; MBlack, An Aramaic Approach[3], '67, 93–95.—DELG. M-M.

ὀβελίσκος, ου, ὁ (ὀβελός 'spit'; Aristoph., X. et al.; ins; PEleph 5, 2; Job 41:22; 4 Macc 11:19; Just., 40, 3 ὄρθιος ὀ. 'upright beam' of the cross) dim. of ὀβελός; ***a little skewer*** or ***spit*** w. ξίφος ApcPt 15:30.—DELG s.v. ὀβελός.

ὀγδοήκοντα indecl. (Thu. et al.; ins, pap, LXX; TestJos 16:5; GrBar 4:2; ApcEsdr; ApcSed 12:4; Jos., Bell. 4, 482, Vi. 15; 75) ***eighty*** **Lk 2:37** (IG XII/3, 10, 3 [II BC] an epitaph θνήσκω δὲ ὀγδώκοντα καὶ ἓξ ἐσιδών=I am dead having seen 86 years); **16:7;** MPol 9:3.—M-M.

ὄγδοος, η, ον (s. ὀκτώ; Hom.+) ***eighth*** **Rv 17:11; 21:20;** MPol 21; Hs 9, 1, 8; 9, 25, 1; ἡ ἡμέρα ἡ ὀ. **Lk 1:59; Ac 7:8** (Gen 21:4; cp. Jos., Ant. 1, 192; Just., D. 24, 1 al.); B 15:9 (Wengst, Didache 200 n. 238), cp. vs. 8. ὄγδοον Νῶε δικαιοσύνης κήρυκα ἐφύλαξεν *he preserved Noah as a preacher of righteousness, with seven others* (lit. 'as the eighth') **2 Pt 2:5** (on this expr. cp. Thu. 1, 46, 2; 1, 61, 1; 2, 13, 1; Pla., Leg. 3, 695c λαβὼν τὴν ἀρχὴν ἕβδομος; Plut., Pelop. 284 [13, 7] εἰς οἰκίαν δωδέκατος κατελθών; Ps.-Apollod., Epict. 3, 15 ἡ μήτηρ ἐνάτη=the mother with eight [children]; 2 Macc 5:27 δέκατος γενηθείς 'with nine others').—DELG s.v. ὀκτώ. M-M.

ὄγκος, ου, ὁ (Hom. et al.; PLond I, 130 [=Neugebauer-Hoesen no. 81], 107; 124f p. 136 astrol. term 'magnitude'; SEG VIII, 802; Philo; Jos., Bell. 4, 319; 7, 443. Loanw. in rabb.)

❶ **material that is ponderously large, *bulk*** τῆς κεφαλῆς ὄ. *the bulk of the head* Papias (3:2).

❷ **that which hinders one from doing someth., *weight, burden, impediment*** fig. ext. of 1 ὄγκον ἀποτίθεσθαι πάντα *lay aside every impediment* **Hb 12:1.**—DELG s.v. 2 ὄγκος. M-M. TW. Spicq.

ὀγκόω (ὄγκος; act. in var. senses trag. et al.; ins [e.g. Kaibel 314, 23]; pass. also TestSim 4:1; TestLevi 6:9; ApcEsdr 5:13 p. 30, 8 Tdf.) pass. ***swell*** (through pregnancy as TestLevi 6:9; ApcEsdr 5:13) ἡ γαστὴρ αὐτῆς ὠγκοῦτο GJs 12:3; καὶ εἶδεν τὴν Μαρίαν ὠγκωμένην 15:1; s. also 13:1; 15:2.—DELG s.v. 2 ὄγκος. M-M s.v. ὄγκος.

ὅδε, ἥδε, τόδε (Hom.+; ins, pap [s. Rydbeck 88–97, w. critique of Mayser and Bl-D. on alleged rarity in pap]; LXX [Thackeray p. 191]; En 106:16; TestSol; TestAbr A 8 p. 85, 15 [Stone p. 18]; TestJob, GrBar; ApcMos 22; EpArist 28; Philo; Jos., Ant. 10, 113; apolog.) demonstrative pron. (Schwyzer II 209f; B-D-F §289; Rob. 696f [on needed correction of the two last s. Rydbeck above])

❶ **a ref. to an entity viewed as present or near in terms of the narrrative context, *this***—ⓐ w. ref. to what follows (so predom.), esp. in the formula τάδε λέγει *this is what ... says* (introductory formula in the decrees of the Persian kings: Hdt. 1, 69, 2 al.; IMagnMai 115, 4 [=SIG 22, s. editor's note]; Ps.-Pla., Alcib. II, 12, 14c τ. λ. Ἄμμων; Jos., Ant. 11, 26. In the OT freq. as an introduction to prophetic utterance [Thackeray p. 11]; so also [after LXX] TestAbr A 8 p. 85, 15 [Stone p. 18]; TestJob 4:3; 7:9; GrBar and ApcMos 22 τάδε λέγει Κύριος. Also in wills: PGiss 36, 10 [161 BC] τάδε λέγει γυνὴ Ἑλληνὶς Ἀμμωνία; GRudberg, Eranos 11, 1911, 170–79; Mussies 180. As introd. to a letter Nicol. Dam.: 90 fgm. 5 p. 336, 22 Jac. Cp. GGerhard, Unters. z. Gesch. d. gr. Briefes: I, D. Anfangsformel, diss. Hdlbg 1903) **Ac 21:11; Rv 2:1, 8, 12, 18; 3:1, 7, 14;** B 6:8; 9:2 (Jer 7:3), 5 (Jer 4:3); cp. IPhld 7:2.

ⓑ w. ref. to what precedes (Soph., Hdt. et al.; Aelian, NA 4, 15 p. 85, 28; 9, 63 p. 241, 11; Philostrat., Vi. Apoll. 218, 25; 271, 3 al.; Jos., Ant. 17, 2; 19; Just., A II, 5, 3) γυνή τις ... καὶ τῇδε ἦν ἀδελφή *she had a sister* **Lk 10:39** (cp. Gen 25:24; 38:27; Judg 11:37 B; MJohannessohn, ZVS 66, '39, p. 184, 7); **16:25 v.l.** (Marcion; s. Zahn, Gesch. des ntl. Kanons II/2, 1892, 480) ἥδε ἀπεκρίθη 1 Cl 12:4.

ⓒ w. ref. to time as present context (Just., A I, 45, 6, A II, 12, 6) ἀπὸ Ἀδὰμ ἕως τῆσδε τῆς ἡμέρας *from Adam to the present* 1 Cl 50:3. ἐν τῇδε τῇ ἐπιστολῇ *in this letter* (the one I'm writing) 63:2.

❷ **a ref. to an entity not specified, *such and such*** εἰς τήνδε τὴν πόλιν *into this or that city, into such and such a city* **Js 4:13** (Eur., Orestes 508 et al.; τήνδε for Att. τὴν δεῖνα or τὴν καὶ τήν Epict. 1, 12, 28 [the two forms side by side]; not strictly a vernacular expression, pace MDibelius/HGreeven, Hermeneia Comm. '76 ad loc; s. Rydbeck 96f. Cp. Cyr. Scyth. p. 207, 20 τῆσδε τῆς πόλεως; 185, 13; Plut., Mor. 623e τήνδε τὴν ἡμέραν [W-S. §23, 1c note 2; B-D-F §289; Rob. 696f.—The same expr. in Appian, Liby. 108 §510 and Ael. Aristid. 46 p. 384 D.]; τόνδε τὸν ἄνθρωπον [Hierocles 11, 439]; τόδε 'this and that' [B-D-F loc. cit.; also Plut., Mor. 168d; SIG[2] 737, 62]; τοῦδέ τινος = τοῦ δεῖνος [PMich 154, 24—c. 300 AD]; cp. the Mod. Gk. use of ὁ τάδε(ς) = ὁ δεῖνα [KBrugmann, Die Demonstrativpronomina: ASG[Leipz] 22, 1904, 133 note]; JWackernagel, Syntax I[2] 1928, 108). ὅδε is also found as **v.l. Ac 15:23.**—Rydbeck, 88–99.—DELG. M-M, but s. Rydbeck.

ὁδεύω (ὁδός) 1 aor. 3 sg. ὥδευσε (TestJob 52:10); inf. ὁδεῦσαι (Hom. et al.; OGI 199, 28; POxy 1537, 18; 22; 1771, 10; LXX, Philo, Joseph.; SibOr 3, 367) ***go, travel, make a trip*** w. implication of using an established route ὁδὸν ὁδεύειν *make one's way* B 19:1 (Artem. 2, 12; 37; cp. Philo, Poster. Cai. 155 ἀτραπὸν ὁδ.). δι' ἧς (i.e. ἀνοδίας.—ὁδ. διά as X., An. 7, 8, 8; Jos., Ant. 20, 118) ἄνθρωπος οὐκ ἐδύνατο ὁδεῦσαι *through which a person could not walk* i.e. there was no path or road Hv 1, 1, 3. Abs. (Tob 6:6 BA; Jos., Bell. 1, 264; 3, 115) Σαμαρίτης ὁδεύων *a Samaritan who was on a trip* **Lk 10:33** (ASouter, Exp. 8th ser., 8, 1914, 94). Pass. (Strabo 5, 1, 7) ῥᾳδίως (Lat. raro) ὁδεύεται ὁ τόπος *the place is easily reached* Hv 4, 1, 2.—New Docs 4, 146. DELG s.v. ὁδός. M-M. TW.

ὁδηγέω (ὁδηγός) fut. ὁδηγήσω; 1 aor. ὡδήγησα LXX; pass. aor. 3 sg. ὡδηγήθη (Just.) ([for ὁδαγέω s. B-D-F §29, 3] Aeschyl. et al.; ins fr. Transjordan [NGG Phil.-hist. Kl. Fachgr. V n.s. I/1, '36 p. 3, 1: divine leading]; Kaibel 1041, 1; PSI 332, 6; LXX; Test12Patr, Just.; Tat. 13, 2)

❶ **to assist in reaching a desired destination, *lead, guide,*** lit. (Jos., Vi. 96; ὁ δὲ Μωσῆς ὁ τοὺς Ἰουδαίους Theoph. Ant. 3, 20 [p. 242, 16]) τινά *someone* τυφλὸς τυφλόν (cp. Hesiod, Astron. fgm. 182 Rz. a blind man; Plut., Mor. 139a τυφλούς; TestReub 2:9; Ps.-Phoc. 24) **Mt 15:14; Lk 6:39.** τινὰ ἐπί τι *someone to someth.* (cp. M. Ant. 7, 55, 1 ἐπί τί σε ἡ φύσις ὁδηγεῖ; PSI loc. cit.; Ps 106:30; 22:3; 24:5) ἐπὶ ζωῆς πηγὰς ὑδάτων *to springs of living water* **Rv 7:17.**

❷ **to assist someone in acquiring information or knowledge, *lead, guide, conduct,*** fig. ext. of 1 (Plut., Mor. 954b; Sextus 167 σοφία ψυχὴν ὁδηγεῖ πρὸς θεόν; LXX; Theoph. Ant. 1, 14 [p 90, 12]) of the Spirit ὁδηγήσει ὑμᾶς εἰς τὴν ἀλήθειαν πᾶσαν **J 16:13** (in the Herm. Lit. Hermes-Nous leads the souls to knowledge: Herm. Wr. 10, 21 εἰς τὴν εὐσεβῆ ψυχὴν ὁ νοῦς ὁδηγεῖ αὐτὴν ἐπὶ τὸ τῆς γνώσεως φῶς. Cp. 4, 11; 7, 2; 9, 10; 12, 12. Rtzst., Poim. 23, 5, Mysterienrel[3] 297; PGM 13, 523ff πάντα κινήσεις ... Ἑρμοῦ σε ὁδηγοῦντος.—Wsd 9:11; 10:10, 17; TestJud 14:1 εἰς πλάνην. Theoph. Ant. 3, 15 [p. 234, 118] λόγος ἅγιος ὁ.). Of lying ὁδηγεῖ εἰς τὴν κλοπήν *it leads to theft* D 3:5. Of complaining: εἰς τ. βλασφημίαν 3:6. Of divination: εἰς τὴν εἰδωλολατρείαν 3:4 (cp. TestJud 19:1 ἡ φιλαργυρία πρὸς εἰδωλολατρείαν ὁδηγεῖ). Also ὁδ. πρός τι (TestGad 5:7) 3:2f. Without further qualification: ἐὰν μή τις ὁδηγήσει με *if no one instructs me* **Ac 8:31.**—DELG s.v. ὁδός. M-M. TW.

ὁδηγός, οῦ, ὁ (ὁδός, ἡγέομαι; on ὁδαγός [cod. D and ApcrEzek P2, recto 7] s. B-D-F §29, 3)

❶ **one who leads the way in reaching a desired destination, *guide, leader*** (Polyb. 5, 5, 15; Plut., Alex. 680 [27, 3]; PCairZen 770, 14 [III BC]; Jos., Ant. 12, 305; 1 Macc 4:2; 2 Macc 5:15; cp. Philo, Mos. 1, 178) of Judas as guide for the men who arrested Jesus **Ac 1:16.**

❷ **one who assists another in following a path, *guide, leader,*** in imagery (Wsd 7:15; 18:3; Jos., Ant. 1, 217) ὁδηγὸς τυφλῶν *a guide for the blind* **Ro 2:19.** τυφλοί εἰσιν ὁδηγοὶ τυφλῶν *they are blind leaders of the blind* **Mt 15:14.** ὁδηγοὶ τυφλοί (Paroem. Gr.: Apostol. 11, 50) **23:16, 24.**—DELG s.v. ὁδός. TW.

ὀδμή s. ὀσμή.

ὁδοιπορέω (ὁδοιπόρος 'a traveler', fr. ὁδός + πόρος 'passage'; Soph., Hdt. et al.; Jos., Vi. 157, Ant. 14, 226; SIG 885, 28; PLond I, 121, 181 p. 90 [III AD]=PGM 7, 181; Cat. Cod. Astr. 113, 31 τοῖς ὁδοιποροῦσι καὶ ἀποπλέουσιν) ***travel, be on the way*** ὁδοιπορούντων ἐκείνων *as they were on their way* **Ac 10:9.**—DELG s.v. ὁδός and πόρος.

ὁδοιπορία, ας, ἡ (s. prec. entry; Hom. Hymns, Hdt. et al.; Diod. S. 5, 29, 1; Epict. 3, 10, 11; POxy 118 verso, 6; Wsd 13:18; 18:3; 1 Macc 6:41; TestAbr; Philo, Mut. Nom. 165, Leg. ad Gai. 254; Jos., Ant. 5, 53) ***walking, journey*** κεκοπιακὼς ἐκ τῆς ὁδ. *tired from the journey* **J 4:6** (TestAbr B 2 p. 107, 1 [Stone p. 62] ἐκοπιάθη ἐκ τῆς ὁδ.; Jos., Ant. 2, 321 ὑπὸ τῆς ὁδοιπορίας κεκοπωμένος; 3, 3; 2, 257; Dio Chrys. 77 [27], 1 οἱ διψῶντες τ. ὁδοιπόρων). Pl. (Hdt. 8, 118; X., Oec. 20, 18) *journeys* **2 Cor 11:26.**—DELG s.v. ὁδός and πόρος. M-M.

ὁδοποιέω (ὁδός, ποιέω) 1 aor. ὡδοποίησα LXX (X., An. 3, 2, 24; 4, 8, 8; 5, 1, 13; Appian, Liby. 91 §430, Bell. Civ. 1, 78 §356 al.; Arrian, Anab. 1, 26, 1; Herodian 3, 3, 7; OGI 175, 10 [II BC]; Is 62:10; Ps 79:10; Just., D. 131, 3 ὁδοποιηθεῖσαν θάλασσαν; Ath., R. 11 p. 60, 1) ***make a way/path,*** of the disciples ἤρξαντο ὁδοποιεῖν τίλλοντες τοὺς στάχυας *they began to make a path as they picked the ears* **Mk 2:23 v.l.**—DELG s.v. ὁδός. M-M.

ὁδός, οῦ, ἡ (Hom.+) gener. an established 'way' or 'course' such as a road or channel of a river.

❶ **a way for traveling or moving from one place to another,** ***way, road, highway,*** used by pers. or impers. entities: **Mt 2:12; 21:8ab; Mk 11:8; Lk 3:5** (Is 40:4 v.l.); **19:36** al.; ἑτέρα ὁδ. **Js 2:25.** ἡ ὁδ. ἡ Καμπανή=Lat. Via Campana *the Campanian Way* Hv 4, 1, 2 (s. MDibelius, Hdb. ad loc.; Hülsen, Pauly-W. III 1434); described as ἡ ὁδ. ἡ δημοσία *the public highway* ibid. (s. δημόσιος 1). τὴν βασιλικήν AcPl Ant 13 (τὴν β. ὁδόν Aa I 237, 4). ἡ ὁδ. ἡ καταβαίνουσα ἀπὸ Ἰερουσαλὴμ εἰς Γάζαν **Ac 8:26.** παρέρχεσθαι διὰ τῆς ὁδ. *pass by* (a certain place) *on the road* **Mt 8:28** (on διὰ τ. ὁδ. cp. Philo, Abr. 269; ParJer 3:21). πίπτειν εἰς τὴν ὁδ. *fall on the road* Hv 3, 7, 1a. ἔρχεσθαι εἰς τὴν ὁδ., μένειν ἐν τῇ ὁδ. v 3, 2, 9a. κυλίεσθαι ἐκ τῆς ὁδ. *roll off the road* 3, 2, 9b and 3, 7, 1b. Of a fig tree ἐπὶ τῆς ὁδοῦ *by the roadside* **Mt 21:19.** Of beggars καθῆσθαι παρὰ τὴν ὁδ. *sit by the roadside* **20:30; Mk 10:46; Lk 18:35** (Stephan. Byz. s.v. Εὔτρησις: κώμη . . . κεῖται παρὰ τὴν ὁδόν), but *along the way* also merits attention (cp. παρὰ τὰς ὁδούς Antig. Car. 29). Of seed that is sown πίπτειν παρὰ τὴν ὁδ. *fall along the road* (Dalman, Pj 22, 1926, 121ff) **Mt 13:4; Mk 4:4; Lk 8:5;** cp. **Mt 13:19; Mk 4:15; Lk 8:12.** ἐξέρχεσθαι εἰς τὰς ὁδ. *go out into the streets* **Mt 22:10; Lk 14:23;** for διεξόδους τῶν ὁδ. **Mt 22:9** s. διέξοδος; καταβαίνειν ἐν τῇ ὁδ. *go down the road* **Lk 10:31.** πορεύεσθαι κατὰ τὴν ὁδ. *go on along the highway* **Ac 8:36.** AcPl Ant 13, 20 (sc. ὁδόν after AcPlTh 3=Aa I 237, 4). ἐν τῇ ὁδῷ ᾗ ἤρχου (by attraction for ἣν ἤρ.; X., An. 2, 2, 10) **9:17.** ἑτοιμάζειν τὴν ὁδ. τινος *prepare someone's way* **Mt 3:3; Mk 1:3; Lk 3:4** (all after Is 40:3); cp. **Lk 1:76** and for the pass. **Rv 16:12.** Also κατασκευάζειν τὴν ὁδ. τινος **Mt 11:10; Mk 1:2; Lk 7:27.** εὐθύνειν τὴν ὁδ. τινος **J 1:23.** κατευθύνειν τὴν ὁδ. τινος **1 Th 3:11** (PsSol 8:6).—W. obj. gen. to indicate direction (Gen 3:24) **Mt 10:5** (s. 3a below); **Hb 9:8.**—The acc. ὁδόν, following the Hebr. דֶּרֶךְ, and contrary to customary Gk. usage (but single cases of ὁδός take on the functions of adverbs or prepositions in the Gk. language as well: cp. Diog. L. 7, 156; Synes., Providence 1, 8 ὁδῷ βαδίζειν='go straight forward'; Appian, Hann. 47 §201 ὁδὸν ἐλάσσονα by a shorter [or the shortest] way; Plut., Mor. 371c.—The nearest parallel to the NT usage cited below would be the report of Diog. L. 9, 8 concerning Heraclitus: τὴν μεταβολὴν ὁδὸν ἄνω κάτω γίνεσθαι, if it might be translated: 'Change [in the universe] is accomplished in an upward and downward direction'.) is used as a prep. *toward* (Dt 11:30; 3 Km 8:48; 18:43 ὁδὸν τῆς θαλάσσης. Cp. B-D-F §161, 1) ὁδ. θαλάσσης *toward the sea* **Mt 4:15** (Is 8:23 LXX, Aq., Sym.).—LCasson, Travel in the Ancient World '74; OEANE IV 431–34.

❷ **the action of traveling,** ***way, trip, journey,*** transf. sense of 1 (Hes., Theogon. 754; X., Mem. 3, 13, 5; Herodian 2, 11, 1; JosAs 9:4 al.; Just., D. 85, 5) εἰς (τὴν) ὁδ. *for the trip/journey* (Jos., Ant. 12, 198) **Mt 10:10; Mk 6:8; Lk 9:3;** *on the way* **Mk 10:17.** ἐν τῇ ὁδῷ *on the way* (Gen 45:24; Jos., Ant. 6, 55; Ps.-Clem., Hom. 10, 2, end) **Mt 15:32; 20:17; Mk 8:3, 27; 9:33f; 10:52; Lk 9:57; 12:58; 24:32; Ac 9:27.** τὰ ἐν τῇ ὁδῷ *what had happened to them on the way* **Lk 24:35.** εἶναι ἐν τῇ ὁδῷ **Mt 5:25; Mk 10:32.** ἐξ ὁδοῦ *from a trip* (Appian, Bell. Civ. 1, 91 §418; Damasc., Vi. Isid. 203 p. 138, 8 W.; Jos., Vi. 246; 248 ἐκ τ. ὁδοῦ) **Lk 11:6.** ἔκαμνον ἐκ τῆς ὁδοῦ GJs 15:1. κατὰ τὴν ὁδ. *along the way* (Arrian, Anab. 1, 26, 5; 3, 19, 3; PKöln VI, 245, 20 καθ' ὁδὸν 'on my way'; Jos., Ant. 8, 404; Ps.-Clem., Hom. 10, 2) **10:4; Ac 25:3; 26:13.** ἀνὰ μέσον τῆς ὁδοῦ *halfway* GJs 17:3. τ. ὁδὸν αὐτοῦ πορεύεσθαι *go on his way* **Ac 8:39** (cp. X., Cyr. 5, 2, 22; TestAbr B 2 p. 106, 2 [Stone p. 60]). πορεύεσθαι τῇ ὁδῷ 1 Cl 12:4. ὁδὸν ποιεῖν *make one's way* (Judg 17:8) **Mk 2:23;** s. ὁδοποιέω.—σαββάτου ὁδός *a Sabbath day's trip* could also belong under 1; it signified the distance an Israelite might travel on the Sabbath, two thousand paces or cubits (=about 800 meters.—Mishnah: ᶜErubin 4, 3; 7; 5, 7; Origen, Princ. 4, 17; Schürer II 472f; 484f; Billerb. II 590–94; Moore, Judaism II 32) **Ac 1:12.** ἡμέρας ὁδός *a day's trip* **Lk 2:44** (Diod. S. 19, 17, 3; Appian, Samn. 1 §5; Polyaenus 7, 21, 1; Lucian, Syr. Dea 9; Procop., Aed. 6, 1, 12; cp. Hdt. 4, 101; X., Cyr. 1, 1, 3 παμπόλλων ἡμερῶν ὁδός; Ael. Aristid. 36, 87 K.=48 p. 473 D.: τριῶν ἡμ. ὁδ.; Gen 30:36; 31:23; Ex 3:18; Jdth 2:21; 1 Macc 5:24; 7:45; Demetr.: 722 fgm. 5 Jac.; Jos., Ant. 15, 293).

❸ **course of behavior,** ***way, way of life,*** fig. ext. of 1 and 2, but oft. w. the picture prominently in mind (SibOr 3, 233; ὁδός τις γίνεται *one finds a way (out)* Did., Gen. 228, 7).

ⓐ *way* εἰς ὁδ. ἐθνῶν μὴ ἀπέλθητε *do not go in the way of the Gentiles* i.e. do not turn to the Gentiles **Mt 10:5** (but s. 1.—JJeremias, Jesu Verheissung für d. Völker, '56). εὐρύχωρος ἡ ὁδ. ἡ ἀπάγουσα εἰς τὴν ἀπώλειαν **7:13** (Pla., Gorg. 524a τὼ ὁδώ, ἡ μὲν εἰς μακάρων νήσους, ἡ δ' εἰς Τάρταρον). Also ἡ ὁδ. τῆς ἀπωλείας ApcPt 1:1; ἡ τοῦ μέλανος ὁδ. B 20:1. ἡ τοῦ θανάτου ὁδ. (Herm. Wr. 1, 29) D 5:1. Cp. 1:1 (on this Jer 21:8; TestAsh 1:3, 5 ὁδοὶ δύο, καλοῦ κ. κακοῦ; SibOr 8, 399 ὁδοὶ δύο, ζωῆς θανάτου τε; Ael. Aristid. 30 p. 577 D.: δυοῖν ὁδοῖν τὴν μὲν . . . τὴν δέ.—The two ὁδοί of Heracles: X., Mem. 2, 1, 21ff; Maximus Tyr. 14, 1a; e; k). ὁδ. σκότους B 5:4b. Description of the way B 20; D 5:1ff. τεθλιμμένη ἡ ὁδ. ἡ ἀπάγουσα εἰς τὴν ζωήν **Mt 7:14** (TestAbr A 2 p. 88, 28 [Stone p. 4]). Also ἡ ὁδ. τῆς ζωῆς D 1:2. ἡ ὁδ. τοῦ φωτός B 19:1. Description of the way B 19; D 1–4. ὁδ. εἰρήνης **Lk 1:79; Ro 3:17** (Is 59:8; Ps 13:3). ὁδ. ζωῆς **Ac 2:28** (Ps 15:11); cp. D 1:2 above. ὁδ. σωτηρίας **Ac 16:17.** ὁδ. πρόσφατος κ. ζῶσα **Hb 10:20.** ὁδ. δικαιοσύνης B 1:4; 5:4a (in these two pass. the imagery of 'way' is stronger than in **Mt 21:32** and **2 Pt 2:21,** on the latter two pass. s. below in b). Of love ὁδ. ἡ ἀναφέρουσα εἰς θεόν IEph 9:1 (cp. Orig., C. Cels. 1, 56, 6 [Christ as teacher of the 'way']). αὕτη ἡ ὁδ. ἐν ᾗ εὕρομεν τὸ σωτήριον ἡμῶν 1 Cl 36:1.—Christ calls himself ἡ ὁδ. (i.e., to God) **J 14:6,** cp. **4f** (s. Orig., C. Cels. 6, 66, 28; cp. Iren. 1, 15, 2 [Harv. I 149, 6].—Hdb. and Bultmann [p. 466ff—Engl. 603ff w. other lit.]; JPascher, Η ΒΑΣΙΛΙΚΗ ΟΔΟΣ; D. Königsweg. z. Wiedergeb. u. Vergottung b. Philon v. Alex. '31).

ⓑ *way of life, way of acting, conduct* (Did., Gen. 168, 8) (ἡ) ὁδ. (τῆς) δικαιοσύνης (Pr 21:16, 21; Job 24:13); En 99:10; **Mt 21:32** (ἐν ὁδῷ δικ. [cp. Pr 8:20] denotes either the way of life practiced by the Baptist [Zahn; OHoltzmann] or the type of conduct he demanded [described in Just., D. 38, 2 as ἡ τοῦ βαπτίσματος ὁδ.; cp. HHoltzmann; BWeiss; JWeiss; EKlostermann; Schniewind]. S. JKleist, CBQ 8, '46, 192–96); **2 Pt 2:21.** τῇ ὁδ. αὐτοῦ ἐπλανήθη *he went astray in his path* (='in his conduct') 1 Cl 16:6 (Is 53:6). ἐκ πλάνης ὁδοῦ αὐτοῦ *from his misguided way of life* **Js 5:20.** ἡ ὁδ. τῆς ἀληθείας (Ps 118:30) vs. **19 v.l.** (cp. **2 Pt 2:2** in c below); 1 Cl 35:5. ἀφιέναι τὴν ὁδ. τὴν ἀληθινήν Hv 3, 7, 1. τῇ ὁδ. τοῦ Κάϊν πορεύεσθαι *follow the way of Cain* **Jd 11.** ὁδ. δικαίων, ἀσεβῶν B 11:7 (Ps 1:6). (ἡ) ὁδ. (ἡ) δικαία (Jos., Ant. 13, 290) 12:4; 2 Cl 5:7. τὸ δίκαιον ὀρθὴν ὁδ. ἔχει *the way of righteousness is a straight one* Hm 6, 1, 2. τῇ ὀρθῇ ὁδ. πορεύεσθαι ibid.; cp. 6, 1, 4 (Just., D. 8, 2). Opp. ἡ στρεβλὴ ὁδ. *the crooked way* 6, 1, 3. θέωμεν τὴν ὁδ. τὴν εὐθεῖαν *let us run the straight course* 2 Cl 7:3; cp. **2 Pt 2:15.** Of life in association w. polytheists αὕτη ἡ ὁδ. ἡδυτέρα αὐτοῖς ἐφαίνετο Hs 8, 9, 1. The basic mng. has disappeared to such a degree that one can speak of καρποὶ τῆς ὁδ. 1 Cl 57:6 (Pr 1:31) and ἔργα τῆς πονηρᾶς ὁδ. B 4:10.—Pl. *ways,* of one's total conduct **Ac 14:16; Ro 3:16** (Is 59:7; Ps

13:3a; PsSol 6:2; 10:4 al.; ApcSed 15:5); **Js 1:8;** Hv 2, 2, 6. Esp. of the *ways* of God, referring either to the ways that God initiates: ὡς ... ἀνεξιχνίαστοι αἱ ὁδ. αὐτοῦ *how inscrutable are his ways* **Ro 11:33;** δίκαιαι καὶ ἀληθιναὶ αἱ ὁδ. σου **Rv 15:3;** αἱ ὁδ. τῆς εὐλογίας *the ways of blessing* 1 Cl 31:1; or to the ways that humans should take: οὐκ ἔγνωσαν τὰς ὁδ. μου **Hb 3:10** (Ps 94:10). διαστρέφειν τὰς ὁδοὺς τοῦ κυρίου **Ac 13:10.** διδάσκειν τὰς ὁδ. σου 1 Cl 18:13 (Ps 50:15). Likew. the sing. τὴν ὁδ. τοῦ θεοῦ ἐν ἀληθείᾳ διδάσκειν **Mt 22:16;** cp. **Mk 12:14; Lk 20:21.** ἀφιέναι τὴν ὁδ. τοῦ θεοῦ ApcPt 20:34. παρέβησαν ἐκ τῆς ὁδ. 1 Cl 53:2 (Ex 32:8).

ⓒ **of the whole way of life fr. a moral and spiritual viewpoint, *the way, teaching*** in the most comprehensive sense (Lucian, Hermot. 46 ὁδ. of the doctrine of a philosophical school Just., D. 39, 2 ἀπολείποντας τὴν ὁδ. τῆς πλάνης; 142, 3 διὰ ταύτης τῆς ὁδοῦ), and specif. of teaching and manner of life relating to Jesus Christ (SMcCasland, JBL 77, '58, 222–30: Qumran parallels) κατὰ τὴν ὁδ. ἣν λέγουσιν αἵρεσιν *according to the Way, which they call a (heterodox) sect* **Ac 24:14.** ἐάν τινας εὕρῃ τῆς ὁδ. ὄντας *if he should find people who belonged to the Way* **9:2.** ὁδ. κυρίου, θεοῦ of teaching relating to Jesus and God's purpose **18:25f.** κακολογεῖν τὴν ὁδ. ἐνώπιον τοῦ πλήθους **19:9.** ταύτην τὴν ὁδ. διώκειν *persecute this religion* **22:4.** ἐγένετο τάραχος περὶ τῆς ὁδ. *there arose a disturbance concerning the Way* **19:23.** τὰ περὶ τῆς ὁδ. *(the things) concerning the teaching* **24:22.** ἡ ὁδὸς τ. ἀληθείας of the true Christian teaching (in contrast to that of dissidents vs. 1) **2 Pt 2:2** (OdeSol 11:3). Of the way of love καθ' ὑπερβολὴν ὁδ. *a far better way* **1 Cor 12:31.** ἡ ὁδ. τῆς δικαιοσύνης ApcPt 7:22; 13:28. Likew. the pl. (En 104:13 μαθεῖν ἐξ αὐτῶν [τ. βίβλων] πάσας τ. ὁδοὺς τῆς ἀληθείας) τὰς ὁδούς μου ἐν Χριστῷ Ἰησου *my Christian directives* (i.e. instructions, teachings) **1 Cor 4:17.**—OBecker, D. Bild des Weges u. verwandte Vorstellungen im frühgriech. Denken '37; FNötscher, Gotteswege u. Menschenwege in d. Bibel u. in Qumran, '58; ERepo, D. Weg als Selbstbezeichnung des Urchr., '64 (but s. CBurchard, Der 13te Zeuge, '70, 43, n. 10; JPathrapankal, Christianity as a 'Way' according to the Acts of the Apostles: Les Actes des Apôtres, Traditions, redaction, théologie, ed. JKremer '79, 533–39 [reflects Is 40:3 and the emphasis on דרך in CD and 1QS: the 'dynamism of Christianity' is 'Way of Life']).—B. 717; 720. DELG. M-M. EDNT. TW. Sv.

ὀδούς, ὀδόντος, ὁ (Hom.+; pap, LXX; PsSol 13:3; TestSol; ApcEsdr 4:30 p. 29, 6 Tdf.; ApcMos; Philo; Jos., Bell. 6, 197; Just., D. 57, 2) ***tooth*** **Rv 9:8** (cp. Jo 1:6). δι' ὀδόντων θηρίων ἀλήθεσθαι *be ground by the teeth of wild beasts* IRo 4:1. W. ὀφθαλμός **Mt 5:38** (Ex 21:24). τρίζειν τοὺς ὀδ. *grind one's teeth* **Mk 9:18.** Also βρύχειν τοὺς ὀδ. ἐπί τινα (s. βρύχω) **Ac 7:54.** From this, βρυγμὸς τῶν ὀδ. *gnashing* or *grinding of teeth* (w. κλαυθμός), only in connection w. the tortures of hell **Mt 8:12; 13:42, 50; 22:13; 24:51; 25:30; Lk 13:28** (s. βρυγμός).—B. 231. DELG s.v. ὀδών. M-M.

ὀδυνάω (ὀδύνη) pass. fut. 3 sg. ὀδυνηθήσεται LXX; aor. 3 sg. ὠδυνήθη 4 Macc 18:9 'cause pain', in our lit. only pass. **ὀδυνάομαι** 2 pers. ὀδυνᾶσαι (B-D-F §87; W-S. §13, 17; Mlt-H. 198; Helbing p. 61) 'feel pain' (trag. et al.; Democr. 159; Pla.; Vett. Val. ind.; LXX; TestJob 24:4; TestIss 7:5; ParJer 7:31).

❶ **to undergo physical torment, *suffer pain*** (Aelian, NA 11, 32 p. 286, 28) περί τινος *suffer pain for the sake of someone* 1 Cl 16:4 (Is 53:4). Esp. of the tortures in Hades ὀδ. ἐν τῇ φλογί *suffer torment in the flames* **Lk 16:24;** cp. vs. **25.**

❷ **to experience mental and spiritual pain, *be pained/distressed*** (Dio Chrys. 66 [16], 1; Alciphron 3, 14, 2; Philo, De Jos. 94 ὀδυνώμενος; Jos., Bell. 6, 183 ὀδυνώμενον) ὀδυνώμενοι ζητοῦμέν σε *we have been anxiously looking for you* **Lk 2:48** (two persons of different sex are referred to with a masc. modifier, as Epici p. 20, 3 K. [p. 42, 60 B.] Achilles and Helen with αὐτούς) ὀδυνώμενοι μάλιστα ἐπὶ τῷ λόγῳ *they were especially pained at his saying* **Ac 20:38** (ὀδυνᾶσθαι ἐπί τινι as Philo, Conf. Lingu. 92).—DELG s.v. ὀδύνη. M-M s.v. ὀδυνάομαι. TW.

ὀδύνη, ης, ἡ (s. prec. entry; Hom. et al.; PGrenf I, 1, 2 [II BC]; Sb 4949, 12; 5716, 12; LXX; En 102:11; PsSol 4:15; TestSol 4:9 D; TestJob; Test12Patr; ApcMos 25; EpArist 208; Philo; Jos., Ant. 15, 62, C. Ap. 2, 143)

❶ **physical suffering or misery, *pain, woe*** ἐν ὀδ. AcPl Ha 5, 30 (through wounding); of the tribulations of the last days **Mt 24:8 v.l.** (itacism s. ὠδίν).

❷ **mental pain, *distress*** ἀδιάλειπτος ὀδ. τῇ καρδίᾳ μου (sc. ἐστί) *my heart is continually grieved* **Ro 9:2** (Philo, Aet. M. 63 ὀδ. ψυχῆς). Of the remorse of conscience ἑαυτοὺς περιέπειραν ὀδύναις πολλαῖς *they have pierced themselves to the heart with many pangs* **1 Ti 6:10.**—Schmidt, Syn. II 596–610. DELG. M-M. TW.

ὀδύνω, οῦ, ὁ (ὀδύνη) (ὀδύνομαι TestIss 7:5) ***be in pain*** **Ro 8:22 v.l.** (for συνωδίνω), perh. under influence of ὀδυνάω.

ὀδυρμός, οῦ, ὁ (ὀδύρομαι; Aeschyl., Pla. et al.; Aelian, VH 14, 22; TestSol 4:2 D; Jos., Bell. 5, 31, Ant. 2, 328; 2 Macc 11:6) ***lamentation, mourning*** **2 Cor 7:7.** W. κλαυθμός **Mt 2:18** (Jer 38:15).—DELG s.v. ὀδύρομαι. M-M. TW.

ὀδύρομαι mid. dep. (s. prec. entry; Hom. et al.; ins fr. Gaza: SEG VIII, 269, 8 [III/II BC]; PThéad. 21, 15; Ramsay, Studies in the History and Art of the Eastern Provinces 1906, 144, 5; Jer 38:18; TestAbr A; TestZeb 2:4; 4:6 both v.l.; GrBar 13:1; ApcSed 11:1 p. 134, 9 Ja.; ApcMos 27; Philo, Migr. Abr. 156; Jos., Ant. 11, 222, C. Ap. 2, 243; Just., D. 83, 3; Ath. 21, 2) ***mourn, lament*** w. ἐλεεῖν MPol 2:2.—DELG. TW.

Ὀζίας, ου, ὁ (-είας.—עֻזִּיָּהוּ עֻזִּיָּה Ὀζίας in LXX and Joseph.; s. EKautzsch, Mitteilungen u. Nachrichten des Deutschen Palästina-Vereins 1904, 6f; BHHW III 2068f) ***Uzziah,*** Hebrew king, in the genealogy of Jesus **Mt 1:8f; Lk 3:23ff** D (here, as Jos., Ant. 9, 236, the gen. is Ὀζία).

ὄζος, ου, ὁ (Hom. et al. 'branch') ***the knot*** on a treebranch (so Theophr. et al.; Wsd 13:13) ῥάβδος σκληρὰ λίαν καὶ ὄζους ἔχουσα *a very hard and knotty staff* Hs 6, 2, 5 (cp. Alciphron 3, 19, 5).—B. 523. DELG 1 ὄζος.

ὄζω 1 aor. 3 sg. ὤζεσεν Ex 8:10; ParJer 6:8 (Hom. et al.; Antig. Car. 117; Plut., Phoc. 751 [22] [odor given off by a corpse]; cp. PSI IV, 297, 3 [V AD?]; Epict. 4, 11, 15; 18 [of an unkempt man]) ***emit an odor,*** pleasant or unpleasant, ***to smell;*** ἤδη ὄζει *by this time he's smelling (stinking)* **J 11:39.**—B. 551. DELG. M-M.

ὅθεν adv. (Hom.+)—❶ **extension from a source referenced by the initial element, *from where, whence, from which.***

ⓐ of place (TestAbr A; JosAs; Jos., Ant. 1, 168; 19, 291; Tat. 5:2) GPt 13:56; Hs 9, 4, 7. ὅθ. ἐξῆλθον **Mt 12:44; Lk 11:24.** εἰς Ἀντιόχειαν ὅθ. ἦσαν παραδεδομένοι **Ac 14:26.** εἰς Συρακούσας ... ὅθ. περιελθόντες κατηντήσαμεν **28:13.** W. attraction (Thu. 1, 89, 3.—B-D-F §437; Rob. 548) συνάγων ὅθ. (ἐκεῖθεν ὅπου) οὐ διεσκόρπισας *gathering where you did not winnow* **Mt 25:24, 26.**

ⓑ of deduction from a circumstance *from which fact* (Jos., Ant. 2, 36; Ar 4:2 al.) **1J 2:18.**

❷ **marker of the basis for an action or procedure,** ***for which reason*** (Pla., Aristot.; ins [Meisterhans[3]-Schw. p. 253]; UPZ 162 II, 4 [117 BC]; BGU 731 II, 12; LXX; Demetr.: 722 fgm. 1, 7 Jac.; Ath. 22, 6); at the beginning of a clause *therefore, hence* (Diod. S. 14, 51, 5; Appian, Liby. 47 §202; Ps.-Callisth. 2, 1, 4; Wsd 12:23; Jdth 8:20; TestNapht 1:8; EpArist 110; Jos., Ant. 19, 203, Vi. 338; Ar. 8, 4; Just., A I, 12, 10 al.—B-D-F §451, 6; Rob. 962) **Mt 14:7; Ac 26:19; Hb 2:17; 3:1; 7:25; 8:3; 9:18; 11:19** (or *from among whom,* s. Goodsp.); 2 Cl 5:1; IEph 4:1.—M-M.

ὀθόνη, ης, ἡ (s. next entry; Hom. et al.; pap; JosAs 2:7; Jos., Ant. 5, 290; 12, 117) ***linen cloth, sheet*** (Appian, Bell. Civ. 4, 47 §200) **Ac 10:11; 11:5.** Esp. of a sail (IAndrosIsis [I BC] 153; Lucian, Jupp. Tr. 46, Ver. Hist. 2, 38; TestZeb 6:2) ὀθ. πλοίου *a ship's sail* MPol 15:2.—DELG. M-M. Spicq.

ὀθόνιον, ου, τό (Aristoph., Hippocr. et al.; ins [e.g. the Rosetta Stone: OGI 90, 18 (196 BC)]; pap [e.g. UPZ 85, 8; 42—163/160 BC]; Judg 14:13 B; Hos 2:7, 11; EpArist 320; JosAs 13:5 cod. A [p. 57, 11 Bat.]. Cp. O. Wilck I p. 266ff. On the origin of the word s. HLewy, Die semit. Fremdwörter im Griech. 1895, 124f; Thumb 111; on the flax plant s. Zohary, Plants 78, Geobot. II 628) dim. of ὀθόνη but not necessarily w. dim. force in our lit.; ***(linen) cloth, cloth wrapping*** **J 19:40; 20:5, 6, 7; Lk 24:12.** The applicability of the sense *bandage* (UPZ 85, 8; PGiss 68, 11) to our lit. is questionable. S. AVaccari, in Miscellanea biblica, BUbach '53, 375–86, w. ref. to PRyl 627, 9 (IV AD]. S. also JBlinzler, ΟΘΟΝΙΑ etc.: Philol 99, '55, 158–66; RBrown, AB: John 942 and JFitzmyer, AB: Luke 1548.—DELG s.v. ὀθόνη. M-M. Spicq.

οἶδα (Hom.+) really the perf. of the stem εἰδ- (Lat. video), but used as a pres.; 2 sing. οἶδας (**1 Cor 7:16; J 21:15f**), οἶσθα (Dt 9:2 4 Macc 6:27), 1 pl. οἴδαμεν LXX, 2 pl. οἴδατε, 3 pl. οἴδασιν (ἴσασιν only **Ac 26:4.** The form οἴδασιν is found as early as Hdt. 2, 43, 1; X., Oec. 20, 14; SIG 182, 8 [362/361 BC]; PCairGoodsp 3, 7 [III BC]; οἶδαν GJs 17:1). ἴστε **Eph 5:5; Hb 12:17; Js 1:19** can be indic. (so 3 Macc 3:14) or impv.; subj. εἰδῶ; inf. εἰδέναι; εἰδῆσαι Dt 4:35; Jdth 9:14; ptc. εἰδώς, εἰδυῖα **Mk 5:33; Ac 5:7.** Plpf. ᾔδειν, 2 sg. ᾔδεις **Mt 25:26; Lk 19:22,** 3 pl. ᾔδεισαν (W-S. §13, 20). Fut. εἰδήσω **Hb 8:11** (Jer 38:34) and εἴσομαι (Dg 12:1). B-D-F §99, 2; 101 p. 45 (εἰδέναι); W-S. §14, 7; Mlt-H. 220–22; Helbing p. 108; Mayser 321, 2; 327, 17; 372f; on relation to γινώσκω s. SPorter, Verbal Aspect in the Greek of the NT '89, 282–87.

❶ **to have information about,** ***know***—ⓐ w. acc. of pers. *know someone, know about someone* **Mk 1:34; J 1:26, 31, 33; 6:42; 7:28a; Ac 3:16; 7:18** (Ex 1:8); **Hb 10:30;** B 10:11. (τὸν) θεόν (Herm. Wr. 14, 8; Ar. 3, 2; Just., D. 10, 4; Tat. 19, 2) of polytheists, who *know nothing about God* (the one God described in vss. 6–7, and in contrast to the plurality of gods that have previously enslaved the Galatians vs. 8) **Gal 4:8; 1 Th 4:5** (cp. Jer 10:25).

ⓑ w. acc. of thing: οὐ τὴν ἡμέραν οὐδὲ τὴν ὥραν **Mt 25:13;** cp. 2 Cl 12:1. τὰς ἐντολάς **Mk 10:19; Lk 18:20.** βρῶσιν **J 4:32.** τ. ἐνθυμήσεις **Mt 9:4 v.l.** (cp. Jos., Vi. 283). τὴν ἐπιθυμίαν **Ro 7:7.** τὰ μυστήρια πάντα **1 Cor 13:2.** τὰ ἐγκάρδια 2 Cl 9:9. τὰ κρύφια IMg 3:2. τὴν πόλιν Hs 1:1.

ⓒ w. acc. of pers. and ptc. in place of the predicate (X., An. 1, 10, 16; TestJob 28:5; Just., A I, 12, 7.—B-D-F §416, 2; s. Rob. 1103) οἶδα ἄνθρωπον ἐν Χριστῷ . . . ἁρπαγέντα τὸν τοιοῦτον ἕως τρίτου οὐρανοῦ *I know of a person in Christ . . . that he was transported into the third heaven* **2 Cor 12:2.** Also without the ptc. εἰδὼς αὐτὸν ἄνδρα δίκαιον (sc. ὄντα) *because he knew that he was a just man* **Mk 6:20** (Chion, Ep. 3, 5 ἴσθι με προθυμότερον [ὄντα]). The obj. more closely defined by a declarative or interrog. clause: οἴδατε τὴν οἰκίαν Στεφανᾶ ὅτι ἐστὶν ἀπαρχὴ τῆς Ἀχαΐας = οἴδατε ὅτι ἡ οἰκία Στεφανᾶ ἐστιν ἀπαρχὴ τῆς Ἀ. **1 Cor 16:15.—Ac 16:3 v.l.** An indirect quest. may take the place of ὅτι: οἶδά σε τίς εἶ **Mk 1:24; Lk 4:34.** οὐκ οἶδα ὑμᾶς πόθεν ἐστέ *I do not know where you come from* **13:25;** cp. vs. **27** (ὑμᾶς is not found in all the mss. here); 2 Cl 4:5. τοῦτον οἴδαμεν πόθεν ἐστίν **J 7:27; 9:29b.**

ⓓ foll. by acc. and inf. (Just., A I, 26, 4; 59, 6, D. 75, 4.—B-D-F §397, 1; s. Rob. 1036ff) **Lk 4:41; 1 Pt 5:9;** 1 Cl 62:3.

ⓔ foll. by ὅτι (Aeneas Tact. 579; Dio Chrys. 31 [48], 1; Maximus Tyr. 16, 2b; TestAbr A 6 p. 83, 14 [Stone p. 14]; JosAs 6:6 al.; Just., A I, 12, 11; D. 4, 4 al.—B-D-F §397, 1; Rob. 1035) **Mt 6:32; 9:6; 15:12; 20:25; Mk 10:42; Lk 2:49; 8:53; J 4:25; Ac 3:17** and very oft.; GJs 4:4; 5:1; 17:1; 20:2 codd.; 23:2. εἰδώς (εἰδότες) ὅτι **Ac 2:30;** 1 Cl 45:7; 2 Cl 7:1; 10:5; B 10:11; 19:6; IMg 14; ISm 4:1; Hs 8, 6, 1; 10, 3, 4 [Ox 404 recto, 15]; Pol 1:3; 4:1; 5:1; 6:1; D 3:10; AcPl Ha 1, 25; AcPlCor 2:29.—τοῦτο, ὅτι **1 Ti 1:9; 2 Ti 1:15.** ἓν οἶδα, ὅτι *I know just this one thing, that* **J 9:25b** (Vi. Aesopi I c. 17 p. 269, 16f Eb. οὐκ οἶδα, τί γέγονεν. ἓν δ' οἶδα μόνον, ὅτι . . .).—The formula οἴδαμεν ὅτι is freq. used to introduce a well-known fact that is generally accepted **Mt 22:16; Lk 20:21; J 3:2; 9:31; Ro 2:2; 3:19; 7:14; 8:22, 28; 2 Cor 5:1; 1 Ti 1:8; 1J 3:2; 5:18ff.** Paul also uses for this purpose the rhetorical question (ἢ) οὐκ οἴδατε ὅτι; **Ro 6:16; 1 Cor 3:16; 5:6; 6:2f, 9, 15f, 19; 9:13, 24.**

ⓕ w. indirect quest. foll.: (TestAbr B 2 p. 106, 1 [Stone p. 60] μὴ εἰδὼς τίς ἐστίν; Just., D. 65, 1 οὐκ οἶδα τί φῶ) τίς, τί **Mt 20:22; Mk 9:6** (HBaltensweiler, D. Verklärung Jesu '59, 114f; on the grammar as well as the theme of inappropriateness in the face of transcendence cp. Eur., Bacch. 506, s. also 358); **10:38; 14:40; J 5:13; 6:6; 9:21b; 13:18; 15:15; Ro 8:27; 11:2; 1 Th 4:2; 2 Ti 3:14;** IEph 12:1. ποῖος **Mt 24:42f; Lk 12:39.** ἡλίκος **Col 2:1.** οἷος **1 Th 1:5.** ποῦ (ParJer 5:13) **J 3:8; 8:14; 12:35 14:5; 20:2, 13.** πῶς (BGU 37, 7; ApcMos 31) **J 9:21a; Col 4:6; 2 Th 3:7; 1 Ti 3:15;** GJs 23:3. πότε **Mk 13:33, 35.** πόθεν **J 2:9a; 3:8; 7:28b; 8:14; 9:30.** Foll. by εἰ *whether* (Lucian, Tox. 22) **J 9:25; 1 Cor 7:16ab** (JJeremias, Bultmann Festschr. '54, 255–66 understands τί οἶδας εἰ as 'perhaps'; CBurchard, ZNW 61, '70, 170f); Hm 12, 3, 4.—εἴτε **2 Cor 12:2f.**

ⓖ followed by a relat. (PPetr II, 11 [1], 7 [III BC]) οἶδεν ὁ πατὴρ ὑμῶν ὧν χρείαν ἔχετε **Mt 6:8;** cp. **Mk 5:33; 2 Ti 1:12.**

ⓗ foll. by περί τινος (Just., D. 5, 1) *know about someth.* **Mt 24:36; Mk 13:32** (RBrown, Jesus, God and Man '67, 59–79).

ⓘ abs. (Just., A I, 21, 4 πρὸς εἰδότας λέγειν οὐκ ἀνάγκη) **Mt 21:27; Mk 4:27; Lk 11:44; J 2:9b;** 1 Cl 43:6. καθὼς (αὐτοὶ) οἴδατε *as you (yourselves) know* **Ac 2:22; 1 Th 2:2, 5;** cp. **3:4.** καίπερ εἰδ. *though you know (them)* **2 Pt 1:12.** ὁ θεὸς οἶδεν *God knows* (that I do) **2 Cor 11:11;** cp. B 9:9. ἴστε **Js 1:19** (indic.: HermvSoden; BWeiss; Weymouth; W-S. §14, 7; impv: Hollmann; MDibelius; Windisch; OHoltzmann; Hauck; Meinertz; NRSV 'You must understand this'; B-D-F §99, 2; Mlt. 245).

❷ **be intimately acquainted with or stand in a close relation to,** ***know*** οὐκ οἶδα τὸν ἄνθρωπον *I don't know the man* **Mt 26:72, 74;** cp. **Mk 14:71; Lk 22:57.** ὥστε ἡμεῖς ἀπὸ τοῦ νῦν οὐδένα οἴδαμεν κατὰ σάρκα **2 Cor 5:16.** οὐ γὰρ ᾔδει αὐτὸν ἐν σαρκί AcPl Ant 13, 16 (for this εἶδεν αὐτὸν σαρκί Aa I 237, 2).—*To know* God, i.e. not only to know theoretically of God's existence, but to have a positive relationship with God, or *not to know* God, i.e. wanting to know nothing about God: **2 Th 1:8; Tit 1:16.—J 7:28b; 8:19** al.—οὐκ οἶδα ὑμᾶς *I have nothing to do with you* **Mt 25:12.** Cp. the formula of similar mng.

by which a teacher excluded a scholar for seven days: Billerb. I 469; IV 293.

❸ **to know/understand how, *can, be able*** w. inf. foll. (X., Cyr. 1, 6, 46; Philosoph. Max. p. 497, 7 εἰδὼς εὔχεσθαι; Herodian 3, 4, 8; Jos., Bell. 2, 91; 5, 407) οἴδατε δόματα ἀγαθὰ διδόναι *you know how to give good gifts* **Mt 7:11; Lk 11:13** (cp. TestJob 44:3 ᾔδεισαν εὖ ποιεῖν). οἴδατε δοκιμάζειν *you understand how to interpret* **12:56ab.** οἶδα καὶ ταπεινοῦσθαι, οἶδα καὶ περισσεύειν **Phil 4:12.** εἰδέναι ἕκαστον ὑμῶν τὸ ἑαυτοῦ σκεῦος κτᾶσθαι ἐν ἁγιασμῷ *each one of you is to know how to possess his own vessel* (s. σκεῦος 3) *in consecration* **1 Th 4:4.** τοῦ ἰδίου οἴκου προστῆναι οὐκ οἶδεν *does not know how to manage his own household* **1 Ti 3:5.** εἰδὼς καλὸν ποιεῖν **Js 4:17.** οἶδεν κύριος εὐσεβεῖς ἐκ πειρασμοῦ ῥύεσθαι **2 Pt 2:9.** οἴδασιν διὰ κόπου . . . πορίζειν ἑαυτοῖς τὴν τροφήν B 10:4. εἰδὼς φέρειν μαλακίαν *one who knew how to endure pain* 1 Cl 16:3 (Is 53:3).—Abs. ἀσφαλίσασθε ὡς οἴδατε *make it* (=the tomb) *as secure as you can* **Mt 27:65.**

❹ **to grasp the meaning of someth., *understand, recognize, come to know, experience*** (Just., D. 114, 1 ἣν τέχνην ἐὰν μὴ εἰδῶσιν [of allegorizing]; Sallust. 3 p. 4, 8 τοῖς δυναμένοις εἰδέναι=to those who can understand it) w. acc. of thing τὴν παραβολήν **Mk 4:13.** τὸν ἐπὶ τοῦ πυροῦ σπόρον . . . ὅτι *the sowing of wheat . . . that* AcPlCor 2:26. τὰ τοῦ ἀνθρώπου *understand what is really human* **1 Cor 2:11.** τὰ ὑπὸ τοῦ θεοῦ χαρισθέντα ἡμῖν vs. **12.** τὰ συνέχοντά με IRo 6:3. W. indir. quest. foll. εἰδέναι τίς ἐστιν ἡ ἐλπίς *come to know what the hope is* **Eph 1:18.** οὐκ οἶδα τί λέγεις *I do not understand what you mean* (Philostrat., Vi. Soph. 1, 7, 4; TestAbr A 16, p. 98, 10 [Stone p. 44] οἶδα τί λέγεις) **Mt 26:70;** cp. **J 16:18; 1 Cor 14:16. Lk 22:60** (Oenomaus in Eus., PE 6, 7, 9 οὐκ οἶσθα ἃ λέγεις; Just., D. 9, 1 οὐ γὰρ οἶδας ὃ λέγεις). εἴσεσθε ὅσα παρέχει ὁ θεός *you will experience what God bestows* Dg 12:1.—Esp. of Jesus' ability to fathom people's thoughts: τὰς ἐνθυμήσεις αὐτῶν **Mt 12:25.** τὴν ὑπόκρισιν **Mk 12:15.** τοὺς διαλογισμοὺς αὐτῶν **Lk 6:8;** cp. **11:17.** PEg[2] 50 (=ASyn. 280, 45). W. ἐν ἑαυτῷ added and ὅτι foll. **J 6:61.**

❺ **to remember, *recollect, recall, be aware of*** λοιπὸν οὐκ οἶδα εἴ τινα ἄλλον ἐβάπτισα *I don't recall baptizing anyone else* **1 Cor 1:16** (cp. Lucian, Dial. Meretr. 1, 1 οἶσθα αὐτόν, ἢ ἐπιλέλησαι τὸν ἄνθρωπον; οὐκ, ἀλλ' οἶδα, ὦ Γλυκέριον; Field, Notes 187).

❻ **to recognize merit, *respect, honor*** εἰδέναι τοὺς κοπιῶντας ἐν ὑμῖν *respect the people who work among you* **1 Th 5:12** (εἰδέναι τινά can mean *recognize* or *honor someone* [Ael. Aristid. 35, 35 K.=9 p. 111 D. τοὺς κρείττους εἰδέναι] but can also mean *take an interest in someone, care for someone:* Witkowski 30, 7 οἱ θεοί σε οἴδασιν). θεὸν καὶ ἐπίσκοπον εἰδέναι *honor God and the bishop* ISm 9:1.—τοῦτο ἴστε γινώσκοντες **Eph 5:5** has been viewed as a Hebraism (so ARobinson 1904 ad loc., calling attention to LXX 1 Km 20:3 γινώσκων οἶδεν and Sym. Jer 49 [42]: 22 ἴστε γινώσκοντες), but against this view SPorter, ZNW 81, '90, 270–76.—B. 1209. DELG. M-M. EDNT. TW.

οἰκεῖος, (α,) ον (οἶκος; Hes., Hdt. +) lit. 'belonging to the house'; in our lit. only subst. οἱ οἰκ. **persons who are related by kinship or circumstances and form a closely knit group, *members of a household.***

ⓐ with focus on normal familial connections or association in common cause (Jos., Vi. 183), of all the members of a household MPol 6:2. οἱ οἰκ. τοῦ σπέρματός σου *your blood relatives* B 3:3 (Is 58:7). W. ἴδιοι of *members of one's family* (schol. on Pla. 20e λέγονται οἰκεῖοι καὶ οἱ συγγενεῖς) **1 Ti 5:8** (Diod. S. 5, 18, 1; Appian, Hann. 28 §118; SIG 317, 38; 560, 21; 591, 59 φίλοι καὶ οἰκεῖοι; TestReub 3:5 γένος κ. οἰκεῖοι).

ⓑ with focus on association in common cause or belief (w. συμπολῖται τῶν ἁγίων) οἰκ. τοῦ θεοῦ *members of God's household* (cp. Marinus, Vi. Procli 32 τοῦ θεοφιλοῦς ἀνδρὸς ἡ πρὸς τ. θεὸν οἰκειότης) of the Christians **Eph 2:19.** οἱ οἰκ. τῆς πίστεως *those who belong to the household of faith* **Gal 6:10** (cp. Polyb. 5, 87, 3 οἰκ. τῆς ἡσυχίας; 4, 57, 4; 14, 9, 5; Diod. S. 13, 91, 4; 19, 70, 3 οἰκ. τυραννίδος; Strabo 17, 1, 5 οἰκ. σοφίας.—GWhitaker, Exp. 8th Ser. 23, 1921, 76ff).—S. on ἑταῖρος.—DELG s.v. οἶκος B. M-M.

οἰκετεία, ας, ἡ (cp. οἰκέτης; since SIG 495, 112f [c. 230 BC]; Strabo 14, 5, 2; Lucian, De Merc. Cond. 15; Epict., Ench. 33, 7 [s. Schenkl, app.]; SIG 694, 54f; 695, 61; PTebt 285, 6; Sym. Job 1:3; EpArist 14; 15; Jos., Ant. 12, 30) **complement of slave members of a household, *household slaves*** καταστῆσαί τινα ἐπὶ τῆς οἰκετείας αὐτοῦ *put someone in charge of (the slaves in) his household* **Mt 24:45** (vv.ll. οἰκίας, θεραπείας).—DELG s.v. οἶκος A II 4. M-M.

οἰκέτης, ου, ὁ (fr. οἶκος, cp. prec. entry) lit. 'member of the household,' then specif. ***house slave, domestic,*** and ***slave*** gener. (in the specif. sense Aeschyl., Hdt.+) **Ac 10:7.** Opp. δεσπότης (Dio Chrys. 64 [14], 10; Ael. Aristid. 45 p. 40 D.; Pr 22:7; Philo, Deus Imm. 64) **1 Pt 2:18;** opp. κύριος as master (Philo, Poster. Cai. 138) **Lk 16:13;** 2 Cl 6:1. ἀλλότριος οἰκ. *another's slave* **Ro 14:4.**—B. 1332. DELG s.v. οἶκος A II 4. M-M. Spicq.

οἰκέω (οἶκος) fut. οἰκήσω; aor. ᾤκησα LXX—❶ **to reside in a place, *live, dwell,*** intr. (Hom.+; ins, pap, LXX; pseudepigr.; Philo, Aet. M. 148 [ἐν]; Just., D. 78, 9 [ἐν]; PJena col. 4, 20; Did.) οἰκ. μετά τινος *live with someone* (M. Ant. 1, 17, 15; Gen 24:3; 27:44) Hv 5:2; in marriage (Soph., Oed. R. 990) **1 Cor 7:12f.** ἔν τινι *in someone* or *someth.* (PPetr II, 17 [3], 4 [III BC] οἴκημα ἐν ᾧ οἰκοῦμεν; Sb 6762, 1; PRev 29, 6) of the Christians ἐν κόσμῳ οἰκ. Dg 6:3b. Also of the soul ἐν τῷ σώματι ibid. a. Of the Spirit of God, which dwells in a pers. (cp. TestGad 5:4 ὁ φόβος τ. θεοῦ οἰκεῖ ἐν αὐτῷ; Just., A I, 32, 8) **Ro 8:9, 11; 1 Cor 3:16.** Of the good **Ro 7:18.** Of sin vss. **17** and **20.**

❷ **to inhabit a place, *inhabit, dwell in*** trans. τὶ *someth.* lit. (Mitt-Wilck II/2, 284, 5 οἰκίαν [TestJob 44:1]; PGiss 2, 23; PTebt 104, 21; Gen 24:13; Philo, Conf. Lingu. 106 κόσμον ὡς πατρίδα οἰκ.; Jos., Ant. 14, 88, C. Ap. 1, 9; Orig., C. Cels. τὴν Ἀσίαν . . . οἰκ.; Iren. 1, 10, 2 [Harv. I 92, 3]) πατρίδας ἰδίας Dg 5:5. In a transcendent sense, of God φῶς οἰκῶν ἀπρόσιτον *who dwells in unapproachable light* **1 Ti 6:16.**—On οἰκουμένη see it as a separate entry.—DELG s.v. οἶκος C. M-M. TW.

οἴκημα, ατος, τό (οἰκέω; Pind., Hdt.+; ins, pap, LXX; TestAbr A 4 p. 80, 21, 29f [Stone p. 8]; Philo, Vi. Cont. 25; Joseph.).

❶ **an individual room in a dwelling, *room, apartment*** (Hdt. 1, 9; 10; Menand., Sam. 19; Diod. S. 1, 92, 6; Appian, Bell. Civ. 4, 24 §98; Jos., Ant. 8, 134; 137; 14, 455; TestAbr A) οἰκήματα μάταια *rooms that will pass away* Hs 1:1.

❷ **a room within a prison complex or a separate dwelling used for detention, *quarters*** (Thu. 4, 47, 3 and 4, 48, 1 of a large building used for temporary detention; Demosth. 32, 29 used euphemistically of a cell; Lucian, Tox. 29 of stifling quarters within a prison; Plut., Agis 803–4 [19, 5; 8; 9]; Aelian, VH 6, 1) φῶς ἔλαμψεν ἐν τῷ οἰκ. *a light shone in (Peter's) cell* **Ac 12:7** the usage here is not necessarily euphemistic (pace Haenchen ad loc) for this is one room or cell in a larger detention complex termed φυλακή (vs. 6); apparently the light shines only in Peter's space.—DELG s.v. οἶκος C. M-M.

οἴκησις, εως, ἡ (οἰκέω) ***house, dwelling*** (so Aeschyl., Hdt.+; Diod. S. 1, 50, 6; 17, 105, 5; SIG 1216, 11; PMagd 29, 3 [III BC]; BGU 1113, 19; PTebt 489; Jdth 7:14; 1 Macc 13:48; ViJer 2 [p. 71, 5 Sch.]; Philo; Jos., Vi. 159, Ant. 14, 261; Just., D. 139, 2 ['habitation']) Hs 1:4.—DELG s.v. οἶκος C.

οἰκητήριον, ου, τό (οἰκητήρ = οἰκητής 'inhabitant', cp. οἰκήτωρ; Eur., Democr.+; Cebes 17, 3 εὐδαιμόνων οἰκ.; Plut., Mor. 60b; UPZ 17a, 23 [127 BC]; BGU 1167, 33 [12BC]; POxy 235, 14 astrological term 'house [of Kronos=Saturn]' w. οἶκος lines 15 and 16; POxy 281, 11; ins in GPlaumann, Ptolemais 1910 p. 35 [76/75 BC]; 2 Macc 11:2; En 27:2; TestSol; Jos., C. Ap. 1, 153; Tat. 13, 2) **a place for living, *dwelling, habitation,*** of angels (Ps.-Aristot., De Mundo 2, 2 heaven as the οἰκητήριον θεοῦ or 3, 4 τῶν ἄνω θεῶν) ἀπολιπεῖν τὸ ἴδιον οἰκ. *abandon one's own dwelling* **Jd 6** (cp. POxy 235 above; ἴδιον οἰκ. as Cornutus 24 p. 45, 21; for the subject matter cp. En 15:3ff; Jos., Ant. 1, 73).—The glorified body of a transfigured Christian, *dwelling* (alternating w. οἰκία, οἰκοδομή vs. **1**) **2 Cor 5:2** (s. on σκῆνος and the lit. on γυμνός 1b).—DELG s.v. οἶκος C. M-M. TW.

οἰκήτωρ, ορος, ὁ (s. prec. entry; Aeschyl., Hdt. et al.; Diod. S. 5, 41, 2; Aelian, VH 9, 16; PLond V 1677, 27; PGM 7, 351; T. Kellis 22, 121; LXX; Philo; Jos., Ant. 14, 75, Vi. 230; Just., D. 119, 5) one who uses a place as a dwelling ***inhabitant*** ἔσονται οἰκήτορες γῆς *they will inhabit the earth* 1 Cl 14:4 (Pr 2:21). οἰκήτορες τοῦ τόπου ἐκείνου *inhabitants of that place* (a transcendent locale) ApcPt 4:17.—Frisk s.v. οἶκος.

οἰκία, ας, ἡ (Hdt.+)—**❶ a structure used as a dwelling, *house*—ⓐ** lit., as a building **Mt 2:11; 7:24–27; 24:43; Mk 10:29f; 13:34; Lk 6:48f; 15:8; 18:29; J 12:3; Ac 10:6; 1 Cor 11:22;** 1 Cl 12:6 al. W. ἀγρός Hs 1:4, 8; cp. **Mt 19:29.** W. χωρίον **Ac 4:34.** εἰς τ. οἰκίαν τινός **Mt 8:14; 9:23; Mk 1:29; Lk 4:38; 7:44; 22:54.** εἰς οἰκίαν τινός **Ac 18:7.** εἰς τὴν οἰκίαν *into the house* **Lk 8:51; 10:38 v.l.** (prob. the orig. rdg., reverentially omitted by some copyists: MdeJonge, NThT 34, 308 [against Metzger 153]; s. RBorger, TRu 52, '87, 32f); **22:10;** *(go, come) home* (Appian, Bell. Civ. 5, 68 §288; Jos., Vi. 144) **Mt 9:28; 13:36; 17:25;** AcPl Ha 4, 3; *at home* **Mk 10:10.** εἰς οἰκίαν *into a house* **6:10; 7:24;** *into your house* **2J 10.** ἐν τῇ οἰκίᾳ τινός **Mk 2:15; 14:3; Lk 5:29; 7:37.** ἐν οἰκίᾳ τινός (POxy 51, 13 ἐν οἰκίᾳ Ἐπαγαθοῦ) **Mt 26:6; Ac 9:11; 10:32;** ἐν τῇ οἰκίᾳ *in the house* **J 8:35; 11:31;** *at home* **Mt 8:6; 9:10; Mk 9:33.** ἐν οἰκίᾳ *in a house* or *at home* **Lk 8:27.** οἱ ἐν τῇ οἰκίᾳ *those who are in the house* **Mt 5:15** (πάντες οἱ ἐν τ. οἰκ. as Dio Chrys. 64 [14], 7); cp. **Ac 16:32.** ὁ κύριος τῆς οἰκίας *the master of the house* **Mk 13:35.** ὁ οἰκοδεσπότης τῆς οἰκίας **Lk 22:11.** κατεσθίειν τὰς οἰκ. τῶν χηρῶν *devour widow's houses* i.e., rob widows of their houses (and household goods; s. οἶκος 4) **Mt 23:13 [14] v.l.; Mk 12:40; Lk 20:47** (Maximus Tyr. 14, 4e κείρειν [=devour] οἶκον βασιλέως). κατοικεῖν οἰκίας πηλίνας *live in houses of clay* 1 Cl 39:5 (Job 4:9).—KJäger, D. Bauernhaus in Palästina, m. Rücksicht auf d. bibl. Wohnhaus untersucht 1912; Dalman, Arbeit VII: D. Haus, Hühnerzucht, Taubenzucht, Bienenzucht '42.

ⓑ in imagery, of the body as the habitation of the soul (cp. σαρκικὸς οἶκος ParJer 6:6) ἡ ἐπίγειος ἡμῶν οἰκ. τοῦ σκήνους *the earthly tent we live in* **2 Cor 5:1a.** In contrast to this the glorified body is called οἰκία ἀχειροποίητος *a dwelling not made with hands* **2 Cor 5:1b.**—S. on οἰκητήριον.—Of heaven as God's dwelling-place (cp. Artem. 2, 68 p. 159, 13 ὁ οὐρανὸς θεῶν ἐστιν οἶκος; schol. on Aeschin. 2, 10: acc. to Timaeus, a woman dreamed that she had been snatched up into heaven and had seen there τὰς τῶν θεῶν οἰκήσεις; Sappho 1, 7 D.[2]: Aphrodite inhabits πατρὸς [Zeus'] δόμον.—Purely formal UPZ 18, 8 [163 BC] ἡ οἰκία τοῦ πατρὸς ἡμῶν) **J 14:2** (difft. OSchaefer, ZNW 32, '33, 210–17, against him Bultmann 464, 5).

❷ social unit within a dwelling, *household, family* (X., Mem. 2, 7, 6; Diod. S. 12, 14, 3; 13, 96, 3; PPetr II, 23 [4], 2 καταγράψας τὴν οἰκίαν τοῦ Ὥρου; Philo, Abr. 92; Jos., Ant. 17, 134) **Mt 12:25** (w. πόλις, as Synes., Providence 1, 4 p. 9d); **Mk 3:25** (w. βασιλεία). ἐπίστευσεν αὐτὸς καὶ ἡ οἰκ. αὐτοῦ ὅλη *he and his whole household came to believe* **J 4:53** (Appian, Bell. Civ. 1, 13 §55 Γράκχος αὐτοῦ σὺν ὅλῃ τῇ οἰκίᾳ κατάρχοιτο). ἡ οἰκ. Στεφανᾶ *the family of Stephanas* **1 Cor 16:15.** ἄτιμος εἰ μὴ . . . ἐν τῇ οἰκ. αὐτοῦ *without honor except . . . in his family* **Mt 13:57; Mk 6:4.**

❸ a kind of middle position betw. mngs. 1 and 2 is held by **Mt 10:12f:** εἰσερχόμενοι εἰς τὴν οἰκίαν ἀσπάσασθε αὐτήν. καὶ ἐὰν ᾖ ἡ οἰκία ἀξία . . . —οἱ ἐκ τῆς Καίσαρος οἰκίας **Phil 4:22** means, whether it be translated *those in the house* or *those in the household of the Emperor,* according to prevailing usage, not members of the emperor's family or relationship, but servants at his court; in early imperial times they were ordinarily slaves or freedpersons (cp. Philo, In Flacc. 35; Jos., Ant. 17, 142; παντὶ τῷ οἴκῳ τῶν Σεβαστῶν PHerrmann, Inschriften von Sardeis: Chiron 23, '93, 234 no. 1 ln. 5; MartPl 1 [Aa I 104, 8; 106, 15]. Cp. also Diog. L. 5, 75 the explanation for the 'ignoble' origin of Demetrius of Phalerum: ἦν γὰρ ἐκ τῆς Κόνωνος οἰκίας. On the other hand Diod. S. 17, 35, 3 αἱ τῆς βασιλικῆς οἰκίας γυναῖκες=the women of the royal family.—AdeWaal, Οἱ ἐκ τῆς Καίσαρος οἰκίας [Phil 4:22]: Röm. Quartalschr. 26, 1912, 160–63; Zahn, Einl.[3] 391; GDuncan, St. Paul's Ephesian Ministry 1929 [where the theory of Paul's Ephesian imprisonment is set forth]. S. also Καῖσαρ ad loc.).—B. 133; 458. DELG s.v. οἶκος A I. M-M. TW.

οἰκιακός, οῦ, ὁ (οἶκος; Plut., Cic. 870 [20, 3]; POxy 294, 17 [22 AD]; PGiss 88, 4) ***member of a household*** **Mt 10:25** (opp. οἰκοδεσπότης), **36** (here extended family rather than those residing together).—DELG s.v. οἶκος A I. M-M.

οἰκοδεσποτέω (οἰκοδεσπότης; late word [Lob., Phryn. p. 373]; esp. astrolog. t.t. 'rule' of the planet that influences human life: Plut., Mor. 90b; Ps.-Lucian, Astrol. 20; POxy 235, 16 [20/50 AD] οἰκοδεσποτεῖ Ἀφροδίτη; PLond I, 130, 163 p. 137: Stilbon, the planet Mercury, 'will dominate the theme [of the nativity]'; Cat. Cod. Astr. IX/1 p. 158, 7) ***manage one's household, keep house*** **1 Ti 5:14.**—M-M. TW.

οἰκοδεσπότης, ου, ὁ (οἶκος, δεσπότης; later word [Lob., Phryn. p. 373]; Alexis Com. [IV BC] 225; Plut., Mor. 271e; SIG 888, 57f; New Docs 2, 58 no. 18,12 [75/76 AD]; Isaurian ins in PASA III p. 150 υἱοὺς τοὺς οἰκοδεσπότας; PLond I, 98 recto, 60 p. 130 [I/II AD]; PSI 158, 80 (for astrol. pap [incl. PParis 19, 42; 75, 10f; PLond I, 110, 41 p. 132 [138 AD]] s. Neugebauer-Hoesen index); TestJob 39:2; Philo; Jos., C. Ap. 2, 128) ***master of the house, householder*** **Mt 24:43; Mk 14:14; Lk 12:39.** Pleonast. οἰκ. τῆς οἰκίας **Lk 22:11** (cp. SIG 985, 52 [II/I BC]; s. B-D-F §484). Used w. ἄνθρωπος in a figure **Mt 13:52; 20:1; 21:33.** In parables and figures, of God (cp. Epict. 3, 22, 4; Philo, Somn. 1, 149) **13:27** (interpreted as the Human One in vs. 37); **20:1, 11; 21:33; Lk 14:21;** Hs 5, 2, 9; cp. IEph 6:1. Christ of himself **Mt 10:25; Lk 13:25** (δεσπότης P^{75}).—DELG s.v. δεσπότης. M-M. TW.

οἰκοδομέω (οἰκοδόμος; Hdt.; ins, pap, LXX, En, EpArist, Philo, Joseph., Test12Patr) impf. ᾠκοδόμουν; fut. οἰκοδομήσω; 1 aor. ᾠκοδόμησα also without augment οἰκοδόμησα (ApcMos 40; on the augment s. W-S. §12, 5a; Mlt-H. 191); pf. ᾠκοδόμηκα LXX; plpf. 3 sg. ᾠκοδομήκει (Just., D. 127, 3). Pass.: impf. 3 sg. ᾠκοδομεῖτο; 1 fut. οἰκοδομηθήσομαι; 1 aor. ᾠκοδομήθην (v.l.) or οἰκοδομήθην (other edd., **J 2:20**); perf. inf. ᾠκοδομῆσθαι (οἰ- **Lk 6:48b**); ptc. οἰκοδομημένος (Ox 1 recto, 15f [GTh 32]); ᾠκοδομημένος Hv 3, 2, 6; plpf. 3 sg. ᾠκοδόμητο.

❶ **to construct a building, *build*—ⓐ** w. obj. acc. *build, erect* (oft. pap [Mayser II/2 p. 315, 30ff]; Jos., Ant. 15, 403 al.; Did., Gen 29, 7) οἰκίαν (Diod. S. 14, 116, 8; Lucian, Charon 17) **Lk 6:48a.** τὰς οἰκοδομάς GJs 9:3; pass. (Sb 5104, 2 [163 BC] οἰκία ᾠκοδομημένη; PAmh 51, 11; 23) **Lk 6:48b.** πύργον (Is 5:2) **Mt 21:33; Mk 12:1; Lk 14:28;** Hs 9, 3, 1; 4; 9, 12, 6; pass. Hv 3, 2, 4ff; 3, 3, 3; 3, 5, 5; 3, 8, 9; Hs 9, 3, 2; 9, 5, 2; 9, 9, 7; cp. 9, 9, 4. ναόν **Mk 14:58;** B 16:3 (Is 49:17); pass. **J 2:20** (Heliodorus Periegeta of Athens [II BC]: 373 fgm. 1 Jac. says of the Acropolis: ἐν ἔτεσι ε̅ παντελῶς ἐξεποιήθη; Orig., C. Cels. 5, 33, 13); B 16:6 (cp. below; the 'scripture' pass. is interpreted spiritually). ἀποθήκας **Lk 12:18** (opp. καθαιρεῖν; s. this 2aα). τοὺς τάφους τῶν προφητῶν *the tombs of the prophets* **Mt 23:29** (s. EKlosterman[2] ad loc.). τὰ μνημεῖα τῶν προφητῶν *the monuments for the prophets* **Lk 11:47** (μνημεῖον 1).—οἰκ. τινί τι *build someth. for someone* (Gen 8:20; Ex 1:11; Ezk 16:24) συναγωγὴν οἰκ. τινί **Lk 7:5.** οἰκ. τινὶ οἶκον **Ac 7:47, 49;** B 16:2 (the last two Is 66:1).—W. the obj. acc. and foll. by ἐπί w. acc. or w. gen: τὴν οἰκίαν ἐπὶ τὴν πέτραν *build the house on the rock* **Mt 7:24.** ἐπὶ τὴν ἄμμον *on the sand* vs. **26** (proverbial: Plut. VII p. 463, 10 Bern. εἰς ψάμμον οἰκοδομεῖς). πόλις ἐπὶ τ. ὄρους **Lk 4:29** (cp. Jos., Ant. 8, 97). ἐπὶ τὴν γῆν **6:49.** πόλις οἰκοδομημένη ἐπ' ἄκρον ὄρους ὑψηλοῦ *a city that is built on the top of a high mountain* Ox 1 recto, 15f (GTh 32). πύργος ἐπὶ ὑδάτων Hv 3, 3, 5; ἐπὶ τὴν πέτραν s 9, 14, 4 (opp. χαμαὶ οὐκ ᾠκοδόμηται).

ⓑ abs.—**α.** when the obj. can be supplied fr. the context (Did., Gen. 33, 27) **Lk 11:48; 14:30.**—Cp. Hv 3, 1, 7; 3, 4, 1a; 3, 10, 1; s 9, 4, 1.

β. but also entirely without an obj. (Theoph. Ant. 2, 13 [p. 132, 4f]) ᾠκοδόμουν *they erected buildings* **Lk 17:28.** οἱ οἰκοδομοῦντες *the builders, the masons* (after Ps 117:22) **Mt 21:42; Mk 12:10; Lk 20:17; Ac 4:11 v.l.; 1 Pt 2:7;** B 6:4. Also with no ref. to the Ps passage: Hs 9, 4, 4; 9, 6, 6.

γ. οἱ λίθοι οἱ ἤδη ᾠκοδομημένοι *the stones already used in the building* Hv 3, 5, 2; cp. s 9, 6, 3.

ⓒ *build up again, restore,* a sense that οἰκ. can receive fr. the context (Josh 6:26; Ps 50:20; 68:36) **Mt 26:61; 27:40; Mk 15:29;** B 16:3 (Is 49:17).—S. also 2.

❷ **to construct in a transcendent sense** (as in Hermas passages given under 1, where the tower is a symbol of the church) ***build:*** of the building up of the Christian congregation/church (cp. Ruth 4:11; θεμελιώσαντες καὶ οἰκοδομήσαντες οἱ μακάριοι ἀπόστολοι τὴν ἐκκλησίαν Iren. 3, 3, 3 [Harv. II 10, 1]) ἐπὶ ταύτῃ τῇ πέτρᾳ οἰκοδομήσω μου τὴν ἐκκλησίαν *on this rock I will build my congregation/church* **Mt 16:18.** ὡς λίθοι ζῶντες οἰκοδομεῖσθε οἶκος πνευματικός *like living stones let yourselves be built up* (pass.) or *build yourselves up* (mid., so Goodsp., Probs. 194f) *into a spiritual house* **1 Pt 2:5.** Paul refers to missionary work where another Christian has begun activities as ἐπ' ἀλλότριον θεμέλιον οἰκ. *building on another's foundation* **Ro 15:20.** He also refers to his negative view of law in relation to the Christ-event as a building, and speaks of its refutation as a tearing down (καταλύειν), and of returning to it as a *rebuilding* (s. 1c above) **Gal 2:18.** This is prob. where B 11:1 belongs, where (followed by citations of Scripture) it is said of the Israelites that they do not accept the baptism that removes sin, but ἑαυτοῖς οἰκοδομήσουσιν *will build up someth. for themselves.* In another pass. B calls the believer a πνευματικὸς ναὸς οἰκοδομούμενος τῷ κυρίῳ *a spiritual temple built for the Lord* 16:10; cp. vs. 6f.—Hermas' temple-building discourse mentions angels entrusted by God with οἰκοδομεῖν *building up* or *completion* of his whole creation Hv 3, 4, 1b.—(In this connection cp. Orig., C. Cels. 4, 38, 16 γυνὴ οἰκοδομηθεῖσα ὑπὸ τοῦ θεοῦ [of Eve]).

❸ **to help improve ability to function in living responsibly and effectively, *strengthen, build up, make more able.*** οἰκ. is thus used in a nonliteral sense and oft. without consciousness of its basic mng. (Straub p. 27), somewhat like *edify* in our moral parlance (this extended use is found as early as X., Cyr. 8, 7, 15 and in LXX: Ps 27:5; Jer 40:7. Also TestBenj 8:3.—JWeiss on 1 Cor 8:1). Of the Lord, who is able to *strengthen* the believers **Ac 20:32.** Of the congregation, which *was being built up* **9:31.**—Esp. in Paul: ἡ ἀγάπη οἰκοδομεῖ *love builds up* (in contrast to γνῶσις, which 'puffs up') **1 Cor 8:1** (=Dg 12:5). πάντα ἔξεστιν, ἀλλ' οὐ πάντα οἰκοδομεῖ *everything is permitted, but not everything is beneficial* **10:23.** ὁ λαλῶν γλώσσῃ ἑαυτὸν οἰκοδομεῖ· ὁ δὲ προφητεύων ἐκκλησίαν οἰκοδομεῖ **14:4;** cp. vs. **17.** οἰκοδομεῖτε εἷς τὸν ἕνα *strengthen one another* **1 Th 5:11.** In **1 Cor 8:10** the apostle is prob. speaking ironically, w. ref. to the 'strong' party at Corinth, who declare that by their example they are *benefiting* the 'weak': οὐχὶ ἡ συνείδησις αὐτοῦ οἰκοδομηθήσεται εἰς τὸ τὰ εἰδωλόθυτα ἐσθίειν; *will not his conscience be 'strengthened' so that he will eat meat offered to idols?* (difft. MargaretThrall, TU 102, '68, 468–72).—Of Paul's letters, by which δυνηθήσεσθε οἰκοδομεῖσθαι εἰς τὴν δοθεῖσαν ὑμῖν πίστιν *you will be able to build yourselves up in the faith that has been given you* Pol 3:2.—HCremer, Über den bibl. Begriff der Erbauung 1863; HScott, The Place of οἰκοδομή in the NT: PT 2, 1904, 402–24; HBassermann, Über den Begriff 'Erbauung': Zeitschr. für prakt. Theol. 4 1882, 1–22; CTrossen, Erbauen: ThGl 6, 1914, 804ff; PVielhauer, Oikodome (d. Bild vom Bau vom NT bis Clem. Alex.), diss. Hdlbg. '39; PBonnard, Jésus-Christ édifiant son Église '48.—B. 590. DELG s.v. δέμω. M-M. TW. Sv.

οἰκοδομή, ῆς, ἡ (οἶκος, δέμω 'build'; rejected by the Atticists [Lob., Phryn. 421; 487ff; WSchmid, Der Attizismus III 1893, 248], but found since Aristot., EN 5, 14, 7; Diod. S. 1, 46, 4; Plut., Lucull. 518 [39, 2]; IG XIV, 645, 146 [Dorian]; OGI 655, 2 [25 BC]; PGrenf I, 21, 17 [126 BC]; BGU 699, 3; 894, 2; LXX; En; TestSol; Philo, Mos. 1, 224 v.l., Spec. Leg. 1, 73 v.l.; Joseph. [Schmidt 528f]; Just., D. 86, 6).

❶ **process of building, *building, construction*—ⓐ** lit. (2 Ch 3:2 v.l.; Sir 40:19; Jos., Ant. 11, 59; ViHg 1 [p. 87, 18 Sch.]; Jos., Ant. 11, 59; Theoph. Ant. 3, 22 [p. 246, 24]; Did., Gen. 33, 27) ἐτελέσθη ἡ οἰκοδομή *the construction was at an end* Hs 9, 5, 1a. ἀνοχὴ τῆς οἰκ. *a delay in the building* ibid. b; 9, 14, 2. Hv 3, 2, 8 prob. belongs in 2a.

ⓑ fig., of spiritual strengthening (s. οἰκοδομέω 3) *edifying, edification, building up.*

α. act., w. obj. gen. πρὸς τὴν οἰκ. τῆς ἐκκλησίας *for the building up of the church* **1 Cor 14:12.** ὑπὲρ τῆς ὑμῶν οἰκ. **2 Cor 12:19.** Abs. πρὸς οἰκοδομήν *for edification* **Ro 15:2; 1 Cor 14:26;** cp. **Eph 4:29** (Straub 36). Paul has received his authority fr. the Lord εἰς οἰκοδομὴν καὶ οὐκ εἰς καθαίρεσιν **2 Cor 13:10;** cp. **10:8.** τὰ τῆς οἰκ. τῆς εἰς ἀλλήλους *what makes for the edification of each other* **Ro 14:19.** The letters of

Ignatius contain πᾶσαν οἰκοδομήν Pol 13:2. Abstr. for concr. ὁ προφητεύων λαλεῖ οἰκοδομήν *the one who prophesies speaks words that edify* **1 Cor 14:3.**

β. pass. οἰκοδομὴν λαβεῖν *receive edification, be edified* **1 Cor 14:5.** εἰς οἰκ. τ. σώματος τ. Χριστοῦ *that the body of Christ might be built up* **Eph 4:12.** εἰς οἰκ. ἑαυτοῦ *for its own edification* vs. **16** (for the grammar cp. TestJob 11:5 εἰς οἰκονομίαν τῶν πτωχῶν).

❷ a building as result of a construction process, *building, edifice*—ⓐ lit.; pl., of secular buildings (Diod. S. 16, 76, 2; 20, 8, 3) Hs 1:1 (w. ἀγροί, παρατάξεις, οἰκήματα); GJs 9:3; 13:1. Esp. of temple buildings (1 Esdr 5:70) εἰς τὴν οἰκ. ἐλπίζειν *put one's hope in the building alone* B 16:1. Pl. of various buildings in the temple area **Mk 13:1f.** αἱ οἰκοδομαὶ τοῦ ἱεροῦ **Mt 24:1.** Esp. freq. in the imagery of the tower in Hermas (v 3; s 9). Yet in many pass. mng. 1a is also prob.: ἡ οἰκ. τοῦ πύργου *the tower building* (or *the building of the tower*) Hv 3, 2, 6b; 3, 4, 1f; 3, 5, 1b; 3, 12, 3; s 9, 1, 2; 9, 3, 3; 9, 4, 2ff; 9, 5, 2; 9, 17, 4 al. τὰ ἐξώτερα μέρη τῆς οἰκ. *the outside of the building* s 9, 9, 3b. Of the stones: εὔχρηστοι εἰς (τὴν) οἰκ. v 3, 5, 5; 3, 6, 1; 6; also εὔχρηστοι τῇ οἰκ. s 9, 15, 6. χρήσιμοι εἰς τὴν οἰκ. τοῦ πύργου v 4, 3, 4. ἀπενεχθῆναι εἰς τὴν οἰκ. s 9, 8, 3a. ἀπέρχεσθαι εἰς τὴν οἰκ. s 9, 5, 3f; 9, 7, 4a; 6f; 9, 10, 2. ἀποβάλλεσθαι ἐκ (ἀπὸ) τῆς οἰκ. s 9, 7, 1; 9, 8, 3b; 9, 9, 5. ἀποδοκιμάζειν ἐκ τῆς οἰκ. s 9, 12, 7; pass. (without ἐκ) 9, 23, 3; ἁρμόζειν εἰς τὴν οἰκ. v 3, 6, 5; 3, 7, 5; pass. s 9, 4, 3; 9, 8, 5ff; 9, 9, 4; 9, 15, 4. βάλλειν εἰς τὴν οἰκ. s 9, 7, 4; 6; 9, 8, 2a; pass. 9, 7, 5; 9, 10, 1; 9, 30, 2. δοκιμάζειν τὴν οἰκ. s 9, 5, 2b. εἰσέρχεσθαι εἰς τὴν οἰκ. s 9, 12, 4; 9, 13, 4. ἐκλέγεσθαι εἰς τὴν οἰκ. s 9, 9, 3a. ἐπιδιδόναι εἰς τὴν οἰκ. s 9, 4, 5; 8; 9, 15, 5; pass. 9, 4, 6. ἐπιθυμεῖν τὴν οἰκ. s 9, 9, 7. ἐπιτίθεσθαι εἰς τὴν οἰκ. v 3, 5, 2. ἐργάζεσθαι εἰς τὴν οἰκ. *work at the building* s 9, 6, 2b. εὑρεθῆναι εἰς τὴν οἰκ. s 9, 6, 4. ὁ ἐφεστὼς εἰς τὴν οἰκ. s 9, 6, 2a. κατανοεῖν τὴν οἰκ. *examine the building* s 9, 5, 7; 9, 6, 3. συναρμόζεσθαι εἰς τὴν οἰκ. τοῦ πύργου s 9, 16, 7. τιθέναι εἰς τὴν οἰκ. v 3, 2, 6a; 7; s 9, 7, 2; 9, 8, 2b; pass. v 3, 5, 4; s 9, 6, 8; 9, 8, 4; 9, 9, 2; 9, 13, 6; 9, 16, 1; 9, 17, 3; 9, 29, 4; 9, 30, 1. τίθεσθαι ἐκ τῆς οἰκ. s 9, 8, 1. ὑπάγειν εἰς τὴν οἰκ. v 3, 5, 1a; 3; 3, 6, 2; s 9, 3, 3f. χρᾶσθαι εἰς τὴν οἰκ. v 3, 2, 8.

ⓑ Hermas hesitates betw. the literal and nonliteral uses of οἰκ. but the fol. passages are quite nonliteral (οἱ τοῦ χριστιανισμοῦ Orig., C. Cels. 3, 28, 8): θεοῦ οἰκοδομή ἐστε *you are God's building* **1 Cor 3:9** (AFridrichsen [s. γεώργιον]; on the imagery Straub 85–88). In **Eph 2:21** the Christian community is called an οἰκοδομή, more definitely a ναὸς ἅγιος ἐν κυρίῳ that is erected on the foundation of the apostles and prophets w. Christ Jesus as cornerstone (HSchlier, Christus u. d. Kirche im Eph 1930).—Of Christians ὄντες λίθοι ναοῦ πατρὸς ἡτοιμασμένοι εἰς οἰκοδομὴν θεοῦ πατρός *since you are stones for the Father's temple, made ready for the building of God the Father* IEph 9:1.—Fig., in another way, of the glorified body of the departed Christian οἰκοδομὴν ἐκ θεοῦ ἔχομεν, οἰκίαν ἀχειροποίητον *we have a building fr. God, a house not made w. hands* **2 Cor 5:1; Rv 21:18 v.l.** (for ἐνδώμησις). S. on οἰκητήριον 2.—Lit. on οἰκοδομέω end.—DELG s.v. δέμω. M-M. EDNT. TW. Sv.

οἰκοδομητός, ή, όν (οἰκοδομή; Strabo 3, 3, 7; 8, 6, 2; Etym. Mag. p. 282, 46; 453, 33) ***built*** οἰκ. ναὸς διὰ χειρός *a temple built with hands* B 16:7.

οἰκοδομία, ας, ἡ (οἰκοδομέω; since Thu. 1, 93, 1; 2, 65, 2; Pla.; Polyb. 10, 22, 7; Plut., Pomp. 654 [66, 1]; Lucian, Hist. Conscr. 4; Jos., Ant. 11, 7; 118; SIG 144, 32 [IV BC]; 204, 26f al.; OGI 483, 104; 107; PHal 1, 181 [III BC]; PSI 500, 3; 4.—Lob., Phryn. p. 487) ***building,*** both as process and result, in our lit. only once as v.l., and in a fig. sense *edification* ἐκζητήσεις παρέχουσιν μᾶλλον ἢ οἰκοδομίαν θεοῦ **1 Ti 1:4 v.l.** (for οἰκονομίαν; D, Irenaeus et al. have οἰκοδομήν).—M-M.

οἰκοδόμος, ου, ὁ (οἶκος, δέμω 'build'; Hdt. et al.; Galen, Protr. 13 p. 42, 17, John [w. τέκτων]; Lucian, Icarom. 19; OGI 770, 7; pap, LXX; Jos., Ant. 7, 66 [w. τέκτων]) ***builder* Ac 4:11.**—DELG s.v. δέμω. M-M. TW.

οἰκονομέω (οἰκονόμος, fr. οἶκος + νέμω) pf. ptc. οἰκονομηκώς (on the mng. of οἰκ. and derivatives s. ARobinson on Eph 1:10)

❶ to manage a household, *manage, administer,* abs., hold the office of an οἰκονόμος (q.v. 1), *be manager* (Astrampsychus p. 8 Dec. 1, 9) **Lk 16:2.**

❷ to administrate achievement of a project, *manage, regulate, administer, plan* (Soph., Pla. et al.; ins, pap; 3 Macc 3:2; TestSol, EpArist, Iren.) τὶ *someth.* (Jos., Ant. 1, 19) of God (οἱ. τὰ τοῦ κόσμου πράγματα ὁ θεός Orig., C. Cels. 6, 79, 38; Did.) πάντα σὺν τῷ παιδὶ οἰκονομηκώς *after (God) had planned everything with the Son* Dg 9:1 (Maximus Tyr. 27, 8a ὁ θεὸς οἰκ. τὸ πᾶν τοῦτο; M. Ant. 5, 32; Philo, Decal. 53 [θεὸς] οἰκονομεῖ σωτηρίως ἀεὶ τὰ σύμπαντα)—New Doc 4, 144. DELG s.v. νέμω. M-M. TW. Spicq.

οἰκονομία, ας, ἡ (οἰκονομέω; X., Pla.+; ins., pap; Is 22:19, 21; TestJob, ParJer, Philo, Joseph.)

❶ responsibility of management, *management* of a household, *direction, office* (X., Oec. 1, 1; Herodian 6, 1, 1; Jos., Ant. 2, 89; PTebt 27, 21 [114 BC]; PLond III, 904, 25 p. 125 [104 AD]; Orig., C. Cels. 8, 57, 22).

ⓐ lit., of the work of an οἰκονόμος 'estate manager' **Lk 16:2–4** (this passage shows that it is not always poss. to draw a sharp distinction betw. the office itself and the activities associated w. it).—WPöhlmann, Der verlorene Sohn u. das Haus '93.

ⓑ Paul applies the idea of administration to the office of an apostle οἰκονομίαν πεπίστευμαι *I have been entrusted with a commission/task* **1 Cor 9:17** (cp. Theoph. Ant. 1, 11 [p. 82, 8]); ἀνθρωπίνων οἰκονομίαν μυστηρίων πεπίστευνται *they have been entrusted with the administration of merely human mysteries* Dg 7:1. Of a supervisor (bishop): ὃν πέμπει ὁ οἰκοδεσπότης εἰς ἰδίαν οἰκ. (οἰκ. ἰδίου οἴκου) *the one whom the master of the house sent to administer his own household* IEph 6:1. This is prob. also the place for κατὰ τὴν οἰκ. τοῦ θεοῦ τὴν δοθεῖσάν μοι εἰς ὑμᾶς *according to the divine office which has been granted to me for you* **Col 1:25,** as well as ἠκούσατε τὴν οἰκονομίαν τ. χάριτος τ. θεοῦ τῆς δοθείσης μοι εἰς ὑμᾶς *you have heard of the administration of God's grace that was granted to me for you* **Eph 3:2** (on the other hand, this latter vs. may be parallel to the usage in vs. **9;** s. 2b below).

❷ state of being arranged, *arrangement, order, plan* (X., Cyr. 5, 3, 25; Polyb. 4, 67, 9; 10, 16, 2; Diod. S. 1, 81, 3)**—ⓐ** ἡ τῆς σαρκὸς οἰκονομία of the *arrangement* or *structure* of the parts of the body beneath the skin; they are laid bare by scourging MPol 2:2.—(Iren. 5, 3, 2 [Harv. II, 326, 3]).

ⓑ of God's unique plan *private plan, plan of salvation,* i.e. *arrangements for redemption of humans* (in the pap of arrangements and directions of authorities: UPZ 162 IX, 2 [117 BC]; CPR 11, 26, and in PGM [e.g. 4, 293] of the measures by which one wishes to attain some goal by extrahuman help.—Just., D. 31, 1 τοῦ πάθους . . . οἰκ.; Hippol., Did.) ἡ οἰκ. τοῦ μυστηρίου *the plan of the mystery* **Eph 3:9** (v.l. κοινωνία; on the thought cp. vs. **2** and s. JReumann, NovT 3, '59, 282–92.—Just., D. 134, 2 οἰκονομίαι

. . . μυστηρίων). Also in the linguistically difficult passage **1:10** οἰκ. certainly refers to the *plan of salvation* which God is bringing to reality through Christ, in the fullness of the times. κατ' οἰκονομίαν θεοῦ *according to God's plan of redemption* IEph 18:2 (cp. Ath. 21, 4 κατὰ θείαν οἰκ.—Pl.: Iren. 1, 10, 1 [Harv. I 90, 8]) προσδηλώσω ὑμῖν ἧς ἠρξάμην οἰκονομίας εἰς τὸν καινὸν ἄνθρωπον Ἰησοῦν Χριστόν *I will explain to you further the divine plan which I began (to discuss), with reference to the new human being Jesus Christ* IEph 20:1. AcPl Ha 3, 23 of God's marvelous *plan = way of doing things;* 6, 26 ο̣ἰ̣κο̣ν̣[ομίαν πληρώσω κτλ.] *(so that I might carry out God's) plan for me;* pl. 5, 27 [ὡς καὶ ἐκεῖ τὰς τοῦ κυρίου οἰκο]νομίας πληρῶσε (=πληρῶσαι) *[Paul has gone off to carry out God's] purpose [also there]* (in Macedonia) (apparently a ref. to the various missionary assignments given by God to Paul; for the formulation cp. τὴν οἰκ. τελέσας Orig., C. Cels. 2, 65, 4).

ⓒ also of God's *arrangements* in nature pl. αἱ οἰκ. θεοῦ Dg 4:5 (cp. Tat. 12, 2; 18, 2 ὕλης οἰκ.; Did., Gen. 92, 6 πάντα ὑπὸ τὴν αὐτοῦ οἰκ. ἐστίν.—Of the order in creation Theoph. Ant. 2, 12 [p. 130, 2]).

❸ **program of instruction, *training*** (in the way of salvation); this mng. (found also Clem. Alex., Paed. 1, 8, 69, 3; 70, 1 p. 130 St.) seems to fit best in **1 Ti 1:4,** where it is said of the erroneous teachings of certain persons ἐκζητήσεις παρέχουσιν μᾶλλον ἢ οἰκονομίαν θεοῦ τὴν ἐν πίστει *they promote useless speculations rather than divine training that is in faith* (οἰκοδομήν and οἰκοδομίαν [q.v.] as vv.ll. are simply 'corrections' to alleviate the difficulty). If οἰκ. is to be taken in the sense of 1b above, the thought of the verse would be somewhat as follows: 'endless speculative inquiry merely brings about contention instead of the realization of God's purpose which has to do with faith.'—OLillger, Das patristische Wort, diss. Erlangen '55; JReumann, The Use of OIKONOMIA and Related Terms etc., diss. U. of Pennsylvania '57.—DELG s.v. νέμω. M-M. EDNT. TW. Spicq. Sv.

οἰκονόμος, ου, ὁ (οἶκος, νέμω 'manage'; Aeschyl.+; ins, pap, LXX; TestJos 12:3 [mss. bdg]; ParJer 7:2; Philo, Praem. 113; Joseph.; Just.. D. 125, 2; Tat.; loanw. in rabb.)

❶ **manager of a household or estate, *(house) steward, manager*** (Diod. S. 36, 5, 1) ὁ πιστὸς οἰκ. ὁ φρόνιμος **Lk 12:42.** Sim. ζητεῖται ἐν τοῖς οἰκ. ἵνα πιστός τις εὑρεθῇ **1 Cor 4:2.** He manages his master's property (cp. Jos., Ant. 12, 200; Artem. 4, 28. The οἰκ. of various persons are mentioned in the pap: PTebt 402, 1; POxy 929, 25; οἰκ. of female employers, s. New Docs, end of entry) **Lk 16:1, 3.** ὁ οἰκ. τῆς ἀδικίας *the dishonest manager* (cp. Lucian, Ep. Sat. 2, 26 ὁ οἰκ. ὑφελόμενος; ÉDelebecque, Études grecques sur l'Évangile de Luc '76, 89–97) vs. **8** (s. on the 'unjust steward' Jülicher, Gleichn. 495–514; LFonck, D. Parabel[3] 1919 [lit. here 675f]; ARücker, Bibl. Studien XVII/5, 1912; JKögel, BFCT XVIII/6, 1914; ERiggenbach, Schlatter Festschr. 1922, 17ff; FTillmann, BZ 9, 1911, 171–84; GKrüger, ibid. 21, '33, 170–81; FHüttermann, ThGl 27, '35, 739–42; HPreisker, TLZ 74, '49, 85–92; JJeremias, Gleichnisse Jes[2] '52, 30–33; JDerrett, Law in the NT, '70, 48–77; DFletcher, JBL 82, '63, 15–30; JFitzmyer, Theological Studies 25, '64, 23–42; DIreland, Stewardship and the Kingdom of God: An Historical, Exegetical, and Contextual Study of the Parable of the Unjust Steward in Luke 16:1–3 '92). With ἐπίτροπος **Gal 4:2** (SBelkin, JBL 54, '35, 52–55).

❷ **public treasurer, *treasurer*** ὁ οἰκ. τῆς πόλεως *the city treasurer* (SIG 1252 πόλεως Κῴων οἰκονόμος; other exx. in PLandvogt, Epigr. Untersuchungen üb. den οἰκονόμος, diss. Strassb. 1908; HCadbury, JBL 50, '31, 47ff) **Ro 16:23.**

❸ **one who is entrusted with management in connection with transcendent matters, *administrator*** (Aristot., Rhet. 3, 3 p. 1406a, 27 οἰκ. τῆς τῶν ἀκουόντων ἡδονῆς; Tat. 9, 3 τῆς εἱμαρμένης οἰκ.) of the administrators of divine things (Βαροὺχ ὁ οἰκ. τῆς πίστεως ParJer 7:2; of an office in the Serapeum UPZ 56, 7 [160 BC]; religious associations also had οἰκ.: OGI 50, 12; 51, 26): the apostles are οἰκονόμοι μυστηρίων θεοῦ *administrators of God's secret counsels/plans* **1 Cor 4:1.** So the overseer of a Christian community must conduct himself as a θεοῦ οἰκ. **Tit 1:7.** But Christians gener. are also θεοῦ οἰκ. (καὶ πάρεδροι καὶ ὑπηρέται) IPol 6:1 or καλοὶ οἰκ. ποικίλης χάριτος θεοῦ *good administrators of God's varied grace* **1 Pt 4:10** (cp. X., Mem. 3, 4, 7 οἱ ἀγαθοὶ οἰκ.).—JReumann, JBL 77, '58, 339–49 (pre-Christian), 'Jesus the Steward', TU 103, '68, 21–29.—New Docs 4, 160f. DELG s.v. νέμω. M-M. EDNT. TW. Spicq. Sv.

οἶκος, ου, ὁ (Hom.+)—❶ ***house***—ⓐ lit.—α. *a dwelling* **Lk 11:17** (cp. πίπτω 1bβ); **12:39; 14:23** (unless οἶκ. means *dining room* here as Phryn. Com. [V BC] 66 Kock; X., Symp. 2, 18; Athen. 12, 54a); **Ac 2:2;** (w. ἀγροί, κτήματα) Hs 1:9. εἰς τὸν οἶκόν τινος *into* or *to someone's house* (Judg 18:26) ἀπέρχεσθαι **Mt 9:7; Mk 7:30; Lk 1:23; 5:25;** εἰσέρχεσθαι **Lk 1:40; 7:36; 8:41; Ac 11:12; 16:15b;** ἔρχεσθαι **Mk 5:38;** καταβαίνειν **Lk 18:14;** πορεύεσθαι **5:24;** ὑπάγειν **Mt 9:6; Mk 2:11; 5:19;** ὑποστρέφειν **Lk 1:56; 8:39.**—κατοικεῖν εἰς τὸν οἶκόν τινος *live in someone's house* Hm 4, 4, 3; s 9, 1, 3. οἱ εἰς τὸν οἶκόν μου *the members of my household* **Lk 9:61.** εἰς τὸν . . . οἶκον ἐγένετο χαρά AcPl Ha 6, 2.—εἰς τὸν οἶκον *into the house; home:* ἀνάγειν **Ac 16:34.** ἀπέρχεσθαι Hs 9, 11, 2. ἔρχεσθαι **Lk 15:6.** ὑπάγειν Hs 9, 11, 6. ὑποστρέφειν **Lk 7:10.**—εἰς τὸν οἶκον (w. ὑποδέχεσθαι) **Lk 10:38 v.l.** (s. οἰκία 1a).—εἰς οἶκόν τινος *to someone's house/home* **Mk 8:3, 26.** εἰς οἶκόν τινος τῶν ἀρχόντων **Lk 14:1** (on the absence of the art. s. B-D-F §259, 1; Rob. 792).—εἰς οἶκον *home* (Aeschyl., Soph.; Diod. S. 4, 2, 1): εἰσέρχεσθαι **Mk 7:17; 9:28.** ἔρχεσθαι **3:20.**—ἐκ τοῦ οἴκου ἐκείνου **Ac 19:16.**—ἐν τῷ οἴκῳ τινός *in someone's house* **Ac 7:20; 10:30; 11:13;** Hs 6, 1, 1.—ἐν τῷ οἴκῳ *in the house, at home* **J 11:20;** Hv 5:1.—ἐν οἴκῳ *at home* (Strabo 13, 1, 38; UPZ 59, 5 [168 BC]; 74, 6; POxy 531, 3 [II AD]; 1 Km 19:9) **Mk 2:1** (Goodsp., Probs. 52); **1 Cor 11:34; 14:35.**—κατὰ τοὺς οἴκους εἰσπορεύεσθαι *enter house after house* **Ac 8:3.** κατ' οἴκους (opp. δημοσίᾳ) *from house to house* i.e. in private **20:20.** In the sing. κατ' οἶκον (opp. ἐν τῷ ἱερῷ) *in the various private homes* (Jos., Ant. 4, 74; 163.—Diod. S. 17, 28, 4 κατ' οἰκίαν ἀπολαύσαντες τῶν βρωτῶν=having enjoyed the food in their individual homes) **2:46; 5:42.** ἡ κατ' οἶκόν τινος ἐκκλησία *the church in someone's house* **Ro 16:5; 1 Cor 16:19; Col 4:15; Phlm 2** (s. ἐκκλησία 3bα; EJudge, The Social Pattern of Christian Groups in the First Century '60; LWhite, House Churches: OEANE III 118–21 [lit.]). τὰ κατὰ τὸν οἶκον *household affairs* (Lucian, Abdic. 22) 1 Cl 1:3.

β. *house* of any large building οἶκος τοῦ βασιλέως *the king's palace* (Ael. Aristid. 32, 12 K.=12 p. 138 D.; 2 Km 11:8; 15:35; 3 Km 7:31; Jos., Ant. 9, 102) **Mt 11:8.** οἶκος ἐμπορίου (s. ἐμπόριον) **J 2:16b.** οἶκος προσευχῆς *house of prayer* **Mt 21:13; Mk 11:17; Lk 19:46** (all three Is 56:7). οἶκ. φυλακῆς *prison-house* B 14:7 (Is 42:7).—Esp. of *God's house* (Herodas 1, 26 οἶκος τῆς θεοῦ [of Aphrodite]; IKosPH 8, 4 οἶκος τῶν θεῶν.—οἶκ. in ref. to temples as early as Eur., Phoen. 1372; Hdt. 8, 143; Pla., Phdr. 24e; ins [cp. SIG ind. IV οἶκος d; Thieme 31]; UPZ 79, 4 [II BC] ἐν τῷ οἴκῳ τῷ Ἄμμωνος; POxy 1380, 3 [II AD]; LXX; New Docs 1, 6f; 31; 139) οἶκος τοῦ θεοῦ (Jos., Bell. 4, 281) **Mt 12:4; Mk 2:26; Lk 6:4.** Of the temple in Jerusalem (3 Km 7:31 ὁ οἶκος κυρίου; Just., D. 86, 6 al.) ὁ οἶκός μου

Mt 21:13; Mk 11:17; Lk 19:46 (all three Is 56:7). ὁ οἶκ. τοῦ πατρός μου **J 2:16a;** cp. **Ac 7:47, 49** (Is 66:1). Specif. of the temple building (Eupolem.: 723 fgm 2, 12 Jac. [in Eus., PE 9, 34, 14]; EpArist 88; 101) μεταξὺ τοῦ θυσιαστηρίου καὶ τοῦ οἴκου *between the altar and the temple building* **Lk 11:51.** Of the heavenly sanctuary, in which Christ functions as high priest **Hb 10:21** (sense bα is preferred by some here).

γ. in a wider sense οἶκ. occasionally amounts to *city* (cp. the note on POxy 126, 4.—Jer 22:5; 12:7; TestLevi 10, 5 οἶκος . . . Ἰερουσ. κληθήσεται) **Mt 23:38; Lk 13:35.**

ⓑ fig. (Philo, Cher. 52 ὦ ψυχή, δέον ἐν οἴκῳ θεοῦ παρθενεύεσθαι al.)

α. of the Christian community as the spiritual temple of God ὡς λίθοι ζῶντες οἰκοδομεῖσθε οἶκος πνευματικός *as living stones let yourselves be built up into a spiritual house* **1 Pt 2:5** (ESelwyn, 1 Pt '46, 286–91; JHElliott (s. end) 200–208). The tower, which Hermas uses as a symbol of the Christian community, is also called ὁ οἶκ. τοῦ θεοῦ: ἀποβάλλεσθαι ἀπὸ τοῦ οἴκ. τοῦ θ. Hs 9, 13, 9. Opp. εἰσέρχεσθαι εἰς τὸν οἶκ. τοῦ θεοῦ 9, 14, 1.—The foll. pass. are more difficult to classify; mng. 2 (the Christians as God's family) is poss.: ὁ οἶκ. τοῦ θεοῦ **1 Pt 4:17;** ἐν οἴκῳ θεοῦ ἀναστρέφεσθαι ἥτις ἐστὶν ἐκκλησία θεοῦ ζῶντος **1 Ti 3:15.**

β. *dwelling, habitation,* of the human body (Just., D. 40, 1 τὸ πλάσμα . . . οἶκ. ἐγένετο τοῦ ἐμφυσήματος; Mel., P. 55, 402 τοῦ σαρκίνου οἴκου; Lucian, Gall. 17) as a habitation of hostile spirits **Mt 12:44; Lk 11:24.** Corresp. the gentiles are called an οἶκ. δαιμονίων B 16:7.

❷ ***household, family*** (Hom. et al.; Artem. 2, 68 p. 161, 11 μετὰ ὅλου τοῦ οἴκου; Ath. 3, 2 τὸν ὑμέτερον οἶκον) **Lk 10:5; 19:9; Ac 10:2; 11:14; 16:31; 18:8.** ὅλους οἴκους ἀνατρέπειν *ruin whole families* **Tit 1:11** (cp. Gen 47:12 πᾶς ὁ οἶκος='the whole household'). ὁ Στεφανᾶ οἶκ. *Stephanas and his family* **1 Cor 1:16;** ὁ Ὀνησιφόρου οἶκ. **2 Ti 1:16; 4:19.** ὁ οἶκ. Ταουΐας ISm 13:2. Esp. freq. in Hermas: τὰ ἁμαρτήματα ὅλου τοῦ οἴκου σου *the sins of your whole family* Hv 1, 1, 9; cp. 1, 3, 1; 2, 3, 1; s 7:2. . . . σε καὶ τὸν οἶκ. σου v 1, 3, 2; cp. m 2:7; 5, 1, 7; s 7:5ff. W. τέκνα m 12, 3, 6; s 5, 3, 9. Cp. **1 Ti 3:4, 12** (on the subj. matter, Ocellus Luc. 47 τοὺς ἰδίους οἴκους κατὰ τρόπον οἰκονομήσουσι; Letter 58 of Apollonius of Tyana [Philostrat. I 362, 3]). ἡ τοῦ Ἐπιτρόπου σὺν ὅλῳ τῷ οἴκῳ αὐτῆς καὶ τῶν τέκνων *the* (widow) *of Epitropus together with all her household and that of her children* IPol 8:2 (Sb 7912 [ins 136 AD] σὺν τῷ παντὶ οἴκῳ). ἀσπάζομαι τοὺς οἴκους τῶν ἀδελφῶν μου σὺν γυναιξὶ καὶ τέκνοις *I greet the households of my brothers (in the faith), including their wives and children* ISm 13:1. In a passage showing the influence of Num 12:7, **Hb 3:2–6** contrasts the οἶκος of which Moses was a member and the οἶκος over which Christ presides (cp. SIG 22, 16f οἶκος βασιλέως; Thu 1, 129, 3 Xerxes to one ἐν ἡμετέρῳ οἴκῳ; sim. οἶκος of Augustus IGR I, 1109 [4 BC], cp. IV, 39b, 26 [27 BC]; s. MFlory, TAPA 126, '96, 292 n. 20). Hence the words of vs. **6** οὗ (i.e. Χριστοῦ) οἶκός ἐσμεν ἡμεῖς *whose household we are.*—On Christians as God's family s. also 1bα above. τοῦ ἰδίου οἴκ. προστῆναι *manage one's own household* **1 Ti 3:4f;** cp. vs. **12** and **5:4.**—On management of an οἶκος s. X., Oeconomicus. On the general topic of family MRaepsaet-Charlier, La femme, la famille, la parenté à Rome: L'Antiquité Classique 62, '93, 247–53.

❸ **a whole clan or tribe of people descended fr. a common ancestor, *house=descendants, nation,*** transf. sense fr. that of a single family (Appian, Bell. Civ. 2, 127 §531 οἶκοι μεγάλοι=famous families [of Caesar's assassins]; Dionys. Byz. 53 p. 23, 1; LXX; Jos., Ant. 2, 202; 8, 111; SibOr 3, 167) ὁ οἶκ. Δαυίδ (3 Km 12:19; 13:2) **Lk 1:27, 69** (on the probability of Semitic inscriptional evidence for the phrase 'house of David' s. articles pro and con in BAR 20/2, '94, 26–39; 20/3, '94, 30–37; 20/4, '94, 54f; 20/6, '94, 47; 21/2, '95, 78f). ἐξ οἴκου καὶ πατριᾶς Δ. **2:4.**—οἶκ. Ἰσραήλ **Mt 10:6; 15:24; Ac 2:36; 7:42** (Am 5:25); **Hb 8:10** (Jer 38:33); 1 Cl 8:3 (quot. of unknown orig.). AcPlCor 2:10. πᾶς οἶκ. Ἰσραήλ GJs 7:3 (Jer 9:25). ὁ οἶκ. Ἰσ. combined w. ὁ οἶκ. Ἰούδα **Hb 8:8** (Jer 38:31). οἶκ. Ἰακώβ (Ex 19:3; Is 2:5; Just., A I, 53, 4;, D. 135, 6) **Lk 1:33; Ac 7:46.** οἶκ. τοῦ Ἀμαλήκ B 12:9.

❹ **a house and what is in it, *property, possessions, estate*** (Hom. et al.; s. also Hdt. 3, 53; Isaeus 7, 42; Pla., Lach. 185a; X., Oec. 1, 5; Demetr.: 722 fgm. 1, 15 Jac.; Jos., Bell. 6, 282; Just., D. 139, 4) ἐπ' Αἴγυπτον καὶ ὅλον τὸν οἶκον αὐτοῦ *over Egypt and over all his estate* **Ac 7:10** (cp. Gen 41:40; Artem. 4, 61 προέστη τοῦ παντὸς οἴκου).—S. the lit. on infant baptism, e.g. GDelling, Zur Taufe von 'Häusern' im Urchrist., NovT 7, '65, 285–311=Studien zum NT '70, 288–310.— JHElliott, A Home for the Homeless '81. B. 133; 458. Schmidt, Syn. II 508–26. DELG. M-M. EDNT. TW. Sv.

οἰκουμένη, ης, ἡ (the pres. fem. part. pass. of οἰκέω; sc. γῆ. Hdt.+; loanw. in rabb.).

❶ **the earth as inhabited area, exclusive of the heavens above and nether regions, *the inhabited earth, the world*** (Ps 23:1 and often; Iren., Orig., Hippol., Did., Theoph. Ant.): πάσας τ. βασιλείας τ. οἰκουμένης **Lk 4:5.** Cp. **21:26; Ro 10:18** (Ps 18:5); **Hb 1:6** (but s. FSchierse, Verheissung u. Heilsvollendung '55: 'heavenly realm'). ὅλη ἡ οἰκ. *the whole inhabited earth* (Diod. S. 12, 2, 1 καθ' ὅλην τὴν οἰκουμένην; EpArist 37.—Diod. S. 3, 64, 6 and Jos., Bell. 7, 43 πᾶσα ἡ οἰκ.) **Mt 24:14; Ac 11:28; Rv 3:10; 16:14;** GJs 4:1. W. πᾶσα as qualifier AcPl Ha 9, 5. οἱ κατὰ τὴν οἰκ. ἄνθρωποι PtK 15:20. αἱ κατὰ τὴν οἰκ. ἐκκλησίαι *the congregations throughout the world* MPol 5:1; cp. 8:1; 19:2.

❷ **the world as administrative unit, *the Roman Empire*** (in the hyperbolic diction commonly used in ref. to emperors, the Rom. Emp. equalled the whole world [as e.g. Xerxes' empire: Ael. Aristid. 54 p. 675 D., and of Cyrus: Jos., Ant. 11, 3]: OGI 666, 4; 668, 5 τῷ σωτῆρι κ. εὐεργέτῃ τῆς οἰκουμένης [Nero]; 669, 10; SIG 906 A, 3f τὸν πάσης οἰκουμένης δεσπότην [Julian]; cp. Artapanus: 726 fgm. 3, 22 Jac., in Eus., PE 9, 27, 22: God as ὁ τῆς οἰκ. δεσπότης; POxy 1021, 5ff; Sb 176, 2.—Cp. 1 Esdr 2:2; Philo, Leg. ad Gai. 16; Jos., Bell. 4, 656, Ant. 19, 193; Just., A I, 27, 2; Ath. 1, 1)

ⓐ as such **Ac 24:5** (as Jos., Ant. 12, 48 πᾶσι τοῖς κατὰ τὴν οἰκουμένην Ἰουδαίοις, except that οἰκ. here is used in the sense of 1 above as surface area. Cp. PLond VI, 1912, 100).

ⓑ its inhabitants **17:6.**—GAalders, Het Romeinsche Imperium en het NT '38.

❸ all inhabitants of the earth, fig. extension of 1 (cp. γῆ) : *world, humankind* **Ac 17:31** (cp. Ps 9:9; Artapanus: 726 fgm. 3:22 Jac., God as ὁ τῆς οἰκ. δεσπότης); **19:27.** Of Satan: ὁ πλανῶν τὴν οἰκ. ὅλην *who deceives all humankind* **Rv 12:9.** The passage ἐξῆλθεν δόγμα παρὰ Καίσαρος Αὐγούστου ἀπογράφεσθαι πᾶσαν τὴν οἰκουμένην (cp. κόσμον . . . πάντα LBW II, 1192, 6) **Lk 2:1** belongs here also. For the evangelist considers it of great importance that the birth of the world's savior coincided w. another event that also affected every person in the 'world'. But it can also be said of Augustus that he ruled the οἰκ., because the word is used also in the sense of 2 above. For connection of the birth of a ruler with the fortunes of humanity s. IPriene 105, 4–11 on the significance of the birth of Caesar Augustus.

❹ an extraordinary use: τὴν οἰκ. ἔκτισας 1 Cl 60:1, where οἰκ. seems to mean *the* whole *world* (so far as living beings inhabit it, therefore the realm of transcendent beings as well). S. Johnston s.v. κόσμος.—Also ἡ οἰκ. ἡ μέλλουσα **Hb 2:5**=ὁ μέλλων αἰών (6:5); JMeier, Biblica 66, '85, 504–33; s. αἰών 2b.—JKaerst, Die antike Idee der Oekumene 1903; JVogt, Orbis terrarum 1929; MPaeslack, Theologia Viatorum II, '50, 33–47.—GHusson, OIKIA: Le vocabulaire de la maison privée en Égypte d'après les papyrus Grecs '83; Pauly-W. XVII 2123–74; Kl. Pauly IV 254–56; B. 13.—DELG s.v. οἶκος C. M-M. EDNT. TW. Sv.

οἰκουργέω (οἰκουργός) **to carry out responsibilities in a household, *be domestic, tend to things in the house*** τὰ κατὰ τὸν οἶκον οἰκ. *fulfill one's household responsibilities* 1 Cl 1:3 (trag., et al. use the verb οἰκουρεῖν, which the Jerus. ms. restores by erasure in Clement's text). Not to be equated with οἰκοδεσποτέω 'manage a household' 1 Ti 5:14 (s. the distinction between οἰκουρός and οἰκονόμος Cass. Dio 56, 3 [s. next entry]). Both the Semitic and Hellenic ideal was for women to remain at home and discharge domestic duties. Appropriate to the role of a respectable woman was observance of οἰκουρίαν καὶ τὸν σέμνον βίον 'tending to things at home and leading a sedate life' Alciphron 3, 22 [58]; in the OT, contrast the 'virtuous' woman who is busy at home Pr 31 and the 'loose' woman who does not remain at home 7:11.—S. DELG s.v. ἔργον I 2 p. 364. M-M. s.v. -ός; Field, Notes, 220–21.

οἰκουργός, όν (οἶκος, ἔργον; for οἰκουρός Aristoph. et al.; the form w. γ is found elsewh. only in Soranus p. 18, 2 v.l. [for οἰκουρός]: οἰκουργὸν καὶ καθέδριον διάγειν βίον) **pert. to carrying out household responsibilities, *busy at home, carrying out household duties,*** of women **Tit 2:5** (cp. Philo, Exsecr. 139 σώφρονας κ. οἰκουροὺς κ. φιλάνδρους; Cass. Dio 56, 3). S. the preceding entry; also Field, Notes, 220–22 and foll. entry.—S. DELG s.v. ἔργον I 2 p. 364. M-M.

οἰκουρός, όν (οἶκος, οὖρος 'watcher, guardian'; Aeschyl. et al.; PGM 11a, 11; Philo, Rer. Div. Her. 186) ***staying at home, domestic*** **Tit 2:5** t.r. (s. οἰκουργέω and οἰκουργός for lit.).—DELG s.v. ὁράω.

οἰκοφθόρος, ον (οἶκος, φθείρω; Eur., Pla.; Philo, Agr. 73; SibOr 2, 257; Suda s.v. Ἰλάριος refers οἰκ. to an act of adultery that destroys a household; cp. Plut., Mor. 12b γυναικῶν οἰκοφθορίαι γαμετῶν 'seducers of married women') **pert. to being a cause of corruption in a household, *destroyer of houses or families,*** as subst. IEph 16:1. The fate of the seducers (Hesych. completes the equation οἰκοφθόρος = μοιχός) serves as a premise in an argument from the lesser to the greater: 'The argument is that if such adulterers perished, how much more those who corrupt faith by their evil teaching.' WSchoedel, Ignatius of Antioch '85, 79.—WBauer concluded that the term was used specif. (citing connection with the imagery of IEph 15:3; s. οἶκος 1aβ) in the sense of *temple-destroyer,* arguing that since Ign. is 'plainly dependent' on 1 Cor 6 (vs. 19; cp. also 1 Cor 3:16f) here, he is prob. thinking of the introduction of immorality as the particular means of destruction; in support Bauer compares Plut., Mor. (s. above) and PGrenf I, 53, 19f.—DELG s.v. φθείρω.

οἰκτείρω (οἶκτος 'pity') s. οἰκτίρω the Attic form (B-D-F §23; 101; W-S. §5, 13a and 15; Mlt-H. 78; 250; 402; Kühner-Bl. II 498; Meisterhans[3]-Schw. 179).—DELG s.v. οἶκτος.

οἰκτιρμός, οῦ, ὁ (οἰκτείρω; Pind., Pyth. 1, 85 [164]; PCairMasp 7, 19 [VI AD]; LXX) rarely in sing. (which is not common in the LXX) **display of concern over another's misfortune, *pity, mercy, compassion*** ἐνδύσασθαι σπλάγχνα οἰκτιρμοῦ (gen. of quality) *put on heartfelt compassion* **Col 3:12.** Almost always pl., partly to express the concrete forms of expression taken by the abstract concept (B-D-F §142; cp. Rob. 408), but more oft. without any difference fr. the sing., due to the influence of the Hebr. pl. רַחֲמִים (2 Km 24:14; Ps 24:6; Is 63:15; TestJos 2:3). Quite gener. χωρὶς οἰκτιρμῶν *without pity* **Hb 10:28.**—Of humans: w. σπλάγχνα (hendiadys) **Phil 2:1.** ἡ . . . μετ' οἰκτιρμῶν μνεία *remembrance with compassion* 1 Cl 56:1.—Of God (Ps 24:6; 39:12; Ps.-Clem., Hom. 3, 29) οἰκ. τοῦ θεοῦ **Ro 12:1.** τὸ πλῆθος τῶν οἰκ. σου *your abundant mercy* 1 Cl 18:2 (Ps 50:3). ἐπιστρέφειν ἐπὶ τοὺς οἰκ. αὐτοῦ *turn to his (God's) compassion* 9:1. προσφεύγειν τοῖς οἰκ. αὐτοῦ *take refuge in his (God's) mercies* 20:11. God as πατὴρ τῶν οἰκ. *merciful Father* **2 Cor 1:3** (s. B-D-F §165; Mlt-H. 440f).—DELG s.v. οἶκτος. M-M. TW.

οἰκτίρμων, ον (οἰκτείρω; Gorgias, Palam. 32 Blass; Theocr. 15, 75; Anth. Pal. 7, 359, 1; Sb 3923 οἰκτείρμων; LXX; TestJud 19:3; JosAs ch. 11 cod. A [p. 54, 7 Bat.]; Anth. Pal. 364) **pert. to being concerned about another's unfortunate state or misery, *merciful, compassionate*** of God (so almost always LXX and, in addition, always combined w. ἐλεήμων; Did., Gen. 83, 5 οἰκ. θεός; w. ἀγαθός and χρηστός Theoph. Ant. 1, 3 [p. 62, 23]) w. πολύσπλαγχνος **Js 5:11.** W. εὐεργετικός 1 Cl 23:1. W. ἐλεήμων 60:1.—Of humans also (Memnon Hist. [I BC/I AD]: 434 fgm. 1, 3, 2 Jac.; Ps 108:12; La 4:10) **Lk 6:36.**—DELG s.v. οἶκτος. TW.

οἰκτίρω fut. οἰκτιρήσω; aor. 2 sg. οἰκτίρησας Ps 59:3; aor. inf.: οἰκτιρῆσαι Ps 76:10; 3 Macc 5:51 (Hom. et al.; ins; pseudepigr.; Ps.-Phoc. 25; Philo, Migr. Abr. 122; Jos., Bell. 4, 384; 5, 418, Ant. 7, 153; 14, 354; for the spelling s. on οἰκτείρω) only in one pass. in our lit., a quot. ***have compassion*** τινά *on someone* (Pla., Laws 2, 1, 653c θεοὶ οἰκτείραντες τὸ τῶν ἀνθρώπων γένος; Epict. 4, 6, 21; Appian, Bell. Civ. 4, 22 §89; Lucian, Tim. 42, Dial. Mort. 28, 2; Ezk. Trag. 125 [in Eus., PE 9, 29, 11]; TestAsh 2:2) **Ro 9:15** (Ex 33:19.—οἰκτίρω of the deity Cypris: Apollon. Rhod. 4, 917; beside ἐλεέω Pla., Euthyd. 288d).—DELG s.v. οἶκτος. TW.

οἶμαι s. οἴομαι.

οἴμοι (=οἴ μοι; since Theognis, trag., Aristoph., also LXX; ins [on gravestones Renehan '75, 1148]; TestSol; TestAbr B 10 p. 115, 9 [Stone p. 78]; ApcEsdr 6:24 p. 32, 3 Tdf. and 7:4 p. 32, 14 Tdf. [both οἴμμοι]; ApcMos 10; ApcrEzk [Epiph. 70, 13]; Schwyzer II 601) *woe is me* GJs (3:1–3 [6 times]).—Schwyzer I 716; ESchwenter, Die primären Interjektionen in den indogermanischen Sprachen (Indogermanische Bibliothek III/5) 1924. DELG.

οἰνόμελι, ιτος, τό (οἶνος, μέλι; Carneades [II BC] in Diog. L. 4, 64; Polyb. 12, 2, 7; Diod. S. 5, 34, 2; Plut., Mor. 196e; 733e; Diosc., Mat. Med. 5, 8 W; Sext. Emp., Adv. Math. 6, 44, 9. Loanw. in rabb.) ***wine mixed with honey,*** a drink someth. like mead. In our lit. only fig., of dissidents: θανάσιμον φάρμακον διδόναι μετὰ οἰνομέλιτος *give a deadly poison mixed with honeyed wine* (Miambi 7, 45 in Herodas p. 50 C. [=Select Papyri, ed. DPage '41, III p. 356, 42] φάρμακον θανάσιμον μετ' οἰνομέλιτος) ITr 6:2.

οἰνοπότης, ου, ὁ (οἶνος, πότης 'drinker'; Anacr. 99 Diehl; Callim. [?], Epigr. 36 Pf.; Polyb. 20, 8, 2 of one socially irresponsible; Anth. Pal. 7, 28, 2 here jocosely; UPZ 81 IV, 21 [II BC]; Pr

23:20; contrast ὑδροπότης teetotaler: Xen., Cyr. 6, 2, 29) ***wine-drinker, drunkard*** (w. φάγος) **Mt 11:19; Lk 7:34** (the point being that Jesus is considered a fool, cp. Pr 23:19–21).—DELG s.v. πίνω. M-M.

οἶνος, ου, ὁ (Hom.+)—**❶ a beverage made from fermented juice of the grape, *wine;*** the word for 'must', or unfermented grape juice, is τρύξ (Anacr. et al.; pap); lit. **J 2:3, 9f** (on abundance of wine in the anticipated future s. Jo 2:19, 24; Am 8:13–15; En 10:19. HWindisch, Die joh. Weinregel: ZNW 14, 1913, 248–57. Further material on the marriage at Cana Hdb.[3] '33, exc. after 2:12. S. also HNoetzel, Christus u. Dionysos '60); **4:46.** οἶνος (v.l. ὄξος) μετὰ χολῆς μεμιγμένος *wine mixed with gall* **Mt 27:34** (s. χολή 1). ὄξος καὶ οἶν. μεμιγμένα ἐπὶ τὸ αὐτό *vinegar and wine mixed together* Hm 10, 3, 3. ἐσμυρνισμένος οἶν. *wine mixed with myrrh* **Mk 15:23.** W. ἔλαιον D 13:6; used medicinally (Theophr., HP 9, 12; Diosc., Mat. Med. 5, 9) **Lk 10:34;** stored in a cellar Hm 11:15. W. other natural products **Rv 18:13.** John the Baptist abstains fr. wine and other alcoholic drink (cp. Num 6:3; Judg 13:14; 1 Km 1:11) **Lk 1:15;** to denote the extraordinary degree of his abstinence it is said of him μὴ ἐσθίων ἄρτον μήτε πίνων οἶνον **7:33** (Diod. S. 1, 72, 2 the Egyptians in mourning for their kings abstain from wheat bread [πυρός] and from wine). Abstinence fr. wine and meat for the sake of 'weak' Christians **Ro 14:21** (Ltzm., Hdb. exc. before Ro 14. Lit. on ἀσθενής 2c and λάχανον). ἡ ἡδονὴ τοῦ οἴνου *the flavor of the wine* Hm 12, 5, 3. οἶν. νέος *new wine* (s. νέος 1a) **Mt 9:17** (WNagel, VigChr 14, '60, 1–8: [GTh]); **Mk 2:22; Lk 5:37f.**—μεθύσκεσθαι οἴνῳ *get drunk with wine* **Eph 5:18** (on bad effects of wine on the mind as viewed by early Gk. poets, s. SDarcusSullivan, L'AntCl 65, '96, 31–51, esp. 47–49). οἶνος πολύς (Ps.-Anacharsis, Ep. 3 p. 103 H.): οἴνῳ πολλῷ προσέχειν *be addicted to much wine* **1 Ti 3:8.** οἴνῳ πολλῷ δεδουλωμένη *enslaved to* drink **Tit 2:3** (cp. the stereotyped 'anus' in Lat. lit. VRosivach, Classical World 88, '94, 113f). οἴνῳ ὀλίγῳ χρῆσθαι *take a little wine* **1 Ti 5:23** (perh. w. implication of contrast to a ὑδροπότης: s. ὑδροποτέω; the moderate use of wine is recommended fr. the time of Theognis [509f]; Plut., Mor. 353b of οἶνος: χρῶνται μέν, ὀλίγῳ δέ; Ps.-Plut., Hom. 206; Crates, Ep. 10).—KKircher, D. sakrale Bed. des Weines im Altertum 1910; VZapletal, D. Wein in d. Bibel 1920; JDöller, Der Wein in Bibel u. Talmud: Biblica 4, 1923, 143–67, 267–99; JBoehmer, D. NT u. d. Alkohol: Studierstube 22, 1926, 322–64; EZurhellen-Pfleiderer, D. Alkoholfrage im NT 1927; IRaymond, The Teaching of the Early Church on the Use of Wine, etc. 1927. S. also ἄμπελος a and ἄρτος 1c.

❷ punishments that God inflicts on the wicked, *wine* fig. ext. of 1, in apocalyptic symbolism, to 'drink' as wine: ὁ οἶνος τοῦ θυμοῦ τοῦ θεοῦ *the wine of God's wrath* **Rv 14:10.** Also ὁ οἶν. τοῦ θυμοῦ τῆς ὀργῆς τοῦ θεοῦ **19:15;** cp. **16:19.** Of Babylon the prostitute ὁ οἶνος τοῦ θυμοῦ τῆς πορνείας αὐτῆς **14:8; 18:3.** Cp. θυμός on all these passages. οἶν. τῆς πορνείας **17:2.**

❸ the plant that makes the production of wine possible, *vine* or ***vineyard,*** eventually the product ***wine,*** effect for cause: **Rv 6:6;** s. ἔλαιον 2. The preservation of olive orchards and vineyards is a striking exhibition of divine mercy, given the social context in which consumption of wine and olives and use of olive oil played a significant role.—RHalberstsma, Wine in Classical Antiquity: Minerva 7/1 Jan/Feb '96, 14–18; NPurcell, Wine and Wealth in Ancient Italy: JRS 75, '85, 1–19.—B. 390. DELG. M-M. TW.

οἰνοφλυγία, ας, ἡ (οἶνος, φλύω 'bubble up'; X.; Aristot., EN 3, 5, 15; Stoic. III 397 οἰνοφλυγία δὲ ἐπιθυμία οἴνου ἄπληστος) ***drunkenness*** pl. (X., Oec. 1, 22; Polyb. 2, 19, 4; Musonius p. 14, 15 H.; Philo, Mos. 2, 185, Spec. Leg. 4, 91) w. ἀσέλγειαι, κῶμοι, πότοι et al., of the individual occurrences of drunkenness **1 Pt 4:3.**—DELG s.v. φλύω. M-M.

οἴομαι contracted οἶμαι; impf. ᾤμην, ᾤου, ᾤετο (all LXX); 1 aor. ᾠήθην ITr 3:3 (Hom.+) **to consider someth. to be true but with a component of tentativeness, *think, suppose, expect*** foll. by acc. and inf. (PEleph 13, 6; POxy 1666, 2; Gen 37:7; Job 34:12; Jos., Ant. 1, 323; Just., D. 114, 3; Tat. 16, 1; Ath. 36, 1) **J 21:25;** 2 Cl 14:2; Dg 3:1. W. inf. foll. (PEleph 12, 1; PFlor 332, 8; POxy 898, 24; 1 Macc 5:61; 2 Macc 7:24; Jos., C. Ap. 2, 117; Just., D. 2, 6; 10, 3; Ath. 36, 1) **Phil 1:17;** 1 Cl 30:4 (Job 11:2); PtK 2 p. 14, 25; Dg 2:7; 3:4f; 10:3. W. ὅτι foll. (Dio Chrys. 65 [15], 22; Epict. 2, 19, 26; Lucian, Ind. 7 p. 106, Alex. 61 p. 265 al.; Ps.-Aeschines, Ep. 4, 2; Is 57:8; EpArist 227; Tat. 26, 1) **Js 1:7;** 2 Cl 6:6; 15:1. The passage . . . εἰς τοῦτο ᾠήθην, ἵνα κτλ. ITr 3:3 is difficult, no doubt because of text damage; in their efforts to make tolerable sense of it, Zahn, Funk, and Bihlmeyer remain closer to the text tradition than does Lghtf. They read οὐκ εἰς τ. ᾠ., ἵνα κτλ. *I do not consider myself entitled to,* etc.—DELG. M-M s.v. οἶμαι.

οἷος, α, ον relative pron. (Hom.+) **pert. to being similar to someth. or belonging to a class, *of what sort (such)*** οἷος . . . τοιοῦτος *as . . . so* (Oenomaus in Eus., PE 5, 27, 5; Sir 49:14) **1 Cor 15:48ab; 2 Cor 10:11.** τὸν αὐτὸν ἀγῶνα . . . οἷον εἴδετε *the same struggle . . . as you saw* (οἷον refers to significance, as GDI 4999 II, 10 [Crete] θάνατος οἷος διακωλυσεῖ=an instance of death whose significance hinders) in its severity **Phil 1:30.** οἷοι ἐτέθησαν τοιοῦτοι καὶ ἦσαν Hs 9, 4, 6; cp. 9, 8, 1; 9, 17, 2. μὴ . . . γενηθῇς τοιοῦτος, οἵους ἀκούομεν *you are not . . . to become like those of whom we hear, that* B 10, 8.—The correlative can oft. be supplied fr. the context (POxy 278, 18; PRyl 154, 28; Gen 44:15; Jos., Ant. 10, 13): θλῖψις, οἵα οὐ γέγονεν **Mt 24:21** (Da 12:1 Theod.); **Mk 9:3; 2 Cor 12:20ab; 2 Ti 3:11a; Rv 16:18** (cp. Da 12:1 LXX and Theod.: the latter smooths the text with a redundant θλῖψις). ὑγιὲς ἦν οἷον καὶ ἑωράκειν αὐτό *the (tree) was as healthy as I had (earlier) seen it* Hs 8, 1, 3; cp. 8, 3, 8; 8, 4, 6; 9, 17, 5. The pleonastic θλῖψις, οἵα οὐ γέγονεν τοιαύτη **Mk 13:19** is to be explained on the basis of Hebr. In an indir. quest. (Epict. 4, 6, 4; Maximus Tyr. 18, 4e) **Lk 9:55 v.l.; 1 Th 1:5;** *how great* GPt 7:25; 2 Cl 10:4. In exclamations (Tat. 22, 1; B-D-F §304) οἵους διωγμοὺς ὑπήνεγκα *what persecutions I endured!* **2 Ti 3:11b.**—οὐχ οἷον ὅτι **Ro 9:6** is a mixture of οὐχ οἷον (Hellenistic=οὐ δή που 'by no means' [Alexis Com., fgm. 201 Kock πέτεται, οὐχ οἷον βαδίζει; Diod. S. 1, 83, 4 οὐχ οἷον . . . , τοὐναντίον 'by no means . . . , on the contrary'; Field, Notes 158]; Jos., C. Ap. 2, 238; s. Phryn. p. 372 Lob.; B-D-F §304; Rob. 732) and οὐχ ὅτι 'not as if' (B-D-F 480, 5; Rob. 1034).—**οἱοσδηποτοῦν,** also written οἷος δή ποτ' οὖν (Vett. Val. p. 339, 26; 354, 23; BGU 895, 28 [II AD] οἵῳ δήποτε οὖν τρόπῳ; Just., D. 125, 2 οἱανδηποτοῦν), is found only in the textually doubtful vs. **J 5:3 [4] v.l.:** οἵῳ δηποτοῦν κατείχετο νοσήματι *no matter what disease he had.*—DELG. M-M.

οἱοσδηποτοῦν s. οἷος, end. M-M.

οἴσω s. φέρω.

οἰωνοσκόπος, ου, ὁ (οἰωνός 'a bird of omen', σκοπός 'watcher'; Eur., Suppl. 500; Strabo 16, 2, 39; Herm. Wr. 480, 7 Sc.; ins, Philo.—οἰωνοσκοπέω Jos., Ant. 18, 125) **one who obtains omens fr. the behavior of birds, *soothsayer, augur*** D 3:4.—DELG s.v. σκέπτομαι.

ὀκνέω 1 aor. ὤκνησα (s. next entry; Hom.+; pap, LXX) **to hold back from doing someth.,** ***hesitate, delay*** w. inf. foll. (Diod. S. 10, 33, 1 ὀκ. ἀποθνήσκειν; Appian, Mithrid. 57 §230; Oenomaus in Eus., PE 5, 21, 2; Just., D. 142, 1; Tat 23, 1) μὴ ὀκνήσῃς διελθεῖν ἕως ἡμῶν *come over to us without delay* **Ac 9:38** (sim. Num 22:16 μὴ ὀκνήσῃς ἐλθεῖν πρός με. Field, p. 118: 'a courteous mode of pressing a request'; Sir 7:35; cp. Lucian, Necyom. 11 μὴ ὀκνήσῃς εἰπεῖν; POxy 1769, 7; Philo, Aet. M. 84; Jos., Vi. 251, C. Ap. 1, 15; Field, Notes 118). οὐκ ὀκνήσω . . . συγκατατάξαι ταῖς ἑρμηνείαις *I will not hesitate to include in my expositions* Papias (2:3).—DELG s.v. 1 ὄκνος. M-M. Spicq.

ὀκνηρός, ά, όν (ὀκνέω; Pind., Hippocr. et al.; LXX; Philo; Jos., Ant. 2, 236).

❶ **possessing ὄκνος (a state involving shrinking from someth., 'holding back, hesitation. reluctance'),** ***idle, lazy, indolent*** (Hierocles Scriptor Facetiarum, ed. AEberhard 1869, Facetiae 211) of a slave (w. πονηρός) **Mt 25:26** (voc. as Pr 6:6, 9). W. dat. τῇ σπουδῇ μὴ ὀκ. *never let your zeal flag* (Moffatt) **Ro 12:11.**

❷ **pert. to involvement in ὄκνος, causing hesitation, reluctance,** ***(such as) to shrink from*** ἐμοὶ οὐκ ὀκνηρόν *it is not troublesome to me* w. inf. **Phil 3:1** (the verb with γράφειν PLeid XVII, 14, 20f; Sb 7353, 14 [c. 200 AD]; PSI 621, 5).—AFridrichsen, StKr 102, 1930, 300f.—B. 315. DELG s.v. 1 ὄκνος. M-M. TW. Spicq.

ὀκταήμερος, ον (ὀκτώ, ἡμέρα; s. Mlt-H. p. 176; Gregor. Naz., Or. 25, 465d Λάζαρος τετραήμερος; 40 p. 715d, Χριστὸς ἀνίσταται τριήμερος) ***on the eighth day*** περιτομῇ ὀκ.= *circumcised on the eighth day* **Phil 3:5** (lit. 'a person-of-eight-days relative to circumcision'; on the dat. of reference s. B-D-F §197; Rob. 523).—DELG. M-M.

ὀκτώ indecl. (Hom.+; loanw. in rabb.) ***eight*** B 9:8. ὀκ. ψυχαί **1 Pt 3:20;** ἡμέραι ὀκ. **Lk 2:21;** cp. **9:28; Ac 25:6.** μεθ' ἡμέρας ὀκ. *after eight days* **J 20:26.** ἐξ ἐτῶν ὀκ. *for eight years* **Ac 9:33.**—δεκαοκτώ *eighteen* **Lk 13:4, 11.** Also δέκα καὶ ὀκ. vs. **16** (B-D-F §63, 2; Rob. 282f). τριάκοντα καὶ ὀκ. *thirty-eight* **J 5:5.**—DELG. M-M.

ὀλεθρευτής, ὀλεθρεύω s. ὀλοθρευτής, ὀλοθρεύω.

ὀλέθριος, ον (s. next entry; Hom. et al.; s. Crönert 186; LXX) act. sense (so mostly, incl. Polyb. 2, 68, 10; 3 Km 21:42) **pert. to being totally destructive,** ***deadly, destructive*** τίνειν ὀλέθριον δίκην *undergo lethal punishment* **2 Th 1:9 v.l.**—DELG s.v. ὄλλυμι.

ὄλεθρος, ου, ὁ (ὄλλυμι 'destroy'; Hom.+; SIG 527, 82 [c. 220 BC]; BGU 1027 XXVI, 11; LXX; PsSol 8:1; TestReub 4:6; 6:3; Philo; Jos., Ant. 17, 38, Vi. 264; SibOr 3, 327; 348)

❶ **a state of destruction,** ***destruction, ruin, death*** in our lit. always w. some kind of transcendent coloring (hostile spirits work ἐπ' ὀλέθρῳ τοῦ γένους τῶν ἀνθρώπων Orig., C. Cels. 8, 54, 32): ἔρχεταί τινι ὄλ. *ruin comes upon someone* 1 Cl 57:4 (Pr 1:26). αἰφνίδιος αὐτοῖς ἐφίσταται ὄλ. *sudden destruction will come upon them* **1 Th 5:3.** βυθίζειν τινὰ εἰς ὄλ. *plunge someone headlong into ruin* **1 Ti 6:9.** ὄλ. αἰώνιος *eternal death* (TestReub 6:3) **2 Th 1:9** (s. ὀλέθριος).

❷ **act of destruction,** ***destruction*** παραδοῦναί τινα τῷ σατανᾷ εἰς ὄλ. τῆς σαρκός *hand someone over to Satan for the destruction of his flesh* **1 Cor 5:5** (handing over to Satan will result in the sinner's death.—EvDobschütz, Die urchristl. Gemeinden 1902, 269–72; Lietzmann, Hdb. '49, 28; and s. παραδίδωμι 1b.—Hierocles 14, 451b has the thought that the soul of the sinner in Hades is purified by the tortures of hell, and is saved thereby). Destruction brought about by Satan is mentioned also IEph 13:1 ὅταν πυκνῶς ἐπὶ τὸ αὐτὸ γίνεσθε, καθαιροῦνται αἱ δυνάμεις τοῦ σατανᾶ καὶ λύεται ὁ ὄλ. αὐτοῦ *when you come together frequently, the (spirit-) powers of Satan are destroyed, and his destructiveness is nullified.*—DELG s.v. ὄλλυμι. M-M. TW.

ὀλιγόβιος, ον (ὀλίγος, βίος; Aristot., HA 8, 28; Sext. Emp., Math. 1, 73; Job) ***short-lived*** γεννητὸς γυναικὸς ὀλ. *he that is born of woman and is short-lived* 1 Cl 30:5 (Job 11:2).

ὀλιγοπιστία, ας, ἡ (cp. ἀπιστία and s. next entry; only in Christian wr.; Leontius 7 p. 14, 18; 21; 15, 6; Cos. and Dam. 26, 71; s. RAC XI 48–122) ***littleness/poverty of faith*** **Mt 17:20.**—DELG s.v. πείθομαι. TW.

ὀλιγόπιστος, ον (s. prec. entry; Sextus 6; elsewh. only in Christian wr. e.g. AcThom 28 [Aa II 2 p. 145]) ***of little faith/trust,*** in our lit., in the NT only in the synoptics and only in addressing the disciples **Mt 6:30; 8:26; 16:8; Lk 12:28;** Peter alone **Mt 14:31.**—To the Christians in Corinth AcPlCor 2:31.—TW.

ὀλίγος, η, ον (Hom.+.—For the NT the spelling ὁλίγος is not infrequently attested [exx. in B-D-F §14; Mlt-H., 98f; cp. Schwyzer I 226; II 201]; like ἑλπίς, ἵδιος and a few others of this kind, this form is found in ins and pap as early as pre-Christian times, and is more freq. later [Crönert 148–53; Helbing 25f; Thackeray 126f; Hauser 60]).

❶ **pert. to being relatively small in number,** ***few*** pl.

ⓐ used w. a noun ἐργάται **Mt 9:37; Lk 10:2.** ἰχθύδια *a few (small) fish* **Mt 15:34; Mk 8:7.** ἄρρωστοι **6:5.** ἄφρονες *a few foolish* persons ITr 8:2. ὀνόματα **Rv 3:4.** πρόσωπα *persons* 1 Cl 1:1. W. κεράμια to be understood fr. the immediate context Hm 12, 5, 3. ἡμέραι ὀλίγαι (PFay 123, 10 [c. 100 AD]; Gen 29:20; cp. Ps 108:8; Philo, Somn. 1, 46; Jos., Ant. 1, 91): ἐν ἡμ. ὀλίγαις (Diod. S. 36, 4, 4) **Ac 15:30** D. πρὸς ὀλ. ἡμέρας *for a few days* **Hb 12:10;** μετὰ ἡμέρας ὀλ. *after a few days* Hs 7:1; 8, 4, 1. μετ' ὀλ. ἡμέρας (Teles p. 19, 5; Diod. S. 13, 8, 1) 8, 11, 5; 9, 5, 5f. μετὰ ὀλ. ἡμέρας 5, 2, 9; 8, 2, 9. ὀλ. ῥήματα *a few words* m 4, 2, 1; 12, 5, 1. δι' ὀλ. γραμμάτων *in a few lines* (s. γράμμα 1) IRo 8:2; IPol 7:3.

ⓑ abs. ὀλίγοι *(a) few* (opp. πολλοί as Menand., Mon. 670 Jäkel [443 Meineke]; Polyb. 18, 53, 1; Diod. S. 15, 37, 1; Plut., Mor. 188e; Porphyr., Vi. Pyth. 22; Tat. 3, 2) **Mt 7:14** (Cebes 15, 2f there are ὀλίγοι who travel the στενὴ ὁδός . . . , ἡ ἄγουσα to the goal; TestAbr A 11 p. 90, 11 [Stone p. 28] ὀλίγοι . . . οἱ σῳζόμενοι); **20:16 v.l.; 22:14**=B 4:14; **Lk 13:23.**—*a few* **1 Pt 3:20;** MPol 5:1 (cp. Just., A I, 44, 13). Used w. the partitive gen. (Arrian, Anab. 5, 15, 4 ὀλίγοι τῶν ἐλεφάντων) and a neg. *not a few, a number (of)* (Jos., Bell. 7, 438) γυναικῶν **Ac 17:4.** γυναικῶν . . . καὶ ἀνδρῶν vs. **12.**—ὀλ. ἐξ αὐτῶν Hs 9, 8, 6.—ὀλίγα *(a) few things* **Lk 10:42 v.l.** (opp. πολλά as Menand., Mon. 311 Jäkel [226 Meineke]; Ath. 12, 3; s. ABaker, CBQ 27, '65, 127–37); **Rv 2:14;** ὑποδείξω ὀλ. *I shall point out a few things* B 1:8. ὀλ. ἐπερωτᾶν τινα *ask someone a few questions* Hm 4, 1, 4. ἐπὶ ὀλίγα ἧς πιστός *you were trustworthy in managing a few things* **Mt 25:21, 23.** δαρήσεται ὀλίγας *he will receive few lashes* **Lk 12:48** (s. δέρω). δι' ὀλίγων γράφειν **1 Pt 5:12** (βραχέων P[72], cp. **Hb 13:22;** s. διά A 3b).

❷ **pert. to being relatively small on a scale of extent,** ***little, small, short,*** sing.—ⓐ of amount (3 Km 17:10 ὀλ. ὕδωρ) οἶνος ὀλ. *a little wine* (Artem. 1, 66 p. 59, 25) **1 Ti 5:23;** πῦρ ὀλ. *a little fire* **Js 3:5 v.l.** οὐκ ὀλ. ἐργασία *no small profit* **Ac 19:24;** of fruit *little* Hs 2:4; of a country *small* 1 Cl 10:2.—Subst. τὸ ὀλίγον *a small amount* ὁ τὸ ὀλ. *one who gathered a small amount* (opp. ὁ τὸ πολύ) **2 Cor 8:15** (cp. Num 11:32; Ex 16:18). ᾧ ὀλίγον ἀφίεται *the one to whom little is forgiven* **Lk 7:47a** (cp. the use in vs. 47b and s. 3 below).

ⓑ of duration—α. (Musaeus vs. 291 ὀλίγον ἐπὶ χρόνον= for a short time; TestAbr B 2 p. 106, 5 [Stone p. 60] ὀλίγην ὥραν) ὀλ. καιρός *a short time* **Rv 12:12.** χρόνος οὐκ ὀλ. *a long time* (Jos., Bell. 2, 62) **Ac 14:28.** ὀλίγον χρόνον *for a short while* (Menand., fgm. 567 Kö.) 2 Cl 19:3; Hs 7:6; ἐν καιρῷ ὀλ. *in a short time* 1 Cl 23:4.

β. The neut. ὀλίγον used adverbially (Hom. et al.; Pr 6:10; Sir 51:16, 27) w. preps. *in a short time, quickly* (Pind.; Pla., Apol. 22b; Jos., Ant. 18, 145; Lucian, Toxaris 24) **Ac 26:28** (s. πείθω 1b; 3a and reff. there). καὶ ἐν ὀλ. καὶ ἐν μεγάλῳ *whether in a short or a long time* vs. **29** (s. B-D-F §195; GWhitaker, The Words of Agrippa to St. Paul: JTS 15, 1914, 82f; AFridrichsen, SymbOsl 14, '35, 50; Field, Notes 141–43; s. Rob. 653).—μετ' ὀλίγον *after a short while* (Diod. S. 14, 9, 6; 15, 6, 5; Appian, Liby. 98 §465; SIG 1170, 25f; PRyl 77, 41; Jdth 13:9; Wsd 15:8; TestAbr A 7 p. 84, 8 [Stone p. 16]; GrBar 9:3; Jos., Vi. 344; Just., D. 56, 18) MPol 11:2.—πρὸς ὀλίγον *for a short time* (Lucian, Dial. Deor. 18, 1; Aelian, VH 12, 63; POxy 67, 14; Jos., Bell. 4, 642, Ant. 4, 128; Just., A I, 12, 2) **Js 4:14.**—Without a prep. (Ps 36:10; TestJob 40:4; ParJer 5:2) **Mk 6:31; 1 Pt 1:6; 5:10; Rv 17:10.**

ⓒ of distance, the neut. ὀλίγον used adverbially *a little* of distance, etc. (Pla., Prot. 26, 339d ὀλίγον προελθών; ApcMos 19 περιπατήσας ὀλίγον) **Mk 1:19; Lk 5:3.**

❸ **relatively low on a scale of extent or existing only to a small degree, *little, slight*** οὐκ ὀλ. *great, severe:* τάραχος **Ac 12:18; 19:23.** στάσις κ. ζήτησις **15:2.** χειμών **27:20.**—*Only a little* (Ael. Aristid. 33, 6 K.=51 p. 573 D.) ὀλίγον ἀγαπᾷ *he loves only* (to) *a little* (extent) **Lk 7:47b.**—W. prep. ἐν ὀλίγῳ (cp. TestGad 4:6='slightly') *in brief* (Aristot., Rhet. 3, 11 p. 1412b, 23; Dionys. Byz. §3) **Eph 3:3.** πρὸς ὀλίγον ὠφέλιμος *profitable for (a) little* (=has some value) **1 Ti 4:8.** GJs19, 2 (s. deStrycker 279).—B. 925f. DELG. M-M. EDNT. TW.

ὀλιγοχρόνιος, ον (Hdt. et al.; Polyb. 2, 35, 6; Epict. in Stob. p. 463, 1 Sch.; oft. Vett. Val., s. index; Wsd 9:5; Philo) ***of short duration, short-lived*** ἡ ἐπιδημία ἡ ἐν τῷ κόσμῳ τούτῳ τῆς σαρκὸς ταύτης μικρά ἐστιν καὶ ὀλ. 2 Cl 5:5. τὰ ἐνθάδε (w. μικρά and φθαρτά) 6:6.—DELG s.v. ὀλίγος.

ὀλιγοψυχέω (Isocr. 19, 39; ins fr. Pamphylia: JHS 32, 1912, 273; PPetr II, 40 [a], 12; UPZ 63, 1 [158 BC]; POxy 1294, 13; LXX; JosAs 11 [p. 53, 8 Bat.] cod. A) opp. ἀνδρίζομαι ***be faint-hearted, discouraged*** οἱ ὀλιγοψυχοῦντες *those who are discouraged* 1 Cl 59:4.—Cp. DELG s.v. ψυχή.

ὀλιγόψυχος, ον (Artem. 3, 5; PMilan [I '37] 24, 50 [117 AD] ὀλιόψυχος [sic] of a woman; LXX; cp. Cat. Cod. Astr. X 222, 16; 226, 8) ***faint-hearted, discouraged,*** subst. **1 Th 5:14.**—DELG s.v. ὀλίγος. M-M. TW.

ὀλιγωρέω (ὀλίγος, ὥρα 'care') aor. subj. 3 sg. ὀλιγωρήσῃ ParJer 5:5 (Thu. et al.; ins, pap; PsSol 3:4; TestJob 13:5; ParJer) **have little esteem for someth., *think lightly, make light*** τινός of *someth.* (Diod. S. 1, 39, 13 τῆς ἀληθείας; 8, 30, 1 τῆς εὐσεβείας; 20, 14, 2 τοῦ δαιμονίου; PFlor 384, 86; Philo; Jos., Ant. 5, 132, C. Ap. 2, 172.—B-D-F §176,2; Rob. 508) παιδείας κυρίου **Hb 12:5** (Pr 3:11; cp. SEG XXVII, 261 B, 19 παιδοτριβῶν; s. New Docs 2, 105).—DELG s.v. ὥρα. M-M.

ὀλίγως adv. of ὀλίγος (Hippocr., Aphorisms 2, 7; Ps.-Pla., Alcibiades II 149a v.l.; Strato [II AD]: Anth. Pal. 12, 205, 1; OGI 669 II, 11: ὀλ[ίγ]ω[ι] in the text; s. note 20 on the rdg. ὀλ[ίγ]ω[ς]; POxy 1223, 16; Is 10:7 Aq.) ***scarcely, barely*** ὀλ. ἀποφεύγειν **2 Pt 2:18** (v.l. ὄντως).—M-M.

ὄλλυμι fut. ὀλῶ; aor. ὤλεσα JosAs 12:9 cod. A; inf. ὀλέσαι (Just.). Mid. fut.: 3 sg., ὀλεῖται, pl. ὀλοῦνται LXX; aor. 3 sg., ὤλετο, pl. ὤλοντο LXX (Hom. et al.; LXX; Just., A I, 25, 2) ***destroy*** τινά *someone* (SibOr 5, 509 πάντας κακούς) ἀσεβεῖς 1 Cl 57:7 (Pr 1:32).—DELG.

ὀλοθρευτής, οῦ, ὁ (only in Christian wr.; cp. AcPh 130 [Aa II/2, 59, 9]. On the spelling [N.[25] ὀλε-] s. ὀλοθρεύω) ***destroyer*** **1 Cor 10:10** (the OT speaks of ὁ ὀλεθρεύων Ex 12:23=הַמַּשְׁחִית; Wsd 18:25; cp. Hb 11:28); the one meant is the destroying angel as the one who carries out the divine sentence of punishment, or perh. Satan (MDibelius, Geisterwelt 44f).—DELG s.v. ὄλλυμι. TW.

ὀλοθρεύω (Vett. Val. 123, 11 ὀλεθρεύει; LXX; TestLevi 13:7; TestJud 6:5; 7:3; Philo, Leg. All. 2, 34; SibOr 5, 304. On its spelling, beside ὀλεθρεύω [LXX w. the forms ὀλεθρεύσω and aor. ὠλέθρευσα], s. B-D-F §32, 1; W-S. §5, 20d; Mlt-H. 71; Reinhold 40; KBuresch, RhM 46, 1891, 216f) **to cause utter destruction, *destroy, ruin*** τινά *someone* ὁ ὀλοθρεύων *the destroying angel* (s. ὀλοθρευτής) **Hb 11:28** (after Ex 12:23).—DELG s.v. ὄλλυμι. M-M. TW.

ὁλοκαύτωμα, ατος, τό (ὅλος, καίω; not in general Gk. usage [but ὁλοκαυτόω X. et al.]. In LXX; TestJob; TestLevi 9:7; Philo, Sacr. Abel. 110; Jos., Bell. 5, 565, Ant. 10, 70. On word formation s. Dssm., B 135 [BS 138]).

❶ **a cultic sacrifice in which the animal was entirely consumed by fire, *whole burnt offering, holocaust*** lit. (w. θυσία and sim. terms) **Mk 12:33;** 1 Cl 18:16 (Ps 50:18); B 2:4, 5 (Is 1:11), 7 (Jer 7:22). W. περὶ ἁμαρτίας *'sin-offering'* **Hb 10:6, 8** (both Ps 39:7). ὁλ. ὑπὲρ ἁμαρτιῶν B 7:6 (cp. Lev 16:5). θυσίας αὐτῷ δι' αἵματος καὶ κνίσης καὶ ὁλοκαυτωμάτων ἐπιτελεῖν *offer sacrifices to (God) with blood, burning fat, and whole burnt offerings* Dg 3:5.

❷ **a person punished with death by fire because of personal conviction, *whole burnt offering, holocaust*** fig. ext. of 1: of Polycarp ὁλ. δεκτὸν τῷ θεῷ ἡτοιμασμένον MPol 14:1.—S. DELG s.v. καίω and ὅλος. M-M.

ὁλοκληρία, ας, ἡ (ὁλόκληρος; Chrysipp. [Stoic. III 33]; Plut., Mor. 1041e; 1047e τοῦ σώματος; 1063f ὑγεία καὶ ὁλ.; Diog. L. 7, 107; SIG 1142, 2 [I/II AD] ὁλ. τῶν ποδῶν; POxy 123, 6; 1478, 3; BGU 948, 4 w. ὑγία; Is 1:6 v.l.) **state of soundness or well-being in all parts, *wholeness, completeness:*** of the healing of a lame man ἡ πίστις . . . ἔδωκεν αὐτῷ τὴν ὁλ. ταύτην *faith . . . has given him this perfect health* **Ac 3:16.** ADebrunner, Philol. 95, '42, 174–76.—DELG s.v. ὅλος. M-M. TW. Spicq.

ὁλόκληρος, ον (ὅλος, κλῆρος; Pla.; Polyb. 18, 45, 9; Ps.-Lucian, Macrob. 2; Epict. 3, 26, 7; 25; 4, 1, 66; 151; OGI 519, 14; SIG 1009, 10; 1012, 9 al., s. New Docs 4, 161f; PLond III, 935, 7 p. 30 [216/17 AD]; POxy 57, 13; LXX; Philo, Abr. 47, Spec. Leg. 1, 283; Jos., Ant. 3, 228; 278; 14, 366; Just., D. 69, 7) **pert. to being complete and meeting all expectations, *with integrity, whole, complete, undamaged, intact, blameless*** πίστις *undiminished faith* Hm 5, 2, 3; GJs 16:2. In an ethical sense: ὁλ. ὑμῶν τὸ πνεῦμα . . . τηρηθείη *may your spirit . . . be preserved complete* or *sound* **1 Th 5:23** (PGM 7, 590 διαφύλασσέ μου τὸ σῶμα, τὴν ψυχὴν ὁλόκληρον.—PvanStempvoort, NTS 7, '60/61, 262–65: connects πνεῦμα and ἁγιάσαι in 1 Th 5:23). W. τέλειος **Js 1:4.**—B. 919. DELG s.v. ὅλος. M-M. TW. Spicq. Sv.

ὀλολύζω fut. ὀλολύξω LXX; aor. ὠλόλυξα (Hom. et al.; PGM 11a, 30; LXX; cp. the similarly onomatopoetic Hb. hiphil form ילל) **to cry out with a loud voice, either in joy or pain,** ***cry out*** (ἐπί τινι as Lucian, Dial. Deor. 12, 1) κλαύσατε ὀλολύζοντες ἐπὶ ταῖς ταλαιπωρίαις ὑμῶν *wail and cry aloud over your tribulations* **Js 5:1.** Of a temple roof GJs 24:3.—LDeubner, Ololyge u. Verwandtes: ABA '41 no. 1.—DELG. M-M. TW.

ὅλος, η, ον (Pind.+ [Hom. and Hes. have the Ion. οὖλος]) in the NT never in attributive position, mostly predicate (W-S. §20, 12a; B-D-F §275, 2; 4; Rob. 774, cp. 656)

❶ **pert. to being complete in extent,** ***whole, entire, complete***

ⓐ used w. a noun that has no art., somet. preceding it, somet. coming after it: ὅλ. οἴκους *whole families* **Tit 1:11.** ὅλ. ἄνθρωπον ὑγιῆ ἐποίησα *I have healed a man's whole body* **J 7:23.**—ἐνιαυτὸν ὅλ. *for a whole year* **Ac 11:26.** διετίαν ὅλ. *for two full years* **28:30.**—δι' ὅλης νυκτός *the whole night through* **Lk 5:5; J 21:6 v.l.** (Appian, Liby. 134 §636; Lucian, Ver. Hist. 1, 29; Just., D. 1, 4.—SIG 1171, 6 δι' ὅλης ἡμέρας; cp. Jos., Ant. 6, 37, Vi. 15 δι' ὅλης τῆς νυκτός; InsPriene 112, 98 διὰ τοῦ χειμῶνος ὅλου). Likew. w. names of cities without the art. ὅλη Ἰερουσαλήμ *all Jerusalem* **Ac 21:31.**

ⓑ used w. a noun that has the art.—**α.** coming before the noun: ὅλ. ἡ περίχωρος ἐκείνη **Mt 14:35;** cp. GJs 8:3; AcPl Ha 8, 30. ὅλ. ἡ χώρα ἐκείνη **Mk 6:55.** ὅλ. ἡ πόλις **1:33.** ὅλ. τὸ σῶμά σου **Mt 5:29f; 6:22f.** ὅλ. ὁ βίος **Lk 8:43.** [ἐφ'] ὅλον τὸν οἶκον **Ac 7:10.** ὅλ. τὴν ἡμέραν *the whole day (through)* (Jos., Ant. 6, 22) **Mt 20:6; Ro 8:36** (Ps 43:23); **10:21** (Is 65:2). ἐξ ὅλης τῆς ἰσχύος ἡμῶν *with all our strength* 1 Cl 33:8. εἰς ὅλην τὴν Γαλιλαίαν **Mk 1:39;** εἰς ὅλον τὸν κόσμον Hs 9, 25, 2 (ὅλ. ὁ κόσμος: Wsd 11:22; Aristobulus in Eus., PE 13, 12, 9 [Denis 224, 4; Holladay 176, 5]; EpArist 210; ApcEsdr 1:11 p. 25, 4 Tdf.). ἡ πίστις ὑμῶν καταγγέλλεται ἐν ὅλῳ τῷ κόσμῳ **Ro 1:8** (on the hyperbole cp. PLond 891, 9 ἡ εὐφημία σου περιεκύκλωσεν τὸν κόσμον ὅλον). ὅλον τὸ πλῆθος AcPl Ha 4, 20.

β. after the noun ὁ κόσμος ὅλ. **Mt 16:26; Lk 9:25; 1J 5:19;** AcPl Ha 3, 7 (TestJob 33:4; Just., D. 127, 2). τὸ συνέδριον ὅλ. **Mt 26:59;** τὸ σῶμά σου ὅλ. **Lk 11:36a;** ἡ οἰκία αὐτοῦ ὅλ. **J 4:53;** ἡ πόλις ὅλ. **Ac 21:30;** ἡ οἰκουμένη ὅλ. **Rv 3:10.**

γ. The noun can also be supplied fr. the context ἕως οὗ ἐζυμώθη ὅλον (i.e. τὸ ἄλευρον) *until (the) whole (batch of flour) was leavened* **Mt 13:33; Lk 13:21.** ἔσται φωτεινὸν ὅλον (i.e. τὸ σῶμά σου) **Lk 11:36b.**—Sim. the subst. ptc. ἔστιν καθαρὸς ὅλος (ὁ λελουμένος) *(the one who has bathed) is clean all over* **J 13:10.**

❷ **pert. to a degree of completeness,** ***wholly, completely,*** w. a pron. σὺ ὅλος *you altogether, wholly* **J 9:34.** τοῦτο ὅλον *all this* **Mt 1:22; 21:4 v.l.; 26:56.** ὅλον ἑαυτὸν ἐπιδείξας *exposed himself completely* (to the lion) AcPl Ha 4, 29.—W. a prep. δι' ὅλου *throughout, through and through* (Philo Mech. 60, 25; POxy 53, 10; 1277, 8; PGM 5, 154) **J 19:23** (cp. New Docs 3, 63, no. 26).

❸ **everything that exists,** ***everything,*** subst. neut. pl. (3 Macc 6:9; EpArist 201; TestAbr A 20 p. 103, 27 [Stone p. 54]; ApcMos, Philo, Joseph., Just., Tat., Ath.) [ὁ τῶν ὅλ]ων δεσπότης Ox 1081, 36 (as TestAbr A, s. above; ApcMos 37; Jos., Ant. 1, 72; Tat. 5, 1; cp. Just., D. 140, 4). ὁ θεὸς ὁ τῶν ὅλων ὁ παντοκράτωρ AcPlCor 2:9. ὁ . . . δεσπότης καὶ δημιουργὸς τῶν ὅλων Dg 8:7.—Cp. πᾶς, s. Schmidt, Syn. IV 549. B. 919. DELG. M-M. TW. Sv.

ὁλοτελής, ές (ὅλος, τέλος; since [dismissing Aristot., De Plantis 817b, in the late Gk. tr. of a Latin version]; Plut., Mor. 909b; Galen XIX p. 162 K.; SIG 814, 45 [67 AD]) **pert. to being totally complete, with implication of meeting a high standard,** ***in every way complete, quite perfect,*** of stones Hv 3, 6, 4. ἀποκάλυψις *a revelation that is in every way complete* 3, 10, 9; 3, 13, 4b. ὁλ. ἐν τῇ πίστει m 9:6. ὁ θεὸς ἁγιάσαι ὑμᾶς ὁλοτελεῖς *may God make you completely holy in every way* **1 Th 5:23.** αἱ ῥάβδοι ὁλοτελεῖς χλωραί *sticks very green* Hs 8, 5, 2.—M-M. TW.

ὁλοτελῶς adv. of ὁλοτελής (Petosiris, fgm. 21 ln. 260; Peripl. Eryth. 30; Vett. Val. 155, 3; Dt 13:16 [17] Aq.) ***wholly, altogether*** μετανοεῖν *repent fully* Hv 3, 13, 4a.

Ὀλοφέρνης, ου, ὁ ***Holofernes,*** Assyrian commander-in-chief, slain by Judith in his own tent when he laid siege to her native city of Bethulia (Jdth 2ff) 1 Cl 55:5.—On the name and pers. of H. s. JMarquart, Philol. 54, 1895, 507ff; Pauly-W. VIII 1167–71; Schürer III/1, 216–18.

Ὀλυμπᾶς, ᾶ, ὁ (IG III 1080, 28.—CIL XIV 1286. Etym. uncertain, but s. W-S. §16, 9; Rouffiac 91) ***Olympas,*** recipient of a greeting **Ro 16:15.** The vv.ll. Ὀλυμπίδα and Olympiadem are prob. due to a Latin copyist's error.—LGPN I. M-M.

ὄλυνθος, ου, ὁ (Hes. et al.; Theophr., Caus. Pl. 5, 9, 12; Diosc. 1, 185; SSol 2:13; loanw. in rabb.) ***late/summer fig*** **Rv 6:13.** VHehn, Kulturpflanzen u. Haustiere[8] 1911, 95ff; RAC VII 641, 675.—DELG. TW.

ὅλως adv. of ὅλος (Pla.+)—❶ **a marker of highest degree on a scale of extent,** ***completely, wholly, everywhere.*** ὅλως ἀκούεται *it's bandied about everywhere = it's a matter of general knowledge, it's the talk of the town* **1 Cor 5:1** (cp. AFridrichsen, Symb Osl 13, '34, 43f: 'to say it at once'; Diod. S. 13, 16, 2 'continually', 'again and again'; Ps.-Demetr., El. c. 175; 199 R. ὅλως='regularly', 'generally', 'everywhere' and can be parallel w. παντοδαποῦ; difft., s. 2 below); ἤδη οὖν ὅλως ἥττημα *believe me, it's an utter disaster* **6:7** (REB: Indeed, you suffer defeat; difft., s. 2 below). Rather oft. w. a neg. *not at all* (X., Mem. 1, 2, 35; Dio Chrys. 53 [70], 5; 8; Philostrat., Vi. Apoll. 1, 39 p. 41, 9; Philo, Op. M. 170, Praem. 40; Jos., Vi. 221, Ant. 8, 241; TestJud 16:3; Ar. 11, 7; Just., A I, 16, 5; 43, 2 al.; Ath. 1, 2; 4, 1) μὴ ὅλ. **Mt 5:34.**—**1 Cor 15:29;** Hv 4, 1, 9; m 4, 2, 1 al. *totally, altogether* κατέλιπον ὁδὸν τοῦ θεοῦ *they have totally abandoned God's way* ApcPt Bodl.

❷ **pert. to being really so, with implication of being generally known,** ***actually, in fact*** (POxy 1676, 31 [III AD] καλῶς ποιήσεις ἐλθοῦσα . . . πρὸς ἡμᾶς ἵνα ὅ. ἴδωμέν σε=you will do us a favor by coming to us . . . so that we actually get to see you) ὅλως ἀκούεται *it is actually reported* (NRSV) **1 Cor 5:1.** ὅλως ἥττημα *already a defeat* (NRSV) **6:7.** For a difft. interp. of these passages s. 1 above.—M-M.

ὁμαλίζω (ὁμαλός) Att. fut. ὁμαλιῶ (X. et al.; SIG 313, 10; 22; PTebt 375, 30; LXX; PsSol 8:17) ***make level*** ὄρη B 11:4 (Is 45:2).—DELG s.v. ὁμός.

ὁμαλός, ή, όν (ὁμός, cp. ἅμα; Hom. et al.; ins; PCairZen 769, 6 [III BC]; Aq., Sym., Theod., Philo; Ath., R. 16, 67, 17)

❶ **pert. to being consistently flat at the surface,** ***level, smooth, even*** lit. ὁμαλὸν γίνεσθαι *become level* Hs 9, 10, 1; τὰ ὁμ. *the level ground* v 1, 1, 3.

❷ **pert. to being without deviation for proper behavior or ease of performance,** ***level,*** fig. ext. of 1: τῇ ὀρθῇ ὁδῷ πορεύεσθαι καὶ ὁμ. *walk in the straight and level way* Hm 6, 1, 2. πάντα ὁμ. γίνεται τοῖς ἐκλεκτοῖς *all things will become level for (his) chosen* v 1, 3, 4; cp. m 2:4 (w. ἱλαρός).—DELG s.v. ὁμός.

ὁμαλῶς adv. of ὁμαλός (Thu. et al.; Ath., R. 11 p. 63, 2) ***smoothly, evenly*** ὁμ. περιπατεῖν *walk smoothly* Hm 6, 1, 4.

ὄμβρος, ου, ὁ (Hom. et al.; ins, also IAndrosIsis, Kyme 54; pap, LXX, En, Philo; Jos., Ant. 1, 101; 2, 343 al.) ***rainstorm, thunderstorm*** **Lk 12:54.**—DELG. M-M.

ὁμείρομαι (also ἱμείρομαι v.l., but prob. not related etym., s. DELG; CIG III 4000, 7 [IV AD] ὁμειρόμενοι περὶ παιδός [Ramsay, JHS 38, 1918, 157; 160]; Job 3:21 οἳ ὁμείρονται τοῦ θανάτου [v.l. ἱμείρ.]; Ps 62:2 Sym. Hesychius explains it w. ἐπιθυμεῖν.—Thackeray 97; GMilligan, Exp. 9th Ser. II 1924, 227f) **to have a strong yearning,** ***long for*** τινός *someone* **1 Th 2:8** (W-H. write ὁμ. [s. Schwyzer I 715 n. 10], s. app. 152; Mlt-H. 251; ADebrunner, IndogF 21, 1907, 203f; W-S. §16, 6; B-D-F §101 p. 53f, on the constr. s. §171, 1; Rob. 508).—DELG ὁμείρομαι. M-M. TW.

ὁμιλέω (ὅμιλος) impf. ὡμίλουν; fut. 3 sg. ὁμιλήσει Pr 15:12; 1 aor. ὡμίλησα; pf. inf. ὡμιληκέναι Just., D. 62, 2 (Hom.+, prim. mng. 'be in association with' someone, and then 'converse') **to be in a group and speak,** ***speak, converse, address*** (Hom., Pla., et al.; LXX. Cp. our use of 'meet' in the sense 'have a discussion' about someth.) τινί *(with) someone* (Philemo Com. 169 K. ἐὰν γυνὴ γυναικὶ κατ' ἰδίαν ὁμιλεῖ; Ael. Aristid. 28, 116 K.=49 p. 529 D.: θεῷ; POxy 928, 5 ὡμείλησας δέ μοί ποτε περὶ τούτου; Da 1:19; GrBar 7:3; ApcMos 16; Jos., Ant. 17, 50; Just., D. 59, 1 al.—Of God's intimate association with the Logos τῷ λόγῳ αὐτοῦ διὰ πάντος ὁμιλῶν Theoph. Ant. 2, 22 [p. 154, 20]) ὡμίλει αὐτῷ *he used to talk with him* **Ac 24:26** (Himerius, Or. 48 [=Or. 14], 18 ὁμ. τινι=confer with someone). Of Christ talking to martyrs (cp. Herm. Wr. 12, 19 [τῷ ἀνθρώπῳ] μόνῳ ὁ θεὸς ὁμιλεῖ) παρεστὼς ὁ κύριος ὡμίλει αὐτοῖς *the Lord was standing by and conversing with them* MPol 2:2. Also πρός τινα (X., Mem. 4, 3, 2; Jos., Ant. 11, 260 τούτων πρὸς ἀλλήλους ὁμιλούντων): ὡμίλουν πρὸς ἀλλήλους περὶ πάντων *they were conversing w. each other about all the things* **Lk 24:14.** W. acc. of thing οὐ ξένα ὁμιλῶ *I have nothing strange to say* Dg 11:1. ἃ λόγος ὁμιλεῖ 11:7. Abs. (Diod. S. 13, 83, 1) **Lk 24:15.** ἐφ' ἱκανὸν ὁμιλήσας ἄχρι αὐγῆς *after talking a long time until daylight* **Ac 20:11.**—RAC IX, 1100–45.—DELG s.v. ὅμιλος. M-M.

ὁμιλία, ας, ἡ (ὅμιλος) As with the verb, this noun is used of a group and then of what a group ordinarily engages in: conversation (schol. Soph., El. 420: ἡ ὁμιλία λέγεται καὶ ἐπὶ συνουσίας καὶ ἐπὶ διαλέξεως 'the term ὁ. is used both of association and conversation').

❶ **state of close association of persons,** ***association, social intercourse, company*** (trag., Thu.+; X., Mem. 1, 2, 20 ὁμιλία τῶν χρηστῶν; Herm. Wr. in Stob. I 277, 21 W.=432, 20 Sc. τὰς πρὸς τοὺς πολλοὺς ὁμιλίας παραιτοῦ; PTebt 703, 273f [III BC]; POxy 471, 76; PYadin 15, 6; 22: s. editor's note p. 63; Wsd 8:18; 3 Macc 5:18; TestAbr B 2 p. 107, 4 [Stone p. 62]; Jos., Ant. 11, 34, Vi. 67; Tat. 26, 4; Ath. 22, 4 ὁμιλίαν τοῦ ἄρρενος πρὸς τὸ θῆλυ) ὁμιλίαι κακαί *bad company* **1 Cor 15:33** (s. ἦθος and also EpArist 130).

❷ **engagement in talk, either as conversation** (so Diod. S. 16, 55, 2. The Hellenistic term acc. to Moeris [276f=203f P.] is λαλιά q.v.) **or as a speech or lecture to a group** (Ael. Aristid. 42, 9 K.=6 p. 68 D.; Lucian, Demon. 12; Philostrat., Vi. Apoll. 3, 15 p. 93, 20, Imag. Prooem. p. 295, 11; Dositheus 1, 1; TestSol D 4, 14; TestAbr A 5 p. 82, 4 [Stone p. 12]; Jos., Ant. 15, 68; Ps.-Clem., Hom. p. 6, 28; 12, 11; 28 al. Lag.). The latter sense, ***speech, lecture,*** appears in our lit. in ref. to presentation of a monologue before a congregation: ὁμιλίαν ποιεῖσθαι *deliver a sermon, preach* (as Just., D. 28, 2; 85, 5.—On ὁμ. ποιεῖσθαι cp. Jos., Vi. 222) περί τινος *about someth.* IPol 5:1.—DELG s.v. ὅμιλος. M-M. EDNT.

ὅμιλος, ου, ὁ (ὁμός 'common, joint', ἴλη 'band'; Hom. et al.; 1 Km 19:20 Aq.; Philo, Agr. 23) ***crowd, throng*** πᾶς ἐπὶ τῶν πλοίων ὁ ὅμ. *the whole throng* (of those traveling) *on ships* **Rv 18:17 v.l.** (s. Charles, ICC Rv ad loc.; Jos., Ant. 5, 17 ὁ πᾶς ὅμιλος).—DELG. M-M.

ὁμίχλη, ης, ἡ (the etym. correct form is ὀμίχλη, so Hom.; Schwyzer I 411; DELG; B. 66; L-S-J-M ὀμίχλη) (Hom. et al.; Plut., Mor. 460a; Ael. Aristid. 51, 19 K.=27 p. 539 D.; PGM 4, 3024; LXX, En; SibOr 3, 806) **an atmospheric condition that darkens the sky** (but not so thick as νέφος or νεφέλη, Aristot., Mete. 346b, 33), ***mist, fog*** pl. ὁμίχλαι ὑπὸ λαίλαπος ἐλαυνόμεναι *mists driven by the storm* **2 Pt 2:17** (w. ζόφος and σκότος as Lucian, Catapl. 2).—B. 66. Schmidt, Syn. I 611–15. DELG s.v. ὀμίχλη. M-M.

ὄμμα, ατος, τό (Hom.+, more common in poetry than in prose; SIG 1168, 120; PLond III, 678, 6 p. 18 [99/98 BC]; BGU 713, 9; PGM 4, 703; LXX; En 106:5; 10; TestSol; Jos., Bell. 6, 288)

❶ **organ of bodily sight,** ***eye,*** lit., pl. (Diod. S. 3, 46, 2) **Mt 20:34; Mk 8:23.**

❷ **medium of transcendent perception,** ***eye,*** fig. ext. of 1: τὸ ὄμμα τῆς ψυχῆς *the eye of the soul* (Pla., Rep. 7, 533d, Soph. 254a; Porphyr., Vi. Pyth. 47; Philo, Sacr. Abel. 36, Abr. 70.—PGM 4, 517 ἀθανάτοις ὄμμασι; 3, 474.—Rtzst., Mysterienrel.[3] 296f; 318f) ἐμβλέπειν τοῖς ὄμμ. τῆς ψυχῆς εἴς τι *gaze at someth. with the eyes of the soul* 1 Cl 19:3.—B. 225. DELG s.v. ὄπωπα B. M-M.

ὀμνύω (a by-form of ὄμνυμι which is predominant in H. Gk. and therefore in the NT as well; in the form ὄμνυμι Hom. et al.; ins, pap; Just.; the by-form in Hdt., X. et al.; ins, pap, LXX, En, Philo; Jos., Ant. 3, 271, C. Ap. 2, 121. In the NT the older form occurs only in the inf. ὀμνύναι **Mk 14:71** [v.l. ὀμνύειν]; B-D-F §92; W-S. §14, 8; Mlt-H. 251) 1 aor. ὤμοσα; pf. ὀμώμοκα LXX **to affirm the veracity of one's statement by invoking a transcendent entity, freq. w. implied invitation of punishment if one is untruthful,** ***swear, take an oath*** w. acc. of pers. or thing by which one swears (Hom. et al.; X., An. 7, 6, 18; Diod. S. 1, 29, 4 τὴν Ἶσιν; Appian, Syr. 60 §317 πάντας τ. θεούς, Bell. Civ. 4, 68, §289; UPZ 70, 2 [152/151 BC] τὸν Σάραπιν; POxy 239, 5 [66 AD] Νέρωνα; B-D-F §149; Rob. 484. On the LXX s. Johannessohn, Kasus 77; Jos., Ant. 5, 14; 13, 76; Orig., Hippol.) τὸν οὐρανόν, τὴν γῆν *swear by heaven, by the earth* (Apollon. Rhod. 3, 699 and schol. on Apollon. Rhod. 3, 714 ὄμοσον Γαῖάν τε καὶ Οὐρανόν; cp. διομνύω Aesop, Fab. 140 H.=89 P.//91 [I, III] H-H.) **Js 5:12.** τὴν Καίσαρος τύχην MPol 9:2; 10:1. Abs., in the same sense (cp. Jos., Ant. 4, 310) 9:3; (w. ἐπιθῦσαι) MPol 4.—Instead of the acc., ἐν w. dat. of pers. or thing is used (as נִשְׁבַּע בְּ in the OT; ἐν ὑμῖν En 5:6; s. Johannessohn, loc. cit.) ἐν τῷ οὐρανῷ, ἐν τῇ γῇ **Mt 5:34–35** (cp. the contrary advice

1QS 5, 8; MDelcor, VetusT 16, '66, 8–25 [heaven and earth]); cp. **23:22** (GHeinrici, Beiträge III 1905, 42–5; ERietschel, Das Verbot des Eides in d. Bergpredigt: StKr 79, 1906, 373–418; ibid. 80, 1907, 609–18; OProksch, Das Eidesverbot Jesu Christi: Thüringer kirchl. Jahrbuch 1907; HMüller, Zum Eidesverbot d. Bergpred. 1913; OOlivieri, Biblica 4, 1923, 385–90; GStählin, Zum Gebrauch von Beteuerungsformeln im NT, NovT 5, '62, 115–43; Billerb. I 321–36; ULuz, Mt, transl. WLinss '89 ['85], 311–22.—Warning against any and all oaths as early as Choerilus Epicus [V BC] fgm. 7 K.=10 B.: Stob., Flor. 3, 27, 1 vol. III p. 611, 3 H. ὅρκον δ' οὔτ' ἄδικον χρεὼν ὀμνύναι οὔτε δίκαιον; Nicol. Dam.: 90 fgm. 103i Jac.: the Phrygians do not swear at all; Pythagoreans acc. to Diog. L. 8, 22; Essenes in Jos., Bell. 2, 135; cp. Soph., Oed. Col. 650f: a good man's word is sufficient; sim. Aeschyl., fgm. 394 TGF p. 114; s. also Plut., Mor. 275c). ἐν τῇ κεφαλῇ σου *by your head* **5:36.** ἐν τῷ ναῷ, ἐν τῷ χρυσῷ τοῦ ναοῦ **23:16; 21.** ἐν τῷ θυσιαστηρίῳ, ἐν τῷ δώρῳ τῷ ἐπάνω vss. **18, 20.** ἐν τῷ ζῶντι εἰς τ. αἰῶνας τ. αἰώνων **Rv 10:6.** ἐν is replaced by εἰς **Mt 5:35** (B-D-F §206, 2). Also κατά τινος *by someone* or *someth.* (Aristoph.; Demosth. [exx. in FBleek, Hb II/2, 1840, 245a]; Longus, Past. 4, 20, 2; Porphyr., Abst. 3, 16; Ps.-Lucian, Calumn. 18; SIG 526, 8; 685, 27; BGU 248, 12 [I AD]; Gen 22:16; 31:53; Ex 32:13; 1 Km 30:15; Am 6:8; Zeph 1:5) ἐπεὶ κατ' οὐδενὸς εἶχεν μείζονος ὀμόσαι, ὤμοσεν καθ' ἑαυτοῦ *since (God) could swear by no one greater, he swore by himself* **Hb 6:13;** cp. vs. **16** (Philo, Leg. All. 3, 203 οὐ καθ' ἑτέρου ὀμνύει θεός, οὐδὲν γὰρ αὐτοῦ κρεῖττον, ἀλλὰ καθ' ἑαυτοῦ, ὅς ἐστι πάντων ἄριστος, De Abr. 273; on the topic cp. Hom., Il. 1, 524–27). ὤμοσεν ὁ δεσπότης κατὰ τῆς δόξης αὐτοῦ *the Master took an oath by his glory* Hv 2, 2, 5. It is even said that God ὄμ. κατὰ τοῦ υἱοῦ αὐτοῦ v 2, 2, 8. Foll. by direct discourse **Hb 7:21** (Ps 109:4). Dir. disc. is preceded by ὅτι **Mt 26:74** (w. καταθεματίζειν); **Mk 14:71** (w. ἀναθεματίζειν); **Rv 10:6f.** As a quot. fr. Ps 94:11 w. εἰ preceding dir. disc. **Hb 3:11; 4:3** (s. εἰ 4).—W. dat. of pers. *confirm someth.* (τὶ) *for someone with an oath* B 6:8 (Ex 33:1); **Ac 7:17 v.l.** (ἧς by attraction, for ἥν). W. inf. foll. (Just., A I, 21, 3 ὀμνύντα . . . ἑωρακέναι) τίσιν ὤμοσεν μὴ εἰσελεύσεσθαι εἰς τὴν κατάπαυσιν αὐτοῦ; *whom did he assure by an oath that they should not enter his rest?* **Hb 3:18** (dat. w. fut. inf. as Plut., Galba 1063 [22, 12]). διαθήκη ἣν ὤμοσεν τοῖς πατράσι δοῦναι τ. λαῷ *the covenant which he swore to the fathers to give to the people* B 14:1. Foll. by dir. disc. introduced by ὅτι recitative **Mk 6:23** (JDerrett, Law in the NT, '70, 339–58). ὅρκῳ ὀμ. τινί w. inf. foll. **Ac 2:30.** Though the dat. ὅρκῳ is rare in this combination (cp. En 6:4; TestJud 22:3), the acc. (Hom. et al.; Gen 26:3; Num 30:3) is quite common: ὅρκον ὀμ. πρός τινα (ὀμ. πρός τινα Od. 14, 331; 19, 288) *swear an oath to someone* foll. by gen of the aor. inf. **Lk 1:73.**—RHirzel, D. Eid 1902; LWenger, D. Eid in d. griech. pap: ZSavRG, Rom. Abt. 23, 1902, 158ff; JPedersen, Der Eid bei den Semiten 1914; ESeidl, Der Eid in röm.-ägypt. Provinzialrecht, '33.—B. 1437. DELG s.v. ὄμνυμι. M-M. TRE IX, 379–82. EDNT. TW. Sv.

ὁμοήθεια, ας, ἡ (ὁμός 'one and the same, common', ἦθος 'character'; Nicol. Dam.: 90 fgm. 139 Jac.; Philostrat., Vi. Apoll. 2, 11 p. 53, 11; Pollux 3, 62) ***similarity in character, agreement in convictions*** ὁμοήθειαν θεοῦ λαβόντες *you who have received a divine agreement in your convictions* IMg 6:2. κατὰ ὁμοήθειαν θεοῦ λαλεῖν *speak on the basis of a divine unity in convictions* IPol 1:3.

ὁμοθυμαδόν (ὁμός 'one and the same, common', θυμός, and adv. termination) adv. (Aristoph., X. et al. On its formation s. Kühner-Bl. II 307γ; Schwyzer I 626; Mlt-H. 164) ***with one mind/purpose/impulse*** **Ac 1:14; 2:1 v.l., 46; 4:24; 7:57; 8:6; 12:20; 18:12; 19:29; 20:18 v.l.;** MPol 12:3. (W. ἐν ἑνὶ στόματι) δοξάζειν τὸν θεόν **Ro 15:6;** γενόμενοι ὁμ. *unanimously* **Ac 15:25.** The weakened mng. *together* (NRSV et al.) is probable in **5:12** and elsewhere (so EHatch, Essays in Biblical Greek, 1889, 63f; HCadbury, JBL 44, 1925, 216–18; NRSV et al.).—DELG s.v. θυμός. M-M. TW. Spicq.

ὁμοιάζω (ὅμοιος + -άζω; only as v.l. in Mt and Mk) ***be like, resemble*** w. dat. (Leontius 43 p. 88, 6 τὸ παιδίον ὁμοιάζον αὐτῷ) τάφοις κεκονιαμένοις **Mt 23:27 v.l.** Abs. ἡ λαλιά σου ὁμοιάζει *your speech is like* (sc.: τῇ λαλιᾷ τῶν Γαλιλαίων) **Mt 26:73 v.l.;** likew. **Mk 14:70 v.l.**

ὁμοιοπαθής, ές (ὅμοιος, πάσχω; Pla., Rep. 3, 409b, Tim. 45c; Theophr., HP 5, 7, 2; Wsd 7:3; 4 Macc 12:13; Philo, Conf. Lingu. 7; Just.; Tat. 35, 2) **pert. to experiencing similarity in feelings or circumstances,** ***with the same nature*** τινί *as someone* **Ac 14:15; Js 5:17.**—DELG s.v. ὅμοιος. M-M. TW.

ὅμοιος, οία, οιον (ὁμός, 'common'; Hom.+.—On the accent s. B-D-F §13; Mlt-H. 58. On ἡ ὅμοιος **Rv 4:3b** s. a below and B-D-F §59, 2; Mlt-H. 157) ***of the same nature, like, similar.***

ⓐ w. dat. of pers. or thing compared (this is the rule Hom. et al.) ὅμ. αὐτῷ ἐστιν *he looks like him* **J 9:9.**—χρυσῷ ἢ ἀργύρῳ . . . τὸ θεῖον εἶναι ὅμ. *divinity is like gold or silver* **Ac 17:29.** τὰ ὅμ. τούτοις *things like these* **Gal 5:21;** cp. Hm 8:5, 10; 12, 3, 1; (w. παραπλήσιος) 6, 2, 5. ὅμ. ὁράσει λίθῳ ἰάσπιδι *similar in appearance to jasper* **Rv 4:3a;** cp. **3b** (here ὅμ. is an adj. of two endings, as Aesop, Fab. 63a H.=59a, 4 Ch. στήλην ὅμοιον). ὅμ. τῇ ἰδέᾳ *similar in appearance* Hs 9, 3, 1.—**Rv 1:15; 2:18; 4:6f; 9:7, 19; 11:1; 13:2; 21:11, 18;** 1 Cl 35:9 (Ps 49:21); B 7:10a; Dg 2:2f; Hs 9, 19, 2; 9, 21, 2. ὑπὸ ἀνθρώπων σκεύη ὅμοια γενέσθαι τοῖς λοιποῖς *to be made by human hands into vessels like the others* Dg 2:4. ἄλλος ὅμ. ἐμοί *any other like me* Pol 3:2. ὅμ. τοῖς φαρμάκοις *like the poisoners* or *magicians* Hv 3, 9, 7 (cp. the vice list Physiogn. I 327, 15). ἡ καταστροφὴ ὅμ. καταιγίδι *the downfall is like a wind-storm* 1 Cl 57:4 (cp. Pr 1:27). ὅμοιοι αὐτῷ ἐσόμεθα *we shall be like (God)* **1J 3:2** (cp. Herm. Wr. 11, 5 ὅμ. τῷ θεῷ; Orig., C. Cels. 4, 30, 10). ὁ τούτοις τὰ ὅμ. ποιῶν *the one who does such things as these* Hs 6, 5, 5. τὸν ὅμοιον τρόπον τούτοις *in the same way as they* **Jd 7.** ἔσομαι ὅμοιος ὑμῖν ψεύστης *I should be like you, a liar* **J 8:55** (ὅ. αὐτῷ every living thing has affection for 'what is akin to itself' Sir 13:15; 28:4 of one who has no pity for a fellow human). Freq. in parables *like* ὅμ. ἐστίν *it is like* (Aristippus in Diog. L. 2, 79 in a parable: τίς ὅμοιός ἐστί τινι; Philosoph. Max 485, 2 M ἡ παιδεία ὁμοία ἐστὶ χρυσῷ στεφάνῳ) **Mt 11:16; 13:31, 33, 44f, 47, 52; 20:1; Lk 6:47–49; 7:31f; 12:36; 13:18f, 21.** οἵτινές εἰσιν ὅμοιοι χοίροις (-ρων v.l.) *like swine* B 10:3. In brachylogy **Rv 9:10.** κέρατα δύο ὅμοια ἀρνίῳ **13:11.**—In a special sense *equally great* or *important, as powerful as, equal (to)*(Gen 2:20; Jos., Ant. 8, 364; cp. the Lat. motto 'nec pluribus impar') τίς ὅμ. τῷ θηρίῳ, καὶ τίς δύναται πολεμῆσαι μετ' αὐτοῦ; *who is a match for the beast, and who is able to fight it?* **Rv 13:4.** τίς ὅμ. τῇ πόλει τῇ μεγάλῃ; **18:18.** δευτέρα (i.e. ἐντολή) ὁμοία αὐτῇ (i.e. τῇ πρώτῃ) *a second, just as great as this one* **Mt 22:39; Mk 12:31 v.l.**

ⓑ w. gen. of comparison (Theophr., HP 9, 11, 11; Hero Alex. I p. 60, 16; Aelian, HA 8, 1 τέτταρας ὁμοίους ἐκείνου κύνας; PIand VI, 97, 9 [III AD]; Cat. Cod. Astr. VIII/3 p. 197, 16 ὅμ. ὄφεως; Sir 13:16; Tat. 14:2.—Kühner-G. I 413, 10; B-D-F §182, 4; Rob. 530) ἔσομαι ὅμ. ὑμῶν ψεύστης **J 8:55 v.l.** (for ὑμῖν; cp. a above; Rydbeck, 46–49). φεῦγε ἀπὸ παντὸς πονηροῦ καὶ ἀπὸ παντὸς ὁμοίου αὐτοῦ *avoid evil of any kind, and everything resembling it* D 3:1 v.l.; B 10:3 s. above.

ⓒ The acc. of comparison appears to be a solecism and nothing more in ὅμ. υἱὸν ἀνθρώπου *one like a human being* **Rv 1:13; 14:14** (both have υἱῷ as v.l.), but s. RCharles, comm. ad loc.—B-D-F §182, 4; Rob. 530.

ⓓ abs. τράγοι ὅμ. *goats that are alike* B 7:6, 10b (Just., D. 40, 4). ὅμοιοι ἐγένοντο λευκοί *they all alike became white* Hs 9, 4, 5. (τὰ δένδρα) ξηρά εἰσι καὶ ὅμοια *(the trees) are all alike dry = one is as dry as the other* 3:2a; cp. vs. 1b. ὅμοια ἦν πάντα *they* (the trees) *were all alike* 3:1a; cp. vs. 2b and 3ab. (Of dissidents: ὅμοια μὲν [viz. ἡμῖν, to us] λαλοῦντες, ἀνόμοια δὲ φρονοῦντες Iren. 1, prol. 2 [Harv. I 4, 5].)—B. 912. Schmidt, Syn. IV 471–87, cp. ἴσος. DELG. M-M. TW.

ὁμοιότης, ητος, ἡ (ὅμοιος; Pre-Socr., Pla., Isocr.+; Polyb. 6, 53, 5; 13, 7, 2; Plut., Mor. 25b; 780e; Epict. 4, 11, 28; Lucian, Dial. Deor. 6, 5; pap, LXX; ParJer 9:26f; Philo; Ath. 17, 2; κατὰ ἀναλογίαν ἢ ὁ ληπτέα Did., Gen. 57, 18; ὁμ. πρὸς τὴν … εἰκόνα Hippol., Ref. 4, 27, 2) **state of being similar to someth., *likeness, similarity, agreement*** πάντας ὑμᾶς αὐτῷ ἐν ὁμ. εἶναι *you are all to be like (Jesus Christ)* IEph 1:3. ἐκπλήττεσθαι ἐπὶ τῇ ὁμ. τινος *be amazed at the similarity w. someth.* B 7:10. καθ᾽ ὁμοιότητα (Philo, Fuga 51; Herm. Wr. 464, 29; 518, 13 Sc.; BGU 1028, 15; PSI 107, 2; PGM 1, 211; Gen 1:11, 12) *in quite the same way* **Hb 4:15.** W. gen foll. (Dionys. Byz. §29; BGU 1028, 15 [II AD]; POxy 1202, 24; PSI 107, 2; Philo, Rer. Div. Her. 232, Spec. Leg. 1, 296; Iren., 1, 15, 5 [Harv. I 154, 7]) κατὰ τὴν ὁμ. Μελχισέδεκ *in the same way as M.* **7:15.**—DELG s.v. ὅμοιος. M-M. TW.

ὁμοιοτρόπως adv. of ὁμοιότροπος 'of like manner' (Thu. 6, 20, 3; Aristot., Gen. An. 3, 5; Philo, Aet. M. 20 [all three w. dat.]) ***in the same way*** ὁμ. τοῖς προειρημένοις *in the same way as those already mentioned* Dg 3:2.—DELG s.v. ὅμοιος.

ὁμοιόω fut. ὁμοιώσω; 1 aor. ὡμοίωσα LXX; aor. subj. 1 pl. ὁμοιώσωμεν **Mk 4:30.** Pass.: 1 fut. ὁμοιωθήσομαι; 1 aor. ὡμοιώθην (on the form ὁμοιώθην **Ro 9:29 v.l.,** s. W-H., app. 161); pf. ptc. pl. ὡμοιώμενοι (EpJer 38) (Hom.+).

❶ ***make like*** τινά τινι *make someone like a person* or *thing;* pass. *become like, be like* τινί *someone* (Ps.-Apollod. 1, 4, 1, 1; Herm. Wr. 1, 26a; PGM 4, 1859; 2500; Sir 13:1; Ps 48:13; Philo, Deus Imm. 48; TestBenj 7:5; τῷ θεῷ Did., Gen. 145, 6; Hippol., Ref. 6, 53, 7) τοῖς ἀδελφοῖς **Hb 2:17** (s. Merki at ὁμοίωσις end). Of deities (Diod. S. 1, 86, 3 ὁμοιωθῆναί τισιν ζῴοις) ὁμοιωθέντες ἀνθρώποις κατέβησαν *they have come down in the form of human beings* **Ac 14:11** (Aesop, Fab. 89 P.=140 H.//111 Ch.//91 H-H. Ἑρμῆς ὁμοιωθεὶς ἀνθρώπῳ). ἀνδρί **Mt 7:24, 26.** αὐτοῖς **6:8;** B 4:2; cp. vs. 6. ἀνθρώποις τοιούτοις 10:4f. τοῖς τοιούτοις vs. 6f. ὡμοιώθη ἡ βασιλεία τ. οὐρανῶν *the kingdom of heaven is like, may be compared to* **Mt 13:24; 18:23; 22:2.** Also, w. a glance at the future parousia, ὁμοιωθήσεται ἡ β. τ. οὐρ. **25:1.** On these Mt pass. in the sense of 'has become like' or 'will be like' s. DCarson, NTS 31, '85, 277–82. Used w. ὡς instead of the dat. (cp. Ezk 32:2) ὡς Γόμορρα ἂν ὡμοιώθημεν *we would have resembled Gomorrah* **Ro 9:29** (Is 1:9). Ten times w. the dat. ὡμοιώθην GJs 3:2 in Anna's lament.

❷ ***compare*** τινά τινι *someone with* or *to someone* or *someth.* (τίῳ σ᾽, ὦ φίλε γάμβρε, καλῶς εἰκάσδω [=ὁμοιόω]; 'to what, dear bridegroom, can I properly compare you?' Sappho, fgm. 127 D.[2] [=115 Campbell]; ins: AnnBSA 29 p. 35 [IV AD]; Did., Gen. 72, 2) τί τινι *someth. with someth.* (Plut., Cim. et Lucull. 1, 5; SSol 1:9; La 2:13; Wsd 7:9; Is 40:18) **Mt 7:24 v.l.** τίνι … ὁμοιώσω τὴν γενεὰν ταύτην; *to what shall I compare this generation?* **Mt 11:16;** cp. **Lk 7:31.** τίνι ὁμοιώσω τὴν βασιλείαν τοῦ θεοῦ; **13:20;** cp. vs. **18.** W. combination of two thoughts πῶς ὁμοιώσωμεν τὴν βασιλείαν τοῦ θεοῦ; *how shall I portray God's Reign?* and *to what shall I compare God's Reign?* **Mk 4:30** (πῶς here equivalent to τίνι: s. HLjungvik, Eranos 62, '64, 33; for the verb cp. Is 40:18 and s. HBartsch, TZ, 15, '59, 126–28).—DELG s.v. ὅμοιος. TW.

ὁμοίωμα, ατος, τό (ὁμοιόω; Pla., Parm. 132d; 133d, Phdr. 250b; Ps.-Aristot., Int. 1, 16a, 7f; SIG 669, 52; PFay 106, 20; LXX; En 31:2; Just., D. 94, 3).

❶ **state of having common experiences, *likeness*** (ἐν ὁμ. τυγχάνειν 'liken' Theoph. Ant. 2, 16 [p. 140, 12])οὗ (Χριστοῦ) καὶ κατὰ τὸ ὁμοίωμα ἡμᾶς … οὕτως ἐγερεῖ ὁ πατὴρ αὐτοῦ *in accordance with whose likeness* (=just as God raised him) *his Father will also raise us in this way* ITr 9:2. This is prob. the place for **Ro 6:5** εἰ σύμφυτοι γεγόναμεν τῷ ὁμοιώματι τ. θανάτου αὐτοῦ *if we have been united* (i.e. αὐτῷ *with him;* cp. vs. 4 συνετάφημεν αὐτῷ) *in the likeness of his death* (=in the same death that he died); but s. PGächter, ZKT 54, 1930, 88–92; OKuss, D. Römerbr. I, '63, 301. On the syntax, B-D-F §194, 2; Rob. 528. ἁμαρτάνειν ἐπὶ τῷ ὁμοιώματι τῆς παραβάσεως Ἀδάμ *sin in the likeness of Adam's transgression* (=just as Adam did, who transgressed one of God's express commands) **5:14.**—Abstr. for concr. τὰ ὁμοιώματα = τὰ ὅμοια: ὃς ἂν τὰ ὁμοιώματα ποιῇ τοῖς ἔθνεσιν *whoever does things similar to (the deeds of) the gentiles = acts as the gentiles do* Hm 4, 1, 9. περὶ τοιούτων τινῶν ὁμοιωμάτων πονηρῶν *(thoughts) about any other wicked things similar to these* 4, 1, 1.—ἐν τίνι ὁμοιώματι παραβάλωμεν αὐτήν; *with what corresponding thing can we compare it?* **Mk 4:30 v.l.**

❷ **state of being similar in appearance, *image, form***

ⓐ *image, copy* (Dt 4:16ff; 1 Km 6:5; 4 Km 16:10; 1 Macc 3:48; Just., D. 94, 3) ὁμοίωμα εἰκόνος φθαρτοῦ ἀνθρώπου (s. εἰκών 3; pleonasm as Maximus Tyr. 27, 3c εἰς μορφῆς εἶδος) **Ro 1:23** (cp. Ps 105:20).

ⓑ *form, appearance* (schol. on Apollon. Rhod. 4, 825–31a ὁμ. κ. πρόσωπον γυναικός=figure and face of a woman; Dt 4:12; Josh 22:28; Ezk 1:16; Jos., Ant. 8, 195; Hippol., Ref. 5, 19, 20; 7, 28, 3) τὰ ὁμοιώματα τῶν ἀκρίδων ὅμοια (v.l.ὅμοιοι) ἵπποις *the locusts resembled horses in appearance* **Rv 9:7.**

❸ There is no general agreement on the mng. in two related passages in which Paul uses our word in speaking of Christ's earthly life. The expressions ἐν ὁμοιώματι ἀνθρώπων (P[46], Marcion, Orig.: ἀνθρώπου) **Phil 2:7** and ἐν ὁμοιώματι σαρκὸς ἁμαρτίας **Ro 8:3** could mean that the Lord in his earthly ministry possessed a completely human form and that his physical body was capable of sinning as human bodies are, or that he had the form of a human being and was looked upon as such (cp. En 31:2 ἐν ὁμ. w. gen.='similar to', 'looking like'; Aesop, Fab. 140 H. of Hermes ὁμοιωθεὶς ἀνθρώπῳ), but without losing his identity as a divine being even in this world. In the light of what Paul says about Jesus in general it is prob. that he uses our word to bring out both that Jesus in his earthly career was similar to sinful humans and yet not totally like them (s. JWeiss, Das Urchristentum1917, 376ff; cp. FGillman, CBQ 49, '87, 597–604).—S. the lit. on ἁρπαγμός.—DELG s.v. ὅμοιος. M-M. EDNT. TW. Sv.

ὁμοίως adv. of ὅμοιος (Pind., Hdt.+) **pert. to being similar in some respect, *likewise, so, similarly, in the same way*** **Mk 4:16 v.l.; Lk 3:11; 10:37; 13:3, 5 v.l.** (see ὡσαύτως) al. ὁμ. καί *and so, so also* **Mt 22:26; 26:35; Mk 15:31; Lk 5:33;** IPol

5:1. ὁμ. μέντοι καί in *the same way, too* **Jd 8.** ὁμ. δὲ καί (pap, EpArist; Jos., Bell. 2, 575, Ant. 14, 216) **Lk 5:10; 10:32; 1 Cor 7:3f; Js 2:25.** In **Ro 1:27** the rdg. varies betw. ὁμ. τε καί and ὁμ. δὲ καί (v.l.). Sim. **Mt 27:41** ὁμοίως καί (vv.ll. ὁμ. δὲ καί and simply ὁμ.).—καθὼς θέλετε . . . , ποιεῖτε ὁμοίως *as you wish . . . , do so* **Lk 6:31.** ὁμ. καθώς *in the same way as* **17:28.** ὁμ. πάλιν *similarly, again* B 12:1. W. the dat. foll. ὁμ. πλανᾶσθαι ἐκείνοις *to go astray as they did* 2:9. Somet. the idea of similarity can fade into the background so that ὁμ. means *also* (UPZ 70, 8 [152/151 BC] ὀμνύω, ὅτι ψευδῆ πάντα καὶ οἱ παρὰ σὲ θεοὶ ὁμοίως; 65, 8f ὁμ. καὶ Κότταβος, ὁμ. καὶ Χεντοσνεύς; TestJob 47:6 ἀφανεῖς ἐγένοντο . . . οἱ σκώληκες . . . , ὁμ. καὶ αἱ πληγαί; GrBar 9:3; Ath. 9, 2 [to introduce additional Scriptural evidence]) ταῦτα καὶ ὁ υἱὸς ὁμ. ποιεῖ *this the Son also does* **J 5:19;** cp. **6:11; 21:13.**—As a connective (Hierocles 26 p. 480 [ὁμοίως δὲ καί]; oft. pap); more than one ὅμ. *in the same way . . . also* (an edict of Augustus fr. Cyrenaica, SEG IX, 8, 108; 110 [lit.]=DocsAugTib 311) **1 Pt 3:1, 7.** Cp. **5:5.**—M-M. TW.

ὁμοίωσις, εως, ἡ (ὁμοιόω) **state of being similar, *likeness, resemblance*** (so since Pla., Theaet. 176b; Aristot., De Plant. 2, 6, 826b, 32f; Plut., Mor. 53c; Sext. Emp., Hyp. Pyrrh. 75 καθ' ὁμοίωσιν κρίνειν; LXX; TestNapht 2:2; Hippol. Ref. 1, 20, 17 ὁμ. θεῷ; Jos., Ant. 13, 67 καθ' ὁμοίωσιν; Just., D. 77, 4; Tat.) καθ' ὁμοίωσιν (w. κατ' εἰκόνα in Gen 1:26, as also in Philo; Iren. 5, 16, 2 [Harv. II 368, 4]; Did., Gen. 59, 5; Theoph. Ant. 2, 18 [p. 144, 7]). The pass. in Genesis is quoted 1 Cl 33:5; B 5:5; 6:12, and **Js 3:9** uses it freely (cp. Did., Gen. 56, 28). HMerki, ΟΜΟΙΩΣΙΣ ΘΕΩ '52 (Pla. to Greg. of Nyssa).—DELG s.v. ὅμοιος. M-M. TW. Sv.

ὁμολογέω (ὁμόλογος 'of one mind') impf. ὡμολόγουν; fut. ὁμολογήσω; 1 aor. ὡμολόγησα. Pass.: aor. 3 sg. ὡμολογήθη (Just.); pf. ὡμολόγηται (Just.) (Soph., Hdt.+)

❶ **to commit oneself to do someth. for someone, *promise, assure*** (Hdt., Pla. et al.; IGR IV, 542, 6f [Phryg.] εὐχὴν . . . , ἣν ὡμολόγησεν ἐν Ῥώμῃ; Jos., Ant. 6, 40 'consent') ἐπαγγελίας ἧς (by attr. of the rel. for ἥν) ὡμολόγησεν ὁ θεὸς τῷ Ἀβραάμ *promise that God had made to Abraham* **Ac 7:17;** μεθ' ὅρκου ὁμ. w. aor. inf. foll. (B-D-F §350; Rob. 1031f) *promise with an oath* **Mt 14:7.** *Solemnly promise, vow* ὁ . . . ὁμολογήσας μὴ γῆμαι ἄγαμος διαμενέτω Agr 18.

❷ **to share a common view or be of common mind about a matter, *agree*** (Hdt. 2, 81 of similarity in cultic rites; Pla., Sym. 202b ὁμολογεῖταί γε παρὰ πάντων μέγας θεὸς εἶναι=there is general agreement that [Love] is a great god; prob. Cleanthes in his definition of τὸ ἀγαθόν: Coll. Alex. p. 229, no. 3, 7; 4 Macc 13:5 reach a conclusion together; pap; Sext. Emp., Adv. Eth. 218 agreement on a subject; Iren. 1, 26, 2 [Harv. I 212, 5] οἱ . . . Ἐβιωναῖοι ὁμ. μὲν τον κόσμον ὑπὸ τοῦ ὄντως θεοῦ γεγονέναι; Theoph. Ant. 2, 4 [p. 102, 10]) ὁμολογοῦσιν τὰ ἀμφότερα *they agree (with one another) on all of them* **Ac 23:8** (but s. 3a below). This meaning readily shades into

❸ **to concede that something is factual or true, *grant, admit, confess*** (Just., D. 80, 1 admission of someth. in an argument; sim. 110, 1)

ⓐ gener., to admit the truth of someth. (Pla., Prot. 317b ὁμολογῶ σοφιστὴς εἶναι; Jos., Ant. 3, 322 an admission of factuality by enemies; Just., D. 2, 5 ὡμολόγησα μὴ εἰδέναι admission of ignorance) *agree, admit* καθάπερ καὶ αὐτὸς ὡμολόγησας Dg 2:1. ὁμολογήσαντες ὅτι ξένοι εἰσίν *admitting that they were* (only) *foreigners* **Hb 11:13.** ὁμολογοῦμεν χάριν μὴ εἰληφέναι *we admit that we have not received grace* IMg 8:1. For **Ac 23:8** s. 2 above.

ⓑ w. a judicial connotation: *make a confession, confess* abs. MPol 6:1; 9:2. τί τινι: ὁμολογῶ δὲ τοῦτό σοι, ὅτι **Ac 24:14.** Foll. by acc. and inf. ὡμολόγησεν ἑαυτὸν Χριστιανὸν εἶναι MPol 12:1 (cp. w. inf. foll.: Just., A II, 13, 2 Χριστιανὸς εὑρεθῆναι . . . ὁμολογῶ; Theoph. Ant. 2, 8 [p. 118, 7] ὁμ. αὐτὰ τὰ πλάνα πνεύματα εἶναι δαίμονες). Cp. John the Baptist's action in reply to questioning by the authorities καὶ ὡμολόγησεν καὶ οὐκ ἠρνήσατο καὶ ὡμολόγησεν ὅτι (dir. disc. follows) **J 1:20** (cp. Plut., Mor. 509e in interrogation; the contrast ὁμ. and ἀρνεῖσθαι as Thu. 6, 60, 3; Phalaris, Ep. 147, 3 ὁμολογοῦμεν κ. οὐκ ἀρνησόμεθα; Aelian, NA 2, 43; Jos., Ant. 6, 151; cp. MPol 9:2 and many of the passages given below).

ⓒ w. focus on admission of wrongdoing (X., An. 1, 6, 7; Ps.-Aristot., Mirabilia 152 ὁμολογοῦντες ἃ ἐπιώρκησαν; Arrian, Anab. 7, 29, 2 [s. ἴασις 2]; Jos., Ant. 6, 151) ἐὰν ὁμολογῶμεν τὰς ἁμαρτίας ἡμῶν *if we confess our sins* **1J 1:9** (cp. Appian, Liby. 79 §369 ὁμολογοῦντες ἁμαρτεῖν; Sir 4:26; ApcSed 13:3 [abs.]; ὁμ. τὸ ἁμάρτημα Did., Gen. 93, 6; ins fr. Sardis: ὁμολογῶ τ[ὸ] ἁμάρτημ]α Μηνί=I confess my sin to Men, s. FSteinleitner, Die Beicht 1913, p. 46 no. 20, 4f=ILydiaKP p. 15, no. 25). S. ἐξομολογέω 2a.

❹ **to acknowledge someth., ordinarily in public, *acknowledge, claim, profess, praise***—ⓐ of a public declaration as such (Herodian. 4, 4, 5 [fr. Steinleitner, p. 109, s. 3c] expression of thanks) ὁμολογήσω αὐτοῖς ὅτι (w. dir. disc. foll.) *I will say to them plainly* **Mt 7:23.** W. inf. foll. (X., Mem. 2, 3, 9; Jos., Ant. 9, 254) θεὸν ὁμολογοῦσιν εἰδέναι *they claim to know God* **Tit 1:16** (opp. ἀρνεῖσθαι, s. 3b).

ⓑ of profession of allegiance (ὁμολογῶ εἶναι χριστιανός Theoph. Ant. 1, 1 [p. 58, 11]) —Esp. of confessing Christ, or the teaching of his community/church; w. double acc. (B-D-F §157, 2; 416, 3; Rob. 480.—Jos., Ant. 5, 52; Just., A II, 5, 1 εἰ θεὸν ὡμολογοῦμεν βοηθόν, D. 35, 2 Ἰησοῦν ὁμολογεῖν καὶ κύριον καὶ χριστόν) ἐὰν ὁμολογήσῃς κύριον Ἰησοῦν *if you confess Jesus as Lord* **Ro 10:9** (cp. τὸν Δία ὁμ. θεόν Orig., C. Cels. 5, 46, 7). αὐτὸν ὁμ. Χριστόν *confess that he is the Messiah* **J 9:22.** ὁμ. αὐτὸν σαρκοφόρον ISm 5:2. ὁμ. Ἰησοῦν Χριστὸν ἐν σαρκὶ ἐληλυθότα *acknowledge that Jesus Christ has come in the flesh* **1J 4:2;** cp. **2J 7.** W. acc. and inf. (Isocr., Or. 4, 100, 61d; Aelian, VH 1, 27; Orig., C. Cels. 1, 41, 9) ὁμ. Ἰησοῦν Χρ. ἐν σαρκὶ ἐληλυθέναι Pol 7:1a; **1J 4:2 v.l.** ὁμ. τὴν εὐχαριστίαν σάρκα εἶναι τοῦ σωτῆρος ἡμῶν Ἰ. Χρ. ISm 7:1. W. ὅτι foll. (Isocr., Or. 11, 5, 222d, but w. mng. 2; Just., D. 39, 6) ὁμ. ὅτι Ἰησοῦς ἐστιν ὁ υἱὸς τοῦ θεοῦ **1J 4:15.** ὁμ. ὅτι κύριον ἔχετε Hs 9, 28, 7 (opp. ἀρν.). W. a single acc. of the pers. whom one confesses, or whom one declares to be someth. that is revealed by the context (Just., D. 35, 1, 2 Ἰησοῦν . . . ὁμολογεῖν; Did., Gen. 176, 13 ὁ γὰρ ὁμολογῶν τὸν θεὸν ἐν Χριστῷ τοῦτο ποιεῖ; Theoph. Ant. 3, 9 [p. 222, 13] θεὸν ὁμ.): ὁμ. τὸν υἱόν **1J 2:23** (opp. ἀρν. as Mel., P. 73, 537 ἀπαρνήσω τὸν ὁμολογήσαντά σε). μὴ ὁμ. τὸν Ἰησοῦν **4:3** (s. λύω 4, end). Cp. 2 Cl 3:2a. τινὰ ἔν τινι *someone by someth.* ἐν τοῖς ἔργοις 4:3; cp. 3:4. ἐὰν ὁμολογήσωμεν δι' οὗ ἐσώθημεν *if we confess him through whom we were saved* 3:3. The acc. (αὐτόν) is supplied fr. the context **J 12:42;** cp. Hs 9, 28, 4.—W. acc. of thing ὁμ. τὸ μαρτύριον τοῦ σταυροῦ Pol 7:1b. ὁμ. τὴν καλὴν ὁμολογίαν **1 Ti 6:12** (ὁμ. ὁμολογίαν='make a promise': Pla., Crito 52a; Jer 51:25; but = 'bear testimony to a conviction': Philo, Mut. Nom. 57, Abr. 203).—Instead of acc. of pers. we may have ἔν τινι *confess someone,* an Aramaism (s. Mlt-H. 463f; B-D-F §220, 2; EbNestle, ZNW 7,1906, 279f; 8, 1907, 241; 9, 1908, 253; FBurkitt, Earliest Sources for the Life of Jesus 1910, 19f). ὅστις ὁμολογήσει ἐν ἐμοὶ ἔμπροσθεν τῶν ἀνθρώπων *whoever confesses me before people* **Mt 10:32a;** sim. **Lk 12:8a.** But

2 Cl 3:2 uses the acc. when it quotes this saying (s. above.—In these last three pass. opp. ἀρν.). Jesus' acknowledgment of the believer on judgment day complements this confession: ἐν αὐτῷ **Mt 10:32b; Lk 12:8b.** αὐτόν 2 Cl 3:2b (opp. ἀρν. in all these pass.—GBornkamm, D. Wort Jesu vom Bekennen [Mt 10:32]: Pastoraltheologie 34, '39, 108–18). τὸ ὄνομα αὐτοῦ **Rv 3:5.**—Abs. pass. στόματι ὁμολογεῖται *with the mouth confession is made* **Ro 10:10.**

ⓒ *praise* w. dat. (Dio Chrys. 10 [11], 147; B-D-F §187, 4; Rob. 541. In the LXX ἐξομολογεῖσθαι τῷ θεῷ. S. ἐξομολογέω 4.) καρπὸς χειλέων ὁμολογούντων τῷ ὀνόματι αὐτοῦ *the fruit of lips that praise his name* **Hb 13:15.**—B. 1267. DELG s.v. ὁμός. M-M. TW. Sv.

ὁμολόγησις, ήσεως, ἡ (ὁμολογέω; Diod. S. 17, 68, 4) **act of professing allegiance, *confessing*** (opp. ἄρνησις) Hs 9, 28, 7.—TW.

ὁμολογία, ας, ἡ (ὁμολογέω; Hdt., Thu. et al.; ins, pap, LXX, Philo; Jos., Bell. 4, 92, Ant. 15, 52, C. Ap. 1, 89 al.; Just., Did., Hippol.; loanw. in rabb.)

❶ **expression of allegiance as an action, *professing, confessing*** (s. ὁμολογέω 4b; θανάτου καταφρονεῖν ὑπὲρ τῆς ὁμολογίας τοῦ Χριστιανισμοῦ=to disdain death in favor of confessing allegiance to Christ, Orig., C. Cels. 2, 15, 16) act. ἡ ὑποταγὴ τῆς ὁμ. ὑμῶν εἰς τὸ εὐαγγέλιον *the subjection of your professing of the gospel* (=your professing of the gospel finds expression in obedient subjection to its requirements) **2 Cor 9:13.**

❷ **statement of allegiance, as content of an action, *confession, acknowledgment that one makes:*** Jesus as the ἀρχιερεὺς τῆς ὁμ. ἡμῶν *the high priest of (whom) our confession (speaks)* **Hb 3:1.** κρατεῖν τῆς ὁμ. *hold fast (to) the confession* **4:14.** κατέχειν τὴν ὁμ. τῆς ἐλπίδος ἀκλινῆ *hold fast the confession of hope without wavering* **10:23.** ὁμολογεῖν τὴν καλὴν ὁμ. *make the good profession of faith* **1 Ti 6:12** (ὁμολογέω 4b). Jesus, the first Christian martyr (s. μαρτυρέω 1c), bore witness or testified to the same *good profession of faith* vs. **13** (s. CTurner, JTS 28, 1927, 270–3).—ASeeberg, Der Katechismus der Urchristenheit 1903, 143; 172; 186; PFeine, D. Gestalt d. apostolischen Glaubensbekenntnisses in d. Zeit des NTs 1925; EvDobschütz, D. Apostolicum in bibl.-theol. Beleuchtung '32; GBornkamm, Ὁμολογία: Her 71, '36, 377–93, also ThBl 21, '42, 56–66 (Hb); AHunter, Paul and His Predecessors '40; PCarrington, The Primitive Christian Catechism '40; OCullmann, Les premières confessions de foi chrétiennes '43; VNeufeld, The Earliest Christian Confessions '63; HvCampenhausen, Das Bekenntnis im Urchristentum, ZNW 63, '72, 210–53.—DELG s.v. ὁμός. M-M. TW. Sv.

ὁμολογουμένως (ὁμολογέω) adv. (Thu. et al.; pap, 4 Macc) **pert. to being a matter on which there is general agreement, *uncontestable, undeniably, most certainly, beyond question*** (Thu. 6, 90, 3; X., An. 2, 6, 1; Pla., Menex. 243c; Diod. S. 9, 11, 2; 13, 27, 4; Epict. 1, 4, 7; Vett. Val. 168, 17; UPZ 161, 65 [119 BC]; 162 V, 32; 4 Macc 6:31; 7:16; 16:1; EpArist 24 [s. p. xxix Wendl.]; Jos., Ant. 1, 180; 2, 229.—Crönert 241; Hippol., Ref. 5, 7, 22; 9, 10, 6) **1 Ti 3:16;** Dg 5:4.—M-M. TW. Spicq. Sv.

ὁμονοέω (Thu. et al.; Dio Chrys. 4, 42; 11 [12], 74; Epict. 2, 20, 31; 2, 22, 24; ins; Sb 4827, 5; LXX; EpArist 185; Jos., Ant. 12, 283, C. Ap. 2, 294) **to be like-minded, *be in agreement, live in harmony*** ὁμ. ἐν ἀγάπῃ κτλ. 1 Cl 62:2.—Renehan '75, 150. DELG s.v. ὁμός. M-M.

ὁμόνοια, ας, ἡ (ὁμονέω; Thu. et al.; Diod. S. 12, 75, 3; Epict. 4, 5, 35; Plut., Ages. 5, 5; Dio Chrys. 21 [38] περὶ ὁμονοίας al.; Ael. Aristid. 23 and 24 K.=42 and 44 D.: περὶ ὁμονοίας; ins, e.g. IPriene 54, 40 of reconciled parties; late pap; LXX; Ps.-Phoc. 74; 219: other reff. Horst p. 164 and 253; Philo; Jos., Bell. 2, 345, Ant. 13, 67, C. Ap. 2, 179; TestJos 17:3; SibOr 3, 375; loanw. in rabb.) **a state of like-mindedness, *oneness of mind, unanimity, concord, harmony.*** W. ἀγάπη IEph 4:1. W. εἰρήνη (q.v., 1b) 1 Cl 60:4; 63:2; 65:1; w. still other sim. concepts 61:1. W. πίστις and ἀγάπη IPhld 11:2; w. still other Christian virtues Hm 8:9; ἐνδύσασθαι τὴν ὁμ. *put on harmony* i.e. *be in agreement* 1 Cl 30:3. ἡ ὁμ. ὑμῶν τῆς πίστεως *your unanimity in the faith* IEph 13:1; ἐν ὁμ. *harmoniously, in agreement* (Ps 54:15; 82:6; Wsd 18:9) 1 Cl 9:4; 11:2; 20:3; 34:7 (ἐν ὁμ. ἐπὶ τὸ αὐτό as Ps 82:6); also μεθ' ὁμονοίας 21:1. ἐν ὁμ. καὶ εἰρήνῃ 20:10; cp. vs. 11. ἀγάπη πάντα ποιεῖ ἐν ὁμ. *love does everything in harmony* 49:5. Hence ποιεῖν τι ἐν ὁμ. ἀγάπης *do someth. in loving harmony* 50:5. διαμένετε ἐν τῇ ὁμ. ὑμῶν *continue in your (present) unanimity* ITr 12:2. ἐν ὁμ. θεοῦ *in godly harmony* (i.e., h. brought about by God) IMg 6:1; 15; IPhld ins.; σύμφωνοι ὄντες ἐν ὁμ. *being harmoniously in concord* IEph 4:2 (cp. Philo, Mut. Nom. 200 τὸ σύμφωνον τῆς ὁμονοίας).—Personified as a virtue Hs 9, 15, 2 (cp. the deity Ὁμόνοια: Apollon. Rhod. 2, 718; Nicol. Dam.: 90 fgm. 130, 69 Jac.; Paus. 5, 14, 9; Chariton 3, 2, 16; CIG 4342, 3; OGI 479, 4; 11; 536, 6; SIG ind. III p. 179b).—HKramer, Quid valeat ὁμόνοια in litteris Graecis, diss. Gött. 1915; JdeRomilly, Vocabulaire et propaganda ou les premiers emplois du mot ὁμόνοια: Mélanges . . . offerts à PChantraine '72, 199–209, AErskine, The Hellenistic Stoa '90, 90–95.—DELG s.v. ὁμός. Sv.

ὁμόσε (ὁμός 'one and the same, common') adv. (Hom. et al.; pap) ***to one and the same place,*** also for ὁμοῦ=*together* (Polyb. 6, 7, 5 al.; Vett. Val. ind.; PGiss 4, 6 [II AD]; Jos., Ant. 12, 292.—B-D-F §103; Rob. 299f) ὁμόσε ὄντων αὐτῶν **Ac 20:18 v.l.**—DELG s.v. ὁμός.

ὁμότεχνος, ον (ὁμός 'one and the same', τέχνη; since Hdt. 2, 89; Appian, Bell. Civ. 4, 27 §119; Lucian; Alciphron 3, 25, 4; Philostrat., Vi. Soph. 1, 9 p. 11, 27; Ps.-Phocyl. 88; Jos., Ant. 8, 334; IKosPH 324; PFouad 37, 7 [48 AD]) ***practicing the same trade*** **Ac 18:3.**—DELG s.v. ὁμός. M-M.

ὁμοῦ adv. (Hom.+; loanw. in rabb.)—❶ **pert. to being together in the same place, *together*** ἦσαν ὁμ. Σίμων Πέτρος καὶ Θωμᾶς . . . *Simon Peter, Thomas . . . were together* **J 21:2.** ἦσαν πάντες ὁμ. ἐπὶ τὸ αὐτό *they were all together in one place* **Ac 2:1** (πάντες ὁμ. as Jos., Ant. 7, 276). ἐστάθησαν ὅμ. *they had stood together* Hs 9, 4, 1. συναχθέντες ὁμοῦ *gathered as a group* GJs 9:1.

❷ **pert. to being simultaneous, *together at the same time (as), in company (with)*** ἔτρεχον οἱ δύο ὁμ. *the two were runnning together* **J 20:4** (cp. TestNapht 5:3). τὰ δύο ὁμ. *these two things at the same time* IMg 5:1. πάντες ὁμ. εὐφρανθήσονται *they will all rejoice together* Hv 3, 4, 2; cp. GPt 8:32 (cp. En 6:5; Jos., Ant. 7, 276 ὁμοῦ πάντες μιᾷ γνώμῃ). ἵνα ὁ σπείρων ὁμ. χαίρῃ καὶ ὁ θερίζων *so that the sower and the reaper may rejoice together* **J 4:36** (the double ptc. as Jos., Bell. 6, 271). πάντα ὁμ. καλά ἐστιν *all things together are good* IPhld 9:2. ἐβάσταζον ὁμ. *they carried together* Hs 9, 3, 5.—DELG s.v. ὁμός. M-M.

ὁμόφρων, ον (ὁμός 'common', φρήν; Hom.+; Plut., Mor. 432c; OGI 515, 4; Kaibel adv. 'in sympathy' 493, 5f; Ps.-Phocyl. 30, s. ὁμόνοια) **pert. to being like-minded, *united in spirit,***

harmonious (w. συμπαθής et al.) **1 Pt 3:8** (Strabo 6, 3, 3 ὁμόφρονας ὡς ἂν ἀλλήλων ἀδελφούς).—DELG s.v. φρήν. M-M. Spicq.

ὁμόφυλος, ον (ὁμός 'common', φῦλον 'tribe', cp. φυλή; Eur., Pla. X. et al.; pap; Jos., Ant. 17, 313) **pert. to belonging to the same tribe,** ***fellow-tribesman, compatriot*** subst. ὁ ὁμ. (Eth. Epic. col. 20, 19; Alciphron 1, 10, 5; 2 Macc 4:10; 3 Macc 3:21; Philo; Jos., Ant. 17, 285; Just., A I, 14, 3) 1 Cl 4:10.—DELG s.v. φῦλον.

ὁμοφωνία, ας, ἡ (ὁμός 'common', φωνή; Aristot., Pol. 2, 5; Philo, Conf. Lingu. 6). From the basic mng. 'state of harmony in expression' (s. L-S-J-M s.v.) derives the fig. ext.: **state of being in accord w. others,** ***harmony*** (Ecphantus in Stob. 4, 7, 64) 1 Cl 51:2.—DELG s.v. φωνή.

ὄμφαξ, ακος (Hom. et al.; ins, LXX), **ἡ** and later also **ὁ** (e.g. Plut., Mor. 138e; 648f; Jer 38:30; Ezk 18:4 v.l.) *unripe grape* (fr. a quot. of unknown origin) 1 Cl 23:4=2 Cl 11:3.—DELG.

ὅμως adversative particle (ὁμός 'common'; Hom.+; Schwyzer II 582f) ***all the same, nevertheless, yet*** strengthened ὅμ. μέντοι (s. μέντοι 2) **J 12:42.**—Paul's two-fold epistolary use of the word is peculiar, yet analogous to J's use: ὅμως τὰ ἄψυχα φωνὴν διδόντα … ἐὰν διαστολὴν τοῖς φθόγγοις μὴ δῷ, πῶς γνωσθήσεται … **1 Cor 14:7** and ὅμως ἀνθρώπου κεκυρωμένην διαθήκην οὐδεὶς ἀθετεῖ **Gal 3:15.** As a rule these passages are explained on the basis of hyperbation or displacement of ὅμως, retaining the mng. 'nevertheless'; so for **Gal 3:15** the transl. would be 'even though it involves only a person's last will and testament, nevertheless no one annuls it' (so, gener., EBurton, ICC, Gal 1920, 178f; cp. passages like X., Cyr. 5, 1, 26 [Kühner-G. II 85f]). But since ὁμ. introduces a comparison both times in Paul (οὕτως follows it in 1 Cor 14:9), we do better (with B-D-F §450, 2) to understand ὅμ. as influenced by the older ὁμῶς 'equally, likewise' (cp. the ambivalent use Od. 11, 565). The transl. would be greatly simplified, and we can render ὅμ. simply *likewise, also* (JJeremias, ZNW 52, '61, 127f agrees).—DELG s.v. ὁμός. M-M.

ὀναίμην s. ὀνίνημι.

ὄναρ, τό (Hom. et al.; Herodas 1, 11; Pherecyd. 24; ins; Philo; Jos., Bell. 2, 112, Ant. 2, 63; 10, 195; Ath. 13, 1 οὐδ' ὄναρ, but only in nom. and acc. sing.) ***dream,*** in our lit. only Mt chapters 1, 2, 27, and in the expr. κατ' ὄναρ *in a dream* (rejected by Photius, Lex. p. 149, 25f as a barbarism [Lob., Phryn. p. 422ff], but attested fr. the time of Conon [I BC/I AD]: 26 fgm. 1, 35, 3 Jac., Apollo gives orders; Strabo 4, 1, 4; Anth. Pal. 11, 263, 1; Diog. L. 10, 32; Eunap. 55; CIG 4331 χρηματισθεὶς κατὰ ὄναρ='after an oracle had been given me in a dream' [sim. of Sarapis IG XI/4, 13f ὁ θεός μοι ἐχρημάτισεν κατὰ τὸν ὕπνον]. Also SIG 1147; 1148/9; IPergamon 357, 8 [Schweizer 157]; IG XII/1, 979, 4f, but here means 'as a result of a dream' [Dssm., NB 81=BS 253], as Paus. Attic. λ, 28.—S. OWeinreich, θεοὶ ἐπήκοοι MAI 37, 1912, 43, n. 1) **Mt 1:20; 2:12f, 19, 22; 27:19.**—EEhrlich, D. Traum im AT '53, D. Traum im Talmud: ZNW 47, '56, 133–45; AWikenhauser, Pisciculi=Antike u. Christentum, Erg.-Bd. I '39, 320–33; other lit. OSchönberger, Longos[4] '60, 178 n. on Longus 7, 1. On incubation oracles s. JGriffiths, Apuleius of Madauros 75, 139; EDodds, The Greeks and the Irrational '51, 107–11.—B. 269. New Docs 1, 31; 3, 23. DELG. M-M. TW.

ὀνάριον, ου, τό (ὄναρ; Diphilus Com. [IV/III BC] 89 K.; Machon [III BC] vs. 390 Gow [in Athen. 13, 582c]; Epict. 2, 24, 18; 4, 1, 79; pap) lit. 'little donkey', but in many cases plainly a dim. in form only (of ὄνος), ***donkey*** (Celsus 4, 43; Vi. Aesopi I c. 33 p. 304, 1; 4; 9 [Eb,]; POxy 63, 11; hence the possibility of a double dim. μικρὸν ὀναρίδιον PRyl. 239, 21), prob. *young donkey* **J 12:14.**—DELG s.v. ὄναρ. M-M. TW.

ὀνειδίζω impf. ὠνείδιζον; fut. 3 sg. ὀνειδιεῖ Sir 18:8; Ps 73, 10 and ὀνειδίσει Sir 20:15; 1 aor. ὠνείδισα. Pass: fut. 3 pl. ὀνειδισθήσονται Sir 41:7; 1 aor. ὠνειδίσθην LXX (ὄνειδος; Hom.; Pla. [on contrast w. λοιδορεῖν s. Pla., Ap. 38c] +; BGU 1024 VII, 21; PGiss 40 II, 5; LXX; PsSol 2:19; Test12Patr; GrBar 1:2; Philo, Joseph., Just.).

❶ **to find fault in a way that demeans the other,** ***reproach, revile, mock, heap insults upon*** as a way of shaming; w. acc. of the pers. affected (trag.; Pla., Apol. 30e; Lucian, Tox. 61; Ps 41:11; 54:13 al. LXX; Jos., Ant. 14, 430; 18, 360) of the reviling/mocking of Jesus **Mk 15:32;** cp. **Ro 15:3** (Ps 68:10) and of Jesus' disciples **Mt 5:11; Lk 6:22.** W. double acc. (Soph., Oed. Col. 1002 ὀν. τινὰ τοιαῦτα; Ael. Aristid. 28, 155 K.=49 p. 542 D.; Heliod. 7, 27, 5) τὸ αὐτὸ καὶ οἱ λῃσταὶ ὠνείδιζον αὐτόν *the robbers also reviled/mocked him in the same way* **Mt 27:44.**—Pass. εἰ ὀνειδίζεσθε ἐν ὀνόματι Χριστοῦ *if you are (being) reviled for the name of Christ* **1 Pt 4:14.**—Only as v.l. in the two foll. pass.: εἰς τοῦτο κοπιῶμεν καὶ ὀνειδιζόμεθα *it is for this* (i.e., what precedes) *that we toil and suffer reproach* **1 Ti 4:10 v.l.** (for ἀγωνιζόμεθα). εἰς τί ὠνείδισάς με; *why have you reproached me?* or *what have you reproached me for?* (ὀν. τινὰ εἴς τι as Appian, Bell. Civ. 2, 104 §430 ὠνείδισεν ἐς δειλίαν=he reproached him for cowardice; 5, 54 §224; 5, 96 §400; Jos., Bell. 1, 237) **Mk 15:34** D and Macarius Magnes 1, 12 (the text has ἐγκατέλιπες. S. Harnack, SBBerlAk 1901, 262ff=Studien I '31, 98ff; JSundwall, D. Zusammensetzung des Mk '34, 83).—A special kind of reproach is the suggestion of reluctance that too often accompanies the giving of a gift (Sextus 339 ὁ διδοὺς μετ' ὀνείδους ὑβρίζει; difft. Plut., Mor. 64a; s. also Sir 20:15; 41:25.—ὀν. can also mean *charge* or *reproach* someone with someth., a kind of verbal extortion, with the purpose of obtaining someth. from a pers., e.g., Maximus Tyr. 5, 7h τῷ θεῷ the building of a temple); God does not do this **Js 1:5.**

❷ **to find justifiable fault with someone,** ***reproach, reprimand,*** w. acc. of pers. (Pr 25:8; Philo, Fuga 30; Jos., Ant. 4, 189; Just., D. 37, 2 ὀνειδίζει ὑμᾶς τὸ πνεῦμα ἅγιον al.) and ὅτι foll. to give the reason for the reproach **Mt 11:20.** W. acc. of pers. and λέγων foll. w. dir. discourse (cp. BGU 1141, 23 [14 BC] ὀνειδίζει με λέγων) GPt 4:13. W. acc. of the thing censured (Isocr., Or. 15, 318, 345a; Herodian 3, 8, 6; Wsd 2:12; Jos., Ant. 10, 139) τὴν ἀπιστίαν αὐτῶν καὶ σκληροκαρδίαν **Mk 16:14.**—Schmidt, Syn. I 136–49. DELG s.v. ὄνειδος. M-M. TW. Spicq.

ὀνειδισμός, οῦ, ὁ (s. prec. entry; Dionys. Hal.; Plut., Artax. 22, 12; Vett. Val. 65, 7; 73, 10; LXX; En 103:4; TestSol 26:8 H; Test12Patr; Jos., Ant. 19, 319. Late word: Lob., Phryn. p. 511f) **act of disparagement that results in disgrace,** ***reproach, reviling, disgrace, insult*** εἰς ὀν. ἐμπίπτειν *fall into disgrace* **1 Ti 3:7.** ἀφεῖλεν ἀπ' ἐμοῦ ὀνειδισμὸν τῶν ἐχθρῶν μου *(God) took away from me the reproach of my enemies* GJs 6:3.—**Hb** speaks of the ὀν. τοῦ Χριστοῦ and holds that even Moses took upon himself the *reproach of Christ* **11:26,** and he calls upon believers: ἐξερχώμεθα πρὸς αὐτὸν … τὸν ὀν. αὐτοῦ φέροντες **13:13** (ὀν. φέρειν as Ezk 34:29; TestReub 4:7 v.l.).—Pl. (TestReub. 4:2; TestJud 23:3) οἱ ὀν. *reproaches, insults* **Ro 15:3** (Ps 68:10; s. ὀνειδίζω 1). W. θλίψεις: ὀνειδισμοῖς καὶ θλίψεσιν θεατριζόμενοι *exposed as a public spectacle to insults and persecutions* **Hb 10:33.**—DELG s.v. ὄνειδος. M-M. TW. Spicq.

ὄνειδος, ους, τό (Hom.+; Diod. S. 1, 93, 1; PCairMasp 97 II, 76; LXX; TestReub 4:7; 6:3; TestLevi 10:4; 15:2; EpArist 249; SibOr 3, 607; Philo; Jos., C. Ap. 1, 285 al.; Just.) **loss of standing connected with disparaging speech, *disgrace, reproach, insult*** ἀφελεῖν ὄν. μου ἐν ἀνθρώποις *take away my disgrace among people* **Lk 1:25** (cp. Gen 30:23; ViJon 3 [Sch. p. 83, 8; cp. 56, 22; 100, 10]).—*Object of reproach* (Ps.-Callisth. 2, 18, 4) ὄν. ἀνθρώπων καὶ ἐξουθένημα λαοῦ 1 Cl 16:15 (Ps 21:7).—B. 1187. DELG. M-M. TW. Spicq.

ὄνειρον, ου, τό and ὄνειρος, ου, ὁ (cp. ὄναρ; Hom.+; ins, pap, LXX; EpArist 192 and 315; En 13:8 [ὄνειροι]; TestLevi 8:18; TestAbr; SibOr 3, 293; Philo, Joseph.; Just., A I, 14, 1; Tat.) ***dream*** ἄγγελος κυρίου φαίνεται αὐτῷ κατ᾿ ὄνειρον *an angel of the Lord appeared to (Joseph) in a dream* GJs 14:2 (cp. κατ᾿ ὄναρ **Mt 1:20**). Cp. the def. Artem. 1, 2 p. 5 H. ὄνειρός ἐστι κίνησις ἢ πλάσις ψυχῆς πολυσχήμων σημαντικὴ τῶν ἐσομένων ἀγαθῶν ἢ κακῶν 'a dream is a movement or formation of the soul signifying in a variety of ways those things that will be good or bad.'—DELG s.v. ὄναρ.

᾿Ονήσιμος, ου, ὁ ***Onesimus,*** lit. 'useful' (s. the play on words in **Phlm 11**), a name freq. found (ins, pap: Mel. HE 4, 26, 13; reff. in Thieme 40; Preisigke, Namenbuch 1922 and in the lit. below), esp. for slaves (Menand., Epitr. 1 [p. 975] al.; Galen, De Optima Doctr. 1 p. 82 JMarquardt [1884] ᾿Ον. ὁ Πλουτάρχου δοῦλος; Lghtf., St. Paul's Ep. to the Col. and to Phlm. 308f; Hatch 146; Zahn, Einleitung I^3 325).

❶ A slave of Philemon, in whose interest Paul wrote Phlm. **Phlm 10; subscr.;** πιστὸς καὶ ἀγαπητὸς ἀδελφός **Col 4:9.** Cp. **Col subscr.**—ARobertson, Exp. 8th ser., 19, 1920, 29ff; EGoodenough, HTR 22, 1929, 181–83; PHarrison, ATR 32, '50, 268–93; BHHW II 1343; JNordling, JSNT 41, '91, 97–119 a runaway slave.

❷ An *Onesimus* appears as bishop of Ephesus in IEph 1:3; 2:1; 6:2; CIG 2983 attests the name for this city (cp. EGoodsp., Introd. to the NT '37, 121f and ref. there to JKnox).—DELG s.v. ὀνίνημι. LGPN I. M-M.

᾿Ονησίφορος, ου, ὁ (ins; Aa [s. index I 301 and II/2, 344]) ***Onesiphorus*** **2 Ti 1:16; 4:19.**—NPlum, TT 3, R. 10, 1919, 193–200.—Cp. DELG s.v. ὀνίνημι. LGPN I. M-M.

ὀνικός, ή, όν (ὄνος; OGI 629, 30; PSI 527, 2 [III BC]; BGU 912, 24 [33 AD] τὰ ὀνικὰ κτήνη; PGen 23, 4 [70 AD]) ***pert. to an ass/donkey,*** in our lit. only in the combination μύλος ὀν. *a millstone worked by donkey-power* (hence heavier than the one used by women; s. μύλος 2) **Mt 18:6; Mk 9:42** (s. λίθος 1c). **Lk 17:2 v.l.** (certainly the upper moving millstone, rather than the animal itself: ὄνος ἀλέτης [X., An. 1, 5, 5; Alexis Com. [IV BC], fgm. 13 K.; Herodas 6, 83; GDI 4992a II, 7 Crete; cp. Ael. Dion. ο, 23, in ref. to Aristotle's apparent application of the action to the lower, stationary millstone: Problemata 35, 3, 964b]).—DELG s.v. ὄνος. M-M.

ὀνίνημι (Hom. et al.; TestSol 13:14 C [?]; Jos., Ant. 16, 242) mid.-pass. 2 aor. sg. ὠνάσθης Tob 3:8. In our lit. only mid. (as Sir 30:2 [fut. 3 sg. ὀνήσεται]; Philo, Agr. 126) **to be the recipient of a favor or benefit or to have someth. for one's use, *have benefit of, enjoy.*** Only in the 2 aor. opt., in the formulation (IDefixAudollent 92, 3 [III BC] ὄναιντο; Kaibel 502, 27) ὀναίμην *may I have joy* or *profit* or *benefit, may I enjoy* w. gen. of the pers. or thing that is the source of the joy (Eur., Hec. 978 ὀναίμην τοῦ παρόντος; Aristoph., Thesm. 469 οὕτως ὀναίμην τῶν τέκνων; Lucian, Philops. 27; Philostrat., Vi. Apoll. 4, 16 p. 135, 3) ἐγώ σου ὀναίμην ἐν κυρίῳ *let me have some benefit from you in the Lord* **Phlm 20.** ὀναίμην ὑμῶν διὰ παντός *may I have joy in you continually* IEph 2:2; IPol 6:2. ὀν. ὑμῶν κατὰ πάντα *let me have joy of you in all respects* IMg 12. ὀν. τῶν θηρίων *may I enjoy the wild animals* IRo 5:2; οὗ ἐγὼ ὀν. IMg 2; οὗ ὀν. ἐν θεῷ IPol 1:1.—DELG. M-M.

ὄνομα, ατος, τό (Hom.+).—❶ **proper name of an entity, *name***—ⓐ gener. τῶν ἀποστόλων τὰ ὀνόματα ἐστιν ταῦτα **Mt 10:2;** cp. **Rv 21:14.** τῶν παρθένων τὰ ὀν. Hs 9, 15, 1. τὸ ὄνομα τοῦ πατρός **Lk 1:59.** ὄν. μοι, sc. ἐστίν, *my name is* (Od. 9, 366) **Mk 5:9b.** τί ὄν. σοι; *what is your name?* vs. **9a;** w. copula **Lk 8:30.**—The expressions ᾧ (ᾗ) ὄν., οὗ τὸ ὄν., καὶ τὸ ὄν. αὐτοῦ (αὐτῆς), ὄν. αὐτῷ (parenthetic) are almost always without the copula (B-D-F §128, 3; Rob. 395): ᾧ (ᾗ) ὄν. (Sb 7573, 13 [116 AD]; Demetr.: 722 fgm. 1, 5 Jac.; Just., A I, 53, 8 ᾧ ὄν. Λώτ) **Lk 1:26, 27a; 2:25; 8:41; 24:13, 18 v.l.; Ac 13:6.**—οὗ τὸ ὄν. (without a verb as BGU 344, 1) **Mk 14:32.** Cp. ὧν τὰ ὀνόματα ἐν βίβλῳ ζωῆς **Phil 4:3** (ὧν τὰ ὀν. is a formula [Dssm., LO 95=LAE 121]. S. esp. BGU 432 II, 3 ὧν τὰ ὀν. τῷ βιβλιδίῳ δεδήλωται).—καὶ τὸ ὄν. αὐτῆς **Lk 1:5b.** καὶ τὸ ὄν. τῆς παρθένου Μαριάμ vs. **27b.**—ὄν. αὐτῷ (Demosth. 32, 11 ᾿Αριστοφῶν ὄνομ᾿ αὐτῷ; Dionys. Hal. 8, 89, 4; Aelian, NA 8, 2 γυνὴ . . . ῾Ηρακληὶς ὄν. αὐτῇ; LXX) **J 1:6; 3:1.** ὁ καθήμενος ἐπάνω αὐτοῦ (i.e. τοῦ ἵππου), ὄν. αὐτῷ (ὁ) θάνατος **Rv 6:8;** cp. **9:11a.**—W. the copula ἦν δὲ ὄν. τῷ δούλῳ Μάλχος **J 18:10** (POxy 465, 12 ὁ δὲ κραταιὸς αὐτοῦ, ὄν. αὐτῷ ἐστιν Νεβύ, μηνύει; Jos., Ant. 19, 332). ἄγγελος . . . , οὗ τὸ ὄν. ἐστιν Θεγρί Hv 4, 2, 4.—The dat. is quite freq. ὀνόματι *named, by name* (X., Hell. 1, 6, 29 Σάμιος ὀνόματι ῾Ιππεύς; Tob 6:11 BA; 4 Macc 5:4; Just., D. 85, 6; 115, 3; B-D-F §160; 197; Rob. 487) ἄνθρωπον ὀν. Σίμωνα **Mt 27:32;** cp. **Mk 5:22; Lk 1:5a; 5:27; 10:38; 16:20; 23:50; 24:18; Ac 5:1, 34; 8:9; 9:10–12, 33, 36; 10:1; 11:28; 12:13; 16:1, 14; 17:34; 18:2, 7, 24; 19:24; 20:9; 21:10; 27:1; 28:7;** MPol 4. Also the acc. τοὔνομα (on the crasis s. B-D-F §18; Mlt-H. 63; FPreisigke, Griech. Urkunden des ägypt. Mus. zu Kairo [1911] 2, 6 γυνὴ Ταμοῦνις τοὔνομα; Diod. S. 2, 45, 4 πόλιν τοὔνομα Θ.; Lucian, Dial. Deor. 3; Philo, Leg. All. 1, 68; Jos., Ant. 7, 344, Vi. 382) *named, by name* (the acc. as X. et al., also 2 Macc 12:13; Demetr.: 722 fgm. 1, 5 Jac. υἱὸν ὀ. Δάν.—B-D-F §160; Rob. 487) **Mt 27:57.** (Cp. ὄν. gener. as 'mode of expression' εἰ καὶ διάφορα ὀνόματα ἐστιν, ἀλλ᾿ . . . οἰκείαν . . . δέχεται τὴν νόησιν *although there are various ways of expressing it, it nevertheless has a definite sense* Did., Gen. 86, 22 [of various metaphors and images for the soul].)

ⓑ used w. verbs—**α.** as their obj.: ὄν. ἔχειν Did., Gen. 29, 6 *bear the name* or *as name, be named* ὄν. ἔχει ᾿Απολλύων **Rv 9:11b** (in this case the name ᾿Α. stands independently in the nom.; B-D-F §143; Rob. 458). καλεῖν τὸ ὄν. τινος w. the name foll. in the acc. (after the Hb.; B-D-F §157, 2; Rob. 459) καλέσεις τὸ ὄν. αὐτοῦ ᾿Ιησοῦν *you are to name him Jesus* **Mt 1:21; Lk 1:31.**—**Mt 1:25.** καλέσεις τὸ ὄν. αὐτοῦ ᾿Ιωάννην **Lk 1:13.** καλέσουσιν τὸ ὄν. αὐτοῦ ᾿Εμμανουήλ **Mt 1:23** (Is 7:14). διδόναι GJs 6:2. Pass. w. the name in the nom. (cp. GrBar 6:10 Φοῖνιξ καλεῖται τὸ ὄν. μου) ἐκλήθη τὸ ὄν. αὐτοῦ ᾿Ιησοῦς **Lk 2:21;** cp. **Rv 19:13.** Also τὸ ὄν. τοῦ ἀστέρος λέγεται ὁ ῎Αψινθος **Rv 8:11.**—ἐπιθεῖναι ὄν. τινι w. acc. of the name **Mk 3:16f;** cp. B 12:8f; κληρονομεῖν ὄν. *receive a name* **Hb 1:4**=1 Cl 36:2. κληροῦσθαι τὸ αὐτὸ ὄν. *obtain the same name* (s. κληρόω 2) MPol 6:2.—τὰ ὀν. ὑμῶν ἐγγέγραπται ἐν τοῖς οὐρανοῖς **Lk 10:20.**—**Rv 13:8; 17:8.** ἐξαλείψω τὸ ὄν. αὐτῶν 1 Cl 53:3 (Dt 9:14); **Rv 3:5a** (perh. to be placed in 4 below); s. ἐξαλείφω.

β. in another way (εἰ δέ τις ὀνόματι καλέσει *but if anyone is so named* Hippol., Ref. 6, 20, 2): ὃς καλεῖται τῷ ὀνόματι τούτῳ *who is so named* **Lk 1:61.** ἀνὴρ ὀνόματι καλούμενος

Ζακχαῖος *a man whose name was Zacchaeus* **19:2.** καλεῖν τι (i.e. παιδίον) ἐπὶ τῷ ὀνόματί τινος *name someone after someone* **1:59.** Cp. IMg 10:1. This leads to

ⓒ used w. prepositions: ἐξ ὀνόματος (Ctesias, Ind. p. 105 M.: Diod. S. 13, 15, 1; 37, 15, 2; Appian, Mithrid. 59, §243, Bell. Civ. 3, 21 §77; 4, 73 §310; PGM 4, 2973; Jos., Ant. 2, 275) *by name, individually, one by one* (so that no one is lost in the crowd) ἐξ ὀν. πάντας ζήτει IPol 4:2. ἀσπάζομαι πάντας ἐξ ὀνόματος 8:2. πάντες ἐξ ὀν. συνέρχεσθε (parallel to κατ' ἄνδρα) IEph 20:2.—κατ' ὄν. *by name, individually* (Diod. S. 16, 44, 2; Gen 25:13; EpArist 247; Jos., Bell. 7, 14) **J 10:3** (New Docs 3, 77f; animals called individually by name: Ps.-Aristot., Mirabil. 118.—HAlmqvist, Plut. u. das NT '46, 74). Esp. in greetings (BGU 27, 18 [II AD] ἀσπάζομαι πάντας τοὺς φιλοῦντάς σε κατ' ὄν.; POxy 1070, 46; pap in Dssm., LO 160/1, ln. 14f [LAE 193, ln. 15, note 21]; New Docs 3, 77f) **3J 15;** ISm 13:2b. ῥάβδους ἐπιγεγραμμένας ἑκάστης φυλῆς κατ' ὄν. *staffs, each one inscribed with the name of a tribe* 1 Cl 43:2b.

ⓓ used in combination with God and Jesus. On the significance of the Divine Name in history of religions s. FGiesebrecht, Die atl. Schätzung des Gottesnamens 1901; Bousset, Rel.^{3} 309ff; ADieterich, Eine Mithrasliturgie 1903, 110ff; FConybeare, JQR 8, 1896; 9, 1897, esp. 9, 581ff; JBoehmer, Das bibl. 'im Namen' 1898, BFCT V 6, 1901, 49ff, Studierstube 2, 1904, 324ff; 388ff; 452ff; 516ff; 580ff; BJacob, Im Namen Gottes 1903; WHeitmüller, 'Im Namen Jesu' 1903; WBrandt, TT 25, 1891, 565ff; 26, 1892, 193ff; 38, 1904, 355ff; RHirzel, Der Name: ASG 36, 2, 1918; Schürer III^4 409–11; HObbink, De magische betekenis van den naam inzonderheid in het oude Egypte 1925; OGrether, Name u. Wort Gottes im AT '34; HHuffman, Name: DDD 1148–52.—The belief in the efficacy of the name is extremely old; its origin goes back to the most ancient times and the most primitive forms of intellectual and religious life. It has exhibited an extraordinary vitality. The period of our lit. also sees—within as well as without the new community of believers—in the name someth. real, a piece of the very nature of the personality whom it designates, expressing the person's qualities and powers. Accordingly, names, esp. holy names, are revered and used in customary practices and ritual (σέβεσθαι θεῶν ὀνόματα Theoph. Ant., 1, 9 [p. 76, 7]), including magic. In Israelite tradition the greatest reverence was paid to the holy name of God and to its numerous paraphrases or substitutes; the names of angels and patriarchs occupied a secondary place. The syncretistic practices of the period revered the names of gods, daemons, and heroes, or even magic words that made no sense at all, but had a mysterious sound. The Judeo-Christians revere and use the name of God and, of course, the name of Jesus. On magic in Jewish circles, s. Schürer III 342–79; for the NT period in general s. MSmith, Clement of Alexandria and a Secret Gospel of Mark '73, 195–230.—The names of God and Jesus

α. in combination w. attributes: διαφορώτερον ὄν. *a more excellent name* **Hb 1:4**=1 Cl 36:2 (διάφορος 2). ἅγιον τὸ ὄν. αὐτοῦ **Lk 1:49** (cp. Ps 110:9; Lev 18:21; 22:2; PGM 3, 570; 627; 4, 1005; 3071; 5, 77; 13, 561 μέγα κ. ἅγιον). τὸ μεγαλοπρεπὲς καὶ ἅγιον ὄν. αὐτοῦ 1 Cl 64; τὸ μέγα καὶ ἔνδοξον ὄν. Hv 4, 1, 3; 4, 2, 4 (on ἔνδοξον ὄν., cp. EPeterson, Εἷς θεός 1926, 282.—ὄν. μέγα κ. ἅγ. κ. ἐνδ.: PGM 13, 183f; 504f). τὸ μέγα καὶ θαυμαστὸν καὶ ἔνδοξον ὄν. Hs 9, 18, 5; τὸ πανάγιον καὶ ἔνδοξον ὄν. 1 Cl 58:1a; τοῦ παντοκράτορος καὶ ἐνδόξου ὄν. Hv 3, 3, 5; τὸ πανάρετον ὄν. 1 Cl 45:7; τῷ παντοκράτορι καὶ ἐνδόξῳ ὀνόματι 60:4; τὸ ὁσιώτατον τῆς μεγαλωσύνης αὐτοῦ ὄν. 58:1b. τὸ ὄν. μου θαυμαστὸν ἐν τοῖς ἔθνεσι D 14:3 (cp. Mal 1:14). The words ὄν. θεοπρεπέστατον IMg 1:2 are difficult to interpret (s. Hdb. ad loc.; θεοπρεπής b).

β. in combination w. verbs: ἁγιάζειν τὸ ὄν. **Mt 6:9** (AFridrichsen, Helligt vorde dit naun: DTT 8, 1917, 1–16). **Lk 11:2;** D 8:2 (ἁγιάζω 3). βλασφημεῖν (q.v. bγ) τὸ ὄν. **Rv 13:6; 16:9;** pass. βλασφημεῖται τὸ ὄν. (Is 52:5) **Ro 2:24;** 2 Cl 13:1f, 4; ITr 8:2. βλασφημίας ἐπιφέρεσθαι τῷ ὀν. κυρίου *bring blasphemy upon the name of the Lord* 1 Cl 47:7. πφοσέθηκαν κατὰ ὄν. τοῦ κυρίου βλασφημίαν Hs 6, 2, 3; βεβηλοῦν τὸ ὄν. 8, 6, 2 (s. βεβηλόω). ἀπαγγελῶ τὸ ὄν. τ. ἀδελφοῖς μου **Hb 2:12** (cp. Ps 21:23). ὅπως διαγγελῇ τὸ ὄν. μου ἐν πάσῃ τῇ γῇ **Ro 9:17** (Ex 9:16). δοξάζειν τὸ ὄν. (σου, τοῦ κυρίου, τοῦ θεοῦ etc.) **Rv 15:4;** 1 Cl 43:6; IPhld 10:1; Hv 2, 1, 2; 3, 4, 3; 4, 1, 3; s 9, 18, 5 (s. δοξάζω 1; cp. GJs 7:2; 12:1[w. ref. to name of Mary]). ὅπως ἐνδοξασθῇ τὸ ὄν. τοῦ κυρίου ἡμῶν Ἰησοῦ **2 Th 1:12.** ἐλπίζειν τῷ ὀν. **Mt 12:21** (vv.ll. ἐν or ἐπὶ τῷ ὀν.; the pass. on which it is based, Is 42:4, has ἐπὶ τῷ ὀν.). ἐπικαλεῖσθαι τὸ ὄν. κυρίου (as PsSol 6:1) or αὐτοῦ, σου etc. (w. ref. to God or Christ) *call on the name of the Lord* **Ac 2:21** (Jo 3:5); **9:14, 21; 22:16; Ro 10:13** (Jo 3:5); **1 Cor 1:2.** ψυχὴ ἐπικεκλημένη τὸ μεγαλοπρεπὲς καὶ ἅγιον ὄν. αὐτοῦ *a person who calls upon his exalted and holy name* 1 Cl 64.—Pass. πάντα τὰ ἔθνη ἐφ' οὓς ἐπικέκληται τὸ ὄν. μου ἐπ' αὐτούς **Ac 15:17** (Am 9:12). τὸ καλὸν ὄν. τὸ ἐπικληθὲν ἐφ' ὑμᾶς **Js 2:7** (on καλὸν ὄν. cp. Sb 343, 9 and the Pompeian graffito in Dssm., LO 237 [LAE 276]). πάντες οἱ ἐπικαλούμενοι τῷ ὀν. αὐτοῦ *all those who are called by (the Lord's) name* Hs 9, 14, 3; cp. οἱ κεκλημένοι τῷ ὀν. κυρίου *those who are called by the name of the Lord* 8, 1, 1. ἐπαισχύνεσθαι τὸ ὄν. κυρίου τὸ ἐπικληθὲν ἐπ' αὐτούς *be ashamed of the name that is named over them* 8, 6, 4. ὁμολογεῖν τῷ ὀν. αὐτοῦ *praise his name* **Hb 13:15** (cp. PsSol 15:2 ἐξομολογήσασθαι τῷ ὀνόματι σου). ὀνομάζειν τὸ ὄν. κυρίου **2 Ti 2:19** (Is 26:13). ψάλλειν τῷ ὀν. σου **Ro 15:9** (Ps 17:50). οὐ μὴ λάβῃς ἐπὶ ματαίῳ τὸ ὄν. κυρίου B 19:5 (Ex 20:7; Dt 5:11).—Although in the preceding examples the name is oft. practically inseparable fr. the being that bears it, this is perh. even more true of the foll. cases, in which the name appears almost as the representation of the Godhead, as a tangible manifestation of the divine nature (Quint. Smyrn. 9, 465 Polidarius, when healing, calls on οὔνομα πατρὸς ἑοῖο 'the name of his father' [Asclepius]; τοσοῦτον . . . δύναται τὸ ὄ. τοῦ Ἰησοῦ κατὰ τῶν δαιμόνων Orig., C. Cels. 1, 56, 11; Dt 18:7; 3 Km 8:16; Ps 68:37; Zech 13:2 ἐξολεθρεύσω τὰ ὀν. τῶν εἰδώλων; Zeph 1:4; PsSol 7:6; Just., D. 121, 3 ὑποτάσσεσθαι αὐτοῦ ὀν.): the 'name' of God is ἀρχέγονον πάσης κτίσεως 1 Cl 59:3. Sim. τὸ ὄν. τοῦ υἱοῦ τοῦ θεοῦ μέγα ἐστὶ καὶ τὸν κόσμον ὅλον βαστάζει Hs 9, 14, 5. λατρεύειν τῷ παναρέτῳ ὀν. αὐτοῦ *worship the most excellent name (of the Most High)* 1 Cl 45:7. ὑπακούειν τῷ παναγίῳ καὶ ἐνδόξῳ ὀν. αὐτοῦ *be obedient to his most holy and glorious name* 58:1a. ὑπήκοον γενέσθαι τῷ παντοκρατορικῷ καὶ παναρέτῳ ὀν. 60:4. κηρύσσειν τὸ ὄν. τοῦ υἱοῦ τοῦ θεοῦ Hs 9, 16, 5. ἐπιγινώσκειν τὸ ὄν. τοῦ υἱοῦ τοῦ θεοῦ 9, 16, 7. φοβεῖσθαι τὸ ὄν. σου **Rv 11:18.** φανεροῦν τινι τὸ ὄν. σου **J 17:6.** γνωρίζειν τινὶ τὸ ὄν. σου vs. **26.** πιστεύειν τῷ ὀν. τοῦ υἱοῦ αὐτοῦ *believe in the name of (God's) son* **1J 3:23.** Also πιστεύειν εἰς τὸ ὄν. (s. γב below and s. πιστεύω 2aβ).—Of the name borne by followers of Jesus Christ (cp. Theoph. Ant. 1, 1 [p. 58, 13]): κρατεῖς τὸ ὄν. μου *you cling to my name* **Rv 2:13.** The same mng. also holds for the expressions: λαμβάνειν τὸ ὄν. τοῦ υἱοῦ αὐτοῦ Hs 9, 12, 4; 8; 9, 13, 2a; 7. τοῦ βαστάσαι τὸ ὄν. μου ἐνώπιον ἐθνῶν *to bear my name before (the) Gentiles* **Ac 9:15.** τὸ ὄν. ἡδέως βαστάζειν *bear the name gladly* Hs 8, 10, 3; cp. 9, 28, 5b. τὸ ὄν. τοῦ υἱοῦ τοῦ θεοῦ φορεῖν 9, 13, 3; 9, 14, 5f; 9, 15, 2; cp. 9, 13, 2b. Christians receive this name at their baptism: πρὶν φορέσαι τὸν ἄνθρωπον τὸ ὄν. τοῦ υἱοῦ τοῦ θεοῦ νεκρός ἐστιν *before a* *person bears the name of God's Son* (which is given the candidate at baptism), *he is dead* 9, 16, 3. Of dissemblers and false teachers ὄν. μὲν ἔχουσιν, ἀπὸ δὲ τῆς πίστεως κενοί εἰσιν *they have the* (Christian) *name, but are devoid of faith* 9, 19, 2. Of Christians in appearance only ἐν ὑποκρίσει φέροντες τὸ ὄν. τοῦ κυρίου *who bear the Lord's name in pretense* Pol 6:3. δόλῳ πονηρῷ τὸ ὄν. περιφέρειν *carry the name about in wicked deceit* (evidently of wandering preachers) IEph 7:1. τὸ ὄν. ἐπαισχύνονται τοῦ κυρίου αὐτῶν *they are ashamed of their Lord's name* Hs 9, 21, 3. More fully: ἐπαισχύνονται τὸ ὄν. αὐτοῦ φορεῖν 9, 14, 6.

γ. used w. prepositions—**א.** w. διά and the gen. διὰ τοῦ ὀνόματός μου πιστεύειν PtK 3 p. 15 ln. 12; σωθῆναι διὰ τοῦ μεγάλου καὶ ἐνδόξου ὀν. *be saved through the great and glorious name* Hv 4, 2, 4. εἰς τὴν βασιλείαν τοῦ θεοῦ εἰσελθεῖν διὰ τοῦ ὀν. τοῦ υἱοῦ (τοῦ θεοῦ) s 9, 12, 5. ἄφεσιν ἁμαρτιῶν λαβεῖν διὰ τοῦ ὀν. αὐτοῦ **Ac 10:43** (cp. Just., D. 11, 4 al.). σημεῖα … γίνεσθαι διὰ τοῦ ὀν. … Ἰησοῦ *by the power of the name* **4:30.** Differently παρακαλεῖν τινα διὰ τοῦ ὀν. τοῦ κυρίου *appeal to someone by the name* (*=while calling on the name*) *of the Lord* **1 Cor 1:10.**—W. διά and the acc. μισούμενοι … διὰ τὸ ὄν. μου *hated on account of my name* (i.e., because you bear it) **Mt 10:22; 24:9; Mk 13:13; Lk 21:17** (Just., A I, 4, 2 al.). ποιεῖν τι εἴς τινα διὰ τὸ ὄν. μου **J 15:21.** ἀφέωνται ὑμῖν αἱ ἁμαρτίαι διὰ τὸ ὄν. αὐτοῦ *your sins are forgiven on account of (Jesus') name* **1J 2:12.** βαστάζειν διὰ τὸ ὄν. μου *bear* (hardship) *for my name's sake* **Rv 2:3** (s. βαστάζω 2bβ). πάσχειν διὰ τὸ ὄν. (also w. a gen. like αὐτοῦ) Pol 8:2; Hv 3, 2, 1b; s 9, 28, 3.

ב. w. εἰς: somet. evidently as rendering of rabb. לְשֵׁם *with regard to, in thinking of* δέχεσθαί τινα εἰς ὄν. Ἰ. Χρ. *receive someone in deference to Jesus Christ* IRo 9:3. δύο ἢ τρεῖς συνηγμένοι εἰς τὸ ἐμὸν ὄν. *two or three gathered and thinking of me,* i.e., so that I am the reason for their assembling **Mt 18:20;** but here the other mng. (s. ג below) has had some influence: 'while naming' or 'calling on my name'. τῆς ἀγάπης ἧς ἐνεδείξασθε εἰς τὸ ὄν. αὐτοῦ (i.e. θεοῦ) **Hb 6:10** is either *the love that you have shown with regard to him,* i.e. *for his sake,* or we have here the frequently attested formula of Hellenistic legal and commercial language (s. Mayser II/2 p. 415; Dssm. B 143ff, NB 25, LO 97f [BS 146f; 197; LAE 121]; Heitmüller, op. cit. 100ff; FPreisigke, Girowesen im griech. Ägypt. 1910, 149ff. On the LXX s. Heitmüller 110f; JPsichari, Essai sur le Grec de la Septante 1908, 202f): εἰς (τὸ) ὄν. τινος *to the name=to the account* (over which the name stands). Then the deeds of love, although shown to humans, are dedicated to God.—The concept of dedication is also highly significant, in all probability, for the understanding of the expr. βαπτίζειν εἰς (τὸ) ὄν. τινος. Through baptism εἰς (τὸ) ὄν. τ. those who are baptized become the possession of and come under the dedicated protection of the one whose name they bear. An additional factor, to a degree, may be the sense of εἰς τὸ ὄν.='with mention of the name' (cp. Herodian 2, 2, 10; 2, 13, 2 ὀμνύναι εἰς τὸ ὄν. τινος; Cyranides p. 57, 1 εἰς ὄν. τινος; 60, 18=εἰς τὸ ὄν. τ.; 62, 13. Another ex. in Heitmüller 107): **Mt 28:19; Ac 8:16; 19:5;** D 7:1, (3); 9:5; Hv 3, 7, 3; cp. **1 Cor 1:13, 15.** S. βαπτίζω 2c and Silva New, Beginn. I/5, '33, 121–40.—πιστεύειν εἰς τὸ ὄν. τινος *believe in the name of someone* i.e. have confidence that the person's name (rather in the sense of a title, cp. **Phil 2:9**) is rightfully borne and encodes what the person really is **J 1:12; 2:23; 3:18; 1J 5:13.**

ג. with ἐν: ἐν ὀνόματι of God or Jesus means in the great majority of cases *with mention of the name, while naming* or *calling* on *the name* (PsSol 11:8; JosAs 9:1; Just., D. 35, 2 al.; no corresponding use has been found in gener. Gk. lit.; but cp. ἐν ὀν. τοῦ μεγάλου καὶ ὑψίστου θεοῦ Hippol., Ref. 9, 15, 6.—Heitmüller p. 13ff, esp. 44; 49). In many pass. it seems to be a formula. ἐν τῷ ὀν. Ἰησοῦ ἐκβάλλειν δαιμόνια **Mk 9:38; 16:17; Lk 9:49.** τὰ δαιμόνια ὑποτάσσεται ἡμῖν ἐν τῷ ὀν. σου *the demons are subject to us at the mention of your name* **10:17.** ποιεῖν τι ἐν τῷ ὀνόματι **Ac 4:7;** cp. **Col 3:17.** Perh. **J 10:25** (but s. below). ἐν τῷ ὀν. Ἰησοῦ … οὗτος παρέστηκεν ὑγιής **Ac 4:10.** ὄν. … ἐν ᾧ δεῖ σωθῆναι ἡμᾶς vs. **12.** παραγγέλλω σοι ἐν ὀν. Ἰ. Χρ. **16:18;** cp. **2 Th 3:6;** IPol 5:1. σοὶ λέγω ἐν τῷ ὀν. τοῦ κυρίου **Ac 14:10** D. Peter, in performing a healing, says ἐν τῷ ὀν. Ἰησοῦ Χρ. περιπάτει **3:6** (s. Heitmüller 60). The elders are to anoint the sick w. oil ἐν τῷ ὀν. τοῦ κυρίου *while calling on the name of the Lord* **Js 5:14.**—Of prophets λαλεῖν ἐν τῷ ὀν. κυρίου **5:10.** παρρησιάζεσθαι ἐν τῷ ὀν. Ἰησοῦ *speak out boldly in proclaiming the name of Jesus* **Ac 9:27f.** βαπτίζεσθαι ἐν τῷ ὀν. Ἰ. Χ. *be baptized* or *have oneself baptized while naming the name of Jesus Christ* **Ac 2:38 v.l.; 10:48.** At a baptism ἐν ὀν. χριστοῦ Ἰησοῦ AcPl Ha 3, 32. αἰτεῖν τὸν πατέρα ἐν τῷ ὀν. μου (=Ἰησοῦ) *ask the Father, using my name* **J 15:16;** cp. **14:13, 14; 16:24, 26.** W. the latter pass. belongs vs. **23** (ὁ πατὴρ) δώσει ὑμῖν ἐν τῷ ὀν. μου *(the Father) will give you, when you mention my name.* τὸ πνεῦμα ὃ πέμψει ὁ πατὴρ ἐν τῷ ὀν. μου *the Spirit, whom the Father will send when my name is used* **14:26.** To thank God ἐν ὀν. Ἰησοῦ Χρ. *while naming the name of Jesus Christ* **Eph 5:20.** ἵνα ἐν τῷ ὀν. Ἰησοῦ πᾶν γόνυ κάμψῃ *that when the name of Jesus is mentioned every knee should bow* **Phil 2:10.** χαίρετε, υἱοί, ἐν ὀν. κυρίου *greetings, my sons, as we call on the Lord's name* B 1:1. ὁ ἐρχόμενος ἐν ὀν. κυρίου *whoever comes, naming the Lord's name* (in order thereby to give evidence of being a Christian) D 12:1. ἀσπάζεσθαι ἐν ὀν. Ἰ. Χρ. *greet, while naming the name of J. Chr.* w. acc. of pers. or thing greeted IRo ins; ISm 12:2. Receive a congregation ἐν ὀν. θεοῦ IEph 1:3. συναχθῆναι ἐν τῷ ὀν. τοῦ κυρίου Ἰ. *meet and call on the name of the Lord Jesus*=as a Christian congregation **1 Cor 5:4.** μόνον ἐν τῷ ὀν. Ἰ. Χρ. *only* (it is to be) *while calling on the name of J. Chr.* ISm 4:2.—Not far removed fr. these are the places where we render ἐν τῷ ὀν. with *through* or *by the name* (s. ἐν 4c); the effect brought about by the name is caused by its utterance ἀπελούσασθε, ἡγιάσθητε, ἐδικαιώθητε ἐν τῷ ὀν. τοῦ κυρίου Ἰ. Χρ. **1 Cor 6:11.** ζωὴν ἔχειν ἐν τῷ ὀν. αὐτοῦ (=Ἰησοῦ) **J20:31.** τηρεῖν τινα ἐν τῷ ὀν. (θεοῦ) **17:11f.**—ἐν τῷ ὀν. *at the command (of), commissioned by* ἔργα ποιεῖν ἐν τῷ ὀν. τοῦ πατρός **J 10:25** (but s. above). ἔρχεσθαι ἐν τῷ ὀν. τοῦ πατρός **5:43a;** in contrast ἔρχ. ἐν τῷ ὀν. τῷ ἰδίῳ vs. **43b.** εὐλογημένος ὁ ἐρχόμενος ἐν ὀν. κυρίου **12:13** (Ps 117:26). The Ps-passage prob. has the same sense (despite Heitmüller 53f) in **Mt 21:9; 23:39; Mk 11:9; Lk 13:35; 19:38.**—OMerlier, "Ονομα et ἐν ὀνόματι dans le quatr. Év.: RevÉtGr 47, '34, 180–204; RBratcher, BT 14, '63, 72–80.

ד. w. ἕνεκα (and the other forms of this word; s. ἕνεκα 1): of persecutions for one's Christian faith ἀπάγεσθαι ἐπὶ βασιλεῖς ἕνεκεν τοῦ ὀν. μου **Lk 21:12.** πάσχειν or ὑποφέρειν εἵνεκα τοῦ ὀνόματος Hv 3, 1, 9; 3, 2, 1; s 9, 28, 5. ἕνεκεν τοῦ ὀν. (τοῦ) κυρίου v 3, 5, 2; s 9, 28, 6. ἀφιέναι οἰκίας … ἕνεκεν τοῦ ἐμοῦ ὀν. *for my name's sake* **Mt 19:29.** ἔκτισας τὰ πάντα ἕνεκεν τοῦ ὀν. σου *you created all things for your name's sake,* i.e. that God's name might be praised for the benefits which the works of creation bring to humankind D 10:3.

ה. w. ἐπί and the dat.: ἐπὶ τῷ ὀν. τινος *when someone's name is mentioned* or *called upon,* or *mentioning someone's name* (LXX; En 10:2; Just., D. 39, 6; Ath. 23, 1; s. Heitmüller 19ff; 43ff; s. also 47ff; 52ff; 87ff) in the NT only of the name of Jesus, and only in the synoptics and Ac. ἐλεύσονται ἐπὶ τῷ ὀν. μου *they will come using my name* **Mt 24:5; Mk 13:6; Lk 21:8.** κηρύσσειν ἐπὶ τῷ ὀν. αὐτοῦ μετάνοιαν **24:47.** λαλεῖν ἐπὶ τῷ ὀν. τούτῳ *to speak using this name* **Ac 4:17; 5:40.** διδάσκειν **4:18; 5:28.** ποιεῖν δύναμιν ἐπὶ τῷ ὀν. μου **Mk 9:39.** ἐπὶ τῷ ὀν. σου ἐκβάλλειν δαιμόνια **Lk 9:49 v.l.** ἐπὶ τῷ σῷ ὀν. τὰς θεραπείας ἐπετέλουν GJs 20:2 (codd.). Of the (spiritual) temple of God: οἰκοδομηθήσεται ναὸς θεοῦ ἐνδόξως ἐπὶ τῷ ὀν. κυρίου *the temple of God will be gloriously built with the use of the Lord's name* B 16:6f, 8 (quot. of uncertain orig.). βαπτίζεσθαι ἐπὶ τῷ ὀν. Ἰ. Χρ. **Ac 2:38.** Baptism is also referred to in καλεῖσθαι ἐπὶ τῷ ὀν. τοῦ υἱοῦ τοῦ θεοῦ *receive a name when the name of God's son is named* Hs 9, 17, 4. The words δέχεσθαι (παιδίον) ἐπὶ τῷ ὀν. μου can also be classed here *receive* (a child) *when my name is confessed, when I am called upon* **Mt 18:5; Mk 9:37; Lk 9:48** (s. Heitmüller 64); but s. also 3 below.—ἐπί w. acc.: πεποιθέναι ἐπὶ τὸ ὁσιώτατον τῆς μεγαλωσύνης αὐτοῦ ὄν. *have confidence in (the Lord's) most sacred and majestic name* 1 Cl 58:1b; ἐλπίζειν ἐπὶ τὸ ὄν. *hope in the name* (of the Lord) B 16:8b.

ו. w. περί and the gen.: εὐαγγελίζεσθαι περὶ τοῦ ὀν. Ἰ. Χ. *bring the good news about the name of J. Chr.* **Ac 8:12.**—(W. acc.: ἔχομεν δέος τὸ ὄ. τοῦ θεοῦ Orig., C. Cels. 4, 48, 34).

ז. w. πρός and acc.: πρὸς τὸ ὀν. Ἰησοῦ . . . πολλὰ ἐναντία πρᾶξαι *do many things in opposing the name of Jesus* **Ac 26:9.**

ח. w. ὑπέρ and gen.: ὑπὲρ τοῦ ὀν. (Ἰησοῦ) ἀτιμασθῆναι **Ac 5:41.** πάσχειν **9:16;** Hs 9, 28, 2. Cp. **Ac 15:26; 21:13.** The activity of the apostles takes place ὑπὲρ τοῦ ὀν. αὐτοῦ *to the honor of (Jesus') name* **Ro 1:5.** Cp. **3J 7.** Of thankful praying at the Lord's Supper εὐχαριστοῦμεν σοι . . . ὑπὲρ τοῦ ἁγίου ὀν. σου, οὗ κατεσκήνωσας ἐν ταῖς καρδίαις ἡμῶν *we thank you . . . for your holy name, which you caused to dwell in our hearts* D 10:2.

δ. ὄν. w. ref. to God or Christ not infreq. stands quite alone, simply *the Name:* **Ac 5:41; Phil 2:9** (cp. Diod. S. 3, 61, 6); **3J 7;** 2 Cl 13:1, 4; IEph 3:1; 7:1; IPhld 10:1; Hv 3, 2, 1; s 8, 10, 3; 9, 13, 2; 9, 28, 3; 5.

❷ ***a person*** (Phalaris, Ep. 128; POxy 1188, 8 [13 AD]; BGU 113, 11; Jos., Ant. 14, 22; other exx. in Dssm., NB 24f [BS 196f]; LXX) τὸ ποθητόν μοι ὄν. *my dear friend*: Alce ISm 13:2; IPol 8:3; Crocus IRo 10:1. Pl. (PThéad 41, 10; PSI 27, 22; Num 1:18 al.) *people* **Ac 1:15; Rv 3:4.** ὀνόματα ἀνθρώπων **11:13** (cp. Ael. Aristid. 50, 72 K.=26 p. 523 D.: ὀνόματα δέκα ἀνδρῶν). This is prob. the place for περὶ λόγου καὶ ὀνομάτων καὶ νόμου *about teaching and persons and (the) law* **Ac 18:15.**

❸ **the classification under which one belongs, noted by a name or category, *title, category*** (cp. Cass. Dio 38, 44; 42, 24 καὶ ὅτι πολλῷ πλείω ἔν τε τῷ σχήματι καὶ ἐν τῷ ὀνόματι τῷ τῆς στρατηγίας ὢν καταπράξειν ἤλπιζε=he hoped to effect much more by taking advantage of his praetorial apparel and title; ins: Sb 7541, 5 [II AD] Νύμφη ὄνομ' ἐστί σοι; POxy 37 I, 17 [49 AD] βούλεται ὀνόματι ἐλευθέρου τὸ σωμάτιον ἀπενέγκασθαι=she claims to have carried off the infant on the basis of its being free-born; Jos., Ant. 12, 154 φερνῆς ὀνόματι; 11, 40; Just., A II, 6, 4 καὶ ἀνθρώπου καὶ σωτῆρος ὄνομα. Other exx. in Heitmüller 50); the possibility of understanding ὄν. as *category* made it easier for Greeks to take over rabb. לְשֵׁם (s. 1dγב above) in the sense *with regard to a particular characteristic,* then simply *with regard to, for the sake of* ὁ δεχόμενος προφήτην εἰς ὄν. προφήτου *whoever receives a prophet within the category 'prophet',* i.e. because he is a prophet, *as a prophet* **Mt 10:41a;** cp. vss. **41b, 42.**—ὃς ἂν ποτίσῃ ὑμᾶς ἐν ὀνόματι, ὅτι Χριστοῦ ἐστε *whoever gives you a drink under the category that you belong to Christ,* i.e. *in your capacity as a follower of Christ* **Mk 9:41.** εἰ ὀνειδίζεσθε ἐν ὀν. Χριστοῦ *if you are reviled for the sake of Christ* **1 Pt 4:14.** δοξαζέτω τὸν θεὸν ἐν τῷ ὀν. τούτῳ *let the person praise God in this capacity* (=ὡς Χριστιανός) vs. **16.** δέδεμαι ἐν τῷ ὀν. *I am imprisoned for the sake of the Name* IEph 3:1.—δέχεσθαι (παιδίον) ἐπὶ τῷ ὀν. μου *for my (name's) sake* **Mt 18:5; Mk 9:37; Lk 9:48** (cp. Heitmüller 113. But s. 1dγח above).

❹ **recognition accorded a person on the basis of performance, *(well-known) name, reputation, fame*** (Hom. et al.; 1 Ch 14:17; 1 Macc 8:12) φανερὸν ἐγένετο τὸ ὄν. αὐτοῦ *his fame was widespread* **Mk 6:14.** ὄν. ἔχειν (Pla., Apol. 38c, Ep. 2, 312c) w. ὅτι foll. *have the reputation of* **Rv 3:1** perh. also **3:5** (s. 1bα; JFuller, JETS 26, '83, 297–306).

❺ **name in terms of office held, *office*** (POxy 58, 6) στασιαζουσῶν τ. φυλῶν, ὁποία αὐτῶν εἴη τῷ ἐνδόξῳ ὀνόματι κεκοσμημένη *when the tribes were quarreling as to which one of them was to be adorned with that glorious office* 1 Cl 43:2. τὸ ὄν. τῆς ἐπισκοπῆς *the office of supervision* 44:1.—B. 1263f. OEANE IV 91–96 on Mesopotamian practices. Schmidt, Syn. I 113–24. DELG. M-M. EDNT. TW. Sv.

ὀνομάζω (ὄνομα) fut. 3 sg. ὀνομάσει Is 62:2; 1 aor. ὠνόμασα. Pass.: 1 fut. 3 sg. ὀνομασθήσεται Jer 3:16; 1 aor. ὠνομάσθην; pf. ptc. ὠνομασμένος (Just.) (Hom.+)

❶ **to give a name to, *call, name*** w. double acc. (Aelian, NA 12, 2; Wsd 2:13; Philo, Gig. 6 al.; Iren. 1, 1, 3 [Harv. I, 12, 1]; τὸν βλάπτοντα μοιχὸν ὀνομάζει 'the one who harms her [the soul, described as bride] [God] calls an adulterer' Did., Gen. 86, 22) οὓς ἀποστόλους ὠνόμασεν *to whom he gave the name 'apostles'* **Mk 3:14** (on the rdg. s. JMeier, JBL 116, '97, 639 n. 11); **Lk 6:13.** ὃν ὠνόμασεν Πέτρον *whom he named Peter* vs. **14** (cp. Jos., Ant. 1, 213 ὃν Ἴσακον ὠνόμασε.—Olympiodorus, Life of Plato p. 1 Westerm.: the man whose name was formerly Aristocles μετωνομάσθη Πλάτων by his teacher; the reason for this is then given). ὠνόμασεν τὸ ὄνομα αὐτῆς Μαρία *she gave her the name Mary* GJs 5:2. Passive w. nom. (Diod. S. 17, 87, 2 ὠνομάζετο, Ἐμβύσαρος; Jos., Vi. 3) ὠνομάσθη τὸ ὄνομα Ἰ. **Lk 2:21** D. τὶς ἀδελφὸς ὀνομαζόμενος *one who is called a member, a so-called member* **1 Cor 5:11** (cp. 3 Macc 7:17). ἐξ οὗ (i.e. τοῦ πατρός) πᾶσα πατριὰ . . . ὀνομάζεται *from whom every family . . . receives its name* **Eph 3:15** (for ὀνομάζειν ἐκ cp. Il. 10, 68; for ὀνομάζεσθαι ἐκ X., Mem. 4, 5, 12).

❷ **to pronounce a name or word, *name a name, use a name/word*** πορνεία . . . μηδὲ ὀνομαζέσθω ἐν ὑμῖν *sexual vice . . . is not even to be mentioned among you* (much less is it actually to be practiced) **Eph 5:3.** ὀν. τὸ ὄνομα κυρίου *name the name of the Lord* (almost='call on') **2 Ti 2:19** (cp. Is 26:13; Jer 20:9; pass.: Orig., C. Cels. 1, 6, 12; 7, 35, 24). πᾶν ὄνομα ὀνομαζόμενον *every name* (of a transcendent being) *that is named* (i.e. called upon) **Eph 1:21** (difft. TAllen, NTS 32, '86, 470–75 God is the namer). ὀν. τὸ ὄνομα τοῦ κυρίου Ἰησοῦ ἐπί τινα *pronounce the name of the Lord Jesus over someone* (to heal him) **Ac 19:13** (cp. Jer 32:29).—*Mention by name* PtK 4 p. 15, 32.

❸ the pass. 'be named' in the sense ***be known*** (cp. Esth 9:4; 1 Macc 3:9; 14:10; EpArist 124) οὐχ ὅπου ὠνομάσθη Χριστός *not where Christ is already known* **Ro 15:20.—1 Cor 5:1 v.l.**—DELG s.v. ὄνομα. M-M. TW.

ὀνομαστός, ή, όν (ὀνομάζω; Hom. et al.; LXX; En 16:1; TestJob; Philo; Jos., C. Ap. 1, 36. On the formation s. Schwyzer I 503) **pert. to having one's name used widely, *illustrious, famous*** δὸς αὐτῇ ὄνομα ὀν. *give her an illustrious name* GJs 6:2; ὄνομα ὀν. (TestJob 4:6; 53:8).—DELG s.v. ὄνομα. M-M. s.v. ὀνομάζω.

ὄνος, ου (Hom.+; loanw. in rabb.), **ὁ** and **ἡ** ***(domesticated) ass, donkey*** (male or female) πῶλος ὄνου *colt of an ass* **J**

12:15 (Just., A I, 32, 6). W. πῶλος **Mt 21:2** (Iambl. Erot. p. 222, 38 εὑρόντες ὄνους δύο), **5, 7** (KPieper, Zum Einzug Jesu in Jerusalem: BZ 11, 1913, 397–402; FVogel, Mt 21:1–11: Blätter für d. Bayerische Gymnasialschulwesen 59, 1923, 212f; ELittmann, ZNW 34, '35, 28; CSmith, The Horse and the Ass in the Bible: ATR 27, '45, 86–97; W-S. §27, 3c; s. JSauer s.v. κάμηλος). W. βοῦς (Is 1:3) **Lk 13:15; 14:5 v.l.** ὄνῳ καθίσαντες αὐτόν ἤγαγον εἰς τὴν πόλιν *they set (Polycarp) on an ass and led him into the city* MPol 8:1. ἔστρωσεν τὸν ὄν. *he saddled his ass* GJs 17:2. κατάγαγέ με ἀπὸ τοῦ ὄνου *take me down from the ass* 17:3.—B. 172. DELG. M-M. TW. Spicq.

ὄντως adv. of the ptc. ὤν (Eur., X., Pla.+; loanw. in rabb.) **pert. to being actually so, *really, certainly, in truth*—ⓐ** lit., as adv. (PGiss 22, 6; Num 22:37; Jer 3:23; Jos., Bell. 1, 68; Just., D. 74, 2; Ath. 23, 4 τὸ ὄντως ὄν) **Lk 23:47; 24:34; J 8:36; 1 Cor 14:25; Gal 3:21;** PtK 4 p. 16, 5. εἶχον τὸν Ἰωάννην ὄν. ὅτι προφήτης ἦν *they held that John was really a prophet* **Mk 11:32.**

ⓑ Used attributively (Pla., Phdr. 260a, Clit. 409e; SIG 893b, 8f τὸν ὄν. Ἡρακλείδην; PStras 53 in Novae Comoed. fgm. ed. OSchröder=Kl. T. 135 p. 47, 14 ὄν. θεός; Sb 3924, 39; Philo, Poster. Cai. 167; Jos., Ant. 15, 63 οἱ ὄν. βασιλεῖς; Ar. 4, 1 τοῦ ὄν. θεοῦ Just., Ath.; Schwyzer II 415) ἡ ὄν. χήρα *the real widow* (one without resources, in contrast to one who has resources, such as relatives, or is still of marriageable age, or, as some hold, has been married several times) **1 Ti 5:3, 5, 16.** ἡ ὄν. ζωή *real, true life* **6:19.** Opp. ὁ ὄν. θάνατος Dg 10:7. οἱ ὄν. ἀποφεύγοντες **2 Pt 2:18 v.l.**—DELG s.v. εἰμί. M-M.

ὀξίζω (fr. ὄξος via ὀξίς 'vinegar cruet') 1 aor. ὤξισα (Soranus p. 69, 25; 70, 14; Diosc. 1, 115, 2; 5, 6, 14; Paradoxogr. Flor. 20; Geopon. 5, 29, 4; 7, 15, 6) ***become sour, taste of vinegar*** of half-empty wine jars ὀξίζουσι *they turn sour* Hm 12, 5, 3b. Therefore their owner fears μήποτε ὤξισαν *that they have become sour* 12, 5, 3a.—DELG s.v. ὀξύς.

ὄξος, ους, τό (on relation to ὀξύς s. Schwyzer I 512, cp. 463; since Solon 26, 7 Diehl[3], Aeschyl., Hippocr.; pap, LXX, ApcEsdr; Philo, Aet. M. 113; Mel., P. 80, 582 al.) ***sour wine, wine vinegar,*** it relieved thirst more effectively than water and, being cheaper than regular wine, it was a favorite beverage of the lower ranks of society and of those in moderate circumstances (Athen. 4, 173e; Plut., Cato Major 336 [1, 13]; Ruth 2:14), esp. of soldiers (PLond III, 1245, 9 p. 228 [357 AD]). Given to Jesus on the cross **Mt 27:48; Mk 15:36; Lk 23:36; J 19:29f** (the contrast to the wine of high quality J 2:40 is prob. designed). In **19:29** (s. vs. 28) scripture is fulfilled (prob. Ps 68:22 ἐπότισάν με ὄξος). This act is interpreted as being due to the malice of some Judeans who committed it, and it is expanded to an offering of gall and vinegar (cp. Ps 68:22; so also Mel., P. 80, 582f; 93, 706f) in GPt 5:16; B 7:5 (both ποτίζειν χολὴν μετὰ ὄξους), 3. Betw. 7:3 and 5 B quotes, as proof that vinegar was given, an otherwise unknown prophetic pass. that directs the priests to eat the goat's ἔντερον ἄπλυτον μετὰ ὄξους (s. ἔντερον) 7:4. W. οἶνος (PLond 856, 28; 1159, 49; other exx. New Docs 1, 85) and mixed w. it Hm 10, 3, 3.—B. 383. Frisk s.v. ὄξος. DELG s.v. ὀξύς. M-M. TW.

ὀξύπτερος, ον (ὀξύς, πτερόν 'wing'; Aesop, Fab. 8 H.=2 P.) 'swift-winged', as subst. ὁ ὀξ. ***hawk*** (Cyranides p. 95, 27) B 10:1, 4.

ὀξύς, εῖα, ύ—❶ pert. to having a keen edge for cutting, *sharp* (so Hom. et al.; LXX; TestJud 1:4; JosAs 16:13; EpArist 60 and 276; Philo; Jos., Ant. 14, 422; Just., D. 127, 2 ὀξὺ ὁρῶν καὶ ὀξὺ ἀκούων [of God]; Mel., P. 78, 522 ἥλους ὀξεῖς) ῥομφαία *a sharp sword* (Ezk 5:1) **Rv 1:16; 2:12; 19:15.** δρέπανον *a sharp sickle* **14:14, 17f.**

❷ pert. to being rapid in motion, *quick, swift* (trag., Hdt. et al.; POxy 900, 7; 1412, 18 ὀξέως; LXX, Philo; Jos., Ant. 5, 261) w. aor. inf. (Ael. Aristid. 34 p. 665 D.: τὰ βέλτιστα πρᾶξαι ὀ.), in an elegantly precise aphorism: ὀξεῖς οἱ πόδες αὐτῶν ἐκχέαι αἷμα *their feet are swift (='sharp' with their feet) when it comes to shedding blood* **Ro 3:15** (Ps 13:3)—B. 1034; 1069. DELG. M-M.

ὀξυχολέω (ὀξύχολος) 1 aor. ptc. ὀξυχολήσας **to be of bad temper, *be irritable, easily moved to anger*** ὁ ἄνθρ. ὁ ὀξυχολήσας *the person who is easily moved to anger* Hm 10, 2, 3.—DELG s.v. χόλος.

ὀξυχολία, ας, ἡ (ὀξύχολος; Cat. Cod. Astr. XII 143, 16; Christian wr.) ***irritability, bad temper*** Hm 5, 1, 3; 6f; 5, 2, 1; 4; 10, 2, 3. ἀπέχεσθαι ἀπὸ τῆς ὀξ. 5, 2, 8a; ἀντιστῆναι τῇ ὀξ. *resist bad temper* 5, 2, 8b. ὀξ. προσπίπτει τινί *irritability comes over someone* 6, 2, 5. ἐὰν ὀξ. τις προσέλθῃ *if bad temper enters in* 5, 1, 3. Called a sister of λύπη and of διψυχία 10, 1, 1f. ἡ ὀξ. λυπεῖ τὸ πνεῦμα *bad temper makes the Spirit sad* 10, 2, 4. Personified among the vices s 9, 15, 3.—DELG s.v. χόλος.

ὀξύχολος, ον (ὀξύς, χόλος 'gall, bitter anger'; the adv. in Soph., Ant. 955, the adj. Solon 1, 26 Diehl[3]; Anth. Pal. 9, 127, 4) **pert. to being readily given to anger, *irritable, irascible, bad-tempered*** w. πικρός and ἄφρων Hm 6, 2, 4. Subst. (cp. Lucian, Fugit. 19 τὸ ὀξύχολον = ἡ ὀξυχολία) ὁ ὀξ. *the irascible, bad-tempered person* 5, 2, 7; s 6, 5, 5.—DELG s.v. χόλος.

ὀπή, ῆς, ἡ (Aristoph. et al.; LXX; TestSol 6:4 D; Philo; Jos., Ant. 9, 163) ***opening, hole*** w. gen. (Herodas 2, 42; Ex 33:22 ὀπ. τῆς πέτρας; Ob 3) τῆς γῆς (Alciphron 2, 1, 2) *in the ground* **Hb 11:38.** Abs. (Aesop, Fab. 353 P.=Babr. 112 Cr. of a mousehole) of the opening out of which a spring flows **Js 3:11.** B. 909.—DELG.

ὄπισθεν adv. (Hom. et al. [ὄπιθεν; s. Kühner-Bl. II 309f; Schwyzer I 628; cp. the adv. ὀπίσω]; ins, pap, LXX, pseudepigr., Joseph.; Ath. 20, 1).

❶ pert. to extension that is behind, *from behind, to the rear, after*—ⓐ as adv. (Appian, Syr. 24 §119; 63 §334, Bell. Civ. 4, 55 §239) **Mt 9:20; Mk 5:27; Lk 8:44.**

ⓑ functioning as prep. w. the gen. (Hom. et al.; SIG 46, 65; 969, 5f; PGM 4, 1230 ὄπισθεν αὐτοῦ σταθείς; LXX)

α. of place *behind, after* someone (Menand., Kolax 47 S. ὄπισθ' ἐβάδιζέ μου; B-D-F §215, 1; Rob. 645) κράζειν ὄπ. τινος *cry out behind/after someone* **Mt 15:23.** ἤκουσα … ὄπ. μου *I heard behind me* **Rv 1:10 v.l.** φέρειν (τι) ὄπ. τινος *carry (someth.) behind someone* **Lk 23:26.**

β. of time *after* someone or someth. ὄπισθεν αὐτῶν *after them* B 4:4 v.l. (cp. Da 7:24).

❷ pert. to position on the back/rear of an object, *behind* opp. ἔμπροσθεν (q.v. 2 and cp. Hes., Shield 132f πρόσθεν … ὄπισθε; Jos., Ant. 13, 30 ἔμπροσθεν αὐτῶν … ὄπισθεν) **Rv 4:6.** Of a scroll w. writing, ἔσωθεν καὶ ὄπισθεν *inside and on the back,* i.e. on the recto and verso **5:1** (cp. PTebt 58 recto, 37 [III BC] τἀπίλοιπα ὀπείσωι='the rest is on the back'; ostracon of the Deissmann collection in PMeyer 107 ff, no. 61, 15 [III BC] ὀπίσω='turn'; PGM 12, 267; 276;). The Revelator evidently draws on Ezk 2:10 to express fullness of communication. On the type of roll ὀπισθόγραφον, s. Pliny, Ep. 3, 5, 17; al. in Wetstein; RCharles, comm. ad loc.

❸ **pert. to coming later in time, *afterwards*** (Hom. et al.) B 4:4 (difft. Da 7:24).—DELG. M-M.

ὀπίσω adv. (Hom. [ὀπίσσω]+).—❶ **marker of a position in back of someth., *behind*—ⓐ** as adv.—**α.** in answer to the quest. 'where?' *behind,* in our lit. only w. art. τὸ ὀπ.: εἰς τοὐπίσω *back* (Pla., Phdr. 254b, Rep. 528a; Diod. S. 1, 32, 5; Lucian, De Merc. Cond. 21; Dionys. Byz. 53 p. 21, 16; Jos., Ant. 7, 15) ἀφορμᾶν *start back* 1 Cl 25:4. Mostly pl. τὰ ὀπ. *what lies behind* (ἐκ τῶν ὀπίσω: PPetr. III, 23 [246 BC]; BGU 1002, 16) in imagery, of a footrace: the part of the course already covered **Phil 3:13.** εἰς τὰ ὀπ. (1 Macc 9:47; Philo, Leg. All. 2, 99 [=Gen 49:17]): ἀπέρχεσθαι *shrink back* **J 18:6;** fig. *draw back* **6:66.** στρέφεσθαι *turn back, turn around* **20:14;** GJs 15:5 (Antimachus Coloph. [V/IV BC] ed. BWyss '36, fgm. 60 στρέφεσθαι εἰς τοὐπίσω; cp. Ps 113:3). Also ἐπιστρέφεσθαι Hv 4, 3, 7 (cp. 4 Km 20:10). ἐπιστρέφειν *return* (home) **Mt 24:18; Mk 13:16; Lk 17:31.** βλέπειν *look back(wards)* (cp. Plut., Nic. 532 [14, 2] ὀπίσω βλ.; Artem. 1, 36 p. 37, 23 τὰ ὀπίσω βλέπειν; Gen 19:17, 26) in imagery **Lk 9:62.** *Cast backward = reject* 1 Cl 35:8 (Ps 49:17).

β. in answer to the quest. 'whither', 'where to?' *back, behind* (Lucian, Dea Syr. 36; Appian, Maced. 18 §3, Mithrid. 104 §489; Polyaenus 7, 27, 1; Gen 24:5; 3 Km 18:37; Jos., Ant. 6, 15) στῆναι ὀπ. παρὰ τ. πόδας αὐτοῦ *come and stand behind him at his feet* **Lk 7:38.** ὀπίσω τὰς χεῖρας ποιεῖν *put* one's *hands behind one* MPol 14:1.

ⓑ functioning as prep. w. gen. (POxy 43 B IV, 3 ὀπίσω Καπιτολείου; LXX) *behind* (OGI 56, 62 [237 BC] ταύτης δ' ὀπίσω=behind this one; Ps.-Lucian, Asin. 17; 29; Chion, Ep. 4, 3; SSol 2:9.—Gen 19:6) ἤκουσα ὀπ. μου *I heard behind me* **Rv 1:10.** τὰ ὀπ. σου Hs 9, 2, 7.—ὕπαγε ὀπ. μου *get behind me! get out of my sight!* **Mt 4:10 v.l.; 16:23; Mk 8:33** (CDodd, JTS 5, '54, 246f); **Lk 4:8 v.l.** (cp. 4 Km 9:19). Subst. τὰ ὀπ. σου ἰδεῖν οὐ δύνῃ Hs 9, 2, 7 (s. 1aα, end).—VHarlow, Jesus' Jerusalem Expedition '36, 20–37: Ὀπίσω μου, esp. 31f.

❷ **marker of position behind an entity that precedes, *after*** functions as prep. w. gen.—ⓐ of place *after* (Ex 15:20; 2 Km 3:16; JosAs 26:7; 27:6) **Lk 19:14.** ὀπ. τῆς γυναικός *after the woman* **Rv 12:15.** ἔρχεσθαι ὀπ. τινός *come after someone, follow someone* (at the same time in the transf. sense 'be an adherent/follower') **Mt 16:24; Mk 8:34 v.l.; Lk 9:23; 14:27.** Also ἀκολουθεῖν (q.v. 2; also s. Gulin s.v. μιμητής a) **Mt 10:38; Mk 8:34.** ἀπέρχεσθαι **Mk 1:20; J 12:19.** πορεύεσθαι ὀπ. τινός **Lk 21:8.** The two latter verbs combine w. ὀπίσω τινός in our lit. in another connection: ἀπέρχεσθαι ὀπ. σαρκὸς ἑτέρας *go after strange/alien flesh* i.e. human beings in Sodom were lusting after beings of a different order, viz. angels (according to En 12:4 al., the reverse took place when angels visited earthly women) **Jd 7.** The parallel pass. **2 Pt 2:10,** on the other hand, has ὀπ. σαρκὸς ἐν ἐπιθυμίᾳ μιασμοῦ πορεύεσθαι, where the σάρξ seems rather to be the power of the defiling desire, to which (σάρξ) the sinners have pledged allegiance. Cp. Hv 3, 7, 3.—δεῦτε ὀπ. μου *come, follow me* (s. δεῦτε) **Mt 4:19; Mk 1:17.** ἀποσπᾶν τινα ὀπ. τινός (s. ἀποσπάω 2a) **Ac 20:30.** ἀφιστάναι λαὸν ὀπ. αὐτοῦ (s. ἀφίστημι 1) **5:37.** ἐκτρέπεσθαι ὀπ. τοῦ σατανᾶ (s. ἐκτρέπω) **1 Ti 5:15** (cp. Ar. 3, 2 ἐπλανήθησαν ὀπ. τῶν στοιχείων; 7, 4). θαυμάζεσθαι ὀπ. τινός (s. θαυμάζω 2) **Rv 13:3.**

ⓑ of time *after* (3 Km 1:6, 24; Eccl 10:14) ἔρχεσθαι ὀπ. τινός **Mt 3:11; Mk 1:7; J 1:15, 27, 30** (CLindeboom, 'Die na mij komt, is voor mij geworden': GereformTT 16, 1916, 438–46; difft. ['a follower of mine'] KGrobel, JBL 60, '41, 397–401).—DELG s.v. ὄπισθεν. M-M. TW.

ὁπλή, ῆς, ἡ (Hom. et al.; LXX; EpArist 150) ***hoof,*** including the split hoof of cattle (Hom. Hymns, Merc. 77; Hes., Works 491; Pind., Pyth. 4, 226; Hdt. 2, 71; SIG 1026, 19 [IV/III BC]) ἐκφέρειν ὁπλάς *grow hoofs* 1 Cl 52:2 (Ps 68:32).—DELG.

ὁπλίζω (ὅπλον) 1 aor. mid. ὡπλισάμην (gener. 'to get someth. ready', or 'equip w. someth.', freq. in contexts indicating military preparation; Hom. et al.; Jer 52:25 Sym.; Jos., Vi. 45; SibOr 2, 119) **to get ready, esp. by equipping, *equip, arm,*** mid. *prepare* or *equip oneself,* in our lit. only fig. τί *with someth.* τὴν αὐτὴν ἔννοιαν *equip oneself with the same insight* **1 Pt 4:1** (cp. Soph., Electra 996 τοιοῦτον θράσος αὐτή θ' ὁπλίζει='you arm yourself with such rashness'; Anth. Pal. 5, 93, 1 ὥπλισμαι πρὸς Ἔρωτα περὶ στέρνοισι λογισμόν='I have armed myself against Love with reason about my breast'; Jos., Ant. 6, 187 τ. θεὸν ὥπλισμαι David faces Goliath). Military imagery is not so evident here (s. next entry 1) as in the next pass. W. the dat. τινί *with someth.* (Eur., Andr. 1118; X., Cyr. 6, 4, 4 w. specific reference to armor; Cornutus 31 p. 63, 17) τοῖς ὅπλοις τῆς δικαιοσύνης Pol 4:1. Here the accompanying dat. establishes a miltary metaphor.—DELG s.v. ὅπλον. M-M. s.v. ὁπλίζομαι. TW.

ὅπλον, ου, τό (s. prec. entry; Hom.+; ins, pap, LXX; TestSol 8:6; TestLevi 5:3; EpArist, Philo, Joseph.; Tat. 31, 1; Ath. 35, 1)

❶ **any instrument one uses to prepare or make ready, *tool*** ὅπλα ἀδικίας *tools of wickedness,* i.e. tools for doing what is wicked **Ro 6:13a** (cp. Aristot., Pol. 1253a). Opp. ὅπλα δικαιοσύνης vs. **13b.** But mng. 2 is also prob.; it is found in all the other pass. of our lit., and specif. in Paul.

❷ **an instrument designed to make ready for military engagement, *weapon*—ⓐ** lit., pl. (Demetr.: 722 fgm. 5 Jac. ὅπλα εἶχον; Jos., Vi. 99 ἧκον μεθ' ὅπλων) **J 18:3.** Riders μετὰ τῶν συνήθων αὐτοῖς ὅπλων *with their usual arms* MPol 7:1. Sing. τίθησιν Μωϋσῆς ἓν ἐφ' ἓν ὅπλον *Moses placed one weapon=shield* (so as early as Hdt.; Diod. S. 17, 21, 2; 17, 43, 9 [interchanged with ἀσπίδες 8]; 17, 57, 2; Sb 7247, 24 [296 AD]; TestLevi 5:3 ὅπλον καὶ ῥομφαίαν) *on the other one,* to stand on them and gain a better view of the battlefield B 12:2.

ⓑ in imagery, pl. of a Christian's life as a battle against evil τὰ ὅπ. τῆς στρατείας ἡμῶν οὐ σαρκικά *the weapons of my warfare are not physical* **2 Cor 10:4.** ἐνδύσασθαι τὰ ὅπ. τοῦ φωτός *put on the weapons of light* **Ro 13:12.** τὰ ὅπ. τῆς δικαιοσύνης τὰ δεξιὰ καὶ ἀριστερά *the weapons of righteousness for offense and defense* (s. ἀριστερός) **2 Cor 6:7.** ὁπλίζεσθαι τοῖς ὅπλοις τῆς δικαιοσύνης Pol 4:1 (s. ὁπλίζω). Of evil desire: φοβουμένη τὰ ὅπ. σου (*your weapons,* i.e. those of the Christian who is equipped for the good fight) Hm 12, 2, 4. Of baptism: τὸ βάπτισμα ὑμῶν μενέτω ὡς ὅπλα *let baptism remain as your arms* ('remain' in contrast to the deserter, who throws his weapons away) IPol 6:2. Of Christ himself ὅπλον εὐδοκίας (God's) *shield of good pleasure* AcPl Ha 8, 23 = Ox 1602, 34f//BMM recto, 30.—B. 1383. DELG. M-M. TW.

ὁπόθεν adv. of place (Hom. et al.; not LXX; PPar I, 125 and 165 [IV AD]; Just.) ***where,*** lit. 'from where' Papias (3:2).—DELG s.v. πο-. Frisk s.v. πόθεν.

ὁποῖος, οἷα, οἷον (Hom.+) correlative pron. ***of what sort, as*** τοιοῦτος, ὁπ. (X., Cyr. 1, 6, 36; Ael. Aristid. 45, 1 K.=8 p. 81 D.; IGR III, 89, 12–14 [69 AD]; Jos., Ant. 7, 385; Just., A I, 19, 5 al.; Tat. 21, 2) **Ac 26:29;** cp. Hm 11:15. Used as a pron. in indirect questions (Hom. et al.; s. B-D-F §300, 1; Rob. 732; in dir. question Tat. 32, 13) τὸ ἔργον ὁπ. ἐστιν *what sort of work* (each has done) **1 Cor 3:13.** ὁπ. εἴσοδον ἔσχομεν πρὸς ὑμᾶς *what* *sort of welcome we had among you* **1 Th 1:9.** ἐπελάθετο ὁποῖος ἦν *he forgets what sort of person he is* **Js 1:24.** Almost equal to the relative 1 Cl 43:2. ὁποῖοί ποτε ἦσαν οὐδέν μοι διαφέρει *it makes no difference to me what sort of people they were* **Gal 2:6** (cp. Just., A I, 21, 4; s. B-D-F §303; Rob. 732; VWeber, Erklärung von Gal 2:6a: Der Katholik 80, 1900, 481–99).—DELG s.v. πο-. Frisk s.v. ποῖος. M-M.

ὁπόσος, η, ον (Hom. et al.; ins; PHal 1, 206; BGU 1074, 6; Jos., Ant. 16, 351; 17, 30; SibOr 3, 480; Just., A I, 23, 1; Ath., R. 23 p. 76, 31 πᾶν ὁπόσον) **interrogative ref. to degree of quantity or quality, *how great, how much*** neut. ὁπόσον (SIG 400, 18) *how much* ὁπ. δίκαιός ἐστιν *how righteous he is* GPt 8:28 (ms.: οτιποσον).—DELG s.v. πο-. Frisk s.v. πόσος.

ὁπόταν temporal particle (Pind.+ [Hom. separates it ὁπότ᾽ ἄν]; SIG 344, 75; pap; Job 29:22; TestSol; SibOr 5, 464; Jos., Ant. 6, 166; 16, 387 al.; Just., Tat., Mel.; Ath., R. 21 p. 74, 28 [all only with subj.]) ***whenever*** εἶτα, ὁπόταν καθεῖλεν *then, whenever he let* (his hands) *drop* B 12:2 (cp. Mel., P. 11, 74 ὁπόταν βούλεται; s. also B-D-F §381; Rob. 971; Reinhold p. 108).

ὁπότε temporal particle (Hom.+) ***when*** w. ind., w. ref. to past concrete events (Hom.; POxy 243, 10; PRyl 245, 3; Tob 7:11 Sin.; Just., D. 28, 5 al.; Mel., P. 42, 287; Ath. 21, 4) B 12:9; **Lk 6:3 v.l.** (for ὅτε).—B-D-F §455, 1; Rob. 971.—DELG s.v. πο-. M-M.

ὅπου particle denoting place (Hom.+), that can also take on causal and temporal mng.

❶ marker of a position in space, *where*—ⓐ of a specific location in the present**—α.** used in connection w. a designation of place, w. ind. foll. **Mt 6:19f; 13:5; 28:6; Mk 2:4b; 4:5; 9:48; 16:6; Lk 12:33; J 1:28; 4:20, 46; 7:42** al.; **Ac 17:1; Rv 11:8; 20:10** (here the verb is supplied fr. the context). πρὸς Καϊάφαν, ὅπου οἱ γραμματεῖς συνήχθησαν *to Caiaphas,* i.e. to his palace, *where the scribes were gathered* **Mt 26:57.** παρ᾽ ὑμῖν ὅπ. **Rv 2:13b;** οὗτοι ... ὅπου σπείρεται ὁ λόγος *those ... in whom* (=*in whose hearts*) *the word is sown* **Mk 4:15.** Looking toward an ἐκεῖ (Jos., C. Ap. 1, 32) **Mt 6:21; Lk 12:34; 17:37; J 12:26.**—Not infreq. ὅπ. is related to an ἐκεῖ that is omitted but is easily supplied (ἐκεῖ) ὅπ. *(there) where* (Maximus Tyr. 31, 5b) **Mt 25:24, 26; Mk 2:4a; 13:14; J 3:8; 14:3; 17:24; 20:12, 19; Ro 15:20; Rv 2:13a;** *(thither) where* **Mk 5:40; 6:55; J 6:62; 7:34, 36; 11:32; 18:1.**—On the pleonastic use of the pers. pron. after ὅπου s. B-D-F §297; Rob. 683; 722f: ὅπ. ἡ γυνὴ κάθηται ἐπ᾽ αὐτῶν **Rv 17:9.** Corresp. ὅπου ... ἐκεῖ (שָׁם... אֲשֶׁר) **12:6, 14.** Cp. **Mk 6:55 v.l.**

β. ὅπ. ἄν w. impf. expresses repetition in past time, *whenever* **Mk 6:56** (s. B-D-F §367; Rob. 969; 972f).

γ. subjunctive is used in a final relative clause ποῦ ἐστιν τὸ κατάλυμα ὅπου τὸ πάσχα φάγω; **Mk 14:14b; Lk 22:11** (s. B-D-F §378; Rob. 969).

δ. ὅπου ἄν (or ἐάν) w. subj. *wherever, whenever* (SIG 1218, 23; PEleph 1, 5 [311/310 BC]; POxy 484, 20; 1639, 20; TestAbr B 4 p. 109, 10f [Stone p. 66] ὅπου ἄν κοιμηθῇ) w. the aor. subj. **Mt 26:13; Mk 6:10; 9:18; 14:9** (s. KBeyer, Semitische Syntax im NT, '62, 196), **14a.** W. the pres. subj. (and ἐκεῖ to correspond) **Mt 24:28.**

ⓑ of a place reached by being in motion, *whither* (Soph., Trach. 40; X., An. 2, 4, 19, Cyr. 8, 3, 23 al. in codd.; Epict. 4, 7, 14; OdeSol 11:5; Jos., Ant. 16, 325).

α. w. ind. foll., related to a 'there (thither)' to be supplied, *where* (O. Wilck II, 1162, 5 ὅπου θέλει) **J 8:21f; 13:33, 36; 14:4; 21:18; Js 3:4.**

β. ὅπου ἄν (or ἐάν) w. pres. subj. *wherever* (POxy 728, 11; TestAbr B 2 p. 106, 8 [Stone p. 60] πορεύου ὅπου ἄν βούλῃ. W. aor. subj. Ruth 1:16; Tob 13:5 S; Jos., Ant. 6, 77) **Mt 8:19; Lk 9:57; Rv 14:4.**

❷ marker of more immediate circumstance or expressing a premise, *where,* transf. sense of 1 (X., Cyr. 6, 1, 7) ὅπου οὐκ ἔνι Ἕλλην καὶ Ἰουδαῖος *where* (i.e. granting the premise involving the idea of the 'new person') *there is no* (longer) *Greek and Judean* **Col 3:11.** Or ὅπου introduces a subordinate clause that indicates the circumstances resulting in what is said in the main clause following it (cp. Pr 26:20; EpArist 149; TestZeb 7:10): ὅπ. διαθήκη, θάνατον ἀνάγκη φέρεσθαι τοῦ διαθεμένου *where there is a will, the death of the one who made it must be established* **Hb 9:16.** ὅπ. ἄφεσις τούτων, οὐκέτι κτλ. **10:18.** The main clause can use ἐκεῖ to refer back to the ὅπ. of the subord. clause *where ..., there* **Js 3:16.**—Used to express an opposite circumstance ὅπου ἄγγελοι οὐ φέρουσιν κρίσιν *where* (i.e. in a situation in which) *angels pronounce no judgment* **2 Pt 2:11.**

❸ marker of cause or reason, *in so far as, since* (Hdt. 1, 68 al.; Thu. 8, 96, 2; Chariton 5, 6, 10; 4 Macc 2:14; somet. also in the combination ὅπου γε as Dionys. Hal., Comp. Verb. 4; Jos., C. Ap. 2, 154) **1 Cor 3:3;** B 16:6.—*whereas* 1 Cl 43:1.—DELG s.v. πο-. M-M.—S. entry οὗ.

ὀπτάνομαι (a new present modeled after αἰσθάνομαι [s. ὄπωπα in DELG and Frisk, cp. B-D-F §101 p. 54 under ὁρᾶν; Mlt-H. 214; 382]. This form is found UPZ 62, 32 [161/160 BC]; PTebt 24, 5 [117 BC]; PGM 4, 3033; Herm Wr. 3, 2; 3 Km 8:8; Tob 12:19 BA.—SPsaltes, Gramm. der Byz. Chroniken 1913, 242; Schwyzer I 700) **be visible to, *appear*** τινί *to someone* (B-D-F §191, 1; 313; Rob. 820) of the risen Christ **Ac 1:3.**—HCadbury, JBL 44, 1925, 218f.—DELG s.v. ὄπωπα. M-M. TW.

ὀπτασία, ας, ἡ (ὀπτάζομαι; pass. 'to be seen'; Anth. Pal. 6, 210, 6; LXX, Just.; Hesychius; Leontius 8 p. 16, 12=vision, phantom [s. also the word-list on p. 182a])

❶ an event of a transcendent character that impresses itself vividly on the mind, *a vision, celestial sight,* of that which a deity permits a human being to see, either of the deity personally or of someth. else usu. hidden fr. mortals (Theod. Da 9:23; 10:1, 7f; Psellus p. 132, 19 of a transcendent phenomenon) ὀπτασίαι (w. ἀποκαλύψεις) κυρίου *visions of the Lord* **2 Cor 12:1** (ELombard, Les extases et les souffrances de l'apôtre Paul. Essai d'une interprétation de II Cor 12:1–10: RTP 36, 1903, 450–500). οὐράνιος ὀπ. **Ac 26:19.** ὀπτασίαν ὁρᾶν *see a vision* (Pel.-Leg. 18, 17) **Lk 1:22.** W. gen. of what is seen: ὀπ. ἀγγέλων ὁρᾶν *see a vision of angels* **24:23** (ViZach 2 [p. 97, 4 Sch.]). ἡ φανερωθεῖσα ὀπ. *the vision that appeared* MPol 12:3. διὰ τὴν ὀπ. τὴν γενομένην Παύλῳ AcPl Ha 3,15.

❷ state of being that is experienced by one who has a vision, *trance* ἐν ὀπτασίᾳ *in a trance* MPol 5:2.—DELG s.v. ὄπωπα. TW.

ὀπτάω (ὀπτός) aor. ὤπτησα LXX; pass subj. 3 sg. ὀπτηθῇ (Ar.) (Hom. et al.; PSI 402, 5 [III BC]; PLond III, 131, 115 p. 173; LXX; Jos., Ant. 1, 197; 3, 255; Ar. 4, 3; Just.) ***bake*** (so Hdt. 8, 137; X., An. 5, 4, 29 ἄρτους ὀπτῶντες) MPol 15:2 ἄρτος ὀπτώμενος.—DELG s.v. ὀπτός.

ὀπτός, ή, όν (Hom. et al.; pap; Ex 12:8, 9; Jos., Ant. 3, 255) **pert. to preparation of food by direct fire** (opp. ἕψω boil), ***roasted, baked, broiled*** ἰχθὺς ὀπ. *broiled fish* (Hippocr., Aff. 52 vol. VI p. 264 L. ἰχθύες ὀπτοί; Plut., Mor. 353d; PCairZen 66,

13; 16 [III BC]; PGiss 93, 6 [II AD]) **Lk 24:42.**—S. the lit. s.v. μελίσσιος.—DELG. M-M.

ὄπυσις, εως, ἡ (hapax. derived fr. ὀπυίω, orig. 'to marry', in later Gk. 'to have intimate relations with a woman' Luc., Eun. 12) perh.= ***fornication*** (CWessely, PatrOr 18, 1924, 482 and KPrümm, Biblica 10, 1929, 62–80) εἰς πόλιν ἄρχουσαν ὀπύσεως *in a city* (i.e. Rome) *that presides over whoring/fornication* ApcPt Rainer 4, 1 p. 278 J. (the reading of the ms.; but cj. by James p. 273 after the Ethiopic version: δύσεως '[rules over] the west').—DELG s.v. ὀπυίω.

ὀπώρα, ας, ἡ properly the time beginning w. the rising of the star Sirius (in July), corresp. to late summer and early fall, when fruit ripens (so Hom. et al.); then the ***fruit*** itself (so trag., X., Pla. et al.; POxy 298, 38 [I AD]; PGM 5, 231; Jer 31:32; 47:10, 12; TestIss 3:6; JosAs 4:4; Philo, Agr. 15; Jos., Bell. 3, 49; loanw. in rabb.) ἡ ὀπ. σου τῆς ἐπιθυμίας τῆς ψυχῆς *the fruit for which your soul longed* **Rv 18:14.**—B. 375. DELG. M-M.

ὅπως (Hom.+)**—❶** as adv. **marker of the manner in which an event develops, *how, that*** (B-D-F §300, 1; Rob. 985) w. the aor. ind. (Jos., Bell. 1, 6; 17) ὅπως τε παρέδωκαν αὐτὸν οἱ ἀρχιερεῖς **Lk 24:20;** w. the pres. ind. (Pherecrates Com. [V BC], fgm. 45 K.; Tat. 22, 2 ὅπως δεῖ μοιχεύειν) ὅπως κολάζονται 2 Cl 17:7. But here the mng. of ὅπως prob. shows a development analogous to that of πῶς in colloq. usage, which comes to resemble ὡς (so Lk 24:20 D)= ὅτι=*that* (X., Hier. 9, 1; Diod. S. 11, 46, 3; Lucian, Dial. Deor. 6, 2; BGU 846, 16 [II AD] γνοῦναι, ὅπως ὀφείλω='to know that I owe'; Dssm., LO 155, 26 [LAE 179, 28]; B-D-F §396; s. Rob. 1045).

❷ as a conj. **marker expressing purpose for an event or state, *(in order) that*** w. the subj. (the transition fr. 1 to 2 is observable SIG 741, 23), predom. the aor. (the fut. ind. [as early as Homer; freq. in V BC and later: Andocides 1, 43; Demosth. 19, 316; Herodas 7, 90; s. Meisterhans[3]-Schw. 255, 32; Nicol. Dam.: 90 fgm. 16 p. 398, 5 Jac.; Hero Alex. I 368, 23 ὅπ. κινήσει; TestAbr B 1 p. 105, 4=Stone p. 58; TestJob 18:2; Jos., Ant. 11, 101] is given in several places as v.l. [e.g. **Mt 26:59**], but prob. should be changed everywhere to the aor. subj.).

ⓐ with numerous types of verbs *(in order) that,* neg. ὅπ. μή *in order that . . . not* (B-D-F §369; Rob. 985–87).

α. without ἄν (this is the rule) after a pres. (ApcSed 16:2; Ar. 9:6; Just., A I, 47, 6 al.) **Mt 5:45** (impv.); **6:2, 5; Hb 9:15; 1 Pt 2:9;** 2 Cl 9:6. After a perf. **Ac 9:17; Hb 2:9; Lk 16:26** (w. μή). After the impf. **Ac 9:24.** After the aor. vss. **2, 12; 20:16** (w. μή); **25:26; Ro 9:17ab** (Ex 9:16); **1 Cor 1:29** (w. μή); **Gal 1:4;** 1 Cl 10:2; 35:4; after the aor. impv. (TestAbr B 13 p. 117, 12 [Stone p. 82]; TestReub 1:4; JosAs 24:5; after the aor. ptc. Demetr.: 722 fgm. 1, 1 Jac.) **Mt 2:8; 5:16; 6:4, 18** (w. μή); **Ac 23:15, 23; 2 Cor 8:11** (here γένηται or ᾖ is to be supplied as the predicate of the ὅπως-clause); GJs 21:2 codd.; AcPlCor 2:16. After the plpf. **J 11:57** (ὅπως is found only here in J, prob. for variety's sake, since ἵνα is used a few words before). After the fut. **Mt 23:35.** In accord w. God's purpose as revealed in Scripture, an event can be presented w. the formula (this or that has happened) ὅπ. πληρωθῇ τὸ ῥηθὲν διὰ τ. προφητῶν (and sim. exprs.) **Mt 2:23; 8:17; 12:17 v.l.; 13:35.**—Alternating w. ἵνα (s. also **J 11:57** above) **2 Cor 8:14; Lk 16:27f** (the ἵνα-clause gives the content of the plea; the ὅπως-clause gives the purpose of the gift requested; so also Ex 23:20; TestAbr B 10 p. 114, 10 [Stone p. 76]; ApcMos 29; Just., D. 108, 1); **2 Th 1:11f** (the ἵνα-clause gives the content, the ὅπως-clause the purpose of the prayer).

β. with ἄν and the aor. subj. (B-D-F §369, 5; Rdm.[2] 194; Rob. 986; EHermann, Die Nebensätze in d. griech. Dialekten 1912, 276f; JKnuenz, De enuntiatis Graecorum finalibus 1913, 13ff; 26ff; Meisterhans[3]-Schw. 254; Mayser II/1 p. 254 f.—X., Cyr. 8, 3, 6 ἐπιμεληθῆναι ὅπως ἂν οὕτω γένηται; Pla., Gorg. 523d; PSI 435, 19 [258 BC]; 438, 19; PMagd 23, 7; LXX) **Mt 6:5 v.l.; Lk 2:35; Ac 3:20; 15:17** (Am 9:12 v.l.); **Ro 3:4** (Ps 50:6).

ⓑ more and more replacing the inf. after verbs of asking *that* (B-D-F §392, 1) αἰτέομαι (Jos., Ant. 19, 288) **Ac 25:3.** δέομαι (Ps.-Aeschines, Ep. 3, 1; Par Jer 7, 24; 32; ApcMos 9 al.; Jos., Ant. 7, 191; 9, 9) **Mt 9:38; Lk 10:2; Ac 8:24** (w. μή). ἐρωτάω (PTebt 409, 4 ff [5 AD]) **Lk 7:3; 11:37; Ac 23:20.** παρακαλέω (Jos., Ant. 8, 143) **Mt 8:34** (v.l. ἵνα). προσεύχομαι or εὔχομαι (cp. PGM 3, 107; Jon 1:6; Jos., Ant. 11, 17) **Ac 8:15; Js 5:16.** So perh. also **Phlm 6,** where ὅπ. could be thought of as depending on προσεύχομαι derived in sense fr. vs. 4, unless ὅπως here=ὥστε (Archimed. I p. 16, 18 Heiberg ὅπως γένηται τὸ ἐπίταγμα al.).—Likew. after verbs of deciding (LXX) συμβούλιον λαμβάνειν ὅπ. *resolve to* **Mt 12:14; 22:15** (D πῶς), where many scholars prefer the transl. *consult with a view to.* Also συμβούλιον διδόναι ὅπ. **Mk 3:6.**—DELG s.v. πο-. M-M.

ὅραμα, ατος, τό (ὁράω; X. et al.) in our lit. of extraordinary visions, whether the pers. who has the vision be asleep or awake.

❶ **someth. that is viewed with one's eye, *someth. seen, sight, vision*** (acc. to Artem. 1, 2 p. 5, 19 ὅραμα is someth. that can actually be seen, in contrast to 5, 17 φάντασμα=a figment of the imagination; PCairGoodsp 3, 5 [III BC]; PParis 51, 38 [160 BC]=UPZ 78 τὸ ὅραμα τοῦτο ὃ τεθέαμαι; Ex 3:3; Dt 4:34; Da 7:1; En 99:8; TestAbr A 4 p. 81, 13 [Stone p. 10] ἀναγγελεῖ τὸ ὅραμα; TestLevi 8:1 εἶδον ὅραμα; 9:2) of the Transfiguration **Mt 17:9.** Of God's appearance in the burning bush **Ac 7:31.** Cp. **Ac 10:17, 19; 11:5; 12:9; 16:9f** (Appian, Bell. Civ. 4, 134 §565 Brutus, when he is about to cross over ἐκ τῆς Ἀσίας ἐς τὴν Εὐρώπην . . . νυκτός sees someth. that appeared to him [ὄψιν ἰδεῖν]: a φάσμα—not a human being, not a god, but a δαίμων κακός—stands at his side and speaks to him; cp. Philostrat., Life of Apollonius 4, 34 on a change of plan prompted by a dream [ὄναρ]); Hv 4, 2, 2. ἐπιδεικνύναι τινὶ ὅραμα *show someone a vision* 3, 2, 3. δεικνύναι τινὶ ὁράματα (w. ἀποκαλύψεις) 4, 1, 3. ἀποκαλύπτειν τὰ ὁράματα *reveal the visions* (double sense, as in the original, which can be understood of the visions themselves or of the interpretation of their mng.) 3, 4, 3.

❷ **the act by which the recipient of a vision is granted a vision, or the state of being in which the pers. receives a vision, *vision*** (SIG 1128 καθ' ὅραμα; LXX) of the Lord: εἰπεῖν ἐν νυκτὶ δι' ὁράματος *say at night in a vision* **Ac 18:9.** ἐν ὁράματι (Gen 15:1; 46:2 εἶπεν ὁ θεὸς ἐν ὁρ. τῆς νυκτός; Da 7:13) εἶδεν ἐν ὁρ. ἄγγελον (cp. TestJud 3:10) **Ac 10:3.** Cp. **9:10, 12.** βλέπειν ἐν ὁρ. τῆς νυκτός Hv 3, 10, 6. [τοῦ παιδὸς] τ̣ο̣υ̣ [διελ]θόντος ἐν ὁρό(=ά)ματι διὰ [τοῦ κεκλεισμένου] κοιτῶ[νος] *[the youth] who, in (Paul's) vision, had entered through [the closed] bedroom* AcPl Ha 5, 31f. ἐν ὁράματι ἰδ[ούσῃ] τὸν κύριον *having seen the Lord in a vision* Ox 3525, 19. Ox 1224 fgm. 2 recto, II, 3 (=Kl. T. 8[3], p. 26, 10) Ἰῆς [ἐ]ν ὁράμα[τι λέγει]. S. ὅρασις 3, ὄναρ, and πνεῦμα 6f.—DELG s.v. ὁράω. M-M. TW. EDNT.

ὅρασις, εως, ἡ (ὁράω; Aristot.+; ins, pap, LXX, En; PsSol 6:3; TestAbr A 4 p. 80, 27 [Stone p. 8]; Test12 Patr; JosAs 18 [p. 68, 13 Bat.]; GrBar 4:3; AscIs 3, 13, 31; EpArist 142; Philo).

❶ **organ of sight, *eye*** (mostly pl. 'eyes' Diod. S. 2, 6, 10; Plut., Mor. 88d; PGM 13, 582. But also the sg. ὅρασις Diod. S. 3, 37, 9; 5, 43, 1; Proclus on Pla., Cratyl. p. 7, 25 Pasqu.; Iren. 1, 18, 1 [Harv. I, 171, 1]; Orig., C. Cels. 1, 48, 31; Hippol., Ref.

6, 15, 1), and hence ***sight, appearance, face*** (Ramsay, CB I/2, 653 no. 564 εἰς ὅρασιν καὶ εἰς ὅλον τὸ σῶμα; PGM 4, 308; 5, 147; Sir 11:2; 25:17; 3 Macc 5:33) in imagery, of mental and spiritual perception ἀχλύος γέμοντες ἐν τῇ ὁράσει *with eyes full of mistiness* 2 Cl 1:6.

❷ **that which is seen, *appearance, sight*—ⓐ** *appearance* (Philo Mech. 51, 10; 62, 23; Ezk 1:5; 1 Km 16:12; Hippol., Ref. 4, 20, 1) ὅμοιος ὁράσει λίθῳ ἰάσπιδι *like jasper in appearance* **Rv 4:3a;** cp. vs. **3b.**

ⓑ *spectacle* ἔσονται εἰς ὅρ. πάσῃ σαρκί *they will be a spectacle for all flesh* (Is 66:24) 2 Cl 7:6; 17:5.

❸ **vision in a transcendent mode** (in this case the distinction made betw. ὅραμα 1 and 2 cannot be carried through w. certainty, so that the focus in 1 will certainly predominate.—Critodemus, a Hellenistic astrologer, wrote a book Ὅρασις in vision form [Vett. Val. 150, 11; 329, 18f]; Herm. Wr. 1, 30 ἀληθινὴ ὅρ.; Tob 12:19; Zech 10:2; Pel.-Leg. 18, 20) ***vision*** (cp. Da 7:1 Theod.; Iren. 4, 28, 3 [Harv. II 296, 16]) ἰδεῖν τι ἐν τῇ ὁρ. **Rv 9:17.** ὅρασιν ἰδεῖν or ὁρᾶν **Ac 2:17** (Jo 3:1); Hv 2, 4, 2. Of the visions of Hermas Hv 2, 1, 1; 3, 10, 3ff; 3, 11, 2; 4; 3, 12, 1; 3, 13, 1; 4, 1, 1. Titles Hv 2; 3; 4.—DELG s.v. ὁράω. M-M. TW.

ὁρατός, ή, όν (ὁράω; Hippocr., Pla. et al.; PGrenf I, 47, 14; LXX; TestReub 4:10; 6:12; Just., D. 3, 7; Tat.) verbal adj. of ὁράω **pert. to capability of being seen, *visible*** (w. ἀόρατος; cp. TestReub 6:12; Philo, Op. M. 12, Migr. Abr. 183 ἀόρατος ὡς ἂν ὁρ. ὤν; Ar. 13, 8; Tat. 5, 1) σῶμα Dg 6:4. ἄρχοντες ISm 6:1. Of Christ ὁ ἀόρατος, ὁ δι᾽ ἡμᾶς ὁρ. IPol 3:2. τὰ ὁρατά (Ps.-Clem., Hom. 2, 7): τὰ ὁρ. καὶ τὰ ἀόρατα *things visible and invisible* **Col 1:16;** cp. ITr 5:2; IRo 5:3.—DELG s.v. ὁράω. M-M. TW.

ὁράω (Hom.+) impf. 3 pl. ἑώρων (**J 6:2** v.l. for ἐθεώρουν); pf. ἑώρακα and ἑόρακα (s. B-D-F §68), 3 pl. ἑώρακαν beside ἑόρακαν and ἑωράκασιν (Mlt-H. 221); plpf. ἑωράκειν Hv 2, 1, 3; fut. ὄψομαι, 2 sg. ὄψῃ (W-S. §13, 18). Pass.: 1 fut. ὀφθήσομαι; 1 aor. ὤφθην, by-form ὠράθην Ezk 12:12; 21:29; Da 1:15 Theod.; pf. 3 sing. ὦπται Ex 4:1, 5; Hv 3, 1, 2, inf. ὦφθαι or ἑωρᾶσθαι (Just.); plpf. 3 sg. ὦπτο. (Just.). In Byz. times there was an aor. mid. ὠψάμην (Lob. on Phryn. p. 734). There is a subjunctive form corresponding to this in one place in the NT, though not without a v.l.; it is ὄψησθε (v.l. ὄψεσθε) **Lk 13:28.** The functions of the aor. active are taken over by εἶδον and the forms belonging to it (s. εἶδον). βλέπω is, for the most part, used for the pres. and impf. On the use of ὁράω and βλέπω s. Reinhold p. 95ff.

A. trans.—❶ **to perceive by the eye, *catch sight of, notice***

ⓐ w. acc. of pers. **Mt 28:7, 10; Mk 16:7; Lk 16:23; J 8:57; 9:37; 14:9; 16:16f, 19, 22; 20:18** (PPerkins, Int 46, '92, 31–41), **25, 29; 1J 4:20a; Rv 1:7;** AcPl Ha 6, 17; Κλαύδιε ὅ[ρα Παῦλον] 8, 1. θεὸν οὐδεὶς ἑώρακεν πώποτε (s. PGM 5, 101f of Osiris ὃν οὐδεὶς εἶδε πώποτε) **J 1:18;** cp. **6:46ab; 1J 4:20b** (on seeing God and its impossibility for mortals s. WGrafBaudissin, 'Gott schauen' in d. atl. Rel.: ARW 18, 1915, 173–239; RBultmann, ZNW 29, 1930, 169–92; EFascher: Marb. Theol. Studien '31, 1, 41–77).—Also of the perception of personal beings that become visible in a transcendent manner (UPZ 78, 8 [159 BC] of a dream in the Sarapeum ὁρῶ τ. διδύμας; 69, 6; Just., D. 115, 3), of the vision of Christ that Paul had **1 Cor 9:1.** The acc. is to be supplied fr. the context **Hb 11:27; 1 Pt 1:8.** W. acc. of the ptc. (B-D-F §416, 1; Rob. 1123.—UPZ 69, 6 [152 BC] ὁρῶ ἐν τῷ ὕπνῳ τὸν Μενέδημον ἀντικείμενον ἡμῖν; Ex 2:11, 13; TestJob 26, 6; ParJer 9:20; GrBar 1:3; Philo, Leg. All. 3, 38; Just., A I, 10, 1 al.) ὄψονται τὸν υἱὸν τοῦ ἀνθρώπου ἐρχόμενον **Mt 24:30; Mk 13:26; Lk 21:27.** ὄψεσθε τὸν υἱὸν τοῦ ἀνθρώπου καθήμενον **Mk 14:62** (NPerrin, The End-product of the Christian Pesher Trad., NTS 12, '66, 150–55).

ⓑ w. acc. of thing ὀπτασίαν ὁρ. *see a vision* (s. ὀπτασία 1.—SIG 1169, 6; UPZ 68, 6 [152 BC] ἐνύπνια ὁρῶ πονηρά) **Lk 1:22; 24:23.** ὁράσεις **Ac 2:17** (Jo 3:1). ταῦτα **Lk 23:49.** πάντα **J 4:45.** σημεῖα **6:2 v.l.** (for ἐθεώρουν). S. also Hv 3, 2, 4. W. acc. of the ptc. (SIG 685, 75; 1169, 15; Ex 33:10; TestJob 37:8; Just., A I, 53, 9 al.) τὸν οὐρανὸν ἀνεῳγότα **J 1:51.**—Hv 3, 8, 9. W. attraction of the relative ὧν=τούτων ἅ **Lk 9:36; Ac 22:15.** The attraction may be due to colloq. breviloquence in μάρτυρα ὧν τε εἶδές με ὧν τε ὀφθήσομαί σοι *a witness to the things in which you saw me and to those in which I shall appear to you* **Ac 26:16b** (difft. MDibelius, Aufsätze zur Apostelgeschichte, ed. HGreeven '51, 83). Of God τ. πάντα ὁρᾷ PtK 2 p. 13, 24 (Ar. 4, 1; cp. 13, 8).—ὁρ. is a favorite word w. J, when he speaks of that which the preëxistent Son saw when he was with the Father (JSchneider, D. Christusschau des Joh.-ev. '35; difft. LBrun, D. Gottesschau des joh. Christus: SymbOsl 5, 1927, 1–22) ὃ ἑώρακεν **J 3:32;** cp. vs. **11.** ἃ ἑώρακα παρὰ τῷ πατρί **8:38** (since this deals w. witness and speaking, the 'perceiving' could be thought of as 'hearing'; what is heard is interpreted as an event. Cp. Diod. S. 13, 28, 5 ὁρᾷς;=do you hear [the outcry]?; schol. on Nicander, Ther. 165 ὁρῶ οἷα λέγεις; Polyaenus 7, 14, 2; Ex 20:18 λαὸς ἑώρα τὴν φωνήν, 22; Dt 4:9; also Philo, Migr. Abr. 47; SibOr 8, 125 βρυγμὸν ὁρ.). Of that which the apostolic witnesses saw of Christ **1J 1:1–3.** Abs. ὁ ἑωρακώς *the eye-witness* **J 19:35.**

ⓒ ὁρ. τὸ πρόσωπόν τινος as a periphrasis for *see someone* (cp. Gen 43:3, 5; 46:30) **Ac 20:25; Col 2:1.** ὁρ. το πρόσωπον τοῦ θεοῦ (=רָאָה אֶת־פְּנֵי יי) **Rv 22:4** (πρόσωπον 1bα). ὁρ. τὴν δόξαν τοῦ θεοῦ (=רָאָה אֶת־כְּבוֹד יי) *see the majesty of God* (Is 66:18f; GkBar 6:12 al.) **J 11:40.** Simply ὁρ. τὸν θεόν *see God* **Mt 5:8.** ὀψόμεθα αὐτὸν καθώς ἐστιν **1J 3:2** (Maximus Tyr. 11, 11a τὸ μὲν ὅλον ὄψει τ. θεὸν τότε, ἐπειδὰν πρὸς αὐτὸν καλῇ). ὁρ. τὸν κύριον **Hb 12:14.**—On ἃ ἑόρακεν ἐμβατεύων **Col 2:18** s. ἐμβατεύω.

ⓓ pass. in act. sense *become visible, appear* (Ael. Aristid. 51, 22 K.=27 p. 539 D.: ὤφθη τοιάδε; LXX) abs. **Rv 11:19; 12:1, 3.** τινί *to someone* **Ac 2:3.** ὅραμα διὰ νυκτὸς τ. Παύλῳ ὤφθη *a vision appeared to Paul at night* **16:9** (Jos., Ant. 2, 70 τὰ διὰ νυκτὸς ὀφθέντα).—Of pers. who appear in a natural way (Appian, Syr. 21 §96 ὤφθησαν=they made an appearance, Bell. Civ. 2, 130 §542; UPZ 145, 5 [164 BC]; 3 Km 3:16 ὤφθησαν δύο γυναῖκες τῷ βασιλεῖ) (Μωϋσῆς) ὤφθη αὐτοῖς **Ac 7:26.** Mostly of beings that make their appearance in a transcendent manner, almost always w. dat. of the pers. to whom they appear: God (Gen 12:7; 17:1 [cp. 1QapGen 22:27 God appears to Abraham]; PGM 4, 3090 ἕως ὁ θεός σοι ὀφθῇ; ParJer 7:20; Just., D. 56, 4 al.) **Ac 7:2.** Angels (Ex 3:2; Judg 6:12) **Lk 1:11; 22:43** (LBrun, ZNW 32, '33, 265–76); **Ac 7:30, 35.** Moses and Elijah **Mt 17:3; Mk 9:4; Lk 9:31** (without the dat. in this pass.: ὀφθέντες ἐν δόξῃ). The risen Christ **Lk 24:34; Ac 9:17; 13:31; 26:16a; 1 Cor 15:5–8** (cp. Ox 1 verso, 13; Unknown Sayings, 69–71); **1 Ti 3:16** (ὤφθη ἀγγέλοις: the triumphant Christ appears to the angelic powers); **Hb 9:28** (Christ at his Second Coming).—οὐκ ἔτι σοι ὀφθήσεται *it will be seen by you no longer* (of evil desire) Hm 12, 2, 4 (Antig. Car. 11 ὁρᾶται=there is; Aristot. in Apollon. Paradox. 39 ὄφις ὤφθη=there was a snake).

❷ **to see someone in the course of making a friendly call, *visit*** (1 Km 20:29; JosAs 22:3) ὄψομαι ὑμᾶς **Hb 13:23.**

❸ **to experience a condition or event, *experience, witness*** (cp. POxy 120, 4f τινὰ ὁρῶντα αἱαυτὸν [= ἑαυτὸν] ἐν δυστυχίᾳ; JosAs 6:5 τί … ἐγὼ ὄψομαι ἡ ταλαίπωρος; s. also Just., D. 61, 2) **Lk 17:22** (s. εἶδον 4). ζωήν **J 3:36** (cp.

Lycophron 1019 βίον; Ps 88:49 θάνατον). μείζω τούτων **1:50.** ὄψεται πᾶσα σὰρξ τὸ σωτήριον τοῦ θεοῦ **Lk 3:6** (Is 40:5).

❹ **to be mentally or spiritually perceptive, *perceive*** (Polystrat. p. 5 ὁρ. τῷ λογισμῷ; Simplicius, In Epict. p. 110, 47 Düb. τὸ ἀληθές), fig. ext. of 1:

ⓐ sensory aspect felt: w. acc. of the ptc. (Diod. S. 2, 16, 5; 4, 40, 2; Appian, Syr. 14 §55, Bell. Civ. 2, 14 §50; PHib 44, 4 [253 BC] ὁρῶντες δέ σε καταραθυμοῦντα; 4 Macc 4:24; 9:30; Jos., Vi. 373 ὄντα με ὁρ.; Just., A I, 43, 5; Ath. 2, 3) *notice, perceive, understand* εἰς χολὴν πικρίας … ὁρῶ σε ὄντα *I perceive that you have fallen into the gall of bitterness* (i.e. *bitter jealousy*) **Ac 8:23.** οὔπω ὁρῶμεν αὐτῷ τὰ πάντα ὑποτεταγμένα *we do not yet see everything subjected to him* **Hb 2:8.** W. acc. and inf. foll. Dg 1. W. ὅτι foll. (M. Ant. 9, 27, 2; Philo, Migr. Abr. 46; Just., D. 23, 3 al.) **Js 2:24;** 1 Cl 12:8; 23:4; 44:6. W. indir. quest foll. 1 Cl 16:17; 41:4; 50:1; B 15:8; Dg 7:8. W. direct discourse foll. ὁρᾶτε 1 Cl 4:7.

ⓑ w. focus on cognitive aspect: *look at* or *upon* ὄψονται οἷς οὐκ ἀνηγγέλη περὶ αὐτοῦ *they who have never been told of (Christ) shall look upon him* **Ro 15:21** (Is 52:15).—*Consider* ὅρα τοῦ ἀγγέλου τῆς πονηρίας τὰ ἔργα Hm 6, 2, 4.—*Become conscious of* ὁ κακοποιῶν οὐχ ἑώρακεν τ. θεόν **3J 11.** Cp. **1J 3:6.**

B. intr.—❶ **to fix one's gaze, *look*** εἴς τινα *on* or *at someone* (Il. 24, 633; Od. 20, 373; Just., D. 112, 1) **J 19:37** (s. ἐκκεντέω). ἄνω ὁρᾶν Dg 10:2 (cp. Cicero, De Natura Deorum 2, 140; Ovid, Matamorphoses 1, 85; other reff. EBlakeney, The Epistle to Diognetus '43, 77f).

❷ **to be alert or on guard, *pay attention, see to it that*** foll. by μή and the aor. subj. (Diod. S. 27, 17, 3 ὁρᾶτε μήποτε ποιήσωμεν; Epict., Ench. 19, 2; Lucian, Dial. Deor. 8, 2; BGU 37, 5 [50 AD]; POxy 532, 15 ὅρα μὴ ἄλλως πράξῃς; 531, 9 ὅρα μηδενὶ ἀνθρώπων προσκρούσῃς.—B-D-F §364, 3) **Mt 8:4; 18:10; Mk 1:44; 1 Th 5:15;** 1 Cl 21:1; D 6:1.—W. μή and impv. (B-D-F §461, 1; Rob. 996) **Mt 9:30; 24:6.**—Elliptically (B-D-F §480, 5; Rob. 949) ὅρα μή (sc. ποιήσῃς) *watch out! don't do that!* **Rv 19:10; 22:9.**—Used w. ἀπό τινος *look out for someth.* (B-D-F §149; Rob. 472) ὁρᾶτε καὶ προσέχετε ἀπὸ τῆς ζύμης τῶν Φαρισαίων *look out (for) and be on your guard against the yeast of the Pharisees* **Mt 16:6.** ὁράτε, βλέπετε ἀπὸ τῆς ζύμης τῶν Φαρ. **Mk 8:15.** ὁράτε καὶ φυλάσσεσθε ἀπὸ πάσης πλεονεξίας **Lk 12:15.**

❸ **to accept responsibility for causing someth. to happen, *look, see to, take care*** σὺ ὄψῃ *see to that yourself! that's your affair!* **Mt 27:4** (Men., Epitr. 493 S. [317 Kö.]; cp. the response of Titus and declaration of innocence at the time of Jerusalem's destruction Jos., Bell. 6, 215); cp. vs. **24; Ac 18:15** (on this Latinism = videris s. DHesseling in B-D-F §362; Rob. 109f). Impv. followed by imperatival fut. ὅρα ποιήσεις πάντα *see to it that you do everything* **Hb 8:5** (Ex 25:40; cp. 4:21). Foll. by indir. quest. (Ael. Aristid. 45 p. 121 D.: ὅρα τί ποιεῖς) ὅρα τί μέλλεις ποιεῖν *take care what you are doing* **Ac 22:26 v.l.**—B. 1042. Schmidt, Syn. I 244–70. DELG. M-M. EDNT. TW. Sv.

ὄργανον, ου, τό (Soph., Pla. et al.; pap, LXX; PsSol 15:3; TestSol 8:2 L; EpArist 101; Philo; Jos., Bell. 2, 230; Just., D. 110, 3 πολεμικὰ ὄρ.; Ath.) ***tool*** τὰ ὄρ. τοῦ διαβόλου *the tools of the devil* 2 Cl 18:2. Lightfoot proposed a military metaph. for this passage, cp. 2 Macc 12:27; Eph 6:16.—Also of that which is used to bring about an event (e.g. wood for a structure: Pla., Leg. 3, 678d of tools used for cutting of wood; Ps.-Aristot., Mirabilia 108 of tools designed for the wooden horse) τὰ πρὸς τὴν πυρὰν ἡρμοσμένα ὄρ. *materials prepared for the pile (to be burned)* MPol 13:3. Since the pyre itself has taken shape out of wood that was gathered (vs. 2), the ὄρ. must refer to the incendiary material placed around Polycarp (αὐτῷ περιετίθετο) and designed to produce an intense flame (for ἅρμοζω w. πρός in the sense 'suited to, designed for' cp. Isoc. 2, 34; s. ἁρμόζω 2, and for the phrase ἡρμ. ὄρ. s. 2 Km 6:5, 14).—Fig. of the animals in the arena as the implements through which the martyr becomes a perfect sacrifice to God IRo 4:2.—B. 586. DELG.

ὀργή, ῆς, ἡ (Hes. et al. in the sense of 'temperament'; also 'anger, indignation, wrath' (so trag., Hdt.+)

❶ **state of relatively strong displeasure, w. focus on the emotional aspect, *anger*** GPt 12:50 (s. φλέγω 2). W. πικρία and θυμός **Eph 4:31;** cp. **Col 3:8** (on the relationship betw. ὀργή and θυμός, which are oft., as the product of Hebrew dualism, combined in the LXX as well, s. Zeno in Diog. L. 7, 113; Chrysipp. [Stoic. III fgm. 395]; Philod., De Ira p. 91 W.; PsSol 2:23; ParJer 6:23). W. διαλογισμοί **1 Ti 2:8.** W. μερισμός IPhld 8:1. ἡ ἀθέμιτος τοῦ ζήλους ὀρ. *the lawless anger caused by jealousy* 1 Cl 63:2. ἀπέχεσθαι πάσης ὀρ. *refrain from all anger* Pol 6:1. μετ' ὀργῆς angrily (Pla., Apol. 34c; Esth 8:12x; 3 Macc 6:23; JosAs 4:16 μετὰ ἀλαζονείας καὶ ὀργῆς) **Mk 3:5;** βραδὺς εἰς ὀρ. *slow to be angry* **Js 1:19** (Aristoxenus, fgm. 56 Socrates is called τραχὺς εἰς ὀργήν; but s. Pla., Phd. 116c, where S. is called πρᾳότατος 'meekest'). ἐλέγχετε ἀλλήλους μὴ ἐν ὀρ. *correct one another, not in anger* D 15:3 (ἐν ὀργῇ Is 58:13; Da 3:13 Theod.). Anger ἄφρονα ἀναιρεῖ 1 Cl 39:7 (Job 5:2); leads to murder D 3:2. δικαιοσύνην θεοῦ οὐκ ἐργάζεται **Js 1:20;** originates in θυμός and results in μῆνις Hm 5, 2, 4.—Pl. *outbursts of anger* (Pla., Euthyphro 7b ἔχθρα καὶ ὀργαί, Rep. 6, 493a; Maximus Tyr. 27, 6b; 2 Macc 4:25, 40; Jos., Vi. 266) 1 Cl 13:1; IEph 10:2 (B-D-F §142; W-S. §27, 4d). JStelzenberger, D. Beziehgen der frühchristl. Sittenlehre zur Ethik der Stoa '33, 250ff. S. also Ps.-Phocyl. 57f; 63f and Horst's annotations 153, 155–57.

❷ **strong indignation directed at wrongdoing, w. focus on retribution, *wrath*** (Πανὸς ὀργαί Eur., Med. 1172; Parmeniscus [III/II BC] in the schol. on Eur., Medea 264 Schw. τῆς θεᾶς ὀργή; Diod. S. 5, 55, 6 διὰ τὴν ὀργήν of Aphrodite; Philostrat., Vi. Apoll. 6, 29; SIG 1237, 5 ἕξει ὀργὴν μεγάλην τοῦ μεγάλου Διός; OGI 383, 210 [I BC]; LXX; En 106:15; TestReub 4:4; ApcEsdr 1:17 p. 25, 11 Tdf.; ApcrEzk pap. fgm. 1 recto, 6 [Denis, p. 125]; SibOr 4, 162; 5, 75f; Philo, Somn. 2, 179, Mos. 1, 6; Just., D. 38, 2; 123, 3; oft. Jos., e.g. Ant. 3, 321; 11, 127; Theoph. Ant. 1, 3 [p. 62, 21].—EpArist 254 θεὸς χωρὶς ὀργῆς ἁπάσης) as the divine reaction toward evil (παιδεύει ἡ καλουμένη ὀρ. τοῦ θεοῦ Orig., C. Cels. 4, 72, 4) it is thought of not so much as an emotion (οὐ πάθος δ' αὐτοῦ αὐτὴν [sc. ὀργὴν] εἶναί φαμεν Orig., C. Cels. 4, 72, 1) as the outcome of an indignant frame of mind (*judgment*), already well known to OT history (of the inhabitants of Nineveh: οἳ τὴν ὀρ. διὰ μετανοίας ἐκώλυσαν Did., Gen. 116, 22), where it somet. runs its course in the present, but more oft. is to be expected in the future, as God's final reckoning w. evil (ὀρ. is a legitimate feeling on the part of a judge; s. RHirzel, Themis 1907, 416; Pohlenz [s. below, b, end] 15, 3; Synes. Ep. 2 p. 158b).—S. Cat. Cod. Astr. V/4 p. 155.

ⓐ of the past and pres.: of judgment on the desert generation ὤμοσα ἐν τῇ ὀργῇ μου (Ps 94:11) **Hb 3:11; 4:3.** In the present, of Judeans ἔφθασεν ἐπ' αὐτοὺς ἡ ὀρ. *the indignation* (ὀργή abs.= ὀρ. θεοῦ also **Ro 12:19**—AvanVeldhuizen, 'Geeft den toorn plaats' [Ro 12:19]: TSt 25, 1907, 44–46; [on 13:4; 1 Th 1:10]. Likew. Jos., Ant. 11, 141) *has come upon them* **1 Th 2:16** (cp. TestLevi 6:11; on 1 Th 2:13–16 s. BPearson, HTR 64, '71, 79–94). Of God's indignation against sin in the pres. ἀποκαλύπτεται ὀρ. θεοῦ ἐπὶ πᾶσαν ἀσέβειαν **Ro 1:18**

(JCampbell, ET 50, '39, 229–33; SSchultz, TZ 14, '58, 161–73). Of God's indignation against evildoers as revealed in the judgments of earthly gov. authorities **13:4f** (here ὀρ. could also be *punishment,* as Demosth. 21, 43). *The indignation of God remains* like an incubus upon the one who does not believe in the Son **J 3:36** (for ἡ ὀρ. μένει cp. Wsd 18:20). Of the Lord's wrath against renegade Christians Hv 3, 6, 1. The Lord ἀποστρέφει τὴν ὀρ. αὐτοῦ ἀπό τινος *turns away (divine) indignation from someone* (ἀποστρέφω 2a) Hv 4, 2, 6.—Of the wrath of God's angel of repentance Hm 12, 4, 1.

ⓑ of God's future *judgment* specifically qualified as punitive (ἐκφυγεῖν τὴν ὀρ. καὶ κρίσιν τοῦ θεοῦ Theoph. Ant. 2, 14 [p. 136, 16]) ἔσται ὀρ. τῷ λαῷ τούτῳ **Lk 21:23;** ἡ μέλλουσα ὀρ. **Mt 3:7; Lk 3:7;** IEph 11:1. ἡ ὀρ. ἡ ἐρχομένη **1 Th 1:10;** cp. **Eph 5:6; Col 3:6.** σωθησόμεθα ἀπὸ τῆς ὀρ. **Ro 5:9.** οὐκ ἔθετο ἡμᾶς ὁ θεὸς εἰς ὀρ. *God has not destined us for punitive judgment* **1 Th 5:9.** θησαυρίζειν ἑαυτῷ ὀργήν (s. θησαυρίζω 2b and PLond VI 1912, 77–78 ταμιευόμενος ἐμαυτῷ . . . ὀργήν and 81 εἰς ὀργὴν δικαίαν [opp. internal hostility, line 80]; s. SLösch, Epistula Claudiana 1930, 8. Claudius reserves to himself punitive measures against ringleaders of civil unrest; the par. is merely formal: in our pass. it is sinners who ensure divine indignation against themselves) **Ro 2:5a.** This stored-up wrath will break out ἐν ἡμέρᾳ ὀργῆς (s. ἡμέρα 3bβ) vs. **5b.** Elsewhere, too, the portrayal of the wrath of God in Paul is predom. eschatological: ὀρ. καὶ θυμός (s. θυμός 2) **Ro 2:8** (cp. 1QS 4:12); cp. 1 Cl 50:4; δότε τόπον τῇ ὀρ. **Ro 12:19** (s. 2a above; τόπος 4). Cp. **9:22a.** ἐπιφέρειν τὴν ὀργήν *inflict punishment* **3:5** (s. **13:4f** under a above; s. Just., A I, 39, 2). Humans are τέκνα φύσει ὀργῆς *by nature children of wrath,* i.e. subject to divine indignation **Eph 2:3** (JMehlman, Natura Filii Irae etc. '57). τέκνα ὀργῆς AcPlCor 2:19 (on gnostic opponents of Paul). Cp. σκεύη ὀργῆς κατηρτισμένα εἰς ἀπώλειαν *objects of wrath prepared for destruction* **Ro 9:22b.** Of the law: ὀργὴν κατεργάζεται *it effects/brings* (only) *wrath* **4:15.**—In Rv the term is also used to express thoughts on eschatology **6:16; 11:18.** ἡ ἡμέρα ἡ μεγάλη τῆς ὀρ. αὐτῶν *the great day of their* (God's and the Lamb's) *wrath* (s. above) **6:17.** On τὸ ποτήριον τῆς ὀρ. αὐτοῦ *the cup of his wrath* **14:10** and οἶνος τοῦ θυμοῦ τῆς ὀρ. τοῦ θεοῦ **16:19; 19:15,** s. θυμός 1 and 2 (AHanson, The Wrath of the Lamb, '57, 159–80).—ARitschl, Rechtfertigung u. Versöhnung II[4] 1900, 119–56; MPohlenz, Vom Zorne Gottes 1909; GWetter, D. Vergeltungsgedanke bei Pls1912; GBornkamm, D. Offenbarung des Zornes Gottes (Ro 1–3): ZNW 34, '35, 239–62; ASchlatter, Gottes Gerechtigkeit '35, 48ff; GMacGregor, NTS 7, '61, 101–9; JHempel, Gottes Selbstbeherrschung, H-WHertzberg Festschr., '65, 56–66. S. also κρίσις, end: Braun 41ff and Filson.—B. 1134. DELG 1 ὀργή. M-M. DLNT 1238–41. EDNT. TW.

ὀργίζω (ὀργή; the act. in Aristoph., X., Pla. et al.; Job 12:6 v.l.; Pr 16:30 v.l.) in our lit. only pass. (Soph., Thu.+; SIG 1170, 5; UPZ 144, 3 [II BC]; LXX, En; PsSol 7:5; TestSol 5:6 L; TestJob 34:2; Test12Patr; JosAs 25:8 [ὀργίσθησαν]; ParJer 9:21; GrBar; ApcMos, Philo, Joseph., Just., Tat., Ath.) **ὀργίζομαι** 1fut. ὀργισθήσομαι (LXX); 1 aor. ὠργίσθην, ptc. ὀργισθείς ***be angry,*** foll. by dat. of pers. (Diod. S. 10, 7, 4; Ael. Aristid. 38 p. 721 D.; Ps 84:6; Is 12:1; En 18:16; JosAs 25:8; GrBar 9:7; ApcMos 8; Jos., Ant. 4, 130; 16, 263; Just., D. 136, 1; of God: Theoph. Ant. 1, 3 [p. 62, 22]) **Mt 5:22;** AcPl Ha 3, 2. Foll. by dat. of pers. and ὅτι *be angry at someone because* Hv 1, 1, 6 (for ὅτι cp. Arrian, Anab. 4, 23, 5; 3 Km 11:9; TestZeb 7:11). ὀρ. τινὶ ἕνεκά τινος *at someone because of someth.* (Jos., Ant. 12, 221) 1, 3, 1a. διά τι ibid. b (cp. X., An. 1, 2, 26). ἐπί τινι *be angry at or with someone* (Andoc. 5, 10; Lysias 28, 2; Num 31:14; TestSim 2:11) **Rv 12:17** (B-D-F §196; s. Rob. 605). Abs. (X., Hell. 4, 8, 30; Aelian, VH 12, 54; TestJob 34:2; TestLevi 6:6; ParJer 9:21; Jos., Ant. 6, 222; Tat. 10, 1; Ath. 18, 4) **Mt 18:34; 22:7; Mk 1:41 v.l.** (for σπλαγχνισθείς.—On the v.l. ὀργισθείς s. CTurner, JTS 28, 1927, 145–58); **Lk 14:21; 15:28; Rv 11:18** (cp. Ps 98:1); GJs 22:1; 23:2; AcPl Ha 1, 21; 6, 22. ὀργίζεσθε καὶ μὴ ἁμαρτάνετε (Ps 4:5) *be angry, but do not sin* **Eph 4:26.**—DELG s.v. ὀργή. M-M s.v. ὀργίζομαι. TW.

ὀργίλος, η, ον (ὀργή; Hippocr.; Pla., Rep. 2, 405c; 411b; X., De Re Equ. 9, 7; Aristot., EN 2, 7, 10; 4, 5, 8 οἱ ὀργίλοι ταχέως ὀργίζονται καὶ οἷς οὐ δεῖ καὶ ἐφ' οἷς οὐ δεῖ καὶ μᾶλλον ἢ δεῖ 'quick-tempered persons lose no time being angry, and do so with those they ought not, over things they ought not, and far more than they ought'; Herodian 4, 9, 3; Ps 17:49; Pr 21:19; 22:24; 29:22; TestAbr A 19 p. 101, 5 [Stone p. 50]; Jos., Ant. 19, 19; Ar.; Theoph. Ant. 1, 2 [p. 60, 28]) ***inclined to anger, quick-tempered*** (w. αὐθάδης et al.) **Tit 1:7.** μὴ γίνου ὀρ. D 3:2.—Subst. τὸ ὀρ. *hotheadedness* Πέτρε, ἀεί σοι τὸ ὀ. παράκειται *Peter, you have a penchant for hotheadedness* GMary 463, 19. Cp. ὀργιλότης Hdt. 2, 181; Aristot., EN 4, 5, 1–4; Rhet. 2, 3; Epict., Ench. 42.—DELG s.v. ὀργή. M-M. TW.

ὀργίλως adv. of ὀργίλος (Demosth. 21, 215 al.; Menand., Dysc. 102; 4 Macc 8:9) ***angrily*** Hm 12, 4, 1.

ὀργυιά (or ὄργυια, but in the pl. prob. ὀργυιαί; s. Kühner-Bl. I 392f; Mlt-H. 58. Derived fr. ὀρέγω 'stretch'; Hom., Hdt. et al.; ins; POxy 669, 39; Jos., Bell. 1, 411) **ᾶς, ἡ the distance measured by a person's arms stretched out horizontally, *fathom*** reckoned at 1.85 meters, a nautical t.t., used to measure the depth of water (Diod. S. 3, 40, 3) **Ac 27:28ab.**—DELG s.v. ὄργυια. M-M.

ὀρέγω (the act. Hom. et al. 'reach, stretch out') in our lit. only mid. **ὀρέγομαι** (Hom.et al., lit. 'stretch oneself, reach out one's hand') and only fig.: **to seek to accomplish a specific goal, *aspire to, strive for, desire*** (also Just., Tat.; Ath., R. 15 p. 66, 33 al.) aor. opt. 3 sg. ὀρεχθείη (Ath., R. 21 p. 74, 29) w. gen. of thing (Thu. 2, 65, 10; X., Mem. 1, 2, 15; Pla., Rep. 6, 485d, Leg. 7, 807c; Polyb. 5, 104, 7; Diod. S. 4, 40, 5 δόξης ὀρεγόμενος=eager for glory; Plut. Phoc. 17, 1, Sol. 29, 4; Lucian, Bis Accus. 29; Epict. 2, 1, 10; 3, 26, 13. Oft. Philo; Jos., Vi. 70; Just., A I, 12, 5.—B-D-F §171, 1; Rob. 508) ἐπισκοπῆς ὀρ. *aspire to the office of supervision/oversight* **1 Ti 3:1** (on the combination of ὀρέγομαι and ἐπιθυμέω cp. EpArist 211). κρείττονος *long for a better* (home) **Hb 11:16.** ἡ φιλαργυρία ἧς τινες ὀρεγόμενοι **1 Ti 6:10** is a condensed expr.; it is the ἀργύριον rather than the φιλαργυρία that is desired.—DELG. M-M s.v. ὀρέγομαι. TW. Spicq.

ὀρεινός, ή, όν (ὄρος) ***hilly, mountainous*** (so Hdt.+; ins, pap, LXX, EpArist, Philo, Joseph.) ἡ ὀρεινή (sc. χώρα, which is added in Hdt. 1, 110; X., Cyr. 1, 3, 3; SIG 633, 78.—ἡ ὀρεινή alone e.g. in Aristot., HA 5, 28, 4 and oft. in LXX; Philo, Aet. M. 63) *hill country, mountainous region* πορεύεσθαι εἰς τὴν ὀρ. *go into the hill country* **Lk 1:39** (cp. Jos., Bell. 4, 451); ἀνέβη ἐν τῇ ὀρ. GJs 22:3. ἐν ὅλῃ τῇ ὀρ. τῆς Ἰουδαίας *in all the hill country of Judea* vs. **65** (Jos., Ant. 5, 128 ὀρ. τῆς Χαναναίας; 12, 7 ἀπὸ τ. ὀρεινῆς Ἰουδαίας). GJs 16:2 v.l. (for ἔρημον).—DELG s.v. ὄρος. M-M.

ὄρεξις, εως, ἡ a condition of strong desire, *longing, desire* (ὀρέγω; Pla. et al.; LXX; Ath. 21, 1 and R. 21 p. 74, 19 al.; Hippol., Ref. 5, 14, 10); in its only occurrence in our lit. it is used in an unfavorable sense (Democr., fgm. 219; Epicurus p. 161, 26 Us.; Lucian, Tyr. 4 τὰς τῶν ἡδονῶν ὀρέξεις χαλιναγωγεῖν; Herodian 3, 13, 6; Herm. Wr. 12, 4; Sir 23:6; Philo.—Of sexual desire Jos., Ant. 7, 169; Ps.-Clem., Hom. 3, 68; Orig, C. Cels. 3, 56, 24) οἱ ἄρσενες … ἐξεκαύθησαν ἐν τῇ ὀρ. αὐτῶν εἰς ἀλλήλους *males … were inflamed with (their) desire for each other* **Ro 1:27.**—DELG s.v. ὀρέγω. M-M. TW. Spicq.

ὀρθοποδέω (ὀρθόπους [ὀρθός, πούς]; Soph. et al.; cp. Nicander, Alexiph. 419 [II BC] ὀρθόποδες βαίνοντες.—ὀρθοποδία='progress': Papiri della Univers. di Milano, ed. AVogliano no. 24, 8 [117 AD]) basic mng. 'walk straight, upright', fig. ext. ***act rightly, be straightforward*** ὀρθοποδεῖν πρὸς τὴν ἀλήθειαν τοῦ εὐαγγελίου *be straightforward about the truth of the gospel* **Gal 2:14** (cp. OGI 48, 9 μὴ ὀρθῶς ἀναστρεφομένους [restoration certain]). But perh. *progress, advance in the direction of the truth* (CRoberts, JTS 40, '39, 55f. Also JWinter, HTR 34, '41, 161f, after an unpubl. pap in the Michigan collection [no. 337: III AD] ὀρθοποδεῖ τὸ παιδίον 'the child is getting on, growing up').—GKilpatrick, NT Studien f. RBultmann '54, 269–74 ('they were not on the right road toward the truth of the gospel'; includes informative survey).—M-M. TW. Spicq.

ὀρθός, ή, όν (Hom.+) superl. ὀρθότατος (EpilMosq 2).

❶ **pert. to being in a straight line or direction, in contrast to being crooked, *straight***—ⓐ *straight up, upright* (Hom. et al.; ins, pap, LXX; Jos., Ant. 20, 67; Just., A I, 55, 4) ἀνάστηθι ἐπὶ τ. πόδας σου ὀρθός *stand upright on your feet* **Ac 14:10.** αἱ τρίχες μου ὀρθαί *my hair stood on end* Hv 3, 1, 5 (Ael. Aristid. 48, 33 K.=24 p. 474 D.: τρίχες ὀρθαί).—In imagery of the resurrected body (simile of the grain of wheat) σῶμα … πολλοστὸν ὀρθὸν ηὐλογήμενον *a body … teeming, erect, blessed* AcPl Cor 2:27.

ⓑ *straight, in a straight line* (Hes. et al.; LXX) τροχιαὶ ὀρ. **Hb 12:13** (Pr 4:26). Of a way (Theognis, Soph. et al.; Pr 12:15; 16:25; Philo; Jos., Ant. 6, 13) in imagery (Aesop, Fab. 287 P.=Babr. 8 Cr. and L-P. [a road]; Philo, Fuga 131 al.) τὸ δίκαιον ὀρ. ὁδὸν ἔχει *has a straight path* Hm 6, 1, 2a (cp. PGrad 4, 9 ὀρθῶς καὶ δικαίως). τῇ ὀρ. ὁδῷ πορεύεσθαι *walk in the straight path* 6, 1, 2b; cp. 4 (Just., D. 8, 2).

❷ **pert. to being in line with belief or teaching, *correct, true,*** fig. extension of 1 (Pind., Hdt. et al.; LXX; TestBenj 3:2; EpArist 244; Just., A II, 2, 2 and D. 3, 3) συγγράμματα κάλλιστα καὶ ὀρθότατα EpilMosq 2. γνώμη ὀρ. IEph 1:1 v.l. (cp. φρόνημα ὀρθόν Polemo B 12 p. 136 Reader, s. also p. 270).—B. 896. DELG. M-M. TW. Sv.

ὀρθοτομέω (ὀρθός, τέμνω) found elsewh. independently of the NT only Pr 3:6; 11:5, where it is used w. ὁδούς and plainly means 'cut a path in a straight direction' or 'cut a road across country (that is forested or otherwise difficult to pass through) in a straight direction', so that the traveler may go directly to his destination (cp. Thu. 2, 100, 2 ὁδοὺς εὐθείας ἔτεμε; Hdt. 4, 136 τετμημένη ὁδός; Pla., Leg. 7, 810e; Plut., Galba 24, 7; Jos., C. Ap. 1, 309). Then ὀρθοτομεῖν τὸν λόγον τῆς ἀληθείας would prob. mean ***guide the word of truth along a straight path*** (like a road that goes straight to its goal), without being turned aside by wordy debates or impious talk **2 Ti 2:15.** For such other mngs. as *teach the word aright, expound (it) soundly, shape rightly,* and *preach fearlessly,* s. M-M.—DELG s.v. τέμνω. TW. Spicq.

ὀρθόω (ὀρθός) fut. 3 sg. ὀρθώσει Sir 27:14; 1 aor. ὤρθωσα. Pass.: aor. ὠρθώθην LXX; pf. 3 sg. ὤρθωται Esth 7:9, ptc. ὠρθώμενος 2 Esdr 6:11; (Hom. et al.; LXX; PsSol 10:3; Philo) ***set upright*** σταυρόν GPt 4:11 (cp. of a mast, Lucian, Catapl. 1; ξύλον=gallows, Esth 7:9).—DELG s.v. ὀρθός.

ὀρθρίζω (so in LXX and NT; O. Amst 22, 8; PMilVogl II, 50, 13; Moeris p. 272 ὀρθρεύει Ἀττικῶς. ὀρθρίζει Ἑλληνικῶς) impf. ὤρθριζον; fut. 2 sg. ὀρθρίσεις and ὀρθριεῖς Judg. 9:33; 1 aor. ὤρθρισα LXX ***be up or get up very early in the morning*** (s. three next entries; Ex 24:4; 4 Km 6:15; SSol 7:13) ὁ λαὸς ὤρθριζεν πρὸς αὐτὸν ἐν τῷ ἱερῷ ἀκούειν αὐτοῦ *the people used to get up very early in the morning (to come) to him in the temple and hear him* **Lk 21:38** (ὀρ. πρός τινα also means gener. *seek someone diligently:* Job 8:5; Ps 77:34; Sir 4:12; 6:36; Wsd 6:14; Test Jos 3:6).—DELG s.v. ὄρθρος. New Docs 1, 86 no. 43. M-M.

ὀρθρινός, ή, όν (s. prec. and next two entries; late substitute for ὄρθριος [Anecd. Gr. p. 54, 7; Lob., Phryn. p. 51], almost only in poets [Arat. 948; Posidippus Epigrammaticus, III BC, in Athen. 13, 69 p. 596d; several times Anth. Pal.]; LXX) ***early in the morning*** γυναῖκες … γενόμεναι ὀρθριναὶ ἐπὶ τὸ μνημεῖον **Lk 24:22.** τί ὀρ. ὧδε ἐλήλυθας; *why have you come here so early?* Hs 5, 1, 1.—**Rv 22:16** t.r. (Erasmian rdg.)—DELG s.v. ὄρθρος. M-M.

ὄρθριος, ία, ιον (s. prec. two and next entries; Hom. Hymns et al.; pap, LXX; Jos., Ant. 5, 330; 7, 195) ***early in the morning*** **Lk 24:22 v.l.** (s. ὀρθρινός).—DELG s.v. ὄρθρος. M-M.

ὄρθρος, ου, ὁ (s. prec. three entries; Hes. et al.; pap, LXX; En 100:2; Test Sol; Test Jos. 8:1; JosAs 11:1 cod. A; ParJer 5:5; Joseph.) **period relatively early in the morning, *dawn, early morning*** ὄρθρου βαθέως *very early in the morning* **Lk 24:1** (s. βαθύς 3b and cp. Heraclit. Sto. 16 p. 24, 16; 68 p. 88, 16; Polyaenus 4, 9, 1 ὄρθρος ἦν βαθύς). In the same sense φαίνοντος ἤδη τοῦ ὄρ. AcPl Ha 4, 3. ὄρθρου *early in the morning* (Hes., Op. 577; Diod. S. 14, 104, 1; PFlor 305, 11; LXX; ParJer 5:5; Jos., Ant. 11, 37) **J 8:2;** AcPl Ha 4, 6; 11, 11. ὄρθρου τῆς κυριακῆς *on Sunday at dawn* GPt 12:50. ὑπὸ τὸν ὄρ. *about daybreak* (Cass. Dio 76, 17; PFay 108, 10; Jos., Ant. 8, 382) **Ac 5:21.**—B. 993. DELG. M-M.

ὀρθῶς adv. of ὀρθός (Hes., Aeschyl., Hdt.+; ins, pap, LXX; Test Sol 24:5 Q; Test12Patr; ParJer 7:11; GrBar 4:10; EpArist, Philo; Jos., Ant. 1, 251; Just.; Tat. 18, 2; Ath. 7, 1 and R. 21 p. 74, 26) **pert. to acting in conformity with a norm or standard, *rightly, correctly*** λαλεῖν *speak correctly = normally* ('properly' TBaird, ET 92, '81, 337f) **Mk 7:35.** ὀρ. προσφέρειν, διαιρεῖν *offer rightly, divide rightly* 1 Cl 4:4 (after Gen 4:7; s. διαιρέω). δουλεύειν αὐτῷ (=τῷ θεῷ) ὀρ. *serve God in the right way*=κατὰ τὸ θέλημα αὐτοῦ Hm 12, 6, 2. τελεῖν τὴν διακονίαν τοῦ κυρίου ὀρ. *perform the service of the Lord properly* s 2:7; ἐργάζεσθαι ὀρ. *act rightly* 8, 11, 4 (cp. ὀρ. ποιεῖν: SIG 116, 10; 780, 37; PEleph 9, 3; 1 Macc 11:43; Just., D. 5, 2; 67, 4; ὀρ. πράσσειν: Jos., Vi. 298; Just., A I, 4, 8). ὀρ. κρίνειν *judge, decide correctly* **Lk 7:43** (cp. Wsd 6:4; Ps.-Clem., Hom. 10, 9.—Diod. S. 18, 56, 3 ὀρθῶς γινώσκειν=think rightly). ὀρ. ἀποκρίνεσθαι *answer correctly* (Herm. Wr. 13, 3; Just., D. 3, 6; cp. ὀρ. ἐρωτᾷς GrBar 4:10) **10:28.** ὀρ. λέγειν καὶ διδάσκειν **20:21** (cp. Aristoxenus, fgm. 33 p. 18, 2 ὀρθῶς λέγοντες; Alex. Aphr., An. II/1 p. 20, 29 ὀρθῶς λέγειν=teach rightly. Of Cercidas [III BC] in Diehl[3], fgm. 11a, 4 [=Coll. Alex. p. 213 no. 16] ὀρθῶς λέγει που Κερκίδας; Dt 5:28). ὀρ. διδάσκεσθαι *be properly taught* Dg 11:2. ἀγαπᾶν ὀρ. *love* (someone) *in the right way* 12:1. ὀρ. ἀπέχεσθαί τινος *be right in abstaining from someth.* 4:6.—M-M.

ὁρίζω (ὅρος) fut. 3 sg. ὁριεῖ LXX; 1 aor. ὥρισα, pf. 3 pl. ὁρίκασιν (Tat. 17, 3). Pass.: 1 aor. 3 sg. ὡρίσθη (Just., A I, 44, 12); ptc. ὁρισθείς; pf. ptc. ὡρισμένος (Aeschyl., Hdt.+)

❶ from the basic mng., 'to separate entities and so establish a boundary', derives the sense 'to define ideas or concepts': ***set limits to, define, explain*** (X. et al. [as Ath. 6, 1] in act. and mid.) περί τινος *give an explanation concerning someth.* B 12:1. τὸ ὕδωρ καὶ τὸν σταυρὸν ἐπὶ τὸ αὐτὸ ὥρισεν *he defined the water and the cross together* (i.e. in the section on the tree by the streams of water Ps 1:3) 11:8. Sim.

❷ **to make a determination about an entity, *determine, appoint, fix, set*—ⓐ** of things**—α.** expressed by the acc. προφήτης ὁρίζων τράπεζαν *a prophet who orders a meal* (s. τράπεζα 2) D 11:9 (w. double acc.: Πυθαγόρας … ἔσχατον ὁρίζει φύσιν Theoph. Ant. 3, 7 [p. 216, 12]).—Of time (Pla., Leg. 9 p. 864e; Demosth. 36, 26 ὁ νόμος τὸν χρόνον ὥρισεν; Epict., Ench. 51, 1; PFlor 61, 45 [85 AD]; Jos., C. Ap. 1, 230; Just., D. 102, 4 χρόνους; more freq. pass., s. below) ἡμέραν **Hb 4:7.** ὁρ. προστεταγμένους καιρούς *set appointed times* **Ac 17:26.**—μηδὲν ὁρίζοντες μηδὲ νομοθετοῦντες *without making rules or ordinances* GMary 463, 29.—Pass. (SIG 495, 171; PFay 11, 16 [c. 115 BC]; PAmh 50, 15; PTebt 327, 12 al.) ὡρισμένοι καιροί (Diod. S. 1, 41, 7; cp. 16, 29, 2; Jos., Ant. 6, 78) *appointed times* 1 Cl 40:2. ὡρισμένης τῆς ἡμέρας ταύτης *after this day has been fixed* Hv 2, 2, 5 (Diod. S. 2, 59, 5; 20, 110, 1 ὡρισμένη ἡμέρα; Herodian 1, 10, 5 ὡρισμένης ἡμέρας; Pollux 1, 67).—ὁ ὡρισμένος τόπος *the appointed place* B 19:1 (cp. Iren. 5, 31, 2 [Harv. II 412, 1]). οἱ ὡρισμένοι νόμοι *the established laws* Dg 5:10. ὁ ὡρισμένος τῆς λειτουργίας κανών *the established limits of (one's) ministry* 1 Cl 41:1. ἡ ὡρισμένη βουλή *the definite plan* **Ac 2:23.**—Subst. (cp. SIG 905, 14 τῶν ὁρισθέντων ἄγνοια) κατὰ τὸ ὡρισμένον *in accordance with the* (divine) *decree* **Lk 22:22.**

β. by an inf. (Appian, Bell. Civ. 5, 3 §12 ἀντιδοῦναι=to give as recompense; ApcMos 28 φυλάττειν; B-D-F §392, 1a) ὥρισαν … πέμψαι *they determined* (perh. *set apart;* so Field, Notes 119f and TGillieson, ET 56, '44/45, 110) … *to send* **Ac 11:29;** by an indirect quest. 1 Cl 40:3.

ⓑ of persons *appoint, designate, declare:* God judges the world ἐν ἀνδρὶ ᾧ ὥρισεν *through a man whom he has appointed* **Ac 17:31.** Pass. ὁ ὡρισμένος ὑπὸ τοῦ θεοῦ κριτής *the one appointed by God as judge* **10:42.** Of eccl. superintendents or overseers οἱ κατὰ τὰ πέρατα ὁρισθέντες *those who are appointed in distant lands* IEph 3:2. W. double acc. *declare someone to be someth.* (Meleag. in Anth. Pal. 12, 158, 7 σὲ γὰρ θεὸν ὥρισε δαίμων) pass. τοῦ ὁρισθέντος υἱοῦ θεοῦ ἐν δυνάμει *who has been declared to be the powerful son of God* **Ro 1:4.**—DELG s.v. ὅρος. M-M. TW.

ὅριον, ου, τό (ὅρος; Soph., Thu. et al.; ins, pap, LXX; TestJud, JosAs) **marker of division between two areas, *boundary*** mostly, in our lit. exclusively, pl. *boundaries = region, district* (Gen 10:19; Ex 10:4, al. in LXX; TestJud 2:6; JosAs) **Mt 8:34; 15:22; Mk 5:17; Ac 13:50.** ἐν ὁρ. Ζαβουλὼν καὶ Νεφθαλίμ *in the region of Zebulun and Naphtali* **Mt 4:13.** τὰ ὁρ. Μαγαδάν **15:39.** τὰ ὁρ. τῆς Ἰουδαίας **19:1; Mk 10:1** (Jos., C. Ap. 1, 251 τὰ ὁρ. τῆς Συρίας). Of the region around a city (Jos., Ant. 6, 191) τὰ ὁρ. Τύρου (καὶ Σιδῶνος) **7:24** (v.l. μεθόρια); cp. vs. **31a.** ἀπὸ τῶν ὁρ. ἐκείνων *from that district* **Mt 15:22.** ἀνὰ μέσον τῶν ὁρ. Δεκαπόλεως *through the region of the Decapolis* **Mk 7:31b.** ἐν Βηθλέεμ καὶ ἐν πᾶσι τοῖς ὁρ. αὐτῆς in *Bethlehem and all the region around it* **Mt 2:16.** ἔστησεν ὁρ. ἐθνῶν *he established the regions* (perh. *boundaries*) *for the nations* 1 Cl 29:2 (Dt 32:8).—The mng. *boundaries* is certain in ὅρια πατέρων παρορίζειν *transgress the boundaries set by the fathers* Dg 11:5 v.l. (but Wengst in text).—B. 1311f. DELG s.v. ὅρος. M-M.

ὁρισμός, οῦ, ὁ (ὁρίζω; Hippocr. et al.; IMakedD 592, 2 [XIII AD] 'ordinance'; pap, LXX; Philo, Leg. All. 2, 63) lit. 'marking out by boundaries', then ***a fixed course.*** Heavenly bodies ἐξελίσσουσιν τοὺς ἐπιτεταγμένους αὐτοῖς ὁρ. *roll on through their appointed courses* 1 Cl 20:3.—DELG s.v. ὅρος. M-M s.v. ὁρίζω.

ὁρκίζω (ὅρκος) fut. 3 sg. ὁρκιεῖ; 1 aor. ὥρκισα; aor. pass. ptc. ὁρκισθείς: all forms LXX (in the sense 'cause someone to swear' X. et al.; ins, pap, LXX, TestSol; ParJer 8:10; Jos., Ant. 18, 124; Hippol.) **to give a command to someone under oath, *adjure, implore*** (so pap; Jos., Vi. 258; LXX) τινὰ κατά τινος *someone by someone* (PGM 3, 36f; 4, 289; 7, 242 ὁρκίζω σε, δαίμων, κατὰ τῶν ὀνομάτων σου; 3 Km 2:42; 2 Ch 36:13.—IDefixAudollent p. 473ff; ParJer 8:10) **Mt 26:63 v.l.** αὐτὸν ὁρ. κατὰ τοῦ κυρίου w. ἵνα foll. Hs 9, 10, 5. Also w. double acc. (Orphica: Fgm., K. p. 313 no. 299 οὐρανὸν ὁρκίζω σε; lead tablet fr. Hadrumetum in Dssm., B 28 [BS 274] ὁρκίζω σε, δαιμόνιον πνεῦμα, τὸν θεὸν τοῦ Αβρααν κτλ.; PGM 4, 3045; B-D-F §149; Rob. 483f) ὁρ. σε τὸν θεόν *I implore you by God* w. μή foll. **Mk 5:7.** ὁρ. ὑμᾶς τὸν Ἰησοῦν **Ac 19:13** (cp. PGM 4, 3019 ὁρκίζω σε κατὰ τοῦ τῶν Ἑβραίων Ἰησοῦ). W. double acc. and foll. by acc. and inf. (B-D-F §392, 1d; Rob. 1085) **1 Th 5:27 v.l.**—B. 1437. M-M. EDNT. TW.

ὅρκιον, ου, τό (=ὅρκος; Hom.+; OGI 453, 25 [39/35 BC]; SIG 581, 91 al.; Philo, Conf. Lingu. 43; SibOr 3, 654) **a solemn promise, *oath, vow, pledge*** ὅρκια πίστεως *pledges of faith* Dg 11:5 (a cj. by Lachmann, s. Bihlmeyer's app.).

ὅρκος, ου, ὁ (Hom.+) ***oath*** **Hb 6:16.** ὅρκον ὀμνύειν *swear an oath* (Hyperid. 5, 1; Lucian, Dial. Mer. 2, 1; PHal 1, 226; 230 ὀμόσας τὸν ὅρκον) **Js 5:12** (Delphic commands: SIG 1268 I, 8 [III BC] ὅρκῳ μὴ χρῶ). ὅρκῳ ὀμνύειν τινί *swear to someone with an oath* (TestJud 22:3; ApcMos 19) **Ac 2:30.** ὁρ. ὃν ὤμοσεν πρὸς Ἀβραάμ **Lk 1:73** (cp. OGI 266, 19 ὅρκος ὃν ὤμοσεν Παράνομος; for the foll. inf. w. the art. cp. Pel.-Leg. p. 13, 9 ἐν ὅρκῳ εἶχεν τοῦ μὴ γεύσασθαί τι). ὁρ. ψευδής *a false oath* (Theoph. Ant. 2, 34 [p. 186, 10]) B 2:8 (Zech 8:17). ἀποδιδόναι τῷ κυρίῳ τοὺς ὅρκους *perform oaths to the Lord* **Mt 5:33** (s. ἀποδίδωμι 2c. But ἀποδοῦναι τινι ὅρκον also means 'give an oath': Demosth. 19, 318; Aeschin. 3, 74; SIG 150, 15). μεσιτεύειν ὅρκῳ *guarantee by means of an oath* **Hb 6:17.** μεθ' ὅρκου *with an oath* (PRev 42, 17 [258 BC] μεθ' ὅρκου; Lev 5:4: Num 30:11; Cornutus 24 p. 46, 8 μεθ' ὅρκων; Just., D. 33, 2) **Mt 14:7; 26:72;** 1 Cl 8:2.—Pl. ὅρκη, even when basically only one oath is involved (cp. X., Hell. 5, 4, 54; Diod. S. 4, 46, 4; 17, 84, 1; Polyaenus 2, 19; Athen. 13, 557a; 2 Macc 4:34; 7:24; 14:32; EpArist 126; Jos., Ant. 3, 272; 7, 294) διὰ τοὺς ὅρκους *because of his oath* **Mt 14:9; Mk 6:26.**—ESanders, Jewish Law fr. Jesus to the Mishnah '90, 51–57, 337f (note). Lit. on ὀμνύω Kl. Pauly II, 209f.—B. 1438. DELG s.v. ὅρκος. M-M. TW. Sv.

ὁρκωμοσία, ας, ἡ (composed of ὅρκον ὀμόσαι [ὄμνυμι] 'to take an oath') Doric.—The neut. ὁρκωμόσιον SIG 1007, 29 [130–100 BC] and its pl. OGI 229, 82 [III BC]. Pollux 1, 38; 1 Esdr 8:90; Ezk 17:18f; Jos., Ant. 16, 163.—B-D-F §2; 119, 3; s. Mlt-H. 338f; EFraenkel, Geschichte der griech. Nomina agentis auf -τήρ, -τωρ, -της I 1910, 200) **the process of taking an oath, *oath-taking, oath*** **Hb 7:20f** (no oath-taking is involved), **28** (oath-taking is involved).—DELG s.v. ὅρκος. M-M. TW.

ὁρμάω (ὁρμή) 1 aor. ὥρμησα; mid. plpf. ὥρμηντο (Just., A I, 29, 4) in our lit. used only intr. (so Hom.+; SIG 709, 19 [c. 107 BC]; PStras 100, 17 [II BC]; PTebt 48, 24; LXX, Test12Patr, Philo, Joseph., Just.; Ath. 2, 2 and R. 1 p. 48, 5) **to make a rapid movement from one place to another, *rush (headlong)*** ὁρ. κατὰ τοῦ κρημνοῦ εἰς τὴν θάλασσαν *rush down the slope into the lake* **Mt 8:32; Mk 5:13;** cp. **Lk 8:33** (cp. POxy 901, 6 of two swine τὴν ὁρμὴν ποιούμενοι). Of a crowd of people ὥρμησαν εἰς τὸ θέατρον *they rushed into the theater* **Ac 19:29** (cp. Jos., Ant. 11, 147). ὁρ. ἐπί τινα *rush at, fall upon someone* (X., An. 4, 3, 31; Alciphron 3, 7, 3; 3, 18, 2; 2 Macc 12:32; Jos., Ant. 12, 270, Vi. 245; TestJud 7:5) **7:57.**—Frisk s.v. ὁρμή. M-M. TW.

ὁρμή, ῆς, ἡ ('rapid motion forwards' [s. ὁρμάω] Hom. et al.; SIG 700, 23 [117 BC]) in our lit. **a psychological state of strong tendency, *impulse, inclination, desire*** (so Hom. et al.; PGrenf II 78, 15; 3 Macc 1:16) of the pilot of a ship ὅπου ἡ ὁρ. τοῦ εὐθύνοντος βούλεται *wherever the impulse of the steersman leads him* **Js 3:4.** καταδιαιρεῖν τι πρὸς τὰς αὐτῶν ὁρμάς *make a distinction betw. some things in accord with their (own) inclinations* Dg 4:5. ἐγένετο ὁρ. τῶν ἐθνῶν *an attempt was made by the gentiles* foll. by aor. inf. **Ac 14:5** (cp. Jos., Ant. 9, 161 ὁρμὴ ἀνακαινίσαι and 15, 52 ὁρ. ἐγένετο).—Frisk. M-M. TW.

ὅρμημα, ατος, τό (ὁρμάω; Hom. et al.; Plut., LXX) ***violent rush, onset*** ὁρμήματι βληθήσεται Βαβυλών *Babylon will be thrown down with violence* **Rv 18:21** (Charles, Rv ad loc. 'indignation' cp. Hos 5:10 and s. ὁρμή)—Frisk s.v. ὁρμή. M-M. TW.

ὄρνεον, ου, τό (a dim. form=ὄρνις; Hom. et al.; IG IV^2/1, 93, 17 [III/IV AD]; PPetr III, 71 [III BC]; PRyl 98[a], 9; PLond III, 1259, 16 p. 240 [IV AD]; LXX; TestSol; JosAs 11:1 cod. A; GrBar, Philo; Jos., Ant. 1, 184; 3, 25; 18, 195) ***bird*** **Rv 19:17, 21.** πᾶν ὄρ. ἀκάθαρτον καὶ μεμισημένον *every bird that is unclean and detestable* (for cultic reasons, e.g. the owl, heron, pelican, great horned owl) **18:2** (cp. Dt 14:11 πᾶν ὄρνεον καθαρόν). Of the phoenix 1 Cl 25:2; 26:1. Pl., of various unclean birds (cp. Dt 14:11ff) B 10:4. W. κτῆνος Hs 9, 1, 8.—DELG s.v. ὄρνις. M-M.

ὄρνιξ (so as nom., Athen. 9, 374d; Herodian Gramm. I p. 44, 7 L.; PCairZen 375, 1. The dat. pl., ὄρνιξι also PLond I, 131 recto, 125 p. 173; 202 p. 175 al. [78/79 AD]; s. Mayser 531.—On this Doric form s. Kühner-Bl. I 510; Thumb 90f; APF 4, 1908, 490; Crönert 174, 5; FRobert, Les noms des Oiseaux en grec ancien, diss. Basel 1911, 17; B-D-F §47, 4; DELG s.v. ὄρνις) **Lk 13:34 v.l.** for the Att. ὄρνις, q.v. W-S. §9, 10; Mlt-H. 130f; 133.—M-M.

ὄρνις, ιθος, ὁ and **ἡ** (Hom.+; pap; 3 Km 5:3 [Swete 4:23; s. Thackeray p. 152f]; SibOr 2, 208 [ὄρνεις]; Philo; Jos., Bell. 2, 289 [ὄρνεις], C. Ap. I, 203f [τὸν ὄρνιθα], Ant. 18, 185 [τὸν ὄρνιν]; Tat.) gener. 'bird', specif. 'cock' or 'hen' (Aeschyl.; X., An. 4, 5, 25; Polyb. 12, 26, 1 al.; TAM II/1, 245, 8; pap); in NT only fem. ***hen.*** The action of the mother bird or specif. of the hen as a symbol of protecting care **Mt 23:37; Lk 13:34.**—D'Arcy Thompson, A Glossary of Greek Birds '36; AParmelee, All the Birds of the Bible '69. B. 175. DELG. M-M.

ὁροθεσία, ας, ἡ (ὅρος, τίθημι; IPriene 42 II, 8 [133 BC] δικαίαν εἶναι ἔκριναν τὴν Ῥωδίων κρίσιν τε καὶ ὁροθεσίαν; BGU 889, 17 [II AD].—B-D-F §119, 3; Mlt-H. 340) ***fixed boundary*** ὁρίσας … τὰς ὁροθεσίας τῆς κατοικίας αὐτῶν (=τ. ἀνθρώπων) *(God) determined the boundaries of their habitation* **Ac 17:26** (s. HCadbury, JBL 44, 1925, 219–21, 'fixed the term of residence'.—MDibelius, SBHeidAk 1938/39 2. Abh, p, 7f; 15: 'limited areas to be colonized'; WEltester, RBultmann Festschr., '54, 209ff).—DELG s.v. ὅρος. M-M. Spicq.

ὄρος, ους, τό (Hom.+) pl. τὰ ὄρη; gen., uncontracted ὀρέων (as early as X., An. 1, 2, 21 [Kühner-Bl. I 432]; SIG 646, 18 [170 BC]; LXX [Thackeray 151; Helbing 41f]; EpArist 119. Joseph. prefers ὀρῶν.—Schweizer 153; B-D-F §48; Mlt-H. 139) **Rv 6:15;** 1 Cl; Hermas (Reinhold 52); **a relatively high elevation of land that projects higher than a βοῦνος** ('a minor elevation, hill'), ***mountain, mount, hill*** (in Eng. diction what is considered a 'mountain' in one locality may be called a 'hill' by someone from an area with extremely high mountain ranges; similar flexibility prevails in the use of ὄρος, and the Eng. glosses merely suggest a comparative perspective; in comparison w. Mt. Everest [8848 meters] or Mount McKinley [6194 meters] any mountain in Palestine is a mere hill) w. βουνός **Lk 3:5** (Is 40:4); **23:30** (Hos 10:8). W. πέτρα **Rv 6:16;** cp. vs. **15.** W. πεδίον (SIG 888, 120f) Hs 8, 1, 1; 8, 3, 2. W. νῆσος **Rv 6:14; 16:20.** As the scene of outstanding events and as places of solitude (PTebt 383, 61 [46 AD] ὄρος denotes 'desert'; Dio Chrys. 19 [36], 40 Zoroaster withdraws fr. among men and lives ἐν ὄρει; Herm. Wr. 13 ins. Hermes teaches his son Tat ἐν ὄρει) mountains play a large part in the gospels and in the apocalypses: Jesus preaches and heals on 'the' mountain **Mt 5:1** (HCarré, JBL 42, 1923, 39–48; Appian, Mithrid. 77 §334 understands τὸ ὄρος in ref. to the Bithynian Olympus, but without naming it.—On the Sermon on the Mount s. GHeinrici, Beiträge II 1899; III 1905; JMüller, D. Bergpredigt 1906; KProost, De Bergrede 1914; HWeinel, D. Bergpr. 1920; KBornhäuser, D. Bergpr. 1923, ^{2}1927; PFiebig, Jesu Bergpr. 1924; GKittel D. Bergpr. u. d. Ethik d. Judentums: ZST 2, 1925, 555–94; ASteinmann, D. Bergpr. 1926; AAhlberg, Bergpredikans etik 1930; MMeinertz, Z. Ethik d. Bergpr.: JMausbach Festschr. '31, 21–32; HHuber, D. Bergpredigt '32; RSeeberg, Z. Ethik der Bergpr. '34; JSchneider, D. Sinn d. Bergpr. '36; ALindsay, The Moral Teaching of Jesus '37; MDibelius, The Sermon on the Mount '40; TSoiron, D. Bergpr. Jesu '41; DAndrews, The Sermon on the Mount '42; HPreisker, D. Ethos des Urchristentums^2 '49; HWindisch, The Mng. of the Sermon on the Mount [tr. Gilmour] '51; WManson, Jesus the Messiah '52, 77–93; TManson, The Sayings of Jesus '54; GBornkamm, Jesus v. Naz. '56, 92–100, 201–4 [Eng. tr. by JRobinson et al. '60, 100–109, 221–25]; JJeremias, Die Bergpredigt '59; JDupont, Les Béatitudes, I, rev. ed. '58; II, '69; W Davies, The Setting of the Sermon on the Mount, '64; JManek, NovT 9, '67, 124–31; HD-Betz, The Sermon on the Mt [Hermeneia] '95.—On the site of the Sermon, CKopp, The Holy Places of the Gosp., '63, 204–13); **8:1; 15:29;** calls the twelve **Mk 3:13;** performs oustanding miracles **J 6:3;** prays **Mt 14:23; Mk 6:46; Lk 6:12; 9:28;** ApcPt 2:4. On an ὄρος ὑψηλόν (Lucian, Charon 2) he is transfigured **Mt 17:1; Mk 9:2** and tempted **Mt 4:8;** the risen Christ shows himself on a mountain (cp. Herm. Wr. 13, 1) **Mt 28:16.** Jesus is taken away by the Holy Spirit εἰς τὸ ὄρος τὸ μέγα τὸ Θαβώρ GHb 20, 61 (cp. Iren. 1, 14, 6 [Harv. I 139, 8: gnostic speculation]); likew. the author of Rv ἐπὶ ὄρος μέγα κ. ὑψηλόν **Rv 21:10.** From the top of one mountain the angel of repentance shows Hermas twelve other mountains Hs 9, 1, 4; 7ff. On the use of mt. in apocalyptic lang. s. also **Rv 8:8; 17:9** (ἑπτὰ ὄρ. as En 24:2. Cp. JohJeremias, D. Gottesberg 1919; RFrieling, D. hl. Berg im A u. NT 1930). GJs 22:3 ὄρ. θεοῦ, where follows ἐδιχάσθη τὸ ὄρ. and ἦν τὸ ὄρ. ἐκεῖνο διαφαῖνον αὐτῇ φῶς *the mt. split* and *that mt. was a bright light for her.* On theophanies and mountain motif s. JReeves, Heralds of That Good Realm '96, 148f.—Of the mt. to which Abraham brought his son, to sacrifice him there 1 Cl 10:7 (cp. Gen 22:2; Demetr.: 722 fgm. 7 Jac.).

Esp. of Sinai (over a dozen sites have been proposed for it) τὸ ὄρος Σινά (LXX.—τὸ Σιναῖον ὄρ. Jos., Ant. 2, 283f) **Ac 7:30, 38; Gal 4:24f;** B 11:3 (cp. Is 16:1); 14:2 (cp. Ex 31:18); 15:1; also without mention of the name: **Hb 8:5** (Ex 25:40); **12:20** (cp. Ex 19:13); 1 Cl 53:2; B 4:7. Of the hill of Zion (Σιών) **Hb 12:22; Rv 14:1.** τὸ ὄρ. τῶν ἐλαιῶν *the Hill* or *Mount of Olives* (s. ἐλαία 1; about 17 meters higher than Jerusalem) **Mt 21:1; 26:30; Mk 14:26; Lk 19:37; 22:39; J 8:1** al. τὸ ὄρ. τὸ καλούμενον Ἐλαιῶν **Lk 19:29; 21:37; Ac 1:12** (s. ἐλαιών). Of Mt. Gerizim, about 868 meters in height (without mention of the name) **J 4:20f** (cp. Jos., Ant. 12, 10; 13, 74).—πόλις ἐπάνω ὄρους κειμένη *a city located on an eminence* or *hill* **Mt 5:14** (cp. Jos., Ant. 13, 203 πόλις ἐπ᾽ ὄρους κειμένη). Also πόλις οἰκοδομημένη ἐπ᾽ ἄκρον ὄρους ὑψηλοῦ Ox 1 recto, 17 (GTh 32) (Stephan. Byz. s.v. Ἀστέριον says this city was so named ὅτι ἐφ᾽ ὑψηλοῦ ὄρους κειμένη τοῖς πόρρωθεν ὡς ἀστὴρ φαίνεται).—Pl. τὰ ὄρη *hills, mountains, hilly* or *mountainous country* (somet. the sing. also means *hill-country* [Diod. S. 20, 58, 2 an ὄρος ὑψηλὸν that extends for 200 stades, roughly 40 km.; Polyaenus 4, 2, 4 al. sing. = hill-country; Tob 5:6 S]) AcPl Ha 5, 18; as a place for pasture **Mt 18:12.—Mk 5:11; Lk 8:32.** As a remote place (s. above; also Dio Chrys. 4, 4) w. ἐρημίαι **Hb 11:38.** As a place for graves (cp. POxy 274, 27 [I AD]; PRyl 153, 5; PGrenf II, 77, 22: the grave-digger is to bring a corpse εἰς τὸ ὄρος for burial) **Mk 5:5.** Because of their isolation an ideal refuge for fugitives (Appian, Bell. Civ. 4, 30 §130 ἐς ὄρος ἔφυγεν=to the hill-country; 1 Macc 9:40) φεύγειν εἰς τὰ ὄρ. (Plut., Mor. 869b οἱ ἄνθρωποι καταφυγόντες εἰς τὰ ὄρη διεσώθησαν; Jos., Bell. 1, 36, Ant. 14, 418) **Mt 24:16; Mk 13:14; Lk 21:21.**—Proverbially ὄρη μεθιστάνειν *remove mountains* i.e. do something that seems impossible **1 Cor 13:2;** cp. **Mt 17:20; 21:21; Mk 11:23.** Of God: μεθιστάνει τοὺς οὐρανοὺς καὶ τὰ ὄρη καὶ τοὺς βουνοὺς καὶ τὰς θαλάσσας *(God) is moving from their places the heavens and mountains and hills and seas* Hv 1, 3, 4 (cp. Is 54:10 and a similar combination PGM 13, 874 αἱ πέτραι κ. τὰ ὄρη κ. ἡ θάλασσα κτλ.).—B. 23. DELG. M-M. TW. Spicq. Sv.

ὅρος, ου, ὁ (Hom.+) ***boundary, limit*** of space τ. θάλασσαν ἰδίοις ὅροις ἐνέκλεισεν Dg 7:2 (Arrian, Anab. 5, 26, 2 τῆς γῆς ὅρους ὁ θεὸς ἐποίησε). Of time ὁ ὅρος τῶν ἐτῶν **ending of Mk in the Freer ms. 7.**—DELG. M-M. Sv.

ὀρύσσω fut. 2 and 3 sg. ὀρύξεις and -ει LXX; 1 aor. ὤρυξα; 2 aor. pass. ὠρύγην (Hs 9, 6, 7; s. OGI 672, 7; 673, 6 ὠρύγη; POxy 121, 8 ὀρυγῆναι; Ps 93:13; En 98:13; Joseph.; Just., D. 97, 4)

➊ **to loosen material by digging, w. focus on the activity as such, *dig (up)*** τὶ *someth.* γῆν (cp. Pla., Euthyd. 288e; Achmes 94, 14) to hide someth. **Mt 25:18.** Pass. ὠρύγη τὸ πεδίον *the plain was dug up* and there were found . . . Hs 9, 6, 7.

➋ **to prepare a place for someth. by digging, *dig out, prepare by digging*** τὶ *someth.* (X., Cyr. 7, 3, 5; Diod. S. 1, 50, 5; Gen 26:21, 25; Jos., Ant. 8, 341; TestSol; TestZeb 2:7; ApcMos 40) ληνόν *a wine-press* **Mt 21:33.** Also ὑπολήνιον **Mk 12:1** (cp. Is 5:2). βόθρον θανάτου *a pit of death* B 11:2 (cp. Jer 2:13 and for ὀρ. βόθρ. Eccl 10:8; Pr 26:27).

➌ **make a hole in someth. by digging, *dig (a hole)*** (X., Oec. 19, 2) ἐν τῇ γῇ (i.e. to hide τὸ ἓν τάλαντον) **Mt 25:18 v.l.**—B. 497. DELG. M-M.

ὀρφανός, ή, όν (cp. Lat. orbus, 'bereft (of)'; in var. senses relating to loss of a relationship Hom. et al.)

➊ **pert. to being deprived of parents, *without parents, orphan*** (so Hom.+; ins [New Docs 4, 162–64, w. texts relating to loss of only one parent], pap, LXX; JosAs 12:11 [freq. cod. A: p. 53, 16; 55, 15 Bat.]; Philo; Jos., Ant. 18, 314 al.), used so in our lit. only as a subst. (as Pla., Leg. 6, 766c; 11, 926c, al.; pap, LXX, TestJob, Ar., Just., Tat.) in sing. and pl. *orphan(s)*, mostly grouped w. χήρα (or χῆραι) as typically in need of protection (Liban., Or. 62 p. 379, 2 F. χήρας οἰκτείρων, ὀρφανοὺς ἐλεῶν; PCairMasp 6 recto, 2; 2 Macc 3:10; Just., A I, 67, 6; freq. in the LXX, but more commonly in the sing. fr. Ex 22:22 on, πᾶσαν χήραν κ. ὀρφανόν) ἐπισκέπτεσθαι ὀρφανοὺς καὶ χήρας **Js 1:27;** Hs 1:8. διαρπάζειν χηρῶν καὶ ὀρφανῶν τὴν ζωήν *rob widows and orphans of their living* 9, 26, 2. κατεσθίειν τὰς οἰκίας τῶν χηρῶν καὶ ὀρφανῶν **Mk 12:40 v.l.;** νουθετεῖν τὰς χήρας καὶ τοὺς ὀρ. *instruct the widows and orphans* Hv 2, 4, 3. W. χῆραι and ὑστερούμενοι m 8:10; in the sing. s 5, 3, 7. W. χήρα and πένης Pol 6:1. W. χήρα and others in need of help ISm 6:2. Collectively κρίνειν ὀρφανῷ *see to it that justice is done (to) the orphan* 1 Cl 8:4 (Is 1:17). χήρᾳ καὶ ὀρφανῷ προσέχειν *be concerned about (the) widow and orphan* B 20:2.

➋ **pert. to being without the aid and comfort of one who serves as associate and friend, *orphaned,*** fig. ext. of 1: Jesus says to his disciples that upon his departure οὐκ ἀφήσω ὑμᾶς ὀρφανούς *I will not leave you orphaned* (or *[as] orphans*) **J 14:18** (for this usage s. Pla., Phd. 65, 116a, where the feelings of Socrates' friends are described thus: ἀτεχνῶς ἡγούμενοι ὥσπερ πατρὸς στερηθέντες διάξειν ὀρφανοὶ τὸν ἔπειτα βίον ='thinking that we would have to spend the rest of our lives just like children deprived of their father'. Sim. the followers of Peregrinus in Lucian, Peregr. 6. Cp. Epict. 3, 24, 14; 15).—B. 130. RE VI/1, 224–25. DELG. M-M. TW.

ὀρχέομαι mid. dep., impf. ὠρχούμην; 1 aor. ὠρχησάμην (Hom.+; LXX; TestAbr A 10 p. 87, 23 [Stone p. 22]; Jos., Ant. 7, 87) ***dance*** (the verb does not of itself indicate a specific type or style of dance) of actual dancing **Mt 14:6; Mk 6:22** (on the dancing of Herodias' daughter s. reff. cited by Wetstein; s. also GDalman, Pj 14, 1918, 44–46 and s.v. Ἰωάννης 1.—FWeege, D. Tanz in d. Antike 1926); Hs 9, 11, 5. Of children at play (w. αὐλεῖν; cp. Aesop, Fab. 27 H.=11 P.; H-H.//24 Ch. ὅτε μὲν ηὔλουν, οὐκ ὠρχεῖσθε) **Mt 11:17; Lk 7:32.**—B. 689. DELG. M-M.

ὅς, ἥ, ὅ—➊ as relative pron. ***who, which, what, that*** (Hom.+). On its use s. B-D-F §293–97; 377–80; Rydbeck 98–118; W-S. §24; Rob. 711–26, and for ancient Gk. in gener. Kühner-G. II 399ff; Schwyzer II 639–41.

ⓐ As a general rule, the relative pron. agrees in gender and number w. the noun or pron. to which it refers (i.e. its antecedent); its case is determined by the verb, noun, or prep. that governs it: ὁ ἀστήρ, ὃν εἶδον **Mt 2:9.** ὁ Ἰησοῦς, ὃν ἐγὼ καταγγέλλω ὑμῖν **Ac 17:3.** Ἰουδαῖον, ᾧ (sc. ἦν) ὄνομα Βαριησοῦς **13:6.** ὁ Ἰουδαῖος . . . , οὗ ὁ ἔπαινος **Ro 2:29.** Ἰσραηλίτης, ἐν ᾧ δόλος οὐκ ἔστιν **J 1:47.** οὗτος, περὶ οὗ ἀκούω τοιαῦτα **Lk 9:9** and very oft.

ⓑ A demonstrative pron. is freq. concealed within the relative pron.:

α. in such a way that both pronouns stand in the same case: ὅς *the one who* ὃς οὐ λαμβάνει **Mt 10:38;** sim. **Mk 4:9; 9:40** (the three w. implied condition). οὗ *of the one whose* **J 18:26.** ᾧ *to the one to whom* **Ro 6:16.** ὅν *the one whom* (or someth. sim.) **Mk 15:12; J 1:45.** οἷς *to those for whom* **Mt 20:23.** οὕς *those whom* **Mk 3:13; J 5:21.** ὅ *that which, what* **Mt 10:27.**—A prep. governing the relative belongs in certain pass. to the (omitted) demonstr. pron. alone: παρ᾽ ὅ **Ro 12:3; Gal 1:8;** ὑπὲρ ὅ (ἅ) **1 Cor 10:13; 2 Cor 12:6; Phlm 21;** πρὸς ἅ **2 Cor 5:10;** εἰς ὅν **J 6:29.** In others it must be added to both pronouns: ἐν ᾧ *in that in* *which* **2 Cor 11:12; 1 Pt 2:12; 3:16** (these passages in 1 Pt may be classed under 1kγ also). ἐν οἷς **Phil 4:11.** ὑπὲρ οὗ *because of that for which* **1 Cor 10:30.** ἀφ' ὧν *from the persons from whom* **2 Cor 2:3.**—The much disputed pass. ἑταῖρε, ἐφ' ὃ πάρει **Mt 26:50** would belong here if we were to supply the words necessary to make it read about as follows: *friend,* (are you misusing the kiss) *for that* (purpose) *for which you are here?* (Wlh.; EKlostermann) or thus: *in connection with that* (=the purposes), *for which* (=for the realization of which) *you have appeared* (do you kiss me)? (Rdm.[2] 78). *Friend, are you here for this purpose?* FRehkopf, ZNW 52, '61, 109–15. But s. βב and iβ below.

β. But the two pronouns can also stand in different cases; in such instances the demonstr. pron. is nearly always in the nom. or acc.

א. in the nom. οὗ *one whose* **Ac 13:25.** ὧν *those whose* **Ro 4:7** (Ps 31:1). ᾧ *the one to* or *for whom* **Lk 7:43; 2 Pt 1:9.** οἷς *those to whom* **Mt 19:11; Ro 15:21** (Is 52:15). ὅ *that* (nom.) *which* (acc.) **Mt 13:12; 25:29; 26:13; Mk 11:23; Lk 12:3.** Likew. ἅ **Lk 12:20.** ὅν *he whom* **J 3:34; 4:18; Ac 10:21.** ἐφ' ὅν *the one about whom* **Hb 7:13.**

ב. in the acc. ὧν *the things of which* **J 13:29.** ᾧ *the one (in) whom* **2 Ti 1:12.** So also w. a prep.: ἐν ᾧ *anything by which* **Ro 14:21.** ἐν οἷς *things in which* **2 Pt 2:12.** ἐφ' ὅ *that upon which* **Lk 5:25.** περὶ ὧν *the things of which* **Ac 24:13.** ἐφ' οἷς *from the things of which* **Ro 6:21** (this passage perh. uses a commercial metaphor, for pap s. Mayser II/2, 434f §121). εἰς ὃν *the one in whom* **Ro 10:14a.**—So **Mt 26:50** (s. bα above), if the words to be supplied are about as follows: *friend,* (do that) *for which you have come!* (so ESchwartz, ByzZ 25, 1925, 154f; EOwen, JTS 29, 1928, 384–86; WSpiegelberg, ZNW 28, 1929, 341–43; FZorell, VD 9, 1929, 112–16; sim. PMaas, Byz.-Neugriech. Jahrb. 8, '31, 99; 9, '32, 64; WEltester: OCullmann Festschr., '62, 70–91; but s. iβ end.—S. Jos., Bell. 2, 615 at πάρειμι 1a).

ג. Only in isolated instances does the demonstr. pron. to be supplied stand in another case: οὗ = τούτῳ, οὗ *in him of whom* **Ro 10:14b.** παρ' ὧν = τούτοις, παρ' ὧν **Lk 6:34.**

ⓒ Constructions peculiar in some respect—**α.** The pleonastic use of the pers. pron. after ὅς (Mlt. 94f; B-D-F §297) γυνὴ ἧς εἶχεν τὸ θυγάτριον αὐτῆς **Mk 7:25** is found in older Gk. (Hyperid., Euxen. 3 ὧν ... τούτων.—Kühner-G. II 433f), and is not unknown in later Gk. (POxy 117, 15), but above all is suggested by Semitic languages (LXX; GrBar 2:1; Thackeray 46; JHudson, ET 53, '41/42, 266f); the omission of αὐτῆς in the v.l. is in line w. Gk. usage. οὗ τὸ πτύον ἐν τῇ χειρὶ αὐτοῦ **Mt 3:12; Lk 3:17.** οὗ ... τῶν ὑποδημάτων αὐτοῦ **Mk 1:7; Lk 3:16.** οὗ τῷ μώλωπι αὐτοῦ **1 Pt 2:24 v.l.** οὗ καὶ πολλὰ αὐτοῦ συγγράματα EpilMosq 2. In a quot. ἐφ' οὓς ἐπικέκληται ... ἐπ' αὐτούς **Ac 15:17** = Am 9:12. οὗ ἡ πνοὴ αὐτοῦ 1 Cl 21:9. Esp. freq. in **Rv 3:8; 7:2, 9; 9:11 v.l.; 13:8, 12; 20:8.**

β. constructions 'ad sensum'—**א.** a relative in the sing. refers to someth. in the pl. οὐρανοῖς ... ἐξ οὗ (οὐρανοῦ) **Phil 3:20.**

ב. a relative in the pl. refers to a sing. (Jdth 4:8 γερουσία, οἵ) πλῆθος πολύ ..., οἳ ἦλθον **Lk 6:17f.** κατὰ πόλιν πᾶσαν, ἐν αἷς **Ac 15:36.** Cp. ἤδη δευτέραν ἐπιστολήν, ἐν αἷς (i.e. ἐν ταῖς δυσὶν ἐπιστ.) **2 Pt 3:1.**

ג. the relative conforms to the natural gender rather than the grammatical gender of its antecedent noun τέκνα μου, οὓς **Gal 4:19;** cp. **2 J 1; Phlm 10.** ἔθνη, οἵ **Ac 15:17** (Am 9:12); cp. **26:17.** παιδάριον, ὅς **J 6:9.** θηρίον, ὅς **Rv 13:14.** ὀνόματα, οἵ **3:4 v.l.** γενεᾶς σκολιᾶς, ἐν οἷς **Phil 2:15.** W. ref. to Christ, τὴν κεφαλήν, ἐξ οὗ **Col 2:19.**

ⓓ Attraction (or assimilation) of the relative. Just as in Hdt. and freq. Att., ins, pap, LXX, the simple relative ὅς, ἥ, ὅ is somet. attracted to the case of its antecedent, even though the relationship of the relative within its own clause would demand a different case.

α. In most instances it is the acc. of the rel. that is attracted to the gen. or dat. of the antecedent: περὶ πράγματος οὗ ἐὰν αἰτήσωνται **Mt 18:19.** τῆς διαθήκης ἧς ὁ θεὸς διέθετο **Ac 3:25.** Cp. **Mt 24:50b; Mk 7:13; Lk 2:20; 3:19; 5:9; 9:43; 15:16; J 4:14; 7:31; 15:20; 17:5; 21:10; Ac 1:1; 2:22; 22:10; 1 Cor 6:19; 2 Cor 1:6; 10:8, 13; Eph 2:10; 2 Th 1:4; Jd 15** al.—When the antecedent is an understood but unexpressed demonstr. pron. (s. b, beg.) that would stand in the gen. or dat., the acc. of a relative pron. can be attracted to this gen. or dat.: οὐδὲν ὧν ἑώρακαν is really οὐδὲν τούτων ἃ ἑώρακαν **Lk 9:36** (Schwyzer II 641); ἅ takes on the case of τούτων which, in turn, is omitted (so already Soph., Pla., et al.).—**23:14, 41; Ac 8:24; 21:19, 24; 22:15; 25:11; 26:16; Ro 15:18; 1 Cor 7:1; Eph 3:20; Hb 5:8.** ὧν = τούτων, οὓς **J 17:9; 2 Cor 12:17.** οἷς = τούτοις, ἅ **Lk 24:25.**

β. The dat. of the relative is less frequently attracted (B-D-F §294, 2; Rob. 717) ἕως τῆς ἡμέρας ἧς (=ᾗ) ἀνελήμφθη **Ac 1:22** (cp. Lev 23:15; 25:50; Bar 1:19); **Eph 1:6; 4:1; 1 Ti 4:6 v.l.;** κατέναντι οὗ ἐπίστευσεν θεοῦ = κατέν. τοῦ θεοῦ ᾧ ἐπίστ. **Ro 4:17.** διὰ τῆς παρακλήσεως ἧς παρακαλούμεθα **2 Cor 1:4.**

γ. In relative clauses that consist of subject, predicate, and copula, the relative pron. somet. agrees in gender and number not w. the noun to which it refers, but w. the predicate if it is the subj. and, conversely, w. the subj. if it is the pred. of its own clause: πνεύματι ..., ὅς ἐστιν ἀρραβών **Eph 1:14 v.l.** τῷ σπέρματί σου, ὅς ἐστιν Χριστός **Gal 3:16.** τὴν μάχαιραν τοῦ πνεύματος, ὅ ἐστιν ῥῆμα θεοῦ **Eph 6:17.**—**Rv 4:5; 5:8.**

δ. Inverse attraction occurs when the relative pronoun attracts its antecedent to its own case (as early as Hom.; also Soph., Oed. Rex 449; s. Kühner-G. II 413; Schwyzer II 641; B-D-F §295; Rob. 717f); τὸν ἄρτον ὃν κλῶμεν, οὐχὶ κοινωνία ... ἐστιν; = ὁ ἄρτος ὅν ... **1 Cor 10:16.** λίθον, ὃν ἀπεδοκίμασαν ... οὗτος ἐγενήθη (Ps 117:22) **Mt 21:42; Mk 12:10; Lk 20:17; 1 Pt 2:7 v.l.**—παντὶ ᾧ ἐδόθη πολύ, πολὺ ζητηθήσεται παρ' αὐτοῦ **Lk 12:48.** ὅρκον, ὃν ὤμοσεν (=μνησθῆναι ὅρκου ὅν) **1:73** (s. W-S. §24, 7 note). τοὺς λίθους, οὓς εἶδες, ἀποβεβλημένους, οὗτοι ... ἐφόρεσαν Hs 9, 13, 3. Cp. **1J 2:25.**

ε. Attraction can, as in earlier Gk. (Thu. 2, 70, 4), fail to take place when the relative clause is more distinctly separated fr. its antecedent by additional modifiers of the noun and by the importance attaching to the content of the relative clause itself (B-D-F §294, 1; Rob. 714f): τῆς σκηνῆς τῆς ἀληθινῆς, ἣν ἔπηξεν ὁ κύριος, οὐκ ἄνθρωπος **Hb 8:2.** But s. also **Mk 13:19; J 2:22; 4:5; Ac 8:32; 1 Ti 4:3; Tit 1:2; Phlm 10; Hb 9:7; Rv 1:20.**

ⓔ The noun which is the antecedent of a relative clause can be incorporated into the latter

α. without abbreviating the constr. and without attraction of the case: ᾗ οὐ δοκεῖτε ὥρᾳ = τῇ ὥρᾳ ᾗ οὐ δοκ. **Mt 24:44;** cp. **Lk 12:40; 17:29, 30.** ἃ ἡτοίμασαν ἀρώματα **24:1.** ὃ ἐποίησεν σημεῖον **J 6:14.** ὃ θέλω ἀγαθόν **Ro 7:19.**

β. w. abbreviation, in that a prep. normally used twice is used only once: ἐν ᾧ κρίματι κρίνετε κριθήσεσθε = ἐν τῷ κρίματι, ἐν ᾧ κρίνετε, κριθήσεσθε **Mt 7:2a.** Cp. vs. **2b; Mk 4:24.** ἐν ᾧ ἦν τόπῳ = ἐν τῷ τόπῳ ἐν ᾧ ἦν **J 11:6.** καθ' ὃν τρόπον = κατὰ τὸν τρόπον, καθ' ὃν **Ac 15:11.**

γ. w. a change in case, due mostly to attraction—**א.** of the relative pron. περὶ πάντων ὧν ἐποίησεν πονηρῶν = περὶ πάντων πονηρῶν, ἃ ἐπ. **Lk 3:19.** περὶ πασῶν ὧν εἶδον δυνάμεων = περὶ πασῶν δυνάμεων, ἃς εἶδον **19:37.** αἰτίαν ... ὧν ἐγὼ ὑπενόουν πονηρῶν **Ac 25:18.**—The dat. of the relative is also attracted to other cases: ἄχρι ἧς ἡμέρας = ἄχρι τῆς ἡμέρας, ᾗ **Mt 24:38; Lk 1:20; 17:27; Ac 1:2.** ἀφ' ἧς ἡμέρας **Col 1:6, 9.**

ב. of the noun to which the rel. refers: ὃν ἐγὼ ἀπεκεφάλισα Ἰωάννην, οὗτος ἠγέρθη = Ἰωάννης ὃν κτλ. **Mk 6:16** εἰς ὃν παρεδόθητε τύπον διδαχῆς = τῷ τύπῳ τῆς διδαχῆς εἰς ὃν παρεδόθητε **Ro 6:17.**

δ. The analysis is doubtful in passages like περὶ ὧν κατηχήθης λόγων = περὶ τῶν λόγων οὓς κατηχήθης or τῶν λόγων, περὶ ὧν κατηχήθης **Lk 1:4.** ἄγοντες παρ' ᾧ ξενισθῶμεν Μνάσωνι **Ac 21:16** must acc. to the sense =ἄγοντες πρὸς Μνάσωνα, ἵνα ξενισθῶμεν παρ' αὐτῷ. S. B-D-F §294, 5; Rob. 719.

ⓕ The prep. can be omitted before the relative pron. if it has already been used before the antecedent noun: ἐν παντὶ χρόνῳ ᾧ (=ἐν ᾧ.) **Ac 1:21.** εἰς τὸ ἔργον ὅ (=εἰς ὅ) **13:2.** ἀπὸ πάντων ὧν (=ἀφ' ὧν) vs. **38.** Cp. **26:2.** ἐν τῷ ποτηρίῳ ᾧ (=ἐν ᾧ) **Rv 18:6.**

ⓖ The neut. is used—**α.** in explanations, esp. of foreign words and of allegories: ὅ ἐστιν *which* or *that is, which means:* βασιλεὺς Σαλήμ, ὅ ἐστιν βασιλεὺς εἰρήνης **Hb 7:2;** cp. **Mt 27:33; Mk 3:17; 7:11, 34; 15:42.** Also ὅ ἐστιν μεθερμηνευόμενον **Mt 1:23; Mk 5:41; Ac 4:36;** cp. **J 1:38, 41f.** ὅ ἐστιν μεθερμηνευόμενος κρανίου τόπος **Mk 15:22 v.l.** (for μεθερμηνευόμενον).τόπος, ὃ λέγεται, Ἑβραϊστὶ Γολγοθά **J 19:17.**—S. also αὐλῆς, ὅ ἐστιν πραιτώριον **Mk 15:16.** λεπτὰ δύο, ὅ ἐστιν κοδράντης **12:42.** τοῦ σώματος αὐτοῦ, ὅ ἐστιν ἡ ἐκκλησία **Col 1:24.** πλεονέκτης ὅ ἐστιν εἰδωλολάτρης **Eph 5:5.** τὴν ἀγάπην ὅ ἐστιν σύνδεσμος τῆς τελειότητος **Col 3:14.**—B-D-F §132, 2.

β. when the relative pron. looks back upon a whole clause: τοῦτον τ. Ἰησοῦν ἀνέστησεν ὁ θεός, οὗ πάντες ἡμεῖς ἐσμεν μάρτυρες **Ac 2:32;** cp. **3:15; 11:30; 26:9f; Gal 2:10; Col 1:29; 1 Pt 2:8; Rv 21:8.**

γ. ὅ is to be understood as an obj. acc. and gains its content fr. what immediately follows in these places (s. W-S. §24, 9; Rob. 715): ὃ ἀπέθανεν, τῇ ἁμαρτίᾳ ἀπέθανεν ἐφάπαξ = τὸν θάνατον, ὃν ἀπέθανεν κτλ. *what he died,* i.e. the death he suffered, *he suffered for sin* **Ro 6:10a;** cp. vs. **10b.** ὃ νῦν ζῶ ἐν σαρκί *the life that I now live in the flesh* **Gal 2:20.**

ⓗ The relative is used w. consecutive or final mng. (result or purpose): τίς ἔγνω νοῦν κυρίου, ὃς συμβιβάσει αὐτόν; *who has known the mind of the Lord, so that he could instruct him?* **1 Cor 2:16** (cp. Is 40:13). ἄξιός ἐστιν ᾧ παρέξῃ τοῦτο *he is worthy that you should grant him this* **Lk 7:4.** ἀποστέλλω τὸν ἄγγελόν μου . . . , ὃς κατασκευάσει **Mt 11:10.** ἔπεμψα Τιμόθεον . . . , ὃς ὑμᾶς ἀναμνήσει **1 Cor 4:17.** ἔχετε μεθ' ἑαυτῶν, εἰς οὓς ἐργάσεσθε τὸ καλόν B 21:2.

ⓘ taking the place of the interrogative pron.—**α.** in indirect questions (Soph., Oed. Rex 1068; Thu. 1, 136, 4; Attic ins of 411 BC in Meisterhans[3]-Schw.; pap [Witkowski 30, 7]; oft. Joseph. [Schmidt 369]; Just., D. 44, 4 δι' ἧς ὁδοῦ). ὃ ἐγὼ ποιῶ *what I am doing* **J 13:7.** ἃ λέγουσιν **1 Ti 1:7** (Just., D. 9, 1 οὐ γὰρ οἶδας ὃ λέγεις).—**J 18:21.**

β. NT philology has generally dismissed the proposition that ὅς is used in direct questions (Mlt. 93; B-D-F §300, 2; Radermacher[2] 78; PMaas [see 1bβב above]). An unambiguous example of it is yet to be found. Even the ins on a goblet in Dssm., LO 100ff [LAE 125–31], ET 33, 1922, 491–93 leaves room for doubt. Therefore also the translation of ἐφ' ὃ πάρει **Mt 26:50** as 'what are you here for?' (so Goodsp., Probs. 41–43; similarly, as early as Luther, later Dssm.; JWilson, ET 41, 1930, 334) has been held suspect. S. ZNW 52, '61, 109ff.—Rob. 725 doubts the interrogative here, but Mlt-Turner 50 inclines toward it. If further proof for interrogative use of ὅς can be found, lit.-crit. considerations (s. vv. 14–16) invite attention to the v.l. (s. Tdf. app.) ἐφ' ᾧ, a combination used in commercial documents (PGrenf II, 17, 2; 5; Mayser II/1 p. 215); the colloquial use suggests the sense: *What deal did you make?*—See also 1bβב above.

ⓙ combined w. particles—**α.** with ἄν (ἐάν), s. ἄν I. b.

β. with γέ (s. γέ aβ and cp. PFlor 370, 9) **Ro 8:32.**

γ. w. δήποτε *whatever* **J 5:3(4) v.l.** (the vv.ll. vary betw. οἵῳ and ᾧ, δηποτοῦν and δήποτε).

δ. w. καί *who also* **Mk 3:19; Lk 6:13f; 7:49** al.

ε. with περ = ὅσπερ, ἥπερ, ὅπερ (TestSol, TestAbr; TestJob 7:13; JosAs 14:12; GrBar; ApcSed 2:1; Jos., Ant. 2, 277, Vi. 95; apolog. [exc. Mel.]) *just the one who* **Mk 15:6 v.l.** ὅπερ *which indeed* Ox 840, 35; ISm 4:1. πάντα ἅπερ *whatever* GPt 11:45.

ⓚ used w. preposition (s. also above: 1bα; 1bβב; 1eβ,γ; 1f, and s. Johannessohn, Präp. 382f [ind.]), whereby a kind of conjunction is formed:

α. with ἀντί: ἀνθ' ὧν (s. ἀντί 4) *because* **Lk 1:20; 19:44; Ac 12:23; 2 Th 2:10;** *therefore* **Lk 12:3.**

β. w. εἰς: εἰς ὅ *to this end* **2 Th 1:11.**

γ. with ἐν: ἐν οἷς connects w. the situation described in what precedes *under which circumstances = under these circumstances* **Lk 12:1; Ac 24:18 v.l.; 26:12.** So also perh. ἐν ᾧ **1 Pt 1:6; 2:12; 3:16, 19; 4:4.** S. also ἐν 7 and cp. 1bα above.

δ. w. ἐπί: ἐφ' ᾧ (normally, 'for which': Plut., Cimon 483 [8, 6] Cimon receives honors in requital for his generous deed [cp. the pl. ἐφ' οἷς IPriene 114, 22 of honors heaped on a gymnasiarch for his numerous contributions]; cp. Plut., Mor. 522e and Diog. L. 7, 173. Conversely Plut., Aratus 1048 [44, 4]: A. suffers some dishonor 'for what' he did to one of his associates) has freq. been interpreted=ἐπὶ τούτῳ ὅτι *for the reason that, because* **Ro 5:12** (lit. on ἁμαρτία 3a); **2 Cor 5:4; Phil 3:12;** *for* **4:10.** But a commercial metaphor may find expression in the first 3 passages cited here; s. ἐπί 6c. Difft. on Ro 5:12 JFitzmyer, NTS 39, '93, 321–39; also comm. (Anchor), ad loc.: 'with the result that, so that'

ε. οὗ χάριν *therefore* **Lk 7:47.**

ζ. in indications of time: ἀφ' ἧς (s. ἀπό 2bγ and cp. BGU 252, 9 [98 AD]) *from the time when; since* **Lk 7:45; Ac 24:11; 2 Pt 3:4;** Hs 8, 6, 6 v.l.; *as soon as, after* 8, 1, 4.—ἀφ' οὗ (s. ἀπό 2bγ) *when once, since* **Lk 13:25; 24:21; Rv 16:18.** ἄχρι οὗ (s. ἄχρι 1bα) *until (the time when)* **Ac 7:18; Ro 11:25; 1 Cor 11:26; Gal 3:19.** Also ἕως οὗ *until* **Mt 1:25; 13:33; 14:22; 17:9; Lk 13:21;** D 11:6 al. μέχρις οὗ *until* **Mk 13:30; Gal 4:19.**—On the gen. οὗ as an adv. of place s. it as a separate entry.

❷ Demonstrative pron. ***this (one)*** (Hom.+; prose of Hdt. et al. [Kühner-G. II 228f]; pap, LXX).—ⓐ ὃς δέ *but he* (Ps.-Lucian, Philopatris 22; PRyl 144, 14 [38 AD]) **Mk 15:23; J 5:11 v.l.** Mostly

ⓑ ὃς μὲν . . . ὃς δέ *the one . . . the other* (Hippocr.+; very oft. in later wr.; POxy 1189, 7 [c. 117 AD]; SibOr 3, 654) the masc. in var. cases of sing. and pl. **Mt 22:5; Lk 23:33; Ac 27:44; Ro 14:5; 1 Cor 11:21; 2 Cor 2:16; Jd 22f.** ὃ μὲν . . . ὃ δέ *this . . . that* **Ro 9:21.** ἃ μὲν . . . ἃ δέ (Lucian, Rhet. Praec. 15) *some . . . others* **2 Ti 2:20.** ὃς μὲν . . . ὃς δὲ . . . ὃς δέ **Mt 21:35; 25:15** (Lucian, Tim. 57 διδοὺς . . . ᾧ μὲν πέντε δραχμάς, ᾧ δέ μνᾶν, ᾧ δὲ ἡμιτάλαντον).ὃ μὲν . . . ὃ δὲ . . . ὃ δέ **Mt 13:8b, 23.** ᾧ μὲν . . . ἄλλῳ δὲ . . . ἑτέρῳ (ἄλλῳ δέ is then repeated five times, and before the last one there is a second ἑτέρῳ) **1 Cor 12:8–10.** ὃ μὲν . . . καὶ ἄλλο κτλ. **Mk 4:4.** ὃ μὲν . . . καὶ ἕτερον (repeated several times) **Lk 8:5.** ἃ μὲν . . . ἄλλα δέ (repeated several times) **Mt 13:4–8a.** In anacoluthon οὓς μέν without οὓς δέ **1 Cor 12:28.** ὃς μὲν . . . ὁ δὲ ἀσθενῶν **Ro 14:2.**—B-D-F §250. MBlack, An Aramaic Approach[3], '67, 100f.—DELG 1 ὅς. M-M.

ὁσάκις adv. (in Hom. ὁσσάκι; in the form ὁσάκις Lysias, Pla., X. et al.; ins, pap; Jos., Vi. 160; Just.; Tat. 14, 1) ***as often as*** w. ἐάν (SIG 972, 124; BGU 1115, 22 [13 BC]; PHamb 37, 3; PGiss 12, 5) **1 Cor 11:25f; Rv 11:6.**—M-M.

ὅσγε for ὅς γε s. ὅς 1jβ.—M-M.

ὅσιος, ία, ον (Aeschyl., Hdt.+ [the noun ὁσίη is found as early as Hom.]. Mostly of three endings, but -ος, ον Pla., Leg. 8, 831d; Dionys. Hal. 5, 71; **1 Ti 2:8.** B-D-F §59, 2; W-S. §11, 1; Mlt-H. 157). Superl. ὁσιώτατος (Pla.; OGI 718, 1; Philo; 1 Cl 58:1). In the Gr-Rom. world this term for the most part described that which helps maintain the delicate balance between the interests of society and the expectations of the transcendent realm. For example, the ὅσιος pers. prays and sacrifices to the gods (Pl., Euthyph. 14b), is conscious of basic taboos (hence wary of pollution because of bloodshed [ibid. 4de; cp. Od. 16, 423]), and observes traditions of hospitality (on Zeus as protector of the stranger, s. Od. 9, 270f). For contrast of τὸ ὅσιον and τὸ δίκαιον s. Pla., Gorgias 507b, Polit. 301d; X., Hell. 4, 1, 33 al.

❶ **pert. to being without fault relative to deity, *devout, pious, pleasing to God, holy*—ⓐ** of ordinary human beings: w. δίκαιος (cp. Pla., Leg. 2, 663b, Gorg. 507b; Polyb. 22, 10, 8 παραβῆναι καὶ τὰ πρὸς τοὺς ἀνθρώπους δίκαια καὶ τὰ πρὸς τ. θεοὺς ὅσια; SIG 800, 20f: ἀναστρέφεται πρός τε θεοὺς καὶ πάντας ἀνθρώπους ὁσίως κ. δικαίως; En 104:12; TestGad 5:4; TestBenj 3:1 and 5:4; Jos., Ant. 9, 35; Just., D. 96, 3 [after Mt 5:45]; Theoph. Ant. 2, 9 [p. 120, 3]) 1 Cl 45:3; 2 Cl 15:3; and still other virtues **Tit 1:8.** ἔργα ὅσια κ. δίκαια (Jos., Ant. 8, 245) 2 Cl 6:9. δίκαιον κ. ὅσιον w. acc. and inf. foll. (Dicaearchus. p. 408, line 2 fr. bottom, Fuhr; cp. ὅσιον εἶναι w. acc. and inf., Orig., C. Cels. 5, 26, 13) 1 Cl 14:1. ὀφείλομεν ὅσια 2 Cl 1:3. (W. ἄμωμος) ἐν ὅσ. κ. ἀμώμῳ προθέσει δουλεύειν τῷ θεῷ *serve God with a holy and blameless purpose* 1 Cl 45:7. ἄνδρες 45:3. ὅσ. βουλή 2:3.—ὅσιοι χεῖρες (Aeschyl., Choëph. 378; Soph., Oed. Col. 470: 'consecrated', 'ceremonially pure') **1 Ti 2:8** transferred to the religio-ethical field (Philip of Perg. [II AD]: 95 fgm. 1 Jac. writes ὁσίῃ χειρί).—The word was prob. used in a cultic sense in the mysteries (ERohde, Psyche[9/10], 1925 I 288, 1): Aristoph., Ran. 335 ὅσιοι μύσται. The mystae of the Orphic Mysteries are called οἱ ὅσιοι: Pla., Rep. 2, 363c; Orph., Hymn. 84, 3 Qu.; cp. Ps.-Pla., Axioch. 371d. Sim. the Essenes are called ὅσιοι in Philo, Omn. Prob. Liber 91; cp. 75 ὁσιότης; PParis 68c, 14 ὅσιοι Ἰουδαῖοι (s. Dssm., B 62, 4 [BS 68, 2]); PGM 5, 417 of a worshiper of Hermes.

ⓑ of Christ, the Heavenly High Priest (w. ἄκακος; cp. the opposition Od. 16, 423) **Hb 7:26.** As subst. ὁ ὅσιός σου (after Ps 15:10) **Ac 2:27; 13:35** (cp. ὁ ὅσιος of Abraham Did., Gen. 228, 8).

❷ **pert. to being the standard for what constitutes holiness, *holy*** of God (rarely of deities outside our lit.: Orph., Hymn. 77, 2 Qu.; Arg. 27; CIG 3594; 3830).

ⓐ as adj., of God (Dt 32:4; Ps 144:17) *holy* μόνος ὅσιος **Rv 15:4.** ἡ ὅσ. παιδεία *holy* (i.e. divine) *discipline* 1 Cl 56:16. τὸ ὁσιώτατον ὄνομα *most holy name* 58:1.

ⓑ as subst. ὁ ὅσιος **Rv 16:5.**

❸ The ref. to ὅσ. in δώσω ὑμῖν τὰ ὅσ. Δαυὶδ τὰ πιστά *I will grant to you* (pl.) *the unfailing divine assurances* or *decrees relating to David* **Ac 13:34** is of special interest (for τὰ ὅσ. in the sense of divine decrees or ordinances s. Wsd 6:10; Jos., Ant. 8, 115—). This quot. fr. Is 55:3 is evidently meant to show that the quot. fr. Ps 15:10, which follows immediately, could not refer to the Psalmist David, but to Christ alone (cp. a sim. line of argument relating to a referent Hb 2:6–9). The promises to David have solemnly been transferred to 'you'. But David himself served not you, but his own generation (vs. 36). So the promises of God refer not to him, but to his Messianic descendant.—Lit. s.v. ἅγιος. JBolkestein, Ὅσιος en Εὐσεβής, diss. Amsterdam '36; WTerstegen, Εὐσεβής en Ὅσιος in het Grieksch taalgebruik na de 4[e] eeuw, diss. Utrecht '41; JMontgomery, HTR 32, '39, 97–102; MvanderValk, Z. Worte ὅσιος: Mnemosyne 10, '41; Dodd 62–64.—B. 1475. DELG. M-M. EDNT. TW. Sv.

ὁσιότης, τητος, ἡ (ὅσιος; X., Pla., Isocr. et al.; Epict. 3, 26, 32 δικαιοσύνη καὶ ὅσ. [this combination also Cat. Cod. Astr. V/4 181, 22]; ins; UPZ 33, 10 [162/161 BC]; 36, 13; LXX; En 102:5; EpArist 18 ἐν ὅσ.; Philo, Abr. 208 ὅσ. μὲν πρὸς θεόν, δικαιοσύνη δὲ πρὸς ἀνθρώπους, Spec. Leg. 1, 304, Virt. 47 δικ. καὶ ὅσ.; Jos., Ant. 19, 300; δι' ὁσιότητα ἀποθνήσκειν Orig., C. Cels. 8, 54, 43) **state of proper attitude toward God as exhibited in action, *devoutness, piety, holiness*** ἐν ὅσ. καὶ δικαιοσύνῃ **Lk 1:75** (the combination is an indication of a high degree of ἀρετή, the mark of an exceptional citizen, cp. Pla., Prot. 319c; SIG 800, 21 ὁσίως καὶ δικαίως, as also **1 Th 2:10**) 1 Cl 48:4. Of a new human being: created in the likeness of God ἐν δικαιοσύνῃ καὶ ὅσ. τῆς ἀληθείας *in true righteousness and holiness* **Eph 4:24.** ἐν ὅσ. ψυχῆς 1 Cl 29:1 (cp. Philo, Abr. 198). ἐν ὅσ. καρδίας (3 Km 9:4; Dt 9:5; Theoph. Ant. 2, 35 [p. 186, 19]) 32:4; 60:2.—DELG s.v. ὅσιος. M-M. TW.

ὁσίως adv. of ὅσιος (Eur., X., Pla.+; ins, pap, LXX; EpArist 306; 310; Philo, Aet. M. 10 εὐσεβῶς κ. ὅσ.; Ar.; Just., A I, 21, 6 ὅσ. καὶ ἐναρέτως. W. εὐαγῶς Orig., C. Cels. 4, 10, 3) pert. to a manner pleasing to God *devoutly* 1 Cl 21:8. δουλεύειν τῷ θεῷ 26:1. ἐπικαλεῖσθαι θεόν 60:4 (acc. to the Lat., Syr. and Coptic versions; the word is lacking in the only Gk. ms. that includes this pass.). θεῷ ὅσ. εὐαρεστεῖν 62:2. τὴν ἀγάπην . . . ὅσ. παρέχειν τινί 21:7. ὅσ. πολιτεύσασθαι 6:1. W. δικαίως (s. ὅσιος 1a and δικαίως 2): PtK 2 p. 15, 2; ἀναστρέφεσθαι 2 Cl 5:6 (SIG 800, 20f ἀναστρέφεται πρός τε θεοὺς καὶ πάντας ἀνθρώπους ὁσίως καὶ δικαίως=he comports himself towards the gods and all persons in a devout and upright manner; ζῆν Theoph. Ant. 2, 16 [p. 140, 20]). W. δικ. and ἀμέμπτως: γενέσθαι (cp. 1 Cl 40:3) **1 Th 2:10.** ἀμέμπτως καὶ ὅσ., προσφέρειν τὰ δῶρα 1 Cl 44:4.—M-M. TW.

ὀσμή, ῆς, ἡ (ὄζω; trag., Thu. et al.; PGM 13, 365; LXX, En; TestAbr, Test12Patr; JosAs 16:4 [ὀσ. ζωῆς]; SibOr 3, 462; Philo; Jos., Ant. 2, 297) and **ὀδμή** (Hom. et al.; later prose [s. L-S-J-M s.v. ὀσμή; Phryn. p. 89 Lob.]) gener. 'odor, smell'

❶ **quality of someth. that stimulates sense of smell, *odor, smell*** (the term itself does not denote whether it is agreeable or disagreeable)

ⓐ of a pleasant odor *fragrance:* of ointment **J 12:3** (cp. Achilles Tat. 2, 38, 3 ὀσμή of the fragrance of ointment and Plut., Alex. 676 [20, 13] ὀδώδει ὑπ' ἀρωμάτων καὶ μύρων ὁ οἶκος).

ⓑ of an unpleasant odor *stench* (Tob 6:17 S; 8:3; Job 6:7) Papias (3:3 ὀδμή)

❷ **the quality of someth. that affects the mind as with an odor, *odor*** fig. ext. of 1 (Sir 24:15 of Wisdom; Porphyr., Adv. Christ. [ABA 1916] 69, 20 speaks of the ὀσμὴ τῆς λέξεως, the [bad] odor [ὀσμή=stench; s. Artem. below] of the saying J 6:53) ἡ ὀσμὴ τῆς γνώσεως αὐτοῦ *the fragrance of the knowledge of him* (=of God) **2 Cor 2:14.** This fragrance is spread throughout the world by the apostolic preaching and works οἷς μὲν ὀσμὴ ἐκ θανάτου εἰς θάνατον, οἷς δὲ ὀσμὴ ἐκ ζωῆς εἰς ζωήν vs. **16** (JosAs 16:4 ὀσ. ζωῆς; s. εὐωδία).ἀπὸ τῆς ὀσμῆς ἐλεγχθήσεσθε *you will be convicted* (or *tested*) *by the odor* (whether you have been corrupted or not [Soph., Ant. 412 the odor coming from the corpse]; Artem. 1, 51 τὰ κρυπτὰ ἐλέγχει διὰ τ. ὀσμήν) IMg 10:2. ὀσμὴ εὐωδίας (Gen 8:21; Ex 29:18; Lev 1:9, 13 al.) *fragrant offering* fig., in reference to the Philippians' gift **Phil 4:18,** to Jesus' sacrifice of himself **Eph 5:2,** to a heart full of praise B 2:10.—ELohmeyer, Vom göttlichen Wohlgeruch: SBBerlAk IX 1919; SLilja, The Treatment of Odours in the Poetry of Antiquity '72.—B. 1022f. Straub 41. DELG s.v. ὄζω. M-M. TW.

ὅσος, η, ον (Hom.+) correlative w. πόσος, τοσοῦτος (Jos., Ant. 1, 318)

❶ **pert. to an extent of space or time that is of the same extent as another extent of the same order, *as great, as far, as long***

ⓐ of space τὸ μῆκος αὐτῆς (τοσοῦτόν ἐστιν), ὅσον τὸ πλάτος *its length is as great as its breadth* **Rv 21:16.**—ὅσον ὅσον *a short distance* (for ὅσον doubled s. Aristoph., Vesp. 213; Leonidas: Anth. Pal. 7, 472, 3; Hesych. 1421) **Lk 5:3** D.

ⓑ of time ἐφ' ὅσ. χρόνον *as long as* (UPZ 160, 12 [119 BC]) **Ro 7:1; 1 Cor 7:39; Gal 4:1.** Also ἐφ' ὅσον (X., Cyr. 5, 5, 8; Polyaenus 4, 7, 10; UPZ 162 I, 23 [117 BC]; Jos., Ant. 13, 359) **Mt 9:15; 2 Pt 1:13.** ὅσ. χρόνον (X., Cyr. 5, 3, 25; Josh 4:14) **Mk 2:19.** ἔτι μικρὸν ὅσον ὅσον (B-D-F §304; Rob. 733; JWackernagel, Glotta 4, 1913, 244f; OLagercrantz, Eranos 18, 1918, 53ff) *in a very little while* **Hb 10:37;** 1 Cl 50:4 (both after Is 26:20).—ἐν ὅσῳ (Aristoph., Pax 943; Thu. 8, 87, 4) *while* Dg 8:10.

❷ **pert. to a comparative quantity or number of objects or events; *how much (many), as much (many) as*** (Aelian, VH 1, 4) ὅσον ἤθελον *as much as they wanted* **J 6:11** (Appian, Bell. Civ. 4, 11 §173 ὅσον ἐβούλετο; Just., A I, 45, 1 ὅσα βούλει ἐξέταζε).—W. πάντες (ἅπαντες) *all who* (Jos., Ant. 18, 370; Just., D. 11, 2) ἅπαντες ὅσοι *all who* **Lk 4:40; J 10:8; Ac 3:24; 5:36f.** πάντα ὅσα *everything that* (Job 1:12; GrBar 7:2; Philo, Op. M. 40; Jos., Ant. 10, 35) **Mt 7:12; 13:46; 18:25; 28:20; Mk 6:30a; 11:24; 12:44; Lk 18:12, 22.**—Even without πάντες/πάντα, ὅσοι/ὅσα has the mng. *all that* (Polyaenus 17, 15, 2; Jos., Ant. 12, 399; Just., D. 26, 1; 87, 4) οἱ πιστοὶ ὅσοι συνῆλθαν τῷ Πέτρῳ *all the believers who came with Peter* **Ac 10:45.** ἱμάτια ὅσα *all the garments that* **9:39.** ὅσα κακὰ ἐποίησεν *all the harm that he has done* vs. **13.** ὅσα εἶδες παράδοξα GJs 20:4. ὅσοι . . . , αὐτοῖς *all who . . . , to them* **J 1:12.** ὅσοι . . . , ἐπ' αὐτούς **Gal 6:16.** ὅσοι . . . , οὗτοι *all who . . . , (these)* (Herm. Wr. 4, 4) **Ro 8:14; Gal 6:12.** ὅσα . . . , ταῦτα **Phil 4:8** (for ὅσα repeated six times cp. Liban., Or. 20 p. 443, 1, where ὅσοι is repeated three times. Also Appian, Liby. 117 §554 ὅσα περιττὰ καὶ μάταια καὶ τρυφερὰ ἦν). W. οὗτοι preceding **Hb 2:15.**—Abs. ὅσοι (cp. Pla., Rep. 3, 415a) *all those who* **Mt 14:36; Mk 3:10; Ac 4:6, 34; 13:48; Ro 2:12ab; 6:3 al.** ὅσα *everything that, whatever* **Mt 17:12; Mk 3:8; 5:19f; 9:13; 10:21; Lk 4:23; 8:39ab; Ac 14:27; 2 Ti 1:18 al.** W. ἄν (ἐάν) making the expr. more general *all those who, whoever,* lit. *as many as ever* (pap, LXX) ὅσοι w. ind. foll. **Mk 6:56;** w. subjunctive foll. **Mt 22:9; Lk 9:5; Ac 2:39.** ὅσα ἐάν (PGM 12, 71 ὅσα ἐὰν θέλω; Mel., P. 35, 237 πάντα ὅσα ἐὰν γίνεται) **Mt 18:18ab,** or ἄν **J 11:22.** Likew. πάντα ὅσα ἐάν (or ἄν) w. subj. foll. **Mt 7:12; 21:22; 23:3** (s. on this HGrimme, BZ 23, '35, 171–79); **Ac 3:22.**

❸ **pert. to degree of correlative extent:** ὅσον . . . , μᾶλλον περισσότερον as *much as . . . , so much the more* **Mk 7:36;** cp. Hs 9, 1, 8. ὅσον . . . , πλειόνως *the more . . . , the more* IEph 6:1. πλείονος . . . , καθ' ὅσον πλείονα as *much more . . . as* **Hb 3:3.** καθ' ὅσον . . . , κατὰ τοσοῦτο *to the degree that . . . , to the same degree* **7:20, 22.** καθ' ὅσον . . . , οὕτως *just as . . . , so* **9:27f.** τοσούτῳ . . . , ὅσῳ *(by) as much . . . , as* **1:4.** τοσούτῳ μᾶλλον, ὅσῳ *all the more, as* **10:25** (s. τοσοῦτος 5). τοσοῦτόν με ὠφελεῖν . . . , ὅσον Papias (2:4). Without τοσούτῳ *to the degree that* (Polyb. 4, 42, 5; Plut., Alex. M. 5, 5) **Hb 8:6.** ὅσα . . . τοσοῦτον *to the degree that . . . to the same degree* **Rv 18:7.** ὅσον *as far as* B 19:8; D 12:2. On ἐφ' ὅσον s. ἐπί 13 and 18cβ.—DELG. M-M.

ὅσπερ s. ὅς 1jε.—M-M.

ὀστέον, ου (Hom. et al., and again in Hellenistic times, e.g. Plut., Pyrrh. 3, 6; PsSol; TestSol 18:35 [cp. PVindobBosw]) pl. ὀστέα (SIG 624, 7; Just., A I, 19, 1.—**Lk 24:39**); gen. ὀστέων (Soph., Trach. 769; Pla., Phd. 47, 98cd; Dionys. Hal. 13, 4, 4; Jos., Bell. 6, 304; Tat.).—**Mt 23:27; Hb 11:22; Eph 5:30 v.l.;** 1 Cl 6:3b (Gen 2:23); IRo 5:3 and contracted **ὀστοῦν, οῦ, τό** (Att.) **J 19:36** (Ex 12:46; Num 9:12); 1 Cl 6:3a (Gen 2:23). Pl. ὀστᾶ (Diod. S. 22, 12; Epict. 4, 7, 32; OGI 599, 1; PLond III, 1170 verso, 486 p. 204 [258/59 AD]; PGM 5, 460; PsSol; TestSol 18:11 P; TestJob, Test12Patr; JosAs ch. 16 and 29 cod. A; Jos., Ant. 5, 125; 8, 232; Just., D. 103, 8 ὀστῶν; Mel., P. 12, 81) 1 Cl 18:8 (Ps 50:10); 25:3; MPol 18:2 (s. B-D-F §45; W-S. §8, 7; Mlt-H. 121). The LXX uses the contracted forms in nom. and acc., the uncontracted in gen. and dat. (Thackeray 144) ***bone;*** of the above-mentioned places the following are of interest in respect to content: σὰρξ καὶ ὀστέα *flesh and bone* **Lk 24:39; Eph 5:30 v.l.** (Od. 11, 219; Epict. 4, 7, 32 οὐ σὰρξ οὐδ' ὀστᾶ; Gen 29:14; Judg 9:2; 2 Km 5:1; Mi 3:2; Just., A I, 19, 1). σκορπισμοὶ ὀστέων *scattering(s) of bones* (in connection w. violent destruction of the human body) IRo 5:3 (influenced by Ps 21:15). ὀστᾶ τεταπεινωμένα *battered bones* 1 Cl 18:8 (Ps 50:10). τὰ Ἐλισαίου ὀστά AcPlCor 2:32.—B. 207. DELG. M-M.

ὅστις, ἥτις, ὅ τι (Hom.+.—On the orthography of ὅ τι s. W-S. §5, 6; Mlt-H. 179); in our lit. as well as in the pap occurring usu. in the nom.

❶ **any person, *whoever, every one who,*** in a generalizing sense:—ⓐ w. pres. ind. foll. **Mt 5:39; 13:12ab; Mk 4:20; 8:34 v.l.; Lk 14:27; Gal 5:4.** Pleonastically πᾶς ὅστις **Mt 7:24.**

ⓑ w. the aor. ind. **Ro 11:4; Rv 1:7; 20:4.** πᾶς ὅστις **Mt 19:29.**

ⓒ w. fut. ind. **Mt 5:41; 18:4; 23:12ab;** πᾶς ὅστις **10:32.**

ⓓ w. aor. subj. (ApcSed 16:5) **Mt 10:33 v.l.; Js 2:10.** But s. on this B-D-F §380, 4; Rob. 959; Kühner-G. II 426, 1.

ⓔ w. ἄν (ἐάν), whereby the indefiniteness of the expr. is heightened:

α. w. the pres. subj. **J 2:5; 1 Cor 16:2; Gal 5:10; Col 3:17** (πᾶν ὅ τι ἐάν).

β. w. the aor. subj. **Mt 10:33** (s. d above); **12:50; Mk 6:23; Lk 10:35; J 14:13; 15:16; Ac 3:23.**

❷ **undetermined person belonging to a class or having a status, *who, one who*—ⓐ** to indicate that persons (or things) belong to a certain class *(such a one) who* ἡγούμενος, ὅστις ποιμανεῖ *a leader who will shepherd* **Mt 2:6.** εὐνοῦχοι οἵτινες **19:12abc;** γεωργοὶ οἵτινες **21:41.** παρθένοι, αἵτινες **25:1.** τινὲς τῶν ὧδε ἑστώτων, οἵτινες **16:28; Mk 9:1.** προφήτας, οἵτινες τὴν ἀπλανῆ θεοσέβειαν ἐκήρυσσον *prophets who proclaimed the correct devotion to God* AcPlCor 2:10.

ⓑ to emphasize a characteristic quality, by which a preceding statement is to be confirmed *who (to be sure, by his very nature), in so far as* προσέχετε ἀπὸ τῶν ψευδοπροφητῶν οἵτινες ἔρχονται ἐν ἐνδύμασι προβάτων *beware of the false prophets, who come in sheep's clothing* **Mt 7:15.** βαπτισθῆναι τούτους οἵτινες τὸ πνεῦμα ἔλαβον *who (indeed)* **Ac 10:47.** οἵτινες ἐδέξαντο τὸν λόγον *in so far as they received the* *word* **17:11.** οἵτινες μετήλλαξαν *since indeed they had exchanged* **Ro 1:25;** cp. vs. **32; 2:15; 6:2.** ἀσπάσασθε Μαρίαν ἥτις *remember me to Mary, who certainly* **16:6;** cp. vss. **4, 7, 12.** ψευδαδέλφους, οἵτινες παρεισῆλθον *bogus members, the kind who sneaked in* **Gal 2:4.** Cp. **Phil 2:20; Eph 4:19; 1 Ti 1:4; Tit 1:11** al. in Paul (B-D-F §293, 4; Rob. 728); **Hb 8:5; 10:11; 13:7;** AcPlCor 2:19, 25 (condemnation of gnostics, with samples of their positions); 2:21 (an urgent warning to avoid them). Sim. Ἀβραάμ, ὅστις ἀπέθανεν *who died, as you know* **J 8:53.** φονεῖς ἐγένεσθε, οἵτινες ἐλάβετε . . . *who, to be sure, received* . . . **Ac 7:53.** σαρκικαὶ ἐπιθυμίαι, αἵτινες στρατεύονται κατὰ τῆς ψυχῆς **1 Pt 2:11.** οἵτινες οὐκ ἔγνωσαν *who, to be sure, have not learned* **Rv 2:24.**—Yet many of the passages already mentioned may be classed under the following head (3), and some that are classed there may fit better in this one (2).

❸ Quite oft. ὅστις takes the place of the simple rel. ὅς, ἥ, ὅ; this occurs occasionally in ancient Gk. usage (s. Hdt. 4, 8, 1 al.; Thu. 6, 3, 1; Demosth. 38, 6; 17; Kühner-G. II 399f; Schwyzer II 643 lit.), but more freq. in later Gk. (W-S. §24, 14d; B-D-F §293; Mlt. 91f; Rdm.[2] 75; 77; 226; Psaltes, Grammatik [Byz.] 198; POxy 110, 3; PFay 108, 7 [both II AD]; Mayser II/3, 57. On the LXX s. Thackeray 192; TestJob 47:1; ParJer 7:8; Just., D. 88, 1; Tat. 41, 1), esp. in Luke's writings: to explain a word or a thing εἰς πόλιν Δαυὶδ ἥτις καλεῖται Βηθλέεμ **Lk 2:4** (Hdt. 2, 99 πόλιν ἥτις νῦν Μέμφις καλέεται). τὴν χώραν τ. Γερασ. ἥτις ἐστὶν ἀντιπέρα τ. Γαλιλαίας **8:26.** ἄνδρες δύο . . . οἵτινες ἦσαν Μωϋσῆς κ. Ἠλίας **9:30.** Cp. **12:1; Ac 16:12; Hb 9:2, 9; Rv 11:8.** τῇ δὲ ἐπαύριον ἥτις ἐστὶν μετὰ τὴν παρασκευήν **Mt 27:62** (POxy 110, 3 αὔριον ἥτις ἐστὶν ιε').τὸν Βαραββᾶν ὅστις ἦν . . . βληθεὶς ἐν τῇ φυλακῇ **Lk 23:19.** μετὰ τῶν στασιαστῶν δεδεμένος οἵτινες . . . φόνον πεποιήκεισαν **Mk 15:7.** οἰκοδεσπότης ὅστις ἐφύτευσεν ἀμπελῶνα **Mt 21:33.** οἰκοδεσπότης ὅστις ἐξῆλθεν **20:1.** Cp. **27:55; Lk 7:39; 8:43; Ac 8:15; 11:20, 28; 12:10; 13:43; 17:10; 21:4; 23:14, 21, 33; 24:1; 28:18; 2 Ti 2:18.** βλέπειν τὴν φωνὴν ἥτις ἐλάλει **Rv 1:12.** τὴν γυναῖκα ἥτις ἔτεκεν **12:13.**

❹ The use of ὅ τι as an interrogative term in the NT is complicated by textual variants (s. PKatz, TLZ 82, '57, 114; 83, '58, 318; B-D-F §300).

ⓐ In an indir. quest. (Just., D. 5, 1; 23, 2 λαληθήσεταί σοι ὅ τί σε δεῖ ποιεῖν **Ac 9:6** is well attested, but was rejected by Blass (s. B-D-F §300, 1), though not by Rob. 730f.

ⓑ As dir. quest. (also written ὅτι in scriptio continua: s. the vv.ll., orig. prob. glosses marking the question, Ath. 34, 1 ὅτι ἂν εἴποιμι τὰ ἀπόρρητα; For LXX s. B-D-F §300, 2) ὅτι οὗτος οὕτως λαλεῖ; *why does this man/fellow speak this way?* **Mk 2:7 v.l.** ὅτι μετὰ τῶν τελωνῶν . . . ἐσθίει; *why does (Jesus) eat with tax-collectors?* **Mk 2:16b** (vv.ll. τί ὅτι, διὰ τί or διατί); **9:11a, 28;** ὅτι δὲ τὸ ἔριον ἐπὶ τὸ ξύλον; *why the wool on the wood?* B 8:5; ὅτι οὖν . . . πάντες οὐ μετενόσαν; *why, then, . . . did they not all repent?* Hs 8, 6, 2 (on debate relating to these pass. s. B-D-F §300, 2; s. also Field, Notes 33; Mlt-Turner 49; MBlack, An Aramaic Approach[3], '67, 119–212.—ὅτι='why' in indir. questions Thu. 1, 90, 5; Jos., Ant. 6, 236; 12, 213; Gen 18:13 A; Black, 119, cites Turner, JTS 27, 1925, 58ff in support of this usage in Mk 8:16f; 14:60 v.l.; cp. B-D-F §300, 2).

❺ On τὴν ἀρχὴν ὅ τι καὶ λαλῶ ὑμῖν **J 8:25** s. ἀρχή 1a, end.—B-D-F §300, 2; Rob. 730.

❻ The prepositional phrases ἀφ' ὅτου (Diod. S. 2, 31, 9) **Lk 13:25** D, ἕως ὅτου (s. ἕως 1bβב; PGen 56, 19), and μέχρις ὅτου (ἐξ ὅτου 'ever since' Just., D. 52, 3; s. μέχρι 2b) are fixed expressions.—HCadbury, The Relative Pronouns in Acts and Elsewhere: JBL 42, 1923, 150ff; Rydbeck, 98–118.—M-M.

ὀστράκινος, η, ον (ὄστρακον; Hippocr. et al.; PLond III, 1177, 75; 92 p. 183 [113 AD]; POxy 1648, 63; LXX; En 99:7; GrBar 3:7) ***made of earth/clay*** used w. σκεῦος (PLond I, 77, 22 p. 233 [VIII AD]; Lev 6:21; 11:33 al.; cp. Epict. 3, 9, 18) *earthen(ware) vessels* (w. those made of other materials) **2 Ti 2:20.** In imagery, denoting breakableness ἔχειν τὸν θησαυρὸν ἐν ὀσ. σκεύεσιν **2 Cor 4:7** (cp. Artem. 5, 25 εἶναι ἐν ὀστρακίνῳ σκεύει).—Of cultic images made of clay θεοὶ . . . ὀστράκινοι Dg 2:7 (SibOr 5, 495; cp. En 99:7).—M-M.

ὄστρακον, ου, τό (Hom. Hymns et al.; SIG 1168, 82; 86 [IV BC]; POxy 234 II, 3; 1450, 4; O. Wilck II, 1152, 5; LXX; JosAs 13:8; Philo, Somn. 2, 57; Ar. 4, 3) ***baked clay, pottery*** of polytheists' deities ὁ δὲ ὄστρακον *another is a piece of pottery* Dg 2:2. Collectively ὄσ. λεπτόν *little pieces of broken pottery* Hs 9, 10, 1 (difft. EGoodspeed, JBL 73, '54, 85f).—DELG. M-M s.v. ὀστράκινος.

ὄσφρησις, εως, ἡ ***sense of smell*** (fr. ὀσφραίνομαι 'catch scent of, smell'; Pla., Phd. 111b al.; Philo; TestReub 2:5) or organ of smell, ***nose*** (sing. Ptolem., Apotel. 3, 15, 5; M. Ant 10, 35, 2 w, ἀκοή='ear'; Diog. L. 6, 39 as a saying of Diogenes the Cynic; PRyl. 63, 5 [III AD] γλῶσσα ὄσφρησις ἀκοή) **1 Cor 12:17** (ἀκοή 3).—B. 1022f. DELG s.v. ὀσφραίνομαι. M-M.

ὀσφῦς (nom. not used in NT; acc. -ύν all edd. On the accent s. PKatz, TLZ 83, '58, 315: ὀσφῦν; B-D-F §13; Mlt-H. 141f) **ύος, ἡ** (Aeschyl., Hdt.+; ins, pap, LXX; PsSol 8:4; TestSol 1, 12 D; TestJob; TestNapht 2:8; JosAs; GrBar 2:3; Jos., Ant. 8, 217=3 Km 12:10).

❶ **the place where a belt or girdle is worn, *waist, loins*** (4 Km 1:8) **Mt 3:4; Mk 1:6.** Since the garment was worn ungirded about the house, girding denotes preparation for activity, esp. for a journey; freq. used in imagery: περιζώννυσθαι τὴν ὀσ. *have a belt around one's waist* (Jer 1:17) **Eph 6:14;** cp. **Lk 12:35** (cp. Ex 12:11). Also ἀναζώννυσθαι τὰς ὀσ. **1 Pt 1:13,** where the gen. τῆς διανοίας shows the extraordinary imagistic use of the expr. The gen. is lacking Pol 2:1.

❷ **the place of the reproductive organs, *the loins*** in line w. the Hebr. phrase יָצָא מֵחֲלָצֵי פ׳ (cp. Gen 35:11; 2 Ch 6:9) as: ἐξέρχεσθαι ἐκ τῆς ὀσ. τινός *come forth from someone's loins* = *be someone's son* or *descendants* **Hb 7:5.** ἐν τῇ ὀσ. τινὸς εἶναι vs. **10.** καρπὸς τῆς ὀσ. τινός *the fruit of someone's loins* = *someone's descendants* **Ac 2:30;** AcPl Ha 8, 14 (ἰσχύος Ox 1602 recto, 12f; cp. Ps 131:11 v.l. [ARahlfs, Psalmi cum Odis '31].—καρπὸς ὀσφύος also Theodor. Prodr. 6, 370 H. Cp. Psellus p. 61, 33 τῆς βασιλείου ὀσφύος=of royal descent). The loins are prob. also thought of as an inmost source of power in αἱ ὀσ. ὑμῶν μὴ ἐκλυέσθωσαν *do not let your loins become powerless* D 16:1 (cp. TestNapht 2:8 ὀσφ. εἰς ἰσχύν).—DELG. M-M. TW.

ὅταν temporal particle (since Hom. who, however, always separates it [ὅτ' ἄν]; ins, pap, LXX, pseudepigr., Philo, Joseph., apolog.)

❶ **pert. to an action that is conditional, possible, and, in many instances, repeated, *at the time that, whenever, when***

ⓐ w. the subj., in which case ὅτ. oft. approaches the mng. of ἐάν, since the time-reference also indicates the conditions under which the action of the main clause takes place (Kühner-G. II 447f). **1J 2:28** the mss. vary betw. ὅτ. and ἐάν (as e.g. also Judg 6:3)

α. w. the pres. subj., when the action of the subordinate clause is contemporaneous w. that of the main clause. Usually of (regularly) repeated action *whenever, as often as, every time that* (PFay 109, 1 ὅταν θέλῃς='every time that you want'; likew. POxy 1676, 26; Just., D. 128, 3 ὅταν βούληται. Cp. ἄν I, cα) ὅταν ποιῇς ἐλεημοσύνην **Mt 6:2;** cp. **5f, 16; 10:23; Mk 13:11.** ὅταν θέλητε **14:7.—Lk 12:11; 14:12f** al. W. τότε foll. *whenever . . . , then* (Hero Alex. III p. 214, 5) ὅταν ἀσθενῶ, τότε δυνατός εἰμι **2 Cor 12:10.** Also without the idea of repetition *when* **1 Th 5:3.**—Looking back upon a preceding time-reference ἕως τῆς ἡμέρας ἐκείνης ὅταν πίνω **Mt 26:29; Mk 14:25.** Introducing an epexegetical statement **1J 5:2** (B-D-F §394).

β. w. the aor. subj., when the action of the subordinate clause precedes that of the main clause (IMaronIsis 9 [ὅτ]αν οἷς ἔβλεψα τὸν ἥλιον='whenever with what [eyes] I have seen the sun' [corrected restoration of editio princeps]; PLips 104, 16 [96/95 BC]; PRyl 233, 2; Is 28:19; 57:13; Ath. 1, 4): ὅταν ὀνειδίσωσιν *when they (have) revile(d)* **Mt 5:11.** Cp. **12:43** (s. KBeyer, Semitische Syntax im NT, '62, 285f); **13:32; 23:15; 24:32f; Mk 4:15f, 31f; 13:28; Lk 6:22, 26** and oft. W. τότε foll. *when* (someth. has happened), *then* (Sir 18:7; Jos., Bell. 6, 287, Ant. 10, 213; TestJob 38:3; ApcEsdr 3:13 p. 27, 24) **Mt 24:15f; 25:31; Mk 13:14; Lk 5:35** (different in the parallels **Mt 9:15; Mk 2:20,** where ἡμέραι ὅταν *days when* belong together and τότε is connected w. καί); **Lk 21:20; J 8:28; 1 Cor 15:28, 54; Col 3:4.**

ⓑ w. the ind. (on this late development s. B-D-F §382, 4; Rob. 972f; also Schwyzer II 304).

α. w. fut. ind. (1 Km 10:7; SibOr 4, 70; 11, 219) *when* 2 Cl 12:2 (GEg 252, 57 has the aor. subj. in the corresponding pass.); 17:6; B 15:5 (s. Reinhold 108 and 2 below); **Lk 13:28 v.l.** (for ὄψησθε). *Whenever* **Rv 4:9** (Mussies 343–47).

β. w. pres. ind. (Strabo 12, 27 p. 555 ὅταν δείκνυται; Ps.-Lucian, Philop. 26; PHamb 70, 19 ὅταν τὸν λόγον δίδομεν; Ps 47:4 v.l. [ARahlfs, Psalmi cum Odis '31]; Philo, Poster. Cai. 15 v.l.—ADebrunner, Glotta 11, 1920, 26f) **Mk 11:25** (in addition to στήκετε, στήκητε and στῆτε are also found in the mss.). As a v.l. in **Lk 11:2** and **J 7:27.**

γ. w. impf. ind. (Polyb. 4, 32, 5f ὅταν . . . ἦσαν; ins in Ramsay, CB I/2, 477 no. 343, 8; Gen 38:9; I Km 17:34; Ps 119:7; Da 3:7 Theod. v.l.; ParJer 2:3) ὅταν αὐτὸν ἐθεώρουν **Mk 3:11.**

δ. w. aor. ind., in place of ὅτε *when* (Ex 16:3; Ps 118:32; GrBar 4:11; 8:1; ApcMos 17:37) **Rv 8:1** (v.l. ὅτε); *whenever* (Ex 17:11; Num 11:9) ὅταν ὀψὲ ἐγένετο, ἐξεπορεύοντο ἔξω τῆς πόλεως **Mk 11:19** (s. B-D-F §367; difft. Mlt. 248); Hs 9, 4, 5; 9, 17, 3.

ε. w. the plpf. ind. *as soon as* Hs 9, 1, 6.

❷ marker of a point of time simultaneous with an action and functioning with causal force, *inasmuch as* ὅταν βλέπετε *since you see* B 4:14 (s. Reinhold 108f).—M-M.

ὅτε (Hom.+) temporal particle.**—❶ marker of a point of time that coincides with another point of time, *when***

ⓐ as a conjunction, w. the ind.**—α.** pres. (ApcSed 16:2) **Mk 11:1** (here the historical present).

β. impf. **Mk 14:12; Ac 12:6; 22:20.**

γ. predom. w. the aor. (B-D-F §382, 1; Rob. 971) **Mt 9:25; 13:48; 21:34; Mk 1:32; 4:10; Lk 2:21, 42; 15:30; J 1:19; 2:22; Ac 1:13; 8:39; Gal 1:15; 2:11; Tit 3:4; Hb 7:10.** ὅτε ἐπιστεύσαμεν *when we first believed* **Ro 13:11** al.; GJs 12:3; 25:1.—W. τότε foll. (ApcMos 19; Jos., C. Ap. 1, 127; w. τότε preceding, D. 141, 3) **Mt 13:26; 21:1; J 12:16.** Mt not infreq. has the transitional formula καὶ ἐγένετο ὅτε in narrative passages *and (it came about that) when . . .* (4 Km 14:5) **7:28; 11:1; 13:53; 19:1; 26:1.** ἀφότε (cp. 2 Esdr 5:12 ἀφ' ὅτε) Hs 8, 6, *ever since.* μέχρι ὅτε *until* GJs 10:2.

δ. perf. ὅτε γέγονα ἀνήρ *when I became a man* **1 Cor 13:11b.**

ⓑ as a substitute for a relative pron. after a noun denoting time

α. pres. ind. ἔρχεται νὺξ ὅτε οὐδεὶς δύναται ἐργάζεσθαι **J 9:4.**

β. fut. (Just., D. 14, 8; 40, 2) ἐλεύσονται ἡμέραι ὅτε ἐπιθυμήσετε *(the) days will come, in which you will desire* **Lk 17:22.** ἐν ἡμέρᾳ ὅτε κρινεῖ ὁ θεός **Ro 2:16** ἔρχεται ὥρα, ὅτε . . . προσκυνήσετε **J 4:21.** Cp. vs. **23; 5:25; 16:25.** καιρὸς ὅτε **2 Ti 4:3.**

γ. w. the aor. subj. (ὅτε w. subj. Hom.+ in epic [SibOr 8, 50] and lyric poetry; but also Vett. Val. 106, 36 ὅτε ἄρξηται; TestAbr A 9 p. 87, 5 [Stone p. 22] ὅτε ἴδω ταῦτα, τότε . . .; 11 p. 89, 24) ἕως ἥξει ὅτε εἴπητε *until the time comes when you say* **Lk 13:35** (text uncertain; s. B-D-F §382, 2; Rob. 971f).

❷ marker of a period of time coextensive with another period of time, *as long as, while* Mk 15:41; J 21:18; Ro 6:20; 7:5; 1 Cor 12:2; 13:11a; Hb 9:17; Hv 3, 6, 7 al.—DELG. M-M.

ὁτέ adv. (Hom. et al.; ins) **marker of a point of time that coincides w. another point of time, anticipating a correlative, *at one point, on one occasion.*** This use is ordinarily found in the structure ὁτὲ μὲν . . . ὁτὲ δὲ . . . 'now' . . . 'now' . . . (Aristot., Pol. 2, 2, 16; Parthenius 27, 2; Dio Chrys. 50 [67], 5; Polyaenus 5, 22, 4; SIG 679, 83f), but ὁτὲ μὲν . . . *at one point* B 2:4 has as its correlative λέγει δὲ πάλιν (for variations in earlier Gk. s. L-S-J-M s.v. ὅτε C; on the text s. Hdb, ad loc.).

ὅτι (Hom.+) conjunction (B-D-F §396f; 408; 416; 470, 1 al.; Rob. 1032–36, al. [s. index]; HPernot, Études sur la langue des Évang. 1927, 41ff) originally the neuter of ὅστις.

❶ marker of narrative or discourse content, direct or indirect, *that.* Used after verbs that denote mental or sense perception, or the transmission of such perception, or an act of the mind, to indicate the content of what is said, etc.

ⓐ after verbs of saying, indicating, etc.: ἀπαγγέλλω, ἀποκρίνομαι, δείκνυμι, δῆλόν (ἐστιν), διδάσκω, εἶπον, ἐμφανίζω, λέγω, μαρτυρέω, ὁμολογέω, φημί etc.; s. the entries in question. Likew. after verbs of swearing, affirming and corresponding formulae: μαρτύρομαι **Ac 20:26; Gal 5:3.** μάρτυρα τὸν θεὸν ἐπικαλοῦμαι **2 Cor 1:23.** ὀμνύω **Rv 10:6.** Cp. the sim. exprs. πιστὸς ὁ θεός **2 Cor 1:18.** ἰδοὺ ἐνώπιον τοῦ θεοῦ **Gal 1:20.—2 Cor 11:10.** Cp. also φάσις . . . ὅτι **Ac 21:31.** αἱ γραφαὶ ὅτι *the Scriptures* (which state) *that* **Mt 26:54.**—On **1J 2:12–14** s. BNoack, NTS 6, '60, 236–41.

ⓑ after verbs that denote sense perception ἀκούω, θεάομαι, θεωρέω (q.v. 1); s. these entries.

ⓒ after verbs that denote mental perception ἀγνοέω, ἀναγινώσκω, βλέπω (perceive), γινώσκω, γνωστόν ἐστιν, ἐπιγινώσκω, ἐπίσταμαι, θεωρέω (q.v. 2a), καταλαμβάνω, μιμνήσκομαι, μνημονεύω, νοέω, οἶδα, ὁράω (q.v. A4a), συνίημι, ὑπομιμνήσκω; s. these entries. In **Gal 1:11** ὅτι comes later in the sentence so as to permit the emphatic portion of the subordinate clause to come to the forefront.

ⓓ after verbs of thinking, judging, believing, hoping: δοκέω (q.v. 1d), ἐλπίζω (q.v. 2), κρίνω, λογίζομαι, νομίζω (q.v. 2), οἶμαι, πέπεισμαι, πέποιθα, πιστεύω (q.v. 1aβ), ὑπολαμβάνω; s. these entries. εἶχον τὸν Ἰωάννην ὅτι προφήτης ἦν *they held that John was a prophet* **Mk 11:32** (s. B-D-F §330; 397, 2; Rob. 1029; 1034).

ⓔ after verbs that denote an emotion and its expression ἀγανακτέω, ἐξομολογέομαι, ἐπαινέω, εὐχαριστέω, θαυμάζω, μέλει μοι, συγχαίρω, χαίρω, χάριν ἔχω τινί; s. these entries.

ⓕ Very oft. the subj. of the ὅτι-clause is drawn into the main clause, and becomes the object of the latter: ἐπεγίνωσκον αὐτοὺς ὅτι (=ὅτι αὐτοὶ) σὺν τῷ Ἰησοῦ ἦσαν **Ac 4:13.** οἴδατε τὴν οἰκίαν Στεφανᾶ ὅτι (=ὅτι ἡ οἰκία Σ.) ἐστὶν ἀπαρχή **1 Cor 16:15.** Cp. **Mt 25:24; Mk 12:34; J 8:54; 9:8; Ac 3:10; 1 Cor 3:20** (Ps 93:11); **1 Th 2:1; Rv 17:8.** Somet. the subj. is repeated by a demonstrative pron. in the ὅτι-clause: ἐκήρυσσεν τὸν Ἰησοῦν ὅτι οὗτός ἐστιν ὁ υἱὸς τοῦ θεοῦ **Ac 9:20.**—Pass. εἰ Χριστὸς κηρύσσεται ὅτι ἐκ νεκρῶν ἐγήγερται (=εἰ κηρύσσεται ὅτι Χρ. ἐκ νεκ. ἐγ.) **1 Cor 15:12.**

❷ marker of explanatory clauses, *that*—ⓐ as a substitute for the epexegetical inf. (acc. w. inf.) after a preceding demonstrative (B-D-F §394; cp. Rob. 1034) αὕτη δέ ἐστιν ἡ κρίσις, ὅτι τὸ φῶς ἐλήλυθεν *the judgment consists in this, that the light has come* **J 3:19.** ἔστιν αὕτη ἡ ἀγγελία . . . , ὅτι ὁ θεὸς φῶς ἐστιν **1J 1:5.** Cp. **3:16; 4:9, 10.** ἐν τούτῳ . . . , ὅτι ἐκ τοῦ πνεύματος αὐτοῦ δέδωκεν ἡμῖν vs. **13; 5:11.** περὶ τούτου . . . ὅτι *about this . . . , that* **J 16:19.** In ἔχω κατὰ σοῦ ὅτι . . . **Rv 2:4,** ὅτι is epexegetical to a τοῦτο that remains unexpressed. Cp. vs. **6.** Of the same order is the use

ⓑ in ellipses τί ὅτι; *what* (is it) *that? why?* **Lk 2:49; Ac 5:4, 9; Mk 2:16 v.l.** (JosAs 16:5).—οὐχ ὅτι (=οὐ λέγω ὅτι) *not that, not as if* **J 6:46; 7:22; 2 Cor 1:24; 3:5; Phil 3:12; 4:11; 2Th 3:9** (so μὴ ὅτι PLond I 42, 43 p. 30 [II BC]). ἐπεὶ οὐχ ὅτι *since it is not the case that* IMg 3:2.—οὐχ οἷον ὅτι **Ro 9:6** (s. οἷος).—ὅτι alone is used for εἰς ἐκεῖνο ὅτι *with regard to the fact that, in consideration of the fact that* (Gen 40:15; Ruth 2:13) ποταπός ἐστιν οὗτος ὅτι; *what sort of person is this,* (in consideration of the fact) *that?* **Mt 8:27** (but it is prob. that in this and sim. passages the causal force of ὅτι [s. 4 below] comes to the fore). τίς ὁ λόγος οὗτος ὅτι; **Lk 4:36.** Cp. **16:3; Mk 4:41; J 2:18; 8:22; 9:17; 11:47; 16:9–11.**—ὅτι =ἐν τούτῳ ὅτι *in that* **Ro 5:8.** ὅτι =περὶ τούτου ὅτι *concerning this, that* **Mt 16:8; Mk 8:17.**—On ὅτι=*why?* (cp. Jos. Ant. 12, 213) **Mk 9:11, 28** s. ὅστις 4b.

❸ marker introducing direct discourse. In this case it is not to be rendered into English, but to be represented by quotation marks (ὅτι recitativum.—B-D-F §397, 5; 470, 1; EKieckers, IndogF 35, 1915, 21ff; Rob. 1027f. As early as Pla. [Apol. 23, 34 d.—Kühner-G. II, 366f]; Epict. 1, 9, 16; Arrian, Alex. An. 2, 12, 4; 2, 26, 4; 4, 8, 9; Philostrat., Vi. Apoll. 1, 38 p. 40; POxy 744, 11 [1 BC]; 119, 10; 1064, 5; LXX; TestAbr A 8 p. 85, 10 [Stone p. 18]; TestJob 6:7; 35:1; 36:3; ParJer 1:6; 2:7; ApcEsdr; AscIs 3:9; Jos. Ant. 11, 5; 18, 326, Vi. 55) ὑμεῖς λέγετε ὅτι 'βλασφημεῖς' ὅτι εἶπον **J 10:36.** ὁμολογήσω αὐτοῖς ὅτι 'οὐδέποτε ἔγνων ὑμᾶς' **Mt 7:23.** So after var. verbs of saying as direct discourse: **Mt 26:72–75; 27:43; Mk 1:37; 2:16; 5:28; 12:29; 13:6** (JSundwall, Om bruket av ὅτι recit. i Mk: Eranos 31, '33, 73–81; MZerwick, Untersuchgen z. Mk-Stil '37, 39–48); **Lk 1:25, 61** (PWinter, HTR 48, '55, 213–16); **4:41a; 5:26; 15:27a; J 1:20, 32; 4:17; 6:42; 16:17; Ac 5:23; 15:1; Ro 3:8** (B-D-F §470, 1; Rob. 1033; AFridrichsen, ZNW 34, '35, 306–8); **2 Th 3:10; 1J 4:20** al. Scripture quotations are also introduced in this way (Appian, Bell. Civ. 62 §260 a saying of Caesar in direct discourse is introduced by ὅτι): Μωϋσῆς ἔγραψεν ἡμῖν ὅτι 'ἐάν τινος κτλ.' **Mk 12:19.—Mt 2:23; 21:16; Lk 2:23; J 10:34; Ro 8:36; 1 Cor 14:21; Hb 11:18.**—On ὅτι foll. by the acc. and inf. in direct discourse **Lk 4:43** s. 5a below.

❹ marker of causality—ⓐ subordinating, ***because, since*** ὅτι ἑώρακάς με, πεπίστευκας **J 20:29.—Mt 2:18** (Jer 38:15); **5:3ff; 13:16; Mk 1:34; 5:9; Lk 4:41b; 6:20ff; 8:30; 10:13; 11:42ff; 13:2b; 15:27b;** perh. **18:9** (TManson, The Sayings of Jesus '54, 309); **19:17; J 1:30, 50a; 2:25; 3:18; 5:27; 9:16, 22; Ro 6:15; 1 Cor 12:15f.** On **1J 2:12–14** s. BNoack, NTS 6, '60, 236–41 (opposes causal mng.).—Used w. demonstr. and interrog. pronouns διὰ τοῦτο . . . ὅτι *for this reason . . . ,* (namely) *that* **J 8:47; 10:17; 12:39; 1J 3:1** al. διὰ τί; ὅτι . . . *why? because . . .* **Ro 9:32; 2 Cor 11:11.** χάριν τίνος; ὅτι . . . *for what reason? because . . .* **1J 3:12.** Foll. by διὰ τοῦτο *because . . . for this reason* **J 15:19.** οὐχ ὅτι . . . ἀλλ' ὅτι *not because . . . but because* **6:26; 12:6.**

ⓑ The subordination is oft. so loose that the transl. ***for*** recommends itself (B-D-F §456, 1; Rob. 962f). Naturally the line betw. the two groups cannot be drawn with certainty: **Mt 7:13; 11:29; Lk 7:47** (on this pass. and 1J 3:14 s. Schwyzer II 646, w. ref. to Il. 16, 34f: 'infer this from the fact that'); **9:12; 13:31; 16:24; J 1:16f; 9:16; 1 Cor 1:25; 4:9; 10:17; 2 Cor 4:6; 7:8, 14; 1J 3:14.**—MBlack, An Aramaic Approach[3], '67, 70ff.

❺ special uses—ⓐ ὅτι w. acc. and inf. after θεωρεῖν **Ac 27:10** (on the mingling of constructions cp. POxy 237 V, 8 δηλῶν ὅτι . . . δεῖσθαι τὸ πρᾶγμα; EpArist 125; schol. on Clem. of Alex., Protr. p. 296, 11f Stäh.—B-D-F §397, 6; Rob. 1036; Rdm.[2] 195; MArnim, De Philonis Byzantii dicendi genere, diss. Greifswald 1912, 88 [but s. on this Rdm.[2] 196, 1]). Less irregular is καὶ ὅτι w. a finite verb as the second member dependent on παρακαλεῖν after the inf. ἐμμένειν **Ac 14:22.**—S. also c, below and HCadbury, JBL 48, 1929, 412–25.

ⓑ ὡς ὅτι is found three times in Pauline letters and simply means 'that' in the later vernacular (exx. in Mlt. 212; B-D-F §396; Rob. 1033). But the subjective mng. of ὡς must be conceded for the NT, since the Vulgate renders ὡς ὅτι twice w. 'quasi' (2 Cor 11:21; 2 Th 2:2) and the third time (2 Cor 5:19) w. 'quoniam quidem': δι' ἐπιστολῆς . . . , ὡς ὅτι ἐνέστηκεν ἡ ἡμέρα τοῦ κυρίου *by a letter . . .* (of such content) *that* (in the opinion of its writer) *the day of the Lord is* (now) *here* **2 Th 2:2.** Paul says ironically: κατὰ ἀτιμίαν λέγω, ὡς ὅτι ἡμεῖς ἠσθενήκαμεν *I must confess to my shame that we have conducted ourselves as weaklings* (as I must concede when I compare my conduct w. the violent treatment you have had fr. others [vs. 20]) **2 Cor 11:21** (for the thought cp. Demosth. 18, 320: 'I confess it. I am weak, but all the more loyal than you [Aeschines] to my fellow citizens'). Likew. **5:19;** we are a new creation in Christ (vs. 17). This does not alter the fact that everything has its origin in God, who reconciled us w. himself through Christ (vs. 18), ὡς ὅτι θεὸς ἦν ἐν Χριστῷ κόσμον καταλλάσσων ἑαυτῷ *that is* (acc. to Paul's own conviction), *(that) it was God who was reconciling the world to himself in Christ.*

ⓒ consecutive ὅτι *so that* (Pel.-Leg. p. 20 τί διδοῖς τοῖς ἀμνοῖς σου ὅτι ζωὴν αἰώνιον ἔχουσιν;=what do you give your sheep so that they have eternal life? Acta Christophori p. 68, 18 Usener τοιοῦτοι γάρ εἰσιν οἱ θεοὶ ὑμῶν, ὅτι ὑπὸ γυναικὸς ἐκινήθησαν. Gen 20:9; Judg 14:3; 1 Km 20:1; 3 Km 18:9) ποῦ οὗτος μέλλει πορεύεσθαι, ὅτι ἡμεῖς οὐχ εὑρήσομεν αὐτόν; **J 7:35.** τί γέγονεν ὅτι . . . ; *what has happened, so that* (=to bring it about that) . . . ? **14:22** (so Rob. 1001; difft. Rdm.[2] 196 and B-D-F §480, 6). This is prob. also the place for οὐδὲν εἰσηνέγκαμεν εἰς τὸν κόσμον, ὅτι οὐδὲ ἐξενεγκεῖν τι δυνάμεθα *we have brought nothing into the world, so that* (as a result) *we can take nothing out of it* **1 Ti 6:7.** τί ἐστιν ἄνθρωπος, ὅτι μιμνήσκῃ αὐτοῦ; **Hb 2:6** (Ps 8:5).—DELG. M-M.

ὅτου gen. sing. masc. and neut. of ὅστις (q.v. 6).

οὗ really the gen. of ὅς, became an adv. of place (Aeschyl. et al.; ins, pap, LXX, En, EpArist, Philo, Joseph.).

❶ marker of a position in space, *where*—ⓐ of a location without ref. to an entity's movement

α. without ref. to a preceding noun οὗ . . . , ἐκεῖ *where . . . , there* **Mt 18:20; Ro 9:26** (Hos 2:1). Without ἐκεῖ IPhld 8:1.

β. mostly after a noun that denotes a locality, in place of the relative pron., *in, at,* or *on which* (Jos., Ant. 8, 349) εἰς Ναζαρά, οὗ ἦν τεθραμμένος **Lk 4:16.** Cp. vs. **17; 23:53; Ac 1:13; 2:2; 7:29; 12:12; 16:13** al.—*The place in which:* ἐπάνω οὗ ἦν τὸ παιδίον **Mt 2:9** (cp. X., An. 1, 7, 6 μέχρι οὗ διὰ καῦμα οὐ δύνανται οἰκεῖν).

ⓑ of a location as destination *where, to which* (GDI 1758, 8; 1766, 7 [both Delphi]; SIG 374, 25; Bar 2:4, 13; GrBar 10:5 [οὗπερ]; EpArist 269) εἰς πᾶσαν πόλιν . . . οὗ ἤμελλεν αὐτὸς ἔρχεσθαι *into every city where he was about to come* **Lk 10:1.** ἐπορεύθησαν . . . εἰς τὸ ὄρος οὗ ἐτάξατο αὐτοῖς ὁ Ἰησοῦς *to the mountain to which Jesus had directed them* (to go) **Mt 28:16.** εἰς τὴν κώμην οὗ ἐπορεύοντο **Lk 24:28.**—οὗ ἐάν w. the pres. subj. of future time (IG IV²/1, 68, 71; 73 [302 BC]; PSI 902, 4 [I AD]) ἄπειμι οὗ ἐὰν βούλησθε 1 Cl 54:2. οὗ ἐὰν πορεύωμαι **1 Cor 16:6.**

❷ **marker of situation or set of circumstances,** someth. like ***(in a situation) where*** fig. ext. of 1 (Jos., Ant. 2, 272) οὗ δὲ οὐκ ἔστιν νόμος οὐδὲ παράβασις *where no law exists, there is no transgression, either* **Ro 4:15.** Cp. **5:20.** οὗ δὲ τὸ πνεῦμα κυρίου ἐλευθερία **2 Cor 3:17.**—M-M.

οὐ (Hom.+; s. Schwyzer II 591–94) objective (as opp. to subjective μή) negative adv., denying the reality of an alleged fact; in the NT used w. the ind. (μή serves as the neg. for the other moods, including inf. and ptc.—w. certain exceptions, which will be discussed below. S. B-D-F §426; Rob. 1168f; Mlt-Turner 281f). Before vowels w. the smooth breathing it takes the form οὐκ; before those w. the rough breathing it is οὐχ; in the mss. this rule is freq. disregarded (W-S. §5, 10bc; B-D-F §14; Rob. 224). On its use s. B-D-F §426–33; Rdm.² p. 210ff; Rob. 1155–66.

❶ **a negative response to a question or statement, as accented form,** οὔ: ***no*** **Mt 13:29** (Schwyzer II 596f); **J 1:21; 7:12; 21:5.** ἤτω ὑμῶν τὸ οὒ οὔ *let your 'no' be 'no'* **Js 5:12.** Doubled for emphasis (s. ναί e.—οὒ οὔ Nicetas Eugen. 5, 76 H. Likew. μὴ μή=no, no! [Herodas 3, 71; Meleager, I BC, in Anth. Pal. 12, 80, 3; Psellus p. 268, 15 μὴ μὴ μάγιστρε]) **Mt 5:37; 2 Cor 1:17ff.** On οὐ μὲν οὖν s. οὐμενοῦν.

❷ **marker of negative propositions,** ***not***—ⓐ used to negative single words or clauses (Ar. 13, 7 μῦθοί εἰσι καὶ οὐκ ἄλλο τι; Just., A II, 2, 2 οὐ σωφρόνως; Tat. 5, 1 οὐ κατὰ ἀποκοπήν;—as earlier Gk.: Hom. et al.; s. Kühner-G. II, 182; Schwyzer II 593f)

α. οὐ πᾶς *not every one* **Mt 7:21.** οὐ πάντες **19:11; Ro 9:6; 10:16.** πάντες οὐ κοιμηθησόμεθα *we shall not all fall asleep* **1 Cor 15:51** (s. JBurn, ET, 1926, 236f; POppenheim, TQ 112, '31, 92–135; AVaccari, Biblica 13, '32, 73–76; B-D-F §433, 2; Rob. 753). Likew. transposed διατί πάντες οὐ μετενόησαν; *why have not all repented?* Hs 8, 6, 2. οὐ πᾶσα σάρξ **1 Cor 15:39.** οὐ πάντως **Ro 3:9; 1 Cor 5:10.**—καλέσω τὸν οὐ λαόν μου λαόν μου *those who were not my people I will call my people* **Ro 9:25a** (Hos 2:25b); cp. **1 Pt 2:10.** οὐκ ἔθνος *no nation at all* **Ro 10:19** (Dt 32:21).

β. freq. in litotes (cp. Lysias 13, 62 εἰ μὲν οὐ πολλοὶ ἦσαν Tat. 3, 2) οὐ πολλοί, πολλαί **J 2:12; Ac 1:5** (οὐ μετὰ πολλὰς ἡμέρας = μετ' οὐ πολλ. ἡμ.; cp. οὐκ ἐξ ὄντων =ἐξ οὐκ ὄντων 2 Macc 7:28). οὐκ ὀλίγος, ὀλίγη, ὀλίγοι, ὀλίγαι **Ac 17:4, 12; 19:23f; 27:20.** οὐκ ἄσημος **21:39.** οὐχ ἁγνῶς **Phil 1:17.** οὐ μετρίως **Ac 20:12.** οὐκ ἐκ μέτρου **J 3:34.** μετ' οὐ πολύ *soon (afterward)* **Ac 27:14** S. also δ below.

γ. *not* in a contrast τῷ κυρίῳ καὶ οὐκ ἀνθρώποις **Col 3:23.** τρέχω ὡς οὐκ ἀδήλως **1 Cor 9:26.**

δ. as a periphrasis for some concepts expressed by verbs: οὐκ ἀγνοεῖν *know quite well* **2 Cor 2:11.** οὐκ ἐᾶν *prevent* **Ac 16:7** (cp. Il. 2, 132); **19:30.** οὐκ ἔχειν *be in need* **Mt 13:12; Mk 4:25** (on these two pass. s. Schwyzer II 593, w. ref. to Kühner-G. II 189–92; contrast the use of μή in Lk 8:18). οὐ θέλειν *refuse* **2 Th 3:10.** οὐ πταίειν **Js 3:2.** οὐχ ὑπακούειν *be disobedient* **2 Th 3:14.** οὐ φιλεῖν *be unfriendly to, disesteem* **1 Cor 16:22.**

ⓑ used sometimes w. the ptc. From a above are derived the points under which this is done, contrary to the rule given at beg. of entry. In addition, it is prob. that in individual cases earlier literary influence is still at work (for earlier Gk. s. Kühner-G. II 198–203. μή suggests contingency).—B-D-F §430; Mlt. 231f (w. pap exx.; cp. Just., A I, 33, 4 οὐ συνουσιασθεῖσαν τὴν παρθένον; 67, 5 τοῖς οὐ παροῦσι al.); Rdm.² 212; Mlt-Turner 284f.

α. to negative a single concept: πράγματα οὐ βλεπόμενα *things not seen* **Hb 11:1.** οὐχ ὁ τυχών *extraordinary* **Ac 19:11; 28:2** (cp. Com. Att. Fgm. III 442 no. 178 οὐδὲ τοῖς τυχοῦσι).θλιβόμενοι ἀλλ', οὐ στενοχωρούμενοι **2 Cor 4:8;** cp. vs. **9.**

β. in strong emphasis or contrast: ἄνθρωπον οὐκ ἐνδεδυμένον ἔνδυμα γάμου (emphasizing the fact that his dress was improper) **Mt 22:11.** οὐ προσδεξάμενοι τὴν ἀπολύτρωσιν (emphasizing the great heroism of their act) **Hb 11:35.** οὐ βλέπων **Lk 6:42.** οὐκ ἰδόντες **1 Pt 1:8.** οὐκ ὄντος αὐτῷ τέκνου **Ac 7:5.**—Contrast: **Ac 28:19.** τότε μὲν οὐκ εἰδότες θεὸν . . . νῦν δέ **Gal 4:8.** καὶ οὐ introducing a contrast is also used w. the ptc. καὶ οὐκ ἐν σαρκὶ πεποιθότες **Phil 3:3.** καὶ οὐ κρατῶν **Col 2:19.** ὁ μισθωτὸς καὶ οὐκ ὢν ποιμήν **J 10:12.**

γ. In quotations fr. the LXX in the NT we notice the tendency of the OT translators regularly to render לֹא w. the ptc. by οὐ: ἡ οὐ τίκτουσα, ἡ οὐκ ὠδίνουσα **Gal 4:27** (Is 54:1). τὴν οὐκ ἠγαπημένην **Ro 9:25b** (Hos 2:25a). οἱ οὐκ ἠλεημένοι **1 Pt 2:10** (Hos 1:6).

δ. τὰ οὐκ ἀνήκοντα **Eph 5:4 v.l.** is presumably a mingling of τὰ μὴ ἀνήκοντα and (the rdg. in the text itself) ἃ οὐκ ἀνῆκεν (as early as P⁴⁶).

ⓒ in main clauses—α. in simple statements w. the indic. οὐκ ἐγίνωσκεν αὐτήν **Mt 1:25.** οὐ δύνασθε θεῷ δουλεύειν καὶ μαμωνᾷ **6:24.** οὐκ ἤφιεν λαλεῖν τὰ δαιμόνια **Mk 1:34.** οὐκ ἦν αὐτοῖς τέκνον **Lk 1:7.** οὐχ ὑμῶν ἐστιν **Ac 1:7.** οὐ γὰρ ἐπαισχύνομαι τὸ εὐαγγέλιον **Ro 1:16** and very oft. οὐ γάρ σου ἠκούσαμέν ποτε AcPlCor 1:14.

β. used to negative the prohibitive future (Hebr. לֹא w. the impf.—Synes., Ep. 67 p. 211b οὐκ ἀγνοήσεις) οὐ φονεύσεις **Mt 5:21;** cp. vs. **27; Mt 19:18; Ro 7:7; 13:9** (all commandments fr. the Decalogue: Ex 20:13–17; Dt 5:17–21). Also οὐκ ἐπιορκήσεις **Mt 5:33.** οὐκ ἐκπειράσεις κύριον **Lk 4:12** (Dt 6:16); **Ac 23:5** (Ex 22:27); **1 Cor 9:9** (Dt 25:4).—**Mt 6:5.**

ⓓ in subordinate clauses—α. in relative clauses w. indic. (in the NT, μή is found in such clauses only Tit 1:11; 2 Pt 1:9; 1J 4:3 [but s. B-D-F §428, 4 and Rob. 1158]; Ac 15:29 D; Col 2:18 v.l.): **Mt 10:38; 12:2; Mk 4:25** (s. 2aδ above) **Lk 6:2; J 6:64; Ro 15:21** (Is 52:15); **Gal 3:10** (Dt 27:26) al.

β. in declarative clauses w. ὅτι, likew. in temporal and causal clauses w. ind.: ὅτι οὐ **J 5:42; 1 Th 2:1.** ὁ ἀρνούμενος ὅτι Ἰησοῦς οὐκ ἔστιν ὁ Χριστός **1J 2:22** (on the negative here s. ἀρνέομαι 2).—ἐπεὶ οὐ **Lk 1:34.** ὅτε οὐ **2 Ti 4:3.**—εἰ οὐ w. indic.: εἰ οὐ δώσει αὐτῷ **Lk 11:8;** cp. ὅστις (ὅς) οὐκ ἔχει **Mt 13:12** and **Mk 4:25**=ὃς ἂν μὴ ἔχει **Lk 8:18** (Schwyzer II 593).εἰ ἐν τῷ ἀλλοτρίῳ πιστοὶ οὐκ ἐγένεσθε **16:12; Mk 11:26; Lk 18:4; J 1:25; 10:37; Ro 8:9b; 11:21; Hb 12:25.**—Once actually in a contrary-to-fact condition: καλὸν ἦν αὐτῷ εἰ οὐκ ἐγεννήθη **Mt 26:24=Mk 14:21**=1 Cl 46:8 (B-D-F §428, 2; Rob. 1160; Mlt-Turner 284).

ⓔ in combination w. other negatives, strengthening the negation (Mel. Chor. Adesp., fgm. no. 11 Diehl[2] ['42] οὐ μήποτε τὰν ἀρετὰν ἀλλάξομαι ἀντ' ἀδίκου κέρδεος 'I shall never exchange virtue for unjust gain'; GrBar 13:3 οὐκ . . . οὐδέν; Just., D. 26, 1) **Mt 22:16; Mk 5:37; Lk 4:2; 23:53** (οὐκ ἦν οὐδεὶς οὔπω); **J 6:63; 11:49; 12:19; 15:5; Ac 8:39; 2 Cor 11:9.** οὐ μηκέτι (s. μηκέτι fα) **Mt 21:19 v.l.** For use in questions s. 3 below.

α. On the combination of οὐ and μή s. μή 4.

β. The combining of οὐδέ and οὐ μή to form οὐδ' οὐ μή instead of οὐδὲ μή is a late development (a barbarism?; B-D-F §431, 3; Rob. 1175; Mlt-Turner 286.—Prayer to the god Socnopaeus: Mitt-Wilck I/2, 122, 2ff εἰ οὐ δίδοταί μοι συμβιῶσαι Ταπεθεῦτι Μαρρείους οὐδ' οὐ μὴ γένηται ἄλλου γυνή [Rdm.[2] 211f]; LXX) **Mt 24:21.** οὐ μή σε ἀνῶ οὐδ' οὐ μή σε ἐγκαταλίπω **Hb 13:5** (Dt 31:6 A, 8 A οὐδ οὐ μή; 1 Ch 28:20 A).—οὐδὲν . . . οὐ μὴ ἀδικήσει instead of οὐδὲν . . . μὴ . . . **Lk 10:19.** οὐδὲν οὐ μὴ λήψῃ Hm 9:5.

ⓕ w. one of two clauses that are either coordinate or contrasted.—**α.** οὐ . . . ἀλλά s. ἀλλά 1ab.—**1 Th 2:4** the οὐ w. the ptc. is prob. to be explained under this head (s. 3 above).

β. οὐ . . . , . . . δέ **Ac 12:9, 14; Hb 4:13, 15.**

γ. . . . , ἀλλ' οὐ looking back upon a 'to be sure' **1 Cor 10:5, 23.**

δ. οὐ μόνον, ἀλλὰ (καί) s. μόνος 2c.

ε. οὐ . . . εἰ μή s. εἰ 6i.

❸ **marker of expectation of an affirmative answer, *not so?***

ⓐ to a direct question (Hom. et al.):—**α.** *do . . . not? does . . . not?* (B-D-F §427, 2; Rob. 917): οὐκ ἀκούεις, πόσα σου καταμαρτυροῦσιν; *you hear, do you not . . .?* **Mt 27:13.** οὐχ ὑμεῖς μᾶλλον διαφέρετε αὐτῶν; **6:26.** Cp. vs. **30.** ὁ διδάσκαλος ὑμῶν οὐ τελεῖ δίδραχμα; *your teacher pays the two-drachma tax, does he not?* **Mt 17:24.**—**Mk 6:3; 7:18; 12:24; Lk 11:40; J 4:35; 6:70; 7:25; Ac 9:21** and oft. οὐ μέλει σοι ὅτι ἀπολλύμεθα; *does it make no difference to you that we are perishing?* **Mk 4:38.** In a related sense

β. destroying the force of the negation (cp. Hdt. et al.; Schwyzer II 598): **Ac 4:20; 1 Cor 12:15** (B-D-F §431, 1; Rob. 1164).—In questions, if the verb itself is already negatived (by οὐ), the negation can be invalidated by the interrogative particle μή (s. μή 3a), which expects the answer 'no', so that the stage is set for an affirmative answer (Aesop, Fab. 374 P.=404aH. μὴ οὐκ ἔστι χλόη;=certainly there is grass, is there not?) μὴ οὐκ ἤκουσαν; *surely they have heard, have they not?* **Ro 10:18;** cp. vs. **19.** μὴ οὐκ ἔχομεν ἐξουσίαν; *we have the right, do we not?* **1 Cor 9:4;** cp. vs. **5.** μὴ οἰκίας οὐκ ἔχετε; *you have houses, do you not?* **11:22.**

ⓑ to a question expressed impatiently in the second pers. of the fut. indic. and functioning as an imperative οὐ παύσῃ;=παῦσαι! *will you not stop? = stop!* **Ac 13:10.**—DELG. M-M.

οὐά (also οὐᾶ, t.r. οὐαί; cp. Proleg. Syllog. p. 101) interjection denoting amazement (Epict. 3, 23, 24 εἰπέ μοι 'οὐά' καὶ 'θαυμαστῶς'; 32; 3, 22, 34; Cass. Dio 63, 20.—Kühner-Bl. II 252; Schwyzer II 601) ***aha!*** As an expression of scornful wonder **Mk 15:29.** An expr. of joy, as read by the Marcosians Mt 11:26 (Iren. 1, 20, 2 [Harv. I 180, 3]).—M-M.

οὐαί (LXX; cp. הוֹי, אוֹי and Lat. vae; En; TestAbr B 9, 16 [Stone p. 74]; TestJob 22:2; 53:2; ParJer 9:8; ApcEsdr. But also Epict. 3, 19, 1; ibid. and 3, 22, 32 οὐαί μοι; Vi. Aesopi W 37 οὐαὶ τῇ ἀτυχίᾳ; POxy 413, 184f οὐαί σοι, ταλαίπωρε . . . οὐαί σοι: οὐαί μοι. Schwyzer II 143; B-D-F §4, 2a; ALowe, The Origin of οὐαί: Hermathena 105, '67, 34–39. Loanw. in rabb.).

❶ **interjection denoting pain or displeasure, *woe, alas***

ⓐ w. dat. of pers. or thing concerning whom (which) pain is expressed (s. above; oft. LXX; cp. Jos., Bell. 6, 306 αἰαὶ Ἱεροσολύμοις) οὐαί σοι Χοραζίν, οὐαί σοι Βηθσαϊδά(ν) **Mt 11:21; Lk 10:13** (cp. Jer 13:27).—**Mt 18:7b; 23:13–16, 23, 25, 27, 29** (on the severe tone in these pass. s. ASaldarini, Understanding Matthew's Vitriol, BRev 13/2, '97, 32–39, 45); **24:19; 26:24; Mk 13:17; 14:21; Lk 21:23; 22:22;** 1 Cl 46:8 (Mt 26:24); Hv 4, 2, 6; D 1:5; GPt 7:25; GJs 20:1 (codd.).—Doubled for emphasis (Am 5:16.—Procop. Soph., Ep. 36 and 62 ἰοὺ ἰού=alas, alas!): three times w. dat. foll. **Rv 8:13 v.l.**—οὐαὶ δι' οὗ ἔρχεται (=τούτῳ δι' οὗ ἐρχ.) **Lk 17:1;** cp. 2 Cl 13:2; ITr 8:2.—W. ὅτι foll. to give the reason **Lk 6:24f; 11:42–44, 47, 52;** also vs. **46,** only w. the difference that here οὐαί follows: ὑμῖν τοῖς νομικοῖς οὐαί, ὅτι. Cp. **Jd 11;** 2 Cl 17:5; B 6:2, 7 (Is 3:9).—W. the prep. ἀπό foll., also to give the reason: οὐαὶ τῷ κόσμῳ ἀπὸ τῶν σκανδάλων **Mt 18:7a;** w. ὅταν foll. **Lk 6:26.**—The transition to the next group is marked by οὐαὶ ὑμῖν, οἱ ἐμπεπλησμένοι vs. **25a.**

ⓑ w. the nom. and article as a voc.: οὐαὶ οἱ γελῶντες νῦν **Lk 6:25b** (cp. Am 5:18; Hab 2:6, 12; Zeph 2:5). οὐαὶ οὐαὶ ἡ πόλις ἡ μεγάλη **Rv 18:10, 16, 19** (to Greeks such interjection would suggest nemesis, cp. Hes., Op. 200f). οὐαὶ οἱ συνετοί B 4:11 (Is 5:21). Also without the art. οὐαὶ τυφλοὶ μὴ ὁρῶντες Ox 840, 31f (Unknown Sayings 36–49).

ⓒ w. acc. of pers. (B-D-F §190, 2; Rob. 1193; cp. Lat. vae me) **Rv 12:12.** οὐαί repeated three times **8:13** (the reason for the 'woe' is introduced by ἐκ).

❷ **a state of intense hardship or distress, *woe,*** subst. (Ezk 2:10; 7:26; Kephal. I 105, 3) indecl. (B-D-F §58; Rob. 302) οὐαί μοί ἐστιν **1 Cor 9:16** (cp. Hos 9:12). As a fem. ἡ οὐαί *woe, calamity* **Rv 9:12a; 11:14ab.** Pl. ἔρχεται ἔτι δύο οὐαί **9:12b** (the lack of agreement in number [B-D-F §136, 5] as Hes., Theog. 321 τῆς δ' [of the Chimaera] ἦν τρεῖς κεφαλαί. The schol. on Hes. explains this characteristic as Doric; for critique of B-D-F s. PKatz, TLZ 82, '57, 112).—DELG. M-M. EDNT. Spicq.

Οὐαλέριος, ου, ὁ ***Valerius,*** freq. found as the name of a Roman gens (Diod. S. 11, 41, 1; 11, 60, 1; 13, 76, 1; 16, 46, 1) *Valerius* w. the cognomen Bito 1 Cl 65:1.

οὐδαμῶς adv. of οὐδαμός 'not one' (Aeschyl., Hdt.+; also SIG 679, 80; PTebt 24, 53 [117 BC]; 27, 41 [113 BC]; 58, 4 [111 BC]) **marker of emphatic negation, *by no means* Mt 2:6;** Papias (2:2).—M-M.

οὐδέ negative conjunction, combination of οὐ and δέ (Hom.+).

❶ ***and not, nor*** joins neg. sentences or clauses to others of the same kind. οὐδὲ . . . οὐδὲ . . . οὐδέ at the beg. of a sentence B 10:4. After οὐ: κλέπται οὐ διορύσσουσιν οὐδὲ κλέπτουσιν **Mt 6:20;** cp. vs. **28; 5:15; 7:18; 10:24; 25:13; Mk 4:22; Lk 6:43f; 12:24, 27; J 6:24; Ac 2:27** (Ps 15:10); **Ro 2:28; Gal 1:1; 3:28ab; 1 Th 5:5; Hb 9:25; 1 Pt 2:22** (cp. Is 53:9); **Rv 21:23;** AcPlCor 1:4. οὐ . . . οὐδὲ . . . οὐδέ **Mt 6:26; J 1:13, 25; 1 Th 2:3;** AcPlCor 1:11, 15. After οὔπω **Mt 16:9; Mk 8:17.** After οὐδείς **Mt 9:17; 11:27; 22:46; Rv 5:3** (οὐδεὶς . . . οὐδὲ . . . οὐδέ). ἵνα μὴ . . . οὐδὲ . . . οὐδέ **9:4.**—οὐδὲ γάρ *for . . . not* **Lk 20:36; J 7:5; 8:42; Ac 4:12, 34; Ro 8:7.** οὐδὲ γὰρ . . . οὐδένα *for . . . not . . . anyone* **J 5:22.** οὐδὲ μὴ πέσῃ (cp. Is 49:10 A) **Rv 7:16.**

❷ ***also not, not either, neither*** ἐὰν μὴ ἀφῆτε . . . , οὐδὲ ὁ πατὴρ ὑμῶν ἀφήσει τὰ παραπτώματα ὑμῶν *if you do not forgive . . . , your Father will not forgive your transgressions (either)* **Mt 6:15.** Cp. **21:27; 25:45; Mk 16:13; Lk 16:31; J 15:4; Ro 4:15; 11:21; 1 Cor 15:13, 16;** GJs 16:3. οὐδὲ γὰρ ἐγὼ . . .

παρέλαβον αὐτὸ οὔτε (v.l. οὐδέ) . . . *for I did not receive it . . . nor . . .* **Gal 1:12.** ἀλλ' οὐδέ *and neither* **Lk 23:15.**

❸ ***not even,*** Lat. ne . . . quidem (B-D-F §445, 2; Rob. 1185; Libanius, Or. 11 p. 439, 14 F. οὐδὲ συγγνώμη=not even forbearance; Just., D. 12, 2 οὐδὲ νῦν *not even now;* Tat. 30, 1; Ath. 13, 1 οὐδ' ὄναρ) οὐδὲ Σολομὼν περιεβάλετο ὡς ἓν τούτων *not even Solomon was dressed like one of them* **Mt 6:29.** Cp. **Lk 7:9; 12:26; J 21:25; 1 Cor 5:1.** οὐδ' ἄν (X., Cyr. 8, 8, 3; Herodian 2, 8, 2) **Hb 8:4.** οὐδ' οὕτως *not even then* **1 Cor 14:21.** οὐδεὶς . . . οὐδὲ . . . οὐδὲ . . . *no one . . . not even . . . and not even . . .* **Mt 24:36; Mk 13:32.** οὐδὲ τὴν γραφὴν ταύτην ἀνέγνωτε; *have you never (even) read this passage of Scripture?* **Mk 12:10.** Cp. **Lk 6:3.** Likew. in other questions **Lk 23:40** (cp. Lucian, Asin. 24 οὐδὲ τὰ δαιμόνια δέδοικας;) **1 Cor 11:14.**—καὶ οὐδέ **Mk 6:31.** καὶ οὐδὲ ἁλύσει (οὐκέτι οὐδεὶς ἐδύνατο αὐτὸν δῆσαι) **5:3.**—ἀλλ' οὐδέ (TestJob 47:10; ApcEsdr 4:4; Just., D. 3, 6) *but not even* **Ac 19:2; 1 Cor 3:2; 4:3; Gal 2:3.**—οὐδὲ εἷς *not even one* (X., Mem. 3, 5, 21; Dionys. Hal. 1, 73; Nicol. Dam.: 90 fgm. 103m, 2 Jac. οὐδὲ εἷς κλέπτει; 2 Km 13:30; Philo, Rer. Div. Her. 66; Jos., C. Ap. 1, 66; 2, 141.—B-D-F §302, 2; Rob. 751) **Mt 27:14; J 1:3; 3:27; Ac 4:32; Ro 3:10** (s. below).—After οὐ, strengthening it (Appian, Liby. 90 §424 οὐ γὰρ οὐδὲ δίδοτε=you do not even allow) οὐκ ἤθελεν οὐδὲ τοὺς ὀφθαλμοὺς ἐπᾶραι *he would not even raise his eyes* **Lk 18:13;** cp. **Ac 7:5; Ro 3:10** (s. above).—GValley, Üb. d. Sprachgebr. des Longus, diss. Ups. 1926, 36–44: on οὔτε and οὐδέ in later times.—M-M.

οὐδείς, οὐδεμία, οὐδέν (Hom.+.—The forms οὐθείς [Hs 9, 5, 6], οὐθέν [**Lk 23:14; Ac 15:9; 19:27; 26:26; 1 Cor 13:2;** Hm 4, 2, 1], οὐθενός [**Lk 22:35; Ac 20:33 v.l.; 2 Cor 11:9**] for which οὐδ- is freq. read as v.l. in mss. and edd., appear in the lit. since Aristotle [Jos., Ant. 5, 250; 6, 47 al.], in ins [Meisterhans[3]-Schw. 258f], and in pap [Mayser 181f], PStras II, 125, 4 [5/4 BC]; on the forms s. B-D-F §33; W-S. §5, 27f and note 62; Mlt-H. 111f; JWackernagel, Hellenistica 1907, 23; New Docs 2, 83; 4, 164f.—The LXX usage in Thackeray p. 58–62).

❶ as an adj. ***no*** οὐδεὶς προφήτης **Lk 4:24.** Cp. **16:13.** παροιμία οὐδεμία **J 16:29.** Cp. **18:38; Ac 25:18; 27:22.** οὐδὲν εἴδωλον **1 Cor 8:4a.** οὐδὲν χρείαν ἔχω **Rv 3:17.** Cp. **J 10:41.** οὐδεὶς ἄλλος (UPZ 71, 15 [152 BC]) **15:24.**—οὐδεμία ἐκκλησία . . . εἰ μὴ ὑμεῖς **Phil 4:15.**—W. other negatives: οὐ . . . οὐδεμίαν δύναμιν **Mk 6:5.**

❷ as a subst.—ⓐ οὐδείς ***no one, nobody*** **Mt 6:24; 8:10; 9:16; Mk 2:21f; 5:4; 7:24; Lk 5:36f, 39; J 1:18** (οὐδεὶς πώποτε as PGM 5, 102 Osiris, ὃν οὐδεὶς εἶδε πώποτε; Jos., C. Ap. 2, 124); **Ro 14:7b; 1 Cor 2:11; 3:11** and oft.—W. partitive gen. (Epict. 4, 1, 3 οὐδεὶς τ. φαύλων; Jos., Ant. 3, 321 οὐδεὶς τ. ἱερέων; Just., D. 16, 3 οὐδεὶς γὰρ ὑμῶν; Tat. 6:1 οὐδεμία τῶν ψυχῶν) οὐδεὶς ἀνθρώπων *no one at all* **Mk 11:2.** Cp. **Lk 14:24.** οὐδεὶς τ. ἀνακειμένων **J 13:28.** τῶν λοιπῶν οὐδεὶς *none of the others* **Ac 5:13.** οὐδ. ὑμῶν **27:34** (Diod. S. 14, 65, 2 οὐδεὶς ἡμῶν). Cp. Ro. **14:7a.** Instead of the part. gen. we may have ἐκ (Jos., Bell. 7, 398) **Lk 1:61; J 7:19; 16:5.**—οὐδεὶς . . . εἰ μὴ *no one . . . except* **Mt 11:27; 17:8; Mk 10:18; Lk 10:22; 18:19; J 14:6; 1 Cor 1:14; 8:4b; Rv 2:17; 14:3; 19:12.** οὐδεὶς ἐξ αὐτῶν ἀπώλετο εἰ μὴ **J 17:12.**—Also οὐδεὶς . . . ἐὰν μὴ **J 3:2; 6:44, 65.** Used w. other negatives (Appian, Samn. 11 §4 οὐδένα λαβεῖν οὐδέν, οὔτε . . . οὔτε=nobody accepted anything, neither . . . nor) οὐ . . . οὐδείς (Appian, Bell. Civ. 1. 19 §80=nobody; Diog. L. 1, 53) **Mt 22:16; Mk 3:27; 5:37; 12:14; Lk 8:43; J 8:15; 18:31; Ac 4:12; 1 Cor 6:5.** οὓς δέδωκάς μοι οὐκ ἀπώλεσα ἐξ αὐτῶν οὐδένα **J 18:9.** οὐκέτι . . . οὐδεὶς **Mk 9:8.** οὐδεὶς οὔπω *no one yet* **Lk 23:53** (v.l. οὐδέπω); οὐδεὶς οὔπω ἀνθρώπων **Mk 11:2.** οὐδέπω οὐδεὶς **J 19:41; Ac 8:16.** οὐδεὶς οὐκέτι **Mk 12:34; Rv 18:11.** οὐδὲ ἁλύσει οὐκέτι οὐδεὶς **Mk 5:3.**—οὐδενὶ οὐδέν **16:8** (Appian, Liby. 128 §613 οὐδὲν οὐδείς=no one [set fire to] anything [ruling out all exceptions]; Just., D. 44, 2 οὐδεὶς γὰρ οὐδέν . . . οὐδαμόθεν λαβεῖν ἔχει. For lit. on the silence of women s. FNeirynck, Evangelica '82, 247–51). Cp. **Lk 9:36.** οὐδὲ . . . οὐδεὶς **J 5:22.**

ⓑ οὐδέν ***nothing***—α. lit. οὐδὲν ἀδυνατήσει ὑμῖν **Mt 17:20.** Cp. **10:26; 26:62; 27:12; Mk 7:15; J 1:3 v.l.** Foll. by partitive gen. **Lk 9:36b; 18:34; Ac 18:17; Rv 3:17 v.l.** (Mussies 183). Foll. by εἰ μή *nothing but* **Mt 5:13; 21:19; Mk 9:29; 11:13.** οὐδὲν ἐκτὸς ὧν *nothing but what* **Ac 26:22.** οὐδὲν αὐτοῦ διεφθάρη *no part of (Jonah) was damaged* AcPlCor 2:30. Used w. other negatives: οὐ . . . οὐδέν **Mk 14:60f; 15:4; Lk 4:2; J 3:27 v.l.** (for οὐδὲ ἕν); **5:30; 9:33; 11:49.** οὐ . . . οὐδενὶ τούτων **1 Cor 9:15a.** οὐ . . . οὐδέν, ἂν (=ἐὰν) μὴ **J 5:19.** οὐκέτι . . . οὐδέν **Mk 7:12; 15:5; Lk 20:40.** οὐδὲν ὑμᾶς οὐ μὴ ἀδικήσει **Lk 10:19** (s. ἀδικέω 2).

β. nonliterally *worthless, meaningless, invalid* (X., Cyr. 6, 2, 8; Diod. S. 14, 35, 5; Dio Chrys. 4, 60; 15 [32], 101 οὐδέν ἐστι=it means nothing, is unimportant; Tat. 27, 2 τῶν πολλῶν θεῶν ἡ ὁμήγυρις οὐδέν ἐστιν 'the assembly of many gods amounts to nothing') ὃς ἂν ὀμόσῃ ἐν τ. ναῷ, οὐδέν ἐστιν *(the oath of) one who who swears by the temple is not binding* **Mt 23:16, 18.** Cp. **J 8:54; 1 Cor 7:19ab.** εἰ καὶ οὐδέν εἰμι **2 Cor 12:11b.** οὐθέν εἰμι **1 Cor 13:2** ([Tat. 26, 3 οὐδέν ἐστε] on the neut. referring to a masc. subj. s. B-D-F §131; Rob. 751).—**Ac 21:24; 25:11.**—γενέσθαι εἰς οὐδέν **5:36.** εἰς οὐδὲν δὲ συνέβη τελευτῆσαι τὴν τάξιν αὐτῶν *ultimately the (angels') status was terminated* Papias (4). εἰς οὐθὲν λογισθῆναι **Ac 19:27.** Antonym τίς 2.

γ. the acc. οὐδέν *in no respect, in no way* (Dio Chrys. 52 [69], 6; Just., D. 14, 1 οὐδὲν ὑμῖν χρήσιμοι; 68, 1 οὐδὲν ἂν βλαβείην.—B-D-F §154; 160; Rob. 751) οὐδὲν διαφέρει *(the heir) differs in no respect* **Gal 4:1.** οὐθὲν διέκρινεν **Ac 15:9.** Ἰουδαίους οὐδὲν ἠδίκηκα **25:10;** cp. **Gal 4:12.** οὐδὲν ὑστέρησα **2 Cor 12:11a.** οὐδὲν ὠφελοῦμαι **1 Cor 13:3.** οὐδὲν γάρ σε ταῦτα ὠφελήσει AcPl Ha 2, 23. ἡ σὰρξ οὐκ ὠφελεῖ οὐδέν **J 6:63.** οὐδὲν οὐδενὸς χρῄζει εἰ μὴ *(the Lord) requires nothing at all, except* 1 Cl 52:1. οὐδὲν ἥμαρτεν Μάρκος οὕτως ἔνια γράψας ὡς ἀπεμνημόνευσεν *Mark was not at fault in recording some things as he remembered them* Papias (2:15). On οὐδέν μοι διαφέρει **Gal 2:6** s. διαφέρω 3.—W. the same mng. ἐν οὐδενί **Phil 1:20.**—Somet. the later usage οὐδέν = οὐ (Aristoph., Eccl. 644; Dionys. Hal. [Rdm. 32, 5]; Epict. 4, 10, 36; POxy 1683, 13; BGU 948, 13) suggests itself, e.g. **Ac 18:17; Rv 3:17.**—M-M. Sv.

οὐδέποτε adv. (Hom.+; Epict.; SIG 800, 29 οὐδέποτε μὴ λειφθῇ; PHib 78, 5 [244/243 BC]; POxy 1062, 11 [II AD]; LXX; pseudepigr.; Philo, Op. M. 12; Joseph., Just.) **an indefinte negated point of time, *never,*** w. pres. (Just., D. 121, 2) **1 Cor 13:8** (the topic and temporal aspect cp. Maximus Tyr. 14, 6e φιλία χρόνῳ αὔξεται=friendship matures over time); **Hb 10:1, 11.** W. a past tense (Diod. S. 14, 6, 1; Appian, Bell. Civ. 2, 139 §578; Jos., Bell. 5, 399, Ant. 13, 311) **Mt 7:23; 9:33; Mk 2:12; Lk 15:29ab; J 7:46; Ac 10:14; 11:8; 14:8;** IRo 3:1; Hm 3:3f; s8, 10, 3; D 16:4. W. fut. **Mt 26:33;** Hm 4, 1, 1.—In questions: οὐδέποτε ἀνέγνωτε . . .; *have you never read . . . ?* **Mt 21:16, 42; Mk 2:25.**—M-M.

οὐδέπω adv. (Aeschyl., Pla.+; POxy 275, 8 [66 AD]; 273, 13; PRyl 178, 7; Ex 9:30; Jos., Bell. 2, 138, Ant, 14, 350) **the negation of extending time up to and beyond an expected point, *not yet, still not*** **J 7:8** P[66] (for οὐκ), **39** (v.l. οὔπω);

20:9; Hm 3:3. οὐ … οὐδεὶς οὐδέπω *no one ever* **Lk 23:53 v.l.** (for οὔπω).οὐδέπω οὐδείς (Jos., Ant. 6, 91) **J 19:41;** cp. **Ac 8:16.**—M-M.

οὐθείς s. οὐδείς.—DELG s.v. οὐ. M-M.

οὐκέτι adv. (οὐκ ἔτι Tdf. Phlm 16; both spellings t.r.—Hom.+)

❶ **the extension of time up to a point but not beyond,** ***no more, no longer, no further*** lit., of time (TestBenj 11:1; JosAs 15:6; Jos., Ant. 7, 16; Just., D. 56,23; Tat. 26, 3) οὐκέτι εἰμὶ ἄξιος κληθῆναι υἱός σου **Lk 15:19, 21.—Mt 19:6; Mk 10:8; J 4:42; 6:66; 11:54; 15:15; Ro 6:9b; Gal 2:20; Eph 2:19; Phlm 16; Rv 10:6;** GJs 4:4.—*Never … again* (Jos., Ant. 6, 156; Artem. 3, 13 ἀθάνατοι οἱ ἀποθανόντες, ἐπεὶ μηκέτι τεθνήξονται) Χριστὸς ἐγερθεὶς … οὐκέτι ἀποθνήσκει **Ro 6:9a.** Cp. **Ac 20:25, 38; 2 Cor 1:23.**—W. the pres., of an event in the very near fut. (cp. ApcEsdr 3:6 οὐκέτι ἦ κόσμος): ὁ κόσμος με οὐκέτι θεωρεῖ *the world will see me no longer* **J 14:19; 16:10, 16; 17:11.**—Used w. another negative: οὐ … οὐκέτι (Zeph 3:15; En 100:5) **Ac 8:39,** οὐδὲ … οὐκέτι **Mt 22:46.** οὐδὲ … οὐκέτι οὐδείς **Mk 5:3.** οὐκέτι οὐδέν **7:12; 15:5; Lk 20:40.** οὐκέτι οὐδείς (UPZ 42, 30 [162 BC]) **Mk 9:8.** οὐδεὶς οὐκέτι **12:34; Rv 18:11.** οὐκέτι οὐ μή *never again* (Am 9:15; TestJob 7:10 οὐκέτι οὐ μη φάγῃς) **Mk 14:25; Lk 22:16 v.l.; Rv 18:14.** οὐκέτι … οὐκέτι no *longer … no longer* B 8:2 (Polyaenus 1, 41, 2 οὐκέτι three times).

❷ **marker of inference in a logical process,** ***not*** (Melissus [V BC] B 9, Vorsokrat.[5] I 275 εἰ … οὐκέτι ἓν εἴη, cp. B 7, 2 ibid. p. 270; Empedocles B 17, 31, I 317 εἴτε … οὐκέτ' ἂν ἦσαν; Ocellus c. 2 Harder; Ps.-Aristot., de Melisso etc. [ed. HDiels, ABA 1900] 1, 4; schol. on Apollon. Rhod. 2, 498–527a [p. 168, 23] οὐκέτι δὲ καὶ θυγάτηρ αὐτοῦ ἦν=then, accordingly, she was not his daughter; Ar. 13, 6 εἰ … , οὐκέτι μία φύσις ἐστίν=certainly, then, they do not share a common characteristic) *then* (accordingly) *not* εἰ δὲ χάριτι οὐκέτι ἐξ ἔργων *if by grace, then not by deeds* **Ro 11:6a.** Cp. **7:20; 14:15; Gal 3:18.** Likew. νυνὶ οὐκέτι **Ro 7:17.**—DELG s.v. ἔτι. M-M.

οὐκοῦν adv. (οὐκ, οὖν; trag., Pla., X. et al.; 4 Km 5:23 v.l.)

❶ inferential ***therefore, so, accordingly*** (Jos., C. Ap. 1, 171; 2, 226; Just., Tat., Ath.) B 5:3, 11, 12; 6:16; 7:1, 10; 9:4; 15:4; Dg 2:9; Hs 9, 28, 6.

❷ interrogative, when the question has inferential force, ***so then*** (Menand., Epitr. 361 S. [185 Kö.]; 553 S. [377 Kö.]; Epict. 1, 7, 6; 8; 2, 24, 3 al.; PHib 12, 4 [III BC]) οὐκοῦν βασιλεὺς εἶ σύ; *so you are a king?* **J 18:37** (s. B-D-F §451, 1; Rob. 1175; Kühner-G. II 163f; Schwyzer II 587–89).—M-M.

Οὐλαμμαούς **Lk 24:13** D for Ἐμμαοῦς; influenced by the earlier name of Bethel, Gen 28:19 (s. Rahlfs' ed. 1926, 36).

οὖλος, η, ον (Hom. et al.) ***curly*** of hair (Plut., Cim. 481 [5, 3] οὔλῃ τριχί; Achilles Tat. 1, 4, 3; En 106:2; SibOr 13, 105) ApcPt 3:10.

οὐ μεν οὖν (so Aristoph., Plu. 870, Ran. 556; 1188; also οὐμενοῦν Paus. 1, 21, 1) adv. (Aristoph., Pla. et al.; incl. Luc., Jupp. Tr. 35 twice.—Kühner=G. II 158) **a marker introducing a negative statement in contradiction of discourse that precedes,** ***not at all, by no means*** (expressing a strong negation to a question) Dg 7:4.

οὐ μή s. μή 4.

οὖν (Hom.+) a particle, never found at the beginning of a sentence. In our lit. it is an inferential and then mainly a transitional conjunction (so Hdt.+ [Kühner-G. II p. 326].—B-D-F §451, 1; Rob. 1191f; Mlt-Turner 337f).

❶ **inferential, denoting that what it introduces is the result of or an inference fr. what precedes,** ***so, therefore, consequently, accordingly, then.***

ⓐ in declarative sentences (PTebt 37, 15 [73 BC] ἐγὼ οὖν … γέγραφα='consequently I … am writing'; difft. 4 below) **Mt 1:17; 3:10** (s. also 3 below); **7:24; Lk 3:9; 11:35; J 6:13; Ac 1:21; 5:41; Ro 5:1; 6:4; 11:5; 13:10; 16:19; 1 Cor 4:16; 7:26; 2 Cor 3:12; Eph 4:1, 17; Phil 2:28; 1 Pt 2:7; 3J 8** al.; AcPlCor 2:10, 19.—ἀπόδοτε οὖν *well, then, give back* **Mt 22:21** (here οὖν=mod. Gk. λοιπόν).

ⓑ in commands and invitations, with intensive force (PTebt 33, 2 [φρόν]τισον οὖν ἵνα γένη(ται) ἀκολύθως='take care, then, that its (the letter's) stipulations are followed'. Here οὖν picks up on the suggestion of the letter's importance because of the prestige of the addressee; difft. 3 below) ποιήσατε οὖν καρπὸν ἄξιον τῆς μετανοίας **Mt 3:8** (also s. 3 below); ἔσεσθε οὖν ὑμεῖς τέλειοι **5:48.** μὴ οὖν φοβεῖσθε **10:31** (cp. ApcEsdr 7:2; Just., D. 9, 2). προσερχώμεθα οὖν μετὰ παρρησίας **Hb 4:16.** Cp. **Mt 6:8, 9, 31; 9:38; Mk 10:9; 13:35; Lk 8:18; 10:2, 40; Ac 2:36; 3:19; 8:22; 23:15, 21** (also s. 4 below); **Ro 6:12** (WNauck, Das οὖν-paräneticum: ZNW 49, '58, 134f); **1 Cor 10:31; 2 Cor 7:1; Gal 5:1; Phil 2:29; Col 2:16** al. νῦν οὖν πορεύεσθε ἐν εἰρήνῃ **Ac 16:36.**

ⓒ in questions—**α.** in real questions θέλεις οὖν; *do you want, then?* **Mt 13:28.** σὺ οὖν εἶ; *are you, then?* **Lk 22:70.** Cp. **J 18:39.** νόμον οὖν καταργοῦμεν; μὴ γένοιτο **Ro 3:31;** cp. **Gal 3:21.—1 Cor 6:15.** τί οὖν; *why then?* (Menand., Her. 40, Epitr. 313 S. [137 Kö.]; Dio Chrys. 2, 9; Just., D. 3, 2) **Mt 17:10;** cp. **19:7; J 1:25;** *what then?* (Menand., Epitr. 226 S. [50 Kö], Peric. 744 [321 Kö.]; TestJob 38:7; Just., D. 3, 6; 67, 10) **Mt 27:22; Mk 15:12; Lk 3:10; 20:15, 17; J 6:30b.** τίς οὖν; (Menand., Epitr. 221 S. [45 Kö.]; TestJob 38:3; Just., D. 7, 1; Ath. 35, 1) **Lk 7:42.** διὰ τί οὖν οὐκ ἐπιστεύσατε; **Mt 21:25; Mk 11:31** (TestJob 38:1; Just., D. 47, 2). πῶς οὖν; (Menand., Epitr. 441 S. [265 Kö.]; TestJob 19:2; Ar. 9, 9; 10, 7 al.) **Mt 22:43; J 9:19; Ro 4:10;** Ox 1081, 25=Otero p. 83 (SJCh 90, 2); AcPl Ha 10, 9. πότε οὖν; **Lk 21:7.** πόθεν οὖν; **Mt 13:27, 56; J 4:11.** ποῦ οὖν; (TestJob 32:2ff) **Ro 3:27; Gal 4:15.**

β. Certain formulas are favorite expressions, esp. in Paul: τί οὖν; *what, then, are we to conclude?* (Dio Chrys. 14 [31], 55; 60; 17 [34], 28; Jos., Bell. 2, 364) **J 1:21; Ro 3:9; 6:15; 11:7.** τί οὖν ἐστιν; *what, then, is to be done?* **Ac 21:22; 1 Cor 14:15, 26.** τί οὖν ἐστιν Ἀπολλῶς; *what is Apollos, really?* **3:5** (s. 3 below). τί οὖν φημι; **1 Cor 10:19.** τί οὖν ἐροῦμεν; *what, then, are we to say?* **Ro 6:1; 7:7; 9:14, 30.** τί οὖν ἐροῦμεν πρὸς ταῦτα; **8:31.** τί οὖν ὁ νόμος; **Gal 3:19.**

γ. in rhetorical questions πόσῳ οὖν διαφέρει ἄνθρωπος προβάτου *how much more, then, is a human being worth than a sheep?* **Mt 12:12.** πῶς οὖν σταθήσεται ἡ βασιλεία αὐτοῦ; *how then will (Beelzebul's) kingdom endure?* vs. **26.—26:54; Lk 7:31; Ro 10:14** (s. also 4 below).

❷ **marker of continuation of a narrative,** ***so, now, then*** (s. Rob. 1191: 'a transitional particle relating clauses or sentences loosely together by way of confirmation')

ⓐ οὖν serves to resume a subject once more after an interruption: *so, as has been said* ἔλεγεν οὖν τοῖς ἐκπορευομένοις **Lk 3:7** (connecting w. vs. 3). Cp. **19:12; J 4:6, 9, 28; Ac 8:25; 12:5;** cp. **25:4** (s. 4 below).—Cp. **1 Cor 8:4** (reaching back to vs. 1); **11:20.**

ⓑ οὖν serves to indicate a transition to someth. new. So esp. in the Gospel of John (Rob. 1191: 'John boldly uses οὖν alone and needs no apology for doing so. It just carries along the narrative with no necessary thought of cause or result'.) *now, then, well* **J 1:22; 2:18, 20; 3:25; 4:33, 46, 48; 5:10, 19; 6:60, 67; 7:25, 28, 33, 35, 40; 8:13, 21, 22, 25** (καὶ ἔλεγον P[66]), **31, 57; 9:7f, 10, 16; 20:30** (s. also 3 below); and oft.; **Ac 25:1; 26:9** (also s. 3 below) al. Prob. also **J 9:18** οὐκ ἐπίστευσαν οὖν οἱ Ἰουδαῖοι *Well, the Judeans refused to believe* (s. 4 below). Cp. **1 Cor 3:5** (s. also 3 below).

ⓒ οὖν serves to indicate a response (HDana and JMantey, Manual Grammar of the Gk. NT 1927, p. 254) where the transl. *in reply, in turn* (Ex 8:6) is prob. **J 4:9, 48; 6:53** al. In **Ac 28:5** (s. also 4 below) Paul's action is a response in narrative terms to the perception of the islanders: ὁ μὲν οὖν ἀποτινάξας τὸ θηρίον *he, in turn, shook off the creature.*

ⓓ Frequently used w. other particles in continuation of discourse or narrative: ἄρα οὖν s. ἄρα 2b. ἐὰν οὖν **Mt 5:19, 23; 24:26; J 6:62; 2 Ti 2:21; Js 4:4; Rv 3:3b;** 2 Cl 3:3. ἐάν τε οὖν **Ro 14:8.** εἰ οὖν s. εἰ 6k. εἰ μὲν οὖν s. εἰ 6g. εἴτε οὖν . . . εἴτε **1 Cor 10:31; 15:11.** ἐπεὶ οὖν s. ἐπεί 2. μὲν οὖν . . . δέ (Jos., Ant. 13, 76f; Just., D. 43, 7) **Mk 16:19f; Lk 3:18f; J 19:24f; Ac 8:4f; 11:19f; 1 Cor 9:25.**—Also without δέ denoting contrast (TestJob 40:14; Jos., Ant. 19, 337; Just., A I, 8, 3; Tat. 15, 1) **Ac 1:6, 18; 2:41; 5:41; 8:25** al. νῦν οὖν (TestJob 23:7; ApcMos 11:30) **Ac 10:33b; 23:15;** also **15:10** (s. νῦν 2a).—ὅταν οὖν (Just., D. 138, 2; Ath. 7, 1; 13, 1; 32, 1 al.) **Mt 6:2; 21:40; 24:15.** ὅτε οὖν **J 2:22; 4:45; 6:24; 13:12, 31; 19:6, 8, 30; 21:15.** τότε οὖν (ApcEsdr 3:14; Just., D. 56, 19) **11:14; 19:1, 16; 20:8.** ὡς οὖν (Jos., Ant. 6, 145, Vi. 292; Just., D. 43, 1; 49, 7) **4:1, 40; 11:6; 18:6; 20:11; 21:9;** AcPlCor 1:6. ὥσπερ οὖν **Mt 13:40.**—οὐκ οὖν s.οὐκοῦν.

❸ It has been proposed that some traces of older Gk. usage in which οὖν is emphatic, = *certainly, really, to be sure* etc. (s. L-S-J-M s.v. 1) remain in the pap (e.g. PLond I, 28, 4, p. 43 [c. 162 BC]; PTebt 33, 2 [on this s. 1b above]) and in the NT (so M-M., s.v. 3 and Dana and Mantey, op. cit. p. 255f) **Mt 3:8** (s. also 1b above), **10; J 20:30** (s. also 2b above); *indeed, of course* **Ac 26:9** (s. also 2b above); **1 Cor 3:5** (s. also 1cβ above) al. On the other hand, as indicated by the cross references, there is little semantic justification for making a separate classification. (On this s. esp. Rob. 1191–92.)

❹ It has also been proposed that οὖν may be used adversatively (M-M., s.v. 4: 'slightly adversative sense', and w. ref. to PTebt 37, 15 [73 BC]; cp. 1b above; so also Dana and Mantey, op. cit. p. 256f) in some NT pass., e.g. **J 9:18** (s. 2b above); **Ac 23:21; 25:4; 28:5; Ro 10:14** (s. 1cγ above) in the sense *but, however*—JMantey, Newly Discovered Mngs. for οὖν: Exp., 8th ser., 22, 1921, 205–14. But s. Rob. 1191–92; B-D-F §451, 1.—Denniston 415–30.—DELG. M-M.

οὔπω adv. of time (Hom. et al.; pap, LXX; ParJer 5:21; Philo, Joseph.) **the negation of extending time up to and beyond an expected point, *not yet*** **Mt 24:6; Mk 13:7; J 2:4; 6:17; 7:6, 8a v.l.** (for οὐκ), **8b** (v.l. οὐδέπω P[66]) **30, 39a** (Aesop, Fab. 466 P. οἶνος γὰρ οὔπω ἦν [people still drank nectar]), **39b v.l.** (for οὐδέπω); **8:20, 57; 11:30; 20:17; 1 Cor 3:2; 8:2; Phil 3:13 v.l.; Hb 2:8; 12:4; 1J 3:2; Rv 17:10, 12;** IEph 3:1; Hv 3, 9, 5; s 9, 5, 2. οὐδεὶς οὔπω *no one ever* (Maximus Tyr. 39, 3i) **Mk 11:2** (v.l. without οὔπω); **Lk 23:53** (v.l. οὐδέπω). οὔπω (for οὐδέπω) . . . ἐπ' οὐδενί **Ac 8:16 v.l.** In questions: **Mt 16:9; Mk 4:40** (v.l. πῶς οὐκ); **8:17, 21.** οὔπω γάρ introducing a digression (Jos., Bell. 1, 39; 6, 80) **J 3:24.**—M-M.

οὐρά, ᾶς, ἡ (Hom. et al.; ins, pap, LXX; TestJud 2:6; Jos., Bell. 4, 6, Ant. 3, 228) ***tail*** **Rv 9:10** (of a scorpion as schol. on Nicander, Ther. 885; SibOr 5, 525), **19ab** (cp. Ael. Dion. α, 109 ὄφις ὁ καὶ ἐπὶ τῆς οὐρᾶς κεφαλὴν ἔχων); **12:4.**—B. 209. M-M.

οὐράνιος, ον (οὐρανός; Hom.+.—An adj. of two endings B-D-F §59, 2; W-S. §11, 1; Mlt-H. 157; Attic wr. predom. form the fem. in -ία) **belonging to heaven, coming from or living in heaven, *heavenly*** (Diod. S. 6, 2, 8 τοὺς οὐρανίους θεούς; IAndrosIsis, Hymn to Anubis fr. Chios 1 p. 139; SEG VIII, 2 [117/18 AD] θεοῦ ἁγίου οὐρανίου; other exx. of οὐ. as a designation of gentile deities: Syria 6, 1925, p. 355, 4; Philo, Omn. Prob. Lib. 130; Jos., C. Ap. 1, 254f τ. οὐρανίους θεούς; SibOr 3, 19; 286 θεὸς οὐ.—ἡ οὐ. φωνή Iren. 3, 12, 7 [Harv. II 60, 1]; παράδειγμα πόλεως οὐρανίας Orig., C. Cels. 5, 43, 18; ἀναστὰς . . . οὐράνιον ἕξεις πολιτείαν Did., Gen. 104, 19) ὁ πατὴρ ὑμῶν (or μου) ὁ οὐράνιος (Just., A I, 15, 8) **Mt 5:48; 6:14, 26, 32; 15:13; 18:35** (v.l. ἐπουράνιος); **23:9.** Cp. **1 Cor 15:47** v.l. στρατιὰ οὐράνιος *the heavenly host* or *army* (=צְבָא הַשָּׁמַיִם 3 Km 22:19 ἡ στρατιὰ τοῦ οὐρανοῦ; ἡ οὐρανία στρατιά Orig., C. Cels. 8, 67, 15) **Lk 2:13** (v.l. οὐρανοῦ). ἡ οὐράνιος ὀπτασία *the heavenly vision* **Ac 26:19.** ἡ οὐράνιος βασιλεία = ἡ βασ. τῶν οὐρανῶν MPol 22:3.—M-M. TW.

οὐρανόθεν adv. of place fr. οὐρανος (Hom., Hes.; Iambl., Vi. Pyth. 32, 216; PGM 2, 95; 4 Macc 4:10; Philo, Somn. 1, 112; SibOr 8, 341; cp. μακρόθεν.—Lob., Phryn. p. 93f). In the ancient Mediterranean world the vast expanse of sky was also understood as a transcendent realm for divine activity (e.g. Il. 8, 558). The rendering ***from heaven*** therefore does justice to the meteorological as well as transcendent aspect (Apollon. Rhod. 1, 547 = from heaven [as the abode of the divine]) **Ac 14:17** (the rain comes from the sky, but God is the ultimate source); **26:13** (an exceptionally bright light appears in the sky and is intimately associated with a vision).—TW.

οὐρανός, οῦ, ὁ 24:31 (Hom.+; 'heaven' in various senses)

❶ **the portion or portions of the universe gener. distinguished from planet earth, *heaven*** (so mostly in the sing.; s. B-D-F §141, 1)

ⓐ mentioned w. the earth—**α.** forming a unity w. it as the totality of creation (Pla., Euthyd. 296d οὐρανὸς καὶ γῆ; Gen 1:1; 14:19, 22; Tob 7:17 BA; Jdth 9:12; Bel 5; 1 Macc 2:37 al.; PsSol 8:7; ParJer 5:32; Just., D. 74, 1; PGM 13, 784 ὁ βασιλεύων τῶν οὐρανῶν κ. τῆς γῆς κ. πάντων τῶν ἐν αὐτοῖς ἐνδιατριβόντων; Orig., C. Cels. 6, 59, 6; Theoph. Ant. 1, 4 [p. 64, 13]) ὁ οὐρανὸς καὶ ἡ γῆ **Mt 5:18; 11:25; 24:35; Mk 13:31; Lk 10:21; 16:17; 21:33; Ac 4:24; 14:15; 17:24** (on the absence of the art. s. B-D-F §253, 3); **Rv 14:7; 20:11;** Dg 3:4; AcPlCor 2:9; 19.

β. standing independently beside the earth or contrasted w. it: **Mt 5:34f; Ac 7:49** (cp. on both Is 66:1). ἐν (τῷ) οὐρανῷ καὶ ἐπὶ (τῆς) γῆς **Mt 6:10; 28:18; Lk 11:2 v.l.; Rv 5:13.**—**1 Cor 8:5; Rv 5:3;** ISm 11:2. τὸ πρόσωπον τ. γῆς καὶ τ. οὐρανοῦ **Lk 12:56.** Cp. **Hb 12:26** (Hg 2:6); **Js 5:12.**—τὰ ἔσχατα τ. γῆς as extreme contrast to heaven 1 Cl 28:3. By God's creative word the heaven was fixed and the earth founded on the waters Hv 1, 3, 4. Neither heaven nor earth can be comprehended by human measure B 16:2 (Is 40:12). On ἀπ' ἄκρου γῆς ἕως ἄκρου οὐρανοῦ **Mk 13:27** s. under ἄκρον. ὁ πρῶτος οὐρ. καὶ ἡ πρώτη γῆ will give way in the last times to the οὐρ. καινός and the γῆ καινή **Rv 21:1** (cp. Is 65:17; 66:22).

ⓑ as firmament or *sky* over the earth; out of reach for humans Hm 11:18. Hence ἕως οὐρανοῦ (ApcEsdr 4:32) **Mt 11:23; Lk 10:15** or εἰς τὸν οὐρ. Hv 4, 1, 5 as an expr. denoting a great height. Likew. ἀπὸ τ. γῆς ἕως τ. οὐρανοῦ 1 Cl 8:3 (scripture quot. of unknown origin); GPt 10:40 (for a transcendent being who walks on the earth and whose head touches the sky, s. Il. 4, 443). Since the heaven extends over the whole earth, ὑπὸ τὸν οὐρ. *under (the) heaven = on earth, throughout the earth* (Pla., Tim. 23c, Ep. 7, 326c; UPZ 106, 14 [99 BC]; Eccl 1:13; 3:1; Just., A II, 5, 2) **Ac 2:5; 4:12; Col 1:23;** Hs 9, 17, 4; m 12, 4, 2. ὑποκάτωθεν τοῦ οὐρανοῦ *throughout the earth* 1 Cl 53:3 (Dt 9:14). ἐκ τῆς (i.e. χώρας) ὑπὸ τὸν οὐρ. εἰς τὴν ὑπ' οὐρανόν *from one place on earth to another* **Lk 17:24** (cp. Dt 29:19; Bar 5:3; 2 Macc 2:18 ἐκ τῆς ὑπὸ τὸν οὐρ. εἰς τὸν ἅγιον τόπον).—In the last days there will appear τέρατα ἐν τ. οὐρανῷ ἄνω *wonders in the heaven above* **Ac 2:19** (Jo 3:3 v.l.). σημεῖον ἐν τῷ οὐρ. **Rv 12:1, 3** (cp. Diod. S. 2, 30, 1 τὰ ἐν οὐρανῷ γινόμενα=what takes place in the heavens; Ael. Aristid. 50, 56 K.=26 p. 519 D., where the statue of Asclepius from Pergamum appears ἐν τῷ οὐρανῷ). The sky can even be rolled up; s. ἑλίσσω.—Rain falls fr. heaven (X., An. 4, 2, 2) and heaven *is closed* to bring about a drought **Lk 4:25.—Rv 11:6; Js 5:18** (cp. 2 Ch 6:26; 7:13; Sir 48:3). Lightning also comes fr. heaven (Bacchylides 17, 55f ἀπ' οὐρανοῦ . . . ἀστραπάν [=Attic -ήν]) **Lk 10:18.** Likew. of other things that come down like rain to punish sinners: fire **Lk 9:54** (cp. 4 Km 1:10; TestAbr A 10 p. 88, 14 [Stone p. 24]); **Rv 20:9;** fire and brimstone **Lk 17:29** (cp. Gen 19:24); apocalyptic hail **Rv 16:21;** AcPl Ha 5, 7.

ⓒ as starry heaven IEph 19:2. τὰ ἄστρα τοῦ οὐρ. (cp. ἄστρον and s. Eur., Phoen. 1; Diod. S. 6, 2, 2 ἥλιον κ. σελήνην κ. τὰ ἄλλα ἄστρα τὰ κατ' οὐρανόν; Ael. Aristid. 43, 13 K.=1 p. 5 D.; TestAbr A 1 p. 78, 1 [Stone p. 4]; JosAs 2:11) **Hb 11:12.** οἱ ἀστέρες τοῦ οὐρ. 1 Cl 32:2 (Gen 22:17); cp. 10:6 (Gen 15:5). In the time of tribulation at the end of the world the stars will fall fr. heaven **Mt 24:29a; Mk 13:25a; Rv 6:13; 12:4.** Cp. **8:10; 9:1.** ἡ στρατιὰ τοῦ οὐρ. (s. οὐράνιος) *the host of heaven,* of the stars, which some Israelites illicitly worshipped **Ac 7:42** (worship of the στρατιὰ τοῦ οὐρ. in enmity to Yahweh also Jer 7:18; 19:13; Zeph 1:5; 2 Ch 33:3, 5). These are also meant by the δυνάμεις τῶν οὐρανῶν **Mt 24:29b; Lk 21:26;** cp. **Mk 13:25b** (cp. δύναμις 4).

ⓓ as place of atmosphere (cp. TestAbr A 9 p. 87, 15 [Stone p. 22] εἰς τὴν αἰθέρα τοῦ οὐρανοῦ); clouds hover in it, the νεφέλαι τοῦ οὐρ. (s. νεφέλη) **Mt 24:30b; 26:64; Mk 14:62;** D 16:8. Likew. the birds, τὰ πετεινὰ τοῦ οὐρανοῦ (Gen 1:26; Ps 8:9; Jdth 11:7; ParJer 7:3; cp. Bar 3:17) **Mt 6:26; 8:20; 13:32; Mk 4:32; Lk 8:5; 9:58; Ac 10:12; 11:6;** B 6:12 (Gen 1:26), 18; Hs 9, 24, 1; GJs 3:2 codd.; 18:2 codd.—πυρράζει ὁ οὐρανός **Mt 16:2, 3.**—In connection w. τὸν σατανᾶν ἐκ τοῦ οὐρανοῦ πεσόντα **Lk 10:18** the atmosphere may well be thought of as an abode of evil spirits. On Satan as the ἄρχων τῆς ἐξουσίας τοῦ ἀέρος, s. ἀήρ. Cp. also the λεγόμενοι θεοὶ εἴτε ἐν οὐρ. εἴτε ἐπὶ γῆς **1 Cor 8:5.** In any case **Rv 12:7f** speaks of the dragon and his angels as being in heaven.

ⓔ The concept of more than one heaven (the idea is Semitic; but s. FTorm, ZNW 33, '34, 48–50, who refers to Anaximander and Aristot. Also Ps.-Apollod. 1, 6, 1, 2 ms. and Achilles Tat. 2, 36, 4 and 37, 2 ms. have οὐρανοί; Himerius, Or. 66 [=Or. 20], 4 οὐρανοί as the abode of the gods; also Hesychius Miles. [VI AD] c. 66 JFlach of the 'godless heathen' Tribonian.—Schlatter, Mt[2] p. 58 on 3:2: 'The pl. οὐρανοί is found neither in Philo nor Joseph.' Cp. PKatz, Philo's Bible '50, 141–46; Mussies 84) is also found in our lit. (s. 1aα; Theoph. Ant. 1, 4 [p. 64, 15]), but it is not always possible to decide with certainty just where the idea is really alive and where it simply survives in a formula (in J's Gospel the pl. is entirely absent; **Rv** has it only **12:12** [fr. LXX]. **Eph** always has the pl. In others the sing. and pl. are interchanged for no apparent reason [cp. **Hb 9:23** w. 24 or Hv 1, 1, 4 w. 1, 2, 1; also GPt 10:40f; Ps. 113:11 lines 1 and 2; TestAbr, TestJob, Just., Tat.]): *the third heaven* (cp. Ps.-Lucian, Philopatris 12 ἐς τρίτον οὐρανὸν ἀεροβατήσας [s. on ἀνακαινίζω and πνεῦμα 8]; PSI 29, 2ff [IV AD?] ἐπικαλοῦμαί σε τὸν καθήμενον ἐν τῷ πρώτῳ οὐρανῷ . . . ἐν τῷ β' οὐρ. . . . ἐν τῷ γ' οὐρ.; Simplicius, In Epict. p. 100, 13 Düb. ὀκτὼ οὐρανοί; TestLevi 3:3; GrBar 11:1 εἰς πέμπτον οὐ. Combination of the third heaven and paradise, GrBar 10:1ff; ApcMos 37. S. τρίτος 1a) **2 Cor 12:2** (s. JohJeremias, Der Gottesberg 1919, 41ff; Ltzm., Hdb.[4] '49, exc. on 2 Cor 12:3f [lit.]). ὑπεράνω πάντων τῶν οὐρανῶν **Eph 4:10.** τ. πάντα ἐν τ. οὐρανοῖς κ. ἐπὶ τ. γῆς **Col 1:16;** cp. vs. **20.** ἔργα τ. χειρῶν σού εἰσιν οἱ οὐρ. **Hb 1:10** (Ps 101:26).—**4:14; 7:26; 2 Pt 3:5, 7, 10, 12f** (of the heavens, their destruction in the final conflagration, and their replacement by the καινοὶ οὐρ.); 1 Cl 20:1; 33:3. τακήσονταί τινες τῶν οὐρανῶν 2 Cl 16:3.—S. also Lampe s.v. 2.—From the concept of various celestial levels a transition is readily made to

❷ **transcendent abode,** ***heaven*** (the pl. is preferred for this mng.: B-D-F §141, 1; Rob. 408)**—ⓐ** as the dwelling-place (or throne) of God (Sappho, fgm. 56 D.[2] [=Campbell 54] of Eros; Solon 1, 22 D.[3] of Zeus; Hom. Hymn to Aphrodite 291 [all three οὐρ. in the sing. as the seat of the gods]; Pla., Phdr. 246e ὁ μέγας ἐν οὐρανῷ Ζεύς; Ps.-Aristot., De Mundo 2, 2; 3, 4 ὁ οὐρ. as οἰκητήριον θεοῦ or θεῶν; Dio Chrys. 19[36], 22 θεῶν μακάρων κατ' οὐρανόν; Artem. 2, 68 p. 159, 13 ὁ οὐρανὸς θεῶν ἐστιν οἶκος; Ael. Aristid. 43, 14 K.=1 p. 5 D.; Maximus Tyr. 11, 11b; ins from Saïtaï in Lydia [δύναμις 5]; IAndrosIsis, Cyrene 8 p. 129.—On the OT: GWestphal, Jahwes Wohnstätten 1908, 214–73) **Mt 23:22; Ac 7:55f; Hb 8:1;** B 16:2b (Is 66:1); Dg 10:7. ὁ θεὸς ὁ ἐν τοῖς οὐρ. Hv 1, 1, 6 (cp. Tob 5:17 S). ὁ θεὸς τοῦ οὐρ. (Gen 24:3) **Rv 11:13; 16:11.** ὁ κύριος ἐν οὐρανοῖς **Eph 6:9;** cp. **Col 4:1.** ὁ πατὴρ ὑμῶν (μου, ἡμῶν) ὁ ἐν (τοῖς) οὐρ. (silver tablet fr. Amisos: ARW 12, 1909, 25 ἐγώ εἰμι ὁ μέγας ὁ ἐν οὐρανῷ καθήμενος) **Mt 5:16, 45; 6:1, 9; 7:11, 21b; 10:33; 12:50; 16:17; 18:10b, 14, 19; Mk 11:25f; Lk 11:2 v.l.;** D 8:2 (here the sing. ὁ ἐν τῷ οὐρ. Cp. PGM 12, 261 τῷ ἐν οὐρανῷ θεῷ).ὁ πατὴρ ὁ ἐξ οὐρανοῦ *the Father who* (gives) *from heaven* **Lk 11:13** (Jos., Ant. 9, 73 ἐκχέαι τὸν θεὸν ἐξ οὐρανοῦ). God dwells in τὰ ὕψη τῶν οὐρ. 1 Cl 36:2. Therefore the one who prays looks up toward heaven: ἀναβλέπειν εἰς τὸν οὐρ. (s. ἀναβλέπω 1) **Mt 14:19; Mk 6:41; 7:34; Lk 9:16;** MPol 9:2; 14:1. ἀτενίσας εἰς τὸν οὐρ. εἶδεν δόξαν θεοῦ **Ac 7:55;** ἐπάρας τ. ὀφθαλμοὺς αὐτοῦ εἰς τὸν οὐρ. **J 17:1.**—The Spirit of God comes fr. (the open) heaven **Mt 3:16; Mk 1:10; Lk 3:21; J 1:32; Ac 2:2(–4); 1 Pt 1:12;** AcPlCor 2:5. The voice of God resounds fr. it (Maximus Tyr. 35, 7b Διὸς ἐξ οὐρανοῦ μέγα βοῶντος, the words follow) **Mt 3:17; Mk 1:11; Lk 3:22; J 12:28; Ac 11:9;** MPol 9:1 (cp. Just., D. 88, 8), and it is gener. the place where divine pronouncements originate **Ac 11:5** and their end vs. **10.** The ὀργὴ θεοῦ reveals itself fr. heaven **Ro 1:18** (s. Jos., Bell. 1, 630 τὸν ἀπ' οὐρανοῦ δικαστήν). Also, a σημεῖον ἐκ (ἀπὸ) τοῦ οὐρ. is a *sign given by God* **Mt 16:1; Mk 8:11; Lk 11:16;** cp. **21:11.**—Lampe s.v. 4.

ⓑ Christ is ἐξ οὐρανοῦ *from heaven, of a heavenly nature* **1 Cor 15:47** (s. ἄνθρωπος 1d. On this HKennedy, St. Paul and the Conception of the 'Heavenly Man': Exp. 8th ser., 7, 1913, 97–110; EGraham, CQR 113, '32, 226) and *has come down from heaven* **J 3:13b, 31; 6:38, 42, 50** (Ar. 15, 1 ἀπ' οὐρανοῦ καταβάς; Mel., P. 66, 467 ἀφικόμενος ἐξ οὐρανῶν), as ὁ ἄρτος ἐκ τοῦ οὐρανοῦ (s. ἄρτος 2). Cp. **Ro 10:6.** He returned to heaven (τὴν ἔνσαρκον εἰς τοὺς οὐρανοὺ ἀνάληψιν Iren. 1, 10, 1 [Harv. I 91, 2]; on the ascension s. CHönn, Studien zur Geschichte der Hf. im klass. Altertum: Progr. Mannheim 1910; EPfister, Der Reliquienkult im Altertum II 1912, 480ff;

HDiels, Himmels u. Höllenfahrten v. Homer bis Dante: NJklA 49, 1922, 239–53; RHolland, Zur Typik der Himmelfahrt: ARW 23, 1925, 207–20; JKroll, Gott u. Hölle '32, 533 [ind.: Ascensus]; WMichaelis, Zur Überl. der Hf.s-geschichte: ThBl 4, 1925, 101–9; AFridrichsen, D. Hf. bei Lk: ibid. 6, 1927, 337–41; GBertram, Die Hf. Jesu vom Kreuz: Deissmann Festschr. 1927, 187–217 [UHolzmeister, ZKT 55, '31, 44–82]; HSchlier, Christus u. d. Kirche im Eph 1930, 1ff; VLarrañaga, L'Ascension de Notre-Seigneur dans le NT '38 [fr. Spanish]. S. also at ἀνάστασις 2 end, and διά A 2a) to live there in glory: **Mk 16:19; Lk 24:51; Ac 1:10f** (AZwiep, The Ascension of the Messiah in Lukan Christology '97); **2:34; 7:55f; 9:3; 22:6; 1 Pt 3:22;** B 15:9. Christians await his return fr. heaven: **Ac 1:11; Phil 3:20; 1 Th 1:10; 4:16; 2 Th 1:7** (Just., A I, 51, 8 al.).—When Messianic woes have come to an end, τότε φανήσεται τὸ σημεῖον τοῦ υἱοῦ τ. ἀνθρώπου ἐν οὐρανῷ *then the sign of the Human One (who is) in heaven will appear;* acc. to the context, the sign consists in this, that he appears visibly in heavenly glory **Mt 24:30.**—Lampe s.v. 10b.

ⓒ as the abode of angels (Gen 21:17; 22:11; Ps.-Clem., Hom. 8, 12; TestAbr A 4 p. 80, 34 [Stone p. 8]; ParJer 3:2; ApcMos 38; Just., D. 57, 2) **Mt 18:10a; 22:30; 24:36; 28:2; Mk 12:25; 13:32; Lk 2:15; 22:43; J 1:51; Gal 1:8; Rv 10:1; 18:1; 19:14; 20:1.** Cp. **Eph 3:15.**—Lampe s.v. 7.

ⓓ Christians who have died also dwell in heaven (cp. Dio Chrys. 23 [40], 35 οὐρανοῦ καὶ τῶν ἐν αὐτῷ θείων κ. μακαρίων αἰώνιον τάξιν; Libanius, Or. 21 p. 459, 9 F. πόρρω τοῦ τὸν οὐρανὸν οἰκοῦντος χοροῦ; Oenomaus in Eus., PE 5, 33, 5; 12; Artem. 2, 68 p. 160, 25 τὰς ψυχὰς ἀπαλλαγείσας τῶν σωμάτων εἰς τὸν οὐρανὸν ἀνιέναι τάχει χρωμένας ὑπερβάλλοντι; Himerius, Or. 8 [=23], 23: the daemon of the dead holds the σῶμα of the dead person, τὴν ψυχὴν ὁ οὐρανός; Quintus Smyrn. 7, 88; TestAbr A 20 p. 103, 26 [Stone p. 54]; TestJob 39:13; ApcEsdr 7:3). Their life, τὸ ἀληθῶς ἐν οὐρανῷ ζῆν, stands in strong contrast to the ὄντως θάνατος, that leads to the everlasting fire Dg 10:7b. Rhoda, who *greets* Hermas *from heaven* Hv 1, 1, 4, need not have died (s. MDibelius, Hdb. ad loc.), and still she shows us that heaven is open to the devout. Furthermore, the true citizenship of Christians is *in heaven* (Tat. 16, 1 τὴν ἐν οὐρανοῖς πορείαν; s. πολίτευμα) **Phil 3:20;** cp. Dg 5:9. Their names are enrolled *in heaven* (s. βίβλος 2) **Lk 10:20; Hb 12:23.** In heaven there await them their glorified body **2 Cor 5:1f,** their reward **Mt 5:12; Lk 6:23,** their treasure **Mt 6:20; Lk 12:33,** the things they hoped for **Col 1:5,** their inheritance **1 Pt 1:4.** It is a place of peace **Lk 19:38.**—ἐκ τοῦ οὐρανοῦ the New Jerusalem (s. Ἱεροσόλυμα 2) will come down to earth **Rv 3:12; 21:2, 10.**

ⓔ The concept of a heaven in which God, attendant spirits of God, and the righteous dead abide, makes it easy to understand the taking over of certain OT expressions in which heaven is personified εὐφραίνεσθε οἱ οὐρανοί (cp. Is 44:23; 49:13; Mel., P. 98, 747) **Rv 12:12;** cp. **18:20;** B 9:3 (Is 1:2); 11:2 (Jer 2:12); 1 Cl 27:7 (Ps 18:2).

❸ **an indirect reference to God,** ***God*** fig. ext. of 2 (s. βασιλεία 1b.—A common Hebrew practice, but not unknown among polytheists: Philippides Com. [IV/III BC] 27 νὴ τὸν οὐρανόν. Acc. to Clem. Al., Protr. 5, 66, 4 Θεόφραστος πῇ μὲν οὐρανὸν, πῇ δὲ πνεῦμα τὸν θεὸν ὑπονοεῖ=Theophrastus at one time thinks of God as heaven and at another time as spirit; Appian, Hann. 56 §233 σημεῖα ἐκ Διός [ln. 14 Viereck-R.]=ἐξ οὐρανοῦ [ln. 16]; JosAs 19:2; SEG XXVIII, 1251, 3 [III/IV AD; s. New Docs 3, 49f]). ἁμαρτάνειν εἰς τὸν οὐρ. *sin against God* **Lk 15:18, 21.** ἐξ οὐρανοῦ ἢ ἐξ ἀνθρώπων **Mt 21:25; Mk 11:30f; Lk 20:4f.** βασιλεία τῶν οὐρ. (GrBar 11:2) in Mt=βασιλεία τοῦ θεοῦ **3:2; 4:17; 5:3, 10, 19f; 7:21; 8:11; 10:7; 11:11f; 13:11, 24, 31, 33, 44f, 47, 52; 16:19; 18:1, 3f, 23; 19:12, 14, 23; 20:1; 22:2; 23:13; 25:1: J 3:5** v.l.; AcPl Ha 8, 31 (restored)=BMM verso 3.—B. 53; 1484. DELG. M-M. DLNT 439–43. EDNT. TW. Sv.

Οὐρβανός, οῦ, ὁ (lead tablet fr. Hadrumetum 13 [Dssm., B 29; 37—BS 275; 283] τὸν Οὐρβανὸν ὃν ἔτεκεν Οὐρβανά; PSI 27, 7 al. The Lat. Urbanus in ins, e.g. ILS 7566; 7986 and Lghtf., Phil p. 174) ***Urbanus,*** addressee of a greeting, described as συνεργὸς ἡμῶν ἐν Χριστῷ **Ro 16:9.**—M-M.

Οὐρίας, ου, ὁ (אוּרִיָּה) ***Uriah,*** husband of Bathsheba who, after his death, married David and bore Solomon to him (2 Km 11; 12:24; TestSol; Jos., Ant. 7, 131–41; 144; 146; 153f; Just., D. 141, 4.—The name is also found elsewh. in the OT and Joseph. [gen. Οὐρία: Ant. 7, 141; 144]) ἡ τοῦ Οὐρίου *the wife of Uriah* **Mt 1:6.**—TW.

οὖς, ὠτός, τό (Hom.+)—❶ **the auditory organ,** ***ear*** **Mk 7:33.** δεξιόν **Lk 22:50** (MRostovzeff, ZNW 33, '34, 196–99 after PTebt 793 XI, 1ff [183 BC] Ἡσίοδος . . . τὸν Δωρίωνος δεξιὸν ὦτα εἰς τέλος ἐξέτεμεν. Also Leo Gramm. 118, 10 IBekker [1842] ἀπετμήθη τὸ δεξιὸν ὦς [=οὖς]; s. JDoeve, Die Gefangennahme Jesu, Studia Evangelica 73, '59, 457–80: connects w. Am 3:12; for another view s. SHall, ibid. 501f); **1 Cor 12:16.** ἃ οὖς οὐκ ἤκουσεν in the apocr. saying of unknown origin (s. Hdb. z. NT6 [J][3] '33, 4f) **1 Cor 2:9;** 1 Cl 34:8; 2 Cl 11:7; MPol 2:3. πρὸς τὸ οὖς λαλεῖν τι *say someth. into someone's ear,* i.e. *secretly* or in *confidence, whisper* (Plut., Demetr. 895 [14, 3]; Jos., Ant. 6, 165; cp. Diog. L. 9, 26 εἰπεῖν πρὸς τὸ οὖς; JosAs 24:2 εἶπον . . . εἰς τὸ οὖς αὐτοῦ) **Lk 12:3.** εἰς τὸ οὖς ἀκούειν (Eur., Or. 616, Andr. 1091) **Mt 10:27.** Differently λαλεῖν εἰς τὰ ὦτα τῶν ἁγίων, where there is no suggestion of secrecy (cp. 2 Km 3:19) Hv 3, 8, 11; 4, 3, 6. ὦτα κυρίου εἰς δέησιν αὐτῶν *the ears of the Lord are open to their prayer* **1 Pt 3:12;** cp. 1 Cl 22:6 (both Ps 33:16; cp. GrBar 1:5). συνέχειν τὰ ὦτα αὐτῶν *hold their ears shut* **Ac 7:57.** βύειν τὰ ὦτα *stop the ears* IEph 9:1 (s. βύω). εἰσέρχεσθαι εἰς τὰ ὦτά τινος *come to someone's ears* (Paroem. Gr.: Zenob. [II AD] 3, 49 εἰς θεῶν ὦτα ἦλθεν; Ps 17:7; GrBar 1:5) **Js 5:4** (cp. Is 5:9); also γίνεσθαι **Lk 1:44.** ἠκούσθη τι εἰς τὰ ὦτά τινος *someth. came to someone's ears* (Is 5:9) **Ac 11:22.** ἐν τοῖς ὠσί τινος *in someone's hearing* (Dt 5:1; 2 Km 3:19; Bar 1:3f) **Lk 4:21.** If **Mt 13:16** is to be interpreted fr. the vantage point of vs. 17, it belongs here. If, on the other hand, it is to be explained on the basis of what precedes, it belongs under 2.

❷ **mental and spiritual understanding,** ***ear, hearing,*** transference fr. οὖς as sense perception (cp. Just., A I, 53, 1 τοῖς τὰ ἀκουστικὰ καὶ νοερὰ ὦτα ἔχουσιν): τοῖς ὠσὶ βαρέως ἀκούειν *be hard of hearing*=comprehend slowly (or, rather, not at all) **Mt 13:15a; Ac 28:27a** (both Is 6:10a); cp. **Mt 13:15b; Ac 28:27b** (both Is 6:10b). θέσθε ὑμεῖς εἰς τὰ ὦτα ὑμῶν τοὺς λόγους τούτους *receive the following words into your ears,* i.e. *take them to heart* **Lk 9:44** (cp. Ex 17:14 δὸς εἰς τὰ ὦτα Ἰησοῖ); ὦτα τοῦ μὴ ἀκούειν **Ro 11:8** (cp. Dt 29:3). W. ἔχειν (Hermocles [IV/III BC] p. 174, 16 Coll. Alex. [=Athen. 6, 63, 253e] images of the gods οὐκ ἔχουσιν ὦτα) ὦτα ἔχοντες οὐκ ἀκούετε; **Mk 8:18** (cp. Jer 5:21; Ezk 12:2). ὁ ἔχων οὖς ἀκουσάτω **Rv 2:7, 11, 17, 29; 3:6, 13, 22;** cp. **13:9.** ὁ ἔχων ὦτα ἀκουέτω **Mt 11:15; 13:9, 43.** ὃς (εἴ τις) ἔχει ὦτα ἀκούειν ἀκουέτω **Mk 4:9, 23; 7:16.** ὁ ἔχων ὦτα ἀκούειν ἀκουέτω **Lk 8:8; 14:35;** Ox 1081, 35f, sim. 6–8f=Otero p. 83 (SJCh 90, 13f, sim. 89, 4–6) (MDibelius, 'Wer Ohren hat zu hören, der höre': StKr 83, 1910, 461–71. Cp. Heraclitus [Vorsokrat.[5] 22b 34] ἀξύνετοι ἀκούσαντες κωφοῖσιν ἐοίκασιν). ἀπερίτμητοι καρδίαις καὶ τοῖς ὠσίν *uncircumcised in hearts and ears* i.e. impervious to moral instruction **Ac 7:51** (ἀπερίτμητος 2).—B. 226. DELG. M-M. TW.

οὐσία, ας, ἡ (εἰμί 'to exist') **that which exists and therefore has substance,** ***property, wealth*** (so Eur., Hdt.+; ins, pap; Tob 14:13 BA; 3 Macc 3:28; ApcSed 6:7 p. 132, 2 Ja.; Philo; Jos., Bell. 4, 241, Ant., 7, 114; Just., Ath.; Mel., fgm. 6, 12) **Lk 15:12f** (Diog. L. 9, 35 three brothers, one of whom wishes to move to a distant land, divide the οὐσία among them. Acc. to ApcSed 6:7 [= p. 132, 2 Ja.], the father takes possession of his son's property and evicts him).—HBerger, Ousia in de dialogen van Plato, '61.—B. 769. DELG s.v. εἰμί. M-M. Sv.

οὔτε adv. (Hom.+. In the mss. freq. exchanged w. οὐδέ: as **v.l.,** e.g. **Mk 5:3; Lk 12:26; 20:36; J 1:25; Ac 4:12; 1 Cor 3:2; Gal 1:12a; 1 Th 2:3; Rv 5:3; 9:20; 12:8; 20:4;** as text: **Gal 1:12b** οὔτε ἐδιδάχθην; **Js 3:12; Rv 5:3, 4** (both οὔτε βλέπειν αὐτό). In several places only οὐδέ is attested, where one should expect οὔτε: Rv 7:16; 9:4; 21:23.—Mayser p. 177; B-D-F §445, 1; Valley s.v. οὐδέ, end.—SIG 747, 27 [73 BC] οὔτε stands for οὐδέ; cp. **Rv 12:8 v.l.** and **20:4 v.l.;** s. also **5:4** [οὐδέ as v.l. for correct οὔτε]) ***and not.*** οὔτε … οὔτε *neither … nor* (Jos., Ant. 3, 16; 15, 182) ὅπου οὔτε σὴς οὔτε βρῶσις ἀφανίζει **Mt 6:20.** Cp. **22:30; Mk 12:25; 14:68; Lk 12:24 v.l., 27 v.l.** (for οὐ … οὐδέ); **14:35; 20:35; J 4:21; 5:37; 8:19; 9:3; Ac 2:31; 15:10; 19:37; 28:21; 1 Cor 3:7; 8:8; 11:11; Gal 5:6; 6:15; Rv 3:15f;** AcPlCor 2:30. οὔτε … οὔτε … οὔτε *neither … nor … nor* (ParJer 5:7 and Just., D. 127, 2 four members; Apc4Esdr fgm. b five members; Xenophon Eph. 1, 7, 1 p. 335, 28–30 six members) **Ac 25:8; Ro 8:38f** (οὔτε ten times); **1 Cor 6:9f** (οὔτε seven times, continued and concluded by οὐ three times); **1 Th 2:5f** (οὔτε three times, then twice in a new series: οὔτε ἀφ' ὑμῶν οὔτε ἀπ' ἄλλων); **Rv 9:20.**—οὔτε several times after οὐ vs. **21;** before (and after) οὐ **21:4.** In **Ac 24:12f** οὔτε threefold *neither … nor … nor* is continued by οὐδέ *and … not at all.* οὐδὲ γάρ … οὔτε *for … not, … nor* **Gal 1:12** (v.l. has οὐδέ twice). οὐκ ἀφεθήσεται αὐτῷ οὔτε ἐν τούτῳ τ. αἰῶνι οὔτε ἐν τ. μέλλοντι **Mt 12:32** (the second οὔτε here is perhaps felt as intensifying = nor, I assure you, in the age to come. Cp. Arrian, Anab. 7, 14, 3 οὔτε βασιλεῖ οὔτε Ἀλεξάνδρῳ=neither for a king nor especially for Alex.). Solitary οὔτε (TestJob 22:2 τάχα οὔτε ἄρτου χορτάζεται=soon [Job] will starve for want of bread; Just., A I, 43, 2) οὐδεὶς ἄξιος εὑρέθη ἀνοῖξαι τὸ βιβλίον οὔτε βλέπειν αὐτό **Rv 5:4.**—οὔτε … καί (very rare in older Gk. [Kühner-G. II 291, 3a: Eur., I. T. 591f]. More freq. later: Plut., Mor. 1115b; Polyaenus 1, 30, 8; Lucian, Jupp. Trag. 5, Dial. Meretr. 2, 4 οὔτε πάντα ἡ Λεσβία, Δωρί, πρὸς σὲ ἐψεύσατο καὶ σὺ τἀληθῆ ἀπήγγελκας Μυρτίῳ; Aelian, NA 1, 57; 11, 9; Longus, Past. 1, 17; 4, 28; ApcSed 14:10; Jos., Bell. 2, 403; 463.—B-D-F §445, 3; s. Rob. 1189) οὔτε ἄντλημα ἔχεις καὶ τὸ φρέαρ ἐστὶν βαθύ *you have no bucket, and the well is deep* **J 4:11.** οὔτε αὐτὸς ἐπιδέχεται τοὺς ἀδελφοὺς καὶ τοὺς βουλομένους κωλύει **3J 10.**—**Js 3:12** οὔτε can scarcely be correct, and perh. the text is faulty (s. B-D-F §445, 1; without critique Rob. 1189).—M-M.

οὗτος, αὕτη, τοῦτο (Hom.+) demonstrative pron., used as adj. and subst. On its use s. B-D-F §290 al.; W-S. §23; Rob. 697–706; Mlt-Turner 192f; cp. Schwyzer II 208–10.

❶ as subst., **the person or thing comparatively near at hand in the discourse material,** ***this, this one*** (contrast ἐκεῖνος referring to someth. comparatively farther away; cp. **Lk 18:14; Js 4:15;** Hm 3:5)

ⓐ gener.—**α.** w. ref. to someth. here and now, directing attention to it (Appian, Liby. 62 §276 οὗτος=this man here [referring to one who is present; s. Schwyzer II 208]. Cp. Pherecrates Com. 134 K. οὗτος πόθεν ἦλθες;='you there, where did you come from?'; cp. ὦ οὗτος οὗτος Aristoph., Vesp. 1364; TestAbr B 6 p. 110, 17 [Stone p. 68] οὗτός ἐστιν τῶν τριῶν ἀνδρῶν εἷς 'he is one of the three men'; TestJob 30:2 οὗτός ἐστιν *he's the one*) οὗτός ἐστιν ὁ υἱός μου **Mt 3:17; 17:5; Mk 9:7; Lk 7:44ff; J 1:15, 30; Ac 2:15; 4:10; 2 Pt 1:17** and oft. τοῦτό ἐστιν τὸ σῶμά μου *this is my body* (s. εἰμί 2cα end) **Mt 26:26; Mk 14:22; Lk 22:19** (ÉDelebecque, Études grecques sur l'évangile de Luc '76, 109–21); **1 Cor 11:24.** τοῦτό ἐστιν τὸ αἷμά μου **Mt 26:28; Mk 14:24.**—W. a connotation of contempt (Ael. Aristid. 53 p. 628 D.: ὦ οὗτος=O you poor fellow! Likew. Maximus Tyr. 37, 8d; in refutation Just., D. 39, 4; 128, 2) **Lk 5:21; 7:39, 49; 15:30** (Reader, Polemo 325); **22:59; J 6:42, 52.** Contexts suggest a related nuance in **Mt 13:55f** (JosAs 4:13 οὐχ οὗτός ἐστιν ὁ υἱὸς τοῦ ποιμένος … ;); **21:10; Mk 6:2f; J 7:15.** (Other reff. Rob. 697; s. also 2a below.)—Cp. **Mt 21:11; Ac 9:21.**

β. w. ref. to someth. that has immediately preceded, *this one* (who has just been mentioned) **Lk 1:32; J 1:2; 6:71; 2 Ti 3:6, 8.** —At the beginning of a narrative concerning a pers. already mentioned **Mt 3:3; Lk 2:36, 37 v.l., 38 v.l.; 7:12 v.l.; 8:42 v.l.; 16:1; J 1:41; 3:2; 12:21; 21:21a; Ac 21:24; Ro 16:2 v.l.; 1 Cor 7:12** (on the interchange of αὐτή and αὕτη s. B-D-F §277, 3).—Emphasizing a pers. already mentioned *this (very) one* **Mt 21:11; J 9:9; Ac 4:10** (ἐν τούτῳ); **9:20; 1J 5:6; 2 Pt 2:17.** καὶ τοῦτον ἐσταυρωμένον *and him as the crucified one* **1 Cor 2:2.** καὶ τούτους ἀποτρέπου *avoid such people* (as I have just described) **2 Ti 3:5.** καὶ οὗτος *this one* (just mentioned) *also* **Hb 8:3** (JosAs 7:3 καὶ αὕτη).

γ. w. ref. to a subject more remote in the paragraph, but closer to the main referent under discussion (W-S. §23, 2; Rob. 702f) **Ac 4:11; 7:19; 2J 7; Jd 7** rebellious angels vs. 6).

δ. w. ref. to what follows: w. a relative foll. οὗτος ὅς **Lk 5:21.** οὗτοί εἰσιν οἵτινες **8:15.** οὗτοί εἰσιν οἱ ἐπὶ τὰ πετρώδη σπειρόμενοι, οἵ … *these are the ones sowed on the rocky ground, who* … **Mk 4:16.** ταύτην … εἰς ἣν στῆτε **1 Pt 5:12.** οὗτοι … ὅπου **Mk 4:15** s. ὅπου 1aα.—W. ὅτι foll.: αὕτη ἐστὶν ἡ κρίσις ὅτι **J 3:19;** cp. **1J 1:5; 5:11, 14.**—W. ἵνα foll.: αὕτη ἐστὶν ἡ ἐντολὴ ἡ ἐμή, ἵνα **J 15:12;** cp. **17:3; 1J 3:11, 23; 5:3; 2J 6ab.** τοῦτό ἐστι τὸ ἔργον, τὸ θέλημα τοῦ θεοῦ, ἵνα **J 6:29, 39f.**—W. inf. foll. **Js 1:27.**—W. ptc. foll. (ApcSed 15:5; Just., D. 2, 1; Mel., P. 68, 486) οὗτος ὁ ἀνοίξας **J 11:37.** οὗτοί εἰσιν οἱ τὸν λόγον ἀκούσαντες *these are the ones who have heard the word* **Mk 4:18.** ἀδελφοί μου οὗτοί εἰσιν οἱ … ἀκούοντες καὶ ποιοῦντες **Lk 8:21.**—W. subst. foll. αὕτη ἐστὶν ἡ νίκη … ἡ πίστις ἡμῶν **1J 5:4.**

ε. Resuming someth. previously mentioned, w. special emphasis—a subst.: Μωϋσῆν, ὃν ἠρνήσαντο … τοῦτον ὁ θεὸς … *Moses, whom they rejected, … is the very one whom God* **Ac 7:35** (Ps.-Callisth. 2, 16, 10 Δαρεῖος …, οὗτος). τῶν ἀνδρῶν … ἕνα τούτων *of the men … one of these (very men)* **Ac 1:21f.** οὐ τὰ τέκνα τ. σαρκὸς ταῦτα τέκνα τ. θεοῦ **Ro 9:8;** cp. vs. **6.** ἕκαστος ἐν τῇ κλήσει ᾗ ἐκλήθη, ἐν ταύτῃ μενέτω *in this (very one)* **1 Cor 7:20.** Cp. **J 10:25; Ac 2:23; 4:10; Ro 7:10; Gal 3:7.**—A relative clause: ὃς ἂν ποιήσῃ καὶ διδάξῃ, οὗτος … **Mt 5:19.**—**Mk 3:35; 6:16; Lk 9:24b, 26; J 3:26; Ro 8:30.** δι' ἧς σαρκὸς … διὰ ταύτης AcPl Ha 2, 15. ὃ …, τοῦτο **Ac 3:6; Ro 7:15f, 19f; Gal 6:7.** ἃ …, ταῦτα **J 8:26; Gal 5:17b; Phil 4:9; 2 Ti 2:2.** ὅστις …, οὗτος **Mt 18:4.** ἅτινα …, ταῦτα **Phil 3:7.** ὅσοι …, οὗτοι **Ro 8:14; Gal 6:12.**—A ptc.: ὁ ὑπομείνας, οὗτος σωθήσεται **Mt 10:22.**—**13:20, 22; 24:13; 26:23; Mk 12:40; Lk 9:48; J 6:46; 15:5; Ac 15:38; 1 Cor 6:4.**—After εἴ τις **Ro 8:9; 1 Cor 3:17; 8:3; Js 1:23; 3:2.**—ὅσα ἐστὶν ἀληθῆ, ὅσα σεμνά, ὅσα … (ὅσα six times altogether), εἴ τις ἀρετὴ καὶ εἴ τις ἔπαινος, ταῦτα λογίζεσθε **Phil 4:8.**—After ἐάν τις **J 9:31.** After ὅταν **Ro 2:14.** After καθώς **J 8:28.**—After the articular inf. εἰ τὸ ζῆν ἐν σαρκί, τοῦτο . . . **Phil 1:22.**

ζ. used w. αὐτός: αὐτὸς οὗτος *he himself* **Ac 25:25.** Pl. **24:15, 20.** On αὐτὸ τοῦτο **2 Pt 1:5** s. αὐτός 1g and Schwyzer II 211.

η. As a subject, the demonstr. can take on the gender of its predicate (W-S. §23, 5; Rob. 698): τὸ καλὸν σπέρμα, οὗτοί εἰσιν οἱ υἱοὶ τῆς βασιλείας **Mt 13:38.** Cp. **Lk 8:14f.**—**Mt 7:12; Lk 2:12; 8:11; 22:53; J 1:19; Ro 11:27** (Is 59:21); **1 Cor 9:3; Gal 4:24.**

ⓑ In particular, the neut. is used (for the fem. sg. **Mk 12:11; Mt 21:42** [both Ps 117:23] s. B-D-F 138, 2)

α. w. ref. to what precedes: **Lk 5:6; J 6:61; Ac 19:17.** As the obj. of a verb of saying (Jos., Vi. 291, Ant. 20, 123 al.) **Lk 24:40; J 6:6; 7:9; 8:6; 12:33; 18:38** al.—Freq. w. preposition (cp. Johannessohn, Präp. 383 [index]): διὰ τοῦτο cp. διά B 2b. εἰς τοῦτο cp. εἰς 4f. ἐκ τούτου cp. ἐκ 3e (='for this reason' also PRyl 81, 24). ἐν τούτῳ *for this reason* **J 16:30; Ac 24:16; 1 Cor 4:4; 2 Cor 5:2;** *by this* **1J 3:19.** ἐπὶ τούτῳ s. ἐπί 18b. μετὰ τοῦτο cp. μετά B 2c. τούτου χάριν (PAmh 130, 6 [I AD]; Just., D. 1, 2) **Eph 3:14.**—The pl. summarizes what precedes: **Lk 8:8; 11:27; 24:26; J 5:34; 15:11; 21:24** and oft.—On Midrashic use in Ac, s. EEllis, BRigaux Festschr., '70, 303–12.

β. w. ref. to what follows, esp. before clauses that express a statement, purpose, result, or condition, which it introduces: τοῦτο λέγω w. direct discourse foll. *this is what I mean* **Gal 3:17;** in ellipsis τοῦτο δέ *the point is this* **2 Cor 9:6;** w. ὅτι foll. **1 Cor 1:12.** τοῦτό φημι ὅτι **7:29 v.l.; 15:50.** τοῦτο γινώσκειν, ὅτι **Lk 10:11; 12:39; Ro 6:6; 2 Ti 3:1; 2 Pt 1:20; 3:3.** (Just., D. 110, 1). λογίζῃ τοῦτο, ὅτι . . .; **Ro 2:3;** ὁμολογῶ τοῦτο, ὅτι **Ac 24:14.** εἰδὼς τοῦτο, ὅτι *understanding this, that* **1 Ti 1:9.** τοῦτο ἔχεις, ὅτι **Rv 2:6.**—W. ἵνα foll.: πόθεν μοι τοῦτο, ἵνα ἔλθῃ ἡ μήτηρ . . . ; **Lk 1:43.** Cp. **J 6:29, 39.**—W. a prep. ἐν τούτῳ, ὅτι **Lk 10:20; J 9:30** (v.l. τοῦτο); **1J 3:16, 24; 4:9, 10.** περὶ τούτου, ὅτι **J 16:19.** διὰ τοῦτο, ὅτι *for this reason, (namely) that* **5:16, 18; 8:47.** εἰς τοῦτο, ἵνα **J 18:37; Ac 9:21; Ro 14:9; 2 Cor 2:9** al. διὰ τοῦτο, ἵνα **13:10; 1 Ti 1:16; Phlm 15.** ἐν τούτῳ, ἵνα **J 15:8; 1J 4:17.** ἐν τούτῳ ἐάν **J 13:35; 1J 2:3.** ἐν τούτῳ, ὅταν **5:2.**—Before an inf. τοῦτο κέκρικεν . . . , τηρεῖν τὴν ἑαυτοῦ παρθένον **1 Cor 7:37.** Cp. **2 Cor 2:1.** Before an inf. w. acc. **Eph 4:17.** Even introducing a foll. subst.: τοῦτο εὐχόμεθα, τὴν ὑμῶν κατάρτισιν **2 Cor 13:9.**—On αὐτὸ τοῦτο cp. αὐτός 1g.

γ. καὶ τοῦτο *and at that, and especially* (B-D-F §290, 5; 442, 9; W-S. §21, 4; Rob. 1181f) **Ro 13:11; 1 Cor 6:6, 8; Eph 2:8.** καὶ ταῦτα (also Pla. et al.; s. Kühner-G. I 647) passing over fr. *and at that* to *although* (Jos., Ant. 2, 266) **Hb 11:12.**

δ. indicating a correspondence: τοῦτο μὲν . . . τοῦτο δέ *sometimes . . . sometimes, not only . . . but also* (Att.) **Hb 10:33** (Tat. 23, 2).

ε. τοῦτ' ἔστιν, τουτέστι(ν) (on the orthography s. B-D-F §12, 3; 17) *that is* or *means* (B-D-F §132, 2; Rob. 705. S. also εἰμί 2cα) **Mt 27:46; Mk 7:2; Ac 1:19; 19:4; Ro 7:18; 9:8; 10:6, 7, 8; Phlm 12. Hb 2:14** al. Cp. **Ro 1:12** (w. δέ).

ζ. An unfavorable connotation (this tone is noticed by Ps.-Demetr. c. 289 in the Κρατερὸν τοῦτον [in Demetrius of Phalerum]) is assumed (after GBernhardy, Wissenschaftl. Syntax der griech. Sprache 1829, 281, by Heinrici; JWeiss; EFascher, V. Verstehen d. NT 1930, 126 al. ad loc.; differently W-S. §23, 9; cp. Rob. 704) καὶ ταῦτά τινες ἦτε *and that is the sort of people you were, at least some of you* **1 Cor 6:11.**

❷ as adj., **pert. to an entity perceived as present or near in the discourse, *this***—ⓐ coming before a subst. (or subst. expr.) with the article (B-D-F §292; W-S. §23, 10; Rob. 700f) ἐν τούτῳ τῷ αἰῶνι **Mt 12:32.** Cp. **16:18; 20:12; Mk 9:29; Lk 7:44; J 4:15; Ac 1:11; Ro 11:24; 1 Ti 1:18; Hb 7:1; 1J 4:21; Rv 19:9; 20:14** al. W. a touch of contempt **Lk 18:11;** cp. **14:30; 15:30** (s. also 1aα).

ⓑ following the subst. that has the art.: ἐκ τῶν λίθων τούτων **Mt 3:9.** Cp. **5:19; Mk 12:16; Lk 11:31; 12:56; J 4:13, 21; Ac 6:13; Ro 15:28; 1 Cor 1:20; 2:6; 11:26; 2 Cor 4:1, 7; 8:6; 11:10; Eph 3:8; 5:32; 2 Ti 2:19; Rv 2:24.** (Freq. the position of οὗτος varies, somet. before, somet. after the noun, in mss.; s. the apparatus in Tdf. on the following **vv.ll.: Mk 14:30; J 4:20; 6:60; 7:36; 9:24; 21:23** al.) Somet. another adj. stands w. the noun ἀπὸ τῆς γενεᾶς τῆς σκολιᾶς ταύτης **Ac 2:40.** ἡ χήρα αὕτη ἡ πτωχή **Lk 21:3.** Cp. πάντα τὰ ῥήματα ταῦτα **2:19, 51 v.l.**

ⓒ The art. is sometimes lacking: μάθημα τοῦτ' αὐτοῖς ἐστιν εὑρημένον Dg 5:3. In such case there is no real connection betw. the demonstrative and the noun, but the one or the other belongs to the predicate (B-D-F §292; W-S. §23, 12; Rob. 701f) ταύτην ἐποίησεν ἀρχὴν τῶν σημείων **J 2:11** (s. **4:54** below). τοῦτο ἀληθὲς εἴρηκας **4:18.**—So esp. in combination w. numerical statement; the noun without the art. is to be taken as part of the predicate: οὗτος μὴν ἕκτος ἐστίν *this is the sixth month* **Lk 1:36.** αὕτη ἀπογραφὴ πρώτη ἐγένετο *this was the first census* **2:2.** τοῦτο πάλιν δεύτερον σημεῖον ἐποίησεν **J 4:54** (s. **2:11** above). τρίτην ταύτην ἡμέραν *this is the third day* (s. ἄγω 4) **Lk 24:21** (Achilles Tat. 7, 11, 2 τρίτην ταύτην ἡμέραν γέγονεν ἀφανής; Menand., Epitr. 244f S.=68f Kö.; Lucian, Dial. Mort. 13, 3). τοῦτο τρίτον ἐφανερώθη *this was the third time that he appeared* **J 21:14.** τρίτον τοῦτο ἔρχομαι *this will be the third time that I am coming* **2 Cor 13:1;** cp. **12:14** (cp. Hdt. 5, 76 τέταρτον δὴ τοῦτο; Gen 27:36 δεύτερον τοῦτο.—Num 14:22; Judg 16:15).—More intricate: οὐ μετὰ πολλὰς ταύτας ἡμέρας *not many days from now* **Ac 1:5** (Alciphron 1, 14, 2; Achilles Tat. 7, 14, 2 ὡς ὀλίγων πρὸ τούτων ἡμερῶν; POxy 1121, 12 [295 AD]; B-D-F §226; Rob. 702). Most difficult of all περὶ μιᾶς ταύτης φωνῆς **Ac 24:21** (cp. POxy 1152, 5 βοήθι ἡμῖν καὶ τούτῳ οἴκῳ. B-D-F §292; W-S. §20, 10c; Rob. 702 ins).—DELG. M-M.

οὑτοσί (trag., Aristoph. et al.; Joseph.; Just., A II, 14, 1) **a position described as relatively near rather than remote in present discourse, *this (here)*** ἐπὶ ταυτησὶ τῆς γῆς *here on this earth* Papias (2:12).

οὕτω/οὕτως adv. of οὗτος (Hom.+ gener. 'so'); the form οὕτως is most used, before consonants as well as before vowels; the form οὕτω (En 98:3 before a vowel; EpArist only before consonants) in the NT only **Ac 23:11; Phil 3:17; Hb 12:21; Rv 16:18** w. really outstanding attestation and taken into the text by most edd.; by others, with t.r., also **Mt 3:15; 7:17; Mk 2:7; Ac 13:47; Ro 1:15; 6:19** (B-D-F §21; W-S. §5, 28b; Mlt-H. 112f; W-H. appendix 146f. Also in ins [s. Nachmanson 112], pap [Mayser 242f; Crönert 142] and LXX [Thackeray p. 136] οὕτως predominates)

❶ **referring to what precedes, *in this manner, thus, so***

ⓐ w. a correlative word καθάπερ . . . οὕτως (s. καθάπερ) *(just) as . . . so* **Ro 12:4f; 1 Cor 12:12; 2 Cor 8:11.** καθὼς . . . οὕτως *(just) as . . . so* **Lk 11:30; 17:26; J 3:14; 12:50; 14:31; 15:4; 2 Cor 1:5; 10:7; Col 3:13; 1 Th 2:4.** ὡς . . . οὕτως *as . . . so* **Ac 8:32** (Is 53:7); **23:11** (οὕτω); **Ro 5:15, 18; 1 Cor 7:17a; 2 Cor 7:14.** ὥσπερ . . . οὕτως (ParJer 7:26f; GrBar 4:16; ApcEsdr 1:14; Jos., Vi. 1; Just., D. 6, 2; Tat. 5, 2 [οὕτω]) **Mt 12:40; 13:40; Lk 17:24; J 5:21, 26; Ro 5:12, 19, 21; 6:4;** GJs 13:1 (end). καθ' ὅσον . . . οὕτως *as . . . so* **Hb 9:27f.** ὃν τρόπον . . . οὕτως **2 Ti 3:8** (TestJob 27:3ff; Just., A I, 7, 3 al.).

ⓑ w. ref. to what precedes, abs. **Mt 5:19; 6:30; Ro 11:5; 1 Cor 8:12** al. τὸν οὕτως (namely ἐν σαρκί) ἀναστάντα AcPlCor 2:25. ταῦτα οὕτως *so much for that* B 17:2. οὐδὲ οὕτως *not even thus* **Mk 14:59** (Just., D. 12, 2; 46, 6). Pointing the moral after figures of speech, parables, and examples (Aristot., Rhet. 1393b [II, 20]) **Mt 5:16; 12:45; 13:49; 18:14; 20:16; Lk 12:21; 15:7, 10; J 3:8.**—οὕτως can take on a specif. mng. fr. what precedes: οὕτως ἀποκρίνῃ τῷ ἀρχιερεῖ; *is that the way (=so shamelessly) you answer the high priest?* **J 18:22;** *so basely* **1 Cor 5:3;** *so intensely* (of love) Dg 10:3; *unmarried* **1 Cor 7:26, 40.** ἐὰν ἀφῶμεν αὐτὸν οὕτως *if we let him (go on) this way* (performing miracle after miracle) **J 11:48.** Cp. **Ro 9:20.** οὕτως προοδοιπορούντων *those who thus precede* AcPlCor 2:37 (restored).—οὕτως καί **Mt 17:12; 18:35; 24:33; Mk 13:29; Lk 17:10.** οὐχ οὕτως ἐστὶν ἐν ὑμῖν *it is not so among you* **Mt 20:26; Mk 10:43.** Elliptically (B-D-F §480, 5) ὑμεῖς οὐχ οὕτως *you (are) not (to act) in this way* **Lk 22:26** (ὑμεῖς δὲ μὴ οὕτως [v.l. οὕτως μὴ ποιεῖτε] TestNapht 3:4). οὐχ οὕτως, Μαρία (you are not to conceive a child) *in that way* i.e. the normal way of women GJs 11:3. Summarizing a thought expressed in what precedes: **Mt 11:26; Ac 7:8; 1 Cor 14:25; 1 Th 4:17; 2 Pt 1:11.**—Drawing an inference fr. what precedes *so, hence* (Horapollo 1, 34 οὕτω ὀνομασθήσεται; En 98:3) **Ro 1:15; 6:11.** οὕτως ὅτι *as it is, since* **Rv 3:16.**—Introducing a question *so:* **Mt 26:40** οὕτως οὐκ ἰσχύσατε μίαν ὥραν γρηγορῆσαι μετ' ἐμοῦ; *so, you were not able to remain awake with me for only one hour?;* **Mk 7:18** οὕτως καὶ ὑμεῖς ἀσύνετοί ἐστε; *are you so dense, too?* (i.e. like the crowd); **1 Cor 6:5** οὕτως οὐκ ἔνι ἐν ὑμῖν οὐδεὶς σοφός *is it so* (=our colloq. 'do you mean to tell me'), *that there's not one person among you wise enough* to settle a dispute between members?—Summarizing the content of a preceding participial constr. (Att.: Lysias 2, 79; also Jos., Bell. 2, 129, Ant. 8, 270; B-D-F §425, 6) **Ac 20:11; 27:17.**—ὁ μὲν οὕτως, ὁ δὲ οὕτως *the one in one way, the other in another* **1 Cor 7:7.**

❷ **pert. to what follows in discourse material,** ***in this way, as follows*** **J 21:1.** Of spoken or written words: what is so introduced follows immediately after οὕτως γέγραπται **Mt 2:5.** Cp. **6:9; Ac 7:6; 13:34, 47; Ro 10:6; Hb 4:4;** GJs 21:2 (codd.); w. ὅτι recitative **Lk 19:31; Ac 7:6; 13:34** (TestAbr A 8 p. 85, 15 [Stone p. 18]). W. inf. foll. (Gen 29:26) **1 Pt 2:15.** Correlatively: οὕτως . . . καθώς **Lk 24:24; Ro 11:26; Phil 3:17.** οὕτως . . . ὃν τρόπον **Ac 1:11;** cp. **27:25.** οὕτως . . . ὡς *thus . . .* as (Jos., Ant. 12, 304; Just., A I, 12, 10; 66, 1 al.) **Mk 4:26** ('it's like when . . . '); **J 7:46; 1 Cor 3:15; 4:1; 9:26ab; Eph 5:33; Js 2:12.** οὕτως . . . ὥστε (Hdt. 7, 174; Epict. 1, 11, 4; 4, 11, 19; SIG 1169, 57f ἔμπυος ἦς οὕτω σφόδρως, ὥστε . . . ἐνέπλησε πύους=he was suffering to such an extent from a suppurating wound, that . . . he was filled with matter; Jos., Ant. 8, 206; 9, 255) **J 3:16** (s. B-D-F §391, 2; Mlt. 209; Rob. 1000); **Ac 14:1.** οὕτως . . . ἵνα: οὕτως τρέχετε ἵνα καταλάβητε **1 Cor 9:24.**—Functions as an adj. (B-D-F) §434, 1; HLjungvik, Eranos 62, '64, 26–31) ἡ γένεσις οὕτως ἦν (=τοιαύτη ἦν) **Mt 1:18.—19:10; Ro 4:18** (Gen 15:5). Cp. **Rv 9:17.**—Also as subst. *something like this:* as subj. **Mt 9:33;** as obj. **Mk 2:12.** οὕτως ποιεῖν τινι *do thus and so to/for someone* **Lk 1:25; 2:48.**

❸ **marker of a relatively high degree,** ***so,*** before adj. and adv. (Soph., Aristoph. et al.) σεισμὸς οὕτω μέγας *an earthquake so great* **Rv 16:18.** οὕτως ἀνόητοί ἐστε; **Gal 3:3** (s. ἀνόητος a). οὕτως φοβερόν **Hb 12:21.**—οὕτως ταχέως (Jos., Vi. 92; cp. οὕτω δρομαίως TestAbr A 7 p. 83, 33 [Stone p. 14]) **Gal 1:6;** AcPlCor 2:2.—Before a verb *so intensely* (X., Cyr. 1, 3, 11; TestAbr B 4 p. 108, 11 [Stone p. 64]; Tat. 19, 1) **1J 4:11.**

❹ **to the exclusion of other considerations,** ***without further ado, just, simply:*** οὕτως (Soph., Phil. 1067 ἀλλ' οὕτως ἄπει; 'then will you go away without further ado?'; Ael. Aristid. 51, 49 K.=27 p. 546 D.; Aesop, Fab. 308 P.=Babr. 48 Cr.//48 L-P.; Jos., Ant. 14, 438) Ἰησοῦς . . . ἐκαθέζετο οὕτως ἐπὶ τῇ πηγῇ **J 4:6** (cp. Ammonius, Catena in ev. S. Ioa. p. 216, 21 Cramer τὸ δὲ 'οὕτως' ἀντὶ τοῦ 'ὡς ἁπλῶς' καὶ 'ὡς ἔτυχε'). Likew. **8:59 v.l.** and prob. ἀναπεσὼν ἐκεῖνος οὕτως ἐπὶ τὸ στῆθος τοῦ Ἰησοῦ **J 13:25** (but here οὕτως can also refer to what precedes *accordingly*=following Peter's nod).—DELG s.v. οὗτος. M-M.

οὐχ s. οὐ.

οὐχί (a strengthened form of οὐ; Hom.+; Attic wr.; SIG 646, 41 [170 BC]; 834, 18; PSI 499, 4 [257/256 BC]; PEdg 111 [=Sb 6994], 27; LXX; En; TestSol, TestJob, JosAs; ApcEsdr 2:13=p. 26, 6 Tdf.; ApcMos; Jos., Ant. 17, 312 al.; Just., Tat.) 'not' (B-D-F §432; 427, 2; Rob. 296; 917 al.).

❶ **a simple negative,** ***not*** (so in many of the pass. mentioned above) οὐχὶ πάντες καθαροί ἐστε **J 13:11;** cp. vs. **10** (ἀλλ' οὐχί as Jos., Ant. 8, 279; Just., A I, 6, 1); **14:22; 1 Cor 6:1.** οὐχὶ μή **Lk 18:30.** οὐχὶ μᾶλλον *not rather* **1 Cor 5:2** (cp. Just., D. 95, 1f). Foll. by ἀλλά *not . . . but* (TestJob 38:6; Just., A I, 23, 1) **10:29; 2 Cor 10:13 v.l.** (for οὐκ); B 12:10.

❷ **a negative reply,** ***no, by no means*** w. ἀλλά foll. (X., Cyr. 1, 3, 4 codd.; Gen 18:15; 19:2; 42:12; TestAbr A 5 p. 82, 5 [Stone p. 12] al.; JosAs 1:14) **Lk 1:60; 16:30; J 9:9; Ro 3:27.** οὐχί, λέγω ὑμῖν, ἀλλά *no, I tell you, but rather* **Lk 12:51; 13:3, 5.** (S. Schwyzer II 597.)

❸ **an interrogative word in questions that expect an affirmative answer,** ***not?*** (X., Cyr. 8, 3, 46; PGrenf I, 1 I, 25 [II BC]; Gen 40:8; Judg 4:6; TestAbr B 10 p. 115, 5 [Stone p, 78]; JosAs 6:5; ApcEsdr 2:13; Just., D. 49, 2) οὐχὶ καὶ οἱ τελῶναι τὸ αὐτὸ ποιοῦσιν; **Mt 5:46.** Cp. vs. **47; 6:25; 10:29; Lk 6:39; 12:6; 15:8; 17:17** (v.l. οὐχ); **24:26; J 11:9; Ro 3:29; 1 Cor 1:20; Hb 1:14;** 1 Cl 31:2; D 1:3. ἀλλ' οὐχὶ ἐρεῖ αὐτῷ . . . ; *will he not rather say to him . . . ?* **Lk 17:8.** ἢ οὐχὶ . . . ; 1 Cl 46:6.—διὰ τί οὐχὶ μᾶλλον ἀδικεῖσθε; **1 Cor 6:7a;** cp. vs. **7b.** πῶς οὐχὶ . . . ; (1 Esdr 4:32; Just., D. 18, 3; 89, 3) **Ro 8:32.**—DELG s.v. οὐ. M-M.

ὀφειλέτης, ου, ὁ (ὀφείλω; Soph. et al.; BGU 954, 22; En 6:3 ἐγὼ μόνος ὀφειλέτης ἁμαρτίας μεγάλης; TestJob 11:12).

❶ **one who is in debt in a monetary sense,** ***debtor*** (Pla., Leg. 5, 736d; Plut. et al.) w. the amount of the debt given in the gen. ὀφ. μυρίων ταλάντων *who owed ten thousand talents* **Mt 18:24** (s. τάλαντον).

❷ **one who is under obligation in a moral or social sense,** ***one under obligation, one liable for,*** ext. of 1.—ⓐ *debtor* πάντες ὀφειλέται ἐσμὲν ἁμαρτίας *we are all debtors in the matter of sin* Pol 6:1.

ⓑ *one who is obligated* to do someth. ὀφειλέτην εἶναι *be under obligation* w. gen. or dat. of pers. or thing to whom (which) one is obligated (B-D-F §190, 1; Rob. 537 al.): w. gen. of pers. *obligated to someone* **Ro 15:27.** W. dat. of pers. **1:14; 8:12.** That which one is obligated to do stands in the gen. ὀφειλέται ἐσμὲν οὐ τ. σαρκὶ τοῦ κατὰ σάρκα ζῆν *we are under obligation but not to the flesh, to live according to its demands* **Ro 8:12** (s. B-D-F §400, 2; Rob. 1076). The simple inf. (Soph., Aj. 590) is found instead of the articular inf. in the gen.: ὀφ. ἐστὶν ὅλον τὸν νόμον ποιῆσαι **Gal 5:3.**

ⓒ *one who is guilty of a misdeed, one who is culpable, at fault*

α. in relation to pers., w. gen. of the one against whom the misdeed was committed ἀφήκαμεν τοῖς ὀφ. ἡμῶν *we have forgiven our debtors,* i. e., those who are guilty of sin against us **Mt 6:12;** cp. D 8:2.

β. in relation to God, *sinner* (cp. **Lk 13:4** w. vs. 2 ἁμαρτωλοί) abs. ὅτι αὐτοὶ ὀφειλέται ἐγένοντο παρὰ πάντας τοὺς ἀνθρώπους *that they were sinners to a greater degree than all the other people* **Lk 13:4.**—Betz, SM p. 400 n. 479 (lit). DELG s.v. ὀφείλω. M-M. TW.

ὀφειλή, ῆς, ἡ (ὀφείλω, cp. ὀφείλημα) rarely used accord. to Etym. Mag., w. ref. to X., De Vect. (Ways and Means).

❶ **that which one owes in a financial sense, *obligation;*** as *debt* (so oft. in pap and ostraca [since III BC]) **Mt 18:32.** Pl., of taxes and imposts **Ro 13:7.** This pass. demonstrates the easy transference to

❷ **that which one ought to do, *duty*—ⓐ** of that which is appropriate in a social relationship: *obligation* of pleasing one's spouse conjugally **1 Cor 7:3.** Pl., of respect and honor, **Ro 13:7** (also s. 1 above).

ⓑ of failure to meet moral obligations ἄφες ἡμῖν τὴν ὀφ. ἡμῶν *forgive us our debt* D 8:2.—DELG s.v. ὀφείλω. M-M. TW.

ὀφείλημα, ατος, τό (ὀφείλω, cp. ὀφειλή; Thu. et al.; ins, pap, LXX).

❶ **that which is owed in a financial sense, *debt, one's due*** (Pla., Leg. 4, 717b; Aristot., EN 8, 15, 1162b, 28; 9, 2, 1165a, 3; SIG 1108, 10 [III/II BC]; PHib 42, 10 [262 BC]; PLond III, 1203, 4 p. 10 [113 BC]; POxy 494, 10 ὀφειλήματα; Dt 24:10; I Esdr 3:20; 1 Macc 15:8) of wages for work done οὐ λογίζεται κατὰ χάριν ἀλλὰ κατὰ ὀφείλημα *it is considered not as a favor, but as a person's due* **Ro 4:4** (on the contrast χάρις–ὀφείλημα cp. Thu. 2, 40, 4 οὐκ ἐς χάριν, ἀλλ' ἐς ὀφείλημα='not as a favor but as payment of an obligation'. The ref. here is to reciprocity in general).

❷ **obligation in a moral sense, *debt*=**sin (as Aram. חוֹבָא in rabb. lit.; s. MBlack, Aramaic Approach[3], '67, 140) ἄφες ἡμῖν τὰ ὀφ. ἡμῶν *forgive us our debts* (=sins) **Mt 6:12** (the parallel Lk 11:4 has τὰς ἁμαρτίας ἡμῶν). Betz, SM 400–404.—DELG s.v. ὀφείλω. M-M. TW.

ὀφείλω impf. ὤφειλον; fut. ὀφειλήσω LXX; our lit. has only the pres. and impf. (Hom.+).

❶ **to be indebted to someone in a financial sense, *owe someth. to someone, be indebted to*** τινί τι **Mt 18:28a; Lk 16:5.** W. acc. of debt (Appian, Bell. Civ. 2, 8 §26; Jos., Ant. 13, 56) **Mt 18:28b; Lk 7:41; 16:7; Phlm 18** (CMartin, in: Persuasive Artistry, ed. DWatson, '91, 321–37). τὸ ὀφειλόμενον *the sum that is owed* (X.; Pla.; CPR I, 228, 5. In pap. the pl. is more freq. found in this mng.) **Mt 18:30.** πᾶν τὸ ὀφ. αὐτῷ *the whole amount that he owed him* vs. **34.**

❷ **to be under obligation to meet certain social or moral expectations, *owe*—ⓐ** gener.—**α.** *owe, be indebted* τινί τι *(to) someone (for)someth.* (Alciphron 4, 13, 1 Νύμφαις θυσίαν ὀφ.; Jos., C. Ap. 2, 295) πόσα αὐτῷ ὀφείλομεν ὅσια; *for how many holy deeds are we indebted to (Jesus Christ)?* 2 Cl 1:3. μηδενὶ μηδὲν ὀφείλετε εἰ μὴ τὸ ἀλλήλους ἀγαπᾶν *owe nothing to anyone except to love each other* **Ro 13:8** (AFridrichsen, StKr 102, 1930, 294–97. For initiative in kindness cp. Thu. 2, 40 'we acquire friends not by receiving benefits but by conferring them'). τὴν ὀφειλομένην εὔνοιαν *the goodwill that one owes,* a euphemism for pleasing one's spouse conjugally **1 Cor 7:3 v.l.** εἰς τὸν ὀφειλόμενον τόπον τῆς δόξης *to the glorious place that he deserved* 1 Cl 5:4. εἰς τὸν ὀφειλόμενον αὐτοῖς τόπον εἰσὶ παρὰ τῷ κυρίῳ Pol 9:2,—Subst. τὰ ὀφειλόμενα (s. 1 above) *duties, obligations* ποιεῖν *fulfill* GPt 12:53.

β. *be obligated.* w. inf. foll. *one must, one ought* (Hom. [Il. 19, 200] et al.; ins, pap; 4 Macc 11:15; 16:19; Philo, Agr. 164, Spec. Leg. 1, 101; TestJos 14:6; Just., A I, 4, 4 al.; Mel., P. 76, 550; Iren., Did.) ὃ ὠφείλομεν ποιῆσαι πεποιήκαμεν **Lk 17:10.** κατὰ τ. νόμον ὀφείλει ἀποθανεῖν **J 19:7.** Cp. **13:14; Ro 15:1, 27; 1 Cor 7:36; 9:10; 11:10; Eph 5:28; 2 Th 1:3; 2:13; Hb 2:17; 5:3, 12; 1J 2:6; 3:16; 4:11; 3J 8;** 1 Cl 38:4; 40:1; 48:6; 51:1; 2 Cl 4:3; B 1:7; 2:1, 9f; 4:6; 5:3; 6:18; 7:1, 11; 13:3; Pol 5:1; 6:2; Hs 8, 9, 4 v.l.; 9, 13, 3; 9, 18, 2; 9, 28, 5. Negat. *one ought not, one must not* (Jos., Vi. 149; Ar. 13, 5) **Ac 17:29; 1 Cor 11:7;** 1 Cl 56:2; Hm 4, 1, 3; 8; s 5, 4, 2; 9, 18, 1. Cp. 2 Cl 4:3. οὐκ ὀφείλει τὰ τέκνα τ. γονεῦσι θησαυρίζειν *children are under no obligation to lay up money for their parents* **2 Cor 12:14.**

ⓑ Rabbinic usage has given rise to certain peculiarities

α. ὀφ. used absolutely [חַיָּב]: ὀφείλει *he is obligated, bound* (by his oath) **Mt 23:16, 18.**

β. *commit a sin* (s. ὀφείλημα 2; but cp. also SIG 1042, 15 ἁμαρτίαν ὀφιλέτω Μηνὶ Τυράννῳ) w. dat. *against someone* ἀφίομεν παντὶ ὀφείλοντι ἡμῖν **Lk 11:4.**

❸ **to be constrained by circumstance,** (best rendered by an auxiliary verb) ***have to, ought*** ἐπεὶ ὠφείλετε ἄρα ἐκ τοῦ κόσμου ἐξελθεῖν *then you would have to come out of the world altogether* **1 Cor 5:10.**—ἐγὼ ὤφειλον ὑφ' ὑμῶν συνίστασθαι *I ought to have been recommended by you* **2 Cor 12:11** (B-D-F §358, 1; Rob. 920). For the semantic perspective of Paul as creditor instead of debtor cp. the use of ὀφείλημα Ro 4:4. Paul's sophisticated use here of diction that was in common use in reciprocity discourse is of a piece with the context in which irony plays a decisive role.—B. 641. DELG. M-M. EDNT. TW.

ὄφελον (prob. not the first pers. 2 aor. of ὀφείλω [ὤφελον] without the augment [so most scholars, incl. Mlt. 201, n. 1; Mlt-H. 191], but a ptc., originally w. ἐστίν to be supplied [JWackernagel, Sprachl. Untersuchungen. zu Homer 1916, 199f; B-D-F §67, 2; so also L-S-J-M s.v. ὀφείλω, end], ὄφελον: OGI 315, 16 [164/163 BC]; Epict. 2, 18, 15 v.l. Sch.; 2, 22, 12 as a correction in ms. S; LXX; En 104:11) a fixed form, functioning as a particle to introduce unattainable wishes (B-D-F §359, 1; Rob. 1003f) **an expression of a wish that someth. had taken place or would take place, *o that, would that*** w. the impf. to express present time (Epict. 2, 22, 12; Dio Chrys. 21 [38], 47 vArnim [ed. Budé has ὤφελον]) **Rv 3:15** (Schwyzer II 346); **2 Cor 11:1.** καὶ ὄφελον ἐμιμοῦντο ISm 12:1. W. the opt. (Ps 118:5) **Rv 3:15 v.l** (Erasmian rdg.).—W. the aor. indic. to express past time (Epict. 2, 18, 15; Chariton 4, 4, 2; Achilles Tat. 2, 24, 3; 5, 15, 5; Ex 16:3; Num 14:2; 20:3) ὄφελόν γε ἐβασιλεύσατε *indeed, I wish that you had become kings* **1 Cor 4:8.**—W. the fut. indic. (acc. to Lucian, Soloec. 1, end, ὄφελον … δυνήσῃ is a solecism) ὄφ. καὶ ἀποκόψονται **Gal 5:12** (s. ἀποκόπτω a and B-D-F §384; Rob. 923).—DELG s.v. ὀφείλω. M-M.

ὄφελος, ους, τό (ὀφέλλω 'increase'; Hom.+; OGI 519, 26 οὐδὲν ὄφελος ἡμεῖν; POxy 118 verso, 30 οὐδὲν ὄφ.; 1468, 6; Job 15:3; ApcSed 1, 3 [after 1 Cor 13:2]; Jos., Ant. 17, 154; Just.; Ath. 22, 8) **an advantage derived from someth., *benefit, good*** τί τὸ ὄφ.; *what good does it do?* **Js 2:16** (Hierocles 14, 451; Philo, Migr. Abr. 55 and Just., D. 14, 1 τί γὰρ ὄφ.;). W. ἐάν foll. (cp. Ael. Aristid. 53 p. 640 D.; M. I. Brutus, Ep. 4) vs. **14;** 2 Cl 6:2 (a saying of Jesus; in Mt 16:26 τί ὠφεληθήσεται ἄνθρωπος, ἐὰν … ;). τί μοι τὸ ὄφ.; *what good is it to me?* **1 Cor 15:32.** τί μοι ὄφελος ταῦτα ἑωρακότι καὶ μὴ γινώσκοντι … ; *how does it benefit me to have seen this and not to understand … ?* Hv 3, 3, 1 (τί μοι ὄφελος; Chariton 7, 4, 10).—DELG s.v. 2 ὀφέλλω. M-M.

ὀφθαλμοδουλία, ας, ἡ (B-D-F §115, 1; also s. Mlt-H. 271; FGingrich, JBL 52, '33, 263; Achmes p. 18, 12 says of a slave κατ' ὀφθαλμὸν δουλεύειν) **service that is performed only to make an impression in the owner's presence,** *eye-service* (CMoule, ET 59, '47/48, 250), not for its own sake nor to please God or one's own conscience (s. Theodoret III p. 437 Schulze on Eph 6:6f ὀφθαλμοδουλείαν δὲ καλεῖ τὴν οὐκ ἐξ εἰλικρινοῦς καρδίας προσφερομένην θεραπείαν, ἀλλὰ τῷ σχήματι κεχρωσνένην=he applies the term 'eye-slavery' to service that is not sincerely rendered but functions only for sake of appearance) κατ' ὀφθαλμοδουλίαν *only when your owner is watching* **Eph 6:6.** Pl., of more than one occurrence of this kind of service ἐν ὀφθαλμοδουλίᾳ (v.l. -λίαις) **Col 3:22.**—S. DELG ὄπωπα F 2. TW.

ὀφθαλμός, οῦ, ὁ (Hom.+)—**❶ eye as organ of sense perception,** *eye* **Mt 5:29, 38** (Ex 21:24; s. DDaube, JTS 45, '44, 177–89.—The principle ἐάν τίς τινος ὀφθαλμὸν ἐκκόψῃ, ἀντεκκόπτεσθαι τὸν ἐκείνου in early Gk. legislation in Diod. S. 12, 17, 4; Diog. L. 1, 57 [Solon]); **6:22; 7:3ff** (s. δοκός); **Mk 9:47; Lk 6:41f; 11:34; J 9:6; 1 Cor 12:16f; Rv 1:14; 2:18; 7:17; 19:12; 21:4;** 1 Cl 10:4 (Gen 13:14) and oft.; GJs 19:2. More than two eyes in the same creature (Artem. 1, 26 p. 28, 13ff) **Rv 4:6, 8** (after Ezk 1:18; 10:12); **5:6** (cp. Lucian, Dial. Deor. 3 and 20, 8: Argus w. many eyes, who sees w. his whole body, and never sleeps; Ath. 20, 1 [of Athena]).—εἶδον οἱ ὀφ. μου (cp. Sir 16:5) **Lk 2:30;** cp.**4:20; 10:23; 1 Cor 2:9** (=1 Cl 34:8; 2 Cl 11:7; MPol 2:3. On possible Gnostic associations s. UWilcken, Weisheit u. Torheit, '59, 77–80 and Hippolytus 5, 26, 16); **Rv 1:7.**—ἰδεῖν τοῖς ὀφ. Dg 2:1 (Philo, Sacr. Abel. 24). ὃ ἑωράκαμεν τοῖς ὀφ. ἡμῶν **1J 1:1** (cp. Zech 9:8 A). βλέπειν ἐν τοῖς ὀφ. GJs 17:2. ὀφ. πονηρός *an evil eye* i.e. one that looks w. envy or jealousy upon other people (Sir 14:10; Maximus Tyr. 20:7b) **Mt 6:23** (opp. ἁπλοῦς; s. this entry, the lit. s.v. λύχνος b and πονηρός 3a, and also PFiebig, Das Wort Jesu v. Auge: StKr 89, 1916, 499–507; CEdlund, Das Auge der Einfalt: ASNU 19, '52; HCadbury, HTR 47, '54, 69–74; JHElliott, The Evil Eye and the Sermon on the Mt: Biblical Interpretation 2, '94, 51–84). Cp. **20:15.** By metonymy for *envy, malice* **Mk 7:22** (but the mng. *stinginess, love for one's own possessions* is upheld for all the NT pass. w. ὀφ. πον. by CCadoux, ET 53, '41/42, 354f, esp. for **Mt 20:15,** and w. ref. to Dt 15:9 al. *Envy,* etc. is preferred by CSmith, ibid. 181f; 54, '42/43, 26 and JPercy, ibid. 26f).—ἐν ῥιπῇ ὀφθαλμοῦ *in the twinkling of an eye* **1 Cor 15:52.** ἀγαπήσεις ὡς κόρην τοῦ ὀφ. σου *you are to love as the apple of your eye* B 19:9 (s. κόρη).—Used w. verbs: αἴρω ἄνω (αἴρω 1b). ἀνοίγω (q.v. 5b). ἐξαιρέω (q.v. 1). ἐξορύσσω (q.v.). ἐπαίρω (q.v. 1). κρατέω (q.v. 5). ὑπολαμβάνειν τινὰ ἀπὸ τῶν ὀφ. τινός *take someone up out of sight of someone* **Ac 1:9.**—ἡ ἐπιθυμία τῶν ὀφθαλμῶν **1J 2:16** (Maximus Tyr. 19, 21m ἐπιθυμία goes through the ὀφθαλμοί). ὀφθαλμοὶ μεστοὶ μοιχαλίδος **2 Pt 2:14** (on the imagery cp. Sir 26:9; s. μεστός 2b).—It is characteristic of the OT (but s. also Hes., Op. 267 πάντα ἰδὼν Διὸς ὀφθαλμός; Polyb. 23, 10, 3 Δίκης ὀφ.; Aristaen, Ep. 1, 19 at the beginning, the pl. of the eyes of Tyche. ὄμματα is also found of a divinity: Alciphron 3, 8, 2; 4, 9, 4) to speak anthropomorphically of God's eyes **Hb 4:13; 1 Pt 3:12;** 1 Cl 22:6 (the last two Ps 33:16). A transference is readily made to

❷ mental and spiritual understanding, ***eye, understanding,*** ὀφθαλμοὺς ἔχοντες οὐ βλέπετε **Mk 8:18.**—**Mt 13:15b; J 12:40b; Ac 28:27b** (all three Is 6:10); **Mt 13:16.** ἔδωκεν αὐτοῖς ὁ θεὸς ὀφθαλμοὺς τοῦ μὴ βλέπειν *the kind of eyes with which they do not see* (s. B-D-F §393, 6; 400, 2; Rob. 1061; 1076) **Ro 11:8** (cp. Dt 29:3). οἱ ὀφ. τῆς καρδίας *the eyes of the heart* (s. καρδία 1bβ and cp. Herm. Wr. 7, 1 ἀναβλέψαντες τοῖς τῆς καρδίας ὀφθαλμοῖς; 10, 4 ὁ τοῦ νοῦ ὀφθαλμός; Just., D. 134, 5 οἱ τῆς ψυχῆς ὀφθαλμοί.—Sir 17:8) **Eph 1:18;** 1 Cl 36:2; 59:3; MPol 2:3. Cp. also the entries καμμύω, σκοτίζω, τυφλόω.—W. a prep.: ἀπέναντι τῶν ὀφ. τινος s. ἀπέναντι 1bβ. ἐκρύβη ἀπὸ ὀφθαλμῶν σου *it is hidden from the eyes of your mind* **Lk 19:42** (cp. Sir 17:15). ἐν ὀφθαλμοῖς (LXX; s. Thackeray 43): ἔστιν θαυμαστὴ ἐν ὀφθαλμοῖς ἡμῶν *it is marvelous in our sight* (=in our judgment) **Mt 21:42; Mk 12:11** (both Ps 117:23), but ἐν ὀφθαλμοῖς ἡμῶν GJs 16:1 (as Lucian, Tox. 39) means 'before our eyes' (likew. Apollon. Rhod. 4, 1619 τέρας ἐν ὀφθαλμοῖσιν ἰδόντες=gaze with their eyes on the portent; Diod. S. 3, 18, 5 ἐν ὀφθαλμοῖς=before their eyes). κατ' ὀφθαλμούς τινος *before someone's eyes, in someone's sight* (2 Km 12:11; 4 Km 25:7; Jer 35:5; Ezk 20:14, 22, 41; 21:11; 22:16; 36:23): οἷς κατ' ὀφθαλμοὺς Ἰ. Χριστὸς προεγράφη *before whose eyes Jesus Christ was portrayed* **Gal 3:1.** πρὸ ὀφθαλμῶν *before (someone's) eyes* (Hyperid. 6, 17; SIG 495, 120 [c. 230 BC]; BGU 362 V, 8; LXX; EpArist 284): πρὸ ὀφθαλμῶν λαμβάνειν (Polyb.; Diod. S. 26, 16b [s. FKrebs, Die Präp. bei Polyb. 1882, 38]; 2 Macc 8:17; 3 Macc 4:4) *place before one's eyes* 1 Cl 5:3. πρὸ ὀφθαλμῶν ἔχειν (JosAs 7:6; Lucian, Tyrannici. 7; OGI 210, 8; PGiss 67, 10; Just., D. 20, 1 al.) *keep one's eyes on* someth. MPol 2:3. πρὸ ὀφθαλμῶν τινος εἶναι (Dt 11:18) *be before someone's eyes* 1 Cl 2:1; 39:3 (Job 4:16).—B. 225. DELG s.v. ὄπωπα. M-M. EDNT. TW.

ὀφθείς, ὀφθήσομαι s. ὁράω.

ὄφις, εως, ὁ (Hom.+; SIG 1168, 113 of the snake that functioned in healings in the temple of Asclepius at Epidaurus; PGM 8, 11; 13, 261; 881; LXX; pseudepigr., Philo; Jos., Bell. 5, 108, Ant. 1, 41; 2, 287; Just.; Ath. 1, 1) 'snake, serpent'

❶ a limbless reptile, ***snake, serpent*** **Mt 7:10** (s. BHjerl-Hansen, RB 55, '48, 195–98); **Mk 16:18; Lk 11:11; 1 Cor 10:9** (Diod. S. 5, 58, 4 ὑπὸ τῶν ὄφεων διαφθαρῆναι); **Rv 9:19** (cp. Achilles Tat. 1, 3, 4 ὄφεις αἱ κόμαι). ὄφεις καὶ σκορπίοι (Procop. Soph., Ep. 136; Sb 6584, 6; Cat. Cod. Astr. VII 177, 21; Dt 8:15; Philo, Praem. 90) **Lk 10:19** (cp. Dt 8:15; Ps 90:13 on protection fr. snakes). Symbol of cleverness (cp. Gen 3:1; symbol of another kind Hyperides, fgm. 80) **Mt 10:16;** IPol 2:2. Of the brass serpent in the desert (Num 21:6–9; Wsd 16:5f) χαλκοῦς ὀφ. (Num 21:9; cp. 4 Km 18:4; Just., D. 94, 3) B 12:6. This serpent, raised aloft, as a type of Jesus **J 3:14;** B 12:5–7 (a typological evaluation of Num 21:6–9 also in Philo, Leg. All. 2, 77ff, Agr. 95; Just., D. 91, 4 al.—Appian, Mithrid. 77 §335 tells of a χαλκοῦς ὄφις in memory of Philoctetes; Diod. S. 2, 9, 5 of ὄφεις ἀργυροί on the temple of Zeus in Babylon).

❷ a person perceived as dangerous, ***snake*** fig. ext. of 1 (cp. SibOr 5:29 of Nero) ὄφεις γεννήματα ἐχιδνῶν *you snakes, you brood of vipers* **Mt 23:33.**

❸ a symbolic figure, frequent in mythology, ***serpent*** (Apollon. Rhod. 4, 128 the serpent guarding the golden fleece; 4, 1434 the Lernaean Hydra; PGM 4, 1638 the sun-god as ὁ μέγας ὄφις.—WGrafBaudissin, Studien zur semitischen Religionsgesch. I 1876, 257ff, RE V 1898, 3ff; XVII 1906, 580ff; HGunkel, Schöpfung u. Chaos 1895, 29ff; 320ff; JFrazer, The Golden Bough[3] IV 1, 1919, 80ff; Pauly-W. 2nd series II/1, 508f; EKüster, D. Schlange in der griech. Kunst u. Religion 1913; EUlback, The Serpent in Myth and Scripture: BS 90, '33, 449–55), as a designation for the devil (s. δράκων) *serpent* **Rv 12:14f;** Dg 12:3, 6, 8 (here in vs. 6 the serpent of Paradise is clearly the devil; Did., Gen. 96, 18). ἦλθεν ὁ ὄφ. . . . καὶ ἐμίανεν αὐτήν *the devil came and defiled (Eve)* GJs 13:1. τοῦ ὄφεως πίστιν ἔχουσιν *they* (the Gnostics) *have the faith of a snake* AcPlCor 2:20. ὁ ὄφ. ὁ ἀρχαῖος (s. ἀρχαῖος 1) **Rv 12:9; 20:2.** In speaking of the serpent that seduced Eve, Paul evidently has the devil in mind **2 Cor 11:3** (Just., A I, 28, 1 al.; cp. 4 Macc 18:8; ApcMos 17.—Ltzm. and Windisch on 2 Cor 11:3; Dibelius, Geisterwelt 50f; SReinach, La Femme et la Serpent: L'Anthropologie 35, 1905, 178ff).—B. 194. BHHW III 1699–1701. Kl. Pauly VI 12–17. DELG. M-M. TW.

ὀφλισκάνω (Aeschyl., Hdt. et al.; ins, pap, Just.) w. the rare and late 1 aor. ὤφλησα (Lysias 13, 65 mss. Schwyzer I 709, 746, 752; Hippocr., Ep. 27 ed. Littré IX p. 426; Ael. Aristid. [s. below]; Just.) **to incur liability,** ***become a debtor*** (w. more focus, compared to ὀφέλλω, on the negative implications of indebtedness) w. acc. *incur the charge of, become guilty of a thing* (Soph., Oed. R. 512 κακίαν; Eur., Heracl. 985 δειλίαν, Ion 443 ἀνομίαν; Ael. Aristid. 39 p. 732 D.: αἰσχύνην ὀφλῆσαι; Philo, Agr. 93 γέλωτα ὀφ.=be laughed at) συμφέρει ἡμῖν ὀφλῆσαι μεγίστην ἁμαρτίαν ἔμπροσθεν τοῦ θεοῦ καὶ μή *it is better for us to become guilty of the greatest sin before God, than* GPt 11:48.—DELG s.v. ὀφείλω.

ὀφρῦς (on the accent s. Mlt-H. 141f), **ύος, ἡ** lit. 'eyebrow' (so Hom. et al.; PPetr I, 11, 17 [220 BC]; PFay 107, 15; BASP XXXII p. 129 ln. 7 [PBer inv. 25576: II AD]; Lev 14:9; EpArist 98; Philo), then ***brow, edge*** of a cliff or hill (Il. 20, 151; Polyb. 7, 6, 3; Diod. S. 22, 13, 4; Plut., Numa 67 [10, 8]; Strabo 5, 3, 7; PAmh 68, 9; 34 [I AD]) ἤγαγον αὐτὸν ἕως ὀφρύος τοῦ ὄρους *they led him to the brow of the hill* **Lk 4:29.** On the circumstances s. MBrückner, Pj 7, 1911, 82.—B. 219. DELG. M-M.

ὀχετός, οῦ, ὁ (in var. senses Pind. et al.; Sym.) 'canal, watercourse' (Hdt.+; ins, pap; ApcSed 14:3 p. 136, 1 Ja. ἐν δάκρυσιν ὀχετοῦ; Philo, Leg. All. 1, 13, Poster. Cai. 50), then ***drain, sewer*** (Antonin, Liberal. 24, 3; Herodian 5, 8, 9; 7, 7, 3; Acta S. Apollonii §21a Klette); so **Mk 7:19** D (for ἀφεδρῶνα [q.v.]). The mng. *intestinal canal* (quotable since Hippocr.; X., Mem. 1, 4, 6) is not applicable here because of the proximity of κοιλία.—DELG s.v. ὀχέω. M-M.

ὀχλέω (ὄχλος; Aeschyl., Hdt. et al.; ins, pap, ostraca, LXX; ApcrEzk P 1 verso, 11 restored, Denis p. 126) **to cause trouble by harassment,** ***trouble, disturb*** (so mostly) pass. (TestSol L; Jos., Ant. 6, 217, Vi. 275 [ὀχ. ὑπό τινος]) ὀχλούμενος ὑπὸ πνευμάτων ἀκαθάρτων *tormented by unclean spirits* **Ac 5:16.** Cp. **Lk 6:18 v.l.** (Tob 6:8 BA ἐάν τινα ὀχλῇ δαιμόνιον ἢ πνεῦμα πονηρόν; AcThom 12 [Aa II/2, 117, 8] ὑπὸ δαιμονίων ὀχλούμενοι).—DELG s.v. ὄχλος. M-M.

ὀχλοποιέω (ὄχλος, ποιέω) 1 aor. ptc. ὀχλοποιήσας (not found elsewh. But cp. Hippocr., Mul. 1, 14 ed. Littré VIII p. 52 ὄχλον ποιέει) ***form a mob*** **Ac 17:5.**—S. DELG s.v. ὄχλος. M-M.

ὄχλος, ου, ὁ (Pind., Hdt.+; ins, pap, LXX; TestJob 24:10; TestJud 7:1; ApcrEzk [Epiph. 70, 8]; EpArist, Philo, Joseph.; Ath. 1, 4; on relation of ὄχλος to ὀχλέω s. MMeier-Brüjger, Glotta 71, '93, 28 [basic idea: a 'pile' that requires a 'heap' of workers, but s. DELG and Frisk s.v. ὄχλος]; loanw. in rabb.—In the NT only in the gospels [in Mk most freq. in sg. in contrast to Mt and Lk, s. RBorger, TRu 52, '87, 28], Ac, and Rv).

❶ **a relatively large number of people gathered together,** ***crowd***—ⓐ a casual gathering of large numbers of people without reference to classification *crowd, throng* **Mt 9:23, 25; 15:35; Mk 2:4** (s. DDaube, ET 50, '38, 138f); **3:9; Lk 5:1; J 5:13; 6:22; Ac 14:14; 21:34f** and oft.; AcPl Ha 5, 11. τὶς ἐκ τοῦ ὄχλου *someone from the crowd* **Lk 12:13;** cp. **11:27.** ἀνὴρ ἀπὸ τοῦ ὄχ. **9:38.** τινὲς τῶν Φαρισαίων ἀπὸ τοῦ ὄχλου *some of the Pharisees in the crowd* **19:39.** ἀπὸ τοῦ ὄχλου *away from the crowd* **Mk 7:17, 33.** οὐκ ἠδύνατο ἀπὸ τοῦ ὄχλου *he could not because of the crowd* **Lk 19:3** (s. ἀπό 5a). οὐ μετὰ ὄχλου *without a crowd* (present) **Ac 24:18** (cp. vs. **12**). This is equivalent in mng. to ἄτερ ὄχλου (s. ἄτερ) *when there was no crowd present* **Lk 22:6** (s. WLarfeld, Die ntl. Evangelien nach ihrer Eigenart 1925, 190), unless ὄχ. means *disturbance* (Hdt.+) here (so Goodsp.). ἐν τῷ θεάτρῳ μετὰ τοῦ ὄχλου AcPl Ha 1, 24.—πᾶς ὁ ὄχλος (Aelian, VH 2, 6) *the whole crowd, all the people* **Mt 13:2b; Mk 2:13; 4:1b; 9:15; Lk 13:17; Ac 21:27;** MPol 9:2; 16:1. Also ὅλος ὁ ὄχλος AcPl Ha 4, 35.—πολὺς ὄχ. (Jos., Vi. 133; 277) **Mt 14:14; Mk 6:34.** ὄχ. πολύς (Cebes 1, 2; IG IV^2/1, 123, 25; several times LXX) **Mt 20:29; Mk 5:21, 24; 9:14; Lk 8:4; J 6:2.** ὁ πολὺς ὄχ. **Mk 12:37.** ὁ ὄχ. πολύς **J 12:9, 12.**—ὄχ. ἱκανός *a considerable throng* **Mk 10:46; Lk 7:12; Ac 11:24, 26;** cp. **19:26.** ὄχ. τοσοῦτος **Mt 15:33.** ὁ πλεῖστος ὄχ. *the great throng* or *greater part of the crowd* **21:8** (the verb in the pl. with a collective noun as Memnon [I BC/I AD]: 434 fgm. 1, 28, 6 Jac. εἷλον . . . ἡ Ῥωμαίων δύναμις. Cp. B-D-F §134, 1). Cp. **Mk 4:1a.** τὸ πλεῖον μέρος τοῦ ὄχ. *the greater part of the throng* Hs 8, 1, 16; τὸ πλῆθος τοῦ ὄχ. 9, 4, 4; αἱ μυριάδες τοῦ ὄχ. *the crowd in myriads* **Lk 12:1.**—The pl. is common in Mt, Lk, and Ac (acc. to later usage: X., Mem. 3, 7, 5; Dionys. Hal.; Ael. Aristid. 34, 47 K.=50 p. 564 D.; Jos., Ant. 6, 25 al. Schwyzer II 43; cp. Mussies 71 and 85) οἱ ὄχλοι *the crowds, the people* (the latter plainly Posidon.: 87 fgm. 36, 51 Jac. συλλαλήσαντες αὐτοῖς οἱ ὄχ.; Diod. S. 1, 36, 10; 1, 83, 8 ἐν ταῖς τῶν ὄχλων ψυχαῖς; 1, 72, 5 μυριάδες τῶν ὄχλων; 4, 42, 3; 14, 7, 2 ὄχλων πλῆθος=a crowd of people; 36, 15, 2 οἱ κατὰ τὴν πόλιν ὄχλοι=the people in the city; Artem. 1, 51 p. 59, 13 Pack; Vi. Aesopi G 124 P; Ps.-Aeschines, Ep. 10, 4 ἡμεῖς ἅμα τ. ἄλλοις ὄχλοις; Ps.-Demetr., Form. Ep. p. 7, 11; OGI 383, 151 [I BC]; Jos., Ant. 9, 3) **Mt 5:1; 7:28; 9:8, 33, 36** and oft. **Lk 3:7, 10; 4:42; 5:3; 8:42, 45** and oft. **Ac 8:6; 13:45; 14:11, 13, 18f; 17:13.** Mk only **6:33 v.l.** J only **7:12a** (v.l. ἐν τῷ ὄχλῳ). MPol 13:1. Without art. **Mk 10:1** (on the textual problem RBorger, TRu 52, '87, 28); ὄχ. πολλοί (s. πολύς 2αα☐) **Mt 4:25; 8:1; 12:15; 13:2a; 15:30; 19:2; Lk 5:15; 14:25.** πάντες οἱ ὄχ. **Mt 12:23.**—A linguistic parallel to the pl. ὄχλοι and a parallel to the type of political maneuvering in **Mk 15:15** (ὁ Πιλᾶτος βουλόμενος τῷ ὄχλῳ τὸ ἱκανὸν ποιῆσαι ἀπέλυσεν αὐτοῖς τὸν Βαραββᾶν καὶ παρέδωκεν τὸν Ἰησοῦν φραγελλώσας ἵνα σταυρωθῇ) is offered by PFlor 61, 59ff [85 AD], where, according to the court record, G. Septimius Vegetus says to a certain Phibion: ἄξιος μὲν ἦς μαστιγωθῆναι . . . χαρίζομαι δέ σε τοῖς ὄχλοις (s. Dssm., LO 229 [LAE 266f], and on the favor of the ὄχλοι PGM 36, 275).

ⓑ a gathering of people that bears some distinguishing characteristic or status.

α. a large number of people of relatively low status *the (common) people, populace* (PJoüon, RSR 27, '37, 618f) in contrast to the rulers: **Mt 14:5; 15:10; 21:26; Mk 11:18, 32** (v.l. λαόν, q.v. 2); **12:12.** Likew. the pl. οἱ ὄχ. (EpArist 271) **Mt 21:46.** *The lower classes* (X., Cyr. 2, 2, 21, Hier. 2, 3 al.) ἐπίστασις ὄχλου *a disturbance among the people* **Ac 24:12.** Contemptuously *rabble* **J 7:49** (Bultmann ad loc. [w. lit.]).

β. a group or company of people with common interests or of distinctive status *a large number (company, throng),* w. gen. (Eur., Iph. A. 191 ἵππων al.; Jos., Ant. 3, 66; Ath, 1, 4 ὄχλον ἐγκλημάτων) ὄχ. τελωνῶν *a crowd of tax-collectors* **Lk 5:29.** ὄχ. μαθητῶν **6:17.** ὄχ. ὀνομάτων **Ac 1:15.** ὄχ. τῶν ἱερέων **6:7**

❷ **a large mass of people, without ref. to status or circumstances leading to its composition,** ***horde, mass*** pl. ὄχλοι as a synonym beside λαοί and ἔθνη **Rv 17:15** (cp. Da 3:4).—VHunter, Thucydides and the Sociology of the Crowd: ClJ 84,

'88, 17–30, esp. 17 n. 5 (lit. on study of crowds); WCarter, CBQ 55, '93, 56 n. 9 (lit. on sociological perspective).—B. 929. DELG. M-M. TW.

Ὀχοζίας, ου, ὁ (אֲחַזְיָה) ***Ahaziah,*** a Hebrew king (4 Km 8:24; 9:16; 2 Ch 22:1; AscIs 2:13–16=MartIs, Denis p. 111 ln. 9, 13, 19, 25 [king of Gomorrah]; Joseph.) in the genealogy of Jesus **Mt 1:8 v.l.; Lk 3:23ff** D.—BHHW I 50.

ὀχυρός, ά, όν (Hes. et al.; LXX; PsSol 2:1; Jos., Ant. 11, 89; TestJud 9:4; πόλεις ὀχ. Theoph. Ant. 3, 20 [p. 244, 6]) **pert. to being firm/stable, *strong, firm, sturdy*** μακροθυμία Hm 5, 2, 3.—Of firm adherence to an opinion τινὲς δὲ ἐξ αὐτῶν ἐλάλησεν ὀχυροὶ λέγοντες **Lk 11:15 v.l.** S. next entry.—DELG s.v. ἐχυρός.

ὀχύρωμα, ατος, τό (ὀχυρόω 'fortify'; in various senses: 'stronghold, fortress, prison' since X., Hell. 3, 2, 3; SIG 502, 39 [III BC]; OGI 455, 14 [39 AD]; PPetr II, 13 [3], 2 [III BC]; PStras 85, 23; LXX; Jos., Ant. 13, 27) **a strong military installation, *fortress,*** in imagery (Hybreas [I BC] in Seneca Rhet., Suas. 4, 5; Pr 21:22 καθεῖλεν τὸ ὀχύρωμα ἐφ' ᾧ ἐπεποίθεισαν; 10:29 ὀχύρωμα ὁσίου φόβος κυρίου) of spiritual weapons that are δυνατὰ ... πρὸς καθαίρεσιν ὀχυρωμάτων *powerful ... to tear down fortresses,* i.e. to destroy λογισμοί, sophistries, and everything that opposes the γνῶσις θεοῦ **2 Cor 10:4** (cp. Philo, Conf. Lingu. 129; 130 τὴν τοῦ ὀχ. τούτου καθαίρεσιν).—DELG s.v. ἐχυρός. M-M. TW.

ὀψάριον, ου, τό dim. of ὄψον (Hom. et al.; Tob 2:2 BA; 7:8 BA)='cooked food' eaten w. bread. ὀψάριον also has this mng. (PRyl 229, 21; s. below). As food eaten w. bread ὀψάριον can mean 'tidbit' in general (so Tob 2:2 S; Plut., Mor. 126a; Philemo Com. fgm. 98, 5 K.; POxy 531, 18; PFay 119, 31) or specif. ***fish*** (cp. Num 11:22 πᾶν τὸ ὄψος τῆς θαλάσσης; Iambl., Vi. Pyth. 21, 98 θαλασσίων ὄψων.—Suda: ὀψάριον· τὸ ἰχθύδιον. This mng. of ὀψάριον is found in several comic wr. in Athen. 9, 35 p. 385f; Lucian, Jupp. Conf. 4; Cyranides p. 109, 4; 5; GDI 4706, 191 [Thera]; OGI 484, 12; 16; BGU 1095, 16 [57 AD] λαγύνιον ταριχηροῦ [=ῶν] ὀψαρίων=preserved fish; PLond II, 483, 77 p. 328 [616 AD] ὀψάρια ἐκ τῶν παντοίων ὑδάτων. In Mod. Gk. ψάρι=fish). It has the latter mng. in our lit., where it occurs only in J: δύο ὀψάρια **J 6:9** (the synoptic parallels have δύο ἰχθύας: Mt 14:17, 19; Mk 6:38, 41; Lk 9:13, 16. Cp. PRyl 229, 21 [38 AD] τ. ἄρτους κ. τὸ ὀψάριον); **J 6:11; 21:9f, 13.**—JKalitsunakis, Ὄψον und ὀψάριον: PKretschmer Festschr 1926, 96–106; opp. ADebrunner, IndogF 24, 1927, 336–43; s. further JKalitsunakis, Philol. Wochenschrift 1928, 1357f; M-EBoismard, RB 54, '47, 478 n. 2; APitta, Biblica 71, '90, 348–64.—S. also B. 184. New Docs 2, 92. DELG s.v. ὄψον. M-M. Sv.

ὀψέ adv. (Hom. et al.; ins, pap, LXX; En, TestSol, TestAbr A 6 p. 83, 19 and 22 [Stone p. 14]; SibOr 5, 51; Philo, Joseph.; Just., D. 52, 4).

❶ **pert. to an advanced point of time in the day (usually between sunset and darkness), *late*** w. gen. ὀψὲ τῆς ὥρας *at a late hour* (Demosth. 21, 84; Chariton 1, 14, 5; UPZ 6, 15 [163 BC]; Jos., Ant. 16, 218) MPol 7:1.

❷ **pert. specif. to the period between late afternoon and darkness, *late in the day, evening*** i.e. *in the evening* **Mk 13:35.** ὀψὲ οὔσης τῆς ὥρας (s. B-D-F §129) **11:11 v.l.** (for ὀψίας). As a predicate (B-D-F §434, 1; also s. Rob. 973) ὅταν ὀψὲ ἐγένετο *when it became evening, when evening came* **11:19.**—Used almost like an indecl. subst. (Thu. 3, 108, 3 al. ἐς ὀψέ)μέχρις ὀψέ *until evening* Hs 9, 11, 1; also ἕως ὀψέ (PLond III, 1177, 66 p. 183 [113 AD]) 9, 11, 2.—TMartin, BR 38, '93, 55–69.

❸ **marker of a point of time subsequent to another point of time, *after,*** w. special ref. to lateness, funct. as a prep. w. gen. ὀψὲ σαββάτων *after the Sabbath* **Mt 28:1** (Aelian, VH 2, 23; Polyaenus 5, 2, 5 ὀψὲ τῆς ὥρας=later than the hour [decided upon]; Philostrat., Vi. Apoll. 4, 18, 138, 8 ὀψὲ μυστηρίων; 6, 10, 213, 24 ὀψὲ τούτων, Her 12, 190, 10 ὀψὲ τῆς μάχης.—B-D-F §164, 4; Rob. 645f; ETobac, RHE 20, 1924, 239–43; JMaiworm, ThGl 27, '35, 210–16; Goodsp., Probs. 43–45; JGrintz, JBL 79, '60, 32–47).—B. 961. DELG. M-M.

ὀψία, ας, ἡ s. ὄψιος 2.

ὄψιμος, ον (ὀψέ; Hom. et al.; pap, LXX; as proper name Ath. 6, 1) prim. pert. to a period of time that is relatively late (Il. 2, 325), and esp. in connection with agricultural activity (s. L-S-J-M s.v.); in our lit. of rain that comes in spring (March to April), after the normal rains of the winter season have passed (מַלְקוֹשׁ Dt 11:14; s. Dalman, Arbeit I 122ff; 302 ff al.) ὑετὸς ὄψιμος (w. πρόϊμος, as Dt 11:14; Jer 5:24 al.) ***late rain, spring rain*** **Js 5:7 v.l.** for the subst. (ὁ) ὄψιμος in the same mng. S. πρόϊμος.—DELG s.v. ὀψέ. M-M.

ὄψιος, α, ον (ὀψέ)—❶ as adj. (Pind. [Isth. 4, 38f ὀψίᾳ ἐν νυκτί=late in the night] et al.; PTebt 304, 5 ὀψίας τῆς ὥρας γενομένης; BGU 380, 3) **pert. to a point in time that is relatively later than another point of time, *late,*** ὀψίας ἤδη οὔσης τῆς ὥρας *since the hour was already late* **Mk 11:11** (s. ὀψέ 2).

❷ In our lit. mostly subst. ἡ ὀψία (sc. ὥρα; B-D-F §241, 3) **the period between late afternoon and darkness, *evening*** (Ael. Aristid. 48, 50 K.=24 p. 478 D.; POxy 475, 16 [182 AD] ὀψίας 'in the evening'; 528, 5 καθ' ἑκάστης ἡμέρας καὶ ὀψίας; PGM 1, 69; Jdth 13:1 ὡς ὀψία ἐγένετο) usu. in the combination ὀψίας δὲ γενομένης *when evening came* (Syntipas p. 49, 11; TestSol 1:42; Jos., Ant. 5, 7) **Mt 8:16; 14:15, 23; 20:8; 26:20; 27:57; Mk 1:32** (the double expr. ὀψ. γενομένης, ὅτε ἔδυσεν ὁ ἥλ. is like Herm. Wr. 1, 29); Hs 9, 11, 6. ὀψίας γενομένης *in the evening* **Mt 16:2; Mk 4:35; 6:47; 14:17.** ἤδη ὀψ. γενομένης **15:42.** Also οὔσης ὀψίας (Jos., Ant. 5, 140) **J 20:19.** ὡς ὀψ. ἐγένετο (s. Jdth above) **6:16.** The context oft. makes it easier to decide just what time is meant, whether before or after sundown.—B. 997. DELG s.v. ὀψέ. M-M.

ὄψις, εως, ἡ (fr. ὄπωπα, 2 pf. of ὁράω; Hom.+).—❶ **the experience of seeing someth., *seeing, sight*** (Paus. 3, 14, 4 ὄψις ὀνείρατος=the seeing of a dream; PFay 133, 11; Jos., Ant. 3, 38; Just., A I, 30, 1 al.) ἡ ὄψις ὑμῶν *the sight of you* B 1:3 (cp. Arrian, Anab. 6, 26, 3 ἐν ὄψει πάντων; Wsd 15:5 ὧν ὄψις).

❷ **external or physical aspect of someth., *outward appearance, aspect*** (Thu. 6, 46, 3; Timaeus Hist. [IV/III BC]: 566 fgm. 13b Jac.; Diod. S. 4, 54, 5; Appian, Liby. 96 §454; Polyaenus 7, 6, 6; Gen 24:16; EpArist 77) τὴν ὄψιν νεωτέραν ἔχειν *look younger* Hv 3, 10, 4; 3, 12, 1. ἀνήρ τις ἔνδοξος τῇ ὄψει *a man of splendid appearance* 5:1 (TestAbr A 12 p. 90, 15 [Stone p. 28]; cp. SIG 1169, 30 ἔδοξε τὰν ὄψιν εὐπρεπὴς ἀνήρ). Perh. **Rv 1:16** (s. 3 below).—κατ' ὄψιν κρίνειν *judge by the outward appearance* **J 7:24** (cp. Lysias, Orat. 16, 19 p. 147 οὐκ ἄξιον ἀπ' ὄψεως, ὦ βουλή, οὔτε φιλεῖν οὔτε μισεῖν οὐδένα, ἀλλ' ἐκ τῶν ἔργων σκοπεῖν; POxy 37 II, 3; 1 Km 16:7; Jos., Bell. 3, 79).

❸ **the front portion of the head or expression thereof, *face, countenance*** (Pla., Phdr. 254b; Phlegon: 257 fgm. 36, 1, 3 Jac.; Diog. L. 6, 91f; PGiss 22, 5; PAmh 141, 12; BGU 451, 13; PGM 4, 746; 774; Jos., Ant. 6, 189; Iren 5, 30, 1 [Hv II 406, 3]) **J 11:44;** ApcPt 3:7a; τὸ κάλλος τῆς ὄψ. 3:7b. Perh. **Rv 1:16** (s. 2 above). Of the face of God (cp. POxy 1380, 127 of Isis τὴν ἐν

Λήθῃ ἱλαρὰν ὄψιν; BGU 162, 4; 8 ὄψις θεοῦ Σοκνοπαίου; 590, 19; Iren. 5, 31, 2 [Hv II 413, 2]) 1 Cl 36:2.—Also the pl. αἱ ὄψεις, chiefly *the eyes* (Pla., Theaet., 156b; Musonius p. 106, 8 H.; Vett. Val. 228, 6; 268, 1; 279, 30; POxy 911, 6; Tob 14:2 BA; Philo, Decal. 68, Ebr. 44; Orig., C. Cels. 7, 39, 47; ὄψεις τῆς ψυχῆς 51, 29), prob. means more gener. *face* (Jos., Ant. 12, 81; TestReub 5:5; ApcMos 37 ἐπ' ὄψεσι κείμενοι) ἐνέπτυον αὐτοῦ ταῖς ὄψεσι GPt 3:9.—DELG s.v. ὄπωπα D. M-M. Sv.

ὄψομαι s. ὁράω.

ὀψώνιον, ου, τό (since Menand., fgm. 1051 J.=fgm. 896 Kö.; freq. used fr. Polyb. on, in sing. and pl.; oft. in ins; pap; ostraca; only three times in LXX, all pl. The Atticists rejected it [Lob., Phryn. p. 420]) 'ration-(money)' paid to a soldier, then

❶ ***pay, wages*** (a dominant usage; s. also SIG 410, 19 pl.; LXX; EpArist 20:22=Jos., Ant. 12:28 pl.). The more general mng. *provisions* may fit 1 Macc 14:32 (cp. SIG 700, 25) and all NT occurrences (CCaragounis, NovT 16, '74, 35–37).

ⓐ lit. ἀρκεῖσθε τ. ὀψωνίοις ὑμῶν (said by J. the Baptist to στρατευόμενοι) **Lk 3:14.** στρατεύεσθαι ἰδίοις ὀψωνίοις *serve as a soldier at one's own expense* **1 Cor 9:7.**

ⓑ in imagery of Christians as soldiers (on the Christian life as military service s. πανοπλία 2), whose wages are paid by the heavenly general: ἀρέσκετε ᾧ στρατεύεσθε, ἀφ' οὗ καὶ τὰ ὀψώνια κομίζεσθε IPol 6:2.—The military viewpoint seems to pass over into a more general one in λαβὼν ὀψώνιον πρὸς τὴν ὑμῶν διακονίαν *accepting support so that I might serve you* **2 Cor 11:8** (on λαμβάνειν ὀψώνιον cp. Polyb. 6, 39, 12; OGI 266, 7 [III BC]; PPetr II, 13 [17], 6 [258–253 BC]; PLond I, 23 [a], 26f, p. 38 [158–157 BC]; POxy 744, 7; cp. PWisc 68, 4 al. 'allowance').—**Ro 6:23** is still further fr. the military scene, and it is prob. better to class it under the foll.

❷ ***compensation*** (IPriene 121, 34 [I BC], public services χωρὶς ὀψωνίων; 109, 94; 106 [II BC] ἄτερ ὀψωνίου) τὰ ὀψώνια τ. ἁμαρτίας θάνατος *the compensation paid by sin* (for services rendered to it) *is death* **Ro 6:23.**—DELG s.v. ὄψον. M-M. TW. Spicq.

Π

παγιδεύω (παγίς) 1 aor. subj. παγιδεύσω LXX a hunting term Eccl 9:12 ***set a snare*** or ***trap, entrap*** fig. (1 Km 28:9; TestJos 7:1) ὅπως αὐτὸν παγιδεύσωσιν ἐν λόγῳ *in order that they might entrap him with something that he said* (s. λόγος 1aγ) **Mt 22:15** (cp. Atumano, Graec. Venet. Pr 6:2 τοῖς λόγοις. Also in the same, Dt 7:25; 12:30).—M-M. TW.

παγίς, ίδος, ἡ (πήγνυμι, cp. prec. entry; Aristoph. et al.; pap, LXX; En 103: 8) prim. 'trap, snare'.

❶ **a device used to catch animals, *trap, snare*** (Aristoph., Aves 527, Ranae 115; Anth. Pal. 6, 109; Pr 6:5; 7:23; Eccl 9:12) ὡς π. *like a trap,* i.e. unexpectedly **Lk 21:35.** As a piece of equipment for a bird-catcher (Aesop, Fab. 323 P.=152 Babr; cp. 13 L-P.) Mt 10:29 read for ἐπὶ τὴν γῆν by Orig. et al. (Tdf. app.).

❷ **that which causes one to be suddenly endangered or unexpectedly brought under control of a hostile force, *trap, snare,*** fig. ext. of 1 (Aristoph. et al.; LXX): γενηθήτω ἡ τράπεζα αὐτῶν εἰς παγίδα *let their table become a snare* (to them) **Ro 11:9** (Ps 68:23). παγὶς θανάτου *a deadly snare* (Tob 14:10a; Ps 17:6): of being double-tongued D 2:4; B 19:7 Funk; of the mouth gener. B 19:8 (cp. Pr 11:9; 18:7). ἐμπίπτειν εἰς παγίδα *fall into the snare* (Tob 14:10b; Pr 12:13; Sir 9:3): abs. εἰς πειρασμὸν καὶ παγίδα καὶ ἐπιθυμίας **1 Ti 6:9.** τοῦ διαβόλου **3:7.** ἀνανήφω ἐκ τῆς διαβόλου παγίδος **2 Ti 2:26;** s. ἀνανήφω.—IScheftelowitz, Das Schlingen u. Netzmotiv 1912.—DELG s.v. πήγνυμι. M-M. TW.

πάγκαρπος, ον (πᾶς, καρπός; Pind. et al.; Ps.-Pla., Axioch. 13, 371c; EpArist 63) ***bearing much fruit*** π. ξύλον *a tree laden with fruit* fig. Dg 12:1.

πάγος s. Ἄρειος πάγος. M-M.

παθεῖν, παθών s. πάσχω.

πάθημα, ατος, τό (πάσχω; Soph., Hdt. et al.; Philo, Joseph.; Just., A II, 2, 16 [v.l.]; Ath. 28, 4)

❶ **that which is suffered or endured, *suffering, misfortune,*** in our lit. almost always in pl. (Orig., C. Cels. 8, 599, 10. The pl. is also predom. in non-biblical wr.: Plut., Mor. 360d; Appian, Bell. Civ. 2, 64 §269; 4, 1 §2; Jos., Ant. 2, 299) τὰ π. τοῦ νῦν καιροῦ *what we suffer at the present time* **Ro 8:18.—2 Cor 1:6f** (on παθ. . . . πάσχειν cp. Lamellae Aur. Orphicae ed. AOlivieri 1915 p. 16, 4 [IV/III BC]). τὰ παθήματα ὑπὲρ ὑμῶν *the sufferings* (that I, Paul, am enduring) *for you* (the Colossians) **Col 1:24** (JSchneider [s. below] 54–61; JSchmid, BZ 21, '33, 330–44; GKittel, ZST 18, '41, 186–91; SHanson, The Unity of the Church, '46, 119f). W. διωγμοί **2 Ti 3:11.** ἄθλησις παθημάτων *a struggle w. suffering* **Hb 10:32.** Of the sufferings of persecuted Christians gener. **1 Pt 5:9;** ISm 5:1.—Of the sufferings of Christ **Hb 2:10.** They are ever before the eyes of Christians 1 Cl 2:1. τὰ παθήματα τοῦ Χριστοῦ *Christ's sufferings* **2 Cor 1:5; 1 Pt 4:13; 5:1** (θεοῦ P[72]). παθήματα αὐτοῦ (=τοῦ Χρ.) **Phil 3:10.** τὰ εἰς Χριστὸν παθήματα *the sufferings of Christ* **1 Pt 1:11** (s. εἰς 4cβ; CScott, Exp. 6th ser., 12, 1905, 234–40). Suffering Christians stand in close relation to the suffering Christ. They suffer as Christ did, or for Christ's sake, or in mystic unity w. Christ. Cp. ASteubing, Der paul. Begriff 'Christusleiden', diss. Heidelb. 1905; TSchmidt, Der Leib Christi 1919, 210ff; RPaulus, Das Christusproblem der Gegenwart 1922, 24f; RLiechtenhan, ZTK 32, 1922, 368–99; OSchmitz, Das Lebensgefühl d. Pls, 1922, 50ff, 105ff; J Schneider, D. Passionsmystik des Pls 1929; ASchweitzer, D. Mystik des Ap. Pls 1930, 141–58 (The Mysticism of Paul the Ap., tr. WMontgomery '31, 141–59); BAhern, CBQ 22, '60, 1–32, al.—The sing. (Arrian, Anab. 4, 22, 2=suffering, misfortune; 6, 11, 2; 3 of the wounding of Alexander) only **Hb 2:9** of Christ διὰ τὸ πάθημα τοῦ θανάτου (epexegetic gen.) *because of the death he suffered.*

❷ **an inward experience of an affective nature,** ***feeling, interest*** (like πάθος, but less frequent than the latter. Pla., Phd. 79d [of the state of the soul when engaged in purest inquiry] al.; Aristot. [HBonitz, Index Aristot. 1870, 554]; Plut., Pomp. 622 [8, 6]) in a bad sense (Plut., Mor. 1128e) in our lit. only in Paul and only in the pl. *interests, desires* τὰ π. τῶν ἁμαρτιῶν *(the) sinful desires* (not limited to sexual interest) **Ro 7:5.** W. ἐπιθυμίαι **Gal 5:24.**—B. 1089f. DELG s.v. πάσχω. M-M. EDNT. TW.

παθητός, ή, όν (πάσχω, cp. πάθημα; Aristot.+) verbal adj. fr. πάσχω (B-D-F §65, 3; Rob. 1097) ***subject to suffering*** (Plut., Mor. 765b; 1026d, Pelop. 286 [16, 5], Numa 65 [8, 7], oft. in contrast to ἀπαθής; Herm. Wr. 6, 2ab; 10, 17; Sallust. 4 p. 8, 7; Philo, Spec. Leg. 3, 180; Ath. 16, 3; R. 10 p. 59, 3) of the Messiah **Ac 26:23.** Opp. ἀπαθής (s. Proclus, Theol. 80 p. 74, 32) IEph 7:2; IPol 3:2.—DELG s.v. πάσχω. M-M. TW.

πάθνη, ἡ s. φάτνη

πάθνωμα, ους, τό s. φάτνωμα, ατος, τό.

πάθος, ους, τό (πάσχω; trag., Hdt.+)—❶ **that which is endured or experienced,** ***suffering*** (trag., Hdt. et al.; Diod. S. 1, 97, 4 τὰ πάθη τῶν θεῶν [various painful experiences of the gods: the battle against the Titans, etc.]; Jos., Ant. 15, 57; 16, 315; Just., A I, 22, 4; Ath. 30, 4), so in our lit. only in B 6:7 and in Ign. (but freq. in his wr.), and always in the sing., w. ref. to the physical sufferings of Christ (so also B 6:7; cp. Just., D. 97, 3 εἰς τὸ πάθος καὶ τὸν σταυρόν; Iren. 3, 18, 3 [Harv. II 97, 3]; Orig., C. Cels. 1, 54, 2). IEph 20:1; IMg 5:2; ITr ins; 11:2; IPhld 9:2. τὸ θεομακάριστον π. ISm 1:2. τὸ π. τοῦ θεοῦ μου IRo 6:3. By his own baptism and by his suffering Christ consecrated the baptismal water for the Christians IEph 18:2. ἀγαλλιᾶσθαι ἐν τῷ π. τοῦ κυρίου *rejoice in the Passion of the Lord* IPhld ins. μετανοεῖν εἰς τὸ π. *change the mind about the suffering* ISm 5:3. Of the church ἐκλελεγμένη ἐν πάθει ἀληθινῷ *chosen by the real Passion* IEph ins. Used beside ἀνάστασις, so that it is equivalent to θάνατος (Appian, Bell. Civ. 1, 28 §129 the death of Nonius; 1, 38 §169 of Drusus; 5, 59 §250. S. πάσχω 3aα) IMg 11: ISm 7:2; 12:2. τῷ π. συγκατατίθεσθαι *agree with, have a share in the Passion* (of Christ) IPhld 3:3.

❷ **experience of strong desire,** ***passion*** (Pla. et al.; oft. 4 Macc; Philo; Jos., C. Ap. 1, 214; Ar. 8, 2; Just., A I, 53, 12; Tat. 19, 3; Ath.; οὐ π. τοῦ θεοῦ ἐστιν ἡ ὀργή Orig., C. Cels. 4, 72, 1), esp. of a sexual nature (Pla.; PMich 149 VI, 30 [II AD] π. αἰσχρόν; Ps.-Phoc. 194; Jos., Ant. 2, 53; Did., Gen. 138, 1) ἐν πάθει ἐπιθυμίας *in lustful passion* **1 Th 4:5** (Ath. 21, 1 πάθη ὀργῆς καὶ ἐπιθυμίας). Abs. (w. other vices, some of which are also sexual in character) **Col 3:5.** Of an adulterous woman: ἐπιμένειν τῷ π. τούτῳ *persist in this passion* Hm 4, 1, 6. Pl. πάθη ἀτιμίας *disgraceful passions* **Ro 1:26.**—Also of the passion of anger Hs 6, 5, 5 v.l. (Cp. τὸ τῆς φιλαργυρίας π. Did., Gen. 126, 15.)—RRabel, Diseases of the Soul in Stoic Psychology: Greek, Roman, and Byzantine Studies 22, '81, 385–93. S. on πάσχω, end.—B. 1089f. DELG s.v. πάσχω. M-M. TW. Sv.

παιδαγωγός, οῦ, ὁ (παῖς, ἄγω) since Eur.; Hdt. 8, 75; Plut.; ins [reff. in SIG 1253 n. 1]; pap, Philo; Jos., Ant. 1, 56; 18, 202, Vi. 429. Common as a loanw. in rabb. [SKrauss, Griech. u. lat. Lehnwörter im Talmud usw. II 1899, 421]). Orig. 'boy-leader', the man, usu. a slave (Plut., Mor. 4ab), whose duty it was to conduct a boy or youth (Plut., Mor. 439f) to and from school and to superintend his conduct gener.; he was not a 'teacher' (despite the present mng. of the derivative 'pedagogue' [s. OED s.v. 1a as opposed to 2]; παιδαγωγός and διδάσκαλος are differentiated: X., De Rep. Lac. 3, 2; Pla., Lys. 208c [JCallaway, JBL 67, '48, 353–55]; Diog. L. 3, 92; Philo, Leg. ad Gai. 53). When the young man became of age, the π. was no longer needed (cp. Gaius' complaint about Macro's intentions Philo, In Facc. 3 (15); s. JMarquardt[2]-AMau, D. Privatleben der Römer 1886, 114; WBecker-HGöll, Charikles II[3] 1878, 46ff [Eng. tr. FMetcalfe, 1889, 226f]; ABaumeister, Denkmäler d. klass. Altertums 1885–88 II, 1125f). In our lit. **one who has responsibility for someone who needs guidance,** ***guardian, leader, guide.*** As a pers. to whom respect is due, beside the father (as Plut., Lyc. 50 [17, 1]) **1 Cor 4:15.** The law as a π. (so Plut., Mor. 645bc τοῦ νόμου καθάπερ παιδαγωγοῦ). Paul evaluates the Mosaic law as a παιδ. εἰς Χριστόν **Gal 3:24,** where the emphasis is on the constrictive function of the law in contrast to freedom in the gospel. Humankind remains under its constraints, ὑπὸ παιδαγωγόν vs. **25,** until God declares, by sending his Son, that it has come of age (s. υἱοθεσία).—DLull, JBL 105, '86, 481–98 the law had temporal limitations; TGordon, NTS 35, '89, 150–54 role of guardian; NYoung, Paidagogos, The Social Setting of a Pauline Metaphor: NovT 29, '87, 150–76.—Pauly-W. 18/2, 2375–85; Kl. Pauly IV 408. Straub 61. DELG s.v. ἄγω. M-M. TW. Spicq.

παιδάριον, ου, τό (παῖς; in a variety of senses Aristoph., Pla. et al.; ins, pap, LXX, TestSol; TestAbr B 2 p. 107, 2 [Stone p. 62]; JosAs; Jos., Ant. 17, 13) dim. of παῖς.

❶ ***child*** (also a female: Aristoph., Th. 1203; Hyperid., fgm. 164; Menand., fgm. 361 Kö.)—ⓐ *children* playing about **Mt 11:16 v.l**—ⓑ *a youth,* who is no longer a child (Gen 37:30 and cp. vs. 2, where Joseph is said to be seventeen years old; Tob 6:3; JosAs 27:2 of Benjamin, aged nineteen); so perh. **J 6:9.** But this pass. could also belong under

❷ ***young slave*** (Callixenus [III BC]: 627 fgm. 2 p. 173, 14, 17 Jac.; X., Ag. 1, 21; Diog. L. 6, 52. Oft. pap.; 1 Km 25:5; Ruth 2:5, 9) MPol 6:1; 7:1. GSimpson, Semantic Study of Words for Young Person, Servant and Child in the Septuagint and Other Early Koine Greek, diss. Sydney '76.—New Docs 1, 87. Schmidt, Syn. II 429f. DELG s.v. παῖς. M-M. TW.

παιδεία, ας, ἡ (παιδεύω; 'cultural nurture' Aeschyl., Thu.+)

❶ **the act of providing guidance for responsible living,** ***upbringing, training, instruction,*** in our lit. chiefly as it is attained by ***discipline, correction*** (LXX, PsSol; TestZeb 2:3), of the holy *discipline* of a fatherly God 1 Cl 56:16. πᾶσα παιδεία *all discipline* **Hb 12:11.** τὰ λόγια τῆς παιδείας τοῦ θεοῦ *the oracles of God's teaching* 1 Cl 62:3. ἐκτρέφειν τινὰ ἐν π. καὶ νουθεσίᾳ κυρίου *bring someone up in the discipline and instruction of the Lord* (=Christian disc. and instr.) **Eph 6:4.** μισεῖν παιδείαν *hate discipline* 1 Cl 35:8 (Ps 49:17; cp. Pr 5:12). ὀλιγωρεῖν παιδείας κυρίου **Hb 12:5** (Pr 3:11). ἀναλαμβάνειν παιδείαν *accept correction* (cp. λαμβάνειν παιδείαν Pr 8:10; Jer 39:33; 42:13) 1 Cl 56:2. παιδεύειν τινὰ παιδείαν (X., Cyr. 8, 3, 37; Aeschin., Or. 3, 148; Ps.-Demosth. 35, 42; s. also παιδεύω 2a): παιδεύειν τινὰ τὴν π. τοῦ φόβου τοῦ θεοῦ *bring someone up with a training that leads to the fear of God* 21:6=Pol 4:2. παιδεύειν παιδείᾳ (Pla., Leg. 5 p. 741a; X., Cyr. 1, 1, 6): παιδεύεσθαι παιδείᾳ δικαίᾳ *be corrected with just discipline* Hv 2, 3, 1. παραδίδοσθαί τινι εἰς ἀγαθὴν π. *be handed over to someone for good instruction* Hs 6, 3, 6. τῆς ἐν Χριστῷ παιδείας μεταλαμβάνειν *share in a Christian upbringing* 1 Cl 21:8. ὠφέλιμος πρὸς παιδείαν τὴν ἐν δικαιοσύνῃ *useful for training in righteousness* **2 Ti 3:16.** Of discipline by

God (PsSol 7:9 al.; Cyrill. Scyth. p. 38, 8; 23): χωρὶς παιδείας εἶναι *be* (left) *without* (divine) *discipline* **Hb 12:8.** εἰς παιδείαν ὑπομένετε *you must endure* (your trials) *as* (divine) *discipline* vs. **7** (GBornkamm, Sohnschaft u. Leiden, '60, 188–98). π. εἰρήνης ἡμῶν ἐπ' αὐτόν *the chastisement that brought peace to us came upon him* 1 Cl 16:5 (Is 53:5).

❷ **the state of being brought up properly,** ***training*** (Diod. S. 12, 13, 4; 12, 20, 1; OGI 504, 8 ἐπὶ παιδείᾳ τε καὶ τῇ ἄλλῃ ἀρετῇ; Sir 1:27; Jos., Vi. 196; 359, C. Ap. 1, 73; Just., A I 1, 1 al.; Tat. 12, 5 ἡμετέρας παιδείας al.; Ath.) μὴ ἔχειν παιδείαν *have no training* Hv 3, 9, 10. The word could have this mng. in some of the places dealt w. under 1.—WJaeger, Paideia I–III '34–47 (Eng. tr. by GHighet, '39–44); HvArnim, Leb. u. Werke des Dio v. Prusa mit e. Einleitung: Sophistik, Rhetorik, Philosophie in ihrem Kampf um d. Jugendbildung 1898; GBertram, Der Begriff d. Erziehung in d. griech. Bibel: Imago Dei (GKrüger Festschr.) '32, 33–52; WJentzsch, Urchristl. Erziehungsdenken '51. MHengel, Judaism '74, esp. I 65–78.—DELG s.v. παῖς. M-M. TW. Sv.

παιδευτής, οῦ, ὁ (παιδεύω; Pla. et al.; ins; Sb 5941, 2; LXX; PsSol 8:29; Tat. 22, 1) ***instructor, teacher*** (Pla., Leg. 7, 811d; Plut., Lyc. 46 [12, 4], Camill. 134 [10, 3], Mor. 4c; Diog. L. 7, 7; ins; Sir 37:19; 4 Macc 5:34; Philo, Omn. Prob. Lib. 143) π. ἀφρόνων **Ro 2:20.**—Somet. the emphasis is on the idea of correcting or disciplining *corrector, one who disciplines* (s. παιδεύω 2 and cp. Hos 5:2; PsSol 8, 29) **Hb 12:9.**—M-M. TW. Spicq.

παιδεύω (s. prec. entry) impf. ἐπαίδευον; fut. παιδεύσω LXX; 1 aor. ἐπαίδευσα. Pass.: 1 fut. παιδευθήσομαι LXX; 1 aor. ἐπαιδεύθην; pf. ptc. πεπαιδευμένος.

❶ **to provide instruction for informed and responsible living,** ***educate*** (trag.+; Pla.; X.; ins, pap; TestSol 1:13 D [ἐπαιδεύθη ταύτην τὴν σοφίαν]; EpArist, Philo; Jos., C. Ap. 1, 22 γράμμασιν ἐπαιδεύθησαν; Tat. τοῦτο ὁ σωτὴρ παιδεύει λέγων; Did., Gen. 102, 18) ἐπαιδεύθη Μωϋσῆς ἐν πάσῃ σοφίᾳ Αἰγυπτίων *Moses was educated in all the culture of the Egyptians* **Ac 7:22.** πεπαιδευμένος κατὰ ἀκρίβειαν τοῦ πατρῴου νόμου *educated strictly according to the law of our fathers* **22:3** (cp. Jos., Bell. 7, 343). CBurchard, ZNW 61, '70, 168f prefers a comma after πεπαιδ.

❷ **to assist in the development of a person's ability to make appropriate choices,** ***practice discipline.***—ⓐ *correct, give guidance* (LXX) τινά (*to*) *someone* (TestZeb 2:3; Aelian, VH 1, 34) τοὺς ἀντιδιατιθεμένους **2 Ti 2:25.** τοὺς ἐκλεκτούς, ἀλλήλους Hv 3, 9, 10. δι' οὗ ἡμᾶς ἐπαίδευσας *through whom* (i.e. Christ) *you* (i.e. God) *have led us to the right way* 1 Cl 59:3 in wordplay w. παῖς preceding. παιδευθῆναι παιδείᾳ δικαίᾳ Hv 2, 3, 1. παιδεύειν τὴν παιδείαν (Ammonius, Vi. Aristot. p. 10, 20 Westerm; s. also παιδεία 1) 1 Cl 21:6=Pol 4:2. W. ἵνα foll. *lead to* **Tit 2:12.**

ⓑ *discipline* w. punishment—**α.** mostly of divine discipline (Cyrill. Scyth. p. 37, 23; 73, 3 παιδευόμενος ὑπὸ τοῦ δαίμονος; LXX; ApcSed 3:7 [cp. 4:1]; ApcrEzk P 1 recto, 6; Theoph. Ant. 2, 26 [p. 162, 17]) **Hb 12:6;** 1 Cl 56:4 (both Pr 3:12). W. ἐλέγχειν (Ps 6:2; 37:2) 1 Cl 56:5 (Ps 140:5); **Rv 3:19** (cp. Pr 3:12 w. v.l.). παιδεύων ἐπαίδευσέν με ὁ κύριος 1 Cl 56:3 (Ps 117:18). Cp. also **Hb 12:10b.**—Pass. (PsSol 3:4; 13:8; Laud. Therap. 19 τὸ σῶμα παιδεύεται=is disciplined [by God]) **1 Cor 11:32; 2 Cor 6:9;** 1 Cl 56:16. παιδευθῆναι εἰς μετάνοιαν *accept correction so as to repent* 57:1. Wholesome discipline can be exerted even through Satan; pass. w. inf. foll. (B-D-F §392, 2) **1 Ti 1:20.**

β. of discipline by human fathers (Pr 19:18; 28:17a; 29:17) **Hb 12:7, 10a.**

γ. *discipline by whipping* or *scourging* (Vi. Aesopi G 61 P.; 3 Km 12:11, 14; 2 Ch 10:11, 14) **Lk 23:16, 22** (contrast φραγγελόω ASherwin-White, Rom. Society and Rom. Law in the NT, '63, 27f).—B. 1446f. DELG s.v. παῖς. M-M. TW. Sv.

παιδιόθεν adv. ***from childhood*** ἐκ π. (Gen 47:3 A; MartPtPl 39 [Aa I 152, 12].—B-D-F §104, 3; Rdm.[2] 32; Mlt-H. 164) **Mk 9:21.**—MLejeune, Les adverbes grecs en -θεν '39. S. παιδόθεν.—DELG s.v. παῖς. M-M.

παιδίον, ου, τό (Hdt., Aristoph.+) dim. of παῖς (Reader, Polemo 274, w. ref. to Hippocr., Sept. 5 and Philo, Op. 105: a very young child 'up to seven years'; B-D-F §111, 3; Mlt.-H. 345).

❶ **a child, normally below the age of puberty,** ***child***

ⓐ *very young child, infant,* used of boys and girls. Of a newborn child (Diod. S. 4, 20, 3; Just., D. 34, 2 al. [after **Mt 2:8f**]; Tat. 33, 3) **Lk 2:21 v.l.** (eight days old, as Gen 17:12); **J 16:21.** Infants are fed honey, then milk B 6:17 (cp. Diod. S. 5, 70, 3 αὗται [αἱ Νύμφαι] δὲ μέλι καὶ γάλα μίσγουσαι τὸ παιδίον [τὸν Δία] ἔθρεψαν.—HUsener [at γάλα b]). Those who are born again have ὡς παιδίων τὴν ψυχήν *a soul like that of newborn children* B 6:11.—**Mt 2:8, 9, 11, 13f, 20f; Lk 1:59, 66, 76, 80; 2:17, 27, 40; Hb 11:23** (cp. Ex 2:2f). GJs 20:3f; 21:3; 22:1 v.l. (for βρέφος); 22:2 v.l. (for παῖς).

ⓑ w. ref. to age (ApcEsdr 4:33, 35 p. 29, 9 and 12 Tdf. παιδίον ... γέρων): **Mt 18:2, 4f; Mk 9:36f; 10:15; Lk 9:47f; 18:17;** 1 Cl 16:3 (Is 53:2). Pl. **Mt 11:16; 19:13f; Mk 7:28; 10:13f; Lk 7:32; 18:16** (on **Mk 10:14, 15** and parallels s. JBlinzler, Klerusblatt '44, 90–96). γυναῖκες καὶ παιδία (Num 14:3; Jdth 7:23; 4 Macc 4:9; cp. Jos., Bell. 4, 115) **Mt 14:21; 15:38.** παιδία ... πατέρες ... νεανίσκοι **1J 2:14.**—B 8:1ab. Of girls **Mk 5:39–41; 7:30.**

ⓒ w. ref. to relationship; the father is indicated by a gen. (μου as TestJob 39:12; cp. Epict. 4, 1, 141 σου; TestJob 4:5) **J 4:49.** Pl. **Lk 11:7.** The child indicated by a gen., w. the father ὁ πατὴρ τοῦ παιδίου **Mk 9:24.**

❷ **one who is open to instruction,** ***child,*** fig. ext. of 1 παιδία ταῖς φρεσίν *children as far as the mind is concerned* **1 Cor 14:20.**—W. ref. to their attitude toward the truth (Artem. 2, 69 p. 162, 7: τὰ παιδία ἀληθῆ λέγει: οὐδέπω γὰρ οἶδε ψεύδεσθαι καὶ ἐξαπατᾶν) **Mt 18:3.**

❸ **one who is treasured in the way a parent treasures a child,** ***child,*** fig. ext. of 1—ⓐ of the children of God **Hb 2:13f** (vs. **13** after Is 8:18, but understood in a NT sense).

ⓑ as a form of familiar address on the part of a respected pers., who feels himself on terms of fatherly intimacy w. those whom he addresses (Cornutus 1 p. 1, 1 ὦ π.; Athen. 13, 47, 584c) **1J 2:18; 3:7 v.l.** Used by the risen Christ in addressing his disciples **J 21:5.**— B. 92. M-M. TW.

παιδίσκη, ης, ἡ dim. of παῖς 'girl', in our lit. always of the slave class, ***female slave*** (so Hdt.+; pap [also Dssm. LO 167, 6=LAE 200, 18; others New Docs 2, 87f], LXX, TestAbr A; TestJob 21:2; Test12Patr, JosAs; Philo, Congr. Erud. Gr. 1=Gen 16:1 [PKatz, Philo's Bible '50, 36]; Jos., Ant. 18, 40; Ar. [Milne 74, 8]; Just., A I, 9, 4) **Mt 26:69; Mk 14:66, 69; Lk 22:56; Ac 12:13; 16:16, 19** D; GJs 2:2f. ἡ π. ἡ θυρωρός *the slave who kept the door* **J 18:17.** W. παῖς (Lev 25:44; Dt 12:12, 18; TestAbr A 15 p. 95, 22 [Stone p. 38]; Pel-Leg. 12, 24f) **Lk 12:45.** W. δοῦλος (2 Esdr 2:65; Eccl 2:7; Ar.; w. δούλη JosAs 6:8) B 19:7; D 4:10; of God's *female slaves* (w. δοῦλοι 'male slaves') 1 Cl 60:2. In specific contrast to ἐλευθέρα of Hagar **Gal 4:22f** (Gen 16:1ff;

Philo, Leg. All. 3, 244); w. a turn in the direction of a more profound sense vss. **30ab** (=Gen 21:10ab), **31.**—JWackernagel, Glotta 2, 1909, 1–8; 218f; 315.—Lob., Phryn. 239f. Schmidt, Syn. II 429f. DELG s.v. παῖς. M-M.

παιδόθεν adv. (Sb 5294, 8; Ps.-Lucian, Philopatr. 19; Themist., Or. 25 p. 310d; evidence for use Ibycus [VI BC] 1, 10 Bergk [=Diehl[2] 6, 12 v.l.], in Athen. 13, 601b, is questionable [L-S-J-M Suppl. deletes the ref.]; Sb 5294, 8 [III AD]) ***from childhood*** ἐκ π. (Laud. Therap. E, ln. 8) **Mk 9:21 v.l.** S. παιδιόθεν.

παιδοφθορέω (fr. παιδοφθόρος: παῖς, φθορέω 'to seduce boys') fut. παιδοφθορήσω (Christian usage: Just., D. 95, 1; Tat. 8, 1) **to engage in same-sex activity with a young male, *commit sodomy*** B 19:4; D 2:2.—For anc. and modern lit. s. PvanderHorst, The Sentences of Pseudo-Phocylides '78, 250f; cp. 111; 237–39.—S. DELG s.v. φθείρω.

παιδοφθόρος, ου, ὁ (παῖς, φθόρος 'seducer of boys'; cp. prec. entry; Physiogn. I 327, 16; TestLevi 17:11) **one who sodomizes a boy, *pederast*** B 10:6.

παίζω (παῖς) aor. subj. 3 sg. παίξῃ Job 40:29, impv. 3 sg. and pl. παιξάτω, -τωσαν LXX (Hom.+; Kaibel 362, 5; BGU 1024 VII, 26; PGM 7, 428; LXX; TestAbr A 10 p. 87, 23 [Stone p. 22]; EpArist 284; Philo; Jos., Bell. 4, 157; Tat. 8, 1; Ath. 31, 1) **to engage in some activity for the sake of amusement, *play, amuse oneself*** (Ion of Chios [V BC], Eleg. 1, 15f [=Campbell 26] καλῶν ἐπιήρανε ἔργων | πίνειν καὶ παίζειν καὶ τὰ δίκαια φρονεῖν [in address to Dionysus] 'O Ruler of all fine deeds, grant me a long age of drinking, fun, and giving thought to what is just'; 2, 7 Diehl[3] [=Campbell 27] πίνωμεν, παίζομεν 'let's drink, let's have fun' [dancing is a part of the merry-making but is expressed w. a different verb: ὀρχείσθω τις ln. 8]; Appian, Syr. 26, 125 παίζοντας καὶ μεθύοντας) **1 Cor 10:7** (Ex 32:6). π. μετά τινος *play with someone* (Gen 21:9; 26:8) Hs 9, 11, 4f.—DELG s.v. παῖς. M-M. TW.

παῖς, παιδός, ὁ or **ἡ** (Hom. et al.) *child.*—❶ **a young pers. normally below the age of puberty, w. focus on age rather than social status, *boy, youth*** (Hom. et al.; ins, pap, LXX; Philo, Op. M. 105; Jos., Ant. 12, 210; Just., D. 78, 2 and 7; s. VLeinieks, The City of Dionysos '96, 199–210 on age-classes) **Mt 17:18; Lk 9:42; Ac 20:12.** Ἰησοῦς ὁ παῖς **Lk 2:43.** In ref. to Jesus GJs 20:4; 22:2.—Pl. (as פְּדַיָּא a loanw. in rabb.) **Mt 2:16; 21:15;** B 8:3f.—ἐκ παιδός *from childhood* (Diod. S. 1, 54, 5; 1, 73, 9; 1, 92, 5; 19, 40, 2 al. Simplicius in Epict. p. 129, 26; UPZ 144, 19 [165 BC] τῆς ἐκ παιδὸς φιλίας; cp. Just., A I, 15, 6 ἐκ παίδων) **Mk 9:21** D.

❷ **one's own immediate offspring, *child*** as 'son' or 'daughter'—ⓐ of a son ὁ παῖς (Hom.+; Diod. S. 20, 22, 1 οἱ παῖδες αὐτοῦ; ins, pap, LXX; TestAbr A 7 p. 84, 19 [Stone p. 16]; JosAs 23:9; ApcMos 42; Jos., Bell. 4, 646, Ant. 20, 140 al.; Just., A II, 2, 16 al.; Tat. 41, 1; Mel., HE 4, 26, 7, P. 53, 389; Ath. 20, 2 al.) ὁ παῖς αὐτοῦ **J 4:51** (=υἱός vss. 46f, 50; υἱός v.l. for παῖς vs. **51**). This sense is also poss. in **Mt 8:6, 8, 13,** but these pass. prob. belong in 3a.

ⓑ of a daughter ἡ παῖς (for the feminine term, but not limited to 'daughter', s. Pind., fgm. 107, 7 [122 Sch.] ὦ παῖδες=girls!; Hyperid., fgm. 144; Phalaris, Ep. 142, 1; Chariton 1, 8, 2; Philostrat., Her. 19, 11 p. 204, 31; Gen 24:28; 34:12; TestJob 7:7f; Jos., Ant. 1, 254; 5, 266 al.; Tat. 8, 3; 33, 2) **Lk 8:51;** GJs fifteen times for Mary. ἡ παῖς *(my) child* (nom. w. art. for voc.; s. B-D-F §147, 3; Rob. 465f; 769) **Lk 8:54.**

❸ **one who is committed in total obedience to another, *slave, servant***—ⓐ of slaves and personal attendants *slave, servant* (since Hipponax [VI BC] 16 D.[3]; Aeschyl., Cho. 652. Also HUsener, Epicurea 1887 p. 168, 10; Plut., Alcib. 193 [4, 5], Mor. 65c; 70e; SIG 96, 26. Oft. pap. and LXX; TestAbr B; JosAs 99:3 al.; AscIs 3:5; Jos., Ant. 18, 192, Vi. 223.—Even an especially trusted male servant is termed ὁ παῖς: Diod. S. 15, 87, 6 Epaminondas' armor-bearer; Appian, Iber. 27, 107 Scipio's groom; Gen 24:2ff Abraham's chief servant, vs. 5 ὁ παῖς) **Lk 7:7** (=δοῦλος vss. 2f, 10); **15:26;** AcPt Ox 849, 15 [Aa I 73, 21 Lat.]. W. παιδίσκη (q.v.) **12:45.** Prob. **Mt 8:6, 8, 13** also belong here (s. 2a).—Of those at a ruler's court οἱ παῖδες *courtiers, attendants* (Diod. S. 17, 36, 5; Gen 41:10, 37f; 1 Km 16:17; Jer 43:31; 44:2; 1 Macc 1:6, 8) **Mt 14:2.**

ⓑ of special relationships—**α.** humans as God's *servants, slaves* (Ael. Aristid. 45 p. 152 D.: θεῶν παῖδες [or 'sons of gods' as Polyb. 3, 47, 8; Chariton 2, 1, 5 and Diog. L. 9, 72]; LXX; ParJer 6:24 [Jeremiah]) Israel (Is 41:8f; PsSol 12:6; 17:21) **Lk 1:54.** David (Ps 17:1; Is 37:35) **1:69; Ac 4:25;** D 9:2a.—Of guileless pers. τοὺς κατὰ θεὸν ἀκακίαν ἀσκοῦντας παῖδας ἐκάλουν, ὡς καὶ Παπίας δηλοῖ *as Papias points out, those who led a godly life without guile were called children* Papias (8).

β. angels as servants of God *(God) does not trust his servants* 1 Cl 39:4 (Job 4:18). Of the young man from heaven who released Paul from his chains παῖς λείαν (=λίαν) εὐειδὴς ἐν χάριτι AcPl Ha 3, 13f.

γ. of Christ in his relation to God. In this connection it has the mng. *servant* because of the identification of the 'servant of God' of certain OT pass. w. the Messiah (Is 52:13 et al.; BJanowski/PStuhlmacher, edd., Der Leidende Gottesknecht '96 [lit.]; DBS XII 1000–1016) **Mt 12:18** (cp. Is 42:1); B 6:1; 9:2 (on the last two cp. Is 50:10). So prob. also D 9:2b (because of the immediate proximity of Δαυὶδ ὁ παῖς σου 9:2a); 9:3; 10:2f.—In other places (cp. Ath. 10, 2; 12, 2 al.; Iren. 3, 12, 5 [Harv. II 58, 8]) the mng. *son* is certainly to be preferred (παῖς was so understood in the Gk. world, when it expressed a relationship to a divinity: Il. 2, 205 Κρόνου παῖς; Sappho 1, 2 Diehl; Alcaeus 1; Bacchylides 17, 70 Minos, a παῖς of Zeus; Hermocles [IV/III BC] p. 174 Coll. Alex.=Athen. 6, 63, 253d: Demetrius Poliorcetes as π. Ποσειδῶνος θεοῦ; Diod. S. 17, 51, 1 the god Ammon has his prophet address Alexander thus χαῖρε, ὦ παῖ; what follows makes it clear that procreation is meant; Plut., Mor. 180d; Maximus Tyr. 14, 1d; Paus. 2, 10, 3 Ἄρατος Ἀσκληπιοῦ π.; Diogenes, Ep. 36, 1; Philostrat., Vi. Apoll. 7, 24 p. 279, 4; Porphyr., Vi. Plot. 23; Iambl., Vi. Pyth. 2, 10; IG IV[2], 128, 50 [280 BC] and oft.; Sb 8314, 9 Hermes conducts the dead man to the Elysian fields ἅμα παισὶ θεῶν. S. above bα the παῖδες θεῶν. Cp. also Herm. Wr. 13, 2 ὁ γεννώμενος θεοῦ θεὸς παῖς; 13, 4; 14; Rtzst., Poim. 223f.—Celsus 7, 9) παῖς αὐτοῦ ὁ μονογενὴς Ἰησοῦς Χρ. MPol 20:2. God as ὁ τοῦ ἀγαπητοῦ κ. εὐλογητοῦ παιδὸς Ἰησοῦ Χρ. πατήρ 14:1. Corresp. Christ as God's ἀγαπητὸς παῖς 14:3; Dg 8:11. The same is true of the other pass. in Dg: 8:9; 9:1.—In the case of the rest of the pass. it is hardly poss. to decide which mng. is better: **Ac 3:13,26; 4:27, 30** (unless the παῖς σου *your servant* of **4:25** should demand the same transl. for the other pass. as well; JMénard, CBQ 19, '57, 83–92 [Acts]); 1 Cl 59:2–4 (in wordplay w. παιδεύω; but here the word ἠγαπημένος repeated in vss. 2 and 3 [cp. the magical pap of c. 300 AD in TSchermann, TU 34, 2b, 1909, 3: Christ as ἠγαπημένος παῖς] could suggest the transl. *son*).—WBousset, Kyrios Christos[2] 1921, 56f; AvHarnack, Die Bezeichnung Jesu als 'Knecht Gottes' u. ihre Geschichte in d. alten Kirche: SBBerlAk 1926, 212–38; Jeremias, ZNW 34, '35, 115–23; KEuler, D. Verkündigung v. leidenden Gottesknecht aus

Jes 53 in d. griech. Bibel '34; PSeidelin, D. ᶜEbed J. u. d. Messiasgestalt im Jesajatargum: ZNW 35, '36, 194–231; HWolff, Jes 53 im Urchristent. '50[2]; EMcDowell, Son of Man and Suffering Servant '44; ELohmeyer, Gottesknecht u. Davidssohn '45, esp. 2–8; TNicklin, Gospel Gleanings '50, 268f; OCullmann, Dieu Vivant 16, '50, 17–34; HHegermann, Jes 53 in Hexapla, Targum u. Peschitta '54; ELohse, Märtyrer u. Gottesknecht '55; WGrundmann, Sohn Gottes: ZNW 47, '56, 113–33; OCullmann, Die Christologie des NT '57; JPrice, Interpretation 12, '58, 28–38 (Synoptics); MHooker, Jesus and the Servant '59; BvanIersel, 'D. Sohn' in d. synopt. Jesusworten, '61, 52–65 (bibliog.); HOrlinsky, The So-called Suffering Servant in Isaiah 53, '64 (s. review in CBQ 27, '66, 147); EKränkl, Jesus der Knecht Gottes, '72 (Acts); FDanker, Proclamation Comm.: Luke '87, 82–86. WZimmerli/JJeremias, The Servant of God (tr. HKnight), '65=Studies in Bibl. Theol. 20.—B. 87f. Schmidt, Syn. II 422–31. DELG. M-M. EDNT. TW. Sv.

παίω 1 aor. ἔπαισα (Aeschyl., Hdt. et al.; pap, LXX; PsSol 8:15; TestSol 2:12 D; Ath.; B-D-F §101 p. 55 s.v. τύπτειν)

❶ **to make violent contact by thrusting with someth., *strike***

ⓐ w. a body part *strike, hit* w. acc. of pers. (Philostrat., Vi. Soph. 2, 10, 6; PSI 168, 15 [II BC] ἔπαισάν με; 2 Km 14:6; Jos., Bell. 2, 176) **Mt 26:68; Lk 22:64.**

ⓑ w. sharp instruments *strike, wound* w. acc. of pers. (X., Cyr. 8, 5, 12; Diod. S. 11, 69, 5 παίει τῷ ξίφει τὸν Ἀρταξέρξην; 2 Km 20:10; TestJud 9:3 (Ch.); Jos., Ant. 4, 153) **Mk 14:47; J 18:10.**

ⓒ w. a stinger *sting,* of scorpions (Aelian, NA 10, 23; Ael. Dion. ε, 8) w. acc. of pers. **Rv 9:5.**

❷ **to inflict punishment, *strike,*** fig. ext. of 1 (in quotations fr. Job in 1 Cl) : ἔπαισεν αὐτοὺς σητὸς τρόπον 1 Cl 39:5 (Job 4:19). Abs. ἔπαισεν, καὶ αἱ χεῖρες αὐτοῦ ἰάσαντο 56:7 (Job 5:18).—B. 553. DELG. M-M.

Πακατιανός, ή, όν ***Pacatian, in Pacatia*** a later (post-Constantine) name for a part of Phrygia, used in the **subscription to 1 Ti v.l.** (Still other forms of the word are attested.) The capital of this district was Laodicea where, acc. to the subscr., 1 Ti was written.

πάλαι adv. denoting past time in contrast to the present (Hom. et al.; ins, pap, LXX; Just.; Tat. 6, 2, Ant. 4, 153).

❶ **pert. to a point of time in the past, *long ago, formerly*** (Philo, Sacr. Abel. 134 πάλαι, νῦν, αὖθις, ἀεί; Jos., Ant. 16, 40 and Just., A I, 14, 2 π. . . . νῦν) πάλαι ἂν μετενόησαν *they would have repented long ago* **Mt 11:21; Lk 10:13; Hb 1:1.** ταῦτα πάλαι ἠκούσαμεν *these things we heard long ago* 2 Cl 11:2 (prophetic quot. of unknown origin). ἐκεῖνοι οἱ π. ἠρνημένοι *those who denied in time past* Hs 9, 26, 6. ἄνθρωποι οἱ π. προγεγραμμένοι **Jd 4** (mng. 2 is also poss.). αἱ π. ἁμαρτίαι *the former sins, sins committed in time past* **2 Pt 1:9** (cp. Appian, Bell. Civ. 4, 124 §521 ὁ πάλαι Καῖσαρ; BGU 747, 9 [II AD] οἱ πάλαι στρατιῶται). οἱ π. θεῖοι ἄγγελοι *angels who were originally holy* Papias (4).

❷ **pert. to a relatively long period of time, looking back fr. the present to a point of time in the past, *for a long time*** (Pla., Phd. 8, 63d; Esth 3:13g; Jos., Ant. 11, 32, Vi. 226; Just., D. 13, 1; 51, 3) πάλαι δοκεῖτε *you imagine all along* **2 Cor 12:19** (v.l. πάλιν). Perh. **Jd 4** (s. 1 above) and **Mk 6:47 v.l.** (s. 3 below).

❸ **pert. to a point of time within a relatively short time looking back from the present** (somewhat longer than the time span suggested by the use of ἤδη, q.v.), ***already*** (Appian, Syr. 66, 348) **Mk 6:47 v.l.** (looks back to the moment of departure.—Mng. 2 is also prob.). εἰ πάλαι ἀπέθανεν (looks back to the moment of crucifixion) *whether he was already dead* **Mk 15:44** (v.l. ἤδη).—DELG. M-M. TW.

παλαιός, ά, όν (πάλαι; Hom.+; loanw. in rabb.) oft. w. the connotation of being antiquated or outworn (so Soph., Oed. R. 290; Lysias, fgm. 6 Thalh.; Diod. S. 3, 46, 4). Comp. παλαιότερος (LXX, Just., Tat.). Superl. παλαίτατος (Tat.).

❶ **pert. to being in existence for a long time, *old*** PtK 2 p. 15, 7. μυθεύματα IMg 8:1. βασιλεία IEph 19:3. διαθήκη **2 Cor 3:14** (*=of long ago;* s. διαθήκη 2). ἐντολή (ἡ) π. **1J 2:7ab** (cp. Pla., Leg. 1, 636b π. νόμιμον; 2, 659b, Lys. 6, 51; PGiss 4, 9 [118 AD] παλαιὸν πρόσταγμα; Just., D. 11, 2 νόμος). οἶνος (opp. νέος) **Lk 5:39ab** (Od. 2, 340; Diod. S. 2, 14, 4; Lucian, De Merc. Cond. 26; PSI 191, 2; 193, 3; JosAs 15:14 [p. 62, 19 Bat. and Pal. 364]). ἱμάτιον (TestZeb 4:10) **Mt 9:16; Mk 2:21a; Lk 5:36a;** w. ἱμάτιον to be supplied, ibid. vs. **36b.** ἀσκοί (Josh 9:4) **Mt 9:17; Mk 2:22; Lk 5:37** (HImmerwahr, New Wine in Ancient Wineskins, The Evidence fr. Attic Vases: Hesperia 61, '92, 121–32). Of an old rock, which is interpreted to mean Christ in Hermas s 9, 2, 2; 9, 12, 1. Of the υἱὸς τοῦ θεοῦ himself 9, 12, 2. Of the Logos οὗτος ὁ ἀπ᾽ ἀρχῆς, ὁ καινὸς φανεὶς καὶ παλαιὸς εὑρεθεὶς καὶ πάντοτε νέος ἐν ἁγίων καρδίαις γεννώμενος Dg 11:4 (καινός and π. contrasted as Hdt. 9, 26. S. also Mel., P. 2, 8 al.).—Subst. (Hippocr., Ep. 12, 5; ApcEsdr 5:5) τὸ καινὸν τοῦ παλαιοῦ *the new from the old* **Mk 2:21b.** παλαιά (opp. καινά: Hdt. 9, 27 παλαιὰ κ. καινὰ λέγειν; Socrat., Ep. 28 [30], 9; Procop. Soph., Ep. 122 μίγνυσι παλαιὰ καινοῖς) **Mt 13:52.**

❷ **pert. to that which is obsolete or inferior because of being old, *old, obsolete*** fig. ὁ π. ἄνθρωπος *the old* (i.e. earlier, unregenerate) *person* or *self* (ἄνθρωπος 5b) **Ro 6:6; Eph 4:22; Col 3:9.** ἡ π. ζύμη *the old leaven* (s. ζύμη 2) **1 Cor 5:7f** (opp. νέον φύραμα). π. πράγματα *obsolete* (i.e. Judean) *ways of life* (παλ. πράγματα oft. in Vett. Val.; s. index) IMg 9:1 (opp. καινότης ἐλπίδος).—OLinton, 'Gammalt' och 'nytt': Svensk Ex. Årsbok 5, '40, 43–55.—B. 958. DELG s.v. πάλαι. M-M. EDNT. TW.

παλαιότης, ητος, ἡ (παλαιός; Eur., Aeschin., Pla. et al.) **state of being superseded or obsolete, *age, obsolescence*** δουλεύειν . . . παλαιότητι γράμματος *serve the obsolete letter* (of the law; opp. καινότης πνεύματος) **Ro 7:6.**—DELG s.v. πάλαι. M-M. TW.

παλαιόω (παλαιός) fut. 3 sg. παλαιώσει Da 7:25 Theod.; aor. 3 sg. ἐπαλαίωσεν; pf. πεπαλαίωκα. Pass.: 1 fut. παλαιωθήσομαι LXX; 1 aor. ἐπαλαιώθην; pf. πεπαλαίωμαι LXX (Pla. et al.; pap, LXX; En; Ath., R. 9 p. 7, 26; outside the Bible only in the pass.).

❶ act. (La 3:4; Is 65:22; Da 7:25 Theod.) ***make old, declare/treat as obsolete*** τὴν πρώτην (i.e. διαθήκην) *treat the first covenant as obsolete* **Hb 8:13a.**

❷ pass. ***become old*** (oft. w. the connotation of becoming useless: Pla., Symp. 208b; Diog. L. 7, 159; Sb 5827, 11 [69 BC]; APF 2, 1903, 441 no. 55, 4 τείχη παλαιωθέντα 'walls that have become ruinous'; LXX; En 104, 2; Philo, Sobr. 56; Ath., R. 9 p. 57, 26) βαλλάντια μὴ παλαιούμενα *purses that do not wear out* **Lk 12:33.** ὡς ἱμάτιον παλαιοῦσθαι (Dt 29:4; Josh 9:5; 2 Esdr 19:21; Sir 14:17; Is 51:6) **Hb 1:11** (Ps 101:27); B 6:2 (Is 50:9). ζύμη παλαιωθεῖσα *leaven that has become old* (cp. 1 Cor 5:7) IMg 10:2. παλαιοῦσθαι ταῖς λύπαις *be made old by sorrows* Hv 3, 11, 3. τὸ παλαιούμενον (w. γηράσκον) *what has become obsolete* **Hb 8:13b** (ins [218 BC]: ΕΛΛΗΝΙΚΑ 7, '34 p. 179, 14 παλαιούμενα=things that have become useless).—DELG s.v. πάλαι. M-M. TW.

παλαίω 1 aor. ἐπάλαισα (Hom. et al.; LXX; TestAbr A 10 p. 87, 24 [Stone p. 22]; Demetr.: 722 fgm. 1, 7 Jac.; Philo; Jos., B. 1, 657; Just., Tat.) ***wrestle*** μετά τινος *w. someone* (Gen 32:25f; Just., D. 125, 3) οἱ μετὰ τοῦ διαβόλου παλαίσαντες *those who wrestled with the devil* Hs 8, 3, 6.

πάλη, ης, ἡ (παλαίω 'wrestle'; Hom. et al.; ins; Sb 678, 6) **engagement in a challenging contest** (orig. 'wrestling' Il. 23, 635 al., then of fights or battles Aeschyl., Ch. 866; Eur., Heracl. 159) ***struggle against,*** fig. ext. (Longus 3, 19, 2 of love; Philo, Sobr. 65 πρὸς πάθη π., here w. wrestling imagery), of Christians' fight against powers of darkness **Eph 6:12** (the opponent is introduced by πρός w. the acc. as in Philo above, but the context suggests military imagery).—DELG s.v. παλαίω. M-M. TW.

παλιγγενεσία, ας, ἡ (Plut., Mor. 722d does not, as some have affirmed, assign the use of this word to Democritus [fgm. 158 Diels]; it is found in Neanthes [200 BC]: 84 fgm. 33 Jac.; Memnon [I BC/I AD]: 434 fgm. 1, 40, 2 Jac.; Cicero, Ad Attic. 6, 6, also a t.t. of the Pythagoreans and Stoics [EZeller, Philosophie der Griechen I^5 1892, 442; III 1^4 1902, 158; HDiels, Doxographi Graeci 1879, p. 469, 11ff] as well as of the Mysteries of Dionysus [Orph. Fragmente 205 p. 225 OKern 1922] and of Osiris [Plut., Mor. 389a; also 364f; 379f; 438d; 996c; 998c; cp. Lucian, Musc. Enc. 7]. It is found in the Herm. Wr. [3, 3; 13, 1 ὁ τῆς παλιγγενεσίας λόγος; 13, 3 al.—JKroll, Die Lehren des Hermes Trismegistos 1914, 360ff; Prümm 559–61]; IDefixWünsch 4, 18 ὁ θεὸς ὁ τῆς παλινγενεσίας Θωβαρραβαυ; PLond 878 δῶρον παλινγενεσίας; Philo, Cher. 114, Poster. Caini 124, Leg. ad Gai. 325; Jos., Ant. 11, 66)

❶ **state of being renewed, w. focus on a cosmic experience, *renewal*—ⓐ** after the Deluge (so Philo, Mos. 2, 65, but the idea of the παλιγγενεσία of the κόσμος is gener. Stoic and originated w. the Pythagoreans: M. Ant. 11, 1, 3; Philo, Aet. M. 47; 76) Νῶε παλ. κόσμῳ ἐκήρυξεν 1 Cl 9:4.

ⓑ of the renewing of the world in the time of the Messiah, an eschatol. sense (Schürer II 537f; Bousset, Rel.[3] 280ff) ἐν τῇ παλ. *in the new* (Messianic) *age* or *world* **Mt 19:28.**

❷ **experience of a complete change of life, *rebirth*** of a redeemed person (cp. Heraclit., Ep. 4, 4 ἐκ παλιγγενεσίας ἀναβιῶναι; Herm. Wr., loc. cit. and PGM 4, 718 where the initiate calls himself πάλιν γενόμενος. Theoph. Ant. 2, 16 [p. 140, 9] λαμβάνειν ... ἄφεσιν ἁμαρτιῶν διὰ ὕδατος καὶ λουτροῦ παλιγγενεσίας): λουτρὸν παλιγγενεσίας καὶ ἀνακαινώσεως πνεύματος ἁγίου *bath of regeneration and renewal by the Holy Spirit* **Tit 3:5** (MDibelius, Hdb., exc. ad loc.; ESelwyn, I Pt '46, 306f; ANock, JBL 52, '33, 132f).—PGennrich, Die Lehre v. d. Wiedergeburt in dogmengeschichtl. und religionsgeschichtl. Beleuchtung 1907; AvHarnack, Die Terminologie der Wiedergeburt: TU 42, 3, 1918, p. 97–143; ADieterich, Eine Mithrasliturgie 1903, 157ff; Rtzst., Mysterienrel.[3] indices; HWilloughby, Pagan Regeneration 1929; VJacono, La παλιγγενεσία in S. Paolo e nel ambiente pagano: Biblica 15, '34, 369–98; JDey, Παλιγγενεσία (on Tit 3:5) '37; JYsebaert, Gk. Baptismal Terminology, '62, 90; FBurnett, CBQ 46, '84, 447–70 (Philo, the rebirth of the soul into incorporeal existence).—Kl. Pauly IV 428f; BHHW III 2171f.—S. DELG s.v. πάλιν. M-M s.v. παλινγενεσία. EDNT. TW. Sv.

πάλιν adv. (Hom.+). On the spelling s. B-D-F §20, end; Mlt-H. 113).

❶ **pert. to return to a position or state, *back*—ⓐ** w. verbs of going, sending, turning, calling etc. πάλιν ἄγειν *go back, return* **J 11:7.** ἀναβαίνειν **Gal 2:1.** ἀναχωρεῖν **J 6:15.** ἀποστέλλειν *send back* **Mk 11:3.** διαπερᾶν **5:21.** ἔρχεσθαι (Jos., Ant. 2, 106; 11, 243) **Mt 26:43; Mk 11:27; J 4:46; 2 Cor 1:16.** ἀπέρχεσθαι **Mk 14:39; J 4:3.** εἰσέρχεσθαι **Mk 2:1** (ParJer 7:22). ἐξέρχεσθαι **7:31** (ParJer 9:12). ἐπιστρέφειν *turn back* **Gal 4:9a.** παραγίνεσθαι **J 8:2,** etc. πάλιν λαβεῖν *take back* (X., An. 4, 2, 13) **10:17f.** παραλαβὼν πάλιν τοὺς δώδεκα *he brought the twelve back* (after he had been separated fr. them for a time, and had preceded them) **Mk 10:32.** ἀνεσπάσθη πάλιν ἅπαντα εἰς τ. οὐρανόν *everything was drawn back into heaven* **Ac 11:10.**—ἡ ἐμὴ παρουσία πάλιν πρὸς ὑμᾶς *my return to you* **Phil 1:26.**—Also pleonastically w. verbs that express the component 'back' (Eur., Ep. 1, 1 ἀναπέμπω πάλιν) πάλιν ἀνακάμπτειν (Bacchylides 17, 81f πάλιν ἀνεκάμπτετ'; Synes., Kingship p. 29b) **Ac 18:21.** πάλιν ὑποστρέφειν **Gal 1:17** (s. B-D-F §484; cp. Rob. 1205).

ⓑ in expressions that denote a falling back into a previous state or a return to a previous activity (TestAbr A 6 p. 89, 13 [Stone p. 14] ἠγέρθη πάλιν ὁ μόσχος; ApcMos 41 πάλιν τὴν ἀνάστασιν ἐπαγγέλομαί σοι; Just., A I, 18, 6; Tat. 11, 2). In Engl. mostly *again.* εἰ ἃ κατέλυσα ταῦτα πάλιν οἰκοδομῶ **Gal 2:18.** ἵνα πάλιν ἐπὶ τὸ αὐτὸ ἦτε **1 Cor 7:5.** διψήσει πάλιν **J 4:13.** πάλιν εἰς φόβον **Ro 8:15.** Cp. **11:23; Gal 5:1; Phil 2:28; Hb 5:12; 6:6; 2 Pt 2:20.**

❷ **pert. to repetition in the same (or similar) manner, *again, once more, anew*** of someth. a pers. has already done (TestAbr A 15 p. 96, 7 [Stone p. 40, 7]; TestJob 15:9; 44:2; JosAs 10:19; ParJer 9:21; Jos., Ant. 12, 109; Just., D. 3, 5 al.), of an event, or of a state or circumstance (Dicaearch., fgm. 34 W. Pythagoras flees first to Καυλωνία ... ἐκεῖθεν δὲ πάλιν εἰς Λοκρούς; ApcEsdr 4:13 κατήγαγόν με ... καὶ πάλιν κατήγαγόν με βαθμοὺς τριάκοντα). πάλιν παραλαμβάνει αὐτὸν ὁ διάβολος εἰς ὄρος **Mt 4:8** (cp. vs. 5). πάλιν ἐξελθὼν **20:5** (cp. vs. 3). πότε πάλιν ὄψονται αὐτόν *when they would see (Paul) again* AcPl Ha 6, 17. ἵνα παρά σου πάλιν ἀκούσωμεν AcPlCor 1:6.—**Mt 21:36** (cp. vs. 34); **26:44** (cp. vs. 42), **72; 27:50; Mk 2:13; 3:1; 4:1.** πάλιν πολλοῦ ὄχλου ὄντος **8:1** (cp. 6:34).—**8:25; 10:1, 24; Lk 23:20** (cp. vs. 13); **J 1:35** (cp. vs. 29); **8:8; 20:26; Ac 17:32; Gal 1:9; Phil 4:4; Js 5:18;** Hv 3, 1, 5 al.; GJs 17:2; 23:2; AcPl Ha 4, 1.—Somet. w. additions which, in part, define πάλιν more exactly: πάλ. δεύτερον (cp. P. Argentor. Gr. 53, 5: Kl. T. 135 p. 47 τὸ δεύτερον πάλιν) **J 21:16.** πάλ. ἐκ δευτέρου (Ctesias: 688 fgm. 14, 31 Jac.; 4 [6] Esdr [POxy 1010]; PCairMasp 24, 12) **Mt 26:42; Ac 10:15.** Also pleonastically πάλ. ἄνωθεν **Gal 4:9b** (s. ἄνωθεν 4). αὖ πάλιν Papias (2:9) (cp. Just., A I, 20, 2). πάλιν ἐξ ἀρχῆς (Mnesimachus Com. [IV BC] 4, 24; Diod. S. 17, 37, 5) B 16:8.—εἰς τὸ πάλιν= πάλιν **2 Cor 13:2** (on this s. WSchmid, Der Attizismus 1887–97, I 167; II 129; III 282; IV 455; 625).

❸ **marker of a discourse or narrative item added to items of a related nature, *also, again, furthermore, thereupon*** (Ps.-Pla., Eryx. 11, 397a καὶ π. with a series of examples): very oft. in a series of quotations fr. scripture (cp. Diod. S. 37, 30, 2 καὶ πάλιν ... καὶ ... followed both times by a poetic quotation; a third one had preceded these. All three deal with riches as the highest good and probably come from a collection of quotations; Ps.-Demetr. c. 184 καὶ πάλιν ... καὶ π. with one quotation each. Cp. also Diod. S. 1, 96, 6; Diog. L. 2, 18; 3, 16; Athen. 4, 17, 140c; 14, 634d; Plut., Mor. 361a καὶ πάλιν ... καὶ ... ; a quotation follows both times; Just., A I, 35, 5; 38, 2 al.; Ath. 9, 1 al.) **J 12:39; 19:37; Ro 15:10–12; 1 Cor 3:20; Hb 1:5; 2:13ab; 4:5; 10:30;** 1 Cl 10:4; 15:3f; 16:15; 17:6; 26:3; B 2:7; 3:1; 6:2, 4, 6, 14, 16 and oft. In a series of parables (Simplicius, In Epict. p. 111, 13–34 connects by means of π. two stories that are along the same lines as the Good Samaritan and the Pharisee and the publican; Kephal. I 76, 34; 77, 8 [a series of proverbs]) **Lk 13:20** (cp. vs. 18). Also a favorite expr. when a speaker takes up a formula previously used and continues: πάλιν ἠκούσατε **Mt 5:33** (cp. vs. 27). πάλιν ὁμοία ἐστὶν ἡ βασιλεία **13:45** (cp. vs. 44), **47.—18:19** (cp. vs. 18); **19:24** (cp. vs. 23).

❹ **marker of contrast or an alternative aspect, *on the other hand, in turn*** (Pla., Gorg. 482d; Theocr. 12, 14; Polyb. 10, 9, 1; Diod. S. 4, 46, 3; Chariton 7, 6, 9; Wsd 13:8; 16:23; 2 Macc 15:39; TestJob 26:4; GrBar 4:15; Just., D. 41, 4 al.) πάλιν γέγραπται *on the other hand, it is written* **Mt 4:7.** πάλ. Ἀνδρέας *Andrew in turn* **J 12:22 v.l.—1 Cor 12:21.** τοῦτο λογιζέσθω πάλ. ἐφ' ἑαυτοῦ *let him remind himself, on the other hand* **2 Cor 10:7;** *on the other hand* **Lk 6:43; 1J 2:8.**

❺ A special difficulty is presented by **Mk 15:13,** where the first outcry of the crowd is reported w. the words οἱ δὲ πάλιν ἔκραξεν. Is it simply a connective (so δὲ πάλιν Ps.-Callisth. 2, 21, 22; POxy 1676, 20 ἀλλὰ καὶ λυποῦμαι πάλιν ὅτι ἐκτός μου εἶ)? Is it because a different source is here used? Or is the meaning *they shouted back?* (so Goodsp.); s. 1a. Or is this really a second outcry, and is the first one hidden behind vs. 8 or 11? Acc. to the parallel Mt 27:21f, which actually mentions several outcries, one after the other, the first one may have been: τὸν Βαραββᾶν. The πάλιν of **J 18:40** is also hard to explain (Bultmann 502; 509, 3). Could there be a connection here betw. Mk and J?—Another possibility would be to classify **Mk 15:13** and **J 18:40** under 4 above, with the meaning *in turn* (Aristoph., Acharn. 342 et al.; s. L-S-J-M). On a poss. Aram. background s. JHudson, ET 53, '41/42, 267f; Mlt-H. 446; Mlt-Turner 229; MBlack, An Aramaic Approach^3, '67, 112f.—B. 989. DELG. M-M.

παλινγενεσία s. παλιγγενεσία.

παλίουρος, οῦ, ὁ and **ἡ** (Eur., Cyclops 394; Theopomp.: 115 fgm. 133 Jac. [=Hell. Oxy. 129 G-H.]; Theophrast., HP 1, 3, 2; 4, 3, 3 al.; BGU 1120, 16 [I BC]) ***bramble, thicket*** AcPl Ha 4, 25 (restoration in a fragmentary context).—DELG.

παμβότανον, ου, τό (πᾶς, βοτάνη) **herbage that covers an entire area, *all(-covering) herbage*** π. τοῦ ἀγροῦ *herbage that covers all the field* 1 Cl 56:14 (Job 5:25). The imagery is that of a field covered in every direction with herbage too thick to count piece by piece. So great in number will be Job's offspring. Others interpret *all the plants of the field.*—DELG s.v. βόσκω.

παμμεγέθης, ες (πᾶς, μέγεθος 'greatness'; Pla., X. et al.; Polyb. 5, 59, 4; Lucian, Charon 20; Herm. Wr. 2, 4a; OGI 619, 6; Ps 67:31 Sym.; TestAbr B 7 p. 111, 10 [Stone p. 70]; 10 p. 114, 22 [Stone p. 76]; GrBar; Philo De Op. Mundi 134 al.; Jos., Ant. 15, 364) ***immense*** ἄστερα παμμεγέθη *a prodigious star* GJs 21:2 (not pap.). Superl. παμμεγεθέστατος (Suda on Γολιάθης) *infinitely great, surpassing* τὸ παμμεγεθέστατον κράτος (of God.—π. is a divine attribute also in Aberciusins. 14: ἰχθὺς π.) 1 Cl 33:3. Subst. τὸ παμμέγεθες *by far the greatest* 33:4 (on κατὰ διάνοιαν here s. διάνοια 3).—DELG s.v. μέγας.

παμπληθεί adv. of παμπληθής (Cass. Dio 75, 9, 1; Just., D. 107, 2) **pert. to a multitude in unison, *all together*** ἀνέκραγον παμπληθεί **Lk 23:18.**—DELG s.v. πίμπλημι. M-M. s.v. πανπληθεί.

παμπληθής, ές (πᾶς, πλῆθος; X.; Diod. S. 4, 33, 5 and 6; 14, 13, 4; Plut., Sull. 35, 1; 2 Macc 10:24; EpArist 90; Philo; Jos., Bell. 3, 69, Ant. 14, 461) **pert. to being abnormally excessive in condition or amount, *in full abundance, a vast amount of*** τὴν π. τροφήν 1 Cl 20:4. χάλαζα παμπληθής *severe hailstorm* AcPl Ha 5, 7.—DELG s.v. πίμπλημι.

πάμπολυς, παμπόλλη, πάμπολυ (πᾶς, πολύς; Aristoph., Pla. et al.; Plut.; ins; BGU 731 II, 8 [II AD]; 836, 3; POxy 718, 11; Sym.; Philo, Aet. M. 119; Jos., Bell. 4, 529, Ant. 7, 106, C. Ap. 1, 107; Ath. 15, 1) **pert. to being very high on a scale of extent, *very great*** (used w. πλῆθος: Pla., Leg. 3, 677e; Paradoxogr. Flor. 39; SIG 1169, 45f) παμπόλλου ὄχλου ὄντος **Mk 8:1 v.l.** (for πάλιν πολλοῦ ὄχλου ὄντος).—M-M.

Παμφυλία, ας, ἡ (Strabo 14, 3, 1; Appian, Mithrid. 56 §226; Cass. Dio 69, 14; Philo, Leg. ad Gai. 281; Joseph. [Niese index]; ins; 1 Macc 15:23.—On the use of the art. s. B-D-F §261, 6) ***Pamphylia,*** a province in the southern part of Asia Minor, along the Mediterranean seacoast. On the Jewish population s. Schürer III 4, 5, 33. Visited by Paul several times. **Ac 2:10; 13:13; 14:24; 15:38; 16:6 v.l.** (for Φρυγίαν); **27:5** (cp. Jos., Ant. 2, 348 Παμφύλιον πέλαγος).—KGrafLanckoroński, Städte Pamphyliens u. Pisidiens 1890/92; IAsMinLyk I. Pauly-W. 354–407; Kl. Pauly IV 441–44; BHHW III 1381. DELG s.v. φῦλον.

πανάγιος, ον (πᾶς, ἅγιος; Iambl., in Nicomach. p. 126, 23 Pistelli; 4 Macc 7:4; 14:7; TestSol 1:3 C) **pert. to being at the acme of holiness on a scale of extent, *all-holy*** ὁ π. of God 1 Cl 35:3. τὸ π. ὄνομα 58:1.

πανάρετος, ον (πᾶς, ἀρετή; Philod., Rhet. 2, 203 Sudh.; Lucian, Philops. 6; TestAbr A 5 p. 82, 4 [Stone p. 12]; Philo, Migr. Abr. 95; OGI 583, 8; Sb 330; 331) **pert. to being at the acme of excellence on a scale of extent, *most excellent*** (i.e. *pervaded with all that is most excellent*) ὄνομα (of God) 1 Cl 45:7; 60:4 v.l. (for ἔνδοξος). πίστις 1:2 (w. βέβαιος). πολιτεία 2:8 (w. σεβάσμιος). Of the wisdom of God, speaking in the book of Proverbs: 1 Cl 57:3.

πανδοκεῖον s. πανδοχεῖον.

πανδοκεύς s. πανδοχεύς.

πανδοχεῖον, ου, τό (πανδοχεύς 'innkeeper'; Strabo 5, 3, 9; 12, 8, 17; Epict., Ench. 11; Philostrat., Vi. Apoll. 4, 39 p. 157, 28; TestJud 12:1; PSI 99, 3; PEg^2, 35=ASyn. 42, 31.—The older form πανδοκεῖον in Aristoph., Ran. 550, but also in Theophr., Char. 11, 2; Polyb. 2, 15, 5; Epict. 2, 23, 36; 4, 5, 15; Appian, Mithrid. 20, §76; Plut., Crass. 556 [22, 4]; Palaeph. 45; Aelian, VH 14, 14; Polyaenus 4, 2, 3; ins [Nachmanson 81]; Phrynichus rejects the form with χ, p. 307 Lob.; cp. B-D-F §33; W-S. §5, 27e; Mlt-H. 108. Though lacking in Philo [except in a fgm., s. JRoyse, NovT 23, '81, 13f] and Joseph., the word was taken over by Jews as a loanw. [Billerb. II 183; Dalman, Gramm.^{2} 187] and has survived to the pres. day in Arabic) ***inn,*** where a traveler may find a night's lodging **Lk 10:34.**—Pauly-W. 36, 3, '49, 520–29. M-M.

πανδοχεύς, έως, ὁ (πᾶς, δέχομαι; Polyb. 2, 15, 6 and Plut., Mor. 130e in mss.; Iambl., Vi. Pyth. 33, 238 [LDeubner, SBBerlAk '39 XIX p. 15]. The Att. πανδοκεύς in Pla., Leg. 11, 918b et al.; Epict. 1, 24, 14; Polyb. [Büttner-W.] and Plut. [Paton-Wegehaupt 1925], loc. cit. in the text. Taken over by Jews [Billerb. II 183f], but not found in Philo and Joseph.—B-D-F §33; W-S. §5, 27e; Mlt-H. 108) ***inn-keeper*** **Lk 10:35.**—Kl. Pauly V 1384–86; BHHW II 693f. M-M.

πανήγυρις, εως, ἡ (πᾶς, ἄγυρις [=ἀγορα] 'gathering'; Pind., Hdt.+; ins, pap, LXX; Philo, In Flacc. 118 al.; Jos., Bell.

5, 230, Ant. 2, 45; Tat., Ath.) **an assemblage of many pers. for a special occasion,** ***festal gathering*** (w. ἐκκλησία) **Hb 12:22.**—M-M. TW. Spicq.

πανθαμάρτητος, ον (πᾶς [*παντ], ἁμάρτημα) ***altogether sinful,*** subst. pl. *people steeped in sin* B 20:2; D 5:2.

πανθαμαρτωλός, όν (πᾶς [*παντ], ἁμαρτωλός) ***utterly sinful*** 2 Cl 18:2.

πανοικεί/πανοικί (πᾶς, οἶκος; it is difficult to decide which sp. to choose; s. Kühner-Bl. II 303; B-D-F §23, 122; Schwyzer I 623; Mlt-H. 279) adv. (Ps.-Pla., Eryx. 392c; PRyl 434, 12; PIand 8, 15; PFay 129, 9; 130, 20; addtl. exx. New Docs 2, 93; Ex 1:1 v.l.; Philo, De Jos. 251, Mos. 1, 5; Jos., Ant. 4, 300; 5, 11) *with one's whole household* **Ac 16:34;** MPol 20:2.—M-M.

πανοπλία, ας, ἡ (πᾶς, ὅπλον; Hdt., Aristoph. et al.; Polyb. 3, 62, 5; 4, 56, 3; Diod. S. 20, 84, 3; ins, LXX)

❶ the complete equipment of a heavy-armed soldier, ***full armor*** (2 Km 2:21; 2 Macc 3:25; Jos., Bell. 2, 649, Ant. 7, 104; 20, 110) **Lk 11:22** (on vss. 21f cp. 4 Macc 3:12 A τὰς πανοπλίας καθωπλίσαντο [s. SLegasse, NovT 5, '62, 5–9]).

❷ IPol 6:2 marks a transition in the direction of a nonliteral mng.; here endurance is compared with πανοπλία in a context that uses many concepts fr. the life of a soldier, and specif. mentions separate parts of his equipment. Purely metaphoric is πανοπλία τοῦ θεοῦ *full armor of God* **Eph 6:11, 13** (fig. use of π. also Wsd 5:17; Sir 46:6; Philo, Somn. 1, 103; 108; other reff. Straub 91f). On ἀναλαβεῖν τὴν πανοπλίαν vs. **13** s. ἀναλαμβάνω 2.—On a Christian's 'military service' and 'warfare' s. AHarnack, Militia Christi 1905; MMeinertz, D. Ap. Pls und d. Kampf: Internat. Monatsschr. 11, 1917, 1115–50; MDibelius, Hdb. exc. on Eph 6:10 and 1 Ti 1:18; AVitti, Militum Christi Regis arma iuxta S. Paulum: Verbum Domini 7, 1927, 310–18; Cumont[3] '31, xiif; 207f; HEmonds: Hlg. Überliefg. (ed. by OCasel) '38, 21–50 (anc. philos.); EFavier, L'armure du soldat de dieu d'après s. Paul '38; CBond, Winning w. God (on Eph 6:10–18) '40.—B. 1398. M-M. TW.

πανουργία, ας, ἡ (πανοῦργος; Aeschyl., X., Pla. et al.; Polyb. 29, 8, 8; Plut., Mor. 91b [w. ἀπάτη]; Herodian 2, 9, 11 [w. δόλος]; OGI 515, 47 [w. κακουργία]; POxy 237 VIII, 12 [II AD]; LXX; Philo, De Op. Mund. 155 al.; Jos., Bell. 4, 503 al.; Test 12Patr) quite predom., and in our lit. exclusively, in an unfavorable sense (rascally, evil) ***cunning, craftiness, trickery,*** lit. 'readiness to do anything' **Lk 20:23; 1 Cor 3:19** (in Job 5:12, 13, which is basic to this pass., vs. 12 has the adj. πανοῦργος); **2 Cor 4:2; 11:3** (in Gen 3:1 Aq. and Sym. have the adj. πανοῦργος); **Eph 4:14.**—M-M. TW.

πανοῦργος, ον (on the form s. Schwyzer I 437; trag., Pla. et al.; first in a bad sense, and that predominately so [sim. TestJob 17:2; Philo; Jos., Bell. 1, 223; Just., D. 123, 4]; later [Aristot. et al. occasionally, also LXX] in a good sense as well) in our lit. never without an unfavorable connotation ***clever, crafty, sly*** lit. 'ready to do anything'. Paul says, taking up an expr. used by his opponents, ὑπάρχων πανοῦργος *crafty fellow that I am* **2 Cor 12:16.** Hermas is called πανοῦργος (w. αὐθάδης), because he is *crafty* enough to want to pry into secret things Hv 3, 3, 1; s 5, 5, 1. μήπως τοῦτο πανοῦργος ἔδωκέν σοι (I fear) *lest some scoundrel has given you this* GJs 2:3.—M-M. TW.

πανούργως adv. of πανοῦργος (Aristoph., Equ. 317; Pla., Soph. 239c et al.; Sb 8026, 14; Ps 82:4 Sym.; Philo, Poster. Cai. 82) ***deceitfully*** πάντοτε πανούργως ἔζησα μετὰ πάντων Hm 3:3 (on the wordplay s. B-D-F §488, 1; Rob. 1201).—TW.

πανπληθεί (so Tdf., W-H.) s. παμπληθεί.—M-M.

πανπληθής s. παμπληθής.

πάνσεμνος, ον (πᾶς, σεμνός; Lucian, Vit. Auct. 26, Anach. 9) ***greatly revered*** πνεῦμα Hv 1, 2, 4 (the text is not certain; s. MDibelius ad loc.).—S. DELG s.v. πᾶς.

πανταχῆ (on the form s. Schwyzer I 622; for spelling B-D-F §26; W-S. §5, 11c; Mlt.-H. 84; Meisterhans[3]-Schw. p. 145) adv. (Hdt. et al.; Pla., Ep. 7, 335c πάντως π.; ins, pap, LXX; Jos., Bell. 1, 149) ***everywhere*** πάντας π. διδάσκων *who is teaching everyone everywhere* **Ac 21:28.** μετὰ πάντων π. τῶν κεκλημένων *with all those everywhere who are called* 1 Cl 65:2.—DELG s.v. πᾶς. M-M.

πανταχόθεν adv. (Hdt., Thu., Pla. et al.; Diod. S. 17, 82, 3; Strabo 8, 6, 15; Jos., Ant. 4, 133; 12, 353; ins, pap; 4 Macc 13:1; 15:32) ***from every direction*** **Mk 1:45 v.l.** (for πάντοθεν).—DELG s.v. πᾶς. M-M.

πανταχοῦ (on the form Schwyzer I 621) adv. (Soph., Thu. et al.; pap; Is 42:22; JosAs 3:10; Jos., Bell. 1, 165, Ant. 14, 137; Just.; Ath. 35, 2) **pert. to positions in any direction,** ***everywhere*** (so almost always) **Mk 16:20; Lk 9:6; Ac 28:22;** 1 Cl 41:2. πάντῃ τε καὶ π. *in every way and everywhere* (B-D-F §103; cp. Rob. 300) **Ac 24:3.** Used in paronomasia w. πᾶς (B-D-F §488, 1a; Dio Chrys. 11 [12], 19; Philo, Aet. M. 68; Jos., Bell. 5, 310, Ant. 17, 143) ἀπαγγέλλει . . . πάντας π. μετανοεῖν **17:30.** π. ἐν πάσῃ ἐκκλησίᾳ **1 Cor 4:17.** Perh. w. the specific nuance *in all directions* **Mk 1:28** (so Bauer, with ref. to Aristoph., Lys. 1230; Lucian, Bis Accus. 27).—DELG s.v. πᾶς. M-M.

παντελής, ές (πᾶς, τέλος; trag., Hdt.+; ins, pap; 3 Macc 7:16; GrBar 4:10; Tat. 6, 1; Ath., R. 19 p. 72, 13 al.) in our lit. in the form εἰς τὸ π. for the adv. παντελῶς (Philo, Joseph., Tat., Aelian)

❶ pert. to meeting a very high standard of quality or completeness, ***completely.***—ⓐ with respect to an action *(quite) complete, perfect, absolute,* the same thing as παντελῶς, i.e. *completely, fully, wholly.* The Armen. version understands σῴζειν εἰς τὸ π. δύναται **Hb 7:25** in this sense; so also many later interpreters. μὴ δυναμένη ἀνακῦψαι εἰς τὸ π. **Lk 13:11** is also understood in this sense by many: *she could not stand completely straight* (εἰς τὸ π. in this mng. Aelian, NA 17, 27; Cyranides 57, 4; Philo, Leg. ad Gai. 144; Jos., Ant. 1, 267; 3, 264; 274; 6, 30; 7, 325).

ⓑ with respect to ability *completely, at all* so **Lk 13:11,** if εἰς τὸ π. is taken w. μὴ δυναμένη instead of w. ἀνακῦψαι *she was completely unable to straighten herself up = she could not straighten herself up at all* (Goodsp.; so the Vulg., but the ancient Syriac gospel transl. [both Sinaitic and Curetonian] permits both this sense and a above.—Ael. Aristid. 26, 72 K.=14 p. 351 D.: παράδειγμα εἰς τὸ π. οὐκ ἔχει).

❷ pert. to unlimited duration of time, ***forever, for all time*** (Aelian, VH 7, 2; 12, 20 [parall. to διὰ τέλους]; OGI 642, 2 εἰς τὸ παντελὲς αἰώνιον τειμήν; RB 39, '30, 544 lines 18f; 546 ln. 6; PLond III, 1164*f*, 11 p. 161 [212 AD]. Perh. Jos., Ant. 3, 274) **Hb 7:25** is understood in this sense by the Vulg., Syr. and Copt. versions, and many moderns, including Rohr, Windisch, Montefiore, NRSV.—DELG s.v. τέλος. M-M. TW.

παντελῶς adv. (s. παντελής; trag., Hdt.+; Polyb., Epict., ins, pap; 2 Macc; TestSol 5:7 P; ApcSed 14:9 p. 136, 15 Ja.; EpArist, Philo; Jos., Ant. 4, 121; Just., A II, 10, 8; Ath., R. 20 p. 73, 11 al.) **to the fullest degree,** ***fully, completely, altogether*** in answers (cp. Pla., Rep. 2, 379b; 3, 401a; 6, 485d al.) οὐ παντελῶς *not at all; by no means* (Lucian, Catapl. 4) Hs 7:4.

παντεπόπτης, ου, ὁ (πᾶς [*παντ], ἐπόπτης 'watcher') ***one who sees all, one who is all-seeing*** (Sb 4127, 18 Ἥλιον τὸν παντεπόπτην δεσπότην; Vett. Val. 1, 4; 331, 20 [Ἥλιος]; magical pap [TSchermann, Griech. Zauberpap. 1909, 28f]; 2 Macc 9:5; Ps.-Clem., Hom. 4, 14; 23; 5, 27; 8, 19; SibOr, fgm. 1, 4 v.l.—The Greeks call Zeus ὁ πανόπτης [e.g. Aeschyl., Eum. 1045] or παντόπτης [e.g. Aeschyl., Suppl. 139; Soph., Oed. C. 1085]) of God ὁ π. δεσπότης 1 Cl 55:6. ὁ π. θεός 64; Pol 7:2.—S. DELG s.v. ὄπωπα.

πάντῃ (πᾶς; on its spelling s. Mlt.-H. p. 84; B-D-F §26; W-S. §5, 11c) adv. (Hom.+; esp. Περὶ ὕψους 1, 4 al.; ins, pap; Sir 50:22; 3 Macc 4:1; Jos., Ant. 14, 183; Just., A II, 13, 2; 15, 4; Ath., R. 1 p. 48, 15 al.) **pert. to all possible considerations or positions,** ***in every way*** π. τε καὶ πανταχοῦ *in every way and everywhere* (B-D-F §103; Rob. 300) **Ac 24:3.**—DELG s.v. πᾶς. M-M.

πάντοθεν adv. (πᾶς; Hom.+; ins, pap, LXX, En; JosAs 3:10; EpArist; Jos., Ant. 14, 442) **pert. to extension fr. a source on all sides,** ***from all directions*** **Mk 1:45; Lk 19:43;** ***on all sides, entirely*** **Hb 9:4;** cp. PAmh 51, 27 [88 BC]; 3 Macc 3:25; EpArist 69; 115; 142; esp. 57; Jos., Bell. 4, 587).—DELG s.v. πᾶς. M-M.

παντοκρατορικός, όν (formed fr. παντοκράτωρ as a result of the idea that this noun, since it denotes an agent [s. EFraenkel, Geschichte der griech. Nomina agentis auf -τήρ, -τωρ, -της, 1910/12], cannot be used w. a neuter [s. παντοκράτωρ]) ***almighty,*** in reference to God τὸ π. βούλημα αὐτοῦ 1 Cl 8:5. τῷ παντοκρατορικῷ (conjecture for the παντοκράτορι of the ms.) καὶ παναρέτῳ ὀνόματί σου 60:4 (as read in G-H-Z).

παντοκράτωρ, ορος, ὁ (πᾶς, κρατέω; Kaibel 815 s. below; Porphyr., Philos. Ex. Orac. ed. GWolff 1856, p. 145 ln. 157=Theosophien 27 p. 174, 4; SEG VIII, 548, 2 [I BC], the fem.; CIG 2569, 12; Sb 4127, 19 of the Egypt. sun-god Mandulis; of Hermes PGM 7, 668; likew. Kaibel 815, 11 [II AD] π. Ἐριούνιε [Hermes]; PMich 155, 3 [II AD]; PLips 40 II, 13; PGM 4, 272; 969 [s. New Docs 3, 118]; HGraillot, Les Dieux tout-puissants, Cybèle et Attis: RevArch 58, 1904 I 331ff; Cumont[3] 230f.—Much more freq. in Jewish [LXX.—S. ZTalshir, JQR 78, '87, 57–75; TestSol, TestAbr, ParJer; GrBar 1:3; EpArist, Philo; SibOr 1, 66 and fgm. 1, 8.—Not in Joseph.] and Christian wr.: Iren. 1, 9, 2 [Harv. I 82, 4]; Theoph. Ant. 2, 3 [p. 100, 1]. π. of the Demiurge in gnostic speculation Iren. 1, 11, 1 [Harv. I 101, 2]) the ***Almighty, All-Powerful, Omnipotent (One)*** only of God (as transl. of צְבָאוֹת [Orig., C. Cels. 5, 45, 46] and שַׁדַּי) π. θεός (3 Macc 6:2; Just., D. 38, 2 al.; Mel., P. 45, 322) 1 Cl ins; ὁ π. θεός (2 Macc 8:18) 2:3; 32:4; 62:2; AcPl Ha 6, 14; ὁ θεὸς ὁ π. **Rv 16:14; 19:15;** AcPlCor 2:12. ὁ θεὸς ὁ τῶν ὅλων ὁ π. 2:9. θεὸς π. (Jer 3:19) Pol ins; AcPlCor 1:11. ὁ π. καὶ παντοκτίστης καὶ ἀόρατος θεός Dg 7:2; κύριος π. (oft. LXX) **2 Cor 6:18.** (ὁ) κύριος ὁ θεὸς ὁ π. (=יְיָ אֱלֹהֵי הַצְּבָאוֹת.—Hos 12:6; Am 3:13; 4:13; 5:14) **Rv 1:8; 4:8; 11:17; 15:3; 16:7; 21:22;** MPol 14:1; κύριος ὁ θεὸς ἡμῶν ὁ π. **Rv 19:6;** ὁ θεὸς καὶ πατὴρ π. MPol 19:2 (cp. Just., D. 139, 4). God is addressed in eucharistic prayer as δέσποτα π. D 10:3 (cp. 3 Macc 2:2 μόναρχε παντοκράτωρ).—νουθέτημα παντοκράτορος 1 Cl 56:6 (Job 5:17).—We find the gen. and dat. (sing.), which is the same in all genders, used w. the neut. ὄνομα. This becomes possible (s. παντοκρατορικός) because of the fact that God's name is almost equivalent to God's being (s. ὄνομα 1d). τῷ ῥήματι τοῦ παντοκράτορος καὶ ἐνδόξου ὀνόματος Hv 3, 3, 5. The ms. rdg. τῷ παντοκράτορι καὶ παναρέτῳ ὀνόματί σου 1 Cl 60:4 (s. παντοκρατορικός) is more difficult, since here the name and God are separated by σου.—FKattenbusch, Das apostolische Symbol II 1900, 520ff; Dodd 19; HHommel, TLZ 79, '54, 283f. Pantokrator: Theologia Viatorum 5, '53/54; OMontevecchi, Studi in Onore di ACalderini e RParibeni II, '56, 401–32.—DELG s.v. πᾶς. M-M. DDD 'Almighty' 36–41. EDNT. TW. Sv.

παντοκτίστης, ου, ὁ (πᾶς [*παντ], κτίστης) ***creator of the universe*** w. παντοκράτωρ Dg 7:2.

πάντοτε adv. (on the formation Schwyzer I 629) of time (Hellenist. and Mod. Gk.; Dionys. Hal.+; Peripl. Eryth. 29; Epict., Ench. 14, 1; Dio Chrys. 15 [32], 37; Herodian 3, 9, 8; Artem. 4, 20; Plut.; Athen.; Diog. L.; OGI 458, 76 [I BC], SIG 814, 37 [67 AD]; BGU 1123, 8 [I BC]; PGiss 17, 4; 72, 11 [II AD]; Wsd 11:21; 19:18; TestSol, Test12Patr; JosAs 7:6; SyrBar 12:2; Jos., Bell. 3, 42; Just., D. 49, 7; 93, 4; Ath., R. 1 p. 49, 1 al.—The Atticists preferred ἑκάστοτε, διαπαντός, or ἀεί [Phryn. 103 Lob.]) ***always, at all times*** **Mt 26:11ab; Mk 14:7ab; Lk 15:31; 18:1; J 6:34; 7:6** (seven times in J); **Ro 1:10; 1 Cor 1:4; 15:58; 2 Cor 2:14** (27 times in Paul); **Hb 7:25** (not found in Ac and Cath. Epistles; B-D-F §105; cp. Rob. 300); Dg 11:4; IEph 4:2; Hv 1, 1, 7 (24 times in Hermas).—B. 984. DELG s.v. πᾶς. DDD 35–41. M-M.

πάντως adv. (πᾶς; Hom.+; esp. Περὶ ὕψους 1, 2; ins, pap, LXX; TestAbr B 13 p. 117, 25 [Stone p. 82]; TestJos 10:4; Philo, Joseph.; Ar. 13, 7; Just.; Tat. 16, 2; Ath., R. 5 p. 53, 15 al.; loanw. in rabb.).

❶ **pert. to strong assumption,** ***by all means, certainly, probably, doubtless*** w. ὡς appearing to retain its force (Pla., Gorg. 527a; Herodas 7, 89; Diod. S. 20, 29, 3; Ps.-Demetr. 84; Ps.-Callisth. 2, 32, 3; SIG 762, 30; BGU 248, 12; PFlor 262, 11; POxy 1676, 15; Tob. 14:8 BA; 2 Macc 3:13; Jos., Vi. 48, C. Ap. 2, 140; Ar. 13, 7; Just.; Tat. 16, 2) πάντως φονεύς ἐστιν ὁ ἄνθρωπος οὗτος **Ac 28:4.** πάντως ἐρεῖτέ μοι **Lk 4:23.** Cp. **Ac 18:21 v.l.; 21:22** (on all these except **Ac 18:21 v.l.** see 3 below). ἢ δι' ἡμᾶς πάντως λέγει; *or is he* (not) *certainly speaking in our interest?* **1 Cor 9:10.** πάντως διὰ πειρασμόν τινα . . . βραδύτερον λαμβάνεις *surely it is on account of some temptation . . . that you receive (an answer) slowly* Hm 9:7. πάντως θέλει ὁ δεσπότης *by all means the Master wishes* s 9, 9, 4. Prob. 5, 7, 4; 7:4b belong here (but s. 3 below). In 7:5 καὶ τοῦτο πάντως prob.=*and especially so.*

❷ **pert. to thoroughness in extent,** ***totally, altogether*** Hs 1:5; B 1:4. πάντως . . . εἰδὼς αὐτήν *inasmuch as (Jesus) knew her through and through* GMary 463, 23f.

❸ **expression of inevitable conclusion in view of data provided,** ***of course.*** This sense has been suggested for Hv 1, 2, 4; s 5, 7, 4; 7:4b (but *perhaps* [Lat. fortasse in both Hs passages] acc. to HCadbury, JBL 44, 1925, 223ff, who suggests the same transl. for **Lk 4:23; Ac 21:22; 28:4;** s. 1 above), but mng. 1 appears to do justice to the context.

❹ **expression of lowest possible estimate on a scale of extent,** ***at least*** ἵνα πάντως τινὰς σώσω *in order to save at least some* **1 Cor 9:22** (though *by [any and] all means* is also prob. here).

❺ with a negating marker—ⓐ *not at all* (Theognis 305 D-B. τοὶ κακοὶ οὐ πάντως κακοὶ ἐκ γαστρὸς γεγόνασιν; Just., D. 57, 2) πάντως οὐκ ἦν θέλημα *he was quite unwilling* **1 Cor 16:12.** Cp. Dg 9:1. Also in answer to a question *not at all* (so PVat. A, 15=Witkowski[2] p. 65) **Ro 3:9** (the text is not certain; s. B-D-F §433, 2; Rob. 423). Hs 7:4a.

ⓑ *by no means* (B-D-F §433, 2 and 3 with ref. to Ps.-Clem., Hom. 4, 8; 19, 9; 20, 5) **1 Cor 5:10.**—DELG s.v. πᾶς. M-M.

πάνυ adv. of πᾶς (Aeschyl., Thu.+) **a high degree on a scale of extent,** ***altogether, very*** used w. other terms—ⓐ w. verbs (Aeschyl. et al.; SIG 798, 5; PGen 74, 23; PFlor 252, 12; TestGad 1:5) π. σωφρονεῖν *show good sense in all respects* 1 Cl 1:3.

ⓑ w. adjectives (Aeschyl. et al.; SIG 890, 15; PHib 27, 19 [III BC]; 2 Macc 15:17; TestAbr A 1 p. 77, 3 [Stone p. 2], B 2 p. 105, 9 [Stone p. 58]; TestJos 9:5; Philo, Aet M.; Jos., Bell. 3, 367; Just., D. 131, 3; Tat. 6, 1 al.) πάνυ ἱλαρός *very well pleased* Hs 6, 1, 6.

ⓒ w. adv. (Aristoph., X. et al.; 2 Macc 9:6; 12:43; 13:8; Jos., Vi. 91; Tat. 1, 1; 34, 3) π. σαφῶς καὶ ἐπιμελῶς Dg 1.

ⓓ w. art. Παπία τοῦ πάνυ *of the renowned Papias* Papias (6). S. L-S-J-M s.v. πάνυ II (e.g. Thu. 8, 1).—DELG s.v. πᾶς.

Παπίας, α and **ου** (proper name in Asia Minor, s. PKretschmer, Einleitung in die Geschichte der griechischen Sprache, 1896, 345f [=1970, 375f]; OGI ind.; pap) ***Papias,*** bishop of Hierapolis in Phrygia (I/II AD) Papias (1:4 al.).—Zahn, Forsch. 6, 109–57; Bihlmeyer, xlvf.

παρά (Hom.+. On elision s. B-D-F §17; Rob. 208) prep. w. three cases (Kühner-G. §440; Schwyzer II 491–98; B-D-F §236–38; Rob. 612–16. Further lit. s.v. ἀνά, beg.; also HRau, De praepositionis παρά usu: GCurtius, Studien etc. III 1870).

A. W. gen., which nearly always as in Hom., Hdt., Pla., X. et al. denotes a pers., and indicates that someth. proceeds fr. this pers. (Hs 2:3 is an exception):

❶ **marker of extension from the side of,** ***from (the side of)*** w. local sense preserved, used w. verbs of coming, going, sending, originating, going out, etc. (TestAbr A 2 p. 78, 30 [Stone p. 4] παρὰ τοῦ μεγάλου βασιλέως ἀπεστάλην; Lucian, Demon. 13 ἀπιὼν παρ' αὐτοῦ) ἐκπορεύεσθαι **J 15:26b.** ἐξέρχεσθαι **16:27; 17:8; Lk 2:1; 6:19.** ἔρχεσθαι **8:49.** παραγίνεσθαι **Mk 14:43.** πέμπειν τινὰ παρά τινος **J 15:26a.** πνεύματος ἁγίου . . . παρὰ τοῦ πατρὸς ἀποσταλέντος εἰς αὐτήν (=Μαρίαν) AcPlCor 2:5. εἶναι παρά τινος *be from someone* (cp. Job 21:2, 9) **J 6:46; 7:29; 9:16, 33; 17:7.**

❷ **marker of one who originates or directs,** ***from*** (Appian, Bell. Civ. 4, 100 §420 παρὰ τ. θεῶν; TestJob 38:8 παρὰ θεοῦ) παρὰ κυρίου ἐγένετο αὕτη *this was the Lord's doing* **Mt 21:42; Mk 12:11** (both Ps 117:23). W. a double negative: οὐκ ἀδυνατήσει παρὰ τ. θεοῦ πᾶν ῥῆμα (s. ἀδυνατέω) **Lk 1:37.** τὰ λελαλημένα αὐτῇ παρὰ κυρίου *what was said to her* (by the angel) *at the Lord's command* vs. **45.** ἀπεσταλμένος παρὰ θεοῦ John the Baptist was not, like Jesus, sent out fr. the very presence of God, but one whose coming was brought about by God **J 1:6** (cp. 2 Macc 11:17). παρ' ἑαυτῆς φέρει καρπὸν καὶ παρὰ τῆς πτελέας *it* (i.e. the vine) *bears fruit which comes both from itself and from the elm* Hs 2:3. On **2 Pt 2:11** s. κρίσις 1bβ.

❸ **marker of the point fr. which an action originates,** ***from***

ⓐ after verbs—**α.** of asking, demanding αἰτεῖν and αἰτεῖσθαι (cp. X., An. 1, 3, 16, Hell. 3, 1, 4; SIG 785, 9f; PFay 121, 12ff; Tob 4:19 BA al.; LXX; TestAbr A 9 p. 87, 2 [Stone p. 22]; TestJob 20:2; ParJer 7:14; Jos., Ant. 15, 92) **Mt 20:20 v.l.** (for ἀπ' αὐτοῦ); **J 4:9; Ac 3:2; 9:2; Js 1:5; 1J 5:15 v.l.** (for ἀπ' αὐτοῦ); 1 Cl 36:4 (Ps 2:8); Hm 9:2, 4; Dg 1. ζητεῖν (Tob 4:18; Sir 7:4; cp. 1 Macc 7:13) **Mk 8:11; Lk 11:16; 12:48.**

β. of taking, accepting, receiving λαμβάνειν (class.; Appian, Mithrid. 88 §397; SIG 546 B, 23 [III BC]; Jdth 12:15; Sus 55 Theod.; 1 Macc 8:8; 11:34; 4 Macc 12:11; TestJob 11:5; JosAs 24:11; Just., A I, 39, 5 al.) **Mk 12:2; Lk 6:34; J 5:34, 41, 44; 10:18; Ac 2:33; 3:5; 17:9; 20:24; 26:10** (Jos., Ant. 14, 167 λαβὼν ἐξουσίαν παρά σου [= τ. ἀρχιερέως]; 11, 169); **Js 1:7; 2 Pt 1:17; 2J 4; Rv 2:28;** Hs 1:8; 8, 3, 5; GJs 20, 2 codices. ἀπολαμβάνειν (SIG 150, 19f [restored text; IV BC]; 4 Macc 18:23) Hv 5:7. παραλαμβάνειν (Hdt. et al.; oft. ins; POxy 504, 14 al. in pap) **Gal 1:12; 1 Th 2:13; 4:1; 2 Th 3:6.** δέχεσθαι (Thu. 1, 20, 1 et al.; 1 Macc 15:20; TestJob 11:12; cp. διαδέχεσθαι Ath. 37, 1) **Ac 22:5; Phil 4:18a.** κομίζεσθαι (SIG 244 I, 5ff [IV BC]; Gen 38:20; 2 Macc 7:11; Ath. 12, 1) **Eph 6:8.** εὑρεῖν (SIG 537, 69; 1099, 28; cp. εὑρίσκω 3, end) **2 Ti 1:18.** ἔχειν τι παρά τινος *have received someth. fr. someone* (1 Esdr 6:5) **Ac 9:14;** cp. Hv 3, 9, 8. γίνεταί μοί τι παρά τινος *I receive someth. from someone* (Att.) **Mt 18:19.** ἔσται μεθ' ἡμῶν χάρις . . . παρὰ θεοῦ πατρὸς καὶ παρὰ Ἰησοῦ **2J 3** (cp. X., An. 7, 2, 25). οἱ πιστευθέντες παρὰ θεοῦ ἔργον *those who were entrusted by God with a task* 1 Cl 43:1 (cp. Polyb. 3, 69, 1; SIG 1207, 12f). παρὰ τοῦ κυρίου πλουτίζεσθαι *receive one's wealth fr. the Lord* Hs 2:10.—Sim. in the case of a purchase the seller is introduced by παρά: *buy fr. someone* ἀγοράζειν (s. ἀγοράζω 1, end) **Rv 3:18.** ὠνεῖσθαι **Ac 7:16.** ἄρτον φαγεῖν παρά τινος *receive support from someone* **2 Th 3:8.**

γ. of learning, coming to know, hearing, asking ἀκούειν (s. ἀκούω 1bβ and 3) **J 1:40; 6:45; 7:51; 8:26, 40; 15:15; Ac 10:22; 28:22; 2 Ti 1:13; 2:2;** AcPlCor 1:6; ἀκριβοῦν **Mt 2:7, 16.** ἐξακριβάζεσθαι Hm 4, 2, 3. ἐπιγινώσκειν **Ac 24:8.** μανθάνειν (since Aeschyl., Ag. 858; Jos., C. Ap. 2, 176; Sir 8:8f; 2 Macc 7:2 v.l.; 3 Macc 1:1; Just., A I, 23, 1 and D. 78, 1 al.; Ath. 7, 2; 22, 8) **2 Ti 3:14.** πυνθάνεσθαι (Hdt. 3, 68; X., Cyr. 1, 6, 23; Pla., Rep. 5, 476e; SIG 1169, 30; 2 Ch 32:31) **Mt 2:4; J 4:52** (without παρά v.l.); B 13:2 (Gen 25:22).

ⓑ w. adjectival function ὁ, ἡ, τὸ παρά τινος *made, given,* etc., *by someone*

α. w. a noun (funct. as a gen.: Pla., Symp. 197e ὁ παρά τινος λόγος 'the expression made by someone'; X., Hell. 3, 1, 6 δῶρον παρὰ βασιλέως, Mem. 2, 2, 12 ἡ παρά τινος εὔνοια, Cyr. 5, 5, 13 τὸ παρ' ἐμοῦ ἀδίκημα 'the crime committed by me'; Polyb. 3, 69, 3 ἡ παρ' αὐτοῦ σωτηρία; Polyaenus 3, 9, 28 ἡ παρὰ στρατηγοῦ ἀρετή; SIG 543, 27; Ex 4:20; 14:13; Philo, Plant. 14; Jos., Ant. 12, 400; Just., A I, 32, 8 and D. 92, 1 al.; Ath. 7, 1) ἡ παρ' ἐμοῦ διαθήκη **Ro 11:27** (Is 59:21).—**Ac 26:12 v.l.; 22 v.l.**

β. w. subst. function—**א.** τὰ παρά τινος *what someone gives, someone's gifts* (X., Mem. 3, 11, 13; Jos., Bell. 2, 124, Ant. 8, 175; Tat. 32, 1 τὰ παρὰ θεοῦ) **Lk 10:7; Phil 4:18b.** τὰ παρ' αὐτῆς *her property, what she had* **Mk 5:26** (cp. IPriene 111, 177). τὰ παρὰ ζώσης καὶ μενούσης *(the help that I received) from a living, contemporary voice* Papias (2:4).

ב. οἱ παρά τινος *someone's envoys* (οἱ παρὰ βασιλέως πρέσβεις X., Hell. 1, 3, 9; oft. in ins.: see, e.g., OGI 5, 50 from Ptolemy; the full expression οἱ παρ' ὑμῶν πρεσβείς OGI 8 VI, 108–9; Schwyzer II 498; B-D-F §237, 2) οἱ παρὰ τοῦ βασιλέως (1 Macc 2:15; 1 Esdr 1:15) 1 Cl 12:4.—The Koine also uses this expr. to denote others who are intimately connected w. someone, e.g. *family, relatives* (PGrenf II, 36, 9 [II BC]; POxy 805 [I BC]; 298, 37 [I AD]; CPR I, 179, 16; 187, 7; Sb 5238, 19 [I AD]; Sus 33; 1 Macc 13:52; Jos., Ant. 1, 193. Further exx. fr. pap in Mlt.

106f; Rossberg [s. ἀνά, beg.] 52) **Mk 3:21** (s. CBruston/PFarel: RTQR 18, 1909, 82–93; AWabnitz, ibid. 221–25; SMonteil, ibid. 19, 1910, 317–25; JMoulton, Mk 3:21: ET 20, 1909, 476; GHartmann, Mk 3:20f: BZ 11, 1913, 248–79; FZorell, Zu Mk 3:20, 21: ZKT 37, 1913, 695–7; JBelser, Zu Mk 3:20f: TQ 98, 1916, 401–18; Rdm.[2] 141; 227.—S. also at ἐξίστημι 2a).

B. w. dat., the case that exhibits close association—**❶ marker of nearness in space,** ***at/by (the side of), beside, near, with,*** acc. to the standpoint fr. which the relationship is viewed

ⓐ *near, beside*—**α.** w. things (Synes., Ep. 126 p. 262a; Kaibel 703, 1; POxy 120, 23; 2 Km 10:8; 11:9; Jos., Ant. 1, 196) εἱστήκεισαν παρὰ τῷ σταυρῷ **J 19:25.** κεῖσθαι παρὰ τῷ πύργῳ Hv 3, 5, 5.

β. w. persons ἔστησεν αὐτὸ παρ᾽ ἑαυτῷ *he had him* (i.e. the child) *stand by his side* **Lk 9:47.**

ⓑ *in (someone's) house, city, company,* etc. (Demetr.: 722 fgm. 1, 5 al. παρὰ Λάβαν)

α. house: ἀριστᾶν **Lk 11:37.** καταλύειν **19:7** (Pla., Gorg. 447b; Demosth. 18, 82). μένειν (JosAs 20:8; Jos., Ant. 1, 298; 299) **J 1:39; Ac 9:43; 18:3; 21:8.** ξενίζεσθαι **10:6; 21:16** (ξενίζω 1). So prob. also ἕκαστος παρ᾽ ἑαυτῷ *each one at home* **1 Cor 16:2** (cp. Philo, Cher. 48 παρ᾽ ἑαυτοῖς, Leg. ad Gai. 271). ὃν ἀπέλιπον ἐν Τρῳάδι παρὰ Κάρπῳ **2 Ti 4:13.**

β. city: **Rv 2:13.** So prob. also ἦσαν παρ᾽ ἡμῖν ἑπτὰ ἀδελφοί **Mt 22:25.**—**J 4:40; Col 4:16** (where the congregation at Laodicea is contrasted w. the one at Col.).

γ. other uses: παρὰ Ἰουδαίοις *among Judeans* **Mt 28:15.** παρ᾽ αὐτοῖς ἐπιμεῖναι *remain with them* **Ac 28:14;** cp. **21:7.** οἱ παρ᾽ ὑμῖν πρεσβύτεροι *the elders among you* 1 Cl 1:3.—παρὰ τῷ πατρί *with* (of spatial proximity) *the Father* **Mt 6:1; J 8:38a;** cp. **17:5** (Synes., Kingship 29 p. 31d: philosophy has her abode παρὰ τῷ θεῷ and if the world refuses to receive her when she descends to earth, μένει παρὰ τῷ πατρί). Of Jesus: παρ᾽ ὑμῖν μένων *while I was with you* (on earth) **J 14:25.** Of the Spirit: παρ᾽ ὑμῖν μένει vs. **17.** Of the Father and Son in their relation to the faithful Christian: μονὴν παρ᾽ αὐτῷ ποιησόμεθα *we will take up our abode with him* vs. **23.**

δ. fig. παρά τινι *before someone's judgment seat* (Demosth. 18, 13 εἰς κρίσιν καθιστάναι παρά τινι; Appian, Maced. 11 §8 παρ᾽ ὑμῖν ἐς κρίσιν) **2 Pt 2:11 v.l.** Closely related is

❷ marker of one whose viewpoint is relevant, ***in the sight or judgment of someone*** (Soph., Hdt.; PSI 435, 19 [258 BC] παρὰ τῷ βασιλεῖ) παρὰ τῷ θεῷ: δίκαιος παρὰ τῷ θεῷ *righteous in the sight of God* **Ro 2:13** (cp. Job 9:2; Jos., Ant. 6, 205; Ath. 31, 2 εὐδοξοῦμεν … παρὰ τῷ θεῷ).—Cp. **1 Cor 3:19; Gal 3:11; 2 Th 1:6; Js 1:27; 1 Pt 2:4; 2 Pt 3:8.** θυσία δεκτὴ παρὰ τῷ θεῷ Hs 5, 3, 8. ἔνδοξος παρὰ τῷ θεῷ m 2:6; s 5, 3, 3; 8, 10, 1; 9, 27, 3; 9, 28, 3; 9, 29, 3.—9, 7, 6.—Acc. to the judgment of humans (Jos., Ant. 7, 84; Just., A I, 20, 3) 8, 9, 1. τί ἄπιστον κρίνεται παρ᾽ ὑμῖν; **Ac 26:8.** ἵνα μὴ ἦτε παρ᾽ ἑαυτοῖς φρόνιμοι **Ro 11:25;** cp. **12:16** (s. Pr 3:7 μὴ ἴσθι φρόνιμος παρὰ σεαυτῷ).—'In the judgment' passes over into a simpler *with* (PsSol 9:5 παρὰ κυρίῳ; Jos. Himerius, Or. 8 [=23], 10 παρὰ θεοῖς=with the gods) εὑρεῖν χάριν παρά τινι *find favor with someone* (Ex 33:16; cp. Num 11:15) **Lk 1:30;** Hs 5, 2, 10. τοῦτο χάρις παρὰ θεῷ **1 Pt 2:20.** χάριν ἔχειν (Ex 33:12) m 5, 1, 5. προέκοπτεν ἐν τῇ χάριτι παρὰ θεῷ καὶ ἀνθρώποις **Lk 2:52.** τί ταπεινοφροσύνη παρὰ θεῷ ἰσχύει, τί ἀγάπη ἁγνὴ παρὰ θεῷ δύναται *how strong humility is before God, what pure love before God can do* 1 Cl 21:8.

❸ marker of personal reference, ***at the side of, with*** almost equivalent to the dat. as such (Ps 75:13): δυνατόν or ἀδύνατον παρά τινι *possible* or *impossible for someone* (Gen 18:14; Just., A I, 33, 2; Ath., R. 9 p. 58, 6) **Mt 19:26ab; Mk 10:27abc; Lk 1:37 v.l.; 18:27ab;** 1 Cl 27:2.—AFridrichsen, SymbOsl 14, '35, 44–46. Closely related in mng. is

❹ marker of connection of a quality or characteristic w. a pers., ***with*** (οὐκ) ἔστιν τι παρά τινι *someth. is (not) with* or *in someone, someone has someth. (nothing) to do w. someth.* (Demosth. 18, 277 εἰ ἔστι καὶ παρ᾽ ἐμοί τις ἐμπειρία; Gen 24:25; Job 12:13; Ps 129:4 παρὰ σοι ὁ ἱλασμός ἐστιν; Just., D. 82, 1 παρὰ … ἡμῖν … χαρίσματα) οὐκ ἔστιν προσωπολημψία παρὰ τ. θεῷ **Ro 2:11** (TestJob 43, 13). Cp. **9:14; Eph 6:9; Js 1:17.** Sim. **Mt 8:10; 2 Cor 1:17.**

❺ marker of a relationship w. a narrow focus, ***among, before*** παρ᾽ ἑαυτοῖς *among themselves* (Philo, Cher. 48) διαλογίζεσθαι **Mt 21:25 v.l.** (cp. Demosth. 10, 17 γιγνώσκειν παρ᾽ αὐτῷ; Epict., Ench. 48, 2).—In ἐν τούτῳ μενέτω παρὰ θεῷ **1 Cor 7:24,** the mng. of παρὰ θεῷ is not certain: *let the pers. remain in that position* (the same one in which he was when called to salvation) *before God;* it is prob. meant to remind Christians of the One *before whom* they cannot even have the appearance of inferiority (ins: Mitt-Wilck, I/2, 4, 4 [13 BC] παρὰ τῷ κυρίῳ Ἑρμῇ='before, in the sight of'; Sb 7616 [II AD] τὸ προσκύνημά σου ποιῶ παρὰ τῷ κυρίῳ Σαράπι='before the Lord' S.; 7661, 3 [c. 100 AD]; 7932, 7992, 6 [letter II/III AD]). Or perh. it simply means that no matter what the situation may be, one is to be focused on God.

C. w. acc. of pers. or thing—**❶ marker of a position viewed as extended** (w. no difference whether παρά answers the question 'where?' or 'whither?' See B-D-F §236, 1; Rob. 615).

ⓐ *by, along* περιπατεῖν παρὰ τὴν θάλασσαν (Pla., Gorg. 511e. Cp. SIG 1182; Jos., Ant. 2, 81) **Mt 4:18;** cp. **Mk 1:16.**

ⓑ *at the edge* or *to the edge of*—**α.** παρὰ (τὴν) θάλασσαν *by the sea* (or *lake*) , *at the shore* **Mt 13:1; Mk 4:1; 5:21; Ac 10:6, 32;** cp. **Lk 5:1, 2.** παρὰ τὴν ὁδόν *by the side of the road* (X., An. 1, 2, 13; Plut., Lysander 450 [29, 4] a tomb παρὰ τ. ὁδόν=beside the road) **Mt 20:30; Mk 10:46; Lk 18:35** (but *on the road* is also poss. in these three places; s. d below).

β. παρὰ τὴν θάλασσαν *to (the side of) the sea (lake)* **Mt 15:29; Mk 2:13.** παρὰ ποταμόν *to the river* **Ac 16:13.**

ⓒ gener. *near, at* παρὰ τοὺς πόδας τινός *at someone's feet* (sit, fall, place etc.; TestAbr A 17 p. 98, 16 [Stone p. 44]) **Mt 15:30; Lk 7:38; 8:35, 41; 10:39 v.l.; 17:16; Ac 4:35, 37 v.l.; 5:2; 7:58; 22:3** (s. ET 30, 1919, 39f). παρὰ τὸν πὺργον *beside the tower* Hs 9, 4, 8; 9, 6, 5; 8; 9, 7, 1; 9, 11, 6.—παρὰ τὴν ἰτέαν 8, 1, 2 (cp. TestAbr A 6 p. 83, 10 [Stone p. 14] παρὰ τὴν δρῦν τὴν Μαμβρῆ).

ⓓ *on* παρὰ τὴν ὁδόν *on the road* (w. motion implied; Aesop, Fab. 226 P.=420 H.: πεσὼν παρὰ τὴν ὁδόν; Phot., Bibl. 94 p. 74b on Iambl. Erot. [Hercher I p. 222, 22] πίπτουσι παρὰ τὴν ὁδόν) **Mt 13:4, 19; Mk 4:4; Lk 8:5;** *on the road* (w. no motion implied; Theophr., HP 6, 6, 10: the crocus likes to be trodden under foot, διὸ καὶ παρὰ τὰς ὁδοὺς κάλλιστος; Phot. p. 222, 29 H. [s. above]) **Mk 4:15; Lk 8:12.** Perh. also **Mt 20:30; Mk 10:46; Lk 18:35** (s. bα above).—παρὰ τὸ χεῖλος τῆς θαλάσσης *on the seashore* **Hb 11:12** (TestAbr A 1 p. 78, 1 [Stone p. 4]; ApcEsdr 3:10; ApcSed 8:9).

❷ marker of extension in time, ***during, from … to*** (Lucian, Catapl. 24 παρὰ τ. βίον=during his life; POxy 472, 10; TestAbr A 20 p. 102, 26 [Stone p. 52] παρὰ μίαν ὥραν; Tat. 14, 2 παρ᾽ ὃν ἔζων χρόνον) παρ᾽ ἐνιαυτόν *from year to year* (Plut., Cleom. 15, 1; cp. ἐνιαυτός 1) B 10:7.

❸ marker of comparative advantage, ***in comparison to, more than, beyond*** ἁμαρτωλοί, ὀφειλέται π. πάντας **Lk 13:2,**

4 (PSI 317, 6 [95 AD] παρὰ πάντας; Jos., C. Ap. 2, 234 παρὰ τ. ἄλλους ἅπαντας; JosAs 10:6 παρὰ πάσας τὰς παρθένους; Just., A I, 20, 3 παρὰ πάντας ἀδίκως μισούμεθα). κρίνειν ἡμέραν παρ' ἡμέραν (s. κρίνω 1) **Ro 14:5.** π. πᾶσαν τὴν γῆν B 11:9 (prophetic quot. of unknown orig.). π. πάντα τὰ πνεύματα *more than all other spirits* Hm 10, 1, 2. ἐλαττοῦν τινα π. τινα *make someone inferior to someone* **Hb 2:7, 9** (s. ἐλαττόω 1 and cp. PGrenf I, 42, 12 [II BC] ἐλαττουμένων ἡμῶν παρὰ τοὺς δεῖνα). εἶδος ἐκλεῖπον π. τὸ εἶδος τῶν ἀνθρώπων (s. ἐκλείπω 4) 1 Cl 16:3.—After a comp. (Thu. 1, 23, 3; ApcEsdr 1:22; Tat. 2, 2) **Lk 3:13; Hb 1:4; 3:3; 9:23; 11:4; 12:24;** B 4:5 (cp. Da 7:7); Hv 3, 12, 1; s 9, 18, 2.—When a comparison is made, one member of it may receive so little attention as to pass fr. consideration entirely, so that 'more than' becomes *instead of, rather than, to the exclusion of* (Plut., Mor. 984c; PsSol 9:9; EpArist 134; Just., A I, 22, 2) λατρεύειν τῇ κτίσει παρὰ τὸν κτίσαντα *serve the creation rather than the Creator* **Ro 1:25** (cp. EpArist 139: the Jews worship τὸν μόνον θεὸν παρ' ὅλην τὴν κτίσιν). δεδικαιωμένος παρ' ἐκεῖνον *justified rather than the other* **Lk 18:14.** ἔχρισέν σε . . . παρὰ τοὺς μετόχους *(God) has anointed you and not your comrades* **Hb 1:9** (Ps 44:8). ὑπερφρονεῖν παρ' ὃ δεῖ φρονεῖν **Ro 12:3** (Plut., Mor. 83f παρ' ὃ δεῖ).παρὰ καιρὸν ἡλικίας **Hb 11:11** (Plut., Rom. 25, 6 παρ' ἡλικίαν; cp. ἡλικία 2a).—παρὰ δύναμιν *beyond their means* (s. δύναμις 2) **2 Cor 8:3.**—After ἄλλος (Pla., Lach. 178b, Leg. 3, 693b; X., Hell. 1, 5, 5; Demosth. 18, 235) *another than* **1 Cor 3:11.**

❹ **marker of degree that falls slightly short in comparison, *except for, almost*** παρὰ μικρόν *except for a little, almost* (s. μικρός 1eγ) Hs 8, 1, 14. Likew. παρά τι (cp. Vett. Val. 228, 6) **Lk 5:7** D; Hs 9, 19, 3.

❺ **marker of causality, *because of*** (cp. Pind., O. 2, 65 κενεὰν παρὰ δίαιταν 'in the interest of' or 'for the sake of a scanty livelihood', the scantiness here contrasting with the immense labor involved; Demosth. 4, 11; 9, 2; PRyl 243, 6; POxy 1420, 7) παρὰ τό w. acc. foll. *because* (SIG 495, 130; UPZ 7, 13 [163 BC] παρὰ τὸ Ἕλληνά με εἶναι.—Mayser II/1, 1926, 331; Gen 29:20; Ex 14:11) 1 Cl 39:5f (Job 4:20f). π. τοῦτο *because of this* (Kühner-G. I 513, 3; Synes., Ep. 44 p. 185a; 57 p. 192d) ITr 5:2; IRo 5:1 (quot. fr. 1 Cor 4:4, where Paul has ἐν τούτῳ). οὐ παρὰ τοῦτο οὐ (double neg. as a strengthened affirmative) *not for that reason any the less* **1 Cor 12:15f.**

❻ **marker of that which does not correspond to what is expected, *against, contrary to*** (Hom., Alc. et al.; ins, pap, LXX; Just., Tat., Ath.—Schwyzer II 497) π. τὴν διδαχήν **Ro 16:17.** παρ' ἐλπίδα *against hope* (s. ἐλπίς 1a) in wordplay w. ἐπ' ἐλπίδι **4:18.** παρὰ φύσιν (Thu. 6, 17, 1; Pla., Rep. 5, 466d; Tat. 22, 2; Ath. 26, 2, R. 6 p. 54, 13) **1:26; 11:24.** παρὰ τὸν νόμον (Just., A II, 2, 4; Ath. 1, 3; cp. X., Mem. 1, 1, 18 παρὰ τοὺς νόμους; PMagd 16, 5 [222 BC] παρὰ τοὺς νόμους; Jos., C. Ap. 2, 233; Just., A I, 68, 10) **Ac 18:13.** παρ' ὃ *contrary to that which* **Gal 1:8f** (Just., A I, 43, 8).

❼ **marker of something that is less, *less*** (Hdt. 9, 33; Plut., Caesar 722 [30, 5]; Jos., Ant. 4, 176; POxy 264, 4 [I AD]) τεσσεράκοντα παρὰ μίαν *forty less one*=thirty-nine (i.e. lashes) **2 Cor 11:24** (cp. Makkoth 3, 10 [tr. HDanby, The Mishnah '33, 407]).—On παρ' αὐτά ITr 11:1 s. παραυτά.—DELG. M-M. TW.

παραβαίνω fut. παραβήσομαι LXX; 2 aor. παρέβην; pf. part. παραβεβηκώς LXX (Hom.+; ins, pap, LXX, En, PsSol 18:10; TestJud 13:7; ApcSed 5:3; EpArist, Philo, Joseph., apolog.)

❶ intr. ***go aside*** fig. ἐκ τῆς ὁδοῦ *deviate from the way* 1 Cl 53:2 (Ex 32:8; Dt 9:12). *Turn aside* fr. an office ἀποστολή, ἀφ' ἧς παρέβη Ἰούδας **Ac 1:25** (on the constr. w. ἀπό cp. Dt 9:16; 17:20).

❷ trans. ***transgress, break***—ⓐ w. acc. τὶ *someth.* (Aeschyl. et al.; Thu. 4, 97, 2; oft. in ins, pap, LXX; Ar. 4, 2 τοὺς ἰδίους ὅρους of heavenly bodies; Just., A II, 5, 3 τὴν τάξιν; Ath. 25, 3; π. τὴν πρώτην πίστιν Hippol., Ref. 9, 12, 16) τὸν νόμον (Eur., Ion 231; Pla., Crito 53e; Sir 19:24; 1 Esdr 8:24, 84; 3 Macc 7:12; SibOr 3, 599f; Jos., C. Ap. 2, 176; Ath. 25, 4; Theoph. Ant. 2, 16 [p. 140, 17]) Hs 8, 3, 5. τὴν ἐντολὴν τοῦ θεοῦ (Epict. 3, 5, 8; Tob 4:5; 4 Macc 13:15; 16:24; Mel., P. 48, 343) **Mt 15:3.** τὴν παράδοσιν vs. **2;** AcPlCor 2:37.

ⓑ abs. (w. 'commandments' to be supplied: Did., Gen. 101, 27. Cp. Iren. 1, 10, 1 [Harv. I 91, 11] of fallen angels) παρέβησαν *they became transgressors* B 9:4. Ptc. ὁ παραβαίνων *the transgressor* **2J 9 v.l.** (Aristot., Pol. 1325b; pl.: POxy 34 III, 12 [II AD]; Sir 40:14; Philo, Mos. 2, 49; Jos., C. Ap. 2, 215; Just., A II, 9, 1, D. 141, 1).—S. παράβασις.—M-M. TW.

παραβάλλω fut. παραβαλῶ; 2 aor. παρέβαλον; pf. ptc. παραβεβλημένος 2 Macc 14:38 (Hom.+).

❶ **to throw to a point where an entity is positioned, *throw to,*** trans. esp. of throwing fodder to animals (Il. 5, 369 al.; Pla., Phdr. 247e; Cass. Dio 59, 14) of the martyrs: τούτοις (i.e. τοῖς θηρίοις) σε παραβαλῶ MPol 11:1. Pass. (cp. παραβληθῆναι τοῖς θηρίοις: Cass. Dio 59, 10; Athen. 3, 84e; Just.) Dg 7:7.

❷ **to expose to hazard, *give up,*** trans. (Aristoph. et al.; Polyb. 40, 4, 2; POxy 533, 13 [II AD]; EpArist 281.—Likew. the mid.) κινδύνῳ ἑαυτόν *expose oneself to danger* 1 Cl 55:6.

❸ **to put someth. beside someth. for the sake of comparison, *compare,*** trans., fig. ext. of 1: (Hdt. et al.; PFlor 312, 8 [I AD]; Philo, Leg. All. 3, 249 al.; Jos., C. Ap. 2, 150; 279) ἐν (instrumental) ποίᾳ παραβολῇ παραβάλωμεν αὐτήν; *what comparison/parable can we use in comparing it* (i.e. the Reign of God)? **Mk 4:30 v.l.**

❹ **to come near to someone or someth., *approach,*** intr. (Pla. et al.; oft. pap; w. εἰς Polyb. 12, 5, 1; 16, 37, 7; 21, 8, 13; Diod. S. 1, 46, 7; 8; Plut., Demetr. 907 [39, 2]; PRyl 153, 5), specif. as a seaman's term *come near by ship, cross over* (Hdt. 7, 179; Ep. Phil. in Demosth. 12, 16; Jos., Ant. 18, 161 εἰς Ποτιόλους παραβαλών) παρεβάλομεν εἰς Σάμον **Ac 20:15.**—M-M.

παράβασις, εως, ἡ (παραβαίνω; see next entry; Strabo et al.; pap, LXX, En, Test12 Patr, GrBar; ApcEsdr 2:12 p. 26, 6 Tdf.; ApcMos, Philo, Joseph., Just.; Tat. 7:3) **act of deviating from an established boundary or norm, *overstepping, transgression*** w. objective gen. (Plut., Mor. 122d, Ages. et Pomp. 662 [1, 5]; 2 Macc 15:10) ἡ π. τοῦ νόμου *the violation of the law* (Porphyr., Abst. 2, 61 Nauck ἡ τοῦ νόμου παράβασις; Alex. Aphr., An. Mant. II 1 p. 158, 37 δικαίων π.=violation of the laws.—Philo, Somn. 2, 123; Jos., Ant. 8, 129 τ. νομίμων π.; 13, 69 ἡ τ. νόμου π.; 18, 263; 340) **Ro 2:23.** W. subjective gen. (Wsd 14:31) ἡ π. Ἀδάμ *Adam's transgression* **5:14.** ἡ π. αὐτῶν B 12:5b. Pl. αἱ π. τοῦ οἴκου σου *the transgressions of your family* Hv 2, 3, 1. Abs. (Plut., Mor. 209a; 746c; Ps 100:3; 4 Km 2:24 v.l.; En 98:5.—Of the Adamic fall into sin: Iren. 4, 40, 3 [Harv. II 303, 6]; Orig., C. Cels. 4, 40, 23; ὁ ἄνθρωπος πρὸ παραβάσεως Did., Gen. 82, 8) **Ro 4:15; Hb 9:15;** B 12:5a W. παρακοή **Hb 2:2.** Among many other vices in a catalogue of vices B 20:1. ἐν π. γίνεσθαι *become a transgressor* **1 Ti 2:14.** τῶν παραβάσεων χάριν *in the interest of transgressions* i.e. to make them poss. and numerous **Gal 3:19.**—DELG s.v. βαίνω. M-M. EDNT. TW.

παραβάτης, ου, ὁ (παραβαίνω; s. prec. entry; in non-bibl. wr. mostly a warrior beside the charioteer, or a certain kind of foot-soldier) in our lit. only ***violator, transgressor*** (so Aeschyl., Eum. 553 [on the rdg. παρβάδαν s. Schwyzer II 492]; Pythag., Ep. 3, 7 παραβάται τᾶν ὁμολογιᾶν γινόμεθα; Polemo [Macrobius, Saturnalia 5, 19, 29] π. θεῶν; perh. PMich 478, 16 [II AD]; Suda on Ἀμάχιος; Sym.; π. τῆς τοῦ θεοῦ ἐντολῆς Did., Gen. 84, 27; Theoph. Ant. 2, 16 [p. 140, 13]) (τοῦ) νόμου **Ro 2:25, 27; Js 2:11; Lk 6:4** D. Abs. *sinner* (Ps.-Clem., Hom. 3, 39) **Gal 2:18** (WMundle, ZNW 23, 1924, 152f); **Js 2:9.**—DELG s.v. βαίνω. M-M. TW.

παραβιάζομαι mid. dep. Att. fut. 3 pl. παραβιῶνται Am 6:10; 1 aor. παρεβιασάμην (Epicurea p. 36, 5 Us.; Polyb., Plut. et al.; LXX; TestSol 26:4; s. Anz 359f). From the mng. 'use force' to accomplish someth. (Polyb. 24, 8, 3; Philo, Congr. Erud. Grat. 125; Jos., C. Ap. 2, 233) w. acc. ('do violence to' Plut., Mor. 19f μύθους, Cleom. 16, 2 τ. Ἀχαιούς; Gen 19:9; cp. Dt 1:43) develops the sense: ***urge strongly, prevail upon*** (4 Km 2:17 al.) **Lk 24:29; Ac 16:15** (cp. 1 Km 28:23). Foll. by acc. and inf. ὁ παραβιασάμενος ἑαυτόν τε καί τινας προσελθεῖν ἑκοντάς *the one who prevailed upon himself and others to come forward of their own free will* MPol 4.—DELG s.v. βία. M-M.

παραβλέπω (Aristoph. et al.; LXX; TestSol 22:5; ApcSed 16:1 [impf. ἐπαράβλεπον]; Philo, Virt. 173) **to look aside so as not to see, *overlook, neglect, despise*** (Polyb. 6, 46, 6 τὰς διαφοράς; Sir 38:9) τινά *someone* of needy persons, widows and orphans Hs 1:8.

παραβολεύομαι (Sb 7562 [II AD];=the pass. use of παραβάλλω Thu. et al.) 1 aor. παρεβολευσάμην ***expose to danger, risk*** (IPontEux I[2], 39, 26–28 [=IGR I/II, 856] ἀλλὰ καὶ [μέχρι] περάτων γῆς ἐμαρτυρήθη τοὺς ὑπὲρ φιλίας κινδύνους μέχρι Σεβαστῶν συμμαχίᾳ παραβολευσάμενος='but also to the ends of the earth witness was borne to him that in the interests of friendship he exposed himself to dangers by his aid in [legal] strife, [taking his clients' cases] even up to the emperors'. Dssm., LO 69 [LAE 84]) τινί *someth.* (on the dat. s. Mlt. 64 and cp. παραβάλλεσθαι τοῖς ὅλοις 'risk everything' Polyb. 2, 26, 3; 3, 94, 4) τῇ ψυχῇ *one's life* (cp. Diod. S. 3, 36, 4 ταῖς ψυχαῖς παραβάλλεσθαι; SIG 762, 39 ψυχῇ καὶ σώματι παραβαλλόμενος) **Phil 2:30.**—DELG s.v. βάλλω. M-M.

παραβολή, ῆς, ἡ (παραβάλλω; Pla., Isocr.+; ins, pap, LXX; En; TestSol 20:4; Just.; Mel., P.—JWackernagel, Parabola: IndogF 31, 1912/13, 262–67)

➊ **someth. that serves as a model or example pointing beyond itself for later realization, *type, figure*** παραβολὴ εἰς τὸν καιρὸν τὸν ἐνεστηκότα *a symbol (pointing) to the present age* **Hb 9:9.** ἐν παραβολῇ *as a type* (of the violent death and of the resurrection of Christ) **11:19.** λέγει ὁ προφήτης παραβολὴν κυρίου B 6:10, where the mng. may be *the prophet is uttering a parable of the Lord* (Goodsp.), or *the prophet speaks of the Lord in figurative language* (Kleist), or *the prophet speaks in figurative language given him by the Lord.* W. αἴνιγμα PtK 4 p. 15, 31. The things of the present or future cannot be understood by the ordinary Christian διὰ τὸ ἐν παραβολαῖς κεῖσθαι *because they are expressed in figures* B 17:2.

➋ **a narrative or saying of varying length, designed to illustrate a truth especially through comparison or simile, *comparison, illustration, parable, proverb, maxim.***

ⓐ in the synoptics the word refers to a variety of illustrative formulations in the teaching of Jesus (in Mt 17 times, in Mk 13 times, in Lk 18 times; cp. Euclides [400 BC] who, acc. to Diog. L. 2, 107, rejected ὁ διὰ παραβολῆς λόγος; Aristot., Rhet. 2, 20, 2ff; Περὶ ὕψους 37; Vi. Aesopi II p. 307, 15 Eb.; Biogr. p. 87 Ὁμήρου παραβολαί; Philo, Conf. Lingu. 99; Jos., Ant. 8, 44. The Gk. OT also used παραβολή for various words and expressions that involve comparison, including riddles [s. Jülicher below: I[2] 32–40].—En 1:2; 3. Cp. π. κυριακαί Iren. 1, 8, 1 [Harv I 67, 1]). For prob. OT influence on the use of comparison in narrative s. Ezk 17. λέγειν, εἰπεῖν παραβολήν: **Lk 13:6; 16:19** D; **19:11** (begins the longest 'parable' in the synoptics: 17 verses). τινί to *someone* **4:23** (the briefest 'parable': 3 words; here and in the next passage π.=*proverb,* quoted by Jesus); **6:39; 18:1; 21:29.** πρός τινα to *someone* **5:36; 12:16, 41; 14:7; 15:3; 18:9; 20:9;** *with reference to someone* **Mk 12:12; Lk 20:19.** παραβολὴν λαλεῖν τινι **Mt 13:33.** παραβολὴν παρατιθέναι τινί *put a parable before someone* vss. **24, 31.** τελεῖν τὰς παραβολάς *finish the parables* vs. **53.** διασαφεῖν (v.l. φράζειν) τινι τὴν παραβολήν vs. **36.** φράζειν τινὶ τὴν παρ. *explain the parable* **15:15.** ἀκούειν **Mt 13:18; 21:33, 45.** γνῶναι and εἰδέναι *understand* **Mk 4:13b** et al. μαθεῖν τὴν παρ. ἀπό τινος *learn the parable from someth.* **Mt 24:32; Mk 13:28.** (ἐπ)ερωτᾶν τινα τὴν παρ. *ask someone the mng. of the parable* **Mk 7:17** (in ref. to vs. 15); cp. **4:10.** Also ἐπερωτᾶν τινα περὶ τῆς παρ. **7:17 v.l.;** ἐπηρώτων αὐτὸν τίς εἴη ἡ παρ. *they asked him what the parable meant* **Lk 8:9;** the answer to it: ἔστιν δὲ αὕτη ἡ παρ. *but the parable means this* vs. **11.**—παραβολαῖς λαλεῖν τινί τι **Mk 4:33.** W. the gen. of that which forms the subj. of the parable ἡ παρ. τοῦ σπείραντος **Mt 13:18.** τῶν ζιζανίων vs. **36** (cp. ἡ περὶ τοῦ . . . τελώνου παρ. Orig., C. Cels. 3, 64, 11).—W. a prep.: εἶπεν διὰ παραβολῆς **Lk 8:4** (Orig., C. Cels. 1, 5, 11).—χωρὶς παραβολῆς οὐδὲν ἐλάλει αὐτοῖς **Mt 13:34b; Mk 4:34.**—Mostly ἐν: τιθέναι τὴν βασιλείαν τοῦ θεοῦ ἐν παραβολῇ *present the Reign of God in a parable* vs. **30.** ἐν παραβολαῖς λαλεῖν τινι **Mt 13:10, 13; Mk 12:1.** ἐν παραβολαῖς λέγειν τινί **Mt 22:1; Mk 3:23.** λαλεῖν τινί τι ἐν παραβολαῖς **Mt 13:3, 34a.** διδάσκειν τινά τι ἐν παραβολαῖς **Mk 4:2.** ἀνοίξω ἐν παραβολαῖς τὸ στόμα μου **Mt 13:35** (Ps 77:2). γίνεταί τινί τι ἐν παραβολαῖς *someth. comes to someone in the form of parables* **Mk 4:11;** cp. **Lk 8:10.** According to Eus. (3, 39, 11), Papias *presented some unusual parables of the Savior,* i.e. ascribed to Jesus: Papias (2:11).—AJülicher, Die Gleichnisreden Jesu I[2] 1899; II 1899 [the older lit. is given here I 203–322]; GHeinrici, RE VI 688–703, XXIII 561f; CBugge, Die Hauptparabeln Jesu 1903; PFiebig, Altjüdische Gleichnisse und d. Gleichnisse Jesu 1904, D. Gleichnisse Jesu im Lichte der rabb. Gleich. 1912, D. Erzählungsstil der Ev. 1925; LFonck, Die Parabeln des Herrn[3] 1909 (w. much lit. on the individual parables), The Parables of the Gospel[3] 1918; JKögel, BFCT XIX 6, 1915; MMeinertz, Die Gleichnisse Jesu 1916; 4th ed. '48; HWeinel, Die Gleichnisse Jesu[5] 1929; RBultmann, D. Geschichte der synoptischen Tradition[2] '31, 179–222; MDibelius, D. Formgeschichte des Ev.[2] 33; EBuonaiuti, Le parabole di Gesù: Religio 10–13, '34–37; WOesterly, The Gospel Parables in the Light of Their Jewish Background '36; EWechssler, Hellas im Ev. '36, 267–85; CDodd, The Parables of the Kgdm.[3] '36; BSmith, The Par. of the Syn. Gosp. '37; WMichaelis, Es ging e. Sämann aus. zu säen '38; OPiper, The Understanding of the Syn. Par.: EvQ 14, '42, 42–53; CMasson, Les Paraboles de Marc IV '45; JJeremias, D. Gleichn. Jesu[4] '56 (Eng. tr. '55); ELinnemann, Jesus of the Parables, tr. JSturdy, '66; AWeiser, D. Knechtsgleichnisse der synopt. Evv. '71; JKingsbury, The Parables of Jesus in Mt 13, '69; FDanker,

Fresh Persp. on Mt, CTM 41, '70, 478–90; JKingsbury, ibid. 42, '71, 579–96; TManson, The Teaching of Jesus, '55, 57–86; JSider, Biblica 62, '81, 453–70 (synoptists); ECuvillier, Le concept de ΠΑΡΑΒΟΛΗ dans le second évangile '93.

ⓑ Apart fr. the syn. gospels, παρ. is found in our lit. freq. in Hermas (as heading: Hs 1:1; 2:1; 3:1; 4:1; 5:1; [6:1; 7:1; 8:1]) but not independently of the synoptic tradition. Hermas uses παρ. only once to designate a real illustrative (double) parable, in m 11:18. Elsewh παρ. is for Hermas an enigmatic presentation that is somet. seen in a vision, somet. expressed in words, but in any case is in need of detailed interpretation: w. gen. of content (s. a above) τοῦ πύργου *about the tower* Hv 3, 3, 2. τοῦ ἀγροῦ *about the field* s 5, 4, 1. τῶν ὀρέων 9, 29, 4. δηλοῦν τὴν παραβολήν 5, 4, 1a. παρ. ἐστιν ταῦτα 5, 4, 1b. ἀκούειν τὴν παραβολήν v 3, 3, 2; 3, 12, 1; s 5, 2, 1. παραβολὰς λαλεῖν τινι 5, 4, 2a. τὰ ῥήματα τὰ λεγόμενα διὰ παραβολῶν 5, 4, 3b; γράφειν τὰς παρ. v 5:5f; s 9, 1, 1; συνιέναι τὰς παρ. m 10, 1, 3. γινώσκειν s 5, 3, 1a; 9, 5, 5. νοεῖν m 10, 1, 4; s 5, 3, 1b. ἐπιλύειν τινὶ παρ. 5, 3, 1c; 5, 4, 2b; 3a. συντελεῖν 9, 29, 4. ἡ ἐπίλυσις τῆς παρ. *explanation, interpretation of the parable* 5, 6, 8; αἱ ἐπιλύσεις τῶν παρ. 5, 5, 1. ὁ υἱὸς τοῦ θεοῦ εἰς δούλου τρόπον κεῖται ἐν τῇ παρ. *the Son of God appears in the parable as a slave* 5, 5, 5. ἡ παρ. εἰς τοὺς δούλους τοῦ θεοῦ κεῖται *the par. refers to the slaves of God* 2:4.—S. also the headings to the various parts of the third division of Hermas (the Parables) and on Hermas gener. s. Jülicher, op. cit. I 204–209.—εἰ δὲ δεῖ ἡμᾶς καὶ ἀπὸ τῶν σπερμάτων μὴ ποιεῖσθαι τὴν παρ. *but if we are not to draw our comparison from the (action of) the seeds* AcPlCor 2:28.—BScott, Profiles of Jesus, Parables: The Fourth R 10, '97, 3–14.—B. 1262. DELG s.v. βάλλω. M-M. EDNT. TW. Sv.

παραβουλεύομαι 1 aor. παρεβουλευσάμην (Cat. Cod. Astr. XII 188, 27; Hesych., prob. w. ref. to Phil 2:30) ***be careless*** τινί *in relation to someth.* τῇ ψυχῇ *have no concern for one's life* **Phil 2:30 v.l.** (for παραβολ. q.v.).—DELG s.v. βούλομαι.

παραβύω (βύω 'to stuff') 1 aor. παρέβυσα (Hippocr. et al.) ***plunge into*** π. ξιφίδιον *plunge a dagger into (a body)* MPol 16:1 (Lucian, Toxar. 58 παραβύειν ἐς τὴν πλευρὰν τὸν ἀκινάκην).—DELG s.v. βυνέω.

παραγγελία, ας, ἡ (παραγγέλλω; X. et al.; Diod. S. 4, 12, 3; pap, Philo, In Flacc. 141; Jos., Ant. 16, 241) **an announcement respecting someth. that must be done, *order, command, precept, advice, exhortation*** παραγγελίαν λαμβάνειν *receive an order* **Ac 16:24;** 1 Cl 42:3. παραγγελίᾳ παραγγέλλειν τινί (B-D-F §198, 6; Rdm.[2] 128; Rob. 531) foll. by μή and the inf. *give someone strict orders* **Ac 5:28.** Of apostolic *instructions* παραγγελίας διδόναι τινί **1 Th 4:2;** παρατίθεσθαί τινι **1 Ti 1:18;** cp. vs. **5.**—GMilligan, St. Paul's Epistles to the Thess. 1908, 47.—DELG s.v. ἄγγελος. M-M. TW. Spicq.

παραγγέλλω (παρά, ἀγγέλλω) impf. παρήγγελλον; 1 aor. παρήγγειλα. Pass.: pf. ptc. παρηγγελμένος 3 Macc 4:14 (Aeschyl., Hdt.+; ins, pap, LXX; TestSol 26:4 B; Test12 Patr; ApcSed 9:5; ApcEsdr 4:28 p. 29, 2 Tdf.; Philo, Joseph., Just.) **to make an announcement about someth. that must be done, *give orders, command, instruct, direct*** of all kinds of persons in authority, worldly rulers, Jesus, the apostles. Abs. παραγγέλλων *in giving my instructions* **1 Cor 11:17.** W. pres. inf. foll. **Ac 15:5;** w. acc. and aor. inf. foll. **1 Ti 6:13f v.l.** τὶ *direct, urge, insist on* (Philo, Spec. Leg. 3, 80) **2 Th 3:4; 1 Ti 4:11; 5:7.** τινί (Jos., Ant. 2, 311) *urge* παραγγείλαντες αὐτοῖς **Ac 15:5 v.l.;** *direct, command someone* καθὼς ὑμῖν παρηγγείλαμεν **1 Th 4:11;** pass. τὰ παρηγγελμένα τινί *what someone was told* (to do) **short ending of Mk.** τινί w. λέγων and dir. discourse foll. **Mt 10:5.** τινί τι w. ὅτι and dir. disc. foll. **2 Th 3:10.**—τινί w. aor. inf. foll. (Philo, Poster. Cai. 29; Jos., C. Ap. 1, 244; Just., D. 14, 3; Hippol., Ref. 5, 26, 22. S. also Iren. 1, prol. 2 [Harv. I 4, 5]) **Mt 15:35; Mk 8:6; Lk 8:29; Ac 10:42; 16:18** (s. Mlt. 119). τινί w. pres. inf. foll. (1 Km 23:8) **Ac 16:23; 23:30;** 1 Cl 1:3; IPol 5:1. παραγγέλλειν w. an inf. and μή comes to mean *forbid to do someth.*: π. τινί w. aor. inf. **Lk 5:14; 8:56;** without the dat., which is easily supplied fr. the context **Ac 23:22.** π. τινί w. pres. inf. (cp. an ins fr. Dionysopolis [Ramsay, ET 14, 1903, 159] παραγγέλλω πᾶσι, μὴ καταφρονεῖν τοῦ θεοῦ; Philo, Leg. All. 1, 98; Just., D. 112, 4) **Lk 9:21; Ac 1:4** (for the transition from indirect discourse to direct cp. Arrian, Anab. 5, 11, 4: Alexander παρηγγέλλετο Κρατέρῳ μὴ διαβαίνειν τὸν πόρον ... ἢν Πῶρος ἐπ᾽ ἐμὲ ἄγῃ [the last clause is spoken by Alexander]); **1 Ti 1:3; 6:17** (s. B-D-F §409, 1); without dat. (Jos., Ant. 19, 311) 1 Cl 27:2, which can be supplied fr. the context **Ac 4:18; 5:40.** παραγγελίᾳ παρηγγείλαμεν ὑμῖν μὴ διδάσκειν vs. **28.**—τινί w. acc. and 1 aor. inf. foll. **1 Cor 7:10; 1 Ti 6:13f;** pres. inf. **Ac 17:30; 23:30; 2 Th 3:6.**—W. ἵνα foll. (s. ἵνα II 1aδ) **2 Th 3:12.** παρήγγειλεν αὐτοῖς ἵνα μηδὲν αἴρωσιν *he forbade them to take anything* **Mk 6:8.**—DELG s.v. ἄγγελος. M-M. TW. Spicq.

παράγγελμα, ατος, τό (Aeschyl., Thu.+; SIG 985, 12; 34; PAmh 50, 5; PLond III, 904, 36 p. 126 [AD 104]; PGM 4, 749; 1 Km 22:14; Philo; Jos., Ant. 16, 43, C. Ap. 1, 178; Just., D. 10, 2; Tat.) **an order directing that someth. must be done, *order, direction, instruction, precept,*** esp. of the edict of a ruler (Jos., Bell. 6, 383) 1 Cl 13:3 (w. ἐντολή). ποιεῖν τὰ τοῦ Χριστοῦ π. *follow the precepts of Christ* 49:1.—DELG s.v. ἄγγελος. M-M s.v. παραγγελία.

παραγίνομαι impf. 3 pl. παρεγίνοντο; 2 aor. παρεγενόμην and παρεγενήθην LXX; pf. παραγέγονα LXX; plpf. 3 sg. παραγεγόνει; inf. παραγεγενῆσθαι (Just) (Hom.+).

❶ **to be in movement so as to be present at a particular place, *draw near, come, arrive, be present*** (Aristoph., Hdt. et al.; Vi. Aesopi G 7 Isis; ins, pap, LXX)

ⓐ of pers. foll. by εἰς and acc. of place (Hdt.; SIG 474, 13f παραγεγονὼς δὲ [καὶ εἰς τὴν πό]λιν; POxy 743, 23 [2 BC]; PRyl 232, 3; Ex 16:35; Josh 24:11; Philo, Mos. 1, 86) **Mt 2:1; J 8:2; Ac 9:26; 13:14** (w. ἀπὸ τ. Πέργης; cp. Jos., Ant. 18, 110); **15:4;** AcPl Ant 13, 1 (=Aa I 236, 6); AcPl Cor 1:2. Also ἐν w. dat. of place (POxy 1185, 26; BGU 286, 6; Just., D. 51, 2) **Ac 9:26 v.l.;** ITr 1:1. Foll. by ἐπί τινα *come against someone,* mostly w. hostile purpose (Thu. 2, 95, 3; 2 Macc 4:34; 8:16; 11:2; 12:6; 15:24.—ἐπί 12b) **Lk 22:52.** Foll. by πρός τινα (Lucian, Philops. 6; PCairZen 214, 5 [254 BC] πρὸς ἡμᾶς; PSI 341, 4; PEleph 9, 4; Ex 2:18; Judg 8:15; Jos., Ant. 6, 131) **Lk 7:4, 20; 8:19; 22:52 v.l.; Ac 20:18.** φίλος παρεγένετο ἐξ ὁδοῦ πρός με **Lk 11:6** (παραγίνεσθαι ἐκ as SIG 663, 4; PMagd 1, 10 [III BC]; Gen 35:9; 1 Macc 5:14; Jos., Vi. 248 ἐκ τῆς ὁδοῦ παρεγενόμην). παραγίνεται ὁ Ἰησοῦς ἀπὸ τῆς Γαλιλαίας ἐπὶ τὸν Ἰορδάνην πρὸς τὸν Ἰωάννην **Mt 3:13** (π. ἐπί w. acc. of place as SIG 633, 85 al.; Sb 3925, 4; Jdth 6:11; 14:13; Bel 15). ἐνθάδε AcPlCor 1:16. Abs. **Mk 14:43; Lk 14:21; 19:16; J 3:23; Ac 5:21f, 25; 9:39; 10:33; 11:23; 14:27; 17:10; 18:27; 21:18; 23:16, 35; 24:17, 24; 25:7; 28:21; 1 Cor 16:3;** 1 Cl 12:6; IRo 6:2; Hs 9, 5, 7; AcPlCor 1:7.

ⓑ of things taught: ἐντολὰς ... τὰς ... ἀπ᾽ αὐτῆς παραγινομένας τῆς ἀληθείας *instructions which proceed directly from the truth* Papias (2:3). Somet. the coming has rather the sense

❷ **make a public appearance, *appear*** of J. the Baptist **Mt 3:1.** Of Jesus, w. inf. of purpose foll. (cp. 1 Macc 4:46) **Lk 12:51.** Χριστὸς παραγενόμενος ἀρχιερεύς **Hb 9:11.**

❸ **to come to help,** ***stand by, come to the aid of*** (trag.; Thu. 3, 54, 4; Pla., Rep. 2, 368b) οὐδείς μοι παρεγένετο **2 Ti 4:16.**—DELG s.v. γίγνομαι. M-M.

παράγω impf. παρῆγον; 2 aor. παρήγαγον LXX. Pass.: aor. 3 sg. παρήχθη LXX (Pind., Hdt.+).

❶ **to move along and so leave a position,** ***go away*** παρῆγεν οὕτως *so he went away* **J 8:59 v.l.** (given this v.l., the παράγων of **9:1** [s. 3 below] would belong here). ἐκεῖθεν **Mt 9:9, 27.**

❷ **to bring in someth. of a type foreign to the present condition or circumstance,** ***bring in, introduce*** παράγουσι φόβους ἀνθρωπίνους 2 Cl 10:3 (s. φόβος 2aα). (The trans. act. in various senses: BGU 1139, 19 [5 BC]; 1 Km 16:9f; Jos., Ant. 5, 97; 20, 200).

❸ **to go past a reference point,** ***pass by*** (Polyb. 5, 18, 4; Appian, Bell. Civ. 2, 62 §259 θεοῦ παράγοντος=as though a god passed by [and struck Labienus with blindness]; Coll. Alex., Lyr. Adesp. 37, 25 ἐὰν . . . μνήματα κωφὰ παράγῃς; Menand., Dyscol. 556 al.; CIG 2129, 2; PTebt 17, 4; 2 Km 15:18; Ps 128:8; 3 Macc 6:16) **Mt 20:30; Mk 2:14; 15:21; J 9:1.** π. παρὰ τὴν θάλασσαν *pass by along the lake* **Mk 1:16.** Cf. ELohmeyer, 'Und Jesus ging vorüber': NThT 23, '34, 206–24.

❹ **to go out of existence,** ***pass away, disappear,*** in imagery

ⓐ act. (Ps 143:4) **1 Cor 7:31.**

ⓑ pass., w. act. sense (cp. 2 Esdr 9:2 παρήχθη σπέρμα τὸ ἅγιον) ἡ σκοτία παράγεται *the darkness is passing away* **1J 2:8;** cp. vs. **17** (ὁ κόσμος παραλεύσεται TestJob 33:4).—M-M. TW.

παραδειγματίζω (παράδειγμα 'model') 1 aor. subj. παραδειγματίσῃς GJs 20:2 codd.; 1 aor. inf. παραδειγματίσαι. Pass.: fut. 2 pl. παραδειγματισθήσεσθε Da 2:5; 1 aor. inf. παραδειγματισθῆναι LXX (Polyb. et al.; LXX; PsSol 2:12). (Mostly = 'make a public example of' by punishment [Polyb. 2, 60, 7; 29, 19, 5; LXX]; then also without the idea of punishment) **to disgrace someone publicly,** ***expose, make an example of*** (Plut., Mor. 520b of Archilochus, who sullied his reputation by scurrilous attacks on women) τινά *someone* **Mt 1:19 v.l.** (s. δειγματίζω); Salome prays μὴ παραδειγματίσῃς με τοῖς υἱοῖς Ἰσραήλ GJs 20:2 codd.; w. ἀνασταυροῦν *hold up to contempt* **Hb 6:6.**—DELG s.v. δείκνυμι. M-M. TW. Spicq. Sv.

παράδεισος, ου, ὁ (Old Persian pairidaêza [Avestan form; s. WHinz, Altiranisches Sprachgut der Nebenüberlieferungen, '75, 179]='enclosure'; Hebr. פַּרְדֵּס. In Gk. X.+; gener. 'garden'; freq. pap., s. also New Docs 2, 201) in our lit., except GJs 2:4, not of any formal garden (as also TestAbr A 4 p. 80, 23 [Stone p. 8, 23] ApcrEzk fgm. a) or park, but only

❶ **the garden of Eden,** ***paradise*** (Gen 2f; Philo; Jos., Ant. 1, 37; SibOr 1, 24; 26; 30; Iren. 5, 5, 1 [Harv. II 331, 3]; Orig., C. Cels. 7, 50, 31; Hippol., Did., Theoph. Ant. 2, 22 [p. 154, 21]), lit. Dg 12:3, and in the same connection fig., of those who love God, οἱ γενόμενοι παράδεισος τρυφῆς *who prove to be a luscious paradise,* in so far as they allow fruit-laden trees to grow up within them 12:1 (cp. PsSol 14:3).

❷ **a transcendent place of blessedness,** ***paradise*** (ὁ παράδεισος τῆς δικαιοσύνης appears as such En 32:3; cp. 20:7; TestLevi 18:10; SibOr fgm. 3, 48 and other passages in the OT pseudepigrapha not preserved in Gk., as well as other sources in the lit. given below.—Dssm., B 146 [BS 148]) **Lk 23:43** (JWeisengoff, EcclRev 103, '40, 163–67). ὡς ἐν π. AcPl Ha 3, 23. More fully ὁ π. τοῦ θεοῦ (Gen 13:10; Ez 28:13; 31:8; PGM 4, 3027 ἐν τῷ ἁγίῳ ἑαυτοῦ [=τ. θεοῦ] παραδείσῳ) **Rv 2:7.** ἁρπάζεσθαι εἰς τὸν π. *be caught up into Paradise* **2 Cor 12:4.**—S. on οὐρανός 1e and τρίτος 1a. Further, Bousset, Rel.[3] 282ff; 488ff; PVolz, D. Eschatologie der jüd. Gemeinde im ntl. Zeitalter '34, 417f; Billerb. IV 1118–65; Windisch on 2 Cor 12:4; AWabnitz, Le Paradis du Hadès: RTQR 19, 1910, 328–31; 410–14; 20, 1911, 130–38.—DELG. M-M. TW.

παραδέχομαι fut. παραδέξομαι; 1 aor. παρεδεξάμην. Pass.: 1 fut. pass. παραδεχθήσομαι; 1 aor. παρεδέχθην (Hom.+)

❶ **to acknowledge someth. to be correct,** ***accept,*** w. a thing as obj. in the acc. (Epict. 3, 12, 15; BGU 1119, 54 [I AD] τὴν συντίμησιν; PRyl 229, 16; PFay 125, 10; Ex 23:1; 3 Macc 7:12; Just., D. 12, 2) τὸν λόγον **Mk 4:20** (Diocles 112 p. 163, 18 παραδ. τὸν λόγον; Plut., Mor. 47e; Philo, Leg. All. 3, 199). ἔθη **Ac 16:21.** μαρτυρίαν **22:18.** τὶ ἄλλο AcPlCor 2:34. κατηγορίαν **1 Ti 5:19** (Sextus 259 διαβολὰς κατὰ φιλοσόφου μὴ παραδέχου). *Receive* erroneous teachings IEph 9:1. (Opp. παραιτεῖσθαι) τὰ κτισθέντα Dg 4:2.

❷ **to accept the presence of someone in a hospitable manner,** ***receive, accept,*** w. a pers. as obj. in the acc. (POxy 492, 8; 14; 1676, 28; BGU 27:10; Jos., C. Ap. 2, 256; 258) dissidents ISm 4:1. θεὸν τὸν παραδεχόμενον ἡμᾶς (w. καλεῖν) 2 Cl 16:1. Pass. (2 Macc 4:22 Cod. V) **Ac 15:4** (v.l. ἀπεδέχθησαν). *Take back* a wife who was dismissed for adultery Hm 4, 1, 8a; pass. 4, 1, 7; 8b. Of a citizen who wishes to return to his home city after living in a strange land, pass. s 1:5.—Corresp. to רָצָה *receive favorably*=love (Pr 3:12) **Hb 12:6;** 1 Cl 56:4.—M-M.

παραδιατριβή, ῆς, ἡ **waste of time in unimportant matters,** ***useless occupation*** pl. **1 Ti 6:5 v.l.** (cp. Field, Notes 211).—M-M.

παραδίδωμι (Pind., Hdt.+) pres. 3 sg. παραδίδει (-δίδη cod. [ApcEsdr 3:12 p. 27, 23 Tdf.]), subj. 3 sg. παραδιδῷ and παραδιδοῖ 1 Cor 15:24 (B-D-F §95, 2; W-S. §14, 12; Mlt-H. 204), ptc. παραδιδούς; impf. 3 sg. παρεδίδου **Ac 8:3** and **1 Pt 2:23,** pl. παρεδίδουν **Ac 16:4 v.l.; 27:1** and παρεδίδοσαν **16:4** (B-D-F §94, 1; Mlt-H. 202); fut. παραδώσω; 1 aor. παρέδωκα; 2 aor. indic. παρέδοσαν **Lk 1:2;** 2 aor. subj. 3 sg. παραδῷ and παραδοῖ Mk 4:29; 14:10, 11; J 13:2 (B-D-F §95, 2; Mlt-H. 210f), impv. παράδος, ptc. παραδούς; pf. παραδέδωκα, ptc. παραδεδωκώς (Ac 15:26); plpf. 3 pl. παραδεδώκεισαν **Mk 15:10** (on the absence of augment s. B-D-F §66, 1; Mlt-H. 190). Pass.; impf. 3 sg. παρεδίδετο **1 Cor 11:23b** (-δίδοτο is also attested; B-D-F §94, 1; Mlt-H. 206); 1 fut. παραδοθήσομαι; 1 aor. παρεδόθην; perf. 3 sg. παραδέδοται **Lk 4:6,** ptc. παραδεδομένος (Ac 14:26).

❶ **to convey someth. in which one has a relatively strong personal interest,** ***hand over, give (over), deliver, entrust***

ⓐ a thing τινί τι (Jos., Ant 4, 83; Mel., P. 42, 290; 292; 294) τάλαντά μοι **Mt 25:20, 22.** αὐτοῖς τὰ ὑπάρχοντα αὐτοῦ vs. **14.** ὑμῖν τὴν γῆν 1 Cl 12:5. τινὶ τὴν κτίσιν Hv 3, 4, 1; λίθους s 9, 7, 1; ἀμπελῶνα 5, 6, 2. Also in the sense *give back, restore, give up* (X., Hell. 2, 3, 7 τινί τι) αὐτῷ τὴν παρακαταθήκην ἣν ἔλαβον Hm 3:2.—Pass., w. the thing easily supplied fr. the context ἐμοὶ παραδέδοται **Lk 4:6.**—παρέδωκεν τὸ πνεῦμα **J 19:30** (ApcMos 42; cp. TestAbr B 12 p. 117, 4f [Stone p. 82] Σαρρα . . . παρέδωκε τὴν ψυχήν; ParJer 9:8; ApcEsdr 7:14) needs no dat.: *he gave up his spirit* voluntarily. ἄνθρωποι παραδεδωκότες τὰς ψυχὰς αὐτῶν ὑπὲρ τοῦ ὀνόματος τοῦ κυρίου *men who have risked* (*pledged* Field, Notes 124) *their lives for the name of the Lord* **Ac 15:26.** καὶ ἐὰν παραδῶ τὸ σῶμά μου ἵνα καυθήσομαι *and if I give up my body to be burned* **1 Cor 13:3** (Maximus Tyr. 1, 9i τῇ Αἴτνῃ αὐτοῦ παραδοὺς σῶμα; Syntipas p. 60, 11 πυρὶ σεαυτὴν παραδίδως). ὅταν παραδιδοῖ τ. βασιλείαν τῷ θεῷ *when (Christ) delivers the kingship to God* **15:24.**

ⓑ *hand over, turn over, give up* a person ([Lat. trado] as a t.t. of police and courts 'hand over into [the] custody [of]' OGI 669, 15; PHib 92, 11; 17; PLille 3, 59 [both pap III BC]; PTebt 38, 6 [II BC] al.—As Military term 'surrender': Paus. 1, 2, 1; X., Cyr. 5, 1, 28; 5, 4, 51.) τινά *someone* **Mt 10:19; 24:10; 27:18; Mk 13:11; Ac 3:13.** Pass. **Mt 4:12; Mk 1:14; Lk 21:16.** τινά τινι **Mt 5:25** (fr. one official to another, as UPZ 124, 19f [II BC]; TestAbr B 10 p. 115, 11 [Stone p. 78]); **18:34; 27:2; Mk 10:33b;** cp. **15:1; Lk 12:58; 20:20; J 18:30, 35; Ac 27:1; 28:16 v.l.;** Hs 7:5; 9, 10, 6; Pass. **Lk 18:32; J 18:36;** Hv 5:3f; m 4, 4, 3; s 6, 3, 6b; 9, 11, 2; 9, 13, 9; 9, 20, 4; 9, 21, 4. τὸν Ἰησοῦν παρέδωκεν τῷ θελήματι αὐτῶν **Lk 23:25.**—Esp. of Judas (s. Brown, Death I 211f on tendency of translators to blur the parallelism of Judas' action to the agency of others in the passion narrative), whose information and action leads to the arrest of Jesus, w. acc. and dat. ἐγὼ ὑμῖν παραδώσω αὐτόν **Mt 26:15.** Cp. **Mk 14:10; Lk 22:4, 6; J 19:11.** Pass. **Mt 20:18; Mk 10:33a.** Without a dat. **Mt 10:4; 26:16, 21, 23; Mk 3:19; 14:11, 18; Lk 22:48; J 6:64, 71; 12:4; 13:21.** Pass. **Mt 26:24; Mk 14:21; Lk 22:22; 1 Cor 11:23b** (NRSV et al. render 'betrayed', but it is not certain that when Paul refers to 'handing over', 'delivering up', 'arresting' [so clearly Posidon.: 87 fgm. 36, 50 Jac. παραδοθείς 'surrendered'] he is even thinking of the action taken against Jesus by Judas much less interpreting it as betrayal; cp. **Ac 3:13** παρεδώκατε). ὁ παραδιδοὺς αὐτόν (παραδιδούς με) *his (my) informer* (on the role of a מסור in Israelite piety s. WKlassen, Judas '96, 62–66; but Ac 1:18 the action of Judas as ἀδικία) **Mt 26:25, 46, 48; Mk 14:42, 44; Lk 22:21; J 13:11; 18:2, 5.** Cp. **Mt 27:3, 4; J 21:20.** The article w. pres. ptc. connotes the notoriety (cp. the use of traditor in Tacitus, Histories 4, 24) of Judas in early tradition. His act is appraised as betrayal **Lk 6:16,** s. προδότης.—τινὰ εἰς χεῖράς τινος *deliver someone/someth. into someone's hands* (a Semitic construction, but paralleled in Lat., cp. Livy 26, 12, 11; Dt 1:27; Jer 33:24; Jdth 6:10; 1 Macc 4:30; 1 Esdr 1:50. Pass. Jer 39:4, 36, 43; Sir 11:6; Da 7:25, 11:11; TestJob 20:3; ParJer 2:7 τὴν πόλιν; AscIs 2:14; cp. Jos., Ant. 2, 20) **Ac 21:11.** Pass. **Mt 17:22; 26:45; Mk 9:31; 14:41; Lk 9:44; 24:7** (NPerrin, JJeremias Festschr., '70, 204–12); **Ac 28:17.** ἡ γῆ παραδοθήσεται εἰς χεῖρας αὐτοῦ D 16:4b. Also ἐν χειρί τινος (Judg 7:9; 2 Esdr 9:7; cp. 2 Ch 36:17; 1 Macc 5:50; Just., D. 40, 2 ὁ τόπος τοῖς ἐχθροῖς ὑμῶν παραδοθήσεται) 1 Cl 55:5b.—W. indication of the goal, or of the purpose for which someone is handed over: in the inf. (Jos., Bell. 1, 655) παραδιδόναι τινά τινι φυλάσσειν αὐτόν *hand someone over to someone to guard him* (X., An. 4, 6, 1) **Ac 12:4.** W. local εἰς (OGI 669, 15 εἰς τὸ πρακτόρειόν τινας παρέδοσαν; PGiss 84 II, 18 [II AD] εἰς τ. φυλακήν): εἰς συνέδρια *hand over to the local courts* **Mt 10:17; Mk 13:9.** εἰς τὰς συναγωγὰς καὶ φυλακάς *hand someone over to the synagogues and prisons* **Lk 21:12.** εἰς φυλακὴν *put in prison* **Ac 8:3;** cp. **22:4.** Also εἰς δεσμωτήριον (of a transcendent place of punishment: cp. PGM 4, 1245ff ἔξελθε, δαῖμον, … παραδίδωμί σε εἰς τὸ μέλαν χάος ἐν ταῖς ἀπωλείαις) Hs 9, 28, 7. ἑαυτοὺς εἰς δεσμά *give oneself up to imprisonment* 1 Cl 55:2a. W. final εἰς (cp. En 97:10 εἰς κατάραν μεγάλην παρα[δο]θήσεσθε): ἑαυτοὺς εἰς δουλείαν *give oneself up to slavery* 55:2b (cp. Just., D. 139, 4). εἰς τὸ σταυρωθῆναι *hand over to be crucified* **Mt 26:2.** εἰς τὸ ἐμπαῖξαι κτλ. **20:19.** εἰς θλῖψιν **24:9.** εἰς κρίμα θανάτου **Lk 24:20.** εἰς κρίσιν **2 Pt 2:4.** εἰς θάνατον *hand over to death* (POxy 471, 107 [II AD]): **Mt 10:21** (Unknown Sayings, 68 n. 3: by informing on the other); **Mk 13:12;** Hm 12, 1, 2f; pass.: **ending of Mk in the Freer ms.; 2 Cor 4:11;** 1 Cl 16:13 (Is 53:12); B 12:2; Hs 9, 23, 5. π. ἑαυτὸν εἰς θάνατον *give oneself up to death* 1 Cl 55:1; fig. *hand oneself over to death* Hs 6, 5, 4. εἰς θλῖψιν θανάτου παραδίδοσθαι *be handed over to the affliction of death* B 12:5. π. τὴν σάρκα εἰς καταφθοράν *give up his flesh to corruption* 5:1.—ἵνα stands for final εἰς: τὸν Ἰησοῦν παρέδωκεν ἵνα σταυρωθῇ *he handed Jesus over to be crucified* **Mt 27:26; Mk 15:15;** cp. **J 19:16.**—π. alone w. the mng. *hand over to suffering, death, punishment,* esp. in relation to Christ: κύριος παρέδωκεν αὐτὸν ὑπὲρ τῶν ἁμαρτιῶν ἡμῶν 1 Cl 16:7 (cp. Is 53:6).—**Ro 8:32.** Pass. **4:25;** cp. B 16:5. π. ἑαυτὸν ὑπέρ τινος **Gal 2:20** (GBerényi, Biblica 65, '84, 490–537); **Eph 5:25.** παρέδωκεν ἑαυτὸν ὑπὲρ ἡμῶν προσφορὰν καὶ θυσίαν τῷ θεῷ *he gave himself to God for us as a sacrifice and an offering* vs. **2.**—π. τινὰ τῷ σατανᾷ εἰς ὄλεθρον τῆς σαρκός *hand someone over to Satan for destruction of his physical body* **1 Cor 5:5.** οὓς παρέδωκα τῷ σατανᾷ, ἵνα *whom I have turned over to Satan, in order that* **1 Ti 1:20** (cp. INikaia I, 87, 4f of someone handed over to the gods of the netherworld for tomb violation [New Docs 4, 165]; also the exorcism PGM 5, 334ff νεκυδαίμων, … παραδίδωμί σοι τὸν δεῖνα, ὅπως … ; s. the lit. s.v. ὄλεθρος 2; also CBruston, L'abandon du pécheur à Satan: RTQR 21, 1912, 450–58; KLatte, Heiliges Recht 1920; LBrun, Segen u. Fluch im Urchr. '32, 106ff). The angel of repentance says: ἐμοὶ παραδίδονται εἰς ἀγαθὴν παιδείαν *they are turned over to me for good instruction* Hs 6, 3, 6a (Demetr. Phaler. [IV/III BC] fgm. 164 FWehrli '49: Demosthenes παραδίδωσι ἑαυτὸν τῷ Ἀνδρονίκῳ to be initiated into dramatic art).—ἑαυτοὺς παρέδωκαν τῇ ἀσελγείᾳ *they gave themselves over to debauchery* **Eph 4:19.** ταῖς ἐπιθυμίαις τ. αἰῶνος τούτου Hs 6, 2, 3. ταῖς τρυφαῖς καὶ ἀπάταις 6, 2, 4. παρεδώκατε ἑαυτοὺς εἰς τὰς ἀκηδίας Hv 3, 11, 3 (s. ἀκηδία). Of God, who punishes evil-doers: παρέδωκεν αὐτοὺς εἰς ἀκαθαρσίαν *he abandoned them to impurity* **Ro 1:24** (for the thought cp. 1QH 2:16–19. See also EKlostermann, ZNW 32, '33, 1–6 [retribution]). εἰς πάθη ἀτιμίας *to disgraceful passions* vs. **26.** εἰς ἀδόκιμον νοῦν vs. **28.** παρέδωκεν αὐτοὺς λατρεύειν τῇ στρατιᾷ τοῦ οὐρανοῦ **Ac 7:42.** God, the All-Gracious One, is the subject of the extraordinary (s. lit. διδαχή 2) expression εἰς ὃν παρεδόθητε τύπον διδαχῆς = τῷ τύπῳ δ. εἰς ὃν π. (obedient) *to the form of teaching, for the learning of which you were given over* i.e. by God **Ro 6:17** (cp. the ins. fr. Transjordania in Nabataean times NGG Phil.-hist. Kl. Fachgr. V n.s. I, 1, '36, p. 3, 1 Abedrapsas thanks his paternal god: παρεδόθην εἰς μάθησιν τέχνης='I was apprenticed to learn a trade'. AFridrichsen, ConNeot 7, '42, 6–8; FBeare, NTS 5, '59, 206–10; UBorse, BZ 12, '68, 95–103; FDanker, Gingrich Festschr., '72, 94).

❷ **to entrust for care or preservation, *give over, commend, commit*** w. dat. (cp. PFlor 309, 5 σιωπῇ παραδ. 'hand over to forgetfulness'; Just., A II, 5, 2 τὴν … τῶν ἀνθρώπων … πρόνοιαν ἀγγέλοις … παρέδωκεν '[God] entrusted angels with concern for humans'; Tat. 7, 3 τῇ σφῶν ἀβελτερίᾳ παρεδόθησαν 'they were handed over to their own stupidity') παραδίδοσθαι τῇ χάριτι τοῦ κυρίου ὑπό τινος *be commended by someone to the grace of the Lord* **Ac 15:40.** Ἀντιόχεια, ὅθεν ἦσαν παραδεδομένοι τῇ χάριτι τοῦ θεοῦ εἰς τὸ ἔργον *Antioch, from which (city they had gone out) commended to the grace of God for the work* **14:26.**—παρεδίδου τῷ κρίνοντι *he committed his cause to the one who judges* **1 Pt 2:23.**

❸ **to pass on to another what one knows, of oral or written tradition, *hand down, pass on, transmit, relate, teach*** (Theognis 1, 28f passes on what he himself learned as παῖς, ἀπὸ τῶν ἀγαθῶν; Pla., Phil. 16c, Ep. 12, 359d μῦθον; Demosth. 23, 65; Polyb. 7, 1, 1; 10, 28, 3; Diod. S. 12, 13, 2 π. τινί τι pass on someth. to future generations εἰς ἅπαντα τὸν αἰῶνα; Plut., Nic. 524 [1, 5]; Herm. Wr. 13, 15; Jos., C. Ap. 1, 60 τὴν κατὰ νόμους παραδεδομένην εὐσέβειαν; PMagd 33, 5 of a report to the police concerning the facts in a case; Just.; A I, 54, 1 τὰ μυθοποιηθέντα) **Lk 1:2.** παραδόσεις **Mk 7:13** (of the tradition of the Pharisees, as Jos., Ant. 13, 297; cp. the rabbinic term מָסַר); **1 Cor 11:2.** ἔθη **Ac 6:14.** ὁ ἡμῖν παραδοθεὶς λόγος *the teaching handed down to us* Pol 7:2 (Just., D. 53, 6). ἡ παραδοθεῖσα αὐτοῖς ἁγία ἐντολή **2 Pt 2:21** (ApcMos 23 τὴν ἐντολήν μου ἣν παρέδωκά σοι). ἡ παραδοθεῖσα τοῖς ἁγίοις πίστις **Jd 3.** τὰ παραδοθέντα (Philo, Fuga 200) Dg 11:1. παρεδίδοσαν αὐτοῖς φυλάσσειν τὰ δόγματα *they handed down to them the decisions to observe* **Ac 16:4.**—(In contrast to παραλαμβάνειν [the same contrast in Diod. S. 1, 91, 4; 3, 65, 6; 5, 2, 3; PHerm 119 III, 22; BGU 1018, 24; PThéad 8, 25]) *pass on* **1 Cor 11:23a; 15:3;** AcPlCor 2:4; EpilMosq 2. W. a connotation of wonder and mystery (of mysteries and ceremonies: Theon Smyrn., Expos. Rer. Math. p. 14 Hiller τελετὰς παραδιδόναι; Diod. S. 5, 48, 4 μυστηρίων τελετὴ παραδοθεῖσα; Strabo 10, 3, 7; Wsd 14:15 μυστήρια καὶ τελετάς. ParJer 9:29 τὰ μυστήρια . . . τῷ Βαρούχ; Just., D. 70, 1 τὰ τοῦ Μίθρου μυστήρια παραδιδόντες; cp. 78, 6. Cp. Herm. Wr. 13, 1 παλιγγενεσίαν; PGM 4, 475) πάντα (πᾶς 1dβ) μοι παρεδόθη ὑπὸ τ. πατρός μου **Mt 11:27; Lk 10:22** (cp. Herm. Wr. 1, 32 πάτερ . . . παρέδωκας αὐτῷ [ὁ σὸς ἄνθρωπος is meant] τὴν πᾶσαν ἐξουσίαν; in Vett. Val. 221, 23 astrology is ὑπὸ θεοῦ παραδεδομένη τ. ἀνθρώποις.—For lit. on the saying of Jesus s. under υἱός 2dβ).—S. παράδοσις, end.

❹ **to make it possible for someth. to happen,** ***allow, permit*** (Hdt. 5, 67; 7, 18 [subj. ὁ θεός]; X., An. 6, 6, 34 [οἱ θεοί]; Isocr. 5, 118 [οἱ καιροί]; Polyb. 22, 24, 9 τῆς ὥρας παραδιδούσης) ὅταν παραδοῖ ὁ καρπός *when the* (condition of the) *crop permits* **Mk 4:29.**—On the whole word: WPopkes, Christus Traditus, '67.—M-M. EDNT. TW. Spicq. Sv.

παράδοξος, ον (παρά, δόξα; X., Pla.+; ins, pap, LXX; JosAs 28:1 cod. A π. θαῦμα [Bat.]; ApcSed 11:1 p. 134, 10 Ja.; EpArist 175; Philo; Jos., C. Ap. 1, 53 al; Just.; loanw. in rabb.) **contrary to opinion or exceeding expectation,** ***strange, wonderful, remarkable.*** κατάστασις τῆς πολιτείας Dg 5:4. σημεῖον 1 Cl 25:1. Subst. in pl. παράδοξα *wonderful things* (Lucian, Somn. 14; Aelian, VH 13, 33; Celsus 1, 6; Philo, Mos. 1, 212; Jos., Bell. 4, 238) **Lk 5:26;** GJs 19:2; 20:3.—OWeinreich, Antike Heilungswunder 1909, 198f.—DELG s.v. δοκάω. M-M. TW.

παράδοσις, εως, ἡ (παρά, δίδωμι; Thu.+; ins, pap, LXX, Philo, Joseph.; Just., D. 38, 2; Tat. 39, 1) 'handing down/over'.

❶ **handing over of someone to authorities,** ***surrender, arrest*** (Diod. S. 11, 33, 4) PEg[2], 29.

❷ **the content of instruction that has been handed down,** ***tradition,*** of teachings, commandments, narratives et al., first in the act. sense (Pla., Leg. 7 p. 803a; Ps.-Pla., Def. 416; Epict. 2, 23, 40; Philo, Ebr. 120; Jos., Vi. 361), but in our lit. only pass., of that which is handed down (SIG 704e, 12 εἰσαγαγὼν τὴν τῶν μυστηρίων παράδοσιν; Herm. Wr. 13, 22b τῆς παλιγγενεσίας τὴν παράδοσιν; Tat. 39, 1 τὴν τῶν Ἑλλήνων παράδοσιν; Orig., C. Cels. 1, 52, 15; Hippol., Ref. 9, 23, 1): of the tradition preserved by the scribes and Pharisees (Orig., C. Cels. 2, 1, 46; Hippol., Ref. 9, 28, 4). They themselves called it ἡ παράδοσις τῶν πρεσβυτέρων **Mt 15:2; Mk 7:5;** cp. vs. **3.** In conversation w. them Jesus calls it ἡ παράδοσις ὑμῶν **Mt 15:3, 6; Mk 7:9, 13** or even ἡ παράδοσις τῶν ἀνθρώπων vs. **8** (on Pharisaic π. s. ABaumgarten, HTR 80, '87, 63–77). Paul uses the latter term to characterize dissident teaching at Colossae **Col 2:8.** In looking back upon his Judean past he calls himself a ζηλωτὴς τῶν πατρικῶν παραδόσεων **Gal 1:14** (cp. Jos., Ant. 13, 297 τὰ ἐκ παραδόσεως τῶν πατέρων; 408. By this is meant the tradition of the rabbis ['fathers'; s. Pirqe Aboth], accepted by Pharisees but rejected by Sadducees). Of Christian teaching ὁ τῆς π. ἡμῶν κανών 1 Cl 7:2. Of Paul's teaching **2 Th 3:6** (used w. παραλαμβάνειν; cp. Iren. 3, 3, 3 [Harv. II, 11, 2]). ἀποστόλων π. Dg 11:6. Pl. of individual teachings **1 Cor 11:2** (w. παραδιδόναι); **2 Th 2:15** (s. ASeeberg, D. Katechismus d. Urchristenheit 1903, 1ff; 41f).—WKümmel, Jesus u. d. jüd. Traditionsgedanke: ZNW 33, '34, 105–30; ADeneffe, D. Traditionsbegriff '31, 1ff; JRanft, D. Ursprung des kath. Traditionsprinzips '31; LGoppelt, Tradition nach Paulus, Kerygma u. Dogma 4, '58, 213–33; BGerhardsson, Memory and Manuscript, etc. '61 (rabb. Judaism and Early Christianity); PFannon, The Infl. of Trad. in St. Paul, TU 102, '68, 292–307.—ὡς ἐκ παραδόσεως ἀγράφου εἰς αὐτὸν ἥκοντα παρατέθειται *he transmits (some other) things that came to him apparently from unwritten tradition* Papias (2:11); cp. Papias (2:7f; 14).—DELG s.v. δίδωμι A 1. M-M. EDNT. TW. Sv.

παραζηλόω fut. παραζηλώσω; 1 aor. παρεζήλωσα (Hesych. = παροξύνω) ***provoke to jealousy, make jealous*** (LXX; GrBar 16:2) τινὰ ἐπί τινι *someone of someone* **Ro 10:19** (Dt 32:21; cp. 4Q 372 I, 12). τινά *someone* (3 Km 14:22; Sir 30:3) **11:11** (RBell, Provoked to Jealousy '94). τὴν σάρκα *(brothers in the) flesh* vs. **14.** It is this mng., rather than a more general one such as *make angry,* that we have **1 Cor 10:22** ἢ παραζηλοῦμεν τ. κύριον *or shall we provoke the Lord to jealousy?* i.e. by being untrue to him and turning to second-rate divinities (daemons). The rhetorical structure here relies heavily on Gr-Rom. understanding that a δαίμων is a service-oriented divinity of a second order, a 'satrap', as Celsus later called it (Orig., C. Cels. 8, 35, 6). With sharp satire Paul says that God has reason to be jealous if the Corinthians engage in civil feasts where sacrifice is made to mere secondary divinities καὶ οὐ θεῷ (vs. 20), which is designedly ambiguous, referring either to deity generically (a god) or to the supreme deity of biblical tradition. The Corinthians are in effect insulting 'the Lord'.—DELG s.v. ζῆλος. M-M. TW.

παραθαλάσσιος, ία (θάλασσα; B-D-F §59, 1; Mlt-H. 158), **ον** (Hdt. et al.; SIG 709, 20 [107 BC]; IEph III, 680, 17; LXX.—B-D-F §123, 1; Mlt-H. 320) ***(located) by the sea/lake,*** of places (Hdt. 7, 109; Polyb. 1, 20, 6; 22, 11, 4; Ezk 25:9; 1 Macc 7:1; 11:8; 2 Macc 8:11; Jos., Bell. 1, 257) Καφαρναοὺμ ἡ παραθαλασσία **Mt 4:13;** cp. **Lk 4:31** D. Perh. AcPl BMM verso 13.—New Docs 4, 165. DELG s.v. θάλασσα. M-M.

παραθαρσύνω (Thu. 4, 115, 1; Diod. S. 14, 115, 3; Plut., Fab. 184 [17, 7], Crass. 560 [27, 1]; Herodian 3, 12, 4; 4 Macc 13:8; Jos., Ant. 12, 290; 14, 440. The later Attic wr. have παραθαρρύνω) ***encourage, embolden,*** w. acc. of the pers. to be encouraged (X., An. 3, 1, 39; 4 Macc 13:8; Jos., Ant. 12, 305) ApcPt 2, 5.—DELG s.v. θάρσος B.

παραθεωρέω (X.+) **to pay insufficient attention, with resulting deficiency in response,** ***overlook, leave unnoticed, neglect*** (so Hero Alex. I p. 410, 5; Diod. S. 40, 5; Dionys. Hal., De Isae. 18; Sb 1161, 38f [57/56 BC]=Mitt-Wilck. I/2, 70, 24;

BGU 1786, 5 [50 BC]) τινά *someone* pass. **Ac 6:1.**—DELG s.v. θεωρός. M-M.

παραθήκη, ης, ἡ (Hdt. et al.; Plato Comicus [V/IV BC], fgm. 158 K.; Polyb. 33, 6, 4; 9; Sext. Emp., Hyp. 3, 25, 189; Vett. Val. 39, 16; 67, 24; ins, pap, LXX; TestBenj 12:2; Ps.-Phoc. 135.—Instead of this, Attic prose has παρακαταθήκη; cp. Phryn. p. 312 Lob.; Nägeli 27) **property entrusted to another,** ***deposit*** (cp. our 'to lay by') in imagery (so as early as Hdt. 9, 45 ἔπεα; also Sextus 21, the soul), in our lit. only in the pastorals and always used w. φυλάσσειν, of the spiritual heritage entrusted to the orthodox Christian. τὴν π. φυλάσσειν *guard what has been entrusted* (acc. to CSpicq, S. Paul et la loi des dépôts: RB 40, '31, 481–502 [also s. lit. below], a legal t.t.) **1 Ti 6:20; 2 Ti 1:12, 14** (in the first and last passages v.l. παρακαταθήκη, q.v.). JRanft, art. 'Depositum' in RAC III, 778–84; RLeonhard, art. 'Depositum', Pauly-W. V/1, 233–36; WBarclay, ET 69, '58, 324–27.—DELG s.v. τίθημι. M-M. TW. Spicq.

παράθου, παραθῶσιν s. παρατίθημι.5

παράθυρος, ου, ἡ (since PMichZen 38, 11 [III BC] ***side entrance*** ἐλθὼν κατὰ τὴν παράθυρον τοῦ σταδίου *the lion approached the side door of the arena* AcPl Ha 2, 5.—S. DELG s.v. θύρα.

παραινέω impf. παρῄνουν; aor. παρῄνεσα LXX, ptc. παραινέσας LXX (Pind., Hdt. et al.; ins, pap, LXX, Philo, Joseph.; TestGad 6:1) **to advise strongly,** ***recommend, urge*** τινά (instead of the st. dat.; s. B-D-F §152, 3; Rob. 475; and s. Ps.-Callisth. 3, 4, 16 παρῄνουν τὸν Ἀλέξανδρον οἱ Μακεδόνες) w. inf. foll. (Jos., Bell. 5, 87f, Ant. 1, 201.—B-D-F §392, 1d; 409, 5; Rdm.[2] 121; 226) **Ac 27:22.** Abs. (SIG 89, 42) w. direct disc. foll. IMg 6:1; foll. by λέγων αὐτοῖς and direct disc. **Ac 27:9** (on the impf. παρῄνει s. B-D-F §328). τινί τι *recommend someth. to someone* (Oenomaus in Eus., PE 5, 25, 1; Philo, Poster. Cai. 13) ISm 4:1. τὶ (Chion, Ep. 16, 1 παρῄνουν ταῦτα) **Lk 3:18** D.—KWeidinger, Die Haustafeln: Ein Stück urchristlicher Paränese, 1928.—DELG s.v. αἶνος. M-M.

παραιτέομαι mid. dep.; impv. παραιτοῦ; impf. παρῃτούμην; 1 aor. παρῃτησάμην. Pass.: pf. 3 sg. παρῄτηται 1 Km 20:28; ptc. παρῃτημένος (Pind., Hdt.+).

➊ **to make a request,** ***ask for, request*** (for oneself).—ⓐ to ask for someth. in behalf of another *intercede for* τινά *someone* (Polyb. 4, 51, 1; Plut., Demetr. 893a [9, 8], Thes. 8 [19, 9]. Cp. BGU 625, 7) δέσμιον **Mk 15:6** (Appian, Bell. Civ. 2, 24 §91 Σκαῦρον τοῦ πλήθους παραιτουμένου=the crowd interceded for Scaurus).

ⓑ foll. by inf. w. the neg. μή (Thu. 5, 63, 3; s. B-D-F §429; Rob. 1094) παρῃτήσαντο μὴ προστεθῆναι αὐτοῖς λόγον *they begged that no further message be given them* **Hb 12:19** (the v.l. lacks μή). Although the net effect is a refusal, the focus of π. is on the request, which is not the case in 2, below.

➋ **to avert someth. by request or entreaty**—ⓐ If π. is used in connection w. an invitation, it becomes a euphemism in the sense ***excuse*** (Polyb. 5, 27, 3) pass. ἔχε με παρῃτημένον *consider me excused* (s. ἔχω 6) **Lk 14:18b, 19;** as a reflexive *excuse oneself* (Jos., Ant. 7, 175; 12, 197) vs. **18a** (for the various excuses used for declining an invitation, s. Aristot., fgm. 554 [VRose 1886]=Paus. Att., τ. 37:1: my wife is sick; 2: the ship is not ready to sail).

ⓑ ***decline, refuse, avoid, reject*** (CMRDM I, 164, 16f a wrestler is declared the victor when his opponents decline to engage him upon seeing his unclothed physique; Diod. S. 13, 80, 2 abs.)

α. w. acc. of pers. *reject, refuse someone* or *refuse to do someth. to someone* (EpArist 184; Philo, Det. Pot. Ins. 38; Jos., Ant. 7, 167) **Hb 12:25ab** (to hear someone). νεωτέρας χήρας παραιτοῦ *refuse (to enroll) widows who are younger* (than 60 years of age), when they apply for help **1 Ti 5:11.** αἱρετικὸν ἄνθρωπον παραιτοῦ **Tit 3:10;** but here the word prob. has the sense *discharge, dismiss, drive out* (cp. Diog. L. 6, 82 οἰκέτην; Plut., Mor. 206a γυναῖκα).

β. w. acc. of thing *reject, avoid* (Pind., Nem. 10, 30 χάριν; Epict. 2, 16, 42; PLond 1231, 3 [II AD]; Philo, Poster. Cai. 2 τὴν Ἐπικούρειον ἀσέβειαν; Jos., Ant. 3, 212; 5, 237) Dg 4:2; 6:10. γραώδεις μύθους παραιτοῦ **1 Ti 4:7.** ζητήσεις παραιτοῦ **2 Ti 2:23** (cp. Herm. Wr. in Stob. I 277, 21 W.= p. 432, 20 Sc. τὰς πρὸς τοὺς πολλοὺς ὁμιλίας παραιτοῦ).—οὐ παραιτοῦμαι τὸ ἀποθανεῖν *I am not trying to escape death* **Ac 25:11** (cp. Jos., Vi. 141).—New Docs 3, 78. DELG s.v. αἰτέω. M-M. TW.

παρακαθέζομαι mid. dep.; 1 aor. pass. ptc. παρακαθεσθείς (Aristoph., Pla., X. et al.) ***sit beside*** (Jos., Ant. 8, 241) παρακαθεζόμενοι *as they sat beside* (him) MPol 8:2. The aor. pass. w. act. reflexive sense (as Jos., Ant. 6, 235) *have seated oneself beside, have taken one's place beside* ἣ καὶ παρακαθεσθεῖσα πρὸς τοὺς πόδας τοῦ κυρίου ἤκουεν τὸν λόγον αὐτοῦ *who, after she had taken her place at the Lord's feet, kept listening to what he said* **Lk 10:39.** W. dat. of the pers. beside whom one sits down (Chariton 3, 3, 17; TestSol; TestJob 9:8 τῇ θύρᾳ; Jos., Ant. 6, 235 αὐτῷ; 16, 50) GPt 12:53.—DELG s.v. ἕζομαι. M-M.

παρακάθημαι (Aristoph., Thu. et al.; ins, pap, LXX) ***sit beside*** τινί (so mostly; the acc. is rare) *sit beside someone* Hs 5, 1, 1; 6, 1, 2; AcPl Ha 2, 10; 3, 2.—DELG s.v. ἧμαι.

παρακαθίζω (Pla. et al., mostly in the mid., as Jos., Ant. 19, 264) in our lit. only in act. ***sit down beside*** τινί *someone* (Diod. S. 23, 9, 5; Plut., Mar. 415 [17, 3], Cleom. 823 [37, 16], Mor. 58d; Job 2:13; TestSol 17:2 P [π. ἐμαυτόν]; TestJob) Hv 5:2. πρὸς τοὺς πόδας τινός **Lk 10:39 v.l.**—DELG s.v. ἕζομαι.

παρακαθίστημι (Isocr. et al.; ins, pap; 2 Macc 12:3; Jos., Ant. 14, 438) **to place or station beside,** ***to post*** φύλακας *guards* Dg 2:7 (cp. Diod. S. 4, 63, 3 φύλακας; Demosth. 4, 25; Plut., Fab. 7, 4 φυλακήν).—DELG s.v. ἵστημι.

παρακαλέω impf. παρεκάλουν; fut. παρακαλέσω LXX; 1 aor. παρεκάλεσα. Pass.: 1 fut. παρακληθήσομαι; 1 aor. παρεκλήθην; pf. παρακέκλημαι (Aeschyl., Hdt.+).

➊ **to ask to come and be present where the speaker is,** ***call to one's side***—ⓐ τινά w. inf. foll., to indicate the purpose of the call; so perh. παρεκάλεσα ὑμᾶς ἰδεῖν *I have summoned you to see you* **Ac 28:20** (but s. 3 below).

ⓑ *invite* τινά *someone* w. inf. foll. (this can be supplied fr. context) παρεκάλει αὐτὸν εἰσελθεῖν εἰς τὸν οἶκον **Lk 8:41.** παρεκάλει αὐτόν (i.e. εἰσελθεῖν) **15:28** (but s. 5 below). παρεκάλεσεν τὸν Φίλιππον καθίσαι **Ac 8:31** (cp. Jos., Ant. 12, 172). The content of the invitation follows in direct discourse **9:38;** introduced by λέγουσα **16:15.** Cp. ἀνὴρ Μακεδών τις ἦν παρακαλῶν αὐτὸν καὶ λέγων . . . βοήθησον ἡμῖν vs. **9.** Pass., w. inf. foll. παρακληθέντες δειπνῆσαι *when you are invited to dine* **Mt 20:28** D.—Some of the passages in 5 may fit here.

ⓒ *summon to one's aid, call upon for help* (Hdt. et al.) so esp. of God, upon whom one calls in time of need (Thu. 1, 118, 3; Pla., Leg. 2, 666b; 11 p. 917b; X., Hell. 2, 4, 17; Epict. 3, 21,

12; Jos., Ant. 6, 25; SIG 1170, 30f in an account of a healing: περὶ τούτου παρεκάλεσα τὸν θεόν. POxy 1070, 8f [III AD] τὸν μέγαν θεὸν Σάραπιν παρακαλῶ περὶ τῆς ζωῆς ὑμῶν; cp. the restoration in the pap letter of Zoilus, servant of Sarapis, in Dssm., LO 121, 11 [LAE 153, 4; the letter, ln. 8: ἐμοῦ δὲ π[α]ρ[ακαλέσαντος τὸν θεὸν Σάραπιν]) τινά: τὸν πατέρα μου **Mt 26:53.** ὑπὲρ τούτου τὸν κύριον παρεκάλεσα, ἵνα **2 Cor 12:8.** θεὸς . . . παρακαλούμενος ἀκούει *God heeds, when called upon* AcPt Ox 849, 27.

❷ **to urge strongly,** ***appeal to, urge, exhort, encourage*** (X. et al.; LXX) w. acc. of pers. **Ac 16:40; 2 Cor 10:1; 1 Th 2:12** (but s. 5 below); **5:11; Hb 3:13;** ITr 12:2; IRo 7:2. The acc. is found in the immediate context **Ac 20:1; 1 Ti 5:1** (but s. 5 below). Pass. **1 Cor 14:31.** τινὰ λόγῳ πολλῷ *someone with many words* **Ac 20:2;** also τινὰ διὰ λόγου πολλοῦ **15:32.** τινὰ δι᾽ ὀλίγων γραμμάτων IPol 7:3. W. acc. of pers. and direct discourse **1 Cor 4:16; 1 Th 5:14; Hb 13:22; 1 Pt 5:1;** direct discourse introduced by λέγων (B-D-F §420) **Ac 2:40.** W. acc. of pers. and inf. foll. (SIG 695, 43 [129 BC]) **11:23; 27:33f; Ro 12:1** (EKäsemann, Gottesdienst im Alltag, '60 [Beih. ZNW], 165–71); **15:30; 16:17; 2 Cor 2:8; 6:1; Eph 4:1; Phil 4:2; Tit 2:6; 1 Pt 2:11** (cp. Phlegon: 257 fgm. 36 II, 4 Jac. p. 1172, 19; ELohse, ZNW 45, '54, 68–89); **Jd 3** (the acc. is found in the immediate context, as Philo, Poster Cai. 138); ITr 6:1; IPhld 8:2; IPol 1:2a; Pol 9:1 al. W. inf. (acc. in the context), continued by καὶ ὅτι (s. B-D-F §397, 6; Rob. 1047) **Ac 14:22.** W. acc. of pers. and ἵνα foll. (PRyl 229, 17 [38 AD]; EpArist 318; Jos., Ant. 14, 168.—B-D-F §392, 1c; Rob. 1046) **1 Cor 1:10; 16:15f; 2 Cor 8:6; 1 Th 4:1** (π. w. ἐρωτάω as BGU 1141, 10; POxy 294, 29) **2 Th 3:12;** Hm 12, 3, 2; AcPl Ha 7, 32. The ἵνα-clause expresses not the content of the appeal, as in the pass. referred to above, but its aim: πάντας παρακαλεῖν, ἵνα σῴζωνται IPol 1:2b.—Without acc. of pers.: w. direct discourse foll. ὡς τοῦ θεοῦ παρακαλοῦντος δι᾽ ἡμῶν· δεόμεθα *since God as it were makes his appeal through us: 'We beg'* **2 Cor 5:20.** Paul serves as God's agent (like a 'legate of Caesar' Dssm. LO 320 [LAE 374]) and functions as mediator (like Alexander the Great, Plut., Mor. 329c διαλλακτής; cp. also the mediatorial role of a judge IPriene 53, esp. 10f; s. also CBreytenbach, Versöhnung '89, 64–66). W. inf. foll. **1 Ti 2:1.** Abs. **Ro 12:8** (mng. 4 is also poss.); **2 Ti 4:2; Tit 1:9; Hb 10:25; 1 Pt 5:12** (w. ἐπιμαρτυρεῖν); B 19:10.—W. acc. of thing *impress upon someone, urge, exhort* πολλὰ ἕτερα **Lk 3:18.** ταῦτα δίδασκε καὶ παρακάλει **1 Ti 6:2.** ταῦτα λάλει καὶ παρακάλει καὶ ἔλεγχε **Tit 2:15.** In the case of several of the passages dealt with in this section, it is poss. that they could as well be classed under

❸ **to make a strong request for someth.,** ***request, implore, entreat*** (H. Gk.: Polyb., Diod. S., Epict., Plut., ins, pap, LXX, EpArist, Philo; Jos., Ant. 6, 143; 11, 338) w. acc. of pers. **Mt 8:5; 18:32; Mk 1:40; 2 Cor 12:18.** πολλά *implore urgently* (4 Macc 10:1) **Mk 5:23.** τινὰ περί τινος *someone concerning someone* or *for someone* **Phlm 10** (for the constr. w. περί cp. POxy 1070, 8). Acc. w. direct discourse foll. (s. BGU 846, 10 παρακαλῶ σαι [= σε], μήτηρ· διαλλάγηθί μοι; PGiss 12, 4; ParJer 1:4 al.), introduced w. λέγων: **Mt 8:31; 18:29; Mk 5:12; Lk 7:4** (v.l. ἠρώτων). W. acc. of pers. and inf. foll. (PTebt 12, 21 [II BC]; 1 Macc 9:35; Jos., Ant. 6, 25) **Mk 5:17;** cp. **Ac 19:31.** Pass. **Ac 28:14.** W. acc. of pers. (easily supplied fr. the context, if not expressed) and ὅπως foll. (Plut., Demetr. 907 [38, 11]; SIG 563, 4; 577, 44f [200/199 BC]; UPZ 109, 9 [98 BC]; PFlor 303, 3; 4 Macc 4:11; Jos., Ant. 13, 76) **Mt 8:34** (v.l. ἵνα); **Ac 25:2;** IEph 3:2. W. acc. of pers. and ἵνα foll. (Epict. 2, 7, 11; PRyl 229, 17; EpArist 318.—B-D-F §392, 1c; Rob. 1046) **Mt 14:36; Mk 5:18; 6:56; 7:32; 8:22; Lk 8:31f; 2 Cor 9:5.** πολλά τινα, ἵνα *beg someone earnestly to* (cp. TestNapht 9:1) **Mk 5:10; 1 Cor 16:12.** W. acc. of pers. and μή w. subj. foll. IRo 4:1. W. acc. and inf. foll. **Ac 24:4;** pass. **13:42** (Just., D. 58, 1). Foll. by subst. inf. w. acc. (B-D-F §400, 7; 409, 5; Rob. 1068; 1085) **21:12.** παρεκάλεσα ὑμᾶς ἰδεῖν *I have requested to be permitted to see you* **28:20** (but s. 1a above). Abs., but in such a way that the acc. is easily restored fr. the context **Phlm 9** (ParJer 9:4; Just., D. 46, 2; 74, 2 [always παρακαλῶ 'please']; cp. New Docs 8 p. 24 ln. 7 [I BC]).

❹ **to instill someone with courage or cheer,** ***comfort, encourage, cheer up*** (Plut., Otho 1074 [16, 2]; Gen 37:35; Ps 118:50; Job 4:3) w. acc. of pers. (Sir 48:24; Jos., Bell. 1, 667; TestReub 4:4) **2 Cor 1:4b; 7:6a;** 1 Cl 59:4; B 14:9 (Is 61:2); Hm 8:10. παρακαλεῖν τινα ἔν τινι *comfort someone with someth.* **2 Cor 7:6b.** π. τινα ἐπί τινι *comfort someone w. regard to someth.* **1:4a.** π. τινα ὑπέρ τινος *encourage someone in someth.* **1 Th 3:2.** παρακαλεῖτε ἀλλήλους ἐν τοῖς λόγοις τούτοις *comfort one another w. these words* **4:18.**—Pass. *be comforted, receive comfort* through words, or a favorable change in the situation **Mt 5:4; Lk 16:25; Ac 20:12; 2 Cor 1:6; 7:13; 13:11;** *let oneself be comforted* **Mt 2:18** (Jer 38:15 v.l.). παρεκλήθημεν ἐφ᾽ ὑμῖν *we have been comforted concerning you* **1 Th 3:7.** ἐν τῇ παρακλήσει ᾗ παρεκλήθη ἐφ᾽ ὑμῖν **2 Cor 7:7.** διά τῆς παρακλήσεως, ἧς (on attraction, for ᾗ, s. B-D-F §294, 2; Rob. 716) παρακαλούμεθα αὐτοί *by the comfort with which we ourselves are comforted* **1:4c.**—W. acc. of thing τὰς καρδίας **Eph 6:22; Col 4:8; 2 Th 2:17;** pass. **Col 2:2.**—Abs. **2 Cor 2:7; Ro 12:8** (but s. 2 above). παρακαλεῖν ἐν τῇ διδασκαλίᾳ *encourage* (others) *with the teaching* **Tit 1:9.**—ἐλθόντες παραεκάλεσαν αὐτούς *(the officials) came and reassured them* **Ac 16:39** (s. 5 below).

❺ In several places παρ. appears to mean simply **treat someone in an inviting or congenial manner,** someth. like our 'be open to the other, have an open door': ***invite in, conciliate, be friendly to*** or ***speak to in a friendly manner*** (cp. 2 Macc 13:23; Ar. 15, 5 [χριστιανοὶ] τοὺς ἀδικοῦντας αὐτοὺς παρακαλοῦσιν) **Lk 15:28** (but s. 1b: the father tries repeatedly [impf.] to get the son to join the party); **Ac 16:39** (the officials are conciliatory, but 'apologize to' may be overinterpretation; s. 4); **1 Cor 4:13** (somewhat like our 'keep the door open'); **1 Th 2:12; 1 Ti 5:1.** These last three pass. may also fit in 1b.—CBjerkelund, Parakalō '67.—M-M. EDNT. TW.

παρακαλύπτω pf. pass. ptc. παρακεκαλυμμένος (Pla., Plut., LXX, Philo, Just.; Tat. 40, 1; Ath. 33, 2) ***hide, conceal*** fig. (as Ezk 22:26; Philo, Decal. 91 τ. ἀλήθειαν; Just., D. 107, 1; adv. παρακεκαλυμμένως: Just., D. 52, 1; 76, 2 and 6) ἦν παρακεκαλυμμένον ἀπ᾽ αὐτῶν*it was hidden from them* **Lk 9:45** (B-D-F §155, 3).

παρακαταθήκη, ης, ἡ (παρακατατίθημι; Hdt. et al. This is the real Attic form [s. παραθήκη], but is also found in Aristot., EN 5, 8, 5, 1135b, 4; Polyb. 5, 74, 5; Diod. S. 4, 58, 6; 15, 76, 1; Plut., Anton. 924 [21, 4]; Aelian, VH 4, 1; Vett. Val. p. 60, 21; ApcEsdr 6:3 p. 31, 7 Tdf. al. [in sense of 'soul']; Philo, Spec. Leg. 4, 30–38; Jos., Bell. 3, 372, Ant. 4, 285; ins, pap, LXX) **someth. given for safekeeping,** ***deposit*** **1 Ti 6:20; 2 Ti 1:14,** both **v.l.** (for παραθήκην. Used w. φυλάσσω as Socrat., Ep. 28, 6. S. Mishnah: Baba Metzia 3; cp. Ps.-Phocyl. 13 παρθεσίην τήρειν, πίστιν δ᾽ ἐν πᾶσι φυλάσσειν 'keep watch over a deposit, and in everything observe fidelity'; other reff. PvanderHorst, The Sentences of Phocylides '78, 120–21); Hm 3:2.—S. DELG s.v. τίθημι. M-M. TW. Sv.

παράκειμαι (X., Pla.; pap, LXX, JosAs, EpArist, Philo; Just., D. 99, 2; Ath. 6, 1) **to be present and ready for some purpose or action,** ***be at hand, ready*** (so Hom. et al.) in our lit. only w. dat. of pers. (Περὶ ὕψους p. 6, 10 V. [3, 5]; Lucian, De Merc. Cond. 26; PSI 542, 12 [III BC] ἐμοὶ οὔπω παράκειται κέρμα='I do not yet have any money at hand') **Ro 7:18, 21.** Of inclinations GMary 463, 19 (s. ὀργίλος).—JDerrett, Law in the NT, '70 (lit. p. 30, n. 1).—M-M. TW.

παρακέκλημαι, παρακληθῶ s. παρακαλέω.

παρακελεύω 1 aor. παρεκέλευσα (as a mid. dep. Hdt. et al.; pap; Pr 9:16; EpArist, Philo; Jos., Ant. 12, 300; Just., A I, 4, 7; 16, 5.—The act. Hippocr. et al.; Plut., Mor. 195a; Appian, Bell. Civ. 5, 89 §372; 4 Macc 5:2) **to urge strongly,** ***encourage, exhort*** τινά *someone* (Polyb. 16, 20, 8) IMg 14.

παράκλησις, εως, ἡ (παρακαλέω; Thu.+).—**❶ act of emboldening another in belief or course of action,** ***encouragement, exhortation*** (Thu. 8, 92, 11; Ps.-Pla., Def. 415e; Polyb. 1, 67, 10; 1, 72, 4; 22, 7, 2; Diod. S. 15, 56, 2; 2 Macc 7:24; Philo, Vi. Cont. 12; Jos., Vi. 87) **1 Th 2:3; 1 Ti 4:13; Hb 12:5.** W. οἰκοδομή: λαλεῖν παράκλησιν *speak words of exhortation* **1 Cor 14:3.** παράκλησις ἐν Χριστῷ *Christian exhortation* **Phil 2:1** (mng. 3 is also prob.). Likew. interpretation varies betw. 1 and 3 for **Ro 12:8** (s. παρακαλέω 2 and 4).—**2 Cor 8:17** could stand under 1, but prob. may better be classed w. 2. λόγος τῆς π. *word of exhortation* (cp. 2 Macc 15:11 ἡ ἐν τοῖς λόγοις παράκλησις; 7:24; Dio Chrys. 1, 9) **Hb 13:22;** cp. **Ac 13:15.** ἰσχυρὰν παράκλησιν ἔχειν *be greatly encouraged* **Hb 6:18.**

❷ strong request, ***appeal, request*** (Strabo 13, 1, 1; Appian, Liby. 51 §221; PTebt 392, 26; 36 [II AD]; PLond III, 1164d, 10 p. 159 [212 AD]; in pap VI AD oft. w. δέησις; 1 Macc 10:24; Jos., Ant. 3, 22) μετὰ πολλῆς π. δεόμενοι *request earnestly* **2 Cor 8:4** (μετὰ παρακλήσεως as Astrampsychus p. 28 Dec. 53, 5). παράκλησιν ἐδέξατο *he has accepted (my) appeal* vs. **17** (Jos., Vi. 193; s. 1 above; but also Betz p. 70f).

❸ lifting of another's spirits, ***comfort, consolation*** (Epict. 3, 23, 28; Dio Chrys. 80 [30], 6; Phalaris, Ep. 103, 1; Jer 16:7; Hos 13:14; Na 3:7; Job 21:2) **Ac 9:31; 2 Cor 1:4–7; 7:4, 13; Phil 2:1** (s. 1 above); **Phlm 7.** παράκλησις αἰωνία *everlasting* (=inexhaustible) *comfort* **2 Th 2:16.** ἡ π. τῶν γραφῶν *the consolation that the sciptures give* **Ro 15:4** (cp. 1 Macc 12:9 παράκλησιν ἔχοντες τὰ βιβλία τὰ ἅγια). ὁ θεὸς τῆς π. vs. **5;** cp. **2 Cor 1:3.** Of comforting circumstances, events, etc. **Lk 6:24; Ac 15:31; 2 Cor 7:7.**—In an eschatol. sense (Ps.-Clem., Hom. 3, 26 ἐν τῷ μέλλοντι αἰῶνι) προσδεχόμενος π. τοῦ Ἰσραήλ *looking for the consolation of Israel* (i.e. Messianic salvation; s. Is 40:1; 61:2) **Lk 2:25** (s. Dalman, Worte 89f; Billerb. II 124–26.—In later times Jews occasionally called the Messiah himself מְנַחֵם='comforter'; s. Billerb. I 66; Bousset, Rel.[3] 227).—**Ac 4:36** The name Barnabas is translated υἱὸς παρακλήσεως (s. βαρναβᾶς and s. also Dalman, Gramm.[2], 178, 4).—DELG s.v. καλέω. M-M. TW. Sv.

παράκλητος, ου, ὁ (παρακαλέω) originally meant in the passive sense (BGU 601, 12 [II AD] παράκλητος δέδωκα αὐτῷ='when I was asked I gave to him', but π. is restored from παρακλος, and the restoration is uncertain), 'one who is called to someone's aid'. Accordingly Latin writers commonly rendered it, in its NT occurrences, with 'advocatus' (Tertullian, Prax. 9; Cyprian, De Domin. Orat. 3, Epist. 55, 18; Novatian, De Trin. 28; 29; Hilary, De Trin. 8, 19; Lucifer, De S. Athanas. 2, 26; Augustine, C. Faust. 13, 17, Tract. in Joh. 94; Tractatus Orig. 20 p. 212, 13 Batiffol. Likew. many [Old Latin] Bible mss.: a c e m q J 14:16; a m q 14:26; e q r 15:26; e m q 16:7. Eus., HE 5, 1, 10 παράκλητος=advocatus, Rufinus. Field, Notes 102f; cp. the role of the 'patronus' in legal proceedings: J-MDavid, Le patronat judicaire au dernier siècle de la république romaine '92). But the technical mng. 'lawyer', 'attorney' is rare (e.g. Bion of Borysthenes [III BC] in Diog. L. 4, 50; SEG XXXVIII, 1237, 18 [235/36 AD]). Against the legal association: KGrayston, JSNT 13, '81, 67–82. In the few places where the word is found in pre-Christian and extra-Christian lit. as well it has for the most part a more general sense: **one who appears in another's behalf,** ***mediator, intercessor, helper*** (Demosth. 19, 1; Dionys. Hal. 11, 37, 1; Heraclit. Sto. 59 p. 80, 19; Cass. Dio 46, 20, 1; POxy 2725, 10 [71 AD]; cp. π. as the name of a gnostic aeon Iren. 1, 4, 5 [Harv. I 38, 8]; Hippol.; s. also the comments on 2 Cor 5:20 s.v. παρακαλέω 2). The pass. idea of παρακεκλῆσθαι retreated into the backgound, and the active idea of παρακαλεῖν took its place (on the justification for equating παράκλητος with παρακαλῶν s. Kühner-Bl. II 289). Jews adopted it in this sense as a loanw. (פְּרַקְלִיט. Pirqe Aboth 4, 11.—SKrauss, Griech. u. latein. Lehnwörter in Talmud, Midrasch u. Targum 1898/99 I 210; II 496; Dalman, Gramm.[2] 185; Billerb. II 560–62). In Job 16:2 Aq. and Theod. translate מְנַחֲמִים (=comforters) as παράκλητοι; LXX has παρακλήτορες. In Philo our word somet. means 'intercessor' (De Jos. 239, Vi. Mos. 2, 134, Spec. Leg. 1, 237, Exsecr. 166, Adv. Flacc. 13; 22), somet. 'adviser', 'helper' (Op. M. 23; 165). The Gk. interpreters of John's gosp. understood it in the active sense=παρακαλῶν or παρακλήτωρ (s. Lampe s.v. παράκλητος, esp. Eusebius of Caesarea, Theodore of Mopsuestia, and Ammonius; s. also Ephraem the Syrian in RHarris, Fragments of the Comm. of Ephrem Syr. 1895, 86). In our lit. the act. sense *helper, intercessor* is suitable in all occurrences of the word (so Goodsp, Probs. 110f). τίς ἡμῶν παράκλητος ἔσται; 2 Cl 6:9. πλουσίων παράκλητοι *advocates of the rich* B 20:2; D 5:2.—In **1J 2:1** (as AcJ in a damaged fragment: POxy 850, 10) Christ is designated as παράκλητος: παράκλητον ἔχομεν πρὸς τὸν πατέρα Ἰησοῦν Χριστὸν δίκαιον *we have Jesus Christ the righteous one, who intercedes for us.* The same title is implied for Christ by the ἄλλος παράκλητος of **J 14:16.** It is only the Holy Spirit that is expressly called παρ.=*Helper* in the Fourth Gosp.: **14:16, 26; 15:26; 16:7.**—HUsener, Archiv für lat. Lexikographie 2, 1885, 230ff; HSasse, Der Paraklet im J: ZNW 24, 1925, 260–77; HWindisch, Johannes u. die Synoptiker 1926, 147f, Die fünf joh. Parakletsprüche: Jülicher Festschr. 1927, 110–37; RAsting, 'Parakleten' i Johannesevangeliet: Teologi og Kirkeliv. Avh. etc. '31, 85–98; SMowinckel, D. Vorstellungen d. Spätjudentums v. Hl. Geist als Fürsprecher u. d. joh. Paraklet: ZNW 32, '33, 97–130 (supported now by 1QS 3:24f; 1QM 17:6–8); JMusger, Dicta Christi de Paracleto '38; EPercy, Untersuchungen üb. den Ursprung d. joh. Theol. '39; Bultmann, J '40, 437–40; NJohansson, Parakletoi: Vorstellgen. v. Fürsprechern f. d. Menschen vor Gott in d. atl. Rel., im Spätjudent. u. Urchristent. '40.; NSnaith, ET 57, '45, 47–50 ('Convincer'); WHoward, Christianity acc. to St. John '47, 71–80; WMichaelis, Con. Neot. 11, '47, 147–62; GBornkamm, RBultmann Festschr. '49, 12–35; CBarrett, JTS, n.s. 1, '50, 8–15; JDavies, ibid. 4, '53, 35–8; TPreiss, Life in Christ, '54, 19–25; OBetz, Der Paraklet, '63; MMiguens, El Paráclito (Juan 14–16) '63; GJohnston, The Spirit-Paraclete in J, '70; RBrown, The Paraclete in Modern Research, TU 102, '68, 158–65; JVeenhof, De Parakleet '77.—DELG s.v. καλέω. M-M. EDNT. TW. Sv.

παρακοή, ῆς, ἡ (cp. παρακούω 2; Pla., Ep. 7, 341b; Galen: CMG V 4, 2 p. 178, 14, Suppl. III p. 30, 2) **refusal to listen and so be disobedient,** ***unwillingness to hear, disobedience***

(so ApcEsdr 2:12 p. 26, 5 Tdf. [w. παράβασις]; Just.; Ps.-Clem., Hom. 2, 31; Synes., Ep. 67; Syntipas p. 97, 2; Photius, Bibl. p. 503, 5; PLond IV, 1345, 36; IV, 1393, 51 [both VIII AD]; Iren., 4, 37, 4 [Harv. II 288, 5]; Did., Gen. 90, 17; Theoph. Ant. 2, 25 p. 160, 3) **Ro 5:19** (cp. Just., D. 100, 4); **2 Cor 10:6;** Dg 12:2. W. παράβασις **Hb 2:2.**—DELG s.v. ἀκούω. M-M. TW. Spicq.

παρακολουθέω fut. παρακολουθήσω; 1 aor. παρηκολούθησα; pf. παρηκολούθηκα (Aristoph., X., Pla.+; ins, pap, 2 Macc, TestSol; JosAs 29:6; ApcMos 8; Philo, Joseph., Just.; Tat. 12, 5; Ath.) 'follow'.

❶ **to be closely associated w. someone viewed as an authority figure,** ***follow*** lit. of direct discipleship τοῖς πρεσβυτέροις Papias (2, 4); αὐτῷ: Jesus (2, 15).—Otherw.

❷ **to be attendant upon,** ***follow, accompany, attend*** w. dat. of pers. (τύχη ἡμῖν π. Demosth. 42, 21; Plut., Mor. 207e; πυρετοί μοι π. Demosth. 54, 11; βλάβη μοι π. PReinach 18, 15 [II BC]; 19, 12; PTebt 28, 2; PStras 22, 20. Cp. 2 Macc 8:11; Philo, Sacr. Abel. 70; Ath. 31, 1 [w. acc. and inf.]) σημεῖα τοῖς πιστεύσασιν ταῦτα παρακολουθήσει *these signs will attend those who have come to believe* **Mk 16:17** (v.l. ἀκολουθήσει).

❸ **to conform to someone's belief or practice by paying special attention,** ***follow faithfully, follow as a rule*** (SIG 885, 32 π. τῇ περὶ τὸ θεῖον τῆς πόλεως θεραπείᾳ; PTebt 124, 4 [I BC] τῇ αὐτῶν π. πίστει; 2 Macc 9:27 π. τῇ ἐμῇ προαιρέσει) διδασκαλίᾳ **1 Ti 4:6; 2 Ti 3:10.** This sense involves only a slight transference from 'follow with the mind, understand, make one's own' (Demosth. et al.; esp. a t.t. of the Stoics) w. dat. of thing (Polyb. 3, 32, 2; Epict. 1, 6, 13 of intelligent awareness as opposed to mere functioning, the diff. between animals and humans; Vett. Val. 276, 23; SIG 718, 9 [c. 100 BC]; Just., D. 114, 1).

❹ **to pay careful attention to someth. in a segment of time,** ***follow a thing, follow a course of events, take note of*** w. dat. of thing (Demosth. 18, 172 παρηκολουθηκότα τοῖς πράγμασιν ἐξ ἀρχῆς=one well acquainted with the affairs from the very beginning; 19, 257 ἀκριβέστατ᾽ εἰδὼς ἐγὼ καὶ παρηκολουθηκὼς ἅπασι κατηγορῶ=I bring my charges as one who has accurate knowledge and has followed everything; UPZ 71, 20 [152 BC] τῇ ἀληθείᾳ; Jos., C. Ap. 1, 53 personal acquaintance as opposed to information secured secondhand; 218 of inability to have a thorough grasp of certain writings: μετὰ πάσης ἀκριβείας … παρακολουθεῖν) ἐμοὶ παρηκολουθηκότι ἄνωθεν πᾶσιν ἀκριβῶς *to me, with a firm grasp of everything from the beginning* **Lk 1:3** (s. HCadbury, Beginn. II 501f; Exp. 8th ser., 144, 1922, 401–20; NTS 3, '56/57: 128ff *having been familiar with,* and M-M.; JRopes, JTS 25, 1924, 67–71.—GWhitaker, Exp. 8th ser., 118, 1920, 262–72; 119, 1920, 380–84; 121, 1921, 239ff; BBacon, Le témoignage de Luc sur lui-même: RHPR 8, 1928, 209–26. Luke does not specify the means whereby he was able to assert his thorough familiarity [a rendering such as 'research' or 'investigate' depends on interpretation of the context and not on the semantic content of π.]. It can be assumed that some of it was derived from the kinds of sources cited in vs. 2. S. also s.v. ἀνατάσσομαι).—LAlexander, The Preface to Luke's Gospel '93, 127–31.—DELG s.v. ἀκόλουθος. M-M. TW.

παρακούω (cp. παρακοή) fut. παρακούσομαι; 1 aor. παρήκουσα (Aristoph., Hdt. +).

❶ **to listen to something when one is not personally addressed,** ***hear what is not intended for one's ears, overhear*** (Aristoph., Frogs 750; Pla., Euthyd. 300d) τὶ *someth.* Ἰησοῦς π. τὸν λόγον *Jesus overheard what was said* to the centurion **Mk 5:36.** But some comm. prefer sense 2a.

❷ **to pay no attention to something that has been heard.**

ⓐ ***ignore*** τὶ *someth.* (Plut., Philop. 378 [16, 1] καὶ παριδεῖν τι καὶ παρακοῦσαι τῶν ἁμαρτανομένων, Mor. 522b ἔνια παρακοῦσαι κ. παριδεῖν) *Jesus ignored what they said* (s. 1).

ⓑ ***refuse to listen to, disobey*** w. gen. of pers. or thing (Polyb. 24, 9, 1; Epict. 2, 15, 4 τῶν λόγων; Lucian, Prometh. 2; PHib 170 [247 BC] ἡμῶν; Esth 3:8; TestSol 25:8 B μου; Jos., Ant. 1, 190; 6, 141; Mel., P. 48, 343 τοῦ θεοῦ) **Mt 18:17ab;** STellan: Laurentianum 35, '94, 91–134. τῶν ἐντολῶν (Tob 3:4; cp. UPZ 110, 130 [164 BC]) 2 Cl 3:4; 6:7. ἐπὶ τῷ ῥήματι **Lk 5:5** D. Abs. (TestDan 2:3) 2 Cl 15:5; Hv 4, 2, 6.—M-M. TW.

παρακύπτω 1 aor. παρέκυψα; inf. παρακύψαι (Aristoph., Hippocr. et al.; pap, LXX, En; JosAs 7:2 [cod. A and Pal. 364]; ApcMos 17; Philo) prim. 'bend over' (to see someth. better. Field, Notes 80f).

❶ **to bend over for the purpose of looking, w. focus on satisfying one's curiosity,** ***take a look*** (Phlegon: 257 fgm. 36, 1, 3 Jac.; POxy 475, 23 [II AD]; LXX) εἰς τὸ μνημεῖον *she stooped to look into the tomb* **J 20:11** (on π. εἴς τι cp. Lucian, Tim. 13; Pr 7:6; Sir 21:23). ἐκεῖ GPt 13:55. Abs. (Epict. 1, 1, 16; Aesop, Fab. 145 P.=251 H.; 203 Ch.; H-H. 150) παρακύψας βλέπει **Lk 24:12; J 20:5.** Cp. GPt 13:56.

❷ **to try to find out someth. intellectually,** ***look (in, into)*** fig. ext. of 1; εἴς τι *into someth.* (Philo, Leg. ad Gai. 56) εἰς νόμον τέλειον **Js 1:25** (here the expr. is suggested by the image of one who looks at oneself in a mirror vss. 23f). Of angels (cp. En 9:1), who strive to παρακύπτειν into the gospel of the suffering and glorified Christ, either: *gain a clear glance,* or: *steal a glance* at it (so POxy s. 1 above; cp. Demosth. 4, 24) **1 Pt 1:12.**—M-M. TW.

παραλαμβάνω (Eur., Hdt.+) 2 aor. παρέλαβον, 1 pl. παρελάβαμεν (AcPlCor 1:5), 3 pl. παρελάβοσαν **2 Th 3:6 v.l.** (B-D-F §84, 2; 14; Mlt-H. 209); 1 aor. inf. παραλάβαι (GJs 9:1); pf. inf. παρειληφέναι Papias (2, 2); fut. mid. παραλήμψομαι (on the spelling with μ s. Mayser p. 194f; Thackeray p. 108ff; B-D-F §101 p. 53; §Mlt-H. 246f; Reinhold 46f; WSchulze, Orthographica 1894.—On the mid. s. B-D-F §77; Rob. 356). Pass.: 1 fut. παραλημφθήσομαι **Lk 17:34f** (on the spelling with μ s. above on the fut. mid.); 1 aor. ptc. acc. sg. fem. παραλημφθεῖσαν Wsd 16:14; pf. παρείλημμαι Num 23:20.

❶ **to take into close association,** ***take (to oneself), take with/along*** (Gen 47:2; 2 Macc 5:5; TestAbr A 15 p. 95, 8f [Stone p. 38]; Jos., Vi. 66) **Mt 2:13f, 20f; 17:1; 26:37; Mk 4:36; 5:40; 9:2; Lk 9:28; Ac 15:39; 16:33; 21:24, 26, 32** (v.l. λαβών); **23:18;** Ox 840, 7; Hs 6, 3, 3. παραλαμβάνει ἕτερα πνεύματα ἑπτά *(the evil spirit) brings along seven other spirits (to help him)* **Lk 11:26** (Menand., Col. 123 S. [112 Kö.] ἐξήκονθ᾽ ἑταίρους παραλαβών). Pass. (Diod. S. 2, 40, 2) εἷς παραλαμβάνεται καὶ εἷς ἀφίεται *the one is taken* (by angels s. Mt 24:31), *the other is left* **Mt 24:40;** cp. vs. **41; Lk 17:34f.** π. τινὰ μεθ᾽ ἑαυτοῦ (μετὰ σοῦ, μετ᾽ αὐτοῦ. Cp. Gen 22:3) **Mt 12:45; 18:16; Mk 14:33.** W. acc. of pers., and w. goal indicated by εἰς *take (along) to, into* (Aelian, VH 2, 18; Num 23:27; Just., D. 99, 2) **Mt 4:5, 8; 27:27.** παραλήμψομαι ὑμᾶς πρὸς ἐμαυτόν *I will take you to myself* **J 14:3** (s. Dssm., LO 144 [LAE 166]; *with me to my home* AHumphries, ET 53, '41/42, 356). π. τινὰ κατ᾽ ἰδίαν *take someone aside* **Mt 20:17.** Also without κατ᾽ ἰδίαν w. the same purpose of private instruction **Mk 10:32; Lk 9:10** (here κατ᾽ ἰδίαν does not belong grammatically with παραλ.); **18:31.**—Of one's wife: *take* (her) *into one's home* **Mt 1:20, 24** (cp. Hdt. 4, 155; Lucian, Toxar. 24; SSol 8:2; Jos., Ant 1, 302; 17, 9). Joseph takes Mary from the temple and brings her into his own house GJs 9:1, 3; 13:1; 15:2; 16:1, 3.—*Take into custody, arrest* **Ac 16:35** D. Pass., GPt 1:2 παρ[αλη]μφθῆναι (another poss. restoration: παρ[απε]μφθῆναι, s. app. and παραπέμπω).

❷ **to gain control of or receive jurisdiction over,** ***take over, receive***—ⓐ τινά *someone,* a prisoner **J 19:16b** (cp. παρέδωκεν ibid. vs. 16a.—Both verbs in this sense in Appian, Bell. Civ. 6, 76 §310f).

ⓑ τὶ someth.—**α.** τὴν διακονίαν **Col 4:17** (SIG 663, 12 [c. 200 BC] the office of priest). τὶ ἀπό τινος Hs 6, 2, 6.

β. βασιλείαν ἀσάλευτον *receive a kingship that cannot be shaken* **Hb 12:28** (βασ. π.: Hdt. 2, 120; OGI 54, 5ff [III BC]; 56, 6; 90, 1; 8; 47; 2 Macc 10:11; Da 6:1, 29; Jos., Ant. 15, 16, C. Ap. 1, 145; Just., D. 32, 1. Of the ἅγιοι ὑψίστου Da 7:18).

γ. of a mental or spiritual heritage (Hdt., Isocr., Pla. et al., esp. of mysteries and ceremonies that one receives by tradition [s. παραδίδωμι 3]: Theon Smyrn., Expos. Rer. Math. p. 14 Hiller τελετὰς παραλ. Cp. Plut., Demetr. 900 [26, 1]; Porphyr., Abst. 4, 16; Herm. Wr. 1, 26b; CIA III 173; also the rabbinic term קִבֵּל) τὶ *someth.* **1 Cor 15:3** (w. παραδίδωμι, as Jos., Ant. 19, 31). B 19:11; D 4:13. παρελάβετε τὸν λόγον*you received the pronouncement* or *teaching* AcPl Ha 8, 25=Ox 1602, 38 and BMM recto 32 (on variations in the textual tradition s. Sander's note p. 85). παρ' ὃ παρελάβετε (=παρὰ τοῦτο ὅ) **Gal 1:9.** τὰ νόμιμα τοῦ θεοῦ Hv 1, 3, 4. τὸ πνεῦμα τὸ ἅγιον s 9, 25, 2. ἃ παρέλαβον κρατεῖν *things that have come down to them to observe* **Mk 7:4** (s. B-D-F §390, 3). τί παρά τινος (Pla., Lach. 197d, Euthyd. 304c σοφίαν παρά τινος. The constr. w. παρά is common in ins and pap; cp. Philo, Cher. 68) **Gal 1:12; 1 Th 2:13; 2 Th 3:6** (παράδοσιν παραλ.). AcPlCor 1:5. παρελάβετε παρ' ἡμῶν τὸ πῶς δεῖ περιπατεῖν. *you have learned from us how you ought to comport yourselves* **1 Th 4:1.** παρὰ τῶν ἐκείνοις γνωρίμων Papias (2, 2). ὡς παρέλαβεν παρὰ τοῦ ἁγίου EpilMosq 2 (w. παραδίδωμι).παρέλαβον ἀπὸ τοῦ κυρίου, ὃ καὶ παρέδωκα ὑμῖν **1 Cor 11:23** (s. ἀπό 5d). ἀπὸ (ὑπὸ) τῶν θυγατέρων Φιλίππου Papias (11:2; cp. 2:9). ὑπὸ τοῦ πρὸ ἐμοῦ ἀποστόλων AcPlCor 2:4 (w. παραδίδωμι).—παραλ. τὸν Χριστὸν Ἰησ. *accept Christ Jesus,* i.e. the proclamation of him as Lord **Col 2:6.**

❸ Somet. the emphasis lies not so much on receiving or taking over, as on the fact that the word implies agreement or approval, ***accept***

ⓐ w. regard to persons: οἱ ἴδιοι αὐτὸν οὐ παρέλαβον *his own people did not accept him* **J 1:11.**

ⓑ w. regard to teaching and preaching (Just., A I, 13, 1 μόνην ἀξίαν αὐτοῦ τιμὴν ταύτην παραλαβόντες) *accept:* τὸ εὐαγγέλιον ὃ εὐηγγελισάμην ὑμῖν ὃ καὶ παρελάβετε **1 Cor 15:1.** ἃ καὶ ἐμάθετε καὶ παρελάβετε **Phil 4:9.**—M-M. EDNT. TW.

παραλέγομαι (cp. λέγομαι in sense of 'choose, pick out'; Lat. lego as nautical term Vergil, Georgics 2, 44; sim. in Engl. 'pick' OED vb. IV, 7, b) ***coast along*** (Strabo 13, 1, 22) w. acc. of the place that one passes (Hanno [IV BC], Periplus 11: CMüller, GGM I [1855] p. 9=ln. 57 Oik., s. also appendix p. 35, 11; Diod. S. 13, 3, 3 τὴν Ἰταλίαν; 14, 55, 2) αὐτήν **Ac 27:8.** τὴν Κρήτην vs. **13.**—Field, Notes 144. DELG s.v. λέγω. M-M.

παραλείπω 2 aor. παρέλιπον; pf. παραλέλοιπα. Pass.: aor. ptc. gen. pl. παραλειφθέντων (Just., D. 14, 3). From the sense 'leave to one side, neglect' (Eur., Thu.+) it is a short step to ***leave out, omit,*** esp. in ref. to speech or writing (Eur., Hel. 773; 976; Thu. 2, 51, 1; Pla., Meno 97b; Strabo 1, 1, 23; Plut., Mor. 114b; Just., A I, 61, 1 al.) τὶ *someth.* (Diod. S. 3, 66, 5; Jos., Ant. 1, 17, Vi. 261) B 17:1; Papias (2:15).—M-M.

παραλημφθήσομαι s. παραλαμβάνω.

παράλιος, ον (ἅλς 'sea'; Aeschyl. et al.; ins, LXX; Philo, Agr. 81; Joseph.—Also of three endings: SibOr 3, 493) pert. to being (located) alongside the sea, as subst. ἡ παράλιος, sc. χώρα (Jos., C. Ap. 1, 60) ***the seacoast*** (Polyb. 3, 39, 3; Diod. S. 3, 15, 41; Arrian, Anab. 1, 24, 3; 2, 1, 1; Dt 33:19; Jos., Bell. 1, 409; TestZeb 5:5 w. v.l.—ἡ παραλία as early as Hdt. 7, 185 and predom. in Polyb.; Diod. S. 20, 47, 2; Arrian, Anab. 3, 22, 4; 6, 15, 4; LXX; Jos., Ant. 12, 292) ἀπὸ τῆς παραλίου Τύρου καὶ Σιδῶνος *from the seacoast district of Tyre and Sidon* **Lk 6:17** (cp. Diod. S. 11, 14, 5 ἡ παράλιος τ. Ἀττικῆς; Jos., C. Ap. 1, 61 ἡ παράλιος τ. Φοινίκης).—B. 32. DELG s.v. ἅλς. M-M.

παραλλαγή, ῆς, ἡ (παραλλάσσω; Aeschyl., Pla. et al.; 4 Km 9:20; EpArist 75. Rarely as an astronom. t.t. [Cat. Cod. Astr. VIII/3, 113]) ***change, variation*** **Js 1:17** (cp. TestJob 33:5 ἐν τῷ . . . αἰῶν . . . τοῦ ἀπαραλλάκτου).—DELG s.v. ἄλλος. M-M.

παραλλάσσω aor. impv. 2 sg. παράλλαξον and inf. παραλλάξαι LXX; pf. pass. ptc. παρηλλαγμένος (trag., Hdt. et al.; PHib 27, 50 [III BC]; Sb 4947, 4; LXX) **to change, with focus on being different,** ***change*** παρηλλαγμένος *strange, extraordinary, peculiar* (Polyb. 2, 29, 1; 3, 55, 1; Diod. S. 14, 70, 4; 17, 90, 1; Plut., Thes. 16 [34, 3], Them. 124 [24, 3]; Lucian, Dial. Deor. 10, 2; TestSol 1:3 L; Philo, Poster. Cai. 9) διάλεκτος παρηλλαγμένη *a peculiar language* Dg 5:2.—M-M. s.v. παραλλαγή.

παραλογίζομαι mid. dep.; 1 aor. παρελογισάμην (Isocr., Demosth. et al.; ins, pap, LXX; PsSol 4:11).

❶ w. acc. of pers. (Aeschin. et al.; Epict. 2, 20, 7; Dio Chrys. 10 [11], 108; PMagd 29, 5 [III BC]; PAmh 35, 12; LXX; Jos., Ant. 11, 275) ***deceive, delude*** **Col 2:4;** IMg 3:2. ἑαυτόν *deceive oneself* **Js 1:22.**

❷ w. acc. of thing ***reckon fraudulently, defraud,*** perh. *distort* (OGI 665, 15 δαπάνας . . . παραλογισ[θεί]σας of expenses fraudulently reckoned; Gen 31:41 τὸν μισθόν) τὰς ἐντολὰς Ἰησοῦ Χριστοῦ 2 Cl 17:6.—DELG s.v. λέγω. M-M.

παραλόγως adv. of παράλογος (Thu., Aristot. et al.; OGI 665, 33; TestAbr A 19 p. 102, 21 [Stone p. 52]; Jos., Bell. 4, 49) ***in an unreasonable manner*** (Polyb. 1, 74, 14; Celsus 5, 14; TestAbr A 20 p. 102, 21 [Stone p. 52]; Ath., R. 11 p. 59, 15) Dg 11:1.—DELG s.v. λέγω.

παραλυτικός, ή, όν (παραλύω; Diosc. 1, 16; Vett. Val. 110, 34; 127, 21; Hippiatr. I 433, 6; Papiri letterari greci, ed. ACarlini et al. '78, no. 32, 17: New Docs 3, 79; Just., A I, 22, 6) ***lame*** only subst. (ὁ) π. *lame person, paralytic* (Rufus [II AD] in Oribas. 8, 39, 8; Geopon. 8, 11) **Mt 4:24; 8:6; 9:2ab, 6** (on Mt 8 and 9 s. JKingsbury, CBQ 40, '79, 559–73); **Mk 2:3–5, 9f; Lk 5:24 v.l.; J 5:3** D; AcPl [Ha 8, 37] //BMM verso, 11 παρ[αλυτι]κοὺς ἐγ[είρων].—PSchmidt, Die Geschichte Jesu II 1904, 205ff; 261.—DELG s.v. λύω. M-M.

παράλυτος, ον (παραλύω) ***lame*** (Artem. 4, 67 p. 244, 2), only subst. ὁ π. *the paralytic* (Artem. 4, 67 p. 244, 4) **Mk 2:9** D; AcPl [Ha 8f]//BMM verso 40 (=PMich 3788 verso 9; παραλύτους for παραλυτικούς).

παραλύω (Eur., Hdt.+) fut. 3 sg. παραλύσει Gen 4:15; aor. 3 sg. παρέλυσε LXX. Pass.: fut. 3 pl. παραλυθήσονται; aor. 3 sg., pl. παρελύθη, -θησαν LXX; pf. ptc. παραλελυμένος **to cause to be feeble,** ***undo, weaken, disable*** (Hdt. et al.—Diod. S. 20, 72, 2 παραλελυμένος by old age) in imagery τὰ παραλελυμένα γόνατα *the weakened knees* **Hb 12:12** (Is 35:3; Sir 25:23; cp. PsSol 8:5.—Diod. S. 18, 31, 4 παραλελυμένος of a man who was lamed by a blow at the back of the knee). ἄνθρωπος ὃς ἦν παραλελυμένος **Lk 5:18; Ac 9:33** (Artem. 5, 51 ἐνόσησε κ. παρελύθη; 1, 50 p. 48, 11). Subst. ὁ παραλελυμένος *the paralytic* **Lk 5:24** (v.l. τῷ παραλυτικῷ); **Ac 8:7.**—M-M.

παραμένω fut. παραμενῶ; 1 aor. παρέμεινα, impv. παράμεινον (Hom.+) prim. 'remain, stay' (at someone's side).

❶ **to remain in a state or situation, *remain, stay (on)***

ⓐ abs. εὔχομαι παραμεῖναι αὐτόν *I wish him to stay on* IEph 2:1 (s. FPreisigke, Griech. Urkunden d. ägypt. Mus. in Kairo 1911 no. 15, 9).

ⓑ w. dat. of pers. *stay* or *remain with someone* (Hom. et al.; SIG 1209, 24f; 1210, 7f; PPetr III, 2, 21 [III BC]; PTebt 384, 21; 32; POxy 725, 43f; Gen 44:33) μενῶ καὶ παραμενῶ πᾶσιν ὑμῖν *I will remain and continue with you all* **Phil 1:25;** AcPl Ha 6, 35 (παραμ. has the sense *remain alive, go on living* Hdt. 1, 30; Dio Chrys. 3, 124; Artem. 2, 27; 67. For the connotation *serve* in Phil 1:25 s. 2 below). παρέμειναν τὰ πνεύματα αὐτοῖς *the spirits remained with them* Hs 9, 15, 6.—W. a prep.: παραμ. πρός τινα *stay with someone* **1 Cor 16:6** (v.l. καταμ.); μετά τινος Ox 404 (Hs 10, 3, 2, s. Whittaker p. 109) recto [μετὰ σοῦ παρα]μ̣ένουσι[ν (cp. σὺν Τρύφωνι παραμεινάντων Just., D. 56, 13). παραμ. εἰς ζωὴν αἰώνιον *endure to eternal life* Hv 2, 3, 2.

❷ **to continue in an official capacity, *continue in an occupation/office*** (Diod. S. 2, 29, 5) abs., of priests in the earthly sanctuary, who are prevented by death fr. remaining in office **Hb 7:23** (cp. Jos., Ant. 9, 273; cp. New Docs 4, 98). Of one who has showed interest in the perfect law **Js 1:25** (perh. w. the connotation of *serving;* s. Vitelli on PFlor 44, 19 and M-M.).—*Continue* in a state of being or quality παραμένουσα πραεῖα καὶ ἡσύχιος *it remains meek and quiet* Hm 5, 2, 3. παράμεινον ταπεινοφρονῶν *continue to be humble-minded* s 7:6.—M-M. TW.

παράμονος ον (παραμένω; a rare form of παραμόνιμος 'constant, steadfast'; Pind. et al.)

❶ **pert. to being of enduring quality, *lasting, constant, enduring,*** of things or circumstances (Plut., Mor. 114f πένθος; Vett. Val. p. 292, 30; Geopon. 1, 12, 5) δόξα (w. ἄτρεπτος) IEph ins; (w. αἰώνιος) χαρά IPhld ins; ἀφροσύνη Hs 6, 5, 2.

❷ of pers. (Hesych.=καρτερός), prim. pert. to being consistent in character, 'steadfast, constant'; in our lit. in an unfavorable sense, ***stubborn, persistent*** Hs 5, 5, 1. W. the dat. of that in which someone is persistent παράμονοι ταῖς καταλαλιαῖς αὐτῶν *stubborn slanderers* 9, 23, 3.—DELG s.v. μένω.

παραμυθέομαι mid. dep. (Hom. et al.; ins, pap; TestJob; TestAsh 6:6 [s. Denis app.]; ParJer 7:26; 2 Macc 15:9; Jos., Bell. 1, 627, Ant. 6, 38; Ath., R. 12 p. 61, 19) ***console, cheer up*** τινά *someone* (Thu. 2, 44, 1 al.) **1 Th 2:12** (JChapa, NTS 40, '94, 150–60). τοὺς ὀλιγοψύχους **5:14** (Arrian, Anab. 4, 9, 7 consolation for Alexander when he was depressed).—Esp. in connection w. death or other tragic events *console, comfort* w. acc. of pers. (Thu. 2, 44, 1 al.; Plut., Mor. 104c; SIG 796b, 13; 39f; 889, 20; IG V/2 no. 517, 13.—KBuresch, Consolationum a Graecis Romanisque scriptarum historia critica: Leipz. Studien z. klass. Phil. 9, 1886; FDanker, Threnetic Penetration in Aeschylus and Sophocles, diss. Chicago, '63) **J 11:31.** τινὰ περί τινος *console someone concerning someone* vs. **19.**—PJoüon, RSR 28, '38, 311–14. CClassen, WienerStud 107/8, '94/95, 327f, notes the rhetorical usage of π. and link w. παρακαλεῖν in var. pass.—M-M. TW. Spicq. Sv.

παραμυθία, ας, ἡ (παραμυθέομαι; Pla. et al.; ins, pap, LXX; TestSol 4:11 D π. τῶν θλιβομένων; JosAs ch. 11 cod. A [p. 54, 16 Bat.] τεθλιμμένων π.) **that which serves as encouragement to one who is depressed or in grief, *encouragement, comfort, consolation*** (Ps.-Pla., Axioch. 365a; Dio Chrys. 77 [27], 9 [the philosopher is sought out as a comforter]; Lucian, Dial. Mort. 15, 3; Aelian, VH 12, 1 end; SIG 796b, 44; PFlor 382, 65; IGA II, 318, 10=Sb 4313, 11; Wsd 19:12; Philo, Mos. 1, 137; Jos., Bell. 3, 194, Ant. 20, 94; cp. our 'talk it out' in coping w. grief) λαλεῖν παραμυθίαν (w. οἰκοδομή, παράκλησις) **1 Cor 14:3.**—New Docs 3, 79. DELG s.v. μῦθος. M-M. TW. Spicq.

παραμύθιον, ου, τό (παραμυθέομαι) **pert. to that which offers encouragement,** esp. as ***consolation, means of consolation, alleviation*** (Soph., El. 129; Thu. 5, 103, 1; Appian, Mithrid. 28 §110 πενίας τὴν σοφίαν ἔθεντο παραμύθιον='they used philosophy [only] as a means of consoling themselves for their poverty', or 'to alleviate their poverty'; Kaibel 951, 4; PFlor 332, 19; Wsd 3:18; Philo, Praem. 72; Jos., Bell. 6, 183; 7, 392) εἴ τι π. ἀγάπης *if there is any solace afforded by love* **Phil 2:1** (SEG 28, 953, 30 [I AD].—DELG s.v. μῦθος. M-M. TW. Spicq. Sv.

παράνοια, ας, ἡ (παρά, ἄνοια; Aeschyl., Hippocr. et al.; Plut., Cato Min. 68, 6; Ps.-Lucian, Macrob. 24; Philo, Cher. 69 al.) **state of being disordered mentally, *madness, foolishness*** **2 Pt 2:16 v.l.** (Vulg. has 'vesania', w. the same mng.).—DELG s.v. νόος.

παρανομέω aor. subj. 2 pl. παρανομήσητε Tat.; ptc. pl. dat. παρανομήσασιν 4 Macc 8:14 (Hdt.+) ***break the law, act contrary to the law*** abs. (Thu. 3, 67, 5; Pla., Rep. 1, 338e; SIG 218, 21f; POxy 1106, 9; LXX) παρανομῶν κελεύεις *in violation of the law you order* **Ac 23:3.** οἱ παρανομοῦντες *those who violate the law, the evil-doers* (Diod. S. 1, 75, 2; Artem. 1, 54 p. 51, 21; Ps 25:4; 74:5; Philo, Spec. Leg. 1, 155) 1 Cl 14:4 (cp. Ps. 36:38).—DELG s.v. νέμω. M-M. TW.

παρανομία, ας, ἡ (Thu.+; Diod. S. 20, 101, 2 [punished by a deity]; PSI 222, 6; BGU 389, 8; POxy 1119, 8; 10; 18; LXX, Test12Patr; ApcMos 21; Philo; Jos., Bell. 1, 226, Ant. 3, 314; Ath., R. 23 p. 76, 8) ***lawlessness, evil-doing*** ἔλεγξιν ἔχειν ἰδίας π. *be rebuked for his evil-doing* **2 Pt 2:16 v.l.** (for παραφρονίαν).—DELG s.v. νέμω. M-M. TW.

παράνομος, ον (trag., Thu.+; ins, pap, LXX; TestSol 6:4 P [adv. -νόμως TestSol 4:2 D]; TestLevi 14:6; ParJer 4:8; 21; EpArist 240; Philo; Jos., Ant. 18, 38, Vi. 26; 80; Ar., Just.; Mel., P.; Ath., R. 23 p. 76, 24) **pert. to being contrary to the law, *lawless.*** In our lit. only of pers., and subst. in pl. οἱ παράνομοι *the evil-doers* (Menand., Peric. 186 S. [=66 Kö.]; Socrat., Ep. 28, 6; Job 27:7; Ps 36:38; Pr 2:22 al.) 1 Cl 45:4 (w. ἄνομοι, ἀνόσιοι); Hs 8, 7, 6 (w. διχοστάται).—DELG s.v. νέμω. M-M s.v. παρανομία.

παραπέμπω (Hom.+ in var. senses) ***take away, escort*** (Demosth. et al.) GPt 1:2 παρ[απε]μφθῆναι (for this restoration s. app. In text a difft. restoration: παρ[αλη]μφθῆναι, s. παραλαμβάνω 1 end).

παραπικραίνω 1 aor. παρεπίκρανα, pass. παρεπικράνθην (s. πικρός and next entry; LXX; GrBar 16:2; Philo, Hesych.).

❶ **to incite to anger,** ***embitter, make angry, provoke,*** w. acc. of pers. (oft. LXX w. an acc. referring to God. Also Philo, Somn. 2, 177 παραπικραίνειν καὶ παροργίζειν θεόν). Pass. *become embittered, be made angry* (La 1:20 v.l.; Philo, Leg. All. 3, 114) Hs 7:2f.

❷ also without an acc., almost like an intransitive, ***be disobedient, rebellious*** (toward God; cp. Dt 31:27; Ps 67:7; 105:7; Ezk 3:9; 12:9 al.) **Hb 3:16** (KJV, Moffatt *provoke*).—DELG s.v. πικρός. M-M. TW.

παραπικρασμός, οῦ, ὁ (παραπικραίνω; 1 Km 15:23 Aq.; Job 7:11 Sym.; Pr 17:11 Theod.; Achmes 238, 5) 'embitterment', then ***revolt, rebellion*** against God (s. παραπικραίνω 2) ἐν τῷ π. *in the rebellion* (referring to the story of the Exodus, e.g. Ex 15:23; 17:7; Num 14; 20:2–5) **Hb 3:8, 15** (both Ps 94:8).—EbNestle, ET 21, 1910, 94.—DELG s.v. πικρός. M-M. TW.

παραπίπτω 2 aor. παρέπεσον, 1 pl. παρεπέσαμεν (B-D-F §81, 3; s. Mlt-H. 208f); pf. 2 sg. παραπέπτωκας Ezk 22:4 (trag., Hdt. et al.; pap, LXX; TestSol 10:8 P; Jos., Ant. 19, 285. In the pap mostly = become lost) lit. 'fall beside', then 'go astray, miss' (Polyb. 3, 54, 5 τῆς ὁδοῦ; fig. 12, 12, 2 τῆς ἀληθείας; 8, 11, 8 τοῦ καθήκοντος); abs. (X., Hell. 1, 6, 4; Polyb. 18, 36, 6=make a mistake) and in the sense **to fail to follow through on a commitment,** ***fall away, commit apostasy*** (Wsd 6:9; 12:2; Ezk 22:4) **Hb 6:6** (s. KBornhäuser, Empfänger u. Verf. des Hb '32). Also w. acc. of inner content (cognate; B-D-F §154; Rob. 477f) ὅσα παρεπέσαμεν *whatever sins we have committed* 1 Cl 51:1.—M-M. TW.

παραπλέω 1 aor. inf. παραπλεῦσαι ***sail past*** (so Thu. 2, 25 end; X., An. 6, 2, 1, Hell. 1, 3, 3; Pla., Phdr. 259a; Jos., Bell. 1, 456.—The word is found in the sense 'steer toward' Thu. et al., also Mitt-Wilck. I/2, 1 II, 2f [c. 246 BC]) w. acc. of place (Diod. S. 3, 40, 1 π. τοὺς τόπους=sail past the places 3, 45, 1) τὴν Ἔφεσον **Ac 20:16.**—M-M.

παραπλήσιος, ία, ιον (s. πλησίον; Hdt. et al.; PTebt 5, 240 [II BC]; 27, 72 [II BC]; PSI 491, 13; EpArist; Philo, Aet. M. 23; 90; Jos., Bell. 3, 82; 6, 388, Ant. 13, 63.—Also of two endings, as Polyb. 9, 41, 2; 18, 54, 2) **pert. to coming alongside or near,** ***coming near, resembling, similar*** (w. ὅμοιος, as Demosth. 19, 196 παρ. τούτῳ κ. ὅμοιον) ὅσα τούτοις π. Hm 6, 2, 5 (Polyb. 3, 111, 11 ταῦτα κ. τούτοις παραπλήσια). Neut. used as adv. (Thu. 7, 19, 2; Polyb. 3, 33, 7; 4, 40, 10; PTebt 5, 71 [II BC]='similarly') ἠσθένησεν παραπλήσιον θανάτῳ *he was so ill that he nearly died* **Phil 2:27** (v.l. θανάτου. Polyb. 1, 23, 6; Rydbeck 46–50.—B-D-F §184; Rob. 646. Cp. PMich 149, 4, 27 [II AD] παραπλήσιον νεκρῷ.)—DELG s.v. πέλας IV. Frisk s.v. πέλας. M-M. Spicq.

παραπλησίως adv. of παραπλήσιος (Hdt. et al.; Hos 8:6 [Quinta]; Papiri letterari greci, ed. ACarlini et al. '78, no. 32, 14: New Docs 3, 79; Tat.) ***similarly, likewise*** **Hb 2:14.** The word itself does not show clearly just how far the similarity goes. But it is used in contexts where no differentiation is intended, in the sense ***in just the same way*** (Hdt. 3, 104, 3; Diod. S. 1, 55, 5; 4, 48, 3; 5, 45, 5; Dio Chrys. 67 [17], 3; Maximus Tyr. 7, 2a; Philostrat., Vi. Apoll. 4, 18 p. 138, 21; Jos., Vi. 187, 233. Cp. Philo, Rer. Div. Her. 151 τὸ παραπλήσιον, Abr. 162; Arrian, Exped. 7, 1, 6 of Alexander the Great ἄνθρωπος ὢν παραπλήσιος τοῖς ἄλλοις).—M-M. Spicq.

παραποιέω aor. ptc. παραποιήσας (Just., D. 69, 1); pf. pass. ptc. παραπεποιημένος (Thu. et al.) **to produce an imitation designed to mislead,** ***imitate, falsify, counterfeit*** (Philostrat., Vi. Apoll. 2, 30 p. 72, 12; Just.) παραπεποιημένος (w. ἄδικος) *falsified* 1 Cl 45:3.

παραπόλλυμι act. in the sense 'destroy' (Plut. et al.), mid. **παραπόλλυμαι** 2 aor. subj. παραπόλωμαι ***perish, be lost*** (so Aristoph. et al.; Lucian, Nigrin, 13; PSI 606, 3 [III BC]; BGU 388 II, 10; POxy 705, 73; Philo, Ebr. 14; Jos., Ant. 11, 293) 2 Cl 17:1.—DELG s.v. ὄλλυμι.

παραπορεύομαι mid. dep.; impf. παρεπορευόμην; fut. 2 sg. παραπορεύσῃ Dt 2:18; aor. 1 pl. παρεπορεύθημεν Dt 2:14 (Aristot. et al.; pap, LXX; PsSol 2:11).

❶ **to move past a ref. point,** ***go/pass by*** (Polyb. 10, 29, 4; 10, 30, 9 al.; PPetr II, 13 [5], 3 [III BC]; PSI 354, 13; LXX) abs. **Mt 27:39; Mk 11:20; 15:29.**

❷ **to make a trip,** ***go (through)*** (Dt 2:14, 18; Josh 15:6) w. διά and the gen. (Dt 2:4; Zeph 2:15 v.l.) διὰ τῶν σπορίμων *go through the grain-fields* **2:23.** This does not mean that the party trampled grain in the process, but that they had grain on either side as they walked, quite prob. on a path. διὰ τῆς Γαλιλαίας **9:30.** From the perspective of the narrator the travelers would have Galilee on either side of them as they went.—DELG s.v. πόρος. M-M.

παράπτωμα, ατος τό—(s. next entry; Polyb. et al.; Diod. S. 19, 100, 3; PTebt 5, 91 [118 BC]; LXX; PsSol) in imagery of one making a false step so as to lose footing: **a violation of moral standards,** ***offense, wrongdoing, sin*** (Polyb. 9, 10, 6 of an offense with political implications; LXX).

ⓐ of offenses against humans **Mt 6:14, 15a v.l.; 18:35 v.l.**

ⓑ ordinarily of offenses against God—**α.** sing., of Adam's one offense (Wsd 10:1) **Ro 5:15ab, 17f.**—προλαμβάνεσθαι ἔν τινι π. *be detected in some wrongdoing* **Gal 6:1.** οἱ ἔν τινι π. ὑπάρχοντες *those who are involved in any wrongdoing* 1 Cl 56:1. ἐλέγχειν τινὰ ἐπὶ παραπτώματι *rebuke someone for wrongdoing* B 19:4 (s. D 4:3 in γ below). W. πειρασμός Hm 9:7.

β. sing., but collectively ἵνα πλεονάσῃ τὸ π. **Ro 5:20.** Of Israel's unbelief **11:11f.**

γ. mostly pl. **Mt 6:15b; Mk 11:25, 26; Ro 4:25; 5:16; 2 Cor 5:19; Eph 1:7; 2:5; Col 2:13ab; Js 5:16 v.l.;** 1 Cl 2:6; 51:3; 60:1; Hm 4, 4, 4; D 4:3 (s. α above), 14; 14:1. παραπτώματα κ. ἁμαρτίαι **Eph 2:1.**—DELG s.v. πίπτω C 1. M-M. TW.

παράπτωσις, εως, ἡ (s. prec. entry; Aristot. et al.) **a fall away from accepted standards of conduct,** ***wrongdoing, sin*** (Polyb. 15, 23, 5 al.) abs. (Polyb. 16, 20, 5 of an historian's blunder; Jer 22:21; Just., D. 141, 3f) 1 Cl 59:1.—DELG s.v. πίπτω C 2.

παραρρέω (Soph., X., Pla. et al.; LXX) 2 aor. pass. subj. παραρυῶ (Pr 3:21.—W-S. §5, 26b; Rob. 212) in imagery of flowing water ('flow by'), ***be washed away, drift away*** μήποτε παραρυῶμεν *lest we drift away* (intr.) **Hb 2:1** (CSpicq, L'Epître aux Hébreux, II '35, 25 disclaims a nautical metaphor, but s. EHilgert, The Ship and Related Symbols in the NT, '62, 133f).—DELG s.v. ῥέω. M-M.

παράσημον, ου, τό s. παράσημος 2.

παράσημος, ον (σῆμα 'mark, sign'; trag. et al.; 2 Macc 2:29; BGU V, 1, 194=Jur. Pap. no. 93, 194; Philo; cp. Jos., Ant. 18, 241)

❶ **pert. to being out of the ordinary,** ***peculiar, odd*** βίος *queer kind of life* Dg 5:2.

❷ pert. to being marked (on the side) so as to be distinguished, *marked* ἐν πλοίῳ . . . Ἀλεξανδρινῷ παρασήμῳ Διοσκούροις *in an Alexandrian ship that was marked by the Dioscuri* i.e. that had the Dioscuri (twin sons of Zeus, Castor and Pollydeuces) as its insignia **Ac 28:11** (on the dat. cp. Plut., Mor. 823b ἐπιφθόνοις παράσημος=making oneself noticed by hateful deeds). Yet it is hard to escape the suspicion that the text here, as so oft. in Ac, is damaged, and that it originally contained the noun τὸ παράσημον *emblem, insignia* situated on both sides of the prow of a ship (Plut., Mor. 162a τῆς νεὼς τὸ παράσημον; PLond II, 256a, 2 p. 99 [11–15 AD]; PTebt 486; Mitt-Wilck., I/2, 248, 19; Sb 423, 5. Note esp. CIL 3=ILS 4395 [22 AD] navis parasemo sopharia=a ship with sopharia as insignia). LCasson, Ships and Seamanship in the Ancient World, '71, 344f. S. Διόσκουροι.—B-D-F §198, 7. DELG s.v. σῆμα. M-M. (dat. absolute).

παρασκευάζω fut. 3 sg. παρασκευάσει (Just., D. 2, 4), inf. παρασκευάσειν (Ath. 31, 1); aor. παρεσκεύασα LXX. Mid.: fut. παρασκευάσομαι; aor. παρεσκευασάμην LXX. Mid. and pass.: pf. παρεσκεύασμαι. Pass.: aor. ptc. pl. neut. παρασκευασθέντα (2 Macc 6:21; Just., D. 57, 3) (s. next entry; trag., Hdt.+) **to cause someth. to be ready, *prepare,*** act. and abs. ἤθελεν γεύσασθαι. παρασκευαζόντων αὐτῶν *(Peter) desired to eat. While they were making preparations* (sc. τὸ δεῖπνον [the meal], which is used w. the verb Hdt. 9, 82; Athen. 4, 15, 138c; Jos., Ant. 1, 269; 7, 347; cp. also παρασκ. συμπόσιον Hdt. 9, 15; 2 Macc 2:27) **Ac 10:10.** Of pers. π. ἑαυτὸν εἴς τι *prepare oneself for someth.* (Horapollo 1, 11 p. 17) **1 Pt 2:8 v.l.**—Mid., to make oneself ready for some purpose *prepare (oneself)* εἰς πόλεμον (Diod. S. 18, 2, 4; Jer 6:4; 27:42.—Hdt. 3, 105; 9, 96; 99 παρασκευάζεσθαι ἐς μάχην, ἐς ναυμαχίην, ἐς πολιορκίην; Appian, Bell. Civ. 2, 105 §434 ἐς μάχην; Brutus, Ep. 29) **1 Cor 14:8.** Perf. *be ready* **2 Cor 9:2f.**—DELG s.v. σκεῦος. M-M.

παρασκευή, ῆς, ἡ (s. prec. entry; trag., Hdt.+; Ath. 15, 2) prim. sense 'preparation' (Hdt. 9, 82 and Polyaenus 7, 21, 6 τοῦ δείπνου; 7, 27, 3 πολέμου), in our lit. only of a definite day, as the *day of preparation* for a festival; acc. to Israel's usage (in this sense only in late pap, s. New Docs 3, 80; Jos., Ant. 16, 163; Synes., Ep. 4 p. 161d) it was Friday, on which day everything had to be prepared for the Sabbath, when no work was permitted **Mt 27:62** (CTorrey, ZAW 65, '53, 242= JBL 50, '31, 234 n. 3, 'sunset'. Against Torrey, SZeitlin, JBL 51, '32, 263–71); **Mk 15:42; J 19:31.** ἡμέρα παρασκευῆς **Lk 23:54** (D ἡμ. πρὸ σαββάτου, cp. **Mk 15:42**). παρασκευὴ τῶν Ἰουδαίων **J 19:42.** παρασκευὴ τοῦ πάσχα *day of preparation for the Passover* (or *Friday of Passover Week*) vs. **14.** For Christians as well παρασκευή served to designate the sixth day of the week (ESchürer, ZNW 6,1905, 10; 11f) *Friday* MPol 7:1; AcPl Ha 7, 14., and so in Mod. Gk. For Christians it is a fast day, as the day of Jesus' death D 8:1. On the chronology s. bibliog. in SPorter, Can Traditional Exegesis Enlighten Literary Analysis of the Fourth Gospel, in CEvans/JSanders, edd., Studies in Scripture in Early Judaism and Christianity '94, 416f n. 3.—B. 1008. Schürer index. M-M. TW.

παραστάτις, ιδος, ἡ (Soph., X. et al.; ins, Philo) fem. of ὁ παραστάτης prim. 'one who stands by or near'; a relatively high status term, the masc. form is used of various types of aides or officials. **One who lends support, *supporter, benefactor,*** of Phoebe **Ro 16:2 v.l.** S. προστάτις.—CPJones, Phoenix 39, '85, 30–35. New Docs 4, 241f. DELG s.v. ἵστημι.

παρασχών s. παρέχω.

παράταξις, εως, ἡ (τάσσω; Aeschin., Isocr., Demosth. et al.; ins, pap, LXX; Jos., Vi. 341 al.) prim. 'placing in order'.

❶ a line of marshalled persons, *array, procession* (lit. of soldiers: Lat. agmen. As a military term Diod. S. 1, 18, 5; TestSol 10:9 C) π. ἀνδρῶν Hs 9, 6, 1.

❷ an array of things, *outfit* pl. (w. ἀγροί and οἰκοδομαί) παρατάξεις πολυτελεῖς *costly establishments* or *furnishings* Hs 1:1. (W. ὁ πλοῦτος ὑμῶν) αἱ παρατάξεις πᾶσαι *all your furnishings,* perh. even more gener. *all your possessions* 1:8.—DELG s.v. τάσσω.

παρατείνω fut. 3 sg. παρατενεῖ Gen 49:13; 1 aor. παρέτεινα (Hdt. et al.; pap, LXX, Philo; Jos., Ant. 1, 105 χρόνον) ***extend, prolong*** τὸν λόγον *the speech* **Ac 20:7** (Aristot. Poet. 17, 5, 1455b, 2 λόγους; 9, 4, 1451b, 38 μῦθον).—DELG s.v. τανυ- E. M-M.

παρατηρέω impf. παρετήρουν; 1 aor. παρετήρησα. Mid.: impf. παρετηρούμην; fut. 3 sg. παρατηρήσεται Ps 36:12 (s. next entry; X. et al.; pap, LXX; TestSol 6:4 D; EpArist; Philo, Sacr. Abel. 98; Joseph.) gener. 'watch closely, observe carefully' (act. and mid. are used side by side w. the same mng.; B-D-F §316, 1; cp. Rob. 804–6).

❶ observe someone to see what the pers. does, *watch* (X., Mem. 3, 14, 4 w. indirect question foll.). Fr. the context this can take on the mng. *watch maliciously, lie in wait for.*

ⓐ τινά *someone*—**α.** act. (Polyb. 11, 9, 9; UPZ 64, 9 [156 BC]; Sus 16 Theod.) foll. by indirect question **Mk 3:2; Lk 6:7 v.l.**

β. mid. (Ps 36:12) **Lk 14:1.** W. indirect question foll. **6:7.**

ⓑ abs. (Vett. Val. 205, 13) *watch one's opportunity* (Field, Notes 74) **Lk 20:20** (v.l. ἀποχωρήσαντες).

❷ to stand guard, *watch, guard* τὰς πύλας *the gates*

ⓐ act. **Ac 9:24 v.l.**—ⓑ mid. **Ac 9:24.**

❸ to carefully observe custom or tradition, *observe scrupulously,* mid. w. acc. (Cass. Dio 53, 10, 3 ὅσα προστάττουσιν οἱ νόμοι; EpArist 246.—Pass. Jos., C. Ap. 2, 282) ἡμέρας καὶ μῆνας καὶ καιροὺς **Gal 4:10** (cp. the act. Jos., Ant. 3, 91 παρατηρεῖν τὰς ἑβδομάδας; 14, 264 παρατηρεῖν τὴν τῶν σαββάτων ἡμέραν; 11, 294). The use of the verb in Ox 654, 35 (Logion 5=GTh 6) seems to belong here also, but the badly damaged state of the text permits no certainty in interpretation.—M-M. TW.

παρατήρησις, εως, ἡ (παρατηρέω; since Pythag., Ep. 5, 1; Polyb., ins; Aq. Ex 12:42).

❶ act of watching or keeping an eye on someth. closely, *observation* (Polyb. 16, 22, 8; Diod. S. 1, 9, 6; 1, 28, 1 [both τῶν ἄστρων and in a technical sense]; 5, 31, 3 [observ. of the future by certain signs; for critique of such practice, s. Herod's comments to his troops Jos., B. 1, 377]; Περὶ ὕψους 23, 2 [observ. in the field of language]; Epict. 3, 16, 15; Plut., Mor. 266b; M. Ant. 3, 4, 1; Proclus on Pla., Cratyl. p. 40, 2 Pasqu.; Medical wr. of the observ. of symptoms [Heraclit. Sto. 14, p. 22, 10; Hobart 153]; IG IV^2/1, 687, 14 [II AD]; Jos., Bell. 1, 570) μετὰ παρατηρήσεως *with observation* (schol. on Soph., Ant. 637 p. 249 Papag.) οὐκ ἔρχεται ἡ βασιλεία τοῦ θεοῦ μετὰ παρατηρήσεως *God's Reign is not coming with observation,* i.e. in such a way that its rise can be observed **Lk 17:20** (HAllen, Exp. 9th ser., 4, 1925, 59–61; s. also ἐντός 1, esp. BNoack '48; AStrobel, ZNW 49, '58, 157–96, cp. AMerx, Die 4 kanonischen Evangelien II, 2, 1905, 345: cp. Ex 12:42).

❷ **act of following rules,** ***observance*** of legal prescriptions (Jos., Ant. 8, 96 παρατήρησις τῶν νομίμων; Ath., R. 15 p. 67, 1 δικαιοσύνης π.), esp. of festivals Dg 4:5 (παρατηρέω 3).—DELG s.v. τηρέω. M-M. TW. Sv.

παρατίθημι (s. παραθήκη; Hom.+) fut. παραθήσω; 1 aor. παρέθηκα; 2 aor. subj. παραθῶ, inf. παραθεῖναι **Lk 9:16** and -θῆναι **Mk 8:7 v.l.** Mid.: fut. παραθήσομαι Ps 30:6; 2 aor. παρεθέμην, impv. παράθου **2 Tim 2:2.** Pass.: 1 aor. παρετέθην. Prim. mng.: 'place beside, place before'.

❶ **to place someth. before someone,** ***set before,*** freq. of food (Hom. et al.; LXX; Abercius ins 13 τροφήν) τινί *someone* (Gen 18:8) **Mk 6:41; 8:6b; Lk 9:16.** τί *someth.* (Gen 43:31) **Mk 8:7.** τινί τι *someth. to someone* (Theophr., Char. 10; 30 ἄρτους ἱκανούς; Diod. S. 21, 12, 5; Gen 24:33; 2 Km 12:20; Demetr.: 722 fgm. 1, 14 Jac.) **Lk 11:6.** Abs. **Mk 8:6a.** π. τράπεζαν *set food* before one who is being entertained (Od. 5, 92; 21, 29; JosAs 7:1; TestAbr A 6 p. 83, 11 [Stone p. 14]; Jos., Ant. 6, 338; cp. Epici, "Alcmaeon" [VI BC] 2, 2 p. 33 B.=p. 76 K.; s. also 2a below) **Ac 16:34.** Pass. αὐτοῖς ἐκέλευσε παρατεθῆναι φαγεῖν κ. πιεῖν MPol 7:2. τὰ παρατιθέμενα *the food that is served/set before* (X., Cyr. 2, 1, 30; Aristot., Pol. 1, 6; Bel 21, cp. 18; Pr 23:1) τὰ παρατιθέμενα ὑμῖν **Lk 10:8;** cp. the sing. **1 Cor 10:27.**—Mid., of hospitality *set, spread* τράπεζαν (Diod. S. 34 + 35, fgm. 2, 35; Jos., Bell. 7, 264; TestAbr A 4 p. 81, 17 [Stone p. 10]) Dg 5:7.

❷ **to set forth in teaching—**ⓐ act. ***put before*** τὶ *someth.* (X., Cyr. 1, 6, 14; Lucian, Rh. Pr. 9 παραδείγματα al.; Ex 19:7; 21:1; Just., A I, 12, 11) παραβολὴν παρέθηκεν αὐτοῖς **Mt 13:24, 31.**

ⓑ mid., ***demonstrate, point out*** (POxy 33 verso III, 12; Jos., Vi. 6) διανοίγων καὶ παρατιθέμενος ὅτι **Ac 17:3.—28:23 v.l.**

❸ **to entrust for safekeeping,** ***give over, entrust, commend,*** mid. (Ps.-X., Rep. Ath. [the Old Oligarch] 2, 16; Polyb. 33, 12, 3; Plut., Num. 66 [9, 10]; oft. pap; Tob 1:14; 4:1, 20; 1 Macc 9:35; ApcEsdr 6:17).

ⓐ τί τινι *entrust someth. to someone* ᾧ παρέθεντο πολύ **Lk 12:48.** For safekeeping or transmission to others **1 Ti 1:18; 2 Ti 2:2.**

ⓑ τινά τινι *entrust someone to the care* or *protection of someone* (Diod. S. 16, 2, 2; 17, 23, 5; PGiss 88, 5 Ἀπολλωνοῦν παρατίθεμαί σοι; PSI 96, 2; Tob 10:13; Jos., Ant. 7, 387) Hs 9, 10, 6. Of divine protection παρέθεντο αὐτοὺς τῷ κυρίῳ **Ac 14:23;** cp. **20:32.** Sim. εἰς χεῖράς σου παρατίθεμαι τὸ πνεῦμά μου **Lk 23:46;** AcPl Ha 10, 22 (cp. Ps 30:6.—With this saying of Jesus cp. the subject matter of Ps.-Callisth. 3, 30, 15: in the face of death, Alexander prays: ὦ Ζεῦ, δέχου κἀμέ); cp. **1 Pt 4:19** and GDalman, Jesus-Jeshua, tr. PLevertoff, 1929, 209f.

❹ **to cause someth. to happen to someone,** ***do (to)*** φοβοῦμαι, μὴ ... ὑμῖν βλάβην παραθῶ *I fear that I may cause you harm* ITr 5:1.—M-M. TW.

παρατυγχάνω (Hom. et al.; ins, pap; Jos., Ant. 3, 100) ***happen to be near/present*** (PTebt 703, 242 [III BC]; POxy 113, 14; 76, 11; Jos., Ant. 2, 226; 17, 37 al.) ὁ παρατυγχάνων *anyone who comes by* (Polyb. 10, 15, 4) pl. οἱ παρατυγχάνοντες *those who happened to be there* (or simply *those who were there,* cp. PLond VI, 1912, 4 of a population that could not be present) **Ac 17:17.**—M-M.

παραυτά (also πάραυτα) adv. (for πάρ' αὐτά sc. πράγματα; Aeschyl., Demosth. et al.; Vett. Val. 152, 10; PTebt 13, 15 [II BC]; PLips 36, 6; New Docs 3, no. 101, 11; PGM 4, 2071 al. in pap) **pert. to a point of time immediately subsequent to another point of time,** ***on the spot, at once*** ITr 11:1.—KKontos in Ἀθηνᾶ 6, 1894, 369.—M-M s.v. παραυτίκα.

παραυτίκα adv.=παραυτά (trag., Hdt. et al.; SIG 495, 62; 68; oft. pap; Tob. 4:14; Ps 69:4; Jos., Ant, 9, 147; 12, 138; SibOr 13, 143; Just., D. 120, 6. On the spelling s. B-D-F §12, 3; Rob. 297) **pert. to a point of time immediately subsequent to another point of time,** ***on the spot, immediately, for the present*** used w. the art. preceding, as an adj. (Thu. 8, 82, 1 τὴν παραυτίκα ἐλπίδα; X., Cyr. 2, 2, 24 αἱ π. ἡδοναί; Pla., Phdr. 239a τὸ π. ἡδύ; Appian, Bell. Civ. 3, 127 §531 ἡ π. ὀργή=the anger of the moment; Philo, Praem. 103; POxy 1381, 191f τ. π. καιρόν) τὸ π. ἐλαφρὸν τῆς θλίψεως *slight momentary trouble* **2 Cor 4:17.**—M-M.

παραφέρω (trag., Hdt.+; ins, pap, LXX; TestAbr B 6 p. 110, 17 [Stone p. 68]; TestJob 46:1; EpArist 316; Philo, Joseph., Just.) impf. παρέφερον; 2 aor. παρήνεγκον, inf. παρενέγκαι **Lk 22:42 v.l.** (s. B-D-F §81, 2; Mlt-H. 211). Pass.: 1 aor. παρηνέχθην; pf. ptc. παρενηνεγμένος Hs 9, 4, 6. Lit. 'carry beside' or 'to the side'.

❶ **to convey someth. to a designated point,** ***bring up*** (pap; Judg 6:5 A; Jos., Ant. 7, 168) λίθους Hv 3, 2, 5; 3, 4, 2; s 9, 4, 4; 8a. Pass. s 9, 4, 5f; 8b v.l.

❷ **to take someth. away from a position,** ***take/carry away***

ⓐ lit. (of being carried off by the force of the wind or a stream of water: Diod. S. 18, 35, 6; Plut., Timol. 250 [28, 9]; Lucian, Hermot. 86; M. Ant. 4, 43; 12, 14) and pass. νεφέλαι ὑπὸ ἀνέμων παραφερόμεναι **Jd 12.**

ⓑ fig. *lead* or *carry away* fr. the path of truth, and so *mislead* (Pla., Phdr. 265b; Plut., Timol. 238 [6, 1]) pass. *be carried away* διδαχαῖς ποικίλαις (instrum. dat.) μὴ παραφέρεσθε **Hb 13:9.**

ⓒ *take away, remove* (Theophr., CP 2, 9, 9) τὶ ἀπό τινος *someth. from someone,* in imagery παρένεγκε τὸ ποτήριον τοῦτο ἀπ' ἐμοῦ *remove this cup from me* **Mk 14:36; Lk 22:42.**—M-M. Spicq.

παραφίημι (Theophr., HP 7, 4, 12; BGU 1011 III, 10 [II BC]) ***set aside, neglect*** **Lk 11:42 v.l.**

παραφρονέω (παρά, φρήν; Aeschyl., Hdt. et al.; Diod. S. 16, 78, 5; Mitt-Wilck I/2, 14 III, 14f; Zech 7:11; Just.; Cat. Cod. Astr. V/4 141, 31) **conduct oneself in an irrational manner,** ***be beside oneself*** (Aristoxenus, fgm. 35 a disgrace for an old man) παραφρονῶν λαλῶ *I am talking as if I were beside myself* or *irrational* **2 Cor 11:23.**—Schmidt, Syn. IV 228–48. DELG s.v. φρήν. M-M.

παραφρονία, ας, ἡ (παράφρων 'senseless') (hapax leg.) **state or condition of irrationality,** ***madness, insanity*** of Balaam **2 Pt 2:16** (vv.ll. παράνοια, παρανομία, παραφροσύνη).—DELG s.v. φρήν. M-M.

παραφροσύνη, ης, ἡ (παράφρων 'senseless'; Hippocr., Pla., Plut., Philo; Jos., Ant. 19, 284) **state or condition of irrationality,** ***madness, insanity*** **2 Pt 2:16 v.l.**—DELG s.v. φρήν.

παραφυάδιον, ου, τό (Hesych. s.v. ἑρμαῖ; SibOr 3, 396–400) dim. of παραφυάς (q.v.), **someth. little growing off the side,** ***a little offshoot*** μικρὸν κέρας παραφυάδιον *a little horn as an offshoot* B 4:5 (cp. Da 7:8).

παραφυάς, άδος, ἡ (παραφύω 'produce at the side', s. prec. entry; Hippocr., Aristot. et al.; LXX; En 26:1) **someth. growing off the side,** ***offshoot, side growth.***

ⓐ (Theophr., HP 2, 2, 4; Nicander, fgm. 80 π. of a palm tree; Philo, Plant. 4) Hs 8, 1, 17f; 8, 2, 1f; 8, 3, 7; 8, 4, 6; 8, 5, 2; 5f.

ⓑ in imagery (Aristot., EN 1, 4 [1096] al.; 4 Macc 1:28), of sectarians who, as side growths of a plant created by God, can bear nothing but death-dealing fruit ITr 11:1.—DELG s.v. φύομαι.

παραχαράσσω (-ττω Tat. 40, 1; fig.='counterfeit', 'debase' Plut., Mor. 332b; Lucian, Demon. 5; Herm. Wr. 488, 12 Sc.; Philo, Omn. Prob. Lib. 4 v.l.; Jos., Bell. 1, 529, Ant. 15, 315; Just., D. 82, 3; Tat. 40, 1. PCairMasp 353, 20. Lit.: 'to stamp beside') **to debase money by altering the original impression,** ***debase/counterfeit*** lit. (Dio Chrys. 14 [31], 24 οἱ παραχαράττοντες τὸ νόμισμα; Cecaumen. p. 51, 22) Hs 1:11.—Fig. τῶν χαρασσόντων τὰ λόγια αὐτοῦ *who falsify his words* AcPlCor 2:3.

παραχειμάζω fut. παραχειμάσω; 1 aor. παρεχείμασα; pf. ptc. παρακεχειμακώς (s. next entry; since Hyperid., fgm. 260; Demosth.; Polyb. 2, 64, 1; Diod. S. 19, 34, 8; Plut., Sertor. 569 [3, 5]; Cass. Dio 40, 4; OGI 544, 30f) ***spend the winter, to winter*** abs. **Ac 27:12.** W. the place given: πρὸς ὑμᾶς **1 Cor 16:6.** ἐκεῖ **Tit 3:12;** of a ship ἐν τῇ νήσῳ **Ac 28:11.**—DELG s.v. χεῖμα. M-M.

παραχειμασία, ας, ἡ (s. παραχειμάζω; Polyb. 3, 34, 6; 3, 35, 1; Diod. S. 19, 68, 5; Jos., Ant. 14, 195; SIG 762, 16 [48 BC]; s. also New Docs 4, 166) **experience of spending winter in a place,** ***wintering*** ἀνεύθετος πρὸς παραχειμασίαν *not suitable for wintering* **Ac 27:12.**—DELG s.v. χεῖμα. M-M.

παραχέω inf. παραχέειν; impf. παρέχεον (Hdt. et al.; PMagd 33, 2 [III BC]) ***pour near/on*** ὕδωρ (Plut., Mor. 235a) w. dat. *pour water on someth.* Hs 8, 2, 7f.

παραχράομαι 1 aor. παρεχρησάμην (Hdt. et al.; PRyl 144, 17 [I AD]) ***misuse*** (Arist. in Plut., Mor. 527a; Just., A I, 49, 5) w. dat. of thing αὐτῇ (of human σάρξ) Hs 5, 7, 2 (cp. Polyb. 13, 4, 5 τῷ σώματι). Abs. *misuse* it (Philo, De Jos. 144) **1 Cor 7:31 v.l.** for καταχρ-.—DELG s.v. χρή p. 1274.

παραχρῆμα adv. (Hdt., Thu., Aristoph.+. On the spelling s. B-D-F §12, 3; Rob. 297; on its use §102, 2; Rob. 550) **pert. to a point of time that is immediately subsequent to an action,** ***at once, immediately*** **Mt 21:19f.** Elsewh. in the NT only in Lk and Ac: **Lk 1:64; 4:39; 5:25; 8:44, 47, 55; 13:13; 18:43; 19:11; 22:60; Ac 3:7; 5:10; 12:23; 13:11; 16:26, 33; 22:29 v.l.**—B 12:7; MPol 13:1; GJs 19:2; 20:4 codd.; 22:3. Pleonastically εὐθέως παραχρῆμα (X. et al.; PStras 35, 17 εὐθὺς καὶ παραχρῆμα) **Ac 14:10** D (B-D-F §484; cp. Rob. 1205).—DDaube, The Sudden in Scripture '64, 38–46 (but s. Rydbeck 174–76). S. εὐθέως.—DELG s.v. χρῆμα. M-M.

πάρδαλις, εως, ἡ (Hom. et al.; Herm. Wr. 510, 2 Sc.; PGM 7, 783; LXX; TestAbr A 19 p. 102, 12 [Stone p. 52]; Philo; Jos., Ant. 12, 146; Test12Patr; Sib Or 3, 737; 789; loanw. in rabb.) ***leopard,*** an apocalyptic θηρίον ὅμοιον παρδάλει **Rv 13:2** (cp. Da 7:6).—DELG. M-M.

παρέβην s. παραβαίνω.

παρεγγυάω (ἐγγυάω 'hand over as a pledge') 1 aor. παρηγγύησα (trag., Hdt. et al.; pap; not LXX.—Used in var. senses of something entrusted or passed on to another) ***exhort, command*** (so X. et al.) Papias (4).—DELG s.v. *γύη. Frisk s.v. ἐγγύη.

παρεδρεύω (πάρεδρος, cp. ἕδρα 'seat'; Eur. et al.; ins, pap; TestAbr A 2 p. 78, 14 [Stone p. 4]; TestDan 5:6; Pr 1:21; 8:3; EpArist 81) 'sit beside, wait on', then ***apply oneself to, concern oneself with*** τινί *someth.* (Athen. 7, 283c οἱ ταῖς κητείαις παρεδρεύοντες ἄνδρες; IG XIV, 1728, 7 of one who applied himself to the liberal arts) of Judeans π. ἄστροις καὶ σελήνῃ *watch the stars and moon closely* Dg 4:5. τῷ θυσιαστηρίῳ π. *serve regularly at the altar* i.e. do the work of a priest (παρεδρεύω in cultic use Diod. S. 4, 3, 3 π. τῷ θεῷ; Vett. Val. 210, 3 ἐν ἱεροῖς τόποις ἢ ναοῖς παρεδρεύειν; SIG 633, 20 [180 BC] τοῦ ταμίου τοῦ παρεδρεύοντος ἐν τῷ ἱερῷ θυσίας ποιήσασθαι; 695, 27f [II BC] παρεδρευέτωσαν ἐν τῷ ἱερῷ τὴν ἐπιβάλλουσαν τιμὴν καὶ παρεδρείαν ποιούμεναι τῆς θεοῦ) **1 Cor 9:13.**—In a fragmentary context AcPl Ha 5, 33f.—DELG s.v. ἕζομαι. M-M.

πάρεδρος, ον (s. παρεδρεύω; Pind. et al.; OGI 185, 9 [I BC] 'assessor'; Wsd 6:14; 9:4; TestSol 3:5; Just., A I, 18, 3 [of familiar spirits, on these s. MSmith, HTR 73, '80, 241–49]) 'sitting beside'; subst. **πάρεδρος, ου, ὁ** ***attendant, assistant*** (Hdt. et al.; ins; PGM 1, 54; 96; 4, 1841; 1850; 7, 884 al.) of believers θεοῦ (οἰκονόμοι καὶ) πάρεδροι (καὶ ὑπηρέται) IPol 6:1 (Sextus 230a the pious man as πάρεδρος θεῷ; cp. PGM 4, 1347 transcendent beings as πάρεδροι τοῦ μεγάλου θεοῦ; Ael. Aristid. 37, 5 K.=2 p. 14 D.: Athena as π. of Zeus; Philo, Spec. Leg. 4, 201).—DELG s.v. ἕζομαι. M-M s.v. παρεδρεύω.

παρεῖδον s. παροράω.

παρειμένος s. παρίημι.

πάρειμι (εἰμί) ptc. παρών; impf. 3 sg. παρῆν, pl. παρῆσαν; fut. 3 sing. παρέσται **Rv 17:8.**—(Hom.+).

❶ ***be present***—ⓐ of pers. **J 11:28; Rv 17:8;** GPt 10:38. ἰδοὺ πάρειμι *here I am* (En 106:8) 2 Cl 15:3; B 3:5 (both Is 58:9). παρών (opp. ἀπών; Wsd 11:11; 14:17) *(being) present* (Himerius, Or. 44 [=Or. 8], 1 παρὼν μόνῳ τῷ σώματι) **1 Cor 5:3ab; 2 Cor 10:2, 11; 13:2, 10;** ISm 9:2; IRo 7:2; IMg 15. ἀκούσας αὐτοὺς παρόντας *when he heard that they were present* MPol 7:2. μηδεὶς τῶν παρόντων ὑμῶν *none of you who are present* IRo 7:1 (Just., A I, 65, 4 ἑκάστῳ τῶν παρόντων).—W. a prep.: ἐνώπιον τοῦ θεοῦ πάρεσμεν *we are here in the presence of God* **Ac 10:33.** ἐπὶ σοῦ παρεῖναι *be here before you* **24:19.** π. πρός τινα *be present with someone* (UPZ 71, 18 [152 BC]) **2 Cor 11:9; Gal 4:18, 20.** οἱ παρόντες *those (who were) present* (Appian, Hann. 39 §166; SIG 665, 38; 1044, 43 τῶν τε παρόντων καὶ τῶν ἀπόντων; 1047, 19; 3 Macc 1:13) MPol 9:1. παρόντες εἰς δόξαν θεοῦ *who are present for the glory of God* IMg 15. μετ' ἐμοῦ πάρεστιν *(Paul) is here with me* AcPl Ha 8, 2.—The pres. 'be here' can take on the perf. sense *have come* (B-D-F §322; Rob. 881; cp. 1 Macc 12:42 v.l., 45; 2 Macc 3:9; Jos., Ant. 3, 84 πάρεστι εἰς, Vi. 115; SIG 814, 4f [I AD]) τίς ἡ αἰτία δι' ἣν πάρεστε; *why have you come?* **Ac 10:21.** οὗτοι καὶ ἐνθάδε πάρεισιν *these men have come here too* **17:6.** πάρεστιν ἀπ' ἀγροῦ *has come from the country* **Lk 11:6** D.—Hv 5:3; s 7:1. On ἑταῖρε, ἐφ' ὃ πάρει (Jos., Bell. 2, 615 John ἐφ' ὃ παρῆν διεπράττετο) **Mt 26:50** s. ὅς 1iβ and RBrown, Death of the Messiah '94, II 1385–88. παρὼν ἤγειρεν αὐτούς *he came and raised them from the dead* IMg 9:3.—The impf. παρῆν *he had come,* or *he came* (Diod. S. 19, 59, 1 παρῆν=he came) Hs 9, 11, 8. Pl. παρῆσαν *they had come, they came* **Lk 13:1** (w. ἐν in indication of time + ἀπαγγέλλειν Plut., Mor. 509c; cp. Diod. S. 17, 8, 2 and 20, 113, 1; with temporal indication without ἀπαγγέλλειν X., Cyr. 1, 2, 4); πρός τινα (Jos., Ant. 14, 451) **Ac 12:20.**

ⓑ of impersonals, τοῦ εὐαγγελίου τοῦ παρόντος εἰς ὑμᾶς *of the gospel that has come to you* **Col 1:6** (π. εἰς as X., An. 1, 2,

2; Jos., Ant. 1, 285; 337). Of time (Hdt. et al.; SIG 700, 10 ἐν τῷ παρόντι καιρῷ; La 4:18 πάρεστιν ὁ καιρὸς ἡμῶν; Hab 3:2) ὁ καιρὸς πάρεστιν *the time has come* **J 7:6.** ἡ καταστροφὴ πάρεστιν 1 Cl 57:4 (Pr 1:27). τοῦ σωτῆρος ἔργα ἀεὶ παρῆν *the Savior's deeds remained apparent* i.e. they had permanent efficacy Qua 2.—Subst. τὸ παρόν *the present* (Hdt. et al.; ins, pap; 3 Macc 5:17; Philo, Spec. Leg. 2, 175) πρὸς τὸ παρόν *for the present, for the moment* (Thu. 2, 22, 1; 3, 40, 7; Pla., Leg. 5, 736a; Lucian, Ep. Sat. 2, 28; Cass. Dio 41, 15; Herodian 1, 3, 5; PGiss 47, 15; Sb 5113, 28; Jos., Ant. 6, 69; Just., A I 46, 6) **Hb 12:11.** κατὰ τὸ π. (Diod. S. 15, 47, 4; SIG 814, 46f; PTebt 28, 9; POxy 711, 2; 3 Macc 3:11) *for the present* MPol 20:1. τὰ παρόντα *the present situation* (Hdt. 1, 113; Pla., Theaet. 186a; Philo, Spec. Leg. 1, 334; PYale 42, 34) ἐν τοῖς παροῦσιν *under the present circumstances* B 1:8.

❷ **to be available for use,** ***at one's disposal,*** πάρεστίν τί μοι *someth. is at my disposal, I have someth.* (trag., Hdt. et al.; Wsd 11:21) ᾧ μὴ πάρεστιν ταῦτα **2 Pt 1:9.** ἡ παροῦσα ἀλήθεια *the truth that you have* vs. **12.** τὰ παρόντα *what one has, one's possessions* (X., Symp. 4, 42 οἷς τὰ παρόντα ἀρκεῖ, Cyr. 8, 4, 6, An. 7, 7, 36. Further exx. under ἀρκέω 2.) **Hb 13:5.** S. παρουσία.—M-M. TW.

παρεισάγω fut. παρεισάξω; 2 aor. παρεισήγαγον (Ar., Tat.); pf. pass. inf. παρεισῆχθαι (Tat. 21, 3) (s. next entry; Isocr. et al.; Polyb. 3, 63, 2; UPZ 162 VIII, 4 [117 BC]; EpArist 20; Ar., Tat.) **to bring in someth. that becomes an addition to someth.,** ***bring in, introduce*** of beliefs (Polyb. 6, 56, 12 of theological views; Diod. S. 1, 96, 5 of the introduction of Egyptian doctrines into Greece; Heraclit. Sto. 30 p. 45, 7; 43 p. 64, 17; Plut., Mor. 328d of alien divinities; sim. Ar. 8, 2 al. In none of these passages does the word connote malicious or secretive procedures; for such connotation, which is not necessarily implied in **2 Pt 2:1,** s. Polyb. 1, 18, 3; 2, 7, 8; Diod. S. 12, 41, 4 οἱ προδόται τοὺς στρατιώτας παρεισαγαγόντες ἐντὸς τῶν τειχῶν κυρίους τῆς πόλεως ἐποίησαν; cp. next entry and the context of Gal 2:4, where semantic qualifiers differ from those within the Petrine passage) οἵτινες παρεισάξουσιν αἱρέσεις ἀπωλείας *who will introduce/bring in destructive opinions* **2 Pt 2:1** (of sectarians also, Hegesippus in Eus., HE 4, 22, 5; Hippol., Ref. 5, 17, 10; 7, 29, 8).—M-M. TW.

παρείσακτος, ον (παρεισάγω; Strabo 17, 1, 8 p. 794 as the nickname of Ptolemy XI. In some mss. the prologue of Sir is called πρόλογος παρείσακτος ἀδήλου. Hesych.=ἀλλότριος) **pert. to coming into a group in a surreptitious manner,** ***secretly brought in, smuggled in, sneaked in*** παρείσακτοι ψευδάδελφοι of Judaizers who, as Paul felt, had come into congregations consisting of a large number of uncircumcised converts in a dishonorable fashion, in order to spy on them **Gal 2:4.** That others had a hand in encouraging their activities is not to be excluded, but their own initiative is indicated by the context. On the qu. of the pass. element in π. understood in a mid. sense s. Burton, comm., p. 78. Also s. WSchmithals, D. Häretiker in Galatien: ZNW 47, '56, 25–67; HBetz, Gal [Hermeneia] ad loc. for reff.—DELG s.v. ἄγω. TW.

παρεισδύ(ν)ω (mostly in the mid., Hippocr. et al.; Plut., Herodian, Philo) ***slip in stealthily, sneak in*** (s. next entry; Plut., Agis 796 [3, 1], Mor. 216b; in the same sense Jos., Bell. 1, 468 παραδύνομαι). In **Jd 4** the v.l. παρεισεδύησαν is 2 aor. pass. 3 pl. w. intrans. sense (s. W-S. §13, 11; B-D-F §76, 2; Rob. 1214 s.v. δύνω; Helbing p. 96f). Beside this the act. aor. 3 pl. παρεισέδυσαν is attested; the first pers. sing. of this could be either the 1 aor. 1 sg. παρεισέδυσα or the 2 aor. παρεισέδυν (s. δύνω).—On the rhetorical use of vituperation s. AduToit, Biblica 75, '94, 408f.—M-M.

παρείσδυσις, εως, ἡ ***slipping in (stealthily), sneaking in*** (παρεισδύω; Theophr., CP 1, 7, 1; Chrysippus: Stoic. III 199; Plut., Mor. 476c; 879e) ὁ πονηρὸς παρείσδυσιν πλάνης ποιήσας ἐν ἡμῖν *the evil one, having caused error to creep in among us* B 2:10. παρείσδυσιν ἔχειν (Vett. Val. 345, 8) *have opportunity to slip in, find a loophole* ἵνα μὴ σχῇ παρείσδυσιν ὁ μέλας 4:10 (cp. PStras 22, 30 [I AD] οὐδεμίαν παρείσδυσιν ἔχεις).—DELG s.v. δύω. M-M. s.v. -δύω.

παρεισενέγκας s. παρεισφέρω.

παρεισέρχομαι mid. dep.; 2 aor. παρεισῆλθον (Epicurus et al.; Diod. S. 17, 105, 1; Vett. Val. 357, 9; Sb 5761, 3 [91–96 AD]) **to come in beside,** ***slip in, come in*** as a side issue, of the law, as having no primary place in the divine plan **Ro 5:20.**—*Slip in* w. unworthy motives, *sneak in* (Polyb. 1, 7, 3; 1, 8, 4; 2, 55, 3; Plut., Popl. 106 [17, 2]; Lucian, Dial. Mer. 12, 3; Ps.-Lucian, Asin. 15 εἰ λύκος παρεισέλθοι; TestSol 11:2 P; Philo, Op. M. 150, Abr. 96; Test Jud 16:2) of the Judaizing false associates **Gal 2:4.**—M-M. TW.

παρειστήκειν s. παρίστημι.

παρεισφέρω Hellenistic aor. παρεισήνεγκα (B-D-F §81, 2; Rob. 338) (Demosth. et al.; PTebt 38, 12; 14 [113 BC]) ***apply, bring to bear*** σπουδὴν πᾶσαν *make every effort, do your best* **2 Pt 1:5** (σπουδὴν [πᾶσαν] εἰσφέρειν is a formal expr. in the Koine in ref. to benefactors and other civic-minded pers: Polyb 21, 29, 12; Diod. S. 1, 83, 8; SIG [index s.v. σπουδή]; Jos., Ant. 20, 204).—M-M. Spicq.

παρεκβαίνω (Hes.+; OGI 573, 17) lit. 'to go beyond' or 'outside' a boundary. In our lit. in transf. sense, to exceed limits of established authority ***go beyond, transgress*** τὶ *someth.* (EpArist 112) *overstep* τὸν ὡρισμένον τῆς λειτουργίας κανόνα 1 Cl 41:1. Of the sea οὐ παρεκβαίνει τὰ περιτεθειμένα αὐτῇ κλεῖθρα 20:6.

παρέκβασις, εως, ἡ (παρεκβαίνω; Theophr., Aristot. et al.; Jos., C. Ap. 1, 57; 183, Vi. 367; Just., D. 32, 5 ἐν παρεκβάσεσι 'in excursuses') ***deviation*** fr. a prescribed course 1 Cl 20:3.—DELG s.v. βαίνω.

παρεκδέχομαι (Polyb., M. Ant., Orig.) 1 aor. ptc. παρεκδεξάμενος ***misinterpret*** Papias (2:12).

παρεκτός adv. (=παρέκ Hom. et al., fr. παρά, ἐκ)

❶ **pert. to being different and in addition to someth. else, w. focus on being external,** ***besides, outside,*** abs. χωρὶς τῶν π. (sc. γινομένων) *apart from what I leave unmentioned* or *what is external* (i.e. sufferings, etc.) **2 Cor 11:28.**

❷ used as prep. w. gen., **pert. to someth. left out of other considerations,** ***apart from, except for*** (Dositheus 45, 3 παρεκτὸς ἐμοῦ, Lat. praeter me; Cyrill. Scyth. p. 34, 4 π. σαββάτου=except on the Sabbath; Geopon. 13, 15, 7; Etym. Magn. p. 652, 18; TestJob 30:5; TestZeb 1:4; Dt 1:36 Aq.) **Mt 5:32; 19:9 v.l.** (AOtto, Die Eheschdg. im Mt '39; KStaab, D. Unauflöslichkeit d. Ehe u. d. sog. 'Ehebruchsklauseln' b. Mt 5:32 u. 19:9: EEichmann Festschr. '40, 435–52, ZKT 67, '43, 36–44; HBaltensweiler, D. Ehe im NT '67, 59–102; GStrecker, ZNW 69, '78, 52–56. S. also πορνεία 2); **Ac 26:29.** π. θεοῦ *without God, leading away from God* D 6:1.—DELG s.v. ἐξ. M-M. EDNT.

παρεκφέρω (Plut., Mor. 102c; SIG 834, 18) *bring* to a place λίθους Hs 9, 4, 8.

παρεμβάλλω fut. παρεμβαλῶ; 2 aor. παρενέβαλον LXX; pf. ptc. παρεμβεβληκώς 1 Km 26:5; plpf. 3 pl. παρεμβεβλήκεισαν Judg 7:12 A and 1 Km 13:16 (Aristoph., Demosth. et al.; pap, LXX; Jos., C. Ap. 1, 229).

❶ **to enclose an object or area on all sides,** ***put around, surround.*** The word is used freq. (even in the LXX) as a military t.t. (cp. παρεμβολή), but w. var. mngs., depending on tactics used. παρεμβαλοῦσιν οἱ ἐχθροί σου χάρακά σοι *your enemies will throw up a palisade against you* **Lk 19:43** (v.l. περιβαλοῦσιν; D has βαλοῦσιν ἐπὶ σέ). Cp. Is 29:3 βαλῶ περὶ σὲ χάρακα; 37:33 οὐδὲ μὴ κυκλώσῃ ἐπ᾽ αὐτὴν χάρακα. Interpretations differ, depending on whether one views the text as actual prophecy (patterned after texts like those of Is cited above) or as prophecy after the event, in which case the earthworks constructed by soldiers under Titus (Jos., B. 5, 11, 4: 466) might be meant.

❷ **to put someth. in between,** ***insinuate,*** fig., of anger παρεμβάλλει ἑαυτὴν εἰς τὴν καρδίαν *it insinuates itself into the heart* Hm 5, 2, 2.—M-M.

παρεμβολή, ῆς, ἡ (παρεμβάλλω; Aeschin.+). Mostly used as a military t.t. (Polyb. et al.; ins, pap, LXX; En 1:4; TestSol 25:7; Test12Patr); so always in our lit.

❶ ***a (fortified) camp*** (Polyb. 3, 75, 5; 9; Diod. S. 13, 87, 2; 15, 84, 1 al.; SIG 700, 20; POxy 736; LXX; Jos., Ant. 6, 110; 20, 152) ἡ παρεμβολὴ τῶν ἀλλοφύλων 1 Cl 55:4 (s. ἀλλόφυλος). Of the Israelite camp (LXX) ἔξω τῆς παρεμβολῆς (Ex 29:14. Cp. Lev 4:12, 21; 10:4f al.) **Hb 13:11;** 1 Cl 4:11.—To the ἔξω τῆς π. **Hb 13:11,** vs. **13** adds the appeal ἐξερχώμεθα ἔξω τῆς π., giving as a reason that we have no 'lasting city' here. In this pass. the words ἔξω τῆς π. seem to refer to separation fr. worldly things in general (cp. Philo, Gig. 54 Μωϋσῆς ἔξω τῆς παρεμβολῆς καὶ τοῦ σωματικοῦ παντὸς στρατοπέδου πήξας τὴν ἑαυτοῦ σκηνήν); but s. GBarton, JBL 57, '38, 204f, Rome.—HKoester, HTR 55, '62, 299–315. Of Jerusalem **Hb 13:12 v.l.** (for πύλης).—ἡ παρεμβολὴ τῶν ἁγίων **Rv 20:9** is also to be understood fr. the OT use of the word.

❷ ***barracks/headquarters*** of the Roman troops in Jerusalem **Ac 21:34, 37; 22:24; 23:10, 16, 32.** Also of the barracks in Rome where the soldiers who accompanied Paul were quartered **Ac 28:16 v.l.**

❸ **an army in battle array,** ***battle line*** (Polyb.; Aelian, VH 14, 46; Ex 14:19f; Judg 4:16; 8:11; 1 Km 14:16; TestSol 25:7 π. τῶν Αἰγυπτίων) **Hb 11:34.**—FFensham, RevQ 4, '63, 557–62.—DELG s.v. βάλλω. M-M.

παρεμπλέκω (Diphilus, physician [III BC] in Athen. 2, 49, 57c; Hero Alex. I p. 20, 11; Oribasius, Ecl. 40: CMG VI 2, 2 p. 202, 7 π. τῷ ποτῷ τὴν τροφήν; schol. on Pind., Eustath., Prooem. 9; PTurin 8, 28 [116 BC]) med. t.t. ***mix, mingle, blend with,*** in ext. sense of false teachers ἑαυτοῖς παρεμπλέκουσιν Ἰησοῦν Χριστόν *they mingle Jesus Christ with themselves (=their teaching)* ITr 6:2 (s. the vv.ll. in Bihlmeyer's app.).—DELG s.v. πλέκω.

παρέμπτωσις, εως, ἡ (cp. πτῶσις and the pf. of πίπτω: πέπτωκα; Aristot. et al.) **throwing of someth. in besides,** ***insidious plot*** διά τινας παρεμπτώσεις, in wordplay 1 Cl 51:1 (the word is not found in the Gk. ms. trad., but Clem. Alex. has it, Strom. 4, 113, 1, in a paraphrase of our pass., and the Lat. and Copt. versions of 1 Cl agree w. him. S. Bihlmeyer, app.).—DELG s.v. πίπτω C.

παρεμφέρω (Galen and Vett. Val. in various mngs.) **to bring in from a position,** ***bring in*** Hs 9, 4, 8.

παρένεγκε s. παραφέρω.

παρενθυμέομαι 1 aor. pass. παρενεθυμήθην (M. Ant. 5, 5, 5; 6, 20, 2; Iambl., In Nicom. p. 83, 15 Pistelli; TAM II/1, 245, 13; POxf 3, 12 [142 AD]; Sb 7404, 39 [II AD]; Philo) **to view some matter as unworthy of serious consideration,** ***disregard, neglect, forget*** τὶ *someth.* (Philo, Spec. Leg. 4, 53) of commands Hm 5, 2, 8 (τὴν ἐντολὴν ταύτην); 12, 3, 6 (ταύτας, i.e. ἐντολάς). Referring to a good thought (τὸ καλόν) and w. αὐτό to be supplied *make light of* s 5, 2, 7. W. ref. to the sins of the members of Hermas' family, w. αὐτάς to be supplied v 2, 3, 1.—DELG s.v. θυμός.

παρενοχλέω fut. 3 sg. παρενοχλήσει Job 16:3; 1 aor. παρενώχλησα LXX. Pass.: fut. 3 sg. παρενοχληθήσεται 2 Macc 11:31 (Hippocr. et al.; ins, pap, LXX) **to cause unnecessary trouble,** ***cause difficulty (for), trouble, annoy*** w. dat. of pers. (Polyb. 1, 8, 1; Plut., Timol. 237 [3, 1]; Epict. 1, 9, 23; PGen 31, 4; LXX) **Ac 15:19.** Anything beyond the requests noted vs. 20 would be an extra (παρα-) imposition.—New Docs 4, 166f. DELG s.v. ὄχλος. M-M.

παρεπιδημέω 1 aor. ptc. παρεπιδημήσας (s. next entry; Polyb. 27, 6, 3; Diod. S. 1, 83, 8; 19, 61, 1; Aelian, VH 8, 7 p. 90, 29; ins freq.; PPetr II, 13, 19 [258–253 BC]; UPZ 196 I, 13; 19 [119 BC]; EpArist 110; Philo, Conf. Lingu. 76, Agr. 65) **to stay for a short time in a strange place,** ***visit*** πρός τινα *(with) someone* 1 Cl 1:2.—New Docs 4, 145. DELG s.v. δῆμος. M-M. s.v. παρεπίδημος.

παρεπίδημος, ον (s. prec. entry; Polyb. 32, 6, 4; Athen. 5, 196a; OGI 383, 150; PPetr I, 19, 22 [225 BC]; III, 7, 15; LXX; Just., A I, 67, 6.—Dssm., B 146f [BS 149]) **pert. to staying for a while in a strange or foreign place,** ***sojourning, residing temporarily*** in our lit. subst. ὁ παρεπίδημος *stranger, sojourner, resident alien,* of Christians, who are not at home in this world ἐκλεκτοὶ π. *chosen sojourners* **1 Pt 1:1.** (W. πάροικοι [cp. Gen 23:4; Ps 38:13]) **2:11.** (W. ξένοι) π. ἐπὶ τῆς γῆς *sojourners on the earth* **Hb 11:13** (cp. Ps.-Pla., Axioch. 365b παρεπιδημία τίς ἐστιν ὁ βίος.—MMeister, De Axiocho Dial., diss. Breslau 1915, 86ff). The cognates παρεπιδημέω and παρεπιδημία are used in ins (s. SIG index, s.v.) in connection w. civil servants who distinguish themselves for exemplary conduct while on international duty. Sim. the author of 1 Pt makes an intimate connection between the status of the addressees (as virtual visitors in the world because of their special relation to God through Jesus Christ) and their moral responsibility. S. πάροικος and lit. cited there.—DELG s.v. δῆμος. M-M. TW. Spicq.

παρέρχομαι mid. dep.; fut. παρελεύσομαι; 2 aor. παρῆλθον, impv. in H. Gk. παρελθάτω **Mt 26:39** (also v.l. -ετω; B-D-F §81, 3; Mlt-H. 209); pf. παρελήλυθα (Hom.+).

❶ **to go past a reference point,** ***go by, pass by*** w. acc. *someone* or *someth.* (Aelian, VH 2, 35; Lucian, Merc. Cond. 15) an animal Hv 4, 1, 9; 4, 2, 1; a place Papias (3, 3). Of Jesus and his disciples on the lake: ἤθελεν παρελθεῖν αὐτούς **Mk 6:48** (s. HWindisch, NThT 9, 1920, 298–308; GEysinga, ibid. 15, 1926, 221–29 al.; Lohmeyer s.v. παράγω 3; BvanIersel, in The Four Gospels, Neirynck Festschr., ed. FvanSegbroeck et al. '92, II 1065–76). διὰ τῆς ὁδοῦ ἐκείνης *pass by along that road* **Mt 8:28** (constr. w. διά as PAmh 154, 2; Num 20:17; Josh 24:17). παρὰ τὴν λίμνην GEb 34, 60. Abs. (X., An. 2, 4, 25) **Lk 18:37;**

1 Cl 14:5 (Ps 36:36). Of someth. impers. *get by unnoticed, escape notice* (Theognis 419; Sir 42:20) Hs 8, 2, 5ab.

❷ of time: **to be no longer available for someth.,** ***pass*** (Soph., Hdt.+; ins, pap, LXX; JosAs 29:8 cod. A; Tat. 26, 1 πῶς γὰρ δύναται παρελθεῖν ὁ μέλλων, εἴ ἐστιν ὁ ἐνεστώς;) ἡ ὥρα ἤδη παρῆλθεν *the time is already past* **Mt 14:15.** Of a definite period of time (SSol 2:11 ὁ χειμὼν π.; Jos., Ant. 15, 408) διὰ τὸ τὴν νηστείαν ἤδη παρεληλυθέναι *because the fast was already over* **Ac 27:9.** ὁ παρεληλυθὼς χρόνος *the time that is past* **1 Pt 4:3** (cp. Isocr. 4, 167 χρόνος . . . ἱκανὸς γὰρ ὁ παρεληλυθώς, ἐν ᾧ τί τῶν δεινῶν οὐ γέγονεν; PMagd 25, 3 παρεληλυθότος τοῦ χρόνου). τὰ παρεληλυθότα (beside τὰ ἐνεστῶτα and τὰ μέλλοντα; cp. Herm. Wr. 424, 10ff Sc.; Demosth. 4, 2; Jos., Ant. 10, 210) *things past, the past* (Demosth. 18, 191; Sir 42:19; Philo, Spec. Leg. 1, 334, Leg. All. 2, 42) B 1:7; 5:3.—ἡ γενεὰ αὕτη **Mt 24:34** belongs here, if γ. is understood temporally.

❸ **to come to an end and so no longer be there,** ***pass away, disappear*** (Demosth. 18, 188 κίνδυνον παρελθεῖν; Theocr. 27, 8; Ps 89:6; Wsd 2:4; 5:9; Da 7:14 Theod.; TestJob 33:4 ὁ κόσμος ὅλος παρελεύσεται) of pers. ὡς ἄνθος χόρτου παρελεύσεται **Js 1:10.** ὁ οὐρανὸς καὶ ἡ γῆ **Mt 5:18a; 24:35a; Mk 13:31a; Lk 16:17; 21:33a;** cp. **2 Pt 3:10; Rv 21:1 t.r.** ὁ κόσμος οὗτος D 10:6 (cp. TestJob 33:4). ἡ γενεὰ αὕτη **Mt 24:34** (but s. 2); **Mk 13:30; Lk 21:32.** αἱ γενεαὶ πᾶσαι 1 Cl 50:3. ἡ ὀργή vs. 4 (Is 26:20). τὰ ἀρχαῖα παρῆλθεν **2 Cor 5:17.**—*Pass away* in the sense *lose force, become invalid* (Ps 148:6; Esth 10:3b τῶν λόγων τούτων: οὐδὲ παρῆλθεν ἀπ᾽ αὐτῶν λόγος) οἱ λόγοι μου οὐ μὴ παρέλθωσιν (or οὐ [μὴ] παρελεύσονται) **Mt 24:35b; Mk 13:31b; Lk 21:33b.** ἰῶτα ἓν ἢ μία κεραία οὐ μὴ παρέλθῃ ἀπὸ τοῦ νόμου **Mt 5:18b.** οὐδὲν μὴ παρέλθῃ τῶν δεδογματισμένων ὑπ᾽ αὐτοῦ 1 Cl 27:5.

❹ **to ignore someth. in the interest of other matters,** ***pass by, transgress, neglect, disobey*** τὶ *someth.* (Hes., Theog. 613; Lysias 6, 52 τὸν νόμον; Demosth. 37, 37; Dionys. Hal. 1, 58; Dt 17:2; Jer 41:18; Jdth 11:10; 1 Macc 2:22; ApcEsdr 5:17 τὴν διαθήκην μου; Jos., Ant. 14, 67) **Lk 11:42; 15:29.**

❺ **to pass by without touching,** ***pass*** of suffering or misfortune (Jos., Ant. 5, 31 fire) ἀπό τινος *from someone* (for the constr. w. ἀπό cp. 2 Ch 9:2) **Mt 26:39; Mk 14:35.** Abs. **Mt 26:42.**

❻ **to pass through an area,** ***go through*** (Appian, Bell. Civ. 5, 68 §288 ὁ Ἀντώνιος μόλις παρῆλθεν=Antony made his way through [to the Forum] with difficulty; 1 Macc 5:48 διελεύσομαι εἰς τὴν γῆν σου, τοῦ ἀπελθεῖν εἰς τὴν γῆν ἡμῶν· καὶ οὐδεὶς κακοποιήσει ὑμᾶς, πλὴν τοῖς ποσὶν παρελευσόμεθα) παρελθόντες τὴν Μυσίαν κατέβησαν εἰς Τρῳάδα **Ac 16:8** (lack of knowledge of this mng., and recognition of the fact that passing by is impossible in this case, gave rise to the v.l. διελθόντες D); cp. **17:15** D.

❼ **to stop at a place as one comes by,** ***come to, come by, come here*** (trag., Hdt. et al.; ins, pap, LXX, EpArist 176; Philo; Jos., Bell. 3, 347, Ant. 1, 337) παρελθὼν διακονήσει αὐτοῖς *he will come by and serve them* **Lk 12:37;** 'παρελθὼν ἀνάπεσε'=*'come here, recline'* **17:7;** of Lysias who came with a substantial force **Ac 24:6[7] v.l.**—M-M. TW.

πάρεσις, εως, ἡ (παρά + ἵημι; Hippocr.+; BGU 624, 21 [s. Dssm., NB 94=BS 266]; Philo; Jos., Ant. 11, 236; Ath., R. 16 p. 68, 4) **deliberate disregard,** ***passing over, letting go unpunished*** (Dionys. Hal. 7, 37 ὁλοσχερῆ πάρεσιν οὐχ εὕροντο, τὴν δὲ εἰς χρόνον ἀναβολὴν ἔλαβον; Dio Chrys. 80 [30], 19 πάρεσίν τινα ἔχειν ἐκ τ. θεοῦ.—Corresp. the verb παριέναι means 'leave unpunished': X., Hipp. 7, 10; Dionys. Hal. 2, 35; Sir 23:2; Jos., Ant. 15, 48 παρῆκεν τὴν ἁμαρτίαν.) διὰ τὴν π. τῶν προγεγονότων ἁμαρτημάτων **Ro 3:25.**—The verb is also used of 'remitting' debts and other obligations (Phalaris, Ep. 81, 1 χρημάτων; SIG 742, 33; 39; OGI 669, 50.—JCreed, JTS 41, '40, 28–30; SLyonnet, Biblica 38, '57, 35–61), but in **Ro 3:25** Paul appears to argue that God's apparent winking at sin puts God's own uprightness at risk (cp. WBeck tr. '76 'patiently passed by'; NRSV, REB, with many scholars).—WKümmel, Πάρεσις u. ἔνδειξις: ZTK 49, '52, 154–67. See s.v. ἔνδειξις 2. JFitzmyer comm. (Anchor) s.v.—DELG s.v. ἵημι. M-M. TW.

παρέχω impf. παρεῖχον, also 3 pl. παρεῖχαν **Ac 28:2 v.l.** (H. Gk.; s. B-D-F §82; Mlt-H. 194); fut. παρέξω; 2 aor. παρέσχον; pf. παρέσχηκα. Mid.: impf. παρειχόμην; fut. 1 sg. παρέξομαι (ApcPt Rainer), 2 sg. παρέξῃ, 1 pl. παρεξόμεθα Esth 8:12h; 2 aor. impv. 2 sg. παράσχου Ps 29:8, inf. παρασχέσθαι 4 Macc 3:2. Pass.: aor. subj. 3 sg. παρασχεθῇ (Just., A I, 68, 7) (Hom.+).

❶ **to make available,** ***give up, offer, present*** (schol. on Nicander, Alexiph. 204 παρέχειν πίνειν=offer to drink) τί τινι *someth. to someone* τὴν σιαγόνα **Lk 6:29.** τὸ πλοῦτος Hs 2:7.

❷ **to cause to experience someth.,** ***grant, show***—ⓐ act. *grant, show* τινί τι *someth. to someone* (Vi. Aesopi G 124 P. οὐδὲν αὐτῷ παρεῖχον; Aesop, Fab. 396 P.=170 H.; Jos., Ant. 2, 329; 11, 2) Dg 12:1. ἀγάπην 1 Cl 21:7. φιλανθρωπίαν **Ac 28:2.** Of God (Appian, Bell. Civ. 3, 65 §265 ἣν οἱ θεοὶ παρέχωσιν εὐπραγεῖν; Alex. Aphr., Quaest. 1, 14 Bruns) ἡμῖν πάντα **1 Ti 6:17;** cp. Dg 8:11. ὅσα . . . αὐτοῖς παρέσχεν AcPl Ha 8, 16//Ox 1602, 18//BMM recto 20 (cp. Just., A I, 10, 1 θεὸν . . . παρέχοντα πάντα) ὧν (attraction of the rel. fr. ἅ) τοῖς οἰομένοις διδόναι παρέχει αὐτός *which he himself supplies to those who think they are giving* Dg 3:4. πίστιν παρασχὼν πᾶσιν **Ac 17:31** (s. πίστις 1c).—Without a dat. (Pind., Paeanes 4, 24 Sch.=OxfT 4, 21 μοῖσαν; Just., D. 3, 6 τὴν ἐπιστήμην) νοῦν *grant understanding* Dg 11:5. ἡσυχίαν **Ac 22:2** (cp. Jos., Ant. 5, 235). δεῖγμά τινος Dg 3:3 (s. δεῖγμα 2 and 1).—Without the acc., which is to be supplied fr. the context Dg 3:5; ISm 11:3.—W. dat. and inf. foll. MPol 18:2.

ⓑ mid. (B-D-F §316, 3; Rob. 810) ἑαυτόν τι *show oneself to be someth.* (X., Cyr. 8, 1, 39; SIG 333, 10f [306 BC]; 442, 8f; 620, 5f; 748, 31f; 1068, 6f; 1104, 18f; UPZ 144, 15 [164/163 BC]; POxy 281, 13; CPR 27, 14.—Dssm., NB 81f [BS 254]; Thieme 24; Rouffiac 52. In earlier Gk., e.g. Antiphon, Pla. et al., the act. would be used, as it is Jos., C. Ap. 2, 156) σεαυτὸν παρεχόμενος τύπον **Tit 2:7.**

❸ **to cause to happen or be brought about,** ***cause, make happen***—ⓐ act. *cause, bring about* τινί τι *someth. for someone* (Hdt. 1, 177 πόνον; Socrat., Ep. 14, 1 κακά; Arrian, Anab. 2, 21, 3 φόβον; EpArist 96 ἔκπληξιν ἡμῖν π.; Jos., Ant. 18, 175 ὄχλον [=annoyance] μοι π.; Just., A I, 4, 7 ἀφορμάς, A II, 4, 1 πράγματα) κόπους *cause trouble* (s. κόπος 1) **Mt 26:10; Mk 14:6; Lk 11:7; 18:5** (κόπον, as Sir 29:4); **Gal 6:17;** AcPlCor 2:34 (κόπους μοι μηδεὶς παρεχέτω in connection w. PGM 14b [ἐάν μοι ὁ δεῖνα κόπους παράσχῃ] is taken as a formula of adjuration by Dssm., B 262ff [BS 352–60], LO 256 [LAE 301]); Hv 3, 3, 2 (περί τινος *about someth.*). χαρὰν ἡμῖν π. *give us joy* 1 Cl 63:2. ἐργασίαν πολλὴν *bring great gain* **Ac 16:16** (Jos., Ant. 15, 332 πλείστην ἐργασίαν παρασχόν).—Without the dat. (s. ref. to Hdt. above.—Sir 29:4 v.l.) Hm 11:20. ξενισμόν *cause astonishment* IEph 19:2. ἐκζητήσεις *give rise to speculations* **1 Ti 1:4.**

ⓑ mid. (B-D-F §316, 3; Rob. 810) *grant* τινί τι *someth. to someone* (Diod. S. 20, 62, 1 παρείχετο τοῖς ἐμπόροις τὴν ἀσφάλειαν; Jos., Ant. 9, 255; cp. τὰ ἑαυτῶν δίκαια παρέσχοντο=they submitted their claims: letter of MAurelius ln. 33 in ZPE 8, ’71, 170f) τοῖς τεχνίταις ἐργασίαν *business to the artisans* **Ac 19:24.** τὸ δίκαιον καὶ τὴν ἰσότητα *what is just and fair* **Col 4:1.** ἄξιός ἐστιν ᾧ παρέξῃ τοῦτο *he deserves that you grant him this* **Lk 7:4.** τὸ πλοῦτος π. τῷ πένητι Hs 2, 7. πλέον *more* IRo 2:2. παρέξομαι τοῖς κλητοῖς μου καὶ ἐκλέκτοις μου ὃν ἐὰν αἰτήσωνταί με ἐκ τῆς κολάσεως *to all my called and elect ones who petition me, I will grant release of the sinner of their choice from torment* ApcPt Rainer (as emended by James; cp. SibOr 2, 330–33). *Offer* 1 Cl 20:10.—Larfeld I 501f. M-M.

παρηγορία, ας, ἡ (παρηγορέω ‘exhort, console’; Aeschyl. et al.; 4 Macc 5:12; 6:1) **a source of encouragement, *comfort*** (Aeschyl., Ag. 95; Plut., Per. 170 [34, 3], Mor. 599b; Vett. Val. 183, 9f; 209, 25; Philo, Deus Imm. 65, Somn. 1, 112; Jos., Ant. 4, 195; Kaibel 204, 12 [I BC]) of pers. ἐγενήθησάν μοι παρηγορία *they have become a comfort to me* **Col 4:11.**—DELG s.v. ἀγορά. M-M.

παρθενία, ας, ἡ (παρθένος; Sappho, Pind., trag.+) **state of being a virgin, *virginity*** (Callim., Hymn. 3, 6 of Artemis: παρθενίη αἰώνιος; Aristocritus [III BC]: 493 fgm. 5 Jac. of Hestia; Diod. S. 5, 3, 4) ἡ π. Μαρίας IEph 19:1. Of the time of virginity (w. focus on time of entry into married status) ἀπὸ τῆς π. αὐτῆς **Lk 2:36** (ἀπό 2bα. Also ἐκ παρθενίας in Chariton 3, 7, 5; cp. cum quo vixit ab virginitate sua ad finem vitae suae=‘with whom she lived from her virginity to the end of her life’ CIL 10, 3720). S. εὐνοῦχος.—DELG s.v. παρθένος. M-M. Spicq.

παρθένος, ου, ἡ (s. prec. entry; Hom.+, gener. of a young woman of marriageable age, w. or without focus on virginity; s. esp. PKöln VI, 245, 12 and ASP 31, ’91 p. 39) and **ὁ** (s. reff. in b) in our lit. **one who has never engaged in sexual intercourse, *virgin, chaste person***

ⓐ female of marriageable age w. focus on virginity ἡ παρθένος **Mt 25:1, 7, 11; 1 Cor 7:25** (FStrobel, NovT 2, ’58, 199–227), **28, 34;** Pol 5:3; Hv 4, 2, 1; s 9, 1, 2; 9, 2, 3; 5; 9, 3, 2; 4f; 9, 4, 3; 5f; 8 al.; AcPl Ox 6, 16 (cp. Aa I 241, 15); GJs 13:1. After Is 7:14 (הָעַלְמָה הָרָה; on this ASchulz, BZ 23, ’35, 229–41; WBrownlee, The Mng. of Qumran for the Bible, esp. Is, ’64, 274–81) **Mt 1:23** (cp. Menand., Sicyonius 372f παρθένος γ’ ἔτι, ἄπειρος ἀνδρός). Of Mary also **Lk 1:27ab;** GJs 9:1; 10:1; 15:2; 16:1; 19:3; ISm 1:1 and prob. Dg 12:8 (the idea that the spirit of a god could father a child by a woman, specifically a virgin, was not foreign to Egyptian religion: Plut. Numa 62 [4, 6], Mor. 718ab; Philo, Cher. 43–50 [on this ENorden, D. Geburt des Kindes 78–90; ELeach, Genesis as Myth, and Other Essays ’69, 85–112; RBrown, The Virginal Conception and Bodily Resurrection of Jesus ’73, 62, esp. n. 104; idem, The Birth of the Messiah ’77, 522f, esp. n. 17]. S. further the lit. on Ἰωσήφ 4 and OBardenhewer, Mariä Verkündigung 1905; EPetersen, Die wunderbare Geburt des Heilandes 1909; HUsener, Das Weihnachtsfest[2] 1911; ASteinmann, D. jungfräul. Geburt des Herrn[3] 1926, D. Jungfrauengeburt u. die vergl. Religionsgeschichte 1919; GBox, The Virgin Birth of Jesus 1916; OCrain, The Credibility of the Virgin Birth 1925; JMachen, The Virgin Birth of Christ[2] ’32 [on this FKattenbusch, StKr 102, 1930, 454–74]; EWorcester, Studies in the Birth of Our Lord ’32; KSchmidt, D. jungfrl. Geb. J. Chr.: ThBl 14, ’35, 289–97; FSteinmetzer, Empfangen v. Hl. Geist ’38; RBratcher, Bible Translator 9, ’58, 98–125 [Heb., LXX, Mt]; TBoslooper, The Virg. Birth ’62; HvCampenhausen, D. Jungfrauengeburt in d. Theol. d. alten Kirche ’62; JMeier, A Marginal Jew I, ’91, 205–52 [lit.].—RCooke, Did Paul Know the Virg. Birth? 1927; PBotz, D. Jungfrausch. Mariens im NT u. in der nachap. Zeit, diss. Tüb. ’34; DEdwards, The Virg. Birth in History and Faith ’43.—Clemen[2] 114–21; ENorden, D. Geburt des Kindes[2] ’31; MDibelius, Jungfrauensohn u. Krippenkind ’32; HMerklein, Studien zu Jesus und Paulus [WUNT 105] ’98; in gener., RBrown, The Birth of the Messiah ’77, 133–63, esp. 147–49. As a contrast to Dibelius’ Hellenistic emphasis s. OMichel and OBetz, Beih., ZNW 26, ’60, 3–23, on Qumran parallels.). Of the daughters of Philip παρθένοι προφητεύουσαι **Ac 21:9.** Of virgins who were admitted to the church office of ‘widows’ ISm 13:1 (s. AJülicher, PM 22, 1918, 111f. Differently LZscharnack, Der Dienst der Frau 1902, 105 ff).—On **1 Cor 7:36–38** s. γαμίζω 1 and s. also PKetter, Trierer Theol. Ztschr. 56, ’47, 175–82 (παρθ. often means [virgin] daughter: Apollon. Rhod. 3, 86 παρθ. Αἰήτεω and the scholion on this has the following note: παρθένον ἀντὶ τοῦ θυγατέρα; Lycophron vss. 1141, 1175; Diod. S. 8, 6, 2; 16, 55, 3; 20, 84, 3 [pl. beside υἱοί]. Likewise Theod. Prodr. 1, 293 H. τὴν σὴν παρθένον=‘your virgin daughter’; in 3, 332 τ. ἑαυτοῦ παρθένον refers to one’s ‘sweetheart’; likew. 6, 466, as well as the fact that παρθ. can mean simply ‘girl’ [e.g. Paus. 8, 20, 4]). On Jewish gravestones ‘of age, but not yet married’ CIJ I, 117. RSeeboldt, Spiritual Marriage in the Early Church, CTM 30, ’59, 103–19; 176–86.—In imagery: the Corinthian congregation as παρθένος ἁγνή (ἁγνός a) **2 Cor 11:2** (on this subj. s. FConybeare, Die jungfräul. Kirche u. die jungfräul. Mutter: ARW 8, 1905, 373ff; 9, 1906, 73ff; Cumont[3] 283, 33).—ἡ τοιαύτη παρθένος AcPl Ox 6, 15f (of Thecla; cp. Aa I 241, 15 ἡ τοιαύτη αἰδὼς τῆς παρθένου).

ⓑ male virgin ὁ παρθένος *virgin, chaste man* (CIG IV, 8784b; JosAs 8:1 uses π. of Joseph; Pel.-Leg. 27, 1 uses it of Abel; Suda of Abel and Melchizedek; Nonnus of the apostle John, who is also called ‘virgo’ in the Monarchian Prologues [Kl. T. 1[2] 1908, p. 13, 13]) **Rv 14:4** (on topical relation to 1 En 15:2–7 al., s. DOlson, CBQ 59, ’97, 492–510).—JFord, The Mng. of ‘Virgin’, NTS 12, ’66, 293–99.—B. 90. New Docs 4, 224–27. DELG. M-M. EDNT. TW. Spicq. Sv.

Πάρθοι, ων, οἱ (since Hdt 3, 93, 3; OGI 544, 32; Joseph. index; SibOr, index of names) ***Parthians*** (successors to the Persians; Parthia was southeast of the Caspian, but in NT times its empire extended to the Euphrates) **Ac 2:9** (Ps.-Callisth. 2, 4, 9 . . . Πάρθων καὶ Ἐλυμαίων καὶ Βαβυλωνίων καὶ τῶν κατὰ τὴν Μεσοποταμίαν . . . χώραν. Cp. 1, 2, 2 Σκύθαι καὶ Ἄραβες καὶ . . . ; 14 names in all; on Ac 2:9–11 s. SWeinstock, JRS 38, ’48, 43–46).—Lit. in Schürer I 351, 40; JBrinkman, CBQ 25, ’63, 418–27.

παρίημι fut. παρήσω LXX; 2 aor. inf. παρεῖναι; pf. pass. παρεῖμαι LXX; pass. ptc. παρειμένος (Hom.+)

❶ **to avoid doing someth., *neglect*** (Pind., Hdt. et al.; 4 Macc 5:29) τὶ *someth.* (Jos., Bell. 2, 202, Ant. 8, 218) ταῦτα ἔδει ποιῆσαι κἀκεῖνα μὴ παρεῖναι **Lk 11:42** (v.l. ἀφεῖναι et al.; cp. πάρεσις).

❷ **to be weak, *let fall at the side, slacken, weaken*** pf. pass. ptc. *weakened, listless, drooping* (Eur. et al.; Pla., Leg. 11, 931d; Diod. S. 14, 105, 2 τὰ σώματα παρειμένοι; Plut., Mor. 102a; LXX; TestJob 18:4 παρειμένη τὰς ὀσφύας; ApcMos 26 τοὺς παρειμένους τῇ καρδίᾳ; Philo, in Flacc. 10 διανοίας παρειμένης; Jos., Ant. 6, 35) παρειμέναι χεῖρες (Sir 2:12; cp. Jos., Ant. 13, 343; Cornutus 16 p. 23, 18): w. παραλελυμένα γόνατα (as Is 35:3; Sir 25:23) **Hb 12:12.**

❸ **to be lax in effort, *careless, indolent*** pf. pass. ptc. w. νωθρός (as Sir 4:29) 1 Cl 34:1. (W. ἀργός) π. ἐπὶ πᾶν ἔργον ἀγαθόν *careless in every good work* 34:4.—M-M. TW.

παριστάνω s. παρίστημι.

παρίστημι/παριστάνω (the word since Hom.+; the later form παριστάνω [**Ro 6:13, 16;** but παρίστησι **1 Cor 8:8 v.l.;** Ath. 33, 1] since Polyb. et al.; Epict. 3, 22, 87; SIG 589, 46 [196 BC]; 814, 36 [67 AD]; 1109, 76.—B-D-F §93; Mlt-H. 202) pres. inf. παραστᾶν (Tat. 33, 1; Ath. 11, 3), ptc. pl. παριστῶντες (Tat. 1, 3—B-D-F §93); fut. παραστήσω; 1 aor. παρέστησα; 2 aor. παρέστην; pf. παρέστηκα, ptc. παρεστηκώς or παρεστώς; plpf. παρειστήκειν; inf. παρεστάναι (Dt 18:5; PsSol 2:36). Mid.: fut. παραστήσομαι. Pass.: 1 aor. παρεστάθην.

❶ trans. (pres., impf., fut., 1 aor. act.) **to cause to be present in any way—ⓐ** ***place beside, put at someone's disposal*** τινά *or* τί τινι *someone* or *someth. to someone* (Demetr.: 722 fgm. 7 Jac.; Socrates of Rhodes [I BC]: 192 fgm. 1 p. 927, 25 Jac. [in Athen. 4, 148b]; Lucian, D. Mar. 6, 2) παραστήσει μοι λεγιῶνας **Mt 26:53.** τὶ *someth.* (cp. 2 Macc 12:3 v.l. σκάφη) κτήνη *provide riding animals* **Ac 23:24.** For protection παρέστησεν αὐτῇ τοὺς υἱοὺς αὐτοῦ *he placed his sons at her side*=Joseph placed Mary in the care of his sons GJs 18:1. Here belongs παραστήσατε ἑαυτοὺς τῷ θεῷ **Ro 6:13b.** W. dat. and double acc. (of the obj. and the pred.) ᾧ παριστάνετε ἑαυτοὺς δούλους (εἰς ὑπακοήν) *to whomever you yield yourselves as slaves* (*to obey him;* w. acc., followed by εἰς=*to* or *for* [s. MTreu, Alkaios '52, p. 12]) vs. **16;** μηδὲ παριστάνετε τὰ μέλη ὑμῶν ὅπλα ἀδικίας τῇ ἁμαρτίᾳ vs. **13a;** cp. vs. **19ab.**

ⓑ ***present, represent*—α.** lit. τινά τινι *someone to someone* παρέστησαν τὸν Παῦλον αὐτῷ **Ac 23:33.** παρθένον ἁγνὴν παραστῆσαι τῷ Χριστῷ **2 Cor 11:2.** Of the 'presentation' of Jesus in the Temple **Lk 2:22** (Billerb. II 120–23. Cp. also Olympiodorus, Life of Plato, ed. AWestermann 1850 p. 1: of Plato, said to be of transcendent origin, λαβόντες οἱ γονεῖς βρέφος ὄντα τεθείκασιν ἐν τῷ Ὑμηττῷ βουλόμενοι ὑπὲρ αὐτοῦ τοῖς ἐκεῖ θεοῖς . . . θῦσαι=his parents took him when he was an infant and placed him on Hymettus with the intent to sacrifice . . . to the gods there). W. dat. of pers., acc. of obj., and pred. acc. οἷς παρέστησεν ἑαυτὸν ζῶντα *to whom he presented himself alive* **Ac 1:3;** without a dat., which is supplied fr. the context παρέστησεν αὐτὴν ζῶσαν **9:41.**

β. fig. παραστήσω σε κατὰ πρόσωπόν σου *I will show you to yourself face to face* 1 Cl 35:10 (Ps 49:21).

ⓒ 'present' becomes almost equivalent to ***make, render*** (Plut., Mor. 676c [ἡ πίσσα] τὸν οἶνον εὔποτον παρίστησι) ἵνα παραστήσῃ αὐτὸς ἑαυτῷ ἔνδοξον τὴν ἐκκλησίαν *that (Christ) might render the church glorious before himself* **Eph 5:27.** σπούδασον σεαυτὸν δόκιμον παραστῆσαι τῷ θεῷ **2 Ti 2:15.** παραστῆσαι ὑμᾶς ἁγίους κατενώπιον αὐτοῦ *to make you holy before him* **Col 1:22.** ἵνα παραστήσωμεν πάντα ἄνθρωπον τέλειον ἐν Χριστῷ *that we may make everyone complete in Christ* vs. **28.**

ⓓ as a t.t. in the language of sacrifice ***offer, bring, present*** (παριστάναι θυσίαν, θύματα etc.: Epici p. 41, 49 B.=p. 19, 16 K.; Polyb. 16, 25, 7; Diod. S. 3, 72, 1; Lucian, Sacr. 13; Jos., Bell. 2, 89, Ant. 4, 113; SIG 589, 46 [196 BC]; 694, 49; 736, 70; OGI 456, 20; 764, 23; 38. The mid. is also used in this way since X., An. 6, 1, 22) fig. παραστῆσαι τὰ σώματα θυσίαν ζῶσαν *offer bodies as a living sacrifice* **Ro 12:1.**

ⓔ as a legal t.t. ***bring before*** (a judge) (Sb 4512, 82 [II BC]; OGI 669, 49; BGU 163, 3; 341, 14; 747 II, 26; 759, 22; 1139, 18). Some would prefer to understand **1 Cor 8:8** in this sense: βρῶμα ἡμᾶς οὐ παραστήσει τῷ θεῷ *food will not bring us before (the judgment seat of) God.* Likew. ἡμᾶς ἐγερεῖ καὶ παραστήσει σὺν ὑμῖν *he will raise us and bring us, together with you, before him* (=before his judgment seat) **2 Cor 4:14.** But the forensic mng. is not certain in either of these places, and the sense is prob. *bring before God* = *bring close to God* (cp. Rtzst., ZNW 13, 1912, 19f).

ⓕ ***prove, demonstrate*** (Lysias 12, 51; X., Oec. 13, 1; Epict. 2, 23, 47; 2, 26, 4; Jos., Ant. 4, 47, Vi. 27; PLips 64, 34) οὐδὲ παραστῆσαι δύνανταί σοι περὶ ὧν νυνὶ κατηγοροῦσίν μου *nor can they prove to you the accusations they are now making against me* **Ac 24:13.**—On the 1 aor. pass. Hs 8, 4, 1 s. 2aγ end.

❷ intr. (mid. and perf., plpf., 2 aor. act., but s. also aγ end) **to be present in any way,** ***be present*—ⓐ** pres., fut., aor. (TestJos 2:6; 20:6; TestSol 6:1 and C 12:1; TestAbr A 20 p. 103, 19 [Stone p. 54]; ApcMos 35; Mel., P. 62, 450).

α. *approach, come* τινί *(to) someone* (Philo, De Jos. 94) **Ac 9:39; 27:23** (Plut., Lysander 444 [20, 7] αὐτῷ κατὰ τοὺς ὕπνους παραστῆναι τὸν Ἄμμωνα).—Also as a t.t. of legal usage *appear before, come before* (s. 1e above.—Chariton 6, 6, 4 παρέστην δικαστηρίῳ) Καίσαρί σε δεῖ παραστῆναι *you must appear before the Emperor* (as judge) **Ac 27:24;** cp. **2 Ti subscr.** πάντες παραστησόμεθα τῷ βήματι τοῦ θεοῦ (v.l. Χριστοῦ) **Ro 14:10.** πάντας δεῖ παραστῆναι τῷ βήματι τοῦ Χριστοῦ Pol 6:2.

β. of appearing with hostile intent (Appian, Illyr. 17 §51) abs. παρέστησαν οἱ βασιλεῖς τῆς γῆς **Ac 4:26** (Ps 2:2).

γ. *come to the aid of, help, stand by* τινί *someone* (Hom. et al.; X., Cyr. 5, 3, 19 al.; PKöln VI, 245, 22 σὺ δὲ θεὰ παρίστασο 'and you, Goddess, be at my side', w. suggestion of a relationship between Athena and Odysseus [for parallels and lit. s. 'Ptocheia' or 'Odysseus in Disguise at Troy' (=ASP 31), ed. MParca '91, 59]; Mitt-Wilck. II/2, 372 VI, 7; 12; Jos., Bell. 2, 245; SibOr 8, 407) **Ro 16:2.** ὁ κύριός μοι παρέστη **2 Ti 4:17** (cp. PHerm 125b, 8 [III AD] θεὸς παρίσταταί σοι; Jos., Ant. 1, 341; SibOr 3, 705).—The 1 aor. pass. παρεστάθην αὐτῷ Hs 8, 4, 1 is prob. used in act. sense *I took a position beside him (so as to be ready for service).*

ⓑ perf. and plpf. (En 14:22; PsSol 2:36; TestSol 14:2 al.; TestAbr A 7 p. 84, 29 [Stone p. 16]; Just., D. 9, 1)

α. of personal beings *stand* (*near* or *by*), *be present* τινί *(with) someone* (LXX; TestJob 24:10; Jos., Bell. 2, 281) **Ac 1:10;** 1 Cl 34:6 (Da 7:10 Theod.). ἐνώπιόν τινος *stand before someone* (1 Km 16:21; TestAbr A 7 p. 84, 29f [Stone p. 16]) οὗτος παρέστηκεν ἐνώπιον ὑμῶν ὑγιής **Ac 4:10.**—Mostly in the ptc.: modifying a noun and followed by an indication of place: ὁ κεντυρίων ὁ παρεστηκὼς ἐξ ἐναντίας αὐτοῦ **Mk 15:39** (cp. 1 Macc 11:68 S). Γαβριὴλ ὁ παρεστηκὼς ἐνώπιον τοῦ θεοῦ **Lk 1:19** (cp. Jdth 4:14; Tob 12:15 S). Without indication of place (Diod. S. 17, 66, 7 παρεστὼς Φιλώτας=Philotas, who stood nearby; Diog. L. 2, 102; Aberciusins. 17; EpArist 19) εἷς παρεστηκὼς τῶν ὑπηρετῶν *one of the servants who was standing by* **J 18:22.** ἰδὼν τὸν μαθητὴν παρεστῶτα *when he saw the disciple standing near* **19:26.** (ἄγγελοι) λειτουργοῦσιν παρεστῶτες 1 Cl 34:5. παρεστὼς ὁ κύριος MPol 2:2. οἱ παρεστῶτες αὐτῷ *those standing near him* **Ac 23:2.**—Subst. οἱ παρεστηκότες (PPetr II, 4, 6, 13 [III BC]) or οἱ παρεστῶτες (Diog. L. 9, 27) *the bystanders, the spectators, those present* **Mk 14:47, 69f; 15:35** (vv.ll. παρεστώτων, ἑστηκότων); **Lk 19:24; Ac 23:4;** in vs. **2** the widely attested rdg. adds a dat.: τοῖς παρεστῶσιν αὐτῷ (cp. POxy 1204, 13 ὁ παρεστώς σοι).

β. of a point of time *be here, have come* (Il. 16, 853; Demosth. 18, 90; 21, 101) παρέστηκεν ὁ θερισμός *the time for the harvest is here* **Mk 4:29.**

γ. as an agricultural t.t. (cp. OGI 56, 68 ὅταν ὁ πρώϊμος σπόρος παραστῇ; PLille 8, 5) someth. like *be fully grown* σταφυλὴ παρεστηκυῖα *a ripe grape* (in contrast to ὄμφαξ)

1 Cl 23:4=2 Cl 11:3 (quot. of unknown orig.).—M-M. DELG s.v. ἵημι. TW.

Παρμενᾶς, ᾶ, ὁ acc. -ᾶν (Sb 2489) ***Parmenas*** (short form of Παρμενίδης, Παρμενίων, Παρμενίσκος etc.—B-D-F §125, 1; W-S. §16, 9; Rob. 173), one of the seven appointees in Jerusalem **Ac 6:5.**—M-M.

παροδεύω 1 aor. 3 sg. παρώδευσεν Wsd 5:14; ptc. παροδεύσας (Theocr. 23, 47; Heraclit. Sto. 68, p. 88, 6; Plut., Mor. 973d; Lucian, Scyth. 10; OGI 544, 32; Kaibel 810, 11; PMich 149, 12; 21 [an astrol. text]; Wsd; Jos., Bell. 5, 426, Ant. 19, 331) **to go past a point of reference, *pass, pass by,*** ἔγνων παροδεύσαντάς τινας ἐκεῖθεν *I learned to know certain people who had passed by on their way from that place* IEph 9:1. Subst. (Anton. Lib. 23, 6) ὡς παροδεύοντα *as one who is passing by* IRo 9:3.—DELG s.v. ὁδός. M-M s.v. πάροδος.

παρόδιος, ον (πάροδος; Hyperid., fgm. 261; Plut., Mor. 521d al.; PTebt 45, 22; 47, 14 [113 BC]) **to stay (somewhere) in the course of a journey,** subst. ὁ π. ***one who is travelling by*** (otherw. παροδίτης or πάροδος.—Thackeray, The LXX and Jewish Worship 1921, 26–28) D 12:2.—DELG s.v. ὁδός. M-M s.v. πάροδος.

πάροδος, ου, ἡ (s. prec. entry; Thu. et al.; ins, pap, LXX; PsSol 11:5; EpArist; Philo, Praem. 112; Joseph.).

❶ **a way for travelers, *passage, thoroughfare*** (X., An. 4, 7, 4 al.; Diod. S. 20, 23, 2; EpArist 118; Jos., Ant. 14, 46) πάροδός ἐστε τῶν . . . *you are the highway for those . . .* IEph 12:2. ἡ πάροδος μετὰ τῶν ἀγγέλων *the way to the angels* Hv 2, 2, 7 (s. Joly's note); s 9, 25, 2.

❷ **the act of moving to a point of reference and continuing on one's course, but with possibility of a stopover, *passing by*** ἐν π. (Thu. 1, 126, 11; Polyb. 5, 68, 8; Cicero, Ad Att. 5, 20, 2; Lucian, D. Deor. 24, 2; PSI 354, 8; PLond III, 1041, 2 [VII AD]; Jos., Ant. 14, 38) ἰδεῖν τινα *see someone in passing* **1 Cor 16:7.**—DELG s.v. ὁδός. M-M.

παροικέω fut. παροικήσω LXX; 1 aor. παρῴκησα; pf. 3 pl. παρῳκήκασιν Ex 6:4 (s. next entry; Thu. et al.; ins, pap, LXX; PsSol 17:28; Demetr.: 722 fgm. 1, 19 Jac.; Philo; Jos., Ant. 1, 121)

❶ **to dwell or reside near, *live nearby, dwell beside*** w. dat. (Thu. 1, 71, 2 πόλει ὁμοίᾳ παρακοῦντες=neighbors inhabiting a city-state like yours; 3, 93, 2; Plut., Mor. 4a; Lucian, Catap. 16; Philo, Sacr. Abel. 44; OGI 666, 13 [I AD] near the pyramids). In **Lk 24:18** σὺ μόνος παροικεῖς Ἰερουσαλὴμ . . . ; the context suggests that the indeclinable form Ἰερουσαλήμ is to be taken as dat. *are you the only one living near Jerusalem* (who doesn't know what happened there these last few days?). Cleopas speaks somewhat sarcastically in a narrative designed to convey irony. For difft. views s. 2 and 3.

❷ **to inhabit a place as a foreigner, *be a stranger.*** In LXX mostly of strangers who live in a place without holding citizenship (so also PSI 677, 2 [III BC]; Diod. S. 13, 47, 4; cp. SIG 709, 9; IPriene index; s. Elliott, 3 below). Also of persons who live as strangers on earth, far fr. their heavenly home (Philo, Cher. 120, Rer. Div. Her. 267 al.):

ⓐ in a certain place *live as a stranger, inhabit* (a place) *as a stranger* w. acc. of place (Isocr. 4, 162; Gen 17:8; Ex 6:4) 1 Cl ins ab; MPol ins a.—Many take Ἰερουσαλήμ **Lk 24:18** σὺ μόνος παροικεῖς Ἰερουσαλήμ as an acc. and interpret somewhat as follows: *are you the only one new in Jerusalem?* But s. 1 and 3.—. Prob. Pol ins belongs here too, since Φιλίπποις is certainly to be changed to Φιλίππους w. Lghtf. and Bihlmeyer (π. w. dat. means *live beside, be a neighbor* s. 1), and the formulation semantically=Eus., HE 4, 23, 5 τῇ ἐκκλησίᾳ τῇ παροικούσῃ Γόρτυναν (s. παροικία 2).

ⓑ in the midst of others *live as a stranger,* w. ἐν (Gen 20:1; 21:34; 26:3 al.; Philo, Conf. Lingu. 78) **Lk 24:18 v.l.;** MPol ins b. Χριστιανοὶ παροικοῦσιν ἐν φθαρτοῖς Dg 6:8.

ⓒ *migrate* w. εἰς *to* **Hb 11:9.**

❸ also simply ***inhabit, live in*** without the connotation of being a stranger (Ps.-Scylax, Peripl. §93 at the beg. [ed. BFabricius 1878] π. τὰ ἔξω τῆς Σύρτιδος; Sus 28 LXX) perh. **Lk 24:18** but (s. 1 and 2a above).—For lit. s. esp. JHElliott, s.v. πάροικος 2.—DELG s.v. οἶκος. M-M. TW.

παροικία, ας, ἡ (παροικέω; TestLevi 11:2; PdeLabriolle, Paroecia: RSR 18, 1928, 60–72).

❶ **the state of being in a strange locality without citizenship, *sojourn, stay,*** also in transf. sense of the ***foreign country*** itself.

ⓐ lit. (2 Esdr 8:35; prol. to Sir ln. 34; 3 Macc 7:19) of the stay of the Israelites in Egypt (Wsd 19:10) ἐν τῇ παροικίᾳ ἐν γῇ Αἰγύπτου **Ac 13:17** (ἐν γῇ Βαβυλῶνος Theoph. Ant. 3, 28 [p. 264, 9]).

ⓑ fig., of a Christian's earthly life, far fr. the heavenly home (Ps 118:54; 119:5; cp. παροικέω 1) ὁ τῆς π. ὑμῶν χρόνος *the time of your stay here in a strange land* **1 Pt 1:17.** καταλείπειν τὴν π. τοῦ κόσμου τούτου *give up their stay in the strange land of this world* 2 Cl 5:1 (cp. CIG 9474; IG XIV, 531, 7 τούτου τοῦ βίου τὴν παροικίαν; Philo, Conf. Lingu. 80 ἡ ἐν σώματι παροικία).

❷ **a cultic (Christian) group perceived as strangers, *congregation, parish*** (the word is derived fr. π.) in so far as it represents a community of such 'strangers' (Eus., HE 4, 23, 5 τῇ ἐκκλησίᾳ τῇ παροικούσῃ Γόρτυναν ἅμα ταῖς λοιπαῖς κατὰ Κρήτην παροικίαις; Irenaeus in Eus. 5, 24, 14; Apollonius in Eus. 5, 18, 9. παροικία means a community of persons in PsSol 17:17) MPol ins., s. παροικέω 2a.—M-M. TW.

πάροικος, ον (Aeschyl., Thu.+) **pert. to being a resident foreigner, *strange,*** in our lit. almost always subst. **πάροικος, ου, ὁ *stranger, alien,*** one who lives in a place that is not one's home (oft. ins [OGI and SIG indices; Dssm., NB 54=BS 227f]; LXX; PsSol 17:28; TestLevi 11:2; ApcSed 11:8 p. 134, 22 Ja.; Philo, Cher. 121; Jos., Ant. 8, 59).

❶ lit., w. the place indicated by ἐν **Ac 7:6** (adj., after Gen 15:13), **29** (cp. Ex 2:22 πάροικός εἰμι ἐν γῇ ἀλλοτρίᾳ).

❷ fig., of Christians, whose real home is in heaven Dg 5:5. W. ξένοι (this combination twice in Diod. S. 20, 84, 2) **Eph 2:19.** W. παρεπίδημοι **1 Pt 2:11** (on the topic of estrangement cp. M. Ant. 2, 17. Differently JHElliott, with emphasis on the inferior socio-political status of the recipients: Home for the Homeless, '81, 50, n. 10, w. lit. on the verb and cognates).—KSchmidt, Israels Stellung zu d. Fremdlingen u. Beisassen usw.: Judaica 1, '46, 269–96; RFeldmeier, Die Christen als Fremde '92.—PGauthier, in RLonis, L'étranger dans le monde grec '88, 23–46 [SEG XXXVIII no. 2032]. M-M. TW.

παροιμία, ας, ἡ (fr. παρ' οἶμον?=side-remark [s. Schwyzer II 498; Frisk s.v. "semantically unclear"])

❶ **a pithy saying, *proverb, saw, maxim*** (so Aeschyl. et al.; Herodas 2, 61; Socrat., Ep. 36 παροιμίαι κ. παραβολαί; Sir 6:35; Philo, Abr. 235, Vi. Mos. 1, 156; 2, 29, Exsecr. 150) τὸ τῆς παροιμίας (Lucian, Dial. Mort. 6, 2; 8, 1) *what the proverb says*

2 Pt 2:22.—LBieler, Die Namen d. Sprichworts in den klass. Sprachen: RhM n.s. 85, '36, 240–47; GDalman, Jesus (Engl. tr.) 1929, 223–36.

❷ **a brief communication containing truths designed for initiates,** ***veiled saying, figure*** of speech, in which esp. lofty ideas are concealed: in Johannine usage (Suda: παροιμία = λόγος ἀπόκρυφος; Sir 39:3 ἀπόκρυφα παροιμιῶν ἐκζητήσει. Acc. to 47:17 ἑρμηνεία is an adjunct of παροιμίαι) **J 10:6; 16:25ab, 29.**—JQuasten, CBQ 10, '48, 8f.—M-M. TW.

πάροινος, ον (Lysias 4, 8; Menand., Peric. 1022 S. [444 Kö.]; Diog. L. 1, 92; Lucian, Tim. 55; the emendation TestJud 14:4 Ch. rests on a misunderstanding of the lit. structure in that book; π. is used of people in all these exx.) **pert. to one who is given to drinking too much wine,** ***addicted to wine, drunken*** **1 Ti 3:3; Tit 1:7.**—DELG s.v. οἶνος. M-M.

παροίχομαι pf. ptc. neut. παρῳχηκός (Tat. 26, 1) and παρῳχημένος mid. dep. ***to be past,*** of time (οἴχομαι 'go, come'; Hom. et al.; Dionys. Hal. 11, 5 χρόνος; SIG 885, 5 διὰ τῶν παρῳχημένων χρόνων; CPR 10, 6; PRyl 153, 35; Jos., Ant. 8, 301) ἐν ταῖς παρῳχημέναις γενεαῖς **Ac 14:16.**—M-M.

παρομοιάζω (παρόμοιος; only Christian wr.) **to be quite similar to,** ***be like*** τινί *someth.* **Mt 23:27** (v.l. ὁμοιάζετε).—DELG s.v. ὁμός. M-M. TW.

παρόμοιος, (α), ον (s. παρομοιάζω; Hdt. et al.; GrBar 4:6; Tat. 15, 2) **pert. to being quite similar,** ***like, similar*** παρόμοια τοιαῦτα πολλὰ ποιεῖτε *you do many such things* **Mk 7:8 v.l., 13.**—DELG s.v. ὁμός. M-M. TW.

παρόν, τό s. πάρειμι 1b.

παροξύνω (ὀξύνω 'sharpen', then 'provoke'; s. next entry) fut. 3 sg. παροξυνεῖ LXX; aor. παρώξυνα LXX. Pass.: impf. παρωξυνόμην; fut. 3 sg. παροξυνθήσεται Da 11:10; aor. 3 sg. παρωξύνθη LXX (trag., Thu.; OGI 48, 15; BGU 588, 7; LXX; pseudepigr.; Mel., P. 93, 699) **to cause a state of inward arousal,** ***urge on, stimulate,*** esp. *provoke to wrath, irritate* (Eur., Thu. et al.; LXX; PsSol 4:21; TestSim 4:8; TestAsh 2:6; GrBar 1:6; Philo, Joseph.; Mel., P. 93, 699); pass. *become irritated, angry* (Thu. 6, 56, 2 et al.; M. Ant. 9, 42, 7; Arrian, Anab. 4, 4, 2; Sb 8852, 15 [III BC] παροξυνόμενοι οἱ νεώτεροι; Hos 8:5; Zech 10:3; TestDan 4:2; Jos., Bell. 2, 8, Ant. 7, 33) of love **1 Cor 13:5.** παρωξύνετο τὸ πνεῦμα αὐτοῦ ἐν αὐτῷ *his spirit was aroused within him* (by anger, grief, or a desire to convert them) **Ac 17:16** (s. Nock, Essays I 824, w. ref. to X., Cyr. 6, 2, 5; cp. MDibelius, Aufsätze zur Apostelgeschichte[2] '53, 61).—DELG s.v. ὀξύς. M-M s.v. παροξύνομαι. TW.

παροξυσμός, οῦ, ὁ (παρόξυνω; Demosth. et al.; LXX)

❶ **rousing to activity,** ***stirring up, provoking*** (so the verb παροξύνω in act. and pass.; X., Mem. 3, 3, 13 πρὸς τὰ καλά, Oec. 13, 9; Isocr., Ad Demonic. 46) εἰς π. ἀγάπης *for encouragement in love,* i.e. *to encourage someone in love* **Hb 10:24.**

❷ **a state of irritation expressed in argument,** ***sharp disagreement*** ('irritation, exasperation': Demosth. 45, 14; Ael. Aristid. 37 p. 709 D.; 52 p. 600; Dt 29:27; Jer 39:37) ἐγένετο π. *a sharp disagreement arose* **Ac 15:39.**

❸ **a severe fit of a disease,** ***attack of fever,*** esp. at its high point: ***convulsion*** (Hippocr., Aph. 1, 11; 12; 2, 13; Galen XIII p. 210; Artem. 3, 56; PTebt 272, 6.—Hobart 233) IPol 2:1.—DELG s.v. ὀξύς. M-M. TW.

παροράω fut. 3 sg. παρόψεται Job 11:11; aor. παρεῖδον. Pass.: fut. inf. παροραθήσεσθαι 2 Macc 3:9; pf. 3 sg. παρῶπται (Ath., R. 19 p. 71, 29), ptc. παρεωράμενος LXX (X., Pla.+) **to look at only by the way,** ***overlook, take no notice of*** (Aristot. et al.; BGU 1140, 23 [I BC]; Wsd 11:23 παρορᾷς ἁμαρτήματα ἀνθρώπων εἰς μετάνοιαν; Philo, Rer. Div. Her. 109) **Ac 17:30** D.

παροργίζω Att. fut. παροργιῶ (but 2 pl. παροργίσετε TestZeb 9:9); 1 aor. παρώργισα. Pass.: fut. 3 sg. παροργισθήσεται Da 11:36; pf. ptc. fem. acc. παρωργισμένην Sir 4:3 ***make angry*** (so in the pass. in Theophr., HP 9, 16, 6; Strabo 7, 2, 1; OGI 610, 4 [VI AD]) τινά *someone* (LXX; TestJob 43:9; Test12Patr; GrBar 16:2; TestLevi 3:10 [rdg. weakly attested]; Philo, Somn. 2, 177; Just., D. 130, 4) **Ro 10:19** (Dt 32:21); **Eph 6:4** (cp. Pla., Leg. 7, 823cd on effective nurture through praise rather than threats); **Col 3:21 v.l.;** Hv 3, 6. 1.—DELG s.v. 1 ὀργή. M-M. TW.

παροργισμός, οῦ, ὁ (PsSol 8:9; LXX mostly act. 'provoking to anger': 3 Km 15:30; 4 Km 23:26 or 'an action that calls forth anger' in someone: 2 Esdr 19:18) **state of being intensely provoked,** ***angry mood, anger,*** pass. (Jer 21:5 w. θυμός and ὀργή) **Eph 4:26** (cp. the Pythagorean saying Plut., Mor. 488bc; also 1QS 5:26–6:1; CD 9:6–8).—DELG s.v. ὀργή. M-M. TW.

παρορίζω **to go beyond a limit or boundary,** ***overstep, transgress*** (so Ammianus Epigr. [II AD]: Anth. Pal. 11, 209, 1; Anecd. Gr. p. 293, 16. As 'move the boundary' IPriene 37, 142 [II BC]; BGU 616, 4; PTebt 410, 5 [I AD]) pass. οἷς (*by whom*) ὅρια παρορίζεται Dg 11:5.—DELG s.v. ὅρος.

παροτρύνω (ὀτρύνω 'rouse') 1 aor. παρώτρυνα **stir up strong emotion against,** ***arouse, incite*** τινά *someone* (Pind., O. 3, 38 in late mss. [s. BGildersleeve, Pindar '85, 161 and ABoeckh on the pass.]; Lucian, Tox. 35, Deor. Concil. 4; Ael. Aristid. 53 p. 633 D.; Jos., Ant. 7, 118) **Ac 13:50.**—M-M.

παρουσία, ας, ἡ (πάρειμι; trag., Thu.+)—❶ **the state of being present at a place,** ***presence*** (Aeschyl. et al.; Herm. Wr. 1, 22; OGI 640, 7, SIG 730, 14; Did.; cp. Hippol., Ref. 7, 32, 8 'existence') **1 Cor 16:17; Phil 2:12** (opp. ἀπουσία). ἡ π. τοῦ σώματος ἀσθενής *his bodily presence is weak* i.e. when he is present in person, he appears to be weak **2 Cor 10:10.**—Of God (Jos., Ant. 3, 80; 203; 9, 55) τῆς παρουσίας αὐτοῦ δείγματα *proofs of his presence* Dg 7:9 (cp. Diod. S. 3, 66, 3 σημεῖα τῆς παρουσίας τοῦ θεοῦ; 4, 24, 1).

❷ **arrival as the first stage in presence,** ***coming, advent*** (Soph., El. 1104; Eur., Alc. 209; Thu. 1, 128, 5. Elsewh. mostly in later wr.: Polyb. 22, 10, 14; Demetr.: 722 fgm. 11, 18 Jac.; Diod. S. 15, 32, 2; 19, 64, 6; Dionys. Hal. 1, 45, 4; ins, pap; Jdth 10:18; 2 Macc 8:12; 15:21; 3 Macc 3:17; TestAbr A 2 p. 78, 26 [Stone p. 4]; Jos., Bell. 4, 345, Vi. 90; Tat. 39, 3).

ⓐ of human beings, in the usual sense **2 Cor 7:6f.** ἡ ἐμὴ π. πάλιν πρὸς ὑμᾶς *my coming to you again, my return to you* **Phil 1:26.**—RFunk, JKnox Festschr. '67, 249–68.

ⓑ in a special technical sense (difft. JWalvoord, BiblSacr 101, '44, 283–89 on παρ., ἀποκάλυψις, ἐπιφάνεια) of Christ (and the Antichrist). The use of π. as a t.t. has developed in two directions. On the one hand the word served as a sacred expr. for the coming of a hidden divinity, who makes his presence felt by a revelation of his power, or whose presence is celebrated in the cult (Diod. S. 3, 65, 1 ἡ τοῦ θεοῦ π. of Dionysus upon earth; 4, 3, 3; Ael. Aristid. 48, 30; 31 K.=24 p. 473 D.; Porphyr., Philos.

Ex Orac. Haur. II p. 148 Wolff; Iambl., Myst. 2, 8; 3, 11; 5, 21; Jos., Ant. 3, 80; 203; 9, 55; report of a healing fr. Epidaurus: SIG 1169, 34).—On the other hand, π. became the official term for a visit of a person of high rank, esp. of kings and emperors visiting a province (Polyb. 18, 48, 4; CIG 4896, 8f; SIG 495, 85f; 741, 21; 30; UPZ 42, 18 [162 BC]; PTebt 48, 14; 116, 57 [both II BC]; O. Wilck II, 1372; 1481. For the verb in this sense s. BGU XIII, 2211, 5.—O. Wilck I 274ff; Dssm., LO 314ff [LAE 372ff]; MDibelius, Hdb. exc. after the expl. of 1 Th 2:20). These two technical expressions can approach each other closely in mng., can shade off into one another, or even coincide (Ins. von Tegea: BCH 25, 1901 p. 275 ἔτους ξθ' ἀπὸ τῆς θεοῦ 'Αδριανοῦ τὸ πρῶτον ἰς τὴν Ἑλλάδα παρουσίας).—Herm. Wr. 1, 26 uses π. of the advent of the pilgrim in the eighth sphere.

α. of Christ, and nearly always of his Messianic Advent in glory to judge the world at the end of this age: **Mt 24:3** (PSchoonheim, Een semasiolog. onderzoek van π. '53); **1 Cor 1:8 v.l.; 15:23; 2 Th 2:8** (on the expr. ἐπιφάνεια παρουσίας s. FPfister, Pauly-W. Suppl. IV '24, 322); **2 Pt 3:4; 1J 2:28;** Dg 7:6; Hs 5, 5, 3. ἡ π. τοῦ υἱοῦ τ. ἀνθρώπου **Mt 24:27, 37, 39** (cp. the suggestion of retribution SIG 741, 21–23; 31f). ἡ π. τοῦ κυρίου **1 Th 4:15; Js 5:7f.** ἡ π. τοῦ κυρίου ἡμῶν 'Ιησοῦ **1 Th 3:13;** cp. **2:19.** ἡ π. τοῦ κυρίου ἡμῶν 'Ιησοῦ Χριστοῦ **5:23; 2 Th 2:1** (on the use in 1 and 2 Th s. RGundry, NTS 33, '87, 161–78); **2 Pt 1:16** (δύναμις w. παρουσία as Jos., Ant. 9, 55; cp. Ael. Aristid. 48, 30 K. [both passages also b above]).—This explains the expr. ἡ π. τῆς τοῦ θεοῦ ἡμέρας *the coming of the Day of God* **2 Pt 3:12.**—EvDobschütz, Zur Eschatologie der Ev.: StKr 84, 1911, 1–20; FTillmann, D. Wiederkunft Christi nach den paulin. Briefen 1909; FGuntermann, D. Eschatol. des hl. Pls '32; BBrinkmann, D. Lehre v. d. Parusie b. hl. Pls u. im Hen.: Biblica 13, '32, 315–34; 418–34; EHaack, E. exeg.-dogm. Studie z. Eschatol. über 1 Th 4:13–18: ZST 15, '38, 544–69; OCullmann, Le retour de Christ[2] '45; WKümmel, Verheissg. u. Erfüllg.[2] '53; TGlasson, The Second Advent '45; AFeuillet, CHDodd Festschr. '56 (Mt and Js).—On delay of the Parousia WMichaelis, Wikenhauser Festschr. '53, 107–23; EGrässer, D. Problem der Parousieverzögerung (synopt and Ac), '57.—JATRobinson, Jesus and His Coming, '57.

β. in our lit. prob. only in a few late pass. of Jesus' *advent* in the Incarnation (so TestLevi 8:15; TestJud 22:2; Just., A I, 52, 3, D. 14, 8; 40, 4; 118, 2 ἐν τῇ πάλιν παρουσίᾳ; Ps.-Clem., Hom. 2, 52; 8, 5; Orig., C. Cels. 6, 68, 5; Hippol., Ref. 9, 30, 5) τὴν παρουσίαν τοῦ σωτῆρος, κυρίου ἡμῶν 'Ιησοῦ Χριστοῦ, τὸ πάθος αὐτοῦ καὶ τὴν ἀνάστασιν IPhld 9:2; PtK 4 p. 15, 33. But **2 Pt 1:16** (s. α above) can hardly be classed here.

γ. Sense α gave rise to an opposing use of π. to designate the *coming* of the Antichrist (s. ἄνομος 4; Iren. 3, 7, 2 [Harv. II 26f]; Orig., C. Cels. 6, 45, 5) in the last times οὗ ἐστιν ἡ π. κατ' ἐνέργειαν τοῦ σατανᾶ *whose coming is in keeping with / in line with Satan's power* **2 Th 2:9.** KThraede, Grundzüge griechisch-römischer Brieftopik '70, 95–106.—New Docs 4, 167f. DELG s.v. εἰμί. M-M. EDNT. TW. Spicq. Sv.

παροψίς, ίδος, ἡ (ὄψον 'prepared food'; since Magnes Com. [V BC] 2; Pherecrates Com. [V BC] 147; X., Cyr. 1, 3, 4 in the sense 'side-dish' [food]) ***dish, plate*** (=vessel. Antiphanes et al.; Plut., Mor. 828a; Epict. 2, 20, 30; Artem. 1, 74 p. 67, 6; Alciphron 2, 17, 3; BGU 781, 2; 6; 14 [I AD]. The Atticists rejected the use of the word in this transferred sense: Phryn. p. 176 Lob.; Moeris p. 297 et al.) **Mt 23:25, 26 v.l.**—DELG s.v. ὄψον. M-M.

παρρησία, ας, ἡ (πᾶς, ῥῆσις; Eur., Pla.+; Stob., Flor. III 13 p. 453 H. [a collection of sayings περὶ παρρησίας]; ins, pap, LXX; TestReub 4:2; JosAs 23:10 cod. A [Bat. p. 75, 2] and Pal. 364; EpArist, Philo, Joseph.; Ath. 11, 2; loanw. in rabb.—On the spelling s. B-D-F §11, 1; Mlt-H. 101; s. also Schwyzer I 469).

❶ **a use of speech that conceals nothing and passes over nothing, *outspokenness, frankness, plainness*** (Demosth. 6, 31 τἀληθῆ μετὰ παρρησίας ἐρῶ πρὸς ὑμᾶς καὶ οὐκ ἀποκρύψομαι; Diod. S. 4, 74, 2; 12, 63, 2; Pr 1:20; a slave does not have such a privilege: Eur., Phoen. 390–92) παρρησίᾳ *plainly, openly* (EpArist 125) **Mk 8:32; J 7:13; 10:24; 11:14; 16:25** (opp. ἐν παροιμίαις.—On the subject matter cp. Artem. 4, 71 οἱ θεοὶ πάντως μὲν ἀληθῆ λέγουσιν, ἀλλὰ ποτὲ μὲν ἁπλῶς λέγουσι, ποτὲ δὲ αἰνίσσονται=the gods always speak the truth, but sometimes directly, sometimes indirectly), **29 v.l.** (opp. παροιμία); Dg 11:2. Also ἐν παρρησίᾳ **J 16:29.** μετὰ παρρησίας (s. Demosth. above; Ael. Aristid. 30 p. 571 D.; Appian, Bell. Civ. 3, §15 λέγω μετὰ π.; 3 Macc 4:1; 7:12; JosAs 23:10 [s. above]; Philo; Jos., Ant 6, 256) *plainly, confidently* **Ac 2:29;** μετὰ παρρησίας ἄκουε MPol 10:1. This is also the place for πολλῇ παρρησίᾳ χρώμεθα (opp. Moses' veiling of his face) **2 Cor 3:12** (παρρησίᾳ χράομαι as Appian, Maced. 11 §3; Cass. Dio 62, 13; Philo, De Jos. 107; Jos., Ant. 2, 116).—RPope, ET 21, 1910, 236–38; HWindisch, exc. on **2 Cor 3:12.**

❷ 'Openness' somet. develops into ***openness to the public,*** before whom speaking and actions take place (Philo, Spec. Leg. 1, 321 τοῖς τὰ κοινωφελῆ δρῶσιν ἔστω παρρησία) παρρησίᾳ *in public, publicly* **J 7:26; 11:54; 18:20.** δειγματίζειν ἐν παρρησίᾳ *make a public example of* **Col 2:15.** ἐν παρρησίᾳ εἶναι *to be known publicly* **J 7:4** (opp. ἐν κρυπτῷ). This is prob. also the place for παρρησίᾳ **Ac 14:19 v.l.** and μετὰ πάσης παρρησίας ἀκωλύτως *quite openly and unhindered* **28:31.** Also ἐν πάσῃ παρρησίᾳ **Phil 1:20.** This is prob. the place also for **2 Cor 7:4** (but sense 3 is preferred by some): *I am speaking to you with great frankness* (REB; i.e. without weighing every word).

❸ **a state of boldness and confidence, *courage, confidence, boldness, fearlessness,*** esp. in the presence of persons of high rank.

ⓐ in association with humans (Socrat., Ep. 1, 12; Cass. Dio 62, 13; EpArist 125 παρρησίᾳ; Philo, De Jos. 107; 222, Rer. Div. Her. 5f; Jos., Ant. 9, 226; 15, 37; TestReub 4:2f. Cp. also OGI 323, 10; POxy 1100, 15; PGM 12, 187; OEger, Rechtsgeschichtliches zum NT: Rektoratsprogr. Basel 1919, 41f) **Ac 4:13.** Some would put πολλή μοι παρρησία πρὸς ὑμᾶς (sc. ἐστίν and cp. Diod. S. 14, 65, 4 πρὸς τύραννον π.) **2 Cor 7:4** here, but the context appears to favor 2 above. πολλὴν παρρησίαν ἔχων ἐπιτάσσειν σοι **Phlm 8** (π. ἔχω as Dio Chrys. 26 [43], 7). ἐν παρρησίᾳ *fearlessly* **Eph 6:19** (DSmolders, L'audace de l'apôtre: Collectanea Mechlinensia 43, '58, 16–30; 117–33; RWild, CBQ 46, '84, 284–98; the verb w. ἅλυσις vs. 20, cp. Paul's situation Ac 28:30f). μετὰ παρρησίας (Aristoxenus, fgm. 32; Appian, Bell. Civ. 5, 42 §178; Jos., Ant. 6, 256; Ps.-Clem., Hom. 1, 11; 5, 18; μετὰ π. καὶ οὐ κρύβδην Orig., C. Cels. 3, 57, 20) **Ac 2:29** (cp. Chion 16, 7 H. ἀνέξῃ γὰρ μετὰ παρρησίας μοῦ λέγοντος); **4:31;** 1 Cl 34:1. μετὰ παρρησίας πάσης (Jos., Ant. 16, 379) **Ac 4:29; 6:10** D; **16:4** D.

ⓑ in relation to God (Job 27:10; Philo, Rer. Div. Her. 5–7; Jos., Ant. 5, 38) w. προσαγωγή **Eph 3:12.** Here *joyousness, confidence* is the result or the accompaniment of faith, as **1 Ti 3:13; Hb 10:35.** W. καύχημα **3:6;** 1 Cl 34:5. παρρησίαν ἔχειν πρὸς τὸν θεόν (Jos., Ant. 2, 52) **1J 3:21;** cp. **5:14.** μετὰ παρρησίας *with joyful heart* **Hb 4:16;** 2 Cl 15:3. ἀλήθεια ἐν παρρησίᾳ 1 Cl 35:2. ἔχοντες παρρησίαν εἰς τὴν εἴσοδον τῶν ἁγίων *since we have confidence to enter the sanctuary* **Hb 10:19.**—W. expressly forensic and eschatological coloring (as Wsd 5:1) παρρησίαν ἔχειν **1J 2:28** (opp. αἰσχύνεσθαι); **4:17.**—EPeterson, Z. Bedeutungsgesch. v. π.: RSeeberg Festschr. I 1929, 283–97; WvUnnik, The Christian's Freedom of Speech: BJRL '62, 466–88; HCombrink, Parresia in Handelinge: GereformTT '75, 56–63; WBeilner, ΠΑΡΡΗΣΙΑ '79 (lit.); SMarrow, CBQ 44, '82, 431–46; PMiguel, Parrhēsia: Dictionnaire de spiritualité 12, '83, 260–67; also articles by DFredrickson, SWinter, AMitchell, WKlassen, in Friendship, Flattery, and Frankness of Speech '96, 163–254; RAC VII 839–77.—DELG s.v. 2 εἴρω. M-M. EDNT. TW. Spicq. Sv.

παρρησιάζομαι (παρρησία) mid. dep. (Pla. et al.; LXX, Philo) impf. ἐπαρρησιαζόμην; fut. παρρησιάσομαι and mid.-pass. 2 sg. παρρησιασθήσῃ Job 22:26; 1 aor. ἐπαρρησιασάμην (on the augment s. B-D-F §69, 4; Mlt-H. 192, n. 3), mid.-pass. inf. παρρησιασθῆναι GrBar 9:8.

❶ **express oneself freely, *speak freely, openly, fearlessly*** abs. (X., Ages. 11, 5; Aeschines 1, 172; 2, 70; Diod. S. 14, 7, 6; Jos., Ant. 16, 377) **Ac 18:26; 19:8;** likew. in the ptc. w. a verb of saying foll. (Appian, Bell. Civ. 1, 56 §247 παρρησιαζόμενον καὶ λέγοντα) παρρησιασάμενοι εἶπαν **13:46.**—**26:26.** π. πρός τινα *speak freely to* or *with someone* (X., Cyr. 5, 3, 8; Diod. S. 23, 12, 1; Lucian, Ind. 30. Cp. π. ἐπὶ Ἰουδαίων Orig., C. Cels. 2, 45, 11) 1 Cl 53:5. W. ἐν the reason for the παρρησία is given, and at the same time the object of the free speech: π. ἐν τῷ ὀνόματι Ἰησοῦ **Ac 9:27;** cp. vs. **28; Eph 6:20.** Likew. w. ἐπί and dat. (Phalaris, Ep. 139 ἐπ᾽ αὐτοῖς π.—B-D-F §235, 2) π. ἐπὶ τῷ κυρίῳ **Ac 14:3.**

❷ When used w. the inf. π. gains (on the analogy of τολμᾶν, s. B-D-F §392, 3) the sense ***have the courage, venture*** **1 Th 2:2** (so w. the ptc., Ps.-Clem., Hom. 4, 17).

❸ The quot. fr. Ps 11:6: παρρησιάσομαι ἐν αὐτῷ is unique, someth. like ***I will deal openly (boldly) with him*** 1 Cl 15:7.—DELG s.v. εἴρω. M-M. TW.

πᾶς, πᾶσα, πᾶν gen. παντός, πάσης, παντός (dat. pl. πᾶσι and πᾶσιν vary considerably in the mss.; s. W-S. §5, 28; cp. Rob. 219–21; on the use of the art. s. B-D-F § 275) (Hom. +).

❶ **pert. to totality with focus on its individual components, *each, every, any*—ⓐ** adj., used w. a noun without the art.—**α.** in the sing. emphasizing the individual members of the class denoted by the noun *every, each, any,* scarcely different in mng. fr. the pl. 'all': πᾶν δένδρον **Mt 3:10; Lk 3:9.** πᾶσα φυτεία **Mt 15:13.** πᾶσα φάραγξ, πᾶν ὄρος **Lk 3:5** (Is 40:4). πᾶς τόπος **4:37.** πᾶς ἄνθρωπος **J 1:9; 2:10; Ro 3:4** (Ps 115:2); **Gal 5:3; Col 1:28abd; Js 1:19.** πᾶσα γυνή GJs 11:2. πᾶν ἔθνος **Ac 17:26a.** πᾶσα ψυχή (Pla., Phdr. 249e) **2:43; 3:23** (cp. Lev 23:29); **Ro 2:9; Jd 15.** πᾶσα ἡμέρα **Ac 5:42; 17:17.** πᾶν σάββατον **18:4.** πᾶσα ἀρχὴ καὶ πᾶσα ἐξουσία **1 Cor 15:24** (cp. Just., D. 111, 2 οὗ τὸ ὄνομα πᾶσα ἀρχὴ δέδιεν). πᾶσα συνείδησις **2 Cor 4:2.** πᾶς ἅγιος **Phil 4:21.** πᾶς οἶκος **Hb 3:4** (GJs 7:3). πᾶσα ἀντιλογία **7:7.** πᾶσα παιδεία *all discipline* **12:11.** πᾶς ὀφθαλμός **Rv 1:7a.** πᾶν κτίσμα **5:13a.**—**Mt 23:35; Lk 2:23** (Ex 13:2); **4:13; 21:36; 2 Th 2:4** (Da 11:36). πᾶσα κτίσις *every creature* **Col 1:15;** ἐν πάσῃ κτίσει *to every creature* vs. **23.** πᾶσα γραφή **2 Ti 3:16** (s. γραφή 2a).—πᾶσα σάρξ (כָּל־בָּשָׂר; used in the OT, also En 1:9; TestGad 7:2; GrBar 4:10; but not in EpArist, Philo, nor Joseph.) *all flesh* **Lk 3:6** (Is 40:5); AcPlCor 2:6 and 16 (s. also 3b below). Mostly w. a neg. (so also En 14:21; 17:6) οὐ (or μή)… πᾶσα σάρξ *no flesh = no one* **Mt 24:22; Mk 13:20; Ro 3:20; 1 Cor 1:29; Gal 2:16** (cp. GrBar 8:7 οὐκ ἂν ἐσώθη πᾶσα πνοή). Other sim. neg. expressions are also Hebraistic (s. B-D-F §302, 1; Mlt-H. 433f) οὐ … πᾶν ῥῆμα *not a thing, nothing* **Lk 1:37** (cp. PRyl 113, 12f [133 AD] μὴ … πᾶν πρᾶγμα). οὐδέποτε ἔφαγον πᾶν κοινόν *I have never eaten anything common* **Ac 10:14.** Cp. **Rv 7:1, 16; 9:4; 21:27.** Also in reverse order, πᾶς … οὐ or μή (Ex 12:16; Sir 8:19; 10:6, but s. also GLee, ET 63, '51f, 156) **18:22; Eph 4:29; 5:5; 2 Pt 1:20; 1J 2:21; 3:15b.**—Only rarely is a ptc. used w. πᾶς in this way: παντὸς ἀκούοντος *when anyone hears* **Mt 13:19.** παντὶ ὀφείλοντι **Lk 11:4** (Mlt-Turner 196f).

β. w. a noun in the pl., without the art. πάντες ἄνθρωποι *all people/men, everyone* (Lysias 12, 60; Andoc. 3, 25; X., Cyr. 7, 5, 52, Mem. 4, 4, 19; Demosth. 8, 5; 18, 72) **Ac 22:15; Ro 5:12a, 18ab; 12:17, 18; 1 Cor 7:7; 15:19; 2 Cor 3:2; Phil 4:5; 1 Th 2:15; 1 Ti 2:4; 4:10; Tit 2:11.** πάντες ἄγγελοι θεοῦ **Hb 1:6** (Dt 32:43; cp. Demosth. 18, 294 πάντες θεοί).

ⓑ adj. used with a noun or ptc. with the art.—**α.** in the sing. Oft. πᾶς ὁ, πᾶσα ἡ, πᾶν τό is used w. a ptc. (B-D-F §413, 2 and 3) *every one who, whoever* πᾶς ὁ (Soph., Aj. 152; Demosth. 23, 97; Sir 22:2, 26; 1 Macc 1:52; 2:27) πᾶς ὁ ὀργιζόμενος **Mt 5:22.** Cp. vss. **28, 32; 7:8, 26** (=πᾶς ὅστις vs. **24;** s. below); **Lk 6:47; 11:10; 14:11; 16:18; 18:14; 19:26; J 3:8, 15f, 20; 4:13; 6:40; 8:34; 18:37; Ac 10:43b; 13:39; Ro 2:1, 10; 10:4, 11; 1 Cor 9:25; Gal 3:13; 2 Ti 2:19; Hb 5:13; 1J 2:23, 29** al.; **2J 9; Rv 22:18.**—πᾶν τό *everything that* (1 Macc 10:41): πᾶν τὸ εἰσπορευόμενον **Mt 15:17; Mk 7:18.** πᾶν τὸ ὀφειλόμενον **Mt 18:34.** πᾶν τὸ πωλούμενον **1 Cor 10:25;** cp. vs. **27.** πᾶν τὸ φανερούμενον **Eph 5:14.** πᾶν τὸ γεγεννημένον **1J 5:4.**—An equivalent of this expr. is πᾶς ὅς (or ὅστις), πᾶν ὅ *every one who, whatever* (s. above and s. B-D-F §293, 1; 413, 2; Rob. 727; 957), masc.: **Mt 7:24; 10:32; 19:29; Lk 12:8, 10** (RHolst, ZNW 63, '72, 122–24), **48; 14:33; Ac 2:21** (πᾶς ὃς ἐάν, s. Jo 2:32); **Ro 10:13** (πᾶς ὃς ἄν, s. Jo 3:5); **Gal 3:10.** Neut. (Jdth 12:14.—Jos., Ant. 5, 211 πᾶν ὅ = πάντες οἵ): **J 6:37, 39; 17:2b; Ro 14:23; Col 3:17** (πᾶν ὅ τι ἐάν).

β. w. a noun in the pl., w. the art. *all*—**א.** w. substantives: πᾶσαι αἱ γενεαί **Mt 1:17; Lk 1:48; Eph 3:21;** GJs 6:2 al. πάντας τοὺς ἀρχιερεῖς **Mt 2:4.** Cp. vs. **16; 4:8; 11:13; Mk 4:13, 31f; 6:33; Lk 1:6; 2:51; 6:26; J 18:20; Ac 1:18; 3:18; 10:12, 43a; 14:16; Ro 1:5; 15:11** (Ps 116:1); **16:4; 1 Cor 12:26ab; 2 Cor 8:18; 11:28; Eph 4:10; 6:16b; Col 2:13; 1 Ti 6:10; Hb 4:4** (Gen 2:2 and 3); **9:21; Js 1:8; Rv 1:7b; 7:11; 15:4** al.—Used w. a demonstr. pron.: πᾶσαι αἱ παρθένοι ἐκεῖναι **Mt 25:7.** πάντας τοὺς λόγους τούτους **26:1.** πάντα τὰ ῥήματα ταῦτα **Lk 1:65; 2:19.**—Somet. following the noun: τὰς πόλεις πάσας **Mt 9:35; Ac 8:40.** οἱ μαθηταὶ πάντες *the disciples, one and all* **Mt 26:56.** αἱ θύραι πᾶσαι **Ac 16:26a.** Cp. **Ro 16:16; 1 Cor 7:17; 13:2a; 15:7; 16:20; 1 Th 5:26; 2 Ti 4:21; Rv 8:3.** οἱ Ἱεροσολυμῖται πάντες **Mk 1:5.**—On the position of ἐκεῖνος, ἕνεκα, πᾶς s. NTurner, VetusT 5, '55, 208–13.

ב. w. participles πάντες οἱ: πάντες οἱ κακῶς ἔχοντες **Mt 4:24.** πάντες οἱ κοπιῶντες **11:28;** cp. **21:12; 26:52; Lk 1:66; 2:47; 13:17; Ac 1:19; 2:44; 4:16; 5:5, 11; 6:15; 9:14; 28:30; Ro 1:7; 4:11; 1 Cor 1:2; Eph 6:24; 1 Th 1:7; 2 Th 1:10; 2 Ti 3:12; 4:8; Hb 5:9; 13:24; 2J 1; Rv 13:8; 18:24.** Following the ptc. οἱ κατοικοῦντες πάντες **Ac 2:14.** ἐν τοῖς ἡγιασμένοις πᾶσιν **20:32.**—πάντα τά: πάντα τὰ γενόμενα **Mt 18:31.** πάντα τὰ ὑπάρχοντα **24:47; Lk 12:44; 1 Cor 13:3.** Cp. **Lk 17:10; 18:31; 21:36; J 18:4; Ac 10:33b.** Used w. a demonstr. pron.: περὶ πάντων τῶν συμβεβηκότων τούτων **Lk 24:14.** Following: τὰ γινόμενα πάντα **9:7.**

ג. w. prepositional expressions, w. which ὄντες (ὄντα) is to be supplied (TestAbr A 4 p. 81, 24 [Stone p. 10] πάντα τὰ ἐπὶ τῆς τραπέζης; 4 [6] Esdr [POxy 1010] πάντες σου οἱ ἐν τοῖς πεδίοις): πάντες οἱ ἐν τῇ οἰκίᾳ **Mt 5:15; Ac 16:32.** πάντες οἱ σὺν αὐτῷ **Lk 5:9.** πάντες οἱ ἐν τοῖς μνημείοις **J 5:28.** πάντες οἱ εἰς μακράν **Ac 2:39.** Cp. **5:17.** πάντες οἱ ἐξ Ἰσραήλ **Ro 9:6.** Cp. **2 Ti 1:15; 1 Pt 5:14.** πάντα τὰ ἐν αὐτοῖς **Ac 4:24; 14:15** (Ex 20:11); cp. **17:24.** Following: οἱ μετʼ ἐμοῦ πάντες **Tit 3:15a** (πάντες οἱ μετʼ αὐτοῦ JosAs 27:7).

ⓒ π. used w. pronouns—**α.** w. personal pronouns: πάντες ἡμεῖς *we all* **Ac 2:32; 10:33a; 26:14; 28:2; Ro 4:16b.** πάντες ὑμεῖς **Mt 23:8; 26:31; Lk 9:48; Ac 4:10a; 22:3; Ro 1:8; 15:33; 2 Cor 7:15; Gal 3:28; Phil 1:4, 7ab, 8; 1 Th 1:2; 2 Th 3:16c, 18; Tit 3:15b; Hb 13:25.** πάντες αὐτοί **Ac 4:33; 19:17b; 20:36.** Following the pron.: ἡμεῖς πάντες **J 1:16; Ro 8:32a; 2 Cor 3:18; Eph 2:3.** ὑμεῖς πάντες **Ac 20:25.** αὐτοὶ πάντες **Mt 12:15; 1 Cor 15:10.** W. art. οἱ πάντες ἡμεῖς **2 Cor 5:10.**

β. w. a demonstr. pron.: πάντες οὗτοι *these all, all these* **Ac 2:7 v.l.** Mostly following the pron.: οὗτοι πάντες **1:14; 17:7; Hb 11:13, 39.** πάντα ταῦτα **Mt 6:32; 24:8; Lk 7:18; Ac 24:8; 1 Cor 12:11; Col 3:14; 1 Th 4:6;** Hm 5, 2, 5 cj. Joly. ταῦτα πάντα **Mt 4:9; 6:33; 13:34, 51; Lk 12:30; Ac 7:50; Ro 8:37; 2 Pt 3:11.**

γ. πάντες ὅσοι, πάντα ὅσα *all who, everything that,* masc.: **Lk 4:40 v.l.** (for ἅπαντες); **J 10:8.** Neut. (TestAbr A 9 p. 86, 17 [Stone p. 20]; TestJob 4:2; GrBar 7:2; Philo, Aet. M. 15; 28; Jos., Ant. 8, 242; Just., A I, 44, 9) **Mt 7:12; 13:46; 18:25; 21:22; Mk 11:24; 12:44b; Lk 18:12, 22; J 10:41.** πάντες, ὃς ἄν Hs 7:7.

ⓓ subst.—**α.** πάντες, πᾶσαι *all, everyone* (even when only two are involved = both: Appian, Bell. Civ. 2, 27 §105 [Caesar and Pompey]) **Mt 10:22; 14:20; 15:37; 21:26; 26:27; Mk 1:37; 5:20; Lk 1:63** and oft. πάντες ἥμαρτον **Ro 5:12** (on the sinfulness of πάντες cp. the saying of Bias s.v. πολύς 1aβℵ; FDanker, Ro 5:12, Sin under Law, NTS 14, '68, 430, n. 1).—οὐ πάντες *not everyone* **Mt 19:11.** Cp. **J 13:10; Ro 10:16.**—πάντων as partitive and comparative gen. ὕστερον πάντων *last of all* **Mt 22:27;** cp. **Mk 12:22, 43.** Even in ref. to a fem. (Thu. 4, 52, 3; Aristoph., Av. 472) ἐντολὴ πρώτη πάντων **Mk 12:28** (but s. B-D-F §164, 1).

β. πάντα *all things, everything.* Abs. (Chrysippus in Stob., Ecl. 1, 1, 26 p. 31 W.; Ps.-Aristot., De Mundo 6; M. Ant. 4, 23; Ael. Aristid. 43, 9 K.=1 p. 3 D.: ἀρχὴ ἁπάντων Ζεύς τε καὶ ἐκ Διὸς πάντα; Herm. Wr. 5, 10; Hymn to Selene in PGM 4, 2838f ἐκ σέο γὰρ πάντʼ ἐστὶ καὶ εἰς σʼ, αἰώνιε, πάντα τελευτᾷ [s. 4dβ]; PGM 5, 139; PKöln VI, 245, 16 of Athena [s. ed.'s comments]) **Mt 11:27 = Lk 10:22** (s. the lit. on this pass. s.v. υἱός 2dβ. The word πάντα here is variously understood of authority and power [so ASchlatter (Mt), FBüchsel (TW II 173) et al.] or of knowledge and teaching: ENorden [Agn. Th. 288], TZahn [Mt], Grundmann [Lk] et al.; also JFitzmyer: "the knowledge of the mutual relation of himself and God" [AB Comm. Luke II 874]. IMarshall [Lk] follows BReicke [TW V 993 n. 289] and opts for both power and knowledge); **J 1:3; 3:35; 21:17; 1 Cor 2:10; 15:27a** (Ps 8:7), **b, 28cd** (πάντα ἐν πᾶσιν w. a somewhat different coloring: Dio Chrys. 54 [71], 1); **Eph 1:22a** (Ps 8:7); **Rv 21:5.** Here we may class ὁ ὢν ἐπὶ πάντων θεός (cp. Aristobulus in Eus., PE 8, 10, 10; 13, 12, 4 ἐπὶ πάντων εἶναι τ. θεόν; Porphyr., Vi. Plot. 23 τῷ ἐπὶ πᾶσι θεῷ) *God, who rules over all* **Ro 9:5** (θεός 2). ὁ πάντων δεσπότης GJs 20:3 (codd.); cp. 11:2.—Of a 'whole' that is implied fr. the context: πάντα ἀποδώσω σοι **Mt 18:26.** Cp. **22:4; Mk 4:34; Lk 1:3; Ro 8:28** (s. Black s.v. συνεργέω); **2 Cor 6:10; Gal 4:1; Phil 2:14; 1 Th 5:21; 2 Ti 2:10; Tit 1:15; 1J 2:27;** GJs 18:3 codd. πάντα ὑμῶν ἐστιν *everything is yours, belongs to you* **1 Cor 3:21,** cp. **22** (Plut., Cic. 873 [25, 4] πάντα τοῦ σοφοῦ εἶναι; Diog. L. 6, 72). πάντα ὑμῶν *everything you do* **16:14.** πρῶτον πάντων **1 Ti 2:1.** πάντα four times as anaphora (rhetorical repetition) **1 Cor 13:7** (cp. Libanius, Or. 3 p. 275, 4 πάντα φθεγγόμενοι, πάντα ἐργαζόμενοι, πάντα χαριζόμενοι).—The acc. of specification stands almost in the sense of an adv. (B-D-F §154; Rob. 487) πάντα *in all respects, in every way, altogether* (Hom. et al.; Aelian, VH 12, 25; Jos., Ant. 9, 166; SibOr 3, 205; Ath. 35, 2) **Ac 20:35** (perh. *always,* as Ps.-Lucian, Asin. 22 p. 590); **1 Cor 9:25b.** πάντα πᾶσιν ἀρέσκω (s. ἀρέσκω 2a) **10:33; 11:2.** Cp. KGrobel, JBL 66, '47, 366 and s. τὰ πάντα in 4dβ below.—W. a prep.: εἰς πάντα *in all respects, in every way* (Pla., Charm. 6, 158a, Leg. 5, 738a; Appian, Iber. 17 §64, Bell. Civ. 4, 92 §385; BGU 798, 7) **2 Cor 2:9.** ἐν πᾶσιν *in all respects, in every way* (PGiss 69, 8; Appian, Bell. Civ. 2, 112 §467 [here ἐν ἅπασιν=in all respects]; Just., D. 80, 1 ἀσφαλὴς ἐν πᾶσι); **1 Ti 3:11; 2 Ti 2:7; 4:5; Tit 2:9, 10b; Hb 13:4, 18; 1 Pt 4:11.** Perh. also **Eph 1:23b.** ἐν πᾶσι τούτοις *in* (or *besides*) *all this* (Sir 48:15; Job 2:10; 12:9; cp. Plut., Mor. 98f) **Lk 16:26.** κατὰ πάντα, s. κατά B 6. περὶ πάντων *in every way* (Mitt-Wilck I/2, 6, 9; SibOr 1, 198) **3J 2.** πρὸ πάντων *above all, especially* (PRein 18, 27 [II BC]; BGU 811, 3; PAmh 135, 2; Just., D. 7, 3) **Js 5:12; 1 Pt 4:8.**

❷ **any entity out of a totality,** ***any and every, every***—ⓐ as adj. w. a noun in the sing. without the article *every, any and every, just any, any at all* μὴ παντὶ πνεύματι πιστεύετε *do not believe just any spirit* **1J 4:1.** περιφερόμενοι παντὶ ἀνέμῳ τῆς διδασκαλίας **Eph 4:14.** περὶ παντὸς πράγματος *about anything* **Mt 18:19.** κατὰ πᾶσαν αἰτίαν *for any reason at all* **19:3.** Cp. **4:4=Lk 4:4 v.l.** (Dt 8:3); **Mt 12:31; 2 Cor 1:4b** (on ἐπὶ πάσῃ τῇ θλίψει ἡμῶν vs. **4a** see 3b below).

ⓑ as subst. without the art.—**α.** πᾶς *everyone without exception* **Lk 16:16.**

β. πᾶν, w. prep.: διὰ παντός s. διά A 2a. ἐν παντί *in every respect* or *way, in everything* (Pla., Symp. 194a; X., Hell. 5, 4, 29; SIG 1169, 27; Sir 18:27; 4 Macc 8:3; GrBar 9:8) πλουτίζεσθαι **1 Cor 1:5; 2 Cor 9:11.** Cp. **2 Cor 4:8; 7:5, 11, 16; 8:7; 9:8b; 11:6a, 9; Eph 5:24; Phil 4:6; 1 Th 5:18.**

❸ **marker of the highest degree of someth.,** ***all***—ⓐ as adj. w. a noun in the sing. without the art. *full, greatest, all* (Pla., Rep. 9, 575a; Demosth. 18, 279 al.; ins, freq. in accolades; pap.: New Docs 8 p. 62, 10 μετὰ πάσης πίστεως καὶ ἐπιμελείας 'with all fidelity and care'; LXX; Tat. 39, 1 μετὰ πάσης ἀκριβείας) μετὰ παρρησίας πάσης **Ac 4:29.** ἐν πάσῃ ἀσφαλείᾳ **5:23.** πάσῃ συνειδήσει ἀγαθῇ *in all good conscience* **23:1.** Cp. **17:11; 24:3; 2 Cor 9:8b; 12:12; Eph 4:2.** ἐν πάσῃ προσκαρτερήσει *with the greatest perseverance* **6:18c.** Cp. **Phil 1:20; 2:29; Col 1:11ab; 1 Ti 2:2b, 11; 3:4; 4:9; 5:2; Tit 2:15; Js 1:2; 2 Pt 1:5; Jd 3** al. ὑπομένειν πᾶσαν ὑπομονήν *practice patient endurance to the limit* Pol 9:1.

ⓑ in related vein as adj. with noun in the sing. w. the art. *all* ἐπὶ πάσῃ τῇ θλίψει ἡμῶν *in all our trouble* **2 Cor 1:4a** (on ἐν πάσῃ θλίψει vs. **4b** s. 2a above); **7:4; 1 Th 3:7.** ἐπὶ πάσῃ τῇ μνείᾳ ὑμῶν *in all remembrance of you* **Phil 1:3.** πᾶσαν τὴν μέριμναν ὑμῶν *all your care* **1 Pt 5:7.** τὸν πάντα χρόνον AcPlCor 2:4; τὴν πᾶσαν σάρκα 2:11 (cp. 1aα).

❹ **pert. to a high degree of completeness or wholeness,** ***whole***—ⓐ as adj. w. a noun in the sing., without the art. *all, the whole* before proper names, mostly geographic (X., Hell. 4, 8, 28 προστάται πάσης Λέσβου ἔσονται al.; LXX) πᾶσα Ἱεροσόλυμα **Mt 2:3** (s. Ἱερ.). πᾶς Ἰσραήλ (3 Km 8:65; 11:16; 1 Esdr 1:19; 5:45, 58; Jdth 15:14) **Ro 11:26** (s. W-S. §20, 11a and b; Rob. 772). The OT is also the source of πᾶς οἶκος Ἰσραήλ (1 Km 7:2, 3) **Ac 2:36** and, in subject matter, ἐπὶ παντὸς προσώπου τῆς γῆς **17:26b** (but Gen 2:6 has πᾶν τὸ πρόσωπον τῆς γῆς, and 7:23; 11:4, 8, 9 ἐπὶ προσώπου [or πρόσωπον] πάσης τῆς γῆς).—Perh. πᾶσα οἰκοδομή **Eph 2:21** (s. W-S. §20:11 b; Rob.

772; Mlt-Turner 199f; MDibelius, Hdb. ad loc.; M. Ant. 6, 36, 1; OGI 383, 86ff).

ⓑ w. a noun in the sing., w. the art. *the whole, all (the).* Preceding the noun that has the art.: πᾶσα ἡ Ἰουδαία καὶ πᾶσα ἡ περίχωρος **Mt 3:5.** πᾶσα ἡ ἀγέλη *the whole herd* **8:32.** Cp. vs. **34; 13:2; 21:10; 27:25, 45; Mk 2:13; 4:1.** πᾶσα ἡ ἀλήθεια **5:33.** πᾶσα ἡ κτίσις *the whole creation* (TestAbr A 13 p. 92, 7 [Stone p. 32]) **Mk 16:15; Ro 8:22.** Cp. **Lk 1:10; 2:1, 10; Ac 3:9, 11; 5:21; 15:12.** πᾶς ὁ κόσμος **Ro 3:19b; Col 1:6.** πᾶν τὸ σπέρμα **Ro 4:16.** πᾶσα ἡ γῆ **9:17** (Ex 9:16); **Lk 4:25.** πᾶσα ἡ γνῶσις, πᾶσα ἡ πίστις **1 Cor 13:2bc.** πᾶν τὸ πλήρωμα **Eph 3:19; Col 1:19; 2:9.** πᾶν τὸ σῶμα **Eph 4:16; Col 2:19.** Cp. **Hb 9:19bc.** W. a demonstrative pron. πᾶς ὁ λαὸς οὗτος *all these people* **Lk 9:13.** πᾶσα ἡ ὀφειλὴ ἐκείνη **Mt 18:32.**—Following the noun that has the article: τὴν κρίσιν πᾶσαν *the whole matter of judgment* **J 5:22.** εἰς τὴν ἀλήθειαν πᾶσαν *into truth in all its outreach* **16:13.** τὴν ἐξουσίαν . . . πᾶσαν **Rv 13:12.**

ⓒ πᾶς and πάντες stand attributively betw. art. and noun, when the noun is regarded as a whole, in contrast to its individual parts (cp. Kühner-G. I 632f).

α. sing. (Thu. 2, 7, 2 ὁ πᾶς ἀριθμός='the whole number'; 8, 93, 2 τὸ πᾶν πλῆθος; X., Mem. 1, 2, 8 εἰς τὸν πάντα βίον; Pla., Gorg. 470e ἡ πᾶσα εὐδαιμονία; 2 Macc 2:17; 3 Macc 1:29; 6:14; 4 Macc 3:8) ὁ πᾶς νόμος *the whole law* **Gal 5:14.** τὸν πάντα χρόνον **Ac 20:18.**

β. pl. (X., An. 5, 6, 7 οἱ πάντες ἄνθρωποι; Pla., Theaet. 204a τὰ πάντα μέρη) αἱ πᾶσαι ψυχαί *all the souls* **Ac 27:37.** οἱ κατὰ τὰ ἔθνη πάντες Ἰουδαῖοι **21:21.** οἱ σὺν αὐτοῖς πάντες ἅγιοι **Ro 16:15.** οἱ σὺν ἐμοὶ πάντες ἀδελφοί **Gal 1:2.**—W. numerals (Hdt. 7, 4; Thu. 1, 60, 1) οἱ πάντες ἄνδρες ὡσεὶ δώδεκα *the whole number of the men was about twelve* **Ac 19:7.**—JBover, Uso del adjetivo singular πᾶς en San Pablo: Biblica 19, '38, 411–34.

ⓓ as subst.—**α.** οἱ πάντες *all (of them) (in contrast to a part)* **Ro 11:32ab; 1 Cor 9:22** (s. HChadwick, NTS 1, '55, 261–75); **Phil 2:21.** *(We, they) all* **Mk 14:64; 1 Cor 10:17; 2 Cor 5:14b.** μέχρι καταντήσωμεν οἱ πάντες *until we all attain* **Eph 4:13.**

β. τὰ πάντα. In the abs. sense of the whole of creation *all things, the universe* (Pla., Ep. 6, 323d τῶν πάντων θεός; hymn to Selene in EAbel, Orphica [1885] 294, 36 εἰς σὲ τὰ πάντα τελευτᾷ [s. 1dβ beg.]; Herm. Wr. 13, 17 τ. κτίσαντα τὰ πάντα; JosAs 8:2 ζωοποιήσας τὰ πάντα; Philo, Spec. Leg. 1, 208, Rer. Div. Her. 36, Somn. 1, 241; Just., A I, 67, 2 τὸν ποιητὴν τῶν πάντων; PGM 1, 212 κύριε τῶν πάντων; 4, 3077) **Ro 11:36** (Musaeus: Vorsokr. 2 A 4 [in Diog. L. 1, 3] ἐξ ἑνὸς τὰ πάντα γίνεσθαι καὶ εἰς ταὐτὸν ἀναλύεσθαι. Cp. Norden, Agn. Th. 240–50); **1 Cor 8:6ab; 15:28ab; Eph 3:9; 4:10b; Phil 3:21; Col 1:16ab, 17b** (HHegermann, D. Vorstellung vom Schöpfungsmittler etc., TU 82, '61, 88ff); **Hb 1:3; 2:10ab; Rv 4:11;** 1 Cl 34:2; PtK 2 (four times).—In the relative sense, indicated by the context, *everything* (Κυπρ. I p. 42 no. 29 τὰς στοὰς καὶ τὰ ἐν αὐταῖς πάντα; PGiss 2, 14 [II BC] in a bill: τὰ π.=everything taken together) ἐν παραβολαῖς τὰ πάντα γίνεται *everything* (=all the instruction) *is in parables* **Mk 4:11.** Cp. **Ac 17:25b; Ro 8:32b.** Of everything in heaven and earth that is in need of uniting and redeeming **Eph 1:10** (EWalter, Christus u. d. Kosmos [Eph 1:10] '48); **Col 1:20.** τὰ πάντα *they all* (of the members of the body) **1 Cor 12:19.** The neut. is also used of persons: **Gal 3:22;** cp. **1 Ti 6:13** (here including humankind and everything else that possesses life).—As acc. of specification, almost like an adv.: τὰ πάντα *in all respects* (Appian, Prooem. 6 §23) **Eph 4:15** (s. 1dβ).—As a summation of what precedes *all this* (PCairZen 741, 16; 742, 22; BGU 1509 [all III BC]) **2 Cor 4:15; Phil 3:8b; Col 3:8.**—Furthermore, πάντες can also have the limited sense *nearly all* (Xenophon Eph. 2, 13, 4 πάντας ἀπέκτεινεν, ὀλίγους δὲ καὶ ζῶντας ἔλαβε. μόνος δὲ ὁ Ἱππόθοος ἠδυνήθη διαφυγεῖν).—Mlt-Turner 199–201.

❺ **everything belonging, in kind, to the class designated by the noun,** ***every kind of, all sorts of,*** adj. for the words παντοδαπός and παντοῖος, which are lacking in our lit.: πᾶσα νόσος καὶ πᾶσα μαλακία **Mt 4:23.** γέμουσιν πάσης ἀκαθαρσίας *they are full of all kinds of uncleanness* **23:27** (Ar. 15, 6). πᾶσα ἐξουσία **28:18.** ἀπὸ παντὸς ἔθνους *from every kind of nation* **Ac 2:5.** Cp. **7:22; 13:10ab; Ro 1:18, 29.** πᾶσα ἐπιθυμία (evil) *desire of every kind* **7:8.** ἐν παντὶ λόγῳ καὶ πάσῃ γνώσει **1 Cor 1:5b.** πᾶν ἁμάρτημα *every kind of sin* **6:18.** Cp. **2 Cor 7:1; 9:8bc; 10:5ab; Eph 1:3, 8, 21a; 4:19; 5:3; Phil 1:9; 2 Th 2:17.** πᾶν ἔργον ἀγαθόν **Tit 1:16; 3:1.** Cp. **2:14; Hb 13:21.** πᾶσα δόσις, πᾶν δώρημα **Js 1:17** (W-S. §20, 11b). Cp. vs. **21; 1 Pt 2:1ab; Rv 8:7** al.—B. 919. Schmidt, Syn. IV, 540–54, s. ἕκαστος and ὅλος. DELG. M-M. EDNT. TW. Sv.

πάσχα, τό indecl. (Aram. פַּסְחָא or פִּסְחָא for Hebr. פֶּסַח.—LXX, Philo, Joseph., Just., Mel., Did.)

❶ **an annual Israelite festival commemorating Israel's exodus from Egypt,** ***the Passover,*** celebrated on the 14th of the month Nisan, and continuing into the early hours of the 15th (Jos., Ant. 3, 284f; s. also Ex 12–13; cp. Mishnah, Pesahim). This was followed immediately by the Feast of Unleavened Bread (Mazzoth; ἄζυμος 2) on the 15th to 21st. Popular usage merged the two festivals and treated them as a unity, as they were for practical purposes (s. **Lk 22:1** and **Mk 14:12** below.—So also Philo and Joseph.: GAmadon, ATR 27, '45, 109–115; cp. BWambacq, Biblica 62, '81, 499–518). τὸ π. *the Passover (Festival)* **Mk 14:1; J 2:23; 11:55b; 12:1; 18:39; Ac 12:4.** τοῦτο τὸ π. *on this Passover* GEb 311, 48; 50f (a rewording of Lk 22:15 fr. the Encratite perspective). τὸ π. τῶν Ἰουδαίων **J 2:13; 11:55a.** τὸ π., ἡ ἑορτὴ τῶν Ἰουδαίων **6:4;** ἡ ἑορτὴ τοῦ π. **Lk 2:41; J 13:1.** παρασκευὴ τοῦ π. (s. παρασκευή) **J 19:14.** ἡ ἑορτὴ τῶν ἀζύμων ἡ λεγομένη πάσχα **Lk 22:1** (Jos., Ant. 14, 21 τῆς τῶν ἀζύμων ἑορτῆς, ἣν πάσχα λέγομεν; 17, 213; 18, 29, Bell. 2, 10. HSchürmann, Der Paschamahlbericht, Lk 22:7–14, 15–18, '53). τὸ π. γίνεται *the Passover is being celebrated* **Mt 26:2.**

❷ **the lamb sacrificed for observance of the Passover,** ***the Passover lamb*** θύειν τὸ π. (שָׁחַט הַפֶּסַח.—Ex 12:21; Dt 16:2, 6; 1 Esdr 7:12; Just., D. 40, 1) *kill the Passover lamb* **Mk 14:12a; Lk 22:7;** fig. of Christ and his bloody death **1 Cor 5:7** (ELohse, Märtyrer u. Gottesknecht, '55, 141–46). φαγεῖν τὸ π. (אָכַל הַפֶּסַח.—2 Ch 30:18 [φασεκ]; 2 Esdr 6:21) *eat the Passover* **Mt 26:17; Mk 14:12b, 14; Lk 22:11, 15; J 18:28;** GEb 311, 47 (here the word ἑτοιμάζειν is found, taken fr. Passover terminology [s. 3], but π. still retains its specific sense 'Passover lamb'.—Mel., P. 16, 101 τὸ π. βιβρώσκεται; Orig., C. Cels. 1, 70, 4).—For lit. s. ἐσθίω 1a.

❸ ***the Passover meal*** ἑτοιμάζειν τὸ π. *prepare the Passover meal* **Mt 26:19; Mk 14:16; Lk 22:8, 13.** ποιεῖν τὸ π. (oft. LXX) *hold* or *celebrate the Passover* **Mt 26:18; Hb 11:28.**

❹ in later Christian usage ***the Easter festival*** (τὸ π. Hippol., Ref. 8, 5) τὸ κυρίου π. Dg 12:9.—GBeer, Pesachim 1912 (p. 1, 1 lit.); Elbogen³ '31; HGuthe, Z. Passah der jüd. Religionsgem.: StKr 96/97, 1925, 144–71; Billerb. IV 1928, 41–76: D. Passamahl; JJeremias, D. Passahfeier der Samaritaner '32, D. Abendmahlsworte Jesu² '49, ³'60, Eng. tr., The Eucharistic Words of Jesus, OEhrhardt '55, 86–184, also ³ tr. NPerrin '64; Dalman, Jesus 80–160; JPedersen, Passahfest u. Passahlegende:

ZAW 52, '34, 161–75; PHeawood, ET 53, '41/42, 295–97; FBussby, ibid. 59, '47/48, 194f; GWalther, Jesus, d. Passalamm '50; ESchweizer, TLZ 79, '54, 577–91; AJaubert, La date de la Cène '57; JSegal, The Hebrew Passover to AD 70 '63; HGrass Ostergeschehen u. Osterberichte[2] '62; NFüglister, Die Heilsbedeutung des Pascha '63; ERuckstuhl, Die Chronologie des letzten Mahles, etc. '63 (Eng. tr. VDrapela '65); RLeDéaut, La nuit pascale '63; JvGoudoever, Studia Evangelica III, '64, 254–59. The work of AJaubert above has been transl. as The Date of the Last Supper by IRafferty '65; Jaubert's thesis rejected by EKutsch, VetusT 11, '61, 39–47; NTheiss, Int 48, '94, 17–35 in relation to the Seder.—EDNT. ABD VI 764f (lit.). TW. Sv.

πάσχω fut. 3 sg. παθεῖται (2 Cl 7:5; v.l. πείσεται; cp. Reinhold p. 74; B-D-F §74, 3), 3 pl. παθοῦνται Hs 8, 10, 4; 2 aor. ἔπαθον; pf. πέπονθα, ptc. πεπονθώς; plpf. 3 pl. ἐπεπόνθεισαν Wsd 18:1 (Hom.+) 'to experience someth., be treated' (π. expresses the passive idea corresponding to the active idea in ποιέω) of everything that befalls a person, whether good or ill. Yet its usage developed in such a way that π. came to be used less and less frequently in a good sense, and never thus without some clear indication, at least fr. the context, that the good sense is meant. In our lit. it is found

❶ only once in the sense ***experience someth. (pleasant)*** (of one who experiences special blessing, Pind., P. 3, 104 εὖ πασχέμεν, N. 1, 32 εὖ παθεῖν; Antiphanes 252, 2b ἀγαθὸν πάσχει; Diod. S. 20, 102, 2 εὖ πάσχειν; Dionys. Hal. 7, 51; Plut., Mor. 1110d; Arrian, Ind. 34, 1, Peripl. 2, 4; Jos., Ant. 3, 312; POxy 1855, 8; 10; 14 πάσχω ἀπόκρισιν of favorable information) τοσαῦτα ἐπάθετε εἰκῇ; *have you had such remarkable experiences in vain?* **Gal 3:4** (Procop. Soph., Ep. 18 τοσοῦτον παθών; Ps.-Aristot., Mirabilia 112 τὸ αὐτὸ πάσχει=he experiences the same thing.—Differently Zahn et al.; in their opinion this pass. belongs to 3b below; in support of their view s. τοσαῦτα παθών Ep. 56 of Apollonius of Tyana [Philostrat. I 359, 16], but the assoc. w. ἐπιχορηγέω Gal 3:5 suggests receipt of beneficence).—On probability of wordplay (παθεῖν . . . μαθεῖν) s. Betz, Gal. 134.

❷ Likew. there is only one place in which π. has a neutral mng. Even here the addition of κακῶς gives it an unfavorable connotation: κακῶς πάσχειν ***be badly off, in an evil plight*** (Hom et al.; Hdt. 3, 146 et al.; Wsd 18:19; JosAs 7:4; 24:1; Philo, In Flacc. 124, Spec. Leg. 4, 3) **Mt 17:15** (v.l. ἔχει).

❸ In all other places, as always in LXX, in an unfavorable sense ***suffer, endure.***—ⓐ *suffer*—**α.** abs. (also in the sense *suffer death, be killed, [have to] die:* Appian, Bell. Civ. 1, 70 §321; 3, 87 §359; Arrian, Anab. 6, 10, 3; Paroem. Gr.: Zenob. 4, 60 the crow ἔπαθε from the scorpion's poison; Herodian 1, 17, 7; Just., D. 52, 3; Mel., P. 8, 65; sim. Callinus [VII BC], fgm. 1, 17 G-B.[=D.[3]] ἤν τι πάθῃ='if he fell'; Demosth. 4, 11f; Straton of Lamps., fgm. 10 [in Diog. L. 5, 61] ἐάν τι πάσχω='if anything happens to me'; Diod. S. 13, 98, 2; Lucian, Dial. Meretr. 8, 3; Iambl., Vi. Pyth. 33, 238; Jos., Ant. 15, 65; 18, 352; Ramsay, CB I/2, 391 no. 254; Iren. 1, 3, 3 [Harv. I, 27, 1]) πρὸ τοῦ με παθεῖν *before I suffer* **Lk 22:15.** Cp. **24:46; Ac 1:3; 3:18; 17:3; 1 Cor 12:26; Hb 2:18** (on ἐν ᾧ s. ἐν 7); **9:26; 1 Pt 2:20, 23; 3:17;** B 7:2a; Hs 8, 10, 4. The expr. γῆ πάσχουσα B 6:9 seems to transfer the philosoph. concept of suffering matter to the γῆ (Hefele, Hilgenfeld, Veil): *earth capable of suffering* (Goodsp.), *earth capable of being molded into a human being* (Kleist, note ad loc.).

β. w. additions: ὑπό τινος *at the hands of someone* denotes the one who caused the suffering (Antiphon Orat., fgm. 34; Ael. Aristid. 45 p. 134 D.; PAmh 78, 4; Jos., Bell. 5, 19, Ant. 10, 92; Mel., P. 75, 546ff; B-D-F §315) **Mt 17:12** (s. also b below). Also ὑπὸ χειρός τινος B 5:5b (cp. Mel., fgm. 7 ὑπὸ δεξιᾶς Ἰσραηλίτιδος). ὑπέρ τινος *for someone* or *someth.* (Appian, Bell. Civ. 1, 15 §63 π. ὑπέρ τινος=suffer for someone; Just., D. 121, 2 ὑπὲρ τοῦ μὴ ἀρνεῖσθαι αὐτόν as military metaphor: EKrentz, in Origins and Method, JHurd Festschr. '93, 126) **Phil 1:29; 2 Th 1:5; 1 Pt 2:21** (περί τινος v.l.), ὑπὲρ τ. ὀνόματος τοῦ υἱοῦ τοῦ θεοῦ Hs 9, 28, 2a. ὑπὲρ τοῦ νόμου 8, 3, 6. ὑπὲρ τῆς σωτηρίας, ὑπὲρ ἁμαρτωλῶν MPol 17:2. ὑπὲρ τῶν ἁμαρτιῶν ἡμῶν ISm 7:1. Also περί τινος (Nicol. Dam.: 90 fgm. 130, 29 p. 415, 29 Jac. περὶ τῶν διαδόχων αὐτοῦ ἅπαν . . . παθεῖν) περὶ ἁμαρτιῶν **1 Pt 3:18** (v.l. ἀπέθανεν). περι τῆς ψυχῆς ἡμῶν B 5:5a. διά w. acc. *for the sake of:* διὰ δικαιοσύνην **1 Pt 3:14.** διὰ τὸ ὄνομα (αὐτοῦ) Pol 8:2; Hv 3, 2, 1; s 9, 28, 3. δι' ἡμᾶς B 7:2b. διὰ τὸν θεόν Hs 9, 28, 6a. εἵνεκα or ἕνεκεν τοῦ ὀνόματος v 3, 1, 9; 3, 5, 2; s 9, 28, 5; 6b. κατὰ τὸ θέλημα τοῦ θεοῦ **1 Pt 4:19.** ἔξω τῆς πύλης **Hb 13:12.** ἐπὶ ξύλου *on the tree* B 5:13b.—Used w. an instrumental (?) dat.: αἰκίαις καὶ βασάνοις π. 1 Cl 6:1 v.l. πολλαῖς πράξεσι Hs 6, 3, 4. W. dat. to denote manner (B-D-F §198) π. σαρκί *suffer in the body* **1 Pt 4:1ab** (in b v.l. ἐν σαρκί).—Used w. an adverb: ἀδίκως **1 Pt 2:19.** ἀληθῶς ISm 2b. δικαίως (TestSim 4:3; Just., D. 110, 6) Hs 6, 3, 6a. ἡδέως 8, 10, 4. προθύμως 9, 28, 2b and 4. οὕτω GPt 4:13; B 5:13a. ὀλίγον (s. ὀλίγος 2bβ) **1 Pt 5:10.** τὸ δοκεῖν (δοκέω 2αα) *in semblance, seemingly* ITr 10; ISm 2c.—ὡς φονεύς *undergo punishment* (cp. SIG 1016, 7 π. ὡς ἱερόσυλος) *as a murderer* **1 Pt 4:15.**

ⓑ *endure, undergo* τί *someth.* (Orig., C. Cels. 7, 13, 7; π. καταστροφήν; Did., Gen. 232, 11; Theoph. Ant. 2, 23 [p. 156, 6]) παθήματα π. *endure sufferings* **2 Cor 1:6** (ὧν by attraction of the rel. fr. ἅ; sim. Iren. 1, 8, 2 [Harv. I 70, 4]). αἰκίσματα 1 Cl 6:2. πολλὰ π. (Jos., Ant. 13, 268; 403) **Mt 27:19; Mk 8:31; 9:12; Lk 9:22** (s. further below); **17:25;** B 7:11; AcPl Ha 8, 19. τὰ ὅμοιά τινι *the same things as someone* Ox 840, 3. οὐδὲν κακόν *suffer no harm* **Ac 28:5.** οὐδὲν τῶν πονηρῶν Hs 6, 3, 6b. ὡς οὐδὲν πεπονθώς *as if nothing had happened to him* MPol 8:3 (cp. TestJob 47:7 ὡς οὐδὲν ὅλως πεπονθώς). ταῦτα **Lk 13:2; 24:26; 2 Ti 1:12;** 1 Cl 45:5. τί παθεῖται; *what will he have to endure?* 2 Cl 7:5 (πάσχειν τι=endure punishment, as Pla., Leg. 10, 1, 885ab). μὴ φοβοῦ ἃ μελλεις πάσχειν *do not be afraid of what you are about to undergo* **Rv 2:10.** W. attraction ἔμαθεν ἀφ' ὧν ἔπαθεν τὴν ὑπακοήν= ἔμαθεν τὴν ὑπακοὴν ἀπὸ τούτων ἃ ἔπαθεν *he learned obedience from what he endured* (i.e. despite his being God's son, Jesus experienced suffering as the medium for exhibiting the ultimate extent of his obedience) **Hb 5:8** (for the consonance or wordplay s. the reff. cited s.v. μανθάνω 3). π. τι ὑπό τινος *endure someth. at someone's hands* (X., Hiero 7, 8, Symp. 1, 9; Jos., Ant. 7, 209; 12, 401; s. 3aβ above) **Mk 5:26; 1 Th 2:14;** B 7:5. Also π. τι ἀπό τινος (Dio Chrys. 67 [17], 11; Lucian, D. Deor. 6, 4; Orig., C. Cels. 8, 27, 5) **Mt 16:21;** perh. **Lk 9:22.** π. τι ἕνεκά τινος *endure someth. for someone's sake* 2 Cl 1:2. Also π. τι διά τινα ISm 2a (Just., D. 117, 3; Mel., P. 59, 435). ὅσα δεῖ αὐτὸν ὑπὲρ τοῦ ὀνόματός μου παθεῖν **Ac 9:16** (π. τι ὑπέρ τινος as Jos., Ant. 13, 199).—WWichmann, D. Leidenstheologie, e. Form der Leidensdeutung im Spätjudentum 1930; HVondran, D. Leidensgedanke im Spiegel d. Selbstbewusstseins Jesu: NKZ 43, '32, 257–75; RLiechtenhan, D. Überwindung d. Leidens b. Pls. u. in d. zeitgen. Stoa: ZTK n.s. 3, 1922, 368–99; WMichaelis, Herkunft u. Bed. des Ausdrucks 'Leiden u. Sterben J. Chr.' '45; HRiesenfeld, Jésus Transfiguré, '47, 314–17 (Le Messie Souffrant . . .); ELohse, Märtyrer u. Gottesknecht (Sühntod Jesu Christi), '55; EGüttgemanns, D. leidende Apostel, '66.—K Schelkle, Die Passion Jesu etc., '49; JGreen, The Death of Jesus '88; RBrown, The Death of the Messiah, 2 vols.

'94; ACollins, From Noble Death to Crucified Messiah, NTS 40, '94, 481–503; on alleged anti-Judaism in Luke's passion narrative, s. HMerkel, NTS 40, '94, 394–95 (lit.).—Schmidt, Syn. I 424–441. DELG. M-M. EDNT. DLNT. TW. Sv.

Πάταρα, ων, τά neut. pl. ***Patara*** (Hdt. 1, 182; Strabo 14, 3, 3; OGI 441, 209; SibOr 3, 441; 4, 112.—On the spelling s. B-D-F §42, 3; Rob. 183) a city in Lycia, on the southwest coast of Asia Minor. Paul stopped there on his journey fr. Corinth to Jerusalem **Ac 21:1.**—Pauly-W. XVIII 2555–61; Kl. Pauly IV 544f; BHHW III 1400; PECS 679f.

πατάσσω fut. πατάξω; 1 aor. ἐπάταξα. Pass.: fut. 3 sg. παταχθήσεται (Just., D. 53, 5); aor. inf. παταχθῆναι (Mel., P. 34, 233), ptc. neut. παταχθέν (AcPl Ha 5, 11); (cp. πάταγος 'crash'; Hom.+; ins, pap LXX; PsSol 17:35; TestJob 20:6; TestLevi, JosAs; GrBar 3:8; AssMos fgm. j; Hecataeus Hist.: 264 fgm. 21 Jac. [in Jos., C. Ap. 1, 203]; Just., Mel.)

❶ to physically strike a blow, *strike, hit*—ⓐ of a light blow or push τὶ *someth.* (Aesop, Fab. 246 P.=108 H.; 88 Ch.; 278 H-H. τὸ στῆθος) τὴν πλευράν τινος *strike someone's side* in order to waken him **Ac 12:7.** τοῦ πατάξαι αὐτά *to drive (sheep) forward* GJs 18:3 codd. Abs., but w. the acc. easily supplied fr. the context, of touching w. a staff Hs 9, 6, 4.

ⓑ of a heavy blow; w. acc. of the pers. (Demosth. 21, 33 τὸν ἄρχοντα; Appian, Bell. Civ. 2, 17 §64 δᾳδοῦχον ἐπάταξε ξίφει) π. τὸν δοῦλον **Mt 26:51; Lk 22:50.** τὸ ὠτίον παταχθέν *the ear hit* (by hail) AcPl Ha 5, 11. Abs. *strike* ἐν μαχαίρῃ **Lk 22:49** (cp. TestLevi 6:5 τὴν πόλιν . . . ἐν στόματι μαχαίρας).

ⓒ of a blow that kills, *strike down, slay* τινά *someone* (PHal 1, 196; UPZ 19, 8 [159 BC]; BGU 1024 III, 17; JosAs 23:7) **Mt 26:31; Mk 14:27;** B 5:12 (all three after Zech 13:7; for the subject-matter s. Jos., Ant. 8, 404); **Ac 7:24** (Ex 2:12).

❷ to inflict someth. disastrous, *strike,* fig. ext. of 1. Used in ref. to transcendent beings, it cannot be determined whether any actual touching or striking is involved, nor how far it goes (cp. Gen 8:21; Ex 9:15; 12:23; Num 14:12; Dt 28:22; 4 Km 6:18; 2 Macc 9:5 and oft. in LXX; PsSol 17:35; TestJob 20:6 [of Satan]. S. also SIG 1240, 11; PHamb 22, 7) ἐπάταξεν αὐτὸν ἄγγελος κυρίου *an angel of the Lord struck him* **Ac 12:23.** Used w. instrumental ἐν and dat.: of the two witnesses π. τὴν γῆν ἐν πάσῃ πληγῇ **Rv 11:6** (PGM 12, 368 θεόν, τὸν πατάξαντα γῆν; 2 Macc 9:5 π. πληγῇ). Of the Logos as judge of the world ἐν αὐτῇ (i.e. the ῥομφαία proceeding fr. his mouth) π. τὰ ἔθνη **19:15.**—DELG s.v. πάταγος. M-M. TW.

πατέω fut. πατήσω; 1 aor. ἐπάτησα LXX. Pass. fut. 3 sg. πατηθήσεται (TestZeb); aor. ἐπατήθην (Hom. et al.; pap, LXX; En 1:4; TestLevi 18:12; TestZeb 9:8 v.l.; JosAs 23:8 [cod. A for ἐπάταξε]; AscIs 3:3; Philo, Just.) *tread (on)* w. feet.

❶ to set foot on, *tread, walk,* trans.—ⓐ *tread* τὶ *someth.* (Herodas 8, 74) τὴν ληνόν (s. ληνός) **Rv 19:15;** pass. **14:20.** Of a stone ὁ πατούμενος *what is trodden under foot* Dg 2:2.

ⓑ *set foot on, tread* of a place (Aeschyl. et al.; LXX) τὴν αὐλήν *the court* B 2:5 (Is 1:12). τὸ ἁγνευτήριον Ox 840 12; τὸ ἱερόν ibid. 17; 20.

❷ to tread heavily with feet, with implication of destructive intent, *trample,* trans.—ⓐ *tread on, trample* (Iambl., Vi. Pyth. 31, 193) of the undisciplined swarming of a victorious army through a conquered city. Its heedlessness, which acknowledges no limits, causes π. to take on the sense 'mistreat, abuse' (so πατέω in Plut., Tim. 14, 2; Lucian, Lexiph. 10 al.; Philo, In Flacc. 65) and 'tread contemptuously under foot' (s. 2b; in Heliod. 4, 19, 8 π. πόλιν actually means *plunder a city*). τὴν πόλιν πατήσουσιν **Rv 11:2;** pass. (Jos., Bell. 4, 171 πατούμενα τὰ ἅγια) **Lk 21:24** (ὑπὸ ἐθνῶν).

ⓑ fig. ext. of a: *trample in contempt* or *disdain* (Il. 4, 157 ὅρκια; Soph., Aj. 1335, Antig. 745 al.; Herodian 8, 5, 9; Jos., Bell. 4, 258 τ. νόμους) τὸ τῆς αἰσχύνης ἔνδυμα πατεῖν *despise* (=throw away w. disdain) *the garment of shame* (s. αἰσχύνη 1) GEg 252, 57.

❸ *move on foot, walk, tread* (not in the sense of 'taking a walk') (since Pind., P. 2, 85 ἀλλ' ἄλλοτε πατέων ὁδοῖς σκολιαῖς, of one who moves against an opponent like a fox, stepping now here and now there, in no straight line) with implication that the experience is not planned, intr. πατεῖν ἐπάνω ὄφεων **Lk 10:19** (ἐπάνω 1b and cp. TestLevi 18:12.—Diod. S. 3, 50, 2f speaks of the danger of death in πατεῖν on ὄφεις).—DELG. M-M. TW.

πατήρ, πατρός, ὁ (Hom.+) acc. somet. πατέραν (ApcEsdr 2:6 p. 25, 26 Tdf.); voc. πάτερ; for this the nom. w. the art. ὁ πατήρ **Mt 11:26; Mk 14:36; Lk 10:21b; Ro 8:15; Gal 4:6.**—The vv.ll. πατήρ without the art. for the voc., in **J 17:11, 21, 24,** and **25** is regarded by B-D-F §147, 3 as a scribal error (but as early as II AD BGU 423, 11 has κύριέ μου πατήρ. Perh. even PPar 51, 36 [159 BC]). S. also W-S. §29, 4b and Mlt-H. 136; 'father'.

❶ the immediate biological ancestor, *parent*—ⓐ male, *father* (of Noah Did., Gen. 165, 6) **Mt 2:22; 4:21f; 8:21; 10:21; Mk 5:40; 15:21; Lk 1:17** (after Mal 3:23); **J 4:53; Ac 7:14; 1 Cor 5:1;** B 13:5 al. οἱ τῆς σαρκὸς ἡμῶν πατέρες *our physical fathers* **Hb 12:9a.**

ⓑ male and female together as parents οἱ πατέρες *parents* (Pla., Leg. 6, 772b; Dionys. Hal. 2, 26; Diod. S. 21, 17, 2; X. Eph. 1, 11; 3, 3; Kaibel 227) **Hb 11:23.—Eph 6:4; Col 3:21** (Apollon. Rhod. 4, 1089 of parents who are inclined to become λίην δύσζηλοι toward their children).

❷ one from whom one is descended and generally at least several generations removed, *forefather, ancestor, progenitor, forebear:* of Abraham (Jos., Ant. 14, 255 Ἀ., πάντων Ἑβραίων πατήρ; Just., D. 100, 3) **Mt 3:9; Lk 1:73; 16:24; J 8:39, 53, 56; Ac 7:2b.** Of Isaac **Ro 9:10.** Jacob **J 4:12** (JosAs 22:5). David **Mk 11:10; Lk 1:32.** Pl. οἱ πατέρες *the forefathers, ancestors* (Hom. et al.; oft. LXX; En 99:14; PsSol 9:10; ParJer 4:10; Jos., Ant. 13, 297; Just., D. 57, 2 and 136, 3; Mel., P. 87, 654) **Mt 23:30, 32; Lk 1:55; 6:23, 26; 11:47f; J 4:20; 6:31; Ac 3:13, 25; Hb 1:1; 8:9** (Jer 38:32); B 2:7 (Jer 7:22); 5:7; 14:1; PtK 2 p. 15, 6 (Jer 38:32).

❸ one who provides moral and intellectual upbringing, *father*—ⓐ in a positive sense (Epict. 3, 22, 81f: the Cynic superintends the upbringing of all pers. as their πατήρ; Procop. Soph., Ep. 13; Ael. Aristid. 47 p. 425 D.: Pla. as τῶν ῥητόρων π. καὶ διδάσκαλος; Aristoxenus, fgm. 18: Epaminondas is the ἀκροατής of the Pythagorean Lysis and calls him πατήρ; Philostrat., Vi. Soph. 1, 8 p. 10, 4 the διδάσκαλος as πατήρ) ἐὰν μυρίους παιδαγωγοὺς ἔχητε ἐν Χριστῷ, ἀλλ' οὐ πολλοὺς πατέρας **1 Cor 4:15** (cp. GrBar 13:4 εἰς πνευματικοὺς πατέρας; on the subject matter ADieterich, Mithraslit. 1903, 52; 146f; 151; Rtzst., Mysterienrel.[3] 40: 'he [the "mystes"] by these teachings becomes the parent of the novice. We find undoubted examples of πατήρ as a title in the Isis cult in Delos, in the Phrygian mystery communities, in the Mithras cult, in the worshipers of the θεὸς ὕψιστος and elsewh.'). Of Jesus ὡς πατὴρ υἱοὺς ἡμᾶς προσηγόρευσεν *as a father he called us* (his) *sons* 2 Cl 1:4 (cp. Ps.-Clem., Hom. 3, 19; ὁ Χριστὸς π. τῶν πιστευόντων ὑπάρχει Did., Gen. 106, 6.—ὁ Ἰησοῦς, ὁ π. [=founder] τῆς τοιαύτης διδασκαλίας Orig., C. Cels. 2, 44, 32).

ⓑ in a neg. sense of the devil (for patristic trad. s. Lampe s.v. πατήρ D)

α. as father of a group of Judeans **J 8:44ab,** as verdict on the sin of the opposition to God's purpose in Jesus, not on the person (cp. descriptions of dissidents at Qumran, esp. 1QS and 1QH, w. focus on aspect of deception).

β. as father of lies (Celsus 2, 47 as π. τῆς κακίας) vs. **44c** (on πατήρ in the sense of 'originator' cp. Caecil. Calact., fgm. 127 ὁ π. τοῦ λόγου=the author of the book). On the view that in **44a** and **c** there might be a statement about the *father of the devil* s. Hdb.[3] ad loc. (NDahl, EHaenchen Festschr. '64, 70–84 [Cain]).—LDürr, Geistige Vaterrschaft in: Herwegen Festschr. '38, 1–30.

❹ **a title of respectful address,** ***father***—ⓐ as an honorary title (Diod. S. 21, 12, 2; 5; Ps.-Callisth. 1, 14, 2 πάτερ; 4 Km 2:12; 6:21; 13:14; Test Abr B 2 p. 106, 3 [Stone p. 60] καλὲ πάτερ; Jos., Ant. 12, 148; 13, 127; Just., D. 3, 7. Also PGen 52, 1; 5 κυρίῳ καὶ πατρὶ Ἀμιννναίῳ Ἀλύπιος; UPZ 65, 3 [154 BC]; 70, 2; BGU 164, 2; POxy 1296, 15; 18; 1592, 3; 5; 1665, 2) **Mt 23:9a;** specif. in addressing the members of the High Council **Ac 7:2a;** cp. **22:1** (of Job in TestJob 53:3 ὁ πατὴρ τῶν ὀρφανῶν).

ⓑ as a designation of the older male members of a church (as respectful address by younger people to their elders Hom. et al. S. also a.) **1J 2:13, 14b.**

❺ **revered deceased persons with whom one shares beliefs or traditions,** ***fathers, ancestors***—ⓐ generation(s) of deceased Christians **2 Pt 3:4;** 1 Cl 23:3=2 Cl 11:2 (an apocryphal saying, at any rate interpreted in this way by the Christian writers). Christians of an earlier generation could also be meant in 1 Cl 30:7; 60:4; 62:2; 2 Cl 19:4. Yet it is poss. that these refer to

ⓑ the illustrious religious heroes of the OT, who are 'ancestors' even to gentile Christians, who are validated as Israelites (Just., D. 101, 1). In **1 Cor 10:1** Paul calls the desert generation of Israelites οἱ πατέρες ἡμῶν (the 'philosophers' of earlier times are so called in Cleopatra 114f). Likew. **Ro 4:12b** Abraham ὁ πατὴρ ἡμῶν (on this s. c below). The latter is also so referred to **Js 2:21;** 1 Cl 31:2; likew. the patriarch Jacob 4:8.

ⓒ the 'fatherhood' can also consist in the fact that the one who is called 'father' is the prototype of a group or the founder of a class of persons (cp. Pla., Menex. 240e οὐ μόνον τῶν σωμάτων τῶν ἡμετέρων πατέρας ἀλλὰ καὶ τῆς ἐλευθερίας; 1 Macc 2:54). Abraham who, when he was still uncircumcised, received the promise because of his faith, and then received circumcision to seal it, became thereby πατὴρ πάντων τῶν πιστευόντων δι᾽ ἀκροβυστίας *father of all those who believe, though they are uncircumcised* **Ro 4:11** and likew. πατὴρ περιτομῆς *father of those who are circumcised* vs. **12a,** insofar as they are not only circumcised physically, but are like the patriarch in faith as well. Cp. **4:16, 17** (Gen 17:5).

❻ **the supreme deity, who is responsible for the origin and care of all that exists,** ***Father, Parent*** (Just., A II, 6, 2 τὸ δὲ πατὴρ καὶ θεὸς καὶ κτίστης καὶ κύριος καὶ δεσπότης οὐκ ὀνόματά ἐστιν, ἀλλ᾽ … προσφήσεις 'the terms, father, god, founder, lord, and master are not names but . . . modes of address [in recognition of benefits and deeds])

ⓐ as the originator and ruler (Pind., O. 2, 17 Χρόνος ὁ πάντων π.; Pla., Tim. 28c; 37c; Stoa: Epict. 1, 3, 1; Diog. L. 7, 147; Maximus Tyr. 2, 10a; Galen XIX p. 179 K. ὁ τῶν ὅλων πατὴρ ἐν θεοῖς; Job 38:28; Mal 2:10; Philo, Spec. Leg. 1, 96 τῷ τοῦ κόσμου πατρί; 2, 6 τὸν ποιητὴν καὶ πατέρα τῶν ὅλων, Ebr. 30; 81, Virt. 34; 64; 179; 214; Jos., Ant. 1, 20 πάντων πατήρ; 230; 2, 152; 7, 380 πατέρα τε καὶ γένεσιν τῶν ὅλων; Herm. Wr. 1, 21 ὁ πατὴρ ὅλων … ὁ θεὸς κ. πατήρ; 30 al., also p. 476, 23 Sc. δεσπότης καὶ πατὴρ καὶ ποιητής; PGM 4, 1170; 1182; Just., A I, 45, 1 ὁ π. τῶν πάντων θεός; D. 95, 2 ὁ πατὴρ τῶν ὅλων; Ath. 27, 2; Iren.; Orig., C. Cels. 1, 46, 34; Hippolyt.; π. δὲ δια τὸ εἶναι πρὸ τῶν ὅλων Theoph. Ant. 1, 4 [p. 64, 8]) ὁ πατὴρ τῶν φώτων *the father of the heavenly bodies* **Js 1:17** (cp. ApcMos 36 v.l. [MCeriani, Monumenta Sacra et Profana V/1, 1868] ἐνώπιον τοῦ φωτὸς τῶν ὅλων, τοῦ πατρὸς τῶν φώτων; 38).

ⓑ as ὁ πατὴρ τῶν πνευμάτων **Hb 12:9b** (cp. Num 16:22; 27:16 and in En the fixed phrase 'Lord of the spirits').—SeeP-Katz, Philo's Bible '50, p. 33, 1.

ⓒ as father of humankind (since Hom. Ζεύς is called πατήρ or πατὴρ ἀνδρῶν τε θεῶν τε; Diod. S. 5, 72, 2 πατέρα δὲ [αὐτὸν προσαγορευθῆναι] διὰ τὴν φροντίδα καὶ τὴν εὔνοιαν τὴν εἰς ἅπαντας, ἔτι δὲ καὶ τὸ δοκεῖν ὥσπερ ἀρχηγὸν εἶναι τοῦ γένους τῶν ἀνθρώπων='[Zeus is called] father because of his thoughtfulness and goodwill toward all humanity, and because, moreover, he is thought of as originator of the human race', cp. 3, 61, 4; 5, 56, 4; Dio Chrys. 36 [53], 12 Zeus as π. τῶν ἀνθρώπων, not only because of his position as ruler, but also because of his love and care [ἀγαπῶν κ. προνοῶν]. Cp. Plut., Mor. 167d; Jos., Ant. 4, 262 πατὴρ τοῦ παντὸς ἀνθρώπων γένους. In the OT God is called 'Father' in the first place to indicate a caring relationship to the Israelite nation as a whole, or to the king as the embodiment of the nation. Only in late writers is God called the Father of the pious Israelite as an individual: Sir 23:1, 4; Tob 13:4; Wsd 2:16; 14:3; 3 Macc 5:7.—Bousset, Rel.[3] 377ff; EBurton, ICC Gal 1921, 384–92; RGyllenberg, Gott d. Vater im AT u. in d. Predigt Jesu: Studia Orient. I 1925, 51–60; JLeipoldt, D. Gotteserlebnis Jesu 1927; AWilliams, 'My Father' in Jewish Thought of the First Century: JTS 31, 1930, 42–47; TManson, The Teaching of Jesus, '55, 89–115; HMontefiore, NTS 3, '56/57, 31–46 [synoptics]; BIersel, 'D. Sohn' in den synopt. Ev., '61, 92–116).

α. as a saying of Jesus ὁ πατήρ σου **Mt 6:4, 6b, 18b.** ὁ πατὴρ ὑμῶν **Mt 6:15; 10:20, 29; 23:9b; Lk 6:36; 12:30, 32; J 20:17c.** ὁ πατὴρ αὐτῶν (=τῶν δικαίων) **Mt 13:43.** ὁ πατὴρ ὑμῶν ὁ ἐν (τοῖς) οὐρανοῖς (the synagogue also spoke of God as 'Father in Heaven'; Bousset, Rel.[3] 378) **Mt 5:16, 45; 6:1; 7:11; Mk 11:25.** ὁ πατὴρ ὑμῶν ὁ οὐράνιος **Mt 5:48; 6:14, 26, 32.** Cp. **23:9b.** ὁ πατὴρ ὁ ἐξ οὐρανοῦ **Lk 11:13.** ὁ πατήρ σου ὁ ἐν τῷ κρυπτῷ (or κρυφαίῳ) **Mt 6:6a, 18a.**—For the evangelist the words πάτερ ἡμῶν ὁ ἐν τοῖς οὐρανοῖς **Mt 6:9** refer only to the relation betw. God and humans, though Jesus perh. included himself in this part of the prayer. The same is true of πάτερ ἁγιασθήτω τὸ ὄνομά σου **Lk 11:2** (for invocation in prayer cp. Simonides, fgm. 13, 20 Ζεῦ πάτερ).—ELohmeyer, D. Vaterunser erkl. '46 (Eng. tr. JBowden, '65); TManson, The Sayings of Jesus, '54, 165–71; EGraesser, Das Problem der Parusieverzögerung in den synopt. Ev. usw., Beih. ZNW 22, '57, 95–113; AHamman, La Prière I, Le NT, '59, 94–134; JJeremias, Das Vaterunser im Lichte der neueren Forschung, '62 (Eng. tr., The Lord's Prayer, JReumann, '64); WMarchel, Abba, Père! La Prière '63; also bibl. in JCharlesworth, ed., The Lord's Prayer and Other Prayer Texts fr. the Greco-Roman Era '94, 186–201.

β. as said by Christians (Sextus 59=222; 225 God as π. of the pious. The servant of Sarapis addresses God in this way: Sb 1046; 3731, 7) in introductions of letters ἀπὸ θεοῦ πατρὸς ἡμῶν: **Ro 1:7; 1 Cor 1:3; 2 Cor 1:2; Gal 1:3,** cp. vs. **4; Eph 1:2; Phil 1:2; Col 1:2; Phlm 3; 2 Th 1:2** (v.l. without ἡμῶν); without ἡμῶν **1 Ti 1:2** (v.l. with ἡμῶν); **2 Ti 1:2; Tit 1:4; 2J 3a** (here vs 3b shows plainly that it is not 'our' father, but the Father of Jesus Christ who is meant).—πατὴρ ἡμῶν also **Phil 4:20; 1 Th 1:3;**

3:11, 13; 2 Th 2:16; D 8:2; 9:2f. τὸν ἐπιεικῆ καὶ εὔσπλαγχνον πατέρα ἡμῶν 1 Cl 29:1. Likew. we have the Father of the believers **Ro 8:15** (w. αββα, s. JBarr, Abba Isn't Daddy: JTS 39, '88, 28–47; s. also JFitzmyer, Ro [AB] ad loc.); **2 Cor 1:3b** (ὁ πατὴρ τῶν οἰκτιρμῶν; s. οἰκτιρμός); **6:18** (cp. 2 Km 7:14); **Gal 4:6; Eph 4:6** (πατὴρ πάντων, as Herm. Wr. 5, 10); **1 Pt 1:17.** ὁ οἰκτίρμων καὶ εὐεργετικὸς πατήρ 1 Cl 23:1. Cp. 8:3 (perh. fr. an unknown apocryphal book). πάτερ ἅγιε D 10:2 (cp. 8:2; 9:2f).

γ. as said by Judeans ἕνα πατέρα ἔχομεν τὸν θεόν **J 8:41b.** Cp. vs. **42.**

ⓓ as Father of Jesus Christ—**α.** in Jesus' witness concerning himself ὁ πατήρ μου **Mt 11:27a; 20:23; 25:34; 26:29, 39, 42, 53; Lk 2:49** (see ὁ 2g and Goodsp., Probs. 81–83); **10:22a; 22:29; 24:49; J 2:16; 5:17, 43; 6:40** and oft. in J; **Rv 2:28; 3:5, 21.** ἡ βασιλεία τοῦ πατρός μου 2 Cl 12:6 in an apocryphal saying of Jesus. ὁ πατήρ μου ὁ ἐν (τοῖς) οὐρανοῖς **Mt 7:21; 10:32, 33; 12:50; 16:17; 18:10, 19.** ὁ πατήρ μου ὁ οὐράνιος **15:13; 18:35** (Just., A I, 15, 8). Jesus calls himself the Human One (Son of Man), who will come ἐν τῇ δόξῃ τοῦ πατρὸς αὐτοῦ **16:27; Mk 8:38.** Abs. ὁ πατήρ, πάτερ **Mt 11:25, 26; Mk 14:36** (s. GSchelbert, FZPhT 40, '93, 259–81; response ERuckstuhl, ibid. 41, '94, 515–25; response Schelbert, ibid. 526–31); **Lk 10:21ab; 22:42; 23:34, 46** (all voc.); **J 4:21, 23ab; 5:36ab, 37, 45; 6:27, 37, 45, 46a, 65** and oft. in J. Father and Son stand side by side or in contrast **Mt 11:27bc; 24:36; 28:19; Mk 13:32; Lk 10:22bc; J 5:19–23, 26; 1J 1:3; 2:22–24; 2J 9;** B 12:8. WLofthouse, Vater u. Sohn im J: ThBl 11, '32, 290–300.

β. in the confession of the Christians π. τοῦ κυρίου ἡμῶν Ἰησοῦ Χριστοῦ **Ro 15:6; 2 Cor 1:3a; Eph 1:3; Col 1:3; 1 Pt 1:3.** π. τοῦ κυρίου Ἰησοῦ **2 Cor 11:31.** Cp. **1 Cor 15:24; Hb 1:5** (2 Km 7:14); **Rv 1:6;** 1 Cl 7:4; IEph 2:1; ITr ins 12:2; MPol 14:1; AcPl Ha 2, 33; 6, 34; AcPlCor 2:7 (cp. Just., D. 30, 3; 129, 1 al.).

ⓔ Oft. God is simply called (ὁ) πατήρ *(the) Father* (e.g. TestJob 33:9, s. DRahnenführer, ZNW 62, '71, 77; ApcMos 35 τοῦ ἀοράτου πατρός; Just., D. 76, 3 al. On the presence or absence of the art. s. B-D-F §257, 3; Rob. 795) **Eph 2:18; 3:14; 5:20; 6:23; 1J 1:2; 2:1, 15; 3:1;** B 14:6; Hv 3, 9, 10; IEph 3:2; 4:2; IMg 13:2; ITr 12:2; 13:3; IRo 2:2; 3:3; 7:2; 8:2; IPhld 9:1; ISm 3:3; 7:1; 8:1; D 1:5; Dg 12:9; 13:1; AcPlCor 2:5, 19; MPol 22:3; EpilMosq 5. θεὸς π. **Gal 1:1** (for the formulation Ἰ. Χρ. καὶ θεὸς πατήρ cp. Diod. S. 4, 11, 1: Heracles must obey τῷ Διὶ καὶ πατρί; Oenomaus in Eus., PE 5, 35, 3 Λοξίας [=Apollo] καὶ Ζεὺς πατήρ); **Phil 2:11; Col 3:17; 1 Th 1:1, 2 v.l.; 2 Pt 1:17; Jd 1;** IEph ins a; ISm ins; IPol ins; MPol ins. ὁ θεὸς καὶ π. **Js 1:27; Col 3:17 v.l.;** MPol 22:1; ὁ κύριος καὶ π. **Js 3:9.**—Attributes are also ascribed to the πατήρ (Zoroaster acc. to Philo Bybl.: 790 fgm. 4, 52 Jac. [in Eus., PE 1, 10, 52] God is π. εὐνομίας κ. δικαιοσύνης) ὁ πατὴρ τῆς δόξης **Eph 1:17.** πατὴρ ὕψιστος IRo ins. ὁ θεὸς καὶ πατὴρ παντοκράτωρ MPol 19:2.—B. 103. DELG. M-M. EDNT. TW. Sv.

Πάτμος, ου, ὁ (Thu. 3, 33, 3; Strabo 10, 5, 13; Pliny, HN 4, 23; CIG 2261; 2262; SIG 1068, 2) ***Patmos,*** a small rocky island in the Aegean Sea, famous for the tradition that John had his 'revelation' here **Rv 1:9.** His exile to Patmos (cp. Artem. 5, 21 εἰς νῆσον κατεδικάσθη) is an old tradition: Clem. Alex., Quis Div. Salv. 42; Origen, In Matth. vol. 16, 6 p. 486, 10 Kl.; Eus., HE 3, 18, 1–3; Tertullian, De Praescr. Haer. 36. See JFrings, D. Patmosexil des Ap. Joh. nach Apk 1:9: TQ 104, 1923, 23–30.—Pauly-W. XVIII 2174–91; Kl. Pauly IV 549; BHHW III 1400f; PECS 681.

πατραλῴας s. πατρολῴας.

πατριά, ᾶς, ἡ (πατήρ; Hdt. et al.; GDI 5501, 7 [Miletus]; Jos., Ant. 7, 365; 11, 68; LXX; TestDan 1:2; 7:3; Mel., P. 13, 83 al.)

❶ **people linked over a relatively long period of time by line of descent to a common progenitor,** ***family, clan, relationship*** (so, as subdivision of the φυλή Tob 5:12; Jdth 8:2, 18 al. LXX; Jos., Ant. 6, 51) ἐξ οἴκου καὶ πατριᾶς Δαυίδ *from the house and family of David* **Lk 2:4.**

❷ **a relatively large body of people existing as a totality at a given moment and linked through ancestry and sociopolitical interests,** ***people, nation*** (αἱ πατριαὶ τῶν ἐθνῶν Ps 21:28; 1 Ch 16:28) πᾶσαι αἱ πατριαὶ τῆς γῆς **Ac 3:25.**

❸ **a division of a total people entity existing at a given moment,** ***family*** (SIG^2 438, 26; 61f; in ref. to 'clans' of the Babylonian empire [Hdt. 1, 200 al.]) in wordplay ἐξ οὗ (i.e. τοῦ πατρός) πᾶσα πατριὰ ἐν οὐρανοῖς καὶ ἐπὶ γῆς ὀνομάζεται *from whom every family in heaven and on earth receives its name* **Eph 3:15** (on the idea of families of angels cp. En 69:4; 71:1; 106:5).—On this and the following entry see JWackernagel, Kl. Schr. 468–93: Über einige lat. u. griech. Ableitungen aus den Verwandschaftswörtern.—DELG s.v. πατήρ. M-M. TW.

πατριάρχης, ου, ὁ (LXX; TestAbr A 20 p. 104, 6 [Stone p. 56]; ApcEsdr 5:22 p. 30, 25 Tdf.; Just., Mel., Iren., Hippol.) **prime ancestor of a national entity,** ***father of a nation, patriarch,*** of Hebr. patriarchs: ApcPt Rainer 9, so of Abraham (cp. 4 Macc 7:19; TestAbr A; Just., D. 84, 4; Did., Theoph. Ant.) **Hb 7:4;** GJs 1:3. Of the 12 sons of Jacob **Ac 7:8f** (Mel., P. 83, 627); *ancestor,* of David **2:29** (Theoph. Ant. 2, 29).—DELG s.v. πατήρ. M-M. Sv.

πατρικός, ή, όν (πατήρ; since Soph., Ichneutae [POxy 9, 40f col. 3, 12]; Thu.; ins, pap, LXX; TestJob 50:3; TestLevi 18:6; Philo; Jos., C. Ap. 1, 109; Just.; Wackernagel, Kl. Schr. 480) **pert. to one's ancestors,** ***derived from / handed down by one's father, paternal*** (Cratinus Com. 116 K. ἐν πατρικοῖσι νόμοις; Just., D. 134, 6 π. θεοί) αἱ πατρικαί μου παραδόσεις *the traditions of my forefathers,* prob. of the traditions of his father's house, adhering strictly to the law **Gal 1:14.**—DELG s.v. πατήρ. M-M. TW.

πατρίς, ίδος, ἡ (πατήρ; really fem. of πάτριος 'of one's fathers', but used as subst. even in Hom. So also ins, pap, LXX; TestLevi 13:8; EpArist 102; Philo, Joseph.; Just., D. 39, 5)

❶ **a relatively large geographical area associated with one's familial connections and personal life,** ***fatherland, homeland*** (Hom. et al.; 2 Macc 8:21; 13:14; Philo; Jos., Bell. 1, 246, Ant. 19, 233) Dg 5:5. Of Galilee as Jesus' homeland **J 4:44** (JPryor, CBQ 49, '87, 254–63 [all Israel]). Fig. (for early extended use s. Eur., fgm. 1047, 2 [Stob. 40:9] TGF p. 692 ἅπασα δὲ χθὼν ἀνδρὶ γενναίῳ πατρίς 'all the earth is homeland to a noble man'; cp. Ovid, Fast. 1, 493), of the heavenly home (cp. Ael. Aristid. 43, 18 K.=1 p. 7 D.: τὴν πρώτην πατρίδα τὴν οὐράνιον; Anaxagoras in Diog. L. 2, 7; Epict. 2, 23, 38; Philo, Agr. 65) **Hb 11:14.** ἀγάπη τῆς πατρίδος *love of one's country* 1 Cl 55:5.

❷ **a relatively restricted area as locale of one's immediate family and ancestry,** ***home town, one's own part of the country*** (oft. ins, pap; Appian, Bell. Civ. 1. 48 §207; 210; Phlegon: 257 fgm. 36, 3, 14 Jac.; Herodian 8, 3, 1; Philo, Leg. ad Gai. 278; Jos., Ant. 6, 67; 10, 114) **Mt 13:54; Mk 6:1; Lk 2:3** D; **4:23; Ac 18:25** D, **27** D. As a proverb: οὐκ ἔστιν προφήτης ἄτιμος εἰ μὴ ἐν τῇ πατρίδι αὐτοῦ (Dio Chrys. 30 [47], 6 πᾶσι τοῖς φιλοσόφοις χαλεπὸς ἐν τῇ πατρίδι ὁ βίος; Ep. 44 of Apollonius of Tyana [Philostrat. I 354, 12] ἡ πατρὶς ἀγνοεῖ; Epict. 3, 16, 11 the philosopher avoids his πατρίς) **Mk 6:4;** cp. **Mt 13:57; Lk 4:24;** Ox 1 recto, 11 (cp. GTh 31). Also **J 4:44;** s. 1 above.—B. 1303. DELG s.v. πατήρ. M-M. Sv.

Πατροβᾶς, ᾶ, ὁ (CIG 6864. Short form of Πατρόβιος. B-D-F §125; Rob. 173) ***Patrobas*** recipient of a greeting **Ro 16:14.**—BHHW III1402; Pauly-W. XVIII 2253; Kl. Pauly IV 555.

Πάτροκλος, ου, ὁ (Hom. et al.; Jos., Ant. 14, 222; OGI 44, 3; 45, 4; pap) ***Patroclus*** Nero's cupbearer AcPl Ha 11, 10.

πατρολῴας, ου, ὁ (also πατραλῴας; Aristoph., Pla. et al.; Jos., Ant. 16, 356. On the formation of the word see s.v. μητρολῴας) ***one who kills his father, a patricide*** (w. μητρολῴας) **1 Ti 1:9** (M. Ant. 6, 34 in a list of the grossest sins).—DELG s.v. ἀλωή. M-M.

πατροπαράδοτος, ον ***inherited, handed down from one's father or forefathers/ancestors*** (Dionys. Hal. 5, 48; Diod. S. 4, 8, 5 [εὐσέβεια]; 15, 74, 5 [εὔνοια]; 17, 4, 1 [ἡγεμονία]; OGI 331, 49 [s. Welles p. 270]; PGM 33, 23; TestSol 13, 4 C) ἡ ματαία ἀναστροφὴ π. *the futile way of life inherited from your ancestors* **1 Pt 1:18** (WvUnnik, De verlossing 1 Pt 1, 18, 19, '42, The Critique of Paganism in 1 Pt 1:18, Neotestamentica et Semitica [MBlack Festschr.], '69, 129–42).—DELG s.v. δίδωμι. M-M.

πατρώνυμος, ον ***named after the father*** (QDAP 1, '31, 155 [Gaza, III AD]) IRo ins (on the subject matter cp. **Eph 3:14f;** s. Lghtf. on IRo ins), where God the Father is meant.—DELG s.v. ὄνομα.

πατρῷος, α, ον (since Hom. [πατρώϊος]; ins, pap, LXX, Philo, Joseph.; Just., D. 63, 5.—Wackernagel, Kl. Schr. 478f.) ***paternal, belonging to one's father, inherited or coming from one's father/ancestors*** ὁ πατρῷος νόμος **Ac 22:3** (Aelian, VH 6, 10; 3 Macc 1:23; 4 Macc 16:16; Jos., Ant. 13, 54 v.l.); τὰ ἔθη τὰ πατρῷα **28:17** (Aelian, VH 7, 19 v.l.; Just., D. 63, 5). ὁ π. θεός (Aeschyl. et al. oft., in sing. and pl.—OGI 194, 6 τὰ τῶν μεγίστων καὶ πατρῴων θεῶν ἱερά; 654, 8; SIG 711 L, 13 τὸν πατρῷιον Ἀπόλλω; PLond III, 973b, 6 p. 213 [III AD]; POxy 483, 24; 715, 28; PHermWess 125 B, 7 ὁ πατρῷος ἡμῶν θεὸς Ἑρμῆς; 4 Macc 12:17; Ezech. Trag. vs. 35 [in Eus., PE 9, 29, 14 p. 444d]; Jos., Ant. 9, 256) *the God of my ancestors* **Ac 24:14.**—DELG s.v. πατήρ. M-M. TW. Sv.

Παῦλος, ου, ὁ ***Paul,*** a Roman surname (never a praenomen), found in lit. (e.g. Diod. S. 14, 44, 1; 15, 76, 1), ins, pap; Mel., HE 4, 26, 3)

❶ Sergius Paulus s. Σέργιος.

❷ Paul, the apostle of Jesus Christ; fr. the beginning he bore the Israelite name Saul as well as the Graeco-Roman Paul (difft. e.g. HDessau, Her 45, 1910, 347–68 and EMeyer III 197; s. GHarrer, HTR 33, '40, 19–33.—Σαούλ 2 and Σαῦλος), prob. born in Tarsus (s. Ταρσός), and perh. brought up there (but s. WvUnnik, Tarsus or Jerusalem, '62), born a Roman citizen. He was educated in Mosaic tradition, but was not untouched by the syncretistic thought-world in which he lived. At first he was a zealous Pharisee and as such a vehement foe of Christians, but his perspective was changed by a vision of Jesus Christ (OKietzig, D. Bekehrg. d. Pls '32; EPfaff, Die Bekehrg. d. hl. Pls in d. Exegese des 20. Jahrh. '42; CBurchard, Der Dreizehnte Zeuge, '70, 126 n. 278 [lit. since '54]). Most prominent of the apostles to the nations/gentiles. As such he worked in Nabataean Arabia, Syria, and Cilicia, traveled through Cyprus, Asia Minor, Macedonia, and Greece, and planned a missionary journey via Italy to Spain (s. Σπανία). He was prevented fr. carrying out this plan (at least at this time) by his subsequent arrest in Jerusalem and the lawsuit connected w. it (NVeldhoen, Het Proces van den Ap. Pls 1924; ESpringer, D. Proz. des Ap. Pls: PJ 218, 1929, 182–96; HCadbury, Roman Law and the Trial of Paul: Beginn. I/5, '33, 297–338). He reached Rome only as a prisoner (on the journey FDavies, St. Paul's Voyage to Rome '31), and was prob. executed there: **Ac 9** and **13–28; Ro 1:1; 1 Cor 1:1, 12f; 3:4f, 22; 16:21; 2 Cor 1:1; 10:1; Gal 1:1; 5:2; Eph 1:1; 3:1; Phil 1:1; Col 1:1, 23; 4:18; 1 Th 1:1; 2:18; 2 Th 1:1; 3:17; 1 Ti 1:1; 2 Ti 1:1; Tit 1:1; Phlm 1, 9, 19; 2 Pt 3:15;** Pol 9:1; (11:2, 3). AcPl Ant 13, 9 recto and 15 verso (= Aa I 237, 1f) and 66 times AcPl Ha, including once ὁ μακάριος Π. AcPl Ha 3, 27; the same 4 times in AcPlCor. ὁ μακάριος Π. ὁ ἀπόστολος 1 Cl 47:1. Π. ὁ ἡγιασμένος, ὁ μεμαρτυρημένος, ἀξιομακάριστος IEph 12:2. ὁ μακάριος καὶ ἔνδοξος Π. Pol 3:2. Mentioned w. Peter 1 Cl 5:5; IRo 4:3.—S. also ApcEsdr 5:22 p. 30, 24 Tdf.; with John ApcEsdr 1:19 p. 25, 13 Tdf.—CClemen, Paulus 1904, where the older lit. is given. Other lit. in RBultmann, TRu n.s. 6, '34, 229–46; 8, '36, 1–22; WLyons and MParvis, NT Literature 1943–45, '48, 225–39; GBornkamm, RGG³ V, '61, 189f; ABD s.v.—ADeissmann, Pls² 1925 (Eng. tr. WWilson 1926); EvDobschütz, Der Ap. Pls I 1926; LMurillo, Paulus 1926; KPieper, Pls., Seine missionarische Persönlichkeit u. Wirksamkeit²,³ 1929; EBaumann, Der hl. Pls 1927; PFeine, Der Ap. Pls 1927; RLiechtenhan, Pls 1928; HLietzmann, Gesch. d. Alten Kirche I '32, 102–31; JStewart, A Man in Christ '36; CScott, St. Paul, the Man and the Teacher '36; ANock, St. Paul '38; TGlover, Paul of Tarsus '38; CYver, S. Paul '39; VGrÿnbech, Paulus '40; WvLoewenich, Pls '40; DRiddle, Paul, Man of Conflict '40; EBuonaiuti, San Paolo '41; JBover, San Pablo '41; EAllo, Paul '42; JKlausner, Fr. Jesus to Paul '43; EGoodspeed, Paul '47; JKnox, Chapters in a Life of Paul '50; MDibelius, Paulus '51; ²'56, with WKümmel (Eng. tr. FClarke '53); EFascher, Pauly-W. Suppl. VIII 431–66, '57.—FPrat, La théologie de S. Paul 1924f (Eng. tr. JStoddard '57); CScott, Christianity Acc. to St. Paul 1928; OMoe, Apostolen Pls' Forkyndelse og Laere 1928; AKristoffersen, Åpenbaringstanke og misjonsforkynnelse hos Pls, diss. Upps. '38; RGuardini, Jes. Chr. I (in Paul) '40; ChGuignebert, Le Christ '43, 3 (Paulinisme).—A Schweitzer, D. Mystik des Ap. Pls 1930 (Eng. tr. WMontgomery '31); MGoguel, La Mystique Paulin.: RHPhr 11, '31, 185–210; MDibelius, Pls u. d. Mystik '41; AFaux, L' Orphisme et St. Paul: RHE 27, '31, 245–92; 751–91; HWindisch, Pls u. Christus, E. bibl.-rel. gesch. Vergleich '34.—EEidem, Det kristna Livet enligt Pls I 1927; MEnslin, The Ethics of Paul 1930; LMarshall, The Challenge of NT Ethics '46; DWhiteley, The Theol. of St. Paul, '64.—APuukko, Pls u. d. Judentum: Studia Orientalia 2, 1928, 1–86; HWindisch, Pls u. d. Judentum '35; NMansson, Paul and the Jews '47; WKnox, St. Paul and the Church of the Gentiles '39.—ASteinmann, Z. Werdegang des Pls. Die Jugendzeit in Tarsus 1928; EBarnikol, D. vorchristl. u. frühchristl. Zeit des Pls 1929; AOepke, Probleme d. vorchristl. Zeit des Pls: StKr 105, '33, 387–424; GBornkamm, D. Ende des Gesetzes, Paulusstudien '52.—WKümmel, Jes. u. Pls: ThBl 19, '40, 209–31; ASchlatter, Jes. u. Pls '40; WDavies, Paul and Rabbinic Judaism ⁴'80.—GRicciotti, Paul the Apostle (Eng. tr. AlZizzamia) '53; JSevenster, Paul and Seneca, '61; H-JSchoeps, Paulus '59 (Engl. tr. HKnight, '61); BMetzger, Index to Periodical Lit. on Paul '60; Wv Loewenich, Paul: His Life and Works (transl.

GHarris), '60; WSchmithals, Paul and James (transl. DBarton), '65; EGüttgemanns, D. Leidende Apostel, '66; HBraun, Qumran u. d. NT '66, 165–80; SPorter, The Paul of Acts '99; additional lit. HBetz, ABD V 199–201.—LGPN I. M-M. EDNT. TW.

παύω (Hom.+) fut. 1 sg. παύσω (JosAs 28:5), 2 sg. παύσεις (Is 58:12), 3 sg. παύσει (Job 6:26); 1 aor. ἔπαυσα, impv. 2 sing. παῦσον (GrBar 1:6; ApcSed 12:1), 3 sing. παυσάτω. Mid.: impf. ἐπαυόμην; fut. παύσομαι; 1 aor. ἐπαυσάμην, impv. παῦσαι; pf. πέπαυμαι; plpf. ἐπεπαύμην (Just., D. 66, 1). Pass.: fut. 3 sg. παυθήσεται (Just., A I, 52, 8); 2 aor. inf. παῆναι (Hv 1, 3, 3; 3, 9, 1.—Reinhold p. 78; StBPsaltes, Grammatik 225; B-D-F §76, 1; 78; W-S. §13, 9).

❶ **to cause someth. to stop or keep someth. from happening,** ***stop, cause to stop, quiet, relieve,*** act. (JosAs 28:5 τὴν ὀργήν; Jos., Ant. 20, 117 στάσιν, Vi. 173; Just., D. 11, 2 νόμον) τὶ ἀπό τινος *hinder, keep someth. from someth.* τὴν γλῶσσαν ἀπὸ κακοῦ *keep the tongue from evil* **1 Pt 3:10;** 1 Cl 22:3 (both Ps 33:14). *Relieve, cure* (SIG 1168, 72) τί τινι *someth. with someth.* τοὺς παροξυσμοὺς ἐμβροχαῖς IPol 2:1.

❷ **to cease doing someth.,** ***stop (oneself), cease,*** mid. (on the syntax s. DHesseling, ByzZ 20, 1911, 147ff) w. pres. act. ptc. foll. (Hom.+), or pres. pass. ptc. (Ath. 1, 3 al.) ἐπαύσατο λαλῶν (Gen 18:33; Num 16:31; Judg 15:17 B) *he stopped speaking* **Lk 5:4.** μετ' ἐμοῦ λαλοῦσα Hv 3, 10, 1. ἐπαυσάμην ἐρωτῶν *I stopped asking* v 3, 8, 1; cp. v 3, 1, 6. π. τύπτων τινά *stop beating someone* **Ac 21:32.** ἀναβαίνων Hs 9, 4, 4a.—οὐ π. foll. by pres. act. ptc. *not to stop doing someth., do someth. without ceasing* (X., Cyr. 1, 4, 2; Herodian 1, 6, 2; Philostrat., V.S. 2, 1, 6 οὐκ ἐπαύσαντο μισοῦντες; Jos., Ant. 9, 255) διδάσκων **Ac 5:42.** λαλῶν **6:13.** διαστρέφων **13:10.** νουθετῶν **20:31.** εὐχαριστῶν **Eph 1:16.** Followed by the pres. mid. ptc. (cp. Himerius, Or. 74 [=Or. 24], 5 μὴ παύονται ἐργαζόμενοι) προσευχόμενος **Col 1:9.** αἰτούμενος Hv 3, 3, 2. Foll. by pres. pass. ptc. (Antiphon Or. 5, 50; Pla., Rep. 9, 583d), in ref. to αἱ θυσίαι: ἐπεὶ οὐκ ἂν ἐπαύσαντο προσφερόμεναι; *otherwise would they not have ceased to be offered?* **Hb 10:2.**—W. gen. of thing (Hom. et al.; Ex 32:12; TestSim 3:6; Philo, Dec. 97; Jos., Ant. 7, 144; Just., A II, 2, 7) *cease from, have done with someth.* τῶν ἀρχαίων ὑποδειγμάτων *leave the old examples,* i.e. mention no more 1 Cl 5:1. πέπαυται ἁμαρτίας *he is through with sin* **1 Pt 4:1.** W. gen. of the inf. (ApcEsdr 4:1; Jos., Ant. 3, 218; Just., D. 56, 2; Ath. 24, 2) π. τοῦ θύειν GEb 54, 20. π. ἀπό τινος *cease from, leave* (Ps 36:8) ἀπὸ τῶν πονηριῶν 1 Cl 8:4 (Is 1:16). ἀπὸ τῆς πονηρίας Hv 3, 9, 1. π. ἀφ' ὑμῶν ἡ ὀργή *the wrath will cease from you* GEb 54, 20 (ParJer 7:28 οὐκ ἐπαύσατο ἡ λύπη ἀφ' ἡμῶν).—Abs. *stop, cease, have finished, be at an end* (Hom. et al.; EpArist 293; SibOr 5, 458; Just., D. 51, 1; 52, 3; Ath. 19, 1) of Jesus at prayer ὡς ἐπαύσατο *when he stopped* **Lk 11:1.** ἐπαύσαντο οἱ οἰκοδομοῦντες μικρόν *the builders stopped for a little while* Hs 9, 4, 4b. οὐ παύσεται ὁ ζητῶν, ἕως ἂν εὕρῃ (for the constr. cp. Sir 23:17) *the one who seeks will not give up until he has found* GHb 70, 17; cp. Ox 654, 6 (GTh 2). Of the raging wind and waves ἐπαύσαντο *they stopped* **Lk 8:24** (cp. Od. 12, 168; Hdt. 7, 193; Arrian, Ind. 22, 1 ὁ ἄνεμος ἐπαύσατο; TestNapht 6:9 ἐπαύσατο ὁ χειμών). Of an uproar **Ac 20:1** (cp. IAndrosIsis, Kyme 26 φόνους); GJs 25:1 (pap, s. entry καταπαύω). Of speaking in tongues, which will come to an end **1 Cor 13:8.** Also of time *elapse, come to an end* (Herodian 1, 16, 2; PGrenf II, 69, 21 τῆς πεπαυμένης τριετηρίδος) τῆς ἑορτῆς παυσαμένης *since the festival was over* GPt 14:58. μετὰ τὸ παῆναι αὐτῆς τὰ ῥήματα ταῦτα *after these words of hers had come to an end* Hv 1, 3, 3.—B. 981. M-M.

Πάφος, ου, ἡ (Hom. et al.; ins; SibOr 4, 128; 5, 451) ***Paphos*** (Nea Paphos), a city on the west coast of Cyprus less than 2 km. fr. the shore (not to be confused w. Palaipaphos, which is east of Nea Paphos) the seat of the Rom. proconsul. Paul visited the city on his so-called first missionary journey **Ac 13:6, 13.**—Lit. s.v. Κύπρος; JHS 9, 1889, 158ff.; Pauly-W. XVIII 937ff; Kl. Pauly IV 484–87; BHHW III 1382f; PECS 673f (lit.); FMaier, Alt-Paphos auf Cypern '85; OEANE IV 245f.

παχύνω aor. 3 sg. ἐπάχυνεν 2 Km 22:12. Pass.: fut. 2 sg. παχυνθήσει (ApcMos 24); aor. ἐπαχύνθην (Aeschyl., Hippocr. et al.; PTebt 273, 31; Philo, Aet. M. 103); pf. 3 sg. πεπάχυται (Just., D. 12, 2; 1); in our lit. only in OT quotations.

❶ lit. ***make fat, well-nourished*** (Pla., X. et al.). Pass. in act. sense *become fat* (X., Conv. 2, 17; Plut., Sol. 89 [20, 8]; LXX; ApcMos 24) ἔφαγεν καὶ ἔπιεν καὶ ἐπλατύνθη καὶ ἐπαχύνθη 1 Cl 3:1 (Dt 32:15).

❷ fig. ***make impervious*** (orig. to water), ***make gross, dull*** (Plut., Mor. 995d τὰς ψυχάς; Philostrat., Vi. Apoll. 1, 8 νοῦν). Pass. in act. sense *become dull* (Herm. Wr. in Stob.=508, 32 Sc. of the ψυχή; SibOr 7, 106; Synes., Dreams 6 p. 136d; 137a 'become dull' [of eyes]) ἐπαχύνθη ἡ καρδία τοῦ λαοῦ τούτου **Mt 13:15; Ac 28:27** (s. βαρύνω; both Is 6:10).—B. 887. DELG. M-M. TW.

πεδάω (fr. πέδη, cp. πέζα 'instep' Pollux 2, 192) aor. ptc. acc. pl. πεδήσαντες Da 3:20 Theod. Pass.: aor. ἐπεδήθην Da 4:33a, ptc. πεδήθεις (Tat. 9, 3); pf. 3 sg. πεπέδηται (Ath., R. 15 p. 66, 33), ptc. πεπεδημένος (Hom. et al.; also Paus. 8, 49, 6; LXX) 'bind the feet with fetters', then gener. ***bind, fetter, shackle*** (En 21:4; Philo, Aet. M. 129; SibOr 1, 371) ἐξαγαγεῖν ἐκ δεσμῶν πεπεδημένους καὶ ἐξ οἴκου φυλακῆς καθημένους ἐν σκότει *to free prisoners from their bonds and from their dungeon those who sit in darkness* B 14:7 (here, as in Just., the word πεπεδημένους, which occurs in sim. LXX passages [e.g. Ps 67:7 ἐξάγων πεπεδημένους], has come into the context of Is 42:7). The emendation πεπεδημένοι (for πεπηδημένοι) has been suggested for AcPl BMM verso 5, but Sanders, favoring Septuagint usage of ἐκπηδάω (q.v. 3) restores: [οἱ ἐ]ν σκοτίᾳ θαν[άτου ἐκ]|πεπηδημένοι lines 4f (s. his note). The text continues: φῶς ἀνέτειλεν ὑμῖν and with the form πεπεδημένοι (which also fits in the lacuna of AcPl Ha 8, 32f) can be rendered *for you, fettered in the darkness of death, the light has shined* (cp. τοὺς νεκροὺς . . . πεπεδημένους καὶ τεθλιμμένους ἐν σκότῳ καὶ γνόφῳ ἐντὸς τοῦ ῞Αιδου Cleopatra p. 15 ln. 44). But Sanders is reluctant to "accept an emendation in a manuscript so carefully written and belonging to the third century" (HTR 31, '38, 87) and interprets 'those who are living (sinfully) in the darkness of death'.—DELG s.v. πέδη.

πέδη, ης, ἡ (s. πεδάω; Hom. et al.; PSI 406, 24; PGM 5, 488; LXX; TestJos 8:5; MartIs 3:6 p. 112 D.; Jos., Ant. 19, 295) ***fetter, shackle*** in pl. w. ἁλύσεις (sim. Dionys. Hal. 6, 27, 2; ἅλυσις 1) **Mk 5:4ab; Lk 8:29.**—DELG. M-M.

πεδινός, ή, όν (πέδιον; Hdt. et al.; LXX) ***flat, level*** either as opposed to 'steep', 'uneven' (Aristot., Probl. 5, 1; Cass. Dio 68, 16; Dt 4:43; Jos., Ant. 13, 217) or in contrast to 'high', 'elevated' (Aristot, HA 9, 32; Jer 17:26; EpArist 107) τόπος π. *a level place* **Lk 6:17.**—B. 893. DELG s.v. πέδον. M-M.

πεδίον, ου, τό (s. prec. entry; Hom.+; ins, pap, LXX, Test12-Patr; GrBar 4:3; 4 [6] Esdr=POxy 1010 recto 8f; SibOr 2, 337; EpArist 23; Philo, Det. Pot. Ins. 1; Jos., Ant. 5, 63, Vi. 207; Tat. 10, 3; Mel., P. 26, 189) ***level place, plain, field*** Hs 6, 1, 5; 7:1;

8, 4, 2; 9, 1, 4; 9, 2, 1; 9, 6, 6f; 9, 9, 4; 9, 29, 4; 9, 30, 1. πεδία καὶ ὄρη *plains and mountains* Hs 8, 1, 1; 8, 3, 2.—1 Cl 4:6ab (Gen 4:8ab). ἐν τῷ Ἠλυσίῳ πεδίῳ ApcPt Rainer 5f (cp. Tat. 10, 3).—B. 26.DELG s.v. πέδον. M-M s.v. πεδινός.

πεζεύω (πεζός) ***travel by land*** in contrast to a sea-journey (so X., An. 5, 5, 4; Polyb. 16, 29, 11; 10, 48, 6; Plut., Cato Maj. 9, 9 al.; OGI 199, 14; PBrem 15, 22; Philo, Ebr. 158 πεζ. κ. πλεῖν) **Ac 20:13.** But the orig. mng. *travel on foot* is not impossible here (Aristot. De Part. An. 3, 6; cp. TestAbr A 2 p. 79, 13 [Stone p. 6]; Jos., Ant. 13, 208; SibOr 4, 78).—DELG s.v. πεζός. M-M.

πεζῇ adv. (Hdt. et al.; PTebt. 5, 28; PSI 446, 13; 2 Km 15:17. On the spelling s. B-D-F §26; W-S. §5, 11 n. 22; Mlt.-H. 163) ***by land*** (opp. ἐν πλοίῳ.—So since Hdt., Thu.; Sb 7600, 10 [16 AD]; Jos., Bell. 4, 659; orig. 'on foot') **Mt 14:13** (v.l. πεζοί); **Mk 6:33.**—M-M.

πεζός, ή, όν (s. πεζεύω; Hom. et al.; ins, pap, LXX) ***going by land*** (Hom. et al.; Jos., Bell. 3, 8) (opp. ἐν πλοίῳ, as Pind., P. 10, 29 ναυσί) **Mt 14:13 v.l.** πεζοὺς πέμπειν *send messengers* (who travel on the highway) IPol 8:1.—M-M.

πειθαρχέω fut. 3 pl. πειθαρχήσουσιν Da 7:27; 1 aor. ptc. πειθαρχήσας (Soph., Hdt.+; M. Ant. 5, 9; ins, pap, LXX, Did. Oft. in Philo; Jos., Bell. 1, 454, C. Ap. 2, 293 τ. νόμοις) ***obey*** θεῷ **Ac 5:29** (cp. Pla., Apol. 17, 29d πείσομαι μᾶλλον τῷ θεῷ ἢ ὑμῖν; Socrat., Ep. 1, 7 ᾧ [= τ. θεῷ] πειστέον μᾶλλον; Jos., Ant. 17, 159; Theoph. Ant. 1, 14 [p. 90, 2]), vs. **32.** τῷ λόγῳ τῆς δικαιοσύνης *obey the word of righteousness* Pol 9:1. ἔδει μὲν . . . πειθαρχήσαντάς μοι μὴ ἀνάγεσθαι *you ought to have followed my advice and not to have sailed* **Ac 27:21** (cp. Polyb. 3, 4, 3.—On the topic cp. the unavailing protest of a passenger Ael. Aristid. 48, 47f K.=24 p. 483 D.). Fig. of the heavenly bodies that obey the Creator Dg 7:2. Abs. (as OGI 483, 70f) *be obedient* **Tit 3:1** (w. ἀρχαῖς ἐξουσίαις ὑποτάσσεσθαι).—ENachmanson, D. Konstruktionen v. πειθαρχεῖν in d. κοινή: Eranos 10, 1910, 201–3.—New Docs 2, 105. DELG s.v. ἄρχω. M-M. TW. Spicq.

πειθός, ή, όν (fr. πείθ[ω]) ***persuasive*** ἐν πειθοῖς σοφίας λόγοις *in persuasive words of wisdom* **1 Cor 2:4.** The word is found nowhere but here; its attestation is extremely good (as early as P[46]), though it is in a context that is subject to considerable variation in detail (the situation is well reviewed in Ltzm., Hdb. ad loc.). The word is formed quite in accordance w. st. Gk. usage (cp. φειδός 'sparing' fr. φείδομαι), and the Gk. Fathers let it pass without comment (so Ltzm., Bachmann, Sickenberger, HermvSoden; Mlt-H. 78). Despite this, many (e.g. Heinrici, Schmiedel, JWeiss) reject this word because of its rarity and prefer the explanation that it originated in dittography of the σ (or perh. through an error in hearing the passage dictated): ἐν πειθοῖ σοφίας, s. πειθώ; B-D-F §47, 4; 112; W-S. §16, 3 n. 20; Rob. 157; GZuntz, The Text of the Epistles '53, 23–25.—Rdm.[2] p. 63 takes πειθοῖς as a rare genitive formation from πειθώ, influenced by the dat. πειθοῖ; the mng. then would be 'words of persuasion from wisdom (herself)'.—DELG s.v. πείθομαι B. M-M. TW. Spicq.

πειθώ, οῦς, ἡ the gift or art of persuasion, ***persuasiveness*** (cp. πειθός; Aeschyl., Thu. et al.; Ps.-Phoc. 78; Philo; Jos., Bell. 2, 8, C. Ap. 2, 186; 223; Just., A I, 53, 12, D. 53, 6; Jos.) ἐν πειθοῖ ἀνθρωπίνης σοφίας λόγοις (others λογῶν, -γοῦ, which is somet. lacking; s. JWeiss ad loc.) *with the persuasiveness of wisdom* **1 Cor 2:4 v.l.** (s. πειθός. On the 'persuasive power' of words cp. Περὶ ὕψους 17, 1 πειθὼ τῶν λόγων; Philo, Virt. 217 τοῖς λόγοις πειθώ; Jos., Ant. 2, 272).—DELG s.v. πείθομαι B. M-M. s.v. πειθός. TW.

πείθω (Hom. et al.; ins, pap, LXX, EpArist, Philo, Joseph., Test12Patr) impf. ἔπειθον; fut. πείσω; 1 aor. ἔπεισα, impv. πεῖσον; 1 pf. 3 sg. πέπεικε(ν) (Just., D. 53, 5; 58, 2); 2 pf. πέποιθα; plpf. ἐπεποίθειν **Lk 11:22** and ἐπεποίθησα Job 31:24 (cp. Judg 9:26 A; Zech 3:3). Mid. and pass. impf. ἐπειθόμην. Pass.: 1 fut. πεισθήσομαι; 1 aor. ἐπείσθην; pf. πέπεισμαι; plpf. 1 pl. (ἐ)πεπείσμεθα (Ath. 31, 2).

❶ act., except for 2 perf. and plpf.: **to cause to come to a particular point of view or course of action.—ⓐ** ***convince*** w. acc. of pers. (X., Mem. 1, 2, 45 al.) ISm 5:1. ἔπειθεν Ἰουδαίους καὶ Ἕλληνας *he tried to convince Jews and Gentiles* **Ac 18:4.** πείθων αὐτοὺς περὶ τοῦ Ἰησοῦ *trying to convince them about Jesus* **28:23** (π. τινὰ περί τινος as Jos., C. Ap. 2, 153). Without acc. πείθων περὶ τῆς βασιλείας **19:8 v.l.** With acc. of thing τὰ περὶ τοῦ Ἰησοῦ **28:23 v.l.** and τῆς βασιλείας **19:8** (on acc. of thing cp. Hdt. 1, 163; Pla., Apol. 27, 37a). Abs. (Jos., Vi. 19) πείθων, οὐ βιαζόμενος *convincing, not compelling* Dg 7:4.—Also of convincing someone of the correctness of the objectionable teachings, almost=*mislead* (Ps.-Clem., Hom. 1, 22) **Ac 19:26.** τινά τινι *someone with someth.* Hs 8, 6, 5.

ⓑ ***persuade, appeal to,*** also in an unfavorable sense ***cajole, mislead*** (so TestDan 1:8; ApcMos 21; Jos., C. Ap. 2, 201) τινά *someone* ἀνθρώπους (Ael. Aristid. 34, 19 K.=50 p. 552 D.) **2 Cor 5:11;** perh. also **Gal 1:10** (but s. c below). Cp. MPol 3:1; 8:2, 3. τινά w. inf. foll. (X., An. 1, 3, 19; Polyb. 4, 64, 2; Diod. S. 12, 39, 2; 17, 15, 5; Herodian 2, 4, 2; Jos., Ant. 8, 256; Just., A II 2, 10, D. 112, 3; Tat. 21, 3) **Ac 13:43;** MPol 4; 5:1. ἔπειθεν (sc. αὐτὸν) ἀρνεῖσθαι *he tried to induce him to deny* 9:2. Perh. this is the place for the textually uncertain pass. **Ac 26:28** ἐν ὀλίγῳ με πείθεις Χριστιανὸν ποιῆσαι *you lose no time trying to make me play the Christian* (cp. the tr. in Beginn. IV 322, w. reff. to 3 Km 20:7 and patristic authors cited in Soph., Lex. s.v. ποιέω 3; s. also Lampe s.v. ποιέω C). Because of apparent misunderstanding of the idiom, this wording is simplified in a widespread v.l. in which ποιῆσαι is replaced with γενέσθαι *in a short time you are persuading* (or *trying to persuade*) *me to become a Christian* (cp. Jos., Vi. 151 πρὸς ὀλίγον ἐπείθοντο='they were nearly persuaded'), prob. meant ironically. Bauer considered it prob. that the rdg. of the text be understood as a combination of the two expressions 'in a short time you are persuading me to become a Christian' and 'in a short time you will make me a Christian', so that the sense is someth. like *you are in a hurry to persuade me and make a Christian of me* (so Goodsp, Probs. 137f [but it is not clear whether "make" here is to be understood in the sense 'play the part of']. S. the lit. s.v. ὀλίγος 2bβ and under 3a below, also AFridrichsen, SymbOsl 14, '35, 49–52, ConNeot 3, '39, 13–16 [w. ref. to X., Mem. 1, 2, 49; cp. PBenoit, RB 53, '46, 303]; DHesseling, Neophilol 20, '37, 129–34; JHarry, ATR 28, '46, 135 f; EHaenchen ad loc.). Instead of the inf. we have ἵνα (Plut., Mor. 181a πείθωμεν ἵνα μείνῃ) **Mt 27:20** (B-D-F §392, 1e; Rob. 993).

ⓒ ***win over, strive to please*** (X., Cyr. 6, 1, 34; 2 Macc 4:45) **Ac 12:20.** τοὺς ὄχλους **14:19.** So perh. also **Gal 1:10** (s. b above.—π. τὸν θεόν=persuade God: Jos., Ant. 4, 123; 8, 256; Ps.-Clem., Hom. 3, 64).—BDodd, NTS 42, '96, 90–104.

ⓓ ***conciliate, pacify, set at ease/rest*** (Hom. et al.) τὸν δῆμον (cp. X., Hell. 1, 7, 7 τοιαῦτα λέγοντες ἔπειθον τὸν δῆμον) MPol 10:2. τὴν καρδίαν (v.l. τὰς καρδίας) ἡμῶν **1J 3:19** (but the text is not in good order). *Conciliate, satisfy* **Mt 28:14** (unless π. ἀργυρίῳ *bribe* is meant: schol. on Pla. 18b; 2 Macc 10:20; Jos., Ant. 14, 281; 490).

❷ The 2 pf. (w. plpf.) has pres. mng. (B-D-F §341; Rob. 881), **to be so convinced that one puts confidence in someth.**

ⓐ ***depend on, trust in*** w. dat. of pers. or thing (Hom. et al.; 4 Km 18:20; Pr 14:16; 28:26; Sir 32:24; Wsd 14:29; Is 28:17) τίνι θεῷ *(in) which God* Dg 1 (here πέπ. w. dat. almost =*believe in,* a sense which πέπ. also approximates in the LXX; cp. Jos., Ant. 7, 122). τοῖς δεσμοῖς μου **Phil 1:14.** τῇ ὑπακοῇ σου **Phlm 21.** ἐπί τινι *(in) someone* or *someth.* (PSI 646, 3 ἐπὶ σοὶ πεποιθώς; LXX; SibOr 3, 545; Syntipas p. 52, 5; Just., D. 8, 2) **Mt 27:43 v.l.; Mk 10:24 v.l.; Lk 11:22; 2 Cor 1:9; Hb 2:13** (Is 8:17); B 9:4; ἐπ᾽ ἐλπίδι 1 Cl 57:7; w. ὅτι foll. (Syntipas p. 32, 6; 35, 7) **Lk 18:9.** ἐπί τινα (Ps 117:8; Acta Christophori [ed. HUsener 1886] 68, 10) **Mt 27:43;** 1 Cl 60:1, cp. 58:1; Hm 9:6; s 9, 18, 5; w. ὅτι foll. **2 Cor 2:3; 2 Th 3:4.** ἔν τινι (Jdth 2:5) *(in) someone* or *someth.* **Phil 3:3f;** w. ὅτι foll. **2:24.** εἴς τινα (Wsd 16:24 v.l.) w. ὅτι foll. **Gal 5:10.**

ⓑ ***be convinced, be sure, certain*** foll. by acc. and inf. **Ro 2:19.** W. ὅτι foll. **Hb 13:18 v.l.** πεποιθὼς αὐτὸ τοῦτο ὅτι *being sure of this very thing, that* **Phil 1:6.** τοῦτο πεποιθὼς οἶδα ὅτι *convinced of this, I know that* **1:25.** εἴ τις πέποιθεν ἑαυτῷ Χριστοῦ εἶναι *if anyone is convinced within of belonging to Christ* **2 Cor 10:7** (cp. BGU 1141, 17 [14 BC] πέποιθα γὰρ ἐμαυτῷ).

❸ pass. and mid., except for the pf.: **to be won over as the result of persuasion.**—ⓐ ***be persuaded, believe*** abs. (Pr 26:25) **Lk 16:31; Ac 17:4; Hb 11:13 v.l.** μὴ πειθομένου αὐτοῦ *since he would not be persuaded* **Ac 21:14.** πεισθεὶς ὑπὸ τῆς γυναικὸς τοῦ Νάβαλ AcPl Ha 6, 23. W. dat. of the thing by which one is persuaded (opp. ἀπιστεῖν; τοῖς γραώδεσι μύθοις Iren. 1, 16, 3 [Harv. I 162, 8]) τοῖς λεγομένοις (Hdt. 2, 146, 1; Jos., Bell. 7, 415) **Ac 28:24.** πείθομαι *I believe* w. ὅτι foll. **Hb 13:18;** Hs 8, 11, 2. **Ac 26:28 v.l.** (s. 1b above), construed w. inf. ἐν ὀλίγῳ με πείθῃ Χριστιανὸν ποιῆσαι *in too short a time you believe you are making a Christian of me* (so Bachmann, Blass). οὐ πείθομαι w. acc. and inf. *I cannot believe* **Ac 26:26.**

ⓑ ***obey, follow*** w. dat. of pers. or thing (Hom. et al.; Diod. S. 4, 31, 5 τῷ χρησμῷ=the oracle; Maximus Tyr. 23, 2d τῷ θεῷ; 36, 6g τ. νόμῳ τοῦ Διός; Appian, Iber. 19 §73 θεῷ; pap; 4 Macc 10:13; 15:10; 18:1; Just., D. 9, 1; Mel., P. 93, 705; π. θεῷ Did., Gen. 225, 17; τῇ ἀδικίᾳ Theoph. Ant. 1, 14 [p. 92, 5]) **Ro 2:8** (opp. ἀπειθεῖν, as Himerius, Or. 69 [=Or. 22], 7); **Gal 3:1 v.l.; 5:7; Hb 13:17; Js 3:3;** 2 Cl 17:5; Dg 5:10; IRo 7:2ab; Hm 12, 3, 3.

ⓒ Some passages stand betw. a and b and permit either transl., w. dat. ***be persuaded by someone, take someone's advice*** or ***obey, follow someone*** **Ac 5:36f, 39; 23:21; 27:11** (objection of a passenger, to which the crew paid no attention and suffered harm as a result: Chion, Ep. 4, 1 οἱ δ᾽ οὐκ ἐπείθοντο. Of relation between heretical leaders and their adherents Iren. 3, 12, 5 [Harv. II 58, 10]).

❹ perf. pass. πέπεισμαι **to attain certainty in ref. to something, *be convinced, certain*** (Pla.+; pap, LXX) πεπεισμένος τοῦτο *convinced of this* B 1:4. πέπεισμαί τι περί τινος *be convinced of someth. concerning someone* **Hb 6:9.** περί τινος *be sure of a thing* IPol 2:3. Foll. by acc. and inf. (Diod. S. 12, 20, 2 πεπεῖσθαι θεοὺς εἶναι; PPetr II, 11, 4 [III BC]; EpArist 5; Just., D. 58, 2; Mel., HE 4, 26, 11; Ath. 36, 1f) **Lk 20:6.** W. περί τινος and acc. w. inf.: περὶ ὧν πέπεισμαι ὑμᾶς οὕτως ἔχειν *concerning this I am certain that it is so with you* ITr 3:2. W. ὅτι foll. (X., Oec. 15, 8; Just., D. 65, 2; Tat., 20, 2) **Ro 8:38; 14:14** (w. οἶδα); **2 Ti 1:5, 12** (cp. w. ὡς foll. Did., Gen. 131, 8); Pol 9:2. πέπεισμαι περὶ ὑμῶν ὅτι **Ro 15:14.**—B. 1206; 1339. DELG s.v. πείθομαι. M-M. EDNT. TW. Spicq.

Πειλᾶτος s. Πιλᾶτος.—M-M.

πεῖν s. πίνω.

πεινάω (πεῖνα 'hunger'; Hom.et al.; PFlor 61, 54; LXX; TestJob 23:8; ParJer 9:20; Philo, Joseph.; Tat. 23, 1) pres. ptc. acc. by-form πεινοῦντα (TestJob 23:8; s. B-D-F §90); fut. πεινάσω; 1 aor. ἐπείνασα (on the forms in α, which our lit. shares w. the LXX, in contrast to earlier Gk., s. Phryn. p. 61 Lob.; B-D-F §70, 2; §88; Mlt-H. 195; 253)

❶ **to feel the pangs of lack of food, *hunger, be hungry*** (Iren. 3, 22, 2 [Harv. II 122, 6]) **Mt 4:2; 12:1, 3; 21:18; 25:35, 37, 42, 44; Mk 2:25; 11:12; Lk 4:2; 6:3, 25; Ro 12:20** (Pr 25:21); **1 Cor 11:34;** B 10:3. Opp. μεθύειν **1 Cor 11:21.** Opp. χορτάζεσθαι **Phil 4:12.** ὁ πεινῶν, οἱ πεινῶντες *the one who is hungry, those who are hungry* **Lk 1:53** (cp. Ps 106:9; Tat. 23, 1); **6:21;** 1 Cl 59:4; B 3:3 (Is 58:7), 5 (Is 58:10); Hv 3, 9, 5. W. διψᾶν (διψάω 1) **1 Cor 4:11; Rv 7:16** (Is 49:10); ISm 6:2.

❷ **desire someth. strongly, *hunger for someth.*** fig. ext. of 1 (X., Pla. et al., but w. gen. of thing. For the acc. cp. διψάω 2 and Zosimus: Hermet. IV p. 111, 3 πεῖν. τὴν σὴν ψυχήν) w. acc. of thing **Mt 5:6** (w. διψᾶν, as Plut., Mor. 460b; Jer 38:25). Of the longing for spiritual food **J 6:35** (also w. διψᾶν. Cp. ParJer 9:20 ἐμπλήσει τὰς πεινώσας ψυχάς [Jer 38, 25]).—DELG s.v. πείνη. M-M. TW.

πεῖρα, ας, ἡ (s. πειράζω; Pind.+)—❶ **an effort to accomplish someth., *attempt, trial, experiment,*** act. sense (Jos., C. Ap. 2, 183) πεῖραν λαμβάνειν *make an attempt* or *make trial of* (trag. et al.; POxy 1681, 10; Dt 28:56) τινός *someone* or *someth.* (X., Cyr. 6, 1, 54, Mem. 1, 4, 18; Pla., Protag. 342a, Gorg. 448a; Polyb. 2, 32, 5; Jos., Ant. 8, 166; SEG VIII, 574, 21 [III AD]; UPZ 110, 129 [164 BC]) ἧς πεῖραν λαβόντες *when they tried (to do) it* **Hb 11:29.** On θεοῦ ζῶντος πεῖραν ἀθλῶμεν 2 Cl 20:2 s. ἀθλέω.

❷ **experience won by attempting someth., *experience,*** pass. sense (X. et al.; IMagnMai 115, 21; Philo; Test Gad 5:2 ἐκ πείρας) πεῖράν τινος λαμβάνειν *have experience with* or simply *experience someth.* (Polyb. 6, 3, 1; 28, 9, 7; Diod. S. 12, 24, 4 τὴν θυγατέρα ἀπέκτεινεν, ἵνα μὴ τῆς ὕβρεως λάβῃ πεῖραν; Vett. Val. 74, 23; 82, 1; 84, 28 al.; Jos., Ant. 2, 60, Vi. 160) μαστίγων πεῖραν ἔλαβον *they experienced scourgings* **Hb 11:36.**—DELG. M-M. TW. Spicq. Sv.

πειράζω impf. ἐπείραζον; fut. πειράσω; 1 aor. ἐπείρασα, mid. 2 sg. ἐπειράσω. Pass.: 1 aor. ἐπειράσθην; pf. ptc. πεπειρασνένος (fr. πεῖρα; Hom., then Apollon. Rhod. 1, 495; 3, 10. In prose since Philo Mech. 50, 34; 51, 9; also Polyb.; Plut., Cleom. 808 [7, 3], Mor. 230a; Vett. Val. 17, 6; schol. on Aristoph., Pl. 575; PSI 927, 25 [II AD]; LXX; TestJos 16:3 v.l.; ApcSed 8:5 p. 133, 5 Ja.; Joseph.; Just., D. 103, 6; 125, 4.—B-D-F §101 p. 54; Mlt-H. 387 n. 1; 404).

❶ **to make an effort to do someth., *try, attempt*** at times in a context indicating futility (ὁ θεὸς τῷ πειράζοντι δοὺς ἐξουσίαν τὴν τοῦ διωκειν ἡμᾶς Orig., C. Cels. 8, 70, 11) w. inf. foll. (Polyb. 2, 6, 9; Dt 4:34.—B-D-F §392, 1a) **Ac 9:26; 16:7; 24:6;** Hs 8, 2, 7. Foll. by acc. w. inf. IMg 7:1. Abs. Hs 8, 2, 7.

❷ **to endeavor to discover the nature or character of someth. by testing, *try, make trial of, put to the test***—ⓐ gener. τινά *someone* (Epict. 1, 9, 29; Ps 25:2) ἑαυτοὺς πειράζετε εἰ ἐστὲ ἐν τῇ πίστει **2 Cor 13:5** (π. εἰ as Jos., Bell. 4, 340).

ἐπείρασας τοὺς λέγοντας ἑαυτοὺς ἀποστόλους **Rv 2:2.** προφήτην οὐ πειράσετε οὐδὲ διακρινεῖτε D 11:7.

ⓑ of God or Christ, who put people to the test, in a favorable sense (Ps.-Apollod. 3, 7; 7, 4 Zeus puts τὴν ἀσέβειαν of certain people to the test), so that they may prove themselves true **J 6:6; Hb 11:17** (Abraham, as Gen 22:1). Also of painful trials sent by God (Ex 20:20; Dt 8:2 v.l.; Judg 2:22; Wsd 3:5; 11:9; Jdth 8:25f) **1 Cor 10:13; Hb 2:18ab; 4:15** (s. πειράω); **11:37 v.l.; Rv 3:10** (SBrown, JBL 85, '66, 308–14 π.=*afflict*). Likew. of the measures taken by the angel of repentance Hs 7:1.

ⓒ The Bible (but s. the Pythia in Hdt. 6, 86, 3 τὸ πειρηθῆναι τοῦ θεοῦ κ. τὸ ποιῆσαι ἴσον δύνασθαι 'to have tempted the deity was as bad as doing the deed'; cp. 1, 159) also speaks of a trial of God by humans. Their intent is to put God to the test, to discover whether God really can do a certain thing, esp. whether God notices sin and is able to punish it (Ex 17:2, 7; Num 14:22; Is 7:12; Ps 77:41, 56; Wsd 1:2 al.) **1 Cor 10:9; Hb 3:9** (Ps 94:9). τὸ πνεῦμα κυρίου **Ac 5:9.** In **Ac 15:10** the πειράζειν τὸν θεόν consists in the fact that after God's will has been clearly made known through granting of the Spirit to the Gentiles (vs. 8), some doubt and make trial to see whether God's will really becomes operative. τὸν διά σου θεὸν πειράσαι θέλων, εἰ *since I want to put the god (you proclaim) to a test, whether* AcPt Ox 849, 20–22 followed by οὐ πειράζεται ὁ θεός *God refuses to be put to a test.*—ASommer, D. Begriff d. Versuchung im AT u. Judentum, diss. Breslau '35. S. πειράω.

❸ **to attempt to entrap through a process of inquiry, *test.*** Jesus was so treated by his opponents, who planned to use their findings against him **Mt 16:1; 19:3; 22:18, 35; Mk 8:11; 10:2; 12:15; Lk 11:16; 20:23 v.l.; J 8:6.**

❹ **to entice to improper behavior, *tempt* Gal 6:1; Js 1:13a** (s. ἀπό 5eβ) and **b, 14** (Aeschin. 1, 190 the gods do not lead people to sin). Above all the devil works in this way; hence he is directly called ὁ πειράζων *the tempter* **Mt 4:3; 1 Th 3:5b.** He tempts humans **Ac 5:3 v.l.; 1 Cor 7:5; 1 Th 3:5a; Rv 2:10.** But he also makes bold to tempt Jesus (Just.. D. 103, 6; Orig., C. Cels. 6, 43, 28) **Mt 4:1; Mk 1:13; Lk 4:2** (cp. use of the pass. without ref. to the devil: ἐν τῷ πειράζεσθαι . . . καὶ σταυροῦσθαι Iren. 3, 19, 3 [Harv. II 104, 3].—Did., Gen. 225, 2). On the temptation of Jesus (s. also Hb 2:18a; 4:15; 2b above) s. HWillrich, ZNW 4, 1903, 349f; KBornhäuser, Die Versuchungen Jesu nach d. Hb: MKähler Festschr. 1905, 69–86; on this Windisch, Hb[2] '31, 38 exc. on Hb 4:15; AHarnack, Sprüche u. Reden Jesu 1907, 32–37; FSpitta, Zur Gesch. u. Lit. des Urchristentums III 2, 1907, 1–108; AMeyer, Die evangel. Berichte üb. d. Vers. Christi: HBlümner Festschr. 1914, 434–68; DVölter, NThT 6, 1917, 348–65; EBöklen, ZNW 18, 1918, 244–48; PKetter, D. Versuchg. Jesu 1918; BViolet, D. Aufbau d. Versuchungsgeschichte Jesu: Harnack Festschr. 1921, 14–21; NFreese, D. Versuchg. Jesu nach den Synopt., diss. Halle 1922, D. Versuchlichkeit Jesu: StKr 96/97, 1925, 313–18; SEitrem/AFridrichsen, D. Versuchg. Christi 1924; Clemen[2] 1924, 214–18; HVogels, D. Versuchungen Jesu: BZ 17, 1926, 238–55; SelmaHirsch [s. on βαπτίζω 2a]; HThielicke, Jes. Chr. am Scheideweg '38; PSeidelin, DTh 6, '39, 127–39; HHoughton, On the Temptations of Christ and Zarathustra: ATR 26, '44, 166–75; EFascher, Jesus u. d. Satan '49; RSchnackenburg, TQ 132, '52, 297–326; K-PKöppen, Die Auslegung der Versuchungsgeschichte usw.'61; EBest, The Temptation and the Passion (Mk), '65; JDupont, RB 73, '66, 30–76.—B. 652f. DELG s.v. πεῖρα. M-M. EDNT. DLNT 1166–70. TW. Spicq. Sv.

πειρασμός, οῦ, ὁ (πειράζω; in extra-Biblical usage only Diosc., Mat. Med. Praef. 5; Cyranides; Syntipas [s. 2b].—LXX; TestJos 2:7).

❶ **an attempt to learn the nature or character of someth., *test, trial*** (Sir 6:7; 27:5, 7) πρὸς πειρασμόν *to test you* **1 Pt 4:12.** διὰ πειρασμόν τινα *because you are being tried in some way* Hm 9:7. Perh. **Js 1:2** and **1 Pt 1:6** belong here (cp. Pind., O. 4, 22 διά πειρά τοι βροτῶν ἔλεγχος=trial is the test of mortals; sim. N. 3, 70f). Here also belongs the *testing* (s. πειράζω 2c) of God by humans (cp. Dt 6:16; 9:22) **Hb 3:8** where vs. **9** shows that it is God who is being tested, and not the Israelites (Ps 94:8f).

❷ **an attempt to make one do someth. wrong, *temptation, enticement*** to sin.—ⓐ act. *tempting* συντελέσας πάντα πειρασμὸν ὁ διάβολος *when the devil had exhausted every way of tempting* **Lk 4:13.**

ⓑ pass. *being tempted* **Js 1:12.** *Temptation,* fr. without or fr. within, that can be an occasion of sin to a person (Sir 33:1; 44:20; 1 Macc 2:52; Orig., C. Cels. 8, 56, 9) μὴ εἰσενέγκῃς ἡμᾶς εἰς πειρασμόν **Mt 6:13; Lk 11:4** (s. bibliog. in The Lord's Prayer and Other Prayer Texts fr. the Gr-Roman Era, ed. JCharlesworth '94, 186–201); D 8:2; cp. Pol 7:2.—KKnoke, Der ursprüngl. Sinn der sechsten Bitte: NKZ 18, 1907, 200–220; AHarnack, Zur sechsten Bitte des Vaterunsers: SBBerlAk 1907, 942–47; AKleber, CBQ 3, '41, 317–20; GVerity, ET 58, '46/47, 221f; FGrant, Introd. to NT Thought, '50, 208.—μέγας ἐπίκειται π. *a great temptation is before me* AcPl Ha 8, 22=Ox 1602, 31 as corrected HTR 31 '38, 58 n. 2, ln. 10=BMM recto 28.—(εἰσ)έρχεσθαι εἰς πειρασμόν (Did., Gen. 225, 8) **Mt 26:41; Mk 14:38** (Unknown Sayings, tr. Fuller '57, p. 59 n. 1 and s. the agraphon fr. Tertullian, pp. 57–59); **Lk 22:40** (HBate, JTS 36, '35, 76f), **46.** ἐμπίπτειν εἰς πειρασμόν **1 Ti 6:9.** ἐν καιρῷ πειρασμοῦ *in a time of temptation* **Lk 8:13.** ἡ ὥρα τοῦ π. **Rv 3:10.** ἐκ πειρασμοῦ ῥύεσθαι **2 Pt 2:9.** Cp. also **Ac 15:26 v.l.; 1 Cor 10:13ab;** 2 Cl 18:2.—Also in the pl. *temptations* (Cyranides p. 40, 24 πειρασμοὶ ἐν γῇ κ. θαλάσσῃ; Syntipas p. 124, 18; TestJos 2:7) **Lk 22:28.** μετὰ ταπεινοφροσύνης καὶ δακρύων καὶ πειρασμῶν **Ac 20:19.** ἐν ποικίλοις πειρασμοῖς **1 Pt 1:6;** cp. **Js 1:2** (*trial* is also prob. in the last two passages, s. 1 above).—**2 Pt 2:9 v.l.**—On the difficult saying τὸν πειρασμὸν ὑμῶν ἐν τῇ σαρκί μου οὐκ ἐξουθενήσατε **Gal 4:14** s. on ἐξουθενέω 1 and 2 and s. JdeZwaan, ZNW 10, 1909, 246–50.—HKorn, ΠΕΙΡΑΣΜΟΣ. Die Versuchg. des Gläubigen in der griech. Bibel, '37; MAndrews, Peirasmos, A Study in Form-Criticism, ATR 24, '42, 229–44; KKuhn, πειρασμός im NT, ZTK 49, '52, 200–222, New Light on Temptation, etc., in The Scrolls and the NT, ed. Stendahl, '57, 94–113.—M-M. TW. Spicq. Sv.

πειράω in our lit. only **πειράομαι** (Hom.+) fut. mid. πειράσομαι; 1 aor. pl. ἐπειράθημεν 1 Macc 12:10; pf. πεπείραμαι 1 Km 17:39; in one place perh. as pass.: impf. 3 sg. ἐπειρᾶτο **Ac 9:26 v.l.;** pf. ptc. πεπειραμένος.

❶ **to try to do someth., *try, attempt, endeavor*** w. inf. foll. (Hom.+; ins, pap, 2 Macc 2:23; 10:12; 3 Macc 2:32; 4 Macc 12:2; EpArist 297; Philo, Sacr. Abel. 123; Jos., C. Ap. 1, 70; 2, 283) Ἰουδαῖοί με ἐπειρῶντο διαχειρίσασθαι **Ac 26:21.** Cp. **9:26 v.l.** (for ἐπείραζεν); 2 Cl 17:3; MPol 13:2; Qua 1.

❷ **to have an experience, *to experience.*** The sense of the wording is difficult in **Hb 4:15 v.l.** (for πεπειρασμένον), which describes Christ as πεπειραμένος κατὰ πάντα. Starting fr. the mng. 'put someone or someth. to the test, in order to know the same better', the mid. can = *go through an experience* and learn someth. by it (Aesop, Fab. 105 H.//437 P.//p. 190 ln. 6 H-H.) and the perf. mid.=*have experienced, know from experience, know* (Hes., Hdt. et al.; X., Hiero 1, 2; 2, 6; Pla., Ep. 6 p. 323a). For our pass. this would result in the mng. *who was experienced in all respects.* The pass. sense *tried, tested, tempted* is hardly in accord w. Gk. usage. S. πειράζω 2b and 4 on the Hb pass.—B. 652f. DELG s.v. πεῖρα. M-M. TW.

πεισμονή, ῆς ἡ (fr. πείθω via πεῖσμα 'persuasion'; Apollon. Dysc.=Gramm. Gr. II 2 p. 429, 9 U.; 299, 17; Eustathius on Hom. several times; Just., A I, 53, 1; Iren. 4, 33, 7 [Harv. II 262, 2] and other eccl. writers, s. Lampe s.v.) ***persuasion*** (Apollon.; Justin, loc. cit.; PLond V, 1674, 36 [VI AD]) οὐ πεισμονῆς τὸ ἔργον, ἀλλὰ μεγέθους ἐστὶν ὁ Χριστιανισμός *Christianity is not a matter of persuasiveness, but of* (true) *greatness* IRo 3:3. ἡ π. οὐκ ἐκ τοῦ καλοῦντος *that persuasion,* that draws you away fr. the truth, *does not come from the one who calls you* **Gal 5:8** (EBurton, ICC Gal 1920, 282f). B-D-F §488, 1b favor the mng. 'obedience' [Folgsamkeit] here (also §109, 6), but must depart fr. the Gk. text as handed down by the great majority of witnesses.—DELG s.v. πείθομαι. M-M. TW. Spicq.

πέλαγος, ους, τό (Hom. et al.; OGI 74, 3; IG XII/2, 119, 7; 2 Macc 5:21; TestSol; TestAbr A 17 p. 98, 27 [Stone p. 44]; TestNapht 6:5; EpArist 214; Philo, Joseph.; loanw. in rabb.).

❶ **open sea (as opposed to stretch of water near land),** ***the open sea, the depths (of the sea)*** (Aristot., Probl. Sect. 23 Quaest. 3, 931b, 14 f. ἐν τῷ λιμένι ὀλίγη ἐστὶν ἡ θάλασσα, ἐν δὲ τῷ πελάγει βαθεῖα; Jos., Bell. 1, 409) τὸ πέλαγος τῆς θαλάσσης (Apollon. Rhod. 2, 608. Cp. also Eur., Tro. 88 πέλαγος Αἰγαίας ἁλός. Hesych.: πέλαγος . . . βυθός, πλάτος θαλάσσης): ἐν τῷ π. τῆς θαλάσσης *in the open (deep) sea* **Mt 18:6** (Jos., C. Ap. 1, 307 of lepers ἵνα καθῶσιν εἰς τὸ πέλαγος); sim. ἐν τῷ μεγάλῳ πέλαγει AcPl Ha 7, 25.

❷ **independent part of a whole body of water,** ***sea*** (mostly so: Aeschyl. et al.; Diod. S. 4, 77, 6 τὸ πέλ. Ἰκάριον; Philo, Op. M. 63; Jos., Ant. 2, 348) τὸ π. τὸ κατὰ τὴν Κιλικίαν *the sea along the coast of Cilicia* **Ac 27:5.**—DELG. M-M.

πέλας adv. (Hom. et al.) ***near*** ὁ π. *the neighbor* (so Alcaeus 137 D.[2]; trag., Hdt.; Sextus 17; POxy 79 II, 9; Pr 27:2; Ath., 32, 2, R. 23 p. 76, 14) MPol 1:2 (after **Phil 2:4,** but with τὸ κατὰ τοῦ πέλας instead of τὰ ἑτέρων).—DELG.

πελεκίζω pf. pass. ptc. πεπελεκισμένος ***behead (with an ax)*** (πέλεκυς), normally an act of capital punishment (Polyb. 1, 7, 12; 11, 30, 2; Diod. S. 19, 101, 3; Strabo 16, 2, 18; Plut., Ant. 36, 4; Jos., Ant. 20, 117; loanw. in rabb.) **Rv 20:4.**—B. 561. DELG s.v. πέλεκυς. M-M.

πεμπταῖος, α, ον (cp. πέμπτος; Hom. et al.; pap; EpArist 175) **pert. to the fifth (day),** ***on the fifth (day)*** ἤλθομεν πεμπταῖοι *we came in five days* **Ac 20:6** D (Diod. S. 14, 103, 2 π.='on the fifth day'; Arrian, Anab. 1, 29, 1 ἀφικνεῖται πεμπταῖος).—DELG s.v. πέντε.

πέμπτος, η, ον (πέντε; Hom. et al.) ordinal ***fifth*** **Rv 6:9; 9:1; 16:10; 21:20;** Hv 3, 1, 2; s 9, 1, 7; 9, 22, 1. ἡ πέμπτη, i.e. ἡμέρα *the fifth day* (Hes., Aristoph. et al.; Jos., Vi. 47) σαββάτων πέμπτῃ *on the fifth day of the week* i.e. *on Thursday* acc. to Judeo-Christian reckoning D 8:1.—DELG s.v. πέντε. M-M.

πέμπω fut. πέμψω; 1 aor. ἔπεμψα; pf. πέπομφα IEph 17:2. Pass.: fut. inf. πεμφθήσεσθαι (Just., A I, 28); 1 aor. ἐπέμφθην; 1 pf. ptc. πεπεμμένος (Just., D. 126, 6); plpf. 3 sg. ἐπέπεμπτο Just., D. 56, 5).

❶ **to dispatch someone, whether human or transcendent being, usually for purposes of communication,** ***send*** τινά *someone* **J 1:22; 13:16; 20:21b; Phil 2:23, 28;** ISm 11:3. δοῦλον **Lk 20:11;** cp. vs. **12f.** τ. ἀδελφούς **2 Cor 9:3.** ἄνδρας πιστούς 1 Cl 63:3. ὑπηρέτην Dg 7:2. ἐπισκόπους IPhld 10:2. W. double acc. π. τινὰ κατάσκοπον *send someone out as a spy* B 12:9; w. acc. of a ptc. π. τινὰ κρίνοντα *send someone as a judge* Dg 7:6. π. τινὰ πρεσβεύσοντα *send someone to be a representative* Pol 13:1. W. a destination indicated (the ref. to a legation somet. being omitted as self-evident, like the Engl. 'send to someone'= 'send a messenger to someone'): π. (τινὰ) εἴς τι *send (someone) to, into* (X., Hell. 7, 4, 39; Jos., C. Ap. 1, 271 εἰς Ἱεροσ.) **Mt 2:8; Lk 15:15; 16:27; Ac 10:5, 32** (without acc.); **15:22;** IEph 6:1; GJs 16:2. W. the point of departure and the destination given ἀπὸ τῆς Μιλήτου εἰς Ἔφεσον **Ac 20:17** (without acc.). W. indication of the pers. to whom someone is sent π. (τινὰ) πρός τινα *send (someone) to someone* (X., Cyr. 1, 5, 4; Demetr.: 722 fgm. 1:13 Jac.; Diod. S. 20, 72, 1 π. τινὰ εἰς Συρακούσας πρὸς τ. ἀδελφόν; PHib 127 descr. 3 [III BC] π. τινὰ πρός τινα; Sb 6769, 5; 2 Esdr 5:17; En 10:2; TestJos 9:1; Manetho: 609 fgm. 10 Jac. [in Jos., C. Ap. 1, 241]) **Lk 7:19** (αὐτούς *them* is supplied by the immediate context); **Ac 10:33** (without acc.); **15:25; 19:31** (without acc.); **23:30** (the acc. αὐτόν *him* is supplied by the context.—S. further below, where this pass. is cited again); **Eph 6:22; Phil 2:25; Col 4:8; Tit 3:12;** GJs 21:2 codd. In several of these places π. is used w. another verb that tells the purpose of the sending. This verb can be in the ptc.: ἔπεμψεν λέγων *he sent to ask* (cp. Gen 38:25; 2 Km 14:32; Jos., C. Ap. 1, 262) **Lk 7:19;** cp. vs. **6.** Or the verb w. π. is in a finite mood and π. stands in the ptc. (Appian, Bell. Civ. 5, 9 §34 πέμψας ἀνεῖλε=he sent and had [her] put to death; 5, 118 §489 ἤρετο πέμπων=he sent and asked; Gen 27:42; Jos., Ant. 7, 149) πέμψαντες παρεκάλουν *they sent and advised* **Ac 19:31;** cp. πέμψας ἀπεκεφάλισεν *he sent and had* (John) *beheaded* **Mt 14:10.—22:7.** Differently πέμψας αὐτοὺς εἶπεν *he sent them and said* **2:8.** W. indication of the one who is to receive someone, in the dat. π. τινά τινι *send someone to someone* **1 Cor 4:17; Phil 2:19.**— ὁ Ἰω. πέμψας δύο τῶν μαθητῶν αὐτοῦ εἶπεν αὐτῷ='sent two of his disciples and had them say to him' **Mt 11:2 v.l.** (cp. Appian, Bell. Civ. 1, 96 §449 πέμψας τινὰς ὁ Πομπήιος συνέλαβεν [Κάρβωνα]=Pompey sent certain men and had Carbo taken into custody). W. purpose indicated by the inf. (Just., D. 45, 4) **Lk 15:15; 1 Cor 16:3;** cp. also **J 1:33; Rv 22:16.** By subst. inf. w. εἰς **1 Th 3:2, 5.** By εἰς (Appian, Mithrid. 108 §516 ἔπεμπεν τὰς θυγατέρας ἐς γάμους=in order to marry them [to Scythian princes]) εἰς αὐτὸ τοῦτο *for this very purpose* **Eph 6:22; Col 4:8.** εἰς ἐκδίκησιν κακοποιῶν **1 Pt 2:14.** W. εἰς twice: εἰς θεοῦ τιμὴν εἰς Σμύρναν IEph 21:1. W. purpose indicated by ἵνα **Lk 16:24.**—Esp. of sending forth of God's representatives (Aberciusins. 7; Philosoph. Max. 497, 8, the wise man is ἀποσταλείς, his πέμψας is God) Moses 1 Cl 17:5; Elijah **Lk 4:26.** The angel of repentance Hs 8, 11, 1. Above all the Father sends the Son (upon the earth) **Ro 8:3;** IMg 8:2. πέμψω τὸν υἱόν μου τὸν ἀγαπητόν **Lk 20:13** (cp. Hdt. 1, 119, 2f ἦν οἱ παῖς εἷς μοῦνος . . . τοῦτον ἐκπέμπει . . . ἐς Ἀστυάγεος . . . Ἀστυάγης σφάξας αὐτόν). John's gospel is dominated by the thought that Jesus is sent by God fr. heaven (s. Hdb. exc. on J 3:17) **J 4:34; 5:23f, 30, 37; 6:38f, 44; 7:16, 28, 33; 8:16, 18, 26, 29; 9:4; 12:44f, 49; 13:20; 14:24; 15:21; 16:5.** Jesus, or God in his name, will send the Paraclete or Holy Spirit **J 14:26; 15:26** (ὃν ἐγὼ πέμψω ὑμῖν παρὰ τοῦ πατρός); **16:7.** Sim. πέμπει αὐτοῖς ὁ θεὸς ἐνέργειαν πλάνης *God sends them a deluding influence* **2 Th 2:11.**—The idea of moving from one place to another, which is inherent in 'sending', can retreat into the background, so that π. takes on the mng. *instruct, commission, appoint:* ὁ πέμψας με βαπτίζειν ἐν ὕδατι **J 1:33.** Cp. **7:18** and the pass. **1 Pt 2:14.** Elsewh., too, π. takes on a particular mng.

fr. the context: πέμψον ἡμᾶς εἰς τοὺς χοίρους *eject us into the swine* **Mk 5:12.** Of one under arrest: *have* him *transported* to his destination **Ac 25:25, 27;** cp. **23:30** (on these pass. s. TGagos/PSijpesteijn, BASP 33, '96, 77–97).—Abs. οἱ πεμφθέντες *those who were sent* **Lk 7:10.**—In several of the places already mentioned (**Ac 23:30; Eph 6:22; Phil 2:28; Col 4:8**) ἔπεμψα is an epistolary aorist (Thu. 1, 129, 3; Chion, Ep. 15, 3 ἔπεμψα δὲ τὸ ἀντίγραφον; POxy 937, 21.—B-D-F §334; Rob. 845f).

❷ **to dispatch someth. through an intermediary,** ***send*** τινί τι *someth. to someone* **Rv 11:10;** Hv 2, 4, 3a; s 5, 2, 9; 5, 5, 3. The thing that is the object of the sending can remain unmentioned if it is easily supplied fr. the context πέμψον ταῖς ἑπτὰ ἐκκλησίαις, εἰς Ἔφεσον καὶ εἰς . . . *send* (the book) *to the seven churches, to Ephesus and to* . . . **Rv 1:11.** πέμψει Κλήμης εἰς τὰς ἔξω πόλεις *Clement is to send* (*it*=his copy or rescripts of it) *to the cities abroad* Hv 2, 4, 3b. ὥρισαν εἰς διακονίαν πέμψαι τοῖς ἀδελφοῖς *they decided to send* (someth.) *to the brethren for their support* **Ac 11:29.** εἰς τὴν χρείαν μοι ἐπέμψατε *you have sent me* (what was necessary) *to satisfy my needs* **Phil 4:16** (cp. vv.ll. without the prep. εἰς and s. Ar. Milne p. 74 ln. 26: πέμπουσιν αὐτοῖς ἃ χρέαν ἔχουσιν). Fig. μερίσας . . . ἀπὸ τοῦ πνεύματος τοῦ Χριστοῦ ἔπεμψεν εἰς τοὺς προφήτας *(God) sent a portion of Christ's spirit into the prophets* AcPlCor 2:10.—On π. τὸ δρέπανον **Rv 14:15, 18** s. δρέπανον.—π. διά τινος could come fr. the OT (=שָׁלַח בְּיַד פ׳ 1 Km 16:20; 2 Km 11:14; 3 Km 2:25) and could have given rise to the expr. πέμψας διὰ τῶν μαθητῶν εἶπεν αὐτῷ *he sent word by his disciples and said to him* **Mt 11:2** ([Just., D. 53, 1]; yet a similar expr. is found in Appian, Mithrid. 108 §516 ἔπεμπεν δι' εὐνούχων).—π. abs. means *send, write* a document, letter, etc. (Ps.-Callisth. 3, 18, 4; PGiss 13, 5 [II AD] Ἀρσινόη μοι ἔπεμψε περὶ τῶν δύο ταλάντων; 17, 8; 13; 27, 8 οὗ ἕνεκα πρὸς σὲ ἔπεμψα ἵνα ἐπιγνῶ; 81, 6; 14 πέμψον μοι οὖν περὶ τῆς σωτηρίας σου and oft. in pap) ἐσπούδασα κατὰ μικρὸν ὑμῖν πέμπειν *I have taken pains to write to you briefly* B 1:5.—DELG. M-M. EDNT.

πένης, ητος (πένομαι 'to work, toil'; Soph., Hdt. et al.; Jos., Ant. 14, 31) **pert. to being obliged to work for a living, but not being reduced to begging,** for the latter aspect πτωχός, q.v., is ordinarily used (s. Aristoph., Plut. 552f πτωχοῦ μὲν γὰρ βίος, ὃν σὺ λέγεις, ζῆν ἐστι μηδὲν ἔχοντα: τοῦ δὲ πένητος ζῆν φειδόμενον καὶ τοῖς ἔργοις προσέχοντα=for the life of a beggar that you describe means existence with nothing, but that of the poor means sparse living and sticking to the job), opp. πλούσιος ***poor, needy*** in our lit. only subst. ὁ π. *the poor person* (Pla., X. et al.; PRyl 62, 11; PRein 47, 11; LXX; pseudepigr.; Philo; Jos., Bell. 4, 379, Ant. 7, 149; Ar., Tat.) **2 Cor 9:9** (Ps 111:9); 1 Cl 15:6 (Ps 11:6. For the juxtaposition here and elsewhere in the LXX of πένης and πτωχός [s. also PsSol 5:11; TestJob 12:1; 32:2; TestAsh 2:6]; Ammonius Gr. [100 AD] p. 108 Valck.; PFlor 296, 18); GJs 20:1 codd. Opp. ὁ πλούσιος (X., An. 7, 7, 28; Pla., Prot. 319d; Plut., Pericl. 155 [7, 3]; PSI 120, 47; 2 Km 12:1; 1 Esdr 3:19; Pr 23:4; EpArist 249; TestAbr A; TestReub 4:7; Tat. 11, 1) Hs 2:5ff; B 20:2; D 5:2. W. χήρα, ὀρφανός Pol 6:1.—JHemelrijk, Πενία en Πλοῦτος, diss. Utrecht 1925; JJvanManen, Πενία en Πλοῦτος in de periode na Alexander, diss. Utrecht '31.—B. 782. Schmidt, Syn. II 611–25. DELG s.v. πένομαι. M-M. TW.

πενθερά, ᾶς, ἡ (Demosth. et al.; ins, pap, LXX; Jos., Ant. 5, 323) ***mother-in-law*** **Mt 8:14; Mk 1:30; Lk 4:38.** W. νύμφη (Mi 7:6) **Mt 10:35; Lk 12:53.**—B. 124. DELG s.v. πενθερός. M-M.

πενθερός, οῦ, ὁ (Hom.+; ins, pap LXX; Jos., Ant. 13, 120; 14, 71; TestJud 13:4) ***father-in-law*** **J 18:13.**—B. 124. DELG. M-M

πενθέω fut. πενθήσω; 1 aor. ἐπένθησα (fr. πάσχω, s. two next entries; Hom. et al.; LXX; pseudepigr., Philo; Jos., Ant. 17, 206; Mel., P. 17, 117).

❶ intr., **to experience sadness as the result of some condition or circumstance,** ***be sad, grieve, mourn*** (Hom. et al.; SIG 1219, 5; 8; UPZ 18, 21 [163 BC]; POxy 528, 9; LXX in most occurrences) in contrast to joy, inward and outward **Mt 9:15.** Before a festive day οὐκ ἔξεστί σοι πενθεῖν GJs 2:2. παρακαλέσαι πάντας τοὺς πενθοῦντας B 14:9 (Is 61:2). Of sorrow for sins one has committed **1 Cor 5:2** (in the OT of sorrow for the sins of others: 1 Esdr 8:69; 9:2; 2 Esdr 10:6. TestReub 1:10 has πενθῶν ἐπὶ τῇ ἁμαρτίᾳ μου, but this has no counterpart in the LXX). Also, the πενθοῦντες **Mt 5:4** mourn not for their own sins, but because of the power of the wicked, who oppress the righteous. W. κλαίειν (POxy 528, 9; 2 Km 19:2; 2 Esdr 18:9): **Mk 16:10; Lk 6:25; Js 4:9; Rv 18:15, 19;** GPt 7:27. οὐ μικρῶς ἐπένθουν νηστεύουσαι AcPl Ha 5, 19. π. ἐπί τινι *mourn over someth.* ἐπὶ τοῖς παραπτώμασιν τῶν πλησίον ἐπενθεῖτε 1 Cl 2:6 (cp. Aeschin. 3, 211; Epict. 3, 3, 15; 1 Esdr 8:69 ἐμοῦ πενθοῦντος ἐπὶ τῇ ἀνομίᾳ; 2 Esdr 10:6). ἐπί τινα *over someone* (2 Ch 35:24) **Rv 18:11.**

❷ trans. (B-D-F §148, 2; Rob. 475) **to engage in mourning for one who is dead, ordinarily w. traditional rites,** ***mourn over*** w. acc. of pers. (Hom. et al.; Lysias 2, 66; Lucian, Dial. Deor. 14, 1; Gen 37:34; 50:3; 1 Esdr 1:30; Bel 40; 1 Macc 12:52; 13:26; TestJos 20, 5; JosAs 29:9; Jos., Bell. 2, l) **2 Cor 12:21;** GJs 24:3. EdeMartino, Morte e pianto rituale nel mondo antico '58.—DELG s.v. πάσχω. M-M. TW.

πενθικός, ή, όν (πένθος; Plut.; 2 Km 14:2; JosAs 10:11 [cod. A]; Jos., Ant. 11, 231; adv. -ῶς X.) ***of/for mourning*** τὰ ἱμάτια αὐτῆς τὰ πενθικά *her mourning garments* GJs 2:4.—DELG s.v. πάσχω.

πένθος, ους, τό (s. prec. two entries; Hom.+) **sorrow as experience or expression,** ***grief, sadness, mourning*** (opp. ὁ γέλως) **Js 4:9.** W. θάνατος and λιμός **Rv 18:8** (on the topic cp. Is 35:10; in the Gk. world: Pind., P. 10, 41–44). W. κραυγή and πόνος **21:4.** W. βασανισμός **18:7a.** π. ἰδεῖν *see, have, experience sorrow* **18:7b.** Pl. (Ptolem., Apotel. 2, 9, 5; in contrast to ἑορταί=joyful feasts, as Philo, Exsecr. 171) *times of mourning* Dg 4:5.—B. 1118. DELG s.v. πάσχω. M-M. TW. Sv.

πενιχρός, ά, όν (on the suffix -χρος s. DELG s.v. μέλι; Hom. et al.; Plut., Pyrrh. 405 [34, 1], Mor. 242b; Vett. Val. 166, 18; CIJ II, 1123; PPetr III, 36a, 6; BGU 1024 VIII, 12; Ex 22:24; Pr 28:15; 29:7; Philo, Somn. 2, 213; Jos., Bell. 4, 207, Ant. 13, 72) **pert. to being in need of things relating to livelihood,** ***poor, needy*** χήρα π. **Lk 21:2.** MHengel, Property and Riches in the Early Church '74.—New Docs 3, 80 (addtl. pap and ins). DELG s.v. πένομαι. M-M. TW.

πεντάκις adv. ***five times*** (Pind. et al.; ins, pap; 4 Km 13:19) **2 Cor 11:24.**—DELG s.v. πέντε.

πενταϰισχίλιοι, αι, α (πέντε + χίλιοι; Hdt., Pla. et al.; ins, LXX; EpArist 82; Jos., Bell. 1, 172, Ant. 11, 16, Vi. 212; Just., A I, 31, 8) ***five thousand*** **Mt 14:21; 16:9; Mk 6:44; 8:19; Lk 9:14; J 6:10.**—GKittel, Rabbinica: Arbeiten z. Religionsgesch., ed. JLeipoldt I/3, 1920, 39ff.—DELG s.v. πέντε.

πεντακόσιοι, αι, α (Hom. et al.; ins; PRyl 129, 13; LXX, En,TestJob; TestJud 9:8; JosAs, ApcEsdr; EpArist 104; Jos., Bell. 2, 477, Ant. 11, 16; Just., A I, 42, 3; Tat.31, 3) ***five hundred*** **Lk 7:41; 1 Cor 15:6** (PKearney, NovT 22, '80, 264–80 [symbolic value]); 1 Cl 25:2.—DELG s.v. πέντε. M-M.

πεντακοσιοστός, ή, όν (Aristoph., Lysias et al.; Philo, Mos. 1, 316) ***five hundredth*** ἔτος 1 Cl 25:5.—DELG s.v. πέντε.

πέντε indecl. (Hom.+) ***five*** **Mt 14:17, 19; 16:9** and oft. πέντε ἄνδρας ἔσχες **J 4:18** (acc. to Lycophron vs. 143; 146ff Helen had five husbands).—GKittel (s. above under πεντακισχίλιοι) and EHommel, ZNW 23, 1924, 305–10.—DELG. M-M. TW.

πεντεκαιδέκατος, η, ον (Aristot.; Diod. S. 12, 81, 5; Plut., Mor. 1084d; ins; PAmh 131, 7; LXX; Jos., Bell. 5, 282; 7, 401, Ant. 15, 89) ***fifteenth*** **Lk 3:1.**—M-M.

πεντήκοντα indecl. (Hom. et al.; IMagnMai 16, 29; pap, LXX, TestJob, JosAs, EpArist; Jos., Bell. 4, 482, Ant. 11, 15; Just.; Tat. 21, 1) ***fifty*** **Lk 7:41; 16:6; J 8:57** (MEdwards, NTS 40, '94, 449–54, cp. Jubilees 23:10f, 15); **21:11; Ac 13:20.** ὡσεὶ ἀνὰ πεντήκοντα **Lk 9:14** s. ἀνά 3. κατὰ π. **Mk 6:40** s. κατά 3a.—DELG s.v. πέντε. M-M.

πεντηκόνταρχος, ου, ὁ (Ps.-X., Rep. Athen. 1, 2 al.; pap, LXX) **leader of a company of fifty,** military t.t. ***company commander*** 1 Cl 37:3.—DELG s.v. πέντε and ἄρχω C.

πεντηκοστή, ῆς, ἡ (the subst. fem. of πεντηκοστός 'fiftieth' [this term Pla.+; LXX; Tat. 41, 2 and 4], found in Hyperides, fgm. 106; Andoc. 1, 133; Demosth. 14, 27 al., also in ins and ostraca as t.t. in taxation ἡ πεντηκοστή [i.e. μερίς] 'the fiftieth part'=two percent) in our lit. ***Pentecost*** (really ἡ π. ἡμέρα, because it means the festival celebrated on the fiftieth day after Passover [=חַג שָׁבֻעוֹת 'feast of weeks' Dt 16:10]; rabb. חַג חֲמִשִּׁים יוֹם 'feast of 50 days'.—Tob 2:1; 2 Macc 12:32; Philo, Decal. 160, Spec. Leg. 2, 176; Jos., Ant. 3, 252; 13, 252; 14, 337; 17, 254, Bell. 1, 253; 2, 42; 6, 299) ἕως τῆς π. *until Pentecost* **1 Cor 16:8.** ἡ ἡμέρα τῆς π. *the Day of Pentecost* **Ac 2:1; 20:16.**—WRoscher, Die Zahl 50: Abh. der Sächs. Ges. d. Wiss. XXXIII 5, 1917; Billerb. II 597ff; CErdman, The Mng. of Pentecost: Bibl. Review 15, 1930, 491–508; KLake, Gift of the Spirit on the Day of Pentecost: Beginn. I/5, '33, 111–21; NAdler, D. erste chr. Pfingstfest '38; Haenchen ad loc.—DELG s.v. πέντε. M-M. EDNT. TW.

πέπειρος, ον (Soph. et al.) ***ripe*** (Theophr., CP 3, 6, 9; Artem. 2, 25; JosAs 2:19) τὸ πέπειρον *ripeness* (Herm. Wr. 1, 17: Rtzst., Poim. 333) εἰς πέπειρον καταντᾶν *come to ripeness* of the fruit of the vine (cp. Gen 40:10) 1 Cl 23:4.

πέποιθα s. πείθω.

πεποίθησις, εως, ἡ (fr. πείθω via the pf. πέποιθα; a word of later Gk. rejected by Phryn. p. 294 Lob.; LXX only 4 Km 18:19, somewhat more freq. in the other Gk. translations of the OT; Philo, Virt. 226; Jos., Ant. 1, 73; 3, 45; 10, 16; 11, 299; Philod., Περὶ παρρησίας p. 22 Ol.; Hermogenes, De Ideis 1, 9 p. 265 Rabe; 2, 7 p. 355; Sext. Emp., Hypotyp. 1, 14, 60; 23, 197; Syntipas p. 125, 12 ἡ ἐπὶ τ. θεῷ π.; Simplicius In Epict., Ench. 79 p. 329; Eustath., In Od. p. 114; 717)

❶ **a state of certainty about someth. to the extent of placing reliance on, *trust, confidence.***—ⓐ of trust or confidence in others. In humans, abs. **2 Cor 1:15.** Esp. of trust in God (occasionally almost=*faith*) μετ' εὐσεβοῦς πεποιθήσεως *with devout confidence* 1 Cl 2:3. ὑπομένοντες ἐν πεποιθήσει 45:8. ἐν π. πίστεως ἀγαθῆς 26:1; πίστις ἐν π. 35:2; ἔχειν προσαγωγὴν ἐν π. *have access* (to God) *in confidence* **Eph 3:12.**—W. prep.: π. εἴς τινα *trust, confidence in someone* **2 Cor 8:22.** Also ἔν τινι: ἔχειν πεποίθησιν ἐν σαρκί *put one's trust in physical matters* **Phil 3:4.**

ⓑ of trust or confidence in oneself θαρρῆσαι τῇ πεποιθήσει *be bold with confidence* (in his position as an apostle) **2 Cor 10:2.** πεποίθησιν τοιαύτην ἔχομεν διὰ τοῦ Χριστοῦ πρὸς τὸν θεόν *such* (as explained in what precedes) *is the self-confidence we have through Christ toward God* (who, acc. to what follows, is the real basis for the apostle's self-confidence) **3:4.** ἡ κενὴ π. *vain self-confidence* Hs 9, 22, 3.

❷ **assurance about an outcome, *confidence,*** μετὰ πεποιθήσεως *with confidence* 1 Cl 31:3. ποίᾳ πεποιθήσει εἰσελευσόμεθα εἰς τὸ βασίλειον; *what basis for confidence* (=prospect) *do we have for getting into the Kingdom?* 2 Cl 6:9.—DELG s.v. πείθομαι. M-M. TW. Spicq.

πέπονθα s. πάσχω.

πέπραγμαι s. πράσσω.

πέπρακα s. πιπράσκω.

πέπραμαι s. πιπράσκω.

πέπραχα s. πράσσω.

πέπτωκα s. πίπτω.

πέπωκα s. πίνω.

περ enclitic particle, w. intensive and extensive force (B-D-F §107; Rob. 1153); s. the words compounded w. it: διόπερ, ἐάνπερ (s. ἐάν 1cγ), εἴπερ (s. εἰ 6l), ἐπειδήπερ, ἐπείπερ, ἤπερ (s. ἤ 2eβ), καθάπερ, καίπερ, ὅσπερ (s. ὅς 1jε), ὥσπερ (ὡσπερεί).—DELG.

Περαία, ας, s. πέραν bγ.

περαιτέρω (πέρα 'beyond , further'; Aeschyl., Thu. et al.; Jos., Bell. 4, 107, Ant. 18, 301; 19, 141; BGU 372 II, 12 [154 AD]) adv. of περαίτερος, α, ον, the comp. of πέρα: **pert. to being in addition to what is already expressed in the context, *further, beyond*** εἰ δέ τι π. ἐπιζητεῖτε *if there is anything further that you want to know* (cp. Pla., Phd. 107b οὐδὲν ζητήσετε περαιτέρω) **Ac 19:39** (v.l. περὶ ἑτέρων).—DELG s.v. πέρα. M-M.

πέραν adv. of place (Hom. [πέρην] et al.; ins, pap, LXX) **marker of a position across from someth. else, with intervening space, *on the other side.***

ⓐ funct. as adv., and subst. w. the art. τὸ πέραν *the shore* or *land on the other side* (X., An. 4, 3, 11; Sb 7252, 19) εἰς τὸ πέραν (Pla.; Polyb.; SIG 495, 84; 619, 27; 709, 6; BGU 1022, 25; 1 Macc 9:48) **Mt 8:18, 28; 14:22; 16:5; Mk 4:35; 5:21; 6:45; 8:13.**

ⓑ funct. as prep. w. gen. (B-D-F §184; Rob. 646)**—α.** answering the question 'whither?' ἀπῆλθεν ὁ Ἰησοῦς πέραν τῆς θαλάσσης *Jesus went away to the other side of the lake* **J 6:1.** ἤρχοντο πέραν τ. θαλάσσης εἰς Καφαρναούμ vs. **17.** Cp. **10:40; 18:1.**

β. answering the question 'where?' ταῦτα ἐν Βηθανίᾳ ἐγένετο πέραν τοῦ Ἰορδάνου *this took place in Bethany on the other side of the Jordan* **J 1:28** (PParker, JBL 74, '55, 257–61 [not 'beyond'=west, but 'across from'=east]). τὰ ὅρια τῆς Ἰουδαίας πέραν τοῦ Ἰορδάνου **Mt 19:1.** Cp. **J 3:26; 6:22, 25.**—πέραν w. gen. can also be used w. the art. as a subst. (X., An. 3, 5, 2 εἰς τὸ πέραν τοῦ ποταμοῦ; Jos., Ant. 7, 198) ἦλθον εἰς τὸ πέραν τῆς θαλάσσης *they came to the* (land on the) *other side of the lake* **Mk 5:1.** Cp. **Lk 8:22.**—The improper restoration τ[ὰ ὄντα]| πέραν τῶν [ἀ]κο[ῶ]ν Ox 1081, 6f fails to take account of the Coptic duplicate, s. ἀκούω 7, ἀπέραντος.

γ. In a number of places πέραν τοῦ Ἰορδάνου (Is 8:23; cp. Jos., Ant. 12, 222) functions as an indecl. name for the territory on the other (eastern) side of the Jordan, i.e. *Perea* ἀπὸ τ. Γαλιλαίας καὶ Ἰουδαίας καὶ πέραν τοῦ Ἰορδάνου *from Galilee and Judea and Perea* **Mt 4:25.** ἀπὸ τῆς Ἰδουμαίας καὶ πέραν τοῦ Ἰορδάνου **Mk 3:8.** Cp. **Mt 4:15** (Is 8:23); **Mk 10:1** (v.l. διὰ τοῦ πέραν τοῦ Ἰορδάνου).—Περαία, ας (oft. in Joseph.) is found in our lit. only as v.l.: **Lk 6:17.** (The expression is by no means limited to Palestine: ἐν τῇ περαίᾳ in Appian, Bell. Civ. 2, 42 §168 refers to the land on the other side of the river. In addition, the region of the Carian mainland opposite the island of Rhodes was called Perea: Appian, op. cit. 4, 72 §305; also Livy 32, 33; 33, 18.)—Meistermann (Καφαρναούμ, end) 93ff. DELG s.v. πέρα. M-M.

πέρας, ατος, τό (cp. πεῖραρ 'end, limit'; Aeschyl.+) 'limit, end'.

❶ a set point as farthest end of a space, *end, limit, boundary.* Pl. τὰ πέρατα *end, limit, boundary,the ends, limits* τῆς γῆς *of the earth* (Alcaeus [c. 600 BC] 50, 1 Diehl[2]; Thu. 1, 69, 5; X., Ages. 9, 4; IPontEux I, 39, 26f (μέχρι) περάτων γῆς; Ps 2:8; 21:28; Da 4:21; En 1:5; 31:2; Philo; Jos., Bell. 4, 262; TestNapht 6:7) **Mt 12:42; Lk 11:31** (on both these passages cp. Apollon. Rhod. 2, 165 ἐκ περάτων; DDD 573–76); **Ac 13:33** D (Ps 2:8); 1 Cl 36:4 (Ps 2:8); IRo 6:1; Hs 8, 3, 2; D 9:4. τὰ πέρατα τῆς οἰκουμένης (Diod. S. 3, 53, 1 τὰ πέρατα τῆς οἰκουμένης; 1, 19, 6 τὸ πέρας τῆς οἰκ.; Jos., Ant. 8, 116; cp. ApcEsdr 3:6 p. 27, 12 Tdf.) **Ro 10:18** (Ps 18:5). Also τὰ πέρατα abs. in the same sense (Vett. Val. 226, 18; Philo, Leg. ad Gai. 18; 173; Ps 64:9) οἱ ἐπίσκοποι, οἱ κατὰ τὰ πέρατα ὁρισθέντες *the overseers/bishops who are appointed in the most distant lands* IEph 3:2.—JGeyer, VetusT 20, '70, 87–90, replying to MTreves, ibid. 19, '69, 235.

❷ the end point of a process, *end, conclusion* (Aeschyl., Pers. 632 τῶν κακῶν; Demosth. 18, 97 πέρας τοῦ βίου ὁ θάνατος; Polyb. 5, 31, 2; 7, 5, 5; Epict. 3, 26, 37; 4, 1, 106; OGI 669, 40; PGiss 25, 7; BGU 1019, 7; POxy 237 VIII, 16; 1 Esdr 9:17; 2 Macc 5:8; 3 Macc 5:5; TestAbr A 1 p. 77, 11 [Stone p. 2] τοῦ βίου πέρας; Philo, Op. M. 150 al.; Jos., Bell. 7, 157, Ant. 7, 374; Just., D. 137, 4 π. ποιεῖσθαι; Tat. 12, 4 π. λαβών) πάσης ἀντιλογίας πέρας *(as) an end to all disputing* **Hb 6:16.**

❸ as adv., πέρας **marker of someth. that is additional in a series, *finally, in conclusion, further(more)*** (since Aeschin. 1, 61; Polyb. 2, 55, 6; Alciphron 4, 17, 3; Manetho: 609 fgm. 8 [77] Jac. [in Jos., C. Ap. 1, 77]; Jos., Bell. 7, 393, Ant. 16, 352) π. γέ τοι B 5:8; 10:2; 12:6; 15:6, 8; 16:3; π. γοῦν MPol 16:1.—DELG s.v. πεῖραρ. M-M. Sv.

Πέργαμος, ου, ἡ (cp. πύργος 'tower' X., Hell. 3, 1, 6; Paus. 7, 16, 1) or **Πέργαμον, ου, τό** (Polyb. 4, 48, 11; Diod. S. 28, 5; Strabo 13, 4, 1; 2; Appian, Mithrid. 52 §210; Jos., Bell. 1, 425 τὸ κατὰ Μυσίαν Πέργαμον.—In the NT, as in many other instances [e.g. OGI ind. II p. 595a] the gender cannot be determined) ***Pergamus*** or ***Pergamum,*** an important city in Mysia, in northwest Asia Minor. It was the center of several cults: Zeus Soter, Asclepius Soter, and Athena Nicephorus had famous temples here. It was also a center of the imperial cult; as early as 29 BC the provincial assembly erected a sanctuary to Augustus and Roma. Christians seem to have been persecuted here at an early date (s. Ἀντιπᾶς). **Rv 1:11; 2:12.**—Altertümer von Pergamon I–VIII 1885–1930; of this vol. VIII=IPergamon; EPontremoli and MCollignon, Pergame 1900; VSchultze, Altchristliche Städte u. Landschaften II 2, 1926; AvSalis, D. Altar v. P. 1912; Pauly-W. XIX 1235–63; Kl. Pauly IV 626–31; BHHW III 1420f; PECS 688–92 (lit.).—DELG. M-M.

Πέργη, ης, ἡ (Callim., Hymn to Diana 187; Strabo 14, 4, 2; Philostrat., V. S. 2, 6; ins; coins) ***Perga,*** a city in Pamphylia, near the south coast of Asia Minor. Visited by Paul on his so-called first missionary journey **Ac 13:14; 14:25.** Π. τῆς Παμφυλίας **13:13.**—WRuge, Pauly-W. XIX 694–704; Kl. Pauly IV 631f; BHHW III 1421; PECS 692f.

περί (Hom.+) prep. w. gen. and acc., in our lit. not w. dat. (B-D-F §203; Rob. 617; see the lit. s.v. ἀνά, beg.) lit. 'round about'

❶ w. the gen. **to denote the object or pers. to which (whom) an activity or esp. inward process refers or relates, *about, concerning***

ⓐ after verbs that denote an oral or written expression or its reception, a mental action, knowing, thinking, recognizing, etc., *about, concerning;* s. the entries ἀκούω 1c and 3c, ἀναγγέλλω 2 end, ἀπαγγέλλω 1, ἀπολογέομαι, γνωρίζω 1, γογγύζω, γράφω 2c, δηλόω, διαβεβαιόομαι, διαλέγομαι 1, διδάσκω 2d, διηγέομαι, εἶπον 1a, ἐντέλλω, ἐπιστέλλω, κατηχέω, λαλέω 2aγ, λέγω 1bδ; λόγον αἰτεῖν, ἀποδιδόναι, διδόναι, ποιεῖσθαι (s. λόγος 2a); μαρτυρέω 1b, μνημονεύω 1c, ὁμιλέω, πυνθάνομαι, προκαταγγέλλω, προφητεύω, ὑπομιμνήσκω, χρηματίζομαι; ἀγνοέω 1a, ἀπορέω, ἐπινοέω, ἐπίσταμαι 2, οἶδα 1h, πέπεισμαι (s. πείθω 4), πιστεύω 1aβ. Also used w. the substantives belonging to these verbs or verbs w. similar mngs.: ἀπολογία 2a, γογγυσμός; διήγησις, εὐαγγέλιον, ἦχος 2, πρόφασις, φήμη; s. these entries. γινώσκω **J 7:17.** συμφωνέω **Mt 18:19.** τί ὑμῖν δοκεῖ περὶ τοῦ Χριστοῦ; *what do you think of the Christ?* **22:42.**

ⓑ after verbs that express considering, asking, examining, charging, judging, censuring, punishing, praising, etc., *on account of, because of, for, concerning.* S. the entries ἀποστοματίζω, ἀπορέω, διαπορέω, ἐγκαλέω, εἶδον (3: *deliberate concerning*), ἐκζητέω 1, ἐλέγχω 2 and 3, ἐξετάζω 1 and 2b, ἐπερωτάω 1a, ἐπιζητέω 1b, ἐρωτάω 1, ζητέω 2, κατηγορέω, παραμυθέομαι.—διαλογίζομαι **Lk 3:15.** κρίνω **J 8:26.** λιθάζω **10:33.** θεὸν αἰνέω **Lk 19:37.** περὶ οὗ … οἱ κατήγοροι οὐδεμίαν αἰτίαν ἔφερον *his accusers brought no charge of this kind* **Ac 25:18** (BWeiss, Preuschen take περὶ οὗ w. σταθέντες, which immediately follows it, and understand it to mean 'around him', 'near him' [περί τινος in this sense IG XIV, 2508, 4]).—S. also the entry ζήτημα.

ⓒ after verbs that denote emotion. S. the entries ἀγανακτέω, θαυμάζω 1aβ, καυχάομαι, σπλαγχνίζομαι.

ⓓ after verbs of caring (for). S. the entries μέλει 1b, μεριμνάω, προβλέπω.

ⓔ after other verbs and expressions, mostly *with regard to, with reference to, in relation to, w. respect to* εὐλογεῖν **Hb 11:20.** ἀναβαίνειν περὶ τοῦ ζητήματος *go up about the question* **Ac 15:2.** ἐντολὰς λαμβάνειν **Col 4:10.** ἐξουσίαν ἔχειν **1 Cor 7:37** (s. ἐξουσία 1). περὶ πάντων εὐοδοῦσθαι *be well off in all respects* **3J 2** (περὶ π.='in all resp.': Pla., Gorg. 23, 467d.—Others take it as 'above all'; cp. Il. 1, 287; 21, 566).

ⓕ w. certain verbs and nouns such as 'ask', 'pray', 'prayer', etc., περί introduces the pers. or thing in whose interest the petition is made. Thus it takes the place of ὑπέρ (B-D-F §229, 1; Rob. 618; WSchulze, Zeitschr. für vergl. Sprachforschung 44, 1911, 359: Callim., Epigr. 55, 3.—SIG 1170, 30 περὶ τούτου παρεκάλεσα τὸν θεόν; POxy 1298, 4; 1494, 6; JosAs 28:5 ἐξιλάσομαι αὐτοὺς περὶ ὑμῶν; EpArist 273) *for.* S. the entries δέομαι b, δέησις, ἐρωτάω 2, παρακαλέω 3. προσεύχεσθαι (Gen 20:7; 1 Km 7:5; 2 Macc 1:6; 15:14) **Lk 6:28; Col 1:3** (v.l. ὑπέρ); **4:3; 1 Th 5:25; 2 Th 1:11; 3:1; Hb 13:18.** προσευχὴ γίνεται **Ac 12:5.** Παῦλος ἐσταυρώθη περὶ ὑμῶν; **1 Cor 1:13 v.l.** (for ὑπέρ). τὸ αἷμα τὸ περὶ πολλῶν ἐκχυννόμενον **Mt 26:28** (cp. Nicol. Dam.: 90 fgm. 730, 29 p. 415, 29 Jac. περὶ τῶν διαδόχων αὐτοῦ ἅπαν … παθεῖν). ἀγῶνα ἔχω περὶ ὑμῶν **Col 2:1 v.l.** (for ὑπέρ).

ⓖ when used w. ἁμαρτία the word 'for' has the sense *to take away, to atone for* περὶ ἁμαρτίας (Num 8:8) **Ro 8:3** (difft. TThornton, JTS 22, '71, 515–17). Ἰ. Χρ. τοῦ δόντος ἑαυτὸν περὶ τῶν ἁμαρτιῶν ἡμῶν **Gal 1:4 v.l.** (for ὑπέρ; CBreytenbach, Versöhnung '89, 197). περὶ ἁμαρτιῶν ἔπαθεν **1 Pt 3:18** (v.l. ἀπέθανεν). Cp. **Hb 5:3c.** προσφορὰ περὶ ἁμαρτίας **10:18.** θυσία περὶ ἁμαρτιῶν vs. **26.** εἰσφέρεται τὸ αἷμα περὶ ἁμαρτίας **13:11.** τὸ περὶ τῆς ἁμαρτίας (i.e. προσφερόμενον) *the sin-offering* (Lev 6:23; 14:19) **Hb 10:6, 8** (both Ps 39:7).

ⓗ περί τινος abs. at the beginning of a sentence *concerning, with reference to* (GrBar 8:6; Just., A I, 15, 1 al.; SIG 736, 1; PEleph 13, 4f; BGU 246, 13; 17; 1097, 5 [c. 50 AD]; 1095, 9 [57 AD]) περὶ ὧν (=περὶ τούτων ἅ) ἐγράψατε *concerning the things you wrote* (to me) **1 Cor 7:1** (s. γράφω 2c). Cp. **8:1; 16:1, 12.** In other, seemingly similar, places it is to be connected w. the verb that follows: **Mt 22:31; 24:36; Mk 12:26; 13:32; 1 Cor 7:25; 8:4; 12:1; 2 Cor 9:1; 1 Th 4:9; 5:1.** (Cp. the formulation of answers by Claudius in PLond 1912; on Paul's rhetorical use, cp. Demosth. 7, 1; 14; 18; 30; 39; MMitchell NovT 31, '89, 229–56.)

ⓘ w. the art. τὰ περί τινος *what concerns someone* or *someth., his* or *its circumstances, situation, condition* (X., An. 2, 5, 37 ὅπως μάθοι τὰ περὶ Προξένου; Sir 19:30; TestJob 41:3; JosAs 19:2; GrBar 4:12; Just., A I, 33, 5; Tat. 36, 2) τὰ περὶ (τοῦ) Ἰησοῦ *the reports about Jesus,* concerning his miracles **Mk 5:27;** of Jesus' passion experiences **Lk 24:19;** of the preaching about Jesus **Ac 18:25;** cp. **28:31.** τὰ περὶ ἑαυτοῦ (αὐτοῦ, ἐμοῦ, ἐμαυτοῦ, ἡμῶν, ὑμῶν) **Lk 24:27; Ac 23:11, 15; 24:10; 28:15; Eph 6:22; Phil 1:27; 2:19f; Col 4:8.**—τὰ περὶ τῆς βασιλείας τοῦ θεοῦ *the things concerning the Kgdm. of God* **Ac 1:3; 19:8** (v.l. without the art.). τὰ περὶ τῆς ὁδοῦ **24:22** (ὁδός 3c).

❷ w. the acc., gener. **in ref. to position** rather than mental or emotional considerations as in the use of the gen., ***about***—ⓐ of place *around, about, near* (TestJob 40:6 περί τινα φάτνην; 12 περὶ τὴν οἰκίαν; Ath. 25, 1 ἄγγελοι … περὶ τὸν ἀέρα ἔχοντες καὶ τὴν γῆν)

α. *(all) around* ἕως ὅτου σκάψω περὶ αὐτήν *until I dig (all) around it* **Lk 13:8.** περιαστράψαι φῶς περὶ ἐμέ **Ac 22:6b.** αἱ παρθένοι ἑστηκυῖαι περὶ τὴν πύλην *who stood about the door* Hs 9, 3, 2.

β. of a part of the body around which someth. goes (Heraclid. Pont. fgm. 55 W. περὶ τὸ μέτωπον; PsSol 2:20 περὶ τὴν κεφαλήν; TestJob 46:9 περὶ τὸ στῆθος; JosAs 3:9 περὶ τὰς χεῖρας): a belt περὶ τὴν ὀσφύν *around the waist* **Mt 3:4; Mk 1:6** (JosAs 14:16); cp. **Rv 15:6.** A millstone περίκειται περὶ τὸν τράχηλον **Mk 9:42; Lk 17:2** (JosAs 18:5); cp. **Mt 18:6.**

γ. of nearby places: αἱ περὶ αὐτὰς πόλεις *the towns near them* (Sodom and Gomorrah) **Jd 7.** τὰ περὶ τὸν τόπον *the region around the place* **Ac 28:7** (Diod. S. 1, 50, 6 τὰ π. τὴν Μέμφιν; Strabo 12, 7, 3). Without the art. περὶ Τύρον καὶ Σιδῶνα *the neighborhood of T. and S.* **Mk 3:8.**

δ. of persons who are standing, sitting, working or staying close to someone ὄχλον περὶ αὐτόν **Mt 8:18;** cp. **Mk 9:14.** τοὺς περὶ αὐτὸν κύκλῳ καθημένους **Mk 3:34;** cp. vs. **32.** οἱ περὶ αὐτόν *those about him, his followers* **Mk 4:10; Lk 22:49.** The central person in the group can be included: οἱ περὶ Παῦλον *Paul and his companions* **Ac 13:13; 21:8 v.l.** οἱ περὶ τὸν Πέτρον *Peter and those with him* short ending of Mark; GHb 356, 38f= ISm 3:2; cp. GHb 22, 39 (Pla., Thu., X.; Diod. S. 11, 40, 3; 11, 61, 3 οἱ περὶ τὸν Κίμωνα=Cimon and his men; ins, pap; 2 Macc 1:33; 8:30; 4 Macc 2:19; JosAs 26:5; Jos., Bell. 5, 10, Ant. 18, 354 al.; Tat. 36, 1 al.; B-D-F §228; Rob. 620). οἱ περὶ τὸν κεντυρίωνα *the centurion and his men* GPt 11:45. πρὸς τὰς περὶ Μάρθαν καὶ Μαριάμ **J 11:19 v.l.** prob. means only the two sisters *to Martha and Mary* (cp. Phalaris, Ep. 136; Polyb. 4, 36, 6; 21, 11, 2; Diod. S. 1, 16, 1; 1, 37, 3; 16, 85, 2 οἱ περὶ Χάρητα καὶ Λυσικλέα=Chares and Lysicles [are made generals]; Plut., Tib. Gracch. 825 [2, 3] οἱ περὶ Δροῦσον = Δροῦσος, Pyrrh. 395 [20, 1] οἱ περὶ Γάϊον Φαβρίκιον = Γάϊος Φαβρίκιος; Diog. L. 2, 43 οἱ περὶ Αἰσχύλον=Aeschylus; 2, 105; EpArist 51; Philo, Vi. Cont. 15; Jos., Ant. 13, 187; 15, 370, C. Ap. 1, 17). οἱ π. τὸν Παῦλον **Ac 27:1a v.l.**=Παῦλος vs. 1b.

ⓑ of time *about, near* (Hdt., Thu., X. et al.; PGen 17, 10; PGiss 70, 7; Gen 15:12; Ex 11:4) περὶ τρίτην ὥραν (Appian, Bell. Civ. 2, 45 §182; TestAbr A 5 p. 82, 11 [Stone p. 12] and B 6 p. 109, 27 [Stone p. 66]; Jos., Vi. 239; cp. 243; PSI 184, 5 χθὲς περὶ ἕκτην ὥραν) *about the third hour* **Mt 20:3.** Likew. w. the hour given vs. **5f, 9; 27:46; Ac 10:3** (ὡσεὶ περὶ ὥραν ἐνάτην; ApcMos 17 περὶ ὥραν, ὅταν), **9;** cp. **Mk 6:48; Ac 22:6a.**

ⓒ of being occupied *with* (Just., D. 2, 5 χρόνον ἐκτρίβειν περὶ ἐκεῖνα τὰ μαθματα; 8, 3 τῆς περὶ τὸ θεῖον ὁρμῆς; Tat. 27, 3; Ath. 17, 3) περισπᾶσθαι (q.v. 2), θορυβάζεσθαι περί τι **Lk 10:40f.** οἱ π. τὰ τοιαῦτα ἐργάται *the workers who were occupied with such things* (s. ἐργάτης 1a) **Ac 19:25.**

ⓓ *with regard* or *respect to* (Diod. S. 2, 18, 2 ἡ περὶ αὐτὴν ἀρετή=her valor; Lucian, Vit. Auct. 17 οἱ περὶ μοιχείαν νόμοι; ApcEsdr 1:6 δικάσασθαι … περὶ τὸ γένος τῶν χριστιανῶν; Jos., Ant. 5, 259; Mel., HE 4, 26, 13 σου τὸ σπουδαῖον περὶ τὴν πίστιν) ἀστοχεῖν **1 Ti 6:21; 2 Ti 2:18.** ναυαγεῖν **1 Ti 1:19.** νοσεῖν *have a morbid craving for someth.* (s. νοσέω) **6:4.** περὶ πάντα *in all respects* **Tit 2:7.**—Pol 4:3; παράδοξον περὶ Ἰοῦστον … γέγονος *a miracle that took place involving Justus* Papias (2:9). On 2 Cl 17:2 s. ἀνάγω 5.—τὰ περὶ ἐμέ *my situation, how I am getting along* (Menand., Sam. 623 S. [Kö. 278]; UPZ 68, 6 [152 BC] τὰ περὶ Ἀπολλώνιον; Just., A I, 54, 2 τὰ περὶ τὸν Χριστόν; Tat. 8, 4 τὰ περὶ σέ; Jos., Ant. 2, 60) **Phil 2:23.** αἱ π. τὰ λοιπὰ ἐπιθυμίαι *desires for other things* **Mk 4:19.**—DELG. M-M. TW.

περιάγω impf. περιῆγον; fut. 3 sg. περιάξει Is 28:27; 2 aor. περιήγαγον (Eur., Hdt. et al.; ins, pap, LXX, Philo)

❶ **to take or bring along, *lead around,*** trans. (Eur., Hdt. et al.; ins, LXX, Joseph.) τινά *take someone about* or *along with oneself, have someone with oneself (constantly)* or *accompanying oneself* (X., Cyr. 2, 2, 28; Demosth. 36, 45 τρεῖς παῖδας ἀκολούθους π.; Diod. S. 2, 38, 6 γυναικῶν πλῆθος περιάγειν; 17, 77, 6 codd. τὰς παλλακίδας='the concubines') ἀδελφὴν γυναῖκα π. *take about a sister* (i.e. a Christian woman) *as wife* **1 Cor 9:5** (Diog. L. 6, 97 Crates the Cynic takes his like-minded wife with him on his philosophical journeys).

❷ **to travel about in various directions, *go around, go about,*** intr. (Cebes 6, 3 codd.; rare in this sense, but s. L-S-J-M s.v. II [B-D-F §150; 308; Rob. 477].—Intr. also Is 28:27) perh. *go around* κύκλῳ τοῦ πύργου Hs 9, 11, 4. *Go about* of a blind man feeling his way **Ac 13:11.** W. the place given: of wanderings *go about* ἐν ὅλῃ τῇ Γαλιλαίᾳ **Mt 4:23.** W. acc. of the district travelled through (PCairZen 33, 3 [257 BC] π. πάντας τοὺς παραδείσους) τὰς πόλεις πάσας *in all the cities* **9:35.** τὰς κώμας κύκλῳ *in the nearby villages* **Mk 6:6.** τὴν θάλασσαν καὶ τὴν ξηράν *travel about on sea and land* **Mt 23:15.**—M-M.

περιαιρέω fut. περιελῶ LXX; 2 aor. περιεῖλον LXX, inf. περιελεῖν, ptc. περιελών. Mid.: fut. 3 sing. περιελοῦνται (EpJer 57); 2 aor. 3 sg. περιείλατο (Jon 3:6; GJs 2:4). Pass.: impf. 3 sg. περιῃρεῖτο; fut. 3 sg. περιαιρεθήσεται LXX; pf. 3 pl. περιῄρηνται (TestJob 43, 4) (Hom. et al.; pap, LXX).

❶ **take away from around someth.,** ***take away, remove*** (τείχη: Hdt. 3, 159; 6, 46; Thu. 1, 108, 3; δέρματα σωμάτων Pla., Polit. 288e; τὸν χιτῶνα Aristot., HA 5, 32) Ἅννα . . . περιείλατο τὰ ἱμάτια αὐτῆς τὰ πενθικά *Hannah* (Anna) *took off her mourning garments* GJs 2:4. Pass., also gener. *take away* (PTebt 5, 146; 165 [118 BC]; Jos., Bell. 1, 179, Ant. 20, 212) περιαιρεῖται τὸ κάλυμμα *the veil is removed* **2 Cor 3:16** (cp. Ex 34:34). τὰς ἀγκύρας περιελόντες εἴων *they cast off* or *slipped the anchors and let them go* (i.e. they let go the ropes that held the anchors and thus abandoned them) **Ac 27:40.**—If the rdg. of the text **28:13** περιελόντες abs. is to be retained, the sense *we got underway* requires that τὰς ἀγκύρας be supplied='we weighed anchor' (so NRSV; AAcworth, JTS 24, '73, 193, favors the reading, but renders 'fetched a compass'=made a change in direction). But Blass ad loc. rejects this rdg., and the sense assigned to it here is admittedly speculative (Metzger ad loc.). Haenchen suggests παρελθόντες 'sailing along (the coast)'. REB: 'we sailed up the coast' (perh. rdg. περιελθόντες v.l. [so NRB 'we sailed round', s. The Greek NT, ed. RTasker '64]; this v.l. also HConzelmann, Hermeneia: Acts, 'we sailed along the coast').

❷ **to do away with,** ***take away, remove*** (Ex 8:4, 27) ἁμαρτίας **Hb 10:11** (the 'removal' of sin by God is also mentioned: 1 Ch 21:8; Zeph 3:11, 15. Cp. PCairZen 147, 3 [256 BC] π.=cancel an entry, a right, and for the fig. use also M. Ant. 12, 2 τὸν πολὺν περισπασμὸν σεαυτοῦ περιαιρήσεις; Alciphron 2, 25, 2 φόβον; Diog. L. 6, 7: to make it unnecessary to unlearn [anything]; 6, 10). Pass. περιῃρεῖτο ἐλπὶς πᾶσα *all hope was gradually abandoned* (impf.) **Ac 27:20.**—M-M. Spicq.

περιάπτω 1 aor. 3 pl. περιῆψαν 3 Macc 3:7; ptc. περιάψας; pf. pass. inf. περιῆφθαι (EpArist 159) (Pind. et al.; PTebt 735, 11 [II BC]; TestSol P [PVindob 18, 37]; Philo; Jos., Ant. 12, 260) ***kindle*** πῦρ (Phalaris, Ep. 122, 2 Herch. v.l.) **Lk 22:55.**—M-M.

περιαστράπτω (ἀστράπτω 'lighten' as of lightning) 1 aor. περιήστραψα (Galen: CMG V 9, 1 p. 392, 2; 4 Macc 4:10; Christian wr. [Lampe s.v.], as well as Rhet. Gr. I 616, 1)

❶ **to shine brightly on an area that is all around a pers.,** ***shine around,*** trans. τινά *someone* **Ac 9:3; 22:6** D.

❷ **to shine brightly,** ***shine,*** intr. (*around*) (Psellus p. 37, 19) περί τινα *around someone* **22:6.** The focus is on Paul.—M-M.

περιβάλλω fut. περιβαλῶ; 2 aor. περιέβαλον, impv. περίβαλε, inf. περιβαλεῖν. Mid.: fut. περιβαλοῦμαι; 2 aor. περιεβαλόμην. Pass.: aor. ptc. pl. περιβληθέντες Wsd 19:17; pf. ptc. περιβεβλημένος (Hom.+)

❶ **to encompass by erecting someth. around,** ***lay, put around,*** of an encircled city (περιβ. of the walling of a city by its inhabitants: Aelian, VH 6, 12; Palaeph. 17; SIG 344, 14; Pr 28:4. Of a piece of ground that is fenced in: POxy 707, 32) περιβαλοῦσιν οἱ ἐχθροί σου χάρακά σοι *throw up an embankment around you* **Lk 19:43 v.l.** (for παρεμβαλοῦσιν; cp. Nearchus of Crete [c. 300 BC]: 133 fgm. 1, 33, 10 Jac.; Arrian, Anab. 5, 23, 6 Ἀλέξανδρος χάρακι περιβάλλει τ. πόλιν; Ezk 4:2; s. χάραξ).

❷ **to put on, esp. of articles of clothing,** ***put on***—ⓐ τί τινι *someth. on someone* (TestLevi 8:7; cp. Plut., Popl. 99 [5, 3] ἱμάτια τοῖς τραχήλοις; Ps.-Clem., Hom. 8, 22); hence (or fr. d below) the mid. περιβάλλομαί τι *put someth. on (oneself)* (Hom. et al.; 1 Km 28:8; 4 Km 19:1; Jon 3:8; Is 37:1; TestAbr A 17 p. 99, 14 [Stone p. 46]; TestNapht 6:8; JosAs 3:9; 15:10) τί περιβαλώμεθα; **Mt 6:31.** Cp. **Ac 12:8; Rv 19:8.** περιβέβλημαί τι *have put someth. on, wear* as a garment (EpJer 11; Da 12:6f; AscIs 2:10; Jos., Ant. 8, 207; Mel., P. 19, 132) νεανίσκον περιβεβλημένον στολὴν λευκήν **Mk 16:5** (Lucian, Philops. 25 of a messenger from heaven: νεανίας λευκὸν ἱμάτιον περιβεβλημένος). Cp. **Rv 7:9, 13; 11:3; 17:4; 18:16; 19:13;** GPt 13:55. ἄγγελον περιβεβλημένον νεφέλην **Rv 10:1.** γυνὴ περιβεβλημένη τὸν ἥλιον **12:1.** περιβεβλημένος σινδόνα ἐπὶ γυμνοῦ *who wore* (nothing but) *a linen cloth on his naked body* **Mk 14:51.**

ⓑ τινά τινι *clothe someone in someth.* (Eur. et al.) περιβεβλημένη πορφυρᾷ καὶ κοκκίνῳ **Rv 17:4** t.r. (Erasmian rdg.; cp. Pla., Critias 116c περιβεβλημένος περιβόλῳ χρυσῷ; 3 Km 11:29).

ⓒ περιβάλλεσθαι ἔν τινι *clothe oneself in* or *with someth.* (Dt 22:12; 1 Ch 21:16; Ps 44:10, 14) **Rv 3:5; 4:4.**

ⓓ w. a double acc. τινά τι *put someth. on someone* (Ezk 27:7.—B-D-F §155, 5; Rob. 483) ἱμάτιον πορφυροῦν περιέβαλον αὐτόν **J 19:2.** Cp. GPt 3:7. The acc. of pers. is easily supplied **Lk 23:11.**

ⓔ with no mention of the garment περιβάλλω τινά *clothe someone* (Ezk 18:7, 16; TestJob 39, 7) **Mt 25:36, 43;** B 3:3 (Is 58:7); w. the acc. supplied **Mt 25:38.** Mid. περιβάλλομαι *dress oneself* (Hg 1:6; Lev 13:45) **Mt 6:29; Lk 12:27; Rv 3:18.**

❸ to envelop someone in torture, thereby involving the pers. in misfortune (Eur. et al.; PSI 330, 7 [258/257 BC]; 3 Macc 6:26 τοὺς . . . περιέβαλεν αἰκίαις; Jos., Ant. 2, 276; cp. EpArist 208; 167; Tat. 19, 1 θανάτῳ περιβαλεῖν), fig. ext. of the prim. mng. 'put around', τοὺς δουλεύοντας τῷ θεῷ εἰς αἰκίαν περιβαλεῖν *treat cruelly those who serve God* 1 Cl 45:7.—M-M.

περιβλέπω (Soph., X., Pla. et al.; BGU 1097, 3; LXX; Jos., Bell. 1, 627 al.) in our lit. only mid. περιβλέπομαι (Polyb.; Περὶ ὕψους 55, 18 V. al.; LXX; TestJos 7:1; cp. B-D-F §316, 1; Rob. 809; 813) impf. 3 sg. περιεβλέπετο; fut. 3 sg. περιβλέψεται Job 7:8; 1 aor. 3 sg. περιεβλέψατο 3 Km 21:40; ptc. περιβλεψάμενος.

❶ **to glance at or look around in various directions,** ***look around (at)*** abs. (Diod. S. 16, 32, 2; Plut., Cato Min. 777 [37; 8]; Ex 2:12; 3 Km 21:40) **Mk 9:8; 10:23.** W. final inf. foll. (B-D-F §392, 3; cp. Rob. 989 f) περιεβλέπετο ἰδεῖν *he looked* (or *kept looking) around to see* **Mk 5:32.** W. acc. of pers. (Polyb. 9, 17, 6; Job 7:8) περιβλεψάμενος τοὺς περὶ αὐτὸν κύκλῳ καθημένους *he looked around at those* etc. **Mk 3:34.** Cp. vs. **5; Lk 6:10.** περιβλεψάμενος πάντα *when he had looked around at everything* **Mk 11:11.** περιέβλεπεν τὰ δεξιὰ καὶ τὰ ἀριστερά *she looked to the right and to the left* GJs 11:1. περιβλεψάμενος [γὰρ κύκλῳ ὁ λέων] AcPl Ha 4, 29.

❷ **be on the lookout for,** ***look for, hunt,*** w. loss of the literal mng. (w. acc. Epict. 3, 22, 65; M. Ant. 7, 55; Lucian, Vit. Auct. 12) περιβλέπονται τίνα ἐκδύσωσιν *they are looking for someone to plunder* B 10:4. Ἐλισάβεδ . . . περιεβλέπετο ποῦ αὐτὸν ἀποκρύψῃ *Elizabeth looked about to see where she could hide (John)* GJs 22:3.—M-M s.v. περιβλέπομαι.

περιβόητος, ον (βοάω; Soph., Thu. et al.) **pert. to being acclaimed far and wide,** ***well known, far famed, celebrated*** (so Demosth. 34, 29; Menand., fgm. 402, 3 Kö.; Plut., Ages. 609c

[24, 5], Themist. 119 [15, 4]; 2 Macc 2:22; Philo, Mos. 2, 284 εὐσέβεια; Jos., Ant. 6, 165, C. Ap. 1, 315) φιλαδελφία 1 Cl 47:5; (w. σεμνός and πᾶσιν ἀνθρώποις ἀξιαγάπητος) ὄνομα 1:1.—DELG s.v. βοή.

περιβόλαιον, ου, τό (περιβολή 'garment'; Eur.+; PStrass 91, 9 [I BC]; LXX; En 14:20; EpArist 158) 'that which is thrown around': **an article of apparel that covers much of the body, *covering, wrap, cloak, robe*** (Diod. S. 36, 2, 4; Dionys. Hal. 3, 61, 1; PStrass [s. above]; Dt 22:12; Is 50:3) someth. like a *cloak* or *mantle* ὡσεὶ π. ἑλίσσειν *roll up as a cloak* **Hb 1:12** (Ps 101:27). ἡ κόμη ἀντὶ περιβολαίου δέδοται αὐτῇ *her* (the woman's) *hair is given to her as a covering* **1 Cor 11:15** (s. OMotta, ET 44, '33, 139–41 and s. on κατακαλύπτω, end).—DELG s.v. βάλλω. M-M.

περιγέλως, ωτος, ὁ (περιγελάω 'deride'; hapax leg.) ***derision*** μήπως ἔσομαι περιγέλως τοῖς υἱοῖς Ἰσραήλ *(I fear) becoming a laughing-stock among the Israelites* GJs 9:2 (καταγέλως v.l.; s. LXX).—DELG s.v. γελάω.

περιγίνομαι aor. 3 sg. περιεγένετο (TestIss 3:5); pass. aor. ptc. fem. acc. sg. περιγενηθεῖσαν 1 Ch 28:19 (Hom. et al.; ins, pap, LXX; En 102:6; Test12Patr; Philo, Op. M. 155; Tat. 11, 2; T. Kellis 22, 97) **to prevail over, *overcome*** w. gen. (Hdt., Aristoph. et al.; Aelian, VH 1, 3; Vett. Val. p. 38, 20; 4 Macc 13:3; Jos., Ant. 7, 165) Hv 1, 3, 2.—DELG s.v. γίγνομαι.

περιδάκρυτος, ον (δακρύω) ***weeping bitterly*** π. γενάμενος ὁ Ἰωσήφ GJs 16:1 (v.l. περίδακρυς).—S. deStrycker 301f.—DELG s.v. δάκρυ.

περιδέω aor. 3 sg. περιέδησε Job 12:18. Pass.: aor. inf. περιδεθῆναι (TestSol); plpf. 3 sg. περιεδέδετο (Hdt., Aristoph. et al.; SIG 1168, 62; TestSol 15:5) ***bind/wrap around*** τί τινι *someth. w. someth.* (Plut., Mor. 825e; Job 12:18) ἡ ὄψις αὐτοῦ σουδαρίῳ π. *his face was wrapped in a cloth* **J 11:44.**—DELG s.v. 1 δέω. M-M.

περιέδραμον s. περιτρέχω.

περιεζωσμένος s. περιζώννυμι.

περιέθηκα s. περιτίθημι.

περιελαύνω impf. περιήλαυνον (since Hom. [where it is found in tmesis]; pap; Jos., Bell., 3, 17; 4, 115) ***drive about*** of livestock (Palaeph. p. 26, 9; PTebt 53, 18 [II BC]) ὧδε καὶ ἐκεῖ (v.l. κἀκεῖσε) περιήλαυνεν αὐτά (i.e. τὰ πρόβατα) *he was driving them about, here and there* Hs 6, 2, 7.

περιελεῖν s. περιαιρέω.

περιελθών s. περιέρχομαι.

περιελών s. περιαιρέω.

περιέπεσον s. περιπίπτω.

περιεργάζομαι (περίεργος) mid. dep. (Hdt. et al.; ins, pap, LXX, Test12Patr) **to be intrusively busy, *be a busybody, meddler*** (Hdt. 3, 46; Pla., Apol. 3 p. 19b; Demosth. 26, 15; 32, 28; Polyb. 18, 51, 2; IG III/1, 74 [=SIG 1042], 14ff; PLond 1912, 58ff; Sir 3:23; EpArist 315; Philo, In Flacc. 5; Jos., Ant. 12, 112. W. πολυπραγμονέω e.g. Aelian, VH 12, 1; SIG 1042, 15) abs. (in wordplay w. ἐργάζεσθαι, as Demosth., Phil. 4, 72 ἐργάζῃ καὶ περιεργάζῃ) **2 Th 3:11.** Also *concern oneself* (Himerius, Or. 64 [=Or. 18], 3) περί τινος *about someth.* περὶ τῶν λοιπῶν μὴ περιεργάζου *do not concern yourself about the rest* Hs 9, 2, 7.—DELG s.v. ἔργον. M-M.

περίεργος, ον (s. prec. entry; Lysias et al.; Menand., Epitr. 262 S. [86 Kö.]; Philo, Joseph.)

❶ pert. to paying attention to matters that do not concern one, of persons, ***meddlesome, officious, curious,*** subst. *a busybody* (X., Mem. 1, 3, 1; Epict. 3, 1, 21; Herodian 4, 12, 3; POsl 49, 7 [c. 100 AD]; TestIss 3:3; Jos., C. Ap. 1, 16; Just., A II, 10, 4) **1 Ti 5:13** (w. φλύαρος). περίεργος εἶ περὶ τοιούτων πραγμάτων *you are inquisitive about such things* Hv 4, 3, 1.

❷ pert. to undue or misdirected curiosity (Ath. 17, 4 π. τέχνη 'excessive, superfluous'; cp. 36, 2), **as in the practice of magic, *belonging to magic*** (cp. Plut., Alex. 665 [2, 5]; Vett. Val. index; Aristaen., Ep. 2, 18, 2; Dssm., B p. 5, 5 [BS 323, 5]; περιεργάζεσθαι in this sense: PGM 12, 404. Cp. our coll. 'fool around with') τὰ περίεργα πράσσειν *practice magic* **Ac 19:19.**—HMette, Curiositas: BSnell Festschr. '66, 227–35. DELG s.v. ἔργον. M-M. Sv.

περιέρχομαι fut. 3 sg. περιελεύσεται LXX; 2 aor. περιῆλθον (Hom. et al.; ins, pap, LXX; TestJob 24:2 [1:1 cod. A, Pal. 364 for κυκλεῦσαι]; Jos., Vi. 397 al.)

❶ to go about in various directions, *go about,* w. a personal subj. *go about* GPt 5:18; *go from place to place* (Cornutus 31 p. 63, 16) of wandering exorcists *be an itinerant* **Ac 19:13.** π. ἐν μηλωταῖς *wander about in sheepskins* **Hb 11:37.** W. acc. of place (X., Ages. 9, 3 πᾶσαν γῆν; Pla., Phd. 112d; PGen 49, 8; POxy 1033, 12; Job 1:7; Jos., Ant. 9, 2) π. τὰς οἰκίας *go about from house to house* **1 Ti 5:13** (cp. Appian, Mithrid. 59 §242 τὰς σκηνὰς περιῄει=he ran about from tent to tent; POxy 1033, 12 περιερχόμενοι τὴν πόλιν; Job 2:9d οἰκίαν ἐξ οἰκίας περιερχομένη).

❷ to go around a reference point, *make a circuit.* W. acc. of place (s. 1) π. ὅλην τὴν νῆσον **Ac 13:6** D. Of the passengers on a ship περιελθόντες *we sailed around, made a circuit* (along the east coast of Sicily) **Ac 28:13 v.l.** (for περιελόντες [s. περιαιρέω 1 and Haenchen ad loc.]).—M-M. TW.

περιέστησαν s. περιίστημι.

περιεστώς s. περιίστημι.

περιέτεμον s. περιτέμνω.

περιετμήθην s. περιτέμνω.

περιέχω fut. 3 pl. περιέξουσιν TestSol 8:7; 2 aor. περιέσχον (Hom.+)

❶ to enclose on all sides, *surround, encircle*—ⓐ of things, one of which surrounds the other (Pla. et al.; SIG 685, 75; 1169, 20 τόπον κύκλῳ πέτραις περιεχόμενον; Job 30:18; Ath. 6, 1) of water τὴν γῆν *flow around the earth* 1 Cl 33:3.

ⓑ of persons, *encircle* w. hostile intent (Hdt. et al.; oft. LXX) περιέσχεν με συναγωγὴ πονηρευομένων B 6:6 (Ps 21:17).

❷ to take hold of completely, fig. ext. of 1: of circumstances, emotions, moods, that ***seize, come upon*** or ***befall someone*** w. acc. of pers. (PTebt 44, 8 [114 BC] χάριν τῆς περιεχούσης με ἀρρωστίας; 2 Macc 4:16; 3 Macc 5:6; Jos., Bell. 4, 585; 6, 182; Mel., P. 30, 203 συμφορά) θάμβος περιέσχεν αὐτόν *amazement seized him,* i.e. *he was amazed* **Lk 5:9** (cp. Da 7:28 ἐκστάσει περιειχόμην).

❸ to have someth. as content, *contain* of a document

ⓐ trans., w. acc. (Diod. S. 2, 1, 1; Jos., C. Ap. 1, 39; 2, 37; 276; SIG 683, 12f [140 BC] ἐπιστολὰν περιέχουσαν τὰν κρίσιν; BGU 1047 III, 11; PGiss 57, 1) ἐπιστολὴν περιέχουσαν τάδε **Ac 15:23** D. ἐπιστολὴν περιέχουσαν τὸν τύπον τοῦτον **23:25 v.l.** Cp. Pol 13:2. ἱστοριαν … ἣν τὸ καθ' Ἑβραίους εὐαγγέλιον περιέχει Papias (2:17).

ⓑ intr. (SIG 685 [139 BC], 21 καθότι τὰ γράμματα περιέχει; 41; 730, 31 [I BC]; 820, 11; POxy 95, 33 [95 BC]; BGU 19, 10 περιέχων οὕτως; 191, 8; 10; 1 Macc 15:2; 2 Macc 11:16 τὸν τρόπον τοῦτον=οὕτως 2 Macc 11:22; TestLevi 10:5) περιέχει ἐν γραφῇ *it stands* or *says in the scripture* **1 Pt 2:6** (ἐν as Jos., Ant. 11, 104; the quot. foll. as SIG 685, 51).—B-D-F §308; Rob. 800. M-M.

περιζώννυμι and **περιζωννύω** 1 aor. 3 sg. περιέζωσεν LXX. Mid.: 1 fut. περιζώσομαι; 1 aor. περιεζωσάμην, impv. περίζωσαι. Pass.: pf. ptc. περιεζωσμένος (since Theopompus [s. 2 below] and Aristoph; PFay 12, 20 [103 BC]; LXX; PsSol 2:20; TestJob 47, 6 and 11 al.; JosAs; Mel., P. 19, 134)

➊ **to put a belt or sash around, *gird about,*** act. (Jos., Ant. 6, 184) w. double acc. *gird someone (about) with someth.* (Ps 17:33, 40; 29:12; Sir 45:7). The pass. w. acc. of thing can be understood as a development of this *be girded with someth.* (Diod. S. 1, 72, 2 σινδόνας; 4 Km 3:21 ζώνην; PGM 5, 157 ὄφιν) περιεζωσμένον ζώνην χρυσᾶν *with a gold belt around him* **Rv 1:13;** cp. **15:6** (but s. 2b below). Certainly pass. is the abs. ἔστωσαν ὑμῶν αἱ ὀσφύες περιεζωσμέναι *let your waists* or *loins be well-girt* **Lk 12:35** (Ex 12:11; Philo, Sacr. Abel. 63). The abs. perf. ptc. can also be understood as a pass. in Hv 3, 8, 4; s 8, 4, 2; 9, 9, 5 and περιεζωσμέναι εὐπρεπῶς 9, 2, 4 (s. εὐπρεπῶς). But the passages in Rv and Hermas can also be taken as

➋ ***gird oneself,*** mid. (since the comic wr. Theopompus [V BC], fgm. 37 K.: περιζωσάμενος ᾤαν [sheepskin]; oft. LXX).

ⓐ abs. (Polyb. 30, 13, 10; Paus. 1, 44, 1; Ps 92:1; Jo 1:13; 1 Macc 3:58; TestJob 47:6 al.) **Lk 12:37; 17:8; Ac 12:8** t.r.

ⓑ w. acc. of the thing girded about one *gird oneself w. someth., bind someth. about oneself* (Theopompus [s. above]; Aristoph., Pax 670; Plut., Rom. 27 [16, 4], Coriol. 217 [9, 3]; 2 Km 3:31; Is 3:24; Jer 4:8; PsSol 2:20; TestJob 47:11; JosAs 10:11 al.; Jos., Ant. 11, 177; Mel., P. 19, 134) περίζωσαι ὠμόλινον Hs 8, 4, 1a; cp. b. This may also be the place for **Rv 1:13; 15:6** (s. 1 above).

ⓒ w. acc. of the part of the body that is girded τὴν ὀσφῦν (Jer 1:17; Is 32:11; JosAs 10:16) *gird one's waist;* that with which one is girded is added w. ἐν (1 Ch 15:27. Such girding is an indication that one is prepared for some activity.) περιζωσάμενοι τὴν ὀσφὺν ἐν ἀληθείᾳ *after you have girded your waists with truth* **Eph 6:14.**—Arnott, Alexis 536–38.—M-M. TW.

περίθεσις, εως, ἡ (περιτίθημι; Arrian, Anab. 7, 22; Sext. Emp., Pyrrh. 3, 15; Jos., Ant. 19, 30; Sym. Ps 31:9) **putting on or around as an act of wearing, *putting on*** π. χρυσίων *the putting on* or *wearing of gold ornaments* **1 Pt 3:3.**—DELG s.v. τίθημι.

περιΐστημι 1 aor. subj. 3 pl. περιστήσωσιν; EpJer 36; 2 aor. περιέστην; pf. ptc. περιεστηκώς (1 Km 4:15; TestSol 6:11 D) and περιεστώς; pres. mid. impv. 2 sg. περιΐστασο (W-S. §15; B-D-F §93; Mlt-H. 207) (Hom. et al.; ins, pap, LXX; pseudepigr.).

➊ **to encircle by standing around some entity, *stand around*** act. (cp. act. 'cause to stand around, place around' of cavalry posted for action Jos., Bell. 3, 148)

ⓐ 2 aor. *stand around* abs. **Ac 25:7 v.l.** W. acc. of pers. (Appian, Hann. 28 §118 περιστάντες τὸ βουλευτήριον=they stood about the senate-house; Jos., Ant. 7, 16; 13, 169) περιέστησαν αὐτὸν οἱ Ἰουδαῖοι *the Judeans stood around him* **25:7.**

ⓑ pf. *stand around* (2 Km 13:31; Jdth 5:22; TestSol 6:11 D; Jos., Vi. 109) ὁ ὄχλος ὁ περιεστώς *the crowd standing by* (Appian, Hann. 19 §84 ἡ στρατιὰ περιεστῶσα) **J 11:42.** οἱ π. *the bystanders* MPol 2:2.

➋ **to go around so as to avoid, *avoid, shun*** mid. (Philod., Rhet. I 384 S. τὰς ἁμαρτίας; M. Ant. 3, 4, 2; Sext. Emp., Math. 11, 93; Lucian, Herm. 86 κύνας; Diog. L. 9, 14; Iambl., Vi. Pyth. 31, 189 τὸ παράνομον; Philo, Ebr. 205; Jos., Bell. 2, 135, Ant. 1, 45; 10, 210) τὶ *someth.* τὰς κενοφωνίας **2 Ti 2:16.** μάχας νομικάς **Tit 3:9.**—M-M.

περικαθαίρω aor. 3 sg. περιεκάθαρεν Josh 5:4 (s. καθαρός; Pla. et al.; Phlegon: 257 fgm. 36, 1, 11 Jac. [περικαθαίρεσθαι=have oneself purified by rites of propitiation]; LXX; Philo, Plant. 112) ***purify completely*** περικαθαίρων (w. οἰωνοσκόπος, ἐπαοιδός, μαθηματικός) *one who performs purificatory rites* of propitiatory magic for gain, *magician* D 3:4 (s. WKnox, JTS 40, '39, 146–49, who proposes the transl. 'the one who performs circumcision').—DELG s.v. καθαρός.

περικάθαρμα, ατος, τό fr. περικαθαίρω='cleanse all around' or 'on all sides'; **that which is removed as a result of a thorough cleansing, *dirt, refuse, off-scouring,*** also as a designation of the 'off-scouring' of humanity (Epict. 3, 22, 78; Vi. Aesopi G 14 P.; cp. 1QH 5:21). Since purification is achieved by the removal of the περικάθαρμα, the word can take on the mng. *propitiatory offering, ransom* (Pr 21:18). ὡς περικαθάρματα τοῦ κόσμου ἐγενήθημεν *we have become like the off-scourings of the world* **1 Cor 4:13.** But since π. is pl. in contrast to the foll. περίψημα (q.v., as well as κάθαρμα) it has been proposed to transl. (s. earlier edd. of this lexicon and Spicq. III 94f) *scapegoats for the world.* On the other hand, the expr. is similar to τὰ γὰρ λύματα καὶ καθάρματα τῆς χώρας ὅλης Jos., Bell. 4, 241, a description of unsavory characters, and the initial ὡς suggests the perception, wholly negative, that Paul's activity generates in the 'world'.—DELG s.v. καθαρός. M-M. TW. Spicq.

περικαθίζω fut. 2 sg. περικαθιεῖς Dt 20:12 (Diod. S. 20, 103, 5 Fischer v.l.; Mitt-Wilck I/2, 11 B. fgm. a, 10 [123 BC]; LXX; Jos., Ant. 13, 151; TestJud 9:4, but mostly in a hostile sense = 'besiege') ***sit around*** (Maximus Tyr. 21, 6d περικαθίσαντες ἐν κύκλῳ τῇ πυρᾷ) **Lk 22:55** D.—DELG s.v. ἕζομαι. M-M.

περικαλύπτω 1 aor. ptc. περικαλύψας; pf. pass. ptc. περικεκαλυμμένος (Hom. et al.; LXX; En 13:9 τὴν ὄψιν; Philo, Leg. All. 2, 62; Jos., Bell. 2, 148) **to cover by putting someth. around, *cover, conceal*** τὶ *someth.* (3 Km 7:5) περικαλύπτειν αὐτοῦ τὸ πρόσωπον **Mk 14:65** (s. on προφητεύω 2); shortened περικαλύψαντες αὐτόν **Lk 22:64.** Pass. ἡ κιβωτὸς περικεκαλυμμένη πάντοθεν χρυσίῳ *the ark, covered on all sides with gold* **Hb 9:4** (cp. Ex 28:20).

περίκειμαι mid. dep. (Hom.+; ins, pap, LXX; TestSol 4:13 D; TestAbr A; JosAs ch. 18 cod. A [p. 68, 19 Bat.]; Philo, Mos. 2, 182; Just., Mel.)

➊ **to be positioned around some object or area, *be around, surround.*—**ⓐ lit., *lie* or *be placed around* περίκειται μύλος ὀνικὸς περὶ τὸν τράχηλον αὐτοῦ *a millstone is hung about his neck* **Mk 9:42;** cp. **Lk 17:2.**

ⓑ fig., of a crowd of people surrounding someone (Herodian 7, 9, 1 τὸ περικείμενον πλῆθος) τοσοῦτον ἔχοντες περικείμενον ἡμῖν νέφος μαρτύρων **Hb 12:1** (s. νέφος).

➋ **to put someth. around, *wear someth., have someth. on*** περίκειμαί τι (for περιτέθειμαί τι as pass. of περιτίθημί τινί τι *put someth. on someone*)

ⓐ lit. (Hdt. 1, 171, 4; Dionys. Hal. 2, 19; Strabo 15, 3, 15; Plut., Arat. 1034 [17, 6]; Polyaenus 1, 20, 2; Herodian 2, 13, 8 ἐσθῆτας στρατιωτικάς; OGI 56, 66; EpJer 23; TestAbr A 17 p. 99, 14 [Stone p. 46]; Jos., Ant. 14, 173, Vi. 334; Just., D. 1, 2.—B-D-F §159, 4; Rob. 485) δέρμα λευκόν *wear a white (goat) skin* Hv 5:1; cp. s 6, 2, 5. Of fetters (4 Macc 12:2 τὰ δεσμά) τὴν ἅλυσιν ταύτην περίκειμαι *I am bearing this chain* **Ac 28:20.**

ⓑ fig. (SibOr 5, 228) νέφος *be clothed in or surrounded by a cloud* 2 Cl 1:6b.—ἀσθένειαν *be beset by weakness,* perh. with suggestion of various kinds **Hb 5:2** (cp. Theocr. 23, 14 ὕβριν 'clad in insolence', but the text may be corrupt, s. app.). ἀμαύρωσιν *blanketed in darkness* 2 Cl 1:6a.

❸ In τοῦ κλήρου, οὗ περίκειμαι ἐπιτυχεῖν ITr 12:3 the text can hardly be in good order, and it is only w. reservations that the transl. *the lot which is incumbent upon me to obtain* (Goodsp.) is suggested (s. Hdb. ad loc.; IHeikel, StKr 106, '35, 317), but s. CStory, VigChrist 33, '79, 319–23 (οὗ πέρι κεῖμαι *[to obtain the lot] for which I am appointed*).—M-M. TW.

περικεφαλαία, ας, ἡ (Aeneas Tact. 1376; Philo Mech. 93, 46; Polyb. 3, 71, 4; 6, 23, 8; Diod. S. 14, 43, 2; SIG 958, 29 [III BC]; PPetr III, 140a, 3 [III BC]; LXX; Jos., Ant. 6, 184) ***helmet*** in our lit. only in imagery, in which Christian virtues are compared to pieces of armor ἡ πίστις ὡς περικεφαλαία IPol 6:2. ἡ π. τοῦ σωτηρίου *the helmet of salvation* **Eph 6:17** (after Is 59:17). Sim. ἐνδυσάμενοι περικεφαλαίαν ἐλπίδα σωτηρίας **1 Th 5:8.**—B. 1401. M-M. TW.

περικόπτω fut. περικόψω (Ps 74:11 Aq.); 1 aor. περιέκοψα (Zech 11:10 Aq.; Just.) pf. inf. περικεκοφέναι (Just, D. 73, 6); 2 aor. pass. περιεκόπην, ptc. περικοπείς (Thu. et al.; pap) in our lit. only in Hermas in the allegory of the tower; pass.

❶ **to cut around an object, of shaping of stones, *hew all around*** (Plut., Mor. 74d) Hs 9, 7, 5.

❷ **to cut away in a trimming process, *cut away, take away*** τὶ *someth.* (Pla., Rep. 7, 519a et al.; Just., D. 72, 2 and 4; 73, 6) ὅταν περικοπῇ αὐτῶν ὁ πλοῦτος *when the wealth is cut off from them* (i.e. fr. the stones, which represent a class of people) Hv 3, 6, 6 (for the fig. use cp. Diod. S. 20, 77, 3 of hopes that were cut off; Porphyr., Antr. Nymph. c. 34 ὅπως τὰ ἐπίβουλα τῆς ψυχῆς αὐτοῦ περικόψῃ; Sb 6787, 23 [257 BC] of plundering property; Philo, Cher. 95).

περικρατής, ές pert. to having control in a situation, *having power, being in command* (Simias [III BC] 1, 11 [ed. HFränckel 1915=Coll. Alex. p. 109, ln. 11]) τινός (Ps.-Callisth. 2, 4, 3; Sus 39 Theod. A ἐκείνου οὐκ ἠδυνήθημεν περικρατεῖς γενέσθαι) *over* or *of a thing* ἰσχύσαμεν μόλις περικρατεῖς γενέσθαι τῆς σκάφης *we were scarcely able to get the boat under control* **Ac 27:16.**—DELG s.v. κράτος. M-M.

περικρύβω (κρύβω is a new formation in H. Gk., cp. the Hellenistic aor. ἐκρύβην. Kühner-Bl. II p. 467; B-D-F §73; Mlt-H. 245; Thackeray §19, 3 p. 227; Lob. on Phryn. p. 317f.—The compound verb in Lucian, D. Mort. 10, 8; Eunap., Hist. Fgm. 55 p. 248f [HGM I 1870]; mid., Diog. L. 6, 61) impf. περιέκρυβον **to keep private, *hide, conceal (entirely)*** περιέκρυβεν ἑαυτήν *she kept herself hidden* or *she lived in seclusion* (REB) **Lk 1:24.**—DELG s.v. κρύπτω. M-M. s.v. -κρύπτω.

περικυκλόω fut. περικυκλώσω; aor. 3 pl. περιεκύκλωσαν LXX; impv. 2 pl. περικυκλώσατε (TestJob 1:6 w. ptc. περικυκλώσαντες). Pass.: fut. 3 sg. περικυκλωθήσεται Jer 38:39; pf. ptc. περικεκυκλωμένος LXX (Hdt., Aristoph. et al.; Jos., Ant. 8, 282, mostly used in the mid. In the act. in Aristot., HA 4, 8 [533b, 11]; Appian, Bell. Civ. 4, 55 §238; PLond 681, 9; LXX; En 24:3; TestAbr A, TestJob; ParJer 1:2; Philo, Leg. All. 1, 68) ***surround, encircle*** w. acc. of a beleaguered city (Josh 6:13; 4 Km 6:14) **Lk 19:43.**—DELG s.v. κύκλος. M-M.

περιλάμπω 1 aor. περιέλαμψα (Diod. S. 3, 69, 3; Lucian et al.) in our lit. only trans. ***shine around*** τινά *someone* (Plut., Artox. 1017 [13, 1] φωτὶ πολλῷ περιλαμπόμενος; Appian, Bell. Civ. 5, 117 §486) **Lk 2:9; Ac 26:13.** τὶ *someth.* (Plut., Cic. 878 [35, 5] τὴν ἀγοράν; Synes., Calvit. 11 p. 74d; Philo, Somn. 1, 90; Jos., Bell. 6, 290) τὸν τόπον GEb 18, 38.

περιλείπομαι occurs only in pass. (Hom. [in tmesis] et al.; Eur.; Pla.; IG XII/3, 326, 24; SIG 852, 46; BGU 1132, 12 [13 BC]; PSI 409, 12; 571, 14; LXX; Just.) aor. pass. ptc. περιλειφθείς (LXX, Just.); pf. ptc. neut. pl. περιλελειμμένα 2 Macc 8:14 ***remain, be left behind*** of pers. (Eur., Hel. 426; Plut., Ages. 608 [22, 8]; Herodian 2, 1, 7; PGiss 82, 23 ἡμᾶς τοὺς ἔτι περιλειπομένους; 4 Macc 12:6; 13:18; Jos., C. Ap. 1, 35) **1 Th 4:15, 17.** See AvVeldhuizen, ThStud 29, 1911, 101–6; Unknown Sayings, 64–67.—DELG s.v. λείπω. M-M. TW. Spicq.

περιλείχω (Aristoph. et al.) ***lick all around, lick off*** **Lk 16:21 v.l.** (for ἐπέλειχον Hippiatr. I 251, 19 ἐν αὐτῇ τῇ γλώσσῃ περιλείχων τὰ ἕλκη).—περιλιχμάω of dogs, which lick wounds: Aelian, HA 8, 9; Philostr., Vi. Ap. 6, 43 p. 253, 22 K.

περίλυπος, ον (λύπη; Hippocr.; Isocr.; Aristot., EN 4, 7, 1124a, 16; Plut.; LXX) ***very sad, deeply grieved*** περίλυπον γενέσθαι (Isocr. 1, 42; Plut., Mor. 634c; Da 2:12) **Mk 6:26; Lk 18:23;** 1 Cl 4:4 (Gen 4:6). περίλυπός ἐστιν ἡ ψυχή μου (cp. Plut., Mor. 1101e; Ps 41:6, 12; 42:5) **Mt 26:38; Mk 14:34** (JHéring, Cullmann Festschr. '62, 64–69 [Gethsemane]). π. εἶναι περί τινος *be very unhappy about someth.* Hv 3, 10, 6 (here π. is further strengthened by λίαν).—DELG s.v. λύπη. TW.

περιμένω fut. 3 pl. περιμενοῦσιν Wsd 8:12; 1 aor. περιέμεινα, impv. περίμεινον (Soph., Hdt. et al.; pap, LXX, Joseph.) ***wait for*** w. acc. τινά *someone* (Aristoph., Plut. 643; Thu. 5, 64, 4; X., An. 2, 1, 3; 2, 4, 1; POxy 1762, 10; PGiss 73, 4; Wsd 8:12; Jos., Ant. 12, 193) Hs 9, 11, 1. τὶ *someth.* (Pla., Phd. 63, 115a, Ep. 7, 327e; Gen 49:18; Jos., Ant. 1, 219; 2, 69, Vi. 176; Ath., R. 16 p. 67, 24) **Ac 1:4.** Foll. by ἵνα *wait to* MPol 1:2. Abs. *wait* (Appian, Syr. 9 §35; Jos., Ant. 6, 100) **Ac 10:24** D.—M-M. TW.

πέριξ adv. strengthened for περί (Aeschyl., Hdt. et al.; Jos., Ant. 11, 19 τὰ π. ἔθνη; SIG 880, 43f ἐκ τῶν π. κωμῶν; PSI 317, 5; Schwyzer II 552f) ***(all) around*** αἱ π. πόλεις *the cities in the vicinity* **Ac 5:16** (as Dio Chrys. 17 [34], 27; Jos., Bell. 4, 241, Vi. 81).—DELG s.v. περί. M-M.

περιοικέω to live near and around, *be in the neighborhood of* w. acc. of pers. (Hdt. 5, 78; Aristoph., Equ. 853; Jos., Bell. 1, 63) οἱ περιοικοῦντες αὐτούς *their neighbors* **Lk 1:65.**—Renehan '82, 116.

περίοικος, ον pert. to living in the vicinity of others, *living around, in the neighborhood;* subst. in pl. οἱ περίοικοι *the neighbors* (Hdt. 1, 175; 4, 161; Thu. 1, 101, 2; Jos., Vi. 78, Ant. 16, 272; Dt 1:7 in various senses) **Lk 1:58** (w. συγγενεῖς).—DELG s.v. οἶκος. SEG XXXVIII, 2032 (lit.).

περιούσιος, ον (περί+εἰμί, περίειμι 'to be over and above') **pert. to being of very special status, *chosen, especial*** (PGen 11, 17 the married man is called ὁ περιούσιος 'the chosen one'. Herm. Wr. 1, 19: Rtzst., Poim. 334; LXX) λαὸς π., a transl. of עַם סְגֻלָּה Ex 19:5; 23:22 (here only in the LXX); Dt 7:6; 14:2 (λ. π. ἀπὸ πάντων τῶν ἐθνῶν or παρὰ πάντα τὰ ἔθνη); 26:18; following these, **Tit 2:14;** 1 Cl 64 *a chosen people* (B-D-F §113, 1; Mlt-H. 322; Lghtf., On a Fresh Revision of the Engl. NT 1891, 260ff).—DELG s.v. εἰμί. M-M.

περιοχή, ῆς, ἡ (Theophr. et al.; Herm. Wr. 8, 5; pap, LXX; Philo, Aet. M. 4; Jos., Bell. 5, 169; 203) ἡ π. τῆς γραφῆς **Ac 8:32** can mean either

❶ *content/wording of a written text/scripture* (περιοχή in this sense, schol. on Thu. 1, 131 ἡ περ. τῶν γραμμάτων; schol. on Apollon. Rhod. 4 superscr. Cp. also Suda s.v. Ὅμηρος Σέλλιος)—or

❷ *portion of written text/scripture* (Dionys. Hal., de Thu. c. 25; Cicero, Ad Attic. 13, 25, 3).—Blass on **Ac 8:32.**—DELG s.v. 1 ἔχω. M-M.

περιπατέω impf. περιεπάτουν; fut. περιπατήσω; 1 aor. περιεπάτησα and ἐπεριπάτησα ApcEsdr s. 1a; plpf. 3 sg. περι(ε)πεπατήκει **Ac 14:8 v.l.** (on augm. in the plpf. s. B-D-F §66, 1; Mlt.-H. 190f) (Aristoph., X., Pla.+)

❶ **to go here and there in walking,** ***go about, walk around***

ⓐ w. an indication of the place where one walks about (Demosth. 54, 7 ἐν ἀγορᾷ; ApcEsdr 6:12 p. 31, 17 Tdf. ἐν τῷ ὄρει; Jos., C. Ap. 2, 117 ἐπὶ τῆς γῆς; Just., D. 1, 1 ἐν τοῖς τοῦ ξυστοῦ περιπάτοις 'on the walkways of the Xystos') ἐν τριβόλοις γυμνοῖς ποσὶ περιπατεῖν *walk among thistles barefoot* Hs 9, 20, 3. ἐν τῇ γῇ ταύτῃ GJs 6:1. In several places one might translate *stay, spend some time, be,* though without the idea of remaining on the same spot (Chion, Ep. 13, 1 ἐν τῷ Ὠιδείῳ; 2 Km 11:2; Da 3:92 of the men in the fiery furnace; 4:29; En 17:6; Jos., Ant. 7, 130): ἐν τῷ ἱερῷ (Cebes 1, 1.—Diog. L. 4, 24 refers to Crantor walking about in the temple of Asclepius) **Mk 11:27; J 10:23;** Ox 840, 9. ἐν τῇ Γαλιλαίᾳ **J 7:1a;** cp. vs. **1b.** ὁ περιπατῶν ἐν μέσῳ τῶν ἑπτὰ λυχνιῶν **Rv 2:1.** π. ἐν τοῖς Ἰουδαίοις *appear among the Judeans* **J 11:54.**

ⓑ *go about* w. indication of the way one is clothed ἐν στολαῖς **Mk 12:38; Lk 20:46.** ἐν λευκοῖς *clothed in white* **Rv 3:4** (Epict. 3, 22, 10 ἐν κοκκίνοις περιπ.; Tat. 2:1 ἐν πορφυρίδι περιπατῶν). ἐν δέρμασιν αἰγείοις 1 Cl 17:1.

ⓒ gener. *walk, go* π. διὰ τοῦ φωτός *walk in the light* **Rv 21:24.** π. εἰς τὸν ἀγρόν *(go for a) walk in the country* Hs 2:1. ἐπὶ τῆς θαλάσσης (ἐπί 1a and cp. Job 9:8.—GBertram, Le chemin sur les eaux: Congr. d'Hist. du Christ. I 1928, 137–66) **Mt 14:26; Mk 6:48f; J 6:19.** AcPl Ha 7, 27 and 34. ἐπὶ τὴν θάλασσαν **Mt 14:25; J 6:19** P[75]. ἐπὶ τὰ ὕδατα **Mt 14:29** (ἐπί 4bβ). παρὰ τὴν θάλασσαν **4:18** (παρά C1a). π. μετά τινος *go about w. someone* **J 6:66;** *walk with someone* Hs 9, 6, 2a; 9, 10, 1. π. περί τι *walk around someth.* s 9, 12, 7; also κύκλῳ τινός s 9, 6, 2b. μετά τινος κύκλῳ τινὸς π. *walk with someone around someth.* s 9, 11, 5. π. ἐπάνω *walk over* **Lk 11:44** (ἐπάνω 1a). More closely defined ὁμαλῶς π. καὶ ἀπροσκόπως Hm 6, 1, 4. γυμνὸν π. *go naked* **Rv 16:15.** μόνον π. *walk alone* Hv 4, 1, 3 (cp. Jos., C. Ap. 1, 281). περιεπάτεις ὅπου ἤθελες *you used to go where you pleased* **J 21:18** (En 17:6 ὅπου πᾶσα σὰρξ οὐ περιπατεῖ).—Abs. *walk (about)*(Diocles 141 p. 180, 19f; Diod. S. 1, 70, 10; EpArist 175; Just., D. 127, 2) **Mt 9:5; 11:5; 15:31; Mk 2:9; 5:42; 8:24; Lk 5:23; 7:22; J 5:8f, 11f; 11:9f; Ac 3:6, 8ab, 9, 12; 14:8, 10; 1 Pt 5:8; Rv 9:20** (cp. Ps 113:15); Hv 2, 1, 3; *(go for a) walk, be out walking* **Mk 16:12; Lk 24:17;** *walk by* **J 1:36.** περιπατῶν ἀφύπνωσα *as I walked along I fell asleep* Hv 1, 1, 3. περιπατῶν ἀνεμνήσθην *as I was walking along I remembered* 2, 1, 1.

ⓓ in imagery, and far on the way toward the nonliteral use of the word: doubters are περιπατοῦντες ἐν ταῖς ἀνοδίαις Hv 3, 7, 1. Esp. in John: περιπατεῖν ἐν τῇ σκοτίᾳ **J 8:12; 12:35b; 1J 2:11;** cp. **1:6.** Corresp. ἐν τῷ φωτί vs. **7;** ἐν αὐτῇ (=ἐν τῇ ὁδῷ τοῦ φωτός) B 19:1 (but it may also refer to ἡ γνῶσις; then the pass. would belong under 2aδ below). μέγα δὲ ἀσεβείας ὑπόδειγμα ἐν τούτῳ τῷ κόσμῳ περιεπάτησεν ὁ Ἰούδας *Judas went about in this world as a notable example of impiety* Papias (3:2). Abs. περιπατεῖτε ὡς τὸ φῶς ἔχετε *walk while you have the light* **J 12:35a.**

❷ **to conduct one's life,** ***comport oneself, behave, live*** as habit of conduct; fig. ext. of 1:—ⓐ of 'walk of life', *go about* (Philod., Περὶ παρρησίας p. 12 Ol.; Epict. 1, 18, 20; s. Simplicius in Epict. p. 125, 52 Düb. Esp. acc. to OT models: 4 Km 20:3 ἐν ἀληθείᾳ; Pr 8:20 ἐν ὁδοῖς δικαιοσύνης.—Eccl 11:9). In the NT this use of the word is decidedly Pauline (the pastoral epp. do not have the word at all); elsewh. it is reasonably common only in 2J and 3J, *live, conduct oneself, walk,* always more exactly defined

α. by an adv. ἀξίως τινός **Eph 4:1; Col 1:10; 1 Th 2:12;** Pol 5:1. ἀτάκτως **2 Th 3:6, 11.** εὐσχημόνως **Ro 13:13; 1 Th 4:12.**

β. by the dat. to denote attendant circumstance, kind, or manner (TestIss 5:8 ἁπλότητι.—B-D-F §198, 5; s. Rob. 528–32) κώμοις καὶ μέθαις **Ro 13:13.** τοῖς ἔθεσιν **Ac 21:21;** cp. **15:1** D; πνεύματι π. **Gal 5:16.** τῷ αὐτῷ πνεύματι **2 Cor 12:18.**

γ. by a comparison ἕκαστον ὡς κέκληκεν ὁ θεός, οὕτως περιπατείτω **1 Cor 7:17.** περιπατεῖν καθὼς τὰ ἔθνη περιπατεῖ **Eph 4:17;** ὡς τέκνα φωτός **5:8.**—**Phil 3:17; 1J 2:6.** The comparison is implied fr. the context (ὡς ἐχθροὶ τοῦ σταυροῦ τοῦ Χριστοῦ) **Phil 3:18.**—πῶς (καθὼς) περιπατεῖτε **Eph 5:15; 1 Th 4:1ab.**

δ. by a prepositional expr. The sphere in which one lives or ought to live, so as to be characterized by that sphere, is designated by ἐν: pl. in sins **Eph 2:2; Col 3:7;** in good deeds **Eph 2:10;** in the Lord's ordinances B 21:1 (Philo, Congr. Erud. Gr. 87 π. ἐν ταῖς τοῦ θεοῦ κρίσεσι κ. προστάξεσιν). Cp. **Hb 13:9.** Sing. ἐν καινότητι ζωῆς **Ro 6:4.** ἐν πανουργίᾳ **2 Cor 4:2.** ἐν ἀγάπῃ **Eph 5:2.** ἐν σοφίᾳ **Col 4:5.** ἐν (τῇ) ἀληθείᾳ **2J 4; 3J 3f;** ἐν ἀκεραιοσύνῃ B 10:4; cp. 19:1 (s. 1d above). ἐν ἀλλοτρίᾳ γνώμῃ IPhld 3:3. ἐν ἀμώμῳ … συνειδήσει Pol 5:3. ἐν αὐτῇ (=ἐν τῇ ἐντολῇ) **2J 6b.** ἐν αὐτῷ (=ἐν τῷ κυρίῳ) **Col 2:6.**—The norm of conduct is designated by κατά w. acc. (s. κατά B5bγ) κατὰ ἄνθρωπον *like ordinary* (unregenerate) *persons* **1 Cor 3:3.** κατὰ σάρκα *according to the old self* viz. the 'flesh' as opposed to the new self under the 'spirit' **Ro 8:4; 2 Cor 10:2.** κατὰ ἀγάπην **Ro 14:15.** κατὰ τὴν παράδοσιν τῶν πρεσβυτέρων **Mk 7:5.** κατὰ τὰς ἐντολὰς αὐτοῦ **2J 6a.**—BEaston, NT Ethical Lists: JBL 51, '32, 1–12; SWibbing, D. Tugend- u. Lasterkataloge im NT, '59; EKamlach, Die Form der katalogischen Paränese im NT, '64; HBraun, Qumran u. das NT II, '66, 286–301; JHolloway III, ΠΕΡΙΠΑΤΕΩ as a Thematic Marker for Pauline Ethics '92.

ⓑ rarely of physical life gener.: ἐν τούτῳ τῷ κόσμῳ περιπατεῖν (formulation as in Papias [3:2]) B 10:11. ἐν σαρκὶ **2 Cor 10:3.** διὰ πίστεως περιπατοῦμεν, οὐ διὰ εἴδους **5:7.**—B. 690. M-M. EDNT. TW.

περιπείρω 1 aor. περιέπειρα ***pierce through, impale*** (lit. in Diod. S.; Lucian; Plut., C. Gracch. 842 [17, 5] κεφαλὴ περιπεπαρμένη δόρατι; Philo; Jos., Bell. 3, 296) fig. ἑαυτὸν π. ὀδύναις πολλαῖς *pierce oneself through with many a pang* **1 Ti 6:10** (Philo, In Flacc. 1 ἀθρόους ἀνηκέστοις περιέπειρε κακοῖς.—Sim. imagery Pind., P. 2, 91 ἐνέπαξαν ἕλκος ὀδυναρὸν ἑᾷ πρόσθε καρδίᾳ=plant in their heart a painful wound).—M-M.

περίπικρος, ον (Philod., Ira [=Περὶ ὀργῆς PHercul. 182] p. 6 Wilke; Vi. Aesopi I G 38 P. and other later wr.) ***very bitter*** fig., of a glance βλέμμα π. *a very bitter look* Hs 6, 2, 5.—DELG s.v. πικρός.

περιπίπτω fut. 2 pl. περιπεσεῖσθε Da 2:9; 2 aor. περιέπεσον (trag., Hdt.+) freq. w. dat. answering the quest. 'whither?' (B-D-F §202 ; s. Rob. 528f).

❶ **to move toward someth. and hit against it,** ***strike*** εἰς τόπον διθάλασσον *strike a point (of land)* **Ac 27:41** (for the use w. εἰς cp. Oxy 3314, 7; s. also διθάλασσος).

❷ **to encounter at hazard,** ***fall in with, fall into***—ⓐ of hostile pers. λῃσταῖς *fall among* or *into the hands of robbers* **Lk 10:30** (Diod. S. 14, 93, 4 λῃσταῖς περιέπεσον; Conon [I BC/I AD]: 26 fgm. 1, 22 Jac. λῃσταῖς περιπ.; Diog. L. 4, 50 λῃσταῖς περιέπεσε; Artem. 3, 65; cp. 1, 5; 2, 22; Simplicius In Epict. p. 111, 13 Düb. δύο εἰς Δελφοὺς ἀπιόντες λῃσταῖς περιπεπτώκασι).

ⓑ fig. of discomfiting circumstances (as oft. since Hdt. 6, 106, 2; Thu. 8, 27, 3 κινδύνῳ. Also in ins, pap, LXX; TestDan 4:5; ApcMos 5 εἰς νόσον; Philo, Leg. All. 2, 77; Jos., Ant. 10, 25; 20, 48; Just., D. 32, 1 4:5 τῇ ἐσχάτῃ κατάρᾳ) πειρασμοῖς ποικίλοις *become involved in various trials* **Js 1:2.** αἰκίαις π. *suffer tortures* 1 Cl 51:2 (Diod. S. 1, 74, 7 περιπίπτει τιμωρίαις=he incurs [lit. falls into] punishment).—M-M. TW. Spicq.

περιπλέκω impf. περιέπλεκον (Hom. et al.; LXX; TestSol 21:3 Q; JosAs 16:14 cod. A [p. 69, 4 Bat.]; Philo, Poster. Cai. 156) ***weave/twine around*** fig. (schol. on Soph., Ant. 244 p. 230 Papag. τὸν λόγον) of a deceitful tongue περιέπλεκεν δολιότητα (s. δολιότης) 1 Cl 35:8 (Ps 49:19).—Mid. 2 aor. ptc acc. pl. περιπλακομένους (TestAbr A 5 p. 82, 25 [Stone p. 12]). Pass.: 2 aor. περιεπλάκην LXX, ptc. περιπλακείς; pf. ptc. περιπεπλεγμένος LXX. In act. sense *embrace* τινί *someone* (Hom. et al.; TestAbr A; Jos., Ant. 8, 7) Hs 9, 11, 4ab. περιπλακὶς (=εἰς) τῷ Παύλῳ AcPl Ha 8, 3 (cp. TestAbr A 15 p. 95, 16f [Stone p. 38] περιεπλάκη ἐπὶ τὸν τράχηλον αὐτοῦ).

περιποιέω (Hdt. et al.; ins, pap, LXX; EpArist 121) in our lit. only mid. (Thu. et al.; LXX; TestSol 9:2 P; Joseph.) act. fut. 2 pl. περιποιήσετε Ex 22:17; 1 aor. inf. περιποιῆσαι 1 Macc 6:44, ptc. dat. περιποιήσαντι 2 Macc 3:35. Mid.: fut. περιποιήσομαι; 1 aor. περιεποιησάμην; pf. περιπεποίημαι 1 Ch 29, 3. Prim.: 'to cause to remain over and above.'

❶ **to make secure for oneself,** ***save/preserve (for oneself)*** τί *someth.* τὴν ψυχήν *preserve one's own life* **Lk 17:33** (cp. X., Cyr. 4, 4, 10 τὰς ψυχάς=his life).

❷ **to gain possession of someth.,** ***acquire, obtain, gain for oneself*** (Thu. 1, 9, 2; X., Mem. 2, 7, 3; Polyb. 3, 6, 13; 24, 9, 6; Is 43:21; Jos., Bell. 1, 180) τὸν αἰῶνα τοῦτον Hv 1, 1, 8. τὴν ἐκκλησίαν τοῦ θεοῦ, ἣν περιεποιήσατο διὰ τοῦ αἵματος τοῦ ἰδίου **Ac 20:28** (s. Haenchen, AG, ad loc.; Danker, Benefactor, 335f).—Oft. w. a reflexive pron. pleonastically added (X., An. 5, 6, 17 ἑαυτῷ δύναμιν περιποιήσασθαι; Demosth. 19, 240; PTor II, 8, 70 [119 BC]; Pr 7:4) βαθμὸν ἑαυτοῖς καλὸν περιποιοῦνται **1 Ti 3:13.** Cp. ἑαυτῷ μέγα κλέος 1 Cl 54:3. σεαυτῷ ζωήν Hm 3:5. σεαυτῷ δόξαν περισσότεραν s 5, 3, 3. ἑαυτῷ τιμήν m 4, 4, 2. θάνατον ἑαυτοῖς s 6, 5, 7c. Also without an acc., which is easily supplied ἑαυτοῖς π. *enrich oneself* s 9, 26, 2.

❸ **to effect some circumstance,** ***bring (about)*** τινί τι *someth. for someone* (Aristot., Pol. 3, 16; PAmh. 34d, 2 [II BC] πλεῖόν τι περιποιούμενοι τῷ βασιλεῖ; 2 Macc 15:21; Jos., Ant. 14, 386.—Mayser II/1, 1926 p. 101) αὕτη ἡ τρυφὴ ζωὴν περιποιεῖται τῷ ἀνθρώπῳ Hs 6, 5, 7a. τιμωρίας αὐτοῖς περιποιοῦνται ibid. vs. 7b.—M-M. Spicq.

περιποίησις, εως, ἡ (περιποιέω; since Ps.-Pla., Defin. 451c; PTebt 317, 26 [174/75 AD]; PRein 52, 2).

❶ **experience of security,** ***keeping safe, preserving, saving*** (s. περιποιέω 1; so Ps.-Pla., loc. cit. σωτηρία: π. ἀβλαβής; 2 Ch 14:12; TestZeb 2:8) εἰς π. ψυχῆς **Hb 10:39** (opp. εἰς ἀπώλειαν).

❷ **experience of an event of acquisition,** ***gaining, obtaining*** (περιποιέω 2) w. obj. gen. foll. (Alex. Aphr., An. Mant. p. 164, 17 Bruns [1887]) **1 Th 5:9; 2 Th 2:14.**

❸ **that which is acquired,** ***possessing, possession, property*** (PTebt loc. cit.) λαὸς εἰς περιποίησιν *a people that has become (God's own) possession* **1 Pt 2:9** (cp. Mal 3:17). ἀπολύτρωσις τῆς π. **Eph 1:14** (s. ἀπολύτρωσις 2a).—DELG s.v. ποιέω. M-M. Spicq.

περίπτωσις, εως, ἡ (πτῶσις; Stoic. II p. 29; Ammonius Gr. [100 AD] p. 60 Valck.: 'misfortune'; M. Ant. 6, 41, 1 π. τοῦ κακοῦ al.) ***experience,*** in this case an unpleasant one, *calamity* (w. συμφορά) 1 Cl 1:1.—DELG s.v. πίπτω.

περι(ρ)ραίνω fut. 3 sg. περιρρανεῖ LXX. Pass.: pf. ptc. περιρεραμμένος (on the reduplication s. Kühner-Bl. II p. 23; B-D-F §68; Rob. 211f), neut. περιρεραμμένον (Aristoph. et al.; ins; Lev; Num; Philo; Jos., Ant. 9, 123; 13, 243) ***sprinkle around, on all sides*** (Diogenes the Cynic is of the opinion [Diog. L. 6, 42] that no matter how extensive the περι(ρ)ραίνειν, it is impossible to get rid of the ἁμαρτήματα) ἱμάτιον περιρεραμμένον αἵματι *a robe sprinkled on all sides with blood* **Rv 19:13 v.l.** (for βεβαμμένον; other vv.ll. ῥεραντισμένον, ἐρραμένον).—DELG s.v. ῥαίνω. M-M.

περι(ρ)ρήγνυμι 1 aor. ptc. περιρήξας (or περιρρήξας, s. B-D-F §11, 1), inf. περιρῆξαι (TestJob 39:7) (Aeschyl. et al.) ***tear off*** (all around) τὶ *someth.*, esp. clothes (Aeschyl., Sept. 329; Demosth. 19, 197 τὸν χιτωνίσκον; Polyb. 15, 33, 4; Diod. S. 17, 35, 7; 2 Macc 4:38 τοὺς χιτῶνας; Philo, De Jos. 16 [mid.]; cp. Jos., Bell. 2, 601, Ant. 6, 357) περιρήξαντες αὐτῶν τὰ ἱμάτια **Ac 16:22.**—M-M.

περισπάω fut. 3 sg. περισπάσει (Just.); aor. 3 sg. περιέσπασε 2 Km 6:6; impf. pass. 3 sg. περιεσπᾶτο (Eur., X. et al.; ins, pap, LXX, Joseph.; Just., D. 2, 4; s. Phryn. p. 415 Lob.); in our lit. only pass. The primary sense ('draw off from around' Isoc., Ep. 9, 10) is apparent in the foll.

❶ **to be pulled away from a reference point,** ***be pulled/dragged away*** (the act. in Polyb., Diod. S., Dionys. Hal., Plut. et al. The pass. Cebes 33, 3; PTebt 124, 39 [I BC] εἰς ἑτέρας λειτουργίας; Jos., Ant. 5, 46) περισπώμενος ὧδε κἀκεῖσε ἀπὸ τῶν πνευμάτων τῶν πονηρῶν Hm 5, 2, 7 (on the constr. w. ἀπό cp. Epict. 1, 8, 5). Closely related to it is mng.

❷ **to have one's attention directed from one thing to another,** ***become*** or ***be distracted, quite busy, overburdened*** (Polyb. 4, 10, 3; Diod. S. 2, 29, 5; Epict. 3, 9, 19; Jos., Bell. 1, 232 al.; UPZ 59, 30 [168 BC]; PTebt 37, 15 [I BC]; POxy 743, 36 [I BC]) περί τι *with* or *by someth.* (Polyb. 3, 105, 1; Diod. S. 1, 74) περὶ πολλὴν διακονίαν **Lk 10:40.** περὶ τὸν πλοῦτον Hs 2:5. περὶ τὰς πραγματείας 4:5.—M-M.

περισσεία, ας, ἡ (s. next entry; Herodian, Gr. I 291, 9 al.; schol. on Nicander, Ther. 266) **that which is beyond the regular or expected amount,** ***surplus, abundance*** (IG V/1, 550, 6 π. χρημάτων; VII, 3221, 5 [ἐκ τῆς] περισσήας; ins fr. Syria: BCH 21, 1897 p. 65. In LXX only several times in Eccl.—Dssm.,

LO 66 [LAE 80]) ἡ π. τῆς χάριτος **Ro 5:17.** ἡ π. τῆς χαρᾶς **2 Cor 8:2.** μεγαλυνθῆναι εἰς π. *be greatly enlarged* **10:15.** π. κακίας *all the evil prevailing* (around you) **Js 1:21.** τὸ τῆς π. μου *the excess (of my offerings)* i. e. Joachim brought gifts beyond cultic requirements for the benefit of the people GJs 1:1 (v.l. περιουσίας).—DELG s.v. περί. M-M. TW.

περίσσευμα, ατος, τό (s. prec. entry)—**❶ a condition of great plenty,** ***abundance, fullness*** (Eratosth. [III BC], Cat. 44 Olivieri; Plut., Mor. 310c; 962f.—The LXX of Eccl 2:15 has the word in line 6, but this line is lacking in the Hebr. text, and hence is prob. a Christian addition: AMcNeile, An Introd. to Eccl 1904, 157; PKatz, TLZ 63, '38, 34) **2 Cor 8:14ab** (opp. ὑστέρημα). ἐκ (τοῦ) περισσεύματος (τῆς) καρδίας *from the abundance of the heart, what the heart is full of* **Mt 12:34; Lk 6:45.**

❷ that which remains above and beyond, ***what remains*** (Artem. 3, 52 'scraps') περισσεύματα κλασμάτων *pieces that were left* (apparently out of the total number of pieces that were broken off in the course of distribution, not scraps left by the diners) **Mk 8:8.**—DELG s.v. περί.

περισσεύω impf. ἐπερίσσευον; fut. περισσεύσω; 1 aor. ἐπερίσσευσα (on the augment B-D-F §69, 4; Mlt-H. 192). Pass.: 1 fut. περισσευθήσομαι (s. prec. two entries; Hes., Thu. et al.; ins, pap, LXX, Philo, Joseph.).

❶ intr., **to be in abundance,** ***abound*****—ⓐ** of things—**α.** *be more than enough, be left over* (SIG 672, 19 [II BC]; Theophil.: 733 fgm. 1 Jac. [in Alex. Polyhist.: Eus., PE 9, 34, 19]; Jos., Ant. 3, 229, Vi. 333) τὰ περισσεύσαντα κλάσματα **J 6:12.** ὁ χρόνος ὁ περισσεύων εἰς τὴν παρουσίαν αὐτοῦ *the time that remains before his coming* Hs 5, 5, 3. οἱ περισσεύοντες *the others, the remainder* 9, 8, 7; w. gen. οἱ π. αὐτῶν vs. 4; strengthened οἱ λοιποὶ οἱ περισσεύσαντες 9, 9, 4. τὸ περισσεῦον *what was left over* τῶν κλασμάτων **Mt 14:20; 15:37** (cp. Jos., Ant. 13, 55). περισσεύει μοί τι *I leave someth.* (cp. Tob 4:16) **J 6:13.** τὸ περισσεῦσαν αὐτοῖς κλασμάτων *what they left in the way of fragments* **Lk 9:17.**

β. *be present in abundance* (X., Cyr. 6, 2, 30; PFlor 242, 2; PLond II, 418, 4 p. 303 [c. 346 AD] ἵνα περισσεύῃ ὁ φόβος τοῦ θεοῦ ἐν σοί) **2 Cor 1:5b; Phil 1:26** ἐὰν μὴ περισσεύσῃ ὑμῶν ἡ δικαιοσύνη πλεῖον τῶν γραμματέων *unless your righteousness far surpasses that of the scribes* **Mt 5:20** (for the omission of 'that' in the Gk. text cp. Maximus Tyr. 15, 8d: their life is different in no respect σκωλήκων=fr. 'that' of the worms). περισσεύει τί τινι (cp. Thu. 2, 65, 13) *someone has someth. in abundance* (Tob 4:16) ISm 9:2. τὸ περισσεῦόν τινι (opp. ὑστέρησις) *someone's abundance* **Mk 12:44.** (Opp. ὑστέρημα) **Lk 21:4.** ἐν τῷ περισσεύειν τινί *in this, namely that one has an abundance* **12:15.** περισσεύει τι εἴς τινα *someth. comes* or *is available to someone in great abundance:* ἡ χάρις τοῦ θεοῦ εἰς τοὺς πολλοὺς ἐπερίσσευσεν **Ro 5:15.** περισσεύει τὰ παθήματα τοῦ Χριστοῦ εἰς ἡμᾶς *we share abundantly in Christ's sufferings* **2 Cor 1:5a.**

γ. *be extremely rich* or *abundant, overflow* **2 Cor 9:12.** εἰ ἡ ἀλήθεια τοῦ θεοῦ ἐν τῷ ἐμῷ ψεύσματι ἐπερίσσευσεν εἰς τὴν δόξαν αὐτοῦ *if by my falsehood the truthfulness of God has shown itself to be supremely great, to his glory* **Ro 3:7.** The thing in which the wealth consists is added in the dat. (Philistion [IV BC], fgm. 9 ln. 13 Wellmann πάσαις τ. ἀρεταῖς περιττεύει [in Athen. 3, 83, 115e]) π. δόξῃ *be extremely rich in glory* **2 Cor 3:9** (v.l. ἐν δόξῃ). In oxymoron ἡ πτωχεία αὐτῶν ἐπερίσσευσεν εἰς τὸ πλοῦτος τῆς ἁπλότητος αὐτῶν *their poverty has overflowed into the wealth of their ingenuousness* **8:2** (s. ἁπλότης 1; NRSV et al. *liberality*).

δ. *grow* αἱ ἐκκλησίαι ἐπερίσσευον τῷ ἀριθμῷ καθ' ἡμέραν **Ac 16:5.** ἵνα ἡ ἀγάπη ὑμῶν ἔτι μᾶλλον καὶ μᾶλλον περισσεύῃ ἐν ἐπιγνώσει **Phil 1:9.**

ⓑ of persons—**α.** *have an abundance, abound, be rich* τινός *of* or *in someth.* (B-D-F §172; Rob. 510) ἄρτων **Lk 15:17 v.l.** (the text has the mid. περισσεύονται [unless it should be pass., s. 2b below], but that is prob. not orig.; s. Jülicher, Gleichn. 346). παντὸς χαρίσματος IPol 2:2. Also ἔν τινι Dg 5:13 (opp. ὑστερεῖσθαι). ἐν τῇ ἐλπίδι **Ro 15:13.** Abs. (opp. ὑστερεῖσθαι) περισσεύομεν *we have more* (divine approval) **1 Cor 8:8.** ζητεῖτε ἵνα περισσεύητε *strive to excel* **14:12.** Cp. **Phil 4:12a** (opp. ταπεινοῦσθαι), vs. **12b** (opp. ὑστερεῖσθαι). ἀπέχω πάντα καὶ περισσεύω *I have received full payment, and have more than enough* vs. **18.** π. εἰς πᾶν ἔργον *have ample means for every enterprise* **2 Cor 9:8b.**

β. *be outstanding, be prominent, excel* (1 Macc 3:30) ἔν τινι *in someth.* ἐν τῷ ἔργῳ τοῦ κυρίου **1 Cor 15:58.** Cp. **2 Cor 8:7ab; Col 2:7.** Abs. w. μᾶλλον added *progress more and more* **1 Th 4:1, 10.**

❷ trans. (Athen. 2, 42b) **to cause someth. to exist in abundance,** ***cause to abound*****—ⓐ** of things that one greatly increases, τὴν εὐχαριστίαν **2 Cor 4:15.** τὶ εἴς τινα *grant someth. to someone richly* **9:8a; Eph 1:8** (ἧς by attraction of the relat. for ἥν). Pass. w. dat. of pers. ὅστις γὰρ ἔχει, δοθήσεται αὐτῷ καὶ περισσευθήσεται *to the one who has* (more) *will be given, and that person will have a great abundance* **Mt 13:12.** Cp. **25:29.**

ⓑ of persons who receive someth. in great abundance ὑμᾶς ὁ κύριος περισσεύσαι τῇ ἀγάπῃ *may the Lord cause you to abound in love* **1 Th 3:12.** πόσοι μίσθιοι περισσεύονται ἄρτων **Lk 15:17** *how many day laborers get more than enough bread* (s. 1bα above).—DELG s.v. περί. M-M. EDNT. TW.

περισσός, ή, όν (cp. πέριξ and s. three next entries; Hes., Hdt.+. Prim.: 'exceeding the usual number or size'; Gignac I 146)

❶ pert. to that which is not ordinarily encountered, ***extraordinary, remarkable*** (Pla., Apol. 20c οὐδὲν τῶν ἄλλων περισσὸν πραγματεύεσθαι; BGU 417, 22 περισσὸν ποιήσω=I am going to do someth. extraordinary; En 102:7) τί περισσὸν ποιεῖτε; *what are you doing that is remarkable?* **Mt 5:47** (cp. Plut., Mor. 233a τί οὖν μέγα ποιεῖς; what, then, are you doing that is so great?—ELombard, L'Ordinaire et l'Extraordinaire [Mt 5:47]: RTP 15, 1927, 169–86). Subst. τὸ περισσόν *the advantage* (WSchubart, Der Gnomon des Idios Logos 1919, 102 [II AD]) τὸ π. τοῦ Ἰουδαίου *the advantage of the Judean (Jew)* **Ro 3:1** (s. Ἰουδαῖος 2a). LCerfaux, Le privilège d'Israël sel. s. Paul: ETL 17, '40, 5–26.

❷ pert. to being extraordinary in amount, ***abundant, profuse*****—ⓐ** *going beyond what is necessary* περισσὸν ἔχειν *have (someth.) in abundance* **J 10:10** (cp. X., Oec. 20, 1 οἱ μὲν περισσὰ ἔχουσιν, οἱ δὲ οὐδὲ τὰ ἀναγκαῖα δύνανται πορίζεσθαι; Plut., Mor. 523d). For περισσότερον **J 10:10** P^{75} s. περισσότερος c.

ⓑ *superfluous, unnecessary* (trag. et al.; cp. 2 Macc 12:44; TestJob 47:1) περισσόν μοί ἐστιν τὸ γράφειν ὑμῖν *it is unnecessary for me to write to you* **2 Cor 9:1** (Mitt-Wilck. I/2, 238 II, 4 περισσὸν ἡγοῦμαι διεξοδέστερον ὑμῖν γράφειν). περισσὸν ἡγοῦμαι *I consider it superfluous* (Appian, Prooem. 13 §50; Jos., Ant. 3, 215; cp. Philo, Agr. 59) Dg 2:10. W. ἄχρηστος 4:2.

❸ in the comparative sense; περισσός together w. its adv. and comp. is a colloquial substitute for μᾶλλον, μάλιστα as well as for πλείων, πλεῖστος (B-D-F §60, 3; Rob. 279; KKrumbacher, ByzZ 17, 1908, 233). τό περισσὸν τούτων *whatever is more than this, whatever goes beyond this* **Mt 5:37** (on the gen. s. B-D-F §185, 1; Rob. 660).—ἐκ περισσοῦ (Περὶ ὕψους 34, 2; Vi.

Aesopi I G 43 P.; Dositheus 40, 4; Da 3:22 Theod.) **Mk 6:51** s. ἐκ 6c and λίαν a.—DELG s.v. περί. M-M. TW.

περισσότερος, τέρα, ον comp. of περισσός (s. prec. entry; since Hdt.; Pla., Apol. 20c οὐδὲν τῶν ἄλλων περιττότερον πραγματεύεσθαι; PFlor 127, 22; TestAbr B 8 p. 113, 11 [Stone p. 74]; Da 4:36 Theod. μεγαλωσύνη περισσοτέρα) **pert. to being beyond a standard of abundance,** ***greater, more, even more***

ⓐ used w. a subst. ἀγαθά 1 Cl 61:3 (s. ἀγαθός 1bα). τιμή **1 Cor 12:23a, 24;** Hm 4, 4, 2. δόξα s 5, 3, 3. κρίμα *more severe punishment* **Mt 23:13 v.l.; Mk 12:40; Lk 20:47.** εὐσχημοσύνη **1 Cor 12:23b.** λύπη *excessive sorrow* **2 Cor 2:7.**

ⓑ w. focus on incremental aspect περισσότερον *even more* (=more than the πολύ that was entrusted to him) **Lk 12:48.** W. gen. of comparison περισσότερον αὐτῶν ἐκοπίασα **1 Cor 15:10.**—περισσότερόν τί *someth. more* or *further* (Lucian, Tyrannic. 3) **Lk 12:4** (s. on this KKöhler, ZNW 18, 1918, 140f); **2 Cor 10:8.** W. gen. of comparison (Jos., Ant. 5, 23; 8, 410) περισσότερόν ἐστιν πάντων τῶν ὁλοκαυτωμάτων *is much more than all whole burnt offerings* **Mk 12:33.** περισσότερον προφήτου **Mt 11:9; Lk 7:26** might be taken as a neut. *someth. greater than a prophet.* But it may be understood as a masc. one *who is more than a prophet* (cp. Plut., Mor. 57f περιττότερος φρονήσει; Gen 49:3 Sym. οὐκ ἔσῃ περισσότερος).

ⓒ the neut. sing. as adv. (Hdt. 2, 129 al.; Vett. Val. p. 74, 6; PFlor 127, 22; BGU 380, 10; PGM 13, 12) ζωὴν π. ἔχωσιν **J 10:10** P[75]. π. ἐπιδεῖξαι *point out even more clearly* **Hb 6:17.** π. ἔτι κατάδηλόν ἐστιν *it is even more evident* **7:15.** Strengthened *so much more* **Mk 7:36.**—B. 924. DELG s.v. περί. M-M s.v. περισσός.

περισσοτέρως adv. of περισσότερος (s. two prec. entries; Diod. S. 13, 108; Athen. 5, 19f; PGiss 25, 12 [II AD]).

❶ ***(even) more*** comp. **Mk 15:14 v.l.;** *to a much greater degree, far more, far greater* (than Paul's opponents) **2 Cor 11:23;** (than those of his own age) **Gal 1:14.** (Opp. ἧσσον) **2 Cor 12:15** (ἀγαπάω 1aα). Intensifying *so much (the) more* **Phil 1:14; Hb 2:1; 13:19.**

❷ ***especially,*** elative, **2 Cor 1:12; 2:4; 7:15;** *(all) the more* **1 Th 2:17.** Strengthened περισσοτέρως μᾶλλον *even much more* **2 Cor 7:13.**—DELG s.v. περί. M-M.

περισσῶς adv. **marker of exceptionally high degree on a scale of intensity,** ***exceedingly, beyond measure, very*** (s. three prec. entries; Eur., Hdt. et al.; Polyb. 1, 29, 7; 32, 15, 4; Athen. 11 p. 501d; PTebt 488; LXX; Theod.; Philo, Det. Pot. Ins. 15 al.; Jos., Ant. 1, 258) **Ac 26:11.**—Comp. (περισσός 3) *more, even more* περισσῶς ἔκραζον *they cried out even louder* **Mt 27:23;** cp. **Mk 15:14.** π. ἐξεπλήσσοντο *they were even more astounded* **10:26.**—M-M.

περιστέλλω fut. περιστελῶ; 2 aor. sg. περιέστειλες (Tob 12:13 ℵ), impv. 2 sg. περίστειλον Sir 38:16; 2 aor. pass. subj. 2 sg. περισταλῇς Ezk 29:5, ptc. neut. περισταλέν (TestJob) (Hom. et al.; Herm. Wr. 492, 21 Sc.; PGM 4, 3138; LXX; PsSol 16:10; TestJob 52:11; Jos., Ant. 19, 237, C. Ap. 2, 269) **to cover all around,** ***clothe*** τινά *someone* of apparel (Diod. S. 19, 11, 7 τὸν ἄνδρα περιέστειλεν; Jos., Ant. 17, 59) B 3:4 (Is 58:8).

περιστερά, ᾶς, ἡ (Hdt., Aristoph.+) a bird of the family Columbidae (Aristot., HA 562b, 3–7 differentiates from τρυγών [turtle-dove] and φάττα: s. also 593a, 16. The rock-dove is the species generally seen in public places.) freq. glossed either as ***pigeon*** or ***dove*** (but the use of the latter term in preference to the former suggests a difference that cannot precisely be determined from usage in our texts), used for sacrifice, hence sold in the temple **Mt 21:12; Mk 11:15; J 2:14, 16.** Dalman, Arbeit VII (s. οἰκία 1a end).—On the δύο νοσσοὶ περιστερῶν **Lk 2:24** s. νοσσός. The pigeon which, fr. the viewpoint of natural science in ancient times, has no bile, was for the early Christians the symbol of all kinds of virtues (s. WBauer, D. Leben Jesu 1909, 117): ἀκέραιοι ὡς αἱ περιστεραί **Mt 10:16;** cp. IPol 2:2. Hence the Holy Spirit, in appearing at Jesus' baptism, took the form of a pigeon/dove (WTelfer, The Form of a Dove: JTS 29, 1928, 238–42; LKeck, NTS 17, '70/71, 41–67 'dove-like descent') **Mt 3:16; Mk 1:10; Lk 3:22; J 1:32;** GEb 18, 36.—HUsener, Das Weihnachtsfest[2] 1911, 56ff; HGressmann, Die Sage v. d. Taufe Jesu und d. vorderoriental. Taubengöttin: ARW 20, 1920/21, 1–40; 323–59.—On the symbolism cp. use of Gen 1:2 at Qumran (4Q521, 2:6), s. DAllison, BAR 8, '92, 58–60; JMarcus, NTS 41, '95, 512–21. ὡσεὶ π. (of Mary) GJs 8:1. π. ἐξῆλθεν ἀπὸ τῆς ῥάβδου *a pigeon went forth from (Joseph's) staff* 9:1 (symbolic of the birth of a king). In MPol 16:1 the rdg. περὶ στύρακα, a conjectural insertion by Wordsworth, generated some undeserved approval. The Gk. mss. have περιστερὰ καί, which is bracketed by Bihlmeyer (s. JKleist, tr. '48, note ad loc.). The concept of the pigeon as representing the soul underlies this (cp., in a way, Quint. Symyrn. 8, 202f ψυχὴ δι' ἕλκεος ἐξεποτήθη ἐκ μελέων=the soul flew out of his body through the wound).—GWeicker, D. Seelenvogel 1902, 26f; HGünter, Die christl. Legende des Abendlandes 1910, 13; 45; 86; 142; 148; 191; FSühling, D. Taube als. relig. Symbol im christl. Altertum 1930.—Kl. Pauly V 534–36; BHHW III 1934. SEG XLII, 1789 (ins and bibliog. on pigeons, incl. their religious functions; s. FChamoux, CRAI '92, 623–42).—DELG. M-M. TW.

περισχίζω 1 aor. mid. περιεσχισάμην (mid. since Hdt., Pla.; also Ezk 47:15; 48:1; TestZeb 4:5; Mel, P. 17, 116 al.; pap) **tear someth. all around,** ***tear, rip*** περιεσχίσαντο ἐπάνωθεν ἕως κάτω *they rent (their garments) from top to bottom* GJs 24:3 (s. deStrycker p. 266 n. 4 and p. 240).

περισῴζω (X. et al.; 1 Km 30:17 v.l.; Ps 114:4 Aq.; ViOb 3 [p. 82, 6 Sch.]; Joseph.) ***rescue (from death)*** **Mk 6:51 v.l.**—DELG s.v. σῶς.

περιτειχίζω 1 aor. περιετείχισα; pf. pass. περιτετείχισμαι (Thu., Aristoph. et al.; pap, LXX; Jos., Bell. 6, 323).

❶ **to construct a solid wall around a place,** ***surround with a wall,*** of a city περιτετειχισμένη κύκλῳ *walled around* Hs 9, 12, 5 (BGU 993 III, 1 [II BC] τόπος περιτετειχισμένος).

❷ **to surround with someth. that envelopes,** ***surround,*** fig. ext. of 1: τούτοις (i.e. ἀγγέλοις) περιτετείχισται ὁ κύριος s 9, 12, 6. Of the sea of flames coming fr. the pyre κύκλῳ περιετείχισε τὸ σῶμα τοῦ μάρτυρος *completely surrounded the martyr's body* MPol 15:2 (w. κύκλῳ as Thu. 2, 78).—DELG s.v. τεῖχος.

περιτέμνω 2 aor. περιέτεμον; pf. περιτέτμηκα LXX. Pass.: 1 fut. περιτμηθήσομαι; 1 aor. περιετμήθην; pf. 3 sg. περιτέτμηται (Just., D. 28, 4); ptc. περιτετμημένος LXX; plpf. 3 sg. περιετέτμητο (Just., D. 46, 3) (Hom. et al.) 'to cut off around'; in our lit. and the LXX, somet. fig., only in the sense: to cut off the foreskin of the male genital organ, ***circumcise*** (so somet. as act., somet. as mid. ['circumcise oneself'], since Hdt. 2, 36, 2; 2, 104, 1 [of the Egyptians and several other peoples], also Diod. S. 1, 28, 3; 1, 55, 5; 3, 32, 4 [Egyptians, Colchians, Ἰουδαῖοι]; Ptolemaeus, Περὶ Ἡρώδου τ. βασιλέως [I AD]: 199 fgm. 1 Jac.; Strabo 17, 2, 5; Philo Bybl. [c. 100 AD]: 790 fgm.

2, 33 p. 812, 8 Jac. [in Eus., PE 1, 10, 33]; Sallust. 9 p. 18, 17; PLond I, 24, 12f p. 32 [163 BC]; PTebt 291, 33; 292, 7; 20; 293, 12; 14; 19; Mitt-Wilck. I/2, 77 I, 11; III, 11 [149 AD]; OdeSol 11:2; TestLevi 6:3; Philo Alex.; Joseph.; Just.) in our lit. prob. only in act. and pass.

ⓐ lit., w. acc. of pers. **Lk 1:59; 2:21** (s. Schwyzer II 372); **J 7:22; Ac 7:8; 15:5; 16:3; 21:21;** B 9:8 (Gen 17:23ff). Pass. *be circumcised, have oneself circumcised* (Orig., C. Cels. 1, 22, 4; Did., Gen. 75, 6; B-D-F §314) **Ac 15:1, 24 v.l.; 1 Cor 7:18b; Gal 2:3** (Ptolemaeus, Περὶ Ἡρώδου τ. βασιλέως: 199 Jac. [I AD] Ἰδουμαῖοι ἀναγκασθέντες περιτέμνεσθαι. S. SBelkin, JBL 54, '35, 43–47); **5:2f; 6:12, 13b.** οἱ περιτεμνόμενοι *those who have themselves circumcised* vs. **13a.** περιτετμημένος *circumcised, in the state of being circumcised* **1 Cor 7:18a; Gal 6:13a v.l.**

ⓑ fig.—**α.** of baptism περιετμήθητε περιτομῇ ἀχειροποιήτῳ **Col 2:11** (OCullmann, D. Tauflehre des NT '48, 50–63).

β. Barnabas maintains strongly that the scripture does not require a physical circumcision: περιέτεμεν ἡμῶν τὴν καρδίαν 9:1a. The κύριος says περιτμήθητε τὰς καρδίας ὑμῶν vs. 1b. Obviously Jer 4:4 (cp. Dt 10:16; OdeSol 11:2) is meant; B comes closer to it in περιτμήθητε τῷ κυρίῳ ὑμῶν *let yourselves be circumcised for your Lord* 9:5a, and in the explanation of it περιτμήθητε τὴν σκληροκαρδίαν ὑμῶν vs. 5b. What is true of the heart is also true of the ears περιέτεμεν ἡμῶν τὰς ἀκοάς 9:4. Cp. 10:12. In 9:6 it is acknowledged that circumcision is somet. justified thus: περιτέτμηται ὁ λαὸς εἰς σφραγῖδα, and it is explained that Ἀβραὰμ ἐν πνεύματι προβλέψας εἰς τὸν Ἰησοῦν περιέτεμεν vs. 7.—Schürer I 536ff–40; Dssm., B 149ff [BS 151–3]; UWilcken, HGunkel and PWendland, APF 2, 1903, 4–31; WOtto, Priester u. Tempel im hellenist. Ägypten I 1905, 213ff; JMatthes, De Besnijdenis: Teylers Theol. Tijdschrift 6, 1908, 163–91; FDölger, Sphragis 1911, 51ff; Billerb. IV 1928, 23–40; FBryk, D. Beschneidung b. Mann u. Weib '31; JSasson, JBL 85, '66, 473–76; JLieu, Circumcision, Women, and Salvation: NTS 40, '94, 358–70.—RAC II, 159–69; BHHW I 223–25; TRE V 714–24. New Docs 3, 81; M-M. EDNT. TW.

περιτίθημι fut. 3 sg. περιθήσει LXX; 1 aor. περιέθηκα; 2 aor. impv. 2 pl. περίθετε, ptc. περιθείς. Mid.: fut. 3 sg. περιθήσεται Wsd 5:18; aor. περιεθέμην LXX. Pass.: impf. περιετιθέμην; 1 aor. περιετέθην; pf. ptc. περιτεθειμένος (Hom. [in tmesis]+).

❶ ***put/place around/on*** τί τινι *someth. around someone* or *someth.* φραγμὸν αὐτῷ (=τῷ ἀμπελῶνι) περιέθηκεν *a fence around a vineyard* **Mt 21:33; Mk 12:1** (the dat. is to be supplied here, as Is 5:2.—SIG 898, 7f. τὸν περίβολον ὃν περιέθηκε τῷ τεμένει). αὐτῷ περιετίθετο τὰ ὄργανα *the wooden instruments* (or *firewood*) *were placed around him* MPol 13:3 (Appian, Iber. §132 ξύλα περιθέντες αὐτῇ. Likew. Appian, Mithrid. 108 §512 ξύλα περιθέντες in order to ignite someth.). The bars or limits set for the sea 1 Cl 20:6 (cp. Job 38:10). σπόγγον καλάμῳ *put a sponge on a reed* **Mt 27:48; Mk 15:36;** cp. **J 19:29.** *Put* or *lay* pieces of clothing *around, on someone* (Herodian 3, 7, 5 χλαμύδα; OGI 383, 137; PSI 64, 17 [I BC]; Job 39:20; Jos., Ant. 6, 184; TestLevi 8:5, 6) χλαμύδα περιέθηκαν αὐτῷ **Mt 27:28.** Esp. of headbands, wreaths etc. (Ps.-Pla., Alcib. 2, 151a στέφανόν τινι. Several times LXX; PsSol 2:21; TestLevi 8:9; Philo, Mos. 2, 243) **Mk 15:17; Lk 23:37 v.l.** (RBorger, TRu 52, '87, 33f). κρεῖττον ἦν αὐτῷ περιτεθῆναι μύλον 1 Cl 46:8.—Var. prep. constrs. take the place of the dat.: π. τὸ ἔριον ἐπὶ ξύλον *put the wool on a stick* B 8:1 (cp. Gen 41:42). π. τὸ ἔριον περὶ τὴν κεφαλήν 7:8 (a quot. that cannot be identified w. certainty.—On π. περὶ τὴν κεφ. cp. Pla., Rep. 3, 406d).

❷ **to cause a state to exist relative to an object,** ***put on/around, grant/bestow*** τί τινι *someth. to/on someone* ext. of 1 w. image of investiture in force (Hdt.+; SIG 985, 51; LXX; Philo, Aet. M. 41; Just., A II, 11, 7) τιμὴν π. w. the dat. *show honor* (OGI 331, 23; BGU 1141, 19 [14 BC]; Esth 1:20; cp. also Thu. 6, 89, 2 ἀτιμίαν τινὶ π.) **1 Cor 12:23.** περιθεὶς τὴν εὐπρέπειαν τῇ κτίσει αὐτοῦ Hv 1, 3, 4.—M-M.

περιτομή, ῆς, ἡ (s. s.v. περιτέμνω) 'circumcision' of the foreskin (Agatharchides [II BC] FHG 61; Timagenes [I BC]: 88 fgm. 5 Jac.; Strabo 16, 2, 37 [in the pl.]; PTebt 314, 5 [II AD]; Gen 17:13; Ex 4:25f; OdeSol 11:3; Artapanus [II BC]: 726 fgm. 3, 10 Jac. [in Eus., PE 9, 27, 10]; Philo, Spec. Leg. 1, 8; 9; Jos., Ant. 1, 192; 214 [here in pl.], C. Ap. 2, 137; 143; TestLevi 6:6; Just.).

❶ ***circumcision***—ⓐ *circumcision* as a cultic rite (Iren. 1, 18, 3 [Harv. I 172, 16]; Orig., C. Cels. 5, 47, 1; Did., Gen. 237, 28) **J 7:22.** διαθήκη περιτομῆς *covenant* or *decree of circumcision* **Ac 7:8.** εἰ περιτομὴν ἔτι κηρύσσω **Gal 5:11.**—B 9:4a, 7. Cp. **Phil 3:5** (s. ὀκταήμερος); Dg 4:1 which can also be classed under

ⓑ pass. *the state of having been circumcised*=τὸ περιτετμῆσθαι (Diod. S. 3, 32, 4; Jos., Ant. 12, 241, C. Ap. 2, 137) **Ro 2:25ab, 26; 3:1; 1 Cor 7:19; Gal 5:6; 6:15.** ἡ ἐν τῷ φανερῷ ἐν σαρκὶ περιτομή **Ro 2:28.** διὰ περιτομῆς vs. **27** (s. διά A 3c). περιτομὴν ἔχειν IPhld 6:1. περιτομὴν λαμβάνειν **J 7:23.** εἶναι ἐν περιτομῇ **Ro 4:10a;** cp. vs. **10b,** where ὄντι is to be supplied. On vs. **11** s. σημεῖον 1. οἱ Αἰγύπτιοι ἐν π. εἰσίν B 9:6.

ⓒ fig., of spiritual circumcision (Just., D. 14, 4 δευτέρας . . . περιτομῆς; s. περιτέμνω bβ) περιτομὴ . . . οὐ σαρκὸς B 9:4b. περιτομὴ καρδίας (s. περιτέμνω bβ) **Ro 2:29** (cp. OdeSol 11:1f; JBarclay, NTS 44, '98, 536–56 [Paul and Philo]). περιτομὴ ἀχειροποίητος **Col 2:11a**=περ. τοῦ Χριστοῦ **11b,** by which baptism is meant (s. vs. **12**).

❷ ***one who is circumcised,*** abstr. for concr. (cp. e.g., Appian, Bell. Civ. 3, 61 §249 ἐπεξέρχεσθαι τὸν φόνον=proceed against the murder [i.e. the murderers]), usu. pl. *those who are circumcised.*

ⓐ lit., of *Judeans* **Ro 3:30; 4:9; Col 3:11** (opp. ἀκροβυστία='non-Judeans' in all three).—**Ro 4:12a; 15:8; Gal 2:7–9.** οἱ λεγόμενοι ἀκροβυστία ὑπὸ τῆς λεγομένης περιτομῆς ἐν σαρκὶ χειροποιήτου *those who are called the 'uncircumcision' by the so-called 'circumcision'* (whose circumcision is) *a purely physical one* (and is) *made by hands* **Eph 2:11.** οἱ οὐκ ἐκ περιτομῆς μόνον *who not only belong to the 'circumcised'* **Ro 4:12b.**—οἱ ἐκ περιτομῆς πιστοί *those of the 'circumcised' who believe*=the Judean (Jewish) Christians **Ac 10:45.** Likew. οἱ ἐκ περιτομῆς (ὄντες) **11:2; Gal 2:12; Col 4:11; Tit 1:10** (cp. ὁ ἐκ π. . . . ὁ ἀπὸ ἐθνῶν Did., Gen. 182, 19).—EEllis, TU 102, '68, 390–99.

ⓑ fig. of believers in Jesus Christ (as truly circumcised people of the promise) ἡμεῖς ἐσμεν ἡ περιτομή **Phil 3:3.**—For lit. s. under περιτέμνω.—DELG s.v. τέμνω. M-M. TW.

περιτρέπω (Lysias, Pla. et al.; Wsd 5:23; Philo) **to turn from one state to its opposite,** ***turn*** τινὰ εἴς τι (BGU 1831, 8 [51 BC] εἰς ἄπορον; Vett. Val. 250, 9f; Jos., Ant. 9, 72 τοὺς παρόντας εἰς χαρὰν περιέτρεψε; Tat. 22, 1 εἰς ἀδοξίαν.—Niese reads the simplex in Jos., Ant. 2, 293) τὰ πολλά σε γράμματα εἰς μανίαν περιτρέπει **Ac 26:24** (s. μανία and cp. the expression εἰς μανίαν περιτρέπειν in Lucian, Abdic. 30 and Vi. Aesopi I G 55 P.).—M-M.

περιτρέχω impf. περιέτρεχον; 2 aor. περιέδραμον, ptc. περιδραμών (Hom. et al.).

❶ **to be in motion around,** ***run/move around*** w. the acc. of the thing or pers. one moves around (Hdt. 8, 128; Aristoph., Ran. 193 τὴν λίμνην κύκλῳ; Athen. 5, 208b; PFlor 120, 7; GrBar 6:2) ἄγγελοι περιέτρεχον αὐτοὺς ἐκεῖσε *angels were moving about them there* ApcPt 5:18. ὧδε κἀκεῖσε περιτρ. κύκλῳ τῆς πύλης *run here and there around the gate* Hs 9, 3, 1.

❷ **to be in rapid motion here and there in an area,** ***run about, go about in*** (Cebes 14, 1; Am 8:12; Jer 5:1 ἐν ταῖς ὁδοῖς) w. acc. (Aristoph., Thesmoph. 657 τὴν πύκνα πᾶσαν) ὅλην τὴν χώραν **Mk 6:55.** ἐν τοῖς πρόβασι (v.l. προβάτοις) π. *run about among the sheep* Hs 6, 1, 6.—M-M.

περιφέρω aor. ptc. fem. acc. sg. περιενέγκασαν 2 Macc 7:27 ***carry about, carry here and there***—ⓐ lit., w. acc. (Eur., Pla. et al.; Plut., Mor. 331c; SIG 1169, 65f, a spearhead in the face; Josh 24:33a; 2 Macc 7:27; TestSol; Ar. 5:3; Tat.) the sick **Mk 6:55.** τὰ δεσμά *the chains* IEph 11:2; cp. IMg 1:2; ITr 12:2. τὴν νέκρωσιν τοῦ Ἰησοῦ ἐν τῷ σώματι π. **2 Cor 4:10** (s. νέκρωσις 1).

ⓑ fig. (Epict. 2, 8, 12 θεὸν π.=carry God about within oneself; 2, 16, 33; TestSol 12:3 C οἴησιν ('opinion') περιφερόμενοι; Philo, Omnis Prob. Lib. 117 τὴν ἀρετήν; POxy 1664, 7 a dear person in one's heart) τὸ ὄνομα *carry the name* (of Christ, or of a Christian) *about* (prob. as wandering preachers) IEph 7:1. The pass., in vivid imagery (Jos., Ant. 19, 46 διὰ λογισμῶν περιφερόμενος) περιφερόμενοι παντὶ ἀνέμῳ τῆς διδασκαλίας *carried here and there by* (any and) *every wind of doctrine* **Eph 4:14** (or does περιφέρεσθαι mean *turn around* here, and is the idea of a weathervane in the background?); cp. **Hb 13:9 v.l.**—M-M.

περιφρονέω aor. 3 sg. περιεφρόνησε ApcrEzk (Epiph. 70, 7) **to have disdain for,** ***disregard, look down on, despise*** (so since Thu. 1, 25, 4; POxy 71 II, 16; ApcrEzk [s. above]; Jos., Ant. 4, 260) w. gen. (Ps.-Pla., Axioch. 372a τοῦ ζῆν; Plut., Thes. 1 [1, 5], Per. 169 [31, 1], Mor. 762e; 4 Macc 6:9; 7:16; 14:1) **Tit 2:15.**—DELG s.v. φρήν. M-M. TW. Spicq.

περιχαρής, ές (χαίρω; Soph., Hdt. et al.; 3 Macc 5:44; TestSol; Philo, Rer. Div. Her. 3; Jos., Ant. 7, 206) ***very glad*** π. γενέσθαι (Diod. S. 20, 76, 6 π. γενόμενος; Chariton 6, 5, 1; Ael. Aristid. 50, 50 K.=26 p. 517 D.; Job 3:22; 29:22; TestSol 1:8; Jos., Ant. 1, 284; 16, 358; PSI 887, 5 [VI AD]) Hv 3, 12, 2; foll. by the inf. in the gen. v 3, 8, 1.—DELG s.v. χαίρω IB.

περίχωρος, ον pert. to being around an area, ***neighboring*** (Gen 19:28) quite predom. used as a subst. (οἱ περίχωροι 'the neighbors' Demosth. 19, 266; Plut., Cat. Maj. 351 [25, 3], Eum. 593 [15, 13]; Aelian, NA 10, 46; Cass. Dio 36, 33) ἡ π. (sc. γῆ; B-D-F §241, 1) *region around, neighborhood* (LXX, which also has τὸ περίχωρον and τὰ περίχωρα. Loanw. in rabb.) **Mt 14:35; Mk 6:55 v.l.; Lk 4:14, 37; 7:17; Ac 14:6;** 1 Cl 11:1; GPt 9:34. Used w. gen.: of a river, whose neighboring region to the right and left is designated as ἡ π.: ἡ π. τοῦ Ἰορδάνου (Gen 13:10f) **Mt 3:5** (s. below); **Lk 3:3.** ἡ περίχωρος τῶν Γερασηνῶν *the Gerasenes and the people living around them* **Lk 8:37.** ὅλη ἡ π. τῆς Γαλιλαίας **Mk 1:28** is either epexegetic gen. *the whole region around, that is, Galilee* or *the region around Galilee* (Mt understands it in the latter sense, and 4:24 inserted ὅλη ἡ Συρία for it); the epexegetical gen. is prob. exhibited in GJs 8:3 καθόλου τῆς π. τῆς Ἰουδαίας *throughout the Judaean countryside* (s. deStrycker ad loc.). By metonymy for the inhabitants **Mt 3:5.**—DELG s.v. χώρα. M-M.

περίψημα, ατος, τό (Vi. Aesopi G 35 P.; from περιψάω= 'wipe all around, wipe clean') **that which is removed by the process of cleansing,** ***dirt, off-scouring*** (Jer 22:28 Sym.) πάντων περίψημα *the off-scouring of all things* **1 Cor 4:13.** But reflection on the fact that the removal of the περίψ. cleanses the thing or the pers. to which (whom) it was attached, has given the word the further mng. *ransom, scapegoat, sacrifice* (cp. Tob 5:19. Hesychius equates it w. περικατάμαγμα [cp. καταμάσσω 'wipe off'] and ἀντίλυτρα, ἀντίψυχα. Photius p. 425, 3 explains περίψ. w. ἀπολύτρωσις and then continues, referring to the custom of making a human sacrifice every year for the benefit of the rest of the people [s. on this Ltzm. and JWeiss on 1 Cor 4:13]: οὕτως ἐπέλεγον τῷ κατ' ἐνιαυτὸν ἐμβαλλομένῳ τῇ θαλάσσῃ νεανίᾳ ἐπ' ἀπαλλαγῇ τῶν συνεχόντων κακῶν· περίψημα ἡμῶν γενοῦ· ἤτοι σωτηρία καὶ ἀπολύτρωσις. καὶ οὕτως ἐνέβαλον τῇ θαλάσσῃ ὡσανεὶ τῷ Ποσειδῶνι θυσίαν ἀποτιννύντες 'in this wise they spoke over the young man who was being cast into the sea in accordance with annual custom for deliverance from afflictions: "Be our means of cleansing; in truth, our salvation and deliverance." And so they cast him into the sea, a sacrificial payment in full, as it were, to Poseidon.'). But it must also be observed that περίψ. had become more and more a term of polite self-depreciation, common enough in everyday speech (Dionys. of Alex. in Eus., HE 7, 22, 7 τὸ δημῶδες ῥῆμα. S. also the grave-inscription [in WThieling, D. Hellenismus in Kleinafrika 1911, p. 34] in which a wife says w. reference to her deceased husband ἐγώ σου περίψημα τῆς καλῆς ψυχῆς); the sense would then be someth. like *most humble servant.* So certainly in περίψ. τοῦ σταυροῦ IEph 18:1. But prob. also 8:1; B 4:9; 6:5 (s. HVeil: EHennecke, Hdb. zu den ntl. Apokryphen 1904, 218; also JToutain, Nouvelles Études '35, 144–46).—Frisk s.v. ψῆν. M-M. TW. Spicq.

περπερεύομαι (πέρπερος 'vainglorious'; M. Ant. 5, 5, 4; Etym. Mag. p. 665, 37; Hesych.=κατεπαίρομαι. The compound ἐμπερπερεύομαι is more common: Epict. 2, 1, 34; Cicero, Ad Attic. 1, 14, 4) **to heap praise on oneself,** ***behave as a πέρπερος*** ('braggart, windbag': Polyb. 32, 2, 5; 39, 1, 2; Epict. 3, 2, 14), *boast, brag* **1 Cor 13:4.**—DELG s.v. πέρπερος. TW.

Περσίς, ίδος, ἡ (Palest. ins: IPeters/HThiersch, Painted Tombs of Marissa 1905, nos. 38 and 41 [II BC]; name used esp. for female slaves: BGU 895, 29; 31 [II AD]; IG VII, 2074; CIL V, 4455) ***Persis,*** recipient of a greeting **Ro 16:12.**—M-M.

πέρυσι before vowels πέρυσιν Hv 2, 1, 3 (on the ν cp. Lex. Rhet. in RReitzenstein, Index Lect. Rostock 1892/93 p. 6; Schwyzer I 405; B-D-F §20.—Mlt-H. 279) adv. of time (Simonides et al.) ***last year, a year ago*** (Aristoph., Pla. et al.; Plut., Mor. 15f; Philostrat., Her. 33 p. 139, 14 K.; ins, pap) Hv 2, 1, 1; 3. ἀπὸ π. (BGU 531 II, 1 [70–80 AD]; Dssm., NB 48f [BS 221]) *a year ago, since last year* **2 Cor 8:10; 9:2.** —DELG. M-M.

περυσινός, ή, όν (πέρυσι; Aristoph., Pla., X. et al.; PSI 560, 8 [III BC]; PTebt 112, 19 [II BC]; al. in pap) ***of last year*** ἡ περυσινὴ ὅρασις *the vision of the previous year* Hv 2, 1, 1; cp. 3, 10, 3.—DELG and M-M s.v. πέρυσι.

πεσεῖν, -ών, πεσοῦμαι s. πίπτω.

πέταλον, ου, τό (w. var. mngs. since Hom., also LXX; TestSol 4:14, 16 D; TestLevi 8:2; Philo, Joseph.) lit. 'leaf', here ***fillet, headband,*** worn by a priest as symbol of his office τὸ π. τοῦ ἱερέως GJs 5:1 (twice; cp. Ex 28:36; Lev 8:9).

πετάομαι (doubtful form for ποτάομαι ['fly hither and thither, flutter'], the frequentative form of πέτομαι [q.v.].—Lob. on Phryn. p. 581; B-D-F §101 p. 54; Helbing 83f; Reinhold

100.—The act. πετάω='fly' in Achmes 236, 6. πετάομαι in Aristot., Metaph. 1009b, 38 [WChrist '38] **v.l.** [false reading, s. L-S-J-M]; Syntipas 79, 28 v.l.) **to be on the wing,** ***fly*** in our lit. only in **Rv**, and in the pres. ptc. πετώμενος, as **v.l.** in **4:7; 8:13; 14:6; 19:17.**

πετεινόν, οῦ, τό (πέτομαι) subst. neut. of πετεινός, ή, όν (Theognis, trag., Hdt. et al.; LXX; TestLevi 9:13; Jos., Ant. 2, 245; 3, 137) **any kind of bird (wild or domestic),** ***bird,*** B 11:3 (Is 16:2). Mostly pl. (Hdt.; O. Wilck II, 1523 [127 BC]; LXX; En 7:5; PsSol 5:9; TestSol C prol. 3; TestJob 27:1; ParJer; Jos., Ant. 8, 40; SibOr 3, 224) **Mt 13:4; Mk 4:4; Lk 12:24.** W. κτήνη (Gen 8:17; Lev 7:26) Hs 9, 1, 8; 9, 24, 1. W. τετράποδα, ἑρπετά **Ac 10:12; Ro 1:23.** W. τετράποδα, θηρία, ἑρπετά (Herm. Wr. 1, 11b) **Ac 11:6;** w. still others PtK 2 p. 14, 17. W. θηρία, ἑρπετά, ἐνάλια **Js 3:7.** W. θηρία, ἰχθύες B 6:12, 18 (s. ἑρπετόν on these combinations). τὰ π. τοῦ οὐρανοῦ (s. οὐρανός 1d) *the birds in the sky*=wild birds **Mt 6:26; 8:20; 13:32** (cp. 1QH 8:9); **Mk 4:32; Lk 8:5; 9:58; 13:19; Ac 10:12; 11:6;** B 6:12 (Gen 1:28), 18; Hs 9, 24, 1; GJs 3:2; 18:2 codd. Of birds of prey B 10:10.—BHHW III 2111. DELG s.v. πέτομαι. M-M s.v. πετεινός.

πέτομαι (Hom.+; ins, pap, LXX; ParJer; ApcSed 8:3 p. 132, 28 Ja.; Philo, Gig. 6; Hecataeus: 264 fgm. 21, 203 Jac. [in Jos., C. Ap. 1, 203]. S. πετάομαι.) w. the aor. ἐπετάσθην derived fr. πεταζω (cp. Aristot., HA 624b, 6 [εἰς πετάσθῃ]; also Is 11:14; JosAs 16 cod. A [p. 65, 11 Bat.]) ***fly*** **Rv 4:7; 8:13; 12:14; 14:6; 19:17.** Aor. 3 sg. GJs 9:1 v.l. (codd. Tdf. for ἐπεστάθη).—B. 682. DELG. M-M.

πέτρα, ας, ἡ (Hom. [πέτρη as 'massive stone' Il. 15, 273; Od. 10, 87f]+; loanw. in rabb.).

❶ **bedrock or massive rock formations,** ***rock*** as distinguished from stones (s. 2 below)—ⓐ lit., of the rock in which a tomb is hewn (s. λατομέω 1) **Mt 27:60; Mk 15:46.** The rocks split apart during an earthquake **Mt 27:51** (cp. PGM 12, 242). αἱ πέτραι w. τὰ ὄρη (PGM 13, 872; all the elements are in disorder) **Rv 6:16;** likew. vs. **15,** where πέτρα rather takes on the mng. *rocky grotto* (as Il. 2, 88; 4, 107; Soph., Phil. 16 al.; Judg 15:13; 1 Km 13:6; Is 2:10; Pr 30:26. Cp. Diod. S. 5, 39, 5 ἐν ταῖς κοίλαις πέτραις καὶ σπηλαίοις). πέτρα *rocky ground* with a thin layer of topsoil **Lk 8:6, 13** (Maximus Tyr. 20, 9g ἐπὶ πετρῶν σπείρεις; Pla., Leg. 8, 838e; Ael. Aristid. 46 p. 302 D.; PSI 433, 6 [260 BC] οὐκ ἐφυτεύθη ἐπὶ τῆς πέτρας). It forms a suitable foundation for the building of a house **Mt 7:24f; Lk 6:48ab v.l.**—Used w. an adj.: of Sinai π. ἔρημος *a barren rock* B 11:3 (Is 16:1). στερεὰ πέτρα 5:14; 6:3 (both Is 50:7; cp. En 22:1; 26:5; OdeSol 11:5). π. ἰσχυρά 11:5 (Is 33:16). π. ἀκίνητος IPol 1:1.—The rock in the vision of Hermas: Hs 9, 2, 1f; 9, 3, 1; 9, 4, 2; 9, 5, 3; 9, 9, 7; 9, 12, 1 (the interpretation); 9, 13, 5; 9, 14, 4.—The rock at various places in the desert fr. which Moses drew water by striking it (Ex 17:6; Num 20:8ff; Ps 77:15f, 20; Philo, Mos. 1, 210; Jos., Ant. 3, 86; Just., D. 86, 1; Mel.—Apollon. Rhod. 4, 1444–46: Heracles, when thirsty, struck a πέτρη at the suggestion of a divinity, and a great stream of water gushed forth at once). Paul calls it πνευματικὴ πέτρα **1 Cor 10:4a** and identifies it w. the preexistent Christ vs. **4b** (EEllis, JBL 76, '57, 53–56; Philo, Leg. All. 2, 86 πέτρα = σοφία, Det. Pot. Ins. 118=λόγος θεῖος).

ⓑ in wordplay (as symbol of firmness Reader, Polemo p. 265) w. the name Πέτρος (GGander, RTP n.s. 29, '41, 5–29). The apostle so named, or the affirmation he has just made, is the rock on which Christ will build his church (for the figure s. Od. 17, 463: Antinous fails to shake Odysseus, who stands firm as rock.—Arrian, Anab. 4, 18, 4ff; 4, 21, 1ff; 4, 28, 1ff πέτρα is a rocky district [so also Antig. Car. 165] as the foundation of an impregnable position or a rocky fortress; 4, 28, 1; 2 this kind of πέτρα could not be conquered even by Heracles.—Diod. S. 19, 95, 2 and 4; 19, 96, 1; 19, 97, 1 and 2; 19, 98, 1 al. ἡ πέτρα [always with the article] is the rock [Petra] that keeps the Nabataeans safe from all enemy attacks; Stephan. Byz. s.v. Στάσις: πόλις ἐπὶ πέτρης μεγάλης of a city that cannot be taken) **Mt 16:18** (s. ADell, ZNW 15, 1914, 1–49; 17, 1916, 27–32; OImmisch, ibid. 17, 1916, 18–26; Harnack, SBBerlAk 1918, 637–54; 1927, 139–52; RBultmann, ZNW 19, 1920, 165–74, ThBl 20, '41, 265–79; FKattenbusch, Der Quellort der Kirchenidee: Festgabe für Harnack 1921, 143–72, Der Spruch über Pt. u. d. Kirche bei Mt: StKr 94, 1922, 96–131; SEuringer, D. Locus Classicus des Primates: AEhrhard Festschr. 1922, 141–79; HDieckmann, Die Verfassung der Urkirche 1923; JJeremias, Αγγελος II 1926, 108–17; ECaspar, Primatus Petri 1927; KGoetz, Pt. als Gründer u. Oberhaupt der Kirche 1927; JGeiselmann, D. petrin. Primat (Mt 16:17ff) 1927; BBartmann, ThGl 20, 1928, 1–17; HKoch, Cathedra Petri 1930; TEngert, 'Tu es Pt': Ricerche relig. 6, 1930, 222–60; FSeppelt, Gesch. d. Papsttums I '31, 9–46; JTurmel, La papauté '33, 101ff; VBurch, JBL 52, '33, 147–52; JHaller, D. Papsttum I '34, 1–31; ACotter, CBQ 4, '42, 304–10; WKümmel, Kirchenbegr. u. Gesch.-bewusstsein in d. Urgem. u. b. Jesus: SymbBUps 1, '43; OSeitz, JBL 69, '50, 329–40. OCullmann, TManson mem. vol., '59, 94–105; OBetz, ZNW 48, '57, 49–77; cp. 1QH 6:26–28; HClavier, Bultmann Festschr., '54, 94–107.—OCullmann, TW VI 94–99: πέτρα. S. also the lit. under Πέτρος, end).

❷ **a piece of rock,** ***rock*** (in an OT quot., where πέτρα is used in parallelism w. λίθος) π. σκανδάλου **Ro 9:33; 1 Pt 2:8** (both Is 8:14).—B. 51. DELG. M-M. TW.

Πέτρος, ου, ὁ (ὁ πέτρος='stone' Hom.+; Jos., Bell. 3, 240, Ant. 7, 142.—Π. as a name can scarcely be pre-Christian, as AMerx, D. vier kanon. Ev. II/1, 1902, 160ff, referring to Jos., Ant. 18, 156 [Niese did not accept the v.l. Πέτρος for Πρῶτος], would have it. But s. ADell [πέτρα 1b] esp. 14–17. Fr. the beginning it was prob. thought of as the Gk. equivalent of the Aram. כֵּיפָא= Κηφᾶς: J 1:42; cp. Mt 16:18 and JWackernagel, Syntax II[2] 1928, 14f, perh. formed on the analogy of the Gk. male proper name Πέτρων: UPZ 149, 8 [III BC]; 135 [78 BC]; Plut., Mor. 422d.—A gentile named Πέτρος in Damasc., Vi. Isid. 170. S. also the Praeses Arabiae of 278/79 AD Aurelius P.: Publ. Princeton Univ. Arch. Expedition to Syria III A, 1913, 4 no. 546) ***Peter,*** surname of the head of the circle of Twelve Disciples, whose name was orig. Simon. His father was a certain John (s. Ἰωάννης 4) or Jonah (s. Ἰωνᾶς 2). Acc. to **J 1:44** he himself was from Bethsaida, but, at any rate, when he met Jesus he lived in Capernaum (Mk 1:21, 29). Fr. that city he and his brother Andrew made their living as fishers (Mk 1:16). He was married (Mk 1:30; cp. 1 Cor 9:5), but left his home and occupation, when Jesus called, to follow him (Mk 1:18; **10:28**). He belonged to the three or four most intimate of the Master's companions (**Mk 5:37; 9:2; 13:3; 14:33**). He stands at the head of the lists of the apostles (**Mt 10:2; Mk 3:16; Lk 6:14; Ac 1:13**). Not all the problems connected w. the conferring of the name Cephas-Peter upon Simon (s. Σίμων 1) have yet been solved (the giving of a new name and the reason for it: Plato [s. ὀνομάζω 1] and Theophrastus [Vi. Platonis 2 ln. 21 in Biog. p. 388 W.= Prolegom. 1 in CHermann, Pla. VI 196 Θεόφραστος, Τύρταμος καλούμενος πάλαι, διὰ τὸ θεῖον τῆς φράσεως Θ. μετεκλήθη]; CRoth, Simon-Peter HTR 54, '61, 91–97). He was at least not always a model of rock-like (πέτρος is a symbol of imperturbability Soph., Oed. Rex 334; Eur., Med. 28 al.) firmness (note Gethsemane, the denial, the unsuccessful attempt at walking on water; his conduct at Antioch Gal 2:11ff which, though, is fr. time to time referred to another Cephas; s. KLake, HTR 14,

1921, 95ff; AVöllmecke, Jahrbuch d. Missionshauses St. Gabriel 2, 1925, 69–104; 3, 1926, 31–75; DRiddle, JBL 59, '40, 169–80; NHuffman, ibid. 64, '45, 205f; PGaechter, ZKT 72, '50, 177–212; but s. HBetz, Gal [Hermeneia] p. 105f w. n. 442). Despite all this he was the leader of Jesus' disciples, was spokesman for the Twelve (e.g. **Mt 18:21; 19:27; Mk 8:27ff; Lk 12:41; 18:28**) and for the three who were closest to Jesus (**Mk 9:5**); he was recognized as leader even by those on the outside (**Mt 17:24**). He is especially prominent in the pronouncement made **Mt 16:18.** Only in the Fourth Gospel does Peter have a place less prominent than another, in this case the 'disciple whom Jesus loved' (s. Hdb. exc. on J 13:23). In connection w. the miraculous events after Jesus' death (on this ELohmeyer, Galiläa u. Jerusalem '36; WMichaelis, D. Erscheinungen d. Auferstandenen '44; MWerner, D. ntl. Berichte üb. d. Erscheinungen d. Auferstandenen: Schweiz. Theol. Umschau '44) Pt. played a unique role: 1 Cor 15:5; Lk 24:34; **Mk 16:7.** He was one of the pillars of the early church (Gal 2:9 [Κηφᾶς]). Three years after Paul was converted, on his first journey to Jerusalem as a Christian, he established a significant contact w. Peter: Gal 1:18. At least until the time described in Gal 2:1–10 (cp. **Ac 15:7**) he was prob. the head of the early Christian community/church. He was also active as a missionary to Israel **Gal 2:8;** cp. 1 Cor 9:5 (Κηφᾶς).—MGoguel, L'apôtre Pierre a-t-il joué un role personnel dans les crises de Grèce et de Galatie?: RHPR 14, '34, 461–500.—In **1 Pt 1:1** and **2 Pt 1:1** he appears as author of an epistle. On Paul's journey to Rome: Ἀρτέμων ὁ κυβερνήτης τοῦ πλοίου ἦν λελουμένος ὑπὸ Πέτρου *Artemon, the ship's captain, was baptized by Peter* AcPl Ha 7, 20. It is probable that he died at Rome under Nero, about 64 AD.—In the NT he is somet. called Σίμων (q.v. 1; in Ac 15:14 and **2 Pt 1:1** more exactly Συμεών=שִׁמְעוֹן); except for **Gal 2:7f** Paul always calls him Κηφᾶς (q.v.). Both names Σίμων Π. **Mt 16:16; Lk 5:8; J 1:40; 6:8, 68; 13:6, 9, 24, 36; 18:10, 15, 25; 20:2, 6; 21:2f, 7b, 11, 15.** Σίμων ὁ λεγόμενος Π. **Mt 4:18; 10:2.** Σίμων ὁ ἐπικαλούμενος Π. **Ac 10:18; 11:13.** Σίμων ὃς ἐπικαλεῖται Π. **10:5, 32.**—Outside the NT it is found in our lit. GEb 34, 59; GPt 14:60 (Σίμων Πέτρος); ApcPt Rainer; GMary 463 (2 times); AcPt Ox 849 (4 times); 1 Cl 5:4 (Paul follows in 5:5); 2 Cl 5:3f (a piece fr. an apocr. gosp.); IRo 4:3 (Πέτρος καὶ Παῦλος); ISm 3:2=GHb 356, 39; Papias (2:4, w. other disciples; 15, w. Mark as his ἑρμηνευτής).—Zahn, Einl. II §38–44; KErbes, Petrus nicht in Rom, sondern in Jerusalem gestorben: ZKG 22, 1901, 1ff; 161ff (against him AKneller, ZKT 26, 1902, 33ff; 225ff; 351ff); PSchmiedel, War der Ap. Petrus in Rom?: PM 13, 1909, 59–81; HLietzmann, Petrus u. Pls in Rom[2] 1927; GEsser, Der hl. Ap. Petrus 1902; CGuignebert, La primauté de St. Pierre et la venue de Pierre à Rome 1909; FFoakes-Jackson, Peter, Prince of Apostles 1927; HDannenbauer, D. röm. Pt-Legende: Hist. Ztschr. 146, '32, 239–62; 159, '38, 81–88; KHeussi, War Pt. in Rom? '36, War Pt. wirklich röm. Märtyrer? '37, Neues z. Pt.-frage '39, TLZ 77, '52, 67–72; HLietzmann, Pt. röm. Märt.: SBBerlAk '36, XXIX; DRobinson, JBL 64, '45, 255–67; HSchmutz, Pt. war dennoch in Rom: Benedikt. Monatsschr. 22, '46, 128–41.—On Mt 16:17–19 s., in addition to the lit. on κλείς 1 and πέτρα 1b: JSchnitzer, Hat Jesus das Papsttum gestiftet? 1910, Das Papsttum eine Stiftung Jesu? 1910; FTillmann, Jesus u. das Papsttum 1910; AKneller, ZKT 44, 1920, 147–69; OLinton, D. Problem der Urkirche '32, 157–83; KPieper, Jes. u. d. Kirche '32; AEhrhard, Urkirche u. Frühkatholizismus I 1, '36.—JMunck, Pt. u. Pls in der Offenb. Joh. '50 (Rv 11:3–13).—OCullmann, Petrus[2], '60 (Eng. tr. Peter, FFilson[2], '62), L'apôtre Pierre: NT Essays (TManson memorial vol.), '59, 94–105; OKarrer, Peter and the Church: an examination of the Cullmann thesis, '63; RO'Callaghan, Vatican Excavations and the Tomb of Peter: BA 16, '53, 70–87; AvGerkan, D. Forschung nach dem Grab Petri, ZNW 44, '52/53, 196–205, Zu den Problemen des Petrusgrabes: JAC '58, 79–93; GSnyder, BA 32, '69, 2–24; JGwynGriffiths, Hibbert Journal 55, '56/57, 140–49; TBarnes, JTS 21, '70, 175–79; GSchulze-Kadelbach, D. Stellung des P. in der Urchristenheit: TLZ 81, '56, 1–18 (lit.); PGaechter, Petrus u. seine Zeit, '58; EKirschbaum, The Tombs of St. Peter and St. Paul (transl. JMurray) '59; EHaenchen, Petrus-Probleme, NTS 7, '60/61, 187–97; SAgourides, Πέτρος καὶ Ἰωάννης ἐν τῷ τετάρτῳ Εὐαγγελίῳ, Thessalonike, '66; DGewalt, Petrus, diss. Hdlbg, '66; RBrown, KDonfried, JReumann edd., Peter in the NT, '73; CCaragounis, Peter and the Rock (BZNW 58) '89.—Pauly-W. XIX '38, 1335–61; Kl. Pauly IV 674–76; BHHW III 1430f. LGPN I. M-M. EDNT. TW. Sv.

πετρώδης, ες (πέτρος + -ώδης; Soph. et al.) **pert. to rocky area with little topsoil,** ***rocky, stony*** (so Hippocr., Aristot.; Jos., Bell. 7, 166, Vi. 187) subst. τὸ πετρῶδες **Mk 4:5** and τὰ πετρώδη (Aristot., HA 5, 17) **Mt 13:5, 20; Mk 4:16** *rocky ground,* over which a thin layer of soil is spread (ὅπου οὐκ εἶχεν γῆν πολλήν). GDalman, Pj 22, 1926, 124ff.—DELG s.v. πέτρα.

Πετρώνιος, ου, ὁ rather freq. name (cp. e.g. OGI 538, 4; pap; Philo, Leg. ad Gai. 209; Jos., Ant. 15, 307) ***Petronius,*** the centurion who commanded the guard at the grave of Jesus GPt 8:31 (s. ASyn. 351, 10, where Klostermann's rdg. Πειρώνιον remains uncorrected).—LVaganay, L'Évang. de Pierre 1930, 283f.

πεφίμωσο s. φιμόω.

πήγανον, ου, τό (Aristoph. et al.; Theophr., HP 1, 3, 4; Diosc. 3, 45 al.; POxy 1675, 4; PTebt 273 introd.; CWessely, StudPal 20 [1921], 27, 5; Jos., Bell. 7, 178; loanw. in rabb.) ***rue*** (ruta chalepensis: Zohary 90), mentioned among the garden herbs that are tithed **Lk 11:42** (the parallel Mt 23:23 has ἄνηθον, hence EbNestle, ZNW 7, 1906, 260f suspects an interchange of שברא and שבתא). Acc. to the Mishnah (Shebi'ith IX 1; s. Billerb. II 189) it was not necessary to tithe it.—RStrömberg, Griech. Pflanzennamen '40, 144; EBishop, ET 59, '47/48, 81; DCorrens, ΧΑΡΙΣ ΚΑΙ ΣΟΦΙΑ (KRengstorf Festschr.), '64, 110–12. —DELG. M-M.

πηγή, ῆς, ἡ (Hom.+; loanw. in rabb.)—**❶ a source of someth. that gushes out or flows,** ***spring, fountain, flow*** (on distinction fr. κρηνή 'artificially constructed fountain' s. L-S-J-M Suppl.; RWycherly, ClR 51, '37, 2f; Renehan '75, 164f)

ⓐ ordinarily of water *spring, fountain* **Js 3:11, 12 v.l.;** Hs 9, 1, 8; 9, 25, 1. (αἱ) πηγαὶ (τῶν) ὑδάτων *(the) springs of water* (cp. Lev 11:36; Num 33:9; 3 Km 18:5; Jdth 7:7; Ps 17:16; Jos., Ant. 2, 294; Just., A I, 64, 1) **Rv 8:10; 14:7; 16:4.** ἀέναοι πηγαί *everflowing springs* 1 Cl 20:10 (ἀέναος 1). As typical of sinners πηγαὶ ἄνυδροι (s. ἄνυδρος) **2 Pt 2:17.** Of a specific source, *well* (called φρέαρ in J 4:11f; cp. Mod. Gk. πηγάδι='well'.—WHutton, ET 57, '45/46, 27) π. τοῦ Ἰακώβ, at the foot of Mt Gerizim (on the location of Jacob's well s. Dalman, Orte[3] 226ff) **J 4:6a;** cp. vs. **6b** (Paus. 8, 23, 4 ὀλίγον ὑπὲρ τ. πόλιν π. ἐστιν καὶ ἐπὶ τῇ π. . . .).

ⓑ of blood ἡ πηγὴ τοῦ αἵματος αὐτῆς (Lev 12:7) **Mk 5:29** (Alex. Aphr., An. p. 40, 2 Bruns πηγὴ τ. αἵματος. Cp. πηγὴ δακρύων: Soph., Ant. 803; Chariton 1, 3, 6; 2, 3, 6; 6, 7, 10; Achilles Tat. 7, 4, 6).

ⓒ Quite symbolic (s. Hdb. exc. on J 4:14 and cp. Dio Chrys. 15 [32], 15 τὸ σῷζον [ὕδωρ] ἄνωθέν ποθεν ἐκ δαιμονίου τινὸς πηγῆς κάτεισι. In schol. on Pla. 611c ἀθάνατος πηγή is a spring whose water bestows immortality) is its usage in some NT pass.: ἡ πηγὴ τοῦ ὕδατος τῆς ζωῆς *the spring of the water of life* **Rv 21:6;** in the pl. ζωῆς πηγαὶ ὑδάτων **7:17;** πηγὴ ὕδατος ἁλλομένου εἰς ζωὴν αἰώνιον *a spring of water welling up for eternal life* **J 4:14** (Essenes apply this figure to the Torah, e.g. CD 6:4; also s. Hdb. ad loc.).

❷ **the place of origin or the cause of a full abundance of someth.,** ***fountainhead,*** fig. ext. of 1 (Pind. et al; Epict. 3, 1, 18 Apollo as πηγὴ τῆς ἀληθείας [πηγὴ ἀληθ. also in Himerius, Or. 48=Or. 14, 35; Maximus Tyr. 12, 6c; 13, 9c; Philo, Mos. 1, 84); πηγὴ ζωῆς *source of life* (Pr 10:11; 13:14; 14:27) of God B 11:2 (Jer 2:13 and 17:13; cp. Ps 35:10); cp. B 1:3 Funk; s. πλούσιος 2.—B. 44. DELG. M-M. TW.

πήγνυμι fut. πήξω LXX; 1 aor. ἔπηξα, ptc. πήξας; pf. 3 sg. and pl. πέπηγεν and πεπήγασιν LXX, ptc. πεπηγώς GJs, LXX. Pass.: 2 fut. παγήσομαι LXX; 2 aor. ἐπάγην; pf. ptc. πεπηγμένος (TestJob 13:3; JosAs 2:4) (Hom.+; prim. 'stick or fix in').

❶ **to make firm or stable by fixing in a place,** ***make firm, fix*** of God's creative activity (Ps.-Lucian, Philopatr. 17 [θεὸς] γῆν ἐφ' ὕδατος ἔπηξεν) τὸν οὐρανόν *the heaven* Hv 1, 3, 4 (cp. Is 42:5).

❷ **to set up or erect a construction,** ***put together, build*** σκηνήν *pitch a tent* (Pla., Leg. 7, 817c; Polyb. 6, 27, 2; 6 al.; Gen 26:25; 31:25; Num 24:6; Judg 4:11; Jos., Ant. 3, 247; TestAbr A 1 p. 77, 4 [Stone p. 2]); GPt 8:33; GJs 1:4. Of the tabernacle (Ex 33:7; 38:26; Josh 18:1; Philo, Leg. All. 2, 54) *set up* **Hb 8:2.**

❸ **to make solid or stiff,** esp. of liquids, pass., intr. sense, of milk ***curdle*** (Aristot., Part. An. 3, 15, 676a, 14 γάλα πήγνυται; Cyranides p. 63, 13) ApcPt fgm. 2 p. 12, ln. 24f; αἷμα πεπηγός *congealed blood* GJs 24:2.—DELG. M-M.

πηδάλιον, ου, τό (πηδόν 'blade of an oar'; Hom. et al.; IG^2, 1607; POxy 1449, 14; 1650, 11; Lat. gubernaculum 'steering oar') ***steering paddle, rudder*** **Js 3:4** (w. χαλινός vs. 3; cp. the combination of rudder and bridle Plut., Mor. 33f καθάπερ ἱππεὺς διὰ χαλινοῦ καὶ [διὰ] πηδαλίου κυβερνήτης [H-Almqvist, Plut. u. das NT '46, 132f]; cp. Aristot., Mech. 5, 850b). Pl. (as PLond III, 1164h, 8 p. 164 [212 AD]) **Ac 27:40,** since each ship had two rudders, connected by a crossbar and operated by one man (LCasson, Ships . . . in the Ancient World '71, 224 n.2).—B. 734. DELG s.v. πηδόν. M-M.

πηδάω (Hom. et al.; LXX; Philo, In Flacc. 162) ***leap, spring*** also of someth. inanimate (Theocrit. 25, 251); of a bolt of fire (Pla., Ep. 7, 341c) ἀπό τινος *from someone* ApcPt fgm. 1 p. 12, ln. 15. Unless we are to follow HSanders in reading [ἐκ]πεπηδημένοι AcPl BMM verso 5//AcPl Ha 8, 33 [καθήμ]ενοι as restored by the ed., the simplex πεπηδημένοι in AcPl BMM suggests a bold image of rapid, and therefore hazardous, movement in the 'darkness of death'; s. ἐκπηδάω, πεδάω.—B. 688. DELG.

πηλίκος, η, ον (Pla. et al.; LXX; EpArist 52; Jos., Ant. 13, 1) correlative pron. 'how large?' but in our lit., in both places where it occurs, in an exclamation (for the older ἡλίκος [Pla. et al]; s. B-D-F §304; Rob. 741).

❶ **pert. to large size,** ***how large*** ἴδετε πηλίκοις ὑμῖν γράμμασιν ἔγραψα *see with what large letters I am writing to you* **Gal 6:11** (Dssm., B 264 [BS 358]. Against him KClarke, ET 24, 1913, 285 and JClemens, ibid. 380; s. the comm.—CStarcke, D. Rhetorik des Ap. Pls im Gal u. die 'πηλίκα γράμματα': Progr. Stargard i. P. 1911).

❷ **pert. to extraordinary importance,** ***how great,*** fig. ext. of 1: of Melchizedek θεωρεῖτε πηλίκος οὗτος *consider how great this man must have been* **Hb 7:4.** πηλίκα μεγαλεῖα ἐδόθη αὐτῷ *what great deeds (God) did (in behalf of Paul)* AcPl Ha 6, 12.—DELG. M-M.

πήλινος, η, ον (πηλός; Demosth. et al.; PPetr III, 48, 9 [241 BC]; LXX; SibOr 3, 589; Tat. 22, 1) ***made of clay*** οἰκίας π. *houses of clay* 1 Cl 39:5 (Job 4:19).—DELG s.v. πηλός.

πηλός, οῦ, ὁ (Aeschyl., Hdt.+; OGI 483, 61; CPR 232, 17; POxy 1450, 4; LXX, pseudepigr., Philo, Joseph.; Mel., P. 36, 247; Ath.)

❶ ***clay***—ⓐ used in making pottery (trag. et al.; Polyb. 15, 35, 2: the potter deals with ὁ τροχός [=potter's wheel] and ὁ πηλός; Is 29:16; 41:25; Jer 18:6; Sir 33:13) **Ro 9:21** (cp. esp. Wsd 15:7).—In a comparison that has allegorical traits humankind is called πηλὸς εἰς τὴν χεῖρα τοῦ τεχνίτου 2 Cl 8:2 (= ἐν τῇ χειρί, s. εἰς 1aδ).

ⓑ Like the pliable material which the artist uses (TestNapht 2:2; Jos., C. Ap. 2, 252; Mel.), clay is also the material fr. which humankind is made (cp. Aristoph., Av. 686 πηλοῦ πλάσματα of humans; Callim. fgm. 493; Herodas 2, 28f; Epict. 4, 11, 27; Lucian, Prom. 13; Themist., Or. 32 after Aesop; Job 10:9) 1 Cl 39:5 (Job 4:19).

❷ ***mud, mire*** (Pla., Parm. 130c π. καὶ ῥύπος; Plut., Marius 414 [16, 7], Mor. 993e; 1059f οἱ πηλὸν ἢ κονιορτὸν ἐπὶ τοῦ σώματος ἔχοντες), esp. of the soft mass produced when the ground is wet, e.g. on the roads (Aeneas Tact. 1421; Herodas 1, 14; Arrian, Anab. 5, 15, 2; 2 Km 22:43; Zech 9:3; 10:5; Jos., Ant. 1, 244; cp. JosAs 13:6). Jesus ἔπτυσεν χαμαὶ καὶ ἐποίησεν πηλὸν ἐκ τοῦ πτύσματος **J 9:6a** (π. ποιεῖν like Chariton 1, 3, 2); cp. vss. **6b, 11, 14, 15.** For the use of πηλός in the healing art of ancient times, even on the part of benevolent divinities s. Hdb. ad loc. and KRengstorf, Die Anfänge der Auseinandersetzung zw. Christusglaube u. Asklepiosfrömmigkeit '53, 39f, n. 61.—B. 20. Schmidt, Syn. II 191–99, s. βόρβορος. DELG. TW.

πήρα, ας, ἡ (Hom. et al.; Jdth 10:5; 13:10, 15; SibOr 6, 15 Joseph.; Tat. 25, 1) **a leather pouch used by travelers,** ***knapsack, traveler's bag,*** which Jesus' disciples were directed not to take w. them when they were sent out, since it was not absolutely necessary (s. on ὑπόδημα) **Mt 10:10; Mk 6:8; Lk 9:3; 10:4; 22:35;** cp. vs. **36.** But perh. this instruction has in mind the more specialized mng. ***beggar's bag*** (Diog. L. 6, 33; Gk. ins fr. Syria: BCH 21, 1897, 60; PGM 4, 2381; 2400. Cp. Const. Apost. 3, 6. Such a bag was part of a Cynic itinerant preacher's equipment [PWendland, Kultur 84. Crates the Cynic wrote a piece titled Πήρα: HDiels, Poetae Philosophi 1902 fgm. 4 p. 218. See Dio Chrys. 49 (66), 21; Lucian, Dial. Mort. 1, 3; Alciphron 3, 19, 5].—Acc. to Diog. L. 6, 13 Antisthenes the Cynic was the first to fold his cloak double [so he could sleep on it] and take a staff and πήρα with him; cp. 6, 22 of Diogenes.—Dssm., LO 87 [LAE 108ff]; SKrauss, Αγγελος I 1925, 96ff; KRengstorf, Jebamot 1929, 214f). οἱ μάγοι . . . ἐξέβαλον ἀπὸ τῆς πήρας αὐτῶν δῶρα GJs 21:3 (after Mt 2:11).—Such a bag was also used by shepherds (Ammon. Gramm. [I/II AD], diff. 112 πήρα . . . φέρουσιν οἱ ποιμένες; Longus 1, 13, 1; 3, 15, 3; Aesop, Fab. 31b H. [s. H-H. 24 II app.]; Babr. 86, 2; Jos., Ant. 6, 185 π. ποιμενική; s. the statue of the Good Shepherd in the Lateran) Hv 5:1; s 6, 2, 5; 9, 10, 5.—DELG. M-M. TW.

πηρός, ά, όν (s. two next entries; Hom. et al.; pap; ApcrEzk [Epiph 70, 15]; SibOr 3, 793; Philo; Just.; Mel., P. 78, 564) **pert. to being impaired in any part of the body, *maimed, disabled, weakened;*** w. ref. to the eyes *blind* (Appian, Samn. 9 §5; Aesop, Fab. 37 P.=57 H.; 37 H-H.; 54 Ch.), fig. (Philo, Somn. 1, 27 πρὸς αἴσθησιν πηροί; Ps.-Lucian, Am. 46 πηροὶ οἱ τῆς διανοίας λογισμοί) πηροὶ τῇ διανοίᾳ *blind in mind* 2 Cl 1:6.—DELG.

πηρόω (πηρός) aor. 3 sg. ἐπήρωσεν 4 Macc 18:21; pf. pass. πεπήρωνται Job 17:7 v.l. (Aristoph., Hippocr. et al.; Job 17:7 v.l.; 4 Macc 18:21; Philo; Jos., C. Ap. 2, 15; Just., D. 12, 2) **to cause physical impairment, *disable, maim*** in our lit. in several places as v.l. for πωρόω (the witnesses also vary in the same way in Job 17:7) in imagery ἐπήρωσεν αὐτῶν τὴν καρδίαν=*closed their mind* **J 12:40** v.l. Pass. (M. Ant. 5, 8, 13) **Mk 8:17** D*. οἱ λοιποὶ ἐπηρώθησαν **Ro 11:7** v.l. (poorly attested by one late ms. 66** [s. Tdf.]=Gregory 1911; here the mng. is surely ***to blind,*** which πηρόω signifies as early as Aristot., HA 620a, 1 and Ephorus [IV BC]: 70 fgm. 1 Jac.; likew. schol. on Apollon. Rhod. 2, introd. and 2, 182). On **Ac 5:3 v.l.** see πληρόω 1a.—DELG s.v. πηρός. M-M. TW.

πήρωσις, εως, ἡ (πηρόω; since Democr. 296; Hippocr.; Maximus Tyr. 29, 2f; Dt 28:28 Aq.; Philo; Jos., Ant. 1, 267; Ath., R. 21 p. 75, 3 al.) **state of physical impairment, *disabling,*** esp. also *nearsightedness, blindness* (Dio Chrys. 47 [64], 6; Artem. 2, 36 p. 134, 28 ὀφθαλμῶν π.; Lucian, Dom. 29) fig. (Manetho, Apot. 4, 518 π. ψυχῆς; Philo, Ebr. 160, Omn. Prob. Lib. 55 λογισμοῦ π.) π. τῆς καρδίας **Mk 3:5 v.l.** (s. πώρωσις).—DELG s.v. πηρός. TW.

πηχυαῖος, α, ον (πῆχυς; Hdt. et al.; ins) ***a cubit*** (about 18 inches) ***long,*** of sticks Hs 8, 1, 2.

πῆχυς, εως, ὁ (Hom.+; ins, pap, LXX, En, TestSol, TestAbr; TestJud 3:7; GrBar, ApcEsdr, EpArist, Philo, Joseph., apolog.) gen. pl. πηχῶν (un-Att.: X., An. 4, 7, 16; Polyb., Diod. S., Hero Alex., Plut.; SIG 1231, 14; pap [Mayser p. 267]; LXX [s. Thackeray p. 151, 21]; En 7:2; Jos., Bell. 6, 166, C. Ap. 2, 119; SibOr 5, 57.—Phryn. p. 245 Lob.; Schwyzer I 573; Dssm., B 152 [BS 153f]; B-D-F §48; Mlt-H. 140f) orig. 'forearm' then ***cubit*** or ***ell*** as a measure of length (Poll. 2, 158: ἀπὸ δὲ τοῦ ὠλεκράνου πρὸς τὸ τοῦ μέσου δακτύλου ἄκρον, τὸ διάστημα πῆχυς=a cubit is the distance from the elbow to the end of the middle finger; about 45–52 cm.—KHermann, Lehrb. der griech. Antiquitäten IV[3] 1882, 438ff; FHultsch, APF 3, 1906, 438ff) **Rv 21:17** (Lucian's marvelous city [Ver. Hist. 2, 11] is measured not by the ordinary human cubit, but by the πῆχυς βασιλικός). ὡς ἀπὸ πηχῶν διακοσίων *about ninety meters away* (s. ἀπό 4) **J 21:8.** προσθεῖναι πῆχυν (cp. Epicharmus in Diog. L. 3, 11 μέτρον παχυαῖον ποτθέμειν): προσθεῖναι ἐπὶ τὴν ἡλικίαν αὐτοῦ π. (ἕνα) **Mt 6:27; Lk 12:25** (Damasc., Vi. Isid. 166 of spiritual growth: αὔξεσθαι κατὰ πῆχυν; Epict. 3, 2, 10 γέγονέ σου τὸ ψυχάριον ἀντὶ δακτυλιαίου δίπηχυ=your little soul, as long as a finger, has become two cubits in length [because you were praised]). This expression has produced two major lines of interpr.: as ref. to length of life (s. ἡλικία 1a and cp. Mimnermus 2, 3 Diehl[2] πήχυιον ἐπὶ χρόνον='for only a cubit of time') *add a single hour to your span of life* NRSV; cp. Betz, SM p. 475f; as ref. to bodily growth *add one cubit to your height / add a cubit to your stature* NRSV mg. The former has been commended because the addition of a cubit in the sense of time appears to be a small matter, whereas a πῆχυς of bodily stature is monstrously large (Alcaeus, fgm. 50 D.[2] gives the measurement of an enormous giant as less than 5 cubits). But this objection fails to take account of freq. use of hyperbole in the dominical discourse. Moreover, the context of both pass. deals with food and clothing. Food provides the nourishment that sustains growth as well as life. Disciples do not grow to their present heights by worrying. The description ἐλάχιστον (Lk 12:26) appears to be an exquisite bit of irony climaxing the hyperbole.—B. 236f. DELG. M-M.

πιάζω 1 aor. ἐπίασα. Pass.: fut. πιασθήσεται Sir 23:1; aor. ἐπιάσθην (Alcman 28 D.[2]; Theocr. 4, 35; Sethianische Verfluchungstafeln 49, 58; 59 Wünsch [1898]; POxy 812, 5 [5 BC]; PHamb 6, 16; LXX [s. Thackeray 282.—B-D-F §29, 2; 101 p. 48; Mlt-H. 69; 254; 405]; TestNapht 5:2, 3) Doric and colloq. for Attic πιέζω (s. Thumb 67 note) in our lit. only in the foll. senses

❶ **to take firm hold of, *grasp*** neutral *take (hold of)* τινά τῆς χειρός *someone by the hand* **Ac 3:7** (cp. Theocr. 4, 35 τὸν ταῦρον ὁπλᾶς).

❷ **to seize with intent to overpower or gain control**—ⓐ of humans ***seize, arrest, take into custody*** (cp. BGU 325, 2 λῃστοπιαστής) τινά *someone* (PGM 5, 172 κλέπτην) **J 7:30, 32, 44; 8:20; 10:39; 11:57;** PEg[2], 26 and 28; **2 Cor 11:32.** ὃν πιάσας ἔθετο εἰς φυλακήν **Ac 12:4.**

ⓑ of animals ***catch*** (SSol 2:15) of fish (PLond II, 483, 76 p. 328 [616 AD]) **J 21:3, 10.** Pass. ἐπιάσθη τὸ θηρίον **Rv 19:20.** On πιάζω and corresponding form πιέζω, s. GShipp, Modern Greek Evidence for the Ancient Greek Vocabulary '79, 454f.—B. 575; 744. New Docs 3, 82.—DELG s.v. πιέζω. M-M.

πίε, πιεῖν, πίεσαι s. πίνω.

πιέζω pass.: pf. ptc. πεπιεσμένος; 3 sg. aor. ἐπιέσθη Papias (v.l.) (Hom.+; Hero Alex. I p. 58, 4; SIG 904, 7; PCairZen 378, 11 [III BC]; PBerlZill 1, 41; Mi 6:15 πιέσεις ἐλαίαν; TestSol 1:2 C; Philo, Migr. Abr. 157, Aet. M. 129; Jos., Ant. 17, 28. See πιάζω) ***press*** μέτρον πεπιεσμένον *a measure that is pressed down* **Lk 6:38.** ὑπὸ τῆς ἁμάξης … ἐπιέσθη ὥστε τὰ ἔγκατα αὐτοῦ ἐκκενωθῆναι *Judas was so pinned by the wagon that his entrails came out* Papias (3:2 v.l. [Preuschen p. 98 app. for ln. 8]).—S. Shipp, πιάζω, end. B. 575; 744. New Docs 3, 82.—DELG. M-M.

πιθανολογία, ας, ἡ (πιθανός 'persuasive, plausible', cp. πείθω) ***persuasive speech, art of persuasion*** (so Pla., Theaet. 162e) in an unfavorable sense in its only occurrence in our lit. ἐν πιθανολογίᾳ *by specious arguments* **Col 2:4** (cp. PLips 40 III, 7 διὰ πιθανολογίας).—DELG s.v. πείθομαι. M-M.

πίθηκος, ου, ὁ (Aristoph., Pla. et al.; Lucian, Philops. 5; Plut., Mor. 52b; pap [Sb 2009; 2629]; 2 Ch 9:21; Jos., Ant. 8, 181; Ar. 12, 7; Tat. 18, 2) ***ape*** PtK 2 p. 14, 20. DELG.

πιθός the spelling preferred by edd. for πειθός (q.v.).

πικραίνω fut. πικρανῶ; aor. ἐπίκρανα LXX. Pass: fut. 3 pl. πικρανθήσονται Jer 40:9; 1 aor. ἐπικράνθην; prim. 'make sharp' esp. to the taste (s. three next entries).

❶ **to cause to become bitter, *make bitter*** in physical sense (Hippocr. et al.) πικρανεῖ σου τὴν κοιλίαν (κοιλία 1b) **Rv 10:9.** Pass., of the stomach ἐπικράνθη ἡ κοιλία vs. **10.** Of someth. that has been swallowed: (τὰ ὕδατα) ἐπικράνθησαν **8:11** (prob. not in ref. to οἱ ἄνθρωποι, in the sense 'made bitter'=poisoned?). Of honey when wormwood is mixed w. it Hm 5, 1, 5.

❷ **to cause bitter feelings, *embitter, make bitter,*** in affective sense (Pla.+; LXX; ApcrEzk Denis p. 122, 3 [Epiph. 70, 14]) pass., intr. sense *become bitter* or *embittered* abs. (Demosth., Ep. 1, 6; Ep. 6 of Apollonius of Tyana: Philostrat. I 346, 19; Is 14:9; Philo, Mos. I, 302) Hm 10, 2, 3. π. πρός τινα *be embittered* *against someone* **Col 3:19** (πρός τινα as Lynceus in Athen. 6, 242b).—DELG s.v. πικρός. M-M. TW.

πικρία, ας, ἡ (πικρός; Demosth., Aristot. et al.; pap, LXX; TestSol 5:13; TestAbrA; TestLevi 11:7; TestNapht 2:8; ApcMos 24; Just., D. 120, 2)

❶ **state of being bitter to the taste, *bitterness*** (Theophr., CP 6, 10, 7; Plut., Mor. 897a), but used in imagery, of a βοτάνη πικρίαν ἔχουσα *a plant that has a bitter taste* GEg 252, 54 (Diog. L. 9, 80 πικρός is 'inedible' in contrast to ἐδώδιμος. Likew. Jos., Ant. 3, 30 πικρία='inedibility'). A reprehensible pers. is called χολὴ πικρίας= χολὴ πικρά (on the close connection of χολή w. πικρία s. Vett. Val. 249, 16; Dt 29:17; La 3:19; TestNapht 2:8) *bitter gall* **Ac 8:23.** ῥίζα πικρίας *a bitter root,* a root that bears bitter fruit **Hb 12:15** (cp. Dt 29:17; Hippocr., Ep. 16, 4 τ. πικρὴν ῥίζαν ἐκκόψαι).

❷ **state of being bitter in an affective sense, *bitterness, animosity, anger, harshness*** fig. ext. of 1 (cp. Demosth. et al.; Bion of Borysthenes [III BC] in Diog. L. 4, 46 [of a slaveholder's inhuman cruelty]; LXX, Philo); it is associated with ὀξυχολία Hm 5, 2, 4; 5, 2, 8; 6, 2, 5. ἐν π. γίνεσθαι *become embittered* m 5, 2, 2. ἐπιτάσσειν τινὶ ἐν π. *give an order to someone harshly* B 19:7; cp. D 4:10. W. θυμός, ὀργή al. (cp. Philo, Ebr. 223; Jos., Ant. 17, 148) in a list of vices **Eph 4:31.** τὸ στόμα ἀρᾶς καὶ πικρίας γέμει *the mouth is full of curses and of bitter words* **Ro 3:14** (Ps 13:3; cp. 9:28. π. γέμειν as Philo, Migr. Abr. 36).—DELG s.v. πικρός. M-M. TW.

πικρός, ά, όν (Hom. et al.; pap, LXX, pseudepigr., apolog.)

❶ **pert. to being bitter to taste, *bitter*** (opp. γλυκύς; cp. Pla., Theaet. 166e πικρῷ γλυκὺ μεμιγμένον; Pr 27:7) of water that is not potable (as Appian, Iber. 88, §385; Ex 15:23; Demetr.: 722 fgm. 4 Jac.; Philo, Rer. Div. Her. 208; Jos., Bell. 4, 476; 7, 186 [opp. γλυκύς]) **Js 3:11** (τό[ν θ]υμ[όν], so the ed. P[74], but perh. τὸ [ἁλ]υκ[όν] is to be read, s. N. app.).

❷ **pert. to being bitter in feeling or attitude, *bitter, embittered, harsh,*** fig. ext. of 1: ζῆλον π. ἔχειν ἐν τῇ καρδίᾳ *have bitter jealousy in one's heart* **Js 3:14.** Of ὀξυχολία (πικρία 2) Hm 5, 1, 6. Of the commandments of the devil m 12, 4, 6. Of humans (trag. et al.; Diod. S. 14, 65, 4 π. τύραννος; Aelian, fgm. 74 p. 222, 27; 103 p. 235, 24; Alciphron 1, 15, 5; Philo, Omn. Prob. Lib. 106; Jos., C. Ap. 2, 277; Ath. 31, 1) *harsh* (w. ὀξύχολος and ἄφρων) m 6, 2, 4; (w. ἄσπλαγχνος) s 6, 3, 2. λέοντα … π. λίαν *a very ferocious lion* AcPl Ha 4, 20. Of patience μηδὲν ἐν ἑαυτῇ ἔχουσα πικρόν *it has no bitterness in it* Hm 5, 2, 3.—B. 1033.—DELG. M-M. TW.

πικρῶς adv. of πικρός (Aeschyl. et al.; pap e.g. PPetr III p. 115, 42 H (8)f, 8 [III BC]; LXX, TestSol, TestAbr A; JosAs, ApcEsdr; Ar. 12, 2; Mel., P. 26, 181) ***bitterly,*** fig. (Diod. S. 3, 71, 3 of the painful oppression of Cronus' rule; Appian, Liby. 100 §472 π. κολάζειν=punish severely; Jos., Ant. 9, 118 βλασφημεῖν) κλαίειν (Is 22:4; 33:7; TestAbr A 11 p. 90, 6 [Stone p. 28]; JosAs 10:17; ApcrEsdr 5:8 p. 30, 1 Tdf.) *weep bitterly* **Mt 26:75; Lk 22:62;** GJs 13:1, 3; 15:3. ὁ λέων … ὠρύετο πικρῶς *the lion roared ferociously* AcPl 2, 7 Ha.—M-M. TW.

Πιλᾶτος, ου, ὁ (also -άτος; on the form Πειλᾶτος, which is preferred by Tdf. and W-H., s. Tdf., Proleg. 84f; W-H., app. 155. On the use of the art. w. it W-S. §18, 6d) ***Pilate*** (Pontius P.), prefect (on the Lat. insc. var. restored, but here cited accord. to the text in Ehrenberg-Jones no. 369, TIBERIEVM [. . PON]TIVS PILATVS [. . . . PRAEF]ECTVS IVDA[EA]E, s. Schürer I 358 n. 22; JVardaman, JBL 81, '62, 70f; Boffo, Iscrizioni no. 25 [lit.]; s. also Mason 142f on the nomenclature) of Judea 26–36 AD (s. PHedley, s. lit cited s.v. Φῆλιξ). He played the decisive role in Jesus' trial and gave the order for his crucifixion. **Mt 27:2ff; Mk 15:1ff; Lk 3:1; 13:1** (this is the only place in our lit. where a detail is given fr. his life outside the Passion Narrative. SJohnson, ATR 17, '35, 91–95; JBlinzler, NovT 2, '58, 24–49); **23:1ff; J 18:29ff; 19:1ff; Ac 3:13; 4:27; 13:28, 29** D; **1 Ti 6:13** (s. μαρτυρέω 1c); IMg 11; ITr 9:1; ISm 1:2; GPt 1:1; 2:3–5; 8:29, 31; 11:43, 45f, 49. (Cp. Just.; Mel., P. 92, 693.—Non-Christian sources, esp. Tacitus, Ann. 15, 44; Philo, Leg. ad Gai. 299–305 based on a letter of Agrippa I; Jos., Bell. 2, 169–77, Ant. 18, 35; 55–64; 85–89; 177.)—Schürer I 383–87, 438–40; HPeter, Pontius Pilatus: NJklA 19, 1907, 1–40; KKastner, Jesus vor Pilatus 1912; MDibelius, 'Herodes u. Pilatus': ZNW 16, 1915, 113–26; BEaston, The Trial of Jesus: AJT 19, 1915, 430–52; RHusband, The Prosecution of Jesus 1916; FDoerr (attorney), Der Prozess Jesu in rechtsgesch. Beleuchtung 1920; GBertram, Die Leidensgesch. Jesu u. der Christuskult 1922, 62–72; GLippert (attorney), Pil. als Richter 1923; PRoué, Le procès de Jésus 1924; GRosadi, D. Prozess Jesu 1926, Il processo di Gesù[14] '33; GAicher, D. Proz. Jesu 1929; MRadin, The Trial of Jes. of Naz. '31; SLiberty, The Importance of P. P. in Creed and Gosp.: JTS 45, '44, 38–56; JBlinzler, D. Prozess Jesu[4] '69, Münchener Theol. Ztschr. 5, '54, 171–84.—On Pilate's wife: EFascher, TLZ 72, '47, 201–4; AOepke, ibid. 73, '48, 743–46.—S. also s.v. ἀποκτείνω 1a, and Feigel, Weidel and Finegan s.v. Ἰούδας 6.—EStauffer, Zur Münzprägung u. Judenpolitik des Pontius Pilatus: La Nouvelle Clio 9, '50, 495–514; EBammell, Syrian Coinage and Pilate: JJS 2, '51, 108–10.—Pauly-W. XX, 1322f; Kl. Pauly IV 1049; BHHW III 1472f. M-M. s.v. Πειλ. EDNT. TW.

πίμπλημι fut. πλήσω LXX; 1 aor. ἔπλησα; pf. mid. ptc. πεπλησμένα (Just.). Pass.: 1 fut. πλησθήσομαι; 1 aor. ἐπλήσθην, ptc. πλησθείς (Hom. et al., pap, LXX, En; TestSol 6:5 D; TestJob 27:3; JosAs; SibOr 3, 311; Joseph.; Just., D. 73, 6.—On the spelling B-D-F §93; 101; Thackeray p. 110; Mlt-H. 106. Trans. in pres. and impf., whereas the corresp. πλήθω is intr. in these tenses.)

❶ **to cause to be completely full, *fill, fulfill***—ⓐ lit.—α. of external, perceptible things τὶ *someth.* **Lk 5:7.** τί τινος *someth. with someth.* (Hom. et al.; PLond II, 453, 6 p. 319 [IV AD]; LXX) a sponge w. vinegar **Mt 27:48; Mk 15:36 v.l.; J 19:29 v.l.** Pass. (Jos., Ant. 3, 299) ἐπλήσθη ὁ γάμος [v.l. νυμφών] ἀνακειμένων **Mt 22:10.** ἐπλήσθη ἡ πόλις τῆς συγχύσεως **Ac 19:29.**—ἡ οἰκία ἐπλήσθη ἐκ τῆς ὀσμῆς **J 12:3 v.l.** (Hom. Hymns, Dem. 280 αὐγῆς ἐπλήσθη δόμος).

β. of a pers. inner life (Hom. et al.; Diod. S. 15, 37, 2 φρονήματος [with enthusiasm] ἐπίμπλαντο; PGM 13, 234 πλησθεὶς τῆς θεοσοφίας; LXX) pass. ἐπλήσθησαν φόβου (Appian, Bell. Civ. 4, 48 §204) **Lk 5:26;** ἀνοίας **6:11;** θάμβους καὶ ἐκστάσεως **Ac 3:10;** ζήλου **5:17; 13:45;** θυμοῦ (Da 3:19) **Lk 4:28;** χαρᾶς AcPl Ha 2, 15; 8, 7. Of the Holy Spirit (cp. Sir 48:12a; Pr 15:4.—Dio Chrys. 55 [72], 12 the Pythia is ἐμπιμπλαμένη τοῦ πνεύματος): πνεύματος ἁγίου πλησθήσεται **Lk 1:15;** cp. vss. **41, 67; Ac 2:4; 4:8, 31; 9:17; 13:9;** AcPl Ha 6, 17. τῷ πνεύματι Hm 11, 9 (w. Ox 5 recto, 5; v.l. πληρωθείς).

ⓑ fig.—α. of prophecies, pass. *be fulfilled* **Lk 1:20 v.l.; 21:22.**

β. of a period of time that passes or comes to an end, pass. ἐπλήσθησαν αἱ ἡμέραι *the days came to an end* **Lk 1:23.** A gen. added denotes the event that follows upon the expiration of the time: ἐπλήσθη ὁ χρόνος τοῦ τεκεῖν αὐτήν *the time came for her to give birth* **Lk 1:57** (cp. Hdt. 6, 63, 1; 69, 5 on period of gestation). Cp. **2:6, 21, 22.**

γ. ἐπλήσθησαν αἱ ἀνομίαι αὐτῶν *the measure of their iniquities has become full* Hv 2, 2, 2.

❷ **to satisfy a need totally,** ***satiate*** pass. *be satiated, have one's fill* τινός *with* or *of someth.* (Soph., Ant. 121; Epigram of Ptolemaeus: Anth. Pal. 9, 577 πίμπλαμαι ἀμβροσίης) τῆς ἀσεβείας 1 Cl 57:6 (Pr 1:31).—DELG. M-M. TW.

πίμπρημι pass.: πίμπραμαι, inf. πίμπρασθαι; 1 aor. ptc. πρησθείς (Hom. et al.; ins, LXX; Tat. 24, 1.—On the spelling s. B-D-F §93; 101; Mlt-H. 106; Thackeray p. 110) a medical term (Hobart 50), but by no means confined to that profession; nevertheless rare in older Gk. prose, which prefers the cmpd. ἐμπίμπρημι. The pass. means either

❶ ***burn with fever*** (Pherecrates Com. [V BC], fgm. 80, 4 Kock; SIG 1179, 15 [s. n. 6]; 1180, 3) or

❷ ***become distended, swell up*** (Hippocr. et al.; SIG 1169, 123; Num 5:21, 27; Jos., Ant. 3, 271. Field, Notes 149). Of Judas, Papias (3:2). Either mng. is poss. in προσεδόκων αὐτὸν μέλλειν πίμπρασθαι **Ac 28:6.**—B. 75. DELG. M-M.

πινακίδιον, ου, τό (s. next entry; Hippocr., Aristot. et al.) dim. of πίναξ ***little (wooden) tablet*** esp. of a writing-tablet for notes (Epict. 3, 22, 74; Ezk 9:2 Sym.) **Lk 1:63.**—DELG s.v. πίναξ. M-M.

πινακίς, ίδος, ἡ ***little (wooden) writing tablet*** (s. prec. entry; Macho [III BC] in Athen. 13, 582c al.; WSchubart, Der Gnomon d. Idios Logos 1919 [=BGU V] 36; PRyl 144, 19 [38 AD]; Sym. Ezk 9:11; Artapanus in Eus., PE 9, 27, 26) **Lk 1:63 v.l.**—DELG s.v. πίναξ. M-M s.v. πινακίδιον.

πίναξ, ακος, ὁ (in var. senses Hom. et al.; ins [e.g. SEG XLIII, 773, 31f: II BC of a portrait painted on a wooden tablet], pap; Ath. 17, 2) **a relatively flat large dish,** ***platter, dish*** (Hom. et al.; BGU 781 V, 16; StudPal 67, 22; Jos., Bell. 5, 562, Ant. 8, 91; loanw. in rabb.) ἐπὶ πίνακι *on a platter* (s. φέρω 2αα) **Mt 14:8, 11; Mk 6:25, 28.** W. ποτήριον **Lk 11:39.**—B. 345; 599. DELG. M-M.

πίνω (Hom.+) impf. ἔπινον; fut. πίομαι (W-S. 13, 6; 17; B-D-F §74, 2; 77; Rob. 354), 2 sg. πίεσαι (Ruth 2:9; B-D-F §87; Thackeray p. 218; 282; Rob. 340; Mlt-H. 198); 2 aor. ἔπιον (on ἔπιαν **1 Cor 10:4** D s. B-D-F §81, 3; Mlt-H. 208), impv. πίε, πιέτω, inf. πιεῖν (edd. contracted πεῖν [πῖν]; s. B-D-F §101 p. 48; §31, 2; W-S. §5, 23b; Rob. 72; 204; Mayser 365; Thackeray p. 63f; W-H., app. 170); perf. πέπωκα; plpf. 3 sg. πεπώκει 1 Km 30:12 (W-S. §13, 15; B-D-F §83, 1).

❶ **to take in a liquid internally,** ***drink,*** w. acc. of someth. that is drunk **Mt 6:25; Mk 16:18; Lk 12:29.** αἷμα (Num 23:24; 1 Ch 11:19 al.; 4 [6] Esdr [POxy 1010]): **J 6:53f, 56** (cp. the imagery in Jos., Bell. 5, 344 ἐσθίειν . . . καὶ τὸ τῆς πόλεως αἷμα πίνειν). οἶνον **Lk 1:15** (cp. Dt 29:5); **5:39;** cp. **Mt 26:29b; Ro 14:21** (Is 22:13) al. τί πίωμεν; *what will we have to drink?* **Mt 6:31.** φαγεῖν καὶ πιεῖν ὅσον ἂν βούλωνται MPol 7:2.ἐσθίειν καὶ πίνειν τὰ παρά τινος *eat and drink what someone sets before one* **Lk 10:7.** Foll. by ἀπό τινος *drink* (of) *someth.* (Ctesias: 688 fgm. 11β p. 433 Jac. [Sotion fgm. 17 in Παραδοξογράφοι W. p. 185] π. ἀπ' αὐτῆς [a spring], resulting in confession of things perpetrated in secret; Ael. Aristid. 39, 4 K.=18 p. 409 D.; Jer 28:7; GrBar 4:6; Just., D. 140, 1) **22:18.** μηδεὶς φαγέτω μηδὲ πιέτω ἀπὸ τῆς εὐχαριστίας D 9:5. Foll. by ἔκ τινος (of) *someth.* (Gen 9:21; TestJos 19:5; GrBar 5:2; Syntipas p. 43, 15 ἐκ τοῦ δηλητηρίου πίομαι) **Mt 26:29a; Mk 14:25a; J 4:13f.** Foll. by acc. of the vessel fr. which one drinks, in which case the vessel and its contents are identified (ποτήριον a) ποτήριον κυρίου πίνειν **1 Cor 10:21;** cp. **11:26f.** The vessel can also be introduced by ἐκ (Hipponax [VI BC] 16 and 17 D.[2]; Aristoph., Equ. 1289; Pla., Rep. 417a; X., An. 6, 1, 4 ἐκ ποτηρίων; SIG 1168, 80) ἐκ τοῦ ποτηρίου πινέτω (s. 2 Km 12:3) **1 Cor 11:28;** cp. **Mt 26:27; Mk 14:23.** Likew. ἐξ αὐτοῦ (=ἐκ τοῦ φρέατος.—Paus. Attic. κ, 56 κρήνη, ἐξ ἧς ἔπινον; Num 21:22; Philo, Deus Imm. 155) *from it* **J 4:12.** ἐκ πέτρας **1 Cor 10:4b.**—On the acc. κρίμα ἑαυτῷ ἐσθίει καὶ πίνει **11:29b** cp. κρίμα 4b.—Abs. **Mt 27:34b.** W. ἐσθίειν **11:18f; Lk 5:33; 12:19** (Phoenix Col. 1, 9 [Coll. Alex. p. 231]), **45** al.; cp **17:8** (on the protocol in 17:7 cp. ViAesopi G 61 P.). ἔφαγεν καὶ ἔπιεν 1 Cl 3:1 (cp. Dt. 32:15); I Tr 9:1. οὔτε ἐπὶ τὸ φαγεῖν οὔτε ἐπὶ τὸ πεῖν (=πιεῖν) AcPl Ox 6, 7f (=Aa 1, 241, 12f). τρώγειν καὶ π. **Mt 24:38;** cp. **1 Cor 15:32.** ἐσθίειν καὶ π. μετά τινος *eat and drink w. someone* **Mt 24:49; Mk 2:16 v.l.; Lk 5:30.** δοῦναί τινι πιεῖν (τι) *give someone someth. to drink* (numerous exx. of δοῦναι πιεῖν in AKnox and WHeadlam, Herodas 1922 p. 55f; Jos., Ant. 2, 64) **Mt 27:34a; Mk 15:23 v.l.; J 4:7** (δὸς πεῖν as POxy 1088, 55 [I AD] and Cyranides p. 49, 16. Cp. Lamellae Aur. Orphicae ed. AOlivieri 1915 p. 12 σοι δώσουσι πιεῖν θείης ἀπὸ κρήνης [IV/III BC]), vs. **10.** πῶς παρ' ἐμοῦ πεῖν αἰτεῖς, *how can you ask me for a drink?* vs. **9.**—In imagery, of the earth: γῆ ἡ πιοῦσα τὸν ὑετόν **Hb 6:7** (this figure and corresp. exprs. trag. et al.; cp. Hdt. 3, 117; 4, 198; Anacreontea 21, 1; Dt 11:11; SibOr 3, 696). In J, Jesus calls those who are thirsty to him, that they may drink the water he gives them and never thirst again (cp. Lucian, Dial. Deor. 4, 5 πίνειν τῆς ἀθανασίας) **J 4:14; 7:37.**

❷ In an idiom πιεῖν τὸ ποτήριον w. added words that make the sense clear ***drink the cup***=submit to a severe trial, or death (ποτήριον b) **Mt 20:22f; Mk 10:38f; J 18:11;** cp. **Mt 26:42;** ApcPt Rainer 16 (for the fig. use cp. Herodas 1, 25 π. ἐκ καινῆς=from the new cup. Then, as **Mt 20:22f; Mk 10:38f** of those who suffer the same fate: Aristoph., Eq. 1289 οὔποτ' ἐκ ταὐτοῦ μεθ' ἡμῶν πίεται ποτηρίου=he will never drink from the same cup as we do; Libanius, Ep. 355, 4 F. μνήμη τῶν ἐκ ταὐτοῦ κρατῆρος πεπωκότων). Sim. πίεται ἐκ τοῦ οἴνου τοῦ θυμοῦ τοῦ θεοῦ **Rv 14:10;** cp. **18:3** (on the rdg. s. RBorger, TRu 52, '87, 50f; θυμός 1; 2; cp. w. acc. τρώγειν καὶ π. τὸν λόγον τοῦ θεοῦ, τὸν τῆς ἀθανασίας ἄρτον Iren. 4, 38, 1 [Harv. II 293, 12]).—B. 331. DELG s.v. πίνω. M-M. EDNT. TW.

Πιόνιος, ου, ὁ *Pionius,* one of those who gathered and edited accounts of Polycarp's martyrdom MPol 22:3; EpilMosq 5.—PCorssen, ZNW 5, 1904, 266ff; ESchwartz, De Pionio et Polycarpo, Progr. Göttingen 1905.

πιότης, τητος, ἡ (Hippocr.; LXX, Philo) **state of oiliness,** ***fatness.*** Use of the term in ref. to plants (Theophr., HP 9, 1, 3; cp. Jos., Bell. 3, 516 of the fertile area of Lake Genesserat) appears in the imagery in **Ro 11:17** ἡ ῥίζα τῆς πιότητος *the root with its oily richness* i.e. its 'sap'=*the root with its rich sap* (REB: 'share the same root and sap as the olive') of the cultivated olive tree (cp. Judg 9:9; TestLevi 8:8; TestIss 5:5. Since oil is the prized product of the olive tree, the root is described as source).—DELG s.v. πίαρ. M-M.

πιπράσκω (Aeschyl., Hdt.+.—B-D-F §101 p. 48; s. Mlt-H. 254) impf. ἐπίπρασκον; pf. πέπρακα (**Mt 13:46** and Hv 1, 1, 1 it has aorist aspect; s. B-D-F §343, 1; Rob. 900). Pass.: fut. πραθήσομαι LXX; 1 aor. ἐπράθην; pf. ptc. πεπραμένος **to engage in vending,** ***sell,*** w. acc. of thing **Mt 13:46; Ac 2:45.** Pass. **4:34; 5:4.** W. gen. of price (Isaeus 7, 31; Lysias 18:20; Dt 21:14) **Mt 26:9; J 12:5;** πραθῆναι ἐπάνω δηναρίων τριακοσίων **Mk**

14:5 (s. ἐπάνω 2). W. acc. of pers. *sell someone* (as a slave) Hv 1, 1, 1. Pass. **Mt 18:25.** In imagery (Ps.-Demosth. 17, 13 τοῖς πεπρακόσιν ἑαυτοὺς εἰς τἀναντία='to those who have sold themselves to what is opposed' [to their country's interests]) of a pers. who is sold as a slave to sin πεπραμένος ὑπὸ τὴν ἁμαρτίαν **Ro 7:14** (sim. 3 Km 20:25; 4 Km 17:17; 1 Macc 1:15 ἐπράθησαν ποιῆσαι πονηρόν).—DELG s.v. πέρνημι. M-M. TW.

πίπτω (Hom.+) impf. ἔπιπτον; fut. πεσοῦμαι (B-D-F §77; Rob. 356); 2 aor. ἔπεσον and ἔπεσα (B-D-F §81, 3; W-S. §13, 13; Mlt-H. 208; W-H., app. p. 164; Tdf., Prol. p. 123); pf. 2 sg. πέπτωκας **Rv 2:5** (πέπτωκες v.l.; B-D-F §83, 2; W-S. §13, 16; Mlt- H 221), 3 pl. πέπτωκαν **Rv 18:3 v.l.** (W-S. §13, 15; Mlt-H. 221)

❶ **to move w. relative rapidity in a downward direction,** ***fall,*** the passive of the idea conveyed in βάλλω.—ⓐ *fall (down)* from a higher point, w. the 'point from which' designated by ἀπό (Hom. et al.) ἀπὸ τῆς τραπέζης *from the table* **Mt 15:27; Lk 16:21.** ἀπὸ τοῦ οὐρανοῦ **Mt 24:29.** ἀπὸ τῆς κεφαλῆς **Ac 27:34 v.l.** (of the falling out of hair, as Synes., Calvit. 1, p. 63b). The direction or destination of the fall is expressed by an adv. ἀπὸ τοῦ τριστέγου κάτω *down from the third story* **Ac 20:9.** ἀπὸ τοῦ κεράμου χαμαί *from the roof to the ground* Hm 11:20. ἔκ τινος *from someth.*: ἐκ τοῦ οὐρανοῦ (Sallust. 4 p. 8, 19; Job 1:16; 3 Km 18:38.—SibOr 5, 72 ἐξ ἄστρων) **Mk 13:25;** of lightning (Ps.-Plut., Vi. Hom. 111 εἰ ἐκπίπτοι ἡ ἀστράπη; Ps.-Clem., Hom. 9, 5; 6) **Lk 10:18** (Lycophron, vs. 363 of the image of Athena ἐξ οὐρανοῦ πεσοῦσα. Cp. σατάν; *be thrown* is also possible here); **Rv 8:10a;** the destination is added ἐκ τοῦ οὐρανοῦ εἰς τὴν γῆν **9:1** (Ps.-Callisth. 2, 10, 10 ἐξ οὐρανοῦ εἰς τὸ ἔδαφος πεπτωκότες). W. only the destination given ἐν μέσῳ τῶν ἀκανθῶν *among the thorns* **Lk 8:7.** ἐπί τι *on someth.* **Rv 8:10b.** ἐπὶ τὴν γῆν (Aeschyl., Ag. 1019; Am 3:5; JosAs 16:16) **Mt 10:29** (with the patristic v.l. εἰς παγίδα cp. Am 3:5 and Aesop, Fab. 193 P.=340 H.//284 Ch.//207 H-H. of a bird: ἐμπίπτειν εἰς τοὺς βρόχους); **13:8;** Hm 11:21 (here the 'place from which' is designated by an adv.: ἄνωθεν).—ἐπὶ τὰ πετρώδη **Mt 13:5;** cp. **Mk 4:5** (ἐπί 4bγ). ἐπὶ τὰς ἀκάνθας **Mt 13:7** (ἐπί 4bδ). A pers. falls down ἐπὶ τὸν λίθον *on the stone* **Mt 21:44a; Lk 20:18a.** Conversely the stone falls on a pers. **Mt 21:44b; Lk 20:18b.** Likew. ἐπί τινα **23:30; Rv 6:16** (cp. on both Hos 10:8).—In imagery ὁ ἥλιος π. ἐπί τινα *the (heat of the) sun falls upon someone* **Rv 7:16** (Maximus Tyr. 4, 1a ἡλίου φῶς πίπτον εἰς γῆν; Alex. Aphr., An. Mant. p. 146, 9 Br. τὸ φῶς ἐπὶ πάντα πίπτει). ὁ κλῆρος π. ἐπί τινα (κλῆρος 1) **Ac 1:26.** *come (upon)* ἐπί τινα *someone* ἀχλὺς καὶ σκότος **Ac 13:11. Rv 11:11 v.l.** (φόβος 2a).—εἴς τι (Hes., Op. 620) εἰς τὴν γῆν (Phlegon: 257 fgm. 36, 1, 5 Jac. πίπτειν εἰς τὴν γῆν) **Mk 4:8; Lk 8:8; J 12:24; Rv 6:13;** 1 Cl 24:5. εἰς τὴν ὁδόν Hv 3, 7, 1. εἰς βόθυνον **Mt 15:14;** cp. **Lk 14:5.** εἰς τὰς ἀκάνθας **Mk 4:7; Lk 8:14.** εἰς τὸ πῦρ Hv 3, 7, 2. παρά τι *on someth.* παρὰ τὴν ὁδόν (Iambl. Erot. p. 222, 22) **Mt 13:4; Mk 4:4; Lk 8:5.** ἐγγύς τινος *near someth.* ἐγγὺς (τῶν) ὑδάτων Hv 3, 2, 9; 3, 7, 3.

ⓑ of someth. that, until recently, has been standing (upright) *fall (down), fall to pieces*

α. of persons—א. *fall to the ground, fall down (violently)* εἰς τὸ πῦρ καὶ εἰς τὸ ὕδωρ **Mt 17:15** (but HZimmern, Die Keilinschriften u. d. AT[3] 1903, 366; 363f, and JWeiss ad loc. take the falling into fire and water to mean fever and chills). ἐπὶ τῆς γῆς (SibOr 4, 110; 5, 100) **Mk 9:20** (π. under the infl. of a hostile spirit; sim. Jos., Ant. 8, 47). ἐπὶ τὴν γῆν (SibOr 4, 110 v.l.) **Ac 9:4;** cp. **22:7** (s. ἔδαφος). χαμαί (Job 1:20; Philo, Agr. 74) **J 18:6.** ἔπεσα πρὸς τοὺς πόδας αὐτοῦ ὡς νεκρός **Rv 1:17.**—Abs. *fall down* GPt 5:18 v.l. *Fall* dead (Paradox. Vat. 37 Keller πίπτει; Mel., P. 26, 184 πρηνὴς δὲ ἔπιπτε σιγῶν) **Ac 5:5, 10; 1 Cor 10:8** (cp. Ex 32:28); **Hb 3:17** (Num 14:29). Specifically *fall* in battle (Ael. Aristid. 46 p. 233 D.; Appian, Hann. 56 §236; Jos., Vi. 341; 354) **Lk 21:24** (cp. στόμα 4 and Sir 28:18; 4 [6] Esdr [POxy 1010, 3–11 σὺ ἐν ῥομφαίᾳ πεσῇ … πεσοῦνται ἐν μαχαίρῃ]).

ב. *fall down, throw oneself to the ground* as a sign of devotion or humility, before high-ranking persons or divine beings, esp. when one approaches w. a petition (LXX; TestAbr A 18 p. 100, 29 [Stone p. 48]; JosAs 14:4; ApcSed 14:2), abs. **Mt 2:11; 4:9; 18:26, 29; Rv 5:14; 19:4; 22:8** (in all these places [except **Mt 18:29**] π. is closely connected w. προσκυνεῖν [as Jos., Ant. 10, 213 after Da 3:5 and ApcMos 27]. Sim. in many of the places already mentioned). W. var. words added (Jos., Ant. 10, 11 πεσὼν ἐπὶ πρόσωπον τ. θεὸν ἱκέτευε; Gen 17:3, 17; Num 14:5) ἐπὶ πρόσωπον (αὐτοῦ, αὐτῶν) **Mt 17:6; 26:39; Lk 5:12; 17:16** (ἐπὶ πρόσωπον παρὰ τοὺς πόδας αὐτοῦ); **1 Cor 14:25;** ἐπὶ τὰ πρόσωπα αὐτῶν **Rv 7:11; 11:16;** ἐπὶ τῆς γῆς **Mk 14:35.** Further, the one to whom devotion is given can be added in var. ways: ἐνώπιόν τινος (cp. 2 Km 3:34) **Rv 4:10; 5:8; 7:11.** ἔμπροσθεν τῶν ποδῶν τινος **19:10.** εἰς τοὺς πόδας τινός (Diog. L. 2, 79) **Mt 18:29 v.l.; J 11:32 v.l.** ἐπὶ τοὺς πόδας **Ac 10:25** (v.l. adds αὐτοῦ). παρὰ τοὺς πόδας τινός **Lk 8:41; 17:16** (s. above). πρὸς τοὺς πόδας τινός **Mk 5:22; J 11:32; Ac 10:25 D;** Hv 3, 2, 3.

β. of things, esp. structures *fall, fall to pieces, collapse, go down* (Appian, Iber. 54 §228; Jos., C. Ap. 1, 192, Ant. 16, 18) of the σκηνὴ Δαυίδ (σκηνή end) **Ac 15:16** (Am 9:11). Of a house *fall (in)* (Diod. S. 11, 63, 2 τῶν οἰκιῶν πιπτουσῶν; Dio Chrys. 6, 61; 30 [47], 25; Aristeas Hist.: 725 fgm. 1, 3 Jac. [in Eus., PE 9, 25, 3]; Job 1:19) **Mt 7:25, 27; Lk 6:49 v.l.** (Diod. S. 15, 12, 2 τῶν οἰκιῶν πιπτουσῶν because of the influx of the ποταμός). τὰ τείχη Ἰεριχὼ ἔπεσαν **Hb 11:30** (cp. Josh 6:5, 20.—Appian, Bell. Civ. 1, 112 §524; Ael. Aristid. 25, 42 K.=43 p. 813 D.: τὰ τείχη π.). ἐφ᾽ οὓς ἔπεσεν ὁ πύργος *upon whom the tower fell* **Lk 13:4** (of a πύργος X., Hell. 5, 2, 5; Arrian, Anab. 6, 7, 5; Polyaenus 6, 50; Jos., Bell. 5, 292; SibOr 11, 12.—π. ἐπί τινα Job 1:19). οἶκος ἐπὶ οἶκον πίπτει *house falls upon house* **11:17** (Jülicher, Gleichn. 221f). Of a city (Oenomaus in Eus., PE 5, 25, 6) Ox 1, 18f (=GTh 32); cp. **Rv 11:13; 16:19.**—Fig. *become invalid, come to an end, fail* (Pla., Euthyphr. 14d; Philostrat., Ep. 9) **Lk 16:17** (cp. Josh 23:14 v.l.; Ruth 3:18); **1 Cor 13:8.**

❷ **to experience loss of status or condition,** ***fall, be destroyed,*** in ext. sense of 1.—ⓐ *fall, be destroyed* ἔπεσεν, ἔπεσεν Βαβυλών (B. as symbol of humans in opposition to God and God's people; cp. Is 21:9; Jer 28:8.; Just., D. 49, 8.—Repetition of the verb for emphasis as Sappho, fgm. 131 D.[2] οὐκέτι ἴξω … οὐκέτι ἴξω [Campbell 114 p. 138: οὐκέτι ἥξω … οὐκέτι ἥξω]; Aristoph., Equ. 247; M. Ant. 5, 7; Ps.-Libanius, Char. Ep. p. 33, 5 ἐρῶ, ἐρῶ. This is to remove all possibility of doubt, as Theod. Prodr. 5, 66 εἶδον, εἶδον='I have really seen'; Theocr. 14, 24 ἔστι Λύκος, Λύκος ἐστί=it really is a wolf; in Rv w. focus on lamentation, s. reff. Schwyzer II 60) **Rv 14:8; 18:2.**

ⓑ *fall* in a transcendent or moral sense, *be completely ruined* (Polyb. 1, 35, 5; Diod. S. 13, 37, 5; Pr 11:28; Sir 1:30; 2:7; TestGad 4:3)=fall from a state of grace **Ro 11:11** (fig. w. πταίω [q.v. 1]), **22; Hb 4:11** (perh. w. ref. to the final judgment). Also in a less severe sense=*go astray morally* τοὺς πεπτωκότας ἔγειρον 1 Cl 59:4.—In wordplay 'stand and fall' (cp. Pr 24:16) **Ro 14:4; 1 Cor 10:12;** 2 Cl 2:6. μνημόνευε πόθεν πέπτωκες *remember (the heights) from which you have fallen* **Rv 2:5.**

ⓒ ὑπὸ κρίσιν π. *fall under condemnation* **Js 5:12** (on π. ὑπό τι cp. Diod. S. 4, 17, 5 π. ὑπ' ἐξουσίαν [Just., D. 105, 4]; Herodian 1, 4, 2; 2 Km 22:39; Tat. 8, 2 ὑπὸ τὴν εἱμαρμένην; Hippol., Ref. 4, 3, 5 ὑπὸ τὴν ἐπίσκεψιν *fall under scrutiny;* Did., Gen. 211, 5 ὑπὸ κατάραν; Theoph. Ant. 2, 25 [p. 162, 12] ὑπὸ θάνατον).

ⓓ π. . . . εἰς νόσον καὶ ἔσχατον κίνδυνον *in sickness and extreme peril* AcPl Ha 4, 15.

ⓔ *fall, perish* (Philo, Aet. M. 128) πίπτοντος τοῦ Ἰσραήλ B 12:5. οἱ πέντε ἔπεσαν *five have perished, disappeared, passed from the scene* **Rv 17:10** (cp. also π.='die' Job 14:10).—B. 671. DELG. M-M. TW. Spicq.

Πισιδία, ας, ἡ (Diod. S. 33, 5a; Strabo 12, 8, 14 Ἀντιόχεια ἡ πρὸς Πισιδίᾳ; Ptolemaeus 5, 4, 11; 5, 5, 4; OGI 535, 5 al. in ins) ***Pisidia,*** a mountainous region in central Asia Minor, west of the Taurus Mts., traversed by Paul, **Ac 14:24.** Ἀντιόχεια τῆς Πισ. **13:14 v.l.**—Zahn, Einl.[3] I 130ff; VSchultze, Altchristl. Städte und Landschaften II 2, 1926; Hemer, Acts 228; Pauly-W. XX 1793–97; Kl. Pauly IV 868f; BHHW III 1475f. See also on Παμφυλία.

Πισίδιος, ία, ιον ***Pisidian*** εἰς Ἀντιόχειαν τὴν Πισιδίαν **Ac 13:14.** But since the adj. Πισίδιος is found nowhere else (s. also FBlass ad loc.), and 'Pisidian' is rather expressed by Πισιδικός, ή, όν (Diod. S. 18, 25, 6; 18, 44, 1; 18, 45, 3.—Strabo refers to this Antioch as located πρὸς (τῇ) Πισιδίᾳ 12, 3, 31; 12, 6, 4; 12, 8, 14), this reading must probably be abandoned in favor of the v.l. εἰς Ἀντιόχειαν τῆς Πισιδίας.—M-M.

πιστεύω (trag.+) impf. ἐπίστευον; 1 aor. ἐπίστευσα; pf. πεπίστευκα; plpf. πεπιστεύκειν **Ac 14:23** (on the omission of the augment s. B-D-F §66, 1; Mlt-H. 190). Pass.: fut. 3 pl. πιστευθήσονται Gen 42, 20; 1 aor. ἐπιστεύθην; pf. πεπίστευμαι (the word does not occur in Phlm, 2 Pt, 2 and 3J, Rv, MPol, or D. But it is a special favorite of J and 1J, where it is found 96 times and 9 times respectively; πίστις is not found in the gospel at all, and occurs in 1J only once, 5:4. Our lit. uses it quite predominantly in a transcendent sense, or at least w. transcendent coloring).

❶ **to consider someth. to be true and therefore worthy of one's trust, *believe*—ⓐ** *believe (in) someth., be convinced of someth.*, w. that which one believes (in) indicated

α. by acc. of thing (Soph., Oed. Rex 646 τάδε; Aristot., Analyt. Pr. 2, 23, 68b, 13 ἅπαντα; PSI 494, 14 μηθέν; UPZ 70, 29 [152/151 BC] π. τὰ ἐνύπνια; ApcEsdr 7:12 p. 32, 26 τὸ βιβλίον τοῦτο) ἡ ἀγάπη πάντα πιστεύει **1 Cor 13:7.** πεπιστεύκαμεν τὴν ἀγάπην *we believe in the love* **1J 4:16.** πιστεύεις τοῦτο; **J 11:26b.** Cp. **Ac 13:41** (Hab 1:5). Pass. ἐπιστεύθη τὸ μαρτύριον ἡμῶν *our testimony was believed* **2 Th 1:10b** (cp. Aristot., EN 10, 2 p. 1172b, 15 ἐπιστεύοντο οἱ λόγοι; Gen 42:20).

β. by means of a ὅτι-clause *believe that* (Plut., Mor. 210d; Aelian, VH 1, 16 p. 8, 9; Herm. Wr. 4, 4: Porphyr., Ad Marcellam 24; PLond III, 897, 12 p. 207 [I AD]; Tob 10:8 S; Job 9:16; 15:31; 39:12; La 4:12; 4 Macc 7:19; TestAbr A 18 p. 100, 18 [Stone p. 48]; ParJer 6:7; Just., A I, 18, 2 al.; Orig., C. Cels. 4, 89, 16) μακαρία ἡ πιστεύσασα ὅτι ἔσται τελείωσις **Lk 1:45** (ὅτι here may=*for:* s. ὅτι 4b).—**Mk 11:23;** cp. vs. **24; J 8:24** (ὅτι ἐγώ εἰμι as Is 43:10); **11:27, 42; 13:19; 14:10; 16:27, 30; 17:8, 21; 20:31a; Ac 9:26; Ro 6:8; 10:9; 1 Th 4:14; Hb 11:6; Js 2:19a; 1J 5:1, 5;** Hv 3, 8, 4; 4, 2, 4; m 1:1; 6, 2, 10b; s 2:5.—[ὅτι εἷς θεός] καὶ εἷς χριστός AcPl Ha 1, 17; AcPlCor 1:8. π. περί τινος ὅτι *believe concerning someone that* **J 9:18** (M. Ant. 1, 15, 5 πιστεύειν περὶ ὧν λέγοι ὅτι οὕτως φρονεῖ=believe concerning whatever he might say, that it was what he actually thought; Just., D. 10, 1 π. ἡμῶν· ὅτι ἐσθίομεν ἀνθρώπους.—π. περί τινος as Plut., Lyc. 19, 4; Jos., Ant. 14, 267).

γ. by the acc. and inf. (pres. Pla., Gorg. 524a; PTebt 314, 3 [II AD]; 4 Macc 5:25; Jos., C. Ap. 2, 160; Just., A I, 8, 2 al.; Ath. 20, 3) πιστεύω τὸν υἱὸν τοῦ θεοῦ εἶναι τὸν Ἰησοῦν **Ac 8:37b.**—GMary 463, 8.—IRo 10:2.—By the inf. (Thu 2, 22, 1; Job 15:22; AscIs 2:10 εἰς οὐρανὸν ἀναβῆναι) πιστεύομεν σωθῆναι **Ac 15:11** (difft. JNolland, NTS 27, '80, 112f [inf. of result: 'we *believe* (in order) to be saved']).—By the acc. and ptc. ἐν σαρκὶ αὐτὸν πιστεύω ὄντα *I believe that he was in the flesh* ISm 3:1.

δ. by means of the dat. of thing *give credence to, believe* (Aeschyl., Pers. 786 θεῶν θεσφάτοισιν; Soph., Phil. 1374 τοῖς ἐμοῖς λόγοις, El. 886; Pla., Phd. 88c, Leg. 7, 798d; Polyb. 5, 42, 9; 9, 33, 1; Herodian 7, 5, 5 ἐλπίδι κρείττονι; BGU 674, 6 τῷ λόγῳ; 2 Ch 9:6 τοῖς λόγοις; Ps 105:24; Pr 14:15; Sir 19:15; En 104:13 ταῖς βίβλοις; Philo, Leg. All. 3, 229 τοῖς κενοῖς λογισμοῖς, Virt. 68 the sayings of God; Jos., C. Ap. 2, 286, Ant. 10, 39 τ. λόγοις; Tat. 18, 2 ὕλης οἰκονομίᾳ; Ath. 30, 2 ταῖς γοναῖς τοῦ Διός; Iren. 1, 10, 2 [Harv. I 92, 4] ἡ ἐκκλησία . . . π. τούτοις [sc. κήρυγμα and πίστις]) οὐκ ἐπίστευσας τοῖς λόγοις μου **Lk 1:20** (cp. Iambl., ViPyth. 28, 148 περὶ θεῶν μηδὲν θαυμαστὸν ἀπιστεῖν 'concerning the gods nothing is so marvelous that it should occasion unbelief'). τῇ γραφῇ καὶ τῷ λόγῳ **J 2:22.** Cp. **4:50; 5:47ab.** τοῖς γεγραμμένοις **Ac 24:14** (Diod. S. 16, 52, 7 πιστεύσαντες τοῖς γεγραμμένοις). τῇ ἐπαγγελίᾳ τοῦ θεοῦ 2 Cl 11:1 (Diod. S. 1, 53, 10 τῇ τοῦ προρρήσει πιστεύειν; 19, 90, 3). τῷ ψεύδει, τῇ ἀληθείᾳ **2 Th 2:11, 12.** τῇ καταλαλιᾷ Hm 2:2. τῇ ἀκοῇ ἡμῶν (Is 53:1; cp. Jos., C. Ap. 2, 14 π. ἀκοῇ πρεσβυτέρων) **J 12:38; Ro 10:16;** 1 Cl 16:3. τοῖς ἔργοις **J 10:38b** (=their testimony); Hm 6, 2, 10a (that they are good and must be followed).—Pass. ἐπιστεύθη τῷ λόγῳ μου *they believed my word* Hm 3:3.

ε. w. prepositional expressions: εἰς **Ro 4:18,** if εἰς τὸ γενέσθαι αὐτόν here is dependent on ἐπίστευσεν. πιστεύειν εἰς τὴν μαρτυρίαν *believe in the witness* **1J 5:10c.** ὁ Χριστιανισμὸς οὐκ εἰς Ἰουδαϊσμὸν ἐπίστευσεν *the Christian way of life/Christianity did not commit itself to the Judean way/Judaism* (s. Hdb. ad loc.) I Mg 10:3a; cp. b (Χριστιανισμόν, εἰς ὃν πᾶσα γλῶσσα πιστεύσασα). On πιστεύειν εἰς τὸ ὄνομά τινος s. 2aβ below. πιστεύετε ἐν τῷ εὐαγγελίῳ *believe in the gospel* (so Ps 105:12 ἐπίστευσαν ἐν τοῖς λόγοις αὐτοῦ. Rather in the sense 'put one's trust in' Sir 32:21 μὴ πιστεύσῃς ἐν ὁδῷ ἀπροσκόπῳ. See B-D-F §187, 6; Rob. 540. ALoisy, Les Évangiles synopt. I 1907, 430; 434; comm.) **Mk 1:15** (Hofmann understands it as 'on the basis of', Wohlenberg 'bei'; Lohmeyer is undecided; Dssm. and Mlt. 67f 'in the sphere of'; s. p. 235). ἐν τῷ εὐαγγελίῳ οὐ πιστεύω IPhld 8:2 (s. Bihlmeyer ad loc.).—ἐπί τινι: πιστεύειν ἐπὶ πᾶσιν οἷς ἐλάλησαν οἱ προφῆται **Lk 24:25; Ro 9:33** (Is 28:16).

ⓑ w. the pers. to whom one *gives credence* or whom one *believes,* in the dat. (Demosth. 18, 10; Aristot., Rhet. 2, 14 p. 1390a, 32; Polyb. 15, 26, 6 τοῖς εἰδόσι τὴν ἀλήθειαν; Herodian 2, 1, 10; PHib 72, 18; POxy 898, 29; PTebt 418, 15; Ex 4:1, 5; 3 Km 10:7; 2 Ch 32:15; Tob 2:14; Jer 47:14; JosAs 13:10; Philo, Praem. 49; Just., A I, 33, 5, D 7, 2 al.) τοῖς θεασαμένοις αὐτὸν ἐγηγερμένον οὐκ ἐπίστευσαν *they did not believe those who saw him after he was raised from the dead* **Mk 16:14.** Cp. **Mt 21:25, 32abc; Mk 11:31; 16:13; Lk 20:5; J 5:46a; Ac 8:12; 26:27a** (τ. προφήταις as Jos., Ant. 11, 96); **1J 4:1;** Hm 6, 1, 2ab.—Also of Jesus and God whom one *believes,* in that one accepts their disclosures without doubt or contradiction: Jesus:

Mt 27:42 v.l.; J 5:38, 46b; 6:30; 8:45, 46; 10:37, 38a. God: **J 5:24; Ro 4:3** (Gen 15:6), **17** κατέναντι οὗ ἐπίστευσεν θεοῦ (= κατέναντι θεοῦ ᾧ ἐπίστευσεν); **Gal 3:6; Js 2:23;** 1 Cl 10:6 (all three Gen 15:6). ὁ μὴ πιστεύων τῷ θεῷ ψεύστην πεποίηκεν αὐτόν **1J 5:10b.** AcPl Ha 3, 7.

ⓒ w. pers. and thing added π. τινί τι *believe someone with regard to someth.* (X., Apol. 15 μηδὲ ταῦτα εἰκῇ πιστεύσητε τῷ θεῷ) Hm 6, 2, 6.—W. dat. of pers. and ὅτι foll. (ApcEsdr 4:35 p. 29, 12 Tdf.): πιστεύετέ μοι ὅτι ἐγὼ ἐν τῷ πατρί **J 14:11a.** Cp. **4:21; Ac 27:25.**

ⓓ abs. (in which case the context supplies the obj., etc.; cp. ParJer 7:19 γέγονε δὲ τοῦτο, ἵνα πιστεύσωσιν) ἐάν τις ὑμῖν εἴπῃ· ἰδοὺ ὧδε ὁ Χριστός, μὴ πιστεύσητε *do not believe* (him or it [the statement]) **Mt 24:23;** cp. vs. **26; Mk 13:21; Lk 22:67; J 3:12ab; 10:25f; 12:47 v.l.; 14:29; 16:31; 19:35; 20:8, 25;** cp. GJs 19:3. **J 20:29ab** πιστεύσαντες *those who have nevertheless believed* (*it*=the fact of the Resurrection); **Ac 4:4; 26:27b; 1 Cor 11:18** πιστεύω *I believe* (*it*=that there are divisions among you); **15:11; Js 2:19b** *even the daemons believe this*; **Jd 5.** Pass. καρδίᾳ πιστεύεται *with* (or *in*) *the heart men believe* (*it*=that Jesus was raised fr. the dead) **Ro 10:10.**

ⓔ *believe = let oneself be influenced* κατά τινος *against someone* Pol 6:1.

ⓕ πιστεύομαι *I am believed, I enjoy confidence* (X., An. 7, 6, 33; Diod. S. 5, 80, 4 τοῖς μάλιστα πιστευομένοις ἐπηκολουθήσαμεν; 17, 32, 1; 1 Km 27:12; Jos., Ant. 10, 114; PGM 12, 279 πιστευθήσῃ=you will be believed) of Eve παρθένος πιστεύεται *people believe that she is a virgin* Dg 12:8, or perh. *a virgin is entrusted* (to someone without fear). S. 3 below.

❷ **to entrust oneself to an entity in complete confidence, *believe (in), trust,*** w. implication of total commitment to the one who is trusted. In our lit. God and Christ are objects of this type of faith that relies on their power and nearness to help, in addition to being convinced that their revelations or disclosures are true. The obj. is

ⓐ given—**α.** in the dat. (cp. Soph., Philoct. 1374 θεοῖς πιστ.; X., Mem. 1, 1, 5; Ps.-Pla., Epinom. 980c πιστεύσας τοῖς θεοῖς εὔχου; Ptolem. Lagi [300 BC]: 138 fgm. 8 Jac.; Maximus Tyr. 3, 8k τῷ Ἀπόλλωνι; Epict., app. E, 10 p. 488 Sch. θεῷ; Himerius, Or. 8 [=23], 18 πῶς Διονύσῳ πιστεύσω; how can I trust D.?; UPZ 144, 12 [164 BC] τ. θεοῖς; Jdth 14:10; Wsd 16:26; 4 Macc 7:21 al. in LXX; Philo, Leg. All. 3, 229 πιστεύειν θεῷ, Rer. Div. Her. 92 μόνῳ θεῷ, Op. M. 45, Sacr. Abel. 70 τῷ σωτῆρι θεῷ, Abr. 269, Mos. 1, 225, Virt. 216 [on faith in Philo s. Bousset, Rel.[3] 446ff; EHatch, Essays in Biblical Gk. 1889, 83ff; ASchlatter, D. Glaube im NT[4] 1927; EBréhier, Les idées philosophiques et religieuses de Philon d'Alexandrie 1908, [2]1925; HWindisch, Die Frömmigkeit Philos 1909, 23ff; HWolfson, Philo '47 I, 143–56, esp. II, 215–18; WPeisker, D. Glaubensbegriff bei Philon, diss. '36]; Jos., Ant. 2, 117; 333; 3, 309; 20, 48, Bell. 3, 387 [s. ASchlatter, D. Theol. d. Judentums nach d. Bericht des Jos. '32, 104ff]; Just., A I, 18, 6 al.). Some of the passages referred to in 1b above, end, are repeated, since they may be classified here or there w. equal justification. Of God: π. τῷ θεῷ (Orig., C. Cels. 4, 89, 15) **Ac 16:34; 13:12** D; **Tit 3:8;** PtK 4 p. 16, 2; B 16:7; Hm 12, 6, 2; s 5, 1, 5. Cp. m 1:2; AcPl Ha 10, 13f. τῷ κυρίῳ (Sir 11:21; 2:8) Hv 4, 2, 6. οἱ πιστεύσαντες τῷ κυρίῳ διὰ τοῦ υἱοῦ αὐτοῦ s 9, 13, 5. τῷ θεῷ w. ὅτι foll. m 9:7; cp. s 1:7.—Of Christ: **Mt 27:42 v.l.** (for ἐπ' αὐτόν); **J 6:30** (σοί=vs. **29** εἰς ὃν ἀπέστειλεν ἐκεῖνος); **J 8:31** (αὐτῷ=vs. **30** εἰς αὐτόν, but see Mlt. 67f; JSwetnam argues for a plpf. sense here: Biblica 61, '80, 106–9); **Ac 5:14; 18:8a** (both τῷ κυρίῳ); **Ro 10:14b** (οὗ οὐκ ἤκουσαν = τούτῳ [about equivalent to εἰς τοῦτον; cp. vs. **14a**] οὗ οὐκ ἤκ.); **2 Ti 1:12;** ITr 9:2; Hs 8, 3, 2.—Pass. *be believed in* (X., Cyr. 4, 2, 8; 6, 1, 39; Pla., Lach. 181b; Ps.-Demosth. 58, 44 al.; 1 Km 27:12; Just., D. 7, 3; Tat. 10, 2. S. B-D-F §312, 1; also s. Rob. 815f) ἐπιστεύθη ἐν κόσμῳ **1 Ti 3:16.**—π. τῷ ὀνόματι τοῦ υἱοῦ *believe in the name of the* Son, i.e. believe in the Son and accept what his name proclaims him to be **1J 3:23.**

β. w. εἰς (cp. Hippol., Elench. 6, 19, 7 W. οἱ εἰς τὸν Σίμωνα καὶ τὴν Ἑλένην πεπιστευκότες; Just., D. 35, 8 al.) God (BGU 874, 11 π. εἰς τὸν θεόν): **J 12:44b; 14:1a** (cp. ET 21, 1910, 53–57; 68–70; 138f); **1 Pt 1:21 v.l.**=Pol 2:1.—Christ: **Mt 18:6; Mk 9:42; J 2:11; 3:15 v.l., 16, 18a, 36; 4:39; 6:29, 35, 40, 47 v.l.; 7:5, 31, 38f, 48; 8:30; 9:35f; 10:42; 11:25, 26a, 45, 48; 12:11, 36** (εἰς τὸ φῶς), **37, 42, 44a, 46; 14:1b, 12; 16:9; 17:20; Ac 10:43; 14:23; 18:8** D; **19:4; Ro 10:14a; Gal 2:16; Phil 1:29; 1 Pt 1:8; 1J 5:10a;** AcPlCor 2:31; Hs 8, 3, 2.—εἰς τὸ ὄνομα Ἰησοῦ (or αὐτοῦ, etc.) **J 1:12; 2:23; 3:18c; 1J 5:13** (s. ὄνομα 1dβ and s. 2aα above, end). π. εἰς τὸν θάνατον αὐτοῦ ITr 2:1. π. εἰς τὸ αἷμα Χριστοῦ ISm 6:1.

γ. w. ἐπί and dat., of God **Ac 11:17** D. Of Christ: **Mt 27:42 v.l.; J 3:15 v.l.; Ro 9:33; 10:11; 1 Pt 2:6** (the last three Is 28:16); **1 Ti 1:16.**

δ. w. ἐπί and acc. (Wsd 12:2; Just., D. 46, 1 al.) of God: **Ac 16:34** D; **Ro 4:5, 24;** PtK 3 p. 15, 12. Of Christ: **Mt 27:42; J 3:15 v.l.; Ac 9:42; 11:17; 16:31; 22:19.**

ε. π. ἔν τινι *believe in someone* (Jer 12:6; Da 6:24 Theod.; Ps 77:22) is questionable in our lit.: in **J 3:15** the best rdg. is ἐν αὐτῷ and is prob. to be construed w. ἔχῃ (in J πιστεύω usually takes the prep. εἰς when expressing the obj. of belief, as in 3:16); in **Eph 1:13** both occurrences of ἐν ᾧ are prob. to be construed w. ἐσφραγίσθητε (='in connection with whom you have been sealed' [cp. 4:30]); the acts of hearing and believing are coordinate, and πιστεύσαντες, along w. ἀκούσαντες, is used abs. (so REB; less clearly NRSV). But s. 1aε above: π. ἐν τῷ εὐαγγελίῳ **Mk 1:15;** IPhld 8:2.

ⓑ not expressed at all (the abs. πιστεύειν in a transcendent sense: Aeschin., In Ctesiph. 1 ἐγὼ πεπιστευκὼς ἥκω πρῶτον τοῖς θεοῖς; Aristot., Rhet. 2, 17, 1391b, 1ff; Plut., Mor. 170f; Porphyr., Ad Marcellam 24 πιστεῦσαι δεῖ, ὅτι [=because] μόνη σωτηρία ἡ πρὸς τὸν θεὸν ἐπιστροφή; Herm. Wr. 9, 10ab ἐπίστευσε καὶ ἐν τῇ καλῇ πίστει ἐπανεπαύσατο; cp. 1, 32 πιστεύω καὶ μαρτυρῶ=PapBerl 9795 [RReitzenstein, Studien z. antiken Synkretismus 1926, p. 161, 2]; Num 20:12; Ps 115:1; Is 7:9; Sir 2:13; 1 Macc 2:59; Philo, Rer. Div. Her. 14; 101, Deus Imm. 4, Mut. Nom. 178; τότε πιστεύσεις θέλων καὶ μὴ θέλων Theoph. Ant. 1, 8 [p. 74, 7]) **Mk 15:32; 16:16f; Lk 8:12f; J 1:7, 50; 3:15, 18b; 4:41f, 48, 53; 5:44; 6:36, 47, 64ab,** perh. **69** (MEnslin, The Perf. Tense in the Fourth Gosp.: JBL 55, '36, 121–31, esp. 128); **9:38; 10:26; 11:15, 40; 12:39; 20:31b; Ac 4:4; 8:13, 37a; 11:21; 13:12, 39, 48; 14:1; 15:5, 7; 17:12, 34; 18:8b, 27; 19:2; 21:25; Ro 1:16; 3:22; 4:11; 10:4; 13:11; 15:13; 1 Cor 1:21; 3:5; 15:2; Gal 3:22; Eph 1:13, 19; 1 Th 2:10, 13; Hb 4:3; 1 Pt 2:7;** 1 Cl 12:7; 2 Cl 17:3; 20:2; B 9:3; 11:11; ISm 3:2; Hs 8, 10, 3; 9, 17, 4; 9, 22, 3. τὸ πιστεύειν *faith* IMg 9:2. ἐν ἀγάπῃ πιστεύειν IPhld 9:2 (ἐν ἀγάπῃ is here used adv.).—Participles in the var. tenses are also used almost subst.: (οἱ) πιστεύοντες *(the) believers, (the) Christians* (Orig., C. Cels. 1, 13, 34; Did., Gen. 106, 6) **Ac 2:44; Ro 3:22; 1 Cor 14:22ab** (opp. οἱ ἄπιστοι); **1 Th 1:7;** Hs 8, 3, 3. (οἱ) πιστεύσαντες *(those) who made their commitment = (those) who became believers, (the) Christians,* **Ac 2:44 v.l.; 4:32; 2 Th 1:10**a; 2 Cl 2:3; Hs 9, 19, 1. οἱ πεπιστευκότες *those who became* (and remained) *believers*

Ac 19:18; 21:20 (Just., D. 122, 2).—οἱ μέλλοντες πιστεύειν *future believers* 1 Cl 42:4; Hm 4, 3, 3a. οἱ νῦν πιστεύσαντες *those who have just come to believe* ibid. 4, 3, 3b.

ⓒ A special kind of this faith is the confidence that God or Christ is in a position to help suppliants out of their distress, *have confidence* (some of the passages already mentioned might just as well be classified here) abs. ὡς ἐπίστευσας γενηθήτω σοι *may it be done to you in accordance with the confidence you have* **Mt 8:13.** ὅσα ἂν αἰτήσητε πιστεύοντες *whatever you pray for with confidence* **21:22.** Cp. **Mk 5:36; 9:23f; Lk 8:50; 2 Cor 4:13a** (Ps 115:1), **b.** W. ὅτι foll.: πιστεύετε ὅτι δύναμαι τοῦτο ποιῆσαι; *do you have confidence that I am able to do this?* **Mt 9:28.—Mk 11:23.**

❸ ***entrust*** τινί τι *someth. to someone* (X., Mem. 4, 4, 17; Plut., Mor. 519e; Athen. 8, 341a; Lucian, Dial. Deor. 25, 1; SIG[2] 845, 7, see for numerous other examples index VI p. 384b. Cp. Wsd 14:5; 1 Macc 8:16; 4 Macc 4:7; TestJob 11:11; Jos., Bell. 4, 492; Hippol., Ref. 9, 12, 6) τὸ ἀληθινὸν τίς ὑμῖν πιστεύσει; **Lk 16:11.** αὐτῷ τοσούτων πιστευομένων *since so many* (or *so much*) *were* (*was*) *entrusted to him* AcPl Ha 7, 21 (connection uncertain). αὐτόν (so N. and Tdf.; v.l. ἑαυτόν) τινι *trust oneself to someone* (Brutus, Ep. 25; Plut., Mor. 181d ἀνδρὶ μᾶλλον ἀγαθῷ πιστεύσας ἑαυτὸν ἢ ὀχυρῷ τόπῳ=entrusting himself to a good man rather than to a stronghold; EpArist 270; Jos., Ant. 12, 396) **J 2:24** (EStauffer, CDodd Festschr., '56, 281–99.—Diod. S. 34 + 35 fgm. 39a οὐ τοῖς τυχοῦσι φίλοις ἑαυτὸν ἐπίστευσεν=he did not trust himself to casual friends).—Pass. πιστεύομαί τι (B-D-F §159, 4) *I am entrusted with someth.* (Pla., Ep. 1, 309a; Polyb. 8, 17, 5; 31, 26, 7; Diod. S. 20, 19, 2; Appian, Bell. Civ. 2, 136 §568 ἃ ἐπιστεύθην; ins; pap [e.g. PLond I, 121, 608 p. 203]; Jos., Bell. 5, 567, Vi. 137; Ath. 24, 3. Cp. Esth 8:12e.—Dssm., LO 320f [LAE 379]). ἐπιστεύθησαν τὰ λόγια τοῦ θεοῦ **Ro 3:2.** πεπίστευμαι τὸ εὐαγγέλιον **Gal 2:7** (PGM 13, 140 ὁ ὑπό σου πάντα πιστευθείς; 446); cp. **1 Th 2:4; 1 Ti 1:11.—Tit 1:3.** οἰκονομίαν πεπίστευμαι **1 Cor 9:17;** cp. Dg 7:1. S. also 7:2; IMg 6:1; IPhld 9:1ab. πιστεύομαί τι παρά τινος *I am entrusted by someone with someth.* (Polyb. 3, 69, 1; Jos., Bell. 1, 667): οἱ πιστευθέντες παρὰ θεοῦ ἔργον τοιοῦτο 1 Cl 43:1.

❹ ***be confident about,*** a unique use found in ὃς μὲν πιστεύει φαγεῖν πάντα, someth. like *the one is confident about eating anything* **Ro 14:2** (a combination of two ideas: 'the pers. is so strong in the faith' and: 'the pers. is convinced that it is permissible to eat anything'; in brief: not cultically fussy. See Ltzm., Hdb. ad loc.; but also B-D-F § 397, 2). Another probability is the sense

❺ ***think/consider (possible),*** in **Ro 14:2** perh. *holds everything possible;* cp. **J 9:18** οὐκ ἐπίστευσαν *they refused to entertain the possibility,* and **Ac 9:26.** S. 4 above.—For lit. s. πίστις, end. DELG s.v. πείθομαι. M-M. EDNT. TW.

πιστικός, ή, όν (πίστις; since Pla., Gorg. 455a) only as modifying νάρδος, w. πολυτελής or πολύτιμος **Mk 14:3; J 12:3;** variously interpreted, but evidently suggesting exceptional quality.

❶ ***genuine, unadulterated.*** In later writers π. means that which belongs to πίστις, 'faithful, trustworthy' (Artem. 2, 32; Vett. Val. p. 10, 14; pap 'trusted pers.'; Celsus 1, 39 λόγος πιστικός). Fr. this basis π. has become interpreted to mean *genuine, unadulterated* (Eus., Dem. Ev. 9, 8, 9 τοῦ πιστικοῦ τῆς καινῆς διαθήκης κράματος. Given as a possibility by Theophyl. Sim., s. 3 below. See B-D-F §113, 2; Mlt-H. 379f).

❷ The derivation fr. πίνω (so L-S-J-M), w. the sense ***drinkable, liquid,*** is very improbable (Frisk II 541).

❸ Some derive π. from a name of some kind (Theophyl. Sim. [MPG CXXIII 645b] πιστικὴν νάρδον νοεῖ ἤτοι εἶδος νάρδου οὕτω λεγόμενον πιστικὴν ἢ τὴν ἄδολον νάρδον); e.g. the Gk. form of the Lat. spicatum (Galen XII 604 K. τὰ πολυτελῆ μύρα τῶν πλουσίων γυναικῶν ἃ καλοῦσιν αὗται σπίκατα other reff. Wetstein on Mk 14:3.—EbNestle, ZNW 3, 1902, 169ff), or fr. πιστάκια 'pistachio tree' (AMerx on Mk 14:3; MBlack, An Aramaic Approach[3], '67, 223–25) or the East-Indian picçita, the name of the plant Nardostachys Jatamansi.—UvWilamowitz, Reden u. Vorträge[2] 1902, 204; AJannaris, ClR 16, 1902, 9; RKöbert, Biblica 29, '48, 279–81. W-S. §16, 3b note 24. S. also νάρδος.—DELG s.v. πείθομαι. M-M. Spicq.

πίστις, εως, ἡ (Hes., Hdt.+; ranging in meaning from subjective confidence to objective basis for confidence).

❶ **that which evokes trust and faith—ⓐ** the state of being someone in whom confidence can be placed, ***faithfulness, reliability, fidelity, commitment*** (X., An. 1, 6, 3; 3, 3, 4; Aristot., Eth. Eud, 7, 2, 1237b, 12; Polyb. 7, 12, 9; 38, 1, 8 al.; Herodian 2, 14, 4 al.; SIG 675, 22; OGI 557, 16; PTebt 27, 6; 51 [II BC]; POxy 494, 9; 705, 32; other pap M-M. s.v.; Ps 32:4; Pr 12:22; Jos., Ant. 2, 61; TestAsh 7:7) w. κρίσις and ἔλεος **Mt 23:23.** (Opp. ἀπιστία as Hes., Op. 370) τὴν πίστιν τοῦ θεοῦ καταργεῖν *nullify the faithfulness/commitment of God* (cp. Ps 32:4; Hos 2:22) **Ro 3:3.** πᾶσαν π. ἐνδείκνυσθαι ἀγαθήν *show all good faith(fulness)* **Tit 2:10** (cp. BGU 314, 19 μετὰ πίστεως ἀγαθῆς). W. other virtues **Gal 5:22** (on πίστις, πραΰτης cp. Sir 45:4; 1:27). W. ὑπομονή **2 Th 1:4.** τὴν πίστιν τετήρηκα *I have remained faithful* or *loyal* (πίστιν τηρεῖν as Polyb. 6, 56, 13; 10, 37, 5; Jos., Bell. 2, 121; 6, 345; OGI 339, 46f; IBM III, 587b, 5f [Dssm., LO 262=LAE 309, esp. note 3]) **2 Ti 4:7,** though this would be classified by some under 3 below. S. also 1c below.

ⓑ a solemn promise to be faithful and loyal, ***assurance, oath, troth*** (X., Cyr. 7, 1, 44; 8, 8, 3, Hell. 1, 3, 12; Diod. S. 14, 9, 7; Appian, Bell. Civ. 4, 86 §362 μεγάλας πίστεις ἔδωκεν=solemn assurances; 3 Macc 3:10; Jos., Ant. 12, 382) τὴν πρώτην πίστιν ἠθέτησαν **1 Ti 5:12** (s. also ἀθετέω 1 and cp. CIA app. [Wünsch, Praef. p. xv] of a woman who πρώτη ἠθέτησεν τὴν πίστιν to her husband). Cp. Rv 2:3.

ⓒ a token offered as a guarantee of someth. promised, ***proof, pledge*** (Pla., Phd. 70b; Isocr. 3, 8; Aristot., Rhet. 1, 1; 3, 13; Epicurus in Diog. L. 10, 63; 85: πίστις βεβαία=dependable proof; Polyb. 3, 100, 3; Περὶ ὕψους 39, 3=p. 74, 20 V.; Epict. 1, 28, 3; Appian, Bell. Civ. 4, 119 §500; Jos., Ant. 15, 69) πίστιν παρασχὼν πᾶσιν ἀναστήσας αὐτόν (God has appointed a man [Jesus] to be judge of the world, and) *he has furnished proof* (of his fitness for this office) *to all people by raising him* (on πίστιν παρέχειν cp. Jos., Ant. 2, 218 πίστιν παρεῖχε; 15, 260; Polyb. 2, 52, 4 πίστιν παρέσχετο=gave a pledge, security; Vett. Val. 277, 29f) **Ac 17:31.** JBarton, Biblica 40, '59, 878–84: π. in **2 Ti 4:7**=*bond* deposited by an athlete. But see 3 below.—WSchmitz, Ἡ Πίστις in den Papyri, diss. Cologne, '64.

❷ **state of believing on the basis of the reliability of the one trusted, *trust, confidence, faith*** in the active sense='believing', in ref. to deity (Soph. Oed. R. 1445 νῦν γ' ἂν τῷ θεῷ πίστιν φέροις; Pla., Leg. 12, 966de; Plut. Mor. 402e; 756b; Dio Chrys. 3, 51 παρὰ θεῶν τιμὴ κ. πίστις; Ael. Aristid. 13 p. 226 D.: πίστιν ἐν τ. θεοῖς ἔχειν; Appian, Liby. 57 §248 ἐς θεοὺς πίστις; Ep. 33 of Apollonius of Tyana [Philostrat. I 352, 14]; Herm. Wr. 9, 10 ἐπίστευσε καὶ ἐν τῇ καλῇ πίστει ἐπανεπαύσατο; Porphyr., Ad Marcellam 21 τῆς βεβαίας πίστεως, τὸ μεμαθηκέναι, ὅτι ὑπὸ τοῦ θεοῦ προνοεῖται πάντα. The divinity Πίστις in Plut., Num. 70 [16, 1] and in magic [exx. in Rtzst., Mysterienrel.[3] 234f, among them Aberciusins. 12; PGM 4, 1014 ἀλήθεια καὶ πίστις; 12, 228]; Wsd 3:14; 4 Macc 15:24; 16:22; 17:2; Philo, Abr. 270; 271; 273, Mut. Nom. 182, Migr. Abr. 43f, Conf. Lingu. 31, Poster. Cai. 13 [on faith in Philo s. the lit. given under πιστεύω 2aα]; Jos, C. Ap. 2, 163; 169; Just., A I, 52, 1 πίστιν ἔχειν; 53, 11 πειθὼ καὶ πίστιν . . . ἐμφορῆσαι), in our lit. directed toward God and Christ, their revelations, teachings, promises, their power and readiness to aid.

ⓐ God: πίστις θεοῦ (cp. Jos., Ant. 17, 179.—Cp. π. καὶ φόβος ὁ τοῦ θεοῦ Theoph. Ant. 1, 7 [p. 72, 26]) *faith, trust, confidence in God* **Mk 11:22;** cp. **Ac 19:20** D; 1 Cl 3:4; 27:3. π. θείου πνεύματος *faith in the divine spirit* Hm 11:9. ἡ π. τοῦ κυρίου s 6, 3, 6. π. (καὶ ἐλπὶς) εἰς θεόν **1 Pt 1:21.** π. ἐπὶ θεόν **Hb 6:1.** ἡ πίστις ἡ πρὸς τὸν θεόν **1 Th 1:8** (on the constr. w. πρὸς τ. θ. cp. Philo, Abr. 268; 271; 273; Just., D. 121, 2 διὰ τὴν πρὸς τὸν ἥλιον π.).—πίστις can also be characterized as faith in God by the context, without the addition of specific words; so in connection w. OT personalities: Abraham **Ro 4:5, 9, 11–13, 16, 19f** (s. also 2dα below); 1 Cl 10:7; 31:2; of Rahab 12:1, 8; of Esther 55:6 (ἡ τελεία κατὰ πίστιν). The OT heroes of faith **Hb 11:4–33, 39** (w. this catalogue of heroes cp. Il. 4, 457–538; 2 Km 23:8–39; 1 Ch 11:10–12:18; CGordon, Homer, and the Bible: HUCA 26, '55, 83).—But in Hb it is also true that God is specifically the object of the Christian's faith, and Christ **12:2** is ὁ τῆς πίστεως ἀρχηγὸς καὶ τελειώτης. Cp. **10:38; 11:3; 13:7.** (On faith in Hb s. Schlatter, Der Glaube im NT[4] 1927, 520ff; BHeigl, Verfasser u. Adresse des Hb 1905, 109–18; GHoennicke, Die sittl. Anschauungen des Hb: ZWT 45, 1902, 26ff; Windisch, Hdb. exc. on Hb 11; Riggenbach and Michel on Hb 11; Strathmann on 10:38. S. ὑπόστασις end.)—ἐὰν ἔχητε πίστιν **Mt 17:20.** Opp. doubt **21:21.** αἰτεῖν ἐν πίστει μηδὲν διακρινόμενος **Js 1:6.** ἡ εὐχὴ τῆς πίστεως **5:15** (εὐχή 1). ἡ πίστις τῆς ἐνεργείας τοῦ θεοῦ τοῦ ἐγείραντος αὐτὸν ἐκ νεκρῶν *faith in the working of God, who raised him from the dead* **Col 2:12.**

ⓑ Christ—α. of belief and trust in the Lord's help in physical and spiritual distress; oft. in the synopt. gospels: **Mt 8:10; 9:2, 22, 29** (κατὰ τὴν πίστιν ὑμῶν); **15:28; Mk 2:5; 4:40; 5:34; 10:52; Lk 5:20; 7:9, 50; 8:25, 48; 17:19; 18:42.**—Cp. ἔχει πίστιν τοῦ σωθῆναι (the lame man) *had faith that he would be cured* **Ac 14:9.**

β. of faith in Christ, designated by the addition of certain words. By the obj. gen. (s. Just., D. 52, 4 διὰ τῆς πίστεως τῆς τοῦ χριστοῦ) πίστις Ἰησοῦ Χριστοῦ *faith in Jesus Christ* (and sim. exprs. On interp. as obj. gen. s. AHultgren, NovT 22, '80, 248–63 [lit.]; response SWilliams, CBQ 49, '87, 431–47.) **Ro 3:22, 26; Gal 2:16ab, 20; 3:22; Eph 3:12; Phil 3:9a; Js 2:1; Rv 14:12;** cp. **2:13** (ἡ πίστις μου=*faith in me,* the Human One [Son of Man]); IMg 1:1. (The πίστις Χριστοῦ in Paul is taken as a subj. gen. by JHaussleiter, Der Glaube Jesu Christi 1891, Was versteht Paulus unter christlichem Glauben?: Greifswalder Studien für HCremer 1895, 161–82 and GKittel, StKr 79, 1906, 419ff. See also Schläger, ZNW 7, 1906, 356–58; BLongenecker, NTS 39, '93, 478–80 [lit. since '81]; DCampbell, JBL 113, '94, 265–85; response BDodd, 114, '95, 470–73.—ADeissmann, Paulus[2] 1925, 125f [Paul, tr. WWilson, 1926, 162ff], speaks of the mystical gen., 'faith in Christ'. Likew. HWeber, Die Formel 'in Christo Jesu': NKZ 31, 1920, 213ff, esp. 231, 3; WWeber, Christusmystik 1924, 82. S. also LAlbrecht, Der Glaube Jesu Christi 1921; OSchmitz, Die Christusgemeinschaft des Pls im Lichte seines Genetivgebr. 1924, 91–134; OHoltzmann, D. Glaube an Jes.: Stromata 1930, 11–25; GTaylor, JBL 85, '66, 58–76: the passages in Gal=Christ's reliability as a trustee. Cp. GHoward, HTR 60, '67, 459–65; MHooker, NTS 35, '89, 321–42.)—By prepositional phrases: πίστις εἰς Χριστόν (and sim. exprs.) *faith in Christ* **Ac 20:21; 24:24; 26:18; Col 2:5** (Just., D. 40, 1).—Also πίστις ἐν Χριστῷ (and sim.) **Gal 3:26; Eph 1:15; Col 1:4; 1 Ti 3:13; 2 Ti 3:15;** 1 Cl 22:1. In ἱλαστήριον διὰ πίστεως ἐν τῷ αὐτοῦ αἵματι **Ro 3:25,** ἐν κτλ. prob. goes not w. πίστις, but w. ἱλαστήριον (s. Ltzm., Hdb. ad loc.; W-S. §20, 5d).—πίστις, ἣν ἔχεις πρὸς τ. κύριον Ἰησοῦν **Phlm 5.**—πίστις διὰ τοῦ κυρίου ἡμῶν Ἰ. Χριστοῦ **Ac 20:21** D; sim. ἡ πίστις ἡ δι' αὐτοῦ **3:16b** (cp. **1 Pt 1:21**).—Jesus Christ is called ἡ τελεία πίστις ISm 10:2.

ⓒ πίστις can also be characterized by an objective gen. of the thing: ἡ πίστις τοῦ ὀνόματος αὐτοῦ *faith in his* (Jesus') *name* **Ac 3:16a.** ἡ πίστις τοῦ εὐαγγελίου **Phil 1:27.** εὐαγγελίων πίστις Dg 11:6. πίστις ἀληθείας **2 Th 2:13.**

ⓓ πίστις is found mostly without an obj., *faith, firm commitment*

α. as true piety, genuine devotion (Sextus 7a and 7; ParJer 6:7), which for our lit. means being a Christian (τὸ ἀληθινὸν πάσχα . . . πίστει νονούμενον Hippol., Ref. 8, 18, 1; Did., Gen. 54, 11) **Lk 18:8** (s. Jülicher, Gleichn. 288); **22:32; Ac 6:5**=vs. **8 v.l.;** cp. **11:24.—6:7; 13:8; 14:22; 15:9; 16:5; Ro 1:5, 8, 12, 17ab** (ἐκ πίστεως εἰς πίστιν does not mean a gradation [as, in a way, Appian, Mithrid. 40 §154: Sulla came upon ἕτερον ὅμοιον ἐξ ἑτέρου=one wall, i.e. fortification, after another similar one] or a transition from one kind to another [Himerius, Or.=Ecl. 10, 6 ἐκ ᾠδῆς εἰς ᾠδὴν ἄλλην μετέβαλον=they changed from one kind of song to another], but merely expresses in a rhetorical way that πίστις is the beginning and the end; s. Ltzm., Hdb. ad loc., and a grave-ins [ANock, Sallust. p. xxxiii, 94] ἐκ γῆς εἰς γῆν ὁ βίος οὗτος='dust is the beginning and the end of human life'.—AFridrichsen, ConNeot 12, '48, 54); **17c** (here and in **Gal 3:11** the LXX of Hab 2:4 [DCampbell, JBL 116, '97, 713–19] is not followed literally, since it has ἐκ πίστεώς μου='as a result of my faithfulness'; even in **Hb 10:38,** where μου does occur, it goes w. δίκαιος, not w. πίστεως); **Ro 3:27f** (Luther's addition of the word 'alone' in vs. 28 is hard to contest linguistically. Cp., e.g., Diog. L. 9, 6: Heraclitus wrote his work in very obscure language ὅπως οἱ δυνάμενοι προσίοιεν αὐτῷ=in order that only the capable might approach it. S. also Fitzmyer, ABComm. 360–64), **30f; 4:5–20** (s. also 2a above); **5:1f; 9:30, 32; 10:6, 17; 11:20** (opp. ἀπιστία); **12:3, 6** (s. ἀναλογία; for a difft. view 3 below); **14:1, 22** (s. ἐνώπιον 2b; others would place in 2dε), **23ab** (but s. ε below); **16:26; 1 Cor 2:5; 15:14, 17; 16:13; 2 Cor 1:24ab; 4:13; 10:15; 13:5; Gal 3:7–26; 5:5, 6** (s. ἐνεργέω 1b); **6:10** (οἱ οἰκεῖοι τῆς πίστεως, s. οἰκεῖος b); **Eph 2:8; 3:17; 4:5, 13; 6:16; Phil 1:25** (χαρὰ τῆς πίστεως); **2:17; 3:9b; Col 1:23; 2:7; 1 Th 3:2, 5, 7, 10; 2 Th 1:3, 11; 3:2; 1 Ti 1:2, 4, 5** (π. ἀνυπόκριτος), **19ab; 4:1; 5:8; 6:10, 12, 21** (but s. 3 below); **2 Ti 1:5** (ἀνυπόκριτος π.); **2:18; 3:8; Tit 1:1, 4, 13; 3:15; Phlm 6** (s. κοινωνία 4); **Hb 6:12; 10:22, 39** (opp. ὑποστολή); **Js 1:3; 2:5; 1 Pt 1:5, 7, 9; 5:9; 2 Pt 1:1; 1J 5:4;** 1 Cl 1:2 (ἡ πανάρετος κ. βεβαία π.); ISm 1:1 (ἀκίνητος π.); Hm 5, 2, 1; 12, 5, 4 (both πλήρης ἐν τῇ πίστει *full of faith*); 5, 2, 3 (π. ὁλόκληρος); 9:6 (ὁλοτελὴς ἐν τ. π.), 7 (opp. διψυχία), 12 (π. ἡ ἔχουσα δύναμιν); 12, 6, 1; s 9, 19, 2 (ἀπὸ τῆς π. κενοί); 9, 26, 8 (κολοβοὶ ἀπὸ τῆς π. αὐτῶν).—τὸ ῥῆμα τ. πίστεως **Ro 10:8.** οἱ λόγοι τῆς π. **1 Ti 4:6.** τὸ μυστήριον τῆς π. **3:9.** ὁ θεὸς ἤνοιξεν τοῖς ἔθνεσιν θύραν πίστεως *God has opened the door of faith to the Gentiles,* i.e. opened the way for them to participate in a new relationship w. God **Ac 14:27** (s. also θύρα 1bγ). ἀκοὴ πίστεως **Gal 3:2, 5** (s. ἀκοή 2 and 4b). (τὸ) ἔργον (τῆς) π. **1 Th 1:3; 2 Th 1:11** (s. ἔργον 1b). οἱ ἐκ πίστεως *the people of faith* (s. ἐκ 3b) **Gal 3:7, 9.** πῶς οὖν [πίστιν εὑρ]ίσκομεν; Ox 1081,

25f (but here [ταῦτα γιγν]ώσκομεν is the preferable restoration w. Till after the Coptic SJCh 90, 2); 32. Of gnostics τοῦ ὄφεως πίστιν ἔχουσιν AcPlCor 2:20.—If the principal component of Christianity is faith, then π. can be understood as *the Gospel* in terms of the commitment it evokes (cp. SIG 932, 7 [II/I BC]) νῦν εὐαγγελίζεται τὴν πίστιν ἥν ποτε ἐπόρθει **Gal 1:23** (s. 3 below). Perh. also **Ro 1:5.**

β. Hb 11:1 defines πίστις as ἐλπιζομένων ὑπόστασις, πραγμάτων ἔλεγχος οὐ βλεπομένων. There is here no qu. about the mng. of π. as confidence or assurance (s. 2a above), but on its relation to ὑπόστασις as its predication s. under that word.—(Ps.-Aristot., De Mundo 6, 18 interprets πιστεύειν in someth. as incapability to see someth. that is apparent only to God.) Paul contrasts walking διὰ εἴδους (εἶδος 3) as the lower degree, with διὰ πίστεως περιπατεῖν **2 Cor 5:7** (s. KDeissner, Pls. u. die Mystik seiner Zeit[2] 1921, 101ff). On the other hand πίστις is on a higher level than merely listening to Christian preaching **Hb 4:2.**

γ. πίστις abs., as a Christian virtue, is often coupled w. others of the same kind, esp. oft. w. ἀγάπη: **1 Th 3:6; 5:8; 1 Ti 1:14; 2 Ti 1:13; Phlm 5;** B 11:8; IEph 1:1; 9:1; 14:1; 20:1; IMg 1:2; 13:1; IRo ins; ISm ins; 6:1; 13:2; AcPl Ha 8, 35. W. ἀγάπη and other abstracts **2 Cor 8:7; Gal 5:22; Eph 6:23; 1 Ti 2:15; 4:12; 6:11: 2 Ti 2:22; 3:10; Tit 2:2; Rv 2:19;** IPhld 11:2; Pol 4:2; Hm 8:9; cp. v 3, 8, 2–5. The triad πίστις, ἐλπίς, ἀγάπη **1 Cor 13:13;** cp. also **Col 1:4f; 1 Th 1:3; 5:8;** B 1:4 (on this triad see s.v. ἀγάπη 1αα). W. ἐλπίς only (cp. **1 Pt 1:21**) 1 Cl 58:2. The ζωῆς ἐλπίς is called ἀρχὴ καὶ τέλος πίστεως ἡμῶν B 1:6.—W. ἀλήθεια (TestLevi 8:2) **1 Ti 2:7** (cp. the combination POxy 70, 4f [III AD]); 1 Cl 60:4. W. δικαιοσύνη Pol 9:2. W. ὑπομονή **Rv 13:10;** w. ὑπομ. and other abstracts **2 Pt 1:5f;** Pol 13:2 (cp. also the following passages already referred to in this section: **1 Ti 6:11; 2 Ti 3:10; Tit 2:2** and **Js 1:3** [α above]). W. γνῶσις (Just., D. 69, 1) et al. **2 Pt 1:5**f [s. above]; D 10:2. ἵνα μετὰ τῆς πίστεως ὑμῶν τελείαν ἔχητε τὴν γνῶσιν B 1:5. W. φόβος and ἐγκράτεια Hm 6, 1, 1.—(Distinguished from θεία σοφία: Orig., C. Cels. 6, 13, 23.)

δ. *faith* as fidelity to Christian teaching. This point of view calls for ἔργα as well as the kind of πίστις that represents only one side of true piety: **Js 2:14ab, 17, 18abc, 20, 22ab, 24, 26** (ἔργον 1a); Hv 3, 6, 5; s 8, 9, 1ab.

ε. Ro 14:22 and **23** π. as *freedom* or *strength in faith, conviction* (s. Ltzm., Hdb. ad loc.; but s. α above).

ζ. In addition to the πίστις that every Christian possesses (s. 2dα above) Paul speaks of a special gift of faith that belongs to a select few **1 Cor 12:9.** Here he understands π. as an unquestioning belief in God's power to aid people with miracles, the faith that 'moves mountains' **13:2** (cp. **Mt 17:20.—21:21;** s. 2a above). This special kind of faith may be what the disciples had in mind when they asked πρόσθες ἡμῖν πίστιν **Lk 17:5;** cp. vs. **6.** τῇ πίστει φερόμενος ὁ Παυλος AcPl Ha 5, 1.

❸ that which is believed, ***body of faith/belief/teaching*** (Diod. S. 1, 23, 8 ἰσχυρὰν πίστιν καὶ ἀμετάθετον=an article of faith that was firm and unshakable [concerning Orpheus and Dionysus]; Mel., HE 4, 26, 13; Ath. 8, 1; Iren., 1, 10, 2 [Harv. I, 92, 1]; Orig., C. Cels., 1, 42, 26; Did., Gen. 156, 23). So clearly **Jd 3** (τῇ ἅπαξ παραδοθείσῃ τοῖς ἁγίοις πίστει), **20** (τῇ ἁγιωτάτῃ ὑμῶν πίστει.—ἅγιος 1αα). πίστις θεοῦ=that which, acc. to God's will, is to be believed IEph 16:2.—This objectivizing of the term πίστις is found as early as Paul: **Ro 1:5; Gal 1:23** (s. 2dα end) and perh. **Gal 3:23–25** (s. Ltzm., Hdb. ad loc.). ASeeberg, D. Katechismus der Urchristenheit 1903, 110f, understands **1 Ti 1:19; 4:1, 6; 6:10,** cp. **21; 2 Ti 2:18** in this manner. **Ro 12:6** (but s. ἀναλογία) and **2 Ti 4:7** are also interpreted in this way by many.—EBurton, ICC Gal 1921, 475–86; ASchlatter, D. Glaube im NT[4] 1927; APott, Das Hoffen im NT in seiner Beziehung zum Glauben1915; ANairne, The Faith of the NT 1920; RGyllenberg, Pistis 1922; WKümmel, D. Glaube im NT: ThBl 16, '38, 209–21; Dodd 65–68; TTorrance, ET 68, '57, 111–14; CMoule, ibid. 157.—Synoptics: TShearer, ET 69, '57, 3–6.—Esp. for Paul: BBartmann, Pls, die Grundzüge seiner Lehre u. die moderne Religionsgeschichte 1914; WMorgan, The Religion and Theology of Paul 1917; WHatch, The Pauline Idea of Faith in Its Relation to Jewish and Hellenistic Religion 1917; Ltzm., Hdb. exc. after Ro 4:25; FKnoke, Der christl. Glaube nach Pls 1922; ERohde, Gottesglaube u. Kyriosglaube bei Pls: ZNW 22, 1923, 43–57; EWissmann, Das Verh. v. πίστις und Christusfrömmigkeit bei Pls 1926; MDibelius, Glaube u. Mystik b. Pls: Neue Jahrb. f. Wissensch. u. Jugendbildg. 7, '31, 683–99; WMundle, D. Glaubensbegriff des Pls '32 (p. xi–xvi extensive bibliog.); RGyllenberg, Glaube b. Pls: ZWT 13, '37, 612–30; MHansen, Om Trosbegrebet hos Pls '37; LMarshall, Challenge of NT Ethics, '47, 270–77; 298–300; RBultmann, Theologie des NT '48, 310–26 (Engl. tr. KGrobel I '51, 314–30; for the Johannines II, 70–92, '55)); MMassinger, BiblSacra 107, '50, 181–94 et al. S. also δικαιοσύνη 3a.—For the Fourth Gosp.: JBuswell, The Ethics of 'Believe' in the Fourth Gospel: BiblSacra 80, 1923, 28–37; JHuby, De la connaissance de foi chez S. Jean: RSR 21, '31, 385–421; RSchnackenburg, D. Glaube im 4. Ev., diss. Breslau '37; WHatch, The Idea of Faith in Christ. Lit. fr. the Death of St. Paul to the Close of the Second Century 1926.—EGraesser, D. Glaube im Hebräerbrief, '65.—ABaumeister, D. Ethik des Pastor Hermae, 1912, 61–140.—ESeidl, π. in d. griech. Lit. (to Peripatetics), diss. Innsbruck, '53; HLjungman, Pistis, '64; DLührmann, Pistis im Judent., ZNW 64, '73, 19–38. On faith in late Judaism s. Bousset, Rel.[3] 534a (index); also DHay, JBL 108, '89, 4611–76; DLindsay, Josephus and Faith '93. On the Hellenistic concept πίστις Rtzst., Mysterienrel.[3] 234–36.—DELG s.v. πείθομαι. M-M. EDNT. TW. Spicq. Sv.

πιστός, ή, όν (πείθω; Hom.+).**—❶ pertaining to being worthy of belief or trust,** ***trustworthy, faithful, dependable, inspiring trust/faith,*** pass. aspect of πιστεύω (Hom.+).

ⓐ of pers.**—α.** of human beings (and Christ) δοῦλος (1 Km 22:14; 2 Macc 1:2; OdeSol 11:22; Jos., Ant. 6, 256; SIG 910 A, 5 [Christian]; PLond II, 251, 14 p. 317 [IV AD] δούλους πιστοὺς καὶ ἀδράστους): δοῦλε ἀγαθὲ καὶ πιστέ **Mt 25:21a, 23a;** cp. **24:45;** Hs 5, 2, 2 πιστότατος (v.l. πιστός). οἰκονόμος **Lk 12:42; 1 Cor 4:2.** μάρτυς (Pind., P. 1, 88; 12, 27; Pr 14:5, 25; Ps 88:38; Jer 49:5; Philo, Sacr. Abel. 17) ὁ μάρτυς μου ὁ πιστός μου **Rv 2:13** (μάρτυς 3); in this 'book of martyrs' Christ is ὁ μάρτυς ὁ πιστὸς (καὶ ὁ ἀληθινός) **1:5; 3:14;** cp. **19:11** (the combination of ἀληθινός and πιστός in the last two passages is like 3 Macc 2:11). Cp. **Rv 17:14.** πιστὸς ἀρχιερεύς *a faithful* or *reliable high priest* **Hb 2:17** (of Christ); cp. **3:2** (ἀρχιερέα … πιστὸν ὄντα τῷ ποιήσαντι αὐτόν). σύμβουλοι πιστοί B 21:4. πιστοὶ ἄνθρωποι *reliable persons* **2 Ti 2:2** (cp. Is 8:2; sing. Tob 5:3 S; 10:6 S; ApcEsdr 2:2). Paul honors his co-workers w. π. as a designation: Timothy **1 Cor 4:17.** Tychicus **Eph 6:21; Col 4:7** (both πιστὸς διάκονος ἐν κυρίῳ). Onesimus **Col 4:9.** Epaphras **1:7** (πιστὸς ὑπὲρ ὑμῶν διάκονος τοῦ Χριστοῦ). Cp. **1 Pt 5:12** (διὰ Σιλουανοῦ τ. πιστοῦ ἀδελφοῦ).—Moses was πιστὸς ἐν ὅλῳ τῷ οἴκῳ αὐτοῦ **Hb 3:5** (Num 12:7). πιστόν τινα ἡγεῖσθαι *consider someone trustworthy* (Aristoph., Plut.

27) **1 Ti 1:12** (cp. **Hb 11:11**; s. β below); s. PtK 3 p. 15, 18. γίνου πιστός (γίνομαι 7 and cp. Jos., Vi. 110, Ant. 19, 317) **Rv 2:10.**—πιστὸς ἔν τινι *faithful, reliable, trustworthy in someth.* (TestJos 9:2 π. ἐν σωφροσύνῃ) ἐν τῷ ἀδίκῳ μαμωνᾷ *in matters relating to unrighteous wealth* **Lk 16:11.** ἐν τῷ ἀλλοτρίῳ in *connection with what belongs to someone else* vs. **12.** ὁ π. ἐν ἐλαχίστῳ καὶ ἐν πολλῷ π. ἐστιν *one who is trustworthy in a very small matter is also trustworthy in a large one* vs. **10;** 2 Cl 8:5; cp. **Lk 19:17.** π. ἐν πᾶσιν *trustworthy in every respect* **1 Ti 3:11.** Also ἐπί τι *in* (connection w.) *someth.* **Mt 25:21b, 23b.**—When Paul explains in **1 Cor 7:25** that the Lord graciously granted him the privilege of being πιστός, and uses this as a basis for his claim to be heard w. respect, πιστός can hardly mean 'believing' (s. 2 below); the apostle rather feels that in a special sense he has been called and commissioned because of the confidence God has in him (πιστός is almost like a title='trusted man, commissioner', oft. in ins of distinguished pers.: ISyriaW 2022a; 2029; 2034; 2045f; 2127f; 2130; 2219; 2238–40; 2243; 2394; cp. SEG XLII, 1484, 1599.—Corresp. πίστις='position of trust': Achilles Tat. 8, 15, 1 οἱ ἄρχοντες οἱ ταύτην ἔχοντες τὴν πίστιν).

β. of God as the One in whom we can have full confidence (Pind., N. 10, 54; Dt 7:9; 32:4; Is 49:7; PsSol 14:1; 7:10; Philo, Rer. Div. Her. 93, Sacr. Abel. 93, Leg. All. 3, 204) **1 Cor 1:9; 10:13; 2 Cor 1:18; 1 Th 5:24; Hb 10:23; 11:11; 1 Pt 4:19; 1J 1:9;** 1 Cl 60:1; ITr 13:3. π. ἐν ταῖς ἐπαγγελίαις 1 Cl 27:1 (cp. Ps 144:13a πιστὸς κύριος ἐν τοῖς λόγοις αὐτοῦ). πιστός ἐστιν ὁ ἐπαγγειλάμενος *(God) is trustworthy, who has promised* 2 Cl 11:6.—Also of the 'Lord' (Christ), who is spoken of in the same way as God **2 Th 3:3; 2 Ti 2:13.**

ⓑ of things, esp. of words (Hdt. 8, 83; Pla., Tim. 49b; Aristot., Rhet. 2, 1, 1377b, 23; Polyb. 3, 9, 4; 15, 7, 1; Plut., Mor. 160e; Cass. Dio 37, 35; Jos., Ant. 19, 132; Just., D. 11, 2 διαθήκη; Ath., R. 17 p. 69, 16 τὸ πιστόν; Aberciusins. 6 γράμματα πιστά [of a divine teacher]) πιστὸς ὁ λόγος (Dionys. Hal. 3, 23, 17; Dio Chrys. 28 [45], 3) *it is a trustworthy saying* **1 Ti 1:15; 3:1; 4:9; 2 Ti 2:11; Tit 3:8;** cp. **1:9** (JBover, Biblica 19, '38, 74–79). οἱ λόγοι πιστοὶ καὶ ἀληθινοί **Rv 21:5; 22:6.** Opp. ψευδής Hm 3: 5ab. On τὰ ὅσια, Δαυὶδ τὰ πιστά **Ac 13:34** s. ὅσιος 3.—Of water *dependable* (i.e. not likely to dry up suddenly; cp. Dt 28:59 νόσοι πισταί), *unfailing, plentiful* B 11:5 (Is 33:16). πιστὸν ποιεῖν τι *act loyally* **3J 5.**

❷ **pert. to being trusting, *trusting, cherishing faith/trust*** act. aspect of πιστεύω (Aeschyl., Pers. 55, Prom. 916; Soph., Oed. Col. 1031; Pla., Leg. 7, 824; Cass. Dio 37, 12, 1; Just., A I, 53, 10 al.), also *believing, full of faith, faithful* (cp. POxy 1380, 152 ὁρῶσί σε [=Isis] οἱ κατὰ τὸ πιστὸν ἐπικαλούμενοι [on this s. AFestugière, RB 41, '32, 257–61]; Sextus 1; 8; Wsd 3:9; Sir 1:14, 24 v.l.; Ps 100:6; SibOr 3, 69; 724) of OT worthies: Abraham (who is oft. called πιστός; cp. Philo, Post. Cai. 173 Ἀβρ. ὁ πιστὸς ἐπώνυμος; 2 Macc 1:2; 1 Macc 2:52; Sir 44:20) **Gal 3:9;** 1 Cl 10:1; Νῶε πιστὸς εὑρεθείς 9:4; Moses 17:5; 43:1 (both Num 12:7) and s. 1aα above (**Hb 3:5**). Of believers in contrast to doubters Hm 11:1ab. Of belief in the resurrection of Jesus μὴ γίνου ἄπιστος ἀλλὰ πιστός **J 20:27.** Of one who confesses the Christian faith *believing* or *a believer in the Lord, in Christ, in God* π. τῷ κυρίῳ **Ac 16:15.** Also π. ἐν κυρίῳ Hm 4, 1, 4. π. ἐν Χριστῷ Ἰησοῦ **Eph 1:1.** πιστοὶ ἀδελφοὶ ἐν Χρ. **Col 1:2.** δι' αὐτοῦ (=Χριστοῦ) πιστοὶ (πιστεύοντες v.l.) εἰς θεόν **1 Pt 1:21.**—The abs. πιστός also means *believing (in Christ), a (Christian) believer* and is used both as adj. (Just., D. 110, 4) and as subst. **Ac 16:1; 2 Cor 6:15; 1 Ti 4:10; 5:16; 6:2ab; Tit 1:6;** 1 Cl 48:5; 62:3; 63:3; Hm 9:9; s 8, 7, 4; 8, 9, 1; 8, 10, 1; 9, 22, 1. οἱ πιστοί *the believers = the Christians* **Ac 12:3** D; **1 Ti 4:3, 12;** IEph 21:2; IMg 5:2 (opp. οἱ ἄπιστοι); MPol 12:3; 13:2; AcPl Ha 7, 7 (cp. Just., D. 47, 2 τοῖς Χριστιανοῖς καὶ πιστοῖς). οἱ ἅγιοι καὶ πιστοὶ αὐτοῦ ISm 1:2. οἱ ἐκ περιτομῆς πιστοί=*the Israelite* (s. Ac 10:36) *believers/Christians* **Ac 10:45.** Without the art. (Orig., C. Cels., prol. 6, 5) Dg 11:2, 5. νέοι ἐν τῇ πίστει καὶ πιστοί *young in the faith, but nevertheless believers* Hv 3, 5, 4.—πιστὸς εἶναι *be a believer* IRo 3:2. ἐὰν ᾖ τις πιστότατος ἀνήρ *even though a man is a firm believer* Hm 6, 2, 7.—LFoley, CBQ 1 '39, 163–65.—B. 1167. New Docs 2, 94, w. reff. to Christian ins. DELG s.v. πείθομαι. M-M. ENDT. TW.

πιστόω (πιστός) 1 aor. pass. ἐπιστώθην (the word since Hom. et al.; ins, LXX, EpArist, Philo; Jos., Bell. 4, 213, Ant. 15, 85; Ath.—Apart fr. our lit. mostly mid., rarely pass., and act. only Thu. 4, 88; 2 Km 7:25; 1 Ch 17:14; 2 Macc 7:24; 12:25; Philo, Leg. All. 3, 206) in our lit. only 1 aor. pass., in act. sense.

❶ **to act in a faithful manner, *show oneself faithful*** ἔν τινι *prove oneself faithful to someth.* 1 Cl 15:4 (Ps 77:37).

❷ **to be sure about someth. because of its reliability, *feel confidence, be convinced*** (so the 1 aor. pass. Od. 21, 218; Soph., Oed. Col. 1039; EpArist 91) σὺ μένε ἐν οἷς (=τούτοις, ἃ) ἔμαθες καὶ ἐπιστώθης *but you must stand by what you have learned and become convinced of* **2 Ti 3:14.** πιστωθέντες ἐν τῷ λόγῳ τοῦ θεοῦ (w. πληροφορηθέντες διὰ τῆς ἀναστάσεως τοῦ κυρίου Ἰ. Χρ.) *full of faith in* or *by the word of God* 1 Cl 42:3.—DELG s.v. πείθομαι. M-M. TW.

πιστῶς adv. of πιστός (since Antiphon Or. 2, 47; ins [SEG XLII, 1215, 6], pap [PLond II, 301, 7f p. 256: II AD]; 4 Km 16:2; Jos., C. Ap. 2, 44) **pert. to being reliable, *faithfully*** στηρίζεσθαι 1 Cl 35:5; φυλάσσειν Dg 7:2.—M-M s.v. πιστός.

πίων, πῖον gen. πίονος (Hom. et al.; LXX; Philo, Aet. M. 100; Jos., Bell. 4, 468; Sib Or 3, 639; Just., D. 28, 3) ***fat*** θυσία MPol 14:2 (w. προσδεκτή).—DELG s.v. πῖαρ.

πλανάω fut. πλανήσω; 1 aor. ἐπλάνησα. Pass.: 1 aor. ἐπλανήθην; perf. πεπλάνημαι (s. four next entries; Hom., Aeschyl., Hdt.+; gener. notion: without fixed goal or apparent rationale).

❶ **to cause to go astray from a specific way,** act.—ⓐ ***lead astray, cause to wander*** τινά *someone* (Aeschyl., Prom. 573; Hdt. 4, 128 et al.) in imagery πλ. τινὰ ἀπὸ τῆς ὁδοῦ *cause someone to wander from the right way* D 6:1 (for πλ. ἀπὸ τ. ὁδοῦ cp. Dt 11:28; Wsd 5:6).

ⓑ ***mislead, deceive*** τινά *someone* trans. sense of 1a without imagistic detail (Pla., Prot 356d, Leg. 655d al.; pap, LXX; TestAbr A 20 p. 103, 17 [Stone p. 54, 17] death deceived Abraham; TestLevi 10:2; TestJud 15:5; GrBar 4:8; Just., D. 103, 6; Orig., C. Cels. 5, 5, 29; Hippol., Ref. 6, 20, 2) **Mt 24:4f, 11, 24; Mk 13:5f; J 7:12; 1J 2:26; 3:7; Rv 2:20; 12:9; 13:14; 19:20; 20:3, 8, 10;** IMg 3:2; IPhld 7:1a. πλ. ἑαυτόν *deceive oneself* **1J 1:8.** Abs. **2 Ti 3:13a.**—S. 2cδ below.

❷ **to proceed without a sense of proper direction, *go astray, be misled, wander about aimlessly,*** pass. freq. in act. sense

ⓐ lit. (since Il. 23, 321; Gen 37:15; PsSol 17:17; ParJer 5:9; ApcrEzk P 1 verso 12; Jos., Bell. 7, 160; Iren. 1, 8, 4 [Harv. I 73, 3]) ἐπὶ (v.l. ἐν) ἐρημίαις πλανώμενοι **Hb 11:38.** Of sheep who have become lost (Ps 118:176) **Mt 18:12ab, 13.** ὡς πρόβατα πλανώμενα **1 Pt 2:25 v.l.**

ⓑ in imagery of people who strayed fr. the right way (cp. 1a), ὡς πρόβατα πλανώμενοι **1 Pt 2:25.** ὡς πρόβατα ἐπλανήθημεν 1 Cl 16:6a (Is 53:6a; cp. also Ps 118:176). καταλείποντες εὐθεῖαν ὁδὸν ἐπλανήθησαν **2 Pt 2:15.** ἄνθρωπος . . . ἐπλανήθη *everyone . . . went astray* 1 Cl 16:6b (Is 53:6b). πλανῶνται καὶ ταλαιπωροῦσιν περιπατοῦντες ἐν ταῖς ἀνοδίαις *they wander about and are miserable as they go through trackless country* Hv 3, 7, 1 (ἐν as Lucian, Calumn. 1 ἐν σκότῳ; **Hb 11:38 v.l.**).

ⓒ fig. without the imagistic detail of 2b (cp. 1b)—**α.** *go astray, be deluded* (Cebes 6, 3; 24, 2; Orig., C. Cels. 6, 79, 41) **Tit 3:3** (Dio Chrys. 4, 115 πλανῶνται . . . δεδουλωμέναι ἡδοναῖς); **Hb 5:2;** 1 Cl 39:7 (Job 5:2); 59:4; 2 Cl 15:1 (of the ψυχή as Pr 13:9a; Wsd 17:1); B 2:9; 16:1. πλανῶνται τῇ καρδίᾳ *their minds are going astray* **Hb 3:10** (Ps 94:10). τινὲς δὲ τῶν ἀνθρώπων ἐπλανήθησαν . . . μὴ εἰδότες *but some people went astray . . . because they did not know* Ox 1081, 21 (as restored).

β. *wander away* ἀπὸ τῆς ἀληθείας (Theoph. Ant. 2, 14 [p. 136, 26]) **Js 5:19** (cp. Wsd 5:6).

γ. *be mistaken* in one's judgment, *deceive oneself* (Isocr., Ep. 6, 10 al.; Jos., Bell. 1, 209, Ant. 10, 19; PFlor 61, 16; 2 Macc 7:18; ApcEsdr 2:28 [p. 26, 22 Tdf.]; Ar. 4, 2 al.; Hippol., Ref. 5, 8, 1; Theoph. Ant. 1, 11 [p. 82, 13]) **Mt 22:29; Mk 12:24;** Hv 2, 4, 1. πολὺ πλανᾶσθε *you are very much mistaken* **Mk 12:27.** μὴ πλανᾶσθε *make no mistake* (Epict. 4, 6, 23) **1 Cor 6:9; Gal 6:7; Js 1:16.** ἐν πᾶσιν πεπλανήμεθα *we are wholly mistaken* B 15:6 (cp. Hero Alex. III p. 214, 2 ἐν μηδενὶ πλανᾶσθαι).

δ. *be deceived, be misled* πλανῶντες καὶ πλανώμενοι *deceivers* (of others) *and* (themselves) *deceived* **2 Ti 3:13** (cp. Herm. Wr. 16, 16 ὁ πλανώμενος κ. πλανῶν).—*Let oneself be misled, deceived* (s. Gildersleeve, Syntax I§167 on the 'permissive' pass.; Bel 7 Theod.; JosAs 13:10; Just., D. 118, 3) **Mt 24:24 v.l.; Lk 21:8; J 7:47; Rv 18:23.** μὴ πλανᾶσθε **1 Cor 15:33;** IEph 16:1; IMg 8:1; IPhld 3:3. μηδεὶς πλανάσθω IEph 5:2; ISm 6:1. τὸ πνεῦμα οὐ πλανᾶται *the Spirit is not led into error* IPhld 7:1b. ὑπὸ τοῦ ὄφεως πλανᾶται *he is deceived by the serpent* or *he lets himself be misled by the serpent* Dg 12:6 (UPZ 70, 28 [152/151 BC] πλανώμενοι ὑπὸ τ. θεῶν; Alex. Aphr., Fat. 12 p. 180, 25 Br. ὑπὸ τ. φύσεως).—Schmidt, Syn. I 547–62. DELG s.v. πλανάομαι. M-M. EDNT. TW.

πλάνη, ης, ἡ (πλανάω; Aeschyl., Hdt.+; BGU 1208, 6 [27/26 BC]; s. New Docs 2, 94 on freq. use in pap in sense of 'deceit'; PWisc II, 10 [III AD] 'mistake'; LXX; En 99:7; TestSol [personified]; Test12Patr; JosAs 8:10; AscIs 2:10; 3:28; Philo; Jos., Ant. 4, 276; apolog. exc. Mel.; Orig.). In our lit. only as fig. ext. of the primary mng. ('roaming, wandering', e.g. Hdt. 1, 30 of Solon, who roamed the earth in search of new information): **wandering fr. the path of truth, *error, delusion, deceit, deception*** to which one is subject (Pla. et al., also Diod. S. 2, 18, 8; Herm. Wr. 1, 28 οἱ συνοδεύσαντες τῇ πλάνῃ; Tob 5:14 BA; Pr 14:8; Jer 23:17; Just., A I, 56, 3; w. φαντασία Theoph. Ant. 2, 8 [p. 118, 4]) **Mt 27:64.** Of an erroneous view of God, as exhibited in polytheism, resulting in moral degradation (Wsd 12:24; Ar. 2, 1 al.; Just., D. 47, 1; Tat. 29, 1; Iren., 1, 1, 3 [Harv. I 11, 10]; Did., Gen. 217, 30) **Ro 1:27;** cp. τερατεία καὶ πλάνη τῶν γοήτων Dg 8:4 (Jos., Ant. 2, 286 κατὰ γοητείαν κ. πλάνην). διὰ τὴν ἐν κόσμῳ πλάνην AcPl Ha 1, 15 (cp. Just., D. 113, 6 ἀπὸ τῆς πλάνης τοῦ κόσμου).—**Eph 4:14** (s. μεθοδεία); **1 Th 2:3; 2 Th 2:11** (opp. ἀλήθεια vs. **10**). ἡ τῶν ἀθέσμων πλ. *the error of unprincipled pers.* **2 Pt 3:17;** τῶν ἁμαρτωλῶν B 12:10. Cp. IEph 10:2. ἡ τῆς πλ. ἀνομία B 14:5 (ἀνομία 1). ἡ πλ. τοῦ νῦν καιροῦ 4:1. παρείσδυσιν πλάνης ποιεῖν 2:10 (s. παρείσδυσις). W. ἀπάτη Dg 10:7. W. ἀπώλεια 2 Cl 1:7. ἡ κενὴ ματαιολογία καὶ ἡ τῶν πολλῶν πλάνη Pol 2:1. μῦθος καὶ πλάνη *a mere story and a delusion* 2 Cl 13:3. οἱ ἐν πλάνῃ ἀναστρεφόμενοι **2 Pt 2:18.** τὸ πνεῦμα τῆς πλάνης (Test12Patr.—Opp. to τὸ πνεῦμα τῆς ἀληθείας: TestJudah 20:1) *the spirit of error* **1J 4:6.** ἐκ πλάνης ὁδοῦ αὐτοῦ **Js 5:20** (ὁδός 3b). τῇ πλάνῃ τοῦ Βαλαὰμ μισθοῦ ἐξεχύθησαν *for gain they have wholly given themselves up to Balaam's error* **Jd 11** (s. μισθός 1 and ἐκχέω 3).—πλάνη τοῦ ὄφεως Dg 12:3 (cp. Just., D. 88, 4 and Hippol., Ref. 5, 6, 3) is prob. not act., meaning deceiving by the serpent, but the deceit or error originated by it; cp. 12:8.—B. 1185. DELG s.v. πλανάομαι. M-M. TW. Sv.

πλάνης, ητος, ὁ (πλανάω; Soph. et al.; X., Mem. 4, 7, 5; Dio Chrys. 30 [47], 8; Vett. Val. 64, 6; Philo; loanw. in rabb.) **Jd 13 v.l.** The word is equivalent in mng. to πλανήτης, q.v.—DELG s.v. πλανάομαι. TW.

πλανήτης, ου, ὁ (πλάνης; Soph. et al.; Vett. Val. 65, 4; Hos 9:17; Jos., Ant. 3, 145; Tat.; Ath. 23, 2) ***wanderer, roamer*** used as subst. and adj. in our lit. only in the combination ἀστέρες πλανῆται (Aristot., Meteor. 1, 6; Plut., Mor. 604a; 905c f; Ps.-Lucian. Astrol. 14, Salt. 7 al.; PGM 7, 513, mostly of the planets, which appeared to 'wander' across the skies among the fixed stars) in imagery, w. tradition such as En 18:15f as background: *wandering stars* **Jd 13** (the v.l. πλάνητες [s. πλάνης] is by no means rare in other lit., e.g. X., Mem. 4, 7, 5; Aristot., Met. 342b, 28 in just this combination).—S. ἀστήρ end. DELG s.v. πλανάομαι. M-M. TW.

πλάνος, ον (πλανάω; trag. et al.; LXX, Philo, Joseph.) in our lit. only in the transf. sense.: **pert. to causing someone to be mistaken**

ⓐ as adj., ***leading astray, deceitful*** (so Menand., fgm. 288 Kö.; Theocr. 21, 43; Moschus 1, 28; 5, 10; Jos., Bell. 2, 259; Just., A II, 15, 1, D. 70, 5 al.) πνεύματα πλάνα *deceitful spirits* **1 Ti 4:1** (cp. TestBenj 6:1; Just., D. 7, 3 al.) τούτων εἰδώλων τῶν πλάνων *these seductive images* ApcPt Bodl.

ⓑ as subst. ὁ πλάνος ***deceiver, impostor*** (Diod. S. 34 + 35, fgm. 2, 14; Vett. Val. 74, 18; Ps.-Clem., Hom. 4, 2) of Jesus **Mt 27:63** (cp. TestLevi 16:3). W. ὁ ἀντίχριστος **2J 7b;** pl. vs. **7a.** ὡς πλάνοι καὶ ἀληθεῖς *considered impostors, and* (yet are) *true* **2 Cor 6:8.**—DELG s.v. πλανάομαι. M-M. TW.

πλάξ, πλακός, ἡ (Pind. et al.; ins, pap, LXX, En, Test 12 Patr; ApcMos prol.) gener. 'someth. with a flat surface'; in our lit. **a flat stone on which inscriptions could be made, *tablet,*** of the tablets of the law (LXX; Philo, Migr. Abr. 85; Jos., Ant. 3, 90; SibOr 3, 257; on the custom of inscribing on πλάκες of stone s. Mitt-Wilck. I/2, 54, 1ff [III BC]; OGI 672, 12) B 14:2 (cp. Ex 31:18; 34:4). πλάκες λίθιναι γεγραμμέναι τῷ δακτύλῳ τῆς χειρὸς τοῦ κυρίου 4:7 (Ex 31:18). αἱ πλάκες τῆς διαθήκης (διαθήκη 3) **Hb 9:4.** Thrown to the ground and broken in pieces by Moses (Ex 32:19; Dt 9:17) B 4:8; 14:3. Paul speaks, w. Ex 32:16; 34:1 in mind and alluding to Ezk 11:19; 36:26, of an ἐπιστολὴ . . . ἐγγεγραμμένη οὐκ ἐν πλαξὶν λιθίναις ἀλλ᾽ ἐν πλαξὶν καρδίαις (the v.l. has the easier καρδίας) σαρκίναις **2 Cor 3:3** (cp. Theodor. Prod. 8, 353 Hercher ζωγραφεῖν πρὸς καρδίας πινακίῳ). S. πλάτος.—DELG. M-M.

πλάσις, εως, ἡ (πλάσσω; Theophr. et al.; pap; ApcEsdr 2:23 p. 26, 16 Tdf. τὴν σὴν πλάσιν; Ath. 25:4 τῇ κατὰ τὴν πλάσιν διαθέσει) **the forming of someth. by shaping a soft substance, *formation, molding, creation*** (w. gen. Polyb. 6, 53, 5; Plut., Cic. 862 [4, 4]; PSI 712, 5 πλάσις ὀπτῆς πλίνθου) ἡ πλ. τοῦ Ἀδάμ B 6:9. τὴν πλ. τὴν τῶν ἀνθρώπων AcPlCor

1:13. δευτέρα πλ. of the spiritual new creation through Christ B 6:13 (cp. Diod. S. 1, 16, 1).—DELG s.v. πλάσσω.

πλάσμα, ατος, τό (πλάσσω; Aristoph., Pla.+; PGM 4, 212; 304; 5, 378; LXX; En 104:10; TestSol 18:20; TestNapht 2:5; ApcSed; ApcMos 37; Philo; Jos., C. Ap. 1, 254; 2, 122; Just., D. 40, 1) **that which is formed or molded, *image, figure*** μὴ ἐρεῖ τὸ πλάσμα τῷ πλάσαντι; *can what is molded say to its molder?* **Ro 9:20** (Is 29:16; Ro 9:21 proceeds to mention κεραμεὺς τοῦ πηλοῦ; cp. Aristoph., Av. 686 πλάσματα πηλοῦ). ὁ παντοκράτωρ … μὴ βουλόμενος ἀκυρῶσαι τὸ ἴδιον πλάσμα *the Almighty … not wishing to spoil (invalidate) his own handiwork* AcPlCor 2:12. The account of the creation (Gen 1:26) is interpreted w. ref. to regeneration, and the Christians speak of themselves as τὸ καλὸν πλ. ἡμῶν *our beautiful creation* B 6:12. The words φθορεῖς πλάσματος θεοῦ 20:2 need not be understood fr. this as a background; as the parallel D 5:2 shows, it comes fr. a different complex of ideas. Beside φονεῖς τέκνων it could mean *those who destroy what God has formed* in the womb, by abortion (but s. φθορεύς).—M-M. TW. Sv.

πλάσσω 1 aor. ἔπλασα; pf. ptc. πεπλακώς. Pass.: 1 aor. ἐπλάσθην; pf. ptc. neut. πεπλασμένον LXX (s. two prec. entries; Hes. et al.; ins [e.g. IAndrosIsis 94]; pap, LXX; pseudepigr.; Philo; Jos., C. Ap. 1, 293; apolog. [Tat. 1, 1 πλάττειν])

❶ **to manufacture someth. by molding a soft substance, *form, mold***—ⓐ of the manufacture of certain objects **Ro 9:20** (s. πλάσμα); Dg 2:3.

ⓑ esp. of God's creative activity in forming humankind (cp. Semonides of Amorgos 7, 21 of a woman as obj. πλάσαντες γηίνην Ὀλύμπιοι; Babrius 66, 2f πλάσσασθαι ἄνθρωπον ἐκ γῆς. Cp. Cornutus 18 p. 31, 20.—Artem. 3, 17 it is said of Prometheus πλ. τοὺς ἀνθρώπους).

α. of the first parents, Adam and Eve (Gen 2:7f, 15; cp. 2 Macc 7:23; TestAbr B 8 p. 113, 4 [Stone p. 74]; Philo, Op. M. 137; Jos., Ant. 1, 32; SibOr 3, 24; Just., D. 19, 3 al.) ἄνθρωπον ταῖς ἱεραῖς χερσὶν ἔπλασεν *(God) formed humankind with holy hands* 1 Cl 33:4 (ἄρσεν καὶ θῆλυ vs. 5). Pass. **1 Ti 2:13** 'Adam' and 'Eve'.

β. of humans in gener., w. the first parents in mind: οὓς (i.e. the humans) ἐκ τῆς ἰδίας εἰκόνος ἔπλασεν *whom (God) formed in his own image* Dg 10:2 (Himerius, Or. 64 [=Or. 18], 4 πλ. of forming of figures by a sculptor).

γ. of humankind gener., with no special ref. to Adam and Eve (oft. LXX; ApcEsdr 3:9 p. 27, 17 Tdf.; Ath. 31, 3) 1 Cl 38:3; B 19:2; AcPlCor 2:7. Specif. the human heart was formed by God B 2:10 (cp. Ps 32:15).

❷ **to direct personal character or cultural formation, *shape,*** in fig. ext. of 1: formation of mental things, in the difficult pass. δεῖξαι αὐτῷ φῶς καὶ πλάσαι τῇ συνέσει *show him light and shape him with understanding* (?) 1 Cl 16:12 (Is 53:11 LXX, without support in the orig. text as handed down to us.—For the figurative meaning cp. Pla., Rep. 377c πλάττειν τὰς ψυχάς [through education], Leg. 671c παιδεύειν καὶ πλάττειν; Theocr. 7, 44).—B. 617. DELG. M-M. TW.

πλαστός, ή, όν (πλάσσω; Hes. et al.) **pert. to being mentally constructed without a basis in fact, *fabricated, false*** (so since Eur., Bacch. 218; Hdt. 1, 68; Lycophron 432 ἐν πλασταῖς γραφαῖς, also PSI 494, 13 [III BC]; POxy 237 VIII, 14 [II AD]; Philo, Somn. 2, 140; Jos., Vi. 177; 337) πλ. λόγοι **2 Pt 2:3** (Ael. Aristid. 36, 91 K.=48 p. 474 D.: ὁ λόγος πέπλασται; cp. POxy 237 VIII, 14 [II AD] of a forged contract).—DELG s.v. πλάσσω. M-M. TW.

πλατεῖα, ας, ἡ (really the fem. of πλατύς, w. ὁδός to be supplied: Sext. Emp., Pyrrh. 1, 188 ὅταν λέγωμεν πλατεῖαν, δυνάμει λέγομεν πλατεῖαν ὁδόν) ***wide road, street*** (Ps.-Eur., Rhes. 283; Diod. S. 12, 10, 7; 17, 52, 3; Plut., Dio 978 [46, 2], Thes. 27, 4; OGI 491, 9; Lyc. ins [Hauser 96]; pap, LXX; TestAbr B 8 p. 113, 11f [Stone p. 74]; Jos., Bell. 1, 425, Ant. 16, 148; Mel., P. 94, 724; loanw. in rabb.) **Mt 12:19** (Is 42:2); **Mk 6:56** D; **Lk 10:10; 13:26; Ac 5:15** (Maximus Tyr. 6, 2 people put their sick out in the street so that passersby can advise them or influence them for good); **Rv 11:8; 21:21; 22:2.** W. ῥύμη (Tob 13:17, 18 BA; Is 15:3) **Lk 14:21.** ἐν ταῖς γωνίαις τῶν πλ. *at* or *on the street-corners* **Mt 6:5.**—B. 720. DELG s.v. 1 πλατύς. M-M.

πλάτος, ους, τό (πλατύς; Hdt.+; ins, pap, LXX; En 21:7; TestSol 11:8 C; TestAbr A 12 p. 91, 2 [Stone p. 30]; GrBar 11:8; EpArist; Philo; Jos., Bell. 7, 312, Ant. 8, 65, C. Ap. 2, 119.—ὁ πλάτος only as an oversight **Eph 3:18** P[46]) **extent from side to side, *breadth, width,*** w. τὸ μῆκος **Rv 21:16a** as well as τὸ μῆκος and τὸ ὕψος vs. **16b.** On τὸ πλάτος καὶ μῆκος καὶ ὕψος καὶ βάθος **Eph 3:18** s. βάθος 1.—τὸ πλάτος τῆς γῆς **Rv 20:9** comes fr. the OT (Da 12:2 LXX. Cp. Hab 1:6; Sir 1:3), but the sense is not clear: *breadth = the broad plain of the earth* is perh. meant to provide room for the countless enemies of God vs. 8, but the 'going up' is better suited to Satan (vs. 7), who has recently been freed, and who comes up again fr. the abyss (vs. 3).—In imagery (cp. Procop. Soph., Ep. 65; Nicetas Eugen. 2, 10 H. καρδίας πλάτος) τὰ δικαιώματα τοῦ κυρίου ἐπὶ τὰ πλάτη τῆς καρδίας ὑμῶν ἐγέγραπτο *the ordinances of the Lord have been written on your heart from side to side* 1 Cl 2:8 (s. Pr 7:3; 22:20; 3:3 A; sim. metaphors Aeschyl., Prom. 789; Soph., fgm. 540 TGF; cp. s.v. πλάξ.—Renehan '75, 165).—DELG s.v. 1 πλατύς.

πλατύνω (πλατύς) aor. ἐπλάτυνα LXX. Pass.: 1 fut. 3 sg. πλατυνθήσεται Gen. 28:14; 1 aor. ἐπλατύνθην; pf. 3 sg. πεπλάτυνται (X. et al.; ins, LXX; TestSol 13:7 C; Jos., Ant. 9, 206; Ath., R. 19 p. 71, 24) **to cause someth. to be broad, *make broad, enlarge,*** lit. τὶ *someth.* τὰ φυλακτήρια **Mt 23:5** (s. φυλακτήριον); **Rv 7:14 v.l.** (for ἔπλυναν). Pass. (w. παχύνεσθαι; s. παχύνω 1) *be enlarged* 1 Cl 3:1 (Dt 32:15).—Fig., of warm affection ἡ καρδία ἡμῶν πεπλάτυνται *my heart is open wide* **2 Cor 6:11** (the expr. also occurs Dt 6:12 v.l.; 11:16; Ps 118:32. Cp. Epict., fgm. Stob. 60 τὰς ψυχὰς αὔξειν); πλατύνθητε καὶ ὑμεῖς *you must open your hearts (wide), too* vs. **13;** cp. SIG 783, 12.—DELG s.v. 1 πλατύς. M-M.

πλατύς, εῖα, ύ (s. three prec. entries and next entry; Hom.+; ins, pap, LXX, TestAbr; TestZeb 4:6 v.l.; JosAs, Philo, Joseph.; Mel., P. 45, 318; Ath., R. 19 p. 72, 9 [γέλως πλατύς]) **pert. to great extent from side to side, *broad, wide*** **Mt 7:13** of a gate πλατεῖα ἡ πύλη καὶ … (rdg. of the text; cp. Plut., Caes. 723 [33, 1] πλατεῖαι πύλαι; PFlor 333, 11 μέχρι πλατείας πύλης; Jos., Bell. 3, 81), or of a road, accord. to the v.l. πλατεῖα καὶ εὐρύχωρος ἡ ὁδός (cp. X., Cyr. 1, 6, 43 ἢ στενὰς ἢ πλατείας ὁδούς; Arrian, Anab. 1, 1, 8 ὁδὸς πλατεῖα; SIG 57, 25 [V BC]; 313, 19f; Jos., Bell. 6, 149).—B. 885. DELG. M-M.

πλατυσμός, οῦ, ὁ (πλατύς; Diosc. 5, 6 al.; LXX; Philo, Somn. 2, 36).

❶ **state of increasing development, *extension, enlargement, expansion*** (schol. on Pind., Eustath., Prooem. 4) of a congregation (w. δόξα) 1 Cl 3:1.

❷ **state of being ample,** ***amplitude, extent*** (2 Km 22:20; Ps 17:20; 118:45), in imagery of patience, which prospers through broad application Hm 5, 2, 3 (εὐθηνέω b).—DELG s.v. 1 πλατύς.

πλέγμα, ατος, τό (Eur., Pla., X.; Is 28:5 Aq. and Theod.; Philo; Jos., Ant. 2, 220: 'someth. that is plaited/woven, braided') ***braided hair,*** w. focus on stylish coiffure **1 Ti 2:9.**

πλείων, πλειόνως, πλεῖστος s. πολύς.—M-M.

πλέκω 1 aor. ἔπλεξα. Pass.: aor. ptc. πλακείς Is 28:5; pf. ptc. πεπλεγμένος (Hom. et al.; POsl 159, 10; 19 [III AD]; LXX; TestSol; JosAs ch. 11 cod. A [p. 53, ln. 11 Bat.]; ApcrEzk [Epiph. 70, 10]; EpArist 70; Philo, Aet. M. 105; Jos., Ant. 3, 170) ***weave, plait*** στέφανον *a wreath* (Epici p. 23, Cypria fgm. 4, 2 K.=fgm 5 p. 47 B.; Pind. et al.) **Mk 15:17.** τὶ ἔκ τινος (Alciphron 2, 35, 1; Paus. 2, 35, 5 στεφ. ἐκ) **Mt 27:29; J 19:2;** pass. ApcPt 3:10.—B. 622. DELG. M-M.

πλέον s. πολύς 1b; 2b (πλείων).

πλεονάζω (πλέον) fut. πλεονάσω LXX; 1 aor. ἐπλεόνασα, aor. pass. 3 pl. ἐπλεονάσθησαν 1 Ch 5:23 (Thu., Hippocr. et al.; ins, pap, LXX; PsSol 5:4; ApcEsdr 3:6 p. 27, 11 Tdf.; EpArist 295 [cj. by Wendl.]; intr. Thu. 1, 120, 4 et al.; in earlier Gk. mostly in neg. sense relating to excess).

❶ **to become more and more, so as to be in abundance,** ***be/become more*** or ***be/become great, be present in abundance, grow, increase,*** intr. (Strabo 4, 1, 13; Appian, Bell. Civ. 5, 89 §370; Ael. Aristid. 33 p. 616 D.; schol. on Nicander, Ther. 553; 2 Ch 24:11; Philo, Rer. Div. Her. 245; Jos., Ant. 19, 319) **2 Pt 1:8.** *Increase* in number, *multiply* Dg 6:9; cp. 7:8. Of sin (cp. Sir 23:3 ὅπως μὴ αἱ ἁμαρτίαι μου πλεονάσωσι) **Ro 5:20a** (cp. Philistion [IV BC] 4 p. 110, 8 Wellmann [s. Diocles] ἐπειδὰν πλεονάσῃ τὸ θερμόν), vs. **20b.** Of grace **6:1; 2 Cor 4:15** (in remarkable violation of the Hellenic principle μηδὲν ἄγαν). Of love **2 Th 1:3.** ἐπιζητῶ τὸν καρπὸν τὸν πλεονάζοντα *I seek the fruit that increases* **Phil 4:17.**

❷ **to have more than is necessary,** ***have too much,*** intr. (Diod. S. 2, 54, 7; 11, 59, 4; 19, 81, 3; Appian, Bell. Civ. 4, 108 §454 of legions with more than the usual number of men) **2 Cor 8:15** (Ex 16:18).

❸ **to be responsible for increase,** trans.—ⓐ ***to bring forth in abundance, increase*** τὶ *someth.* (Ps 70:21; Jos., Ant. 1, 32) τὸ στόμα σου ἐπλεόνασεν κακίαν 1 Cl 35:8 (Ps 49:19).

ⓑ ***to cause increase*** (w. περισσεύειν) ὑμᾶς ὁ κύριος πλεονάσαι τῇ ἀγάπῃ *may the Lord cause you to increase (=become rich) in love* **1 Th 3:12.**—DELG s.v. πλείων. M-M.TW.

πλεονεκτέω (s. πλεονέκτης) 1 aor. ἐπλεονέκτησα, pass. ἐπλεονεκτήθην (since Hdt. 8, 112; ins, pap, LXX; Test12 Patr; EpArist 270; Philo; Jos., Bell. 6, 79, Ant. 1, 66; 2, 260 al.; Just., A I, 16, 4; predom. intr., s. B-D-F §148, 1; Mlt. 65). In our lit. only trans.

❶ **to take advantage of,** ***exploit, outwit, defraud, cheat*** τινά *someone* (Dionys. Hal. 9, 7; Dio Chrys. 67 [17], 8 τὸν ἀδελφόν; Plut., Marc. 315 [29, 7]; Ps.-Lucian, Amor. 27).

ⓐ of humans who take advantage of others **2 Cor 7:2** (w. ἀδικεῖν [cp. PCairMasp 151, 242f ἀδικῶς πλεονεκτεῖσθαι] and φθείρειν); **12:18.** πλ. τινὰ διά τινος *take advantage of someone through someone* vs. **17.** πλ. τινὰ ἐν τῷ πράγματι **1 Th 4:6** (s. πρᾶγμα 2).

ⓑ of Satan, pass. (Demosth. 41, 25 πλεονεκτεῖσθαι χιλίαις δραχμαῖς; OGI 484, 27 πλεονεκτεῖσθαι τοὺς ὀλίγους ὑπ' αὐτῶν ἀνθρώπους) ἵνα μὴ πλεονεκτηθῶμεν ὑπὸ τοῦ σατανᾶ *that we may not be outwitted by Satan* **2 Cor 2:11** ('robbed' by Satan of a member of our group: BNoack, Satanas u. Soteria '48, 98f).

❷ ***increase the number of*** τὶ *someth.* (PCairMasp 3, 9 πλεονεκτῆσαι τὰ πράγματα) of the hare κατ' ἐνιαυτὸν πλ. τὴν ἀφόδευσιν B 10:6 (s. ἀφόδευσις).—DELG s.v. ἔχω and πλείων. M-M. TW.

πλεονέκτης, ου, ὁ (=ὁ πλέον ἔχων; since Hdt. [7, 158 adj.]; PMagd 5, 7 [221 BC]; Sir 14:9; Philo, Mos. 1, 56; Ar. 10, 3; Just., A I, 12, 1) **one who desires to have more than is due,** ***a greedy person,*** whose ways are judged to be extremely sinful by Christians and many others. (S. πλεονεξία and JWeiss on 1 Cor 5:11. In Hellenic society this was a violation of the basic principle of proportion and contrary to the idea of beneficent concern for the citizenry.) Among the sinners of the 'two ways' B 19:6; D 2:6. Also elsewh. w. those who are burdened w. serious vices (as M. Ant. 11, 18, 6; Philo, Sacr. Abel. 32) **1 Cor 5:10f; 6:10; Eph 5:5** (here characterized as εἰδωλολάτρης; s. on πλεονεξία); Hs 6, 5, 5 (Thu. 1, 40, 1; X., Mem. 1, 2, 12 [both w. βίαιος]; 1, 5, 3, Cyr. 1, 6, 27 [w. κλέπτης and ἅρπαξ]; Aristot., EN 5, 2 [w. ὁ παράνομος and ὁ ἄνισος]; Diod. S. 20, 106, 4; Plut., Ages. 607 [20, 6] [w. ἐν ταῖς ἐξουσίαις πονηρός], Mor. 57c [w. κακοῦργος]; Vett. Val. 42, 28 [w. ἀλλοτρίων ἐπιθυμητής]).—DELG s.v. ἔχω and πλείων. M-M. TW.

πλεονεξία, ας, ἡ (πλεονέκτης) **the state of desiring to have more than one's due,** ***greediness, insatiableness, avarice, covetousness*** (so Hdt., Thu.+; Aristoxenus, fgm. 50 p. 23, 36ff [πλ. as the vice pure and simple]; Diod. S. 21, 1, 4 [πλ. as the μητρόπολις τῶν ἀδικημάτων]; Musonius 72, 9; 90, 10 H.; Dio Chrys., Or. 67 [17] περὶ πλεονεξίας: 6 μέγιστον κακῶν αἴτιον; 7 μέγιστον κακόν; Ael. Aristid. 39 p. 733 D.: πλ. is among the three most disgraceful things; Herm. Wr. 13, 7; pap, LXX; Test12Patr; GrBar 13:3; ApcMos 11; EpArist 277; Philo, Spec. Leg. 1, 173, Praem. 15 al.; Jos., Bell. 7, 256, Ant. 3, 67; 7, 37 al.; Just., D. 14, 2; Tat. 19, 2; Ath., R. 21 p. 74, 9; Theoph. Ant. 1, 14 [p. 92, 7]) B 10:4; w. other vices (as Diod. S. 13, 30, 4 in catalogues of vices. On these s. AVögtle, Die Tugend- u. Lasterkataloge im NT '36) **Ro 1:29;** 1 Cl 35:5; B 20:1; D 5:1; Pol 2:2; Hm 6, 2, 5; 8:5. Used w. ἀκαθαρσία **Eph 4:19; 5:3.** Characterized as εἰδωλολατρία **Col 3:5** (s. εἰδωλολατρία, πλεονέκτης and cp. TestJud 19:1. Chaeremon the Stoic, Nero's teacher, in Porphyr., Abst. 4, 6 [=Chaeremon, fgm. 10, p. 16 Horst] contrasts πλεονεξία with θεία γνῶσις). Of false teachers **2 Pt 2:3, 14** (s. γυμνάζω end). πρόφασις πλεονεξίας (subj. gen.) *pretext for avarice* **1 Th 2:5** (cp. Philostrat. I 362, 14 πρόσχημα τ. πλεονεξίας). φυλάσσεσθαι ἀπὸ πάσης πλ. *guard against every form of greed* **Lk 12:15.**—The pl. of the individual expressions of greed (B-D-F §142.—X., Cyr. 1, 6, 29; Plut., Pomp. 640 [39, 6]; 2 Macc 4:50; Philo, Agr. 83, Vi. Cont. 70; Jos., Ant. 17, 253; Tat. 19, 2) **Mk 7:22.**—In **2 Cor 9:5** the context calls for the pregnant mng. *a gift that is grudgingly granted by avarice* (εὐλογία 4); *extortion* (Plummer, ICC ad vs. 10c).—WSedgwick, ET 36, 1925, 478f; TManson, JTS 44, '43, 86f; EKlaar, Πλεονεξία, -έκτης, -εκτεῖν TZ 10, '54, 395–97.—DELG s.v. ἔχω and πλείων. M-M. TW. Spicq. Sv.

πλευρά, ᾶς, ἡ (Hom.+) ***side,*** mostly of the human body **Mt 27:49 v.l.; J 19:34** (on both s. νύσσω 1); **20:20, 25, 27; Ac 12:7** (s. πατάσσω 1a).—Of the flat side of a stone Hs 9, 4, 1.—B. 862. DELG. M-M.

πλέω impf. 1 pl. ἐπλέομεν; fut. 3 sg. πλευσεῖται Ath. 22, 8; aor. 3 sg. ἔπλευσεν 4 Macc 7:3 and Ath. 22:8; inf. πλεῦσαι Jon 1:3 (Hom.+) ***travel by sea, sail*** abs. (X., An. 5, 1, 4; Herodian 8, 2, 3) **Lk 8:23; Ac 27:24;** AcPl Ha 5, 16. W. the destination given (X., Hell. 1, 1, 8; Jos., Ant. 18, 111 εἰς τὴν Ῥώμην) εἰς Συρίαν **21:3.** εἰς τὴν Ἰταλίαν **27:6.** εἰς τοὺς κατὰ τὴν Ἀσίαν τόπους vs. **2.** W. the point of departure given as well as the destination (Appian, Liby. 113 §535 ἀπὸ Σικελίας ἐς Ἰτύκην [Utica]) ἀπὸ Τρῳάδος εἰς Νεάπολιν IPol 8:1.—As subst. πᾶς ὁ ἐπὶ τόπον πλέων *everyone who sails to a place = seafarer, sea traveler* (prob. a ref. to tourists who travel to take in the sights at 'Babylon' [on touring in the Roman world, s. LFriedländer, Roman Life and Manners under the Early Empire[7], tr. LMagnus, 1907, I 323–94]). These are mentioned beside sailors and merchants **Rv 18:17.** The vv.ll. (τὸν ποταμόν, τῶν πλοίων, πόντον [for the textual problems, s. RBorger, TRu 52, '87, 51–53]) have led to various interpretations. Some render: *everyone who sails along the coast* (deWette, HHoltzmann, Bousset, Lohmeyer et al. For πλ. ἐπί w. acc. of place s. Thu. 1, 53, 2; 4 Macc 7:3. In FPhGr I 489, 28 we have πλέοντες παρὰ τόπον. On the v.l. ὁ ἐπὶ τῶν πλοίων πλέων cp. Lucian, Ver. Hist. 1, 34; SIG 409, 5f ἔπλευσεν ἐπὶ τῶν νεῶν. Ms. 469 has ἐπὶ πόντον, partially supported by Primasius' 'super mare'. See EbNestle, Einführung in das Griech. NT 1909, 182; AFridrichsen, K. Hum. Vetensk.-Samf. i Upps. Årsb. '43, 31 note ὁ ἐπίτοπον πλέων=one who sails occasionally, a passenger. S. also IHeikel, StKr 106, '34/35, 317).—LCasson, Travel in the Ancient World '74. B. 680f. DELG. M-M.

πληγή, ῆς, ἡ (πλήσσω; Hom.+; ins, pap, LXX; En, TestJob, Test12Patr; JosAs 17:3 cod. A [p. 66, 4 Bat.]; ApcMos 8; Just., D. 132, 2 ['plague' of mice, s. 1 Km 6]; Mel., P. 18, 120; 87, 657) 'blow'.

❶ **a sudden hard stroke with some instrument, *blow, stroke*** lit. (Diod. S. 4, 43, 3 [blow of a whip]; Jos., Vi. 335) **Lk 12:48** (on the omission of πληγάς with πολλάς, ὀλίγας vs. 47f, s. δέρω and cp. Pla., Leg. 9, 854d; 879e; Demosth. 19, 197; Herodas 3, 77; 5, 33; Diod. S. 36, 8, 3 τρίτην [i.e. πληγὴν] λαβών; B-D-F §241, 6; Rob. 653); **2 Cor 6:5; 11:23.** ἐπιθεῖναί τινι πληγάς (ἐπιτίθημι 1aβ) **Ac 16:23;** cp. **Lk 10:30.**

❷ **wound caused by a blow, *wound, bruise*** (Diod. S. 15, 55, 4; Nicol. Dam.: 90 fgm. 130, 26 p. 410, 24 Jac.; Appian, Iber. 74 §314 al.; schol. on Pla., Rep. 566a; Jos., Ant. 7, 128; 10, 77) **Ac 16:33** (Appian, Bell. Civ. 2, 26 §98 πλ.=weal, scar caused by being beaten with rods). ἡ πλ. τῆς μαχαίρης *the sword-wound* (cp. Philosoph. Max. 496, 151 ξίφους πληγή) **Rv 13:14** (πλ. alone=fatal wound: Diod. S. 16, 12, 3; Jos., Ant. 9, 121.—πλ. ἔχειν: Anaxandrides Com. 72). ἡ πλ. τοῦ θανάτου *mortal wound* (cp. Lucian, Dial. Deor. 14, 2; Plut., Anton. 951 [76, 10] πλ. εὐθυθάνατος) vss. **3, 12.** The sg. collectively ἡ πληγή *wounding=wounds* B 5:12; 7:2.

❸ **a sudden calamity that causes severe distress, *blow*** in the sense 'a blow of fate', etc. (Aeschyl. et al.; Polyb. 14, 9, 6; Appian, Bell. Civ. 3, 72 §295; LXX; En 10:7; TestJob 4:4 al.; Philo, Joseph.) fig. ext. of 1 and 2: *plague, misfortune* (sent by God: Διὸς πλ. Aeschyl., Ag. 367; Soph., Aj. 137. πληγαὶ θεοῦ Plut., Mor. 168c.—Ex 11:1 and oft.; Test12Patr; ApcMos 8; Jos., Bell. 1, 373, Ant. 6, 94; SibOr 3, 306; 519; Mel., P. 87, 657 τὰς δέκα πλ.) **Rv 9:18, 20; 11:6; 15:1, 6, 8; 16:9, 21ab; 18:4, 8; 21:9; 22:18.** Of God's suffering Servant ἐν πληγῇ εἶναι *be struck down with misfortune* 1 Cl 16:3, 4 (Is 53:3, 4; TestJob 27:5; cp. 2 ἐν πλ. ὑπάρχεις and 35:1); καθαρίσαι αὐτὸν τῆς πλ. *free him from misfortune* vs. 10 (Is 53:10).—B. 305. DELG s.v. πλήσσω. M-M.

πλῆθος, ους, τό (πίμπλημι; Hom.+.—In our lit. it is lacking in Mt, the Pauline epp., the catholic epp. [except Js and 1 Pt], Rv, and D [B has it only in a quot. fr. the OT]; in the NT the large majority of occurrences are in Lk and Ac).

❶ **the fact or condition of being many, *quantity/number*** καθὼς τὰ ἄστρα τοῦ οὐρανοῦ τῷ πλήθει **Hb 11:12** (cp. Josh 11:4; Da 3:36 v.l.; TestJob 13:2.—S. also Hdt. 6, 44 al.).

❷ **a large amount, *large number, multitude,*** in concrete sense—ⓐ of things, w. gen. (Diod. S. 15, 3, 3 σίτου; 15, 9, 3; Polyaenus 8, 28, Exc. 15, 9; TestJob 18:4 τῶν ὠδίνων; JosAs 5:7 καρποῦ; SEG VIII, 467, 15f [217 BC] πολὺ πλ. χρυσίου κτλ.) πλ. ἰχθύων (Eparchides [III BC]: 437 fgm. 1 Jac.; Diod. S. 3, 44, 8; 5, 19, 4) πολύ **Lk 5:6;** cp. **J 21:6.** πλ. ἁμαρτιῶν *a host of sins* (cp. Sir 5:6; Ezk 28:17f; ParJer 1:1, 8; Jos., Ant. 12, 167) **Js 5:20; 1 Pt 4:8;** 1 Cl 49:5; 2 Cl 16:4. φρυγάνων πλ. *a bundle of sticks* **Ac 28:3.** πλ. αἵματος *a great quantity of blood* MPol 16:1. πλ. τῆς χαλάζης *density of the hail* AcPl Ha 5, 10. πλ. τῶν θυσίων B 2:5 (Is 1:11). τὸ πλ. τῶν οἰκτιρμῶν σου *the abundance of your compassion* 1 Cl 18:2 (Ps 50:3). τὸ πλ. τῶν σχισμάτων *the large number of cracks* Hs 9, 8, 3.

ⓑ of persons—α. gener. *crowd (of people), throng, host,* also specif. a disorganized crowd (as Maximus Tyr. 39, 2eh) πολὺ πλ. **Mk 3:7f.** W. gen. of pers. (Diod. S. 15, 14, 4 στρατιωτῶν; Cebes 1, 3 γυναικῶν; Appian, Bell. Civ, 1. 81 §370 στρατιᾶς πολὺ πλ.=a large number of military personnel; Jos., Bell. 7, 35, Ant. 18, 61; Just., D. 120, 2) πλῆθος πολὺ τοῦ λαοῦ *a great throng of people* **Lk 6:17; 23:27** (a πλ. at an execution Jos., Ant. 19, 270). τὸ πλ. τοῦ λαοῦ **Ac 21:36** (πλῆθος … κράζοντες is constructio ad sensum as Diod. S. 13, 111, 1 συνέδριον … λέγοντες; Polyb. 18, 9, 9 σύγκλητος … ἐκεῖνοι and similar expressions). τὸ πλ. τοῦ ὄχλου Hs 9, 4, 4. πλ. τῶν ἀσθενούντων *a large number of sick people* **J 5:3.** Ἑλλήνων πολὺ πλ. **Ac 14:1; 17:4.** πλῆθός τι ἀνδρῶν *a large number of* (other) *men* Hs 9, 3, 1 (Diod. S. 15, 76, 2 and Appian, Iber. 59 §248 πλ. ἀνδρῶν, Bell. Civ. 2, 67 §276 πολὺ πλ. ἀνδρῶν). πολὺ πλ. ἐκλεκτῶν 1 Cl 6:1.—Of angels πλ. στρατιᾶς οὐρανίου *a throng of the heavenly army* **Lk 2:13** (πλ. of military personnel Diod. S. 20, 50, 6; Appian, Bell. Civ. 1, 81 §370 στρατιᾶς πλ.; Jos., Ant. 14, 482). τὸ πᾶν πλ. τῶν ἀγγέλων αὐτοῦ 1 Cl 34:5.—Pl. (cp. Socrat., Ep. 1, 2; Diod. S. 1, 64, 5; 1, 85, 2; Appian, Bell. Civ. 2, 120 §503; 2 Macc 12:27; 3 Macc 5:24; EpArist 15; 21. S. Mayser II/1, 1926, 38f) πλήθη ἀνδρῶν τε καὶ γυναικῶν *large numbers of men and women* **Ac 5:14.**

β. *a* (stated) *meeting, assembly* ἐσχίσθη τὸ πλ. **Ac 23:7.** πᾶν τὸ πλ. MPol 3:2. ἅπαν τὸ πλ. αὐτῶν **Lk 23:1** (the verb is in the pl. as Polyaenus 7, 1; 8, 46; Xenophon Eph. 1, 3, 1 ἦλθον ἅπαν τὸ πλῆθος).

γ. *people, populace, population* (Diod. S. 5, 15, 2; Appian, Samn. 4 §14; SIG 581, 95 [c. 200 BC] τὸ πλῆθος τὸ Ῥοδίων; 695, 20 [II BC] τὸ πλ. τὸ Μαγνήτων; IG XII/1, 846, 10; 847, 14 [cp. SIG 765, 129 note 5: τὸ πλέθος τὸ Λινδίων]; 1 Macc 8:20; 2 Macc 11:16; EpArist 308, the last three: τὸ πλ. τῶν Ἰουδαίων; Jos., Vi. 198 τὸ πλ. τῶν Γαλιλαίων; Just., D. 119, 4 Ἀμμανιτῶν πολὺ πλ.) τὸ πλῆθος *the populace* abs. (as Polyaenus 8, 47; 50) **Ac 2:6;** 1 Cl 53:5 (=ὁ λαός vss. 3, 4). ὅλον τὸ πλ. **Ac 14:7** D; AcPl Ha 4, 21. W. gen. τὸ πλ. τῆς πόλεως (Sir 7:7) **Ac 14:4.** τὸ πλ. τῶν πέριξ πόλεων **5:16.** ἅπαν τὸ πλ. τῆς περιχώρου **Lk 8:37.** ἅπαν τὸ πλ. τῶν Ἰουδαίων **Ac 25:24;** cp. MPol 12:2.

δ. in the usage of cultic communities as a t.t. for the whole body of their members, *fellowship, community, congregation* (cp. 1QS 5:2, 9, 22; 6:19; IG XII/1, 155, 6; 156, 5; SIG 1023, 16f τὸ πλ[ῆθος] τῶν μετεχόντων τοῦ ἱεροῦ; OGI 56, 71 [237 BC];

Lucian, Syr. Dea 50) abs. τὸ πλ. *the community, the church* **Ac 15:30; 19:9; 21:22 v.l.;** 1 Cl 54:2; ISm 8:2; Hm 11:9. πᾶν τὸ πλ. *the whole community, group* **Ac 6:5; 15:12.** Also τὸ πᾶν πλ. IMg 6:1. τὸ ἐν θεῷ πλ. ITr 8:2. W. gen. τὸ πᾶν πλ. ὑμῶν 1:1. πᾶν το πλ. τοῦ λαοῦ **Lk 1:10.** ἅπαν τὸ πλ. τῶν μαθητῶν *the whole community of his disciples* **Lk 19:37;** cp. **Ac 6:2.** τὸ πλ. τῶν πιστευσάντων **4:32.**—Dssm., NB 59f [BS 232f].—B. 929. DELG s.v. πίμπλημι. M-M. EDNT. TW. Sv.

πληθύνω (cp. πλῆθος) fut. πληθυνῶ; 1 aor. opt. 3 sg. πληθύναι (Gen 28:3; **2 Cor 9:10 t.r.**). Pass.: impf. ἐπληθυνόμην; fut. 3 sg. πληθυνθήσεται, 3 pl. πληθυνθήσονται LXX; 1 aor. ἐπληθύνθην; pf. 3 sg. πεπλήθυνται, ptc. πεπληθυμμένος LXX (Aeschyl.+; LXX; pseudepigr.; Jos., C. Ap. 2, 139 al.; Ath. 6, 4).

❶ **to cause to become greater in number** trans.—ⓐ ***increase, multiply*** act. (En 16:3; TestJos 11:7; JosAs 21 p. 71, 21 Bat.), in our lit. always of God: τὶ *someth.* τὸν σπόρον ὑμῶν **2 Cor 9:10.** ἔθνη 1 Cl 59:3. Of God's promise to Abraham πληθύνων πληθυνῶ σε *I will surely multiply you* **Hb 6:14** (Gen 22:17). κύριος ἐπλήθυνεν αὐτοὺς ἐν τοῖς κόποις τῶν χειρῶν αὐτῶν *the Lord has given them abundance in the works of their hands* Hs 9, 24, 3. ὁ θεὸς κτίσας τὰ ὄντα καὶ πληθύνας καὶ αὐξήσας v 1, 1, 6.

ⓑ ***be multiplied, grow, increase*** pass. (En 5:5, 9) in number ἐπληθύνετο ὁ ἀριθμὸς τῶν μαθητῶν **Ac 6:7.** ηὔξησεν ὁ λαὸς καὶ ἐπληθύνθη **7:17** (cp. Ex 1:7).—**9:31;** D 16:3. αὐξάνεσθε καὶ πληθύνεσθε (Gen 1:28; cp. SibOr 1, 57; Herm. Wr. 3, 3 εἰς τὸ αὐξάνεσθαι ἐν αὐξήσει καὶ πληθύνεσθαι ἐν πλήθει) 1 Cl 33:6; B 6:12; cp. vs. 18.—Of the growth of Christian preaching, expressed in the number of converts ὁ λόγος τοῦ κυρίου ηὔξανεν καὶ ἐπληθύνετο **Ac 12:24.** Of the spread of godlessness τὸ πληθυνθῆναι τὴν ἀνομίαν **Mt 24:12.** As a formula in devout wishes (cp. Da 4:1 Theod., 37c LXX; 6:26 Theod.) χάρις ὑμῖν καὶ εἰρήνη πληθυνθείη *may grace and peace be yours in ever greater measure* **1 Pt 1:2; 2 Pt 1:2.** Cp. **Jd 2;** 1 Cl ins; Pol ins; MPol ins. Cp. also Dg 11:5.

❷ **to increase greatly in number, *grow, increase*** intr. (Herodian 3, 8, 8; TestIss 1:11; AscIs 2:5; Jos., Bell. 5, 338; Ex 1:20; Sir 16:2; 23:3; 1 Macc 1:9. Cp. Anz 296f; Thackeray 282) πληθυνόντων τ. μαθητῶν *when the disciples were increasing (in number)* **Ac 6:1; 19:20** D.—DELG s.v. πίμπλημι. M-M. EDNT. TW.

πλήκτης, ου, ὁ (πλήσσω; Aristot., Eth. Eud. 2, 3; Plut., Dio 971 [30, 4], Marcell. 298 [1, 2]; Diog. L. 6, 38; Ps 34:15 Sym.) ***pugnacious person, bully*** in a list of qualities relating to a superintendent **1 Ti 3:3; Tit 1:7.**—DELG s.v. πλήσσω.

πλημμέλεια, ας, ἡ (πλημμελέω 'err'; Democr. 46; Pla. et al.; LXX) the prim. sense, 'false note' in music, leads to the fig. ext.: **someth. that is contrary to a generally recognized standard,** freq. of cultic or legal violation: ***fault, error, sin, offense*** (Aristot. 1251a, 31 ἀσέβεια ἡ περὶ θεοὺς πλ.; Jos., C. Ap. 2, 250; restored in POxy 850 [AcJ], 30) θυσίαι περὶ ἁμαρτίας καὶ πλημμελείας *sin and offense (trespass) offerings* (LXX, esp. Lev 7:37) 1 Cl 41:2. Pl. (Plut., Mor. 168d ἁμαρτίαι κ. πλημμέλειαι; Philo, Mos. 2, 230; Jos., Bell. 5, 392) 60:1 (w. ἀνομίαι, ἀδικίαι, παραπτώματα).—Dodd 76.—DELG s.v. πλημμελής.

πλήμμυρα, ης (on the formation s. Schwyzer I 475, 3 and L-S-J-M s.v. πλημυρίς 'rise of the sea, flood'; on the form of the gen. [-ας t.r., Sod., Vog., Bov.] s. B-D-F §43, 1; Mlt-H. 118; on the spelling Mlt-H. 101; 274; s. also PKatz, TLZ 83, '58, 315), ἡ (Dionys. Hal. 1, 71; Crinagoras no. 33, 1; Plut., Rom. 19 [3, 6], Caes. 726 [38, 4], Mor. 897bc; Arrian, Ind. 21, 3; 6; POxy 1409, 17; Job 40:23 ἐὰν γένηται πλήμμυρα; Philo, Op. M. 58, Leg. All. 1, 34, Abr. 92, Mos. 1, 202; 2, 195) **the overflowing of a body of water, *high water, flood*** πλημμύρης γενομένης **Lk 6:48.**—On the spelling with one μ (v.l.), which belongs to the older period of the language, see Mlt-H. p. 101; 274f; JWackernagel, Kl. Schr. '53, 1164, 1.—DELG s.v. πλημυρίς. M-M.

πλήν—❶ adv. used as conj. (trag.+), coming at the beginning of a sentence or clause: **marker of someth. that is contrastingly added for consideration**

ⓐ adversative ***but:*** μὲν ... πλήν *(indeed)* ... *but* (s. B-D-F §447, 6; Rob. 1187) **Lk 22:22.**

ⓑ ***only, nevertheless, but*** (πλήν rather than ἀλλά is the real colloq. word for this idea [Schmid I 133]), so in Mt and Lk but not in Ac (B-D-F §449, 1.—See L-S-J-M s.v. B III 2) πλὴν λέγω ὑμῖν *nevertheless I tell you* **Mt 11:22, 24** (ἀμὴν λέγω ὑμῖν in the corresp. pass. Mt 10:15); **26:64** (Mt 17:12 λέγω δὲ ὑμῖν; Mk 9:13 ἀλλὰ λέγω ὑμῖν; cp. ApcMos 39 πλὴν οὖν λέγω σοι). πλὴν οὐαί **Mt 18:7; Lk 17:1** (οὐαὶ δὲ v.l.). πλὴν οὐχ ὡς ἐγὼ θέλω, ἀλλ' ὡς σύ **Mt 26:39;** cp. **Lk 22:42** (Mk 14:36 ἀλλ' οὐ τί ἐγὼ θέλω).—**Lk 6:24, 35; 10:11, 14, 20; 11:41; 13:33; 18:8; 19:27; 22:21.**—Also looking back at a neg. (TestZeb 1:5; JosAs 23:15; ApcMos 19; Just., D. 44, 2; 88, 7; 93, 1): μὴ κλαίετε ἐπ' ἐμέ, πλὴν ἐφ' ἑαυτὰς κλαίετε *do not weep for me, but (rather) weep for yourselves* **Lk 23:28.** μὴ ζητεῖτε ... πλὴν ζητεῖτε **12:**(29–) **31.**

ⓒ ***only, in any case, on the other hand, but,*** breaking off a discussion and emphasizing what is important (JosAs 14:9; Mel., P. 95, 729; UPZ 110, 207 [164 BC]; Sb 6994, 28; B-D-F §449, 2; Rob. 1187; s. L-S-J-M s.v. B III 2), so in Paul **1 Cor 11:11; Eph 5:33; Phil 3:16; 4:14.** Perh. **1:18** τί γάρ; πλὴν ὅτι ... *what then? In any case* ... (but the text is not certain; s. also d); **Rv 2:25.**

ⓓ πλὴν ὅτι ***except that*** (Aristoph., Pla., Hdt. et al.; Hero Alex. I p. 188, 1; Dionys. Hal., Comp. Verb. 14, end; Plut., Cato Maj. 350 [23, 6]; Just., A I, 21, 4; D. 71, 3; Schwyzer II 543) **Ac 20:23.** Perh. also **Phil 1:18** (s. c above) τί γὰρ πλὴν ὅτι ... ; *what then will come of it, except that* ... ?

ⓔ breaking off and passing to a new subject ***only, but*** (exx. in L-S-J-M πλήν B III 2.—Polyb. 2, 17, 1; Plut., Pericl. 170 [34, 1]; Tat. 36, 1 begin new sections with πλήν) πλὴν ἰδοὺ ἡ χεὶρ κτλ. *but here is (my informer's) hand* with mine on the table (the narration passes from the institution of the Eucharist to a prediction of Judas's role as informer) **Lk 22:21.**

❷ used as prep. w. gen. as **marker denoting an exception, *except,*** in ref. to pers. or thing (since Od. 8, 207; ins, pap, LXX [Johannessohn, Präp. 342–44; Schwyzer II 542]; TestSol 13:12 C; TestAbr A 8 p. 85, 22 [Stone p. 18]; TestIss 7:2; JosAs 2:16; 5:10; ApcSed; Ar. 15, 3; Just., A I, 53, 6 al.; B-D-F §216, 2; Rob. 646 [cp. the use of παρά w. acc. in this sense Plut., Cat. Min. 768 (20), Ant. 918 (5); s. L-S-J-M παρά C III 5b]) mostly after neg. statements: **Mk 12:32** (οὐκ ἄλλος πλήν as Jos., Ant. 1, 182); **J 8:10 v.l.; Ac 15:28; 27:22.** After a positive statement (Thu. 4, 54, 2; X., An. 2, 4, 27; Appian, Liby. 14 §59; Jos., Ant. 12, 422 ἔφυγον πάντες πλὴν ὀκτακοσίων) **Ac 8:1.**—DELG. M-M.

πλήρης, ες (Aeschyl., Hdt.+).—❶ **pert. to containing within itself all that it will hold, *filled, full*—ⓐ** of things

α. τινός *with* or *of someth.* (Diod. S. 2, 4, 2 λίμνη πλήρης ἰχθύων; Appian, Hann. 15 §66; PSI 422, 14 [III BC] ἡ γῆ ῥηγμῶν [fissures] πλ. ἐστίν; Num 7:26; Dt 6:11; Diog. L. 6, 37 πάντα ἐστὶ αὐτοῦ [= θεοῦ] πλήρη) baskets κλασμάτων πλ. *full of pieces* **Mk 8:19;** cp. **6:43 v.l.** A vineyard βοτανῶν πλ. *full of weeds* Hs 5, 2, 3. Of a mountain ἀκανθῶν καὶ τριβόλων πλ. 9, 1, 5; πηγῶν πλ. vs. 8. Trees καρπῶν πλ. 9, 28, 1. πλήρης πᾶσα ἡ κτίσις τ. δόξης αὐτοῦ 1 Cl 34:6 (Is 6:3). εἰς συναγωγὴν πλήρη ἀνδρῶν δικαίων Hm 11:14.

β. abs. ἑπτὰ σπυρίδες πλήρεις **Mt 15:37;** cp. **14:20** (GrBar 15:2 τὰ κανίσκια πλήρη). Of jars Hm 12, 5, 3ab.—ἐκ πλήρους (SIG 1104, 21 ἐποίησεν ἐκ πλήρους τὰ δίκαια; PTebt 106, 20 [II BC]; 281, 22; BGU 584, 6 and oft. in pap='in [the] full [amount]'. Acc. to CTurner, JTS 21, 1920, 198, note 1 this is a Latinism for 'in pleno') *in full, in all fullness* τι ἐκ πλ. Hv 2, 2, 6.

ⓑ of persons, w. gen. ἀνὴρ πλήρης λέπρας **Lk 5:12** (=all covered w. it, as 4 Km 7:15; Is 1:15). Mostly *full* of a power, gift, feeling, characteristic quality, etc. (Eur., El. 384; Pla., Plt. 310d; Jos., Vi. 192 πλ. συνέσεως; Just., D. 93, 2.—Procop. Soph., Ep. 68 πλ. τοῦ θεοῦ) πλ. πνεύματος ἁγίου **Lk 4:1; Ac 7:55.** πλ. πνεύματος ἁγίου καὶ πίστεως **11:24;** cp. **6:5.** πλ. πνεύματος καὶ σοφίας vs. **3.** πλ. χάριτος καὶ ἀληθείας **J 1:14** (s. this entry, end). πλ. χάριτος καὶ δυνάμεως **Ac 6:8.** πλ. τῆς χάριτος τοῦ θεοῦ MPol 7:3. πλ. ἔργων ἀγαθῶν *rich in good deeds* **Ac 9:36.** πάσης κακίας πλ. 1 Cl 45:7 (Maximus Tyr. 34, 3a πλ. κακῶν. Similarly Appian, Bell. Civ. 3, 19 §69, who calls the murderers of Caesar φόνου πλήρεις). πλ. παντὸς δόλου **Ac 13:10** (πλήρης δόλου Sir 1:30; 19:26; Jer 5:27). γενόμενοι πλήρεις θυμοῦ **19:28** (cp. Petosiris, fgm. 21, ln. 29 πλῆρες τὸ ἀγαθὸν γενήσεται). πλ. ἁμαρτιῶν (cp. Is 1:4) Hs 9, 23, 4. πλ. πάσης ἁπλότητος Hv 1, 2, 4.—Of a heart (cp. 2 Ch 15:17; 1 Esdr 1:21) πλ. εἰδωλολατρίας B 16:7.—*Surfeited (with)* πλ. εἰμὶ ὁλοκαυτωμάτων *I am surfeited with whole burnt offerings* B 2:5 (Is 1:11).

❷ **pert. to being complete and w. nothing lacking,** ***complete, full, in full*** (Hdt. et al.; LXX; AssMos fgm. e, Denis p. 65) μισθὸς πλ. (X., An. 7, 5, 5; Ruth 2:12. πλ. is a favorite word in the pap for a sum that is complete) **2J 8.** πλ. σῖτος *fully ripened grain* (cp. the 'fully developed' στάχυες Gen 41:7, 22, 24) **Mk 4:28 v.l.** (other mss. πλήρης σῖτον, πλήρη σ.). νηστεία πλ. *a complete fast* Hs 5, 1, 3. πλ. πνεύματος ἔκχυσις *a full outpouring of the Spirit* 1 Cl 2:2.—Of persons who are complete in a certain respect or who possess someth. fully πλ. ἔν τινι: ἐν τούτοις πλ. 2 Cl 16:4. πλ. ἐν τῇ πίστει Hm 5, 2, 1; 12, 5, 4.—In some of the passages already mentioned πλήρης is indecl., though never without v.l., and almost only when it is used w. a gen., corresponding to an Engl. expression such as 'a work full of errors': τὴν δόξαν αὐτοῦ . . . πλήρης (referring to αὐτοῦ) χάριτος καὶ ἀληθείας **J 1:14** (cp. CTurner, JTS 1, 1900, 120ff; 561f). ἄνδρα πλήρης πίστεως **Ac 6:5** (v.l. πλήρη). It is found as an itacistic **v.l.** in **Mk 8:19; Ac 6:3, 5; 19:28,** and without a gen. **2J 8 v.l.** (s. N.[25] app.). Examples of this use of πλήρης w. the gen. are found fr. the second century BC, and fr. the first century AD on it is frequently found in colloq. H.Gk.: PLeid C II, 14 (160 BC). Wooden tablet fr. Egypt fr. the time of Augustus in RevArch 29, 1875, 233f=Sb 3553, 7; BGU 707, 15; POxy 237 IV, 14 (all three II AD); Mitt-Wilck. I/2, 499, 9 (II/III AD); En 21:7. S. the exx. in Crönert 179, 4 and also s. Mayser 63f (w. lit.); 297; Dssm., LO 99f (LAE 125ff); Thackeray 176f; Reinhold 53; Borger, GGA 139 (lit.); B-D-F §137, 1; Mlt. 50; Rob. 275f.—B. 931. Frisk. M-M. TW.

πληροφορέω (*πληροφόρος [πλήρης, φέρω via φορέω]) 1 aor. impv. πληροφόρησον, inf. πληροφορῆσαι. Pass.: 1 aor. inf. πληροφορηθῆναι, ptc. πληροφορηθείς; pf. πεπληροφόρημαι, ptc. πεπληροφορημένος (Ctesias: 688 fgm. 14 (42) Jac. p. 467, 9f [=fgm. 29, 39 Müller]; elsewh. since LXX Eccl 8:11; TestAbr A 1 p. 78, 7f [Stone p. 4], B 7 p. 112, 5 v.l. [Stone p. 72; NTS 1, '54/55, 223]; TestGad 2:4; BGU 665 II, 2 [I AD]; APF 5, 1913, 383 no. 69b, 5 [I/II AD]; BGU 747 I, 22 [139 AD]; PAmh 66 II, 42; POxy 509, 10 [both II AD]; Vett. Val. 43, 18; 226, 20.—Dssm., LO 67f [LAE 82f]).

❶ ***fill (completely), fulfill,*** a synonym of πληρόω, which occasionally appears as v.l. for it. In our lit. only fig.—ⓐ w. a thing as obj. τὶ *someth.*, adding to someth. that which it lacks, someth. like *fill out, complement, aid* τὸν πλοῦτον Hs 2:8a. τὰς ψυχάς 8b.—τὴν διακονίαν σου πληροφόρησον *fulfill your ministry* **2 Ti 4:5.** Also the pass. ἵνα δι' ἐμοῦ τὸ κήρυγμα πληροφορηθῇ vs. **17.**—Of a request that is *fulfilled* Hm 9:2 (the pap use the word mainly in the sense 'fully satisfy a demand').—*Accomplish* τὰ πεπληροφορημένα ἐν ἡμῖν πράγματα *the things that have been accomplished among us* **Lk 1:1** (s. M-JLagrange, Le sens de Luc 1:1 d'après les papyrus: Bull. d'ancienne Litt. et d'Arch. chrét. 2, 1912, 96–100; OPiper, Union Sem. Rev. 57, '45, 15–25: Lk [and Ac] as 'fulfillment' of the OT.—S. also the lit. given s.v. παρακολουθέω, end). Some (e.g. KRengstorf, Das NT Deutsch '37 ad loc.) would here transl. *on which there is full conviction among us,* and put the pass. under 2. But in view of Lk's thematic emphasis on God's βουλή (q.v. 2b), the idea of accomplishment of things planned seems more prob. (s. Lagrange).

ⓑ of pers. πεπληροφορημένος τινός *filled w. someth.* ἀγάπης *love* 1 Cl 54:1 (w. εὔσπλαγχνος). Perh. also ἔν τινι (πληρόω 1b) πεπληροφορημένοι ἐν παντὶ θελήματι τ. θεοῦ *full of everything that is (in accord with) God's will* **Col 4:12** (s. also 2 below).

❷ ***convince fully*** (Ctesias: 688 fgm. 14, 42 Jac. p. 467, 9f; AcPh 9 [Aa II, 2 p. 5, 20]; Ps.-Clem., Hom. 1, 20 al.) pass. *be fully convinced, assured, certain* (cp. Test Gad 2:4 ἐπληροφορήθημεν τῆς ἀναιρέσεως αὐτοῦ='we were quite filled w. the intention to kill him'.—Hegesippus in Eus., HE 2, 23, 14; Martyr. Pionii 4, 17 in HMusurillo, The Acts of the Christian Martyrs '72) foll. by ὅτι *be fully convinced that* (Ps.-Clem., Hom. p. 9, 22 Lag.) **Ro 4:21;** IMg 8:2. *Have perfect faith* (i.e. limited by no doubt at all) εἰς τὸν κύριον *in the Lord* ISm 1:1. ἔν τινι *in someth.* IMg 11; IPhld ins.—Abs. (in case ἐν παντὶ κτλ. [s. 1b above] belongs to σταθῆτε) *be fully assured* τέλειοι καὶ πεπληροφορημένοι **Col 4:12** (but in that case it may also mean here *complete, finished*). πληροφορηθέντες διὰ τῆς ἀναστάσεως τοῦ κυρίου *be fully assured by the Lord's resurrection* 1 Cl 42:3. ἕκαστος ἐν τῷ ἰδίῳ νοῒ πληροφορείσθω *every one must be fully convinced in the person's own mind* **Ro 14:5** (JBeckler, Biblica 65, '84, 364).—Ltzm., Hdb. on Ro 4:21; Dssm. LO[4] 67f [LAE 86f].—DELG s.v. πίμπλημι. M-M. EDNT. TW. Spicq.

πληροφορία, ας, ἡ (πληροφορέω) **state of complete certainty,** ***full assurance, certainty*** (PGiss 87, 25 [II AD]; Rhet. Gr. VII 108, 3; Hesychius=βεβαιότης; cp. πληροφορέω 2); this mng. is prob. in the word's occurrences in our lit. πλοῦτος τῆς πληροφορίας τῆς συνέσεως *a wealth of assurance, such as understanding brings* **Col 2:2.** ἐν . . . πλ. πολλῇ, *with full conviction* **1 Th 1:5.** ἡ πλ. τῆς ἐλπίδος **Hb 6:11.** πλ. πίστεως **10:22.** πλ. πνεύματος ἁγίου *the assurance that the Holy Spirit gives* 1 Cl 42:3; but in **Col 2:2; Hb 6:11; 10:22;** 1 Cl 42:3 the mng. *fullness* also merits attention. Likew. **Ro 15:29 v.l.**—DELG s.v. πίμπλημι. M-M. TW. Spicq.

πληρόω impf. 3 sg. ἐπλήρου; fut. πληρώσω; 1 aor. ἐπλήρωσα; pf. πεπλήρωκα; plpf. 3 sg. πεπληρώκει (on the omission of the augm. B-D-F §66, 1; Mlt-H. 190). Pass.: impf. ἐπληρούμην; 1 fut. πληρωθήσομαι; 1 aor. ἐπληρώθην; pf.

πεπλήρωμαι; plpf. 3 sg. πεπλήρωτο (s. B-D-F §66, 1; Mlt-H. 190) (Aeschyl., Hdt.+).

➊ **to make full,** ***fill (full)***—ⓐ of things τὶ *someth.* τὴν γῆν (Orig., C. Cels. 3, 8, 29) B 6:12 (Gen 1:28; cp. Ocellus [II BC] c. 46 Harder [1926] τὸν πλείονα τῆς γῆς τόπον πληροῦσθαι with their descendants). Pass., of a net ἐπληρώθη **Mt 13:48.** πᾶσα φάραγξ πληρωθήσεται **Lk 3:5** (Is 40:4). ὀθόνη πλοίου ὑπὸ πνεύματος πληρουμένη *a ship's sail filled out by the wind* MPol 15:2.—τόπον πληρῶσαι *fill a space* Hs 9, 7, 5. ἐπλήρωσεν τοὺς τύπους τῶν λίθων *he filled in the impressions of the stones (that had been removed)* 9, 10, 2.—Also of sounds and odors (as well as light: schol. on Pla. 914b) ἦχος ἐπλήρωσεν τὸν οἶκον *a sound filled the house* **Ac 2:2** (Diod. S. 11, 24, 4 αἱ οἰκίαι πένθους ἐπληροῦντο=with cries of grief). ἡ οἰκία ἐπληρώθη ἐκ τῆς ὀσμῆς *the house was filled with the fragrance* **J 12:3** (cp. Diod. S. 4, 64, 1 τὴν οἰκίαν πληρώσειν ἀτυχημάτων; Ael. Aristid. 36, 84 K.=48 p. 471 D.: ὅταν οἴκημα πληρωθῇ; TestAbr A 4 p. 80, 23f [Stone p. 8] πλήρωσον τὸν οἶκον ἡμῶν [with aromatic plants]).—Also in other ways of the filling of impers. objects with real but intangible things or qualities: τὸ πρόσωπον αὐτοῦ (i.e. of the martyr Polycarp) χάριτος ἐπληροῦτο MPol 12:1 (χάρις 1 and 4). πεπληρώκατε τὴν Ἰερουσαλὴμ τῆς διδαχῆς ὑμῶν *you have filled Jerusalem with your teaching* **Ac 5:28.** ὑμεῖς πληρώσατε (aor. impv. as a rhetor. demand; vv.ll. πληρώσετε, ἐπληρώσατε) τὸ μέτρον τῶν πατέρων ὑμῶν of filling the measure of sins (cp. Da 8:23) **Mt 23:32;** cp. ἐπεὶ πεπλήρωτο ἡ ἡμετέρα ἀδικία Dg 9:2. θεὸς πληρώσει πᾶσαν χρείαν ὑμῶν **Phil 4:19** (cp. Thu. 1, 70, 7). πλ. τὴν καρδίαν τινός *fill someone's heart,* i.e. take full possession of it (cp. Eccl 9:3) ἡ λύπη πεπλήρωκεν ὑμῶν τ. καρδίαν **J 16:6.** διὰ τί ἐπλήρωσεν ὁ σατανᾶς τ. καρδίαν σοῦ; **Ac 5:3** (Ad'Alès, RSR 24, '34, 199f; 474f prefers the v.l. ἐπήρωσεν; against him LSt.-Paul Girard, Mém. de l'inst. franc. du Caire 67, '37, 309–12). ὁ ψευδοπροφήτης πληροῖ τὰς ψυχάς Hm 11:2 (θείου πνεύματος πληρώσαντος … τὰς ψυχάς Orig., C. Cels. 3, 81, 20).—Of Christ, who passed through all the cosmic spheres ἵνα πληρώσῃ τὰ πάντα **Eph 4:10** (cp. Jer 23:24; Philo, Leg. All. 3, 4 πάντα πεπλήρωκεν ὁ θεός, Vita Mos. 2, 238, Conf. Lingu. 136; Ath. 8, 3 πάντα γὰρ ὑπὸ τούτου πεπλήρωται). The mid. in the sense of the act. (B-D-F §316, 1; Rob. 805f. Cp. X., Hell. 6, 2, 14; 35 al.; Plut., Alc. 211 [35, 6]) τὸ πλήρωμα τοῦ τὰ πάντα ἐν πᾶσιν πληρουμένου **Eph 1:23** (πλήρωμα 2).

ⓑ of persons *fill* w. powers, qualities, etc. τινὰ *someone* ὁ ἄγγελος τοῦ προφητικοῦ πνεύματος πληροῖ τὸν ἄνθρωπον Hm 11:9a. τινά τινος *someone with someth.* (OdeSol 11:2; B-D-F §172; Rob. 510) πληρώσεις με εὐφροσύνης **Ac 2:28** (Ps 15:11). Cp. **Ro 15:13** (cp. POxy 3313, 3 χαρ[ᾶς ἡμ]ᾶς ἐπλήρωσας). τινά τινι *someone with someth.* (B-D-F §195, 2) ὁ διάβολος πληροῖ αὐτὸν τῷ αὐτοῦ πνεύματι Hm 11:3.—Mostly pass., in pres., impf., fut., aor. *become filled* or *full* (Scholiast on Pla. 856e of μάντις: ἄνωθεν λαμβάνειν τὸ πνεῦμα καὶ πληροῦσθαι τοῦ θεοῦ); in the perf. *have been filled, be full:* w. gen. of thing (Diod. S. 20, 21, 3 τῶν βασιλείων πεπληρωμένων φόνων=when the palace was full of murderous deeds; Diog. L. 5, 42 τὸ πάσης ἀρετῆς πεπληρῶσθαι) **Lk 2:40 v.l.; Ac 13:52** (Jos., Ant. 15, 421 ἐπληρώθη χαρᾶς; cp. Just., A I, 49, 5); **Ro 15:14; 2 Ti 1:4;** Dg 10:3; IRo ins; Ox 840, 40f.—W. dat. of thing (Aeschyl., Sept. 464 et al.; Parthenius 10, 4 ἄχει ἐπληρώθη; 2 Macc 7:21; 3 Macc 4:16; 5:30; Just., D. 7, 1 πνεύματι. Cp. BGU 1108, 12 [I BC]) **Lk 2:40; Ro 1:29; 2 Cor 7:4;** Hm 5, 2, 7; 11:9b v.l. (for πλησθείς).—W. acc. of thing (pap use the act. and pass. w. acc. of thing in the sense 'settle in full by [paying or delivering] someth.': PLond II, 243, 11 p. 300 [346 AD]; 251, 30; POxy 1133, 8; 1134, 6; PFlor 27, 3 al.; B-D-F §159, 1; Rob. 510) πεπληρωμένοι καρπὸν δικαιοσύνης **Phil 1:11.** Cp. **Col 1:9.**—W. ἐν and dat. of thing ἐν πνεύματι *with the Spirit* **Eph 5:18.** ἐν πίστει καὶ ἀγάπῃ ISm ins. Cp. **Col 4:12 v.l.,** in case ἐν κτλ. here belongs to πεπληρωμένοι (s. πληροφορέω 1b); but mng. 3 also merits attention. ἐστὲ ἐν αὐτῷ πεπληρωμένοι **Col 2:10** is prob. different, meaning not 'with him', but *in him* or *through him.*—Abs. **Eph 3:19** (εἰς denotes the goal; s. πλήρωμα 3b). πεπλήρωμαι *I am well supplied* **Phil 4:18** (cp. Diod. S. 14, 62, 5 πληροῦν τινα=supply someone fully).

➋ **to complete a period of time,** ***fill (up), complete*** (Pla., Leg. 9, 866a, Tim. 39d; Plut., Lucull. 516 [35, 8]; POxy 275, 24 [66 AD] μέχρι τοῦ τὸν χρόνον πληρωθῆναι; 491, 6; PTebt 374, 10; BGU 1047 III, 12 al. in pap; Gen 25:24; 29:21; Lev 8:33; 12:4; 25:30; Num 6:5; Tob 10:1; 1 Macc 3:49 al.; TestAbr B; TestJob 28:1 ἐπλήρωσα εἴκοσι ἔτη; ApcMos 13; Jos., Ant. 4, 78; 6, 49) in our lit. only pass. (Ps.-Callisth. 3, 17, 39; 41 πεπλήρωται τὰ τῆς ζωῆς ἔτη; Did., Gen. 195, 23) πεπλήρωται ὁ καιρός **Mk 1:15;** cp. **J 7:8.** χρόνος instead of καιρός Hs 6, 5, 2; cp. πληρωθέντος τοῦ χρόνου (pl.: Iren. 1, 17, 2 [Harv. I 168, 13]) *when the time has elapsed* 1 Cl 25:2. πεπλήρωνται αἱ ἡμέραι *the days are over, have come to an end* Hv 2, 2, 5. πληρωθέντων … τῶν ἡμερῶν GJs 5:2 (TestAbr B 1 p. 105, 4 [Stone p. 58]).—**Ac 9:23.** πεπλήρωται ὁ ὅρος τῶν ἐτῶν **ending of Mk in the Freer ms.** 6f. πληρωθέντων ἐτῶν τεσσερακοντα *when forty years had passed* **Ac 7:30** (TestJud 9:2).—**24:27;** 1 Cl 25:5. ὡς ἐπληροῦτο αὐτῷ τεσσερακονταετὴς χρόνος *when he had reached the age of 40* **Ac 7:23** (PFlor 382, 6; 11 ἑβδομήκοντα ἔτη ἐπλήρωσας). ἐπληρώθησαν οἱ μῆνες αὐτῆς ὡς εἶπεν ἕξ *(Anna) had passed her sixth month as (the angel) said* GJs 5:2 (but s. deStrycker ad loc.).

➌ **to bring to completion that which was already begun,** ***complete, finish*** (X., Hell. 4, 8, 16; Herodian 1, 5, 8; Olympiodorus, Life of Plato p. 2 Westerm.: the hymn that was begun; Himerius, Or. 6 [2], 14 πληρῶσαι τὴν ἐπιθυμίαν=fully gratify the desire, in that the Persians wished to incorporate into their great empire a small piece of the west, i.e. Greece; ApcSed 13:1 τὴν μετάνοιαν) τὸ εὐαγγέλιον τοῦ Χριστοῦ *bring* (the preaching of) *the gospel to completion* by proclaiming it in the most remote areas **Ro 15:19;** sim. πλ. τ. λόγον τοῦ θεοῦ **Col 1:25.** πληρώσατέ μου τ. χαράν **Phil 2:2.** Cp. **2 Th 1:11.**—Pass. **2 Cor 10:6; Col 4:12 v.l.** (s. 1b above). ὁ πᾶς νόμος ἐν ἑνὶ λόγῳ πεπλήρωται **Gal 5:14** because of its past tense is prob. to be translated *the whole law has found its full expression in a single word* or *is summed up under one entry* (s. s.v. λόγος 2a; some would put this passage under 4b). οὐχ εὕρηκά σου ἔργα πεπληρωμένα **Rv 3:2.** Johannine usage speaks of *joy that is made complete* (the act. in **Phil 2:2,** s. above) **J 3:29; 15:11; 16:24; 17:13; 1J 1:4; 2J 12.**

➍ **to bring to a designed end,** ***fulfill*** a prophecy, an obligation, a promise, a law, a request, a purpose, a desire, a hope, a duty, a fate, a destiny, etc. (Pla., Gorg. 63, 507e ἐπιθυμίας [cp. TestJos 4:7 ἐπιθυμίαν]; Herodian 2, 7, 6 ὑποσχέσεις; Epict. 2, 9, 3; 8 ἐπαγγελίαν; Plut., Cic. 869 [17, 5] τὸ χρεών [=destiny]; Procop. Soph., Ep. 68 τ. ἐλπίδας; Spartan ins in BSA 12, 1905/6, p. 452 [I AD] τὰ εἰθισμένα; pap, LXX; Philo, Praem. 83 τὰς θείας παραινέσεις μὴ κενὰς ἀπολιπεῖν τῶν οἰκείων πράξεων, ἀλλὰ πληρῶσαι τοὺς λόγους ἔργοις ἐπαινετοῖς=the divine exhortations it [God's people] did not leave devoid of appropriate performance, but carried out the words with praiseworthy deeds; Jos., Ant. 5, 145; 14, 486).

ⓐ of the fulfillment of divine predictions or promises. The word stands almost always in the passive *be fulfilled* (Polyaenus 1, 18 τοῦ λογίου πεπληρωμένου; Alex. Aphr., Fat. 31, II 2 p. 202, 21 ὅπως πληρωθῇ τὸ τῆς εἱμαρμένης δρᾶμα; 3 Km 2:27; TestBenj 3:8 προφητεία; Ps.-Clem., Hom. 8, 4) and refers mostly to the Tanach and its words: τοῦτο γέγονεν ἵνα πληρωθῇ τὸ ῥηθὲν ὑπὸ κυρίου διὰ τοῦ προφήτου (cp. 2 Ch 36:21) **Mt 1:22;** cp. **2:15, 17, 23; 4:14; 8:17; 12:17; 13:35; 21:4; 26:54, 56; 27:9** (PNepper-Christensen, D. Mt-evangelium, '58, 136–62); **Mk 14:49; 15:27(28) v.l.** (after Lk 22:37); **Lk 1:20; 4:21; 21:22 v.l.; 24:44; J 12:38; 13:18; 15:25; 17:12; 19:24, 36; Ac 1:16** (cp. Test Napht 7:1 δεῖ ταῦτα πληρωθῆναι); **Js 2:23.** A vision ἔδει γὰρ τὸ τῆς . . . ὀπτασίας πληρωθῆναι *for what (Polycarp) had seen in his vision was destined to be fulfilled* MPol 12:3.—The OT type *finds its fulfillment* in the antitype **Lk 22:16** (cp. MBlack, ET 57, '45/46, 25f, An Aramaic Approach[3], '67, 229–36). At times one of Jesus' predictions is fulfilled: **J 18:9, 32.** The act. *bring to fulfillment,* partly of God, who brings divine prophecies to fulfillment **Ac 3:18;** MPol 14:2, partly of humans who, by what they do, help to bring divine prophecies to realization (Vi. Thu. 1, 8 [=OxfT p. xii, 8] οὗτος ἐπλήρωσε τὰ μεμαντευμένα) **Ac 13:27.** Jesus himself *fulfills* his destiny by dying, as God's messengers Moses and Elijah foretell **Lk 9:31.**—GPt 5:17.

ⓑ a prayer (Chariton 8, 1, 9 πεπληρώκασιν οἱ θεοὶ τὰς εὐχάς; Aristaen., Ep. 1, 16 the god πεπλήρωκε τ. εὐχήν [=prayer]; IBM 894, 8 of answered prayer) πληρῶσαί μου τὴν αἴτησιν *answer my prayer* ITr 13:3 (cp. Ps 19:5; TestAbr A 15 p. 96, 4 [Stone p. 40]). A command(ment) (Herodian 3, 11, 4 τὰς ἐντολάς; POxy 1252A, 9 πλήρωσον τὸ κεκελευσμένον; 1 Macc 2:55; SibOr 3, 246) πεπλήρωκεν ἐντολὴν δικαιοσύνης Pol 3:3. νόμον (Ps.-Demetr., Form. Ep. p. 12, 9; cp. Hdt. 1, 199 ἐκπλῆσαι τὸν νόμον) **Ro 13:8;** pass. **Gal 5:14** (but s. 3 above and cp. Aeschyl., Ag. 313). τὸ δικαίωμα τοῦ νόμου **Ro 8:4.** πᾶσαν δικαιοσύνην (cp. 4 Macc 12:14 πλ. τὴν εὐσέβειαν) **Mt 3:15** (s. AFridrichsen: Congr. d'Hist. du Christ. I 1928, 167–77; OEissfeldt, ZNW 61, '70, 209–15 and s. βαπτίζω 2a, end); pass. ISm 1:1 (s. δικαιοσύνη 3b). Also ἐστὶ πρέπον πληρωθῆναι πάντα *it is fitting that all things should be fulfilled* GEb 18, 40 (cp. APF 3, 1906, 370 II, 7 [II AD] ἕως ἅπαντα τὰ κατ' ἐμὲ πεπληρῶσθαι).—A duty or office βλέπε τὴν διακονίαν . . . , ἵνα αὐτὴν πληροῖς *pay attention to your duty . . . and perform it* **Col 4:17** (cp. CIG 2336 πλ. πᾶσαν ἀρχὴν κ. λειτουργίαν; PFlor 382, 40 πληρῶσαι τὴν λειτουργίαν; ISardRobert I p. 39 n. 5).—Abs., in the broadest sense and in contrast to καταλύειν (s. καταλύω 3a): οὐκ ἦλθον καταλῦσαι ἀλλὰ πληρῶσαι **Mt 5:17;** depending on how one prefers to interpret the context, πληρόω is understood here either as *fulfill*=do, carry out, or as *bring to full expression*=show it forth in its true mng., or as *fill up*=complete (s. AKlöpper, ZWT 39, 1896, 1ff; AHarnack, Aus Wissenschaft u. Leben II 1911, 225ff, SBBerlAk 1912, 184ff; JHänel, Der Schriftbegriff Jesu 1919, 155ff; Dalman, Jesus 56–66 *confirm;* WHatch, ATR 18, '36, 129–40; HLjungman, D. Gesetz Erfüllen, '54; WKümmel, Verheissung u. Erfüllung[3], '56; JO'Rourke, The Fulfilment Texts in Mt, CBQ 24, '62, 394–403).

❺ **to bring to completion an activity in which one has been involved from its beginning, *complete, finish*** (1 Macc 4:19) πάντα τὰ ῥήματα **Lk 7:1** (cp. TestBenj 12:1 τοὺς λόγους). τὴν διακονίαν **Ac 12:25.** [τὰς τοῦ κυρίου οἰκο]νομίας πληρῶσε (=πληρῶσαι) *to carry out to the end God's designs* (i.e. Paul's life as programmed by God is about to be concluded) AcPl Ha 5, 27; cp. the restoration in 6, 26 ο̣ἰκο̣ν̣[ομίαν πληρώσω] (cp. the description of Jeremiah's death ParJer 9:31 ἐπληρώθη αὐτοῦ οἰκονομία); τὸν δρόμον **Ac 13:25;** cp. the abs. ἕως πληρώσωσιν *until they should complete (their course)* **Rv 6:11 v.l.** (s. 6 below). τὸ ἔργον **Ac 14:26.** τὴν εὐχήν MPol 15:1. τὰ κυνηγέσια 12:2 (another probability here is the quite rare [Hdt. 2, 7 al.] intr. sense *be complete, be at an end*). Pass. *be accomplished, be finished, at an end* (Ps.-Callisth. 1, 24, 9 as a saying of Philip as he lay dying: ἐμοῦ τὸ πεπρωμένον πεπλήρωται = my destiny has been fulfilled; Mel., P. 43, 297 ὁ νόμος ἐπληρώθη τοῦ εὐαγγελίου φωτισθέτος) ὡς ἐπληρώθη ταῦτα **Ac 19:21.** ἄχρι οὗ πληρωθῶσιν καιροὶ ἐθνῶν **Lk 21:24.** αἱ ἀποκαλύψεις αὗται τέλος ἔχουσιν· πεπληρωμέναι γάρ εἰσιν *these revelations have attained their purpose, for they are completed* Hv 3, 3, 2.

❻ ***complete*** a number, pass. *have the number made complete* (since Hdt. 7, 29; Iren. 1, 16, 2 [Harv. I 161, 6]; Hippol., Ref. 6, 51, 2) ἕως πληρωθῶσιν οἱ σύνδουλοι **Rv 6:11** (s. 5 above).—CMoule, Fulfilment Words in the NT, NTS 14, '68, 293–320. DELG s.v. πίμπλημι. M-M. EDNT. TW.

πλήρωμα, ατος, τό (πληρόω; Eur., Hdt. et al.; ins, pap, LXX, Philo; Mel., P. 40, 279).

❶ **that which fills—**ⓐ ***that which fills (up)*** (Eur., Ion 1051 κρατήρων πληρώματα; Hippocr., Aër. 7 τὸ πλ. τῆς γαστρός. Esp. oft. of a crew or cargo of ships since Thu. 7, 12, 3; 14, 1) ἡ γῆ καὶ τὸ πλ. αὐτῆς *the earth and everything that is in it* **1 Cor 10:26;** 1 Cl 54:3 (both Ps 23:1, as also Did., Gen. 74, 8). ἦραν κλάσματα δώδεκα κοφίνων πληρώματα *they gathered (enough) pieces to fill twelve baskets, twelve basketfuls of pieces* **Mk 6:43;** cp. **8:20** (s. Eccl 4:6; EBishop, ET 60, '48, 192f).

ⓑ ***that which makes someth. full/complete, supplement, complement*** (Appian, Mithr. 47 §185 τὰ τῶν γυναικῶν πάντα ἐς τὸ πλήρωμα τῶν δισχιλίων ταλάντων συνέφερον) lit. of the *patch* on a garment **Mt 9:16; Mk 2:21** (FSynge, ET 56, '44/45, 26f).—Fig., perh., of the church which, as the body, is τὸ πλ., *the complement* of Christ, who is the head **Eph 1:23** (so Chrysostom. The word could be understood in a similar sense Pla., Rep. 2, 371e πλ. πόλεώς εἰσι καὶ μισθωτοί). Much more probably the Eph passage belongs under

❷ ***that which is full of someth.*** (Lucian, Ver. Hist. 2, 37; 38 and Polyaenus 3, 9, 55 the manned and loaded ship itself [s. 1a above]; Philo, Praem. 65 γενομένη πλ. ἀρετῶν ἡ ψυχὴ . . . οὐδὲν ἐν ἑαυτῇ καταλιποῦσα κενόν; Herm. Wr. 12, 15 God is called πλήρωμα τῆς ζωῆς; 6, 4 ὁ κόσμος πλήρωμά ἐστι τῆς κακίας, ὁ δὲ θεὸς τοῦ ἀγαθοῦ; 16, 3 τ. πάντων τὸ πλ. ἕν ἐστι.—Rtzst., Poim. 25, 1) *(that) which is full of him who* etc. (so as early as Severian of Gabala [KStaab, Pls-Kommentare '33, 307] and Theodoret, who consider that it is God who fills the church.—Cp. CMitton, ET 59, '47/48, 325; 60, '48/49, 320f; CMoule, ibid. 53 and Col and Phil '57, 164–69).

❸ **that which is brought to fullness or completion**

ⓐ ***full number*** (Hdt. 8, 43; 45 of ships; Aristot., Pol. 2, 7, 22 of citizens; Iren. 1, 1, 3 [Harv. I 11, 11] and Hippol., Ref. 6, 38, 4 as Gnostic t.t.) τὸ πλ. τῶν ἐθνῶν **Ro 11:25** (cp. Ael. Aristid. 13 p. 262 D.: πλήρωμα ἔθνους). For **11:12,** which is also classed here by many, s. 4 below.

ⓑ ***sum total, fullness,*** even *(super)abundance* (Diod. S. 2, 12, 2 καθάπερ ἔκ τινος πηγῆς μεγάλης ἀκέραιον διαμένει τὸ πλήρωμα=as if from a great source the abundance [of bitumen] remains undiminished. As gnostic t.t. Iren. 1, 8, 4 [Harv. I, 73, 3]; Hippol., Ref. 8, 10, 3—s. also a) τινός *of someth.* πλ. εὐλογίας Χριστοῦ *the fullness of Christ's blessing* **Ro 15:29.** πᾶν τὸ πλ. τῆς θεότητος *the full measure of deity* (s. θεότης) **Col 2:9;** without the gen., but in the same sense **1:19.**—W. gen.

to denote the one who possesses the fullness: θεοῦ πατρὸς πλ. IEph ins (s. Hdb. ad loc.). εἰς πᾶν τὸ πλ. τοῦ θεοῦ *that you may be filled with all the fullness of God* **Eph 3:19** (s. πληρόω 1b). Of Christ: ἐκ τοῦ πληρώματος αὐτοῦ **J 1:16** (s. Bultmann 51, 7).—Abs. ἀσπάζομαι ἐν τῷ πληρώματι *I greet in the fullness* of the Christian spirit ITr ins.—On εἰς μέτρον ἡλικίας τοῦ πληρώματος τοῦ Χριστοῦ **Eph 4:13** s. μέτρον 2b.

❹ **act of fulfilling specifications, *fulfilling, fulfillment*** (=πλήρωσις, as Eur., Tro. 824; Philo, Abr. 268 π. ἐλπίδων) τὸ πλήρωμα αὐτῶν *their* (the people of Israel) *fulfilling* (the divine demand) **Ro 11:12** (opp. παράπτωμα and ἥττημα). But this pass. is considered by many to belong under 3a above. πλ. νόμου ἡ ἀγάπη **13:10** (on the semantic field relating to love s. TSöding, ETL 68, '92, 284–330, and Das Liebesgebot bei Paulus '95).

❺ **the state of being full, *fullness*** of time (πληρόω 2) τὸ πλήρωμα τοῦ χρόνου **Gal 4:4** (s. ASP VI, 587, 34 [24/25 AD] τοῦ δὲ χρόνου πληροθέντος). τὸ πλ. τῶν καιρῶν **Eph 1:10.**—Lghtf., Col and Phlm 255–71; ARobinson, Eph 1904, 255ff; HMaVallisoleto, Christi 'Pleroma' iuxta Pli conceptionem: Verbum Domini 14, '34, 49–55; FMontgomery-Hitchcock, The Pleroma of Christ: CQR 125, '37, 1–18; JGewiess: MMeinertz Festschr. '51, 128–41; PBenoit, RB 63, '56, 5–44 (prison epp.); AFeuillet, Nouvelle Revue Theol. (Tournai) 88, '56, 449–72; 593–610 (Eph 1:23); GMünderlein NTS 8, '62, 264–76 (Col 1:19); HSchlier, D. Brief an die Epheser[4], '63, 96–99; POverfield, NTS 25, '79, 384–96; CEvans, Biblica 65 '84, 259–65 (Nag Hammadi).—DELG s.v. πίμπλημι. M-M. EDNT. TW.

πλήσας, πλησθείς, πλησθῆναι s. πίμπλημι.

πλησίον (in form, the neut. of πλησίος, α, ον, an adj. that goes back to Hom.; Schwyzer I 461) adv. (Hom.+)

❶ **marker of a position quite close to another position, *nearby, near, close***—ⓐ abs. (Diod. S. 11, 4, 1 πλησίον εἶναι; Dionys. Byz. §102; SIG 344, 83; 888, 127; Mitt-Wilck. I/2, 11, 6 ἐκ τῶν πλ[ησίο]ν κωμῶν; 2 Macc 6:11; Ath. 35, 2 πλ. εἶναι) πλ. ἑκάτερον πεφύτευται *they were planted close to each other* Dg 12:4.

ⓑ functions as prep. w. gen. (Hom.+; Schwyzer II 548) *near, close to someth.* πλ. τοῦ χωρίου (Menand., Epitr. 242 πλ. τῶν χωρίων S. [=66 Kö.]) **J 4:5.** πλ. τοῦ τόπου ἐκείνου ApcPt 11:26. πλ. ἐκείνων 13:28.

❷ as subst. ὁ πλησίον: **the one who is near or close by, *neighbor, fellow human being*** (Theognis et al.; X., Mem. 3, 14, 4; Pla., Theaet. 174b ὁ πλησίον καὶ ὁ γείτων; Polyb. 12, 25, 5; Plut., Mor. 40c; 57d; Ael. Aristid. 23, 28 K.=42 p. 777 D. al.; Epict. 4, 13, 2; 9; M. Ant. 4:18 al.; Ps.-Lucian, Philopatr. 16 ἐὰν κτάνῃς τὸν πλησίον, θανατωθήσῃ παρὰ τ. δίκης; LXX; En 99:15; PsSol 8:10; TestIss 5:1f; Philo, Virt. 116; Jos., Bell. 7, 260; Just., Tat.; Schwyzer II 547) with and without gen., of a compatriot **Ac 7:27** (cp. Ex 2:13). Of fellow-Christians **Ro 15:2; Eph 4:25** (Zech 8:16); **Js 4:12;** 1 Cl 38:1; Dg 10:6; IMg 6:2; ITr 8:2; Pol 3:3. In the teaching about the Two Ways: B 19:3, 5f, 8; D 1:2 (cp. Lev 19:18); 2:3 (cp. Ex 20:17), vs. 6. Quite freq. as a quot. from or in close connection with the OT: B 2:8 (Zech 8:17). Esp. oft. the passage involved is Lev 19:18 (Philosoph. Max., FPhGr I, 489, 27 warns against λυπεῖν τὸν πλησίον): **Mt 5:43** (here the NT introduces the contrast ὁ πλησίον … ὁ ἐχθρός); **19:19; 22:39; Mk 12:31, 33; Lk 10:27; Ro 13:9;** cp. vs. **10; Gal 5:14; Js 2:8.** Without the art., as pred. (s. B-D-F §266; Rob. 547 and SSol 5:16) καὶ τίς ἐστίν μου πλησίον; *and who is my neighbor?* **Lk 10:29;** cp. vs. **36.**—Pl. οἱ πλησίον (Ar. 10, 8; 15, 4; Ath. 11, 3; Alex. Aphr., An. Mant. p. 162, 19 Br.) of fellow Christians 1 Cl 2:6; 51:2; Dg 10:5.—Billerb. I 353–68, Nathanael 34, 1918, 12ff; JGspann, Die Nächstenliebe im NT: Der Katholik 87, 1907, 376–91; MRade, Der Nächste: Jülicher Festschr. 1927, 70–79; RBultmann, Aimer son prochain: RHPR 10, 1930, 222–41; EFuchs, ThBl 11, '32, 129–40; HWeinel, D. Nächstenliebe: Arch. f. d. gesamte Psychol. 86, '33, 247–60; ANikolainen, D. Nächste als rel. Frage im NT '37 (s. Theol. Fennica 1, '39, 13–22); HPreisker, D. Ethos des Urchristentums '49, 68–81; JBowman, ET 59, '47/48, 151–3; 248 f.; ANissen, Gott u. der Nächste im Antiken Judentum, '74.—B. 867.—DELG s.v. πέλας IV. M-M. EDNT. TW.

πλησμονή, ῆς, ἡ (πίμπλημι; Eur., Pla., X. et al.; GVI I, 1946, 3=New Docs 4 no. 6, 3; Plut., LXX; PsSol 5:17; Philo; Jos., Ant. 11, 34; Just., D. 126, 6) **process of securing complete satisfaction, *satiety*** esp. w. food and drink, but also w. other types of enjoyment, ***satisfaction, gratification*** (Pla., Leg. 837 c; cp. Ps.-Clem., Hom. 8, 15 πρὸς τὴν ἑαυτῶν πλησμονήν). In our lit. the word is found only **Col 2:23** in a difficult saying (Theodore of Mops. I 296 Swete) πρὸς πλησμονὴν τ. σαρκός. The Gk. exegetes understood this to mean *for the gratification of physical needs.* But σάρξ, acc. to vs. 18, is surely to be taken in a pejorative sense, and πρός has the force 'against'. The transl. is prob. best made along the lines of NRSV: *of no value in checking self-indulgence.*—BHall, ET 36, 1925, 285; PHedley, ZNW 27, 1928, 211–16; GBornkamm, TLZ 73, '48, 18.—DELG s.v. πίμπλημι. M-M.

πλήσσω impf. ἔπλησσον; fut. 3 sg. πλήξει 3 Km 14:14 Aq.; 1 aor. 3 sg. ἔπληξεν 1 Km 11, 11 v.l.; pf. ptc. πεπληγώς LXX. Pass.: fut. πληγήσομαι LXX; 2 aor. ἐπλήγην; pf. ptc. πεπληγμένος (3 Macc 2:22 v.l.; Just., D. 132, 2) (Hom.+) **to strike with force, *strike*** of flames of fire (Lucian, Jupp. Conf. 15 of lightning) τινὰ κατὰ τῶν ὀφθαλμῶν (κατά A 1b) ApcPt 11, 26.—Of divinely-adminstered 'blows' or disasters that come to persons or things (Ex 9:31f; Ps 101:5; TestReub 1:7 ἔπληξέ με πληγῇ μεγάλῃ); pass. (Diod. S. 17, 117, 2 ὑπό τινος πληγῆς πεπληγμένος; Ael. Aristid. 13 p. 206 D.: ἐκ θεοῦ πληγείς; EpArist 313 ὑπὸ τ. θεοῦ; Tat. 16, 3 λόγῳ θεοῦ δυνάμεως πληττόμενοι) of heavenly bodies, which lose one third of their light as the result of a blow **Rv 8:12.**—DELG. M-M.

πλοιάριον, ου, τό (Aristoph., X.+; Diod. S. 14, 30, 4; PEdg 39 [=Sb 6745], 3 [253/252 BC]; BGU 812, 5; PGen 14, 8; Ostraka II 1051, 4) dim. of πλοῖον, **any kind of relatively small boat, *small ship, boat, skiff*** **Mk 3:9** (πλοῖον is used for the same kind of vessel 4:1; hence it is prob. no longer thought of as a dim.; this is plainly the case in Ael. Aristid. 50, 35 K.=26 p. 512 D., where there are nothing but πλοιάρια in the harbor); **4:36 v.l.; Lk 5:2 v.l.** (for πλοῖα); πλοιάριον ἄλλο **J 6:22; 23** (s. the text and vv.ll. with interchange of πλοῖα and πλοιάρια), **24.** οἱ μαθηταὶ τῷ πλοιαρίῳ (comitative-instrum. dat.; s. Kühner-G. I 430ff. Locative, perh. instrum.: Rob. 520f; 533) **21:8.**—Dalman, Arbeit VI 351–56, 363–70.—DELG s.v. πλέω. M-M.

πλοῖον, ου, τό (Aeschyl., Hdt.+; esp. freq. in later times, when ναῦς [in our lit. only Ac 27:41; on the differentiation s. Didymus p. 321 MSchmidt] became rare; ins, pap, LXX; En 101:4; OdeSol 11:9; TestSol; TestJob 18:7; TestNapht 6:2, 3, 5; EpArist 214; Joseph.—Prim.: 'ship' of any kind, though esp. a merchant ship).

❶ **a rather large sea-faring ship, *ship*** **Ac 20:13, 38; 21:2f, 6; 27:2–44** (on vs. **44** s. FZorell, BZ 9, 1911, 159f); **28:11; Js 3:4; Rv 8:9; 18:19.**

❷ **a relatively small fishing vessel, such as would be used on Lake Gennesaret,** ***boat*** (Jos., Vi. 163; 165) **Mt 4:21f; Mk 1:19f; Lk 5:2f, 7; J 6:19, 21ab, 23;** w. ἐμβαίνω and without the art. ἐμβαίνειν εἰς πλ. *get into a boat* **Mt 9:1; 13:2; Mk 4:1; Lk 8:22, 37** (these five last reff. w. τό as v.l.: s. N. and Tdf.); w. ἐμβαίνω and the art. ἐμβαίνειν εἰς τὸ πλ. **Mt 14:22** (v.l. without τό); **15:39; Mk 5:18; 8:10** (v.l. without τό); **J 21:3;** ἀναβαίνειν εἰς τὸ πλ. **Mt 14:32; Mk 6:51; Ac 21:6.** συνεισέρχεσθαι εἰς τὸ πλ. **J 6:22.** ἐξέρχεσθαι ἐκ τοῦ πλ. *get out of the boat* **Mk 6:54.** κατάγειν τὰ πλ. ἐπὶ τὴν γῆν (s. κατάγω) **Lk 5:11.**—On the 2000-year-old 'Galilee Boat' discovered in '86, s. OEANE II 377–79.

❸ quite gener. ***a ship*** ὀθόνη πλοίου *the sail of a ship* MPol 15:2.—EHilgert, The Ship and Related Symbols in the NT, '60.—B. 727; 729. DELG s.v. πλέω. M-M.

πλόκαμος, ου, ὁ (πλέκω; Hom. et al.; also Tat. 10, 1 ὁ Βερενίκης πλόκαμος) ***braid/lock of hair*** predom. of women (so in pl. since Il. 14, 176; also 3 Macc 1:4) ApcPt 9:24.—DELG s.v. πλέκω.

πλοκή, ῆς, ἡ (πλέκω; Eur., Pla. et al.; pap; Ex 28:14; TestSol 21, 3 Q; EpArist) **the condition of being braided,** ***braiding, braid*** ὁ ἔξωθεν ἐκ πλοκῆς (ἐκπλοκῆς?) τριχῶν κόσμος **1 Pt 3:3 v.l.** (for ἔξωθεν ἐμπλοκῆς τ. κ.).—DELG s.v. πλέκω.

πλόος (Hom. et al.) or contracted **πλοῦς** (Att.; ins, pap, Wsd 14:1; Philo, Joseph., Just.), **ὁ** orig. belonging to the second declension. In Hellenistic times it passed over to the third decl. and is declined like βοῦς (s. B-D-F §52; W-S. §8, 11, end; Mlt-H. 127; 142). In our lit. the word is limited to Ac, where it has the gen. πλοός (Peripl. Eryth. 61; Xenophon Eph. 1, 14; 5, 12; OGI 572, 21 [c. 200 AD]; but πλοῦ Just., D. 142, 3) and the acc. πλοῦν (Jos., Bell. 2, 40, Ant. 8, 181; Just., D. 142, 1) **movement of a boat through water,** ***voyage, navigation*** (so Hom. et al.) **Ac 27:9f.** τὸν πλ. διανύειν (s. διανύω 1) **21:7.** Also ἐτελέσθη ὁ πλ. AcPl Ha 7, 35.—DELG s.v. πλέω. M-M.

πλούσιος, ία, ιον (πλοῦτος; Hes., Hdt.+)—❶ **pert. to having an abundance of earthly possessions that exceeds normal experience,** ***rich, wealthy,*** ἦν Ἰωακεὶμ πλ. σφόδρα GJs 1:1 (Sus 4 Theod.); ἄνθρωπος πλ. *a rich man* (i.e. one who does not need to work for a living) **Mt 27:57; Lk 12:16;** cp. **16:1, 19** (here, in P[75], the rich man's name is given as Νευης, q.v. as a separate entry); **18:23; 19:2.** γείτονες πλ. *wealthy neighbors* **14:12.**—Subst. ὁ πλ. *the rich man* (oft. in contrast to the poor; cp. TestAbr A 19 p. 101, 20, [Stone p. 50; opp. πένης, who must work for a living].—S. PFurfey, CBQ 5, '43, 241–63) **Lk 16:21f; Js 1:10f;** 1 Cl 13:1 (Jer 9:22); 38:2; Hs 2:5–7 (vs. 4 εἰς πτωχὸν καὶ πλούσιον the art. is omitted after the prep.). Pl. οἱ πλ. (Menand., Cith. fgm. 1, 1 Kö. [=fgm. 281, 1]) **Lk 6:24; 21:1; 1 Ti 6:17; Js 2:6; 5:1; Rv 6:15; 13:16;** 1 Cl 16:10 (Is 53:9); Hs 2:8; 9, 20, 1f. Without the art. πλούσιος *a rich man* **Mt 19:23f; Mk 10:25; Lk 18:25** (cp. Sextus 193 χαλεπόν ἐστιν πλουτοῦντα σωθῆναι; s. also Pla., Laws 5, 743a). Pl. **Mk 12:41;** B 20:2; D 5:2.—Of the preexistent Christ δι' ὑμᾶς ἐπτώχευσεν πλούσιος ὤν *for your sake he became penniless, though he was rich* **2 Cor 8:9** (here the emphasis on wealth vs. poverty relates esp. to status, cp. Phil 2:6–11; some place the pass. in 2 below; opp. Demosth 18, 131).

❷ **pert. to being plentifully supplied with someth.,** ***abound (in), rich (in),*** fig. ext. of 1 (Menand., fgm. 936 Kö. and EpArist 15 πλουσία ψυχή; PsSol 5:14 δόμα … πλούσιον; CIG IV, 9688, 4f τέκνα) *rich* ἔν τινι *in someth.* of God ἐν ἐλέει **Eph 2:4;** of humans ἐν πίστει **Js 2:5.** πλ. τῷ πνεύματι (analogous, but not in contrast to πτωχὸς τῷ πνεύματι Mt 5:3) *rich in spirit* (paralleling ἁπλοῦ τῇ καρδίᾳ) B 19:2. Abs., of those who are rich in a transcendent sense **Rv 2:9; 3:17;** cp. (ἡ ἔντευξίς ἐστιν) πλουσία πρὸς κυρίον Hs 2:6. ἀπὸ τοῦ πλουσίου τῆς ἀγάπης κυρίου *from the Lord, who is rich in love* B 1:3 (on the text which, perhaps, is damaged, s. Windisch, Hdb. ad loc.). The text is also uncertain in vs. 2, where μεγάλων ὄντων καὶ πλουσίων τῶν τοῦ θεοῦ δικαιωμάτων εἰς ὑμᾶς is prob. to be rendered: *since the righteous deeds of God toward you are great and generous.* For **2 Cor 8:9** s. 1 above.—For lit. s. under πλοῦτος, πτωχός.—DELG s.v. πλοῦτος. M-M. EDNT. TW.

πλουσίως adv. of πλούσιος (since Eur.; Hdt. 2, 44; OGI 767, 18; Philo) ***richly, abundantly*** ἐκχέειν **Tit 3:6.** ἐνοικεῖν **Col 3:16.** ἐπιχορηγεῖν **2 Pt 1:11.** μανθάνειν B 9:7. παρέχειν **1 Ti 6:17.** Comp. πλουσιώτερον (X., Oec. 9, 13) *more richly, more abundantly* (w. ὑψηλότερον) B 1:7.—M-M. TW.

πλουτέω fut. 3 sg. πλουτήσει Da 11:2; 1 aor. ἐπλούτησα; pf. πεπλούτηκα (πλοῦτος; Hes., Hdt. et al.; SIG 1268, 30; PGiss 13, 19; LXX, pseudepigr., Philo, Joseph., Tat.)

❶ **to be relatively high on a scale of opulence,** ***be rich*** aor. *become rich;* pf. *have become rich.* lit., abs. (Artem. 4, 59; En 97:8 πλούτῳ πεπλουτήκαμεν; ApcMos 24; Philo, Virt. 166; Jos., Ant. 4:14; Tat. 11:1; Orig., C. Cels. 8, 38, 17) **Lk 1:53; 1 Ti 6:9;** 2 Cl 20:1; Dg 10:5; Hv 3, 6, 7; ApcPt 15:30. οἱ πλουτοῦντες ἐν τούτῳ τῷ αἰῶνι *those who have riches in this age* Hv 3, 6, 6.—Aor. Hs 8, 9, 1. The source fr. which the wealth comes is indicated by ἀπό τινος (Aristoph., Plut. 569; Lucian, Dial. Deor. 16, 1; Sir 11:18) οἱ ἔμποροι οἱ πλουτήσαντες ἀπ' αὐτῆς **Rv 18:15.** Also ἔκ τινος (Lysias 32, 25) vss. **3, 19.**

❷ **to be plentifully supplied with someth.,** ***be rich,*** in imagery ἔν τινι in *someth.* (Synes., Ep. 130 p. 265b; OdeSol 11:9) ἐν ἔργοις καλοῖς **1 Ti 6:18.** ἐν ἐντεύξει Hs 2:7. εἰς θεὸν πλ. *be rich in God* or *toward God,* in any case, in the things that are worthy in the sight of God **Lk 12:21.** The εἰς-constr. in **Ro 10:12** is different: κύριος πλουτῶν εἰς πάντας *the Lord, who is rich* (and *generous*) *toward all,* i.e. who gives of his wealth generously to all (Philostrat., Vi. Apoll. 4, 8 p. 129, 16 εἰς τὸ κοινόν).—Abs., of being rich in transcendent values **1 Cor 4:8; 2 Cor 8:9** (τῇ ἐκείνου πτωχείᾳ is dat. of instrument or of cause); **Rv 3:18.** Pf. πλούσιός εἰμι καὶ πεπλούτηκα vs. **17** (cp. also Hos 12:9).—DELG s.v. πλοῦτος. M-M. TW.

πλουτίζω (πλοῦτος) fut. 3 sg. πλουτίσει 1 Km 17:25 Theod.(?) and inf. πλουτιεῖν 2 Macc 7:24; 1 aor. ἐπλούτισα. Pass.: 1 fut. 3 sg. πλουτισθήσεται Sir 19:1; 1 aor. ἐπλουτίσθην (Aeschyl., X. et al.; ins, LXX; Anz 297)

❶ **to cause to be relatively high on a scale of opulence,** ***make wealthy*** τινά someone (Gen 14:23; Sir 11:21; Jos., Ant. 17, 147) Hs 1:9. Abs. (w. πτωχίζω) of God 1 Cl 59:3 (cp. 1 Km 2:7). Pass. παρὰ τοῦ κυρίου πλουτίζεσθαι *receive one's riches from the Lord* Hs 2:10.

❷ **to cause to abound in someth.,** ***make rich,*** in imagery, of spiritual riches: τινά someone, of the apostle Paul, to whom alone the pl. prob. refers in ὡς πτωχοὶ πολλοὺς πλουτίζοντες *as poor, though making many rich* **2 Cor 6:10;** cp. of the Christians πτωχεύουσι καὶ πλουτίζουσι πολλούς Dg 5:13. Pass. ὁ υἱός, δι' οὗ πλουτίζεται ἡ ἐκκλησία 11:5. πλουτίζεσθαι ἔν τινι *be made rich in someth.* ἐν παντί in *everything* **1 Cor 1:5;** it is resumed w. ἐν παντὶ λόγῳ and given content. The ἐν αὐτῷ in the same verse denotes that this rich possession is dependent upon a close relationship to Christ. ἐν παντὶ πλουτιζόμενοι εἰς πᾶσαν ἁπλότητα *being made rich in every way for every (demonstration of) generosity* i.e. so that you might demonstrate generosity in every way **2 Cor 9:11.**—DELG s.v. πλοῦτος. M-M. TW.

πλοῦτος, ου, ὁ (s. prec. four entries; Hom.+) Paul, who also uses the masc., in eight passages (**2 Cor 8:2; Eph 1:7; 2:7; 3:8, 16; Phil 4:19; Col 1:27; 2:2**) has in the nom. and acc. the neuter **τὸ πλοῦτος** (AcPh 109 [Aa II/2, 42, 5]; Is 29:2 [acc. to SA; s. Thackeray 159]); Tdf., Proleg. 118; W-H., app. 158; B-D-F §51, 2; Mlt-H. 127; Gignac II 100; 'wealth, riches'.

❶ abundance of many earthly goods, ***wealth*** (Iren. 1, 8, 3 [Harv. I 71, 9]; Orig., C. Cels. 3, 9, 8; καὶ τὰ ἀνθρώπινα Did., Gen. 150, 8) **Mt 13:22; Mk 4:19; Lk 8:14; 1 Ti 6:17; Js 5:2; Rv 18:17;** 1 Cl 13:1 (Jer 9:22); Hv 3, 6, 5b; 6b; m 10, 1, 4; s 1:8; 2:5, 7f (τὸ πλ.); ApcPt 15, 30. Leading souls (astray) Hv 3, 6, 6a (restored). πλ. τοῦ αἰῶνος τούτου 3, 6, 5a. πολυτέλεια πλούτου m 8:3; 12, 2, 1. γαυριᾶν ἐν τῷ πλούτῳ *glory in wealth* 1, 1, 8. Also γαυροῦσθαι ἐν τῷ πλ. 3, 9, 6. ἐπιλάθου τοῦ πλούτου καὶ τοῦ κάλλους σου AcPl Ha 2, 21; πλ. καταναλίσκεται 2, 24f; the restoration in 9, 9 is based on 2:24f.—OSchilling, Reichtum u. Eigentum in der altkirchl. Lit. 1908 (p. ix–xii for lit.); ETroeltsch, D. Soziallehren der christl. Kirchen u. Gruppen 1912; MWeber, D. Wirtschaftsethik der Weltreligionen: Archiv f. Sozialwissensch. 44, 1918, 52ff; FHauck, Die Stellung des Urchristentums zu Arbeit u. Geld 1921; ELohmeyer, Soziale Fragen im Urchristentum 1921; HGreeven, D. Hauptproblem der Sozialethik in der neueren Stoa u. im Urchristentum '35 (slavery, property, marriage); KBornhäuser, D. Christ u. s. Habe nach dem NT '36; HvCampenhausen, D. Askese im Urchristentum '49. Cp. πτωχός 1.

❷ plentiful supply of someth., ***a wealth, abundance,*** fig. ext. of 1, w. gen. of thing (Pla., Euthyphr. 12a π. τῆς σοφίας; Theoph. Ant. 2, 12 [p. 130, 6] τῆς σοφίας τοῦ θεοῦ) τῆς ἁπλότητος; **2 Cor 8:2.** τῆς δόξης **Ro 9:23; Eph 1:18; 3:16; Col 1:27.** τῆς πληροφορίας **2:2.** τῆς χάριτος **Eph 1:7; 2:7.** τῆς χρηστότητος **Ro 2:4** (Simplicius In Epict. p. 12, 7 πλοῦτος τῆς αὐτοῦ [God] ἀγαθότητος). The genitives in **Ro 11:12,** πλ. κόσμου, πλ. ἐθνῶν are different: *(an) abundance (of benefits) for the world, for the gentiles.* Of that which God or Christ possesses in boundless abundance: βάθος πλούτου vs. **33** (s. βάθος 2 and cp. Jos., Bell. 6, 442 ὁ πλοῦτος ὁ βαθύς).—**Phil 4:19.**—**Eph 3:8; Rv 5:12** (w. δύναμις, σοφία, ἰσχύς, τιμή, δόξα, εὐλογία. Cp. Aristot., Pol. 1323a, 37f πλοῦτος, χρήματα, δύναμις, δόξα; Herodas 1, 28 πλοῦτος, δύναμις, δόξα; Crantor [IV/III BC]: FPhGr III 148 πλοῦτος κ. δόξα; Diod. S. 4, 74, 1 πλ. κ. δόξα).—μείζονα πλ. ἡγησάμενος τῶν Αἰγύπτου θησαυρῶν τὸν ὀνειδισμὸν τοῦ Χριστοῦ *he considered the reproach suffered on behalf of the Christ to be greater wealth than the treasures of Egypt* **Hb 11:26.**—TESchmidt, Hostility to Wealth in Philo of Alexandria: JSNT 19, '83, 85–97; for other lit. s. πένης. B. 772. DELG. M-M. TW. Sv.

πλύνω impf. ἔπλυνον; fut. πλυνῶ; 1 aor. ἔπλυνα, impv. πλῦνον. Pass.: fut. 3 sg. πλυθήσεται LXX; aor. inf. πλυθῆναι Lev 13:55 (Hom. et al.; OGI 483, 169 ἱμάτια; PStras 91, 8; PSI 599, 7; PLond V, 1695, 18; LXX; TestSol 18:15; TestAbr B 6 p. 110, 24 [Stone p. 68]; Philo, Leg. All. 3, 144; 147; Just.)

❶ to wash someth. other than a part of the body (for this s. λούω 1b), ***wash.*** τὶ *someth.* τὰ δίκτυα *wash the nets* **Lk 5:2** (cp. Mk 1:19 καταρτίζειν 'mend'). Washing of clothes (Artem. 2, 3 p. 88, 23) as a symbol of cleansing fr. sins ἔπλυναν τὰς στολὰς αὐτῶν **Rv 7:14** (on πλύνειν τ. στολ., at times w. ἔν τινι, cp. Gen 49:11.—Appian, Samn. 7 §6 of a defiled garment ἐκπλυνεῖτε τοῦτο αἵματι πολλῷ=you will wash this out with a great deal of blood); cp. **22:14.** This affords an easy transition to

❷ free someth. of someth., ***free from,*** i.e. from the impurity of sin; fig. ext. of 1, although the original mng. of πλ. is still felt (cp. Artem. 2, 4) πλῦνόν με ἀπὸ τῆς ἀνομίας μου 1 Cl 18:3 (Ps 50:4) and in the continuation of the quot. πλυνεῖς με vs. 7 (Ps 50:9).—B. 579. DELG. M-M.

πνεῦμα, ατος, τό (πνέω; Aeschyl., Pre-Socr., Hdt.+. On the history of the word s. Rtzst., Mysterienrel.[3] 308ff).

❶ air in movement, ***blowing, breathing*** (even the glowing exhalations of a volcanic crater: Diod. S. 5, 7, 3)—ⓐ *wind* (Aeschyl. et al.; LXX, EpArist, Philo; Jos., Ant. 2, 343; 349; SibOr 8, 297) in wordplay τὸ πνεῦμα πνεῖ *the wind blows* **J 3:8a** (EpJer 60 πνεῦμα ἐν πάσῃ χώρᾳ πνεῖ. But s. TDonn, ET 66, '54f, 32; JThomas, Restoration Qtrly 24, '81, 219–24). ὀθόνη πλοίου ὑπὸ πνεύματος πληρουμένη MPol 15:2. Of God ὁ ποιῶν τοὺς ἀγγέλους αὐτοῦ πνεύματα *who makes his angels winds* **Hb 1:7;** 1 Cl 36:3 (both Ps 103:4).

ⓑ *the breathing out of air, blowing, breath* (Aeschyl. et al.; Pla., Tim. 79b; LXX) ὁ ἄνομος, ὃν ὁ κύριος Ἰησοῦς ἀνελεῖ τῷ πνεύματι τοῦ στόματος αὐτοῦ **2 Th 2:8** (cp. Is 11:4; Ps 32:6).

❷ that which animates or gives life to the body, ***breath, (life-)spirit*** (Aeschyl. et al.; Phoenix of Colophon 1, 16 [Coll. Alex. p. 231] πν.=a breathing entity [in contrast to becoming earth in death]; Polyb. 31, 10, 4; Ps.-Aristot., De Mundo 4 p. 394b, 8ff; PHib 5, 54 [III BC]; PGM 4, 538; 658; 2499; LXX; TestAbr A 17 p. 98, 19 [Stone p. 44] al.; JosAs 19:3; SibOr 4, 46; Tat. 4:2) ἀφιέναι τὸ πνεῦμα *give up one's spirit, breathe one's last* (Eur., Hec. 571; Porphyr., Vi. Plotini 2) **Mt 27:50. J** says for this παραδιδόναι τὸ πν. **19:3** (cp. ApcMos 31 ἀποδῶ τὸ πν.; Just., D. 105, 5). Of the return of the *(life-)spirit* of a deceased person into her dead body ἐπέστρεψεν τὸ πν. αὐτῆς **Lk 8:55** (cp. Jdg 15:19). εἰς χεῖράς σου παρατίθεμαι τὸ πν. μου *into your hands I entrust my spirit* **23:46** (Ps 30:6; for alleged focus on ἐλπίζειν s. EBons, BZ 38, '94, 93–101). κύριε Ἰησοῦ, δέξαι τὸ πνεῦμά μου **Ac 7:59;** composite of both passages AcPl Ha 10, 23 (cp. ApcMos 42). τὸ πν. μου ὁ δεσπότης δέξεται GJs 23:3 (on the pneuma flying upward after death cp. Epicharm. in Vorsokrat. 23 [=13, 4th ed.], B 9 and 22; Eur., Suppl. 533 πνεῦμα μὲν πρὸς αἰθέρα, τὸ σῶμα δ' ἐς γῆν; PGM 1, 177ff τελευτήσαντός σου τὸ σῶμα περιστελεῖ, σοῦ δὲ τὸ πνεῦμα . . . εἰς ἀέρα ἄξει σὺν αὐτῷ 'when you are dead [the angel] will wrap your body . . . and take your spirit with him into the sky'). τὸ σῶμα χωρὶς πν. νεκρόν ἐστιν **Js 2:26.** πν. ζωῆς ἐκ τ. θεοῦ εἰσῆλθεν ἐν αὐτοῖς (i.e. the prophet-witnesses who have been martyred) **Rv 11:11** (cp. Ezk 37:10 v.l. εἰσῆλθεν εἰς αὐτοὺς πνεῦμα ζωῆς; vs. 5). Of the *spirit* that animated the image of a beast, and enabled it to speak and to have Christians put to death **13:15.**—After a person's death, the πν. lives on as an independent being, in heaven πνεύματα δικαίων τετελειωμένων **Hb 12:23** (cp. Da 3:86 εὐλογεῖτε, πνεύματα καὶ ψυχαὶ δικαίων, τὸν κύριον). According to non-biblical sources, the πν. are in the netherworld (cp. En 22:3–13; Sib Or 7, 127) or in the air (PGM 1, 178), where evil spirits can prevent them from ascending higher (s. ἀήρ2b). τοῖς ἐν φυλακῇ πνεύμασιν πορευθεὶς ἐκήρυξεν **1 Pt 3:19** belongs here if it refers to Jesus' preaching to the spirits of the dead confined in Hades (so Usteri et al.; s. also JMcCulloch, The Harrowing of Hell, 1930), whether it be when he descended into Hades, or when he returned to heaven (so RBultmann, Bekenntnis u. Liedfragmente im 1 Pt: ConNeot11, '47, 1–14).—CClemen, Niedergefahren zu den Toten 1900; JTurmel, La

Descente du Christ aux enfers 1905; JMonnier, La Descente aux enfers 1906; HHoltzmann, ARW 11, 1908, 285–97; KGschwind, Die Niederfahrt Christi in die Unterwelt 1911; DPlooij, De Descensus in 1 Pt 3:19 en 4:6: TT 47, 1913, 145–62; JBernard, The Descent into Hades a Christian Baptism (on 1 Pt 3:19ff): Exp. 8th ser., 11, 1916, 241–74; CSchmidt, Gespräche Jesu mit seinen Jüngern: TU 43, 1919, 452ff; JFrings, BZ 17, 1926, 75–88; JKroll, Gott u. Hölle '32; RGanschinietz, Katabasis: Pauly-W. X/2, 1919, 2359–449; Clemen[2] 89–96; WBieder, Die Vorstellung v. d. Höllenfahrt Jesu Chr. '49; SJohnson, JBL 79, '60, 48–51; WDalton, Christ's Proclamation to the Spirits '65. S. also the lit. in Windisch, Hdb.[2] 1930, exc. on 1 Pt 3:20; ESelwyn, The First Ep. of St. Peter '46 and 4c below.—This is prob. also the place for θανατωθεὶς μὲν σαρκὶ ζωοποιηθεὶς δὲ πνεύματι: ἐν ᾧ καὶ . . . **1 Pt 3:18f** (some mss. read πνεύματι instead of πνεύμασιν in vs. **19**, evidently in ref. to the manner of Jesus' movement; πνεῦμα is that part of Christ which, in contrast to σάρξ, did not pass away in death, but survived as an individual entity after death; s. ἐν 7). Likew. the contrast κατὰ σάρκα . . . κατὰ πνεῦμα **Ro 1:3f.** Cp. **1 Ti 3:16.**

❸ **a part of human personality, *spirit*—ⓐ** when used with σάρξ, the flesh, it denotes the immaterial part **2 Cor 7:1; Col 2:5.** *Flesh and spirit*=the whole personality, in its outer and inner aspects, oft. in Ign.: IMg 1:2; 13:1a; ITr ins; 12:1; IRo ins; ISm 1:1; IPol 5:1; AcPl Ant 13, 18 (=Aa I 237, 3).—In the same sense beside σῶμα, the body (Simplicius, In Epict. p. 50, 1; Ps.-Phoc. 106f; PGM 1, 178) **1 Cor 5:3–5; 7:34.**—The inner life of humans is divided into ψυχὴ καὶ πνεῦμα (cp. Ps.-Pla., Axioch. 10 p. 370c τι θεῖον ὄντως ἐνῆν πνεῦμα τῇ ψυχῇ=a divine spirit was actually in the soul; Wsd 15:11; Jos., Ant. 1, 34; Tat. 13, 2; 15, 1 et al.; Ath. 27, 1. S. also Herm. Wr. 10, 13; 16f; PGM 4, 627; 630. ἐκ τριῶν συνεστάναι λέγουσι τὸν ἄνθρωπον ἐκ ψυχῆς καὶ σώματος καὶ πνεύματος Did., Gen. 55, 14) **Hb 4:12.** Cp. **Phil 1:27.** τὸ πνεῦμα καὶ ἡ ψυχὴ καὶ τὸ σῶμα **1 Th 5:23** (s. GMilligan, Thess. 1908, 78f; EvDobschütz in Meyer X[7] 1909, 230ff; EBurton, Spirit, Soul, and Flesh 1918; AFestugière, La Trichotomie des 1 Th 5:23 et la Philos. gr.: RSR 20, 1930, 385–415; CMasson, RTP 33, '45, 97–102; FGrant, An Introd. to NT Thought '50, 161–66). σαρκί, ψυχῇ, πνεύματι IPhld 11:2.

ⓑ as the source and seat of insight, feeling, and will, gener. as the representative part of human inner life (cp. PGM 4, 627; 3 Km 20:5; Sir 9:9 al.; Just., D. 30, 1; Did., Gen. 232, 5) ἐπιγνοὺς ὁ Ἰησοῦς τῷ πν. αὐτοῦ **Mk 2:8.** ἀναστενάξας τῷ πν. αὐτοῦ λέγει **8:12** (s. ἀναστενάζω). ἠγαλλίασεν τὸ πν. μου **Lk 1:47** (in parallelism w. ψυχή vs. 46, as Sir 9:9). ἠγαλλιάσατο τῷ πν. **10:21 v.l.,** Ἰησοῦς ἐνεβριμήσατο τῷ πν. **J 11:33** (s. ἐμβριμάομαι 3); Ἰησ. ἐταράχθη τῷ πν. **13:21.** παρωξύνετο τὸ πν. αὐτοῦ ἐν αὐτῷ **Ac 17:16;** ζέων τῷ πν. *with spirit-fervor* **18:25** (s. ζέω). τὸ παιδίον ἐκραταιοῦτο πνεύματι **Lk 1:80; 2:40 v.l.;** ἔθετο ὁ Παῦλος ἐν τῷ πν. *Paul made up his mind* **Ac 19:21** (some would put this pass. in 6c, but cp. **Lk 1:66** and analogous formulations Hom. et al. in L-S-J-M s.v. τίθημι A6). προσκυνήσουσιν τῷ πατρὶ ἐν πνεύματι of the *spiritual,* i.e. the pure, inner worship of God, that has nothing to do w. holy times, places, appurtenances, or ceremonies **J 4:23;** cp. vs. **24b.** πν. συντετριμμένον (Ps 50:19) 1 Cl 18:17; 52:4.—2 Cl 20:4; Hv 3, 12, 2; 3, 13, 2.—This usage is also found in Paul. His conviction (s. 5 below) that the Christian possesses the (divine) πνεῦμα and thus is different fr. all other people, leads him to choose this word in preference to others, in order to characterize a believer's inner being gener. ᾧ λατρεύω ἐν τῷ πν. μου **Ro 1:9.** οὐκ ἔσχηκα ἄνεσιν τῷ πν. μου **2 Cor 2:13.** Cp. **7:13.** As a matter of fact, it can mean simply a person's *very self* or *ego:* τὸ πνεῦμα συμμαρτυρεῖ τῷ πνεύματι ἡμῶν *the Spirit* (of God) *bears witness to our very self* **Ro 8:16** (cp. PGM 12, 327 ἠκούσθη μου τὸ πνεῦμα ὑπὸ πνεύματος οὐρανοῦ). ἀνέπαυσαν τὸ ἐμὸν πν. καὶ τὸ ὑμῶν *they have refreshed both me and you* **1 Cor 16:18.** ἡ χάρις τοῦ κυρίου ἡμῶν Ἰ. Χρ. μετὰ τοῦ πν. (ὑμῶν) **Gal 6:18; Phil 4:23; Phlm 25.** Cp. **2 Ti 4:22.** Likew. in Ign. τὸ ἐμὸν πν. *my* (unworthy) *self* IEph 18:1; IRo 9:3; cp. **1 Cor 2:11a**—On the relation of the divine Spirit to the believer's spiritual self, s. SWollenweider, Der Geist Gottes als Selbst der Glaubenden: ZTK 93, '96, 163–92.—Only a part of the inner life, i.e. that which concerns the will, is meant in τὸ μὲν πνεῦμα πρόθυμον, ἡ δὲ σὰρξ ἀσθενής **Mt 26:41; Mk 14:38;** Pol 7:2. That which is inferior, anxiety, fear of suffering, etc. is attributed to the σάρξ.—The mng. of the expr. οἱ πτωχοὶ τῷ πνεύματι **Mt 5:3** is difficult to determine w. certainty (cp. Pla., Ep. 7, 335a πένης ἀνὴρ τὴν ψυχήν. The dat. as τῇ ψυχῇ M. Ant. 6, 52; 8, 51). The sense is prob. *those who are poor in their inner life,* because they do not have a misdirected pride in their own spiritual riches (s. AKlöpper, Über den Sinn u. die ursprgl. Form der ersten Seligpreisung der Bergpredigt bei Mt: ZWT 37, 1894, 175–91; RKabisch, Die erste Seligpreisung: StKr 69, 1896, 195–215; KKöhler, Die ursprgl. Form der Seligpreisungen: StKr 91, 1918, 157–92; JBoehmer, De Schatkamer 17, 1923, 11–16, TT [Copenhagen] 4, 1924, 195–207, JBL 45, 1926, 298–304; WMacgregor, ET 39, 1928, 293–97; VMacchioro, JR 12, '32, 40–49; EEvans, Theology 47, '44, 55–60; HLeisegang, Pneuma Hagion 1922, 134ff; Betz, SM 116 n. 178 for Qumran reff.).

ⓒ *spiritual state, state of mind, disposition* ἐν ἀγάπῃ πνεύματί τε πραΰτητος *with love and a gentle spirit* **1 Cor 4:21;** cp. **Gal 6:1.** τὸ πν. τοῦ νοὸς ὑμῶν **Eph 4:23** (s. νοῦς 2a). ἐν τῷ ἀφθάρτῳ τοῦ ἡσυχίου πνεύματος *with the imperishable (gift) of a quiet disposition* **1 Pt 3:4.**

❹ **an independent noncorporeal being, in contrast to a being that can be perceived by the physical senses, *spirit*** (ELangton, Good and Evil Spirits '42).

ⓐ God personally: πνεῦμα ὁ θεός **J 4:24a** (Ath. 16, 2; on God as a spirit, esp. in the Stoa, s. MPohlenz, D. Stoa '48/49. Hdb. ad loc. Also Celsus 6, 71 [Stoic]; Herm. Wr. 18, 3 ἀκάματον μέν ἐστι πνεῦμα ὁ θεός).

ⓑ good, or at least not expressly evil *spirits* or *spirit-beings* (cp. CIG III, 5858b δαίμονες καὶ πνεύματα; Proclus on Pla., Cratyl. p. 69, 6; 12 Pasqu.; En 15:4; 6; 8; 10; TestAbr A 4 p. 81, 15f [Stone p. 10, 15f] πάντα τὰ ἐπουράνια πνεύματα; TestAbr B 13 p. 117, 26 [Stone p. 82] ὑψηλὸν πν.; PGM 3, 8 ἐπικαλοῦμαί σε, ἱερὸν πνεῦμα; 4, 1448; 3080; 12, 249) πνεῦμα w. ἄγγελος (cp. Jos., Ant. 4, 108; Ps.-Clem., Hom. 3, 33; 8, 12) **Ac 23:8f.** God is ὁ παντὸς πνεύματος κτίστης καὶ ἐπίσκοπος 1 Cl 59:3b.—Pl., God the μόνος εὐεργέτης πνεύματων 1 Cl 59:3a. Cp. 64 (s. on this Num 16:22; 27:16. Prayers for vengeance fr. Rheneia [Dssm., LO 351–55=LAE 423ff=SIG 1181, 2] τὸν θεὸν τὸν κύριον τῶν πνευμάτων; PGM 5, 467 θεὸς θεῶν, ὁ κύριος τῶν πν.; sim. the magic pap PWarr 21, 24; 26 [III AD]); the πατὴρ τῶν πνευμάτων **Hb 12:9.** Intermediary beings (in polytheistic terminology: δαίμονες) that serve God are called λειτουργικὰ πνεύματα **Hb 1:14.** In **Rv** we read of the ἑπτὰ πνεύματα (τοῦ θεοῦ) **1:4; 3:1; 4:5; 5:6;** s. ASkrinjar, Biblica 16, '35, 1–24; 113–40.—*Ghost* **Lk 24:37, 39.**

ⓒ evil *spirits* (PGM 13, 798; 36, 160; TestJob 27, 2; ApcSed [both Satan]; AscIs 3:28; Just., D. 39, 6 al.; Ath. 25, 3), esp. in accounts of healing in the Synoptics: (τὸ) πνεῦμα (τὸ) ἀκάθαρτον (Just., D. 82, 3) **Mt 12:43; Mk 1:23, 26; 3:30; 5:2, 8; 7:25; 9:25a; Lk 8:29; 9:42; 11:24; Rv 18:2.** Pl. (TestBenj 5:2) **Mt 10:1; Mk 1:27; 3:11; 5:13; 6:7; Lk 4:36; 6:18; Ac**

5:16; 8:7; Rv 16:13; ending of Mk in the Freer ms.—τὸ πν. τὸ πονηρόν Ac 19:15f. Pl. (En 99:7; TestSim 4:9; 6:6, TestJud 16:1; Just., D. 76, 6) Lk 7:21; 8:2; Ac 19:12f.—πν. ἄλαλον Mk 9:17; cp. vs. 25b (s. ἄλαλος). πν. πύθων Ac 16:16 (s. πύθων). πν. ἀσθενείας Lk 13:11. Cp. 1 Ti 4:1b. πνεῦμα δαιμονίου ἀκαθάρτου (s. δαιμόνιον 2) Lk 4:33. πνεύματα δαιμονίων Rv 16:14 (in effect = personified 'exhalations' of evil powers; for the combination of πν. and δαιμ. cp. the love spell Sb 4324, 16f τὰ πνεύματα τῶν δαιμόνων τούτων).—Abs. of a harmful *spirit* Mk 9:20; Lk 9:39; Ac 16:18. Pl. Mt 8:16; 12:45; Lk 10:20; 11:26.—1 Pt 3:19 (s. 2 above) belongs here if the πνεύματα refer to hostile spirit-powers, evil spirits, fallen angels (so FSpitta, Christi Predigt an die Geister 1890; HGunkel, Zum religionsgesch. Verständnis des NT 1903, 72f; WBousset, ZNW 19, 1920, 50–66; Rtzst., Herr der Grösse 1919, 25ff; Knopf, Windisch, FHauck ad loc.; BReicke, The Disobedient Spirits and Christian Baptism '46, esp. 54–56, 69).—Hermas also has the concept of evil spirits that lead an independent existence, and live and reign within the inner life of a pers.; the Holy Spirit, who also lives or would like to live there, is forced out by them (cp. TestDan 4) Hm 5, 1, 2–4; 5, 2, 5–8; 10, 1, 2. τὸ πν. τὸ ἅγιον . . . ἕτερον πονηρὸν πν. 5, 1, 2. These πνεύματα are ὀξυχολία 5, 1, 3; 5, 2, 8 (τὸ πονηρότατον πν.); 10, 1, 2; διψυχία 9:11 (ἐπίγειον πν. ἐστι παρὰ τοῦ διαβόλου); 10, 1, 2; λύπη 10, 1, 2 (πάντων τῶν πνευμάτων πονηροτέρα) and other vices. On the complicated pneuma-concept of the Mandates of Hermas s. MDibelius, Hdb. exc. on Hm 5, 2, 7; cp. Leutzsch, Hermas 453f n. 133.

❺ **God's being as controlling influence, with focus on association with humans, *Spirit, spirit*** as that which differentiates God fr. everything that is not God, as the divine power that produces all divine existence, as the divine element in which all divine life is carried on, as the bearer of every application of the divine will. All those who belong to God possess or receive this spirit and hence have a share in God's life. This spirit also serves to distinguish Christians fr. all unbelievers (cp. PGM 4, 1121ff, where the spirit is greeted as one who enters devotees and, in accordance w. God's will, separates them fr. themselves, i.e. fr. the purely human part of their nature); for this latter aspect s. esp. 6 below.

ⓐ the Spirit of God, of the Lord (=God) etc. (LXX; TestSim 4:4; JosAs 8:11; ApcSed 14:6; 15:6; ApcMos 43; SibOr 3, 701; Ps.-Phoc. 106; Philo; Joseph. [s. c below]; apolog. Cp. Plut., Numa 4, 6 πνεῦμα θεοῦ, capable of begetting children; s. παρθένος a) τὸ πν. τοῦ θεοῦ 1 Cor 2:11b, 14; 3:16; 6:11; 1J 4:2a (Just., D. 49, 3; Tat. 13, 3; Ath. 22, 3). τὸ τοῦ θεοῦ πν. 1 Pt 4:14 (Just., A I, 60, 6). τὸ πν. τὸ ἐκ τοῦ θεοῦ 1 Cor 2:12b. τὸ πν. κυρίου Ac 5:9; B 6:14; 9:2 (cp. Mel., P. 32, 222). τὸ πνεῦμά μου or αὐτοῦ: Mt 12:18 (Is 42:1); Ac 2:17f (Jo 3:1f.—Cp. 1QS 4:21); 1 Cor 2:10a v.l.; Eph 3:16; 1 Th 4:8 (where τὸ ἅγιον is added); 1J 4:13.—τὸ πν. τοῦ πατρὸς ὑμῶν Mt 10:20. τὸ πν. τοῦ ἐγείραντος τὸν Ἰησοῦν Ro 8:11a.—Without the art. πν. θεοῦ (JosAs 4:9; Tat. 15:3; Theoph. Ant. 1, 5 [p. 66, 18]) *the Spirit of God* Mt 3:16; 12:28; Ro 8:9b, 14, 19; 1 Cor 7:40; 12:3a; 2 Cor 3:3 (πν. θεοῦ ζῶντος); Phil 3:3. πν. κυρίου Lk 4:18 (Is 61:1); Ac 8:39 (like J 3:8; 20:22; Ac 2:4, this pass. belongs on the borderline betw. the mngs. 'wind' and 'spirit'; cp. Diod. S. 3, 60, 3 Ἕσπερον ἐξαίφνης ὑπὸ πνευμάτων συναρπαγέντα μεγάλων ἄφαντον γενέσθαι 'Hesperus [a son of Atlas] was suddenly snatched by strong winds and vanished fr. sight'. S. HLeisegang, Der Hl. Geist I 1, 1919, 19ff; OCullmann, TZ. 4, '48, 364); 1 Cl 21:2.

ⓑ the Spirit of Christ, of the Lord (=Christ) etc. τὸ πν. Ἰησοῦ Ac 16:7. τὸ πν. Χριστοῦ AcPlCor 2:32. τὸ ἐν αὐτοῖς πν. Χριστοῦ 1 Pt 1:11. πν. Χριστοῦ Ro 8:9c. πν. τοῦ Χριστοῦ AcPl Ha 8, 18. ἀπὸ τοῦ πν. τοῦ χριστοῦ AcPlCor 2:10. τὸ πν. Ἰησ. Χριστοῦ Phil 1:19. τὸ πν. κυρίου 2 Cor 3:17b (JHermann, Kyrios und Pneuma, '61). τὸ πν. τοῦ υἱοῦ αὐτοῦ (=θεοῦ) Gal 4:6. As possessor of the divine Spirit, and at the same time controlling its distribution among humans, Christ is called κύριος πνεύματος *Lord of the Spirit* 2 Cor 3:18 (s. Windisch ad loc.); but many prefer to transl. *from the Lord who is the Spirit.*—CMoule, OCullmann Festschr., '72, 231–37.

ⓒ Because of its heavenly origin and nature this Spirit is called *(the) Holy Spirit* (cp. PGM 4, 510 ἵνα πνεύσῃ ἐν ἐμοὶ τὸ ἱερὸν πνεῦμα.—Neither Philo nor Josephus called the Spirit πν. ἅγιον; the former used θεῖον or θεοῦ πν., the latter πν. θεῖον: Ant. 4, 118; 8, 408; 10, 239; but ἅγιον πνεῦμα Orig. C. Cels 1, 40, 16).

α. w. the art. τὸ πνεῦμα τὸ ἅγιον (Is 63:10f; Ps 50:13; 142:10 v.l.; cp. Sus 45 Theod.; TestAbr A 4 p. 81, 10 [Stone p. 10]; JosAs 8:11 [codd. ADE]; AscIs 3, 15, 26; Just., D. 36, 6 al.) Mt 12:32 = Mk 3:29 = Lk 12:10 (τὸ ἅγιον πνεῦμα; on the 'sin against the Holy Spirit' s. HLeisegang, Pneuma Hagion 1922, 96–112; AFridrichsen, Le péché contre le Saint-Esprit: RHPR 3, 1923, 367–72). Mk 12:36; 13:11; Lk 2:26; 3:22; 10:21; J 14:26; Ac 1:16; 2:33; 5:3, 32; 7:51; 8:18 v.l.; 10:44, 47; 11:15; 13:2; 15:8, 28; 19:6; 20:23, 28; 21:11; 28:25; Eph 1:13 (τὸ πν. τῆς ἐπαγγελίας τὸ ἅγιον); 4:30 (τὸ πν. τὸ ἅγιον τοῦ θεοῦ); Hb 3:7; 9:8; 10:15; 1 Cl 13:1; 16:2; 18:11 (Ps 50:13); 22:1; IEph 9:1; Hs 5, 5, 2; 5, 6, 5–7 (on the relationship of the Holy Spirit to the Son in Hermas s. ALink, Christi Person u. Werk im Hirten des Hermas 1886; JvWalter, ZNW 14, 1913, 133–44; MDibelius, Hdb. exc. following Hs 5, 6, 8 p. 572–76).—τὸ ἅγιον πνεῦμα (Wsd 9:17; OdeSol 11:2; TestJob 51:2; ApcEsdr 7:16; Just. D. 25, 1 al.) Mt 28:19; Lk 12:10 (s. above), 12; Ac 1:8; 2:38 (epexegetic gen.); 4:31; 9:31; 10:45; 13:4; 16:6; 1 Cor 6:19; 2 Cor 13:13; 1J 5:7 v.l. (on the Comma Johanneum s. λόγος 3); GJs 24:4 (s. χρηματίζω 1bα). As the mother of Jesus GHb 20, 61 (HLeisegang, Pneuma Hagion 1922, 64ff; SHirsch, D. Vorstellg. v. e. weibl. πνεῦμα ἅγ. im NT u. in d. ältesten christl. Lit. 1927. Also WBousset, Hauptprobleme der Gnosis 1907, 9ff).

β. without the art. (s. B-D-F §257, 2; Rob. 761; 795) πνεῦμα ἅγιον (PGM 3, 289; Da 5:12 LXX; PsSol 17:37; AssMos fgm. b; Just., D. 4, 1 al.; Ath. 24, 1. S. also Da Theod. 4:8, 9, 18 θεοῦ πνεῦμα ἅγιον or πνεῦμα θεοῦ ἅγιον) Mk 1:8; Lk 1:15, 35, 41, 67; 2:25; 4:1; 11:13; J 20:22 (Cassien, La pentecôte johannique [J 20:19–23] '39.—See also 1QS 4:20f); Ac 2:4a; 4:8; 7:55; 8:15, 17, 19; 9:17; 10:38; 11:24; 13:9; 19:2ab; Hb 2:4; 6:4; 1 Pt 1:12 v.l.; 1 Cl 2:2; AcPl 6:18; 9:4 (restored after Aa I 110, 11); AcPlCor 2:5.—So oft. in combination w. a prep.: διὰ πνεύματος ἁγίου Ac 1:2; 4:25; Ro 5:5; 2 Ti 1:14; 1 Cl 8:1 (cp. διὰ πν. αἰωνίου Hb 9:14). διὰ φωνῆς πν. ἁγίου AcPl Ha 11, 6. ἐκ πνεύματος ἁγίου (Eus., PE 3, 12, 3 of the Egyptians: ἐκ τ. πνεύματος οἴονται συλλαμβάνειν τὸν γῦπα. Here πνεῦμα= 'wind'; s. Horapollo 1, 11 p. 14f. The same of other birds since Aristot.—On the neut. πνεῦμα as a masc. principle cp. Aristoxenus, fgm. 13 of the two original principles: πατέρα μὲν φῶς, μητέρα δὲ σκότος) Mt 1:18, 20; IEph 18:2; GJs 14:2; 19:1 (pap). ἐν πνεύματι ἁγίῳ (PsSol 17:37; ApcZeph; Ar. 15, 1) Mt 3:11; Mk 1:8 v.l.; Lk 3:16; J 1:33b; Ac 1:5 (cp. 1QS 3:7f); 11:16; Ro 9:1; 14:17; 15:16; 1 Cor 12:3b; 2 Cor 6:6; 1 Th 1:5; 1 Pt 1:12 (without ἐν v.l.); Jd 20. ὑπὸ πνεύματος ἁγίου 2 Pt 1:21. Cp. ἐν δυνάμει πνεύματος ἁγίου Ro 15:13, 19 v.l. (for πνεύματος θεοῦ). μετὰ χαρᾶς πνεύματος ἁγίου 1 Th 1:6. διὰ ἀνακαινώσεως πνεύματος ἁγίου Tit 3:5.

ⓓ abs.—**α.** w. the art. τὸ πνεῦμα. In this connection the art. is perh. used anaphorically at times, w. the second mention of a word (s. B-D-F §252; Rob. 762); perh. **Mt 12:31** (looking back to vs. **28** πν. θεοῦ); **Mk 1:10, 12** (cp. vs. **8** πν. ἅγιον); **Lk 4:1b, 14** (cp. vs. **1a**); **Ac 2:4b** (cp. vs. **4a**).—As a rule it is not possible to assume that anaphora is present: **Mt 4:1; J 1:32, 33a; 3:6a, 8b** (in wordplay), **34; 7:39a; Ac 8:29; 10:19; 11:12, 28; 19:1** D; **20:3** D, **22; 21:4; Ro 8:23** (ἀπαρχή 1bβ; 2), **26a, 27; 12:11; 15:30; 2 Cor 1:22** and **5:5** (KErlemann, ZNW 83, '92, 202–23, and s. ἀρραβών); **12:18** (τῷ αὐτῷ πν.); **Gal 3:2, 5, 14** (ἐπαγγελία 1bβ); **Eph 4:3** (gen. of the author); **6:17** (perh. epexegetic gen.); **1 Ti 4:1a; Js 4:5; 1J 3:24; 5:6ab** (some mss. add καὶ πνεύματος to the words δι' ὕδατος κ. αἵματος at the beg. of the verse; this is approved by HvSoden, Moffatt, Vogels, Merk, and w. reservations by CDodd, The Joh. Epistles '46, TManson, JTS 48, '47, 25–33), vs. **8; Rv 2:7, 11, 17, 29; 3:6, 13, 22; 14:13; 22:17;** B 19:2, 7= D 4:10 (s. ἑτοιμάζω b). ἐν τῷ πνεύματι *(led) by the Spirit* **Lk 2:27.**—Paul links this Spirit of God, known to every Christian, with Christ as liberating agent in contrast to legal constraint ὁ κύριος τὸ πνεῦμα ἐστιν *the Lord means Spirit* **2 Cor 3:17a** (UHolzmeister, 2 Cor 3:17 Dominus autem Spiritus est 1908; JNisius, Zur Erklärung v. 2 Cor 3:16ff: ZKT 40, 1916, 617–75; JKögel, Ὁ κύριος τὸ πνεῦμά ἐστιν: ASchlatter Festschr. 1922, 35–46; C Guignebert, Congr. d'Hist. du Christ. II 1928, 7–22; EFuchs, Christus u. d. Geist b. Pls '32; HHughes, ET 45, '34, 235f; CLattey, Verb. Dom. 20, '40, 187–89; DGriffiths ET 55, '43, 81–83; HIngo, Kyrios und Pneuma, '61 [Paul]; JDunn, JTS 21, '70, 309–20).

β. without the art. πνεῦμα B 1:3. κοινωνία πνεύματος **Phil 2:1** (κοινωνία 1 and 2). πνεύματι *in the Spirit* or *through the Spirit* **Gal 3:3; 5:5, 16, 18; 1 Pt 4:6.** εἰ ζῶμεν πνεύματι, πνεύματι καὶ στοιχῶμεν *if we live by the Spirit, let us also walk by the Spirit* **Gal 5:25.** Freq. used w. a prep.: διὰ πνεύματος **1 Pt 1:22 v.l.** ἐξ (ὕδατος καὶ) πνεύματος **J 3:5.** ἐν πνεύματι *in, by, through the Spirit* **Mt 22:43; Eph 2:22; 3:5; 5:18; 6:18; Col 1:8** (ἀγάπη ἐν πνεύματι *love called forth by the Spirit*); B 9:7. κατὰ πνεῦμα **Ro 8:4f; Gal 4:29.** ἐν ἁγιασμῷ πνεύματος **2 Th 2:13; 1 Pt 1:2** (s. ἁγιασμός).—In neg. expressions: οὔπω ἦν πνεῦμα *the Spirit had not yet come* **J 7:39b.** ψυχικοὶ πνεῦμα μὴ ἔχοντες *worldly people, who do not have the Spirit* **Jd 19.**—ἓν πνεῦμα *one and the same Spirit* **1 Cor 12:13; Eph 2:18; 4:4;** *one (in) Spirit* **1 Cor 6:17.**

ⓔ The Spirit is more closely defined by a gen. of thing: τὸ πν. τῆς ἀληθείας (TestJud 20:5) **J 14:17; 15:26; 16:13** (in these three places the *Spirit of Truth* is the Paraclete promised by Jesus upon his departure); **1J 4:6** (opp. τὸ πνεῦμα τῆς πλάνης, as TestJud 20:1; PsSol 8:14 πλ. πλανήσεως; Just., D. 7, 3 πλάνου καὶ ἀκαθάρτου πνεύματος; cp. 1QS 4:23); τὸ τῆς δόξης πν. **1 Pt 4:14.** τὸ πν. τῆς ζωῆς *the Spirit of life* **Ro 8:2.** το πν. τῆς πίστεως **2 Cor 4:13.** πν. σοφίας καὶ ἀποκαλύψεως **Eph 1:17** (cp. Just., D. 87, 4). πν. υἱοθεσίας **Ro 8:15b** (opp. πν. δουλείας vs. **15a**). πν. δυνάμεως AcPl Ha 8, 25. πν. δυνάμεως καὶ ἀγάπης καὶ σωφρονισμοῦ **2 Ti 1:7** (opp. πν. δειλίας). τὸ πν. τῆς χάριτος (s. TestJud 24:2) **Hb 10:29** (Zech 12:10); cp. 1 Cl 46:6.

ⓕ Of Christ 'it is written' in Scripture: (ἐγένετο) ὁ ἔσχατος Ἀδὰμ εἰς πνεῦμα ζῳοποιοῦν **1 Cor 15:45.** The scripture pass. upon which the first part of this verse is based is Gen 2:7, where Wsd 15:11 also substitutes the words πνεῦμα ζωτικόν for πνοὴν ζωῆς (cp. Just., D. 6, 2). On the other hand, s. Philo, Leg. All. 1, 42 and s. the lit. s.v. Ἀδάμ ad loc.

ⓖ The (divine) Pneuma stands in contrast to everything that characterizes this age or the finite world gener.: οὐ τὸ πν. τοῦ κόσμου ἀλλὰ τὸ πν. τὸ ἐκ τοῦ θεοῦ **1 Cor 2:12;** cp. **Eph 2:2** and **1 Ti 4:1ab.**

α. in contrast to σάρξ, which is more closely connected w. sin than any other earthly material (Just., D. 135, 6): **J 3:6; Ro 8:4–6, 9a, 13; Gal 3:3; 5:17ab; 6:8.** Cp. B 10:9. πᾶσα ἐπιθυμία κατὰ τοῦ πνεύματος στρατεύεται Pol 5:3.

β. in contrast to σῶμα (=σάρξ) **Ro 8:10** and to σάρξ (=σῶμα, as many hold) **J 6:63a** (for τὸ πν. ἐστιν τὸ ζῳοποιοῦν cp. Philo, Op. Mund. 30; Herm. Wr. in Cyrill., C. Jul. I 556c=542, 24 Sc. the pneuma τὰ πάντα ζῳοποιεῖ καὶ τρέφει. S. also f above). Cp. **Ro 8:11b.**

γ. in contrast to γράμμα, which is the characteristic quality of God's older declaration of the divine will in the law: **Ro 2:29; 7:6; 2 Cor 3:6ab, 8** (cp. vs. 7).

δ. in contrast to the wisdom of humans **1 Cor 2:13.**

❻ the Spirit of God as exhibited in the character or activity of God's people or selected agents, ***Spirit, spirit*** (s. HPreisker, Geist u. Leben '33).

ⓐ πνεῦμα is accompanied by another noun, which characterizes the working of the Spirit more definitely: πνεῦμα καὶ δύναμις *spirit and power* **Lk 1:17; 1 Cor 2:4.** Cp. **Ac 10:38; 1 Th 1:5.** πνεῦμα καὶ ζωή **J 6:63b.** πνεῦμα κ. σοφία **Ac 6:3;** cp. vs. **10** (cp. TestReub 2:6 πνεῦμα λαλίας). πίστις κ. πνεῦμα ἅγιον **6:5** (cp. Just., D. 135, 6). χαρὰ καὶ πνεῦμα ἅγ. **13:52.**

ⓑ Unless frustrated by humans in their natural condition, the Spirit of God produces a spiritual type of conduct **Gal 5:16, 25** and produces the καρπὸς τοῦ πνεύματος vs. **22** (s. Vögtle under πλεονεξία).

ⓒ The Spirit inspires certain people of God B 12:2; 13:5, above all, in their capacity as proclaimers of a divine revelation (Strabo 9, 3, 5 the πνεῦμα ἐνθουσιαστικόν, that inspired the Pythia; Περὶ ὕψους 13, 2; 33, 5 of the divine πν. that impels prophets and poets to express themselves; schol. on Pla. 856e of a μάντις: ἄνωθεν λαμβάνειν τὸ πνεῦμα καὶ πληροῦσθαι τοῦ θεοῦ; Aristobulus in Eus., PE 8, 10, 4 [=fgm. 2, 4 p. 136 Holladay] τὸ θεῖον πν., καθ' ὃ καὶ προφήτης ἀνακεκήρυκται '[Moses possessed] the Divine Spirit with the result that he was proclaimed a prophet'; AscIs 1:7 τὸ πν. τὸ λαλοῦν ἐν ἐμοί; AssMos fgm. f εἶδεν πνεύματι ἐπαρθείς; Just., A I, 38, 1 al.; Ath. 10, 3 τὸ προφητικὸν πν. Cp. Marinus, Vi. Procli 23 of Proclus: οὐ γὰρ ἄνευ θείας ἐπινοίας ... διαλέγεσθαι; Orig., C. Cels. 3, 28, 23). προφητεία came into being only as ὑπὸ πνεύματος ἁγίου φερόμενοι ἐλάλησαν ἀπὸ θεοῦ ἄνθρωποι **2 Pt 1:21;** cp. **Ac 15:29 v.l.;** cp. 1 Cl 8:1. David **Mt 22:43; Mk 12:36;** cp. **Ac 1:16; 4:25.** Isaiah **Ac 28:25.** Moses B 10:2, 9; the Spirit was also active in giving the tables of the law to Moses 14:2. Christ himself spoke in the OT διὰ τοῦ πνεύματος τοῦ ἁγίου 1 Cl 22:1. The ἱεραὶ γραφαί are called αἱ διὰ τοῦ πν. τοῦ ἁγίου 45:2.—The Christian prophet Agabus also ἐσήμαινεν διὰ τοῦ πν. **Ac 11:28;** cp. **Ac 21:11.** Likew. Ign. IPhld 7:2. In general *the Spirit* reveals the most profound secrets to those who believe **1 Cor 2:10ab.**—1 Cl claims to be written διὰ τοῦ ἁγ. πν. 63:2. On **Ac 19:21** s. 3b.

ⓓ The Spirit of God, being one, shows the variety and richness of its life in the different kinds of spiritual gifts which are granted to certain Christians **1 Cor 12:4, 7, 11;** cp. vs. **13ab.**—Vss. **8–10** enumerate the individual *gifts of the Spirit,* using various prepositions: διὰ τοῦ πν. vs. **8a;** κατὰ τὸ πν. vs. **8b;** ἐν τῷ πν. vs. **9ab.** τὸ πν. μὴ σβέννυτε *do not quench the Spirit* **1 Th 5:19** refers to the gift of prophecy, acc. to vs. 20.—The use of the pl. πνεύματα is explained in **1 Cor 14:12** by the varied nature of the Spirit's working; in vs. **32** by the number of persons who possess the prophetic spirit; on the latter s. **Rv 22:6** and **19:10.**

ⓔ One special type of spiritual gift is represented by ecstatic speaking. Of those who 'speak in tongues' that no earthly person can understand: πνεύματι λαλεῖ μυστήρια *expresses secret things in a spiritual way* **1 Cor 14:2.** Cp. vss. **14–16** and s. νοῦς 1b. τὸ πνεῦμα ὑπερεντυγχάνει στεναγμοῖς ἀλαλήτοις *the Spirit pleads in our behalf with groans beyond words* **Ro 8:26b.** Of speech that is ecstatic, but expressed in words that can be understood λαλεῖν ἐν πνεύματι D 11:7, 8; cp. vs. 9 (on the subject-matter **1 Cor 12:3;** Jos., Ant. 4, 118f; TestJob 43:2 ἀναλαβὼν Ἐλιφᾶς πν. εἶπεν ὕμνον). Of the state of mind of the seer of the Apocalypse: ἐν πνεύματι **Rv 17:3; 21:10;** γενέσθαι ἐν πν. **1:10; 4:2** (s. γίνομαι 5c, ἐν 4c and EMoering, StKr 92, 1920, 148–54; RJeske, NTS 31, '85, 452–66); AcPl Ha 6, 27. On the Spirit at Pentecost **Ac 2:4** s. KLake: Beginn. I 5, '33, 111–21. κατασταλέντος τοῦ πν. τοῦ ἐν Μύρτῃ *when the Spirit (of prophecy) that was in Myrta ceased speaking* AcPl Ha 7, 9.

ⓕ The Spirit leads and directs Christian missionaries in their journeys (Aelian, NA 11, 16 the young women are led blindfolded to the cave of the holy serpent; they are guided by a πνεῦμα θεῖον) **Ac 16:6, 7** (by dreams, among other methods; cp. vs. 9f and s. Marinus, Vi. Procli 27: Proclus ἔφασκεν προθυμηθῆναι μὲν πολλάκις γράψαι, κωλυθῆναι δὲ ἐναργῶς ἔκ τινων ἐνυπνίων). In **Ac 16:6–7** τὸ ἅγιον πν. and τὸ πν. Ἰησοῦ are distinguished.

❼ **an activating spirit that is not fr. God,** ***spirit:*** πν. ἕτερον *a different* (kind of) *spirit* **2 Cor 11:4.** Cp. **2 Th 2:2; 1J 4:1–3.** Because there are persons activated by such spirits, it is necessary to test the var. kinds of *spirits* (the same problem Artem. 3, 20 περὶ διαφορᾶς μάντεων, οἷς δεῖ προσέχειν καὶ οἷς μή) **1 Cor 12:10; 1J 4:1b.** ὁ διάβολος πληροῖ αὐτὸν αὐτοῦ πν. Hm 11:3. Also οὐκ οἴδατε ποίου πνεύματός ἐστε **Lk 9:55 v.l.** distinguishes betw. the spirit shown by Jesus' disciples, and another kind of spirit.—Even more rarely a spirit divinely given that is not God's own; so (in a quot. fr. Is 29:10) a πνεῦμα κατανύξεως **Ro 11:8.**

❽ **an independent transcendent personality,** ***the Spirit,*** which appears in formulas that became more and more fixed and distinct (cp. Ath. 12, 2; Hippol., Ref. 7, 26, 2.—Ps.-Lucian, Philopatr. 12 θεόν, υἱόν πατρός, πνεῦμα ἐκ πατρὸς ἐκπορευόμενον ἓν ἐκ τριῶν καὶ ἐξ ἑνὸς τρία, ταῦτα νόμιζε Ζῆνα, τόνδ' ἡγοῦ θεόν='God, son of the father, spirit proceeding from the father, one from three and three from one, consider these as Zeus, think of this one as God'. The entire context bears a Christian impress.—As Aion in gnostic speculation Iren. 1, 2, 5 [Harv. I 21, 2]): βαπτίζοντες αὐτοὺς εἰς τὸ ὄνομα τοῦ πατρὸς καὶ τοῦ υἱοῦ καὶ τοῦ ἁγίου πνεύματος **Mt 28:19** (on the text s. βαπτίζω 2c; on the subject-matter GWalther, Die Entstehung des Taufsymbols aus dem Taufritus: StKr 95, 1924, 256ff); D 7:1, 3. Cp. **2 Cor 13:13;** 1 Cl 58:2; IEph 9:1; IMg 13:1b, 2; MPol 14:3; 22:1, 3; EpilMosq 5. On this s. HUsener, Dreiheit: RhM 58, 1903, 1ff; 161ff; 321ff; esp. 36ff; EvDobschütz, Zwei- u. dreigliedrige Formeln: JBL 50, '31, 116–47 (also Heinrici Festschr. 1914, 92–100); Norden, Agn. Th. 228ff; JMainz, Die Bed. der Dreizahl im Judentum 1922; Clemen[2] 125–28; NSöderblom, Vater, Sohn u. Geist 1909; DNielsen, Der dreieinige Gott I 1922; GKrüger, Das Dogma v. der Dreieinigkeit 1905, 46ff; AHarnack, Entstehung u. Entwicklung der Kirchenverfassung 1910, 187ff; JHaussleiter, Trinitarischer Glaube u. Christusbekenntnis in der alten Kirche: BFCT XXV 4, 1920; JLebreton, Histoire du dogme de la Trinité I: Les origines[6] 1927; RBlümel, Pls u. d. dreieinige Gott 1929.—On the whole word FRüsche, D. Seelenpneuma '33; HLeisegang, Der Hl. Geist I 1, 1919; EBurton, ICC Gal 1921, 486–95; PVolz, Der Geist Gottes u. d. verwandten Erscheinungen im AT 1910; JHehn, Zum Problem des Geistes im alten Orient u. im AT: ZAW n.s. 2, 1925, 210–25; SLinder, Studier till Gamla Testamentets föreställningar om anden 1926; AMarmorstein, Der Hl. Geist in der rabb. Legende: ARW 28, 1930, 286–303; NSnaith, The Distinctive Ideas of the OT '46, 229–37; FDillistone, Bibl. Doctrine of the Holy Spirit: Theology Today 3, '46/47, 486–97; TNicklin, Gospel Gleanings '50, 341–46; ESchweizer, CDodd Festschr., '56, 482–508; DLys, Rûach, Le Souffle dans l'AT, '62; DHill, Gk. Words and Hebr. Mngs. '67, 202–93.—HGunkel, Die Wirkungen des Hl. Geistes[2] 1899; HWeinel, Die Wirkungen des Geistes u. der Geister im nachap. Zeitalter 1899; EWinstanley, The Spirit in the NT 1908; HSwete, The Holy Spirit in the NT 1909, The Holy Spirit in the Ancient Church 1912; EScott, The Spirit in the NT 1923; FBüchsel, Der Geist Gottes im NT 1926; EvDobschütz, Der Geistbesitz des Christen im Urchristentum: Monatsschr. für Pastoral-theol. 20, 1924, 228ff; FBadcock, 'The Spirit' and Spirit in the NT: ET 45, '34, 218–21; RBultmann, Theologie des NT '48, 151–62 (Eng. tr. KGrobel, '51, I 153–64); ESchweizer, Geist u. Gemeinde im NT '52, Int 6, '52, 259–78.—WTosetti, Der Hl. Geist als göttliche Pers. in den Evangelien 1918; HLeisegang, Pneuma Hagion. Der Ursprung des Geistbegriffs der syn. Ev. aus der griech. Mystik 1922; AFrövig, Das Sendungsbewusstsein Jesu u. der Geist 1924; HWindisch, Jes. u. d. Geist nach syn. Überl.: Studies in Early Christianity, presented to FCPorter and BWBacon 1928, 209–36; FSynge, The Holy Spirit in the Gospels and Acts: CQR 120, '35, 205–17; CBarrett, The Holy Spirit and the Gospel Trad. '47.—ESokolowski, Die Begriffe Geist u. Leben bei Pls 1903; KDeissner, Auferstehungshoffnung u. Pneumagedanke bei Pls 1912; GVos, The Eschatological Aspect of the Pauline Conception of the Spirit: Bibl. and Theol. Studies by the Faculty of Princeton Theol. Sem. 1912, 209–59; HBertrams, Das Wesen des Geistes nach d. Anschauung des Ap. Pls 1913; WReinhard, Das Wirken des Hl. Geistes im Menschen nach den Briefen des Ap. Pls 1918; HHoyle, The Holy Spirit in St. Paul 1928; PGächter, Z. Pneumabegriff des hl. Pls: ZKT 53, 1929, 345–408; ASchweitzer, D. Mystik des Ap. Pls 1930, 159–74 al. [Mysticism of Paul the Apostle, tr. WMontgomery '31, 160–76 al.]; E-BAllo, RB 43, '34, 321–46 [1 Cor]; Ltzm., Hdb. exc. after Ro 8:11; Synge [s. above], CQR 119, '35, 79–93 [Pauline epp.]; NWaaning, Onderzoek naar het gebruik van πνεῦμα bij Pls, diss. Amsterd. '39; RJewett, Paul's Anthropological Terms, '71, 167–200.—HvBaer, Der Hl. Geist in den Lukasschriften 1926; MGoguel, La Notion joh. de l'Esprit 1902; JSimpson, The Holy Spirit in the Fourth Gospel: Exp., 9th ser., 4, 1925, 292–99; HWindisch, Jes. u. d. Geist im J.: Amicitiae Corolla (RHarris Festschr.) '33, 303–18; WLofthouse, The Holy Spirit in Ac and J: ET 52, '40/41, 334–36; CBarrett, The Holy Spirit in the Fourth Gospel: JTS 1 n.s., '50, 1–15; FCrump, Pneuma in the Gospels, diss. Catholic Univ. of America, '54; GLampe, Studies in the Gospels (RHLightfoot memorial vol.) '55, 159–200; NHamilton, The Holy Spirit and Eschatology in Paul, '57; WDavies, Paul and the Dead Sea Scrolls, Flesh and Spirit: The Scrolls and the NT, ed. KStendahl, '57, 157–82.—GJohnston, 'Spirit' and 'Holy Spirit' in the Qumran Lit.: NT Sidelights (ACPurdy Festschr.) '60, 27–42; JPryke, 'Spirit' and 'Flesh' in Qumran and NT, RevQ 5, '65, 346–60; HBraun, Qumran und d. NT II, '66, 150–64; DHill, Greek Words and Hebrew Meanings, '67, 202–93; WBieder, Pneumatolog. Aspekte im Hb, OCullmann Festschr. '72, 251–59; KEasley, The Pauline Usage of πνεύματι as a Reference to the Spirit of God: JETS 27, '84, 299–313 (statistics).—B. 260; 1087. Pauly-W. XIV 387–412. BHHW I 534–37. Schmidt, Syn. II 218–50. New Docs 4, 38f. DELG s.v. πνέω. M-M. Dict. de la Bible XI 126–398. EDNT. TW. Sv.

πνευματικός, ή, όν (πνεῦμα; Pre-Socr. et al., mostly in the sense 'pert. to wind or breath'; Strabo 1, 3, 5; Cleom. [II AD] 1, 8 p. 84, 22; Vett. Val. p. 1, 11; 231, 20; PLond I, 46, 25 p. 66 [IV AD?]; PGM 5, 25; GrBar 13:4 [π. πατέρας]; Philo; Just.; Tat. 15, 3) predom. in Paul in our lit. (elsewh. only 1 Pt, 2 Cl, B, Ign., D)

❶ **pert. to spirit as inner life of a human being, *spiritual*** (s. πνεῦμα 3.—Plut., Mor. 129c πν. stands in contrast to σωματικόν; Hierocles 27, 483 τὸ πνευματικὸν τῆς ψυχῆς ὄχημα= the spiritual vehicle of the soul; cp. also Philo, Rer. Div. Her. 242); so perh. ἐπιμελείᾳ σαρκικῇ καὶ πνευματικῇ IPol 1:2 (s. ἐπιμέλεια); cp. 2:2; IMg 13:2; ISm 12:2; 13:2. But mng. 2a is not improb.

❷ In the great majority of cases in ref. to the divine πνεῦμα (s. πνεῦμα 5) **having to do with the (divine) spirit, *caused by* or *filled with the (divine) spirit, pert./corresponding to the (divine) spirit*** (Philo, Abr. 113; PGM 4, 1778; Zosimus [2aγ below, end]).

ⓐ adj.—**α.** of Jesus; in his preexistence 2 Cl 14:2. σαρκικός τε καὶ πνευματικός *of flesh and* (at the same time) *of spirit* IEph 7:2. Of the δεύτερος ἄνθρωπος **1 Cor 15:47** P[46] (s. also the addition ὁ κύριος).

β. as a rule it is used of impersonal things (πλήρωμα Iren. 1, 1, 3 [Harv. I 11, 11]; νόμος Orig., C. Cels. 4, 1, 28; βρῶμα 2, 2, 50; ἀρετή Did., Gen. 236, 6): the law given by God **Ro 7:14.** χάρισμα πν. **1:11.** τῆς δωρεᾶς πνευματικῆς χάριν B 1:2 (s. δωρεά). εὐλογία πν. **Eph 1:3** (s. εὐλογία 3bα). ᾠδαὶ πν. *spiritual songs* **5:19; Col 3:16** (cp. Just., D. 118, 2 πν. αἴνους). σύνεσις πν. *understanding given by the Spirit* **1:9.** Christians are to let themselves be built up into an οἶκος πν. **1 Pt 2:5a** and they are to bring πν. θυσίαι vs. **5b** (ESelwyn, 1 Pt '46, 281–85). Using the same figure, B 16:10 characterizes the believer as πν. ναός. Ign. calls his bonds πν. μαργαρῖται IEph 11:2; *the fellowship* that binds him to the Ephesian bishop is συνήθεια οὐκ ἀνθρωπίνη ἀλλὰ πνευματική 5:1; the presbytery he calls ἀξιόπλοκος πνευματικὸς στέφανος *a worthily woven spiritual wreath* IMg 13:1.—Of the Lord's Supper and its OT counterpart: πνευματικὸν βρῶμα **1 Cor 10:3** and πν. πόμα vs. **4a,** the former in the manna granted fr. heaven (s. βρῶμα 1), the latter in the water ἐκ πν. πέτρας vs. **4b** (s. πέτρα 1a). πνευματικὴ τροφὴ καὶ (sc. πνευματικὸν) ποτόν D 10:3.—That which belongs to the transcendent order of being is described as πν.: accordingly, the resurrection body is a σῶμα πν. (the expr.: Cleopatra p. 24 ln. 24) **1 Cor 15:44a;** cp. vs. **44b.** Of the preexistent church 2 Cl 14:1, 2, 3.

γ. ὁ πνευματικὸς (w. ἄνθρωπος to be supplied) **1 Cor 2:15** stands in contrast to ψυχικὸς ἄνθρωπος of vs. **14.** The latter is a person who has nothing more than an ordinary human soul; the former possesses the divine πνεῦμα, not beside his natural human soul, but in place of it; this enables the person to penetrate the divine mysteries. This treatment of ψυχή and πνεῦμα in contrast to each other is also found in Hellenistic mysticism (s. Rtzst., Mysterienrel.[3] 70f; 325ff; 333ff; JWeiss, exc. on 1 Cor 15:44a. See also Zosimus in CALG pt. 2, 230 οὐ δεῖ τὸν πνευματικὸν ἄνθρωπον τὸν ἐπιγνόντα ἑαυτὸν κτλ.=Hermetica IV p. 105, 25 Sc.; s. also p. 107, 7. Iren. 1, 8, 3 [Harv. I 72, 6].—HMüller, Plotinos u. der Ap. Pls: Her 54, 1919, 109f).

ⓑ subst.—**α.** neut. τὰ πνευματικά *spiritual things* or *matters* (in contrast to τὰ σαρκικά *earthly things*) **Ro 15:27; 1 Cor 9:11;** it is characteristic of adherents to sound tradition, as τὰ σαρκ. is of dissidents IEph 8:2 (s. β below).—τὰ πν. *spiritual gifts* **1 Cor 12:1** (the gen. here may also be masc. *those who possess spiritual gifts*); **14:1.** In πνευματικοῖς πνευματικὰ συγκρίνοντες **1 Cor 2:13** the dat. is either to be taken as a neut. (Lghtf., BWeiss, Bachmann, Ltzm., Rtzst. op. cit. 336, HDWendland) or as a masc. (Schmiedel, Heinrici, JWeiss, Sickenberger); s. συγκρίνω and πνευματικῶς 2.—τὸ πνευματικόν (in contrast to τὸ ψυχικόν [s. 2aγ above]) **1 Cor 15:46.**

β. masc. (ὁ) πνευματικός *possessing the Spirit, the one who possesses the Spirit* (w. προφήτης) **1 Cor 14:37.** (οἱ) πνευματικοί (οὐδεὶς ἢ οἱ πν. μόνοι Hippol., Ref. 5, 9, 6) *(the) spirit-filled people* **3:1** (opp. σάρκινοι and νήπιοι ἐν Χριστῷ); **Gal 6:1;** B 4:11; IEph 8:2 (of adherents to sound tradition in contrast to σαρκικοί, dissidents; s. 2bα above). Perh. also **1 Cor 2:13** and **12:1** (2bα).

❸ *pert. to (evil) spirits* (s. πνεῦμα 4c) subst. τὰ πνευματικὰ τῆς πονηρίας *the spirit-forces of evil* **Eph 6:12.**—DELG s.v. πνέω. M-M. TW. Sv.

πνευματικῶς adv. of πνευματικός (Hermogenes [II AD], Inv. 4, 1 in the sense 'in one breath', s. L-S-J-M).

❶ **pert. to transcendent influence, *spiritually, in a spiritual manner, in a manner caused by or filled with the Spirit*** w. ref. to the inner life of a pers. (s. πνευματικός 1) μένετε ἐν Ἰησοῦ Χριστῷ σαρκικῶς καὶ πνευματικῶς *remain in Jesus Christ both in body and in spirit,* i.e. w. one's whole personality (s. πνεῦμα 3a) IEph 10:3. μετὰ τὴν ἀνάστασιν συνέφαγεν αὐτοῖς ὡς σαρκικὸς καίπερ πνευματικῶς ἡνωμένος τῷ πατρί *after his resurrection he dined with them as though being in the body although united with the Father spiritually* ISm 3:3 marks the transition to

❷ **pert. to being consistent with transcendent influence, *in keeping w. the spirit*** w. ref. to the divine πνεῦμα (s. πνευματικός 2) πνευματικῶς ἀνακρίνεται *it must be examined in a manner consistent with the (divine) Spirit* **1 Cor 2:14.**—Vs. **13** (s. πνευματικός 2bα) has πνευματικῶς as a **v.l.** for πνευματικοῖς. It is said of Paul when he wrote 1 Cor that πνευματικῶς ἐπέστειλεν ὑμῖν *full of the* (divine) *Spirit he wrote to you* 1 Cl 47:3.—This is also the place for ἥτις (i.e. the city of Jerusalem) καλεῖται πνευματικῶς Σόδομα **Rv 11:8:** if one follows the *spiritual* (the opp. is σαρκικῶς Just., D. 14, 2) understanding of scripture (cp. Is 1:9f), Jerusalem lies concealed beneath the name Sodom. Someth. more is involved here than mere allegory or figurative usage.—TW.

πνευματοφόρος, ον (πνεῦμα, φέρω; on similar formations s. Hdb. Ergänzungsband 189–91 on Θεοφόρος; Schwyzer I 438f; for detailed list s. CBuck, Reverse Index '44, 335f) ***bearing the (divine) Spirit*** within oneself, subst. (Herm. Wr. 13, 19) *a bearer of the Spirit,* of Christian prophets Hm 11:16 (adj. of OT prophets Hos 9:7; Zeph 3:4; Leutzsch, Hermas 464 n. 271; s. also Lampe s.v.—Cp. DELG s.v. φέρω D.).

πνέω fut. 3 sg. πνεύσει LXX; 1 aor. ἔπνευσα (Hom. et al.; pap, LXX; En 29:2; TestSol; ApcSed 8:9 p. 133, 14 Ja.; Philo, Joseph.)

❶ **to move as wind with relatively rapid motion, *blow,*** abs. (Hom. et al.; Ptolem., Apotel. 1, 11, 4 οἱ πνέοντες ἄνεμοι; PHib 27, 59; Sir 43:20; EpJer 60; ApcSed 8:9; Jos., Bell. 7, 318, Ant. 7, 76; SibOr 5, 375) **Mt 7:25, 27; Lk 12:55; J 3:8** (Diod. S. 24, 1, 2 πνεύματος πνεύσαντος=when a wind blew); **6:18; Rv 7:1.** τῷ ἀνέμῳ ἐπιδόντες τῷ πνέοντι **Ac 27:15 v.l.**—Subst. ἡ πνέουσα (sc. αὔρα; this word is added by Arrian, Peripl. 3, 2) *the wind that was blowing* (Lucian [ἐπιδίδωμι 2]) **Ac 27:40.**

❷ **to emit an odor, *breathe out,*** abs., ὡς λιβανωτοῦ πνέοντος MPol 15:2.

❸ w. acc. (Hom. et al.; schol. on Nicander, Ther. 308 δυσωδίαν πνεοντες; 2 Macc 9:7; En 29:2) ***breathe someth. out.*** The anointing of Jesus had for its purpose ἵνα πνέῃ τῇ ἐκκλησίᾳ ἀφθαρσίαν *that he might breathe immortality upon* and therefore *into the church* IEph 17:1 (on πνέω τινί τι='instill someth. into someone' cp. Ps.-Clem., Hom. 4, 19).—B. 260, 684. DELG. M-M. TW.

πνίγω impf. ἔπνιγον; 1 aor. ἔπνιξα (trag., Hdt.+; ChronLind B, 111; PTebt 278, 40; 1 Km 16:14f; TestSol; Jos., Bell. 2, 327, Ant. 10, 121).

❶ **to apply pressure around the neck in order to kill,** ***strangle*** (since Sophron Com. [V BC] 68; Pla., Gorg. 522a; cp. Vett. Val. 127, 1; 1 Km 16:14) in dramatic narrative κρατήσας αὐτὸν ἔπνιγεν *he seized him and proceeded to strangle him* (=he grabbed him with a choking grip) **Mt 18:28** (Lucian, Dial. Mort. 22, 2 uses the synonym ἄγχω for the treatment of a debtor).

❷ **to cause someth. to be stifled,** ***choke***—ⓐ Anger chokes out the Holy Spirit within the human personality: τὸ πνεῦμα τὸ ἅγιον . . . πνίγεται ὑπὸ τοῦ πονηροῦ πνεύματος Hm 5, 1, 3 (cp. 1 Km 16:14f).

ⓑ of weeds in relation to good seed *choke* (X., Oec. 17, 14) **Mt 13:7.** ὁ ἀμπελὼν μὴ ἔχων βοτάνας τὰς πνιγούσας αὐτόν *the vineyard without the weeds that were choking it* Hs 5, 2, 4b; cp. ibid. a.

ⓒ pass. *be choked,* intr. *choke* (Themistocl., Ep. 12), *drown* (X., An. 5, 7, 25; Plut., Mor. 599b; Jos., Ant. 10, 121; 20, 248) **Mk 5:13.**

ⓓ fig. (Lysippus Com. [V BC], fgm. 7, 9 [I p. 702 Kock] πνίγομαι ἐπ' αὐτοῖς=I choke with disgust at them) πνίγεσθαι ὑπὸ τῶν πράξεων *be choked by one's work* Hs 9, 20, 2.—DELG. M-M. TW.

πνικτός, ή, όν (πνίγω; in non-biblical Gk. only w. another mng.: Pherecrates Com. [V BC] 175 and Alexis Com. 124, 2='steamed, stewed, baked'; Galen VI p. 707, 1 al. It is restored in an ins fr. the Asclepiaeum on Cos A 26f; 41 by RHerzog: ARW 10, 1907, 402; 408f.—Not in LXX nor in Hellenistic Jewish wr.) in Ac it plainly means ***strangled, choked to death*** (so also Ps.-Clem., Hom. 7, 8; 8, 19) of animals killed without having the blood drained fr. them, whose flesh the Israelites were forbidden to eat (Lev 17:13f. In this connection Philo, Spec. Leg. 4, 122 opposes those who are ἄγχοντες and ἀποπνίγοντες animals.—Hierocles 26, 480 the Pythagorean dietary laws forbid τῶν ἀθύτων σαρκῶν μετάληψις=of meat fr. animals that have not been properly slaughtered) **Ac 15:20, 29; 21:25** (D omits it in all three places).—On the questions raised by this word s. Harnack, SBBerlAk 1899, 150ff (=Studien I 1f) and w. another result in: Die Apostelgeschichte 1908, 189ff and Neue Untersuchungen zur AG 1911, 22ff; GResch, D. Aposteldekret: TU n.s. 13, 1905; ASeeberg, Die beiden Wege u. d. Aposteldekret 1906; HvanOort, TT 40, 1906, 97ff; HCoppieters, RB 4, 1907, 31ff; 218ff; WSanday, The Apostolic Decree, Acts 15:20–29: Theol. Studien, TZahn dargebr. 1908, 317–38, The Text of the Apost. Decr.: Exp. 8th ser., 6, 1913, 289–305; HDiehl, ZNW 10, 1909, 277–96; KLake, CQR 71, 1911, 345ff, Jew. Stud. in Mem. of IAbrahams 1927, 244ff, Beginn. I 5, '33, Note 16, esp. p. 206ff; KSix, Das Aposteldekret 1912; FDibelius, StKr 87, 1914, 618ff; AWikenhauser, Die AG 1921, 213ff; LBrun, Apostelkonzil u. Aposteldekret: NorTT 21, 1920, 1–52; JRopes, The Text of Acts (=Beginn. I 3) 1926, 265ff; HLietzmann, Amicitiae Corolla '33, 203–11; HWaitz, D. Problem des sog. Aposteldekrets: ZKG 55, '36, 227–63; MDibelius, D. Apostelkonzil: TLZ 72, '47, 193–98; OCullmann, Petrus '52, 47ff; WKümmel, KKundsin Festschr. '53, 83ff; EHaenchen ad loc.; FBruce, Ac[3] '90 ad loc.—DELG s.v. πνίγω. M-M. TW.

πνοή, ῆς, ἡ (πνέω)—❶ **relatively rapid movement of air,** ***wind*** (Hom. et al.; Job 37:10; TestSol; GrBar 2:1; ApcEsdr 5:23 p. 30, 26 Tdf. 'blowing of the wind'; SibOr 5, 375 [πνοιή]; Ar. 5, 4f [ἀνέμων]) πν. βιαία *a strong wind* **Ac 2:2.**

❷ **the process of breathing,** ***breath*** (trag. et al.; LXX; TestReub 2:5; JosAs [also of things: aroma 15:14 οἴνου; 16:4 κηρίου μέλιτος]; GrBar 8:7) with ζωή (cp. Gen 2:7; 7:22; Philo, Spec. Leg. 4, 123 πνοὴ ζωῆς and Pr 24:12 ὁ πλάσας πνοὴν πᾶσιν) **Ac 17:25** (s. TMitchell, The OT Usage of N[e]Sama, VT 11, '61, 177–87). Abstr. for concr. πᾶσα πν. *everything that breathes* (Ps 150:6; TestAbr A 13 p. 92, 17 [Stone p. 32]; GrBar 8:7) Pol 2:1. It passes over to the mng. of πνεῦμα (PGM 12, 331; 333; Ath. 7, 1) of God's πνοή 1 Cl 21:9 (Knopf, Hdb. ad loc.); 57:3 (Pr 1:23).—B. 260. DELG s.v. πνέω. M-M. TW.

ποδαπός s. ποταπός.

ποδήρης, ες (πούς + -ήρης 'fit') ***reaching to the feet*** (Aeschyl. et al.; LXX; EpArist 96; Philo, Fuga 185) subst. ὁ ποδ. (sc. χιτών; used w. χιτών X., Cyr. 6, 4, 2; Paus. 5, 19, 6; Ex 29:5; Jos., Ant. 3, 153. Without χιτ. Appian, Liby. 66 §296; Ex 25:7; 28:4; Ezk 9:3; EpArist 96; Philo, Leg. All. 2, 56; Jos., Bell. 5, 231; TestLevi 8:2) *a robe reaching to the feet* **Rv 1:13;** B 7:9.—DELG s.v. πούς and -ηρης. M-M.

ποδονιπτήρ, ῆρος, ὁ (Stesichorus 10D [188 Page] in Athen. 10, 451d; Plut., Mor. 151e; Phryn. 689 Lob.) ***basin for washing feet*** **J 13:5** P[66]. More commonly found in the spelling ποδανιπτήρ (Hdt. 2, 172; Aristot., Pol. 1, 12 al.; GDI 3340, 33 [Argolis]; SIG 1169, 33 [III BC]).—DELG s.v. νίζω.

πόθεν interrog. adv. (Hom.+) in direct and indir. questions: 'from where, from which, whence'.

❶ **interrogative expression of extension from a local source,** ***from what place? from where?*** (Hom. et al.; Gen 16:8; 29:4; Tob 7:3; Jos., Ant. 9, 211; 11, 210) **Mt 15:33; Mk 8:4** (QQuesnell, The Mind of Mark '69, 164–68); **Lk 13:25, 27** (2 Cl 4:5); **J 3:8** and sim. IPhld 7:1 (s. EvdGoltz, Ign. v. Ant. 1894, 134–36); **J 4:11;** perh. **6:5,** but s. 3 below; **8:14ab** (πόθεν ἦλθον καὶ ποῦ ὑπάγω. See GWetter, Eine gnost. Formel im vierten Ev.: ZNW 18, 1918, 49–63); **9:29f; 19:9; Rv 7:13.** πόθεν αὕτη εἴη ἡ φωνή *whence this voice might have come* GJs 11:1.—In imagery μνημόνευε πόθεν πέπτωκες *remember from what* (state) *you have fallen* **Rv 2:5.** γινώσκομεν πόθεν ἐλυτρώθημεν *we realize from what* (state) *we have been redeemed* B 14:7. πόθεν ἐκλήθημεν 2 Cl 1:2.

❷ **interrogative expression of derivation fr. a source,** ***from what source? brought about*** or ***given by whom? born of whom?*** (Hom. et al.; Jos., Vi. 334; Just., A I, 29, 4) **Mt 13:27, 54, 56; 21:25; Mk 6:2; Lk 20:7; J 2:9; Js 4:1ab;** B 10:12; IEph 19:2; GJs 13:3. πόθεν ἐστίν **J 7:27ab** could be interpreted in accordance w. **6:42,** and then would mean *of what kind of parents he was born.* But a more general sense is also prob.

❸ **interrogative expression of cause or reason,** ***how, why, in what way?*** (Aeschyl. et al.) **Mk 12:37.** In a question expressing surprise (Att.; Jer 15:18) **Lk 1:43;** GJs 12:2 (πόθεν ἐμοί Plut., Mor. 526f); **J 1:48; 6:5** (Field, Notes 91 'with what', s. 1). [π]ό̣θε̣[ν] ἔχαιτε (=ἔχετε) [τὸν βασιλέα τοῦτον, ὅτι αὐτῷ πιστεύ]ετε *whence do you have this king, so that you believe in him* (=whence does your king come, to invite such commitment from you) AcPl Ha 9, 30f.—DELG s.v. πο-. Frisk. M-M.

ποθέω (cognate w. θέσσασθαι 'pray for', s. Boisacq 342, 799; Schwyzer I 719) 1 aor. ἐπόθησα (s. two next entries; Hom. et al.; LXX; TestSol 1:3 L; Test12Patr, Philo, Jos., Just., Mel.) **to have a strong desire for,** ***desire, wish (for), be anxious, strive after*** τὶ *someth.* (Pr 7:15; TestIss 2:5; SibOr 5, 420; Philo, De Jos. 90 ἀλήθειαν; Jos., Ant. 2, 65; Just., A I, 5, 4; Mel., P. 38, 261) D 4:3 (codd. and Lake; Bihlmeyer and many edd. ποιήσεις, cp. B 19:12); Dg 10:1. Foll. by the aor. inf. (Philo, Fuga 8 μαθεῖν; Jos., Vi. 204; Just., D. 2, 3) B 16:10; Dg 3:1. τὰ παρὰ θεῷ ποθούμενα *what is desirable in the sight of God* 12:8.—DELG.

ποθητός, ή, όν (on the formation s. ποθέω, cp. Hom. ποθή; Aelian, NA 7, 3; Alciphron 3, 39, 2; IG VII 3434; Ramsay, Phrygia I/2 p. 386 ln. 3 τέκνα π.; Just., D. 57, 4; Mel., P. 26, 186) ***longed-for, dearly beloved*** IRo 10:1; ISm 13:2; IPol 8:3.—DELG s.v. ποθέω.

πόθος, ου, ὁ (on the formation s. ποθέω; Hom.+; TestDan 4:5; TestJos 14:4; ApcEsdr 7:16 p. 33, 4 Tdf.; Philo; Jos., Ant. 12, 242; 15, 18; Mel., HE 4, 26, 13) **a deeply felt interest in someth.,** ***longing, wish, desire*** ἀκόρεστος π. εἰς ἀγαθοποιίαν *an insatiable longing to do good* 1 Cl 2:2 (π. εἰς as Ps 9:24 Aq.; SibOr 2, 112).—Schmidt, Syn. III 596–601, ἐπιθυμία. DELG s.v. ποθέω. Sv.

ποῖ interrog. adv. (Theognis et al.; Celsus 6, 11; Jos., Ant. 1, 197; 16, 373) ***where? whither?*** 1 Cl 28:4.—DELG s.v. πο-.

ποία, ας, ἡ (Doric form, quotable since Pind., also SIG 1169, 121 [III BC]; Mal 3:2 v.l.; Jer 2:22 v.l. for Att. πόα, Ion. and epic ποίη. See Lob., Phryn. 496) ***grass, herb, weed;*** this mng. was formerly assumed at times for **Js 4:14** (Exp. 7th ser., 10, 566); but ποία in that pass. is better taken as the fem. of ποῖος (1aγ).—DELG s.v. πόα. M-M.

ποιέω (Hom.+) impf. ἐποίουν; fut. ποιήσω; 1 aor. ἐποίησα; pf. πεποίηκα; plpf. πεποιήκειν **Mk 15:7** (as IMagnMai 93b, 24; on the omission of the augment s. B-D-F §66, 1; Mlt-H. 190). Mid.: impf. ἐποιούμην; 1 aor. ἐποιησάμην; pf. πεποίημαι 1 Cl 1:1. Pass. (has disappeared almost entirely; B-D-F §315): 1 fut. ποιηθήσομαι; 1 aor. 3 pl. ἐποιήθησαν (En 22:9); pf. 3 sg. πεποίηται (Ec 8:14; Tat. 11, 2), ptc. πεποιημένος (Ec 1:14 al.) **Hb 12:27.** A multivalent term, often without pointed semantic significance, used in ref. to a broad range of activity involving such matters as bringing someth. into being, bringing someth. to pass, or simply interacting in some way with a variety of entities.

❶ **to produce someth. material,** ***make, manufacture, produce*** τὶ *someth.* (Gen 6:14ff; 33:17 al.; JosAs 16:8; GrBar 3:5 'build'; ApcMos 20; Mel., P. 38, 261).

ⓐ of human activity: σκεῦος 2 Cl 8:2. χιτῶνας, ἱμάτια **Ac 9:39.** εἰκόνα **Rv 13:14b.** θεούς *make gods* **Ac 7:40** (Ex 32:1). ναοὺς ἀργυροῦς **19:24.** ἀνθρακιάν **J 18:18.** τέσσαρα μέρη **19:23** (s. μέρος 1a). πηλόν **9:11, 14.** σκηνὰς *pitch tents, build huts* (1 Ch 15:1; 2 Esdr 18: 16f; Jdth 8:5; Jos., Ant. 3, 79; Just., D. 127, 3 σκηνήν) **Mt 17:4; Mk 9:5; Lk 9:33.** ἁγίασμα GJs 6:1; καταπέτασμα τῷ ναῷ 10:1; τὴν πορφύραν καὶ τὸ κόκκινον 12:1.—Used w. prepositional expressions ποιῆσαι αὐτὴν (i.e. τὴν σκηνὴν τοῦ μαρτυρίου) κατὰ τὸν τύπον *to make it* (the tent of testimony) *according to the model* (Ex 25:40) **Ac 7:44;** cp. **Hb 8:5.** ποιεῖν τι ἔκ τινος *make someth. from* or *out of someth.* (i.e. fr. a certain material; Hdt. 2, 96; cp. X., An. 4, 5, 14; Theophr., HP 4, 2, 5; Ex 20:24f; 28:15; 29:2) **J 2:15; 9:6; Ro 9:21.**

ⓑ of divine activity, specifically of God's creative activity *create* (Hes., Op. 109; Heraclitus, fgm. 30 κόσμον οὔτε τις θεῶν οὔτε ἀνθρώπων ἐποίησεν, ἀλλ᾽ ἦν ἀεὶ καὶ ἔστιν καὶ ἔσται; Pla., Tim. 76c ὁ ποιῶν 'the Creator'; Epict. 1, 6, 5; 1, 14, 10; 2, 8, 19 σε ὁ Ζεὺς πεποίηκε; 4, 1, 102; 107; 4, 7, 6 ὁ θεὸς πάντα πεποίηκεν; Ael. Aristid. 43, 7 K.=1 p. 2 D.: Ζεὺς τὰ πάντα ἐποίησεν; Herm. Wr. 4, 1. In LXX oft. for בָּרָא also Wsd 1:13; 9:9; Sir 7:30; 32:13; Tob 8:6; Jdth 8:14; Bar 3:35; 4:7; 2 Macc 7:28; Aristobulus in Eus., PE13, 12, 12 [pp. 182 and 184 Holladay]; JosAs 9:5; Philo, Sacr. Abel. 65 and oft.; SibOr 3, 28 and fgm. 3, 3; 16; Just., A II, 5, 2 al.) w. acc. ἡ χείρ μου ἐποίησεν ταῦτα πάντα **Ac 7:50** (Is 66:2). τοὺς αἰῶνας **Hb 1:2** (s. αἰών 3). τὸν κόσμον (Epict. 4, 7, 6 ὁ θεὸς πάντα πεποίηκεν τὰ ἐν τῷ κόσμῳ καὶ αὐτὸν τὸν κόσμον ὅλον; Sallust. 5 p. 10, 29; Wsd 9:9; TestAbr A 10 p. 88, 21 [Stone p. 24]) **Ac 17:24.** τὸν οὐρανὸν καὶ τὴν γῆν (cp. Ael. Aristid. above; Gen 1:1; Ex 20:11; Ps 120:2; 145:6; Is 37:16; Jer 39:17 et al.; TestJob 2:4; Jos., C. Ap. 2, 121; Aristobulus above) **Ac 4:24; 14:15b;** cp. **Rv 14:7.** τὰ πάντα PtK 2 p. 13, 26 (JosAs 12, 2; Just., D. 55, 2; also s. Ael. Aristid. above). **Lk 11:40** is classed here by many. Of the relation of Jesus to God Ἰησοῦν, πιστὸν ὄντα τῷ ποιήσαντι αὐτόν=*appointed him* **Hb 3:2** (cp. Is 17:7).—W. a second acc., that of the predicate (PSI 435, 19 [258 BC] ὅπως ἂν ὁ Σάραπις πολλῷ σὲ μείζω ποιήσῃ) ἄρσεν καὶ θῆλυ ἐποίησεν αὐτούς *(God) created them male and female* **Mt 19:4b; Mk 10:6** (both Gen 1:27c).—Pass. **Hb 12:27.**—ὁ ποιήσας *the Creator* **Mt 19:4a v.l.**

❷ **to undertake or do someth. that brings about an event, state, or condition,** ***do, cause, bring about, accomplish, prepare,*** etc.

ⓐ ἔργα π. *do deeds,* also in sg. (as JosAs 29:3 μὴ ποιήσῃς τὸ ἔργον τοῦτο) τὰ ἔργα τοῦ Ἀβραὰμ π. *do as Abraham did* **J 8:39.** τὰ ἔργα τοῦ πατρὸς ὑμῶν vs. **41;** cp. **10:37.** τὰ πρῶτα ἔργα **Rv 2:5.** ἔργον *commit a deed* **1 Cor 5:2 v.l.** ἔργον ποίησον εὐαγγελιστοῦ **2 Ti 4:5** (s. ἔργον 2).—ἔργον or ἔργα somet. refer to wondrous *deeds:* ἓν ἔργον ἐποίησα *I have done just one* (wondrous) *deed* **J 7:21.** Pl. **14:12a;** cp. vs. **12bc.** This illustrates the transition to

ⓑ *do, perform* miracles δυνάμεις **Mt 7:22; 13:58; Ac 19:11** (Just., A I, 26, 2 al.); sg. **Mk 6:5; 9:39.** θαυμάσια **Mt 21:15** (cp. Sir 31:9). μεγάλα καὶ θαυμάσια AcPl Ha 8, 33=BMM verso 5f (Just., A I, 62, 4). σημεῖα (Ex 4:17) **J 2:23; 3:2; 7:31; 9:16; 11:47b; 20:30; Rv 13:13a; 16:14; 19:20.** Sing. **J 6:30; 10:41.** τέρατα καὶ σημεῖα **Ac 6:8; 7:36.** ὅσα **Mk 3:8; 6:30; Lk 9:10.—Ac 10:39; 14:11.**

ⓒ of conditions *bring about,* etc.: εἰρήνην *make, establish peace* **Eph 2:15; Js 3:18** (cp. 2 Macc 1:4). τὴν ἔκβασιν *provide a way out* **1 Cor 10:13** (on the foll. gen. of the inf. w. the art. s. B-D-F §400, 2; Rob. 1067). ἐπίστασιν ὄχλου *cause a disturbance among the people* **Ac 24:12.** τὰ σκάνδαλα *create difficulties* **Ro 16:17.** On **Mk 6:20 v.l.** KRomaniuk, ETL 69, '93, 140f.—W. dat. of advantage ἐποίουν χαρὰν τοῖς ἀδελφοῖς *they brought joy to the members* **Ac 15:3** (s. ἀδελφός 2a).

ⓓ used w. a noun as a periphrasis for a simple verb of doing (s. 7a below; B-D-F §310, 1.—ποιέω in such combinations as early as IPriene 8, 63 [c. 328 BC], also Plut., Crass. 551 [13, 6]; s. ἑορτή, end). ἐποίησεν ᾆσμα GJs 6:3. διαθήκην π. **Hb 8:9** (Jer 38:32 cod. Q; cp. Is 28:15; TestAbr A 8 p. 86, 6 [Stone p. 20] διάταξιν). π. τὴν ἐκδίκησιν **Lk 18:7f;** cp. **Ac 7:24** (s. ἐκδίκησις 1). ἐνέδραν **25:3.** κοπετόν **8:2.** κρίσιν (s. κρίσις 1aα and β) **J 5:27; Jd 15.** θρῆνον GJs 3:1. κυνηγίαν AcPl Ha 1, 33. λύτρωσιν **Lk 1:68.** ὁδὸν ποιεῖν (v.l. ὁδοποιεῖν) **Mk 2:23** (ὁδός 2). π. (τὸν) πόλεμον (μετά τινος) *wage war* (on *someone*) **Rv 11:7; 12:17; 13:7** (Da 7:8 LXX; 7:21 Theod.; Gen 14:2). πρόθεσιν **Eph 3:11;** συμβούλιον π. **Mk 3:6 v.l.; 15:1;** συστροφήν **Ac 23:12;** cp. vs. **13.** φόνον **Mk 15:7** (cp. Dt 22:8;

Callinicus, Vi. Hyp. 98, 21 Bonn; TestAbr B 10 p. 115, 4 [Stone p. 78, 4]).—τὸ ἱκανὸν ποιεῖν τινι vs. **15** s. ἱκανός 1.

ⓔ what is done is indicated by the neut. of an adj. or pron.: τὸ ἀγαθὸν π. *do what is good* **Ro 13:3;** τὰ ἀγαθὰ π. **J 5:29;** ἀγαθὸν π. *do good* **Mk 3:4; 1 Pt 3:11** (Ps 33:15). τὸ καλὸν **Ro 7:21; 2 Cor 13:7b; Gal 6:9.** τὰ καλὰ (καὶ εὐάρεστα ἐνώπιον αὐτοῦ) 1 Cl 21:1. καλὸν **Js 4:17.** τὸ κακόν **Ro 13:4.** τὰ κακά **3:8.** κακὸν **2 Cor 13:7a** (κακὸν μηδέν; cp. SIG 1175, 20 κακόν τι ποιῆσαι). κακά **1 Pt 3:12** (Ps 33:17). τὰ ἀρεστὰ αὐτῷ (=τῷ θεῷ) **J 8:29;** cp. **Hb 13:21b; 1J 3:22** (TestAbr A 15 p. 96, 12 [Stone p. 40] πάντα τὰ ἀρεστὰ ἐνώπιον σου ἐποίησεν). πάντα **1 Cor 9:23; 10:31b;** IEph 15:3.—ὅ **Mt 26:13; Mk 14:9; J 13:7, 27a.** τοῦτο **Mt 13:28; Mk 5:32; Lk 5:6; J 14:13, 14 v.l.;** AcPl Ha 9, 27; **Ro 7:15f, 20** (cp. Epict. 2, 26, 4 ὃ θέλει οὐ ποιεῖ καὶ ὃ μὴ θέλει ποιεῖ); **1 Cor 11:24f** (the specific sense 'sacrifice' in this passage is opposed by TAbbott [JBL 9, 1890, 137–52], but favored by FMozley [ET 7, 1896, 370–86], AAndersen [D. Abendmahl in d. ersten zwei Jahrh. 1904], and K Goetz [D. Abendmahlsfrage[2] 1907]). αὐτὸ τοῦτο **Gal 2:10.** ταῦτα **Mt 21:23; 23:23; Gal 5:17; 2 Pt 1:10b.** αὐτά **J 13:17; Ro 1:32; 2:3.** τὸ αὐτό **Mt 5:46, 47b.**—τί ποιήσω; **Mk 10:17;** cp. **J 18:35** (TestAbr A 4 p. 81, 19 [Stone p. 10]; ParJer 6:14 τί ποιήσωμεν; ApcEsdr 7:4 p. 32, 14 Tdf.). τί ἀγαθὸν ποιήσω; **Mt 19:16.** τί κακὸν ἐποίησεν; **Mt 27:23; Lk 23:22; Mk 15:14.** τί περισσὸν ποιεῖτε; **Mt 5:47a.** τί ποιεῖτε τοῦτο; *what is this that you are doing?* or *why are you doing this?* **Mk 11:3** (GrBar 2:2 τί ἐποίησας τοῦτο; s. B-D-F §299, 1; Rob. 736; 738; Rdm.[2] 25f). τί ταῦτα ποιεῖτε; **Ac 14:15a** (as Demosth. 55, 5). τί σὺ ὧδε ποιεῖς; Hv 1, 1, 5. W. ptc. foll. (B-D-F §414, 5; Rob. 1121) τί ποιεῖτε λύοντες; *what are you doing, untying?* **Mk 11:5.** τί ποιεῖτε κλαίοντες; *what are you doing, weeping?* or *what do you mean by weeping?* **Ac 21:13.** τί ποιήσουσιν οἱ βαπτιζόμενοι; *what are they to do, who have themselves baptized?* **1 Cor 15:29.**—A statement of what is to be done follows in an indirect question ὃ ποιεῖς ποίησον *do what you must do* **J 13:27** (as Epict. 3, 21, 24 ποίει ἃ ποιεῖς; 3, 23, 1; 4, 9, 18; TestJob 7:13).

ⓕ of meals or banquets, and of festivities of which a banquet is the principal part *give* ἄριστον **Lk 14:12.** δεῖπνον (q.v. bα) **Mk 6:21; Lk 14:12, 16; J 12:2;** Hs 5, 2, 9. δοχήν (s. δοχή) **Lk 5:29; 14:13;** GJs 6:2. γάμους (s. γάμος 1a) **Mt 22:2** (JosAs 20:6).—*Keep, celebrate* (PFay 117, 12) the Passover (feast) **Mt 26:18; Hb 11:28** (s. πάσχα 3). Also in connection w. τὴν ἑορτὴν ποιῆσαι **Ac 18:21** D the Passover is surely meant. But π. is also used of festivals in general (cp. X., Hell. 4, 5, 2 ποιεῖν Ἴσθμια; 7, 4, 28 τὰ Ὀλύμπια).

ⓖ of the natural processes of growth; in plant life *send out, produce, bear, yield* καρπόν, καρπούς (Aristot., Plant. 1, 4, 819b, 31; 2, 10, 829a, 41; LXX [καρπός 1αα]) **Mt 3:10; 7:17ab, 18, 19; 13:26; Lk 3:9; 6:43ab; 8:8; 13:9; Rv 22:2;** also in imagery **Mt 3:8; 21:43; Lk 3:8.** κλάδους **Mk 4:32.** ἐλαίας **Js 3:12a** (cp. Jos., Ant. 11, 50 ἄμπελοι, αἳ ποιοῦσιν τὸν οἶνον). π. ὕδωρ *produce water* vs. **12b** (but s. ἁλυκός).—Of capital yielding a return ἡ μνᾶ ἐποίησεν πέντε μνᾶς *the mina has made five minas* **Lk 19:18.** Also of a person who operates w. capital *make money* (Ps.-Demosth. 10, 76; Polyb. 2, 62, 12) ἐποίησεν ἄλλα πέντε τάλαντα **Mt 25:16 v.l.**

ⓗ with focus on causality—**α.** The result of the action is indicated by the acc. and inf.; *make (to), cause (someone) to, bring it about that* (Hom. et al.; also ins [SIG IV p. 510a index], pap, LXX; TestJob 3:7; 42:6; ParJer 9:16f; ApcMos 16; Just., A I, 26, 5, D. 69, 6; 114, 1; Ath. 13, 2) ποιεῖ αὐτὴν μοιχευθῆναι **Mt 5:32.** ποιήσω ὑμᾶς γενέσθαι ἁλεεῖς ἀνθρώπων **Mk 1:17.** Cp. **7:37b; Lk 5:34** (*force* someone *to fast*); **J 6:10; Ac 17:26; Rv 13:13b.**—ἵνα takes the place of the inf.: ποιήσω αὐτοὺς ἵνα ἥξουσιν **Rv 3:9;** cp. **13:12b, 16.** ἵνα without acc. (TestAbr B 6 p. 110, 20 [Stone p. 68] ποίησον ἵνα φαγῶμεν) **J 11:37; Col 4:16; Rv 13:15.**—ἡμῖν ὡς πεποιηκόσιν τοῦ περιπατεῖν αὐτόν *us, as though we had caused him to walk* **Ac 3:12** (s. B-D-F §400, 7).

β. w. a double accusative, of the obj. and the pred. (Hom. et al.; LXX; ApcEsdr 4:27 p. 38, 32 Tdf. λίθους ἄρτους ποιήσας; Mel., P. 68, 494 ποιήσας ἡμᾶς ἱεράτευμα καινόν), *make someone* or *someth.* (into) *someth.* W. noun as predicate acc.: ποιήσω ὑμᾶς ἁλιεῖς ἀνθρώπων **Mt 4:19.** ὑμεῖς αὐτὸν (i.e. τὸν οἶκον τοῦ θεοῦ) ποιεῖτε σπήλαιον λῃστῶν **21:13; Mk 11:17; Lk 19:46.** Cp. **Mt 23:15b; J 2:16; 4:46, 54;** cp. **2:11; Ac 2:36; 2 Cor 5:21; Hb 1:7** (Ps 103:4); **Rv 1:6; 3:12** al. ποίησόν με ὡς ἕνα τ. μισθίων σου **Lk 15:19, 21 v.l.** (cp. Gen 45:8; 48:20 and s. B-D-F §453, 4; Rob. 481). If the obj. acc. is missing, it may be supplied fr. the context as self-evident ἁρπάζειν αὐτὸν ἵνα ποιήσωσιν βασιλέα *take him by force, in order to make (him) king* **J 6:15.**—**1 Cor 6:15.** *Claim that someone is someth., pretend that someone is someth.* **J 8:53; 10:33; 19:7, 12; 1J 1:10; 5:10.** Cp. 5b.—W. adj. as predicate acc.: εὐθείας ποιεῖτε τὰς τρίβους (Is 40:3) *make the paths straight* **Mt 3:3; Mk 1:3; Lk 3:4.** τρίχα λευκὴν π. **Mt 5:36.** Cp. **12:16; 20:12b; 26:73; 28:14; Mk 3:12; J 5:11, 15; 7:23; 16:2; Ac 7:19; Eph 2:14** ὁ ποιήσας τὰ ἀμφότερα ἕν; **Rv 12:15; 21:5.** ἴσον ἑαυτὸν ποιῶν τῷ θεῷ (thereby) *declaring that he was equal to God* or *making himself equal to God* **J 5:18.**—Cp. use of the mid. 7b below.

γ. w. adv. of place *send outside* ἔξω ποιεῖν τινα *put someone out* (=send outside; cp. X., Cyr. 4, 1, 3 ἔξω βελῶν ποιεῖν='put outside bowshot') **Ac 5:34.**

❸ **to carry out an obligation of a moral or social nature, *do, keep, carry out, practice, commit*—ⓐ** *do, keep* the will or law obediently τὸ θέλημα τοῦ θεοῦ etc. (JosAs 12:3; s. θέλημα 1cγ) **Mt 7:21; 12:50; Mk 3:35; J 4:34; 6:38; 7:17; 9:31; Eph 6:6; Hb 10:7, 9** (both Ps 39:9), **36; 13:21; 1J 2:17;** Pol 2:2; τὰ θελήματα **Mk 3:35 v.l.; Ac 13:22;** GEb 121, 34. π. τὰ θελήματα τῆς σαρκός **Eph 2:3.** Cp. **Mt 21:31.**—π. τὸν νόμον **J 7:19; Gal 5:3;** cp. **Mt 5:19; Ro 2:14; Gal 3:10** (Dt 27:26); vs. **12** (cp. Lev 18:5).—**Mt 7:24, 26; Lk 6:46; J 2:5; 8:44.** ἐκεῖνο τὸ προσταχθὲν ἡμῖν ποιήσωμεν *let us do what has been commanded us* GMary 463, 27f (ParJer 6:9).—ὃ ἐὰν φανηρώσῃ … ὁ θεός, τοῦτο ποιήσομεν GJs 8:2.—ἐξουσίαν ποιεῖν *exercise authority* **Rv 13:12a.**

ⓑ *do, practice* virtues (cp. SIG 304, 41f τὰ δίκαια): π. τὴν ἀλήθειαν (ἀλήθεια 2b) *live the truth* **J 3:21** (cp. 1QS 1:5 al.); **1J 1:6.** (τὴν) δικαιοσύνην (δικαιοσύνη 3a) **1J 2:29; 3:7, 10; Rv 22:11;** 2 Cl 4:2; 11:7. τὰς ἐντολάς **Ro 22:14 v.l.** (SGoranson, NTS 43, '97, 154–57). Differently **Mt 6:1** (δικαιοσύνη 3b), which belongs with ποιεῖν ἐλεημοσύνην vs. **2a** and **3a** (s. ἐλεημοσύνη 1); cp. **Ac 9:36; 10:2; 24:17.** π. ἐγκράτειαν 2 Cl 15:1. π. χρηστότητα **Ro 3:12** (Ps 13:1, 3; 52:4 v.l.). π. ἔλεος *show mercy* **Js 2:13;** μετά τινος *to someone* **Lk 1:72; 10:37a** (JosAs 23:4; s. ἔλεος a and μετά A2γℶ).

ⓒ *do, commit, be guilty of* sins and vices (τὴν) ἁμαρτίαν (ἁμαρτία 1a) **J 8:34; 2 Cor 11:7; 1 Pt 2:22; 1J 3:4a, 8, 9;** pl. **Js 5:15** (TestAbr B 10 p. 115, 10 [Stone p. 78, 10]). ἁμάρτημα (TestJob 11:3; ParJer 2:2; s. ἁμάρτημα) **1 Cor 6:18.** (τὴν) ἀνομίαν (ἀνομία 2) **Mt 13:41; 1J 3:4b;** 1 Cl 16:10 (Is 53:9). βδέλυγμα καὶ ψεῦδος **Rv 21:27.** τὸ πονηρὸν τοῦτο GJs 13:1; cp. 13:2; 15:3f; ταῦτα 15:2. τὰ μὴ καθήκοντα **Ro 1:28.** ὃ οὐκ ἔξεστιν **Mk 2:24;** cp. **Mt 12:2.**

ⓓ The manner of action is more definitely indicated by means of an adv. (Jos., C. Ap. 2, 51). καλῶς ποιεῖν *do good* or *well*

Mt 12:12; 1 Cor 7:37, 38a (ApcMos 17). κρεῖσσον π. **7:38b; Js 2:8** (s. 5d below), **19;** φρονίμως π. *act wisely* **Lk 16:8;** π. οὕτως *do so* (Chariton 8, 6, 4 ποιήσομεν οὕτως=this is the way we will proceed; JosAs 10:20; ApcMos 40; Mel., P. 13, 82) **Mt 24:46; Lk 9:15; 12:43; J 14:31** (καθὼς . . . οὕτως π.); **Ac 12:8; 1 Cor 16:1; Js 2:12;** B 12:7; GJs 7:2. π. ὡσαύτως *proceed in the same way* **Mt 20:5;** ὁμοίως π. **Lk 3:11; 10:37b.** ὥσπερ οἱ ὑποκριταὶ ποιοῦσιν *as the dissemblers do* **Mt 6:2b.** καθὼς ποιεῖτε **1 Th 5:11.**—ποιεῖν foll. by a clause beginning w. ὡς: ἐποίησεν ὡς προσέταξεν *he did as (the angel) had ordered* **Mt 1:24;** cp. **26:19.** Or the clause begins w. καθὼς **Mt 21:6; J 13:15b** (TestJob 7:9). For GJs 17:1 s. 5e.

ⓔ The manner of the action is more definitely indicated by a prepositional expr. ποιεῖν κατά τι *do* or *act in accordance w. someth.* (SIG 915, 13 π. κατὰ τὰς συνθήκας; 1016, 6; PLille 4, 6; 22 [III BC]; BGU 998 II, 12 [II BC] π. κατὰ τὰ προγεγραμμένα) κατὰ τὰ ἔργα αὐτῶν *as they do* **Mt 23:3b.**—**Lk 2:27.** Also π. πρός τι: πρὸς τὸ θέλημα **12:47.**

❹ **to do someth. to others or someth.,** ***do someth. to/with,*** of behavior involving others, π. τι w. some indication of the pers. (or thing) with whom someth. is done; the action may result to the advantage or disadvantage of this person:

ⓐ neutral π. τί τινα *do someth. with someone* (double acc. as Demosth. 23, 194 τὶ ποιεῖν ἀγαθὸν τὴν πόλιν) τί ποιήσω Ἰησοῦν; *what shall I do with Jesus?* **Mt 27:22.** τί οὖν αὐτὴν ποιήσωμεν; *what, then, shall I do about (Mary)?* GJs 8:2; cp. 14:1; 17:1. τί ποιήσεις τὸν ἀγρόν; *what will you do with the land?* Hs 1:4 (ParJer 3:9 τί θέλεις ποιήσω τὰ ἅγια σκεύη). Cp. **Mk 15:12.**—B-D-F §157, 1; Rob. 484.—Neutral is also the expr. π. τί τινι *do someth. to someone* **J 9:26; 12:16; 13:12; Ac 4:16.** Likew. the passive form of the familiar saying of Jesus ὡς ποιεῖτε, οὕτω ποιηθήσεται ὑμῖν *as you do* (whether it be good or ill), *it will be done to you* 1 Cl 13:2.

ⓑ to someone's advantage: π. τί τινι (Diod. S. 18, 51, 3; TestAbr B 12 p. 116, 19 [Stone p. 80]; ParJer 3:12; ApcMos 3): ὅσα ἐὰν θέλητε ἵνα ποιῶσιν ὑμῖν οἱ ἄνθρωποι **Mt 7:12a.** τί θέλετε ποιήσω ὑμῖν; *what do you want me to do for you?* **Mt 20:32.—25:40;** cp. vs. **45; Mk 5:19f; 7:12; 10:35f, 51; Lk 1:49; 8:39ab; J 13:15a.**—π. τι εἴς τινα **1 Th 4:10.** π. τι μετά τινος (B-D-F §227, 3, add. reff. B-D-R) **Ac 14:27; 15:4** (TestJob 1:4; on the constr. w. μετά s. 3b above and cp. BGU 798, 7; 948, 8).

ⓒ to someone's disadvantage: π. τί τινι (Gen 20:9; JosAs 28:10 μὴ ποιήσητε αὐτοῖς κακόν; ApcMos 42) τί ποιήσει τοῖς γεωργοῖς; *what will he do to the vine-dressers?* **Mt 21:40.—Mk 9:13; Lk 6:11; 20:15; Ac 9:13; Hb 13:6** (Ps 117:6); GJs 9:2.—π. τι εἴς τινα (PSI 64, 20; 22 [I BC] μηδὲ ποιήσειν εἰς σὲ φάρμακα) **J 15:21.** π. τι ἔν τινι **Mt 17:12; Lk 23:31.**

ⓓ w. dat. and adv. ἐποίησαν αὐτοῖς ὡσαύτως *they treated them in the same way* **Mt 21:36.** οὕτως μοι πεποίηκεν κύριος *the Lord has dealt thus with me* **Lk 1:25;** cp. **2:48; Mt 18:35.** εὖ ποιεῖν τινι **Mk 14:7.** καλῶς π. τινι **Mt 5:44 v.l.; Lk 6:27.** ὁμοίως π. τινι **6:31b.**—In a condensed colloquialism (ποιεῖν) καθὼς ἐποίει αὐτοῖς *(to do) as he was accustomed to do for them* **Mk 15:8** (s. εὔποιΐα 1).

ⓔ w. dat. and prep. κατὰ τὰ αὐτὰ ἐποίουν τοῖς προφήταις οἱ πατέρες αὐτῶν **Lk 6:23;** cp. vs. **26.**

❺ ***do, make,*** with variations in specialized expressions

ⓐ *get* or *gain* someth. for oneself, *provide oneself* with someth. ποιήσατε ἑαυτοῖς βαλλάντια **Lk 12:33;** φίλους **16:9** (cp. X., An. 5, 5, 12 φίλον ποιεῖσθαί τινα).—Without a dat. Ἰησοῦς μαθητὰς ποιεῖ *Jesus was gaining disciples* **J 4:1.**

ⓑ of mental construction *assume, suppose, take as an example* (Hdt. et al.) w. double acc. (Pla., Theaet. 197d) ποιήσατε τὸ δένδρον καλόν *suppose the tree is good* **Mt 12:33a;** cp. vs. **33b.**

ⓒ w. an acc. of time *spend, stay* (Anth. 11, 330; PSI 362, 15 [251/250 BC]; UPZ 70, 21; PFlor 137, 7 [III AD] ἡμέραν, ἥν ποιεῖ ἐκεῖ; PGen 54, 18 τρεῖς ἡμέρας; Pr 13:23; Ec 6:12; Tob. 10:7 BA; TestJob 20:5; 31:4; ParJer 6:16; ApcMos 37 ὥρας τρεῖς; Jos. Ant. 6, 18 μῆνας τέσσαρας; cp. our colloquial 'do time'. Demosth. 19, 163 and Pla., Phileb. 50d are wrongly cited in this connection, as shown by WSchulze, Graeca Latina 1901, 23f) χρόνον (Dionys. Hal. 4, 66; ParJer 7:33; ApcMos 31) **Ac 15:33; 18:23.** μῆνας τρεῖς **20:3.** τρεῖς μῆνας GJs 12:3. νυχθήμερον **2 Cor 11:25.** ἐνιαυτόν **Js 4:13** (TestJob 21:1 ἔτη).

ⓓ καλῶς ποιεῖν w. ptc. foll. *do well if, do well to,* as a formula somet.=*please* (s. καλῶς 4a and cp. SIG 561, 6f καλῶς ποιήσειν τοὺς πολίτας προσδεξαμένους; UPZ 110, 11 [164 BC]; POxy 300, 5 [I AD]; 525, 7; Hdt. 5, 24 εὖ ἐποίησας ἀφικόμενος; SIG 598e, 8f) **Ac 10:33; Phil 4:14; 2 Pt 1:19; 3J 6;** GEg 252, 53.—Sim. καλῶς ποιεῖν, εἰ . . . **Js 2:8** (cp. PPetr II, 11 [1], 1 καλῶς ποιεῖς εἰ ἔρρωσαι).

ⓔ αὕτη ἡ ἡμέρα κυρίου ποιήσει ὡς βούλεται *this day of the Lord will turn out as (the Lord) wills* GJs 17:1 (deStrycker cites Mt 6:34 for the construction); if the accentuation αὐτή is adopted, render: *the day of the Lord shall itself bring things about as (the Lord) wills.*

❻ **to be active in some way,** ***work, be active,*** abs. (X., An. 1, 5, 8; Ruth 2:19) w. acc. of time (Socrat., Ep. 14, 8 ποιήσας ἡμέρας τριάκοντα) μίαν ὥραν ἐποίησαν *they have worked for only one hour* **Mt 20:12a.** ποιῆσαι μῆνας *be active for months* **Rv 13:5.**—Somet. it is not a general action or activity that is meant, but the doing of someth. quite definite. The acc. belonging to it is easily supplied fr. the context: λέγουσιν καὶ οὐ ποιοῦσιν *they say* (it), *but do not do* or *keep* (it) **Mt 23:3c** (the contrast is not betw. speaking [λαλεῖν] and acting in general).—**2 Cor 8:10f** (s. Betz, 2 Cor p. 64); **1 Th 5:24.**

❼ ***make/do someth. for oneself*** or ***of oneself*** mid.

ⓐ mostly as a periphrasis of the simple verbal idea (s. 2d) ἀναβολὴν ποιεῖσθαι **Ac 25:17** (s. ἀναβολή). ἐκβολὴν ποιεῖσθαι **27:18** (s. ἐκβολή); αὔξησιν π. **Eph 4:16;** δέησιν or δεήσεις π. **Lk 5:33; Phil 1:4; 1 Ti 2:1** (s. δέησις). διαλογισμοὺς π. 1 Cl 21:3; τὰς διδασκαλίας Papias (2:15); τὴν ἕνωσιν π. IPol 5:2; ἐπιστροφὴν π. 1 Cl 1:1 (ἐπιστροφή 1); καθαρισμὸν π. **Hb 1:3** (καθαρισμός 2). κοινωνίαν **Ro 15:26.** κοπετόν **Ac 8:2 v.l.;** λόγον (Isocr., Ep. 2, 2; Just., D. 1, 3 al.) **1:1; 11:2** D; **20:24 v.l.** (on these three passages s. λόγος: 1b; 1aγ and 1aα, end). μνείαν **Ro 1:9; Eph 1:16; 1 Th 1:2; Phlm 4** (μνεία 2). μνήμην **2 Pt 1:15** (s. μνήμη 1). μονήν **J 14:23** (μονή 1). νουθέτησιν 1 Cl 56:2 (Just., A I, 67, 4). ὁμιλίαν IPol 5:1 (ὁμιλία 2). ποιεῖσθαι τὴν παραβολήν AcPlCor 2:28. πορείαν π. (=πορεύεσθαι; cp. X., An. 5, 6, 11, Cyr. 5, 2, 31; Plut., Mor. 571e; Jos., Vi. 57; 2 Macc 3:8; 12:10; Ar. 4, 2) **Lk 13:22.** πρόνοιαν π. *make provision, care* (Isocr. 4, 2 and 136; Demosth., Prooem. 16; Ps.-Demosth. 47, 80; Polyb. 4, 6, 11; Dion. Hal. 5, 46; Aelian, VH 12, 56. Oft. in ins and pap [esp. of civic-minded people]; Da 6:19 προν. ποιούμενος αὐτοῦ; Jos., Bell. 4, 317, C. Ap. 1, 9; Ar. 13, 2) **Ro 13:14;** Papias (2:15). προσκλίσεις π. 1 Cl 47:3; σπουδὴν π. *be eager* (Hdt. 1, 4; 5, 30 πᾶσαν σπουδὴν ποιούμενος; 9, 8; Pla., Euthyd. 304e, Leg. 1, 628e; Isocr. 5, 45 πᾶσαν τὴν σπ. περὶ τούτου ποιεῖσθαι; Polyb. 1, 46, 2 al.; Diod. S. 1, 75, 1; Plut., Mor. 4e; SIG 539A, 15f; 545, 14 τὴν πᾶσαν σπ. ποιούμενος; PHib 71, 9 [III BC] τ. πᾶσαν σπ. ποίησαι; 44, 8) **Jd 3.** συνελεύσεις ποιεῖσθαι *come together, meet* 1 Cl 20:10 (Just., A I, 67, 7). συνωμοσίαν ποιεῖσθαι *form a conspiracy* (Polyb. 1, 70, 6; Herodian 7, 4, 3; SIG 526, 16) **Ac 23:13.**—Cp. use of the act. 2d.

ⓑ w. double acc., of the obj. and pred. (Lucian, Prom. Es in Verb. 6 σεμνοτάτας ἐποιεῖτο τὰς συνουσίας; GDI 4629, II, 22; 25 [Laconia]; Jos., Ant. 2, 263; s. 2hβ) βεβαίαν τὴν κλῆσιν ποιεῖσθαι *make the calling certain* **2 Pt 1:10.** οὐδενὸς λόγου ποιοῦμαι τὴν ψυχὴν τιμίαν ἐμαυτῷ *I don't consider my life as something of value for myself* **Ac 20:24.** Cp. use of the act. 2hβ.—B. 538. Cp. πράσσω. Schmidt, Syn. I 397–423. DELG. M-M. EDNT. TW. Sv.

ποίημα, ατος, τό (ποιέω; Hdt. et al.; SIG 532, 5; LXX; TestSol 2:1 L; TestAbr; TestJob 49:2f; ApcEsdr 2:24 p. 26, 17 Tdf.; ApcMos; apolog. exc. Mel.) **that which is made, *work, creation,*** in our lit. only of the works of divine creation (Aesop, Fab. 444 P.=142 H. ποιήματα; Ps 142:5; TestSol 2:1 L; ApcEsdr; Philo, Det. Pot. Ins. 125 θεοῦ ποιήματα; Just., Tat., Ath. Cp. Aelian, NA 1, 53 π. Προμηθέως; Alex. Aphr., An. Mant. II 1 p. 112, 1 of the creations of Nus; difft. Ar. 13, 5 and Tat. 33, 1: poem) τὰ ἀόρατα αὐτοῦ τοῖς ποιήμασι νοούμενα καθορᾶται *(God's) invisible nature is perceived with the mind's eye by the things (God) created* **Ro 1:20** (on this s. the lit. under ἀόρατος and γνωστός 2). Of Christians αὐτοῦ ἐσμεν π. *we are (God's) creation,* i.e. *(God) has made us what we are* **Eph 2:10.**—DELG s.v. ποιέω. M-M. TW. Sv.

ποίησις, εως, ἡ (ποιέω. Hdt. et al.; ins, pap, LXX)

❶ **the process of activity, *doing, working*** (Pla., Soph. 266d θείας ἔργα ποιήσεως, Charm. 163e; Jos., Ant. 17, 94) μακάριος ἐν τῇ ποιήσει αὐτοῦ ἔσται *that person will be blessed in the doing* **Js 1:25.** Of God: ποίησις χειρῶν αὐτοῦ 1 Cl 27:7 (Ps 18:2; cp. Just., D. 56, 10 πρὸ ποιήσεως κόσμου).

❷ **the product of activity, *work, creation*** of the artist (Aristoph., Pla. et al.; SIG 547, 48 [211/210 BC]; EpArist 57; Jos., C. Ap. 1, 12; Just., Tat., Ath.; of poetry and ships Tat. 1, 1 al.; Ath. 29, 1), in our lit. of the Divine Artist (Proclus on Pla., Cratylus p. 21, 18f Pasqu.): God is merciful ἐπὶ τὴν ποίησιν αὐτοῦ (Da 9:14 Theod.) Hm 4, 3, 5; 9:3.—DELG s.v. ποιέω. M-M. TW. Sv.

ποιητής, οῦ, ὁ (ποιέω)—❶ **one who does someth. by producing someth., *maker*** (of God Pla., Tim. 28c; Just., D. 56, 4 al. ὁ τῶν ὅλων ποιητής; Tat., Ath.), then specif. *poet* (so Aristoph., Ran. 96; 1030; Pla., Phd. 61b al.; oft. ins [SIG IV 510b index; OGI II 694b ind.]; PHerm 125 B, 6; POsl 189, 13 [III AD]; TestSol; EpArist 31; Philo; Jos., Ant. 12, 38; 110 al.; Just., A I, 4, 9 al.; Tat., Ath.) **Ac 17:28.**

❷ **one who does what is prescribed, *a doer*** w. obj. gen. (cp. 1 Macc 2:67) **Ro 2:13; Js 4:11.** (Opp. ἀκροατής) π. λόγου **1:22f.** π. ἔργου *a doer that acts* (opp.: a forgetful hearer) vs. **25.**—B. 1299. DELG s.v. ποιέω. M-M. TW.

ποικιλία, ας, ἡ (ποικιλός; Pla., X. et al.; ins, PTebt 703, 93 [III BC]; LXX; EpArist 56; Philo, Tat.) **state of variations in aspect, *many-colored appearance, variety, diversity*** τῶν ὀρέων ἡ π. Hs 9, 18, 5. Pl. (Isocr. 5, 27) αἱ ποικιλίαι τοῦ νοὸς τῶν ἐθνῶν *the diversity of mental attitudes among the nations* 9, 17, 2. αἱ ποικιλίαι τῶν λίθων *the various appearances of the stones* 9, 6, 4.—DELG s.v. ποικίλος.

ποικίλος, η, ον (Hom.+)—❶ **pert. to existence in various kinds or modes, *diversified, manifold*** (Pind. et al.; 2 Macc 15:21; EpArist 78; Philo; Jos., Bell. 3, 393, Ant. 10, 142) ἄνθη (Ps.-Pla., Axioch. 13 p. 371c) ApcPt 3:10. ἀρνήσεις Hs 8, 8, 4. ἀσθένειαι 6, 3, 4c. βάσανοι *many/various kinds of torments* **Mt 4:24;** Hs 6, 3, 4b; of torture MPol 2:4. βοτάναι Hm 10, 1, 5. δυνάμεις **Hb 2:4.** ἔθνη Hs 9, 17, 2b; ἐπιθυμίαι **2 Ti 3:6;** cp. **Tit 3:3.** ἰδέαι Hs 9, 17, 1. καρποί 9, 28, 3; Dg 12:1. νόσοι (Tat. 20, 2; Philo, Omn. Prob. Lib. 58 νοσήματα) **Mt 4:24; Mk 1:34; Lk 4:40.** ὄρη Hs 9, 17, 2ac; 3. πειρασμοί **Js 1:2; 1 Pt 1:6** (πολλοῖς P^{72}). πονηρίαι Hs 9, 18, 3. πραγματεῖαι (cp. Philo, In Flacc. 3) 9, 20, 1. τιμωρίαι 6, 3, 3; 4a. τρυφαί m 6, 2, 5. π. χάρις θεοῦ *the grace of God, that manifests itself in various ways* **1 Pt 4:10.** χρόαι Hs 9, 4, 5ac. W. ξένος: διδαχαί **Hb 13:9** (s. also 2b below). W. πολύς (Diod. S. 5, 62, 1 πολλοὶ κ. ποικίλοι λόγοι=many and varied reports; 17, 13, 1; Maximus Tyr. 11, 11e; Ps.-Plut., Hom. 122) Hm 4, 2, 3; s 9, 20, 2. ἐν πολλαῖς θλίψεσι π. *in many kinds of afflictions* 7:4.

❷ **pert. to existence in various aspects**—ⓐ of things, ***many-colored, variegated*** (Hom.+; Polyaenus 6, 1, 4; Lucian, Deor. Conc. 10; PGM 4, 2709; LXX [Gen 37:3 al.]; TestJob 46:7; TestZeb 1:3; Jos., Ant. 11, 235). This mng. is to be preferred in οἱ λίθοι οἱ π. *the many-colored stones* (JosAs 2:3; 13:5; IG $IV^2/1$, 106 I, 96; 113 [IV BC]) Hs 9, 4, 5b.

ⓑ of persons, esp. w. ref. to devious ways of thinking, words, actions, fig. ext. of 2a: ***ambiguous, crafty, sly, deceitful*** (Hes. et al.; trag.; Pind., N. 5, 28 βουλεύματα; Aristoph., Thesm. 438 λόγοι; Polyb. 8, 18, 4 Κρὴς ὑπάρχων καὶ φύσει ποικίλος; Just., D. 134, 5) **Hb 13:9** (s. also 1 above). ἀπατη[λοὺς] καὶ π. . . . λόγους AcPl Ox 6, 12 (restored after Aa I 241, 14).—DELG. M-M. TW.

ποιμαίνω (ποιμήν) fut. ποιμανῶ; 1 aor. ἐποίμανα Ps 77:72, impv. 2 pl. ποιμάνατε **1 Pt 5:2;** fut. pass. 2 sg. ποιμανθήσῃ Ps 36:3 (Hom.+) 'to herd, act as a shepherd'.

❶ **to serve as tender of sheep, *herd, tend, (lead to) pasture*** (Did., Gen. 60, 12), w. acc. (Jos., Ant. 2, 264) π. ποίμνην *tend a flock* **1 Cor 9:7.** Abs. (Demetr.: 722 fgm. 1, 13 Jac.; Jos., Ant. 1, 309) δοῦλος ποιμαίνων *a slave tending sheep* **Lk 17:7.**—Dalman (as cited under ἀμφιβάλλω).

❷ **to watch out for other people, *to shepherd,*** of activity that protects, rules, governs, fosters, fig. ext. of 1:—ⓐ in the sense of lead, guide, or rule (Eur., fgm. 744 TGF στρατόν; Ps.-Lucian, Amor. 54 τ. ἀμαθεῖς).

α. w. imagistic detail prominently in mind: of the direction of a congregation ποιμαίνειν τὸ ποίμνιον τοῦ θεοῦ *tend God's flock* **1 Pt 5:2** (PsSol 17:40 ποιμαίνων τὸ ποίμνιον κυρίου ἐν πίστει κ. δικαιοσύνῃ). ποίμαινε τὰ πρόβατά μου **J 21:16.**

β. w. imagistic detail retreating into the background (cp. 1 Ch 11:2; Mi 7:14; Jer 23:2): of the administration of a congregation ποιμ. τὴν ἐκκλησίαν τοῦ θεοῦ **Ac 20:28.**—Of the Messiah ποιμανεῖ τὸν λαόν μου Ἰσραήλ (cp. 2 Km 5:2; 7:7.—Himerius, Or. 39 [=Or. 5], 8 Ἀττικὴ Μοῦσα ποιμαίνει τὴν πόλιν, i.e. Thessalonica) **Mt 2:6.** Of death: θάνατος ποιμανεῖ αὐτούς 1 Cl 51:4 (Ps 48:15). The latter pass. forms a transition to several others in which

γ. the activity as 'shepherd' has destructive results (cp. Jer 22:22 and s. ELohmeyer, Hdb. on Rv 2:27) ποιμανεῖ αὐτοὺς ἐν ῥάβδῳ σιδηρᾷ (after Ps 2:9) **Rv 2:27; 12:5; 19:15** (cp. Heraclitus fgm. 11 πᾶν ἑρπετὸν πληγῇ νέμεται=everything that creeps is shepherded by a blow [from God]. Pla., Critias 109b alludes to this).

ⓑ *protect, care for, nurture* (Aeschyl., Eumen. 91 ἱκέτην; Pla., Lys. 209a τὸ σῶμα) αὐτούς **Rv 7:17** (cp. Ps 22:1; Ezk 34:23). π. ἑαυτόν *look after oneself* i.e. care for oneself alone (cp. Ezk 34:2) **Jd 12.**—B. 146. DELG s.v. ποιμήν. M-M. TW.

ποιμενικός, ή, όν (ποιμήν; Pla. et al.; poets since Theocr. 1, 23. In prose: Maximus Tyr. 20, 6b; 38, 2a; Philostrat., Imag.

2, 18 p. 370, 9; LXX; Philo; Jos., Ant. 6, 185) ***pertaining to a shepherd*** (Vi. Aesopi W 75 P. τὸ ποιμενικὸν σχῆμα) σχήματι ποιμενικῷ *in the garb of a shepherd* Hv 5:1.—DELG s.v. ποιμήν.

ποιμήν, ένος, ὁ (s. prec. two entries; Hom.+; pap, LXX; JosAs; ApcEl [PSI I, 7 verso, 1]; AscIs, ApcrEzk, Philo; Jos., Ant. 8, 404 al.)

➊ **one who herds sheep, *shepherd, sheep-herder*** (Demetr.: 722 fgm. 1, 13 Jac. nomads; Theoph. Ant. 2, 35 [p. 190, 8]. In imagery or parable: Orig., C. Cels. 4, 17, 21) **Mt 9:36=Mk 6:34** (Num 27:17); **Mt 25:32;** GJs 4:3; 18:3 (codd.). Of the shepherds at Jesus' birth **Lk 2:8, 15, 18, 20** (s. HGressmann, Das Weihnachtsevangelium 1914 [on this CClemen, StKr 89, 1916, 237–52]; JGeffcken, D. Hirten auf dem Felde: Her 49, 1914, 321–51 [against him JKroll, Her 50, 1915, 137ff]; Clemen[2] 1924, 195; 203ff; IHarrie, Die Anbetung der Hirten: ARW 23, 1925, 369–82; RBultmann, Gesch. d. syn. Trad.[2] '31, 323–6; GErdmann, D. Vorgesch. d. Lk u. Mt '32; ADeissmann, D. Anbetung d. Hirten u. d. Anbetung d. Weisen: Lutherring 16, '35, 377–82).—In imagery, w. detail predominating: πατάξω τὸν ποιμένα, καὶ διασκορπισθήσονται (v.l. and also more grammatically correct: -θήσεται) τὰ πρόβατα τῆς ποίμνης (cp. Zech 13:7) **Mt 26:31; Mk 14:27;** B 5:12. Of Christ in extended imagery **J 10:2, 7 v.l., 16;** (opp. ὁ μισθωτός) vs. **12;** ὁ ποιμὴν ὁ καλός vs. **11ab, 14** (Maximus Tyr. 6, 7d Cyrus is called ποιμὴν ἀγαθός, because he protects the Persian 'flock' fr. the barbarian 'wolves').

➋ **one who serves as guardian or leader, *shepherd,*** fig. ext. of 1 (Diog. L. 9, 40 Democritus is called ποιμὴν [=guardian] μύθων)

ⓐ esp. freq. in Hermas (Leutzsch, Hermas 439f n. 546)

α. as the angel of repentance and bearer of a revelation (MDibelius, Der Offenbarungsträger im 'Hirten' des H.: Harnack-Ehrung 1921, 105–18; Rtzst., Erlösungsmyst. 1921, 149) Hv 5:3, 7; s 2:1; 5, 1, 1; 8, 1, 4; 18; 8, 2, 5f; 8; 8, 4, 1; 8, 5, 1; 6; 8, 6, 1; 9, 1, 1; 9, 2, 6; 9, 5, 1; 7; 9, 7, 1; 3f; 9, 8, 1; 9, 9, 5–7; 9, 10, 1; 4; 6; 9, 11, 1; 8; 10, 3, 4f [=POxy 404 recto C, 15; 20 restored].

β. in the vision of the shepherds Hs 6, 1, 5f; 6, 2, 1; 5f; 6, 3, 2; 7:1.

ⓑ of those who lead Christian communities/congregations/churches

α. God (Philo, Agr. 51; Aberciusins. 3 π. ἁγνός) IRo 9:1.

β. Christ τὸν ποιμένα τῶν προβάτων τὸν μέγαν **Hb 13:20** (RGyllenberg, D. Christol. des Hb: ZST 11, '34, 662–90). τὸν ποιμένα καὶ ἐπίσκοπον τῶν ψυχῶν ὑμῶν **1 Pt 2:25** (cp. Philo, Mut. Nom. 116 of the θεῖος λόγος; Ezk 34:23). ποιμ. τῆς ἐκκλησίας MPol 19:2. S. above 1, end, and Hdb. exc. after J 10:21; Bultmann 276–93; JQuasten, Hlg. Überliefg. (edited by OCasel) '38, 51–58 (Hellenistic and early Christian); WJost, Poimen. D. Bild v. Hirten in d. bibl. Überl. u. s. christol. Bed., diss. Giessen '39; TKempf, Christus der Hirt '42; VMuller, Prehistory of the Good Shepherd: JNES 3, '44, 87–90.

γ. human leaders (on 'shepherds' as the founders and temporary thiasarchs [leaders] of Gk. religious guilds s. EMaass, Orpheus 1895, 181; Himerius, Or. 54 [=Or. 15] when greeting his newly arrived students, compares the teachers to shepherds [ἀγελάρχαι] and the pupils to the flock [ἀγέλη alternating with ποίμνιον §2]. S. also Jer 2:8; 3:15; Ezk 34:2) *pastor* **Eph 4:11** (w. other church leaders). ὅπου ὁ ποιμήν (i.e. the superintendent/supervisor) ἐστιν, ἐκεῖ ὡς πρόβατα ἀκολουθεῖτε IPhld 2:1. S. also IRo 9:1 (Ign. as 'shepherd' of the Syrian church).—EHatch/AHarnack, D. Gesellschaftsverf. der christl. Kirchen im Altertum 1883, 230; HBruders, D. Verfassung der Kirche bis zum Jahr 175 n. Chr. 1904, 190f; 371f; Harnack, D. Mission[4] I 1923, 350f; NCavatassi, De Munere Pastoris in NT: Verb. Domini 29, '51, 215–27; 275–85.—B. 149. DELG. EDNT. RAC XV 577–607. M-M. TW.

ποίμνη, ης, ἡ (ποιμήν; Hom. et al.; PAmh 127, 39; Gen 32:17; TestGad 1:3; TestJos 19: 5, 6 [A]; Jos., Ant. 6, 295) ***flock,*** esp. of sheep (Diod. S. 4, 26, 2 ποίμνας προβάτων; 5, 65, 2; 20, 8, 4) **Lk 2:8; 1 Cor 9:7b.** ποιμαίνειν ποίμνην vs. **7a.**—In imagery: w. ref. to Jesus' disciples **Mt 26:31;** B 5:12 (both=Zech 13:7 A); to the church and to Jesus as its head μία ποίμνη εἷς ποιμήν **J 10:16** (Maximus Tyr. 35, 2g ἐν ἀγέλῃ μιᾷ ὑπὸ ποιμένι ἑνί; Philo, Agr. 51 God as ποιμήν leads the whole world as ποίμνη).—DELG s.v. ποιμήν. M-M. TW.

ποίμνιον, ου, τό (fr. ποιμήν via ποίμνη; Soph., Hdt. et al.; PRyl 114, 20; LXX; PsSol 17:40; TestSol 10, 52 C; Test12Patr, Philo)

➊ **an assemblage of a specific kind of animal, *flock,*** esp. of sheep (Ps.-Apollod., Epit. 7, 5, 8; Tzetzes on Lycophron 344; EpArist 170; Jos., Ant. 8, 404; 18, 316; Test12Patr) MPol 14:1; GJs 4:2, 4.

➋ **a defined group of persons under a leader, *flock*** fig. ext. of 1 (Hippocr., Ep. 1, 2; Themist., Or. 23 p. 289)—ⓐ in the vision of the shepherds (ποιμήν 2aβ) Hs 6, 1, 6.

ⓑ of the Christian community (as of the people of Israel in the OT: Jer 13:17 τὸ π. κυρίου; Zech 10:3 al.) **Ac 20:28f; 1 Pt 5:3.** τὸ π. τοῦ θεοῦ vs. **2.** τὸ π. τοῦ Χριστοῦ 1 Cl 44:3; 54:2; 57:2; cp. 16:1. Of Jesus' disciples (Liban., Or. 58, 36 of a sophist's pupils; Himerius, Or. 54 [=Or. 15], 2 of the hearers) τὸ μικρὸν π. (nom. w. art. for voc. B-D-F §147 app.; Rob. 465) **Lk 12:32.**—DELG s.v. ποιμήν. TW.

ποῖος, α, ον (Hom.+) interrog. pron., in direct and indir. interrog. sentences.

➊ **interrogative ref. to class or kind, *of what kind?***

ⓐ used w. a noun (B-D-F §298, 2; cp. Rob. 740)—**α.** beside τίς (Hdt. 7, 21, 1; Herodas 6, 74f; Maximus Tyr. 33, 5a τίνα καὶ ποῖον τύραννον; PTebt 25, 18 [117 BC]; BGU 619, 8) εἰς τίνα ἢ ποῖον καιρόν *to what time or what kind of time* **1 Pt 1:11** (cp. UPZ 65, 52 [154 BC] ἀπὸ ποίου χρόνου=since what time). ποῖον οἶκον . . . ἢ τίς τόπος . . . ; **Ac 7:49;** B 16:2 (both Is 66:1; s. ed. JZiegler). τίς μοι ἐγέννησεν; ποία δὲ μήτρα ἐξέφυσέν με; *who begot me, and what kind of womb delivered me?* GJs 3:1.

β. in a direct question (3 Km 22:24) διὰ ποίου νόμου; *by what kind of law?* **Ro 3:27.** ποίῳ σώματι; *with what kind of body?* **1 Cor 15:35.** ποίῳ προσώπῳ; *with what kind of look* or *expression?* GJs 13:1. ποῖον κλέος; ironically *what kind of credit?* **1 Pt 2:20;** sim. ποία ὑμῖν χάρις ἐστίν; **Lk 6:32, 33, 34;** cp. D 1:3.—1 Cl 28:2; 2 Cl 1:5; 6:9; Hv 1, 2, 1; m 12, 1, 3a; s 6, 5, 5; 9, 13, 3.—For **Js 4:14** see γ.

γ. in an indir. quest. (Archimed. II 416, 6 Heib. ποῖαι γωνίαι) ποίῳ θανάτῳ *(by) what sort of death* **J 12:33; 18:32; 21:19** (cp. Just., D. 104, 1 διὰ ποίου θανάτου).—**Lk 9:55 v.l.; Js 4:14** (this may be taken as a direct quest.; s. Windisch ad loc.); 1 Cl 38:3a; Hm 4, 2, 3; 12, 1, 3b.

ⓑ without a noun ποῖοι καὶ τίνες 1 Cl 38:3b. In the predicate οἱ καρποὶ φανεροῦνται ποῖοί τινές εἰσιν Hs 4:3.

➋ (=τίς) ***which, what?***—ⓐ w. a noun—**α.** in a dir. question (Theopomp. [IV BC]: 115 fgm. 263a Jac.; 2 Km 15:2; 3 Km 13:12; Jon 1:8; Jos., Ant. 15, 137) ποία ἐντολή; *which commandment?* **Mt 22:36;** cp. **Mk 12:28; J 10:32.** ποίῳ τρόπῳ; *in what way?* Hv 1, 1, 7; cp. m. 12, 3, 1. εἰς ποῖον τόπον v 3, 1, 3.

β. in an indir. quest. (Aeschin., In Ctesiph. 24; Tob 5:9) **Mt 24:42f; Lk 12:39; Rv 3:3.** ἐκ ποίας ἐπαρχίας ἐστίν **Ac 23:34.**—Hv 4, 3, 7; m 12, 3.

γ. In some cases π. takes the place of the gen. of the interrog. τίς (in dir. as well as indir. questions. Cp. Chariton 4, 4, 3 Blake ποίᾳ δυνάμει πεποιθώς;) ἐν ποίᾳ δυνάμει ἢ ἐν ποίῳ ὀνόματι; *by whose power or by whose name?* **Ac 4:7.** ἐν ποίᾳ ἐξουσίᾳ(;) **Mt 21:23, 24, 27; Mk 11:28, 29, 33; Lk 20:2, 8.**

ⓑ without a noun—**α.** which can, though, be supplied fr. the context (Jos., C. Ap. 1, 254 ποίους;): ποίας; (i.e. ἐντολάς) **Mt 19:18.** ποῖα (i.e. γενόμενα) **Lk 24:19.** ποίαν; (i.e. ἀντιμισθίαν) 2 Cl 9:8. ποίους (i.e. ἀνθρώπους) βαστάζει Hs 9, 14, 6. In the predicate: τὰ ξηρὰ (i.e. δένδρα) ποῖά ἐστιν 3:3.

β. gen. of place, w. ellipsis (B-D-F §186, 1; Mlt. 73) ποίας (i.e. ὁδοῦ) *by what way* **Lk 5:19.**—DELG s.v. πο-. M-M.

πολεμέω (πόλεμος) fut. πολεμήσω; 1 aor. ἐπολέμησα. Pass.: 1 fut. πολεμηθήσομαι; aor. 3 pl. ἐπολεμήθησαν Judg 5:20 v.l. (Soph., Hdt.+).

❶ ***wage war***—ⓐ act. *make war, fight* μετά τινος *on* or *with (against) someone* (μετά A2cβ) **Rv 12:7a; 13:4; 17:14.** π. μετά τινος ἐν τῇ ῥομφαίᾳ *war against someone with the sword* **2:16** (for πολ. ἐν τῇ ῥομφ. cp. 1 Macc 3:12). πολ. κατά τινος *war against someone* **Rv 12:7a** t.r. W. acc. μέλλει] γὰρ [ἐν μιᾷ ἡμέρᾳ] πολεμῖν τὸ[ν κόσμον ἐν πυρί] AcPl Ha 9, 14 (prob. erroneously for ἀπολλύειν; s. Schmidt ad loc.) Abs. **Rv 12:7b;** (w. κρίνειν) **19:11.** διὰ τὸ πολεμεῖν αὐτούς *because they went to war* B 16:4.

ⓑ pass. *be warred upon, be fought against* ὑπό τινος (Demosth. 9, 9; Jos., Ant. 9, 255; Just., D. 49, 8) B 12:2a. Abs. (Thu. 1, 68, 3; X., Hell. 7, 4, 20) ibid. vs. 2b.

❷ **to be in opposition to,** ***be hostile,*** in military imagery, of the hostile attitude of Judeans toward Christians ὑπὸ Ἰουδαίων ὡς ἀλλόφυλοι πολεμοῦνται Dg 5:17 (of perpetrating hostile actions Vi. Aesopi I c. 127; Jos., Vi. 244; of persecution by gentiles Just., A II, 12, 6); **Gal 1:13, 23** (both **v.l.**).—Of impenitent Israelites εἰς τὸν αἰῶνα πολεμηθήσονται B 12:2c. Of the disputes of Christians among themselves **Js 4:2** (Diod. S. 13, 84, 4; Sb 4317, 12).—τὸ ζῆλος ἐμὲ πολεμεῖ *the passionate desire* (for martyrdom) *is pressing me hard* ITr 4:2 (the acc. as Dinarchus 1, 36; Diod. S. 2, 37, 3; Chariton 7, 5, 3).—Of the hostile attitude of the σάρξ toward the ψυχή Dg 6:5 (Herm. Wr. 392, 3 Sc. of the ψυχή: αὐτὴν ἑαυτῇ πολεμῆσαι δεῖ).—B. 1370. DELG s.v. πελεμίζω II. Frisk s.v. πόλεμος. M-M. TW.

πόλεμος, ου, ὁ (s. prec. entry; Hom.+; loanw. in rabb.).

❶ **military conflict**—ⓐ ***war*** **Hb 11:34.** πόλεμοι καὶ ἀκοαὶ πολέμων *wars and rumors of wars* **Mt 24:6; Mk 13:7.** W. ἀκαταστασίαι **Lk 21:9.** W. λιμός 1 Cl 56:9 (Job 5:20). συμβαλεῖν τινι εἰς πόλεμον *make war on someone* **Lk 14:31** (συμβάλλω 5a). ποιεῖν πόλεμον μετά τινος (s. μετά A2cβ) **Rv 11:7; 12:17; 13:7** (Da 7:21 Theod.); **19:19.** AFridrichsen, Krig och fred i Nya Testamentet '40.

ⓑ of a single engagement ***battle, fight*** (Hom., Hes.; Diod. S. 22, 13, 5; Appian, Bell. Civ. 3, 67 §278; Polyaenus, Exc. 13, 3; 9; 3 Km 22:34; 1 Macc 4:13; 10:78; JosAs 26:5; Jos., Bell. 3, 189) παρασκευάζεσθαι εἰς π. *prepare for battle* **1 Cor 14:8.** Of horses (Dio Chrys. 46 [63], 4) ἑτοιμάζεσθαι εἰς π. *be made ready for battle* **Rv 9:7.** τρέχειν εἰς π. *rush into battle* vs. **9.** Cp. **12:7; 16:14; 20:8.**

❷ **a state of hostility/antagonism,** ***strife, conflict, quarrel*** fig. ext. of 1 (since Soph., El. 218; Pla. [e.g. Phd. 66c]; Epict. 3, 20, 18; TestJob 4:4; TestGad 5:1; ApcMos 28; Philo, Praem. 91, Gig. 51; Tat. 26, 3) of earthly and heavenly powers IEph 13:2 (opp. εἰρήνη).—Of the situation in Corinth 1 Cl 3:2; 46:5. Pl. (w. μάχαι; cp. Dio Chrys. 11 [12], 78; Himerius, Or. [Ecl.] 3, 7) **Js 4:1.**—B. 1374. DELG s.v. πελεμίζω II. Frisk. M-M. EDNT. TW.

πολιά, ᾶς, ἡ (fem. subst. of the adj. [in use since Hom.] πολιός, ά, όν 'gray') ***old age*** (Cornutus 23 p. 44, 19; Lucian, Philops. 23; Ps.-Lucian, Amor. 12; Themist. p. 163d; 182b; LXX; Philo, Spec. Leg. 2, 238) ἀγαθὴ πολ. (cp. Judg 8:32 A πολιὰ ἀγαθή) MPol 13:2 v.l. (for πολιτεία).—DELG s.v. πολιός.

πολιορκία, ας, ἡ (πόλις, cp. ἕρκος 'enclosure'; Hdt. et al.; ins; Sb 3776, 4 [I BC]; LXX; TestSol 10:36 C; TestJud 23:3; Jos., Bell. 3, 183, Vi. 329) **hostile surrounding of an area for a protracted period,** ***siege,*** w. θλῖψις 1 Cl 57:4 (Pr 1:27). The later metaph. use *distress, tribulation* (Plut., Sulla 25, 4 Z. v.l.) is certainly to be understood here.—DELG s.v. πόλις.

πόλις, εως, ἡ (Hom.+. Gener. a population center in contrast to a relatively uninhabited or rural area. In the Gr-Rom. world the term gener. implied strong political associations, esp. in the sense 'city-state').

❶ **population center of varying size,** ***city, town,*** lit. **Mt 5:14; Lk 10:8, 10.** Pl. **Mt 11:20; Lk 5:12; 19:17, 19.** ἡ πόλις *the city* or *the town* designated in the context **Mt 8:33; 21:17f; 26:18; Mk 11:19; 14:13, 16; Lk 4:29a; 7:12ab; J 4:8, 28, 30; Ac 8:9; 14:4; Rv 11:13;** B 16:5; AcPl Ha 4, 18; 5, 17. Likew. αἱ πόλεις **Ac 16:4.** ἡ πόλις *the city* can also be *the capital city, the main city* (Mayser II/2 p. 28; Jos., C. Ap. 2, 125) **Ac 8:5;** cp. **Mk 5:14** (s. vs. 1); **Lk 8:27** (s. vs. 26). ἡ πόλις ἐκείνη **Mt 10:14f; Lk 9:5; 10:12; 18:3; J 4:39; Ac 8:8;** Hs 9, 12, 5b. ἡ πόλ. αὕτη **Mt 10:23a; Ac 4:27; 18:10; 22:3;** Hs 1:3. ἔν τινι πόλει *in a certain city* **Lk 18:2;** cp. Hs 9, 12, 5a. εἰς τήνδε τὴν πόλιν **Js 4:13** (s. ὅδε 2). πᾶσα πόλις **Lk 10:1.** αἱ πόλεις πᾶσαι **Mt 9:35; Ac 8:40;** cp. **Mk 6:33.**—πόλις (πόλεις) beside κώμη (κῶμαι) **Mt 9:35; 10:11; Lk 8:1; 13:22.** W. κῶμαι and ἀγροί **Mk 6:56.** ἡ πόλις καὶ οἱ ἀγροί **5:14; Lk 8:34.** W. τόπος **10:1.** In contrast to the open plain or the desert, where no cities are found **Mt 14:13; Mk 1:45; 2 Cor 11:26;** to the interior of a building **Ac 12:10.**—Used w. the gen.: to denote the region in which it is located πόλ. τῆς Γαλιλαίας **Lk 1:26; 4:31.** πόλ. Ἰούδα (Ἰούδας 1c) **1:39.** Cp. **J 4:5; Ac 14:6; 21:39;** to denote the inhabitants (Diod. S. 34 and 35 fgm. 23 ἡ τῶν Γαλατῶν πόλις; Jos., Ant. 1, 200) ἡ πόλ. Δαμασκηνῶν **2 Cor 11:32.** π. Σαμαριτῶν **Mt 10:5; Lk 9:52 v.l.** Cp. **23:51; Ac 19:35;** EpilMosq 4; AcPl Ox 6, 20 (=Aa I 242, 1). αἱ πόλεις τοῦ Ἰσραήλ *the cities in which the people of Israel live* **Mt 10:23b** (Ἰσραήλ 2).—**Rv 16:19b.** ἡ πόλ. αὐτῶν **Mt 22:7; Lk 4:29b.**—**2:39.** Also w. the gen. sg. πόλ. Δαυίδ *city of David* **2:4b, 11;** ἡ ἑαυτοῦ πολ. *the person's own town* (=ancestral locale; but **2:39** Nazareth = their place of residence) **2:3.**—**J 1:44.** Also ἡ ἰδία πόλ. (s. ἴδιος 1b) **Mt 9:1; Lk 2:3 v.l.;** Hs 1:2b (in imagery, s. 2 below). Pl. 1 Cl 55:1. The πόλεις ἴδιαι of the Christians Dg 5:2 are those inhabited by them alone; they are contrasted w. πόλεις Ἑλληνίδες *Greek cities* (cp. SIG 761, 15 [48/47 BC]; 909, 2), π. βάρβαροι Dg 5:4.—π. μεγάλαι *great cities* 1 Cl 6:4; AcPl Ha 2, 25f. In Rv ἡ πόλ. ἡ. μεγάλη (Tat. 19, 1; 29, 1 Rome) is almost always 'Babylon' (s. Βαβυλών) **16:19a; 17:18; 18:16, 18f, 21;** ἡ πόλις ἡ μεγάλη, Βαβυλὼν ἡ πόλις ἡ ἰσχυρά **18:10.** On the other hand ἡ πόλ. ἡ μεγάλη **11:8** is clearly Jerusalem (as SibOr 5, 154; 226). Elsewh. Jerus. is called ἡ πόλ. ἡ ἠγαπημένη **20:9** (cp. ApcSed 8:3 πρῶτον ἠγάπησας . . . εἰς τὰς πόλεις τὴν Ἰερουσαλήμ); ἡ ἁγία πόλ. **Mt 4:5; 27:53; Rv 11:2** (ἅγιος 1aα); πόλ. τοῦ μεγάλου βασιλέως *the city of the Great King* **Mt 5:35** (βασιλεύς 2b). εἰς πόλιν ἄρχουσαν ὀπύσεως *in the city that sponsors fornication* ApcPt Rainer 4,

1 (Ja. p. 278; s. also ὄπυσις).—The name of the town or city that goes w. πόλις stands either in the epexegetic gen. (Aeschyl. et al.; also Demetr.: 722 fgm. 1, 8 Jac. πόλιν Σικίμων) πόλεις Σοδόμων καὶ Γομόρρας **2 Pt 2:6** or in the case in which πόλις itself is found, ἐν πόλει Ἰόππῃ **Ac 11:5;** πόλις Λασαία **27:8.** From the construction πόλεως Θυατίρων **Ac 16:14** no determination of the nom. of Θυ- can be made: either πόλις Θυατίρων or πόλις Θυάτιρα (B-D-R §167, 3). W. indecl. place names **Lk 2:4a, 39.** πόλις λεγομένη or καλουμένη w. the name following **Mt 2:23; Lk 7:11; 9:10.** Cp. **J 11:54.**—ἀπὸ πόλεως εἰς πόλιν (Aesop, Fab. 228 P.//421 H.//354 Ch.//H-H. 256 μεταβαίνουσιν ἀπὸ πόλεως εἰς πόλιν) **Mt 23:34.** κατὰ τὴν πόλιν *anywhere in the city* **Ac 24:12.** Cp. **Lk 8:39** (κατά B1a). κατὰ πόλιν *from city to city* IRo 9:3; pl. **Lk 13:22;** *in every city* (Appian, Bell. Civ. 1. 39 §177) **Ac 15:21, 36** (κατὰ πόλιν πᾶσαν); **20:23; Tit 1:5** (Diod. S. 5, 78, 2 Crete has, indeed, 'not a few' cities). Cp. **Lk 8:1, 4** (κατά B1d). αἱ ἔξω πόλεις **Ac 26:11** (ἔξω 1aβ). αἱ πέριξ πόλεις **5:16** (s. πέριξ). αἱ περὶ αὐτὰς (i.e. Sodom and Gomorrah) πόλεις **Jd 7.** πρὸ τ. πόλεως (Jos., Bell. 1, 234, Ant. 10, 44) **Ac 14:13.**

❷ *the (heavenly) city = the New Jerusalem* (Bousset, Rel.[3] 283ff; RKnopf, GHeinrici Festschr. 14, 213–19; McQueen, Exp. 9th ser., 2, 1924, 220–26; FDijkema, NThT 15, 1926, 25–43) **Hb 11:10, 16** (cp. TestJob 18:8; TestAbr A 2 p. 78, 30 [Stone p. 4] ἀπὸ τῆς μεγάλης πόλεως ἔρχομαι [of Michael]). πόλ. θεοῦ ζῶντος **12:22** (SibOr 5, 250 θεοῦ π. of Jerus.). ἡ μέλλουσα (opp. οὐ ... μένουσα πόλις) **13:14.** Esp. in Rv: ἡ πόλις ἡ ἁγία Ἰερουσαλὴμ (καινή) **21:2, 10** (CBouma, GereformTT 36, '36, 91–98). Further vss. **14–16, 18f, 21, 23; 22:14, 19;** also **3:12.** (Cp. Lucian's description of the wonder-city in Ver. Hist. 2, 11f: ἡ πόλις πᾶσα χρυσῆ, τὸ τεῖχος σμαράγδινον. πύλαι ... ἑπτά, πᾶσαι μονόξυλοι κινναμώμιναι ... γῆ ἐλεφαντίνη ... ναοὶ βηρύλλου λίθου ... βωμοὶ ... ἀμεθύστινοι ... ποταμὸς μύρου τοῦ καλλίστου ... οἶκοι ὑάλινοι ... οὐδὲ νὺξ οὐδὲ ἡμέρα.) On the topic s. JMorwood, Aeneas, Augustus, and the Theme of the City: Greece and Rome new ser. 38, '91, 212–23.—Hs 1:1, 2.

❸ **inhabitants of a city,** ***city*** abstr. for concrete (X., Cyr. 1, 4, 25; Herodian 3, 2, 7; Jos., Ant. 5, 357) **Lk 4:43; Ac 14:21; 16:20** (cp. Jos., Bell. 7, 41; DWhitehead, MusHelv 53/1, '96, 1–11 [on identification of citizens and place cp. Thu. 2, 2, 1; X., Hell. 2, 2, 9]). πᾶσα ἡ πόλις (Diod. S. 18, 70, 2; Appian, Numid. 1) **Mt 8:34; 21:10** (w. λέγουσα foll.); **Ac 13:44;** ὅλη ἡ π. (Diod. S. 10, 3, 2) **Mk 1:33; Ac 21:30.** πόλις μερισθεῖσα καθ' ἑαυτῆς **Mt 12:25.** ἐθριαμβεύετο ὑπὸ τῆς πόλεως *(Paul) was derided by the city* AcPl Ha 4, 13 (s. θριαμβεύω 5). HConn, Lucan Perspective and the City: Missiology 13, '85, 409–28 (Lk-Ac contains half of the 160+ occurrences of π. in the NT).—B. 1308. Schmidt, Syn. II 495–507. DELG. M-M. EDNT. TW.

πολιτάρχης, ου, ὁ (on the form cp. πολίαρχος Mason 76f; found only in ins and pap, but Aeneas Tact. 26, 12 has a dialectical variant πολίταρχος) **a magistrate who formed part of a town or city council,** ***city official.*** No precise job description is extant, but administration of security measures, as indicated Aeneas Tact. 26, 12 and suggested by the circumstances recorded Ac 17:5–13, was certainly assigned to such office, which predates 167 BC. A number of π. (five or six in Thessalonica) formed the city council in Macedonian cities, and occasionally in others (s. EBurton, The Politarchs in Macedonia and Elsewhere: AJTh 2, 1898, 598–632 w. exx. fr. ins; s. also SIG 700, 1; 48 [the Maced. city of Letae, 118/117 BC]; POxy 745, 4 [I BC/I AD]; Sb 5765, 7), specif. in Thessalonica (CIG II 1967; BCH 18, 1894, 420; 21, 1897, 161 al.; fr. Berea SEG XXVII, 261 [II BC] παρὰ τῶν πολιταρχῶν οὐ εἷς=one 'no' vote from among the politarchs) **Ac 17:6, 8.**—Ins in IMakedD; EBurton, AJT 2, 1898, 598–632; Ferguson, Legal Terms 65f and index, p. 103 w. reff. to Demitsas; CSchuler, ClPh 55, '60, 90–100 [w. list of all then-known ins referring to Macedonia, most from Thess.]; JOliver, ClPh 58, '63, 164f; Pauly-W., Suppl. 13, '73, 483–500; BLaourdas/CMakaronas, edd., Ancient Macedonia II '77, 139–50 [JCormack, 'Gymnasiarchal Law of Beroea'], 531–44 [BHelly, 'Politarques, Poliarques et Polito-phylaques']; MHatzopoulos, in Dritter internationaler Thrakologischer Kongress zu Ehren WTomascheks, 2–6 Juni 1980, '84, 137–49; GHorsley, ABD V, 384–89, w. list of ins and bibl.; Boffo, Iscrizioni no. 27 (lit.); Hemer Acts 115; s. also New Docs, '82, 34f; SEG XLIV, 499.—S. DELG s.v. ἄρχω C. M-M.

πολιτεία, ας, ἡ (πολίτης; Hdt.+; ins, pap; 2, 3, 4 Macc; TestAbr A 20 p. 104, 7 [Stone p. 56]; ApcMos prol.; Philo, Joseph., Just., Tat.)

❶ **the right to be a member of a sociopolitical entity,** ***citizenship*** (Hdt. 9, 34; X., Hell. 1, 1, 26; 1, 2, 10; 4, 4, 6; Polyb. 6, 2, 12; Diod. S. 14, 8, 3; 14, 17, 3; Cyr. Ins. 57; 59; Gnomon [=BGU V 1] 47; 3 Macc 3:21, 23; Jos., Ant. 12, 119) lit., of Roman citizenship (Dio Chrys. 24 [41], 2 Ῥωμαίων π.; Ael. Aristid. 30, 10 K.=10 p. 117 D.; IG IV^2/1, 84, 33 [40/42 AD]; Jos., Bell. 1, 194 and Vi 423 π. Ῥωμαίων.—WRamsay, The Social Basis of Roman Power in Asia Minor '41) πολιτείαν ἐκτησάμην **Ac 22:28.**—In a transf. sense, this transl. is poss. (EHaupt, PEwald et al.) for **Eph 2:12,** but not very probable (s. 2 below).

❷ **a sociopolitical unit or body of citizens,** ***state, people, body politic*** (Thu. 1, 127, 3; Pla., Rep. 10, 619c; Diod. S. 5, 45, 3; Appian, Bell. Civ. 2, 19 §68; Just., A II, 10, 6) ἀπηλλοτριωμένοι τ. πολιτείας τοῦ Ἰσραήλ *alienated from the people of Israel* Eph **2:12** (so HvSoden, MDibelius, NRSV et al.; s. 1 above).

❸ **behavior in accordance with standards expected of a respectable citizen,** ***way of life, conduct*** (Athen. 1, 19a; Herm. Wr. in Stob. p. 486, 24 Sc. ἡ τῶν ἀνθρώπων ἄγριος πολιτεία; Ps.-Liban., Charact. Ep. p. 34, 2; 47, 8; 10; Biogr. p. 261; TestAbr A 20 p. 104, 7 [Stone p. 56]; ApcMos prol.; Just., A I, 4, 2 al.; Tat.) Dg 5:4; ἀγαθὴ πολ. MPol 13:2; ἡ ἀπ' ἀρχῆς ἀνεπίληπτος πολ. 17:1; ἡ πανάρετος καὶ σεβάσμιος πολ. 1 Cl 2:8. οἱ πολιτευόμενοι τὴν ἀμεταμέλητον πολιτείαν τοῦ θεοῦ *those who follow God's way of life, that brings no regrets* 54:4 (πολιτεύεσθαι πολιτείαν in Nicol. Dam.: 90 fgm. 126 Jac. and in the Synagogue ins fr. Stobi [c. 100 AD] lines 6f: ZNW 32, '33, 93f).—DELG s.v. πόλις. M-M. TW. Spicq.

πολίτευμα, ατος, τό (πολίτης, cp. the prec. and next entry; Pla. et al.; ins, pap) ***commonwealth, state*** (so Polyb. 1, 13, 12; 35, 5; Diod. S. 19, 75, 4; ins; 2 Macc 12:7; Jos., Ant. 1, 13, C. Ap. 2, 257; fig. Philo, Agr. 81 τῷ τῆς ἀρετῆς ἐγγεγραμμέναι πολιτεύματι, Conf. Lingu. 78 πατρίδα τὸν οὐράνιον χῶρον ἐν ᾧ πολιτεύονται.—Schürer III 88f; PBöttger, ZNW 60, '69, 244–53) ἡμῶν τὸ πολ. ἐν οὐρανοῖς ὑπάρχει *our commonwealth is in heaven* **Phil 3:20** (πολίτευμα oft. denotes a colony of foreigners or relocated veterans CIG 5361, III add. 5866c; PTebt 32, 9; 17 [II BC]; EpArist 310. Cp. OGI 737, 2 with note 2 and the lit. in MDibelius, Hdb. ad loc.; JdeZwaan, Philippenzen 3:20 en de Κοινή: TSt 31, 1913, 298–300; LFuchs, D. Juden in Ägypten 1924, 89; MEngers, Πολίτευμα: Mnemosyne 54, 1926, 154–61; WRuppel, Politeuma: Philol. 82, 1927, 268–312; 433–52; EPeterson s.v. ἐκκλησία, end; 'Our home is in heaven, and here on earth we are a colony of heavenly citizens' MDibelius.—The sense seems to be more general in Menand. Rhet. [II AD] III 421, 16 Spengel: the deceased, so the word of consolation goes, πολιτεύεται μετὰ τῶν θεῶν; Hierocles, 3, 2 p. 424: 'heroes' convey the souls of the righteous πρὸς τὴν θείαν πολιτείαν. Olympiodorus In Platonis Phaedonem, ed. WNorvin 1913 p. 122, 8 [on Pla., Phd. 69c] of the philosopher: συμπολιτεύεσθαι τοῖς θεοῖς καὶ συνοικονομεῖν).—DELG s.v. πόλις. M-M. TW. Spicq. Sv.

πολιτεύομαι (πολίτης; the mid., which is the only voice found in our lit., since Thu., Aristoph.+) 1 aor. ἐπολιτευσάμην, subj. 1 pl. πολιτευσώμεθα; pf. πεπολίτευμαι.

❶ **to be a citizen,** ***have one's citizenship/home*** (Philo, Conf. Lingu. 78 [s. πολίτευμα]) of Christians ἐν οὐρανῷ Dg 5:9 (Himerius, Or. 8 [=23], 23 of a deceased person: μετὰ θεῶν πολιτεύεσθαι; Hippol., Ref. 6, 34, 3 of angels: π. ἐν Ἱερουσαλὴμ τῇ ἄνω; cp. Iren. 4, 5, 3 [Harv. II 156, 8; here opposite ξενιτεύω 'live away from home']).

❷ **to administrate a corporate body,** ***rule***—ⓐ of a head of state, *govern a state* abs. (Thu. 2, 15, 1 al.; Jos., Ant. 14, 91 π. ἐν Ἱεροσ.) of God, who ἐν οὐρανοῖς πολιτεύεται *rules in heaven* Dg 10:7.

ⓑ of church officials (Orig., C. Cels. 3, 30, 15) 1 Cl 44:6.

❸ **to conduct one's life,** ***live, lead one's life*** (UPZ 144, 14 [164/163 BC] ὁσίως κ. δικαίως; Hierocles 11, 444; Ps.-Liban., Charact. Ep. p. 31, 5 σεμνῶς; 34, 1; 2 Macc 6:1; 11:25; 3 Macc 3:4; 4 Macc 2:8 al.; ApcEsdr 2:9; Philo, Virt. 161, Spec. Leg. 4, 226; Jos., Ant. 12, 142, Vi. 12; Just., Tat., Ath.; Did., Gen. 153, 28 καλῶς) καλῶς κ. ἁγνῶς Hs 5, 6, 6. ὁσίως 1 Cl 6:1. ἀξίως τινός **Phil 1:27** (RBrewer, JBL 73, '54, 76–83: 'discharge your obligations as citizens'; EMiller, JSNT 15, '82, 86–96; EKrentz, in Origins and Method, JHurd Festschr., ed. BMcLean '93, 114–17); 1 Cl 21:1; Pol 5:2. μετὰ φόβου καὶ ἀγάπης 1 Cl 51:2. (W. πορεύεσθαι) πολιτεύεσθαι κατὰ τὸ καθῆκον τῷ Χριστῷ 3:4 (πολ. κατά τι as SIG 618, 12 [188 BC]; 2 Macc 11:25; 4 Macc 2:23; EpArist 31; Jos., Ant. 12, 142; Did., Gen. 196, 29); π. πολιτείαν 54:4 (πολιτεία 3). W. a double dat. συνειδήσει ἀγαθῇ πεπολίτευμαι τῷ θεῷ *I have lived my life with a clear conscience before God* **Ac 23:1** (for the dat. τῷ θεῷ cp. PHib 63, 10 [III BC] εἰ οὕτως πολιτευσόμεθα ἀλλήλοις).—Straub p. 30. DELG s.v. πόλις. M-M. TW. Spicq. Sv.

πολίτης, ου, ὁ (πόλις; Hom. et al.; ins, pap, LXX, TestJob 29, 1; EpArist, Philo, Joseph.)

❶ **one who lives in or comes fr. a city or country,** ***citizen*** of πόλεως **Ac 21:39.** τῆς χώρας ἐκείνης **Lk 15:15.** (Opp. ξένοι, as Philo, Poster. Cai. 109) Dg 5:5; AcPl Ha 4, 6.

❷ **a member of one's own sociopolitical group,** ***fellow-citizen, compatriot*** (Pla., Apol. 37c, Prot. 339f; Diod. S. 11, 47, 3; 11, 62, 1 al.; Phlegon: 257 fgm. 36, 2, 4 Jac.; Appian, Bell. Civ. 4, 127 §531 al.; Chion, Ep. 15, 1; Pr 11:9; 24:28; TestJob 29:1; Jos., Ant. 1, 21, Vi. 274) **Hb 8:11** (Jer 38:34). The *compatriots* or *subjects* of a ruler are likew. so called (Schol. on Nicander, Ther. 15 [p. 5, 34]; Jos., Ant. 12, 162) 1 Cl 55:1. Cp. **Lk 19:14.**—DELG s.v. πόλις. M-M. TW. Spicq.

πολῖτις, ιδος, ἡ fem. of πολίτης (Soph., Eur., Pla.; also Menand., Sicyonius 197 S.; ins, Philo, Joseph.) ***citizen,*** of Artemilla ἡ τῆς τρυφῆς πολλῆς π. *citizen of great luxury* AcPl Ha 2, 19f.—DELG s.v. πόλις.

πολλά s. πολύς 1aβב.

πολλάκις adv. (Hom.+) **pert. to a number of related points of time,** ***many times, often, frequently*** **Mt 17:15; Mk 5:4; 9:22; J 18:2; Ac 26:11; Ro 1:13; 15:22 v.l.; 2 Cor 11:23, 26, 27ab; Phil 3:18; 2 Ti 1:16; Hb 6:7; 9:25f; 10:11;** Hv 3, 1, 2. In wordplay (Dio Chrys. 11 [12], 50; 71; Theodor. Prodr. 6, 93 H. πολλοῖς πολλαχοῦ κ. πολλάκις; SIG 888, 138f πολλοὶ πολλάκις στρατιῶται; Esth 8:12e πολλάκις δὲ καὶ πολλοὺς κτλ.; Jos., C. Ap. 2, 219; 231) ἐν πολλοῖς πολλάκις *often in many ways* **2 Cor 8:22** (πολύ and πολλῇ follow in the same sentence).—B. 986. M-M.

πολλαπλασιάζω (πολύς, πλάσσω; Aristot., Ph. 237b, 33; Polyb. 30, 4, 13; Diod. S. 1, 1, et al.) ***multiply, increase*** π. τὴν ἐργασίαν *increase the proceeds* (=*make much profit on an investment*) GHb 297, 21.

πολλαπλασίων, ον, gen. ονος (Isocr. 15, 177; Archimed. II 134, 13 Heib.; Polyb. 35, 4, 4; Philodem., Π. σημ. 9, 32; Plut., Mor. 191c; 215b; Jos., Bell. 1, 514; Ael. Aristid. 27, 20 K.=16 p. 390 D. for earlier πολλαπλάσιος [Hdt., Pla. et al.; so also Philo, Somn. 1, 53; Jos., Bell. 5, 553]) **far in excess of a quantity normally expected,** ***many times as much, manifold*** λαμβάνειν neut. pl. πολλαπλασίονα (Jos., Bell. 1, 514; TestZeb 6:6) **Mt 19:29 v.l.; Lk 18:30.**—ESchwyzer, Museum Helveticum 2, '45, 137–47; Renehan '75, 167.—M-M.

πολλοστός, ή, όν formed from πολύς on the analogy of εἰκοστός (s. L-S-J-M; Schwyzer I 584.—In non-bibl. Gk. freq. in ref. to relative remoteness on a scale of extent or degree Aristoph., X., Pla.; Philo, De Somn. 1, 204, De Praem. 128; πολλοστὸν μέρος 'smallest part' or 'very small fraction' Andoc. et al. Used like πολύς to denote degree 2 Km 23:20 πολλοστὸς ἔργοις='noted for many deeds'; Ps 54:19 Sym.; cp. Pr 5:19) ***abounding*** of the resurrected body (in imagery of a grain of wheat) σῶμα … π., ὀρθόν, ηὐλογημένον *a body … abounding/teeming* (because it is productive), *upright, and blessed* AcPlCor 2:27.—DELG s.v. πολύς.

πόλος, ου, ὁ (πέλομαι 'become, be'; Aeschyl., Hdt., Pla. et al.; Philo; Jos., Ant. 3, 184) **vault of heaven,** ***firmament*** ἀνέβλεψα εἰς τὸν π. *I looked up to the firmament* GJs 18:2 (codd.).—DELG s.v. πέλομαι.

πολυαγάπητος, ον (Hesychius s.v. πολύθεστος) ***much-loved*** ὄνομα IEph 1:1.

Πολύβιος, ου, ὁ (Dit., Syll. 686; 1115, 30) ***Polybius,*** bishop of Tralles ITr 1:1.

πολυευσπλαγχνία, ας, ἡ (cp. πολυεύσπλαγχνος) ***richness in mercy*** π. τοῦ κυρίου Hs 8, 6, 1 v.l.—DELG s.v. σπλήν.

πολυεύσπλαγχνος, ον ***rich in compassion,*** of God **Js 5:11 v.l.;** Hs 5, 4, 4.—DELG s.v. σπλήν.

πολυεύτακτος, ον ***very well ordered/disciplined*** subst. ὑμῶν τὸ π. τῆς κατὰ θεὸν ἀγάπης *how well-ordered your God-like love is* IMg 1:1.—DELG s.v. τάσσω.

Πολύκαρπος, ου, ὁ (references for the name in the Hdb. on Pol ins) ***Polycarp,*** bishop of Smyrna, and acc. to Irenaeus (3, 3, 4 [Harv. II 12–15]) a disciple of the Apostle John. He died as a martyr, prob. Feb. 22, 156 AD (so ESchwartz, De Pionio et Polycarpo 1905, Christl. und jüd. Ostertafeln: AGG n.s. VIII 6 [1905] 125ff). Other calculations conclude that the date is Feb. 23 of 155 or 166 AD (s. Harnack, Chronologie I 1897, 325ff; PCorssen, ZNW 3, 1902, 61ff; NBonwetsch, RE XV 1904, 535ff). We possess a letter to the Philippians written by him (Pol.—S. PHarrison, Polycarp's Two Epistles to the Philippians '36 [bibliogr.]); MPol is a contemporary report of his martyrdom. IEph 21:1; IMg 15; IPol ins; 7:2; 8:2; Pol ins; MPol 1:1 al. Acc. to Iren.,

Eus., and Philip of Side (in Pamphylia), Papias was a contemporary: Papias (1:4; 11:1).—RGrant, Polycarp of Smyrna: ATR 28, '46, 137–48; Altaner/Stuiber, Patrologie[8] '78 (lit.); Pauly-W. XXI 1662–93; Kl. Pauly IV 998f; BHHW III 1479; ABD V 389f.

πολύλαλος, ον (Cleobulus [VI BC] in Stob. III p. 112, 3 H.; Ael. Dion. κ, 8; Vi. Aesopi G 26 P.; schol. on Soph., Ant. 324 p. 234 Papag.; Plotinus 6, 2, 21; Job 11:2 Sym.) **engaged in much purposeless talk, *talkative, garrulous*** w. ἀναιδής Hm 11:12. VandeSande Bakhuyzen suspects that πολύλαλοι was once read **Js 3:1** for πολλοὶ διδάσκαλοι (B-D-F §115, 1).—DELG s.v. λαλέω.

πολυλογία, ας, ἡ (X., Cyr. 1, 4, 3; Pla., Leg. 1, 641e; Plut., Mor. 6c; 519c; Vett. Val. 108, 8; 23; Herm. Wr. 14, 5; Sextus 155; Pr 10:19) **speech of tedious length, *much speaking, wordiness, long-windedness*** ἐν τῇ π. αὐτῶν *with their many words* **Mt 6:7; Lk 11:2** D (Ael. Aristid. 45, 8 K.=8 p. 85 D.: θεοὺς ἄνευ μέτρων προσαγορεύοντες οὐκ αἰσχυνόμεθα=we are not ashamed of addressing gods without mantras/incantations).—DELG s.v. λέγω B. M-M. TW.

πολυμερῶς (μέρος) adv. (Diod. S. 5, 37, 2; Plut., Mor. 537d; several times in Vett. Val. [index III]; Jos., Ant. 12, 54) of πολυμερής, ές (Aristot.; Plut., Mor. 427b; 757d; PGM 13, 304; Wsd 7:22; Ar. 13, 5 body consists of 'of many parts'; Tat. 15, 1 the soul is composite; s. also Porph., Sent. 34) of prophetic writing, ***in various parts*** w. πολυτρόπως='in various ways' (the two words together also Maximus Tyr. 1, 2b; 11, 7a) **Hb 1:1** (on the alliteration cp. the beginning of Philo, περὶ μετανοίας; for extreme fondness of π sounds s. e.g. Gorgias 11, 11). Many render *in many ways* (L-S-J-M cite Plut., Mor. 537d in support, but this pass. refers to the numerous aspects of Thersites' deformed body, whose various parts are described in Il. 2, 217–19) so NRSV: 'in many and various ways'. If 'many ways' in such rendering refers to a variety of Scripture passages, the translators have the support of the Vulgate: multifariam. But to avoid a suggestion of banality, it is best to render along the line suggested above. Also, the rhetorical structure of Hb requires some preparation in the prol. for the numerous reff. to the OT.—DELG s.v. μείρομαι II. M-M.

πολυπλάσιος, α, ον (on the form s. Schwyzer I 446; 2 Macc 9:16; Philo; Agis, Anth. Pal. 6, 152; PPanop 2, 232 [III AD]) ***manifold*** καρπὸν δικαιοσύνης αὐτοῦ μονοούσιον πολυπλάσιον *his harvest of uprightness, unique and diverse* GJs 6:3 (codd.; s. deStrycker 225–27. The pap and other codd. have the otherwise unknown πολυπλούσιον 'abundantly rich').—DELG s.v. πέλας.

πολυπλήθεια, ας, ἡ (πολύς, πλῆθος; Hippocr. et al.; Menand., Dysc. 166; Περὶ ὕψους 32, 1 p. 56, 5 V.; Ps.-Plut., Hom. 85; Dit., Syll. 880, 40; 2 Macc 8:16) ***large crowd*** **Ac 14:7 v.l.** (in an addition in codex E; codex D has πλῆθος). τὴν π. (πολυπληθίαν is to be rejected, w. Lghtf., and πολυπλήθειαν, which is also attested, is to be inserted) ὑμῶν ἀπείληφα *I have received your whole (large) congregation* IEph 1:3.—DELG s.v. πίμπλημι.

πολυπλοκία, ας, ἡ (πολύπλοκος 'tangled, complex' [πλέκω]; Theognis 67) **practice of complex intrigue, *cunning, craftiness*** τοῦ διαβόλου Hm 4, 3, 4.—DELG s.v. πλέκω B.

πολυπλούσιος s. πολυπλάσιος.

πολυποίκιλος, ον (s. ποικίλος; Eur. et al.) **pert. to being diversified, *(very) many-sided*** (so Orph. Hymn., 6, 11; 61, 4 [λόγος]; TestSol 4:4 and C 11:4 [τρόπος]; SibOr 8, 120 [ὀργή]) σοφία **Eph 3:10.**—M-M. TW.

πολύπους, ποδος, ὁ *octopus* (Hom. et al.; Ps.-Phoc. 49; Philo, Ebr. 172; Tart. 2, 1) w. sea-eel and cuttle-fish B 10:5 (vGebhardt's edition has πώλυπα [s. πῶλυψ]. πολύποδα is also attested; Bihlmeyer ad loc.; cp. Lev 11:10; also s. σηπία and σμύραινα).

πολυπραγμοσύνη, ης, ἡ (s. next entry; Thu., Aristoph. et al., mostly in an unfavorable sense such as 'inquisitiveness, officiousness, meddlesomeness'; s. esp. Plut., Mor. 515b–23) **state of being overly interested in minor details, *fussiness,*** ἡ Ἰουδαίων πολυπρ. Dg 4:6.—AAdkins, ClPh 71, '76, 301–27.—DELG s.v. πράσσω.

πολυπράγμων, ον, gen. **ονος** (cp. prec. entry; since Eupolis Com. [V BC] 222, Lysias, Aristoph.; Philo Bybl. [100 AD]: 790 fgm. 1 [24] Jac. [in Eu., PE 1, 9, 24]; Philo Alex., Abr. 20, Spec. Leg. 1, 69; Jos., Ant. 15, 182) if in the rarer good sense (Polyb. 9, 4, 4; cp. πολυπραγμονέω 'inquire' New Docs 1 no. 12, 15) ***inquisitive*** π. ἄνθρωποι Dg 5:3.—DELG s.v. πράσσω.

πολύς, πολλή, πολύ, gen. **πολλοῦ, ῆς, οῦ** (Hom.+; ins, pap, LXX, pseudepigr., Philo, Joseph., apolog.) 'much'.—Comparative **πλείων, πλεῖον** (18 times in the NT, 4 times in the Apost. Fathers [including Hv 3, 6, 4; s 8, 1, 16] and Ath. 12, 3) or **πλέον** (**Lk 3:13** and **Ac 15:28** μηδὲν πλέον; otherwise, πλέον in the NT only **J 21:15;** 14 times in the Apost. Fathers [incl. μηδὲν πλέον Hs 1, 1, 6]; Ar. twice; Just. 6 times; Tat. once; Ath. 7 times), **ονος ;** pl. πλείονες, and acc. πλείονας contracted πλείους, neut. πλείονα and πλείω (the latter **Mt 26:53** [πλεῖον, πλείους vv.ll.]; B-D-F §30, 2; Mlt-H. 82; Thackeray p. 81f; Mayser p. 68f) 'more' (Hom.+; ins, pap, LXX; TestAbr B 7 p. 111, 27=Stone p. 70 [πλείον]; TestJob 35:2; TestGad 7:2 [πλεῖον]; AscIs 3:8; [πλέον]; EpArist; apolog. exc. Mel.).—Superlative **πλεῖστος, η, ον** 'most' (Hom.+).

❶ pert. to being a large number, *many, a great number of* ⓐ positive πολύς, πολλή, πολύ—**α.** adj., preceding or following a noun (or ptc. or adj. used as a noun) in the pl. *many, numerous* δυνάμεις πολλαί *many mighty deeds* **Mt 7:22b.** δαιμονιζόμενοι πολλοί **8:16.** Cp. vs. **30; 9:10; 13:17; 24:11; 27:52, 55; Mk 2:15a; 6:13; 12:41; Lk 4:25, 27; 7:21b; 10:24; J 10:32; 14:2; Ac 1:3; 2:43; 8:7b; 14:22; Ro 4:17f** (Gen 17:5); **8:29; 12:4; 1 Cor 8:5ab; 11:30; 12:12a, 20; 1 Ti 6:12; 2 Ti 2:2; Hb 2:10; 1J 4:1; 2J 7; Rv 5:11; 9:9; 10:11;** 1 Cl 55:3ab. ἔτη πολλά *many years:* **Lk 12:19b** (εἰς ἔτη π.); **Ac 24:10** (ἐκ π. ἐτῶν); **Ro 15:23** (ἀπὸ π. [v.l. ἱκανῶν] ἐτῶν).—αἱ ἁμαρτίαι αἱ πολλαί **Lk 7:47a.** αἱ εὐεργεσίαι αἱ π. 1 Cl 21:1.—πολλὰ καὶ βαρέα αἰτιώματα *many serious charges* **Ac 25:7** (cp. Ps.-Pla., Sisyph. 1, 387a πολλά τε καὶ καλὰ πράγματα; B-D-F §442, 11; Rob. 655). πολλὰ καὶ ἄλλα σημεῖα **J 20:30** (on the form X., Hell. 5, 4, 1 πολλὰ μὲν οὖν . . . καὶ ἄλλα λέγειν καὶ Ἑλληνικὰ καὶ βαρβαρικά; Dionys. Hal. 2, 67, 5; Ps.-Demetr. 142 πολλὰς κ. ἄλλας χάριτας; Jos., Ant. 3, 318; Tat. 38, 1. On the subject-matter Bultmann 540, 3; also Porphyr., Vi. Pyth. 28 after a miracle-story: μυρία δ' ἕτερα θαυμαστότερα κ. θειότερα περὶ τἀνδρὸς . . . εἴρηται κτλ.).—ἄλλοι πολλοί *many others* IRo 10:1. ἄλλαι πολλαί **Mk 15:41.** ἄλλα πολλά (Jos., Bell. 6, 169, Ant. 9, 242; Just., D. 8, 1) **J 21:25.** ἕτεροι πολλοί **Ac 15:35.** ἕτερα πολλά (Jos., Vi. 39) **Lk 22:65.**—Predicative: πολλοί εἰσιν οἱ εἰσερχόμενοι **Mt 7:13.—Mk 5:9; 6:31; Gal 4:27** (Is 54:1). AcPl Ha 5, 16.—οὐ πολλοί *not many=(only) a few* οὐ πολλαὶ ἡμέραι (Jos., Ant. 5, 328, Vi. 309) **Lk 15:13; J 2:12;**

Ac 1:5; AcPl Ha 11, 1. οὐ πολλοὶ σοφοί *not many wise (people)* **1 Cor 1:26a;** cp. **bc.** οὐ πολλοί πατέρες *not many fathers* **4:15.**

β. subst.—**א.** πολλοί *many* i.e. persons—without the art. **Mt 7:22; 8:11; 12:15; 20:28; 24:5ab; 26:28; Mk 2:2; 3:10** (Mt 12:15 has ascensive πάντας; other passages to be compared in this connection are **Mk 10:45=Mt 20:28** πολλῶν and 1 Ti 2:6 πάντων. Cp. the double tradition of the saying of Bias in Clem. of Alex., Strom. 1, 61, 3 πάντες ἄνθρωποι κακοὶ ἢ οἱ πλεῖστοι τ. ἀνθρώπων κακοί.—On **Mk 10:45** s. OCullmann, TZ 4, '48, 471–73); **6:2; 11:8; Lk 1:1** (cp. Herm. Wr. 11, 1, 1b and see JBauer, NovT 4, '60, 263–66), **14; J 2:23; 8:30; Ac 9:42; Ro 16:2; 2 Cor 11:18; Gal 3:16** (πολλοί=*a plurality*); **Tit 1:10; Hb 12:15; 2 Pt 2:2.** AcPl Ha 5, 8; 7, 5; 11, 3. Opp. ὀλίγοι **Mt 22:14; 20:16 v.l.** (cp. Pla., Phd. 69c ναρθηκοφόροι μὲν πολλοί, βάκχοι δέ τε παῦροι=the thyrsus-bearers [officials] are many, but the truly inspired are few)—W. a partitive gen. πολλοὶ τῶν Φαρισαίων **Mt 3:7.** π. πῶν υἱῶν Ἰσραήλ **Lk 1:16.—J 4:39; 12:11; Ac 4:4; 8:7a; 13:43; 18:8; 19:18; 2 Cor 12:21; Rv 8:11.**—W. ἐκ and gen. (AscIs 3:1; Jos., Ant. 11, 151) πολλοὶ ἐκ τῶν μαθητῶν **J 6:60, 66.—10:20; 11:19, 45; 12:42; Ac 17:12.** ἐκ τοῦ ὄχλου πολλοί **J 7:31** (Appian, Iber. 78 §337 πολλοὶ ἐκ τοῦ πλήθους).

ב. πολλά—*many things, much* without the art.: γράφειν *write at length* B 4:9. διδάσκειν **Mk 4:2; 6:34b.** λαλεῖν **Mt 13:3.** μηχανᾶσθαι MPol 3. πάσχειν (Pind., O. 13, 63 al.; Jos., Ant. 13, 268; 403) **Mt 16:21; Mk 5:26a; 9:12; Lk 9:22; 17:25;** B 7:11; AcPl Ha 8, 19. ποιεῖν **Mk 6:20 v.l.** United w. another neut. by καί (Lucian, Icar. 20 πολλὰ κ. δεινά; Ael. Aristid. 46 p. 345 D.: πολλὰ κ. καλά; Ps.-Demetr., El. 70 πολλὰ κ. ἄλλα; likew. Appian, Bell. Civ. 5, 13 §53; Arrian, Anab. 6, 11, 2) πολλὰ κ. ἕτερα *many other things* **Lk 3:18.** πολλὰ ἂν κ. ἄλλα εἰπεῖν ἔχοιμι Dg 2:10 (Eur., Ep. 3, 2, πολλὰ κ. ἕτερα εἰπεῖν ἔχω; Diod. S. 17, 38, 3 πολλὰ δὲ καὶ ἄλλα . . . διαλεχθείς). ἐν πολλοῖς *in many ways* (Diod. S. 26, 1, 2; OGI 737, 7 [II BC]; Just., D. 124, 4 [of line of proof]) **2 Cor 8:22a.** ἐπὶ πολλῶν (opp. ἐπὶ ὀλίγα) *over many things* **Mt 25:21, 23.**—W. art. (Pla., Apol. 1, 17a) τὰ πολλὰ πράσσειν *transact a great deal of business* Hs 4:5b.

γ. elliptical δαρήσεται πολλά (sc. πληγάς) *will receive many (lashes)* **Lk 12:47** (B-D-F §154; 241, 6).

ⓑ comparative πλείων, πλεῖον—**α.** adj. w. a plural (Diod. S. 14, 6, 1 μισθοφόρους πλείους=many mercenaries) πλείονας πόνους (opp. οὐχ ἕνα οὐδὲ δύο) 1 Cl 5:4. ἐπὶ ἡμέρας πλείους *for a (large) number of days, for many days* (Jos., Ant. 4, 277; cp. Theophr. in Apollon. Paradox. 29 πλείονας ἡμ.) **Ac 13:31.—21:10** (Jos., Ant. 16, 15); **24:17; 25:14; 27:20.** οἱ μὲν πλείονές εἰσιν γεγονότες ἱερεῖς *the priests of former times existed in greater numbers* **Hb 7:23.** ἑτέροις λόγοις πλείοσιν *in many more words* (than have been reported) **Ac 2:40.** ταῦτα καὶ ἕτερα πλείονα MPol 12:1.—W. a gen. of comparison (Just., A I 53, 3; Tat. 3, 2) ἄλλους δούλους πλείονας τῶν πρώτων *other slaves, more than* (he had sent) *at first* **Mt 21:36.** πλείονα σημεῖα ὧν *more signs than those which* **J 7:31.** Also w. ἤ: πλείονας μαθητὰς ἢ *more disciples than* **4:1.** After πλείονες (-α) before numerals the word for 'than' is omitted (B-D-F §185, 4; Kühner-G. II 311; Rob. 666; Jos., Ant. 14, 96) ἐτῶν ἦν πλειόνων τεσσεράκοντα ὁ ἄνθρωπος *the man was more than 40 years old* **Ac 4:22.** πλείους τεσσεράκοντα **23:13, 21.** Cp. **24:11; 25:6** (Jos., Ant. 6, 306 δέκα οὐ πλείους ἡμέρας).—The ref. is to relative extent (cp. 2bα) in τὰ ἔργα σου τὰ ἔσχατα πλείονα τῶν πρώτων *your deeds, the latter of which are greater than the former* **Rv 2:19.**

β. subst.—**א.** (οἱ) πλείονες, (οἱ) πλείους *the majority, most* (Diog. L. 1, 20; 22; Jos., Ant. 10, 114) **Ac 19:32; 27:12.** W. ἐξ: ἐξ ὧν οἱ πλείονες *most of whom* **1 Cor 15:6.** W. gen. and a neg. (litotes) οὐκ ἐν τ. πλείοσιν αὐτῶν ηὐδόκησεν ὁ θεός *God was pleased with only a few of them* **10:5.** This is perh. (s. ג below) the place for **1 Cor 9:19; 2 Cor 2:6; 9:2. Phil 1:14;** MPol 5:1.

ב. (οἱ) πλείονες, (οἱ) πλείους *(even) more* πλείονες *in even greater numbers* **Ac 28:23.** πολλῷ πλείους ἐπίστευσαν *many more came to believe* **J 4:41.**—διὰ τῶν πλειόνων *to more and more people*=those who are still to be won for Christ **2 Cor 4:15.**

ג. (οἱ) πλείονες, (οἱ) πλείους. In contrast to a minority οἱ πλείονες can gain the sense *the others, the rest* (so τὰ πλείονα Soph., Oed. Col. 36; τὸ πλέον Thu. 4, 30, 4; Jos., Ant. 12, 240; B-D-F §244, 3). So perh. (s. א above) ἵνα τ. πλείονας κερδήσω (opp. the apostle himself) **1 Cor 9:19; 2 Cor 2:6** (opp. the one who has been punished too severely.—In this case [s. א above] his punishment would have been determined by a unanimous vote of the Christian assembly rather than by a majority). Cp. **9:2; Phil 1:14;** MPol 5:1.

ד. πλείονα (for πλεῖον) *more* **Mt 20:10 v.l.;** *various things* **Lk 11:53.** ἐκ τοῦ ἑνὸς πλείονα 1 Cl 24:5 (s. as adv. ParJer 7:26).

ⓒ superl. adj. πλείστη w. a plural *most of* αἱ πλεῖσται δυνάμεις **Mt 11:20** (difft. B-D-F § 245, 1).

❷ pert. to being relatively large in quantity or measure, *much, extensive*

ⓐ positive πολύς, πολλή, πολύ—**α.** adj. preceding or following a noun (or ptc. or adj. used as a noun)

א. in the sg. *much, large, great* πολὺς ἀριθμός **Ac 11:21.** W. words that in themselves denote a plurality (Appian, Bell. Civ. 5, 80 §338 στρατὸς πολύς) πολὺς ὄχλος (s. ὄχ. 1a) **Mt 14:14; 20:29; 26:47; Mk 5:21, 24; 6:34a; 8:1; 9:14; 12:37** (ὁ π. ὄχ.); **Lk 5:29; 6:17a; 8:4; J 6:2, 5** (for the expression ὁ ὄχλος πολύς, in which π. follows the noun, **J 12:9, 12,** cp. Arrian, Anab. 1, 9, 6 ὁ φόνος πολύς); **Ac 6:7; Rv 7:9; 19:1, 6.** πολὺ πλῆθος (s. πλ. 2bα) **Mk 3:7f; Lk 5:6; 6:17b; 23:27; Ac 14:1; 17:4;** 1 Cl 6:1. λαὸς πολύς *many people* **Ac 18:10.** Of money and its value, also used in imagery μισθὸς πολύς **Mt 5:12; Lk 6:23, 35** (all three predicative, as Gen 15:1). ἐργασία π. **Ac 16:16.** π. κεφάλαιον **22:28.** χρυσοῦ πολλοῦ . . . τρυφῆς πολλῆς AcPl Ha 2, 19.—Of things that occur in the mass or in large quantities (Diod. S. 3, 50, 1 πολλὴ ἄμπελος) γῆ πολλή **Mt 13:5; Mk 4:5;** θερισμὸς π. **Mt 9:37; Lk 10:2** (both pred.). χόρτος π. **J 6:10;** καρπὸς π. (Cyranides p. 121, 11) **12:24; 15:5, 8.**—λόγος π. *a long speech* (Diod. S. 13, 1, 2; Just., D. 123, 7) **Ac 15:32; 20:2.** περὶ οὗ πολὺς ἡμῖν ὁ λόγος *about this we have much to say* **Hb 5:11** (cp. Pla., Phd. 115d).—Of time: πολὺς χρόνος *a long time* (Hom. et al.; Demetr.(?): 722 fgm. 7; Jos., Ant. 8, 342; 19, 28; Just., A II, 2, 11) **J 5:6** (s. ἔχω 7b); Hs 6, 4, 4 (pred.). μετὰ πολὺν χρόνον (Jos., Ant. 12, 324) **Mt 25:19.** Differently **Mk 6:35ab** (s. 3aα).

ב. adj. w. a noun in the pl. *many, large, great, extensive, plentiful* ὄχλοι πολλοί *great crowds* or probably better *many people* (as Diod. S. 20, 59, 2; Ps.-Clem., Hom. 10, 3. For the corresponding mng. of ὄχλοι s. ὄχλος 1a) **Mt 4:25; 8:1; 13:2; 15:30a; 19:2; Lk 5:15; 14:25.** κτήματα πολλά *a great deal of property* **Mt 19:22; Mk 10:22** (cp. Da 11:28 χρήματα π.). ὕδατα πολλά *much water, many waters* (Maximus Tyr. 21, 3g of the Nile ὁ πολὺς ποταμός, likew. Procop. Soph., Ep. 111) **J 3:23; Rv 1:15; 14:2; 17:1; 19:6b.** θυμιάματα πολλά *a great deal of incense* **8:3.** τὰ πολλὰ γράμματα **Ac 26:24.** πολλοὶ χρόνοι *long periods of time* (Plut., Thes. 6, 9). πολλοῖς χρόνοις *for long periods of time* (SIG 836, 6; pap) **Lk 8:29;** 1 Cl 44:3. χρόνοις πολλοῖς AcPlCor 2:10. ἐκ πολλῶν χρόνων (Diod. S. 3, 47, 8; Jos., Ant. 14, 110; 17, 204) 1 Cl 42:5.

β. subst.—א. πολλοί *many* i.e. pers.—w. the art. οἱ πολλοί *the many,* of whatever appears in the context **Mk 6:2 v.l.** (the many people who were present in the synagogue); **9:26b** (the whole *crowd*). Opp. ὁ εἷς **Ro 5:15ac, 19ab;** *the many* who form the ἓν σῶμα *the one body* **12:5; 1 Cor 10:17.** Paul pays attention to the interests of *the many* rather than to his own vs. **33** (cp. Jos., Ant. 3, 212).—*The majority, most* (X., An. 5, 6, 19; Appian, Maced. 7, Bell. Civ. 4, 73 §309; 2 Macc 1:36; En 104:10; AscIs 3:26; Jos., Ant. 17, 72; Just., D. 4, 3) **Mt 24:12; Hb 12:15 v.l.** W. a connotation of disapproval *most people, the crowd* (Socrat., Ep. 6, 2; Dio Chrys. 15 [32], 8; Epict. 1, 3, 4; 2, 1, 22 al.; Plut., Mor. 33a; 470b; Plotinus, Enn. 2, 9, 9; Philo, Rer. Div. Her. 42) **2 Cor 2:17;** Pol 2:1; 7:2.—Jeremias, The Eucharistic Words of Jesus[3], tr. NPerrin, '66, 179–82; 226–31, and TW VI 536–45: πολλοί.

ב. πολύ *much* ᾧ ἐδόθη πολύ, πολὺ ζητηθήσεται παρ' αὐτοῦ, καὶ ᾧ παρέθεντο πολὺ κτλ. **Lk 12:48** (Just., A I, 17, 4 twice πλέον). Cp. **16:10ab;** 2 Cl 8:5; καρποφορεῖν π. *bear much fruit* Hs 2:3. πολὺ κατὰ πάντα τρόπον *much in every way* **Ro 3:2** (Ael. Aristid. 34, 43 K.=50 p. 562 D. gives answer to a sim. quest. asked by himself: πολλὰ καὶ παντοῖα).—**Js 5:16.**—As gen. of price πολλοῦ *for a large sum* of money (Menand., fgm. 197 Kö.; PRyl 244, 10. S. στρουθίον.) **Mt 26:9.**—Of time: ἐπὶ πολύ *(for) a long time* (JosAs 19:3; Ar. 65, 3; s. also ἐπί 18cβ) **Ac 28:6;** AcPl Ha 10, 21. μετ' οὐ πολύ *soon afterward* **Ac 27:14** (μετά B 2c).—ἐπὶ πολύ *more than once, often* (Is 55:7) Hm 4, 1, 8.—Before a comp. (as Hom. et al.; B-D-F §246; Rob. 664) in the acc. πολὺ βέλτιον *much better* Hs 1:9. π. ἐλάττων v 3, 7, 6 (Ar. 6, 2). π. μᾶλλον *much more, to a much greater degree* (Dio Chrys. 2, 10; 17; 64 al.; Ael. Aristid. 34, 9 K.=50 p. 549 D.; Just., A II, 8, 3; D. 95, 1 al.) **Hb 12:9, 25** (by means of a negative it acquires the mng. *much less;* cp. Diod. S. 7, 14, 6 πολὺ μᾶλλον μὴ . . . =even much less); Dg 2:7b. π. πλέον 2:7a (Ar. 11, 7). π. σπουδαιότερος **2 Cor 8:22b.** Cp. π. τιμώτερον **1 Pt 1:7 v.l.;** in the dat. of degree of difference πολλῷ μᾶλλον (Thu. 2, 51, 4; UPZ 42, 48 [162 BC]; EpArist 7; 24 al.; Sir prol. ln. 14; Jos., Ant. 18, 184; Just., A I, 68, 9; Tat. 17, 4) **Mt 6:30; Mk 10:48b; Lk 18:39; Ro 5:9f, 15b, 17; 1 Cor 12:22; 2 Cor 3:9, 11; Phil 2:12.** πολλῷ μᾶλλον κρεῖσσον **1:23** (v.l. without μᾶλλον). πολλῷ πλείους **J 4:41.** πολλῷ στρουθίων as **v.l. Mt 20:31** and **Lk 12:7** (both N.[25] app.; on the strong ms. support for this rdg. s. RBorger, TRu 52, '87, 21–24).—W. the art. τὸ πολύ (opp. τὸ ὀλίγον as X., An. 7, 7, 36) **2 Cor 8:15** (cp. Ex 16:18).

ג. πολύς (Diod. S. 14, 107, 4 πολὺς ἦν ἐπὶ τῇ τιμωρίᾳ=he was strongly inclined toward punishing) μὴ πολὺς ἐν ῥήμασιν γίνου *do not be profuse in speech, do not gossip* 1 Cl 30:5 (Job 11:3).—Παπίας ὁ πολύς Papias (7), prob. to be understood as ὁ πάνυ; s. πάνυ d.

ⓑ comp. πλείων, πλεῖον; adv. πλειόνως—α. adj., w. a singular (TestJob 35:2 διὰ πλείονος εὐωδίας) καρπὸν πλείονα *more fruit* **J 15:2, 8** P[66]; Hs 5, 2, 4. τὸ πλεῖον μέρος τοῦ ὄχλου *the greater part of the throng* 8, 1, 16. ἐπὶ πλείονα χρόνον *for a longer time* (PTebt 6:31 [II BC]) **Ac 18:20.** Foll. by gen. of comparison: πλείονα τιμήν *more honor* **Hb 3:3b.**—IPol 1:3a. Foll. by παρά τινα for comparison **Hb 3:3a; 11:4;** Hs 9, 18, 2. ὅσῳ πλείονος κατηξιώθημεν γνώσεως, τοσούτῳ μᾶλλον 1 Cl 41:4.—τὸ πλεῖον μέρος as adv. acc. *for the greater part* Hv 3, 6, 4a.

β. as subst. πλεῖον, πλέον *more* τὸ πλεῖον *the greater sum* (cp. Diod. S. 1, 82, 2=the greater part; Ps 89:10) **Lk 7:43.** πλεῖον λαμβάνειν *receive a larger sum* **Mt 20:10.** W. partitive gen. ἐπὶ πλεῖον προκόψουσιν ἀσεβείας *they will arrive at an ever greater measure of impiety*=become more and more deeply involved in impiety **2 Ti 2:16.** W. a gen. of comparison πλεῖον τῆς τροφῆς *someth. greater (more important) than food* **Mt 6:25; Lk 12:23.** πλεῖον Ἰωνᾶ **Mt 12:41;** cp. vs. **42; Lk 11:31, 32.** ἡ χήρα πλεῖον πάντων ἔβαλεν *the widow put in more than all the rest* **Mk 12:43; Lk 21:3.** μηδὲν πλέον *nothing more* (Jos., Bell. 1, 43; cp. Just., D. 2, 3 οὐδὲν πλέον); the words *than, except* following are expressed by παρά and the acc. **Lk 3:13** or by πλήν w. gen. **Ac 15:28,** w. εἰ μή Hs 1:6.—The acc. is used as an adv. *more, in greater measure, to a greater degree* (Herm. Wr. 13, 21 Nock after the mss.) **Lk 7:42;** IRo 1:1; IEph 6:2; w. a gen. of comparison **Mt 5:20** (περισσεύω 1aβ); **J 21:15;** IPol 5:2 (s. Ad'Alès, RSR 25, '35, 489–92). τριετίαν ἢ καὶ πλεῖον *for three years or even more* **Ac 20:18** D (cp. TestAbr B 7 p. 111, 27 [Stone p. 70, 27]).—ἐπὶ πλεῖον *any farther* (of place) **Ac 4:17** (TestGad 7:2; Ath. 12 [ἐπί 4bβ]); (of time) *at length* **Ac 20:9** (ἐπί 18cβ) or *any longer, too long* **24:4;** 1 Cl 55:1 (ἐπί 18cβ); *any more, even more* (ἐπί 13) **2 Ti 3:9;** 1 Cl 18:3 (Ps 50:4). Strengthened πολὺ πλέον *much more, much rather* (4 Macc 1:8; cp. X., An. 7, 5, 15; BGU 180, 12f [172 AD] πολλῷ πλεῖον; Ar. 11, 7 πολλῷ πλεῖον) Dg 2:7; 4:5.—Also w. indications of number (s. 1bα) πλεῖον ἢ ἄρτοι πέντε **Lk 9:13** (the words πλ. ἢ outside the constr. as X., An. 1, 2, 11). In πλείω δώδεκα λεγιῶνας ἀγγέλων *more than twelve legions of angels* **Mt 26:53** the text is uncertain (B-D-F §185, 4; s. Rob. 666).—The adv. can also be expressed by **πλειόνως** (Aeneas Tact. 237; Jos., Ant. 17, 2; Leontios 24, p. 52, 10) *more* ὅσον . . . πλειόνως *the more . . . the more* IEph 6:1.

ⓒ superl. πλεῖστος, ον—α. adj.—א. superlative proper τὸ πλεῖστον μέρος *the greatest part* w. partitive gen. Hs 8, 2, 9; 9, 7, 4. As adv. acc. *for the greatest part* 8, 5, 6; 8, 10, 1 (s. μέρος 1d).

ב. elative (s. Mayser II/1, 1926, 53) *very great, very large* (ὁ) πλεῖστος ὄχλος **Mt 21:8** (ὁ πλεῖστος ὄχλος could also be *the greatest part of the crowd,* as Thu. 7, 78, 2; Pla., Rep. 3, 397d); **Mk 4:1.**

β. subst. οἱ πλεῖστοι *the majority, most* **Ac 19:32** D (Just., D. 1, 4; cp. D. 48, 4 πλεῖστοι).

❸ **pert. to being high on a scale of extent**—ⓐ positive πολύς, πολλή, πολύ—α. as simple adj., to denote degree *much, great, strong, severe, hard, deep, profound* (Diod. S. 13, 7, 4 πολὺς φόβος; schol. on Apollon. Rhod. 4, 57; 58 p. 265, 3 πολλὴ δικαιοσύνη; Eccl 5:16 θυμὸς π.; Sir 15:18 σοφία; TestAbr A 20 p. 103, 4 [Stone p. 54] ἀθυμία; Just., D. 3, 1 ἠρεμία) ἀγάπη **Eph 2:4.** ἀγών **1 Th 2:2.** ἄθλησις **Hb 10:32.** ἁπλότης Hv 3, 9, 1. ἀσιτία **Ac 27:21.** βία **24:6 [7] v.l.** γογγυσμός **J 7:12.** διακονία **Lk 10:40.** δοκιμή **2 Cor 8:2.** δόξα **Mt 24:30;** Hv 1, 3, 4; 2, 2, 6. δύναμις **Mk 13:26.** ἐγκράτεια *strict self-control* Hv 2, 3, 2. εἰρήνη *complete* or *undisturbed peace* (Diod. S. 3, 64, 7; 11, 38, 1) **Ac 24:2.** ἔλεος **1 Pt 1:3.** ἐπιθυμία **1 Th 2:17.** ζημία **Ac 27:10.** ζήτησις **15:7.** θλῖψις **2 Cor 2:4a; 1 Th 1:6.** καύχησις **2 Cor 7:4b** (pred.). μακροθυμία **Ro 9:22.** ὀδυρμός **Mt 2:18.** παράκλησις **2 Cor 8:4.** παρρησία (Wsd 5:1) **3:12; 7:4a** (pred.); **1 Ti 3:13; Phlm 8.** πεποίθησις **2 Cor 8:22c.** πλάνη 2 Cl 1:7. πληροφορία **1 Th 1:5.** πόνος **Col 4:13.** σιγή *a great* or *general hush* (X., Cyr. 7, 1, 25; Arrian, Anab. 5, 28, 4) **Ac 21:40.** στάσις **23:10.** τρόμος **1 Cor 2:3.** φαντασία **Ac 25:23.** χαρά **8:8; Phlm 7.** ὥρα πολλή *late hour* (Polyb. 5, 8, 3; Dionys. Hal. 2, 54; Jos., Ant. 8, 118) **Mk 6:35ab.**

β. subst. πολλά in the acc. used as adv. *greatly, earnestly, strictly, loudly, often* etc. (X., Cyr. 1, 5, 14; Diod. S. 13, 41, 5; Lucian, Dial. Deor. 19, 2; Aelian, VH 1, 23; 4 Km 10:18; Is 23:16; TestSol 1:1; GrBar; ApcMos; Jos., Ant. 14, 348) ἀλαλάζειν πολλά **Mk 5:38** (s. ἀλαλάζω). πολλὰ ἁμαρτάνειν Hs 4:5c

(ApcMos 32). π. ἀνακρίνειν **Ac 28:18 v.l.** π. ἀπορεῖν **Mk 6:20** (Field, Notes 29). π. ἀσπάζεσθαι **1 Cor 16:19** (s. ἀσπάζομαι 1a). δεηθῆναι π. (GrBar 4:14; Jos., Vi. 173; 343) Hs 5, 4, 1. διαστέλλεσθαι **Mk 5:43** (s. διαστέλλω). π. ἐπιτιμᾶν **3:12.** π. ἐρωτᾶν *earnestly pray* Hv 2, 2, 1. κατηγορεῖν π. **Mk 15:3** (s. κατηγορέω 1a). κηρύσσειν π. *talk freely* **1:45.** κλαίειν *bitterly* **Ac 8:24** D (ApcMos 39). κοπιᾶν (ApcMos 24; CIG IV 9552, 5 . . . μοι πολλὰ ἐκοπίασεν, cp. Dssm., LO 266, 5 [LAE 317]) *work hard* **Ro 16:6, 12;** 2 Cl 7:1b. νηστεύειν π. *fast often* **Mt 9:14a.** ὀμνύναι π. **Mk 6:23.** παρακαλεῖν **Mk 5:10, 23; Ac 20:1** D; **1 Cor 16:12.** π. πταίειν *make many mistakes* **Js 3:2.** π. σπαράσσειν *convulse violently* **Mk 9:26a.**—W. the art. ἐνεκοπτόμην τὰ πολλά *I have been hindered these many times* (cp. Ro 1:13 πολλάκις) **Ro 15:22** (v.l. πολλάκις here too).

γ. subst. πολύ in the acc. used as adv. *greatly, very much, strongly* (Da 6:15, 24 Theod.) ἀγαπᾶν πολύ *show much affection, love greatly* **Lk 7:47b.** κλαίειν π. *weep loudly* **Rv 5:4.**—**Mk 12:27; Ac 18:27.**

ⓑ superlative, the neut. acc. πλεῖστον, α as adv. (sing. Hom. et al.; pl. Pind. et al.)

α. pl. πλεῖστα in the formula of greeting at the beginning of a letter πλεῖστα χαίρειν (POxy 742; 744; 1061 [all three I BC]; PTebt 314, 2 [II AD] and very oft. in pap.—Griech. pap ed. Ltzm.: Kl. Texte 14^2, 1910, p. 4, 5, 6, 7 al.; Preis. II s.v. πλεῖστος) *heartiest greeting(s)* IEph ins; IMg ins; ITr ins; IRo ins; ISm ins; IPol ins.

β. sing. τὸ πλεῖστον *at the most* (Aristoph., Vesp. 260; Diod. S. 14, 71, 3 πεμπταῖοι ἢ τὸ πλ. ἑκταῖοι; POxy 58, 17; PGiss 65:9) κατὰ δύο ἢ τὸ πλ. τρεῖς (word for word like Περὶ ὕψους 32, 1) **1 Cor 14:27.**—B. 922f. DELG. M-M. EDNT. TW.

πολυσπλαγχνία, ας, ἡ (s. πολύσπλαγχνος) **a very high degree of affection and compassion for someone,** ***sympathy, compassion, mercy*** (Just., D. 55, 3) as a divine attribute Hv 1, 3, 2; 2, 2, 8; 4, 2, 3; m 9:2.—DELG s.v. σπλήν.

πολύσπλαγχνος, ον pert. to a very high degree of affection and compassion for someone, ***sympathetic, compassionate, merciful*** (cp. prec. entry; Clem. Alex., Quis Div. Salv. 39, 6; AcThom 119 [Aa II/2 p. 229, 11f]) of God (cp. πολυέλεος Ps 102:8) **Js 5:11;** Hm 4, 3, 5; s 5, 7, 4.—M-M. TW.

πολυτέλεια, ας, ἡ (τέλος; Hdt. et al.; Diod. S. 5, 42, 6; ins [OGI 383, 69: I BC]; EpArist 80; Philo; Jos., Ant. 11, 200, C. Ap. 2, 234) **expenditure in maintaining a life style that far exceeds what is considered normal,** ***extravagance, luxury, richness.*** In Hs 1:10f. π. is first used lit. τὴν οὖν πολυτέλειαν τῶν ἐθνῶν μὴ πράσσετε *so then, do not practice the extravagance of the nations (unbelievers)* and then metaph. τὴν δὲ ἰδίαν πολυτέλειαν πράσσετε *but practice your own kind of extravagance* (as described vss. 8f). π. ἐδεσμάτων πολλῶν *luxury of many (kinds of) food(s)* Hm 6, 2, 5. π. πλούτου *extravagance of wealth* (i.e. such as wealth affords) m 8:3; 12, 2, 1.—DELG s.v. τέλος. M-M.

πολυτελής, ές (τέλος; Hdt. et al.; ins, pap, LXX; En; TestSol 5:1 D; TestJob; TestJud 26:3; JosAs) **pert. to being of great value or worth, ordinarily of relatively high degree on a monetary scale,** ***(very) expensive, costly*** (so Thu.+; ins, pap, LXX, Philo; Jos., C. Ap. 2, 191) of ointment **Mk 14:3.** Of clothing (X., An. 1, 5, 8; Diod. S. 4, 53, 3; 17, 35, 2; Polyaenus 6, 1, 4; Philo, Sacr. Abel. 21; Jos., Bell. 1, 605) **1 Ti 2:9.** Of stones (Diod. S. 1, 33, 3; 2, 16, 4; OGI 90, 34; 132, 8 [s. note 7]; SEG VIII 467, 16 [217 BC]; PGM 5, 239. So mostly LXX; En 18:6; EpArist 60 al.) λίθος π. B 6:2 (Is 28:16); pl. MPol 18:2. παρατάξεις π. *costly establishments* (s. παράταξις 2) Hs 1:1.—Metaph., of inward adornment ἐνώπιον τοῦ θεοῦ πολυτελές (i.e. God appraises it at high value) **1 Pt 3:4.**—DELG s.v. τέλος. M-M. Spicq.

πολυτελῶς adv. of πολυτελής (since Eupolis Com. 335 K. [V BC]; Lysias 7, 31; Diod. S. 5, 41, 2; OGI 524, 7; Philo, Mos. 2, 95; Jos., Ant. 8, 95; 18, 92) **pert. to expenditure very high on a scale of degree,** ***abundantly, lavishly,*** metaph. (cp. the metaph. usage s.v. πολυτέλεια and πολυτελής) τὸ ἀγαθὸν π. ἐργάζεσθαι *do good lavishly* Hm 4, 2, 2.

πολύτιμος, ον (cp. τιμάω; Cornutus 16 p. 21, 16; Plut., Pomp. 621 [5, 2]; Alciphron 3, 10, 4; Herodian 1, 17, 3; POxy 1121, 20 [II AD]; PHerm 9, 7; TestSol 22:16 P; TestAbr; JosAs 7:4; 3:9 cod. A; Jos., Ant. 7, 161; Tat. 30, 1 [comp.]) **pert. to being very high on a monetary scale,** ***very precious, valuable*** of a pearl **Mt 13:46.** Of an ointment **26:7 v.l.; J 12:3.** Comp. τὸ δοκίμιον τῆς πίστεως πολυτιμότερον χρυσίου *the genuineness* (δοκίμιον 2) *of* (your) *faith which is more precious than gold* **1 Pt 1:7.**—DELG s.v. τιμή. M-M.

πολυτρόπως adv. (πολύτροπος 'various, manifold'; Philo, Aet. M. 129; Geopon. 9, 11, 4; 4 Macc 3:21 v.l.) fr. πολύτροπος (Hom.+; PFlor 33, 15; Job 5:13 v.l.; 4 Macc; ApcMos 24; Philo, Vi. Mos. 1, 117, Dec. 83; Jos., Ant. 10, 142) **pert. to a variety of modes of expressing someth.,** ***in many ways*** (w. πολυμερῶς, q.v.) **Hb 1:1.**—DELG s.v. τρέπω. M-M.

πόμα, ατος, τό (πίνω; so Pind., Hdt. and later writers, also Kaibel 244, 10; LXX; TestReub 2:7; Philo; Just., A I, 66, 2 for Att. πῶμα. Kühner-Bl. II 286) **someth. that satisfies thirst,** ***a drink***

ⓐ pl., of usual things to drink (w. βρώματα; s. βρῶμα 1) **Hb 9:10;** GJs 1:4.

ⓑ in imagery (Ael. Aristid. 28, 114 K.=49 p. 528 D.: π. ἐξ Ἀπόλλωνος πηγῶν; Philo, Somn. 2, 248 θεῖον π.; SibOr 5, 240) ἓν πόμα ἐποτίσθημεν **1 Cor 12:13 v.l.,** prob. in ref. to the Eucharist. The typological predecessor of the Eucharist in the OT is seen (beside manna as the πνευματικὸν βρῶμα) as τὸ πνευματικὸν πόμα *the spiritual drink* (fr. the spiritual rock that followed them) **1 Cor 10:4.** Ign. describes the joys of communion w. Christ that accompany martyrdom by means of expressions taken fr. the liturgy of the Eucharist, among them πόμα IRo 7:3 (Hdb. ad loc.).—DELG s.v. πίνω B. M-M. TW.

πονέω (πόνος) fut. πονέσω LXX; 1 aor. ἐπόνεσα LXX, inf. πονέσαι (Just., D. 90, 2) and πονῆσαι (TestSol 6:13 D); pf. ptc. pl. gen. πεπονηκότων (Ath., R. 17 p. 69, 11). Pass.: aor. ptc. neut. pl. πονηθέντα (Just., A II, 10, 2) (Pind. et al. [the mid. as dep. as early as Hom.]; ins, pap, LXX; PsSol 2:14; TestSol; JosAs 25:3; Jos., Ant. 12, 240; 15, 33; Just.; Ath., R. 17 p. 69, 11) **to engage in any kind of hard work,** ***toil, undergo trouble*** ἐπί τινι *about* or *in behalf of someone* ἐπὶ καταπονουμένῳ (s. καταπονέω) B 20:2; D 5:2. πονεῖ ἡ ψυχή μου ἐπὶ τοῖς υἱοῖς τῶν ἀνθρώπων Ox 1 verso, 17f (GTh 28) (of the ψυχή as Philo, Somn. 1, 255). An uncertain restoration εἰ πονε[ῖ]ς AcPl Ha 7, 30.—DELG s.v. πένομαι.

πονηρεύομαι mid. dep.; fut. πονηρεύσομαι; aor. ἐπονηρευσάμην LXX; pf. inf. πεπονηρεῦσθαι Ex 22:7, 10 (πονηρός; Heraclit. et al.; Demosth. 19, 32; Menand., Epitr. 133; Plut., Pomp. 640 [39, 5], Cic. 7, 4, Cato Maj. 9, 10; Ael. Aristid. 39 p. 745 D.; LXX; Test12Patr; JosAs; Philo, Spec. Leg. 2, 11; 4, 76; Jos., Ant. 15, 348; Just.) gener. 'be wicked, act wickedly', with implication of being contrary to the interests of a well-ordered society (s. πόνηρος beg.) **to be of wicked disposition or act in a wicked manner,** ***do wrong, commit sin*** Hm 10, 3, 2ab. Opp.

ἀγαθοποιεῖν Hs 9, 18, 1f. π. εἴς τινα *act wickedly toward someone, do harm to someone* m 4, 3, 4; 9:9; s 9, 22, 4. π. ἔν τινι *(commit) sin with someth.* (Mi 3:4): w. the tongue Hv 2, 2, 3. μηδὲν πονηρεύσῃ *you must do no evil* s 5, 1, 5. οἱ πονηρευόμενοι ποικίλαις πονηρίαις *doers of various kinds of wickedness = sinners of every description* 9, 18, 3.—The subst. ptc. in the pl. οἱ πονηρευόμενοι *the evil-doers, the sinners* (OGI 515, 58; LXX; Philo, Virt. 227) B 5:13; 6:6 (cp. on both Ps 21:17).—DELG s.v. πένομαι. TW.

πονηρία, ας, ἡ (πονηρός; Soph., Hippocr. et al.) in our lit. only in the ethical sense: **state or condition of a lack of moral or social values, *wickedness, baseness, maliciousness, sinfulness*** (Soph.; Lysias 22, 16 et al.; OGI 519, 10; PLips 119 recto and verso I, 7; LXX; En 10:16; OdeSol 11:20; Test12Patr; Philo, De Jos. 212; Jos., Ant. 10, 37; 13, 120; Just., Tat.; Mel., P. 50, 369 Bo.; Orig., Did., loanw. in rabb.) **Mt 22:18;** Hv 3, 5, 4; 3, 6, 1. W. ἁρπαγή **Lk 11:39;** w. ἄνοια 2 Cl 13:1; w. δολιότης Hs 8, 6, 2; w. κακία **1 Cor 5:8.** In the Lord's Prayer **Mt 6:13 v.l.** In a catalogue of vices (s. Philo, Ebr. 223) **Ro 1:29;** 1 Cl 35:5. Cp. Hs 9, 15, 3, where πονηρία and other vices are personified. πονηρία μεγάλη Hv 2, 2, 2a. Of children μὴ γινώσκοντα τὴν πονηρίαν τὴν ἀπολλύουσαν τὴν ζωὴν ἀνθρώπων *who know nothing of the wickedness that ruins the life of people* Hm 2:1 (s. παιδίον 2).—In the objective gen. κόλασις τῆς π. *punishment for wickedness* Hs 9, 18, 1; ὁ μισθὸς τῆς π. B 4:12. In gen. of quality (to be rendered as adj.; respectable Gk. [cp. ὁ τᾶς ἡσυχίας βίοτος Eur., Bacch. 389], but strongly influenced in our lit. by Semitic tradition, s. Leutzsch, Hermas 383 n. 44; cp. Schwyzer II 122): ἡ ἐπιθυμία τῆς π. *evil desire* Hv 1, 1, 8; m 11:2; συμφυρμοὶ πονηρίας v 2, 2, 2b; διδάσκαλοι πονηρίας *evil teachers* or obj. gen. *teachers of wickedness* s 9, 19, 2; τὰ πνευματικὰ τῆς π. (Iren. 1, 5, 4 [Harv. I 47, 2]) **Eph 6:12** (s. πνευματικός 3); ὁ ἄγγελος τῆς πονηρίας (opp. ἄγγ. τῆς δικαιοσύνης) Hm 6, 2, 1; 4f; 7; 9f (cp. 1QS 3:18f). πλείονα πονηρίαν ποιεῖν *act more wickedly* Hs 9, 18, 2.—Pl., of the various kinds of evil-mindedness and individual expressions of it (Demosth. 21, 19; Aristot. 1389a, 18; Jer 39:32; B-D-F §142; W-S. §27, 4; s. Rob. 408) **Mk 7:22; Ac 3:26;** 1 Cl 8:4 (Is 1:16); Hv 3, 7, 2; m 8:3. αἱ π. ἐν ταῖς καρδίαις ἐμμένουσιν *wickedness remains in their hearts* Hv 3, 6, 3 (here the pl. could refer to the plurality of persons involved, since virtually only one kind of wickedness is meant). On πονηρεύεσθαι ποικίλαις πονηρίαις s 9, 18, 3 see πονηρεύομαι.—S. also ἁγιάζω 4, ἀποβάλλω 1b, ἀφαιρέω 2a, κατισχύω 2, παύω 2.—DELG s.v. πένομαι. M-M. TW.

πονηρός, ά, όν (s. πονέω, πόνος; Hes., Thu.+) comp. πονηρότερος **Mt 12:45; Lk 11:26;** superl. πονηρότατος (Diod. S. 14, 4, 2; PRyl III, 493, 89) Hm 3:5.—Freq. in Gk. lit. the opp. of ἀγαθός/καλός or χρηστός.

❶ **pert. to being morally or socially worthless, *wicked, evil, bad, base, worthless, vicious, degenerate*—ⓐ** as adj.—**α.** of humans or transcendent beings (since trag. and Ps.-X., Rep. Ath. 1, 1; Is 9:16; Sir 25:16, 25; TestJob 43:5; ApcMos 21 γύναι; Philo, Joseph., Just.) ὁ πον. ἄνθρωπος (Plut., Alcib. 196 [13, 4]; cp. GrBar 13:1, 3; Philo, Exsecr. 149; Jos., Ant. 7, 291; Just., A II, 12, 3) **Mt 12:35a; Lk 6:45a** (where ἄνθρωπος is to be supplied); cp. **2 Th 3:2; 2 Ti 3:13.** δοῦλος πον. (Comp. 120; Jos., Ant. 2, 55; 16, 296) **Mt 18:32; 25:26; Lk 19:22** (cp. PFouad 25 verso I, 2 [II AD] address to an incompetent helper); γενεὰ πον. **Mt 12:39, 45b; 16:4; Lk 11:29.—Mt 12:34.** ἄνδρες πον. *rowdies, ruffians* **Ac 17:5.** People are called πονηροί in contrast to God **Mt 7:11** (here the component of class distinction finds dramatic expression); **Lk 11:13** (Iambl., Vi. Pyth. 18, 82 ἀληθέστατον … πονηροὶ οἱ ἄνθρωποι).—Of hostile spirits τὸ πνεῦμα τὸ πονηρόν (Cat. Cod. Astr. X 180, 16; 186, 4; cp. EGoodspeed, The Harrison Papyri, no. 1, 7: ClPh 5, 1910, 321) **Ac 19:15f.** Pl. (Cyranides p. 51, 14; Just., D. 30, 2 al.) **Lk 7:21; 8:2; Ac 19:12f.** Of the *evil spirit* that contends w. the Holy Spirit for a place in the human soul (cp. 1 Km 16:14–23) Hm 5, 1, 2 and 3. ἄγγελος πον. B 9:4 (Just., A II, 9, 4, D. 105, 3; cp. Paus. Attic. τ, 18 and Just., A I, 66, 4 πονηροὶ δαίμονες; Julian p. 371, 5; 11 Hertlein δαίμονες πονηροί; PLips 34 recto, 8 [375 AD] π. δαίμων. Did., Gen. 45, 4 αἱ π. δυνάμεις). ὁ πονηρὸς ἄρχων 4:13 (ἄρχων 1c).

β. of things βουλή (Menand., Mon. 134 [568 Mei.]) B 6:7 (Is 3:9); 19:3; D 2:6; Hv 1, 2, 4b (βουλή 1). διαλογισμοί **Mt 15:19; Js 2:4** (διαλογισμός 2). διδαχή Hm 6, 2, 7 (παντὶ ἔργῳ is dat. of disadvantage [Schwyzer II 150f]). δόλος (SIG 693, 6 [129 BC]) IEph 7:1. ἐπιθυμία (-αι: Dio Chrys. 4, 89) 2 Cl 16:2; Hv 1, 1, 8b; 1, 2, 4c; s 6, 2, 1 and oft. ἔργον **2 Ti 4:18;** Hv 1, 2, 4b. (TestAbr A 6 p. 83, 28 [Stone p. 14] w. opp. ἀγαθόν.) ἔργα **J 3:19; 7:7; Col 1:21; 1J 3:12b; 2J 11;** Hv 3, 7, 6; 3, 8, 4 al. θησαυρός **Mt 12:35b; Lk 6:45b** (here θησ. is to be supplied fr. the context). καρδία (ApcMos 13; cp. Menand., fgm. 540, 8 [=538 Kö.], ψυχή) 1 Cl 3:4; καρδία πονηρὰ ἀπιστίας (gen. of quality; s. Schwyzer under πονηρία; B-D-F §165; definition Mlt. 74) **Hb 3:12.** καταλαλιά Hm 2:3. *Arrogant* καύχησις **Js 4:16;** λόγοι π. *malicious words* (Menand., Mon. 822 [542 Mei.]) **3J 10.** Of the ὁδὸς τοῦ θανάτου D 5:1; cp. B 4:10 (PsSol 10:1). ὀφθαλμὸς π. (ὀφθαλμός 1 and s. 3 below) **Mt 20:15; Mk 7:22.** πρᾶγμα (Menand., Epitr. 1107 S. [749 Kö.]; fgm. 530 Kö.; TestAbr A 4 p. 81, 5 [Stone p. 10]; Tat. 17, 3) Hv 1, 1, 8a; ῥᾳδιούργημα π. **Ac 18:14.** ῥῆμα π. *slanderous, evil word* (SIG 1175, 16; Jdth 8:8, 9) **Mt 5:11 v.l.** (the ῥ. is 'bad' because of the content consisting, as the context indicates, of false charges); Hs 5, 3, 6; συνείδησις π. *evil, guilty conscience* **Hb 10:22** (the conscience is not itself intrinsically bad, but evil deeds load it with a bad content; B 19:12; D 4:14; Hm 3:4; ὑπόνοιαι π. **1 Ti 6:4.** Cp. **Ac 25:18 v.l.** τὸ πονηρότατον ψεῦσμα *the most wicked sin of lying* Hm 3:5. Of a Christian's name ἐκβάλλειν τὸ ὄνομα ὡς πονηρόν *spurn the name as vile* (i.e as held only by worthless persons) **Lk 6:22** (cp. Ath. 2, 2).—In the judgment of Christians a close connection w. sin is the chief characteristic of this age: ἐκ τοῦ αἰῶνος τοῦ ἐνεστῶτος πονηροῦ **Gal 1:4.** Cp. αἱ ἡμέραι πονηραί εἰσιν **Eph 5:16.**—B 2:1. Sg. **Eph 6:13.**

ⓑ as subst.—**α.** *wicked* or *evil-intentioned person, evildoer* (Dt 21:21; Esth 7:6; Just., A I, 27, 1; Ath. 2, 3; Theoph. Ant. 2, 37 [p. 198, 22]) ὁ πονηρός (the art. is generic) **Mt 5:39; 1 Cor 5:13** (Dt 17:7, cp. 19:19 al.; PZaas, JBL 103, '84, 259–61); B 19:11 v.l. (but τὸ πον. in text).—Pl. πονηροὶ καὶ ἀγαθοί (cp. Philo, Praem. 3; Jos., Ant. 6, 307; 8, 314 God ἀγαπᾷ τ. ἀγαθούς, μισεῖ δὲ τ. πονηρούς; Iren. 1, 24, 2 [Harv. I 198, 4]) **Mt 5:45; 22:10.** Opp. οἱ δίκαιοι **13:49** (cp. T. Kellis 22, 48f). W. οἱ ἀχάριστοι (s. ἀχάριστος; also Lucian, Timon 48, perh. fr. comedy [III p. 654 Kock]) **Lk 6:35.** W. ἁμαρτωλοί B 4:2.

β. ὁ πονηρός *the evil one*=the devil (who is not defined as a sinner but as one who is morally destructive) **Mt 13:19; J 17:15; Eph 6:16; 1J 2:13f; 5:18, 19** (κεῖμαι 3d); B 2:10; 21:3; MPol 17:1; AcPlCor 2:2, 15) ἐκ τοῦ πονηροῦ εἶναι *be a child of the evil one* (ἐκ 3a, end) **1J 3:12a;** cp. οἱ υἱοὶ τοῦ πονηροῦ **Mt 13:38,** in case πον. is masc. here.—The gen. τοῦ πονηροῦ **Mt 5:37; 6:13** can also be taken as masc. (it is so taken by Ps.-Clem., Hom. 3, 55 p. 51, 19; 21; Tertullian, Cyprian, Origen, Chrysostom; KFritzsche, JWeiss; s. also Schniewind on **Mt 6:13;** Weymouth, Goodsp.;—it is taken as a neut. [s. γ] by Augustine: WMangold, De Ev. sec. Mt 6:13, 1886; BWeiss, Zahn, Wlh.; Harnack, SBBerlAk 1907, 944; PFiebig, D. Vaterunser 1927, 92;

Betz, SM 380f; 405–13; Mft., NRSV marg.); **Lk 11:4 v.l.; 2 Th 3:3;** D 8:2. These passages may also belong under

γ. τὸ πονηρόν *(that which is) evil* **Lk 6:45c; Ro 12:9; 1 Th 5:22** (sim. Plut., Mor. 82c; s. also εἶδος 2); B 19:11. πᾶν πον. *every kind of evil* **Mt 5:11;** ποιεῖν τὸ πονηρὸν ἔμπροσθεν τοῦ κυρίου (cp. Dt 17:2; 4 Km 21:2, 20) Hm 4, 2, 2; cp. **Ac 5:4 v.l.;** 1 Cl 18:4 (Ps 50:6). τὸ πονηρὸν τοῦτο *this shameful deed* GJs 13:1. ἀγρυπνεῖν εἰς τὸ π. D 5:2 and ἐπὶ τὸ π. B 20:2 s. ἀγρυπνέω 2. ἐλάλησέν τι περὶ σοῦ πονηρόν **Ac 28:21** (cp. JosAs 6:6).—Pl. *wicked thoughts, evil deeds* (Gen 6:5; 8:21) **Mt 9:4; 12:35c; Mk 7:23; Lk 3:19; J 3:20 v.l.; Ac 25:18;** 2 Cl 8:2. δύο καὶ πονηρά *two evil things* B 11:2 (Jer 2:13 v.l.).—πονηρόν ἐστίν τινι *it is bad for someone* Hm 5, 1, 4.—ῥύσασθαι ἀπὸ παντὸς πονηροῦ D 10, 5.

❷ **pert. to being so deficient in quality in a physical sense as to be worthless,** ***of poor quality, worthless*** (X., Pla. et al.) καρποί (Ael. Aristid. 23, 57K.=42 p. 787 D.) **Mt 7:17f** (the same idea 13:48; cp. Jer 24:8 τὰ σῦκα τὰ πονηρά).

❸ **pert. to being in an unhealthy condition physically**

ⓐ in ref. to a part of the body ***sick*** (Pla., Prot. 313a σῶμα; πονηρῶς ἔχειν 'be badly off', 'be ill' since Thu. 7, 83, 3) of the eye (cp. Pla., Hipp. Min. 374d πονηρία ὀφθαλμῶν) **Mt 6:23; Lk 11:34** (Weizsäcker, BWeiss, HHoltzmann, Fitzmyer, Goodsp., NRSV. But see s.v. ἁπλοῦς, λύχνος b, ὀφθαλμός 1, also 1aβ above and the four articles ET 53, '42, 181f; 354f; 54, '42, 26; 26f).

ⓑ in ref. to the status of some ailment ***painful, virulent, serious*** (since Theognis 274) ἕλκος *sore, ulcer* (Dt 28:35; Job 2:7) **Rv 16:2.**—See Lofthouse s.v. κακός, end; WBrandt, ZNW 14, 1913, 189ff.—DELG s.v. πένομαι. M-M. TW.

πονηρόφρων, ον, (πονηρός, φρήν) gen. ονος **pert. to having one's mind directed in a morally or socially destructive way,** ***evil-minded*** w. αὐθάδης D 3:6 (the word is found only here and in Apost. Constit. 7, 7, which is dependent upon this pass.).—DELG s.v. φρήν II.

πονηρῶς adv. of πονηρός (Thu., Aristoph. et al.) ***basely, wickedly*** w. ἀφρόνως Hv 5:4.

πόνος, ου, ὁ (πένομαι 'toil'; Hom.+)—❶ **work that involves much exertion or trouble,** ***(hard) labor, toil*** (Onesicritus [c. 310 BC]: 134 fgm. 17a Jac.: because of the ὕβρις of humans, Zeus brought the utopian state of affairs in India to an end, and sent πόνος into the life of humans [cp. ἐν λύπαις Gen 3:17]; Ps 89:10; Philo; Jos., Ant. 3, 49; 18, 244) πόνον ἔχειν ὑπέρ τινος **Col 4:13** (πόνον ἔχειν: Il. 15, 416; Hes., Shield 305; Paus. 4, 16, 3. As mark of distinction, SJohnstone, Virtuous Toil, Vicious Work—Xenophon on Aristocratic Style: ClPh 89, '94, 219–40.—Theocr. 7, 139 has π. with a ptc. in the sense 'take pains'). μετὰ πόνου *with difficulty, laboriously, painstakingly* (Pla., Soph. 230a μετὰ πολλοῦ πόνου) Dg 11:8. According to ABoegehold (Greek, Roman, and Byzantine Studies 23, '82, 147–56), the years 424–421 BC mark a trend in the direction of

❷ **experience of great trouble,** ***pain, distress, affliction*** (Thu. 2, 49, 3; X., Mem. 2, 2, 5; Aelian, NA 7, 30 p. 190, 9, VH 5, 6 [CPJones, ClPh 79, '84, 43f]; SIG 708, 11; POxy 234 II, 24; 37; Is 65:14; Job 4:5; TestJob 52:1; JosAs; ApcMos 5; Just., A I, 21, 2 φυγῇ πόνων) w. πένθος and κραυγή **Rv 21:4** (cp. Is 35:10; Pind., P. 10, 42 in a description of the blissful Hyperboreans). εἶναι ἐν πόνῳ (cp. Gen 34:25; TestJob 24:6 ἐν πόνοις; Just., D. 125, 5) 1 Cl 16:3f (Is 53:4). ἀφαιρεῖν ἀπὸ τ. πόνου τῆς ψυχῆς (ἀφαιρέω 2a.—πόνος τ. ψυχῆς: Maximus Tyr. 1, 4b) vs. 12 (Is 53:10f). Of the Crucified One ὡς μηδὲ πόνον ἔχων *as though he felt no pain at all* GPt 4:10. Of a hailstone πῶς πόνον παρέχει *how much pain it causes, how much it hurts* Hm 11:20. ἐκ τοῦ π. *in pain* (Appian, Iber. 97 §423) **Rv 16:10;** pl. (Gen 41:51; Jos., C. Ap. 2, 146; Test Jud 18:4) ἐκ τῶν π. (Eur., fgm. 364 Nauck[2]) *because of their sufferings* vs. **11.** πόνους ὑποφέρειν *undergo hardships* 1 Cl 5:4.—HKuist, Biblical Review 16, '32, 415–20 (πόνος, μόχθος).—B. 540. Schmidt, Syn. II 611–25 πονηρός. DELG s.v. πένομαι. M-M. Spicq. Sv.

Ποντικός, ή, όν ***from Pontus*** (s. Πόντος; Hdt. et al.; Just., A I, 26, 5 [Marcion]) subst. (Socrat., Ep. 30, 14) of Aquila Π. τῷ γένει *a native of Pontus* **Ac 18:2.**

Πόντιος, ου, ὁ (Diod. S. 14, 116, 3; Plut.; SIG 797, 2 [37 AD]; OGI 656, 4) ***Pontius,*** the name of a Roman, originally Samnite gens, going as far back as the Samnite Wars (Cic., De Off. 2, 21, 75; Livy 9, 1), the nomen (middle, or tribal [gentile] name) of Pilate (s. Πιλᾶτος) **Mt 27:2 v.l.; Lk 3:1; Ac 4:27; 1 Ti 6:13;** IMg 11:1; ITr 9:1; ISm 1:2; Just., A I, 13, 3 al. WSchulze, Zur Geschichte latein. Eigennamen: GGAbh. V/5, 1904; JOllivier, Ponce Pilate et les Pontii: RB 5, 1896, 247–54; 594–600; MStern, The Province of Judaea: CRINT I/1, 68–70; J-PLémonon, Pilate et le gouvernement de la Judée:Textes et monuments, '81. See Kl. Pauly IV 1048–50.

πόντος, ου, ὁ (Hom. et al.; Arrian, Anab. 6, 19, 4; 5; Ex 15:5) ***the (high/open) sea*** ὁ ἐπὶ πόντον πλέων **Rv 18:17 v.l.** (on the numerous witnesses to this rdg s. RBorger, TRu 52, '87, 51–53; cp. Diod. S. 20, 25, 2 οἱ πλέοντες τὸν Πόντον=those who sail the Pontus).—DELG.

Πόντος, ου, ὁ (Aeschyl., Hdt. et al.; ins; Philo, Deus Imm. 174; Joseph.; Just., A I, 58, 1) ***Pontus,*** orig. the name of a sea (the Euxine, or Black Sea), then the designation of an empire founded by the Achaemenid Persians in northeast Asia Minor, extending fr. the Black Sea to the Caucasus. After Pompey's conquest a part of it was made a Roman province. Acc. to Appian, Mithrid. 15 §53 many Ἕλληνες had settled there. **Ac 2:9; 1 Pt 1:1** (on the address Ps.-Callisth. 2, 11, 2, an encyclical letter of Alexander [s. Καππαδοκία]). JMarquardt, Römische Staatsverwaltung I[2], 1881, 349ff; VSchultze, Altchristl. Städte u. Landschaften II/1, 1922; Pauly-W. III 507–42; Kl. Pauly IV 1050f; BHHW III 1480.

Πόπλιος, ου, ὁ (Diod. S. 11, 41, 1; 13, 7, 1; 14, 47, 1 al.; Plut.; ins, pap; Philo, Leg. ad Gai. 333; Jos., Ant. 14, 236) ***Publius,*** a Roman praenomen (first or personal name; s. AWalde, Latein. etymolog. Wörterbuch[2] 1910 s.v. poplicus; B-D-F §41, 2; cp. Mlt-H. 155). **Ac 28:7f** mentions a Π. as πρῶτος τῆς νήσου for the island of Malta. The title is also attested elsewh. for Malta: IG XIV, 601 [=IGR I, 512] Λ. Κα[στρί]κιος Κυρ(είνᾳ) Προύδηνς ἱππεὺς Ῥωμ(αίων), πρῶτος Μελιταίων καὶ πάτρων, ἄρξας καὶ ἀμφιπολεύσας θεῷ Αὐγούστῳ; CIL X, 7495 [munic]ipi Mel(itensium) primus omnium (but s. Bruce, Acts 532f on this ins). As a rule it is taken for granted that it was a designation for the highest Roman official on the island (Holtzmann, Wendt, Bruce et al.). It has also been thought to refer to any office that was non-Roman in origin (AMayr, Die Insel Malta im Altertum 1909, 116; AWikenhauser, Die AG 1921, 345f; Beginn. IV 342; s. Haenchen and other comm. ad loc.). Difft. Warnecke [Romfahrt, 119–33 esp. 123], who associates a Publius Alf(ius) Primus w. the island of Cephallenia.—BHHW III 1531. Boffo, Iscrizioni 177–81 (lit). LGPN I. M-M.

πορεία, ας, ἡ (πόρος 'passage, path'; Aeschyl., X., Pla.+) gener. 'going'

❶ **a planned movement over a considerable distance,** ***journey, trip*** πορείαν ποιεῖσθαι (X., An. 5, 6, 11; Diod. S. 14, 39, 4; Cornutus 19 p. 33, 20; Plut., Mor. 162f; 2 Macc 3:8; Jos., Ant. 7, 49; 14, 128; Ar. 4:2) w. the destination given (Jos., Ant. 14, 358 εἰς Μ.) εἰς Ἱεροσόλυμα **Lk 13:22.** Many think that **Js 1:11** also belongs here: ὁ πλούσιος ἐν ταῖς πορείαις αὐτοῦ *the rich man* on *his* (business) *journeys* or more gener. *in his undertakings* or *pursuits* (NRSV: 'in the midst of a busy life'). The pl. is a strong indication that this transl. is correct; but the pl. may be thought of as parallel to vs. 8 ἐν ταῖς ὁδοῖς αὐτοῦ, so that we cannot finally exclude the sense

❷ **way of life,** ***conduct*** (Pr 2:7.—Of the 'way' that one should take: Socrat., Ep. 27, 5) Hs 5, 6, 6. κατευθύνοντες τὴν πορείαν αὐτῶν ἐν ὁσιότητι 1 Cl 48:4. The cj. by Lightf. at 62:1 draws on 48:4. Fr. this point of view **Js 1:11** would be translated *in all his ways* (Ropes, MDibelius, et al.).—DELG s.v. πόρος II. M-M.

πορεύω (Pind.+; ApcSed 15:5=p. 136, 32 Ja. οἱ πορεύοντες) in our lit. only as mid. and pass. **πορεύομαι** (trag., Hdt.+) impf. ἐπορευόμην; fut. πορεύσομαι; 1 aor. ἐπορεύθην; pf. ptc. πεπορευομένος. On the fut. aspect of the pres. s. B-D-F §323, 3; Rob. 869. On the durative sense of the pres. impv. πορεύου in contrast to the aor. πορεύθητι s. B-D-F §336, 1; also Rob. 855f; 890.

❶ **to move over an area, gener. with a point of departure or destination specified,** ***go, proceed, travel,*** w. indication of the point of departure: ἀπό τινος *depart from someone* (cp. X., An. 4, 4, 17 'from the camp of Tiribazus') **Mt 25:41** (impv.); **Lk 4:42b.** ἐντεῦθεν **13:31** (impv.). ἐκεῖθεν **Mt 19:15.** W. indication of place to which: εἴς τι (X., Hell. 7, 4, 10; Is 22:15 εἴς τι πρός τινα; JosAs 28:5 εἰς τὴν ὕλην; ApcMos 10; Just., A II, 2, 6) *to, in, into, toward* **Mt 2:20; 17:27; Mk 16:12; Lk 1:39; 4:42a; 9:56** (εἰς ἑτέραν κώμην, cp. Jos., Vi. 231); **22:33** (εἰς φυλακήν); **J 7:35b; Ac 1:11; 19:21; 20:1, 22** (πορεύομαι=*I am going, I am about to go*); **22:5, 10; Ro 15:24, 25** *(I am going, I am about to go);* IPol 7:2; 8:2; Hv 1, 1, 3; 2, 1, 1. εἰς τὸν οἶκόν σου **Lk 5:24;** cp. AcPl Ha 4, 3 εἰς τὴν οἰκίαν. Of fish π. εἰς τὸ βάθος *dive into the depth* B 10:10b. Also of passing into the beyond, in a good sense of Paul and Peter: π. εἰς τὸν ἅγιον τόπον 1 Cl 5:7 v.l.; εἰς τὸν ὀφειλόμενον (ὀφείλω 2aα) τόπον τῆς δόξης 5:4 (so of Peter in **Ac 12:17:** WSmaltz, JBL 71, '52, 211–16; s. Bruce, Acts on var. traditions), and in a bad sense of Judas the informer εἰς τὸ τόπον τὸν ἴδιον **Ac 1:25.** εἰς τὰ ἔθνη *to the gentiles* **18:6.** ἐπὶ Καίσαρα π. *go to Caesar, appear before the Emperor* (ἐπί 10) **25:12.** πρός τινα *to someone* (Soph., Ant. 892; Pla., Clit. 410c; Theophr., Char. 2, 1; Diog. L. 8, 43; Gen 26:26; TestAbr B 4 p. 109, 9 [Stone p. 66]; Just., A II, 2, 19) **Mt 25:9; 26:14; Lk 11:5; 15:18; 16:30; J 14:12, 28; 16:28** (pres. w. fut. aspect in the three J pass. *I am about to go*); **Ac 27:3;** 1 Cl 31:4. σύν τινι *with someone* **Lk 7:6; Ac 10:20; 26:13; 1 Cor 16:4b.** ἐπί τι *after someth.* (ἐπί 4bα) **Lk 15:4;** *(up) to someth.* (ἐπί 4bγ) **Mt 22:9; Ac 8:26; 9:11,** also ἕως ἐπί τι **17:14.** W. ἕως and gen. of place **23:23** (TestAbr A 2 p. 79, 1 [Stone p. 6,1]). W. διά and gen. of place *through* (X., An. 4, 7, 15) **Mt 12:1; Mk 9:30 v.l.** ποῦ (instead of ποῖ) **J 7:35a.** οὗ (instead of ὅποι, as 1 Macc 13:20) **Lk 24:28a; 1 Cor 16:6.** π. τῇ ὁδῷ *go one's way, proceed on one's journey* 1 Cl 12:4; also ἐπορεύετο τὴν ὁδὸν αὐτοῦ **Ac 8:39** (cp. Josh 3:4; X. An. 2, 2, 11 πορεύεσθαι μακροτέραν [sc. ὁδόν]; Jos., Ant. 1, 282). π. ἐν τῇ ὁδῷ *go along the road* **Lk 9:57;** also π. κατὰ τὴν ὁδόν **Ac 8:36;** AcPl Ant 13, 19f(=Aa I 237, 4).—W. purpose indicated by an inf. (Gen 37:25; JosAs 25:2) **Lk 2:3; 14:19, 31; J 14:2.** Also ἵνα **11:11.**—Somet. the place fr. which or to which is easily supplied fr. the context: θέλετε πορεύεσθαι *you wish to go* (i.e. to the house of the non-believer/non-Christian who has invited you) **1 Cor 10:27.** πορ. (i.e. εἰς Ἰερουσαλήμ) **16:4a.** πορ. (i.e. εἰς Δαμασκόν) **Ac 22:6.**—The aor. ptc. of πορ. is oft. used pleonastically to enliven the narrative (B-D-F §419, 2.—4 Km 5:10; Josh 23:16; GrBar 15:4; Jos., Ant. 7, 318); in any case the idea of going or traveling is not emphasized **Mt 9:13; 11:4; 18:12; 21:6; 22:15; 25:16; 27:66; 28:7; Mk 16:10; Lk 7:22; 9:13; 13:32; 14:10** al.—Abs. (X., An. 5, 3, 2; TestAbr B 3 p. 107, 5 [Stone p. 62] καὶ ἀναστάντες ἐπορεύοντο) ἐπορεύθησαν *they set out* **Mt 2:9.** πορεύθητι καὶ πορεύεται *go!, and he goes* (cp. PGM 1, 185 πορεύου καὶ ἀπελεύσεται) **8:9; Lk 7:8** (opp. ἔρχεσθαι, as Epict. 1, 25, 10 Ἀγαμέμνων λέγει μοι 'πορεύου . . .'. πορεύομαι. 'ἔρχου'. ἔρχομαι; TestJob 34:5 ἐγὼ πορεύσομαι ἐληλύθημεν γὰρ ἵνα . . .).—**Lk 10:37;** *be on the way, be journeying* **Lk 10:38; 13:33; Ac 9:3.**—ἔμπροσθέν τινος (UPZ 78, 15 [159 BC] ἔμπροσθεν αὐτῶν ἐπορευόμην; Josh 3:6): ἔ. αὐτῶν πορεύεται *he goes in front of them* **J 10:4** (schol. on Apollon. Rhod. 1, 577 προπορεύεται ὁ ποιμήν); cp. B 11:4 (Is 45:2). μὴ πορευθῆτε ὀπίσω αὐτῶν *do not go after them* **Lk 21:8** (ὀπίσω 2a). προθύμως (+ μετὰ σπουδῆς v.l.) ἐπορεύετο *he walked on with alacrity* MPol 8:3.—πορεύου=go your way (Diog. L. 4, 11): πορεύου εἰς εἰρήνην **Lk 7:50; 8:48** or ἐν εἰρήνῃ **Ac 16:36** s. εἰρήνη 2a.—In imagery, of life gener. (Dio Chrys. 58 [75], 1 διὰ τ. βίου); abs. πορευόμενοι *as they pass by* (Jülicher, Gleichn. 529) **Lk 8:14** (another mng.: *step by step*).—GKilpatrick, JTS 48, '47, 61–63 (in synopt. gosp.).

❷ **to conduct oneself,** ***live, walk*** (cp. Soph., Oed. Rex 884; LXX; PsSol 18:10) w. ἔν τινι foll.: (En 99:10 ἐν ὁδοῖς δικαιοσύνης; TestReub 1:6; 4:1 ἐν ἁπλότητι καρδίας; TestIss 3:1; TestAsh 4:5) ἐν ὁδῷ θανάτου B 19:2. ἐν ἀληθείᾳ (Tob 3:5 BA; Pr 28:6) Hm 3:4. ἐν ἀκακίᾳ καὶ ἁπλότητι v 2, 3, 2. ἐν ἀσελγείαις κτλ. **1 Pt 4:3.** ἐν τῇ ἁγνότητι ταύτῃ Hm 4, 4, 4. ἐν ὁσιότητι 1 Cl 60:2. ἐν ταῖς ἐντολαῖς τοῦ κυρίου (cp. Ps 118:1 ἐν νόμῳ κυρίου) **Lk 1:6;** cp. Pol 2:2; 4:1; Hs 6, 1, 1–4. ἐν τοῖς προστάγμασιν 5, 1, 5.—κατά τι (Num 24:1; Wsd 6:4) κατὰ τὰς ἐπιθυμίας *according to the* passions **2 Pt 3:3; Jd 16, 18.**—τῇ ὀρθῇ ὁδῷ πορ. *follow the straight way* Hm 6, 1, 2 (on the dat. s. B-D-F §198, 5; Rob. 521 and SIG 313, 20; LXX [reff. in Johannessohn, Kasus 57f]). ταῖς ὁδοῖς αὐτῶν **Ac 14:16.** τῇ ὁδῷ τοῦ Κάϊν **Jd 11.** τῷ φόβῳ τοῦ κυρίου *live in the fear of the Lord* **Ac 9:31.** ταῖς ἐντολαῖς μου Hs 7, 6f. ταῖς ἐπιθυμίαις τοῦ αἰῶνος τούτου 8, 11, 3.—πορ. ὀπίσω τινός in the sense 'seek a close relation with' (cp. Judg 2:12; 3 Km 11:10; Sir 46:10) οἱ ὀπίσω σαρκὸς ἐν ἐπιθυμίᾳ μιασμοῦ πορευόμενοι *follow* (i.e. indulge) *their physical nature in desire that defiles* **2 Pt 2:10.** ὀπίσω τῶν ἐπιθυμιῶν Hv 3, 7, 3.

❸ **go to one's death,** a euphemistic fig. ext. of 1 (cp. **Lk 22:33** εἰς θάνατον πορεύεσθαι): ***die*** (SyrBar 14:2; Julian, Letter 14 p. 385d) **Lk 22:22.** (For the figure of death as a journey s. RLattimore, Themes in Gk. and Lat. Epitaphs: Illinois Studies in Language and Literature 28 nos. 1–2, §43 [=ed. 1962, 169–71]).—DELG s.v. πόρος II. M-M s.v. πορεύομαι. TW.

πορθέω impf. ἐπόρθουν; 1 aor. ἐπόρθησα (Hom.+; OGI 201, 17; BGU 588, 3 πορθοῦντες ὑμᾶς; 4 Macc 4:23; 11:4; GrBar 1:1; Jos., Bell. 4, 405, Ant. 10, 135 τὰ Ἱεροσόλυμα) **to attack and cause complete destruction,** ***pillage, make havoc of, destroy, annihilate*** τὶ *someth.* ἐπόρθουν αὐτήν (i.e. τὴν ἐκκλησίαν τοῦ θεοῦ) *I tried to destroy God's congregation* **Gal 1:13.** τὴν πίστιν ἥν ποτε ἐπόρθει *the faith which he once tried to annihilate* vs. **23.** τινά *someone* (Aeschyl. et al.; Diod. S. 11, 32, 1; s. BGU above) π. τοὺς ἐπικαλουμένους τὸ ὄνομα τοῦτο **Ac 9:21.**—P-HMenoud, EHaenchen Festschr. '64, 178–86 (Ac, Gal).—DELG s.v. πέρθω. M-M. Spicq. Sv.

πορία s. πορεία.

πορίζω (trag., Thu.+) **to cause someth. to become available,** ***procure, provide*** ἑαυτῷ τὴν τροφήν *food for oneself* (Horapollo 1, 42 αἱ τροφαὶ πορίζονται; PGrenfII, 14a, 11 [III BC] πόρισόν μοι εἰς τὴν τροφήν; Aelian, VH 13, 26 and Jos., Ant. 8, 13 π. αὑτῷ τι) B 10:4.—DELG s.v. πόρος II.

πορισμός, οῦ, ὁ (πορίζω; Polyb. et al.; ins [New Docs 4, 169]; Wsd 13:19; 14:2; EpArist 111; Philo, Op. M. 128; Jos., Bell. 2, 603) ***means of gain*** (so Plut., Cato Maj. 351 [25, 1] δυσὶ μόνοις πορισμοῖς, γεωργίᾳ καὶ φειδοῖ=he had only two means of gain: farming and frugality; TestIss 4:5 v.l.; cp. the use of πορίζω of a swindling magician Aesop, Fab. 112a H.=56 H-H. v.l.) **1 Ti 6:5,** followed by wordplay vs. **6.**—DELG s.v. πόρος. M-M.

Πόρκιος, ου, ὁ (Polyb., Plut.; Jos., Ant. 20, 182) ***Porcius,*** name of a Roman gens to which, among others, the Catos belonged. Festus the procurator belonged to it (s. Φῆστος) **Ac 24:27.**—Pauly-W. XXII 220–27; Kl. Pauly IV 1059.

πορνεία, ας, ἡ (of various kinds of 'unsanctioned sexual intercourse': Demosth. et al.; LXX, En, Test12Patr; GrBar [in vice lists]; AscIs, Philo, apolog. exc. Ar. W. φθορά Iren. 1, 28, 1 [Harv. I 220, 14])

❶ **unlawful sexual intercourse,** ***prostitution, unchastity, fornication,*** **1 Cor 5:1ab** (CdeVos, NTS 44, '98, 104–14); **6:13** (on 1 Cor 5–6 s. PTomson, Paul and the Jewish Law: CRINT III/1, '90, 97–102); Hm 4, 1, 1. In a vice list (cp. AscIs 2:5) **Ro 1:29 v.l.** W. ἀκαθαρσία **2 Cor 12:21; Gal 5:19; Eph 5:3; Col 3:5.** Differentiated fr. μοιχεία (Philo, Mos. 1, 300; s. also πορνεύω 1) **Mt 15:19; Mk 7:21** (WGabriel, Was ist 'porneia' im Sprachgebr. Jesu?: Ethik 7, '31, 106–9; 363–69); Hm 8:3; D 5:1 (the pl. denotes individual acts). On the other hand μοιχεία appears as πορνεία (cp. Sir 23:23) Hm 4, 1, 5. Of the sexual unfaithfulness of a married woman **Mt 5:32; 19:9** (for the view that ref. is made in these pass. to forbidden degrees of marriage, s. 2 below.—JSickenberger, TQ 123, '42, 189–206, ZNW 42, '49, 202ff; KStaab [παρεκτός 2]; AAllgeier, Angelicum 20, '43, 128–42. Cp. AFridrichsen, SEÅ 9, '44, 54–58; AIsaksson, Marriage and Ministry in the New Temple, '65, 127–42 [lit.]; s. also JFitzmyer, TS 37, 76, 197–226). Caused by lust D 3:3. διὰ τὰς πορνείας **1 Cor 7:2** (the pl. points out the various factors that may bring about sexual immorality; PTomson [s. above] 103–8). BMalina, Does Porneia Mean 'Fornication'? NovT 14, '72, 10–17. φεύγειν τὴν π. **6:18.** Also ἀπέχεσθαι ἀπὸ τῆς π. **1 Th 4:3** (cp. Tobit 4:12). ἐκ π. γεννηθῆναι *be an illegitimate child, a bastard* (cp. Cephalion [II AD]: 93 fgm. 5 p. 444, 5 Jac. ἐγέννησε ἐκ πορ.; Gen 38:24) **J 8:41.** On ἀπέχεσθαι τῆς πορνείας καὶ πνικτοῦ **Ac 15:20** (cp. vs. **29; 21:25** and s. 2 below) s. the lit. s.v. πνικτός and in BBacon, The Apost. Decree against πορνεία: Exp. 8th ser., 7, 1914, 40–61.

❷ **participation in prohibited degrees of marriage,** ***fornication*** (s. Lev. 18:16–18; cp. Acts 15:20–29, s. Bruce, comm. Ac; **21:25**) **Mt 5:32; 19:9** (w. some favor RSmith, Matthew [Augsburg] '89,100; RGundry, Matthew '82, 91: "no need to adopt obscure definitions of πορνείας, such as marriage within the forbidden degrees. . . . The specific word for adultery does not appear in the exceptive phrase simply because a general expression occurs in Deuteronomy" [24:1], but s. BWitherington, NTS 31, '85, 571–76: 'except in the case of incest'. On these pass. s. 1.).

❸ **immorality of a transcendent nature,** ***fornication,*** in imagery, of polytheistic cult in the mystic city Babylon, which appears in Rv as a prostitute with an international clientele. Fr. the time of Hosea the relationship betw. God and his people was regarded as a marriage bond. This usage was more easily understandable because some Semitic and Graeco-Roman cults were at times connected w. sexual debauchery (cp. Hos 6:10; Jer 3:2, 9; 4 Km 9:22; on the positive side, for concern about propriety on the part of some cults s. e.g. SIG 820 [83/84 AD], in which an Ephesian official assures Rome that the annual autumn fertility festival is conducted 'with much chastity and due observance of established customs'. This level of conduct prob. stands up well against activities associated with celebration of a modern Mardi Gras.) **Rv 19:2.** μετανοῆσαι ἐκ τῆς π. αὐτῆς *repent of her immorality* **2:21;** cp. **9:21.** ὁ οἶνος τοῦ θυμοῦ τῆς π. *the wine of her passionate immorality* **14:8; 18:3** (on these passages s. θυμός 1 and 2). ὁ οἶνος τῆς π. **17:2.** τὰ ἀκάθαρτα τῆς π. vs. **4** (ἀκάθαρτος 2).—V.l. for πονηρίας Hv 1, 1, 8 (Leutzsch, Hermas 447 n. 53). S. next entry 2.—DELG s.v. πέρνημι. M-M. EDNT.

πορνεύω fut. πορνεύσω; 1 aor. ἐπόρνευσα; pf. 3 pl. πεπορνεύκασιν Ezk 16:34 (Hdt. et al.; LXX, En; TestAbr A 10 p. 88, 8 [Stone p. 24]; Test12Patr; Ar. 15, 4; Just.; Tat. 34, 3) of a variety of 'unsanctioned sexual intercourse'.

❶ **to engage in sexual immorality,** ***engage in illicit sex, to fornicate, to whore,*** in Gk. lit. freq. in ref. to prostitution (s. L-S-J-M s.v.). In a gener. sense **1 Cor 10:8ab.** Distinguished fr. μοιχεύειν 'commit adultery' (Did., Job 133, 22ff [quote fr. Hos 4:14], 25ff); D 2:2; B 19:4; **Mk 10:19 v.l.** Regarded as a sin against one's own body **1 Cor 6:18.** W. φαγεῖν εἰδωλόθυτα 'eat meat offered to idols' **Rv 2:14, 20.**

❷ **engagement in polytheistic cult,** ***fornication,*** in imagery (Phalaris, Ep. 121, 1), of polytheistic cult in the sense 'practice image-worship/idolatry' (πορνεία 3 and cp. Hos 9:1; Jer 3:6; Ezk 23:19; 1 Ch 5:25; Ps 72:27; En 8:2) **Rv 17:2; 18:3, 9.** —DELG s.v. πέρνημι. M-M. TW.

πόρνη, ης, ἡ (cp. πέρνημι 'export for sale' [s. Schwyzer I 362] as of captive women exported for slavery Hom. et al.) (Alcaeus, Hipponax; Aristoph., and X., Mem. 1, 5, 4; PSI 352, 4 [254/253 BC]; POxy 528, 18 [II AD]; BGU 1024 VI, 4; LXX; PsSol 2:11; TestLevi 14:5, 6; Philo, Just.; Tat. 34, 2; loanw. in rabb.) 'prostitute'.

❶ **one engaged in sexual relations for hire,** ***prostitute, whore*** lit. (since Alcaeus 109 + 110, 26 D.[2] [115 fgm. 3b 26 L-P.]) **Lk 15:30** (cp. Pr 29:3; Test Levi 14:5 μετὰ πορνῶν); **1 Cor 6:15.** Of Rahab (Josh 2:1; 6:17, 23, 25) **Hb 11:31; Js 2:25;** 1 Cl 12:1 (a πόρνη rewarded for a rescue also in Neanthes [200 BC]: 84 fgm. 9 Jac.). W. tax-collectors as the lowest class of people, morally speaking **Mt 21:31f.** W. female flutists Ox 36. κολλᾶσθαι τῇ π. *have to do with a prostitute* (Sir 19:2) **1 Cor 6:16.**

❷ **a political entity hostile to God,** ***prostitute, whore,*** fig. ext. of 1 (s. πορνεία and πορνεύω; Is 1:21; 23:15f; Jer 3:3; Ezk 16:30f, 35) as the designation of a government that is hostile to God and God's people **Rv 17:15f.** ἡ πόρνη ἡ μεγάλη vs. **1; 19:2.** Βαβυλὼν (q.v.) ἡ μεγάλη ἡ μήτηρ τῶν πορνῶν **17:5** (unless masc. πόρνων is to be read, s. next entry).—For the woman sitting on the beast cp. Cebes 5, 1, a beautifully adorned woman sitting on a throne. She is called Ἀπάτη, ἣ ἐν τῇ χειρὶ ἔχει ποτήριόν τι, from which she gives men to drink (ποτίζει Cebes 5, 2 as Rv 14:8), in order to lead them astray (πλανάω as Rv 18:23).—B. 1368. RAC III 1149–1212. DELG s.v. πέρνημι. M-M. EDNT. TW.

πόρνος, ου, ὁ (cp. πόρνη; Aristoph., X.+ in the sense 'male whore/prostitute' and related terms; Sir 23:17; Philo, Leg. All. 8; Just.; Tat. 34, 3)

❶ **one who practices sexual immorality,** ***fornicator*** **1 Cor 5:9, 11; Hb 12:16; Rv 17:5,** if accented as masc. (in N.[27] as fem.; s. app. in Tdf. and early edd. of Nestle incl. 25th ed), but s. also 2. οἱ π. τοῦ κόσμου τούτου *the (sexually) immoral persons in this world* **1 Cor 5:10.** W. other sinners **Eph 5:5; 1 Ti 1:10; Rv 21:8; 22:15.** Differentiated fr. an adulterer **1 Cor 6:9; Hb 13:4.** Excluded fr. the Reign of God, w. others guilty of grave sins **1 Cor 6:9** (=Pol 5:3).

❷ **a political entity hostile to God,** ***fornicator,*** fig. ext. of 1: ἡ μητὴρ τῶν πόρνων *mother of fornicators* **Rv 17:5 v.l.,** s. 1.—RBorger TRu 52, '87, 48–50.—DELG s.v. πέρνημι. M-M. EDNT. TW.

πόρρω adv. (the att. form [=πόρσω, cp. πρόσω in the same sense]; Pla., X.+; LXX; En; EpArist 31; Just., D. 10, 2; Tat.—Thackeray p. 123; B-D-F §34, 2) **pert. to a position that is relatively distant,** ***far (away).***

ⓐ used as an adv. 1 Cl 3:4; Hv 3, 6, 1. π. εἶναι *be far away* (B-D-F §434, 1; Rob. 546) **Lk 14:32.** π. ἀπό (En 32:4; Jos., Vi. 281): π. γίνεσθαι ἀπό τινος *be* or *remain far from someone* or *someth.* fig. (cp. Bar 3:21) 1 Cl 23:3; 30:3 (some would put in b); 39:9 (Job 5:4). π. ἀπέχειν ἀπό τινος *be far removed fr. someone,* fig. **Mt 15:8; Mk 7:6;** 1 Cl 15:2; 2 Cl 3:5 (all four Is 29:13).

ⓑ used as a prep. w. gen. (Isocr., Ep. 6, 13 κινδύνων π.; Περὶ ὕψους 17, 3; Ael. Aristid. 28, 103 K.=49 p. 525 D.: π. θεῶν; Philo, Op. M. 63; Jos., Ant. 7, 71, Vi. 167; Just., D. 10, 2; Tat. 15, 2) ὧν μακρὰν καὶ πόρρω πραΰτης B 20:2. S. a for 1Cl 30:3.

ⓒ as comp. of the adv. we have in the text of **Lk 24:28** πορρώτερον (Aristot. et al.), and as v.l. πορρωτέρω (X., Pla.; Jos., Bell. 4, 108, Vi. 326.—Thumb 77): πορρ. πορεύεσθαι *go farther.*—B. 868. DELG s.v. πόρσω. M-M.

πόρρωθεν adv. (s. πόρρω; Pla. et al.; LXX; KDieterich, Untersuchungen zur Gesch. der griech. Sprache 1898, 183f) **pert. to a position as point of reference for determining someth. as distant,** ***from a distance*** (Aen. Tact. 540; 1199; Diod. S. 1, 83, 4; Jos., Bell. 3, 113; 4, 157, Ant. 3, 9) **Hb 11:13.** W. substitution of one concept for another *from a distance*=***at a distance*** (Herodian 2, 6, 13 π. ἑστῶτες) οἳ ἔστησαν πόρρωθεν *who stood at a distance* (ἵστημι B 1) **Lk 17:12** (Aesop, Fab. 1 P.=5 H.; 3 Ch.; 1 H-H. πόρρωθεν στᾶσα). οἱ πόρρωθεν *those who are at a distance* (Jos., Bell. 3, 394) B 9:1 (Is 33:13).—DELG s.v. πόρσω. M-M.

πορρώτερον/πορρωτέρω s. πόρρω, end.

πορφύρα, ας, ἡ (Aeschyl., Hdt.et al.; ins, pap, LXX; TestAbr A 4 p. 80, 21 [Stone p. 8]; TestLevi 8:7; JosAs, EpArist; Philo, Congr. Erud. Gr. 117; Jos., Bell. 6, 390; loanw. in rabb.) the purple fish (a shell-fish, murex), then a purple dye obtained fr. it, finally the cloth, clothing, etc. In our lit. only in the last-named sense (so Aeschyl. et al.; Aristot., Polyb., Lucian; Jos., Ant. 8, 185; EpArist 320; LXX) ***purple*** **(*cloth*)** w. βύσσος (q.v.) **Lk 16:19;** GJs 10:(2), twice w. κόκκινον (s. the Bodmer pap and deStrycker's ed. on this disputed text); 12:1. ἔλαβεν τὴν π. . . . καὶ ἧλκεν τὴν π. 11:1. *Purple garment* (Appian, Liby. 66, 297) w. τὸ βύσσινον (s. βύσσινος and cp. JosAs 5:6 πορφύρα ἐκ βύσσου χρυσοϋφής) **Rv 18:12.** Cp. **17:4 v.l.** (w. κόκκινον). Of the red garment which the soldiers put on Jesus **Mk 15:17, 20;** GPt 3:7 (Appian, Bell. Civ. 2, 150 the Roman soldier's cloak is called ἡ πορφύρα; s. χλαμύς.—Dio Chrys. 4, 71 and Jos., Ant. 11, 256; 257 of a royal purple garment; cp. 1 Macc 10:62).—Lit. s. κόκκινος, also RGradwohl, Die Farben im AT, Beih. ZAW 83, '63, 66–73 and lit.; Pauly-W. XXIII 2200–220; Kl. Pauly IV 1243f; BHHW III 1532f; ABD s.v. 'Purple' (V 557–60) and 'Zoology (Animal Profiles)' (VI 1149f); New Docs 2, 25–27 (lit.); CHemer, New Docs 3, 53–55; also Hemer, Acts 114; HStulz, Die Farbe Purpur im frühen Griechentum '90.—Schmidt, Syn. III 44–51. DELG. M-M.

πορφυρόπωλις, ιδος, ἡ (πωλέω; the fem., found in CIG 2519 [where it is restored, but is surely correct], and PFlor 71, 641 [IV AD] of πορφυροπώλης, ου, ὁ [e.g. IHierapJ 156]=dealer in purple [woolen] cloth [s. WSchmidt, Forschungen aus dem Gebiete des Altertums I 1842, 163ff]) ***a merchant dealing in purple cloth,*** of Lydia of Thyatira (s. Θυάτιρα) at Philippi **Ac 16:14.**—M-M.

πορφυροῦς, ᾶ, οῦν (the form preferred in Attic Gk., also in LXX, Joseph. [e.g. Bell. 7, 124, Ant. 10, 235; Schmidt 492] for the older [Hom. et al.; SIG 999, 5; SibOr 3, 659] πορφύρεος, έα, εον) ***purple*** in color ἱμάτιον πορφυροῦν (Diod. S. 2, 59, 4; Num 4:14; EpJer 11; cp. PRyl 151, 14 [40 AD] χιτῶνα πορφυροῦν) *a purple cloak* **J 19:2, 5.** Subst. τὸ πορφυροῦν (i.e. ἱμάτιον) *purple clothing* w. κόκκινον (s. κόκκινος) **Rv 17:4;** cp. **18:16.**—GEuler, πορφυροῦς, purpureus, Progr. Weilburg 1907.—DELG s.v. πορφύρα. M-M s.v. πορφύρεος.

ποσάκις (on the formation s. Schwyzer I 597f) adv. Pla. et al.; POxy 528, 24; LXX; TestJos 3:1) **reference to a number of related points of times,** in a question or exclamation ***how many times? how often?*** **Mt 18:21; 23:37; Lk 13:34;** AcPl Ha 8, 10.—S. DELG s.v. πο- and -κις. M-M.

πόσις, εως, ἡ (πίνω; Hom. et al.; BGU 1191, 3 [I BC]; O. Theb 3, 1; Ath 22, 2) in our lit. always w. βρῶσις (as Da 1:10; TestAbr B 13 p. 117, 23 [Stone p. 82]; τὰς τρυφὰς καὶ τὰς π. ApcSed 11:11 p. 134, 27 Ja.).

❶ **act of drinking,** ***drinking*** (Hdt. 1, 172; Pla., Leg. 1, 637d al.) lit. βρῶσις καὶ πόσις (βρῶσις 1) **Ro 14:17; Col 2:16.**

❷ **that which one drinks,** ***a drink*** (Aeneas Tact. 589; Da 1:10; Philo, Op. M. 38) of Jesus' blood ἀληθής ἐστιν πόσις **J 6:55.**—DELG s.v. πίνω C 4. M-M. TW.

πόσος, η, ον (Aeschyl.+) a correlative pron. in dir. and indir. questions.

❶ **pert. to degree or magnitude:** as interrogative or exclamation, ***how great(?)*** in the sing. **Ac 22:28** D (indir.); 1 Cl 56:16 (indir.). πόσ. χρόνος ἐστίν; *how long is it?* **Mk 9:21** (on πόσ. χρόν. cp. Soph., Oed. R. 558; Pla., Rep. 7, 546a; ApcMos 31; Just., D. 32, 4). In an exclamation (Appian, Mithrid. 58 §237 πόσην ὠμότητα, πόσην ἀσέβειαν—B-D-F §304; Rob. 741) πόσην κατειργάσατο ὑμῖν σπουδήν *how much zeal it has called forth in you!* **2 Cor 7:11;** postpositive use τὸ σκότος πόσον; *how great must the darkness be?* **Mt 6:23.** πόσῳ; *to what degree? how much?* πόσῳ διαφέρει ἄνθρωπος προβάτου; **Mt 12:12.** W. a comp. foll. (Polyaenus 3, 9, 25 πόσῳ φοβερώτεροι;) πόσῳ δοκεῖτε χείρονος ἀξιωθήσεται τιμωρίας; *how much greater a punishment do you think one will deserve?* **Hb 10:29.** πόσῳ μᾶλλον; *how much more?* (PFlor 170, 8 [III AD] εἰ . . . πόσῳ μᾶλλον=if . . . how much more; Syntipas 19, 15; Jos., Bell. 2, 365; Diod. S. 1, 2, 2) **Mt 7:11; 10:25; Lk 11:13; 12:24, 28; J 13:14 v.l.; Ro 11:12, 24; Phlm 16; Hb 9:14;** B 19:8; D 4:8; IEph 5:1f; 16:2; AcPl Cor 2:31. πόσῳ μᾶλλον οὐ; *how much less?* (Ps.-Clem., Hom. 10, 20) 2 Cl 17:1.—JBonsirven, Exégèse rabbinique et exégèse paulinienne '39; HMüller, Der rabbinische

Qal-Wachomer-Schluss in paul. Typologie (Ro 5), ZNW 58, '67, 73–92.

❷ **pert. to quantity:** as interrogative, ***how many, how much(?)***—ⓐ w. a noun in the pl. (Aeschin. 2, 95; X., Mem. 1, 2, 35; 2 Km 19:35; ApcSed 8:7ff; Just., A I, 21, 2) πόσους ἄρτους ἔχετε; *how many loaves do you have?* **Mt 15:34; Mk 6:38; 8:5.** Cp. **Mt 16:9, 10; Mk 8:19, 20; Lk 15:17** (exclam. like Ps 118:84); **Ac 21:20** (Jos., Ant. 7, 318 πόσαι μυριάδες εἰσὶ τοῦ λαοῦ); 2 Cl 1:3.

ⓑ without a noun—**α.** in the pl. πόσοι; *how many?* (TestBenj 3:4; Ps.-Clem., Hom. 9, 18; 10, 23) Hs 8, 6, 1.—πόσα; *how many things?* (TestJos 10:1; Ps.-Clem., Hom. 9, 18; Just., D. 85, 5) **Mt 27:13; Mk 15:4.**

β. in the sing. πόσον; *how much?* (TestNapht 2:2 οἶδεν ὁ κεραμεὺς τὸ σκεῦος πόσον χωρεῖ; BGU 893, 26 ἐπύθετο, πόσον ἔχει) πόσον ὀφείλεις; **Lk 16:5, 7.**—DELG s.v. πο-. M-M.

ποσότης, ητος, ἡ (πόσος; Aristot., Metaph. 1028a, 19; Polyb. 16, 12, 10 al.; ins, pap, Philo) **quality of greatness in degree or number, *quantity, amount*** w. καλλονή 1 Cl 35:3. συνοψίσας τὴν π. τῆς δαπάνης *estimating the amount of the cost* Hs 5, 3, 7.—DELG s.v. πο-.

ποταμός, οῦ, ὁ (Hom.+) ***river, stream***—ⓐ lit., of the Jordan (Jos., Ant. 20, 97, Vi. 399; SibOr 6, 5) **Mt 3:6; Mk 1:5.** Of the Euphrates (s. Εὐφράτης) **Rv 9:14; 16:12.** Of the Tiber (SibOr 5, 170; Just., A I, 26, 2) Hv 1, 1, 2ab; but the ποταμός of 1, 1, 3 cannot be identified (cp. Hdb. ad loc.). ἦν π. ἕλκων ἐκ δεξιῶν (ἕλκω 3) B 11:10. Cp. **Ac 16:13; 2 Cor 11:26; Rv 8:10; 12:15f; 16:4.** ἐπέβλεψα ἐπὶ τὸν χείμαρρον τοῦ ποταμοῦ *I watched the flow of the river* GJs 18:3 (codd.).—**Lk 6:48f** ὁ ποταμός means a river that flows continuously near the house in question, but in the parallel **Mt 7:25, 27** οἱ ποταμοί are to be understood as the *mountain torrents* or *winter torrents* which arise in ravines after a heavy rain and carry everything before them (so the pl. in Heraclit. Sto. 38 p. 55, 9; Quint. Smyrn. [400 AD] 8, 384; 14, 5). The *river of living water* in the heavenly Jerusalem **Rv 22:1;** cp. vs. **2.** In a fragmentary context AcPl BMM verso 15.

ⓑ The pl. of large amounts of flowing water. Fig. ποταμοὶ ἐκ τῆς κοιλίας αὐτοῦ ῥεύσουσιν ὕδατος ζῶντος *streams of living water will flow from his* (the Redeemer's—s. κοιλία 3) *body* **J 7:38** (scripture quot. of unknown orig. See Hdb. ad loc.; Bultmann 229, 2; LKöhler, Kleine Lichter '45, 39–41; CGoodwin, JBL 63, '54, 72f).—B. 42. DELG. M-M. TW.

ποταμοφόρητος, ον (φορητός 'borne, carried' [φέρω]; PAmh 85, 16 [78 AD]; PTebt 610; PStras 5, 10; PFlor 368, 12 al. in pap) **pert. to being borne along involuntarily by a flow of water, *swept away by a river, overwhelmed by a stream*** ἵνα αὐτὴν π. ποιήσῃ *that he might sweep her away with the stream* i.e. drown her **Rv 12:15.**—AWikenhauser, BZ 6, 1908, 171; 7, 1909, 48. —DELG s.v. φέρω. M-M. TW.

ποταπός, ή, όν a substitute for the older ποδαπός (the latter occurs Aeschyl., X., Pla.+; Jos., Bell. 4, 169, Ant. 6, 345; so D **Mk 13:1; Lk 1:29; 7:39;** s. Lob., Phryn. p. 56f; Schwyzer I 604, 1), but only in the sense quotable for ποδαπός (Demosth.+) **interrogative reference to class or kind, *of what sort* or *kind(?)*** (Dionys. Hal.; Lucian; ApcSed 7:1; Philo; Jos., Bell. 2, 32, C. Ap. 1, 255 al.; POxy 1678, 16 [III AD]; Sus 54 LXX; B-D-F §298, 3; Rob. 741) of persons **Mt 8:27; 2 Pt 3:11;** Hs 8, 6, 3. τίς καὶ ποταπὴ ἡ γυνή *who and what kind of woman* **Lk 7:39** (cp. Jos., Ant. 7, 72 and the related formulation εἰς τίνα ἢ ποῖον καιρόν 'to what or what sort of time' 1 Pt 1:11 [s. καιρός 1a]). ποταποὶ τὴν μορφὴν *what kind of form* they have ApcPt 2:5.—ποταπός ἐστιν τῇ εἰδέᾳ ὁ Παῦλος *how Paul looked* AcPl Ant 13, 13–15 (=Aa I 237, 2). Of things **Lk 1:29;** Hv 3, 4, 3; s 4:3; 6, 3, 4. Somet. the context calls for the sense *how great, how wonderful* **Mk 13:1ab;** *how glorious* **1J 3:1.**—In ποταπαὶ . . . εἰσὶν αἱ πονηρίαι; Hm 8:3 ποταπαί=τίνες: *what are the vices?*—DELG s.v. πο- B4. M-M. Spicq.

ποταπῶς adv. of ποταπός (q.v.) ***in what way, how(?)*** **Ac 20:18** D.

πότε interrog. adv. of time (Hom.+) ***when(?)*** predom. in direct questions, but also in indirect: **Mt 24:3** (perh. indir.); **25:37–39, 44; Mk 13:4** (perh. indir.), **33** (indir.), **35** (indir.); **Lk 12:36** (indir.); **17:20** (indir.); **21:7; J 6:25;** 2 Cl 12:2 (indir.; apocryphal saying of Jesus); B 12:1 (prophetic quot. of uncertain orig.); Hv 1, 1, 7; 3, 6, 6; AcPl Ha 6, 17. Elliptic (indir.) εἴρηκεν πότε *he has told* (us) *when* (it will happen) B 6:19. ἕως π.; (LXX; ApcSed 12:1.—Jos., Ant. 2, 309 ἄχρι π.) *how long?,* lit. *until when?* **Mt 17:17ab; Mk 9:19ab; Lk 9:41; J 10:24; Rv 6:10;** GJs 2:2; Hv 3, 6, 5. ἀπὸ πότε *since* **Mk 8:2** D (B-D-F §203).—DELG s.v. πο- A. M-M.

ποτέ enclitic particle (Hom. et al.; pap, LXX, TestSol, TestAbr,TestJob, JosAs, GrBar; ApcEsdr 4:33 p. 29, 9 Tdf.; ApcMos; apolog. [Mel., P. 37, 253 al.])

❶ **pert. to generalization of time, *at some time or other*** of the past *once, formerly* (Jos., Bell. 7, 112; Mel.) **J 9:13; Ro 7:9; 11:30** (on ποτὲ . . . νῦν [νυνί] δέ, s. νῦν 1aβℷ); **Gal 1:13, 23; Eph 2:2f** al.; B 7:9; MPol 8:1; EpilMosq 3; Papias (2:3).—Of the future (Appian, Bell. Civ. 3, 63 §257=at last; Jos., Bell. 5, 19; Just., D. 65, 2) σύ ποτε ἐπιστρέψας *when once you (will) have turned* **Lk 22:32;** Hm 9, 7.—ποτὲ μὲν . . . ποτὲ δέ *now . . . now, at times . . . at times* (X., Mem. 4, 2, 32; Pla., Theaet. 170c; Diod. S. 1, 32, 2; 2, 59, 5; Wsd 16:18f; TestSol; GrBar 3:5; ApcEsdr 4:33; Ar. 7, 2; Just., A I, 14, 1 al.) B 10:7; GJs 17:2. *Finally, at last* MPol 8:1. On ἤδη ποτέ *now at last* **Ro 1:10; Phil 4:10;** 2 Cl 13:1 s. ἤδη 2.—After negatives *ever* οὐ . . . ποτέ *not . . . ever, never* **2 Pt 1:21;** AcPlCor 1:4. οὔτε . . . ποτὲ . . . οὔτε **1 Th 2:5;** IRo 2:1. MPol 17:2. μήτε . . . ποτὲ B 16:10. οὐδείς ποτε **Eph 5:29** (X., Mem. 1, 4, 19 μηδέν ποτε). οὐ μὴ . . . ποτέ **2 Pt 1:10.** On μή ποτε s. μήποτε; on δή ποτε s. δήποτε. In rhetorical questions that expect a neg. answer τίς . . . ποτέ; **1 Cor 9:7.** Cp. **Hb 1:5, 13;** Dg 8:1.

❷ **indicating a supposition, *presumably*** ἐν τῇ φιλοξενίᾳ εὑρίσκεται ἀγαθοποίησίς ποτε Hm 8:10. Cp. s 6, 5, 4 v.l.

❸ **pert. to generalizing, *ever*** after relatives (ὅπου ποτέ Just., D., 127, 2) ὅσοι ποτέ *whatever, whoever* Hs 9, 6, 7; 9, 28, 3. On ὁποῖοί ποτε ἦσαν **Gal 2:6** s. ὁποῖος and cp. Epict. 2, 20, 5 τίνες ποτέ; οἱ 'Ακαδημαϊκοὺς αὑτοὺς λέγοντες=who are they then? Those who call themselves Academics? Demetr.: 722 fgm. 1, 14 διὰ τί ποτε; 'why, in the world?'—On τί δή ποτε Dg 1 s. δήποτε.—DELG s.v. πο- A. M-M.

πότερος, α, ον (Hom.+) in our lit. (and in the LXX, but only in Job; Thackeray p. 192) only in the fixed form **πότερον** as an interrog. word (B-D-F §64, 6; 298, 1; Rob. 741; 1177) ***whether:*** in a disjunctive question πότερον . . . ἤ *whether . . . or whether* (Pind.; X., Mem. 2, 7, 4; Appian, Bell. Civ. 3, 53 §220; SIG 977, 24–29 ἐπερωτᾷ . . . πότερον . . . ἤ; cp. 987, 14–19; PTebt 289, 6 [23 AD]; Job 7:12; Jos., Ant. 6, 71, C. Ap. 2, 120; Tat. 21, 2; Ath. 26, 3) **J 7:17;** B 19:5; D 4:4; Hs 9, 28, 4.—DELG s.v. πο-B 4. M-M s.v. πότερον.

ποτήριον, ου, τό (dim. of ποτήρ [πίνω]; Alcaeus, Sappho, Hdt.+) **a vessel used for drinking, *cup*** (in Gk. lit. mostly for drinking of wine)

ⓐ lit. **Mt 23:25f; Mk 7:4, 8 v.l.; Lk 11:39.** π. χρυσοῦν (ChronLind B, 42) **Rv 17:4** (s. on πόρνη 2). W. gen. of its contents: π. ὕδατος **Mk 9:41** (Just., D. 65, 3; 66, 4). π. ψυχροῦ *a cup of cold water* **Mt 10:42** (on the ellipsis s. B-D-F §241, 7; Rob. 1202). Oft. in the language of the Eucharist λαβὼν ποτήριον **Mt 26:27; Mk 14:23;** cp. **Lk 22:17, 20a; 1 Cor 11:25a;** IPhld 4; D 9:2.—The cup stands, by metonymy, for what it contains (Pr 23:31) **Lk 22:20b; 1 Cor 11:25b, 26** (τὸ ποτ. corresponds to τὸν ἄρτον).—ἐκ τοῦ ποτηρίου πίνειν vs. **28** (Alcaeus 34 D.[2]). τὸ ποτήριον τῆς εὐλογίας (JosAs 8:11; s. εὐλογία 3bβ) **1 Cor 10:16.** W. gen. of the pers. who bestows the drink (τὸ) ποτήριον (τοῦ) κυρίου πίνειν vs. **21a; 11:27.** Opp. ποτήριον δαιμονίων **10:21b** (FDölger, D. Kelch der Dämonen: AC IV 266–70).

ⓑ fig. (in the OT ποτήριον is an expr. for destiny in both good and bad senses, for death in general TestAbr A 1 al. On the concept of drinking a cup of suffering cp. Is 51:17, 22; La 4:21; Ps 10:6; 74:9.—WLotz, D. Sinnbild des Bechers: NKZ 28, 1917, 396–407; F-JLeenhardt, Le Sacrement de la Sainte Cène '48, 43–45) of undergoing a violent death; first of Christ himself τὸ ποτήριον ὃ δέδωκέν μοι ὁ πατὴρ οὐ μὴ πίω αὐτό; *shall I not drink the cup which the Father has given me?* **J 18:11.** Cp. **Mt 20:22; 26:39, 42 v.l.; Mk 10:38; 14:36** (Cranfield, ET 59, '47/48, 137f; DDaube, A Prayer Pattern in Judaism, Studia Evangelica 73, '59, 539–45); **Lk 22:42.** Of Peter's martyrdom πίε τὸ ποτήριον . . . ἐν χειροῖν τοῦ υἱοῦ τοῦ ἐν Ἅιδου *drink the cup from the hands of the son, (who is) in Hades* ApcPt Rainer 16–18 (on the quest. of the identity of the υἱός s. the comments by Ja. p. 274). The martyrdom of a Christian is corresp. described as a λαβεῖν μέρος ἐν τῷ ποτηρίῳ τοῦ Χριστοῦ *share in the cup of Christ* MPol 14:2. Cp. **Mt 20:23; Mk 10:39** (s. on these pass. ESchwartz, Über den Tod der Söhne Zebedaei: GGAbh. n.s. VII/5, 1904, NGG 1907, 266ff, ZNW 11, 1910, 89–104; FSpitta, ibid. 39–58; CBruston, RTQR 19, 1910, 338–44, RHPR 5, 1925, 69–71; VWeber, Der Katholik 92, 1912, 434–45; JBernard, ET 39, 1928, 456–58).—On τὸ ποτήριον τοῦ οἴνου τοῦ θυμοῦ τῆς ὀργῆς αὐτοῦ **Rv 16:19** s. θυμός 1 and 2. On the pass. connected w. it, i.e. **Rv 14:10; 18:6,** s. κεράννυμι 1.—B. 348. DELG s.v. C 7. M-M. EDNT. TW.

ποτίζω impf. ἐπότιζον; fut. ποτιῶ LXX, and 3 sg. ποτίσει Sir 15:3; 1 aor. ἐπότισα; pf. πεπότικα. Pass.: impf. ἐποτιζόμην B 7:3 (in Hs 9, 1, 8; 9, 25, 1 prob. mid., s. 2 below); 1 fut. 3 sg. ποτισθήσεται Ezk 32:6; 1 aor. ἐποτίσθην; pf. ptc. πεποτισμένος (ποτόν, πότος; Hippocr., X.+)

❶ **make it possible for someone or someth. to drink**

ⓐ of persons ***give to drink*** τινά *to someone* **Mt 25:35, 37, 42; 27:48; Mk 15:36; Ro 12:20** (Pr 25:21). W. double acc. *cause someone to drink someth.*, τινά τι π. *give someone someth. to drink* (Pla., Phdr. 247e; Gen 19:32; Judg 4:19a; 1 Km 30:11 al.; B-D-F §155, 7; Rob. 484) water (ποτίζειν τινὰ ποτήριον as Jer 16:7) **Mt 10:42; Mk 9:41.** ὕδωρ τῆς ἐλέγξεως *water of conviction* in ref. to trial by water to expose sin GJs 16:1; cp. 16:2. χολὴν μετὰ ὄξους GPt 5:16; B 7:5. In imagery π. τινὰ γάλα *give someone milk to drink* **1 Cor 3:2** (οὐ βρῶμα is added in zeugma; B-D-F §479, 2; Rob. 1200f). Instead of the acc. of thing we have ἔκ τινος **Rv 14:8** (in imagery). ἐπότιζεν ῥήματι *(Paul) gave (Artemilla) the word to drink* AcPl Ha 4, 5. Pass. *be given (someth.) to drink* w. dat. of thing (for the act. w. dat. of thing s. OGI 200, 16; Cebes 5, 2; 3 Macc 5:2) ἐποτίζετο ὄξει καὶ χολῇ *he was given vinegar and gall to drink* B 7:3. Also acc. of thing (TestAbr A, ApcEsdr; B-D-F §159, 1; Rob. 485) in imagery (cp. e.g. Sir 15:3; Is 29:10) πάντες ἓν πνεῦμα ἐποτίσθημεν *we have all been made to drink* (or *been imbued with*) *the same Spirit* **1 Cor 12:13** (difft., GCuming NTS 27, '81, 283–85, under c).

ⓑ of animals ***water*** (Diod. S. 19, 94, 9; Polyaenus 6, 4, 2; OGI 483, 169; oft. LXX) **Lk 13:15.**

ⓒ of plants ***water*** (X., Symp. 2, 25 et al.; Ezk 17:7; Cleopatra ln. 93 τ. βοτάνας. The sense 'irrigate' a field, garden, etc. is much more common; oft. so in pap, LXX, OdeSol, JosAs) τὰς ῥάβδους *the sticks* that have been planted Hs 8, 2, 9a. Pass. 8, 2, 9b (ὕδατι); 8, 3, 8. GCuming (s. a above) interprets **1 Cor 12:13** of 'watering' with the Spirit through baptismal affusion; response by ERogers, NTS 29, '83, 139–42 ('cause to drink'). Abs., in imagery of the founding of a church, w. φυτεύειν (as Hs 8, 3, 8) **1 Cor 3:6–8.**

❷ **to provide a drink for oneself, *drink*** mid. πᾶν γένος τῆς κτίσεως τοῦ κυρίου ἐποτίζετο ἐκ τῶν πηγῶν Hs 9, 1, 8; cp. 9, 25, 1.—DELG s.v. πίνω C 1. M-M. TW. Spicq.

Ποτίολοι, ων, οἱ (Strabo 5, 4, 6; Porphyr., Vi. Plot. 2; Jos., Ant. 18, 161, Vi. 16; ins [OGI II, index p. 595]; on the sp. s. B-D-F §41, 1; Mlt-H. 76) ***Puteoli,*** a highly cosmopolitan city on the Gulf of Naples in Italy, 12 km. fr. Naples. Paul landed there on his journey to Rome, and spent a week w. the Christians there **Ac 28:13.**—MRostovtzeff, The Social and Economic History of the Roman Empire[2] '57, II 610 n. 25 (reff.); Hemer, Acts 155; Pauly-W. XXIII 2036–60; Kl. Pauly IV 1244f; DACL XIV 1673–87; BHHW III 1533; PECS 743f; Haenchen ad loc.

ποτόν, οῦ, τό (Hom.+; PSI 64, 21 [I BC]; PGiess 19, 6; LXX; TestSol 11: 7, 9 C; SibOr 3, 746; Philo; Jos., Bell. 3, 183, Ant. 1, 245f; Ar.; subst. neut. of ποτός, ή, όν=drinkable) **that which one drinks, *drink*** w. τροφή (food and) *drink* (Longus 2, 7, 4; Jos., Ant. 7, 159) gener. D 10:3a, then of the Eucharist πνευματικὴ τροφὴ καὶ ποτόν 3b. W. βρωτόν GJs 1:4. Pl. βρώματα καὶ ποτά (βρῶμα 1 and cp. PSI loc. cit. μήτε ἐν ποτοῖς μήτε ἐν βρωτοῖς; EpArist 128 al.) ITr 2:3. Also σιτία καὶ ποτά (cp. Hdt. 5, 34, 1; X., An. 7, 1, 33; oft. Philo) Dg 6:9.—DELG s.v. πίνω C. TW.

πότος, ου, ὁ (X., Pla. et al.; Sb 7452, 21 [III AD?]; LXX; JosAs 21:6 [cod. A p. 71, 25 Bat.]; EpArist 262; Philo, Vi. Cont. 46; Jos., Ant. 5, 289; TestJud 8:2) **a social gathering at which wine was served, *drinking party*** (X., Symp. 8, 41, as synonym of κλῆσις 'banquet' 1, 7) pl. (Aristoph., Pla. et al.; Pr 23:30) w. κῶμοι (q.v. and Synes., Providence 1, 14 p. 107c) **1 Pt 4:3** here prob. in the sense of 'carousal'. In the Gr-Rom. world it was customary for literati to hold banquets at which topical discussions were featured, with participants well lubricated with wine (s. the dialogues of Pl. and esp. X., Symp.). These would not properly be rendered 'carousals'. It is prob. that the Petrine pass. has less sophisticated participants in mind.—TW.

ποῦ interrog. marker of place (Hom.+).—❶ **interrogative reference to place without suggestion of movement, *where(?), at which place(?)***

ⓐ in direct questions **Mt 2:2; 26:17; Mk 14:12, 14; Lk 17:17, 37; 22:9, 11; J 1:38; 7:11; 8:10, 19; 9:12; 11:34** al.; **1 Cor 1:20;** IEph 18:1 (both Is 19:12); H 9, 11, 3; GJs 21:1, 2 (codd.); 23:1a, 2. In rhetorical questions that expect a neg. answer *where is?* (Il. 5, 171; Diod. S. 14, 67, 1 ποῦ . . . ; ποῦ . . . ; Lucian, Dial. Deor. 4, 4; TestJob 32:2ff; ApcEsdr 2:8 p. 28, 19 Tdf. al.; pap, LXX; Jos., Ant. 10, 156 al.; Ath., R. 21 p. 74, 16) **Lk 8:25; Ro 3:27; 1 Cor 1:20abc** (ποῦ in several direct questions consecutively as Libanius, Or. 61 p. 337, 18 F.); **12:17ab,**

19; 15:55ab (Hos 13:14ab); **Gal 4:15; 1 Pt 4:18** (Pr 11:31); **2 Pt 3:4.**

ⓑ in indir. questions instead of ὅπου w. indic. foll. (En 12:1b; ParJer 7:14) **Mt 2:4; Mk 15:47; J 1:39; 11:57; 20:2, 13, 15; Rv 2:13;** 1 Cl 40:3; GJs 23:1. W. subj. foll.: οὐκ ἔχειν ποῦ (Epict. 2, 4, 7) *have no place, have nowhere* **Mt 8:20; Lk 9:58; 12:17.** ποῦ αὐτὸν ἀποκρύψῃ *where (Elizabeth) could hide (John)* GJs 22:3.

❷ **interrogative reference to place with implication of movement** (for ποῖ [q.v.], which is not found in Bibl. Gk.) ***where(?), whither(?), to what place(?)*** (Antiphon 2, 4, 8; X., Cyr. 1, 2, 16; Epict. [index Sch.]; Vett. Val. 137, 35; 341, 6; Alciphron 4, 13, 2; Gen 16:8; Judg 19:17; Jdth 10:12; 1 Macc 3:50; En, JosAs, ParJer, ApcMos—Kühner-G. I 545, 4; B-D-F §103; Rob. 298; AMaidhof, Z. Begriffsbestimmung der Koine: Beiträge zur histor. Syntax der Griech. Sprache 20, 1912, 298ff).

ⓐ in direct questions (Cebes 6, 2; 20, 1; En 102:1; JosAs 6:2f; GrBar 9:2) **J 7:35; 13:36; 16:5** (cp. the amulet of a polytheist in ABarb, Der Österreich. Limes XVI 54f ποῦ ὑπάγεις; also Rtzst., ARW 24, 1926, 176–78); 1 Cl 28:2, 3 (Ps 138:7), 4. ποῦ σε ἀπάξω *where should I bring you?* GJs ποῦ πορεύῃ 19:1 (codd.).

ⓑ in indir. questions (En 12:1a; ParJer 5:13; ApcMos 42) **J 3:8; 8:14ab; 12:35; 14:5; Hb 11:8; 1J 2:11;** IPhld 7:1; Hm 12, 5, 4.—DELG s.v. πο-. M-M.

πού enclitic adv. (Hom.+; pap, LXX; TestSol 1, 46; Just.; Tat. 37, 1; Mel., P. 72, 530.)

❶ **marker of an undetermined position or place, *somewhere*** w. quotations (Diod. S. 1, 12, 10 'the poet' [=Homer] says πού κατὰ τὴν ποίησιν=somewhere in his poem. Of Cercidas [III BC] [ed. Diehl[3] fgm. 11a, 4] ὀρθῶς λέγει που Κερκίδας [quot. follows]. Lucian, Ver. Hist. 2, 42 φησὶ γάρ που κἀκεῖνος [i.e. Antimachus IV BC], then a quot.; Appian, Bell. Civ. 1, 97 §452 [with a quot.]; Plut., Mor. 553b [Homeric quot.]; Philo, Ebr. 61 εἶπε γάρ πού τις, and Gen 20:12 follows; Just. A I, 3, 3 ἔφη γάρ που καί τις) **Hb 2:6; 4:4;** 1 Cl 15:2; 21:2; 26:2; 28:2; 42:5.—After a neg.=*nowhere* Dg 5:2. W. weakening of the local mng. εἰ δέ που παρηκολουθώς τις τοῖς πρεσβυτέροις ἔλθοι *when perchance someone came who had been associated with the 'elders'* Papias (2:4).

❷ **marker of numerical approximation, *about, approximately*** (Paus. 8, 11, 14 περὶ εἴκοσί που σταδίους; Aelian, VH 13, 4; Jos., C. Ap. 1, 104) **Ro 4:19.**—On δή π., μή π. s. δήπου, μήπου.—μή που (some edd. μήπου; v.l. μήπως. Hom. et al.; BGU 446, 15; Jos., Bell. 7, 397, Ant. 18, 183) conj. *lest* φοβεῖσθαι μ. π. **Ac 27:29.**—DELG s.v. πο-. M-M.

Πούδης, εντος, ὁ (BGU 455, 4 [I AD] al. in pap; Jos., Bell. 6, 172) ***Pudens,*** Roman personal name (the *n* was lost, as on Rom. ins, because it was nasalized in pronunciation: B-D-F §41, 2; 54;; s. Mlt-H. 134). An otherw. unknown Christian **2 Ti 4:21** (identification w. the husband of Claudia mentioned CIL VI 15066 is uncertain).—Lghtf., St. Clement I 1890, 76ff; GEdmundson, The Church in Rome 1913, 244–49; Kl. Pauly IV 1240. M-M.

πούς, ποδός, ὁ (Hom.+ 'foot' in various senses)—❶ ***foot,*** of persons or (rarely in our lit.) animals, or the strange creatures of Rv

ⓐ w. focus on a body part: **Mt 4:6** (Ps 90:12); **7:6; Mk 9:45ab** al. W. κεφαλή **J 20:12; 1 Cor 12:21;** 1 Cl 37:5ab. W. χείρ or χεῖρες (Ps 21:17) **Mt 18:8ab; 22:13; Lk 24:39, 40 v.l.; J 11:44; 1 Cor 12:15** (for the speculation about foot and hand concerning their relation to the whole body cp. Epict. 2, 10, 4). ὑποδήσασθαι τοὺς π. *put shoes on the feet* **Eph 6:15** (in vivid imagery). Of listeners and pupils καθῆσθαι παρὰ τοὺς π. τινός *sit at someone's feet* **Lk 8:35;** cp. **10:39.** W. non-lit. mng. ἀνατεθραμμένος παρὰ τοὺς πόδας Γαμαλιήλ **Ac 22:3** (schol. on Pla. 467b παρὰ πόδας τοῦ Σωκράτους). W. partial imagery (Synes., Ep. 17 p. 175c παρὰ πόδας ἀποδίδως τὴν χάριν) ἐτίθουν παρὰ τοὺς πόδας τῶν ἀποστόλων **4:35;** cp. vs. **37; 5:2.** πίπτειν (q.v. 1baב) εἰς τοὺς πόδας τινός **Mt 18:29 v.l.; J 11:32 v.l.;** ἔμπροσθεν τῶν ποδῶν τινος **Rv 19:10;** ἐπὶ τοὺς πόδ. **Ac 10:25;** παρὰ τοὺς π. τινός **Lk 8:41; 17:16.** πρὸς τοὺς π. τινός **Mk 5:22; 7:25** (προσπίπτειν πρὸς κτλ.); **J 11:32; Ac 5:10; 10:25** D (the gen. is easily supplied); **Rv 1:17;** Hv 3, 2, 3. προσπίπτειν πρὸς τοὺς π. τινί **Ac 16:29** D. προσκυνεῖν ἐνώπιον (or ἔμπροσθεν) τῶν ποδῶν τινος **Rv 3:9; 22:8.** To wash feet, as expression of hospitality or humility (Gen 18:4; 19:2; TestAbr A 3 p. 80, 2 [Stone p. 8]; B 3 p. 107, 21 [St. p. 62] al.; JosAs 7:1): **J 13:5f, 8–10, 12, 14ab** (cp. λούω 2a); **1 Ti 5:10;** cp. **Lk 7:44a.**—See HAlmqvist, Plutarch u. d. NT '46, 75. Anoint feet (Anaxandrides Com. [IV BC] 40 μύρῳ … ἀλείφει τ. πόδας Καλλιστράτου; Eubulus Com. [IV BC] 90, 5f) **Lk 7:46;** cp. vs. **38c; J 12:3a;** cp. **11:2.** Kiss feet: **Lk 7:38c, 45.**—In **Rv 10:1** πούς clearly means *leg* (cp. Lucian, Zeuxis 4, Pseudomant. 59 πούς μέχρι τοῦ βουβῶνος [groin]; Achilles Tat. 1, 1, 10; Aëtius p. 86, 2; PGiss 43, 14; PFlor 42, 9 and s. Charles, ICC Rv ad loc.).

ⓑ in special imagery: the one who is vanquished lies beneath the victor's feet (Diod. S. 17, 100, 8 ῥιφέντος ἐπὶ γῆν ἐπιβὰς ἐπὶ τὸν τράχηλον τῷ ποδί=[the victor] placed his foot on the neck of his foe, who had been thrown to the ground) τιθέναι τοὺς ἐχθροὺς ὑποκάτω τῶν ποδῶν σου **Mt 22:44; Mk 12:36;** here Ps 109:1 is quoted; its wording acc. to the LXX is quoted more exactly as ὑποπόδιον τῶν ποδῶν σου **Lk 20:43; Ac 2:35; Hb 1:13; 10:13;** 1 Cl 36:5; B 12:10. For this in the same Ps.-quot. τιθ. ὑπὸ τοὺς πόδας (αὐτοῦ) **1 Cor 15:25** (Plut., Mor. 1197c ὑπὸ πόδας τιθ.). πάντα ὑπέταξεν ὑπὸ τοὺς πόδας αὐτοῦ **1 Cor 15:27; Eph 1:22;** these passages quote Ps 8:7, the exact wording of which in the LXX appears in ὑποκάτω τῶν ποδῶν αὐτοῦ **Hb 2:8.**—συντρίψει τὸν σατανᾶν ὑπὸ τοὺς πόδας ὑμῶν **Ro 16:20.**—The earth as God's footstool (Is 66:1) ὑποπόδιον τῶν ποδῶν αὐτοῦ (or, as LXX, μου) **Mt 5:35; Ac 7:49;** B 16:2. Cp. **Rv 12:1** (on prob. anti-Isis thrust s. lit. cited EDNT III 144).—Acc. to a usage common also in the OT (Eur., Hipp. 661, Or. 1217) the feet represent the person who is in motion: οἱ πόδες τῶν θαψάντων *those who have buried* **Ac 5:9.** ὀξεῖς οἱ πόδες αὐτῶν ἐκχέαι αἷμα *they are quick to shed blood* **Ro 3:15** (cp. Is 59:7). τοῦ κατευθῦναι τοὺς πόδας ὑμῶν εἰς ὁδὸν εἰρήνης *to guide us in the way of peace* **Lk 1:79.** Cp. **Ro 10:15** (cp. Is 52:7).

❷ **leg of a piece of furniture, *leg*** (so Aristoph. et al.; Arrian, Anab. 6, 29, 5; SIG 996, 9f; PLond II, 402, verso 27; 30 pp. 10 and 12; POxy 520, 17) Hv 3, 13, 3.

❸ **measurement based on length of a human foot, *foot*** (Hdt., also ins, pap) Hv 4, 1, 6; 4, 2, 1; cp. **Ac 7:5** s. βῆμα.—RAC VIII 743–77; BHHW I 505f; B. 243. DELG. M-M. EDNT. TW.

πρᾶγμα, ατος, τό (πράσσω; Pind., Hdt.+) gener. 'someth. that one is engaged in'.

❶ **that which is done or happens, *deed, thing, event, occurrence, matter*** (Jos., Ant. 16, 376; Ps.-Clem., Hom. 9, 5; Just., D. 23, 4) περὶ τῶν πεπληροφορημένων πραγμάτων *concerning events that have taken place* **Lk 1:1** (cp. Jos., Vi. 40 τ. ἱστορίαν τ. πραγμάτων τούτων ἀναγράφειν, C. Ap. 1, 47). τὸ πρᾶγμα τοῦτο *this deed* **Ac 5:4.** ἁγνοὶ τῷ πράγματι *guiltless in the matter* under discussion **2 Cor 7:11.** διὰ δύο πραγμάτων ἀμεταθέτων *through two unchangeable things* (i.e. the promise and the oath) **Hb 6:18.**

❷ that which is to be done, *undertaking, occupation, task* (Appian, Mithrid. 103 §477 μεγάλα πράγματα=great undertakings; Lucian, Nav. 41; Eccl 3:1; TestJob 6:3 περὶ πράγματος ἀναγκαίου) βιωτικὰ πράγματα *tasks of everyday life* Hv 3, 11, 3; m 5, 2, 2. ἐν ᾧ ἂν ὑμῶν χρῄζῃ πράγματι *in whatever undertaking she may need you* **Ro 16:2.** πλεονεκτεῖν ἐν τῷ πράγματι τὸν ἀδελφόν **1 Th 4:6** (but s. 3 below). ἄξιον πρᾶγμα *a task that is worthy* ISm 11:3.

❸ matter or concern of any kind, *thing, matter, affair* (Fgm. Iamb. Adesp. 12 Diehl οὐκ ἔστ᾽ ἐμὸν τὸ πρ.; Dio Chrys. 13 [7], 53; 16 [33], 36; 19 [36], 18; Ath. 15, 1 δύο ὀνόματα καθ᾽ ἑνὸς πράγματος) περὶ παντὸς πράγματος *about anything at all* **Mt 18:19.** Cp. **Hb 10:1; 11:1** (RTaylor, ET 52, '40/41, 256–59: 'affair'); Hv 3, 4, 1; m 9:10; 10, 2, 3; s 5, 6, 6; 9, 29, 2. Pl. Hv 3, 3, 1; 4, 1, 4; 4, 3, 1. μέγα π. *something great* Hv 3, 2, 4; cp. s 9, 2, 5; ἔνδοξα π. Hv 4, 1, 4; πονηρὸν π. *an evil thing* 1, 1, 8; s 5, 1, 5; 7:5; πᾶν φαῦλον π. *every evil thing, everything that is evil* **Js 3:16.** περιγίνεσθαι τοῦ π. *master the thing* Hv 1, 3, 2. τὰ πρ. *relationships, ways, circumstances* (Diod. S. 14, 97, 3; 19, 50, 2; 19, 52, 1; 6; Appian, Bell. Civ. 5, 3 §12; Artem. 4, 27; Jos., Bell. 4, 318) ἐν παλαιοῖς π. ἀναστραφῆναι *live in old, obsolete ways* IMg 9:1. Also w. an unfavorable connotation *difficulties, troubles* (Soph., Aj. 314; X., An. 2, 1, 16; 7, 6, 24, Mem. 2, 7, 2; Socrat., Ep. 3; Diod. S. 13, 12, 1; 13, 97, 6; Jos., Ant. 13, 7; Just., A II, 4, 1) 1 Cl 1:1 (s. ἐπιζητέω 1c).—Cp. IMg 5:1; Hv 1, 2, 4.—Prob. as euphemism=*(illicit sexual) affair* **1 Th 4:6** (cp. Aeschin. 1, 132), but s. 4.

❹ a matter of contention, *dispute, lawsuit* (X., Mem. 2, 9, 1 al.; Polyaenus 6, 36; Cyr.-Ins. 54; 67; 123. Oft. pap; Jos., C. Ap. 2, 177) πρᾶγμα ἔχειν πρός τινα *have a lawsuit with someone* (POxy 743, 19 [I BC]; 706, 4; BGU 22, 9) **1 Cor 6:1** (LVischer, Die Auslegungsgeschichte von 1 Cor 6:1–11, '55). Perh. *legal process* **1 Th 4:6** (cp. Ps.-Clemens, Hom. 10, 1).—B. 634. DELG s.v. πράσσω. M-M. TW. Sv.

πραγματεία, ας, ἡ (πραγματεύομαι; Hippocr., X., Pla. et al.; pap, LXX; AscIs 2, 5 [pl.]; Philo; Jos., Ant. 1, 5; 14, 218; loanw. in rabb.) ***activity, occupation,*** in our lit. only pl. *undertakings, business, affairs* Hm 10, 1, 4; s 9, 20, 1f. αἱ τοῦ βίου π. *the affairs of everyday* (civilian) *life* **2 Ti 2:4** (Philo, Spec. Leg. 2, 65 αἱ περὶ βίον π.). π. πονηραί Hv 2, 3, 1. Under persecution, leading to denial of Christ v 3, 6, 5; s 8, 8, 2. Enticing people to lie m 3:5. Separating fr. the saints s 8, 8, 1.—DELG s.v. πράσσω. M-M. TW. Spicq.

πραγματεύομαι (πρᾶγμα) mid. dep.; 1 aor. ἐπραγματευσάμην (Hdt.+; ins, pap, LXX, Philo; Jos., Bell. 2, 594, Ant. 4, 149; 16, 180 al.) 'conduct / be engaged in a business' (so Plut., Sull. 462 [17, 2], Cato Min. 788 [59, 3]; PEdg 32 [=Sb 6738], 11 [255 BC]; UPZ 106, 5 [99 BC]; BGU 246, 8; PLond V, 1674, 84; 1855, 3; Philo, In Flacc. 57), ***do business, trade*** **Lk 19:13.**—B. 819. DELG s.v. πράσσω. M-M. Spicq.

πραθείς, πραθῆναι s. πιπράσκω.

πραιτώριον, ου, τό (Lat. loanw.: praetorium. Attested in Gk. in ins and pap s. CWessely, WienerStud 24, 1902, 144; UWilcken, APF 2, 1903, 138; 4, 1908, 116; 121; s. also PPetaus 47, 44; 48, 2; B-D-F §5, 1; Rob. 109) ***the praetorium,*** orig. the praetor's tent in camp, w. its surroundings. In the course of its history (sketched by MDibelius, exc. on Phil 1:13) the word also came to designate the governor's official residence (IG XIV, 2548 τοῦ ἡγεμονικοῦ πραιτωρίου; SIG 880, 63; BGU 288, 14; POxy 471, 110). This is the mng. of the word in the gospels **Mt 27:27; Mk 15:16; J 18:28ab, 33; 19:9.** But it is a matter of dispute whether it refers to the palace of Herod in the western part of the city (Schürer I 361 w. reff. to Jos., Bell. 2, 14, 8; 15, 5 and Philo, Leg. 38; REckardt, Das Praetorium des Pilatus: ZDPV 34, 1911, 39–48; Dalman, Orte[3] 355–63 [Eng. tr. 335–45]; JBlinzler, Der Prozess Jesu[3], '60, 183–86; PBenoit, RB 59, '52, 531–50, HTR 64, 71, 135–67; RMackowski; Jerusalem, City of Jesus '80, 102–11; JMurphy-O'Connor, The Holy Land, rev. ed. '86) or to the fortress Antonia northwest of the temple area (so the later trad. and SMeistermann, Le Prétoire de Pilate et la forteresse Antonia 1902; CSachsse, ZNW 19, 1920, 34–38; CLattey, JTS 31, 1930, 180–82; HVincent, L'Antonia et le Prétoire: RB 42, '33, 83–113, Autour du Prétoire: ibid. 46, '37, 563–70; JFinegan, Archaelogy of the NT '69, 156–62). On the Hasmonean royal palace as site of Pilate's praetoruim s. BPixner, ZDPV 95, '79, 65–86, also ABD s.v. 'Praetorium' (lit.); against this ancient identification s. Dalman above. Of a palace of Herod GJs 21:2 (codd.). In Caesarea, at any rate, the palace of Herod served as the 'praetorium'. Paul was imprisoned ἐν τῷ πραιτωρίῳ τοῦ Ἡρῴδου **Ac 23:35.** ELohmeyer (Phil 1930, 3; 40f) places **Phil 1:13** here; this conclusion is variously regarded, depending on one's conception of the place where Paul was imprisoned. If the letter was written fr. Rome, the words ἐν ὅλῳ τῷ πραιτωρίῳ are best taken to mean *in the whole praetorian* (or *imperial*) *guard* (EHaupt, PEwald, et al.). If it belongs to a non-Roman imprisonment, τὸ πραιτώριον beside οἱ λοιποί includes those who live in the governor's palace (s. PFeine [s.v. Φίλιπποι] p. 72f; 88 and the other lit. given there).—Pauly-W. XXII 2535–37, Suppl. IX 1180f; Kl. Pauly IV 1117; BHHW III 1482; ABD V 322f, 447f. M-M. EDNT.

πραίφεκτος, ου, ὁ (Polyb. 6, 26, 5; ins [IG XIV, 680, II AD; IGR 1, 10]; Lydus, Mag. 2, 6) **a person appointed to administrate in a civil or military capacity, *prefect*** (Lat. praefectus) ὁ πραίφεκτος ἀτενίζων τῷ Πέτρῳ *the prefect* (of the city of Rome, Agrippa) *looking at Peter (said)* AcPl Ox 849, 12f (Aa I 73, 20). [τῷ] προφέκτῳ (for πραιφέκτῳ) Λογ[γίνῳ] *(eagerly sharing the Word) w. the (military) prefect Long[inus]* AcPl Ha 9, 18.—Mason 78 (ins); Boffo, Iscrizioni p. 219.

πράκτωρ, ορος, ὁ (Aeschyl. et al.; Is 3:12) a t.t. designating certain officials, esp. tax-collectors and other finance officials (Antiphon et al.; ins, pap [Dssm., B 152=BS 154; BGU 530, 36; O. Wilck. 1599, II AD]. Also oft. Sb [word-list sect. 8 p. 339]). In **Lk 12:58ab,** the only place where it occurs in our lit., the word refers to a court functionary who is under a judge's orders, someth. like a ***bailiff*** or ***constable,*** who is in charge of a debtor's prison (πρακτόρειον: OGI 669, 15; 17. In UPZ 118, 15; 24 πρ. is the constable; it is his duty, after sentence is passed, to collect [by force, if necessary] debts, under orders fr. the judge. The τοῦ κριτηρίου ὑπηρέτης 'servant of the court' ln. 18 is differentiated fr. him).—DELG s.v. πράσσω. M-M. Spicq.

πρᾶξις, εως, ἡ (πράσσω; Hom.+).—**❶ a function implying sustained activity, *acting, activity, function*** κατὰ τὴν πρᾶξιν αὐτοῦ *in accordance with his activity* or *what he did* **Mt 16:27.** τὰ μέλη πάντα οὐ τὴν αὐτὴν ἔχει πρᾶξιν *the parts do not all have the same function* **Ro 12:4.** ἐν πάσῃ πράξει αὐτοῦ Hm 5, 2, 7; cp. 7:1; s 4:4.

❷ way of conducting oneself, *way of acting, course of action* αὕτη ἡ πρᾶξις ἐπὶ γυναικὶ καὶ ἀνδρὶ κεῖται *this is the proper course of action for the wife and for the husband* Hm 4, 1, 8; cp. 11.

❸ **engagement in a project that involves planning, *plan of action, undertaking*** (Jos., Bell. 1, 230, Vi. 271) περὶ πράξεώς τινος *concerning any undertaking* Hm 11:4.

❹ **performance of some deed, *act, action, deed*—ⓐ** gener. (Diod. S. 10, 19, 5=deed; Just., A I, 17, 4 κατ' ἀξίαν τῶν πράξεων) Hm 10, 2, 2 and 4b. ἡ ἀγαθὴ πρᾶξις 1 Cl 30:7. μεγάλαι καὶ ἔνδοξοι πράξεις *great and glorious deeds* 19:2.—This is also the place for the title of Ac πράξεις (ἀποστόλων); cp. 2 Ch 12:15; 13:22; 28:26 and the transl. of Res Gestae Divi Augusti: IGR III, 159 πράξεις τε καὶ δωρεαὶ Σεβαστοῦ Θεοῦ; Socrat., Ep. 28, 1 [Malherbe p. 284, 23f] Ἀντίπατρος . . . γράφει τὰς Ἑλληνικὰς πράξεις; Diod. S. 3, 1, 1 of the first two books of Diodorus ἡ πρώτη contains the πράξεις τῶν βασιλέων; 16, 1, 1 πόλεων ἢ βασιλέων πράξεις=the story of cities or kings; Jos., Ant. 14, 68 οἱ τὰς κατὰ Πομπήιον πράξεις ἀναγράψαντες; Tat. 38, 1 τὰς τῶν βασιλέων πράξεις. Also the exx. in AWikenhauser, Die AG 1921, 94–104: D. antike Praxeis-Lit. The sing., πρᾶξις (ἀποστόλων), which is also attested, views the deeds collectively, *work*.—For lit. on Ac s. EGrässer, TRu 26, '60, 91–167; also comm.

ⓑ *evil* or *disgraceful deed* (Polyb. 2, 7, 9; 2, 9, 2; 4, 71, 6; Diod. S. 3, 57, 4; 4, 49, 3; 4, 63, 4) **Lk 23:51;** Hm 4, 2, 2. Pl. **Ro 8:13; Col 3:9;** Hm 4, 2, 1.—In **Ac 19:18,** because of the context, it is poss. that πρᾶξις is specif. a t.t. for certain magical practices (PGM 4, 1227 πρᾶξις γενναία ἐκβάλλουσα δαίμονας. Cp. PGM 1, 276; 4, 159; 1317 and oft.; Ps.-Clem., Hom. 2, 26; Acta Pilati A 1, 1 [Ea 215, 2]; πράσσειν='practice magic' PGM 3, 125).

❺ **customary daily activity, *undertaking, business*** (so Aesop, Fab. 236 P.=312 H.//256 Ch//227 H-H.; very oft. in Vett. Val., s. index; PGM 4, 2366; loanw. in rabb.) pl. Hm 6, 2, 5; 10, 1, 4; s 6, 3, 5. αἱ βιωτικαὶ πρ. *the affairs of everyday living* Hv 1, 3, 1 (Ps-Lucian, Halc. 5 αἱ κατὰ τὸν βίον πρ.).

❻ **a state of being, *state, condition, situation*** (Pind., Hdt. et al.) τὴν πρᾶξιν, ἣν ἔχουσιν ἐν ἑαυτοῖς Hs 9, 26, 8; also in the pl. (Soph., Ant. 1305 κακαὶ πράξεις) ἀπὸ τῶν προτέρων αὐτοῦ πράξεων *from his former condition* Hv 3, 12, 2. ἑτέραις πολλαῖς πράξεσι πάσχοντες *suffering in many other situations* s 6, 3, 4.—DELG s.v. πράσσω. M-M. Sv.

πρᾶος (without ι subscr.; s. W-S. §5, 11a; Mlt-H. 84; Mayser 121) s. πραΰς.

πραότης s. πραΰτης.

πρασιά, ᾶς, ἡ (πράσον 'leek' [prop. 'bed of leeks']; Hom. [πρασιή] et al.; PTebt 703, 198 [III BC: πρασιά]; BGU 530, 27 [πρασεά]; Sir 24:31) fr. the lit. sense 'garden plot, garden bed' it is but a short step to the imagistic πρασιαὶ πρασιαί ***group by group,*** picturing the groups of people contrasted w. the green grass **Mk 6:40** (on the distributive force of the repetition cp. Hs 8, 2, 8 τάγματα τάγματα and s. B-D-F §493, 2; Mlt. 97; Rob. 673).—DELG s.v. πράσον. M-M.

πράσσω impf. ἔπρασσον; fut. πράξω; 1 aor. ἔπραξα; pf. πέπραχα. Pass.: 1 aor. ἐπράχθην; pf. ptc. πεπραγμένος (Hom.+ [the Attic form πράττω **Ac 17:7v.l.; 19:36 v.l.; Col 4:9 v.1.,** cp. Gignac I 151; for ins Threatte II 650f]; ins, pap, LXX, EpArist, Philo, Joseph., Test12Patr; Just., D. 35, 7 opp. λόγος).

❶ **to bring about or accomplish someth. through activity,** trans.—ⓐ ***do, accomplish*** (oft. used without distinction betw. itself and ποιεῖν, as Diod. S. 16, 27, 1 ἔξεστιν αὐτῷ πράττειν ὃ βούλεται. Cp. **Ro 1:32; 2:3;** IMg 7:1). τὶ *someth.* προσέχετε ἑαυτοῖς . . . τί μέλλετε πράσσειν **Ac 5:35;** πάντα πρ. IMg 4; 6:1; cp. 7:1; ITr 2:2 al. πρᾶξιν πράσσειν (s. also farther below) *do a deed, do someth.* Hs 5, 2, 11; τὰ πνευματικὰ πρ. *do spiritual things* IEph 8:2a. ἄξια τῆς μετανοίας ἔργα πρ. *do deeds that are consistent with repentance, act in a manner consistent* etc. **Ac 26:20.** τὴν δικαιοσύνην 2 Cl 19:3 (cp. Xenophanes 1, 16 Diehl[2] τὰ δίκαια πρήσσειν). εἴτε ἀγαθὸν εἴτε φαῦλον **2 Cor 5:10;** cp. **Ro 9:11.—1 Cor 9:17; Eph 6:21; Phil 4:9.**—Pass. οὐ γάρ ἐστιν ἐν γωνίᾳ πεπραγμένον τοῦτο **Ac 26:26.**—Mostly of actions that are not praiseworthy (TestAbr B 10 p. 115, 8 [Stone p. 78] εἴ τι ἔπραξεν ἐκ νεότητος αὐτῆς; ApcEsdr 4:24 μικρὸν θέλημα πράξας) *do, commit* τὶ *someth.* **Lk 22:23; 23:41a; Ro 1:32ab; 2:1–3; 7:15; 2 Cor 12:21** (ἧ by attraction for ἥν); **Gal 5:21;** 1 Cl 35:6; 2 Cl 4:5; 10:5; Hm 3:3; D 1:5 (περὶ ὧν = περὶ τούτων ἅ). τὸ ἔργον τοῦτο πρ. **1 Cor 5:2** (Herodas 3, 62; cp. 82 ἔργα πράσσειν=commit evil deeds; τὸ ἔργον πρ. as Jos., Vi. 47). τὴν πολυτέλειαν τῶν ἐθνῶν πρ. Hs 1:10; ἄτοπόν τι πρ. **Lk 23:41b** (ἄτοπος 2). (τὸ) κακόν (Pr 13:10 κακά; Jos., Ant. 19, 193) **Ro 7:19; 13:4.** τὸ πονηρόν Hm 10, 2, 4. πονηρά 2 Cl 8:2; 19:2. πονηρὰ ἔργα Hs 6, 3, 5; cp. 6. πονηρίαν 8, 8, 2. προπετές τι **Ac 19:36.** (τὰ) φαῦλα **J 3:20; 5:29.** πρᾶξιν πράσσειν *commit a(n evil) deed* (πρᾶξις 4b) Hm 4, 2, 2; 10, 2, 3 (ἧ by attraction for ἥν); pl. Hs 8, 9, 4; 8, 10, 4. ἄλλα τινὰ πράσσοντες ἀνάξια θεοῦ *while doing certain other things unworthy of God* IEph 7:1. ἄξιον θανάτου πράσσειν τι *do someth. worthy of death* **Ac 25:11, 25; 26:31;** pass. οὐδὲν ἄξιον θανάτου ἐστὶν πεπραγμένον αὐτῷ (*by him,* B-D-F §191; Rob. 534; cp. Demosth. 29, 1 τὰ τούτῳ πεπραγμένα; Diod. S. 17, 1, 2; Appian, Bell. Civ. 3, 44 §180 τὰ Καίσαρι πεπραγμένα; Chariton 2, 5, 8 πέπρακταί σοί τι δεινόν=a terrible deed has been committed by you; Syntipas p. 17, 1 τὰ πραχθέντα μοι; PTebt 23, 8 [119 or 114 BC] πέπρακταί σοι; Jos., Ant. 14, 161 τὰ Ἡρώδῃ πεπραγμένα; Ath. 20, 2 τὰ πραχθέντα αὐτοῖς. Other exx. in Mlt-H. 459; Schmid IV 612) **Lk 23:15.** πρὸς τὸ ὄνομα Ἰησοῦ πολλὰ ἐναντία πρᾶξαι **Ac 26:9** (ἐναντία πρ. as X., Cyr. 8, 7, 24). μηδὲν πράξῃς σεαυτῷ κακόν *do yourself no harm* **16:28.**—Ign. is fond of combinations w. κατά and the acc. μηδὲν κατ' ἐριθείαν πρ. IPhld 8:2; κατὰ θεόν τι πρ. 4; κατὰ σάρκα τι πρ. *do someth. in the* (physical) *body* IEph 8:2b; likew. 16:2 *do someth. that involves the physical* i.e. in contrast to corruption of the gospel, as false teachers do.—More in the sense *practice, busy oneself with, mind* τὶ *someth.* τὰ περίεργα *magic* **Ac 19:19.** τὰ ἴδια *one's own affairs* **1 Th 4:11** (ἴδιος 4b and Soph., El. 678 σὺ μὲν τὰ σαυτῆς πρᾶσσε; X., Mem. 2, 9, 1 τὰ ἑαυτοῦ πρ.). τὰ πολλὰ πρ. *busy oneself with many things* Hs 4:5; νόμον πρ. *observe the law* **Ro 2:25.**

ⓑ ***collect*** taxes, duties, interest (Hdt. et al.; Theophr., Char. 6, 10; ins, pap, LXX; Jos., Ant. 9, 233 al.) τὶ *someth.* **Lk 19:23.** W. connotation in the direction of 'extort' **3:13** (cp. OGI 519, 22 τὰ μὴ ὀφειλόμενα αὐτοῖς παραπράσσουσιν).

❷ **to engage in activity or behave in a certain way,** intr. ***act, behave*** κατὰ ἄγνοιαν πρ. **Ac 3:17;** ἀπέναντι τῶν δογμάτων πρ. *act contrary to the decrees* **17:7** (opp. εὖ πράσσειν); καθὰ πράσσομεν *in our actions* IMg 10:1. εὖ πράσσειν *act rightly, do well* (Just., A I, 28, 3 [-ττ-]; cp. POxy 1067, 3 [III AD] καλῶς πρ. and Appian, Hann. 2, §3 πρ. κακῶς) IEph 4:2; ISm 11:3; prob. also **Ac 15:29** because of the focus on performance of decretal specifications (cp. the formulation εὖ ποιήσετε . . . ἀποδεχάμενα IMagnMai 91d, 8–10; Danker, Benefactor 311f; s. εὖ and 3 below).

❸ **to experience what is going on, *be, be situated,*** intr. (Pind., Hdt.; pap) εὖ πρ. *be well off* (s. εὖ 1) so perh. **Ac 15:29** (cp. POxy 120, 27 [IV AD]; s. 2 above; w. either interp. there is envisaged a positive effect on the beneficiaries resulting from their compliance). ἵνα εἰδῆτε . . . τί πράσσω *in order that you may know . . .*

how (lit. 'in respect to what') *I am getting along* **Eph 6:21** (Soph., Oed. R. 74 τί πράσσει; Pla., Tht. 174b; BGU 93, 32 δήλωσόν μοι, τί ἔπραξας; 821, 8; Jos., Ant. 6, 176; 19, 239).—B. 537f. DELG. Schmidt, Syn. I 397–423. M-M. TW. Sv.

πραϋπαθία, ας, ἡ (πραΰς, πάθος via παθεῖν [aor. of πάσχω; Philo, Abr. 213; Hesychius explains it by using the words ἡσυχία and πραΰτης as synonyms, hence the opp. of an overbearing attitude) ***gentleness*** **1 Ti 6:11** (v.l. πραότητα). Also πραϋπάθεια ITr 8:1. On the sp. cp. κακοπάθεια, -ία s. Kühner-Bl. II 276, 1. See also ADebrunner, Griech. Wortbildungslehre 1917, §299.—DELG s.v. πάσχω. M-M. Spicq.

πραΰς, πραεῖα, πραΰ (Hom.+; Crinagoras [I BC / I AD] in Anth. Pal. 10, 24, 4; 16, 273, 6; PGM 4, 1046; LXX; Jos., Ant. 19, 330; SibOr 4, 159 with v.l.) gen. πραέως (**1 Pt 3:4;** cp. W-S. §9, 5 p. 87; Kühner-Bl. I §126, 3 n. 9; B-D-F §46, 3; Mayser I/2 §68, 2, 1e p. 55f) and πραέος; pl. πραεῖς (on πραΰς and πρᾶος Kühner-Bl. I 532f; B-D-F §26 app.; Mlt-H. 160; Thackeray 180f; Crönert 290, 2.—But in our lit. πρᾶος [2 Macc 15:12; Philo; Jos., C. Ap. 1, 267] occurs only **Mt 11:29 v.l.**) **pert. to not being overly impressed by a sense of one's self-importance,** ***gentle, humble, considerate, meek*** in the older favorable sense (cp. OED s.v. 1b; Pind., P. 3, 71 describes the ruler of Syracuse as one who is π. to his citizens, apparently the rank and file [Gildersleeve]), *unassuming* D 3:7a; **Mt 21:5** (Zech 9:9). W. ταπεινός (Is 26:6) **Mt 11:29** (THaering, Schlatter Festschr. 1922, 3–15; MRist, JR 15, '35, 63–77). W. ἡσύχιος (and occasionally other characteristics) **1 Pt 3:4;** 1 Cl 13:4 (cp. Is 66:2); B 19:4; Hm 5, 2, 3; 6, 2, 3; 11:8 (Leutzsch, Hermas 452, n. 122). Among the qualities required of church officials D 15:1. πρὸς τὰς ὀργὰς αὐτῶν ὑμεῖς πραεῖς *gentle in the face of their wrath* IEph 10:2 (cp. PLond 1912, 83f εἵνα 'Αλεξανδρεῖς πραέως καὶ φιλανθρόπως προσφέροντε [=προσφέρωνται] 'Ιουδαίοις=therefore we affirm that the Alexandrines are to conduct themselves with kindness and goodwill toward the Judeans/Jews [41 AD]).—οἱ πραεῖς (Ps 36:11) **Mt 5:5** (WClarke, Theology 47, '44, 131–33; NLohfink, Die Besänftigung des Messias, Gedanken zu Ps. 37 [Mt]: FKamphous Festschr., ed. JHainz et al. '97, 75–87; Betz, SM 124–27); D 3:7b.—LMarshall, Challenge of NT Ethics '47, 80ff; 300ff. —DELG s.v. πρᾶος. M-M. EDNT. Spicq. Sv.

πραΰτης, ητος, ἡ (πραΰς; Appian, Bell. Civ. 4, 123 §518 διὰ πραΰτητα; Aesop, Fab. 168 P.=94b H.//247 Ch.//H-H. 178; CIG 2788; LXX [Thackeray p. 91; 181]; Sextus 545) and older Gk (since Thu., also Appian, Basil. 1 §5; PLond 1912, 101 [41 AD]; Philo; Jos., Bell. 6, 383, Ant. 19, 334; IPol 2:1; 6:2), **πραότης, ητος, ἡ** (so in Ign. and Hermas, while in the NT πραΰτης is the predom. form and πραότης appears as v.l.; for the lit. s. πραΰς) **the quality of not being overly impressed by a sense of one's self-importance,** ***gentleness, humility, courtesy, considerateness, meekness*** in the older favorable sense (s. πραΰς) w. ἐπιείκεια (Plut., Caesar 734 [57], and, occasionally, other qualities, as Lucian, Somn. 10; s. also Plut., Pyrrh. 398[23, 3]) **2 Cor 10:1** (RLeivestad, NTS 12, '66, 156–64); 1 Cl 30:8; Dg 7:4; cp. **Tit 3:2;** 1 Cl 21:7. W. other virtues (Ps 44:5) **Gal 5:23; Col 3:12; Eph 4:2;** B 20:2; D 5:2; Hm 12, 3, 1. ἐν π. *with* or *in gentleness* (Sir 3:17; 4:8) **2 Ti 2:25;** IPol 2:1; 6:2; *with humility* **Js 1:21; 3:13** (ἐν πραΰτητι σοφίας *in wise gentleness;* cp. Appian, Bell. Civ. 3, 79 §323 ἐπὶ σοφίᾳ τε καὶ πραότητι); ἐν εἰρήνῃ καὶ π. 1 Cl 61:2. Also μετὰ π. (so in PLond above) **1 Pt 3:16;** Hm 5, 2, 6. As a characteristic of a bishop ITr 3:2 (as political virtue, s. LRobert, Hellenica 13, '65, 223). The devil is thwarted by humility 4:2. πνεῦμα πραΰτητος **1 Cor 4:21; Gal 6:1.**—AvHarnack, 'Sanftmut, Huld und Demut' in der alten Kirche: JKaftan Festschr. 1920, 113ff; JdeRomilly, La douceur dans la pensée grecque '79; RAC III 206–31.—DELG s.v. πρᾶος. M-M. TW. Spicq. Sv.

πρέπω (Hom.+ in var. senses) ***be fitting, be seemly/suitable*** (Pind.+) impf. 3 sing. ἔπρεπεν: τοιοῦτος ἡμῖν ἔπρεπεν ἀρχιερεύς *it was fitting that we should have such a high priest* **Hb 7:26.** Cp. **1 Ti 2:10; Tit 2:1.** μηδὲν ὑμῖν πρεπέτω *let nothing be pleasing to you* IEph 11:2.—The impers. constr. πρέπει τινί *it is fitting for someone* (X., Hell. 4, 1, 37; TestAbr B 14 p. 119, 3 [Stone p. 86] αὐτῷ πρέπει δόξα; ApcEsdr 7:16; ApcMos 43) καθὼς πρέπει ἁγίοις **Eph 5:3.** ὡς πρέπει ἀγαπῶντι B 4:9. W. dat. and inf. foll. (Chariton 7, 6, 12; Philo, Leg. All. 1, 48 πρέπει τῷ θεῷ φυτεύειν) **Hb 2:10;** IEph 4:1; IMg 3:1; ITr 12:2; IPol 5:2. W. inf. foll., in which case the dat. is to be supplied ISm 11:2; IPol 7:2.—πρέπον ἐστίν *it is fitting, proper, right* (POxy. 120, 24 ὡς πρέπον ἐστίν; 1 Macc 12:11; 3 Macc 7:13; Just., A I, 3, 1) w. dat. of pers. and inf. foll. (Isocr., Ep. 5, 3) **Mt 3:15;** IRo 10:2; IPhld 10:1. W. inf. foll. and dat. to be supplied IEph 2:2; IMg 3:2; 4:1; ISm 7:2. W. acc. and inf. foll. (Lysias 19, 59) **1 Cor 11:13.**—MPohlenz, Τὸ πρέπον: NGG '33, 53–92.—B. 641. DELG. M-M.

πρεσβεία, ας, ἡ (πρεσβεύω; Aeschyl. et al. in var. senses, incl. 'embassy' Aristoph., Pla.) abstract for concrete ***ambassador, ambassadors*** (Aristoph., X., Pla.+; ins, pap; Orig., C. Cels. 8, 6, 13) π. ἀποστέλλειν (SIG 412, 6 al. [index IV p. 526a]; cp. 2 Macc 4, 11; Philo, Leg. ad Gai. 239; Jos., Ant. 4, 296) **Lk 14:32; 19:14.** πρεσβεύειν θεοῦ πρεσβείαν *travel as an ambassador of God* IPhld 10:1 (πρεσβεύειν πρεσβείαν as Philo, Congr. Erud. Gr. 111).—DELG s.v. πρέσβυς. M-M.

πρεσβευτής, οῦ, ὁ (πρεσβεύω; Thu., Pla. et al.; ins, pap) ***ambassador*** RBentley's cj. in place of πρεσβύτης (q.v.) **Phlm 9.**—DELG s.v. πρέσβυς.

πρεσβεύω fut. πρεσβεύσω; 1 aor. ἐπρέσβευσα (trag., Hdt. et al., prim. sense 'be older' or 'in the first rank') ***be an ambassador/envoy, travel/work as an ambassador*** (so Aristoph., X., Pla. et al.; ins, pap; ApcSed 14:1 p. 135, 35 Ja. πρέσβευσαι 'be my spokesman'; Philo; Jos., Ant. 12, 163f, Vi. 65. Used esp. of the emperor's legates: Magie 89; Dssm., LO 320 [LAE 378f]; s. also SEG XXXIX, 1865 for ins) πέμπειν τινὰ πρεσβεύσοντα περί τινος *send someone as a representative for someone* Pol 13:1. πρεσβεύειν θεοῦ πρεσβείαν IPhld 10:1, s. πρεσβεία. Paul speaks of his apostolic work as ὑπὲρ Χριστοῦ πρεσβεύειν *work as an ambassador for Christ* **2 Cor 5:20;** cp. **Eph 6:20** (πρεσβεύειν ὑπέρ τινος: OGI 339, 6; SIG 591, 5; 656, 19; 805, 7ff; on mediatorial role of envoys s. CBreytenbach, Versöhnung '89, 64–66).—M-M. DELG s.v. πρέσβυς.

πρεσβυτέριον, ου, τό (πρεσβύτερος) **an administrative group concerned with the interests of a specific community,** ***council of elders***

ⓐ of the highest Judean council in Jerusalem, in our lit. usu. called συνέδριον (Schürer II 206–8) τὸ πρεσβυτέριον τοῦ λαοῦ **Lk 22:66.** ὁ ἀρχιερεὺς καὶ πᾶν τὸ πρ. **Ac 22:5.**

ⓑ as a council in connection with adminstration of Christian congregations, including all the πρεσβύτεροι (s. πρεσβύτερος 2b), *presbytery.* So, except for **1 Ti 4:14** (JJeremias, ZNW 48, '57, 127–32: 'honor' or 'privilege of an elder'; cp. Sus 50 [Theodotion] and rabb.), in our lit. only in Ign.: w. ἐπίσκοπος and διάκονοι IMg 13:1; ITr 7:2; IPhld 4; 7:1; ISm 12:2. W. ἐπίσκοπος IEph 2:2; 20:2; IMg 2; ITr 13:2. The ἐπίκοπος and πρ. belong together as the strings to the harp IEph 4:1. The πρ.

is to be obeyed as the apostles ITr 2:2; ISm 8:1. The apostles are described as πρ. ἐκκλησίας IPhld 5:1.—Sv.

πρεσβύτερος, α, ον (Hom.+; comp. of πρέσβυς)

❶ pert. to being relatively advanced in age, *older, old*

ⓐ of an individual person *older* of two ὁ υἱὸς ὁ πρ. (cp. Aelian, VH 9, 42; TestJob 15:2 τῷ ἀδελφῷ τῷ πρεσβυτέρῳ; JosAs; Just., A II, 6, 1) **Lk 15:25;** of Manasseh (w. Ephraim) B 13:5. In contrast to the younger generation οἱ πρεσβύτεροι *the older ones* **J 8:9.** Opp. οἱ νεανίσκοι **Ac 2:17** (Jo 3:1). Opp. νεώτεροι (s. νεός 3aβ) **1 Ti 5:1** (similar advice, containing a contrast betw. πρ. and νεώτ., from ins and lit. in MDibelius, Hdb. ad loc.); **1 Pt 5:5** (though here the πρεσβύτεροι are not only the older people, but at the same time, the 'elders'; s. 2bβ). The same double mng. is found for πρεσβύτεροι in 1 Cl 1:3 beside νέοι, while in 3:3; 21:6, beside the same word, the concept of being old is the dominant one (as Jos., C. Ap. 2, 206). On the disputed pass. Hv 3, 1, 8 (οἱ νεανίσκοι… οἱ πρεσβύτεροι) cp. MDibelius, Hdb. ad loc.—Fem. πρεσβυτέρα *old(er) woman* (opp. νεωτέρα, as Gen 19:31) **1 Ti 5:2.**—With no ref. to younger persons, w. complete disappearance of the comparative aspect: πρεσβύτερος *an old man* (Jos., Ant. 13, 226; 292 [as a witness of events in the past, as Ps.-Pla., Virt. 3, 377b; 4, 377c]) Hv 3, 12, 2; cp. 3, 11, 3. The personified church is called λίαν πρεσβυτέρα *very old* 3, 10, 3; cp. 3, 11, 2. She appears as ἡ πρ. *the elderly woman* 2, 1, 3; 3, 1, 2; 3, 10, 6; 9 and has τὰς τρίχας πρεσβυτέρας *the hair of an old woman* 3, 10, 4; 5; 3, 12, 1.

ⓑ of a period of time (Petosiris, fgm. 3 and 4 mention οἱ πρεσβύτεροι and οἱ νεώτεροι. In both instances the context shows that the reference is to astrologers from earlier and more recent times) οἱ πρεσβύτεροι *the men of old, our ancestors* **Hb 11:2.** ἡ παράδοσις τῶν πρεσβυτέρων *the tradition of the ancients* (cp. Iambl., Vi. Pyth. 35, 253 τῶν π. συγγράμματα) **Mt 15:2; Mk 7:3, 5** (ELohse, D. Ordination im Spätjudentum u. NT, '51, 50–56: *scholars*).

❷ an official (cp. Lat. senator), ***elder, presbyter*—ⓐ** among the Jews (the congregation of a synagogue in Jerusalem used πρεσβύτεροι to denote its officers before 70 AD: SEG VIII, 170, 9; cp. Dssm., LO 378–80 [LAE 439–41]).

α. for members of local councils in individual cities (cp. Josh 20:4; Ruth 4:2; 2 Esdr 10:14; Jdth 8:10; 10:6) **Lk 7:3;** 1 Cl 55:4.—Schürer II, 185.

β. for members of a group in the Sanhedrin (Schürer II, 206–8; JJeremias, Jerusalem z. Zt. Jesu II B 1: Die gesellschaftl. Oberschicht 1929, 88ff). They are mentioned together w. (the) other groups: ἀρχιερεῖς (**Ac 4:5** has ἄρχοντες for this), γραμματεῖς, πρεσβύτεροι (the order is not always the same) **Mt 16:21; 26:3 v.l.; 27:41; Mk 8:31; 11:27; 14:43, 53; 15:1; Lk 9:22; 20:1.**—Only ἀρχιερεῖς (**Ac 4:8** has for this ἄρχοντες τοῦ λαοῦ) and πρεσβύτεροι (τοῦ λαοῦ: cp. Ex 19:7; Num 11:16b, 24; 1 Macc 7:33; 12:35; Just., D. 40, 4 al.) **Mt 21:23; 26:3, 47, 59 v.l.; 27:1, 3, 12, 20; 28:(11), 12; Lk 22:52** (here, as an exception, οἱ στρατηγοὶ τοῦ ἱεροῦ); **Ac 4:23; 23:14; 25:15;** cp. **24:1.** Also οἱ πρεσβύτεροι καὶ οἱ ἱερεῖς GPt 7:25 (for this combination cp. Jos., Ant. 11, 83; 12, 406).—Only πρεσβύτεροι and γραμματεῖς **Mt 26:57; Ac 6:12.**—The use of πρεσβύτερος as a title among the Jews of the Diaspora appears quite late, except for the allusions in the LXX (cp. Schürer III/1, 102; MAMA III [Cilicia], 344; 448 [cp. ZNW 31, '32, 313f]. Whether πρεσβύτερος is to be understood in the older Roman inscriptions [CIJ 378] as a title [so CIJ p. lxxxvi], remains doubtful).

ⓑ among the Christians (for their use of the word as a title one must bear in mind not only the Jewish custom, but also its use as a t.t. among the ἔθνη, in connection w. associations of the 'old ones' [FPoland, Geschichte des griech. Vereinswesens 1909, 98ff] and to designate civic as well as religious officials [Dssm., B 153ff=BS 154–57, NB 60ff=BS 233–35, also LO 315, 5; HHausschildt, ZNW 4, 1903, 235ff; MStrack, ibid. 213ff; HLietzmann, ZWT 55, 1914, 116–32 [=Kl. Schr. I '58, 156–69]; MDibelius, exc. on 1 Ti 5:17ff; RAlastair-Campbell, The Elders, Seniority within Earliest Christianity '94.].—BGU 16, 6 [159 AD] πρεσβύτεροι ἱερεῖς θεοῦ Σοκνοπαίου; 347, 6; PVindBosw 1, 31 [87 AD].—As honorary title: Iren. 4, 26, 5 [Harv. II 238, 3]. The Engl. word 'priest' comes fr. πρεσβύτερος via Lat. presbyter; later Christian usage is largely, if not entirely, responsible for this development; s. OED s.v. 'priest' B).

α. **Ac 11:30; 14:23; 15:2, 4, 6, 22f; 16:4** (in all the places in Ac 15 and 16 mention is made of οἱ ἀπόστολοι καὶ οἱ πρεσβύτεροι in the Jerusalem church); **20:17; 21:18; 1 Ti 5:17, 19** (Nicol. Dam.: 90 fgm. 103a Jac. νεωτέρῳ πρεσβυτέρου καταμαρτυρεῖν οὐκ ἔξεστι); **Tit 1:5; Js 5:14; 1 Pt 5:1, 5** (s. 1a above); 1 Cl 44:5; 47:6; 54:2; 57:1. WWrede, Untersuchungen zum 1 Cl 1891, 8ff.—Acc. to 2 Cl 17:3, 5 exhortation and preaching in the church services were among their duties.—In Ign. the πρεσβύτεροι come after the bishop, to whom they are subordinate IMg 2; 3:1; 6:1, or betw. the bishop and the deacons IPhld inscr.; 10:2; IPol 6:1, or the higher rank of the bishop in comparison to them is made plain in some other way ITr 3:1; 12:2 (s. πρεσβυτέριον b; cp. Hippol., Ref. 9, 12, 22).—Polycarp—an ἐπίσκοπος, accord. to the title of the ep. bearing his name—groups himself w. πρεσβύτεροι in Pol inscr., and further takes the presence of presbyters in Philippi for granted (beside deacons, though no ἐπίσκοπος is mentioned; cp. Hdb. on Pol inscr.) Pol 5:3.

β. Just how we are to understand the words ὁ πρεσβύτερος, applied to himself by the author of the two smallest Johannine letters **2J 1; 3J 1,** remains in doubt. But in any case it is meant to indicate a position of great dignity *the elder.*—HWindisch, exc. on 3J, end; ESchwartz, Über den Tod der Söhne Zebedaei 1904, 47; 51; HWendt, ZNW 23, 1924, 19; EKäsemann, ZTK 48, '51, 292–311; DWatson, NTS 35, '89, 104–30, rhetorical analysis of 2J.—ὁ πρ. and οἱ πρ. are mentioned by Papias in these much-discussed passages: 2:3, 4, 5, 7, 14, 15. For some of the lit. s. the note on JKleist's transl. '48, p. 207 n. 18.

γ. In Rv there are 24 elders sitting on thrones about the throne of God; they form a heavenly council of elders (cp. Is 24:23) **4:4, 10; 5:5–14; 7:11, 13; 11:16; 14:3; 19:4.** The elders have been understood as glorified human beings of some kind or astral deities (or angels) (for the var. views s. RCharles, ICC Rv I 128–33; JMichl, D. 24 Ältesten in d. Apk. d. hl. J. '38); the number 24 has been referred to the following: the 24 priestly classes of the Jews (1 Ch 24:7–18; Jos., Ant. 7, 365–67) whose heads were called 'elders' (Yoma 1, 5; Tamid 1, 1; Middoth 1, 8); the 24 stars which, according to Babylonian belief, stood half on the north and half on the south of the zodiac (Diod. S. 2, 31, 4; POsl 4, 19: HGunkel, Z. religionsgesch. Verständnis des NT 1903, 42f; Boll 35f); the 24 hours of the day, represented as old men w. shining garments and w. crowns (acc. to the Test. of Adam [ed. CBezold, TNöldeke Festschr. 1906, 893–912]: JWellhausen, Analyse der Offb. Joh. 1907, p. 9, 1; NMorosof, Offb. Joh. 1912, 32); the 24 Yazatas in the state of the gods in heaven, acc. to Persian thought (Bousset). It is certainly an open question whether, or how far, the writer of Rv had any of these things in mind.—On the presbyters, and esp. on the question how ἐπίσκοπος and πρεσβύτερος were originally related to each other (a question which is raised particularly in the pastorals; cp. MDibelius, Hdb. exc. after 1 Ti 3:7 section 2 [w. lit.] and before 5:17), s. the lit. s.v. ἐπίσκοπος.—BEaston, Pastoral Epistles '47, 188–97; WMichaelis, Das Ältestenamt '53;

GBornkamm, πρεσβύτερος; RCampbell, The Elders '94.—B. 1472. DELG s.v. πρέσβυς. M-M. EDNT. TW.

πρεσβύτης, ου, ὁ (Aeschyl., Hippocr. et al.; IG IV²/1, 123, 120; pap; LXX; Jos., Bell. 1, 312) ***old man, aged man*** (Philo, Op. M. 105, after Hippocr.: a man of 50–56 years; Dio Chrys. 57 [74], 10 πρεσβύτης immediately follows the series παῖς, μειράκιον νεανίσκος; Aristoxenus fgm. 35 has the steps νήπιος, παῖς, νεανίσκος, ἀνήρ, πρεσβύτης; cp. VLeinieks, The City of Dionysos '96, 199–209) **Lk 1:18; Tit 2:2; Phlm 9** (but many accept RBentley's conjecture πρεσβευτής *ambassador,* i.e. of Christ: Lghtf.; W-H., app.; EHaupt; Lohmeyer; REB; RSV; Goodsp., Probs. 185–87; against this point of view HermvSoden, MDibelius, Meinertz, NRSV; JBirdsall, NTS 39, '93, 625–30. On this pass. cp. also RSteck, PM 18, 1914, 96–100; 192f; PSchmidt, ibid. 156–58.—Polyaenus 8, 9, 1 πρεσβύτης and πρεσβευτής are found as variants); MPol 7:2 (used attributively w. ἀνήρ: πρ. ἀνήρ as Theophyl. Sim., Ep. 60); Hm 8:10.—FBoll (s. νεανίας) 116f. DELG s.v. πρέσβυς. M-M.

πρεσβῦτις, ιδος, ἡ (Aeschyl., Pla.+; perh. CIJ 400 [I BC–III AD], s. BBrooten, Inscriptional Evidence for Women as Leaders in the Ancient Synagogue: SBLSP 20, '81, 4; B's rendering: 'Here lies Sara Ura, elder [or aged woman]'; Diod. S. 4, 51, 1; 4 Macc 16:14; Philo, Spec. Leg. 2, 33; Jos., Ant. 7, 142; 186) ***old(er) woman, elderly lady*** **Tit 2:3;** Hv 1, 2, 2 (γυνὴ πρ., as Aeschines 3, 157).—DELG s.v. πρέσβυς. M-M.

πρήθω (Hom. et al.; LXX; Jos. Ant. 3, 271) 1 aor. inf. πρῆσαι (Num 5:22), pass. ptc. πρησθείς; lit. 'blow out, distend'; pass. ***swell up*** Ἰούδας πρησθεὶς ἐπὶ τοσοῦτον τὴν σάρκα, ὥστε ... *Judas, whose flesh was so swollen, that* .... Papias (3:2); v.l. ἐπρήσθη γάρ; other vv.ll. in Preuschen, Antilegomena, and AHilgenfeld, ZWT 18, 1875, 262–65.

πρηνής, ές, gen. **οῦς** (On the form Schwyzer I 189; Hom. et al.; PGM 4, 194; LXX; Just., D. 90, 5; Mel., P. 26, 184.—X. has πρανής, which is found in later Attic usage beside πρηνής) ***forward, prostrate, head first, headlong*** πρηνὴς γενόμενος *being (falling) headlong* **Ac 1:18** (cp. πρ. πεσών Theophyl., MPG CXXIII 146; Posid.: 87 fgm. 5 Jac. πρ. προσπεσών; Diod. S. 34+35, fgm. 28a πρηνὴς ἐπὶ τὴν γῆν; Appian, Celts 10 κατέπεσε πρηνής; Philo, Op. M. 157 πρηνὲς πεπτωκός; Jos., Bell. 1, 621 and Vi. 138 πρ. πεσών, Bell. 6, 64, Ant. 18, 59; SibOr 4, 110). The mng. *swollen, distended* was first proposed by FChase, JTS 13, 1912, 278–85; 415, and accepted by Harnack, TLZ 37, 1912, 235–37; EbNestle, ZNW 19, 1920, 179f; HWendt and GHoennicke, ad loc.; JMoffatt, transl. 1913; RHarris, AJT 18, 1914, 127–31; Goodsp., Probs. 123–26; L-S-J-M gives it as a possibility s.v. πρανής, w. ref. to πρησθείς; in this case it would be derived fr. the root πρη-, πίμπρημι (q.v.), which is linguistically questionable. Other exx. of πρηνής in the sense 'swollen' are lacking, unless the word be given this mng. in Wsd 4:19 (so Goodsp.), but 'prostrate and silent' makes good sense in this passage. Lake (below) points out harmonizing interests of later writers such as Ps-Zonaras and Euthymius Zigabenus.—Bursting as a result of a violent fall is also found Aesop, Fab. 177b H.=181 P.//192 H-H.//142f Ch. κατακρημνισθεὶς διερράγη.—S. further Zahn, Forsch. VI 1900, 126; 153–55; IX 1916, 331–33; AKnox, JTS 25, 1924, 289f; HCadbury, JBL 45, 1926, 192f; KLake, Beginn. I 5, '33, 22–30; Beyer, Steinmann, and Bruce ad loc.; REB; NRSV.—DELG. M-M.

πρίζω (πρίω 'saw'; [Ps.-?]Pla., Theag. 124b; Diod. S. 3, 27, 3; 4, 76, 5; PHerm 28, 11 φοίνικες πεπρισμένοι; Am 1:3; designated as un-Attic by Pollux 7, 114) or **πρίω** (trag., Thu. et al.) 1 aor. ἔπρισα (Sus 59 Theod.; Just., D. 120, 5), pass. ἐπρίσθην ***saw (in two)*** as a method of execution (Sus 59 Theod.); acc. to tradition (MartIs 3:14, 16, 19 Gebh. [=Denis p. 113 lines 18 and 30, p. 114 ln. 14]; ViIs rec. Dor. [p. 41, 18 Sch.; Torrey p. 20]; Justin, Dial. 120 et al.; MGaster and BHeller, Monatsschr. f. Gesch. u. Wissensch. des Judent. 80, '36, 32–44) Isaiah met his death in this manner, **Hb 11:37.**—DELG s.v. πρίω. M-M.

πρίν (Hom.+; ins, pap, LXX) lit. an adv. of time 'before, formerly', then a **marker of a point of time prior to another point of time,** ***before***

ⓐ as temporal conjunction (the ms. tradition oft. varies betw. πρίν, which is predom. Attic, and πρὶν ἤ [s. ἤ 2d], which is Ionic [Schwyzer II 313], and predominates in the Koine [Schwyzer II 656]).

α. w. the aor. subj. (Plut., Caes. 735 [58, 2]; Lucian, Ver. Hist. 2, 18) or opt. (B-D-F §383, 3; Rob. 977) πρὶν ἀκουσθῶσι τὰ ῥήματα Hs 5, 7, 3. **Lk 2:26** is text-critically uncertain πρὶν ἢ ἂν ἴδῃ, but ἤ is omitted (cp. Cyr.-Ins. 123 πρὶν ἄν w. aor. subj.) as well as ἄν in some mss., and one v.l. has ἕως ἂν ἴδῃ. Likew. in **22:34** ἕως, ἕως οὗ, ἕως ὅτου are also attested instead of πρὶν ἤ; the corrector has been at work in all these passages, so that the original rdg. can no longer be determined w. certainty.—Only once w. the opt., in indirect discourse after a past tense (B-D-F §386, 4; Rob. 970) πρὶν ἢ ὁ κατηγορούμενος ἔχοι **Ac 25:16** (cp. Jos., Ant. 20, 210).

β. foll. by the acc. and the aor. inf. (B-D-F §395; Rob. 977.—Plut., Lysander 448 [27, 1] πρὶν ἐπανελθεῖν τὸν Ἀγησίλαον; Lucian, Dial. Deor. 20, 16 πρίν; Jos., Ant. 11, 1 πρὶν ἤ) **Mt 1:18** (πρὶν ἤ); **J 8:58; Ac 7:2** (πρὶν ἤ); 1 Cl 38:3: Dg 2:3 (πρὶν ἤ); 8:1; Hs 9, 16, 3. Also of future things (Arrian, Ind. 24, 6 πρὶν ταχθῆναι τὴν φάλαγγα=before the phalanx will have been drawn up) πρὶν ἀλέκτορα φωνῆσαι *before the cock will have crowed* **Mt 26:34, 75; Mk 14:30** (πρὶν ἤ), **72; Lk 22:61.** Cp. **J 4:49; Ac 2:20** (Jo 3:4); Hs 9, 26, 6.—Without the acc., which is understood fr. the context (Menand., Epitr. 264 S. [88 Kö.]; 508 S. [332 Kö.]; Diod. S. 13, 10, 1; 14, 52, 1; Chion, Ep. 4, 4; Ps.-Apollod. 3, 3, 2; Jos., Bell. 6, 213; Just., A I, 4, 4) **J 14:29;** Hv 3, 1, 3.

ⓑ funct. as prep. w. gen. (since Pind., P. 4, 43, also Plut., Mor. 883b; Arrian, Anab. 3, 18, 6; PGM 7, 418; 420 πρὶν ἡλίου ἀνατολῆς; En 14:6; Jos., Ant. 4, 269 πρὶν ἡλίου δυσμῶν; Sus 35a LXX=42 Theod.; for contrast w. πρότερον cp. the epitath οὐ τὸ θανεῖν ἄλγεινόν, ἐπεὶ τό γε Μοῖρ' ἐπέκλωσεν, | ἀλλὰ πρὶν ἡλικίας καὶ γονέων πρότερον EpigrAnat 13, '89, 128f, no. 2=dying is not itself to be deplored, for Fate decrees it so, but when before one comes of age and then before one's parents) πρὶν ἀλεκτοροφωνίας **Mt 26:34 v.l.;** πρὶν Ἀβραὰμ ἐγὼ εἰμί **J 8:58 v.l.**—Even πρίν w. the acc. occurs as v.l. πρὶν τὸ πάσχα **J 11:55** D; πρὶν σάββατον **Mk 15:42** D (cp. B-D-F §395 app.; JWackernagel, Syntax II² 1928, 215).—ATschuschke, De πρίν particulae apud scriptores aet. August. prosaicos usu, diss. Bresl. 1913.—DELG. M-M.

Πρίσκα (Πρῖσκα? s. B-D-F §41, 3; cp. Mlt-H. 155) and its dim. **Πρίσκιλλα, ης, ἡ** (Preisigke, Namenbuch. A priestess of Zeus named Πρίσκιλλα is mentioned in an honorary ins fr. the city of Olbasa: Ramsay, Phrygia I p. 309 no. 122) ***Prisca, Priscilla,*** tentmaker (s. Ἀκύλας and the lit. there), named before her husband in the majority of cases (Harnack [s.v. Ἀκ.] concludes fr. this that she was a more important pers. than her husband and that she may have played the major part in the writing of Hb: ZNW 1, 1900, 16ff.—In Ramsay, op. cit. p. 637 no. 530

[70–80 AD] Julia Severa is named before her husband Tyrronius Rapon, prob. because she was of higher rank) **Ac 18:2, 18, 26.** The forementioned passages have the name Πρίσκιλλα (likew. **Ro 16:3 v.l.; 1 Cor 16:19 v.l.**), but Πρίσκα is the predominant form in the Pauline letters **Ro 16:3; 1 Cor 16:19; 2 Ti 4:19.**—IReimer, Women in the Acts of the Apostles '95. M-M.

πρίω s. πρίζω.

πρό prep. w. gen. (Hom.+—S. the lit. s.v. ἀνά, beg.; also Rydbeck 62–77) 'before'.

❶ **marker of a position in front of an object,** ***before, in front of, at*** πρὸ τῆς θύρας *at the door* **Ac 12:6;** cp. **5:23 v.l.;** πρὸ τοῦ πυλῶνος **12:14;** perh. **J 10:8** belongs here (Jesus is the door, vs. 7). πρὸ τῆς πόλεως (Jos., Bell. 1, 234, Ant. 10, 44): ὁ ἱερεὺς τοῦ Διὸς τοῦ ὄντος πρὸ τῆς πόλεως *the priest of* (the temple of) *Zeus just outside the city* (gate) **14:13** (CIG 2963c τῆς μεγάλης Ἀρτέμιδος πρὸ πόλεως ἱερεῖς [restored]. Cp. the sim. inscriptions w. πρὸ πόλεως 2796; 3194; 3211; BCH 11, 1887 p. 464 no. 29 ὁ πρὸ πόλεως Ἀπόλλων [Thyatira]; TWiegand, SBBerlAk 1906, 259 Ἀσκληπιοῦ πρὸ πόλεως [Miletus]; cp. αἱ προκαθήμεναι θεαὶ τῆς πόλεως SIG 694, 50f; lit. s.v. Λύστρα).—In vivid imagery ὁ κριτὴς πρὸ τῶν θυρῶν ἕστηκεν **Js 5:9.** Fig. πρὸ ὀφθαλμῶν ἔχειν, λαμβάνειν and πρὸ ὀφθαλμῶν τινος εἶναι; on these s. ὀφθαλμός 2.—πρὸ προσώπου τινός (= לִפְנֵי פ׳; s. Johannessohn, Präp. 184f) *before* or *ahead of someone* **Mt 11:10; Mk 1:2; Lk 7:27** (on all three cp. Mal 3:1; Ex 23:20; TestAbr A 12 p. 91, 4 [Stone p. 30]; GrBar 1:4); **1:76 v.l.; 9:52; 10:1;** 1 Cl 34:3 (cp. Is 62:11); *in front of someone* IEph 15:3 (JosAs 24:6 πρόκειται πρὸ προσώπου ὑμῶν). W. transition to a temporal mng. *prior to* προκηρύξαντος Ἰωάννου πρὸ προσώπου τῆς εἰσόδου αὐτοῦ *after John had preached as his forerunner before his* (i.e. Jesus') *appearance* **Ac 13:24.**

❷ **marker of a point of time prior to another point of time,** ***earlier than, before*** πρὸ τοῦ ἀρίστου *before the meal* (X., Cyr. 6, 2, 21) **Lk 11:38.** πρὸ τοῦ βαπτίσματος D 7:4a. πρὸ χειμῶνος **2 Ti 4:21.** πρὸ τοῦ πάσχα **J 11:55.** πρὸ τῆς ἑορτῆς τοῦ πάσχα **13:1.** πρὸ τοῦ κατακλυσμοῦ **Mt 24:38.** πρὸ καταβολῆς κόσμου **J 17:24; Eph 1:4; 1 Pt 1:20.** πρὸ ἡλίου καὶ σελήνης 2 Cl 14:1 (s. ἥλιος). πρὸ πάντων **Col 1:17;** cp. πρὸ τούτων πάντων **Lk 21:12.** πρὸ τῶν αἰώνων (Ps 54:20) **1 Cor 2:7;** cp. IEph ins; IMg 6:1. πρὸ χρόνων αἰωνίων **2 Ti 1:9; Tit 1:2.** πρὸ παντὸς τοῦ αἰῶνος **Jd 25.** πρὸ καιροῦ *before the proper time* or *the last times* (καιρός 3b; cp. Sir 51:30; Theodor. Prodr. 1, 281 H.) **Mt 8:29; 1 Cor 4:5.** πρὸ τούτων τῶν ἡμερῶν **Ac 5:36; 21:38;** Hm 4, 3, 4. πρὸ ἐτῶν **2 Cor 12:2.** πρὸ τῆς μεταθέσεως **Hb 11:5.** Latinizing (on the use of the Rom. calendar among the Gks. s. Hahn 245; EBickerman, Chronology of the Ancient World[2], '80, 47–51; on calculation of a date, 43–44) πρὸ ἐννέα καλανδῶν Σεπτεμβρίων *on August twenty-fourth* IRo 10:3. πρὸ ἑπτὰ καλανδῶν Μαρτίων *on February twenty-third* MPol 21 (cp. IPriene 105, 23 πρὸ ἐννέα καλανδῶν Ὀκτωβρίων).—On the expr. πρὸ ἓξ ἡμερῶν τοῦ πάσχα **J 12:1** s. ἡμέρα 2c and cp. Am 1:1; 4:7. πρὸ τριῶν ἡμερῶν τοῦ συλληφθῆναι αὐτόν *three days before he was arrested* MPol 5:2. πρὸ μιᾶς τῶν ἀζύμων *one day before the feast of unleavened bread* GPt 2:5 (Plut., Lucull. 510 [27, 9] πρὸ μιᾶς νωνῶν Ὀκτωβρίων, Publ. 101 [9, 8]; Appian, Bell. Civ. 2, 115 §479 πρὸ μιᾶς τοῦδε τοῦ βουλευτηρίου). πρὸ μιᾶς (sc. ἡμέρας [Polyaenus 7, 10 and Just., D. 27, 5 πρὸ μιᾶς ἡμέρας]; cp. Lucian, Alex. 46; Dositheus 40, 2; PGM 13, 350) *one day before* D 7:4b; *the day before* Hs 6, 5, 3.—Rydbeck 62–77; Mlt-Turner 260.—W. gen. of the personal pron. (PsSol 1:8 τὰ πρὸ αὐτῶν ἔθνη; Just., D. 16, 4 πρὸ αὐτοῦ; PTebt 61b, 384 [118/117 BC]) πρὸ ὑμῶν (Lev 18:28) **Mt 5:12;** cp. **Ac 7:4** D. πρὸ ἐμοῦ (1 Macc 15:5) **J 5:7; 10:8** (s. also 1 above); **Ro 16:7; Gal 1:17** (s. AcPlCor 2:4). Cp. 1 Cl 19:1.—πρὸ τοῦ w. acc. and inf. (En 9:11; TestAbr A 9 p. 87, 10 [Stone p. 22]; ParJer 7:31; Just., D. 92, 3. Cp. B-D-F §403; Rob. 1074f) πρὸ τοῦ ὑμᾶς αἰτῆσαι **Mt 6:8.** Cp. **Lk 2:21; 22:15; J 1:48; 13:19** (here the acc. is missing, but can easily be supplied); **17:5; Ac 23:15; Gal 2:12; 3:23;** B 16:7.

❸ **marker of precedence in importance or rank** (Pind. et al.; pap; Jos., Ant. 16, 187 πρὸ ἐκείνων; Just., A I, 2, 1 πρὸ τῆς ἑαυτοῦ ψυχῆς) πρὸ παντός *above all, especially* Pol 5:3. Also πρὸ πάντων (Ar. 9, 2; Just., D. 7, 3; POxy 292, 11; 294, 30) **Js 5:12; 1 Pt 4:8;** D 10:4.—DELG. M-M. EDNT. TW.

προαγαπάω 1 aor. προηγάπησα **to be beforehand in expression of affection,** ***love before, love first*** τινά *someone* Dg 10:3.

προάγω impf. προῆγον; fut. προάξω; 2 aor. προήγαγον; 1 aor. pass. προήχθην LXX (Hdt.+).

❶ trans. **to take or lead from one position to another by taking charge,** ***lead forward, lead*** or ***bring out*** τινά *someone:* προαγαγὼν αὐτοὺς ἔξω *after he had led them out* **Ac 16:30** (Diod. S. 4, 44, 3 τῆς φυλακῆς προαγαγεῖν=lead out of the prison). αὐτοὺς προαγαγεῖν εἰς τὸν δῆμον **17:5** (Jos., Ant. 16, 320 εἰς τὸ πλῆθος). Cp. **12:6** (Jos., Ant. 2, 105 al.).—In the language of the law-court *bring before* (Jos., Bell. 1, 539, Ant. 16, 393; Just. A I, 21, 3.—ἐπί 3) **Ac 25:26.**

❷ intr. **to move ahead or in front of,** ***go before, lead the way, precede***—ⓐ in place τινά *go before someone* (2 Macc 10:1; B-D-F §150; Rob. 477) **Mt 2:9** (GJs 21:3); **21:9;** AcPl Ha 3, 29. Abs. (Diod. S. 17, 19, 1 προῆγε=he pushed on; Jos., Bell. 1, 673, Ant. 14, 388) **Mt 21:9 v.l.; Mk 11:9** (opp. ἀκολουθεῖν); **Lk 18:39.** *Walk ahead of* those who are going slowly and w. hesitation ἦν προάγων αὐτοὺς ὁ Ἰησοῦς . . . οἱ δὲ ἀκολουθοῦντες **Mk 10:32.** κατὰ πόλιν με προῆγον *they went before me from city to city* IRo 9:3.—In imagery πᾶς ὁ προάγων καὶ μὴ μένων ἐν τῇ διδαχῇ *anyone who goes too far and does not remain in the teaching* **2J 9.** Of πίστις (cp. Aberciusins. 12 πίστις προῆγε), which is followed by ἐλπίς (ἐπακολουθεῖν), προαγούσης τῆς ἀγάπης *love leads the way* Pol 3:3.

ⓑ in time *go* or *come ahead of* someone w. acc. of pers. προάγειν αὐτὸν εἰς τὸ πέραν *go on ahead of him to the other shore* **Mt 14:22.** προάξω ὑμᾶς εἰς τὴν Γαλιλαίαν *I will go on ahead of you to Galilee* **26:32; Mk 14:28** (CEvans, JTS 5, '54, 3–18); cp. **Mt 28:7; Mk 16:7.** Without acc. (which can be supplied fr. the ἕως-clause [cp. SIG 684, 25]) προάγειν εἰς τὸ πέραν πρὸς Βηθσαϊδάν **Mk 6:45.** οἱ τελῶναι προάγουσιν ὑμᾶς εἰς τὴν βασιλείαν τοῦ θεοῦ *the tax-collectors will get into the kingdom of God ahead of you* **Mt 21:31.** Fig. of sins προάγουσαι εἰς κρίσιν *they go ahead of* (sinners) *to judgment* **1 Ti 5:24** (cp. Oenomaus in Eus., PE 5, 24, 1 εἰς τ. κρίσιν προάγειν='come before the court').—πάντα τὰ προάγοντα *everything that had gone before* MPol 1:1. κατὰ τὰς προαγούσας προφητείας *in accordance with the prophecies that were made long ago* (i.e. in reference to Timothy) **1 Ti 1:18** (IG XII/3, 247 τὰ προάγοντα ψαφίσματα; PFlor 198, 7 [III AD] κατὰ τὸ προάγον ἔθος; POxy 42, 3 ἡ πανήγυρις προάγουσα; Just., D. 33, 1 καὶ τὰ ἐπαγόμενα καὶ τὰ προάγοντα [in the psalm]). ἀθέτησις προαγούσης ἐντολῆς **Hb 7:18** (ἀθέτησις 1).—M-M. TW.

προαδικέω (since Aeschin. and Menand., Her. prol. 7; Diod. S. 4, 53, 1; 13, 30, 2; Plut., Dion 979 [47, 8], Mor. 1090e; Wsd

18:2; Philo, Mos. 1, 303) ***be first in wrong-doing, injure beforehand.*** It appears in a mutilated context at the beginning of Ox 840, where its meaning cannot be determined w. certainty.

προαθλέω pf. ptc. προηθληκώς (schol. on Pind., O. 8, 71c p. 256) **to be involved in an earlier contest, *compete in former times*** in a transf. sense of the martyrs of earlier ages (opp. οἱ μέλλοντες) ἡ τῶν προηθληκότων μνήμη *the memory of those who have already competed* MPol 18:3.

προαίρεσις, εως, ἡ (αἱρέω; Pla., Demosth., Aristot., ins, pap, LXX, Test12Patr, EpArist, Philo, Joseph., Just., Tat., Ath.) **a choosing of one thing before another, *choice, commitment*** (freq. w. a political connotation, of one who chooses the correct side and manifests loyalty, s. Welles, ind.; also a favorite term of moral philosophers, e.g. Diogenes 21, 5 p. 114 Malherbe) λ[ά]βετε π[ροαίρ]|εσιν ἀγαθήν *make the right commitment,* that is, from polytheism to Christianity AcPl Ha 1, 20 (for the use of ἀγαθ. w. προαίρεσις s. Welles, no. 75, 10, of a treasurer who is commended for his 'exemplary dedication' or 'commitment' to his responsibilities); s. the ed's. note on the lacuna in 2, 2f.—M-M s.v. προαιρέω.

προαιρέω (Hdt., Aristoph. et al.; ins, pap, LXX) 2 aor. προεῖλον. Mid. 2 aor. προειλόμην, 3 pl. προείλαντο (Schwyzer I 753; B-D-F §80; 81, 3; cp. Mlt-H. 212; OGI 383, 46 [I BC] προειλάμην); pf. προήρημαι, ptc. προῃρημένος.

❶ act. **to set someth. forth, *bring*** or ***take out*** (Aristoph., Thu. et al.; PTebt 112, 31 [II BC]; PFay 119, 21; Jdth 13:15) τὶ *someth.* 1 Cl 43:5.

❷ mid. **to reach a decision beforehand, *choose (for oneself), commit oneself to, prefer*** (X., Pla.+) τὸν φόβον τοῦ κυρίου οὐ προείλαντο *they did not choose the fear of the Lord* 1 Cl 57:5 (Pr 1:29). πρ. τι μᾶλλον ἤ τι *prefer one thing to another* (X., Mem. 2, 1, 2) 2 Cl 10:3. *Undertake, determine, decide, make up one's mind* (Pla. et al.; Diod. S. 1, 72, 3; 19, 78, 2 ins, pap; Pr 21:25; 2 Macc 6:9; 3 Macc 2:30; 7:2; EpArist 33; 45 al.) w. inf. foll. (Diod. S. 3, 55, 3; Ael. Aristid. 38 p. 721 D.; Philo, Mos. 1, 325; Jos., C. Ap. 1, 257, Vi. 103) IMg 1:1. Abs. (Demosth. 18, 190) καθὼς προήρηται τῇ καρδίᾳ *as he has made up his mind* **2 Cor 9:7.** Cp. Larfeld I 499.—M-M.

προαιτιάομαι mid. dep.; 1 aor. προῃτιασάμην **to reach a charge of guilt prior to an implied time, *accuse beforehand*** followed by acc. and inf. (B-D-F §397, 3; Rob. 1036) προῃτιασάμεθα *we* (=I) *have already charged that* **Ro 3:9.**—M-M.

προακούω 1 aor. προήκουσα (Hdt. et al.; Philo, Ebr. 160) ***hear beforehand*** τὶ *someth.* (Nicol. Dam. 90 fgm. 66, 24 Jac. τὶ παρά τινος) ἐλπίδα ἣν προηκούσατε *what you hope for* (ἐλπίς 3), *about which you have heard before* (i.e. before you receive it or before you received this letter) **Col 1:5** (Diod. S. 16, 66, 4 Τιμολέων προακηκοὼς ἦν=he had heard before it happened; 19, 38, 6 πρ. τὸ μέλλον; Jos., Ant. 8, 301 Βασάνης προακηκοὼς τὰ μέλλοντα αὐτῷ συμβήσεσθαι).

προαμαρτάνω 2 aor. 1 pl. προημάρτομεν (Just., A I, 61, 10); pf. ptc. προημαρτηκώς (OGI 751, 10 [II BC] w. μετανοεῖν; Herodian 3, 14, 4; Jos., Bell. 1, 481; Just., s. above) ***sin beforehand*** πολλοὺς τῶν προημαρτηκότων (prob. for πολλοὺς τοὺς προημαρτηκότας, Ltzm. ad loc.) *many who sinned before* **2 Cor 12:21;** cp. **13:2.**—M-M.

προαύλιον, ου, τό (Themist., Or. 33 p. 443, 13 fig. τὸ πρ. τοῦ λόγου) **place in front of a house, *forecourt, gateway*** (Pollux 1, 77; 9, 16; Suda) **Mk 14:68.**—M-M.

προβαδίζω (Plut., Mor 707b; cp. Hippiatr. 1, 13; PCairCat 10735 verso 9f; patr. ref. Lampe) ***go before*** [ἔδει δὲ προκηρύσ]σειν τὸν ἀρχιστρά[τηγον Ἰωάννην τὸ]ν οἰκέτην προβαδί[ζοντα τῆς τοῦ κυρίου αὐτοῦ] παρουσίας *the commander-in-chief [is to announce John as] servant who goes in advance [of his Lord's] appearing* PCairCat 10735 verso, 8–10 (as restored by Dssm. LO 368–70)=A Syn. 3, 24 and Otero I 86 no. 6.

προβαίνω 2 aor. προέβην, ptc. προβάς; pf. ptc. προβεβηκώς (Hom. et al.; pap, LXX; En 22:5; Joseph.; Ath. 32, 3)

❶ **to make a forward movement, *go ahead, advance*** lit. *go on* (X., Ages. 6, 7; Herodian 7, 12, 4) οὐ προέβαινον, ἀλλ' ἵσταντο *(the sheep) did not come forward, but stood still* GJs 18:3 (codd.). ὀλίγον *a little* (distance) **Mk 1:19.** Also μικρόν Hv 4, 1, 5; s 6, 2, 5. ἐκεῖθεν **Mt 4:21.**

❷ **to make an advance in time, *advance in years*** fig. ext. of 1: προβεβηκέναι ἐν ταῖς ἡμέραις *be advanced in years* **Lk 1:7, 18;** cp. **2:36** (ἡμέρα, end; also Lysias 24:16 προβεβηκὼς τῇ ἡλικίᾳ; Diod. S. 12, 18, 1; 13, 89, 2; UPZ 161, 61 [119 BC] πρ. τοῖς ἔτεσιν; Mitt-Wilck. II 2, 31; VII, 29 [116 BC]; Jos., Vi. 266, Ant. 7, 182; abs. προβεβηκώς: ViZech 1 [p. 88, 3 Sch.]; Ath. 32, 3).—M-M.

προβάλλω impf. προέβαλλον; 2 aor. προέβαλον. Mid.: fut. 2 pl. προβαλεῖσθε (Just., D. 64, 2). Pass.: aor. subj. 3 sg. προβληθῇ (Just., D. 65, 2); pf. ptc. fem. προβεβλημένη (Tat.) (Hom. +) 'throw/put before'

❶ **to cause to come forward, *put forward*** (cp. Jos., Bell. 4, 230) τινά *someone* (Demosth. 18, 149; Vi. Aesopi G 85 push someone forward to speak in the theater; 86) **Ac 19:33.** τὴν γλῶσσαν πρ. *thrust out the tongue* (schol. on Nicander, Ther. 206 πρ. τ. γλ. of a serpent thrusting out its tongue; 2 Macc 7:10) Hv 4, 1, 9.

❷ **to send out new growth, *put out*** foliage or fruit (w. acc. Epict. 1, 15, 7 τὸν καρπόν; likew. Jos., Ant. 4, 226. Cp. SSol 2:13 Aq. Of the Logos: Just., D. 62, 4 ἀπὸ τοῦ πατρὸς προβληθὲν γέννημα) abs. (but v.l. addition τὸν καρπὸν αὐτῶν) ὅταν προβάλωσιν ἤδη *when they* (i.e. the trees) *put out (their leaves)* **Lk 21:30.**—M-M. Spicq.

προβάς s. προβαίνω.

προβατικός, ή, όν *pert. to (a) sheep* (PCairGoodsp 30 VI, 5; XXXI, 9 al. [II AD]; 2 Esdr [s. below]) ἡ προβατική (sc. πύλη, as Life of Polycarp by Pionius in the phrase ἐπὶ τὴν καλουμένην Ἐφεσιακήν [Lghtf. II/3 p. 434 n. on ln. 23; s. also p. 450 n. on related phrase in ch. 20 p. 451 ln. 49]. The Christian POxy 1151 [V AD]=PGM II p. 212 P 5b, 7f and the ostrakon 3 p. 234, 1 add κολυμβήθρα: sheep pool) *sheep gate,* a gate in the north city wall of Jerusalem ([ἡ] πύλη ἡ προβατική 2 Esdr 13:1, 32; 22: 39; s. HGuthe, RE VIII 680, 24ff) **J 5:2** (s. Hdb. ad loc. and on Βηθζαθά; also JJeremias, D. Wiederentdeckung v. Bethesda '49).—M-M.

προβάτιον, ου, τό (Aristoph., Pla.+; Plut., Fab. 174 [1, 4]; PTebt 793, 1; 28 [183 BC]) dim. of πρόβατον; 'lamb' though it is oft. used without dim. sense=***sheep*** (Menand., Her. 26; Plut., Publ. 103 [11, 4] v.l., interchanged w. πρόβατον; Philostrat., Her. p. 133, 5; Celsus 4, 43) **J 21:16f v.l.** (for the juxtaposition of βόσκειν, ἀρνία, ποιμαίνειν and προβάτια cp. IPriene 362, 17f [IV BC] φέρειν τοὺς τὰ πρόβατα βόσκοντας ἀπὸ τῆς ποίμνης ἄρνα). 10:3 P[66].—TW.

πρόβατον, ου, τό (Hom.+; on the dat. pl. πρόβασι Hs 6, 1, 6 s. Herodian, Gramm. 1414, 10. πρόβασι βοσνήμασι Hesych p. 275 MSchmidt, as Schwyzer I 499)

❶ *sheep* (on this mng. s. O. Wilck I 286; B-D-F §126, 1aα; L-S-J-M s.v. I. The more general senses 'cattle' or 'small cattle' scarcely merit serious attention for our lit., though they are barely poss. in certain passages.) **Mt 12:11f; 18:12; Lk 15:4, 6** (on this parable: GNordberg, SEÅ 1, '37, 55–63); **Rv 18:13;** B 16:5 (En 89:54ff); GJs 18:3 (codd.). As a sacrificial animal 1 Cl 4:1 (Gen 4:4); **J 2:14f.** πρόβατα σφαγῆς *sheep to be slaughtered* **Ro 8:36** (Ps 43:23). Defenseless in the midst of wolves **Mt 10:16.** In danger without a shepherd **Mt 9:36; Mk 6:34** (both Num 27:17; cp. Ezk 34:5 and Jdth 11:19); **Mt 26:31; Mk 14:27;** B 5:12 (the three last Zech 13:7); 1 Cl 16:6f (Is 53:6f). ἐν ἐνδύμασι προβάτων (cp. ἔνδυμα 2; Proverbia Aesopi 123 P. κρύπτειν τὸν λύκον προβάτου δορᾷ) **Mt 7:15.** The first fruits of the sheep belong to the prophets D 13:3. Jesus ὡς πρόβατον ἐπὶ σφαγὴν ἤχθη . . . ἄφωνος (after Is 53:7) **Ac 8:32** (cp. Vi. Aesopi G 48 P. a dispute over the question: διὰ τί τὸ πρόβατον ἐπὶ θυσίαν ἀγόμενον οὐ κέκραγεν;); B 5:2 (Is 53:7); 1 Cl 16:7.

❷ **people of God, *sheep.*** The lit. usage passes over to the nonliteral, or the sheep appear for the most part as symbols of certain people (En 89:42ff; Did., Gen 215:24): in the extended allegory of the Good Shepherd and the sheep **J 10:1–16, 26f** (in vs. **3** P[66] reads προβάτια). Jesus is ὁ ποιμὴν τῶν προβάτων ὁ μέγας **Hb 13:20.** Cp. **1 Pt 2:25.** The bishop is the shepherd, the church members the sheep IPhld 2:1. Cp. **J 21:16, 17** (Porphyr., Adv. Chr. fgm. 26: the ἀρνία are the catechumens, but the πρόβατα are οἱ πιστοὶ εἰς τὸ τῆς τελετώσεως προβάντες μυστήριον). The Christians are called πρόβατα τῆς νομῆς σου (=God's) 1 Cl 59:4 (cp. Ps 78:13; 94:7; 99:3). In the last times under the influence of lying prophets τὰ πρόβατα will be turned εἰς λύκους D 16:3. At the last judgment people will be divided as the shepherd separates τὰ πρόβατα from οἱ ἔριφοι **Mt 25:32f** (s. ἔριφος; PAmh 73, 6 [129/30 AD] differentiates πρόβ. and αἶγες), and the πρόβατα, representing those blessed by the Father, will stand at the right hand of the Human One (Son of Man) vs. **33** (HGraffmann, D. Gericht nach d. Werken im Mt: KBarth Festschr. '36, 124–36). Jesus knows that he is (divinely) sent **15:24,** and sends his disciples **10:6** πρὸς τὰ πρόβατα τὰ ἀπολωλότα οἴκου Ἰσραήλ.—In Hermas sheep appear (w. shepherds) as symbolic of all kinds of persons Hs 6, 1, 5f; 6, 2, 3f; 6f; 6, 3, 2; 9, 1, 9; 9, 27, 1.—B. 144. DELG s.v. πρόβατα. M-M. EDNT. TW.

προβεβηκώς s. προβαίνω.

προβιβάζω (Aristoph., Soph., Pla. et al.; PBad 39 II, 4 [IV AD]; Just., D. 90, 1) fut. 2 sg. προβιβάσεις Dt 6:7; 1 aor. προεβίβασα; pass. ptc. προβιβασθείς ***cause to come forward*** (Soph., Oed. Col. 180; Kaibel 947, 1) ἐκ τοῦ ὄχλου προεβίβασαν Ἀλέξανδρον *they made Alexander come out from the crowd* **Ac 19:33 v.l.** ἡ δὲ προβιβασθεῖσα ὑπὸ τῆς μητρός *but she, pushed forward by her mother* **Mt 14:8** (here many prefer the mng. 'incite, urge on [beforehand], prompt'. But προβιβ. εἴς τι in places like X., Mem. 1, 5, 1 εἰς ἐγκράτειαν, Pla., Prot. 328b εἰς ἀρετήν, Musonius p. 60, 5 H. νέους εἰς φιλοσοφίαν means 'lead on to', 'train in'. Even more compelling is usage in the LXX, where the word='instruct, teach, inculcate': Ex 35:34; Dt 6:7; Just., D. 90, 1 ἡμᾶς . . . προβίβασον ἐκ τῶν γραφῶν). 'Coached' may best express the mng.—DELG s.v. βαίνω. M-M. Spicq.

προβλέπω impf. προέβλεπον; 1 aor. προέβλεψα (Dionys. Hal. 11, 20; somet. in Vett. Val. [ind.]; Kaibel 326; Ps 36:13)

❶ act. **to see beforehand, *foresee*** ὧν (=τούτων, οὓς) προέβλεπεν τὸ πνεῦμα κυρίου B 6:14. ἐν πνεύματι προβλέψας εἰς τὸν Ἰησοῦν *looking forward in the spirit to Jesus* 9:7. προβλέψας, ὡς *foreseeing that* 3:6.

❷ mid. **to make provision for, *provide*** (in the act. Kaibel 326) τὶ περί τινος *select* or *provide someth. for someone* **Hb 11:40.**—M-M s.v. προβλέπομαι.

προγενής, ές gen. οὗς **born in early times,** ***primeval*** comp. προγενέστερος, α, ον *older* (Hom. et al.; Theodotus [II BC] in Eus., PE 9, 22, 3=Denis p. 205, 27; Tat. 41, 1 [comp.]) τινός *than someth.* of the Son of God πάσης τῆς κτίσεως αὐτοῦ προγενέστερος *older than his whole creation* Hs 9, 12, 2.—DELG s.v. γίγνομαι.

προγίνομαι (Hom. et al.) aor. ptc. pl. προγενόμενοι (Just., A I, 46, 4); pf. ptc. προγεγονώς, mid.-pass. pl. προγεγενημένοι (Just.) **to originate in time before, *be born earlier, happen*** or ***be done before*** (Hdt.+; ins, pap, LXX, Just.) τὰ προγεγονότα ἁμαρτήματα *the sins that were committed in former times,* in the time when God also showed forbearance **Ro 3:25** (schol. on Apollon. Rhod. 4, 411–13 τὰ προγεγενημένα ἁμαρτήματα; Diod. S. 19, 1, 3 τὰ προγεγενημένα ἀδικήματα; cp. X., Mem. 2, 7, 9 τ. προγεγονυῖαν χάριν).τὰ προγεγονότα πονηρά Hv 1, 3, 1. ὁ προγεγονώς *the former one* (i.e. the Phoenix), *predecessor* 1 Cl 25:3.—DELG s.v. γίγνομαι. M-M.

προγινώσκω (Eur., X., Pla. et al.; BGU 1141, 39 [14 BC]; Wsd) 2 aor. προέγνων, ptc. προγνούς. Pass.: aor. 3 sg. προεγνώσθη Wsd 18:6; pf. ptc. προεγνωσμένος; plpf. 3 sg. προέγνωστο (Just., D. 70, 5)

❶ **to know beforehand or in advance, *have foreknowledge (of)*** τί *someth.* (Philo, Somn. 1, 2; Jos., Vi. 106; Tat. 8, 4) affliction Hs 7:5. Abs. (Jos., Ant. 2, 86) προγινώσκοντες *since you know* this (i.e. what the context makes clear) *in advance* **2 Pt 3:17.** Of God (Alex. Aphr., An. p. 1, 7 Br. τὰ μέλλοντα, Fat. 30 p. 200, 29; Just.) πάντα Hm 4, 3, 4.—Closely connected is the idea of choice that suggests foreknowledge

❷ ***choose beforehand*** τινά *someone* **Ro 8:29.** τὸν λαὸν αὐτοῦ **11:2** (EWeber, D. Problem der Heilsgesch. nach Ro 9–11, 1911; THoppe, D. Idee d. Heilsgesch. b. Pls 1926; FMaier, Israel in d. Heilsgesch. nach Ro 9–11, 1929; EvDobschütz, Prädestination: StKr 106, '35, 9–19; JMunck, Christus u. Israel: Ro 9–11, '56; EDinkler, Prädestination bei Paulus, GDehn Festschr., '57, 61–102; s. also on προορίζω). Pass. of Christ προεγνωσμένος πρὸ καταβολῆς κόσμου **1 Pt 1:20.**—*Know from time past* (Jos., Bell. 6, 8) προγινώσκοντές με ἄνωθεν **Ac 26:5.**—DELG s.v. γιγνώσκω. M-M. TW.

πρόγλωσσος, ον (Ptolem., Apotel. 3, 14, 31 Boll-B.; Ps.-Polemon Physiogn. 37 Förster et al.) **pert. to ready use of the tongue, *hasty of tongue, talkative*** (Pythag., Ep. 12, 2 of the ideal nurse, who is to set an example of composure by not being garrulous) B 19:8. As suggested by the clause that follows: παγὶς γὰρ τὸ στόμα θανάτου, perh. with implication of being gossipy.

πρόγνωσις, εως, ἡ (cp. προγνώστης; Hippocr. et al. as a medical t.t.; Plut., Mor. 399d; 982c; Phlegon of Tralles [time of Hadrian]: 257 fgm. 16e Jac. [in Orig., C. Cels. 2, 14]; Lucian, Alex. 8; Vett. Val. 220, 9; 221, 25; 355, 9; Jos., Ant. 15, 373 πρόγνωσιν ἐκ θεοῦ τῶν μελλόντων ἔχων; 17, 43; PGM 7, 294; Jdth 11:19; Just.; Tat. 1, 1)

❶ ***foreknowledge*** πρ. λαμβάνειν τελείαν *receive complete foreknowledge* 1 Cl 44:2.

❷ *predetermination,* of God's omniscient wisdom and intention (so Alex. Aphr., Fat. 30 p. 200, 31 Br.; Proverbia Aesopi 131 P.; Jdth 9:6; Just., D. 92, 5 πρόγνωσιν ἔχων) w. βουλή **Ac 2:23.** κατὰ πρόγνωσιν θεοῦ πατρός *destined by God the Father* (NRSV) **1 Pt 1:2** (Just., D. 134, 4; s. WArndt, CTM 9, 1929, 41–43).—DELG s.v. γιγνώσκω. M-M. TW.

προγνώστης, ου, ὁ (cp. πρόγνωσις; PGM 5, 410) *one who knows someth. beforehand,* of God (Just. A I, 44, 11; D. 16, 3; 23, 2 al. Theoph. Ant. 2, 15 [p. 138, 2].—Of Apollo: Tat. 19, 3) πρ. τῶν πάντων *one who knows everything beforehand* 2 Cl 9:9.—DELG s.v. γιγνώσκω.

πρόγονος, ον (Hom. et al.) 'born early' or 'before' (Mel., HE 4, 26, 7) in our lit. only subst. in the pl. οἱ πρόγονοι (Pind.+; ins, pap, LXX; EpArist 19; Philo; Jos., Ant. 12, 150, C. Ap. 2, 157; Just.; Mel.; Ath. 30, 2, R. 16 p. 68, 9) ***parents, forebears, ancestors:*** ἀμοιβὰς ἀποδιδόναι τοῖς προγόνοις *to requite their (living) forebears* (i.e. parents/grandparents etc.) **1 Ti 5:4.** ἀπὸ προγόνων *from my ancestors = as my ancestors did* (OGI 485, 3; 529, 1; IMagnMai 163, 2; 164, 3) **2 Ti 1:3.**—B. 119. DELG s.v. γίγνομαι B p. 223. M-M.

προγράφω 1 aor. προέγραψα. Pass.: 2 aor. προεγράφην; pf. 3 sg. προγέγραπται (Just., D. 43, 3), ptc. προγεγραμμένος (Aristoph., Thu. et al.; ins, pap, LXX, Joseph., Just.).

❶ **to write in advance or before, *write before(hand)*—ⓐ** in the same document in which the word is found (so oft. pap) καθὼς προέγραψα *as I have written above* **Eph 3:3** (Ins of Sinuri no. 46, 17 LRobert '45 καθότι προγέγραπται; Just., A I, 63, 2 ὡς προεγράψαμεν). τὰ προγεγραμμένα *what I have written above* (Ins of Sinuri no. 46, 5; PPetr III, 61, 17 [III BC]; BGU 1107, 30; 1131, 55 al.) Hv 4, 3, 6; s 5, 3, 7. ὁ προγεγραμμένος, τὸ προγεγραμμένον *the person* or *thing mentioned above* (POxf 8, 13 [104/5 AD] ὁ πρ. μου ἀνήρ; 10, 10; 16) τὰ προγεγραμμένα πρόσωπα *the persons mentioned above* IMg 6:1 (cp. also Da 3:3). τὸ πρ. (ἀντίγραφον) *the forementioned copy* MPol 22:3.

ⓑ What is written before, is found in an older document (by another author, as well; cp. Ps.-Clem., Hom. p. 12, 31 Lag.) ὅσα προεγράφη *what was written in earlier times* (in the γραφή) **Ro 15:4.**—εἴς τι *mark out, designate for someth.* (Appian, Bell. Civ. 4, 1 §2 τ. ἐχθροὺς ἐς θάνατον πρ.) of false teachers: οἱ πάλαι προγεγραμμένοι εἰς τοῦτο τὸ κρίμα *who for a long time have been marked out* (or *written about*) *for this judgment* (described in what follows) **Jd 4.**

❷ **to set forth for public notice, *show forth/portray publicly, proclaim*** or ***placard in public*** (γράφω='draw, paint' Hdt., Aristoph. et al.; here and there in Pla.; Jos., C. Ap. 2, 252; PGM 2, 47; 36, 265.—PGM 2, 60 προγράφω of a figure 'drawn above') οἷς κατ' ὀφθαλμοὺς Ἰ. Χρ. προεγράφη ἐσταυρωμένος *before whose eyes Jesus Christ was portrayed on a cross* **Gal 3:1** (many would prefer to transl. *placard publicly, set forth in a public proclamation* so that all may read: Aristoph., Demosth. et al.; Plut., Demetr. 912 [46, 10], Mor. 408d; Just., A I, 15, 2; IG X, 4, 24; PFlor 99, 11).—M-M. TW.

πρόδηλος, ον (Soph., Hdt. et al.; ins; POxy 237 VII, 9; LXX; EpArist 133; Philo, Gig. 39; Jos., Vi. 22; 212; SibOr 5, 37) **pert. to someth. that is quite obvious, *clear, evident, known (to all)* 1 Ti 5:24f;** 1 Cl 51:3. προδήλων ἡμῖν ὄντων τούτων *since this is quite plain to us* 40:1. πρόδηλον ποιεῖν foll. by ὅτι *reveal, make clear* 11:1; 12:7. πρόδηλον (sc. ἐστίν) foll. by ὅτι *it is known to all* (X., Hell. 6, 4, 9; Hero Alex. III p. 312, 17) **Hb 7:14** (B-D-F §397, 4; Rob. 1034).—M-M.

προδηλόω 1 aor. προεδήλωσα; aor. ptc. n. pl. gen. προδηλωθέντων; pf. pass. ptc. προδεδηλωμένος (Thu. 6, 34, 7; ins, pap; 3 Macc 4:14; Philo, Decal. 45; 50) **to make known beforehand, *reveal*** τὶ *someth.* (Diod. S. 20, 37, 1; Plut., Pomp. 636 [32, 6]; Jos., Bell. 2, 629) τὴν θλῖψιν Hs 7:5. Pass. οἱ προδεδηλωμένοι πατέρες *the fathers, whom we have previously mentioned* (cp. IG XII/7, 239, 23; 3 Macc 4:14) 1 Cl 62:2.—DELG s.v. δῆλος. M-M s.v. πρόδηλος.

προδημιουργέω 1 aor. προεδημιούργησα (Philop. [VI AD], on Aristot., De Generat. Anim. 61, 14) ***create beforehand*** 1 Cl 33:3 v.l. (for προετοιμάσας).—DELG s.v. δημιουργός.

προδίδωμι fut. ptc. προδώσων 4 Macc. 4:1; 1 aor. προέδωκα; 2 aor. ptc. προδούς

❶ **to be beforehand in giving, *give in advance*** (X.; Aristot.; Polyb. 8, 18, 7; ins, pap) τινί *to someone* **Ro 11:35** (cp. Is 40:14 v.l., which is taken from **Ro 11:35**).

❷ **to hand over in a treacherous manner, *betray*** (Aeschyl., Hdt. et al.; ins; PThéad 17, 16; LXX; Test12Patr; Jos., Bell. 2, 594; 4, 228, C. Ap. 2, 263) τινά *someone* **Mk 14:10** D. Of betrayal in persecutions MPol 4 v.l. 6:2ab; Hv 2, 2, 2ab.—M-M.

προδότης, ου, ὁ (προδίδωμι; Aeschyl., Hdt. et al.; 2 and 3 Macc; TestSol 9:3; EpArist 270; Philo, Leg. All. 2, 10, Spec. Leg. 3, 164; Jos., Bell. 3, 354, Vi. 133) ***traitor, betrayer*** in a catalogue of vices **2 Ti 3:4.** W. φονεύς of the chief priests and asssociates **Ac 7:52.** W. revilers of the Lord Hs 9, 19, 3b. W. apostates and revilers (for the gen. cp. Diod. S. 11, 3, 1 τῆς ἐλευθερίας; cp. Sextus 365 προδότης θεοῦ) προδόται τῆς ἐκκλησίας Hs 8, 6, 4 or προδόται τῶν δούλων τοῦ θεοῦ 9, 19, 1; cp. 3a. ἤκουσαν προδόται γονέων *they were called* or *were known to be betrayers of their parents* Hv 2, 2, 2. Of Judas **Lk 6:16** (πρ. γίν. as Diod. S. 8, 6, 3; Jos., Ant. 19, 61; on the role of Judas s. the lit. s.v. Ἰούδας 6 and esp. WKlassen, Judas, Betrayer or Friend of Jesus '96).—DELG s.v. δίδωμι. M-M.

πρόδρομος, ον pert. to being a precursor, *going* (lit. running) ***before, going ahead,*** also subst. (Aeschyl., Hdt. et al.; Ael. Aristid. 38, 21 K.=7 p. 78 D.; LXX) fig ext. of the mng. 'to run on ahead', which is not found in our lit. for the verb προτρέχω (but s. προβαδίζω): of Jesus, who entered the Holy of Holies as the ***forerunner*** of his followers **Hb 6:20.**—DELG s.v. δραμεῖν. M-M. TW.

προέγνων s. προγινώσκω.

προέδραμον s. προτρέχω.

προέδωκα s. προδίδωμι.

προεθέμην s. προτίθημι.

πρόειμι ptc. προών (εἰμί; cp. Il. 1, 70 τά τ' ἐόντα τά τ' ἐσσόμενα πρό τ' ἐόντα; Hes., Theog. 32 τὰ τ' ἐσσόμενα πρό τ' ἐόντα and later wr.; pap, EpArist) ***be preexistent*** (Herm. Wr. 422, 25 Sc. ὁ προὼν θεός) of the Holy Spirit Hs 5, 6, 5.—Renehan '82, 121.

προεῖπον defective verb, used as 2 aor. of προλέγω; fut. expressed by προερῶ fr. a difft. stem (M-M.); pf. προείρηκα; pf. pass. ptc. προειρημένος (Hom. [in tmesis], Hdt., Pla.+). On προεῖπα s. B-D-F §81, 1; Mlt-H. 208.

❶ **to tell beforehand, *foretell, tell/proclaim beforehand, warn,*** of prophetic utterances concerning future events and circumstances, of a scripture pass. (Jos., Bell. 6, 109) τὴν γραφήν, ἣν προεῖπεν τὸ πνεῦμα τὸ ἅγιον **Ac 1:16.** τινί τι *tell someone someth. beforehand* (Dio Chrys. 28 [45], 4 τ. θεοῦ προείποντος τ. ἡγεμονίαν αὐτῷ; Philostrat., Vi. Soph. 2, 11, 3 πρ. αὐτῷ ταῦτα. Cp. Ael. Aristid. 46 p. 191 D.: ὁ θεὸς πρ. τῇ μητρὶ . . .) **Mk 13:23** (cp. **Mt 24:25,** where the context supplies the acc.); **1 Th 4:6** w. connotation of warning. Pass. (Jos., Ant. 2, 17 τὰ προειρημένα) τὰ ῥήματα τὰ προειρημένα ὑπὸ τῶν ἀποστόλων **Jd 17;** cp. **2 Pt 3:2;** 1 Cl 58:1. W. a quot. foll. καθὼς προείρηκεν Ἠσαΐας (Is 1:9 follows) **Ro 9:29.** Cp. **Gal 1:9.** W. ὅτι foll.: προλέγω ὑμῖν καθὼς προεῖπον **Gal 5:21.** προείρηκα καὶ προλέγω **2 Cor 13:2.** But some would place these three last pass. and **1 Th 4:6** in 2.

❷ **to have already stated someth.,** the aor. or pf. in contrast to the present—ⓐ ***have said someth. before*** or ***previously*** (Appian, Samn. 10 §11 προεῖπε Κινέας=Cineas had said previously; cp. Plut., Peric. 170 [33, 3]) w. ref. to a previous visit (cp., in a way, Sb 8247, 17 [I AD] ἐν τῇ παρεμβολῇ εἶπα ὑμῖν καὶ νῦν τὸ αὐτὸ λέγω) ὡς προειρήκαμεν καὶ ἄρτι πάλιν λέγω **Gal 1:9.** καθὼς προείπαμεν ὑμῖν as *we have told you before* **1 Th 4:6.** W. ὅτι foll. προλέγω ὑμῖν, καθὼς προεῖπον **Gal 5:21.** προείρηκα καὶ προλέγω **2 Cor 13:2.** Some would place these pass. in 1 because of the connotation of warning. μετὰ τὸ προειρηκέναι (i.e. τὸ πνεῦμα τὸ ἅγιον) is followed by Jer 38:33, and in such a way that λέγει κύριος (in the LXX φησὶν κύριος) introduces the main clause *after he* (the Holy Spirit) *said . . . , the Lord said* (as follows) **Hb 10:15 v. l.** Of the act of baptism ταῦτα πάντα προειπόντες βαπτίσατε *after you have stated all these things* (the prescribed admonitions), *baptize* D 7:1.

ⓑ ***have already said*** (in the same document), ***have mentioned previously*** (Appian, Syr. 66, §349 προεῖπον=I have mentioned earlier; Artem. 4, 69; Just., D. 64, 7; oft. pap) προείρηκα ὅτι *I have already said* **2 Cor 7:3** (s. 3:2; 6:12). Redundantly προειρήκαμεν ἐπάνω B 6:18 (cp. vs. 12). Pass. καθὼς προείρηται (cp. Diod. S. 2, 32, 5 and PTebt 27, 74 [II BC] καθότι προείρηται) **Hb 4:7** (s. 3:15).—The pf. pass. ptc. *already mentioned, aforementioned* (Polyb. 1, 20, 7; 3, 51, 8 al.; Diod. S.4, 66, 1; 11, 20, 3 al.; Ps.-Demetr. 264; 288; 2 Macc 3:28; 4:1; 3 Macc 6:35b; Jos., Vi. 45) with and without a name 1 Cl 41:2; 43:1; 44:2; Dg 3:2; Hm 9:4; 10, 1, 5; s 6, 5, 7; 8, 11, 3; 9, 29, 3; D 11:1. Uncertain rdg. προειρημένων AcPl Ha 1, 13.—DELG s.v. ἔπος. M-M.

προείρηκα s. προλέγω.

προέλαβον s. προλαμβάνω.

προελεύσομαι s. προέρχομαι.

προελθών s. προέρχομαι.

προελπίζω pf. προήλπικα (Posidippus Com. [III BC], fgm. 27, 8 Kock [in Athen. 9, 377c]; Simplicius, In Epict. p. 29, 51) **to be prior in hoping, *hope before, be the first to hope*** ἐν τῷ Χριστῷ **Eph 1:12** (in such case πρ. is to be understood syntagmatically: hope is prior to realization [cp. giving, προδιδόναι, as prior to recompense, ἀνταποδοῦναι, Ro 11:35]; if ἡμεῖς here refers to Jewish Christians, as most scholars [fr. Chrysostom to MDibelius[2] 1927; this interpr. opposed by EPercy, D. Probleme der Kolosser u. Epheserbriefe, '46, 266f] prefer to take it, then προ would suggest 'before the Gentiles' or even 'before Christ appeared'. If the ἡμεῖς are the Christians as a whole [EHaupt; PEwald; Meinertz; HRendtorff; HGreeven in Dibelius[3] '53], then προ looks forward to the fulfillment of the hope in the future).—DELG s.v. ἔλπομαι. TW.

προενάρχομαι 1 aor. προενηρξάμην (hapax leg., cp. Lampe s.v.) ***begin (beforehand)*** so that the beginning lies in the past as contrasted w. the present τὶ *someth.* **2 Cor 8:10** (where προ is explained by ἀπὸ πέρυσι, and νυνί vs. 11 forms the contrast). Abs. (opp. ἐπιτελεῖν) vs. **6.**—DELG s.v. ἄρχω.

προεξομολογέομαι 1 aor. προεξωμολογησάμην (an emend. by AvHarnack; see the apparatus in Bihlmeyer) ***confess (one's sins) beforehand*** D 14:1 (i.e. before the Lord's Supper; the ms. has προσεξομολογησάμενοι [=at the same time confessing your sins]).—DELG s.v. ὁμός.

προεπαγγέλλω (the act. in Cass. Dio) 1 aor. mid. προεπηγγειλάμην; in our lit. only mid. and pass. ***promise before(hand), previously*** (so mid. in Cass. Dio 42, 32; 46, 40) τὶ *someth.* **Ro 1:2.** Pf. pass. ptc. (IPriene 11, 71 [84 BC] τὰ προεπηγγελμένα) ἡ προεπηγγελμένη εὐλογία *the bountiful gift which was (previously) promised* **2 Cor 9:5.**—M-M s.v. προεπαγγέλλομαι. TW.

προεπικαλέω **to call on somone for someth.,** ***request*** τινά *someone* to do someth. Pol 3:1 v.l.; s. προεπιλακτίζω.

προεπιλακτίζω 1 aor. mid. προεπελακτισάμην. The word προεπελακτίσασθε='you have forced me' Pol 3:1 is Zahn's restoration of the text on the basis of four different Gk. readings that are alike in that they yield no sense. Until now the word is not attested lexically; neither is ἐπιλακτίζειν nor προλακτίζειν. The form προεπεκαλέσασθε, preferred by Lghtf., Funk, Hilgenfeld, Krüger, Bihlmeyer means 'you have invited' or 'requested' but it has no more lexical attestation than Zahn's conjecture. Conversely, ἐπικαλεῖν and προκαλεῖν were in current use and the 'provocastis' of the Latin version seems to presuppose it.—DELG s.v. λαξ.

προέρχομαι mid. dep.; impf. προηρχόμην; fut. προελεύσομαι; 2 aor. προῆλθον; pf. 3 sg. προελήλυθεν (Just.) (Hdt.+; ins, pap, LXX; TestSol; TestJob 10:3; TestJos 19:3 [8]; EpArist 235 πρ. εἰς='go over to'; Philo, Joseph., Just.; Tat. 5, 2; Mel., P. 66, 469; Ath., 10, 3, R. 17 p. 69, 8).

❶ **to continue to advance, *go forward, advance, proceed*** w. acc. of degree or way (Pla., Rep. 1, 328e; 10, 616b ὁδόν) μικρόν *a little* (Plut., Thes. 11, 1; cp. Jos., Vi. 304 πρ. ὀλίγον) **Mt 26:39** (v.l. προσελθών); **Mk 14:35** (v.l. προσελθών). ῥύμην μίαν *go along one lane* or *go one block farther* **Ac 12:10.** πρ. ὡσεὶ πόδας λ' Hv 4, 2, 1.—Of time *advance, come on* (Iambl., Vi. Pyth. 35, 251) τὸ κυρίου πάσχα προέρχεται Dg 12:9.—Of Christ ἵνα εἰς κόσμον προέλθῃ *that he might come into this world* AcPlCor 2:6.

❷ **to precede as leader/guide, *go before.*** W. acc. of pers. (Plut., Brut. 995 [25, 4] ὁ Βροῦτος πολὺ προῆλθε τοὺς κομίζοντας τὸ ἄριστον=Brutus went before the bearers) Ἰούδας προήρχετο αὐτοὺς **Lk 22:47** (v.l. αὐτῶν; for the gen. cp. X., Cyr. 2, 2, 7; Jdth 2:19; Just., A I, 23, 1). For **Lk 1:17** s. 3.

❸ **to precede so as to be ahead, *come/go before*** someone, ***go on before*** or ***ahead*** (cp. Sir 32:10) abs. (Herodian 1, 5, 2) **Ac 20:5** (v.l. προσελθόντες). πρ. ἐπὶ τὸ πλοῖον *go on board the ship beforehand* vs. **13** (v.l. προσελθόντες). πρ. εἰς ὑμᾶς *go on to you ahead (of me)* **2 Cor 9:5.** οἱ προελθόντες με ἀπὸ Συρίας εἰς Ῥώμην *those who have gone ahead of me from Syria to Rome* IRo 10:2.—*Arrive at a place before* τινά *someone* προῆλθον αὐτούς **Mk 6:33** (vv.ll. προσῆλθον αὐτοῖς et al.).

προελεύσεται (v.l. προσελεύσεται) ἐνώπιον αὐτοῦ **Lk 1:17** (cp. Gen 33:3, 14).

❹ **to come to the fore,** ***come out, proceed*** (2 Macc 4:34; Philo, Op. M. 161; Jos., Bell. 4, 651; Just., D. 30, 1 al.)

ⓐ abs. *come out of the house* (Ps.-Lucian, De Asin. 47; POxy 472, 5 [II AD]) **Ac 12:13 v.l.** (for προσῆλθεν). Of Christ *come out* (of the womb) GJs 17:3.

ⓑ ***come forth, proceed,*** of Christ's transcendent origin ἀπό *from* (πρ. ἀπό as 2 Macc 10:27 v.l.; Just., D. 64, 7 al.) ἀφ' ἑνὸς πατρός IMg 7:2; ἀπὸ σιγῆς 8:2 (Proclus on Pla., Cratyl. p. 67, 9 Pasqu.: God ἀπ' ἄλλου προῆλθεν; 100, 6).—M-M.

προετοιμάζω 1 aor. προητοίμασα, mid. προητοιμασάμην; pf. pass. fem. ptc. προητοιμασμένην (Just., D. 131, 2) (Hdt. et al.; Wsd 9:8; Is 28:24; Philo, Op. M. 77; Jos., Ant. 17, 121) ***prepare beforehand;*** the act. is used in our lit. only of God; τὶ *someth.* τὰ ἐν τῇ θαλάσσῃ ζῷα 1 Cl 33:3; τὰς εὐεργεσίας αὐτοῦ 38:3. W. indication of the goal: ἃ προητοίμασεν εἰς δόξαν **Ro 9:23.** οἷς (by attraction for ἅ) προητοίμασεν ὁ θεὸς ἵνα **Eph 2:10.** The martyr's self-description is that of a sacrifice prepared by God acc. to God's good pleasure. In this sense the context fills out the expr. καθὼς προητοίμασας MPol 14:2.—IEph 9:1 cj. Lightf.—Mid. prepare oneself w. μετανοεῖν Hv 4, 2, 5.—DELG s.v. ἑτοῖμος. TW.

προευαγγελίζομαι 1 aor. προευηγγελισάμην ***proclaim good news in advance*** (schol. on Soph., Trach. 335 p. 299 Papag.; Philo, Op. M. 34, Mut. Nom. 158) τινί *to someone,* foll. by direct discourse introduced by ὅτι **Gal 3:8.**—DELG s.v. ἄγγελος. M-M. TW.

προέχω aor. ptc. προσχών TestSol (Hom. et al.; pap; Job 27:6 v.l. [s. Swete], προσέχων in text; En; TestSol 5:3; Just., D. 2, 6; Tat.; Ath. 7, 2)

❶ **to be in a prominent position,** ***jut out, excel, be first*** (Jos., C. Ap. 2, 186) w. gen. of the thing that is exceeded (Memnon [I BC / I AD]: 434 fgm. 1, 34, 7 Jac.; Cebes 34, 1; Dio Chrys. 44 [61], 11; Ael. Aristid. 30 p. 581 D.; EpArist 235; Tat. 15, 3; T. Kellis 22, 28f; w. acc. Ath. 7, 2) πάντων προέχουσα ἐπιθυμία *above all there is (the) desire* Hm 12, 2, 1.—Much is to be said for taking προεχόμεθα **Ro 3:9** as a pass., meaning ***are we excelled?*** i.e. *are we in a worse position (than they)?* or *have we lost our advantage?* (s. Field, Notes 152f; Goodsp.; NRSV mg.; cp. Plut., Mor. 1038d οὐθὲν πρ. ὑπὸ τοῦ Διός of the philosopher whose majesty is not excelled by that of Zeus. A link with vs. 1 is suggested by the v.l. προκατέχομεν περρισόν; s. προκατέχω; FDanker, Gingrich Festschr. 100f). S. 2.

❷ In **Ro 3:9,** which is text-critically uncertain (s. 1), the mid. either has the same mng. as the act. (the act. is so used in X., Cyr. 2, 1, 16; Jos., Ant. 7, 237) ***have an advantage*** (Vulgate)—a mng. not found elsewh. for the mid.—or its customary sense ***hold someth. before oneself for protection*** (so also En 99:3). In that case, if the 'we' in προεχόμεθα refers to Judeans, the οὐ πάντως that follows vigorously rejects the idea that they possess anything that might shield them fr. God's wrath. But if the 'we' in 9a must of necessity be the same as in 9b, i.e. Paul himself, he is still dealing w. the opponents whom he has in mind in vss. 7, 8, and he asks ironically: *am I protecting myself? am I making excuses?* He is able to answer this question w. a flat no, since his explanation in vs. 9b is no less clear and decisive than his earlier statements (for προέχεσθαι='put up as a defense' cp. Soph., Ant. 80; Thu. 1, 140, 4).—M-M. TW.

προηγέομαι mid. dep.; fut. προηγήσομαι (Hdt., Aristoph. et al.; ins, pap, LXX; TestJob 43:14; 52:12; ApcMos 38 [w. dat.]; Philo, Op. M. 28)

❶ **to go first and lead the way,** ***go before and show the way*** τινός *(to) someone* (X., Hipparch. 5, 4; 2 Macc 11:8) in vivid imagery of righteousness that goes before the good man to judgment B 4:12.

❷ **to be in a position of leadership,** ***preside*** (SIG 1109, 87; PLips 63, 6) οἱ προηγούμενοι *the officials* (cp. Dt 20:9; 1 Esdr 5:8f; 9:12 [τοῦ πλήθους]) of the Christian congregations 1 Cl 21:6. More definitely οἱ πρ. τῆς ἐκκλησίας Hv 2, 2, 6. W. πρωτοκαθεδρῖται 3, 9, 7.

❸ The difficult passage τῇ τιμῇ ἀλλήλους προηγούμενοι **Ro 12:10** is understood by the versions (It., Vulg., Syr., Armen.) to mean *try to outdo one another in showing respect.* Others make an association w. ἡγεῖσθαι=*consider, esteem* and prefer the sense ***consider better, esteem more highly*** for προηγ.: *as far as honor is concerned, let each one esteem the other more highly* (than oneself); cp. Kaibel 716, 5 φίλους ὑπὲρ ἀτὸν ἐτίμα=he valued his friends above himself; s. B-D-F §150.—M-M. TW.

πρόθεσις, εως, ἡ (προτίθημι)—❶ **setting forth of someth. in public,** ***setting forth, putting out, presentation*** (Pla. et al.; ins; Sb 5252 [pap. of 65 AD regarding the farming out of the fees fr. a temple of Isis: ln. 19 φαγεῖν ἐκθέτου οὔσης τῆς προθέσεως]. On the cultic use of the verb προτίθημι in Diocles [Athen. 3, 110b] cp. Dssm., B 155f [BS 157]; on πρόθεσις τ. ἄρτων s. UPZ 149, 21, vol. I pp. 638–40) of the 'sacred bread', lit. *loaves of presentation* οἱ ἄρτοι τῆς προθέσεως (ἄρτος 1b) **Mt 12:4; Mk 2:26; Lk 6:4** (all three 1 Km 21:7). ἡ πρ. τῶν ἄρτων in a concrete usage, the furniture for the presentation of the bread, *the table for the sacred bread,* despite the presence of τράπεζα in the immediate context, with which it is identical (cp. Ex 25:23–30; Lev 24:6) **Hb 9:2.** Some exegetes here take πρ. in the abstract sense = presentation of the showbread.

❷ **that which is planned in advance,** ***plan, purpose, resolve, will*** (Aristot. et al; Polyb. 1, 26, 1 and oft.; Plut., Mor. 960f; ins, pap; 2 and 3 Macc; EpArist, Philo; Jos., Ant. 18, 272; 19, 190).

ⓐ of humans **2 Ti 3:10** (here perh. w. a turn toward the mng. *way of thinking;* cp. Polyb. 4, 73, 2 ἡ πρ., ἣν ἔχει πρός τινα; cp. PTebt 27, 81 [113 BC]). ὁσία καὶ ἄμωμος πρ. 1 Cl 45:7. ἡ πρ. τῆς καρδίας *purpose of heart,* i.e. *devotion* **Ac 11:23** (cp. the Stoic thrust Epictet. 2, 8, 29; 4, 6, 26). τῆς πρ. κρατεῖν *obtain one's purpose* **27:13.** κατὰ πρόθεσιν *according to purpose* (Polyb.; PTebt 27, 81 [II BC]; 3 Macc 5:29; EpArist 199) w. gen. κατὰ πρόθεσιν εὐνουχίας *in accordance with the resolve to remain unmarried* Agr 18.

ⓑ of divine purpose (s. lit. s.v. προγινώσκω 2) οἱ κατὰ πρόθεσιν κλητοὶ ὄντες *those who are called in accordance with (God's) purpose* **Ro 8:28** (EBlackman, ET 50, '39, 378f). ἡ κατ' ἐκλογὴν πρόθεσις τοῦ θεοῦ *God's purpose which operates by selection* **9:11.** κατὰ πρόθεσιν (Philo, Mos. 2, 61) *according to design* **Eph 1:11.** Cp. **2 Ti 1:9.** κατὰ πρόθεσιν τῶν αἰώνων *according to the eternal purpose* **Eph 3:11** (s. αἰών 1b).—B. 1240f. DELG s.v. τίθημι. M-M. EDNT. TW.

προθεσμία, ας, ἡ (Lysias, Pla.+; ins [e.g. IG V/1, 550, 12; also the ins in JZingerle, Hlg. Recht: JÖAI 23, 1926, col. 23f οὐκ ἐτήρησε τὴν προθεσμίαν τῆς θεοῦ]; pap [e.g. POxy 2732, 19: 154 AD; 2754, 6: III AD πάλαι τοῦ διαλογισμοῦ τὴν προθεσμίαν εἰδότες=having known long ago the time fixed for the circuit court]; Sym.; Philo; Jos., Bell. 2, 633, Ant. 12, 201. Loanw. in rabb.—Subst. fem. of προθέσμιος, α, ον; ἡμέρα is to be supplied) **a point of time set in advance,** ***appointed day, fixed/limited time,*** of the day when a son reaches his majority ἄχρι τῆς προθεσμίας τοῦ πατρός *until the time set by the father* **Gal 4:2.** It is uncertain whether Paul is referring here to certain legal measures which gave the father the right to fix the date when his son would come of age, or whether he is rounding out his comparison w. details that occur to him at the moment, as he so oft. does (though there was a προθεσμία τοῦ πατρός for the coming of age of humankind in general; the parallel phrase, τὸ πλήρωμα τοῦ χρόνου, vs. 4 is used oft. in the pap of contractual termination; see s.v. πληρόω 2).—DELG s.v. τίθημι.

προθυμία, ας, ἡ (πρόθυμος; Hom. et al.; ins, pap; Sir 45:23; TestSol; TestJob 11:1; EpArist, Philo, Joseph.) **exceptional interest in being of service, *willingness, readiness, goodwill* 2 Cor 8:19; 9:2;** Dg 1. W. ἐκτένεια 1 Cl 33:1; ἐν ἀγαθῇ πρ. 2:3. μετὰ πάσης προθυμίας (as Hdt. 4, 98; Pla., Rep. 412e; Philo, Abr. 246; Jos., Ant. 15, 124; in ins esp. of benefactors SIG 532, 6f; IMagnMai 97, 74; IGerasaWelles 192; OGI 229, 98; 669, 13 μετὰ προθυμίας) **Ac 17:11** here w. emphasis on *goodwill* and absence of prejudice (FDanker, NTS 10, '64, 366f). εἰ ἡ πρ. πρόκειται *if willingness is present,* i.e. *if a person is willing* **2 Cor 8:12.** προθυμίαν ἔχειν *have zeal* (Hdt. et al.) Hs 5, 3, 4b; foll. by gen. *for someth.* 5, 3, 4a. ἡ προθυμία τοῦ θέλειν (as Pla., Leg. 3, 697d) **2 Cor 8:11.**—Larfeld I 499. DELG s.v. θυμός. M-M. TW. Spicq.

πρόθυμος, ον (cp. προθυμία; Soph., Hdt.+. Freq. of public-spirited pers.) **pert. to being eager to be of service, *ready, willing, eager,*** of the spirit (opp. ἡ σὰρξ ἀσθενής) **Mt 26:41; Mk 14:38**=Pol 7:2. πρ. εἴς τι (Thu. et al.; OGI 221, 61; Hab 1:8) πρόθυμος εἰς ἀγαθοποιΐαν *eager for doing good* 1 Cl 34:2 (the formulation πρ. . . . εἰς, with some term expressive of public service is common in honorary decrees, e.g. IMagnMai 89, 38; IPriene 99, 23; 108, 313 al. τὰ συμφέροντα). πρόθυμον εἶναι w. inf. foll. Hm 12, 5, 1. Gener. *willing, eager* w. ἱλαρός Hs 9, 2, 4 (cp. IK XXX, 14, 22f).—The subst. neut. τὸ πρόθυμον *desire, eagerness* (Eur., Med. 178; Thu. 3, 82, 8; Pla., Leg. 9, 859b; Herodian 8, 3, 5; Jos., Ant. 4, 42; 213; 3 Macc 5:26) τὸ κατ' ἐμὲ πρόθυμον *my eagerness* (κατά B 7b) **Ro 1:15.**—M-M. TW. Spicq.

προθύμως adv. fr. πρόθυμος (Aeschyl., Hdt.+) **pert. to being eager to be of service, *willingly, eagerly, freely*** opp. αἰσχροκερδῶς **1 Pt 5:2,** the contrast indicating that officials are to be eager to meet the needs of others rather than seek gain for themselves. μάλιστα προθύμως *with the greatest eagerness* MPol 13:1. *Readily* πάσχειν Hs 9, 28, 2; 4. *Eagerly* MPol 8:3.—M-M. TW. Spicq.

πρόθυρον, ου, τό (Hom., Hdt. et al.; LXX, TestSol; Mel., P. 14, 89 pap; cp. πρόθυροι 'doorkeepers' TestJob 6:2) ***forecourt*** εἰς τὰ πρόθυρα τοῦ ναοῦ GJs 23:3.—DELG s.v. θύρα.

προϊδών s. προοράω.

προΐημι fut. mid. προήσομαι; aor. mid. inf. προέσθαι Pr 17:27, subj. προῶμαι Job 27:6 (Hom. et al.; ins, pap, LXX, Philo, Joseph.; Ar. 15:10) in our lit. only mid. **to send forward from oneself, *bring forth, express*** (Demosth. 19, 118 ῥῆμα; Ps.-Pla., Tim. Locr. 100c λόγον; Jos., C. Ap. 1, 43 ῥῆμα) τινί τι *someth. to someone* (Alciphron 3, 18, 3) προήσομαι ὑμῖν ἐμῆς πνοῆς ῥῆσιν 1 Cl 57:3 (Pr 1:23).

πρόϊμος, ον (the standard sp. is πρώϊμος [X., Oec. 17, 4 al.; OGI 56, 68 πρώϊμος σπόρος: III BC; PTebt 27, 25; 76: 113 BC; L-S-J-M s.v.; DGeorgacas, ClPh 76, '81, 156; s. RPfeiffer's note in Callimachus I '49, 392, on fgm. 550/482]; on LXX usage s. Thackeray p. 90.—B-D-F §35, 1; Mlt-H. 73). The subst. (s. B-D-F §241, 5; W-S. §5, 19) πρόϊμος **Js 5:7** (opp. ὄψιμος; s. Tdf. app. on the rdg. πρώϊμον, and add P[74]) is usu. understood to mean ***early rain*** in line w. t.r. and many mss. that add ὑετός (Hollmann, Windisch, MDibelius, et al., w. ref. to Dt 11:14; Hos 6:3; Jo 2:23; Zech 10:1; Jer 5:24.). Others think of the ***early crops*** based on the v.l. πρ(ό)ϊμον καρπόν (cp. Petosiris, fgm. 6, ln. 45 πρώϊμοι καρποί; Geopon. 1, 12, 32 οἱ πρώϊμοι καρποὶ κ. οἱ ὄψιμοι).—In B 3:4, τότε ῥαγήσεται πρόϊμον τὸ φῶς σου is quoted fr. Is 58:8. The LXX might better have translated the Hebr. orig. w. πρωϊνός, but it seems likely that the translator meant 'early'=soon.—DELG s.v. πρώην. M-M.

προϊνός Rv 2:28 v.l.; 22:16 v.l. is prob. a faulty spelling of πρωϊνός (q.v.).

προΐστημι (Hom.+; ins, pap, LXX, TestJos 2:6; Joseph.; Just.; Mel., P. 42, 288 [Bo.]: 'come forward') in our lit. only intr.; pres. and impf. mid.; also 2 aor. inf. προστῆναι; pf. 3 pl. προεστήκασιν 4 Macc 11:27, προεστᾶσιν Dg 5:3, ptc. προεστηκώς LXX, προεστώς Pr 26:17; **1 Ti 5:17** (also Just.). By-form προιστανόμενος **Ro 12:8 v.l.; 1 Th 5:12 v.l.** (s. B-D-F 93, 1).

❶ to exercise a position of leadership, *rule, direct, be at the head (of),* w. gen. of pers. or thing (Hdt., Thu. et al.; ins, pap; Am 6:10; 1 Macc 5:19), manage, conduct τοῦ ἰδίου οἴκου **1 Ti 3:4f.** τέκνων, οἴκων vs. **12.** Of officials and administrators in congregations (cp. Diod. S. 40, 3, 4 of suitable men δυνησομένους τοῦ σύμπαντος ἔθνους [=τῶν Ἰουδαίων] προΐστασθαι; Jos., Ant. 8, 300 πρ. τοῦ πλήθους, Vi. 168). So perh. (s. 2 below) οἱ προϊστάμενοι ὑμῶν **1 Th 5:12** and the abs. ὁ προϊστάμενος (cp. Jos., Vi. 93) **Ro 12:8** (s. 2 below). Certainly οἱ καλῶς προεστῶτες πρεσβύτεροι **1 Ti 5:17** (s. Nicol. Dam.: 90 fgm. 130, 28 p. 414, 2 Jac. τοῦ κοινοῦ προεστῶτες; Plut., Mor. 304a οἱ προεστῶτες τῆς πολιτείας; Just., A I, 65, 3 al.). οἱ πρεσβύτεροι οἱ προϊστάμενοι τῆς ἐκκλησίας Hv 2, 4, 3.—HGreeven, ZNW 44, '52/53, 31–41.

❷ to have an interest in, *show concern for, care for, give aid* (Demosth. 4, 46; Epict. 3, 24, 3; PFay 13, 5; PTebt 326, 11 τοῦ παιδίου; BGU 1105, 6; EpArist 182; Jos., Ant. 14, 196 τ. ἀδικουμένων) w. gen. δόγματος ἀνθρωπίνου Dg 5:3 (for the sense 'to champion' someth. s. Aeschin. 2, 161 peace). So perh. (s. 1) οἱ προϊστάμενοι ὑμῶν (betw. κοπιῶντες and νουθετοῦντες) **1 Th 5:12** and ὁ προϊστάμενος (betw. μεταδιδούς and ἐλεῶν) **Ro 12:8** (s. vDobschütz on 1 Th 5:12 and the exc. after 5:13; against him vHarnack, ZNW 27, 1928, 7–10). *Busy oneself with, engage in* w. gen. (Soph., Elect. 980 φόνου; Athen. 13, 612a τέχνης; Ep. 53 of Apollonius of Tyana [Philostrat. I 358, 8] προϊστάμενοι φιλοσοφίας; Pr 26:17; Jos., Ant. 5, 90; ins freq. of public service, e.g. IPriene 50, 14f) καλῶν ἔργων **Tit 3:8, 14** (cp. SIG 593, 5f προεστηκότες τοῦ ἐνδόξου, as indication of exceptional merit).—M-M. TW.

προκάθημαι (Hdt. et al.; ins)—**❶ to be in an office of leadership, *preside (over), lead*** (Pla. et al.; Polyb. 12, 16, 6; Plut., Rom. 14, 5; Cass. Dio 49, 40 et al.; SIG 694, 50f [129 BC] προκαθημέναις θεαῖς τ. πόλεως; UPZ 110, 165 [164 BC]; 1 Esdr). lit. of the ἐπίσκοπος IMg 6:1. Of other church officials beside the overseer/bishop οἱ προκαθήμενοι *the leaders* 6:2. Of the Roman congregation προκάθηται ἐν τόπῳ (s. τύπος, end) χωρίου Ῥωμαίων *it presides in the land of the Romans* IRo ins a (s. on this Lghtf. and Hdb. ad loc.; Harnack, SBBerlAk 1896, 111–31; JChapman, Rev. Bénéd. 13, 1896, 385ff; FFunk, Kirchengeschichtl. Abhandlungen u. Untersuchungen I 1897, 1–23; HAchelis, Das Christentum in den ersten drei Jahrhunderten 1912, I 210ff).

❷ **to exercise preeminence,** ***take the lead*** fig. ext. of 1: of the Roman church προκαθημένη τῆς ἀγάπης *preeminent in love* IRo ins b (s. AJülicher, GGA 1898, 4).

προκαλέω mostly mid. (Hom. et al.; ins, pap; 2 Macc 8:11; Jos., Ant. 7, 315; 18, 369; Just., D. 123, 7; Tat. 23, 1) **to call out to someone to come forward,** freq. in a hostile sense ***provoke, challenge*** τινά *someone* **Gal 5:26** (Diod. S. 4, 17, 4 προκαλεῖσθαί τινα εἰς μάχην; Arrian, Cyneg. 16, 1; Lucian, Conv. 20 ἐς ἀγῶνα προκαλέσασθαι αὐτόν).—M-M. TW. Sv.

προκαταγγέλλω 1 aor. προκατήγγειλα; pf. pass. ptc. προκατηγγελμένος (Jos., Ant. 1, 219; 2, 218) **to announce beforehand,** ***foretell*** of prophetic utterance τί *someth.* (Jos., Ant. 10, 67) **Ac 3:24 v.l.** Acc. of thing foll. by aor. inf. (B-D-F §350; 397, 3; Rob. 1036) **3:18.** περί τινος *give information concerning someth. beforehand,* i.e. *foretell someth.* **7:52.** Pass. **2 Cor 9:5 v.l.**—M-M.

προκαταρτίζω 1 aor. subj. προκαταρτίσω (Hippocr. et al.) ***get ready, make arrangements for in advance*** τί *someth.* (SEG IV, 449, 13 [II BC] λίθους) **2 Cor 9:5.**—Frisk s.v. ἄρτι.

προκατέχω (Hom. Hymns, Thu. et al.; pap; Jos., Bell. 4, 503) ***gain possession of previously*** or ***occupy previously*** τί *someth.* fig. (cp. Polyb. 8, 33, 3 προκατέχεσθαι τῇ πρὸς Ῥωμαίους εὐνοίᾳ; 27, 4, 9) ἀπὸ τῶν προκατεχόντων σου τὴν διάνοιαν λογισμῶν=(cleanse yourself) *of all the thoughts that have taken over your mind up till now* Dg 2:1. The word is also found **Ro 3:9 v.l.** προκατέχομεν περισσόν; *do we have a previous advantage?* (s. προέχω).

πρόκειμαι (Hom.+; prim. 'be set before one') defective dep.

❶ **to be open to public view,** ***be exposed*** (of corpses lying in state Aeschyl., Sept. 965 al.) of Sodom and Gomorrah πρόκεινται δεῖγμα *they are exhibited as an example* **Jd 7** (cp. Jos., Bell. 6, 103 καλὸν ὑπόδειγμα πρόκειται).

❷ **to be present before one,** ***lie before, be present*** (Ps.-Clem., Hom. 3, 51) ἡ προθυμία πρόκειται *willingness is present* **2 Cor 8:12** (w. ἐπιτελεῖν [s. vs. 11], cp. SIG 671 B5 of royal goodwill). ἀντὶ τῆς προκειμένης αὐτῷ χαρᾶς *instead of* (ἀντί 1) *the joy that was set before him,* i.e. instead of the joy that was within his grasp he endured the cross **Hb 12:2** (ERiggenbach; JNisius, Zur Erklärung v. Hb 12:2: BZ 14, 1917, 44–61); s. also 3 below. ἡ προκειμένη ἐλπίς *the hope that is set before* **6:18** (cp. Jos., Ant. 1, 14 εὐδαιμονία πρόκειταί τινι παρὰ θεοῦ). πρόκειται *it lies before (us),* i.e. *that is the question at issue* (Diod. S. 8, 11, 4; Περὶ ὕψους 2, 3; 16, 1; Just., A II, 9, 5 τὸ προκείμενον=the subject under discussion) IPhld 8:2. οὐ γὰρ μικρὸς ἀγὼν πρόκειται περὶ σοῦ *there is no small dispute concerning you* GJs 20:11 (codd.; for the wording s. Hb 12:1 below).

❸ **to be subsequent to some point of time as prospect,** of a goal or destination, w. dat. of pers. ***lie or be set before someone*** (Ael. Aristid. 31, 2 K.=11 p. 127 D.: μητρὶ πένθος πρόκειται; Ath. 18, 1 οὐ … προκείμενον μοι ἐλέγχειν τὰ εἴδωλα) ὁ προκείμενος ἡμῖν σκοπός *the goal that is set before us* 1 Cl 63:1 (s. σκοπός). ὁ προκείμενος ἡμῖν ἀγών (s. ἀγών 1) **Hb 12:1.** Without a dat. (Diod. S. 4, 42, 7) IMg 5:1. τὸ προκείμενον ζῆν *the life that is set before* (you) IEph 17:1.—Also *be in prospect* (Jos., Ant. 1, 14; 8, 208.—Diod. S. 15, 60, 1 [a prize] and Περὶ ὕψους p. 66, 20 V. of wages that have been allowed; Tat. 23, 1): so perh. (s. 2) **Hb 12:2:** *for* (ἀντί 1 and 3) *the joy that was in prospect for him* (so Windisch[2], Strathmann; cp. Moffatt; NRSV).—M-M. TW.

προκηρύσσω 1 aor. 3 sg., pl. προεκήρυξε, -ξαν (Just.); ptc. προκηρύξας; plpf. 3 sg. προκεκηρύχει (Just., D. 78, 6). Pass.: aor. 3 sg. προκεκηρύχθη (Mel., P. 39, 275), ptc. acc. sg. προκηρυχθέντα (Just., A I, 58, 1); pf. ptc. προκεκηρυγμένος, inf. προκεκηρύχθαι (thus Just., A I, 52, 1); plpf. 3 sg. προκεκεκήρυκτο (Just., A I, 36, 3 al.) (since Soph.; X., De Rep. Lac. 11, 2; ins, pap, Philo, Joseph.; Just., Mel.) in our lit. the prefix προ obviously gives the word the sense ***proclaim publicly*** (Lucian, Tyrannic. 9; Alex. Aphr., An. p. 1, 6 Br.; Jos., Bell. 6, 385) τί *someth.* of John the Baptist βάπτισμα μετανοίας **Ac 13:24.** Of OT prophets (Jos., Ant. 10, 79 Ἱερεμίας τὰ μέλλοντα τῇ πόλει προεκήρυξε; Just., D. 84, 2 [of Isaiah] al.) τὴν ἔλευσιν τοῦ κυρίου Pol 6:3. Pass. **Ac 3:20 v.l.** (for προκεχειρισμένον).—DELG s.v. κῆρυξ. M-M. TW.

προκοιμάομαι pf. pass. ptc. προκεκοιμημένος **to fall asleep prior to a temporal reference point,** ***fall asleep before or earlier*** euphemism for *die before now* (s. κοιμάω 2, προοδοιπορέω; Cat. Cod. Astr. VIII/3, 110; Leontius 45 p. 94, 18) προκεκοιμημένοι *those who fell asleep before* Hs 9, 16, 5f.—DELG s.v. κεῖμαι.

προκοπή, ῆς, ἡ (Polyb.+; Bion in Diog. L. 4, 50; Posidonius in Diog. L. 7, 91; Diod. S. 16, 6, 3; Epict. [index Sch.]; OGI 627, 2; PRyl 233, 16; PGiss 27, 7; PMert 24, 9f; Sir 51:17; 2 Macc 8:8; EpArist 242; Philo; Jos., Ant. 4, 59; Test12Patr; loanw. in rabb. Rejected by Atticists: Phryn. p. 85 Lob.; Theoph. Ant. 2, 24 [p. 158, 16]) **a movement forward to an improved state,** ***progress, advancement, furtherance*** **Phil 1:25; 1 Ti 4:15.** εἰς πρ. τινος ἔρχεσθαι *help to advance someth.* **Phil 1:12.**—New Docs 4, 36. DELG s.v. κόπτω. M-M. TW. Spicq. Sv.

προκόπτω (Eur., Hdt. et al.) in our lit. only intr. (Polyb. et al.; ins, pap; Ps 44:5 Sym.; TestJud 21:8; Philo, Joseph., Just.) impf. προέκοπτον; fut. προκόψω; 1 aor. προέκοψα.

❶ **to move forward to a final stage,** of time ***be advanced, be far gone*** (Chariton 2, 3, 9; Appian, Bell. Civ. 2, 78 §325 ἡ ἡμέρα προύκοπτεν; Just., D. 56, 16) ἡ νὺξ προέκοψεν (Jos., Bell. 4, 298) **Ro 13:12.**

❷ **to move forward to an improved state,** ***progress, advance*** in what is good or in what is bad τινί *in someth.* (Diod. S. 11, 87, 5; SIG 708, 18 [II BC] ἡλικίᾳ προκόπτων; Philo, Sacr. Abel. 7) **Lk 2:52 v.l.** Also ἔν τινι (Diod. S. 17, 69, 4; Epict. 2, 17, 4; Lucian, Hermot. 63; M. Ant. 1, 17, 8; Vett. Val. 60, 15; 19) **Lk 2:52.** ἐν τῷ Ἰουδαϊσμῷ **Gal 1:14.** ἐν ταῖς ἐντολαῖς 2 Cl 17:3; ἐπὶ πλεῖον πρ. (Diod. S. 14, 98, 3) *make further progress* **2 Ti 3:9;** w. gen. foll. (Ael. Aristid. 46 p. 405 D. τ. σοφίας) ἐπὶ πλεῖον πρ. ἀσεβείας **2:16** (cp. Jos., Ant. 20, 205). πρ. ἐπὶ τὸ χεῖρον *go on from bad to worse* **3:13** (Paroem. Gr.: Zenob. 3, 82 τῶν ἐπὶ τὸ χεῖρον προκοπτόντων; Jos., Bell. 6, 1 τὰ πάθη προύκοπτεν καθ' ἡμέραν ἐπὶ τὸ χεῖρον, Ant. 4, 59; 18, 340; TestJud 21:8 v.l. ἐπὶ τὸ κακόν; schol. on Soph., El. 875 p. 142 ἐπὶ τὸ βέλτιον).—M-M. TW. Spicq.

πρόκριμα, ατος, τό (προκρίνω; as a legal term t.t. IG V/1, 21 II, 7 [II BC]; Mitt-Wilck. II/2, 88 II, 30) **a judgment that involves taking a side beforehand,** ***prejudgment, discrimination*** χωρὶς πρ. (PFlor 68, 13; 16f three times) **1 Ti 5:21.**—M-M. TW.

προκρίνω aor. προέκρινα Wsd 7:8; pf. pass. προκέκριμαι (Eur., Hdt.; ins, pap, Wsd 7:8; Just., D. 5, 5; Mel., HE 4, 26, 13) **to make a selection based on a preference,** ***prefer*** τινός *to someth.* (Herm. Wr. 4, 8a) pass. *be preferred* (Arrian, Anab. 1, 16, 4; Mitt-Wilck. I/2, 27, 6 [II AD] προκρίνονται παντὸς οὕτινοσοῦν [cj. by Schubart for οὕτινος οὐχ]οἱ νόμοι the laws supersede anything else [such as decrees]; Philo, Cher. 46; Jos., Ant. 11, 196; 18, 46) of faith and love ὧν οὐδὲν προκέκριται *to which nothing is preferred* or *superior* ISm 6:1 (Diog. L. 1, 82 Βίας προκεκριμένος τῶν ἑπτά=Bias, who surpassed the others of the seven [wise men]); cp. IMg 1:2.

προκυρόω pf. pass. ptc. προκεκυρωμένος ***make valid/ ratify in advance*** (SEG III, 674A, 28 [II BC]) διαθήκη προκεκυρωμένη ὑπὸ τοῦ θεοῦ *a will* or *covenant* (διαθήκη 1) *previously ratified by God* **Gal 3:17.**—New Docs 4, 171. DELG s.v. κύριος. M-M. TW.

προλαμβάνω 2 aor. προέλαβον; 1 aor. pass. προελήμφθην (on the sp. s. B-D-F §101 p. 53; Mlt-H. 246f) (trag., Hdt.+; ins, pap, LXX, EpArist; SibOr 3, 569; Philo, Joseph., Just.; Ath., R. 25 p. 78, 23) prim. 'take before(hand)'.

❶ **to do someth. that involves some element of temporal priority—**ⓐ w. temporal force of προ felt rather strongly πρ. τι ***do someth. before the usual time, anticipate someth.*** (cp. Theophr., HP 8, 1, 4 πρ. ταῖς εὐδίαις τὴν αὔξησιν 'begin the growth beforehand in favorable weather'; IG XIV, 2014, 1; Philo, Somn. 1, 2; Just., D. 131, 4 πάντα [of God]) w. inf. foll. (Jos., Ant. 6, 305; B-D-F §392, 2; Rob. 1120) προέλαβεν μυρίσαι τὸ σῶμά μου *she had anointed my body beforehand* **Mk 14:8.**

ⓑ w. temporal force of προ still felt ***take it upon oneself, undertake*** (in the sense 'anticipate mentally' in Polyb. and Plut.; EpArist 206; w. inf. foll. Hippocr., Ep. 27, 41) προέλαβον παρακαλεῖν ὑμᾶς IEph 3:2.

ⓒ ***take, get*** of a meal (SIG 1170, 7; 9; 15 of the taking of food [ἄρτον, γάλα et al.] in the temple of Asclepius in Epidaurus. S. also vWilamowitz in note 4 to the ins) prob. w. the temporal force of προ felt to a degree ἕκαστος τὸ ἴδιον δεῖπνον προλαμβάνει ἐν τῷ φαγεῖν *in eating, each goes on ahead to take one's own supper* **1 Cor 11:21** (s. ἴδιος 1b).

❷ **to ascertain someth. by surprise, *detect, overtake, surprise*** τινά *someone* (TestJud 2:5 running down a boar) pass. (POxy 928, 8; Wsd 17:16) ἐὰν προλημφθῇ ἄνθρωπος ἔν τινι παραπτώματι **Gal 6:1.** See Field, Notes 190; JRobb, ET 57, '45/46, 222.—M-M. TW.

προλέγω pf. pass. 3 sing. προλέλεκται (Aeschyl., Hdt.+; ins; Is 41:26; TestSol; GrBar 8:7; EpArist 8; Just., Tat.).

❶ **to say someth. in advance of an event, *tell beforehand/ in advance*** (Demetr. of Phal. [300 BC]: 228 fgm. 39 Jac. p. 970, 2f τὶς θεῶν αὐτοῖς προὔλεγε τὸ μέλλον; Apollon. Paradox. 3 τὰ μέλλοντα; TestSol 10:10 C; Jos., Ant. 7, 226; cp. Ramsay, CB I/2 p. 386 no. 232, 8: Gaius, an attorney, before his death expresses his thoughts in an epitaph for his tomb; s. προεῖπον 1) w. ὅτι foll. (Pla., Rep. 1, 337a) **2 Cor 13:2; Gal 5:21** (corresponding to the words προλέγω καθὼς προεῖπον, Appian, Bell. Civ. 2, 139 §579 has the doublet προλέγομεν . . . καὶ προεροῦμεν); in warning (Nicol. Dam.: 90 fgm. 130, 97 Jac.) **1 Th 3:4** (in the above-mentioned passage from Appian, Brutus says προλέγομεν 'we', as Paul says προελέγομεν). Of a prophetic saying προλέγει ἡμῖν (a quot. fr. Is follows) 1 Cl 34:3 (Appian, Bell. Civ. 1. 71 §326 the priests in charge of the sacrifices foretell what is to happen; Just., D. 41, 3 [fr. Mal.]).

❷ **to say/express someth. at a point of time that is prior to another point of time, *state beforehand/earlier*** (προεῖπον 2b) pf. pass. ὡς προλέλεκται *as has been stated above* (Ps.-Demetr., Eloc. 89) EpilMosq 5.—M-M.

προμαρτύρομαι mid. dep. (PLond IV, 1356, 32 [710 AD]) **to speak with solemn assurance about someth. that is to happen, *bear witness to beforehand, predict*** τὶ *someth.* **1 Pt 1:11** (the form in the v.l. fr. προμαρτυρέομαι, is found PLond IV, 1343, 27 [709 AD]).—DELG s.v. μάρτυς. M-M. TW.

προμελετάω (Aristoph.; Ps.-X., Rep. Ath. 1, 20; Pla. et al.; Philo, Fuga 36) **to prepare beforehand by giving careful thought and attention, *practice beforehand, prepare*** (of practicing a speech Aristoph., Eccl. 116) w. inf. foll. (B-D-F §392, 2) πρ. ἀπολογηθῆναι *prepare one's defense* (for a court appearance) **Lk 21:14.**—DELG s.v. μέλω. TW.

προμεριμνάω **to worry beforehand, *concern oneself*** or ***be anxious beforehand*** w. indir. quest. foll. **Mk 13:11.**—DELG s.v. μέριμνα. TW.

προνηστεύω 1 aor. προενήστευσα (Hdt. 2, 40; Hippocr. ed. Littré VII 412; VIII 178) ***fast beforehand*** D 7:4.—DELG s.v. 1 νῆστις.

προνοέω 1 aor. 3 sg. προενόησεν Wsd 13:16, inf. προνοῆσαι (Just., D. 116, 2); mid. pf. 2 pl. προνενόησθε (Ath. 1, 3); aor. mid.-pass. impv. 2 sg. προνοήθητι 2 Macc 14:9, subj. 3 sg. προνοηθῇ Da 11:37 (Hom. et al.; ins, pap, LXX; Just.; Tat. 2, 2; Ath.) 'to think about someth. beforehand'

❶ **to give careful thought to, *take thought for, take into consideration, have regard for*** w. gen. foll. (Jos., Ant. 1, 53 ἀρετῆς) ἁγνείας Pol 5:3. τοῦ καλοῦ ἐνώπιον θεοῦ 6:1. W. acc. καλὰ ἐνώπιον κυρίου (cp. Pr 3:4 for this and Pol 6:1) **2 Cor 8:21.** Foll. by πῶς so *that* D 12:4.—The mid. in the same sense (Thu.+; ins, pap, LXX, Philo; Jos., Ant. 9, 3; 19, 309 al.; Just., A I, 44, 11; Ath. 1, 3), w. acc. (X., Mem. 4, 3, 12) καλὰ ἐνώπιον πάντων ἀνθρώπων **Ro 12:17;** cp. **2 Cor 8:21 v.l.**

❷ **to think about beforehand in a solicitous manner, *care for, provide for someone/someth.*** w. gen. (X.+; Maximus Tyr. 5, 4c [προνοεῖ ὁ θεὸς τοῦ ὅλου]; ins [e.g. New Docs 7, 234 no. 10, 23], pap; Wsd 13:16; Philo, Virt. 216; Just., D. 1, 4 al.) τῶν ἰδίων καὶ μάλιστα οἰκείων *his own people and especially the members of his family* **1 Ti 5:8** (Horapollo 2, 108 ὑπὸ τ. οἰκείων προνοούμενος; New Docs 8, 113–16); the v.l. has the mid. in the same sense (Horap., loc. cit. προνοούμενος ἑαυτοῦ).—M-M. DELG s.v. νόος. TW.

πρόνοια, ας, ἡ (πρόνοος 'prudent'; Aeschyl., Ag. 683, Ch. 606; Hdt.+; ins, pap, LXX; TestSol 1:13 D; EpArist, Philo, Joseph., apolog. exc. Mel.) **thoughtful planning to meet a need, *forethought, foresight, providence***

ⓐ of God esp. with reference to divine beneficence (trag.; Hdt, 3, 108, 1; X., Mem. 1, 4, 6; 4, 3, 6; Pla., Tim. 30b; 44c; Polyb. 23, 17, 10; Posidonius in Diog. L. 7, 138; Diod. S. 1, 1, 3; 3, 57, 5; 4, 47, 1 θεῶν πρόνοια al.; Diog. L. 3, 24; Plut., Mor. 425f; 436d; Achilles Tat. 7, 10, 1; Herm. Wr. 1, 19; 12, 14; 21; in Stob. p. 514, 24; 516, 5 Sc. ἡ ἄνω πρόνοια p. 418, 28 Sc.; SIG 700, 29 [117 BC] μετὰ τῆς τῶν θεῶν προνοίας; POslo 148 [II/I BC] τῇ τ. θεῶν προνοίᾳ; POxy 1682, 6; SJCh 78, 5; Wsd; 3 and 4 Macc; EpArist 201; SibOr 5, 227; 323. Philo wrote a work titled Περὶ προνοίας [Eus., PE 2, 18, 6; 7, 20, 9; 8, 13, 7]; Jos., Bell. 3, 391; 7, 453, Ant. 2, 60; 349 al.; Ar. 1, 1; Just.; Tat. 2, 1; Ath.; cp. Cicero, De Natura Deorum 2, 73f; New Docs 3, 143f numerous pap reff.) 1 Cl 24:5; AcPlCor 2:19. W. σοφία (Ael. Aristid. 36, 123 K.=48 p. 488 D.) Hv 1, 3, 4 (Leutzsch, Hermas 391 n. 119).

ⓑ of humans **Ac 24:2.** πρόνοιαν ποιεῖσθαί τινος *make provision for someth., be concerned for* or *about someth.* (Demosth.; Polyb.; Dionys. Hal. 10, 1; Plut.; SIG 734, 5 τᾶς εὐσεβείας and oft. of pers. distinguished for ἀρετή or excellence [s. index];

POxy 899, 17; PFlor 2, 207; PLond 1912 [letter of Claudius], 103 [41 AD] and oft.; Da 6:19; EpArist 80; Jos., C. Ap. 1, 9, Vi. 62) τῆς σαρκὸς πρόνοιαν μὴ ποιεῖσθε εἰς ἐπιθυμίας **Ro 13:14** (Philo, Ebr. 87 σαρκῶν ποιεῖσθαι πρόνοιαν). ἑνὸς γὰρ ἐποιήσατο πρ., τοῦ μηδὲν ... παραλιπεῖν *(Mark) was primarily concerned ... to omit nothing* or *made provision for one thing, to omit* ... Papias (2:15).—JAmann, D. Zeusrede d. Ail. Arist. '31, 73ff.—Renehan '75. Larfeld I 499. New Docs 8, 109–116. DDD 1263–66. DELG s.v. νόος. M-M. TW. Sv.

προοδοιπορέω 1 aor. ptc. προοδοιπορήσας (Lucian, Hermot. 27; Diog. L. 7, 176; Jos., Ant. 3, 2; Mel., P. 54, 396) prim. 'travel, go on before'. Euphemist. (as consolatory component suggesting that the departed have some control over their destiny) for ***die before now*** οἱ προοδοιπορήσαντες πρεσβύτεροι 1 Cl 44:5; τῶν οὕ]τως προοδυπορ[ούντω]ν=προοδοιπορούντων (restoration by Testuz) *those (false teachers) who thus go on before him (to final judgment)* AcPlCor 2:37. S. κοιμάω 2.—DELG s.v. ὁδός.

προοδοιπόρος, ον (late and rare; s. prec. entry and Hesychius s.v. ὁδουρός) ***going before,*** subst. ὁ, ἡ προοδοιπόρος of vice as (ἡ) προοδοιπόρος τῶν ἁμαρτιῶν ἡμῶν *the forerunner of our sins* 2 Cl 10:1.

προοιδα (Hdt. et al.; Epict. 2, 10, 5; PSI 349, 8 [III BC]; Wsd 19:1; 4 Macc 4:25; Just., D. 103, 4; Ath. 21, 5) perf. (w. pres. mng.), ptc. προειδώς; plpf. προῄδειν ***know beforehand/previously*** w. gen. (Menand., Peric. 472 S. [222 Kö.]; Polyb. 5, 13, 5 τὸ μέλλον; Herodian 7, 1, 9) **Ac 2:31 v.l.;** IPhld 7:2 v.l. (s. Bihlmeyer ad loc.). Foll. by acc. and inf. 1 Cl 43:6.

προοικονομέω (Aristot. et al.; Joseph.) ***arrange beforehand/previously*** w. acc. of thing and dat. of pers. Χριστὸν Ἰησοῦν τὸν προοικονομοῦντα Παύλῳ *Christ Jesus, who was looking out for Paul* AcPl Ha 7, 24.—DELG s.v. οἶκος.

προοράω (Hdt. et al.; ins, pap, LXX, JosAs 23:8; Philo, Joseph.) 2 aor. προεῖδον (Hom. et al.); pf. προεώρακα; impf. mid. προορώμην **Ac 2:25** (on this form B-D-F §66, 2; Mlt-H. 190); aor. pass. ptc. n. προοραθέν (Mel., P. 57, 418 Ch.) (Hdt., Thu., X. et al. in various senses).

➊ **to see in advance, *foresee*** w. an eye to the future τὶ (X., Cyr. 2, 4, 21 τοῦτο προϊδὼν ὡς; Jos., Ant. 10, 142; JosAs 23:8) ITr 8:1. W. ὅτι foll. **Gal 3:8.** Abs. (Jos., Bell. 2, 619) προϊδὼν ἐλάλησεν **Ac 2:31.**

➋ **to see at a time prior to the present, *see previously*** ἦσαν προεωρακότες Τρόφιμον ἐν τῇ πόλει σὺν αὐτῷ *they had previously seen Trophimus in the city with (Paul)* **Ac 21:29.** The perf. tense and the temporal sense of προ- provide the basic components for this mng.

➌ mid. **have before one's eyes, *see before one,*** w. acc. (Menand., Peric. 132 S. [12 Kö.]; SIG 569, 13; UPZ 42, 22 [162 BC]; Philo) τινά *someone* προορώμην τὸν κύριον ἐνώπιόν μου **Ac 2:25** (Ps 15:8).—M-M.

προορίζω 1 aor. προώρισα, pass. προωρίσθην (Demosth. 31, 4 codd.; Heliod. 7, 24, 4; TestSol 12:3; Sopater Rhet. [V AD]: Rhet. Gr. V p. 152, 20; var. pap fr. VI AD in non-Christian usage) **decide upon beforehand, *predetermine,*** of God (Iren. 2, 33, 5 [Harv. I 380, 5]) τινά *someone* **Ro 8:30.** Foll. by acc. w. inf. **Ac 4:28.** W. final εἰς foll.: τὶ *someth.* **1 Cor 2:7;** τινά *someone* **Eph 1:5.** τινά τι *someone as someth., to be someth.* **Ro 8:29.** Pass. w. inf. foll. IEph ins Foll. by εἰς τὸ εἶναι **Eph 1:11 (12).**—RLiechtenhan, D. göttl. Vorherbestimmung bei Pls u. in d. posidonianischen Philosophie 1922; HBraun, Qumran u. d. NT II, '66, 243–50. S. also προγινώσκω.—DELG s.v. ὅρος. TW.

προπάσχω 2 aor. προέπαθον (Soph., Hdt.+; Appian, Liby. 51 §223; 52 §225; Jos., Vi. 250) ***suffer previously*** προπαθόντες *after we had already suffered* **1 Th 2:2.**—M-M. TW.

προπάτωρ, ορος, ὁ (Pind., Hdt.+; Cass. Dio 44, 37; Lucian, Alex. 43; Ps.-Plut., Mor. 106f; OGI 446, 3; PGiss. 25, 16 [II AD]; 3 Macc 2:21 [of God]; TestAbr A 8 p. 85, 28 [Stone p. 18, 28]; TestLevi 9:1; Philo, Op. M. 145; Jos., Ant. 4, 26; 19, 123; Just., A I, 32, 3 and 14 Ἰούδας γὰρ προπάτωρ Ἰουδαίων, ἀφ' οὗ καὶ τὸ Ἰουδαῖοι καλεῖσθαι ἐσχήκασι=Judah was the ancestor of the Judeans, and fr. him they got to be called Judeans).

➊ **primary founder of a family, *ancestor,*** of Abraham as ancestral founder (Jos., Bell. 5, 380) **Ro 4:1** (the Cynics call Diogenes προπάτωρ: ADieterich, E. Mithrasliturgie 1903, p. 161, 1).

➋ **archetypal founder, *ultimate ancestor*** ὁ τῶν ὅλ]ων δεσπότης ο[ὐκ ἔστ]ι (πατὴρ) ἀλλὰ προπά[τωρ κτλ.] Ox 1081 36–38//SJCh 90, 17 (s. WTill TU 60, 5 ['55] p. 57).—DELG s.v. πατήρ. M-M.

προπέμπω impf. προέπεμπον; fut. 3 pl. προπέμψουσιν Judth 10:15; 1 aor. προέπεμψα, pass. προεπέμφθην (Hom. et al.; ins, pap, LXX; TestSol 22:16 P; JosAs 22:7; Ar. [Milne p. 76 ln. 38]; Just., D. 19, 4) 'send forth'.

➊ **to conduct someone who has a destination in mind, *accompany, escort*** (Soph., Hdt.+; PFlor 206, 2; LXX; JosAs; Jos., Bell. 2, 631, Ant. 20, 50; Just.) προέπεμπον αὐτὸν εἰς τὸ πλοῖον *they accompanied him to the ship* **Ac 20:38.** ἕως ἔξω τῆς πόλεως *escort outside the city* **21:5.**

➋ **to assist someone in making a journey, *send on one's way*** with food, money, by arranging for companions, means of travel, etc. (1 Macc 12:4; 1 Esdr 4:47; EpArist 172) τινά *someone* **1 Cor 16:11.** W. δέχεσθαι Pol 1:1. σπουδαίως **Tit 3:13.** ἀξίως τοῦ θεοῦ **3J 6.** W. the destination given οὗ ἐὰν πορεύωμαι **1 Cor 16:6.** Pass. w. ὑπό τινος **Ac 15:3.** Also w. the destination: εἰς τὴν Ἰουδαίαν **2 Cor 1:16;** ἐκεῖ **Ro 15:24.**—M-M.

προπετής, ές (πρό, πίπτω) gen. **οῦς** (Pind.+), lit. 'falling down or forward'; in our lit. only fig. **pert. to being impetuous, *rash, reckless, thoughtless*** (Isocr., Pla.; Appian, Bell. Civ. 3, 43 §176; et al.; Pr 10:14; 13:3; Sir 9:18; Jos., Ant 5, 106, Vi. 170) **2 Ti 3:4.** W. αὐθάδης 1 Cl 1:1. μηδὲν π. πράσσειν *do nothing rash* **Ac 19:36** (schol. on Soph., Aj. 32 p. 5 μὴ προπετές τι πράσσειν; Menand., Peric. 1017 S. [439 Kö.] προπετὲς ποιεῖν μηδέ; 1019 S. [441 Kö.] τί πράξω προπετές; Jos., Ant. 15, 82).—DELG s.v. πίπτω. M-M. Spicq.

προπορεύομαι fut. προπορεύσομαι (X. et al.; POxy 1144, 3; 5; 9 [I/II AD]; LXX) ***go on before*** w. gen. of pers. (Aristot. 844b, 5; LXX) **Ac 7:40** (Ex 32:1, 23). ἐνώπιόν τινος **Lk 1:76** shows the influence of OT usage, though the v.l. πρὸ προσώπου τινός is also found in the LXX.—The metaph. προπορεύσεται ἔμπροσθέν σου ἡ δικαιοσύνη B 3:4 (Is 58:8) also has an OT background (but cp. X., Cyr. 4, 2, 23 πορεύεσθε ἔμπροσθεν).—DELG s.v. πόρος. M-M.

πρός prep. expressing direction 'on the side of', 'in the direction of': w. gen. 'from', dat. 'at', or acc. (the most freq. usage in our lit.) 'to' (s. the lit. s.v. ἀνά. beg.) (Hom.+).

➊ w. gen. (pseudepigr. only TestSol 10:4 C; apolog. exc. Ar.) **marker of direction or aspect from which someth. is determined, *to the advantage of, advantageous for*** (Thu. 3, 59, 1 οὐ πρὸς τῆς ὑμετέρας δόξης τάδε; Hdt. 1, 75; Dionys. Hal. 10,

30, 5; Diod. S. 18, 50, 5; Lucian, Dial. Deor. 20, 3; Mel., HE 4, 26, 8; Ath. 36, 1; B-D-F §240; Rob. 623f) οἱ πρ. ζωῆς μαζοί *the life-giving breasts* 1 Cl 20:10. πρ. τῆς σωτηρίας *in the interest of safety* **Ac 27:34** (πρὸς τῆς σ. as Jos., Ant. 16, 313).

❷ w. dat. (pesudepigr. only TestSol 6:4 D; TestAbr [s. below]; JosAs 19:1.—Just.; Mel., HE 4, 26, 7; Ath., R. 22 p. 75, 10) **marker of closeness of relation or proximity**

ⓐ of place ***near, at, by*** (Hom. et al. incl. Aristarch. Samos 398, 20; LXX; TestSol 6:4 D; Jos., Ant 8, 349; 381) **Mk 5:11;** *around* **Rv 1:13.** πρ. τῇ θύρᾳ ἑστηκέναι *stand at the door* (Menand., fgm. 420, 1; 830 K.=352, 1; 644 Kö.; JosAs 19:1) **J 18:16;** cp. **20:11.** πρὸς τῇ πύλῃ GJs 4:4; ἐγγίζοντος αὐτοῦ πρ. τῇ καταβάσει τοῦ ὄρους *when he came close to the slope of the mountain* **Lk 19:37** (s. κατάβασις). πρ. τῇ κεφαλῇ, τοῖς ποσίν *at the head, at the feet* **J 20:12.** τὰ πρ. ταῖς ῥίζαις *the parts near the roots* Hs 9, 1, 6; 9, 21, 1. In geographical designations Μαγνησία ἡ πρ. Μαιάνδρῳ *Magnesia on the Maeander* IMagnMai ins.—(Cp. the temporal use: πρὸς ἑσπέρᾳ ἐστίν *it takes place at evening* TestAbr B 2 p. 106, 7 [Stone p. 60]; cp. Just., D. 105, 3 and 5; 142, 1.)

ⓑ ***in addition to*** (Hom. et al.; Polyb., Just.; Mel., HE 4, 26, 7; Ath., R. 22 p. 75, 10; ins) πρὸς τούτοις (SIG 495, 105; 685, 70 and 100; 796 B, 30; 888, 35 al.; UPZ 26, 18; 25 [163 BC]; 2 Macc 4:9; 5:23; 9:17, 25; 14:4, esp. 12:2; Philo, Aet. M. 67 al.; Just., A I, 40, 5; D. 93, 4 al.) 1 Cl 17:1.

❸ w. acc. (pseudepigr. and apolog. throughout) **marker of movement or orientation toward someone/someth.—ⓐ** of place, pers., or thing ***toward, towards, to,*** after verbs

α. of going; s. ἄγω 5, ἀναβαίνω 1αα, ἀνακάμπτω 1a, ἀπέρχομαι 1b, διαβαίνω, διαπεράω, εἴσειμι, εἰσέρχομαι 1bα, ἐκπορεύομαι 1c, also ἐπισυνάγομαι **Mk 1:33,** ἔρχομαι 1aβ, ἥκω 1d et al.—προσαγωγὴ πρὸς τὸν πατέρα **Eph 2:18.** εἴσοδος **1 Th 1:9a.**

β. of sending; s. ἀναπέμπω **Lk 23:7, 15; Ac 25:21,** ἀποστέλλω 1bα, πέμπω.

γ. of motion gener.; s. βληθῆναι (βάλλω 1b), ἐπιστρέφω 1a, 4ab, κεῖμαι 2, πίπτω 1bαא and ב, προσκολλάω, προσκόπτω 1, προσπίπτω.

δ. of leading, guiding; s. ἄγω 1a, ἀπάγω 2a and 4, also ἕλκω 2 end **J 12:32,** κατασύρω, etc.

ε. of saying, speaking; s. ἀποκρίνομαι 1, also δημηγορέω **Ac 12:21,** εἶπον 1a, λαλέω 2aγ and 2b, λέγω 1bγ et al. Hebraistically λαλεῖν στόμα πρὸς στόμα *speak face to face* (Jer 39:4; ApcEsdr 6:6 p. 31, 10 Tdf.) **2J 12b; 3J 14** (cp. PGM 1, 39 τὸ στόμα πρὸς τὸ στόμα). πρὸς ἀλλήλους *to one another, with each other, among themselves:* s. ἀντιβάλλω, διαλαλέω, also διαλέγομαι **Mk 9:34,** διαλογίζομαι **8:16; Lk 20:14,** εἶπον **24:32; J 16:17; 19:24,** λαλέω, λέγω et al. πρὸς ἑαυτούς *to themselves, to each other:* s. διαλογίζομαι 1; εἶπον **Mk 12:7; J 7:35;** λέγω (Ps.-Callisth. 2, 15, 7 πρὸς ἑαυτὸν ἔλεγεν; Just., D. 62, 2) **Mk 10:26; 16:3.** διαθήκην ὁ θεὸς διέθετο πρὸς τοὺς πατέρας ὑμῶν, λέγων πρὸς Ἀβραάμ *God made a covenant with your fathers, when he said to Abraham* **Ac 3:25** (διατίθημι 1). ὅρκον ὀμνύναι πρ. τινα (ὀμνύω, end) **Lk 1:73.**

ζ. of asking, praying δέομαι **Ac 8:24.** εὔχομαι (s. εὔχομαι 1; cp. 2 Macc 9:13) **2 Cor 13:7.** προσεύχομαι (cp. 1 Km 12:19; 2 Esdr 12:4; 2 Macc 2:10) Hv 1, 1, 9. γνωρίζεσθαι πρὸς τὸν θεόν **Phil 4:6** (γνωρίζω 1).—Also after nouns like δέησις, λόγος et al. **Ro 10:1; 15:30; 2 Cor 1:18** al.

ⓑ of time ***near, at,*** or ***during (a certain time)*—α.** denoting approach *toward* (X., Pla. et al.) πρὸς ἑσπέραν *toward evening* **Lk 24:29** (so Just., D. 97, 1; s. ἑσπέρα).

β. of temporal duration *for* πρὸς καιρόν *for a time, for a while* (καιρός 1a) **Lk 8:13; 1 Cor 7:5.** πρὸς καιρὸν ὥρας (καιρός 1a) **1 Th 2:17.** πρὸς ὥραν *for an hour,* i.e. for a short time **J 5:35; 2 Cor 7:8; Gal 2:5a; Phlm 15;** MPol 11:2. πρὸς ὀλίγας ἡμέρας **Hb 12:10.** Also πρὸς ὀλίγον **Js 4:14;** GJs 19:2 (ὀλίγος 3). πρὸς τὸ παρόν *for the present* **Hb 12:11** (πάρειμι 1b).

ⓒ of goal ***(aiming) at*** or ***(striving) toward*—α.** with conscious purpose *for, for the purpose of, on behalf of* οὗτος ἦν ὁ πρὸς τὴν ἐλεημοσύνην καθήμενος *this was the one who sat (and begged) for alms* **Ac 3:10.** πρὸς τὴν ἔνδειξιν τῆς δικαιοσύνης αὐτοῦ **Ro 3:26.** τοῦτο πρὸς τὸ ὑμῶν αὐτῶν σύμφορον λέγω **1 Cor 7:35a;** cp. **35b.** ἐγράφη πρὸς νουθεσίαν ἡμῶν **10:11.** Cp. **Ro 15:2; 1 Cor 6:5; 2 Cor 4:6; 7:3; 11:8; Eph 4:12.**—W. acc. of the inf. (Polyb. 1, 48, 5; PRyl 69, 16; BGU 226, 22; Jer 34:10; 2 Macc 4:45; TestJob 45:4; Jos., Ant. 14, 170; 15, 148 al.; Just., D. 132, 1) πρὸς τὸ θεαθῆναι τοῖς ἀνθρώποις *in order to be seen by men* **Mt 23:5;** cp. **6:1.** πρὸς τὸ κατακαῦσαι αὐτά **13:30.** πρὸς τὸ ἐνταφιάσαι με **26:12.** πρὸς τὸ ἀποπλανᾶν εἰ δυνατὸν τοὺς ἐκλεκτούς **Mk 13:22.** πρὸς τὸ μὴ ἀτενίσαι υἱοὺς Ἰσραήλ **2 Cor 3:13.** Cp. **Eph 6:11a; 1 Th 2:9; 2 Th 3:8; Js 3:3 v.l.**

β. gener. of design, destiny (Demetr.[?]: 722 fgm. 7 Jac. πρὸς τὴν κάρπωσιν; TestJob 42:7 τὰ πρὸς θυσίαν; Jos., Bell. 4, 573 τὸ πρ. σωτηρίαν φάρμακον) τῷ θεῷ πρὸς δόξαν *for the glory of God* **2 Cor 1:20** (on πρὸς δόξαν cp. SIG 456, 15; 704e, 21; 3 Macc 2:9; Just., A I, 15, 10 μηδὲν πρὸς δόξαν ποιεῖν). τῇ πυρώσει πρὸς πειρασμὸν ὑμῖν γινομένῃ **1 Pt 4:12.**—After adjectives and participles *for* ἀγαθὸς πρὸς οἰκοδομήν **Eph 4:29** (ἀγ. 1a) ἀδόκιμος **Tit 1:16.** ἀνεύθετος πρὸς παραχειμασίαν **Ac 27:12.** γεγυμνασμένος **Hb 5:14.** δυνατός **2 Cor 10:4.** ἐξηρτισμένος **2 Ti 3:17.** ἕτοιμος (q.v. b) **Tit 3:1; 1 Pt 3:15.** ἱκανός (q.v. 2) **2 Cor 2:16.** ὠφέλιμος **1 Ti 4:8ab; 2 Ti 3:16.**

γ. of the result that follows a set of circumstances *(so that)* πάντα πρὸς οἰκοδομὴν γινέσθω *everything is to be done in such a way that it contributes to edification* **1 Cor 14:26;** cp. vs. **12; Col 2:23** (but see εδ below); **1 Ti 4:7.** ὁ βλέπων γυναῖκα πρὸς τὸ ἐπιθυμῆσαι αὐτήν *one who looks at a woman with sinful desire* **Mt 5:28,** but s. εε below. λευκαί εἰσιν πρὸς θερισμόν *they* (the fields) *are white, so that the harvest may begin* **J 4:35.** αὕτη ἡ ἀσθένεια οὐκ ἔστιν πρὸς θάνατον *this disease is not of the kind that will lead to death* **11:4.** Cp. ἁμαρτία πρὸς θάνατον **1J 5:16f.**

ⓓ of relationship (hostile or friendly), ***against, for*—α.** hostile *against, with* after verbs of disputing, etc.; s. ἀνταγωνίζομαι, γογγύζω, διακρίνομαι (διακρίνω 5b), διαλέγομαι 1, πικραίνομαι (πικραίνω 2), στασιάζω, ἔστην (ἵστημι B3). ἐστίν τινι ἡ πάλη πρός **Eph 6:12.** ἔχειν τι πρός τινα *have anything (to bring up) against someone* **Ac 24:19.** μομφὴν ἔχειν πρός τινα **Col 3:13.** πρᾶγμα ἔχειν πρός τινα **1 Cor 6:1** (πρᾶγμα 4). ἐγένετο γογγυσμὸς τῶν Ἑλληνιστῶν πρὸς τοὺς Ἑβραίους **Ac 6:1.** τὸ στόμα ἡμῶν ἀνέῳγεν πρὸς ὑμᾶς **2 Cor 6:11** (ἀνοίγω 7). ἐν ἔχθρᾳ ὄντες πρὸς αὐτούς **Lk 23:12.** βλασφημίαι πρὸς τὸν θεόν **Rv 13:6** (cp. TestJob 25:10 εἰπὲ ἓν ῥῆμα πρὸς τὸν θεόν). ἀσύμφωνοι πρ. ἀλλήλους *unable to agree among themselves* **Ac 28:25** (Tat. 25, 2); cp. the structure of **Col 2:23.**

β. friendly *to, toward, with, before* ἐργάζεσθαι τὸ ἀγαθόν **Gal 6:10ab** (ἐργάζομαι 2a). μακροθυμεῖν **1 Th 5:14.** εἰρήνην ἔχειν πρὸς τὸν θεόν **Ro 5:1** (s. εἰρήνη 2b). παρρησίαν ἔχειν πρὸς τ. θεόν **1J 3:21;** cp. **5:14.** πίστιν ἔχειν πρὸς τ. κύριον Ἰ. **Phlm 5.** πεποίθησιν ἔχειν πρὸς τ. θεόν **2 Cor 3:4.** ἔχειν χάριν πρὸς ὅλον τὸν λαόν **Ac 2:47** (FCheetham, ET 74, '63, 214f). πραΰτητα ἐνδείκνυσθαι **Tit 3:2.** ἐν σοφίᾳ περιπατεῖν **Col 4:5.** ἤπιον εἶναι πρὸς πάντας **2 Ti 2:24.**—After substantives: πίστις **1 Th 1:8** (cp. 4 Macc 15:24; Just., D. 121, 2); παρρησία **2 Cor 7:4;** κοινωνία **6:14;** συμφώνησις vs. **15** (cp. Is 7:2).

ⓔ to indicate a connection by marking a point of reference, ***with reference/regard to*****—α.** *with reference to* (Ocellus Luc. c. 42 πρὸς ἡμᾶς=with reference to us) ἔγνωσαν ὅτι πρὸς αὐτοὺς τὴν παραβολὴν εἶπεν *they recognized that he had spoken the parable with reference to them* **Mk 12:12; Lk 20:19;** cp. **12:41** (Vita Aesopi cod. G 98 P. οἱ Σάμιοι νοήσαντες πρὸς ἑαυτοὺς εἰρῆσθαι τοὺς λόγους; Just., D. 122, 3 ταῦτα … πρὸς τὸν χριστὸν … εἴρηται). ἔλεγεν παραβολὴν πρὸς τὸ δεῖν προσεύχεσθαι *he told them a parable about the need of praying* **18:1** (Just., D. 90, 5 σύμβολον … πρὸς τὸν χριστόν). οὐδεὶς ἔγνω πρὸς τί εἶπεν αὐτῷ *nobody understood with respect to what (=why) he said (this) to him* **J 13:28.** πρὸς τὴν σκληροκαρδίαν ὑμῶν *with reference to* (i.e. *because of*) *your perversity* **Mt 19:8; Mk 10:5** (Just., D. 45, 3). Cp. **Ro 10:21a; Hb 1:7f.** οὐκ ἀπεκρίθη αὐτῷ πρὸς οὐδὲ ἓν ῥῆμα *he did not answer him a single word with reference to anything* **Mt 27:14** (s. ἀποκρίνομαι 1). ἀνταποκριθῆναι πρὸς ταῦτα **Lk 14:6** (s. ἀνταποκρίνομαι). ἀπρόσκοπον συνείδησιν ἔχειν πρὸς τὸν θεόν *have a clear conscience with respect to God* **Ac 24:16.**

β. as *far as … is concerned, with regard to* (Maximus Tyr. 31, 3b) πρὸς τὴν πληροφορίαν τῆς ἐλπίδος **Hb 6:11.** συνιστάνοντες ἑαυτοὺς πρὸς πᾶσαν συνείδησιν ἀνθρώπων *we are recommending ourselves as far as every human conscience is concerned = to every human conscience* (πρός w. acc. also stands simply for the dative; s. Mayser II/2 p. 359) **2 Cor 4:2.** τὰ πρὸς τὸν θεόν *that which concerns God* or as adverbial acc. *with reference to what concerns God* (Soph., Phil. 1441; X., De Rep. Lac. 13, 11; Ps.-Isocr. 1, 13 εὐσεβεῖν τὰ πρὸς τ. θεούς; SIG 204, 51f; 306, 38; Mitt-Wilck. I/2, 109, 3 εὐσεβὴς τὰ πρὸς θεούς; Ex 4:16; 18:19; Jos., Ant. 9, 236) **Ro 15:17; Hb 2:17; 5:1.** τὰ πρός τι *that which belongs to someth.; that which is necessary for someth.* (Plut., Mor. 109b; Jos., Ant. 12, 405 τὰ πρὸς τὴν μάχην; 14, 27; a standard term in state documents) τὰ πρὸς ἀπαρτισμόν **Lk 14:28 v.l.** τὰ πρὸς εἰρήνην (TestJud 9) vs. **32;** *what makes for peace* **19:42.** Cp. **Ac 28:10; 2 Pt 1:3.**

γ. elliptically τί πρὸς ἡμᾶς (sc. ἐστιν); *what is that to us?* **Mt 27:4.** τί πρὸς σέ; *how does it concern you?* **J 21:22f** (cp. Epict. 4, 1, 10 τί τοῦτο πρὸς σέ; Plut., Mor. 986b; Vi. Aesopi I 14 p. 265, 4 Eberh. τί πρὸς ἐμέ; ApcMos 11 οὐ πρὸς ἡμᾶς ἡ πλεονεξία σου).

δ. *in accordance with* ὀρθοποδεῖν πρὸς τὴν ἀλήθειαν **Gal 2:14.** πρὸς τὸ κένωμα *in accordance with the emptiness* Hm 11:3. πρὸς τὸ θέλημα in *accordance w. the will* **Lk 12:47;** Hs 9, 5, 2. πρὸς ἃ ἔπραξεν **2 Cor 5:10.** πρὸς ὅ **Eph 3:4.**—*In comparison with, to be compared to* (Pind., Hdt. et al.; Ps.-Luc., Halc. 3 πρὸς τὸν πάντα αἰῶνα=[life is short] in comparison to all eternity; Sir 25:19; TestJob 18:8; 23:8; Just., D. 19, 2 οὐδὲν … πρὸς τὸ βάπτισμα τοῦτο τὸ τῆς ζωῆς ἐστι; Tat. 29, 1 ὀρθοποδεῖν πρὸς τὴν ἀλήθειαν) ἄξια πρός **Ro 8:18** (RLeaney, ET 64, '52f; 92 interprets Col 2:23 in the light of this usage). Cp. IMg 12.

ε. expressing purpose πρὸς τό w. inf. (s. Mayser II/1 p. 331f) *in order to, for the purpose of* **Mk 13:22; Ac 3:19 v.l.** Perh. **Mt 5:28** (s. cγ above).

ⓕ in adverbial expressions (cp. πρὸς ὀργήν = ὀργίλως Soph., Elect. 369; Jos., Bell. 2, 534. πρὸς βίαν = βιαίως Aeschyl., Prom. 208, 353, Eum. 5; Menand., Sam. 559 S. [214 Kö.]; Philo, Spec. Leg. 3, 3. πρὸς ἡδονήν Jos., Ant. 7, 195; 12, 398; Just., A II, 3, 2 πρὸς χάριν καὶ ἡδονὴν τῶν πολλῶν) πρὸς φθόνον prob.=φθονερῶς *jealously* **Js 4:5** (s. φθόνος, where the lit. is given). πρὸς εὐφρασίαν *w. joy* AcPl Ox 6, 9f (cp. Aa 1 p. 241, 1 ὑπερευφραινομένη).

ⓖ ***by, at, near*** πρός τινα εἶναι *be (in company) with* someone **Mt 13:56; Mk 6:3; 9:19a; 14:49; Lk 9:41; J 1:1f; 1 Th 3:4; 2 Th 2:5; 3:10; 1J 1:2.** διαμένειν **Ac 10:48** D; **Gal 2:5b.** ἐπιμένειν **1:18; 1 Cor 16:7.** παραμένειν **16:6** (v.l. κατα-). μένειν **Ac 18:3** D. παρεῖναι **12:20; 2 Cor 11:9; Gal 4:18, 20;** cp. παρουσία πρὸς ὑμᾶς **Phil 1:26.** παρεπιδημεῖν 1 Cl 1:2. ἐποίησεν τρεῖς μῆνας πρὸς τὴν Ἐλισάβεδ GJs 12:3. πρὸς σὲ ποιῶ τὸ πάσχα **Mt 26:18b.** Cp. also **2 Cor 1:12; 7:12; 12:21; 2 Th 3:1; Phlm 13; 1J 2:1;** Hm 11:9b v.l.—πρὸς ἑαυτούς *among* or *to themselves* **Mk 9:10** (in case πρὸς ἑ. belongs w. τὸν λόγον ἐκράτησαν; B-D-F §239, 1). πρὸς ἑαυτὸν προσηύχετο *he uttered a prayer to himself* **Lk 18:11.** Cp. **24:12.**—δεδεμένον πρὸς θύραν *tied at a door* **Mk 11:4.** τὴν πᾶσαν σάρκα ἀνθρώπων πρὸς ἡδονὴν ἐδέσμευεν *(Satan) bound all humankind to self-gratification* AcPlCor 2:11. πρὸς τ. θάλασσαν *by the seaside* **Mk 4:1b.** On πρὸς τὸ φῶς *at the fire* **Mk 14:54; Lk 22:56** s. B-D-F §239, 3; Rob. 625 (perh. w. the idea of turning toward the fire; s. also 4 Km 23:3). πρὸς ἓν τῶν ὀρέων *at one of the mountains* 1 Cl 10:7. τὰ πρὸς τὴν θύραν *the place near the door* **Mk 2:2.** πρὸς γράμμα *letter by letter* Hv 2, 1, 4.—On πρός τι terms s. PWouters, The Treatment of Relational Nouns in Ancient Grammar: Orbis 38, '95, 149–78 (lit.). M-M. EDNT. TW. Sv.

προσάββατον, ου, τό (Jdth 8:6; Ps 91:1 S; Ps 92:1; Bull. de l'Inst. franç. d'Archéol. orient. 30, '31, pp. 4–6) **the day before the Sabbath,** i.e. ***Friday,*** used to explain the word παρασκευή **Mk 15:42.** Also in the fgm. of the Diatessaron fr. Dura (CKraeling, A Gk. Fgm. of Tatian's Diatessaron fr. Dura: Studies and Documents [ed. KLake and SLake] III '35; s. ASyn. 348, 30).—DELG s.v. σάββατα. M-M.

προσαγορεύω fut. 2 sg. προσαγορεύσεις Dt 23:7; 1 aor. προσηγόρευσα. Pass.: 1 aor. προσηγορεύθην; pf. 3 sg. προσηγόρευται; plpf. 3 sg. προσηγόρευτο (Just.).

❶ **to say hello,** ***greet*** (Aeschyl., Hdt. et al.; OGI 771, 48; oft. in pap; cp. Dt 23:7? [w. dat. as JosAs 7:9]) τινά *someone* MPol 20:2ab.

❷ **to refer to someone by name or some other term,** ***call, name, designate*** (X., Pla. et al.; ins, pap, LXX; TestSol 6:2; TestLevi 16:3; AscIs 3:10) w. acc. of obj. and also of predicate (X., Mem. 3, 2, 1; Plut., Aem. 258 [8, 3]; ins; Wsd 14:22; 2 Macc 1:36) of Christ as bestower of numerous bounties υἱοὺς ἡμᾶς προσηγόρευσεν *he addresssed us as a father does his sons* 2 Cl 1:4. Pass. (Pla. et al.; Diod. S. 1, 4, 7; 13, 98, 3; 40, 3, 3; 1 Macc 14:40; 2 Macc 4:7; 14:37; Demetr.: 722 fgm. 1, 3 Jac.; Philo, Agr. 66, Abrah. 121, Mos. 2, 109; 112; Jos., Bell. 3, 35, Ant. 15, 293, C. Ap. 1, 250) **Hb 5:10.** Of Abraham φίλος προσηγορεύθη τοῦ θεοῦ 1 Cl 17:2; cp. 10:1 (s. Ἀβραάμ and φίλος 2aβ).—DELG s.v. ἀγορά. M-M.

προσάγω 2 aor. προσήγαγον, impv. προσάγαγε, inf. προσαγαγεῖν; pf. 3 pl. προσαγειόχασιν Lev 10:19. Pass.: impf. προσηγόμην; 1 fut. 3 sg. προσαχθήσεται Lev 14:2; 1 aor. προσήχθην (Hom.+; ins, pap, LXX, EpArist, Philo, Joseph., Test12Patr, apolog.).

❶ trans. **bring into someone's presence,** ***bring (forward)***

ⓐ lit. τινά *someone* **Ac 12:6 v.l.;** B 13:5a. Pass. MPol 9:1f. προσάγαγε ὧδε τὸν υἱόν **Lk 9:41.** W. acc. to be supplied Ἰωσὴφ προσήγαγεν (αὐτόν) εἰς … B 13:5b (πρ. τινὰ εἴς τι Herodian 1, 5, 1). τινά τινι *bring someone to someone* **Ac 16:20;** B 13:4 (Gen 48:9); pass. **Mt 18:24 v.l.**

ⓑ fig.**—α.** of Christ, who brings people to God (X., Cyr. 1, 3, 8 of admission to an audience with the Great King) ἵνα ὑμᾶς προσαγάγῃ τῷ θεῷ **1 Pt 3:18** (Just., D. 2, 1 al.; Jos., Ant. 14, 272 the mid. conveys the sense 'negotiate peace', 'reconcile').

β. as a t.t. of sacrificial procedure (Hdt. 3, 24 et al.; LXX; EpArist 45 π. θυσίας) *bring, present,* of Isaac προσήγετο θυσία 1 Cl 31:3. προσάξω αὐτὸ δῶρον κυρίῳ *I will present* *it* (the child, Mary) *to the Lord as a gift* GJs 4:1. τὴν θρησκείαν πρ. αὐτῷ (=τῷ θεῷ) *offer (cultic) worship to God* Dg 3:2 (cp. Tob 12:12; Ath. 13, 2). Abs. ὀφείλομεν πλουσιώτερον καὶ ὑψηλότερον προσάγειν τῷ φόβῳ αὐτοῦ *we ought to sacrifice all the more bountifully and richly out of fear of (God)* B 1:7; but s. 2b.

❷ intr. **to move toward a reference point,** ***come near, approach*** (Theocr. et al.; Plut., Mor. 800a, Pomp. 643 [46, 1]; SIG 1042, 3; PTebt 47, 15; Josh 3:9; 1 Km 9:18; 3 Km 18:30ab; Sir 12:13; 2 Macc 6:19; EpArist 59; Jos., Ant. 6, 52.—Anz 335).

ⓐ lit. ὑπενόουν προσάγειν τινὰ αὐτοῖς χώραν *they suspected that land was near* (lit. 'approaching them') **Ac 27:27** (vv.ll. προσανέχειν, προσεγγίζειν, προσαχεῖν).

ⓑ fig., of pers. approaching God B 2:9. προσάγειν τῷ φόβῳ αὐτοῦ (= τοῦ θεοῦ) *approach (the fear of) God* 1:7, unless πρ. here means *bring an offering* (so Lghtf. et al.; s. 1bβ).—M-M. TW.

προσαγωγή, ῆς, ἡ (Hdt. et al.; ins, pap, EpArist 42) intr. **a way of approach,** ***access*** (the intr. aspect is certain in Polyb. 10, 1, 6 access point for ships; Plut., Aem. Paul. 261 [13, 3] of ground that offered no access to enemy forces) abs. **Eph 3:12.** εἴς τι *to someth.* **Ro 5:2.** πρός τινα *to someone* **Eph 2:18.** A status factor is implied (cp. X., Cyr. 7, 5, 45 of access to Cyrus for an audience).—DELG s.v. ἄγω p. 18. M-M.

προσαιτέω fut. 3 pl. προσαιτήσουσιν Job 27:14 (Pind. et al.; PSI 349, 6; TestJob 22:3 [ἄρτον]) abs. ***beg*** (Aristoph., X., Pla. et al.; Plut., Mor. 471a; 1058d; Job 27:14) **Mk 10:46 v.l.; Lk 18:35 v.l.; J 9:8.**—M-M.

προσαίτης, ου, ὁ (Plut., Mor. 294a; Diog. L. 6, 56; Lucian, Navig. 24; cp. αἴτης· πτωχός Hesych. I 78) ***beggar*** **Mk 10:46; J 9:8.**

προσαναβαίνω fut. mid. 3 sg. προσαναβήσεται LXX; 2 aor. προσανέβην, impv. προσανάβηθι (since Plato Com. [V/IV BC], fgm. 79 K.; X.; pap, LXX) **to go up from one level to another,** ***go up, move up*** ἀνώτερον *move up (higher)* to one of the places of honor at the table **Lk 14:10.**—DELG s.v. βαίνω. M-M.

προσαναλαμβάνω (Polyb.; Diod. S. 13, 3, 3; pap) **take in besides,** ***welcome*** πάντας ἡμᾶς *us all* to the fire **Ac 28:2 v.l.**

προσαναλίσκω/προσαναλόω 1 aor. ptc. προσαναλώσας (Kühner-Bl. II p. 367. The word used since X., Pla. et al.; SIG 497, 7; cp. PCairZen 569, 152 [III BC]) **spend in addition,** ***spend lavishly*** τὶ τινι *someth. on someth.* or *someone* (Diog. L. 6, 98; Cass. Dio 43, 18; cp. Philo, Agr. 5 τί ὑπέρ τινος) ἰατροῖς προσαναλώσασα ὅλον τὸν βίον *who had spent all her assets on physicians* **Lk 8:43.**—DELG s.v. ἁλίσκομαι. M-M.

προσαναπληρόω 1 aor. προσανεπλήρωσα (Aristot.; Diod. S. 5, 71, 1; 14, 2, 4; Athen. 14, 654d; PTebt 946, 4 [III BC]; Wsd 19:4; Philo, Praem. 103. The mid. as early as Pla., Meno 84d; Ath. 17, 2) **to fill up or replenish besides,** ***supply*** τὶ *someth.* τὰ ὑστερήματά (or τὸ ὑστέρημά) τινος *supply someone's wants* **2 Cor 9:12; 11:9** (schol. on Soph., El. 32 p. 100: διὰ τ. διηγήσεως ταύτης τὸ λεῖπον τ. ἱστορίας προσανεπλήρωσεν ἡμῖν).—M-M.

προσανατίθημι 2 aor. mid. προσανεθέμην (X. et al.; ins; PTebt 99, 5 [II BC]) in our lit. only mid.

❶ **to add someth. to an existing amount,** ***add*** or ***contribute*** τινί τι *someth. to someone* (cp. X., Mem. 2, 1, 8) **Gal 2:6.** Another probability is simply ***lay before, submit*** (Vi. Aesopi W 37 P. αὐτῷ προσανάθου τὸ ζήτημα=submit the question to him; c. 83–85).

❷ **to take up a matter with,** ***consult with*** τινί *someone* (Clearchus, fgm. 76b ὀνειροκρίτῃ [Chrysipp.: Stoic. II 344]; Diod. S. 17, 116, 4 τοῖς μάντεσι; Lucian, Jupp. Tr. 1) **Gal 1:16.**—M-M. TW.

προσανέχω (Polyb.; Jos., Bell. 4, 84, Ant. 1, 15; Tat. 18, 1) ***rise up toward*** τινί *someone* (Synes., Ep. 82 p. 229a τῷ θεῷ of one distinguished for piety) **Ac 27:27 v.l.** (for προσάγειν) of land coming into sight; s. προσεγγίζω.—M-M.

προσαπειλέω 1 aor. mid. ptc. προσαπειλησάμενος (Demosth. 21, 93; Synes., Ep. 47 p. 186d; Sir 13:3 v.l.; Jos., Ant. 14, 170) ***threaten further / in addition*** **Ac 4:21.**

προσαχέω (Doric form for προσηχέω [Plut. et al.]; see Mlt-H. 71) ***resound*** of the surf, indicating that land is near by **Ac 27:27 v.l.** (resonare in mss. gig s; s. προσάγω 2a).—DELG s.v. ἠχή.

προσβαίνω 2 aor. προσέβην (Hom., Hdt., trag. X., ins, pap; 1 Esdr 4:53; 8:1; Jdth 4:7; 7:10; Joseph.) ***approach*** in our lit. only abs. (Soph., Phil. 42) προσέβην μικρόν *I drew a little closer* Hv 4, 1, 5.

προσβιάζομαι mid. dep.; fut. προσβιάσομαι; 1 aor. ptc. προσβιασάμενος (Aristoph., Pla.) **to force to do someth.,** ***compel, use force*** in our lit. only of the conduct of a martyr in the arena toward animals which show no inclination to attack him; abs. προσβιάσομαι *I will use force* IRo 5:2. προσβιασάμενος *by force* MPol 3:1.—DELG s.v. βία.

προσβλέπω fut. προσβλέψω (Ps 83:10 Sym.); 1 aor. impv. 2 sg. πρόσβλεψον (Jon 2:5 Sym., Theod.)

❶ **to fix one's gaze upon,** ***gaze at, look at*** (X., Symp. 3, 14; Plut., Cato Min. 791 [65, 11]; Lucian, Alex. 42, Dial. Mer. 11, 4; Philo, Abr. 76. In earlier Gk. [Soph. et al.] in this sense usually w. the acc., so also Philo, Op. M. 152; Just., D. 94, 3.) *look at* τοῖς ἁγίοις σκεύεσιν Ox 840, 29.

❷ **to consider from a special point of view,** ***look upon, regard,*** w. the acc. (Aeschyl., Pla., X. et al.; Vett. Val. 114, 25; SIG 1168, 44) τὸν ἐπίσκοπον ὡς αὐτὸν τὸν κύριον προσβλέπειν *regard the overseer as the Lord himself* IEph 6:1.

προσδαπανάω 1 aor. προσεδαπάνησα ***spend in addition*** (freq. used of philanthropists: Lucian, Epist. Sat. 4, 39; SIG 661, 10; 691, 8f; IPriene 118, 11) **Lk 10:35.**—DELG s.v. δάπτω. M-M.

προσδεκτός, ή, όν (προσδέχομαι; Pr 11:20; 16:15; Wsd 9:12) **pert. to being received as completely satisfactory,** ***acceptable*** ἐνώπιον τοῦ ποιήσαντος ἡμᾶς 1 Cl 7:3. θυσία MPol 14:2. ἔντευξις Hs 2:6.—DELG s.v. δέχομαι A.

προσδέομαι (Hdt. et al.) pass. dep. fut. 3 sg. προσδεηθήσεται (Sir 13:3); 1 aor. 3 sg. προσεδεήθη (Sir 42:21) orig. 'need in addition / further' (so Thu. et al.; ins; pap; Pr 12:9; Sir; Jos., Ant. 7, 340; Ar. 10, 2—but the force of the προσ is no longer felt e.g. in Epict. 1, 16, 1; SIG 313, 11 [IV BC]; UPZ 110, 154 [164 BC]; PTebt 59, 8 [99 BC]) **to have need of someth.,** ***need,*** w. gen. of what is needed (Thu. 2, 41, 4 al.; EpArist 11; 113) Dg 3:4a. Of God, who has need of nothing 3:5; **Ac 17:25** (s. New Docs 4, 86 for the view that the force of πρός may be felt here: 'God needs nothing [beyond what he has] from anyone . . .'.); cp. Dg 3:3, 4b (a Gr-Rom. commonplace: Pla., Tim. 34b; Aristot., Eth. Eud. 7, 12; 'Onatas' the Pythagorean in Stob., Ecl.

1, 1, 39 vol. I 49, 20 W. [Norden, Agn. Th. 14]; Philo, Op. M. 13; 46; cp. Eur., Herc. Furens 1345f: H. asks, δεῖται γὰρ ὁ θεὸς, εἴπερ ἔστ' ὀρθῶς θεός, οὐδενός;=Is God, if he is indeed God, in need of anything?).—DELG s.v. 2 δέω. M-M. TW.

προσδέχομαι (Hom. et al.; ins, pap, LXX; TestJob 42:8; TestLevi 16:5; TestAsh 4:3; Just.) mid. dep.; impf. προσεδεχόμην; fut. προσδέξομαι (LXX); 1 aor. προσεδεξάμην; pass. προσεδέχθην.

❶ **to receive favorably, *take up, receive, welcome*** (Aeschyl., Hdt. et al.; also EpArist 257).—ⓐ w. acc. of pers. ***receive in a friendly manner*** (Pla., Leg. 4, 708a; Jos., Ant. 6, 255; TestLevi 16:5; Just., A I, 10, 1 and D 33, 2) ἁμαρτωλούς **Lk 15:2.** τινὰ ἐν κυρίῳ *welcome someone in the Lord,* i.e. as a Christian brother or sister (cp. 1 Ch 12:19) **Ro 16:2; Phil 2:29.** ἵνα ἡμᾶς προσδέξηται ὡς υἱούς 2 Cl 9:10 (Diod. S. 17, 37, 4 Ἀλέξανδρον ὡς θεὸν προσεδέξαντο). Pass. MPol 14:2.

ⓑ w. acc. of thing (Jos., Ant. 14, 30) ***receive*** οἱ δὲ ὡς περὶ βρώσεως προσεδέξαντο (i.e. τὰ δόγματα) *they took* (the decrees) *as if they really dealt with food* B 10:9.—*Receive willingly, put up with* (Hdt. et al.; see Pla., Phileb. 15b ὄλεθρον) τὴν ἁρπαγὴν τῶν ὑπαρχόντων **Hb 10:34.** τὰ ἐνεργήματα ὡς ἀγαθά B 19:6; D 3:10. ἐλπίδα, ἣν καὶ αὐτοὶ οὗτοι προσδέχονται.—W. a negative *refuse to accept, reject* (Jos., Ant. 6, 42; Just., D 117, 2) τὸ βάπτισμα B 11:1. τὴν ἀπολύτρωσιν **Hb 11:35** (ἀπολύτρωσις 1).

❷ **to look forward to, *wait for*** (Hom. et al.; Jos., Ant. 14, 451)—ⓐ w. acc. of pers. (X., Cyr. 4, 5, 22) **Lk 1:21** D; **Ac 10:24** D. τὸν κύριον **Lk 12:36.**

ⓑ w. acc. of thing (X., Hiero 1, 18, Apol. Socr. 33; Herodian 3, 1, 1; SIG 1268 [Praecepta Delphica: III BC] II 21 καιρὸμ προσδέχου=wait for the [right] time) τὴν βασιλείαν τοῦ θεοῦ **Mk 15:43; Lk 23:51.** λύτρωσιν Ἰερουσαλήμ **2:38.** παράκλησιν τοῦ Ἰσραήλ vs. **25.** τὴν ἐπαγγελίαν (ἐπαγγελία 2) **Ac 23:21.** ἐλπίδα *look forward to the fulfillment of our expectation* **Tit 2:13** (cp. Job 2:9a); *await* (the realization of) **Ac 24:15.** τὸ ἔλεος τοῦ κυρίου **Jd 21.** τὴν ἐσχάτην ἡμέραν Hv 3, 12, 2; cp. 3, 13, 2. ἀφθαρσίαν Dg 6:8.

ⓒ abs. ***wait*** ἡμέραν ἐξ ἡμέρας *wait day after day* 2 Cl 11:2 (prophetic saying of unknown origin).—M-M. TW.

προσδέω 1 aor. προσέδησα; pass. pf. 3 impv. pl. προσδεδέσθωσαν 1 Cl 27:1; ptc. fem. acc. προσδεδεμένην (Just., D. 53, 2 [on Mk 11:4]) **to fasten by binding, *tie, bind***

ⓐ lit. (Hdt.; Hippocr.; Diod. S. 17, 41; Lucian, Dial. Deor. 6, 5; Ps.-Lucian, Asinus 38; Plut., Pericl. 167 [28, 2]; SIG 1169, 41; 4 Macc 9:26; TestSol 10:8 P; Just., D. 53, 2 [on Mk 11:4]) τινά MPol 14:1 to a stake.

ⓑ fig., pass. (Sir 18:32; Jos., Ant. 5, 135 ἡδονῇ προσδεδεμένοι) ***be bound securely*** τινί *to someone* 1 Cl 27:1.—DELG s.v. 1 δέω.

προσδηλόω fut. προσδηλώσω (Aristot., Anal. Post. 2, 7, 92b, 23) **to clarify in addition, *explain further*** (in a second letter) IEph 20:1 (w. a rel. clause foll.).—DELG s.v. δῆλος.

προσδίδωμι (trag., Isocr., X. et al.; ins, pap, LXX) **to distribute in shares, *give (over), apportion*** (s. L-S-J-M s.v. II) **Lk 24:30** D.

προσδοκάω impf. προσεδόκων; fut. προσδοκήσω (Just.); 1 aor. προσεδόκησα. Pass.: impf. προσεδοκώμην; aor. inf. προσδοκηθῆναι (Just. D, 142, 1) (s. προσδοκία; Aeschyl., Hdt. et al.; pap, LXX; TestSol 13:8 C [προσδοκέω] Philo, Joseph.) **to give thought to something that is viewed as lying in the future, *wait for, look for, expect*** the context indicates whether one does this in longing, in fear, or in a neutral state of mind.

ⓐ w. acc. of pers. (Jos., Bell. 5, 403; Just.) **Mt 11:3; Lk 1:21; 7:19f; 8:40; Ac 10:24;** 1 Cl 23:5 (Mal 3:1); IMg 9:3; IPol 3:2; GJs 24:1.

ⓑ w. acc. of thing (La 2:16; Ps 118:166; TestJob 12:3; Philo; Jos., Bell. 5, 528 φαῦλον, Ant. 7, 114 τὰ βελτίω; Ar. 15:3 ἀνάστασιν νεκρῶν) **2 Pt 3:12–14;** Dg 8:11; 12:6; Hv 3, 11, 3. Pass. (Appian, Illyr. 17 §51 προσδοκωμένου τοῦ πολέμου=since the war was to be expected) θάνατος προσεδοκᾶτο *death was to be expected* Dg 9:2 (act.: Achilles Tat. 3, 2, 1 τ. θάνατον πρ.).

ⓒ abs., though the obj. is to be supplied fr. the context (Himerius, Or. 62 [Or. 16], 8; Philo, Leg. All. 2, 43) **Mt 24:50; Lk 3:15; 12:46; Ac 27:33; 28:6b.**

ⓓ foll. by acc. and inf. (Appian, Bell. Civ. 4, 51 §220; 2 Macc 12:44; Jos., Ant. 5, 340; 7, 213; Just., A I, 18, 6 al.) **Ac 28:6a.**

ⓔ w. inf. foll. (TestJob 7:4;Jos., Ant. 15, 358; Just., D. 125, 5 al.) **Ac 3:5;** Dg 4:6; Hs 1:2 (B-D-F §350; 397, 2; Rob. 1036).—M-M. TW.

προσδοκία, ας, ἡ (προσδοκάω; Thu., X., Pla. et al.; pap, LXX; PsSol ins; TestJos 7:6; Philo; Jos., Ant. 15, 58 al.) **expectation of someth. that is to happen, whether good or bad, *expectation*** w. obj. gen. (cp. for the obj. gen. and use w. φόβος Plut., Anton. 951 [75, 4] φόβος καὶ προσδοκία τοῦ μέλλοντος, Demetr. 895 [15, 4]; Philo, Abr. 14; Jos., Ant. 3, 219 κακοῦ πρ.) τῶν ἐπερχομένων **Lk 21:26.** W. subj. gen. πρ. τοῦ λαοῦ **Ac 12:11.**—DELG s.v. δοκάω. M-M. TW.

προσδραμών s. προστρέχω.

προσεάω (PLond V, 1790, 7 in fgm. context [V–VI AD 'permit as well') ***permit to go farther*** τινά *someone* **Ac 27:7.**—M-M.

προσεγγίζω fut. 3 sg. προσεγγιεῖ LXX, 1 pl. προσεγγιοῦμεν (TestJob 31:1); 1 aor. προσήγγισα **to move toward a reference point, *approach, come near*** (Polyb. 38, 7, 4; Diod. S. 3, 16, 4; Hero Alex. III p. 218, 22; Leonidas Tarent. 35, 6 Gef.: Anth. Pal. 7, 442, 6; LXX; TestJob; Test12Patr) **Mk 2:4 v.l.;** of land from the perspective of a sailor whose ship approaches it **Ac 27:27 v.l.** (for προσάγειν; s. προσανέχω). εἰς τὴν Καισάρειαν **10:25** D.—DELG s.v. ἐγγύς. TW.

προσεδρεύω (Eur. et al.; Theosophien 180, §56, 6; 1 Macc 11:40) **to be beside so as to be in attendance, *attend, serve, wait upon,*** lit. 'sit near' w. dat. (Aristot., Pol. 8, 4, 4, 1338b, 25; Demosth. 1, 18; Diod. S. 5, 46, 3 πρ. ταῖς τῶν θεῶν θεραπείαις; Ael. Aristid. 48, 9 K.=24 p. 467 D.: τ. θεῷ. Also ins, pap; TestSol 3:7 C; Jos., C. Ap. 1, 30 τῇ θεραπείᾳ τοῦ θεοῦ; Archäolog.-epigr. Mitteilungen aus Österreich 6, 1882 p. 23 no. 46: an association of Σαραπιασταί has as officials οἱ προσεδρεύοντες τῷ ἱερῷ) τῷ θυσιαστηρίῳ **1 Cor 9:13 v.l.** τῷ ναῷ *serve in the temple* GJs 23:1 (v.l. παρεδρεύω).—DELG s.v. ἕζομαι. Frisk s.v. ἕδρα.

προσεθέμην s. προστίθημι.

προσέθηκα s. προστίθημι.

I. πρόσειμι (from εἰμί; Aeschyl., X., Pla.+; ins, pap; Sir 13:24 v.l.; Jos., C. Ap. 1, 61; Just., Tat.; Ath. 1, 4, R. 20 p. 73, 19ff) pres. ptc. fem. dat. προσούσῃ (Just., A I, 7, 5); n. pl. προσόντα

(Just.); impf. 3 sg. προσῆν (Tat. 32, 3) **to belong to as an addition, *belong to, be present with, be an attribute/custom of*** τινί *someone* (Nicolaus Com. 1, 41 πάντα πρόσεστί μοι; Herodas 1, 19; Diog. L. 2, 37; Dio, Ep. 2 τὰ προσόντα αὐτῷ) βία οὐ πρόσεστι τῷ θεῷ Dg 7:4.

II. πρόσειμι (from εἶμι; Hom.+; ins, pap; 4 Macc; TestSol 20:2 P; Jos., Bell. 2, 324; Ath. R. 11 p. 60, 15) **to make movement towards, *approach, come forward*** MPol 4.

προσεκλίθην s. προσκλίνω.

προσελαβόμην s. προσλαμβάνω.

προσέλευσις, εως, ἡ (POxy 283, 19 [I AD] and oft in pap) ***access*** ἕξομεν τὴν προσέλευσιν *we shall have access (to the Lord)* AcPl Ha 8, 22f (restored fr. Ox 1602, 32f).

προσελεύσομαι s. προσέρχομαι.

προσελήλυθα s. προσέρχομαι.

πρόσελθε s. προσέρχομαι.

προσενέγκαι, προσένεγκε, προσενεγκεῖν, προσένεγκον, προσενεχθείς, προσενήνοχα s. προσφέρω.

προσεξομολογέομαι D 14:1 s. προεξομολογέομαι.—DELG s.v. ὁμός.

προσέπεσον s. προσπίπτω.

προσεργάζομαι 1 aor. προσηργασάμην or προσειργασάμην—B-D-F §67, 3; see also Mlt-H. 189f (Eur., Hdt. et al.; pap; var. senses) **to earn in addition, *make more*** (X., Hell. 3, 1, 28; PCairZen 509, 13) ἡ μνᾶ σου δέκα προσηργάσατο μνᾶς *your mina has made ten minas more* **Lk 19:16.**—DELG s.v. ἔργον. M-M.

προσέρχομαι mid. dep.; impf. προσηρχόμην; fut. προσελεύσομαι; 2 aor. προσῆλθον (also προσῆλθα B-D-F §81, 3; Mlt-H. 208); pf. προσελήλυθα; plpf. 1 pl. προσεληλύθειμεν (Just., A II, 2, 3) (Aeschyl., Hdt.+) prim. 'come, go to, approach'.

➊ **to move towards**—ⓐ of physical movement ***come/go to, approach*** (esp. oft. in Mt, about 50 times; s. JEdwards, JBL 106, '87, 65–74) w. dat. of pers. (X., Cyr. 1, 4, 27; Aelian, VH 9, 3, end; En 14:25; Jos., Ant. 12, 19; Just., D. 2, 4 al.) **Mt 5:1; 8:5; 9:14** al.; **Lk 23:52; J 12:21; Ac 9:1; 10:28** 'visit'; **18:2;** MPol 16:1; GJs 20:4 (deStrycker; without dat. Tdf.). W. dat. of place (Herodian 2, 6, 5) **Hb 12:18, 22;** AcPl Ha 11, 13; εἰς Ἱερουσαλήμ 8, 30. Abs. **Mt 4:11; Lk 9:42; Ac 8:29; 20:5 v.l.** (s. CMaurer, TZ, 3, '47, 321–37). MPol 4. Uncertain AcPl Ha 2, 2. The ptc. is freq. used w. verbs denoting an activity, to enliven the narrative προσελθὼν εἶπεν (cp. BGU 587, 2 [II BC]; Jos., Ant. 9, 194) **Mt 4:3; 8:19; 18:21;** see also **13:10; 15:12; 25:20, 22, 24; Mk 6:35; 14:45; Lk 9:12.** πρ. προσεκύνει **Mt 8:2; 9:18 v.l.,** et al. πρ. ἔπεσεν **26:39 v.l.;** cp. **Mk 14:35 v.l.,** et al. (s. προέρχομαι 1). Foll. by inf. denoting purpose (1 Macc 2:23) προσῆλθον οἱ μαθηταὶ αὐτοῦ ἐπιδεῖξαι *his disciples came up to show* **Mt 24:1.** προσερχομένου αὐτοῦ κατανοῆσαι **Ac 7:31.** Cp. **12:13.**

ⓑ of approach to or entry into a deity's presence, transf. sense of 1a: ***approach*** (Cass. Dio 56, 9, 2 τοῖς θεοῖς προσερχώμεθα; PGiss 20, 24=Mitt-Wilck. I/2, 94; Jer 7:16; Sir 1:28 μὴ προσέλθῃς αὐτῷ [=τῷ κυρίῳ] ἐν καρδίᾳ δισσῇ; Philo, Plant. 64, Deus Imm. 8; Tat. 18, 2; Ath. 18, 1) πρ. τῷ θεῷ **Hb 7:25; 11:6;** cp. 1 Cl 23:1; 29:1. W. dat. of place τῷ θρόνῳ τῆς χάριτος **Hb 4:16.** Also abs. προσέρχεσθαι means *come to* God in a cultic sense. **10:1, 22.** Some hold that πρ. in Hb may connote the forensic idea 'appear in court' (POxy 40, 4 [II/III AD]; 2783, 25 [III AD]; PRyl 234, 6 [II AD]). The cultic aspect prob. furnishes the clue to the abs. πυκνότερον προσερχόμενοι 2 Cl 17:3.—To Jesus **1 Pt 2:3** (of proselytes, FDanker, ZNW 58, '67, 95f; w. πρός as Lucian, Ver. Hist. 2, 28; Ex 34:32; Josh 14:6).

ⓒ of inanimate things, ***come upon*** transf. sense of 1a (Soph. et al.; cp. Eur., Or. 859 προσῆλθεν ἐλπίς; BGU 614, 21) πρ. τινί *someth. comes upon* or *over someone* φρίκη μοι προσῆλθεν Hv 3, 1, 5. ὑμῖν ἰσχυρότης 3, 12, 3. Without a dat., which is easily supplied fr. the context m 5, 1, 3.

➋ **to apply oneself to someth., *turn to, occupy oneself with a thing*** (Diod. S. 1, 95, 1 τοῖς νόμοις; Plut., Cato Min. 764 [12, 2]; Epict. 4, 11, 24; pap; Sir 4:15 v.l.; 6:19, 26; Philo, Agr. 123, Migr. Abr. 86 ἀρετῇ; Just., D. 112, 5 τοῖς προφητικοῖς λόγοις; PYale 83, 15) οὐ προσελεύσῃ ἐπὶ προσευχήν σου D 4:14; *devote onself to* εἴ τις μὴ προσέρχεται ὑγιαίνουσιν λόγοις **1 Ti 6:3** (s. προσέχω 2b). πρ. τῷ θελήματι αὐτοῦ (=τοῦ θεοῦ) 1 Cl 33:8.—M-M. TW.

προσευχή, ῆς, ἡ—➊ **petition addressed to deity, *prayer*** (polyth. pap BGU 1080, 4 [III AD] κατὰ τὰς κοινὰς ἡμῶν εὐχὰς καὶ προσευχάς; LXX; pseudepigr.; Jos., Bell. 5, 388, w. less prob. [s. 2] C. Ap. 2, 10, Ant. 14, 258) IEph 1:2; 5:2; 10:2; 11:2; IMg 14:1; IPhld 5:1; ISm 11:1, 3. αἱ πρ. τῶν ἁγίων **Rv 5:8; 8:3f.**—**1 Pt 3:7.** W. δέησις **Ac 1:14 v.l.; Eph 6:18; Phil 4:6;** IMg 7:1; cp. **1 Ti 2:1; 5:5** (s. δέησις). W. εὐχαριστία ISm 7:1. W. ἐλεημοσύναι **Ac 10:4;** διὰ τὴν πρ. IPol 7:1; διὰ τῶν πρ. **Phlm 22;** ἐν (τῇ) πρ. *through prayer* **Mk 9:29;** IEph 20:1; IPhld 8:2; *in prayer* IRo 9:1; ἐν ταῖς πρ. *in the prayers* IMg 14:1; ITr 13:1; **Col 4:12.** W. the same mng. ἐπὶ τῶν πρ. **Ro 1:10; Eph 1:16; 1 Th 1:2; Phlm 4;** κατὰ τὴν πρ. IPhld 10:1. ἡ πρ. τοῦ θεοῦ *prayer to God* **Lk 6:12.** Also πρ. γινομένη πρὸς τὸν θεόν **Ac 12:5;** cp. πρὸς τὸν κύριον AcPl Ha 6, 9 (πρ. πρός as Ps 68:14). ὥστε … ἐκτενῆ ὑπὸ πάντων πρ. γενέσθαι τῷ Παύλῳ *so that prayers were said fervently by all for Paul* AcPl Ha 6, 7. W. νηστεία **Mt 17:21; Mk 9:29 v.l.** Fasting called better than prayer 2 Cl 16:4a. Prayer fr. a good conscience saves fr. death, vs. 4b; drives out demons **Mk 9:29.** τὰς πρ. ἀναφέρειν πρὸς τὸν θεόν (ἀναφέρειν προσευχάς Orig., C. Cels. 8, 73, 32; s. ἀναφέρω 3) 2 Cl 2:2; προσκαρτερεῖν τῇ πρ. **Ac 1:14; Ro 12:12; Col 4:2;** cp. **Ac 2:42; 6:4** (w. τῇ διακονίᾳ). ἐκπεσεῖν τῆς πρ. AcPl Ha 2, 8. σχολάζειν τῇ πρ. **1 Cor 7:5** (on prayer and abstinence s. TestNapht 8:8); see IPol 1:3. νήφειν εἰς προσευχάς **1 Pt 4:7;** καταπαύειν τὴν πρ. MPol 8:1; ἀναπαύειν τὴν πρ. AcPl Ha 4, 32. αἰτεῖν ἐν τῇ πρ. **Mt 21:22.** προσευχῇ προσεύχεσθαι *pray earnestly* **Js 5:17.** In a kneeling position or prone on the ground; hence ἀναστὰς ἀπὸ τῆς πρ. **Lk 22:45;** ἐγείρεσθαι ἀπὸ τῆς πρ. Hv 2, 1, 3; εἰσηκούσθη ἡ πρ. **Ac 10:31;** ἀκούειν πρ. AcPl Ha 2, 14. τὸ ἴδιον ἔργον τῆς πρ. 4, 28. Public, communal *prayer* ἡ μετ' ἀλλήλων πρ. ITr 12:2. αἱ πρ. ὑπέρ τινος πρὸς τὸν θεόν *intercessions to God on behalf of someone* **Ro 15:30;** ὥρα τῆς πρ. **Ac 3:1** (s. ἔνατος and the lit. there.—On a fixed time for prayer s. Marinus, Vi. Procli 24 καιρὸς τῶν εὐχῶν; also 22, end). οἶκος προσευχῆς (=בֵּית־תְּפִלָּה Is 56:7) *house of prayer* **Mt 21:13; Mk 11:17; Lk 19:46.** On προσέρχεσθαι ἐπὶ προσευχήν D 4:14 s. προσέρχομαι 2. Cp. B 19:12.—For lit. s. προσεύχομαι, end.

➋ **a place of or for prayer, *place of prayer*** **Ac 16:13, 16.** Esp. used among Jews, this word is nearly always equivalent to συναγωγή in the sense of a cultic place (s. συναγωγή 2a; SKrauss, Pauly-W. 2 ser. IV, '32, 1287f; ins New Docs 3, 121f;

4, 201f). But many consider that the πρ. in **Ac 16:13, 16** was not a regular synagogue because it was attended only by women (vs. **13**), and because the word συν. is freq. used elsewh. in Ac (e.g. 17:1, 10, 17); the πρ. in our passage may have been an informal meeting place, perh. in the open air (s. BSchwank VD 3, '55, 279).—In the rare cases in which a polyth. place of prayer is called πρ., Jewish influence is almost always poss. (reff. fr. lit., ins and pap in Schürer II 425f; 439–47; Mayser I/3[2] '36 p. 19; Boffo, Iscrizioni 39–60. See also 3 Macc 7:20 al.; SEG VIII, 366, 6 [II BC], also reff. in XLII, 1849; Dssm., NB 49f [BS 222f]; MStrack, APF 2, 1903, 541f; Philo; perh. Jos., C. Ap. 2, 10 and Ant. 14, 258 [contradictory positions on the latter in Schürer II 441, 65 and 444, 76]; Elbogen[2] 445; 448; 452; SZarb, De Judaeorum προσευχή in Act. 16:13, 16: Angelicum 5, 1928, 91–108; also συναγωγή 2). But such infl. must be excluded in the case of the ins fr. Epidaurus of IV BC (IG IV^2/1, 106 I, 27), where the Doric form of προσευχή occurs in the sense 'place of prayer': ποτευχὰ καὶ βωμός. Hence it is also improbable in IPontEux I^2, 176, 7 and in Artem. 3, 53 p. 188, 27; 189, 2.—RAC VIII 1134–1258; IX 1–36; BHHW I 518–23. MHengel, Proseuche u. Synagoge, KGKuhn Festschr., '71, 157–84; Schürer II 423–63.—DELG s.v. εὔχομαι. M-M. EDNT. TW. Sv.

προσεύχομαι impf. προσηυχόμην; fut. προσεύξομαι; 1 aor. προσηυξάμην (on the augment s. W-H., App. 162; Tdf., Prol. 121; B-D-F §67, 1; Mlt-H. 191f) mid. dep. **to petition deity,** ***pray*** (Aeschyl., Hdt.+; PEdg 7 [=Sb 6713], 10 [257 BC]; Sb 3740 [I AD] Ἄττηος προσεύχεται τοῖς ἐν Ἀβύδῳ θεοῖς; LXX; pseudepigr.; Philo, Joseph.; Ar. [Milne 76, 37f]; Ath. 11, 2) abs. (Demochares [300 BC]: 75 fgm. 2 Jac.; Dio Chrys. 35 [52], 1) **Mt 6:5–7; 14:23; 26:36; Mk 1:35; 6:46; Lk 1:10; 5:16; Ac 1:24; 6:6; 1 Cor 11:4f** (on the topic of head covering s. PTomson, Paul and the Jewish Law [CRINT III/1] '90); **14:14b; 1 Ti 2:8** (on the topic of prayer for gentiles s. Schürer II 311f); **Js 5:13, 18;** MPol 5:2; 7:3; 12:3; Hv 1, 1, 4; 3, 1, 6; 5:1; s 9, 11, 7a; D 8:2. AcPl Ha 1, 32; 2, 12; 4, 23; 7, 19; 11, 14 (restored) and 22; AcPlCor 2:30. Followed by a prayer introduced by λέγων (Is 44:17; cp. Did., Gen. 223, 28) **Mt 26:42; Lk 22:41;** cp. **Mt 26:39; Lk 11:2** (on the Lord's Prayer see TManson, The Sayings of Jesus '54, 165–71; EGrässer, D. Problem der Parusieverzögerung, '57, 95–113; HBetz, Essays on the Sermon on the Mount '85, SM 370–86 [lit.]). W. dat. of pers. to whom the prayer is addressed (so predom. outside our lit.; see B-D-F §187, 4; cp. Rob. 538) πρ. τῷ θεῷ *pray to God* (Diod. S. 13, 16, 7 τοῖς θεοῖς; Chariton 3, 10, 6 θεῷ; Athen. 13, 32, 573d τῇ θεῷ; Philostrat., Vi. Apollon. 5, 28 p. 186, 9 τοῖς θεοῖς; Jos., Ant. 10, 252; cp. 256; τῷ ἐπὶ πᾶσι θεῷ Orig., C. Cels. 8, 26, 17) **1 Cor 11:13;** τῷ κυρίῳ πρ. (TestJos 3:3; 7:4) Hv 1, 1, 3; 2, 1, 2; τῷ πατρὶ πρ. **Mt 6:6b.** Also πρὸς τὸν θεόν (LXX; ParJer 6:1) Hv 1, 1, 9. πρὸς κύριον GJs 20:2 (pap, not codd.; but 2:4 codd., not pap). W. dat. of manner πρ. γλώσσῃ, τῷ πνεύματι, τῷ νοΐ *pray in a tongue, in the spirit, with understanding* **1 Cor 14:14a, 15;** ἐν πνεύματι πρ. **Eph 6:18;** cp. **Jd 20** (s. Borger, GGA 140); προσευχῇ πρ. *pray earnestly* **Js 5:17.** ἀδιαλείπτως **1 Th 5:17;** IEph 10:1; Hs 9, 11, 7b. ἀδεῶς MPol 7:2a. πρ. ὑπέρ τινος *pray for someone* or *someth.* (Philostrat., Vi. Apoll. 8, 26 p. 340, 5; LXX; ApcMos 36; Ath.; Hippol., Ref. 9, 23, 3) **Mt 5:44** (cp. Ro 12:14 and Plut., Mor. 275d); **Col 1:9;** IEph 10:1; 21:2; ISm 4:1; D 1:3. Also πρ. περί τινος (LXX; s. περί 1f) **Lk 6:28; Col 1:3; 1 Th 5:25; Hb 13:18;** ITr 12:3; MPol 5:1; D 2:7; GJs 8:2. Foll. by ἵνα (B-D-F §392, 1c) **Mt 24:20; 26:41; Mk 13:18; 14:38; Lk 22:40, 46.** τοῦτο πρ. ἵνα **Phil 1:9.** περί τινος ἵνα **Col 4:3; 2 Th 1:11; 3:1.** περί τινος ὅπως **Ac 8:15.** ὑπέρ τινος ὅπως **Js 5:16 v.l.** Foll. by gen. of inf. w. art. (B-D-F §400, 7; Rob. 1094) τοῦ μὴ βρέξαι **Js 5:17.** πρ. ἐπί τινα (ἐπί 1cγ) vs. **14** (cp. Marinus, Vi. Procli 20b: Proclus, on his deathbed, has his friends recite hymns to him). W. acc. foll., which refers to the content or manner of the prayer (Philostrat., Vi. Apoll. 6, 18 p. 229, 32) ταῦτα πρ. **Lk 18:11.** μακρὰ πρ. *make long prayers* **Mk 12:40; Lk 20:47.**—W. acc. of the thing prayed for πρ. τι *pray for someth.* (X., Hell. 3, 2, 22 νίκην) **Mk 11:24; Ro 8:26** (on the ability of the ordinary person to pray see Philosoph. Max. p. 497, 7 μόνος ὁ σοφὸς εἰδὼς εὔχεσθαι=only the wise man knows how to pray).—FHeiler, Das Gebet[5] 1923 (lit.); FDölger, Sol Salutis: Gebet u. Gesang im christl. Altert.[2] 1925 (material fr. history of religions); JDöller, Das G. im AT in rel.-gesch. Beleuchtung 1914; AGreiff, Das G. im AT 1915; JHempel, G. u. Frömmigkeit im AT 1922, Gott u. Mensch im AT[2] '36; Elbogen[2] 353ff; 498ff.—EvdGoltz, Das G. in der ältesten Christenheit 1901; IRohr, Das G. im NT 1924; JMarty, La Prière dans le NT: RHPR 10, 1930, 90–98; JNielen, G. u. Gottesdienst im NT '37; HGreeven, G. u. Eschatologie im NT '31. LRuppoldt, D. Theol. Grundlage des Bittgebetes im NT, diss. Leipzig '53; AHamman, La Prière, I (NT), '59.—JoachJeremias, D. Gebetsleben Jesu: ZNW 25, 1926, 123–40; AJuncker, Das G. bei Pls 1905, Die Ethik des Ap. Pls II 1919, 55–72; CSchneider, Αγγελος IV '32, 11–47 (Paul); EOrphal, Das Plsgebet '33; J-AEschlimann, La Prière dans S. Paul '34; GHarder, Pls u. d. Gebet '36; AKlawek, Das G. zu Jesus 1921; AFrövig, D. Anbetung Christi im NT: TTK 1, 1930, 26–44; EDelay, A qui s'adresse la prière chr.? RTP 37, '49, 189–201.—OHoltzmann, Die tägl. Gebetsstunden im Judentum u. Urchristentum: ZNW 12, 1911, 90–107, HWagenvoort, Orare: Precari: Verbum, HWObbink Festschr., '64, 101–11 (prayer among the Romans); RMerkelbach, MTotti, eds., Abrasax: Ausgewählte Papyri religiösen u. magischen Inhalts, I: Gebete '90; FHickson, Roman Prayer Language '93; JCharlesworth, ed., The Lord's Prayer and Other Prayer Texts fr. the Greco-Roman Era '94 (lit. 186–201); MKiley, ed., Prayer fr. Alexander to Constantine (tr. only) '97.— B. 1471. M-M. EDNT. TW.

προσέχω impf. προσεῖχον; fut. προσέξω LXX; 2 aor. προσέσχον (1 Cl 4:2=Gen 4:5); pf. προσέσχηκα; plpf. 2 pl. προσεσχήκειτε (Just., D. 64, 3); verbal adj. n. προσεχτέον (TestSol 13:1 C) (Aeschyl., Hdt.+). In non-biblical wr. the prim. mng. 'have in close proximity to'; freq. act. as mostly in our lit. of mental processes 'turn one's mind to' (so in the phrase πρ. τὸν νοῦν τινι Aristoph. et al.; Just., D. 64, 3 al.; but also freq. without τὸν νοῦν X. et al., likew. Wsd 8:12; 1 Macc 7:11; 4 Macc 1:1).

❶ **to be in a state of alert,** ***be concerned about, care for, take care*** w. dat. χήρᾳ, ὀρφανῷ B 20:2. προσέχετε ἑαυτοῖς καὶ παντὶ τῷ ποιμνίῳ **Ac 20:28** (Sb IV, 7353, 9f [200 AD] a son advises his mother to look out for herself and not to be worried [διστάζειν] about him, for he is in a good place).—προσέχειν ἑαυτῷ *be careful, be on one's guard* (Plut., Mor. 150b νήφων καὶ προσέχων ἑαυτῷ; Gen 24:6; Ex 10:28; 34:12; Dt 4:9; 6:12 al.) **Lk 17:3;** B 4:6. W. inf. foll. 2:1. Foll. by μήποτε *take care that . . . not* or *take care lest . . .* **Lk 21:34.** Foll. by ἀπό τινος *beware of, be on one's guard against someth.* (TestLevi 9:9; TestDan 6:1.—B-D-F §149; Rob. 577) **12:1.** προσέχετε ἑαυτοῖς ἐπὶ τοῖς ἀνθρώποις τούτοις τί μέλλετε πράσσειν *take care what you propose to do with these men* **Ac 5:35** (on the function of ἐπί here, see ἐπί 14a).—The reflexive pron. can also be omitted (cp. UPZ 69, 7 [152 BC] προσέχω μή; 2 Ch 25:16; Sir 13:8) προσέχωμεν μήποτε B 4:14. προσέχετε μήπως Ox 840, 2 (Unknown Sayings 93f). προσέχειν ἀπό τινος *beware of someone* or *someth.* (Sir 6:13; 11:33; 17:14; 18:27; Syntipas p. 94, 28 πρόσεχε ἀπὸ τῶν πολιτῶν) **Mt 7:15; 10:17; 16:6, 11f; Lk 20:46;** D 6:3; 12:5. Foll. by μή and the inf. *take care not* **Mt 6:1.**

❷ **to pay close attention to someth.,** ***pay attention to, give heed to, follow***—ⓐ w. dat. of pers. (Polyb. 6, 37, 7; Cass. Dio 58, 23, 2; Diog. L. 1, 49; Jos., Bell. 1, 32, Ant. 8, 34; 264) τῷ ἐπισκόπῳ IPhld 7:1; IPol 6:1. τοῖς προφήταις ISm 7:2. Cp. **Ac 8:10f.** πρ. τοῖς φυσιοῦσίν με *pay heed to those who puff me up* ITr 4:1. πρ. πνεύμασι πλάνοις **1 Ti 4:1.**

ⓑ w. dat. of thing προσεῖχε τῷ πετάλῳ τοῦ ἱερέως *he (Joachim) took note of the priest's frontlet* GJs 5:1. Heed words or instruction (Mnesimachus Com. [IV BC] 4, 21 πρόσεχ' οἷς φράζω; Plut., Mor. 362b; PPetr II, 20 II, 1 τῇ ἐπιστολῇ; 1 Macc 7:11; Jos., Ant. 8, 241 τ. λόγοις; TestZeb 1:2; Just., D. 10, 1; Tat. 12, 3; Ath. 7, 3) πρ. τοῖς λεγομένοις ὑπὸ τοῦ Φιλίππου *pay attention to what was said by Philip* **Ac 8:6** (λέγω 1bκ); cp. **16:14.** πρ. μύθοις (Ps.-Plut., Pro Nobilitate 21, end τοῖς Αἰσωπικοῖς μύθοις προσέχοντες) **1 Ti 1:4; Tit 1:14.—Hb 2:1; 2 Pt 1:19.** ἐμαῖς βουλαῖς 1 Cl 57:5 (Pr 1:30); cp. 57:4 (Pr 1:24; w. dat. τοῖς λόγοις to be supplied).—1 Cl 2:1; 2 Cl 19:1; MPol 2:3. (τούτοις) ἃ ἐνετείλατο προσέχετε B 7:6.—Mid. *attach oneself to, cling to* w. dat. of thing (lit. and fig. trag., Hdt.+) εἴ τις μὴ προσέχεται ὑγιαίνουσιν λόγοις **1 Ti 6:3 v.l.**

ⓒ abs. *pay attention, be alert, notice* (Demosth. 21, 8; Diod. S. 20, 21, 2 οὐδεὶς προσεῖχεν; PMagd 22, 5 [221 BC]; Sir 13:13) 2 Cl 17:3; B 4:9; 7:9. προσέχετε ἀκριβῶς *pay close attention* 7:4. Foll. by indir. question: πῶς 7:7. τί 15:4. προσέχετε ἵνα *see to it that* 16:8.—προσέχετε as v.l. for προσεύχεσθε **Mt 5:44.**

ⓓ ἐπὶ ταῖς θυσίαις αὐτοῦ οὐ προσέσχεν *(God) took no notice of (Cain's) sacrifices* 1 Cl 4:2 (Gen 4:5).

❸ **to continue in close attention to someth.,** ***occupy oneself with, devote*** or ***apply oneself to*** w. dat. (Hdt. et al.; Demosth. 1, 6 τῷ πολέμῳ; Herodian 2, 11, 3 γεωργίᾳ καὶ εἰρήνῃ; POxy 531, 11 [II AD] τοῖς βιβλίοις σου) τῇ ἀναγνώσει κτλ. **1 Ti 4:13.** τῷ θυσιαστηρίῳ, *officiate at the altar* **Hb 7:13.** οἴνῳ πολλῷ πρ. *be addicted to much wine* **1 Ti 3:8** (Polyaenus, Strateg. 8, 56 τρυφῇ καὶ μέθῃ).—M-M. Sv.

προσήκω fut. προσήξω (Aeschyl., Thu.+; ins, pap, LXX; TestJud 5:2; JosAs; EpArist 29; Philo; Jos., Bell. 7, 450; Just.; Tat. 31, 1; Ath. 9, 2, R. 1 p. 49, 2 al.).

❶ in a spatial sense **to come so as to be present,** ***come to, approach*** w. dat. of pers. (Dio Chrys. 65 [15], 2) IRo 9:3 of congregations that were not on Ignatius' route.—ἐπὶ προσευχήν *come for prayer* B 19:12.

❷ qualitative **to be appropriate in a given circumstance,** ***be fitting, suitable, proper, be one's duty*** (trag., Thu. et al.; Jos., Ant. 13, 432 τὰ μὴ προσήκοντα) κατὰ τὸ προσῆκον *as is fitting* (Plut., Mor. 122a; OGI 90, 18 [196 BC]; PCairMasp 167, 16; freq. in civic documents in ref. to a high level of conduct, s. SIG IV ind.) MPol 10:2.

προσηλόω 1 aor. προσήλωσα; pass. pf. ptc. pl. προσηλωμένοι (3 Macc 4:9) (Pla. et al.; ins; Philo, De Prov. fgm. 2 [Eus., PE 8, 14, 24]; Jos., Ant. 5, 208; Just., A I, 58, 3; Mel., P. 76, 556; 80, 591) ***nail (fast)*** τί τινι *someth. to someth.* (Diod. S. 4, 47, 5) a bond to the cross **Col 2:14** (s. Dibelius, Lohmeyer ad loc.; FDölger, Die Sonne der Gerechtigkeit und d. Schwarze 1918, 129ff.—πρ. σταυρῷ='crucify' Diod. S. 2, 18, 1; Artem. 2, 56; Jos., Bell. 2, 308; Galen, De Usu Part. II 214, 8 Helmr.). *Nail* the condemned man *fast* to the pyre MPol 13:3 (the more general sense 'fasten' [Jos., Bell. 5, 232] is excluded by the specific mention of nails). Perh. here in the sense *chain fast* (cp. Lucian, Prometh. 2 κατάκλειε καὶ προσήλου, Dial. Deor. 1, 1).—DELG s.v. ἧλος. M-M.

προσήλυτος, ου, ὁ (cp. ἦλθον; also ἔλευσις) **one who has come over from polytheism to Judean religion and practice,** ***convert*** (so Goodsp., Probs. 36f; the transliterated form 'proselyte' NRSV, REB, but only **Ac 2:11,** otherwise 'convert' or 'worshiper'), a designation for a gentile won for the Israelite community through missionary efforts (the word is found in Apollon. Rhod. 1, 834 [μετοίκους καὶ προσηλύτους] and in the LXX. Plainly in a technical sense in Philo; cp. Spec. Leg. 1, 51 τούτους δὲ καλεῖ προσηλύτους ἀπὸ τοῦ προσεληλυθέναι καινῇ καὶ φιλοθέῳ πολιτείᾳ=these he [apparently Moses] calls 'proselytes' because they have 'proselyted' to a new state where love of God prevails; Sb 1742 Σάρρα προσήλυτος. Roman grave inscriptions also contain 'proselytus' or 'proselyta' [Schürer III 162, 55].—Perh. πρ. was used as a t.t. in the Isis cult [=Lat. 'advena' in Apuleius, Metam. 11, 26; s. Rtzst., Mysterienrel.[3] 193]). W. Ἰουδαῖοι **Ac 2:11.** Of Nicolaus of Antioch **6:5.** Of Jewish efforts to proselytize **Mt 23:15.**—They are to be differentiated fr. the σεβόμενοι τὸν θεόν, who had obligated themselves only to follow certain commandments; in a mixed expr. **Ac 13:43** speaks of σεβόμενοι πρ.—ABertholet, Die Stellung der Israeliten u. der Juden zu den Fremden 1896, 257ff; KAxenfeld, Die jüd. Propaganda als Vorläuferin der urchristl. Mission: Missionswissenschaftl. Studien für GWarneck 1904, 1–80; ILevi, Le Prosélytisme juif: REJ 50, 1905, 1 ff; 51, 1906, 1ff; 53, 1907, 56ff; Schürer III 150–76; HGressmann, ZMR 39, 1924, 10ff; 169ff; MMeinertz, Jesus u. die Heidenmission[2] 1925; Bousset, Rel.[3] 76ff; Billerb. I 924ff; II 715; IV 353ff; Harnack, Mission I[4] 1923, 1–23 (Eng. tr., JMoffatt[2], 1908, 1–23); GRosen, Juden u. Phönizier 1929; GMoore, Judaism I, 1927, 323–53; FDerwacter, Preparing the Way for Paul 1930; HLietzmann, Gesch. d. Alten Kirche 1, '32, 68–101; CSchneider, Ntl. Zeitgeschichte '34, 173–75; HPreisker, Ntl. Zeitgesch. '37, 290–93; WBraude, Jewish Proselyting in the First Five Centuries of the Common Era '40; SLieberman, Greek in Jewish Palestine '42: Gentiles and Semi-Proselytes, 68–90; JKlausner, From Jesus to Paul (tr. WStinespring)'43, 31–49; ESimon, Verus Israel '48; SZeitlin, Proselytes and Proselytism, etc.: HAWolfson-Festschr. '65, 871–81. Add. bibl., esp. since '65, Schürer III 1–3; ABD V 505.—Pauly-W., Suppl. IX, 1248–83; Kl. Pauly IV, 1187; BHHW IV 1515.—S. also lit. s.v. σέβω 1b.—DELG s.v. ἐλεύσομαι. M-M. EDNT. TW. Sv.

προσηνῶς (cp. Hom. antonym ἀπηνής 'ungentle'; Theophr.; Diod. S. 5, 44, 6 et al.) adv. of προσηνής, ές (Pind., Hdt. et al.; SIG 783, 29; Pr 25:25; Philo; Jos., Bell. 3, 507; Mel., P. 11, 72) **pert. to being kindly disposed,** ***kindly, gently, lovingly*** w. ἠπίως of God (Orph. Hymns 2, 5; 40, 12; 60, 7 Qu. use the adj. to characterize goddesses) 1 Cl 23:1.—DELG s.v. προσηνής.

προσηχέω s. προσαχέω.

πρόσθεν adv. (antonym of ὄπισθεν; Hom. et al.; ins, pap; Jos., Ant. 14, 370; 463; SibOr 3, 391) in our lit. only of time: **pert. to a period of time that is before another period of time,** ***earlier, former*** ὁ πρόσθεν χρόνος *the former time* (X.; SIG 85, 11; 136, 6; 165, 13) Dg 9:1, 6.—DELG.

πρόσθεσις, εως, ἡ (προστίθημι; Thu. et al.; ins, pap, LXX, Philo, in every case in a different sense than in the NT, such as 'application', etc.; e.g. Polyaenus 2, 3, 8 πρόσθεσις τοῦ θεοῦ='God's [supportive] presence') ***presentation*** ἄρτοι τῆς προσθέσεως (for προθέσεως) *(sacred) loaves of presentation* **Mt 12:4** D=**Mk 2:26** D=**Lk 6:4** D, s. πρόθεσις 1.—DELG s.v. τίθημι. Sv.

πρόσκαιρος, ον (Strabo 7, 3, 11; Ael. Aristid. 46 p. 218 D. al.; OGI 669, 14 [I AD]; SIG 1109, 44; pap; 4 Macc 15:2,

8, 23; TestSol 5:5; TestAbr B 1 p. 105, 5 [Stone p. 58]; Jos., Bell. 5, 66, Ant. 2, 51; Just.; Mel., P. 2, 9 al.) **lasting only for a time, *temporary, transitory*** (Appian, Bell. Civ. 5, 43, §179) opp. αἰώνιος (Dionys. Hal., Ars Rhet. 7, 4; 6 ἀθάνατος; Cass. Dio 12 fgm. 46, 1 ἀΐδιος) of the things in the visible world **2 Cor 4:18** (Ps.-Clem., Hom. 2, 15 ὁ μὲν παρὼν κόσμος πρόσκαιρος, ὁ δὲ ἐσόμενος ἀΐδιος; Pel.-Leg. p. 12, 26; JosAs 12:12 ἰδοὺ γὰρ πάντα τὰ χρήματα τοῦ πατρός μου Πεντεφρῆ πρόσκαιρά εἰσι κ. ἀφανῆ, τὰ δὲ δώματα τῆς κληρονομίας σου, κύριε, ἄφθαρτά εἰσι κ. αἰώνια 'behold, all the property of my father P. is transitory and evanescent, but the bounties of your inheritance, Lord, are incorruptible and eternal'). πρ. ἀπόλαυσις (s. ἀπόλαυσις) **Hb 11:25.** Of persecutions τὸ πῦρ τὸ πρ. Dg 10:8. Of a pers.: πρ. ἐστιν *lasts only a little while* (Dalman, Pj 22, 1926, 125f) **Mt 13:21; Mk 4:17.**—M-M. TW.

προσκαλέω (Soph., X., Pla.+; ins, pap, LXX; TestSol, TestAbr, Test12Patr; JosAs 23:2; AssMos fgm. a) in Gk. outside our lit. and in LXX predom. mid., in our lit. exclusively mid.; fut. 3 sg. προσκαλέσεται Ps. 49:4; 1 aor. προσεκαλεσάμην; pf. προσκέκλημαι. Pass.: 1 aor. 3 sg. προσεκλήθη LXX; 'summon'.

❶ **to call to or notify in order to secure someone's presence**

ⓐ of a call issued for presence with the speaker ***summon, call on, call to oneself, invite*** τινά *someone* (Gen 28:1; Esth 4:5; Sir 13:9; EpArist 182; Jos., Ant. 1, 271, Vi. 110; TestReub 4:9; AssMos p. 62 Denis [p. 272 Tromp]) **Mt 10:1; 15:10; Mk 3:13, 23; 6:7; 7:14; 15:44; Lk 7:18; 15:26; Ac 6:2; 23:17f, 23; Js 5:14;** Hv 1, 4, 2; s 5, 2, 2; 6; 9, 7, 1; 9, 10, 6.

ⓑ in transf. sense of God's invitation to share in the benefits of salvation ***call (to)*** God or Christ, to faith, etc. **Ac 2:39** (cp. Jo 3:5). πρ. διὰ τοῦ πνεύματος τοῦ ἁγίου *call through the Holy Spirit* (i.e. through inspired scripture) 1 Cl 22:1. Of Christ δι' οὗ (i.e. τοῦ σταυροῦ) ἐν τῷ πάθει αὐτοῦ προσκαλεῖται ὑμᾶς *by which* (i.e. the cross) *in his suffering* (or *death;* s. πάθος 1, end) *he summons you* ITr 11:2.

❷ **to call in a legal or official sense—**ⓐ as a legal t.t. (so Aristoph., Lysias et al.; pap) ***call in, summon*** for inquiry **Ac 5:40.** Perh. **Mt 18:32.**

ⓑ ***call*** to a special task or office—issued by the Holy Spirit εἰς τὸ ἔργον ὃ (=εἰς ὅ) προσκέκλημαι αὐτούς **Ac 13:2.** τινά foll. by the inf. εὐαγγελίσασθαι **16:10.**—M-M. TW.

προσκαρτερέω aor. ptc. pl. προσκαρτερήσαντες Num. 13:20 (Demosth. et al.; SIG 717, 84; OGI 383, 130; 168 al.; pap, LXX; Jos., Bell. 6, 27)

❶ **to stick by or be close at hand, *attach oneself to, wait on, be faithful to someone,*** w. dat. of pers. and emphasis on continuity (Ps.-Demosth. 59, 120; Polyb. 23, 5, 3; Diog. L. 8, 11, 14; PGiss 79 II, 9 [II AD]; PLond II, 196, 3 p. 153 [II AD]) **Ac 8:13; 10:7** a military aide. Of a boat, ***stand ready* Mk 3:9.**

❷ **to persist in someth.—**ⓐ ***busy oneself with, be busily engaged in, be devoted to,*** w. dat. of thing (τῇ πολιορκίᾳ Polyb. 1, 55, 4; Diod. S. 14, 87, 5; ταῖς θήραις Diod. S. 3, 17, 1; τῇ καθέδρᾳ Jos., Ant. 5, 130; τῇ γεωργίᾳ PAmh 65, 3; BGU 372 II, 15; PLond III, 904, 27 p. 125 [104 AD].—POxy 530, 9; PHamb 34, 9 [all the pap II AD]) τῇ προσευχῇ **Ac 1:14; Ro 12:12; Col 4:2;** cp. **Ac 6:4.** νηστείαις Pol 7:2.—Instead of the dat. εἴς τι **Ro 13:6.**—Foll. by local ἐν *spend much time in* (Sus 6 Theod. ἐν τῇ οἰκίᾳ) ἐν τῷ ἱερῷ **Ac 2:46** (also w. the dat.: τῷ ναῷ *in the temple* Did., Gen. 135, 23; Theoph. Ant. 3, 21 [p. 246, 3]). On προσκαρτερέω in Ac s. ESchürer, SBBerlAk 1897, 214f.

ⓑ ***hold fast to, continue in, persevere in*** *someth.,* w. dat. of thing (Polyb. 1, 59, 12 τῇ ἐπιμελείᾳ) τῇ διδαχῇ κτλ. (Posidon.: 87 fgm. 36, 48 Jac. τοῖς λόγοις=the teaching) **Ac 2:42** (mng. 2a is also prob.). τῇ ἐλπίδι Pol 8:1.—M-M. TW. Spicq.

προσκαρτέρησις, εως, ἡ (s. προσκαρτερέω 2; Philod., Rhet. I 11 S.; IPontEux II, 52; 53 [both end of I AD]; EHicks, JTS 10, 1909, 571f; Dssm., LO 80 [LAE 100f]) **firm persistence in an undertaking or circumstance, *perseverance, patience* Eph 6:18.**—M-M. TW. Spicq.

πρόσκειμαι (Hom.+; ins, pap, LXX; JosAs [τῷ θεῷ 'maintain allegiance to, adhere to God']; Jos., Bell. 2, 450; 542, Ant. 17, 225; Mel., P. 95, 727 [τίτλος πρόσκειται 'the inscription is attached']) defective dep.; w. dat. of thing **to be closely attached to, *be involved in, absorbed in, be devoted to*** (Soph., Ajax 406; Thales in Diog. L. 1, 44; Paus. 4, 9, 3 μαντικῇ; Thu. 7, 50, 4 and Plut., Nic. 525 [4, 1] θειασμῷ; Jos., Ant. 12, 363) Hm 10, 1, 4.—W. dat.of pers. πρόσκειται ἀνδρὶ ξένῳ (Thecla) *is an adherent of a foreigner* AcPl Ox 6, 10f (=Aa 1, 241, 13).

προσκεφάλαιον, ου, τό an object on which one may rest one's head, *pillow* (Aristoph., Hippocr. et al.; Diod. S. 13, 84, 6; Diog. L. 4, 37; pap; 1 Esdr 3:8; Ezk 13:18, 20) MPol 5:2; 12:3. Perh. the word has this mng. in **Mk 4:38** as well. But here the mng. sailor's ***cushion*** is just as likely (Cratinus Com. [V BC] 269; SIG 736, 23 [92 BC]).—DELG s.v. κεφαλή. M-M.

προσκληρόω 1 aor. pass. προσεκληρώθην (Plut., Mor. 738d; Ps.-Lucian, Amor. 3; 'allot, assign') **to be in close association, *be attached to, join,*** w. dat. *someone* (s. OGI 257, 5 [109 BC] τῷ πατρὶ ἡμῶν προσκληθέντας [s. Dittenberger's note]; UPZ 144, 18 [II BC]; Philo, Sacr. Abel. 6, Exsecr. 162, Leg. ad Gai. 3; 68 τῶν μὲν τούτῳ τῶν δὲ ἐκείνῳ προσκληρουμένων; Jos., Bell. 2, 567) **Ac 17:4.**—DELG s.v. κλῆρος. M-M. TW.

πρόσκλησις s. πρόσκλισις.—M-M.

προσκλίνω 1 aor. pass. προσεκλίθην; plpf. 3 sg. pass. προσεκέκλιτο 2 Macc 14:24 (Hom. et al.; ins; TestSol 12:3 C; Jos., Ant. 5, 193) act. 'cause to lean against'; in our lit. only pass. intr. **to incline toward, with a view to association, *attach oneself to, join someone*** w. dat. of pers. (cp. next entry; Sext. Emp., Math. 7, 324; schol. on Aristoph., Plut. 1027 τοῖς δικαίοις προσεκλίθη; 2 Macc 14:24) **Ac 5:36** (s. also προσκολλάω); 1 Cl 47:4; 63:1.—M-M.

πρόσκλισις, εως, ἡ (προσκλίνω; Polyb. 5, 51, 8; 6, 10, 10; Diod. S. 3, 27, 2; Diog. L., Prooem. 20 al.) **a relatively strong preference for someth., *inclination,*** in our lit. only in an unfavorable sense κατὰ πρόσκλισιν *in a spirit of partiality* **1 Ti 5:21** (v.l., as EpArist 5, πρόσκλησιν *summons, invitation*); cp. 1 Cl 21:7. δίχα προσκλίσεως ἀνθρωπίνης *free from human partisanship* 50:2. προσκλίσεις ποιεῖσθαι *engage in partisan strife* 1 Cl 47:3; cp. 4.—DELG s.v. κλίνω. M-M.

προσκολλάω fut. προσκολλήσω Ezk 19:1; aor. opt. 3 sg. προσκολλήσαι Dt 28:21. Pass.: 1 fut. προσκολληθήσομαι; aor. 3 sg. προσεκολλήθη LXX; in our lit. only pass., used intr. with the lit. sense 'stick to' (Jos., Ant. 7, 12, 4 of a sword sticking to the hand of a valiant warrior with the blood of his slain enemies) shifting metaph. to human relationships **to adhere to closely, *be faithfully devoted to, join*** w. dat. (Pla., Phd. 82e, Leg. 5, 728b; POxy 1901, 26; Sir 6:34; 13:16; TestBenj 8:1) **Ac 5:36 v.l.** (for προσεκλίθη).—Of the attachment felt by a husband for his wife (after Gen 2:24) τῇ γυναικί (LXX v.l.) **Mt 19:5 v.l.;** πρὸς τὴν γυν. (LXX, text; Philo, Leg. All. 2, 49) **Mk 10:7; Eph**

5:31 (of a wife in relation to her husband POxy 1901, 26; 41; 43; 63).—DELG s.v. κόλλα. M-M. TW.

πρόσκομμα, ατος, τό (προσκόπτω; 'bruise' as result of stumbling Plut., Mor. 1048c; Athen. 3, 97f; 'stumbling, offense' LXX; TestReub 4:7)

❶ **act of stumbling,** *stumbling* itself—ⓐ λίθος προσκόμματος *a stone that causes people to stumble* (Sir 31:7 ξύλον προσκόμματος; Is 8:14 λίθου πρόσκομμα) metaph., of Christ **Ro 9:32f; 1 Pt 2:8.**

ⓑ fig. διὰ προσκόμματος ἐσθίειν i.e. 'eat and stumble in the process' **Ro 14:20** (διά A 3c). Some would put this under 2.

❷ **opportunity to experience inward pain (take offense) or make a misstep,** ***cause for offense, cause for making a misstep***

ⓐ lit. of things against which one can stumble or that can cause one to lose one's footing *obstacle, hindrance* of a rough road ἔχει ἀνοδίας καὶ προσκόμματα πολλά Hm 6, 1, 3.

ⓑ fig. τιθέναι πρόσκομμα τῷ ἀδελφῷ *give a member an occasion to experience inward pain or offense, put an obstacle in a member's way* (s. ἀδελφός) **Ro 14:13** (w. σκάνδαλον). βλέπετε μή πως ἡ ἐξουσία ὑμῶν πρόσκομμα γένηται τοῖς ἀσθενέσιν *take care that your freedom does not somehow turn out to be a hindrance to the weak,* or *cause the weak to stumble* **1 Cor 8:9.** σεμνότης, ἐν ᾗ οὐδὲν πρόσκομμά ἐστιν πονηρόν *reverence, in which there is no evil cause for offense* Hm 2:4.—JLindblom, Z. Begriff 'Anstoss' im NT: Strena Philologica Upsaliensis 1922, 1–6. S. σκάνδαλον, end.—DELG s.v. κόπτω. EDNT. TW.

προσκοπή, ῆς, ἡ (προσκόπτω; Polyb.)=πρόσκομμα 2b (q.v.) ***an occasion for taking offense*** or ***for making a misstep,*** fig. διδόναι προσκοπήν **2 Cor 6:3.** As the succeeding purpose clause indicates, Christians are not to provide outsiders with any reason for finding fault with the Christian message, either because of conduct contrary to the cultural ethos or alleged undermining of morals.—DELG s.v. κόπτω. TW.

προσκόπτω fut. 3 sg. προσκόψει LXX; 1 aor. προσέκοψα (Aristoph., X. et al.; SIG 985, 41; pap, LXX; En 15:11).

❶ **to cause to strike against someth.,** ***strike against,*** trans. τὶ *someth.* (Aristoph., Vesp. 275 πρ. τὸν δάκτυλον ἐν τῷ σκότῳ) πρός τι *against someth.* πρὸς λίθον τὸν πόδα σου (Ps 90:12) **Mt 4:6; Lk 4:11** (imagery in both).

❷ **to make contact w. someth. in a bruising or violent manner,** ***beat against, stumble,*** intr. (of the blind Tobit, Tob 11:10; Pr 3:23; Jer 13:16) ἐάν τις περιπατῇ ἐν τῇ ἡμέρᾳ, οὐ προσκόπτει **J 11:9;** cp. vs. **10.** Of winds προσέκοψαν τῇ οἰκίᾳ *they beat against the house* **Mt 7:27** (preferred to προσέπεσαν for vs. 25 by JWilson, ET 57, '45, 138).

❸ **to experience or cause offense,** fig. ext. of 1 and 2

ⓐ ***take offense at, feel repugnance for, reject*** (Polyb. 1, 31, 7; 5, 7, 5; 6, 6, 3 and 6; Diod. S. 4, 4, 6; 4, 61, 7 διὰ τὴν ὑπερβολὴν τῆς λύπης προσκόψαντα τῷ ζῆν=reluctant to go on living because of his overwhelming grief; 17, 30, 4; Epict. 1, 28, 10; 3, 22, 89; M. Ant. 6, 20; 10, 30) προσέκοψαν τῷ λίθῳ τοῦ προσκόμματος (πρόσκομμα 1a; προσκόπτω of 'striking one's foot against a stone' Vi. Aesopi I c. 66) **Ro 9:32;** cp. **1 Pt 2:8** (cp. also Diod. S. 15, 6, 3 προσκόπτειν τοῖς ῥηθεῖσι=take offense at the words). ἔν τινι **Ro 14:21** (on πρ. ἐν cp. Sir 32:20).

ⓑ ***give offense*** (Polyb. 5, 49, 5; 7, 5, 6; Epict. 4, 11, 33; Sir 31:17) w. dat. of pers. (Posidippus Com., fgm. 36 K. προσέκοψε τῷ ἀνθρώπῳ; Diod. S. 6, 7, 6 Διί; 17, 77, 7 al.; Aesop, Fab. 417b H.//350b Ch.//39b H-H. πρ. ἀνθρώποις) μᾶλλον ἀνθρώποις προσκόψωμεν ἢ τῷ θεῷ 1 Cl 21:5.—Lit. s.v. πρόσκομμα, end.—M-M. TW.

προσκρούω (Pl. et al.; POxy 531, 10 [AD II]; LXX; TestGad; TestJob 20:5 v.l.; Jos.) **to strike against with force,** ***strike against*** τὶ *someth.* **Mt 7:25 v.l.** (for προσπίπτω); **27 v.l.** (for προσκόπτω, apparently in the interest of the stronger imagery conveyed by κρούω).

προσκυλίω 1 aor. προσεκύλισα (Aristoph., Vesp. 202 al.; Polyaenus 2, 31, 3) ***roll (up to)*** τὶ *someth.* λίθον τῇ θύρᾳ *a stone to the opening* **Mt 27:60;** also ἐπὶ τὴν θ. **Mk 15:46; Lk 23:53 v.l.**—DELG s.v. κυλίνδω.

προσκυνέω (κυνέω 'to kiss') impf. προσεκύνουν; fut. προσκυνήσω; 1 aor. προσεκύνησα (trag., Hdt.+. Freq. used to designate the custom of prostrating oneself before persons and kissing their feet or the hem of their garment, the ground, etc.; the Persians did this in the presence of their deified king, and the Greeks before a divinity or someth. holy.) **to express in attitude or gesture one's complete dependence on or submission to a high authority figure, *(fall down and) worship, do obeisance to, prostrate oneself before, do reverence to, welcome respectfully,*** in Attic Gk., and later (e.g. Appian, Mithrid. 104 §489), used w. the acc. (so **Mt 4:10** and **Lk 4:8** [Dt 6:13 v.l.]; **J 4:22ab, 23b, 24a; Rv 9:20.**—Gen 37:9; Ex 11:8; Judg 7:15 A; pseudepigr.; Philo; Jos., C. Ap. 1, 239, Ant. 2, 13; 7, 250; Just.; Tat.; Mel., P. 92, 690; Ath.); beside it the Koine uses the dat. (Phryn. p. 463 Lob.; JWittmann, Sprachl. Untersuchungen zu Cosmas Indicopl., diss. Munich 1913, 16; KWolf, Studien z. Sprache des Malalas II, diss. Munich 1912, 34; GKilpatrick in: Studies and Documents 29, '67, 154–56; B-D-F §151, 2; Rob. 455; 476f), which the LXX (s. also JosAs; ApcMos 27:33) and our lit. prefer (s. also EpArist 135; Jos., Ant. 6, 55; Just., D. 30, 3; 78, 9; 88, 1.—Jos., Ant. 6, 154 πρ. τῷ θεῷ immediately after τὸν θεὸν πρ.). This reverence or worship is paid

ⓐ to human beings, but by this act they are to be recognized as belonging to a superhuman realm (Appian, Mithrid. 104 §489: Pompey; Galen, Protr. 5 p. 12, 2ff ed. WJohn: Socrates, Homer, Hippocrates, Plato): to a king (so Hdt. et al.; cp. 2 Km 18:28; 24:20; 3 Km 1:16, 53. On proskynesis in the Hellenistic ruler cults s. LTaylor, JHS 47, 1927, 53ff, The Divinity of the Rom. Emperor '31, esp. 256–66; against her WTarn, Alexander the Great II, '50, 347–73) ὁ δοῦλος προσεκύνει αὐτῷ **Mt 18:26** (of a female slave toward her κύριος PGiss 17, 11f=Mitt-Wilck, I/2, 481; s. Jos., Ant. 2, 11); to Peter by Cornelius **Ac 10:25** (cp. Apollonius [c. 197 AD] in Eus., HE 5, 18, 6).—The church at Philadelphia προσκυνήσουσιν ἐνώπιον τῶν ποδῶν σου **Rv 3:9** (on πρ. ἐνώπιόν τινος cp. Ps 21:28; 85:9; Is 66:23; TestAbr B 4 p. 108, 17 [Stone 64, 17]).—Jesus, who is rendered homage as Messianic king and helper: **Mt 2:2, 8, 11.—8:2; 9:18; 14:33; 15:25; J 9:38.—Mt 20:20;** GJs 20:4 (codd.); 21:1, 2 (codd.). A man possessed by an unclean spirit asks a favor of him **Mk 5:6.** Mock worship on the part of soldiers **15:19** (στέφανος 1). S. also be below.

ⓑ to transcendent beings (God: Aeschyl. et al.; X., An. 3, 2, 9; 13; Pla., Rep. 3, 398a; Polyb. 18, 37, 10; Plut., Pomp. 626 [14, 4]; Lucian, Pisc. 21 τῇ θεῷ; PGM 4, 649. Of various divinities in the ins [s. OGI II 700a index VIII; Sb 7911ff]; PFlor 332, 11 θεούς; LXX; Philo, Gig. 54 τὸν θεόν al.; Jos., Ant. 6, 154; 20, 164 al.; Theoph. Ant. 1, 11 [p. 82, 3]).

α. of deity in monotheistic cult (Christians, Judeans, Samaritans) κύριον τὸν θεόν σου προσκυνήσεις (Dt 6:13 v.l.) **Mt 4:10; Lk 4:8.** πρ. τῷ πατρί **J 4:21, 23a;** cp. **23b.** τῷ θεῷ (Jos., Ant. 6, 55; 9, 267; cp. Orig., C. Cels. 5, 11, 38 [w. λατρεύειν]) **Rv 19:4** (w. πίπτειν), **10b; 22:9.** See **Hb 1:6** (Dt 32:43 LXX). τῷ ζῶντι **Rv 4:10.** τῷ ποιήσαντι τὸν οὐρανόν **14:7.** πεσὼν ἐπὶ πρόσωπον προσκυνήσει τῷ θεῷ *he will fall down and worship God* (cp. 2 Km 9:6 of obeisance before David) **1 Cor 14:25;** cp. **Rv 7:11; 11:16.** ἐνώπιόν σου (s. the Ps. reff. in a above) **15:4.** Abs. (SIG 1173, 2; PTebt 416, 7; LXX) **J 4:20ab, 24ab; Ac 8:27.** Used w. ἀναβαίνειν (UPZ 62, 33 [161 BC] ἐὰν ἀναβῶ κἀγὼ προσκυνῆσαι; Jos., Ant. 20, 164) **J 12:20; Ac 24:11;** cp. **Rv 11:1.** W. πίπτειν (s. Jos., Ant. 8, 119) **Rv 5:14.** προσεκύνησεν ἐπὶ τὸ ἄκρον τῆς ῥάβδου αὐτοῦ *he bowed in worship* (or *prayed*) *over the head of his staff* **Hb 11:21** (Gen 47:31).

β. of image worship in polytheistic cult (LXX; Ar. 3, 2; Just.; Ath. 15, 1 τὰ ἀγάλματα) προσκυνεῖν τοῖς νεκροῖς θεοῖς 2 Cl 3:1 or λίθους καὶ ξύλα κτλ. 1:6 (cp. EpArist 135 . . . οἷς πρ.). See **Ac 7:43;** Dg 2:5. τὰ ὑφ᾽ ὑμῶν προσκυνούμενα *the things that are worshiped by you* 2:4. Abs., w. θύειν MPol 12:2.

γ. the devil and Satanic beings (the eschatological opponent Iren. 5, 28, 2) **Mt 4:9; Lk 4:7** (on πρ. ἐνώπιον ἐμοῦ s. α above). τὰ δαιμόνια **Rv 9:20.** τῷ δράκοντι **13:4a;** τῷ θηρίῳ **13:4b.** τὸ θηρίον vss. **8** (αὐτόν), **12; 20:4.** τῇ εἰκόνι (Da 3:5 al.) τοῦ θηρίου **13:15;** cp. **16:2; 19:20.** τὸ θηρίον καὶ τ. εἰκόνα αὐτοῦ **14:9, 11.** See θηρίον 1b; also PTouilleux, L'Apocalypse et les cultes de Domitien et de Cybèle '35.

δ. angels (TestAbr A 3 p. 79, 28 [Stone p. 6]) **Rv 22:8;** cp. **19:10a.**

ε. The risen Lord is esp. the object of worship: **Mt 28:9, 17; Lk 24:52** P[75] et al. Likewise the exalted Christ MPol 17:3. See also a above, end.—Lit. s.v. προσεύχομαι, end; Bolkestein [δεισιδαιμονία, end] 23ff; JHorst, Proskynein: Z. Anbetung im Urchristentum nach ihrer religionsgesch. Eigenart '32; Berthe MMarti, Proskynesis and adorare: Language 12, '36, 272–82; BReicke, Some Reflections on Worship in the NT: TWManson mem. vol. '59, 194–209.—B. 1469; Kl. Pauly IV 1189. New Docs 2, 68; 3, 77–78; 4, 61f. M-M. EDNT. TW. Sv.

προσκυνητής, οῦ, ὁ (προσκυνέω; pre-Christian Syrian pap in OGI 262, 21 [III AD. See Dssm., LO 79f=LAE 99]; Byz. pap) ***worshiper*** ἀληθινοὶ πρ. **J 4:23.**—DELG s.v. κυνέω. M-M. TW.

προσλαλέω fut. 3 sg. προσλαλήσει Ex 4:16; 1 aor. προσελάλησα **to communicate orally with someone, *speak to, speak with, address*** τινί (Antiphanes Com. 218, 3 Kock; Heniochus Com. 4, 3; cp. Ex 4:16; Wsd 13:17; Jos., Bell. 1, 444) **Ac 13:43;** IEph 3:1; IMg 1:1; IPol 5:1. Abs. (Theophr., Char. 7, 5; Mel., P. 24, 173; 53, 387; pap) **Ac 28:20.**—M-M.

προσλαμβάνω 2 aor. προσέλαβον; pf. προσείληφα. Mid.: fut. 3 sg. προσλήψεται (Just., D. 140, 1); 2 aor. προσελαβόμην (Aeschyl., Hdt.+. Prim.: 'take besides, take in addition')

❶ **to take someth. that meets a personal need, *take, partake of*** food, act. (X., Mem. 3, 14, 4 ἄρτον) w. partitive gen. **Ac 27:34 v.l.**—Mid. *take (in),* of food μηθέν **Ac 27:33.** W. partitive gen. τροφῆς vs. **36** (s. Ps.-Clem., Hom. 3, 21).

❷ **to promote one's own ends, *exploit, take advantage of,*** act. (Demosth. 2, 7 τὴν ἄνοιαν) τὴν νεωτερικὴν τάξιν *the youthful appearance* (of a bishop) IMg 3:1.

❸ **to take or lead off to oneself, *take aside,*** mid. τινά *someone* **Mt 16:22; Mk 8:32.** So prob. also **Ac 18:26:** Priscilla and Aquila take Apollos aside to teach him undisturbed.

❹ **to extend a welcome, *receive in(to) one's home or circle of acquaintances,*** mid. τινά *someone* (2 Macc 10:15) of one Christian receiving another **Ro 14:1; 15:7a.** Of God or Christ accepting a believer (cp. Chariton 8, 2, 13 θεῶν προσλαμβανομένων) **14:3; 15:7b;** 1 Cl 49:6 (cp. Ps 26:10; 64:5; 72:24).—**Ac 28:2; Phlm 12 v.l.; 17** (PTebt 61a, 2 [II BC] πρ. εἰς τὴν κατοικίαν; BGU 1141, 37 [14 BC] προσελαβόμην αὐτὸν εἰς οἶκον παρ᾽ ἐμέ). S. πρόσλημψις.

❺ **to take or bring along with oneself, *take along,*** mid.; w. oneself as companion or helper (PFay 12, 10 [103 BC] πρ. συνεργὸν Ἀμμώνιον; PAmh 100, 4; POxy 71 II, 9 προσελαβόμην ἐμαυτῇ εἰς βοήθειαν Σεκοῦνδον; 2 Macc 8:1; Jos., Ant. 18, 4, C. Ap. 1, 241) ἄνδρας τινὰς πονηρούς **Ac 17:5.**—M-M. TW. Spicq.

προσλέγω (Hom. et al., but almost always in the mid. The act. is found now and then in the pap [Mayser 494]) ***answer, reply*** w. dat. of pers., and foll. by direct discourse introduced by ὅτι, **Mk 16:14 v.l.** (in the Freer-Logion).

πρόσλημψις/πρόσληψις (the latter form as v.l.; B-D-F §101 s.v. λαμβάνειν; likew. Mlt.-H. 247), **εως, ἡ** (προσλαμβάνω; Pla.+; PTebt 64b, 6; 72, 246 [II BC]; Jos., Ant. 18, 353; Ath., R. 6 p. 54, 5) **acceptance into a relationship, *acceptance*** (by God) **Ro 11:15.**—DELG s.v. λαμβάνω. TW.

προσμένω fut. προσμενῶ LXX; 1 aor. προσέμεινα; pf. inf. προσμεμενηκέναι (Just., D. 107, 2) (Pind., Hdt.+; ins; UPZ 60, 16 [168 BC]; LXX; GrBar 13:3; SibOr 5, 131; Jos., Vi. 62; 63; Just.).

❶ **to be steadfast in association, *remain/stay with*** τινί *someone* or *someth.*

ⓐ w. dat. of pers.—**α.** lit. **Mt 15:32; Mk 8:2.**

β. transf. sense τῷ κυρίῳ *remain true to the Lord* **Ac 11:23** (Jos., Ant. 14, 20 τῷ Ἀριστοβούλῳ).

ⓑ w. dat. of thing *continue in* ταῖς δεήσεσιν **1 Ti 5:5.** τῇ χάριτι τοῦ θεοῦ **Ac 13:43.** τῇ προθέσει τῆς καρδίας πρ. ἐν τῷ κυρίῳ **11:23 v.l.**

❷ **to stay on at a place beyond some point of time, *remain longer, further*** (Herodas 8, 3) ἡμέρας ἱκανάς **Ac 18:18.** ἐν Ἐφέσῳ **1 Ti 1:3.**—M-M. TW.

προσομιλέω 1 aor. 3 sg. προσωμίλησε(ν) (Just.); inf. προσομιλῆσαι (Eur., Thu.+; Just.; Tat. 5, 2; in a difft. sense Ath., R. 5 p. 53, 10) **to communicate conversationally, *speak to, converse with*** τινί *someone* (Theognis 1, 31 κακοῖσι μὴ προσομίλει ἀνδράσιν; Pla., Gorg. 502e; Vett. Val. 353, 1; Philo, Agr. 60; Just., D. 1, 2 al.) of communication by letter IEph 9:2.—DELG s.v. ὅμιλος.

προσονομάζω aor. 3 pl. προσωνόμασαν (Just., A I, 9, 1), inf. προσονομάσαι 2 Macc 6:2 (since Hdt. 2, 52; Plut., Alex. 696 [54, 6], Thes. 36, 6; Cass. Dio 57, 5; 59, 4; Diog. L. 2, 85; 3, 50; 7, 135; 147; OGI 56, 22; 24 [III BC] ἣ προσονομασθήσεται πέμπτη φυλή; 90, 39; 2 Macc 6:2; EpArist; Philo, Abr. 57; Just.) **to give a name to, *name*** pass. *be named, be called* 'phoenix' bird 1 Cl 25:2 (Just., D. 61, 1).—DELG s.v. ὄνομα.

προσορμίζω 1 aor. pass. προσωρμίσθην (Hdt. et al.; ins, pap); the act., which is rare, means 'bring a ship into harbor', the mid. (Philo, Agr. 64, cp. Somn. 2, 143) or pass. (Arrian, Anab. 6, 4, 6; 20, 7; Aelian, VH 8, 5; Cass. Dio 41, 48; 64, 1) aorist, ***come into harbor, come to anchor*** **Mk 6:53.**—DELG s.v. 2 ὅρμος. M-M.

προσοφείλω (Thu. et al.; ins, pap) ***owe besides, still owe*** (POxy 101, 42 and oft. pap) τινί τι *someth. to someone* of debts outstanding (PHib 63, 14 τὸ λοιπὸν ὃ προσοφείλεις μοι) καὶ σεαυτόν μοι προσοφείλεις *you owe me even your very self (besides)* **Phlm 19.** Though it is not always poss. to find any special force in the prep. and to differentiate the compound fr. the simple verb, in addition to rhetorical structure the concentration of commercial expressions in the letter point to some emphasis on the prefix.—M-M.

προσοχθίζω (ὀχθίζω 'be very angered') fut. προσοχθιῶ LXX; 1 aor. προσώχθισα (-ησα v.l. at **Hb 3:10, 17;** JosAs 9 [cod. A p. 50, 1 Bat.]); pf. προσώχθικα Gen 27:46; aor. 3 sg. pass. προσωχθίσθη 2 Km 1:21 **to be very upset over someth. someone has done,** ***be angry, offended, provoked*** (LXX; TesJud 18:5; SibOr 3, 272) w. dat. of pers. *at someone* (Cass. Dio 7, 21, 3; TestDan 5:4) **Hb 3:17.** W. dat. of thing (SibOr 3, 272) τῇ γενεᾷ ταύτῃ vs. **10** (Ps 94:10). Abs. Hs 9, 7, 6.—DELG s.v. ὀχθέω. M-M.

πρόσοψις, εως, ἡ *appearance, aspect* (so pass. Pind. et al.; Polyb. 9, 41, 2; Diod. S. 1, 91, 6; 13, 27, 6; Lucian, Tim. 41; Kaibel 376, 8; LXX; EpArist 59) Hs 9, 1, 10.—DELG s.v. ὄπωπα D.

προσπαίω 1 aor. προσέπαισα (Soph., fgm. 311 [335 Pearson]; schol. on Aeschyl., Prom. 885; Ps. 90, 12 Sym.) ***strike, beat against*** τινί *someth.* **Mt 7:25 cj.** by Lachmann for προσέπεσαν; favored by SNaber, Mnemosyne 9, 1881, 276 and EbNestle, ZNW 9, 1908, 252f. B-D-F §202.—M-M.

πρόσπεινος, ον (πεῖνα 'hunger'; Demosthenes Ophthalmicus [I AD] in Aëtius p. 74, 26 εἰ πρόσπεινοι γένωνται) ***hungry*** πρόσπεινον γενέσθαι *become hungry* **Ac 10:10.**—DELG s.v. πείνη. M-M.

προσπήγνυμι 1 aor. προσέπηξα (Eur., fgm. 679 Nauck[2]; Philo Mech. 74, 10; Cass. Dio 40, 9; 63, 2) ***fix/fasten to*** abs. *nail to (a cross)* **Ac 2:23.**

προσπίπτω impf. προσέπιπτον; aor. προσέπεσον or προσέπεσα—B-D-F §81, 3; Mlt-H. 208 (Hom.+; pap, LXX; TestAbr A; ApcMos; EpArist 180; Philo, Joseph.).

➊ **to prostrate oneself before someone,** ***fall down before/at the feet of*** freq. in the gesture of a suppliant (Soph. et al.) w. dat. of pers. (Pla., Ep. 7, 349a; Polyb. 10, 18, 7; Plut., Pyrrh. 384 [3, 4]; PPetr II, 1, 4 [III BC]; Ps 94:6; Jos., Bell. 3, 201; 454) **Mk 3:11; 5:33; Lk 8:28, 47; Ac 16:29;** GEb 18, 39.— Before God τῷ δεσπότῃ 1 Cl 48:1; abs. 9:1 (cp. TestAbr A 14 p. 94, 14f [Stone p. 36] τοῖς οἰκτιρμοῖς αὐτοῦ; ApcMos 33 τῷ θεῷ.).—πρ. τοῖς γόνασίν τινος *fall at someone's feet* (Eur., Or. 1332 al.; Plut., Pomp. 621 [5, 2], Mor. 1117b; Chariton 3, 2, 1; Achilles Tat. 5, 17, 3; Jos., Ant. 19, 234. See TestAbr A 3 p. 79, 28 [Stone p. 6] al. τοῖς ποσὶν τοῦ ἀσωμάτου) **Lk 5:8,** unless the ref. here is to the *clasping* of a person's knees by a suppliant, as perh. in the Eur. pass. above (s. L-S-J-M s.v. γόνυ 1 and προσπίπτω III). πρὸς τοὺς πόδας τινός (Esth 8:3; cp. Ex 4:25 and PCairZen 210, 1 [254 BC] πρὸς τὰ γόνατα) **Mk 7:25.**

➋ **to move with force against someth.,** ***fall upon, strike against*** (cp. Thu. 3, 103, 2 et al.; Appian, Bell. Civ. 4, 113 §472; Arrian, Anab. 3, 13, 6; Sir 25:21; Pr 25:20; Jos., Bell. 4, 343) τινί *someth.* of the winds (Ael. Aristid. 36, 8 K.=48 p. 440 D.; schol. on Apollon. Rhod. 4, 26–71a p. 277, 6) that *beat upon* a house w. great force **Mt 7:25** (s. προσπαίω and προσκόπτω 2).—*Come (suddenly) upon* ὀξυχολία προσπίπτει τινί *bad temper comes over someone* Hm 6, 2, 5 (Menand., Epitr. 497 J. χολὴ μέλαινα πρ.).—M-M.

προσποιέω 2 sg. mid. προσποιεῖ (on this Attic form s. Schwyzer I 668; Rob. 339f; B-D-F §27; cp. βούλει Lk 22:42) 1 aor. mid. προσεποιησάμην (Eur., Hdt.+; pap, LXX, Test12Patr) in our lit. only mid.

➊ **to engage in an action or gesture that gives the appearance of conveying specific intent,** ***make/act as though, pretend*** (Thu., Pla. et al.; Diod. S. 1, 94, 1; 15, 46, 2; Plut., Timol. 238 [5, 2]; Aelian, VH 8, 5; PCairZen 534, 44; 61 [III BC]; Philo, In Flacc. 40; 98; Jos., C. Ap. 1, 5, Vi. 319; TestJud 7:2) w. inf. foll. (so mostly in the passages cited, also Jos., Ant. 13, 102; TestJos 3:7) προσεποιήσατο πορρώτερον πορεύεσθαι *he made as though he were going farther* **Lk 24:28.** προσποιεῖ ἀγνοεῖν με *you are pretending that you do not know me* MPol 10:1.

➋ **to act in response to,** *take notice (of)* abs. (Zeno the Eleatic in Diog. L. 9, 29 ἐὰν μὴ προσποιῶμαι=if I do not notice [it].—The thing that one notices is added in the acc.: Diog. L. 1, 20 τί; Job 19:14 με.) μὴ προσποιούμενος *taking no notice* **J 8:6 v.l.**—M-M.

προσπορεύομαι dep. (Aristot., Polyb.; SIG 344, 112; PEleph 18, 5 [223/222 BC]; PMagd 27, 6; PAmh 33, 17; UPZ 79, 3 [159 BC] προσπορεύεταί μοι; LXX) ***to come up to, approach*** τινί **Mk 10:35.**—JLee, Equivocal and Stereotyped Renderings in the LXX: RB 87, '80, 104–17. DELG s.v. πόρος. M-M.

προσρήγνυμι s. προσρήσσω.

προσρήσσω (on the relationship betw. ῥήσσω and ῥήγνυμι s. EFraenkel, Gesch. der griech. Nomina agentis II 1912, 40f; B-D-F §101 under ῥηγνύναι; Mlt-H. 403) fut. 2 sg. προσρήξεις (Ps. 2:9 Aq); 1 aor. προσέρηξα (on the form w. -ρρ- s. W-S. §5, 26b; Mlt-H. 193).

➊ **to break into pieces upon striking against someth.,** ***break to pieces, shatter,*** trans. (Ps 2:9 Aq; Jos., Ant. 6, 182; 9, 91) pass. (schol. on Soph., Trach. 821 Papag.) w. dat. of thing *be broken* or *wrecked on* or *against someth.* (M. Ant. 4, 49, 1 ἄκρᾳ, ᾗ τὰ κύματα προσρήσσεται; Etym. Mag. p. 703, 20 προσρησσομένου τῇ γῇ ὕδατος; Ar. 16, 6 προσρήσσονται ἑαυτοῖς) ἵνα μὴ προσρησσώμεθα τῷ ἐκείνων νόμῳ *that we might not be wrecked on their law* B 3:6.

➋ **to break in force against,** ***burst upon*** intr., w. dat. of thing προσέρηξεν ὁ ποταμὸς τῇ οἰκίᾳ **Lk 6:48;** cp. vs. **49; Mt 7:27 v.l.**—M-M s.v. προσρήγυμι.

πρόσταγμα, ατος, τό (προστάσσω; Pla.+; loanw. in rabb.) **an official directive,** ***order, command(ment), injunction*** (SEG XXXVII, 10 [209 BC]) in our lit. only of divine precepts (πρόσταγμα of a divine command: Dio Chrys. 16 [33], 9; Ael. Aristid. 48, 51 K.=24 p. 478 D.; Ptolem., Apotel. 1, 3, 6 θεῖον πρ.; SIG 1127, 8; 1129; 1131; 1138; IG XI, 1263; PEdg 7 [=Sb 6713], 19 [257 BC] τὰ ὑπὸ τοῦ θεοῦ προστάγματα; Sb 685 [II BC] τοῦ θεοῦ πρόσταγμα ἔχων; UPZ 20, 27; PGM 5, 138; 13, 268; LXX; En 18:15; EpArist 279; Philo; Jos., C. Ap. 2, 231 τὰ τοῦ νόμου πρ., Ant. 2, 291 θεοῦ πρ.; Ar. 4, 1; Just., D. 122, 5) Dg 12:5. Elsewh. always pl. 1 Cl 20:5. τὰ ἄμωμα πρ. αὐτοῦ 37:1; τὰ λαϊκὰ πρ. *rules for non-officiants* 40:5. W. δικαιώματα 2:8; 58:2. τὰ πρ. τοῦ θεοῦ ποιεῖν *keep the commandments of God* 50:5. πορεύεσθαι ἐν τοῖς πρ. αὐτοῦ Hs 5, 1, 5. ἐν τοῖς νομίμοις τῶν προσταγμάτων αὐτοῦ πορεύεσθαι *walk according to the laws of his commandments* 1 Cl 3:4. ὑπακούειν τοῖς πρ. *obey the instructions* 2 Cl 19:3.

προστάσσω fut. 3 sg. προστάξει Lev. 14:4 al.; 1 aor. προσέταξα; pf. προστέταχα LXX; plpf. 3 sg. προσετετάχει (Just., D. 21, 1). Pass.: 1 aor. προσετάχθην; 2 aor. προσετάγην; pf. προστέταγμαι, ptc. προστεταγμένος (s. πρόσταγμα; Aeschyl., Hdt.+) **to issue an official directive or make a determination,** ***command, order, give instructions, determine*** w. dat. of pers. **Mt 1:24; 21:6 v.l.** (for συνέταξεν); AcPl Ha 5, 36. W. acc.

of thing *order, prescribe someth.* (Herodas 6, 2) **Mt 8:4; Mk 1:44;** PtK 4 p. 16, 5. πρ. τὰ περί τινος *give orders concerning someone* Hs 7:1. τινί τι pass. τὰ προστεταγμένα σοι **Ac 10:33.** τὸ προσταχθὲν ἡμῖν GMary Ox 3525, 27 (cp. OGI 664, 15 τὰ ὑπ' ἐμοῦ προσταχθέντα; ParJer 6:9 τὰ προσταχθένται σου ὑπὸ τῶν ἀγγέλων). τοῖς ἱερεῦσιν τόπος προστέτακται *an office is assigned to the priests* 1 Cl 40:5. Without the dat. ἵνα μὴ κατέξω τὰ [πρός]τεταγμένα *so that I do not hinder what has been decreed for me* AcPl Ha 7, 14. Foll. by the acc. and inf. (Eur., X.; PTebt 7, 1; 1 Esdr 8:10; 3 Macc 7:8; TestAbr B 2 p. 106, 5 [Stone p. 60, 5]; Philo, Spec. Leg. 2, 130; Jos., Ant. 10, 213) **Ac 10:48;** 1 Cl 20:11. Pass., w. inf. foll. (Jos., Bell. 1, 488; Just., D. 19, 6; Tat. 4, 1) Hm 4, 1, 10. ποιεῖν τὰ προστασσόμενα ὑπὸ τοῦ πλήθους 1 Cl 54:2. Abs. καθὼς προσέταξεν (TestAbr A 20 p. 103, 2 [Stone p. 54]; cp. Gen 47:11; TestBenj 12:3 [ms. c, s. Charles]; Jos., Ant. 8, 267) **Lk 5:14;** Hs 7:5; cp. IPol 8:1. (οἱ) προστεταγμένοι καιροί *(the) fixed times* **Ac 17:26;** 1 Cl 40:4 (καιρός 2, end.—Jos., Ant. 3, 30 τὸ προστεταγμένον μέτρον).—M-M. TW.

προστάτης, ου, ὁ (cp. προστάτις; Aeschyl., Hdt.+; Eupolis, CGFP 96, 63–66 [twice, both restored]; ins, pap, LXX; ApcSed 14, 1 p. 135, 34 Ja.; EpArist 111; Jos., Bell. 1, 385; Just., D. 92, 2. Prim.: of one who 'stands out in front' [προΐστημι]) **one who looks out for the interest of others, *defender, guardian, benefactor,*** of deities; an important term in a society that attached a great deal of importance to benefaction and patronage (Soph., Oed. Rex 881, Trach. 208; Cornutus 27 p. 51, 15 πρ. κ. σωτήρ; Heraclit. Sto. 11 p. 18, 9; 38 p. 55, 11; Ael. Aristid. 28, 156 K.=49 p. 542 D.; 33, 2 K.=51 p. 572 D.: Ἀσκληπιὸς πρ. ἡμέτερος; schol. on Pind., Isthm. 1, 11c πρ. ὁ θεός; Jos., Ant. 7, 380) of Christ, in each case w. ἀρχιερεύς: 1 Cl 64; πρ. καὶ βοηθός 36:1; προστάτης τῶν ψυχῶν ἡμῶν 61:3.—S. next entry. DELG s.v. ἵστημι. New Docs 4, 242–44. Sv.

προστάτις, ιδος, ἡ (προΐστημι, cp. προστάτης; Cornutus 20 p. 37, 20; Lucian, Bis Accus. 29 θεὰ προστάτις ἑαυτῶν; Cass. Dio 42, 39 al.; PGM 36, 338; also pap ref. New Docs 4, 243) **a woman in a supportive role, *patron, benefactor*** (the relationship suggested by the term πρ. is not to be confused w. the Rom. patron-client system, which was of a different order and alien to Gk. tradition [s. JTouloumakos, Her 116, '88, 304–24]) προστάτις πολλῶν ἐγενήθη καὶ ἐμοῦ αὐτοῦ *she has proved to be of great assistance to many, including myself* **Ro 16:2** (Ltzm., Hdb. ad loc. The masc. προστάτης took on a technical sense and is found w. this mng. in Israelite [Schürer III, 102] as well as in polyth. [OGI 209; SIG 1109, 13; CIG I, 126; GHeinrici, ZWT 19, 1876, 516ff.—EZiebarth, Das griech. Vereinswesen 1896, index s.v.; Poland, Gesch., index s.v.; WOtto, Priester u. Tempel im hellenist. Ägypten II 1908 p. 75, 1] religious circles).—S. preceding entry. On women as benefactors, s. RvanBremen, in Images of Women in Antiquity, ed. ACameron/AKuhrt '83, 223–42; COsiek, Women in the Ancient Mediterranean World: BR 39, '94, 57–61 (NT). New Docs 4, 242–44. M-M.

προστίθημι (Hom.+) impf. 3 sing. προσετίθει **Ac 2:47;** fut. προσθήσω; 1 aor. προσέθηκα; 2 aor. subj. προσθῶ, impv. πρόσθες, inf. προσθεῖναι, ptc. προσθείς; pf. 2 sg. προστέθεικας 3 Km 10:7. Mid.: fut. προσθήσομαι LXX; 2 aor. προσεθέμην. Pass.: impf. 3 pl. προσετίθεντο; 1 fut. προστεθήσομαι; 1 aor. προσετέθην.

❶ **to add to someth. that is already present or exists, *add, put to*—ⓐ** of things that are added to someth. already present: abs. (opp. ἀφαιρεῖν; s. Isocr. 12, 264; Pla., Leg. 5 p. 742d al.; Epict. 1, 6, 10; Dt 4:2; 13:1) *add (someth.)* B 19:11; D 4:13. Pass. **Mk 4:24.** τὶ *someth.* Hs 5, 3, 3; D 11:2. τῇ δὲ παιδὶ προσετίθεντο οἱ μῆνες αὐτῆς lit. *the months were added to her child (=her* [Anna's] *child* [Mary] *grew month by month)* GJs 7:1. Of the addition of a word, sentence, etc. (Demosth. et al.; Just., D. 55, 1; Mitt-Wilck. II/2, 372 V, 11 [the statement follows in direct discourse]; PStras 41, 21) 1 Cl 8:2 of an addition to a written document (EpArist 26; Jos., Ant. 1, 17); ῥήματα Hv 2, 4, 2. Of faith πρόσθες ἡμῖν πίστιν *increase our faith* **Lk 17:5** (others would place this in 2 below.) Pass. (ὁ νόμος) προσετέθη *(the law) was added* to the promise **Gal 3:19.**—πρ. λόγον τινί *speak a further message to someone* (Dionys. Hal. 6, 88, 3; 8, 9, 1) **Hb 12:19** (παραιτέομαι 1b).—τί τινι *someth. to someth.* ταῖς ἁμαρτίαις αὐτῶν τὰς ἀσελγείας Hv 2, 2, 2.—It is oft. used w. dat. alone, fr. which the acc. is easily supplied *add to, increase* πρ. ταῖς ἁμαρτίαις ὑμῶν Hv 5:7; cp. m 4, 3, 7; 12, 6, 2; s 6, 1, 4; 6, 2, 3; 8, 11, 3. προσθεῖναι τῷ δρόμῳ σου *to press on in your course* IPol 1:2.—τὶ ἐπί τι *someth. to someth.* (4 Km 20:6; PsSol 3:10 ἁμαρτίας ἐφ' ἁμαρτίας) **Mt 6:27; Lk 12:25.** τὶ ἐπί τινι (Sir 3:27) προσέθηκεν καὶ τοῦτο ἐπὶ πᾶσιν *he added this to all (his) other (misdeeds)* **3:20** (B-D-F §461, 2; Rob. 605).

ⓑ of persons who are added to a group already existing, or who are attached to an individual, to whom they henceforth belong: *add, associate* (Diod. S. 5, 45, 3) πρ. τινὰ τῇ ἐκκλησίᾳ **Ac 2:47 v.l.** The same dat. is to be supplied in the text which is preferred by the critical editions in this pass.; likew. vs. **41** and **5:14** (if τῷ κυρίῳ is to be taken w. πιστεύοντες here, another dat. is to be supplied w. προσετίθεντο).—προστίθεσθαι τῷ κυρίῳ *be brought to the Lord* **11:24.** Also **5:14** (s. above), in case τῷ κυρ. here belongs w. προσετίθ. (προστίθεσθαι hardly means 'attach oneself to' as in Demosth. 18, 39 al.; 1 Macc 2:43; Jos., Vi. 87, 123).—Of one deceased πρ. πρὸς τοὺς πατέρας αὐτοῦ *be gathered to one's ancestors* (Judg 2:10; 4 Km 22:20; 1 Macc 2:69; ViMal 4 [p. 89, 8 Sch.]) **Ac 13:36.**

ⓒ In accordance w. Hebr. usage (but s. Helbing p. iv, contradicted by AWifstrand, SvTK 16, '40, 257) the adverbs *again, further* and sim. expressions are paraphrased w. πρ. (B-D-F §392, 2; 419, 4; 435a; Mlt-H. 445f). προσθεὶς εἶπεν παραβολήν *again he told a parable,* or *he proceeded to tell a parable* **Lk 19:11;** Ox 1081, 10 (for restoration: προ[σθεὶς ε]ἶπεν s. Wessely, PatrOr 18, 1924, 494, 10=Otero I 83) (Gen 38:5 προσθεῖσα ἔτεκεν υἱόν). οὐ μὴ προσθῶ πεῖν *I shall never again drink* **Mk 14:25 v.l.** προσθήσω τοῦ ἐπερωτῆσαι Hm 4, 3, 1. It is usu. found in the mid. w. the inf. foll. (Gen 8:12; Ex 9:34 Φαραὼ προσέθετο τοῦ ἁμαρτάνειν; 1 Km 18:29) **Lk 20:11f.** προσέθετο συλλαβεῖν καὶ Πέτρον *he proceeded to have also Peter arrested* **Ac 12:3** (cp. AcJ 2 [Aa II/1, 151, 14]). See 1 Cl 12:7; B 2:5 (Is 1:13).

❷ **to add as a benefit, *provide, give, grant, do*** (X., Cyr. 2, 2, 18 τὰς τιμὰς ἑκάστῳ; PRyl 153, 27) τινί τι *someth. to someone* πρόσθες ἡμῖν πίστιν *grant us faith* **Lk 17:5.** W. dat. of thing προσέθηκε τῷ ἀμπελῶνι ἔργον καλόν *he did good work in the vineyard* Hs 5, 2, 7.—Pass. ταῦτα προστεθήσεται ὑμῖν **Mt 6:33; Lk 12:31.** See Agr 10ab (Unknown Sayings, 87–89).—M-M. TW.

πρόστιμον, ου, τό (Hippocr.; Polyb. 1, 17, 11; Diod. S. 1, 65, 3; Lucian, Anach. 21; Plut., Solon 91 [23, 2]; ins, pap; 2 Macc 7:36; Jos., Ant. 4, 248. Prim. 'someth. that is paid in addition', e.g. 'fine') ***penalty*** θάνατον τὸ πρόστιμον ἔχειν *incur the death penalty* 1 Cl 41:3.—DELG s.v. τιμή.

προστρέχω 2 aor. προσέδραμον (Aristoph., X., Pla. et al.; POxy 247, 12 [non-literal]; LXX; ApcEsdr 7:15 p. 33, 3 Tdf.; Jos., Ant. 7, 249, Vi. 140; Just., D. 105, 5) **to run to or towards,**

run up (to); except for the **v.l. J 20:16,** it is used in our lit. only in the ptc., combined w. another verb (Menand., Per. 155 S. [35 Kö.]; Num 11:27; Tob 11:9 BA; Jos., Bell. 1, 662; TestNapht 5:2) προστρέχοντες ἠσπάζοντο αὐτόν **Mk 9:15.** Cp. **10:17; Ac 8:30;** Hs 9, 6, 2.—M-M.

προσφάγιον, ου, τό (fr. φαγεῖν, not to be confused w. the homograph derived fr. προσφάζω 'sacrifice beforehand'; 'a relish' eaten w. bread [Proverbia Aesopi 98 P. πρ. beside ἄρτος; POxy 498, 33; 39 ἄρτον ἕνα καὶ προσφάγιον; 736, 46; 89; 739, 7; 10; 12; 14; BGU 916, 22; PGrenf II, 77, 21; OGI 484, 26. Acc. to Moeris and Hesychius it = ὄψον. But the latter word, as well as its dim. ὀψάριον (q.v.), oft. simply = 'fish']) ***fish (to eat)*** μή τι προσφάγιον ἔχετε; *you have no fish to eat, have you?* or *did you catch anything to eat?* **J 21:5** (the narrative context contrasts the disciples' lack of success in providing a meal with the Lord's role as chef, vss. 9–13).—DELG s.v. φαγεῖν. M-M.

πρόσφατος, ον (Hom. et al.; on the formation s. Boisacq s.v.) ***new, recent*** (Aeschyl. et al.; Michel 1501, 24 [103/102 BC]; POxy 1088, 25; LXX; Jos., Ant. 1, 264. See Phryn. p. 374 Lob.) Hs 9, 2, 2 (opp. παλαιός). Also in the sense 'not previously existing' (cp. Eccl 1:9 οὐκ ἔστιν πᾶν πρόσφατον ὑπὸ τὸν ἥλιον; Ps 80:10) ὁδός **Hb 10:20.**—DELG s.v. θείνω. M-M. TW.

προσφάτως adv. of πρόσφατος, of time ***recently*** (Machon [III BC] vs. 364, in Athen. 13, 581e; Polyb. 3, 37, 11; Alciphron 4, 14, 2; OGI 315, 23 [164/163 BC] ἐληλυθότι προσφάτως; UPZ 144, 10 [164 BC]; LXX; EpArist 5; Jos., Bell. 1, 127, Ant. 10, 264) in our lit. used w. ἐληλυθὼς ἀπό **Ac 18:2;** MPol 4.—M-M. TW.

προσφέρω impf. προσέφερον; fut. προσοίσω LXX; aor. προσήνεγκον and προσήνεγκα (s. B-D-F §81, 2; Rob. 338; 363); pf. προσενήνοχα Hb 11:17; 1 aor. pass. προσηνέχθην (Pind.+).

❶ **to bring someone or someth. to someone, *bring*** act. and pass.—ⓐ *bring (to)* w. acc. of pers. τινά τινι *bring someone to someone,* sick people to Jesus or his disciples **Mt 4:24; 8:16; 9:2, 32; 12:22 v.l.** (for the pass.); **14:35; 17:16.** The acc. is lacking but easily supplied **Mk 2:4.** Children to Jesus **Mk 10:13a;** cp. **b v.l.; Lk 18:15.** Pass. **Mt 19:13.** *Bring someone before* a judge, king, etc. **Lk 23:14;** cp. **12:11 v.l.** (for εἰσφέρωσιν). Pass. **Mt 18:24.**

ⓑ *bring (to)* w. acc. of thing—**α.** *bring (to), offer* (Iren. 1, 13, 2 [Harv. I, 117, 3]; Did., Gen. 123, 25) τί τινι *someth. (to) someone* προσήνεγκαν αὐτῷ δηνάριον **Mt 22:19.** See **Ac 8:18;** 1 Cl 43:2. Without a dat., which is supplied by the context **Mt 25:20;** Hs 8, 1, 12.—Esp. *bring someone* someth. to drink (Menand., Georg. 61 S. and Kö. φαγεῖν πρ.; Jos., Bell. 1, 488, Ant. 4, 72 οἶνον προσφέρεσθαι='take wine', Vi. 225) ὄξος προσφέροντες αὐτῷ **Lk 23:36.** Cp. σπόγγον μεστὸν τοῦ ὄξους ... προσήνεγκαν αὐτοῦ τῷ στόματι *they held a sponge full of vinegar to his mouth* **J 19:29.** Without acc. of thing GJs 18:2 (codd.).—Without dat. ὕδωρ ... προσήνεγκεν *(Paul) then brought water* (after distributing the eucharistic bread) AcPl Ha 4, 4.

β. τὴν χεῖρα τῷ παιδίῳ *reach (your) hand out to the child* GJs 20:3 (codd.).

γ. fig. of partisanship ἥττονα ἁμαρτίαν ὑμῖν προσήνεγκεν *made you less guilty* lit. '(that factionalism) brought less sin on you' 1 Cl 47:4.

❷ **to present someth. to someone by bringing it, *bring, offer, present*** of offerings, gifts etc. (Simplicius In Epict. p. 93, 41 Düb. τὰς ἀπαρχάς [τῷ θεῷ]; oft. LXX; Jos., Bell. 3, 353, Ant. 3, 231).

ⓐ lit. τὶ *someth.* with or without dat. of pers. (of prayers Orig., C. Cels. 8, 13, 21) δῶρον, δῶρα (Jos., Ant. 6, 67), of the gifts brought by the Magi **Mt 2:11** (s. Ps 71:10; on the quality of such gifts cp. Aristot., fgm. 101 οὐθὲν κολοβὸν προσεφέρομεν πρὸς τοὺς θεούς=we don't offer anything shoddy to the gods); of sacrificial gifts **5:23f; 8:4; Hb 8:3f; 9:9** (pass.); GJs 1:1f; 5:1; 1 Cl 44:4. θυσίαν, θυσίας (EpArist 170b; Jos., Ant. 8, 118; Just., D. 41, 2 al. λογικὴν καὶ ἄκαπνον θυσίαν Orig., C. Cels. 7, 1, 15) **Hb 11:4;** D 14:3 (s. Mal 1:11 and vs. 13 v.l.).—**Hb 10:11;** see vss. **1, 2** (pass.), **8** (pass.); 1 Cl 41, 2a (pass.); PtK 2 p. 14, 21. σφάγια καὶ θυσίας προσηνέγκατέ μοι **Ac 7:42** (Am 5:25). προσενέγκαι μοι ὁλοκαυτώματα καὶ θυσίας B 2:7 (s. Jer 7:22f); 7:6 (s. Lev 16:7, 9); 8:1 (TestJob 3:3).—τινά *someone* of the offering up of Isaac προσενήνοχεν (the pf. to denote what 'stands written'; cp. Mlt 129; 142; 238) Ἀβραὰμ τὸν Ἰσαὰκ καὶ τὸν μονογενῆ προσέφερεν (impf., in a conative or inceptive sense, because the sacrifice was not actually made) **Hb 11:17.** Cp. Ἰσαὰκ προσενεχθεὶς ἐπὶ τὸ θυσιαστήριον B 7:3b (on ἐπὶ τὸ θυσ. cp. 1 Esdr 8:15). προσήνεγκεν τὴν παῖδα Ἰωακεὶμ τοῖς ἱερεῦσιν GJs 6:2ab (cp. προσάγω). Of Jesus ἑαυτὸν πρ. **Hb 7:27 v.l.;** cp. **9:14** (τῷ θεῷ); vs. **25.** πρ. αὐτὸν ἐπὶ τὴν σφαγήν B 8:2b. Pass. ὁ Χριστὸς προσενεχθεὶς **Hb 9:28;** here the purpose is indicated by εἰς τό w. the inf. foll. Elsewh. the purpose is expressed by means of other preps.: πρ. (τι) περί τινος (Lev 16:9; Job 1:5) **Mk 1:44;** cp. **Lk 5:14.** περὶ αὐτοῦ (v.l. ἑαυτοῦ) προσφέρειν περὶ ἁμαρτιῶν **Hb 5:3.** Also ὑπέρ τινος (1 Macc 7:33) **Hb 5:1; 9:7; 10:12;** B 7:5. Pass. **Ac 21:26;** B 7:4 ('scripture' quot. of unknown origin). W. double acc. *offer someone/someth. as a* θυσίαν *sacrifice* 1 Cl 10:7; B 7:3a (w. ὑπέρ τινος). πρ. τινί *sacrifice to someone* Dg 3:3. Abs. *make an* offering, *sacrifice* B 8:2a. ὀρθῶς 1 Cl 4:4 (Gen 4:7). αἷς δοκεῖτε τιμαῖς προσφέρειν *by the honors which you think you offer* (them) Dg 2:8. Pass. 1 Cl 41:2b. The pres. ptc. used as a subst. τὸ προσφερόμενον *the offering* 41:2c.—NSnaith, The Sin-Offering and Guilt-Offering, VetusT 15, '65, 73–80.

ⓑ fig. (s. BGU 1024 VII, 25 of a poor girl ζῶσα προσεφέρετο τοῖς βουλομένοις ὡς νεκρά='she offered herself') the killing of Christians will be considered by the Judeans as λατρείαν προσφέρειν τῷ θεῷ **J 16:2** (s. ἀποκτείνω 1a). δεήσεις καὶ ἱκετηρίας πρ. πρὸς (τὸν θεόν) **Hb 5:7** (Achilles Tat. 7:1 προσφέρειν δέησιν; JosAs 12:7 τὴν δέησίν μου; Jos., Bell. 3, 353 προσφέρει τῷ θεῷ εὐχήν; Mel., HE 4, 26, 6 δέησιν).—ἁμαρτίαν 1 Cl 47:4; δῶρα 1 Cl 44:4.

❸ **to behave towards or deal w. someone in a certain way, *meet, deal with*** pass. in act. sense w. dat. of pers. (so oft. Thu.+; Diod. S. 14, 90, 3; Aelian, VH 12, 27; Herodian 1, 13, 7; Philo, Ebr. 69, De Jos. 47; Jos., Bell. 7, 254; 263; OGI 456, 64; SIG 807, 13 [54 AD]; PLond 1912, 65 [41 AD]) ὡς υἱοῖς ὑμῖν προσφέρεται ὁ θεός **Hb 12:7.**—M-M. EDNT. TW.

προσφεύγω 2 aor. προσέφυγον; 2 pf. προσπέφευγα (Plut., Pomp. 643 [46, 7], Cic. 3, 5; Herodian 3, 9, 2; PMagd 13, 13 [III BC]; BGU 180, 16; POxy 488, 23; Sym.; JosAs 12:7 cod. A [p. 55, 16 Bat.]; Philo, Det. Pot. Ins. 62; Jos., Ant. 1, 311, Vi. 154; Just.) **to flee to, *flee for refuge to*** w. dat. of thing or pers. τινί (Cornutus 20 p. 38, 8) 1 Cl 20:11; IPhld 5:1.

προσφιλής, ές (Aeschyl., Hdt. et al.; SEG XXIX, 784, 1 and 3 [s. New Docs 4, 171 for other ins ref.]; pap, LXX act. and pass.; Ar. 15, 5 [act.]) in our lit. only pass. **pert. to causing pleasure or delight, *pleasing, agreeable, lovely, amiable*** (so also Diod. S. 5, 39, 4; PSI 361, 9 [251/250 BC]; BGU 1043, 24; Sir 4:7; 20:13;

Jos., Ant. 1, 258; cp. the adv. use OGI 331, 9) abs. **Phil 4:8.** λόγῳ πρ. *pleasing to the* λόγος Dg 11:2 cj. (s. the crit. apparatus; Diod. S. 2, 49, 2; 6, 7, 6 τ. θεοῖς; Dio Chrys. 16 [33], 28 τοῖς θεοῖς; 70 [20], 21 τῇ θεῷ; Jos., Ant. 1, 258; 17, 149).—DELG s.v. φίλος. M-M.

προσφορά, ᾶς, ἡ (προσφέρω; Soph.+; pap, LXX; TestLevi 3:6; 14:5; EpArist 170; Joseph., Just.; Hippol., Ref. 6, 16, 2)

➊ the act of bringing as a voluntary expression ('presenting, offering': Pla., Aristot., Polyb.; Did., Gen. 125, 8), in our lit. in the literal as well as fig. sense of ***sacrificing, offering*** (Sir 46:16 προσφορὰ ἀρνός) foll. by the obj. gen. διὰ τῆς προσφορᾶς τοῦ σώματος Ἰησοῦ *through the offering of Jesus' body in sacrifice* **Hb 10:10.** Cp. vss. **14, 18** (s. Windisch, Hdb., exc. on Hb 10:18). προσφορὰς ποιεῖν *have sacrifices made* **Ac 24:17;** 1 Cl 40:4 (Just., D. 29, 8; 67, 8). W. λειτουργίαι vs. 2. ἀνθρωποποίητος πρ. *an offering made by man* B 2:6 (mng. 2 is also prob.). προσφορᾶς γενομένης ὑπὸ τοῦ Παύλου *when a sacrifice had been made by Paul* AcPl Ha 6, 37.

➋ that which is brought as a voluntary expression ('present, gift': Theophr., Char. 30, 19) in our lit. in fig. and literal use ***offering*** (Sir 14:11; 34:18, 19 al.; TestLevi 14:5) w. ὁλοκαύτωμα MPol 14:1. W. θυσία **Eph 5:2; Hb 10:5** (Ps 39:7). W. θυσίαι, ὁλοκαυτώματα κτλ. (s. Da 3:38; Jos., Ant. 11, 77) vs. **8** (Ps 39:7); B 2:4; ἀνθρωποποίητος προσφορά *a sacrifice made by a human being* vs. 6 (mng. 1 is also prob.; s. above). προσηνέχθη ἡ προσφορά **Ac 21:26** (προσφέρω 2a). Jesus is called ὁ ἀρχιερεὺς τῶν προσφορῶν ἡμῶν *the High Priest of our offerings* in that he brings the prayers of the Christians into God's presence 1 Cl 36:1. ἡ προσφορὰ τῶν ἐθνῶν *the offering that consists of the gentiles* (i.e. those from 'the nations' who have become Christian) **Ro 15:16.** For the interpretation of ἐθνῶν as subjective, *the offering that the Gentiles make* s. AMDenis, RSPT 42, '58, 405f.—DELG s.v. φέρω D. M-M. TW.

προσφωνέω impf. προσεφώνουν; 1 aor. προσεφώνησα; aor. pass. inf. προσεφωνηθῆναι 1 Esdr. 6:6 (Hom. et al.; ins, pap, LXX; EpArist 306; Joseph.).

➊ to call out or speak to, *call out, address* (Hom. et al., as a rule w. acc. of pers.) w. dat. of pers. (Diod. S. 4, 48, 1; Diog. L. 7, 7; PPetr II, 38b, 3 [242 BC]; PTebt 27, 109; Mitt-Wilck I/2, 27 verso, 15.—Cp. Eus., HE 4, 3 [introd. to Qua.]) **Mt 11:16; Lk 7:32; 23:20.** τῇ Ἑβραΐδι διαλέκτῳ προσεφώνει αὐτοῖς **Ac 22:2;** without dat. of pers., **21:40; 22:2** D. Likew. abs. **Lk 23:20 v.l.**

➋ to call to oneself, *call to, summon,* with implication of shared interests τινά *someone* (Jos., Ant. 7, 156) **Lk 6:13** (D ἐφώνησεν); **13:12; Ac 11:2** D.—DELG s.v. φωνή. M-M.

προσχαίρω (Plut., Ant. 29, 4; Pr 8:30) ***be glad*** **Mk 9:15** D.

πρόσχυσις, εως, ἡ (Just., A II, 12, 5; Ps.-Clem., Hom. 2, 44. From προσχέω [Ex 24:6; 29:21 al.]) **act of putting liquid on someth., *pouring, sprinkling, spreading*** ἡ πρόσχυσις τοῦ αἵματος *the sprinkling of blood* (on the doorposts) **Hb 11:28** (s. Ex 12:22).—DELG s.v. χέω.

προσψαύω (Pind. et al.; TestSol 2:6; Jos., Bell. 7, 348) **to reach out to touch, *touch*** τινί *someth.* (Herophil. [300 BC] in Galen II p. 570, 12 K.) ἑνὶ τῶν δακτύλων ὑμῶν οὐ προσψαύετε τοῖς φορτίοις *you do not touch the burdens with one of your fingers* **Lk 11:46:** the hyperbole accents a lack of concern for the one who is oppressed.

προσωπολημπτέω (edd. also -ληπτέω; this word and the two words following, which are closely related, have so far been found only in Christian writers. They are based on the πρόσωπον λαμβάνειν of the LXX, which in turn is modeled on the Hebr. [s. πρόσωπον 1bα, end]. On the spelling with or without μ s. λαμβάνω, beg.) ***show partiality*** **Js 2:9.**—DELG s.v. πρόσωπον. M-M. TW.

προσωπολήμπτης, ου, ὁ (s. προσωπολημπτέω.—Leontius 4 p. 10, 14 uses προσωπολήπτης [which is, in the final analysis, a biblical word] apart from a scriptural context, as an element of popular speech) ***one who shows partiality*** of God οὐκ ἔστιν πρ. *he is not one to show partiality* **Ac 10:34** (cp. Ro 2:11).—TW.

προσωποληµψία, ας, ἡ (edd. also -ληψία; s. προσωπολημπτέω) ***partiality*** named as a sin, w. other sins Pol 6:1. Not found in God (TestJob 43:13) **Ro 2:11; Eph 6:9; Col 3:25.** Pl. τὴν πίστιν ἔχειν ἐν προσωποληµψίαις *hold the faith while showing partiality* **Js 2:1** (Goodsp, Probs. 142f).—EDNT. TW.

πρόσωπον, ου, τό (Hom.+; loanw. in rabb.).**—➊ the front part of the head—ⓐ** lit. ***face, countenance*** **Mt 6:16f; 17:2; Mk 14:65; Lk 9:29** (s. εἶδος 1); **Ac 6:15ab** (Chariton 2, 2, 2 θαυμάζουσαι τὸ πρόσωπον ὡς θεῖον; Damasc., Vi. Isid. 80 Πρόκλος ἐθαύμαζε τὸ Ἰσιδώρου πρόσωπον, ὡς ἔνθεον ἦν; Marinus, Vi. Procli 23); **2 Cor 3:7** twice, **13** (JMorgenstern, Moses with the Shining Face: HUCA 2, 1925, 1–28); cp. vs. **18; 4:6;** but in the last two passages there is a transition from the face of Moses to a symbolic use of πρ. (s. 1bβℶ below); **Rv 4:7; 9:7ab; 10:1;** IEph 15:3 (cp. 1bβℵ); MPol 12:1; Hv 3, 10, 1; B 5:14; GJs 17:2; 18:2 (codd.). ἐμβριθεῖ τῷ πρ. MPol 9:2 (s. ἐμβριθής). ποίῳ προσώπῳ GJs 13:1b. πρόσωπον τῆς γενέσεως αὐτοῦ *the face he was born with* **Js 1:23** (γένεσις 2a). ἐμπτύειν εἰς τὸ πρ. τινος *spit in someone's face* (s. ἐμπτύω) **Mt 26:67.** εἰς πρ. δέρειν τινά *strike someone in the face* **2 Cor 11:20.** τύπτειν τὸ πρ. GJs 13:1a. συνέπεσεν τὸ πρόσωπον αὐτοῦ *his face fell* or *became distorted* 1 Cl 4:3; cp. vs. 4 (Gen 4:6 and 5; JosAs 13:8). πίπτειν ἐπὶ (τὸ; the art. is usu. lacking; B-D-F §255, 4; 259, 1; cp. Rob. 792) πρ. αὐτοῦ *fall on one's face* as a sign of devotion (=נָפַל עַל פָּנָיו; cp. Gen 17:3; Ruth 2:10; TestAbr A 9 p. 86, 16 [Stone p. 20]; JosAs 14:4 al.; ApcSed 14:2) **Mt 17:6; 26:39; Rv 7:11; 11:16.** Without αὐτοῦ (Gen 17:17; Num 14:5; Jos., Ant. 10, 11) **Lk 5:12; 17:16; 1 Cor 14:25.**

ⓑ *personal presence or relational circumstance,* fig.**—α.** in all kinds of imagery which, in large part, represent OT usage, and in which the face is oft. to be taken as the seat of the faculty of seeing. Βλέπειν πρόσωπον πρὸς πρόσωπον *to see face to face* **1 Cor 13:12** (cp. Gen 32:31 [Jos., Ant. 1, 334 θεοῦ πρόσωπον]; Judg 6:22. See HRiesenfeld, ConNeot 5, '41, 19; 21f [abstracts of four articles]). κλίνειν τὸ πρ. εἰς τὴν γῆν **Lk 24:5** (κλίνω 1). πρ. κυρίου ἐπὶ ποιοῦντας κακά **1 Pt 3:12;** 1 Cl 22:6 (both Ps 33:17). ἐπίφανον τὸ πρ. σου ἐφ᾽ ἡμᾶς (ἐπιφαίνω 1) 60:3 (s. Num 6:25). ἐμφανισθῆναι τῷ προσώπῳ τοῦ θεοῦ (ἐμφανίζω 1) **Hb 9:24.** βλέπειν τὸ πρ. τινος, i.e. of God (βλέπω 1a, ὁράω A1c and s. JBoehmer, Gottes Angesicht: BFCT 12, 1908, 321–47; EGulin, D. Antlitz Jahwes im AT: Annal. Acad. Scient. Fenn. 17, 3, 1923; FNötscher, 'Das Anges. Gottes schauen' nach bibl. u. babylon. Auffassung 1924) **Mt 18:10;** cp. **Rv 22:4.** ὁρᾶν, ἰδεῖν or θεωρεῖν τὸ πρ. τινος *see someone's face,* i.e. see someone (present) in person (UPZ 70, 5 [152/151 BC] οὐκ ἄν με ἴδες τὸ πρόσωπον. See Gen 32:21; 43:3, 5; 46:30 al.) **Ac 20:25, 38; 1 Th 2:17b; 3:10;** IRo 1:1; s. IPol 1:1. τὸ πρόσωπόν μου ἐν σαρκί **Col 2:1.** τῷ προσώπῳ ἀγνοούμενος *unknown by face,* i.e. *personally* **Gal 1:22** (ἀγνοέω 1b). ἀπορφανισθέντες ἀφ᾽ ὑμῶν προσώπῳ οὐ καρδίᾳ (dat. of specification) *orphaned by separation from you in person, not in heart* (or *outwardly, not inwardly*) **1 Th 2:17a.** ἐκζητεῖν τὰ πρόσωπα τῶν ἁγίων (ἐκζητέω 1) B 19:10; D 4:2. ἀποστρέφειν τὸ πρ. ἀπό τινος (ἀποστρέφω 1) 1 Cl 18:9 (Ps 50:11); 16:3 (Is 53:3). στερεῖν τοῦ προσώπου τινός B 13:4 (Gen 48:11).—τὸ πρόσωπον στηρίζειν (s. στηρίζω 2 and cp. SAntoniades, Neotestamentica: Neophilologus 14, 1929, 129–35) **Lk 9:51.** τὸ πρ. αὐτοῦ ἦν πορευόμενον εἰς Ἰερουσαλήμ *his face was set toward Jerusalem* vs. **53** (cp. 2 Km 17:11).—θαυμάζειν πρόσωπον *flatter* **Jd 16** (PsSol 2:18; s. also θαυμάζω 1bα). λαμβάνειν πρόσωπον (=נָשָׂא פָּנִים; cp. Sir 4:22; 35:13; 1 Esdr 4:39; s. Thackeray p. 43f; B-D-F p. 3, note 5; Rob. 94) *show partiality* or *favoritism* **Lk 20:21; B** 19:4; D 4:3. λαμβ. πρόσωπόν τινος (cp. Mal 1:8) **Gal 2:6.** S. PKatz, Kratylos 5, '60, 161.

β. governed by prepositions, in usages where πρ. in many cases requires a dynamic equivalent

א. ἀπὸ προσώπου τινός *from the presence of someone* (JosAs 28:10; Just., A I, 36, 1; s. Vi. Aesopi W 104 v.l. p. 188 last line P. ἐπιστολὴ ὡς ἐκ προσώπου τοῦ Αἰσώπου) **Ac 3:20;** *(away) from someone* or *someth.* (Ctesias: 688 fgm. 9 Jac. φυγεῖν ἀπὸ προσώπου Κύρου; LXX; PsSol 4:8 al.; Herodas 8, 59 ἔρρ᾽ ἐκ προσώπου=get out of my sight; TestAbr A 2 p. 78, 11 [Stone p. 4] ἐκ προσώπου: here because of the compound ἐξέρχομαι) **5:41; 7:45; 2 Th 1:9; Rv 6:16** (Is 2:10, 19, 21); **12:14; 20:11** (cp. Ex 14:25; Josh 10:11; Sir 21:2; 1 Macc 5:34 and oft.) 1 Cl 4:8 (s. ἀποδιδράσκω), 10 (s. the passages cited for Rv 20:11 above); 18:11 (Ps 50:13; ἀπο[ρ]ρίπτω 2); 28:3 (Ps 138:7).

ב. εἰς πρόσωπον: (Aesop, Fab. 302 P.= εἰς Ζηνὸς πρόσωπον ἔρχεσθαι=before the face of Zeus) εἰς πρόσωπον τῶν ἐκκλησιῶν *before* (lit. 'in the face of') *the congregations* **2 Cor 8:24.** τὰ φαινόμενά σου εἰς πρόσωπον *what meets your eye,* i.e. the visible world IPol 2:2. βλέπειν εἰς πρόσωπόν τινος **Mt 22:16; Mk 12:14** (s. βλέπω 4). *To one's face* i.e. when present Hv 3, 6, 3 cj. (cp. POxy 903, 2; BGU 909, 12).

ג. ἐν προσώπῳ (Maximus Tyr. 38, 1a) ἐν προσώπῳ Χριστοῦ *before the face of Christ* that looks down with approval **2 Cor 2:10** (cp. Pr 8:30; Sir 35:4), or *as the representative of Christ* (REB); difft. **4:6** *on the face of Christ* (s. 1a above).

ד. κατὰ πρόσωπον *face to face, (present) in person* (Polyb. 24, 15, 2; Diod. S. 19, 46, 2; Plut., Caesar 716 [17, 8]; IMagnMai 93b, 11; IPriene 41, 6; OGI 441, 66 [81 BC]; PLond II, 479, 6 p. 256 [III AD?]; POxy 1071, 1) B 15:1. (Opp. ἀπών) **2 Cor 10:1.** Παῦλος, ὃς γενόμενος ἐν ὑμῖν κατὰ πρόσωπον Pol 3:2. πρὶν ἢ ὁ κατηγορούμενος κατὰ πρόσωπον ἔχοι τοὺς κατηγόρους *before the accused meets his accusers face to face* **Ac 25:16,** κατὰ πρόσωπον αὐτῷ ἀντέστην *I opposed him to his face* **Gal 2:11** (cp. Diod. S. 40, 5a of an accusation κατὰ πρόσωπον; 2 Macc 7:6; Jos., Ant. 5, 46; 13, 278).—κατὰ πρόσωπον *with partiality, in favoritism* B 19:7; D 4:10.—τὰ κατὰ πρόσωπον *what is before your eyes* **2 Cor 10:7.**—Used w. the gen. like a prep. (PPetr III, 1 II, 8 κατὰ πρόσωπον τοῦ ἱεροῦ; LXX; Jos., Ant. 3, 144; 9, 8) κατὰ πρ. τινος *before* or *in the presence of someone* (Jos., Ant. 11, 235) **Lk 2:31; Ac 3:13; 16:9** D; 1 Cl 35:10 (Ps. 49:21).

ה. μετὰ προσώπου: πληρώσεις με εὐφροσύνης μετὰ τοῦ προσώπου σου **Ac 2:28** (Ps 15:11); μετά A 2γ ג.

ו. πρὸ προσώπου τινός (LXX; TestAbr A 12 p. 91, 4 [Stone p. 30] πρὸ προσώπου τῆς τραπέζης; GrBar 1:4; s. Johannessohn, Präp. 184–86) *before someone* **Mt 11:10; Mk 1:2; Lk 7:27** (on all three cp. Mal 3:1).—**Lk 1:76 v.l.** (s. Ex 32:34); **9:52** (s. Ex 23:20); **10:1;** 1 Cl 34:3 (s. Is 62:11). IEph 15:3 (cp. 1a).—πρὸ προσώπου τῆς εἰσόδου αὐτοῦ **Ac 13:24** (εἴσοδος 2).

❷ **entire bodily presence,** ***person*** (Polyb. 5, 107, 3; 8, 13, 5; 12, 27, 10; 27, 7, 4; Diod. S. 37, 12, 1; Plut., Mor. 509b; Epict. 1, 2, 7; Vett. Val. s. index; Just., A I, 36, 2; POxy 1672, 4 [37–41 AD] ξένοις προσώποις=to strangers; 237 VII, 34; PRyl 28, 88. Cp. Phryn. p. 379 Lob., also Lob.'s comment p. 380; KPraechter, Philol 63, 1904, 155f) ὀλίγα πρόσωπα *a few persons* 1 Cl 1:1; ἓν ἢ δύο πρ. 47:6. τὰ προγεγραμμένα πρ. *the persons mentioned above* IMg 6:1. Here is surely also the place for ἐκ πολλῶν προσώπων *by many (persons)* **2 Cor 1:11** (from Luther to NRSV et al.; 'face' is preferred by Heinrici, Plummer et al.—With this expr. cp. Diod. S. 15, 38, 4 ἐκ τρίτου προσώπου=[claims were raised] by a third 'party', i.e. Thebes, against Sparta and Athens).

❸ **the outer surface of someth.,** ***face=surface*** πρόσωπον τῆς γῆς (Gen 2:6; 7:23; 11:4, 8 al.) **Lk 21:35; Ac 17:26;** B 11:7 (Ps 1:4); and 6:9 prob. belongs here also.

❹ **that which is present in a certain form or character to a viewer,** ***external things, appearance*** opp. καρδία (1 Km 16:7) **2 Cor 5:12.** πρόσωπον εἰρήνης (opp. πονηρίαι . . . ἐν ταῖς καρδίαις) Hv 3, 6, 3. ἡ εὐπρέπεια τοῦ προσώπου αὐτοῦ (i.e. of grass and flowers) **Js 1:11.** Of the appearance of the sky **Mt 16:3;** cp. **Lk 12:56** (s. Ps 103:30).—SSchlossmann, Persona u. Πρόσωπον im röm. Recht u. christl. Dogma 1906; RHirzel, Die Person; Begriff u. Name derselben im Altertum: SBBayAk 1914, Heft 10; HRheinfelder, Das Wort 'Persona'; Gesch. seiner Bed. 1928; FAltheim, Persona: ARW 27, 1929, 35–52; RAC I 437–40; BHHW I 93f. B. 216.—DELG. M-M. EDNT. TW. Sv.

προτάσσω (Aeschyl. et al.; Thu. 3, 52; ins, pap; TestSol 6:11 L; Jos., Ant. 2, 340; Ath., R. 1 p. 49, 15 al.) **to arrange for someth. before,** ***fix, determine, allot (beforehand)*** (Soph., Trach. 164; Aristot., Probl. 30, 11; 2 Macc 8:36) pf. pass. ptc. προτεταγμένοι καιροί instead of προστετ. κ. **Ac 17:26** D (s. προστάσσω, end).—M-M.

προτείνω 1 aor. προέτεινα (trag., Hdt.+; ins, pap; LXX nearly always in 2 Macc and always of stretching out the hands; EpArist 179; Philo; Jos., Vi. 30; Just., A I, 68, 10) **stretch out before,** ***stretch out, spread out*** a criminal who is to be flogged ὡς προέτειναν αὐτον τοῖς ἱμᾶσιν **Ac 22:25;** the transl. depends on one's understanding of the dat.; s. ἱμάς.—DELG s.v. τανυ-. M-M.

πρότερος, α, ον (Hom.+; cp. πρό)**—❶ pert. to a period of time preceding another period of time,** ***earlier*****—ⓐ** adj. (Hom. et al.) ***former, earlier*** ἡ πρ. ἀναστροφή **Eph 4:22.** οἱ πρ. (sc. λίθοι) Hs 9, 4, 3. τάς χρόας τὰς προτέρας 9, 4, 5; τὰ πρ. ἁμαρτήματα 2 Cl 13:1; Hm 12, 6, 2; s 9, 23, 5. ἡ πρ. ἁμαρτία m 4, 1, 11; pl. v 2, 3, 1; m 4, 3, 3; s 6, 1, 4; 8, 11, 3; αἱ ἁμαρτίαι αἱ πρ. m 4, 3, 1. τὰ πρ. ἀγνοήματα s 5, 7, 3f. τὰ πρ. παραπτώματα m 4, 4, 4. ἡ πρ. ὅρασις v 4, 1, 1. αἱ πρ. λύπαι 3, 13, 2. τὰ πρ. ὁράματα 4, 2, 2. τὰ πρ. χαλεπά 1, 4, 2 v.l. πρῶτα. οἱ πρ. χρόνοι s 9, 20, 4. ἡ ζωὴ ἡ πρ. 9, 16, 2.

ⓑ the neut. πρότερον as adv. ***earlier, formerly, in former times*** (Pind., Hdt.+).

α. without art.; opp. νῦν (Ael. Aristid. 33, 16 K.=51 p. 576 D.; Procop. Soph., Ep. 88) νῦν καὶ οὐ πρότερον *now and not in former times* Dg 1. πρότερον . . . ἔπειτα (Ps.-Clem., Hom. 7, 6; cp. Artem. 2, 39 p. 144, 27f πρότερον . . . εἶτα) **Hb 7:27.** Oft. the time which is later than the one designated by πρ. is not expressed, but is understood fr. the context *earlier, beforehand, previously* (oft. Pind., Hdt. et al.) **J 7:50 v.l., 51 v.l.; 2 Cor 1:15; 1 Ti 1:13 v.l.; Hb 4:6.**—Schwyzer I 533f.

β. w. art. and functioning as an adj. *former* (Hdt. 6, 87; Aristoph., Equ. 1355; Diod. S. 17, 69, 3) αἱ πρότερον ἡμέραι **Hb 10:32.** αἱ πρότερον ἐπιθυμίαι **1 Pt 1:14.**—W. the art. simply adverbially τὸ πρότερον *before, once, formerly* (X., Mem. 3, 8, 1; Menand., Dyscolus 15; Hero Alex. I, 190, 19; TestAbr A 18 p. 100, 9 and 11 [Stone p. 48]; ApcMos 9; Jos., Ant. 20, 173) **J 6:62; 7:50; 9:8; 1 Ti 1:13;** Hv 3, 3, 5. *The first time* Hv 3, 12, 1; s 9, 1, 3. So prob. also **Gal 4:13.** Naturally the transl. *once* is also prob., but from a linguistic point of view it is not poss. to establish the thesis that Paul wished to differentiate betw. a later visit and an earlier one.

❷ prior to someone/someth. else in importance, ***superior, preferable, more prominent*** (Pla., Lach. 183b πρότεροι ἡμῶν; Aristot. Cat. 14b, 5ff εἰώθασι δὲ καὶ οἱ πολλοὶ τοὺς ἐντιμοτέρους καὶ μᾶλλον ἀγαπωμένους ὑπ᾽ αὐτῶν προτέρους φάσκειν εἶναι=ordinary people are accustomed to say that those who are especially esteemed and held in affection by them enjoy priority in their thinking; Wsd 7:29) ἄλλοι σου πρότεροί εἰσιν *others are superior to you* Hv 3, 4, 3.—As equivalent of an ordinal numeral τῆς Ἰωάννου προτέρας ἐπιστολῆς *the first letter of John* Papias (2:17),—DELG. M-M.

προτίθημι 1 aor. προέθηκα LXX; 2 aor. subj. προθῶ; pf. ptc. προτεθεικώς (Just., D. 65, 3). Mid. 2 aor. προεθέμην. Pass.: 1 aor. ptc. gen. pl. προτεθέντων (Ath., R. 15 p. 65, 20); pf. ptc. προτεθειμένος LXX (Hom.+; ins, pap, LXX; TestReub 1:6 v.l.; Philo, Joseph.; Ar. 13, 5; Just.; Ath.).

❶ to set someth. before someone as someth. to be done, ***set before someone as a task/duty,*** act. w. dat. τινί (Soph., Ant. 216; Hdt. 3, 38; 9, 27) ἐὰν σὺ σεαυτῷ προθῇς ὅτι Hm 12, 3, 5.

❷ to set forth publicly, ***display publicly, make available publicly,*** mid. (Appian, Bell. Civ. 3, 26 §101; Just., D. 65, 3 τὸ πρόβλημα) of Christ ὃν προέθετο ὁ θεὸς ἱλαστήριον **Ro 3:25** (s. ἱλαστήριον). But the act., at least, seems to have had the mng. *offer* as well (s. SIG 708, 15 w. the editor's note 5; 714, 16–18, and M-M.; also ZPE 3, '68, 166 n. 9).

❸ to have someth. in mind beforehand, ***plan, propose, intend,*** τὶ *someth.*, mid. (Pla., Phdr. 259d; Polyb. 6, 12, 8; Jos., Vi. 290) **Eph 1:9.** W. inf. foll. (Pla., Rep. 1, 352d, Leg. 1, 638c; Polyb. 8, 13, 3; 11, 7, 3; Jos., C. Ap. 2, 287, Ant. 18, 286; 19, 37) **Ro 1:13** (B-D-F §392, 1a). ὁ καιρὸς ὃν θεὸς προέθετο φανερῶσαι ... *the time that God had appointed to reveal* (as part of a comprehensive plan and design) Dg 9:2.—M-M. TW.

προτρέπω in our lit. only mid. (so Hom.+; the prefix focuses on forward motion) 1 aor. προετρεψάμην; 2 aor. pass. 3 sg. προετράπη (ApcrEzk) **to promote a particular course of action,** ***urge (on), encourage, impel, persuade*** (Soph. et al.) τινά *someone* w. inf. foll. (Hyperid. 6, 24; UPZ 110, 165 [164 BC]; PRyl 77, 48; BGU 164, 17; 450, 15; 2 Macc 11:7; Jos., Ant. 12, 166; Just., D. 106, 1) 1 Cl 34:4. Abs. (Jos., Ant. 5, 171; 7, 262) **Ac 18:27.**—M-M. Spicq.

προτρέχω 2 aor. προέδραμον (Antiphon et al.; LXX) ***run ahead*** **J 20:4** (=outrun; cp. X., An. 1, 5, 2 προδραμόντες ... πολὺ γὰρ τῶν ἵππων ἔτρεχον θᾶττον of asses who 'outran' someone mounted on a horse, 'for they ran much faster than the horses'); **Ac 10:25** D. πρ. εἰς τὸ ἔμπροσθεν *run on ahead* **Lk 19:4** (s. ἔμπροσθεν 1a and cp. Tob 11:3; Job 41:14 v.l.; *progress* AcPlCor 2:2).

προϋπάρχω impf. προϋπῆρχον intr. ***exist before*** (so Thu. et al.; Diod. S. 16, 82, 6; ins, pap; Job 42:18; Philo, Op. M. 130; Jos., Ant. 1, 290; Just.) w. ptc. foll. (B-D-F §414, 1; Rob. 1121) προϋπῆρχεν μαγεύων *he had been practicing magic* **Ac 8:9** (Jos., Ant. 4, 125 ἅ τε καὶ προϋπῆρξεν ἐν τοῖς ἔμπροσθεν χρόνοις γενόμενα τοῖς ἀνθρώποις). προϋπῆρχον ἐν ἔχθρᾳ ὄντες **Lk 23:12** (cp. Diod. S. 19, 7, 2 διὰ τὰς προϋπαρχούσας ἔχθρας; Vett. Val. 283, 24 διὰ τὴν προϋπάρχουσαν ἔχθραν).—DELG s.v. ἄρχω. M-M.

προφανερόω 1 aor. προεφανέρωσα, pass. προεφανερώθην ***reveal beforehand/in advance*** τὸ πάθος pass. B 6:7. τινὶ περί τινος *reveal someth. to someone in advance* 3:6. Without the dat., which is to be supplied fr. the context 11:1. τί τινι *someth. to someone* 7:1. Abs. (w. προετοιμάζειν and followed by πληροῦν, the 'fulfilling' of the revelation) MPol 14:2.—DELG s.v. φαίνω.

πρόφασις, εως, ἡ (προφαίνω; Hom+)**—❶ someth. said in defense of an action,** ***actual motive or reason, valid excuse*** (Pind., Thu. et al.; SIG 888, 137; PLips 64, 8 διὰ τὴν πρόφασιν ταύτην='for this reason'; TestAbr B 3 p. 107, 8 [Stone p. 62], purpose; TestJob 11:11 προφάσει τῶν πενήτων=for the sake of the poor, for the poor; TestJos 8:5; Philo; Jos., Ant. 13, 427, Vi. 167) πρ. ἔχειν περί τινος *have a valid excuse for someth.* **J 15:22.**

❷ falsely alleged motive, ***pretext, ostensible reason, excuse*** (Hom. et al.; OGI 669, 15 προφάσει=under the pretext; pap, LXX, Philo; Jos., Bell. 2, 348, Vi. 79; 282; Just., D. 141, 1; Tat.) προφάσει *with false motives* (opp. ἀληθείᾳ, Thu. 6, 33, 2; cp. Arrian, Anab. 1, 25, 3.—In reality they have other interests.) **Phil 1:18.** *For a pretext, for appearance' sake* (as if they felt an inner need) **Mt 23:14 v.l.; Mk 12:40; Lk 20:47** (JDerrett, NovT 14, '72, 1–9: a display of piety to secure confidence in them). προφάσει ὡς *under the pretext that, pretending that* (Philip in Demosth. 18, 77 πρόφασιν ὡς w. ptc.) **Ac 27:30.** ἐν πρ. πλεονεξίας *with a pretext for* (satisfying) *greed* **1 Th 2:5.**—KDeichgräber, Πρόφασις: Quellen u. Stud. z. Gesch. der Naturwissenschaften u. d. Med. III/4, '33; LPearson, Prophasis and Aitia: TAPA 83, '52, 205–23.—DELG s.v. φαίνω. M-M. TW. Sv.

προφέρω 2 aor. προήνεγκον (-κα) (Hom. et al.; ins, pap, LXX; TestJob 11:1) of productivity **to bring someth. forth,** ***yield (the earth) yields*** τοὺς κάρπους GJs 3:3; of bringing someth. out into the open (Appian, Syr. 59 §309; Jos., Bell. 1, 671) τὶ ἔκ τινος (Alciphron 4, 13, 15; Pr 10:13) **Lk 6:45ab.**—M-M.

προφητεία, ας, ἡ (προφήτης; Lucian, Alex. 40; 60; Heliod. 1, 22, 7; 1, 33, 2; 2, 27, 1; Ps.-Callisth. 2, 1, 3 [prophetic office]; CIG 2880, 4–6; 2881, 4; 5; OGI 494, 8f; PTebt 294, 8; 295, 10; LXX, Test12Patr; AscIs 3:21 and 31; Philo, Joseph., Just.; Ath. 9, 2)

❶ act of interpreting divine will or purpose, ***prophetic activity*** αἱ ἡμέραι τῆς προφητείας αὐτῶν **Rv 11:6.** μισθοὺς λαμβάνει τῆς προφητείας αὐτοῦ *he accepts pay for his activity as prophet* Hm 11:12.

❷ the gift of interpreting divine will or purpose, ***gift of prophesying*** (Iren. 1, 13, 4 [Harv. I 120, 4]), of Rahab 1 Cl 12:8. Of Christians **Ro 12:6; 1 Cor 12:10; 13:2, 8 v.l.; 14:22.** The pl. of various kinds and grades of prophetic gifts **13:8; 1 Th 5:20** (here mng. 3b is also prob.). τὸ πνεῦμα τῆς πρ. *the spirit of prophecy* **Rv 19:10.**

❸ the utterance of one who interprets divine will or purpose, ***prophecy*** (Jos., Ant. 9, 119; Just., D. 30, 2; 54, 2 al. Of the Sibyl: Theoph. Ant. 2, 36 [p. 190, 10]).

ⓐ of OT inspired statement (Orig., C. Cels. 1, 51, 23; Hippol., Ref. 6, 19, 7; Theoph. Ant. 3, 25 [p. 256, 20]) ἡ προφητεία

Ἠσαΐου **Mt 13:14** (Just.. D. 50, 2 al.). αἱ προφητεῖαι beside ὁ νόμος Μωσέως (Μωϋσέως is better; s. Bihlmeyer p. xxxvi) ISm 5:1. Gener. of OT sayings **2 Pt 1:20f** (but P[72] appears to distinguish prophecy and OT writing: προφητεία καὶ γραφή); B 13:4 (Gen. 48:11; Just., A I, 54, 7 Μωϋσέως).

ⓑ of inspired statements by Christian prophets ἐν προφητείᾳ *in the form of a prophetic saying* **1 Cor 14:6; 1 Th 5:20** (s. 2 above); **1 Ti 1:18; 4:14.** οἱ λόγοι τῆς πρ. *the words of the prophecy* **Rv 1:3.** οἱ λόγοι τῆς πρ. τοῦ βιβλίου τούτου *the words of prophecy in this book* **22:7, 10, 18.** οἱ λόγ. τοῦ βιβλίου τῆς πρ. ταύτης *the words of this book of prophecy* vs. **19.**—DELG s.v. φημί II A. M-M. TW.

προφητεύω (προφήτης) impf. ἐπροφήτευον; fut. προφητεύσω; 1 aor. ἐπροφήτευσα (also προεφήτ. [1 Km 18:10; Just.] v.l.; on the augment s. B-D-F §69, 4; W-S. §12, 6; Mlt-H. 192). Pass.: aor. 3 sg. προεφητεύθη; pf. 3 sg. πεπροφήτευται; plpf. 3 sg. ἐπεπροφήτευτο (all Just.) (Pind., Hdt.+; Diod. S. 17, 51, 1; Ps.-Aristot., De Mundo 1, 391a, 16 ἡ ψυχὴ θείῳ ψυχῆς ὄμματι τὰ θεῖα καταλαβοῦσα τοῖς τε ἀνθρώποις προφητεύουσα=the soul comprehending divine things with its divine eye and interpreting them to humans; Plut., Mor. 412b; Lucian, VH 2, 33; Herodian 5, 5, 10; OGI 473, 2; 530, 9; Gnomon [= BGU V] 93; LXX; pseudepigr., Philo, Joseph., Just. Prim.: 'to serve as interpreter of divine will or purpose'; futurity may or may not be indicated)

❶ **to proclaim an inspired revelation,** ***prophesy*** abs. (Diod. S. 17, 51, 1; Jos., Ant. 5, 348) οὐ τῷ σῷ ὀνόματι ἐπροφητεύσαμεν; **Mt 7:22** (s. Jer 34:15).—**Ac 2:17f** (Jo 3:1); **19:6; 21:9; 1 Cor 11:4f** (w. προσεύχεσθαι); **13:9; 14:1, 3–5, 24, 31, 39; Rv 11:3;** B 16:9; Hm 11:12. Of sayings fr. scripture B 9:2; Hv 2, 3, 4 (the quot. here fr. the book of Eldad and Modat has no bearing on the future; naturally that does not exclude the possibility that these 'prophets' practiced their art in the sense of mng. 3 below).

❷ **to tell about someth. that is hidden from view,** ***tell, reveal,*** of the scornful challenge to Jesus that reduces inspired activity to clairvoyance προφήτευσον ἡμῖν, Χριστέ, τίς ἐστιν ὁ παίσας σε; **Mt 26:68;** cp. **Mk 14:65; Lk 22:64** (cp. the mocking of Eunus the soothsayer in Diod. S. 34/35, 2, 46 [GRudberg, ZNW 24, 1925, 307–9] and WCvanUnnik, ZNW 29, '30, 310f; PBenoit, OCullmann Festschr., '62, 92–110).

❸ **to foretell someth. that lies in the future,** ***foretell, prophesy*** (SibOr 3, 163; 699 al.; Iren. 1, 13, 3 [Harv I 118, 15]; Orig., C. Cels. 6, 47, 11. τὸ π. καὶ προλέγειν τὰ ἐσόμενα Hippol., Ref. 9, 27, 3), of prophets and people of God in times past: **Mt 11:13.** πρ. περί τινος *prophesy about someone* or *someth.* (2 Ch 18:7; AscIs 2:14) **Mt 15:7; Mk 7:6; 1 Pt 1:10.** πρ. εἴς τινα *prophesy with reference to someone* B 5:6. Also πρ. ἐπί τινι 5:13. Foll. by direct discourse 12:10. ἐπροφήτευσεν λέγων, foll. by dir. disc. **Lk 1:67** (John the Baptist's father); also τινί *to someone* **Jd 14** (Enoch). W. ὅτι foll.: of the high priest (s. Jos., Bell. 1, 68f=Ant. 13, 299f; s. also 282f; CHDodd, OCullmann Festschr., '62, 134–43.—According to Diod. S. 40, 3, 5; 6 Ἰουδαῖοι considered the ἀρχιερεύς to be an ἄγγελος τῶν τοῦ θεοῦ προσταγμάτων. Whatever is revealed to him he communicates to the people in their assemblies [κατὰ τὰς ἐκκλησίας]) **J 11:51** (cp. ref. to Elijah περὶ Ὀχοζείου ὅτι AscIs 2:14). Of the writer of Rv πρ. ἐπὶ λαοῖς **Rv 10:11.** Of Christian bogus seers Hm 11:13 (s. 11:2 on their identity: they speak with people who ask them τί ἄρα ἔσται αὐτοῖς).—DELG s.v. φημί II A. M-M. TW.

προφήτης, ου, ὁ (πρό, φημί; ind., Hdt.+. Exx. in Fascher, s. end of this entry) a proclaimer or expounder of divine matters or concerns that could not ordinarily be known except by special revelation (a type of person common in polytheistic society, s. e.g. Plato Com. [V/IV BC] 184 [Orpheus]; Ephor. [IV BC]: 70 fgm. 206 Jac. of Ammon, likew. Diod. S. 17, 51, 1; Plut., Numa 9, 8 the pontifex maximus as ἐξηγητὴς κ. προφήτης; Dio Chrys. 19 [36], 42 πρ. τῶν Μουσῶν; Ael. Aristid. 45, 4 K.=8 p. 83 D.: προφῆται τῶν θεῶν; 45, 7 K.=8 p. 84 D.; 46 p. 159 D.: οἱ πρ. κ. οἱ ἱερεῖς, likew. Himerius, Or. 8 [Or. 23], 11; Alciphron 4, 19, 9 Διονύσου πρ.; Himerius, Or. 38 [Or. 4], 9 Socrates as Μουσῶν καὶ Ἑρμοῦ προφήτης, Or. 48 [Or. 14], 8 προφῆται of the Egyptians [on the role of the Egypt. proph. s. HKees, Der berichtende Gottesdiener: ZASA 85, '60, 138–43]; PGM 3, 256).

❶ **a person inspired to proclaim or reveal divine will or purpose,** ***prophet***—ⓐ of prophetic personalities in the OT who bear a message fr. God (cp. GHölscher, Die Profeten v. Israel 1914; BDuhm, Israels Propheten[2] 1922; HGunkel, Die Proph. 1917; LDürr, Wollen u. Wirken der atl. Proph. 1926; JSeverijn, Het Profetisme 1926; HHertzberg, Prophet u. Gott 1923; JHempel, Gott u. Mensch im AT[2] '36, 95–162). Some are mentioned by name (Moses: Orig., C. Cels. 6, 21, 8): Jeremiah **Mt 2:17; 27:9.** Isaiah (Did., Gen. 52, 13) **3:3; 4:14; 8:17; Lk 3:4; J 1:23; 12:38; Ac 28:25** al. Joel **2:16.** Jonah **Mt 12:39.** Daniel **24:15.** Elijah, Elisha, Ezekiel 1 Cl 17:1. Elisha **Lk 4:27;** AcPlCor 2:32; Samuel **Ac 13:20;** cp. **3:24.** David **2:30** (ApcSed 14:4; Just., A I, 35, 6; JFitzmyer, CBQ 34, '72, 332–39). Even Balaam **2 Pt 2:16.**—Somet. the identity of *the prophet* is known only fr. the context, or the reader is simply expected to know who is meant; sim. a Gk. writer says ὁ ποιητής, feeling sure that he will be understood correctly (Antig. Car. 7 [Hom. Hymn to Hermes]; Diod. S. 1, 12, 9; 3, 66, 3 al. [Homer]; schol. on Nicander, Ther. 452; Ps.-Dicaearchus p. 147 F. [Il. 2, 684]; Steph. Byz. s.v. Χαλκίς [Il. 2, 537]—Did., Gen. 25, 20 [Haggai]): **Mt 1:22** (Isaiah, as Just., D. 89, 3); **2:5** (Micah), **15** (Hosea); **21:4** (Zechariah); **Ac 7:48** (Isaiah). See B 6:2, 4, 6f, 10, 13; 11:2, 4, 9; 14:2, 7–9.—The pl. οἱ προφῆται brings *the prophets* together under one category (Iren. 1, 7, 3 [Harv. I 63, 2]; cp. Theoph. Ant. 1, 14 [p. 88, 14]): **Mt 2:23; 5:12; 16:14; Mk 6:15b; Lk 1:70; 6:23; 13:28; J 1:45** (w. Moses); **8:52f; Ac 3:21; 7:52; 10:43; Ro 1:2; 1 Th 2:15; Hb 11:32** (w. David and Samuel); **Js 5:10; 1 Pt 1:10** (classed under e below by ESelwyn, 1 Pt '46, ad loc. and 259–68); **2 Pt 3:2;** 1 Cl 43:1 (Μωϋσῆς καὶ οἱ λοιποὶ πρ.); B 1:7; IMg 9:3; IPhld 5:2; AcPl Ha 8, 16; AcPlCor 1:10; 2:9 and 36. οἱ θειότατοι πρ. IMg 8:2; οἱ ἀγαπητοὶ πρ. IPhld 9:2. οἱ ἀρχαῖοι πρ. (Jos., Ant. 12, 413) D 11:11b. S. 2 below for prophetic figures in association with their written productions.

ⓑ John the Baptist (Just., D. 49, 3) is also called a prophet **Mt 14:5; 21:26; Mk 11:32; Lk 1:76** (προφήτης ὑψίστου; cp. OGI 756, 2 τὸν προφήτην τοῦ ἁγιωτάτου θεοῦ ὑψίστου); **20:6,** but Jesus declared that he was higher than the prophets **Mt 11:9; Lk 7:26.**

ⓒ Jesus appears as a prophet (FGils, Jésus prophète [synoptics], '57 [lit.]) appraised for his surprising knowledge **J 4:19** and ability to perform miracles **9:17.** οὗτός ἐστιν ὁ προφήτης Ἰησοῦς **Mt 21:11.** Cp. vs. **46; Mk 6:15a; Lk 7:16** (πρ. μέγας), **39; 13:33; 24:19; J 7:52.** This proverb is applied to him: οὐκ ἔστιν προφήτης ἄτιμος εἰ μὴ ἐν τῇ πατρίδι αὐτοῦ **Mt 13:57; Mk 6:4;** cp. **Lk 4:24; J 4:44;** Ox 1:10f (GTh 31; EPreuschen, Das Wort v. verachteten Proph.: ZNW 17, 1916, 33–48). He was also taken to be one of the ancient prophets come to life again: **Mt 16:14; Mk 8:28.** πρ. τις τῶν ἀρχαίων **Lk 9:8, 19.**—In **Ac 3:22f** and **7:37** (cp. 1QS 9:11), Dt 18:15, 19 is interpreted w. ref. to the Messiah and hence to Jesus (HSchoeps, Theol. u. Geschichte des Judenchristentums '49, 87–98).—For **J,** Jesus is ὁ προφήτης *the Prophet* **6:14; 7:40,** a title of honor which is disclaimed by the Baptist **1:21, 25** (s. exc. in the Hdb. on J 1:21; HFischel, JBL 65, '46, 157–74). Cp. **Lk 7:39 v.l.**—RMeyer, Der Proph. aus Galiläa '40; PDavies, Jesus and the Role of the Prophet: JBL 64, '45,

241–54; AHiggins, Jesus as Proph.: ET 57, '45/46, 292–94; FYoung, Jesus the Proph.: JBL 68, '49, 285–99.—RSchnackenburg, D. Erwartung des 'Propheten' nach dem NT u. Qumran: Studia Evangelica '59, 622, n. 1; HBraun, Qumran u. das NT, I, '66, 100–106.

ⓓ also of other pers., without excluding the actual prophets, who proclaim the divine message w. special preparation and w. a special mission (1 Macc 4:46; 14:41; Hippol., Ref. 1, prol. 10): **Mt 11:9** and parallels (s. 1b above); **13:57** and parall. (s. 1c above); **23:30, 37; Lk 10:24** (on προφῆται καὶ βασιλεῖς s. Boll 136–42); **13:33f; Ac 7:52.** The two prophets of God in the last times **Rv 11:10** (s. μάρτυς 2c and Πέτρος, end). In several of the passages already mentioned (**1 Th 2:15** [s. a above]; **Mt 23:30, 37; Lk 13:34; Ac 7:52**), as well as others (s. below for **Mt 23:34; Lk 11:49** [OSeitz, TU 102, '68, 236–40]), various compatriots of Jesus are murderers of prophets (cp. 3 Km 19:10, 14; Jos., Ant. 9, 265). HJSchoeps, D. jüd. Prophetenmorde '43.—Jesus also sends to his own people προφήτας καὶ σοφούς **Mt 23:34** or πρ. κ. ἀποστόλους **Lk 11:49;** s. also **Mt 10:41** (πρ. beside δίκαιος, as **13:17**). This brings us to

ⓔ Christians, who are endowed w. the gift of προφητεία **Ac 15:32; 1 Cor 14:29, 32, 37; Rv 22:6, 9;** D 10:7; 13:1, 3f, 6. W. ἀπόστολοι (Celsus 2, 20) **Lk 11:49; Eph 2:20** (though here the ref. could be to the OT prophets, as is surely the case in Pol 6:3. Acc. to PJoüon, RSR 15, 1925, 534f, τῶν ἀπ. καὶ πρ. in Eph 2:20 refer to the same persons); **3:5;** D 11:3. πρ. stands betw. ἀπόστολοι and διδάσκαλοι **1 Cor 12:28f;** cp. **Eph 4:11.** W. διδάσκαλοι **Ac 13:1;** D 15:1f. W. ἅγιοι and ἀπόστολοι **Rv 18:20.** W. ἅγιοι **11:18; 16:6; 18:24.** Prophets foretell future events (cp. Pla., Charm. 173c προφῆται τῶν μελλόντων) **Ac 11:27** (s. vs. 28); **21:10** (s. vss. 11f). True and false prophets: τὸν προφήτην καὶ τὸν ψευδοπροφήτην Hm 11:7; s. vss. 9 and 15 (the rest of this 'mandate' also deals w. this subj.); D 11:7–11.—Harnack, Lehre der Zwölf Apostel 1884, 93ff; 119ff, Mission[4] I 1923, 344f; 362ff; Rtzst., Mysterienrel.[3] 236–40; s. ESelwyn on 1 Pt 1:10 in 1a above; HGreeven, Propheten, Lehrer, Vorsteher b. Pls: ZNW 44, '52/53, 3–15.

ⓕ Only in one place in our lit. is a polytheist called a 'prophet', i.e. the poet whose description of the Cretans is referred to in **Tit 1:12:** ἴδιος αὐτῶν προφήτης *their* (the Cretans') *own prophet* (s. ἀργός 2).

❷ by metonymy, **the writings of prophets.** The prophet also stands for his book ἀνεγίνωσκεν τ. προφήτην Ἠσαΐαν **Ac 8:28, 30;** cp. **Mk 1:2.** λέγει (κύριος) ἐν τῷ προφήτῃ B 7:4. ἐν ἄλλῳ πρ. λέγει 11:6. See 6:14; 12:1 and 4. Pl. of the prophets as a division of scripture: οἱ προφῆται καὶ ὁ νόμος (s. 2 Macc 15:9; Mel., HE 4, 26, 13, P. 72, 530) **Mt 11:13.** Cp. **Lk 16:16; Ac 13:15; 24:14; Ro 3:21;** Dg 11:6. Μωϋσῆς κ. οἱ πρ. **Lk 16:29, 31.** Cp. also **24:27; Ac 28:23.** πάντα τὰ γεγραμμένα ἐν τῷ νόμῳ Μωϋσέως καὶ τοῖς προφήταις καὶ ψαλμοῖς **Lk 24:44.** Now and then οἱ προφῆται alone may mean all scripture **Lk 24:25; J 6:45** (s. JHänel, Der Schriftbegriff Jesu 1919, 21); **Hb 1:1** (s. CBüchel, Der Hb u. das AT: StKr 79, 1906, 508–91).—οἱ πρ. **Mt 5:17; 7:12; 22:40** (all three w. ὁ νόμος) unmistakably refers to the contents of the prophetic books.—EFascher, Προφήτης. Eine sprach- und religionsgeschichtliche Untersuchung 1927; GFohrer, TRu 19, '51, 277–346; 20. '52. 193–271, 295–361; JLindblom, Prophecy in Ancient Israel '67; DAune, Prophecy '83; ASchwemer ZTK 96, '99, 320–50 (prophet as martyr); Pauly-W. XXIII 797ff; Kl. Pauly IV, 1183f; BHHW III 1496–1514.—DELG s.v. φημί II A. EDNT. TW. Sv.

προφητικός, ή, όν (προφήτης; Lucian, Alex. 60; Philo, Migr. Abr. 84 al.; Just., Mel., Ath.; PGM 1, 278; 4, 933) **pert. to inspired interpretation of the divine will,** ***prophetic*** γραφαὶ πρ. *the writings of the prophets*=the OT **Ro 16:26** (cp. AcPh 77 [Aa II/2, 30, 6]). ὁ πρ. λόγος (Philo, Plant. 117; TestSol 1:12 D ἡ -κὴ ῥῆσις) **2 Pt 1:19** (on the true prophetic word vs. the false [s. 2 Pt 2:1] cp. Pind., P. 10, 65f); 2 Cl 11:2 (the origin of *the prophetic word* that follows is unknown); AcPl Ha 8, 27. ὁ ἄγγελος τοῦ πρ. πνεύματος Hm 11:9 (πρ. πνεῦμα, as Philo, Fuga 186; Just., A I, 38, 1; Ath. 10, 3). Of Polycarp διδάσκαλος ἀποστολικὸς καὶ προφητικός MPol 16:2.—DELG s.v. φημί II A. TW.

προφητικῶς adv. of προφητικός, ***prophetically*** εἰπεῖν *speak prophetically* (followed by direct discourse) MPol 12:3 (Ath. 10, 3 after direct discourse).

προφῆτις, ιδος, ἡ (cp. προφήτης; Eur., Pla.+; Diod. S. 14, 13, 3 [Pythia]; ins: CIG 3796; InsMagn 122d, 3 [if it is correctly restored]; LXX: Ex 15:20 Miriam; Judg 4:4 Deborah et al.; Philo; Jos., Ant. 10, 59; SibOr 3, 818; Sextus 441) the form corresponding to προφήτης (s. above) ***prophet*** **Lk 2:36.** Of a Jezebel who was misleading the church at Thyatira ἡ λέγουσα ἑαυτὴν προφῆτιν *who calls herself a prophet* **Rv 2:20** (s. Ἰεζάβελ and the lit. there).—DELG s.v. φημί II A. M-M. TW.

προφθάνω fut. 3 sg. προφθάσει LXX; 1 aor. προέφθασα; pf. 3 sg. προέφθακεν 1 Macc 10:23 (Aeschyl., Pla. et al.; Plut., Mor. 806f; LXX) of temporal priority

❶ **to be ahead of someone in some activity,** ***be ahead of, come before, anticipate*** w. acc. and ptc. foll. (Aristoph., Eccl. 884; B-D-F §414, 4; Rob. 1120; φθάνω w. ptc.: EpArist 137) προέφθασεν αὐτὸν λέγων *he spoke to him first* **Mt 17:25.**

❷ **to do someth. at a point of time prior to another point of time,** ***do before/previously*** w. inf. foll. (B-D-F §392, 2; Rob. 1120) ἐὰν προφθάσῃ εἰς τὴν κάμινον αὐτὸ βαλεῖν *if he has previously* (=*already*) *put it into the furnace* 2 Cl 8:2.—M-M. TW.

προφυλάσσω fut. mid. προφυλάξομαι 2 Km 22:24 (φύλαξ; Hom. Hymns, Hdt. et al.; SIG 730, 15; PWürzburg 9, 8 [II AD])

❶ **to take security measures beforehand,** ***guard, protect*** τινά *someone,* act. ITr 8:1. πρ. τινὰ ἀπό τινος *someone against someone* ISm 4:1 (on ἀπό τινος cp. 2 Km 22:24). S. also 2.

❷ **to be vigilant in the face of danger,** ***be on one's guard,*** mid. (Hdt., Thu. et al.; 2 Km 22:24; SibOr 3, 733) w. μή and inf. IMg 11 (though because of the analogy of the two passages mentioned above the mid. here could have act. mng. [Diogenian. the Epicurean, of II AD, fgm. 4 Gercke: in Eus., PE 4, 3, 7 end, twice; and Philo, Cher. 34 the mid. means 'ward someth. off']; Rdm.[2] 79f).—DELG s.v. φύλαξ.

προχειρίζω in our lit., as mostly, only as mid. dep. **προχειρίζομαι** 1 aor. προεχειρισάμην. Pass.: aor. ptc. pl. masc. προχειρισθέντες Da 3:22; pf. ptc. προκεχειρισμένος **to express preference of someone for a task,** ***choose for oneself, select, appoint*** τινά *someone* (Isocr. et al.; Polyb. 2, 43, 1; 6, 58, 3; Dionys. Hal., De Orat. Ant. 4; Plut., Galba 1056 [8, 3], Caesar 735 [58, 8]; Lucian, Tox. 10; SIG 873, 14f; OGI 339, 46; 50; pap; 2 Macc 3:7; 8:9) foll. by an inf. of purpose **Ac 22:14.** W. two acc., of obj. and pred. (Polyb. 1, 11, 3; Diod. S. 12, 27, 1; PLond 2710 recto, 5; Ex 4:13) προχειρίσασθαί σε ὑπηρέτην **26:16.** Pass. (προκεχειρισμένος as UPZ 117 II, 4 [II BC]; BGU 1198, 2 [I BC]; PFay 14, 1) τὸν προκεχειρισμένον ὑμῖν Χριστὸν Ἰησοῦν *Christ Jesus, who was appointed for you* or *Jesus who was appointed* (or *destined*) *to be your Messiah* **3:20** (the dat. like Josh 3:12; s. προκηρύσσω).—DELG s.v. χείρ III. M-M. TW. Spicq.

προχειροτονέω (cp. χειροτόνος 'stretching out the hands') pf. pass. ptc. προκεχειροτονημένος ***choose/appoint beforehand*** (so Pla., Leg. 6, 765bc al.; Cass. Dio 50, 4; BGU 1191, 6 [I BC] τῷ προκεχειροτονημένῳ) **Ac 10:41.**—DELG s.v. χείρ II. M-M.

Πρόχορος, ου, ὁ (found in later Gk.) ***Prochorus,*** one of the seven appointees for special service in the church at Jerusalem **Ac 6:5.**

προχωρέω (Soph., Hdt. et al.; ins, pap, TestIss 1:11) prim. sense 'go forward, advance', in our lit. only fig. **to advance as state or condition, *turn out, succeed*** w. dat. of pers. for whom someth. goes well (Hdt. 5, 62; Thu. 4, 73, 4; Lucian, Icar. 10; PLond 358, 13 [II AD] προχωρεῖν αὐτοῖς τὰ ἄνομα; Jos., Vi. 122) οὐδὲν αὐτοῖς ὅλως προχωρεῖ *nothing at all turns out well for them* Hs 6, 3, 5.—DELG s.v. χώρα.

πρύμνα, ης, ἡ (Hom. et al.; pap) the after part of a boat ***stern*** (opp. πρῷρα) ἦν ἐν τῇ πρύμνῃ καθεύδων *he was asleep in the stern* **Mk 4:38.—Ac 27:29** (WStammler, AG 27 in nautischer Beleuchtung etc., '31, 3–15; against him FBruce, Acts[3], '90, 523, w. evidence of ships dropping anchor from the stern) (w. πρῷρα as X., An. 5, 8, 20; Ael. Aristid. 44, 13 K.=17 p. 405 D.).—DELG s.v. πρυμνός. M-M.

πρωΐ adv. of time (cp. πρό; Hom.+; in Attic writers as πρῴ) **in the early part of the daylight period, *early, early in the morning*** **Mt 16:3; 21:18; Mk 1:35; 11:20; 16:9;** Hs 9, 11, 2 (opp. ὀψέ). As the fourth watch of the night (after ὀψὲ ἢ μεσονύκτιον ἢ ἀλεκτοροφωνίας) it is the time fr. three to six o'clock **Mk 13:35.** εὐθὺς πρ. *as soon as morning came* **15:1.** ἅμα πρ. (ἅμα 2, end) **Mt 20:1;** λίαν πρ. w. dat., of the day *very early* **Mk 16:2.** ἀπὸ πρ. ἕως ἑσπέρας *from morning till evening* **Ac 28:23** (cp. Jos., Ant. 13, 97). πρωῒ σκοτίας ἔτι οὔσης **J 20:1.** ἦν πρ. *it was early in the morning* (B-D-F §129; 434, 1) **18:28.** τὸ πρωΐ is likew. an adv. (PSI 402, 10 [III BC] τὸ πρωῒ εὐθέως; LXX; TestAbr B 2 p. 106, 7 [Stone p. 60] τῷ πρωί; TestNapht 1:3; JosAs 9:4; ApcEsdr 4:29; B-D-F §160; 161, 3) **Ac 5:21** D. ἐπὶ τὸ πρωΐ *toward morning* **Mk 15:1 v.l.;** for this another v.l. has ἐπὶ τῷ πρ.—Billerb. I 688–91; TMartin, BR 38, '93, 55–69. B. 960. DELG s.v. πρώην. M-M.

πρωΐα, ας, ἡ (cp. πρωΐ; Diod. S.; CIG 1122, 16; BGU 1206, 20 [28 BC]; PLond I, 131, 16 p. 170; 461 p. 183 [78/79 AD]; III, 1177, 66 p. 183 [113 AD] ἀπὸ πρωΐας ἕως ὀψέ; LXX; ParJer; EpArist 304; Philo, Vi. Cont. 89; Jos., Ant. 7, 164; Ar. [Milne 76, 34] κατὰ πρώϊας.—Really the fem. of πρώϊος [since Hom.], sc. ὥρα) **early part of the daylight period, *(early) morning,*** πρωΐας γενομένης *when it was morning* (ParJer 4:1; Syntipas p. 49, 17; 53, 6) **Mt 27:1;** 1 Cl 43:5. Cp. **J 18:28 v.l.; 21:4.** Gen. of time πρωΐας *(early) in the morning* **Mt 21:18 v.l.;** GPt 9:34.—B. 994. DELG s.v. πρώην. M-M.

πρωΐθεν (πρωΐ) adv. of time (LXX; Herodian, Gr. I 501, 9) ***(from) morning,*** ἀπὸ πρ. ἕως ἑσπέρας 1 Cl 39:5 (Job 4:20). The ending -θεν tended to lose its force and become meaningless in many instances: s. exx. B-D-F §104, 2; Rob. 300; MLejeune, Les adverbes grecs en -θεν '39, but in the case of πρ. the traditional force was apparently still felt but strengthened by the prep. ἀπό (cp. Georg. Mon. 179, 16).—DELG s.v. πρώην.

πρώϊμος s. πρόϊμος.

πρωϊνός, ή, όν (PCairZen 207, 36 [III BC]; Babrius 124, 17 w. the v.l. προϊνων fr. cod. V. [L-P.]; Plut., Mor. 726e; Athen. 1, 19 p. 11c; LXX) **pert. to early morning, *early, belonging to the morning*** ὁ ἀστὴρ ὁ πρ. *the morning star,* Venus **Rv 2:28; 22:16** (s. προϊνός for vv.ll.).—DELG s.v. πρώην.

πρῷρα (Hom. et al.; PSI 382, 2 [III BC]; PEdg 9 [=Sb 6715], 15 [257 BC]. On the ι subscript B-D-F §26; Mlt-H. 84), **ης** (PGM 8, 40; B-D-F §43, 1; Mlt-H. 118), **ἡ, the forepart of a boat, *bow, prow*** (opp. πρύμνα) **Ac 27:30, 41** (cp. the description Pind., P. 10, 51f; s. πρύμνα). DELG. M-M.

πρωτεῖος, α, ον (cp. πρωτεύω) **pert. to high degree on a scale of quality or importance, *of first quality/rank*** (BGU 950, 4; PLond V, 1764, 7; Sym.) the neut. subst. in the pl. (Ael. Aristid. 38 p. 720 D.; Stephan. Byz. v. Ἰδουμαῖοι; Sb 6997, 28; PSI 716, 14 where, unfortunately, the text breaks off after τὰ πρωτεῖα. The sing. is found Kaibel 560, 3 [I AD]; Jos., Vi. 37; Proclus, Theol. 98 p. 88, 24) περὶ πρωτείων *for the first places, about preeminence* Hs 8, 7, 4; 6.

πρωτεύω (cp. πρωτεῖος; Pla., X. et al.; ins, incl. IMagnSip [IK VIII, 32, 3f]; pap, LXX; Ath., R. 24 p. 78, 4) **to hold the highest rank in a group, *be first, have first place*** ἵνα γένηται ἐν πᾶσιν αὐτὸς πρωτεύων *that he might come to have first place in everything* **Col 1:18** (ἐν πᾶσιν like Plut., Mor. 9b. The pres. ptc. like PLips 40 II, 16; POxy 1983, 3; 2 Macc 6:18; 13:15; EpArist 275; Jos., Ant. 9, 167; 20, 182).—New Docs 2, 96; 4, 172. DELG s.v. πρῶτος. M-M. TW.

πρωτοκαθεδρία, ας, ἡ (πρῶτος, καθέδρα; schol. on Eur., Orest. 93; Theophanes Conf. 163, 26 de Boor; cp. προεδρία of seats reserved for pers. in recognition of their public service, s. Reader, Polemo 285f) **a position or place indicative of special honor for the pers. occupying it, *seat of honor, best seat*** desired by Pharisees in the synagogue **Mt 23:6; Mk 12:39; Lk 11:43; 20:46.** Likew. by a false prophet θέλει πρωτοκαθεδρίαν ἔχειν Hm 11:12.—DELG s.v. ἕζομαι. TW.

πρωτοκαθεδρίτης, ου, ὁ (s. prec. entry; only in Christian writers) ***one who occupies a seat of honor*** (w. οἱ προηγούμενοι) of congregation leaders Hv 3, 9, 7 (Leutzsch, Hermas 424 n. 420).

πρωτοκλισία, ας, ἡ (ins fr. Delos [II BC]: JHS 54, '34, 142; Suda) ***the place of honor*** at a dinner, beside the master of the house or the host **Mt 23:6; Mk 12:39; Lk 14:7f; 20:46.**—DELG s.v. κλίνω. M-M. TW.

πρωτόμαρτυς, υρος, ὁ of one especially distinguished for testimony to the death, *first martyr,* of Stephen **Ac 22:20 v.l.** (cp. Πράξεις Παύλου Aa I 235 v.l. in the fem. form of Thecla, whose prestige is indicated by the descriptive terms ἀποστολός and ἰσαπόστολος in the ms. tradition; the mss. vary, some qualifying πρ. with ἐν γυναιξί).—Late pap: New Docs 2, 152.

πρῶτον adv. of πρῶτος, s. next entry.

πρῶτος, η, ον (Hom.+; loanw. in rabb.).—**❶ pert. to being first in a sequence, inclusive of time, set (number), or space, *first*** of several, but also when only two persons or things are involved (=πρότερος; exx. in Hdb. on J 1:15; Rdm.[2] 71f; Thackeray 183; s. also Mlt. 79; 245; B-D-F §62; Rob. 516; 662; and s. Mt 21:31 v.l.).

ⓐ of time ***first, earliest, earlier*—α.** as adj. ἀπὸ τῆς πρώτης ἡμέρας ἄχρι τοῦ νῦν **Phil 1:5;** cp. **Ac 20:18** (on the absence of the art. [also **Phil 1:5 v.l.**] s. B-D-F §256; Rob. 793). ἡ πρώτη ἀπολογία **2 Ti 4:16** (MMeinertz, Worauf bezieht sich die πρώτη ἀπολογία 2 Ti 4:16?: Biblica 4, 1923, 390–94). ἡ πρ. διαθήκη **Hb 9:15.** τὰ πρῶτα ἔργα **Rv 2:5.** ἡ ἀνάστασις ἡ πρώτη **20:5f.** ἡ πρώτη ὅρασις Hv 3, 10, 3; 3, 11, 2; 4. ἡ ἐκκλησία ἡ πρ. 2 Cl 14:1.—Subst. τὰ πρ. . . . τὰ ἔσχατα (Job 8:7): γίνεται τὰ ἔσχατα χείρονα τῶν πρώτων **Mt 12:45;** cp. **Lk 11:26; 2 Pt 2:20;** Hv 1, 4, 2. οἱ πρῶτοι (those who came earlier, as Artem. 2, 9 p. 93, 19 those who appeared earlier) **Mt 20:10;** cp. vs. **8.** ἀπέστειλεν ἄλλους δούλους πλείονας τῶν πρώτων **21:36.** Cp. **27:64.** πρῶτος ἐξ ἀναστάσεως νεκρῶν *the first to rise from the dead* **Ac 26:23.** ὁ πρῶτος *the first one* **J 5:4; 1 Cor 14:30.** On the self-designation of the Risen Lord ὁ πρ. καὶ ὁ ἔσχατος **Rv 1:17; 2:8; 22:13;** s. ἔσχατος 2b (πρ. of God: Is 44:6; 48:12).—As a predicate adj., where an adv. can be used in English (ParJer 1:8 εἰ μὴ ἐγὼ πρῶτος ἀνοίξω τὰς πύλας; B-D-F §243; Rob. 657), *as the first one = first* ἦλθεν πρῶτος *he was the first one to come = he came first* **J 20:4;** cp. vs. **8.** πρῶτος Μωϋσῆς λέγει **Ro 10:19.** Ἀβραὰμ πρῶτος περιτομὴν δούς *Abraham was the first to practice circumcision* B 9:7. οἱ ἄγγελοι οἱ πρῶτοι κτισθέντες *the angels who were created first* Hv 3, 4, 1; s 5, 5, 3.—**1 Ti 2:13; 1J 4:19;** AcPlCor 2:9.—ἐν ἐμοὶ πρώτῳ *in me as the first* **1 Ti 1:16.**—Used w. a gen. of comparison (Ocelus Luc. 3 ἐκεῖνο πρῶτον τοῦ παντός ἐστιν=prior to the All; Manetho 1, 329; Athen. 14, 28 p. 630c codd.) πρῶτός μου ἦν *he was earlier than I = before me* **J 1:15, 30** (PGM 13, 543 σοῦ πρῶτός εἰμι.—Also Ep. 12 of Apollonius of Tyana: Philostrat. I p. 348, 30 τὸ τῇ τάξει δεύτερον οὐδέποτε τῇ φύσει πρῶτον). So perh. also ἐμὲ πρῶτον ὑμῶν μεμίσηκεν **15:18** (s. β below) and πάντων πρώτη ἐκτίσθη Hv 2, 4, 1.—As a rule the later element is of the same general nature as the one that precedes it. But it can also be someth. quite different, even its exact opposite: τὴν πρώτην πίστιν ἠθέτησαν **1 Ti 5:12.** τὴν ἀγάπην σου τὴν πρώτην ἀφῆκες **Rv 2:4.**—Used elliptically ἡ πρώτη (i.e. ἡμέρα sim. Polyb. 5, 19, 1; 18, 27, 2 τῇ πρώτῃ) τῶν ἀζύμων **Mt 26:17.** πρώτῃ σαββάτου *on the first day of the week* **Mk 16:9.** In some of the passages mentioned above the idea of sequence could be predom.

β. the neuter πρῶτον as adv., of time ***first, in the first place, before, earlier, to begin with*** (Peripl. Eryth. 4; Chariton 8, 2, 4; ApcEsdr 3:11; Just., D. 2, 4) πρῶτον πάντων *first of all* Hv 5:5a. ἐπίτρεψόν μοι πρῶτον ἀπελθεῖν καὶ θάψαι *let me first go and bury* **Mt 8:21.** συλλέξατε πρῶτον τὰ ζιζάνια *gather the weeds first* **13:30.** Cp. **17:10, 11 v.l.; Mk 7:27; 9:11f; 13:10; Lk 9:59, 61; 12:1** (*first* Jesus speaks to his disciples, and only then [vs. 15] to the people. If one prefers to take πρ. w. what follows, as is poss., it has mng. 2a); **14:28, 31; J 7:51; 18:13; Ac 26:20; Ro 15:24** al. in NT; B 15:7; Hv 3, 1, 8; 3, 6, 7; 3, 8, 11; 5:5b. τότε πρῶτον *then for the first time* **Ac 11:26** D. πρῶτον . . . καὶ τότε *first . . . and then* (Sir 11:7; Jos., Ant. 13, 187) **Mt 5:24; 7:5; 12:29; Mk 3:27; Lk 6:42;** IEph 7:2. τότε is correlative w. πρῶτον without καί **J 2:10 v.l.** Likew. πρῶτον . . . εἶτα (εἶτεν) *first . . . then* (Just., D. 33, 2 al.; s. εἶτα 1) **Mk 4:28; 1 Ti 3:10;** B 6:17. πρῶτον . . . ἔπειτα (ἔπειτα 2) **1 Cor 15:46; 1 Th 4:16.** πρῶτον . . . μετὰ ταῦτα **Mk 16:9,** s. vs. 12. πρῶτον . . . εἶτα . . . μετὰ ταῦτα 1 Cl 23:4; 2 Cl 11:3 (in both cases the same prophetic saying of unknown origin). πρῶτον . . . ἐν τῷ δευτέρῳ **Ac 7:12.**—Pleonastically πρῶτον πρὸ τοῦ ἀρίστου **Lk 11:38.**—W. gen. (Chariton 5, 4, 9 cod. πρῶτον τ. λόγων=before it comes to words) ἐμὲ πρῶτον ὑμῶν μεμίσηκεν *it hated me before (it hated) you* **J 15:18** (but s. 1αα).—W. the art. τὸ πρῶτον (Hom. et al.; Jos., Ant. 8, 402; 14, 205) *the first time* **J 10:40; 19:39;** *at first* (Diod. S. 1, 85, 2; Jos., Ant. 2, 340) **12:16;** 2 Cl 9:5. τὰ πρῶτα (Hom. et al.; Appian, Syr. 15 §64; Ps.-Phoc. 8) *the first time, at first* MPol 8:2.

ⓑ of number or sequence (the area within which this sense is valid cannot be marked off w. certainty from the area 1αα)

α. as adj. **Mt 21:28; 22:25; Mk 12:20; Lk 14:18; 16:5; 19:16; 20:29; J 19:32; Ac 12:10; 13:33 v.l.; Rv 4:7; 8:7; 21:19;** Hs 9, 1, 5. τὸ πρῶτον . . . τὸ δεύτερον (Alex. Aphr., An. p. 28, 9 Br.) **Hb 10:9.** On πρώτης τῆς μερίδος Μακεδονίας πόλις **Ac 16:12** s. μερίς 1 and RAscough, NTS 44, '98, 93–103.—Since πρῶτος can stand for πρότερος (s. 1 at beg.; also Mlt-Turner 32), it by no means follows from τὸν μὲν πρῶτον λόγον **Ac 1:1** that the writer of Luke and of Ac must have planned to write a third book (Zahn, NKZ 28, 1917, 373ff, Comm. 1919, 16ff holds that he planned to write a third volume; against this view s. EGoodspeed, Introd. to the NT '37, 189; Haenchen, et al.—Athenaeus 15, 701c mentions the first of Clearchus' two books on proverbs with the words ἐν τῷ προτέρῳ περὶ παροιμιῶν, but 10, 457c with ἐν τῷ πρώτῳ περὶ παροιμιῶν. Diod. S. 1, 42, 1 the first half of a two-part work is called ἡ πρώτη βίβλος and 3, 1, 1 mentions a division into πρώτη and δευτέρα βίβ. In 13, 103, 3 the designation for the first of two works varies between ἡ πρώτη σύνταξις and ἡ προτέρα σ. See Haenchen on Ac 1:1).—πρῶτος is also used without any thought that the series must continue: τὸν πρῶτον ἰχθύν *the very first fish* **Mt 17:27.** αὕτη ἀπογραφὴ πρώτη ἐγένετο **Lk 2:2,** likewise, does not look forward in the direction of additional censuses, but back to a time when there were none at all (Ael. Aristid. 13 p. 227 D. παράκλησις αὕτη [=challenge to a sea-fight] πρώτη ἐγένετο; for interpolation theory s. JWinandy, RB 104, '97, 372–77; cp. BPearson, CBQ, '99, 262–82).—τὰ τείχη τὰ πρῶτα Hs 8, 6, 6 does not contrast the 'first walls' w. other walls; rather it distinguishes the only walls in the picture (Hs 8, 7, 3; 8, 8, 3) as one edifice, from the tower as the other edifice.

β. adv., the neuter πρῶτον of sequence in enumerations (not always clearly distinguished fr. sense 1αβ) *first* πρῶτον ἀποστόλους, δεύτερον προφήτας, τρίτον . . . **1 Cor 12:28** (Mitt-Wilck. I/2, 20 II, 10ff [II AD] τὸ πρ. . . . τὸ δεύτερον . . . τὸ τρίτον. Without the art. 480, 12ff [II AD]; Diod. S. 36, 7, 3; Tat. 40, 1). See **Hb 7:2; Js 3:17.**—Not infrequently Paul begins w. πρῶτον μέν without continuing the series, at least in form (B-D-F §447, 4; Rob. 1152. For πρ. without continuation s. Plat., Ep. 7, 337b, Plut., Mor. 87b; Jos., Ant. 1, 182; Ath. 27, 1 πρῶτα μέν) **Ro 1:8; 3:2; 1 Cor 11:18.** S. also 2 Cl 3:1.

ⓒ of space ***outer, anterior*** σκηνὴ ἡ πρώτη *the outer tent,* i.e. the holy place **Hb 9:2;** cp. vss. **6, 8.**

➋ **pert. to prominence, *first, foremost, most important, most prominent*—ⓐ** adj.—**α.** of things (Ocellus [II BC] 56 Harder [1926] πρώτη κ. μεγίστη φυλακή; Ael. Aristid. 23, 43 K.=42 p. 783 D.: πόλεις; Ezk 27:22; PsSol 17:43; χρυσίον τὸ πρῶτον τίμιον; JosAs 15:10) ἡ μεγάλη καὶ πρώτη ἐντολή **Mt 22:38;** cp. **Mk 12:29.** ἐντολὴ πρώτη πάντων vs. **28** (OLehmann, TU 73, '59, 557–61 [rabb.]; CBurchard, ZNW 61, '70, cites JosAs 15:10; 18:5). Without superl. force ἐντολὴ πρώτη ἐν ἐπαγγελίᾳ *a commandment of great importance, with a promise attached* **Eph 6:2** (the usual transl. 'first commandment w. a promise' [NRSV, REB et al.] loses sight of the fact that Ex 20:4–6=Dt 5:8–10 has an implied promise of the same kind as the one in Ex 20:12=Dt 5:16. πρ. here is best taken in the same sense as in **Mk 12:29** above). στολὴν τὴν πρώτην *the special robe* **Lk 15:22** (JosAs 15:10).—ἐν πρώτοις *among the first = most important things,* i.e. *as of first importance* **1 Cor 15:3** (Pla., Pol. 522c ὃ καὶ παντὶ ἐν πρώτοις ἀνάγκη μανθάνειν; Epict., Ench. 20; Mitt-Wilck I/2, 14 II, 9 ἐν πρώτοις ἐρωτῶ σε; Josh 9:2d).

β. of persons (Dio Chrys. 19 [36], 35 πρ. καὶ μέγιστος θεός; TestAbr B 4 p. 108, 18 [Stone p. 64]; ApcSed 5:2; Jos., Ant. 15, 398; Just., A I, 60, 5 al. τὸν πρῶτον θεόν) ὃς ἂν θέλῃ ἐν ὑμῖν εἶναι πρῶτος *whoever wishes to be the first among you*

Mt 20:27; Mk 10:44; cp. **9:35.** πρῶτος Σίμων **Mt 10:2** is not meant to indicate the position of Simon in the list, since no other numbers follow, but to single him out as the *most prominent* of the twelve. W. gen. ὧν (=τῶν ἁμαρτωλῶν) πρῶτός εἰμι **1 Ti 1:15.** Pl. (οἱ) πρῶτοι in contrast to (οἱ) ἔσχατοι **Mt 19:30; 20:16; Mk 9:35; 10:31; Lk 13:30;** Ox 654, 25f (cp. GTh 4; sim. Sallust. 9 p. 16, 21f τοῖς ἐσχάτοις . . . τοῖς πρώτοις; s. ἔσχατος 2).—αἱ πρῶται *prominent women* (in the phrase γυναικῶν τε τῶν πρώτων οὐκ ὀλίγαι) **Ac 17:4** (s. New Docs 1, 72). οἱ πρῶτοι *the most prominent men, the leading men* w. gen. of place (Jos., Ant. 7, 230 τῆς χώρας) οἱ πρ. τῆς Γαλιλαίας **Mk 6:21;** cp. **Ac 13:50** (in phrasing sim. to πολλὰς μὲν γυναῖκας εὐγενεῖς καὶ τῶν πρώτων ἀνδρῶν ἤισχυναν='they dishonored many well-born women as well as men of high station' Theopomp.: 115 fgm. 121 Jac. p. 563, 33f), or of a group (Strabo 13, 2, 3 οἱ πρ. τῶν φίλων; Jos., Ant. 20, 180) οἱ πρ. τοῦ λαοῦ (Jos., Ant. 11, 141) **Lk 19:47;** cp. **Ac 25:2; 28:17.** On ὁ πρῶτος τῆς νήσου vs. **7** (πρῶτος Μελιταίων IGR I, 512=IG XIV, 601; cp. Ramsay, CB I/2, 642 no. 535 ὁ πρῶτος ἐν τῇ πόλει; p. 660 no. 616; SEG XLI, 1345, 14f; cp. CIL X, 7495, 1; s. Hemer, Acts 153, n. 152; Warnecke, Romfahrt 119ff) s. Πόπλιος.

ⓑ adv. **πρῶτον** of degree ***in the first place, above all, especially*** (Jos., Ant. 10, 213) ζητεῖτε πρῶτον τὴν βασιλείαν **Mt 6:33.** Ἰουδαίῳ τε πρῶτον καὶ Ἕλληνι **Ro 1:16;** cp. **2:9f.**—**Ac 3:26; 2 Pt 1:20; 3:3.** Of the Macedonian Christians ἑαυτοὺς ἔδωκαν πρῶτον τῷ κυρίῳ καὶ ἡμῖν *they gave themselves first of all to the Lord, and (then) to us* **2 Cor 8:5.** παρακαλῶ πρῶτον πάντων *first of all I urge* **1 Ti 2:1.**—B. 939. DELG. M-M. EDNT. TW. Sv.

πρωτοστάτης, ου, ὁ (πρῶτος, ἵστημι; Thu. et al.; pap [late, New Docs 4, 244]; Job 15:24) 'one who stands first' **a person who is at the head of a group, *leader,*** prob. in the sense *ringleader* πρ. τῆς τῶν Ναζωραίων αἱρέσεως **Ac 24:5.**—DELG s.v. ἵστημι. M-M.

πρωτοτόκια, ων, τά (πρωτότοκος; B-D-F §120, 1; Mlt-H. 279) **privileges associated with being a firstborn, *birthright, right of primogeniture*** of a firstborn son (Gen 27:36; Philo, Leg. All. 2, 47, Sacr. Abel. 120 al. in the Esau story) Ἠσαῦ ἀντὶ βρώσεως μιᾶς ἀπέδοτο τὰ πρωτοτόκια ἑαυτοῦ *Esau sold his birthright for a single meal* **Hb 12:16** (Gen 25:33).—DELG s.v. τίκτω B. M-M. TW.

πρωτότοκος, ον (πρῶτος, τόκος; Sb 6647 [5 BC; s. WMichaelis in 2a: p. 314f]; Kaibel 460, 4; 730, 3; PLips 28, 16; PGM 36, 312; Anth. 8, 34; 9, 213; LXX; TestReub, JosAs; SibOr 3, 627 Philo, Cher. 54 al.; Jos., Ant. 4, 71; Just., Tat., Mel., Iren.) 'firstborn, heir apparent'.

❶ lit. **pert. to birth order, *firstborn*** ὁ υἱὸς ὁ πρ. (PLips loc. cit. υἱὸν γνήσιον καὶ πρωτότοκον; Gen 25:25 al. LXX; JosAs 1:11; Σὴθ τρίτος, οὐ π. ἐστίν Did., Gen 147, 7) **Mt 1:25 v.l.; Lk 2:7** (JFrey, La signification du terme πρ. d'après une inscription juive: Biblica 2, 1930, 373–90; CIJ II 1510, 6; Boffo, Iscrizioni 156–65; New Docs 163); cp. B 13:5 (Gen 48:18). τὰ πρ. *the firstborn*=all the firstborn (τὰ πρ. Ex 22:28; Num 18:15 al.; Just., D. 84, 1; 111, 3) **Hb 11:28** (cp. Ex 11:5). τὰ πρ. τῶν προβάτων the firstborn of the sheep 1 Cl 4:1 (Gen 4:4). The special status enjoyed by a firstborn son as heir apparent in Israel is an implicit component of πρ. in ref. to such a son and plays a dominant role in

❷ **pert. to having special status associated with a firstborn, *firstborn,*** fig. ext. of 1—ⓐ of Christ, as the firstborn of a new humanity which is to be glorified, as its exalted Lord is glorified πρωτότοκος ἐν πολλοῖς ἀδελφοῖς **Ro 8:29.** Also simply πρωτότοκος **Hb 1:6;** cp. **Rv 2:8 v.l.** This expr., which is admirably suited to describe Jesus as the one coming forth fr. God to found the new community of believers, is also used in some instances where the force of the element -τοκος appears at first glance to be uncertain, but s. comment on status at end of 1 (cp. the originally polytheistic Naassene psalm in Hippol., Ref. 5, 10, 1 and also Ex 4:22; Ps. 88:28) (ὁ) πρ. (ἐκ) τῶν νεκρῶν **Col 1:18; Rv 1:5.** πρ. πάσης κτίσεως **Col 1:15** (cp. Orig., C. Cels. 6, 17, 38; Theoph. Ant. 2, 22 [p. 154, 18]; s. JGewiess, Christus u. d. Heil nach d. Kol.: diss. Breslau '32; ECerny, Firstborn of Every Creature [Col 1:15]: diss. Baltimore '38; Romualdus, Studia Cath. 18, '42, 155–71; WMichaelis, D. Beitrag d. LXX zur Bedeutungsgeschichte von πρ.: ADebrunner Festschr. '54, 313–20, ZST 23, '54, 137–57; AArgyle, ET 66, '54, 61f, cp. 124f, 318f; NKehl, D. Christushymnus im Kol., '67, 82–98).

ⓑ of ordinary humans—**α.** of God's people (JosAs 21:3 Ἰωσὴφ . . . ἐστὶν ὁ υἱὸς τοῦ θεοῦ ὁ πρ.) of the *assembly of the firstborn* (s. Ex 4:22) in heaven ἐκκλησία πρωτοτόκων **Hb 12:23.** Some interpret this phrase as a ref. to angels. On the various interpretations s. OMichel, comm. ad loc.

β. of a notorious dissident πρωτότοκος τοῦ Σατανᾶ Pol 7:1 (NDahl, D. Erstgeborene Satans u. d. Vater des Teufels: EHaenchen Festschr., '64, 70–84). Specif. of Marcion acc. to a saying of Polycarp, EpilMosq 3 (cp. Iren. 3, 3, 4 [Harv. II 14, 2]); s. also the corresp. Hebr. expr. in HZucker, Studien z. jüd. Selbstverwaltg. im Altert. '36, 135.—DELG s.v. τίκτω B. M-M. EDNT. TW. Spicq. Sv.

πρώτως adv. (πρῶτος; Aristot. et al.; OGI 602, 4; UPZ 110, 81 [164 BC]; POxy 1023, 3f [II AD]; 1267, 10; ViJer 14 [p. 73, 14 Sch.]; EpArist 4; Ath., R. 25 p. 78, 31) ***for the first time*** (so Polyb. 6, 5, 10; Diod. S. 4, 24, 1; IPriene 117, 39; SIG 797, 16; PRyl 235, 11; Jos., Bell. 2, 25. See Lob., Phryn. p. 311f; Crönert 193; B-D-F §102, 5; Mlt-H. 163) **Ac 11:26** (v.l. πρῶτον).—M-M.

πταίω 1 aor. ἔπταισα; pf. ἔπταικα LXX; aor. pass. ptc. masc. acc. πταισθέντα (Papias v.l.) (Pind. et al.; ins, pap, LXX; TestJob 38:1; ApcSed 1:1; EpArist, Philo, Joseph.; trans. only the Catena on Mt 27:11 [JCramer I 231] in ref. to Papias [3:2] ὑπὸ τῆς ἁμάξης πταισθέντα *struck by the cart*) in our lit. only intr.

❶ **to lose one's footing, *stumble, trip*** (X., An. 4, 2, 3 πρὸς τὰς πέτρας; Polyb. 31, 11, 5 πρὸς τὸν λίθον; Jos., Bell. 6, 64 πρὸς πέτρᾳ), in imagery (as Aeschyl., Hdt. et al.) in which the lit. sense is clearly discernible. Abs. (Maximus Tyr. 34, 2e) μὴ ἔπταισαν ἵνα πέσωσιν; *they did not stumble so as to fall into ruin, did they?* **Ro 11:11.** The 'stumbling' means *to make a mistake, go astray, sin* (Pla., Theaet. 160d al.; abs. Arrian, Anab. 4, 9, 6; M. Ant. 7, 22 ἴδιον ἀνθρώπου φιλεῖν καὶ τοὺς πταίοντας; POxy 1165, 11 εἴτε ἔπταισαν εἴτε οὐκ ἔπταισαν='whether they have committed an error or not'; Dt 7:25; TestJob 38:1; ApcSed 1:1; EpArist 239; Philo, Leg. All. 3, 66) πολλὰ πταίομεν *we commit many sins* **Js 3:2a** (ApcSed 1:1); πτ. ἐν ἑνί *sin in one respect (only)* **2:10.** ἐν λόγῳ *in what one says* **3:2b.**

❷ **to experience disaster, *be ruined, be lost*** (Hdt. 9, 101; Aristot., Rhet. 3 al.; Diod. S. 15, 33, 1 et al.; Philo, De Jos. 144; Jos., Ant. 7, 75; 14, 434) of the loss of salvation **2 Pt 1:10:** the aor., as in reff. cited above, provides the semantic component of climactic disaster. But mng. 1 also has supporters.—DELG. M-M. TW.

πτελέα, ας, ἡ (Hom. [πτελέη] et al.; Sym. Is 41:19) *elm tree* as a support for vines Hs 2:1ff.—DELG.

πτέρνα, ης, ἡ (var. of the earlier form πτέρνη; Hom. et al.; LXX; ApcMos 26; Jos., Ant. 1, 258 [after Gen 25:26]; SibOr 1, 63; s. B-D-F §43, 2) ***heel*** ἐπαίρειν τὴν πτ. ἐπί τινα *raise one's heel against someone* for a malicious kick **J 13:18** (w. some relation to a form of Ps 40:10 which, in the LXX, ends w. ἐπ' ἐμὲ πτερνισμόν).—DELG s.v. πτέρνη.

πτεροφυέω (πτερόν, φύω) fut. 3 pl. πτεροφυήσουσιν Is 40:3 ***get/grow feathers/wings*** (Plut., Mor. 751f of Eros; Lucian, Icar. 10; Olympiodorus, Life of Plato p. 2 Westermann; Horapollo 1, 55; Is 40:31.—In fig. sense as early as Pla.) σκώληξ . . . πτεροφυεῖ 1 Cl 25:3.

πτερύγιον, ου, τό (πτέρυξ; Aristot. et al.; Aeneas Tact. 1440; ins, LXX; TestSol 22:8) dim. of πτέρυξ 'wing'; it serves to denote **the tip or extremity of anything, *end, edge*** τὸ πτερύγιον τοῦ ἱεροῦ someth. like *the pinnacle* or *summit of the temple* **Mt 4:5; Lk 4:9** (also in Hegesippus: Eus., HE 2, 23, 11. Rufinus has for this 'excelsus locus pinnae templi'.—See Theod. Da 9:27 [reading of a doublet; s. ed. JZiegler '54 p. 191] and M-JLagrange, RB 39, 1930, 190). JJeremias, ZDPV 59, '36, 195–208 proposes: 'the lintel or super-structure of a gate of the temple.' But for Greeks the word for this that was most easily understood would be ὑπέρθυρον (Parmenides [VI/V BC], fgm. 1, 12 [28 B Diels]; Hdt. 1, 179 et al.; also Herodas 2, 65; Artem. 2, 10 p. 97, 26; 4, 42 p. 226, 8.—Jos., Bell. 5, 201 in a description of the Jerus. temple).—DELG s.v. πτερόν. M-M. TW.

πτέρυξ, υγος, ἡ (πτερόν 'feather'; cp. πέτομαι; Hom. et al.; SIG 1167, 1–5; POxy 738, 10; LXX, Test12Patr, JosAs, GrBar; ApcSed 2:4; ApcMos 26; Jos., Ant. 8, 72) ***wing,*** of birds **Mt 23:37; Lk 13:34; Rv 12:14** (Test Napht 5:6 πτ. ἀετοῦ). The four strange creatures of Rv have six wings apiece (cp. Is 6:2) **Rv 4:8.** Of apocalyptic locusts ἡ φωνὴ τῶν πτ. *the noise of the wings* **9:9.**—B. 245. DELG s.v. πτερόν. M-M.

πτερωτός, (ή), όν (πτερόν 'feather', πέτομαι; Aeschyl., Hdt. et al.; LXX; TestSol) **pert. to having feathers, *feathered, winged*** subst. τὰ πτερωτά *winged creatures, birds* (Aeschyl., Suppl. 510; Eur., Hel. 747.—Ps 77:27 and 148:10 in the expr. πετεινὰ πτερωτά, πετεινά is clearly the subst. The masc. οἱ πτερωτοί occurs in the same sense: Eur., Bacch. 257) ἐκτείνεται δίκτυα πτερωτοῖς B 5:4 (Pr 1:17).—DELG s.v. πτερόν.

πτηνός, (ή), όν (cp. the aor. ἔπτην of πέτομαι; Pind. et al.) **pert. to having feathers, *feathered, winged*** subst. τὰ πτηνά *the birds* (Aeschyl., Pla. et al.; Aq. Job 5:7; EpArist 145; 146; 147; Philo; SibOr 3, 370) **1 Cor 15:39.**—DELG s.v. πέτομαι. M-M.

πτοέω fut. πτοήσω LXX. Pass.: 1 fut. πτοηθήσομαι LXX; 1 aor. ἐπτοήθην; pf. 3 sg. ἐπτόηται Jer 28:56 (Hom.+; LXX; PsSol 6:3; JosAs 26:2 cod. A [p. 80, 2 Bat.] μηδένα πτοουμένη) ***terrify, frighten*** pass. *be terrified, be alarmed, frightened, startled* (Polyb. 8, 19, 2; 31, 11, 4; Diod. S. 17, 102, 3 πτοηθέντες; LXX; Jos., Bell. 1, 591; 4, 108; TestJos 2:5; PGM 4, 3093; 13, 199; 765) **Lk 12:4 v.l.; 21:9.** W. ἔμφοβοι γενόμενοι **24:37** (cp. En 21:9 φοβεῖσθαι κ. πτ.); for this passage s. also the variants θροηθέντες and φοβηθέντες.—Cp. φοβέω and Schmidt, Syn. III 507–36. DELG. M-M.

πτόησις, εως, ἡ (πτοέω; also πτοίησις; Pla. et al.; LXX; of vehement emotion or excitement). In μὴ φοβούμεναι μηδεμίαν πτόησιν **1 Pt 3:6** (Pr 3:25) two aspects are possible

❶ **act of causing someone to be intimidated, *terrifying, intimidation,*** but more prob.

❷ **experience of being intimidated, *fear, terror*** (Philo, Rer. Div. Her. 251, end; cp. Od. 18, 340–42 on the theme of women frightened by a superior figure). In the case of mng. 2 πτόησιν would be acc. of the inner obj.—DELG s.v. πτοέω.

Πτολεμαΐς, ΐδος, ἡ (on the spelling s. B-D-F §15; 30, 1; 34, 6; Mlt-H. 81) ***Ptolemais,*** a Phoenician seaport city (Polyb. 5, 61f; 71; Strabo 2, 5, 39; also 1 and 2 Macc; EpArist 115; Joseph.) **Ac 21:7.**—Schürer II 121–25 (lit.); Abel, Geographie II 235–37; Kl. Pauly IV 1234; BHHW III 1530.

πτύον, ου, τό (Hom. et al.; Artem. 2, 24 p. 117, 28; PFay 120, 5 [c. 100 AD]; Sym. Is 30:24) **a fork-like shovel, with which the threshed grain was thrown into the wind, thus separating chaff fr. grain, *winnowing shovel*** **Mt 3:12; Lk 3:17.**—See Dalman s.v. ἀλοάω.—B. 500. DELG. M-M.

πτύρω (on the formation s. Schwyzer I 351) 2 aor. pass. 3 sg. ἐπτύρη; act. 'frighten, scare'; almost always pass. and so in our lit. **to let oneself be intimidated, *be frightened, terrified*** (since Hippocr., Mul. Morb. 1, 25; Ps.-Pla., Axioch. 370a; Philo Bybl. [I/II AD]:790 fgm. 2 p. 807, 5 Jac. [in Eus, PE 1, 10, 4]; Plut., Mor. 800c; M. Ant. 8, 45, 2; on the permissive pass. s. Gildersleeve, Syntax I §167) μὴ πτυρόμενοι ἐν μηδενὶ ὑπὸ τῶν ἀντικειμένων *in no way intimidated by your opponents* **Phil 1:28.** Παῦλος οὐκ ἐπτύρη AcPl Ha 4, 33.—M-M.

πτύσμα, ατος, τό (πτύω; Hippocr.+; Polyb. 8, 12, 5; SibOr 1, 365; Pollux 2, 103) ***saliva, spit(tle)*** used by Jesus in the healing of a blind man **J 9:6.**—On this subj. s. EKlostermann, Hdb., exc. on Mk 7:33; Billerb. II 15ff; AJacoby, ZNW 10, 1909, 185–94; OWeinreich, Antike Heilungswunder 1909, 97f; FDölger, D. Exorzismus im altchr. Taufritual 1909, 118ff; 130ff; JHess, ZAW 35, 1915, 130f; SEitrem, Some Notes on Demonology in the NT, SymbOsl 12, '50, 46–49; OBöcker, Dämonenfurcht u. Dämonenabwehr '70.—BHHW III 1826. DELG s.v. πτύω. M-M.

πτύσσω 1 aor. ἔπτυξα (Hom. et al.) **to put something away after use by putting one part over another, *fold up, roll up, close*** (in the sense 'fold' Jos., Ant. 10, 16 ἐπιστολάς; 15, 171. Of the folding of a document PGen 10, 17 [IV AD]; Sb 5174, 23; 5175, 24) πτύξας τὸ βιβλίον *after he had rolled up the scroll* **Lk 4:20** (cp. the act of unrolling vs. 17).—B. 544. M-M.

πτύω 1 aor. ἔπτυσα (Hom. et al.; Num 12:14; Sir 28:12; TestSol; JosAs 29:1) ***spit, spit out*** χαμαί *on the ground* **J 9:6** (also TestSol 7:3). πτύσας εἰς τὰ ὄμματα αὐτοῦ *when he had spit on his eyes* **Mk 8:23** (Jos., Ant. 5, 335 πτ. εἰς τὸ πρόσωπον. On association with magical procedures s. L-S-J-M s.v. 4. Cp. Persius 2, 31–34.). Abs. **7:33.**—Lit. s.v. πτύσμα.—B. 264.

πτῶμα, ατος, τό (πίπτω; Aeschyl.+; LXX; PsSol 3:10 'fall'; TestSol 1:7 D; Philo, Joseph.; SibOr 3, 183; 5, 457; loanw. in rabb.; prim.: 'that which has fallen') **a dead body: animal or human, *(dead) body, corpse,*** esp. of one killed by violence (used w. νεκροῦ or the gen. of a name as early as trag.; without them in Polyb. 15, 14, 2; Plut., Alex. 684 [33, 8]; Vett. Val. 275, 19; Herodian 7, 9, 7; Jos., Bell. 5, 570, Ant. 7, 16 al.; SIG 700, 17 [118 BC]; Kaibel 326, 5; LXX) **Mt 14:12; 24:28** (gathering-point for vultures as Cornutus 21 p. 41, 15f); **Mk 6:29; 15:45; Rv 11:8f** (τὸ πτῶμα αὐτῶν in vss. **8** and **9a,** τὰ πτώματα αὐτῶν **9b**); GJs 24:3a (pap; s. deStrycker).—**Mt 14:12** and **Mk 15:45** have as **v.l.** σῶμα, a more dignified word.—B. 290. DELG s.v. πίπτω C 1. M-M. TW.

πτῶσις, εως, ἡ (πίπτω; Pla.+; LXX; PFamTebt 15, 67 [114/115 AD]; En; TestJob 39:8; GrBar 4:17; ApcEsdr 3:11 p. 27, 21 Tdf.; Jos., Ant. 17, 71; Just., D. 124, 3) **state or condition of falling,** ***fall*** (Diod. S. 5, 31, 3; Lucian, Anach. 28) lit. of the *fall* or *collapse* of a house (Manetho, Apot. 4, 617) **Mt 7:27.** Fig. (Petosiris, fgm. 6 ln. 96=downfall, destruction, i.e. of the barbarians; Diogenian., Ep. 8, 2; oft. LXX; En 100:6) οὗτος κεῖται εἰς πτῶσιν καὶ ἀνάστασιν πολλῶν *he is appointed/destined to cause the fall and rise of many* **Lk 2:34** (the opposition of πτῶσις and ἀνάστασις as Diod. S. 3, 27, 3; cp. 1QH 2:8–10).—DELG s.v. πίπτω C 2. M-M. TW.

πτωχεία, ας, ἡ (πτωχεύω; Hdt., Aristoph. et al.; PGen 14, 23; LXX, Test12Patr; prim.: 'beggarliness') **state of being deficient in means of support,** ***poverty,*** lit., w. θλῖψις **Rv 2:9.** ἡ κατὰ βάθους πτ. (βάθος 2) *extreme poverty* **2 Cor 8:2.** Paradoxically τῇ πτ. τινὸς πλουτῆσαι *become rich through someone's poverty* vs. **9.** In Ox 1 recto, 1 the word πτωχία occurs, but the context is lost.—DELG s.v. πτήσσω III. M-M. TW.

πτωχεύω (πτωχός) fut. 3 sg. πτωχεύσει Pr 23:21; 1 aor. ἐπτώχευσα (='beg' Hom.+; LXX; Tat. 9, 1) **to be or become poor as a beggar,** ***be (extremely) poor*** (Aristot., Rhet. 27 in contrast to πλουτεῖν; Antiphanes Com. 322 Kock; Ps.-Pla., Eryx. 394b) of Christ in ref. to renunciation of transcendent prosperity ἐπτώχευσεν πλούσιος ὤν *he became poor* (for the aor. cp. Tob 4:21; B-D-F §331; Rob. 834) **2 Cor 8:9** (some idea of the contrast can be gained from Ps.-Aristot, De Mundo 6, 398b). Of Christians, w. acc. of ref. πτωχεύουσι καὶ πλουτίζουσι πολλούς Dg 5:13. ὁ πλούσιος τὰ πρὸς τὸν κύριον πτωχεύει Hs 2:5.—Schmidt, Syn. IV 392. DELG s.v. πτήσσω III. TW.

πτωχίζω (πτωχός; s. prec. entry) ***make (extremely) poor*** opp. πλουτίζειν 1 Cl 59:3 (cp. 1 Km 2:7).

πτωχός, ή, όν (s. two prec. entries; Hom.+; PPetr III, 36a, 17f; 140a, 1; LXX; TestSol 10:12 C; TestJob; Test12Patr; JosAs 10:13; Philo, Hypoth. f. 1 [Eus., PE 8, 7, 6]; Joseph.; Tat. 6, 2)

❶ **pert. to being economically disadvantaged,** orig. 'begging' (s. πένης for a differentiation betw. the two words; note the juxtaposition in Ps 39:18; 69:6 al.), ***dependent on others for support,*** but also simply ***poor*** (as Mod. Gk. φτωχός) χήρα πτωχή **Mk 12:42;** cp. vs. **43; Lk 21:3.** Mostly as subst. (Jos., Bell. 5, 570) opp. ὁ πλούσιος one who has more than enough (Pla., Tht. 24, 175a; Maximus Tyr. 1, 9a) **Lk 6:20** (cp. vs. 24); **Rv 13:16;** 1 Cl 38:2; Hs 2:4.—**Mt 26:11; Mk 14:7; Lk 14:13, 21; 16:20, 22; J 12:6, 8; Ro 15:26** (οἱ πτ. τῶν ἁγίων τῶν ἐν Ἰερουσαλήμ, part. gen. On the other hand πτωχοί [in the sense of 2]=ἅγιοι: KHoll, SBBerlAk 1921, 937–39 and Ltzm., exc. on Ro 15:25); **2 Cor 6:10** (in wordplay w. πλουτίζειν); **Gal 2:10; Js 2:2f, 6;** B 20:2; D 5:2. οἱ πτ. τῷ κόσμῳ *those who are poor in the world's estimation* **Js 2:5** (opp. πλούσιοι ἐν πίστει). διδόναι (τοῖς) πτ. **Mt 19:21; Mk 10:21; Lk 19:8;** cp. **18:22; J 13:29;** D 13:4. Pass. **Mt 26:9; Mk 14:5; J 12:5.**

❷ **pert. to being thrust on divine resources,** ***poor.*** At times the ref. is not only to the unfavorable circumstances of these people from an economic point of view; the thought is also that since they are oppressed and disillusioned they are in special need of God's help, and may be expected to receive it shortly (cp. Od. 6, 207f πρὸς γὰρ Διός εἰσιν ἅπαντες ξεῖνοί τε πτωχοί τε=all strangers and needy persons are wards of Zeus; LXX; HBruppacher, D. Beurteilung d. Armut im AT 1924; WSattler, D. Anawim im Zeitalter Jes. Chr.: Jülicher Festschr. 1927, 1–15; A Meyer, D. Rätsel des Jk 1930, 146ff; HBirkeland, ᶜAni u. ᶜanāw in den Psalmen '33; LMarshall, Challenge of NT Ethics '47, 76f; KSchubert, The Dead Sea Community '59, 85–88; 137–39; AGelin, The Poor of Yahweh, '64; FDanker, The Literary Unity of Mk 14:1–25: JBL 85, '66, 467–72; s. πλοῦτος 1). The gospel is preached to them (Is 61:1) **Mt 11:5; Lk 4:18; 7:22;** 1 Cl 52:2 (Ps 68:33); Pol 2:3 (εἶπεν ὁ κύριος διδάσκων).

❸ **lacking in spiritual worth,** fig. ext. of 1 (Tat. 6, 2 of humans ὁ μὲν πτωχός [in contrast to God]) οἱ πτωχοὶ τῷ πνεύματι **Mt 5:3** (cp. 1QM 14:7 עֲנִיֵּי רוּחַ; s. πνεῦμα 3b and Goodsp., Probs. 16f;; EBest, NTS 7, '60/61, 255–58; SLégasse, NTS 8, '61/62, 336–45 (Qumran); HBraun, Qumran u. d. NT I, '66, 13; LKeck, The Poor among the Saints in Jewish Christianity and Qumran, ZNW 57, '66, 54–78; add. lit. Betz, SM 111). The 'messenger' of the church at Laodicea, who says of himself πλούσιός εἰμι καὶ πεπλούτηκα, is termed πτωχός **Rv 3:17.** In 1 Cl 15:6, Ps 11:6 is quoted w. ref. to the situation in the Corinthian church.

❹ **pert. to being extremely inferior in quality,** ***miserable, shabby*** (Dionys. Hal., Comp. Verb. 4 νοήματα; Iren. 2, 33, 5 [Hv I, 380, 2] of God οὐ . . . π. οὐδὲ ἄπορος) of the στοιχεῖα (w. ἀσθενής) **Gal 4:9.** Of the grace of God πτωχὴ οὐκ ἐγενήθη *did not turn out to be shabby* **1 Cor 15:10 v.l.** (this is in keeping with the Aristotelian view that exceptional generosity produces exceptional results Aristot., EN 4, 2, 19).—JRoth, The Blind, the Lame, and the Poor etc. diss. Vanderbilt 1994. B. 782; 784. TRE IV s.v. 'Armut', 69–121. DELG s.v. πτήσσω III. M-M. EDNT. TW. Sv.

πτωχότης, ητος, ἡ (πτωχός) ***poverty*** (Griech . . . Ostraka der . . . Bibl. zu Strassburg, ed. PViereck 1923, 794) Hv 3, 12, 2.

πυγμή, ῆς, ἡ—❶ ***fist*** (so Eur., Hippocr. et al.; PPetr III, 22 (e) 2 [III BC]; LXX) in a difficult pass. ἐὰν μὴ πυγμῇ νίψωνται τὰς χεῖρας lit. *unless they wash their hands with (the) fist* **Mk 7:3** (where the v.l. πυκνά [s. πυκνός] is substituted for π. [Vulgate crebro], thus alleviating the difficulty by focusing on the vigor of the action. Itala codex d has 'primo' [on this and other Itala readings s. AJülicher, Itala II '40, p. 59]). The procedure is variously described and interpreted as a washing: 'in which one clenched fist is turned about in the hollow of the other hand', or 'up to the elbow' or 'the wrist', or 'with a handful' of water. FSchulthess, ZNW 21, 1922, 232f thinks of it simply as a rubbing w. the dry hand. Whatever the actual motion may have been, the emphasis is on the cultic devotion of those who engage in the lustral act.—Palladius, Hist. Laus. 55 νίψασθαι τὰς χεῖρας καὶ τοὺς πόδας πυγμῇ ὕδατι ψυχροτάτῳ. CTorrey, ZAW 65, '53, 233f.—For lit. s. βαπτίζω 1.—Field, Notes 30f; Goodsp., Probs. 59f; MBlack, Aramaic Approach[2], '53, 8f; PWeis, NTS 3, '56/57, 233–36 (Aramaic); SReynolds, JBL 85, '66, 87f (with cupped hands; against him MHengel, ZNW 60, '69, 182–98; reply by Reynolds ibid. 62, '71, 295f).

❷ ***fist-fight, boxing*** (Hom. et al.; ins; Tat. 4, 1; 26, 3) more generally (Jos., Ant. 14, 210) ἐν μέσῳ τῆς πυγμῆς *in the midst of the fight* B 12:2.—DELG s.v. πύξ I. M-M. TW.

πυθόμενος, -εσθαι s. πυνθάνομαι.

πύθων, ωνος, ὁ (fr. Πυθώ, the region in which the city of Delphi lay) orig. 'the Python', acc. to Strabo 9, 3, 12 the serpent or dragon that guarded the Delphic oracle; it lived at the foot of Mt. Parnassus, and was slain by Apollo. Later the word came to designate a ***spirit of divination,*** then also of ventriloquists, who were believed to have such a spirit dwelling in their belly (Plut., Mor. 414e τοὺς ἐγγαστριμύθους νῦν πύθωνας προσαγορευομένους. Sim., Erotiani Vocum Hippocr. Coll. fgm. 21 p. 105, 20 Nachmanson; Hesychius and Suda on ἐγγαστρίμυθος, also L-S-J-M on the same word.—Suda on Πύθωνος: δαιμονίου μαντικοῦ. τάς τε πνεύματι Πύθωνος ἐνθουσιώσας καὶ φαντασίαν κυήσεως παρεχομένας τῇ τοῦ δαιμονίου περιφορᾷ ἠξίου τὸ ἐσόμενον προαγορεῦσαι=of Python: of a soothsaying divinity. It deemed such women worthy of foretelling the future who were in ecstasy with the Python's spirit and exhibited at the whirling of the divinity an appearance of conception; Ps.-Clem., Hom. 9, 16 καὶ πύθωνες μαντεύονται, ἀλλ' ὑφ' ἡμῶν ὡς δαίμονες ὁρκιζόμενοι φυγαδεύονται; Syntipas p. 62, 6; 15; 63, 4 πύθωνος πνεῦμα. So as loanw. in rabb.—On the difference betw. ancient and modern ideas of ventriloquism, s. A-JFestugière, RB 54, '47, 133 and s. OED s.v. ventriloquist) πνεῦμα πύθωνα *a spirit of divination* or *prophecy* (in apposition like ἄνθρωπος βασιλεύς) **Ac 16:16** (v.l. πνεῦμα πύθωνος='the spirit of a ventriloquist.'—Philochoros [300 BC]: 326 fgm. 78 Jac. refers to women w. this ability).—WEbstein, D. Medizin im NT u. im Talmud 1903; JTambornino, De Antiquorum Daemonismo 1909; FDölger, Der Exorzismus im altchristl. Taufritual 1909; AWikenhauser, Die AG 1921, 401ff; TOesterreich, D. Besessenheit 1921, esp. 319–30; RMacMullen, Enemies of the Roman Order '75, 128–51.—Pauly-W. XXIV 609f; Kl. Pauly IV 1280; Haenchen, ad loc. DELG s.v. Πυθώ. DDD 1263–66. M-M. TW.

πυκνός, ή, όν occurring freq. at intervals, *frequent, numerous* (so as early as Od. 14, 36; IG VII, 3073, 104 [II BC]; pap; 3 Macc 1:28; JosAs 22 cod. A [p. 73, 1 Bat.] EpArist 90; Jos., Ant. 13, 139) ἀσθένειαι **1 Ti 5:23.**—Neut. pl. as adv. ***often, frequently*** (Hom.+; X., An. 5, 9, 8, De Rep. Lac. 12, 5; Pla., Rep. 6, 501b; Plut., Mor. 228d) **Mt 9:14** v.l. (for πολλά); **Mk 7:3 v.l.** (s. πυγμή); **Lk 5:33.**—Neut. of the comp. πυκνότερον as adv. *more often, more frequently* and in an elative sense *very often, quite frequently* (Pla., Demosth. et al.; PTebt 41, 3 [II BC]; POxy 717, 16; 3 Macc 4:12) also *as often as possible* (POxy 805 [25 BC] ἀξιῶ δὲ ἀντιφωνεῖν μοι πυκνότερον; PGM 13, 58; 430; EpArist 318; B-D-F §244, 1; Rob. 665) **Ac 24:26;** 2 Cl 17:3; IEph 13:1a; IPol 4:2 (Clidemus [350 BC] : 323 fgm. 7 Jac. of the Athenians: συνῄεσαν εἰς τὴν Πύκνα ὀνομασθεῖσαν διὰ τὸ τὴν συνοίκησιν πυκνουμένην εἶναι=they gathered in Dense, so named because it was so densely settled).—B. 888; 986. DELG s.v. πύκα II. M-M.

πυκνῶς adv. of πυκνός (posthomeric [Hom. has πυκινῶς]) ***frequently, often*** (Ps.-X., Cyneg. 6, 22; Plut., Mor. 229e; JosAs 10:17; ViAm 1 [p. 81, 10 Sch.]; PGM 4, 2569; 2639; Jos., Ant. 7, 22) IEph 13:1b; Hm 11:4; D 16:2.

πυκτεύω (πύκτης 'boxer'; X., Pla. et al.; Dio Chrys. 14 [31], 156; Kaibel 291, 1) **to fight with fists, *box*** metaph. (Reader, Polemo 342f; APapathomas, NTS 43, '97, 237f [lit. n. 63; for pap w. the noun πύκτης s. n. 65]) **1 Cor 9:26.**—DELG s.v. πύξ IV. M-M. TW.

πύλη, ης, ἡ (Hom.+; loanw. in rabb.) ***gate, door*—ⓐ** lit., of gates of cities (X., Mem. 3, 9, 7; Maximus Tyr. 15, 3a; Polyaenus 7, 13; Jos., Vi. 108) **Lk 7:12; Ac 9:24** (a situation as in Appian, Bell. Civ. 4, 12 §48 αἱ πύλαι κατείχοντο in the hunt for proscribed men). ἔξω τῆς πύλης *outside the gate, outside the city* **16:13; Hb 13:12** (crucifixion outside the city was the usual practice: Artem. 2, 53 p. 152, 17); GJs 4:4 (s. deStrycker on the passage). Of a gate of the temple in Jerusalem ἡ ὡραία πύλη **Ac 3:10** (s. ὡραῖος 2). The prison has τὴν πύλην τὴν σιδηρᾶν **12:10** (s. Jos., Bell. 7, 245). πύλας χαλκᾶς συντρίψω B 11:4 (Ps 106:16). In a vision of a rock w. a gate(way) Hs 9, 2, 2f; 9, 3, 1f; 4; 9, 4, 1f; 5f and 8; 9, 5, 3; 9, 6, 7; 9, 12, 1–6; 9, 13, 6; 9, 14, 4; 9, 15, 5. On the πύλαι ᾅδου **Mt 16:18** s. ᾅδης 1 and the lit. s.v. κλείς 1 and πέτρα 1b, also JBernard, The Gates of Hades: Exp. 8th ser., 11, 1916, 401–9; REppel, Aux sources de la tradition Chrétienne: MGoguel Festschr. '50, 71–73; OBetz, ZNW 48, '57, 49–77 (Qumran; cp. 1QH 6:24); CBrown, SBLSP 26, '87, 357–67.

ⓑ in imagery (cp. Pind., O. 6, 27 'gate of song'; Soph., fgm. 360 TGF 'gate of the soul'), of the στενὴ πύλη that leads into life **Mt 7:13a, 14** (s. TestAbr A 11 p. 89, 1f [Stone p. 26], B 9 p. 113, 15 [Stone p. 74]; SibOr 2, 150 π. ζωῆς); s. also vs. **13b; Lk 13:24 v.l.** (cp. Cebes 15, 1–3 the difficult road and the narrow gate, which afford an ἀνάβασις στενὴ πάνυ to the ἀληθινὴ παιδεία). π. δικαιοσύνης *the gate of righteousness* 1 Cl 48:2a; s. also vs. 2b (Ps 117:19). Also ἡ ἐν δικαιοσύνῃ (πύλη) vs. 4b. This gate is also called ἡ πύλη τοῦ κυρίου *the gate to the Lord* (or *of the Lord*) vs. 3 (Ps 117:20). πολλῶν πυλῶν ἀνεῳγυιῶν *since many gates are open* vs. 4a.—Renehan '75. B. 466. DELG. M-M. EDNT. TW.

πυλών, ῶνος, ὁ (πύλη; Polyb.; Diod. S. 13, 75, 7; Cebes 1, 2 al.; ins, pap, LXX, JosAs; GrBar 11:2 [v.l. ὁ πύλος]; ApcEsdr 5:13 p. 30, 12 Tdf.; Joseph.; TestZeb 3:6. Loanw. in rabb.).

❶ **an entrance that contains a gate or gates, *gateway, entrance, gate*** esp. of the large, impressive gateways at the entrance of temples and palaces (Ps.-Aristot., De Mundo 6, 8, 397a; Plut., Tim. 241 [12, 9] contrast πύλη; ins, LXX; Jos., Bell. 1, 617; 5, 202 δύο ἑκάστου πυλῶνος θύραι of Herod's temple=each gateway had two doors) of the entrances of the heavenly Jerusalem (Berosus: 680 fgm. 8, 140 Jac. [in Jos., C. Ap. 1, 140] of the magnificent city gates of Babylon; Cephalion [II AD]: 93 fgm. 5 p. 444, 23f Jac., of Thebes πόλιν μεγάλην πάνυ, δωδεκάπυλον) οἱ πυλῶνες αὐτῆς οὐ μὴ κλεισθῶσιν *its entrances shall never be shut* **Rv 21:25;** cp. vss. **12ab, 13abcd, 15, 21ab; 22:14.** Of the gates of a temple or of a city **Ac 14:13.** At the palace of the rich man (cp. Lucian, Nigr. 23) **Lk 16:20;** at the apparently elegant residence of Mary the mother of John Mark **Ac 12:13:** π. distinct from its θύρα (cp. Jos., 5, 202 s. above). Cp. vs. **14ab;** also of Simon's house **10:17.** The choice of diction contributes to the picture of Mary's and Simon's social status. Of prison gates AcPl Ha 3, 22 and 24 (text restored).

❷ **a gateway consisting of a forecourt, *gateway, entrance*** separated fr. the house by a court (IPontEux I², 32b, 48 [III BC]; Polyb. 2, 9, 3; 4, 18, 2; Diod. S. 1, 47, 1; Ps.-Aristot., De Mundo 6). Peter leaves (ἐξελθόντα) the court (vs. 69) and enters εἰς τὸν πυλῶνα **Mt 26:71,** and finally leaves it (vs. 75).—DELG s.v. πύλη. M-M. TW.

πυνθάνομαι mid. dep. (Hom.+; ins, pap, LXX, En, TestSol, EpArist, Philo, Joseph., Just.) impf. ἐπυνθανόμην; 2 aor. ἐπυθόμην (on the use of the two tenses s. B-D-F §328).

❶ **to seek to learn by inquiry, *inquire, ask*** παρά τινος B 13:2 (Gen 25:22). τὶ παρά τινος (Pla., Gorg. 455c; SIG 1169, 30; 2 Ch 32:31; Jos., C. Ap. 1, 6) **J 4:52** (ἐκείνην v.l.). τι ἀκριβέστερον πυνθάνεσθαι περὶ αὐτοῦ **Ac 23:20** (π. περί τινος as X., An. 5, 5, 25; PHib 72, 11; POxy 930, 12; 1064, 4; Esth 6:4; Just., A I, 31, 2, D. 64, 2.—π. ἀκριβέστερον as PPetr II, 16, 13 [III BC]). π. (καὶ λέγειν) foll. by dir. quest. **Ac 17:19** D (Just., D. 36, 6 al.). Foll. by indir. quest. (w. or without ἄν in the opt.; s. B-D-F §386, 1; Pla., Soph. 216d; 2 Macc 3:9; Jos., Ant. 8, 331 πυθ. τίς εἴη; BGU 893, 26 ἐπύθετο, πόσον ἔχει; POxy 1063, 6) **Lk 15:26; 18:36; J 13:24; Ac 21:33.** π. εἰ w. indic. foll. *inquire whether* . . . **10:18** (s. 2 Macc 3:9; Jos., Ant. 10, 259). π.

παρά τινος w. indir. quest. foll. (Lucian, Nigr. 1; Jos., Vi. 258, Ant. 16, 328) **Mt 2:4.** Foll. by a dir. quest. (Plut., Demetr. 901 [27, 9]) **Ac 4:7; 10:29; 23:19.**

❷ **to determine someth. by inquiry, *learn*** by inquiry w. ὅτι foll. (X., An. 6, 3, 23; PHamb 27, 7 [III BC] πυνθανόμενος αὐτοῦ, ὅτι ἀπῆλθεν) **Ac 23:34.** π. περί τινος (Appian, Bell. Civ. 4, 123 §515 περὶ τοῦ λιμοῦ) foll. by indir. quest. Dg 1.—DELG. M-M.

πυξίς, ίδος, ἡ prim. 'box' made of boxwood, then any kind of box, esp. as a container for medicine (Lucian, Philops. 21; Galen XIII 743 K.; Jos., Bell. 1, 598; BGU 1300, 8 [III/II BC]; PRyl 125, 26f [I AD]; Sb 4324, 17), in our lit. of a container for poison (as Jos., Bell. 1, 598, Ant. 17, 77) ***box, container*** Hv 3, 9, 7.—Frisk s.v. πύξος.

πύον, ου, τό (cp. πύθομαι 'decay'; Hippocr. et al.; Antig. Car. 117) ***pus*** ApcPt 16:31.—DELG s.v. πύθομαι.

πῦρ, ός, τό (Hom.+) ***fire***—ⓐ of earthly fire, as an important element in creation Dg 7:2.—**Mt 17:15; Mk 9:22; Ac 28:5; Js 5:3** (cp. 4 Macc 15:15); ITr 2:3. Melting lead 2 Cl 16:3. Necessary for forging metals Dg 2:3. Testing precious metals for purity **1 Pt 1:7;** Hv 4, 3, 4; in metaphor **Rv 3:18.** For ἄνθρακες πυρός **Ro 12:20** s. ἄνθραξ. For κάμινος (τοῦ) πυρός (Iren. 5, 5, 2 [Harv. II 332, 2) 1 Cl 45:7; 2 Cl 8:2 s. κάμινος. For βάλλειν εἰς (τὸ) π. s. βάλλω 1b.—περιάπτειν πῦρ *kindle a fire* **Lk 22:55.** κατακαίειν τι πυρί *burn someth. (up) with fire,* in a pass. construction **Mt 13:40;** τινὰ ἐν πυρὶ **Rv 17:16** (v.l. without ἐν). Pass. construction **18:8.** ὑπὸ πυρὸς κατακαίεσθαι MPol 5:2 (κατακαίω, end). πῦρ καιόμενον 11:2b (καίω 1a). πυρὶ καίεσθαι **Hb 12:18; Rv 8:8** (καίω 1a). Fire is used in comparisons γλῶσσαι ὡσεὶ πυρός **Ac 2:3** (Ezek. Trag. 234 [in Eus., PE 9, 29, 14] ἀπ' οὐρανοῦ φέγγος ὡς πυρὸς ὤφθη ἡμῖν). φλὸξ πυρός *a flame of fire* (Ex 3:2; Is 29:6; PsSol 15:4; JosAs 14:9): ὀφθαλμοὶ ὡς φλὸξ πυρός **Rv 1:14;** cp. **2:18; 19:12.**—Of a Christian worker who has built poorly in the congregation it is said σωθήσεται ὡς διὰ πυρός *he will be saved as if through (the) fire,* i.e. like a person who must pass through a wall of fire to escape fr. a burning house (Ps.-Crates, Ep. 6 [=Malherbe p. 56] κἂν διὰ πυρός; Jos., Ant. 17, 264 διὰ τοῦ πυρός; Diod. S. 1, 57, 7; 8 διὰ τοῦ φλογὸς … σωθείς from a burning tent) **1 Cor 3:15** (HHollander, NTS 40, '94, 89–104; s. σῴζω 3). Cp. **Jd 23** (ἁρπάζω 2a).—Of the torture of a loyal confessor by fire IRo 5:3; ISm 4:2; MPol 2:3; 11:2a; 13:3; 15:1f; 16:1; 17:2; cp. **Hb 11:34;** in imagery of Rome ἀπέρχομαι εἰς κάμινον πυρός AcPl Ha 6, 20 (cp. b below).

ⓑ of fire that is heavenly in origin and nature (cp. Diod. S. 4, 2, 3 of the 'fire' of lightning, accompanying the appearance of Zeus; 16, 63, 3 τὸ θεῖον πῦρ; Just., D. 88, 3 πῦρ ἀνήφθη ἐν τῷ Ἰορδάνῳ [at Jesus' baptism]. In gnostic speculation Iren. 1, 17, 1 [Harv. I 164, 14]; Hippol., Ref. 6, 9, 5.—Orig., C. Cels. 4, 13, 19): an angel appears to Moses ἐν φλογὶ πυρὸς βάτου *in the flame of a burning thorn-bush* **Ac 7:30** (s. Ex 3:2; cp. Just., A I, 62, 3 ἐν ἰδέᾳ πυρός.—PKatz, ZNW 46, '55, 133–38). God makes τοὺς λειτουργοὺς αὐτοῦ πυρὸς φλόγα (cp. Ps 103:4, esp. in the v.l. [ARahlfs, Psalmi cum Odis '31]) **Hb 1:7;** 1 Cl 36:3. Corresp., there burn before the heavenly throne seven λαμπάδες πυρός **Rv 4:5** and the 'strong angel' **10:1** has πόδες ὡς στῦλοι πυρός, but both of these pass. fit equally well in a. Fire appears mostly as a means used by God to execute punishment: in the past, in the case of Sodom ἔβρεξεν πῦρ καὶ θεῖον ἀπ' οὐρανοῦ **Lk 17:29** (Gen 19:24; cp. 1QH 3:31). Cp. **Lk 9:54** (4 Km 1:10, 12; TestAbr A 10 p. 88, 13 [Stone p. 24, 13] ἐξ οὐρανοῦ; Jos., Ant. 9, 23 πῦρ ἀπ' οὐρανοῦ πεσόν). Quite predom. in connection w. the Last Judgment: the end of the world δι' αἵματος καὶ πυρός Hv 4, 3, 3; cp. **Ac 2:19** (Jo 3:3. Also SibOr 4, 173; 5, 376f); **Rv 8:7.** κόσμος αἴρεται ἐν πυρί AcPl Ha 2, 26; 9, 11. The Judgment Day ἐν πυρὶ ἀποκαλύπτεται *makes its appearance with fire* **1 Cor 3:13a;** cp. **13b** (JGnilka, Ist 1 Cor 3:10–15 … Fegfeuer? '55); **2 Pt 3:7** (on first-century cosmological views s. FDowning, L'AntCl 64, '95, 99–109, esp. 107f). When Jesus comes again he will reveal himself w. his angels ἐν πυρὶ φλογός (cp. Sir 45:19) **2 Th 1:8.** Oft. in Rv: fire is cast fr. heaven upon the earth **8:5; 13:13; 20:9** (καταβαίνω 1b). It proceeds fr. the mouths of God's two witnesses **11:5** and fr. the mouths of plague-bringing horses **9:17f.** See **16:8.** For πυρὸς ζῆλος ἐσθίειν μέλλοντος τ. ὑπεναντίους **Hb 10:27** s. ζῆλος 1, end. ἡ χείρ μου πυρὶ ἀποπίπτει ἀπ' ἐμοῦ *my hand falls off me from (burning in) the fire* GJs 20:1 (codd.).—The fire w. which God punishes sinners (cp. ApcSed 4:1 κόλασις καὶ πῦρ ἐστιν ἡ παίδευσίς σου) οὐ σβέννυται (cp. Is 66:24) **Mk 9:48;** 2 Cl 7:6; 17:5. Hence it is called (s. PGM 5, 147 τὸ πῦρ τὸ ἀθάνατον): (τὸ) πῦρ (τὸ) αἰώνιον (4 Macc 12:12; TestZeb 10:3; GrBar 4:16; Just., A I, 21, 6 al.; Tat. 17, 1; Theoph. Ant. 1, 14 [p. 92, 9]) **Mt 18:8; 25:41; Jd 7;** Dg 10:7 (opp. τὸ πῦρ τὸ πρόσκαιρον 10:8). πῦρ ἄσβεστον (ἄσβεστος 1) **Mt 3:12; Mk 9:43, 45 v.l.; Lk 3:17;** 2 Cl 17:7; IEph 16:2; AcPl Ha 1, 22. It burns in the γέεννα (τοῦ) πυρός (ApcEsdr 1:9 p. 25, 1 Tdf.; s. γέεννα and cp. En 10:13 τὸ χάος τοῦ πυρός) **Mt 5:22; 18:9** (cp. 1QS 2:7f); **Mk 9:47 v.l.;** 2 Cl 5:4 (a saying of Jesus not recorded elsewhere). ἡ λίμνη τοῦ πυρὸς (καὶ θείου) **Rv 19:20; 20:10, 14ab, 15** (cp. Jos As 12, 10 ἄβυσσον τοῦ πυρός); cp. **Rv 21:8; 14:10, 18; 15:2.** The fiery place of punishment as ἡ κάμινος τοῦ πυρός **Mt 13:42, 50** (difft. AcPl Ha 6, 20 see at the end of a, above). τὸ πῦρ ἐστι μετ' αὐτοῦ *fire awaits that person* AcPlCor 2:37. The fire of hell is also meant in certain parables and allegories, in which trees and vines represent persons worthy of punishment **Mt 3:10; 7:19; Lk 3:9; J 15:6.** The one whose coming was proclaimed by John the Baptist βαπτίσει ἐν πνεύματι ἁγίῳ καὶ πυρί; whether πῦρ in **Mt 3:11; Lk 3:16** refers to reception of the Holy Spirit (esp. in **Lk 3:16**) or to the fire of divine judgment is debatable; for association of πῦρ with πνεῦμα s. **Ac 2:3f;** AcPlCor 2:13 (βαπτίζω 3b). As Lord of Judgment God is called πῦρ καταναλίσκον **Hb 12:29** (Dt 4:24; 9:3.—Mesomedes calls Isis πῦρ τέλεον ἄρρητον [IAndrosIsis p. 145, 14]).—Of a different kind is the idea that fire is to be worshiped as a god (Maximus Tyr. 2, 4b of the Persians: πῦρ δέσποτα; Theosophien 14 p. 170, 11 τὸ πῦρ ἀληθῶς θεός) Dg 8:2.

ⓒ fig. (Just., D. 8, 1 πῦρ ἐν τῇ ψυχῇ ἀνήφθη; Chariton 2, 4, 7 πῦρ εἰς τ. ψυχήν; Ael. Aristid. 28, 110 K.=49 p. 527 D.: τὸ ἱερὸν κ. θεῖον πῦρ τὸ ἐκ Διός; Aristaen., Ep. 2, 5; PGrenf I=Coll. Alex. p. 177 ln. 15 [II BC] of the fire of love; Theoph. Ant. 1, 3 [p. 62, 21] of God's wrath) ἡ γλῶσσα πῦρ **Js 3:6** (s. γλῶσσα 1a). The saying of Jesus πῦρ ἦλθον βαλεῖν ἐπὶ τὴν γῆν **Lk 12:49** seems, in the context where it is now found, to refer to the fire of discord (s. vss. 51–53). πῦρ is also taken as fig. in Agr 3, the sense of which, however, cannot be determined w. certainty (s. Unknown Sayings, 54–56) ὁ ἐγγύς μου ἐγγὺς τοῦ πυρός. ὁ δὲ μακρὰν ἀπ' ἐμοῦ μακρὰν ἀπὸ τῆς βασιλείας (cp. ἐγγύς 3; ἐγγὺς εἶναι τοῦ πυρός as someth. dangerous also Chariton 6, 3, 9). On the difficult pass. πᾶς πυρὶ ἁλισθήσεται **Mk 9:49** and its variants s. ἁλίζω and cp. ἅλας b (s. also NColeman, JTS 24, 1923, 381–96, ET 48, '37, 360–62; PHaupt, Salted with Fire: AJP 45, 1924, 242–45; AFridrichsen, Würzung durch Feuer: SymbOsl 4, 1926, 36–38; JdeZwaan, Met vuur gezouten worden, Mc 9:49: NThSt 11, 1928, 179–82; RHarris, ET 48, '37,

185f; SEitrem, Opferritus u. Voropfer der Griechen u. Römer 1915, 309–44. JBauer, TZ 15, '59, 446–50; HZimmermann [Mk 9:49], TQ 139, '59, 28–39; TBaarda [Mk 9:49], NTS 5, '59, 318–21).—B. 71; RAC VII 786–90; BHHW I 479f. DELG. M-M. EDNT. TW. Sv.

πυρά, ᾶς, ἡ (πῦρ; Hom. et al.; PGM 4, 32; LXX; Philo, Conf. Lingu. 157; SibOr 8, 494) in our lit. only of a **pile of combustible or even of burning material,** ***a fire*** ἅπτειν πυράν (Hdt. 1, 86; 2 Macc 10:36) **Ac 28:2;** cp. **Lk 22:55 v.l.; Ac 28:3.**—A *pyre* on which someone is burned (of Croesus: Hdt. 1, 86, 2ff; Ep. 56 of Apollonius of Tyana [Philostrat. I 359, 13]; of Calanus, the wise man of India: Arrian, Anab. 7, 3, 4ff; of Caesar: Just., A I, 21, 3; of Heracles: Ath. 29, 1): of a faithful confessor MPol 13:2f.—DELG s.v. πύρ.

πύργος, ου, ὁ (Hom.+ [a Nordic loanw.: PKretschmer, Glotta 22, '34, 100ff]; loanw. in rabb.).

❶ a tall structure used as a lookout, ***tower*** ὁ πύργος ἐν τῷ Σιλωάμ **Lk 13:4** (Demetr. of Kallatis [200 BC]: 85 fgm. 6 Jac. πεσόντος τοῦ πύργου πεσεῖν κ. αὐτάς [=25 young women]). Of towers such as are built in a vineyard for watchmen (BGU 650, 8 [60/61 AD]: Is 5:2) **Mt 21:33; Mk 12:1;** prob. also **Lk 14:28** (but s. 2 below and s. C-HHunzinger, ZNW Beiheft 26, '60, 211–17 [Gospel of Thomas]).—B 16:5 (scripture quot., presumably fr. En 89:56). In Hermas the Christian community is pictured as a tower (cp. SibOr 5, 424; Leutzsch, Hermas 410–12 n. 282) Hv 3; 4, 3, 4; s 8 and 9 (over 145 times).

❷ a tower-shaped building, ***farm building*** (s. FPreisigke, Her 54, 1919, 93; EMeyer, Her. 55, 1920, 100; AAlt, ibid. 334–36; JHasebroek, Her 57, 1922, 621–23; PMeyer, Ztschr. für vergleichende Rechtswissenschaft 40, 1922, 207. Rejected by WCrönert, Gnomon 4, 1928, 80) so poss. **Lk 14:28** (but s. 1 above).—DELG. M-M. TW. Spicq. Sv.

πυρέσσω (s. next entry; Eur., Hippocr. et al.; Epict. [s. index Sch.]; M. Ant. 8, 15; Diog. L. 6, 1, 6; Jos., Vi. 404; POslo 95, 20 [96 AD]; 152, 4) ***suffer with a fever*** **Mt 8:14; Mk 1:30.**—DELG s.v. πύρ. M-M. TW.

πυρετός, οῦ, ὁ (πῦρ, s. prec. entry) *fever* ([Il. 22, 31 'burning heat']; Aristoph.; Hippocr.; SIG 1239, 20; 1240, 12; IDefixAudollent 74, 6; BGU 956, 2; POxy 924, 6; 1151, 35; Dt 28:22; TestSol 18, 20 and 23; Philo; Jos., Vi. 48) **Lk 4:39.** ἀφῆκεν αὐτὴν (αὐτὸν) ὁ πυρετός **Mt 8:15; Mk 1:31** (JCook, NTS 43, '97, 184–208); **J 4:52.** In the two passages foll. πυρ. is used w. συνέχεσθαι (cp. Diod. S. 36, 13, 3 παραχρῆμα πυρετῷ συνεσχέθη; Jos., Ant. 13, 398 πυρετῷ συσχεθείς; POxy 986, 33 ὄντα πυρετίοις συνεχόμενον), pl. (Demosth. et al.; Hippocr.: CMG I/1 p. 40, 1; 50, 6; w. δυσεντερία p. 57, 27f; 60, 27) πυρετοῖς καὶ δυσεντερίῳ συνεχόμενον **Ac 28:8.** συνεχομένη πυρετῷ μεγάλῳ *suffering with a severe attack of fever* **Lk 4:38** (cp. Diod. S. 32, 10, 3 τῶν πυρετῶν μεγάλων συνεπιγινομένων; Galen, De Diff. Febr. 1, 1 vol. VII 275 Kühn σύνηθες τοῖς ἰατροῖς ὀνομάζειν τὸν μέγαν τε καὶ μικρὸν πυρετόν; Alexander of Aphrodisias, De Febribus Libell. 31 [JIdeler, Physici et Medici Graeci Minores I 1841, 105f] μικρούς τε καὶ μεγάλους ὀνομάζομεν πυρετούς; Aulus Cornel. Celsus 4, 14 magnae febres.—S. on this JSchuster, M.D., BZ 13, 1915, 338ff; HCadbury, JBL 45, 1926, 194f; 203; 207 note); GDunst, ZPE 3, '68, 148–53 (fever-cult); WKirschläger, Fieberheilung in Apg 28 und Lk 4: Les Actes des Apôtres etc., ed. JKremer '79, 509–21. On fever in the Gr-Rom. world s. also PBurke, ANRW II Principat 37/3 '96, 2252–81.—DELG s.v. πύρ. M-M. TW.

πύρινος, η, ον of the color of fire, ***fiery*** (Aristot. et al.; Kaibel 987 [95 AD]; PTebt 1, 16 [I BC]; BGU 590, 1; PGM 4, 589; Sir 48:9 ἐν ἅρματι ἵππων πυρίνων; Ezk 28:14, 16; En 14:11; TestAbr A; ApcEsdr 4:9 p. 28, 8 Tdf. [θρόνος] al.) ἀκρίδες πύριναι *fiery locusts* Hv 4, 1, 6. Spectral riders wear θώρακας πυρίνους **Rv 9:17** (SibOr 3, 673 ῥομφαῖαι πύριναι).—DELG s.v. πύρ. TW.

πυρκαϊά, ᾶς, ἡ (Hom. et al.; trag., Hdt., Aristot.) ***funeral pyre*** MPol 13:2 v.l. (for πυρά).—DELG s.v. καίω 10; πύρ.

πυροειδής, ές (on the formation s. Schwyzer I 440—Pla., Leg. 10, 895c et al.; Cleanthes: Stoic. fgm. 506 et al. Comp. πυρωδέστερος Just., D. 121, 2; Cat. Cod. Astr. IX/2 p. 119, 5 of φῶς) **the color of fire,** ***red as fire***=bright red (w. αἱματώδης, q.v.) Hv 4, 1, 10; 4, 3, 3.—S. αἷμα 3; Leutzsch, Hermas 434f n. 507.

πυρός, οῦ, ὁ (on the formation s. Schwyzer I 58; perh. related to πυρήν 'stone' of a fruit, s. Boisacq 829—Hom., Hdt., Aristoph. et al.; pap, LXX; TestJud 9:8; EpArist 145; Philo; Tat. 9, 2) ***wheat*** τὸν ἐπὶ τοῦ πυροῦ σπόρον *sowing of wheat* AcPlCor 2:26.—DELG s.v. πυρός.

πυρόω fut. πυρώσω LXX; 1 aor. ἐπύρωσα LXX. Pass.: 1 aor. ἐπυρώθην; pf. ptc. πεπυρωμένος (Pind. et al.; ins, LXX, Philo) prim. as act. 'burn someth. with fire', in our lit. only pass. (Ps.-Pla., Axioch. 372a of torments in Tartarus; Philo).

❶ to cause to be on fire, ***burn*****—ⓐ** lit., of the fiery end of the world οὐρανοὶ πυρούμενοι λυθήσονται *the heavens will be set ablaze and dissolved* **2 Pt 3:12.** In imagery τὰ βέλη τὰ πεπυρωμένα (s. βέλος) **Eph 6:16** (s. Cicero, Tusc. Disp. 5, 27, 76).

ⓑ fig. (act. Cornutus 25 p. 47, 11 πυροῦν τ. ψυχάς; pass., Horapollo 1, 22 ἡ καρδία πυροῦται) *burn, be inflamed* w. sympathy, readiness to aid, or indignation **2 Cor 11:29** (cp. 2 Macc 4:38; 10:35; 14:45; 3 Macc 4:2; Philo, Leg. All. 1, 84 πεπύρωται ἐν εὐχαριστίᾳ θεοῦ. So prob. also the Jewish-Gk. ins fr. Tell el Yehudieh ed. Ltzm. [ZNW 22, 1923, 282] 18, 5 πατὴρ καὶ μήτηρ οἱ πυρώμενοι='father and mother, who are burning w. grief'; cp. Sb 6646; 6659; Ltzm. thinks of the burning of the dead and refers to 20, 4, but there the act. is used); *burn with sexual desire* **1 Cor 7:9** (on the topic cp.Hos 7:4; Sir 23:17; for poetic expression of ardent desire s. Anacreontea 11, 15 Preis.: Ἔρως εὐθέως με πύρωσον; cp. Sappho fgm. 36 and 48; a common theme in magical pap, e.g. PGM 4, 2931 βάλε πυρσὸν ἔρωτα; 36, 111; 200 πυρουμένη; PBerlin 9909, 48; cp. Plut., Mor. 138f; 752d; 753a et al.—SGordon, ET 21, 1910, 478f).

❷ to cause to be very hot, ***make red hot, cause to glow, heat thoroughly*** (Lucian, Alex. 21 βελόνην) of metals πεπυρωμένον σίδηρον APt 13:28. By such heating precious metals are tested and refined (Job 22:25; Ps 11:7; 65:10; Pr 10:20) **Rv 1:15** (πεπυρωμένης is one of the linguistic peculiarities of Rv [s. καὶ ἔχων which follows soon thereafter]. All the variant readings [-μένῳ, -μένοι] here are simply efforts at improvement; on Aramaic connection s. Mussies 98f. FRehkopf, JJeremias Festschr. '70, 214–19); **3:18;** MPol 15:2.—Hv 4, 3, 4 makes a comparison betw. the refining influence of fire on metals and the effect that fiery trials have in removing impurities from Christians.—DELG s.v. πύρ. M-M. TW.

πυρράζω (s. next entry; also πυράζω only in Byzantine writers [Psaltes 332]; LXX has πυρρίζω) ***to be (fiery) red*** of the color of the morning or evening sky **Mt 16:2f.**—M-M.

πυρρός, ά, όν (s. prec. entry; Aeschyl., Hdt.+; ins, pap, LXX; En 18:7. On the double ρ s. B-D-F §34, 2; Mlt-H. 101) ***fiery red*** as the apocalyptic color of a horse (Theocr. 15, 53, of a fox standing on its hind legs) **Rv 6:4** (τὸ λευκόν, μέλαν, ἐρυθρόν, χλωρόν are the four basic colors [Theophr., Sens. 13, 73–75]. In Rv, prob. because of the influence of the ἵππος πυρρός of Zech 1:8 and 6:2, the word ἐρ. has been changed to its practical equivalent πυρρ.—Cp. Petosiris, fgm. 12 l. 25f: μέλας … λοιμὸν [better λιμὸν acc. to ln. 187] ποιεῖ, χλωρὸς δὲ νόσους, πυρρὸς δὲ πόλεμον καὶ σφαγάς. RGradwohl, D. Farben im AT, Beih. ZAW 83, '63, 8). Of a dragon **Rv 12:3** (in Diod. S. 1, 88, 4 π. is the color of Typhon, the enemy of the gods. Cp. also Phlegon: 257 fgm. 36, 3, 11 Jac. ὑπὸ λύκου πυρροῦ εὐμεγέθους καταβρωθῆναι=be devoured by a huge red wolf). In imagery of sins πυρρότεραι κόκκου *redder than scarlet* 1 Cl 8:3 (quot. of unknown orig.).—For lit. s. αἷμα 3.—DELG s.v. πύρ. M-M. TW.

Πύρρος, ου, ὁ (Gk. lit.; ins, pap) ***Pyrrhus,*** father of Sopater of Beroea; Sop. accompanied Paul when he took the collection to Jerusalem **Ac 20:4.**—LGPN I. M-M.

πύρωσις, εως, ἡ (πυρόω; Aristot., Theophr. et al.; PGM 2, 110; Am 4:9; TestSol 18:29 P; TestJud 16:1; Just., D. 116, 2)

❶ **process of burning, *burning*** (Jos., Ant. 1, 203) lit. in pass. sense τὸν καπνὸν τῆς πυρώσεως αὐτῆς **Rv 18:9, 18.**

❷ **an intense degree of some painful occurrence or experience, *burning ordeal*** fig. ext. of 1 ἡ π. τῆς δοκιμασίας *the fiery test* D 16:5. π. πρὸς πειρασμὸν γινομένη *fiery ordeal to test you* **1 Pt 4:12** (cp. the πύρωσις for testing metals Pr 27:21). In this sense the focus is on degree of intensity of the trial, but a component of suffering is indicated by the context, and some would prefer to render: *severe suffering.*—DELG s.v. πύρ. M-M. TW.

πωλέω impf. ἐπώλουν; 1 aor. ἐπώλησα (Eur., Hdt.+) ***sell*** τὶ *someth.* **Mt 13:44; 19:21; 21:12**b (on πωλεῖν in the ἱερόν cp. ILegesSacr II, 88, 31); **Mk 10:21; 11:15b; Lk 12:33; 18:22** (PRyl 113, 8 πάντα τὰ ἐμαυτοῦ πωλήσας); **22:36; J 2:14, 16; Ac 5:1.** The obj. is to be supplied **4:34, 37.**—Pass. *be offered for sale, be sold* (Artem. 4, 15) πᾶν τὸ ἐν μακέλλῳ πωλούμενον **1 Cor 10:25** (MIsenberg, The Sale of Sacrificial Meat: ClPh 70, '75, 271–73). W. gen. of price (X., Mem. 1, 2, 36; PPetr II, 38(b), 2 [243 BC] τὸ ἔλαιον πωλεῖσθαι τιμῆς … ; Jos., Vi. 75.—B-D-F §179, 1; Rob. 510f) **Mt 10:29; Lk 12:6.** Abs. (opp. ἀγοράζειν; s. ἀγοράζω 1) **Lk 17:28; Rv 13:17.** οἱ πωλοῦντες *the sellers, dealers* **Mt 25:9; Lk 19:45.** W. οἱ ἀγοράζοντες (cp. Is 24:2) **Mt 21:12a; Mk 11:15a.** On ascetic practices, s. HvCampenhausen, Tradition and Life in the Church, '68, 90–122.—DELG. M-M.

πῶλος, ου, ὁ (Hom.+; ins, pap, LXX; Ps-Phoc. 126; Just; Philo.)

❶ **young animal, *foal*** (orig. 'colt of a horse': Hom. et al.; besides, it refers to a horse that is old enough to use: Hipponax 41 Diehl; Anacr. 88 D.; X., De Re Equ. 1, 6 al.; PGM 2, 95; then any 'young animal' [Aristot. et al.], the term being applied to any young animal born of its kind, from an elephant to a locust, depending on context; WBauer, The 'Colt' of Palm Sunday [Der Palmesel]: JBL 72, '53, 220–29: the German original in WBauer, Aufsätze u. Kleine Schriften, ed. GStrecker, '67, 109–20. For an ass cp. exx. fr. Geopon., 16, 21, 6; PLille and BGU 373, 7; Gen 32:15; 49:11ab) ὄνος κ. πῶλος μετ' αὐτῆς *an ass, and a colt with her* **Mt 21:2;** cp. vs. **7** and the quotation in vs. **5;** also **J 12:15:** all three echoing Zech 9:9, whose ὑποζύγιον is correctly termed an ὄνος: *foal of an ass.* See PNepper-Christensen, Das Mt-evangelium, '58, 143–48.

❷ **horse** is meant when π. stands alone without indication that it is a foal, and it can refer to any age from the time of being a foal to a grown working animal: **Mk 11:2, 4f, 7; Lk 19:30, 33ab, 35.**—Just., A I, 54, 7 τὸ τοῦ πώλου ὄνομα καὶ ὄνου πῶλον καὶ ἵππου σημαίνειν ἐδύνατο='the term π. was able to signify both the foal of an ass and of a horse'; but there is no evidence that the term π. was ever used without further qualification in the sense of 'ass' or 'foal of an ass'; s. Bauer (1 above), who prefers ***horse*** for the passages in Mk and Lk. Most Eng. translations render π. with 'colt', and it is difficult to determine what kind of animal is meant in their versions of Mk and Luke, inasmuch as, similar to Greek usage, 'colt', when unqualified, is ordinarily associated with a young male horse, although such popular limitation was not the case in earlier stages of the Eng. language: s. OED s.v. 'colt'.—HKuhn, Das Reittier Jesu usw., ZNW 50, '59, 82–91; OMichel, Einzugsgeschichte, NTS 6, '59/60, 81f.—S. also the lit. s.v. ὄνος.—B. 171. DELG. M-M. TW.

πῶλυψ, πος, ὁ ***octopus*** (so Epicharmus in Athen. 7, 32f; Diphilus Siphnius [III BC] ibid. 8, 356e) B 10:5 v.l.; s. πολύπους.—DELG s.v. πώλυπος.

πώποτε adv. (Hom.+; ins, pap, LXX; JosAs 7:8 cod. A [p. 48, 8 Bat.]; al.; Joseph.; Philo; Ath. 21, 4; Mel., HE 4, 26, 6) **pert. to an indefinite point of time, *ever, at any time*** Dg 8:11; MPol 8:1. Usu. used w. a neg. As a rule the verb w. it stands in a past tense *never, not ever* οὐδεὶς πώποτε *no one ever* (X., An. 1, 6, 11; Jos., C. Ap. 2, 124, Ant. 17, 310) **Lk 19:30; J 1:18** (Galen II p. 66 K. μηδ' ἑωρακέναι πώποτε; PGM 5, 102 Osiris, ὃν οὐδεὶς εἶδε πώποτε); **8:33; 1J 4:12.** Cp. **J 5:37.**—Only rarely of the future (Batr. 178; 1 Km 25:28; PGM 4, 291) οὐ μὴ διψήσει πώποτε *will never thirst again* **J 6:35.**—M-M.

πωρόω 1 aor. ἐπώρωσα; pf. πεπώρωκα **J 12:40 v.l.** Pass.: 1 aor. ἐπωρώθην; pf. 3 pl. πεπώρωνται Job 17:7, ptc. πεπωρωμένος (s. next entry; Hippocr., Aristot. et al.; Job 17:7 [of eyes=become dim]) prim.: 'harden, petrify'; in our lit. only fig., **to cause someone to have difficulty in understanding or comprehending, *harden, petrify,*** mostly of hearts τὴν καρδίαν τινός *make dull/obtuse/blind, close the mind* **J 12:40** (ἐπήρωσεν v.l.); pass. ἦν αὐτῶν ἡ καρδία πεπωρωμένη **Mk 6:52;** cp. **8:17;** Hm 4, 2, 1; 12, 4, 4.—Of νοήματα **2 Cor 3:14.** Of persons themselves **Ro 11:7.**—Zahn on Ro, exc. III p. 618–20; Windisch on 2 Cor 3:14; KLSchmidt, D. Verstockung des Menschen durch Gott: TZ 1, '45, 1–17.—DELG s.v. πῶρος. M-M. TW.

πώρωσις, εως, ἡ (πωρόω, s. prec. entry; Hippocr., Galen; on the history of the word s. JARobinson, JTS 3, 1902, 81–93, Eph comm. 1904, 264ff) prim.: 'hardening, dulling'; in our lit. only fig. (TestLevi 13:7 πώρωσις ἁμαρτίας) **state or condition of complete lack of understanding, *dullness, insensibility, obstinacy*** ἡ π. τῆς καρδίας (Theoph. Ant. 2, 35 [p. 188, 22]; s. πωρόω and LCerfaux, Muséon 59, '46, 267–79) **Mk 3:5; Eph 4:18.** π. τῷ Ἰσραὴλ γέγονεν *insensibility (=a closed mind) has come over Israel* **Ro 11:25.**—DELG s.v. πῶρος. M-M. TW.

πῶς (Hom.+)—❶ **interrog. reference to manner or way, *in what way? how?***—ⓐ in direct questions—**α.** to determine how someth. has come to be, how someth. is happening, or should happen; w. indic. *how? in what way?* πῶς ἔσται τοῦτο; **Lk 1:34.** πῶς ἀναγινώσκεις; **10:26;** cp. the indirect qu. Mk 12:26 (s. b, below). πῶς οὖν ἠνεῴχθησάν σου οἱ ὀφθαλμοί; **J 9:10.—3:4,**

9; 9:26; **Ro 4:10** (π. οὖν); **1 Cor 15:35** (cp. 1 Ch 13:12); B 5:5 (π. οὖν); IEph 19:2 (π. οὖν); Hm 3:3 (π. οὖν); GJs 17:11 AcPl Ha 5, 3. In ref. to the content of a document πῶς ἀναγινώσκεις; *what do you read?*='What does it say?' **Lk 10:26** (s. HLjungvik, Eranos 62, '64, 31); πῶς γέγραπται; *What does it say (about the Messiah)?* GJs 21:2 (codd.). W. the special mng. *with what right? with what evidence? in what sense?* πῶς λέγουσιν οἱ γραμματεῖς ὅτι ὁ Χριστὸς υἱὸς Δαυίδ ἐστιν; **Mk 12:35.—Mt 22:43** (π. οὖν), **45; Lk 20:41, 44** (cp. Gen 39:9); **J 12:34** (GrBar 10:8).—γέγραπται **Mk 9:12.**

β. in questions indicating surprise *how is it (possible) that? I do not understand how* (Manetho[?] in Jos., C. Ap. 259 a series of questions expressing surprise, introduced again and again by πῶς; Lucian, Deor. Conc. 10 πῶς φέρεις; TestAbr B 6 p. 110, 12f [Stone p. 68]) πῶς παρ' ἐμοῦ πεῖν αἰτεῖς; **J 4:9.—7:15; Ac 2:8; Gal 4:9.** W. οὖν **J 9:19;** AcPl Ha 10, 9. W. a neg. (Isocr. 6, 4) πῶς οὐ νοεῖτε; *how is it possible that you don't understand?* **Mt 16:11; Mk 8:21 v.l.** πῶς οὐκ ἔχετε πίστιν; *how is it that you have no faith?* **Mk 4:40 v.l.** πῶς οὐ συνίετε; **8:21 v.l.** Cp. **Lk 12:56.**

γ. in questions denoting disapproval or rejection *with what right? how dare you?* πῶς ἐρεῖς τῷ ἀδελφῷ σου; **Mt 7:4** (πῶς ἐρεῖς as Jer 2:23). πῶς εἰσῆλθες ὧδε; *how is it that you are bold enough to come in here?* **22:12.** πῶς σὺ λέγεις; *how can you say?* (cp. Job 33:12; TestAbr B 10 p. 115, 4 [Stone p. 78, 4]) **J 14:9.—Lk 6:42;** *what does he mean by saying?* **J 6:42; 8:33; 1 Cor 15:12; Gal 2:14.**

δ. in rhetorical questions that call an assumption into question or reject it altogether *how* (could or should)?=*by no means, it is impossible that* (Job 25:4; Ar. 3, 2 al; Just., D. 51, 2 al.; Tat., 4, 2; Ath. 16, 4; 19, 2) πῶς (οὖν) σταθήσεται ἡ βασιλεία αὐτοῦ; **Mt 12:26; Lk 11:18.** Cp. **Mt 12:29, 34; Mk 3:23; 4:13; J 3:12; 5:44, 47; 6:52; 9:16; 14:5** (KBeyer, Semitische Syntax im NT, '62, 94f). ἐπεὶ πῶς κρινεῖ ὁ θεὸς τὸν κόσμον; *otherwise* (i.e. if he were unjust) *it would be impossible for God to judge the world* **Ro 3:6.** Cp. **6:2; 1 Cor 14:7, 9, 16; 1 Ti 3:5; Hb 2:3; 1J 3:17; 4:20 v.l.;** B 5:10; MPol 9:3; Hv 3, 9, 10.—If πῶς is accompanied by a neg., the 'impossible' becomes *most surely, most certainly* (Hyperid. 3, 35; 5, 15; Pr 15:11 πῶς οὐχί; EpArist 149; Jos., C. Ap. 1, 256; Just., D. 18, 3 πῶς οὐχί; al.; Tat. 8, 1; 32, 2) πῶς οὐχὶ τὰ πάντα ἡμῖν χαρίσεται; **Ro 8:32.—2 Cor 3:8.**—As an exceptional case the opt. w. ἄν (potential; s. B-D-F §385, 1; Rob. 938; 1021f and Ael. Aristid. 29 p. 557 D.; Just., D. 127, 3; Tat. 16, 1; 17, 3f; Ath. 19, 3 al.) πῶς γὰρ ἂν δυναίμην;=it is impossible for me to do so **Ac 8:31** (s. Gen 44:8; Dt 28:67; Sir 25:3).

ε. in questions of deliberation w. a deliberative subjunctive (B-D-F §366, 1; Rob. 934f.—Epict. 4, 1, 100; M. Ant. 9, 40; 2 Km 23:3; Sir 49:11; Ps.-Clem., Hom. 19, 2) πῶς οὖν πληρωθῶσιν αἱ γραφαί; **Mt 26:54.** πῶς ὁμοιώσωμεν τὴν βασιλείαν; *what comparison can we find for the Kingdom?* **Mk 4:30.** πῶς φύγητε; *how are you to escape?*=you will not escape at all **Mt 23:33.** πῶς οὖν w. subj. **Ro 10:14a,** foll. by πῶς δέ and the subj. three times in vss. **14bc, 15.**—Hs 5, 7, 3.

ⓑ in indirect questions—**α.** w. indic. after verbs of knowing, saying, asking etc. ἀκούειν B 7:3 (Just., A I, 40, 1 al.); cp. **Mk 12:26.** ἀπαγγέλλειν **Lk 8:36; 1 Th 1:9.** βλέπειν **1 Cor 3:10; Eph 5:15.** διηγεῖσθαι **Mk 5:16; Ac 9:27ab; 12:17.** εἰδέναι (X., Mem. 1, 2, 36) **J 9:21; Col 4:6; 2 Th 3:7;** GJs 23:3. ἐπέχειν **Lk 14:7;** ἐπιδεικνύειν B 6:13. ἐπισκέπτεσθαι **Ac 15:36.** ἐπίστασθαι **20:18.** ἐρωτᾶν **J 9:15.** θεωρεῖν **Mk 12:41** (TestAbr B 8 p. 113, 10 [Stone p. 74]). καταμαθεῖν **Mt 6:28** (on π. αὐξάνουσιν here s. PKatz, JTS 5, '54; 207–9); ISm 6:2. κατανοεῖν **Lk 12:27;** 1 Cl 24:1; 37:2. μεμνῆσθαι GJs 9:2. μνημονεύειν **Rv 3:3.** νοεῖν 1 Cl 19:3. ὁρᾶν 50:1.—The addition of an article gives the indir. question the value of a noun παρελάβετε τὸ πῶς δεῖ ὑμᾶς περιπατεῖν **1 Th 4:1** (s. also β below).—In some of the passages given above in this section πῶς could have the same mng. as ὅτι *that,* and this equation at the same time suggests how the Hellenic ear grasped the significance of ὅτι *that* (for the synonymity in later Gk. s. Epict. 1, 18, 7; 2, 25, 3; 3, 22, 51; Jos., Ant. 12, 205; BGU 37, 6 [50 AD]; PRyl 235, 6 ἐθαύμασα δὲ πῶς οὐκ ἐδήλωσάς μοι. See GHatzidakis, Einl. in die neugriech. Gramm. 1892, 19; Rdm.[2] 196; B-D-F §396; Rob. 1032). That is clearly the mng. in **Mt 12:4; Mk 2:26; Ac 11:13;** B 11:1; 14:6; 1 Cl 34:5.

β. w. deliberative subjunctive (ParJer 6, 11 and 14) μὴ μεριμνήσητε πῶς ἢ τί λαλήσητε **Mt 10:19.—Mk 11:18; 14:1, 11; Lk 12:11.** μεριμνᾷ πῶς ἀρέσῃ **1 Cor 7:32, 33, 34** (t.r. has the fut. in Mk 11:18 and 1 Cor 7:32–34; s. Herodian 5, 4, 9 ἠγνόουν, πῶς χρήσονται τῷ πράγματι). In this case, too, the article can be added (s. α) **Lk 22:2, 4; Ac 4:21** (ParJer 6:15).

❷ in exclamations (cp. 1aβ; Schwyzer II 626) ***how . . . !*** (X., An. 6, 5, 19 al.; Epict. 1, 16, 13; 4, 1, 115; 116, Ench. 24, 3 πῶς ἄνισοί ἐστε καὶ ἀγνώμονες; M. Ant. 6, 27.—B-D-F §436; Rob. 302; OLagercrantz, Eranos 18, 1918, 26ff; KRupprecht, Philol. 80, 1924, 207) πῶς δύσκολόν ἐστιν **Mk 10:24;** cp. vs. **23; Lk 18:24.** πῶς συνέχομαι **12:50.** πῶς ἐφίλει αὐτόν **J 11:36.**—Hm 11:20; 12, 4, 2.—JBauer, Pōs in der gr. Bibel, NovT 2, '57, 81–91. DELG s.v. πο-. M-M. EDNT.

πώς enclitic particle (Hom. et al.)—❶ as adv.: **marker of undesignated means or manner,** ***somehow, in some way, perhaps*** ἐάν πως (cp. SIG 364, 24 [III BC]; 3 Km 18:5) ISm 4:1. W. a neg. (Il. 2, 203; 4, 158 al.; Hdt. 1, 33; Schwyzer II 580) οὐδ' ἄν πως οἱ ἄνθρωποι ἐσώθησαν *humans could in no way have been saved* B 5:10 v.l.—In combination w. εἰ s. εἰ 6n (also Jos., Bell. 6, 422, Ant. 2, 159; M-M s.v. πως).

❷ as conj.: in the form **μή πως** (or **μήπως**; since Hom., also pap, Sir 28:26; TestSol 6:14 D; TestAbr B 2 p. 106, 8 [Stone p. 60, 8]; TestJob 15:9; TestZeb 4:2; ParJer 5:5) **marker of a negative perspective expressing misgiving,** frequently rendered ***lest.***

ⓐ in clauses that in effect qualify as purpose clauses *so that . . . (perhaps) not, lest somehow* w. aor. subj. **1 Cor 9:27; 2 Cor 2:7; 9:4.** GJs 7:1; 8:2.

ⓑ in object clauses, after verbs of apprehension *that perhaps, lest somehow* w. aor. subj. after φοβεῖσθαι (Test. Zeb. 4:2; ParJer 5:5) **Ac 27:29 v.l.; 2 Cor 11:3; 12:20a;** cp. vs. **20b,** where the verb (γένωνται) is to be supplied. W. ind. GJs 14:1; fut. 9:2 end. After βλέπετε *take care that . . . not somehow* **1 Cor 8:9** (cp. Sir 28:26). Referring to someth. that has already taken place, w. perf. ind. **Gal 4:11** (B-D-F §370, 1; Rob. 995; 1169). Elliptically μ. οὐδὲ σοῦ φείσεται (it is to be feared) *that perhaps he will not spare you, either* **Ro 11:21.** μ. ἐπείρασεν ὑμᾶς ὁ πειράζων καὶ εἰς κενὸν γένηται ὁ κόπος ἡμῶν (in the fear) *that the tempter might really have tempted you* (ind., as **Gal 4:11** above), *and then our work might have been in vain* **1 Th 3:5.** μήπως τοῦτο πανοῦργος ἔδωκέν σοι *lest some mischief-maker has given it to you* GJs 2:3. μ. περίγελος become a laughing-stock 9:2.

ⓒ in introduction to an indirect question (cp. TestJob 15:9) ***(lest) perhaps*** μ. εἰς κενὸν τρέχω ἢ ἔδραμον (fearing) *that perhaps I may be running or had run in vain* **Gal 2:2.**—DELG s.v. πο-. M-M.

Ρ

ρ´ numerical sign=***100*** (ἑκατόν; Jos., C. Ap. 2, 134) Hv 4, 1, 6; GJs 4:3 pap.

Ῥαάβ, ἡ indecl. (רָחָב; LXX; Just., D. 111, 4.—In Joseph. Ῥαάβη [v.l. Ῥαχάβη], ης [Ant. 5, 8]) ***Rahab,*** a prostitute in Jericho who, acc. to Josh 2, saved Israelite spies by hiding them. For this reason she was spared when the city was taken (Josh 6:17, 25). This courageous woman is cited as a model of faith, uprightness, and hospitality **Hb 11:31; Js 2:25;** 1 Cl 12:1, 3. FYoung, JBL 67, '48, 339–45. S. also Ῥαχάβ (B-D-F §39, 3; Mlt-H. 109).

ῥαββί (from רַב 'lord, master', רַבִּי 'my lord'; also ῥαββεί; on the interchange of ει and ι s. B-D-F §38; W-S. §5, 13a; s. Mlt-H. 76f.—EbNestle, ZNW 7, 1906, 184) properly a form of address, and so throughout our lit., then an honorary title for outstanding teachers of the law: ***master, sir, rabbi*** **Mt 23:7f** (here, too, ῥαββί is a form of address). Of John the Baptist, whom his disciples addressed in this manner **J 3:26.** Otherw. always of Jesus: **Mt 26:25, 49; Mk 9:5; 10:51 v.l.; 11:21; 14:45; J 1:49; 4:31; 6:25; 9:2; 11:8.** κύριε ῥ. **Mk 10:51** D; s. the apocryphal gospel fgm. ZNW 22, 1923, 153f=PBerlin 11710 (in the form ῥαμβιού and ῥαμβίς, s. ASyn. 21, 74; 75; 76). With the transl. διδάσκαλε, which paraphrases the sense **J 1:38;** cp. **3:2.**—Schürer II 325f; The Jewish Encyclopedia X 1905, 294ff; Dalman, Worte 272–80; TReinach, REJ 48, 1904, 191–96 (ins fr. Cyprus: εὐχὴ ῥαββὶ Ἀττικοῦ); Billerb. I 916; JNeusner, The Phenomenon of the Rabbi in Later Antiquity, Numen 16, '69, 1–20; Kl. Pauly IV, 1322f; TRE III, 608; BHHW III 1541ff; ABD V 600–602. M-M. EDNT. TW.

ῥαββουνί (also written ῥαββουνεί, ῥαββονί, ῥαββωνί, ῥαββονεί, s. ῥαββί), properly a heightened form of רַב: רַבָּן and beside it רִבּוֹן w. suffix רִבּוֹנִי or רַבּוּנִי ***my lord, my master.*** Jesus is so addressed in **Mk 10:51** and **J 20:16;** in the latter pass. διδάσκαλε is added as a transl.—E Kautzsch, Grammatik des Bibl.-Aramäischen 1884, 10; Dalman, Gramm.[2] §35, 2, Worte 267; 279, Jesus 12; Schürer II 326; Billerb. II 25; PKahle, The Cairo Geniza '47, 129 (exx. fr. Jewish sources); WAlbright, Recent Discoveries in Palestine and J, in CHDodd Festschr. '56, 158 ('my dear [or] little master').—TW.

ῥαβδίζω (ῥάβδος; since Pherecrates Com. [V BC] 50; Aristoph.; Theophr.; PRyl 148, 20; LXX) 1 aor. 3 sg. ἐρράβδισεν Ruth 2:17; pass. ἐραβδίσθην (on the quest. whether to spell it ἐρ- or ἐρρ- s. B-D-F §11, 1; Mlt. H. 101f; 192f) **to beat with a rod,** ***beat*** (Aristoph., Lys. 587; Diod. S. 19, 101, 3) of the punishment known formally in Lat. legal terminology as admonitio (Dig. Just. 48, 19, 7 'veluti fustium'=as in the use of rods [hence the term fustigatio for the beating itself]) as distinct from catigatio (a lashing) and verberatio (flogging with chains); Paul was beaten three times acc. to **2 Cor 11:25;** in his case it was prob. the fustigatio prescribed by city magistrates, cp. **Ac 16:22.**—TMommsen, ZNW 2, 1901, p. 89, 1. BAFCS 3, 123–25. DELG s.v. ῥάβδος. M-M. TW.

ῥαβδίον, ου, τό (ῥάβδος; Theophr. et al.; Ezk 21:26 v.l.) dim. of ῥάβδος **a relatively light piece of wood,** ***stick, twig*** Hs 8, 1, 2f; 8, 2, 9.

ῥάβδος, ου, ἡ (Hom.+; ins; PSI 168, 16; PTebt 44, 20; LXX; TestSol 10:4 [personifed]; Test12Patr; JosAs 14:8 [oft. cod. A]; ApcEsdr 1:4 p. 24, 10 Tdf.; Philo; Jos., Bell. 2, 365f, Ant. 5, 284; Just.; Mel., P. 13, 85; Ath.) **a relatively slender piece of wood varying in length,** ***rod, staff, stick*** gener. **Rv 11:1;** many times in Hs 8. Of the test involving rods (Num 17) 1 Cl 43:2–5; **Hb 9:4** (Num 17:23); GJs 9:1. Of a shepherd's staff (Mi 7:14) Hv 5:1; s 6, 2, 5; GJs 18:3 v.l. In imagery ποιμαίνειν τινὰ ἐν ῥ. σιδηρᾷ (ποιμαίνω 2aγ and cp. PGM 36, 109) **Rv 2:27; 12:5; 19:15.** Of a traveler's staff (lit. s.v. ὑπόδημα) **Mt 10:10; Mk 6:8; Lk 9:3.** Of a ruler's staff, *scepter* (Pind., O. 9, 33 [50]; LXX) **Hb 1:8** (Ps 44:7). Of a 'magic' wand (Lucian, Dial. Deor. 7, 4, Dial. Mort. 23, 3; Ps.-Callisth. 1, 1, 3) Hv 3, 2, 4; s 9, 6, 3 (Leutzsch, Hermas 409f n. 279). Of a stick as a means of punishment (Pla., Leg. 3, 700c; Plut., Mor. 268d; 693f; Ex 21:20; Is 10:24) ἐν ῥάβδῳ ἔρχεσθαι (opp. ἐν ἀγάπῃ) *come with a stick* **1 Cor 4:21** (s. ἐν 5aβ). ῥάβδοι πυρός *fiery rods* APt 19:33. Of an old man's staff **Hb 11:21** (Gen 47:31).—DELG. M-M. TW. Sv.

ῥαβδοῦχος, ου, ὁ (ῥάβδος, ἔχω; Aristoph., Thu. et al.; ins, pap) orig. 'staff-bearer', then of the Roman 'lictor' (Polyb. et al.; Diod. S. 5, 40, 1; Plut., Rom. 34 [26, 3], Mor. 280a διὰ τί λικτώρεις τοὺς ῥαβδούχους ὀνομάζουσι; Herodian 7, 8, 5.—Joseph. does not have the word, but ῥάβδοι in Bell. 2, 365f prob. refers to the fasces or bundles of sticks carried by the lictors), roughly equiv. to ***constable, police officer.*** The στρατηγοί (q.v.) of Philippi had two lictors in attendance on them (JMarquardt, Röm. Staatsverwaltung 1[2] 1881 p. 175, 7; ASherwin-White, Roman Society and Roman Law in the NT '63, 74f) **Ac 16:35, 38** (Mason 82f [literary]; New Docs 2, 18f).—M-M. TW.

ῥαβιθα. In **Mk 5:41** codex D reads ραββι θαβιτα; this is meant for ῥαβιθά, the fem. of râbîâ ***girl;*** accordingly ῥ.=ταλιθά, which is read by the majority of witnesses.—Wlh. ad loc.; FSchulthess, ZNW 21, 1922, 243 note; TRE III 609.

Ῥαγαύ (רְעוּ), **ὁ** indecl. (LXX.—In Jos., Ant. 1, 148 v.l. Ῥάγαους) ***Reu,*** son of Peleg and father of Serug (Gen 11:18–21), in the genealogy of Jesus **Lk 3:35.**

ῥᾳδιούργημα, ατος, τό (ῥᾳδιουργέω 'engage in trickery' via ῥᾳδιουργός 'unscrupulous', which in turn derives from ῥᾴδιος and a verbal root associated w. ἔργον; Dionys. Hal. 1, 77; Plut., Pyrrh. 6, 7, Mor. 860d; Ps.-Lucian, Calumn. 20) orig. the action of one who endeavors to gain some personal end through clever or tricky means. From the sense 'prank, knavery, roguish trick, slick deed' it is but a short step to that of serious misdeed, ***crime, villainy*** (Oenomaus in Eus., PE 5, 26, 2) ῥ. πονηρόν *a serious piece of villainy* **Ac 18:14** (w. ἀδίκημα). DELG s.v. ῥᾶ.

ῥᾳδιουργία, ας, ἡ (s. beg. of prec. entry; X. et al.; Suda: ῥ. =πλατογράφος καὶ ὁ κακοῦργος ἁπλῶς a counterfeiter and, in general, a bad pers.) in its less pejorative sense ῥ. suggests an easygoing approach to things in contrast to serious acceptance of responsibilties: 'frivolity' (the trickery of slaves is a common theme in Gr-Rom. comedy), then **an endeavor to gain some personal end through clever or tricky means,** in effect a mild expr. for ***chichanery, wickedness, villainy, deceit, fraud, unscrupulousness*** (one who looks for an easy and questionable way of doing things to make money may be said, in American parlance, 'to con' others.) (Polyb. 12, 10, 5; Diod. S. 5, 11, 1; Plut., Cato Min. 16, 3; PMagd 35, 11 [216 BC]; BGU 226, 14 [99 AD]; POxy 237 VIII, 15; PStras 40, 30; SB 10929 III, 10; Philo, Cher. 80) w. δόλος **Ac 13:10.**—AWikenhauser, BZ 8, 1910, 273; CBarrett, in Les Actes des Apôtres, ed. JKremer '79, 289, on Elymas.—M-M. TW. Spicq.

ῥᾳδίως adv. of ῥᾴδιος (Att. [Hom. et al. in the form ῥηϊδίως]; OGI 508, 8; PPetr II, 11, 1; 4; PGiss 47, 26; POxy 471, 54; Philo; Jos., Bell. 3, 99; 6, 157, Ant. 11, 240; Just., D. 90, 2; Tat. 14, 1) ***readily, easily*** (i.e. without being impeded) Hv 4, 1, 2; Pa (3, 2).—DELG s.v. ῥᾶ.

ῥαθυμέω 1 aor. ἐραθύμησα (X., Pla.+; OGI 521, 15; pap, LXX; Philo, Migr. Abr. 133; Jos., Ant. 14, 166), freq. ῥᾳθ- in mss. (so also Joly for Hv 1, 3, 2) but better ῥαθυμέω (PEdg 83 [=Sb 6789], 6; PHib 46, 12 [III BC]) **to approach someth. in a light-hearted or nonchalant manner, *be unconcerned, be idle, relax*** Hv 1, 3, 2.—DELG s.v. ῥᾶ.

ῥαίνω (cp. ῥαντίζω) 1 aor. ἔρρανα (Hom.+; ins; pap [Sb 8000, 17: III AD]; LXX; TestSol 18:15; Jos., Ant. 3, 205; 242; 4, 79; 81) ***sprinkle*** τὶ *someth.* ῥ. ὕδωρ *sprinkle water* (Ezk 36:25) in cleaning a place Hs 9, 10, 3. Pass. **Rv 19:13 v.l.** (Lucian, Anach. 11 αἵματι ῥαινόμενος).—DELG.

Ῥαιφάν, ὁ indecl. (the form of the word differs considerably in the mss., freq. w. infixed nasal: Ῥομφάν [-άμ], Ῥεμφάν [-άμ, -α], and the like; the mss. of the LXX are not in full agreement [Ῥαιφαν, Ῥεμφαν; s. ed. JZiegler '43]. Ῥαφάν Just., D. 22, 3). ***Rephan, Rompha,*** a deity worshipped by some Israelites, put by the LXX in Am 5:26 in the place of כִּיּוּן (=Saturn; cp. CD 7:15, 17); this is quoted in **Ac 7:43.**—WGrafBaudissin, RE XVI 1905, 636–49; RBorger, ZAW 100, '88, 70–81 (lit.; Haenchen, Bruce ad loc.).

ῥακά (also written ῥαχά; so as an uncomplimentary, perh. foul epithet in a Zenon pap of 257 BC: Sb 7638, 7 Ἀντίοχον τὸν ῥαχᾶν [s. on this Colwell, JBL 53, '34, 351–54; Goodsp, Probs. 20–23; MSmith, JBL 64, 1945, 502f]) **a term of abuse/put-down relating to lack of intelligence, *numskull, fool*** (in effect verbal bullying) **Mt 5:22,** a term of abuse, as a rule derived fr. the Aramaic רֵיקָא or רֵיקָה 'empty one', found (Billerb. I 278f) in the Talmud (EKautzsch, Gramm. des Biblisch-Aramäischen 1884, 10; Dalman, Gramm.[2] 173f; SFeigin, JNES 2, '43, 195f; Mlt-H. 152 w. note 3), *empty-head.* Doubt as to the correctness of this derivation is expressed by Wlh. and Zahn ad loc.; FSchulthess, ZNW 21, 1922, 241–43. Among the ancient interpreters, the Gk. Onomastica, Jerome, Hilary, and the Opus Imperfectum p. 62 (MPG LVI, 690) take ῥ. as= κενός=Lat. vacuus=*empty-head, numskull, fool.* Chrysostom says (MPG LVII, 248): τὸ δὲ ῥακὰ οὐ μεγάλης ἐστὶν ὕβρεως ῥῆμα … ἀντὶ τοῦ σύ='ῥ. is not an expression denoting a strong put-down … but is used in place of σύ.' The same thing in somewhat different words in Basilius, Regulae 51 p. 432c: τί ἐστί ῥακά; ἐπιχώριον ῥῆμα ἠπιωτέρας ὕβρεως, πρὸς τοὺς οἰκειοτέρους λαμβανόμενον 'what is the mng. of ῥ.? It is a colloquial term of rather gentle cheek and generally used in familiar surroundings'. Sim., Hecataeus: 264 fgm. 4 p. 13, 21f Jac. (in Plut., Mor. 354d) explains the name Ammon as coming fr. a form of address common among the Egyptians: προσκλητικὴν εἶναι τὴν φωνήν.—SKrauss, OLZ 22, 1919, 63; JLeipoldt, CQR 92, 1921, 38; FBussby, ET 74, '64, 26; RGuelich, ZNW 64, '73, 39–52; Betz, SM ad loc. S. the lit. s.v. μωρός.—TRE III 608. EDNT. M-M. TW.

ῥάκος, ους, τό—❶ ***tattered garment, rag*** (Hom. et al.; POxy 117, 14; Is 64:5) ῥάκη ῥυπαρά *filthy rags* (Cebes 10, 1; Plut., Mor. 168d) ApcPt 15:30.

❷ ***piece of cloth, patch*** (Hdt. 7, 76; Hippocr. et al.; Artem. 1, 13; PStras 647, 2 a patch of plaster for healing wounds; PGM 4, 1082; 3192; 7, 208; 359; Jer 45:11; Jos., Ant. 6, 289) ἐπίβλημα ῥάκους ἀγνάφου *a patch made of a piece of new cloth* **Mt 9:16; Mk 2:21** (RLewis, ET 45, '34, 185; FHahn, EvTh 31, '71, 357–75).—B. 398. DELG. M-M.

Ῥαμά, ἡ indecl. (רָמָה; Judg 19:13; 3 Km 15:17.—Jos., Ant. 8, 303f has Ἀρμαθών, ῶνος; Just., D. 78, 8 ἐν Ῥαμᾶ … ἀπὸ Ῥαμᾶ) ***Rama,*** a city in the tribe of Benjamin, about 8 km north of Jerusalem **Mt 2:18** (Jer 38:15). Buhl, Geogr. 172; Dalman, Orte[3] 29. BHHW III 1548f.

ῥαντίζω (Ael. Dion. π. 40 ἐρραντισμένος αἵματι; Athen. 12, 521a; Lev 6:20; 4 Km 9:33; JosAs 13:5; Just., A I, 62, 1.—Thumb 223) fut. ῥαντιῶ; 1 aor. ἐράντισα (on the quest. whether to spell it w. one ρ or two s. B-D-F §11, 1; Mlt-H. 101f). Pass.: 1 aor. 3 sg. ἐρραντίσθη 4 Km 9:33; pf. ptc. ῥεραντισμένος (B-D-F §68; Mlt-H. 100; Kühner-Bl. I p. 278, 5).

❶ to sprinkle liquid on someth., *(be)sprinkle* w. acc., of the rite of purification (Num 19) τὸν λαὸν ἐράντισεν *he sprinkled the people* **Hb 9:19.** Cp. B 8:1 and, without the acc. (supplied fr. the context) 8:3f. τί τινι *someth. w. someth.* **Hb 9:21.** ῥαντιεῖς με ὑσσώπῳ 1 Cl 18:7 (Ps 50:9).—Pass. (s. above) ἱμάτιον ῥεραντισμένον αἵματι *a garment sprinkled with blood* **Rv 19:13 v.l.** (for βεβαμμένον; there are also other variants). The act. is also used of liquids and of other things that *sprinkle someone* **Hb 9:13.**

❷ The mid. is found in our lit. w. the mng. **to cleanse oneself of impurities, *cleanse, purify*—ⓐ** of a cultic action *cleanse* or *wash oneself* ἐὰν μὴ ῥαντίσωνται οὐκ ἐσθίουσιν **Mk 7:4 v.l.** (for βαπτίσωνται; s. βαπτίζω 1).

ⓑ in imagery *purify someth. for oneself,* fig. ῥεραντισμένοι τὰς καρδίας ἀπὸ συνειδήσεως πονηρᾶς *after we have purified our hearts of an evil conscience* **Hb 10:22.**—DELG s.v. ῥαίνω. M-M. TW.

ῥάντισμα, ατος, τό (ῥαντίζω; Vett. Val. 110, 17) ***sprinkling*** ἐν τῷ αἵματι τοῦ ῥαντίσματος αὐτοῦ *by his sprinkled blood* B 5:1.—DELG s.v. ῥαίνω. M-M.

ῥαντισμός, οῦ, ὁ (ῥαντίζω; LXX) ***sprinkling.*** The blood of Jesus is called αἷμα ῥαντισμοῦ *blood of sprinkling,* i.e. *blood that is sprinkled* for atonement **Hb 12:24** (cp. Num 19:9 al. ὕδωρ ῥαντισμοῦ). Christians are destined by God's choice εἰς ῥαντισμὸν αἵματος Ἰησοῦ Χρ. *to be sprinkled with the blood of Christ* and thus have their sins expiated **1 Pt 1:2.**—DELG s.v. ῥαίνω. M-M. TW.

ῥαπίζω (ῥαπίς 'a rod'; since Xenophanes, fgm. 7, 4 [Vorsokr.[8] I 131; in Diog. L. 8, 36]; Hdt.; LXX; AscIs 2:12) fut. ῥαπίσω; 1 aor. ἐράπισα (on the spelling w. one ρ or two s. B-D-F §11, 1; Mlt-H. 101 f) lit., and almost always in non-biblical authors 'strike with a club or rod'; the abs. ἐράπισαν **Mt 26:67** could have this mng. But in the other places in our lit. the sense is clearly **to strike with the open hand,** esp. in the face, ***slap*** (Suda: ῥαπίσαι· πατάσσειν τὴν γνάθον ἁπλῇ τῇ χειρί.—Hyperid., fgm. 97 and Plut., Mor. 713c ῥ. τινὰ ἐπὶ κόρρης; Achilles Tat. 2, 24; 5, 23; 6, 20 κατὰ κόρρης; Jos., Ant. 8, 408 in retelling the story of 3 Km 22:24 uses ῥαπίζειν instead of πατάσσειν ἐπὶ τὴν σιαγόνα; 1 Esdr 4:30; Hos 11:4 ῥ. ἐπὶ τὰς σιαγόνας; Phryn. p. 175 Lob.) ῥ. τινὰ εἰς τὴν σιαγόνα αὐτοῦ *slap someone on* *the cheek* **Mt 5:39** (Lk 6:29 prefers the more elegant τύπτω; s. σιαγών). Also τὰς σιαγόνας τινὸς ῥ. GPt 3:9.—DELG. M-M.

ῥάπισμα, ατος, τό (ῥαπίζω; Antiphon et al.)—**❶ a blow inflicted by some instrument such as a club, rod, or whip,** ***blow*** (Antiphanes in Athen. 14, 623b; Lucian, Dial. Mer. 8, 2) so perh. οἱ ὑπηρέται ῥαπίσμασιν αὐτὸν ἔλαβον **Mk 14:65** (s. λαμβάνω 5). But even here it may have the mng. that is certain for the other passages in our lit.:

❷ a blow on the face with someone's hand, ***a slap in the face*** (s. ῥαπίζω and cp. ῥάπισμα Ael. Dion. ε, 55 [ῥάπισμα τὸ ἐπὶ τῆς γνάθου]; Alciphron 3, 3, 2; schol. on Pla. 508d, also Anth. Pal. 5, 289 [VI AD] ῥ. ἀμφὶ πρόσωπα; AcJo 90 [Aa II/1 p. 195f]) διδόναι ῥάπισμά τινι *give someone a slap in the face* **J 18:22** (but s. Field, Notes 105f); pl. **19:3.** ἐάν τίς σοι δῷ ῥάπισμα εἰς τὴν δεξιὰν σιαγόνα D 1:4. τιθέναι τὰς σιαγόνας εἰς ῥαπίσματα *offer the cheeks to slaps* B 5:14 (Is 50:6).—PBenoit, Les Outrages à Jésus Prophète, OCullmann Festschr., '62, 92–110.—DELG s.v. ῥάπτω. M-M.

ῥάσσω (Demosth. 54, 8; Achilles Tat. 5, 23, 5; LXX) **to use violence and so cause someone to fall down to a surface,** ***strike, dash, throw down,*** τινά *someone* **Mk 9:18** D (for ῥήσσω, q.v. 2a).

ῥαφίς, ίδος, ἡ (ῥάπτω 'sew') ***needle*** esp. one used for sewing (Hippocr., Morb. 2, 66 al.; POxy 736, 75) τρύπημα (v.l. τρῆμα) ῥαφίδος *eye of a needle* **Mt 19:24.** Also τρυμαλιὰ ῥ. **Mk 10:25; Lk 18:25 v.l.** (βελόνη in Lk's text may reflect a higher style, s. New Docs 5, 80).—See s.v. βελόνη, also Field, Notes 196; PMinear, JBL 61, '42, 157–69 and lit. at κάμηλος.—B. 412. DELG s.v. ῥάπτω. M-M.

ῥαχά s. ῥακά.

Ῥαχάβ, ἡ indecl. ***Rahab*** (רָחָב; s. Ῥαάβ.—Jos., Ant. 5, 8; 11; 15 al. has beside Ῥαάβη, ης [Ant. 5, 8], the v.l. Ῥαχάβη), in the genealogy of Jesus **Mt 1:5,** wife of Salmon and mother of Boaz.—S. Θαμάρ. JQuinn, Biblica 62, '81, 225–28.—TW.

ῥαχή, ἡ s. ῥαχία, ῥάχος.

Ῥαχήλ, ἡ indecl. (רָחֵל; LXX; Test12Patr, JosAs; Demetr.: 722 Jac.; Philo, Just.—Joseph. has Ῥάχηλα, ας [Ant. 1, 301]) ***Rachel,*** Jacob's wife, mother of the people of Israel **Mt 2:18** (Jer 38:15).—BHHW III 1548.

ῥαχία, ας, ἡ name of a berry-bush, perh. ***the blackberry*** ἐπὶ φρύγανον τὸ λεγόμενον ῥ. *on a bush called the blackberry* B 7:8 as read by Gebh.-Harn.-Zahn (but s. the textual tradition in Bihlmeyer; s. ῥάχος).—Sv.

ῥάχος (ῥαχός? on the sp. s. DELG and Frisk, both s.v. ῥάχις), **ου, ἡ** (since Hdt. [7, 142 ῥηχός]; ins: ILegesSacr II, 153 [III BC]; BGU 1466, 4 [I BC]; prim.: 'thornbush') **name of a thornbush bearing sweet fruits,** perh. ***the blackberry*** (cp. ῥαχία, w. which the text of Gebh.-Harn.-Zahn interchanges it as an equivalent. Bihlmeyer has ῥαχή in both places) B 7:8 (JHarris, On the Locality of Pseudo-Barnabas, JBL 9, 1890, 60–70).

Ῥεβέκκα, ας, ἡ (רִבְקָה; declined in LXX, Philo, and Joseph.) ***Rebecca,*** wife of Isaac **Ro 9:10;** B 13:2 (Gen 25:21), 3.—BHHW III 1558.

ῥέδη, ης, ἡ (acc. to Quintilian 1, 5, 57 orig. a Celtic word [s. also Caesar, Bell. Gall. 1, 51; 6, 30]. It came into Gk. lit. by way of Lat. authors [in the form 'reda' or 'raeda' in Cicero; Horace, Sat. 1, 5, 86; 2, 6, 42; Suetonius, Jul. 57 al.]. S. on it, as well as on the spelling ῥαίδη, B-D-F §5, 1d; 41, 1; Mlt-H. 81; 155; Hahn 263, 5 [lit.]) **a four-wheeled traveling carriage,** ***carriage*** **Rv 18:13** (sp. v.l. ῥαίδη).—M-M.

Ῥεμφάν, Ῥεφάν s. Ῥαιφάν.

Ῥέος, ου, ὁ ***Rheus*** surnamed Agathopus (s. Ἀγαθόπους) IPhld 11:1 (s. Hdb. on the passage); ISm 10:1.

ῥεραμμαι s. ῥαίνω.

ῥεριμμένος s. ῥίπτω.

ῥέω (Hom.+; ins, pap, LXX; TestJob 13:1; JosAs 29:1; ApcMos; SibOr 3, 54; Philo; Jos., Bell. 6, 105 μνήμη ῥέουσα δι' αἰῶνος; Just.; Mel., HE 4, 26, 9) fut. ῥεύσω (B-D-F §77; Rob. 355); aor. impv. 3 pl. ῥευσάτωσαν SSol 4:16; ptc. gen. sg. ῥεύσαντος (Just., D. 67, 2). Pass.: fut. 3 sg. ῥυήσεται LXX; aor. 3 sg. ἐρρύη LXX, inf. ῥυῆναι (Mel.) **to flow with liquid,** in our lit. only in transf. sense

ⓐ as symbol of transcendent blessing ***flow*** ποταμοὶ ἐκ τ. κοιλίας αὐτοῦ ῥεύσουσιν ὕδατος ζῶντος **J 7:38** (Hdb. ad loc., and s. κοιλία 3).

ⓑ fig. in the sense of 'have more than enough of': ***(over)flow with*** τὶ *someth.* γῆ ῥέουσα γάλα καὶ μέλι *a land flowing w. milk and honey* (LXX) B 6:8, 10, 13 (for a more detailed treatment of this pass. s. Windisch, Hdb. on B 6:8.—S. also γάλα a).—B. 677. DELG. M-M.

Ῥήγιον, ου, τό (Aeschyl., Hdt. et al.; ins; Philo, Aet. M. 139; Jos., Ant. 19, 205) ***Rhegium,*** a city and promontory in Bruttium, at the 'toe' of Italy, opposite the Sicilian city of Messina **Ac 28:13.**—Pauly-W. I 487–502; Kl. Pauly IV 1367; BHHW III 1572; PECS 753f.—M-M.

ῥῆγμα, ατος, τό (ῥήγνυμι; since Archippus Com. [V/IV BC], fgm. 38; Hippocr.; pap, LXX; Jos., Bell. 6, 337) **the event of reduction to a ruined state,** ***wreck, ruin, collapse,*** lit. 'breaking' τῆς οἰκίας (this mng. is not found elsewh.; but the pl. w. ref. to bldgs.: Polyb. 13, 6, 8; PSI 456, 11 τοῦ πύργου ῥήγματα; Am 6:11 v.l. πατάξει τὸν οἶκον ῥήγμασιν.—PLond I, 131 recto, 45; 60 pp. 171f [78/79 AD] uses the word of a break in a dam on the Nile, i.e. of damage by water) **Lk 6:49.**—DELG s.v. ῥήγνυμι. M-M.

ῥήγνυμι (**Mt 9:17** and its by-form ῥήσσω Mt 9:17 D; Lk 5:6 D) fut. ῥήξω; 1 aor. ἔρ(ρ)ηξα, impv. ῥῆξον; pf. 3 pl. ἐρρώγασιν Josh 9:13, ptc. ἐρρηγώς Job 32:19. Pass.: 2 fut. ῥαγήσομαι; 2 aor. ἐράγην LXX; inf. ῥαγῆναι AcPl Ha 3, 11 (Hom.+; LXX; TestSol; TestJob 28:3; TestJud 2:6; Mel., P. 91, 682; Ath., 18, 3)

❶ to cause to come apart or be in pieces by means of internal or external force, ***tear in pieces, break, burst*** τινά or τὶ *someone* or *someth.* (Jos., Ant. 5, 310) of wine τοὺς ἀσκούς *burst the wine-skins* (Alex. Aphr., An. Mant. 124, 20 Br.) **Mk 2:22;** cp. **Mt 9:17** D; **Lk 5:37.** Pass. *be torn, burst* (Diod. S. 3, 34, 2; TestJud 2:6; ViHab 12; PGM 4, 361; 2674; 13, 264) **Mt 9:17.** ὥστε τὰ δίκτυα ῥήσσεσθαι **Lk 5:6** D. ῥαγῆναι τὰ δεσμά AcPl Ha 3, 11. Of ferocious animals *tear in pieces* w. their teeth μήποτε ῥήξωσιν ὑμᾶς **Mt 7:6** (Aesop, Fab. 408a H. of a swine: τοῖς ὀδοῦσιν ἀναρρήξειν τὴν κύνα; cp. the alternate version: 408b H. ἀνατεμεῖν 'cut up'//250 III H-H. ἀνατεμεῖ).

❷ to effect an action or intensify it by initially throwing off restraint, ***tear/break/let loose, break out in*** (Hdt. 2, 2, 3 and Aelian, fgm. 41 p. 203, 2 φωνήν; Plut., Pericl. 172 [36, 7] κλαυθμόν; LXX; Philo, Conf. Lingu. 194. Cp. also Ps.-Oppian,

Cyneg. 1, 226 ῥῆξεν ποτὲ δεσμὰ σιωπῆς) ῥῆξον καὶ βόησον *break forth and cry aloud* (Is 54:1) **Gal 4:27;** 2 Cl 2:1.—Pass. *break forth* (PPetr II, 23, 1, 12 [III BC] ὕδωρ ἐρράγη; SibOr 4, 53) of light B 3:4 (Is 58:8).—S. also ῥήσσω.—DELG. M-M.

ῥηθείς s. εἶπον.

ῥῆμα, ατος, τό (Pind.; Pla., Leg. 840c [w. μῦθος], prob. of edifying maxims; Hdt.+)

❶ **that which is said,** ***word, saying, expression, or statement of any kind*** τὰ ῥήματα *the words* (opp. τὰ ἔργα) 2 Cl 13:3; Hs 9, 21, 2; cp. **Ac 16:38.** πᾶν ῥῆμα *every word* B 11:8. πᾶν ῥῆμα ἀργόν **Mt 12:36.** πᾶν ῥ. πονηρόν Hs 5, 3, 6; οὐδὲ ἓν ῥ. *not even one word* **Mt 27:14;** cp. ῥῆμα ἕν **Ac 28:25.—Lk 2:17, 50; 20:26;** 1 Cl 27:7 (Ps 18:3). φωνὴ ῥημάτων *the sound of words, a voice whose words* **Hb 12:19;** αἰσχρὸν ῥ. Hv 1, 1, 7. ὡσεὶ λῆρος τὰ ῥ. **Lk 24:11.** ἄρρητα ῥήματα (s. ἄρρητος 2) **2 Cor 12:4.** ῥ. ἔκφρικτα Hv 1, 3, 3b. ῥ. ἀληθῆ m 11:3; δεινὰ ῥ. MPol 8:3. ῥ. βλάσφημα **Ac 6:11.** ῥῆμα, ῥήματα ἀκούειν B 16:10; Hv 1, 1, 6; 4, 1, 7; 4, 2, 6 al. τὰ προειρημένα ῥ. (s. προεῖπον 1) **2 Pt 3:2;** s. **Jd 17;** Hm 9:4. πολὺν ἐν ῥήμασιν γενέσθαι *be profuse in speech, be too talkative* 1 Cl 30:5 (Job 11:3).—τὸ ῥ., τὰ ῥ. oft. takes a special significance fr. the context: *prophecy, prediction* **Mt 26:75; Mk 9:32; 14:72; Lk 1:38; 2:29; 9:45ab; 18:34; 22:61** (v.l. λόγος); **24:8; Ac 11:16;** MPol 16:2. *Declaration of scripture* 2 Cl 15:4 (cp. Mel., P. 11, 73 τὰ ῥ. τῆς γραφῆς).—*Command(ment), order, direction* **Lk 5:5;** esp. of God (Dt 1:26) **3:2; Hb 11:3;** 1 Cl 10:1; ῥ. τῆς δυνάμεως αὐτοῦ **Hb 1:3.** τὸ ἰσχυρὸν ῥ. *the mighty creative word* Hv 1, 3, 4; cp. 3, 3, 5. διὰ ῥήματος Χριστοῦ **Ro 10:17.**—*Threat* λαλεῖν ῥήματα κατά τινος *make threats against someth.* **Ac 6:13.**—τὰ ῥ. *speech, sermon, proclamation* πάντα τὰ ῥ. αὐτοῦ *everything he had to say* **Lk 7:1.** ἐνωτίσασθε τὰ ῥήματά μου *pay attention to what I am proclaiming* **Ac 2:14.—10:44; J 8:20.** τὰ ῥήματα αὐτῶν *their preaching* **Ro 10:18** (Ps 18:5).—Of pronouncements of (Christian) teaching or of divine understanding πῶς τοῖς ἐμοῖς ῥήμασιν πιστεύσετε; **J 5:47.** Cp. **6:63; 10:21; 12:47f; 14:10; 15:7; 17:8; Ac 10:22.** ῥήματα ζωῆς αἰωνίου **J 6:68.** τὰ ῥήματα τῆς ζωῆς ταύτης **Ac 5:20.** ῥήματα ἐν οἷς σωθήσῃ **11:14.** ῥήματα ἀληθείας κ. σωφροσύνης **26:25.** τὰ ῥ. τοῦ θεοῦ (Sextus 4, 39 ῥήματα θεοῦ; Marinus, Vi. Procli 32 θεῖα ῥ.) **J 3:34; 8:47.** ἐπὶ παντὶ ῥήματι ἐκπορευομένῳ διὰ στόματος θεοῦ (Dt 8:3) **Mt 4:4.** τὰ ῥήματα τοῦ κυρίου τὰ λεγόμενα διὰ παραβολῶν *the Lord's teachings which were expressed in the form of parables* Hs 5, 4, 3. διάσταλμα ῥήματος *the special meaning of the teaching* B 10:11. Gener. the sing. brings together all the divine teachings as a unified whole, w. some such mng. as *gospel,* or *confession:* ἐγγύς σου τὸ ῥῆμά ἐστιν **Ro 10:8a** (Dt 30:14); cp. vs. **9 v.l.** MSuggs, 'The Word Is Near You' Ro 10:6–10, JKnox Festschr. '67, 289–312. Cp. **Eph 5:26.** ἐπότισεν ῥήματι *he* (Paul) *gave* (Artemilla) *a drink of words to ponder* AcPl Ha 4, 5. τὸ ῥῆμα τὸ εὐαγγελισθὲν εἰς ὑμᾶς **1 Pt 1:25b.** W. objective gen. τὸ ῥῆμα τῆς πίστεως **Ro 10:8b.** W. subjective gen. ῥῆμα θεοῦ **Eph 6:17; Hb 6:5.** τὸ ῥ. κυρίου **1 Pt 1:25a** (cp. Is 40:8).—GKittel, D. Wort Gottes im NT: Pastoralblätter für Predigt etc. 80, '37/38, 345–55.

❷ after the Hebrew **an event that can be spoken about,** ***thing, object, matter, event*** οὐκ ἀδυνατήσει παρὰ τοῦ θεοῦ πᾶν ῥῆμα *nothing will be impossible with God* **Lk 1:37** (Gen 18:14). ἐπὶ στόματος δύο μαρτύρων σταθῇ πᾶν ῥῆμα **Mt 18:16; 2 Cor 13:1** (both Dt 19:15; cp. TestAbr A 13 p. 92, 24 [Stone p. 32]). Cp. the sing. (TestAbr A 15 p. 96, 15 [Stone p. 40]; JosAs 17:1 [CBurchard, A Note on ῥῆμα in JosAs 17:1f; Lk 2:15, 17; Ac 10:3: NovT 27, '85, 281–95]) **Lk 2:15** (cp. 1 Km 4:16); **Ac 10:37.** Pl. **Lk 1:65; 2:19, 51; Ac 5:32; 13:42.**—ERepo, Der Begriff Rhema im Biblisch-griechischen (Academia Scientia Fennica) I '52 (LXX); II '54 (NT and early Christian lit.), but s. critique by GZuntz, L'Antiquité Classique 22, '53, 106–12.—B. 1262. DELG s.v. εἴρω (2). M-M. EDNT. TW.

Ῥησά, ὁ indecl. *Rhesa,* in the genealogy of Jesus **Lk 3:27** (GKuhn, ZNW 22, 1923, 212).

ῥῆσις, εως, ἡ (ἐρῶ; Hom. et al.; pap [e.g. Kl.T. 135 p. 47, 8]; LXX, TestSol 1:12 D; SibOr 5, 258; Philo, Just.) ***word, expression*** ἐμῆς πνοῆς ῥῆσις (πνοή 2) 1 Cl 57:3 (Pr 1:23).—DELG s.v. εἴρω (2).

ῥήσσω—❶ by-form of ῥήγνυμι, q.v.

❷ epic ῥήσσω (s. προσρήσσω and the lit. there)=Att. ῥάττω **to cause to fall down,** ***throw down*** (Artem. 1, 60; Wsd 4:19) τινά *someone*

ⓐ lit., of an evil spirit's treatment of its victim, who is cast to the ground in convulsions **Mk 9:18; Lk 9:42** (cp. Eur., Ba. 633 δώματ᾿ ἔρρηξεν χαμᾶζε)

ⓑ fig., of the devil, who tries *to cause* the righteous man *to fall* Hm 11:3.—DELG s.v. ῥήγνυμι.

ῥήτωρ, ορος, ὁ orig. 'public speaker, orator' (since Soph.; Thu. 8, 1, 1 et al.; ins, pap; Philo, Vi. Cont. 31; Jos., Ant. 17, 226; 19, 208), then specif. **a speaker in court,** ***advocate, attorney*** (Dio Chrys. 59 [76], 4; POxy 37 I, 4 [49 AD]; 237 VII, 25; BGU 969 I, 8; 15 al. in pap; Preisigke, Fachw. 1915) **Ac 24:1,** here as prosecuting attorney; on the form of Tertullus's speech s. BWinter, JTS 42, '91, 505–31.—DELG s.v. εἴρω (2). M-M.

ῥητῶς (adv. of ῥητός 'expressly stated') **pert. to what is stated or has been stated as being precisely so,** ***expressly, explicitly*** (Aristot. 1017b, 1; 3; Stoic. III 219, 45; Polyb. 3, 23, 5; Plut., Brut. 997 [29, 4]; Diog. L. 8, 71; OGI 515, 39; SIG 685, 77 and 83; UPZ 110, 62 [164 BC]; POxy 237 VII, 7; Philo, Leg. All. 1, 60 al.; Jos., Ant. 1, 24, C. Ap. 1, 83; Just.) τὸ πνεῦμα ῥητῶς λέγει **1 Ti 4:1.**—DELG s.v. εἴρω (2). M-M.

ῥίζα, ης, ἡ (on the formation s. Schwyzer I 352, cp. Lat. radix; Hom.+; ins, pap, LXX; OdeSol 11:16b; TestJud 24:5; Philo; Jos., Ant. 3, 174 al.; Tat. 12, 3f).

❶ **the underground part of a plant,** ***root***—ⓐ lit. **Mt 3:10; Lk 3:9;** Hs 9, 1, 6; 9, 21, 1. ἐκ ῥιζῶν *to its roots, root and branch* (Heraclid. Pont., fgm. 50 W.; Plut., Pomp. 629 [21, 3]; Polyaenus 2, 1, 10; Job 31:12; Aesop, Fab. 70 P.=101 Ch.//71 H-H.) **Mk 11:20.** ῥίζαν ἔχειν *have (deep) root(s)* **Mt 13:6; Mk 4:6** (Theophr., HP 6, 6, 7 πολλὴν ἔχουσα ῥίζαν; Reader, Polemo p. 372).

ⓑ in imagery and transferred sense (LXX; oft. Philo; SibOr 3, 396): in the parable οὐκ ἔχειν ῥίζαν (ἐν ἑαυτῷ) *have no firm root* and hence be easily inclined to fall away **Mt 13:21; Mk 4:17; Lk 8:13.**—In Paul's figure of the olive tree, its root and branches **Ro 11:16–18.** On ῥίζας βάλλειν 1 Cl 39:8 (Job 5:3) s. βάλλω 3c.—Of the beginnings fr. which someth. grows (Socrat., Ep. 14, 2; Herm. Wr. 4, 10): a family or nation (Ael. Aristid. 30, 16 K.=10 p. 120 D.; OGI 383, 30f [I BC] ἐμοῦ γένους ῥίζα) ἐκκόπτειν ἐκ ῥιζῶν *root out, destroy root and branch* B 12:9 (cp. ἐκ ῥιζῶν ἐξαιρεῖν Jos, Ant. 9, 181). ῥίζα πικρίας **Hb 12:15** (πικρία 1). ῥ. πάντων τῶν κακῶν **1 Ti 6:10** (cp. SibOr 3, 234; Constantin. Manasses 2, 9 H.: φθόνος ἡ ῥίζα τῶν κακῶν; Himerius, Ecl. 32, 5 W.: παιδεία ῥίζα τῶν ἀγαθῶν; Straub 31). τῆς πίστεως ῥ. Pol 1:2 (cp. Epicurus in Athen. 12, 67 p. 546f [HUsener, Epicurea 1887 p. 278, 10] ἀρχὴ καὶ ῥίζα παντὸς ἀγαθοῦ; Plut.,

Mor., 4b πηγὴ καὶ ῥίζα καλοκἀγαθίας; Sir 1:6, 20 ῥ. σοφίας; Wsd 15:3 ῥ. ἀθανασίας).

❷ **that which grows from a root,** ***shoot, scion,*** in our lit. in imagery ***descendant*** (Diod. S. 26, 16a μηδὲ ῥίζαν ἀπολιπεῖν συγγενείας=not a single scion of the family should survive; Ps.-Apollod. 2, 1, 4, 2 Ἀγήνωρ τῆς μεγάλης ῥίζης ἐγένετο γενεάρχης=the progenitor of the strong offshoot; Sir 40:15; 1 Macc 1:10) of the Messiah ἡ ῥίζα τοῦ Ἰεσσαί *the Scion from Jesse* **Ro 15:12** (Is 11:10); ἡ ῥίζα Δαυίδ (cp. Sir 47:22) **Rv 5:5;** cp. **22:16.** ὡς ῥίζα ἐν γῇ διψώσῃ 1 Cl 16:3 (Is 53:2).

❸ Hs 9, 30, 1f speaks of the ῥίζαι τοῦ ὄρους (of a mountain, hill, etc. as its foot: Aeschyl., Prom. 365 [pl.]; Polyb. 2, 66, 10; Diod. S. 20, 41, 3; Plut., Sulla 461 [16, 1]; Jos., Bell. 5, 239).—B. 523. DELG. M-M. TW.

ῥιζόω (ῥίζα; Hom. et al.; LXX; PsSol 14:4; Philo; Jos., Bell. 4, 471) aor. ἐρρίζωσα Sir 24:12; pf. 3 sg. ἐρρίζωκεν Sir 3:28. Pass.: aor. 3 pl. ἐρριζώθησαν Jer 12:2; pf. ptc. ἐρριζωμένος (w. double ρ; s. Schwyzer I 731f) 'cause to take root', mostly fig., 'put on a firm foundation, fix firmly' (Hom. et al.) pass. ***be/become firmly rooted/fixed*** (Pla., Ep. 7, 336b ἐξ ἀμαθίας πάντα κακὰ ἐρρίζωται; Sext. Emp., Math. 1, 271; Kaibel 1078, 7 of a bridge αἰώνιος ἐρρίζωται) ἐρριζωμένοι: ἐν ἀγάπῃ **Eph 3:17,** ἐν αὐτῷ (the Lord) **Col 2:7** (Nicander, Ther. 183 ῥιζοῦσθαι ἐν=be firmly rooted in; Philosoph. Max. 499, 38 ῥιζωθέντες ἐκ θεοῦ).—DELG s.v. ῥίζα. M-M. TW.

ῥιπή, ῆς, ἡ (ῥίπτω; Hom. et al.; TestAbr A 4 p. 80, 34 [Stone p. 8]; Philo, Somn. 2, 125, Aet. M. 20; SibOr 5, 464) prim.: 'a throwing, the swing or force by which someth. is thrust forward'. The focus on sudden speed readily becomes the major semantic component in ref. to a variety of objects: ***rapid movement,*** e.g. of the eyes; the 'casting' of a glance takes an extremely short time: ἐν ῥιπῇ ὀφθαλμοῦ *in the twinkling of an eye* **1 Cor 15:52** (Billerb. II, 156; TestAbr A 4; s. DDaube, The Sudden in the Scriptures '64, 76–79).—DELG s.v. ῥίπτω.

ῥιπίζω aor. 3 sg. ἐρρίπισεν Da 2:35 (Aristoph. et al.) ***blow here and there, toss,*** of the wind (Da 2:35; EpArist 70), that sets a wave in motion on the water, pass. (Philo, Aet. M. 125 πρὸς ἀνέμων ῥιπίζεται τὸ ὕδωρ; a quot. in Dio Chrys. 15 [32], 23 δῆμος ἄστατον κακὸν καὶ θαλάσσῃ πανθ' ὅμοιον ὑπ' ἀνέμου ῥιπίζεται; Cass. Dio 70, 4 ῥιπιζομένη ἄχνη. See also Epict., fgm. F 2 p. 487 Sch.) ὁ διακρινόμενος ἔοικεν κλύδωνι θαλάσσης ἀνεμιζομένῳ καὶ ῥιπιζομένῳ **Js 1:6.**—DELG s.v. ῥίπτω. M-M.

ῥίπτω, ῥιπτέω the latter Demosth. 19, 231; Dio Chrys. 3, 15; Da 9:18 Theod.; **Ac 22:23;** Hv 3, 5, 5; Just., A I, 18, 4 (the word is found Hom.+; ins, pap, LXX; pseudepigr.; Joseph. [ῥίπτω Bell. 1, 150, Ant. 16, 248—ῥιπτέω Ant. 2, 206; 14, 70]; Just., s. above; Ath. 26, 3) impf. ἐ(ρ)ρίπτουν; fut. 3 sg. ῥίψει LXX; 1 aor. ἔ(ρ)ριψα, impv. ῥῖψον; ptc. n. ῥῖψαν (ῥίψαν). Pass.: fut. ῥιφήσομαι LXX; aor. 3 sg., pl. ἐρρίφη, -σαν LXX, ptc. ῥιφείς LXX; inf. ῥιφῆναι LXX; pf. 3 sg. ἔρριπται; ptc. ἐ(ρ)ριμμένος; plpf. 3 sg. ἔρριπτο 2 Macc 3:29 (on the doubling of the ρ s. W-S. §5, 26b; B-D-F §11, 1; Mlt-H. 101f. Itacistic ptc. ἐρρημένος Tob 1:17 cod. V; TestJob 30:5 [s. 2 below]; ἐρημένοι **Mt 9:36** cod. L).

❶ **to propel someth. with a forceful motion,** ***throw,*** in a manner suited to each special situation: *throw away* (OdeSol 11:10; JosAs 12:9; Achilles Tat. 2, 11, 5) Μωϋσῆς ἔ(ρ)ριψεν ἐκ τῶν χειρῶν τὰς πλάκας B 14:3 (Ex 32:19; Dt 9:17); cp. 4:8. ῥ. τι μακρὰν ἀπό τινος *throw someth. far away from someth.* Hv 3, 2, 7; s 9, 7, 2; without μακράν v 3, 5, 5. Pass. w. μακράν 3, 2, 9; 3, 6, 1; 3, 7, 1.—*Throw* into the sea, fr. a ship (Chariton 3, 5, 5; TestJob 8:7; Achilles Tat. 3, 2, 9) **Ac 27:19, 29;** fr. dry land, pass. εἰς τὴν θάλασσαν **Lk 17:2** (ῥ. εἰς as Polyaenus 8, 48; schol. on Nicander, Ther. 825 [ῥ. εἰς τὴν θαλ.]; Gen 37:20; Ex 1:22; TestZeb 2:7).—ῥίψας τὰ ἀργύρια εἰς τὸν ναόν **Mt 27:5** (Diod. S. 27, 4, 8 the temple-robbers, suffering an attack of conscience ἐρρίπτουν τὰ χρήματα; Appian, Bell. Civ. 2, 23 §86 Πτολεμαίου τὰ χρήματα ῥίψαντος εἰς τὴν θάλασσαν; Ps.-Anacharsis, Ep. 6 ῥίψας τὸ ἀργύριον).—*Take off* clothing (Aristoph., Eccl. 529; Pla., Rep. 5, 474a τὰ ἱμάτια) as a statement of protest **Ac 22:23** (s. Field, Notes 136).—*Throw down* to the floor τινά *someone* **Lk 4:35.**—*Expose* newborn infants (Apollod. [II BC]: 244 fgm. 110a Jac.; POxy 744 [I BC]; Diod. S. 2, 58, 5; Epict. 1, 23, 10; Aelian, VH 2, 7; Ps.-Phoc. 185 [Horst p. 233, lit.]; cp. Wsd 11:14; SibOr 2, 282; other reff. EBlakeney, The Epistle to Diognetus '43, 50f; Christians forbid it Just., A I, 27, 1.—The Family in Ancient Rome, ed. BRawson '86, 172, 246 [lit.]) Dg 5:6 (AvanAarde, SPSBL '92, 441–42).

❷ w. no connotation of violence, but context may indicate some degree of rapidity, ***put/lay someth. down*** (Demosth. 19, 231; Crinagoras 2, 1; Gen 21:15; 2 Macc 3:15) Ἰωσὴφ . . . ῥίψας τὸ σκέπαρνον *Joseph threw down his axe* GJs 9:1. Ἐλισάβεδ ἔρριψεν τὸ κόκκινον 12:2. ἔ(ρ)ριψαν αὐτούς (the sick people) παρὰ τοὺς πόδας αὐτοῦ **Mt 15:30.** Ἰωσὴφ . . . ἔρριψεν αὐτὸν χαμαὶ ἐπὶ τὸν σάκκον *Joseph threw himself down on sackcloth* GJs 13:1 (TestAbr A 11 p. 89, 13 [Stone p. 26]). Pass. pf. ptc. *thrown down, prostrate, scattered,* of position on an extended flat surface such as 'ground, floor' (X., Mem. 3, 1, 7; Polyb. 5, 48, 2; Plut., Galba 1066 [28, 1]; Epict. 3, 26, 6 χαμαὶ ἐρριμμένοι; Chariton 2, 7, 4 ἐρρ. ὑπὸ λύπης; 3 Km 13:24; Jer 14:16; 1 Macc 11:4; TestJob 30:5; Jos., Ant. 3, 7; 6, 362) the vine, without the support of the elm tree, is ἐ(ρ)ριμμένη χαμαί Hs 2:3; cp. 4. Of the crowds of people ἦσαν ἐσκυλμένοι καὶ ἐ(ρ)ριμμένοι ὡσεὶ πρόβατα μὴ ἔχοντα ποιμένα *they were distressed and dejected, like sheep without a shepherd* **Mt 9:36** (of animals lying on the ground Heraclit. Sto. 14 p. 22, 20 τὰ ἐπὶ γῆς ἐρριμμένα ζῷα; Eutecnius 4 p. 42, 25).—B. 673. DELG. M-M. TW. Spicq.

ῥίς, ῥινός, ἡ (Hom. et al.; pap fr. III BC; LXX [only pl. ῥῖνες]; ApcEsdr 6:7f [pl.]; Philo [pl.]) ***nose;*** pl. ***nostrils,*** i.e. *nose* (so Hom. et al.) ἐὰν μὴ τὰς ῥ. ταῖς χερσὶν ἐπιφράξῃ *without covering one's nose with one's hands* Pa (3:3).—DELG.

ῥιψοκινδύνως (ῥίπτω, κίνδυνος; Appian, Bell. Civ. 1, 103 §482; POxy 2131, 16 [III AD]) adv. of ῥιψοκίνδυνος (the adj. as early as X., Mem. 1, 3, 10; Vett. Val. 17, 27; BGU 909, 15; PFlor 36, 2; PSI 686, 5; Philo, Agr. 167; Jos., Bell. 7, 77) **in a foolhardy manner,** ***rashly, recklessly*** 1 Cl 14:2 (cp. the adj. New Docs 3, no. 101, 12 [343 AD]).

Ῥοβοάμ, ὁ indecl. (רְחַבְעָם; 3 Km 12; 1 Ch 3:10; TestSol 26:7 H.—Joseph. has Ῥοβόαμος, ου [Ant. 8, 212]) ***Rehoboam,*** son and successor of Solomon; in the genealogy of Jesus **Mt 1:7ab; Lk 3:23ff** D.—BHHW III 157.

Ῥόδη, ης, ἡ (in myths and comedy [Menand., fgm. 210, 6; 592, 5 Kö.; Philemon Com., fgm. 84]; Longus 4, 36, 3; 4, 37, 2; Sb 392 [III BC]; ins) **Rhoda**

❶ a slave in the house of Mary the mother of John Mark **Ac 12:13** (Dalman, Arbeit I 365; New Docs 2, 88 poses possibility of assignment as doorkeeper [?]).

❷ Hermas' owner Hv 1, 1, 1.—M-M.

ῥόδον, ου, τό (Hom. Hymns et al.; Lucian, Nigrin. 32; ins: BCH 10, 461, 101 [364 BC]; Sb 7541, 10 [II AD]; PIand 66, 7; Sb

1080; a Jewish-Gk. ins fr. Tell el Yehudieh: ZNW 22, 1923, 282 no. 19, 7; LXX; TestSim 6:2; JosAs cod. A 16:8; 18:7 [p. 64, 7; 68, 10 Bat.]) *rose* ἐρυθρότερος παντὸς ῥ. ApcPt 3:8 (cp. En 106:2; 10).—B. 527. DELG.

Ῥόδος, ου, ἡ (Hom. et al.; ins; 1 Macc 15:23; Philo, Aet. M. 120; Joseph.; SibOr 3, 444) ***Rhodes,*** an island off the southwest point of Asia Minor; its main city bears the same name. **Ac 21:1.**—Pauly-W., Suppl. V, 731–840; Kl. Pauly, 1421–23; BHHW III 1596. PECS 755–58.

ῥοιζηδόν (on the formation s. Schwyzer I 626) adv. (in ref. to 'whirring sound made by an obj. going swiftly through the air': Lycophron 66; Nicander, Theriaca 556; Polyaenus, Exc. 18, 5; Geopon. 15, 2, 34) **pert. to noise made by someth. passing with great force and rapidity,** ***with a rushing noise*** οἱ οὐρανοὶ ῥοιζηδὸν παρελεύσονται ***the heavens will pass away with a roar*** **2 Pt 3:10.**—DELG s.v. ῥοῖζος. M-M.

ῥοῖζος, ου, ὁ and **ἡ** (orig. 'noise made by someth. passing swiftly through the air', e.g. an arrow; Hom. et al.; IAndrosIsis 150 [I BC]; PGM 2, 96; LXX; Philo, Aet. M. 128; SibOr 3, 304) **a sound produced by rapid motion,** ***a whoosh*** ἤρχετο τὸ θηρίον ῥοίζῳ *the beast was coming on with a whoosh* (the dat., with various senses for the noun: Cornutus 1 p. 2, 14; Plut., Demetr. 898 [21, 13] of an immense structure designed as a 'taker of a city'; Longus 2, 10, 2 of whistling; 2 Macc 9:7 a swiftly moving chariot; Jos., Bell. 3, 243.—233 and 488 of the irresistible rush of an attack) Hv 4, 1, 8 (if a hissing sound is meant, cp. Apollon. Rhod. 4, 129: the dragon who guards the golden fleece ῥοίζει πελώριον=hisses mightily; the noun follows in 138: ῥοίζῳ=[frightened] by a hissing).—DELG.

Ῥομφά, ὁ, s. Ῥαιφάν.—M-M.

ῥομφαία, ας, ἡ 'a large and broad sword' used by non-Greek-speaking peoples, esp. the Thracians (Phylarch. [III BC]: 81 fgm. 57 Jac.; Plut., Aemil. 264 [18, 5]; Hesychius; Suda). In our lit. simply ***sword*** (so also LXX; pseudepigr.; Jos., Bell. 6, 289, Ant. 6, 254; 7, 299;—In Philo [like ApcMos] always of the angel's flaming sword after Gen 3:24) **Lk 21:24 v.l.; Rv 2:16; 6:8; 19:15, 21.** ῥ. δίστομος καὶ ὀξεῖα *a sharp and double-edged sword* **Rv 2:12;** cp. **1:16.** φείδεσθαι τῆς ψυχῆς τινος ἀπὸ ῥ. *spare someone's life from the sword* (so that he may die on the cross) B 5:13 (Ps 21:21). In imagery for pain or anguish (s. SibOr 5, 260 v.l.) τὴν ψυχὴν διελεύσεται ῥομφαία **Lk 2:35** (ῥ. διελεύσ. cp. SibOr 3, 316; Ezk 14:17.—Artem. 1, 41 p. 39, 19 τιτρώσκεσθαι κατὰ τὸ στῆθος means 'receive sad news').—DELG. M-M. TW.

ῥοπή, ῆς, ἡ (ῥέπω 'to incline'; Aeschyl., Pla.+; Herodas 7, 33; Vett. Val. 301,1; SIG 761, 5 [48/47 BC]; UPZ 110, 73 [164 BC]; PTebt 27, 79; LXX; TestSol 24:2 H; Philo; Jos., Bell. 3, 396; 4, 367; 5, 88 al.; Mel.) **downward movement** (esp. of a scale-pan), ***inclination*** ἐν ῥ. ὀφθαλμοῦ *in the twinkling of an eye* **1 Cor 15:52 v.l.** (ῥοπή, though without ὀφθαλμοῦ, = 'moment': Diod. S. 13, 23, 2; 13, 24, 6 [ῥ. καιροῦ 'decisive moment']; 20, 34, 2; Plut., Ages. 614 [33, 3]; Wsd 18:12 πρὸς μίαν ῥοπήν; 3 Macc 5:49 ὑστάτη βίου ῥοπῇ; EpArist 90; Mel., P. 21, 145 ἐν μιᾷ ῥοπῇ; 26, 185 and 29, 200 ὑπὸ μίαν ῥοπήν).—DELG s.v. ῥέπω. M-M.

Ῥουβήν, ὁ indecl. (רְאוּבֵן; LXX, Philo. Ῥουβήμ Test12Patr [in part]; JosAs 27:6. Ῥουβίμ Test12Patr [in part] and Just., D. 120, 1. Ῥουβίν Demetr.: 722 fgm. 1, 3 al.; Joseph. has Ῥουβῆλος, ου [Ant. 1, 307]) ***Reuben,*** oldest son of Jacob and Leah (Gen 29:32) **Rv 7:5.** Ῥουβήλ (v.l. Ῥουβίμ) GJs 1:2; 6:3.—BHHW III 1624.

Ῥούθ, ἡ indecl. (רוּת; LXX; Mel., HE 4, 20, 14—Joseph. has Ῥούθη) ***Ruth,*** a Moabite, w. leading role in the OT book of the same name. In the genealogy of Jesus as wife of Boaz **Mt 1:5.**—S. θαμάρ. BHHW III 1624. TW.

Ῥοῦφος, ου, ὁ a Latin name found freq. even in its Greek spelling (Diod. S. 11, 60, 1; 14, 107, 1; Ael. Aristid. 48, 15 K.=24 p. 469 D.; Joseph., index; ins, pap) ***Rufus.***

❶ son of Simon of Cyrene and brother of Alexander **Mk 15:21.**

❷ recipient of a greeting **Ro 16:13.**

❸ a steadfast confessor w. Ignatius and Zosimus Pol 9:1 (cp. Eus., HE 3, 36, 13 and s. Lghtf. ad loc.).—BHHW III 1624. M-M. TW.

ῥύμη, ης, ἡ (Thu., Aristoph. et al., in the sense 'swing, rush'; Philo; Jos., Ant. 7, 239) in later Gk. ***narrow street, lane, alley*** (Polyb. 6, 29, 1 al.; oft. in pap since PPetr II, 17, 2, 19 [III BC]; also LXX; SibOr 3, 364) **Ac 12:10.** W. συναγωγαί **Mt 6:2.** W. πλατεῖαι (Is 15:3; Tob 13:18 [17] BA) **Lk 14:21.** Provided w. a name (s. the Alexandrian pap in APF 5, 1913, 37, 1, fr. Augustan times Εὐδαίμων ἐν τῇ Εὐδαίμονος λεγομένῃ ῥύμῃ) **Ac 9:11.**—B. 720.—Frisk. M-M.

ῥύομαι mid. dep. (Hom.+—Anz 275f; FChase, The Lord's Prayer in the Early Church: Texts and Studies I/3, 1891, 71ff) fut. ῥύσομαι; 1 aor. ἐ(ρ)ρυσάμην, impv. ῥῦσαι **Mt 6:13;** pf. 3 sg. ἔρυσται [=εἴρυσται] AcPlCor 1:8. Pass.: fut. ῥυσθήσομαι LXX; 1 aor. ἐ(ρ)ρύσθην (on the spelling w. one ρ or two s. B-D-F §11, 1; 101 p. 48; Mlt-H. 101f; 193) **to rescue from danger,** ***save, rescue, deliver, preserve*** τινά *someone* (Hippol., Ref. 8, 10, 3; Theoph. Ant. 3, 9 [p. 224, 15]) **Mt 27:43;** 1 Cl 16:16 (both Ps 21:9); **2 Pt 2:7;** 1 Cl 8:4 (Is 1:17); 22:8 (Ps 33:20) v.l.; 55:6; 2 Cl 6:8 (Ezk 14:18). τινὰ ἀπό τινος *rescue, save, deliver,* or *preserve someone fr. someone* or *someth.* (B-D-F §180; s. also Rob. 517f.—Pr 2:12; Is 25:4; Ezk 37:23; 1 Macc 12:15; PsSol 4:23 al.; TestReub 4:10; JosAs 12:7; ApcSed 16:7; SibOr 2, 344; ἀπὸ τῆς πλάνης Orig., C. Cels. 5, 33, 39; Did., Gen. 154, 20) **Mt 6:13; Lk 11:4 v.l.** (on the subject matter s. Hierocles 25 [ln. 61], 474 Ζεῦ πάτερ, ἦ πολλῶν κε κακῶν λύσειας ἅπαντας); **2 Ti 4:18;** 1 Cl 60:3b; D 8:2; 10:5. Pass. **Ac 5:15 v.l.; Ro 15:31; 2 Th 3:2;** 1 Cl 60:3a. Also τινὰ ἔκ τινος (Anacreon 111 Diehl; Hdt. 5, 49; Diod. S. 12, 53, 1; hymn to Isis: SEG VIII, 548, 27 [I BC]; PBad 48, 3 [126 BC] ἐκ πολεμίων; LXX; TestSim 2:8; Jos., Ant. 12, 407; Just., D. 111, 3; Mel., P. 68, 489.—Aristoxenus, fgm. 113 ῥύεσθαι καὶ ἐρύεσθαι διαφορὰν ἔχει πρὸς ἄλληλα. τὸ μὲν γὰρ ῥύεσθαι ἐκ θανάτου ἕλκειν, τὸ δὲ ἐρύεσθαι φυλάττειν='ῥύεσθαι and ἐρύεσθαι are different: ῥ. means rescuing fr. death, but ἐ. to ward off [death]') **2 Ti 3:11;** from death (SibOr 2, 81; Just., D. 111, 3) **2 Cor 1:10a;** 1 Cl 56:9 (Job 5:20); 2 Cl 16:4 (w. acc. to be supplied); fr. the power of darkness **Col 1:13** (cp. JosAs 15:13 ἐκ τοῦ σκότους); fr. wrath to come **1 Th 1:10;** fr. blood-guilt 1 Cl 18:14 (Ps 50:16); fr. all afflictions 22:7 (Ps 33:18); fr. eternal punishment 2 Cl 6:7; fr. temptation **2 Pt 2:9.** τίς με ῥύσεται ἐκ τοῦ σώματος τοῦ θανάτου τούτου; *who will set me free from this body of death?* **Ro 7:24.** ἐκ δεσμῶν ἐρύσατο τὸν κόσμον ὅλον (God, who) *rescued the entire world from its chains* AcPl Ha 3, 7. ἐκ χειρὸς ἀνόμου ὁ θεὸς ἐρύσατο τὸν Ἰσραήλ 8, 10. εἴρυσταί σε κύριος ἐκ χειρὸς ἀνόμου *the Lord rescues you from a lawless hand* AcPlCor 1:8 (on the form Schwyzer I 681 n. 1: 'praesentisches Perfekt'). Pass. ῥυσθῆναι ἐκ χειρός τινος *be rescued from someone's power* **Lk 1:74** (cp. Jos., Vi. 83, Ant. 7, 151; JosAs 28:3 ῥῦσαι ἡμᾶς ἐκ τῶν χειρῶν τῶν ἀδελφῶν). ἐκ στόματος λέοντος *be saved from the jaws of the lion* **2 Ti 4:17.** ῥ. τινά τινι *save someone by someth.* (Diod. S. 13, 64, 6 ἐρρύσατο χρήμασι τὴν ἰδίαν ψυχήν=his life by means of money) 2 Cl 6:9. Also ῥ. τινα διά τινος 1 Cl 55:1. Abs. **Mt 27:43** (for a 'divine' rescue of a θεοσεβής fr. extreme danger s. Hdt. 1, 86, 2, Croesus on the pyre: Κῦρος βουλόμενος εἰδέναι εἴ τίς μιν δαιμόνων ῥύσεται τοῦ μὴ ζῶντα κατακαυθῆναι=Cyrus wishing to know whether some divinity would rescue (Croesus) from being burned alive. S. also Ps 21:9); **2 Cor 1:10b;** AcPl Ha 2, 30. ῥυσθείητε ἀπὸ τούτων ἁπάντων *may you be delivered from all these* (*men* or *sins*) D 5:2.—Subst. ὁ ῥυόμενος *the deliverer* **Ro 11:26** (Is 59:20); 1 Cl 35:11 (Ps 49:22).—DELG s.v. ἔρυμαι. M-M. EDNT. TW.

ῥυπαίνω (ῥύπος) 1 aor. pass. ἐ(ρ)ρυπάνθην (since Pherecrates Com. [V BC] 228; X.) fr. the mng. 'to make dirty, befoul, soil' in ref. to someth. external and fig. (Aristot. et al.; Dionys. Hal. 11, 5 of reputation; Vett. Val. 116, 8; Herm. Wr. 9, 5; Philo, Det. Pot. Ins. 20; Jos., C. Ap. 1, 220) it is a short step to expression of internal defilement ***defile, pollute*** pass. (Sotacus in Apollon. Paradox. 36; Plut., Mor. 85f) ὁ ῥυπαρὸς ῥυπανθήτω ἔτι *let one who is defiled continue to be defiled* or *be defiled more and more* **Rv 22:11** (cp. the judgment on Pharaoh).—DELG s.v. ῥύπος. M-M.

ῥυπαρεύω (hapax leg.) ***befoul, defile*** **Rv 22:11 v.l.**—DELG s.v. ῥύπος.

ῥυπαρία, ας, ἡ (since Critias [V BC] in Pollux 3, 116) prim. 'dirt, filth', fig., in ethical aspect **a state of moral defilement or corruption, *moral uncleanness, vulgarity*** (Pel.-Leg. p. 6, 30 ἀφῆκεν ἐν τῷ ὕδατι πᾶσαν αὐτῆς τὴν ῥυπαρίαν; Did., Gen. 89, 9 ἡ ῥ. τῆς ἁμαρτίας), esp. *sordid avarice, greediness* (Teles p. 33, 4; 37, 5 H.; Plut., Mor. 60d; Cass. Dio 74, 5, 7; TestSol 10:12 C) w. κακία **Js 1:21.**—DELG s.v. ῥύπος. M-M. Spicq.

ῥυπαρός, ά, όν (ῥύπος; Teleclides Com. [V BC], fgm. 3; Hippocr. et al.; pap, LXX; Just., D. 116, 1)

❶ **pert. to being dirty, *filthy, soiled,*** a *dirty* area Hs 9, 7, 6; *filthy* clothes (Plut., Phoc. 750 [18, 4]; Cass. Dio 65, 20; Artem. 2, 3 p. 88, 23; Aelian, VH 14, 10; PGiss 76, 2f [II AD]; Zech 3:3f; SibOr 5, 188; Jos., Ant. 7, 267 ῥυπαρὰν τὴν ἐσθῆτα) ἐσθής **Js 2:2.** ῥάκη ῥ. *filthy rags* (s. ῥάκος 1) ApcPt 15, 30. In imagery occasioned by the proximity of ῥύπος: ἡμέραι ῥ. *foul days* B 8:6.

❷ **pert. to moral sordidness, *unclean, defiled,*** fig. ext. of 1 (Dionys. Hal. et al. use the word for 'sordidly avaricious'; s. Vett. Val. 104, 5; 117, 10; Test Jud 14:3 διαλογισμοὶ ῥ.) **Rv 22:11;** IEph 16:2 (cp. ἐν … πάσῃ ῥυπαρᾷ πράξει Just., D. 116, 1).—B. 1081.—DELG s.v. ῥύπος. M-M. Spicq.

ῥύπος, ου, ὁ (Hom. et al.; LXX) prim. 'a filthy substance, dirt'

❶ **dirt as refuse differentiated from soil, *dirt*** (Hom. et al.) σαρκὸς ἀπόθεσις ῥύπου *removing of dirt from the body* **1 Pt 3:21** (on the gen. s. W-S. §30, 12f; on the topic cp. FSokolowski, Lois sacrées des cités grecques, Suppl. '62, no. 108, 4–7).

❷ fig. ext. of 1 (M. Ant. 7, 47 ὁ ῥύπος τοῦ χαμαὶ βίου; Is 4:4), in an ethical sense ***uncleanness*** καθαρὸς ἀπὸ ῥύπου 1 Cl 17:4 (Job 14:4; the Job pass. also in Philo, Mut. Nom. 48). W. ἁμαρτίαι B 11:11.

❸ **a dark viscous juice, *juice*** (for ῥ. in the sense of an effluent, e.g. ear-wax, s. Aristot., fgm. 289 p. 226, 1 Rose; Artem. 1, 24; PGM 36, 332) ῥ. ὑσσώπου *dark juice of the hyssop* perh. in the sense 'foul juice of the hyssop' B 8:6 (but JKleist, transl. '48, p. 175 note 97, refers it to the mixture of water and heifer's ashes sprinkled by means of hyssop).—DELG. M-M. Spicq.

ῥυπόω (ῥύπος) 1 aor. impv. 3 sing. ῥυπωσάτω (Od. 6, 59; schol. on Apollon. Rhod. 2, 301–2a; Themist., Or. 7 p. 112, 6; Achmes 63, 8; 118, 2; Pel.-Leg. 9, 9; Pollux 4, 180; Philo, fgm. 9 RHarris) fig. ext. of the prim. sense 'make dirty, soil': ***defile, pollute*** **Rv 22:11** t.r. (Erasmian rdg.; s. ῥυπαίνω, ῥυπαρεύω).—DELG s.v. ῥύπος. M-M.

ῥύσις, εως, ἡ (ῥέω; Hippocr., Pla. et al.; pap; En 26:2; Philo; SibOr 1, 315) ***flowing, flow*** ῥ. αἵματος *flow of blood* (Lev 15:25; medical wr. [Hobart 15]; Diod. S. 5, 31, 3; Aelian, VH 6, 6 p. 79, 17; Vett. Val. 282, 30 αἵματος πολλὴν ῥύσιν), of a hemorrhage fr. which a woman suffered **Mk 5:25; Lk 8:43f** (Acta Pilati 7=A Syn. 95, 91).—M-M.

ῥυτίς, ίδος, ἡ (Aristoph., Pla. et al.; Plut., Mor. 789d; Lucian) ***a wrinkle,*** in imagery, of the church μὴ ἔχουσα σπίλον ἢ ῥυτίδα **Eph 5:27.**—M-M.

Ῥωμαϊκός, ή, όν (Polyb. et al.; Arrian, Peripl. 10, 1 τὰ Ῥωμαϊκὰ γράμματα=the Latin letter; ins, pap, Philo, Joseph.; Just., A I, 26, 2) ***Roman, Latin*** **Lk 23:38 v.l.**—M-M.

Ῥωμαῖος, α, ον pert. to the city of Rome or the Roman Empire, *Roman* subst. ὁ Ῥ. (Polyb.+) *the Roman, the Roman citizen,* pl. *the Romans* as a people or *Roman citizens* (Appian, Bell. Civ. 2, 26 §98 Ῥωμαίων πολῖται and Ῥωμαῖοι alternate) **J 11:48; Ac 2:10; 16:21, 37f; 22:25–27, 29; 23:27** (on Rom. citizenship s. FSchulz, Rom. Registry of Births, JRS 32, '42, 78–91; 33, '43, 55–64 HTajra, The Trial of St Paul '89, 81–89); **25:16; 28:17** (on Ac 16:37f; 22:25 s. μαστίζω). **Phlm subscr.** In the sense *Roman Christians* **Ro ins.** χωρίον Ῥωμαίων IRo ins (s. Hdb. ad loc.). ἡ Ῥωμαίων πόλις *Rome* (Jos., C. Ap. 1, 66, Ant. 19, 7) EpilMosq 4. ἡ Ῥωμαίων ἡγεμωνία the Roman empire AcPl Ha 9, 3 (cp. τὸ Ῥωμαίων κράτος).—RAC II, 779–86; BHHW III 1610f; EDNT.

Ῥωμαϊστί adv. **in the Latin language, *in Latin*** (Diosc. I 115, 5; Epict. 1, 17, 16; Jos., Ant. 14, 191 ἑλληνιστὶ καὶ ῥωμαϊστί) **J 19:20.**—**Subscr.** after **Mk** in minuscule 13 et al. (the Ferrar group. K and SLake, Studies and Documents XI '41, 116) ἐγράφη ῥωμαϊστὶ ἐν Ῥώμῃ.—M-M.

Ῥώμη, ης, ἡ (Aristot., Polyb. et al.; ins, 1 Macc, SibOr, Philo, Joseph., Just.) **the capital city of the Roman Empire, *Rome*** without the art. **Ac 19:21; 23:11; 28:16; Ro 1:7** (where the words ἐν Ῥ. are missing in many mss.; s. Ltzm., Hdb. exc. on Ro 1:7; Zahn, comm., exc. I p. 615; Harnack, ZNW 3, 1902, 83ff; RSteinmetz, ZNW 9, 1908, 177ff), vs. **15** (here, too, the words ἐν Ῥώμῃ are omitted in a few isolated mss.); **2 Ti 1:17;** 1 Cl ins; IEph 1:2; 21:2; IRo 5:1; 10:2; EpilMosq 2; Hv 1, 1, 1. Also **1 Pt 5:13 v.l.** and the **subscr.** of **Gal, Eph, Phil, Col, 2 Th, 2 Ti, Phlm, Hb;** AcPl Ha 7, 8 and 14.—W. the art. (Just., A I, 56, 2 ἐν τῇ βασιλίδι Ῥώμῃ) **Ac 18:2; 28:14, 16 v.l.;** AcPl Ha 6, 16; 7, 8 and 32; 9, 19. S. prec. entry.—Pauly-W. IV 1441–51; Kl. Pauly IV 1441ff; BHHW III 1606–9; EDNT.

ῥώννυμι in the act. (obsolete in NT times) 'to strengthen'; the perf. pass. (in the sense 'be strong', since Eur., Thu.; also LXX.—Tat. 32, 3; Ath. 27, 1 [both ἐρρωμένος]) ἔρρωμαι, inf. ἐρρῶσθαι, impv. ἔρρωσο, ἔρρωσθε (always w. double ρ: B-D-F §11, 1; Mlt-H. 101f). Gr-Rom. letters gener. included at the beginning inquiries about a recipient's health and at the conclusion a wish for the recipient's well-being. The latter formulation was freq. expressed w. the verb ῥ. in the perf. pass. impv. **be in good health,** ***farewell, goodbye*** (Hippocr., X., Pla.+; ins [SIG 4 p. 549b index]; pap [very oft.; s. FExler, The Form of the Ancient Gk. Letter 1923, 74ff; HLietzmann, Kl. Texte 14,[2] 1910, nos. 3; 4; 6; 7; 8 al.] 2 Macc 11:21, 33; 3 Macc 7:9; TestSol 22:5 B; EpArist 40; 46; Jos., Vi. 227; 365) **Ac 15:29; 23:30 v.l.;** IEph 21:2; IMg 15; ITr 13:2; IRo 10:3; IPhld 11:2; ISm 13:1f; IPol 8:3b (in Ign. the greeting is combined w. various additions fr. Christian usage). ἔρρωσο ἐν κυρίῳ AcPlCor 1:16. Periphrastically ἐρρῶσθαι ὑμᾶς εὔχομαι (oft. pap) IPol 8:3a; MPol 22:1.—DELG. M-M.

Σ

σαβαχθάνι (also σαβαχθανεί; Aram. שְׁבַקְתַּנִי instead of the Hebr. עֲזַבְתָּנִי Ps 22:2; fr. שׁבק) ***you have forsaken me*** **Mt 27:46; Mk 15:34.**—EKautzsch, Gramm. des Bibl.-Aram. 1884, 11; Dalman, Gramm.[2] 147 note 4; 156; 221, Jesus 1922, 185f [Engl. tr. 204f]; DSidersky, RHR 103, '31, 151–54. On the accent s. Wlh. on Mk 15:34.

Σαβαώθ indecl. ***Sabaoth*** (LXX; TestSol; SibOr; Just., D. 64, 2; PGM 4, 1235; 15, 14; 18a, 1; 35, 20; IDefixWünsch 2; 3, 27; 4, 15) Greek transcription of צְבָאוֹת, pl. of צָבָא=*army,* in a name applied to God κύριος Σ.=יהוה צְבָאוֹת ***Yahweh Lord of the Armies, Lord of Hosts*** (on the mng. EKautzsch, RE XXI 1908, 620–27 [lit.]; here 626f a short treatment of the usage in the LXX. Also XXIV 1913, 661f. More detailed information in Thackeray 9; PKatz, Philo's Bible, 146–49; BWambacq, L'épithète divine Jahwe Sebbâôt, '47; BHHW III 2205; ZTalshir, JQR 78, '87, 57–75 [LXX]) **Ro 9:29** (Is 1:9); 1 Cl 34:6 (Is 6:3); **Js 5:4.**—M-M.

σαββατίζω fut. σαββατιῶ LXX; 1 aor. ἐσαββάτισα; pf. 3 sg. σεσαββάτικε (Just., D. 12, 3) (LXX, Just.; Byz. chron. in Psaltes p. 329) ***keep the Sabbath*** ἐὰν μὴ σαββατίσητε τὸ σάββατον, οὐκ ὄψεσθε τὸν πατέρα Ox 1, 8–10 (s. GTh 27; LWright, JBL 65, '46, 180). On the other hand, Judeans who become Christians give up the celebration of the Sabbath in favor of the Lord's Day, Sunday IMg 9:1.

σαββατισμός, οῦ, ὁ (σαββατίζω; Plut., Mor. 166a cj.; Just., D. 23, 3) ***sabbath rest, sabbath observance*** fig. **Hb 4:9** a special period of rest for God's people modeled after the traditional sabbath (CBarrett, CHDodd Festschr. '56, 371f [eschat.]).—S. on κατάπαυσις HWeiss, CBQ 58, '96, 674–89. M-M. TW.

σάββατον, ου, τό (שַׁבָּת) dat. pl. σάββασιν (Meleager [I]: Anth. Pal. 5, 160; 1 Macc 2:38; Jos., Vi. 279, Ant. 16, 163; Just., D. 27, 5; 29, 3) always in NT except that a v.l. at **Mt 12:1** and **12** acc. to codex B has σαββάτοις (so usu. LXX [Thackeray 35]; Jos., Bell. 1, 146, Ant. 3, 294. See W-S. §8, 12; B-D-F §52; Mlt-H. 128; MBlack, BRigaux Festschr. '70, 60f.—The word is found Plut. et al.; pap, LXX; En 10:17; Philo, Joseph.)

❶ **the seventh day of the week in Israel's calendar, marked by rest fr. work and by special religious ceremonies,** ***sabbath***

ⓐ sing. (τὸ) σάββατον (Nepualius [I AD] ed. W Gemoll, Progr. Striegau 1884, 53; LXX; Philo, Cher. 87; Jos., Ant. 3, 143; 255; Just., D. 8, 4 al.) **Mt 12:8; Mk 2:27f** (Alex. Aphr., Eth. Probl. 10, II 2 p. 130, 34ff ὁ ἄνθρωπος τῶν ἀρετῶν χάριν, ἀλλ' οὐκ ἔμπαλιν [=vice versa]); **6:2; 15:42 v.l.; 16:1; Lk 6:5; 23:54; J 5:9f; 9:14;** B 15:1a, 3; GPt 2:5 al. ἁγιάζειν τὸ σ. B 15:1b (s. 2 Esdr 23:22). βεβηλοῦν τὸ σ. **Mt 12:5b;** λύειν τὸ σ. **J 5:18** (s. λύω 4). τηρεῖν τὸ σ. **9:16** (cp. Just., D. 10, 3). σαββατίζειν τὸ σ. (cp. Lev 23:32) Ox 1, 9f (GTh 27) φυλάσσειν τὸ σ. (s. Ex 31:13f; Lev 19:3; Just., D. 8, 4) B 15:2, s. vs. 3. *On the Sabbath* (s. B-D-F §200, 3; Rob. 523): ἐν τῷ σαββάτῳ (2 Esdr 23:15a, 16) **Lk 6:7; J 19:31a;** ἐν σαββάτῳ (2 Esdr 20:32b) **Mt 12:2; Lk 6:1; J 5:16; 7:22f;** τῷ σαββάτῳ **Lk 6:4** D (Unknown Sayings, 49–54); **6:9; 13:14a, 15; 14:3;** τῷ σαββάτῳ ἐπερχομένης τῆς κυριακῆς AcPl Ha 3, 8. σαββάτῳ (Jos., Bell. 2, 456) **Mt 24:20** (s. Boll 134, 1); **Lk 14:1; J 6:59 v.l.;** ἐν ἑτέρῳ σ. **Lk 6:6;** τῷ ἐρχομένῳ σ. **Ac 13:44;** ἐν τῇ ἡμέρᾳ τοῦ σ. (cp. Jer 17:21f) **Lk 14:5 v.l.;** ἐν ἡμέρᾳ τοῦ σ. (2 Esdr 20:32a; 23:15b; cp. Cyranides p. 79, 11 ἐν ἡμ. σαββάτου) **Lk 14:5;** τῇ ἡμέρᾳ τοῦ σ. **Lk 13:14b, 16.** In the acc. of duration of time (B-D-F §161, 2) τὸ σάββατον *throughout the Sabbath* **Lk 23:56.** κατὰ πᾶν σ. *(on) every Sabbath* **Ac 13:27; 15:21; 18:4;** εἰς τὸ μεταξὺ σ. *on the following Sabbath* **13:42.** ἡ ἡμέρα πρὸ σαββάτου **Lk 23:54** D.—σάββατον μέγα *Great Sabbath* MPol 8:1; 21:1; cp. **J 19:31b** (s. ESchwartz, Christl. u. jüd. Ostertafeln: AGG VIII/6, 1905, 127). σ. τὸ λεγόμενον πρῶτον *the so-called first Sabbath* PtK 2, p. 14, 28.—On σαββάτου ὁδός *a Sabbath day's journey* **Ac 1:12** s. ὁδός 2.

ⓑ pl.—**α.** of more than one Sabbath (2 Ch 31:3; Ezk 46; 3; Jos., Ant. 13, 252; Just., D. 10, 3 al.) σάββατα τρία **Ac 17:2.** B 15:8a (Is 1:13), b.

β. τὰ σάββατα for a single Sabbath day (PCairZen 762, 6 [III BC]; Plut., Mor. 169c; 671e τὴν τῶν σαββάτων ἑορτήν; 672a; Ex 20:10; Lev 23:32 al.; Philo, Abr. 28 τὴν ἑβδόμην, ἣν Ἑβραῖοι σάββατα καλοῦσιν; Jos., Ant. 1, 33; 3, 237; 12, 259; 276.—B-D-F §141, 3 ; Rob. 408; ESchwyzer, ZVS 62, '35, 1–16; ASchlatter, Mt 1929, 393) ὀψὲ σαββάτων **Mt 28:1a** (s. ὀψέ 3). Also prob. **Col 2:16.** ἡ ἡμέρα τῶν σαββάτων (Ex 20:8; 35:3; Dt 5:12; Jer 17:21f; Jos., Ant. 12, 274; Just., 27, 5) **Lk 4:16; Ac 13:14; 16:13;** Dg 4:3. (ἐν) τοῖς σάββασιν *on the Sabbath* (Jos., Vi. 279 τοῖς σάββασιν, Ant. 13, 252 v.l. ἐν τοῖς σάββασιν) **Mt 12:1, 5, 10–12; Mk 1:21; 2:23, 24; 3:2, 4; Lk 4:31; 6:2; 13:10.** ἡ περὶ τὰ σάββατα δεισιδαιμονία *fanatical veneration of the Sabbath* Dg 4:1 (only extreme danger to human life can cause the Sabbath law to be suspended: Synes., Ep. 4 p. 162bc). τὰ σάββατα *the Sabbath feasts* B 2:5 (Is 1:13).—JMeinhold, Sabbat u. Woche im AT 1905, Sabbat u. Sonntag 1909; JHehn, Siebenzahl u. Sabbat bei den Babyloniern u. im AT 1907, Der israelit. Sabbat 1909, Zur Sabbatfrage: BZ 14, 1917, 198–213; EMahler, Der Sabbat: ZDMG 62, 1908, 33–79, Handbuch der jüd. Chronologie 1916; GBeer, Schabbath1908; WNowack, Schabbat 1924; MWolff, Het ordeel der helleensch-romeinsche schrijvers over . . . den Sabbath: TT 44, 1910, 162–72; ELohse, Jesu Worte über den Sabbat, Beih. ZNW 26, '60, 79–89; Moore, Judaism s. ind.; Schürer II 424–27; 447–54; 467–75. S. also κυριακός, end.

❷ **a period of seven days, *week*—ⓐ** sing. δὶς τοῦ σαββάτου *two days (in) a week* **Lk 18:12.** πρώτῃ σαββάτου *on the first day of the week* (Sunday) **Mk 16:9.** κατὰ μίαν σαββάτου *every Sunday* **1 Cor 16:2.** πρωῒ μιᾶς σαββάτου *early on Sunday morning* **Mk 16:2** D.

ⓑ pl. (ἡ) μία (τῶν) σαββάτων (i.e. ἡμέρα) *the first day of the week* **Mt 28:1b** (Just., D. 41, 4; s. Dalman, Gramm. 247; SKrauss, Talm. Archäologie II 1911, 428f; PGardner-Smith, JTS 27, 1926, 179–81); **Mk 16:2; Lk 24:1; J 20:1, 19; Ac 20:7; 1 Cor 16:2 v.l.** Judeans fast δευτέρᾳ σαββάτων καὶ πέμπτῃ on *the second and fifth days of the week* (Monday and Thursday) D 8:1 (s. νηστεύω and the lit. there).—ESchürer, Die siebentägige Woche im Gebr. der christl. Kirche der ersten Jahrhunderte: ZNW 6, 1905, 1–66; FColson, The Week 1926; FBoll, Hebdomas: Pauly-W. VII/2, 1912, 2547–48; RNorth, The Derivation of 'Sabbath', Biblica 36, '55, 182–201; WRordorf, Sunday, tr. AGraham, '68; BHHW III 1633–35; TRE III 608.—B. 1005. DELG s.v. σάββατα. M-M. EDNT. TW.

σαγήνη, ης, ἡ (Plut., Mor. 169c; Lucian, Pisc. 51, Tim. 22; Artem. 2, 14, p. 107, 13; Ael. Aristid. 13 p. 200 D.; Aelian, HA 11, 12; PTebt 868, 2 [II BC]; LXX; cp. the metaph. use of the verb σαγηνεύω Hdt. 6, 31) **a large net hanging vertically, with floats on the top and sinkers on the bottom, *seine, dragnet*** σαγήνῃ βληθείσῃ εἰς τὴν θάλασσαν **Mt 13:47** (βάλλειν σαγ. as Is 19:8; Babrius, Fab. 4, 1; 9, 6). S. ἀμφιβάλλω and cp. ἀμφίβληστρον.—DELG. M-M.

Σαδδουκαῖος, ου, ὁ member of a major Israelite group, *Sadducee,* always pl. οἱ Σαδδουκαῖοι *the Sadducees* (s. Joseph.: the passages are printed in Schürer II 382f; s. pp. 384–88 for evidence fr. the Mishnah; cp. Billerbeck IV 339–52; Just., D. 80, 4 beside other Judean sects). **Ac 5:17** associates the high priest and his adherents with this group. Acc. to **Mt 22:23; Mk 12:18; Lk 20:27; Ac 23:8** they denied the resurrection of the dead. S. also **Mt 3:7; 16:1, 6, 11f; 22:34; Ac 4:1; 23:6f.** Many questions concerning the origin, name, and character of the Sadducees cannot yet be satisfactorily answered.—Wlh., Pharisäer u. die Sadd. 1874; GHölscher, Der Sadduzäismus 1906; Schürer II, 404–14; RLeszynsky, Die Sadduzäer 1912; BEerdmans, Farizeën en Saduceën: TT 48, 1914, 1–16; MSegall, Pharisees and Sadducees: Exp. 8th ser., 13, 1917, 81ff; GBox, Who Were the Sadducees in the NT: ibid. 401ff; 16, 1918, 55ff; EMeyer II 1921, 290ff; JLightley, Jewish Sects and Parties in the Time of Jesus 1923; HRasp, Fl. Joseph. u. die jüd. Religionsparteien: ZNW 23, 1924, 27–47; JJeremias, Jerusalem z. Zeit Jesu II 1924/29; Billerb. IV 1928, 334–52: D. Pharis. u. d. Sadd. in d. altjüd. Lit.; TManson, Sadducee and Pharisee—the Origin and Significance of the Names: BJRL 22, '38, 144–59; WStrawson, Jesus and the Future Life '59, 203–20; JLeMoyne, Les Sadducéens, '72; ASaldarini, Pharisees, Scribes and Sadducees in Palestinian Society '88; GStemberger, Pharisees, Sadducees, Essenes '95; Schürer II 381f (lit.).— Kl. Pauly IV 1491f; BHHW III 1639f. EDNT. TW.

Σαδώκ, ὁ (צָדוֹק) indecl., freq. in the OT (Joseph. has Σάδωκος, ου [Ant. 7, 201]; AscIs 2:5 has Σαδδουκ) ***Zadok,*** in the genealogy of Jesus **Mt 1:14ab; Lk 3:23ff** D.—M-M. BHHW III 2220.

σαίνω (Hom. et al.)**—❶** prim., of dogs, 'wag the tail' (Hom. et al.), hence **to try to win favor by an ingratiating manner, *fawn upon, flatter*** (so trag. et al.; Antig. Car. 172 σαίνειν φιλοφρόνως; Jos., Bell. 6, 336). It is in this direction that many prefer to take the mng. of the pass. in the only place in our lit. where the word occurs, **1 Th 3:3** τὸ μηδένα σαίνεσθαι (ἐν ταῖς θλίψεσιν ταύταις) *so that no one might be deceived* (PSchmidt, Schmiedel, Wohlenberg, GMilligan, CWilliams, Frame ad loc., also Zahn, Einl.[3] I 158f). It is prob. that the misfortunes of the new converts would provide opportunity for Paul's opponents to show them exceptional kindness and so perh. beguile them into adopting their own views. Others, following the ancient versions and the Gk. interpreters prefer to understand σ. in the sense

❷ **to cause to be emotionally upset, *move, disturb, agitate*** (Soph., Ant. 1214 παιδός με σαίνει φθόγγος; Diog. L. 8, 41 οἱ σαινόμενοι τοῖς λεγομένοις ἐδάκρυον.—In Stoic. III 231, 8f σαίνεσθαι is = 'be carried away w. someth.'), *so that no one might be shaken* or *disturbed* (Bornemann, vDobschütz [p. 133f n. 3 the material necessary for understanding the word is brought together], MDibelius, Steinmann, Oepke ad loc., NRSV; HChadwick, JTS n.s. 1, '50, 156ff). On the construction s. B-D-F §399, 3; Rob. 1059; also EbNestle, ZNW 7, 1906, 361f; GMercati, ZNW 8, 1907, 242; RPerdelwitz, StKr 86, 1913, 613ff; AKnox, JTS 25, 1924, 290f; RParry, ibid. 405; IHeikel, StKr 106, '35, 316.—DELG. M-M. TW.

σάκκος, ου, ὁ (Hdt., Aristoph.+; ins, pap, LXX; PsSol 20:2; Test12Patr, JosAs; AscIs 2:10; Joseph.; Mel., P. 19, 131.—Semit. loanw.: HLewy, Die semit. Lehnwörter im Griech. 1895, 87 [cp. שַׂק]. On the quest. whether to spell it w. one κ or two s. Mayser 215) **a coarse cloth made of animal (goat or camel) hair, *sack, sackcloth*** ὠμόλινον ἐκ σάκκου γεγονός *a rough linen towel made of (a) sack (cloth)* Hs 8, 4, 1. The fabric from which a sack is made is usu. dark in color ἁμαρτίαι μελανώτεραι σάκκου 1 Cl 8:3 (quot. of unknown orig.). μέλας ὡς σάκκος τρίχινος **Rv 6:12** (cp. Is 50:3). Hence *sackcloth* is esp. suited to be worn as a mourning garment (LXX; PsSol 2:20; JosAs 10:16 al.; Jos., Bell. 2, 237, Ant. 5, 37 al.) περιβεβλημένοι σάκκους **Rv 11:3** (cp. 4 Km 19:2; Is 37:2; AscIs 2:10 σάκκον and s. περιβάλλω 2a). ἔρριψεν αὐτὸν χαμαὶ ἐπὶ τὸν σ. *(Joseph) threw himself down to the ground on sackcloth* JosAs 13:1. W. σποδός (Esth 4:2f; Jos., Ant. 20, 123; TestJos 15:2) ἐν σ. καὶ σποδῷ καθῆσθαι *sit in sackcloth and ashes* **Lk 10:13** (Mel., P. 19, 131). ἐν σ. καὶ σποδῷ μετανοεῖν **Mt 11:21.** ἐπὶ σ. καὶ σποδοῦ κόπτεσθαι (κόπτω 2) B 7:5. καὶ σάκκον ἐνδύσησθε καὶ σποδὸν ὑποστρώσητε 3:2 (Is 58:5).—Menand., fgm. 544 Kock=754 Kö., of Syrian penitents, who sinned against the goddess: ἔλαβον σακίον, εἶτ' εἰς τὴν ὁδὸν ἐκάθισαν αὑτοὺς ἐπὶ κόπρου, καὶ τὴν θεὸν ἐξιλάσαντο τῷ ταπεινοῦσθαι σφόδρα 'they took sackcloth, then seated themselves in the path on a dunghill and propitiated the goddess by humiliating themselves exceedingly'; Plut., Superst. 7 p. 168d: ἔξω κάθηται σακκίον ἔχων καὶ περιεζωσμένος ῥάκεσι ῥυπαροῖς, πολλάκις δὲ γυμνὸς ἐν πηλῷ κυλινδούμενος ἐξαγορεύει τινὰς ἁμαρτίας, ὡς τόδε φαγόντος ἢ πιόντος ἢ βαδίσαντος ὁδόν, ἣν οὐκ εἴα τὸ δαιμόνιον 'he sits outside in sackcloth, girt with filthy rags, and frequently he rolls naked in mire and publicly confesses some sins, such as eating or drinking this or that or taking some path forbidden by Heaven'; cp. Lam. 4:5. On the rags of a penitent cp. ἐν ἱεροῖς ῥακενδύτας: Hermes Trismeg., Cat. Cod. Astr. VIII/4 p. 148, 2; 165, 16.—DELG. M-M. TW.

Σαλά, ὁ (שֶׁלַח) indecl. ***Shelah,*** in Luke's genealogy of Jesus.

❶ son of Nahshon and father of Boaz **Lk 3:32;** here the v.l. has Σαλμών (Mt 1:4f; 1 Ch 2:11; cp. Ruth 4:20f), materially correct, but demonstrably secondary.—EbNestle, Sala, Salma, Salmon: ZNW 11, 1910, 242f.

❷ son of Cainan and father of Eber (Gen 10:24; 11:13–15; 1 Ch 1:18 A) **Lk 3:35.**

Σαλαθιήλ, ὁ (שְׁאַלְתִּיאֵל) indecl. (LXX; ViZech 3 [p. 88, 6 Sch].—Jos., Ant. 11, 73 Σαλαθίηλος) ***Shealtiel, Salathiel,*** father of Zerubbabel (1 Ch 3:19; 2 Esdr 3:2; 5:2; 22:1; Hg 1:1); in the genealogy of Jesus **Mt 1:12** he is a son of Jechoniah (1 Ch 3:17), in **Lk 3:27** a son of Neri.

Σαλαμίς, ῖνος, ἡ (on the v.l. Σαλαμίνη s. B-D-F §57; Mlt-H. 128) ***Salamis,*** a large city on the east coast of the island of Cyprus (Aeschyl., Hdt. et al.; ins; SibOr 4, 128; 5, 452 πόλις μεγάλη) visited by Paul on his 'first' missionary journey **Ac 13:5.**—S. the lit. on Κύπρος.—Pauly-W. II 1832–44; Kl. Pauly IV 1505f; BHHW III 1645f; PECS 794–96.—M-M.

Σαλείμ, τό (also Σαλίμ) indecl. ***Salim.*** John baptized ἐν Αἰνὼν ἐγγὺς τοῦ Σαλίμ **J 3:23.** Acc. to Eus., Onom. p. 40, 1 this place lay 8 Roman miles (=12.4 km.) south of Scythopolis in northern Samaria (so Lagrange and Abel; s. Αἰνών). Today there is a place called Salim 5.5 km. east of Shechem; it is mentioned in Epiph., Haer. 55, 2 (this one is preferred by WAlbright, HTR 17, 1924, 193f). S. in addition for Αἰνών also EbNestle, ZDPV 30, 1907, 210ff; BBacon, Biblical World 33, 1909, 223ff; KKundsin, Topolog. Überlieferungsstoffe im J 1925. Erbes s.v. Βηθανία 2.—BHHW III 1648ff.

σαλεύω fut. 3 sg. σαλεύσει Wsd 4:19; 1 aor. ἐσάλευσα. Pass.: 1 fut. σαλευθήσομαι Wsd 4:19; 1 aor. ἐσαλεύθην; pf. 3 sg. σεσάλευται Ps 93:18; ptc. σεσαλευμένος (σάλος; Aeschyl., Pla., X.+; OGI 515, 47; pap, LXX; En 101:4; TestSol; TestLevi 3:9; GrBar 6:13; Philo; Jos., Bell. 2, 636, Ant. 8, 136 al.; SibOr 3, 675) prim. 'shake'; in our lit. only trans.

❶ **to cause to move to and fro, *shake, cause to waver/totter*** pass. ***be shaken, be made to waver/totter*** (Diod. S. 12, 47, 2 τ. τείχη) οἰκίαν *shake a house* (a flood: Sb 8267, 8 [5 BC]) **Lk 6:48.** τὴν γῆν **Hb 12:26**—Pass. (Hippol., Ref. 1, 8, 12) κάλαμος ὑπὸ ἀνέμου σαλευόμενος *a reed driven to and fro by the wind* (Appian, Bell. Civ. 4, 28 §120 [pass. in act. sense of a swaying reed]; s. Is 7:2; Jos., Ant. 4, 51 ἐξ ἀνέμου σαλευόμενον κῦμα) **Mt 11:7; Lk 7:24.** Cp. **Rv 6:13 v.l.** Of a house ἐσαλεύθη ὁ τόπος *the place shook,* lit. *was shaken* (cp. Ps 17:8; GrBar 6:13) **Ac 4:31** (cp. Lucian, Necyom. 10 ἅπαντα ἐκεῖνα ἐσαλεύετο.—σαλεύεσθαι as a sign of divine presence TestLevi 3:9; Jos., Ant. 7, 76f). Of foundations shaking in an earthquake (cp. Ps 81:5) **16:26.** αἱ δυνάμεις τῶν οὐρανῶν σαλευθήσονται *the armies of heaven will be shaken* **Mt 24:29; Lk 21:26;** cp. **Mk 13:25** (PJoüon, RSR 29, '39, 114f). Also of the heavens *moving* in orderly fashion at God's command, prob. in ref. to the variety of motions exhibited in the heavens οἱ οὐρανοὶ σαλευόμενοι 1 Cl 20:1 (s. HHellfritz, VigChr 22, '68, 1–7).—μέτρον σεσαλευμένον a *measure that is shaken together* **Lk 6:38.**—In imagery: τὰ σαλευόμενα *that which is* or *can be shaken* **Hb 12:27a** forms a contrast (cp. Philo, Leg. All. 38) to τὰ μὴ σαλευόμενα *that which is not* (and *cannot be*) *shaken* vs. **27b;** the former is the heaven and earth of the world as it now exists (vs. 26), the latter the coming Kingdom (vs. 28).

❷ **to disturb inwardly, *disturb, shake,*** fig. ext. of 1 (Appian, Iber. 102 §442 of wavering in loyalty; PsSol 8:33; 15:4) ἵνα μὴ σαλευθῶ *that I may not be shaken* or *disturbed* **Ac 2:25** (Ps 15:8); σαλευθῆναι ἀπὸ τοῦ νοός (Theodor. Prodr. 4, 319 H. τὸν νοῦν σαλευθείς) **2 Th 2:2.** *Incite* perh. to the point of riot **Ac 17:13.**—B. 675. DELG s.v. σάλος. M-M. TW.

Σαλήμ, ἡ (שָׁלֵם; LXX; Philo.—Jos., Ant, 1, 180 has Σολυμᾶ, also indecl.) ***Salem.*** **Hb 7:1f,** following Gen 14:18, calls Melchizedek βασιλεὺς Σαλήμ and interprets it as 'King of peace' (s. Philo, Leg. All. 3, 79 Μελχισεδὲκ βασιλέα τῆς εἰρήνης—Σαλὴμ τοῦτο γὰρ ἑρμηνεύεται).—S. on Μελχισέδεκ and Erbes s.v. Βηθανία 2.—BHHW III 1647–48.

Σαλίμ, τό s. Σαλείμ.

Σαλμών, ὁ indecl. (שַׂלְמוֹן), ***Salmon,*** son of Nahshon and father of Boaz (1 Ch 2:11; cp. Ruth 4:20f [Σαλμάν; but A reads Σαλμών]), in the genealogy of Jesus **Mt 1:4f** husband of Rahab; **Lk 3:32 v.l.** (s. Σαλά 1).

Σαλμώνη, ης, ἡ (this form of the name is found only in our passage. Elsewh. it appears as Σαλμώνιον, Σαμώνιον, Σαμμώνιον, Σαλμωνίς; see the exx. in JWeiss, RE XI 89, 14ff) ***Salmone,*** a promontory on the northeast corner of Crete **Ac 27:7.**—Kl. Pauly IV 1519, 1532f; BHHW III 1650.

σάλος, ου, ὁ a rolling or tossing motion, *surge,* esp. of the *waves* in a rough sea (s. σαλεύω; trag.; Plut., Lucull. 498 [10, 3]; Lucian, Tox. 19, Hermot. 28; Jon 1:15; Ps 88:10; PsSol 6:3.—Philo, Sacr. Abel. 13 al. metaph. w. κλύδων. Metaph. also Jos., Ant. 14, 376), but also of an earthquake (Eur., Iph. Taur. 46; Is 24:20 v.l.; Jos., Ant. 4, 51), although the former is more probable in **Lk 21:25.**—DELG. M-M. TW.

σάλπιγξ, ιγγος, ἡ (s. two next entries; Hom.+; Kaibel 1049, 7; New Docs 4, p. 19, ln. 5 at a gladiatorial contest; PHerm 121, 10; LXX; TestAbr A 12 p. 91, 7 [Stone p. 30, 7]; ParJer 3:2; ApcSed; ApcEsdr 4:36 p. 29, 13 Tdf.; ApcMos; Philo; Jos., Bell. 3, 89 (military use), Ant. 3, 291, 7, 359; Tat. 1, 2; loanw. in rabb.)

❶ **a wind instrument used esp. for communication, *trumpet*** (Artem. 1, 56, p. 52, 15ff: the ἱερὰ σ. is straight, the military trumpet spiral) **1 Cor 14:8; Hb 12:19** (cp. Ex 19:16); **Rv 1:10; 4:1; 8:2, 6, 13; 9:14;** D 16:6; EpilMosq 4. μετὰ σάλπιγγος φωνῆς μεγάλης *with a trumpet giving forth a blast* **Mt 24:31 v.l.** (s. φωνή 1). ἤχησεν σ. κυρίου *the Lord's trumpet sounded* GJs 8:3 (cp. PsSol 8:1 φωνὴν σάλπιγγος ἠχούσης).

❷ **the sound made or signal given by a trumpet, *trumpet-call, trumpet-sound*** (Aristoph., Ach. 1001; X., R. Equ. 9, 11, Hipp. 3, 12; Aristot., Rhet. 3, 6; Polyb. 4, 13, 1; Ael. Aristid. 34, 22 K.=50 p. 554 D.: τῇ πρώτῃ σ.; s. Pollux 4, 88f on its loud sound; could be heard at a distance of 60 stadia Diod. S. 17, 106, 7) μετὰ σάλπιγγος μεγάλης *with a loud trumpet-call* **Mt 24:31.** ἐν τῇ ἐσχάτῃ σάλπιγγι *at the sound of the last trumpet* **1 Cor 15:52.** ἐν σάλπιγγι θεοῦ (καταβήσεται ἀπ' οὐρανοῦ) *at the call of the trumpet blown by God's command* **1 Th 4:16.**—PKrentz, The Salpinx in Gk. Warfare, in Hoplites, The Classical Gk. Battle Experience, ed. VHanson '91; JHale/MTunnell, ClBull 72, '96, 118–24. For add. lit. s. ISBE III 449; TRE XXIII 455 (Israel's musical instruments).—DELG. M-M. EDNT. TW.

σαλπίζω (σάλπιγξ; Hom. et al.; LXX; PsSol 11:1; ParJer 4:2; ApcEsdr 4:36; ApcMos; Philo, Spec. Leg. 2, 188; Jos., Ant. 5, 23) fut. σαλπίσω (Lob. on Phryn. p. 191); 1 aor. ἐσάλπισα (Aelian, VH 1, 26; LXX; Jos., Ant. 7, 279.—On both forms s. B-D-F §71; Mlt-H. 257)

❶ **to produce the sound of a trumpet, *blow a trumpet*** **Rv 8:6–13; 9:1, 13; 10:7; 11:15.**—Impers. (X., An. 1, 2, 17) σαλπίσει *the trumpet will sound* **1 Cor 15:52** (B-D-F §129; Rob. 392).

❷ **to publicize someth. with fanfare,** *to trumpet.* σ. is prob. to be taken metaph. (cp. Ps.-Lucian, Ocypus v. 114 ἀλέκτωρ ἡμέραν ἐσάλπισεν; Achilles Tat. 8, 10, 10 ὑπὸ σάλπιγγι . . . μοιχεύεται=advertises her adultery in public; Synesius, To Paeonius 1 p. 308a τὸ κηρύττειν ἑαυτὸν καὶ πάντα ποιεῖν ὑπὲρ ἐπιδείξεως οὐ σοφίας ἀλλὰ σοφιστείας ἐστί=to trumpet one's own achievements and do everything for the sake of publicity is not the part of wisdom, but of misused wit; cp. M. Ant. 5, 6 ἄνθρωπος εὖ ποιήσας οὐκ ἐπιβοᾶται=one who does a good thing does not advertise it) in μὴ σαλπίσῃς ἔμπροσθέν σου *you must not blow a trumpet before you* **Mt 6:2** (difft. EKlostermann ad loc.; ABüchler, JTS 10, 1909, 266ff. S. Betz, SM 355–58.).—DELG s.v. σάλπιγξ. M-M. TW.

σαλπιστής, οῦ, ὁ (s. two prec. entries; a later form for the older σαλπι(γ)κτής.—Theophr., Char. 25; Polyb. 1, 45, 13; Dionys. Hal. 4, 17, 3; 4, 18, 3; Chariton 8, 2, 6 al.; SIG 1058, 4; 1059 II, 20; Sb 4591, 3.—WRutherford, The New Phrynichus 1881, 279; Lob., Phryn. 191f) ***trumpeter*** **Rv 18:22.**—DELG s.v. σάλπιγξ. M-M. TW.

Σαλώμη, ης, ἡ (SEG VIII, 197 [I AD; Jerusalem]; Joseph. index and s. B-D-F §53, 3; Mlt-H. 144) ***Salome,*** one of a number of Galilean women who followed Jesus, **Mk 15:40; 16:1;** GJs 19:3; 20:1, 2 (codd.); 3:4 (codd.); in case it is permissible to combine **Mk 15:40** w. its parallel Mt 27:56, where the name does not occur, she was the wife of Zebedee and mother of James and John. (The daughter of Herodias mentioned but not named in Mt 14:6ff [on Mk 6:22–24 s. Ἡρῳδίας] was also called *Salome,* cp. Jos., Ant. 18, 136.—HDaffner, Salome, 1912; WSpeyer, D. Tod der Salome, AC 10, '67, 176–80; RGundry, Mark '93, 320f.)—Kl. Pauly IV 1520; BHHW III, 1650f.

Σαλωμών (LXX; s. Thackeray 165; Christian magical pap: PGM II, P 17, 10 p. 226 [Henrichs]) **Ac 7:47** Tdf.; s. Σολομών.

Σαμάρεια, ας, ἡ (to be spelled and accented on the analogy of Ἀλεξάνδρεια etc.; s. B-D-F §38, but also Rob. 197; Mlt-H. 147) ***Samaria*** (the Gk. form of the name in Polyb. 5, 71, 11; Strabo 16, 2, 34; Diod. S. 19, 93, 7; Pliny 5, 13, 17; LXX; ParJer 8:11; AscIs; Joseph. index), orig. the name of the city (Hebr. שֹׁמְרוֹן, Aram. שָׁמְרַיִן), though not so in our lit., then transferred to the whole province which, in NT times, included the region fr. the Plain of Jezreel southward to the border of Judea. **J 4:4** (Jos., Vi. 269 ἔδει δι' ἐκείνης [=τ. Σαμαρείας] πορεύεσθαι, Ant. 20, 118); **4:5; Ac 8:9, 14.** W. Judea **1:8; 8:1;** w. Judea and Galilee **9:31;** w. Galilee **Lk 17:11;** w. Phoenicia **Ac 15:3.** γυνὴ ἐκ τῆς Σαμαρείας a Samaritan woman **J 4:7.** ἡ πόλις τῆς Σαμαρείας *the* (main) *city of Samaria* (s. πόλις 1), i.e. the city of Samaria which, since the time of Herod the Great, was known as Sebaste **Ac 8:5** (on this s. JBoehmer, ZNW 9, 1908, 216–18).—GHölscher, Palästina in der persischen u. hellenist. Zeit 1903; Baedeker, Palästina u. Syrien[7] 1910; HGuthe, RE XVII 1906, 419ff; XXIV 1913, 448f; Schürer index, s. esp. II 16f n. 50; LHaefeli, Gesch. der Landschaft Sam. von 722 BC bis 67 AD 1922; AParrot, Samaria, trans. SHooke, '58.— Kl. Pauly IV 1529f; BHHW III 1655–60; OEANE II 463–67; TRE XXIX, 744–50.—M-M. DBS XI, 740–56. TW.

Σαμαρία s. Σαμάρεια.

Σαμαρίτης, ου, ὁ (also Σαμαρείτης; Σαμαριτάνος Mt 10:5 D [perh. influenced by Latin].— Joseph. index; Damasc., Vi. Isid. 141. For the spelling s. B-D-F §38; Rob. 197.—Stephan. Byz. s.v. Ὠρεός requires Σαμαρείτης and refers s.v. Σαμάρεια to a certain Antiochus as authority.—Appian, Bell. Civ. 5, 75 §319 has, like Just., the form Σαμαρεύς, -έως: Ἰδουμαίων καὶ Σαμαρέων) ***Samaritan*** (masc.) **Lk 17:16.** Main character in a story (on this EBuonaiuti, Religio 11, '35, 117–25; JGordon, ET 56, '45, 302–4; FLeenhardt, Aux sources de la tradition chrétienne [MGoguel Festschr.] '50, 132–38; BGerhardsson, ConNeot 16, '58; JDerrett, Law in the NT, '70, 208–27; DHamm, CBQ 56, '94, 273–87; s. παραβολή 2a, end) **Lk 10:33.** Pl. **J 4:39f.** Avoided by Judeans vs. **9** (s. συγχράομαι; cp. Sir 50:25f; Jos., Ant. 18, 30; 20, 118, Bell. 2, 232f; but Just. A I, 53, 3f links Judeans and Samaritans in contrast to the 'nations'; s. Schürer II 19f on relation to Israel), also despised by them **8:48.** πόλις Σαμαριτῶν **Mt 10:5;** κώμη Σ. **Lk 9:52;** cp. **Ac 8:25.**—Lit. s.v. Σαμάρεια, also EKautzsch, RE XVII 1906, 428ff; JMontgomery, The Samaritans 1907; JEHThomson, The Samaritans 1919; MGaster, The Samaritans 1925; Lightley (Σαδδουκαῖος, end); Billerb. I 538–60; KBornhäuser, ZST 9, '32, 552–66; JJeremias, Jerusalem z. Zeit Jesu II B 1929–37, 224ff: Die Samaritaner; MEnslin, Lk and the Samaritans: HTR 36, '43, 278–97; JBowman, Samaritan Studies: BJRL 40, '58, 298–329; ACrown/RPlummer/ATal, edd., A Companion to Samaritan Studies '93; ACrown, A Bibliography of the Samaritans '93; Schürer index.—RE XVII 428ff; DBS XI 740–56; BHHW III 1660f; OEANE IV 468–72; TRE XXIX 750–56. On Samaritan ins s. New Docs 1, 110; 5, 138; Boffo, Iscrizioni 47–60 (lit.).—M-M. EDNT. TW.

Σαμαρῖτις, ιδος, ἡ (also Σαμαρεῖτις; 1 Macc 10:30; 11:28; EpArist 107; Jos., Bell. 3, 48 al.; IG III, 2892) fem. of Σαμαρίτης adj. and subst., ***Samaritan*** ἡ γυνὴ ἡ Σαμαρῖτις *the Samaritan woman* **J 4:9a;** cp. **9b.**—TW.

Σαμοθρᾴκη, ης, ἡ (oft. in lit. and ins) **an island in *Samothrace,*** the northern part of the Aegean Sea (famous in antiquity for its Sanctuary of the Great Gods, s. SCole, Theoi Megaloi '84) **Ac 16:11.**—Pauly-W. I A, 2162–2218; Kl. Pauly IV 1534–37; BHHW III 1663; PECS 804–6; M-M.

Σάμος, ου, ἡ (Hom. et al.; oft. in ins; 1 Macc 15:23; SibOr 3, 363; Ath. 17, 3) ***Samos,*** an island off the west coast of Asia Minor, opposite the promontory of Mycale, not far fr. Ephesus. Landing-place for ships on the voyage fr. the Hellespont to Syria (Jos., Ant. 16, 23; 62) **Ac 20:15.**—CCurtius, Urkunden zur Gesch. von Samos 1873, Inschriften u. Studien zur Geschichte von S. 1877.—Pauly-W. I A, 2162–2218; Kl. Pauly IV 1534–37; BHHW III 1663; PECS 802–3.—DELG s.v. σάμος.

Σαμουήλ, ὁ indecl. (שְׁמוּאֵל) ***Samuel*** a major OT prophet (1 Km 1:1–25:1, 28; Jer 15:1; Ps 98:6; 1 Ch 6:13, 18; 9:22; 1 Esdr 1:18 ἀπὸ τῶν χρόνων Σαμουὴλ τοῦ προφήτου; Sir 46:13; Philo, Just.—Joseph. has Σαμούηλος, ου [Ant. 6, 51]; s. EpArist 50; Preisigke, Namenbuch); in our lit. he brings the period of the Judges to an end **Ac 13:20,** and begins the line of the prophets **3:24.** περὶ Δαυίδ τε καὶ Σαμουὴλ καὶ τῶν προφητῶν **Hb 11:32.** In addition he is: a priest who serves in place of Zacharias GJs 10:2; a son of Joseph 17:2. On these two passages see deStrycker 317.—BHHW III 1663f. M-M.

Σαμφουριν indecl. *Samphurin* ἀπῆλθεν εἰς τ. χώραν Σαμφουριν ἐγγὺς τῆς ἐρήμου εἰς Ἐφραὶμ λεγομένην πόλιν **J 11:54** D (cp. Josh 19:19 A Ἀφεραΐμ). S. Dalman, Orte u. Wege Jesus[3] 1924, 233 [Eng. tr. 219]; RBrown, comm. ad loc. perhaps a corruption of שֵׁם אֶפְרַיִם 'whose name is Ephraim'. On Sepphoris, which some consider the referent in the v.l., s. PECS 827f, w. lit.

Σαμψών, ὁ indecl. (שִׁמְשׁוֹן) ***Samson,*** a judge in Israel (Judg 13–16.—Jos., Ant. 5, 290–318 has Σαμψών, ῶνος [297]) **Hb 11:32** (B-D-F §39, 5; 8 Mlt-H. 103, BHHW III 1799f).

σανδάλιον, ου, τό (Hdt. et al.; Diod. S. 5, 46, 2; Lucian, Herod. 5; LXX w. the same mng. as in our lit.) dim. of σάνδαλον (Hom. Hymns et al.; Sb 7243, 17 [IV AD]; Jos., Ant. 4, 256; loanw. in rabb.) **footwear consisting of a sole made of leather or other fabric and held on the foot by means of thongs, *sandal*** ὑπόδησαι τὰ σανδάλιά σου *put on your sandals* **Ac 12:8.** ὑποδεδεμένος σανδάλια *with* (nothing but) *sandals on one's feet* **Mk 6:9.**—Pauly-W. I A 2257, II 741–58; Kl. Pauly IV 1541; BHHW III 1738.—DELG s.v. σάνδαλον. M-M. TW.

σανίς, ίδος, ἡ (Hom. et al.; ins; PFlor 69, 21; SSol 8:9; Ezk 27:5; TestNapht 6:6; Philo, De Prov.: Eus., PE 8, 14, 26; Jos., Ant. 8, 134 al.) ***board, plank;*** beside τὰ ἀπὸ τοῦ πλοίου, the pieces of wreckage fr. the ship, the σανίδες of **Ac 27:44** are perh. boards or planks that were used to hold the cargo of grain in place (Breusing 203).—DELG. M-M. Spicq.

Σαούλ, ὁ indecl. (שָׁאוּל) ***Saul*—❶ son of Kish and first king of Israel** (1 Km 9ff; 1 Ch 8:33; 1 Macc 4:30; Philo, Migr. Abr. 196; Just., D. 105, 4.—Joseph. has Σαοῦλος, ου [Ant. 6, 74].—B-D-F §53, 2; Mlt-H. 144) **Ac 13:21;** 1 Cl 4:13; AcPl Ha 6, 22.

❷ **Hebrew name of the Apostle Paul** (s. Παῦλος 2). **Ac**, which is the only book in our lit. that uses the name Saul for the apostle, has it mostly in its Gk. form (s. Σαῦλος). The OT form Σαούλ is found only in the account of his Damascus experience, and as a voc. **9:4, 17; 22:7, 13; 26:14** (cp. TestLevi 2:6 the call of the angel fr. the opened heavens: Λευί, Λευί, εἴσελθε).—BHHW III 1677f.

σαπρός, ά, όν (σήπω 'make putrid'; Hipponax [VI BC] 32 A Diehl;, Aristoph., Hippocr. et al.; TestAbr B 13 p. 118, 13 [Stone p. 84, 13]; SIG[2] 587, 24; pap) prim.: 'rotten, putrid'.

❶ lit. **of such poor quality as to be of little or no value, *bad, not good*—ⓐ** in the prim. sense *spoiled, rotten* (of spoiled fish Antiphanes Com. [IV BC] fgm. 218, 4 K. [in Athen. 6, 225f]) of rotten fruits (PFlor 176, 9 figs; Theophr., HP 4, 14, 10 of worms that infect olives) of grapes that lie on the ground and rot Hs 2:4.

ⓑ of poor quality *bad*—**α.** of living matter, fish **Mt 13:48** (s. BAR 19, '93, 52; it is of semantic significance that these fish have just been caught and would therefore not be rotten or spoiled, whereas Antiphanes in the ref. cited above [1a] declaims about fish that have been in the marketplace too long).—Of plants and their products (Aristoph., Theophr. et al.; PFay 119, 4; 6) that are of inferior quality: trees, **Mt 7:17f; 12:33a; Lk 6:43b;** fruit **Mt 12:33b; Lk 6:43a.** Unless the proverb contains hyperbolic diction, 'rotten' would be an inappropriate rendering, since 'rotten' trees would either not bear any fruit at all or at the most fruit of such poor quality as to be inedible.

β. of stones *unusable, unfit, bad* λίθοι σ. *stones of poor quality* Hs 9, 5, 2; 9, 6, 4 (cp. Herodas 2, 23 worn-out shoes; PLond II, 356, 11f p. 252 [I AD])

❷ **bad or unwholesome to the extent of being harmful, *bad, evil, unwholesome,*** in a moral sense fig. ext. of 1 (Menand., Mon. 722; Epict. 3, 22, 61 σαπρὰ δόγματα; TestAbr B 13 p. 118, 13 [Stone 84, 13] λέγει ὁ θάνατος: οὐκ ἐστὶν ἄλλος σαπρότερός μου; Sb 5761, 23 [I AD] σ. ὄνομα; PSI 717, 4 [II AD] ἐὰν κατ' ἐμοῦ καταψηφίσηταί τι σαπρόν; 312, 13 [IV AD] οὐδὲν σαπρὸν ποιήσει) λόγος σαπρός *an evil word, evil speech* **Eph 4:29** (cp. M. Ant. 11, 15 ὡς σαπρὸς ὁ λέγων).—CLindhagen, Die Wurzel ΣΑΠ im AT u. NT: Upps. Univ. Årsskr. 5, '50, 27–53.—DELG s.v. σήπομαι. M-M. TW.

Σάπφιρα (also Σαπφείρα, Σαμπφ-, Σαφφ-; Aram. שַׁפִּירָא. On the spelling and accentuation s. B-D-F §38; 39, 7; 40; Mlt-H. 145; M-M. Both Aramaic and Gk. forms are found on ossuaries discovered near Jerusalem: SEG VIII 201 [I BC/I AD]; 184 [I AD]; HJCadbury, Amicitiae Corolla [RHarris Festschr.] '33, 54f; KBeyer, Die aramäischen Texte vom Toten Meer '84; JFitzmyer/DHarrington, A Manual of Palestinian Aramaic Texts '78; cp. TRE III 608), gen. **ης**, dat. **ῃ, ἡ** (on its declension s. B-D-F §43, 1; Mlt-H. 118) ***Sapphira,*** wife of Ἁνανίας (q.v. 2 and the lit. s.v. κοινός 1a. PMenoud, La mort d'An. et de Saph.: Aux sources de la tradition chrét. [MGoguel Festschr.] '50, 146–54; DMarguerat, NTS 39, '93, 209–26) **Ac 5:1.**—M-M.

σάπφιρος, ου, ἡ (also -φειρ- [so Michel Psellus, in Lapidaires p. 203, ln. 16]; ins; Semitic loanw., Hebr. סַפִּיר.—Theophr., Lap. 1, 8; 4, 23; 6, 37; Diosc. 5, 157; Aelian, VH 14, 34; PGM 3, 515; LXX; En 18:8 [σάφφ-]; Jos., Bell. 5, 234, Ant. 3, 168) **a transparent precious stone ordinarily blue in color, *the sapphire*** (the ancients prob. understood the σα. to be the lapis lazuli) **Rv 21:19** (s. Tob 13:17; Is 54:11).—RGradwohl, D. Farben im AT: Beih. ZAW 83, '63, 33f; other lit. s.v. ἀμέθυστος.—DELG. M-M.

σαργάνη, ης, ἡ (Aeschyl. et al., in the sense 'plait, braid') ***basket*** (so Aeneas Tact. 1348; Timocl. Com. [IV BC], fgm. 14, 4 Kock [in Athen. 8, 339e; 9, 407e]; Lucian, Lexiph. 6; BGU 417, 14; PFlor 269, 7; PStras 37, 13) **2 Cor 11:33,** where it is 'clearly a rope-basket' (B. 623; s. also FHort, JTS 10, 1909, 567ff [κόφινος, σφυρίς, σαργάνη]).—MSchnebel, D. Landwirtsch. im hellenist. Ägypt. I 1925, 280f. DELG. M-M. Spicq.

Σάρδεις, εων, αἱ (this spelling of the name Aeschyl., Thu. et al.; ins; SibOr 5, 289) ***Sardis,*** the ancient capital city of Lydia, in western Asia Minor **Rv 1:11; 3:1, 4.**—Ramsay, Letters 1905. Its inscriptions are found in Sardis: Publications of the American Soc. for the Excav. of Sardis VII '32; on Jews in Sardis s. ISardRobert I, p. 38. Apollonius of Tyana wrote letters τοῖς ἐν Σάρδεσιν (nos. 38; 75f) and τοῖς Σαρδιανοῖς (56): Philostrat. I p. 353; 359; 366; SJohnson, Christianity in Sardis, HRWilloughby Festschr. '61, 81–90.—Pauly-W. II 2475–78; Kl. Pauly IV 1551f; BHHW III 1670f; OEANE IV 484–88; PECS 808–810. CHemer in New Docs 3, 55f.

σάρδινος, ου, ὁ (An. Ox. IV 229) late form of σάρδιον **Rv 4:3 v.l.;** s. σάρδιον.—DELG s.v. σάρδιον.

σάρδιον, ου, τό (Aristoph.+; Pla., Phd. 110d; Theophr., Lap. 1, 8; 4, 23; Diod. S. 3, 53, 6; SIG[2] 588, 3; PHolm 3, 36; LXX; Jos., Bell. 5, 234) **a reddish precious stone, *carnelian, sard(ius)*** **Rv 4:3 v.l.** (σαρδίνῳ); **21:20.**—Lit. s.v. ἀμέθυστος. BHHW III 362–66. DELG. M-M.

σαρδόνυξ, υχος, ὁ (σάρδιον, ὄνυξ 'a veined gem'; Plut., Mor. 1160f; 1163a; Cyranides p. 34, 2; Jos., Bell. 5, 233, Ant. 3, 165 al.) ***sardonyx,*** a precious stone, w. difft. colors in parallel layers, a variety of agate **Rv 21:20.** Lit. s.v. ἀμέθυστος.—DELG s.v. σάρδιον. M-M.

Σάρεπτα (also Σάραπτα, Σάρεφθα; צָרְפַת On the spelling s. B-D-F §39, 2; Mlt-H. 147), **ων** (declinable in this way at least Ob 20; s. B-D-F §56, 2; Mlt-H. 147), **τά** ***Zarephath,*** a city on the Phoenician coast betw. Tyre and Sidon (Jos., Ant. 8, 320), where Elijah lived during a famine. Σ. τῆς Σιδωνίας (as 3 Km

17:9 in this same account) **Lk 4:26.**—BHHW III 2204; DBS XI 1414f; OEANE IV 488–91.

σαρκικός, ή, όν (σάρξ; Aristot., HA 10, 2, 635a, 11 v.l.; a verse, perh. by Sotades Lyr. [III BC] 19, p. 244 Coll.; Maximus Tyr. 11, 10e v.l. [for σάρκινος]; ParJer 6:6 τῷ σαρκικῷ οἴκῳ [cp. Mel., P. 55, 402 Ch. τοῦ σαρκίνου οἴκου, but σαρκικοῦ B]; Just., Tat.—σαρκικός means 'belonging to the σάρξ' [opp. πνευματικός], 'fleshly'; on the other hand, σάρκινος is 'consisting/composed of flesh', 'fleshy'. Our lit., or at least its copyists, for the most part did not observe this distinction in all occurrences of the word. The forms are generally interchanged in the tradition; for exceptions s. MParsons, NTS 34, '88, 151–55; s. also B-D-F §113, 2; Rob. 158f.)

❶ **pert. to being material or belonging to the physical realm, *material, physical, human, fleshly*—ⓐ** of everyday earthly things, τὰ σαρκικά in ref. to a collection for the poor in Jerusalem **Ro 15:27;** of material means of support **1 Cor 9:11.**

ⓑ of human physical being as such: Polycarp is σαρκικὸς καὶ πνευματικός, i.e. the physical aspect makes it possible to deal with visible phenomena and the spiritual contributes a special dimension to the encounter IPol 2:2. Jesus is called σαρκικός τε καὶ πνευματικός, γεννητὸς καὶ ἀγέννητος IEph 7:2. The Risen Lord συνέφαγεν αὐτοῖς (i.e. the disciples) ὡς σαρκικός *he ate with them as an ordinary human being would* ISm 3:3. ἵνα ἐκ νεκρῶν ἡμᾶς ἐγείρῃ σαρκικούς *that (Jesus Christ) might raise us mere humans from the dead* AcPlCor 2:6.—Sim. ἀγάπη σαρκική τε καὶ πνευματική ISm 13:2. ἕνωσις IMg 13:2. ἐπιμέλεια IPol 1:2. In all these pass. Ignatius expresses his understanding of a human being as consisting of two major parts: material body and inward endowment of spirit. Thus Ignatius's Christians function in two realms. This perspective is different (exc. for the reminiscence IEph 8:2 [s. 2]) from the qualitative judgments expressed in pass. in 2 in which σ. and πνευματικός are in opposition.

❷ **pert. to being human at a disappointing level of behavior or characteristics, *(merely) human.*** Old Testament perspectives respecting the fragility of bodily existence are assumed in our lit., but with a heightening of contrast between the physical and spiritual state or condition and with focus on the physical as being quite mediocre, transitory, or sinful *earthly, mediocre, merely human, worldly* (Anth. Pal. 1, 107; Iren. 1, 6, 3 [Harv. I 56, 2]; Orig., C. Cels. 3, 42, 11; Hippol., Ref. 5, 8, 18; Did., Gen. 62, 3): (ἄνθρωποι) σ. **1 Cor 3:4 v.l.;** ὅπλα **2 Cor 10:4.** σοφία **1:12.** αἱ σαρκικαὶ ἐπιθυμίαι **1 Pt 2:11;** αἱ σαρκικαὶ καὶ σωματικαὶ ἐπιθυμίαι D 1:4. Of immature Christians σαρκικοί ἐστε **1 Cor 3:3ab.** In what appears to be a reminiscence of 2 Cor 2:14–3:3 (s. also Ro 8:5), of dissidents or schismatics in contrast to orthodox believers οἱ σαρκικοὶ τὰ πνευματικὰ πράσσειν οὐ δύνανται, οὐδὲ οἱ πνευματικοὶ τὰ σαρκικά IEph 8:2.—In addition, σαρκικός is found as **v.l.** (σάρκινος is in the text, as Maximus Tyr. 11, 10f; Philo, Sacr. Abel. 63) in **Ro 7:14; 1 Cor 3:1; Hb 7:16;** in all three places the v.l. is the rdg. of the t.r.—S. lit. s.v. σάρξ. DELG s.v. σάρξ. M-M. TW. Spicq.

σαρκικῶς adv., **pert. to external aspect of conduct, *outwardly*** w. πνευματικῶς 'inwardly' IEph 10:3 (σαρκικός 1b).

σάρκινος, η, ον (since Eupolis Com. [V BC] 387; Pla.; PLond III, 1177, 169; 172 p. 186 [II AD]; LXX, En, Philo.—Cp. σαρκικός).

❶ **pert. to being material or belonging to the physical realm, *material, physical, human, fleshly*** (Theocr., Id. 21, 66; Maximus Tyr. 17, 3f σῶμα; Artem. 2, 35 p. 132, 27) καρδία *a human* (opp. λιθίνη), i.e. a heart capable of feeling B 6: l4 (Ezk 11:19; 36:26); cp. **2 Cor 3:3.** νόμος ἐντολῆς σαρκίνης (opp. ζωῆς) *possessing any legal physical qualifications* (Goodsp.) **Hb 7:16.**—Things of flesh in contrast to the non-physical (Epict., App. D, 4 [p. 479f Sch.] εὐχόμενος θεοῖς αἴτει τὰ θεῖα, ὧν οὐδὲν σάρκινον κ. γήινον ψαύει πάθος 'when praying to the gods ask for divine things, which no physical or earthly longing can attain'; Maximus Tyr. 11, 10f; 29, 7g; Cass. Dio 38, 21, 3; Philo, Sacr. Abel. 63; Orig., C. Cels. 6, 70, 35 σ. θυσίαι; Did., Gen. 168, 4 w. γήϊνος; ὀφθαλμοί σ. Theoph. Ant. 1, 3 [p. 62, 9]) in imagery, of humans (TestJob 27:2 of Job as human and Satan as a πνεῦμα; 38:2; Hipparchus the Pythagorean in Stob. IV 980, 15 H. θνατοὶ κ. σάρκινοι; Iambl., Protr. 20 p. 104, 10 Pistelli; SibOr, fgm. 1, 1) **1 Cor 3:1** (opp. πνευματικός). From this mng. it is a short step to Paul's nuanced view of the human condition:

❷ **pert. to being human at a disappointing level of behavior or character, *(merely) human,*** in ref. to the state or condition of a human being, with focus on being weak, sinful, or transitory, in contrast to or in opposition to that which is spiritual: *human* **Ro 7:14.**—σάρκινος as v.l. (for σαρκικός) **2 Cor 1:12.**—DELG s.v. σάρξ. TW. Spicq.

σαρκίον, ου, τό dim. of σάρξ **a part or piece of a body, *piece of flesh, bit of flesh*** (Hippocr. et al.; M. Ant. 2, 2, 1; 2) of an entire body ('bit of flesh' Plut., Brut. 987 [8, 3]) κοινωνῆσαι τῷ ἁγίῳ (κοινωνέω 1bα) *to share some moments with his holy bit of flesh* MPol 17:1.—DELG s.v. σάρξ.

σαρκοφάγος, ον (σάρξ, φαγεῖν; Aristot. et al.; cp. EpArist 146; SibOr 2, 236) ***flesh-eating*** θηρία λεπτὰ σ. of worms ApcPt fgm. 2.

σαρκοφόρος, ον (σάρξ + φέρω via φόρος; Nicetas Eugen. 3, 319 Hercher; of humans SibOr 8, 222; of Christ 1, 325; Clem. of Alex., Strom. 5, 34, 1) ***flesh-bearing*** of Christ's appearing in true human form ὁμολογεῖν αὐτὸν (=κύριον) σαρκοφόρον *confess that he was clothed in flesh* (adj. or subst.) ISm 5:2.—Cp. forms s.v. φέρω in DELG p. 1190.

σάρξ, σαρκός, ἡ (Hom.+; 'flesh').—❶ **the material that covers the bones of a human or animal body, *flesh*** lit. **1 Cor 15:39abcd;** Hv 3, 10, 4; 3, 12, 1. The pl. (which denotes flesh in the mass [Lucian, Dial. Mort. 10, 5], whereas the sing. rather denotes the substance.—Herodas 4, 61; Gen 40:19; 1 Km 17:44; 4 Km 9:36; PsSol 4:19; TestJob 13:5; Philo; Jos., Ant. 12, 211; Just., A I, 26, 7; Mel., P. 52, 383; Ath. 34, 2) **Lk 24:39 v.l.; Rv 19:18, 21** (4 [6] Esdr [POxy 1010, 16] cannibalism out of hunger, sim. Mel., P. 52, 383; Quint. Smyrn. 11, 245: the σάρκες of the slain are food for the birds) B 10:4; metaph. **Rv 17:16.** It decays 1 Cl 25:3; cp. **Ac 2:31** (cp. 2a below). Normally gives forth an evil odor when burned MPol 15:2. W. bones (s. ὀστέον) 1 Cl 6:3 (Gen 2:23); **Lk 24:39; Eph 5:30 v.l.** (metaph.). Paul speaks of his illness as a σκόλοψ τῇ σαρκί (s. σκόλοψ) **2 Cor 12:7.** ἡ ἐν σαρκὶ περιτομή *the physical circumcision* (cp. Just., D. 10, 1 al.) **Ro 2:28;** cp. **Eph 2:11b; Col 2:13** (ἀκροβυστία 2); **Gal 6:13** (ἡ σάρξ=the flesh that is circumcised); B 9:4. Metaph.: the corrosion on the precious metals of the rich φάγεται τὰς σάρκας ὑμῶν ὡς πῦρ **Js 5:3.**—Ign. describes the elements of the Eucharist as σάρξ (or αἷμα) Ἰησοῦ Χριστοῦ IRo 7:3; IPhld 4; ISm 7:1. Also **J 6:51–56** urges that one must eat the flesh (and drink the blood) of the Human One or Son of Man (Just., A I, 66, 2; s. TPhilips, Die Verheissung der hl. Eucharistie nach Joh. 1922; Bultmann ad loc.; AWikenhauser '48, 105f).—His anti-Docetic position also leads Ign. to use the concept 'flesh (and blood) of

Christ' in other contexts as well ITr 8:1; IPhld 5:1.—For **Mt 16:17; Gal 1:16; Eph 6:12;** and **1 Cor 15:50** s. 3a.

❷ **the physical body as functioning entity, *body, physical body*—ⓐ** as substance and living entity (Aeschyl., Sept. 622: opp. νοῦς; Ex 30:32; 4 Km 6:30; TestAbr A 20 p. 103, 6 [Stone p. 54] πάντα τὰ μέλη τῆς σαρκός μου; w. καρδία or ψυχή Alex. Aphr., An. p. 98, 7–10 Br.; Ps 37:8; 62:2; Eccl 2:3; Ezk 11:19; 44:7 al.; Jos., Bell. 6, 47, Ant. 19, 325; Ar.15, 7) οὔτε ἡ σὰρξ αὐτοῦ εἶδεν διαφθοράν **Ac 2:31** (but s. 1). W. ψυχή 1 Cl 49:6 (Tat. 13:2 al.). W. καρδία **Ac 2:26** (Ps 15:9).—**Eph 5:29.** ἑόρακαν τὸ πρόσωπόν μου ἐν σαρκί *they have seen me face to face* **Col 2:1.** ἕως ἂν τὸν χριστὸν ἐν σαρκὶ ἴδῃ *before he had seen the Messiah in person* GJs 24:4 (cp. Lk 2:26). Opp. πνεῦμα (Ath. 31:3; PGM 5, 460 ἐπικαλοῦμαί σε τὸν κτίσαντα πᾶσαν σάρκα κ. πᾶν πνεῦμα) **1 Cor 5:5; 2 Cor 7:1; Col 2:5; 1 Pt 4:6;** Hm 3:1; 10, 2, 6; cp. AcPl Ant 13:17 (=Aa, I 237, 2; s. οἶδα); also in relation to Christ (though this is disputed) **J 6:63;** Hs 5, 6, 5–7; cp. **1 Ti 3:16.**—ἀσθένεια τῆς σαρκός *bodily ailment* **Gal 4:13;** s. vs. **14.** ἀσθενὴς τῇ σαρκί *weak in the body* Hs 9, 1, 2. ὁ ἀλγῶν σάρκα *the one who is ill in body* B 8:6. πάσχειν σαρκί **1 Pt 4:1b.** Cp. **2 Cor 7:5.** ἡ τῆς σαρκὸς καθαρότης *the purity of the body* **Hb 9:13** (opp. καθαρίζειν τὴν συνείδησιν vs. 14). σαρκὸς ἀπόθεσις ῥύπου **1 Pt 3:21** (s. ῥύπος 1). The σάρξ is raised fr. the dead (s. ParJer 6:9; Theoph. Ant. 1, 7 [74, 2]) 1 Cl 26:3; 2 Cl 9:1. ἀνάστασις σαρκός AcPlCor 1:12; 2:24 (σαρκὸς ἀνάστασιν Just., D. 80, 5); cp. ἀναστήσεσθε ἔχοντες ὑγιῆ τὴν σάρκα AcPlCor 2:32. Of the body of Christ during his earthly ministry **Eph 2:14** (JHart, The Enmity in His Flesh: Exp. 6th ser., 3, 1901, 135–41); **Hb 10:20; 1 Pt 3:18; 4:1a; 1J 4:2; 2J 7;** B 5:1, 10f; 6:7, 9; 7:5; 12:10; IEph 7:2; Pol 7:1; AcPlCor 2:6b. Married couples form μία σάρξ (Gen 2:24; s. Ath. 33, 2 τὴν σάρκα πρὸς σάρκα … κοινωνίαν.—GAicher, Mann u. Weib ein Fleisch: BZ 5, 1907, 159–65) **Mt 19:5f; Mk 10:8ab; 1 Cor 6:16; Eph 5:31** (on these passages, TBurkill, ZNW 62, '71, 115–20). δικαιώματα σαρκός behind 'all sorts of ceremonial washings' there are *regulations that concern the physical body* **Hb 9:10.**—On ὑποτάγητε τῷ ἐπισκόπῳ ὡς ὁ Χριστὸς τῷ πατρὶ κατὰ σάρκα IMg 13:2 s. Hdb. ad loc. and MRackl, Die Christologie des hl. Ignatius v. Ant. 1914, 228.—πνεῦμα δυνάμεως … ὁ θεὸς … κατέπεμψεν εἰς σάρκα τουτέστιν εἰς τὴν Μαρίαν *God sent a powerful spirit* (prob. a ref. to the kind of divine breath that brought the first human being to life [Gen 2:7]) *into flesh, that is, into Mary* AcPl Ha 8, 26=BMM recto 34; s. AcPlCor 1:14.

ⓑ as someth. with physical limitations, life here on earth (ApcEsdr 4:4 p. 28, 3 Tdf. σάρκα ἀνθρωπίνην φορῶ) θλῖψιν τῇ σαρκὶ ἕξουσιν **1 Cor 7:28.** Cp. **2 Cor 4:11; Col 1:24.** Of Christ τὸ σῶμα τῆς σαρκὸς αὐτοῦ *his body with its physical limitations* **Col 1:22;** cp. **2:11** and s. cα below (cp. En 102:5 τὸ σῶμα τῆς σαρκὸς ὑμῶν; 1QpHab 9:2; Orig., C. Cels. 6, 29, 25).—Of human life: ἀποδημεῖν τῆς σαρκός MPol 2:2 (s. ἀποδημέω). ἐπιμένειν ἐν τῇ σαρκί **Phil 1:24.** ζῆν ἐν σαρκί vs. **22; Gal 2:20.** ἐν σ. περιπατεῖν **2 Cor 10:3a.** ἐν σ. τυγχάνειν Dg 5:8a. ὄντος ἔτι ἐν σ. σου AcPlCor 1:6. τὸν ἐπίλοιπον ἐν σ. χρόνον **1 Pt 4:2.** ἡ ἐπιδημία τῆς σαρκὸς ταύτης *our sojourn in life* 2 Cl 5:5. ἐν τῇ σαρκί *in our earthly life* 8:2.

ⓒ as instrument of various actions or expressions.**—α.** In Paul's thought esp., all parts of the body constitute a totality known as σ. or *flesh,* which is dominated by sin to such a degree that wherever flesh is, all forms of sin are likew. present, and no good thing can live in the σάρξ **Ro 7:18** (cp. Philo, Gig. 29 αἴτιον δὲ τῆς ἀνεπιστημοσύνης μέγιστον ἡ σὰρξ καὶ ἡ πρὸς σάρκα οἰκείωσις; Sextus 317 ἀγαθὸν ἐν σαρκὶ μὴ ἐπιζήτει. The OT lays no stress on a necessary relationship betw. flesh as a substance, and sin. But for Epicurus the σάρξ is the bearer of sinful feelings and desires as well as the means of sensual enjoyment: Ep. in Plut., Mor. 135c; 1087bf; 1089e; 1096c αἱ τῆς σαρκὸς ἐπιθυμίαι. Also Diog. L. 10, 145. Likew. Plut. himself: Mor. 101b ταῖς τῆς σαρκὸς ἡδοναῖς; 672e; 688d; 734a; Ps.-Plut., Mor. 107f σαρκὶ καὶ τοῖς πάθεσι ταύτης; Maximus Tyr. 33, 7a. Cp. 4 Macc 7:18 τὰ τῆς σαρκὸς πάθη; Philo, Deus Imm. 143 σαρκὸς ἡδονή, Gig. 29; TestJud 19:4; TestZeb 9:7; ApcMos 25 [p. 14, 2 Tdf.] εἰς τὴν ἁμαρτίαν τῆς σαρκός); **Ro 6:19; 7:25** (opp. νοῦς); **8:3a, 4–9** (cp. Persius 2, 63 scelerata pulpa, which contaminates devotion to deity), **12f; Gal 5:13, 24; Col 2:23; Jd 23;** AcPlCor 2:11, 15; Dg 6:5 (opp. ψυχή, as Plut., Mor. 101b). Opp. τὸ πνεῦμα **Ro 8:4, 5, 6, 9, 13; Gal 3:3; 5:16, 17ab; 6:8ab; J 3:6;** B 10:9. τὸ μὲν πνεῦμα πρόθυμον, ἡ δὲ σὰρξ ἀσθενής (cp. Orig., C. Cels. 2, 25, 8) **Mt 26:41; Mk 14:38;** Pol 7:2. σὰρξ ἁμαρτίας *sinful flesh* **Ro 8:3b.** ἐπιθυμία (τῆς) σαρκός (cp. Maximus Tyr. 20, 9f σαρκῶν … ἐπιθυμίας) **Gal 5:16; 1J 2:16;** B 10:9. Pl. **Eph 2:3a,** cp. **b; 2 Pt 2:18;** cp. **Ro 13:14.** τὰ ἔργα τῆς σαρκός **Gal 5:19** (s. Vögtle at πλεονεξία). τὰ θελήματα τῆς σαρκός **Eph 2:3b.** ὁ νοῦς τῆς σαρκός **Col 2:18.** τὸ σῶμα τῆς σαρκός *the body of (sinful)* flesh **2:11;** cp. 1:22 and s. b above (cp. Sir 23:17 σῶμα σαρκὸς αὐτοῦ; En 102:5 τῷ σώματι τῆς σαρκὸς ὑμῶν). τὰ τῆς σαρκός *what pertains to (sinful) flesh* **Ro 8:5b.** ἐν (τῇ) σαρκὶ εἶναι *be in an unregenerate* (and sinful) *state* **Ro 7:5; 8:8f.** τὰ ἔθνη ἐν σαρκί **Eph 2:11a.** κατὰ σάρκα εἶναι **Ro 8:5a;** ζῆν vs. **12b; 13;** Dg 5:8b; περιπατεῖν **Ro 8:4; 2 Cor 10:2;** βουλεύεσθαι **1:17;** στρατεύεσθαι **10:3b;** cp. IRo 8:3 (opp. κατὰ γνώμην θεοῦ).

β. source of the sexual urge. The σάρξ is the source of the sexual urge, without any suggestion of sinfulness connected w. it ἐκ θελήματος σαρκὸς ἐγεννήθησαν **J 1:13.**

ⓓ as someth. attractive **2 Pt 2:10** (a Hebraism, cp. Judg 2:12; 3 Km 11:10; Sir 46:10). S. also 3b.

❸ **one who is or becomes a physical being, *living being with flesh*—ⓐ** of humans *person, human being:* πᾶσα σάρξ *every person, everyone* (LXX; TestAbr B 7 p. 112, 3 [Stone p. 72]; GrBar 4:10; ApcEsdr 7:7; ApcMos 13 [p. 7, 1 Tdf.]; Mel., P. 55, 400: for כָּל־בָּשָׂר; s. πᾶς 1aα) **Lk 3:6** (Is 40:5); **J 17:2; Ac 2:17** (Jo 3:1); **1 Pt 1:24** (Is 40:6); 1 Cl 59:3; 64; 2 Cl 7:6; 17:5 (the last two Is 66:24); AcPlCor 2:6a. οὐ πᾶσα σάρξ *no person, nobody* (En 14:21 end.—W-S. §26, 10a; B-D-F §275, 4; 302, 1; Rob. 752) **Mt 24:22; Mk 13:20; Ro 3:20** (cp. Ps 142:2 πᾶς ζῶν); **1 Cor 1:29** (μή); **Gal 2:16.**—Though σ. in the foll. passages refers to body in its physical aspect, it cannot be divorced from its conjunction with αἷμα, and the unit σὰρξ καὶ αἷμα (cp. Sir 17:31; TestAbr B 13 p. 117, 26 [Stone p. 82]; Philo, Quis Div. Rer. Her. 57; Just., D. 135, 6) refers to *a human being* in contrast to God and other transcendent beings **Mt 16:17; Gal 1:16; Eph 6:12** (here vice versa, αἷ. καὶ σ.). τὰ παιδία κεκοινώνηκεν αἵματος καὶ σαρκός *the children share mortal nature* **Hb 2:14,** but with suggestion of its frailty, as indicated by the context with its ref. to death. Because they are the opposites of the divine nature σὰρξ καὶ αἷμα βασιλείαν θεοῦ κληρονομῆσαι οὐ δύναται **1 Cor 15:50** (JJeremias, NTS 2, '56, 151–59). For **Jd 7** s. b next. Cp. AcPl Ant 13, 17 (=Aa I 237, 2) σαρκί *personally* (s. οἶδα 2).

ⓑ of transcendent entities ὁ λόγος σὰρξ ἐγένετο **J 1:14** (RSeeberg, Festgabe AvHarnack dargebracht 1921, 263–81.—Artem. 2, 35 p. 132, 27 ἐὰν σάρκινοι οἱ θεοὶ φαίνωνται; Synes., Dio 6 p. 45b).—Of flesh other than human: ὀπίσω σαρκὸς ἑτέρας *after another kind of flesh* (cp. Judg 2:12 ὀπίσω θεῶν ἑτέρων) i.e. of divine messengers who take on σ. when they appear to humans (so Windisch et al.; difft. Frame et al. of same-sex activity) **Jd 7.**

❹ **human/ancestral connection, *human/mortal nature, earthly descent*** (Did., Gen. 144, 25) Ἀβραὰμ τὸν προπάτορα ἡμῶν κατὰ σάρκα **Ro 4:1** (Just., D. 43, 7 al.). οἱ συγγενεῖς μου κατὰ σάρκα **9:3.** τοὺς τῆς σαρκὸς ἡμῶν πατέρας **Hb 12:9.** τὸν Ἰσραὴλ κατὰ σάρκα *the earthly Israel* **1 Cor 10:18** (opp. τὸν Ἰσραὴλ τοῦ θεοῦ Gal 6:16). Of natural descent τὰ τέκνα τῆς σαρκός *children by natural descent* **Ro 9:8** (opp. τὰ τέκνα τῆς ἐπαγγελίας). ὁ μὲν ἐκ τῆς παιδίσκης κατὰ σάρκα γεγέννηται **Gal 4:23;** cp. vs. **29.** μου τὴν σάρκα *my compatriots* **Ro 11:14** (s. Gen 37:27).—Of Christ's physical nature **Ro 8:3c; Hb 5:7.** Christ is descended fr. the patriarchs and fr. David (τὸ) κατὰ σάρκα *according to the human side of his nature, as far as his physical descent is concerned* **Ro 1:3** (JDunn, Jesus: Flesh and Spirit [Ro 1:3f], JTS 24, '73, 40–68); **9:5;** 1 Cl 32:2; IEph 20:2. The context of **2 Cor 11:18** includes ancestry as a reason for boasting, but σ. in this pass. applies as well to other aspects of Paul's career and therefore belongs more properly in 5.

❺ **the outward side of life** as determined by normal perspectives or standards, a transf. sense of 1 and 2. Usually w. κατά indicating norm or standard σοφοὶ κατὰ σάρκα *wise (people) according to human standards* **1 Cor 1:26.** καυχᾶσθαι κατὰ (τὴν) σάρκα *boast of one's outward circumstances,* i.e. descent, manner of life, etc. (cp. 11:22) **2 Cor 11:18.** κατὰ σάρκα Χριστόν *Christ (the Messiah) from a human point of view* or *as far as externals are concerned* **5:16b,** cp. **a** (κατά B5bβ and 7a; also VWeber, BZ 2, 1904, 178–88; HWindisch, exc. ad loc.; Rtzst., Mysterienrel.[3], 374–76; FPorter, Does Paul Claim to Have Known the Historical Jesus [2 Cor 5:16]?: JBL 47, 1928, 257–75; RMoxon, CQR 108, 1929, 320–28). οἱ κατὰ σάρκα κύριοι *those who, according to human standards, are masters* **Eph 6:5; Col 3:22.** ὑμεῖς κατὰ τὴν σ. κρίνετε *you judge by outward things, by externals* **J 8:15.** Of the route taken in one's earthly life ἡ ὁδὸς ἡ κατὰ σάρκα IRo 9:3.—ἐν σαρκὶ πεποιθέναι *place one's trust in earthly things* or *physical advantages* **Phil 3:3f.** εὐπροσωπῆσαι ἐν σαρκί **Gal 6:12.** Onesimus is a beloved brother to Philemon καὶ ἐν σαρκὶ καὶ ἐν κυρίῳ *both as a human being* (=*personally,* in the external relationship betw. master and slave) *and as a Christian* **Phlm 16.** ὑμῶν δὲ ἐν σαρκὶ ἐπισκόπῳ IEph 1:3 (cp. IMg 3:2).—HWindisch, Taufe u. Sünde 1908; EBurton, ICC Gal. 1920, 492–95; WSchauf, Sarx 1924; WBieder, Auferstehung des Fleisches od. des Leibes?: TZ 1, '45, 105–20. W. special ref. to Paul: Ltzm., Hdb. exc. on Ro 7:14 and 8:11; Lohmeyer (ἁμαρτία 3a); EKäsemann, Leib u. Leib Christi '33; RGrant, ATR 22, '40, 199–203; RBultmann, Theologie des NTs '48, 228–49 (Engl. tr. by KGrobel, '51 I, 227–59); LMarshall, Challenge of NT Ethics '47, 267–70; E Schweizer, Die hellenist. Komponente im NT sarx-Begriff: ZNW 48, '57, 237–53; two in KStendahl, The Scrolls and the NT, '57: KKuhn, 94–113 and WDavies, 157–82; JPryke, 'Spirit' and 'Flesh' in Qumran and NT: RevQ 5, '65, 346–60; DLys, La chair dans l'AT '67; ASand, D. Begriff 'Fleisch' '67 (Paul); RJewett, Paul's Anthropological Terms '71, 49–166. On Ign.: CRichardson, The Christianity of Ign. of Ant. '35, esp. 49 and 61. S. also the lit. s.v. πνεῦμα, end.—B. 202. DELG. M-M. EDNT. TW. Spicq. Sv.

σάρος, ου, ὁ (a rare masc. [Hesych.] for the usual neut. σάρον. The gender cannot be determined in SIG 1169, 48 σάρῳ τινὶ ἀποκαθαίρειν and Anth. Pal. 11, 207, 4 σάρον acc.) ***broom*** Hs 9, 10, 3.

Σαρούχ v.l. for Σερούχ (q.v.).

σαρόω (later form for σαίρω via σάρον; censured by Phryn., see Lob.) 1 aor. ἐσάρωσα. Pass.: 1 aor. ἐσαρώθην; pf. ptc. σεσαρωμένος **to sweep by using a broom, *sweep*** (so Artem. 2, 33; Apollon. Dysc. p. 253, 7; Geopon. 14, 6, 5; PGiss 11, 19 [II AD]) τὶ *someth.* **Lk 15:8.** Pass. (cp. Sb 8000, 17 [III AD] συνσαρωθῆναι καὶ ῥανθῆναι τὸν οἶκον) **Mt 12:44; Lk 11:25:** Hs 9, 10, 2. Abs. Hs 9, 10, 3 (Leutzsch, Hermas p. 487 n. 313).—B. 580. DELG s.v. 1 σαίρω.

Σάρρα, ας, ἡ (שָׂרָה Gen 17:15; declined as in LXX, TestAbr; TestLevi 6:8; JosAs 1:8; Joseph., Just.; B-D-F §40; Mlt-H. 144) ***Sarah,*** wife of Abraham, mother of Isaac **Ro 4:19; 9:9** (cp. Gen 18:10); **Hb 11:11; 1 Pt 3:6;** GJs 2:4.—BHHW III 1670. M-M.

Σαρ(ρ)ων, ωνος, ὁ (שָׁרוֹן Is 33:9.—The accent cannot be determined, though it was probably on the second syllable, as in Hebr. Further, the form may be indecl. B-D-F §56, 2; Mlt-H. 149) ***Sharon,*** a plain along the coast of Palestine fr. Joppa to Caesarea. **Ac 9:35** (v.l. Ἀσσάρων).

σατάν, ὁ indecl. and **σατανᾶς , ᾶ, ὁ** (the former=Hebr. שָׂטָן 3 Km 11:14; Just., D. 103, 5; the latter Sir 21:27, also TestSol 1:1 D al.; TestJob; Test12Patr; ApcMos 17; Just.=Aram. סָטָנָא; for σατανος **Lk 11:18** P[75] read σατανας) literally 'adversary', in our lit. only as title or name: ***(the) Satan,*** in a very special sense, the enemy of God and all of those who belong to God, simply ***Satan, the Enemy*** (on the concept of Satan s. the lit. s.v. διάβολος 2), almost always w. the art. (B-D-F §254, 1), without it only in **Mk 3:23; Lk 22:3; 2 Cor 12:7** and in personal address.—**Mt 4:10** (here, as well as in the two passages from Mt and Mk near the end of this entry, without the art. and in the voc.); **Mk 1:13; 3:26; Lk 11:18; 22:31.** W. διάβολος of the same being **Rv 20:2;** cp. **2:9f;** Pol 7:1 (Just., A I, 28, 1 al.). The Lawless One (Antichrist) appears κατ' ἐνέργειαν τοῦ σατανᾶ **2 Th 2:9.** He incites people to evil (cp. Homeric usage LfgrE s.v. δαιμόνι[ος] col. 198; TestJob 41:5 Ἐλίους ἐμπνευσθεὶς ἐν τῷ Σ. ; 23:11 ὁ Σ. . . . ἐπλαγίαζεν αὐτῆς τὴν καρδίαν; cp. 26:6) **Mk 4:15; Ac 5:3; 1 Cor 7:5; 2 Cor 2:11; Rv 12:9.** Esp. guilty of instigating Judas' evil deed by entering into this disciple **Lk 22:3; J 13:27.** Causing sickness **Lk 13:16** (s. δέω 1b, end). Hence driven out in healings **Mt 12:26; Mk 3:23.** Hindering the apostle in his work **1 Th 2:18** (cp. Julian., Ep. 40 [68] p. 46, 19 Bidez-Cumont εἰ μή τι δαιμόνιον γένοιτο κώλυμα). Causing false beliefs to arise **1 Ti 5:15;** hence the one who denies the resurrection and judgment is called πρωτότοκος τοῦ σ. Pol 7:1; Polycarp uses the same expr. in speaking of Marcion, Epil Mosq 3. Persecutions of Christians are also inspired by Satan **Rv 2:13ab** (on the θρόνος τοῦ σ. s. θρόνος 1bε); hence certain Judeans who were hostile to Christians are called συναγωγὴ τοῦ σ. **Rv 2:9; 3:9.** God will crush him **Ro 16:20.** Jesus saw Satan falling (or fallen) fr. heaven **Lk 10:18** (Burton, Moods and Tenses §146 [deZwaan §148]; FSpitta, ZNW 9, 1908, 160–63; CWebster, ET 57, '45/46, 52f: πεσ. is timeless and means 'I watched him fall'). Imprisoned, but freed again after a thousand years **Rv 20:7.** ὁ σ. μετασχηματίζεται εἰς ἄγγελον φωτός *Satan disguises himself as an angel of light* **2 Cor 11:14** (TestJob 6:4 μετασχηματισθεὶς εἰς ἐπαίτην a beggar; ApcMos 17 ἐγένετο ἐν εἴδει ἀγγέλου; s. μετασχηματίζω; on the subject s. Windisch ad loc.). ἄγγελος σατανᾶ **2 Cor 12:7** (UHeckel, ZNW 84, '93, 69–75); ἄγγελοι τοῦ σ. B 18:1 (ἄγγελος 2c). αἱ δυνάμεις τοῦ σ. IEph 13:1 (δύναμις 5). τὰ βαθέα τοῦ σ. **Rv 2:24** (s. βαθύς 2). ἡ ἐξουσία τοῦ σ. *the power of Satan* **Ac 26:18; ending of Mk** in the **Freer ms.** ln. 6 (ἐξουσία 2); ibid. ln. 2 ὁ αἰὼν οὗτος . . . ὑπὸ τὸν σ. ἐστιν.—παραδοῦναί τινα τῷ σ. **1 Cor 5:5** (s. ὄλεθρος; cp. the Christ. ins New Docs 3, 83); **1 Ti 1:20** (s. on both passages παραδίδωμι 1b).—In **Mt 16:23; Mk 8:33** Peter is called Satan by Jesus, because his attempt to turn Jesus aside fr.

his divine assignment to accept the consequences of his involvement with humanity has made him a tempter of a diabolical sort, who might thwart the divine plan of salvation. This metaph. usage relates to the striking verdict **Rv 2:9; 3:9** above (cp. διάβολος J 6:70; 8:44).—BNoack, Satanás u. Sotería '48. DDD 1369–80 (lit.). DBS XII 1–47. DNP III 269. DELG. M-M. EDNT. TRE III 608f. TW.

σάτον, ου, τό (Aram. סָאתָא=Hebr. סְאָה.—Hg 2:16; Jos., Ant. 9, 85 ἰσχύει τὸ σάτον μόδιον καὶ ἥμισυ Ἰταλικόν) **a Hebrew dry measure holding about thirteen liters,** ***a seah, a thirteen-liter measure*** (1/30 of a κόρος; s. Joseph. above; also s. μόδιος). ἀλεύρου σάτα τρία *three measures of flour = about thirty-five liters* or *about a bushel of flour,* implying an astonishing baking operation **Mt 13:33; Lk 13:21.** On estimating the size of the measure s. Billerb. I 669f; PYadin p. 69 note.—TRE III 609f M-M.

Σαῦλος, ου, ὁ *Saul,* Grecized form of שָׁאוּל (Joseph. mentions several Judeans w. this name; s. index s.v. Σαοῦλος), the Hebrew name of the Apostle Paul (s. Παῦλος 2 and Σαούλ) **Ac 7:58; 8:1, 3; 9:1, 8, 11, 22, 24; 11:25, 30; 12:25; 13:1f, 7, 9; 22:7** D (Σαῦλε); **26:14 v.l.** (Σαῦλε).—M-M.

σαφῶς (Hom. [σαφέως]+; ins, pap, LXX; TestSol 4:2 D; Philo; Jos., Bell. 2, 104 σ. ἐπίσταμαι, Ant. 4, 41) adv. of σαφής (comp. σαφέστερον Just., A I, 35, 2) **pert. to high degree of exactitude,** ***clearly, exactly, very well*** εἰδέναι (Pla., Ep. 6, 323d, Ep. 7, 324a; Diod. S. 19, 9, 2; Appian, Bell. Civ. 3, 82 §335; PCairZen 110, 12 [257 BC]) 1 Cl 62:3; PtK 3 p. 15, 26. μανθάνειν (Menand., Epitr. 332 S. [156 Kö.]; Mitt-Wilck. I/2, 6, 4) Dg 11:2. (W. ἐπιμελῶς) πυνθάνεσθαι (Menand., Epitr. 877 S. [557 Kö.]) Dg 1.—DELG s.v. σάφα.

σβέννυμι fut. σβέσω; 1 aor. ἔσβεσα, inf. σβέσαι. Pass.: 1 fut. σβεσθήσομαι; 1 aor. ἐσβέσθην LXX; pf. ptc pl. ἐσβεσμένοι 3 Macc. 6:34 (Hom. et al.; Sb 7033, 46; 67; LXX; TestJob 43:5; TestLevi 4:1; Ar. 5, 3; Just., D. 93, 1; Mel., P. 82, 614; Ath., R. 20 p. 73, 11) **to cause an action, state, or faculty to cease to function or exist,** ***quench, put out***

ⓐ lit. ***extinguish, put out*** τὶ *someth.*, fire (Jos., Bell. 7, 405) **Hb 11:34.** In imagery, fiery arrows **Eph 6:16;** a smoldering wick **Mt 12:20** (Is 42:3). Pass. *be extinguished, be put out, go out* (Artem. 2, 9; Pr 13:9; Philo, Leg. All. 1, 46; TestLevi 4:1) of lamps (s. TestJob 43:5 λύχνος … σβεσθείς; PGM 7, 364 σβέσας τὸν λύχνον; Musaeus, Hero and Leander 338) **Mt 25:8.** Cp. D 16:1. Of a pyre μετ' ὀλίγον σβεννύμενον MPol 11:2. Of the fire of hell, that οὐ σβέννυται (Is 66:24) **Mk 9:44, 46, 48;** 2 Cl 7:6; 17:5; μηδέποτε σβεννύμενον πῦρ MPol 2:3.

ⓑ fig. ext. of a, ***quench, stifle, suppress*** (Il. 9, 678 χόλον; epigram in praise of Apollonius of Tyana: New Docs 3, no. 15, 2 [III/IV AD] ἀμπλακίας 'faults'; Pla., Leg. 8, 835d ὕβριν; 10, 888a τὸν θυμόν; Herm. Wr. 12, 6; SSol 8:7 τὴν ἀγάπην; 4 Macc 16:4 τὰ πάθη; Jos., Bell. 6, 31 τ. χαράν, Ant. 11, 40; Just., D. 93, 1 τὰς φυσικὰς ἐννοίας) τὸ πνεῦμα μὴ σβέννυτε **1 Th 5:19** (Plut., Mor. 402b τοῦ πνεύματος ἀπεσβεσμένου; Ps.-Plut., Hom. 127 τὸ πνεῦμα τὸ κατασβεννύμενον).—DELG. M-M. TW. Spicq.

σέ s. σύ.

σεαυτοῦ (not σαυτοῦ [so Jos., Ant. 18, 336; Tat. 25, 1], B-D-F §31, 1 and 64, 1; Mlt-H. 180f; Rob. 287), **ῆς** (Alcaeus [c. 600 BC] et al.; pap, LXX, En, JosAs; ParJer 6:6; EpArist, Just., Tat.) reflexive pron. of the second pers. sing. (Kühner-Bl. I 596ff; B-D-F §283; W-S. §22, 11; Rob. 687–90) used only in the gen., dat., and acc. (on the replacement of σεαυτοῦ by ἑαυτοῦ s. ἑαυτοῦ 1b) ***yourself***

ⓐ gen. **Mt 18:16 v.l.; J 1:22; 8:13; 9:17** א* P[75] (EBammel, NTS 40, '94, 455f); **2 Ti 4:11;** Hv 3, 6, 7; m 1:2.

ⓑ dat. **J 17:5; Ac 9:34; 16:28; Ro 2:5;** Hm 3:5; 9:1b; 12, 3, 5f. Also λογίζεσθαι ἐν σεαυτῷ Hs 9, 2, 6 (a Semitism, cp. TestJob 2:3; Leutzsch, Hermas 486 n. 290).

ⓒ acc. **Mt 4:6; 8:4; Mk 1:44; Lk 5:14; Ro 2:21; Gal 6:1; 1 Ti 4:16b;** B 19:3; Dg 2:1; Hm 9:8.—On the quot. fr. Lev 19:18: **Mt 19:19; 22:39; Mk 12:31; Lk 10:27;** D 1:2, cp. Appian, Bell. Civ. 3, 75 §305: Pansa says to Octavian ἐγὼ τῷ σῷ πατρὶ φίλος ἦν ὡς ἐμαυτῷ; Vi. Aesopi W 31 P.: θέλω (q.v. 3b=love) αὐτὴν (his wife) ὡς ἐμαυτόν=ed. Eberh. I c. 8 p. 247, 1 ταύτην ὡς ἐμαυτὸν στέργω.—M-M.

σεβάζομαι (σέβας 'reverential awe'; s. four next entries; dep. (Hom. et al.) 1 aor. ἐσεβάσθην; =σέβομαι **to show reverence to,** ***worship*** (Orph., Argon. 550; oracular saying in Eus., PE 9, 10, 4 σεβαζόμενοι θεὸν ἁγνῶς; Ar. 12, 7 [of certain polytheists ἐσεβάσθησαν πρόβατον; cp. Hos 10:5 Aq.]) 1 aor. pass. in act. sense (JosAs 12:6 σεβασθεῖσα εἴδωλα νεκρὰ καὶ κωφά; SibOr 5, 405; 8, 46; s. Aristid. above) ἐσεβάσθησαν καὶ ἐλάτρευσαν τῇ κτίσει παρὰ τὸν κτίσαντα **Ro 1:25.**—DELG s.v. σέβομαι II. M-M. TW.

σέβασμα, ατος, τό (σεβάζομαι) **someth. that relates to devotional activity,** ***devotional object*** (so Dionys. Hal. 1, 30; Wsd 14:20; 15:17; Bel 27 Theod.; Jos., Ant. 18, 344; SibOr 8, 57; Ps.-Clem., Hom. 10, 21 and 22; Ar.) w. θεός **2 Th 2:4.** Pl. (ViEzk 2 [p. 74, 8 Sch.=Torrey 23, 1f] ἐπὶ εἰδώλων σεβάσμασι) τὰ σεβάσματα **Ac 17:23.** The pl. together with the verb ἀναθεωρέω refers to the total visual impact of a city full of cultic monuments.—DELG s.v. σέβομαι II. M-M. TW.

σεβάσμιος, ον (σεβάζομαι; Plut.; Vett. Val. 221, 23; Lucian; Herodian; Jos., Bell. 4, 164, Ant. 18, 349; ins; oft. used w. ὅρκος in the pap) **worthy of veneration,** ***honorable*** (w. πανάρετος) πολιτεία 1 Cl 2:8.—DELG s.v. σέβομαι II.

σεβαστός, ή, όν (σεβάζομαι; Dionys. Hal. 2, 75; SIG 820, 6; pap, Philo, Joseph.; loanw. in rabb.) **worthy of reverence,** ***revered, august,*** as a transl. of Lat. Augustus and designation of the Roman emperor (Paus. 3, 11, 4 τὸ δὲ ὄνομα εἶναι τούτῳ Αὔγουστος, ὃ κατὰ γλῶσσαν δύναται τὴν Ἑλλήνων σεβαστός=his name is Augustus, which in Gk. is rendered by σεβαστός; Strabo 3, 3, 8; 12, 13, 14; Lucian, Herodian, Philo; Jos., Ant. 16, 173 al.; CIA III 63 [27 BC] ἱερεὺς θεᾶς Ῥώμης καὶ Σεβαστοῦ σωτῆρος; IG XII/3, 174 [6 BC]; pap. As epithet of Antonius Pius, Ar. ins; Just., A I, ins—EBréhier, ByzZ 15, 1906, 161f; 164f; Hahn 116f; Dssm., LO 306 [LAE 358ff]; HDieckmann, Kaisernamen u. Kaiserbez. bei Lukas: ZKT 43, 1919, 213–34; Goodsp., Probs. 136f) ὁ Σεβαστός *His Majesty the Emperor* **Ac 25:21, 25** (of Nero).—In σπεῖρα Σεβαστή **27:1** (cp. OGI 421), Σεβαστή is likew. an exact transl. of Lat. Augusta, an honorary title freq. given to auxiliary troops (Ptolem. renders it Σεβαστή in connection w. three legions that bore it: 2, 3, 30; 2, 9, 18; 4, 3, 30) *imperial cohort,* but σπεῖρα Σεβαστή cannot be regarded as equivalent to σπεῖρα Σεβαστηνῶν.—For lit. s. on ἑκατοντάρχης.—DELG s.v. σέβομαι. M-M. TW.

σέβω (s. four prec. entries)—**❶ to express in gestures, rites, or ceremonies one's allegiance or devotion to deity,** ***worship***

ⓐ act. (since Pind.) *worship* (X., Mem. 4, 4, 19 θεοὺς σέβειν; Epict. 3, 7, 26 θεὸν σέβειν; POxy 1464, 5; Philo, Virt. 34; Just., Tat.; Ath. 30, 1; Hippol., Ref. 1, preface 1; Orig., C. Cels. 3, 77,

7; on Hellenic view of respect for deity s. e.g. VLeinieks, the city of Dionysos '96, 243–56.—But τὴν ἀρετὴν σ. 5, 39, 14) θεὸν σέβειν Dg 3:2; cp. 2:7. Elsewh. always

ⓑ mid. (Hom.+; ins, pap, LXX, TestSol; TestJos 4:6; JosAs, Ar., Just.) ***worship*** (Pind.+; Pla., Phd. 251a ὡς θεὸν σέβεται, Leg. 11 p. 917b; X., Hell. 3, 4, 18; Diod. S. 1, 35, 6; 2, 59, 2 θεούς; Plut., Mor. 368 [44] σεβόμενοι τὸν Ἄνουβιν; SIG 611, 24 τοὺς θεούς; 557, 7 [207/206 BC] οἱ σεβόμενοι Ἀπόλλωνα; 559, 6; 560, 17; PTebt 59, 10 [I BC] σέβεσθαι τὸ ἱερόν; LXX; TestJos 4:6; JosAs; SibOr fgm. 1, 15; 3, 28; 30; EpArist 16 al.; Jos., Ant. 9, 205 εἴδωλα; 8, 192 θεούς; Ar. 2, 1 al.; Just., A I, 13, 1; 25, 1; Iren. 3, 12, 7 [Harv. II 60, 5]; τὸ πλῆθος ὧν σέβονται ζώων Αἰγύπτοι Theoph. Ant. 1, 10 [p. 80, 1]) w. the acc. of that which is worshiped **Mt 15:9; Mk 7:7** (both Is 29:13); **Ac 18:13; 19:27;** PtK 2.—σεβόμενοι τὸν θεόν *God-fearers, worshipers of God* is a term applied to former polytheists who accepted the ethical monotheism of Israel and attended the synagogue, but who did not obligate themselves to keep the whole Mosaic law; in particular, the males did not submit to circumcision (Jos., Ant. 14, 110 πάντων τῶν κατὰ τὴν οἰκουμένην Ἰουδαίων καὶ σεβομένων τὸν θεόν; RMarcus, The Sebomenoi in Josephus '52.—JBernays, Gesammelte Abhandlungen 1885 II 71–80; EvDobschütz, RE XVI 120f; Schürer III 161–71, Die Juden im Bosporanischen Reiche u. die Genossenschaften der σεβόμενοι θεὸν ὕψιστον: SBBerlAk 1897, 200–225; FCumont, Hypsistos: Suppl. à la Revue de l'instruction publ. en Belgique 1897; Dssm., LO 391f [LAE 451f]; Moore, Judaism I 323–53; JKlausner, From Jesus to Paul, tr. WStinespring, '43, 31–49; New Docs 3, 24f; 54f; GLüdemann, Early Christianity According to the Traditions in Acts '87, 155f; TCallan, CBQ 55, '93, 291–95). In our lit. it is limited to **Ac**, where the expr. takes various forms: σεβ. τὸν θεόν **16:14; 18:7.** Simply σεβ. **13:50; 17:4, 17.** Once σεβόμενοι προσήλυτοι **13:43;** s. φοβέω 2a and προσήλυτος; MWilcox, the 'God-Fearers' in Acts, A Reconsideration: JSNT 13, '81, 102–22 (emphasis on piety, not on a distinct group).—Of the worship of Christ by the faithful MPol 17:2b; cp. vs. 2a.

❷ **to have a reverent attitude toward human beings,** ***show reverence/respect for*** (Aeschyl. et al.; X., Cyr. 8, 8, 1 Κῦρον ὡς πατέρα, Hell. 7, 3, 12; Pla., Leg. 7, 813d; Polyb. 6, 39, 7; Chilon in Stob. III 116, 7 H. πρεσβύτερον σέβου; PSI 361, 9 [III BC] ὅσοι αὐτὸν σέβονται) πρεσβύτας σέβεσθαι Hm 8:10.—AMichels, ClJ 92, '97, 399–416 (on 'pius' and 'pietas' in Rom. lit.).—B. 1469. DELG s.v. σέβομαι. M-M s.v. σέβομαι. TW. S. θεοσεβής.

Σεγρί Hv 4, 2, 4 v.l. Late for Θεγρί.

Σειλέας s. Σιλᾶς.

σειρά, ᾶς, ἡ (Hom. [σειρή] et al.; SIG[2] 588, 200; LXX; TestSol 1:12 D; Jos., Ant. 3, 170) fr. the beginning w. the mng. **pliable length of someth. used for binding,** ***cord, rope, chain*** σειραῖς ζόφου *with chains of hell* (ζόφος 2. See also Wsd 17:16 μιᾷ ἁλύσει σκότους ἐδέθησαν; Pythag. in Diog. L. 8, 31: the ψυχαί ἀκάθαρτοι after their separation from the σῶμα are bound in hell by the Erinyes ἐν ἀρρήκτοις δεσμοῖς) **2 Pt 2:4** (s. σειρός and σιρός).—DELG. M-M.

σειρός: 2 Pt 2:4 v.l. σειροῖς, which is better spelled σιροῖς; s. σιρός.—DELG s.v. σιρός. M-M.

σεισμός, οῦ, ὁ (σείω; Eur. et al. in var. senses) **a violent shaking or commotion,** ***shock, agitation,*** in our lit. only of natural phenomena, w. the specific type qualified by context

ⓐ most commonly ***earthquake*** (Soph., Hdt.+; Diod. S. 25, 19 ed. Dindorf p. 351, ln. 17 σεισμὸς ἐγένετο δεινός, ὡς ὄρη διαστῆναι; SIG 505; 1116, 6; LXX; TestSol 6:10; ApcEsdr 3:11 p. 27, 21 Tdf.; Philo, Op. M. 59; Jos., Ant. 9, 225 σ. μέγας) **Mt 27:54; Ac 16:35** D; **Rv 11:13b.** Pl. in the account of the Messianic woes **Mt 24:7; Mk 13:8;** σεισμοὶ μεγάλοι **Lk 21:11** (cp. the σεισμοί seen in prospect Pherecyd. 18; Cat. Cod. Astr. VII 186, 8; 22; VIII/3, 174, 21; Boll 131). The σεισμός is accompanied by peals of thunder (Esth 1:1d; cp. Is 29:6) **Rv 8:5; 11:19.** σ. μέγας *a severe earthquake* (Lucian, M. Peregr. 39; Jer 10:22; Ezk 38:19) **Mt 28:2** (CWebster, ET 42, '31, 381f); **Ac 16:26; Rv 6:12; 11:13a; 16:18ab.**

ⓑ ***storm*** on a body of water, w. waves caused by high winds σεισμὸς μέγας ἐν τῇ θαλάσσῃ **Mt 8:24** (cp. vs. 26f where ἄνεμοι is found w. θάλ.; schol. on Pla. 25c τὸ τὸν σεισμὸν ποιοῦν πνεῦμα = ἄνεμος; Artem. 2, 38 σεισμὸς κ. ὄμβρος corresponds to 1, 73 p. 66, 7 χειμὼν κ. ὄμβ.; Diod. S. 26, 8 Rhodes is swallowed up by a σεισμός [as a result of a storm? or earthquake at sea?]; cp. σείω Maximus Tyr. 9, 6a; 11, 7h.—GBornkamm, D. Sturmstillg. im Mt: Jahrb. d. Theol. Schule Bethel '48, 49–54).—RAC V 1070–114; BHHW I 425.—DELG s.v. σείω. M-M. EDNT. TW.

σείω fut. σείσω. Pass.: fut. 3 sg. σεισθήσεται LXX; 1 aor. ἐσείσθην (s. σεισμός; Hom. et al.; pap, LXX, Philo; Jos., Ant. 4, 44) **to cause to be in a state of commotion,** ***shake, agitate.***

ⓐ lit. of things, esp. natural phenomena ***shake*** τὶ *someth.* τὴν γῆν, τὸν οὐρανόν **Hb 12:26** (Hg 2:6.—Cp. X., Hell. 4, 7, 4 ἔσεισεν ὁ θεός). Pass. of the earth *be shaken, quake* (Apollon. Rhod. 3, 864 σείετο γαῖα; DioChrys. 46 [63], 3; 80 [30], 11; cp. Vergil, Georg. 1, 475; Judg 5:4; 2 Km 22:8; Ps 67:9) **Mt 27:51;** ἡ γῆ πᾶσα ἐσείσθη GPt 6:21 (s. Jer 8:16; En 102:2; Jos., Ant. 15, 121.—Ps.-Callisth. 1, 12, 9: when Alexander touched the earth, σεισμὸς ἐγένετο, ὥστε τὸν πάντα κόσμον συγκινηθῆναι). Pass., of a tree that is shaken by the wind (s. SibOr 8, 297) **Rv 6:13.**—On the significance of earthquake in the Gk.-Rom. world s. RAC V 1070–1113.

ⓑ fig. ext. of a, ***stir up, set in motion;*** pass. (s. B-D-F §78) *be stirred* of a city, as a result of a striking event **Mt 21:10.** Of mental agitation (Philostrat., Vi. Soph. 2, 1, 11 ἐσείσθη τ. καρδίαν; Philo) *tremble* **28:4.** —B. 675. DELG. M-M. TW.

Σεκοῦνδος, ου, ὁ (Σέκουνδος is also permissible; B-D-F §41, 3; cp. Mlt-H. 59) a name of Latin origin (in the Gk. form e.g. OGI 481, 4, SIG 1063, 3; pap) ***Secundus*** a Christian of Thessalonica **Ac 20:4.**—LGPN I. M-M.

Σελεύκεια, ας, ἡ (less acceptable Σελευκία or Σελευκεία) ***Seleucia,*** the port city of Antioch in Syria (mentioned in Polyb. 5, 58, 4; Strabo 7, 5, 8 al.; ins; 1 Macc 11:8; Jos., Ant. 13, 221–23, C. Ap. 1, 207) **Ac 13:4.**—Kl. Pauly V 85; BHHW III 1764.

σελήνη, ης, ἡ (Hom.+) ***moon*** PtK 2 p. 14, 27 (twice). W. sun and stars (X., Mem. 4, 3, 4; SIG 1267, 18f; Jo 2:10; 4:15; EpJer 59; TestNapht 3:2; Ar. 3, 2; Just., D. 85, 5; Ath. 6, 3) **Lk 21:25; 1 Cor 15:41; Rv 6:12f; 8:12;** 1 Cl 20:3; B 15:5; Dg 7:2; IEph 19:2. W. the sun (Maximus Tyr. 40, 4h; oft. in LXX) **Rv 12:1; 21:23;** 2 Cl 14:1 (cp. ἥλιος, end). W. the stars (Ps 8:4) Dg 4:5. Darkened in the time of tribulation (s. Is 13:10; Ezk 32:7; Jo 2:10; 4:15) **Mt 24:29; Mk 13:24;** changed to blood **Ac 2:20** (Jo 3:4); cp. **Rv 6:12.**—WGrafBaudissin, RE XIII 337–49; ORühle, RGG IV 1930, 161–67 (lit.); Kl. Pauly III 1194–96; 1408f; RE XIII 337–49; BHHW II 1235f; RGG[3] IV 1094–97; DDD 1098–1113 (lit.).—B. 55. M-M. Sv.

σεληνιάζομαι (σελήνη; TestSol 10:35 C; Lucian; Vett. Val. 113, 10; Cat. Cod. Astr. VIII/1 p. 199, 7; Manetho, Apotel. 4, 81; 217, in both cases the act. as v.l. Prim. 'to be moonstruck') **to experience epileptic seizures,** ***be an epileptic*** (in the ancient world epileptic seizure was associated with transcendent powers of the moon; cp. Cat. Cod. Astr. IX/2 p. 156, 10f πρὸς ‹δὲ› δαιμονιζομένους, ἐπιληπτικοὺς καὶ σεληνιαζομένους) **Mt 17:15.** W. δαιμονίζεσθαι **4:24.**—RE IV 412, 25ff; BHHW II 1236.—DELG and M-M s.v. σελήνη.

Σεμεΐν (v.l. Σεμεΐ, Σεμεεί, Σεμείν), ὁ indecl. (שִׁמְעִי, freq. in the OT: Ex 6:17; Num 3:18; 2 Km 16:5; TestLevi 12:1 Σεμεΐ.—Joseph. has var. forms [s. index s.v. Σαμούις]) ***Semein,*** in the genealogy of Jesus **Lk 3:26.**

σεμίδαλις, εως, ἡ (since Hermippus Com. [V BC] 63, 22; Hippocr.; BGU 1067, 15; POxy 736, 82; PSI 580, 3; LXX; EpArist 92; Philo; Jos., Ant. 1, 197; 3, 235; Just.; loanw. in rabb., and prob. orig. a Semit. word; s. L-S-J-M s.v.) **a high-grade wheat flour,** ***flour of the best quality*** B 2:5 (Is 1:13). Cp. similae clarae mundae Papias (1:1 Lat.). W. oil and grain **Rv 18:13.**—DELG. M-M.

σεμνός, ή, όν (σέβομαι; Hom. Hymns+) **pert. to evoking special respect**

ⓐ of living entities—**α.** human beings ***worthy of respect/honor, noble, dignified, serious*** (ὁ σ. φιλόσοφος Orig., C. Cels. 4, 48, 21) of eccl. assistants **1 Ti 3:8.** Of aged men **Tit 2:2.** Of women (s. X., Mem. 1, 2, 24 and the ins in Ramsay, CB I/2, 656 no. 590) **1 Ti 3:11.** W. δίκαιος (Jos., Bell. 4, 319) and other good qualities Hs 8, 3, 8.

β. transcendent beings ***worthy of reverence, august, sublime, holy*** (fr. the beginning an epithet of divine beings; s. Sb 4094, 8 [I AD] ἡ σεμνὴ Ἶσις) ὁ σεμνότατος ἄγγελος *the most reverend angel* (of repentance) Hv 5:2 (SEG VIII, 550, 2 [I BC] Ἶσι σεμνοτάτη); m 5, 1, 7.

ⓑ of characteristics, states of being, and things ***honorable, worthy, venerable, holy, above reproach***—**α.** adj. (Maximus Tyr. 3, 5c νόμοι; Jos., C. Ap. 2, 221; Just., D. 3, 1 ἦθος) **Phil 4:8** (Lucian, Enc. Patr. 1 ὅσα σεμνὰ κ. θεῖα; cp. Cicero, Tusc. Disp. 5, 23 [67]). ἔργα (Philo, Sacr. Abel. 49) Hv 3, 8, 7 (w. ἁγνά [as EpArist 31] and θεῖα). ἐπιθυμία m 12, 1, 1 (w. ἀγαθή; cp. SibOr 5, 262). ἀγωγή 1 Cl 48:1 (w. ἁγνή). συνείδησις 1:3b (w. ἄμωμος and ἁγνή; missing in the ancient versions). κανών 7:2 (w. εὐκλεής). ὄνομα (2 Macc 8:15; Philo, Dec. 136) 1:1 (w. περιβόητον and ἀξιαγάπητον). πνεῦμα Hm 3:4 (w. ἀληθές). κλῆσις (Philo, Leg. ad Gai. 163) m 4, 3, 6 (w. μεγάλη). (On usage in Hermas s. Leutzsch 421 n. 386.)

β. the neut. as subst. (Demosth. 21, 126; BGU 1024 VIII, 7; Philo; Ath. 16, 1; 20, 3) τὸ σεμνὸν τῆς φιλαδελφίας ὑμῶν *the worthy character of your brotherly love* 1 Cl 47:5. Pl. (Menand., Mon. 336 Mei. [461 Jaekel]; Polyb. 15, 7, 6 τὰ σ. καὶ καλά; Philo, Aet. M. 77) μέτρια καὶ σεμνὰ νοεῖν *have moderate and seemly thoughts* 1 Cl 1:3a.—DELG s.v. σέβομαι III. M-M. TW. Spicq. Sv.

σεμνότης, τητος, ἡ (s. σεμνός; Eur., X., Pla. et al.; SIG 807, 8; OGI 567, 19; EpArist 5; 171; Philo; Tat. 34, 2; μεγαλόνοια καὶ σ. θεολογίας Orig., C. Cels. 6, 18, 21) **a manner or mode of behavior that indicates one is above what is ordinary and therefore worthy of special respect**

ⓐ of a human being ***dignity, seriousness, probity, holiness***=Lat. gravitas (Diod. S. 17, 34, 6; Philo; Jos., Vi. 258 μετὰ πάσης σ; Theoph. Ant. 3, 13 [p. 230, 16] περὶ σ. διδάσκειν; Did., Gen. 249, 14 σ. καὶ γνησιότης) **1 Ti 3:4;** 1 Cl 41:1; Hm 4, 1, 3. W. εὐσέβεια **1 Ti 2:2.** W. ἁγνεία Hm 4, 4, 3; s 5, 6, 5. W. ἁγνεία and other virtues m 6, 2, 3. W. ἁπλότης and ἀκακία v 3, 9, 1. W. other καλὰ ἔργα **Tit 2:7.** Loved by the Lord Hm 5, 2, 8; ἐνδύσασθαι τὴν σ. 2:4. Personified w. other virtues v 3, 8, 5; 7; 3, 9, 1.—Neg. reaction to σ. AcPl Ha 4, 14, prob. construed as arrogance by the crowd (cp. Soph., Ajax 1107 on neg. reaction to σέμνα ἔπη).

ⓑ of a deity ***holiness*** (cp. 2 Macc 3:12; Philo, Spec. Leg. 2, 7; Jos., C. Ap. 1, 225) πορεύεσθαι κατὰ τὴν σ. τοῦ θεοῦ *walk in accordance with God's holiness* Hv 3, 5, 1.—DELG s.v. σέβομαι III. RAC XII 752–79 s.v. gravitas. M-M. TW. Spicq.

σεμνῶς adv. of σεμνός (Aeschyl., X., Pla. et al.; ins, pap; 4 Macc 1:17; EpArist; Philo, Op. M. 12) **pert. to manner or mode of behavior that is extraordinary and therefore worthy of special respect,** ***honorably, worthily, in a manner above reproach*** διακονεῖν κτλ. Hv 3, 5, 1; cp. s 9, 25, 2 (both w. ἁγνῶς). W. καλῶς (Alex. Aphr., Eth. Probl. 21 p. 142, 9 Br.) Hs 9, 1, 2. τὰ κατὰ τὸν οἶκον σεμνῶς οἰκουργεῖν *you taught* (the women) *to manage their households with dignity* 1 Cl 1:3.

Σεπτέμβριος, ου, ὁ ***September,*** also used as an adj. (Dionys. Hal. 9, 67 περὶ τὰς καλάνδας τοῦ Σεπτεμβρίου μηνός; 6, 48 καλάνδαις Σεπτεμβρίαις; Plut., Publ. 104 [14, 6] εἰδοῖς Σεπτεμβρίαις. On the use of the Rom. calendar by Greeks s. Hahn 245; EBickerman, Chronology of the Ancient World[2], '80, 47–51) τῇ πρὸ ἐννέα καλανδῶν Σεπτεμβρίων *on the twenty-fourth of August* IRo 10:3.

Σέργιος, ου, ὁ ***Sergius,*** name of a Roman gens (in its Gk. form in Diod. S. 12, 24, 1; 12, 43, 1; 14, 19, 1; SIG 646, 16; pap): Σέργιος Παῦλος ἀνθύπατος *proconsul Sergius Paulus* **Ac 13:7.** Attempts to confirm the identity of this official through ins have not proved convincing (Hemer, Acts 109 n. 17; 166f n. 16). On the principal documents (IGR III, 930, but without the name Sergius, s. HDessau, ZNW 2, 1901, 83 n. 3; Groag, Pauly-W. VI [1909] 1781; for improved rdg. TMitford, ANRW II/7/2 [1980], 1301–4. SEG XX, 302, 10f K]οΐντου Σεργ|[ίου Παύλου ἀνθυπάτου----], which is placed in a restored rdg. under the reign of Gaius [Caligula], not Claudius, by Mitford p. 1300 n. 54 and 1330 n. 195. A terminal stone in the city of Rome CIL VI 31545 [=ILS 5926; s. Mommsen, ZNW 2, 1901, p. 83, 3] w. full name 'L. Sergius Paullus' but without ref. to Cyprus; two inscriptions fr. Pisidian Antioch [Ramsay, Bearing 150; 153f; GCheesman, JRS 3, 1913, 262]) s. Hemer above and Boffo, Iscrizioni 242–46.—TZahn, NKZ 15, 1904, 23–41; 189–200; Ramsay, Bearing 150–72; Cheesman, loc. cit. 253–66; AWikenhauser, Die AG 1921, 338–41; Kl. Pauly V 137; Haenchen p. 77 (Eng. tr. 64); DBS XII 693–99.—LGPN I. M-M.

Σερούχ, ὁ (also Σαρούχ) indecl. (שְׂרוּג; LXX.—Jos., Ant. 1, 148 has Σεροῦγος) ***Serug,*** son of Reu and father of Nahor (Gen 11:20–23; 1 Ch 1:26); in the genealogy of Jesus **Lk 3:35.**

σεσηπός s. σήπω.

Σήθ, ὁ indecl. (שֵׁת; LXX, ApcMos, Philo; TestBenj 10:6.—Joseph. has Σῆθος, ου [Ant. 1, 68]) ***Seth,*** son of Adam and Eve and father of Enos (Gen 4:25f; 5:3-8; 1 Ch 1:1; Sir 49:16); in the genealogy of Jesus **Lk 3:38.**—AKlijn, Seth in Jewish, Christian, and Gnostic Literature '77.

σηκός, οῦ, ὁ (Hom.+; ins, pap; 2 Macc 14:33; SibOr 3, 266; 281) prim. 'pen, enclosure', of birds ***nest*** (Aristot., HA 6, 8), also of humans ***burial-place, sepulcher, tomb*** (Simonides fgm. 5, 6 Diehl[2] [26, 6 Page] in Diod. S. 11, 11, 6; also Diod. S. 17, 71, 7). In the σηκός which the bird Phoenix prepared for itself 1 Cl 25:2f, the mngs. *nest* and *tomb* merge in striking imagery.—DELG.

Σήμ, ὁ indecl. (שֵׁם; LXX; TestBenj 10:6; Philo; Just., D. 139, 2ff.—Joseph. has Σήμας, ᾳ [Ant. 1, 143]) ***Shem,*** son of Noah and father of Arphaxad (Gen 5:32; 9:26f; 10:22; Sir 49:16); in the genealogy of Jesus **Lk 3:36.**—BHHW III 1769.

σημαίνω (σῆμα 'sign', s. three next entries; Hom.+; ins, pap, LXX, TestJob; JosAs 23:8; Just., Tat. 17, 2; Mel., P. 95, 728) impf. ἐσήμαινον; fut. σημανῶ LXX; 1 aor. ἐσήμανα (X., Hell. 1, 1, 2; BGU 1097, 17; Judg 7:21; s. B-D-F §72; Mlt-H. 214f); pf. 1 pl. σεσημάγκαμεν (Aristobul. in Eus., PE 13, 12, 7 [=Holladay p. 172, fgm. 4, lines 85f]). Pass.: aor. 3 sg. ἐσημάνθη LXX; pf. 3 sg. σεσήμανται 2 Macc 2:1.

➊ **to make known,** ***report, communicate*** (trag., Hdt.+; ins, pap., LXX, En; TestJob 6:3; EpArist; Philo, Post. Cai. 155 al.; Jos., Vi. 206; Just., D. 114, 2 al.) τὶ *someth.* indicate charges **Ac 25:27.** τινί *to someone* (En 106:13; 107, 2; TestJob 6:5) **Rv 1:1.**

➋ **to intimate someth. respecting the future,** ***indicate, suggest, intimate*** (Ezk. Trag. 83, in Eus., PE 9, 29, 6; Just., D. 78, 9 al.; cp. Appian, Liby. 104 §491 προσημαίνειν τὰ μέλλοντα of divine prediction of the future) w. acc. and inf. foll. (Jos., Ant. 6, 50; cp. 8, 409) **Ac 11:28.**—Also of speech that simply offers a vague suggestion of what is to happen (Heraclitus 93 in Plut., Mor. 404e w. ref. to the Delphic oracle οὔτε λέγει, οὔτε κρύπτει, ἀλλὰ σημαίνει; Epict. 1, 17, 18f; Jos., Ant. 7, 214; 10, 241) w. an indirect question foll. **J 12:33; 18:32; 21:19.**

➌ **to provide an explanation for someth. that is enigmatic,** ***mean, signify*** (Pla., Cratylus 393A; Aristot., Physics 213b, 30, Rhet. 32f; Dionys. Hal., Thucyd. 31) B 15:4, in ref. to a passage of Scripture (Just., A I, 65, 4 τὸ δὲ Ἀμὴν τῇ Ἑβραΐδι φωνῇ τὸ Γένοιτο σημαίνει) ἡ γὰρ ἡμέρα παρ' αὐτῷ σημαίνει χίλια ἔτη *for a day with the Lord means a thousand years* (s. Ps. 89:4).—DELG s.v. σῆμα. M-M. TW.

σημεῖον, ου, τό (s. prec. entry; Aeschyl., Hdt.+; ins, pap, LXX, pseudepigr., Philo, Joseph., apolog.; loanw. in rabb.; Hippol., Ref. 6, 27, 4; Did., Gen. 115, 9 'symbol'; gener. 'sign')

➊ **a sign or distinguishing mark whereby someth. is known,** ***sign, token, indication*** (Diod. S. 3, 66, 3=evidences τῆς παρουσίας τοῦ θεοῦ; Cornutus 16 p. 21, 9.—Arrian, Anab. 6, 26, 4 of marks in the landscape showing direction; ParJer 5:11 τὰ σ. τῆς πόλεως; Just., A I, 55, 6 al.; Iren. 1, 14, 8 [Harv. I 143, 10]; Orig., C. Cels. 3, 43, 36 σ. τῆς μετὰ θάνατον ἐπιφανείας αὐτοῦ [sc. Ἰησοῦ]; 2, 59, 6 of the scars of the resurrected Lord τὰ σ. τῆς κολάσεως). τοῦτο ὑμῖν σημεῖον *this (will be) a sign for you* **Lk 2:12** (cp. Is 37:30). ὅ ἐστιν σ. ἐν πάσῃ ἐπιστολῇ *this is the mark of genuineness in every letter* **2 Th 3:17** (Ps.-Pla., Ep. 13, 360a has at its beginning the words σύμβολον ὅτι παρ' ἐμοῦ ἐστιν). Of a *signal* previously agreed upon δοῦναί τινι σημεῖον (PFay 128, 7 ἔδωκεν ἡμῖν σημεῖον 'he gave us a signal'; Jos., Ant. 12, 404) **Mt 26:48;** 1 Cl 12:7.—*A sign* of things to come (PsSol 15:9 τὸ … σημεῖον ἀπωλείας ἐπὶ τοῦ μετώπου αὐτῶν; Did., Gen. 191, 6; Philo, Op. M. 58 σημεῖα μελλόντων; Jos., Bell. 6, 285; 296; 297) **Mk 13:4; Lk 21:7.** The event to be expected is added in the gen. τί τὸ σ. τῆς σῆς παρουσίας; **Mt 24:3.** τὸ σ. τοῦ υἱοῦ τοῦ ἀνθρώπου *the sign* by which one can mark the coming *of the Human One* (Son of Man) vs. **30** (TGlasson, JTS 15, '64, 299f [a military metaphor, 'standard'; cp. Is 18:3; 1QM 3f]). τὰ σημεῖα τῶν καιρῶν *the signs of the (end)times* (καιρός 3b) **Mt 16:3.**—*A sign* of warning (Plut., Caes. 737 [63, 1]; SibOr 3, 457; Mel., P. 14, 90) 1 Cl 11:2. Prob. in like manner αἱ γλῶσσαι εἰς σημεῖόν εἰσιν τοῖς ἀπίστοις *the tongues* (γλῶσσα 3) *serve as a (warning) sign to the unbelievers* **1 Cor 14:22.** Likew. the *sign of Jonah* (s. Ἰωνᾶς 1) in Luke: **Lk 11:29, 30.** Here the Human One is to be a sign to his generation, as Jonah was to the Ninevites; cp. οὗτος κεῖται εἰς σημεῖον ἀντιλεγόμενον (s. ἀντιλέγω 2) **2:34** (cp. Is 11:12).—W-S. §30, 10d.—GRunze, Das Zeichen des Menschensohnes u. der Doppelsinn des Jonazeichens 1897 (against him PSchmiedel, Lit. Centralblatt 48, 1897, 513–15; Runze again, ZWT 41, 1898, 171–85; finally PSchm. ibid. 514–25); PAsmussen, Protestantenblatt 37, 1904, 375–8; STyson, Bibl. World 33,1909, 96–101; CBowen, AJT 20, 1916, 414–21; JMichael, JTS 21, 1920, 146–59; JBonsirven, RSR 24, '34, 450–55; HGale, JBL 60, '41, 255–60; PSeidelin, Das Jonaszeichen, StTh 5, '51, 119–31; AVögtle, Wikenhauser Festschr. '53, 230–77; OGlombitza, D. Zeichen des Jona, NTS 8, '62, 359–66.—In the OT circumcision is σημεῖον διαθήκης=a sign or token of belonging to the covenant (Gen 17:11). For Paul this sign becomes a *mark,* or *seal* (so σημεῖον: PRev 26, 5 [III BC]; PRein 9 introd. [II BC]; 35, 3; BGU 1064, 18) σημεῖον ἔλαβεν περιτομῆς σφραγῖδα *he got the mark of circumcision as a seal* **Ro 4:11.** In the difficult pass. B 12:5 ἐν σημείῳ is prob. best taken as *by a sign;* but it is poss. that the text is defective (s. Windisch, Hdb. ad loc.; RKraft, Did. and Barnabas '65, 119 note: 'standard, norm').—τὰ σημεῖα τοῦ ἀποστόλου **2 Cor 12:12a** belongs rather to the next category; *the signs of the* (true) *apostle* (cp. SIG 831, 14 [117 AD] ἡγούμην σημεῖα ἀγαθῶν ἀνδρῶν) are, as is shown by the verb κατειργάσθη and what follows, the wonders or miracles performed by him.

➋ **an event that is an indication or confirmation of intervention by transcendent powers,** ***miracle, portent***

ⓐ ***miracle*****—α.** a miracle of divine origin, performed by God himself, by Christ, or by men of God (cp. Diod. S. 5, 70, 4 πολλὰ σ. of the young Zeus; 16, 27, 2 ἐγένετο αὐτῷ σημεῖον ἐν τῷ ἱερῷ τοῦ Ἀπόλλωνος; Strabo 16, 2, 35 παρὰ τ. θεοῦ σ.; Appian, Ital. 8 §1 σημείων γενομένων ἐκ Διός, Hann. 56 §233; SIG 709, 25 [c. 107 BC] διὰ τῶν ἐν τῷ ἱερῷ γενομένων σαμείων; PGM 1, 65; 74; Jos., Ant. 2, 274; 280; Mel., P. 78, 568): **Mt 12:38f; 16:1** (σ. ἐκ τοῦ οὐρανοῦ), **4; Mk 8:11** (σ. ἀπὸ τοῦ οὐρανοῦ, as Synes., Prov. 1, 7; s. OLinton, The Demand for a Sign from Heaven, StTh 19, '65, 112–29; JGibson, JSNT 38, '90, 37–66, a phenomenon suggesting divine deliverance), **12; 16:17, 20; Lk 11:16** (σ. ἐξ οὐρανοῦ), **29** (s. 1 above); **23:8; J 2:11, 18, 23; 3:2; 4:54; 6:2, 14, 26, 30; 7:31; 9:16; 10:41; 11:47; 12:18, 37; 20:30** (on σημ. as a designation of Jesus' miracles in J s. Hdb. on J 2:11 and 6:26; JBernard, ICC John 1929, I introd. 176–86; CBarrett, The Gosp. acc. to St. John, '55, 62–65); **Ac 4:16, 22** (τὸ σ. τῆς ἰάσεως *the miracle of healing*); **8:6; 1 Cor 1:22;** Agr 9. τί εἴδετε σημεῖον ἐπὶ τὸν γεννηθέντα βασιλέα; *what kind of sign did you see over the newborn king?* GJs 21:2 (codd.). τὸ σημεῖον τὸ ἐνάρετον *the marvelous sign* AcPl Ha 3,16.—σημεῖα καὶ τέρατα (Polyb. 3, 112, 8 σημείων δὲ καὶ τεράτων πᾶν μὲν ἱερόν, πᾶσα δ' ἦν οἰκία πλήρης; Plut., Alex. 706 [75, 1 sing.]; Appian, Bell. Civ. 2, 36 §144 τέρατα καὶ σημεῖα οὐράνια; 4, 4 §14; Aelian, VH 12, 57; Philo, Mos. 1, 95, Aet. M. 2; Jos., Bell. 1, 28, Ant. 20, 168. Oft. in LXX: Ex 7:3; Dt 4:34; 6:22; 7:19 al.; Is 8:18; 20:3; Jer 39:21; Wsd 8:8; 10:16) **J 4:48; Ac 2:43; 4:30; 5:12; 6:8; 7:36; 14:3; 15:12; Ro 15:19; Hb 2:4;** 1 Cl 51:5; B 4:14; 5:8. δυνάμεις καὶ τέρατα κ. σημεῖα **Ac 2:22; 2 Cor 12:12b** (SSchreiber, Paulus als Wundertäter: BZNW 79, '96) σημεῖα καὶ δυνάμεις **Ac 8:13.**—1 Cl 25:1; 2 Cl 15:4. SMcCasland, JBL 76, '57, 149–52; MWhittaker, Studia Evangelica 5, '68, 155–58.

β. worked by Satan or his agents to mislead God's people (s. Iren. 5, 28, 2 [Harv. V 401, 32]) **Rv 13:13f; 16:14; 19:20.**

σημεῖα κ. τέρατα **Mt 24:24; Mk 13:22** (GBeasley-Murray, A Commentary on Mk 13, '57; EGrässer, D. Problem der Parusieverzögerung, '57, 152–70); **2 Th 2:9;** D 16:4.

ⓑ ***portent*** terrifying appearances in the heavens, never before seen, as *portents* of the last days **Lk 21:11, 25** (Appian, Bell. Civ. 4, 4 §14 σημεῖα πολλά around the sun; AscIs 3, 20); **Ac 2:19** (cp. Jo 3:3); s. D 16:6. Of that which the seer of the Apocalypse sees ἐν τῷ οὐρανῷ **Rv 12:1, 3; 15:1.** Of the portentous signs in heaven and earth at the death of Jesus GPt 8:28 (cp. Da 6:28 Theod. σημεῖα κ. τέρατα ἐν οὐρανῷ κ. ἐπὶ τῆς γῆς; Diod. S. 38 + 39 fgm. 5: at the end of each one of the eight ages ordained by God there is a σημεῖον ἐκ γῆς ἢ οὐρανοῦ θαυμάσιον).—On miracles s. SIG 1168–73; RLembert, Das Wunder bei Römern u. Griechen I 1905; RReitzenstein, Hellenist. Wundererzählungen 1906, OWeinreich, Antike Heilungswunder 1909, Gebet u. Wunder: WSchmid Festschr. 1929, 169ff; PWendland, De Fabellis Antiquis earumque ad Christianos Propagatione 1911; FKutsch, Attische Heilgötter u. Heilheroen 1913; WJayne, The Healing Gods of Ancient Civilizations 1925; RHerzog, D. Wunderheilungen v. Epidaurus '31; PFiebig, Jüdische Wundergeschichten des ntl. Zeitalters 1911; ASchlatter, Das Wunder in d. Synagoge 1912.—RLehmann, Naturwissenschaft u. bibl. Wunderfrage 1930; GNaumann, Die Wertschätzung des Wunders im NT 1903; GTraub, Das Wunder im NT[2] 1907; KBeth, Die Wunder Jesu 1908; JThompson, Miracles in the NT 1911; LFonck, Die Wunder des Herrn im Ev.[2] 1907; LFillion, Les miracles de Jésus-Christ 1909/1910; PDausch, Die Wunder Jesu 1912; SEitrem, Nordisk Tidskrift for Filologie 5, 1919, 30–36; RBultmann, Die Gesch. der synopt. Tradition[2] '31, 223–60; RJelke, Die Wunder Jesu 1922; GShafto, The Wonders of the Kingdom 1924; JBest, The Miracles of Christ in the Light of our Present Day Knowledge '37; TTorrance, Expository Studies in St. John's Miracles '38; ARichardson, The Miracle Stories of the Gospels '41; AFridrichsen, Le Problème du Miracle dans le Christianisme primitif: Études d' Hist. et de Phil. rel. XII 1925; HSchlingensiepen, Die Wunder des NT '33; OPerels, D. Wunderüberlieferung der Synoptiker '34; PSaintyves, Essais de folklore biblique 1923; GMarquardt, D. Wunderproblem in d. deutschen prot. Theologie der Gegenwart '33; GDelling, D. Verständnis des Wunders im NT, ZST 24, '55, 265–80, Zur Beurteilung des Wunders durch d. Antike: Studien zum NT '70, 53–71; SMcCasland, Signs and Wonders, JBL 76, '57, 149–52; CBarrett, The Gosp. Acc. to John '55, 62–65; JCharlier, La notion de signe (sêmeion) dans J: RSPT 43, '59, 434–48; PRiga, Signs of Glory (J): Int 17, '63, 402–24; HvanderLoos, The Miracles of Jesus '65; WNicol, The Semeia in the Fourth Gosp. '72; for Acts s. FNeirynck, the Miracle Stories in the Acts of the Apostles, An Introduction, in Les Actes des Apôtres, ed. JKremer '79, 169–213.—Esp. on the healing of demoniacs JWeiss, RE IV 408ff; JJaeger, Ist Jesus Christus ein Suggestionstherapeut gewesen? 1918; KKnur, M.D., Christus medicus? 1905; KDusberger, Bibel u. Kirche '51, 114–17 (foretoken).—RGrant, Miracle and Natural Law in Graeco-Roman and Early Christian Thought '52. S. also the lit. s.v. δαιμόνιον 2.—See further MWestermann, ed. ΠΑΡΑΔΟΞΑΓΡΑΦΟΙ, Scriptores Rerum Mirabilium Graeci, 1839.—B. 914. DELG s.v. σῆμα. M-M. DBS XII 1281–1330. EDNT. ABD IV 869 (lit.). TW. Spicq. Sv.

σημειόω (σημεῖον; since Hippocr. V 672 L.; Theophr.; ins, pap, Ps 4:7; TestSol, EpArist, Philo) 1 aor. mid. ἐσημειωσάμην; usu., and in our lit. exclusively, in the mid.

❶ **to note in writing, *note down, write*** (OGI 629, 168 ὡς καὶ Κουρβούλων ὁ κράτιστος ἐσημειώσατο ἐν τῇ ἐπιστολῇ) τὶ *someth.* πάντα ἐν ταῖς ἱεραῖς βίβλοις 1 Cl 43:1.

❷ **to take special notice of, *mark*** τινά *someone* **2 Th 3:14.**—DELG s.v. σῆμα. M-M. TW.

σημείωσις, εως, ἡ (σημειόω; Chairemon, fgm. 5, p. 32, 8; Plut., Mor. 961c; pap; Ps 59:6; PsSol 4:2; TestJob 51:4; EpArist) ***sign, signal*** εἰς σ. γίνεσθαί τινι *serve as a (sign of) warning to someone* 1 Cl 11:2 (σημεῖον 1).—DELG s.v. σῆμα. M-M.

σήμερον adv. of time (Hom.+ [the Attic τήμερον is not found in our lit.: B-D-F §34, 1; Mlt-H. 279]; loanw. in rabb.) ***today*** **Mt 6:11** (BMetzger, How Many Times Does ἐπιούσιος Occur Outside the Lord's Prayer? ET 60, '57, 52–54; see ἐπιούσιος); **16:3; 21:28; Lk 4:21; 23:43** (=*before today is over* as Philostrat., Vi. Soph. 1, 25, 14); **Ac 4:9** and oft.; **Lk 3:22** D (Ps 2:7); cp. **Hb 1:5; 5:5;** 1 Cl 36:4; GJs 19:2. Opp. αὔριον **Js 4:13.** ἡ σήμερον ἡμέρα (Dio Chrys. 31 [48], 3; SIG 1181, 11=prayer for vengeance fr. Rheneia: Dssm., LO 351ff, esp. 357 [LAE 414 ff]; LXX) *today, this very day:* **Mt 28:15** (μέχρι τῆς σ. ἡμέρας, as 1 Esdr 8:74; Jos., Ant. 10, 265); **Ac 20:26** (ἐν τῇ σ. ἡμέρᾳ, as Phlegon: 257 fgm. 36, 3, 11 Jac.; Josh 5:9; PGM 4, 1580; 1699; 2062; 5, 187; 194); **Ro 11:8** (ἕως τῆς σ. ἡμέρας, as UPZ 57, 3; Gen 19:38 al.; Just., D. 134, 5; Ath. 2, 1); **2 Cor 3:14** (ἄχρι τῆς σ. ἡμέρας, as Jos., Ant. 7, 366). ὡς μεγάλη ἡ σ. ἡμέρα GJs 19:2. W. ellipsis (BGU 598, 6; POxy 121, 6; LXX; JosAs 7:11; 15:4 ἀπὸ τῆς σ. B-D-F §241, 2) ἡ σήμερον: **Mt 11:23; 28:15 v.l.** (both μέχρι τῆς σ. as Jos., Ant. 9, 28); **27:8** (ἕως τῆς σ. as UPZ 5, 5 [163 BC]); **Ac 19:40** (περὶ τῆς σ.).—ἕως σ. **2 Cor 3:15** (ViIs 4 [p. 69, 12 Sch.]; cp. Ps-Callisth. 1, 35, 9 μέχρι σ.).—Since Israelites consider that the day begins at sundown, the whole night belongs to one and the same 24-hour period: σ. ταύτῃ τῇ νυκτί *this very night* **Mk 14:30.** Also simply σ. **Mt 27:19; Lk 2:11; 22:34.** On ἐχθὲς καὶ σήμερον **Hb 13:8** s. ἐχθές. Looking fr. the present to the coming judgment ἄχρις οὗ τὸ σήμερον καλεῖται *as long as 'today' lasts* **Hb 3:13** (cp. Philo, Leg. All. 3, 25 ὁ αἰὼν ἅπας τῷ σήμερον παραμετρεῖται and s. καλέω 1d, end).—Like the Lat. hodie, σ. serves to denote a limited period of time (Appian, Liby. 112 §532): σήμερον … αὔριον=*now … in a little while* **Mt 6:30; Lk 12:28.** The expr. σήμερον καὶ αὔριον καὶ τῇ τρίτῃ (or καὶ τῇ ἐχομένῃ) refers to a short period of time, the exact duration of which the speaker either cannot or does not wish to disclose **Lk 13:32f** (JBlinzler, Klerusblatt '44, 381–83).—See ABonhöffer, Epiktet u. das NT 1911, 329f on σήμερον in the ethical teaching of Epict.—B. 998. DELG s.v. τήμερον. M-M. TW.

σημικίνθιον s. σιμικίνθιον.

σηπία, ας, ἡ (Aristoph. et al.) ***cuttle-fish, sepia*** w. sea-lamprey and octopus (w. octopus: schol. on Pla. 160e) B 10:5 (s. Lev 11:10; also πολύπους and σμύραινα).—DELG.

σήπω (Hom. et al.; pap, LXX; Ath. 36, 2. Act. 'cause to rot/decay', pass. 'rot') 1 aor. impv. 2 sg. σῆψον Job 40:12; 2 pf. σέσηπα, ptc. n. σεσηπός. Pass.: 2 fut. 3 sg. σαπήσεται Ezk 17:9; 2 aor. 3 pl ἐσάπησαν LXX; pf. 3 sg. σέσηπται (TestJob 43:7). The pf. act. 'make rotten' as a rule is used outside our lit. (Hom. et al.) intransitively like the pass. in the sense 'decay', and in our lit. exclusively so. ***Decay, rot*** (TestJob 43:7; Philo, Aet. M. 125; Jos., C. Ap. 2, 143), 2 pf. act. *be decayed* ξύλον σεσηπός *rotten wood* Dg 2:2. σηπομένης τῆς σαρκός *as the flesh decays* 1 Cl 25:3 (Cyranides p. 7, 21 ἐσέσηπτο ἡ σάρξ; Jos., Bell. 6, 164 σηπόμενον σῶμα). ὅπου … Ἱερόνυμος ἐκ τοῦ ὠτίου ἐσήπετο *where … Hieronymus was suffering an aural discharge* AcPl Ha 5, 23. οὐ πάντα σηπόμενα; Dg 2:4. Of a vine creeping along on the ground: σεσηπότα φέρειν *bear rotten fruit* Hs 2:3.

Of the treasures of the rich **Js 5:2.**—DELG s.v. σήπομαι. M-M. TW.

σηρικός s. σιρικός.

σής (since Pind., fgm. 209 [OxfT=222 Sch./M.] Διὸς παῖς ὁ χρυσός. κεῖνον οὐ σὴς οὐδὲ κὶς δάπτει 'gold is the child of Zeus: neither moth nor rust can consume it'; LXX), **σητός** (so Aristot., HA 5, 32; Menand. et al.; LXX; Philo, Abr. 11.—The class. gen. is σεός s. Kühner-Bl. I 510f), **ὁ** ***the moth,*** whose larvae eat clothing (Menand., fgm.538, 5 Kö.=540, 5 Kock; Lucian, Ep. Sat. 1, 21 ἱμάτια ὑπὸ σητῶν διαβρωθέντα) **Mt 6:19f; Lk 12:33.** Being eaten by moths as a symbol of feebleness and destruction 1 Cl 39:5 (Job 4:19); B 6:2 (Is 50:9).—Worms, specific. wood-worms, seem to be meant (cp. Philo, Somn. 1, 77), since the σής is damaging sticks Hs 8, 1, 6f; 8, 4, 5; 8, 6, 4.—DELG. M-M. TW.

σητόβρωτος, ον (σής, βιβρώσκω; Sb 7404, 28 [II AD]; SibOr fgm. 3, 26; Hesych.) ***motheaten*** ἱμάτια (Job 13:28) **Js 5:2.**—New Docs 1, 77. M-M. TW.

σθενόω (σθένος 'strength') fut. σθενώσω (Herodian Gramm. 449, 21; Rhet. Gr. VII 260, 20; Hesych.) ***strengthen, make strong*** **1 Pt 5:10.**—DELG s.v. σθένος. M-M.

σιαγών, όνος, ἡ (cp. ψίω 'chew'; Soph., X., Pla.+; usu. in its orig. sense 'jaw, jawbone', so also LXX [e.g. Judg 15:14–17]; TestAbr A 16 p. 97, 14 [Stone p. 42]; Jos., Ant. 5, 300) ***cheek*** (so fr. III BC [s. L-S-J-M s.v.], pap, LXX [e.g. Is 50:6]) **Mt 5:39; Lk 6:29;** D 1:4 (on the subject-matter JWeismann, ZNW 14, 1913, 175f; JMoffatt, Exp. 8th ser., 7, 1914, 89; 8, 1914, 188f; UHolzmeister, ZKT 45, 1921, 334ff; HBryant, ET 48, '37, 236f); GPt 3:9. τιθέναι τὰς σ. εἰς ῥαπίσματα *give up one's cheeks to blows* B 5:14 (Is 50:6).—B. 222. DELG. M-M.

σιαίνομαι (Hippiatr. II 81, 5; POxy 1837, 2 [VI AD]; 1849, 2; Psaltes, Grammatik p. 333) ***be disturbed/annoyed*** (the act.='cause annoyance' or 'loathing': schol. on Lucian p. 261, 22 Rabe) **1 Th 3:3 v.l.**—S. vDobschütz ad loc. and the lit. s.v. σαίνω.—M-M.

Σίβυλλα, ης, ἡ (Heraclitus [s. Plut., Mor. 397a] and Eur. et al.; SibOr 3, 815; 4, 22; TestSol 5:1 D; Jos., Ant. 1, 118; Just.; Tat. 41, 1; Ath. 30, 1) ***the Sibyl,*** an ecstatic (s. Vergil, Aen. 6, 77–101 on the Cumaean Sibyl associated with Apollo) prophetic figure, first recognized as one pers. and later pluralized (Pauly-W. II 2073ff; Kl. Pauly V 158–61; ABD VI 2–6 [lit.]) Hv 2, 4, 1 (s. MDibelius, Hdb. ad loc., Festgabe für AvHarnack 1921, 118).

σιγάω (s. next entry) fut. σιγήσω LXX; 1 aor. ἐσίγησα; fut. mid. σιγήσομαι Lam 3:49; pf. pass. ptc. σεσιγημένος

❶ to be silent, intr. (Hom. et al.; Sb 7183, 5; LXX; ApcMos 12; Jos., Vi. 175, Ant. 19, 44; Just., Mel.)—**ⓐ** ***say nothing, keep still, keep silent*** (Pind., N. 5, 18 τὸ σιγᾶν πολλάκις ἐστὶ σοφώτατον ἀνθρώπῳ νοῆσαι; Just., D. 137, 3; Mel., P. 94, 723) **Mk 14:61** D; **Lk 19:40** D; **20:26; Ac 12:17; 15:12; 1 Cor 14:28** (ESchüsler-Fiorenza, In Memory of Her '83, 230–33; PTomson, Paul and the Jewish Law '90, 137). Response to accusation Ἰωσὴφ ἐσίγησεν GJs 15:4 (cp. Just., D. 102, 5 [on Mt 26:63]). αἱ γυναῖκες ἐν τ. ἐκκλησίαις σιγάτωσαν **1 Cor 14:34** (cp. the Hellenic attitude Od. 18, 184, also 17, 57; 21, 386; 22, 398; Eur., Heracl. 476f γυναικὶ γὰρ σιγή … κάλλιστον, εἴσω θ' ἥσυχον μένειν δόμων=for a woman silence is best and to remain tranquil in the house; for Hellenic cultural perspective on female aggressiveness s. VLeinieks, the City of Dionysos '96, 277–302; s. the lit. s.v. γυνή 1. Also RSeeberg, Aus Rel. u. Gesch., Ges. Aufs. I 1906, 128–44; HHöpfl, Bened. Monatsschr. 14, '32, 63–77; GDautzenberg, Urchristl. Prophetie, '75, 253–90; GFetzer, Das Weib schweige in der Gemeinde '63.—PSchmiedel, JWeiss, WBousset ad loc., HWindisch [s. γυνή 1], RBultmann [ThBl 12, '33, 362] consider vs. 34f a secondary gloss; on the textual-critical history s. CNiccum, NTS 43, '97, 242–55; cp. PPayne, NTS 44, '98, 152–58; also note gender differentiation in sacred laws SEG XLIII nos. 1293 and 1310); 1 Cl 35:9 (Ps 49:21); IEph 6:1; 15:1f (opp. λαλεῖν, as Alex. Aphr., Fat. 9 p. 175, 23 Br.); IPhld 1:1 (opp. λαλεῖν).—*hold one's tongue* (cp. sense b) **Lk 9:36.**

ⓑ ***stop speaking, become silent*** (ApcMos 12; Just., D. 57, 1 al.; Mel., P. 26, 184; Chariton 5, 7, 8; Synes., Kingship 29 p. 32a; SibOr 3, 473) **Lk 18:39; Ac 13:41** D; 15:13; **1 Cor 14:30;** MPol 7:2 v.l.—In the sense of 'lose one's power of speech' τῷ … καιρῷ ἐκείνῳ Ζαχαρίας ἐσίγησεν GJs 10:2.

❷ to keep someth. from becoming known, ***keep secret, conceal,*** trans. τὶ *someth.* (Pind. et al.; Chariton 3, 10, 1; POxy 471, 41 [II AD]; Jos., Ant. 17, 309) Παῦλος ἦν μὴ σιγῶν (v.l. σιωπῶν) τὸν λόγον *Paul was not reticent about (God's) message* AcPl Ha 9, 17. Pass. μυστήριον χρόνοις αἰωνίοις σεσιγημένον *a secret that was concealed for long ages* **Ro 16:25.** Cp. **Lk 9:36** in 1a.—B. 1259. Schmidt, Syn. I 215–24, s. σιωπάω. DELG s.v. σιγή. M-M.

σιγή, ῆς, ἡ (s. prec. entry; Hom. et al.; Wsd 18:14; 3 Macc 3:23; En 89:46; EpArist; Jos., Vi. 417; Just., D. 103, 9; Ath., R. 19 p. 71, 30) **the absence of all noise, whether made by speaking or by anything else,** ***silence, quiet*** 1 Cl 21:7. σιγῆς ὑπαρχούσης *when it was quiet on ship* AcPl Ha 7, 25. πολλῆς σιγῆς γενομένης *when a great silence had fallen = when they had become silent* **Ac 21:40** (likew. Ps.-Callisth. 2, 15, 6; without πολλῆς Arrian, Anab. 4, 12, 2; Vi. Aesopi W 87 P.; Jos., Vi. 141, Ant. 5, 236); cp. the dramatic silence in **Rv 8:1,** which may imply lack of both verbal and other type of sound, for the opening of six previous seals is accompanied either by verbal declarations or celestial phenomena (s. Clemen[2] 391; WBeet, ET 44, '33, 74–76). σιγὴν ἔχειν *be silent* (Appian, Hann. 14 §60; Arrian, Anab. 5, 1, 4; Paroem. Gr.: App. 3, 7) Hs 9, 11, 5. ἀνάπαυσιν ἐν σιγῇ *rest in silence* GMary 463, 2. Christ is called αὐτοῦ λόγος, ἀπὸ σιγῆς προελθών *(God's) Word, proceeding from silence*=without audible expression IMg 8:2 (cp. the corollary: ἃ … οὖς οὐκ ἤκουσεν 1 Cor 2:9; for other views on the text and subj.-matter s. Hdb. ad loc.; H-WBartsch, Gnost. Gut u. Gemeindetradition b. Ign. v. Ant. '40. On the deity that is silence and that can be rightly worshiped only in silence, s. Mesomedes 1, 1–3 [=Coll. p. 197], addressing the goddess: Ἀρχὰ καὶ πάντων γέννα | πρεσβίστα κόσμου μᾶτερ | καὶ νὺξ καὶ φῶς καὶ σιγά; Porphyr., Abst. 2, 34 διὰ σιγῆς καθαρᾶς θρησκεύομεν [θεόν]; Sextus 578 τιμὴ μεγίστη θεῷ θεοῦ γνῶσις ἐν σιγῇ; PGM 4, 558ff λέγε· σιγή, σιγή, σιγή, σύμβολον θεοῦ ζῶντος ἀφθάρτου· φύλαξόν με, σιγή; 1782. Hermes in Iambl., De Myst. 8, 3 ὃ δὴ διὰ σιγῆς μόνης θεραπεύεται. Herm. Wr. 10, 5 ἡ γὰρ γνῶσις αὐτοῦ βαθεῖα σιωπή ἐστι. Martyr. Petri Aa I 96, 16ff.—HKoch, Ps.-Dionys. Areop. 1900, 128ff; OCasel, De Philosophorum Graecorum Silentio Mystico 1919, Vom hl. Schweigen: Bened. Monatsschr. 3, 1921, 417ff; GMensching, Das hl. Schweigen 1926).—DELG s.v. σῖγα. M-M. Sv.

σίδηρος, ου, ὁ (s. next entry; Hom.+) ***iron*** Dg 2:3. W. χαλκός (as Diod. S. 1, 33, 3; 2, 16, 4; EpArist 119; Philo, Aet. M. 20) **Rv 18:12;** PtK 2 p. 14, 14. Destroyed by rust Dg 2:2. Metonymically for sword (Hom. et al.; Jos., Bell. 3, 364; 6, 273, Ant. 19, 148) 1 Cl 56:9 (Job 5:20). πεπυρωμένος σ. *red-hot* *iron* (Alex. Aphr., Quaest. 2, 17) ApcPt 13:28.—B. 613. DELG. M-M.

σιδηροῦς, ᾶ, οῦν (s. prec. entry; Hom.+ in the form σιδήρεος, whereas the Attic Gks. have the contracted form. The word is also found in ins, pap, LXX; TestJud 9:40; JosAs 10:5; GrBar 3:7; ApcEsdr 4:25 p. 28, 30 Tdf.; Philo, Op. M. 141; Joseph. [in both forms; cp. Schmidt, Joseph. 492]; SibOr 3, 540) ***(made of) iron*** of a bar B 11:4 (Is 45:2; JosAs 10:5; ApcEsdr 4:25). Of a prison door (s. πύλη a) **Ac 12:10.** Of breastplates **Rv 9:9.** In imagery = merciless (Hom.+; cp. Περὶ ὕψους 13, 1 after Pla., Rep. 586a σιδηροῖς κέρασι) ῥάβδος σιδηρᾶ (after Ps 2:9) **Rv 2:27; 12:5; 19:15** (ποιμαίνω 2aγ).—DELG s.v. σίδηρος. M-M s.v. σιδήρεος.

Σιδών, ῶνος, ἡ (צִידוֹן; Hom. et al.; ins, LXX; Philo, Leg. ad Gai. 337; Joseph.; Just., D. 34, 8; SibOr 14, 83) ***Sidon,*** an ancient Phoenician royal city, on the coast betw. Berytus (Beirut) and Tyre. Oft. formulaically combined w. Tyre (Philostrat., Her. 1, 1; Jos., Ant. 8, 320; 15, 95) **Mt 11:21f; Mk 3:8; Lk 6:17; 10:13f** (written Σιδόνι vs. **13** P[75]). τὰ μέρη Τύρου καὶ Σιδῶνος *the region around Tyre and Sidon* **Mt 15:21;** also τὰ ὅρια Τ. καὶ Σ. **Mk 7:24 v.l.;** ἦλθεν διὰ Σιδῶνος εἰς *(Jesus) went by way of Sidon to . . .* **Mk 7:31.** Σάρεπτα τ. Σιδῶνος *Zarephath, which belongs to Sidon* **Lk 4:26 v.l.** Visited by Paul on his journey to Rome **Ac 27:3.**—FEiselen, Sidon: Columbia Univ. Oriental Studies IV 1907; HGuthe, RE XVIII 280ff; XXIV 503f.; Pauly-W. II 2216ff; Kl. Pauly V 175f; BHHW III 1784f; PECS 837; OEANE V 38–41.—M-M.

Σιδώνιος, ία, ιον (Soph., Hdt. et al.; ins, LXX) **pert. to Sidon, *Sidonian.***

ⓐ ἡ Σ. (sc. χώρα) *the country around Sidon* (Od. 13, 285 [Σιδονία]; LXX) Σάρεπτα τῆς Σιδωνίας (3 Km 17:9) *Zarephath in the region of Sidon* **Lk 4:26.**

ⓑ οἱ Σιδώνιοι (Od. 4, 84 al.; ins; SibOr 3, 451; 5, 203 all write Σιδόνιος; but SIG 185, 5 [376–360 BC]; 391, 2; 15; LXX; Jos. [index] Σιδώνιος) *the Sidonians* mentioned w. Tyrians (as Diod. S. 16, 41, 1; 1 Esdr 5:53) **Ac 12:20** (Beginn. ad loc.).

σικάριος, ου, ὁ (Lat. loanw. 'sicarius' pl.'-ii', fr. sica= 'dagger'; s. B-D-F §5, 1; Mlt-H. 347; Rob. 109, and the entry Ἰσκαριώθ.—The word is found several times in Joseph. [s. index].—σικάριον='dagger' POxy 1294, 8 [II/III AD].—Also as a loanw. in the Talmud; s. SKrauss, Griech. u. latein. Lehnwörter im Talmud usw. II 1899, 392) **one who is intent on killing someone as part of an organized subversive political program, *dagger man, assassin, terrorist,*** name of the most extreme group among Judean nationalists, quite hostile to Rome; they did not hesitate to assassinate their political opponents (Jos., Bell. 2, 254–57, Ant. 20, 186) **Ac 21:38.**—Schürer I 463; MHengel, Die Zeloten, '61, 47–54; BHHW II 1209.—M-M. TW.

σίκερα, τό (Aram. שִׁכְרָא=Hebr. שֵׁכָר; Is 5:11, 22; 24:9 make it certain that the gender is neut. See B-D-F §58; Rob. 105. Orig. Akkadian; s. HZimmern, Akkad. Lehnwörter 1915, 39) (Galen XIX 693 K. [though the tractate in question is strongly interpolated by Christians, acc. to PKatz]; Anecdota Astrologica [ALudwich, Maximi et Ammonis Carmina 1877] p. 120, 23 οἶνος κ. σίκερα; LXX, Hesychius, Suda) indecl. (but Eus., PE 6, 10, 14 has σίκερος as a gen.—Also 6, 10, 9 the verb σικερατίζω): **an alcoholic beverage.** As a rule σ. was differentiated fr. wine and mentioned w. it (Lev 10:9; Num 6:3; Dt 29:5; Is 29:9; TestReub 1:10. The Akkadian šikaru='barley beer' [CAD XVII 421]) ***beer*** **Lk 1:15** (s. Judg 13:4 A). It is not possible to determine whether σ. was considered any stronger than wine; the rendering 'strong drink' (so in many versions) may therefore be misleading. Cp. Lampe; Soph., Lex.—TRE III 609. M-M. DDD 1550–53. DELG.

Σιλᾶς, α or **Σίλας, ᾶ** (still other spellings are attested for the NT; s. B-D-F §53, 2; 125, 2), **ὁ** (several times in Joseph. as a Semitic name; OGI 604, 4; IGR III 817, 1. Evidently=שְׁאִילָא, the Aram. form [in Palmyrene inscriptions] of שָׁאוּל Saul) ***Silas.*** This name, which occurs only in **Ac,** is borne by a respected member of the church at Jerusalem who was prophetically gifted **15:22, 27;** he was sent to Antioch and stayed there vss. **32, 33 [34] v.l.;** later he accompanied Paul on his so-called second missionary journey **15:40–18:5** (mentioned nine times). Despite CWeizsäcker, Das apost. Zeitalter[2] 1892, 247 et al., incl. LRadermacher, ZNW 25, 1926, 295, it is hardly to be doubted that this Silas is the same pers. as the Σιλουανός who is mentioned in Paul and 1 Pt. See the next entry and s. AStegmann, Silvanus als Missionär u. 'Hagiograph' 1917. S. also s.v. Ἰωάν(ν)ης 6.—TRE III 609. M-M.

Σιλβανός s. Σιλουανός; **2 Cor 1:19 v.l.**

Σιλουανός, οῦ, ὁ (Diod. S. 11, 27, 1, a Σ. as contemporary with the battle of Salamis [480 BC]; OGI 533, 50 [time of Augustus] and later ins and pap; Jos., Ant. 20:14; in rabbinic lit. סִילְוָנִי CIJ I, 596) ***Silvanus;*** surely the same man who appears in Ac as Σίλας (q.v.). Either he had two names (like Paul), one Semit. and one Lat. (Zahn), or Σιλουανός is the Lat. form of the same name that is Grecized in Σίλας (B-D-F §125, 2; Mlt-H. 109f; 146). **2 Cor 1:19** (v.l. Σιλβανός, which is also found Diod. S. 11, 41, 1); **1 Th 1:1; 2 Th 1:1** (s. also the **subscr.** of **2 Th**); **1 Pt 5:12** (this pass. has given rise to the conclusion that Silvanus was somehow or other [as translator? in Sb 8246, 38 Germanus speaks before the court δι' Ἀνουβίωνος ἑρμηνεύοντος] connected w. the writing of 1 Pt; e.g., Zahn [Einleitung II[3] 10f], GWohlenberg [NKZ 24, 1913, 742–62], WBornemann [Der erste Petrusbrief—eine Taufrede des Silvanus?: ZNW 19, 1920, 143ff], Harnack [Mission I[4] 1923, 85], LRadermacher [Der 1 Pt u. Silvanus: ZNW 25, 1926, 287ff]; ESelwyn, 1 Pt '46, 9–17 but s. WKümmel [Introd. NT, tr. HKee, '75, 416–25]).—M-M.

Σιλωάμ, ὁ indecl. (שִׁלֹחַ; masc.: Is 8:6 τὸ ὕδωρ τοῦ Σιλωάμ; 2 Esdr 13:15 S κολυμβήθρα τοῦ Σιλωάμ; VIs 2:4 [p. 69, 5 and 10 Sch.]; but fem.: Jos., Bell. 5, 505 τὴν Σιλωάμ.—Elsewh. Jos. usu. has declinable forms: τοῦ Σιλωᾶ Bell. 2, 340; 6, 363; ἡ Σιλωά, ᾶς, ᾷ, άν 5, 140; 145 [τὴν Σιλωὰν πηγήν]; 252, 410; 6, 401.—B-D-F §56, 4; s. Rob. 95) ***Siloam,*** name of a water supply system in Jerusalem, through which the water of the spring Gihon became available for the Fortress of David. ἡ κολυμβήθρα τοῦ Σ. *the pool of Siloam* was prob. the basin into which the water was conducted **J 9:7;** cp. vs. **11.**—Vincent/Abel, Jérus.: (s. Ἱεροσόλυμα 1b) II chap. 34 §2; GDalman, Jerus. u. s. Gelände 1930, 386 (index); CKopp, The Holy Places of the Gospels tr. RWalls, '63, 314–20; RBrown, AB ad loc.—ὁ πύργος ἐν τῷ Σ. *the tower near the pool of Siloam* **Lk 13:4.**—BHHW III 1715. M-M.

Σιμαίας, ου, ὁ (שְׁמַעְיָה. The name is freq. in the OT, but the LXX always renders it differently from 2 Ti, even though the LXX does not always spell it in the same way; Schürer II 363, 25) ***Simaias,*** named in **2 Ti 4:19 v.l.** as a son of Aquila.

σιμικίνθιον, ου, τό (Aesop fr. the Cod. Paris. 1277: CRochefort, Notices et Extraits II 1789 p. 718 no. 18. Latin loanw.: semicinctium; B-D-F §5, 1d; 41, 1; Rob. 109; 189; 192) ***apron,*** such as is worn by workers w. σουδάριον **Ac 19:12.** It is not certain just what is meant by this ref. Hesychius took it to be a *band* or *bandage* of some kind. Ammonius and Theophylact thought it was a *handkerchief,* but this does not accord well w. σουδάριον. Suda combined the two ideas: φακιόλιον (towel) ἢ σουδάριον.—On the indirect mediation of miracle-working fr. one pers. to another s. FPfister, Der Reliquienkult im Altertum I 1909, 331ff.—M-M.

Σίμων, ωνος, ὁ (שִׁמְעוֹן. The name is found freq. among Greeks [Aristoph. et al.; ins, pap. See Bechtel p. 30; 251] and Israelites [LXX; EpArist 47; 48; Joseph.; s. GHölscher, ZAW Beihefte 41, 1925, 150f; 155; MNoth, D. israelit. Personennamen 1928, 38; Wuthnow 113; CRoth, Simon-Peter, HTR 54, '61, 91–97—first and second century].—On its declension s. Mlt-H. 146) ***Simon***

❶ surnamed Πέτρος=Κηφᾶς, most prominent of the twelve disciples **Mt 4:18; Mk 1:16; Lk 4:38** and oft. S. Πέτρος.

❷ another of the twelve disciples, called ὁ Καναναῖος **Mt 10:4; Mk 3:18,** or (ὁ) ζηλωτής (s. Καναναῖος) **Lk 6:15; Ac 1:13;** GEb 34, 61 (the two Alexandrian Epicureans named Ptolemaeus are differentiated as ὁ μέλας καὶ ὁ λευκός Diog. L. 10, 25).—KLake, HTR 10, 1917, 57–63; JHoyland, Simon the Zealot 1930.

❸ name of a brother of Jesus **Mt 13:55; Mk 6:3.**

❹ a man of Cyrene, who was pressed into service to carry Jesus' cross to the place of execution **Mt 27:32; Mk 15:21; Lk 23:26** (s. Κυρήνη).—SReinach, S. de Cyrène: Cultes, Mythes et Religions IV 1912, 181ff; on this JHalévy, RevSém 20, 1912, 314–19; AKinsey, Simon the Crucifier and Symeon the Prophet: ET 35, 1924, 84ff.

❺ father of Judas Iscariot **J 6:71; 12:4 v.l.; 13:2, 26.**

❻ Σ. ὁ λεπρός *Simon the leper* owner of a house in Bethany on the Mount of Olives. Jesus paid him a visit fr. Jerusalem, and on this occasion the anointing of Jesus took place, acc. to the first two evangelists **Mt 26:6; Mk 14:3.**—CTorrey, The Four Gospels '33, 296; ELittmann, ZNW 34, '35, 32.

❼ name of a Pharisee who invited Jesus to his home and thereby gave a grateful woman an opportunity to anoint Jesus **Lk 7:40, 43f.**

❽ a tanner in Joppa, w. whom Peter stayed for a while; fr. here he went to Caesarea to visit Cornelius **Ac 9:43; 10:6, 17, 32b.**

❾ a magician **Ac 8:9, 13, 18, 24.** He is portrayed as a Samaritan who μαγεύων vs. 9 or ταῖς μαγείαις vs. 11 led his compatriots to believe that he was the 'Great Power of God'; the miracles of the apostles surprised and disturbed him to such a degree that he tried to buy the gift of imparting the Holy Spirit fr. them.—HWaitz, RE XVIII 1906, 351ff; XXIV 1913, 518ff (lit. in both vols.); KPieper, Die Simon-Magus Perikope 1911; OWeinreich, ARW 18, 1915, 21ff; Ramsay, Bearing 117ff; MLidzbarski, NGG 1916, 86–93; EdeFaye, Gnostiques et Gnosticisme[2] 1925, 216ff; 430f; CSchmidt, Studien zu d. Ps.-Clementinen 1929, 47ff; RCasey: Beginn. I/5, 151–63; ANock, ibid. 164–88; L-HVincent, RB 45, '36, 221–32; HSchoeps, Theol. u. Gesch. des Judenchristentums '49, 127–34; MSmith, Simon Magus in **Ac 8:** HA Wolfson Festschr. '65, 735–49; JSelles-Dabadie, Recherches sur Simon le Mage '69; Haenchen s. index; KRudolph, TRu 42, '77, 279–354 (lit.); RMcLWilson, Simon and Gnostic Origins, in Les Actes des Apôtres etc., ed. JKremer '79, 485–91.

❿ a Gnostic in Corinth AcPlCor 1:2.—LGPN I. M-M.

Σινᾶ indecl. (סִינַי.—LXX Σινα: Ex 16:1; Dt 33:2; Judg 5:5; Ps 67:9; Sir 48:7. τὸ ὄρος τὸ Σινα: Ex 19:11, 20, 23; 24:16. [τὸ] ὄρος Σινα: Ex 19:16; Lev 7:38; 25:1; 26:46; Num 3:1; 2 Esdr 19:13; SibOr 3, 256; Just., D. 127, 3. τὸ Σιν' ὄρος: En 1:4.—Joseph. has Σίναιον ὄρος) ***Sinai,*** name of a rocky mountain on the peninsula named after it. Mountain on which the law was given: **Ac 7:30** (on ἡ ἔρημος τοῦ ὄρους Σινᾶ s. ἡ ἔρημος [τοῦ] Σ. Ex 19:1, 2; Num 33:15, 16 al.), 38; B 11:3; 14:2 (cp. Ex 31:18); 15:1. On **Gal 4:24f** s. Ἁγάρ. Also SRiva, Il Sinai egizio e cristiano: Ricerche Religiose 9, '33, 12–31.—Mlt-H. 148. OEANE V 41–46. TW.

σίναπι, εως, τό (prob. of foreign origin, Schwyzer I 308) Diocles 141 p. 184, 13; PTebt 9, 13; 18 [III BC]; 11, 19 [II BC]; PFay 122, 4; 12; 165; PFlor 20, 21 al. in pap; rejected by Phryn. [Lob. 288] in favor of the Attic νάπυ [νᾶπυ], s. Theophr., HP 7, 1, 2f) ***mustard plant.*** The precise species cannot be determined, and some may grow to a height of three or more meters. κόκκος σινάπεως *mustard seed,* popularly viewed as the smallest of all seeds (s. Antig. Car. 91 and likew. word for word Diod. S. 1, 35, 2 ὁ κροκόδειλος ἐξ ἐλαχίστου γίνεται μέγιστος; cp. Pliny, NH 19, 54, 170; Mishnah, Kilaim 3, 2) **Mt 13:31; 17:20; Mk 4:31; Lk 13:19; 17:6.**—ILöw, D. Flora d. Juden I 1928, 516–27. On the parable of the mustard seed s. in addition to the interpr. of the parables and of the synoptic gospels CBowen, AJT 22, 1918, 562ff; FJehle, NKZ 34, 1923, 713–19; KClark, ClW 37, '43/44, 81–83.—Zohary, Plants p. 93 prob. 'brassica nigra'. BHHW III 1771. DELG s.v. νᾶπυ. M-M. TW.

σινδών, όνος, ἡ (trag., Hdt.+; IG $IV^2/1$, 118, 70 and 71 [III BC]; SIG^2 754, 5; PPetr I, 12, 21 [III BC]; PTebt 182; PPar 18b, 10; LXX; TestAbr A; ApcMos 40; Jos., Ant. 3, 153) gener. 'fine cloth'.

❶ **fabric made from linen, *linen cloth,*** of the cloth in which the body of Jesus was wrapped **Mt 27:59** (on ancient practice Hdt. 2, 86, 6; Vi. Aesopi I G 112 P. σ. καθαράν of a linen garment for a king; TestAbr A 20 p. 103, 21 [Stone 54, 21] for Abraham; ApcMos 40 for Adam and Abel; PGM 13, 653 σ. καθ.; PJoüon, Mt 27:59 σινδὼν καθ.: RSR 24, '34, 93–95); **Mk 15:46; Lk 23:53;** GPt 6:24 (JBlinzler, 'Sindon' in Evangeliis, Verbum Domini 34, '56, 112f).

❷ **a light piece of clothing like a chemise, *shirt,*** by metonymy (cp. Hdt. 2, 95) which was the only piece of clothing worn by the youth who tried to follow Jesus after the latter's arrest **Mk 14:51f** (since σ. was in use in ref. to either linen [usually] or cotton, it is impossible to determine from the scanty context the nature of the fabric; on περιβεβλημένος σινδόνα s. 1 Macc 10:64. For the sense and w. suggestion of scanty attire s. Diog. L. 6, 90, where Crates refers to Theophrastus, who does without a beard; a baptismal initiate receives a σ. after being unclothed AcThom 121 [Aa II/2, 231].—MSmith, Clement of Alexandria and a Secret Gospel of Mark '73, 176.—Appian, Iber. 35 §143: when an unexpected cry from a herald wakened them early in the morning, soldiers ran out ἐν χιτῶσι μόνοις, without dressing fully; contrast ἱμάτιον Mk 10:50 [a garment regularly made of wool, PDickerson, JBL 116, '97, 278f]). S. γυμνός 1a.—M-M.

σινιάζω 1 aor. ἐσινίασα (a late word, for the earlier σήθω; found Syntipas p. 31, 14; 16; Psaltes, Grammatik p. 332; Hesychius; Suda; Etym. Mag.; B-D-F §108, 3; Mlt-H. 405) **to sift by shaking in a sieve, *sift*** metaph. ἐξῃτήσατο ὑμᾶς τοῦ σινιάσαι ὡς τὸν σῖτον (ἐξαιτέω 1) **Lk 22:31** (for the idea cp. Synes., King. 20 p. 24d καθαρτέον τὸ στρατόπεδον, ὥσπερ θημῶνα πυρῶν; Heb. text of Amos 9:9; DCrump, Jesus the Intercessor '92, 154–75).—CPickar, CBQ 4, '42, 135; BNoack, Satanas u. Soteria '48, 101f.—M-M. TW.

σιρικός, ή, όν (the spelling attested by uncials [cp. Peripl. Eryth. 39, p. 13, 11; IG XIV, 785, 4 σιρικοποιός] for the more usual σηρικός [='silken' Strabo 15, 1, 20; Plut., Mor. 396b; Cass.

Dio 57, 15; Jos., Bell. 7, 126 Vespasian and Titus are clothed ἐν ἐσθῆσιν σηρικαῖς].—B-D-F §41, 1; 42, 4; Mlt-H. 72; 378; cp. Σῆρες 'Chinese'; also Paus. 6, 26, 4. Loanw. in rabb.) **pert. to silk fabric from Ser,** subst. τὸ σιρικόν ***silk*** cloth or garments w. other costly materials **Rv 18:12;** GJs 10:2.—B. 403. M-M. Spicq.

σιρός, οῦ, ὁ (Eur., Demosth. et al.; Longus 1, 11, 2; SIG 83, 10 οἰκοδομῆσαι σιρούς; PLond II, 216, 11 p. 186 [I AD]) **a deep hole,** ***pit, cave*** σιροῖς ζόφου **2 Pt 2:4 v.l.** (s. σειρός). On the rdg. σειρά see s.v.—Field, Notes 241.—DELG. M-M.

σιτευτός, ή, όν ***fattened*** (X., An. 5, 4, 32; Polyb. 38, 8, 7; pap, LXX) ὁ μόσχος ὁ σιτευτός *the calf that has been fattened* (Athen. 9, 32, 384a; 14, 74, 657b; Judg 6:28 A; Jer 26:21) **Lk 15:23, 27, 30.** The fatness of the calf would make it a delicacy=prime beef.—DELG s.v. σῖτος. M-M.

σιτία, ας, ἡ (Christian wr.; Hesychius.—σιτεία=feeding, fattening is found as early as PCairZen 534, 1 [III BC]. Is this a different word, from σιτεύω=feed, fatten, or just another spelling?) **a batch of dough,** ***dough*** (so Apophtheg. Patrum [c. VI AD]: MPG LXV 192a; 196b) σ. ποιεῖν *make bread, bake bread* D 13:5.—DELG s.v. σῖτος.

σιτίον, ου, τό (Hdt., Aristoph.+; PGiss 19, 2; POxy 1158, 11; Pr 30:22; TestSol; JosAs 13:7 [codd. AB for σιτιστά]; Philo; Joseph.; prim.: 'grain' or 'food made from grain') dim. of σῖτος; mostly, and in our lit. always, in the pl. τὰ σιτία and in a general ref. to victuals ***food*** (oft. in Hdt. et al.; pap; Jos., Ant. 4, 270; 15, 300) **Ac 7:12.** σιτία καὶ ποτά *food and drink* (s. ποτόν; also HMørland, SymbOsl 13, '34, 103; LDeubner, SBBerlAk '35, XIX, 71) Dg 6:9.—B. 329. DELG s.v. σῖτος. M-M.

σιτιστός, ή, όν (σιτεύω 'to feed, fatten') ***fattened*** (Athen. 14, 656e ὄρνιθες; Herodian. Gramm., Philet. 152 [Dain] σιτευτοὺς ὄρνιθας οὓς οἱ νῦν σιτιστούς; JosAs 10:14; 13:7; Jos., Ant. 8, 40 βόες; Ps 21:13 Sym.; Jer 46:21 Sym. [=Jer 26:21 LXX, which has σιτευτοί]) subst. τὰ σιτιστά *cattle that have been fattened* **Mt 22:4.**—DELG s.v. σῖτος. M-M.

σιτομέτριον, ου, τό (σιτομετρέω 'deal out grain') **a measured allowance of grain/food,** ***food allowance, ration*** (PPetr II, 33a, 5 [s. Dssm., B 156, 5 (BS 158, 1); Mayser 431]; ins fr. Rhodiapolis in Lycia of 149 AD [RHeberdey, Opramoas 1897 p. 50 col. XIX A, 8=IGR III, 739, col. XIX, 8, a billionaire ensures a grain supply for the populace; s. Dssm., LO 82, 1=LAE 104, 1] σειτομέτριον; Rhet. Gr. VI 226, 29.—σιτομετρία is more common) διδόναι τὸ σ. *give out the food allowance* **Lk 12:42.**—New Docs 2, 8. M-M.

σῖτος, ου, ὁ (Hom.+; ins, pap, LXX, JosAs; ApcEsdr 5:12 p. 30, 6 Tdf.; SibOr, Philo Jos., Vi. 71; Ath. 22, 6) ***wheat,*** but also ***grain*** gener. **Mt 13:25, 29** (weeds in it as SibOr 1, 397); **Lk 16:7; Rv 6:6** (on this s. Diod. S. 14, 111, 1 as an indication of severe famine and rising prices πέντε μνῶν γενέσθαι τὸν μέδιμνον τοῦ σίτου=a bushel of grain sold for five minas; Jos., Ant. 14, 28); **18:13.** κόκκος τοῦ σ. **J 12:24; 1 Cor 15:37** (cp. ApcEsdr 5:12 τὸν σπόρον τοῦ σίτου; granum tritici Papias [1, 3]). συνάγειν τὸν σ. εἰς τὴν ἀποθήκην **Mt 3:12; 13:30; Lk 3:17;** cp. **12:18.** σινιάσαι τὸν σ. **22:31.** As a ship's cargo **Ac 27:38.** σ. ὥριμος 1 Cl 56:15 (Job 5:26). For πλήρης σῖτον **Mk 4:28** see πλήρης 2.—Pl. τὰ σῖτα (Hdt.+; Philo, Det. Pot. Ins. 19 and LXX, where this form occurs in Job and Pr; but the pl. is not found in any other book; s. Thackeray 155.—B-D-F §49, 3; Mlt-H. 122; 372) **Ac 7:12 v.l.** Ignatius, in his fervent longing for martyrdom, uses this imagery: σῖτός εἰμι θεοῦ *I am God's wheat* and will be ground by the teeth of the wild beasts IRo 4:1.—B. 514; Pauly-W. Suppl. VI (1935) 819ff; I (1894) 261ff; VII (1912) 1336ff; Kl. Pauly V 217–19; BHHW I 563. DELG. M-M.

σίφων, ωνος, ὁ (since Hipponax [VI BC] 52 D.[3]; Eur., Hippocr.; PEleph 5, 4 [III BC]; PLond 1177, 129; loanw. in rabb.) ***water-pump*** (various types used in agriculture and for fire-fighting Hero Alex. I p. 18, 2; 28, 18 al.) Hm 11:18.—DELG.

σιφωνίζω (σίφων) 1 aor. ἐσιφώνισα (Aristoph., Thesm. 557) ***squirt*** Hm 11:18.

Σιχάρ s. Συχάρ.

Σιών, ἡ indecl. (צִיּוֹן; LXX; PsSol 11:1; TestSol; ParJer 7:33; Mel., P. 7, 47; on the sp. s. B-D-F §38; 56, 3; cp. Mlt-H. 149) **Zion,** of

❶ ***Mt. Zion,*** a hill within the city of Jerusalem (Dalman, Pj 11, 1915, 39ff. S. Ἱεροσόλυμα 1) τὸ ὄρος Σιών, the place where the Lamb is standing w. his people **Rv 14:1.** In imagery as a counterpart to Sinai (cp. Gal 4:24–26; Ps.-Cyprian, De Montibus Sina et Sion: Cyprian III p. 104ff Hartel) **Hb 12:22** (cp. Mel., P. 47 ὁ νόμος λόγος ἐγένετο . . . συνεξελθὼν ἐκ Ζιὼν καὶ Ἱερουσαλήμ).

❷ the city of ***Jerusalem*** (Jer 3:14 et al.; cp. 11 Qps 22:1–15). ἡ θυγάτηρ Σιών of the city of Jerus. and its inhabitants (s. θυγάτηρ 4) **Mt 21:5; J 12:15** (both Zech 9:9; s. SibOr 324).

❸ the ***people of God***—ⓐ the people of Israel, whose center is Jerus. **Ro 9:33;** B 6:2 (both Is 28:16); **Ro 11:26** (Is 59:20).

ⓑ the New Jerus. of prophetic promise **1 Pt 2:6** (Is 28:16).—BHHW III 2242f. M-M. EDNT. TW.

σιωπάω impf. ἐσιώπων; fut. σιωπήσω; 1 aor. ἐσιώπησα; pf. 1 pl. σεσιωπήκαμεν Job 18:3; mid. fut. σιωπήσομαι LXX (Hom. et al.; pap, LXX; TestSol 6:11; TestJob, Test12Patr, ParJer, Philo; Jos., Vi. 195; 338; Mel., P. 25, 177; Ath. 21, 3) prim. 'be silent'.

❶ **to refrain from speaking or making a sound,** ***keep silent, say nothing, make no sound*** **Mt 26:63** (Maximus Tyr. 3, 7e, Socr. before a jury. On the subject-matter cp. Diog. L. 3, 19 Plato before the popular assembly on Aegina, on trial for his life: μηδ' ὁτιοῦν φθέγξασθαι=did not say a single word; Eur. in Plut., Mor. 532f); **Mk 3:4; 9:34; 14:61; Ac 18:9** (opp. λαλεῖν as PGM 5, 292; cp. Theophr., Charac. 7); IEph 15:1 (opp. λαλεῖν); IRo 2:1a; GPt 4:10. σ. περί τινος *be silent concerning someone* IEph 3:2. σ. ἀπό τινος *be silent and leave someone alone* IRo 2:1b.

❷ **to disrupt the process of speaking or making a sound,** ***stop speaking, be/become quiet***—ⓐ of humans (Menand., Georg. 54; Plut., Mor. 434f; Herm. Wr. 1, 16; TestJos 9:4; Jos., Ant. 7, 378; Mel., P. 25, 177) **Mt 20:31; Mk 10:48; Lk 18:39 v.l.; 19:40;** MPol 7:3; GMary 463, 3—*Be silent* in the sense *lose the ability to speak* **Lk 1:20.**

ⓑ not of humans: of swine B 10:3 (opp. κραυγάζειν).—Metaph., of the wind and waves in a storm **Mk 4:39** (cp. the imagery Theocr., Idyll 2, 38 σιγᾷ πόντος).—B. 1259. Schmidt, Syn. I 224. DELG. M-M. S. σιγάω.

σιωπῇ dat. of σιωπή, ῆς, ἡ 'silence' (as a noun Soph., X.+; ins, pap, LXX; TestAbr A 16 p. 98, 11 [Stone p. 44] ἐν σ. γενόμενος; Joseph., Philo; Mel., P. 25, 179 ἡ τοῦ θανάτου σ.) as adv. (as early as Hom.; X., Cyr. 5, 3, 43; Ps.-Demosth. 48, 31; SIG 1218, 11 [V BC]) **pert. to being said out of the hearing of others,** ***quietly, privately*** **J 11:28** D and versions.—DELG s.v. σιωπάω. M-M s.v. σιωπάω.

σκάμμα, ατος, τό (σκάπτω; Pla. et al.) 'someth. that has been dug, trench' (PCol IV, 78 passim [III BC]), then *arena* (surrounded by a trench, or dug up and covered w. sand; CIG 2758), a favorite in metaph. usage (Polyb. 38, 18, 5; Epict. 4, 8, 26) ἐν τῷ αὐτῷ σ. εἶναι *be in the same arena* 1 Cl 7:1.—DELG s.v. σκάπτω.

σκανδαλίζω (σκάνδαλον) 1 aor. ἐσκανδάλισα. Pass.: 1 fut. σκανδαλισθήσομαι; 1 aor. ἐσκανδαλίσθην; pf. ptc. ἐσκανδαλισμένος; (LXX, Aq., Sym., Theod.; PsSol 16:7; TestSol; AscIs 3:14 [but not in Test12Patr, EpArist, Philo, Joseph., apolog.]; Cat. Cod. Astr. X 67, 23; Christian authors).

❶ **to cause to be brought to a downfall,** ***cause to sin*** (the sin may consist in a breach of the moral law, in unbelief, or in the acceptance of false teachings)

ⓐ τινά *someone* (Mal 2:8 Sym., Theod.; PsSol 16:7 γυναικὸς σκανδαλιζούσης ἄφρονα; Palladius 5 p. 21 σκανδαλίσαι ψυχήν) **Mt 5:29f; 18:6, 8f; Mk 9:42f, 45, 47; Lk 17:2; 1 Cor 8:13ab;** 1 Cl 46:8.—Pass. *be led into sin* (Sir 23:8; 32:15; AcJ 82 [Aa II/1, 192, 1]) so perh. **2 Cor 11:29** (s. 2 below).—The abs. pass. can also mean *let oneself be led into sin* (for the 'permissive pass.' s. Gildersleeve, Syntax I §167), *fall away* (Passio Perpet. 20, 10 vGebh.; MartPt 3 [Aa I p. 82, 22]) **Mt 13:21; 24:10; Mk 4:17; 14:27, 29; J 16:1;** D 16:5.—ἐσκανδαλισμένοι Hv 4, 1, 3; m 8:10 are *people who have been led astray,* but who have not altogether fallen away fr. the faith.

ⓑ σκανδαλίζεσθαι ἔν τινι (Sir 9:5; 23:8; 32:15) *be led into sin, be repelled by someone* of Jesus; by refusing to believe in him or by becoming apostate fr. him a person falls into sin **Mt 11:6; 13:57; 26:31, 33** (cp. AscIs 3, 14 δώδεκα οἱ μετ' αὐτοῦ ὑπ' αὐτοῦ σκανδαλισθήσονται); **Mk 6:3; Lk 7:23.** ἐν ᾧ ὁ ἀδελφὸς σκανδαλίζεται **Ro 14:21 v.l.**

❷ **to shock through word or action,** ***give offense to, anger, shock*** (AcJ 56 [Aa II/1 p. 178, 35]; Athanasius, Vita Anton. 81; Palladius 37 p. 115 σκανδαλίζω πολλούς; 46 p. 136) τινά *someone* **Mt 17:27** (JDerrett, NovT 6, '63, 1–15); **J 6:61.** Pass. **Mt 15:12.**—τίς σκανδαλίζεται; perh. *who has any reason to take offense?* **2 Cor 11:29** (s. 1a above).—S. σκάνδαλον, end.—DELG s.v. σκάνδαλον. M-M. EDNT. TW.

σκάνδαλον, ου, τό (s. σκανδαλίζω; non-bibl. pap; PLond 1338, 25; 1339, 10 [both 709 AD]; LXX, Aq., Sym., Theod.; PsSol 4:23 [but not in Test12Patr, EpArist, Philo, Joseph., apolog.], then Christian wr. Later word for σκανδάληθρον [Aristoph. et al.]; s. Hesych. and Phot. s.v.).

❶ **a device for catching someth. alive,** ***trap*** (PCairZen 608, 7 [III BC], where written σκάνδαδον) w. παγίς, used metaph. (Josh 23:13; Ps 140:9; 1 Macc 5:4; Is 8:14 Sym. and Theod.) **Ro 11:9** (Ps 68:23). σκ. ἐν αὐτῷ οὐκ ἔστιν *in such a pers. there is no reason for falling* i.e., as the next vs. indicates, the pers. can see what lies along the path **1J 2:10** (Moffatt 'no pitfall'; s. AVicentCernuda, EstBíbl 27, '68, 153–75, 215–32); but s. 3.

❷ **an action or circumstance that leads one to act contrary to a proper course of action or set of beliefs,** ***temptation to sin, enticement*** to apostasy, false belief, etc., fig. ext. of 1 (Ezk 7:19 Aq. and Sym.; Wsd 14:11) **Mt 18:7abc; Lk 17:1;** B 4:9. τὸ τέλειον σκ. *the final temptation* 4:3. βαλεῖν σκάνδαλον ἐνώπιον τῶν υἱῶν Ἰσραήλ *entice the sons of Israel to sin* **Rv 2:14.** σκάνδαλα ποιεῖν *bring about temptations (to sin)* **Ro 16:17.** τιθέναι τινὶ σκάνδαλον *put a temptation in someone's way* **14:13** (on τιθέναι σκ. cp. Jdth 5:1); in place of the dat. κατά τινος 1 Cl 35:8 (Ps 49:20).—Also of persons (PsSol 4:23; 1 Macc 5:4): Jesus censures Peter, as Satan σκάνδαλον εἶ ἐμοῦ *you are tempting me to sin* **Mt 16:23.** In ἀπεχόμενοι σκανδάλων καὶ τῶν ψευδαδέλφων κτλ. Pol 6:3, σκ. is prob. best taken as *one who tempts others to sin* (cp. Pistis Sophia 105; 106 [p. 173–75 CSchmidt] ὡς σκάνδαλον καὶ ὡς παραβάτης; AcJ 64 [Aa II/1 p. 182, 14f] of a woman ἡ σκάνδαλον γενομένη ἀνδρί; 79 [p. 190, 11]).—To those who cannot come to a decision to believe on him, Jesus is a σκάνδαλον (σκανδαλίζω 1b). In line w. OT imagery (Is 8:14, where Aq., Sym., Theod.—in contrast to the LXX—have our word) Jesus is called πέτρα σκανδάλου **Ro 9:33; 1 Pt 2:8** (on the relation of these two passages to each other s. RHarris, Testimonies I 1916, 18f; 26f).

❸ **that which causes offense or revulsion and results in opposition, disapproval, or hostility,** ***fault, stain*** etc. (Sir 7:6; 27:23). σκ. ἐν αὐτῷ οὐκ ἔστιν *in him there is no stain or fault* **1J 2:10** (cp. Jdth 5:20); but s. 1. Of the cross ὅ ἐστιν σκάνδαλον τοῖς ἀπιστοῦσιν *which is revolting to those who have no faith* IEph 18:1. The crucified Christ is a σκ. to Judeans **1 Cor 1:23.** τὸ σκάνδαλον τοῦ σταυροῦ *the stumbling-block of the cross,* i.e. that which, in the preaching about the cross, arouses opposition **Gal 5:11.** συλλέξουσιν ἐκ τῆς βασιλείας αὐτοῦ πάντα τὰ σκ. *they will gather out of his kingdom everything that is offensive* **Mt 13:41** (this interpr., which refers τὰ σκ. to things, would correspond to the scripture passage basic to this one, i.e. Zeph 1:3, where Sym. has our word in the combination τὰ σκάνδαλα σὺν [τοῖς] ἀσεβέσι. But the fact that Mt continues w. καὶ τοὺς ποιοῦντας τὴν ἀνομίαν could require us to take τὰ σκ. to mean persons; s. 2 above).—To bibl. in TW add RKnox, Trials of a Translator '49, 66–73; AHumbert, Biblica 35, '54, 1–28 (synoptics).—DELG. M-M. DBS XII 49–66. EDNT. TW. Sv.

σκάπτω fut. σκάψω; 1 aor. ἔσκαψα. Pass.: 2 aor. ἐσκάφην; pf. ptc. ἐσκαμμένος (s. σκάμμα; Hom. Hymns, Thu. et al.; ins, pap; Is 5:6; TestJob 39:8, 11)

❶ **to dig into the ground,** ***dig,*** intr. (Aristoph. et al.; BGU 1119, 23 [I BC] σκάπτειν καὶ ποτίζειν) σκάπτειν οὐκ ἰσχύω **Lk 16:3** (s. texts cited in Wetstein; the proverbial expr. Aristoph., Av. 1432 σκάπτειν οὐκ ἐπίσταμαι and Galen, Protr. 13 p. 42, 1ff John: ἰσχύς enough to σκάπτειν. Digging is the hardest kind of work [Chariton 8, 8, 2; Appian, Liby. 15 §61]; an uneducated workman must engage in it [Diog. L. 7, 169; Ps.-Phoc. 158]). σκ. καὶ βαθύνειν (s. βαθύνω) **6:48** (Stephan. Byz. s.v. Ἄργιλος: σκάπτειν εἰς τὸ θεμελίους καταβαλέσθαι).

❷ **to dig for agricultural purposes,** ***cultivate***—ⓐ intr. περὶ αὐτήν *dig around it* (with a hoe or mattock) of a fig tree **Lk 13:8** (cp. Diod. S. 5, 41, 6 περισκαπφείσης τ. γῆς ἀπὸ τῶν ῥίζων).

ⓑ trans. *dig (up), spade (up)* τὶ *someth.* τὸν ἀμπελῶνα (Diod. S. 4, 31, 7; PLond II, 163, 33 p. 183 [I AD]) Hs 5, 2, 4. Pass. (Is 5:6) 5, 2, 5; 5, 6, 2.—B. 497. DELG.

Σκαριώθ the rdg. of D in **Mk 3:19; J 6:71** (for Ἰσκαριώτου). S. next entry.

Σκαριώτης the rdg. of D in **Mt 10:4; 26:14; Mk 14:10.** S. Ἰσκαριώθ. S. prec. entry.

σκάφη, ης, ἡ (σκάπτω; Aeschyl., Hdt. et al.; ins, pap; Bel LXX 33, Theod. 33; [Test12 Patr and Philo σκάφος]; Jos., C. Ap. 2, 11 [a quot. fr. Apion w. σκάφη as fem. sing.]; loanw. in rabb.) gener. someth. that is concave or hollow, such as a 'bowl', 'basin', or 'tub'.

❶ ***dish*** GJs 18:2 (codd.)

❷ ***(small) boat, skiff*** (so Soph. et al.; Polyb. 1, 23, 7; PGradenwitz [SBHeidAk 1914] 9, 5 [III BC]; BGU 1157, 8; 1179; the transference of sense from mng. 1 is readily seen in a pun Ar., Eu. 1315: cp. our 'tub' for an old or slow boat) of a ship's boat (ordinarily in tow, LCasson, Ships and Seamanship in the Ancient World, '71, 248f) **Ac 27:16, 30, 32.**—B. 730. DELG s.v. σκάπτω. M-M.

σκελοκοπέω (prob. not **σκελοκοπάω**) (σκέλος, κόπος 'striking') 1 aor. pass. ἐσκελοκοπήθην ***break the legs*** of someone (s. σκέλος) GPt 4:14 (cp. κατάγνυμι and s. AKirk, NTS 40, '94, 578–83).

σκέλος, ους, τό (Hom.+; ins, pap, LXX, EpArist, Philo; Jos., Ant. 3, 271) *leg* καταγνύναι τὰ σ. *break the legs,* of the breaking of leg-bones as a punishment, known in late Lat. as crurifragium (s. TLL s.v.). Orig. this was a separate form of capital punishment, comparable to torture on a wheel (s. κατάγνυμι and KKohler, Das Verbot d. Knochenzerbrechens: ARW 13, 1910, 153f; a servile punishment fr. at least II BC [Plautus, As. 474 et al.]) **Phlm subscr.**—**J 19:31–33** it accompanied crucifixion, in order to hasten death (s. also Appian, Bell. Civ. 4, 44 §189 ἑνὸς τὸ σκέλος συντριβέντος= one [of the bearers] broke his leg).—GBarton, 'A Bone of Him Shall Not Be Broken' J 19:36: JBL 49, 1930, 13–19; SHarrison, Cicero and 'crurifragium': ClQ n.s. 33, '83, 453–55.—B. 241. DELG. M-M.

σκεπάζω fut. σκεπάσω 1 aor. ἐσκέπασα. Pass.: 1 fut. σκεπασθήσομαι; 1 aor. ἐσκεπάσθην; pf. ptc. n. pl. ἐσκεπασμένα ParJer 6:4 (σκέπας 'covering'; X. et al. Aristot.; pap, LXX, pseudepigr.; Mel., P. 84, 632; Philo, Joseph.).

❶ to spread out over someth. ***cover*** (ApcMos 40; ViJer 13; Jos., Ant. 1, 44) τὶ *someth.* (X. et al.; SibOr 3, 612) of a tree that covers the earth w. its shade Hs 8, 1, 1; 8, 3, 2; cp. 9, 27, 1. Pass. (cp. Philo, Leg. All. 2, 53) 8, 1, 2.

❷ to provide security, ***protect, shelter*** (PSI 440, 14 [III BC]; PTebt 5, 60 [II BC]; PLond III, 897, 6 p. 207 [84 AD]; LXX; SibOr 3, 705) τινά *someone* of bishops σκ. τὰς χήρας τῇ διακονίᾳ *shelter the widows by their ministry* Hs 9, 27, 2 (a play on words w. σκεπάζω 9, 27, 1 [s. 1]). Pass. (PHib 35, 10 [III BC]) 1 Cl 60:3; Hs 9, 27, 3. σκ. ἀπὸ τῶν μελλόντων κριμάτων *be protected from the judgments to come* 1 Cl 28:1.

❸ to keep from view, ***conceal*** ποῦ … σκεπάσω σου τὴν ἀσχημοσύνην; *where shall I conceal your embarrassing condition?*='where shall I keep your pregnancy from public view?' GJs 17:3 (cp. TestAbr A 16 p. 97, 1 [Stone 42, 1] σκέπασόν σου τὴν σαπρίαν).—B. 849. DELG s.v. σκέπας.

σκέπαρνον, ου, τό (also masc.; Hom. et al.; LXX, ins, pap [I AD]) ***axe*** GJs 9:1.—DELG s.v. σκέπαρνος.

σκέπασμα, ατος, τό (σκεπάζω; Pla. et al.) **that which serves as a cover and hence as a protection,** ***covering.*** Chiefly *clothing* (Aristot., Pol. 7, 1336a, 17; Philo, Det. Pot. Ins. 19; Jos., Bell. 2, 129), but also *house* (Aristot., Metaph. 7, 168, 11 οἰκία σκέπασμα ἐκ πλίνθων κ. λίθων) w. διατροφή **1 Ti 6:8.**—DELG s.v. σκέπας. M-M.

σκέπη, ης, ἡ (cp. σκεπάζω; Hdt.+; ins, pap, LXX; JosAs 28:8 [cod. A p. 83, 10 Bat. and Pal 364]; ParJer 6:11; EpArist 140; Manetho: 609 fgm. 10, 237 Jac. [in Jos., C. Ap. 1, 237]; Jos., Ant. 1, 44; Ath., R. 12 p. 61, 12; 23 p. 76, 30) ***shade*** afforded by trees (cp. Diod. S. 5, 65, 1; Philo, Sacr. Abel. 25) suggesting protection or security Hs 8, 1, 1; 8, 3, 2; 9, 1, 9.—DELG s.v. σκέπας.

σκέπτομαι (Hom. et al.; pap, LXX; TestSol 1:1 D; Philo, Ath.) the pass. form is standard, but in the one occurrence in our lit. only act.: fut. ptc. pl. σκέψοντες ***consider***(?) AcPl Ha 1, 12 (text uncertain).—DELG.

Σκευᾶς, ᾶ, ὁ (Plut., Caes. 715 [16, 2]; Appian, Bell. Civ. 2, 60 §247 [a centurion: Lat. Scaeva]; Cass. Dio 56, 16, 1; B-D-F §125, 2) ***Sceva*** a high priest **Ac 19:14** (acc. to EKase, Am. Hist. Review 43, '38, 437f a misunderstanding due to dittography).—BMastin, JTS 27, '76, 405–12 (w. ref. to CIG 2889, on which s. LRobert, Les gladiateurs dans l'orient grec '40, 180ff: an adj. [σκαιός] meaning 'left-handed'); BHHW III 1813; Pauly-W. Suppl. IV 931f; II 471–83; Hemer, Acts 234.—M-M.

σκευή, ῆς, ἡ (Pind., Hdt. et al.; TestSol 5:12; Philo; Jos., Bell. 3, 117, Ant. 4, 301; BGU 775, 6; 11; POslo 187, 6; PWarr 18, 25) **a collective for a variety of items that fall in the category of σκεῦος,** ***equipment*** (used elsewhere of attire, military gear, chorus props, etc.) in our lit. of a *ship's gear* or *equipment* (Diod. S. 14, 79, 4; Appian, Bell. Civ. 5, 88 §367 [= τὰ σκεύη τὰ ἐν τῷ πλοίῳ Jon 1:5]) ἡ σκευὴ τοῦ πλοίου of the equipment of a ship that can be dispensed w. **Ac 27:19** (acc. to CVoigt, Die Romfahrt des Ap. Pls: Hansa 53, 1916, 725–32 *the tackle* or *rigging of a ship*; so NRSV et al.; s. comm.).—DELG s.v. σκεῦος. M-M.

σκεῦος, ους, τό (Aristoph., Thu.+)—**❶ a material object used to meet some need in an occupation or other responsibility,** gener. ***thing, object*** used for any purpose at all (e.g. a table: Diod. S. 17, 66, 5) **Mk 11:16** (PCasey, CBQ 59, '97, 306–32). σκεῦος ἐλεφάντινον or ἐκ ξύλου **Rv 18:12ab.** Pl. (Diod. S. 13, 12, 6) Dg 2:2–4. Of all one has (Jos., Vi. 68; 69) τὰ σκεύη αὐτοῦ *his property* **Lk 17:31.**—**Mt 12:29; Mk 3:27** (both in allusion to Is 49:24f).—By an added statement or via the context σκ. can become an object of a certain specific kind: τὰ σκεύη τῆς λειτουργίας *the equipment used in cultic service* **Hb 9:21** (ParJer 3:9; 11:18; cp. Jos., Bell. 6, 389 τὰ πρὸς τὰς ἱερουργίας σκεύη). Also τὰ ἅγια σκεύη Ox 840, 14; 21; 29f (Jos., Bell. 2, 321; cp. Plut., Mor. 812b σκεῦος ἱερόν; Philo, Mos. 2, 94; Just., D. 52, 3 σκεύη ἱερά). τὸ σκεῦος **Ac 27:17** seems to be the *kedge* or *driving-anchor* (Breusing 17ff; Blass and Haenchen ad loc.; Voigt [s. σκευή]. Differently HBalmer, Die Romfahrt des Ap. Pls 1905, 355ff. See FBrannigan, TGl 25, '33, 182–84; PEdg 6 [=Sb 6712], 10 [258 BC] ἄνευ τῶν ἀναγκαίων σκευῶν πλεῖν τὰ πλοῖα. Pl. also X., Oec. 8, 11f; ; TestJob 18:7 and elsewh. of ship's gear; Arrian, Peripl. 5, 2 τὰ σκεύη τὰ ναυτικά. Eng. tr. have 'gear', 'sails'). **Ac 10:11, 16; 11:5** represent a transitional stage on the way to 2.

❷ a container of any kind, ***vessel, jar, dish,*** etc. (Aristoph., Thesm. 402; X., Mem. 1, 7, 5; Aelian, VH 12, 8; Herodian 6, 7, 7; LXX; Jos., Bell. 7, 106; 8, 89; PsSol 17:38; TestNapth 2:2; JosAs; Just., A I, 9, 2 ἐξ ἀτίμων … σκευῶν) **Lk 8:16; J 19:29; 2 Ti 2:20** (four kinds as Plut., Caes. 730 [48, 7]). τὸ κενὸν σκεῦος Hm 11:13. ποιεῖν σκ. *make a vessel* 2 Cl 8:2. τὰ σκεύη τὰ κεραμικά **Rv 2:27** (s. κεραμικός). σκ. εἰς τιμήν or εἰς ἀτιμίαν (s. τιμή 2b) **Ro 9:21; 2 Ti 2:21** (a fig. sense makes itself felt in the latter pass.).

❸ a human being exercising a function, ***instrument, vessel*** fig. ext. of 1 or 2 (Polyb. 13, 5, 7 Δαμοκλῆς ὑπηρετικὸν ἦν σ.) for Christ Paul is a σκεῦος ἐκλογῆς *a chosen instrument* **Ac 9:15.**—Of the body, in which the Spirit dwells (cp. TestNapht 8:6 ὁ διάβολος οἰκειοῦται αὐτὸν ὡς ἴδιον σκεῦος; ApcMos 16 γενοῦ μοι σκεῦος; and the magical prayer in FPradel, Griech. u. südital. Gebete1907, p. 9, 11f ἐξορκίζω σε ἐξελθεῖν ἀπὸ τοῦ σκεύους τούτου) Hm 5, 1, 2. Christ's body as τὸ σκ. τοῦ πνεύματος *the vessel of the Spirit* B 7:3; 11:9; cp. τὸ καλὸν σκεῦος 21:8 (of the human body, as ApcSed 11:5 [p. 134, 17 Ja.] ὦ χεῖρες … δι' ἃς τὸ σκεῦος τρέφεται; cp. 10 [ln. 25 Ja.]; 11 [ln. 27 Ja.]). On the human body as ὀστράκινα σκεύη **2 Cor 4:7,** s. ὀστράκινος. Those who are lost are σκεύη ὀργῆς **Ro 9:22**

(cp. Jer 27:25.—CDodd, JTS 5, '54, 247f: *instruments of judgment;* sim. AHanson, JTS 32, '81, 433–43), those who are saved σκ. ἐλέους vs. **23.**—**1 Pt 3:7** woman is called ἀσθενέστερον σκεῦος (ἀσθενής 2a). τὸ ἑαυτοῦ σκεῦος **1 Th 4:4** from antiquity has been interpreted to mean *one's own body* (Theodoret, Calvin, Milligan, Schlatter, MDibelius; RKnox, transl. '44; CCD transl. '41, mg.; NRSV) or *one's own wife* (Theodore of Mopsuestia, Schmiedel, vDobschütz, Frame, Oepke; WVogel, ThBl 13, '34, 83–85; RSV et al.). The former interpr. is supported by passages cited at the beg. of this section 3, and the latter is in accord w. rabb. usage (Billerb. III 632f. S. also κτάομαι 1). Also probable for **1 Th 4:4** is 'penis' (so Antistius [I AD] in Anthol. Plan. 4, 243; Aelian, NA 17, 11; cp. the euphemistic Lat. 'vasa' in this sense: Plautus, Poenulus. 863; s. MPoole, Synopsis Criticorum Ali. Sacrae Script., rev. ed.1694, V col. 908; on sim. usage at Qumran s. TElgvin, NTS 43, '97, 604–19; NAB [1970] renders *guarding his member* [difft. rev. ed. of NAB, 1986]. Cp. KDonfried, NTS 31, '85, 342). In such case κτᾶσθαι must mean someth. like 'gain control of', etc.—DELG. M-M. EDNT. TW.

σκηνή, ῆς, ἡ (trag., X., Pla.+; ins, pap, LXX, TestAbr A; TestJud 25:2; ApcMos, Philo, Joseph., Just.; Tat. 22, 2; Orig., C. Cels. 7, 6, 16)

❶ a place of shelter, freq. of temporary quarters in contrast to fixed abodes of solid construction, *tent, hut*

ⓐ gener. *lodging, dwelling,* of the tents of nomads (Gen 4:20; 12:8; TestAbr A 1 p. 77, 4 [Stone p. 2].—Dalman, Arbeit VI '39) **Hb 11:9.** Of a soldier's tent σκηνὴν πηγνύναι *pitch a tent* (πήγνυμι 2) GPt 8:33. Of Joseph in the desert ἔπηξεν τὴν σκηνὴν αὐτοῦ ἐκεῖ GJs 1:4. δίαιτα τῆς σκηνῆς (s. δίαιτα 2) 1 Cl 56:13 (Job 5:24). τρεῖς σκηναί *three huts* (of temporary structures made from brush) in the account of the Transfiguration (w. ποιεῖν as Jos., Ant. 3, 79= pitch tents) **Mt 17:4; Mk 9:5** (RStein, JBL 95, '76, 79–86); **Lk 9:33** (s. σκηνοπηγία and lit. s.v. μεταμορφόω 1; esp. ELohmeyer, ZNW 21, 1922, 191ff; HRiesenfeld, Jésus transfiguré '47, 146–205; HBaltensweiler, Die Verklärung Jesu '59; WSchmithals, ZTK 69, '72, 379–411).—Metaph. ἡ σκηνὴ Δαυὶδ ἡ πεπτωκυῖα *David's fallen dwelling* of his ruined kingdom **Ac 15:16** (Am 9:11). Here σκηνή may perh. mean *king's tent* (Diod. S. 17, 36, 4. More precisely 5 ἡ τοῦ Δαρείου σκηνή; 17, 76, 6 ἡ βασιλικὴ σκηνή): *David's fallen royal tent.*

ⓑ of a movable cultic tent—**α.** Yahweh's tabernacle ἡ σκηνὴ τοῦ μαρτυρίου the *Tabernacle* or *Tent of Testimony* (Ex 27:21; 29:4; Lev 1:1; Num 1:1 and oft.; ViHab 13 [p. 87, 4 Sch.]; Just., D. 36, 2 al.) **Ac 7:44;** 1 Cl 43:2, 5. Also simply ἡ σκηνή (LXX; Jos., Ant. 20, 228; Just., D. 127, 3; s. Iren. 1, 18, 2 [Harv. I 171, 15]) **Hb 8:5; 9:21;** 1 Cl 43:3. οἱ τῇ σκ. λατρεύοντες **Hb 13:10** (s. θυσιαστήριον 1dγ and OHoltzmann, ZNW 10, 1909, 251–60). σκηνὴ ἡ πρώτη *the outer tent,* i.e. the Holy Place **9:2;** cp. vss. **6, 8** (πρῶτος 1c; Jos., C. Ap. 2, 12 has ἡ πρώτη σκηνή of the tabernacle in contrast to Solomon's temple). Hence σκηνὴ ἡ λεγομένη Ἅγια Ἁγίων *the Tabernacle* or *Tent that is called the Holy of Holies* vs. **3,** ἡ δευτέρα (σκηνή) vs. **7.**

β. Moloch's tabernacle ἡ σκηνὴ τοῦ Μολόχ of this deity's portable sanctuary (cp. ἡ ἱερὰ σκηνή of the Carthaginians in Diod. S. 20, 65, 1) **Ac 7:43** (Am 5:26), s. Μόλοχ.

❷ transcendent celestial tent, *tent, dwelling* metaph. ext. of 1. The earthly Tabernacle (s. RKittel, RE XIX 33–42 and GBarton, JBL 57, '38, 197–201) corresponds in Hb to another σκηνή: Christ as High Priest, taking his own blood (rather than that of goats and calves), goes διὰ τῆς μείζονος καὶ τελειοτέρας σκηνῆς ἐφάπαξ εἰς τὰ ἅγια **9:11f.** He is τῶν ἁγίων λειτουργὸς καὶ τῆς σκηνῆς τῆς ἀληθινῆς **8:2. Rv 15:5** speaks of a ναὸς τῆς σκηνῆς τοῦ μαρτυρίου ἐν τῷ οὐρανῷ. God's σκ.=*dwelling* is in heaven **13:6,** and will some time be among humans **21:3.** αἱ αἰώνιοι σκηναί *the eternal dwellings* of the life to come **Lk 16:9** (TestAbr A 20 p. 104, 2 [Stone p. 56] αἱ σκηναὶ τῶν δικαίων; s. RPautrel, 'Aeterna tabernacula' [Lk 16:9]: RSR 30, '40, 307–27; LEby, JBL 58, '39, p. xi).—OScherling, De Vocis σκηνή Significatione et Usu, diss. Marburg 1908; HBornhäuser, Sukka '35, 126–28: Σκηνή u. verwandte Worte im NT.—B. 461. DELG. OEANE V 179–81. M-M. EDNT. TW.

σκηνοπηγία, ας, ἡ (σκηνή, πήγνυμι Aristot., HA 9, 7 of the nest-building of swallows. Elsewh. only as a t.t. of Jewish religious lang.—σκανοπαγέομαι is found as a rel.-technical term in an ins [GDI 3632, 11–16] fr. the island of Cos [II BC.—Dssm., LO 92f=LAE 92f]. On σκηνὴν πηγνύναι s. πήγνυμι 2) prim. 'the setting up of tents' or 'construction of huts'. As name for the ***Festival of Booths/Tabernacles*** (σκ. in this sense, mostly w. ἑορτή: Dt 16:16; 31:10; Zech 14:16, 18, 19; 1 Esdr 5:50; 2 Macc 1:9 [τὰς ἡμέρας τῆς σκ.]; Jos., Ant. 4, 209; 8, 100; 123; 11, 154; 13, 241; 372; 15, 50, Bell. 2, 515. Jewish ins fr. Berenice in the Cyrenaica CIG III 5361 [13 BC]=Schürer III 94, n. 20, ln. 4), a festival celebrated Tishri (roughly=October) 15–21, out of doors when poss., in booths made fr. tree branches (חַג הַסֻּכּוֹת). Joseph. declares (Ant. 15, 50; cp. 8, 123) that it is the most important Jewish festival. **J 5:1 v.l.; 7:2** (CSmith, NTS 9, '63, 130–46).—Billerb. II 774–812; HBornhäuser, Sukka '35, esp. pp. 34–39.—Demetrius of Scepsis in Athen. 4, 141ef tells of the τῶν Καρνείων of the Spartans σκηναῖς ἔχοντες παραπλήσιόν τι. They put up for nine days 'something like a tent'. At times nine men eat together in them.—GMacRae, The Mng. and Evolution of the Feast of Tabernacles, CBQ 22, '60, 251–76.—M-M. TW.

σκηνοποιός, οῦ, ὁ—**❶** ***maker of stage properties*** (acc. to Pollux 7, 189 the Old Comedy used the word as a synonym for μηχανοποιός=either a 'stagehand' who moved stage properties [as Aristoph., Pax 174] or a 'manufacturer of stage properties'. Associated terms include σκηνογράφος Diog. L. 2, 125 and σκηνογραφία Arist., Poet. 1449a and Polyb. 12, 28a, 1, in ref. to painting of stage scenery) **Ac 18:3.** But if one understands σκηνή not as 'scene' but as 'tent' and considers it improbable that Prisca, Aquila, and Paul would have practiced such a trade in the face of alleged religious objections (s. Schürer II 54–55 on Jewish attitudes towards theatrical productions), one would follow the traditional rendering

❷ ***tentmaker.*** This interpretation has long enjoyed favor (s. Lampe s.v.; REB, NRSV; Hemer, Acts 119, 233), but several considerations militate against it. The term σκηνοποιός is not used outside the Bible (and its influence), except for Pollux (above) and Herm. Wr. 516, 10f=Stob. I, 463, 7ff. There it appears as an adj. and in a figurative sense concerning production of a dwelling appropriate for the soul. The context therefore clearly indicates a structure as the primary component, but in the absence of such a qualifier in **Ac 18:3** it is necessary to take account of words and expressions that similarly contain the terms σκηνή and ποιεῖν. A survey of usage indicates that σκηνή appears freq. as the obj. of ποιέω in the sense 'pitch' or 'erect a tent' (s. ποιέω 1a; act. σκηνοποιέω Is 13:20 Sym. οὐδὲ σκηνοποιήσει ἐκεῖ Ἄραψ; 22:15 Sym.; mid. σκηνοποιέομαι Aristot., Meteor. 348b, 35; Clearch., fgm. 48 W.; Polyb. 14, 1, 7; Diod. S. 3, 27, 4; Ps.-Callisth. 2, 9, 8.—Cp. σκηνοποιΐα Aeneas Tact. 8, 3; Polyb. 6, 28, 3; ins, RevArch 3, '34, 40; and acc. to the text. trad. of Dt 31:10 as an alternate expr. for σκηνοπηγία.—Ex 26:1, it is granted, offers clear evidence of use of the non-compounded σκηνή +

ποιέω in the sense 'produce' or 'manufacture [not pitch] a tent', but the context makes the meaning unmistakable; cp. Herodian 7, 2, 4 on the building of rude housing). Analogously σκηνοποιός would mean 'one who pitches or erects tents', linguistically a more probable option than that of 'tentmaker', but in the passages cited for σκηνοποιέω and σκηνοποιΐα components in the context (cp. the case for provision of housing in the Hermetic pass.) clearly point to the denotation 'pitching of tents', whereas **Ac 18:3** lacks such a clear qualifier. Moreover, it is questionable whether residents of nomadic areas would depend on specialists to assist in such a common task (s. Mt 17:4 par. where a related kind of independent enterprise is mentioned).—That Prisca, Aquila, and Paul might have been engaged in the preparation of parts for the production of a tent is also improbable, since such tasks would have been left to their hired help. That they might have been responsible for putting a tent together out of various pieces is ruled out by the availability of the term σκηνορράφος (Ael., VH 2, 1 et al.; Bull. Inst. Arch. Bulg. 8, 69) in the sense of stitching together (the verb ἐπιτελεῖν Hb 8:5 does not support such a view, for it is not an alternate expr. for 'production' of a tent but denotes 'completion' of a project, connoting a strong sense of religious commitment; see ἐπιτελέω 2) in which the component ῥαφ- provides an unmistakable qualifier.—In modern times more consideration has been given to identification of Paul's trade as 'leather-worker', an interpretation favored by numerous versions and patristic writings (s. Zahn, AG, ad loc.; L-S-J-M Suppl., s.v., as replacement for their earlier 'tentmaker'; Haenchen, ad loc., after JJeremias, ZNW 30, '31; Hock, s. below). As such he would make tents and other products from leather (Hock [s. below] 21). But this and other efforts at more precise definition, such as weaver of tent-cloth (a view no longer in fashion) may transmit reflections of awareness of local practice in lieu of semantic precision.—In the absence of any use of the term σκηνοποιός, beyond the pass. in Pollux and the Herm. Wr., and the lack of specific qualifiers in the text of **Ac 18:3,** one is left with the strong probability that Luke's publics in urban areas, where theatrical productions were in abundance, would think of σκηνοποιός in ref. to matters theatrical (s. 1). In addition, Ac 20:34; 1 Cor 4:12; 1 Th 2:9; 2 Th 3:8 indicate that Paul's work was of a technical nature and was carried out in metropolitan areas, where there would be large demand for such kind of work. What publics in other areas might understand is subject to greater question, for the evidence is primarily anecdotal.—JWeiss, Das Urchristentum 1917, 135; FGrosheide, Παῦλος σκηνοποιός: TSt 35, 1917, 241f; Zahn, AG II 632, 10; 634; Billerb. II 745–47; Beginn. IV, 223; PLampe, BZ 31, '87, 211–21; RHock, The Social Context of Paul's Ministry: Tentmaking and Apostleship '80.—M-M. TW.

σκῆνος, ους, τό (Pre-Socr., Hippocr.+; ins; Wsd 9:15) **a temporary abode as opposed to a permanent structure, *tent, lodging*** fig. ext. of the prim. mng. 'tent', which is not found in our lit.: of the body (Democr. [Vorsokrat. index] et al.; Ps.-Pla., Axioch. 365e; 366a; Herm. Wr. 13, 12; 15; Achilles Tat. 2, 36, 3 τὸ οὐράνιον θνητῷ σκήνει δεδεμένον; CIG 1656 σκῆνος μὲν . . . , ψυχὴ δέ; 3123; 6309; PGM 1, 319; 4, 1951; 1970; Wsd 9:15) εἶναι ἐν τῷ σ. *be in one's tent,* i.e. be physically alive **2 Cor 5:4.** ἡ ἐπίγειος ἡμῶν οἰκία τοῦ σ. *the earthly tent we live in* vs. **1** (on the gen.-combination s. B-D-F §168, 1; Rob. 498; on the imagery Straub 84f).—S. γυμνός 3, end.—DELG s.v. σκηνή. M-M. TW.

σκηνόω (σκηνή) fut. σκηνώσω; 1 aor. ἐσκήνωσα (X., Pla. et al.; LXX; Jos., Vi. 244, Ant. 3, 293) ***live, settle, take up residence*** (X., Demosth. 54, 3; SIG 344, 3; PSI 340, 10; 13 [III BC]; LXX) w. ἐν and the dat. of place (X., An. 5, 5, 11; PEdg 68 [=Sb 6774], 7; Gen 13:12) ἐν τ. οὐρανῷ **Rv 13:6;** cp. **12:12** ἐν ἡμῖν *among us* (perh. an expression of continuity with God's 'tenting' in Israel) **J 1:14** (Iren. 1, 9, 2 [Harv. I 82, 9]; Diogenes, Ep. 37, 1 παρὰ τούτοις ἐσκήνωσα='I took up residence w. them'). μετ' αὐτῶν *with them* **Rv 21:3.** ἐπ' αὐτούς *over* or *above them,* i.e. shelter them, of God (s. σκηνή 1bα) **7:15.**—DELG s.v. σκηνή. M-M. TW.

σκήνωμα, ατος, τό (σκηνόω; Eur., X. et al.; LXX; TestJob 43:7, 11; ParJer; ApcSed 9; Jos., Ant. 11, 187) gener. 'lodging, dwelling', in our lit. only metaph. ***habitation***

ⓐ of a people σκήνωμα τῷ οἴκῳ Ἰακώβ *a habitation for the house of Jacob* **Ac 7:46** (after Ps 131:5, but w. οἴκῳ for θεῷ). For this rdg. of the text s. Metzger 351–53, lit. n. 11.

ⓑ of God (Paus. 3, 17, 6; LXX) **Ac 7:46** belongs here if σκήνωμα in the text as cited above is to be understood in ref. to a dwelling shared by God, and esp. so if θεῷ instead of Ἰακώβ is preferred, in which case the dwelling is for God alone.

ⓒ of the body (Ps.-Callisth. 1, 24, 11; Herm. Wr. in Stob., Flor. I 396, 1 W.=p. 476, 3 Sc.; schol. on Nicander, Ther. 694; PGM 19a, 49; Sextus 320; s. σκῆνος) εἶναι ἐν τούτῳ τῷ σκ.=remain alive **2 Pt 1:13** (cp. the late Christ. ins IG X/2, 1, 397, 6f, s. New Docs 4, 172); opp. ἡ ἀπόθεσις τοῦ σκ.=death vs. **14.** ἡ ψυχὴ ἐν θνητῷ σκηνώματι κατοικεῖ Dg 6:8 (Sext., loc. cit. τὸ σ. τῆς ψυχῆς).—DELG s.v. σκηνή. M-M. TW.

σκῆπτρον, ου, τό (σκήπτομαι 'lean (on)', e.g. a staff; Hom.+; ins; PGM 13, 182; 187; LXX; TestSol; Test12Patr)

❶ ***scepter*** as a symbol of the power to rule (TestJud 24:5; JosAs 5:6; Ant. 17, 197) σκ. τῆς μεγαλωσύνης τοῦ θεοῦ *the scepter of the majesty of God* 1 Cl 16:2 (cp. Esth 4:17q; Ezk. Trag. 71 in Eus., PE 9, 29, 5; Philo, Mut. Nom. 136; SibOr 3, 49. The scepter of Zeus Pind., P. 1, 6; Cornutus 9 p. 10, 10; Iambl., Vi. Pyth. 28, 155; of Rhea Pind., N. 11, 4; of Isis IAndrosIsis, Cyrene 6 p. 129; of Selene PGM 4, 2843f.—FdeWaele, The Magic Staff or Rod in Graeco-Italian Antiquity 1927, ch. 1).

❷ ***tribe,*** by metonymy, of the tribes of Israel (1 Km 2:28; 9:21; 3 Km 11:31f, 35f al.; Jos., Ant. 6, 61; TestJud 25:1; TestNapht 5:8) 1 Cl 32:2.—DELG s.v. σκήπτομαι.

σκιά, ᾶς, ἡ (Hom.+; ins, pap, LXX; ParJer 3: 14; 5:1 Philo; Jos., Bell. 2, 28 σκιά-σῶμα, Ant. 5, 238; 10, 29; Just., Mel., Ath.).

❶ **shade or shelter from light and any heat associated with it, *shade* Mk 4:32** (cp. Ezk 17:23; ParJer, Just., Ath.).

❷ **the shape cast by an object as it blocks rays of light, *shadow*—ⓐ** lit. **Ac 5:15**

ⓑ fig. (s. σκότος 3.—Jos., Bell. 1, 215) σκιὰ θανάτου *shadow of death* (Job 12:22; Ps 22:4; 43:20; Jer 13:16; Mel., P. 56, 409 τὰς τοῦ θανάτου σκιάς.—So also σκιά by itself of the shadow of death, which stands beside an old man: Herodas 1, 16) **Mt 4:16** (Is 9:1); w. σκότος (Job 3:5; Ps 106:10, 14) **Lk 1:79** (Ps 106, 10; s. New Docs 4, 149). For σκοτία **1J 2:8 v.l.**

❸ **a mere representation of someth. real, *shadow*** (from the sense of insubstantial aspect, e.g. shades of the dead: Od. 10, 495; Aeschyl., Eum. 302, there develops the idea of a contrast between image and reality: Prodicus [V BC] fgm. 2 [in X., Mem. 2, 1, 22]; Achilles Tat. 1, 15, 6 τὸ ὕδωρ ἦν κάτοπτρον, ὡς δοκεῖν τὸ ἄλσος εἶναι διπλοῦν, τὸ μὲν τ. ἀληθείας, τὸ δὲ τ. σκιᾶς 'the water served as a mirror suggesting that the grove was twofold, one real and the other a reflection'; Phalaris, Ep. 35 λόγος ἔργου σκ. Oft. in Philo: Somn. 1, 206, Plant. 27; Leg. All. 3, 102, Post. Caini 112) σκιὰ τῶν μελλόντων *a shadow of what* *is to come* **Col 2:17** (opp. τὸ σῶμα, as Philo, Conf. Lingu. 190; Jos., Bell. 2, 28; Lucian, Hermot. 79). ὑπόδειγμα καὶ σκιὰ τῶν ἐπουρανίων **Hb 8:5** (Synes., Ep. 44 p. 182d τοῦ θείου σκ. τὸ ἀνθρώπινον; LHurst, JTS 34, '83, 163–65). σκιά forms a contrast to εἰκών (s. εἰκών 3) **10:1.**—B. 62.—DELG. M-M. EDNT. TW.

σκιρτάω fut. 2 pl. σκιρτήσετε Mal 3:20; 1 aor. ἐσκίρτησα (Hom. et al.; PGM 3, 200; LXX; Philo, Spec. Leg. 1, 304) **exuberant springing motion, *leap, spring about*** as a sign of joy (Jer 27:11; Mal 3:20; Jos., Bell. 5, 120) **Lk 6:23;** AcPl Ha 3, 18. Of sheep gaily skipping about (cp. Dio Chrys. 69 [19], 3; Longus 1, 9,1; Theophyl. Sim., Ep. 29; Eutecnius 1 p. 18, 3) Hs 6, 1, 6; 6, 2, 3 f; 6. ἐκκλησίας χάρις σκιρτᾷ Dg 11:6. Of the movements of a child in the womb (Gen 25:22. S. ENorden, Die Geburt des Kindes 1924 p. 104, 1), which are taken as an expression of joy **Lk 1:41, 44;** GJs 12:2.—Metaph. καὶ τὰ ὕδατα ταῦτα γαληνιῶντα καὶ σκιρτῶντα *these waters at once calm and then billowing* with suggestion of life in contrast to Anna's sterility GJs 3:3.—DELG. M-M. TW.

σκληροκαρδία, ας, ἡ (a correct formation, but modeled after עָרְלַת לֵבָב Dt 10:16; Jer 4:4; Sir 16:10; En 16:3; TestSim 6:2 v.l.; Philo, Spec. Leg. 1, 305; Just.; Did., Gen 233, 10.—B-D-F §120, 4; Mlt-H. 279) **an unyielding frame of mind, *hardness of heart, coldness, obstinacy, stubbornness* Mt 19:8; Mk 10:5;** Hv 3, 7, 6 (Leutzsch, Hermas 419 n. 374); B 9:5 (after Dt 10:16; Jer 4:4). W. ἀπιστία **Mk 16:14.**—EDNT. TW. Spicq.

σκληρός, ά, όν (σκέλλομαι 'be parched, be dry'; Hes., Hdt.+; 'hard [to the touch], harsh')

❶ **pert. to being externally hard or rough, *hard*** (to the touch), ***rough,*** of things λίθοι *hard* (OGI 194, 28; Wsd 11:4) Hs 9, 6, 8; 9, 8, 6ab. ῥάβδος *rough,* of a knotty stick (s. Pind., O. 7, 29; Diogenes the Cynic [IV BC] in Diog. L. 6, 21 σκληρὸν ξύλον=a hard staff; Aelian, VH 10, 16) 6, 2, 5.

❷ **pert. to causing an adverse reaction because of being hard or harsh, *hard, harsh, unpleasant,*** fig. ext. of 1, of words (Demetrius in Stob., Flor. 3, 8, 20 vol. III p. 345 H.; Diogenes, Ep. 21; Gen 21:11; 42:7; Dt 1:17; En) **J 6:60; Jd 15** (after En 1:9); s. Hv 1, 4, 2 (w. χαλεπός). ἐντολαί *hard, difficult* (Diod. S. 14, 105, 2 σκ. πρόσταγμα; Porphyr., Vi. Pyth. 8 προστάγματα) Hm 12, 3, 4f; 12, 4, 4 (w. δύσβατος). ἄνεμοι *rough, strong* (Aelian, VH 9, 14; Pollux 1, 110; Procop., Bell. 3, 13, 5; Pr 27:16) **Js 3:4.**

❸ **pert. to being difficult to the point of being impossible, *hard,*** implying an adverse force that is unyielding, the neut.: σκληρόν σοι (sc. ἐστίν) *it is hard for you* w. inf. foll. **Ac 9:4 v.l., 6 v.l.; 26:14.**

❹ **pert. to being unyielding in behavior or attitude—ⓐ** of pers., in dealing with others ***hard, strict, harsh, cruel, merciless*** (Soph., Pla. et al.; OGI 194, 14; 1 Km 25:3; Is 19:4; 48:4; PsSol 4:2; EpArist 289; Mel., P. 20, 138) **Mt 25:24.** Of the devil Hm 12, 5, 1.

ⓑ in response to a call for change of mind, subst. τὸ σκληρόν ***stubbornness*** w. gen. (Polyb. 4, 21, 1; Jos., Ant. 16, 151 τὸ σκ. τοῦ τρόπου) τὸ σκ. τῆς καρδίας *the hardness of heart* B 9:5 v.l. (for σκληροκαρδία, q.v.).—On the history of the word s. KDieterich, RhM, n.s. 60, 1905, 236ff; FDanker, Hardness of Heart, CTM 44, '73, 89–100, Deafness and Hearing in the Bible, in The Word in Signs and Wonders, ed. DPokorny/RHohenstein '77, 25–37.—B. 1064.—DELG s.v. σκέλλομαι. M-M. TW. Spicq.

σκληρότης, ητος, ἡ (σκληρός; Antiphon, Pla. et al.; LXX, Philo; Jos., Ant. 3, 2) ***hardness (of heart), stubbornness*** as a human characteristic (Pla., Rep. 3, 410d; 10, 607b; Aristot., Poet. 15, 11; Dt 9:27; Philo, Spec. Leg. 304) **Ro 2:5.** Of the spirit of *harshness, roughness* w. which the Holy Spirit cannot live Hm 5, 2, 6 (cp. Antiphon Or. 3, 3, 4 σκλ. τοῦ δαίμονος).—DELG s.v. σκέλλομαι. M-M. TW. Spicq.

σκληροτράχηλος, ον (a correct formation, but modeled after קְשֵׁה־עֹרֶף; Aesop 318 H. [=S 30 P. p. 538 and H-H.]; Physiogn. I 368, 4, this and the Aesop pass. are the product of Byzantine editing; LXX; En 98:11; ViDa 6 [p. 77, 11 Sch. τὸ σκλ.]; Mel., P. 17, 115 [Φαραώ].—τράχηλος σκληρός: Hippocr., Coac. Progn. 2, 14, 256 ed. Littré V p. 640) ***stiff-necked, stubborn* Ac 7:51;** 1 Cl 53:3 (Dt 9:13).—M-M. TW. Spicq.

σκληρύνω fut. σκληρυνῶ; 1 aor. ἐσκλήρυνα. Pass.: impf. ἐσκληρυνόμην; 1 aor. ἐσκληρύνθην (σκληρός; Hippocr. et al.; Aristot., Galen; PLeid X II, 28; LXX; PsSol 8:29; TestSol 25:3, 5) prim. 'harden'; in our lit. only in fig. sense: **to cause to be unyielding in resisting information, *harden*** (LXX)

ⓐ act.—**α.** w. a human subject τὶ *something* τὴν καρδίαν 1 Cl 51:3a; τὰς καρδίας (Ps 94:8) **Hb 3:8, 15; 4:7.** τὸν τράχηλον σκλ. *stiffen the neck* B 9:5 (Dt 10:16).

β. w. God as subj. τινά *harden the heart of someone* (cp. Ex 7:3; 9:12 al.) **Ro 9:18.**—KSchmidt, D. Verstockung des Menschen durch Gott: TZ 1, '45, 1–17.

ⓑ pass. *be* or *become hardened* (Sir 30:12) ἐσκληρύνοντο **Ac 19:9;** cp. **Hb 3:13.** ἐσκληρύνθη ἡ καρδία (cp. Ex 8:15; 9:35) 1 Cl 51:3b; cp. 5.—For the Hellenic mode of expressing this topic s. s.v. τίκτω end.—DELG s.v. σκέλλομαι. M-M. TW. Spicq.

σκολιός, ά, όν (σκέλος; Hom. et al.; Kaibel 244, 4; LXX, Joseph.; SibOr 1, 124; prim. 'curved, bent')

❶ **pert. to being bent, curved, or crooked as opposed to straight, *crooked*** (opp. εὐθύς; cp. Jos., Bell. 3, 118 τὰ σκολιὰ τῆς λεωφόρου [=highway] κατευθύνειν) ἔσται τὰ σκολιὰ εἰς εὐθεῖαν **Lk 3:5** (cp. schol. on Nicander, Ther. 478 of the ὁδός in contrast to εὐθύς; Is 40:4; 42:16). In imagery of τοῦ μέλανος ὁδός B 20:1 (cp. Pr 21:8; 28:18).

❷ **pert. to being morally bent or twisted, *crooked, unscrupulous, dishonest,*** etc., fig. extension of 1 (Hom. et al.; Dio Chrys. 58 [75], 1 w. πονηρός; Lucian, Bis Accus. 16 ῥημάτια; LXX; Jos., C. Ap. 1, 179) γενεὰ σκ. (Dt 32:5 γεν. σκ. καὶ διεστραμμένη; Ps 77:8. Also Dionysius Perieg. [GGM II 186 p. 127 v. 392 σκολιὸν γένος]) **Ac 2:40** (difft. MWilcox, The Semitisms of Ac, '65, 30); **Phil 2:15.** δεσπόται *harsh, unjust* **1 Pt 2:18** (opp. ἀγαθοὶ κ. ἐπιεικεῖς).—σκολιόν τι *someth. wrong* 1 Cl 39:4 (Job 4:18).—JPalache, Semantic Notes on the Hebrew Lexicon '59, 55f. B. 897. DELG s.v. σκέλος. M-M. TW.

σκολιότης, ητος, ἡ (σκολιός; Hippocr.+; LXX, Aq., Sym.) fig. (Aristaen., Ep. 1, 28) ***crookedness, perversity, deceit*** (Ezk 16:5 τῇ σκολ. τῆς ψυχῆς σου) w. πονηρία Hv 3, 9, 1.—DELG s.v. σκέλος.

σκόλοψ, οπος, ὁ (Hom. et al.; Artem.; PGM 36, 152; 270; LXX) orig. 'anything pointed' such as a '(pointed) stake', then someth. that causes serious annoyance ***thorn, splinter,*** etc., specif. of an injurious foreign body (SIG 1168, 92; Num 33:55 σκόλοπες ἐν τοῖς ὀφθαλμοῖς; Sext. Emp. in BGU 380, 8 τὸν πόδαν πονεῖς ἀπὸ σκολάπου; Aesop, Fab. 187 P.; 363 P.=Babrius no. 136, 18 L-P.; Artem. 3, 33; Cyranides p. 112, 24 a prescription for removing σκόλοπας κ. ἀκάνθας.—Field, Notes 187). Paul alludes to his illness (s. κολαφίζω 2 and also EMerrins, St. Paul's Thorn in the Flesh: BiblSacr 64, 1907, 661–92. For varying viewpoints s. CBruston, L'Écharde de St. Paul:

RTQR 21, 1912, 441ff; PJoüon, RSR 15, 1925, 532f; CNash, Paul's 'Thorn in the Flesh': RevExp 28, '31, 33–51; PMenoud, Studia Paulina [JdeZwaan Festschr.] '53, 163–71; HClavier, ibid. 66–82; TMullins, JBL 76, '57, 299–303; AHisey and JBeck, Journ. of Bible and Religion 29, '61, 125–29; JThierry, D. Dorn im Fleisch, NovT 5, '62, 301–10; MBarré, CBQ 42, '80, 216–27; VFurnish, II Corinthians (AB) '84, 547–50; DPark, NovT 22, '80, 179–83; UHeckel, ZNW 84, '93, 65–92. Lack of details makes impossible a truly scientific analysis of Paul's σκ.) in ἐδόθη μοι σκ. τῇ σαρκί *a thorn in the flesh was given to me* **2 Cor 12:7.** The fact that Celsus uses the word σκ. (2, 55; 68) w. evident scorn (Origen has σταυρός) to mean the cross of Jesus, can scarcely indicate that Paul is using it in that sense here, since he always says σταυρός elsewh. (against ASchlatter, Pls, d. Bote J. Chr. '34, 666). Lucian also, in Peregr. 13, 337, contemptuously of the ἀνεσκολοπισμένος ἐκεῖνος σοφιστής. Cp. 11, 334 ἄνθρωπος ἀνασκολοπισθείς. A believer does not use that sort of language.—DELG. M-M. TW.

σκοπέω (σκοπός; Hom.+; ins, pap; Esth 8:12g; 2 Macc 4:5; TestNapth 3:1 v.l.; Philo, Joseph., Just.; Ath. 10, 2, R. 2 p. 49, 25 al.—B-D-F §101, p. 48; Mlt.-H. 258) fut. ptc. σκόπησον (Just., D. 3, 2) **to pay careful attention to,** ***look (out) for, notice*** w. acc. of pers. or thing *someone* or *someth.* (Jos., Ant. 12, 30; Just., D. 2, 5) σκοπεῖτε τοὺς οὕτω περιπατοῦντας *notice those who conduct themselves thus,* i.e. in order to imitate them **Phil 3:17.** σκοπεῖν τοὺς τὰς διχοστασίας ποιοῦντας *look out for those who cause divisions,* i.e. avoid them **Ro 16:17.**—σκ. τὰ βλεπόμενα *keep one's eyes on what can be seen* **2 Cor 4:18.**—τὰ ἑαυτῶν *look out for one's own interests* (Pla., Phdr. 232d) **Phil 2:4.** Also τὸ καθ' ἑαυτούς MPol 1:2. τὸ κοινὸν τῆς ἐλπίδος 1 Cl 51:1.—σκ. ἑαυτόν foll. by μή *look to oneself, that . . . not* **Gal 6:1.** σκόπει μὴ τὸ φῶς σκότος ἐστίν *consider whether the light be darkness* **Lk 11:35** (μή interrog. = Lat. 'num' [cp. Zahn ad loc.; difft. Rob. 995] because of the indic.; cp. Epict. 4, 5, 18 ὅρα μὴ Νερωνιανὸν ἔχει χαρακτῆρα).—DELG s.v. σκέπτομαι. M-M. TW.

σκοπός, οῦ, ὁ (since Hom. in var. senses) ***goal, mark*** (Hom.+; ins, pap; Job 16:12; La 3:12; Wsd 5:12; TestJob 9:8; EpArist 251; Jos., Ant. 16, 248; Ath., R. 23 p. 77, 7) ὁ τῆς εἰρήνης σκ. 1 Cl 19:2; ὁ προκείμενος ἡμῖν σκ. 63:1 (Philo, Mos. 1, 48; Jos., Bell. 4, 555 σκοπὸς προύκειτο Ῥωμαίοις). κατὰ σκοπὸν διώκειν *press on toward the goal* (Paul is 'in the stretch'; cp. κατὰ σκόπον ἐκτοξεύειν='shoot right on target' Onosander 17; διώκω 1) **Phil 3:14.** σκοπὸν τιθέναι *set a mark* (cp. Pla., Leg. 12, 961e; Polyb. 7, 8, 9) 2 Cl 19:1.—DLasky, An Examination of the Metaphorical Use of 'Skopos' or Target in the Philosophical Works of Plato and Aristotle through a Study of Archery Imagery in the Greek Literary Tradition, 2 vols. diss. Chicago '94. DELG s.v. σκέπτομαι B. M-M. TW.

σκορπίζω (fr. σκορπίος) fut. σκορπιῶ LXX; 1 aor. ἐσκόρπισα. Pass.: fut. 3 pl. σκορπισθήσονται Tob 14:4 BA; 1 aor. ἐσκορπίσθην; pf. ptc. ἐσκορπισμένος LXX.

❶ **to cause a group or gathering to go in various directions,** ***scatter, disperse*** (Hecataeus Mil.: 1 fgm. 366 Jac. [in Phryn. p. 218 Lob.]; Strabo 4, 4, 6; Ps.-Lucian, Asinus 32; Aelian, VH 13, 45; Jos., Ant. 16, 10; LXX; TestSol; TestAsh 7:6 v.l.; Tat. 30, 1) of a wolf τὰ πρόβατα σκορπίζει *he chases the sheep in all directions* **J 10:12.** Opp. συνάγειν (Artem. 1, 56 p. 52, 17 συνάγει τοὺς ἐσκορπισμένους τὸ ὄργανον; Tob 13:5 BA) ὁ μὴ συνάγων μετ' ἐμοῦ σκορπίζει, prob. w. ref. to a flock rather than to a harvest **Mt 12:30; Lk 11:23** (in Astrampsychus 40 Dec. 83, 8 and Cat. Cod. Astr. II 162, 7 σκ.='squander, waste'.—On the idea s. Polyaenus 8, 23, 27: Καῖσαρ Πομπηΐου κηρύξαντος ἔχθραν καὶ τοῖς μηδετέρῳ προστιθεμένοις ἀντεκήρυξε καὶ φίλους ἡγήσεσθαι κατ' ἴσον τοῖς ἑαυτῷ συμμαχήσασιν 'when Pompey declared hostility, Caesar in turn proclaimed to those who did not choose sides that he equated friends with those who joined forces with himself'. In Lat. in Cicero: AFridrichsen, ZNW 13, 1012, 273–80. Caesar's point of view resembles that of Mk 9:40=Lk 9:50). Pass. (Plut., Timol. 4, 2; Philo; Jos., Ant. 6, 116; 1 Macc 6:54 ἐσκορπίσθησαν ἕκαστος εἰς τὸν τόπον αὐτοῦ) *be scattered* ἵνα σκορπισθῆτε ἕκαστος εἰς τὰ ἴδια **J 16:32.**

❷ **to distribute in various directions,** ***scatter abroad, distribute*** (PLond I, 131, 421 p. 182 [I AD] of spreading fertilizer over an entire field; PFlor 175, 22 τὰ καμήλια ἐσκορπίσαμεν='we have distributed the camels in various places'; Jos., Ant. 16, 10) of God ἐσκόρπισεν, ἔδωκεν τοῖς πένησιν **2 Cor 9:9** (Ps 111:9).—DELG s.v. σκορπίος. M-M. TW.

σκορπίος, ου, ὁ (Aeschyl., Pla. et al.; Sb 1209 ἐτελεύτησεν ὑπὸ σκορπίου; 1267, 7; LXX; TestSol 13:8 P; Philo; Jos., Ant. 8, 217; Tat. 9, 2).

❶ **a species of vermin,** ***scorpion*** (an arachnid, 4 to 5 inches long) common in southern latitudes, much feared because of its sting **Rv 9:3, 5, 10** (κέντρον as Demosth. 25, 52). W. serpents (Dio Chrys. 57 [74], 20; Sb 6584, 6; Dt 8:15) **Lk 10:19; 11:12** (cp. ἀντί 1. HPegg, ET 38, 1927, 468).

❷ **an extremely harmful person,** ***scorpion,*** fig. ext. of 1, of prostitutes ἔνδοθεν πεπλήρωνται σκορπίων καὶ πάσης ἀδικίας Ox 840, 40 (metaph. of evil persons in Ps.-Demosth. 25, 52; Artem. 2, 13 p. 107, 11 et al. See also Ezk 2:6).—S. Eitrem, Der Sk. in Mythol. u. Religionsgesch.: SymbOsl 7, 1928, 53–82; Neugebauer/Hoesen index p. 201.—DELG. M-M.

σκορπισμός, οῦ, ὁ (σκορπίζω; M. Ant. 7, 50, 2; Artem. 2, 30 p. 126, 13; Hippiatr. 70, 6 [of dispersion of fever-heat]; Cat. Cod. Astr. VIII/1, p. 268, 26 σκ. χρημάτων; Jer 25:34 Aq., Sym., Theod.; PsSol 17:18; Philo, Leg. All. 2, 86; SibOr 3, 317) ***scattering*** σκ. ὀστέων *scattering of bones,* prob. a specific ref. to the action of wild beasts wrenching Paul's flesh apart; in the unbridled imagination of Ign. one of the many related tortures accompanying martyrdom, IRo 5:3.—DELG s.v. σκορπίος. TW.

σκοτεινός, ή, όν (σκότος; Aeschyl. et al.; Cebes 10, 1; Cornutus 17, p. 29, 14; UPZ 78, 19 [159 BC] εἰς σκοτινὸν τόπον; LXX; En, TestSol; Jos., Bell. 1, 77, Ant. 2, 344; Just., D. 17, 3; Mel., P. 24, 164 and 169.—W-H. σκοτινός as En 22:2) ***dark*** opp. φωτεινός (cp. X., Mem. 3, 10, 1; 4, 3, 4; Plut., Mor. 610e; 953c; En 22:2): **Mt 6:23; Lk 11:34, 36** (cp. TestBenj 4:2 σκοτεινὸς ὀφθαλμός; Damasc., Vi. Isid. 92 τὸ σκ. τῶν ὀφθαλμῶν). Opp. φανερός *obscure* B 8:7. νεφέλη σκ. dark cloud GJs 19:2 (cp. Ex 19:16 νεφέλη γνοφώδης; s. also φωτεινός). θησαυροὶ σκ. *treasures that lie in darkness* 11:4 (Is 45:3). [καὶ σκότει]νοῦ [τόπου] AcPl Ha 3, 19. Of color ἔνδυμα *a dark garment* ApcPt 6:21.—DELG s.v. σκότος. M-M. TW.

σκοτία, ας, ἡ (cp. prec. and three next entries; Apollon. Rhod. 4, 1698; Anth. 8, 187; 190; Sb 6648, 4; PGM 4, 2472; Job 28:3; Mi 3:6; Is 16:3; TestSol 13:5 D; TestJob 43:6; SibOr 5, 349; Tat. 13, 4)

❶ **state of being devoid of light,** ***darkness, gloom.*** **J 6:17.** σκοτίας ἔτι οὔσης *while it was still dark* **20:1.** Perh. **12:35b** (s. 2). Metaph. ἐν τῇ σκ. λέγειν (εἰπεῖν) τι *say someth. in the dark,* i.e. in secret (opp. ἐν τῷ φωτί) **Mt 10:27; Lk 12:3** (s. HGrimme, BZ 23, '35, 258–60).

❷ **darkening of the mind or spirit,** ***darkness,*** fig. ext. of 1, of ignorance in moral and relig. matters **Mt 4:16 v. l.** (s. Is 9:1). Esp. in Johannine usage as a category including everything that is at enmity w. God, earthly and demonic **J 1:5ab; 8:12; 12:35a;** perh. also **35b** (s. 1), **46; 1J 1:5; 2:8f, 11abc.**—HBakotin, De Notione Lucis et Tenebrarum in Ev. Jo. '43.—DELG s.v. σκότος A 1. M-M. TW.

σκοτίζω (σκότος; since Polyb. 12, 15, 10; TestSol; Test12Patr in act.), in our lit., as well as in LXX; Mel., P. 97, 742 (it is not found in En, EpArist, Philo, Joseph.), only pass. **σκοτίζομαι** : fut. 3 sg. σκοτισθήσεται; 1 aor. ἐσκοτίσθην; pf. ἐσκότισμαι, ptc. ἐσκοτισμένος.

❶ ***be/become dark, be darkened.,*** lit. (Cleomedes [II AD] 2, 4 p. 188, 18; 24 [HZiegler 1891]) of the sun which, in times of tribulation, loses its radiance (Eccl 12:2; Is 13:10) **Mt 24:29; Mk 13:24;** cp. **Rv 8:12; 9:2 v.l.** Of the darkening of the sun at Jesus' death **Lk 23:45 v.l.**

❷ ***be/become inwardly darkened,*** fig. ext. of 1, of the organ of spiritual and moral perception (Polyb. 12, 15, 10 Bütt.-W. v.l.=566 fgm. 124b, 10 Jac. in the text [the pass. of moral darkening]; Plut., Mor. 1120e; TestReub 3:8, TestLevi 14:4, Gad 6:2 τὸν νοῦν): among polytheists ἐσκοτίσθη ἡ ἀσύνετος αὐτῶν καρδία **Ro 1:21.** σκοτισθήτωσαν οἱ ὀφθαλμοὶ αὐτῶν τοῦ μὴ βλέπειν **11:10** (Ps 68:24). σκοτίζεσθαι τὴν διάνοιαν *be darkened in one's understanding* 2 Cl 19:2; cp. ἐσκοτωμένοι τῇ διανοίᾳ **Eph 4:18 v.l.**—DELG s.v. σκότος D 5. M-M. TW.

σκότος, ους, τό (as a masc. word Hom. et al. and so in the Attic writers [EFraenkel, ZVS 43, 1910, 195ff; σκότος and φῶς], as well as Jos., Ant. 19, 216; 217; as a neut. Pind. et al. and H. Gk. gener., also in LXX [Thackeray p. 159]; pseudepigr.; Philo; Jos., Bell. 6, 140, Ant. 1, 27; apolog.; PWarr 21, 25; 30 [III AD].—B-D-F §51, 2; Mlt-H. 127. Only in **Hb 12:18** does ὁ σκ. appear as a v.l. in the t.r.) 'darkness'

❶ ***darkness, gloom,*** lit., of the darkness in the depths of the sea B 10:10. Of dark clouds ApcPt 10:25. Of the darkening of the sun (σκότος at the death of Aeschyl., acc. to Aristoph.: Ael. Aristid. 32, 32 K.=12 p. 145 D. At the death of Alexander ἐγένετο σκότος: Ps.-Callisth. 3, 33, 26. Others HUsener, RhM n.s. 55, 1900, 286f) **Mt 27:45; Mk 15:33; Lk 23:44;** GPt 5:15; **Ac 2:20** (Jo 3:4: here σκ. means 'bearer of darkness'; s. 4, end). Of the darkness of chaos (Gen 1:2; Mel., P. 82, 611; Theoph. Ant. 1, 6 [p. 70, 19]) **2 Cor 4:6.** Of the darkness of nonexistence 1 Cl 38:3 (Sb 8960, 19 [grave-epigram I BC] σκότους πύλας); JosAs 8:10 ἀπὸ τοῦ σκότους εἰς τὸ φῶς). Of the darkness of the place of punishment far removed fr. the heavenly kingdom (Philo, Exsecr. 152 βαθὺ σκότος. Cp. Wsd 17:20; PsSol 14:9.—σκ. κ. βόρβορος 'gloom and muck' await those who are untrue to the Eleusinian Mysteries, Ael. Aristid. 22, 10 K.=19 p. 421 D. Of the darkness of death and the underworld in Hom. and the trag. As the domain of evil spirits PGM 36, 138; Theoph. Ant. 2, 7 [p. 110, 5]) τὸ σκ. τὸ ἐξώτερον *the darkness outside* **Mt 8:12; 22:13; 25:30** (also ApcEsdr 4:37 p. 29, 16 Tdf.; cp. Vi. Aesopi W 31 P., where Aesop advises a man: ῥῖψον αὐτὴν [his wife] εἰς τὸ σκότος.—RTaylor, Theology 33, '42, 277–83). Also ὁ ζόφος τοῦ σκότους (ζόφος 2) **2 Pt 2:17; Jd 13.**—Of the darkness in which the blind live (Soph., Oed. R. 419; Eur., Phoen. 377; 1534; Dt 28:29) w. ἀχλύς (q.v. 1) **Ac 13:11.** [διὰ τὸ] σκότος ἀφα[νής] *unnoticed because of the darkness* AcPl Ha 3, 27 (other restorations suggested in app.).

❷ **the state of being unknown,** ***darkness,*** fig. τὰ κρυπτὰ τοῦ σκότους *the things that are hidden in darkness* and therefore are known to nobody **1 Cor 4:5.**

❸ **the state of spiritual or moral darkness,** ***darkness,*** of darkening by sin, of the state of unbelievers and of the godless, opp. φῶς (Herm. Wr. 7, 2a; Philo, Det. Pot. Ins. 101, Somn. 2, 39; TestLevi 19:1; TestNapht 2:10; OdeSol 11:19; TestAbr B 7 p. 111, 22 [Stone p. 70]; TestJob 43:6; JosAs 15:13; Mel., P. 68, 491; Orig., C. Cels. 6, 67, 6.—S. σκότος as gnostic term Iren. 1, 4, 2 [Harv. I 36, 2]; Hippol., Ref. 10, 16, 4) **Mt 4:16** (Is 9:1; s. σκοτία); **6:23b; J 3:19; Ac 26:18; Ro 2:19; 2 Cor 6:14; 1 Th 5:4f; 1 Pt 2:9; 1J 1:6;** 1 Cl 59:2; B 14:7 (Is 42:7); 18:1; AcPl Ha 8, 32//BMM verso 4. Opp. δικαιοσύνη B 5:4. Cp. 14:5f. W. σκιὰ θανάτου (σκιά 2b) **Lk 1:79** (schol. on Soph., El. 1079 p. 149 P. ἐν σκότει γενέσθαι τ. θανάτου. For σκότος=darkness of death cp. Plut., Mor. 296ab, an oath 'by the σκότος near the oak tree, where the men of Priene had been killed in such great numbers'; s. also New Docs 4, 149).—Sins are τὰ ἔργα τοῦ σκότους **Ro 13:12; Eph 5:11.**—On ἡ ἐξουσία τοῦ σκότους **Lk 22:53; Col 1:13** s. ἐξουσία 6. On οἱ κοσμοκράτορες τοῦ σκότους τούτου **Eph 6:12** s. κοσμοκράτωρ.—In a related sense, and in contrast to φῶς, σκότος has the sense

❹ ***bearer/victim/instrument of darkness*** **Mt 6:23a; Lk 11:35; Eph 5:8** (s. KKuhn, NTS 7, '61, 339f [Qumran]). S. also 3 above.—B. 61. DELG. M-M. EDNT. TW. Sv.

σκοτόω (s. σκότος; Soph., Hippocr., Pla. et al.; POxy 1854, 3; LXX, Test12Patr) pass.: 1 aor. ἐσκοτώθην; pf. ptc. ἐσκοτωμένος; prim. 'to cause to be dark, darken', in our lit. only pass. functioning intr.

❶ ***be/become darkened.,*** lit. ἐσκοτώθη ὁ ἥλιος καὶ ὁ ἀήρ **Rv 9:2** (cp. Job 3:9). Of the kingdom of the 'Beast' **16:10.**

❷ ***be/become darkened in mind*** fig. ext. of 1 (schol. on Nicander, Alexiphar. 27 τοῖς ἐσκοτωμένοις τῇ μέθῃ; TestDan 2:4 σκ. τὴν διάνοιαν) διάνοια ἐσκοτωμένη *darkened understanding* 1 Cl 36:2. ἐσκοτωμένος τῇ διανοίᾳ **Eph 4:18.**—DELG s.v. σκότος D 1. M-M. TW.

σκύβαλον, ου, τό useless or undesirable material that is subject to disposal, ***refuse, garbage*** (in var. senses, 'excrement, manure, garbage, kitchen scraps': Plut. et al.; PSI 184, 7; PRyl 149, 22; PFay 119, 7; Sir 27:4; Philo, Sacr. Abel. 109; 139; Jos., Bell. 5, 571; SibOr 7, 58.—τὰ σκύβαλα specif. of human excrement: Artem. 1, 67 p. 61, 23; 2, 14 p. 108, 21; Jos., Bell. 5, 571 [cp. Epict., Fgm. Stob. 19 ἀποσκυβαλίζω].—MDibelius, Hdb. on Phil 3:8) πάντα ἡγεῖσθαι σκύβαλα *consider everything garbage/crud* **Phil 3:8** (cp. AcPl Ha 2, 23; Spicq. s.v. "to convey the crudity of the Greek . . . : 'It's all crap'.").—DELG. TW.

Σκύθης, ου, ὁ *the Scythian,* living in the region of the Black Sea (Hes., Hdt. et al.; ins, LXX, Philo, Joseph.), frequently viewed as the epitome of unrefinement or savagery (uncouth ways are satirized Aristoph., Lysist. 451ff, Thesm. 1017; cp. Cicero, In Pis. 8, Nat. Deor. 2, 34, 88; Seneca, In Troad. 1104; 2 Macc 4:47; 3 Macc 7:5) w. βάρβαρος (Philostrat., Ep. 5) **Col 3:11.**—THermann, Barbar u. Sk.: ThBl 9, 1930, 106; WKnox, St. Paul and the Church of the Gentiles '39, 175 w. note 4; TRice, The Scythians '57; Reader, Polemo 383; OEANE IV 503–5.—M-M. TW.

σκυθρωπία, ας, ἡ (hapax leg.; σκυθρωπός fr. σκυθρός 'sullen' and ὤψ 'face') **a sorrow that gives a gloomy aspect to one's face,** ***sorrow*** ἐξῆλθεν ὁ Παῦλος μετὰ μεγάλης σκυθρωπίας *Paul went with heavy sadness* AcPl Ha 7, 36. S. next entry.

σκυθρωπός, (ή), όν (cp. σκυθρωπία; Aeschyl., Hippocr., et al.; Plut., Mor. 139f; PGM 13, 259; Cat. Cod. Astr. XII 125, 14 in a list of neg. personal characteristics; LXX; TestSol; TestSim 4:1; GrBar 16:1; Philo; Jos., Ant. 6, 229) **pert. to having a look suggestive of gloom or sadness,** ***sad, gloomy, sullen, dark*** (X., Mem. 2, 7, 12; Menand., Epitr. 260 S. [84 Kö.]; Jos., Bell. 1, 80) **Mt 6:16; Lk 24:17.**—Metaph. of dark garments, reflecting the wearer's state of mind σκυθρωπότερα ἱμάτια *darker garments* AcPl Ha 2, 16.—DELG s.v. σκύζομαι; Frisk s.v. σκυδμαίνω. M-M.

σκύλλω pf. pass. ptc. ἐσκυλμένος (Aeschyl. et al.; ins, pap) orig. 'flay, skin'.

❶ ***weary, harass*** (Herodian 7, 3, 4; UPZ 110, 25 [164 BC] σκύλλεσθαι μὴ μετρίως; En 104:5) pass. ἐσκυλμένοι *dejected* **Mt 9:36.**

❷ ***trouble, bother, annoy*** τινά *someone.* act. (TestAbr B 2 p. 107, 2 [Stone p. 62]; PTebt 421, 11; POxy 295, 5; Sb 4317, 22) **Mk 5:35; Lk 8:49.**

❸ ***trouble oneself (by taking an interest in)*** (cp. pass. POxy 1669, 13 σκύληθι καὶ αὐτὸς ἐνθάδε; 123, 10; 941, 3) mid. μὴ σκύλλου *don't trouble yourself* **Lk 7:6** (cp. the act. μὴ σκύλλε ἑατήν POxy 295, 5; s. Rob. 807).—DELG. M-M.

σκῦλον, ου, τό (Soph., Thu. et al.; ins, pap, LXX; PsSol 5:3) usu., and in our lit. always, pl. τὰ σκῦλα=armor and weapons taken ('stripped') fr. the body of a slain enemy, then gener. ***booty, spoils*** (SIG 61, 1 [V BC]; OGI 332, 8; PHamb 91, 4; Jos., Bell. 2, 464, Ant. 7, 161) μερίζειν σκῦλα *divide the spoils* 1 Cl 16:13 (Is 53:12). Also σκῦλα διαδιδόναι **Lk 11:22** (in apparent allusion to Is 49:24f; cp. PsSol 5:3; WGrundmann, Der Begriff der Kraft in der NTlichen Gedankenwelt, '32, 49f; SLegasse, 'L'Homme Fort' [Lk 11:21f], NovT 5, '62, 5–9).—B. 1415. DELG s.v. σκῦλα. M-M.

σκωληκόβρωτος, ον (σκώληξ, βιβρώσκω) ***eaten by worms*** (used of plants Theophr., HP 3, 12, 6; 4, 11, 1, C. Pl. 5, 9, 1; PSI 490, 14 [258 BC]; PTebt 701, 74 and 81 [235 BC]. Not yet found as a medical t.t., but humans are spoken of as being eaten by σκώληκες: TestJob 20:8 [σῶμα]; Lucian, Alex. 59; 2 Macc 9:9; Jos., Ant. 17, 169) **Ac 12:23** (for the subject-matter s. Jos., Ant. 19, 346–50 and s. φθειρόβρωτος='eaten by lice' [Hesychius Miles. 40], as Plato acc. to Diog. L. 3, 40; cp. reports of the terminal illness [a form of phthiriasis] of Pherecydes of Syros: Pherecyd. nos. 27–37 S.; s. TAfrica, Worms and the Death of Kings, A Cautionary Note on Disease and History: ClAnt 1, '82, 1–17; OAllen, Jr., The Death of Herod [SBL Diss. Ser. 158] '97).—DELG s.v. σκώληξ. M-M.

σκώληξ, ηκος, ὁ (Hom. et al.; SEG XXVIII, 1586; LXX; TestJob, ApcEsdr; Jos., Ant. 3, 30; Tat. 3, 2) ***worm*** 1 Cl 25:3 (on σκ. and the phoenix s. GrBar 6:12; Artem. 4, 47 p. 229, 14). Symbol of insignificance and wretchedness (Maximus Tyr. 15, 8d; Lucian, Vit. Auct. 27) 1 Cl 16:15 (Ps 21:7; cp. Epict. 4, 1, 142). Acc. to Is 66:24 a never-dying worm shall torment the damned (cp. Jdth 16:17; Sir 7:17) **Mk 9:43 [44] v.l., 45 [46] v.l., 48;** 2 Cl 7:6; 17:5. Cp. the σκώληκες ApcPt 10:25 (s. σκωληκόβρωτος). Papias (3:2).—B. 194. New Docs 3, 83 (s. SEG above).—DELG. M-M. TW.

σκωρία, ας, ἡ (Aristot. et al.; Strabo 9, 1, 23; Sym.) **refuse produced when metal is smelted,** ***slag, dross,*** Hv 4, 3, 4.—DELG s.v. σκῶρ.

σμαράγδινος, η, ον (s. next entry) **pert. to emerald,** ***(of) emerald*** (both 'made of emerald' [so Phylarchus—III BC: 81 fgm. 41 Jac., and Lucian, Ver. Hist. 2, 11] and 'emerald in color' [Eutecnius 2 p. 29, 30; CPR 27, 8; PHamb 10, 25]) ἶρις ὅμοιος ὁράσει σμαραγδίνῳ prob. should have λίθῳ supplied w. it *a halo that was like an emerald in appearance* **Rv 4:3.**—DELG s.v. σμάραγδος. M-M.

σμάραγδος, ου, ὁ (s. prec. entry; Hdt.+; ins fr. Delos: BCH 14, 1891, 402, 44 [279 BC]; PGM 5, 239; TestSol 21:2; Jos., Bell. 5, 234, Ant. 3, 168; in the older period it was fem.; so also Theophr., Lap. 1, 4; 8; 6, 34; LXX. As a masc. first in Strabo 16, 4, 20; Philo, Mos. 2, 133; M. Ant. 7, 15; Lucian, Dom. 15) **a bright green transparent precious stone,** ***emerald*** (Michel Psellus, in Lapidaires p. 203 ln. 25 πρασοειδής ἐστι και ἠρέμα χρυσίζουσα 'grass-green with a yellowish cast'), **Rv 21:19** (cp. Tob 13:17; cp. the description of a wondrous city, Lucian, Ver. Hist. 2, 11). Lit. s.v. ἀμέθυστος.—DELG. M-M.

σμῆγμα, ατος, τό (cp. next entry; Plut.; Aëtius p. 14, 4; 16; schol. on Pla. 429e; 430b; pap; Sus 17 Theod.) ***ointment, salve*** **J 19:39 v.l.**—DELG s.v. σμήω; Frisk s.v. σμάω.

σμήχω 1 aor. mid. ἐσμηξάμην (Hom. et al.) orig. 'rub off, wash off', then gener. ***wash, cleanse*** τὶ *someth.* Ox 840, 37. Mid. *wash oneself* (Hippocr.; Jos., Bell. 2, 123 τὸ σῶμα) τὸ ἐκτὸς δέρμα ἐσμήξω *you have washed your outer skin* 840, 35.—DELG s.v. σμήω; Frisk s.v. σμάω.

σμίγμα, ατος, τό for μίγμα (q.v.) **J 19:39 v.l.**

σμύραινα, ης, ἡ (Aristot., HA 1, 5; 2, 13; 15; Nicander, Ther. 823) ***the sea eel,*** which Israelites were forbidden to eat B 10:5 (cp. Lev 11:10, and s. πολύπους, σηπία).—DELG s.v. μύραινα.

Σμύρνα, ης, ἡ (on the spelling Ζμύρνα s. that entry and s. Tdf. app. **Rv 1:11;** Lghtf., Ap. F. II/2, 331 n. 2 [IPol ins]; W-S. §5, 27d; Mlt. 45) ***Smyrna*** (Mimnermus, Hdt.+; ins [s. collection ISmyrna in IK XXIII], SibOr), a prosperous commercial city on the west coast of Asia Minor: **Rv 1:11; 2:8;** IEph 21:1; IMg 15; ITr 1:1; 12:1; IRo 10:1; ISm ins; MPol ins; 12:2; 16:2; 19:1; EpilMosq 4.—JWeiss, RE X 550, 29ff; Ramsay, Letters 1905, ch. 19f; VSchultze, Altchristl. Städte u. Landschaften II/2, 1926; CCadoux, Ancient Smyrna '38; Pauly-W. XII Suppl 690; Kl. Pauly V 244; BHHW III 1816f; PECS 847f.—M-M.

σμύρνα, ης, ἡ (trag., Hdt.+; En 29:2; OGI 214, 58; POxy 234 II; PGM 13, 20 al. [here mostly spelled ζμύρνα, in line w. the tendency for ζ to replace σ in pap and ins after 329 BC: UPohle, D. Sprache des Redners Hypereides 1928, 11f]; PGrenf I, 14, 9; 10; 18; 192, 11; 205, 11; Ps 44:9; SSol 3:6 σμ. καὶ λίβανον; Jos., Ant. 3, 197) **the resinous gum of the bush 'balsamodendron myrrha',** ***myrrh:*** w. incense and other aromatic substances (Diod. S. 5, 41, 4–6) 1 Cl 25:2. W. gold and incense **Mt 2:11** (GJs 21:3). W. aloes (s. ἀλόη) **J 19:39** (for embalming a corpse, as Hdt. 2, 40; 86; 3, 107; Theophr., HP 9, 3f).—ILöw, D. Flora d. Juden I 1928, 305–11; RSteuer, Myrrhe u. Stakte '33; PGrassi, Aromi inutili: Religio 10, '34, 530–33; Zohary, Plants 200; Pauly-W. III A 728–30; Kl. Pauly III 1524f; BHHW II 1263f.—DELG s.v. σμύρνη. M-M. TW.

Σμυρναῖος, α, ον ***coming from Smyrna*** ὁ Σ. *the Smyrnaean* (Pind., Hdt. et al.; ins) pl. **Rv 2:8 v.l.;** IMg 15; ITr 13:1; IPhld 11:2; ISm 13:2 subsc; IPol ins.—New Docs 3, 52f (CHemer).

σμυρνίζω (s. σμύρνα; in the sense 'be like myrrh' Diosc., Mat. Med. 1, 66, 1 W.) perf. pass. ptc. ἐσμυρνισμένος ***treat with myrrh*** (cp. Cyranides p. 89, 13; 97, 20; PGM 36, 313; Cos. and Dam. 33, 115) ἐσμυρνισμένος οἶνος *wine flavored with* *myrrh* **Mk 15:23** (cp. Pliny, NH 14, 13 vina myrrhae odore condita; Chariton 8, 1, 12 οἶνος κ. μύρα). The μυρσινίτης οἶνος (Diosc. 5, 37; Chion, Ep. 6), wine mixed with myrtle juice, was something different.—DELG s.v. σμύρνη. TW.

Σόδομα, ων, τά (סְדֹם.—LXX [Thackeray 168]; TestAbr B 6 p. 111, 1 [Stone p. 70]; Test12Patr, ApcEsdr; AscIs 3:10; 4:1; Philo; Jos., Ant. 1, 174; Strabo 16, 2, 44; Galen XI 694 K.) ***Sodom,*** the city that was destroyed by God w. fire and brimstone because of the sinfulness of its inhabitants (Gen 19:24; Ezk 16:46–49 inhospitality, self-indulgence, and indifference to the poor) **Lk 17:29;** 1 Cl 11:1. As an ex. of extraordinary sinfulness **Mt 11:23f; Lk 10:12.** As such, and as proof of the awesome power of God to punish, beside Gomorrah (cp. the ins fr. Pompeii, 'Sodoma Gomora': AMau, Pompeji^2 1908, 16) **Mt 10:15; Mk 6:11 v.l.: Ro 9:29** (Is 1:9); **2 Pt 2:6; Jd 7** (Just., A I, 53, 8 al.).—Jerusalem is called πνευματικῶς Σόδομα καὶ Αἴγυπτος **Rv 11:8** (cp. SibOr 6, 21ff).—JSimons, Geographical and Topgraphical Texts of the OT, '59; Kl. Pauly V 246f; BHHW III 1817f.—M-M.

Σολομών, ῶνος, ὁ (so predom. in NT and Joseph. [even in quotations of Joseph. fr. Dios, pre-Christian: 785 fgm. 1, 114 Jac. =C. Ap. 1, 114f] and Menander of Ephesus, III BC: 783 fgm. 1, 120 Jac. [C. Ap. 1, 120]; Eupolemus the Jew [II BC]: 723 fgm. 2b 8ff Jac. [in Eus., PE 9, 30, 8ff]; Just., Tat., Mel.; Christian magical pap PGM II, P 17, 10 p. 218 [Henrichs], rare in the LXX) and **Σολομῶν, ῶντος, ὁ** ([for accent cp. Ξενοφῶν] Cass. Dio. 69, 14, 2 τὸ μνημεῖον τοῦ Σολομῶντος; Zosimus: Hermet. IV p. 111, 13; **Ac 3:11** and **5:12** as στοὰ Σολομῶντος); only as v.l. the indecl. Σολομών **Mt 1:6** and Σαλωμών **Ac 7:47** (the latter is the normal form in the LXX) or Σαλομών Sin.; s. Tdf., Proleg. 104; 110: W-H., App. 158; B-D-F §53, 1; 55, 2; W-S. §10, 4; Mlt-H. 146f; Thackeray p. 165 f (שְׁלֹמֹה) ***Solomon,*** son of Bathsheba and David, and the latter's successor, known for his love of splendor **Mt 6:29; Lk 12:27** and for his wisdom **Mt 12:42ab; Lk 11:31ab.** Builder of the first temple in Jerusalem **Ac 7:47.** There was also a colonnade named for him in Herod's temple **J 10:23; Ac 3:11; 5:12** (cp. Jos., Ant. 20, 221, Bell. 5, 185). In the genealogy of Jesus **Mt 1:6f.** Pauly-W. VIII Suppl. 660–704; BHHW III 1651–53.—GKnoppers, The Vanishing Solomon: JBL 116, '97, 19–44 (anc. Israel). M-M. TW.

σορός, οῦ, ἡ (Hom. et al.; pap) *coffin, bier* (so Hdt. 2, 78; Aristoph., Plut. 277 al.; Lucian, Hermot. 78; OGI 526, 2; SIG 1236, 5; PGM 4, 1424; 7, 236; Gen 50:26; TestReub 7:2; TestLevi 19:5; Mel., P. 80, 595; Ath. 30, 3) **Lk 7:14.**—DELG. M-M.

σός, σή, σόν (s. σύ; Hom.+.—B-D-F §285, 1; Rob. 288; 684f) possess. pronoun of the second pers. sing., **pert. to you (the addressee),** ***your, yours*** (sing.). It serves to emphasize or to contrast.

ⓐ used w. nouns (TestAbr A 16 p. 97, 25 [Stone p. 42] ἡ σὴ ἐνδοξότης; Jos., Ant. 2, 67; SibOr 6, 22) τὴν ἐν τῷ σῷ ὀφθαλμῷ δοκὸν οὐ κατανοεῖς; **Mt 7:3.** Cp vs. **22abc; 13:27; Mk 2:18; J 4:42; 18:35; Ac 5:4; 24:2, 4; 1 Cor 8:11; 14:16; Phlm 14;** 1 Cl 60:2; Hs 1:5. παιδίσκη εἰμὶ σὴ GJs 2:2.

ⓑ subst.—**α.** masc. οἱ σοί *your own people* (Soph., Pla., X. et al.; oft. in pap; Jos., Ant. 7, 218; 8, 54) **Mk 5:19**

β. neut. τὸ σόν *what is yours* (Soph., Pla. et al.) **Mt 20:14; 25:25.** Likew. the pl. τὰ σά (Hom. et al.; BGU 1040, 5; POxy 903, 11) **Lk 6:30; J 17:10b.**—S. Kilpatrick, s.v. ἐμός, end.—M-M.

σουδάριον, ου, τό (Lat. loanw.: sudarium [ESchwyzer, NJklA 7, 1901, 242; Hahn 263, 2]; Pollux 7, 71; CPR I, 27, 7f [190 AD]; 21, 19 [230 AD]; PGM 36, 269.—Also as a loanw. in Mishnah and Talmud [SKrauss, Griech. u. lat. Lehnwörter im Talmud II 1899, 373; Schürer II 70]) ***face-cloth*** for wiping perspiration, corresp. somewhat to our 'handkerchief' (s. GustavMeyer, SBAkWien 132/3, 1895, 62), prob. simply *a cloth* **Lk 19:20** (on the slave's legal correctness s. Horst, Ps.-Phoc. 121f); **J 11:44; 20:7; Ac 19:12.**—M-M.

Σουσάννα, ης (this form of the gen. Sus 27; 28 Theod.) or **ας** (so Sus 30 LXX.—Thackeray 161; B-D-F §53, 3), **ἡ** ***Susanna,*** a benefactor in the service of Jesus and The Twelve **Lk 8:3.**—M-M.

σοφία, ας, ἡ (s. σοφίζω, σοφός; Hom., Pre-Socr. et al.; LXX, TestSol; TestJob 37:6; Test12patr, JosAs; AscIs 3:23; AssMos fgm. e; EpArist, Philo, Joseph., Just.,Tat., Ath.)

❶ **the capacity to understand and function accordingly,** ***wisdom.***—ⓐ natural *wisdom* that belongs to this world σοφία Αἰγυπτίων (Synes., Provid. 1, 1 p. 89a; Jos., Ant. 2, 286; cp. Tat. 31, 1 πάσης βαρβάρου σοφίας ἀρχηγόν [of Moses]) **Ac 7:22** (on the subj. s. Philo, Vita Mos. 1, 20ff; Schürer II 350). In contrast to God's wisdom and the wisdom that comes fr. God ἡ σοφία τῶν σοφῶν **1 Cor 1:19** (Is 29:14). ἡ σοφία τοῦ κόσμου (τούτου) vs. **20; 3:19.** σοφία τοῦ αἰῶνος τούτου **2:6b.** ἀνθρωπίνη σοφία **2:13.** σ. ἀνθρώπων vs. **5.** Cp. **1:21b, 22; 2:1.** σοφία λόγου *cleverness in speaking* **1:17.** On ἐν πειθοῖς σοφίας λόγοις **2:4** see πειθός. σοφία σαρκική **2 Cor 1:12.** σ. ἐπίγειος, ψυχική, δαιμονιώδης **Js 3:15** (cp. σ. as ironical referent for dissident teaching: ἡ παμποίκιλος σ. [τῆς] Περατικῆς αἱρέσεως Hippol., Ref. 5, 17, 1).—An advantage that is given to certain persons (like strength and riches, Just., D. 102, 6) 1 Cl 13:1 (Jer 9:22); 32:4; 38:2. So perh. also 39:6 (Job 4:21); but s. 1bα.

ⓑ transcendent wisdom—**α.** wisdom that God imparts to those who are close to God. Solomon (3 Km 5:9; Pr 1:2; Jos., Ant. 8, 168 σ. τοῦ Σ; AssMos fgm. e [Denis p. 65]; Orig., C. Cels. 3, 45, 9) **Mt 12:42; Lk 11:31;** Stephen **Ac 6:10;** Paul **2 Pt 3:15;** Pol 3:2; to those believers who are called to account for their faith **Lk 21:15.** The gift of unveiling secrets (2 Km 14:20; Da 1:17; 2:30. Oenomaus in Eus., PE 5, 27, 1 ἡ σοφία is necessary for the proper use of the oracles) **Ac 7:10; Rv 13:18; 17:9.** τὸν δεσπότην τὸν δόντα μοι τὴν σοφίαν τοῦ γράψαι τὴν ἱστορίαν ταύτην *the Lord, who gave me the wisdom to write this account* GJs 25:1. Good judgment in the face of human and specif. Christian demands *(practical) wisdom* **Ac 6:3; Col 4:5; Js 1:5; 3:13, 17** (for the view that σ. in **Js 1:5; 3:17**=πνεῦμα s. WBieder, TZ 5, '49, 111). The apostle teaches people ἐν πάσῃ σοφίᾳ **Col 1:28,** and Christians are to do the same among themselves **3:16** (ἐν πάσῃ σ. also **Eph 1:8; Col 1:9**).—W. φρόνησις (q.v. 2) **Eph 1:8.** W. ἀποκάλυψις vs. **17.** W. σύνεσις (Jos., Ant. 8, 49): σοφία καὶ σύνεσις πνευματική **Col 1:9.** σοφία, σύνεσις, ἐπιστήμη, γνῶσις (cp. Philo, Gig. 27) B 2:3; 21:5. σοφία καὶ νοῦς τῶν κρυφίων αὐτοῦ *wisdom and understanding of his* (i.e. the Lord's) *secrets* 6:10.—As a spiritual gift the λόγος σοφίας (cp. Just., D. 121, 2) stands beside the λόγος γνώσεως **1 Cor 12:8** (s. γνῶσις 1 and cp. Aesopica 213, 1 P.: Τύχη ἐχαρίσατο αὐτῷ λόγον σοφίας). Paul differentiates betw. his preaching to unbelievers and immature Christians and σοφίαν λαλεῖν ἐν τοῖς τελείοις **2:6a;** the latter he also calls λαλεῖν θεοῦ σοφίαν ἐν μυστηρίῳ *set forth the wisdom that comes fr. God as a mystery* vs. **7** (WBaird, Interpretation 13, '59, 425–32).—The false teachers of Colossae consider that their convictions are σοφία **Col 2:23.**—JdeFinance, La σοφία chez St. Paul: RSR 25, '35, 385–417.

β. *wisdom* of Christ and of God—א. Christ: of Jesus as a boy (s. ἡλικία 1b) **Lk 2:40, 52.** Of him as an adult **Mt 13:54; Mk 6:2.** Of the exalted Christ ἐν ᾧ εἰσιν πάντες οἱ θησαυροὶ τῆς σοφίας καὶ γνώσεως **Col 2:3.**—**Rv 5:12.** By metonymy Χρ. Ἰ., ὃς ἐγενήθη σοφία ἡμῖν ἀπὸ θεοῦ *Christ Jesus, who has become a source of wisdom from God for us* **1 Cor 1:30.** This last makes a transition to

ב. *wisdom* of God (Diog. L. 1, 28 σοφίᾳ πρῶτον εἶναι τὸν θεόν; Theoph. Ant. I, 6 [p. 70, 18] σ. τοῦ θεοῦ): revealed in his creation and rule of the world **1 Cor 1:21a,** or in the measures intended to bring salvation to the believers **Ro 11:33** (here w. γνῶσις; cp. TestJob 37:6 of God's depth of wisdom); **Eph 3:10;** Hv 1, 3, 4 (w. πρόνοια).—**Rv 7:12;** 1 Cl 18:6 (Ps 50:8); B 16:9 (cp. δικαίωμα 1). Christ is called θεοῦ σοφία *the* embodiment of the *wisdom of God* **1 Cor 1:24** (cp. א above; Just., D. 61, 3 ὁ λόγος τῆς σοφίας; Diog. L. 9, 50 Protagoras is called Σοφία.—Lucian in Peregr. 11 speaks ironically of the θαυμαστὴ σοφία τῶν Χριστιανῶν. Orig., C. Cels. 6, 44, 27 τῷ υἱῷ τοῦ θεοῦ ὄντι δικαιοσύνῃ καὶ ἀληθείᾳ καὶ σ.)—UWilckens, Weisheit u. Torheit (1 Cor 1 and 2), '59; FChrist, Jesus Sophia (synopt.) '70.

❷ **personified wisdom,** ***Wisdom*** (Ael. Aristid. 45, 17 K. as a mediator betw. Sarapis and humans; perh.=Isis; AHöfler, D. Sarapishymnus des Ael. Aristid. '35, 50 and 53f; the name of an aeon Iren. 1, 2, 3 [Harv. I 16, 5]; s. also Did., Gen, 213, 12). In connection w. Pr 1:23–33: 1 Cl 57:3 (λέγει ἡ πανάρετος σοφία), 5 (=Pr 1:29); 58:1. On ἐδικαιώθη ἡ σοφία κτλ. **Mt 11:19; Lk 7:35** cp. δικαιόω 2bα and Ps.-Pla., Eryx. 6, 394d ἡ σοφία καὶ τὰ ἔργα τὸ ἀπὸ ταύτης=wisdom and her fruits. ἡ σοφία τοῦ θεοῦ εἶπεν **Lk 11:49** introduces a statement made by 'wisdom' ('wisdom' is variously explained in this connection; on the one hand, it is said to refer to the OT, or to an apocryphal book by this title [s. 3 below]; on the other hand, Jesus is thought of as proclaiming a decree of divine wisdom, or Lk is thinking of wisdom that Jesus has communicated to them at an earlier time).

❸ **a book titled 'The Wisdom of God',** s. 2.—EBréhier, Les idées philosophiques et religieuses de Philon d'Alexandrie 1907, 115ff; JMeinhold, Die Weisheit Israels 1908; GHoennicke, RE XXI 1908, 64ff; HWindisch, Die göttl. Weisheit der Juden u. die paulin. Christologie: Heinrici Festschr. 1914, 220 ff; PHeinisch, Die persönl. Weisheit des ATs in religionsgesch. Beleuchtung[2] 1923; Bousset, Rel.[3] 343ff; FFerrari, Il Progresso religioso 8, 1928, 241–53; MTechert, La notion de la Sagesse dans les trois prem. siècles: Archiv. f. Gesch. d. Philos. n.s. 32, 1930, 1–27; WKnox, St. Paul and the Church of the Gentiles '39, 55–89; BRigaux, NTS 4, '57/58, esp. 252–57 (Qumran); HConzelmann, Pls. u. die Weisheit, NTS 12, '66, 231–44; MSuggs, Wisdom, Christology, and Law in Mt, '70. Other lit. in Schürer III/1, 198–212.—BGladigow, Sophia und Kosmos, Untersuchungen zur frühgeschichte von σοφός und σοφίη '65.—DELG s.v. σοφός. M-M. EDNT. TW. Sv.

σοφίζω (σοφός) impf. ἐσόφιζον; 1 aor. ἐσόφισα. Pass.: 1 fut. σοφισθήσομαι LXX; 1 aor. ἐσοφίσθην LXX; pf. ptc. pl. σεσοφισμένοι LXX

❶ **to cause a pers. to develop understanding to a relatively sophisticated degree,** ***make wise, teach, instruct*** (pass. in Hes., also Diog. L. 5, 90 ironically; POxy 1790, 23 [I BC]; Just., D. 32, 5; act.: Ps 18:8; 104:22; TestSol)

ⓐ act., in a good sense (as also in the pass. cited above) τινά *someone* **2 Ti 3:15;** ISm 1:1. τινὰ ἔν τινι *make someone wise in* or *for someth.* B 5:3 (cp. the pass. w. ἔν τινι Sir 38:31).

ⓑ act., in a pejorative sense (so the mid. elsewh.: Philo, Mut. Nom. 240; Jos., Bell. 4, 103) ἄγγελος πονηρὸς ἐσόφιζεν αὐτούς *a wicked messenger (angel) beguiled them* B 9:4.

❷ **to be skilled in formulating or creating someth. in an artful manner,** freq. w. implication of self-serving cleverness, ***reason out, concoct ingeniously/slyly*** or ***devise craftily*** (cp. 1b), mid. (Hdt., X. et al.; PSI 452, 11; Jos., Bell. 3, 222), as it seems, Ox 840, 1f π̣ά̣ν̣τ̣α̣ σ̣ο̣φ̣ί̣ζεται *reasons it all out quite subtly.* Pass. (Soph., Phil. 77; Demosth. 29, 28) σεσοφισμένοι μῦθοι **2 Pt 1:16.**—DELG s.v. σοφός. M-M. TW.

σοφός, ή, όν (s. two prec. entries; Pind., Hdt.et al.; LXX, TestSol, Test12Patr; JosAs 13:11; ApcSed 14:8 p. 136, 14 Ja; EpArist, Philo, Joseph., apolog. exc. Mel.) prim. a clever pers. who knows how to do someth. or construct someth., such as buildings, poems (so esp. Pind.; many philosophers published their thoughts in verse), speeches.

❶ **pert. to knowing how to do someth. in a skillful manner,** ***clever, skillful, experienced*** (Pind., N. 7, 17 [25] of mariners; τεχνίτης Iren. 1, 8, 1 [Harv. I 68, 1]) σ. ἀρχιτέκτων **1 Cor 3:10** (Is 3:3; cp. Il. 15, 412 σοφία τέκτονος; Eur., Alc. 348 σοφὴ χεὶρ τεκτόνων; Maximus Tyr. 6, 4d ὁ τέκτων σ.; Philo, Somn. 2, 8). Cp. **6:5.** σοφὸς ἐν διακρίσει λόγων *skillful in the interpretation of discourse* 1 Cl 48:5 (σ. ἐν as Maximus Tyr. 24, 6b).

❷ **pert. to understanding that results in wise attitudes and conduct,** ***wise***—ⓐ of humans—α. *wise, learned,* having intelligence and education above the average, perh. related to philosophy (Pind. et al.; Jos., Bell. 6, 313; Just., D. 5, 6; Tat., 33, 4; Ath. 29, 1; w. πεπαιδευμένος and φρόνιμος Orig., C. Cels. 3, 48, 8): ὁ σοφός beside ὁ ἰσχυρός and ὁ πλούσιος 1 Cl 13:1 (Jer 9:22); 38:2. Opp. ἀνόητος **Ro 1:14.** Those who are wise acc. to worldly standards, the σοφὸς κατὰ σάρκα **1 Cor 1:26** (cp. ὁ τοῦ κόσμου σ. Hippol., Ref. 4, 43, 1), stand in contrast to God and God's wisdom, which remains hidden for them **Ro 1:22** (Just., D. 2, 6 ᾤμην σοφὸς γεγονέναι; Oenomaus in Eus., PE 5, 34, 10 οἰομένους εἶναι σοφούς); **1 Cor 1:19** (Is 29:14), **20, 27; 3:19** (cp. Job 5:13), **20** (Ps 93:11); IEph 18:1. W. συνετός (Jos., Ant. 11, 57; 58; Just., D. 123, 4) **Mt 11:25; Lk 10:21** (s. WNestle, Vom Mythos zum Logos '42, 13–17; GKilpatrick, JTS 48, '47, 63f).

β. *wise* in that the wisdom is divine in nature and origin (opp. ἄσοφος) **Eph 5:15.** (Opp. μωρός) **1 Cor 3:18ab.** W. ἐπιστήμων (Philo, Migr. Abr. 58) **Js 3:13;** B 6:10. σοφὸς εἰς τὸ ἀγαθόν (opp. ἀκέραιος εἰς τὸ κακόν) **Ro 16:19.** Jesus intends to send out προφήτας καὶ σοφοὺς κ. γραμματεῖς **Mt 23:34.**

ⓑ of God. In the abs. sense God is called σοφός (Sir 1:8; cp. 4 Macc 1:12; SibOr 5, 360.—Ael. Aristid. 46 p. 409 D.: σοφώτατον εἶναι θεόν.—Orig., C. Cels. 3, 70, 9) μόνος σοφὸς θεός (Ps.-Phoc. 54 εἷς θεὸς σοφ.; Herm. Wr. 14, 3; s. GRudberg, ConNeot 7, '42, 12) **Ro 16:27; 1 Ti 1:17 v.l.; Jd 25 v.l.;** cp. **1 Cor 1:25.** ὁ σοφὸς ἐν τῷ κτίζειν 1 Cl 60:1 (w. συνετὸς ἐν τῷ κτλ.). σοφὴ βουλή God's *wise counsel* Dg 8:10. (On 2aβ and b cp. Sb 6307 [III BC] of Petosiris the astrologer: ἐν θεοῖς κείμενος, μετὰ σοφῶν σοφός.)— B. 1213. DELG. M-M. EDNT. TW. Sv.

Σπανία, ας, ἡ (Diod. S. 5, 37, 2; Athen. 8, 330f; 13 p. 657f; pap [CWessely, WienerStud 24, 1902, 147]; 1 Macc 8:3) ***Spain,*** the goal of a journey planned by Paul **Ro 15:24, 28** (EBarnikol, Spanienreise u. Römerbrief '34). That he reached Spain at some time (cp. 1 Cl 5:7 'the western limit') is maintained w. more or less certainty by BWeiss, FSpitta (Zur Gesch. u. Lit. des Urchristentums I 1893, 1–108), Zahn (Einl. I[3] 1907 §33–37), Harnack (Mission I[4] 1923, 83), JFrey (Die zweimalige röm. Gefangenschaft u. das Todesjahr des Ap. Pls 1900, Die letzten Lebensjahre des Pls 1910), EDubowy (Klemens v. Rom über d. Reise Pauli nach Spanien 1914), JWeiss (Das Urchristentum 1917, 300), ADeissmann (Paulus[2] 1925, 192=Paul 1926, 248) et al.; on the other hand, it is denied by HHoltzmann et al. and by PWendland (Die urchristl. Literaturformen 1912, 366), FPfister (ZNW 14, 1913, 216ff), EMeyer (III 1923, 131f), FHielscher (Forschungen zur Geschichte des Ap. Pls 1925), EvDobschütz (Der Ap. Pls I 1926, 17) et al.; HLietzmann, Gesch. der Alten Kirche I '32, 111 and ANock, St. Paul '38, 142–44 (Paulus '40, 112f) leave the question open.—Paul's interest in Spain accords with his general interest in reaching centers of considerable cultural achievement. See Fontes Hispaniae Antiquae I–IX 1922–59; La grande enciclopédie VIII 'Easpagna'; Pauly-W. VIII 1965–2046; MRostovtzeff, Social and Economic History of the Roman Empire I '57, 83–112; JvanNostrand, 'Roman Spain', in TFrank, ed. Economic Survey of Ancient Rome III '37, 119–24.—M-M.

σπαράσσω 1 aor. ἐσπάραξα. Pass.: aor. 3 pl. ἐσπαράχθησαν 2 Km 22:8; pf. ptc. nom. pl. fem. ἐσπαραγμέναι 3 Macc 4:6 (orig. 'tear, pull to and fro, rend'; Aristoph., Ran. 424 τὰς γνάθους; Diod. S. 8, 32, 3 and 19, 34, 3 τὰς τρίχας; Chariton 3, 10, 4 τὰς κόμας; Jos., Ant. 11, 141 τὴν κεφαλήν; Da 8:7 ἐσπάραξεν αὐτὸν ἐπὶ τὴν γῆν.—The word in another sense goes back to Aeschyl. [Prom. 1018, Zeus will shatter a jagged prominence]; also PPetr II, 17, 4, 2; 6; LXX, Philo) τινά *someone* (Aristoph., Acharn. 688 ἄνδρα σπαράττων καὶ ταράττων; s. Herodas 5, 57 'handle roughly'; JosAs 12:10; Jos., Ant. 13, 233) ***shake to and fro*** an unclean spirit convulses the person in whom it dwells (ἄνθρωπος σπαραττόμενος of an attack: Cyranides p. 59, 15) **Mk 1:26; 9:20 v.l.; Lk 9:39.** W. acc. of pers. to be supplied **Mk 9:26.**—B. 566. DELG. M-M.

σπαργανόω (fr. *σπάργω via σπάργανον ['swathing-band'], found mostly in the pl. σπάργανα [M-M s.v. σπαργανόω]; Eur., Hippocr.+; Posidon.: 87 fgm. 58a Jac.; Plut.; Ps.-Apollod. 1, 1, 7; Job 38:9; Ezk 16:4; Vi. Elij. 2 [p. 93, 10f Sch.]) 1 aor. ἐσπαργάνωσα; pf. pass. ptc. ἐσπαργανωμένος (Cornutus 6 p. 7, 7) **to wrap in pieces of cloth used for swaddling infants, *wrap up in cloths*** τινά *someone* **Lk 2:7** (GJs 22:2). Pass. **Lk 2:12** (s. Goodsp, Probs. 73f: 'wrapped him up' vs. **7,** 'a baby wrapped up' vs. **12**).—DELG s.v. *σπάργω.

σπαρείς s. σπείρω.

σπαταλάω 1 aor. ἐσπατάλησα **to indulge oneself beyond the bounds of propriety, *live luxuriously/voluptuously*** (Polyb. 36, 17, 7; Kaibel 646a, 5; Ezk 16:49; Sir 21:15) **1 Ti 5:6; Js 5:5;** B 10:3. Of sheep in rich pasture *be sportive* Hs 6, 1, 6; 6, 2, 6.—DELG s.v. σπατάλη; s. also Frisk, w. suggestion of deriv. fr. σπάω in the sense 'suck in', e.g. wine. M-M.

σπάω (Hom. et al.; LXX; JosAs, Philo) 1 aor. inf. σπάσαι Ezk 26:15; 1 aor. mid. ἐσπασάμην; pf. pass. ptc. ἐσπασμένος LXX **to exert force so as to pull or draw, *draw, pull (out)*** in our lit. (as almost always in the LXX) only mid. in the sense *draw* a sword (so Od. 22, 74; X., An. 7, 4, 16 al.) τὴν μάχαιραν (PTebt 48, 19 [113 BC]; 1 Ch 21:5; 1 Esdr 3:22; Ps 151:7; Jos., Vi. 303) **Mk 14:47; Ac 16:27.**—B. 571. DELG. M-M.

σπεῖρα (trag.+), **ης** (this form of the gen. in ins [OGI index VIII p. 704a]; BGU 462, 5 [150–56 AD]; 142, 10 [159 AD]; 26, 12; CPR I, 18, 1; POxy 477, 3 al.; B-D-F §43, 1; Mlt-H. 117f; Mayser 12, 4), **ἡ** a military t.t. (Polyb. et al.; ins, pap; 2 Macc 8:23; 12:20; Jdth 14:11; Jos., Bell. 2, 318, Vi. 214). This is the Gk. word used to transl. the Lat. cohors (Polyb. 11, 23, 1; ins, pap [cp. Sb, word-list 10 p. 345; OGI, loc. cit.]; also as loanw. in the Mishnah: SKrauss, Griech. u. lat. Lehnwörter im Talmud II 1899, 408; 497), but also Lat. manipulus (Polyb. 6, 24, 5; cp. 2, 3, 2; 3, 115, 12 al.; Dionys. Hal. 5, 42, 2; Strabo 12, 3, 18). In our lit. prob. always ***cohort,*** the tenth part of a legion (the σπ. thus normally had 600 men, but the number varied; s. Jos., Bell. 3, 67). **Mt 27:27; Mk 15:16; J 18:3, 12; Ac 21:31.** On σπεῖρα ἡ καλουμένη Ἰταλική **10:1** s. Ἰταλικός, on σπεῖρα σεβαστή **27:1** s. σεβαστός and the lit. there. On the whole word s. Schürer I 363–65 and the lit. s.v. ἑκατοντάρχης; cp. Hemer, Acts 132f; Boffo, Iscrizioni 295–96 (lit.).—DELG. M-M.

σπείρω fut. σπερῶ LXX; 1 aor. ἔσπειρα; pf. 2 sg. ἔσπαρκας. Pass.: fut. 3 sg. σπαρήσεται LXX; 2 aor. ἐσπάρην; pf. ptc. ἐσπαρμένος (Hes., Hdt.+).

❶ *sow seed*—ⓐ lit.—**α.** abs., opp. θερίζω **Mt 6:26; Lk 12:24.—Mt 13:3b, 4; Mk 4:3b, 4; Lk 8:5c.** ὁ σπείρων *a sower* **Mt 13:3a** (cp. Cicero, Tusc. Disp. 2, 5 [13]); **Mk 4:3a; Lk 8:5a; 2 Cor 9:10** (Is 55:10); 1 Cl 24:5. Also ὁ σπείρας **Mt 13:18.** On the sower in the parable: UHolzmeister, Verb. Dom. 22, '42, 8–12; KGrayston, ET 55, '44, 138f; SFinlayson, ibid. 306f; DHaugg, TQ 127, '47, 60–81; 166–204.

β. w. acc. of what is sown (X., Oec. 14, 5) **1 Cor 15:36, 37ab;** (τὸ) καλὸν σπέρμα **Mt 13:24, 27, 37.** τὸν σπόρον **Lk 8:5b.** ζιζάνια **Mt 13:39.** Pass. **Mk 4:32.**

γ. w. indication of the place in which or on which someth. is sown (Pla., Leg. 8, 7, 838e εἰς πέτρας κ. λίθους σπ.) εἰς τὰς ἀκάνθας **Mt 13:22; Mk 4:18.** Also ἐπὶ τὰς ἀκ. **4:18 v.l.** ἐν τῷ ἀγρῷ *sow in the field* **Mt 13:24, 31.** ἐπὶ τῆς γῆς **Mk 4:31** (ApcSed 3:4). ἐπὶ τὰ πετρώδη **4:16; Mt 13:20.** ἐπὶ τὴν καλὴν γῆν vs. **23;** cp. **Mk 4:20** (opp. w. acc. Did., Gen. 218, 4; on the problem of identity s. PPayne, NTS 26, 564–68). παρὰ τὴν ὁδόν **Mt 13:19b** (GDalman, Viererlei Acker: Pj 22, 1926, 120–32; gener. Dalman, Arbeit II: D. Ackerbau '32). But in these passages the lit. usage is already passing over into the metaphorical yet w. the idea of sowing at the forefront.

ⓑ in imagery and metaph.—**α.** in proverbial expressions based on the contrast θερίζειν . . . σπείρειν (cp. θερίζω 2a and ἐπί 5) of appropriating the fruits of another's labor, without doing any work θερίζων ὅπου οὐκ ἔσπειρας **Mt 25:24, 26.** Cp. **Lk 19:21f.** ἄλλος ἐστὶν ὁ σπείρων καὶ ἄλλος ὁ θερίζων **J 4:37.** The harvest corresponds to what is sown (Hes., fgm. 174 Rz.; εἰ κακὰ σπείραις, κακὰ κέρδεά κ' ἀμήσαιο; TestLevi 13:6; Gr Bar 15:2 οἱ γὰρ καλῶς σπείραντες καὶ καλῶς ἐπισυνάγουσιν) ὃ ἐὰν σπείρῃ ἄνθρωπος, τοῦτο καὶ θερίσει **Gal 6:7;** cp. vs. **8ab** (here the 'field' is given w. εἰς τὴν σάρκα or τὸ πνεῦμα); **2 Cor 9:6ab.**

β. The word of God, the gospel et al. are sown (Herm. Wr. 1, 29 ἔσπειρα αὐτοῖς τοὺς τῆς σοφίας λόγους) ὁ σπείρων τὸν λόγον σπείρει **Mk 4:14;** cp. (Orig., C. Cels. 4, 9, 6) vs. **15ab; Mt 13:19a; J 4:36.** τὰ πνευματικά **1 Cor 9:11.** The κακὴ διδαχή of the false teachers IEph 9:1ab (cp. AscIs 2:4 τῇ ἀνομίᾳ ἥτις ἐσπάρη ἐν Ἰερουσαλήμ).

γ. μὴ σπείρητε ἐπ' ἀκάνθαις B 9:5 (Jer 4:3). καρπὸς δικαιοσύνης ἐν εἰρήνῃ σπείρεται τοῖς ποιοῦσιν εἰρήνην **Js 3:18** (σπ. καρπόν as Antiphanes 228, 4; Paus. 1, 14, 2).

δ. The body after burial is compared to a seed-grain, for in the resurrection it comes forth fr. the earth. This is the background of the contrast σπείρειν . . . ἐγείρειν **1 Cor 15:42–44.**

❷ *scatter, disperse* (Hdt. et al.; also AscIs 2:4 [s. 1bβ]) ἔσπαρται κατὰ πάντων τῶν τοῦ σώματος μελῶν ἡ ψυχή *the soul is spread throughout all the members of the body* Dg 6:2.—B. 505.—DELG. M-M. TW.

σπεκουλάτωρ, ορος (also ωρος v.l.), **ὁ** (Lat. loanw., speculator: PCairGoodsp 30 VII, 31 [II AD]; POslo 59, 9; POxy 1193, 1; 1223, 21; Martyrium S. Dasii [died 303]: AnalBoll

16, 1897, 15, 5; B-D-F §109, 8.—Also loanw. in the Mishnah: SKrauss, Griech. u. lat. Lehnwörter usw. II 1899, 92; Billerb. II 12) prim. 'spy, scout', then ***courier,*** but also ***executioner*** (Seneca, Benef. 3, 25, Ira 1, 18, 4; Syntipas p. 61, 8; 71, 10; MartPl 5 [Aa I 115, 17]; Acta Alex. XI, col. 2, 26) **Mk 6:27.**—Schürer I 371, esp. notes 84 and 85.—New Docs 2, 174. M-M. Spicq.

σπένδω fut. 2 sg. σπείσεις LXX; 1 aor. ἔσπεισα LXX (Hom.+; ins, pap, LXX; TestJob; Jos., Ant. 6, 22; SibOr 7, 81) ***offer a libation/drink-offering,*** in our lit. only pass. and fig. (s. Philo, Ebr. 152 νοῦν σπένδεσθαι θεῷ) of the apostle who is about *to be offered up,* to shed his blood as a sacrifice **2 Ti 4:6; Phil 2:17** (s. θυσία 1; 2b and CBruston, RTP 42, 1909, 196–228.—In the Apollonaretal., Berl. Gr. Pap. 11 517 [II AD]: Her 55, 1920, 188–95 ln. 26, the putting to death of a prophet of Apollo who was true to his god appears as a σπονδή). S. σπονδίζω.—DELG. M-M. TW. Sv.

σπέρμα, ατος, τό (σπείρω; Hom.+)—❶ **the source from which someth. is propagated, *seed***—ⓐ seed of plants pl. *seeds* 1 Cl 24:5; AcPlCor 2:26, 28 (Ath. 33, 1); *(kinds of) seeds* (ApcMos 29; Mel., P. 48, 341) **Mt 13:32; Mk 4:31; 1 Cor 15:38** (MDahl, The Resurrection of the Body [1 Cor 15], '62, 121–25). Sing., collective (POslo 32, 15 [1 AD] τὸ εἰς τ. γῆν σπέρμα) **Mt 13:24, 27, 37f; 2 Cor 9:10 v.l.** (Is 55:10). See Papias (1:3, Lat.).

ⓑ male seed or semen (Pind. et al.; ApcEsdr 5:12 p. 30, 7 Tdf.; Just., A I, 19, 1 al.; Ath. 21, 1; 22, 4), so perh. **Hb 11:11** (s. καταβολή 2 and s. 2b below, also Cadbury [αἷμα 1a]) and **J 7:42; Ro 1:3; 2 Ti 2:8;** IEph 18:2; IRo 7:3 (s. also 2a below on these passages). Then, by metonymy

❷ **the product of insemination, *posterity, descendants***

ⓐ *descendants, children, posterity* (in Pind. and trag., but mostly of an individual descendant; Pla., Leg. 9, 853c ἀνθρωποί τε καὶ ἀνθρώπων σπέρμασιν νομοθετοῦμεν. The pl. also 4 Macc 18:1; Ps.-Phoc. 18; Jos., Ant. 8, 200) in our lit. (as well as Aeschyl.; Soph., Trach. 1147; Eur., Med. 669 and, above all, LXX; TestAbr A 8 p. 85, 21 [Stone 18, 21]; ApcEsdr 3:10 p. 27, 19 Tdf.; ApcMos 41; Just., A I, 32, 14 al.) collective τῷ Ἀβραὰμ καὶ τῷ σπέρματι αὐτοῦ **Lk 1:55.** See **J 8:33, 37; Ac 7:5, 6** (Gen 15:13); **13:23; Ro 4:13; 11:1; 2 Cor 11:22; Hb 2:16; 11:18** (Gen 21:12); 1 Cl 10:4–6 (Gen 13:15f; 15:5); 16:11 (Is 53:10); 32:2 (cp. Gen 22:17); 56:14 (Job 5:25); B 3:3 (Is 58:7); Hv 2, 2, 2; s 9, 24. Of Salome σπ. εἰμὶ Ἀβραὰμ καὶ Ἰσαὰκ καὶ Ἰακώβ GJs 20:2.—ἀνιστάναι σπ. τινί *raise up children for someone* **Mt 22:24** (s. ἀνίστημι 3 and Dt 25:5); GJs 1:3b. Also ἐξανιστάναι σπ. **Mk 12:19; Lk 20:28** (s. ἐξανίστημι 2). ἔχειν σπ. **Mt 22:25;** ἀφιέναι σπ. **Mk 12:20, 22;** also καταλείπειν σπ. vs. **21.** ποιεῖν σπ. (Is 37:31) GJs 1:2f. ὅπως εὐλογηθῇ τὸ σπ. σου *so that your posterity may be blessed* 15:4.—**Hb 11:11** may belong here (s. καταβολή 1 and s. 1b above); ἐκ (τοῦ) σπέρματος Δαυίδ w. ref. to Jesus may be classed here (s. Ps 88:5 and s. 1b above) **J 7:42; Ro 1:3; 2 Ti 2:8;** IEph 18:2; IRo 7:3; AcPlCor 2:5.—In imagistic use of metonymy σπ. is also used w. ref. to Abraham's spiritual descendants, i.e. those who have faith like his **Ro 4:16, 18** (Gen 15:5); **9:8;** cp. vs. **7ab** (Gen 21:12); **Gal 3:29.**—It is contrary to normal OT usage (for, even if Gen 4:25; 1 Km 1:11 σπέρμα is used w. ref. to a single individual, he stands as the representative of all the descendants) when one person, i.e. the Messiah, is called σπέρμα and thus is exalted above the mass of Abraham's descendants (s. MWilcox, JSNT 5, 79, 2–20 on Targumim and rabbinic sources for application to individuals). In **Ac 3:25** the promise of Gen 22:18 is referred to him, and s. esp. **Gal 3:16, 19** (EBurton, ICC Gal 1921, 505–10).—In **Rv 12:17** the Christians are called οἱ λοιποὶ τοῦ σπέρματος αὐτῆς *the rest* (in addition to the son just born to her) *of her* (the heavenly woman's) *children.*

ⓑ of a few *survivors,* fr. whom a new generation will arise (cp. Wsd 14:6; 1 Esdr 8:85; Jos., Ant. 11, 144; 12, 303; also Pla., Tim. 23c; Phlegon: 257 fgm. 36 II, 3, 8 vs. 21 Jac. [p. 1174] ὅ τί που καὶ σπέρμα λίποιτο) **Ro 9:29** (Is 1:9). Then

❸ **genetic character, *nature, disposition, character,*** of the divine σπέρμα (acc. to BWeiss = the word of God; acc. to EHaupt, Westcott, HHoltzmann, OBaumgarten, OHoltzmann, HHWendt, FHauck = the beginning or germ of a new life, planted in us by the Spirit of God; acc. to HWindisch and THaering, who are uncertain, = word or spirit; acc. to WWrede = the grace that makes us holy; RSV et al. 'nature') that dwells in one who is γεγεννημένος ἐκ τοῦ θεοῦ (γεννάω 1b) and makes it 'impossible for such a pers. to sin' **1J 3:9** (JPainter, NTS 32, '86, 48–71). The imagery suggests a person of exceptional merit, in Greco-Roman circles a model citizen, possesser of ἀρετή (q.v.; on the importance of ancestral virtue s. Pind., O. 7, 90–92; P. 10, 11–14; N. 3, 40–42; 6, 8–16; cp. Epict. 1, 13, 3: the slave has, just as you do, τὸν Δία πρόγονον, ὥσπερ υἱὸς ἐκ τῶν αὐτῶν σπερμάτων γέγονεν; s. also Herm. Wr. 9, 3; 4a; 6 ἀπὸ τ. θεοῦ λαβὼν τὰ σπέρματα; Philo, Ebr. 30 τὰ τοῦ θεοῦ σπέρματα al.; Synes., Ep. 151 p. 289b τὸ σπ. τὸ θεῖον; Just. A I, 32, 8 τὸ παρὰ τοῦ θεοῦ σπέρμα, ὁ λόγος.—Musonius p. 8, 1 ἀρετῆς σπ. Maximus Tyr. 10, 4g σπ. ψυχῆς.—Pind., P. 3, 15 σπέρμα θεοῦ καθαρόν refers to Asclepius, Apollo's son by Coronis.).—B. 505. DELG s.v. σπείρω. M-M. EDNT. TW.

σπερμολόγος, ον (σπέρμα, λέγω, lit. 'picking up seeds'; of birds, Alex. of Myndos [I AD] in Athen. 9, 39 388a; Plut., Demetr. 902 [28, 5]) subst. of a kind of bird, the 'rook' (Aristoph.; Aristot.; Lynceus fr. Samos [280 BC] in Athen. 8, 32, 344c), in pejorative imagery of persons whose communication lacks sophistication and seems to pick up scraps of information here and there ***scrapmonger, scavenger*** (s. Goodsp, Probs. [citing Browning: 'picker-up of learning's crumbs'] 132f, and s. the ref. to Eustath. below.—Demosth. 18, 127 σπερμολ. περίτριμμα ἀγορᾶς; Dionys. Hal. 19, 5, 3 [=17, 8]; Eustath. on Od. 5, 490 σπερμολόγοι: οἱ περὶ τὰ ἐμπόρια καὶ ἀγορὰς διατρίβοντες διὰ τὸ ἀναλέγεσθαι τὰ ἐκ τῶν φορτίων ἀπορρέοντα καὶ διὰ ζῆν ἐκ τούτων = σπερμολόγοι are people who spend their time around stores and markets to pick up scraps from the produce and live off them; Philo, Leg. ad Gai. 203) **Ac 17:18** (Norden, Agn. Th. 333; Beginn. IV, 211.—WSchmid, Philol. 95, '42, 82f). Engl. synonyms include 'gossip', 'babbler', 'chatterer'; but these terms miss the imagery of unsystematic gathering.—DELG s.v. σπείρω. M-M. Spicq.

σπεύδω impf. ἔσπευδον; fut. 3 pl. σπεύσουσιν LXX; 1 aor. ἔσπευσα (Hom. et al.; ins, pap, LXX)

❶ **to be in a hurry, *hurry, hasten,*** intr.—ⓐ w. inf. foll. *make haste, hasten* (Diod. S. 12, 68, 3 ἔσπευδεν κύριος γενέσθαι=hastened to become master [of a city]; Pr 28:22; TestNapht 1:12; TestGad 4:3; GrBar 3:7; Just., A II, 4, 4 al.; Tat..—B-D-F §392, 1a; Rob. 1077f) **Ac 20:16** Paul was in a hurry; 1 Cl 33:1; MPol 6:2. Foll. by acc. w. inf. Hs 9, 3, 2. Abs. (PTebt 19, 8 [114 BC]; JosAs; Jos., Vi. 89) σπεῦσον καὶ ἔξελθε *make haste and go out, leave as quickly as possible* **Ac 22:18.** In asyndeton σπεῦσον κατάβηθι **Lk 19:5** D. In the ptc. w. a finite verb (1 Km 4:14, 16; Jos., Bell. 1, 222) ἦλθαν σπεύσαντες **2:16.** σπεύσας κατέβη **19:6.** σπεύσας κατάβηθι vs. **5.**

ⓑ go *in haste, hasten* πρός τινα *to someone* (Herm. Wr. 4, 8b; Jos., Ant. 7, 222; cp. Philo, Aet. M. 30) πρὸς Πιλᾶτον GPt 11:45.

❷ **to cause someth. to happen or come into being by exercising special effort,** ***hasten,*** trans. (POxy 121, 12 [III AD] σπεῦσον τοῦτο.—Sir 36:7 καιρόν) or *strive for* (Od. 19, 137; Pind., P. 3, 61f [109f] βίον ἀθάνατον; Hdt. 1, 38; Thu. 5, 16, 1, also Is 16:5 δικαιοσύνην) τὶ *someth.* τὴν παρουσίαν τῆς τοῦ θεοῦ ἡμέρας **2 Pt 3:12** (s. Mayor, comm. ad loc.).—B. 971.

❸ **to be very interested in discharging an obligation,** ***be zealous, exert oneself, be industrious,*** in the Gr-Rom. world a mark of civic excellence (σπουδή 2) σπεύσῃ τοῖς ἔργοις αὐτοῦ B 19:1.—DELG. M-M.

σπήλαιον, ου, τό (Pla. et al.; Sb 5295, 7; LXX, TestSol, Just.) prim. 'cave'; as a σπήλαιον λῃστῶν, a robbers' ***hideout*** (Jer 7:11; cp. Jos., Ant. 14, 415; 421; Field, Notes 15) **Mt 21:13; Mk 11:17; Lk 19:46** (s. on ἱερόν b): 2 Cl 14:1. As a place of refuge (Cornutus 27 p. 50, 5; Jos., C. Ap. 1, 292; 300) B 11:4 (Is 33:16); **Hb 11:38; Rv 6:15.** As a place of birth GJs 18:1; 19:1 (codd.), 2f; 20:4; 21:3 (Just., D. 78, 5). Of tombs (TestReub 7:2; TestIss 7:8; ViEzk 4 [p. 74, 10 Sch.]; ViDan 20 [p. 79, 11 Sch.]) **J 11:38.**—HLavagne, Operosa Antra, Recherches sur la grotte à Rome de Sylla à Hadrien '88.—DELG. M-M. Sv.

σπιθαμή, ῆς, ἡ a measure of distance equal to the space betw. the thumb and little finger of the hand when spread out, about 23 cm., ***span*** (Hdt. 2, 106 al.; Diod. S. 3, 47, 2; pap, LXX; ApcEsdr 4:31 p. 29, 7 and 7:5 p. 32, 16 Tdf.) B 16:2 (Is 40:12).—DELG.

σπιλάς, άδος, ἡ used metaph. in **Jd 12.** The interpretation depends on which of two possible mngs. is preferred:

❶ (s. DELG 1 σπίλος) **a rocky hazard hidden by waves,** ***a rock washed by the sea, a (hidden) reef*** (Hom. et al.; Nicander, Alex. 290; Philostrat., Imag. 2, 13 p. 359, 19; Sb 6160, 1; Jos., Bell. 3, 420). Acc. to the Etymol. Magnum it is characteristic of the σπιλάδες that they cannot be seen, and hence a ship can be wrecked on them before any danger is suspected (αἱ ὑπὸ θάλασσαν κεκρυμμέναι πέτραι; Diod. S. 3, 44, 4 σπιλάδας ἐνθαλάττους). This type of interpr. is preferred by deWette, Mayor, Wordsworth, Chase, Weymouth, and conditionally by HvSoden, Windisch, REB 'danger', NRSV (mg. 'reefs'). In its favor is the sequence of unfavorable natural phenomena.

❷ (s. DELG 2 σπίλος) **that which soils or discolors,** ***spot, stain*** (Orpheus, Lithica 614 GHermann=620 Ch-ÉRuelle [1898]: the agate is said to be κατάστικτος σπιλάδεσσι='sprinkled w. spots'. Hesychius explains σπιλάδες in our pass. w. μεμιασμένοι. S. also the par. **2 Pt 2:13** s.v. σπίλος and B-D-F §45; Mlt-H. 360f) so Spitta et al., L-S-J-M., NRSV (text 'blemishes'), and conditionally HvSoden, Windisch, et al.—AKnox, Σπιλάδες: JTS 14, 1913, 547–49; 16, 1915, 78 (dirty, foul wind); HJones, ibid. 23, 1922, 282f.—M-M. Spicq.

σπίλος, ου, ὁ (s. next entry; Dionys. Hal. et al.—On the accent s. B-D-F §13; Mlt-H. 57) ***spot*** (Jos., Bell. 1, 82, Ant. 13, 314) in Hermas in the allegory of the building of the tower, of certain stones, which represent people w. serious faults Hs 9, 6, 4; 9, 8, 7; 9, 26, 2. Fig. ***stain, blemish*** (Lysis in Iambl., Vi. Pyth. 17, 76 Deubner v.l.; Dionys. Hal. 4, 24, 6) **2 Pt 2:13** (w. μῶμος). Of the church **Eph 5:27** (here, beside ῥυτίς, σπίλος means a spot on the body: Diosc. 1, 39; Artem. 5, 67; Ps.-Lucian, Amor. 15; does the exhortation imply a warning against wife-battering?).—DELG s.v. 2 σπίλος. M-M.

σπιλόω aor. pass. ptc. n. σπιλωθέν Wsd 15:4; pf. pass. ptc. ἐσπιλωμένος (s. prec. entry; Dionys. Hal. et al.; TestAsh 2:7) ***stain, defile*** in our lit. only metaph. (Dositheus 68:3) **Js 3:6; Jd 23.**—DELG s.v. 2 σπίλος. M-M.

σπλαγχνίζομαι (σπλάγχνον; Pr 17:5 A; Ex 2:6 Atumano; 1 Km 23:21; Ezk 24:21 Sym.; pseudepigr.; PFlor 296, 23 [VI AD].—The act.= Att. σπλαγχνεύω 2 Macc 6:8; the pass. so ins fr. Cos [IV BC]: ABA 1928, 6 p. 12 no. 4, 14) pass. dep., 1 fut. σπλαγχνισθήσομαι; 1 aor. ἐσπλαγχνίσθην ***have pity, feel sympathy,*** perh. τινός *with* or *for someone* (B-D-F §176, 1; Rob. 509) **Mt 18:27** (the constr. is in doubt; τοῦ δούλου should prob. rather be taken w. ὁ κύριος). Also ἐπί τινι (B-D-F §235, 2) **Mt 14:14; Mk 6:34 v.l.; Lk 7:13;** Hs 8, 6, 3; 9, 14, 3; ἐπί τινα (B-D-F §233, 2; TestAbr B 12 [Stone p. 80]; TestZeb 7:1; ApcMos 9 p. 116, 31f) **Mt 14:14 v.l.; 15:32; Mk 6:34; 8:2; 9:22; Lk 7:13 v.l.;** Hv 3, 12, 3; m 4, 3, 5; 9:3; s 6, 3, 2; 8, 6, 3. W. περί τινος (B-D-F §229, 2) **Mt 9:36.**—Abs. **18:27** (s. above); **20:34; Mk 1:41; Lk 10:33; 15:20;** 2 Cl 1:7; Hs 7:4; 8, 11, 1.—DELG s.v. σπλήν. M-M. TW. Spicq.

σπλάγχνον, ου, τό (s. prec. entry; Hom.+, almost always pl. σπλάγχνα, ων, τά; ins, pap, LXX; PsSol 2:14; TestSol 18:29; TestAbr A 3 p. 80, 7 [Stone p. 8]; A 5 p. 80, 20 [St. p. 12]; Test12Patr)

❶ **the inward parts of a body, including esp. the viscera,** ***inward parts, entrails,*** lit. (Hom. et al.; ins; PRyl 63, 6; 2 Macc 9:5f; 4 Macc 5:30; 10:8; Philo; Jos., Bell. 2, 612) **Ac 1:18** (Appian, Bell. Civ. 2, 99 §410 of Cato's suicide προπεσόντων αὐτῷ τῶν σπλάγχνων).

❷ as often in the ancient world, inner body parts served as referents for psychological aspects (s. καρδία): of the seat of the emotions, in our usage a transference is made to the rendering ***heart,*** fig. (Aeschyl. et al.; Pr 12:10; Sir 30:7; PsSol 2:14; TestAbrA; TestLevi 4:4, al. in Test12Patr; JosAs 6:1; Jos., Bell. 4, 263.—On Engl. 'bowels' in this sense s. OED s.v. bowel sb. 3), in our lit. mostly as the seat and source of love (so Herodas 1, 57; Theocr. 7, 99; Dionys. Hal. 11, 35, 4), sympathy, and mercy (not exclusively Semitic, cp. SEG XXVIII, 541, 14) σπλάγχνα ἐλέους *the merciful heart* (qualitative gen.; TestZeb 7:3; 8:2) **Lk 1:78.** Also σπλάγχνα οἰκτιρμοῦ **Col 3:12.** σπλάγχνα καὶ οἰκτιρμοί *affection and sympathy* **Phil 2:1** (on the constr. s. B-D-F §137, 2; Rob. 130; difft. HNT ad loc.). τὰ σπλ. αὐτοῦ εἰς ὑμᾶς ἐστιν *his heart goes out to you* **2 Cor 7:15.** ἐν τοῖς σπλ. ὑμῶν *in your own hearts* **6:12.** σπλάγχνα ἔχειν ἐπί τινα *have compassion for someone* 1 Cl 23:1. κλείειν τὰ σπλάγχνα αὐτοῦ ἀπό τινος *close one's heart to someone* in need **1J 3:17.** ἀναπαύειν τὰ σπλ. τινός (ἀναπαύω 1) **Phlm 20;** pass., vs. **7.**—On τοὺς λόγους αὐτοῦ ἐνεστερνισμένοι ἦτε τοῖς σπλάγχνοις 1 Cl 2:1 s. ἐνστερνίζομαι. By metonymy

❸ of the feeling itself, pl. ***love, affection*** (Wsd 10:5; TestZeb 8:2; TestNapht 4:5) τὰ σπλ., ἃ ἔχετε ἐν Χρ. Ἰ. IPhld 10:1. ἐπιποθεῖν τινα ἐν σπλάγχνοις Χριστοῦ Ἰ. *long for someone with the affection of Christ Jesus* **Phil 1:8.**—Love=the object of love (Artem. 1, 44; 5, 57) αὐτόν, τοῦτ' ἔστιν τὰ ἐμὰ σπλ. *him, my beloved* **Phlm 12** (or in mng. 2, *my very heart*).—Sing. (Jos., Ant. 15, 359), fig. (occasionally since Soph., Aj. 995; BGU 1139, 17 [5 BC]) *mercy, love* σπλάγχνον ἔχειν ἐπί τινα Hs 9, 24, 2.—B. 1085f. New Docs 3, 84. DELG s.v. σπλήν. M-M. EDNT. TW. Spicq.

σπόγγος, ου, ὁ (Hom. et al.; PSI 535, 20 [III BC]; 558, 7; loanw. in rabb.—On the spelling B-D-F §34, 5; Mlt-H. 109) ***sponge*** (Antig. Car. 158 σπόγγοις πρὸς ξύλοις δεδεμένοις=[water is brought up] by means of sponges tied to poles) **Mt 27:48; Mk 15:36; J 19:29.**—DELG. M-M.

σποδός, οῦ, ἡ (Hom. et al.; ins, LXX, TestJob, TestJos 15:2; Jos., Ant. 20, 89; 123; Just., D. 92, 2) ***ashes*** w. γῆ as a designation for someth. transitory 1 Cl 17:2 (Gen 18:27). On its use w. σάκκος **Mt 11:21; Lk 10:13;** B 3:2; 7:5 s. σάκκος. The ashes of the red heifer (Num 19:9; s. IScheftelowitz, Das Opfer der Roten Kuh [Num 19]: ZAW 39, 1924, 113–23) **Hb 9:13;** B 8:1.—DELG. M-M.

σπονδίζω (derivative of σπονδή; =earlier Gk. σπένδω) 1 aor. pass. ἐσπονδίσθην ***offer a libation/drink-offering*** *pour out (as an offering)* pass. IRo 2:2.—DELG s.v. σπένδω.

σπορά, ᾶς, ἡ (s. σπείρω and two next entries; Aeschyl. et al.; ins, pap, LXX; TestSol 5:3 P; TestReub 2:8; Philo, Joseph., Just.; Tat. 11, 1; Ath. 22, 6 and R. 1 p. 48, 6) prim. 'the activity of sowing' and fig. 'procreation', then by metonymy 'that which is sown' (Eur., Andr. 637; pap; 1 Macc 10:30; Jos., Ant. 2, 306), whence it also comes to mean ***seed*** (SIG 826c, 15 [117 BC] μήτε σπορῶν μήτε καρπῶν; Herm. Wr. 13:2; PGM 1, 32; 13, 176), which is generally accepted for **1 Pt 1:23** (cp. θεοῦ σπορά Ps.-Callisth. 1, 10; 13), though ESelwyn, 1 Pt '46, 307 prefers *origin* or *sowing*.—DELG s.v. σπείρω. M-M. TW.

σπόριμος, ον (s. σπείρω, σπορά, and σπόρος; X. et al.; IG XII, 3, 344; 345; pap, LXX) **pert. to being sown, *sown,*** subst. τὰ σπόριμα ***standing grain, grain fields*** (Ps.-Aeschines, Ep. 9, 1; SibOr 8, 181; Geopon. 1, 12, 37; PLond II, 413, 14f p. 302 ἐπιδὴ τὰ δορκάδια ἀφανίζουσειν τὸ [read τὰ] σπόριμα) **Mt 12:1; Mk 2:23; Lk 6:1.**—BMurmelstein, Jesu Gang durch d. Saatfelder: Αγγελος III, 1930, 111–20.—DELG s.v. σπείρω. M-M. TW.

σπόρος, ου, ὁ (s. σπείρω and two prec. entries)—**❶ the process of sowing, *sowing*** (Hdt. et al.; ins, pap; Philo, Fuga 171; Jos., Ant. 18, 272) 1 Cl 24:4; AcPlCor 2:26.

❷ the kernel part of fruit, *seed* (Apollon. Rhod. 3, 413; 498; Theocr. 25, 25; Diod. S. 5, 68, 2; Plut., Mor. 670b; pap, LXX; En 10:19; Philo; ApcEsdr 5:12 p. 30, 6 Tdf.) **Mk 4:27; Lk 8:11.** βάλλειν τὸν σπ. ἐπὶ τῆς γῆς **Mk 4:26.** Also σπεῖραι τὸν σπ. (cp. Dt 11:10) **Lk 8:5** (on the parable s. GHarder, Theologia Viatorum, '48/49, 51–70; JJeremias, NTS 13, '66, 48–53. On the philosopher as sower of seed, AHenrichs, ZPE 1, '67, 50–53). Cp. **2 Cor 9:10a v.l.**—In imagery πληθυνεῖ τὸν σπόρον ὑμῶν *he will increase your store of seed* (i.e. your store of things to distribute to the needy) **2 Cor 9:10b.** Text uncertain AcPl BMM verso 25 σπό[ρον].—DELG s.v. σπείρω. M-M. TW.

σπουδάζω (s. three next entries; Soph., X., Pla.+; ins, pap, LXX, Test12Patr, Philo, Joseph., apolog.) fut. σπουδάσω (Polyb. 3, 5, 8; Diod. S. 1, 58, 4; EpArist 10; Jos., Ant. 17, 203; B-D-F §77; Mlt-H. 259); 1 aor. ἐσπούδασα; pf. ἐσπούδακα Job 21:6; 23:15.

❶ to proceed quickly, *hurry, hasten* w. inf. foll. (Jdth 13:12 ἐσπούδασαν τοῦ καταβῆναι; ParJer 5:5 εἰ μὴ γὰρ ἐσπούδαζεν *if he were not in a hurry;* Jos., Ant. 8, 202 σπ. καταλιπεῖν) **2 Ti 4:9, 21; Tit 3:12;** IEph 1:2. διὰ τὸ ἕκαστον σπουδάζειν, ὅστις ἅψηται *because each one hastened to touch* MPol 13:2. But mng. 3 is also acceptable in all these places.

❷ to speed up a process, *expedite* w. acc. τὰ θηριομαχία *the combats with wild animals* (Lat. ludus bestiariorum) AcPl Ha 2, 11.

❸ to be especially conscientious in discharging an obligation, *be zealous/eager, take pains, make every effort, be conscientious* w. inf. foll. (X., Ap. 22; Diod. S. 1, 58, 4; Herodian 1, 1, 1; Jos., Ant. 17, 203, C. Ap. 1, 116; TestDan 6:3; TestNapht 3:1; Ar. 15, 5; Just., A II, 8, 2; Mel., HE 4, 26, 13) **Gal 2:10; Eph 4:3; 1 Th 2:17; 2 Ti 2:15; Hb 4:11; 2 Pt 1:10; 3:14;** 2 Cl 10:2; 18:2; B 1:5; 4:9; 21:9; IEph 5:3; 10:2; 13:1; IMg 6:1; 13:1; IPhld 4. Foll. by acc. and inf. (BGU 1080, 14; PFlor 89, 11 and13; 131) **2 Pt 1:15.** W. nom. and inf. (Epict. 2, 22, 34) IEph 10:3 (B-D-F 392, 1a; Rob. 1077f).—περί τινος *concerning someth.* (Ath., R. 14 p. 64, 21) and περί τινος, ἵνα of a benefactor *concern oneself about someone, so that* Hs 2, 6. ἐπί τι: σπουδάζετε ἐπὶ . . . τὴν ἀγάπην AcPl Ha 6, 18='be eager for . . . [text corrupt] and to show affection'.—S. Larfeld at entry σπουδή. DELG s.v. σπεύδω. M-M. TW. Spicq.

σπουδαῖος, α, ον (s. σπουδάζω and the two next entries; σπουδή; Pind., Hdt.+; ins, pap; Ezk 41:25 [σπουδαῖα ξύλα]; TestJud 1:4. Oft. Philo. Jos., Ant. 6, 296 v.l., C. Ap. 1, 214; apolog. exc. Ar.) common in lit. and ins in ref. to exceptional sense of civic responsibility or ἀρετή (cp. Arist., Poetics 1448a; JSmithson, The Moral View of Aristotle's 'Poetics': Journal of the History of Ideas 44, '83, 3–17; σπουδή 2) **pert. to being conscientious in discharging a duty or obligation, *eager, zealous, earnest, diligent*** ἔν τινι **2 Cor 8:22a;** σπ. εἴς τι *eagerly intent upon someth.* Hv 3, 1, 2. πλέον σπουδαῖος *even more diligent* IPol 3:2.—Comp. σπουδαιότερος *very earnest* (B-D-F §244, 2; cp. ILegesSacr II, 7, 34 [III AD] εὐσεβέστερος) **2 Cor 8:17.** πολὺ σπουδαιότερος *much more zealous* vs. **22b.**—For **2 Ti 1:17 v.l.,** s. σπουδαίως 2.—DELG s.v. σπεύδω. M-M. TW. Spicq.

σπουδαίως adv. of σπουδαῖος (X., Pla., Aristot. et al.; PSI 742, 6; Wsd 2:6; TestSol 22:11; Joseph.)

❶ pert. to being quick in doing someth., *with haste,* w. focus on importance of what is done (Pollux 3, 149) comp. σπουδαιοτέρως *with special urgency* **Phil 2:28.**

❷ pert. to being conscientious in discharging a duty or obligation, *diligently, earnestly, zealously* (Diog. L. 6, 27; Jos., Ant. 8, 6; ins: SEG XL, 1770, 16f [196/97 AD Chr.]; Ramsay, CB I/2 no. 480, w. πιστῶς) **2 Ti 1:17; Tit 3:13.** παρακαλεῖν σπ. *urge strongly* **Lk 7:4.**—Comp. *very eagerly* σπουδαιότερον (Pla., Rep. 7, 536c; Jos., Ant. 16, 85; Tat. 33, 2 [w. gen. of comparison]) **2 Ti 1:17 v.l.;** σπουδαιοτέρως (Ps.-Plut., Nobil. 15, ed. Bern. VII 252, 15) ibid. v.l.—DELG s.v. σπεύδω. M-M. TW. Spicq.

σπουδή, ῆς, ἡ (s. three prec. entries; Hom.+)—**❶ swiftness of movement or action, *haste, speed*** μετὰ σπουδῆς *in haste, in a hurry* (Appian, Iber. 27 §105; 28 §110; Polyb. 1, 27, 8; Herodian 3, 4, 1; 6, 4, 3; PTebt 315, 8 [II AD]; Ex 12:11; Wsd 19:2; JosAs 28:8 cod. A [p. 83, 9 Bat.]; Jos., Ant. 7, 223) **Mk 6:25; Lk 1:39** (BHospodar, CBQ 18, '56, 14–18 ['seriously']); MPol 8:3 v.l.

❷ earnest commitment in discharge of an obligation or experience of a relationship, *eagerness, earnestness, diligence, willingness, zeal* oft. in Gr-Rom. lit. and ins. of extraordinary commitment to civic and religious responsibilities, which were freq. intertwined, and also of concern for personal moral excellence or optimum devotion to the interests of others (IMagnMai 53, 61; 85, 12 and 16; s. Thieme, p. 31; Larfeld I 499f; Danker, Benefactor 320f; Herm. Wr. 2, 17 σπουδὴ εὐσεβεστάτη; Jos., Ant. 13, 245; Just., D. 9, 3; Mel., HE 4, 26, 13) **Ro 12:11; 2 Cor 7:11; 8:7, 8** (subj. gen.). μετὰ σπουδῆς *diligently, attentively* (Ps.-Aristot., De Mundo 1; SIG 611, 5; UPZ 110, 131 [164 BC]; 3 Macc 5:24, 27; Philo; Jos., C. Ap. 2, 42) Dg 12:1. Also ἐν σπ. **Ro 12:8.** σπ. ὑπέρ τινος *good will toward, devotion for someone* (cp. Philo, Leg. ad Gai. 242) **2 Cor 7:12; 8:16.** ἐνδείκνυσθαι σπουδὴν πρός τι *show earnestness in* *someth.* **Hb 6:11** (cp. Philo, Somn. 2, 67; Jos., Ant. 12, 134; Ath. 3, 2). σπουδὴν πᾶσαν παρεισενέγκαντες ἐπιχορηγήσατε *make every effort to add* **2 Pt 1:5** (πᾶσα σπ., a freq. formulation in civic decrees [s. the indexes in various ins. corpora]; also, inter alia, PTebt I, 33, 18f; Philo, Leg. ad Gai. 338, Sacr. Abel. 68); πᾶσαν σπ. ποιεῖσθαι (s. ποιέω 7a) *be very eager* w. inf. foll. (Philostrat., Ep. 1) **Jd 3;** πᾶσαν εἰσήγησε (=εἰσήγησαι) σπουδὴν παραγενέσθαι ἐνθάδε *make every effort to come here* AcPlCor 1:16. σπουδὴ τοῦ συλλημφθῆναι τοιοῦτον ἄνδρα MPol 7:2.—DELG s.v. σπεύδω. M-M. TW. Spicq.

σπυρίς, ίδος, ἡ (Hdt., Aristoph. et al.; pap; Philo, Spec. Leg. 3, 160; on the form σφυρίς, which is also attested, s. Schwyzer I 161; B-D-F §34, 5; W-S. §5, 27e; Mlt-H. 109; Mayser 173; Dssm., B 157, NB 13 [BS 158; 185]) ***basket, hamper*** **Ac 9:25.** In connection w. the miracle of feeding (as a basket for edibles: Hdt. 5, 16; Epict. 4, 10, 21; Athen. 8, 365a) **Mt 15:37; 16:10; Mk 8:8, 20.**—S. κόφινος.—B. 623. DELG. M-M.

σταγών, όνος, ἡ (Aeschyl., Hippocr.+; ins, LXX) ***drop*** of water Hm 11:20.—B. 672. DELG s.v. στάζω. M-M.

στάδιον, ου, τό (Jos., Ant. 15, 415; Just., D. 9, 3) pl. τὰ στάδια **J 6:19 v.l.;** Hv 4, 1, 2 and οἱ στάδιοι (TestAbrB 2 p. 106, 20 [Stone p. 60]; TestZeb 7:4; TestGad; Just., A I, 34, 2; both plurals also in Attic Gk.; s. Kühner-Bl. I 500; B-D-F §49, 3; W-S. §8, 12; Mlt-H. 122; Mayser 289; Thackeray 155; Helbing 46f; Reinhold 53f)

❶ **a measure of distance of about 192 meters,** ***stade, one-eighth mile*** (Hdt. et al.; ins, pap; Da 4:12; 2 Macc; pseudepigr.; Jos., Bell. 5, 192 ἓξ σταδίους; 7, 284, Ant. 18, 60; Just., A I, 34, 2) = w. allowance for variations according to locale, 600 Greek (625 Roman; c. 607 English) feet=192 meters. **Mt 14:24; Lk 24:13** (for the v.l. cp. Appian, Bell. Civ. 5, 35 §140 ἑξήκοντα καὶ ἑκατὸν σταδίους); **J 6:19; 11:18; Rv 14:20; 21:16;** Hv 4, 1, 2; 5.—S. ASegré, JBL 64, '45, 369–71.

❷ **an area for public spectacles,** ***arena, stadium*** (Pind. et al.; ins, pap; Philo, Op. M. 78; Jos., Bell. 2, 172, Vi. 331 τὸ στ.; loanw. in rabb.) on or in which foot-races and other public athletic contests were held MPol 6:2; 8:3; 9:1f; 12:1. ἐν στ. τρέχειν *run a race* **1 Cor 9:24.** ἔξω βάλλεσθαι τοῦ στ. *be expelled from the stadium* 2 Cl 7:4 (s. μαστιγόω 1a). Abs. *arena for animal combat* AcPl Ha 2, 5 (restored); 4, 11 and 13; 5, 14.—DELG. M-M.

στάζω 1 aor. ἔσταξα—❶ **to cause to fall drop by drop** (Hom.+; LXX; PsSol 17:18; ParJer) in imagery of divine activity ***instill*** στ. τὴν δικαιοσύνην ἐπί τινα *instill righteousness into someone* Hv 3, 9, 1.

❷ **to fall drop by drop,** ***drip, trickle,*** intr. (since trag.; Hdt. 6, 74; Hippocr.; LXX; SibOr 5, 373) B 12:1 (quot. of uncertain orig.).—DELG. M-M.

σταθμός, οῦ, ὁ (Hom. et al.; ins, pap, LXX; PsSol 5:4; TestNapht 2:3; Philo, Rer. Div. Her. 144; Just., D. 111, 3 and Mel., P. 14, 90 doorposts) the mng. in ἀνέμων σταθμοί 1 Cl 20:10 is uncertain; it may be: ***station*** (?—so Polyaenus 5, 8, 1; Jos., Bell. 1, 308) or ***weight*** (?—so Jos., C. Ap. 2, 216; cp. Job 28:25).—DELG.

στάμνος, ου (Aristoph. et al.; ins, pap, LXX), ἡ (so in Attic Gk.; but ὁ in Doric and LXX: B-D-F §49, 1; Thackeray p. 146; note on PHamb 10, 35; Mlt-H. 124) ***jar,*** in which the manna was kept (Ex 16:33; Philo, Congr. Erud. Grat. 100) **Hb 9:4.**—DELG. M-M.

στασιάζω 1 aor. ἐστασίασα (s. two next entries; Aristoph., Hdt.+; ins, LXX; Jos., Bell. 5, 248, Ant. 17, 27; Acta Alex. XVIII, col. 2, 14) **to be factious and cause public discord,** ***rebel*** πρός τινα *against someone* (X., An. 6, 1, 29, Hell. 1, 1, 28; Pla., Rep. 8, 545d; 566a al.; s. Jos., Ant. 1, 110; 13, 74) 1 Cl 4:12; 46:7; 47:6; 51:3. Abs. (Menand., Epitr. 641 J.; Diod. S. 18, 39, 3; Polyaenus 5, 26; 8, 23, 21; Oenomaus in Eus., PE 5, 28, 8; Philo, Op. M. 33) 43:2; 49:5; 55:1.—DELG s.v. στάσις.

στασιαστής, οῦ, ὁ (στασιάζω; Diod. S. 10, 11, 1; Dionys. Hal. 6, 70, 1; Jos., Bell. 6, 157, Ant. 14, 8; PSI 442, 4 [III BC]) **a factious pers. who causes public discord,** ***rebel, revolutionary*** **Mk 15:7.**—DELG s.v. στάσις. M-M. Spicq.

στάσις, εως, ἡ—❶ **condition of being in a certain position or state of affairs,** ***existence, occurrence*** στάσιν ἔχειν *be in existence, be standing* (Polyb. 5, 5, 3; Plut., Mor. 731b ἔχ. γένεσιν καὶ στάσιν) **Hb 9:8** (also prob. is *place, position* [Hdt. 9, 24 al.; Diod. S. 12, 72, 10; 13, 50, 9; LXX; En 12:4]). Stability was a dominant concern in administration of a state. If the focus is on the process leading up to establishment of a position, change is a dominant component, hence

❷ **movement toward a (new) state of affairs,** ***uprising, riot, revolt, rebellion*** (opp. ἡσυχία [q.v. 1] civil harmony, peaceful conduct; since Alcaeus 46a, 1 D.[2] [ἀνέμων στάσις=tumult of the winds]; Aeschyl., Hdt.; Sb 6643, 18 [88 BC]; PLond VI, 1912, 73 [41 AD]; Philo; Jos., Ant. 20, 117; Tat. 19, 3; loanw. in rabb.) against the civil authority **Mk 15:7; Lk 23:19** (of an uprising: Dio Chrys. 21 [38], 14 γενομένης στάσεως), **25; Ac 19:40.** Against the leaders of a Christian congregation 1 Cl 1:1. W. διχοστασία 51:1. But it is difficult to differentiate in 1 Cl betw. this sense and the foll. one, with focus on the component of discord.

❸ **lack of agreement respecting policy,** ***strife, discord, disunion*** (Diod. S. 12, 14, 3 στάσεις ἐν τ. οἰκίαις; Appian, Bell. Civ. 4, 45 §193 ἡ Καίσαρος κ. ᾿Αντωνίου στάσις; IG IV[2]/1, 687, 13; PStras 20, 10; Jos., Ant. 18, 374 al.; Tat. 16, 3) 1 Cl 46:9. W. ἔρις 3:2; 14:2 (στάσεις). W. ἔρις and σχίσματα 54:2. W. σχίσμα 2:6. W. ζήτησις **Ac 15:2.** τὴν καταβολὴν τῆς στ. ποιεῖν *lay the foundation of the discord* 1 Cl 57:1. ἡσυχάζειν τῆς ματαίας στ. *cease from that futile dissension* 63:1. Specif. of a difference in opinion, *dispute* (Aeschyl., Pers. 738; Apollon. Paradox. 6 τήν γινομένην στάσιν τοῖς Πυθαγορείοις προειπεῖν; Diog. L. 3, 51; Philo, Rer. Div. Her. 248; Jos., Vi. 143 γίνεται στ.; Tat. 1, 1 al.) **Ac 23:7, 10** (Polyaenus, Exc. 40, 3 στάσεως γενομένης). κινεῖν στάσεις (v.l. στάσιν) τισί *create dissension among certain people* **Ac 24:5.**—DELG. M-M. TW. Spicq. Sv.

στατήρ, ῆρος, ὁ (as the name of coins Aristoph., Hdt. et al.; ins, pap, Aq., Sym., Jos., Ant. 7, 379; loanw. in rabb.) ***the stater,*** a silver coin = four drachmas (c. four days' wages) **Mt 17:27** (s. OLZ 40, '37, 665–70; JDerrett, Law in the NT, '70, 248–52; NMcEleney, CBQ 38, '76, 178–92); **26:15 v.l.**—Lit. s.v. ἀργύριον 2c.—DELG. M-M.

Στάτιος, ου, ὁ ***Statius,*** a Roman name, Στάτιος Κοδρᾶτος, *Statius Quadratus,* proconsul of Asia at the time of Polycarp's martyrdom MPol 21. The time when he held office is variously estimated; s. on Πολύκαρπος.

στατίων, ωνος (Lat. loanw. statio, found also in rabb., used w. various mngs. in Strabo 17, 3, 2, 826; ins [OGI index VIII p. 704b; Hahn 227, 14]; BGU 326 II, 10; PRyl 78, 23; O. Wilck I 294f.—See OGI 595 n. 4; JSvennung, ZNW 32, '33, 294–308), ἡ and rarely ὁ (OGI 755, 4) prim. 'a state or position of guard-duty, post, station' στατίωνα ἔχειν= Lat. stationem habere = 'do guard duty, stand sentinel'; this became part of the ecclesiastical vocabulary (Lampe s.v.) and in a transf. sense ***keep a fast*** (cp. Tertullian, Jejun. 13, Orat. 19, Fuga 1, Ad Uxorem 2, 4) Hs 5, 1, 1f (Leutzsch, Hermas 470 n. 51).

σταυρίσκω (σταυρός) ***crucify*** τινά *someone* GPt 2:3.

σταυρός, οῦ, ὁ (Hom. et al. in the sense 'upright, pointed stake' or 'pale'; s. Iren. 1, 2, 4 cj. [Harv. I, 18, 4]; as name of an aeon Hippol., Ref. 6, 31, 6)

❶ **a pole to be placed in the ground and used for capital punishment,** ***cross*** (Diod. S. 2, 18, 1; Plut. et al.; Epict. 2, 2, 20; Diog. L. 6, 45; ApcEsdr 7:1 p. 32, 8 Tdf.; AscIs 3:18; Philo, In Flacc. 84; Jos., Ant. 11, 261; 266f.; Just.; s. also CSchneider, TW III 414, 4 and JCollins, The Archeology of the Crucifixion, CBQ 1, '39, 154–59; JBlinzler, Der Prozess Jesu³, '60, 278–81; EDinkler, Signum Crucis '67; JFitzmyer, CBQ 40, '78, 493–513), a stake sunk into the earth in an upright position; a cross-piece was oft. attached to its upper part (Artem. 2, 53), so that it was shaped like a T or thus: †—MHengel, Crucifixion '77. Lit., w. other means of execution (Diogenes, Ep. 28, 3) IRo 5:3; Hv 3, 2, 1. Used in the case of Jesus **Mt 27:40, 42; Mk 15:30, 32; J 19:25, 31; Phil 2:8** (Just., D. 134, 5); GPt 4:11; 10:39, 42. ὑπομένειν σταυρόν *submit to the cross* **Hb 12:2.** The condemned carried their crosses to the place of execution (Plut., Mor. 554a ἕκαστος κακούργων ἐκφέρει τὸν αὑτοῦ σταυρόν; Chariton 4, 2, 7 ἕκαστος τ. σταυρὸν ἔφερε; Artem. 2, 56.—Pauly-W. IV 1731) **J 19:17;** in the synoptics Simon of Cyrene was made to carry the cross for Jesus (Σίμων 4) **Mt 27:32; Mk 15:21; Lk 23:26.** An inscription on the cross indicated the reason for the execution **J 19:19** (s. τίτλος).—WMichaelis, Zeichen, Siegel, Kreuz, TZ 12, '56, 505–25. B seeks to show in several passages that acc. to the scriptures it was necessary for the Messiah to die on the cross: 8:1 (the ξύλον that plays a part in connection w. the red heifer, Num 19:6, is ὁ τύπος ὁ τοῦ σταυροῦ); 9:8 (in the case of the 318 servants of Abraham Gen 14:14 the number 300 [=T′] points to the cross; cp. Lucian, Jud. Voc. 12: the letter tau has the form of the σταυρός); 11:1, 8a (the ξύλον of Ps 1:3); 12:1 (scripture quot. of uncertain origin), 2.

❷ **the cross, with focus on the fate of Jesus Christ,** ***the cross.*** The cross of Christ is one of the most important elements in Christian cult and proclamation: w. death and resurrection IPhld 8:2 and other details of his life PtK 4 p. 15, 33. For Judeans a σκάνδαλον **Gal 5:11** (cp. Dt 21:23); cp. IEph 18:1. Hence an occasion for persecution **Gal 6:12** (τῷ σταυρῷ *because of the cross;* dat. of cause, s. ἀπιστία 1). But it was for Paul his only reason for boasting vs. **14.** ὁ λόγος ὁ τοῦ σταυροῦ *the message of the cross* **1 Cor 1:18,** w. its mysterious, paradoxical character, is necessarily foolishness to unbelievers. For this reason any attempt to present this message in the form of worldly wisdom would rob the σταυρὸς τοῦ Χριστοῦ of its true content vs. **17.** τὸ μαρτύριον τοῦ σταυροῦ is the testimony rendered by the Passion to the fact of Christ's bodily existence Pol 7:1 (cp. Just., D. 40, 3 πάθος τοῦ σταυροῦ).—Christ's death on the cross brings salvation **Eph 2:16; Col 2:14.** εἰρηνοποιεῖν διὰ τοῦ αἵματος τοῦ σταυροῦ αὐτοῦ *make peace through the shedding of his blood on the cross* **1:20** (s. W-S. §30, 12c; Rob. 226). Hence we may ἐπὶ τὸν σταυρὸν ἐλπίζειν B 11:8b. Paul knows of baptized Christians whom he feels constrained to call ἐχθροὶ τοῦ σταυροῦ τοῦ Χριστοῦ because of their manner of life **Phil 3:18.** On the other hand Ign. speaks of blameless Christians ὥσπερ καθηλωμένους ἐν τῷ σταυρῷ τοῦ κυρίου Ἰησοῦ Χρ. σαρκί τε καὶ πνεύματι *as if nailed to the cross of the Lord Jesus Christ both in the flesh and in the spirit* ISm 1:1 (cp. MartAndr Prius 1, 14 [Aa II/1, 54–55]). In the imagery of Ign. the cross is called ἡ μηχανὴ Ἰησοῦ Χρ. IEph 9:1 (s. HSchlier, Relgesch. Untersuchungen zu d. Ign.-briefen 1929, 110–24), and the orthodox believers are the κλάδοι τοῦ σταυροῦ *branches of the cross* ITr 11:2. Such passages provide a link with the transf. sense

❸ **the suffering/death which believers endure in following the crucified Lord,** ***cross*** λαμβάνειν τὸν σταυρὸν αὐτοῦ **Mt 10:38.** ἆραι τὸν στ. αὐτοῦ **16:24; Mk 8:34; 10:21** t.r.; **Lk 9:23.** βαστάζειν τὸν στ. ἑαυτοῦ **14:27** (s. on these parallel passages AFridrichsen, Festskrift for Lyder Brun 1922, 17–34.—EDinkler, Jesu Wort v. Kreuztragen: Bultmann Festschr. '54, 110–29).—DELG. M-M. EDNT. TW. Sv.

σταυρόω (σταυρός; in the sense 'fence w. stakes' Thu. et al.) fut. σταυρώσω; 1 aor. ἐσταύρωσα. Pass.: 1 aor. ἐσταυρώθην; pf. ἐσταύρωμαι

❶ **to fasten to a cross,** ***crucify*** (Polyb. 1, 86, 4; Diod. S. 16, 61, 2; Epict. 2, 2, 20; Artem. 2, 53; 4, 49; Esth 7:9; 8:12r; Jos., Ant. 2, 77; 17, 295). τινά *someone* w. ref. to Jesus' crucifixion (Orig., C. Cels. 4, 22, 9; s. TestSol 22:20) **Mt 20:19; 23:34; 26:2; 27:22f, 26, 31, 35, 38; 28:5; Mk 15:13ff, 20, 24f, 27; 16:6; Lk 23:21, 23, 33; 24:7, 20; J 19:6ab** (the doubling of the impv. as Anaxarchus [IV BC] in Diog. L. 9, 59 πτίσσε, πτίσσε=pound, pound away [in a mortar]), vs. **6c, 10, 15f, 18, 20, 23, 41; Ac 2:36; 4:10; 13:29** D; **1 Cor 2:8; 2 Cor 13:4; Rv 11:8;** B 7:3, 9; 12:1; IEph 16:2; GPt 4:10; 12:52. Χριστὸς ἐσταυρωμένος **1 Cor 1:23;** cp. **2:2; Gal 3:1.** Also simply ὁ ἐσταυρωμένος MPol 17:2. ὁ σταυρωθείς (Iren. 2, 32, 4 [Harv. I 375, 12]; Orig., C. Cels. 1, 31, 20) GPt 13:56. ἀληθῶς ἐσταυρώθη *he was truly crucified* (in contrast to the Docetic view that the Passion was unreal; Iren. 3, 19, 3 [Harv. II 104, 3]) ITr 9:1. (On the crucifixion of Jesus s. Feigel, Weidel, and Finegan s.v. Ἰούδας 6; also EBickermann, Utilitas Crucis: RHR 112, '35, 169–241; on Mk 15:16–32 as crucifixion narrative in the light of the Roman triumphal s. TSchmidt, NTS 41, '95, 1–18.).—μὴ Παῦλος ἐσταυρώθη ὑπὲρ ὑμῶν; *Was Paul crucifed for you?* **1 Cor 1:13.** ἄνωθεν μέλλω σταυροῦσθαι *I must once again be crucified* AcPl Ha 7, 39 (cp. MartPt 6 [Aa I 88, 7; 8; 9; 12]). This last offers an interesting transition to 2, containing as it does a component expressed in 2 and also anticipation of a literal death.

❷ **destroy through connection with the crucifixion of Christ,** ***crucify,*** a transcendent sense in ext. of 1, of imitation of Christ; fig. οἱ τοῦ Χριστοῦ Ἰ. τὴν σάρκα ἐσταύρωσαν *those who belong to Christ Jesus have crucified the flesh* w. its sinful desires **Gal 5:24.** Pass.: of the cross of Christ, δι᾽ οὗ ἐμοὶ κόσμος ἐσταύρωται κἀγὼ κόσμῳ *through which the world has been crucified to me, and I (have been crucified) to it,* the believer who is inseparably united to the Lord has died on the cross to the kind of life that belongs to this world **Gal 6:14.** ὁ ἐμὸς ἔρως ἐσταύρωται *my passion* (for worldly things) *has been crucified* IRo 7:2.—DELG s.v. σταυρός. M-M. EDNT. TW.

σταφυλή, ῆς, ἡ (Hom.+; ins, pap, LXX; JosAs 4:4) ***(a bunch of) grapes*** **Mt 7:16; Lk 6:44** (w. σῦκον as Epict. 3, 24, 86; 91; Jos., Bell. 3, 519); **Rv 14:18.** στ. παρεστηκυῖα *a bunch of ripe grapes* (παρίστημι 2bγ) 1 Cl 23:4=2 Cl 11:3 (quot. of unknown origin).—B. 378. DELG. M-M.

στάχυς, υος, ὁ—❶ **the fruiting spike of a cereal grain,** ***head*** or ***ear (of grain)*** (Hom. et al.; ins, pap, LXX; EpArist 63; Philo, Aet. M. 98; Jos., Bell. 2, 112, Ant. 5, 213 al.; Just., D. 119,

3) in our lit. only of wheat **Mk 4:28ab.** τίλλειν (τοὺς) στάχυας *pick (the) heads of wheat* **2:23; Mt 12:1;** cp. **Lk 6:1.**

❷ νάρδου στάχυς (Geopon. 7, 13, 1)=ναρδοστάχυς **the flower of the aromatic plant spikenard,** ***(spike)nard flower*** (shaped like a head of grain) ApcPt 3, 10.—DELG. M-M.

Στάχυς, υος, ὁ (several times in PCairZen [III BC]; Mitt-Wilck. I/2, 10, 14 [131/130 BC]; IG III, 1080, 37; 1095, 19; XII/3, 624; 749; IMagnMai 119, 25; CIL VI 8607) ***Stachys,*** recipient of a greeting **Ro 16:9.**—LGPN I. M-M.

στέαρ, ατος, τό (Hom. et al.; pap, LXX, Philo) ***fat*** 1 Cl 4:1 (Gen 4:4); B 2:5 (Is 1:11).—DELG.

στέγη, ης, ἡ (s. στέγω and next entry; Aeschyl., Hdt.+; ins, pap, LXX; En 14:17; JosAs 3:3; Jos., Ant. 8, 67f; Ar. 15, 7; loanw. in rabb.) ***roof*** **Mk 2:4** (on uncovering the roof cp. Jos., Ant. 14, 459 and FSchulthess, ZNW 21, 1922, 220; HJahnow, ibid. 24, 1925, 155ff [s. JDerrett, Law in the NT, '70, xv, n. 1]; against Jahnow: SKrauss, ibid. 25, 1926, 307ff; LFonck, Biblica 6, 1925, 450–54 and PGvanSlogteren, NThT 14, 1925, 361–65. See also CMcCown, JBL 58, '39, 213–16). On εἰσέρχεσθαι ὑπὸ τὴν στ. (τινός) **Mt 8:8; Lk 7:6** s. εἰσέρχομαι 1aγ.—B. 473. DELG s.v. στέγω. M-M.

στέγος, ους, τό (s. prec. entry; Aeschyl. et al.; ins [SIG 1179, 20]; EpJer 9 v.l.) ***roof*** (Diod. S. 19, 45, 7; Jos., Ant. 7, 130 al.) συνάξεις τοὺς σοὺς ὑπὸ τὸ στέγος σου *you are to gather your people under your roof* 1 Cl 12:6.—DELG s.v. στέγω. M-M s.v. στέγη.

στέγω aor. inf. στέξαι (Sir 8:17) (Aeschyl. et al.; ins, pap; freq. in the sense of covering or enclosing in such a way as to keep someth. undesirable from coming in, as water into a ship)

❶ to keep confidential, ***cover, pass over in silence*** (Eur., Electra 273 τἀμὰ ἔπη; Thu. 6, 72, 5; Polyb. 8, 14, 5 τὸν λόγον; Sir 8:17; Jos., Vi. 225; Field, Notes 177f), so perh. ἡ ἀγάπη πάντα στέγει **1 Cor 13:7** of love that throws a cloak of silence over what is displeasing in another person (Harnack, SBBerlAk 1911, 147; but s. 2).

❷ to bear up against difficulties, ***bear, stand, endure*** (Aeschyl. et al.; Polyb.; Diod. S.; Plut.; SIG 700, 23; Philo, In Flacc. 64 στέγειν τὰς ἐνδείας) τὶ *someth.* πάντα **1 Cor 9:12;** perh. (s. 1) **13:7** (GWhitaker, 'Love Springs No Leak': Exp. 8th ser., 21, 1921, 126ff). Abs. (PGrenf I, 1, 18 [II BC]; POxy 1775, 10 καὶ ἔστεξα, ἕως ἔλθῃς) μηκέτι στέγων *since I could not bear it any longer* **1 Th 3:5;** cp. vs. **1.**—B. 849. DELG. M-M. TW. Spicq.

στεῖρα, ας, ἡ (Hom. et al.; IAndrosIsis 82; Philo; LXX; En 98:5; Just.. D. 84, 3 adj. and subst.; B-D-F §43, 1) in our lit. ***incapable of bearing children, barren, infertile*** **Lk 1:7** (on the social implications of a woman's infertility s. Gen 29:31; Lev 20:20f; a similar perspective in the Gk. world: Hdt. 6, 86; but by stressing the uprightness of the couple [Lk 1:6] Lk indicates that sin was not the cause), vs. **36; 23:29; Gal 4:27** (Is 54:1); **Hb 11:11;** 2 Cl 2:1 (Is 54:1); B 13:2 (Gen 25:21).—DELG 1 στεῖρα. M-M s.v. στεῖρος.

στέλλω mid. aor. 3 sg. ἐστείλατο LXX; pf. ptc. fem. pl. ἐσταλμέναι 3 Macc 1:19 (Hom. et al. in the sense 'make ready, send', etc.; ins, pap, LXX, Philo; Jos., Ant. 2, 43) in our lit., as well as in LXX, only mid.

❶ to keep one's distance, ***keep away, stand aloof*** ἀπό τινος (Polyb. 8, 22, 4; cp. Mal 2:5) *from someone* **2 Th 3:6.**

❷ to shun someth., ***avoid, try to avoid*** (Hippocr., π. ἀρχ. ἰητρ. 5 Heib. acc. to codd. οὔτ' ἂν ἀπόσχοιντο οὐδενός, ὧν ἐπιθυμέουσιν οὐδὲ στείλαιντο='not keep away from something [of food] . . . nor avoid what they have their mind set on'; SEG II, 615, 1 στέλλεο Περσεφόνας ζᾶλον. Mal 2:5 uses στ. as a parallel to φοβεῖσθαι, which corresponds to Hesychius: στέλλεται· φοβεῖται) στελλόμενοι τοῦτο, μή τις *avoiding* or *trying to avoid this, lest someone* **2 Cor 8:20** (so It., Vulg., Goth., Chrys., Luther, Calvin, and many in later times).—DELG. M-M. TW.

στέμμα, ατος, τό (Hom. et al.; ins, pap; TestSol 7:4 D) ***wreath/garland of flowers*** (but wool was also necessary for religious purposes: Herodas 8, 11) **Ac 14:13** (IKosPH [s. ἀγαθός 2aα] no. 37, 29–31: ἱερεύς . . . βοῦς . . . στέμμα in a sacrifice to Zeus; s. Field, Notes 122).—DELG s.v. στέφω. M-M.

στεναγμός, οῦ, ὁ (στενάζω; Pind.+; Sb 4949, 12; 5716, 12; PGM 4, 1406; 7, 768; LXX; pseudepigr.; Jos., Bell. 6, 272; Hippol., Ref. 6, 32, 2) **an involuntary expression of great concern or stress,** ***sigh, groan, groaning*** **Ac 7:34** (cp. Ex 2:24 [sim. Philo, Leg. All. 3, 211]; 6:5) 1 Cl 15:6 (Ps 11:6); Hv 3, 9, 6. Pl. (Diod. S. 3, 29, 7 στεναγμοὶ μεγάλοι) στεναγμοὶ ἀλάλητοι (s. ἀλάλητος) **Ro 8:26** (WBieder, TZ 4, '48, 31–33; JSchniewind, Nachgelassene Reden, '52, 81–103; ADietzel, TZ 13, '57, 12–32 [Hodayoth]; EKäsemann, EHaenchen Festschr. '64, 142–55; MDibelius, Formgeschichte des Evangeliums[5] '66, 82f).—DELG s.v. στένω. M-M. TW.

στενάζω fut. στενάξω; 1 aor. ἐστέναξα (trag., Demosth. et al.; Sb 2134, 14; LXX; pseudepigr.; Philo)

❶ to express oneself involuntarily in the face of an undesirable circumstance, ***sigh, groan*** (Herm. Wr. in Stob. I 395, 5 W.=474, 22 Sc.) **2 Cor 5:2** (ἐν τούτῳ=in this earthly body), **4; Hb 13:17;** MPol 2:2; Hv 3, 9, 6; GJs 22:3; AcPl Ha 2, 18. MPol 9:2; στ. ἐν ἑαυτῷ *sigh to oneself* **Ro 8:23** (cp. Lycophron 1462f στ. ἐν καρδίᾳ).—In connection w. a healing, prob. as an expr. of power ready to act **Mk 7:34** (cp. PGM 13, 945).

❷ to express discontent, ***complain,*** fig. ext. of 1: στ. κατά τινος *groan against, complain of someone* **Js 5:9.**—B. 1131. DELG s.v. στένω. M-M. TW.

στενός, ή, όν (Aeschyl., Hdt.+; ins, pap, LXX; TestAbr; EpArist 118; Philo; Jos., Bell. 1, 41; Mel., P. 45, 317) in ref. to dimension ***narrow*** πύλη (q.v. 2) **Mt 7:13f.** θύρα (Arrian, Anab. 6, 29, 5 of the θυρὶς στενή in the grave of Cyrus ὡς μόλις ἂν εἶναι ἑνὶ ἀνδρὶ οὐ μεγάλῳ πολλὰ κακοπαθοῦντι παρελθεῖν=so that it would be difficult for even a relatively small man to pass through without some distress) **Lk 13:24.** Of a prison cell AcPl Ha 3, 19 (restored). στ. ὁδός (Machon vs. 392; Nicol. Dam.: 90 fgm. 66, 38 Jac.; Diod. S. 20, 29, 7; Maximus Tyr. 39, 3n μία [ὁδὸς] στενὴ κ. τραχεῖα κ. οὐ πολλοῖς πάνυ ὁδεύσιμος=one narrow, rough path and not readily passable for a large group; Appian, Syr. 43 §225; Arrian, Anab. 2, 11, 3; 3, 18, 4; Jos., Ant. 19, 116) **Mt 7:14 v.l.**—B. 886. DELG. M-M. EDNT. TW.

στενοχωρέω (στενός, χῶρος 'space') 1 aor. 3 sg. ἐστενοχώρησεν Judg 16:16 B (since Machon [III BC] vs. 396; pap, though intr.)

❶ to confine or restrict to a narrow space, ***crowd, cramp, confine, restrict*** (Diod. S. 20, 29, 7; Lucian, Nigr. 13, Tox. 29 al.; LXX) fig., pass. *be confined, restricted* (Herm. Wr. 2, 11; schol. on Eur., Med. 57 στενοχωρεῖσθαι τῷ κακῷ; Is 28:20; Jos., Bell. 4, 163) οὐ στενοχωρεῖσθε ἐν ἡμῖν, στενοχωρεῖσθε δὲ ἐν τοῖς σπλάγχνοις ὑμῶν *you are not restricted in us* (i.e.

they are not boxed off in a narrow area of Paul's affection; s. vs. 11), *but rather in your own hearts* **2 Cor 6:12.**

❷ **to be in a circumstance that seems to offer no way out, *be distressed*** fig. ext. of 1, pass., as the higher degree beside θλίβεσθαι (Epict. 1, 25, 28) θλιβόμενοι ἀλλ' οὐ στενοχωρούμενοι *hard pressed, but not distressed/crushed* **2 Cor 4:8.** In act. sense, of the Holy Spirit, when anger moves into a person whom he indwells: στενοχωρεῖται *he is distressed* Hm 5, 1, 3. Of the hardships that the slaves of God, in contrast to the unrighteous, must undergo 2 Cl 20:1.—DELG s.v. στενός. M-M. TW.

στενοχωρία, ας, ἡ (s. prec. entry; in the lit. sense, 'narrowness', Thu. et al.) fig. **a set of stressful circumstances, *distress, difficulty, anguish, trouble*** (Polyb. 1, 67, 1; Petosiris, fgm. 7 ln. 22 [w. πόλεμος]; Plut., Mor. 182b; Artem. 3, 14; Aelian, VH 2, 41; Cass. Dio 39, 34; PCairZen 435, 2 [III BC]; Cat. Cod. Astr. VII 169, 21; Sir 10:26; 1 Macc 2:53; 3 Macc 2:10; En 98:10; TestAbr B 7 p. 111, 21 [Stone p. 70]) w. θλῖψις (Artem. 1, 68; 82; 2, 3 al.; Dt 28:53; 55; 57; Is 8:22; 30:6; Esth 1:1g; PLond V, 1677, 11 [VI AD]. Cp. Epict. 1, 25, 26 στενοχωρία . . . θλίβειν) **Ro 2:9; 8:35.** W. λύπη Hv 4, 3, 4; m 10, 2, 6. Pl. *difficulties* (oft. Artem.; 1 Macc 13:3; Cat. Cod. Astr. VIII/1 p. 165, 2) **2 Cor 6:4; 12:10.**—DELG s.v. στενός. TW.

στέργω (Aeschyl., Hdt.+; ins, pap; Sir 27:17; Philo; Jos., Bell. 1, 596, Ant. 8, 249; SibOr 4, 25; Just., Ath.; seldom used for sexual expression) **to have a benevolent interest in or concern for, *love, feel affection for*** τινά *someone,* of the love of a wife for her husband (Theocr. 17, 130; IAndrosIsis, Kyme 27f; cp. Menand., PDidot I, 14f p. 329 S.: of νόμος that applies to husband and wife) 1 Cl 1:3; Pol 4:2. BWarfield, The Terminology of Love in the NT: PTR 16, 1918, 1–45; 153–203.—B. 1110. DELG. Sv.

στερεός, ά, όν (Hom. et al.; ins, pap, LXX, En, EpArist, Philo, Joseph., Just., D. 5, 2)

❶ **pert. to being firm or solid in contrast to being soft or viscous, *firm, hard, solid, strong*** θεμέλιος **2 Ti 2:19.** πέτρα (PPetr II, 4, 1, 3 [III BC]; LXX; En 26:5; OdeSol 11:5) B 5:14; 6:3 (both Is 50:7). (Opp. γάλα) στερεὰ τροφή *solid food* (Theophr., CP 3, 16; Diod. S. 2, 4, 5; Epict. 2, 16, 39; Lucian, Lexiph. 23) **Hb 5:12, 14.**

❷ fig. ext. of 1, of human character (Hom. et al.) ***steadfast, firm*** (Diog. L. 2, 132 of athletes; Quint. Smyrn. [c. 400 AD] 5, 597; 9, 508 Zimmermann [1891] στερεῇ φρενί=w. steadfast mind) στερεοὶ τῇ πίστει **1 Pt 5:9** (ἑδραῖοι P[72]). —DELG s.v. 2 στεῖρα, B στερεός; Frisk s.v. στερεός. M-M. TW.

στερεόω (στερεός) fut. 2 sg. στερεώσεις; 1 aor. ἐστερέωσα. Pass.: impf. ἐστερεούμην; fut. 3 sg. στερεωθήσεται LXX; 1 aor. ἐστερεώθην; pf. ptc. fem. ἐστερεωμένη 1 Km 6:18 (X. et al.; LXX; En 103:15)

❶ **to render physically firm, *make strong, make firm.*** lit., of impotent limbs, pass. *be strengthened, become strong* ἐστερεώθησαν αἱ βάσεις αὐτοῦ **Ac 3:7** (X., De Re Equ. 4, 3 τοὺς πόδας; Hippocr., Epid. 2, 3, 17 ed. Littré V p. 118 τὰ ὀστέα; Hippiatr. II 82, 1). On the basis of this passage the act. is used in referring to the same act of healing τοῦτον ἐστερέωσεν τὸ ὄνομα *the name* (of Christ) *has made this man strong* vs. **16.**

❷ **to cause to become firmer in such matters as conviction or commitment, *strengthen,*** fig. ext. of 1 (1 Km 2:1 ἡ καρδία), pass. αἱ ἐκκλησίαι ἐστερεοῦντο τῇ πίστει *the congregations were continually* (impf.) *being strengthened in the faith* **Ac 16:5.**—DELG s.v. 2 στεῖρα, B στερεός. M-M. TW.

στερέω fut. 3 sg. στερήσει Ps 83:12; 1 aor. ἐστέρησα. Pass.: fut. 3 sg. στερηθήσει (ApcMos 26), 3 pl. στερηθήσονται 4 Macc 4:7; 1 aor. ἐστερήθην LXX; pf. 3 pl. ἐστέρηνται 3 Macc 1:12 (Hom. et al.; pap, LXX; Jos., C. Ap. 2, 277, Ant. 16, 93) ***deprive*** τινά τινος *someone of a thing* B 13:4 (Gen 48:11).—DELG s.v. στέρομαι.

στερέωμα, ατος, τό (στερεόω; in var. senses of someth. solid: Aristot. et al.; Herm. Wr. 514, 12 Sc.; PGM 4, 1210; IDefixWünsch 4, 22; LXX, En; TestSol 20:12, 17; TestAbr B 12 p. 116, 12 [Stone p. 80]; TestJob 8:1; ApcMos; Mel. 82, 615; Ath. 24, 5) prim. 'the solid part'.

❶ **the sky as a supporting structure, *the firmament*** (Gen 1:6ff; En 18:2; Philo, Op. M. 36; TestNapht 3:4; IDefixAudollent 242, 8 [III AD]) 1 Cl 27:7 (Ps 18:2).

❷ **state or condition of firm commitment, *firmness, steadfastness*** τῆς πίστεως **Col 2:5** (cp. 1 Macc 9:14 [military sense]).—DELG s.v. στεῖρα, B στερεός. M-M. TW.

Στεφανᾶς, ᾶ, ὁ (CIG II, 3378; Sb 361, 10 [in the gen. Στεφανᾶτος].—Short form of Στεφανηφόρος? or a development of Στέφανος? B-D-F §125, 1; Rob. 173; 255; W-S. §16, 9; AFick[2]-FBechtel, Griech. Personennamen 1894, 253f) ***Stephanas,*** a member of the church at Corinth who, w. his household, was baptized by Paul himself **1 Cor 1:16** as the 'firstfruits of Achaia' **16:15.** Acc. to vs. **17** he was w. Fortunatus and Achaicus in Paul's company at Ephesus. Together with other presbyters at Corinth addresses a request to Paul AcPlCor 1:1. S. also **1 Cor subscr.**—LGPN I. M-M.

Στέφανος, ου, ὁ (since Andocides 1, 18; Pla, Meno 94c; Demosth.; ins, pap; Jos., Bell. 2, 228) a name freq. found, ***Stephen,*** one of the seven 'assistants' in Jerusalem. Ac relates that he performed miracles and became esp. prominent as a proclaimer. Religious differences w. certain synagogues (s. Λιβερτῖνος) brought him before the Sanhedrin, where he made a speech which so incited his audience that they stoned him in the presence of Saul (Paul) **Ac 6:5, 8f; 7:1 v.l., 59; 8:2; 11:19; 22:20.**—KPahncke, StKr 85, 1912, 1–38; WMundle, ZNW 20, 1921, 133–47; EMeyer III 154ff; JRopes, StKr 102, 1930, 307–15; AFridrichsen, Le Monde oriental 25, '32, 44–52; RSchumacher, Der Diakon Stephanus 1910; MSimon, St. Stephen and the Hellenists in the Primitive Church '58; JBihler, D. Stephanusgeschichte etc. '63; CBarrett, Stephen and the Son of Man, EHaenchen Festschr. '64, 32–38; MScharlemann, Stephen, a Singular Saint '68; MHengel, ZTK 72, '75, 151–206.—Kl. Pauly V 360f [no. 11]; BHHW III 1864f; Haenchen ad loc.—LGPN I. M-M. EDNT.

στέφανος, ου, ὁ (s. next entry; Hom.+)—❶ **a wreath made of foliage or designed to resemble foliage and worn by one of high status or held in high regard, *wreath, crown.*** Hs 8, 2, 1ab. Jesus' 'crown of thorns' **Mt 27:29; Mk 15:17; J 19:2, 5;** GPt 3:8 (on the crowning w. thorns and mocking of Jesus s. FCumont, AnalBoll 16, 1897, 3ff; LParmentier, Le roi des Saturnales: RevPhilol, n.s. 21, 1897, 143ff; PWendland, Jesus als Saturnalienkönig: Her 33, 1898, 175–79; WPaton, ZNW 2, 1901, 339–41; SReinach, Le roi supplicié: L'Anthropologie 33, 1902, 621ff; HReich, D. König m. der Dornenkrone 1905 [=NJklA 13, 1904, 705–33]; HVollmer, ZNW 6, 1905, 194–98, 8, 1907, 320f, Jesus u. das Sacäenopfer 1905; KLübeck, Die Dornenkrönung Christi 1906; JGeffcken, Her 41, 1906, 220–29; KKastner, Christi Dornenkrönung u. Verspottung durch die röm. Soldateska: BZ 6, 1908, 378–92, ibid. 9, 1911, 56; TBirt, PJ 137,1909, 92–104; HAllroggen, Die Verspottung Christi: ThGl 1, 1909, 689–708;

HZimmern, Zum Streit um die Christusmythe 1910, 38ff, Verh. d. Sächs. Ges. d. W., phil.-hist. Kl. 70, 5, 1918, Pauly-W. second ser. II 1, 208; LRadermacher, ARW 28, 1930, 31–35; RDelbrueck, Antiquarisches zu den Verspottungen Jesu: ZNW 41, '42, 124–45). On the wreath for the winner of an athletic contest (Aelian, VH 9, 31; TestJob 4:10; Tat. 11, 1; 23, 1; on the socio-cultural context s. APapathomas, NTS 43, '97, 225–33), cp. the imagery relating to a heavenly reward **1 Cor 9:25;** 2 Cl 7:3 (s. 3 below).—Apart from recognition of athletes and winners of various kinds of competitions, in the Gr-Rom. world the awarding of a crown or wreath signified appreciation for exceptional contributions to the state or groups within it (s. the indexes in ins corpora, and lit. cited at the end of this entry; cp. SEG XXXII, 809, 3f). The recipients were usually public officials or civic-minded pers. serving at their own expense (s. New Docs 7, 240 and the entries beginning λειτουργ-; s. MBlech below). In **Rv** the (golden) crown is worn by beings of high rank (divine beings w. a golden crown: PGM 4, 698; 1027; the high priest w. the στ. χρύσεος: Jos., Ant. 3, 172; the king 17, 197; MParca, ASP 31, '91, 41–44 on the radiant crown in antiquity [cp. PKöln VI, 245, 14]): by the 24 elders **4:4, 10** (perh. the gold crowns or wreaths of the 24 elders simply belong to the usual equipment of those who accompany a divine figure. Cp. Athen. 5, 197f the triumphal procession of Dionysus with 40 σάτυροι wearing golden wreaths; also the whole fantastic procession here described; s. also MGuarducci, Epigraphica 35, '73, 7–23; 39, '77, 140–42); also by the Human One (Son of Man) **14:14** (who at 19:12 wears the real head-dress of the ruler [s. διάδημα]. But s. 2 Km 12:30; 1 Ch 20:2; SSol 3:11); s. also **6:2; 9:7; 12:1** (στεφ. ἀστέρων δώδεκα, s. Boll. 99). In **1 Cor 9:25** σ. does double duty, first in ref. to an earthly crown and then to a heavenly one (cp. 2 Cl 7:3 and s. 3 below).—Ign. refers metaph. to the presbytery as ἀξιόπλοκος πνευματικὸς στέφανος *a worthily-woven spiritual wreath* IMg 13:1, but this pass. belongs equally in 2.

❷ **that which serves as adornment or source of pride, *adornment, pride,*** fig. ext. of 1 (Lycurgus 50 of brave Hellenes who died in behalf of freedom and whose 'souls are the σ. of the homeland'; Hom., Epigr. 13, 1 ἀνδρὸς μὲν στέφανος παῖδες; Eur., Iphig. Aul. 193 Αἴας τᾶς Σαλαμῖνος στέφ.; Pr 12:4; 17:6.—Expr. denoting tender love: HSwoboda et al., Denkmäler aus Lykaonien etc. 1935 p. 78, no. 168) of the Philippians χαρὰ καὶ στέφανός μου **Phil 4:1.** (χαρὰ ἢ) στέφανος καυχήσεως prize *to be proud of* (Goodsp.; cp. Pr 16:31) **1 Th 2:19.** S. IMg 13:1 at 1 above, end.

❸ **award or prize for exceptional service or conduct, *prize, reward*** fig. (LXX; ApcEsdr 6:17, 21 p. 31, 26 and 31 Tdf.; as symbol of victory ANock, ClR 38, 1924, 108 n. 11). In **1 Cor 9:25** (ref. to incorruptibility) and 2 Cl 7:3 (s. 1 above) the ref. to crown or wreath is strongly felt, but in the pass. that follow the imagery of the wreath becomes less and less distinct, yet without loss of its primary significance as a symbol of exceptional merit (Ael. Aristid. 27, 36 K.=16 p. 397 D.: τῶν ἀθανάτων στ.; PSI 405, 3 [III BC]; Danker, Benefactor 468–71). Obj. gen. τ. δικαιοσύνης *for righteousness* (recognition of uprightness is a common topic in Gr-Rom. decrees; s. δικαιοσύνη 3a; on the implied exceptional character of the wearer of a crown s. LDeubner, De incubatione capitula duo, 1899, 26) **2 Ti 4:8** (on posthumous award s. New Docs 2, 50; cp. Soph., Phil. 1421f of glory after suffering). W. epexegetical gen. (this is the sense of στ. δικαιοσύνης EpArist 280; TestLevi 8:2) ὁ στέφ. τῆς ζωῆς (s. ζωή 2bβ) **Js 1:12; Rv 2:10;** cp. **3:11;** ὁ τῆς ἀφθαρσίας στ. MPol 17:1; 19:2; ὁ ἀμαράντινος τῆς δόξης στ. **1 Pt 5:4** (cp. Jer 13:18 στ. δόξης; La 2:15; cp. 1QS 4:7; 1QH 9:25; τῆς βασιλείας στ. Hippol., Ref. 9, 17, 4).—ἐλευθέριος στ. AcPl Ha 2, 31.—MBlech, Studien zum Kranz bei den Griechen 1982 (lit.).—Schürer III/1 103f, n. 60 (lit). Pauly-W. XI 1588–1607; Kl. Pauly III 324f; BHHW II 999f.—New Docs 2, 50. DELG s.v. στέφω. M-M. EDNT. TW. Sv.

στεφανόω (στέφανος) fut. 2 sg. στεφανώσεις Ps 5:13 Aq., Sym.; 1 aor. ἐστεφάνωσα. Pass.: fut. 3 sg. στεφανωθήσεται 3 Macc 3:28; 1 aor. ἐστεφανώθην; pf. ptc. ἐστεφανωμένος (Hom.+)

❶ **to encircle someone's head with ornamental foliage, *wreathe, crown*** τινά (s. στέφανος 1) *someone* (Diod. S. 20, 94, 5) Hs 8, 2, 1. The winner in an athletic contest (who received a wreath of some botanical variety), pass. (Pind., O. 4, 14; Hdt. 8, 59; PCairZen 60, 7 [257 BC]) **2 Ti 2:5;** 2 Cl 7:1; cp. 7:2, 3; 20:2 (where 2 Cl passes over to the crowning of the victor in the immortal contest. See the hymn to Sarapis IG XI/4, 1299, 9f [c. 200 BC] διὰ τὴν εὐσέβειαν ἐστεφανώθη ὑπὸ τοῦ θεοῦ). Hs 8, 3, 6; 8, 4, 6.—One of the two goats on the great Day of Atonement (Lev 16:5ff) is called ἐστεφανωμένος and is taken to be a type of Christ B 7:9.

❷ **to recognize distinguished service or performance with an award, *honor, reward, crown,*** fig. ext. of 1 (Pind., Eur. et al.—Cebes 22, 1 στ. δυνάμει; 23, 4) δόξῃ καὶ τιμῇ ἐστεφάνωσας αὐτόν **Hb 2:7** (Ps 8:6); cp. vs. **9** (Windisch, Hdb. ad loc. [lit.]). Of Polycarp the martyr ἐστεφανωμένος τὸν τῆς ἀφθαρσίας στέφανον MPol 17:1 (Diod. S. 16, 13, 1 στεφάνοις ἐστεφανωμένους; cp. Iren. 5, 29, 1 [Harv. II 404]). Cp. 2 Cl 20:2 (s. 1 above). Pregnant constr. στεφανωθεὶς κατ' αὐτῆς *crowned as victor* (in the struggle) *against it* (i.e., evil desire) Hm 12, 2, 5.—So intimately are the terms τιμή and τιμάω (q.v.) associated with the awarding of a wreath or crown that the usage of these terms suggests the kinds of qualities or deeds that invite such public recognition (s. MBlech, Studien zum Kranz bei den Griechen '82, 161; lit. xvii–xxxiii).—DELG s.v. στέφω. M-M. TW.

στῆθος, ους, τό (Hom.+) ***chest, breast*** **Rv 15:6;** Hv 1, 4, 2 (Leutzsch, Hermas 393 n. 132). ἀναπεσεῖν ἐπὶ τὸ στ. τινος (ἀναπίπτειν 2) **J 13:25; 21:20.** τύπτειν τὸ στῆθος (αὐτοῦ) *beat one's breast* as a sign of grief **Lk 18:13** (v.l. εἰς τὸ στῆθος); **23:48.** Also κόπτεσθαι τὸ στ. (κόπτω 2) GPt 8:28. As the seat of the inner life (as early as Alcaeus [VII/VI BC] fgm. 283, 3 Treu, p. 6 ln. 3]; Iambl., Vi. Pyth. 35, 252) 2 Cl 19:2.—B. 24. DELG. M-M. Sv.

στήκω (found first in the NT; in the LXX only as an untrustworthy v.l. [ADebrunner, GGA 1926, 146f], but also occurs TestSol; TestJob 26:6; Kaibel 970; Hippiatr. 69, 2 and 4 p. 269, 16; 270, 16; PGM 4, 923; 36, 273. A late formation fr. ἕστηκα, the perf. of ἵστημι, and used beside it; s. B-D-F §73; Mlt-H. 220; 259.—εστηκεν J 8:44 is prob. the perf. of ἵστημι, whether written ἔστ. or ἕστ.; s. EAbbott, The Authorship of the 4th Gosp. and Other Critical Essays, 1888, 286–93; B-D-F §14; 73; 97, 1; difft. Rob. 224, after W-H.; s. also Mlt-H. 100. In Rv 12:4 the impf. ἔστηκεν is prob. to be preferred to the perf. ἕστ.).

❶ **to be in a standing position, *stand*** **Mk 11:25;** ἔξω στ. *stand outside* **3:31.** μέσος ὑμῶν στήκει *there is one standing in your midst* **J 1:26 v.l.** ὁ δράκων ἔστηκεν ἐνώπιον τῆς γυναικός **Rv 12:4 v.l.** (s. above).

❷ **to be firmly committed in conviction or belief,** fig. ext of 1: *stand firm, be steadfast* ἔν τινι *in someth.*: ἐν τῇ πίστει **1 Cor 16:13.** ἐν κυρίῳ **Phil 4:1; 1 Th 3:8.** ἐν ἑνὶ πνεύματι *in one spirit* **Phil 1:27.** τῷ ἰδίῳ κυρίῳ στήκειν ἢ πίπτειν *stand or fall to the advantage or disadvantage of his own master* or *to be his own master's concern whether he stands or falls* **Ro 14:4.**

Abs. **2 Th 2:15; Gal 5:1** ('in freedom' is to be supplied).—M-M. TW.

στήλη, ης, ἡ (Hom. et al.; ins, pap, LXX, Philo; Jos., Ant. 14, 188; Just., D. 86, 2; loanw. in rabb.) **a commemorative stone block or pillar,** ***monument, pillar*** from the time of Hom. inscribed and used as a grave marker, or for commemoration of events, proclamation of decrees, recognition of personal achievements (freq. in addition to awarding of a wreath, s. στέφανος 3), and the like; w. τάφοι νεκρῶν *tombstones* IPhld 6:1. στ. ἁλός *a pillar of salt* (Gen 19:26) 1 Cl 11:2 (ironical, as indicated by the subsequent phrase εἰς τὸ γνωστὸν εἶναι πᾶσιν [a formulaic synonym of a common purpose clause in honorific decrees, ἵνα/ὅπως πάντες γινώσκωσιν and variations, e.g. SIG 656, 37; 695, 74] but here expressing condemnation instead of commendation; s. γνωστός 2).—TWujewski, Anatolian Sepulchral Stelae in Roman Times '91. Pauly-W. II/3, 2307–25; 4, 428–34; Kl. Pauly V 255f; BHHW III 1678f. DELG.

στηριγμός, οῦ, ὁ (στηρίζω; Aristot. et al. in the sense 'standing still'.—Is 3:1 Sym. [LXX; En 18:5; TestJud 15:3, 6 have στήριγμα]) in our lit. only fig.

❶ **a state of security,** ***safe position*** τοῦ στ. ἐκπίπτειν *lose one's firm hold* **2 Pt 3:17** (REB: safe foothold; NRSV: stability). But the term σ. may also be understood in the sense

❷ **firm commitment to conviction or belief,** ***steadfastness*** τοῦ στ. ἐκπίπτειν *lose one's firmness of commitment* **2 Pt 3:17.**—DELG s.v. στηρίζω. M-M. TW.

στηρίζω (Hom.+; also OGI 612, 8; 769, 11; InsGolanHeights no. 11* line 11; PSI 452, 3) fut. στηρίξω (beside στηρίσω—B-D-F §71; W-S. §13, 4; Mlt-H. 259; Rob. 1219—and στηριῶ [s. Ezk 14:8; Sir 6:37]); 1 aor. ἐστήριξα (t.r.) and ἐστήρισα (B-D-F §71; W-S. § 13, 4; Mlt-H.; and Rob. as above). Pass.: fut. 3 sg. στηριχθήσεται Sir 15:4 and στηρισθήσεται Sir 15:4 v.l.; 1 aor. ἐστηρίχθην; perf. ἐστήριγμαι, inf. ἐστηρίχθαι (LXX, Just.) and ἐστηρίσθαι 1 Km 26:19.

❶ **to fix firmly in a place,** ***set up, establish, support,*** lit. τὶ *someth.* τοὺς οὐρανούς 1 Cl 33:3 (στ. of the creation of the world: Arat., Phaen. 10; Orphica, fgm. 170, 3; Mel.; s. Hippol, Ref. 6, 32, 2 [w. μορφόω]). Pass., of a city *be well established* Ox 1, 17–18 (GTh 32). Of a chasm ἐστήρικται *has been fixed* **Lk 16:26** (cp. Gen 28:12 κλίμαξ ἐστηριγμένη; En 24:2; ParJer 9:17 τὸ δένδρον τὸ στηριχθέν).

❷ **to cause to be inwardly firm or committed,** ***confirm, establish, strengthen*** fig. ext. of 1 (Apollon. Rhod. 4, 816 hatred; Appian, Bell. Civ. 1, 98 τὴν ἀρχήν; Ps 50:14; Sir 3:9; 1 Macc 14:14) w. acc. οὐ τὰ ἑστῶτα στηρίζειν ἀλλὰ τὰ πίπτοντα 2 Cl 2:6 (s. Sir 13:21).— **Lk 22:32; Ac 18:23; Ro 16:25; 1 Th 3:2; 2 Th 3:3; 1 Pt 5:10; Rv 3:2.** Pass. (Iren. 1, 2, 4 [Harv. I 19, 1]) **Ro 1:11.** τὴν καρδίαν τινός (Judg 19:5, 8; Sir 6:37; 22:16) **Js 5:8;** w. a second acc. στ. ὑμῶν τὰς καρδίας ἀμέμπτους **1 Th 3:13** (s. Rtzst., Erlösungsmyst. 147, 3). τινὰ ἔν τινι *someone in someth.* **2 Th 2:17;** IPhld ins. Pass. **2 Pt 1:12.** τινά τινι *strengthen someone w. someth.* 1 Cl 18:12 (Ps 50:14). τινὶ στ. ἑαυτὸν εἴς τι *strengthen oneself w. someth. in order to do someth.* 13:3; στ. τινί *establish* (someth.) *by someth.* 8:5. ἐὰν ἐστηριγμένη ᾖ ἡ διάνοια ἡμῶν πιστῶς πρὸς τὸν θεόν *if our mind is firmly fixed on God in faith* 35:5. ἐγὼ ὑπὸ κίνδυνον, ὑμεῖς ἐστηριγμένοι *I am in danger, you are secure* IEph 12:1.—In a related sense, but with more evident retention of the imagery of someth. that is fixed, to be determined to accomplish an objective, *resolve:* Hebraistically στηρίζειν τὸ πρόσωπον *set one's face* (Ezk 6:2; 13:17; 14:8; 15:7) to denote firmness of purpose (s. Jer 21:10; cp. our 'set one's jaw') foll. by gen. of inf. w. art. (B-D-F §400, 7; Rob. 1068) **Lk 9:51** (s. πρόσωπον 1b and on 9:51–19:27 HConzelmann, The Theology of St. Luke, tr. GBuswell, '60, esp. 60–73).—DELG. M-M. TW. Spicq.

στιβάζω (στιβάς; exx. in WCrönert, GGA 1909, 656) lit. 'to put on a bed', then of putting someth. down for later use, ***store (up)*** εἰς ἀποθήκην οἶνον *wine in the cellar* Hm 11:15.—DELG s.v. στείβω A 3.

στιβαρός, ά, όν (prob. cogn. with στείβω 'tread upon'; Hom. et al.; IAndrosIsis 170; Ezk 3:6; Herm. Wr II, 2 [Sc. 134]; Jos., Bell. 6, 161; 293; SibOr fgm. 3, 39) ***stout, sturdy*** (w. ἰσχυρός) δύναμις Hm 5, 2, 3.—DELG s.v. στείβω A 4.

στιβάς, άδος, ἡ (Eur., Hdt. et al.; ins, pap, of a kind of bed or mattress made of straw, rushes, reeds, leaves etc.) in the only place where it occurs in our lit. (it is lacking in LXX, EpArist, and Philo, but is a loanw. in rabb.) it obviously means ***leaves, leafy branches*** **Mk 11:8** (on the spelling στοιβάς in the t.r. s. W-S. §5, 16; Mlt-H. 76).—DELG s.v. στείβω A 3. M-M.

στίγμα, ατος, τό (στίζω 'tattoo'; Hdt. et al.; SIG 1168, 48; SSol 1:11) ***mark, brand*** (not only did the master put a στίγμα on his slave [Porphyr., Vi. Pyth. 15; Ps.-Phoc. 225.—Diod. S. 34 + 35 fgm. 2, 32 expresses this with τὰ στίγματα and 34 + 35, fgm. 2, 1 with the sing. στιγμή], but religious tattooing also played a prominent role in antiquity: Hdt. 2, 113 στίγματα ἱερά; Lucian, Syr. Dea 59 στιγματηφορεῖν in honor of the goddess.—Dssm., B 265f [BS 349–52]; WHeitmüller, Heinrici Festschr. 1914, 47; FDölger, Sphragis 1911, 39ff, AC I 1929, 66ff; II 1930, 102ff; III '32, 257ff) τὰ στ. τοῦ Ἰησοῦ ἐν τῷ σώματί μου βαστάζω *I bear on my body the marks of Jesus* **Gal 6:17** (Straub 59f); cp. AcPlCor 2:35 (Lucian, Catapl. 28: the whole [ὅλος] man is covered with στίγματα). Paul is most likely alluding to the wounds and scars which he received in the service of Jesus (Plut., Mor. 566f and Hierocles 12, 445 col. 1 στίγματα are the scars left by the divine rod of discipline).—JMoulton, ET 21, 1910, 283f; TCrafer, The Stoning of St. Paul at Lystra and the Epistle to the Galatians: Exp. 8th ser., 6, 1913, 375–84; OSchmitz, Die Christus-Gemeinschaft des Pls im Lichte seines Genetivgebrauchs 1924, 185ff; UWilcken, Deissmann Festschr. 1927, 8f; OHoltzmann, ZNW 30, '31, 82f against EHirsch, ibid. 29, 1930, 196f; EGüttgemanns, D. leidende Apostel, '66, 126–35; HWindisch, Pls u. Christus '34, 187; 251f.—CPJones, 'Stigma', Tatooing and Branding in Gr-Rom. Antiquity: JRS 77, '87, 139–55. DELG s.v. στίζω. M-M. EDNT. TW.

στιγμή, ῆς, ἡ first 'point' (Aristot. et al.), then of someth. quite insignificant (Demosth. et al.), finally specif. of time, ***a moment*** (Plut.; M. Ant. 2, 17; Vett. Val. 131, 4; 239, 11 ἐν στιγμῇ; Is 29:5; 2 Macc 9:11), more fully στιγμὴ χρόνου (Plut., Mor. 13b; Ps.-Plut., Mor. 104b from Demetr. Phaler., fgm. 79 [ed. FWehrli '49]) **Lk 4:5.** Lit., s. ῥιπή.—DELG s.v. στίζω 2. M-M. TW.

στίλβω **to cast rays of light,** ***shine, be radiant*** of garments (Hom. et al.; Pla., Phd. 59, 110d; Kaibel 918. In LXX almost always of the radiance of stars or the luster of metals) at the Transfiguration **Mk 9:3** (cp. OdeSol 11:14 ἔστιλβον οἱ ὀφθαλμοί μου; Hippiatr. I 287, 16 ὀφθαλμοὶ γίνονται στίλβοντες). Of a gate ἔστιλβεν ὑπὲρ τὸν ἥλιον Hs 9, 2, 2 (cp. Chariton 1, 1, 5 στίλβων ὥσπερ ἀστήρ).—DELG. M-M. TW.

στοά, ᾶς, ἡ (Aristoph., Hdt. et al.; ins, pap, LXX, Joseph.; loanw. in rabb.) **a roofed colonnade open normally on one side,** ***portico*** **J 5:2** (Callicrates-Menecles [before 86 BC]: 370 fgm. 1 Jac. κύκλῳ τοῦ λιμένος στοαὶ πέντε).ἡ στοὰ τοῦ Σολομῶνος (cp. Nicol. Dam.: 90 fgm. 130, 82 Jac. ἡ Πομπηίου στοά) **J 10:23** (Ps.-Pla., Eryx. 1, 392a περιπατοῦντες ἐν τῇ στοᾷ τοῦ Διός); cp. **Ac 3:11; 5:12** (s. Σολομών, end).—DELG. M-M.

στοιβάς s. στιβάς.

Στοϊκός (the form Στωϊκός, which is also attested, is more correct, but not necessarily the original one [Just., Tat., Ath.; s. B-D-F §35, 1; Mlt-H. 73 prefers Στω- as the orig.]), **ή, όν** ***Stoic*** (Dionys. Hal., Comp. Verb. 2 p. 7, 3 Us.-Rad.; Diog. L. 4, 67; Philo; Jos., Vi. 12; Just.) Στοϊκοὶ φιλόσοφοι, mentioned beside Epicureans **Ac 17:18.** MPohlenz, Die Stoa[3] '71/72; WBarclay, ET 72, '61, 5 articles passim, 164–294.—M-M.

στοιχεῖον, ου, τό (since Aristoph., X., Pla.; also BGU 959, 2) in our lit. only pl.

❶ **basic components of someth.,** ***elements***—ⓐ of substances underlying the natural world, the basic ***elements*** fr. which everything in the world is made and of which it is composed (Pla. et al.; PGM 4, 440; Wsd 7:17; 19:18; 4 Macc 12:13; Ath., R. 3 p. 51, 17), to disappear in the world conflagration at the end of time **2 Pt 3:10, 12** (Ath. 22, 3; lit. s.v. καυσόω). The four elements of the world (earth, air, fire, water) Hv 3, 13, 3 (cp. Diog. L. 7, 137 [Zeno the Stoic] ἔστι δὲ στοιχεῖον, ἐξ οὗ πρώτου γίνεται τὰ γινόμενα καὶ εἰς ὃ ἔσχατον ἀναλύεται ... τὸ πῦρ, τὸ ὕδωρ, ὁ ἀήρ, ἡ γῆ; Plut., Mor. 875c; Philo, Cher. 127 τὰ τέσσαρα στοιχεῖα; Jos., Ant. 3, 183.—JKroll, Die Lehren des Hermes Trismegistos 1914, 178ff; ESchweizer, JBL 107, '88, 455–68). πῦρ ... ὕδωρ ... ἄλλο τι τῶν στοιχείων Dg 8:2; cp. 7:2 (s. b).

ⓑ of basic components of celestial constellations, ***heavenly bodies*** (Ar. 3, 2; Just., A II, 5, 2; Diog. L. 6. 102 τὰ δώδεκα στοιχεῖα of the signs of the zodiac; POsl 4, 18 δώδεκα στ. τοῦ οὐρανοῦ; Ps.-Callisth. 13, 1.—PGM 4, 1303 the 'Bear' is called a στοιχεῖον ἄφθαρτον.—Rtzst., Poim. 69ff, Herr der Grösse 13ff; Diels [s. below] 53f; JvanWageningen, Τὰ στοιχεῖα τοῦ κόσμου: ThSt 35, 1917, 1–6; FColson, The Week 1926, 95ff) Dg 7:2.

ⓒ of things that constitute the foundation of learning, ***fundamental principles*** (X., Mem. 2, 1, 1; Isocr. 2, 16; Plut., Lib. Educ. 16, 2; Just., A I, 60, 11) or even *letters of the alphabet, ABC's* (Pla. et al.) τὰ στ. τῆς ἀρχῆς τῶν λογίων τοῦ θεοῦ *the very elements of the truths of God* **Hb 5:12.** This mng. is also prob. for the passages in **Gal** (**4:3, 9** NEB 'elementary ideas belonging to this world'; cp. LBelleville, JSNT 26, '86, 53–78) and Col; s. next.

❷ **transcendent powers that are in control over events in this world,** ***elements, elemental spirits.*** The mng. of στ. in τὰ στοιχεῖα τοῦ κόσμου **Gal 4:3; Col 2:8, 20** (for the expr. στοιχ. τ. κόσμου cp. SibOr 2, 206; 3, 80f; 8, 337) and τὰ ἀσθενῆ καὶ πτωχὰ στοιχεῖα **Gal 4:9** is much disputed. For a survey s. EBurton, ICC Gal 1921, 510–18. Some (e.g. Burton, Goodsp.) prefer to take it in sense 1c above, as referring to the elementary forms of religion, Jewish and polytheistic, which have been superseded by the new revelation in Christ (so also WKnox, St. Paul and the Church of the Gentiles '39, 108f; RGrant, HTR 39, '46, 71–3; ACramer, Stoicheia Tou Kosmou, '61 [the unregenerate tendencies within humans]).—Others (e.g. WBauer, Mft., NRSV) hold that the ref. is to the *elemental spirits* which the syncretistic religious tendencies of later antiquity associated w. the physical elements (Herm. Wr. Κόρη κόσμου in Stob. I 409 W.=Sc. 486ff, esp. 486, 23; 25; 490, 14: the στοιχεῖα, fire, air, water, earth, complain to the deity who is over all; Orph. Hymn. 5, 4; 66, 4 Qu.; Ps.-Callisth. 1, 3 [s. below Pfister p. 416f]; Simplicius In Aristot. De Caelo 1, 3 p. 107, 15 Heiberg.—MDibelius, Geisterwelt 78ff; 228ff, Hdb. z. NT[2] exc. on Col 2:8; ELohmeyer, Col 1930, 4–8; 103–5; FPfister, Die στοιχεῖα τοῦ κόσμου in den Briefen des Ap. Pls: Philol. 69, 1910, 411–27; GMacgregor: ACPurdy Festschr. '60, 88–104); they were somet. worshiped as divinities (Vett. Val. 293, 27; Philo, Vita Cont. 3 τοὺς τὰ στοιχεῖα τιμῶντας, γῆν, ὕδωρ, ἀέρα, πῦρ. Cp. Diels [s. below] 45ff; Schweizer 1a above). It is not always easy to differentiate betw. this sense and that of 1b above, since heavenly bodies were also regarded as personal beings and given divine honors.—HDiels, Elementum 1899; ABonhöffer, Epiktet u. das NT 1911, 130ff; OLagercrantz, Elementum 1911 (p. 41 στοιχεῖα τοῦ κόσμου=θεμέλια τοῦ κόσμου); BEaston, The Pauline Theol. and Hellenism: AJT 21, 1917, 358–82; KDieterich, Hellenist. Volksreligion u. byz.-neugriech. Volksglaube: Αγγελος I 1925, 2–23; on Gal 4 and Col 2, GKurze, D. στοιχεῖα τ. κόσμου: BZ 15, 1927, 335; WHatch, Τὰ στοιχεῖα in Paul and Bardaisân: JTS 28, 1927, 181f; JHuby, Στοιχεῖα dans Bardesane et dans St. Paul: Biblica 15, '34, 365–68; on Gal 4:3, 9 and Col 2:8, 20, LScheu, Die 'Weltelemente' beim Ap. Pls: diss. Cath. Univ., Washington '34; BReicke, JBL 70, '51, 259–76 (Gal 4:1–11); WBrownlee, Messianic Motifs of Qumran and the NT, NTS 3, '56/57, 195–210; MKiley, SBLSP 25, '86, 236–45.—RAC IV 1073–1100; B. 1501. DELG s.v. στείχω. M-M. EDNT. TW. Sv.

στοιχέω (στοῖχος) fut. στοιχήσω (X. et al.; ins, pap; Eccl 11:6) orig. 'be drawn up in line', in our lit. only fig. **to be in line with a pers. or thing considered as standard for one's conduct,** ***hold to, agree with, follow, conform*** w. dat. (Polyb. 28, 5, 6; Dionys. Hal. 6, 65; OGI 339, 51 [II AD]; SIG 685, 18; 734, 6; Michel 544, 14 βουλόμενος στοιχεῖν τοῖς πρασσομένοις; pap not until Byz. times) ὅσοι τῷ κανόνι τούτῳ στοιχήσουσιν *all those who will follow this rule* **Gal 6:16;** cp. **Phil 3:16 v.l.;** στ. τῷ λόγῳ Ἰησοῦ Χρ. MPol 22:1. πνεύματι στ. *follow the Spirit* **Gal 5:25.** εἰς ὃ ἐφθάσαμεν, τῷ αὐτῷ στοιχεῖν *we must hold on to what we have attained* **Phil 3:16.** στ. τοῖς ἴχνεσίν τινος *let our conduct be consistent with what we have already attained* (so REB; s. ἴχνος) **Ro 4:12.**—Abs. (so perh. OGI 308, 21) στοιχεῖς φυλάσσων τὸν νόμον **Ac 21:24** (the ptc. tells what it is that Paul conforms to).—New Docs 2, 97. DELG s.v. στείχω. M-M. TW.

στοῖχος, ου, ὁ (Hdt. et al.; ins; POxy 1119, 12; Philo, Op. M. 141; Jos., Ant. 15, 413) **a row in an ascending series,** ***row, course*** of masonry (so SIG 970, 11) Hs 9, 4, 3.—DELG s.v. στείχω.

στολή, ῆς, ἡ (στέλλω 'robe'; trag., X., Pla. et al.) esp. a ***long, flowing robe*** (SIG 1025, 10; PEdg 9 [=Sb 6715], 32 [258 BC]; 44 [=Sb 6750], 4 al. in pap; Ex 28:2; 2 Ch 18:9; Esth 6:8 al. in LXX; pseudepigr., Philo; Jos., Ant. 20, 7, Vi. 334; Just., A I, 32, 8; Tat., 24, 1; Mel., P. 17, 116 al.; loanw. in rabb.) **Lk 15:22** (πρῶτος 2aα); **Rv 7:14; 22:14** (on the metaph. use in both these places s. πλύνω 1). στολὴ λευκή (PGiss 20, 17) as worn by angels **Mk 16:5** and by glorified believers **Rv 6:11; 7:9, 13.** στ. λαμπροτάτη GPt 13:55 (TestAbr A 16 p. 97, 8 [Stone p. 42]; cp. the priest's sacred robe SIG 1025, 10). Of the scribes ἐν στολαῖς περιπατεῖν *walk about in long robes* (M. Ant. 1, 7, 4 ἐν στολίῳ [v.l. στολῇ] περιπατεῖν) **Mk 12:38; Lk 20:46** (of priests' vestments Philo, Leg. ad Gai. 296; Jos., Ant. 3, 151; 11, 80).—KRengstorf, OMichel Festschr., '63, 383–404. DELG s.v. στέλλω. TW.

στόμα, ατος, τό (Hom.+; loanw. in rabb.).—❶ ***mouth***

ⓐ of humans or of beings whose appearance resembles that of humans: **Mt 15:11a, 17; J 19:29; Ac 11:8; 23:2; 2 Th 2:8** (cp. Is 11:4; Ps 32:6); **Rv 11:5.**—Used in imagery **Rv 1:16; 2:16;**

3:16; 10:9f (cp. Ezk 3:1ff); **19:15, 21.**—As an organ of speech **Mt 15:11b, 18** (cp. Num 32:24); **21:16** (Ps 8:3); **Lk 4:22; 11:54; Ro 10:8** (Dt 30:14); **Eph 4:29; Js 3:10** (cp. Aesop, Fab. 35 P.=64 H.//60 Ch.//35 H-H.: ἐκ τοῦ αὐτοῦ στόματος τὸ θερμὸν καὶ τὸ ψυχρὸν ἐξιεῖς=out of the same mouth you send forth warm and cold [of the person who blows in his hands to warm them, and on his food to cool it off]); 1 Cl 15:3 (Ps 61:5), 4 (Ps 77:36); 2 Cl 9:10; B 11:8; Hm 3:1. ἀπόθεσθε αἰσχρολογίαν ἐκ τοῦ στόματος ὑμῶν *put away shameful speech from your mouth = don't let any dirty talk cross your lips* **Col 3:8.** ἀκούειν τι ἐκ τοῦ στόματός τινος **Ac 22:14;** 2 Cl 13:3; B 16:10 (cp. ParJer 6:24); ἀκ. ἀπὸ τοῦ στ. τινος (Polyaenus 8, 36 ἀπὸ στόματος τῆς ἀδελφῆς) **Lk 22:71;** ἀκ. τι διὰ τοῦ στ. τινος **Ac 1:4** D; **15:7**.—ἀνεῴχθη τὸ στ. αὐτοῦ (of a mute person) *his mouth was opened* (Wsd 10:21) **Lk 1:64,** words could now come out, as REB renders: 'his lips and tongue were freed'. ἀνοίγειν τὸ στόμα τινός open someone's *mouth* for him and cause him to speak 1 Cl 18:15 (cp. Ps 50:17). ἀνοίγειν τὸ (ἑαυτοῦ) στόμα *open one's (own) mouth* to speak (ApcMos 21; ApcrEzk; s. ἀνοίγω 5a) **Mt 5:2; 13:35** (Ps 77:2); **Ac 8:35; 10:34; 18:14;** GEb 34:60. οὐκ ἀνοίγει τὸ στ. αὐτοῦ=he is silent **Ac 8:32;** 1 Cl 16:7 (both Is 53:7; cp. Mel., P. 64; 462). For ἄνοιξις τοῦ στόματος **Eph 6:19** s. ἄνοιξις. On στόμα πρὸς στόμα λαλεῖν *speak face to face* **2J 12; 3J 14** s. πρός 3aε. On ἵνα πᾶν στ. φραγῇ **Ro 3:19** s. φράσσω.—There is no δόλος or ψεῦδος in the mouth of the upright **Rv 14:5;** 1 Cl 50:6 (Ps 31:2); esp. of God's 'Servant' (Is 53:9) **1 Pt 2:22;** 1 Cl 16:10; Pol 8:1.—στόμα stands for the person in the capacity of speaker (3 Km 17:24; 22:22; 2 Ch 36:21f): ἐκ τοῦ περισσεύματος τῆς καρδίας τὸ στόμα λαλεῖ **Mt 12:34** (καρδία . . . στ. as TestNapht 2:6). διὰ στόματός τινος (ApcMos 16f; B-D-F §140) *by (the lips of) someone* **Lk 1:70; Ac 1:16; 3:18, 21.**—ἐν ἑνὶ στόματι *with one voice* (ἓν στόμα Aristoph., Equ. 670; Pla., Rep. 364a, Laws 1, 634e; Ael. Aristid. 51, 40 K.=I p. 544 D.; PGiss 36, 12 [161 BC] αἱ τέτταρες λέγουσαι ἐξ ἑνὸς στόματος; Pla., Rep. 364a) **Ro 15:6;** cp. 1 Cl 34:7.—For **Mt 18:16; 2 Cor 13:1; Lk 19:22; Lk 21:15** s. 2.

ⓑ of God (Dexippus of Athens [III AD]: 100 fgm. 1, 7 Jac. ἡ τοῦ θεοῦ μαρτυρία διὰ στόματος; Theognis18; ParJer 6:12) **Mt 4:4** (Dt 8:3); 1 Cl 8:4 (Is 1:20).

ⓒ of animals and animal-like beings, *mouth, jaws,* of a fish (PGM 5, 280ff) **Mt 17:27.** Of horses **Js 3:3;** cp. **Rv 9:17–9;** a weasel B 10:8; lion (Judg 14:8) **Hb 11:33; Rv 13:2;** in imagery **2 Ti 4:17;** an apocalyptic monster (Diod. S. 3, 70, 4 the Aegis: ἐκ τοῦ στόματος ἐκβάλλον φλόγα) **Rv 12:15, 16b; 16:13abc;** Hv 4, 1, 6; 4, 2, 4 (cp. Da 6:22 Theod.; JosAs 12:10).

❷ **the product of the organ of speech,** ***utterance, mouth.*** By metonymy for what the mouth utters ἐπὶ στόματος δύο μαρτύρων (Dt 19:15) **Mt 18:16; 2 Cor 13:1.** ἐκ τοῦ στόματός σου κρινῶ σε **Lk 19:22.** ἐγὼ δώσω ὑμῖν στόμα καὶ σοφίαν *I will give you eloquence and wisdom* **Lk 21:15.** S. also 1a.

❸ **a geological fissure,** ***mouth*** in imagery of the earth in which a fissure is opened (s. Gen 4:11) ἤνοιξεν ἡ γῆ τὸ στόμα αὐτῆς **Rv 12:16a.**

❹ **the foremost part of someth.,** ***edge*** fig. ext. of 1. The sword, like the jaws of a wild animal, devours people; hence acc. to OT usage (but s. Philostrat., Her. 19, 4 στ. τῆς αἰχμῆς; Quint. Smyrn. 1, 194; 813 and s. μάχαιρα 1; cp. στ.='point' of a sword Hom. et al.; στόμα πολέμου Polemo Soph. B8 Reader p. 134) στόμα μαχαίρης *the edge of the sword = the voracious sword* (Josh 19:48; Sir 28:18; s. also μάχαιρα 1, end) **Lk 21:24; Hb 11:34.**—B. 228; esp. 860. DELG. M-M. TW.

στόμαχος, ου, ὁ (Hom. et al., orig. mng. 'throat'; TestSol 18:18, 21; Philo; TestNapht 2:8; loanw. in rabb.) ***stomach*** (so Plut., Mor. 698ab; Epict. 2, 20, 33; Athen. 3, 79e; PGM 13, 830) **1 Ti 5:23.**—DELG s.v. στόμα. M-M. Spicq.

στραγγαλιά, ᾶς, ἡ (Ptolem., Apotel. 4, 9, 10 Boll-B.; Hippiatr. 51, 3; 4, vol. I 228, 9; 229, 7; LXX) ***knot*** διαλύειν στραγγαλιὰς βιαίων συναλλαγμάτων *untie the knots of forced agreements* (i.e. made under duress) B 3:3 (Is 58:6; cp. Plut., Mor. 1033e on philosophers' knotted arguments).

στραγγαλόω 1 aor. pass. ἐστραγγαλώθην; pf. pass. ptc. ἐστραγγαλωμένος Tob 2:3 BA (Philo Mech. 57, 42; Alex. Aphr., Probl. 1, 76 Ideler) *strangle* (Tob 2:3 BA), pass., w. intr. sense ***choke*** ITr 5:1.—DELG s.v. στράγξ.

στρατεία, ας, ἡ (στρατεύω; Aeschyl., Hdt.+; ins, pap, LXX; TestSol 10:36 C; Jos., Bell. 3, 445, Ant. 16, 343. On the spelling s. Dssm., NB 9f [BS 181f]; B-D-F §23; Mlt-H. 78) **military engagement,** ***expedition, campaign*** in imagery (Epict. 3, 24, 34 στρατεία τίς ἐστιν ὁ βίος ἑκάστου; Maximus Tyr. 13, 4d) τὰ ὅπλα τῆς στρατείας ἡμῶν *the weapons we use in our warfare* **2 Cor 10:4** (v.l. στρατίας is itacism: W-S. §5 A 31). στρατεύεσθαι τὴν καλὴν στρατείαν *fight the good fight* **1 Ti 1:18** (for στρατεύεσθαι στρ. cp. Isaeus 10, 25; Aeschin. 2, 169; Plut., Mor. 204a; Epict. 2, 14, 17 (MAdinolfi, Le imagini militari nelle diatribe de Epitteto un confronto con l'epistolario Paolino, in Atti del IV Simposio di Tarso su S. Paolo Apostolo, ed. LPadovese '96, 59–72); SIG 346, 55; 4 Macc 9:24; Philo, Leg. All. 3, 14).—On the Christian life as military service s. πανοπλία 2.—DELG s.v. στρατός. M-M. TW.

στράτευμα, ατος, τό **a military force,** ***army*** (so trag., Hdt. et al.; ins, pap, LXX; TestJob 30:2 al. [troops] EpArist 37; Philo; Jos., Bell. 3, 162, Ant. 4, 94) sing. **Rv 19:19b;** pl. **19:14, 19a.**—Of a smaller detachment of soldiers, sing. **Ac 23:10, 27.**—τὰ στρατεύματα *the troops* (4 Macc 5:1; Jos., Ant. 13, 131. See AVerrall, JTS 10, 1909, 340f) **Mt 22:7** (MBlack, An Aramaic Approach^3, '67, 128); **Lk 23:11; Rv 9:16.**—B. 1377. DELG s.v. στρατός. M-M. TW.

στρατεύω (var. in the act. or mid. since Aeschyl., Hdt. et al.; ins, pap, LXX, ApkEzk [Epiph 70, 6], Tat.) in our lit. always a mid. dep. **στρατεύομαι** 1 aor. ἐστρατευσάμην; inf. mid.-pass. (s. Schwyzer I 639, II 237f; B-D-F §87) στρατευθῆναι (AcPl Ha 9, 6 restored)

❶ **do military service,** ***serve in the army*** (X., Mem. 1, 6, 9; BGU 1097, 8 [I AD]; Jos., Bell. 2, 520, Ant. 17, 270, Vi. 346; Tat.) **2 Ti 2:4;** 1 Cl 37:2. στ. ἰδίοις ὀψωνίοις *serve as a soldier at one's own expense* **1 Cor 9:7.** στρατευόμενοι=*soldiers* (Thu. 8, 65, 3; Plut., Mor. 274a; Appian, Bell. Civ. 3, 41 §168; 3, 90 §371; Sb 8008, 49 [261 BC]) **Lk 3:14** (SMcCasland, JBL 62, '43, 59–71).

❷ **to engage in a conflict,** ***wage battle, fight*** fig. ext. of 1 (Lucian, Vit. Auct. 8 ἐπὶ τὰς ἡδονάς) of Christians 1 Cl 37:1; w. the dat. for God, Christ IPol 6:2; AcPl Ha 9, 6f; of the apostle's activity **2 Cor 10:3.** On στρατεύεσθαι τὴν καλὴν στρατείαν **1 Ti 1:18** s. στρατεία. Of the struggles of the passions within the human soul **Js 4:1; 1 Pt 2:11;** Pol 5:3.—DELG s.v. στρατός. M-M. TW.

στρατηγός, οῦ, ὁ (στρατός 'army, host', ἄγω; Aeschyl., Hdt.+; ins, pap, LXX; EpArist 280; Philo, Joseph.; Mel., P. 105, 818; loanw. in rabb. Orig. 'general').

❶ **the highest official in a Gr-Rom. city,** ***praetor, chief magistrate*** pl. of the highest officials of the Roman colony of Philippi. This title was not quite officially correct, since these men were properly termed 'duoviri', but it occurs several times in ins as a popular designation for them (JWeiss, RE XII 1903, p. 39, 39f.—στρατηγοί governed Pergamum [Jos., Ant. 14, 247] and Sardis [14, 259]) **Ac 16:20, 22, 35f, 38.**—Mommsen, Röm. Geschichte V 274ff; JMarquardt, Staatsverw. I² 1881, 316ff; Ramsay, JTS 1, 1900, 114–16; FHaverfield, ibid. 434f; Zahn, Einl.³ I 378ff; AWikenhauser, Die AG 1921, 346f. Mason 86f.

❷ ὁ στρατηγὸς τοῦ ἱεροῦ=**commander responsible for the temple in Jerusalem,** ***captain of the temple*** **Ac 4:1; 5:24.** Also simply ὁ στρατηγός (Jos., Bell. 6, 294, Ant. 20, 131) vs. **26.** In the pl. (LXX; s. Schürer II 278, 7) στρατηγοὶ (τοῦ ἱεροῦ) **Lk 22:4, 52.**—Schürer II 277f and s. EBriess, WienerStud 34, 1912, 356f; Kl. Pauly V 388–91 (CIG 3151 στ. ἐπὶ τοῦ ἱεροῦ).—B. 1381f. DELG s.v. στρατός. M-M. TW.

στρατιά, ᾶς, ἡ—❶ *army* (so Pind., Hdt.+; ins, pap, LXX, TestAbr A 2 p. 78, 28 [Stone p. 4]; JosAs 14:7 [τοῦ ὑψίστου]; ApcEsdr 6:16f p. 31, 23 Tdf. [ἀγγέλων]; ApcMos 38 [κύριος στρατιῶν]; Philo; Jos., Bell. 7, 31, Ant. 14, 271; Just.; loanw. in rabb.) of Pharaoh's army 1 Cl 51:5 (cp. Ex 14:4, 9, 17).—στρατιὰ οὐράνιος *the heavenly army* of angels (s. 3 Km 22:19; 2 Esdr 19: 6.—Pla., Phdr. 246e στρατιὰ θεῶν τε καὶ δαιμόνων; Just., D. 131, 2 τοῦ διαβόλου) **Lk 2:13** (for the constr. ad sensum πλῆθος στρατιᾶς … αἰνούντων cp. Appian, Bell. Civ. 5, 64 §272 ὁ στρατὸς αἰσθανόμενοι εἵλοντο). ἡ στρατιὰ τοῦ οὐρανοῦ *the host of heaven* of the heavenly bodies (cp. Ps.-Demetr. c. 91 after an ancient lyric poet ἄστρων στρατόν; Maximus Tyr. 13, 6e; 2 Ch 33:3, 5; Jer 8:2; PGM 35, 13) **Ac 7:42.**

❷ occasionally (poets, pap) in the same sense as στρατεία **2 Cor 10:4 v.l.**, but s. στρατεία on this passage.—DELG s.v. στρατός. M-M. TW.

στρατιώτης, ου, ὁ (Aristoph., Hdt.+; loanw. in rabb.) ***soldier.*—ⓐ** lit. **Mt 8:9; 27:27; 28:12; Mk 15:16; Lk 7:8; J 19:2; Ac 10:7; 28:16;** GPt 8:30–32 al.; AcPl Ha 10, 28.

ⓑ fig., but w. the major component of allegiance to a commander in the central mng. of 'soldier' as defining aspect στ. Χριστοῦ Ἰησοῦ *a soldier of Christ Jesus* **2 Ti 2:3;** AcPl Ha 8, 9; cp. ὁ τοῦ θεοῦ στ. 11, 6 (on the idea cp. the lit. s.v. πανοπλία 2 and s. PGM 4, 193).—B. 1380. DELG s.v. στρατός. M-M. TW.

στρατιωτικός, ή, όν (στρατιώτης; X., Pla. et al.; ins, pap, EpArist; Philo, Virt. 23; Jos., Bell. 1, 340) ***belonging to, or composed of, soldiers*** στρατιωτικὸν τάγμα *a detachment of soldiers* IRo 5:1.—M-M.

στρατολογέω (στρατός 'army, host', λέγω) 1 aor. ἐστρατολόγησα **gather an army,** ***enlist soldiers*** (Diod. S. 12, 67, 5; 14, 54, 6; Dionys. Hal. 11, 24; Plut., Caesar 724 [35, 1]; Jos., Bell. 5, 380) ὁ στρατολογήσας *the one who enlisted (him)* **2 Ti 2:4.**—M-M. TW. Spicq.

στρατοπεδάρχης (στρατόπεδον, ἀρχή; Dionys. Hal. 10, 36; Lucian, Hist. 22; Vett. Val. 76, 13; Jos., Bell. 2, 531; 6, 238; OGI 605, 3; BGU 1822, 13 [I BC]; Mitt-Wilck. II/2, 87, 5 [II AD]) so t.r. **Ac 28:16** (s. Tdf.) or **στρατοπέδαρχος, ου, ὁ** ***military commander,*** *commandant of a camp* **Ac 28:16 v.l.** On the subject-matter s. Mommsen and Harnack, SBBerlAk 1895, 491ff; Zahn, Einl.³ I 392ff; AWikenhauser, Die AG 1921, 358f; Pauly-W. IV 1896ff; Haenchen ad loc.; Mason 87; HTajra, The Trial of St. Paul '89, 177.—M-M. TW.

στρατόπεδον, ου, τό (Aeschyl., Hdt. et al.; ins, LXX, Philo, Joseph.) lit. 'camp' (Jos., Vi. 398), then 'body of troops, army' (Eur., Hdt. et al.; ins, LXX; EpArist 20; Jos., Ant. 14, 271), even specif. ***legion*** (Polyb. 1, 16, 2; 1, 26, 6; 6, 20ff; 27ff; BGU 362 XI, 15 [III AD].—Hahn 46) **Lk 21:20;** Mason 87.—B. 1377. DELG s.v. στρατός. M-M. TW.

στρεβλός, ή, όν (Aristoph., Hippocr. et al.; LXX; used e.g. of a wrinkled brow, or of twisting and turning in athletic competition) in our lit. only fig. ***crooked, perverse,*** of the way of unrighteousness Hm 6, 1, 2f. Of persons (Eupolis Com. [V BC] 182) 1 Cl 46:3 (Ps 17:27).—B. 897. DELG. Cp. στρεβλόω 2.

στρεβλόω (στρέφω, cp. prec. entry) impv. 2 sg. στρέβλου (Hdt., Aristoph. et al.; pap, LXX) orig. 'twist, make taut' of cables, then in various senses of wrenching dislocated limbs for the purpose of setting them, and of the use of tortuous devices in the course of inquiries (s. e.g. BGU 195, 13 [II AD]; 4 Macc; Jos., Bell. 7, 373); in our lit. only fig. (cp. 2 Km 22:27 of perverse pers.)

❶ **to cause inward pain,** ***torture, torment*** (Diod. S. 16, 61, 3 tortured by anxiety) μὴ στρέβλου σεαυτόν *do not trouble yourself* (with the solving of a riddle, as Vi. Aesopi W 78 P.) Hs 9, 2, 7.

❷ **to distort a statement so that a false mng. results,** ***twist, distort*** (2 Km 22:27) τὶ *someth.* (Numenius of Apamea, περὶ τῆς τῶν Ἀκαδημαϊκῶν πρὸς Πλάτωνα διαστάσεως 1, 1 ed. KGuthrie [1917] p. 63) **2 Pt 3:16.**—DELG s.v. στρεβλός. M-M.

στρέφω fut. στρέψω LXX; 1 aor. ἔστρεψα. Pass.: 2 fut. στραφήσομαι LXX; 2 aor. ἐστράφν (Hom. +).

❶ **to change the position of someth. relative to someth. by turning—ⓐ** ***turn*** (SibOr 5, 497 στ. ψυχάς) τί τινι *someth. to someone* **Mt 5:39;** D 1:4.—So perh. also in a nonliteral sense ἔστρεψεν ὁ θεός *God turned* the Israelites toward the heavenly bodies, so that they were to serve them as their gods **Ac 7:42** (s. 3 Km 18:37 σὺ ἔστρεψας τὴν καρδίαν τοῦ λαοῦ τούτου ὀπίσω. But s. 4 below).

ⓑ ***turn around, turn toward*** pass. w. act. force**—α.** lit. στραφείς foll. by a finite verb *he turned (around) and* … (X., Cyr. 3, 3, 63; TestAbr B 12 p. 116, 14 [Stone p. 80]). The purpose of the turning can be to attack someone **Mt 7:6,** or a desire to see or speak w. someone **9:22** (cp. Mitt-Wilck. I/2, 20 I, 6 στραφεὶς καὶ ἰδὼν Ἡλιόδωρον εἶπεν); **16:23; Lk 7:9; 9:55; 14:25; 22:61; J 1:38; 20:16;** MPol 5:2. Finite verb instead of ptc. (ApcMos 19) ἐστράφη … καὶ εἶδεν GJs 15:1; 17:2ab. στρ. πρός w. acc. *turn to* or *toward* (schol. on Nicander, Ther. 677 πρὸς ἥλιον στρέφεσθαι of the heliotrope): στραφεὶς πρός τινα foll. by a finite verb (TestJob 27:1; 29:3; ApcMos 23:25, 28) **Lk 7:44; 10:22 v.l., 23; 23:28.** στρ. εἰς τὰ ὀπίσω *turn around* **J 20:14;** GJs 7:2 (cp. X., De Re Equ. 7, 12 στρέφεσθαι εἰς τὰ δεξιά).

β. in a transf. sense of 1a compounded of change of mind and direction στρεφόμεθα εἰς τὰ ἔθνη *we turn to the Gentiles* **Ac 13:46.** ἐστράφησαν ἐν ταῖς καρδίαις αὐτῶν εἰς Αἴγυπτον *in their hearts they turned back to Egypt* **7:39.**

❷ **to carry someth. back to its previous location,** ***bring back, return*** τὶ *someth.* τὰ τριάκοντα ἀργύρια **Mt 27:3**

❸ **to turn someth. into someth. else,** ***turn, change*** (Just., A I, 59, 1 ὕλην of God) τὶ εἴς τι *someth. into someth.* ὕδατα εἰς αἷμα **Rv 11:6** (cp. Ps 113:8; 29:12). Pass. *be changed, be turned* (1 Km 10:6 εἰς ἄνδρα ἄλλον) στραφήσονται τὰ πρόβατα εἰς λύκους D 16:3a. ἡ ἀγάπη στραφήσεται εἰς μῖσος D 16:3b (cp. La 5:15; 1 Macc 1:39, 40).

❹ **to turn away so as to dissociate oneself,** ***turn*** intr. (X., An. 4, 3, 26; 32, Ages. 2, 3) so perh. ἔστρεψεν ὁ θεός *God turned away* from them **Ac 7:42** (s. 1a above).

❺ **to experience an inward change,** ***turn, change,*** pass. in act. sense. For the better: *make a turn-about, turn around* (Sib-

Or 3, 625) **Mt 18:3** (JDupont, MBlack Festschr., '69, 50–60); **J 12:40** (Is 6:9.—Field, Notes 99.—The Eng. term 'conversion' could suggest a change from one religious persuasion to another, which is not the case in these pass.). For the worse: *turn* to someth. evil, *be perverted* D 11:2.—B. 666. DELG. M-M. TW.

στρηνιάω (στρῆνος) 1 aor. ἐστρηνίασα (Antiphanes in Athen. 3, 127d; Diphilus in Bekker, Anecdot. p. 113, 25; PMeyer 20, 23 [III AD]; Is 61:6 Sym.; POxy 2783, 24 of bulls running wild) ***live in luxury, live sensually*** **Rv 18:7.** W. πορνεύειν vs. **9.**—DELG s.v. στρηνής. M-M.

στρῆνος, ους, τό (in Nicostratus [IV BC]: Com. Att. fgm. p. 230 no. 42 Kock; Lycophron 438 al.; also 4 Km 19:28 in a different sense) ***sensuality, luxury*** (Palladas [VI AD]: Anth. Pal. 7, 686) ἡ δύναμις τοῦ στρήνους (δύναμις 4) **Rv 18:3.**—DELG s.v. στρηνής. M-M.

στρογγύλος, η, ον (Aristoph., Thu., X., Pla.+; ins, pap, LXX; Philo, Leg. All. 3, 57 [opp. τετράγωνος]) ***round*** of stones (X., De Re Equ. 4, 4; Cebes 18, 1 [opp. τετρ.]; JosAs 27:3) Hv 3, 2, 8; 3, 6, 5f; s 9, 6, 7f (opp. τετρ.); 9, 9, 1; 2 (opp. τετρ.); 9, 29, 4ab; 9, 30, 4.—B. 904. DELG.

στρουθίον, ου, τό (Aristot. et al.; LXX; PsSol 17:16; Jos., Bell. 5, 467) dim. of στρουθός ***sparrow*** καλιά στρουθίων GJs 3:1 v.l. *a nest of sparrows;* as an example of an article that has little value **Mt 10:29, 31; Lk 12:6f.** (Vi. Aesopi G 26 P. is of interest grammatically and formally, but expresses a different thought: στρουθία πολλοῦ πωλεῖται; in a restoration concerning 'articulate birds that fetch a high price', s. Perry's note and p. 281 no. 107.)—Dssm., LO 234f (LAE 272ff); HGrimme, BZ 23, '35, 260–2. DELG s.v. στρουθός. M-M. TW.

στρουθός, οῦ, ὁ (Sappho, Hdt. et al.) ***sparrow*** GJs 3:1 v.l., s. στρουθίον.—DELG.

στρωννύω/στρώννυμι impf. ἐστρώννυον; fut. στρώσω (JosAs 13:12 cod. A [p. 58, 10 Bat.]), 3 pl. -σουσιν LXX; 1 aor. ἔστρωσα; pf. ἔστρωκα Pr 7:16. Pass.: pf. 3 sg. ἔστρωται Job 17:13; ptc. ἐστρωμένος (on the two forms of the word: B-D-F §92; Rob. 318.—For the word: Hom. [στορέννυμι, στόρνυμι], Aeschyl., X., Pla.; ins, pap, LXX, TestAbr; JosAs 2:15 [also cod. A 13:12]; Joseph.; SibOr 5, 438)

❶ **to distribute someth. over a surface, *spread*** τὶ *someth.* ἱμάτια κτλ. ἐν τῇ ὁδῷ **Mt 21:8ab;** also εἰς τὴν ὁδόν **Mk 11:8** (for the idea cp. 4 Km 9:13; Jos., Ant. 9, 111 ὑπεστρώννυεν αὐτῷ τὸ ἱμάτιον). χιτῶνας χαμαί Hs 9, 11, 7. στρῶσον σεαυτῷ (i.e. τὴν κλίνην; στρ. is used w. this acc. in Eur., Pla., and Nicol. Dam.: 90 fgm. 44, 2 Jac.; Diod. S. 8, 32, 2; SIG 687, 16; 1022,1f τὴν κλίνην στρῶσαι τῷ Πλούτωνι. Cp. Ezk 23:41; TestAbr B 5 p. 109, 17f [Stone p. 66], cp. A 4 p. 80, 17 [Stone p. 8] δύο κλινάρια; Jos., Ant. 7, 231 κλίνας ἐστρωμένας) *make your own bed* **Ac 9:34.**—Of a room, without an indication of what is being spread or put on over a surface within it: ἀνάγαιον ἐστρωμένον **Mk 14:15; Lk 22:12** may be a *paved upper room* (στρ. has this mng. in an ins APF 2, 1903, 570 no. 150. So Luther et al.—Jos., Ant. 8, 134 ἐστρωμένος means 'floored' or 'panelled'). Others prefer 2a next

❷ **to equip someth. with appropriate furnishing(s)**—ⓐ ***to furnish*** ἀνάγαιον ἐστρωμένον *upper room furnished* w. carpets or couches for the guests to recline on as they ate (EKlostermann, ELohmeyer; Field, Notes 39; somewhat as Plut., Artox. 10 [22, 10]; Artem. 2, 57 codd. Also Diod. S. 21, 12, 4; IG II, 622 ἔστρωσεν refers to a couch at a meal; Dalman, Arbeit VII 185. Eng. transl. gener. prefer this sense.—PGM 1, 107 χώρημα στρῶσαι means to prepare a room for a banquet) **Mk 14:15; Lk 22:12.**

ⓑ ***to saddle*** a riding animal (L-S-J-M στόρνυμι II) ἔστρωσεν τὸν ὄνον Joseph *saddled his donkey.*—B. 573. DELG s.v. στόρνυμι.

στυγητός, ή, όν (Aeschyl., Prom. 592; POxy 433, 28; Philo, Dec. 131; Heliod. 5, 29, 4) ***loathsome, despicable*** **Tit 3:3** w. μισέω; 1 Cl 35:6; 45:7.—DELG s.v. στυγέω. M-M.

στυγνάζω (στυγνός) 1 aor. ἐστύγνασα—❶ **to be in state of intense dismay, *be shocked, appalled*** (Ezk 26:16 [JZiegler '52]; 27:35; 28:19; 32:10 ἐπί τινα) so perh. στυγνάσας ἐπὶ τῷ λόγῳ=*shocked at the prescription* **Mk 10:22** (s. 2a below).

❷ **to have a dark or gloomy appearance, *be* or *become gloomy, dark*** (AcPlTh 35 [Aa 261, 10])—ⓐ of one whose appearance displays sadness or gloom (TestSol 1:4 L; Himerius, Or. [Ecl.] 3, 2; PGM 13, 177; 494; schol. on Aeschyl., Pers. 470; schol. on Soph., Ant. 526; schol. on Apollon. Rhod. 2, 862f; Macrembolites Eustathius 4, 1, 2 Hilberg 1876; Nicetas Eugen. 6, 286 H.) ἐπί τινι *at someth.*, so perh. **Mk 10:22** (but s. 1 above).

ⓑ of the appearance of the sky (s. στυγνός: Heraclit. Sto. 39 p. 56, 18) *lowering* **Mt 16:3** (Cat. Cod. Astr. XI/2 p. 179, 19 is dependent on this).—DELG s.v. στυγέω. M-M.

στυγνός, ή, όν *gloomy, sad* (so since Aeschyl.; X., An. 2, 6, 9. Also PSI 28, 1 στυγνοῦ σκότους; LXX; TestLevi 3:1; Jos., Ant. 19, 318) Hv 1, 2, 3 opp. γελῶν as GJs 17:2. τί ‹οὕ›τως στυγνὸς καὶ κατηφής, κύριε; *Why so sad and downcast, Lord?* AcPl Ha 7, 30.—DELG s.v. στύγεω.

στῦλος, ου, ὁ (Aeschyl., Hdt.+; ins, pap, LXX, En; TestSol 25:8 B; ParJer 1:2; Jos., Ant. 13, 211; Just., D. 38, 1 al.; Mel., P. 84, 631; 88, 658. On the accent [στύλος] s. KLipsius, Gramm. Untersuchungen 1863 p. 43)

❶ **a supporting portion, ordinarily cylindrical, of a structure, *pillar, column*** lit. στῦλοι πυρός (En 18:11; 21:7; sing. Ex 13:21f; 14:24) **Rv 10:1.** In imagery (Philo, Migr. Abr. 124)

❷ **a pers. or community recognized for spiritual leadership, *pillar, support*** ποιήσω αὐτὸν στ. ἐν τῷ ναῷ τοῦ θεοῦ *I will make him a pillar in the temple of God* **Rv 3:12** (στῦλοι in the temple 3 Km 7:3=Jos., Ant. 8, 77). Hence fig. of the leaders of the Jerusalem church: James, Cephas, John **Gal 2:9** (cp. Eur., Iph. Taur. 57 στῦλοι οἴκων εἰσὶ παῖδες ἄρσενες. Vi. Aesopi G 106 P. Aesop is called ὁ κίων [pillar] τῆς βασιλείας. S. CBarrett, Studia Paulina '53, 1–19; RAnnand, ET 67, '56, 178 ['the markers' in a racecourse]). In 1 Cl 5:2 the term is applied to the apostles and other leaders of the primitive church.—The community of Christians is στῦλος καὶ ἑδραίωμα τῆς ἀληθείας *support* (στ. is also used in this general sense Sir 24:4; 36:24) *and foundation of the truth* **1 Ti 3:15.**—DELG. TW.

στύραξ, ακος, ὁ (X., Pla.+; also TestSol 5:13) lit. the spike at the butt end of a spear-shaft, then by synecdoche the ***shaft, spear*** itself; περὶ στύρακα MPol 16:1 as a conjecture instead of the ms. rdg. περιστερὰ καί, which is not transmitted by Eus. (s. περιστερά).—DELG 2 στύραξ.

Στωϊκός s. Στοϊκός.—M-M.

σύ (Hom.+) personal pron. of the second pers. σοῦ (σου), σοί (σοι), σέ (σε); pl. ὑμεῖς, ὑμῶν, ὑμῖν, ὑμᾶς: *you*

ⓐ nominative—α. in contrast to another pers. ἐγὼ … σύ **Mt 3:14; 26:39; Mk 14:36; J 13:7; Js 2:18;** s. **Lk 17:8.** σὺ … ἕτερος **Mt 11:3.** πᾶς ἄνθρωπος … σύ **J 2:10.** Μωϋσῆς … σὺ οὖν **8:5.** οὐδεὶς … σύ **3:2** and oft. αὐτοὶ … σύ **Hb 1:11** (Ps

101:27). ἐγώ . . . ὑμεῖς or vice versa (TestJob 1:5; Mel., P. 103, 789ff) **J 7:34, 36; 8:15, 22f; 13:15; 15:5** al.; **Gal 4:12.** ὑμεῖς . . . ἡμεῖς or vice versa (ParJer 4:9; Just., D. 10, 1 al.) **J 4:22; 1 Cor 4:10abc; 2 Cor 13:9.**—The contrast is evident fr. the context: **Mt 6:6, 17; Ro 2:3.** ὑμεῖς **Mt 5:48; 6:9, 26b.**—On σὺ λέγεις **Mt 27:11; Mk 15:2; Lk 23:3** s. λέγω 2e.

β. for emphasis before a voc. σὺ Βηθλεέμ **Mt 2:6** (Mi 5:1). σὺ παιδίον (Lucian, Dial. Deor. 2, 1) **Lk 1:76.** σὺ κύριε **Ac 1:24** (PsSol 2:23; 17:4). σὺ δὲ ὦ ἄνθρωπε θεοῦ **1 Ti 6:11.** ὑμεῖς οἱ Φαρισαῖοι **Lk 11:39.**

γ. used w. a noun or ptc., by which the pron. is more exactly defined σὺ Ἰουδαῖος ὤν *you as a Jew* **J 4:9;** cp. **Gal 2:14.** ὑμεῖς πονηροὶ ὄντες **Mt 7:11** (cp. ParJer 7:3 σὺ ὁ λαλῶν).—Esp. emphasizing the subj.: σὺ τρίς με ἀπαρνήσῃ *you are the very one who will deny me three times* **Mk 14:30.** δότε αὐτοῖς ὑμεῖς φαγεῖν *you yourselves are to give them someth. to eat = give them some food yourselves* Mft **Mt 14:16.** Cp. **J 13:6; 17:8; 20:15.** εὐλογημένη σὺ ἐν γυναιξίν **Lk 1:42.** σὺ μόνος παροικεῖς **24:18.** So freq. w. forms of εἰμι (TestAbr A 7 p. 84, 19 [Stone p. 16] ὁ ἥλιος . . . σὺ εἶ; A 16 p. 97, 26 [Stone p. 42] τίς εἶ σύ; A 17 p. 98, 21 [Stone p. 44] σὺ εἶ ὁ θάνατος; TestJob 29:3 al.): σὺ εἶ ὁ χριστός **Mt 16:16;** σὺ εἶ Πέτρος vs. **18;** σὺ εἶ ὁ βασιλεὺς τῶν Ἰουδαίων; **27:11.** καὶ σύ *you,* too **26:69, 73; Lk 19:19; 22:58; Gal 6:1** (TestAbr B 4 p. 109, 10 [Stone p. 66]; TestJob 27:5; ParJer 7:9; Just., A II, 2, 17). καὶ ὑμεῖς **Mt 7:12; 15:3, 16; Lk 17:10** (TestJob 27:7). σὺ δέ *but you* **Lk 9:60; Ro 11:17; 2 Ti 3:10** (Just., D. 1, 6 al.; Tat. 19, 3). ὑμεῖς δέ **Mt 21:13; Js 2:6** (TestJob 24:3; ApcMos 30).

δ. pleonastically added to forms that are clear enough by themselves (Semitism? See B-D-F §277, 2; Mlt-H. 431f) σὺ τί λέγεις **Mk 14:68.** μὴ φοβεῖσθε ὑμεῖς **Mt 28:5.** μὴ ἀνελεῖν με σὺ θέλεις; **Ac 7:28** (Ex 2:14). ὑμεῖς **Mt 5:13f.**

ⓑ oblique cases—**α.** The accented forms are used in the oblique cases of the sing. when emphasis is to be laid on the pron. or when a contrast is intended σοῦ δὲ αὐτῆς τὴν ψυχήν **Lk 2:35.** οὐ σὺ ῥίζαν βαστάζεις ἀλλὰ ἡ ῥίζα σέ **Ro 11:18.** καὶ σέ **Phil 4:3.**

β. The accented forms also appear without special emphasis when used w. prepositions (B-D-F §279; Mlt-H. 180) ἐν σοί **Mt 6:23.** ἐπὶ σέ **Lk 1:35.** μετὰ σοῦ vs. **28.** σὺν σοί **Mt 26:35,** but πρός σε **Mt 14:28; 25:39** (cp. PsSol 5:8; s. ἐγώ).

ⓒ σου and ὑμῶν as substitutes for the possessive/adjectival pronouns σός and ὑμέτερος (πάντες σου 4 [6] Esdr [POxy 1010]; as well as for the gen. of the reflexives σεαυτοῦ and ὑμῶν αὐτῶν) come after the word they modify: τὴν γυναῖκά σου **Mt 1:20;** τὸν πόδα σου **4:6** (Ps 90:12); ἡ πίστις ὑμῶν **Ro 1:8;** τὰ μέλη ὑμῶν **6:19;** ἡ ζωὴ ὑμῶν **Col 3:4.** Or before the word they modify (TestAbr A 16 p. 97, 1 [Stone p. 42] σου τὴν ἀγριότητα; B 6 p. 110, 13 [Stone p. 68] σου οἱ ὀφθαλμοί; TestJob 4:5 σου τὰ ὑπάρχοντα; JosAs 4:10; 15:9 al.; ApcMos 12): ἆρόν σου τὴν κλίνην **Mt 9:6;** ἀφέωνταί σου αἱ ἁμαρτίαι **Lk 7:48;** μηδείς σου τῆς νεότητος καταφρονείτω **1 Ti 4:12.** Or betw. the noun and the art. (TestJob 42:5 οἱ δύο σου φίλοι): διὰ τῆς ὑμῶν δεήσεως **Phil 1:19;** εἰς τὴν ὑμῶν προκοπήν vs. **25.**—On τί ἐμοὶ καὶ σοί; s. ἐγώ, end; on τί ἡμῖν κ. σοί; s. τίς 1aβℶ.—M-M.

συγγένεια, ας, ἡ (συγγενής; Eur., Thu.+; ins, pap, LXX; pseudepigr.; Philo; Jos., Bell. 7, 204 ἐκ μεγάλης σ., Ant. 1, 165; Just., D. 4, 2; Tat. 20, 3) **an extended family system, *relationship, kinship*** concr. *the relatives* (Eur., Pla.+; LXX) **Lk 1:61; Ac 7:3;** 1 Cl 10:2f (the two last Gen 12:1); **Ac 7:14** (Diod. S. 16, 52, 3 μετεπέμψατο ἀμφοτέρους μεθ' ὅλης τῆς συγγενείας; 34 + 35 fgm. 23).—DELG s.v. γίγνομαι. M-M. TW. Spicq. Sv.

συγγενεῦσιν s. the following entry.

συγγενής, ές (σύν, γένος)—➊ **belonging to the same extended family or clan, *related, akin to*** (Pind., Thu. et al.; also Ath., R. 20 p. 73, 17 τὸ συγγενές) in our lit. only subst. In the sing., masc. (Jos., Vi. 177; Just., A I, 27, 3) **J 18:26** and fem. (Menand., fgm. 929 K.=345 Kö.; Jos., Ant. 8, 249) **Lk 1:36 v.l.** (for συγγενίς). Predom. pl. (also Demetr.: 722, 1, 13 and 18 Jac.) οἱ συγγενεῖς (the dat. of this form, made on the analogy of γονεῖς . . . γονεῦσιν, is συγγενεῦσιν [a Pisidian ins: JHS 22, 1902, p. 358 no. 118; 1 Macc 10:89 v.l.] **Mk 6:4; Lk 2:44** [both passages have συγγενέσιν as v.l., the form in Diod. S. 1, 92, 1; OGI 177, 7: 97/96 BC; UPZ 161, 21: 119 BC; PTebt 61, 79; 1 Macc 10:89; Jos., Vi. 81, Ant. 16, 382]; B-D-F §47, 4; W-S. §9, 9; Mlt-H. 138; Thackeray 153) **Lk 2:44; 21:16.** W. gen. (B-D-F §194, 2) **Mk 6:4; Lk 1:58; 14:12; Ac 10:24.**

➋ **belonging to the same people group, *compatriot, kin,*** ext. of 1 (Jos., Bell. 7, 262, Ant. 12, 338) οἱ συγγενεῖς μου κατὰ σάρκα **Ro 9:3** (of Andronicus and Junia; on the latter s. Ἰουνία and EEpp, in Handbook to Exegesis of the NT, ed. SPorter '97, 49f); cp. **16:7, 11, 21.**—B. 132. DELG s.v. γίγνομαι. M-M. TW. Spicq.

συγγενικός, ή, όν (συγγενής; Hippocr., Aristot. et al.; ins) orig. in ref. to familial relationships, then more gener. **of a similar nature or character, *related, kindred, of the same kind*** (Diog. L. 10, 129 [Epicurus]; Plut., Mor. 561b, Pericl. 164 [22, 4], Themist. 114 [5, 2]; Vett. Val. index; Herm. Wr. 440, 6 Sc.; EpArist 147; Philo) τὸ συγγενικὸν ἔργον *the task (so) well suited to you* IEph 1:1.—DELG s.v. γίγνομαι.

συγγενίς, ίδος, ἡ (Plut., Mor. 267d; Chariton 5, 3, 7; SEG IV, 452, 4; BCH 24 [1900] 340, 17; IAsMinLyk I, 53 E, 3; OGI index VIII [of cities]; PAmh 78, 9 [II AD]; Mitt-Wilck. II/2, 123, 9; Psaltes, Grammatik 152), a late and peculiar fem. of συγγενής, rejected by the Atticists (Ps.-Herodian in Phryn., p. 451f Lob.): ἡ σ. ***kinswoman, relative*** **Lk 1:36;** GJs 12:2.—B-D-F §59, 3; Mlt-H. 131.—M-M. Spicq.

συγγινώσκω 2 aor. συνέγνων; fut. 3 sg. mid. συγγνώσεται 4 Macc 8:2 (s. next entry; trag., Hdt.+; ins, pap, LXX; TestSim 3:6; TestJud 19:3; JosAs 13:9; Jos., C. Ap. 1, 218; Ath. 18, 1) **to think along with another in a congenial manner, *have the same opinion/purpose/wish, agree*** (Hdt. et al.; BGU 341, 4; 432 III, 8) w. dat. of pers., esp. of understanding and forbearance for someone (Simonides, fgm. 13, 20f Ζεῦ . . . ὅτι θαρσαλέον ἔπος εὔχομαι . . . , σύγγνωθί μοι=because I am using a bold word in my prayer, show me [some] understanding; JosAs 13:9; Philo, Mos. 1, 173; Jos., Vi. 103; TestSim 3:6 v.l.) σύγγνωτέ μοι *understand my position* (lit. 'join your minds w. mine') IRo 6:2 (Lghtf. 'bear w. me').—Less prob. is *forgive* or *pardon me* (Soph. et al.; Mod. Gk.).—DELG s.v. γιγνώσκω.

συγγνώμη, ης, ἡ (συγγινώσκω; Soph., Hdt.+; ins, pap, LXX, EpArist, Philo; Jos., Vi. 227; Just., D. 9, 1; 65, 2; Tat. 20, 1; Ath., R. 21 p. 73, 29) **permission to do someth., *concession, indulgence, pardon*** συγγνώμην ἔχειν *pardon, be indulgent to* τινί *someone* (Soph., Hdt. et al.; PEdg 81 [=Sb 6787], 36–38 [257 BC] συγγνώμην ἡμῖν ἔχων; without dat., Himerius, Or. 36, 17 [=Ecl. 36, 14]; Sir prol. ln. 18 and 3:13; EpArist 295) συγγνώμην μοι ἔχετε IRo 5:3. τοῦτο λέγω κατὰ συγγνώμην οὐ κατ' ἐπιταγήν *I say this as a concession* (to meet you halfway), *not as a command* **1 Cor 7:6** (Tat. 20, 1 κατὰ σ.).—DELG s.v. γιγνώσκω. M-M. s.v. συνγνώμη. TW.

συγγνωμονέω (later form for συγγιγνώσκω) ***make allowance for, pardon*** w. dat. (Sext. Emp., Math. 1, 126; Athen. 4, 177d; Gnomon [BGU V] 63 [II AD] pass.; 4 Macc 5:13; Jos., Ant. 11, 144) *pardon* τινί *someone* (Ps.-Callisth. 1, 40, 5 συγγνωμονέω ὡς θεὸς ἀνθρώποις) ITr 5:1.—DELG s.v. γιγνώσκω.

σύγγραμμα, ατος, τό (Hdt. et al.) **someth. composed in writing, *book, (written) work*** (X., Mem. 2, 1, 21; 4, 2, 10; Pla., Ep. 2, 314c; Philo, Vi. Cont. 29; Jos., C. Ap. 1, 44; 2, 288; Just.) EpilMosq 1, 2,4.—Of the Apology of Quadratus, Eus., HE 4, 3, 1. τοῦ δὲ θεοφίλου . . . τρία τὰ πρὸς Αὐτόλυκον . . . συγγράμματα 4, 24.—DELG s.v. γράφω.

συγγραφή, ῆς, ἡ (Heraclitus, fgm. 129; Hdt. et al.; ins, pap, LXX; Jos., C. Ap. 1, 129; Ar. 13:5 [pl. books]) ***document, contract*** (Thu. et al.; oft. in ins [IAndrosIsis, Kyme, 30: marriage contract], pap) ἄδικον συγγραφὴν διασπᾶν *tear up an unjust contract* B 3:3 (Is 58:6).

συγγράφω 1 aor. mid. συνεγραψάμην (Hdt.+; ins, pap) ***write down, compose*** mid. Papias (2:16) (the rdg. of Gebhardt-Harnack-Zahn), but s. συντάσσω.—DELG s.v. γράφω.

συγκάθημαι (Hdt. et al.; Sb 6796, 98 [258/257 BC]; Jos., Ant. 16, 362) ***sit with*** τινί *someone* (Mitt-Wilck I/2, 14 II, 5f συνκα[θημένων αὐτῷ] [=Caesar] συνκλητικ[ῷ]ν and 13f [συν]καθήμενοι [π]άντες σ[υνκλητικοί] [I AD]) ὁ βασιλεὺς . . . καὶ οἱ συγκαθήμενοι αὐτοῖς **Ac 26:30.** Also μετά τινος (Ps 100:6) **Mk 14:54.**—DELG s.v. ἧμαι.

συγκαθίζω 1 aor. συνεκάθισα; pf. 3 sg. συγκεκάθικεν (OdeSol 11:5)

❶ ***cause to sit down with*** *someone,* trans. ἡμᾶς . . . συνεκάθισεν ἐν τοῖς ἐπουρανίοις *(God) made us sit down with (Christ) in the heavenly realms* or simply *in heaven* **Eph 2:6.**

❷ ***sit down with*** *someone,* intr. (Gen 15:11; Ex 18:13; 1 Esdr 9:6. The mid. so X. et al.) **Lk 22:55.**—DELG s.v. ἕζομαι A. TW.

συγκακοπαθέω 1 aor. impv. συγκακοπάθησον (schol. on Eur., Hecub. 203) ***suffer together with someone*** abs. συγκακοπάθησον ὡς καλὸς στρατιώτης *suffer hardship with (me) as a good soldier* **2 Ti 2:3.** συγκακοπάθησον τῷ εὐαγγελίῳ (dat. of respect) *join with* (*me,* the apostle in prison) *in suffering for the gospel* **1:8.**—DELG s.v. κακός. TW.

συγκακουχέομαι (hapax leg.; cp. κακουχέω 'injure, maltreat') ***suffer/be mistreated with*** someone else τῷ λαῷ τοῦ θεοῦ *with God's people* **Hb 11:25.**—M-M.

συγκαλέω 1 aor. συνεκάλεσα, mid. συνεκαλεσάμην. (Act.: Hom. et al.; SIG 1185, 15f; PLond V, 1711, 53; LXX; JosAs 21:7 cod. A [p. 71, 25 Bat.]; Jos., Ant. 7, 363; 18, 279. Mid.: Hdt. 2, 160, 2; 2 Macc 15:31.)

❶ **to summon pers. to come together, *summon,*** act. foll. by acc. (Arrian, Anab. Alex. 6, 22, 2 ξυγκαλεῖν τὸ πλῆθος) **Mk 15:16; Lk 15:6, 9; Ac 5:21;** 1 Cl 43:5; Hs 5, 2, 11.

❷ **to call to one's side, *summon,*** mid. (on relation to act. s. B-D-F §316, 1) foll. by the acc. **Lk 9:1; 15:6 v.l., 9 v.l.; 23:13; Ac 5:21** D; **10:24; 13:7** D; **28:17;** Hs 5, 2, 11 v.l.—M-M s.v. συνκαλέω. TW.

συγκαλύπτω fut. συγκαλύψω LXX; 1 aor. συνεκάλυψα LXX. Pass.: aor. συνεκαλύφθην (TestSol 25:7); pf. ptc. συγκεκαλυμμένος (Hom. et al.; SIG 1170, 6; BGU 1816, 19 [I BC]; PGM 36, 270; 272; LXX; TestSol; TestNapht 9:2; Jos., Ant. 9, 209) **to keep someth. from being known by concealing it, *conceal*** (opp. ἀποκαλύπτω) pass. **Lk 12:2.**—M-M. s.v. συνκαλύπτω. TW.

συγκάμπτω 1 aor. συνέκαμψα (Hippocr., X., Pla. et al.; SIG 1168, 28 συγκάμψας τὰν χῆρα; LXX) ***(cause to) bend*** τὸν νῶτον αὐτῶν σύγκαμψον *cause their back(s) to bend* **Ro 11:10** (Ps 68:24); **Lk 13:11** D (for συγκύπτω).—M-M. s.v. συνκάμπτω.

συγκαταβαίνω 2 aor. 3 sg. συγκατέβη LXX, ptc. συγκαταβάς; fut. 3 sg. mid. συγκαταβήσεται Ps 48:18 **to accompany someone in going down to, *go down with someone*** fr. a high place to a lower one (Aeschyl., Thu. et al.; LXX; Philo, Abr. 105; Jos., Bell. 6, 132), fr. Jerusalem to Caesarea by the sea **Ac 25:5.**—M-M s.v. συνκαταβαίνω.

συγκατάθεσις, εως, ἡ (σύν, κατά, τίθημι; 'approval, assent': Polyb. 2, 58, 11; 21, 26, 16; Dionys. Hal. 8, 79; Epict. and oft., incl. OGI 484, 32; pap; Philo, Poster. Cai. 175; Just.) ***agreement, union*** (of an agreement BGU 194, 11; 19; PGen 42, 21; PFlor 58, 8 al.) τίς σ. ναῷ θεοῦ μετὰ εἰδώλων; *what agreement is there betw. the temple of God and idols?* **2 Cor 6:16.**—M-M s.v. συνκατάθεσις. Sv.

συγκατανεύω 1 aor. συγκατένευσα ***agree, consent*** (Polyb. 3, 52, 6; 7, 4, 9 al.; Jos., Vi. 22; 124; abs.: Anth. Pal. 5, 287, 8; that the gesture 'nod' suggested by the component νεύω is to be understood in the foregoing reff. cannot be determined, at least not in Jos., Vi 22, but prob. in Anth. Pal. 5, 287, 8) **Ac 18:27** D.

συγκατατάσσω 1 aor. inf. συγκατατάξαι (X. et al.; ins, also s. Lampe) ***to set forth things along with*** other information συγκατατάξαι ταῖς ἑρμηνείαις *set forth (in writing) along with my interpretations* Papias (2:3).

συγκατατίθημι in other Gk lit. almost always mid., and always so in our lit. (as in the LXX) συγκατατίθεμαι (Isaeus, Demosth. et al.; SIG 742, 52f; OGI 437, 43; pap; Ex 23:1, 32; Sus 20 Theod.; Just.); fut. 2 sg. συγκαταθήσῃ Ex 23:1, 32; 2 aor. impv. 2 sg. συγκατάθου Sus 20 Theod.; pf. ptc. συγκατατεθειμένος **Lk 23:51** (so also Just., A I, 65, 1) ***agree with, consent to*** τινί *something* (Demosth. 18, 166; Epict. 1, 28, 4; 2, 8, 24; Jos., Ant. 8, 166; 20, 13 τ. γνώμῃ; w. dat of person Pla., Gorg. 501c 'put down the same vote or opinion as'; Just., D. 5, 1) **Lk 23:51** (the rdg. varies betw. the pres. and the perf. ptc.); **Ac 4:18** D; **15:12** D; *find oneself in agreement* τινί *with someth.* IPhld 3:3.—M-M s.v. συνκατατίθημι.

συγκαταψηφίζομαι (s. ψηφίζω; found only in one other place, Plut., Them. 122 [21, 7], where it is a mid. dep.='join in a vote of condemnation') in our lit. in only one passage and only as pass. (1 aor. συγκατεψηφίσθην) ***be chosen (by a vote) together with*** (for the favorable sense cp. καταψηφίζω Diod. S. 29, 18 of posthumous honors voted for Philopoemen), or gener. ***be added*** μετὰ τῶν ἕνδεκα ἀποστόλων *to the eleven apostles* **Ac 1:26.**—DELG s.v. ψῆφος. M-M s.v. συνκαταψηφίζω. TW.

σύγκειμαι (Soph., Hdt. et al.; SIG 633, 25 [180 BC]; pap, LXX; Jos., C. Ap. 1, 112; 198; Ath. 8, 2 συγκείμενος καὶ διαιρούμενος) ***recline together*** (Soph., Aj. 1309) for συνανάκειμαι (q.v.) **Mt 9:10** D.

συγκεράννυμι (Aeschyl., Hdt. et al.; SIG 783, 32; LXX, Philo; Ath., R. 6 p. 54, 1 al.) 1 aor. συνεκέρασα. Pass.: aor.

opt. 3 sg. συγκραθείη (Ath., R. 7 p. 56, 15), inf. συγκραθῆναι Da 2:43; ptc. συγκειρασθείς 2 Macc. 15:39; pf. ptc. συγκεκερασμένος **Hb 4:2** or συγκεκραμένος **v.l.** (B-D-F §101 p. 52; Mlt-H. 243); plpf. 3 sg. συνεκέκρατο ApcPt 3:9. Prim. 'mix (together)'.

❶ **to bring about a blend by mixing various items, *blend, unite,*** lit., pass., of colors ApcPt 3:9.

❷ **to effect a harmonious unit, *compose,*** fig. ext. of 1 (Maximus Tyr. 16, 4f of the powers granted the soul by God) τὸ σῶμα *compose the body* (by unifying its members so as to form one organism) **1 Cor 12:24** (on the topic s. Περὶ Ὕψους 43, 5). συγκεράσαι ὑμῶν τὴν φρόνησιν ἐπὶ τὸ αὐτό *unite your wisdom harmoniously* Hv 3, 9, 8. οὐκ ὠφέλησεν ὁ λόγος τῆς ἀκοῆς ἐκείνους μὴ συγκεκερασμένους τῇ πίστει τοῖς ἀκούσασιν *the word that they heard did not benefit those who were not united with those who listened in faith* (Libanius, Ep. 571 vol. X, 536 F. συγκεράννυ τῷ νεανίσκῳ σαυτόν) **Hb 4:2.** Instead of the pl. συγκεκερασμένους a **v.l.** has the nom. sg. συγκεκερασμένος, prob.=*because it was not united by faith* (dat. of instrum.; s. B-D-F §202) *w. the hearers.*

συγκινέω 1 aor. συνεκίνησα; pass. impf. συνεκινούμην ***to stir up, move*** τὰ πάντα συνεκινεῖτο *everything was set in commotion* (in ref. to many changes taking place) IEph 19:3 (cp. Philo, Dec. 44 πάντα συγκεκινῆσθαι). τινά *arouse/excite someone* **Ac 6:12** (w. focus on emotional aspect, cp. Polyb. 15, 17, 1 of pers. 'moved' by the utterances of disaster victims; cp. the pass.: Herm. 2, 6b; Epict., Enchir. 33, 10; TestAbr A 5 p. 82, 20 [Stone p. 12], ibid. A 5 p. 83, 2 [Stone p. 14]).—M-M s.v. συνκινέω.

συγκλάω fut. συγκλάσω; 1 aor. συνέκλασα LXX, 3 sg. pass. συνεκλάσθη Jer 27:23 (Aristoph., Pla. et al.; PGronAmst 1, 8 [455 AD]; LXX; TestJob 27:4; JosAs 6:1) ***shatter*** τὶ *someth.* bars B 11:4 (Is 45:2).

συγκλεισμός, οῦ, ὁ (s. συγκλείω; pap, LXX) ***confinement, encirclement*** (Ezk 4:3, 7, 8; 5:2; 1 Macc 6:21; ViIs 3 [p. 69, 8 Sch.]) ἐν συγκλεισμῷ οὔσης τῆς πόλεως *when the city was under siege* 1 Cl 55:4; cp. vs. 5.—DELG s.v. κλείς.

συγκλείω fut. συγκλείσω LXX; 1 aor. συνέκλεισα; pf. 3 sg. συγκέκλεικεν Ex 14:3, ptc. acc. pl. συγκεκλεικότας Jer 21:9; plpf. συνεκεκλείκει (Just., D. 49, 4). Pass.: aor. συνεκλείσθην LXX; pf. ptc. συγκέκλεισμένοι **Gal 3:23** (Eur., Hdt.+; ins, pap, LXX; TestSol; Jos., Vi. 74, Ant. 12, 328; Ar. 3, 2; Just., D. 49, 4)

❶ **to catch by enclosing, *close up together, hem in, enclose*** τὶ *someth.* fish in a net (Aristot., HA 533b, 26; Ael. Aristid. 32 p. 606 D.) **Lk 5:6.**

❷ **to confine to specific limits, *confine, imprison,*** fig. ext. of 1 τινὰ εἴς τι (Polyb. 3, 63, 3 εἰς ἀγῶνα; Diod. S. 12, 34, 5; 19, 19, 8 εἰς τοιαύτην ἀμηχανίαν συγκλεισθεὶς Ἀντίγονος μετεμέλετο; Herm. Wr. 500, 8 Sc.; Ps 30:9 οὐ συνέκλεισάς με εἰς χεῖρας ἐχθροῦ, 77:50 τὰ κτήνη εἰς θάνατον συνέκλεισεν; cp. in the lit. sense PFay 12, 17 [II BC] συνκλείσαντές με εἰς τὴν οἰκίαν) of God συνέκλεισεν τοὺς πάντας εἰς ἀπείθειαν *he has imprisoned them all in disobedience,* i.e. put them under compulsion to be disobedient or given them over to disobedience **Ro 11:32.** τὶ ὑπό τι 'someth. under someth.': συνέκλεισεν ἡ γραφὴ τὰ πάντα ὑπὸ ἁμαρτίαν *the Scripture* (i.e. God's will as expressed in the Scripture) *has locked everything in under the power of sin* **Gal 3:22;** cp. vs. **23.**—DELG s.v. κλείς. M-M s.v. συνκλείω. TW.

συγκληρονόμος, ον inheriting together with, mostly subst. *co-heir* (Philo, Ad Gai. 67; Just., D. 140, 1; ins [IBM III, 633, 6f : Ephesus; ins on a sarcophagus fr. Thessalonica: MAI, Abt. 21, 1896, 98; SEG VIII, 91, 3 (II AD) ἀδελφὸς καὶ σ.]; PLond V, 1686, 35; PByz 6, 12 and other pap of Byz. times) **Eph 3:6.** Foll. by objective gen. of the thing **Hb 11:9; 1 Pt 3:7.** Foll. by gen. of the pers. w. whom one is inheriting (ViDan 17 [79, 6 Sch.] τῶν τέκνων) σ. Χριστοῦ *co-heir with Christ* **Ro 8:17** (cp. PMich 659, 60). W. dat. of the pers. w. whom one inherits (of slaves Lucian, Dial. Mort. 19, 4, Hist. Conscr. 20; Leutzsch, Hermas 471 n. 69) Hs 5, 2, 7f; 11.—New Docs 2, 97. DELG s.v. κλῆρος. M-M s.v. συνκληρονόμος.

συγκοιμάομαι pass. dep. (Aeschyl. et al.) 1 aor. συνεκοιμήθην.

❶ ***sleep with*** τινί *someone,* freq. as euphemism of intimate sexual relationship (trag., Hdt.; En 9:8) ApcPt 17:32.

❷ Before συνεγείρεσθε and after συμπάσχετε, συγκοιμᾶσθε is prob. also a euphemism **to lie together in the sleep of death, *die together*** συμπάσχετε, συγκοιμᾶσθε, συνεγείρεσθε *suffer together, die together, rise together* IPol 6:1 (difft. Lightfoot, to whom such such interp. appears "altogether out of place": he renders 'rest together' [of athletes after vigorous activity]; on the series of compounds w. σύν, among them συγκοιμ., s. Epict. 2, 22, 13 [but here συγκοιμ. of children sleeping together]).

συγκοινωνέω 1 aor. συνεκοινώνησα (Hippocr. et al.)

❶ **to be associated w. someone in some activity, *be connected*** τινί *with someth.* (Herm. Wr. 1, 28 τῇ ἀγνοίᾳ; w. gen. of thing Demosth. 57, 2; τινί τινος=' w. someone in someth.' Cass. Dio 37, 41; 77, 16)

ⓐ in the sense of actually taking part **Eph 5:11; Rv 18:4.**

ⓑ in the sense of taking a sympathetic interest **Phil 4:14**

❷ **to give a portion of what one has to another, *share*** τί τινι *someth. w. someone* συγκοινωνεῖν πάντα τῷ ἀδελφῷ *share everything with one's brother* D 4:8.—DELG s.v. κοινός. TW.

συγκοινωνός, οῦ, ὁ ***participant, partner*** (PBilabel 19, 2 [110 AD]; PCairMasp 158, 11 of business partners οἱ συγκοινωνοί μου) w. gen. of the thing in which one shares (Stephan. of Athens, in Hippocr. 1, 76 Dietz [1834] συγκοινωνὸς τῆς βασιλείας μου) **Ro 11:17.** ἵνα συγκ. αὐτοῦ (i.e. τοῦ εὐαγγελίου) γένωμαι *that I might jointly share in it* (i.e. in the benefits promised by the gospel; difft. EMolland, D. paul. Euangelion '34, 53f: 'fellow-worker in the gospel [Mitarbeiter des Evan.]') **1 Cor 9:23.** συγκοινωνοί μου τῆς χάριτος *sharers of the same grace as myself* **Phil 1:7.** Also συγκ. τινος ἔν τινι *sharer with someone in someth.* **Rv 1:9** (ViJer 15 [p. 42, 2 Sch.] s. Μωϋσέως).—MPol 17:3 v.l.—DELG s.v. κοινός. M-M s.v. συνκοινωνός. TW.

συγκομίζω 1 aor. συνεκόμισα, pass. συνεκομίσθην; orig. 'collect'.

❶ **to gather in as harvest, *bring in*** (so Hdt. et al., in the act. [cp. Jos., Ant. 14, 472], and the mid. X. et al., oft. in pap) pass. θημωνιὰ ἅλωνος καθ' ὥραν συγκομισθεῖσα *a heap of sheaves on the threshing-floor, brought in* (to the barn) *at the right time* 1 Cl 56:15 (Job 5:26).

❷ **to carry out burial arrangements, *bury*** a euphemistic fig. ext. of 1 (Soph., Aj. 1048; Plut., Sulla 475 [38, 5]) τινά *someone* **Ac 8:2.**—DELG s.v. κομέω 2. M-M. s.v. συνκομίζω.

συγκοπή, ῆς, ἡ (κόπτω; Dionys. Hal., Comp. Verb. 15; 22; Peripl. Eryth. 6; Plut.; POxy 1654, 6 [II AD]) ***cutting to pieces, mangling*** συγκοπαὶ (-ὴ v.l.) μελῶν IRo 5:3.—DELG s.v. κόπτω 2.

συγκοπιάω (schol. on Eur., Hecuba 862; SEG VI, 473, 5f [IV AD]) ***labor together*** τινί *with someone* τῷ πνεύματι *with the*

Spirit Hs 5, 6, 6. συγκοπιᾶτε ἀλλήλοις *unite your efforts* IPol 6:1.—DELG s.v. κόπτω 1.

συγκόπτω fut. συγκόψω; 1 aor. συνέκοψα LXX; 2 aor. pass. συνεκόπην (Eur., Hdt. et al.; ins, pap, LXX; TestJud 3:4; SibOr 3, 188; 613)

❶ **to break into pieces, *break*** (X., Cyr. 6, 4, 3; PSI 630, 20; 4 Km 24:13) stones Hv 3, 6, 1.

❷ **to bring an end to someth. as an effective force, *destroy,*** fig. ext. of 1 (Lucian, Cal. 1) τὴν δύναμιν τοῦ διαβόλου *break the power of the devil* Hm 12, 6, 4.

❸ **to be crushed inwardly, *be overcome,*** fig. ext. of 1, pass. intr. sense of a depressed frame of mind ἀπὸ τῆς λύπης *by grief* Hv 5:4.

σύγκρασις, εως, ἡ (συγκεράννυμι; Eur., Pla. et al.; Cornutus 8 p. 8, 15; Vett. Val.; Herm. Wr. 11, 7; PGM 7, 512; Ezk 22:19; Ath., R. 5 p. 53, 13) **state of parts that are combined, *assemblage, combination*** 1 Cl 37:4.—DELG s.v. κεράννυμι.

συγκρατέω fut. συγκρατήσω; 1 aor. pass. συνεκρατήθην (Plut. et al.; Ps 16:5 Sym.; Jos., Ant. 8, 67; Ath. 10, 1)

❶ **to keep parts together, *hold together*** w. acc. (Anaximenes [VI BC] 2 Diels: ἡ ψυχὴ συγκρατεῖ ἡμᾶς) Hs 9, 7, 5.

❷ **to be supportive by surrounding, *surround (and protect)*** τὸν λαόν Hs 5, 5, 3; cp. 9, 12, 8.

❸ **to give suppport to, *support, hold upright*** (cp. Aretaeus 3, 5, 7; 40, 29 Hude ὕπνος συγκ. τὰ μέλεα; Geopon., Prooem. 6) pass., of a sick pers. ἵνα συγκρατηθῇ ἡ ἀσθένεια τοῦ σώματος αὐτοῦ *that the person's weak body might find support* Hv 3, 11, 4.—DELG s.v. κράτος.

συγκρίνω 1 aor. συνέκρινα; aor. subj. 1 pl. pass. συγκριθῶμεν 1 Macc 10:71 (since Epicharmus [V BC] in Plut., Mor. 110a; ins, pap, LXX; JosAs 4:14; Tat.; Ath., R. 8 p. 57, 14).

❶ **to bring things together so as to form a unit, *combine*** (Epicharmus et al.; Pla.; Aristot., Metaph. 1, 4, 985a, 24) so perh. πνευματικοῖς (neut.) πνευματικὰ συγκρίνοντες *giving spiritual truth a spiritual form* (Goodsp., Lghtf., BWeiss, Bousset) **1 Cor 2:13** (s. 2b and 3 below).

❷ **to draw a conclusion by comparing, *compare*** (Aristot. et al.; Polyb., Diod. S., Dionys. Hal., Epict., Philo; Jos., Ant. 5, 77 al.)

ⓐ τινά τινι *someone with someone* (Diod. S. 4, 44, 6; cp. CIG 5002 ὁ ἱερεὺς . . . , πατὴρ τῶν ἱερέων, ᾧ οὐδεὶς τῶν ἱερέων συγκρίνεται; Philo, Ebr. 45) ἑαυτόν τινι *oneself with someone* (Plut., C. Gracch. 836 [4, 6]) **2 Cor 10:12ab.**

ⓑ **1 Cor 2:13** (s. 1 above and 3 below) may also be classified here: *comparing the spiritual gifts and revelations* (which we already possess) *with the spiritual gifts and revelations* (which we are to receive, and judging them thereby; cp. Maximus Tyr. 6, 4a) so Rtzst., Mysterienrel.[3] 336; Ltzm., Hdb. ad loc.; Field, Notes 168.

❸ **to clarify on the basis of a compatible relationship, *explain, interpret*** (Polyb. 14, 3, 7; Gen 40:8, 16, 22; 41:12f, 15; Da 5:12 Theod.; JosAs 4:14 [ἐνύπνιον]) πνευματικοῖς (masc.) πνευματικὰ συγκρίνοντες *interpreting spiritual truths to those who possess the Spirit* **1 Cor 2:13** (s. 1 and 2b above) so NRSV text, PSchmiedel, Heinrici, JSickenberger.—FBlass and JWeiss propose emendation of the text.—M-M. s.v. συνκρίνω. TW.

συγκύπτω aor. ptc. συγκύψας Job 9:27; pf. ptc. συγκεκυφώς Sir 12:11 (Hdt., Aristoph. et al.; LXX) prim. 'bend forwards, stoop', then of a fixed bent-over position, act. intr. ***be bent over*** (Sir 12:11; 19:26; Orig., C. Cels. 4, 36, 7) of a woman possessed by a spirit of illness ἦν συγκύπτουσα *she was bent double* **Lk 13:11.**

συγκυρία, ας, ἡ (κυρέω 'hit, light upon', then 'come to pass'; Hippocr.: CMG I/1 p. 42, 16; 1 Km 6:9 Sym.; Hesych.) **an unexpected conjunction of events, *coincidence, chance*** κατὰ συγκυρίαν *by coincidence* (Eustath., In Il. 3, 23 p. 376, 11) **Lk 10:31** (συγτυχείαν=συντυχείαν P75[c]; τύχᾳ D).—DELG s.v. κύρω. M-M.

συγχαίρω impf. συνέχαιρον; fut. συγχαρήσομαι and 3 sg. συγχαρεῖται Gen 21:6; 2 aor. pass. (with same sense as act. and mid.) συνεχάρην (Aeschyl., X. et al.; ins, pap, LXX)

❶ **to experience joy in conjunction w. someone, *rejoice with*** τινί *someone* (Aristot., EN 1166a, 8; UPZ 148, 3 [II BC]; BGU 1080, 2; Diogenes, Ep. 16 p. 108, 22 Malherbe; Philo, Det. Pot. Ins. 124) **Lk 1:58; Phil 2:17f** (s. also 2 below); ITr 1:1. συνεχάρην ὑμῖν μεγάλως *I rejoiced with you from the bottom of my heart* Pol 1:1. τινί foll. by ὅτι *rejoice w. someone because* (PLond I, 43, 3f p. 48 [II BC]) **Lk 15:6, 9.** Without dat., which is easily supplied (X., Hiero 5, 4; SIG 1173, 5 [138 AD]) **1 Cor 12:26** (metaph.: the 'parts' stand for the believers).—W. dat. of thing as cause of rejoicing (Herm. Wr. 1, 26.—In such case the compound prob. has the same mng. as the simple verb, as Jos., Ant. 15, 210 [opp. ἄχθεσθαι]) οὐ χαίρει ἐπὶ τῇ ἀδικίᾳ συγχαίρει δὲ τῇ ἀληθείᾳ *it does not rejoice over injustice, but rejoices in the truth* **1 Cor 13:6** (EFranz, TLZ 87, '62, 795–98). Cp. Hs 8, 2, 7.

❷ **to express pleasure over another's good fortune, *congratulate*** τινί *someone* (Aeschin. 2, 45; Socrates, Ep. 33, 2 [=p. 300, 15 Malherbe] w. ὅτι foll.; Polyb. 15, 5, 13; 30, 18, 1 al.; Diod. S. 22, 13, 7; Plut., Mor. 231b; PTebt 424, 5; cp. Jos., Ant. 8, 50) B 1:3; IEph 9:2; IPhld 10:1; ISm 11:2; Hs 5, 2, 6.—**Lk 1:58** and **Phil 2:17f** could perh. be classed here as well.—M-M. s.v. συνχαίρω. TW.

συγχέω (Hom.+; ins, PGM 4, 3101; LXX; PsSol 12:3; Philo, Joseph.; Ath. 22, 2), and beside it the Hellenistic συγχύν(ν)ω (B-D-F §73; 101; Mlt-H. 195; 214f; 265; W-S. §15; Thackeray §19, 2; 24) **Ac 21:31** συγχύννεται and Hv 5:5 συγχύννου; impf. συνέχεον **Ac 21:27** (s. W-S. §13, 13 note 13) and συνέχυννεν **Ac 9:22,** v.l. συνέχυνεν; fut. συγχεῶ Am 3:15; 1 aor. συνέχεα **Ac 21:27 v.l.** Pass.: 1 aor. συνεχύθην; pf. συγκέχυμαι **Ac 21:31 v.l.;** lit. 'pour together', then by fig. ext. **to cause dismay, *confuse, confound, trouble, stir up*** w. acc. (Eunap., Vi. Soph. p. 44 Boiss. ἅπαντα; Philo, Mut. Nom. 72 τ. ψυχήν, Spec. Leg. 1, 328 πάντα; Jos., Ant. 11, 140) πάντα τὸν ὄχλον **Ac 21:27.** Pass. w. act. force *be in confusion* (PGM 13, 874) **19:29** D, 32. ὅλη συγχύννεται Ἰερουσαλήμ **21:31.**—*Confound, throw into consternation* w. acc. **Ac 9:22;** cp. **11:26 v.l.** Pass., intr. sense *be amazed, surprised, excited, agitated* (Diod. S. 4, 62, 3 συνεχύθη τὴν ψυχήν=he became distraught in spirit; Phlegon: 257 fgm. 36, 1, 5 Jac.; Achilles Tat. 5, 17, 7; 1 Km 7:10; Jo 2:1; Jos., Bell. 2, 230, Ant. 8, 199; 12, 317) **Ac 2:6;** Hv 5:4f; m 12, 4, 1f.—M-M. s.v. συνχέω.

συγχράομαι mid. dep. (Polyb. et al.; ins, pap) inf. συγχρᾶσθαι IMg 3:1 and συγχρῆσθαι (Tat. 4, 1); 1 aor. ptc. συγχρησάμενος (Tat. 18, 2; Ath. 9, 1).

❶ Related to the gener. sense 'to avail oneself of someth., make use of' (Polyb. 1, 8, 1; 3, 14, 5; Epict. 1, 16, 10; 2, 19, 1; EpArist 162; 266 al.; SIG 685, 45; BGU 1187, 22 [I BC]) is the pejorative application ***take advantage of*** τῇ ἡλικίᾳ τοῦ ἐπισκόπου *the bishop's youth* IMg 3:1.

❷ **to associate on friendly terms with, *have dealings with,*** τινί *someone* (Ps.-Demetr., Eloc. c. 281; Diogenes Oenoand.

[II AD], fgm. 64 W. [=53 III, 9f Ch.]; Ps.-Callisth. 2, 19, 3 συγχρησάμενός μοι='associating with me'; Ps.-Clem., Hom. 9, 22) οὐ συγχρῶνται Ἰουδαῖοι Σαμαρίταις (s. Σαμαρίτης) **J 4:9** (DDaube, JBL 69, '50, 137–47 prefers 'use [vessels for food and drink] together' and discusses the pass. fr. Diogenes Oenoand., also IMg 3:1; on the qu. of omission of the clause by some mss. s. Metzger ad loc.; B-D-F §193, 5).—DELG s.v. χρή. M-M. s.v. συνχράομαι.

συγχρωτίζομαι (cp. the adv. συγχρῶτα, 'body to body'; Hecato on Zeno the Stoic in Diog. L. 7, 2; Herm. Wr. 10, 17) pf. ptc. gen. συγκεχρωτισμένου (Ath. 24, 2) **to be in defiling contact with,** ***defile by touching*** τινός Dg 12:8.—DELG s.v. χρώς.

συγχύν(ν)ω s. συγχέω.

σύγχυσις, εως, ἡ (συγχέω; Eur., Thu.+; Jos., Bell. 4, 129, Ant. 16, 75; ins, pap, LXX; Just., A II, 7, 1; Tat. 5, 3) ***confusion, tumult*** (Diod. S. 1, 75, 2; 20, 9, 5 συγχύσεως τὴν πόλιν ἐχούσης; Chion, Ep. 1; Philo; Jos., Bell. 2, 294 σύγχυσις εἶχεν τὸν δῆμον; 4, 125; SibOr 8, 81; AcPlTh 10 [Aa I 243, 3] of mourning) ἐπλήσθη ἡ πόλις τῆς συγχύσεως **Ac 19:29.**—DELG s.v. χέω III. M-M.

συγχωρέω 1 aor. συνεχώρησα (LXX, Just.); pf. inf. συγκεχωρηκέναι (Just., D. 55, 1). Pass.: fut. 3 sg. συγχωρηθήσεται (Just., D. 77, 2); 1 aor. 3 sg. συνεχωρήθη (GrBar 1:1; 3:5); pf. συγκεχώρηται (Dg 8, 6; Just.); plpf. συγκεχώρητο (Just., D. 20, 1) (trag., Hdt. et al.) prim. 'to include by making room'.

❶ **to display willingness to cooperate,** ***grant a little ground*** τινί *to someone* (Thu. 1, 140, 5 al. in the sense of making some concession) IMg 3:1.

❷ **to permit as a privilege,** ***grant, permit*** τινί *(to) someone* (Bel 26; Jos., Ant. 3, 277) w. dat. and inf. (X., Cyr. 6, 3, 20; Diod. S. 38 + 39 fgm. 8, 1; Appian, Bell. Civ. 5, 62 §260; Jos., Ant. 11, 6) mid. **Ac 21:39** D.—Pass. (Herm. Wr. 1, 13a; cp. the pers. construction GrBar, s. above) pf. συγκεχώρηται *it is granted* Dg 8:6.—DELG s.v. χώρα. Sv.

συζάω (Aeschyl., Pla. et al.; EpArist, Philo; Just., D. 47, 2; Ath., R. 10 p. 54, 9 al.) fut. συζήσω (on the spelling συνζάω s. B-D-F §19, 2; Rob. 217; W-S. §5, 25) ***live with*** τινί *someone* (Demosth. 19, 69; Kaibel 1085, 2; EpArist 130) of living with a sinner Hm 4, 1, 9. Of the believer's life w. the exalted Lord **Ro 6:8** (s. σύμφυτος). Also μετά τινος (Demosth. 18, 314 v.l.; Plut., Pyrrh. 396 [20, 4]; Aristot., EN 8, 3 p. 1156a, 27 μετ' ἀλλήλων) of living w. one's wife Hm 4, 1, 4f; w. polytheists Hs 8, 9, 1; 3. Abs. (w. συναποθνήσκειν as Athen. 6, 54, 249b τούτους [the bodyguards] οἱ βασιλεῖς ἔχουσι συζῶντας καὶ συναποθνήσκοντας): the Corinthians have a place in Paul's heart εἰς τὸ συναποθανεῖν καὶ συζῆν *to live together and die together* **2 Cor 7:3.** The Christians die and live w. their Lord **2 Ti 2:11.**—DELG s.v. ζώω. M-M. s.v. συνζάω. TW.

συζεύγνυμι 1 aor. συνέζευξα; pf. pass. ptc. fem. pl. συνεζευγμέναι Ezk 1:11, 23; lit. 'yoke together' (X., Cyr. 2, 2, 26), then gener. **to make a pair,** ***join together, pair*** (PGiss 34, 3; Ezk 1:11; Philo), specif. of matrimony (Eur. et al.; cp. X., Oec. 7, 30 νόμος συζευγνὺς ἄνδρα καὶ γυναῖκα; Aristot., HA 7, 6; Jos., Ant. 6, 309; PLond V, 1727, 9) ὃ οὖν ὁ θεὸς συνέζευξεν **Mt 19:6; Mk 10:9** (cp. the polytheistic counterpart Nicetas Eugen. 3, 12; 7, 265 Hercher: two lovers οὓς θεὸς [a god] συνῆψε, τίς διασπάσοι;).—M-M. s.v. συνζεύγνυμι.

συζητέω impf. συνεζήτουν; 1 aor. inf. συζητῆσαι (Just., D. 120, 5) (s. two next entries; Pla. et al.; pap freq.; 2 Esdr 12:4 v.l.; Just.)

❶ **to carry on a discussion,** ***discuss,*** περί (the NT never has σ. w. περί) τινος *about someth.* B 4:10. Foll. by indir. question **Mk 9:10.** Abs. **1:27.** ὁμιλεῖν καὶ συζητεῖν **Lk 24:15.**

❷ **to contend with persistence for a point of view,** ***dispute, debate, argue*** (ASP 6, '70, 581, 9 ἀλλὰ καὶ συνζητήσαντό[ς] μου αὐτῶν περὶ τούτων [ca. 126–28 AD]) τινί 'w. someone' (POxy 532, 17; 1673, 20 [II AD]; Just., D. 102, 5 al.) **Mk 8:11; 9:14 v.l.; Ac 6:9;** GMary 463, 20. Also πρός τινα **Mk 9:14, 16** both αὐτούς (vs. 16 v.l. ἑαυτούς [cp. vs. 10], s. Sod. and ASyn. app. ad loc.; Tdf.'s app. contains the typographical error αὐτούς for ἑαυτούς; RBorger, TRu 52, '87, 27f); **Lk 22:23** (w. τό and indir. quest.); **Ac 9:29.** Abs. (Cyranides p. 10, 22) **Mk 12:28.** συζητοῦντες ἀποθνήσκουσιν *they are perishing while they dispute* ISm 7:1.

❸ **to ponder various aspects of a matter,** ***reflect, meditate*** (in solitude) περί τινος Hs 6, 1, 1. Foll. by ὅτι 2:1.—M-M. s.v. συνζητέω. TW.

συζήτησις, εως, ἡ (s. prec. and next entry; Cicero, Ad Fam. 16, 21, 4; Philo, Det. Pot. Ins. 1, Leg. All. 3, 131, Op. M. 54 v.l.) **a discussion in the course of which disputants persistently advocate/sponsor a particular point of view,** ***dispute, discussion*** (collection of Epicurean sayings: CBailey, Epicurus 1926 p. 116, fgm. 74) **Ac 15:2 v.l., 7 v.l.** πολλὴν ἔχοντες ἐν ἑαυτοῖς συζήτησιν *disputing vigorously among themselves* **28:28 [29] v.l.**—DELG s.v. ζητέω. M-M. s.v. συνζήτησις.

συζητητής, οῦ, ὁ (hapax leg.) ***disputant, debater*** (s. συζήτησις and συζητέω 2) **1 Cor 1:20** (=IEph 18:1).—TW.

σύζυγος, ον (Sappho, fgm. 213 [L-P.]; Aeschyl. et al.; Ezk 23:21 Aq.). The corresp. subst. **σύζυγος, ου, ὁ** has not yet been found as a proper name (AFick²/FBechtel, Die griech. Personennamen 1894, 132), but only as a compound common noun (='brother' Eur., Tro. 1001;='comrade, companion' Eur., Iph. T. 250; Aristoph., Plut. 945; Anth. 8, 145; Magnet. Graffiti ed. Kern 321; 328 [I AD] σύζυγοι Βαίβιος Κάλλιπος; Herm. Wr. 6, 1b. In the same sense as Lat. commilito ['fellow-soldier'], a term of flattery used by Julius Caesar and the emperors, and perh. esp. evocative in its Gk. equivalent in a letter addressed to residents of a Rom. colony. The Gk. term is also used of gladiators, each one of whom is his opponent's σύζυγος: RHerzog, Koische Forschungen u. Funde 1899 no. 133; CIG 4175; Kaibel 318, 2.—Thieme 32) γνήσιε σύζυγε ***true comrade,*** lit. 'yoke-fellow' **Phil 4:3.** It is no longer possible to determine w. certainty just whom the apostle has in mind (MDibelius; FTillmann.—Epaphroditus has been conjectured by some fr. Victorinus to Lghtf. and Zahn. JJeremias, NT Essays [TWManson mem. vol.] '59, 136–43, esp. 140 [Silas]). Since ἡ σύζυγος='wife' (Eur., Alc. 314; 342; Anth. 8, 161, 6; 164, 2; Syntipas p. 16, 9; 18, 6; Test Reub 4:1), some have thought that Paul's wife is meant (since Clem. Alex., Strom. 3, 53, 1; Origen, Comm. in Ep. ad Rom. 1, 1). Lohmeyer considers it to mean a 'brother in suffering' who is sharing Paul's imprisonment. Finally, the idea that σ. is a proper name has received considerable support (RLipsius, EHaupt, PEwald, KBarth et al. W-H. mg.).—DELG s.v. ζεύγνυμι IV. M-M. s.v. σύνζυγος. TW.

συζωοποιέω 1 aor. συνεζωοποίησα (only in Christian writers) ***make alive together with someone*** ἡμᾶς τῷ Χριστῷ *us together w. Christ* **Eph 2:5.** ὑμᾶς σὺν αὐτῷ *you together w. him* (=Christ) **Col 2:13.** The ref. is to people who were dead in their sins, but through union w. Christ have been made alive by God together w. him.—TW.

συκάμινος, ου, ἡ (Theophr.; Phaenias in Athen. 2, 51e; Diod. S. 1, 34, 8; Strabo 17, 2, 4; Diosc. 1, 23; ins fr. Sinuri [ed. LRobert '45] no. 47a, 13; BGU 492, 7; 9; PTebt 343, 86 al. In LXX for שִׁקְמָה, the sycamore.—HLewy, Die semit. Fremdwörter bei den Griechen 1895, 23) ***the mulberry tree,*** which is evidently differentiated fr. the sycamore (s. συκομορέα; Zohary, Geobot. II 633, Plants 71: morus nigra) in **Lk 17:6** (cp. 19:4), as well as in the ancient versions.—On the two kinds of trees, and on the question whether Lk may not have differentiated betw. them, s. Löw (s. συκῆ; here also SKlein) I 266–74.—RAC VII 683f, 686. DELG s.v. συκάμινον. M-M.

συκῆ, ῆς, ἡ (Hom. et al.; ins, pap, LXX; TestSol 18:37 P; Jos., Bell. 3, 517, Ant. 5, 236f) ***fig tree,*** ficus carica (Zohary, Plants 58f), much cultivated because of its sweet fruit, also growing wild **Mt 24:32; Mk 13:28; Lk 13:6f; 21:29; J 1:48, 50; Js 3:12; Rv 6:13** (cp. Is 34:4). Jesus execrates a fig tree **Mt 21:19–21; Mk 11:13, 20f;** s. WvandeSandeBakhuyzen, NThT 7, 1918, 330–38; FvanHasselt, NThSt 8, 1925, 225–27; SHirsch, NThT 27, '38, 140–51; ARobin, NTS 8, '61/62, 276–81 (Mi 7:1–6); HBartsch, ZNW 53, '62, 256–60.—On the fig tree s. FGoldmann, La Figue en Palestine à l'époque de la Mišna 1911; SKlein, Weinstock, Feigenbaum u. Sykomore in Palästina: ASchwarz Festschr. 1917; ILöw, D. Flora der Juden I 1928, 224–54; WRauh and HReznik, SBHeidAk, Math.-nat. '51, Abh. 3, 164–74.—RAC VII 640–82. DELG s.v. σῦκον. M-M. TW.

συκομορέα, ας, ἡ (σῦκον + μορέα via μόρον; Hippiatr. II 165, 16; Geopon. 10, 3, 7.—B-D-F §25; 45; Mlt-H. 81. L. writes it συκομωρέα; -μωραία t.r. [s. Tdf. app.]) ***fig-mulberry tree, sycamore fig*** (s. συκάμινος; Zohary, Plants 68f) **Lk 19:4.**—See Löw (s. συκῆ) I 274–80.—RAC VII 683–89.—M-M. TW.

σῦκον, ου, τό (Hom. et al.; ins, pap, LXX; JosAs 4:4; ParJer; ApcMos 20; Jos., Bell. 3, 519, Vi. 14) **fruit of the fig tree,** ***fig*** (s. συκῆ), esp. *ripe fig* **Mt 7:16; Mk 11:13; Lk 6:44; Js 3:12.**—B. 378. M-M. TW.

συκοφαντέω fut. 3 sg. συκοφαντήσει Lev 19:11; 1 aor. ἐσυκοφάντησα; fut. 3 sg. pass. συκοφαντηθήσεται (Just., D. 92, 5) (Aristoph., X., Pla. et al.; pap, LXX; TestJos 8:4; Philo; Jos., Bell. 1, 11, Ant. 10, 114, Vi. 52; SibOr 2, 73). Prim. 'accuse falsely, slander' (for guesses at derivation of the term s. L-S-M-J s.v. συκοφάντης, and lit. below)

❶ **to put pressure on someone for personal gain,** ***harass, squeeze, shake down, blackmail*** τινά *someone* (Pr 14:31; 22:16 πένητα; 28:3 πτωχούς) w. διασείω (BGU 1756, 11 [I BC]; s. διασείω and also cp. Antiphon, Or. 6, 43; UPZ 113, 9f [156 BC]; PTebt 43, 26 συκοφαντηθῶμεν and 36 συκοφαντίας τε καὶ διασισμοῦ χάριν=for the sake of calumny and shakedown) **Lk 3:14.**

❷ **to secure someth. through intimidation,** ***extort*** (Lysias 26, 24 τὶ παρά τινος) εἴ τινός τι ἐσυκοφάντησα *if I have extorted anything from anyone* **Lk 19:8.**—EbNestle, Sykophantia im bibl. Griech.: ZNW 4, 1903, 271f; JLofberg, The Sycophant-Parasite: ClPh 15, 1920, 61–72. On the derivation of the term s. esp. KLatte, Pauly-W. IV A (1932) 1028–31. S. also Arnott, Alexis p. 551f.—DELG s.v. σῦκον. M-M. TW.

συλαγωγέω **to gain control of by carrying off as booty,** ***make captive of, rob*** τινά *someone* (Tat. 22, 2 [fig.]; Heliod. 10, 35 p. 307, 32 Bekker οὗτός ἐστιν ὁ τὴν ἐμὴν θυγατέρα συλαγωγήσας; Aristaen. 2, 22 Hercher) in imagery of carrying someone away fr. the truth into the slavery of error **Col 2:8.**—M-M.

συλάω 1 aor. ἐσύλησα; pf. 2 pl. σεσυλήκατε (Tat. 10, 2). Pass.: aor. subj. 3 pl. συληθῶσι EpJer 17 (Hom. et al.; ins, pap; EpJer 17; Jos., C. Ap. 2, 263) ***rob, sack*** τινά *someone* as a dramatic fig. expr. for Paul's procedure in accepting financial support fr. certain sources ἄλλας ἐκκλησίας ἐσύλησα *I sacked* (or *looted/raided*) *other churches* and thus obtained the money that enabled me to serve you free of charge **2 Cor 11:8.** Perh. the technical sense *use right of seizure* applies here (IG IX/1, 333, 3 [V BC] et al.; s. L-S-J-M 3d and s.v. σύλη I; Spicq s.v.).—M-M.

συλλαβή, ῆς, ἡ (Aeschyl.) ***syllable*** (Pla., Demosth. et al.; Philo, Poster. Cai. 94) Hv 2, 1, 4 (Porphyr., Vi. Plot. 8 ἔγραψε οὔτε εἰς κάλλος ἀποτυπούμενος τὰ γράμματα οὔτε εὐσήμως τὰς συλλαβὰς διαιρῶν=he wrote with no interest in the beauty of the letters, nor giving clear indication of the division of syllables).—DELG s.v. λαμβάνω.

συλλαλέω impf. συνελάλουν; 1 aor. συνελάλησα (Polyb.; OGI 229, 23; pap., LXX) **to exchange thoughts with,** ***talk/discuss/converse with*** τινί *someone* (Polyb. 4, 22, 8; PHib 66, 4 [III BC]; PRainer 18, 23; Ex 34:35; Pr 6:22; Is 7:6; TestJob 30:3 ἀλλήλοις) **Mk 9:4; Lk 9:30; 22:4.** Also μετά τινος **Mt 17:3; Ac 18:12** D; **25:12.** συνελάλουν πρὸς ἀλλήλους λέγοντες **Lk 4:36.**—M-M s.v. συνλαλέω.

συλλαμβάνω fut. συλλήμψομαι and συλλήψεις GJs 4:1 (for the spelling s. λαμβάνω); 2 aor. συνέλαβον; pf. συνείληφα; 2 aor. mid. συνελαβόμην. Pass.: 1 fut. συλλημφθήσομαι LXX; 1 aor. συνελήμφθην (Aeschyl., Hdt.+).

❶ **to take into custody—ⓐ** ***seize, grasp, apprehend*** τινά *arrest someone* (Soph., Thu. et al.; SIG 700, 30; PHib 54, 20; POxy 283, 12 al.; LXX; Jos., Bell. 2, 292, Ant. 15, 124; Just., D. 111, 3) **Mt 26:55; Mk 14:48; Lk 22:54; J 18:12; Ac 1:16; 12:3;** 1 Cl 12:2a. Pass. **Ac 23:27;** 1 Cl 12:2b; MPol 5:2; 7:2; 9:1; 21.

ⓑ mid. ***seize, arrest*** **Ac 26:21;** MPol 6:1.

❷ **to capture (an animal),** ***catch*** (Dio Chrys. 25 [42], 3; Aelian, HA 1, 2; Philo, Omn. Prob. Lib. 147) **Lk 5:9** (s. ἄγρα).

❸ **to become pregnant,** ***conceive,*** of a woman (Aristot., HA 7, 1, 582a, 19, Gen. An. 1, 19, 727b, 8; Plut., Mor. 829b; Lucian, Sacrif. 5; LXX; cp. EpArist 165; for med. writers s. Hobart 91f) abs. *become pregnant* (Gen 4:1; 30:7 al.; Tat. 33, 3; Ath. 22, 4) **Lk 1:24;** B 13:2; GJs 4:1; συλλήμψομαι ἐκ λόγου (θεοῦ) . . . ἀπὸ κυρίου θεοῦ ζῶντος 11:2; ApcP 11:26 mg. as restored by Dieterich et al. Also συλλ. ἐν γαστρί (Hippocr., Aph. 5, 46 ed. Littré IV 548, Mul. 1, 75 vol. VIII 162 [al. in Hipp. and Galen, s. Hobart 92]; Demetr.: 722 fgm. 1, 4 Jac. Cp. Gen 25:21) **Lk 1:31** and alt. (as Gen 25:21; En 7:2) ἐν γαστρὶ λαμβάνειν GJs 4:2, 4. Pass. ἐν ἀνομίαις συνελήμφθην 1 Cl 18:5 (Ps 50:7).—W. the acc. of the child to be born (Lucian, Ver. Hist. 1, 22; LXX; Demetr.: 722 fgm. 1, 3 Jac.) **Lk 1:36.** Pass. πρὸ τοῦ συλλημφθῆναι αὐτὸν ἐν τῇ κοιλίᾳ *before he was conceived in the womb* **2:21.**—In imagery (cp. Περὶ ὕψους 14, 3 τὰ συλλαμβανόμενα ὑπὸ τῆς ψυχῆς; Ps 7:15; TestBenj 7:2 συλλαμβάνει ἡ διάνοια διὰ τοῦ βελιάρ; Philo) ἡ ἐπιθυμία συλλαβοῦσα τίκτει ἁμαρτίαν **Js 1:15.**

❹ **to help by taking part w. someone in an activity** (lit. 'take hold of together'), ***support, aid, help*** (Aeschyl. et al.) w. dat. of the one to whom help is given (Eur., Med. 812; Hdt. 6, 125; Pla., Leg. 10, 905c; POxy 935, 3; 8 συλλαμβάνουσι ἡμῖν οἱ θεοί; 1064, 7; Jos., Ant. 12, 240) συλλάβωμεν ἑαυτοῖς *let us help each other* 2 Cl 17:2. Mid. (Soph., Phil 282; Pla., Theag.

129e; Diod. S. 11, 40, 1; Jos., Ant. 4, 198; 7, 341 τῷ παιδί; PGiss 25, 4 συλλαμβανόμενός μοι; PTebt 448 συλλαβοῦ αὐτῷ; Gen 30:8; s. New Docs 4, 56) *come to the help of* τινί *someone* **Lk 5:7** (βοηθεῖν v.l.); **Phil 4:3.**—M-M. TW.

συλλέγω (λέγω 'gather') fut. συλλέξω; 1 aor. συνέλεξα. Pass.: aor. ptc. gen. pl. συλλεγέντων 3 Macc 1:21; plpf. 3 sg. συνελέλεκτο Jdth 4:3 (Hom. et al.; ins, pap, LXX; Jos., Vi. 119, Ant. 5, 240 τὸν καρπόν; SibOr 8, 55; Just., A I, 67, 6) **to gather by plucking or picking,** ***collect, gather (in), pick*** τι *someth.* weeds **Mt 13:28–30.** Pass. vs. **40.** The place to which what is gathered is taken is indicated by εἰς vs. **48;** the place fr. which it is removed is indicated by ἐκ vs. **41** (σκάνδαλον 3). Hence also ἐξ ἀκανθῶν συλλ. **Lk 6:44** (on the indefinite pl. s. Rydbeck 40); also ἀπὸ ἀκανθῶν **Mt 7:16.**—M-M.

σύλλημμα, ατοσ, τό med. term since Galen (συλλαμβάνω) ***that which is conceived and is in the womb, fetus*** σύλλημμα ἔχει ἐκ πνεύματος ἁγίου *(Mary) is pregnant through the Holy Spirit* GJs 19:1.—DELG s.v. λαμβάνω.

σύλληψις, εως, ἡ (in var. senses since V BC; ins., pap, LXX, Philo; Just., A I, 25, 6) of pregnancy ***conception*** GJs 19:1 Tdf. (for σύλλημμα).

συλλογίζομαι fut. 3 sg. συλλογιεῖται LXX; 1 aor. συνελογισάμην; fut. 3 sg. pass. συλλογισθήσεται Num 23:9 (Hdt. et al.; ins, pap, LXX) **to ponder or discuss various possibilities relating to a matter,** ***reason, discuss, debate*** (Pla., Demosth., Polyb.; Is 43:18; Philo, Leg. All. 2, 99; Jos., Bell. 1, 560; 4, 125) πρὸς ἑαυτόν *to oneself* (Plut., Pomp. 651 [60, 3]) or pl. *among themselves* **Lk 20:5.**—DELG s.v. λέγω. M-M. Spicq. Sv.

συλλυπέω (act. 'to feel hurt or grief with someone or at the same time' Aristot., EN 1171b, 7) in our lit. pass. in an act. sense ***be grieved with, feel sympathy*** (Hdt. et al.; Diod. S. 4, 11, 2; Is 51:19); in συλλυπούμενος ἐπὶ τῇ πωρώσει τῆς καρδίας αὐτῶν **Mk 3:5** the prep. surely has no other force than to strengthen the simple verb *deeply grieved at the hardening of their heart.*—DELG s.v. λύπη. TW.

συμβαίνω impf. συνέβαινον; fut. συμβήσομαι; 2 aor. συνέβην; pf. συμβέβηκα (Aeschyl., Hdt.+)

❶ **to join someone in going somewhere,** ***go along with*** of Paul who went on shipboard with others AcPl Ha 5, 17 (cp. 5, 15 ἀνέβη).

❷ **to occur as event or process,** ***happen, come about*** (trag., Hdt. +) συμβαίνει τί τινι (trag., Thu. et al.; TestSim 2:13) **Mk 10:32** (w. ref. to death: last will and testament of Aristot. in Diog. L. 5, 11; 12); **Ac 20:19; 1 Cor 10:11; 1 Pt 4:12; 2 Pt 2:22;** 1 Cl 23:3 (scripture quot. of unknown origin); B 19:6; D 3:10. οὕτως συμβαίνει πᾶσι Hm 5, 2, 7. οὕτως κἀμοὶ συνέβη *the same thing has happened to me* GJs 13:1. καθὼς φρονοῦσιν καὶ συμβήσεται αὐτοῖς *in accordance w. their opinions, so the outcome shall be for them* ISm 2. W. inf. foll. (Hdt. 6, 103 al.; ins; POxy 491, 10; Ar. 8, 6; Just., D. 23, 1) Hv 3, 7, 6. συνέβη foll. by acc. and inf. (Hdt. 7, 166 al.; SIG 535, 5; 685, 36f; 1 Esdr 1:23; Jos., Ant. 9, 185; Mel., HE 4, 26, 9; Ath. 5, 1) συνέβη βαστάζεσθαι αὐτὸν ὑπὸ τῶν στρατιωτῶν **Ac 21:35** (B-D-F §393, 5; 408; Rob. 392; 1043); εἰς οὐδὲν δὲ συνέβη τελευτῆσαι (τελέσαι v.l.) τὴν τάξιν αὐτῶν *but it came to pass that finally their* (the angels') *status was terminated* Papias (4).—τὸ συμβεβηκός τινι *what has happened to someone* (Sus 26 Theod.; TestJob 1:6 al. [pl.]; Jos., Vi. 51; Just., D. 78, 8) **Ac 3:10.** Sing., without the dat. τὸ συμβάν *what had happened* (Epict. 3, 24, 13; Appian, Hann. 36 §154; TestSol 1:4 [pl.]; Agatharchides: 86 fgm. 20, 211 Jac. [in Jos., C. Ap. 1, 211]; cp. Jos., Ant. 13, 413 τὰ ξυμβάντα) GPt 14:59. Pl. τὰ συμβεβηκότα *the things that had happened* (Isocr. 5, 18; 1 Macc 4:26; EpArist; Jos., Bell. 4, 43, Ant. 13, 194) **Lk 24:14.**—M-M.

συμβάλλω impf. συνέβαλλον; 2 aor. συνέβαλον; pf. συμβέβληκα. Mid.: 2 aor. συνεβαλόμην; pf. 3 sg. συμβέβληται Wsd 5:8. Pass.: aor. 3 sg. συνεβλήθη Sir 22:1f (Hom. et al.; ins, pap, LXX; TestGad 4:4)

❶ **to engage in mutual pondering of a matter,** ***converse, confer*** (w. λόγους added Eur., Iphig. Aul. 830; without λ. Plut., Mor. 222c) τινί *with someone* (Epict. 4, 12, 7; Iambl., Vi. Pyth. 2, 12; PFay 129, 2) **Ac 17:18.** πρὸς ἀλλήλους **4:15.**

❷ **to give careful thought to,** ***consider, ponder*** (Pla., Crat. 384a μαντείαν; Philo, In Flacc. 139; Jos., Ant. 2, 72 συμβαλὼν τῷ λογισμῷ τὸ ὄναρ) τὰ ῥήματα συμβάλλουσα ἐν τῇ καρδίᾳ αὐτῆς **Lk 2:19** (cp. our colloquial 'get it all together').

❸ **to draw a conclusion by comparing,** ***compare*** (Hdt. et al.; pap; Sir 22:1f; Jos., Ant. 1, 105) τινά τινι *someone with someth.* ἑαυτὸν ξύλῳ 1 Cl 23:4=2 Cl 11:3 (quot. of unknown orig.).

❹ **to come together at a point,** ***meet, fall in with*** (Hom. et al.; pap) τινί *someone* (on a journey; cp. Jos., Ant. 1, 219; 2, 184; Just., D. 68, 1; 80, 4) **Ac 20:14.** Cp. MPol 8:1.

❺ **to come into conflict w. someone**—ⓐ ***engage, fight someone*** τινί (Polyb. 1, 9, 7; 3, 111, 1 al.; Mitt-Wilck. I/2, 16, 6; 1 Macc 4:34; 2 Macc 8:23; 14:17) εἰς πόλεμον *meet someone in battle, wage war on someone* **Lk 14:31** (cp. εἰς μάχην Polyb. 3, 56, 6; Jos., Bell. 1, 191, Ant. 12, 342; πρὸς μάχην Polyb. 10, 37, 4).

ⓑ ***quarrel, dispute*** τινί *with someone* (PSI 93, 4 συνέβαλον τοῖς ἐπιτρόποις) συμβάλλειν αὐτῷ περὶ πλειόνων *quarrel with him about many things* **Lk 11:53 v.l.**

❻ **to be of assistance,** ***help, be of assistance,*** mid. (Philo, Migr. Abr. 219; Just., D. 46, 7) τινί *(to) someone* (Pla.; Demosth. 21, 133; Antiphon 5, 79 p. 138, 37 πολλὰ συμβ. τοῖς βουλομένοις; Polyb. 2, 13, 1; Epict. 3, 22, 78 πλειόνά τινι σ.; PLond VI, 1915, 13; Wsd 5:8; Jos., Ant. 12, 312; Ar. [Milne 74, 22]; Tat. 24, 1) Apollos συνεβάλετο πολὺ τοῖς πεπιστευκόσιν **Ac 18:27.** συνεβάλλοντο . . . πάντες οἱ ἀδελφοὶ ὡς μηδὲν λυπηθῆναι Παῦλον *all the fellowship were helping* (as much as possible). . . *that Paul should not be grieved* AcPl Ha 7, 17.—M-M s.v. συνβάλλω. EDNT.

συμβασιλεύω fut. συμβασιλεύσω (Polyb. 30, 2, 4; Dionys. Hal., Strabo; Lucian, Dial. Deor. 16, 2; Plut., Lyc. 42 [5, 5], Num. 61 [3, 6], Anton. 941 [54, 4]; 1 Esdr 8:26 v.l.) **to reign jointly,** ***rule (as king) with someone*** in imagery of the eschatological situation when Christians are to share kingship w. their royal Lord **2 Ti 2:12;** Pol 5:2. Paul ironically states that the Corinthians have achieved kingship; he wishes they had achieved it because then he would be reigning with them; actually he was still enduring a miserable life (cp. vs. 9) **1 Cor 4:8.**—DELG s.v. βασιλεύς. M-M s.v. συνβασιλεύω. TW.

συμβιβάζω fut. συμβιβάσω, Att. συμβιβῶ Ps 31:8; 1 aor. συνεβίβασα, pass. ptc. συμβιβασθείς (βιβάζω 'cause to go'; Hdt. et al.; ins, LXX).

❶ **to bring together into a unit,** ***unite***—ⓐ lit., of the body, which is *held together* by sinews, ligaments, joints τὸ σῶμα συμβιβαζόμενον διὰ πάσης ἁφῆς **Eph 4:16** (GWhitaker, JTS 31, 1930, 48f); cp. **Col 2:19.**

ⓑ fig. *unite, knit together* (Hdt. 1, 74; Thu. 2, 29, 6; Pla., Prot. 337e) pass. συμβιβασθέντες ἐν ἀγάπῃ **Col 2:2** (so Lghtf. et al., NRSV. But s. 4 below).

❷ **to draw a conclusion in the face of evidence,** ***conclude, infer*** (Pla., Hipp. Min. 369d, Rep. 6, 504a) **Ac 16:10** (w. ὅτι foll.).

❸ **to present a logical conclusion,** ***demonstrate, prove*** (Aristot., Top. 7, 5, 150a, 36 [ὅτι]; 8, 3, 154b, 27; 8, 11, 157b, 37; Iambl., Vi. Pyth. 13, 60) συμβιβάζων ὅτι οὗτός ἐστιν ὁ Χριστός **Ac 9:22.**

❹ **to advise by giving instructions,** ***instruct, teach, advise*** τινά *someone* (LXX) **1 Cor 2:16** (Is 40:13f); **Ac 19:33** (vv.ll. προεβίβασαν, κατεβίβασαν; difft. PLampe, BZ 36, '92, 72–74).—Some (e.g. MDibelius, Mft.) classify **Col 2:2** here (s. 1b above).—DELG s.v. βαίνω. M-M. s.v. συνβιβάζω. TW.

σύμβιος, ον 'living together' (Aristot. et al.; TestJud 23:3; TestIss 7:2 v.l. [for γυναικός]; Philo, Poster. Cai. 78) subst. 'companion' then esp. ὁ, ἡ σ. ***husband, wife*** (ins and oft. in pap; New Docs 1 no. 18, 18) IPol 5:1 MMacDonald, NTS 40, '94, 105–25; Hv 2, 2, 3.

συμβουλεύω fut. συμβουλεύσω LXX; 1 aor. συνεβούλευσα (s. four next entries; Theognis, trag., Hdt.+)

❶ **to give advice on a course of action,** ***advise,*** act. τινί someone (Ex 18:19; Jos., C. Ap. 1, 309a; Just., D. 56, 8) **J 18:14.** τινί τι *advise someone (to do) someth.* (Hdt. 7, 237 al.; 3 Km 1:12 συμβουλεύσω σοι συμβουλίαν) MPol 8:2. W. dat. and inf. foll. (Hdt. et al.; BGU 1097, 8 [I AD]; 4 Macc 8:29; Jos., Ant. 12, 384; Tat. 27, 2) **Rv 3:18.** Abs. (Diog. L. 1, 92a; Jos., Bell. 2, 345) 2 Cl 15:1.

❷ **to be involved with others in plotting a course of action,** ***consult, plot,*** mid. (Jos., Ant. 8, 379; TestJud 13:4) w. ἵνα foll. **Mt 26:4; J 11:53 v.l.** Foll. by inf. of purpose **Ac 9:23.**

❸ **to give careful thought to someth.,** ***meditate on, consider,*** mid. (PPetr II, 13, 6, 12; PSI 236, 30) τὶ *someth.* Hv 1, 2, 2.—DELG s.v. βούλομαι. M-M.

συμβουλή, ῆς, ἡ ***advice, counsel*** (s. prec. and three next entries; Hdt. 1, 157 al.; TestSol; GrBar 3:5 σ. δοῦναι; Philo, Fuga 24; Jos., Ant. 19, 192) δέχεσθαι σ. *accept advice* 1 Cl 58:2.—DELG s.v. βούλομαι.

συμβουλία, ας, ἡ ***advice, counsel*** (s. two prec. and two next entries; Hdt. et al.; ins, pap, LXX, Philo; Jos., Ant. 5, 336; 8, 277 al.) συμβουλίαν ποιεῖσθαι περί τινος *give advice about someth.* (Diod. S. 12, 17, 2) 2 Cl 15:1. γνώμης ἀγαθῆς λαμβάνειν συμβουλίαν *accept well-meant advice* B 21:2 (cp. Vi. Aesopi I, 26 Eb. συμβ. λαμβάνειν).—DELG s.v. βούλομαι.

συμβούλιον, ου, τό (s. three prec. entries and next; Plut., Cass. Dio et al.; ins [since II BC]; pap.—Dssm., NB 65 [BS 238])

❶ **the act of consulting or conferring,** ***consultation, meeting*** σ. ἐγένετο τῶν ἱερέων GJs 8:2; cp. 10:1.

❷ **meeting of an official deliberative assembly,** ***council session, meeting*** (Plut., Rom. 25 [14, 3], Luc. 509 [26, 4]; BGU 288, 14 [II AD]; 511 I, 20; PRyl 75, 29) συμβούλιον ἄγειν *convene a council* IPol 7:2. On the restoration [εἰς τὸ συμ]β[ο]ύλιον ἄγεσθαι AcPl BMM verso 19f, see Sander's note p. 89.

❸ **the result reached by a deliberating group,** ***plan, purpose*** σ. λαμβάνειν a Latinism = consilium capere (B-D-F §5, 3b, cp. a; Rob. 109.—Jos., Ant. 6, 38 βουλὰς λ.) *form a plan, decide, consult, plot* **Mt 12:14; 22:15; 27:1, 7; 28:12.** In the same sense σ. διδόναι (s. IHeikel, StKr 106, '35, 314) **Mk 3:6** (v.l. ποιεῖν); σ. ἑτοιμάζειν *reach a decision* **15:1 v.l.;** συμβούλιον ποιεῖν vs. **1.**—ASherwin-White, Roman Society and Roman Law in the NT, '63, 44f.

❹ **an official deliberative assembly as a body,** ***council*** (ins, pap; 4 Macc 17:17; Jos., Ant. 14, 192; 16, 163.—Mommsen, Röm. Staatsrecht[3] 1887 I 307ff; II 249; Schürer I 370 n. 80 [sources and lit.]) Φῆστος συλλαλήσας μετὰ τοῦ συμβουλίου **Ac 25:12.**—M-M.

σύμβουλος, ου, ὁ (s. four prec. entries; trag., Hdt.+) ***adviser, counsellor*** **Ro 11:34** (Is 40:13); B 21:4; Dg 9:6; Hs 5, 2, 6; 5, 4, 1; 5, 5, 3; 5, 6, 4; 7; 9, 12, 2.—M-M.

Συμεών, ὁ indecl. Semitic (שִׁמְעוֹן) name (for which the similar-sounding genuine Gk. name Σίμων [q.v.] is sometimes substituted; B-D-F §53, 2d; Mlt-H. 146.—LXX, Philo, Test12Patr, JosAs; Demetr.: 722 fgm. 1, 3 al. In Joseph. Συμεών, ῶνος: Bell. 4, 159, Ant. 12, 265; Preisigke, Namenbuch) ***Symeon, Simeon.***

❶ son of Jacob (Gen 29:33.—49:5; Jdth 9:2; 4 Macc 2:19). Ancestor of the tribe of the same name (Jdth 6:15; ViHab 1 [p. 85, 19 Sch.]) **Rv 7:7.**

❷ in the genealogy of Jesus **Lk 3:30.**

❸ a devout man in Jerusalem **Lk 2:25, 34.** In GJs 24:4 successor of Zacharias; 10:2 v.l. (for Σαμουήλ).

❹ *Simeon* surnamed Niger, named w. other teachers and prophets of the church at Antioch **Ac 13:1.**

❺ The original name of the apostle Peter (s. Σίμων 1) is occasionally written in this way **Ac 15:14** (SGiet, L'Assemblée apostolique et le Décret de Jérusalem—Qui était Siméon?: RSR 39, '51/52, 203–20). Συμεὼν (v.l. Σίμων) Πέτρος **2 Pt 1:1.**—M-M.

συμμαθητής, οῦ, ὁ (Pla., Euthyd. 1, 272c; Anaxippus Com. [IV BC] 1, 2 vol. III p. 296 K.; Diog. L. 6, 2; Ps.-Callisth. 1, 13, 5; Pollux 6, 159) ***fellow-pupil, fellow-disciple*** **J 11:16;** MPol 17:3.—DELG s.v. μανθάνω. M-M. s.v. συνμαθητής. TW.

συμμαρτυρέω (Soph., Thu. et al.) 'to testify' or 'bear witness with' (Plut., Thes. et Romul. 6, 5, Mor. 64c; BGU 86, 40 [II AD] al.), then also gener. **to provide supporting evidence by testifying,** ***confirm, support by testimony*** (as early as Solon 24, 3 D.[2] the prefix συν- has in the highest degree the effect of strengthening. Likewise trag. et al.; Pla., Hipp. Major 282b συμμαρτυρῆσαι δέ σοι ἔχω ὅτι ἀληθῆ λέγεις; X., Hell. 7, 1, 35 συνεμαρτύρει αὐτῷ ταῦτα πάντα; 3, 3, 2; Jos., Ant. 19, 154. Without dat. and w. ὅτι foll. Plut., Mor. 724d) συμμαρτυρούσης αὐτῶν τῆς συνειδήσεως **Ro 2:15.** συμμαρτυρούσης μοι τῆς συνειδήσεώς μου … ὅτι **9:1** (on the witness of the conscience Jos., C. Ap. 2, 218). τὸ πνεῦμα συμμαρτυρεῖ τῷ πνεύματι ἡμῶν ὅτι **8:16.**—The mid. **Rv 22:18** t.r. (Erasmian rdg.).—DELG s.v. μάρτυς. M-M. s.v. συνμαρτυρέω. TW.

συμμαχέω fut. συμμαχήσω LXX; aor. 3 pl. συνεμάχησαν 1 Ch 12:22. Prim. 'fight at someone's side, be an ally'. In our lit. in the gener. sense ***help, assist*** (Aeschyl., Hdt.+; ins; POxy 705, 33; LXX; TestSol 6:4 P; TestJud 7:6; ApcSed 8:5 p. 133, 4 Ja. [συμμαχᾷ]; Jos., C. Ap. 1, 236 σ. τινί, Ant. 1, 313) τὰ συμμαχοῦντα ἡμῖν (w. βοηθοί) B 2:2.—DELG s.v. μάχομαι.

συμμείγνυμι (frequently written συμμίγνυμι) 1 aor. συνέμιξα LXX. Pass.: fut. 3 pl. συμμιγήσονται Da 11:6 Theod.; 2 aor. ptc. συμμιγείς (since Hom. [συμμίσγω]; ins, pap., LXX) 'mix together' pass. **to be united sexually,** ***join with*** (Hdt. 4, 114; Pla., Symp. 207b, Laws 930d) ApcPt 9:24.

συμμερίζω (Diod. S.; Dionys. Hal.; Diog. L. et al.) mid. **συμμερίζομαι** (IHierapJ 336, 11; Eutecnius 2 p. 23, 12) **to receive a portion in association with,** ***share with*** τινί *someone* or *someth.* (Pr 29:24 v.l. ὃς συμμερίζεται κλέπτῃ; Philopon. in

Aristot., De An. p. 417, 35 H.) τῷ θυσιαστηρίῳ συμμερίζονται *they share with the altar* in the things sacrificed on it **1 Cor 9:13.**—DELG s.v. μείρομαι II μέρος. M-M. s.v. συνμερίζω.

συμμέτοχος, ον (συμμετέχω 'to share in the possession of someth.'; Aristot., Plant. 1, 1; Jos., Bell. 1, 486 συμμέτοχοι τοῦ σκέμματος αὐτῷ; PLond V, 1733, 52; Just., A II, 13, 4) **having a share with another in some possession or relationship,** ***sharing with*** *someone* τινός in *someth.* **Eph 3:6.** Prob. subst. συμμέτοχοι αὐτῶν *sharing with them, casting one's lot with them* **5:7** (s. B-D-F §182, 1; difft., but less prob. HNT ad loc.).—DELG s.v. ἔχω 4. M-M. s.v. συνμέτοχος. TW.

συμμιμητής, οῦ, ὁ one who joins others as an imitator, ***fellow-imitator*** w. obj. gen. foll. συμμιμηταί μου γίνεσθε *join* (w. the others) *in following my example* **Phil 3:17.**—DELG s.v. μῖμος. M-M. s.v. συνμιμητής. TW.

συμμορφίζω (only in Christian wr. but=συμμορφόω below) **to cause to be similar in form or style to someth. else,** ***grant*** or ***invest w. the same form as,*** pass. συμμορφίζεσθαί τινι *be conformed to, take on the same form as* τῷ θανάτῳ αὐτοῦ=the style of Christ's death, i.e. to be like Christ in his death **Phil 3:10.**—DELG s.v. μορφή. M-M. TW.

σύμμορφος, ον (s. prec. and next entry; Ps.-Lucian, Amor. 39 al.) **pert. to having a similar form, nature, or style,** ***similar in form*** τινός *as* or *to someth.* (σ. τοῦ θανάτου αὐτοῦ Orig., C. Cels. 2, 69, 16; B-D-F §182, 1; Rob. 504; 528) σύμμ. τῆς εἰκόνος τοῦ υἱοῦ αὐτοῦ *like his Son in form* or *appearance* **Ro 8:29** (JKürzinger, BZ 2, '58, 294–99). Also w. the dat. (Nicander [II BC], Ther. 321 ed. OSchneider [1856]; Heraclit. Sto. 77 p. 102, 12 σ. τρισὶ θεοῖς of Agamemnon; B-D-F §194, 2; Rob. 528) σύμμ. τῷ σώματι τῆς δόξης αὐτοῦ **Phil 3:21.**—DELG s.v. μορφή. TW.

συμμορφόω 'to give the same form', pass. ***take on the same form*** (s. two prec. entries; Libanius, Descript. 30, 5 vol. VIII 542, 10 F.; Menand. Protector [VI AD]: HGM II p. 67, 8) **Phil 3:10 v.l.**—DELG s.v. μορφή.

συμμύστης, ου, ὁ (cp. μύω 'close', esp. eyes) **one who has been initiated into the same mysteries,** ***fellow-initiate*** (IG XII/8, 173, 13 [66 BC]; OGI 541, 9 οἱ τῶν τῆς θεοῦ μυστηρίων συνμύσται; PGM 4, 732; 12, 94.—Poland 39), fig. of the Christians in Ephesus Παύλου συμμύσται *fellow-initiates of Paul* IEph 12:2. Note the apostolic church discipline in AHilgenfeld, NT Extra Canonem Receptum[2] IV 1884 p. 117, 7: the presbyters are the συμμύσται of the bishop; Origen, Hom. 7, 2 in Lev., Hom. 7 in Jos.—DELG s.v. μύω.

συμπαθέω 1 aor. συνεπάθησα; impv. 2 sg. mid. συμπάθησαι (ApcSed 16:3) **to have/show sympathy with,** ***sympathize with*** (s. next entry; Isocr. et al.; Plut., Timol. 242 [14, 1]; 4 Macc 13:23; Jos., Ant. 16, 404; TestSim 3:6; TestBenj 4:4; ApcSed 16:3 τοὺς ἁμαρτουλούς; SibOr 11, 58; Jos., Ant. 16, 404; Mel., P. 24, 172) w. dat. of pers. or thing that is the obj. of the sympathy (Isocr. 4, 112 v.l.; Dionys. Hal. 10, 6 τῷ ἀνδρί; Plut., Mor. 90f; Philo, Spec. Leg. 2, 115; TestBenj 4:4; 4 Macc 5:25; Just., D. 38, 2; Mel., P. 46, 328): w. dat. of thing ταῖς ἀσθενείαις ἡμῶν **Hb 4:15** (cp. Philistion [Com. II no. 230 Kock] ἐκ τοῦ παθεῖν γίγνωσκε καὶ τὸ συμπαθεῖν. καὶ σοὶ γὰρ ἄλλος συμπαθήσεται παθών); **10:34 v.l.** (δεσμοῖς); w. dat. of pers., **10:34** (δεσμίοις); IRo 6:3. τῇ γραΐδι AcPt Ox 849 verso, 5–6.—WBurkert, Zum altgriech. Mitleidsbegriff, diss. Erlangen '55, 63–66. Cp. the visage of Darius, filled w. concern for a fellow-officer, in the Alexander mosaic fr. Pompeii: LCurtius, Die Wandmalerei Pompejis '60 (1929) 323–35.—DELG s.v. πάσχω. M-M. s.v. συνπαθέω. TW. Spicq.

συμπαθής, ές (since Eur., s. below; Aristot. et al.; CIG 9438; OGI 456, 66; LXX, Philo) ***sympathetic, understanding*** (Eur., TGF 164 ἄριστον ἀνδρὶ κτῆμα συμπαθὴς γυνή='the best thing for a husband is an understanding wife'; Polyb. 2, 56, 7; 8, 22, 9; Plut., Eum. 594 [18, 5], Mor. 536a; Jos., Ant. 19, 330) **1 Pt 3:8.**—TW. Spicq.

συμπαραγίνομαι mid. dep.; 2 aor. συμπαρεγενόμην.

❶ *come together* (Hdt. et al.; PSI 502, 24 [III BC]; Ps 82:9) ἐπὶ τὴν θεωρίαν ταύτην *for this spectacle* **Lk 23:48.**

❷ *come to the aid of* (Thu. 2, 82; 6, 92, 5) τινί *someone* **2 Ti 4:16 v.l.** (for παρεγένετο).—DELG s.v. γίγνομαι. M-M. s.v. συνπαραγίνομαι.

συμπαρακαλέω (X., Pla. et al.) ***encourage together*** (Polyb. 5, 83, 3) pass. συμπαρακληθῆναι ἐν ὑμῖν *receive encouragement* or *comfort together with you* **Ro 1:12.**

συμπαραλαμβάνω 2 aor. συμπαρέλαβον; 1 aor. pass. subj. 2 sg. συμπαραλημφθῇς Gen 19:17 (Pla. et al.; pap, LXX; PsSol 13:5; TestJob 15:3) ***take along with*** oneself τινά *someone* (PLond II, 358, 6 p. 172 [150 AD]; BGU 226, 12; Job 1:4; 3 Macc 1:1; Jos., Ant. 9, 7) prob. as bureaucratic parlance (s. papyri above) ***take along as adjunct*** **Ac 12:25; 15:37f; Gal 2:1.**—M-M.

συμπαραμένω fut. συμπαραμενῶ (Thu. et al.; PSI 64, 3 [I BC]; Ps 71:5) ***stay with someone to help*** w. dat. of pers. (Thu. 6, 89, 4; SIG 567 A, 12f) πᾶσιν ὑμῖν **Phil 1:25 v.l.**

συμπάρειμι ***to be in a place together with others, be together, be present with*** (X., Lac. 2, 2 al.; ins, pap, LXX; TestSol) τινί *someone* (SIG 685, 28 [139 BC]; PSI 439, 29; Jos., Ant. 10, 239) οἱ συμπαρόντες ἡμῖν *all who are here present with us* **Ac 25:24;** *be present (together) with* τινί *someone* (Jos., Ant. 11, 322) of ecclesial representatives ITr 12:1.—DELG s.v. εἰμί. M-M. s.v. συνπάρειμι.

σύμπας, ασα, αν (Hom. et al.) ***all (together), whole,*** ὁ σύμπας κόσμος 1 Cl 19:2 (Diod. S. 3, 61, 5; 6; Just., A I, 19, 5; cp. En. 102:2 ἡ γῆ σύμπασα) τὰ σύμπαντα B 15:4.

συμπάσχω 2 aor. συνέπαθον—❶ **to have the same thing happen to one,** ***suffer with,*** also ***suffer the same thing as*** (Pla., Charm. 169c) w. the dat. (Epict. 1, 14, 2; IG XIV/2, 124, 3 [c. 200 AD]; POxy 904, 7 ἅμα μοι συνπαθεῖν; Herm. Wr. 494, 1 Sc.; Philo, De Prov. in Eus., PE 8, 14, 23; TestZeb 7:5; TestBenj 4:4 v.l.; sim. use of the dat. in 2 below) αὐτῷ (='Ιησοῦ Χριστῷ) ISm 4:2; cp. Pol 9:2. Abs., but also of suffering w. Christ **Ro 8:17.**—συμπάσχει πάντα τὰ μέλη w. one part of the body that suffers **1 Cor 12:26** (Diod. S. 18, 42, 4 συμπασχόντων ἁπάντων τῶν μελῶν=all the members [of the σῶμα] are involved in suffering [or exertion] together; Diog. L. 2, 94 τὴν ψυχὴν συμπαθεῖν τῷ σώματι. Cp. Maximus Tyr. 28, 2c; Alex. Aphr., An. p. 100, 3 Br. πάντα τὰ μόρια ἀλλήλοις ἐστὶν ἐν τῷ σώματι συμπαθῆ; Philo, Spec. Leg. 3, 194; Plut., Solon 88 [18, 6] τ. πολίτας ὥσπερ ἑνὸς σώματος μέρη συναισθάνεσθαι κ. συναλγεῖν ἀλλήλοις).

❷ **to have understanding or sensitivity for others esp. in their troubles,** ***have sympathy for*** τινί (Polyb.; Diod. S. 17, 36, 3 τοῖς ἠτυχηκόσιν; Plut.) IRo 6:3. συμπάσχειν ἀλλήλοις 2 Cl 4:3; IPol 6:1.—M-M. s.v. συνπάσχω. TW.

συμπέμπω 1 aor. συνέπεμψα (Pind., Hdt.+; ins, pap; Jos., C. Ap. 1, 48; Just., D. 56, 17 [v. l. for συμπροπέμπων Gen 18:16]) **to send someone together with someone else,** ***send with or at the same time*** τινά τινι (Hdt. et al.; PCairZen 230, 4 [253 BC]; Mitt-Wilck. I/2, 11 A, 47 [123 BC]) **2 Cor 8:22.** Also τινὰ μετά τινος (cp. X., Hell. 1, 4, 21) vs. **18.**—M-M. s.v. συνπέμπω.

συμπεριέχω (Dionys. Hal. 3, 43) **to be closely packed in a position around,** ***stand around/together*** w. κύκλῳ added **Lk 12:1** D.

συμπεριλαμβάνω fut. 2 sg. συμπεριλήμψῃ Ezk 5:3; 2 aor. ptc. συμπεριλαβών (Pla., Aristot. et al.; ins, pap; Jos., C. Ap. 2, 32) **to throw one's arms around,** ***embrace*** w. acc. to be supplied **Ac 20:10** (like X., An. 7, 4, 10 περιλαβὼν τὸν παῖδα).—M-M.

συμπίνω 2 aor. συνέπιον (Hdt., Aristoph. et al.; Esth 7:1 συμπιεῖν τῇ βασιλίσσῃ; Jos., Vi. 224 ἡμῖν; Just.) ***drink with*** (beside συνεσθίειν as SIG 1179, 18f) τινί *someone* **Ac 10:41** (Just., D. 51, 2 συμπιεῖν πάλιν καὶ συμφαγεῖν); ISm 3:3.—M-M. s.v. συνεσθίω.

συμπίπτω 2 aor. συνέπεσον; pf. συμπέπτωκα LXX (Hom.+; ins, pap, LXX; TestJob 40:12; Test12Patr; JosAs 18:3; Joseph.) 'fall together'.

❶ **to fall together in a heap,** ***fall in, collapse*** (trag.; Thu. 8, 41, 2; Diod. S. 19, 45, 2 houses as a result of a downfall of rain and hail; Jos., Bell. 1, 331 οἶκος; OGI 595, 15; 28; PMagd 9, 3; POxy 75, 27 al. in pap; Sb 5109, 2 [I AD] οἰκίας συμπεπτωκυίας) **Lk 6:49.**

❷ **to experience inward breakdown** fig. ext. of 1—ⓐ (1 Macc 6:10 συνπέπτωκα τῇ καρδίᾳ ἀπὸ τῆς μερίμνης; TestZeb 10:1) ***collapse*** fr. fright MPol 12:1.

ⓑ in OT expression συνέπεσεν τὸ πρόσωπον ***his countenance fell, has become distorted = he was downcast*** 1 Cl 4:3, 4 (Gen 4:5 [συνέπεσεν τῷ προσώπῳ], 6; cp. TestJos 7:2; JosAs cod. A 18 [p. 67, 11f and 14 Bat.; also cod. Pal. 364]).—M-M. s.v. συνπίπτω.

συμπληρόω impf. pass. συνεπληρούμην (Hdt.+; ins, pap; TestSol 22:7; Philo, Joseph.; Just., D. 32, 3; Ath. 8, 1; 18, 3, R. 4 p. 52, 7) 'fill up, fill completely'. In our lit. only pass. 'become quite full'.

❶ **to fill completely** of a ship (equipped w. sailors: Arrian, Anab. 1, 19, 10; Menand. Ephes.: 783 fgm. 4, 285 Jac. [in Jos., Ant. 9, 285]) that is being filled w. water in a storm ***be swamped*** συνεπληροῦντο *they were being swamped* **Lk 8:23.**

❷ fig., of time **to arrive as the timely moment for an event to take place,** ***fulfill, approach, come*** (πληρόω 2.—Herodian 7, 4, 1; BGU 1122, 22 [13 BC] ἐπὶ τοῦ συμπληρωθῆναι τοῦτον [τὸν χρόνον]; Jer 25:12 v.l.; Jos., Ant. 4, 176) ἐν τῷ συμπληροῦσθαι τὰς ἡμέρας τῆς ἀναλήμψεως *when the days of his* ἀνάλημψις (q.v.) *were approaching* **Lk 9:51.** ἐν τῷ συνπληροῦσθαι τὴν ἡμέραν τῆς πεντηκοστῆς *when the day of Pentecost had come* **Ac 2:1** (so NRSV, REB; s. JRopes, HTR 16, 1923, 168–75).—M-M. s.v. συνπληρόω. TW.

συμπλοκή, ῆς, ἡ (Pla. et al.; ins; Philo, Rer. Div. Her. 198; Jos., Bell. 4, 423) gener. 'intertwining'; in our lit. only in the sexual sense ***intimate embrace, intercourse*** (Pla., Symp. 191c; Aristot., HA 5, 5; Cornutus 24 p. 45, 9) μιαραὶ κ. ἄναγναι συμπλοκαί 1 Cl 30:1 (cp. Achilles Tat. 7, 5, 4 μεμιασμένας συμπλοκάς).—DELG s.v. πλέκω. Sv.

συμπνέω (Aeschyl. et al.; pap; lit. 'breathe with') **to be in a harmonious relationship,** ***agree, coincide, coalesce*** (Polyb. 30, 2, 8 συμπ. καὶ μιᾷ γνώμῃ χρῆσθαι; Plut.; Herodian; Herm. Wr. 10, 17; BGU 1024, 8, 20; Philo, Conf. Lingu. 69; Jos., Ant. 7, 105) 1 Cl 37:5.

συμπνίγω impf. συνέπνιγον; 1 aor. συνέπνιξα (Jos., Ant. 12, 275 v.l.)

❶ **to check the growth or well-being of someth. by pressure,** ***choke*** of plants whose food and light is cut off by weeds that crowd together and choke (Theophr., CP 6, 11, 6 δένδρα συμπνιγόμενα) **Mk 4:7.** In imagery in the interpr. of the parable τὸν λόγον **Mt 13:22; Mk 4:19.** Pass. **Lk 8:14.**

❷ as a hyperbolic expr. for ***crowd around, press upon,*** someth. like *almost crush* (Goodsp.) οἱ ὄχλοι συνέπνιγον αὐτόν **Lk 8:42.** ἀλλήλους **12:1** D.—TW.

συμπολιτεύομαι 1 aor. συνεπολιτευσάμην ***live in the same state, be a fellow-citizen/compatriot*** (s. next entry; Thu. et al. in the act. The mid. in Aeschin. 1, 17; Isocr. 3, 4; 5, 20 al.; Epict. 3, 22, 99; ins, pap) τινί *of* or *as someone* (Diod. S. 5, 58, 2; OGI 504, 6 συνπεπολιτευμένος ἡμεῖν; Jos., Ant. 19, 306) MPol 22:2; EpilMosq 1.—DELG s.v. πόλις. M-M. s.v. συνπολίτης.

συμπολίτης, ου, ὁ (s. prec. entry; Eur., Her. 826; Aelian, VH 3, 44; TestJob 16:5; 18:2; Jos., Ant. 19, 175; IG XIV, 1878; pap) ***fellow-citizen/compatriot*** fig. When gentiles believe the Good News, they become συμπολῖται τῶν ἁγίων *fellow-citizens of God's people* and, as Christians, are members of God's household (οἰκεῖοι τοῦ θεοῦ) **Eph 2:19** (cp. 5:5).—M-M.

συμπορεύομαι dep. impf. συνεπορευόμην; fut. συμπορεύσομαι LXX; aor. συνεπορεύθην

❶ **to be in movement together with one or more persons,** ***go (along) with*** (Eur.; Pla.; PSI 353, 13 [III BC]; LXX, Test12Patr) τινί *someone* (Pla., Phdr. 249c; PEdg 42 [=Sb 6748], 2 [253/252 BC]; Tob 5:3, 9; TestZeb 7:4) **Lk 7:11; 14:25; 24:15.**

❷ **to gather with others in the same place,** ***come together, flock*** (Polyb. 5, 6, 1 πρός τινα; 6, 16, 4 al.; Plut., Eum. 591 [13, 8]; ins; Dt 31:11; Job 1:4 πρὸς ἀλλήλους) πρός τινα *to someone* **Mk 10:1.**—GKilpatrick, JTS 48, '47, 63.—DELG s.v. πόρος II. M-M s.v. συνπορεύομαι.

συμποσία, ας, ἡ (Pind.+; 3 Macc 5:15, 16, 17; 7:20; EpArist) ***a common meal*** **Mk 6:39** D.

συμπόσιον, ου, τό (συμπίνω; Theognis et al.; lit. 'drinking-party', which is better understood as 'banquet', at which sparkling conversation was highly prized, as exemplified in the Platonic dialogues and the collection of topics in Athenaeus; sim. J 13–17 and numerous discourses in Lk would be understood by Greco-Romans in the context of a συμπόσιον; for a misconception cp. Lk 7:34 al.; cp. the cognate verb συμπίνω Ac 10:41; on the Hellenic perspective s. RHalbertsma, Wine in Classical Antiquity: Minerva 7, '96, esp. 15–17, citing Poseidippos, Anth. Pal. 5, 183; Athen. 2, 37; for the term συμπόσιον in the sense of 'banquet' s. also Philo, Op. M. 78; Jos., Ant. 8, 137; 12, 231; since X. et al. also = hall where a banquet is held; also pap, LXX in both mngs.) **a party of people eating together,** ***party, group*** (so Plut., Mor. 157d; 704d) repeated, in a distributive sense (B-D-F, §493, 2; Mlt. 97): συμπόσια συμπόσια *in parties* **Mk 6:39** (s. πρασιά).—DELG s.v. πίνω p. 905. M-M.

συμπρεσβύτερος, ου, ὁ (only in Christian sources [SEG VI, 347, 2]. But συμπρεσβευτής='fellow-ambassador' not infreq. in lit. and ins; likew. the pl. συμπρέσβεις w. the same mng.

[Thu. 1, 90, 5; 1, 91, 3; Jos., Vi. 62; 73]) **one who is a ruling elder along with others,** ***fellow-elder, fellow-minister*** (πρεσβύτερος 2bα) **1 Pt 5:1.**—DELG s.v. πρέσβυς. M-M s.v. συνπρ.

συμφέρω impf. συνέφερον; 1 aor. συνήνεγκα, ptc. συνενέγκας (Hom. [mid.]+; Aeschyl., Hdt.; ins, pap, LXX, Test12Patr; ApcEsdr 1:11 p. 25, 3 Tdf.; EpArist, Philo, Joseph.; Ath., 14:2 [mid.]).

❶ **to bring together into a heap,** ***bring together*** τὶ *someth.* (cp. X., An. 6, 4, 9; Jos., Bell. 5, 262, Ant. 16, 45) **Ac 19:19.**

❷ **to be advantageous,** ***help, confer a benefit, be profitable/useful*** (Hdt. et al.; Jos., Ant 1, 162)—ⓐ impers. συμφέρει τι *someth. is good* (*for someone* or *someth.*), *someth. is useful* or *helpful* **1 Cor 6:12; 10:23.** οὐ συμφέρει μοι **2 Cor 12:1 v.l.** (s. Windisch on this pass., which is prob. corrupt). συμφέρει τί τινι (Soph. et al.; Pr 19:10; Sir 30:19; 37:28 οὐ πάντα πᾶσιν συμφέρει) **2 Cor 8:10;** IRo 5:3. συμφέρει τινί foll. by inf. (Epict. 2, 22, 20; Esth 3:8) GPt 11:48; ISm 7:1. συμφ. τινί foll. by ἵνα (B-D-F §393, 1; Rob. 992; POxy 1220, 19) **Mt 5:29f** (foll. by καὶ μή to denote, by way of contrast, what is not advantageous; here and elsewh. it is well translated *it is better . . . than*); **Mt 18:6; J 11:50** (foll. by καὶ μή); **16:7.** οὐ συμφέρει γαμῆσαι *it is better not to marry* **Mt 19:10** (Polyaenus 3, 9, 2 διώκειν οὐ συμφέρει). W. acc. and inf. (s. EpArist 25) συμφέρει ἕνα ἄνθρωπον ἀποθανεῖν **J 18:14.**

ⓑ ptc. συμφέρων *profitable,* etc.—**α.** τὰ συμφέροντα *what advances your best interests* or *what is good for you* **Ac 20:20** (Pla., Rep. 1, 341e; Philo; Jos., Bell. 2, 502, Vi. 370; 3 Macc 6:24).

β. σοὶ συμφέρον ἐστί w. inf. foll. Hs 7:5. οὐ συμφέρον (sc. ἐστίν) *there is nothing to be gained by it* **2 Cor 12:1** (cp. Thu. 3, 44, 2).

γ. subst. τὸ συμφέρον *profit, advantage* (Soph. et al.; ins; 2 Macc 11:15; 4 Macc 5:11; Philo; TestSol 7:2 D; Jos., Ant. 12, 54; 13, 152, τὸ αὑτοῦ σ. 14, 174. A common term, both sg. and pl. in ins in ref. to contributions to the public good by civic-minded pers., e.g. IPriene 119, 23 al.) τὸ ἐμαυτοῦ συμφέρον **1 Cor 10:33 v.l.** τὸ κοινῇ συμφέρον *the common good* (cp. τὸ δημοσίᾳ συμφέρον POxy 1409, 11; Ocellus [II BC] 48 τὸ σ. τῷ κοινῷ) B 4:10. πρὸς τὸ συμφέρον (τινός) *for* (someone's) *advantage* **1 Cor 7:35 v.l.; 12:7** (Aeneas Tact. 469; schol. on Pind., I. 1, 15b; cp. Jos., Ant. 15, 22). Also ἐπὶ τὸ συμφέρον **Hb 12:10** (cp. Appian, Liby. 89 §420 ἐπὶ συμφέροντι κοινῷ, Syr. 41 §217; Jos., Bell. 1, 558 and Vi. 48 ἐπὶ συμφέροντι).—Schmidt, Syn. IV 162–72. M-M. TW.

σύμφημι fut. 2 pl. συμφήσετε (Just., D. A I, 12, 3); pres. mid. ptc. pl. συμφάμενοι (Just., D. 137, 2) (trag., X., Pla. et al.) ***concur, agree with*** σύμφημι τῷ νόμῳ ὅτι καλός *I concur with the law* (and thus bear witness) *that it is good* **Ro 7:16** (σ. ὅτι: Pla., Phd. 9, 64b; Just., D. 77, 1).

συμφθείρω (Eur., Aristot., Polyb., Philo) 2 aor. ptc. n. pl. συμφθαρέντα ***decompose*** of grains of wheat ὅτι . . . συμφθαρέντα κάτω ἠγέρθη *that . . . (the seeds) . . . after they have decomposed in the earth* (through mixture with it) *come up again/are raised* AcPlCor 2:26.—B. 1096.

συμφορά, ᾶς, ἡ (συμφέρω) **an unfortunate occurrence** (in Gk. lit. it is a truism that heaven distributes both good and evil, and a happening or event can therefore be beneficial or unsalutary. The latter characteristic [contrast συμφέρω, σύμφορος, in a positive sense] increasingly became associated w. σ. [s. L-S-J-M s.v. σ. II 2]) ***misfortune, calamity, disaster*** (so in sg. and pl. Pind., Hdt.+). Pl. w. περιπτώσεις 1 Cl 1:1.—B. 1096. DELG s.v. φέρω p. 1190. M-M s.v. σύμφορος.

σύμφορος, ον (συμφέρω) ***beneficial, advantageous, profitable*** (Hes., Hdt. et al.; ins; POxy 1676, 25 τὸ σύνφορόν σοι ποίει; 2 Macc 4:5; Just., D. 8, 1) τινί *to* or *for someone* Hv 1, 3, 3; 5:5; s 6, 1, 3; 6, 5, 7; 7:5. Comp. (Epict. 1, 28, 7; Jos., C. Ap. 2, 294) συμφορώτερόν ἐστι w. inf. foll. Hm 6, 1, 4 (συμφερώτερον Joly, s. his app.).—Subst. τὸ σύμφορον *benefit, advantage* (Thu. 5, 98. The pl. τὰ σύμφορα is more freq. Soph. et al.) τό τινος σύμφορον **1 Cor 7:35; 10:33.**—Frisk s.v. φέρω B 3. M-M. TW.

συμφορτίζω **to burden together with,** ***burden*** συμφορτιζόμενος τῷ θανάτῳ αὐτοῦ *burdened* (together w. him) *by his death* **Phil 3:10 v.l.**—DELG s.v. φόρτος.

συμφύγιον, ου, τό=καταφυγή, the normal Gk term for 'refuge in flight' (Corpus Glossariorum Latinorum II 443, 19 σ. confugium) **a place of refuge,** ***haven in flight, sanctuary, shelter,*** *of Jesus Christ* συνφύγιον καὶ ὅπλον εὐδοκίας *refuge/ally and shield of goodwill* AcPl Ha 8, 23f (=BMM recto 29f; s. mg. in Schubart; for this σύμφυτον Ox 1602, 33f).—DELG s.v. φεύγω.

συμφυλέτης, ου, ὁ (φυλή; Gr-Rom. ins IG XII/2, 505, 18 [II BC]; Doxogr. Gr. 655, 8; Rhet. Gr. VII 49, 22; Isocr. 12, 145 Bl. v.l.; Herodian Gramm., Philetaerus 475 [in the edition of Moeris by JPierson p. 351]; Hesych.) **one who is a member of the same tribe or people group,** ***compatriot;*** pl. one's *people* **1 Th 2:14.**—DELG s.v. φῦλον. M-M.

συμφυρμός, οῦ, ὁ (συμφύρω 'knead together'; hapax leg.—συμφύρομαι 'mix' Eur. et al.; Jos., Bell. 2, 150) **sexual mingling,** ***intercourse*** (w. ἀσέλγειαι) συμφυρμοὶ πονηρίας *improper sexual activities* Hv 2, 2, 2.—DELG s.v. φύρω.

σύμφυτος, ον (φύω; Pind.+; pap, LXX, Philo; Jos., C. Ap. 1, 42, but mostly = 'innate' or someth. sim.; Did., Gen. 215, 11) **pert. to being associated in a related experience** ('grown together' Aristot., HA 5, 32, 557b, 18, Topica 7, 6, 145b, 3; 13) ***identified with*** τινί *someth.* (Antiphon: POxy 1364, 44f) fig. σύμφυτοι γεγόναμεν τῷ ὁμοιώματι τοῦ θανάτου αὐτοῦ **Ro 6:5** (ὁμοίωμα 1; cp. Dio Chrys. 11 [12], 28 of pers. of primitive times in their relationship to the divine: οὐ μακρὰν τ. θείου . . . ἀλλὰ ἐν αὐτῷ μέσῳ πεφυκότες μᾶλλον δὲ συμπεφυκότες ἐκείνῳ=not [living] far from the divine, but growing up in the very midst of it; indeed, one might aver, growing up together with it). SStricker, D. Mysteriengedanke des hl. Pls nach Rö 6:2–11: Liturgisches Leben 1, '34, 285–96; OKuss, D. Römerbrief I, '63, 299f; see also comm. by OMoe[2] '48; ANygren '51; CCranfield '75. On Ox 1602, 33f s. συμφύγιον.—DELG s.v. φύομαι C. M-M. TW. Spicq.

συμφύω 2 aor. pass. ptc. συμφυείς (trans. in Pla. et al.; intr. in Hippocr., Pla. et al., incl. Wsd 13:13; Philo, Dec. 87; Jos., Bell. 6, 155, Ant. 8, 63 [συμφυέντες]) pass. intr. w. act. force ***grow up with*** someth. **Lk 8:7.**—DELG s.v. φύομαι C. M-M. s.v. συνφύω. Spicq.

συμφωνέω fut. συμφωνήσω; 1 aor. συνεφώνησα, pass. συνεφωνήθην (s. three next entries; Pla., Aristot. et al.; ins, pap, LXX, Philo; Jos., Ant. 10, 106, C. Ap. 2, 181; Ath.)

❶ **to be so alike or similar as to match,** of things—ⓐ ***fit (in) with, match (with), agree with*** (Pla., Aristot. et al.; Demetr.: 722 fgm. 2, 2 Jac. [abs.]) w. dat. τούτῳ συμφωνοῦσιν οἱ λόγοι τῶν προφητῶν *with this* (i.e. w. God's call to the nations) *the words of the prophets agree* **Ac 15:15** (cp. Jos., Ant. 1, 107; 15, 174). τῷ παλαιῷ οὐ συμφωνήσει τὸ ἐπίβλημα **Lk 5:36.** (λίθοι) μὴ συμφωνοῦντες τοῖς ἑτέροις λίθοις Hs 9, 6, 4.

ⓑ ***fit together*** συμφωνοῦσιν αἱ ἁρμογαί *the joints* (of the stones) *fit together* Hv 3, 5, 1c. συμφ. ταῖς ἁρμογαῖς αὐτῶν *they fit together at their joints* 3, 5, 1a. συμφ. ταῖς ἁρμογαῖς αὐτῶν μετὰ τῶν ἑτέρων λίθων 3, 5, 2; cp. 3, 2, 6.

ⓒ ***match in sound*** of empty jars that harmonize when knocking against each other συμφωνοῦσιν ἀλλήλοις Hm 11:13.

❷ **to have common interests, *be in agreement, in harmony,*** of pers. τινί *with someone* (Pla., Aristot. et al.; Strabo 12, 3, 25) ἑαυτοῖς συνεφώνησαν *they were in agreement with each other* Hv 3, 5, 1b.

❸ **to have come to an agreement about someth., *be of one mind, agree,*** w. focus on specific result of negotiations, of pers. (Diod. S. 12, 25, 3; 4 Km 12:9; Jos., C. Ap. 1, 17; 2, 255 τινὶ περί τινος) ἐὰν δύο συμφωνήσουσιν περὶ πράγματος **Mt 18:19.** Impers. pass. συνεφωνήθη ὑμῖν πειράσαι; *did you agree to test?,* lit. 'was it agreed by you to test?' **Ac 5:9** (B-D-F §202; 409, 3; cp. Lat. convenit inter vos; Rob. 1084). Of a business arrangement (oft. pap) συμφωνήσας μετὰ τῶν ἐργατῶν ἐκ δηναρίου *he came to an agreement* or *he settled with the workers for a denarius* **Mt 20:2** (on ἐκ w. gen. of price s. ἐκ 4b). Sim. οὐχὶ δηναρίου (gen. of price) συνεφώνησάς μοι; vs. **13,** but the latter pass may also fit in 2.—DELG s.v. φωνή. M-M. TW. Spicq.

συμφώνησις, εως, ἡ (s. συμφωνέω; An. Ox. IV 326, 12) **a state of shared interests, *agreement*** τινὸς πρός τινα *of someone with someone* **2 Cor 6:15.**—DELG s.v. φωνή. M-M. TW. Spicq.

συμφωνία, ας, ἡ (s. σύμφωνος; Pla. et al.; pap, LXX; EpArist 302; Philo; Jos., C. Ap. 2, 170; 179; Tat. 12, 3) in our lit. only in one pass., as a term dealing w. music **Lk 15:25.** It is variously interpreted:

❶ **the sound produced by several instruments, *music*** (Paradoxogr. Flor. 43).

❷ **a group of performing musicians, *band, orchestra*** (PFlor 74, 5; 18; POxy 1275, 9; 12; 24 συμφωνία αὐλητῶν καὶ μουσικῶν).

❸ **a wind instrument** (Polyb. 26, 1, 4 μετὰ κερατίου καὶ συμφωνίας; Athen. 13, 594e χορῷ μεγάλῳ κ. παντοίοις ὀργάνοις κ. συμφωνίαις; Da 3:5, 15 v.l. Loanw. in rabb. w. the mng. 'double flute' [Billerb. IV 396, 400]). Acc. to PBarry, JBL 23, 1904, 180ff; 27, 1908, 99ff a kind of ***bagpipe.*** Against this GMoore, JBL 24, 1905, 166ff. PSchmitt-Pantel, La cité au banquet, histoire des repas publics dans les cités grecques '92 (s. SEG XLII, 1746 on vocabulary of banquets).—DELG s.v. φωνή. M-M. TW. Spicq. Sv.

σύμφωνος, ον (s. συμφωνία; Hom. Hymns, Pla. et al.; ins, pap, 4 Macc; Ar. 13, 5; Tat. 25, 2; Ath.; adv. συμφώνως Ath., R. 23 p. 77, 4)

❶ **pert. to being in tune with, *attuned to, harmonious,*** in imagery IEph 4:1, 2; 5:1.

❷ **pert. to being in agreement, *agreeing*** (EpArist 302; Jos., C. Ap. 2, 169, Ant. 15, 408); subst. τὸ σύμφωνον *agreement* (Philo): ἐκ συμφώνου *by agreement* (PLond II, 334, 19 p. 211 [166 AD]; PHamb 15, 8; PStras 14, 13; BGU 446, 13 al. in pap) **1 Cor 7:5.**—M-M. TW. Spicq. Sv.

συμψέλιον, ου, τό (POxy 921; Sb 4292, 4. Written συμψέλλιον throughout Hermas cod. A [s. Joly's note Hv 3, 1, 4 app.]; so also AcThom 49 [Aa II/2, 165, 19]; σεμψέλλιον: PGrenf II, 111, 37; CWessely, WienerStud 24, 1902, 99f. Lat. loanw. = subsellium. Loanw. in rabb.) ***bench*** Hv 3, 1, 4; 7; 3, 2, 4; 3, 10, 1; 5; 3, 13, 3; m 11:1.

συμψηφίζω (as a mid. Aristoph., X. et al.) in our lit. act. (as PGM 13, 348) 1 aor. συνεψήφισα **to calculate a total, *count up, compute*** τὶ *someth.* τὰς τιμὰς αὐτῶν *the price of them* (=the books) **Ac 19:19.** S. also συνοψίζω.—τὴν ποσότητα τῆς δαπάνης *count up the amount of the cost* Hs 5, 3, 7 v.l. τὰς ὥρας *count the hours* v 3, 1, 4 v.l.—The pass. (cp. Appian, Bell. Civ. 3, 22 §83; Sb 7378, 9 [II AD]; Jer 30:14 v.l.) συνεψηφίσθη μετὰ τ. ἀποστόλων *he was counted as one of the apostles* **Ac 1:26** D (for συγκατεψηφίσθη). (Verbs compounded w. σύν are oft. used w. μετά in the LXX: Johannessohn, Präp. 205.)—DELG s.v. ψῆφος. M-M. TW.

σύμψυχος, ον lit. 'united in spirit', ***harmonious*** (so in Polemo, Decl. 2, 54 p. 34, 19) w. τὸ ἓν φρονῶν **Phil 2:2** (but AFridrichsen, PhilolWoch 58, '38, 910–12 *wholeheartedly*).—DELG s.v. ψυχή. M-M.

σύν (the Koine knows nothing of the Attic form ξύν; B-D-F §34, 4; Rob. 626) prep. w. dat. (Hom.+.—For lit. s. on ἀνά and μετά, beg.; Tycho Mommsen, Beiträge zu der Lehre v. den griech. Präp. 1895, esp. p. 395ff; B-D-F 221; Rob. 626–28) ***with*** (it is hazardous to attempt to establish subtle differences in use of σύν and μετά in ref. to association, for the NT manifests a rather fluid use).

❶ w. dat. of pers. **marker of accompaniment and association—ⓐ** with focus on associative aspect—**α.** be, remain, stand, etc., *with someone* ἀνακεῖσθαι σύν τινι **J 12:2.** διατρίβειν **Ac 14:28.** τὸν ἄνθρωπον σὺν αὐτοῖς ἑστῶτα **Ac 4:14.** μένειν **Lk 1:56; 24:29** (here alternating w. μένειν μετά τινος as its equivalent).

β. go, travel, etc. *with someone* ἔρχεσθαι σύν τινι *go with, accompany someone* (Jos., Vi. 65 Just., D. 78, 6) **J 21:3; Ac 11:12;** *come with someone* **2 Cor 9:4.** ἀπέρχεσθαι **Ac 5:26.** εἰσέρχεσθαι (X., Cyr. 3, 3, 13; JosAs 22:2) **Lk 8:51; Ac 3:8.** ἐξέρχεσθαι **J 18:1; Ac 10:23; 14:20;** AcPl Ant 13, 3 (=Aa I 236, 6). συνέρχεσθαι **21:16.** πορεύεσθαι **Lk 7:6; Ac 10:20.**

γ. In the case of εἶναι σύν τινι the emphasis is sometimes purely on being together (Tat. 5, 1 πᾶσα δύναμις . . .), and somet. upon accompaniment: *be with someone* (X., An. 1, 8, 26; Alexandrian graffito, prob. fr. imperial times [Dssm., LO 257, 4=LAE 303, 1] εὔχομαι κἀγὼ ἐν τάχυ σὺν σοὶ εἶναι [addressed to a deceased person]) **Lk 24:44** (ἔτι ὢν σὺν ὑμῖν as 4 Macc 18:10); **Phil 1:23** (Quint. Smyrn. 7, 698 of Achilles ἐστὶ σὺν ἀθανάτοισι); **Col 2:5;** w. indication of place ἐν τῷ ὄρει **2 Pt 1:18.** *Accompany, follow someone* **Lk 7:12.** *Be someone's companion* or *disciple* **8:38; 22:56; Ac 4:13;** *be among someone's attendants* **13:7.** ἐσχίσθη τὸ πλῆθος καὶ οἱ μὲν ἦσαν σὺν τοῖς Ἰουδαίοις, οἱ δὲ σὺν τοῖς ἀποστόλοις **14:4** (cp. X., Cyr. 7, 5, 77). οἱ σύν τινι ὄντες *someone's comrades, companions, attendants* **Mk 2:26; Ac 22:9.** Without ὄντες (X., An. 2, 2, 1; UPZ 160, 9 [119 BC]; Jos., Vi. 196, Ant. 11, 105; 12, 393; Just., D. 9, 3 al.) **Lk 5:9; 8:45 v.l.; 9:32; 24:10** (αἱ σὺν αὐταῖς); **24:33; Ac 5:17.** In the sing. Τίτος ὁ σὺν ἐμοί **Gal 2:3.**—With a subst. (ParJer 7:9 τοῖς σὺν αὐτῷ δεσμίοις; POxy 242, 33; BGU 1028, 19) οἱ σὺν αὐτῷ τεχνῖται *his fellow-artisans* **Ac 19:38.** Στεφανᾶς καὶ σὺν αὐτῷ πρεσβύτεροι AcPlCor 1, 1. οἱ σὺν αὐτοῖς ἀδελφοί **Ro 16:14;** cp. **Gal 1:2; Ro 16:15; Phil 4:21.** οἱ σὺν αὐτῷ πιστοί MPol 12:3.

δ. γενέσθαι σύν τινι *join someone* **Lk 2:13** (γίνομαι 6f). καθίσαι σύν τινι *sit beside someone* **Ac 8:31.**

ⓑ w. focus on association in activity—α. do: Ἁνανίας σὺν Σαπφίρῃ ἐπώλησεν κτῆμα **Ac 5:1.** ἐπίστευσεν σὺν τῷ οἴκῳ αὐτοῦ **18:8.** προσεύχεσθαι **20:36.** ἁγνίσθητι σὺν αὐτοῖς **21:24.**—**Phil 2:22.**—Have empathy: καὶ ὁ ποιμὴν σὺν αὐτῷ λίαν ἱλαρὸς ἦν ἐπὶ τούτοις *and the shepherd joined the angel in delight over these (fruitbearing cuttings)* Hs 8, 1, 18 (cp. TestAbr B 6 p. 110, 2 [Stone 68] ἔκλαυσεν σὺν τῷ υἱῷ αὐτου; TestJob 53:1)

β. experience, suffer: σύν τινι ἀποθανεῖν **Mt 26:35.** ἀναιρεθῆναι **Lk 23:32.** σταυρωθῆναι **Mt 27:38;** cp. vs. **44.** Cp. **Ac 8:20; 1 Cor 11:32.** οἱ ἐκ πίστεως εὐλογοῦνται σὺν τῷ πιστῷ Ἀβραάμ **Gal 3:9.** ἡ ζωὴ ὑμῶν κέκρυπται σὺν τῷ Χριστῷ ἐν τῷ θεῷ **Col 3:3.**—In mystic union w. Christ the Christian comes to ἀποθανεῖν σὺν Χριστῷ **Ro 6:8; Col 2:20** and to ζῆν σὺν αὐτῷ **2 Cor 13:4;** cp. **1 Th 5:10** (ELohmeyer, Σὺν Χριστῷ: Deissmann Festschr. 1927, 218–57; JDupont, Σὺν Χριστῷ '52).

γ. To the personal obj. acc. of the verb in the act., σύν adds other persons who are undergoing the same experience *at the same time with, just as* (Philochorus [IV/III BC]: 328 fgm. 7a Jac. ὥπλιζε σὺν τοῖς ἄρρεσι τὰς θηλείας) σὺν αὐτῷ σταυροῦσιν δύο λῃστάς **Mk 15:27.** ὁ βεβαιῶν ἡμᾶς σὺν ὑμῖν **2 Cor 1:21.** ἡμᾶς σὺν Ἰησοῦ ἐγερεῖ **4:14;** cp. **Col 2:13; 1 Th 4:14.**

❷ **marker of assistance** (X., Cyr. 5, 4, 37 ἦν οἱ θεοὶ σὺν ἡμῖν ὦσιν, An. 3, 1, 21; Jos., Ant. 11, 259 θεὸς σὺν αὐτῷ) ἡ χάρις τοῦ θεοῦ ἡ σὺν ἐμοί *God's grace, that came to my aid* **1 Cor 15:10.** (The expr. σὺν θεῷ: PGrenf II, 73, 16 ὅταν ἔλθῃ σὺν θεῷ; POxy 1220, 23 et al; Pind., O. 10, 105 [115] σὺν Κυπρογενεῖ 'with the favor of Aphrodite' is not semantically parallel; s. BRees, JEA 36, '50, 94f).

❸ **marker of linkage,** with focus on addition of a pers. or thing—ⓐ ***with, at the same time as***—α. τὸ ἐμὸν σὺν τόκῳ *my money with interest* **Mt 25:27** (POsl 40, 7 [150 AD] κεφάλαιον σὺν τ. τόκοις).αὐτὸν σὺν τῷ κλινιδίῳ **Lk 5:19.** σὺν αὐτῷ τὰ πάντα **Ro 8:32.** σύν τῷ πειρασμῷ καὶ τὴν ἔκβασιν **1 Cor 10:13.**

β. somet. σύν is nearly equivalent to καί (O. Wilck 1535, 5 [II BC] τοῖς συνστρατιώταις σὺν Πλάτωνι; Johannessohn, Präp. 207; AssMos fgm. f Denis p. 65 Ἰησοῦς . . . σὺν καὶ τῷ Χαλέβ) *(together) with* οἱ γραμματεῖς σὺν τοῖς πρεσβυτέροις **Lk 20:1.** Πέτρος σὺν τῷ Ἰωάννῃ **Ac 3:4.** Cp. **Lk 23:11; Ac 2:14; 10:2; 14:5; 23:15; Eph 3:18; Phil 1:1** (cp. POxy 1293, 3 [117–38 AD]); 1 Cl 65:1; IPol 8:2. τὴν σάρκα σὺν τοῖς παθήμασιν **Gal 5:24.** Cp. **Eph 4:31; Js 1:11.**

ⓑ when a new factor is introduced ***besides, in addition to*** (Jos., Ant. 17, 171) σὺν πᾶσιν τούτοις *beside all this, in addition to* or *apart from all this* (cp. σὺν τούτοις='apart fr. this': Galen, CMG V 9, 1 p. 381, 2; 3 Macc 1:22; JosAs 11 cod. A [p. 53, 17 Bat.]; GrBar 16:3) **Lk 24:21.**

ⓒ in combination w. ἅμα (q.v. 2b) **1 Th 4:17; 5:10.**—BMcGrath, CBQ 14, '52, 219–26: 'Syn'-Words in Paul; OGert, D. mit. *syn*-verbundenen Formulierungen in paul. Schrifttum, diss. Berlin, '52.—M-M. DELG. EDNT. TW.

συνάγω fut. συνάξω; 1 aor. συνῆξα (2 Esdr 7:28; 8:15; cp. ParJer 7:16f; D 10:5), inf. συνάξαι **Lk 3:17 v.l.** (on the late aor. form s. Schwyzer I 749, 1; JMoulton, Cambridge Bibl. Essays 1909, 485f); 2 aor. συνήγαγον. Pass.: 1 fut. συναχθήσομαι; 1 aor. συνήχθην; pf. 3 sg. συνῆκται LXX (Hom. et al.)

❶ **to cause to come together, *gather (in)***—ⓐ things: **J 15:6.** κλάσματα **6:12f.** ξύλα MPol 13:1. Of fish of every kind, which the net *gathers up* when it is cast **Mt 13:47.** Of the fragments of a ms. that is wearing out MPol 22:3a; EpilMosq 5a. Of field crops (Ex 23:10; Lev 25:3; JosAs 1:3) **Mt 25:24, 26;** cp. pass. (Jos., Ant. 5, 242) D 9:4a. W. indication of the destination εἴς τι (Diod. S. 19, 100, 2 τ. ἄσφαλτον σ. εἴς τινα τόπον) εἰς τὴν ἀποθήκην **Mt 3:12; 6:26; 13:30; Lk 3:17.** ποῦ **12:17.** ἐκεῖ vs. **18.** συνάγειν πάντα **Lk 15:13** *gather everything together,* perh. with a commercial connotation *turn everything into cash* (cp. Plut., Cato Min. 762 [6, 7] κληρονομίαν εἰς ἀργύριον συναγαγών).—In imagery συνάγειν μετά τινος *join with someone in gathering* (opp. σκορπίζω, q.v. 1) **Mt 12:30; Lk 11:23.** συνάγειν καρπὸν εἰς ζωὴν αἰώνιον **J 4:36.** Of sheep, metaph. **10:16** P^{66}.

ⓑ of persons *bring* or *call together, gather* a number of persons (1 Km 5:11; PsSol 11:3; TestJob 17:2; Jos., C. Ap. 1, 234; IAndrosIsis, Kyme 17 husband and wife) πάντας οὓς εὗρον **Mt 22:10.** πάντας τοὺς ἀρχιερεῖς **2:4** (Appian, Bell. Civ. 4, 4 §15: in view of frightening signs ἡ βουλὴ μάντεις συνῆγεν). πάντα τὰ ἔθνη 2 Cl 17:4; (Is 66:18). συνέδριον (Diod. S. 17, 4, 2 συνέδριον συναγαγών, likew. 17, 30, 1.—Cp. Ex 3:16 τ. γερουσίαν, likew. Jos., Ant. 5, 332; PsSol 8:28 τὴν διασπορὰν Ἰσραήλ) **J 11:47.** τὸ πλῆθος (Diod. S. 4, 53, 1 συναγαγεῖν εἰς ἐκκλησίαν τὰ πλήθη; Jos., Ant. 3, 188; cp. ParJer 7:16f τὸν λαόν) **Ac 15:30.** τὴν ἐκκλησίαν (Aeneas Tact. 431; Lucian, Jupp. Trag. 15) **14:27;** cp. D 10:5. συνάξεις πάντας τοὺς σοὺς ὑπὸ τὸ στέγος σου 1 Cl 12:6. Foll. by εἰς to indicate the place (X., Ages. 1, 25; Jos., Vi. 280 τὸ πλῆθος εἰς τὴν προσευχήν; ApcEsdr 3:6 πάντας εἰς τὴν κοιλάδα τοῦ Ἰωσαφάτ) εἰς τὸν τόπον **Rv 16:16** (Diod. S. 17, 20, 1 συνήγαγεν εἰς ἕνα τόπον τοὺς ἀρίστους; 13, 49, 3). εἰς ἕν **J 11:52** (cp. εἰς 4a). To indicate purpose (Dionys. Hal. 2, 45 ὅπως εἰς φιλίαν συνάξουσι τὰ ἔθνη; Jos., C. Ap. 1, 111) εἰς τὸν πόλεμον **Rv 16:14; 20:8.** Cp. **13:10 v.l.** ἐπί τινα **Mt 27:27.** ἵνα κἀμὲ συναγάγῃ ὁ κύριος Ἰ. Χρ. μετὰ τῶν ἐκλεκτῶν *that the Lord Jesus Christ may gather me also with the chosen* MPol 22:3b; EpilMosq 5b.—Pass., either in the passive sense *be gathered* or *brought together* συναχθήσονται ἔμπροσθεν αὐτοῦ πάντα τὰ ἔθνη **Mt 25:32.** συναχθήτω σου ἡ ἐκκλησία ἀπὸ τῶν περάτων τῆς γῆς εἰς τὴν σὴν βασιλείαν D 9:4b; or w. act. force *gather, come together, assemble* (Gen 29:8; Dt 33:5; Esth 9:18; En 13:9; TestReub 1:2; ApcMos 5:38; ViJer 12 [p. 73, 8 Sch.]) **Mt 22:41; 27:17; Mk 2:2;** MPol 18:2; D 14:1; 16:2. The subject can also be a collective word συνήχθη τὸ πρεσβυτέριον **Lk 22:66;** ἡ πόλις **Ac 13:44.** More closely defined: as to place εἴς τι **Mt 26:3; Ac 4:5 v.l.** εἰς τὸ δεῖπνον **Rv 19:17.** ἔν τινι: **Ac 4:5, 31.** ἐν τῇ ἐκκλησίᾳ *with the congregation* **11:26.** ἐὰν ἦτε μετ᾽ ἐμοῦ συνηγμένοι ἐν τῷ κόλπῳ μου *if you are gathered with me in my bosom* 2 Cl 4:5 (a dominical saying, of unknown origin). παρά τινι *with someone* **Ac 21:18** D. πρός τινα *to* or *with someone* (TestBenj10:11) **Mt 13:2; 27:62; Mk 4:1; 6:30; 7:1.** πρὸς ἀλλήλους GPt 8:28. ἐπί τινα *with* or *around someone* **Mk 5:21;** *against someone* (Gen 34:30; Josh 10:6; Hos 10:10) **Ac 4:27** (=κατά τινος vs. 26 after Ps 2:2). ἐπὶ τὴν ζωήν *into life* 2 Cl 17:3. ἐπὶ τὸ αὐτό (s. αὐτός 3b and ἐπί 1cβ) **Mt 22:34; Ac 4:26** (Ps 2:2); 1 Cl 34:7. συναχθέντες ὁμοῦ GJs 9:1. σύν τινι (Mi 2:12) **1 Cor 5:4.** συναχθέντες μετὰ τῶν πρεσβυτέρων **Mt 28:12;** also of an individual pers. συνήχθη Ἰησοῦς μετὰ τῶν μαθητῶν αὐτοῦ **J 18:2** (HReynen, BZ 5, '61, 86–90 'stay'). W. an adv. of place οὗ **Mt 18:20; Ac 20:8;** ὅπου **Mt 26:57; J 20:19 v.l.;** ἐκεῖ (TestBenj 9:2; Jos., Ant. 6, 23) **Mt 24:28; Lk 17:37 v.l.; J 18:2.** Foll. by inf. of purpose **Ac 13:44; 15:6; 20:7; Rv 19:19.**

❷ **to effect renewed relations, *bring together, reconcile,*** ext. of 1 (Demosth. et al.; Herodian 3, 13, 5; 4, 3, 4; 9) μαχομένους συναγαγών B 19:12.

❸ **to bring together with, *lead* or *bring (to)*** (Hom. et al.) pass. πᾶσα γλῶσσα εἰς θεὸν συνήχθη of Christianity as the one route to God for all IMg 10:3 (the prep. prob. functions here in an associative sense).

❹ **to extend a welcome to,** ***invite/receive as a guest*** (w. εἰς τὴν οἰκίαν or εἰς τὸν οἶκον added Judg 19:18; 2 Km 11:27; Dt 22:2. S. also Gen 29:22; Achilles Tat. 3, 8, 3) **Mt 25:35, 38, 43.**

❺ intr. (so, but w. a different mng., Theocr. 22, 82; Polyb. 11, 18, 4 [both = meet in hostile fashion]) **to move to another position,** ***advance, move*** (Aelian, VH 3, 9 συνάγοντος τοῦ πολέμου) σύναγε ἔτι ἄνω *move farther up* **Mt 20:28** D (the prep. may function here in a deferential and associative sense 'come along up higher').—On Dg 12:9 s. καιρός, end (cp. Jos., C. Ap. 1, 126 συνάγεται πᾶς ὁ χρόνος).—M-M.

συναγωγή, ῆς, ἡ (Thu. et al.; ins, pap, LXX, Just.). The term σ. is fluid, and its use as a loanword in Eng. in connection with cult suggests a technical usage that belies the extraordinary breadth of use of σ. Orig. in act. sense 'a bringing together, assembling', then in LXX and contemporary documents 'a gathering' or 'place of assembly'.—For ins evidence relating to cultic usage s. ROster, NTS 39, '93, 181 n. 14 (the principal corpora); for synonyms, p. 186; cp. New Docs 4, 202f.

❶ **a place where someth. collects,** ***gathering place*** of the basins in which water is gathered at the creation (Gen 1:9; cp. Jos., Ant. 15, 346 σ. ὑδάτων; Did., Gen. 25, 14 σ., ἣν καλεῖν εἰώθασιν ὠκεανόν) 1 Cl 20:6.

❷ **a place of assembly** (Cybele-ins [Bilderatlas z. Religionsgesch. 9–11, 1926 p. xix no. 154] ἐν τῇ τοῦ Διὸς συναγωγῇ; s. New Docs 3, 43. Sb 4981, 6f [restored].—On συναγωγή as a room for meetings cp. συνέδρια of the meeting-houses of the Pythagoreans Polyb. 2, 39, 1).

ⓐ of the Jewish ***synagogue*** (it is used for a place of assembly for Jews in Philo, Omn. Prob. Lib. 81 [w. ref. to the Essenes]; Jos., Bell. 2, 285; 289; 7, 44, Ant. 19, 300; 305; CIG 9894; 9904; BCH 21, 1897 p. 47; Συναγωγὴ Ἑβραίων in Corinth [s. Κόρινθος, end], in Rome [CIG IV, 9909] and ILydiaKP III, 42 p. 32ff.—S. AvHarnack, Mission[4] II 1924, p. 568, 2; GKittel, TLZ 69, '44, 11f.—Orig., C. Cels. 6, 23, 3; Hippol., Ref. 9, 12, 7); people came to the συν. to worship God **Mt 4:23; 6:2, 5; 9:35; 12:9; 13:54; Mk 1:39; 3:1; 6:2; Lk 4:15; 6:6; J 18:20.** In the same buildings court was also held and punishment was inflicted: **Mt 10:17; 23:34; Mk 13:9; Lk 12:11; 21:12; Ac 22:19; 26:11** (HKee, NTS 36, '90, 1–24 perceives Acts as reading a post-70 situation into Paul's career; rejoinder ROster, ibid 39, '93, 178–208, with caution against reliance on mere transliteration of σ. and w. conclusion that Luke is not guilty of anachronism; response by Kee, ibid. 40, '94, 281–83 [also 41, '95, 481–500], w. observation that the inscription from the syngagogue of Theodotus in Jerusalem [s. Dssm. LO 378–80=LAE 439–41; Boffo, Iscrizioni no. 31] may well be no earlier than IV AD; for critique of Kee's views s. also ESanders, Jewish Law from Jesus to the Mishnah, '87, 341–43 notes 28 and 29. For early use in reference to a Jewish synagogue, s. New Docs 4, 202, IBerenike 16, 5 [55 AD] of a building, ln. 3 of members meeting in it). Synagogues are also mentioned as existing in Antioch in Pisidia **13:14;** Athens **17:17;** Berea vs. **10;** Damascus **9:20;** Ephesus **18:19** (GHorsley, The Inscriptions of Ephesus and the NT: NovT 34, '92, 105–68); Capernaum **Mk 1:21; Lk 4:33; 7:5; J 6:59** (HKohl and CWatzinger, Antike Synagogen in Galiläa 1916; HVincent, RB 30, 1921, 438ff; 532ff; GOrfali, Capharnaum et ses ruines 1922); Corinth **Ac 18:4** (s. New Docs 3, 121); Ephesus **19:8;** Nazareth **Lk 4:16;** Salamis on the island of Cyprus **Ac 13:5;** Thessalonica **17:1.**—ESukenik, Ancient Synagogues in Palestine and Greece '34.—On the building of synagogues by patrons s. TRajak, Benefactors in the Greco-Jewish Diaspora, in MHengel Festschr. I '96, 307 n. 7 lit.—On the relationship betw. συναγωγή and προσευχή (q.v. 2) s. SKrauss, Synagogale Altertümer 1922, 11; Boffo, Iscrizioni 39–46; Pauly-W. 2d ser. IV '32, 1284–1316; ERivkin, AHSilver Festschr. '63, 350–54.—AGroenman, De Oorsprong der Joodsche Synagoge: NThT 8, 1919, 43–87; 137–88; HStrack, RE XIX 221–26; Elbogen[2] 444ff; 571ff; Billerb. IV, 115–52 (the syn. as an institution), 153–88 (the syn. services); GDalman, Jesus-Jeshua (tr. PLevertoff) 1929, 38–55; SSafrai, MStern et al., The Jewish People in the 1st Century II, '77, 908–44; LLevine, The Second Temple Synagogue, The Formative Years: The Synagogue in Late Antiquity '87, 7–31; Schürer II 423–63; III 138–49; s. also lit. cited by Oster, Kee, and Boffo above.

ⓑ an assembly-place for Judeo-Christians (Nazarenes) can also be meant in **Js 2:2** (so LRost, Pj 29, '33, 53–66, esp. 54f but s. 4 below). εἰς σ. πλήρη ἀνδρῶν Hm 11:14 (cp. the superscription on a Marcionite assembly-place near Damascus συναγωγὴ Μαρκιωνιστῶν [OGI 608, 1 fr. 318/19 AD]; Harnack, SBBerlAK 1915, 754ff). S. 5 below.

❸ **the members of a synagogue, (the congregation of a) synagogue** (Just., D. 53, 4 al.; references for this usage in Schürer II 423f; III 81–86; EPeterson, Byz.-Neugriech. Jahrbücher 2, 1921, 208)

ⓐ of localized synagogues **Ac 6:9** (Schürer II 428; cp. CIJ 683 [=Corpus Ins. Regni Bosporani '65 no. 70], for translation and ill. see RMackennan, BAR 22/2, '96, 47); **9:2.**

ⓑ in a limited sense, of those who consider themselves Ἰουδαῖοι but are hostile to Christians (who also identify themselves as Ἰουδαῖοι whether Israelite by descent or believers from the nations—on the mixed composition of the followers of Jesus Christ s. Ac 13:43; ISm 1:2), and are called (instead of συναγωγὴ κυρίου: Num 16:3; 20:4; 27:17; Josh 22:16; Ps 73:2) συναγωγὴ τοῦ σατανᾶ *synagogue of Satan* **Rv 2:9; 3:9** (cp. Just., D. 104, 1 ἡ σ. τῶν πονηρευομένων; s. 5 below).

❹ **a synagogal meeting,** ***a meeting, gathering*** for worship, of the Judeans λυθείσης τῆς συναγωγῆς **Ac 13:43** (s. λύω 3).—Transferred to meetings of Judeo-Christian congregations (cp. TestBenj 11:2, 3; Just., D. 63, 5; 124, 1; Theoph. Ant. 2, 14 [p. 136, 12]) ἐὰν εἰσέλθῃ εἰς συναγωγὴν ὑμῶν **Js 2:2** (this is the preferred interpr.: HermvSoden, Ropes, Meinertz, FHauck; s. 2b above). συναγωγὴ ἀνδρῶν δικαίων Hm 11:9, 13, cp. 14. πυκνότερον συναγωγαὶ γινέσθωσαν *meetings* (of the congregation) *should be held more often* IPol 4:2. (συναγ. is also found outside Jewish and Christian circles for periodic meetings; s. the exx. in MDibelius, Jakobus 1921 p. 124, 1. Also Philo Bybl.: 790 fgm. 4, 52 Jac. [in Eus., PE 1, 10, 52] Ζωροάστρης ἐν τῇ ἱερᾷ συναγωγῇ τῶν Περσικῶν φησι; OGI 737, 1 [II BC] σ. ἐν τῷ Ἀπολλωνείῳ; PLond 2710 recto, 12: HTR 29, '36, 40; 51.—Sb 8267, 3 [5 BC] honorary ins of a polytheistic σ.=association. W. ref. to the imperial cult BGU 1137, 2 [6 BC]. On the Christian use of the word s. also ADeissmann, Die Urgeschichte des Christentums im Lichte der Sprachforschung 1910, 35f).

❺ **a group of pers. who band together, freq. with hostile intent,** ***band, gang*** σ. πονηρευομένων (Ps 21:17) B 5:13; 6:6; GJs 15:1 v.l. (for σύνοδος).—SSafrai, The Synagogue: CRINT I/2, 908–44; WSchrage, BHHW III 1906–10; Kl. Pauly V 451f.—S. ἀρχισυναγωγός and New Docs 4, 213–20. DELG s.v. ἄγω. EDNT. DLNT 1141–46. M-M. TW.

συναγωνίζομαι mid. dep.; 1 aor. συνηγωνισάμην (Thu. et al.; ins; TestAsh 6:2; JosAs 23:4 [cod. A p. 74, 8 Bat. and Pal. 364 for συνάρασθε]) **to join w. someone in a common**

effort, ***fight/contend along with*** τινί *someone,* w. focus on a supportive role *help, assist* (Demosth. 21, 190; SIG 651, 14 τοῖς πρεσβευταῖς συναγωνιζόμενος ἐκτενῶς; ZPE 35, '79 no. 42 of a benefactor; Philo, Spec. Leg. 4, 179; Jos., Ant. 12, 18; 17, 220; Tat. 19, 2; Hippol., Ref. 7, 31, 5; noun in POxy 1676, 36f [III AD]: 'fellow-worker') **Ro 15:30** (here perh. w. judicial overtones: a common plea to God in the face of opposition to the Apostle).—DELG s.v. ἄγω. M-M.

συναθλέω 1 aor. συνήθλησα (Diod. S. 3, 4, 1='help') ***contend/struggle along with*** τινί *someone* ἐν τῷ εὐαγγελίῳ συνήθλησάν μοι *they fought at my side in (spreading) the gospel* **Phil 4:3** (with stress on the bravery of Euodia and Syntyche: FMalinowski, BTB 15, '85, 60–64; perh. military imagery: EKrentz, in Origins and Methods, JHurd Festschr. '93, 122f). τῇ πίστει (dat. of advantage) τοῦ εὐαγγελίου *for the faith of the gospel* **1:27.** Abs. IPol 6:1.—DELG s.v. ἄεθλος. TW.

συναθροίζω 1 aor. συνήθροισα. Pass.: fut. 3 pl. συναθροισθήσονται Am 4:8; 1 aor. συνηθροίσθην; pf. ptc. συνηθροισμένος; plpf. 3 sg. συνήθροιστο 3 Macc 5:24 (Thu. et al.; ins; POxy 1253, 5; LXX; JosAs 29 cod. A [epilogue]).

❶ **to cause to gather together as a group, *gather, bring together*** w. acc. of pers. (cp. 2 Km 2:30; Jos., Bell. 4, 645) **Ac 19:25.** Pass. *be gathered, meet* (X., An. 6, 5, 30; Antig. Car. 173; Josh 22:12; 1 Km 8:4; Jo 4:11; Jos., Bell. 5, 533, C. Ap. 1, 308) **Lk 24:33 v.l.; Ac 12:12;** *hold meetings* for purposes of worship IMg 4 (cp. Ex 35:1; Jos., Bell. 2, 289 εἰς τὴν συναγωγήν, Ant. 3, 84).

❷ **to link w. others in a common experience, *unite with, be joined to.*** Pass., w. act. sense w. dat. τοῖς ἀνδράσιν συνηθροίσθη πολὺ πλῆθος ἐκλεκτῶν 1 Cl 6:1.—DELG s.v. ἀθρόος. M-M.

συναινέω 1 aor. συνῄνεσα (αἶνος prim. 'tale, story'; Aeschyl., Hdt. et al.; ins, pap, 3 Macc) ***agree with, be in accord with*** τινί *someone* (EpArist 226; cp. Philo, Op. M. 2; Jos., Ant. 3, 192) IEph 11:2 (συνῄνεσαν is read by Lghtf., Funk, Bihlmeyer et al., whereas Zahn [also Forschungen VI 1900 p. 191, 1] prefers συνῆσαν, though it is less well attested).—DELG s.v. αἶνος.

συναίρω 1 aor. inf. συνᾶραι (Hom.+; Ex 23:5 v.l.; Jos., Ant. 12, 286; TestDan 4:7. Mid. συνάρασθέ μοι 'help me' JosAs 23:4; Just., D. 132, 1 συναίρεται 'it is helpful') lit. 'raise up' or 'bind/yoke together'; in our lit. only in a commercial sense συναίρειν λόγον ***settle accounts, cast up accounts*** (in act. and mid. [B-D-F §310, 1; Mlt. 160]; PFay 109, 6 [I AD]; BGU 775, 19; POxy 113, 27. Now and then in the expr. παντὸς λόγου συνηρμένου='when accounts have been settled in full': PFlor 372, 14 al.) μετά τινος *with someone* (PLond I, 131, 194 p. 175 [I AD]) **Mt 18:23; 25:19.** Without λόγον, which is supplied by the preceding verse, **18:24.** On the legal principles involved s. RSugranyesdeFranch, Études sur le droit Palestinien à l'époque évangélique '46.—DELG s.v. 1 ἀείρω. M-M. Spicq.

συναιχμάλωτος, ου, ὁ (Ps.-Lucian, Asinus 27; Theodor. Prodr. 7, 256 Hercher; Nicetas Eugen. 9, 46; 81) ***fellow-prisoner*** **Ro 16:7; Col 4:10; Phlm 23.**—DELG s.v. αἰχμή. M-M. TW.

συνακολουθέω impf. συνηκολούθουν; 1 aor. συνηκολούθησα (Thu., Aristoph.+; PTebt 39, 14 [II BC]; 2 Macc 2:4, 6; TestSol 25:6; Philo, Omn. Prob. Lib. 94; Jos., Ant. 6, 365; Tat. 7, 3) **to accompany someone, freq. in the interest of maintaining an association, *follow,*** w. dat. of pers. followed (X., Cyr. 8, 7, 5; Diod. S. 14, 39, 5 συνηκολούθουν αὐτοῖς) **Mk 5:37 v.l.; 14:51; Lk 23:49** (here 'follow' has the connotation of being a disciple, as Philostrat., Vi. Apoll. 8, 19 p. 335, 32; s. ἀκολουθέω 3); **J 13:36 v.l.** See also a Diatessaron fgm. fr. Dura (s. on προσάββατον) line 2. W. μετά τινος instead of the dat. (Isocr. 4, 146; Diod. S. 13, 62, 5) **Mk 5:37.**—DELG s.v. ἀκόλουθος. M-M. TW.

συναλίζω in the difficult passage συναλιζόμενος (συναλισκόμενος D) παρήγγειλεν αὐτοῖς **Ac 1:4,** the word is variously understood:

❶ συνᾰλίζω: **to eat at the same table, with focus on fellowship, *eat salt with, eat with*** (s. ἅλς) so the Lat., Syr., Copt. and the other ancient versions, Ephraem (AMerck, Der neuentdeckte Komm. des hl. Ephraem zur AG: ZKT 48, 1924, 228), Chrysost. (s. v.l. in a comment on Ps 140:4); PFeine, Eine vorkanonische Überl. des Lukas 1891, 160; AHilgenfeld, ZWT 38, 1895, 74; BWeiss, Blass, Preuschen; CBowen, ZNW 13, 1912, 247–59 (=Studies in the NT, ed. RHutcheon '36, 89–109); Wendt, Zahn, Jacquier, JMoffatt; Goodsp., Probs. 122f; EGill, Rev. and Expos. 36, '39, 197f 'salt covenant'; OCullmann, Urchristentum u. Gottesdienst '44, 15; EBishop, ET 56, '44/45, 220; PBenoit, RB 56, '49, 191 n. 3; EHaenchen, comm. ad loc. The objections to this point of view are that it fits rather poorly into the context, and also the circumstance that this mng., strictly speaking, is not found elsewh. (in Manetho, Apotel. 5, 339 and Ps.-Clem., Hom. p. 11, 12; 134, 19 Lag. it does not necessarily refer to table fellowship. Yet Libanius V 246, 13 F. ἁλῶν κοινωνεῖν = τραπέζης κ.); besides, Ac 10:41 appears to echo **1:4.**

❷ συνᾱλίζω (σύν + ἁλίζω 'gather'; s. L-S-J-M s.v. ἁλίζω [A]): **to bring together in assembly, *bring together, assemble,*** pass., intr. sense *come together* (both Hdt. et al.; the pass. also Petosiris, fgm. 33, ln. 6 [Πετόσειρις as an ἀνὴρ παντοίαις τάξεσι θεῶν τε καὶ ἀγγέλων συναλισθείς] and Jos., Bell. 3, 429, the act. Ant. 8, 105) so Weizsäcker; WBrandt, Die evangel. Gesch. 1893 p. 371, 1; Field, Notes 110f ('as he was assembling w. them'); HHoltzmann, Knopf; WHatch, JBL 30, 1911, 123–28; ASteinmann, OHoltzmann. The objections to this are the singular number (IHeikel, StKr 106, '35, 315 proposes συναλιζομένοις) and the pres. tense of συναλιζόμενος (a linguistic counterpart may perh. be found in the sing. pres. in Ocellus Luc. 15 πῦρ εἰς ἓν συνερχόμενον).

❸ The difficulties in 1 and 2 have led some to resort to the expedient of finding in συναλιζόμενος simply another spelling of συναυλιζόμενος, which is actually the reading of several minuscules here (the same variation in X., Cyr. 1, 2, 15 and Ps.-Clem., Hom. p. 11, 12): συναυλίζομαι dep., lit. 'spend the night with', then also gener. **to spend time with, *be with, stay with*** (Babrius, Fab. 106, 6; Pr 22:24; Synes., Kingship 19 p. 21 d; Achmes 109, 18). So HCadbury, JBL 45, 1926, 310–17; KLake; NRSV. Cp. CMoule, NTS 4, '57/58, 58–61; MWilcox, The Semitisms of Ac, '65, 106–109.—On the whole question s. also CTorrey, The Composition and Date of Acts 1916, 23f.—M-M s.v. συναλίζομαι.

συναλίσκομαι (Plut. et al.; Aelian, NA 11, 12; Diog. L. 2, 105) pass. ***be taken captive together*** **Ac 1:4** D.

συνάλλαγμα, ατος, τό (s. next entry; Hippocr. et al.) ***contract, agreement*** (Demosth., Aristot. et al.; ins, pap; 1 Macc 13:42; Jos., Ant. 16, 45; PsSol 4:4) βίαια συναλλάγματα *extorted contracts* B 3:3 (Is 58:6).—DELG s.v. ἄλλος.

συναλλάσσω impf. συνήλλασσον (s. prec. entry; Aeschyl. et al.; ins, pap) ***reconcile*** (Thu. et al.) τινά *someone* συνήλλασσεν αὐτοὺς εἰς εἰρήνην *he undertook* (the impf. expressing a course of action undertaken as Diod. S. 20, 37, 3 προῆγεν=she was setting out; 20, 71, 1 ἠνάγκαζε=he was putting pressure on) *to reconcile them, so that they would be peaceful* **Ac 7:26.** (On the qu. of a so-called conative component in the impf. s. the comments of Schwyzer II 277 in ref. to alleged 'inchoative' imperfects; also 256f on the pres. tense.)—M-M.

συναναβαίνω fut. 3 sg. συναναβήσεται; 2 aor. συνανέβην ***come/go up with*** (Hdt.+; LXX) τινί *someone* (PTebt 21, 11 [115 BC]; Ex 12:38) w. the destination given (Ps.-Lucian, Charid. 24 εἰς Ἴλιον σ. τοῖς, Ἀχαιοῖς) εἰς Ἱεροσόλυμα **Mk 15:41;** w. place fr. which and place to which ἀπὸ τῆς Γαλιλαίας εἰς Ἰερουσαλήμ **Ac 13:31.** Instead of dat. μετά τινος (OGI 632, 2 [II AD] μετ' αὐτοῦ; LXX) Hs 9, 16, 7.—DELG s.v. βαίνω. M-M.

συνανάκειμαι (s. ἀνάκειμαι) dep. impf. συνανεκείμην **to recline at table with for the purpose of dining, *eat with*** (3 Macc 5:39) τινί *someone* **Mt 9:10; Mk 2:15; Lk 14:10.** οἱ συνανακείμενοι *the fellow guests/banqueters* **Mt 14:9; Mk 6:22, 26 v.l.; Lk 7:49; 14:15; J 12:2 v.l.** —BHHW III 1991–93. DELG s.v. κεῖμαι. TW.

συναναμίγνυμι (also συναναμείγνυμι) (Hippocr.; Athen. 5, 177b 'mix up together') pass. w. act. sense ***mingle, associate with*** w. dat. of pers. (Clearch. fgm. 19 p. 14, 19 W. [in Athen. 6, 256a]; Plut., Philop. 368 [21, 8]; Hos 7:8, cp. Ezk 20:18; Philo, Mos. 1, 278; Jos., Ant. 20, 165; Just., D. 21, 2 [for συναναμίσγεσθε Ezk 20:18]) **1 Cor 5:9** (echoing the injunctions in vs. 5f); **2 Th 3:14.** Abs. **1 Cor 5:11.**—DELG s.v. μείγνυμι. M-M. TW.

συναναπαύομαι 1 aor. συνανεπαυσάμην **to relax in someone's company, *rest with*** τινί *someone* **Ro 15:32** (perh. w. suggestion of relaxation after the public service, διακονία, described vs. 31, cp. ἀνάπαυσις λειτουργίας PFlor 57, 56—Elsewh. only lit.='lie down, sleep w. somebody' [Arrian, Cyneg. 9, 2], esp. of married couples [Dionys. Hal.; Plut.].—Is 11:6).—M-M.

συναναστρέφω in our lit. only pass.: fut. 2 pl. συναναστραφήσεσθε (TestNapht 4:2); 2 aor. συνανεστράφην LXX (Jos., Bell. 5, 58; TestNapht 4:2; TestDan 5:13 [interpolation?]) **to go about with someone, *associate with*** w. dat. of pers. (Agatharchides [II BC]: 86 fgm. 12 Jac.; Diod. S.3, 58, 3; Epict. 3, 13, 5; SIG 534, 8 [218/217 BC]; Sir 41:5; Jos., Ant. 20, 206) **Ac 10:41** D (the dat. is to be supplied).

συναναφύρω 1 aor. pass. συνανεφύρην (Lucian; Galen: CMG V 9, 1 p. 193, 6; Proclus on Pla., Tim. III p. 49, 13 Diehl; PHolm 26, 39; Ezk 22:6) lit. 'to mix someth. together w. someth. else' fig. ***entangle, involve*** pass., act. sense ταῖς πραγματείαις σου συνανεφύρης ταῖς πονηραῖς *you have involved yourself in your wicked affairs* Hv 2, 3, 1 (the dat. as Lucian, Ep. Sat. 2, 28; difft. Brox ad loc.).

συναναχέω (Heliod. [III AD] 'to pour on together with') pass. συναναχυθῆ[ν]αι **Ac 11:26 v.l.** P^{74} (cp. Tdf. app. for συναχθῆναι, which is prob. a lectio facilior, RBorger, GGA 141) fig. *be received* —DELG s.v. χέω.

συναντάω fut. συναντήσω, mid. συναντήσομαι LXX; 1 aor. συνήντησα

❶ ***meet*** (Hom.+; ins, pap, LXX; TestAbr B 2 p. 106, 8 [Stone p. 60]; GrBar 11:6; Just., D. 1, 1) τινί *someone* (X., An. 7, 2, 5; Diod. S. 3, 65, 1; PLille 6, 6 [III BC]; 1 Macc 5:25; TestAbr B; GrBar; Jos., Ant. 8, 331; Just.) **Lk 9:18 v.l., 37; 22:10; Ac 10:25; Hb 7:1, 10;** EpilMosq 3. Abs. (Jos., Bell. 5, 40) ISm 4:1 (sc. αὐτοῖς).

❷ ***happen,*** of events fig. ext. of 1 (PSI 392, 1 [242/241 BC]; Plut., Sulla 452 [2, 7]; Ex 5:3; Job 30:26; TestLevi 1:1.—The mid. is also used in this way: Polyb. 22, 7, 14; Eccl 2:14; 9:11) τὰ ἐν αὐτῇ συναντήσοντα ἐμοὶ μὴ εἰδώς *without knowing what will happen to me there* **Ac 20:22.**—DELG s.v. ἄντα. New Docs 2, 98. M-M.

συνάντησις, εως, ἡ (s. prec. entry; Eur., Hippocr. et al.; pap) **a coming together at some point, *meeting*** εἰς συνάντησίν τινι *to meet someone* (Ps.-Callisth. 3, 26, 5 σοι εἰς συνάντησιν; oft. LXX, JosAs; ParJer 8:9; w. dat. and also gen., s. Johannessohn, Präp. 295f) **Mt 8:34 v.l.; J 12:13 v.l.;** εἰς σ. Παύλ[ου or -ῳ] AcPl Ant 13, 8f (=Aa I 236, 7). εἰς σ. αὐτῶν GJs 9:1.—DELG s.v. ἄντα. M-M.

συναντιλαμβάνομαι fut. 3 sg. συναντιλήψεται, 3 pl. -ψονται LXX; 2 aor. συναντελαβόμην (Diod. S. 14, 8, 2; SIG 412, 7 [270 BC]; OGI 267, 26; PHib 82, 18 [perh. 238 BC]; PSI 329, 6; 591, 12; LXX; Jos., Ant. 4, 198 [replaced by Niese w. συλλαμβάνομαι].—Dssm., LO 68 [LAE 87f]) 'take part with' (EpArist 123 'collaborate'), gener. **to come to the aid of, be of assistance to, *help*** τινί *someone* (Ex 18:22; Ps 88:22) **Lk 10:40.** τὸ πνεῦμα συναντιλαμβάνεται τῇ ἀσθενείᾳ ἡμῶν *the Spirit helps us in our weakness* **Ro 8:26** (v.l. τῆς ἀσθενείας; B-D-F §170, 3; Rob. 529; 573).—New Docs 3, 84. M-M. TW.

συναπάγω 1 aor. pass. συναπήχθην (X., pap; Ex 14:6 συναπήγαγεν [2 aor.]) in our lit. only pass. and only fig. (Zosimus, Hist. 5, 6, 9 αὐτὴ ἡ Σπάρτη συναπήγετο τῇ κοινῇ τῆς Ἑλλάδος ἁλώσει)

❶ **to cause someone in conjunction with others to go astray in belief, *lead away with.*** Pass. *be led* or *carried away* τινί *by someth.* (instrum. dat.) or *to someth.* (s. Kühner-G. I p. 407) **Gal 2:13; 2 Pt 3:17.**

❷ **to adjust to a condition or circumstance, *accommodate:*** τοῖς ταπεινοῖς συναπαγόμενοι **Ro 12:16** may be taken to refer to things *accommodate yourself to humble ways* (Weymouth; sim. NRSV mg.) in contrast to τὰ ὑψηλὰ φρονοῦντες (so, gener., BWeiss, RLipsius, Lietzmann, Kühl, Sickenberger, OHoltzmann, Althaus, Goodsp, WBallantine, NRSV mg.) or to people:

❸ **to join the company of others, *associate with:*** *associate with humble folk* (Moffatt; so, gener., the ancient versions and Chrysostom; Hilgenfeld, Zahn; KThieme, ZNW 8, 1907, 23ff; Lagrange; REB; NRSV text=20th Cent.; NABRev). Interpretations 2 and 3 are connected insofar as the form is taken to be neuter, but referring to persons (so FSpitta, Zur Gesch. u. Lit. des Urchristentums III 1, 1901, 113. S. also the ambiguous transl. of Weizsäcker: 'sich heruntergeben zur Niedrigkeit', or the sim. Confraternity of Christian Doctrine transl. '41: 'condescend to the lowly'. Cp. PBerlin 9734 of Tyche: τὰ ταπεινὰ πολλάκις εἰς ὕψος ἐξάειρας).—AFridrichsen, Horae Soederblom. I/1, '44, 32.—M-M.

συναποθνῄσκω 2 aor. συναπέθανον (Hdt. et al.; Diod. S. 19, 34, 1 [of the burning of widows in India]; Sir 19:10; Philo, Spec. Leg. 1. 108) ***die with*** τινί *someone* (Clearch., fgm. 28; Diod. S. 18, 41, 3 αὐτῷ; Περὶ ὕψους 44, 2; Polyaenus 8, 39; Chariton 4, 2, 14; Hierocles 11 p. 445 μὴ συναποθνῄσκειν τῷ σώματι τὴν ψυχήν; Orig., C. Cels. 2, 69, 17) **Mk 14:31.** Abs. (opp. συζῆν as Nicol. Dam.: 90 fgm. 80 Jac.) **2 Cor 7:3; 2 Ti 2:11** (dying and living with Christ).—FOlivier, Συναποθνῄσκω: RTP 17, 1929, 103–33; WHahn, D. Mitsterben u. Mitauferstehen mit Chr. bei Pls '37.—DELG s.v. θάνατος. M-M. TW. Spicq.

συναπόλλυμι (act. Thu. et al.; LXX; Jos., Ant. 1, 199) fut. 2 sg. συναπολέσῃς, 3 sg. ἀπολέσῃ LXX; mid. συναπολοῦμαι;

2 aor. συναπωλόμην *destroy with.* Mid. *be destroyed, perish with* (Hdt.+; POxy 486, 35 [131 AD]; LXX; Jos., Ant. 19, 144) w. dat. (Hdt. 7, 221 al.; Plut., Phoc. 758 [36, 3]; Philo, Mut. Nom. 80) **Hb 11:31;** B 21:3. Also μετά τινος *with someth.* 21:1 (cp. Gen 18:23).—DELG s.v. ὄλλυμι. M-M.

συναποστέλλω fut. συναποστελῶ LXX; 1 aor. συναπέστειλα (Thu. et al.; ins, pap, LXX) **to send someone together with someone else,** ***send with*** τινά *someone* (PMich I, 28, 25; 36=Sb 6798 [256 BC]) **2 Cor 12:18.**—M-M.

συναριθμέω pf. pass. ptc. συνηριθμημένος (Isaeus, Pla. et al.; POxy 1208, 17; Ex 12:4 συναριθμήσεται [fut. mid.] συνηριθμημένος) **to include in a group as one among others,** ***count/number together*** (Aristot., Eth. 1, 5; 2, 3; Plut., Mor. 1018f; Philo, Mos. 1, 278) ἔν τινι (Plut., Brut. 997 [29, 10]) ἐν τῷ εὐαγγελίῳ IPhld 5:2.—DELG s.v. ἀριθμός.

συναρμόζω (or συναρμόττω; Pind., Thu.+; ins, pap; ApcSed 11:10 p. 134, 24 Ja.; EpArist 71; Jos., Bell. 7, 307, C. Ap. 2, 173; Ath., R. 5 p. 52, 33; 15 p. 65, 26) 1 aor. pass. συνηρμόσθην; pf. pass. συνήρμοσμαι. In our lit. only pass. w. active force

❶ **to join so as to fit in with,** ***fit in (with)*** συνηρμόσθησαν εἰς τὴν οἰκοδομὴν τοῦ πύργου Hs 9, 16, 7.

❷ **to be associated in a fitting or appropriate manner,** ***be associated with*** w. dat. of pers. pass. w. act. sense (SIG 783, 30 συνηρμόσθη αὐτῷ γυνή; BGU 1103, 23; 1104, 24; PSI 166, 17) τὸ πρεσβυτέριον συνήρμοσται τῷ ἐπισκόπῳ IEph 4:1, though in this context mng. 3 is also poss.

❸ **to be in tune with,** ***attune*** (so the pass., X., Symp. 3, 1); s. 2 above and cp. συνευρυθμίζω.—DELG s.v. ἅρμα.

συναρμολογέω (ἁρμός, λέγω; only in Christian writers) **to join together so as to form a coherent entity,** ***fit/join together*** pass. of a building **Eph 2:21.** Of the body (cp. συμβιβάζω 1a) **4:16.**—M-M. TW.

συναρπάζω 1 aor. συνήρπασα; plpf. συνηρπάκειν; 1 aor. pass. συνηρπάσθην (trag., X. et al.; pap, LXX, Philo, Joseph.; Just., A I, 5, 2; 58, 2) **to take hold of forcibly,** ***seize*** τινά *someone* (Soph. et al.; Diod. S. 37, 27, 2; Dio Chrys. 5, 15; PSI 353, 12 [III BC]) **Ac 6:12; 19:29.** Of a possessed pers. who is seized by an unclean spirit **Lk 8:29.** Pass. (Diod. S. 20, 29, 11; Philo, Plant. 39; Jos., Ant. 7, 177 συναρπαγεὶς ὑπὸ τ. πάθους) of a ship that *was caught, torn away* by the wind **Ac 27:15** (cp. Jos., Vi. 3 βαπτισθέντος . . . του πλοίου). M-M.

συναυλίζομαι s. συναλίζω 3.

συναυξάνω (X. et al.; ins, pap, LXX; Jos., Ant. 14, 116; Just., D. 131, 6) pass. (X., Cyr. 8, 7, 6; Plut., Numa 62 [5, 3]; Philo, Aet. M. 103; Jos., Ant. 1, 32) **to grow side by side,** ***grow together*** **Mt 13:30.**—DELG s.v. αὔξω. M-M.

συνβ- s. συμβ-.

συνγ- s. συγγ-.

σύνδενδρος, ον (Timaeus Hist. [IV/III BC]: 566 fgm. 57 Jac.; Polyb. 12, 4, 2; Diod. S. 5, 65, 1; Sb 4483, 6; EpArist 112) ***covered with trees, forested*** ὄρος Hs 9, 1, 10.—DELG s.v. δένδρεον.

σύνδεσμος, ου, ὁ (συνδέω; Eur., Thu. et al.; LXX; Jos., Ant. 3, 120) and **τὸ σύνδεσμον** B 3:3 (the pl. σύνδεσμα is found occasionally beside σύνδεσμοι) prim. 'that which binds together'.

❶ **that which holds someth. together,** ***fastener*** lit. (Appian, Bell. Civ. 4, 115 §483 οἱ σύνδεσμοι of the fastenings that hold the various ships together; Herm. Wr. 1, 18; EpArist 85='fastening') *ligaments* of the body (Eur., Hipp. 199 al.; on Galen's usage s. Lghtf., Col p. 199; Straub 33f) w. ἁφή **Col 2:19** pl.

❷ **that which brings various entities into a unified relationship,** ***uniting bond*** fig. ext. of 1; σύνδ. τῆς εἰρήνης the *bond of peace,* i.e. that consists in peace (epexegetic gen.; Plut., Numa 63 [6, 4] σύνδεσμος εὐνοίας κ. φιλίας; W-S. §30, 9b) **Eph 4:3.** Love is σύνδεσμος τῆς τελειότητος the *bond that unites* all the virtues (which otherwise have no unity) *in perfect harmony* or *the bond of perfect unity* for the church **Col 3:14** (cp. Simplicius In Epict. p. 89, 15 Düb. οἱ Πυθαγόρειοι . . . τὴν φιλίαν . . . σύνδεσμον πασῶν τ. ἀρετῶν ἔλεγον; Pla., Polit. 310a.—S. also Pla., Leg. 21, 5, 921c of law: τῆς πόλεως σ.).—On σύνδεσμος as a philos. concept: WJaeger, Nemesios v. Emesa 1918, 96–137. KReinhardt, Kosmos u. Sympathie 1926; AFridrichsen, Serta Rudbergiana '31, 26, SymbOsl 19, '39, 41–45; GRudberg, ConNeot 3, '39, 19–21.

❸ **a bond that confines/hinders,** ***fetter*** only fig. σύνδεσμος ἀδικίας (Is 58:6) *fetter that consists in unrighteousness* **Ac 8:23** (s. also 4 below); B 3:3, 5 (in the two last-named passages Is 58:6 and 9 are quoted in context).

❹ **entities that are held together by a bond,** ***bundle*** (of cattle food O. Mich 240, 2 [III–IV AD]; 239, 2 [IV AD]); in imagery **Ac 8:23** according to Mft., Goodsp. et al. (s. 3 above). By fig. ext. ***band, college*** (Herodian 4, 12, 6 ὁ σ. τῶν ἐπιστολῶν) σ. ἀποστόλων ITr 3:1.—DELG s.v. 1 δέω. M-M. TW. Sv.

συνδέω fut. συνδήσω Ezk 3:26; 1 aor. συνέδησα LXX. Pass.: aor. συνεδέθην; pf. ptc. συνδεδεμένος LXX (s. prec. entry; Hom. et al.; pap, LXX; TestSol 8:1; En 101:6) **to bind so as to constrain or confine (with),** ***bind (with)***

ⓐ The force of σύν may be felt: ***bind someone with, put someone in chains with*** (Jos., Ant. 2, 70 δοῦλος συνδεδεμένος τῷ οἰνοχόῳ; 18, 196) ὡς συνδεδεμένοι *as* (though you were) *fellow-prisoners* **Hb 13:3.**

ⓑ But σ. can also mean simply ***bind, imprison,*** so that the force of σύν is no longer felt (Nicol. Dam.: 90 fgm. 4 p. 332, 19 Jac.; Aristaen., Ep. 2, 2, 2 p. 171 [end] Herch.).—M-M.

συνδιδασκαλίτης, ου, ὁ (hapax leg., modeled after numerous Hell. nouns w. -ίτης, e.g. συνθιασίτης 'fellow member of a θίασος [=Bacchus club/society]') apparently in the mng. ***fellow-pupil, fellow-disciple*** IEph 3:1 (s. Hdb. ad loc.).

συνδοξάζω 1 aor. συνεδόξασα, pass. συνεδοξάσθην (Aristot. et al.)

❶ **to join w. others in praising,** ***join in praise*** (s. δόξα 3) w. acc. of thing for which praise is offered ISm 11:3.

❷ **to honor together with,** pass. ***be glorified with someone, share in someone's glory*** (s. δόξα 1), **Ro 8:17.**—DELG s.v. δοκάω. TW.

σύνδουλος, ου, ὁ (Eur., Lysias et al.; ins [New Docs 2, 54]; BGU 1141, 20 [13 BC]; PLond III, 1213a, 4 p. 121 [65–66 AD]; PLips 40 II, 3; 2 Esdr; Jos., Ant. 11, 118. Other reff. in Herodas ed. AKnox and WHeadlam 1922 p. 252f)

❶ **one who, along w. others, is in a relationship of total obedience to one master or owner,** ***fellow-slave*** (e.g. Herodas 5, 56) **Mt 24:49;** Hs 5, 2, 9f.

❷ **a subordinate in total obedience to a ruler,** ***slave,*** esp. typical of eastern social perceptions—ⓐ of the relationship betw. an oriental court official and the ruler (s. δοῦλος 2bα) **Mt 18:28f, 31, 33.**

ⓑ of a relationship to the heavenly κύριος. Paul and Ign. designate certain Christians as their σύνδουλοι: **Col 1:7; 4:7** (σύνδουλος ἐν κυρίῳ); IEph 2:1; IMg 2; IPhld 4; ISm 12:2 (in the last two passages there are no names mentioned; the 'assistants' [διάκοναι] are called σ.). In **Rv 6:11** σύνδουλος also has the sense 'fellow-Christian'. Since it is a truism that one can be a slave to only one master, such self-identification, far from being a declaration of mean servility, served notice that ultimate allegiance was owed to God or Christ alone.

ⓒ In Rv the revealing angel calls himself the *fellow-slave* of the seer and his brothers **19:10; 22:9.**—New Docs 2, 54. M-M. TW.

συνδρομή, ῆς, ἡ (συντρέχω) **formation of a mob by pers. running together,** ***running together*** (Cephisodorus [V/IV BC] in Aristot., Rhet. 3, 10, 1411a, 29; Polyb. 1, 69, 11; Diod. S. 3, 71, 3; 15, 90, 2; 3 Macc 3:8; Ath., R. 21, 74, 5) ἐγένετο σ. τοῦ λαοῦ *the people rushed together* **Ac 21:30** (Polyb. 1, 67, 2; Jdth 10:18 ἐγένετο συνδρομή).—DELG s.v. δραμεῖν. M-M.

συνεγείρω 1 aor. συνήγειρα, pass. συνηγέρθην (in var. senses: 'assist someone in lifting up' Ex 23:5; 4 Macc 2:14; Ps.-Phoc. 140; 'awaken' Ps-Plut., Mor. 117c τὰς λύπας καὶ τοὺς θρήνους συνεγείρειν [=give rise to]; 'revive' Ael. Aristid. 48, 43 K.=24 p. 476 D.; Is 14:9 συνηγέρθησάν σοι πάντες 'all rise up together for you')

❶ **to cause to emerge with from an inactive state,** ***awaken with*** lit. (cp. Ps.-Plut. above) pass. w. act. force συνεγείρεσθε *awaken* or *rise up together (from sleep)* IPol 6:1. But this passage more prob. (pace Lghtf.) belongs in 2 below (s. συγκοιμάομαι).

❷ **to raise up with from death, physical or spiritual,** ***raise with*** fig. ext. of 1—ⓐ pass. w. act. force: of rising up from the dead in conjunction w. others IPol 6:1 (here an athletic metaphor, expressed in the compound verbs preceding συνεγείρεσθε, climaxes in imagery of a winner's award, viz. an awakening fr. the sleep of death).

ⓑ of participating in the resurrection of Jesus; the believer, in mystic union w. him, experiences this ὁ θεὸς . . . ἡμᾶς συνήγειρεν **Eph 2:6.**—Pass. συνηγέρθητε τῷ Χριστῷ **Col 3:1.** ἐν ᾧ συνηγέρθητε **2:12.**—TW.

συνέδριον, ου, τό (ἕδρα 'a seat'; Hdt.+; ins, pap, LXX; PsSol 4:1; EpArist 301; Philo, Joseph.—Schürer II 205, 14) a common administrative term

❶ **a governing board,** ***council*** (Posidon.: 87 fgm. 71 Jac.; Diod. S. 15, 28, 4; συνέδριον ἐν Ἀθήναις συνεδρεύειν; 19, 46, 4; Ael. Aristid. 13 p. 286 D.; Jos., Ant. 20, 200, Vi. 368; cp. Poland 156–58; New Docs 4, 202)

ⓐ of a *local council,* as it existed in individual cities pl. **Mt 10:17; Mk 13:9.**

ⓑ transferred by Ign. to the Christian situation. The elders (presbyters; cp. CIG 3417 the civic συνέδριον τῶν πρεσβυτέρων in Philadelphia; CCurtius, Her 4, 1870: ins fr. Ephesus nos. 11 and 13 p. 199; 203; 224) are to take the place of the συνέδριον τῶν ἀποστόλων *the council of the apostles* in the esteem of the church IMg 6:1. They are called συνέδριον θεοῦ ITr 3:1. συνέδριον τοῦ ἐπισκόπου IPhld 8:1.

ⓒ **the high council in Jerusalem,** ***Sanhedrin,*** the dominant mng. in our lit. (Joseph. [Schürer II 206, 18]; Hebraized in the Mishnah סַנְהֶדְרִין); in Roman times this was the highest indigenous governing body in Judaea, composed of high priests (ἀρχιερεύς 1bα), elders, and scholars (scribes), and meeting under the presidency of the ruling high priest. This body was the ultimate authority not only in religious matters, but in legal and governmental affairs as well, in so far as it did not encroach on the authority of the Roman procurator. The latter, e. g., had to confirm any death sentences passed by the council. (Schürer II 198–226; MWolff, De Samenstelling en het Karakter van het groote συνέδριον te Jeruzalem voor het jaar 70 n. Chr.: ThT 51, 1917, 299–320;—On the jurisdiction of the council in capital cases s. ἀποκτείνω 1a [J 18:31]. Also KKastner, Jes. vor d. Hoh. Rat 1930; MDibelius, ZNW 30, '31, 193–201; JLengle, Z. Prozess Jesu: Her 70, '35, 312–21; EBickermann, RHR 112, '35, 169–241; ESpringer, PJ 229, '35, 135–50; JBlinzler, D. Prozess Jesu '51 [much lit.], [2] '55, Eng. tr., The Trial of Jesus, I and FMcHugh, '59 [3d ed. '60]; JJeremias, ZNW 43, '50/51, 145–50; PWinter, On the Trial of Jesus, in Studia Judaica I, '61.—SZeitlin, Who Crucified Jesus? '42; on this s. CBQ 5, '43, 232–34; ibid. 6, '44, 104–10; 230–35; SZeitlin, The Political Synedrion and the Religious Sanhedrin, '45. Against him HWolfson, JQR 36, '46, 303–36; s. Zeitlin, ibid. 307–15; JDerrett, Law in the NT, '70, 389–460; DCatchpole, The Problem of the Historicity of the Sanhedrin Trial: SHoenig, The Great Sanhedrin, '53; CFD Moule Festschr. '70, 47–65; JFitzmyer, AB: Luke 1468–70 [lit.].—On Jesus before the council s. also Feigel, Weidel, Finegan s.v. Ἰούδας 6). **Mt 5:22** (RGuelich, ZNW 64, '73, 43ff); **26:59; Mk 14:55; 15:1; Lk 22:66** (perh.; s. below); **Ac 5:21, 27, 34, 41; 6:12, 15; 22:30; 23:1, 6, 15, 20, 28** (on the probability of ref. in vv. **20** and **28** to a locality s. κατάγω and 3, below); **24:20.**

❷ **an official session of a council,** ***council meeting*** (cp. Diod. S. 13, 111, 1 συναγαγὼν συνέδριον, of a circle of friends). Of the Sanhedrin συνήγαγον οἱ ἀρχιερεῖς καὶ οἱ Φαρισαῖοι συνέδριον *the high priests and the Pharisees called a meeting of the council* **J 11:47.**

❸ **council meeting room,** ***meeting room*** (SIG 243 D, 47; 249 II, 77f; 252, 71; POxy 717, 8; 11 [II BC]; BGU 540, 25) of the Sanhedrin **Ac 4:15;** perh. (s. 1 above) **Lk 22:66** (GSchneider, Verleugnung etc. [Lk 22:54–71], '69); **Ac 23:20, 28.**—Pauly-W. II 8, 1333–53; Kl. Pauly V 456; DBS XI 1353–1413; BHHW II 740f.—DELG s.v. ἕζομαι B 2. M-M. EDNT. TW.

συνέδριος **Ac 5:35** D, prob. an error, caused by the presence of συνέδριον in vs. 34, for

σύνεδρος, ου, ὁ (s. συνέδριον; Hdt. et al.; Diod. S. 16, 60, 1; 36, 7, 4; Arrian, Tact. 27, 4; ins, LXX; Philo, Sobr. 19; Jos., Ant. 14, 172) ***member of a council*** **Ac 5:35** D.—DELG s.v. ἕζομαι B 2.

συνείδησις, εως, ἡ (συνεῖδον)—❶ **awareness of information about someth.,** ***consciousness*** (Democr., fgm. 297 σ. τῆς κακοπραγμοσύνης; Chrysipp. in Diog. L. 7, 85 τὴν ταύτης συνείδησιν; Eccl 10:20; Sir 42:18 v.l.; Jos., Ant. 16, 212; Just.; Theoph. Ant. 2, 4 [p. 102, 8]) w. obj. gen. συνείδησις ἁμαρτιῶν *consciousness of sin* **Hb 10:2** (Diod. S. 4, 65, 7 διὰ τὴν συνείδησιν τοῦ μύσους; Philo, Det. Pot. Ins. 146 οἱ συνειδήσει τῶν οἰκείων ἀδικημάτων ἐλεγχόμενοι, Virt. 124 σ. ἁμαρτημάτων). συνείδησις θεοῦ *consciousness, awareness of God* **1 Pt 2:19** (s. ESelwyn, 1 Pt '46, 176–78). Opp. σ. τοῦ εἰδώλου *in awareness that this is an idol* **1 Cor 8:7a v.l.** (for συνηθείᾳ).

❷ **the inward faculty of distinguishing right and wrong,** ***moral consciousness, conscience*** (Menand., Monost. 597 ἅπασιν ἡμῖν ἡ συνείδησις θεός comes close to this mng.; cp. 654; Dionys. Hal., De Thuc. 8 μιαίνειν τὴν ἑαυτοῦ συνείδησιν; Heraclit. Sto., 37 p. 54, 8 σ. ἁμαρτόντος ἀνθρώπου; Ps.-Lucian, Amor. 49 οὐδεμιᾶς ἀπρεποῦς συνειδήσεως παροικούσης; Hierocles 14, 451; Stob., Flor. 3, 24 [I 601ff H.]

quotes sayings of Bias and Periander on ὀρθὴ or ἀγαθὴ συνείδησις; PRyl 116, 9 [II AD] θλιβομένη τῇ συνειδήσει περὶ ὧν ἐνοσφίσατο; Mitt-Wilck. II/2, 88 I, 35 [II AD]; BGU 1024 III, 7; PFlor 338, 17 [III AD] συνειδήσει='conscientiously', also s. 3, below; Wsd 17:10; Jos., Ant. 16, 103 κατὰ συνείδησιν ἀτοπωτέραν; TestReub 4:3; TestJud 20:2 v.l.; συνείδησιν μολύνειν Hippol., Ref. 9, 23, 4) w. subj. gen. **Ro 2:15; 9:1; 1 Cor 10:29a; 2 Cor 1:12; 4:2; 5:11; Hb 9:14** al.; ἡ ἰδία σ. **1 Ti 4:2.** Opp. ἄλλη σ. *another's scruples* **1 Cor 10:29b;** διὰ τὴν σ. *for conscience' sake* (cp. OGI 484, 37 διὰ τὸ συνειδός; Ps.-Dio Chrys. 20 [37], 35) **Ro 13:5; 1 Cor 10:25, 27f;** τὸ μαρτύριον τῆς σ. **2 Cor 1:12,** cp. σ. as the subj. of μαρτυρεῖν **Ro 9:1;** cp. **2:15,** or of ἐλέγχειν **J 8:9 v.l.** (s. ἐλέγχω 2). W. attributes: σ. ἀγαθή *a good conscience* (cp. Herodian 6, 3, 4; PRein s.v. καλός 2b) **Ac 23:1; 1 Ti 1:5; 1 Pt 3:21** (on the topic cp. FSokolowski, Lois sacrées des cités grecques, Supplément '62 no. 108, 4–7 'one who enters the temple . . . must be pure, not through bathing but in mind'); ἔχειν ἀγαθὴν σ. (cp. ἐλευθέραν ἐχ. τὴν σ. Did., Gen. 89, 11) **1 Ti 1:19; 1 Pt 3:16.** Also ἐν ἀγαθῇ σ. ὑπάρχειν 1 Cl 41:1. ἐν ἀμώμῳ καὶ ἁγνῇ συνειδήσει περιπατεῖν Pol 5:3 (μετὰ συνειδήσεως ἀγαθῆς τελευτᾶν Hippol., Ref. 9, 26, 4); cp. 1 Cl 1:3. σ. ἀσθενής *a weak conscience,* indecisive because of being bound to old ways **1 Cor 8:7;** cp. vss. **10, 12.** σ. ἀπρόσκοπος **Ac 24:16;** καθαρὰ σ. **1 Ti 3:9; 2 Ti 1:3;** 1 Cl 45:7; καθαρὸς τῇ σ. ITr 7:2; καλὴ σ. **Hb 13:18;** 2 Cl 16:4. σ. πονηρά *a bad conscience* or *a consciousness of guilt* (s. καρδία 1bδ) **Hb 10:22;** D 4:14; B 19:12; Hm 3:4. ἡ σ. μολύνεται **1 Cor 8:7.** μιαίνεται **Tit 1:15** (s. Dionys. Hal. above). καθαριεῖ τ. συνείδησιν ἡμῶν ἀπὸ νεκρῶν ἔργων **Hb 9:14.** κατὰ συνείδησιν (s. on this Vett. Val. 210, 1) τελειῶσαί τινα vs. **9.**

❸ **attentiveness to obligation, *conscientiousness*** (for ins s. New Docs 3, 85; pap.) μετὰ συνειδήσεως *conscientiously* 1 Cl 2:4; ἐν ὁμονοίᾳ συναχθέντες τῇ σ. *assembled in concord, with full consciousness of our duty* 1 Cl 34:7.—MKähler, Das Gewissen I 1, 1878, RE VI 1899, 646ff; RSteinmetz, Das Gewissen bei Pls 1911; MPohlenz, GGA 1913, 642ff, Die Stoa '48; '49 (index), ZNW 42, '49, 77–79; HBöhlig, Das Gewissen bei Seneka u. Pls: StKr 87, 1914, 1–24; FTillmam, Zur Geschichte des Begriffs 'Gewissen' bis zu den paulin. Briefen: SMerkle Festschr. 1922, 336–47; FZucker, Syneidesis-Conscientia 1928; TSchneider, D. paulin. Begriff d. Gewissens (Syneidesis): Bonner Zeitschr. f. Theol. u. Seelsorge 6, 1929, 193–211, D. Quellen d. paul. Gewissensbegr.: ibid. 7, 1930, 97–112; BSnell, Gnomon 6, 1930, 21ff; MDibelius Hdb.[2] '31 exc. on 1 Ti 1:5; HOsborne, Σύνεσις and σ.: ClR 45, '31, 8–10, Συνείδησις: JTS 32, '31, 167–79; GRudberg, JAEklund Festschr. '33, 165ff; GJung, Συνείδησις, Conscientia, Bewusstsein: Archiv f. d. gesamte Psychologie 89, '34, 525–40; WAalders, Het Geweten, '35; CSpicq, La conscience dans le NT: RB 47, '38, 50–80; BReicke, The Disobedient Spirits and Christian Baptism '46, 174–82; JDupont, Studia Hellenistica 5, '48, 119–53; HClavier, Συν., une pierre de touche de l'Hellénisme paulinien, announced in Studia Paulina [JdeZwaan Festschr.] '53, p. 80 n. 1; CPierce, Conscience in the NT, '55; BReicke, TZ 12, '56, 157–61, esp. 159; DMariella Jr., The NT Concept of Conscience, diss. Vanderbilt '59; PDelhaye, Studia Montis Regii (Montreal) 4, '61, 229–51; JStelzenberger, Syneidesis im NT, '61; MThrall, NTS 14, '67/68, 118–25; BHarris, Westminster Theol. Journal 24, '62, 173–86; RJewett, Paul's Anthropological Terms, '71, 402–46; HEckstein, Der Begriff Syneidesis bei Paulus '83; GSelby, The Meaning and Function of σ. in Hb 9 and 10: Restoration Qtrly 28, '86, 145–54 (internal awareness of sin); PGooch, Conscience in 1 Cor 8 and 10: NTS 33, '87, 244–54; PTomson, Paul and the Jewish Law (CRINT III/1) '90, 208–20 ('consciousness'); EBorgh, La notion de conscience dans le NT: Filología Neotestamentaria 10, 1997, 85–98.—RAC X 1025–1107; BHHW I 564f.—New Docs 3 no. 69. DELG s.v. οἶδα C. M-M. EDNT. TW. Spicq. Sv.

συνεῖδον s. συνοράω.

συνειδός, τό s. σύνοιδα 2.

συνειδυῖα s. σύνοιδα.

συνείληφα s. συλλαμβάνω.

I. σύνειμι (fr. εἰμί) impf. 3 sg. συνῆν (συνήμην ApcMos 42) ***be with*** (Hom.+) τινί *someone* (trag., Thu. et al.; Jos., Ant. 3, 75) **Ac 22:11;** IEph 11:2 v.l. (s. συναινέω). συνῆσαν αὐτῷ *joined him* **Lk 9:18.**—M-M.

II. σύνειμι (fr. εἶμι) ***come together*** (Hom. et al.; ins; Jos., Ant. 4, 203; Tat. 23, 2; in late pap as an accounting expr.) συνιόντος ὄχλου εἶπεν *when a crowd gathered, he said* **Lk 8:4** (cp. Jos., Vi. 9).—M-M.

συνεισέρχομαι mid. dep. fut. 3 sg. συνεισελεύσεται LXX; 2 aor. συνεισῆλθον (Eur., Thu. et al.; BGU 388 II, 26; LXX; Jos., Ant. 9, 133 εἰς) ***enter with, go in(to) with*** τινί *someone* εἴς τι *(into) someth.* (Eur., Hel. 1083 ἐς οἴκους τινί; Appian, Iber. 43 §176 συνεσῆλθεν αὐτοῖς ἐς τὸ στρατόπεδον) **J 6:22; 18:15; Mk 6:33 v.l.; Lk 8:51 v.l.**—M-M.

συνέκδημος, ου, ὁ (ἔκδημος 'abroad'; Diod. S.; Plut., Otho 1069 [5, 2], Mor. 100f; Palaeph., 45 p. 67, 7; Jos., Vi. 79; SIG 1052, 9; OGI 494, 13f; cp. Lat. comes) ***traveling companion,*** w. focus on official assignment **Ac 19:29; 2 Cor 8:19.**—DELG s.v. δῆμος. M-M.

συνεκλεκτός, ή, όν pert. to being chosen together with, *also chosen,* only fem. and subst. ἡ ἐν Βαβυλῶνι συνεκλεκτή *the one in Babylon chosen the same as (you)* **1 Pt 5:13.** No individual woman is meant, least of all Peter's wife, but rather a congregation w. whom Peter is staying. Cp. Βαβυλών.—DELG s.v. λέγω. M-M.

συνεκπορεύομαι (Polyb. 6, 32, 5; Judg 11:3 A; 13:25 B) impf. mid. ***go out with*** someone understood **Ac 3:11** D.—DELG s.v. πόρος.

συνελαύνω 1 aor. συνήλασα. Pass.: aor. ptc. gen. pl. συνελασθέντων 2 Macc 5:5; plpf. 3 sg. συνήλαστο 2 Macc 4:26 (Hom. et al.; pap; 2 Macc; Jos., Bell. 2, 526; 4, 567, Ant. 2, 249; 5, 162 [all four times w. εἰς and local acc.]) **to cause movement through constraint, *drive, force, bring*** εἴς τι *to someth.,* in imagery (Aelian, VH 4, 15 εἰς τὸν τῆς σοφίας ἔρωτα; Sb 5357, 13 σ. τινὰ πρὸς εὐγνωμοσύνην=make someone reasonable) **Ac 7:26 v.l.;** GJs 18:3 v.l. (for ἀπελ.).—DELG s.v. ἐλαύνω.

συνέλευσις, εως ἡ (Plut., Ptolemaeus et al.; PSI 450, 10; Judg 9:46 B and 49 B; ParJer 3:11; Jos., Ant. 3, 118; Just.; in var. senses of 'coming together') **coming together in sexual union, *intercourse*** (Vett. Val. 47, 8 et al.) of very small animals 1 Cl 20:10.—DELG s.v. ἐλεύσομαι.

συνεξέρχομαι fut. 3 sg. συνεξελεύσεται Pr 22:10; 2 aor. συνεξῆλθον ***go out with*** τινί *someone* (Eur., Hdt., Thu. et al.; BGU 38, 13; Jdth 2:20; Mel., P. 7, 47) 1 Cl 11:2.

συνεπέρχομαι mid. dep. 2 aor. συνεπῆλθον ***to come together against, attack together*** (Quint. Smyrn. 2, 302; SIG 700,

22 [117 BC]; PLips 40 II, 5; 17) συνεπελθόντες *when they closed in on him* MPol 7:1.

συνεπιμαρτυρέω *testify at the same time* (Petosiris, fgm. 21 ln. 58; Polyb. 25, 6, 4; Ps.-Aristot., De Mundo 6; Sext. Emp., Math. 8, 323; Athen. 13, 595e; EpArist 191; Philo, Mos. 2, 123) foll. by ὅτι 1 Cl 23:5. τινί *by means of someth.* **Hb 2:4,** *to someth.* 1 Cl 43:1.—DELG s.v. μάρτυς. M-M. TW.

συνεπίσκοπος, ου, ὁ *co-supervisor, co-superintendent* **Phil 1:1 v.l.,** apparently an error for σὺν ἐπισκόποις.—DELG s.v. σκέπτομαι.

συνεπιτίθημι mostly, as in its only occurrence in our lit., mid. συνεπιτίθεμαι, 2 aor. (Dt 32:27) συνεπεθέμην *join* w. others ***in an attack*** on pers. or things (Thu., Isaeus, X.; Polyb., Diod. S., Plut.; LXX; Jos., Ant. 10, 116) abs. **Ac 24:9** (cp. Ps 3:7).—M-M.

συνέπομαι mid. dep.; impf. συνειπόμην (Hom.+; POxy 1415, 8; 2 and 3 Macc; Ath., R. 20 p. 73, 15) ***accompany*** τινί *someone* (Jos., Ant. 13, 21; TestJud 3:10) **Ac 20:4.**—M-M.

συνεργέω impf. συνήργουν; 1 aor. συνήργησα (Eur., X.+; ins, pap, LXX, Test12Patr, Philo; Jos., Bell. 6, 38, Ant. 1, 156; Just., D. 142, 2; Orig.) **to engage in cooperative endeavor, *work together with, assist, help*** abs. τοῦ κυρίου συνεργοῦντος (PAmh 152, 5 τοῦ θεοῦ συνεργήσαντος; Did., Gen. 162, 10 συνεργῶν ὁ τῶν ὅλων θεός) **Mk 16:20.** παντὶ τῷ συνεργοῦντι *to everyone who helps* (such people as Stephanas) *in the work* **1 Cor 16:16.** With συνεργοῦντες **2 Cor 6:1** either θεῷ (Hofmann, Windisch, Sickenberger, NRSV) or ὑμῖν (Chrysost., Bengel, Schmiedel, Bachmann) can be supplied. σ. ἐν παντὶ πράγματι *be helpful in every respect* Hs 5, 6, 6. W. dat. of person or thing that is helped (X., Mem. 4, 3, 12; Diod. S. 4, 25, 4 σ. ταῖς ἐπιθυμίαις=assist [him] in his wishes; OGI 45, 11 [III BC]; PSI 376, 4 [250 BC]; 1 Macc 12:1; TestReub 3:6; TestIss 3:7 ὁ θεός): βλέπεις ὅτι ἡ πίστις συνήργει τοῖς ἔργοις αὐτοῦ *you see that faith worked with* (and thereby *aided*) *his good deeds* **Js 2:22.** W. the goal indicated by εἰς (Epict. 1, 9, 26; Appian, Syr. 59 §309 ἐς τὸν θάνατον σ., Bell. Civ. 5, 90 §378; Philo, Agr. 13; TestGad 4:7 εἰς θάνατον, εἰς σωτηρίαν): in τοῖς ἀγαπῶσιν τὸν θεὸν πάντα συνεργεῖ εἰς ἀγαθόν **Ro 8:28,** σ. means *assist* (or *work with*) *someone to obtain someth.* or *bring someth. about* (IG^2, 654, 15f σ. εἰς τ. ἐλευθερίαν τῇ πόλει; Larfeld I 500; Plut., Mor. 769d οὕτως ἡ φύσις γυναικὶ . . . πρὸς εὔνοιαν ἀνδρὸς καὶ φιλίαν μεγάλα συνήργησεν 'thus nature greatly assists a self-controlled woman in securing the goodwill and friendship of her husband'; cp. Polyb. 11, 9, 1). Then the subj. will be either πάντα *everything helps* (or *works with* or *for*) *those who love God to obtain what is good* (Vulg., Zahn, Sickenberger, Althaus, RSV mg.; NRSV), or ὁ θεός, which is actually read after συνεργεῖ in good and very ancient mss. (P^{46} BA; Orig. For ἡμῖν συνεργεῖν of gods: X., Mem. 4, 3, 12; but s. MBlack, The Interpr. of Ro 8:28: OCullmann Festschr. '62, 166–72); in the latter case πάντα is acc. of specification (πᾶς 1dβ) *in everything God helps* (or *works for* or *with*) *those who love him to obtain what is good* (so RSV; NRSV mg.; Syr., Copt., BWeiss, RLipsius, Jülicher, Kühl, Ltzm.; Goodsp., Probs. 148–50.—Cp. OGI 219, 10f on helpful deity. The prep. phrase σ. . . . εἰς would correspond exactly to Alex. Aphr., Fat. 31 p. 203, 8 Br. acc. to cod. H: εἰς ἀγαθὸν οὐδὲν ὁ Πύθιος τῷ Λαΐῳ συνεργεῖ='in no respect does Apollo work w. Laius for good', or 'help L. to obtain what is good'. For the idea cp. Herm. Wr. 9, 4b πάντα γὰρ τῷ τοιούτῳ [=θεοσεβεῖ], κἂν τοῖς ἄλλοις τὰ κακά, ἀγαθά ἐστι 'everything is good for such a [god-fearing] person, even if bad for others'; Plotin. 4, 3, 16, 21. JBauer, ZNW 50, '59, 106–12. Cp. Sext. Emp., Outlines of Pyrrhonism I, 207 'be to one's advantage' [communication fr. EKrentz]).—DELG s.v. ἔργον. EDNT. TW.

συνεργός, όν (Pind., Thu. et al.; ins, pap; 2 Macc 8:7; Mel., P. 54, 396 [ἡ τοῦ θανάτου συνεργός, in ref. to ἁμαρτία]) **pert. to working together with, *helping*,** as subst. and always so in our lit. ***helper, fellow-worker*** (Philo; Jos., Bell. 2, 102, Ant. 7, 346; Orig., C. Cels. 5, 58, 17; Polyb. 31, 24, 10). Paul refers to those who helped him in spreading the gospel as *his fellow-workers* (subjective gen.) **Ro 16:3, 9, 21; Phil 2:25; 4:3; 1 Th 3:2 v.l.; Phlm 1; 24.** Instead of the gen. there may be an indication of the field in which the cooperation took place εἰς *in* (Alex. Aphr., An. Mant. p. 167, 9 Br.) συνεργοὶ εἰς τὴν βασιλείαν τοῦ θεοῦ *co-workers in the Kingdom of God* **Col 4:11.** εἰς ὑμᾶς συνεργός *fellow-worker among you* **2 Cor 8:23.** συνεργὸς τοῦ θεοῦ ἐν τῷ εὐαγγελίῳ *God's helper in the gospel* **1 Th 3:2.** συνεργοί ἐσμεν τῆς χαρᾶς ὑμῶν *we are working with you to bring you joy* **2 Cor 1:24** (on the gen. cp. X., Cyr. 2, 4, 10; 3, 3, 10 συνεργοὺς τοῦ κοινοῦ ἀγαθοῦ). W. the dat. of that which is assisted (Eur., Thu. et al.) ἵνα συνεργοὶ γινώμεθα τῇ ἀληθείᾳ *that we may prove to be helpers of the truth* **3J 8** (σ. γίνεσθαί τινι as UPZ 146, 3 [II BC]). In θεοῦ ἐσμεν συνεργοί **1 Cor 3:9** the συν- refers either to communion w. God *we are fellow-workers with God* or to the community of teachers at Corinth *we are fellow-laborers in the service of God* (so VFurnish, JBL 80, '61, 364–70).—New Docs 3, 154; DELG s.v. ἔργον. M-M. EDNT. TW.

συνέρχομαι (since Il. 10, 224 [in tmesis]; ins, pap, LXX, pseudepigr., Philo, Joseph., Just.; Ath., R. 23, p. 77, 8) impf. συνηρχόμην; fut. συνελεύσομαι; 2 aor. συνῆλθον (συνῆλθα B-D-F §81, 3; W-S. §13, 13; Mlt-H. 208); pf. ptc. συνεληλυθώς; plpf. 3 pl. συνεληλύθεισαν, ptc. fem. pl. συνεληλυθεῖαι.

❶ **to come together w. others as a group, *assemble, gather*** συνέρχεται ὁ ὄχλος **Mk 3:20.** συνέρχονται πάντες οἱ ἀρχιερεῖς **14:53.—Ac 1:6** (s. B-D-F §251; Rob. 695); **2:6, 37** D; **5:16; 10:27; 16:13; 19:32; 21:22 v.l.; 22:30; 28:17; 1 Cor 14:26.** W. the addition of εἰς w. acc. of place (Pla., Leg. 6, 13, 767c; Diod. S. 13, 100, 7 συνῆλθον εἰς Ἔφεσον; Zech 8:21) **Ac 5:16 v.l.;** ἐν w. dat. of place (POxy 1187, 6) ἐν ἐκκλησίᾳ **1 Cor 11:18;** αὐτοῦ **Mk 6:33 v.l.;** ὅπου **J 18:20;** ἐπὶ τὸ αὐτό (s. αὐτός 3b; σ. ἐπὶ τὸ αὐτό Josh 9:2; Syntipas p. 75, 16) **1 Cor 11:20; 14:23;** B 4:10. Foll. by a dat. *come together with someone, assemble at someone's house* (PTebt 34, 4 [I BC] συνελθεῖν Ὥρῳ; Jos., Bell. 2, 411) **Mk 14:53 v.l.;** D 14:2. πρός τινα *come together to (meet) someone* (Ex 32:26) **Mk 6:33 v.l.** Foll. by an inf. of purpose **Lk 5:15;** by εἰς denoting purpose **1 Cor 11:33;** IEph 13:1. εἰς can also introduce a result that was not intended οὐκ εἰς τὸ κρεῖσσον ἀλλὰ εἰς τὸ ἧσσον συνέρχεσθε *you hold your meetings in such a way that they turn out not to your advantage, but to your disadvantage* **1 Cor 11:17.** εἰς κρίμα vs. **34** (on the solemnity of a celebration cp. the schol. on Aristoph., Pax 967f: to the question 'τίς τῇδε;' [="who is here?"] the group answers 'πολλοὶ κἀγαθοί'. τοῦτο δὲ ἐποίουν οἱ σπένδοντες, ἵνα οἱ συνειδότες τι ἑαυτοῖς ἄτοπον ἐκχωροῖεν τ. σπονδῶν="many good men." Now, those who pour the libations were accustomed to do this [ask the question], so that those who were aware of anything inappropriate about themselves might absent themselves from the libation). W. indication of the nature and manner of the meeting συνέρχεσθε ἐν μιᾷ πίστει IEph 20:2.

❷ **to come/go with one or more pers., *travel together with*** someone (BGU 380, 13; 596, 4 [84 AD]) τινί (EpArist 35; Jos.,

Ant. 9, 33) τοὺς συνελθόντας αὐτῇ Ἰουδαίους **J 11:33.** ἦσαν συνεληλυθυῖαι ἐκ τῆς Γαλιλαίας αὐτῷ **Lk 23:55.** Cp. **Ac 1:21; 9:39; 10:23, 45; 11:12.** σ. τινι εἰς τὸ ἔργον **15:38.** σύν τινι instead of the dat. alone **21:16.** συνελθόντων ἐνθάδε prob. means (because of συνκαταβάντες 25:5) *they came back here with (me)* **25:17.**

❸ **to unite in an intimate relationship,** ***come together*** in a sexual context (X., Mem. 2, 2, 4; Diod. S. 3, 58, 4; Ps.-Apollod. 1, 3, 3; Philo, Virt. 40; 111; Jos., Ant. 7, 168; 213) ἐπὶ τὸ αὐτό σ. **1 Cor 7:5 v.l.** In πρὶν ἢ συνελθεῖν αὐτούς **Mt 1:18** domestic and marital relations are combined. (In marriage contracts in pap πρὸς γάμον τινὶ συνελθεῖν means 'marry'. Also without πρὸς γάμον: BGU 970, 13 [II AD] συνηρχόμην τῷ προγεγραμμένῳ μου ἀνδρί).—M-M. TW.

συνεσθίω impf. συνήσθιον; 2 aor. συνέφαγον (Pla. et al.; Plut., Lucian; SIG 1179; LXX; TestSim 6:7 [Christ. interpolation]; JosAs 7:1) ***eat with*** τινί *someone* (Pla., Leg. 9, 881d; Epict., Ench. 36; Ps 100:5) **Lk 15:2; Ac 11:3; 1 Cor 5:11;** PEg[2] 34 (ASyn. 42, 30); w. συμπίνειν (as Polyaenus 6, 24; SIG 1179, 18f) **Ac 10:41;** ISm 3:3. Instead of the dat. μετά τινος (cp. Ex 18:12; Aristoph., Acharn. 277 ξυμπίνειν μετά τινος; JosAs 7:1) **Gal 2:12.** VParkin, Studia Evangelica III, '64, 250–53; CHeil, Die Ablehnung der Speisegebote durch Paulus '94.—DELG s.v. ἔδω. M-M.

σύνεσις, εως, ἡ (συνίημι; Hom. et al.)—❶ **the faculty of comprehension,** ***intelligence, acuteness, shrewdness*** (Pind. et al.; OGI 323, 6 [II BC] συνέσει κ. παιδείᾳ προάγων; LXX, pseudepigr., Philo; Jos., C. Ap. 2, 125; Ath. 1:3 al.; Orig., C. Cels. 4, 76, 6; Did., Gen. 226, 12)

ⓐ gener. **Lk 2:47** (s. Jos., Vi. 8f); D 12:4. ἡ σύνεσις τῶν συνετῶν **1 Cor 1:19** (Is 29:14). W. σοφία (Aristot., EN 1, 13, 20; Diod. S. 9, 3, 3; Dt 4:6) 1 Cl 32:4. The whole field of the inner life is covered by the expr. ἐξ ὅλης τῆς καρδίας καὶ ἐξ ὅλης τῆς συνέσεως καὶ ἐξ ὅλης τῆς ἰσχύος **Mk 12:33.**

ⓑ in the religio-ethical realm (IG IV[2]/1, 86, 18; Iren. 1, 10, 3 [Harv. I 97, 11]) *understanding* such as God grants to God's own (LXX; pseudepigr.; Just., D. 70, 5): w. σοφία, ἐπιστήμη, γνῶσις B 2:3; 21:5 (cp. Ex 31:3; 35:31; Sir 1:19). W. σοφία (as Jos., Ant. 8, 24): σύνεσις πνευματική **Col 1:9.** W. ἐπίγνωσις τ. μυστηρίου τοῦ θεοῦ: πλοῦτος τῆς πληροφορίας τῆς συνέσεως **2:2.** W. πίστις AcPl Ha 8, 34= BMM verso, 7f [συν]έσει. W. φῶς 1 Cl 16:12 (Is 53:11). Personified w. other godly virtues (as gnostic name of an Aeon Iren. 1, 1, 2 [Harv. I 11, 8]) Hs 9, 15, 2. Where the Lord dwells there is σύνεσις πολλή m 10, 1, 6.—σύνεσιν αἰτεῖσθαι IPol 1:3; Hs 5, 4, 3f. σύνεσιν διδόναι Hm 4, 2, 2a. σ. λαμβάνειν (Aristot., EN 1161b, 26) s 9, 2, 6. σ. ἔχειν (Hdt. 2, 5) 9, 22, 2b and 3; D 12:1 (s. Hdb., Suppl. 1 ad loc.; for a difft. int. s. ἀριστερός). ἀπέστη ἀπ' αὐτῶν ἡ σύνεσις *understanding has departed from them* Hs 9, 22, 2a. ἐν τῇ συνέσει *in the correct* (God-given, comprehending the true mng.) *understanding* B 10:1. Repentance is σύν. Hm 4, 2, 2b, c, d.

ⓒ *the wisdom of the creator* (Theoph. Ant. 2, 15 [p. 138, 13]) 1 Cl 33:3; Hv 1, 3, 4.

❷ **the content of understanding or comprehension,** ***insight, understanding*** σύνεσις ἔν τινι *insight into, understanding of someth.* **Eph 3:4; 2 Ti 2:7.**—DELG s.v. ἵημι. M-M. TW. Sv.

συνεστώς s. συνίστημι.

συνετίζω fut. συνετιῶ; 1 aor. impv. συνέτισον; inf. συνετίσαι LXX (Rhet. Gr. I 584, 30; LXX; ApcMos 13) ***cause to understand*** τινά *someone* (TestLevi 4:5; 9:8; Hesych.; Suda) Hm 4, 2, 1. Pass. *be given insight* Dg 12:9.

συνετός, ή, όν (συνίημι) **pert. to being able to understand with discernment,** ***intelligent, sagacious, wise, with good sense*** (Theognis, Pind. et al.; LXX; EpArist 148; Philo, Joseph.; Just.—Adv. συνετῶς [LXX; Just., D. 114, 3]; superl. συνετώτατα [Just., D. 87, 3]) ἀνὴρ σ. **Ac 13:7** (Just., D. 2, 6). συνετὸν εἶναι Hm 12, 1, 2; s 5, 5, 4; 9, 2, 6. W. μακρόθυμος m 5, 1, 1. (οἱ) συνετοί (w. σοφοί; s. σοφός 2αα) **Mt 11:25; Lk 10:21.** ἡ σύνεσις τῶν συνετῶν **1 Cor 1:19** (Is 29:14.—Cp. Maximus Tyr. 16, 4c συνετὰ συνετοῖς). οἱ συνετοὶ ἑαυτοῖς *those who are wise in their own sight* (w. ἐνώπιον ἑαυτῶν ἐπιστήμονες) B 4:11 (cp. Is 5:21). οἱ λεγόμενοι σ. IEph 18:1. Of the Creator συνετὸς ἔν τινι *understanding in someth.* (w. σοφὸς ἔν τινι) 1 Cl 60:1.—DELG s.v. ἵημι. M-M. TW.

συνευδοκέω 1 aor. συνηυδόκησα (Polyb. 32, 6, 9; Diod. S.; SIG 712, 46; pap; 1 and 2 Macc) **to join in approval,** ***agree with, approve of, consent to, sympathize with*** w. dat. of pers. (BGU 834, 24 [II AD]) *approve of someone* **Ro 1:32** (as TestAsh 6:2); 1 Cl 35:6. W. dat. of thing *approve of, give approval to* (BGU 1130, 3 [I BC]; POxy 504, 32; PGen 11, 3 al.; 1 Macc 1:57; 2 Macc 11:24) **Lk 11:48; Ac 8:1;** Dg 9:1. Abs. (Polyb. 23, 4, 13; Diod. S. 4, 24, 1; 11, 57, 5; BGU 1129, 6; 2 Macc 11:35) **Ac 22:20.** συνευδοκησάσης τῆς ἐκκλησίας πάσης *with the consent of the whole assembly (church)* 1 Cl 44:3. W. inf. foll. *be willing* to do someth. (PMich 202, 12 [105 AD]) **1 Cor 7:12f.** W. dat. of pers., foll. by the acc. and inf. Hs 5, 2, 11. ταύτῃ τῇ γνώμῃ ὁ υἱὸς τοῦ δεσπότου συνηυδόκησεν αὐτῷ, ἵνα *the son of the master agreed with him in this decision, namely that* 5, 2, 8 (on the text, which may be corrupt, s. MDibelius, Hdb. ad loc.).—M-M.

συνευρυθμίζω pf. pass. 3 sg. συνευρύθμισται ***bring into harmony with*** συνευρύθμισται ταῖς ἐντολαῖς ὡς χορδαῖς κιθάρα *he is in accord with the* (divine) *commandments as a lyre with its strings* IPhld 1:2 (cp. συναρμόζω 3).—DELG s.v. ῥυθμός.

συνευφραίνομαι aor. impv. 2 sing. συνευφράνθητι (TestAbr A 4 p. 81, 24 [Stone p. 10]) ***rejoice (together) with*** (Ps.-Dionys. Hal., A. Rh. 2, 5; Ael. Aristid. 42, 9 K.=6 p. 68 D.; Pollux 5, 129; Pr 5:18; TestAbr loc. cit.; Philo, Conf. Lingu. 6) w. dat. foll. (Demosth. 18, 217; Herodian 2, 8, 9) B 2:3.—DELG s.v. φρήν.

συνευωχέομαι pass. dep. in act. sense ***feast together*** (Aristot., Eth. Eud. 7, 12, 14, 1245b; Posidonius: 87 fgm. 15, 3 Jac. [in Athen. 4, 152b]; Philo, Spec. Leg. 4, 119 al.) **Jd 12.** τινί *with someone* (Lucian, Ver. Hist. 2, 15, Ep. Sat. 4, 36 al.; Jos., Ant. 1, 92; 4, 203; BGU 596, 10 [I AD] ὅπως συνευωχηθῇς ἡμῖν; PGM 4, 3150) **2 Pt 2:13.**—DELG s.v. εὐωχέω. M-M.

συνέφαγον s. συνεσθίω.

συνεφίστημι 2 aor. συνεπέστην (Thu. et al.) intr. **to join in an uprising,** ***join in an attack*** κατά τινος *against* or *upon someone* **Ac 16:22.**—DELG s.v. ἵστημι.

συνέχω fut. συνέξω; 2 aor. συνέσχον. Pass. impf. συνειχόμην; fut. 3 pl. συσχεθήσονται Job 36:8; En 21:10; aor. συνεσχέθην LXX, AcPl Ha (Hom.+).

❶ **to hold together as a unit,** ***hold together, sustain*** τὶ *someth.* (Ael. Aristid. 43, 16 K.=1 p. 6 D.: τὰ πάντα σ.; PTebt

410, 11. Cp. IG XIV, 1018 to Attis συνέχοντι τὸ πᾶν [s. CWeyman, BZ 14, 1917, 17f]; PGM 13, 843. Other exx. in Cumont[3] 230, 57; Wsd 1:7; Aristobulus in Eus., PE 13, 12, 12 [=Holladay p. 184, 78; s. p. 229 n. 139 for add. reff. and lit.]; Philo; Jos., C. Ap.2, 208) συνέχει αὐτὴ (i.e. ἡ ψυχή) τὸ σῶμα Dg 6:7. Pass. 1 Cl 20:5.

❷ **to close by holding together,** ***stop, shut*** (στόμα Ps 68:16; Is 52:15; PsSol 17:19 πηγαὶ συνεσχέθησαν. The heavens, so that there is no rain Dt 11:17; 3 Km 8:35) συνέσχον τὰ ὦτα αὐτῶν i.e. they refused to listen **Ac 7:57.**

❸ **to press in and around so as to leave little room for movement,** ***press hard, crowd*** τινά *someone* **Lk 8:45.** Of a city (2 Macc 9:2) οἱ ἐχθροί σου συνέξουσίν σε πάντοθεν **19:43.**

❹ **to hold in custody,** ***guard*** (Lucian, Tox. 39; PMagd 42, 7; PLille 7, 15 [III BC]) **Lk 22:63.**

❺ **to cause distress by force of circumstances,** ***seize, attack, distress, torment*** τινά *someone* τὰ συνέχοντά με *that which distresses me* IRo 6:3. Mostly pass. (Aeschyl., Hdt. et al.) *be tormented by, afflicted w., distressed by* τινί *someth.,* of sickness (Pla. et al.; ApcMos 5; Tat. 2, 1; 3; SIG 1169, 50 ἀγρυπνίαις συνεχόμενος; POxy 896, 34 πυραιτίοις συνεχόμενος) νόσοις καὶ βασάνοις **Mt 4:24;** πυρετῷ (Hippiatr. I 6, 23; Jos., Ant. 13, 398; s. also πυρετός) **Lk 4:38;** πυρετοῖς καὶ δυσεντερίῳ **Ac 28:8.** Of unpleasant emotional states (Diod. S. 29, 25 λύπῃ; TestAbr A 16, p. 96, 21 [Stone p. 40] δειλίᾳ πολλῇ; Aelian, VH 14, 22 ὀδυρμῷ; Ps.-Plut., De Fluv. 2, 1; 7, 5; 17, 3; 19, 1) φόβῳ μεγάλῳ συνείχοντο *they were overcome by great fear* **Lk 8:37** (cp. Job 3:24). φόβῳ μεγάλῳ συσχεθεῖσα AcPl Ha 3, 34; cp. 11, 16.—Without the dat. (Leontios 16 p. 33, 13 συνεχόμενος=tormented) πῶς συνέχομαι *how great is my distress, what vexation I must endure* **Lk 12:50.** The apostle, torn betw. conflicting emotions, says συνέχομαι ἐκ τῶν δύο *I am hard pressed* (to choose) *between the two* **Phil 1:23.**

❻ **to occupy someone's attention intensely,** συνέχομαί τινι ***I am occupied with*** or ***absorbed in*** *someth.* (Herodian 1, 17, 9 ἡδοναῖς; Diog. L. 7, 185 γέλωτι; Wsd 17:19) συνείχετο τῷ λόγῳ (Paul) *was wholly absorbed in preaching* **Ac 18:5** (EHenschel, Theologia Viatorum 2, '50, 213–15; cp. Arrian, Anab. 7, 21, 5 ἐν τῷδε τῷ πόνῳ ξυνείχοντο=they were intensively engaged in this difficult task) in contrast to the activity cited in vs. 3. Closely related is the sense

❼ **to provide impulse for some activity,** ***urge on, impel,*** τινά *someone* ἡ ἀγάπη συνέχει ἡμᾶς **2 Cor 5:14** (so Bachmann, Belser, Sickenberger, Lietzmann, Windisch, OHoltzmann, 20th Cent.; NRSV). Pass. συνείχετο τῷ πνεύματι ὁ Παῦλος **Ac 18:5 v.l.**

❽ **to hold within bounds so as to manage or guide,** ***direct, control.*** Many, including RSV and REB, offer this interp. for **2 Cor 5:14** (s. 7 above. Heinrici leaves the choice open betw. 7 and 8. GHendry, ET 59, '47/48, 82 proposes 'include, embrace.').—M-M. TW. Spicq.

συνεχῶς adv. of συνεχής (Just., D. 192, 1; Ath., R. 16 p. 68, 1), of time (Hes. et al.; ins, pap; TestJob 2:3; Test12Patr; EpArist 78 al.; Philo; Jos., Vi. 20, Ant. 19, 318) ***continually, unremittingly*** ἐκζητεῖν B 21:8.

συνζ- s. συζ-.

συνήγορος, ου, ὁ (Aeschyl., Demosth. et al.; ins; PAmh 23, 15; 24 [II BC]; POxy 1479, 5; Philo, Conf. Lingu. 121; Ar. 8, 4; Tat.1, 2; loanw. in rabb.) **one who serves as an advocate in legal matters,** ***attorney*** (Diod. S. 1, 76, 1; Philo, Vi. Cont. 44) ISm 5:1.—DELG s.v. ἀγορά 3.

συνήδομαι pass. dep. (Soph., X. et al.; Dio Chrys. 3, 103; SIG [index]; Philo, Conf. Lingu. 7; Jos., Bell. 4, 656, Ant. 8, 386; POxy 1663a, 4 τινί='rejoice with someone') **to experience joy in connection with,** ***delight in*** συνήδομαι τῷ νόμῳ *I (joyfully) agree with the law* **Ro 7:22** (cp. Simplicius In Epict. p. 53, 5 Düb. τ. ἐπιτάγμασι σ.).—M-M.

συνήθεια, ας, ἡ (ἦθος)—❶ **a relationship in which the participants are compatible because of shared interests,** ***friendship, fellowship, intimacy*** (Isocr., Aeschin. et al.; ins, pap) πρός τινα *with someone* (Polyb. 1, 43, 4; 31, 14, 3; Plut., Crass. 544 [3, 6]; PAmh 145, 10; Jos., Ant. 15, 97) IEph 5:1 (συνήθειαν ἔχ. πρός τινα also Vett. Val. 228, 23). There is a close semantic relationship between 'being accustomed to one another' in the sharing of values in a personal relationship and

❷ **a usage or practice that has become established or standard,** ***custom*** (Hom. Hymns; Pla.; ins, pap, 4 Macc; Philo, Spec. Leg. 3, 35 al.; Joseph.; Mel., HE 4, 26, 9; so as loanw. in rabb.).

ⓐ subjectively ***being*** or ***becoming accustomed*** τῇ συνηθείᾳ ἕως ἄρτι τοῦ εἰδώλου (obj. gen. as SIG 888, 154 διὰ τὴν συνήθειαν τῆς τοιαύτης ἐνοχλήσεως.—τῇ σ. is dat. of cause; s. on ἀπιστία 1) *through being accustomed to idols in former times* **1 Cor 8:7.**

ⓑ objectively ***custom, habit, usage*** (Jos., Ant. 10, 72) Dg 2:1. τὴν συνηθ̣ι̣α̣[ν τῆς]| νη[. . . νη]στίας AcPl Ha 7, 10f (some dittography [?], rdg. uncertain). συνήθειαν ἔχειν (PFlor 210, 15) **1 Cor 11:16;** w. inf. foll. Hm 5, 2, 6. ἔστιν συνήθειά τινι w. ἵνα foll. **J 18:39.**—Renehan '75 p. 185. DELG s.v. ἦθος. M-M. Sv.

συνήθης, ες (ἦθος; Hes. et al.) ***habitual, customary, usual*** (Soph., Thu.+; ins, pap, Sym.; TestSol 1:10; Philo; Jos., Ant. 6, 339; 12, 300; Ath., R. 7 p. 55, 10 [comp.]) μετὰ τῶν συνήθων αὐτοῖς ὅπλων *with the weapons that they usually carried* MPol 7:1 (Callisth.: 124 fgm. 14a Jac. μετὰ τῆς συνήθους στολῆς). σύνηθές ἐστί τινι *it is someone's custom* (Eur., Alc. 40): ὅπερ ἦν σύνηθες αὐτῷ 5:1. καθὰ ἦν αὐτῷ σύνηθες *as was the (lion's) habit* AcPl Ha 5, 18.—DELG s.v. ἦθος. M-M. s.v. συνήθεια. Sv.

συνῆκα s. συνίημι.

συνῆλθον s. συνέρχομαι.

συνηλικιώτης, ου, ὁ (σύν + ἡλικία via ἧλιξ; CIG III 4929; Alciphron 1, 15, 1; Ps.-Callisth. 1, 36, 3; in Diod. S. 1, 53, 10 and Dionys. Hal. 10, 49, 2 the best witnesses have ἡλικιώτης) **a person of one's own age,** ***a contemporary*** **Gal 1:14.**—DELG s.v. ἧλιξ. M-M.

συνηρπάκειν s. συναρπάζω.

συνῆσαν s. σύνειμι.

συνήσω s. συνίημι.

συνῆτε s. συνίημι.

συνήχθην s. συνάγω.

συνθάπτω 2 aor. pass. συνετάφην ***bury (together) with*** (Aeschyl., Hdt. et al.; PEleph 2, 12; ApcMos 42; Jos., Ant. 10, 48) pass. *be buried with* τινί *someone* (Hdt. 5, 5 συνθάπτεται τῷ ἀνδρί; Chariton 6, 2, 9), in our lit. only fig. (Lycurgus, Or. in Leocr. 50 συνετάφη τοῖς τούτων σώμασιν ἡ τῶν Ἑλλήνων ἐλευθερία) of the believers being buried together w. their Lord in baptism συνταφέντες αὐτῷ (=τῷ Χριστῷ) ἐν τῷ βαπτισμῷ (v.l. βαπτίσματι) **Col 2:12** (cp. Diod. S. 18, 22, 7 ἐν ταῖς οἰκίαις συνετάφησαν τοῖς οἰκείοις=they were buried in the houses together with their relatives). διὰ τοῦ βαπτίσματος **Ro 6:4** (s. σύμφυτος.—EStommel, 'Begraben mit Chr.' [Rö 6:4]: Röm. Quartalschr. 49, '54, 1–20).—M-M. TW.

σύνθεσις, εως, ἡ (Pla. et al.; ins, pap, LXX, Philo; Jos., Ant. 14, 173; Ar. 10, 5; Just., D. 86, 3; Tat.) **a putting/placing together,** ***combination,*** of clothing σύνθεσις ἱματίων *a collection (=a suit) of clothing* (POxy 496, 4 [II AD] al. Cp. συνθεσίδιον=garment PGiss 21, 8 [II AD]) Hs 6, 1, 5.—DELG s.v. τίθημι.

συνθλάω fut. συνθλάσω LXX; 1 aor. συνέθλασα LXX. Pass.: 1 fut. συνθλασθήσομαι; pf. ptc. acc. συντεθλασμένον Is 42:3 v.l. (Alexis Com. [IV BC] fgm. 270, 3 Kock [in Athen. 11, 466e]; Eratosth. p. 13, 18; Diod. S. 2, 57, 2; Manetho, Apot.. 5, 201; Plut., Artox. 1021 [19, 9]; Michel 817, 21 [IV BC]; LXX) **to crush in such a way that an object is put in pieces,** ***crush (together), dash to pieces,*** pass., abs. (Aristot., Probl. 1, 38, 863b, 13) **Mt 21:44** (RSwaeles, NTS 6, '60, 310–13); **Lk 20:18.**—M-M.

συνθλίβω impf. συνέθλιβον; aor. pass. subj. 3 sg. συνθλίβῃ Eccl. 12:6 (Pla. et al.; Strabo, Plut.; Philo, Aet. M. 110; Joseph.; LXX) **to crowd around so as to leave little room for movement,** ***press together, press upon*** τινά *someone,* of a crowd of people **Mk 5:24, 31** (cp. Appian, Mithrid. 81 §365 συνθλιβεὶς ἐν πλήθει; Jos., Bell. 3, 393 τ. πλήθους συνθλιβομένου περὶ τῷ στρατηγῷ).

συνθραύω (Eur., X.+; ins; Sym. Eccl 12:6) prim. 'break in pieces'; pass., of one experiencing personal loss (as of prestige) intr. ***be broken, shattered,*** in imagery of a wine jug that when empty can bang against others similarly empty without breaking, but in encounter w. a full one is broken: of a false prophet encountering spirit-filled Christians Hm 11:14 (cp. 11:13 σκεῦος θραύεται). Brox, Hermas 262.

συνθρύπτω (Hippiatr. II 106, 4f.—HCadbury, JBL 52, '33, 61) ***break in pieces*** (Jos., Ant. 10, 207) fig. τὴν καρδίαν τινός *break someone's heart* **Ac 21:13.** —M-M.

συνιδών s. συνοράω.

συνίημι (Hom. et al.; pap, LXX; pseudepigr.; Philo, Aet. M. 27; Jos., Ant. 7, 186 al.; apolog.); the NT has only one quite certain ex. of the conjugation in -μι: the inf. συνιέναι **Ac 7:25a.** In all the other cases the ms. tradition is divided: 3 pl. συνιᾶσιν **2 Cor 10:12** (s. Windisch ad loc.); impf. συνίειν LXX; inf. συνιέναι **Lk 24:45;** ptc. συνιείς, -έντος **Mt 13:19, 23; Eph 5:17 v.l.** Beside συνίημι may also be found **συνίω** Hm 4, 2, 1; 10, 1, 3; 3 pl. συνίουσιν **Mt 13:13; 2 Cor 10:12 v.l.;** Hm 10, 1, 6a (the accentuation συνιοῦσιν is incorrect; s. W-S. §14, 16; Mlt-H. 60). Impv. σύνιε Hm 6, 2, 3 lat. (for συνιεῖς); s 5, 5, 1; 9, 12, 1. Ptc. συνίων **Mt 13:23 v.l.; Mk 4:9** D; **Ro 3:11;** B 12:10 (not συνιῶν or συνιών; s. W-S. loc. cit.). Inf. συνίειν LXX. Either the -μι form or the -ω form could supply the 2 pl. indic. or impv. συνίετε **Mt 15:10; Mk 8:17, 21; Eph 5:17,** the 3 sg. impv. συνιέτω **Mk 4:9** D and, depending on the way the form is accented, the foll. subjunctive forms: 3 pl. συνιωσιν (συνιῶσιν or συνίωσιν) Mk 4:12; Lk 8:10; cp. συνιωμεν B 10:12b, συνιητε 6:5.—Fut. συνήσω, 2d sg. συνιεῖς (?) Hs 6, 2, 2; 1 aor. συνῆκα; 2 aor. subj. συνῶ Ps 72:17, συνῆτε, συνῶσιν, impv. 2 sg. σύνες (LXX; GrBar 1:3), 2 pl. σύνετε.; inf. συνεῖναι (Just.); ptc. συνείς (Just., A II, 3, 3.—B-D-F §94, 2; Mlt-H. 202–207; 325; Reinhold p. 94; Mayser 354, 2; Crönert 258; WSchmid, Der Attizismus II 1889, 26; Thackeray 250f; Rob. 314f) **to have an intelligent grasp of someth. that challenges one's thinking or practice,** ***understand, comprehend*** τὶ *someth.* (Pind., Hdt. et al.; Jos., Ant. 1, 255 τὴν γνώμην τ. θεοῦ; Just., A I, 31, 5) **Mt 13:51; Lk 2:50; 18:34; 24:45; Ac 13:27** D; 1 Cl 35:11 (Ps 49:22); B 10:12b; 12:10; Hm 4, 2, 1; 6, 2, 6; 10, 1, 3; 6a; 6b; s 5, 5, 1. W. ὅτι foll. (Herodian 4, 15, 6; TestLevi 8:18; TestJos 6:2; Jos., C. Ap. 1, 319; Ar. 3, 2; Just., D. 11, 4; Tat. 29, 1) **Mt 16:12; 17:13; Ac 7:25a;** B 14:3; Hm 4, 2, 2; s 2:10; 5, 4, 1. W. indir. quest. foll. **Eph 5:17** (Just., D. 69, 4). σ. ἐπί τινι *understand with regard to, gain an insight (into someth.)* (revealed by the context) ἐπὶ τοῖς ἄρτοις *in connection with the loaves* i.e. to understand that in the person and work of Jesus the disciples have all they need to carry out their mission **Mk 6:52.** ἐπὶ τῷ πλούτῳ αὐτοῦ *(the rich man) shows understanding in connection with his wealth* what the Christian's duty is Hs 2:7. Abs., but w. the obj. easily supplied fr. the context **Mt 13:13f** (Is 6:9), **19, 23; 15:10** (Eupolis Com. [V BC] 357, 1 κ. ἀκούετε κ. ξυνίετε; Iren. 1, 3, 1 [Harv. I 25, 11]); **Mk 4:12** (Is 6:9); **7:14; 8:17, 21; Lk 8:10** (Is 6:9); **Ac 7:25b; 28:26** (Is 6:9); **Ro 3:11** (cp. Ps 13:2); **15:21** (Is 52:15); B 4:6, 8; 6:5; 10:12a; Hm 6, 2, 3; 10, 1, 6a; s 9, 12, 1. συνιέναι τῇ καρδίᾳ (dat. of instr.; cp. καρδία 1bβ) **Mt 13:15; Ac 28:27** (both Is 6:10).—**2 Cor 10:12** (and **13**) the text is in doubt and the words οὐ συνιᾶσιν (συνιοῦσιν v.l.). ἡμεῖς δέ are omitted by some ancient witnesses and numerous scholars, among them Holsten, Schmiedel, Bousset, Windisch, Mft. ('They belong to the class of self-praisers; while I limit myself to my own sphere'); JHennig, CBQ 8, '46, 332–43; B-D-F §416, 2; EbNestle[4]-vDobschütz, Einführung in das Griechische NT 1923, 30. If the words are allowed to stand, since they occur in the best witnesses, incl. P[46] (w. numerous scholars, incl. Goodsp., NRSV), the two preceding participles indicate the ways in which the ignorance of those people is expressed.—B. 1207. M-M. EDNT. TW.

συνίστημι (Hom.+) **Ro 3:5; 5:8; 16:1; 2 Cor 4:2 v.l.; 6:4 v.l.; 10:18b; Gal 2:18 v.l.** Beside it **συνιστάνω** (Polyb. 4, 82, 5; 31, 29, 8; Jos., Bell. 1, 15, Ant. 6, 272.—Schweizer 177; Nachmanson 157; KDieterich, Untersuchungen 1898, 218; B-D-F §93; W-S. §14, 14; Rob. 315f) **2 Cor 3:1; 4:2; 6:4 v.l.; 10:12, 18a; Gal 2:18** and **συνιστάω** (Sb 4512, 77 [II BC] impf. συνίστων) **2 Cor 4:2 v.l.; 6:4 v.l.; 10:18a v.l.**—1 aor. συνέστησα; 2 aor. συνέστην LXX; pf. συνέστηκα, ptc. συνεστηκώς (LXX) and συνεστώς; inf. συνεστάναι (Tat. 30, 1; Ath. 25, 3); 1 aor. mid. συνεστησάμην (s. Schwyzer I 758, 760); 1 aor. pass. ptc. συσταθείς. The basic semantic component refers to coherence or being in a state of close relationship.

A. transitive, act., pass., and mid.—❶ **to bring together by gathering,** ***unite, collect*** pass. of the water of the boundless sea συσταθὲν εἰς τὰς συναγωγάς *collected in its gathering-places* 1 Cl 20:6.

❷ **to bring together as friends or in a trusting relationship by commending/recommending,** ***present, introduce/recommend someone to someone else*** (X., Pla.; PHamb 27, 3; PHib 65, 3; POxy 292, 6; PGiss 71, 4 al.; 1 Macc 12:43; 2 Macc 4:24; 9:25; Jos., Ant. 16, 85; Just., D. 2, 1 θεῷ) τινά τινι *(re)commend someone to someone* (PSI 589, 14 [III BC] σύστησόν με Σώσῳ; PBrem 5, 7 [117–19 AD]) ὑμῖν Φοίβην **Ro 16:1** (in a letter, as Chion, Ep. 8 ὅπως αὐτὸν συστήσαιμί σοι). Self-commendation (ἑαυτὸν/ἑαυτοὺς σ.) may be construed either as inappropriate **2 Cor 3:1;** οὐ πάλιν ἑαυτοὺς συνιστάνομεν ὑμῖν **5:12; 10:12** (ἑαυτούς), **18a** (ἑαυτόν); or as appropriate (ὡς θεοῦ διάκονοι) **6:4** (but s. 3 below). συνιστάνοντες ἑαυτοὺς πρὸς πᾶσαν συνείδησιν ἀνθρώπων *we commend ourselves to every human conscience*

4:2=*to every person's awareness of what is right* (s. πρός w. acc. 3eβ as PMich 210, 4 [c. 200 AD]). (The juxtaposition of apparently contradictory approaches to self-commendation is true to Gr-Rom. perspectives: contrast Pind., O. 9, 38f 'an untimely boast plays in tune with madness' and O. 1, 115f in which the poet celebrates his own power of song. The subject of appropriate and inappropriate self-commendation is discussed at length by Plut., Mor. 539–47 [On Inoffensive Self-Praise]. τινά *someone* ὃν ὁ κύριος συνίστησιν **10:18b.** Pass. συνίστασθαι ὑπό τινος *be recommended by someone* (Epict. 3, 23, 22; PPetr II 2, 4, 4 [III BC]) **12:11.**

❸ **to provide evidence of a personal characteristic or claim through action,** ***demonstrate, show, bring out*** τὶ someth. (Polyb. 4, 5, 6 εὔνοιαν) **Ro 3:5.** Cp. **2 Cor 6:4** (see comm. and 2 above). συνίστησιν τὴν ἑαυτοῦ ἀγάπην εἰς ἡμᾶς ὁ θεός **5:8.** Difficult and perh. due to a damaged text (B-D-F §197) is the constr. w. acc. and inf. (cp. Diod. S. 14, 45, 4) συνεστήσατε ἑαυτοὺς ἁγνοὺς εἶναι τῷ πράγματι **2 Cor 7:11.** W. a double acc. (Diod. S. 13, 91, 4; Sus 61 Theod.; Philo, Rer. Div. Her. 258 συνίστησιν αὐτὸν προφήτην [so in the mss.]; Jos., Ant. 7, 49) παραβάτην ἐμαυτὸν συνιστάνω *I demonstrate that I am a wrongdoer* **Gal 2:18** (WMundle, ZNW 23, 1924, 152f).

❹ **to bring into existence in an organized manner,** ***put together, constitute, establish, prepare,*** mid. τὶ *someth.* (Pla. et al.; Tat. 1, 2; pap) of God's creative activity (Lucian, Hermot. 20 Ἥφαιστος ἄνθρωπον συνεστήσατο; En 101:6; Philo, Leg. All. 3, 10 θεὸν τὸν τὰ ὅλα συστησάμενον ἐκ μὴ ὄντων; Jos., Ant. 12, 22 τὸν ἅπαντα συστησάμενον θεόν) ἐν λόγῳ συνεστήσατο τὰ πάντα 1 Cl 27:4 (Herm. Wr. 1, 31 ἅγιος εἶ, ὁ λόγῳ συστησάμενος τὰ ὄντα).

B. intransitive, in our lit. the pres. mid. and pf. act.—❶ **to stand in close association with,** ***stand with/by*** (1 Km 17:26), perf. act. τινί *someone* **Lk 9:32** (οἱ συνεστῶτες as Apollon. Paradox. 5).

❷ **to be composed or compounded of various parts,** ***consist,*** pres. mid., ἔκ τινος *of someth.* (Pla., X. et al.; Herm. Wr. 13, 2; Jos., Vi. 35; Ar. 4, 2; Ath. 8, 2, R. 25 p. 78, 9) ἡ μῆνις ἐκ τοσούτων κακῶν συνισταμένη Hm 5, 2, 4.

❸ **to come to be in a condition of coherence,** ***continue, endure, exist, hold together,*** pres. mid. and perf. act. (EpArist 154 τὸ ζῆν διὰ τῆς τροφῆς συνεστάναι; Tat. 30, 1; Mel., P. 91, 681) γῆ ἐξ ὕδατος καὶ δι' ὕδατος συνεστῶσα **2 Pt 3:5** (mngs. 2 and 3 are prob. blended here and in the next pass.; s. also Philo, Plant. 6). τὰ πάντα ἐν αὐτῷ συνέστηκεν **Col 1:17** (cp. Pla., Rep. 7, 530a, Tim. 61a; Ps.-Aristot. DeMundo 6, 2 ἐκ θεοῦ τὰ πάντα καὶ διὰ θεὸν συνέστηκεν; Philo, Rer. Div. Her. 58; PGM 4, 1769 τὰ πάντα συνέστηκεν; Ar. 1, 5 δι' αὐτοῦ δὲ τὰ πάντα συνέστηκεν). SHanson, The Unity of the Church in the NT '46, 112.—RWard, Aristotelian Terms in the NT: Baptist Quarterly 11, '45, 398–403 (συνίστημι).—M-M. EDNT. TW.

συνίω, συνίων s. συνίημι.

συνιών, συνιῶσιν s. σύνειμι.

συνκ- s. συγκ-.

συνκεκέραμμαι alt. form of συγκεκέρασμαι, s. συγκεράννυμι.

συνκεκέρασμαι alt. form of συγκεκέρασμαι, s. συγκεράννυμι.

συνκέκραμαι alt. form of συγκεκέρασμαι, s. συγκεράννυμι.

συνλ- s. συλλ-.

συνμ- s. συμμ-.

συνοδεύω fut. συνοδεύσω Wsd 6:23; 1 aor. συνώδευσα **to take the same path,** ***travel together with***—ⓐ lit. τινί; (Plut., Mor. 609d; Lucian, Peregr. 24; Vett. Val. 248, 7; Herodian 4, 7, 6; Achilles Tat. 7, 3, 7; Tob 5:17 S; Jos., Ant. 1, 226) **Ac 9:7;** AcPl Ha 6, 21f. λε̣[προις συν]|οδεύων PEg[2] 33f (ASyn. 42, 30).

ⓑ metaph. (Alex. Aphr., An. p. 80, 11, Fat. c. 6 p. 169, 22 Br.; Herm. Wr. 1, 28 οἱ συνοδεύσαντες τῇ πλάνῃ; Wsd 6:23) of the Lord ἐμοὶ συνώδευσεν ἐν ὁδῷ δικαιοσύνης *he was my traveling companion on the upright way* B 1:4.—DELG s.v. ὁδός. M-M.

συνοδία, ας, ἡ **a group of travelers,** ***caravan*** (so Strabo 4, 6, 6; 11, 14, 4; Epict. 4, 1, 91; OGI 633, 1; 638, 7; 646, 6; Jos., Bell. 2, 587, Ant. 6, 243; loanw. in rabb.—2 Esdr 17:5, 64 συνοδία means 'family') **Lk 2:44.**—New Docs 2, 209;—DELG s.v. ὁδός. M-M.

σύνοδος, ου, ὁ ***traveling companion, fellow-traveler*** (Manetho, Ap. 5, 58; Epict. 4, 1, 97; Anth. Pal. 7, 635, 2) fig. of pers. who are traveling the same way (here the way of love, commanded by God) IEph 9:2 (cp. 9:1).—Frisk s.v. 1 ὁδός. Sv.

σύνοδος, ου, ἡ (in var. senses: Solon, Hdt., SEG XXIX, 1183 trade assoc.; pap, LXX, Philo, Joseph Ant. 14, 257) ***assembly, meeting*** διὰ τί οὐκ ἐφάνης τῇ συνόδῳ ἡμῶν; *why did you not come to our assembly?* GJs 15:1 (v.l. συναγωγῇ).—M-M.

σύνοιδα (Aeschyl., Hdt.+; ins, pap, LXX, Philo, Joseph.; Ath.) a perf. w. pres. mng.; 3 pl., συνίσασιν (Ath. 34, 1); ptc., fem. gen. sg. συνειδυίης (for the form cp. BGU 55; 77 εἰδυίης; Ex 8:17, 20; 1 Km 25:20; Tdf., Prol. 117; W-H., App. 156).

❶ **to share information or knowledge with,** ***be privy to*** (Soph. et al.; PRev 8, 1; 21, 9; PPetr III, 36a, 9 [III BC]; BGU 1141, 50; PFlor 373, 6) in the sense 'be implicated, be an accomplice' **Ac 5:2** (Jos., Ant. 13, 424 ξυνῄδει ἡ γυνὴ μόνη; 16, 330).

❷ **to be aware of information about someth.,** ***to know, be conscious of*** σύνοιδα ἐμαυτῷ *I know with myself;* i.e. *I am conscious* (Eur., Hdt. et al.; Diod. S. 4, 38, 3 συνειδυῖα ἑαυτῇ τὴν ἁμαρτίαν=being conscious of her error; SIG 983, 6f; POxy 898, 20; Job 27:6; Ath. 34, 1) w. ὅτι foll. B 1:4. οὐδὲν ἐμαυτῷ σύνοιδα **1 Cor 4:4** (cp. Polyb. 4, 86 διὰ τὸ μηδὲν αὑτοῖς συνειδέναι; Diod. S. 17, 106, 2 πολλοὶ συνειδότες ἑαυτοῖς ὕβρεις; Demosth., Ep. 2, 15).—τὸ συνειδός (since Demosth. 18, 110) *consciousness* in which one imparts information to oneself, *conscience* (Plut., Mor. 85c; 556a; Epict. 3, 22, 94; Chariton 3, 4, 13; Appian, Bell. Civ. 1, 82 §373 τὸ συνειδὸς τῶν ἄλλων χεῖρον=worse than that of the others; 5, 16 §67 τὸ σ., that punishes the guilty; Philo, Spec. Leg. 1, 235 ὑπὸ τοῦ συνειδότος ἐλεγχόμενος; 4, 6; 40, Op. M. 128; Jos., C. Ap. 2, 218, Bell. 1, 453; 2, 582, Ant. 1, 47; 13, 316; 16, 102 ἐκ τοῦ συνειδότος='fr. a consciousness of guilt, fr. a bad conscience'; OGI 484, 37; POxy 532, 23 [II AD]) ἐκ συνειδότος *because of the witness of my own conscience* (opp. κατὰ θέλημα [θεου] = ἐκ χάριτος θεοῦ) ISm 11:1.—S. on συνείδησις, end.—DELG s.v. οἶδα. M-M. TW. Sv.

συνοικέω fut. 3 sg. συνοικήσει Dt 25:5; aor. συνῴκησα LXX; pf. ptc. fem. συνῳκηκυῖα LXX ***live with*** τινί *someone* (since Hipponax [VI BC] 20 Diehl[3] and Aeschyl.; also Demetr.: 722 fgm. 2, 2 Jac.) of man and wife (Hdt. et al.; OGI 771, 28; pap, LXX; Jos., Ant. 4, 247; 8, 191; Demetr.: 722 fgm. 1, 12;

cp. Philo, Sacr. Abel. 20) **1 Pt 3:7.**—New Docs 3, 85. DELG s.v. οἶκος II C. M-M.

συνοικοδομέω 1 aor. pass. συνῳκοδομήθην (Thu. et al.; SIG 913, 16; POxy 1648, 60; 1 Esdr 5:65) 'build together with', in our lit. only in imagery and exclusively pass. (both as Philo, Praem. 120).

❶ **to build up or construct of various parts,** ***build up,*** of the various parts of a structure, fr. which the latter is *built up (together)* (Περὶ ὕψους 10, 7) **Eph 2:22.**

❷ **to build in with other materials,** ***build in:*** *be built in* (Thu. 1, 93, 5 λίθοι; Diod. S. 13, 82, 3 συνῳκοδομοῦντο οἱ κίονες τοῖς τοίχοις) Hs 9, 16, 7.—DELG s.v. οἶκος. M-M. TW.

σύνολος, η, ον in description of completeness (Pla., Aristot., pap, LXX; ApcEsdr 5, 13 p. 30, 8 Tdf.; adv. συνόλως Ath., R. 15 p. 67, 2) adverbial τὸ σύνολον (LXX) ***at all, whatsoever*** **Ac 23:14 v.l.** (s. pap cited L-S-J-M; Herm. Wr. II, 8 [Sc. 138]).

συνομιλέω—❶ to engage with someone in conversation, ***talk, converse with*** (Cebes 13, 1; Jos., Bell. 5, 533; BGU II, 401, 15) τινί *someone* **Ac 10:27.**

❷ **to live in close association with,** ***live with*** τινί (Antiochus of Athens [II AD]: Cat. Cod. Astr. VII 109, 30) **1 Pt 3:7 v.l.** or

❸ **to be intimate with in a sexual manner,** ***to have intercourse with*** (cp. συνομιλία [not found in our lit.] 'intercourse'; s. L-S-J-M s.v.) τινί **1 Pt 3:7 v.l.** (s. 2 above).—M-M.

συνομορέω (σύν + ὁμός 'common' + ὅρος; elsewh. only in Byz. writers; the simple verb w. the same mng. in Plut.; Herodian 6, 7, 2; ins, pap, LXX) **to border on,** ***be next (door) to*** τινί *someth.* **Ac 18:7.**—DELG s.v. ὅρος. M-M.

συνοράω 2 aor. συνεῖδον (X., Pla. et al.; ins, pap, LXX; TestJob 19:3; Just.) in our lit. only of mental seeing

❶ **to receive information and make an assessment of its significance,** ***become aware of, perceive*** (Polyb. 1, 4, 6; 3, 6, 9 al.; Plut., Themist. 115 [7, 3] τὸν κίνδυνον; SIG 495, 54; PRein18, 17; 19, 12; BGU 1139, 13 [I BC]; 2 Macc 4:41; 14:26, 30; 3 Macc 5:50; EpArist 56; Philo, Sacr. Abel. 76, Somn. 1, 94; Jos., Bell. 4, 338, C. Ap. 2, 153; Just.) συνιδόντες κατέφυγον *when they became aware of (it) they fled* **Ac 14:6.**

❷ **to arrive at an understanding about someth.,** ***comprehend, realize*** (Pla. et al.) συνιδὼν *when he realized (this)* **12:12** (Field, Notes 120).

συνορία, ας, ἡ (Peripl. Eryth. 65; OGI 168, 18 [II BC]; 206, 3; pap) ***neighboring country*** **Mt 4:24 v.l.**—DELG s.v. ὅρος.

συνοχή, ῆς, ἡ (s. συνέχω; Hom. et al.; LXX; EpArist 61; Jos., Ant. 8, 65)

❶ **a place for confinement,** ***prison*** (PLond II, 354, 24 p. 165 [10 BC]) ἐν σ. γενόμενος *when he is put into prison* D 1:5 (in the pl. *bonds, fetters* Manetho, Ap. 1, 313 al., several times in Vett. Val. index).

❷ **a state of distress that involves a high degree of anxiety,** ***distress, dismay, anguish*** (Artem. 2, 3 p. 88, 14; Astrampsychus p. 24 Dec. 42, 8; p. 26 Dec. 48, 10; BGU 1821, 21 and 28 [50 BC]; PLond I, 122, 35 p. 117 [IV AD]; Cat. Cod. Astr. VIII/1 p. 267, 5; Job 30:3; Ps. 24:17 Aq.) **Lk 21:25.** (W. θλῖψις) συνοχὴ καρδίας *anguish of heart = troubled heart* **2 Cor 2:4.**—DELG s.v. 1 ἔχω 4. M-M. TW.

συνοψίζω 1 aor. συνώψισα (σύν + *ὀψίζω 'to engage in seeing', via ὄψις; PTebt 82, 2 [II BC]; StudPal 70 [I AD]; Simplicius in Aristot. Phys. 918, 13) **to make a calculation,** ***estimate, count*** τὰς ὥρας Hv 3, 1, 4 (v.l. συνεψήφισα). τὴν ποσότητα τῆς δαπάνης *calculate the expense* s 5, 3, 7 (some edd. συμψηφίσας).—Cp. DELG s.v. ὄπωπα.

συνπ- s. συμπ-.

συνρ- s. συρρ-.

συνσ- s. συσσ-.

συνσπ- s. συσπ-.

συνστ- s. συστ-.

σύνταξις, εως, ἡ (Thu., X., Pla.+; ins, pap, LXX; X., EpArist 186; TestJob 15:5; Philo, Just.; Tat. 12:5) **a systematic arrangement,** ***an organized account*** (Aristot., Polyb. et al.) οὐχ ὥσπερ σύνταξιν τῶν κυριακῶν ποιούμενος λογίων *not with the thought of producing an organized presentation of the dominical sayings* Papias (2:15) (HRigg, Jr., NovT 1, '56, 161–83: 'any special arrangement').—DELG s.v. τάσσω.

συνταράσσω fut. συνταράξω LXX; 1 aor. συνετάραξα. Pass. 1 fut. 3 pl. συνταραχθήσονται (En 99:4); 1 aor. συνεταράχθην LXX (Hom. [in tmesis] et al.) **to throw into confusion,** ***disturb*** (Hdt., Thu. et al.; Pla., Leg. 7, 798A συνταραχθεὶς ὑπὸ νόσων; OGI 669, 41 [I AD]; PGM 36, 142; LXX; En 99:4; TestJud 14:3; Just., D. 124, 1) **Lk 9:42** D.

συντάσσω fut. 3 sg. συντάξει LXX; 1 aor. συνέταξα, mid. συνεταξάμην (Sus 14 Theod.; Papias [2:16]); pf. συντέταχα Job 38:12. Pass.: 2 aor. ptc. gen. συνταγέντος Da 11:23; pf. 3 sg. συντέτακται LXX (Hdt. et al.; TestSol 22:11 B; TestAbr B 5 p. 109, 19f [Stone p. 66]; Jos., Ant. 3, 213; 7, 305 al.; Just., Tat.)

❶ **to direct that someth. be done in an explicit fashion,** ***order, direct, prescribe*** (X., Cyr. 8, 6, 8; Polyb. 3, 50, 9; ins [e.g. IAndrosIsis, Kyme 14 of origins of paths for sun and moon], pap, LXX) τινί *(for) someone* (PEdg 10 [=Sb 6716], 2 [258/257 BC] Ἀμύντου μοι συντάσσοντος) **Mt 21:6** (προστάσσω v.l., cp. 1:24); **26:19; 27:10** (cp. Ex 37:20; 40:19; Num 27:11 al.; RPesch, Eine ATliche Ausführungsformel im Mt, BZ 10, '66, 220–45).

❷ **to arrange various parts in an organized manner,** ***organize*** Ματθαῖος . . . Ἑβραΐδι διαλέκτῳ τὰ λογία συνετάξατο *M . . . . organized the sayings in Hebrew* (i.e., some form of Aramaic) Papias (2:16).—M-M.

συνταφείς s. συνθάπτω.

συντέλεια, ας, ἡ (orig. 'community contribution' [the basic semantic component relates to someth. that complements someth. already present]; in various senses Pla., Demosth. et al.; ins, pap, LXX; En 106:18; TestSol; TestJob 4:6; Test12Patr; ApcEsdr 2:31 p. 26, 25 Tdf.; Aristobul., in Eus., PE 8, 10, 9[=Denis p. 219 ln. 11f; Holladay fgm. 2, 55 p. 138]; Jos., Ant. 15, 389; 20, 262; Tat.; Ath., R. 12 p. 61, 31 'increment'; Theoph. Ant. 2, 31 [p. 176, 14] 'posterity') in our lit. only in a temporal sense: **a point of time marking completion of a duration,** ***completion, close, end*** (Polyb. 1, 3, 3; 1, 4, 3 al.; SIG 695, 13 [II BC]; POxy 1270, 42 [II AD] σ. τοῦ ἔτους; LXX; Iren. 1, 6, 1 [Harv. I 53, 2]) συντέλεια (τοῦ) αἰῶνος *the end of the* (present; αἰών 2a) *age* (TestBenj 11:3; TestJob 4:6) **Mt 13:39f, 49; 24:3; 28:20.** τοῦ αἰῶνος τούτου *of this age* **13:40 v.l., 49 v.l.** τῶν αἰώνων *of the ages* (TestLevi 10:2; Did., Gen. 115, 19. Cp. in gnostic speculation σ. καὶ ἐκπύρωσις τοῦ παντός Hippol., Ref. 9, 30, 8) **Hb 9:26.** τῶν καιρῶν (Da 9:27) Hv 3, 8, 9. τοῦ κόσμου **Mt 13:49** D. ἐπ' ἐσχάτων τῶν ἡμερῶν τῆς συντελείας *in the last days of the consummation* (of the age) Hs 9, 12, 3 (cp. TestZeb 9:9 καιρὸς συντελείας; ApcEsdr 2:31 τὴν ἡμέραν τῆς συντελείας; cp. Vi-Jer 13).—DELG s.v. τέλος. M-M. TW.

συντελέω fut. συντελέσω; 1 aor. συνετέλεσα LXX. Pass.: 1 fut. συντελεσθήσομαι; 1 aor. συνετελέσθην; pf. 2 pl. συντετέλεσθε Gen 44:5, 3 sg. συντετέλεσται LXX, ptc. συντετελεσμένος LXX, inf. συντετελέσθαι 2 Macc 3:32 (Thu.+).

❶ **to complete someth. that has been in process,** ***bring to an end, complete, finish, close*** τὶ *someth.* (Diod. S. 1, 3, 2; PGM 3, 90 [=RMerkelbach/MTotti, Abrasax '90, p. 88 ln. 90]; Philo, Ebr. 53; Jos., Ant. 15, 269; Just., A I, 65, 3) Hs 8, 11, 1; 9, 7, 1; 9, 29, 4. πάντα πειρασμόν **Lk 4:13.** A teaching, a speech, λόγους **Mt 7:28 v.l.** τὰς ἐντολάς Hm 12, 3, 2. Abs., though the obj. is to be supplied fr. the context B 15:3f (Gen 2:2). Pass., of the building of a tower (cp. PSI 407, 2 [III BC] ἐπειδή σοι [=by you] τὰ ἔργα [s. ἔργον 3] συντετέλεσται; Berosus: 680 fgm. 8 a, 140 Jac. [in Jos., C. Ap. 1, 140]) Hv 3, 4, 2; 3, 8, 9; s 9, 5, 2.

❷ **to carry out or bring into being someth. that has been promised or expected,** ***carry out, fulfill, accomplish*** τὶ *someth.* (Polyb. 4, 81, 3; Diod. S. 4, 53, 2 συντελέσαι τὴν ὑπόσχεσιν=keep one's word; Phlegon: 257 fgm. 36, 1, 11 Jac. perform an act of expiation; Jos., Bell. 7, 392; Just., A I, 32, 6) τὰ προγεγραμμένα Hs 5, 3, 7 (v.l. γεγραμμένα). Of God λόγον *carry out (his) word, bring (his) word to accomplishment* (cp. Sb 717, 2, 25 [217 BC] εὐχαριστῶν τοῖς θεοῖς ἐπὶ τῷ συντελέσαι αὐτοὺς ἃ ἐπηγγείλαντο αὐτῷ; Polystrat. p. 10 τ. θεὸν συντελεῖν ταῦτα κατὰ βούλησιν; La 2:17; the magical ins fr. Ashmunên published by the Soc. Ital. per la Ricerca dei Papiri Greci in Egitto, in Omaggio for the conf. of classical philologists, April 1911, no. 5, 40 ναὶ κύριε βασιλεῦ χθονίων θεῶν συντέλεσον τὰ ἐγγεγραμμένα τῷ πεδάλῳ τούτῳ=Yes, Lord and King of the netherworld deities, bring to pass the things written on this leaf; PGM 3, 121; 57, 2) **Ro 9:28** (Is 10:22). συντελέσω διαθήκην (Jer 41:8, 15) καινήν *I will bring a new covenant to accomplishment* **Hb 8:8** (Jer 38:31 διαθήσομαι), or simply *I will establish a new covenant* (σ.='make' X., Cyr. 6, 1, 50; Demosth. 21, 22).—Perh. **Mk 13:4** (s. 4 below), if it is to be translated *when all this is to be accomplished* (Diod. S. 2, 30, 1 everything is accomplished by a decision of the gods.—In 17, 1, 2 συντελεῖσθαι is simply 'happen'). Cp. B 12:1 (prophetic saying of unknown origin). πρᾶξις συντελεῖται *a course of action finds application* Hm 4, 1, 11 (Diod. S. 26, 7 ἀσεβῆ συνετελέσατο πρᾶξιν=he perpetrated an impious deed).

❸ **to exhaust the supply of someth.,** pass. w. act. sense ***give out*** συνετελέσθη ὁ οἶνος τοῦ γάμου **J 2:3 v.l.** (the act. = 'blot out, destroy' Jer 14:12; Ezk 7:15; TestLevi 5:4; corresp. the pass. Jer 14:15; 16:4; TestDan 6:4).

❹ **to come to the end of a duration,** ***come to an end, be over*** (Dt 34:8; Job 1:5; Tob 10:7) **Lk 2:21 v.l.; 4:2; Ac 21:27;** B 16:6 (quot. of uncertain origin). Perh. this is the place for ὅταν μέλλῃ ταῦτα συντελεῖσθαι πάντα *when all this* (colloq.: *when the time is when all this* cp. vs. 2) *is to come to an end* **Mk 13:4** (s. 2 above).—DELG s.v. τέλος. M-M. TW.

συντέμνω pf. συντέτμηκα. Pass.: aor. 3 pl. συνετμήθησαν Da 9:24 Theod.; pf. 3 sg. συντέτμηται Da 5:27; ptc. συντετμημένος **to put a limit to someth.,** freq. w. implication of abruptness, ***cut short, shorten, limit*** (Aeschyl., Thu. et al.; PCairZen 577, 11 [II BC]; LXX) of time (Philippides [Com. Att. III 308 Kock] 25 [IV/III BC] ὁ τὸν ἐνιαυτὸν συντεμὼν εἰς μῆν' ἕνα; Da 5:26–28 LXX; 9:24 Theod.; Jos., Ant. 1, 152) τοὺς καιρούς B 4:3. A passage not only of uncertain interpretation, but fraught w. textual difficulties as well, is λόγον συντελῶν καὶ συντέμνων ποιήσει ὁ κύριος **Ro 9:28** (Is 10:22b–23; these two compounds of συν- are also combined in Da 5:26–28 LXX; sim. Da 9:24 Theod.) *the Lord will act by accomplishing* (συντελέω 2) *his word and by shortening or cutting off*; in this case the shortening is thought of as referring either to God's promise to Israel, which will be fulfilled only to a limited degree (RLipsius, BWeiss), or to the Israelite nation, which is to enter into salvation trimmed and cut down, as a (vs. 27) 'remnant' (Jülicher, Sickenberger). Others take it to mean: *The Lord will act by closing the account and shortening (the time),* i.e. God will not prolong indefinitely the period of divine patience (Zahn; sim. also Hofmann and Althaus; cp. the NRSV 'the Lord will execute his sentence . . . quickly and decisively'—Mnesimachus [Com. Att. II 436 Kock] 3, 4 [IV BC] σύντεμνε='make it short, come to the point'; Musonius p. 87, 6 ἵνα συντεμὼν εἴπω='in short'; Psellus p. 232, 31 συντεμὼν τὸν λόγον=I will speak concisely; Philostrat., Vi. Apollon. 7, 14 p. 268, 16 λόγους ξυντεμεῖν πάντας='bring the speech to a sudden close'. S. CClassen, WienerStud 107/108, '94/95, 330f on qu. of rhetorical aspect.).—M-M.

συντεχνίτης, ου, ὁ (PAberd 59 III, 3 [IV/V AD], and freq. in late pap) ***one who follows the same trade*** ἄνδρες συντεχνῖται *fellow-craftsman* **Ac 19:25** D.—DELG s.v. τέχνη.

συντηρέω impf. συνετήρουν; fut. συντηρήσω; 1 aor. συνετήρησα LXX and ἐσυνετήρησα GrBar. Pass.: 1 fut. 3 sg. συντηρηθήσεται Da 4:26; 1 aor. 3 pl. συνετηρήθησαν Da 3:23 (Aristot. et al.; ins, pap, LXX; TestLevi 6:2; GrBar 16:4; EpArist, Joseph.; Just., D. 30, 2f).

❶ **to preserve against harm or ruin,** ***protect, defend*** τινά *someone* (PTebt 416, 14; Just., D. 30, 2) **Mk 6:20;** Hm 5, 1, 7; s 5, 6, 2. Pass. (IG XII/5, 860, 44 [I BC]; Jos., Bell. 1, 184) *be saved, preserved* (opp. ἀπόλλυσθαι) **Mt 9:17; Lk 5:38 v.l.**

❷ **to have a marked regard for,** ***keep in mind, be concerned about*** τὶ *someth* (Polyb. 4, 60, 10; ins, pap, LXX) ἀδελφότητα Hm 8:10.

❸ **to store information in one's mind for careful consideration,** ***hold*** or ***treasure up*** *(in one's memory)* (Sir 39:2; Da 7:28 Theod. τὸ ῥῆμα ἐν τῇ καρδίᾳ μου; sim. TestLevi 6:2.—Polyb. 30, 30, 5 the word means 'keep to oneself, conceal', as perh. also Jos., Bell. 2, 142) συνετήρει (διετήρει 2:51) τὰ ῥήματα **Lk 2:19** (Da 7:28 Theod.; Syntipas p. 102, 1; 104, 9 συνετήρουν ἐν τῇ καρδίᾳ πάντα); BMeyer, CBQ 26, '64, 31–49.—M-M. TW.

συντίθημι 1 aor. συνέθηκα LXX. Mid.: 2 aor. συνεθέμην; plpf. συνετεθείμην, ptc. συντεθειμένος (Just.). Pass.: 2 aor. sg. (as mid.) συνετέθης (Just., D. 67, 11), ptc. pl. συντεθέντες (Ar. 13, 7) (Hom.+)

❶ **to place someth. together with someth. else so as to be side by side,** ***put/place with*** σκεῦος κενὸν μετὰ τῶν κενῶν συντιθέμενον pass. *an empty vessel placed beside the* (other) *empty ones* (in such a way that it knocks against them) Hm 11:13 (cp. X., Cyr. 8, 5, 4; POxy 1631, 17; Ar. 13, 7).

❷ **to work out a mutually agreeable contract,** ***agree,*** mid., w. someone (Hdt. et al.) συνέθεντο αὐτῷ ἀργύριον δοῦναι where, no matter how the dat. is construed, the sense is *they came to an agreement with him, to pay him money* **Lk 22:5.**

❸ **to reach a decision in group discussion,** ***decide,*** through agreement among themselves, mid. (Jos., Vi. 196; TestZeb 1:6) foll. by the articular inf. in the gen. (B-D-F §400, 7; Rob. 1068; TestJos 6:9) **Ac 23:20.** W. ἵνα foll. **J 9:22.**

❹ **to be supportive by expressing agreement,** ***agree, affirm,*** mid. (Lysias et al.; Dionys. Hal., Isocr. 18; Paus. 4, 15, 2; PSI 484, 2 [III BC]; 524, 4; Just., A II, 9, 2 al.) **Ac 24:9 v.l.**—M-M. Sv.

σύντομος, ον (Aeschyl., Hdt. et al.; pap, LXX; TestSol 8, 12 P; TestZeb 4:6; Jos., Bell. 4, 228) 'cut short'.

❶ **pert. to being brief or concise about someth.,** ***short, brief*** ('terse and to the point' Aeschin., Or. 2, 51; Philo, Praem. 50) of beasts in action εὔχομαι σύντομά μοι εὑρεθῆναι *I pray that they be found quick for me = I pray that (the beasts) might deal with me speedily* IRo 5:2 (but s. 2 below).

❷ **pert. to being ready for someth. that is to be done,** ***close at hand, ready*** (of Nemesis, Anth. 12, 12, 2.—Jos., Bell. 4, 227) of ravenous beasts in the arena IRo 5:2 (s. 1 above).

συντόμως adv. of σύντομος, cp. συντέμνω (Aeschyl., Hippocr.+. Loanw. in rabb.)

❶ **in a short time,** ***promptly, readily*** (Aeschyl., Hippocr. et al.; pap; Pr 13:23; 3 Macc 5:25; Jos., Ant. 2, 315) 2 Cl 20:4; IRo 5:2; alternative **short ending of Mk.**

❷ **pert. to making someth. short,** ***briefly, concisely*** of discourse (Aeschyl., Isocr.; cp. Jos., C. Ap. 1, 3; 29; Just., Tat., Ath.) IMg 14. ἀκοῦσαί τινος συντόμως *give someone a hearing briefly* (i.e. someone who promises to speak briefly and to the point) **Ac 24:4.**—DELG s.v. τέμνω. M-M.

σύντονος, ον ('stretched tight, intense, vehement' trag. et al.; Philo, Joseph.) the neut. as subst. τὸ σύντονον ***intense desire, zeal*** (Philo, Leg. ad Gai. τὸ σ. τῆς σπουδῆς) ὑμῶν τὸ σύντονον τῆς ἀληθείας *your intense desire for the truth* IPol 7:3.—The neut. of the comp. as adv. (Aristot., Pol. 5, 8, 2; Plut., Cato Maj. 349 [21, 5]; Jos., Bell. 1, 274; 3, 13) συντονώτερον γράφειν *write more sharply* ITr 3:3.—DELG s.v. τείνω.

συντρέχω dep. fut. 3 pl. συνδραμοῦνται Jdth 14:3; 2 aor. συνέδραμον (Hom., Aeschyl., Hdt. et al.; pap, LXX; Test12Patr; ApcSed 11:11 p. 134, 25 Ja.; Philo, Aet. M. 103; Joseph.; Ath., R. 15 p. 66, 5) 'run together'.

❶ **to run together to a place and gather,** ***run together*** (X. et al.; Mitt-Wilck. I/2, 20 III, 8; LXX) πρός τινα (Diod. S. 19, 13, 7 πρὸς ἀλλήλους; Plut., Alc. 209 [32, 3], Mar. 423 [29, 10], Pomp. 423 [60, 5]; Chariton 5, 9, 5; Jos., Bell. 1, 250) **Ac 3:11** (Jos., Ant. 7, 257 ἅπαντα τὸν λαὸν συνδραμεῖν πρὸς αὐτόν). ἐκεῖ (Diod. S. 20, 96, 4) **Mk 6:33.** εἰς ναόν IMg 7:2 (cp. Jdth 6:16; Archilochus fgm. 54 Diehl³; Posidon.: 87 fgm. 36, 51 Jac.; Diod. S. 4, 42, 3, εἰς ἐκκλησίαν).

❷ 'run w. someone' (Appian, Bell. Civ. 2, 49 §200), then by fig. ext. **to be in league with,** ***go with,*** in imagery of close association in some activity, abs. IPol 6:1 (with other συν- compounds). τινί *someone* 1 Cl 35:8 (Ps 49:18). Also μετά τινος B 4:2. εἴς τι to denote the common goal (Himerius, Or. [Ecl. 10, 3 fig.]) συντρέχειν εἰς τὴν αὐτὴν τῆς ἀσωτίας ἀνάχυσιν *dash with (them) into the same stream of debauchery* **1 Pt 4:4.**

❸ **to be in harmony with,** ***agree with*** (Aeschyl. et al.) τινί *someth.* (Soph., Trach. 880; Mitt-Wilck. II/2, 96, 11 τούτῳ τῷ λόγῳ) τῇ γνώμῃ τοῦ θεοῦ IEph 3:2; cp. 4:1.—M-M.

συντριβή, ῆς, ἡ (Vett. Val. 74, 4; Heliod. 10, 28; Sb 5763, 42; LXX) lit. 'rubbing away' ***crushing, destruction,*** of Christ, who is put in place like a firm stone εἰς συντριβήν to destroy those who dash against (=take offense at) him B 6:2 ('polishing' JKleist, transl. '48, p. 172 n. 59).—Sv.

συντρίβω fut. συντρίψω; 1 aor. συνέτριψα. Pass.: 2 fut. συντριβήσομαι; 2 aor. συνετρίβην; perf. inf. συντετρῖφθαι, ptc. συντετριμμένος (Eur., Thu.+)

❶ **to cause destruction of someth. by making it come apart,** ***shatter, smash, crush,*** of things (Diod. S. 14, 58, 3; 15, 86, 2; Arrian, Anab. 6, 9, 4; JosAs 13:10 cultic images; Ath., R. 9 p. 57, 26) ἀλάβαστρον *break an alabaster flask* **Mk 14:3.** πύλας χαλκᾶς *shatter gates of brass* (cp. PTebt 45, 21 [113 BC]) B 11:4 (Is 45:2). Pass. (Diod. S. 4, 62, 3 συντριβῆναι of a wagon; Jos., Bell. 1, 43; 90) of a reed *be bent* **Mt 12:20** (cp. Is 42:3). Of fetters *be broken* **Mk 5:4** (cp. Dionys. Hal. 6, 26, 3). Of bones *be broken* (Hippocr., Ep. 22, 3 ὀστέων συντριβομένων; TestJob 25:10; Himerius, Or. 69 [=Or. 22], 5 of Ibycus' broken hand; Stephan. Byz. s.v. Ἀμαζόνες: σ. τὰ μέλη of people) **J 19:36** (Ps 33:21.—S. σκέλος, end). Of the tables of the law (Ex 32:19; Dt 9:17) B 14:3; cp. 4:8. Vessels (Ael. Aristid. 19, 7 K.=41 p. 765 D.; Aesop, Fab. 190 H. τὰ σκεύη συνέτριψε; SIG 1168, 82) *are broken* **Rv 2:27** (cp. Ps 2:9) or *break* (intr.) 2 Cl 8:2. Of waves *be dashed into foam* 1 Cl 20:7 (Job 38:11).

❷ **to cause damage to by mistreatment,** ***mistreat/beat severely*** of persons *mistreat, beat someone severely* (Eur. et al.), also *wear out, bruise* (PPetr II, 4, 3, 5; PLips 38, 17) **Lk 9:39.**

❸ **to overcome by subduing completely,** ***annihilate, crush*** enemies (Polyb. 5, 47, 1; 1 Macc 3:22 al.; PsSol 17:24; 4 [6] Esdr [POxy 1010] αἱ πόλεις σου συ(ν)τριβήσονται) ὁ θεὸς συντρίψει τὸν σατανᾶν **Ro 16:20.**

❹ **to be severely damaged psychologically,** ***be broken*** pass., fig. of mental and emotional states (συντριβῆναι τῇ διανοίᾳ Polyb. 21, 13, 2; 30, 32, 11; Diod. S. 4, 66, 4 ταῖς ἐλπίσιν= their hopes were shattered; τοῖς φρονήμασιν Diod. S. 11, 78, 4.—Plut., Mor. 47a; 165b; LXX) καρδία συντετριμμένη (καρδία 1bε) 1 Cl 18:17b; B 2:10 (both Ps 50:19b). πνεῦμα συντετριμμένον 1 Cl 18:17a; 52:4 (both Ps 50:19a). οἱ συντετριμμένοι τὴν καρδίαν (Is 61:1; cp. Ps 33:19; 146:3) **Lk 4:18 v.l.;** B 14:9.—DELG s.v. τρίβω. M-M. TW.

σύντριμμα, ατος, τό (συντρίβω; Aristot. et al.; LXX) ***destruction, ruin*** **Ro 3:16** (Is 59:7; Ps 13:3).—DELG s.v. τρίβω. M-M. TW.

σύντροφος, ον (συντρέφομαι 'be brought up together') 'nourished' or 'brought up together with' also 'familiar, on friendly terms' (trag., Hdt. et al.; also LXX, Mel., HE 4, 26, 7) **pert. to being brought up with someone, either as foster-brother or as companion/friend** subst. ὁ σ. ***foster-brother, companion*** (from one's youth), *intimate friend* τινός *of someone* (σύντροφος τοῦ βασιλέως Polyb. 5, 9, 4; Diod. S. 1, 53, 5; 1, 54, 5; OGI 247, 2; 323, 2 al. Cp. Aelian, VH 12, 26; POxy 1034, 2; 7; 2 Macc 9:29; Jos., Bell. 1, 215, Ant 14, 183) **Ac 13:1** (s. Μαναήν.—A Cilician ins in MAMA III, '31 no. 62 [I BC] mentions Hermias as the σύντρ.= 'intimate friend' of the Seleucid King Philip II).—B. 1346. DELG s.v. τρέφω. New Docs 3, 38. M-M.

συντυγχάνω 2 aor. συνέτυχον (trag. et al.; ins, pap; 2 Macc 8:14; TestSol 10:11 C; TestJob, EpArist; Joseph.) **to come together with,** ***meet, join*** (trag., Hdt. et al.; TestJob 6:5; Jos., Ant. 1, 219; 15, 187; pap) **Lk 8:19;** Ox 840, 11. Without the dat., which is to be supplied **Ac 11:26** D.—M-M.

Συντύχη, ης, ἡ *Syntyche* (reff., esp. fr. ins, in Zahn, Einl. I 379=Intr. I 533; see also LBW 722, 1 [204 AD]), a Christian in Philippi **Phil 4:2.**—LGPN I. M-M.

συντυχία, ας, ἡ (lyric poets, Hdt. et al.; TestJob 23:2 [κατὰ σ.]; Philo; Jos., Ant. 15, 187 [κατὰ τὴν σ.]) **the unexpected coinciding of two events,** ***happening, chance*** **Lk 10:31** P[75] (spelled -εία), as v.l. for συγκυρία.

συνυποκρίνομαι dep.; 1 aor. συνυπεκρίθην (Polyb. 3, 92, 5 al.; Plut., Marius 413 [14, 14]; 415 [17, 5]; EpArist 267) **to join in playing a part or pretending,** ***join in pretense/hypocrisy***

w. dat. of the pers. whom one joins in dissimulation **Gal 2:13.**—DELG s.v. κρίνω. M-M. TW.

συνυπουργέω (Hippocr.; Lucian, Bis Acc. 17; TestSol 22, 8) ***join in helping, co-operate with*** τινί *by means of someth.* συνυπουργούντων ὑμῶν ὑπὲρ ἡμῶν τῇ δεήσει *while you join in helping us by your prayers* **2 Cor 1:11.**—DELG s.v. ἔργον.

συνφ- s. συμφ-.

συνχ- s. συγχ-.

συνψ- s. συμψ-.

συνωδίνω (ὠδίνω 'be in pain' as in childbirth; Eur., Hel. 727; Aelian, NA 3, 45 p. 78, 5 after Aristot.; Porphyr., Abst. 3, 10) ***suffer agony together*** πᾶσα ἡ κτίσις συστενάζει καὶ συνωδίνει *all creation lets out a groan in common pain* **Ro 8:22** (on στενάζειν and the ὠδῖνες of the κτίσις cp. Heraclit. Sto. c. 39 p. 58, 9 ἐπειδὰν ἡ μεμυκυῖα γῆ τὰς κυοφορουμένας ἔνδον ὠδῖνας ἐκφήνῃ=when [after the winter's cold] the groaning earth gives birth in pain to what has been formed within her.—Diod. S. 5, 5, 1 quotes the tragic poet Carcinus: all Sicily, filled with fire from Aetna, groaned [στενάξαι] over the loss of Persephone).—DELG s.v. ὠδίς.

συνωμοσία, ας, ἡ (συνόμνυμι 'to swear together with, conspire') ***conspiracy, plot*** (Thu., Aristoph. et al.; ins; PMilVogl 287, 9; Ezk 22:25 Sym.; Jos., Ant. 15, 288; 16, 111) συνωμοσίαν ποιεῖσθαι *form a conspiracy* (Polyb. 1, 70, 6; Diod. S. 3, 57, 5; Herodian 7, 4, 3) **Ac 23:13.**—B. 1363.—DELG s.v. ὄμνυμι. M-M.

Σύρα, ας, ἡ ***Syrian woman*** (Aristoph. et al.) **Mk 7:26** v.l. (s. Συροφοινίκισσα).

Συράκουσαι, ῶν, αἱ (Pind., Hdt. et al.; ins in var. spellings) ***Syracuse,*** a city on the east coast of Sicily **Ac 28:12.**—KFabricius, D. antike S.[21], '63; PECS 871–74 (lit.); Pauly-W. XIII 815ff; Kl. Pauly V 460–69; DACL XV 1840–55; BHHW III, 1918.—M-M.

Συρία, ας, ἡ (Aeschyl., Hdt. et al.; ins, LXX; EpArist 22; SibOr 12, 102 [elsewh. Συρίη, s. index of names]; Philo, Joseph.; Ar. 12, 2; Just., A I, 1; s. B-D-F §261, 6) ***Syria,*** the part of Western Asia bounded on the north by the Taurus Mts., on the east by the lands of the Euphrates, on the south by Palestine, on the west by the Mediterranean Sea. In 64 BC it became a Roman province; its capital was Antioch. **Mt 4:24; Ac 18:18; 20:3; 21:3;** IEph 1:2; IRo 5:1; 10:2; ISm 11:2; IPol 7:2; 8:2; Pol 13:1. Mentioned beside Cilicia, its neighboring province in Asia Minor (X., An. 1, 4, 4; Diod. S. 16, 42, 1; 9 of the two neighboring satrapies of Persian times) **Ac 15:23, 41; Gal 1:21;** IPhld 11:1. Ἀντιόχεια τῆς Σ. (s. Ἀντιόχεια 1) ISm 11:1; IPol 7:1; IPhld 10:1. The province was governed by an imperial legate (s. ἡγεμονεύω and Κυρήνιος) **Lk 2:2.** ἡ ἐκκλησία ἡ ἐν Συρίᾳ *the church in Syria* IEph 21:2; IMg 14; ITr 13:1; IRo 9:1. Ignatius is ὁ ἐπίσκοπος Συρίας IRo 2:2.—GBeer, RE XIX 1907, 281–95 (lit.); RDussaud, Mission dans les régions désertiques de la Syrie moyenne 1903, Topographie historique de la Syrie antique et médiévale 1926; BMaisler, Untersuchungen z. alten Gesch. u. Ethnographie Syriens u. Palätinas I 1929; KBaedeker, Palästina u. Syrien[7] 1910, Syrie-Palestine, Irâq, Transjordanie '32; LHaefeli, Syrien u. sein Libanon 1926; UKahrstedt, Syr. Territorien in hellenist. Zeit 1926. On the relig. situation s. Schürer III 13f; Dussaud, Notes de Mythologie Syrienne 1903–5; FCumont, Études Syriennes 1917, Religionen[3] '31, 94–123; 253–77 (lit.); HPreisker, Ntl. Zeitgesch. '37, 146–57; Prümm 264–68; 651–54. S. also CClermont-Ganneau, Recueil d'archéol. orientale, eight vols. 1888–1924; PHitti, History of S., Lebanon, and Palestine '51; GTchalenko, Villages antiques de la S. du Nord I–III '55–58; AVööbus, History of Asceticism in the Syrian Orient '58–61; GDowney, A History of Antioch in S. fr. Seleucus to the Arab Conquest '61; HGese, Die Religionen Altsyriens '70; EWirth, S., eine geogr. Landeskunde '71. Pauly-W. VII 2157–63; 2d ser. IV 1574–82, 1602–1728; Kl. Pauly V 469–73; RAC I 854–60; DACL XV 1855–1942; BHHW III 1919–22.—M-M.

Σύρος, ου, ὁ ***Syrian man*** (Soph., Hdt. et al.; ins, pap; TestNapht 5:8; SibOr, Philo, Joseph.; Just., D. 103, 5; Ath. 30, 1) of Naaman, the Syrian army commander **Lk 4:27** (cp. 2 Kings 5). Circumcision practiced by the Syrians B 9:6 (s. Windisch, Hdb. ad loc.).—M-M.

Συροφοινίκισσα, ης, ἡ ***Syrophoenician woman*** (masc. Συροφοίνιξ in Lucian, Concil. Deor. 4; Eunap., Vi. Soph. p. 98), an inhabitant of Syrophoenicia, a district which was so called because Phoenicia belonged to the province of Syria (s. Diod. S. 19, 93, 7 ἡ Φοινίκη Συρία; Just., D. 78, 10; s. Συροφοινίκη: EHonigmann, Pauly-W. 2d ser. IV '32, 1788f), and could thus be differentiated fr. Libophoenicia around Carthage (Diod. S. 20, 55, 4 Λιβυφοίνικες; Strabo 17, 19) **Mk 7:26** (v.l. Συροφοίνισσα, Σύρα Φοινίκισσα; s. B-D-F §111, 1; Mlt-H. 279; 349).—DMargoliouth, Exp. 8th ser., 22, 1921, 1–10; AvanVeldhuizen, De Syrofenicische Vrouw: Op den Uitkijk 3, 1926, 65ff; JHalser, The Incident of the Syrophoenician Woman: ET 45, '34, 459–61; TBurkill, NovT 9, '67, 161–77; WStorch, BZ 14, '70, 256f; BHHW III 1922. S. also on Χαναναῖος.—M-M.

συρρέω (Hdt., Pla., X. et al.; pap; Jer 51 [28]:44 Sym.; Philo, Op. M. 38; Jos., Bell. 2, 118) ***flow together*** ἐκ παντὸς τοῦ σώματος συρρέοντας ἰχῶράς τε καὶ σκώληκας *pus and worms coming in one stream out of his body* (in ref. to Judas) Papias (3, 2).

συρρήγνυμι (Hom. et al.; Jos., Bell. 1, 251; 3, 302; SibOr 2, 201) intr. (Hdt. et al.; Jos., Bell. 1, 364) ***dash (together)*** τινί *upon someth.* **Lk 6:49** D.

Σύρτις, εως, ἡ (Hdt. et al.) ***Syrtis;*** name of two gulfs along the Libyan coast which, because of their shallowness and shifting sand-banks, were greatly feared by mariners (Apollon. Rhod. 4, 1235ff; Strabo 17, 3, 20; Dio Chrys. 5, 8–11; Jos., Bell. 2, 381). The Syrtis meant in **Ac 27:17** is the so-called Great one, toward Cyrenaica.—Pauly-W. 2d ser., IV 1796–824; Kl. Pauly V 475; BHHW III 1922–24; Haenchen, comm., ad loc.; Warnecke 35.—M-M.

σύρω impf. ἔσυρον; fut. 1 pl. συροῦμεν 2 Km 17:13; aor. 3 pl. ἔσυραν 4 Macc 6:1; 2 aor. pass. ptc. συρείς Mel. (Aristot.; Theocr. et al.; pap, LXX; TestSol 6:10; Joseph.; Mel., P. 71, 515) ***drag, pull, draw, drag away*** τὶ *someth.* (cp. PFlor 158, 7 τὸ ταυρικὸν σύρει τὰ ξύλα) σύροντες τὸ δίκτυον *dragging in the net* **J 21:8** (σ. in catching fish: Plut., Mor. 977f). Of the dragon in heaven: ἡ οὐρὰ αὐτοῦ σύρει τὸ τρίτον τῶν ἀστέρων *his tail swept away a third of the stars* **Rv 12:4.**—τινά *drag someone away (by force)* (Ps.-Theocr., Hymn to the Dead Adonis ln. 12 [Bucoliques Grecs ed. ELegrand 1925 vol. II p. 112] ἔσυρον αἰχμάλωτον; Epict. 1, 29, 16; 22; Jos., Bell. 1, 452; 2, 491, Ant. 20, 136.—4 Macc 6:1 ἐπί τι; Mel., P. 71, 515 εἰς σφαγήν) **Ac 8:3;** GPt 3:7 (cp. Eutecnius 4 p. 41, 33 σύρειν αἰσχρῶς κατὰ γῆς). ἀδελφοὺς ἐπὶ τοὺς πολιτάρχας **Ac 17:6.**—ὡς δὲ ἐσύρετο *as he* (Paul) *was dragged* (into the amphitheater) AcPl Ha 4, 11.

Of a (supposedly) lifeless human body (Herodian 1, 13, 6; 5, 8, 9) ἔσυρον ἔξω τῆς πόλεως **Ac 14:19.** S. κατασύρω.—DELG. M-M.

συσκέπτομαι impf. συνεσκεπτόμην (σκέπτομαι; Sym. Ps 2:2; 30:14; Just., D. 46, 2) ***contemplate together, determine*** τινί *with someone* (Herodian 1, 17, 7; Iambl., Protr. 21, 31 p. 123, 19 Pistelli) ἀλλήλοις GPt 11:43 (w. inf. foll.).

συσπαράσσω 1 aor. συνεσπάραξα (Maximus Tyr. 7, 5e 'tear to pieces') **to agitate violently, *pull about, convulse*** τινά *someone,* of a hostile spirit, who so treats the person who is in his power **Mk 9:20;** w. ῥήγνυμι **Lk 9:42.**

συσπάω (Pla. et al.; La 5:10) **to draw together or retract so as to be no longer open and extended, *draw together*** τὰς χεῖρας πρὸς τὸ δοῦναι *clench one's fists when it comes to giving* (RKnopf D 4:5) or *keep one's hands closed* (HWindisch B 19:9) B 19:9; D 4:5. But since this expr. is contrasted w. ἐκτείνειν τὰς χεῖρας (s. ἐκτείνω 1), it may be better to translate *pull back, pull in, retract* (cp. Lucian, Tim. 13 συσπ. τοὺς δακτύλους; Aristot., HA 2, 17 τ. γλῶτταν; 5, 20 τὴν κεφαλήν).

σύσσημον, ου, τό (σῆμα; συν- Tdf.; since Menand. [Per. 792 S.=362 Kö], as Phryn. p. 418 Lob. explains in rejecting the word; Diod. S., Strabo, Plut., LXX; loanw. in rabb.)

❶ **an action or gesture previously agreed upon as a signal, *signal, sign*** (freq. in military context of someth. raised up Aeneas Tact. 223; Diod. Sic. 11, 22, 1; 19, 30, 1; a gilded shield 20, 51, 1; a special piece of headware Strabo 6, 3, 3) σ.=giving of a kiss to a potential victim **Mk 14:44.**—M-M. TW.

❷ **a device used as a means of recognition or rallying point for members of a group, *sign, token, standard, banner*** αἴρειν σύσσημον *raise a sign* ISm 1:2 (the idiom αἴρειν σύσσημον is freq. used in ref. to military action [s. pass. cited 1 above; s. also Is 5:26, to which Ignatius prob. alludes]. But our pass. focuses on corporate identity; s. Is 49:22).

σύσσωμος, ον (σῶμα; only in Christian writers) ***belonging to the same body*** w. συγκληρονόμος, συμμέτοχος τῆς ἐπαγγελίας **Eph 3:6.**—EPreuschen, ZNW 1, 1900, 85f.—Cp. Frisk s.v. σῶμα. M-M. TW.

συστασιαστής, οῦ, ὁ (σύστασις, fr. συνίστημι, but in the mid. mng. 'stand together' [as of a group conspiring] Jos., Ant. 14, 22) ***fellow-insurrectionist*** **Mk 15:7 v.l.**—Cp. DELG s.v. ἵστημι.

σύστασις, εως, ἡ (Eur., Hdt.+). All usage in our lit. is associated with usage of the mid. συνίσταμαι (s. prec. entry beg.).

❶ **a group with common interests, *gathering, union, association*** (Appian, Bell. Civ. 5, 132, §547 συστάσεις=gangs [of robbers]) αἱ συστάσεις αἱ ἀρχοντικαί (s. ἀρχοντικός and ἄρχων 1c) ITr 5:2. On the basis of this pass. and the Lat. version, θηρίων συστάσεις IRo 5:3 can be taken to mean *packs of wild beasts.* But mng. 2 is also prob. here.

❷ **a strenuous encounter with a hostile entity, *encounter, struggle*** (Eur., Hdt. et al.; Diod. S. 4, 16, 2): *struggles with wild beasts* IRo 5:3 (s. 1 above).

❸ **the basic way in which someth. is structured, *structure, constitution, nature*** (Diod. S. 15, 32, 1; TestReub 2:4; Tat. 1, 1; 4, 1 al.; Ath. 19, 2 al.; Alex. Aphr., An. p. 3, 19 Br.; T. Kellis 22, 8; 33) τοῦ κόσμου (Cornutus 18 p. 32, 5; cp. Wsd 7:17) 1 Cl 60:1 τοῦ κόσμου σύστασιν (cp. Ath. 25, 3 τοῦ παντὸς κόσμου σύστασιν). The rendering *permanence, duration* has been suggested, but such interp. can only be derived from the qualifier ἀέναος, resulting in an inelegant pleonasm 'eternal permanence'. DELG s.v. ἵστημι. Sv.

συστατικός, ή, όν (συνίστημι; since Aristot. in Diog. L. 5, 18; pap) ***introducing, commendatory*** συστατικὴ ἐπιστολή *a letter of recommendation* (Ammonius, Vi. Aristot. p. 11, 18 Westerm. συστατικαὶ ἐπ.) **2 Cor 3:1** (Epict. 2, 3, 1 γράμματα παρ' αὐτοῦ λαβεῖν συστατικά; Diog. L. 8, 87; POxy 1587, 20; PTebt 315, 29 [II AD] ἔχει συστατικάς, i.e. ἐπιστολάς.—Models: Ps.-Demetr., Form. Ep. p. 3, 16ff; Ps.-Libanius, Charact. Ep. p. 22, 12ff; also p. 58). Paul does not need such letters, for his addressees constitute letters of rec. (cp. Aristot. [Diog. L. 5, 18] on the superiority of personal appearance to letters of rec.).—On this subject s. Dssm., LO 137f (LAE 170–72); Windisch ad loc.; CKeyes, The Gk. Letter of Introduction: AJP 56, '35, 28ff; CKim, Form and Structure of the Pauline Greek Letter of Introduction, SBLDS 4 '72; Betz, 2 Cor 131–39.—Cp. DELG s.v. ἵστημι. M-M. Spicq.

συσταυρόω Pass.: 1 aor. συνεσταυρώθην; pf. συνεσταύρωμαι. In our lit. only pass.

❶ **to crucify together with, *crucify with,*** of one who is nailed to the cross w. one or more persons; lit. σύν τινι, of brigands crucified alongside Jesus **Mt 27:44; Mk 15:32.** Also simply w. the dat. **J 19:32.**

❷ **to crucify with in a transcendent sense, *crucify with,*** fig. ext. of 1, of identification w. Christ's crucifixion ὁ παλαιὸς ἡμῶν ἄνθρωπος συνεσταυρώθη *our old self was jointly crucified* **Ro 6:6.** Χριστῷ συνεσταύρωμαι *I have been crucified w. Christ* **Gal 2:19** (s. GStaffelbach, D. Vereinigung mit Christus als Prinzip der Moral bei Pls, diss. Freiburg, Switzerland, '32).—DELG s.v. σταυρός. TW.

συστέλλω 1 aor. συνέστειλα. Pass. 2 aor. 3 sg. συνεστάλη LXX, ptc. gen. pl. συσταλέντων GrBar 9:1; pf. ptc. συνεσταλμένος (Eur., Thu. et al.; ins, pap, LXX, Philo, Joseph.)

❶ **to draw together so as to be less extended, *limit, shorten*** (Hippocr.: CMG I/1 p. 53, 14; 85, 9; Isocr. 12, 230; X., Vect. 4, 3; Diod. S. 1, 41, 2; Cass. Dio 39, 37; Jos., Ant. 14, 74) of time ὁ καιρὸς συνεσταλμένος ἐστίν **1 Cor 7:29,** where it is not certain whether Paul has a divine act of shortening in mind (JWeiss), or whether there is no reference intended to a time that was originally longer (Diod. S. 4, 20, 1 τοῖς ὄγκοις συνεσταλμένοι=compact in body [of the Ligurians]). σ. τὰ ἱστία *shorten/furl the sails* **Ac 27:15 v.l.,** see s.v. ἱστίον.

❷ **to limit the area of one's presence, *withdraw*** ἐγὼ . . . συνέστελλον ἑαυτὸν ἐν τῇ ἐρήμῳ *I withdrew into the wilderness* GJs 25:1.

❸ **to wrap up by winding someth. around, *cover, wrap up*** (Eur., Tro. 377; Lucian, Imag. 7; Achilles Tat. 8, 1, 5; Ps.-Callisth. 2, 22, 3 ὃν [=Darius when dying] τῇ χλαμύδι συστείλας). So the Syrian and Coptic versions; many comm.; NRSV et al. for the rendering of οἱ νεώτεροι συνέστειλαν αὐτόν **Ac 5:6;** cp. vs. **10** D. Held less in favor are mngs. 4 and 5.

❹ **to gather up, *pack, fold up, snatch up*** (cp. GrBar 8:2 ὄρνεον . . . συστέλλον τὰς πτερύγας αὐτοῦ bird . . . folding its wings; Psellus 50, 31 σ. τὰ παραπετάσματα=gather the curtains together). So the Armenian version and HMeyer, Overbeck, Weizsäcker, Zahn for **Ac 5:6** (s. 3 and 5).

❺ **to remove an object from a place, *take away, remove*** (Philo, Leg. All. 3, 35). So the Vulgate, amoverunt for **Ac 5:6** (but s. 3 and 4).—M-M. TW.

συστενάζω **to groan together with, *lament, groan*** (Eur., Ion 935 and TestIss 17:5 τινί 'with someone'.—Nicetas Eugen. 1,

342 H. without dat.) of creation *groan together* (w. συνωδίνειν, q.v. Also A-MDubarle, RSPT 38, '54, 445–65) **Ro 8:22** (on the pessimistic tone s. GKennedy, The Art of Rhetoric in the Roman World '72, 447f).—DELG s.v. στένω. TW.

συστοιχέω (Polyb. 1:23 of soldiers 'stand in the same line', hence in grammarians and in the Pythagorean tables of categories, s. Aristot., EN 1, 4, 1906b, 6, Metaphys. 1, 5, 986a, 23) ***correspond*** (the members of the same categories in the tables συστοιχοῦσι, while members of opposite categories ἀντιστοιχοῦσι.—Ltzm., Hdb. on Gal 4:25) w. the dat. Ἁγάρ = Σινᾶ ὄρος … συστοιχεῖ τῇ νῦν Ἰερουσαλήμ *corresponds to the present Jerusalem* **Gal 4:25.**—DELG s.v. τεῖχος. M-M. TW.

συστρατιώτης, ου, ὁ (s. στρατιώτης; X., Pla. et al.; BGU 814, 27 [soldier's letter]; O. Wilck II, 1535 [II BC]; Jos., Ant. 4, 177) ***comrade in arms, fellow-soldier,*** in our lit. only fig. of those who devote themselves to the service of the gospel; as a term of honor (which in Polyaenus 8, 23, 22 makes the soldier equal to the commander-in-chief, and in Synes., Kingship 13 p. 12c makes the warrior equal to the king) applied to certain of Paul's associates mentioned in **Phil 2:25; Phlm 2** (on the Christian life as military service s. πανοπλία 2).—DELG s.v. στρατός. M-M. TW.

συστρέφω 1 aor. συνέστρεψα. Pass.: fut. 3 pl. συστραφήσονται En 100:4; 2 aor. 3 sg. συνεστράφη; pf. ptc. masc. pl. συνεστραμμένοι 1 Macc 12:50 (s. next entry; Aeschyl., Hdt. et al.; pap, LXX)

❶ **to cause to come together,** ***gather up, bring together*** τὶ *someth.* a bundle of sticks **Ac 28:3.** τινάς *certain people* **17:5** D (cp. Diod. S. 3, 35; Judg 12:4 B; 2 Macc 14:30; Jos., Ant. 18, 85).

❷ **to come together as a gathering,** ***be gathered, gather, come together*** (Hdt. et al.; En 100:4; Jos., Bell. 3, 302, Ant. 18, 351) **Ac 10:41** D; **11:28** D; **16:39** D. So perh. also **Mt 17:22** (cp. ἀναστρέφω 2). Zahn suggests: 'while they were crowding' (around Jesus), and VHarlow, Jesus' Jerusalem Expedition '36, 38–55 a 'half-military review'.—M-M.

συστροφή, ῆς, ἡ (συστρέφω)—❶ **a tumultuous gathering of people,** ***disorderly/seditious gathering*** or ***commotion*** (Hdt. 7, 9; Polyb. 4, 34, 6; Jos., Bell. 4, 601) **Ac 19:40** (here in contrast to a regularly scheduled assembly, cp. vs. 39). ποιήσαντες συστροφὴν οἱ Ἰουδαῖοι *Judeans came together in a mob* **23:12.** But in the last pass. the word may also mean

❷ **the product of a clandestine gathering,** ***plot, conspiracy*** (Am 7:10 συστροφὰς ποιεῖται; Ps 63:3) **Ac 23:12** (s. 1 above).—DELG s.v. στρέφω. M-M.

συσχηματίζω **to form according to a pattern or mold,** ***form/model after*** *someth.* (Aristot., Top. 6, 14, 151b, 8 τὶ πρός τι; Plut., Mor. 83b) pass. w. act. mng. *be formed like, be conformed to, be guided by* (Plut., Mor. 100f; Eunap., Vi. Soph. p. 111) w. dat. of thing to which one is conformed τῷ αἰῶνι τούτῳ **Ro 12:2.** ταῖς ἐπιθυμίαις **1 Pt 1:14.**—DELG s.v. 1 ἔχω 3.

Συχάρ, ἡ indecl. ***Sychar,*** a city in Samaria; acc. to Jerome, Quaest. in Gen. 66, 6 and Epict. 108, 13, a corrupt form of Συχέμ (Sinaitic Syr. Shechim); s. next entry. Many later scholars reject this conclusion, usu. in favor of identifying Sychar w. Askar (Samaritan Ischar) at the southeast foot of Mt. Ebal. Yet excavations seem to show that Jerome was right (s. RB 37, 1928, 619). A place called Sichar or Suchar in the Babyl. Talmud (Baba Kamma 82b; Menachoth 64b) cannot be identified w. certainty. **J 4:5.**—ESchwartz, NGG 1908, 504f; Zahn, NKZ 19, 1908, 207–18; JBoehmer, ZNW 9, 1908, 218–23; KKundsin, Topolog. Überlieferungsstoffe im Joh. 1925; CKopp, The Holy Places of the Gospels, tr. RWalls '63, 155–66; BHHW III 1896.—EDNT.

Συχέμ (שְׁכֶם) indecl.—❶ fem., ***Shechem*** (Συχέμ TestLevi 5:3=Σίκιμα Gen 48:22; Josh 24:32; Demetr.: 722 fgm. 1, 8 Jac.; Theodotus [II BC]: 732 fgm. 1 p. 692, 23 al. Jac. [in Eus., PE 9, 22, 2]; Joseph.), a city in Samaria, destroyed 128 BC by Hyrcanus I. West of it Vespasian founded a new city, Flavia Neapolis (Eus., Onom. p. 150, 1) **Ac 7:16ab.**—KBaedeker, Pal. u. Syr.[7] 1910, 203ff; FFörster, Sichem, s. Gesch. u. Bed., diss. Leipzig 1923; various articles ZDPV 1926–28; ESellin (earlier material in PThomsen, Palätina u. s. Kultur[3] '31, 116): ZAW 50, '32, 303–8; PThomsen, Reallex. d. Vorgesch. XII 1928, 74ff; TBöhl, De opgraving van Sichem 1927; GWright in BASOR '56–'62, The Biography of a Bibl. City '65; ENielsen, Shechem, A Traditio-Hist. Investigation '55; BHHW III, 1781–83; Kl. Pauly V 163.

❷ masc., **a son of Hamor,** ***Shechem*** (s. Ἑμμώρ) Ἑμμὼρ τοῦ Συχέμ (cp. Gen 33:19; JosAs 23:13) *Hamor the father of Shechem* **Ac 7:16 v.l.** (in Jos., Ant. 1, 337f Συχέμμης).—M-M. EDNT.

σφαγή, ῆς, ἡ (σφάζω; trag., X., Pla. et al.; LXX; En 16:1; PsSol 8:1; TestSol 17:1; Philo; Jos., Ant. 1, 102; 7, 39; Ar. 8, 6 [G]; Mel., P. 3, 17 al.; Ath. 14, 1) ***slaughter*** πρόβατα σφαγῆς *sheep to be slaughtered* (cp. Zech 11:4, 7) **Ro 8:36** (Ps 43:23). προσφέρειν ἐπὶ τὴν σφαγήν *bring to be slain* B 8:2. Pass. ἐπὶ σφ. ἄγεσθαι **Ac 8:32;** 1 Cl 16:7; B 5:2 (in each case Is 53:7. Cp. Lucian, Dem. 40 the question βοῦν ἐπὶ σφαγὴν ἤγομεν; in imagery w. ref. to Demosth.). ἡμέρα σφαγῆς *day of slaughter* (Jer 12:3; En 16:1; cp. Syntipas p. 13, 1 ἡμέρα … τ. σφαγῆς.—σφ.=massacre, blood-bath: Appian, Bell. Civ. 2, 24 §91) of the Day of Judgment (Beyschlag, Spitta, FHauck, Meinertz et al.) or of a day of misfortune, when things turned out badly for the poor, but not for the rich (Windisch, MDibelius) **Js 5:5** ('day of slaughter', in the sense of Rv 18:24; σφ. w. reference to humans: Diod. S. 13, 48, 1; 8).—DELG s.v. σφάζω. TW.

σφάγιον, ου, τό (σφαγή; Aeschyl., Hdt.+; LXX, Philo; Jos., Bell. 6, 434) **someth. that is offered as a sacrifice,** ***victim*** to be sacrificed, ***offering*** pl. (w. θυσίαι) **Ac 7:42** (Am 5:25).—DELG s.v. σφάζω. TW.

σφάζω fut. σφάξω; 1 aor. ἔσφαξα. Pass. 2 fut. 3 pl. σφαγήσονται Num 11:22; 2 aor. 2 sg. ἐσφάγης, 3 pl. ἐσφάγησαν (Ar. 13, 6), ptc. σφαγείς (LXX, Mel.), inf. σφαγῆναι (Is 14:21; Ar. 10, 8); pf. ptc. ἐσφαγμένος (Hom. et al. [Att. σφάττω; Tat. 10, 2; Ath. 1, 3; s. B-D-F §71; Mlt-H. 404]; ins, pap, LXX; pseudepigr., apolog.; Orig., C. Cels. 6, 35, 26; Theoph. Ant.) ***slaughter*** w. acc. ἀρνίον **Rv 5:6, 12; 13:8** (in all these passages pass., ἀρνίον ἐσφαγμένον). Abs. B 8:1. Of the killing of a person by violence (Pind. et al.; Theoph. Ant. 3, 5 [p. 214, 1]) σφάζειν τινά *butcher* or *murder someone* (4 Km 10:7; Jer 52:10; Manetho: 609 fgm. 8, 76 Jac. [in Jos., C. Ap. 1, 76]; Demetr. [?]: 722 fgm. 7; Ar. 10, 9) **1J 3:12; Rv 6:4.** Pass. (Hdt. 5, 5) **5:9; 6:9; 18:24.** κεφαλὴ ὡς ἐσφαγμένη εἰς θάνατον *a head that seemed to be mortally wounded* **13:3.**—DELG. M-M. TW.

σφάλλω fut. 3 pl. σφαλοῦσιν 2 Km 22:46; 1 aor. 3 sg. ἔσφαλε LXX. Pass. 2 fut. σφαλήσομαι; 2 aor. 3 pl. ἐσφάλησαν (LXX; AcPl Ha 8, 20) (Hom. et al.; PGM 36, 221; LXX, Philo; Jos., Bell. 3, 479, Ant. 7, 264; Just., A I, 43, 4) in our lit. only pass., act. sense

❶ **to lose one's footing,** ***slip, stumble, fall,*** lit. (Aristoph., Vesp. 1324; X., Lac. 5, 7; Diod. S. 3, 24, 3; Maximus Tyr. 21, 2b; 34, 2e; Dt 32:35) pass. **Mt 15:14 v.l.**

❷ **to fail to secure someth. that was anticipated,** ***lose out on*** w. gen. (Aeschyl., Soph., Eur., Thu.) ἐσφάλησαν τῆς κληρονομίας τῆς αἰωνίας *they lost out on their eternal inheritance* AcPl Ha 8, 20f=Ox 1602, 27f//BMM recto 26f.

σφόδρα adv. of σφοδρός (Pind., Hdt. et al.) **a very high point on a scale of extent,** ***very (much), extremely, greatly*** (in many contexts with ref. to vehemence or violence) used w. an adj. (Lucian, Nigr. 37; PEdg 11 [= Sb 6717], 6 [257 BC]; pseudepigr.; Jos., Vi. 191; Tat. 32, 2) **Mt 2:10; 14:30 v.l.; Mk 16:4; Lk 18:23; Rv 16:21;** GJs 1:1. Used w. verbs (Aeneas Tact. 1463; TestBenj 1:5; TestAbr A 20 p. 103, 14 [Stone p. 54] and B 3 p. 108, 5 [Stone p. 64]; JosAs 8:8f; 24:12 ἐταράχθησαν σφόδρα; Jos., Vi. 159 ἐταράχθην σφόδρα; Just., D. 2, 6; Herm. Wr. 1, 1) φοβεῖσθαι σφ. **Mt 17:6; 27:54;** GJs 14:1. λυπεῖσθαι (1 Macc 14:16; JosAs 8:8; ParJer 9:23; GrBar 12:8) **Mt 17:23; 18:31; 26:22;** GJs 1:3f; 2:4; AcPl Ha 7, 16. ἐκπλήττεσθαι **19:25.** πληθύνεσθαι **Ac 6:7.** ἐταπείνωσεν . . . σφ. GJs 2:3; εὐλόγησέν με σφ. 4:4; ἠνόμησεν . . . σφ. 15:2.—DELG s.v. σφεδανός. M-M.

σφοδρός, ά, όν (Thu., Pla, X.; LXX; TestNapht 6:4; TestSol 10:37 C) **pert. to being excessive,** ***vehement*** (s. prec. entry) χάλαζα . . . λίαν μεγάλην (read: μεγάλη) σφοδρά *a violent hailstorm* AcPl Ha 5, 7.—DELG s.v. σφεδανός.

σφοδρῶς adv. (Hom. et al.; Aelian, NA 14, 26 p. 359, 23; SIG 1169, 57; LXX; Jos., Ant. 13, 292 al.) ***very much, greatly, violently*** (s. two prec. entries) σφ. χειμάζεσθαι *be violently beaten by a storm* **Ac 27:18** (cp. Jos., Ant. 14, 377 χειμῶνι σφοδρῷ περιπεσών).

σφραγίζω 1 aor. ἐσφράγισα. Mid.: fut. 2 sg. σφραγιῇ Jer 39:44; 1 aor. ἐσφραγισάμην. Pass.: 1 aor. ἐσφραγίσθην; pf. ptc. ἐσφραγισμένος (s. next entry; Aeschyl. et al.; ins, pap, LXX, TestSol; TestJob 5:2; ParJer 3:10; ApcMos 42; Philo, Joseph.; Mel., P. 15, 97 al.)

❶ **to provide with a seal as a security measure,** ***seal*** w. acc. of the obj. that is to be secured or fastened by the seal: of a stone, to prevent its being moved fr. position (Da 6:18=Jos., Ant. 10, 258) **Mt 27:66** (but s. μετά A3b). Likew. GPt 9:34, where the words μνημεῖον ἐσφραγισμένον refer back to the sealing of the stone used to close the tomb (8:32f); cp. ApcMos 42 ὁ θεὸς . . . ἐσφράγισε τὸ μνημεῖον. In the case of a closed building, so that it cannot be opened (Bel 11; 14) τὰς κλεῖδας 1 Cl 43:3. A bundle of rods, that were not to be disturbed 43:2. Abs. ἐσφράγισεν ἐπάνω αὐτοῦ *he sealed* (the closed mouth of the abyss) *over him* **Rv 20:3.**

❷ **to close someth. up tight,** ***seal up*** τὶ *someth.* in order to keep it secret (Solon in Stob., Flor. III p. 114, 8 H. τοὺς λόγους σιγῇ; Cleopatra 73 μυστήριον ἐσφραγισμένον; PTebt 413, 6; Job 14:17; 24:16; Da 9:24 Theod.; Da 12:9 LXX) **Rv 10:4; 22:10.**

❸ **to mark with a seal as a means of identification,** ***mark, seal*** (Eur., Iph. T. 1372; Mel., P. 16, 104 al.; in pap, of all kinds of animals), so that the mark denoting ownership also carries w. it the protection of the owner (on the apotropaic aspect cp. TestSol 14:2): σφραγίσωμεν τοὺς δούλους τοῦ θεοῦ ἐπὶ τῶν μετώπων αὐτῶν **Rv 7:3** (marking w. a seal on the forehead in the cult of Mithra: Tertullian, Praescr. Haer. 40). Corresp. ἐσφραγισμένοι vs. **4ab, 5, 8** (on the concept of sealing eschatologically cp. Ezk 9:4ff; Is 44:5; PsSol 15:6, 9; 4 Esdr 6:5f; 8:51ff. S. also LBrun, Übriggebliebene u. Märtyrer in Apk: StKr 102, 1930, 215–31). This forms a basis for understanding the imagery which speaks of those who enter the Christian community as being sealed with or by the Holy Spirit **Eph 1:13;** cp. **4:30.** Sim. θεός, ὁ σφραγισάμενος ἡμᾶς καὶ δοὺς τὸν ἀρραβῶνα τοῦ πνεύματος ἐν ταῖς καρδίαις ἡμῶν **2 Cor 1:22;** but here the context contributes an additional component in the sense of 'endue with power from heaven', as plainly in **J 6:27** (cp. σφραγίς 4a); but EDinkler, OCullmann Festschr. '62, 183–88 associates **2 Cor 1:22** w. baptism; s. σφραγίς 4b.

❹ **to certify that someth. is so,** ***attest, certify, acknowledge,*** fig. (as a seal does on a document: pap; Jer 39:10f; Esth 8:8, 10.—Anth. Pal. 9, 236 ἐσφράγισαν ὅρκοι) w. ὅτι foll. **J 3:33.**

❺ **to seal someth. for delivery,** ***seal*** σφραγισάμενος αὐτοῖς τὸν καρπὸν τοῦτον **Ro 15:28** is perh. to be understood fr. the practice of sealing sacks of grain (Dssm., NB 65f [BS 238f]). But some have thought that the imagery is rather hard to maintain, since the 'fruit' must not only be sealed, but also forwarded to Jerusalem and delivered there. In any case the sense of the expr. is easier to understand in some such wording as this: *when I have placed the sum that was collected safely (sealed) in their hands* (s. LRadermacher, ZNW 32, '33, 87–89; HBartsch, ZNW 63, '72, 95–107). On the debate s. New Docs 2, 191, w. a late pap in further support of Dssm.'s view.—Straub 29f. DELG s.v. σφραγίς. M-M. TW.

σφραγίς, ῖδος, ἡ (s. prec. entry; trag., Hdt.+; ins, pap, LXX; PsS 2:6; TestPs, ParJer; ApcMos 42; Philo; Jos., Ant. 15, 408; 18, 93 al.; loanw. in rabb.) prim. 'seal, signet'.

❶ **the instrument used for sealing or stamping,** ***signet*** (Aristot., Strabo et al., Appian, Liby. 32 §137; 104 §493, Bell. Civ. 2, 22 §82; pap, LXX; Hippol., Ref. 9, 11, 5) σφραγὶς θεοῦ **Rv 7:2** (against power of demons, etc. RCharles, Comm. I 196).

❷ **the substance which bears the imprint of a signet and seals a document,** ***seal*** (ParJer 3:10) GPt 8:33; 1 Cl 43:5. In Rv a book w. seven seals **5:1** (a last will and testament acc. to EHuschke, Das Buch mit sieben Siegeln 1860, Zahn, JWeiss; cp. JMarquardt, Römisches Privatieben[2] 1886, 805f; TBirt, Die Buchrolle in der Kunst 1907, 243.—On **Rv 5f:** WSattler, ZNW 20, 1921, 231–40; 21, 1922, 43–53; KStaritz, ibid. 30, '31, 157–70; WTaylor, JTS 31, 1930, 266–71). λῦσαι τὰς σφραγῖδας **Rv 5:2, 5 v.l.** (cp. λύω 1a). Also ἀνοῖξαι vs. **5, 9; 6:1, 3, 5, 7, 9, 12** (Aeschyl., Eum. 828); **8:1** (ἀνοίγω 4).

❸ **the impression made by a signet,** ***mark*** (Hdt. et al.; LXX; ApcMos 42) **Rv 9:4** (cp. Martial 3, 21, of a slave 'fronte notata'). In imagery ὁ θεμέλιος τοῦ θεοῦ ἔχων τὴν σφραγῖδα ταύτην κτλ. *God's foundation that bears the following mark (=inscription)* . . . **2 Ti 2:19** (s. Dölger, Sphragis 3; Straub 63).—Cp. Hs 8, 2, 4, prob. of a document bearing a mark that permits passage, a *pass* (cp. Aberciusins. 9 λαὸς λαμπρὰν σφραγεῖδαν ἔχων and the Naasene hymn in Hippol., Ref. 5, 10, 2 σφραγῖδας ἔχων καταβήσομαι; likewise the books of Jeû and the Mandaean wr.; Mani, Kephal. I 225, 13; 15; 18; difft. Leutzsch, Hermas p. 480 n. 201).

❹ **that which confirms or authenticates,** ***attestation, confirmation, certification,*** fig. ext. of 3—ⓐ w. the gen. of that which is confirmed or authenticated ἡ σφραγίς μου τῆς ἀποστολῆς ὑμεῖς ἐστε *you are the certification of my apostleship* **1 Cor 9:2.** σημεῖον ἔλαβεν περιτομῆς σφραγῖδα τῆς δικαιοσύνης τῆς πίστεως *he* (Abraham) *received the sign of circumcision as something that confirms the righteousness through faith* that was already present **Ro 4:11.** σφ. need be no more than a metaphor for *attestation* or *confirmation* in περιτέτμηται ὁ λαὸς εἰς σφραγῖδα B 9:6.

ⓑ as a term for baptism in 2 Cl and Hermas (Theognis ln. 19: the author's name, as a σφρηγίς [Ionic form], ensures his work against all possibility of falsification): ἡ σφραγίς 2 Cl 7:6; 8:6; Hs 8, 6, 3; 9, 16, 3ff al. ἡ σφ. τοῦ υἱοῦ τοῦ θεοῦ Hs 9, 16, 3 (also AcThom 131 [Aa II/2, 239, 3; s. Leutzsch, Hermas

p. 483 n. 239]. Cp. ἡ σφ. τοῦ κυρίου Clem. Alex., Quis Div. Salv. 42, 4. ἡ σφ. τοῦ Χριστοῦ AcPh 134 [Aa II/2, 65, 11]; τῆς ἐν κυρίῳ σφραγῖδος AcPl Ha 3, 24; 11, 23 [s. μυέω]; ἡ ἐν Χριστῷ σφ. AcPlTh 25 [Aa I, 253, 7f]; AcThom, end [Aa II/2, 291, 7f]). Used with the verbs διδόναι τινὶ (τὴν σφ.) Hs 9, 16, 5b (AcThom 49 [Aa II/2, 165, 14]; s. also 27 [Aa II/2, 142f]). λαμβάνειν 8, 6, 3; 9, 16, 3; 9, 17, 4. ἔχειν 9, 16, 5a; 7; κηρύσσειν 9, 16, 4b. τεθλακέναι 8, 6, 3. τηρεῖν 2 Cl 7:6; 8:6= τηρεῖν τὸ βάπτισμα 6:9 (δέχεσθαι AcThom 26 [Aa II/2, 141, 14]; περιτιθέναι Celsus in Origen, C. Cels. 2, 96f).—GAnrich, Das Antike Mysterienwesen 1894, 120ff; GWobbermin, Religionsgesch. Studien 1896, 144ff; ASeeberg, Der Katechismus der Urchristenheit 1903, 232ff; FDölger, Sphragis als Taufbez. 1911, 49ff, AC I 1929, 88–91; AvStromberg, Studien zur Theorie u. Praxis der Taufe 1913, 89ff; WHeitmüller, ΣΦΡΑΓΙΣ: Heinrici Festschr. 1914, 40ff; WBousset, Kyrios Christos[2] 1921, 227ff; FPreisigke, Die Gotteskraft der frühchristl. Zeit 1922, 25f; EMaass, Segnen, Weihen, Taufen: ARW 21, 1922, 241ff; JYsebaert, Greek Baptismal Terminol., '62, 204f.—Kl. Pauly V 309; OEANE IV 509–12; DBS XII 66–228 esp. 213–28 on NT; BHHW III 1786–90.—DELG. EDNT. TW. Sv.

σφυδρόν, οῦ, τό (PFlor 391, 53; 56 [III AD]; Hesych.) ***ankle*** **Ac 3:7** (v.l. σφυρόν, q.v.; B-D-F §34, 6).—DELG s.v. σφυρόν.

σφυρίς, ίδος, ἡ s. σπυρίς.

σφυροκοπέω (σφῦρα 'hammer', cp. κόπτω 'smite'; Philod., Περὶ σημείων 2, 7 Gomp.; Judg 5:26 B) ***beat with a hammer*** τὶ *someth.* of a smith τὸ ἔργον αὐτοῦ *his work* Hv 1, 3, 2.—DELG s.v. σφῦρα.

σφυρόν, οῦ, τό—❶ ***ankle*** (Hom. et al.; EpArist 87; Jos., Ant. 3, 155; 7, 171).**—❷** ***heel*** (Eur., Alc. 586; Ps.-Oppian, Cyn. 3, 143); both are poss. in **Ac 3:7 v.l.** S. σφυδρόν.—DELG.

σχεδόν adv. (Hom. et al.) ***nearly, almost*** (Soph., X., Pla.; ins, pap; 2 Macc 5:2; 3 Macc 5:14, 45; EpArist, Philo, Just.; Tat. 41, 4) **Ac 13:44** (cp. Jos., Ant. 7, 20 πᾶσαν σχεδόν); **19:26; Hb 9:22** (cp. Jos., Ant. 1, 18 πάντα σχ.); B 16:2; MPol 1:1; 22:3; EpilMosq 5.—DELG.

σχῆμα, ατος, τό (fr. the same root as ἔχω, cp. 2 aor. inf. σχεῖν; Aeschyl., Thu.+; loanw. in rabb.; in various senses 'bearing, manner, deportment' cp. Lat. 'habitus')

❶ the generally recognized state or form in which someth. appears, *outward appearance, form, shape* of pers. Hv 5:1 (Menyllus: 295 fgm. 2 Jac. Ἄρης ἐν σχήματι ποιμένος). σχήματι εὑρεθεὶς ὡς ἄνθρωπος **Phil 2:7** (Just., A I, 55, 4 ἀνθρώπειον σχῆμα; cp. Lucian, Somn. 13 ἀφεὶς . . . τιμὴν κ. δόξαν . . . κ. δύναμιν σχῆμα δουλοπρεπὲς ἀναλήψῃ; Jos., Ant. 10, 11 a king who exchanges his kingly robes for sackcloth and takes on a σχῆμα ταπεινόν; for the σχῆμα ταπεινόν cp. also Appian, Syr. 40 §206; for assoc. of σχῆμα and ὄνομα cp. Cass. Dio 42, 24).

❷ the functional aspect of someth., *way of life,* of things (Just., D. 105, 2 al. τοῦ σταυροῦ) παράγει τὸ σχῆμα τοῦ κόσμου τούτου *this world in its present form is passing away* **1 Cor 7:31** (Eur., Bacch. 832 τὸ σχ. τοῦ κόσμου; Philostrat., Vi. Apoll. 8, 7 p. 312, 9 τὸ σχ. τοῦ κόσμου τοῦδε; PGM 4, 1139 σχῆμα κόσμου). S. μορφή.—B. 874. DELG s.v. ἔχω. M-M. TW.

σχηματίζω aor. ἐσχημάτισα (s. prec. entry; Hippocr., Pla., POxy 2267, 13 [IV AD], Philo, Just.—Gener. 'give form' to someth., hence 'make ready' for someth.) **to cause to be in an appropriate position for someth.,** ***position*** (on the freq. use of σ. in ref. to posture s. L-S-J-M) ἐσχημάτισεν αὐτήν *(Salome) positioned (Mary)* for a probe of her virginity GJs 20:1 pap; difft. codd.: σχημάτισον σαυτήν *put yourself into position* (spoken by the midwife), followed by Mary's action ἐσχημάτισεν αὑτήν (for Salome's examination).—DELG s.v. ἔχω.

σχίζω fut. σχίσω; 1 aor. ἔσχισα. Pass.: fut. 3 sg.; aor. ἐσχίσθην; pf. ptc. pl. ἐσχισμένοι Is 36:22 (Hom. Hymns et al.; pap, LXX, Test12Patr; JosAs 14:3; ParJer 2:5; Philo; Jos., Ant. 8, 207; 20, 97)

❶ to divide by use of force, *split, divide, separate, tear apart, tear off* lit. τὶ *someth.*—ⓐ act. τὸ ξύλον *split the wood* (Antig. Car. 142 ξύλον σχίσας; Paradoxogr. Flor. 9; Paroem. Gr.: Apostolius 7, 24a) Ox 1 recto, 8 (GTh 77; cp. Eccl 10:9, also Gen 22:3; 1 Km 6:14 and see ἐγείρω 10).τὸ καινὸν σχίσει *he will tear the new* **Lk 5:36b.** Cp. **J 19:24.** ἐπίβλημα ἀπὸ ἱματίου σχ. *tear (off) a patch from a garment* **Lk 5:36a** (cp. Jos., Ant, 8, 207).

ⓑ pass. *be divided, be torn, be split* αἱ πέτραι ἐσχίσθησαν *the rocks were split* **Mt 27:51b** (cp. Is 48:21; TestLevi 4:1; PTebt 273, 43; 52 λίθος σχισθείς). Of the curtain in the temple (s. καταπέτασμα) ἐσχίσθη *(it) was torn* (cp. Anacr. 95b Diehl; as portent, cp. Plut., Dem. 894 [12, 3] of Athena's robe, which was rent [ἐρράγη] during a procession) **Lk 23:45;** εἰς δύο (cp. schol. on Apollon. Rhod. 4, 282–91b p. 281, 10 W. σχίζεται εἰς δύο; Polyb. 2, 16, 11 εἰς δύο μέρη; PGM 13, 262 σχίσον εἰς δύο=in two) **Mt 27:51a; Mk 15:38** (D +μέρη). Of a net **J 21:11.** Of the dome of heaven **Mk 1:10** (JosAs 14:4 ἐσχίσθη ὁ οὐρανός; Himerius, Or. [Ecl.] 32, 14 οὐρανὸν σχίσας for a divine announcement, to bring from the house of Zeus a pure soul, τῶν θείων φασμάτων παρ' ἡμᾶς τὴν οὐσίαν διαπορθμεύουσαν=who communicates to us the nature of the divine appearances).

❷ to tear apart a group through conflicting aims or objectives, fig. ext. of 1—ⓐ act. ***cause a division/schism*** IPhld 3:3 (cp. Dionys. Alex. in Eus., HE 6, 45).

ⓑ pass. ***become divided/disunited*** (X., Symp. 4, 59 ἐσχίσθησαν, καὶ οἱ μὲν . . ., οἱ δέ) ἐσχίσθη τὸ πλῆθος **Ac 14:4; 23:7** (cp. Diod. S. 12, 66, 2 τοῦ πλήθους σχιζομένου κατὰ τὴν αἵρεσιν; Celsus 3, 10; Ps.-Lucian, Asin. 54 εἰς δύο γνώμας).—B. 564; 845. DELG. M-M. TW.

σχίσμα, ατος, τό (σχίζω; Aristot. et al.; 'split, division')

❶ the condition resulting from splitting or tearing, *tear, crack* (Aristot., HA 2, 1; Physiogn. I 372, 6; En 1:7) in a garment **Mt 9:16; Mk 2:21;** in a stick Hs 8, 5, 1; in a stone 9, 8, 3.

❷ the condition of being divided because of conflicting aims or objectives, *division, dissension, schism* fig. ext. of 1 (PLond 2710 recto, 13 [=Sb 7835—I BC] the ἡγούμενος of the brotherhood of Zeus Hypsistos forbids σχίσματα most strictly; Cat. Cod. Astr. XI/2 p. 122, 24 πολέμους, φόνους, μάχας, σχίσματα; Hippol., Ref. 6, 35, 5 w. διαφορά; Iren. 4, 33, 7 [Harv. II 261, 1], opp.: ἡ ἕνωσις τῆς ἐκκλησίας) **J 7:43; 9:16; 10:19; 1 Cor 1:10; 11:18; 12:25;** 1 Cl 46:9; 49:5 (ἔσονται σχίσματα καὶ αἱρέσεις Just., D. 35, 3 [Gospel quot. of unknown origin; s. Unknown Sayings 59–61]). W. στάσις 2:6; w. στάσις, ἔρις 54:2. ἔρεις, θυμοί, διχοστασίαι, σχίσματα, πόλεμος 46:5. ποιεῖν σχίσμα *cause a division* D 4:3; B 19:12. σχίσματα ἐν ἑαυτοῖς ἐποίησαν *they brought about divisions* (of opinion) *in their own minds* (or *among themselves;* s. ἑαυτοῦ 2) Hs 8, 9, 4.—MMeinertz, BZ n.s. 1, '57, 114–18.—M-M. DELG s.v. σχίζω. TW. Sv.

σχισμή, ῆς, ἡ (σχίζω) ***crack, fissure*** (Rhet. Gr. I 552, 4; LXX) in stones (cp. Is 2:19, 21; SibOr 3, 607) Hv 3, 2, 8; 3, 6,

3; s 9, 6, 4; 9, 8, 3f; 9, 23, 1–3; in sticks Hs 8, 1, 9f; 14; 8, 4, 6; 8, 5, 1; 4f; 8, 7, 1f; 4; 8, 10, 1; in a mountain (Jon 2:6) s 9, 1, 7.—DELG s.v. σχίζω.

σχοινίον, ου, τό (Hdt. et al.; ins, pap, LXX; PsSol 2:20; TestSol 4:12; JosAs; ApcrEzk [Epiph 70, 10]; Jos., Ant. 8, 385; 19, 346) ***rope*** or ***cord*** (orig. of rushes, then gener. of other material); used to elevate someth. IEph 9:1. Of the ropes that hold a ship's boat in place **Ac 27:32.** Jesus uses them to make a whip **J 2:15.**—B. 549. DELG s.v. σχοῖνος. M-M.

σχοίνισμα, ατος, τό (LXX) lit. 'a piece of land measured out by means of a measuring-line (σχοῖνος, σχοινίον)', in our lit. only in imagery ***allotment*** (Hesych.; Etym. Mag. p. 740, 46) σχ. κληρονομίας αὐτοῦ *the allotment that he acquired* 1 Cl 29:2 (Dt 32:9).—DELG s.v. σχοῖνος.

σχολάζω (σχολή) 1 aor. ἐσχόλασα (Aeschyl., Thu. et al.; ins, pap, LXX; TestSol 1:10 L; TestJob 6:3, 7; TestJud 20:1; Philo; in gener. of release from routine or pressing obligation; wars, e.g., permit no leisure Pla., Leg. 694e)

❶ **to have time or leisure for, *busy oneself with, devote oneself to, give one's time to*** τινί *someone* or *someth.* (Lucian, Ver. Hist. 2, 15; Ps.-Lucian, Macrob. 4 φιλοσοφίᾳ; Epict. 2, 14, 28; Herodian 1, 8, 1 al.; SIG 717, 34f [100 BC] τοῖς φιλοσόφοις; OGI 569, 23 θεῶν θρησκείᾳ; Sb 4284, 15 τῇ γῇ; PAmh 82, 6 γεωργίᾳ; Philo, Spec. Leg. 3, 1 al.; TestJud 20:1) τῇ προσευχῇ **1 Cor 7:5** (on this subj. s. TestNapht 8:8); cp. IPol 1:3. Χριστιανὸς θεῷ σχολάζει 7:3 (cp. the letter by a polytheist Sb 4515 οὐ μέλλω θεῷ σχολάζειν, εἰ μὴ πρότερον ἀπαρτίσω τὸν υἱόν μου 'I don't plan on having time for a deity until I first educate my son').

❷ **to be without occupants, *be unoccupied, stand empty*** (Plut., C. Gracch. 840 [12, 6] τόπος; Julian, Caes. 316c καθέδρα; SEG XI, 121, 13) of a house **Mt 12:44; Lk 11:25 v.l.** HNyberg, Ntl. Sem. zu Uppsala 4, '36, 22–35, ConNeot 13, '49, 1–11.—DELG s.v. σχολή. M-M.

σχολή, ῆς, ἡ (Pind.+; ins, pap, LXX, Philo, Joseph., loanw. in rabb.) prim. 'leisure', which freq. implied opportunity for intellectual pursuits, esp. through lectures: ***lecture hall*** (cp. Plut., Mor. 42a of an elementary school; for focus not on locale but on intellectual engagement at a sophisticated level s. Dionys. Hal., Isocrates 1, Demosthenes 44; Plut., Mor. 519f, 605a; Epict. 1, 29, 34; Jos., C. Ap. 1, 53; s. New Docs 1, 129f) **Ac 19:9** (Beginn. IV 239; Bruce, comm.; et al.).—B. 1227. DELG. M-M. Sv.

σχῶ s. ἔχω.

σῴζω fut. σώσω; 1 aor. ἔσωσα; pf. σέσωκα. Pass.: impf. ἐσῳζόμην; fut. σωθήσομαι; 1 aor. ἐσώθην; pf. 3 sing. σέσωται **Ac 4:9** (UPZ 122, 18 [157 BC] σέσωμαι) w. σέσῳσται or σέσωσται as v.l. (s. Tdf. ad loc. and B-D-F §26); ptc. σεσῳσμένος **Eph 2:5, 8** (Hom.+—σῴζω [=σωΐζω] and the forms surely derived fr. it are to be written w. ι subscript. On the other hand, it is not possible to say how far the ι has spread fr. the present to the tenses formed fr. the root σω-. Kühner-Bl. II 544; B-D-F §26; Mlt-H. 84; Mayser 134)

❶ **to preserve or rescue fr. natural dangers and afflictions, *save, keep from harm, preserve, rescue*** (X., An. 3, 2, 10 οἱ θεοὶ . . . ἱκανοί εἰσι κ. τοὺς μεγάλους ταχὺ μικροὺς ποιεῖν κ. τοὺς μικροὺς σῴζειν; Musonius p. 32, 10; Chion, Ep. 11; 12 θεοῦ σῴζοντος πλευσοῦμαι; Ar. [Milne 74, 15]).

ⓐ ***save from death*** (ins [I BC]: Sb 8138, 34 σῴζονθ' οὗτοι ἅπαντες who call upon Isis in the hour of death) τινά *someone* (Apollon. Rhod. 3, 323 θεός τις ἄμμ' [=ἡμᾶς] ἐσάωσεν from danger of death at sea; Diod. S. 11, 92, 3; PsSol 13:2 ἀπὸ ῥομφαίας [cp. Ps 21:21]) **Mt 14:30; 27:40, 42, 49; Mk 15:30f; Lk 23:35ab, 37, 39;** 1 Cl 16:16 (Ps 21:9); 59, 4; AcPl Ha 5, 12. Pass. (TestJob 19:2 πῶς οὖν σὺ ἐσώθης;) **Mt 24:22; Mk 13:20; J 11:12** (ἐγερθήσεται P[75]); **Ac 27:20, 31;** 1 Cl 7:6. Abs., w. acc. easily supplied **Mt 8:25.** ψυχὴν σῶσαι *save a life* (Achilles Tat. 5, 22, 6; PTebt 56, 11 [II BC] σῶσαι ψυχὰς πολλάς; EpArist 292; Jos., Ant. 11, 255) **Mk 3:4; Lk 6:9; 21:19 v.l.** τὴν ψυχὴν αὐτοῦ σῶσαι *save one's own life* (Gen 19:17; 1 Km 19:11; Jer 31:6) **Mt 16:25; Mk 8:35a=Lk 9:24a** (on **Mk 8:35b=Lk 9:24b** s. 2aβ below); **17:33 v.l.** (PGM 5, 140 κύριε [a god] σῶσον ψυχήν).

ⓑ w. ἔκ τινος ***bring out safely*** fr. a situation fraught w. mortal danger (X., An. 3, 2, 11; SIG 1130, 1 ἐκ κινδύνων; OGI 69, 4; JosAs 4:8 ἐκ τοῦ λιμοῦ; 28:16 ἐκ τῆς ὀργῆς; Jos., C. Ap. 1, 286) ἐκ γῆς Αἰγύπτου **Jd 5.** ἐκ χειρὸς Φαραώ AcPl Ha 8, 11; ἐκ Σοδόμων 1 Cl 11:1 (Pla., Gorg. 511d ἐξ Αἰγίνης δεῦρο). ἐκ τῆς ὥρας ταύτης **J 12:27.** ἐκ θανάτου *from (the threat of) death* (Hom. et al.; Pla., Gorg. 511c; UPZ 122, 18 [157 BC]) **Hb 5:7.**—Of the evil days of the last tribulation ἐν αἷς ἡμεῖς σωθησόμεθα B 8:6; cp. 1 Cl 59:4.

ⓒ ***save/free from disease*** (Hippocr., Coacae Praenotiones 136 vol. 5 p. 612 L.; IG[2], 1028, 89 [I BC]; Mitt-Wilck. I/2, 68, 32 [132 BC]: gods bring healing) or *from possession by hostile spirits* τινά *someone* ἡ πίστις σου σέσωκέν σε **Mt 9:22a; Mk 5:34; 10:52; Lk 8:48; 17:19; 18:42.** Cp. **Js 5:15;** AcPl Ha 5, 31. Pass. *be restored to health, get well* (Just., D. 112, 1; Ael. Aristid. 33, 9 K.=51 p. 573 D.) **Mt 9:21, 22b; Mk 5:23, 28; 6:56; Lk 8:36; Ac 4:9; 14:9.** Also of the restoration that comes about when death has already occurred **Lk 8:50.**

ⓓ ***keep, preserve*** in good condition (pap; Did., Gen. 145, 1.—Theoph. Ant. 1, 12 [p. 84, 4]) τὶ *someth.* (Ath. 17, 2 ὁ τύπος . . . σῴζεται, R. 20 p. 73, 10 μνήμην and αἴσθησιν; Eunap., Vi. Soph. p. 107: θειασμός) pass. τὴν κλῆσιν σῴζεσθαι Hs 8, 11, 1.

ⓔ pass. ***thrive, prosper, get on well*** (SibOr 5, 227) σῴζεσθαι ὅλον τὸ σῶμα 1 Cl 37:5. As a form of address used in parting σῴζεσθε *farewell, remain in good health* B 21:9 (cp. TestAbr B 2 p. 106, 1 [Stone p. 60] σῶσόν σε ὁ θεός).

❷ **to save or preserve from transcendent danger or destruction, *save/preserve from eternal death*** fr. judgment, and fr. all that might lead to such death, e.g. sin, also in a positive sense ***bring*** Messianic ***salvation, bring to salvation*** (LXX; Herm. Wr. 13, 19 σῴζειν='endow w. everlasting life'.—Of passing over into a state of salvation and a higher life: Cebes 3, 2; 4, 3; 14, 1. Opp. κολάζειν Orig., C. Cels. 2, 38, 16).

ⓐ act. τινά *someone* or τὶ *someth.*—**α.** of God and Christ: God (ApcEsdr 2:17 p. 26, 9 Tdf. σὺ δὲ ὃν θέλεις σῴζεις καὶ ὃν θέλεις ἀπολεῖς) **1 Cor 1:21; 2 Ti 1:9; Tit 3:5;** AcPlCor 2:10, 16. The acc. is easily supplied **Js 4:12.** ὁ θεὸς ὁ σῴζων **Mt 16:16** D.—Christ (Orig., C. Cels. 3, 14, 9): **Mt 18:11; Lk 19:10; J 12:47; 1 Ti 1:15; 2 Ti 4:18** (εἰς 10d); **Hb 7:25;** MPol 9:3. σώσει τὸν λαὸν αὐτοῦ ἀπὸ τῶν ἁμαρτιῶν αὐτῶν **Mt 1:21** (σ. ἀπό as Jos., Ant. 4, 128); also ἐκ τῶν ἁμαρτιῶν αὐτῶν GJs 11:3; cp. 14:2. The acc. is to be supplied 2 Cl 1:7. διὰ τῶν ἁγνῶν ἀνδρῶν AcPl Ha 1, 16.

β. of persons who are mediators of divine salvation: apostles **Ro 11:14; 1 Cor 9:22; 1 Ti 4:16b.** The believing partner in a mixed marriage **1 Cor 7:16ab** (JJeremias, Die missionarische Aufgabe in der Mischehe, Bultmann Festschr. '54, 255–60). One Christian of another σώσει ψυχὴν αὐτοῦ ἐκ θανάτου **Js 5:20** (on σ. ἐκ θαν. s. 1a above). Cp. **Jd 23.** Of ultimate personal security **1 Ti 4:16a; Mk 8:35b=Lk 9:24b** (for **Mk 8:35a=Lk 9:24a** s. 1a above).

γ. of qualities, etc., that lead to salvation ἡ πίστις σου σέσωκέν σε **Lk 7:50** (s. 1c above). Cp. **Js 1:21; 2:14; 1 Pt 3:21;** Hv 2, 3, 2. οὐ γάρ ἐστιν π[λοῦτος ἢ τὰ νῦν ἐν τῷ βίῳ λαμπ]ρὰ σώσι (=σώσει) σε *it's not [the wealth or pomp in this life] that will save you* AcPl Ha 9, 8 (for the restoration s. corresponding expressions 2, 21–27).

ⓑ pass. *be saved, attain salvation* (TestAbr A 11 p. 90, 3 [Stone p. 28] al.; Just., A I, 18, 8 al.; Theoph. Ant. 2, 14 [p. 136, 15]) **Mt 10:22; 19:25; 24:13; Mk 10:26; 13:13; 16:16; Lk 8:12; 18:26; J 5:34; 10:9; Ac 2:21** (Jo 3:5); **15:1; 16:30f; Ro 10:9, 13** (Jo 3:5); **11:26; 1 Cor 5:5; 10:33; 1 Th 2:16; 2 Th 2:10; 1 Ti 2:4** (JTurmel, Rev. d'Hist. et de Littérature religieuses 5, 1900, 385–415); **1 Pt 4:18** (Pr 11:31); 2 Cl 4:2; 13:1; IPhld 5:2; Hs 9, 26, 6; AcPl Ha 1, 5 and 21.—σωθῆναι διά τινος *through someone* (Ctesias: 688 fgm. 8a p. 452 Jac. [in Ps.-Demetr., Eloc. c. 213] σὺ μὲν δι' ἐμὲ ἐσώθης, ἐγὼ δέ; Herm. Wr. 1, 26b ὅπως τὸ γένος τῆς ἀνθρωπότητος διὰ σοῦ ὑπὸ θεοῦ σωθῇ) **J 3:17;** 2 Cl 3:3; *through someth.* (Mel., P. 60, 440 διὰ τοῦ αἵματος) **Ac 15:11; 1 Cor 15:2; 1 Ti 2:15** (διά A 3c); Hv 3, 3, 5; 3, 8, 3 (here faith appears as a person, but still remains as a saving quality); 4, 2, 4. ἔν τινι *in* or *through someone* 1 Cl 38:1; AcPl Ha 2, 29; *in* or *through someth.* **Ac 4:12; 11:14; Ro 5:10.** ὑπό τινος *by someone* (Herm. Wr. 9, 5 ὑπὸ τ. θεοῦ σ.; Philo, Leg. All. 2, 101 ὑπὸ θεοῦ σῴζεται) 2 Cl 8:2. ἀπό τινος *save oneself by turning away from* **Ac 2:40** (on σ. ἀπό s. 2aα above; ELövestam, ASTI 12, '83, 84–92). διά τινος ἀπό τινος *through someone from someth.* **Ro 5:9.**—χάριτι *by grace* **Eph 2:5;** Pol 1:3. τῇ χάριτι διὰ πίστεως **Eph 2:8.** τῇ ἐλπίδι ἐσώθημεν (only) *in hope have we* (thus far) *been saved* or *it is in the context of this hope that we have been saved* (i.e., what is to come climaxes what is reality now) **Ro 8:24.**—οἱ σῳζόμενοι *those who are to be* or *are being saved* (Iren. 1, 3, 5 [Harv. I 30, 9]) **Lk 13:23; Ac 2:47** (BMeyer, CBQ 27, '65, 37f: cp. Is 37:2); **1 Cor 1:18; 2 Cor 2:15** (opp. οἱ ἀπολλύμενοι in the last two passages); **Rv 21:24** t.r. (Erasmian rdg.); 1 Cl 58:2; MPol 17:2.

❸ Certain passages belong under 1 and 2 at the same time. They include **Mk 8:35=Lk 9:24** (s. 1a and 2a β above) and **Lk 9:[56] v.l.,** where σῴζειν is used in contrast to destruction by fire fr. heaven, but also denotes the bestowing of transcendent salvation (cp. Cornutus 16 p. 21, 9f οὐ πρὸς τὸ βλάπτειν, ἀλλὰ πρὸς τὸ σῴζειν γέγονεν ὁ λόγος [=Ἑρμῆς]). In **Ro 9:27** τὸ ὑπόλειμμα σωθήσεται (Is 10:22) the remnant that is to escape death is interpreted to mean the minority who are to receive the Messianic salvation. In **1 Cor 3:15** escape fr. a burning house is a symbol for the attainment of eternal salvation (πῦρ a; cp. also Cebes 3, 4 ἐὰν δέ τις γνῷ, ἡ ἀφροσύνη ἀπόλλυται, αὐτὸς δὲ σῴζεται).—WWagner, Über σώζειν u. seine Derivata im NT: ZNW 6, 1905, 205–35; J-BColon, La conception du Salut d'après les Év. syn.: RSR 10, 1930, 1–39; 189–217; 370–415; 11, '31, 27–70; 193–223; 382–412; JSevenster, Het verlossingsbegrip bij Philo. Vergeleken met de verlossingsgedachten van de syn. evangeliën '36; PMinear, And Great Shall be your Reward '41; MGoguel, Les fondements de l'assurance du salut chez l'ap. Paul: RHPR 17, '38, 105–44; BHHW II 995, 1068.—B. 752. DELG s.v. σῶς. M-M. EDNT. TW. Spicq. Sv.

Σωκράτης, ους, ὁ *Socrates,* a name freq. found; a Christian in Corinth, who made a copy of the MPol: 22:2. EpilMosq 5 gives his name as Ἰσοκράτης.—DELG s.v. σῶς.

σῶμα, ατος, τό (Hom.+) 'body.'—❶ **body of a human being or animal,** ***body***—ⓐ ***dead body, corpse*** (so always in Hom. [but s. HHerter, σῶμα bei Homer: Charites, Studien zur Altertumswissenschaft, ELanglotz Festschr., ed. KvonSchauenburg '57, 206–17] and oft. later, e.g. Memnon: 434 fgm. 1, 3, 3 Jac. καίειν τὸ σ.=burn the corpse; ins, pap, LXX; PsSol 2:27; TestJob 52:11; ApcMos 34 al.; Philo, Abr. 258; Jos., Bell. 6, 276, Ant. 18, 236; Ar. 4, 3; Mel., P. 28, 196) **Mt 14:12 v.l.; 27:59; Mk 15:45 v.l.; Lk 17:37; Ac 9:40;** GPt 2:4; pl. **J 19:31.** W. gen. **Mt 27:58; Mk 15:43; Lk 23:52, 55; 24:3, 23; J 19:38ab, 40; 20:12; Jd 9;** GPt 2:3. Pl. **Mt 27:52; Hb 13:11.** AcPlCor 2:27.

ⓑ ***the living body*** (Hes. et al.) of animals **Js 3:3.**—Mostly of human beings **Mt 5:29f; 6:22f; 26:12; Mk 5:29; 14:8; Lk 11:34abc; J 2:21; Ro 1:24; 1 Cor 6:18ab;** IRo 5:3. τὰ τοῦ σώματος *the parts of the body* 4:2. Of women αἱ ἀσθενεῖς τῷ σώματι 1 Cl 6:2; cp. Hv 3, 11, 4.—W. and in contrast to πνεῦμα (4 Macc 11:11) **Ro 8:10, 13; 1 Cor 5:3; 7:34; Js 2:26.** W. and in contrast to ψυχή (Pla., Gorg. 47, 493a; Diod. S. 34 + 35 fgm. 2, 30; Appian, Bell. Civ. 5, 112 §467; Ael. Aristid. 45, 17f K.=8 p. 88f D.; Lucian, Imag. 23; PGM 7, 589; Wsd 1:4; 8:19f; 2 Macc 7:37; 14:38; 4 Macc 1:28; ApcEsdr 7:3 p. 32, 13 Tdf.; EpArist 139; Philo; Jos., Bell. 3, 372–78; 6, 55; Just., A I, 8, 4; D. 6, 2 al.; Tat. 13, 1; Ath. 1, 4; Did., Gen. 56, 4; Theoph. Ant. 1, 5 [p. 66, 2]) **Mt 6:25ab; 10:28ab; Lk 12:4 v.l., 22f;** 2 Cl 5:4 (a saying of Jesus, fr. an unknown source); 12:4; MPol 14:2; AcPl Ha 1, 4. τὸ πνεῦμα καὶ ἡ ψυχὴ καὶ τὸ σῶμα (s. the Christian POxy 1161, 6 [IV AD]) **1 Th 5:23.** W. and in contrast to its parts (ApcSed 11:13; Mel., P. 78, 563) **Ro 12:4; 1 Cor 12:12abc** (Ltzm. ad loc.), 14–20 (PMich 149, 4, 26 [II AD] ἧπαρ . . . ὅλον τὸ σῶμα); **Js 3:6;** 1 Cl 37:5abcd. The body as the seat of sexual function **Ro 4:19; 1 Cor 7:4ab** (rights over the σῶμα of one's spouse as Artem. 1, 44 p. 42, 14f; Iren. 1, 13, 3 [Harv. I 119, 10]).—The body as seat of mortal life εἶναι ἐν σώματι *be in the body = alive, subject to mortal ills* (TestAbr A 9 p. 87, 3 [Stone p. 22]; Poryphr., Abst. 1, 38) **Hb 13:3.** ἐνδημεῖν ἐν τῷ σώματι **2 Cor 5:6** (s. ἐνδημέω). ἐκδημῆσαι ἐκ τοῦ σώματος vs. **8** (s. ἐκδημέω). διὰ τοῦ σώματος *during the time of one's mortal life* (cp. Lucian, Menipp. 11, end, Catapl. 23) vs. **10** (s. κομίζω 3, but s. also below in this section). Paul does not know whether, in a moment of religious ecstasy, he was ἐν σώματι or ἐκτὸς (χωρὶς) τοῦ σώματος **12:2f** (of Epimenides [A2: Vorsokrat.[5] I p. 29] it was said ὡς ἐξίοι ἡ ψυχὴ ὁπόσον ἤθελε καιρὸν καὶ πάλιν εἰσῄει ἐν τῷ σώματι; Clearchus, fgm. 7: καθάπερ ὁ Κλέαρχος ἐν τοῖς περὶ ὕπνου φησίν, περὶ τῆς ψυχῆς, ὡς ἄρα χωρίζεται τοῦ σώματος καὶ ὡς εἴσεισιν εἰς τὸ σῶμα καὶ ὡς χρῆται αὐτῷ οἷον καταγωγίῳ [a resting-place]. In fgm. 8 Clearchus tells about Cleonymus the Athenian, who seemed to be dead, but awakened after 3 days and thereupon reported everything that he had seen and heard ἐπειδὴ χωρὶς ἦν τοῦ σώματος. His soul is said finally to have arrived εἴς τινα χῶρον ἱερὸν τῆς Ἑστίας; Maximus Tyr. 38, 3a–f Ἀριστέας ἔφασκεν τὴν ψυχὴν αὐτῷ καταλιποῦσαν τὸ σῶμα in order to wander through the universe. He finds faith everywhere. Similarly 10, 2f. See also the story of Hermotimus in Apollon. Paradox. 3 as well as Lucian, Musc. Enc. [The Fly] 7.—On the two kinds of transcendent vision [with or without the body] s. Proclus, In Pla. Rem Publ. II p. 121, 26ff Kroll: οἱ μὲν μετὰ τοῦ σώματος τῶν τοιούτων [like Ἐμπεδότιμος] ἵστορες [=eyewitnesses], οἱ δὲ ἄνευ σώματος [like Κλεώνυμος]. καὶ πλήρεις αἱ παραδόσεις τούτων.). ἀπὼν τῷ σώματι (παρὼν δὲ τῷ πνεύματι) **1 Cor 5:3.** ἡ παρουσία τοῦ σώματος **2 Cor 10:10** (παρουσία 1). The body is the instrument of human experience and suffering **4:10ab; Gal 6:17** (allusion AcPlCor 2, 35); **Phil 1:20;** the body is the organ of a person's activity: δοξάσατε τὸν θεὸν ἐν τῷ σώματι ὑμῶν *glorify God through your body,* i.e. by leading an upright life **1 Cor 6:20;** cp. **Ro 12:1.** This may be the place (s. above in this section) for διὰ τοῦ σώματος **2 Cor 5:10** which, in that case, would be taken in an instrumental sense *with* or *through the body* (cp. Pla., Phd. 65a; Ps.-Pla., Axioch.

13, 371c; Aelian, NA 5, 26 τὰ διὰ τοῦ σώματος πραττόμενα). In some of the last-named passages (such as **Ro 12:1; Phil 1:20;** also **Eph 5:28** w. parallel in Plut., Mor. 142e: s. HAlmqvist, Plut. u. d. NT '46, 116f) the body is almost synonymous w. the whole personality (as Aeschin., Or. 2, 58; X., An. 1, 9, 12 τὰ ἑαυτῶν σώματα=themselves. Appian, Syr. 41 §218 παρεδίδου τὸ σῶμα τοῖς ἐθέλουσιν ἀπαγαγεῖν=[Epaminondas] gave himself up to those who wished to take him away, Mithr. 27 §107 ἐς τὸ σῶμα αὐτοῦ=against his person, Bell. Civ. 2, 106 §442 Caesar's person [σῶμα] is ἱερὸς καὶ ἄσυλος=sacred and inviolable; 3, 39 §157 ἔργον … σῶμα=course of action … person; Mitt-Wilck. I/2, 55, 7 [III BC] ἑκάστου σώματος=for every person. See Wilcken's note).—Because it is subject to sin and death, man's mortal body as τὸ σῶμα τῆς σαρκός (σάρξ 2ca) **Col 2:11** is a σῶμα τῆς ἁμαρτίας **Ro 6:6** or τοῦ θανάτου **7:24;** cp. **8:11.** In fact, σῶμα can actually take the place of σάρξ **8:13** (cp. Herm. Wr. 4, 6b ἐὰν μὴ πρῶτον τὸ σῶμα μισήσῃς, σεαυτὸν φιλῆσαι οὐ δύνασαι; 11, 21a.—Cp. Hippol., Ref. 5, 19, 6). As a σῶμα τῆς ταπεινώσεως *lowly body* it stands in contrast to the σῶμα τῆς δόξης *glorious body* of the heavenly beings **Phil 3:21.** In another pass. σῶμα ψυχικόν of mortals is opposed to the σῶμα πνευματικόν after the resurrection **1 Cor 15:44abc.**—Christ's earthly body, which was subject to death (Orig., C. Cels. 2, 9, 13) **Ro 7:4; Hb 10:5** (Ps 39:7 v.l.), **10; 1 Pt 2:24;** AcPlCor 2:16f. τὸ σῶμα καὶ τὰ ὀστᾶ καὶ τὸ πνεῦμα Χριστοῦ 2:32. τὸ σῶμα τῆς σαρκὸς αὐτοῦ **Col 1:22.** Esp. in the language of the Eucharist (opp. αἷμα) **Mt 26:26; Mk 14:22; Lk 22:19; 1 Cor 10:16** (GBornkamm, NTS 2, '56, 202–6); **11:24, 27, 29.** S. the lit. s.v. ἀγάπη 2 and εὐχαριστία 3, also JBonsirven, Biblica 29, '48, 205–19.—ἓν σῶμα *a single body* **1 Cor 6:16** (cp. Jos., Ant. 7, 66 Δαυίδης τήν τε ἄνω πόλιν κ. τὴν ἄκραν συνάψας ἐποίησεν ἓν σῶμα; Artem. 3, 66 p. 196, 9; RKempthorne, NTS 14. '67/68, 568–74).

❷ pl. σώματα ***slaves*** (Herodas 2, 87 δοῦλα σώματα; Polyb. et al.; oft. Vett. Val.; ins, pap; Gen 36:6; Tob 10:10; Bel 32; 2 Macc 8:11; Jos., Ant. 14, 321; cp. our colloq. 'get some bodies for the job') **Rv 18:13** (cp. Ezk 27:13; the abs. usage rejected by Atticists, s. Phryn. 378 Lob.).

❸ **plant and seed structure,** ***body.*** In order to gain an answer to his own question in **1 Cor 15:35** ποίῳ σώματι ἔρχονται; (i.e. the dead after the resurrection), Paul speaks of bodies of plants (which are different in kind fr. the 'body' of the seed which is planted.—Maximus Tyr. 40, 60e makes a distinction betw. the σώματα of the plants, which grow old and pass away, and their σπέρματα, which endure.—σώματα of plants also in Apollon. Paradox. 7 [after Aristot.]) vs. **37f,** and of σώματα ἐπουράνια of the heavenly bodies vs. **40** (cp. Ps.-Aristot., De Mundo 2, 2 the stars as σώματα θεῖα; Maximus Tyr. 21, 8b οὐρανὸς κ. τὰ ἐν αὐτῷ σώματα, acc. to 11, 12a οἱ ἀστέρες; 40, 4h; Sallust. 9 p. 18, 5).

❹ **substantive reality,** ***the thing itself, the reality*** in imagery of a body that casts a shadow, in contrast to σκιά (q.v. 3) **Col 2:17.**

❺ **a unified group of people,** ***body*** fig. ext. of 1, of the Christian community or church (cp. Cyr. Ins. 58, 'body of the Hellenes'; Polyaenus, Exc. 18, 4 of the phalanx; Libanius, Or. 1 p. 176, 25 F. τὸ τῆς πόλεως σ.; Plut., Philop. 360 [8, 2]), esp. as the body of Christ, which he fills or enlivens as its Spirit (in this case the head belongs with the body, as Appian, Bell. Civ. 3, 26 §101, where a severed head is differentiated from τὸ ἄλλο σῶμα=the rest of the body), or crowns as its Head (Hdt. 7, 140; Quint. Smyrn. 11, 58; SIG 1169, 3; 15 κεφαλή w. σῶμα as someth. equally independent; Orig., C. Cels. 6, 79, 27): οἱ πολλοὶ ἓν σῶμά ἐσμεν ἐν Χριστῷ **Ro 12:5.** Cp. **1 Cor 10:17; 12:13, 27; Eph** (s. Schlier s.v. ἐκκλησία 3c) **1:23; 2:16; 4:12, 16; 5:23, 30; Col 1:18, 24; 2:19; 3:15;** ISm 1:2; Hs 9, 17, 5; 9, 18, 3f. ἓν σῶμα καὶ ἓν πνεῦμα **Eph 4:4;** cp. Hs 9, 13, 5; 7 (Iambl., Vi. Pyth. 30, 167: all as ἓν σῶμα κ. μία ψυχή; also Just., D. 42, 3) διέλκομεν τὰ μέλη τοῦ Χριστοῦ καὶ στασιάζομεν πρὸς τὸ σῶμα τὸ ἴδιον 1 Cl 46:7.—T Schmidt, Der Leib Christi (σῶμα Χριστοῦ) 1919; EKäsemann, Leib u. Leib Christi '33 (for a critique s. SHanson, Unity of the Church in the NT '46, 113–16); ÉMersch, Le Corps mystique du Christ[2] '36; AWikenhauser, D. Kirche als d. myst. Leib Christi, nach dem Ap. Pls[2] '40; EPercy, D. Leib Christi in d. paulin. Homologumena u. Antilegomena '42; RHirzel, Die Person: SBMünAk 1914 H. 10 p. 6–28 (semantic history of σῶμα); WKnox, Parallels to the NT use of σῶμα: JTS 39, '38, 243–46; FDillistone, How Is the Church Christ's Body?: Theology Today 2, '45/46, 56–68; WGoossens, L'Église corps de Christ d'après St. Paul[2] '49; CCraig, Soma Christou: The Joy of Study '51, 73–85; JRobinson, The Body: A Study in Pauline Theol. '52; RBultmann, Theol. of the NT, tr. KGrobel '51, 192–203; HClavier, CHDodd Festschr. '56, 342–62; CColpe, Zur Leib-Christi Vorstellung im Eph, '60, 172–87; KGrobel, Bultmann Festschr. '54, 52–59; HHegermann, TLZ 85, '60, 839–42; ESchweizer, ibid. 86, '61, 161–74; 241–56; JMeuzelaar, D. Leib des Messias, '61; MDahl, The Resurrection of the Body, '62; RJewett, Paul's Anthropological Terms, '71, 201–304; JZiegler, NovT 25, '83, 133–45 (LXX); JDunn: JSNT Suppl. 100, '94, 163–81 (Col.).—B. 198. New Docs 4, 38f. DELG. M-M. TW. Sv.

σωματεῖον, ου, τό (σῶμα; otherw. only POxy 5 recto, 10f; Codex Iustin. 6, 48, 1, 10, Basilica 2, 5, 24) **mode of functioning as a group,** ***corporate life*** ISm 11:2 (v.l. σωμάτιον). Perh. in this instance we have a common itacistic misspelling of σωμάτιον (q.v.).—DELG s.v. σῶμα.

σωματικός, ή, όν (σῶμα; Aristot. et al.; ins, pap, 4 Macc; Ath. R. 18 p. 70, 32 al.)

❶ **pert. to being corporeal as opposed to noncorporeal,** ***bodily, corporeal,*** σωματικῷ (opp. ἀσώματος Ps.-Pla., Tim. Locr. 96a; Philo, Op. M. 16; 18) εἴδει *bodily form* i.e. the Holy Spirit descended in some kind of physical shape: ὡς περιστεράν 'like a pigeon' **Lk 3:22.**

❷ **pert. to the physical body,** ***body-related, bodily*** (Aristot. et al.; Herm. Wr. 1, 1; ins, pap, Philo; Jos., Bell. 1, 430; 6, 55 σ. ἕξις) ἡ σωματικὴ γυμνασία **1 Ti 4:8.** (σαρκικαὶ καὶ) σωματικαὶ ἐπιθυμίαι D 1:4 cod. (Aristot., EN 7, 7, 1149b, 26 ἐπιθυμίαι καὶ ἡδοναί; 4 Macc 1:32; Ath., R. 18 p. 70, 32).—DELG s.v. σῶμα. M-M. TW.

σωματικῶς adv. of σωματικός (Plut., Mor. 424d; Vett. Val. 231, 2; 269, 28; OGI 664, 17 [54 AD]; pap [Sb 8748, 15–178 AD], others New Docs 3, 86; TestAbr B 7 p. 112, 7 [Stone p. 72]; Philo, Rer. Div. Her. 84) ***bodily, corporeally*** of Christ ἐν αὐτῷ κατοικεῖ πᾶν τὸ πλήρωμα τῆς θεότητος σωματικῶς *in him the whole fullness of Deity dwells bodily* **Col 2:9** (prob. to be understood fr. 2:17 [s. σῶμα 4] as = in reality, not fig.). σωματικῶς τῆς Χριστοῦ βασιλείας ἐπὶ ταυτησὶ τῆς γῆς ὑποστησομένης *when Christ's dominion is to be established materially on this earth* Papias (2:12).—M-M. TW. Spicq.

σωμάτιον, ου, τό (Isocr. et al.; pap) dim. of σῶμα.

❶ ***little body,*** esp. ***poor (little) body*** (Socrat., Ep. 30, 1; 31; Epict. 1, 1, 10; 24; 1, 9, 2 al., s. the index of Schenkl's ed.; Lucian, Jupp. Trag. 41; Philo, Leg. ad Gai. 273) lit., of the tortured body of a martyr MPol 17:1.

❷ **a transcendent body,** ***body,*** fig. ext. of 1, the 'body' of a persecuted church ISm 11:2 v.l. (for σωματεῖον 'corporate body', the rdg. of Bihlmeyer's text; s. L-S-J-M and Lightfoot's note ad loc.).—DELG s.v. σῶμα. M-M. s.v. σῶμα.

Σώπατρος, ου, ὁ (Athen.; Jos., Ant. 14, 241; ins) ***Sopater*** son of Pyrrhus. S. was a Christian in Beroia and Paul's companion on his last journey to Jerusalem **Ac 20:4.** His father's name is lacking in one v.l., and another gives the name itself as Σωσίπατρος (q.v.).—Hemer, Acts 236.—LGPN I.

σωρεύω (σωρός 'heap') fut. σωρεύσω; aor. 3 sg. ἐσώρευσεν Jdth 15:11; pf. pass. ptc. σεσωρευμένος (Aristot. et al.; Cat. Cod. Astr. IX/2 p. 115, 9 ὁ ἀήρ; ApcSed 11:6, 8, 11 p. 134, 18, 22, and 26 Ja.; Philo, De Prov. in Eus., PE 8, 14, 62; Jos., Ant. 12, 211).

❶ **to amass by setting one thing atop another, *heap/pile up*** (Polyb.; Diod. S. 5, 46, 5 et al.; Jos., Bell. 4, 380; 6, 431) τὶ ἐπί τι *someth. on someth.* **Ro 12:20** (Pr 25:22; cp. ἄνθραξ).

❷ **to heap a place with, *load up with*** (Polyb. 16, 8, 9; Maximus Tyr. 35, 3b; Herodian 4, 8, 9 βωμοὺς λιβάνῳ; 5, 5, 8) pass., fig. γυναικάρια σεσωρευμένα ἁμαρτίαις *silly women, overwhelmed by their sins* **2 Ti 3:6.**—DELG s.v. σωρός. M-M. TW.

Σωσθένης, ους, ὁ (Diod. S., Diog. L.; Achilles Tat. 5, 17, 5 al.; ins, pap; on the termination -ης s. Mussies 77) ***Sosthenes***

❶ leader of a synagogue in Corinth at the time of Paul's first missionary work in that city. He was beaten in the presence of Gallio the proconsul **Ac 18:17,** but the account (18:12–17) does not say why. From Theodoret to Zahn many scholars, not without good reason, have identified him with the foll.

❷ a 'brother' mentioned in the salutation **1 Cor 1:1,** beside Paul himself. See also **subscr.** He is known to the Corinthians, but need not have been a Corinthian himself, unless he is to be identified w. 1.—LGPN I. M-M.

Σωσίπατρος, ου, ὁ (Athen.; ins, pap; 2 Macc 12:19, 24) ***Sosipater,*** designated as a συγγενής of Paul in **Ro 16:21,** where he also sends greetings to the church. He is freq. considered to be the same man as Sopater of Beroia (s. Σώπατρος), e.g. by Zahn, Ltzm. Linguistically this is prob.—LGPN I. M-M.

σωτήρ, ῆρος, ὁ (σῴζω) **one who rescues, *savior, deliverer, preserver,*** as a title of divinities Pind., Aeschyl.+; ins, pap; TestSol 17:4. This was the epithet esp. of Asclepius, the god of healing (Ael. Aristid. 42, 4 K. σ. τῶν ὅλων; OGI 332, 9 [138–133 BC], s. note 8; SIG 1112, 2; 1148); Celsus compares the cult of Ascl. w. the Christian worship of the Savior (Origen, C. Cels. 3, 3). Likew. divinities in the mystery religions, like Sarapis and Isis (Σαράπιδι Ἴσιδι Σωτῆρσι: OGI 87; Sb 597 [both III BC]; Sb 169 [Ptolemaic times]; 596; CIG 4930b [I BC]), as well as Heracles (τῆς γῆς κ. τῶν ἀνθρώπων σ.: Dio Chrys. 1, 84) or Zeus (Ael. Aristid. 52 p. 608 D.: Ζεὺς ὁ σ.).—GAnrich, Das antike Mysterienwesen 1894, 47ff; GWobbermin, Religionsgesch. Studien 1896, 105ff.—In gnostic speculation: ὁ σ. = ὁ παράκλητος Iren. 1, 4, 5 (Harv. I, 38, 9). The LXX has σωτήρ as a term for God; so also ApcSed 13:6 p. 135, 29 Ja.; and so do Philo (s. MDibelius, Hdb., exc. on 2 Ti 1:10) and SibOr 1, 73; 3, 35; but σ. is not so found in EpArist, Test12Patr, or Josephus (s. ASchlatter, Wie sprach Jos. von Gott? 1910, 66).—At an early date σωτήρ was used as a title of honor for deserving pers. (s. X., Hell. 4, 4, 6, Ages. 11, 13; Plut., Arat. 53, 4; Herodian 3, 12, 2.—Ps.-Lucian, Ocyp. 78 in an address to a physician [s. θεός 4a]; JosAs 25:6 [of Joseph]; the same phrase IXanthos p. 45 no. 23, 3f, of Marcus Agrippa [I BC]; Jos., Vi. 244; 259 Josephus as εὐεργέτης καὶ σωτήρ of Galilee), and in ins and pap we find it predicated of high-ranking officials and of persons in private life. This is never done in our lit. But outside our lit. it is applied to personalities who are active in the world's affairs, in order to remove them fr. the ranks of ordinary humankind and place them in a significantly higher position. For example, Epicurus is called σωτήρ by his followers (Philod.: pap, Herc. 346, 4, 19 ὑμνεῖν τὸν σωτῆρα τὸν ἡμέτερον.—ARW 18, 1930, 392–95; CJensen, Ein neuer Brief Epikurs: GGAbh. III/5, '33, 80f). Of much greater import is the designation of the (deified) ruler as σ. (Ptolemy I Soter [323–285 BC] Πτολεμαῖος καὶ Βερενίκη θεοὶ Σωτῆρες: APF 5, 1913, 156, 1; see Sb 306 and oft. in later times, of Roman emperors as well [Philo, In Flacc. 74; 126, Leg. ad Gai. 22; cp. Jos., Bell. 3, 459]).—PWendland, Σωτήρ: ZNW 5, 1904, 335ff; Magie 67f; HLietzmann, Der Weltheiland 1909; WOtto, Augustus Soter: Her 45, 1910, 448–60; FDölger, Ichthys 1910, 406–22; Dssm., LO 311f (LAE 368f); ELohmeyer, Christuskult u. Kaiserkult 1919; Bousset, Kyrios Christos[2] 1921, 241ff; EMeyer III 392ff; E-BAllo, Les dieux sauveurs du paganisme gréco-romain: RSPT 15, 1926, 5–34; KBornhausen, Der Erlöser 1927; HLinssen, Θεος Σωτηρ, diss. Bonn 1929=Jahrb. f. Liturgiewiss. 8, 1928, 1–75; AOxé, Σωτήρ b. den Römern: WienerStud 48, 1930, 38–61; WStaerk, Soter, I '33; II '38. S. also GHerzog-Hauser, Soter . . . im altgriech. Epos '31; ANock, s.v. εὐεργέτης.—CColpe, Die Religionsgeschichtliche Schule '61 (critique of some of the lit. cited above); FDanker, Benefactor '82.

ⓐ of God ὁ θεὸς ὁ σωτήρ μου (Ps 24:5; 26:9; Mi 7:7 al.) **Lk 1:47.** θεὸς σ. ἡμῶν **1 Ti 1:1; Jd 25.** ὁ σ. ἡμῶν θεός **1 Ti 2:3; Tit 1:3; 2:10; 3:4.** σ. πάντων ἀνθρώπων μάλιστα πιστῶν **1 Ti 4:10** (cp. PPetr III, 20 I, 15 [246 BC] πάντων σωτῆρα and s. above Heracles as τῶν ἀνθρώπων σ. and in b below Sarapis). ὁ τῶν ἀπηλπισμένων σωτήρ *the Savior of those in despair* 1 Cl 59:3.

ⓑ of Christ (Just., A I, 33, 7 τὸ . . . Ἰησοῦς . . . σωτὴρ τῇ Ἑλληνίδι διαλέκτῳ δηλοῖ) **Lk 2:11; Ac 13:23; Phil 3:20;** Dg 9:6; Ox 840, 12; 21 (restored); 30; GMary 463, lines 4, 8, 18, 22, 31; Ox 1081, 27 (SJCh 90, 4); Qua. W. ἀρχηγός **Ac 5:31;** 2 Cl 20:5 (ἀρχηγὸς τῆς ἀφθαρσίας). σωτὴρ τοῦ σώματος *Savior of the body* (i.e. of his body, the Christian community) **Eph 5:23.** ὁ σωτὴρ τοῦ κόσμου (ins; cp. WWeber, Untersuchungen zur Gesch. des Kaisers Hadrianus 1907, 225f; 222) **J 4:42; 1J 4:14.** σ. τῶν ἀνθρώπων (Ael. Aristid. 45, 20 K.=8 p. 90 D. calls Sarapis κηδεμόνα καὶ σωτῆρα πάντων ἀνθρώπων αὐτάρκη θεόν) GPt 4:13. ὁ σ. ἡμῶν Χρ. Ἰ. **2 Ti 1:10;** ISm 7:1; w. Χρ. Ἰ. or Ἰ. Χρ. preceding **Tit 1:4; 3:6;** IEph 1:1; IMg ins; Pol ins. ὁ μέγας θεὸς καὶ σ. ἡμῶν Χρ. Ἰ. *our great God and Savior Christ Jesus* **Tit 2:13** (cp. PLond III, 604b, 118 p. 80 [47 AD] τῷ μεγάλῳ θεῷ σωτῆρι; but the presence of καί **Tit 2:13** suggests a difft. semantic aspect and may justify the rendering in NRSV mg). S. MDibelius, exc. after Tit 2:14; HWindisch, Z. Christologie der Past.: ZNW 34, '35, 213–38.—ὁ σωτὴρ κύριος ἡμῶν Ἰ. Χρ. IPhld 9:2. ὁ σ. τῶν ψυχῶν MPol 19:2. ὁ θεὸς ἡμῶν καὶ σ. Ἰ. Χρ. **2 Pt 1:1.** ὁ κύριος (ἡμῶν) καὶ σ. Ἰ. Χρ. vs. 11; 2:20; 3:18; without any name (so ὁ σωτήρ [meaning Asclep.] Ael. Aristid. 47, 1 K.=23 p. 445 D.; 66 K.=p. 462 D.; 48, 7 K.=24 p. 466 D.—Orig., C. Cels. 6, 64, 16; Hippol., Ref. 5, 8, 27) **2 Pt 3:2;** AcPl Ha 8, 29 (restored: καὶ σωτῆρα). S. Loewe s.v. σωτηρία end.—Pauly-W. 2, VI 1211–21; Kl. Pauly V 289; RAC VI 54–219; DLNT 1082–84; BHHW I 430–32.—M-M. EDNT. TW. Spicq. Sv.

σωτηρία, ας, ἡ (trag., Hdt.+)—❶ ***deliverance, preservation,*** w. focus on physical aspect: fr. impending death, esp. on the sea (IMaronIsis 11; Diod. S. 3, 40, 1 λιμὴν σωτηρίας; 2 Macc 3:32; GrBar 1:3; Philo, Mos. 1, 317; Jos., Ant. 7, 5; 183; Ar. 3, 2)

Ac 27:34; Hb 11:7. Of the deliverance of the Israelites fr. Egyptian bondage (Jos., Ant. 2, 331) **Ac 7:25** (διδόναι σωτηρίαν on the part of a deity: Menand., Col. fgm. 292, 5=1, 5 Kö.). Survival of a hand punished by fire GJs 20:3. A transition to mng. 2 is found in **Lk 1:71,** where σωτηρία ἐξ ἐχθρῶν ἡμῶν *deliverance from the hand of our enemies* is expected (cp. Ps 105:10 and ApcPt Rainer ἐν σωτηρίᾳ Ἀχερουσίας λίμνης, where the ref. is to a baptism marking the beginning of life in Elysium); 1 Cl 39:9 (Job 5:4).—S. λίμνη, end.

❷ ***salvation,*** w. focus on transcendent aspects (LXX, Just., Iren; cp. Herm. Wr. 7, 2 [on salvation through gnosis s. GLuck, SBLSP 24, '85, 315–20]; Ael. Aristid., Sacr. Serm. 3, 46 p. 424 Keil ἐγένετο φῶς παρὰ τῆς Ἴσιδος καὶ ἕτερα ἀμύθητα φέροντα εἰς σωτηρίαν; the Hymn to Attis in Firmicus Maternus, De Errore Prof. Relig. 22, 1 Θαρρεῖτε μύσται τοῦ θεοῦ σεσωσμένου. Ἔσται γὰρ ὑμῖν ἐκ πόνων σωτηρία [HHepding, Attis, seine Mythen u. sein Kult 1903, 167]. The Lat. 'salus' in the description of the Isis ceremony in Apuleius corresponds to the Gk. σωτηρία [GAnrich, Das antike Mysterienwesen 1894, 47f; Rtzst., Mysterienrel.[3] 39]). In our lit. this sense is found only in connection w. Jesus Christ as Savior. This salvation makes itself known and felt in the present, but it will be completely disclosed in the future. Opp. ἀπώλεια **Phil 1:28** (Mel., P. 49, 356; on the probability of military metaphor s. EKrentz, in Origins and Method, JHurd Festschr., ed. BMcLean, '93, 125f); θάνατος (cp. Damasc., Vi. Isid. 131: through Attis and the Mother of the Gods there comes ἡ ἐξ ᾅδου γεγονυῖα ἡμῶν σωτ.) **2 Cor 7:10;** ὀργή **1 Th 5:9.** W. ζωή 2 Cl 19:1; ζωὴ αἰώνιος IEph 18:1. σωτηρία αἰώνιος (Is 45:17) **Hb 5:9; short ending of Mk;** ἡ κοινὴ ἡμῶν σωτ. **Jd 3** (SIG 409, 33f ἀγωνιζόμενος ὑπὲρ τῆς κοινῆς σωτηρίας); σωτ. ψυχῶν *salvation of souls* **1 Pt 1:9** (σ. τῶν ψυχῶν Hippol., Ref. 10, 19, 3); cp. vs. **10** (ESelwyn, 1 Pt '46, 252f). σωτηρία ἡ τῶν ἐκλεκτῶν MPol 22:1. ἡ τῶν σῳζομένων σωτ. 17:2 (ἡ σ. τῶν μετανοούντων Did., Gen. 71, 28; σωτηρία τῶν ἀγαθῶν Hippol., Ref. 7, 28, 6; ἡ τῶν ἀνθρώπων σ. Orig., C. Cels. 4, 73, 13). On κέρας σωτηρίας **Lk 1:69** s. κέρας 3. σωτηρίας as objective gen. dependent upon various nouns: γνῶσις σωτηρίας **Lk 1:77;** ἐλπὶς σωτ. (TestJob 24:1; cp. Philemo Com. 181 οἱ θεὸν σέβοντες ἐλπίδας καλὰς ἔχουσιν εἰς σωτηρίαν) **1 Th 5:8;** 2 Cl 1:7; ἔνδειξις σωτ. **Phil 1:28** (opp. ἀπώλεια). τὸ εὐαγγέλιον τῆς σωτηρίας ὑμῶν **Eph 1:13.** ὁ λόγος τῆς σωτηρίας ταύτης **Ac 13:26.** ὁδὸς σωτηρίας *way to salvation* **16:17;** περιποίησις σωτ. **1 Th 5:9.** ἡμέρα σωτηρίας (quot. fr. Is 49:8) of the day when the apostle calls them to salvation **2 Cor 6:2ab** (cp. the mystery in Apuleius, Metam. 11, 5 'dies salutaris' = 'day of initiation'). Christ is ὁ ἀρχηγὸς τῆς σωτ. **Hb 2:10** (ἀρχηγός 3). ὁ θεὸς τῆς σωτ. μου 1 Cl 18:14 (Ps 50:16).—Used w. verbs: ἔχειν σωτηρίαν Hv 2, 2, 5; 3, 6, 1; m 10, 2, 4; 12, 3, 6. κληρονομεῖν σωτηρίαν **Hb 1:14.** τὴν ἑαυτοῦ σωτ. κατεργάζεσθαι **Phil 2:12** (κατεργάζομαι 2). σωτηρίας τυχεῖν τῆς ἐν Χριστῷ Ἰ. **2 Ti 2:10** (τυχεῖν σωτηρίας: Diod. S. 11, 4, 4; 11, 9, 1). εἰς σωτηρίαν *for salvation* (i.e. to appropriate it for oneself or grant it to another) **Ro 1:16; 10:1, 10; 2 Cor 7:10; Phil 1:19** (ἀποβαίνω 2); **2 Th 2:13; 2 Ti 3:15; 1 Pt 2:2.** πόρρω . . . ἀπὸ τῆς σωτ. 1Cl 39:9 (Job 3:4).τὰ ἀνήκοντα εἰς σωτηρίαν *the things that pertain to salvation* 1 Cl 45:1; B 17:1 (cp. SIG 1157, 12f).—σωτηρία is plainly expected to be fully culminated w. the second coming of the Lord **Ro 13:11; Hb 9:28; 1 Pt 1:5.**—(ἡ) σωτηρία without further qualification=*salvation* is also found **Lk 19:9** (cp. GJs 19:2); **J 4:22** (ἡ σωτ. ἐκ τῶν Ἰουδαίων ἐστίν); **Ac 4:12** (cp. Jos., Ant. 3, 23 ἐν θεῷ εἶναι τ. σωτηρίαν αὐτοῦ καὶ οὐκ ἐν ἄλλῳ); **Ro 11:11; 2 Cor 1:6; Hb 2:3** (τηλικαύτη σωτ.); **6:9.** ἡ σωτ. ἡμῶν 2 Cl 1:1; 17:5; B 2:10.—Christ died even for the salvation of the repentant Ninevites in the time of Jonah 1 Cl 7:7; cp. vs. 4.—σωτηρία stands by metonymy for σωτήρ (in the quot. fr. Is 49:6) τοῦ εἶναί σε εἰς σωτηρίαν ἕως ἐσχάτου τῆς γῆς **Ac 13:47;** B 14:8. On the other hand, for *a circumstance favorable for our attainment of salvation* ἡγεῖσθαί τι σωτηρίαν **2 Pt 3:15.**—In the three places in **Rv** in which σωτ. appears as part of a doxology we have a Hebraism (salvation as victory intimately associated w. God; PEllingworth, BT 34, '83, 444f; cp. Ps 3:9 and PsSol 10:8 τοῦ κυρίου ἡ σωτηρία) **7:10; 12:10; 19:1.**—LMarshall, Challenge of NT Ethics '47, 248–66; HHaerens, Σωτήρ et σωτηρία dans la religion grecque: Studia Hellenistica 5, '48, 57–68; FDölger, AC 6, '50, 257–63.—DELG s.v. σῶς. RLoewe, JTS 32, '81, 341–68 (ins pp. 364–68). DBS XI 486–739. M-M. TW. Spicq. Sv.

σωτήριος, ον (σωτήρ; trag., Thu.+; ins, pap, LXX; TestJob 51:4; Test12Patr, Philo, Joseph.; Just., D. 13, 1; 24, 1; 74, 3) **pert. to salvation, *saving, delivering, preserving, bringing salvation.***

ⓐ as adj. ἐπεφάνη ἡ χάρις τοῦ θεοῦ σωτήριος πᾶσιν ἀνθρώποις *the grace of God has appeared, bringing salvation to all human beings* (σ. τινι as Thu. 7, 64, 2 τοῖς ξύμπασι σωτήριος) **Tit 2:11.**

ⓑ subst., neut. τὸ σωτήριον *means of deliverance,* then also the *deliverance* itself (Aeschyl. et al.; Plut., Lucian; Herm. Wr. 10, 15 τοῦτο μόνον σωτήριον ἀνθρώπῳ ἐστίν, ἡ γνῶσις τοῦ θεοῦ; LXX; Jos., Bell. 3, 171; 6, 310 [τὰ σωτήρια of God]; Just., D. 74, 3b.—ταπεινοφρονσύνης σ[ω]τ̣ή[ρ]ιον Did., Gen. 70, 26), in our lit. of Messianic *salvation* and the one who mediates it. Dg 12:9. W. gen. τὸ σωτήριον τοῦ θεοῦ (TestSim 7:1; cp. TestDan 5:10) **Lk 3:6** (Is 40:5); **Ac 28:28;** 1 Cl 35:12 (Ps 49:23); cp. 18:12 (Ps 50:14); περικεφαλαία τοῦ σωτηρίου **Eph 6:17** (Is 59:17). θήσομαι ἐν σωτηρίῳ 1 Cl 15:6 (v.l. σωτηρίᾳ=Ps 11:6).—Also of the σωτήρ himself εὕρομεν τὸ σωτήριον ἡμῶν Ἰησοῦν Χρ. 36:1. εἶδον οἱ ὀφθαλμοί μου τὸ σωτήριόν σου **Lk 2:30.**—ELohse, Passafest, '53, 50–56 ('peace-offering' in some LXX passages).—DELG s.v. σῶς. M-M. TW. Spicq.

σωφρονέω (σώφρων, via σῶς + φρήν) 1 aor. ἐσωφρόνησα (trag., X., Pla. et al.; pap) the thematic semantic note in this and cognate terms is the Hellenic ideal of μηδὲν ἄγαν ('nothing to excess').

❶ **to be able to think in a sound or sane manner, *be of sound mind.*** of mental health (in contrast to μαίνεσθαι; Pla., Phdr. 22, 244a, Rep. 331c; Ps.-Apollod. 3, 5, 1; 6; Philo, Cher. 69) *to be in one's right mind,* of a demoniac who was healed **Mk 5:15; Lk 8:35.** Sim., **2 Cor 5:13** (opp. ἐκστῆναι; s. ἐξίστημι 2a).

❷ **to be prudent, with focus on self-control, *be reasonable, sensible, serious, keep one's head*** (X., Cyr. 3, 2, 4; TestSol 8:8; Philo, Det. Pot. Ins. 114; Jos., Ant. 2, 296; Just., Tat.; Ath. 32, 2; Orig., C. Cels. 2, 8, 16) **Tit 2:6.** W. νήφειν **1 Pt 4:7.** Esp. of women *be chaste, virtuous* (Musonius p. 14, 12ff H.; Arrian, Anab. 4, 20, 2; Alciphron, 4, 17, 3; Jos., Ant. 18, 66.—σωφροσύνη 2) 1 Cl 1:3; Pol 4:3.—In contrast to ὑπερφρονεῖν and in a play on words w. it and w. φρονεῖν twice **Ro 12:3** (cp. Plut., Mor. 776d φρονεῖν κ. σωφ.; Socrat., Ep. 36 σωφρονέω . . . συσσωφρονέω; Iren. 1, 16, 3 [Harv. I, 164, 3])—DELG s.v. σῶς. M-M. TW. Spicq.

σωφρονίζω (σώφρων) fut. 2 sg. σωφρονίσεις Is 38:16 Aq. (Eur., Thu. et al.; Philo; Jos., Bell. 2, 493) 'bring to one's senses' τινά *someone* (Demosth. 25, 93; Dio Chrys. 17 [34], 49; Maximus Tyr. 30, 5g; Mitt-Wilck. I/2, 20 IV, 11; Jos., Ant. 5, 256, Bell. 3, 445; 4, 119), **to instruct in prudence or behavior that is becoming and shows good judgment, *encourage, advise, urge*** (s. GGerhard, Phoinix v. Kolophon 1909, 35ff) w. acc. and inf. foll. ἵνα σωφρονίζωσιν τὰς νέας φιλάνδρους εἶναι **Tit 2:4.**—DELG s.v. σῶς. M-M. TW. Spicq.

σωφρονισμός, οῦ, ὁ—❶ in non-biblical Gk. with act. force (=σωφρόνισις) **the teaching of prudence,** ***advice, improvement*** (Strabo 1, 2, 3; Plut., Cato Maj. 338 [5, 1], Mor. 653c; 961d; Appian, Liby. 65 §290; Philo, Leg. All. 3, 193; Jos., Bell. 2, 9, Ant. 17, 210); the Syriac version understands **2 Ti 1:7** in this sense. The Spirit functions in such a way that Christians learn to exercise prudence. But mng. 2 is prob. to be preferred here.

❷ exercise of prudence, ***moderation, self-discipline, prudence*** (=σωφροσύνη. So the Vulgate. σωφρονισμός is used in someth. like this sense in Plut., Mor. 712c; Iambl., Vi. Pyth. 30, 174).—DELG s.v. σῶς. M-M. TW. Spicq.

σωφρόνως adv. of σώφρων (Aeschyl., Hdt. et al.; ins; Wsd 9:11) **pert. to being prudent,** ***soberly, moderately, showing self-control*** ζῆν (Strabo 16, 2, 35; InsMagnMai 162, 6 ζήσαντα σωφρόνως; TestJud 16:3; Jos., Ant. 4, 248; Just., A II, 2, 2 οὐ σωφρόνως) w. δικαίως, εὐσεβῶς **Tit 2:12** (Ps.-Pla., Alcib. 1, 134d and Sextus 399 w. δικαίως).—TW. Spicq.

σωφροσύνη, ης, ἡ (Hom.+; ins, pap, LXX [esp. 4 Macc]; TestJos, EpArist, Philo, Joseph., Just., Ath., R. 22 p. 75, 19; one of the four cardinal virtues; for the Hellenic perspective of general harmony of the κόσμος and φύσις s. JKube, ΤΕΧΝΗ and ΑΡΕΤΗ, '69, 46)

❶ gener. **soundness of mind,** ***reasonableness, rationality*** (s. σωφρονέω 1; in contrast to μανία X., Mem. 1, 1, 16; Pla., Prot. 323b; Iren. 1, 26, 1) ἀληθείας καὶ σωφροσύνης ῥήματα *true and rational words* (opp. μαίνομαι) **Ac 26:25.**

❷ practice of prudence, ***good judgment, moderation, self-control*** as exercise of care and intelligence appropriate to circumstances (Pla., Rep. 4, 430e ἡ σωφροσύνη ἐστὶ καὶ ἡδονῶν τινων καὶ ἐπιθυμιῶν ἐγκράτεια, cp. Phd. 68c, Symp. 196c; Aristot., Rhet. 1, 9, 9 σωφροσύνη δὲ ἀρετὴ δι' ἣν πρὸς τὰς ἡδονὰς τοῦ σώματος οὕτως ἔχουσιν ὡς ὁ νόμος κελεύει, ἀκολασία δὲ τοὐναντίον, De Virt. et Vit. 2; Diog. L. 3, 91; 4 Macc 1:3, 31; Philo; Jos., Ant. 2, 48, C. Ap. 2, 170 [w. other virtues]; Just., A I, 6, 1; 10, 1 al.; Orig., C. Cels. 2, 29, 13; Did., Gen. 27, 15) w. ἁγνεία IEph 10:3. W. still other virtues (Theoph. Ant. 3, 15 [p. 234, 13]) 1 Cl 64. W. ἐγκράτεια (so Ath.) and other virtues 62:2. Esp. as a woman's virtue *decency, chastity* (Diod. S. 3, 57, 3; Phalaris, Ep. 78, 1; Philo, Spec. Leg. 3, 51 w. αἰδώς; Jos., Ant. 18, 73; BGU 1024, 8; 15; grave ins APF 5, 1913, 169 no. 24. S. σωφρονέω 2; TDrew-Bear, Three Inscriptions fr. Kyme: EpigrAnat 1, '83, '97 n. 56 [lit.]) w. αἰδώς (X., Cyr. 8, 1, 30f and Philo, above) **1 Ti 2:9** (EpigrAnat 1, '83, 97 n. 56). W. other virtues vs. **15.**—TBird, CBQ 2, '40, 259–63; AKollmann, Sophrosyne: WienerStud 59, '41, 12–34; HNorth, Sophrosyne '66.—DELG s.v. σῶς. M-M. TW. Spicq. Sv.

σώφρων, ον, gen. **ονος** (σώφρων, φρήν, prim. 'one of sound mind') (Hom. et al.; ins, pap, 4 Macc, Test12Patr; JosAs 4:9; EpArist, Philo, Joseph., Just.; Tat. 10, 3) **pert. to being in control of onself,** ***prudent, thoughtful, self-controlled*** (the Hellenic model is avoidance of extremes and careful consideration for responsible action: Aristot., EN 3, 15, end ἐπιθυμεῖ ὁ σώφρων ὧν δεῖ καὶ ὡς δεῖ καὶ ὅτε=the prudent pers. is intent on the what, the how, and the when of doing what should be done; Aeschin., C. Ctesiph 170 of one moderate in lifestyle so as not to be tempted by bribes) w. πιστός 1 Cl 63:3; w. other virtues **Tit 2:2.** Being a characteristic of persons distinguished for public service, σ. appears in the list of qualifications for an ἐπίσκοπος **1 Ti 3:2** (used w. κόσμιος as Lysias 21, 19; Pla., Gorg. 508a; Menand., Sam. 344 S. [129 Kö.]; Lucian, Bis Accus. 17; IMagnMai 162, 6; cp. MAMA VIII, 412c, 5f ζήσαντα κοσμίως καὶ σωφρόνως); **Tit 1:8** (w. δίκαιος as EpArist 125).—Esp. of women *chaste, decent, modest* (Menand., fgm. 679 Kö.; Diod. S. 10, 20, 2. In ins on women's graves: BCH 22, 1898, 496; 23, 1899, 301; 25, 1901, 88; IXanthos p. 149 no. 57, 5f; Philo; Jos., Ant. 18, 180.—Dssm., LO 267 [LAE 315]. S. σωφρονέω 2 and σωφροσύνη 2) **Tit 2:5** (w. ἀγαθή as Jos., Ant. 6, 296).—ἡ σώφρων καὶ ἐπιεικὴς ἐν Χριστῷ εὐσέβεια 1 Cl 1:2.—B. 1213. DELG s.v. σῶς. M-M. TW. Spicq.

T

τ' numerical sign = ***300*** (τριακόσιοι; SibOr 5, 21; 38; 42). Because of its form (T) a symbol of the cross B 9:8 (cp. Lucian s.v. σταυρός, end), spelled out ταῦ, v.l.

ταβέρναι, ῶν, αἱ (Lat. loanw.: tabernae; s. GMeyer, Die lat. Lehnworte im Neugriech.: SBWienAk 132, vol. 1895, app. 3, p. 64) Lat. taberna refers var. to a hut, inn, or shop. In our lit. only as transliterated pl. in the place name Τρεῖς ταβέρναι ***Three Taverns,*** a station on the Appian Way, located betw. Aricia and Appii Forum at the foot of the Alban Mount. It was 33 Roman miles (c. 49 km.) fr. Rome (Cicero, Ad. Attic. 2, 10.—CIL IX 593; X p. 684). **Ac 28:15.**—TKleberg, Hotels, restaurants et cabarets dans l'antiquité romaine '57; Kl. Pauly V 138; Hemer, Acts 156.

Ταβιθά, ἡ indecl. (also Ταβειθά, s. M-M.; Aram. טְבִיתָא, also טַבְיְתָא; s. EKautzsch, Gramm. des Bibl.-Aram. 1884, 11; Dalman, Grammatik[2] 141) ***Tabitha*** (on this name in rabbin. lit. s. Billerb. II 694. Late pap in Preisigke, Namenbuch), a Christian in Joppa **Ac 9:36, 40.** Her name is interpreted in vs. **36** as Δορκάς (q.v.).—**Mk 5:41** W, for ταλιθά. —S. Haenchen, ad loc.; IRichter, Women in the NT '95.—M-M.

Ταβώρ s. Θαβώρ.

ταγή, ῆς, ἡ (τάσσω; Aristoph. et al.; ins, pap) ***command, decree*** pl. (SEG IV, 467, 3 [263 AD]) of divine authority that prescribes an order for things, such as progression of the seasons 1 Cl 20:8.—New Docs 4, 176. DELG s.v. τάσσω 1.

τάγμα, ατος, τό (τάσσω; X., Pla. et al.; ins, pap, LXX; GrBar 11:6)

❶ a clearly defined group—ⓐ of an orderly arrrangement of personnel, ***division, group*** military t.t. for bodies of troops in various numbers (since X., Mem. 3, 1, 11; Diod. S. 1, 86, 4; 20,

110, 4; Appian, Celt. 1 §7 τὰ τάγματα=the divisions of the army; Polyaenus 3, 13, 1; ins, pap; 2 Km 23:13; EpArist 26; Jos., Bell. 4, 645, Ant. 20, 122 al. So as loanw. in rabb.) στρατιωτικὸν τάγμα (Diod. S. 17, 33, 1 τάγματα τῶν στρατιωτῶν) *a detachment of soldiers* IRo 5:1. Cp. 1 Cl 37:3; because of the latter pass. 41:1 is prob. to be classed here, too.

ⓑ without any special military application ***class, group*** (Epicurus p. 24, 9 Us.; Sext. Emp., Math. 9, 54; ins, pap; Philo, Migr. Abr. 100; Jos., Bell. 2, 164 the Sadducees as a δεύτερον τάγμα; see 2, 122; 143 of the Essenes) Hs 8, 4, 6; 8, 5, 1–6. τάγματα τάγματα *group by group, by groups* 8, 2, 8a; 8, 4, 2b, cp. 6. Likew. κατὰ τάγματα 8, 2, 8b; κατὰ τὰ τάγματα, ὡς 8, 4, 2a.—Acc. to **1 Cor 15:23f** the gift of life is given to various ones in turn (cp. Arrian, Tact. 28, 2 ἐπειδὰν τάγμα τάγματι ἕπηται), and at various times. One view is that in this connection Paul distinguishes three groups: Christ, who already possesses life, the Christians, who will receive it at his second coming, and the rest of humanity (s. τέλος 2), who will receive it when death, as the last of God's enemies, is destroyed: ἕκαστος ἐν τῷ ἰδίῳ τάγματι (ζῳοποιηθήσεται)· ἀπαρχὴ Χριστός, ἔπειτα οἱ τοῦ Χριστοῦ ἐν τῇ παρουσίᾳ αὐτοῦ, εἶτα τὸ τέλος (JWeiss and Ltzm. ad loc. S. also JHéring, RHR 12, '32, 300–320; E-BAllo, RB 41, '32, 187–209.).

❷ **a stage in a sequence, *order, turn*** (Ps.-Pla., Def. 414e; Aristot., Pol. 4, 7 [9], 3; Plut., Mor. 601a) κατὰ τὸ τάγμα, ὡς *in the order in which* Hs 8, 4, 2a (so J.; κατὰ τὰ τάγματα, ὡς W., s. 1 above).—DELG s.v. τάσσω 2. M-M. TW. Sv.

ταχήσομαι s. τήκω.

τακτός, ή, όν (τάσσω; since Thu. 4, 65, 1; pap; Job 12:5; Jos., Ant. 8, 396) ***fixed, appointed*** τακτὴ ἡμέρα (Polyb. 3, 34, 9; Dionys. Hal. 2, 74; PFlor 133, 4 τὰς τακτὰς ἡμέρας) **Ac 12:21.**—DELG s.v. τάσσω 4. M-M.

ταλαιπωρέω (ταλαίπωρος) impf. ἐταλαιπώρουν; fut. 3 pl. ταλαιπωρήσουσιν Hos 10:2; 1 aor. ἐταλαιπώρησα; pf. 3 sg. τεταλαιπώρηκεν LXX; occasionally act. 'torment, afflict' (Isocr. 8, 19; Ps 16:9; Is 33:1); pass. in act./intr. sense (Thu. 3, 3, 1 al.; Philo, In Flacc. 155; Jos., Ant. 2, 334; 5, 147 al.) **to experience distress, *endure sorrow/distress, be miserable*** (Eur., Thu. et al.; Epict. 1, 26, 11; LXX; Manetho in Jos., C. Ap. 1, 237; SibOr 5, 75) 2 Cl 19:4; Hv 3, 7, 1; s 6, 2, 7; 6, 3, 1. To the extent of giving expression to grief: the act. used intr. ταλαιπωρήσατε *feel miserable, lament* (w. πενθεῖν, κλαίειν) **Js 4:9.**—Spicq.

ταλαιπωρία, ας, ἡ (ταλαίπωρος; Hdt.+; PTebt 27, 40 [113 BC]; Libanius, Or. 50 p. 485, 19 F. [opp. ἀσέλγεια]; LXX; TestSol 20:4 [-ορία]; TestJob 3:4; JosAs cod. A ch. 11 [p. 54, 14 Bat.], also Pal. 364; Philo; Jos., Bell. 7, 278, Ant. 2, 257; Ar. 11, 4) ***wretchedness, distress, trouble, misery*** **Ro 3:16** (Is 59:7). ἡ ταλαιπωρία τῶν πτωχῶν 1 Cl 15:6 (Ps 11:6). Pl. *miseries* (Hdt. 6, 11; Diod. S. 1, 36, 5; Galen, Protr. 14 p. 46, 20 J.; EpArist 15; Philo, Somn. 1, 174; Jos., Ant. 14, 379; Iren. 1, 14, 8 [Harv. I 143, 8]) **Js 5:1.**—M-M. Spicq.

ταλαίπωρος, ον (s. prec. entry; τ. approaches Homeric δειλός; Pind. et al.; UPZ 110, 132 [164 BC]; APF 5, 1913, 381 no. 56, 9 [I AD]; Sb 643, 8 [ostracon, Christian]; LXX; TestAbr B 10 p. 115, 4 [Stone p. 78]; JosAs 6:5, 7; ApcSed 11:15 p. 134, 34 and 36 Ja.; EpArist 130; Philo; Jos., Ant. 11, 1; Ar. 12, 8 prayers for vengeance fr. Rheneia [Dssm., LO 352; 354; 356, LAE 413ff; SIG 1181, 4f]; antonym of μακάριος) ***miserable, wretched, distressed*** w. ἐλεεινός and other adjs. **Rv 3:17.** ταλαίπωρος ἐγὼ ἄνθρωπος *wretched creature that I am* **Ro 7:24** (Epict. 1, 3, 5 τί γάρ εἰμί; ταλαίπωρον ἀνθρωπάριον 'What am I? Just a miserable particle of humanity'; ZPE 4, '69, 206: fgm. B 1, 5 of a romance ὦ ταλαίπωρε ἄνθρωπε [restored]; ibid. line 9 ὁ μισητὸς ἔφη ἐγώ); cp. Hs 1:3. In the latter pass. w. δίψυχος, and also of a doubter in the scripture quot. of uncertain origin 1 Cl 23:3=2 Cl 11:2; cp. 2 Cl 11:1. Subst. (Demosth. 18, 121 ὦ ταλαίπωρε; likewise Diogenes the Cynic in Diog. L. 6, 66; Iren. 1, 13, 2 [Harv. I 117, 10]) οἱ ταλαίπωροι *wretched people* (Epict. 3, 22, 44) B 16:1.—S. Eranos 29, '32, 3; 4.—Schmidt, Syn. IV 443–50. DELG. M-M. Spicq.

ταλαντιαῖος, α, ον (τάλαντον) ***weighing a talent*** (so Aristot., Cael. 4, 4; Polyb. 9, 41, 8; Diod. S. 20, 87, 1; Jos., Bell. 5, 270. Cp. SIG 966, 44 note.) χάλαζα μεγάλη ὡς ταλαντιαία *a severe hailstorm* with hailstones *weighing a talent* (the talent=125 librae, or Roman pounds of c. 343 gr. or 12 ounces each) (*weighing about a hundred pounds* NRSV) **Rv 16:21.**—DELG s.v. ταλάσσαι B. M-M.

τάλαντον, ου, τό (Hom. et al.) orig. a measure of weight varying in size fr. about 26 to 36 kg.; then a unit of coinage ***talent*** (lit., ins, pap, LXX, TestSol; TestJud 9:5; TestJos 18:3; EpArist; Jos., Bell. 5, 571, C. Ap. 2, 266), whose value differed considerably in various times and places, but was always comparatively high; it varied also with the metal involved, which might be gold, silver, or copper. In our lit. only in **Mt 18:24; 25:15–28.** In **18:24,** at 6,000 drachmas or denarii to the Tyrian talent, a day laborer would need to work 60,000,000 days to pay off the debt. Even assuming an extraordinary payback rate of 10 talents per year, the staggering amount would ensure imprisonment for at least 1,000 years. The amounts distributed in **25:15–28** are not small change, either (MPowell, ABD VI 907f; ECook, ISBE IV 1053f; s. also JDerrett, Law in the NT '70, 17–47; TMartin, BR 38, '93, 70–72).—Lit. s.v. ἀργύριον 2c.—Kl. Pauly V 502f; BHHW III 1928. DELG s.v. ταλάσσαι B. M-M.

ταλιθα (also ταλιθά, ταλειθά) Aram. טְלִיתָא or טַלְתָא, emphatic state of טְלֵיָה (Dalman, Gramm.[2] 150) ***girl, little girl*** **Mk 5:41.** S. ῥαβιθά.—TRE III 609.

ταμεῖον, ου, τό (this contracted form of the older ταμιεῖον [q.v.] is found as early as the first cent. BC in ins [SIG 783, 37] and pap [BGU 1115, 41], but does not become very common until the beginning of our era. Cp. Plut., Mor. 9d; Babrius, Fab. 108, 2 L-P.; LXX [Thackeray 63.—Rahlfs inserts the uncontracted form into the text every time the word is used]; En 11:1; TestSol 13:2; TestAbr; Philo, Omn. Prob. Lib. 86. S. also Lob., Phryn. 493; Mayser 92; B-D-F §31, 2; W-S. §5:23b; Mlt. 44f; Mlt-H. 89f; Nachmanson 71; PKatz-Walters, The Text of the Septuagint '73, 94f. Rabb. loanw. טמיון).

❶ **a place for the keeping of valuables, *storeroom*** (the word has this sense Thu. et al.; oft. pap, LXX) w. ἀποθήκη **Lk 12:24.**

❷ gener. **a room in the interior of a house, *inner room*** (so X., Hell. 5, 4, 6 v.l.; Gen 43:30; Ex 7:28; SSol 1:4, and freq. in LXX; TestAbr B 5 p. 109, 24 [Stone p. 66]) **Mt 6:6** (TestJos 3:3). ἐν τοῖς ταμείοις *in one of the inner rooms* **Mt 24:26; Lk 12:3.** εἰς τὰ ταμεῖα 1 Cl 50:4 (cp. Is 26:20).—DELG s.v. ταμία. M-M.

ταμιεῖον, ου, τό (cp. prec. entry; Thu.+; older ins and pap; PsSol 4:8; TestSim 8:3; TestJos 3:3; JosAs 2:9; EpArist 111 [on this HMeecham, The Letter of Aristeas '35, 79]; Jos., Bell. 2, 17, Ant. 8, 410; 18, 312) ***hidden, secret room*** fig. τὰ ταμιεῖα τῆς γαστρός 1 Cl 21:2 (Pr 20:21). In the NT only **Mt 24:26** as a poorly attested v.l. (B-D-F §31, 2; Mlt.-H. 89). N[13] through N[25] always print the uncontracted forms.—OGI I p. 278 n. 32. DELG s.v. ταμία. M-M. s.v. ταμεῖον.

ταννῦν s. νῦν 2b.

τάξις, εως, ἡ (Aeschyl., Hdt.+; loanw. in rabb.).—❶ **an arrangement of things in sequence,** ***fixed succession/order*** (Epict. 3, 2, 2; Appian, Bell. Civ. 4, 22 §92; TestNapht 2:8 ἐν τάξει) ἐν τῇ τάξει τῆς ἐφημερίας αὐτοῦ **Lk 1:8** (MAvi-Yonah, The Caesarea Inscription of the Twenty-Four Priestly Courses, in The Teacher's Yoke [in mem. HTrantham], ed. JVardaman/JGarrett, '64, 46–57). Without ἐν: τάξει *in* (strict chronological) *order* Papias (2:15), though JKleist, transl. '48, 207f, note 19, prefers *verbatim.* HRigg, Jr., NovT 1, '56, 171: emends to τάχει=in a slipshod manner.

❷ **a state of good order,** ***order, proper procedure*** πάντα τάξει ποιεῖν 1 Cl 40:1. κατὰ τάξιν *in order, in an orderly manner* prob. 'one after the other' (Lucian, Alex. 46; Alex. Aphr., Quaest. 1, 4, 1 p. 10, 17 Br.) **1 Cor 14:40** (cp. the rules of the Iobakchoi: IG II^2, 1368); Dg 8:7.—**Col 2:5.**—HvCampenhausen, Tradition and Life in the Church, '68, 123–40.

❸ **an assigned station or rank,** ***position, post*** (one has a responsibility in an ordered scheme of things: Hyperid. 3, 30; Demosth. 18, 258; Diod. S. 15, 64, 4; Epict. 1, 29, 39 [assigned by God]; Diog. L. 9, 21, end; 1 Esdr 1:15; ApcMos 38; Jos., Vi. 397, Ant. 7, 36) εἰς τοσαύτην αὐτοὺς τάξιν ἔθετο ὁ θεός *God has appointed them* (i. e. the Christians) *to so great a position* Dg 6:10 (on Gr-Rom. perspective s. Reader, Polemo 345–47).—*Administration* (of a position) Papias (4); s. entry συμβαίνω 2.

❹ **an arrangement in which someone or someth. functions,** ***arrangement, nature, manner, condition, outward aspect*** (2 Macc 1:19 φρέατος τάξιν ἔχοντος ἄνυδρον of a well that had an arrangement for a dry area; Polyb. 3, 20, 5; Diod. S. 1, 25, 5; EpArist 69 κρηπῖδος ἔχουσα τάξιν='it had the appearance of a shoe') ἡ νεωτερικὴ τάξις *the youthful nature* or *appearance* IMg 3:1. Perh. it is in this way that **Hb** understood Ps 109:4b, which the author interprets to mean that Jesus was a high priest κατὰ τὴν τάξιν Μελχισέδεκ *according to the nature of = just like Melchizedek* i.e. like the type of arrangement made for the functioning of M.: **5:6, 10; 6:20; 7:11a, 17, 21 v.l.** In any case the reference is not only to the higher 'rank', but also to the entirely different nature of Melchizedek's priesthood as compared w. that of Aaron **7:11b.** (In Mitt-Wilck. I/2, 81, 16; 19 and al. in pap τάξις=position of a priest.)—AcPl Ha 8, 18=BMM recto 23 (restoration certain, s. Ox 1602, 21).—DELG s.v. τάσσω. M-M. Sv.

Ταουΐα, ας, ἡ ***Tavia,*** an otherw. unknown Christian in Smyrna ISm 13:2 (Ταουΐα is the form of the name in the Gk. ms. and in the Lat. version. It is not found elsewh. But we find Ταους as a woman's name PLond II, 258, 184 p. 33, and Ταουεις PLond II, 257, 212 p. 26; 245 p. 27 as well as the Lat. masc. Tavius e.g. CIL III 6248.—The interpolated Gk. and the Armen. have Γαουΐα.)

ταπεινός, ή, όν (Pind., Aeschyl., Hdt.+; pap, LXX; En 26, 4 and Did., Gen. 220, 7 [ὄρος]; PsSol 5:12; Test12Patr; JosAs 28:3 cod. A al.; ApcSed, EpArist, Philo, Joseph.; Theoph. Ant. 2, 13 [p. 132, 3]) gener. 'low', in our lit. only in a fig. sense.

❶ **pert. to being of low social status or to relative inability to cope,** ***lowly, undistinguished, of no account*** (Hdt. 7, 14; Pla., Phd. 257c; Isocr. 3, 42 al.; 1 Km 18:23; Jos., Bell. 4, 365, Ant. 7, 95; 13, 415; Did., Gen. 244, 14.—Orig., C. Cels. I, 56, 4) ὁ ἀδελφὸς ὁ ταπ. (opp. πλούσιος, one who has more control of life than the τ.) **Js 1:9.**—Subst. (Philo, Poster. Cai. 109; Jos., Bell. 4, 319) B 3:3. Pl. (Heraclides Pont., fgm. 55 W. ταπεινοί beside δοῦλοι; Diod. S. 14, 5, 4; Menand., Monost. 412 Mei. [608 Jaekel]; Ps.-Callisth. 2, 16, 10 of Fortune: ἢ τοὺς ταπεινοὺς ὑπεράνω νεφῶν τιθεῖ ἢ τοὺς ἀφ' ὕψους εἰς ζόφον κατήγαγεν; Zeph 2:3; Is 11:4; 14:32) **Lk 1:52** (opp. δυνάσται, who have the resources to cope). ὁ παρακαλῶν τοὺς ταπεινοὺς *who encourages the downcast* **2 Cor 7:6** (Is 49:13). On τοῖς ταπεινοῖς συναπαγόμενοι **Ro 12:16** s. συναπάγω. 1 Cl 59:3f prob. belongs here (but s. 3 below); also B 14:9 (Is 61:1 v.l.).

❷ **pert. to being servile in manner,** ***pliant, subservient, abject*** a neg. quality that would make one lose face in the Gr-Rom. world, opp. of a free person's demeanor (X., Mem. 3, 10, 5; Pla., Leg. 6, 774c; Demochares [III BC]: 75 fgm. 1 Jac. αἰσχρὰ κ. ταπεινά; Cass. Dio 74, 5; POxy 79 II, 2 [II AD]) in a judgment pronounced by Paul's opponents upon him κατὰ πρόσωπον ταπεινός **2 Cor 10:1.**

❸ **pert. to being unpretentious,** ***humble*** (Aeschyl. et al.; Pla., Leg. 4, 716a; X., Ag. 11, 11 in a description of Agesilaus, who does not let success or station go to his head; PGen 14, 6; LXX; EpArist 263; TestGad 5:3; Orig., C. Cels. 3, 64, 6) ταπεινὸς τῇ καρδίᾳ (w. πραΰς, q.v.) **Mt 11:29.** Subst. pl., opp. (οἱ) ὑψηλοί 1 Cl 59:3 (but s. 1 above); B 19:6; D 3:9. Opp. ὑπερήφανοι (after Pr 3:34) **Js 4:6; 1 Pt 5:5;** 1 Cl 30:2. τὸ ταπεινὸν τῆς ψυχῆς *humility of the soul* 55:6. RLeivestad, ΤΑΠΕΙΝΟΣ - ΤΑΠΕΙΝΟΦΡΩΝ, NovT 8, '66, 36–47. S. πραΰτης.—DELG. M-M. TW. Spicq. Sv.

ταπεινοφρονέω (ταπεινός, φρήν) impf. ἐταπεινοφρόνουν; fut. ταπεινοφρονήσω; 1 aor. ἐταπεινοφρόνησα (Epict. 1, 9, 10 in a pejorative sense) **to be humble in thought or demeanor,** ***be modest, unassuming*** (Ps 130:2; SibOr 8, 480; Rhet. Gr. I 624, 29) 1 Cl 13:3; 16:17; 17:2; 38:2; 48:6; Hs 5, 3, 7; 7:6. Opp. ἀλαζονεύεσθαι 1 Cl 2:1; cp. 13:1; 16:2. Opp. ἐπαίρεσθαι 16:1. W. ἐγκρατεύεσθαι 30:3. ταπ. τὰ πρὸς τὸν θεόν *be humble toward God* 62:2 (s. ὁ 2e and B-D-F §160; also Rob. 486f). ταπεινοφρονῆσαι ἐν πάσῃ πράξει αὐτοῦ *be humble in all that he does* Hs 7:4.—DELG s.v. ταπεινάς. TW.

ταπεινοφρόνησις, εως, ἡ (ταπεινός, φρόνησις) ***humility*** w. μακροθυμία Hs 8, 7, 6 v.l.—TW.

ταπεινοφροσύνη, ης, ἡ (s. prec.; Epict. 3, 24, 56; Jos., Bell. 4, 494, both in a pejorative sense) in our lit. only in a favorable sense (τὸ τῆς τ. δόγμα Orig., C. Cels. 6, 15, 23; ταπεινοφροσύνης σωτήριον Did., Gen. 70, 26) ***humility, modesty*** **Phil 2:3** (in dat. of the motivating cause); **1 Pt 5:5;** 1 Cl 21:8; Hs 5, 3, 7 (of humility that expresses itself in fasting; Leutzsch, Hermas 425f, n. 441). W. ἐπιείκεια 1 Cl 56:1; cp. 58:2. W. ἐπιείκεια and πραΰτης 30:8. W. πραΰτης, μακροθυμία, and other virtues **Col 3:12;** cp. **2:23.** μετὰ πάσης ταπ. *in all humility* **Ac 20:19; Eph 4:2** (+ καὶ πραΰτητος); without πάσης 1 Cl 31:4; 44:3. πᾶσα ἐρώτησις ταπεινοφροσύνης χρῄζει *every prayer requires humility* Hv 3, 10, 6. Humility can also be wrongly directed **Col 2:18, 23.**—Lit. s.v. πραΰτης and ταπεινόω 4. Also KDeissner, D. Idealbild d. stoischen Weisen 1930; Vögtle (s.v. πλεονεξία) word-list; LGilen, Demut des Christen nach d. NT: ZAszMyst 13, '38, 266–84; LMarshall, Challenge of NT Ethics '47, 92–96; ADihle, Demut: RAC III '56, 735–78 [lit.]; SRehol, Das Problem der Demut in der profan-griechischen Literatur im Vergleich zu Septuaginta und NT '61.—DELG s.v. ταπεινός. EDNT. TW.

ταπεινόφρων, ον (ταπεινός, φρήν) gen. **-ονος** (in Plut. Mor. 336e; 475e and Iambl., Protr. 21, 15 p. 115, 23 Pistelli='fainthearted') in our lit. ***humble*** (Pr 29:23; Leontius 26 p. 56, 22) **1 Pt 3:8** (v.l. φιλόφρονες); B 19:3; Hm 11:8 (w. πραΰς and other adjs.). πρὸς τὰς μεγαλορημοσύνας αὐτῶν ὑμεῖς ταπεινόφρονες *you are to be humble in contrast to their boastfulness* IEph 10:2 (w. πραεῖς).—Subst. ὁ ταπεινόφρων 1 Cl 38:2 v.l. τὸ ταπεινόφρον *humility* 19:1. S. Leivestad s.v. ταπεινός.—DELG s.v. ταπεινός. EDNT. TW. Sv.

ταπεινόω (ταπεινός) fut. ταπεινώσω; 1 aor. ἐταπείνωσα. Pass.: 1 fut. ταπεινωθήσομαι; 1 aor. ἐταπεινώθην; pf. ptc. τεταπεινωμένος (Hippocr. et al.; LXX; En 106:1; EpArist 257; Philo, Joseph.) gener. 'lower, make low'

❶ **to cause to be at a lower point, *lower*** (Diod. S. 1, 36, 8; Bar 5:7; En 1:6; PsSol 11:4) ὄρος, βουνόν *level a mountain, hill* **Lk 3:5** (Is 40:4).

❷ **to cause someone to lose prestige or status, *humble, humiliate, abase,*** done esp. to slaves, fig. ext. of 1

ⓐ w. focus on reversal of status ταπ. ἑαυτόν *humble oneself* of Christ, who went voluntarily to his death **Phil 2:8** (s. on the whole pass. the lit. s.v. ἁρπαγμός and κενόω 1b; also KThieme, D. ταπεινοφροσύνη Phil 2 u. Ro 12: ZNW 8, 1907, 9–33). Of Paul, who did not hesitate to work w. his hands *degrade* **2 Cor 11:7.** ὅστις ταπεινώσει ἑαυτὸν ὑψωθήσεται (ταπ. . . . ὑψόω: Chilon in Diog. L. 1, 69) **Mt 23:12b;** cp. **Lk 14:11b; 18:14b** (s. also 2b below). Also the pass. (Hyperid. 6, 10; Jos., Ant. 18, 147) **Mt 23:12a; Lk 14:11a; 18:14a** (cp. X., An. 6, 3, 18 θεὸς τοὺς μεγαληγορήσαντας ταπεινῶσαι βούλεται).

ⓑ w. focus on shaming, w. acc. of pers. or thing treated in this manner (Diod. S. 8, 25, 1; Orig., C. Cels. 3, 62, 29) μὴ ταπεινώσῃ με ὁ θεὸς πρὸς ὑμᾶς *that God may not humiliate me before you* **2 Cor 12:21.** κύριος ὁ θεὸς ἐταπείνωσέν με σφόδρα *the Lord God has profoundly shamed me* GJs 2:3. τί ἐταπείνωσας τὴν ψυχήν σοὺ; *Why have you so disgraced yourself?* GJs 13:2; 15:3.

ⓒ w. focus on punitive aspect (Diod. S. 13, 24, 6 Tyche [Fortune] ταπεινοῖ τοὺς ὑπερηφάνους; Cyranides p. 49, 12 ἐχθρούς) *confound, overthrow* τοὺς ὑψηλούς 1 Cl 59:3b; ὕβριν ὑπερηφάνων vs. 3a. Cp. B 4:4f (Da 7:24).—ταπεινόω can also refer to external losses, approx. = 'hold down, harm' (Petosiris, fgm. 6 ln. 21 [act.] and 24 [pass.]).

❸ **to cause to be or become humble in attitude, *humble, make humble*** in a favorable sense (Philod., περὶ κακιῶν col. 22, 3 = p. 38 Jensen ἑαυτόν; Celsus 3, 62 αὐτόν) ὅστις ταπεινώσει ἑαυτὸν ὡς τὸ παιδίον τοῦτο **Mt 18:4.** So perh. also **23:12b; Lk 14:11b; 18:14b** (s. 2a above). ταπεινοῦσθαι *humble oneself, become humble* (Menand., fgm. 754, 6 Kö.=544, 6 Kock τὴν θεὸν ἐξιλάσαντο τῷ ταπεινοῦσθαι σφόδρα; Sir 18:21; GrBar 7:5 ἐταπεινώθην φόβῳ μεγάλῳ) ταπεινώθητε ἐνώπιον κυρίου **Js 4:10.** ταπεινώθητε ὑπὸ τὴν χεῖρα τοῦ θεοῦ *bow down beneath the hand of God* (cp. Gen 16:9) **1 Pt 5:6.** καρδία τεταπεινωμένη *a humbled heart* 1 Cl 18:17 (Ps 50:19). ψυχὴ τεταπεινωμένη B 3:5 (Is 58:10.—Cp. Diod. S. 20, 53, 3 τῇ ψυχῇ ταπεινωθείς; 20, 77, 3 ἐταπεινώθη τὴν ψυχήν). Corresp. ὀστᾶ τεταπεινωμένα 1 Cl 18:8 (Ps 50:10).—KThieme, D. christl. Demut I (history of the word, and humility in Jesus) 1906; DFyffe, ET 35, 1924, 377–79. S. also πραΰτης, end.

❹ **to subject to strict discipline, *constrain, mortify.*** In accordance w. OT usage, ταπεινοῦν τὴν ἑαυτοῦ ψυχήν (Lev 16:29, 31; 23:27; Ps 34:13; Is 58:3 al.) or ταπεινοῦσθαι (Sir 34:26; 2 Esdr 8:21; the prayers for vengeance fr. Rheneia [Dssm., LO 353f, LAE 413ff=SIG 1181, 11] θεὸς ᾧ πᾶσα ψυχὴ ταπεινοῦται; s. Dssm., LO 357f, LAE 419) means *to mortify oneself* GJs 2:2; B 3:1, 3 (Is 58:5); Hm 4, 2, 2 (s. ταπεινοφροσύνη). οἶδα ταπεινοῦσθαι (opp. περισσεύειν) of an austere regimen: *I know how to do w. little* (cp. ταπεινός Pla. Leg. 762e; s. also Plut., Mor. 7e) **Phil 4:12.**—WCvanUnnik, Zur Bedeutung von ταπεινοῦν τὴν ψυχήν bei den Apost. Vätern, ZNW 44, '52f, 250–55. On the whole word: ESchweizer, Erniedrigung u. Erhöhung bei Jesus u. s. Nachfolgern '55.—DELG s.v. ταπεινός. M-M. EDNT. TW. Spicq. Sv.

ταπείνωσις, εως, ἡ (ταπεινόω; Pla., Aristot. et al.; OGI 383, 201 [I BC]; LXX, Test12Patr; JosAs 11:1; 13:1 cod. A [p. 57, 1 Bat. al.]; Philo, Joseph.).

❶ **experience of a reversal in fortunes, *humiliation*** as an experience (Epict. 3, 22, 104; PsSol 2:35; TestJud 19:2; Jos., Bell. 2, 604, Ant. 2, 234) **Ac 8:33;** 1 Cl 16:7 (both Is 53:8). καυχάσθω ὁ πλούσιος ἐν τῇ ταπεινώσει αὐτοῦ *let the rich man boast* (said in irony) *in his comedown/downfall* **Js 1:10** (BWeiss, Beyschlag, Windisch, MDibelius, FHauck). In Diod. S. 11, 87, 2 ταπείνωσις is the *limitation* placed upon the financial worth of a wealthy man. Petosiris, fgm. 6 lines 5; 11; 29 the word means the humiliation or depression caused by severe external losses, someth. like a *breakdown.*

❷ **an unpretentious state or condition, *lowliness, humility, humble station*** (Diod. S. 2, 45, 2; Horapollo 1, 6; TestAbr B 7 p. 111, 20 [Stone p. 70, opp. ὕψος]) **Hb 11:20** D. ἐπιβλέπειν ἐπὶ τὴν ταπ. τινος *look upon someone's humble station* i.e. show concern for someone in humble circumstances **Lk 1:48** (cp. 1 Km 1:11; 9:16; Ps 30:8.—HToxopeüs, Lc. 1:48a: TT 45, 1911, 389–94). τὸ σῶμα τῆς ταπ. *the humble body,* of the material body in contrast to the glorified body **Phil 3:21.**

❸ **a self-abasing demeanor, *self-abasement, mortification*** (ταπεινόω 4) w. νηστεία (cp. PsSol 3:8; TestJos 10:2; JosAs 11:1) 1 Cl 53:2; 55:6.—DELG s.v. ταπεινός. M-M. TW. Spicq. Sv.

ταράσσω impf. ἐτάρασσον; fut. 3 sg. ταράξει LXX; 1 aor. ἐτάραξα. Pass.: impf. ἐταρασσόμην; fut. 3 sg. ταραχθήσεται; 1 aor. ἐταράχθην; pf. τετάραγμαι, ptc. τεταραγμένος (Hom.+; Ath., R. 3 p. 51, 30 [-ττ]).

❶ **to cause movement by shaking or stirring, *shake together, stir up*** of water (Hom. et al.; Aesop 155 P.=274b Halm//160 H-H; Babrius 166, 5=fgm. 4 p. 144 L-P.; Athen. 7, 52, 298c ταραττομένου τοῦ ὕδατος; Hos 6:8; Is 24:14; Ezk 32:2, 13) **J 5:3 [4] v.l.;** pass. (Solon 11 Diehl[3]) *be moved, be stirred* vs **7.**

❷ **to cause inward turmoil, *stir up, disturb, unsettle, throw into confusion,*** fig. ext. of 1 (Aeschyl., Hdt. et al., pap, LXX; Just., A I, 68, 7 [Hadrian]; Ath., R. 3 p. 51–30), in our lit. of mental and spiritual agitation and confusion (Menand., Epitr. 611 Kö. [but s. 931 S. mg.]; Philo, Conf. Lingu. 69), which can manifest themselves in outward tumult τὸν ὄχλον **Ac 17:8;** cp. vs. **13** (Hyperid. 1, 31, 8; POxy 298, 27; PGiss 40 II, 20 ταράσσουσι τὴν πόλιν). τὴν διάνοιάν τινος ταρ. 2 Cl 20:1 (Epict., Ench. 28 τ. γνώμην σου). Of mental confusion caused by false teachings ταρ. τινά **Ac 15:24** (w. λόγοις foll.); **Gal 1:7; 5:10.** Of Jesus in John's Gospel ἐτάραξεν ἑαυτόν *he was troubled* or *agitated* **J 11:33** (difft. NRSV 'deeply moved'. S. Hdb. ad loc.—Menand., Sam. 672 S. [327 Kö.] σαυτὸν ταράττεις; M. Ant. 4, 26 σεαυτὸν μὴ τάρασσε).—Pass. *be troubled, frightened, terrified* (Ps 47:6; Is 8:12; Jos., Ant. 7, 153; 12, 164; Just., D. 38, 2) **Mt 2:3** (GJs 21:2); **14:26** (cp. Phlegon: 257 fgm. 36, II, 3 w. θαρρεῖν, at a φάσμα); **Mk 6:50; Lk 1:12; 24:38;** MPol 5:1; 12:1; Hm 12, 4, 2. μηδὲ ταραχθῆτε *do not let yourselves be intimidated* **1 Pt 3:14** (Is 8:12). ἡ ψυχή μου τετάρακται **J 12:27** (cp. Diod. S. 17, 112, 4 Alexander ἐταράττετο τὴν ψυχήν at the prediction of his death; Dio Chrys. 23 [40], 20 ταράξαι τὴν ψυχήν; Chion,

Ep. 16, 7 ταράσσειν τὴν ψυχήν; Ps 6:4; TestZeb 8:6; TestDan 4:7b); also ἡ καρδία **14:1, 27** (cp. Ps 108:22; 54:5; TestDan 4:7a). ταραχθῆναι τῷ πνεύματι *be inwardly moved* **13:21;** cp. **11:33 v.l.** (Ps.-Callisth. 2, 12, 5 ἐταράσσετο τῇ ψυχῇ).—DELG. M-M. Spicq.

ταραχή, ῆς, ἡ (ταράσσω; Pind., Hdt.+; ins, pap, LXX; TestSol 10:29 C; TestJob, Test12Patr, EpArist, Philo, Joseph.; loanw. in rabb.) gener. in ref. to a disturbance of the usual order.

❶ **movement of someth. caused by stirring,** ***stirring up*** of water which was usually quiet **J 5:3 [4] v.l.**

❷ **inward disturbance,** ***perplexity, disquietude,*** fig. ext. of 1 (Thu., Pla., LXX; Jos., Ant. 14, 273 w. φόβος) IEph 19:2.

❸ **upset of normal civic relations,** ***disturbance, tumult, rebellion,*** fig. ext. of 1 (Hdt. et al.; OGI 90, 20; PAmh 30, 10 [II BC]; Mitt-Wilck. I/2, 167, 14 [II BC]; 3 Macc 3:24; Jos., Bell. 1, 216) pl. (Diod. S. 5, 40, 1 ταραχαί=confusion; Artem. 1, 17; 52 al.; TestDan 5:2; Jos., Vi. 103) **Mk 13:8 v.l.**—M-M.

τάραχος, ου, ὁ (ταράσσω; since Hippocr. I 604; VI 112 L.; X.; BGU 889, 23 [II AD]; LXX; Jos., Bell. 4, 495)=ταραχή.

❶ **a state of mental agitation** (X., An. 1, 8, 2; Epicurus in Diog. L. 10, 77; 82 ἐν τ. ψυχαῖς; Aretaeus p. 142, 7) **Ac 12:18.**

❷ **a state of civic unrest,** ***disturbance, commotion*** (Appian, Bell. Civ. 5, 87 §365) **Ac 19:23** (in both places τάραχος οὐκ ὀλίγος. In the same sense Chion, Ep. 3, 2 πολὺς τάραχος; PLampe, BZ 36, '92, 69 [ins]).—DELG s.v. ταράσσω. M-M. Spicq. Sv.

Ταρσεύς, έως, ὁ (Apollodorus [II BC]: 244 fgm. 55 Jac.; Strabo 14, 5, 14; Arrian, Anab. 2, 4, 7; Plut., Mar. 433 [46, 2] al.; ins [s. New Docs 4, 173]; 2 Macc 4:30) **a pers. from Tarsus,** ***a Tarsian*** of Paul, who (**Ac 22:3**) was born in Tarsus **Ac 9:11; 21:39.** Schürer III 133, on Paul's citizenship.—M-M.

Ταρσός, οῦ, ἡ (the sing. form of the name in Diod. S. 14, 20, 2; Strabo 14, 5, 9; Dio Chrys. 16 [33], 17; 17 [34], 46; Arrian, Anab. 2, 4, 7; Joseph., ins) ***Tarsus,*** capital of Cilicia in southeast Asia Minor (Diod. S., loc. cit., μεγίστη τῶν ἐν Κιλικίᾳ πόλεων) famous as a seat of Gk. learning **Ac 9:30; 11:25; 21:39** D; **22:3** (T. τῆς Κιλικίας as Diod. S. 20, 108, 2; Xenophon Eph. 2, 13, 5; Jos., Ant. 9, 208).—WRamsay, The Cities of St. Paul 1907, 85–244; HBöhlig, Die Geisteskultur v. Tarsos 1913; HSteinmann, Z. Werdegang d. Pls. D. Jugendzeit in Tarsus 1928; WvanUnnik, Tarsus or Jerusalem '62; AJones, The Cities of the Eastern Roman Provinces[2] '71; Pauly-W. IV 2413–39; Kl. Pauly V 529f; BHHW III 1933; Haenchen on Ac 22:3. S. also CHemer, Acts index.; s. also s.v. Κιλικία.—PECS 883f. Schürer III 33f (lit.).

ταρταρόω (Τάρταρος 'the Netherworld') 1 aor. ἐταρτάρωσα (Acusilaus Hist. [V BC]: 2 fgm. 8 Jac. I p. 50; Lydus, Men. 4, 158 p. 174, 26 W.; cp. Sext. Emp., Pyrrh. Hypot. 3, 24, 210 ὁ Ζεὺς τὸν Κρόνον κατεταρτάρωσεν [this compound several times in Ps.—Apollod.: 1, 1, 4; 1, 2, 1, 2; 1, 2, 3]. Tartarus, thought of by the Greeks as a subterranean place lower than Hades where divine punishment was meted out, and so regarded in Israelite apocalyptic as well: Job 41:24; En 20:2; Philo, Exs. 152; Jos., C. Ap. 2, 240; SibOr 2, 302; 4, 186) ***hold captive in Tartarus*** **2 Pt 2:4.**—DELG s.v. Τάρταρος. M-M.

τάσσω fut. τάξω LXX; 1 aor. ἔταξα; perf. τέταχα. Mid.: 1 aor. ἐταξάμην. Pass.: aor. ptc. n. sg. ταχθέν EpJer 61, pl. ταγέντα (TestJob 16:3); pf. τέταγμαι, ptc. τεταγμένος (Pind., Aeschyl., Pre-Socr., Hdt.+)

❶ **to bring about an order of things by arranging,** ***arrange, put in place***

ⓐ of an authority structure pass. αἱ οὖσαι (ἐξουσίαι) ὑπὸ θεοῦ τεταγμέναι εἰσίν *the (structures of authority) presently existing are put in place by God* **Ro 13:1** (cp. IAndrosIsis, Kyme on the role of Isis in ordering a variety of social, political, and economic structures; some interpret as metonymy for officeholders, cp. Da 4:37b; Horace, Odes 1, 12, 13–16; 49–52; Vergil, Ecl. 3, 60f); of established authority in contrast to a rabble MPol 10:2 (τάσσεσθαι ὑπό τινος as here, Eur., Iph. A. 1363; X., An. 1, 6, 6; 2, 6, 13; Simplicius In Epict. p. 60, 19 Düb. τεταγμένοι ὑπὸ θεοῦ).

ⓑ of a pers. put into a specific position, used w. a prep. τάσσειν τινὰ ἐπί τινος *put someone over* or *in charge of someone* or *someth.* (Polyb. 5, 65, 7; ins; Mitt-Wilck. I/2, 11, 51 [II BC]; PRev 51, 9 [III BC]) pass. (Arrian, Anab. 3, 6, 7 ἐπὶ τῶν χρημάτων=in charge of the finances; En 20:5; Jos., Ant. 2, 70; 7, 370.—ἐπί τινι Ath. 24, 3) ἐφ' ἧς (i.e. the way of light) εἰσὶν τεταγμένοι φωταγωγοὶ ἄγγελοι B 18:1.—On ἄνθρωπος ὑπὸ ἐξουσίαν τασσόμενος **Mt 8:9 v.l.; Lk 7:8** s. ἐξουσία 4 (τάσσεσθαι ὑπό τινα 'be put under someone's command' Polyb. 3, 16, 3; 5, 65, 7; Diod. S. 2, 26, 8; 4, 9, 5; OGI 56, 13 [237 BC] τοῖς ὑπὸ τὴν βασιλείαν τασσομένοις; but Just., D. 126, 5 ὑπὸ τῷ πατρί).—τάσσειν τινά εἰς *assign someone to a (certain) classification,* used also w. an abstract noun (Pla., Rep. 2, 371c, Polit. 289e), pass. *belong to, be classed among those possessing* ὅσοι ἦσαν τεταγμένοι εἰς ζωὴν αἰώνιον **Ac 13:48.**—τάσσειν ἑαυτὸν εἰς διακονίαν *devote oneself to a service* (cp. X., Mem. 2, 1, 11 εἰς τὴν δουλείαν ἐμαυτὸν τάττω; Pla., Rep. 2, 371c τάττειν ἑαυτὸν ἐπὶ τὴν διακονίαν ταύτην) **1 Cor 16:15.**

❷ **to give instructions as to what must be done,** ***order, fix, determine, appoint*** (trag., Hdt. +; ins, pap, LXX; TestJob 17:3; Just., A I, 17, 1 φόρους, A II, 5, 2 νόμον; Ath., R. 14 p. 64, 19 τὰ φύσει τεταγμένα)

ⓐ act. and pass., foll. by acc. w. inf. (X., An. 3, 1, 25) **Ac 15:2; 18:2 v.l.** περὶ πάντων ὧν τέτακταί σοι ποιῆσαι *concerning everything that you have been ordered to do* **22:10** (cp. X., Resp. Lac. 11, 6). ὁ τεταγμένος ὑπ' αὐτοῦ δρόμος *the course which has been fixed by him* (i.e. by God) 1 Cl 20:2 (cp. Philo, Poster. Cai. 144, Rer. Div. Her. 97 τεταγμέναι περίοδοι ἀστέρων). κατὰ καιροὺς τεταγμένους *at appointed times* 40:1 (cp. Polyb. 17, 1, 1).

ⓑ mid.=act. (Hdt. et al.; 2 Km 20:5) εἰς τὸ ὄρος οὗ ἐτάξατο αὐτοῖς ὁ Ἰησοῦς (i.e. πορεύεσθαι) **Mt 28:16.** ταξάμενοι αὐτῷ ἡμέραν ἦλθον *they set a day for him and came* **Ac 28:23** (τασσ. ἡμέραν as Polyb. 18, 19, 1; Jos., Ant. 9, 136).—DELG. M-M. TW.

ταῦ, τό (Hippocr.; Pla., Cratyl. 364c) ***tau,*** numeral for *300* B 9:8; s. τ' (numerical symbol).

ταῦρος, ου, ὁ (Hom.+; ins, pap, LXX, Philo, Joseph.) ***bull, ox*** as a sacrificial animal (Cornutus 22 p. 42, 12; Arrian., Anab. 1, 11, 6; Philo, Omn. Prob. Lib. 102; Jos., Ant. 13, 242) **Ac 14:13** (Diod. S. 16, 91, 3 ταῦρος ἐστεμμένος); **Hb 9:13; 10:4;** B 2:5 (Is 1:11). For great banquets **Mt 22:4.**—B. 154. DELG. M-M.

ταὐτά = τὰ αὐτά, only as v.l. **Lk 6:23, 26; 17:30; 1 Th 2:14** —B-D-F §18; Rob. 208; W-S. §5, 9; W-H. App. 145; HvSoden, D. Schriften des NTs I/2, 1911, 1380f.

ταφή, ῆς, ἡ (θάπτω, cp. τάφος)—❶ ***burial*** (Soph., Hdt.+; OGI 90, 32 [II BC]; PSI 328,2 and 5 [III BC]; PAmh 125, 1; PTebt 479 al.; LXX: TestJob 40:13; AssMos fgm. k Denis p. 67; Philo, Mos. 2, 283; Jos., Bell. 4, 317, Ant. 6, 292; 9, 182; Ath. 22, 6) αἰτεῖν τὸ σῶμα πρὸς ταφήν *ask for the corpse for burial* GPt

2:3 (Diod. S. 10, 29, 1 ἵνα λάβῃ τὸ σῶμα εἰς ταφήν). δώσω τοὺς πονηροὺς ἀντὶ τῆς ταφῆς αὐτοῦ *I will deliver up the wicked for his burial,* i.e. for putting him in the grave (par. to θάνατος) 1 Cl 16:10 (Is 53:9).

❷ ***burial-place*** (2 Ch 26:23 ἡ τ. τῶν βασιλέων; O. Joach 2, 2; 3, 2 al.; 18, 11 [I BC] ταφὴ ἰβίων καὶ ἱεράκων ,α='a burial-place for 1,000 mummies of ibises and falcons'. In the sense 'grave' oft. Hdt. et al.; Dt 34:6; Mel., P. 71, 522) εἰς ταφὴν τοῖς ξένοις *as a burial ground for strangers* **Mt 27:7.**—DELG s.v. θάπτω. M-M.

τάφος, ου, ὁ (θάπτω, cp. ταφή; in Hom.='funeral rites'; gener. 'tomb')

❶ **a site or receptacle for interment, *grave, tomb*** of a dead pers. (Hes.+) **Mt 27:61, 64, 66; 28:1** (EBickermann, Das leere Grab: ZNW 23, 1924, 281–92; Guillaume Baldensperger, Le tombeau vide: RHPR 12, '32, 413–33; 13, '33, 105–44; 14, '34, 97–125; CMasson, Le tomb. v.: RTP 32, '44, 161–74; HvCampenhausen, D. Ablauf der Osterereignisse u. das leere Grab[3] '66; JKennard, Jr., The Burial of Jesus: JBL 74, '55, 227–38; WNauck, ZNW 47, '56, 243–67; LOberlinner, ZNW 73, '82, 159–82; Finegan s.v. Ἰούδας 6; s. also ἀνάστασις 2, end and μνημεῖον 2.—An external parallel to the motif of the empty τάφος in Chariton 3, 3, 1–4.—Phlegon: 257 fgm. 36, 1, 9 Jac.: to ascertain whether a resurrection from the dead had actually occurred, ὁ τάφος is opened and entered to see πότερον εἴη τὸ σῶμα ἐπὶ τῆς κλίνης ἢ κενὸν τόπον εὑρήσομεν); GPt 6:24; 8:31; 9:36f; 10:39; 11:45; 13:55. οἱ τάφοι τῶν προφητῶν **Mt 23:29** (on the cult of graves and veneration of pious pers. among the Jews s. Billerb. I 937f; JJeremias, Heiligengräber in Jesu Umwelt '58). Grave of Paul AcPl Ha 10, 18; 11, 13. On τάφοι κεκονιαμένοι **Mt 23:27;** GNaass 284, 153; s. κονιάω. In the prec. apocryphal gospel τάφ. κεκ. is used metaphorically. Likew. τάφοι νεκρῶν, ἐφ' οἷς γέγραπται μόνον ὀνόματα ἀνθρώπων *graves of the dead, on which only people's names are inscribed* IPhld 6:1. ἔρχεσθαι ἐν τάφῳ *come to the grave* 1 Cl 56:15 (Job 5:26).

❷ **anything that functions as a tomb, *tomb,*** in varied imagery: of the dark place fr. which God introduces us into the world at birth 1 Cl 38:3. Of wild animals who are to be Ignatius' grave ἵνα μοι τάφος γένωνται (i.e. τὰ θηρία) IRo 4:2 (Gorgias, fgm. 5a Diels in Περὶ ὕψους 3, 2 calls vultures ἔμψυχοι τάφοι). Of sinful pers. τάφος ἀνεῳγμένος ὁ λάρυγξ (s. ἀνοίγω 2 and cp. Artem. 1, 80 p. 80, 27 τὸ στόμα τάφῳ ἔοικε) **Ro 3:13** (Ps 5:10; 13:3).—B. 294. DELG s.v. θάπτω. M-M. EDNT.

τάχα adv. (ταχύς; Hom. et al.; also Wsd. 13:6; 14:19; TestJob 22:2 'soon'; ApcSed 4:2 τί τάχα ἐποίησας; 'what, ultimately, did you accomplish?') **marker expressing contingency ranging between probability and bare possibility, *perhaps, possibly, probably*** (Aeschyl., Hdt. et al.; pap, Wsd., Just., D. 5, 2, quite predom. w. ἄν and the opt. Rarely, as in both NT passages, w. the indic. and without ἄν: Dio Chrys. 15 [32], 33; Ps.-Demetr., El. 180; BGU 1040, 41 [II AD] τάχα δύνασαι; POxy 40, 7; Wsd 13:6 αὐτοὶ τάχα πλανῶνται; Philo, Aet. M. 54; Jos., Ant. 6, 33; 18, 277.—MArnim, De Philonis Byz. dicendi genere, diss. Greifswald 1912, 86; JScham, Der Optativgebrauch bei Klemens v. Alex, 1913, 83; B-D-F §385, 1) **Ro 5:7; Phlm 15.**—B. 965. DELG s.v. ταχύς. M-M.

τάχειον (so e.g. POsl 52, 15 [II AD]) itacistic spelling for τάχιον (ταχέως, beg).

ταχέως adv. of ταχύς, positive (Hom.+; pap, LXX; En 98:16; TestSol 6:5 D; TestAbr.; JosAs cod. A 16, 2 and ch. 19 [p. 63, 5; 69, 6 Bat.]; ApcMos 21).—Comp. **τάχιον** ([ταχεῖον Sod. and Vog.; τάχειον t.r. Hippocr., Mul. Morb. 1, 2; Epicurus in Diog. L. 10, 98; Diod. S. 13, 106, 1; oft. in colloq. speech in general, incl. ViHab 8 [p. 86, 11 Sch.]; Jos., Bell. 5, 537, Ant 2, 142 al.; ins, pap; Wsd 13:9; 1 Macc 2:40; TestIss 6:3. This form was rejected by the Atticists; the Attic form θᾶττον [also 2 Macc; AssMos fgm. f; Philo, Aet. M. 30; Jos., Ant. 12, 143—WSchmidt 505], which replaced the Homeric θᾶσσον, is found in our lit. only 1 Cl 65:1a; MPol 13:1.—B-D-F §61, 1; 244, 1; W-S. §11, 3; Mlt-H. 164).—Superl. **τάχιστα** only once (**Ac 17:15** s. 1c below), in an expr. taken fr. the literary lang. (B-D-F §60, 2; 244, 1; 453, 4; Rob. 488; 669.—Alcaeus 70, 15 D.[2]; Menand., Per. 537 S. [287]; Arrian., Anab. 6, 2, 2; Ael. Aristid. 24, 26 K.=44 p. 833 D.; SIG 1168, 4 [IV BC]; PSI 360, 12 [252/251 BC]; 792, 10; 3 Macc 1:8; TestSol 6:3 D; Jos., Vi. 16). In some instances there may be semantic overlap between mngs. 1 and 2.

❶ **pert. to a very brief extent of time, with focus on speed of action—ⓐ** positive**—α.** in a favorable sense ***quickly, at once, without delay, soon*** (Diod. S. 13, 106, 4; 17, 4, 6; En 98:16; EpArist 291; Jos., Bell. 7, 31; Ant.9, 51) **Lk 14:21; 15:22** D; **16:6; J 11:31;** B 3:4; AcPl Ha 3, 4; οὕτως ταχέως AcPlCor 2:2 (cp. Gal 1:6 under β).

β. in a remonstrative sense ***too quickly, too easily, hastily*** (Pr 25:8; Wsd 14:28; SibOr fgm. 1, 2) **Gal 1:6** (cp. AcPlCor 2:2 under α); **2 Th 2:2; 1 Ti 5:22;** Pol 6:1.

ⓑ comp.**—α. *more quickly, faster* Hb 13:19.** τάχ. τοῦ Πέτρου *faster than Peter* **J 20:4.** The comparison is supplied fr. the context, *more quickly* (than the others), *be the first to* . . . MPol 13:2. θᾶττον ἤ *more quickly than* 13:1. *As quickly, as soon as possible* (TestIss 6:3; Ps.-Clem., Hom. 1, 14) 1 Cl 65:1a (θᾶττον) and b (τάχιον). *All the more quickly* MPol 3:1.

β. without any suggestion of comparison ***quickly, soon, without delay*** (PGM 4, 1467 θᾶττον; Jos., Vi. 310 θᾶσσον) **J 13:27;** difft. Mussies 128: 'very quickly'; Hm 10, 1, 6.

ⓒ superl. ὡς τάχιστα ***as soon as possible* Ac 17:15.**

❷ **pert. to a future point of time that is subsequent to another point of time, with focus on brevity of interval rather than on speed of activity, *soon***

ⓐ positive **1 Cor 4:19; Phil 2:19** (τ. πέμπ. as Plut., Mor. 612e), **24; 2 Ti 4:9.**

ⓑ comp. τάχιον without any suggestion of comparison **1 Ti 3:14 v.l.; Hb 13:23.**—DELG s.v. ταχύς. M-M.

ταχινός, ή, όν (poetic and late prose for ταχύς; Theocr. et al.; CIA III 1344, 3; Cat. Cod. Astr. I 137; LXX; Mel., P. 20, 142)

❶ **pert. to a very brief extent of time, with focus on speed of action, *quick, in haste*** ταχινὸς γενέσθω Hs 9, 26, 6.

❷ **pert. to taking place without delay, *coming soon, imminent, swift* 2 Pt 1:14; 2:1.** ἡ μετάνοια αὐτῶν ταχινὴ ὀφείλει εἶναι *they must repent soon* Hs 8, 9, 4; cp. 9, 20, 4.—DELG s.v. ταχύς. M-M.

τάχιον, τάχιστα s. ταχέως.

τάχος, ους, τό (Hom. et al.; ins, pap, LXX; TestSol 7:3 D; Just., D. 68, 3)

❶ **a very brief period of time, with focus on speed of an activity or event, *speed, quickness, swiftness, haste,*** μετὰ τάχους *with speed* (Pla., Prot. 332b, Leg. 944c; POxy 2107, 4 [III AD]) MPol 13:1.—ἐν τάχει (Pind., Aeschyl. et al.; Galen, CMG V/9/2 p. 25, 25 al.; ins, pap, LXX; Jos., Ant. 6, 163; 17, 83) *quickly, at once, without delay* **Ac 10:33** D; **12:7; 17:15** D; **22:18;** 1 Cl 48:1; 63:4.—τάχει (Tetrast. Iamb. 2, 6, 1 p. 287; SibOr 1, 205; in Plut., Caes. 717 [20, 4], Lys. 438 [11, 2] w. the addition of πολλῷ, παντί; cp. Just., D. 68, 3 σὺν τάχει) *quickly* **Rv 2:5 v.l.**

(s. Tdf.).—τὸ τάχος as acc. of specification, adverbially *(very) quickly, without delay* (PHib 62, 13; PPetr II, 9, 2, 9; PSI 326, 12; 495, 17; 18 [all III BC]; LXX; Jos., Ant. 13, 8. Without the art. as early as Aeschyl.) 1 Cl 53:2; B 4:8; 14:3 (w. all three cp. Ex 32:7).

❷ **pert. to a relatively brief time subsequent to another point of time,** ἐν τάχει as adverbial unit ***soon, in a short time*** **Lk 18:8; Ro 16:20; 1 Ti 3:14; Rv 1:1; 22:6;** 1 Cl 65:1; *shortly* **Ac 25:4.** Cp. ταχύς 2.—DELG s.v. ταχύς. M-M.

ταχύνω fut. 3 sg. ταχυνεῖ Gen 41:32; aor. ἐτάχυνα LXX, almost always intr. (Aeschyl., X. et al.; LXX; PsSol 17:45) ***hasten, hurry*** combined w. another verb by means of καί *hasten to do someth.* (Judg 13:10) B 4:3.—DELG s.v. ταχύς.

ταχύς, εῖα, ύ (Hom.+)—❶ **pert. to a very brief period of time, with focus on speed of an activity or event**

ⓐ adj. ***quick, swift, speedy*** ταχ. καρπός *fruit that ripens quickly* 2 Cl 20:3. ταχὺς εἰς τὸ ἀκοῦσαι *quick to hear* **Js 1:19** (Lucian, Epigr. 18 ταχ. εἰς τὸ φαγεῖν; Sir 5:11; Libanius, Or. 33 p. 186, 15 ἐν τῷ δῆσαι ταχύς, ἐν τῷ κρῖναι βραδύς 'quick to arrest but slow in deciding'; cp. PsSol 4:5 ταχὺς εἰσόδῳ εἰς πᾶσαν οἰκίαν).

ⓑ mostly in the neut. sing. as adv. ταχύ (trag., Hdt.+; pap, LXX; En 97:10; TestSol 4:2 P; Jos., Bell. 7, 394, Vi. 149).

α. *quickly, at a rapid rate* ταχὺ ἔφυγον **Mk 16:8 v.l.—Mt 28:8.**

β. *without delay, quickly, at once* (though it is not always poss. to make a clear distinction betw. this mng. and the one in 2) **Mt 5:25; 28:7; Lk 15:22; J 11:29; Ac 14:2** D; 1 Cl 23:5ab (Is 13:22); 53:2 (Ex 32:8; Dt 9:12); Hm 9:7. This is prob. the place for the ἔρχεσθαι ταχύ of **Rv: 2:5 v.l.** (many cursives and printed texts), **16; 3:11; 11:14; 22:7, 12, 20** (P-ÉLangevin, Jésus Seigneur, '67, 209–35).

❷ **pert. to a relatively brief time subsequent to another point of time,** neut. sg. as adv. ***in a short time, soon*** (cp. 1bβ above and τάχος 2). **Mk 9:39** *(soon afterward);* Hv 3, 8, 9; m 12, 5, 3. This is also prob. the place for the μετανοεῖν ταχύ of Hs: 8, 7, 5; 8, 8, 3; 5; 8, 10, 1; 9, 19, 2; 9, 21, 4; 9, 23, 2; εἰς ταχεῖαν (sc. ὥραν) *soon* AcPlCor 2:3.—DELG. M-M.

τέ (Hom.+) enclitic particle (in the NT never elided to τ'. In **Mt** three times, in **Luke's gosp.** nine times, in **John's gosp.** three times ['always textually contestable' B-D-F §443, 1], in Paul [quite predom. in **Ro**] more than twenty times, scarcely less oft. in **Hb,** in 1 Cl forty-three times, in Dg seven times, in **Js** twice, once each in **Jd, Rv,** 2 Cl, B. It is not found at all in Mk, Gal, Col, 1 and 2 Th, 1 and 2 Ti, Tit, 1, 2 and 3 J, 1 and 2 Pt, GJs. By far most freq. [about 150 times] in **Ac** (cp. the frequent usage in Polyb.). The ms. tradition oft. confuses τέ and δέ.—B-D-F §443f; Rdm.[2] p. 5f, 37; Rob. index. p. 1285; Mlt.-Turner 338.

❶ **marker of close relationship between sequential states or events, *and likewise, and so, so*** (B-D-F §443, 3; TestJob 24:1; 53:5; Just., A II, 4, 2) ἑτέροις τε λόγοις πλείοσιν διεμαρτύρατο *and likewise* . . . **Ac 2:40** (here D has the poorer rdg. δέ). κατενύγησαν τὴν καρδίαν, εἶπόν τε . . . , *and so they said* vs. **37.—J 4:42; 6:18; Ac 4:33; 5:19, 35; 6:7, 12f** al.; **Ro 2:19; Hb 12:2; Jd 6.**—The use of τέ to introduce a parenthesis is scarcely admissible; δέ is to be preferred: **Ac 1:15; 4:13** (s. B-D-F §443, 1; 447, 7).

❷ **marker of connection between coordinate nonsequential items**—ⓐ used alone, ***and:*** τέ thus connects single concepts, parts of clauses, or words (Just., A II, 11, 4; s. Kühner-G. II 241; Schwyzer II 574–76; Denniston 497–503) ἐν ἀγάπῃ πνεύματί τε πραΰτητος **1 Cor 4:21.** θεοῦ ῥῆμα δυνάμεις τε μέλλοντος αἰῶνος **Hb 6:5.** Cp. **9:1.** ἔκλασεν ἄρτον ὕδωρ τε προσήνεγκεν AcPl Ha 4, 4; relative clause ἅ τε Ἀριστίων . . . λέγουσιν Papias (2:4). Participles: συναχθέντες συμβούλιόν τε λαβόντες **Mt 28:12;** φοβούμενος τὸν θεὸν μαρτυρούμενός τε **Ac 10:22;** cp. **Mt 27:48; Ac 2:33; 20:11; 28:23a; Hb 1:3; 6:4.** Infinitives: ἁρπάσαι αὐτὸν ἐκ μέσου αὐτῶν ἄγειν τε **Ac 23:10;** cp. **11:26; 24:23; 27:21b; Eph 3:19.**

ⓑ τὲ . . . τέ, used as connecter of sentences and parts of sentences that are closely related to each other ***as . . . so, not only . . . but also*** (Kühner-G. II 243; Schwyzer II 573f; Denniston 503–5; Jos., Ant. 1, 92) μάρτυρα ὧν τε εἶδές με ὧν τε ὀφθήσομαί σοι **Ac 26:16** (on the constr. s. ὁράω A1b). ἐάν τε γὰρ ζῶμεν, τῷ κυρίῳ ζῶμεν, ἐάν τε ἀποθνῄσκωμεν, τῷ κυρίῳ ἀποθνῄσκομεν *for just as when we live, we live to the Lord, so also when we die, we die to the Lord* **Ro 14:8a.** ἐάν τε οὖν ζῶμεν ἐάν τε ἀποθνῄσκωμεν, τοῦ κυρίου ἐσμέν *so, not only if we live, but also if we die* (i.e. *whether we live or die*) *we belong to the Lord* vs. **8b.** Cp. **Ac 2:46; 17:4; 26:10.** τε γάρ 'for the fact is that' is one way of rendering this combination (X., Mem. 1, 1, 3; Just., D. 3, 5; Ath. 2, 4) **Ro 1:26; 7:7; Hb 2:11.**

ⓒ w. the same mng. τὲ . . . καί (Jos., Bell. 2, 142, Ant. 1, 9) and τὲ καί

α. connecting concepts, usu. of the same kind or corresponding as opposites. In these uses τὲ καί can oft. be translated simply ***and:*** δῶρά τε καὶ θυσίας **Hb 5:1.** δεήσεις τε καὶ ἱκετηρίας vs. **7.** ὀνειδισμοῖς τε καὶ θλίψεσιν **10:33.** φόβητρά τε καὶ σημεῖα **Lk 21:11b.** Cp. **22:66; Ac 4:27; 26:3.** ποιεῖν τε καὶ διδάσκειν **Ac 1:1.** ἀσφαλῆ τε καὶ βεβαίαν **Hb 6:19.** πάντῃ τε καὶ πανταχοῦ **Ac 24:3.** ὑμῶν τε καὶ ἐμοῦ **Ro 1:12;** cp. **1 Cor 1:2 v.l.** παρά τε σοῦ κἀκείνων AcPlCor 1:5. πονηρούς τε καὶ ἀγαθούς **Mt 22:10.** ἄνδρες τε καὶ γυναῖκες **Ac 8:12; 9:2; 22:4.** Ἰουδαίοις τε καὶ Ἕλλησιν **1 Cor 1:24.** μικρῷ τε καὶ μεγάλῳ **Ac 26:22a.** When used w. a noun that has the art. τέ comes after the latter: ὅ τε στρατηγὸς . . . καὶ οἱ ἀρχιερεῖς **Ac 5:24;** cp. **Lk 23:12; J 2:15; Ac 8:38; 17:10; 27:1; Hb 2:11.** ἰχῶράς τε καὶ σκώληκας Papias (3:2). ψαλμῶν τε . . . καὶ ᾠδῶν AcPl Ha 7, 11.—τέ can be followed by more than one καί (Ar. 3, 1 ἡλίου τε καὶ σελήνης καὶ τῶν λοιπῶν στοιχείων; 4:1 ἄφθαρτός τε καὶ ἀναλλοίωτος καὶ ἀόρατος; Just., D. 126, 5; Libanius, Or. 2 p. 256, 6 F.) τήν τε Μαριὰμ καὶ τὸν Ἰωσὴφ καὶ τὸ βρέφος **Lk 2:16.** ἐσθίειν τε καὶ πίνειν καὶ μεθύσκεσθαι **12:45.** Cp. **Ac 1:8, 13; Hb 2:4; 9:2.**—In **1 Cor 1:30** τὲ καί connects the second and third members of a series, and another καί joins the fourth one. Sim. **Hb 11:32.** τὲ καί doubled: Ἕλλησίν τε καὶ βαρβάροις, σοφοῖς τε καὶ ἀνοήτοις **Ro 1:14.** θηρίων τε καὶ πετεινῶν ἑρπετῶν τε καὶ ἐναλίων **Js 3:7.**—τὲ καὶ . . . τέ: ἐνώπιον ἐθνῶν τε καὶ βασιλέων υἱῶν τε Ἰσραήλ **Ac 9:15.** Cp. **26:10f.** The τὲ καὶ . . . τὲ . . . καί of vs. **20** seems to be due to a textual error.

β. infrequently connecting whole sentences (Mayser II/3, 160; 163f; 165) ἠνεῴχθησάν τε αἱ θύραι, καὶ πάντων τὰ δεσμὰ ἀνέθη **Ac 16:26 v.l.** καὶ . . . , καὶ . . . τὲ . . . , καί **2:2-4 v.l.** τὲ . . . , καὶ . . . , καί **21:30.**—On εἴτε s. εἰ 6o. On μήτε s. that entry.

❸ **marker w. ascensive stress and serving without copulative force, *even*** ἐάν τε γὰρ περισσότερόν τι καυχήσωμαι *for suppose I (even) do boast a little too much* (Goodsp.) **2 Cor 10:8;** cp. **Ro 7:7** (on Hellen. developments s. Rdm.[2] 5f; B-D-F §443, 3: w. suggestion of probable suppression of a second τε).—CRuigh, Antour de τέ epique, études sur la syntax grecque, Amsterdam '70.—DELG. M-M. EDNT.

τέγος, ους, τό (Hom. [Od.]+; Lucian; Aelian, NA 2, 48 p. 56, 11; Jos., Bell. 1, 337, Ant. 17, 71; Just., A I, 26, 3; SibOr 3, 186) ***roof:*** ὑπὸ τὸ τέγος *under the roof* (guide, as Appian, Bell. Civ.

4, 18 §70) 1 Cl 12:6 (as the rdg. preferred to στέγος by Lghtf.; the same confusion of rdgs. in EpJer 9).

τέθεικα, τεθεικώς, τέθειται, τεθῆναι s. τίθημι.

τεθλιμμένος s. θλίβω.

τεθνάναι, τέθνηκα s. θνήσκω.

τέθραμμαι, τεθραμμένος s. τρέφω.

τεθῶ s. τίθημι.

τεῖχος, ους, τό (Hom.+; loanw. in rabb.; 'wall', freq. designed for defense) ***wall,*** esp. city wall **Ac 9:25; 2 Cor 11:33** (διὰ τοῦ τείχους as Jos., Ant. 5, 15. Cp. Athen. 5, 214a κατὰ τῶν τειχῶν καθιμήσαντας φεύγειν; s. also Plut., Aemil. Paul. 269 [26]); **Hb 11:30; Rv 21:12, 14f, 17–19** (on assoc. w. pers. s. Reader, Polemo 264f, 375). Pl. of several circular walls surrounding the tower in Hermas: Hs 8, 2, 5; 8, 6, 6; 8, 7, 3; 8, 8, 3.—B. 472. DELG. M-M.

τεκεῖν s. τίκτω.

τεκμήριον, ου, τό (Aeschyl., Hdt., Thu.+) **that which causes someth. to be known in a convincing and decisive manner,** ***proof*** (demonstrative proof: Aristot., An. Pr. 70b, 2; Rh. 1357b 4; 1402b 19; Diod. S. 17, 51, 3 τεκμήρια τῆς ἐκ τοῦ θεοῦ γενέσεως; SIG 867, 37 μέγιστον τεκμήριον w. ref. to Artemis; 685, 84; PGiss 39, 9) ἐν πολλοῖς τεκμηρίοις *by many convincing proofs* **Ac 1:3** (DMealand, ZNW 80, '89, 134f [Hell. reff.]; cp. Jos., Ant. 5, 39 διὰ πολλῶν τεκμηρίων.—τεκ. used w. παραστῆσαι Jos., Ant. 17, 128. Cp. Libanius, Or. 18, 13 τὸ τῆς φύσεως βασιλικὸν πολλοῖς καὶ μεγάλοις τεκμηρίοις ἐμηνύετο=his regal nature was attested by many exceptional signs).—DELG. M-M.

τέκνημα, ατος, τό (hapax leg. for γέννημα) ***brood, offspring*** τεκνήματα ἐχιδνῶν *generation of vipers* AcPlCor 2:38.

τεκνίον, ου, τό (Epict. 3, 22, 78; Anth. Pal.; PFlor 365, 15 [III AD]; POxy 1766, 14; TestJob, ApcMos) dim. of τέκνον; ***(little) child*** voc. pl. τεκνία; in our lit. only in the voc. pl., used by Jesus in familiar, loving address to his disciples, or by a Christian apostle or teacher to his spiritual children τεκνία **J 13:33; 1J 2:12, 28; 3:7, 18; 4:4; 5:21.** τεκνία μου (TestReub 1:3; TestJob 5:1 al.; ApcMos 5:30) **Gal 4:19 v.l.; 1J 2:1.**—DELG s.v. τίκτω C. Frisk s.v. τέκνον. M-M. TW.

τεκνογονέω (s. next entry; Philippus Epigr. [I AD]: Anth. Pal. 9, 22, 4 [of an animal]) ***bear/beget children*** (Appian., Basil. 1a §5; Achmes 63, 10) **1 Ti 5:14;** Dg 5:6 (pointing to a normal practice among Christians and in contrast to custom of infanticide; s. ῥίπτω 1).—Cp. DELG s.v. γίγνομαι; Frisk s.v. γονή. M-M.

τεκνογονία, ας, ἡ (s. prec. entry; Hippocr., Ep. 17, 21; Aristot., HA 7, 1, 8, 582a, 28; Stoic. III 158, 5; Galen: CMG V/9, 1 p. 27, 12; Cat. Cod. Astr. IX/1 p. 181, 17) ***the bearing of children*** **1 Ti 2:15** (RFalconer, JBL 60, '41, 375–79; SPorter, JSNT 49, '93, 87–102; NDemand, Birth, Death, and Motherhood in Classical Greece '94).—M-M.

τέκνον, ου, τό (τίκτω 'engender, bear'; Hom.+ 'child')

➊ **an offspring of human parents,** ***child***—ⓐ without ref. to sex **Mt 10:21a** (on the complete dissolution of family ties s. Lucian, Cal. 1; GrBar 4:17; ApcEsdr 3:14 p. 27, 23 Tdf.; Just., A I, 27, 3f; Orig., C. Cels. 6, 43, 25 [Job's children]); **Mk 13:12a; Lk 1:7; Ac 7:5; Rv 12:4.** Pl. **Mt 7:11; 10:21b; 18:25; 19:29; 22:24** (=σπέρμα, cp. Dt 25:5f, but σπ. and τ. are contrasted **Ro 9:7); Mk 13:12b; Lk 1:17; 14:26; 1 Cor 7:14** (on the baptism of children s. HWood, EncRelEth II 392ff; JLeipoldt, D. urchr. Taufe 1928, 73–78; AOepke, LIhmels Festschr. 1928, 84–100, ZNW 29, 1930, 81–111 [against him HWindisch, ZNW 28, 1929, 118–42]; JJeremias, Hat d. Urkirche d. Kindertaufe geübt? '38; 2d ed. '49; Die Kindert. in d. ersten 4 Jhdtn. '58; revisited D. Anfänge d. Kindert. '62; s. also ZNW 40, '42, 243–45. KAland, D. Saülingst. im NT u. in d. alten Kirche '62, 2d ed. '63; Die Stellung d. Kinder in d. frühe christl. Gemeinden, und ihre Taufe '67. KBarth, Z. kirchl. Lehre v. d. Taufe[2] '43; D. Taufe als Begründung d. christlichen Lebens in Kirchliche Dogmatik IV, 4, '67; for discussion of Barth's views, s. EJüngel, K. Barths Lehre v. d. Taufe '68; KViering (ed.), Zu K. Barth's Lehre v. d. Taufe '71; K. Aland, Taufe u. Kindertaufe '71; HHubert, D. Streit um d. Kindertaufe, '72. FFrøvig, TTK 11, '40, 124–31; EMolland, NorTT 43, '42, 1–23; F-JLeenhardt, Le Baptême chrétien '46; OCullmann, D. Tauflehre d. NT '48; P-HMenoud, Verbum Caro 2, '48, 15–26; HSchlier, TLZ 72, '47, 321–26; GFleming, Baptism in the NT '49; GBeasley-Murray, Baptism in the New Testament '62; WKümmel, TRu 18, '50, 32–47; GDelling, D. Taufe im NT '63; EDinkler, Die Taufaussagen d. NT '71 [in: KViering, s. above, 60–153]; JDidier, Le baptême des enfants '59; HKraft, Texte z. Gesch. d. Taufe bes. d. Kindert. i. d. alten Kirche, Kl. T. no. 174, 2d ed. '69); **2 Cor 12:14ab** (simile); **1 Th 2:7** (simile), **11** (simile); **1 Ti 3:4, 12; 5:4** al. In the table of household duties (s. MDibelius Hdb. exc. after Col 4:1; KWeidinger, Die Haustafeln 1928) **Eph 6:1** (τὰ τέκνα voc.), **4; Col 3:20** (τὰ τ. voc.), **21.** In the case of φονεῖς τέκνων B 20:2; D 5:2, what follows shows that *murders of* their own *children* are meant.—The unborn fetus is also called τέκνον B 19:5; D 2:2 (like παιδίον: Hippocr., π. σαρκ. 6 vol. VIII 592 L. On Jesus' attitude toward children, cp. JKalogerakos, Aristoteles' Bild von der Frau: ΠΛΑΤΩΝ 46, '94, 159–83, esp. p. 174 and notes [cp. Aristot., EN 1161b].).

ⓑ The sex of the child can be made clear by the context, *son* (Herodian 7, 10, 7; PGen 74, 1ff; PAmh 136, 1f; POxy 930, 18; Jos., Ant. 14, 196; Just., D. 56, 5; 134, 4) **Mt 21:28a; Phil 2:22** (simile); **Rv 12:5;** GJs 22;3. The voc. τέκνον as an affectionate address to a son **Mt 21:28b; Lk 2:48; 15:31.** In a more general sense the pl. is used for

➋ **descendants from a common ancestor,** ***descendants, posterity*** Ῥαχὴλ κλαίουσα τὰ τέκνα αὐτῆς **Mt 2:18** (Jer 38:15).—**27:25; Ac 2:39; 13:33.** A rich man is addressed by his ancestor Abraham as τέκνον **Lk 16:25.** τὰ τέκνα τῆς σαρκός *the physical descendants* **Ro 9:8a.**

➌ **one who is dear to another but without genetic relationship and without distinction in age,** ***child***—ⓐ in the voc. gener. as a form of familiar address *my child, my son* (Herodian 1, 6, 4; ParJer 5:30; Achilles Tat. 8, 4, 3. Directed to fully grown persons, Vi. Aesopi G 60 P., where a peasant addresses Aesop in this way) **Mt 9:2; Mk 2:5.**

ⓑ of a spiritual child in relation to master, apostle, or teacher (PGM 4, 475.—Eunap. p. 70 the sophist applies this term to his students) **2 Ti 1:2; Phlm 10.** τέκνον ἐν κυρίῳ **1 Cor 4:17.** τέκ. ἐν πίστει **1 Ti 1:2.** τέκ. κατὰ κοινὴν πίστιν **Tit 1:4.** Pl. **1 Cor 4:14; 2 Cor 6:13; 3J 4.** In direct address (voc.): sing. (on dir. address in the sing. cp. Sir 2:1 and oft.; Herm. Wr. 13, 2ab; PGM 13, 226; 233; 742; 755.—S. also Norden, Agn. Th. 290f; Boll 138f): **1 Ti 1:18; 2 Ti 2:1;** D 3:1, 3–6; 4:1. Pl.: **Mk 10:24;** B 15:4.—1 Cl 22:1 understands the τέκνα of Ps 33:12 as a word of Christ to Christians. Cp. B 9:3. The address in **Gal 4:19** is intended metaphorically for *children* for whom Paul is once more undergoing the pains of childbirth.—The adherents of false teachers are also called their τέκνα **Rv 2:23.**

ⓒ of the members of a congregation **2J 1; 4; 13.** In Hermas the venerable lady, who embodies the Christian communities, addresses the believers as τέκνα Hv 3, 9, 1. In **Gal 4:31** οὐκ ἐσμὲν παιδίσκης τέκνα ἀλλὰ τῆς ἐλευθέρας posts a dramatic image = 'we belong not to a community dependent on the rules of Sinai, but to one that adheres to the promises made to Abraham'.

❹ **one who has the characteristics of another being,** ***child*** ⓐ of those who exhibit virtues of ancient worthies: children of Abraham **Mt 3:9; Lk 3:8; J 8:39; Ro 9:7.** True Christian women are children of Sarah **1 Pt 3:6.**

ⓑ of those who exhibit characteristics of transcendent entities: the believers are (τὰ) τέκνα (τοῦ) θεοῦ (cp. Is 63:8; Wsd 16:21; SibOr 5, 202; Just., D. 123, 9; 124, 1. On the subj. matter s. HHoltzmann, Ntl. Theologie I[2] 1911, 54; Bousset, Rel.[3] 377f; ADieterich, Mithrasliturgie 1903, 141ff; Hdb. on J 1:12; WGrundmann, Die Gotteskindschaft in d. Gesch. Jesu u. ihre relgesch. Voraussetzungen '38; WTwisselmann, D. Gotteskindsch. der Christen nach dem NT '39; SLegasse, Jésus et L'enfant [synopt.], '69), in Paul as those adopted by God **Ro 8:16f, 21; 9:7, 8b** (opp. σπέρμα); **Phil 2:15,** s. also **Eph 5:1;** in John as those begotten by God **J 1:12; 11:52; 1J 3:1f, 10a; 5:2.** Corresp. τὰ τέκνα τοῦ διαβόλου **1J 3:10b** (on this subj. s. Hdb. on J 8:44).—Cp. Ac 17:28, where the idea of kinship w. deity is complex because of semantic components not shared by polytheists and those within Israelite tradition.—Cp. 6 below.

❺ **inhabitants of a city,** ***children,*** an Hebraistic expression (Rdm.[2] p. 28; Mlt-H. 441; s. Jo 2:23; Zech 9:13; Bar 4:19, 21, 25 al.; 1 Macc 1:38; PsSol 11:2) **Mt 23:37; Lk 13:34; 19:44; Gal 4:25.**

❻ **a class of persons with a specific characteristic,** ***children of.*** τ. is used w. abstract terms (for this Hebraism s. prec.; ἀνάγκης, ἀγνοίας Just., A I, 61, 10) τέκνα ἀγάπης B 9:7; ἀγ. καὶ εἰρήνης 21:9 (ἀγάπη 1bα). εὐφροσύνης 7:1 (s. εὐφροσύνη). δικαιοσύνης AcPlCor 2:19. κατάρας **2 Pt 2:14** (s. κατάρα). ὀργῆς **Eph 2:3;** AcPlCor 2:19. ὑπακοῆς **1 Pt 1:14.** φωτός **Eph 5:8;** cp. IPhld 2:1. On the 'children of wisdom', i.e. those who attach themselves to her and let themselves be led by her **Mt 11:19 v.l.; Lk 7:35** s. δικαιόω 2bα. Cp. 4b above.—Billerbeck I 219f, 371–74; BHHW II 947–49; III 1935–37.—DELG s.v. τίκτω. Frisk. M-M. EDNT. TW. Sv.

τεκνοτροφέω 1 aor. ἐτεκνοτρόφησα (since Aristot., HA 9, 40, 14, 625b, 20 [of the bee]; IG XII, 5, 655, 8 [II/III AD]; SEG XXVII, 948a, 5f [Christ. VI AD) ***bring up children,*** i.e. care for them physically and spiritually (Epict. 1, 23, 3 after Epicurus) **1 Ti 5:10.**—New Docs 2, 194. DELG s.v. τρέφω. M-M.

τεκνόω 1 aor. ἐτέκνωσα (Just.); aor. pass. subj. τεκνωθῶ Gen 16:2 Sym. (Hes., fgm. 138 R.; trag.; Phalaris, Ep. 103, 2) commonly of the man in the sense 'beget' (ISmyrna I [IK 23] 541, 4; Plut., Pericl. 165 [24, 10]; En 15:5; Jos., Ant. 1, 150; 2, 213; Just.), but also, and only so in our lit., of the woman ***bear (a child)*** (Jos., Ant. 4, 255) in **Hb 11:11 v.l.**—DELG s.v. τίκτω A. Frisk s.v. τέκνον.

τέκτων, ονος, ὁ (cp. τέχνη; Hom. et al.; pap, LXX; Jos., Ant. 15, 390; SibOr 5, 404; Ath., R. 9 p. 57, 28) **one who constructs,** ***builder, carpenter*** (Hom.+; SEG XXVIII, 1186 'worker in wood, carpenter, joiner'. Acc. to Maximus Tyr. 15, 3c, a τ. makes ἄροτρα; Just., D. 88, 8, states that Joseph made ἄροτρα καὶ ζυγά 'plows and yokes'; acc. to Epict. 1, 15, 2 a τ. works w. wood, in contrast to a worker in bronze; for the latter, less freq., Eur., Alc. 5; in Ael. Aristid. 46 p. 211 D. τέκτων signifies worker in stone. GJs 9:3 al. Joseph's work is οἰκοδομῆσαι τὰς οἰκοδομάς; the word. τ. is not used.—CMcCown, ὁ τέκτων: Studies in Early Christ., ed. SCase 1928, 173–89). In **Mt 13:55** Jesus is called ὁ τοῦ τέκτονος υἱός, in **Mk 6:3** ὁ τέκτων (cp. Just., D. 88, 8=ASyn. 18, 55f; the difference may perh. be explained on the basis of a similar one having to do with Sophillus, the father of Sophocles: Aristoxenus, fgm. 115 calls him τέκτων, but the Vita Sophoclis 1 [=OxfT. of Soph., ed. Pearson p. xviii; not printed in NWilson's ed. '90] rejects this and will admit only that he may possibly have possessed τέκτονες as slaves. Considerations of social status may have something to do with the variation in the gospel tradition).—HHöpfl, Nonne hic est fabri filius?: Biblica 4, 1923, 41–55; ELombard, Charpentier ou maçon: RTP '48, 4; EStauffer, Jeschua ben Mirjam (Mk 6:3): MBlack Festschr., '69, 119–28; RBatey, NTS 30, '84, 249–58.—B. 589. BHHW III 2341. DELG. M-M. EDNT.

τέλειος, α, ον (Hom. [e.g. Il. 24, 34 of unblemished sacrificial animals] +) gener. 'attaining an end or purpose, complete'.

❶ **pert. to meeting the highest standard**—ⓐ of things, ***perfect***—α. as acme of goodness, as adj. (ἀρετή Did., Gen. 40, 19.—Of aeons, Iren. 1, 1, 1 [Harv. I 8, 2]; Hippol., Ref. 6, 31, 4) ἔργον **Js 1:4a** (s. ἔργον lb); cp. ISm 11:2. δώρημα **Js 1:17** (s. δώρημα). νόμος vs. **25** (opp. the Mosaic law). ἀγάπη **1J 4:18.** ἀνάλυσις 1 Cl 44:5 (Just., D. 41, 1). γνῶσις 1:2; B 1:5. πρόγνωσις 1 Cl 44:2. μνεία 56:1. ἐλπίς ISm 10:2 (v.l. πίστις); χάρις 11:1. νηστεία Hs 5, 3, 6. ναός B 4:11 (ἐκκλησία Did., Gen. 69, 14). τελειοτέρα σκηνή (s. σκηνή 2) **Hb 9:11.**—Subst. τὸ τέλειον *what is perfect* **Ro 12:2;** perh. **1 Cor 13:10** (opp. ἐκ μέρους. S. EHoffmann, ConNeot 3, '38, 28–31). ἐνάρετον καὶ τέλειον *(someth.) virtuous and perfect* IPhld 1:2. W. gen. τὸ τέλειον τῆς γνώσεως ἡμῶν *the full measure of our knowledge* B 13:7. Pl. (Philo) τέλεια *what is perfect* ISm 11:3b (Tat. 13, 2 τὰ τέλεια).

β. as acme of badness (ApcSed 14:7 ἀπόγνωστοι τὴν τελείαν ἀπόγνωσιν), adj. ἁμαρτίαι B 8:1; Hv 1, 2, 1. σκάνδαλον B 4:3.—Subst. τὸ τέλειον τῶν ἁμαρτιῶν *the full measure of the sins* 5:11.

ⓑ of persons who are fully up to standard in a certain respect and not satisfied with half-way measures ***perfect, complete, expert*** (TAM II/1, 147, 4f ἰατρὸς τέλειος; ZPE 3, '68, 86: Didymus fgm. 281, 7 τέλειος γεώμετρος; Wsd 9:6; 1 Ch 25:8) τέλειος ἀθλητής IPol 1:3. Esther is τελεία κατὰ πίστιν 1 Cl 55:6. Jesus became τέλειος ἄνθρωπος *perfect human* ISm 4:2.

❷ **pert. to being mature,** ***full-grown, mature, adult*** (Aeschyl., Pla., X.+; oft. pap; Philo; Jos., Ant. 19, 362).—ⓐ adj. ἀνὴρ τέλειος **Eph 4:13** (opp. νήπιοι, as Polyb. 5, 29, 2; Philo, Leg. All. 1, 94, Sobr. 9 νήπιον παιδίον πρὸς ἄνδρα τέλειον=an immature child compared to a mature man, Somn. 2, 10). In dazzling wordplay: μὴ παιδία γίνεσθε ταῖς φρεσίν, ἀλλὰ τῇ κακίᾳ νηπιάζετε, ταῖς δὲ φρεσὶν τέλειοι γίνεσθε *do not think like children, yet do be infants as respects evil, while at the same time grown-up in your thinking* **1 Cor 14:20.**

ⓑ subst. (Dio Chrys. 34 [51], 8 οἱ τ.; Diogenes, Ep. 31, 3 οἱ τ. . . . οἱ παῖδες; Ath., R. 17 p. 68, 31) τελείων ἐστὶν ἡ στερεὰ τροφή *solid food is* (only) *for adults* **Hb 5:14** (opp. νήπιος). οἱ τέλειοι **1 Cor 2:6** is contrasted with νήπιοι 3:1 by WBauer, Mündige u. Unmündige bei dem Ap. Paulus, diss. Marburg 1902 (also Aufsätze u. Kleine Schriften, ed. GStrecker, '67, 124–30 et al.; s. also GDelling, TW VIII 76–78.) But this may also belong in the next classification

❸ **pert. to being a cult initiate,** ***initiated.*** As a t.t. of the mystery religions, τέλειος refers to one initiated into mystic rites (τελετή; s. τελειόω 3; cp. Herm. Wr. 4, 4; Philod., Περὶ θεῶν

1, 24, 12 [ed. HDiels, ABA 1915 p. 41; 93]; Iambl., Myst. 3, 7 p. 114 Parthey; Philo, Somn. 2, 234; Gnostics [WBousset, Kyrios Christos[2] 1921 p. 197, 1].—Rtzst., Mysterienrel.[3] 133f; 338f; JWeiss, exc. after 1 Cor 3:3, also p. xviiif, Das Urchristentum 1917, 492; HKennedy, St. Paul and the Mystery Religions 1913, 130ff; Clemen[2] 314; in general, CZijerveld, Τελετή, Bijdrage tot de kennis der religieuze terminologie in het Grieksch '34). **Phil 3:15** and **Col 1:28** prob. belong here (s. MDibelius, Hdb. on both passages. οἱ ὡς ἐν χριστιανισμῷ τ. Orig., C. Cels. 3, 19, 13).—CGuignebert, Quelques remarques sur la Perfection (τελείωσις) et ses voies dans le mystère paulinien: RHPR 8, 1928, 412–29; UWilckens, Weisheit u. Torheit, '59, 53–60 supports Reitzenstein against Bauer.

❹ **pert. to being fully developed in a moral sense—ⓐ** of humans ***perfect, fully developed*** (Hippol., Ref. 1, 19, 16) in a moral sense τέλειος ἀνήρ **Js 3:2** (s. RHöistad, ConNeot 9, '44, p. 22f). τὸν τέλειον ἄνθρωπον GMary 463, 26f (restored). Mostly without a noun εἰ θέλεις τέλειος εἶναι **Mt 19:21** (EYarnold, TU 102, '68, 269–73). Cp. IEph 15:2; D 1:4; 6:2. Pl. **Mt 5:48a;** ISm 11:3a. W. ὁλόκληροι **Js 1:4b.** W. πεπληροφορημένοι **Col 4:12.**

ⓑ of God ***perfect*** (Pind., Aeschyl. et al.; Theocr., Diod. S., Plut. et al.; Tat.4, 2, 12; 4, 15, 2; Theoph. Ant. 2, 15 [p. 138, 12]) **Mt 5:48b** (i.e. God is a role model for unlimited display of beneficence; cp. on this verse Hierocles 18 p. 459: the goal is τὴν πρὸς θεὸν ὁμοίωσιν κτήσασθαι 'attainment of likeness to God' [oft. in Hierocles]; Marinus, Vi. Procli 18 ἵνα τὴν ὁμοίωσιν ἔχῃ πρὸς τὸν θεόν, ὅπερ τέλος ἐστὶ τὸ ἄριστον τῆς ψυχῆς; Betz, SM ad loc.). Restoration in a corrupt context AcPl Ha 1, 11 (ed. indicates τελέσαι or τελεῖν as alternatives).—RFlew, The Idea of Perfection '34; FGrant, The Earliest Gospel, '43; EFuchs, RBultmann Festschr., '54 (Beih. ZNW 21), 130–36; PDuPlessis, Teleios. The Idea of Perfection in the NT '59; KPrümm, Das NTliche Sprach- u. Begriffsproblem der Vollkommenheit, Biblica 44, '63, 76–92; AWikgren, Patterns of Perfection in Hb, NTS 6, '60, 159–67.—Schmidt, Syn. IV 503f. DELG s.v. τέλος. M-M. EDNT. TW. Sv.

τελειότης, ητος, ἡ (τέλειος) ***perfection, completeness*** (Ps.-Pla., Def. 412b; Epict. 1, 4, 4; M. Ant. 5, 15, 2; PGM 7, 778; Wsd 6:15; 12:17; Philo; Iren. 1, 7, 5 [Harv. I 65, 7]) of love in its perfection 1 Cl 50:1; 53:5. Of ***maturity*** in contrast to the stage of elementary knowledge **Hb 6:1.**—On σύνδεσμος τῆς τελειότητος **Col 3:14** s. σύνδεσμος 2.—DELG s.v. τέλος. M-M. TW. Sv.

τελειόω (τέλειος) fut. τελειώσω; 1 aor. ἐτελείωσα; perf. τετελείωκα. Pass.: pf. τετελείωμαι; 1 fut. τελειωθήσομαι; 1 aor. ἐτελειώθην; pf. τετελείωμαι (Soph., Hdt.+; ins, pap, LXX; TestAbr A 15 p. 95, 7 [Stone p. 38]; TestGad 7:1; EpArist, Philo; Jos., Vi. 12 al.; Ath., R. 17 p. 69, 10. The form τελεόω, freq. used outside our lit., occurs only **Hb 10:1 v.l.**—B-D-F §30, 2; Thackeray p. 82).

❶ **to complete an activity, *complete, bring to an end, finish, accomplish*** (Dionys. Hal. 3, 69, 2 τῆς οἰκοδομῆς τὰ πολλὰ εἰργάσατο, οὐ μὴν ἐτελείωσε τὸ ἔργον; Polyb. 8, 36, 2; 2 Ch 8:16; 2 Esdr 16: 3, 16) τὸ ἔργον **J 4:34; 17:4;** pl. **5:36.** πάντα 1 Cl 33:6. ὡς τελειώσω τὸν δρόμον μου καὶ τὴν διακονίαν **Ac 20:24.** ἁγνῶς τελειοῦν τὴν διακονίαν *complete service as deacon in holiness* Hs 9, 26, 2. τὰς ἡμέρας *spend all the days* of the festival **Lk 2:43** (cp. Jos., Ant. 3, 201). Pass. ἵνα τελειωθῇ ἡ γραφή *in order that the scripture might receive its final fulfillment* **J 19:28** (perh. this belongs to 2c.)—τελειῶσαί τινα *allow someone to reach the person's goal* (Hdt. 3, 86) pass. τῇ τρίτῃ τελειοῦμαι *on the third day I will reach my goal* **Lk 13:32** (hardly mid., 'bring to a close' [Iambl., Vi. Pyth. 158] w. 'my work' to be supplied. But s. 2d below and cp. JDerrett, ZNW 75, '84, 36–43 [wordplay involving death]).—This may also be the place for **Hb 7:19** (s. 2eα below); **11:40** (s. 2d below).

❷ **to overcome or supplant an imperfect state of things by one that is free fr. objection, *bring to an end, bring to its goal/accomplishment***

ⓐ of Jesus ἔπρεπεν αὐτῷ (i.e. τῷ θεῷ) διὰ παθημάτων τελειῶσαι (Ἰησοῦν) **Hb 2:10** (i.e., as the context indicates, he receives highest honors via suffering and death in his identification w. humanity); pass., **5:9; 7:28.** This is usu. understood to mean the ***completion*** and ***perfection*** of Jesus by the overcoming of earthly limitations (s. Windisch, Hdb. exc. on Hb 5:9.—JKögel, Der Begriff τελειοῦν im Hb: MKähler Festschr. 1905, 35–68; OMichel, D. Lehre von d. christl. Vollkommenheit nach d. Anschauung des Hb: StKr 106, '35, 333–55; FTorm, Om τελειοῦν i Hb: Sv. Ex. Årsb. 5, '40, 116–25; OMoe, TZ 5, '49, 165ff). S. 3 below.

ⓑ ***bring to full measure, fill the measure of*** τὶ *someth.* τὰς ἀποκαλύψεις καὶ τὰ ὁράματα Hv 4, 1, 3. ἐτελείωσαν κατὰ τῆς κεφαλῆς αὐτῶν τὰ ἁμαρτήματα GPt 5:17 (κατά A 2bγ).

ⓒ ***fulfill*** of prophecies, promises, etc., which arouse expectation of events or happenings that correspond to their wording (τελείωσις 2.—Jos., Ant. 15, 4 θεοῦ τοὺς λόγους τελειώσαντος; Artem. 4, 47 p. 228, 19 ἐλπίδας) ἡ πίστις πάντα ἐπαγγέλλεται, πάντα τελειοῖ Hm 9:10; pass. *be fulfilled* ἐξαίφνης τελειωθήσεται τὸ βούλημα αὐτοῦ 1 Cl 23:5.—MPol 16:2ab. The promises of the prophets find their fulfillment, by implication, in the gospel ISm 7:2. This may be the place for **J 19:28** (so Bultmann.—S. 1 above).

ⓓ of the ***perfection*** of upright pers. who have gone on before, pass. (Wsd 4:13; Philo, Leg. All. 3, 74 ὅταν τελειωθῇς καὶ βραβείων καὶ στεφάνων ἀξιωθῇς) πνεύματα δικαίων τετελειωμένων **Hb 12:23.** So perh. also **11:40** and **Lk 13:32** (s. 1 above).

ⓔ ***make perfect*—α.** *someone* ὁ νόμος οὐδέποτε δύναται τοὺς προσερχομένους τελειῶσαι **Hb 10:1;** likew. perh. (s. 1 above) **7:19** (then οὐδέν would refer to humanity). κατὰ συνείδησιν τελειῶσαι τὸν λατρεύοντα **9:9.** Perh. **10:14** (s. 3 below). Pass. in act. sense *become perfect* (Zosimus: Hermet. IV p. 111, 15f) D 16:2; ἔν τινι in someth. (Jos., Ant. 16, 6) ἐν (τῇ) ἀγάπῃ **1J 4:18;** 1 Cl 49:5; 50:3. W. inf. foll. B 6:19. ἵνα ὦσιν τετελειωμένοι εἰς ἕν *in order that they might attain perfect unity* **J 17:23.**—Also in an unfavorable sense τελειωθῆναι τοῖς ἁμαρτήμασιν B 14:5.—For **Phil 3:12** s. 3 below.

β. *someth.* The Lord is called upon, in the interest of his community τελειῶσαι αὐτὴν ἐν τῇ ἀγάπῃ σου D 10:5. Pass. (Philo, Somn. 1, 131 ψυχὴ τελειωθεῖσα ἐν ἄθλοις ἀρετῶν) ἐκ τῶν ἔργων ἡ πίστις ἐτελειώθη *faith was perfected in good deeds* **Js 2:22.** Of love **1J 2:5; 4:12, 17.** Cp. **2 Cor 12:9 v.l.**

❸ As a term of mystery religions ***consecrate, initiate,*** pass. *be consecrated, become a* τέλειος (s. τέλειος 3) **Phil 3:12** (though mng. 2eα is also prob.). Some of the **Hb-passages** (s. 2a; eα above) may belong here, esp. those in which a *consecration* of Jesus is mentioned **2:10; 5:9; 7:28** (s. THaering, Monatschr. für Pastoraltheol. 17, 1921, 264–75. Against him ERiggenbach, NKZ 34, 1923, 184–95 and Haering once more, ibid. 386–89.—EKaesemann, D. wand. Gottesvolk '39, 82–90; GAvdBerghvEysinga, De Brief aan de Hebreën en de oudchristelijke Gnosis: NThT 28, '39, 301–30).—DELG s.v. τέλος. M-M. EDNT. TW.

τελείως adv. of τέλειος (this form in Isocr. 13, 18; Ps.-Pla., Def. 411d; Aristot. et al.; Polyb. 6, 24, 7; Hero Alex. I p. 20,

25; PPetr III, 42 H 8c, 3 p. 114 [III BC]; PFlor 93, 27; LXX [Thackeray p. 82]; TestSol 26, 7 B and 8 B; TestAbr B 7 p. 112, 5 [Stone p. 72]; TestGad 7:1; Philo; Ath. 26:2 ὁ θεὸς τελείως ἀγαθὸς ὤν) ***fully, perfectly, completely, altogether*** ἔχειν τὴν πίστιν IEph 14:1. ἐλπίζειν **1 Pt 1:13.** Of dedicated service τ. λειτουργεῖν *perform superbly*1 Cl 9:2. φεύγειν B 4:1. μισεῖν τι 4:10. φανεροῦσθαι Dg 9:2. ἔργον ἀπαρτίζειν IEph 1:1. ἀπαρνεῖσθαι ISm 5:2. ἔχειν τελείως περί τινος *have received full enlightenment concerning someth.*—B 10:10.—M-M.

τελείωσις, εως, ἡ (τελειόω; since Hippocr. VII 436; 448 L.; Epicurus p. 38, 5 Us.; Aristot.; ins, pap, LXX, En; TestAbr A 20 p. 103, 24 [Stone p. 54]; TestReub 6:8; EpArist; Philo, Aet. M. 71; 99; Jos., Ant. 19, 199 in a different sense; Ar. [Milne 76, 48]; Ath., R. 17 p. 69, 9)

❶ ***perfection*** (En 25, 4; Ar., Ath.) **Hb 7:11.**

❷ ***fulfillment*** of a promise (Jdth 10:9; Philo, Mos. 2, 288.—τελειόω 2c) **Lk 1:45.**—DELG s.v. τέλος. M-M. TW.

τελειωτής, οῦ, ὁ (τελειόω; Dionys. Hal., Dinarchus 1; otherwise only in Christ. wr. Methodius MPG XVIII, 360b; on morphology Schwyzer I 500) **one who brings someth. to a successful conclusion, *perfecter*** (opp. ἀρχηγός, q.v. 3; Jesus is both) τῆς πίστεως **Hb 12:2** (AWikgren, NTS 6, '60, 159–67; NCroy, JBL 114, '95, 117–19='one not to be transcended by subsequent improvements').—DELG s.v. τέλος.

τέλεον neut. acc. sing. of τέλεος (=τέλειος; cp. SibOr 3, 117) used as an adv. (Περὶ ὕψους 41, 1; Ael. Aristid. 33 p. 635 D.; Lucian, Merc. Cond. 5; Appian, Bell. Civ. 1, 8 §34; BGU 903, 12 [II AD]; PFay 106, 21; 3 Macc 1:22; JosAs. 12:11 cod. A [p. 56, 14 Bat.]; Jos., Bell. 4, 285) **pert. to being at the end of a process, *fully, altogether, in the end*** Dg 2:5.

τελεσφορέω (τέλος, φέρω; Theophr. et al.; 4 Macc 13:20; Philo; Jos., Ant. 1, 140) ***bear fruit to maturity*** (Jülicher, Gleichn. 530.—Cp. Ocellus Luc. [II BC] c. 16 Harder [1926]; Epict. 4, 8, 36) **Lk 8:14, 15 v.l.**—M-M.

τελευταῖος, α, ον (Aeschyl., Hdt. +) **pert. to closure in a series, *final, last,*** as concluding point in time τελευταία ἡμέρα (Demosth. et al.; Epict. 2, 23, 21; IG IV² 1, 123, 128 [IV BC] ἐν ταῖς τελευταίαις ἁμέραις) τῶν ἀζύμων GPt 14:58.—Schmidt, Syn. IV 524–34, cp. ἔσχατος. DELG s.v. τέλος.

τελευτάω (τελευτή; Hom. et al.) fut. τελευτήσω; 1 aor. ἐτελεύτησα; perf. 3 sg. τετελεύτηκεν Josh 1:2, ptc. τετελευτηκώς; in our lit. only intr.

❶ ***come to an end*** (Aeschyl. et al.) Papias (4), s. συμβαίνω 2.

❷ ***die*** (Aeschyl., Hdt. et al.—B-D-F §480, 2) **Mt 2:19** (cp. GJs 25:1); **9:18; 22:25; Lk 7:2; J 11:39; Ac 2:29; 7:15; Hb 11:22;** 1 Cl 39:6 (Job 4:21 v.l.); Papias (3:3). Of the phoenix 1 Cl 25:2f. As in Is 66:24 of the worm in hell: **Mk 9:43 (44)** and **45 (46)** both **v.l.; 48;** 2 Cl 7:6; 17:5. θανάτῳ τελευτάτω *let the pers. die the death = surely die* (=מוֹת יוּמָת Ex 21:17 MT; JosAs cod. A ch. 21 [p. 71, 28 Bat., also Pal. 364]. But s. also schol. on Soph., Ajax 516 p. 46 τελευτᾶν θανάτῳ) **Mt 15:4** (cp. Ex 21:16); **Mk 7:10.**—DELG s.v. τέλος. M-M.

τελευτή, ῆς, ἡ (Hom. et al. in var. senses: 'completion, issue, end') **that which marks the point at which someth. ceases to exist, *end,*** a euphemism for ***death*** (s. prec. entry; Pind., Thu. 11:7 et al.; pap, LXX; TestAbr B 10 p. 115, 5 [Stone p. 78]; Test12Patr; ApcMos 5; SibOr 3:363; Jos., Ant. 8, 190; Just., D. 47, 3; Tat. 6, 1; Ath., R. p. 61, 19, W. βιότοιο as early as Il. 7, 104) **Mt 2:15.**—DELG s.v. τέλος. M-M.

τελέω fut. τελέσω; 1 aor. ἐτέλεσα; pf. τετέλεκα. Pass.: 1 fut. τελεσθήσομαι; 1 aor. ἐτελέσθην; perf. τετέλεσμαι (Hom.+).

❶ **to complete an activity or process, *bring to an end, finish, complete*** τὶ *someth.* ταῦτα Hs 8, 2, 5. τὸν δρόμον (Il. 23, 373; 768; Soph., El. 726) **2 Ti 4:7.** τοὺς λόγους τούτους **Mt 7:28; 19:1; 26:1** (cp. Just., D. 110, 1). τὰς παραβολὰς ταύτας **13:53.** τὴν μαρτυρίαν **Rv 11:7.** τὴν εὐχήν GJs 9:1. τὴν ἐξήγησιν Hv 3, 7, 4. τὰ γράμματα 2, 1, 4. τελέσας τὴν χαράκωσιν *when he had finished the fencing* Hs 5, 2, 3. τελεῖν πάντα τὰ κατὰ τὸν νόμον **Lk 2:39** (τελ. πάντα as Jos., Ant. 16, 318). τελ. τὰς πόλεις τοῦ Ἰσραήλ *finish (going through) the cities of Israel* **Mt 10:23** (on this pass. KWeiss, Exegetisches z. Irrtumslosigkeit u. Eschatologie Jesu Christi 1916, 184–99; JDupont, NovT 2, '58, 228–44; AFeuillet, CBQ 23, '61, 182–98; MKünzi, Das Naherwartungslogion Mt 10:23, '70 [history of interp.]). Foll. by a ptc. to designate what is finished (B-D-F §414, 2; Rob. 1121; cp. Josh 3:17; JosAs 15:12) ἐτέλεσεν διατάσσων **Mt 11:1.** Cp. **Lk 7:1** D; Hv 1, 4, 1.—Pass. *be brought to an end, be finished, completed* of the building of the tower (cp. 2 Esdr 5:16; 16: 15) Hv 3, 4, 1f; 3, 5, 5; 3, 9, 5; s 9, 5, 1; 9, 10, 2 (τὸ ἔργον). τελεσθέντος τοῦ δείπνου GJs 6:3 (TestAbr A 5 p. 81, 32 [Stone p. 10]; JosAs 21:8). ὡς . . . ἐτελέσθη ὁ πλοῦς AcPl Ha 7, 35. Of time *come to an end, be over* (Hom. et al.; Aristot., HA 7, 1, 580a, 14 ἐν τοῖς ἔτεσι τοῖς δὶς ἑπτὰ τετελεσμένοις; Lucian, Alex. 38) **Lk 2:6** D; sim. τοῦ ἐξεῖναι τὸν Παῦλον εἰς τὴν Ῥώμην AcPl Ha 6, 15; τὰ χίλια ἔτη **Rv 20:3, 5, 7.** πάντα τετέλεσται **J 19:28** (GDalman, Jesus-Jeschua 1922, 211–18 [tr. PLevertoff 1929, same pages].—Diagoras of Melos in Sext. Emp., Adv. Math. 9, 55 κατὰ δαίμονα κ. τύχην πάντα τελεῖται='everything is accomplished acc. to divine will and fortune'; an anonymous writer of mimes [II AD] in OCrusius, Herondas[5] [p. 110–16] ln. 175 τοῦτο τετέλεσται); cp. τετέλεσται used absolutely in vs. **30** (if these two verses are to be taken as referring to the carrying out [s. 2 below] of divine ordinances contained in the Scriptures, cp. Diod. S. 20, 26, 2 τετελέσθαι τὸν χρησμόν=the oracle had been fulfilled; Ael. Aristid. 48, 7 K.=24 p. 467 D.: μέγας ὁ Ἀσκληπιός· τετέλεσται τὸ πρόσταγμα. Cp. Willibald Schmidt, De Ultimis Morientium Verbis, diss. Marburg 1914. OCullmann, TZ 4, '48, 370 interprets the two verses in both a chronological and theol. sense. Diod. S. 15, 87, 6 reports the four last sayings of Epaminondas, two in indirect discourse and the other two in direct. S. also the last words of Philip s.v. πληρόω 5).—ἡ δύναμις ἐν ἀσθενείᾳ τελεῖται *power finds its consummation* or *reaches perfection in* (the presence of) *weakness* **2 Cor 12:9.** The passives in **Rv 10:7** (the aor. suggests the 'final clearing up of all the insoluble riddles and problems of human life': EBlakeney, The Epistle to Diognetus '43, '67); **15:1, 8; 17:17** belong under 2 as well as here.

❷ **to carry out an obligation or demand, *carry out, accomplish, perform, fulfill, keep*** τὶ *someth.* (Hom.+. Of rites, games, processions, etc., dedicated to a divinity or ordained by it: Eur., Bacch. 474 τὰ ἱερά; Pla., Laws 775a; X., Resp. Lac. 13, 5; Plut., Mor. 671 al.; Just., A II, 12, 5 μυστήρια; Mel., P. 16, 102 μυστήριον al.; in ins freq. of public service, e.g. IPriene 111, 22 an embassy) τὸν νόμον *carry out the demands of, keep the law* **Ro 2:27; Js 2:8.** τὴν ἐντολήν Hs 5, 2, 4 (Jos., Bell. 2, 495 τὰς ἐντολάς). τὸ ἔργον (Theogn. 914; Apollon. Rhod. 4, 742; Sir 7:25) 2:7a; 5, 2, 7. τὴν διακονίαν m 2:6ab; 12, 3, 3; s 2:7b; pass. m 2:6c. τὰς διακονίας s 1:9. τὴν νηστείαν 5, 1, 5; 5, 3, 8. ἐπιθυμίαν σαρκὸς τελεῖν *carry out what the flesh desires, satisfy one's physical desires* (Artem. 3, 22; Achilles Tat.

2, 13, 3 αὐτῷ τὴν ἐπιθυμίαν τελέσαι) **Gal 5:16.** ὡς ἐτέλεσαν πάντα τὰ περὶ αὐτοῦ γεγραμμένα *when they had carried out everything that was written* (in the Scriptures) *concerning him* **Ac 13:29** (Appian, Bell. Civ. 3, 59 §243 τὸ κεκριμένον τ.=carry out what was decided upon). Pass. **Lk 18:31; 22:37** (cp. pass. cited 1, end). ἕως ὅτου τελεσθῇ *until it* (the baptism) *is accomplished* **Lk 12:50.** ἵνα ὁ τύπος τελεσθῇ *in order that the type might be fulfilled* B 7:3.

❸ **to pay what is due,** *pay* (Hom., Pla., et al.; pap; Jos., Ant. 2, 192 al.) φόρους (Ps.-Pla., Alc. 1, 123a τὸν φόρον; Appian, Syr. 44 §231; PFay 36, 14 [111/12 AD]; Philo, Agr. 58; Jos., Ant. 15, 106; Just., A I, 17, 2 φόρους τελεῖν [Luke 20:22]; Tat. 4:1) **Ro 13:6.** τὰ δίδραχμα **Mt 17:24.** V.l. for τελευτάω Papias (4).—B. 797. DELG s.v. τέλος. M-M. EDNT. TW.

τέλος, ους, τό (Hom.+)—❶ **a point of time marking the end of a duration,** ***end, termination, cessation*** (Nicol. Dam.: 90 fgm. 130 §139 Jac. τέλος τ. Βίου Καίσαρος; TestAbr A 1 p. 78, 5 [Stone p. 4] τῆς ζωῆς; Maximus Tyr. 13, 9d ἀπιστίας) τῆς βασιλείας αὐτοῦ οὐκ ἔσται τέλος **Lk 1:33.** μήτε ἀρχὴν ἡμερῶν μήτε ζωῆς τέλος ἔχων **Hb 7:3.** τὸ τέλος τοῦ καταργουμένου *the end of the fading (splendor)* **2 Cor 3:13.** τέλος νόμου Χριστός **Ro 10:4** (perh. 3 below). πάντων τὸ τέλος ἤγγικεν *the end of all things is near* **1 Pt 4:7.** τὸ τ. Ἰερουσαλὴμ GPt 7:25. τὸ τέλος κυρίου **Js 5:11** is oft. (fr. Augustine to ABischoff, ZNW 7, 1906, 274–79) incorrectly taken to mean *the end*=the death (this is what τέλος means e.g. TestAbr A 4, p. 81, 14 [Stone p. 10]; Appian, Syr. 64 §342, Bell. Civ. 1, 107 §501; 3, 98 §408; Arrian, Anab. 3, 22, 2; 7, 24, 1) *of the Lord* Jesus (s. 3 below). τ̣ὸ̣ [τέλο]ς (or τ̣ε̣[λο]ς) τῶν φαινο[με]νων (Till's rdg. of Ox 1081, 29f after the Coptic SJCh 90, 6, in place of τ̣ὸ̣ [φῶ]ς τῶν φαινο[μέ]νων) *the end of the things that are apparent.* τέλος ἔχειν *have an end, be at an end* (X., An. 6, 5, 2; Pla., Phdr. 241d, Rep. 3, 392c; Diod. S. 14, 18, 8; 16, 91, 2) **Mk 3:26** (opp. στῆναι). The possibility of repenting ἔχει τέλος *is at an end* Hv 2, 2, 5. Of the consummation that comes to prophecies when they are fulfilled (Xenophon Eph. 5, 1, 13; Jos., Ant. 2, 73; 4, 125; 10, 35; SibOr 3, 211): revelations Hv 3, 3, 2. So perh. τὸ περὶ ἐμοῦ τέλος ἔχει *the references* (in the Scriptures) *to me are being fulfilled* **Lk 22:37;** also prob. is *my life's work is at an end* (cp. Diod. S. 20, 95, 1 τέλος ἔχειν of siege-machines, the construction of which entailed a great deal of hard work: *be completed;* Plut., Mor. 615e; Jos., Vi. 154).

❷ **the last part of a process,** ***close, conclusion,*** esp. of the last things, the final act in the cosmic drama (Sb 8422, 10 [7 BC] τοῦτο γάρ ἐστι τέλος; TestAbr A 13 p. 92, 19 [Stone p. 32] τῆς κρίσεως ἐκείνης τὸ τέλος; ApcEsdr 3:13 ἐγγύς ἐστιν τὸ τέλος; Iren., 1, 10, 3 [Harv. I 96, 8] περὶ τοῦ τ. καὶ τῶν μελλόντων)

ⓐ **Mt 24:6, 14; Mk 13:7; Lk 21:9;** PtK 2 p. 13, 22. Perh. **1 Cor 15:24,** if ἔσται is to be supplied w. εἶτα τὸ τέλος *then the end will come* (so JHéring, RHPR 12, '33, 300–320; s. below, bα and 4). ἔχει τέλος *the end is here* Hv 3, 8, 9. On τὰ τέλη τῶν αἰώνων **1 Cor 10:11** s. αἰών 2b and 5 below; also MBogle, ET 67, '56, 246f: τ.='mystery'.—PVolz, D. Eschatologie d. jüd. Gemeinde im ntl. Zeitalter '34; Bousset, Rel.[3] 202–301; EHaupt, Die eschatol. Aussagen Jesu in den synopt. Evangelien 1895; HSharman, The Teaching of Jesus about the Future acc. to the Synopt. Gospels 1909; FSpitta, Die grosse eschatol. Rede Jesu: StKr 82, 1909, 348–401; EvDobschütz, The Eschatology of the Gospels 1910, Zur Eschatol. der Ev.: StKr 84, 1911, 1–20; PCorssen, Das apokalypt. Flugblatt in der synopt. überl.: Wochenschr. für klass. Philol. 32, 1915, nos. 30f; 33f; DVölter, Die eschat. Rede Jesu: SchTZ 32, 1915, 180–202; KWeiss (s. τελέω 1); JWeiss, Das Urchristent. 1917, 60–98; JJeremias, Jesus als Weltvollender 1930; WKümmel, Die Eschatologie der Ev.: ThBl 15, '36, 225–41, Verheissg. u. Erfüllg. '45; CCadoux, The Historic Mission of Jesus '41 (eschat. of the synoptics); HPreisker, Das Ethos des Urchristentums '49; AStrobel, Untersuchungen zum eschat. Verzögerungsproblem, '61. Billerb. IV 799–976. S. also ἀνάστασις 2b, end.—In contrast to ἀρχή: B 1:6ab; IEph 14:1ab; IMg 13:1. Of God **Rv 1:8 v.l.; 21:6; 22:13** (Ar. 4, 2; Just., D. 7, 2; Mel., P. 105, 113f; s. also ἀρχή 2).

ⓑ adverbial expressions—**α.** adv. acc. τὸ τέλος ***finally*** (Pla. et al.; BGU 1024 VII, 23; B-D-F §160; s. Rob. 486–88; Theoph. Ant. 1, 14 [p. 92, 8].—The customary use in this case is τέλος without the art.: ViAm 1 [p. 81, 11 Sch.]) **1 Pt 3:8.** εἶτα τὸ τέλος **1 Cor 15:24** is classed here by Hofmann[2]; FBurkitt, JTS 17, 1916, 384f; KBarth, Die Auferstehung der Toten[2] 1926, 96 (s. 2a above and 4 below).

β. ***to the end, to the last:*** ἄχρι τέλους **Hb 6:11; Rv 2:26;** ἕως τέλους (Da 6:27 Theod.; JosAs 12:3) **1 Cor 1:8; 2 Cor 1:13** (here, too, it means *to the end*=until the parousia [Windisch, Sickenberger, NRSV] rather than 'fully' [Ltzm., Hdb.; RSV '46]); Hs 9, 27, 3; μέχρι τέλους (Phocylides [VI BC] 17 Diehl[3] ἐξ ἀρχῆς μέχρι τέλους; Chariton 4, 7, 8; Appian, Mithrid. 112 §550; Polyaenus 4, 6, 11; POxy 416, 3; PTebt 420, 18; Wsd 16:5; 19:1; Jos., Vi. 406) **Hb 3:6 v.l., 14;** Dg 10:7. S. also εἰς τέλος (γ below).

γ. εἰς τέλος ***in the end, finally*** (Hdt. 3, 40 et al.; PTebt 38, 11 [113 BC]; 49, 12; Gen 46:4; GrBar 13:2; Ps.-Clem., Hom. 18, 2) **Lk 18:5.** σωθῆναι 2 Cl 19:3.—*To the end, until the end* (Epict. 1, 7, 17; Jos., Ant. 19, 96; JosAs 23:5) **Mt 10:22; 24:13; Mk 13:13;** IEph 14:2; IRo 10:3.—*Forever, through all eternity* (Dionys. Hal. 13, 88, 3; Ps 9:19; 76:9; 1 Ch 28:9; Da 3:34) ἔφθασεν ἐπ' αὐτοὺς ἡ ὀργὴ εἰς τέλος **1 Th 2:16** (s. also below and cp. TestLevi 6:11, concerning which there is a variety of opinion). εἰς τέλος ἀπολέσαι τὴν ζωήν *lose one's life forever* Hs 8, 8, 5b.—*Decisively, extremely, fully, altogether* (Polyb. 1, 20, 7; 10; 12, 27, 3 and oft.; Diod. S. 18, 57, 1 ταπεινωθέντες εἰς τ.=ruined utterly; Lucian, Philop. 14; Appian, Bell. Mithr. 44 §174; OGI 90, 12 [II BC]; PTebt 38, 11 [II BC]; 49, 11; 793 [s. οὗς 1]; Josh 8:24; 2 Ch 12:12; Ps 73:1; Job 6:9; PsSol 1:1; TestAbr A 13 p. 92, 23 [Stone p. 32]; ApcMos 19; Jos., Vi. 24; Just., A I, 44, 12; Diodorus on Ps 51:7: MPG 33, 1589b εἰς τέλος τουτέστι παντελῶς) **1 Th 2:16** (*forever* is also prob.; s. above); B 4:7; 10:5; 19:11. ἱλαρὰ εἰς τέλος ἦν *she was quite cheerful* Hv 3, 10, 5. Cp. 3, 7, 2; m 12, 2, 3; s 6, 2, 3; 8, 6, 4; 8, 8, 2; 5a; 8, 9, 3; 9, 14, 2.—For εἰς τέλος ἠγάπησεν αὐτούς **J 13:1** s. εἰς 3.

δ. ἐν τέλει *at the end* (opp. πρὸ αἰώνων) IMg 6:1.

❸ **the goal toward which a movement is being directed,** ***end, goal, outcome*** (Dio Chrys. 67 [17], 3; Epict. 1, 30, 4; 3, 24, 7; Maximus Tyr. 20, 3b; Jos., Ant. 9, 73; TestAsh 1:3; ἡ θεία παίδευσις καὶ εἰσαγωγὴν ἔχει καὶ προκοπὴν καὶ τ. Did., Gen. 69, 9) **Mt 26:58.** τὸ τέλος κυρίου *the outcome which the Lord brought about* in the case of Job's trials **Js 5:11** (Diod. S. 20, 13, 3 τὸ δαιμόνιον τοῖς ὑπερηφάνως διαλογιζομένοις τὸ τέλος τῶν κατελπισθέντων εἰς τοὐναντίον μετατίθησιν=the divinity, in the case of the arrogant, turns the outcome of what they hoped for to the opposite.—On **Js 5:11** s. 1 above). τὸ τέλος τῆς παραγγελίας ἐστὶν ἀγάπη *the instruction has love as its aim* **1 Ti 1:5** (Ἐπίκουρος . . . λέγων τὸ τ. τῆς σοφίας εἶναι ἡδονήν Hippol., Ref. 1, 22, 4. τ.='goal' or 'purpose': Epict. 1, 20, 15; 4, 8, 12; Diog. L. 2, 87; Just., D. 2, 6). Perh. this is the place for **Ro 10:4,** in the sense that Christ is the goal and the termination of the law at the same time, somewhat in the sense of Gal 3:24f (schol. on Pla., Leg. 625d τέλος τῶν νόμων=goal of the laws;

Plut., Mor. 780e δίκη . . . νόμου τέλος ἐστί; FFlückiger, TZ 11, '55, 153–57; difft. RJewett, Int 39, '85, 341–56, Christ as goal but without repudiation of the law; cp. SBechtler, CBQ 56, '94, 288–308); s. 1.—Esp. also of the final *goal* toward which pers. and things are striving, of the *outcome* or *destiny* which awaits them in accordance w. their nature (TestAsh 6:4; Philo, Exs. 162, Virt. 182; Just., A II, 3, 7; Ath., R. 24 p. 77, 19; Aelian, VH 3, 43; Alciphron 4, 7, 8; Procop. Soph., Ep. 154; τὸ τ. ὁρόμου Orig., C. Cels. 7, 52, 6) τὸ τέλος ἐκείνων θάνατος . . . τὸ τέλος ζωὴν αἰώνιον **Ro 6:21f.** Cp. **2 Cor 11:15; Phil 3:19** (HKoester, NTS 8, '61/62, 325f): perh. a play on a mystery term; **1 Pt 4:17** (cp. 2 Macc 7:30–38); **Hb 6:8.** κομιζόμενοι τὸ τέλος τῆς πίστεως **1 Pt 1:9.** τέλος τὰ πράγματα ἔχει *all things have a goal* or *final destiny* (i.e. death or life) IMg 5:1 (τέλος ἔχειν as Plut., Mor. 382e; Polyaenus 4, 2, 11 τέλος οὐκ ἔσχεν ἡ πρᾶξις=did not reach its goal; Jos., C. Ap. 2, 181, Ant. 17, 185.—Ael. Aristid. 52 p. 597 D.: τὸ τέλος πάντων πραγμάτων). εἰς τέλος εἶναι *be at = reach the goal* IRo 1:1 (εἰς for ἐν; s. εἰς 1aδ).

❹ **last in a series,** ***rest, remainder*** (Aristot. De Gen. Anim. 1, 18 p. 725b, 8; Is 19:15. Of a military formation Arrian, Tact. 10, 5; 18, 4), if τὸ τέλος **1 Cor 15:24** is to be taken, w. JWeiss and Ltzm., of a third and last group (τάγμα 1b; s. 2a and 2bα above).

❺ **revenue obligation,** ***(indirect) tax, toll-tax, customs duties*** (X., Pla. et al.; ins, pap; 1 Macc 10:31; 11:35; Jos., Ant. 12, 141) ἀποδιδόναι τὸ τέλος **Ro 13:7b;** cp. **a** (w. φόρος as Appian, Sicil. 2, 6, Bell. Civ. 2, 13 §47; Vi. Aesopi W 92; Ps.-Clem., Hom. 10, 22. Pl. w. εἰσφοραί Theoph. Ant. 1, 10 [p. 80, 19]). λαμβάνειν τέλη ἀπό τινος **Mt 17:25** (w. κῆνσος; Just., A I, 27, 2).—τὰ τέλη τ. αἰώνων **1 Cor 10:11** is transl. *the* (spiritual) *revenues of the ages* by ASouter (Pocket Lex. of the NT 1916, s.v. τέλος) and PMacpherson, ET 55, '43/44, 222 (s. 2a above).—GDelling, TW VIII, 50–88: τέλος and related words, also ZNW 55, '64, 26–42=Studien zum NT, '70, 17–31.—B. 802; 979. Schmidt, Syn. IV 496–523. DELG. M-M. EDNT. TW. Sv.

τελωνεῖον s. τελώνιον.

τελώνης, ου, ὁ (τέλος, ὠνέομαι or the related noun ὠνή 'buying, purchasing'; Aristoph., Aeschin. et al.; ins, pap, ostraca) ***tax-collector, revenue officer*** (cp. τέλος 5; Goodsp., Probs. 28; on the semantic range of τελώνης s. New Docs 5, 103; cp. JVergote, Eos 48, '56, 149–60, s. p. 149). The τελ. in the synoptics (the only part of our lit. where they are mentioned) are not the holders (Lat. publicani) of the 'taxfarming' contracts themselves, but subordinates (Lat. portitores) hired by them; the higher officials were usu. foreigners, but their underlings were, as a rule, taken fr. the native population. The prevailing system of tax collection afforded a collector many opportunities to exercise greed and unfairness. Hence tax collectors were particularly hated and despised as a class (s. these condemnatory judgments on the τελῶναι: Demochares [300 BC] 75 fgm. 4 Jac. τελ. βάναυσος; Xeno Com. III 390 Kock πάντες τελῶναι ἅρπαγες; Herodas 6, 64; Diogenes, Ep. 36, 2; Lucian, Necyom. 11; Artem. 1, 23; 4, 42; 57; Heraclid. Crit., Reisebilder 7 p. 76, 6 Pfister; Ps.-Dicaearchus p. 143, 7 Fuhr.; Iambl. Erot. 34; Cicero, De Off. 1, 150; UPZ 113, 9; 16 [156 BC]; O. Wilck I 568f; PPrinc II, 20, 1ff [on this OReinmuth, ClPh 31, '36, 146–62]; Philo, Spec. Leg. 2, 93ff. Rabbinic material in Schürer I 374–76; Billerb. I 377f, 498f). A strict Israelite was further offended by the fact that tax-collectors had to maintain continual contact w. non-Israelites in the course of their work; this rendered an Israelite tax-collector ceremonially unclean. The prevailing attitude is expressed in these combinations: τελῶναι καὶ ἁμαρτωλοί (s. ἁμαρτωλός bβ) **Mt 9:10f; 11:19; Mk 2:15, 16ab** (RPesch, BRigaux Festschr., '70, 63–87; cp. Theophr., Characters 6, 47); **Lk 5:30; 7:34; 15:1** (JJeremias, ZNW 30, '31, 293–300). ὁ ἐθνικὸς καὶ ὁ τελώνης **Mt 18:17.** οἱ τελῶναι καὶ αἱ πόρναι **21:31f.** As typically selfish **5:46.**—**Lk 3:12** (Sb 8072, 6 [II AD] a prefect reprimands τελ. who demand τὰ μὴ ὀφιλόμενα αὐτοῖς); **5:29; 7:29.** A Pharisee and a tax-collector **Lk 18:10f, 13.** Μαθθαῖος ὁ τελώνης **Mt 10:3** (Jos., Bell. 2, 287 Ἰωάννης ὁ τελώνης). τελ. ὀνόματι Λευί **Lk 5:27** (cp. Λευί 4).—Schürer I 372–76; JMarquardt, Staatsverw. II[2] 1884, 261ff; 289ff; AJones, Studies in Rom. Gov't. and Law, '60, 101–14; JDonahue, CBQ 33, '71, 39–61; EBadian, Publicans and Sinners '72; WWalker, JBL 97, '78, 221–38; FHerrenbrück, ZNW 72, '81, 178–94, Jesus und die Zöllner '90; DBraud, Gabinus, Caesar, and the 'publicani' of Judaea: Klio 65, '83, 241–44; MGoodman, The Ruling Class of Judaea '87. S. κῆνσος.—Kl. Pauly V 1551; BHHW III 2245f.—New Docs 5, 103, also 8, 47–56. DELG s.v. τέλος and ὠνέομαι. Frisk s.v. τέλος and ὦνος. M-M. EDNT. TW.

τελώνιον, ου, τό ***revenue/tax office*** (s. τελώνης; Posidippus Com. [III BC], fgm. 13; Strabo 16, 1, 27 [prob. 'toll-collection operation']; 17, 1, 16 ['toll-office'], difft. L-S-J-M; OGI 496, 9; 525, 10; UPZ 112 VIII, 3 [203/202 BC]; Mitt-Wilck. I/2, 223, 3) **Mt 9:9; Mk 2:14; Lk 5:27;** GEb 34, 61 (PPetr II, 11 [2], 3 ἐπὶ τελώνιον).—M-M.

τέξομαι s. τίκτω.

τέρας, ατος, τό (Hom. et al.) **someth. that astounds because of transcendent association,** ***prodigy, portent, omen, wonder*** in our lit. only pl. and combined w. σημεῖα; s. σημεῖον 2aβ and b, where all the passages containing τέρατα are given (ViZech 2; Appian, Bell. Civ. 1, 83 §377 τέρατα πολλὰ ἐγίνοντο, i.e. terrifying portents caused by a divinity [τὸ δαιμόνιον, ὁ θεός] that foretell the destructive results of Sulla's campaign in Italy).—PStein, ΤΕΡΑΣ, diss. Marburg 1909. DELG. M-M. TW.

τερατεία, ας, ἡ (τέρας; Aristoph., Isocr. et al.; Eus., PE 63; 132) **that which relates to marvelous matters,** ***illusion, jugglery, humbug*** (Aristoph., Isocr. et al.; Polyb. 2, 17, 6; Diod. S. 4, 51, 3; Heraclit. Sto. 27 p. 42, 10; Jos., Bell. 1, 630) in satire Dg 8:4 (w. πλάνη).—EPlümacher ZNW 89, '98, 66–90 (lit.).

Τερέντιος, ου (Lat. gentile name) ***Terence*** **Ro 16:22 v.l.**

τέρμα, ατος, τό (cp. τέρμων 'boundary'; Hom. et al.; GDI 711; PFay 217 βίου τέρμα; Sb 5829, 12; 3 Km 7:32; Wsd 12:27; SibOr 3, 756) **a position on a limit of extent,** ***end, limit, boundary*** (Hdt. 7, 54 ἐπὶ τέρμα τ. Εὐρώπης γίνεσθαι; Philostrat., Vi. Apoll. 5, 4; En 106:8; Philo, Mos. 1, 2 τὰ τ. γῆς τέρματα; Jos., Bell. 7, 284; Tat. 20, 2) τὸ τέρμα τῆς δύσεως *the farthest limits of the west* 1 Cl 5:7 (the var. interpretations of the expr. are dealt w. by Dubowy [s.v. Σπανία] 17–79). On the question of Paul's journey to Spain s. lit. s.v. Σπανία.—DELG s.v. τέρμα A.

τερπνός, ή, όν (Tyrtaeus [VII BC] et al.; LXX; SibOr 4, 191) ***delightful, pleasant, pleasing*** 1 Cl 7:3 (cp. Ps 132:1). Subst. (τὸ τερπνόν Polyb. 1, 4, 11; EpArist 77; Jos., Ant. 19, 181; τὰ τ. Isocr. 1, 21; Philo, Somn. 2, 209) τὰ τερπνὰ τοῦ κόσμου *the delights* or *pleasures of the world* IRo 6:1 (so Zahn, w. the Gk. witnesses to the uninterpolated text, though Lghtf., Funk, Hilgenfeld, GKrüger and Bihlmeyer w. the interpolated Gk. and the Lat. and Syr. versions prefer πέρατα, s. Bihlmeyer app. ad loc.).—DELG s.v. τέρπομαι.

τερπνόω/τερπνέω (not found elsewhere) ***be delighted, be happy*** AcPl Ha 7, 12. S. τερπνός.

Τέρτιος, ου, ὁ (Gk. ins fr. I AD in GEdmundson, The Church in Rome 1913 p. 22, 1) ***Tertius,*** a Christian helpful to Paul; in **Ro 16:22** he is ὁ γράψας τὴν ἐπιστολήν, and sends personal greetings to the church for which the letter is intended. Cp. **Ro subscr.**—LGPN I. M-M.

Τέρτουλλος, ου, ὁ (lit., ins, coins) ***Tertullus.*** The name of the Roman eparch under whom Onesimus suffered martyrdom is spelled this way in **Phlm subscr.**

Τέρτυλλος, ου, ὁ (CIG 3001; 4337; IG VII, 4173; XIV, 826, 44; CIL III, 14, 428; 14, 447. On the spelling s. WDittenberger, Her 6, 1872, 293f; B-D-F §41, 1) ***Tertullus,*** attorney for those who accused Paul before Felix the procurator **Ac 24:1f.**—SLösch, D. Dankesrede des T.: TQ 112, '31, 295–319.—Kl. Pauly V 615; BHHW III 1953. M-M.

τεσσαράκοντα, τεσσαρακονταετής s. τεσσερ-.—M-M.

τέσσαρες (Hom. et al., pseudepigr., apolog.) neut. τέσσαρα or τέσσερα (the latter is practically never found in ins and pap [Mayser p. 57 w. lit.; Rdm.[2] p. 43], but is predom. in LXX-mss.). Gen. τεσσάρων (ApcEsdr 3:6 p. 27, 12 Tdf.; ApcMos 33; EpArist; Jos., Vi. 75.—τὸ διὰ τεσσάρων as a musical expr.: Dionys. Hal., Comp. Verb. 11). Dat. τέσσαρσιν (JosAs 24:15; **Ac 11:5** D τέτρασιν; B-D-F §63, 1). Acc. masc. τέσσαρας (τέσσαρες as acc. [pap, LXX; for both s. Thackeray 148f] is poorly attested for the NT [B-D-F §46, 2; Mlt-H. 130; 170]) ***four*** **Mt 24:31** (ἄνεμος 2); **Mk 2:3** pers.; **13:27** (ἄνεμος 2); **Lk 2:37; J 11:17; 19:23; Ac 10:11** al. (six times in all); **Rv 4:4ab** al. (29 times); Hv 1, 4, 1 al. (11 times). αἱ τ. (παρθένοι) s 9, 2, 3; D 10:5 (ἄνεμος 2). On τέσσερα ζῷα **Rv 4:6** cp. Lohmeyer ad loc.; FDölger, Die Sonne der Gerechtigkeit u. der Schwarze 1918.—DELG. M-M. TW.

τεσσαρεσκαιδέκατος, η, ον (Hippocr., Epid. 6, 3, 2 L.; SIG 1112, 14; PEleph 1, 1 [311 BC]; PYadin 20, 18 al.; POslo 40, 35 [150 AD]; LXX [cp. Thackeray 189]; Demetr.: 722 fgm. 1, 5 Jac.; Jos., Ant. 2, 311 al., C. Ap. 1, 159. The Ionic-Hellenistic form τεσσερεσκαιδέκατος Hdt. 1, 84; SIG 633, 27 [c. 180 BC]; 1017, 10) ***fourteenth*** **Ac 27:27, 33.**—M-M.

τεσσεράκοντα (throughout the NT the oldest witnesses have this Ionic-Hellenistic form; so also SIG 344, 45 [c. 303 BC]; LXX in the uncials [Thackeray 62f; 73]; whether the same can be affirmed for the autographs is questionable since even in I AD the pap almost never have τεσσεράκοντα; for exceptions s. BGU 1170, 6 [10 BC]; PSI 317, 4 [95 AD]. Hence the variation in critical edd., with most of them preferring τεσσεράκοντα.—B-D-F §29, 1; W-S. §5, 20c; Mlt-H. 66f; Tdf., Proleg. 80; W-H., App. 150.—τεσσαράκοντα Hom.+; pseudepigr.; Tat. 31, 3) indecl. ***forty,*** often of days (Dicaearchus, fgm. 35b W. of Pythagoras: ἀποθανεῖν τετταράκοντα ἡμέρας ἀσιτήσαντα; Diod. S. 17, 111, 6 ἐν ἡμ. τεττ.; Jos., Ant. 18, 277; Procop., Bell. 6, 15, 7) **Mt 4:2ab; Mk 1:13; Lk 4:2** (including nights as Ps.-Callisth. 3, 26, 7 p. 127, 3); **Ac 1:3.** Freq. in ref. to Ex 34:28: 1Cl 53:2ab; B 4:7ab; 14:2ab.—In other connections: **J 2:20; Ac 4:22** al. (PMenoud, OCullmann Festschr. '62, 148–56). Cp. **2 Cor 11:24** (cp. Jos., Ant. 4, 238; 248); **Hb 3:10** (Ps 94:10), **17; Rv 7:4** al.; Hs 9, 4, 3; 9, 5, 4; 9, 15, 4; 9, 16, 5 (in these Hermas passages 'forty' appears as a numeral: μ').—EKönig, Die Zahl 40 u. Verwandtes: ZDMG 61, 1907, 913–17; WRoscher, Die Zahl 40 im Glauben, Brauch u. Schrifttum der Semiten: ASGLeipz 27, no. IV 1908, Die Tessarakontaden: BSGLeipz 61, 1909, 21–206; KSchubert, The Dead Sea Community, tr. Doberstein '59 (symbolism of '40' in Qumran).—BHHW III 2109.—DELG s.v. τέσσαρες. M-M. TW.

τεσσερακονταετής, ές (edd. also -έτης.—Sb 8246, 9; 21 [340 AD]) or τεσσαρακονταετής (Hes., Op. 441, see s.v. τεσσεράκοντα; on the accent s. ἑκατονταετής) **pert. to a period of forty years,** ***forty years*** τεσσ. χρόνος (Appian, Mithrid. 118 §583 τεσσαρ. χρ.; cp. διετὴς χρ.: Hdt. 2, 2; Jos., Ant. 2, 74) *forty years old* **Ac 7:23;** *for forty years* **13:18.**—TW.

τεταρταῖος, α, ον (τέταρτος; Hippocr., Pla., X.+; Polyb. 3, 52, 2; Diod. S. 14, 29, 2; 17, 67, 1; Jos., Ant. 13, 398; SIG 1239, 20; PTebt 275, 21; POxy 1151, 37) ***happening on the fourth day*** τεταρταῖός ἐστιν *he has been (dead) four days* (cp. X., An. 6, 4, 9 ἤδη γὰρ ἦσαν πεμπταῖοι=they had already been [dead] for five days) **J 11:39.**—DELG s.v. τέσσαρες. M-M. TW.

τέταρτος, η, ον (Hom.+) ***fourth*** **Mt 14:25; Mk 6:48; Ac 10:30; Rv 4:7** al.; B 4:5 (Da 7:7); Hs 9, 1, 6; 9, 15, 2f; 9, 21, 1. Subst. neut. τὸ τέταρτον (i.e. μέρος) ***the fourth part, quarter*** (Diod. S. 1, 50, 2; POxy 611; 1102, 9; 1293, 25 [II AD]; Jos., Ant. 14, 203) τὸ τέταρτον τῆς γῆς **Rv 6:8.**—DELG s.v. τέσσαρες. M-M. TW.

τετρα- ***four*** in comp. words.

τετρααρχέω (τετραάρχης; some edd. spell it τετραρχέω; on this s. B-D-F §124; W-S.§5, 24b; Mlt-H. 63 al.) ***be tetrarch*** (Jos., Bell. 3, 512 of Philip, Vi. 52) **Lk 3:1** three times w. gen. of the region governed (B-D-F §177; Rob. 510).—DELG s.v. ἄρχω C.

τετραάρχης, ου, ὁ (some edd. spell it τετράρχης; on this s. B-D-F §124; W-S.§5, 24b; Mlt.-H. 63 al.) **a petty prince dependent on Rome and with rank and authority lower than those of a king,** ***tetrarch*** (Strabo, Joseph., ins: s. the reff. in Schürer I 333–35 n. 12. Also Plut., Anton. 942 [56, 7]; 943 [58, 11]; Polyaenus 8, 39), orig., ruler of the fourth part of a region (Strabo 12, 5, 1 [567]); later, when the orig. sense was wholly lost (Appian, Mithrid. 46 §178; 58 §236 there are more than four Galatian tetrarchs), title of a petty prince who ruled by courtesy of Rome. In our lit. Herod Antipas is given this title (as well as in OGI 416, 3; 417, 4; Jos., Ant. 17, 188; 18, 102; 109; 122) **Mt 14:1; Lk 3:19; 9:7; Ac 13:1;** ISm 1:2.—BNiese, RhM n.s. 38, 1883, 583ff; Pauly-W. 2, IV 1089–97; Kl. Pauly V 632f; BHHW III 1956f.—DELG s.v. ἄρχω C. M-M.

τετράγωνος, ον (τέτρα-, γωνία; Hdt. et al.; ins, pap, LXX, JosAs 2:17; Philo; Jos., Ant. 3, 116; 12, 227; loanw. in rabb.) **pert. to having four sides and four right angles,** ***(four)-square*** of a city ἡ πόλις τετράγωνος κεῖται *the city is laid out as a square* **Rv 21:16** (Rome was originally built in this way acc. to Appian, Basil. 1a §9; Strabo 12, 4, 7 of Nicaea: ἔστι τῆς πόλεως ἑκκαιδεκαστάδιος ὁ περίβολος ἐν τετραγώνῳ σχήματι … τετράπυλος ἐν πεδίῳ κείμενος); but s. also below. Of stones that are to be used in a building (Appian, Mithrid. 30 §119; Arrian, Peripl. 2, 1; 1 Macc 10:11 v.l.; Jos., Ant. 20, 221) Hv 3, 2, 4; 3, 5, 1; s 9, 3, 3; 9, 6, 7f; 9, 9, 2; cp. v 3, 6, 6. *Shaped like a cube* of a tremendous rock Hs 9, 2, 1. Perh. **Rv 21:16** (s. above) also has this sense.—Subst. neut. τὸ τετράγωνον ***rectangle, square*** (Pla. et al.; OGI 90, 45 [II BC]; POxy 669, 21) ἐν τετραγώνῳ *in a square* or *rectangle* Hv 3, 2, 5.—DELG s.v. γωνία. M-M.

τετράδιον, ου, τό (cp. τετράς; BGU 956, 3 [III AD]; POxy 2156, 10) as a military t.t. (Philo, In Flacc. 111) ***a detachment/squad of four soldiers*** (s. Goodsp., Probs. 131f) one for each of the four night watches (s. Vegetius, De Re Militari 3, 8 p. 84f Lang) τέσσαρσιν τετραδίοις στρατιωτῶν **Ac 12:4** (on the topic Philostrat., Vi. Apoll. 7, 31).—DELG s.v. τέσσαρες. M-M.

τετρακισχίλιοι, αι, α (Hdt., Aristoph. et al.; LXX; GkBar 6:7; Jos., Bell. 2, 501, Vi. 371) ***four thousand*** **Mt 15:38; 16:10; Mk 8:9, 20; Ac 21:38.**—M-M.

τετρακόσιοι, αι, α (Hdt. et al.; pap, LXX; ParJer 9:15; GrBar; AscIs 2:12; EpArist 20; Jos., Bell. 5, 382, Ant. 11, 15; 18; Tat.) ***four hundred*** **Ac 5:36; 7:6** (Gen 15:13.—The ἔτη τετρακόσια is a round number, not necessarily precise; the same number is used in Appian, Bell. Civ. 1, 98 §459 to indicate approximately the period of time in which there had been no dictator); **13:20; 21:38 v.l.; Gal 3:17.**—DELG s.v. τέσσαρες. M-M.

τετράμηνος, ον ***lasting four months*** (Thu. et al.; ins, pap) in the only occurrence in our lit. subst. (cp. Judg 19:2 A; 20:47 A; B-D-F §241, 3; Mlt-H. 286) ἡ τετράμηνος (sc. ὥρα) *the period of four months, third of a year* (SIG 410, 4 τὴν πρώτην τετράμηνον; 24 [274 BC]; 442, 3; 17; 645, 74; BGU 1118, 8; 1119, 17 [both I BC]) ἔτι τετράμηνός ἐστιν καί *four months more, then* **J 4:35.** The t.r. has τὸ τετράμηνον in the same mng. (JBover, Biblica 3, 1922, 442ff).—DELG s.v. 2 μήν. M-M.

τετραπλοῦς, ῆ, οῦν (contracted fr. τετραπλόος, όη, όον. The word since X., An. 7, 6, 7; also Jos., Ant. 7, 150 al.; as adv. 3 Km 6:33) ***four times, fourfold*** ἀποδιδόναι τετραπλοῦν *pay back four times as much* **Lk 19:8** (cp. PSI 1055, 13 [III AD] τοῦ τετραπλοῦ μισθοῦ; others New Docs 2, 72f).—DELG s.v. πλέω. M-M. Spicq.

τετράποδος, ον (cp. τετράπους) a by-form (since Polyb. 1, 29, 7; also TestAbr A 2 p. 79, 12 [Stone p. 6] ζώου τετραπόδου) of τετράπους (q.v.) ***four-footed*** σὺν κτήνεσι τετραπόδοις PtK 2 p. 14, 19.—DELG s.v. πούς.

τετράπους, ουν (cp. τετράποδος) gen. **-ποδος** 'four-footed' (Hdt. et al.; ins, pap) in our lit. only subst. τὰ τετράποδα ***four-footed animals, quadrupeds*** (Thu. 2, 50, 1; PHib 95, 8 [256 BC]; PStras 5, 15; LXX; TestSol; ApcEsdr 3:11 p. 27, 22 Tdf.; ApcSed; SibOr 3, 692; Philo, Gig. 31; Jos., Ant. 4, 70; Just., A I, 43, 8; Tat. 9, 1) always w. πετεινά and ἑρπετά **Ac 10:12; Ro 1:23.—Ac 11:6** adds θηρία.—M-M.

τετραρχ- s. τετρααρχ-.

τετράς, άδος, ἡ 'the number four' (Aristot., Philo), esp. 'the fourth day' (Hes. et al.; ins, pap, LXX of the fourth day of the month) ***the fourth day of the week, Wednesday*** τετράδα *on Wednesday* D 8:1 (on the acc. in answer to the question 'when?' s. B-D-F §161, 3; Rob. 470f).—DELG s.v. τέσσαρες.

τέτυχα s. τυγχάνω.

τεφρόω (τέφρα 'ashes'; Theophr. et al.; JosAs cod. A 27:8 [p. 82, 10 Bat.] for ἐρρύησαν and 28:10 [p. 83, 16 Bat.] for ἀπετέφρωσε; Philo, Ebr. 223 [of Sodom and Gomorrah]; SibOr 5, 124) 1 aor. ἐτέφρωσα; pass. aor. 3 pl. ἐτεφρώθησαν (JosAs cod. A 27:8; 28:10) ***cover with*** or ***reduce to ashes*** πόλεις Σοδ. καὶ Γομ. **2 Pt 2:6.**—DELG s.v. τέφρα. M-M.

τέχνη, ης, ἡ (Hom.+; loanw. in rabb.) ***skill, trade*** **Ac 17:29; Rv 18:22.** Pl. Dg 2:3. σκηνοποιὸς τῇ τ. α σκ. *by trade* **Ac 18:3.** τέχνην ἔχειν *have and practice a skill* or *trade* (Eur., Suppl. 381; X., Mem. 3, 10, 1 al.) Hs 9, 9, 2; D 12:4.—JKube, ΤΕΧΝΗ und ΑΡΕΤΗ '69.—DELG. M-M. Sv.

τεχνίτης, ου, ὁ (τέχνη; X., Pla.; ins, pap, LXX; TestSol; ApcSed 5:4 p. 131, 26 Ja.; EpArist; Philo; Jos., Ant. 20, 219; Ar. 4:2; Just., Ath.) ***craftsperson, artisan, designer*** Dg 2:3; D 12:3. Of a silversmith **Ac 19:24, 25 v.l., 38** (PLampe, BZ 36, '92, 66f [ins]). Of a potter 2 Cl 8:2 (metaph., cp. Ath. 15:2). πᾶς τεχνίτης πάσης τέχνης **Rv 18:22.**—Of God (Dox. Gr. 280a, 7 [Anaxagoras A 46]; Maximus Tyr. 13, 4c; 41, 4g; Herm. Wr. 486, 30 Sc. al.; Wsd 13:1; Philo, Op. M. 135, Mut. Nom. 31 δημιούργημα τοῦ τῶν καλῶν καὶ ἀγαθῶν μόνων τεχνίτου; Ar. 4, 2; Ath. 16, 1 al.) as the *architect* of the heavenly city (w. δημιουργός) **Hb 11:10.** Of the holy Logos ὁ τεχνίτης καὶ δημιουργὸς τῶν ὅλων Dg 7:2 (cp. Herm. Wr. 490, 34 Sc. ὁ τῶν συμπάντων κοσμοποιητὴς καὶ τεχνίτης).—HWeiss, TU 97, '66, 52–5; s. also lit. s.v. δημιουργός.—DELG s.v. τέχνη. M-M.

τηγανίζω (to fry in a τήγανον 'frying-pan'; Posidippus Com. [III BC], fgm. 5; BGU 665, 3 [I AD]; 2 Macc 7:5; Jos., Ant. 7, 167; loanw. in rabb.) ***fry*** (as in a pan), pass. w. act. sense of those undergoing fiery torments in hell ApcPt 20:34.—DELG s.v. τάγηνον.

τήκω fut. τήξω LXX; 1 aor. ἔτηξα LXX; pf. 3 pl. (intr.) τετήκασι (JosAs). Pass.: 2 fut. τακήσομαι **2 Pt 3:12 v.l.** (2 Cl 16:3); 2 aor. ἐτάκην LXX (Hom. et al.; LXX; En 1:6; Test12Patr; JosAs 28:10 cod. A [p. 83, 16 Bat.]; Apc4Esdr 8:23 [fgm. c]; Jos., Bell. 5, 426; SibOr 7, 77) **to cause someth. to become liquid, *melt*** (trans.); in our lit. pass. ***melt*** (intr.), ***dissolve*** (intr.) (Philo, Aet. M. 110 of the earth) of the στοιχεῖα et al. at the end of the world (Is 34:4 v.l. [quoted ApcPt, fgm. 5]; En 1:6; TestLevi 4:1) στοιχεῖα τήκεται *elements melt/dissolve* **2 Pt 3:12.** τακήσονταί τινες τῶν οὐρανῶν καὶ πᾶσα ἡ γῆ ὡς μόλιβος ἐπὶ πυρὶ τηκόμενος *some of the heavens will melt, with the whole earth melting as does lead over fire* 2 Cl 16:3 (Apollon. Rhod. 4, 1680 τηκομένῳ μολίβῳ). πᾶσα δύναμις ApcPt, fgm. 5 (s. above).—DELG. M-M.

τηλαυγής, ές (τῆλε 'afar', αὐγή; Pind. et al.; LXX, Philo) lit. 'far-shining'; then gener. 'clear, plain' neut. comp. as adv. τηλαυγέστερον (Diod. S. 1, 50, 1; Vett. Val. 54, 7f οἱ παλαιοὶ μυστικῶς καὶ σκοτεινῶς διέγραψαν, ἡμεῖς δὲ τηλαυγέστερον; Philo, Poster. Cai. 65) metaph. in ref. to intellectual understanding (cp. Vett. Val. above) ***more clearly*** Hs 6, 5, 1 (s. also δηλαυγῶς).—DELG s.v. τῆλε. M-M. s.v. τηλαυγῶς.

τηλαυγῶς adv. of τηλαυγής (Strabo 17, 1, 30; POxy 886, 24 [III AD]; Philo, Congr. 24, 25; Cleopatra p. 15, 38) of a visual image ***(very) plainly/clearly*** **Mk 8:25** (v.l. δηλαυγῶς, q.v.—B-D-F §119, 4; Rdm.[2] 37; s. Mlt-H. 283).—M-M.

τηλικοῦτος, αύτη, οῦτο (strengthened form of τηλίκος 'so great'; Aeschyl., X., Pla.; CGFP 340, 1f; et al.; ins, pap, LXX; TestSol 23:4 P; Ath.) a demonstrative pron. correlative to ἡλίκος (as Diod. S. 10, 19, 5; Hero Alex. I p. 396, 26; 416, 1; Jos., Ant. 8, 208; 13, 5).—On the form of the neut. (-ον or -ο) s. B-D-F §64, 4; Rob. 290. For the use of the art. w. it B-D-F §274; Rob. 771.

❶ in ref. to size ***so great, so large*** (Polyaenus 7, 35, 1) θηρίον Hv 4, 2, 3f. κῆτος 4, 1, 9. πλοῖα **Js 3:4.**

❷ in ref. to degree *so great/important/mighty* etc. (Diod. S. 13, 41, 2 χειμών; EpArist 312; Jos., Bell. 4, 157 τὸ τηλικοῦτον ἀσέβημα; 7, 393, Ant. 14, 352; Ath.) σημεῖα καὶ τέρατα B 4:14; 5:8. σεισμός **Rv 16:18** (w. οὕτω μέγας pleonastically added). θόρυβος MPol 8:3. θάνατος *so great a peril of death* (θάνατος 1c) **2 Cor 1:10.** σωτηρία **Hb 2:3.** —DELG s.v. τηλίκος. M-M.

τημελέω (Eur., Pla. et al.; Sym. Ps 30:4 and Is 40:11; Philo; Jos., Ant. 1, 252; 2, 79) ***care for, look after*** τινά *someone* (Eur., Iph. A. 731; Plut., Mor. 148d; Sext. Emp., Math. 1, 249) τὸν ἀσθενῆ 1 Cl 38:2.—DELG.

τημελοῦχος, ον (cp. τημέλεια 'care, attention', ἔχω; for -οῦχος formations s. Buck, Reverse Index 687f) **pert. to providing care, *care-taking, fostering*** τημελοῦχος ἄγγελος *a guardian angel* ApcPt, fgm. 1 and 2 (fr. Clem. Alex., Ecl. Proph. 41, 1; 48, 1 Stählin).—DELG s.v. τημελέω.

τηνικαῦτα adv., the commoner form for τηνίκα, ***at that time, then*** (Soph., Hdt. et al.; Ael. Aristid. 53 p. 624, 23 D.) **Phlm subscr.**—DELG s.v. τηνίκα.

τηρέω impf. ἐτήρουν, 3 pl. ἐτήρουν and ἐτήρουσαν AcPl Ha 8, 11 and 13; fut. τηρήσω; 1 aor. ἐτήρησα; pf. τετήρηκα, 3 pl. τετήρηκαν **J 17:6** (B-D-F §83, 1; W-S. §13, 15; Mlt. 52f; Mlt-H. 221). Pass.: impf. ἐτηρούμην; 1 aor. ἐτηρήθην; pf. τετήρημαι (Pind., Thu.+)

❶ **to retain in custody, *keep watch over, guard*** τινά, τὶ *someone, someth.* a prisoner (Thu. 4, 30, 4) **Mt 27:36, 54; Ac 16:23;** a building (s. PPetr II, 37, 1, 19 [III BC] τηρεῖν τὸ χῶμα; PFlor 388, 32; 1 Macc 4:61; 6:50) Hs 9, 6, 2; 9, 7, 3. Pass. (Jos., Ant. 14, 366) Πέτρος ἐτηρεῖτο ἐν τῇ φυλακῇ **Ac 12:5.** Cp. **24:23; 25:4, 21b.** τηρεῖν τὴν φυλακὴν *guard the jail* **12:6.** ὅπου οἱ κεκλεισμένοι τηροῦνται AcPl Ha 3, 20. Abs. *(keep) watch* (PSI 165, 4; 168, 9; 1 Esdr 4:11; 2 Esdr 8:29) MPol 17:2. οἱ τηροῦντες *the guards* (SSol 3:3) **Mt 28:4.**

❷ **to cause a state, condition, or activity to continue, *keep, hold, reserve, preserve*** *someone* or *someth.* (Aristoph., Pax 201; τὴν ἁρμονίαν τ. τοῦ πατρός Iren. 2, 33, 5 [Harv. I 380, 13])

ⓐ for a definite purpose or a suitable time (Jos., Ant. 1, 97) τετήρηκας τὸν καλὸν οἶνον ἕως ἄρτι **J 2:10** (POxy 1757, 23 τήρησόν μοι αὐτά, ἕως ἀναβῶ). Cp. **12:7** (WKühne, StKr 98/99, 1926, 476f; s. CBarrett, The Gospel According to St. John '60, 346 on the problem of interp.). τηρηθῆναι αὐτὸν εἰς τὴν τοῦ Σεβαστοῦ διάγνωσιν **Ac 25:21a.** κληρονομίαν τετηρημένην ἐν οὐρανοῖς εἰς ὑμᾶς (εἰς 4g) **1 Pt 1:4.—2 Pt 2:4** (cp. TestReub 5:5 εἰς κόλασιν αἰώνιον τετήρηται), **9, 17; 3:7** (cp. Jos., Ant. 1, 97 τηρεῖσθαι κατακλυσμῷ); **Jd 6b, 13;** MPol 2:3; 11:2; 15:1.

ⓑ *keep,* etc., unharmed or undisturbed (Polyb. 6, 56, 13 one's word; Herodian 7, 9, 3) ὁ δὲ ἀγαπῶν με τηρηθήσεται ὑπὸ τοῦ πατρός μου **J 14:21** P^{75}. τὴν σφραγῖδα 2 Cl 7:6. τὴν ἐκκλησίαν 14:3a (opp. φθείρειν). τὴν σάρκα 14:3b. τηρεῖ ἑαυτόν **1J 5:18 v.l.** τηρεῖν τὴν ἑαυτοῦ παρθένον *keep his virgin inviolate* as such **1 Cor 7:37** (Heraclit. Sto. 19 p. 30, 3; Achilles Tat. 8, 18, 2 παρθένον τὴν κόρην τετήρηκα. SBelkin, JBL 54, '35, 52 takes τηρ. here to mean *support* one's fiancée, without having marital relations.—On this subj. s. the lit. s.v. γαμίζω 1).—W. a second acc. (of the predicate, to denote the condition that is to remain unharmed; cp. M. Ant. 6, 30 τήρησαι σεαυτὸν ἁπλοῦν; BGU 1141, 25 [13 BC] ἄμεμπτον ἐμαυτὸν ἐτήρησα; Wsd 10:5; Just., D. 88, 5 ἀτιμωρήτους αὐτοὺς τηρῆσαι) τὴν ἐντολὴν ἄσπιλον **1 Ti 6:14.** τὸ βάπτισμα ἁγνόν 2 Cl 6:9. τὴν σφραγῖδα ὑγιῆ Hs 8, 6, 3. τὴν σάρκα ἁγνήν 2 Cl 8:4, 6. τὴν σάρκα ὡς ναὸν θεοῦ IPhld 7:2. σεαυτὸν ἁγνόν **1 Ti 5:22.—2 Cor 11:9; Js 1:27.** Pass. ὁλόκληρον ὑμῶν τὸ πνεῦμα τηρηθείη **1 Th 5:23.** τηρεῖν τινα ἔν τινι *keep someone (unharmed) by* or *through someth.* **J 17:11f.** ἑαυτοὺς ἐν ἀγάπῃ θεοῦ τηρήσατε *keep yourselves from harm by making it possible for God to show his love for you in the future also* **Jd 21.** τοῖς Χριστῷ τετηρημένοις κλητοῖς *to those who have been called and who have been kept unharmed for Christ,* or, in case the ἐν before θεῷ is to be repeated, *through Christ* **Jd 1.**

ⓒ of holding on to someth. so as not to give it up or lose it (Diod. S. 17, 43, 9 τὰ ὅπλα, the shields; τὴν ἀρετήν Did., Gen. 87, 4. Cp. τ. τὰ μυστήρια . . . καὶ ἐξειπεῖν μηδενί Hippol., Ref. 5, 27, 2) τὴν ἁγνείαν Hm 4, 4, 3. τὴν ἑνότητα τοῦ πνεύματος **Eph 4:3.** τὴν πίστιν **2 Ti 4:7** (cp. Diod. S. 19, 42, 5 τηρεῖν τὴν πίστιν; IBM III, 587b, 5 ὅτι τὴν πίστιν ἐτήρησα; Jos., Bell. 2, 121, Ant. 15, 134). τὰ ἱμάτια αὐτοῦ **Rv 16:15** (or else he will have to go naked). αὐτόν (=τὸν θεόν) **1J 5:18.** W. a neg.: *fail to hold fast = lose* through carelessness or *give up* through frivolity or a deficient understanding of the value of what one has τὶ *someth.* τὸ μικρόν 2 Cl 8:5 (a dominical saying whose literary source is unknown). τὴν ἑαυτῶν ἀρχήν (s. ἀρχή 7) **Jd 6a.**

ⓓ of being protective (Pind. et al.; En 100:5) *keep* τινὰ ἔκ τινος *someone from someone* or *someth.* **J 17:15; Rv 3:10b** (cp. Pr 7:5 τηρεῖν τινα ἀπό τινος).

❸ **to persist in obedience, *keep, observe, fulfill, pay attention to,*** esp. of law and teaching (LXX) τὶ *someth.* (Polyb. 1, 83, 5 legal customs; Herodian 6, 6, 1; Just., A I, 49, 3 τὰ παλαιὰ ἔθη) **Mt 23:3; Ac 21:25 v.l.;** Hs 5, 3, 9. τὸν νόμον (Achilles Tat. 8, 13, 4; Tob 14:9; TestDan 5:1.—τ. νόμους Jos., C. Ap. 2, 273; Orig., C. Cels. 8, 10, 11; Theoph. Ant. 2, 16 [p. 140, 15]) **15:5; Js 2:10;** Hs 8, 3, 3–5. τὰ νόμιμα τοῦ θεοῦ Hv 1, 3, 4 (τηρ. τὰ νόμιμα as Jos., Ant. 8, 395; 9, 222). δικαιώματα κυρίου B 10:11. τὰ πρὸς τὸν κύριον AcPl Ha 8, 11; 13. πάντα ὅσα ἐνετειλάμην ὑμῖν **Mt 28:20.** τὰς ἐντολάς (Ramsay, CB I/2, 566f, nos. 467–69, side A of an altar [313/14 AD] τηρῶν ἐντολὰς ἀθανάτων, i.e. θεῶν; Sir 29:1; Jos., Ant. 8, 120; Just., D. 10, 3; Iren. 1, 10, 1 [Harv. I 91, 14]) **19:17; J 14:15, 21; 15:10ab; 1J 2:3f; 3:22, 24; 5:3; Rv 12:17; 14:12;** Hm 7:5; 12, 3, 4; 12, 6, 3; s 5, 1, 5; 5, 3, 2; 6, 1, 4; 8, 7, 6; 10, 3, 4 (Oxy 404, 17 restoration on basis of Lat. and Ethiopic versions); cp. 5, 3, 3. Pass. 5, 3, 5a. τὸ σάββατον *observe the Sabbath* **J 9:16.** τὴν νηστείαν *keep the fast* Hs 5, 3, 5b v.l.; cp. 5, 3, 9. τὴν παράδοσιν (Jos., Vi. 361b) **Mk 7:9 v.l.** τὸν λόγον **J 8:51f, 55; 14:23; 15:20ab; 17:6; 1J 2:5; Rv 3:8.** τὸν λόγον τῆς ὑπομονῆς μου vs. **10a.** τοὺς λόγους (1 Km 15:11) **J 14:24.** ἃ παρελάβαμεν AcPlCor 1:5. τοὺς λόγους τῆς προφητείας **Rv 22:7,** τοῦ βιβλίου τούτου vs. **9.** τὰ ἐν τῇ προφητείᾳ γεγραμμένα **1:3.** ὁ τηρῶν τὰ ἔργα μου *the one who takes my deeds to heart* **Rv 2:26.** Abs., but w. the obj. easily supplied fr. the context τήρει *pay attention to it* **3:3** (cp. Philo, Leg. All. 3, 184).—DELG. M-M. TW. Sv.

τήρησις, εως, ἡ (τηρέω; Thu. et al.; ins, pap, LXX; Jos., Ant. 17, 205)

❶ **act of holding in custody, *custody, imprisonment*** (Jos., Ant. 16, 321).

❷ **a place for custody, *prison*** (BGU 388 III, 7). This and mng. 1 are prob. (cp. Thu. 7, 86, 2; Jos., Ant. 18, 235) in ἔθεντο εἰς τήρησιν **Ac 4:3.** ἔθεντο αὐτοὺς ἐν τηρήσει δημοσίᾳ **5:18.**

❸ **act of ensuring the well-being of another, *care*** GJs 9:1, 3.

❹ **act of persisting in obedience, *keeping, observance*** (Wsd 6:18) ἐντολῶν (Sir 32:23.—τῶν νόμων Hierocles, Carm. Aur. 2, 2 p. 422 M.) **1 Cor 7:19.**—DELG s.v. τηρέω. M-M. TW.

τηρητής, οῦ, ὁ (since III BC, incl. pap) ***sentry, guard*** in charge of detention AcPl Ha 3, 20.—DELG s.v. τηρέω.

Τιβεριάς, άδος, ἡ (Josephus index) ***Tiberias,*** a city on the west shore of the Lake of Gennesaret, founded by Herod Antipas as the capital of his domain and named in honor of the Emperor Tiberius; **J 6:23.** The Lake of Gennesaret (s. EbNestle, Der Name des Sees Tiberias: ZDPV 35, 1912, 48–50; JDuncan, The Sea of Tiberias and Its Environs: PEF 58, 1926, 15–22; 65–74; RMiddleton, Tiberias: ibid. 162f) is also called θάλασσα τῆς Τιβεριάδος (cp. the more precise λίμνη: Paus. 5, 7, 4 λίμνην Τιβεριάδα ὀνομαζομένην; Jos., Bell. 3, 57 Τιβεριὰς λίμνη; 4, 456 Τιβεριέων λίμνη; SibOr 12, 104 Τιβεριάδος ἅλμη) **J 21:1,** more fully θάλασσα τῆς Γαλιλαίας τῆς Τιβεριάδος **6:1.**—Baedeker, Palästina u. Syrien[7] 1910, 234f; Schürer II 178–82; Dalman, Orte[3] 1924; MAvi-Yonah, The Foundation of Tiberias: Israel Exploration Journ. 1, '50f, 160–69; PECS 920f.—Pauly-W. VI 770–81; Kl. Pauly V 812; BHHW III, 1982f.

Τιβέριος, ου, ὁ ***Tiberius*** (the name is found Diod. S. 15, 51, 1: Τιβέριος, Ἰούλιος a Rom. military tribune IV BC), a Roman emperor (if dated from the death of Augustus, he ruled fr. Aug. 19, 14 AD to March 16, 37; mentioned in Philo and Joseph.; also Just., A I, 13, 3; cp. SibOr 5, 20–23; s. Schürer index); **Lk 3:1** places the first appearance of John the Baptist as a prophet in the fifteenth year of Tiberius' reign. On the chronological matters involved s. Meyer I 46f; III 205f; CCichorius, ZNW 22, 1923, 16ff; HDieckmann, Die effektive Mitregentschaft des T.: Klio 15, 1919, 339–75, Das fünfzehnte Jahr des T.: BZ 16, 1924, 54–65, Das fünfzehnte Jahr des Cäsar T.: Biblica 6, 1925, 63–67; s. s.v. Αὔγουστος. HDessau, Gesch. der röm. Kaiserzeit II 1, 1926; GBaker, Tib. Caesar 1929; ECiaceri, Tiberio '34; CSmith, Tib. and the Rom. Empire '42; WGolub, Tib. '59; EKornemann, Tib. '60; RSeager, Tib. '72; Pauly-W. X 478–536; Kl. Pauly V 814–18; BHHW III 1983f.—On the chronology of the Life of Jesus gener.: OGerhardt, Grundzüge der Chronologie Jesu Christi '34; RHennig, D. Geburts- u. Todesjahr Jesu Christi '36; RJewett, A Chronology of Paul's Life '79; RBrown, The Birth of the Messiah '77, 547–56, The Death of the Messiah '94, 1350–78 (lit.); KDonfried, ABD I 1011–16 (lit. 1022).—M-M.

Τίβερις, εως or **ιδος, ὁ** acc. Τίβεριν (Polyb. 6, 55, 1; Strabo et al.; Just., A I, 26, 2 ἐν τῷ Τίβερι ποταμῷ SibOr 5, 170) ***the Tiber*** river Hv 1, 1, 2.—Kl. Pauly V 813f.

τίθημι (Hom.+) and its by-form **τιθέω** (Hv 1, 1, 3 and 2, 1, 2 as historical present; B-D-F §321; s. Rob. 318); impf. 3 sg. ἐτίθει, 3 pl. ἐτίθεσαν **Mk 6:56** and ἐτίθουν as **v.l.; Ac 3:2; 4:35;** Hv 3, 2, 7 (B-D-F §94, 1; Mlt-H. 202); fut. θήσω; 1 aor. ἔθηκα (B-D-F §95, 1; Rob. 308; 310); 2 aor. subj. θῶ, impv. 2 pl. θέτε, inf. θεῖναι, ptc. θείς; pf. τέθεικα.; plpf. ἐτεθείκει (Just., D. 78, 5). Mid.: fut. θήσομαι; 2 aor. ἐθέμην. Pass.: fut. 3 pl. τεθήσονται Jer 13:16; 1 aor. ἐτέθην; pf. τέθειμαι, ptc. τεθειμένος (Nicol. Dam.: 90 fgm. 130, 18 p. 401, 3 Jac.) **J 19:41;** Hs 9, 15, 4 (on the pf. s. B-D-F §97, 2). The middle is gener. not different in mng. fr. the act. (B-D-F §316, 1; s. Rob. 804f). The semantic boundaries of this multivalent verb are quite flexible.

❶ to put or place in a particular location, *lay, put*—ⓐ act. and pass.: gener.—**α.** w. acc. *lay (away), set up, put (away)* ποῦ τεθείκατε αὐτόν; *where have you laid him?* **J 11:34** (as early as Hom. τιθέναι has the special sense *lay away, bury*); cp. **Mk 16:6; J 19:42; 20:2, 13, 15.** Pass. (ApcMos 42 ποῦ μέλλοι τεθῆναι τὸ σῶμα αὐτῆς) **Mk 15:47; Lk 23:55.** ὅπου ἦν τεθείς GPt 12:51. λίθον **Ro 9:33** (Is 28:16 ἐμβαλῶ); **1 Pt 2:6;** pass. B 6:2. θεμέλιον *lay a foundation* **Lk 14:29; 1 Cor 3:10f** (in imagery).—Of stones ἐξώτεροι ἐτέθησαν *they were placed* on *the outside* Hs 9, 8, 3; 5a (cp. c); 7. ἐν ἰσχύι τέθεικεν τὴν σάρκα αὐτοῦ κύριος *the Lord* (God) *has set his* (Christ's) *flesh in strength* B 6:3a; cp. b (Is 50:7).

β. w. the acc., oft. supplied fr. the context, and a prepositional expr. closely related to the verb (Herodas 4, 34 τιθέναι εἰς τοὺς λίθους ζοήν [*sic*]) εἰς κρύπτην *put someth. in a cellar* **Lk 11:33.** εἰς μνημεῖον *lay in a tomb* **Ac 13:29;** cp. **Rv 11:9.** Of stones τιθ. εἰς τ. οἰκοδομήν *put into the building* Hv 3, 2, 7. Pass. Hs 9, 4, 5; 9, 6, 8; cp. 9, 5, 4. Opp. ἐκ τῆς οἰκοδομῆς ἐτέθησαν *they were put out of the building* 9, 8, 1. ἔμπροσθέν τινος GPt 4:12. ἔν τινι (Gen 50:26; Jos., Ant. 14, 124; TestJob 20:9): ἐν μνημείῳ **Mt 27:60;** cp. **Mk 6:29; 15:46; Lk 23:53; Ac 7:16.** Pass. **J 19:41.—Mk 6:56; Ac 9:37.** ἐνώπιόν τινος (1 Km 10:25) **Lk 5:18.** ἐπί τινος (X., Cyr. 8, 8, 16; Ezk 40:2; JosAs 3:11; Jos., Ant. 6, 15) **8:16b; J 19:19; Ac 5:15; Rv 10:2;** GPt 3:8; 6:21; 12:53. ἐπί τινι 8:32. ἐπί τι (Ps 20:4; 1 Km 6:8; TestAbr B 5 p. 109, 18 [Stone p. 66]; JosAs 16:11; ParJer 9:32; Mel., P. 14, 90) **Mk 4:21b; Lk 6:48** (θεμέλιον; s. α above); **2 Cor 3:13.** Esp. τὰς χεῖρας ἐπί τι or ἐπί τινα (cp. Ps 138:5) **Mk 8:25 v.l.; 10:16:** τὴν δεξιάν **Rv 1:17.** θήσω τὸ πνεῦμά μου ἐπ' αὐτόν **Mt 12:18** (=ἔδωκα Is 42:1; τ. τὸ πνεῦμα as Is 63:11). παρά τι (Plut., Mor. 176e; 3 Km 13:31) **Ac 4:35, 37 v.l.; 5:2.** πρός τι (JosAs 8:4 πρὸς τὸ στῆθος) **3:2; 4:37.** ὑπό τι **Mt 5:15; Mk 4:21;** cp. **1 Cor 15:25** (s. 5aα). ὑποκάτω τινός (Jer 45:12) **Lk 8:16a.—Mt 22:44** (Ps 109:1); **Mk 12:36.**

ⓑ special expressions—**α.** act. ***explain*** *in what figure of speech can we present* (the Reign of God)? (i.e., *how shall I put it?*) **Mk 4:30.**

β. act. ***take off, give up*** in Joh. lit. *take off, remove* τὰ ἱμάτια (Hdt 1, 10, 1 τ. τὰ εἵματα; cp. Herodas 5, 62; Plut., Alc. 195 [8, 2]; Jos., Bell. 1, 390 τ. τὸ διάδημα and s. ἱμάτιον 3) **J 13:4.** τὴν (ἑαυτοῦ) ψυχήν *lay down* or *give (up) one's life* **10:11** and **15** (both v.l. δίδωμι), **17, 18ab** (ApcSed 1:5 τὴν ψυχὴν θῇ ὑπὲρ τῶν φίλων; EFascher, Z. Auslegg. v. J 10:17, 18: Deutsche Theol. '41, 37–66); **13:37f; 15:13; 1 J 3:16ab** (Appian, Bell. Civ. 4, 68 §289 δεξιάς; SibOr 5, 157 τ. simply=δίδωμι).

γ. act. ***show deference to*** τιθέναι τὰ γόνατα (σοι γόνυ τίθημι γαίᾳ Eur., Troad. 1307; also in Lat.: genua ponere Ovid, Fasti 2, 438; Curt. 8, 7, 13; B-D-F §5, 3b) *bend the knee, kneel down* **Mk 15:19; Lk 22:41; Ac 7:60; 9:40; 20:36; 21:5;** Hv 1, 1, 3; 2, 1, 2.

δ. act. ***place before someone, serve*** (X., Mem. 3, 14, 1; JosAs 15:14 τράπεζαν καὶ ἄρτον Just., A I, 66, 4) οἶνον **J 2:10** (Bel 11 Theod. οἶνον θές).

ε. act. and mid. ***have (in mind)*** θέτε ἐν ταῖς καρδίαις w. inf. foll. *make up (your) minds* **Lk 21:14.** Mid. ἔθεντο ἐν τῇ καρδίᾳ αὐτῶν *they kept in mind* (the obj. acc. is supplied by the immediate context) **Lk 1:66** (1 Km 21:13). The same expr.=*come to think of someth., contrive someth. in one's mind* **21:14 v.l.; Ac 5:4.** Likew. ἔθετο ὁ Παῦλος ἐν τῷ πνεύματι w. inf. foll. *Paul resolved* **19:21.** θέσθε εἰς τὰ ὦτα ὑμῶν τοὺς λόγους τούτους **Lk 9:44.**

ζ. act. and mid. ***effect someth., arrange for someth.*** τ. ἐπί τινος foll. by the acc. and inf. *ordain by means of someone that* . . . B 13:6.—τὸ μέρος αὐτοῦ μετὰ τῶν ὑποκριτῶν θήσει (μέρος 2) **Mt 24:51;** cp. **Lk 12:46.** Mid. w. acc. (GrBar 2:1 [of God]; Appian, Bell. Civ. 2, 106 §442 εὐχὰς τίθεσθαι=offer prayers) βουλήν *reach a decision* (βουλή 2a) **Ac 27:12.**

η. mid. ***put (in custody)*** τίθεσθαί τινα ἐν τηρήσει **Ac 5:18;** ἐν (τῇ) φυλακῇ (Gen 41:10; 42:17) **Mt 14:3 v.l.; Ac 5:25;** εἰς φυλακήν (PPetr II, 5a, 3 [III BC]) **12:4;** εἰς τήρησιν (w. the acc. easily supplied) **4:3.** ἐν σωτηρίῳ *place in safety, cause to share salvation* (w. acc. to be supplied) 1 Cl 15:6 (Ps 11:6).

θ. act. ***provide (an example)*** ὑπόδειγμά τινος τιθ. *set up an example of someth.* **2 Pt 2:6** (cp. Jos., Ant. 17, 313 παράδειγμα τῆς ἀρετῆς τιθέναι). Those persons are added, in the dat., to whose advantage or disadvantage the example is given: τιθέναι πρόσκομμα τῷ ἀδελφῷ **Ro 14:13** (πρόσκομμα 2b). σκοπὸν τοῖς νέοις θήσομεν 2 Cl 19:1.

❷ act. **to lay aside/deposit (money),** ***put aside, store up, deposit*** a t.t. term of commercial life (Demosth. 52, 3 ἀργύριον al.; Hyperid. 5, 4; Theocr., Epigr. 14, 2; Plut., Mor. 829b; pap) opp. αἴρειν *you withdraw what you did not deposit* **Lk 19:21;** cp. vs. **22.** ἕκαστος παρ' ἑαυτῷ τιθέτω *each one is to put aside at home* **1 Cor 16:2.**

❸ **to assign to some task or function,** ***appoint, assign***

ⓐ τιθέναι τινὰ εἴς τι *place/appoint someone to* or *for (to function as) someth.* (for the construction cp. Ael. Aristid. 53 p. 636 D.: τοὺς οὐκ ὄντας νόμους εἰς νόμους τ.) τέθεικά σε εἰς φῶς ἐθνῶν **Ac 13:47** (Is 49:6); pass.: εἰς ὃ ἐτέθην ἐγὼ κῆρυξ **1 Ti 2:7; 2 Ti 1:11.** Also τιθ. τινὰ ἵνα *appoint someone to . . .* **J 15:16.**

ⓑ mid. τίθεσθαι τινὰ εἴς τι *appoint someone to* or *for someth.* Dg 6:10. W. acc. easily supplied **1 Ti 1:12.**

❹ **to bring about an arrangement—ⓐ** ***establish, give,*** of a law (τιθέναι νόμον since Soph., El. 580; IAndrosIsis, Kyme 4; the mid. τίθεσθαι νόμον since Hdt. 1, 29. Both oft. in Pla.; likew. Diod. S. 5, 83, 5, where the act. as well as the mid. is used of law. The act. also EpArist 15; Jos., C. Ap. 1, 316, Ant. 16, 1; Ath. 34, 2. The mid. also Appian, Bell. Civ. 3, 55 §228; Jos., C. Ap. 1, 269; 2, 273; Ar. 13, 7) only in the pass. (as Pla., Leg.; 4, 705d al.; Jos., C. Ap. 2, 184; Just., D. 11, 2; Ath. 33, 1) ὁ νόμος ἐτέθη **Gal 3:19** D.

ⓑ mid. w. acc. ***fix, establish, set*** καιροὺς οὓς ὁ πατὴρ ἔθετο *times which the Father has fixed* **Ac 1:7.** θέμενος ἐν ἡμῖν τὸν λόγον τῆς καταλλαγῆς *as he established among us the word of reconciliation* (=*entrusted to us . . .* ; cp. Ps 104:27 ἔθετο ἐν αὐτοῖς τ. λόγους) **2 Cor 5:19.** ὁ θεὸς ἔθετο τὰ μέλη *God has arranged the parts* of the body **1 Cor 12:18.**

❺ **to cause to undergo a change in experience/condition,** ***make, consign*****—ⓐ** act. or pass., either w. a double acc. of the obj. and of the pred. (Hom.+; X., Cyr. 4, 6, 3; Lucian, Dial. Marin. 14, 2; Aelian, VH13, 6; Lev 26:31; Is 5:20; Wsd 10:21; Jos., Ant. 11, 39) or in the form τιθέναι τινὰ εἴς τι (cp. 3a).

α. *make someone* ὃν ἔθηκεν κληρονόμον πάντων **Hb 1:2.** πατέρα πολλῶν ἐθνῶν τέθεικά σε **Ro 4:17** (Gen 17:5). ἕως ἂν θῶ τοὺς ἐχθρούς σου ὑποπόδιον τῶν ποδῶν σου *until I make your enemies a footstool for your feet* (Ps 109:1): **Mt 22:44 v.l.; Lk 20:43; Ac 2:35; Hb 1:13;** the same quotation introduced with ἄχρι οὗ θῇ **1 Cor 15:25;** pass. **Hb 10:13** (on this expr. cp. Plut., Mor. 1097c [HAlmqvist, Pl. u. das NT '46, 104]). *Consign,* act. εἰς κόλασιν 1 Cl 11:1; pass. of those who refuse to believe the word εἰς ὃ καὶ ἐτέθησαν **1 Pt 2:8;** of Paul's obligation to accept his destiny at Rome εἰς τοῦτο γὰρ ἐτέθην AcPl Ha 7, 15. Cp. 3a.

β. *make someth.* (Mimnermus 1, 10 D.[2] cause someth. to become someth. [adj.]: 'God has made old age vexatious') ἀδάπανον θήσω τὸ εὐαγγέλιον **1 Cor 9:18.**

ⓑ mid. w. a double acc. *make someone someth.* (Appian., Illyr. 13 §37 φίλον τίθεσθαί τινα; schol. on Pind., O. 1, 58b; 2 Macc 5:21; Ath. 12, 2. S. also Tyrtaeus [VII BC] 8, 5 D.[3] of the man who is called upon to hate his own life [in battle]: ἀνὴρ ἐχθρὴν ψυχὴν θέμενος) **Ac 20:28** (CClaereboets, Biblica 24, '43, 370–87); **1 Cor 12:28.** τίθεσθαι τινὰ εἴς τι *consign someone to someth.* ὀργήν **1 Th 5:9.**—B. 832. DELG. M-M. EDNT. TW.

τίκτω fut. τέξομαι; 2 aor. ἔτεκον; pf. τέτοκα LXX; plpf. ἐτετόκει (Just., D. 78, 5). Pass.: fut. 3 sg. τεχθήσεται (Just., A I, 54, 8 1), ptc. τεχθησόμενος (LXX; Just., A I, 33, 1); 1 aor. ἐτέχθην (Hom.+) prim. 'bring into the world, engender' (when used of the father 'beget', when used of the mother 'bring forth'); in our lit.

❶ **to cause to be born or come into the world,** ***give birth (to), bear*** w. acc. υἱόν etc. (Demetr.: 722 fgm. 1, 3 al. Jac.; Jos., Ant. 1, 257) **Mt 1:21;** GJs 14:2 (Ps.-Callisth. 1, 8 Philip learns in a dream: ἡ γυνή σου τέξει σοι υἱόν, ὃς κυριεύσει τ. κόσμον πάντα; Apollon. Rhod. 4, 802 according to a saying of Themis, it is destined that Thetis will παῖδα τεκεῖν who will tower over everything); **Mt 1:23** (Is 7:14), **25; Lk 1:31; 2:7; Rv 12:4b, 5, 13.** Abs. **J 16:21; Gal 4:27;** 2 Cl 2:1 (the last two Is 54:1); **Rv 12:2, 4a;** GEg 252, 49, 51, and 53; ὁ χρόνος or αἱ ἡμέραι τοῦ τεκεῖν αὐτήν (acc. as subj.) **Lk 1:57; 2:6.** Pass. (Petosiris, fgm. 9 ln. 93 ἐκ τῆς ἀχλύος [mist] τίκτονται σκώληκες; JosAs 17:4; ViMal 1 [p. 89, 1 Sch.]; Just., A I, 54, 8; Mel., P. 7, 53; Ath., 33, 2—S. B-D-F §76, 2) **Mt 2:2; Lk 2:11.**

❷ **to cause to come into being,** ***bring forth, produce,*** in imagery of the earth (Aeschyl., Cho. 127; Eur., Cycl. 333; Philo, Op. M. 132 γῆς τῆς πάντα τικτούσης) *bring forth* βοτάνην **Hb 6:7.** Of desire συλλαβοῦσα τίκτει (on this combination cp. Gen 4:17, 25; 29:35) ἁμαρτίαν **Js 1:15** (cp. Aeschyl., Ag. 764 φιλεῖ δὲ τίκτειν ὕβρις ὕβριν; Solon in Stob. III p. 114, 7 H. ἡδονὴ λύπην τ.; Pla., Symp. 212a ἀρετήν, Ep. 3, 315c ἡδονὴ ὕβριν τίκτουσα ἐν τῇ ψυχῇ. The imagery is a favorite w. Philo. SibOr 3, 235 κακὰ τ.).— B. 281. DELG. M-M.

τίλλω impf. ἔτιλλον; aor. ptc. τίλας (ApcrEzek [Epiph. 70, 10]). Pass. pf. ptc. gen. τετιλμένου Is 18:7; aor. 3 sg. ἐτίλη Da 7:4 (Hom. et al.; pap, LXX; PsSol 13:3; AscIs 2:11) ***pluck, pick*** τὶ *someth.* (Diod. S. 5, 21, 5 τοὺς παλαιοὺς στάχυς τίλλειν; τίλλ. χόρτον: PFlor 321, 47; 322, 20.—Philo, Leg. ad Gai. 223, De Jos. 16) στάχυας *heads of wheat* **Mt 12:1; Mk 2:23; Lk 6:1.**—Dalman, Arbeit II 339; BCohen, The Rabb. Law Presupp. by Mt 12:1 and Lk 6:1: HTR 23, 1930, 91f; Murmelstein (s. on σπόριμος).—DELG. M-M. Spicq. Sv.

Τιμαῖος, ου, ὁ *Timaeus* **Mk 10:46** (s. Βαρτιμαῖος).—M-M.

τιμάω (τιμή) fut. τιμήσω; 1 aor. ἐτίμησα; perf. 2 pl. τετιμήκατε (Tat.). Mid.: 1 aor. ἐτιμησάμην. Pass.: 1 fut. 3 sg. τιμηθήσεται; 1 aor. 3 sg. ἐτιμήθη LXX; perf. τετίμημαι, ptc. τετιμημένος (τιμή; Hom.+).

❶ **to set a price on,** ***estimate, value*** (Thu. et al.; ins; PSI 382, 15 [I BC]; PFlor 266, 6 al.) pass. τὴν τιμὴν τοῦ τετιμημένου (sc. ἀγροῦ or ἀνθρώπου, the latter referring to Judas) *the price for the field* or *for the man whose price was set* (τιμή 1) **Mt 27:9a.** Mid. *set a price on* or *estimate for oneself* (Hdt. et al.; Mitt-Wilck I/2, 224a, 8; c, 8f; 11 [III BC]; PHal 1, 201; 205 and oft. in pap; Lev 27:8; Jos., Ant. 5, 79; Mel., P. 89, 668ff) ὃν ἐτιμήσαντο *the one* (=field or person) *on which they had set a price* vs. **9b.**

❷ **to show high regard for,** ***honor, revere*** τινά *someone* God (X., Mem. 4, 3, 13; Diod. S. 6, 1, 4; 8 τοὺς θεούς; Strabo 16, 2, 35; Dio Chrys. 16 [33], 45; 58 [75], 8; Ael. Aristid. 13 p. 297 D.: πρὸ τῶν γονέων; freq. in honorific inscriptions, s. indexes in the various corpora, also New Docs 3, 37 no. 9, 3 [96/97 AD]; Is 29:13; EpArist 234; Philo; Jos., Ant. 9, 153; 256; Just., A I, 9, 1; Orig., C. Cels. 8, 56, 35) **Mt 15:8; Mk 7:6;** 1 Cl 15:2; 2 Cl 3:5; cp. 3:4.—**J 5:23bd; 8:49** (Jesus honors his Father). Christ **J 5:23ac.** On GPt 3:9 s. τιμή 2a (cp. Just., A I, 6, 2; 13, 3). Parents (Ex 20:12; also Ar. 15, 4) **Mt 15:4; 19:19; Mk 7:10; 10:19; Lk 18:20; Eph 6:2.** Cp. **Mt 15:6.** Elders (older members of the community) 1 Cl 21:6. The supervisor (ἐπίσκοπος) ISm 9:1a. Teacher of the divine word D 4:1. Those who are really widows

1 Ti 5:3 (though the mng. of τιμή 3 may be influential here; cp. Sir 38:1). πάντας (JWilson, ET 54, '42/43, 193f), τὸν βασιλέα **1 Pt 2:17ab.** (Opp. προσκυνέω Theoph. Ant. 1, 11 [p. 82, 5]). τ. πολλαῖς τιμαῖς (τιμή 2a) **Ac 28:10;** cp. GPt 3:9. Abs. Dg 5:15.—Of God (Soph., fgm. 226 TGF ὃν τιμᾷ θεός; pass. 4 Macc 17:20) or Christ: *(show) honor (to)* or *reward* the Christians (so Isocr. 9, 42; X., An. 1, 9, 14; 5, 8, 25, Cyr. 3, 3, 6; Diod. S. 2, 3, 2 τιμᾶν δώροις; 2, 6, 9; 14, 42, 1; 16, 13, 1; Ps.-Callisth. 2, 1, 2 τιμάω τινὰ χρυσῷ; pass. Hdt. 7, 213; Lys. 12, 64; 19, 18; Diod. S. 15, 74, 1.—On the rewarding of devout persons by God: Ps.-Aristot., Mund. 6, 23 τιμᾶν; Simplicius, In Epict. p. 79, 11 Düb. τιμᾶν κ. κολάζειν; Mel., P. 73, 535 ἠτίμησας τὸν τιμήσαντά σε) **J 12:26;** 1 Cl 59:3; IPhld 11:2; pass. ISm 9, 1b.—The officials of a congregation are called οἱ τετιμημένοι ὑμῶν (partitive gen.) *the honorable men among you* D 15:2 (οἱ τετιμημένοι of persons in high standing: X., Cyr. 8, 3, 9). For ἡ αὐτοῖς τετιμημένη λειτουργία 1 Cl 44:6 s. λειτουργία 1b.—DELG s.v. τιμή. M-M. EDNT. TW.

τιμή, ῆς, ἡ (s. τιμάω; Hom.+; loanw. in rabb.).—**❶ the amount at which someth. is valued, *price, value*** (s. ApcMos 18 νόησον τὴν τιμὴν τοῦ ξύλου Eden's tree) esp. *selling price* (Hdt. et al.; O. Wilck II, 318, 3; POxy 1382, 18 [II AD]) συνεψήφισαν τὰς τιμὰς αὐτῶν (s. συμψηφίζω) **Ac 19:19.** Also concrete *the price received* in selling someth. **5:2.** W. the gen. of that for which the price is paid (Is 55:1; Jos., Vi. 153, Ant. 4, 284; TestZeb 3:2) ἡ τιμὴ τοῦ χωρίου *the price paid for the piece of ground* vs. **3.** ἡ τιμὴ τοῦ τετιμημένου (τιμάω 1) **Mt 27:9.** τιμὴ αἵματος *the money paid for a bloody deed* (αἷμα 2a), *blood money* vs. **6.** Pl. (Diod. S. 5, 71, 3; 6=prize, price, reward) τὰς τιμὰς τῶν πιπρασκομένων **Ac 4:34.** τὰς τιμὰς αὐτῶν *the prices that they received for themselves* 1 Cl 55:2.—W. the gen. of price ᾧ (by attr. of the rel. for ὅ) ὠνήσατο Ἀβραὰμ τιμῆς ἀργυρίου *which Abraham had bought for a sum of silver* **Ac 7:16.** Abs. τιμῆς *at* or *for a price, for cash* (Hdt. 7, 119; PTebt 5, 185; 194; 220 [118 BC]; BGU 1002, 13 δέδωκά σοι αὐτὰ τιμῆς.—B-D-F §179, 1; Rob. 510f; Dssm., LO 275f [LAE 323f]) ἠγοράσθητε τιμῆς **1 Cor 6:20; 7:23** (ἀγοράζω 2).—οὐκ ἐν τιμῇ τινι **Col 2:23** may be a Latinism (cp. Ovid, Fasti 5, 316 nec in pretio fertilis hortus; Livy 39, 6, 9; Seneca, Ep. 75, 11. See Lohmeyer ad loc.) *are of no value* (NRSV). See also s.v. πλησμονή.—GBornkamm, TLZ 73 '48, col. 18, 2 observes that τ. here has nothing to do with 'honor', as it does in the expr. ἐν τιμῇ εἶναι X., An. 2, 5, 38; Herodian 4, 2, 9; Arrian, Anab. 4, 21, 10; Lucian, De Merc. Cond. 17.

❷ manifestation of esteem, *honor, reverence*—ⓐ act., *the showing of honor, reverence,* or *respect* as an action (X., Cyr. 1, 6, 11; Diod. S. 17, 76, 3; Herodian 4, 1, 5; 2 Macc 9:21; Just., A I, 13, 1; Tat. 32, 1; Ath. 30, 2; Theoph. Ant. 1, 11 [p. 82, 5]; usually as a commendation for performance; s. Reader, Polemo 280) **1 Ti 6:1.** ταύτῃ τῇ τιμῇ τιμήσωμεν τ. υἱὸν τοῦ θεοῦ GPt 3:9. So perh. τῇ τιμῇ ἀλλήλους προηγούμενοι **Ro 12:10** (s. προηγέομαι 3). Pl. οἳ πολλαῖς τιμαῖς ἐτίμησαν ἡμᾶς **Ac 28:10** (cp. Diod. S. 11, 38, 5 τιμαῖς ἐτίμησε τὸν Γέλωνα; OGI 51, 13 τοὺς τοιούτους τιμᾶν ταῖς πρεπούσαις τιμαῖς; Jos., Ant. 20, 68. In **1 Th 4:4** τιμή may well be understood in this sense, if σκεῦος refers to a female member of the household; s. also c.—For the τιμαί that belong to the physician, s. Sir 38:1; s. 3 below). Of the demonstrations of reverence that characterize polytheistic worship (OGI 56, 9 αἱ τιμαὶ τῶν θεῶν; Himerius, Or. 8 [=23], 11 ἡ θεῶν τιμή.—S. Orig., C. Cels. 8, 57, 29) Dg 2:8; Judean worship 3:5a.

ⓑ pass. *the respect* that one enjoys, *honor* as a possession. The believers are promised τιμή **1 Pt 2:7** (it is given them w. Christ, the λίθος ἔντιμος vs. 6) but see 4 below; cp. IMg 15. τιμὴν ἔχειν *be honored* (Hdt. 1, 168) **J 4:44; Hb 3:3.** τιμήν τινι (ἀπο)διδόναι **Ro 13:7; 1 Cor 12:24; Rv 4:9** (w. δόξαν). τιμήν τινι ἀπονέμειν (Ath. 32, 3) **1 Pt 3:7;** 1 Cl 1:3; MPol 10:2. τιμήν τινι περιτιθέναι **1 Cor 12:23.** λαβεῖν τιμήν (w. δόξαν) **2 Pt 1:17;** (w. δόξαν and δύναμιν; cp. FPfister, Philol 84, 1929, 1–9) **Rv 4:11; 5:12** (w. δύναμις, as Plut., Mor. 421e: the divinity grants both of them if it is addressed by its various names). τ. τιμῆς μεταλαβεῖν Dg 3:5b. ἑαυτῷ τιμὴν περιποιεῖσθαι Hm 4, 4, 2 (w. δόξαν).—εἰς τιμήν *for honor*=to be honored σκεῦος, *a vessel* that is honored (or dishonored) by the use to which it is put **Ro 9:21; 2 Ti 2:20f.** εἰς τιμήν τινος *for someone's honor*=that the pers. might be honored (Cornutus 28 p. 55, 7 εἰς τιμὴν τῆς Δήμητρος; OGI 111, 26 εἰς τιμὴν Πτολεμαίου; εἰς τιμὴν τῶν Αἰώνων Iren. 1, 5, 1 [Harv. I 42, 16]; εἰς τ. γονέων Did., Gen. 50, 21) IEph 2:1; 21:1, 2; IMg 3:2; ITr 12:2; ISm 11:2; IPol 5:2b; cp. vs. 2a (εἰς τιμὴν τῆς σαρκὸς τοῦ κυρίου). On εἰς λόγον τιμῆς IPhld 11:2 s. λόγος 2c.—An outstanding feature of the use of τ., as already shown in several passages, is its combination w. δόξα (Dio Chrys. 4, 116; 27 [44], 10; Appian, Bell. Civ. 3, 18 §68; Arrian, Ind. 11, 1; Plut., Mor. 486b; Jos., Ant. 12, 118; Iren. 1, 2, 6 [Harv. I 23, 8]): of earthly possessions τὴν δόξαν καὶ τὴν τιμὴν τῶν ἐθνῶν **Rv 21:26** (τιμή concr.=an object of value: Ezk 22:25). Of the unique, God-given position of the ruler 1 Cl 61:1, 2 (in the latter pass. w. ἐξουσία). Mostly of heavenly possessions: **Ro 2:7** (w. ἀφθαρσία), vs. **10** (w. εἰρήνη); **1 Pt 1:7** (w. ἔπαινος); 1 Cl 45:8. Christ is (acc. to Ps 8:6) crowned w. δόξα and τιμή **Hb 2:7, 9.** God is called (amid many other predicates) φῶς, τιμή, δόξα, ἰσχύς, ζωή Dg 9:6.—Hence esp. in the doxological formulas (God as the recipient of τ.: Eur., Bacch. 323 θεῷ τιμὴν διδόναι; Paus. 9, 13, 2; Ps 28:1 [w. δόξα]; 95:7 [w. δόξα]; TestAbr B 14 p. 119, 3 [Stone p. 86]; ApcEsdr 7:16 [w. δόξα, κράτος]; Philo; Jos., C. Ap. 2, 206) **1 Ti 1:17** (w. δόξα); **6:16** (w. κράτος αἰώνιον); w. δόξα and κράτος **Jd 25 v.l.; Rv 5:13** (w. δόξα et al.); **7:12** (w. δόξα et al.); 1 Cl 64 (w. δόξα et al.); 65:2 (w. δόξα et al.); MPol 20:2; 21 (both w. δόξα et al.).

ⓒ as a state of being, *respectability* (cp. τίμιος 1c) **1 Th 4:4** (w. ἁγιασμός). If τιμή is here to be understood as a nomen actionis, the pass. belongs in a.

ⓓ *place of honor, (honorable) office* (Hom. et al. [s. FBleek on Hb 5:4]; pap. In Joseph. of the high-priestly office: Ant. 12:42 Ἐλεαζάρῳ τῷ ἀρχιερεῖ ταύτην λαβόντι τὴν τιμήν; 157 and oft.) οὐχ ἑαυτῷ τις λαμβάνει τὴν τιμήν *no one takes the office of his own accord* **Hb 5:4.**

❸ honor conferred through compensation, *honorarium, compensation* (testament of Lycon [III BC] fgm. 15 W., in Diog. L. 5, 72, a physician's honorarium; Sir 38:1; s. 2a above), so prob. **1 Ti 5:17** (MDibelius, Hdb. ad loc. and see s.v. διπλοῦς).—Mng. 2b is also poss. In that case cp. Ael. Aristid. 32, 3 K.=12 p. 134 D.: διπλῇ τιμῇ τιμῆσαι.—MGreindl (s. δόξα, end).

❹ a right that is specially conferred, *privilege* **1 Pt 2:7** (FDanker, ZNW 58, '67, 96), difft. REB 'has great worth'; NRSV 'is precious'.—B. 825; 1143. DELG. M-M. EDNT. TW. Sv.

τίμιος, α, ον (τιμή; Hom.+) gener. 'held in honor' (Herodas 4, 5 of altars)

❶ pert. to being of exceptional value—ⓐ *costly, precious* Plut., Mor. 486b λίθος **Rv 17:4; 18:12a, 16; 21:19;** AcPl Ha 1, 11 (cp. Tob 13:17 S; JosAs 2:3; 18:4). Superl. (Jos., Ant. 17, 225 φίλον τιμιώτατον) λίθος τιμιώτατος **Rv 21:11.** Pl. λίθοι τίμιοι **1 Cor 3:12** (s. λίθος 2b and the lit. s.v. ἀμέθυστος). ξύλον τιμιώτατον **Rv 18:12b** (on the elative force s. Mussies 71, 128). τίμια ἀρώματα MPol 15:2.

ⓑ ***of great worth/value, precious*** of the blood of Jesus τίμιον αἷμα **1 Pt 1:19;** τίμιον τῷ θεῷ *precious to God* 1 Cl 7:4. τίμιος καρπὸς τῆς γῆς **Js 5:7.** τὰ τίμια καὶ μέγιστα ἐπαγγέλματα **2 Pt 1:4.** τιμίαν ταύτην νηστείαν AcPl Ha 6, 24. Comp. τιμιώτερος w. gen. (Eur., Alc. 301; Menand., Mon. 482; 552 Meinecke [715; 843 Jaekel]): of a martyr's bones τιμιώτερα λίθων πολυτελῶν (Pr 3:15; ApcEsdr 6:15 p. 33, 2 Tdf. τὸ τίμιον . . . αὐτοῦ σῶμα) MPol 18:1. Of the δοκίμιον τῆς πίστεως: πολὺ τιμιώτερον χρυσίου **1 Pt 1:7 v.l.** (on τιμιώτερον χρυσ. cp. Diog. L. 8, 42; EpArist 82; Philo, Sacr. Abel. 83, Det. Pot. Ins. 20; Theophyl. Sim., Ep. 81; cp. PsSol 17:43 χρυσίον τὸ πρῶτον τίμιον).

ⓒ ***held in honor, respected*** (τιμή 2c) τίμιος ὁ γάμος **Hb 13:4.**

ⓓ For οὐδενὸς λόγου ποιοῦμαι τὴν ψυχὴν τιμίαν ἐμαυτῷ **Ac 20:24** cp. λόγος 1aα, end.

❷ **pert. to high status that merits esteem, *held in honor/high regard, respected*** (oft. in the salutations of papyrus letters; cp. the greeting τιμιώτατε πάτερ TestAbr A 2 p. 78, 21 [Stone p. 4]; τ. Ἀβραάμ 7 p. 84, 24 [St. p. 16] and τίμιε Ἀβραάμ 16 p. 97, 21 [St. p. 42]) τινί *by someone* (Jos., Bell. 5, 527 τῷ δήμῳ τίμιος, Ant. 1, 273) **Ac 5:34; 17:34 v.l.**—DELG s.v. τιμή. M-M.

τιμιότης, ητος, ἡ (τίμιος; Aristot. et al.; in pap as an honorary title) ***richness, prosperity*** abstract for concrete *abundance of costly things* **Rv 18:19.**—DELG s.v. τιμή. M-M.

Τιμόθεος, ου, ὁ (freq. found Aristoph., X.+; ins, pap, LXX; Jos., Ant. 12, 329–44) voc. Τιμόθεε **1 Ti 1:18; 6:20.** ***Timothy,*** a friend, traveling companion and co-worker of Paul. **Ac 16:1ff** tells us that he lived in Lycaonia, prob. in Lystra, and was born of a polytheistic father and a monotheistic mother (named Eunice acc. to 2 Ti 1:5). Paul had him circumcised (Ac 16:3) before taking him on one of his important journeys (**2 Cor 1:19; Ac 17:14f; 18:5**), and used him permanently as an associate (συνεργός **Ro 16:21**). He is named as the 'co-writer' of six letters (**2 Cor 1:1; Phil 1:1; Col 1:1; 1 Th 1:1; 2 Th 1:1; Phlm 1**). He was active in Thessalonica (**1 Th 3:2, 6;** s. the **subscr.** to **2 Th**), Corinth (**1 Cor 4:17; 16:10**), and then again in Macedonia (**Ac 19:22**) as Paul's envoy. He also accompanied him on his last journey to Jerusalem (**Ac 20:4**). Later he shared Paul's imprisonment (cp. **Phil 2:19** and also the introductions of the imprisonment epistles except Eph). In 1 and 2 Ti he is mentioned in the salutations (**1 Ti 1:2; 2 Ti 1:2**) and also **1 Ti 1:18; 6:20** (s. above, beg.); **2 Ti subscr.** refers to him as overseer. Finally he appears once more in the NT, **Hb 13:23.** He is mentioned nowhere else in our lit.—AJülicher, RE XIX 1907, 781–88; FPölzl, Die Mitarbeiter des Weltap. Pls 1911, 136ff; ERedlich, St. Paul and His Companions 1913; WHadorn (s.v. ὑπηρέτης); JAlexander, The Character of Tim.: ET 25, 1914, 277–85 (against him GFindlay, ibid. 426); Pauly-W. VI A '37, 1342–54; Kl. Pauly V 851f; BHHW III, 1988–91; WOllrog, Paulus u. s. Mitarbeiter '79; PTrümert, Die Paulustrad. d. Past. '78. On the composition and language of the Pastorals s. PHarrison, The Problem of the Pastoral Epistles 1921; BEaston, The Pastoral Epistles '47; comprehensive comm. by CSpicq '47; MDibelius and HConzelmann, The Pastoral Epistles (Eng. tr.) '72; JWhite, New Testament Epistolary Lit. in the Framework of Ancient Epistolography, ANRW II/25/2 '84, 1730–56. S. also WKümmel, Einleitung[21] '83 —DELG s.v. τιμή. LGPN I. M-M. TW.

Τίμων, ωνος, ὁ (freq. in lit., ins, pap) ***Timon***, one of the seven persons appointed to release the apostles from papyrus-work relating to aid for widows **Ac 6:5** (on the topic cp. Ex 18:13–27).—DELG s.v. τιμή. LGPN I. M-M.

τιμωρέω (τιμωρός 'avenger', fr. τιμή + a root *or* [as in the Dor. τιμάορος, Pind. O. 9, 84, but there in the sense of 'paying honor to']) 1 aor. ἐτιμώρησα Wsd 12:20; pf. 2 pl. τετιμωρήκατε (Tat. 27, 1). Mid.: fut. τιμωρήσομαι LXX; 1 aor. ἐτιμωρησάμην LXX. Pass.: 1 aor. ἐτιμωρήθην; pf. 3 sg. τετιμώρηται 4 Macc 18:5, ptc. τετιμωρημένος (TestSol 5:3) (trag., Hdt. et al.; ins, pap, LXX, En; ParJer 7:26) ***punish*** τινά *someone, have someone punished* (Soph., Oed. Rex 107; Lysias 13, 41; 42; Jos., Ant. 2, 107; 7, 93; TestJos 14:1; Just.; Tat. 27, 1. But the mid. is much more widely used in this sense [it is customary in Philo; Jos., Ant. 1, 195; 17, 211]) **Ac 26:11.** τιμωρεῖν τινα δειναῖς τιμωρίαις *punish someone with terrible punishments* Hs 6, 3, 3. Pass. (X., An. 2, 5, 27; Pla., Gorg. 81, 525b; 2 Macc 7:7; En 22:13) **Ac 22:5;** Hs 6, 3, 4; 6, 5, 3f; 6.—DELG s.v. τιμωρός. M-M.

τιμωρητής, οῦ, ὁ (τιμωρέω; 2 Macc 4:16; Philo, Rer. Div. Her. 109; PCairMasp 5, 16) ***avenger, punisher,*** of the punishing shepherd ὁ ποιμὴν ὁ τιμωρητής Hs 7:1 Joly. ὁ ἄγγελος ὁ τιμ. 7:1, 6 (cp. ὁ τιμωρὸς δαίμων Herm. Wr. 1, 23; Lydus, Mens. 90, 24).—DELG s.v. τιμωρός.

τιμωρία, ας, ἡ (fr. τιμωρός 'avenger', s. τιμωρέω) ***punishment*** (Aeschyl., Hdt.+) in our lit. inflicted by God (Theopompus [IV BC]: 115 fgm. 253, p. 590, 29 Jac. παρὰ θεῶν τιμ.; Eth. Epic. col. 12, 7 τιμ. ἐκ θεῶν; Diod. S. 13, 21, 1 τιμ. παρὰ θεῶν; 16, 64, 1; Aesop, Fab. 1 P.=5 H. ἐκ θεοῦ τιμ. Cp. Jos., Bell. 2, 155 τιμωρίαι ἀδιάλειπτοι) B 20:1; Hs 6, 3, 2b; 6, 4, 4; 6, 5, 3ab. πόσῳ δοκεῖτε χείρονος ἀξιωθήσεται τιμωρίας; *how much more severe a punishment, do you think, will be decreed for . . . ?* **Hb 10:29** (Diod. S. 4, 12, 7 ἕκαστος τιμωρίας ἠξιώθη=each one had punishment inflicted on him; 16, 31, 2; 16, 46, 3). Pl. (Pla., Ep. 7, 335a μεγίστας τ. [of God]; Diod. S. 1, 96, 5 τὰς τῶν ἀσεβῶν ἐν ᾅδου τιμωρίας; Plut., Mor. 566e [in the nether world]; LXX; TestJos 3:1; EpArist 208; Philo; Jos., C. Ap. 2, 292; Just., A II, 20, 4 al.; Tat. 17, 1) Hs 6, 3, 3; 4ab; 6, 5, 7. μετὰ πολλὰς . . . βασάνους καὶ τιμωρίας Papias (3:3). τιμωρίαν ὑπέχειν *undergo punishment* (schol. on Soph., Oed. Col. 1565 p. 460 Papag.; Ath. 2, 1) MPol 6:2. ὁ ἄγγελος τῆς τιμωρίας *the punishing angel* (s. τιμωρητής) Hs 6, 3, 2a; 7:2 (Leutzsch, Hermas 476 n. 157).—DELG s.v. τιμωρός. M-M.

τίνω (Hom. et al.; PHamb 22, 5; Just., A I, 17, 1) fut. τίσω (better τείσω: Kühner-Bl. II 552; Mayser 91, 2; B-D-F §23; Mlt-H. 261) **to experience retribution, *pay, undergo a penalty*** δίκην τίνειν (since Soph., Aj. 113; s. δίκη 1; Pr 27:12 ζημίαν τείσουσιν) **2 Th 1:9;** Hm 2:5; s 9, 19, 3.—DELG. M-M.

τίς, τί gen. **τίνος**, dat. **τίνι**, acc. **τίνα, τί** (Hom.+) interrogative pron. in direct, indirect and rhetorical questions (W-S. §25, 1ff; B-D-F §298f, al.; Rob. 735–40 al.)

❶ **an interrogative ref. to someone or someth., *who? which (one)? what?***—ⓐ as subst.—**α.** τίς;—**א.** *who? which one?* τίς ὑπέδειξεν ὑμῖν; **Mt 3:7; Lk 3:7.** τίς ἐστιν ὁ παίσας σε; **Mt 26:68** (FNeirynck, ETL 63, 5–47; RBrown, The Death of the Messiah '94, II 578–80). τίνος υἱός ἐστιν; *whose son is he?* **22:42b.** τίνα λέγουσιν οἱ ἄνθρωποι εἶναι τὸν υἱὸν τοῦ ἀνθρώπου; **16:13.** Cp. **Mk 11:28; 12:16; 16:3; Lk 9:9, 18; J 18:4, 7** (cp. Jos., Ant. 9, 56). τίς σοφὸς . . . ἐν ὑμῖν; **Js 3:13.** τίς οὖν ἐστιν; who, then, is she? Hs 2, 4, 1.—Esp. in questions to which the answer 'nobody' is expected **Ac 8:33** (Is 53:8); **Ro 7:24; 8:24, 33–35; 9:19b; 10:16** (Is 53:1); **11:34ab** (Is 40:13ab); **1 Cor 9:7abc; 2 Cor 11:29ab.** Likew. τίς . . . εἰ μή; *who . . . except (for), but?* **Mk 2:7; Lk 5:21b; 1J 2:22; 5:5** (PsSol. 5:3, 11). Pl.

ὑμεῖς δὲ τίνες ἐστέ; **Ac 19:15.** Cp. **2 Ti 3:14; Hb 3:16–18; Rv 7:13.**—Foll. by partitive gen. (JosAs 6:7 [τίς . . . ἀνθρώπων;]; Ar. 9, 5; Tat. 2, 1) τίς τούτων τῶν τριῶν; **Lk 10:36.** τίνος ὑμῶν υἱός; **14:5.** τίνι τῶν ἀγγέλων; **Hb 1:5.** τίνα τῶν προφητῶν; **Ac 7:52.** Cp. **Mt 22:28; Mk 12:23; Hb 1:13** al. For the part. gen. τίς ἐξ ὑμῶν; etc. **Mt 6:27; Lk 11:5; 14:28.**—**Mt 21:31.** τίνα ἀπὸ τῶν δύο; **Mt 27:21.**

ב. *who?* in the sense *what sort of person?* (=ποῖος; cp. Ex 3:11; Jdth 12:14; Jos., Ant. 6, 298; Ath. 12, 2) τίς ἐστιν οὗτος ὃς λαλεῖ βλασφημίας; **Lk 5:21a.** Cp. **19:3; J 8:53; Ac 11:17** (cp. 4 Km 8:13); **Ro 14:4; 1 Cor 3:5ab v.l.** (in both); **Js 4:12.** σὺ τίς εἶ; (just) *who are you? what sort of person are you?* (Menand., Epitr. 391 S. [215 Kö.]; Epict. 3, 1, 22; 23; Herm. Wr. 1, 2; Job 35:2; Tat. 6, 2 τίς ἤμην, οὐκ ἐγίνωσκον) **J 1:19; 8:25; 21:12.** τίς εἰμι ἐγὼ ὅτι *who am I, that* GJs 12:2 (Ex 3:11).

ג. *which of two?* (=πότερος) **Mt 27:17; Lk 22:27; J 9:2.**

ד. as a substitute for the rel. pron. (Callimachus 28 [=30], 2; Ptolemaeus Euergetes in Athen. 10, 438e τίνι ἡ τύχη δίδωσι, λαβέτω. Cp. BGU 665 III, 13 [I AD]; 822, 4 [III AD] εὗρον γεοργόν, τίς αὐτὰ ἑλκύσῃ; Gen 38:25; Lev 21:17; Dt 29:17; s. 1aβד below and s. Kühner-G. II 517f; OImmisch, Leipz. Studien z. klass. Philol. 10, 1887, 309ff; KBuresch, RhM n.s. 46, 1891, 231ff; Mlt. 21 n. 1; 93f; Rob. 737f; Dssm., LO 266, 5 [CIG 9552—LAE 313, 6]; Mayser II/1, 1926, 80) τίνα με ὑπονοεῖτε εἶναι οὐκ εἰμὶ ἐγώ **Ac 13:25 v.l.** So also **Js 3:13,** if it is to be punctuated τίς σοφὸς ἐν ὑμῖν, δειξάτω.

β. τί;—א. *what?* τί σοι δοκεῖ; **Mt 17:25a;** cp. **18:12; 21:28.** τί ποιήσει; vs. **40.** Cp. **Mk 9:33; 10:3, 17; Lk 10:26; J 1:22b; 18:38; Ac 8:36; Ro 10:8; 1 Cor 4:7b** al. τίνι; *to what (thing)?* **Lk 13:18ab; 20.**—W. prepositions: διὰ τί; *why? for what reason?* cp. διά B 2b. εἰς τί; *why? for what purpose?* εἰς 4f. ἐν τίνι; *with what? through whom?* **Mt 5:13; 12:27; Mk 9:50; Lk 11:19; 14:34; Ac 4:9.** πρὸς τί; *why?* (X., Cyr. 6, 3, 20; 8, 4, 21) **J 13:28.** χάριν τίνος; *why?* lit. 'because of what thing?' **1J 3:12** (cp. Just., A II, 12, 5; Tat. 34, 3).

ב. *what sort of thing?* (=ποῖον) τί ἐστιν τοῦτο; *what sort of thing is this?* (Ps.-Lucian, Halc. 1 τίς ἡ φωνή; Ex 16:15) **Mk 1:27.** τί τὸ πλοῦτος *what sort of wealth* **Col 1:27;** cp. **Eph 1:19; 3:18.**

ג. *which of two?* (=πότερον; Pla., Phlb. 52d) **Mt 9:5; 23:19; Mk 2:9; Lk 5:23; 1 Cor 4:21; Phil 1:22.**

ד. τί as pred. can go w. a subject that is in the pl. (Pla., Tht. 155c τί ἐστι ταῦτα; [so also TestAbr A 12 p. 91, 16=Stone p. 30, and TestLevi 2:9 v.l.]; Lucian, Dial. Deor. 11, 1; Synes., Prov. 2, 2 p. 118b; Laud. Therap. 18 τί μοι ταῦτα; cp. TestAbr A 7 p. 83, 32 [Stone p. 14] τί τὰ ὁραθέντα; GrBar 2:7 τί εἰσιν οἱ ἄνθρωποι οὗτοι; what's the meaning of these people? Jos., Vi. 296 τί γεγόνασιν;) or that is not neut. gender (B-D-F §299, 1; 2; Rob. 736; cp. X., Hell. 2, 3, 17 τί ἔσοιτο ἡ πολιτεία, Mem. 4, 2, 21; GrBar 6:13 τί ἐστιν ἡ φωνὴ αὕτη; ApcMos 5 τί ἐστιν πόνος καὶ νόσος;): τί ἐστι ἄνθρωπος; (Epict. 2, 5, 26; 2, 9, 2) **Hb 2:6** (Ps 8:5). ταῦτα τί ἐστιν εἰς τοσούτους; **J 6:9.** ἐπυνθάνετο τί ἂν εἴη ταῦτα **Lk 15:26.** τί ἐσόμεθα **1J 3:2.** τί ἄρα ὁ Πέτρος ἐγένετο *what had become of Peter* **Ac 12:18.** οὗτος δὲ τί (ἔσται); *what about this man?* **J 21:21.** This pass. forms a transition to

ה. elliptical expressions: τί οὖν; (X., Mem. 4, 2, 17; Teles p. 25, 13; Diod. S. 13, 26, 1; Ael. Aristid. 28, 17 K.=49 p. 496 D.; schol. on Pind., O. 12, 20c; Jos., Bell. 2, 364; Just., D. 3, 6; Ath. 15, 1.—**1 Cor 14:15, 26** the expr. is given more fully τί οὖν ἐστιν; **Ro 6:1; 7:7; 9:14, 30** τί οὖν ἐροῦμεν; **1 Cor 10:19** τί οὖν φημι;) **J 1:21; Ro 3:9; 6:15** (Seneca, Ep. 47, 15 also introduces an absurd inference w. 'quid ergo'); **11:7.**—τί γάρ; *what, then, is the situation?* (Ps.-Pla., Erx. 1, 392b; Diod. S. 34 + 35 fgm. 2, 38; Dio Chrys. 71 [21], 16; Lucian, Tyrannic. 13; Just., D. 1, 3) **Ro 3:3;** *what does it matter?* **Phil 1:18.** Also τί γάρ μοι (TestJob 23:8 τί γάρ μοι ἡ θρίξ) w. inf. foll. *is it any business of mine?* (Tat. 33, 2 τί γάρ μοι . . . λέγειν why should I take the time . . . to say something?—cp. without γάρ Epict. 2, 17, 14 καὶ τί μοι; 3, 22, 66 τί οὖν σοι; Maximus Tyr. 2, 10c) **1 Cor 5:12.**—On τί πρὸς ἡμᾶς (πρός σε); s. πρός 3eγ. On τί ἐμοὶ καὶ σοί; s. ἐγώ, end; also Schwyzer II 143; Goodsp., Probs. 98–101; MSmith, JBL 64, '45, 512f; JLilly, CBQ 8, '46, 52–57. τί ἡμῖν καὶ σοί; has the same mng.: **Mt 8:29; Mk 1:24a; Lk 4:34a** (cp. Epict. 2, 19, 16; 2, 20, 11).—τί ὅτι;=τί γέγονεν ὅτι; (cp. **J 14:22**) *what* has happened *that? why?* (LXX; JosAs 16:5 τί ὅτι εἶπας . . . ;) **Mk 2:16 v.l.; Lk 2:49; Ac 5:4, 9;** Hs 9, 5, 2.—On ἵνα τί s. the entry ἱνατί.

ו. as a substitute for the relative (SIG 543, 12; 705, 56; 736, 50; s. aαד above) οὐ τί ἐγὼ θέλω ἀλλὰ τί σύ **Mk 14:36.** Cp. **4:24; Lk 17:8; Ac 13:25.** Pl. **1 Ti 1:7.**—οὐκ ἔχουσιν τί φάγωσιν **Mt 15:32; Mk 8:2** (cp. vs. **1**) is prob. to be understood as an indirect question='they do not know what they are to eat' (W-S. §24, 17b).

γ. Two interrog. pronouns stand together without a conjunction (distributive; s. Kühner-G. II 521f; B-D-F §298, 5; Rob. 737) τίς τί ἄρῃ *what each one should receive* **Mk 15:24.** τίς τί διεπραγματεύσατο *what each one gained in trading* **Lk 19:15 v.l.** Cp. Hv 3, 8, 6; m 6, 1, 1 (s. also Ael. Aristid. 31 p. 598 D.: τί τίς ἂν λέγοι; Ps.-Clem., Hom. 2, 33).

ⓑ as adj. (TestAbr A 15 p. 96, 15 [Stone p. 40] τί ῥῆμα γενήσεται; TestJob 47:1 τίς οὖν χρεία; ApcEsdr 5:26 p. 30, 30 Tdf. τίς ἄρα ἄνθρωπος; Just., A I, 53, 2 al.) τίνα *what (sort of)* μισθὸν ἔχετε; **Mt 5:46.** τίς βασιλεύς; **Lk 14:31.** Cp. **15:4, 8; J 2:18; 18:29; Ac 10:29; 1 Cor 15:2; 2 Cor 6:14–16** (five times). **1 Th 4:2** οἴδατε γὰρ τίνας παραγγελίας *for you know what instructions (we gave you).* In **Ac 7:49** τίς replaces ποῖος (as read by D, after Is 66:1); cp. **1 Pt 1:11,** where τίς and the following ποῖος are contrasted. τί περισσόν; etc.: **Mt 5:47; 19:16; 27:23.**

❷ **interrogative expression of reason for, *why?*** adv. τί (Hom., Pla., et al.; LXX; TestAbr A 8 p. 85, 23 [Stone p. 18]; B 7 p. 111, 4 [St. p. 70]; ApcEsdr 5:16 p. 30, 15 Tdf.; ApcSed 3:1; ApcMos 27; Just., A I, 20, 3; Tat. 10, 2; Ath. 17, 4) τί μεριμνᾶτε; *why do you worry?* **Mt 6:28.** Cp. **7:3; 19:17; Mk 2:7a, 8; 4:40; 11:3; Lk 2:48; 6:46; 19:33; 24:38a; J 7:19; 18:23; Ac 1:11; 14:15; 26:8; 1 Cor 4:7c; 10:30; Col 2:20.** τί τοῦτο ἐποίησας; GJs 13:2; 15:3 (GrBar 1:2 τί ἐποίησας τοῦτο;). τί οὖν ὁ νόμος; *why have the law, then*=well then, what's the use of the (Mosaic) law? **Gal 3:19.** τί καί; *why, indeed? for what possible reason?* **1 Cor 15:29b, 30.** τί γινώσκω ποῦ ἐστιν ὁ υἱός μου; *how should I know where my son is?* GJs 23:1.

❸ **exclamatory expression of extent or degree, *how!*** adv. τί (transl. of Hebr. מַה; W-S. §21, 4; B-D-F §299, 4; Rob. 739; 1176; LXX [Ps 3:2; SSol 1:10; 7:7; 2 Km 6:20]; Basilius, Hexaëm. p. 8b MPG τί καλὴ ἡ τάξις [s. JTrunk, De Basilio Magno sermonis Attici imitatore: Wissensch. Beilage z. Jahresber. d. Gymn. Ehingen a. D. 1911, 36]) τί στενή **Mt 7:14;** τί θέλω **Lk 12:49** (s. θέλω 1, end, and Black, Aramaic Approach[3], '67, 121–24).—M-M. EDNT.

τὶς, τὶ, gen. **τινός,** dat. **τινί,** acc. **τινά, τὶ** (Hom.+) enclitic, indefinite pronoun (W-S. §26, 1–4; B-D-F §301 al.; Rob. 741–44)

❶ **a ref. to someone or someth. indefinite, *anyone, anything; someone, something; many a one/thing, a certain one***

ⓐ subst.—**α.** τὶς, τινές—א. *someone, anyone, somebody* **Mt 12:29, 47; Mk 8:4; 9:30; 11:16; Lk 8:46; 9:57; 13:6, 23; J 2:25; 6:46; Ac 5:25; 17:25; Ro 5:7ab; 1 Cor 15:35; 2 Cor**

11:20 (five times); **Hb 3:4; Js 2:18; 2 Pt 2:19** al. Pl. τινές *some, a number of* (people—supplied as in Appian, Hann. 47 §203 λαβών τινας=he received some, i.e. people; TestAbr B 14 p. 118, 20 [Stone p. 84]; TestJob 9:8; Just., A I, 28, 2) **Lk 13:1; Ac 15:1; Gal 2:12; 2 Th 3:11;** *anyone* **2 Pt 3:9b** (TestAbr B 12 p. 116, 24 [Stone p. 80] εἶδεν ... τινὰς ἀπερχομένους εἰς ἔρημον τόπον).—In contrast to a majority made evident by the context *some* of those present (Appian, Bell. Civ. 1, 26 §119 ἔφερόν τινες) **Mk 14:65; J 13:29a;** of all (under consideration) **1 Cor 8:7; 9:22.** ἀνατρέπουσιν τήν τινων πίστιν **2 Tim 2:18;** AcPlCor 1:2.—W. partitive gen. (Diod. S. 2, 24, 4; Plut., Mor. 189a τῶν ἐχθρῶν τις; Epict. 2, 14, 1 τὶς τῶν Ῥωμαϊκῶν; TestReub 4:2 τινὶ τῶν ἀδελφῶν; Ar. 12, 7 τινὲς ... αὐτῶν; Just., A I, 27, 3; Tat. 36, 2) τὶς τῶν Φαρισαίων *(some) one of the Pharisees, a Pharisee* **Lk 7:36.** Cp. **11:45; Ac 5:15.** τὶς ὑμῶν **1 Cor 6:1.** Pl. τινὲς τῶν γραμματέων *some (of the) scribes* **Mt 9:3.** Cp. **12:38; 28:11; Mk 7:1f; 12:13; Lk 6:2; Ac 10:23; 12:1; 17:18a, 28; 1 Cor 10:7–10** al.—Also τὶς ἐκ (Plut., Galba 1065 [27, 2]; Appian, Bell. Civ. 3, 84 §343 τὶς ἐκ τῆς βουλῆς) τὶς ἐξ ὑμῶν **Js 2:16; Hb 3:13;** GJs 24:2. Pl. τινὲς ἐξ αὐτῶν (Jos., Bell. 1, 311; Just., D. 85, 1 τινὲς ἐξ ὑμῶν) **Lk 11:15.** Cp. **J 6:64; 7:25, 44; 9:16; 11:37, 46; Ac 15:24.**—τὶς ἐν ὑμῖν *any one among you, any of you* **Js 5:13a, 14, 19.** ἐν ὑμῖν τινες **1 Cor 15:12.**—ταῦτά τινες ἦτε *some of you were that sort of people* **6:11** (οὗτος 1bζ). τινές described by a rel. clause (Dionysius Com. [IV BC] 11 εἰσίν τινες νῦν, οὓς ...) **Mk 9:1.** τὶς in **14:47** is prob. not original (PDickerson, JBL 116, '97, 302).

ב. with suggestion of non-specificity in a context where an entity is specified to some extent τίς *a certain pers.*, etc., of a definite pers. **Lk 9:49; 2 Cor 2:5; 10:7; 11:21** (of an opponent as UPZ 146, 2 [II BC]; Sallust. 12 p. 24, 20; 24.—Artem. 4, 22 p. 214, 20ff τὶς ... οὗ ἐγὼ καίπερ εὖ εἰδὼς τὸ ὄνομα οὐκ ἐπιμνησθήσομαι; Tat. 27, 1 [of Callimachus]). Pl. τινές *certain people,* etc. (Crates, Ep. 32 [p. 82 Malherbe]; Demosth. 25, 40, Ep. 3, 8; Diod. S. 15, 18, 1; Appian, Bell. Civ. 5, 112 §470 'certain' people who had conspired to cause trouble; Iambl., Myst. 1, 13 p. 43, 2 P.; Sallust. 4 p. 4, 28) **Ro 3:8; 1 Cor 4:18; 15:34; 2 Cor 3:1; 1 Ti 1:3, 19** al.; **2 Pt 3:9a.** W. a name added ἦν δέ τις ἀσθενῶν, Λάζαρος *there was a man who was ill, named L.* **J 11:1** (begins like a story that originally circulated independently; cp. Alcman 84 Diehl[2] ἦσκέ [=ἦν] τις Καφεὺς ἀνάσσων=there was once someone, named Capheus, who ruled). The name is also added in **Ac 18:7.** W. a subst. ptc. τινές εἰσι οἱ ταράσσοντες **Gal 1:7** (cp. Lysias 19, 57 εἰσί τινες οἱ προαναλίσκοντες).

ג. For εἷς τις s. εἷς 3c. For εἴ τις s. εἰ 7. ἐάν τις (TestAbr B 13 p. 118, 7 [Stone p. 84]; Just., D. 46, 1 ἐὰν δέ τινες) **Mt 21:3a; 24:23; Mk 11:3; Lk 16:30; J 6:51** al.; **Ac 13:41** (Hab 1:5); **1 Cor 8:10; 10:28; Col 3:13a; 1 Ti 1:8; 2 Ti 2:5; Js 2:14; 1J 2:1, 15; 4:20; Rv 3:20; 22:18f.** ἐὰν μή τις *if someone ... not* **J 3:3, 5; 15:6;** *if no one* **Ac 8:31.** τὶς w. a neg. *no one, nobody* οὐ ... τὶς **J 10:28.** οὐδὲ ... τὶς **Mt 11:27; 12:19.** οὔτε ... τὶς **Ac 28:21.** οὐ ... ὑπό τινος **1 Cor 6:12.** μή τις *that no one* **Mt 24:4; Mk 13:5; Ac 27:42; 1 Cor 1:15; 16:11; 2 Cor 8:20; 11:16a; Eph 2:9; 1 Th 5:15; Hb 4:11** al. πρὸς τὸ μή τινα **1 Th 2:9.** ὥστε μὴ ... τινά **Mt 8:28.**

ד. The ptc. that belongs directly w. the indef. pron. is added w. the art. πρός τινας τοὺς πεποιθότας *to some who put their trust* **Lk 18:9.** Cp. **2 Cor 10:2; Gal 1:7; Col 2:8.** But it also stands without the art: τινῶν λεγόντων *when some were talking* **Lk 21:5.** Cp. **1 Ti 6:10, 21; Hb 10:28.**

ה. corresponding τὶς ... ἕτερος δέ *someone ... and another* **1 Cor 3:4.** τινὲς (μὲν) ... τινὲς (δὲ) **Lk 9:7f; Phil 1:15** (τινὲς μὲν ... τινὲς δέ as Diod. S. 12, 41, 6; Ar. 8, 2).

ו. *each one* καθώς τις ἄξιός ἐστιν κατοικεῖν *as each one deserves to dwell* Hs 8, 2, 5a. Cp. 8, 4, 2. B-D-F §301, 2.

β. τὶ, τινά—**א.** *something, anything* ὁ ἀδελφός σου ἔχει τι κατὰ σοῦ **Mt 5:23.** Cp. **20:20; Mk 8:23; 9:22; 13:15; Lk 7:40; 11:54; J 13:29a; 1 Cor 10:31** al.—W. partitive gen. (Diod. S. 20, 39, 3 τινὰ τῶν ἀφηρπασμένων=some of what had been seized [by the enemy]; Just., D. 2, 4 τὶ τῶν εἰς εὐδαιμονίαν συντελούντων something that contributes to happiness) τὶ τῶν ὑπαρχόντων **Ac 4:32.** Cp. **Ro 15:18; Eph 5:27.** τὶ ἀγαθοῦ Hs 5, 3, 3.

ב. in negative statements *not (nor) anything =nothing* οὔτε ... τὶ **Ac 25:8.** οὐδὲ ... τὶ **1 Ti 6:7** (TestJob 11:12; cp. JosAs 10:20 μηδὲ ... τινός).

ג. τινὰ μὲν ... τινὰ δέ *some ... others* (w. ref. to πρόβατα and hence neut.) Hs 6, 2, 2.

ד. On εἴ τι s. εἰ 7.

ה. εἶναί τι *be* or *amount to someth.* **Gal 2:6; 1 Cor 3:7.** εἰ δοκεῖ τις εἶναί τι μηδὲν ὤν **Gal 6:3** (s. 2 below and s. W-S. §26, 3).

Ⓑ adj.—**α.** *some, any, a certain,* though oft. omitted in transl. into Engl.; used with

א. a subst. τὶς: ἱερεύς τις **Lk 1:5; 10:31.** ἀνήρ (a narrative begins in this way Syntipas p. 16, 4; 30, 3; 46, 16; 57, 1; Just., D. 81, 4 [of John]) **Ac 3:2; 8:9a; 14:8.** ἄνθρωπος **Mt 18:12** (JosAs 28:4). κώμη **Lk 17:12** (Just., A I, 34, 2). Cp. **7:2, 41; 18:2; J 4:46; Ac 27:8; Hb 4:7.**—τὶ: ὕδωρ **Ac 8:36.** σκεῦος **10:11.**

ב. a proper name (X., Hell. 5, 4, 3; Jos., Ant. 12, 160; Ar. 10, 1 Ἥφαιστόν τινα; Just., A I, 26, 4 Μένανδρον ... τινά; Ath. 12, 1 Μίνως τις) Σίμωνά τινα *a certain Simon* **Lk 23:26; Ac 10:5f; Mk 15:21.** Σίμων τις AcPlCor 1:2. Cp. **Ac 21:16; 22:12; 25:19b.**

ג. an adj. or adjectival pron. μέγας **Ac 8:9b.** ἕτερός τις vs. **34** (GrBar 6:6; Just., D. 128, 4; Mel., P. 26, 180). τὶς ἕτερος Papias (2, 4). τὶς ἄλλος **1 Cor 1:16; Phil 3:4** (TestAbr B 6 p. 110, 7 [Stone p. 68] ἄλλο τι; TestJob 11:2 ἄλλοι τινές; Just., D. 6, 1 ἄλλο τι). τινὲς ἄλλοι (Diod. S. 5, 81, 4 ἄλλοι τινὲς [τ. ποιητῶν]; Jos., Ant. 8, 248; Just., D. 84, 4 ἄλλαι τινές) **Ac 15:2.** τὶ ἀγαθόν **Ro 9:11;** Hs 2, 10. ἀσφαλές τι **Ac 25:26.** Cp. **Hb 11:40.**—In neg. statements (TestAbr A 8 p. 86, 3 [Stone p. 20]) *not any = no* **Lk 11:36; Js 5:12.**

β. serving to moderate or heighten—**א.** to moderate an expr. that is too definite (Just., D. 48, 1 [λόγος] ... παράδοξός τις ... δοκεῖ μοι εἶναι [your statement], in my judgment, does not make much sense; Diod. S. 1, 1, 3; Appian, Bell. Civ. 1, 15 §65 οἱά τινες δορυφόροι=as a kind of bodyguard) ἀπαρχήν τινα *a kind of first-fruits* **Js 1:18** (Appian, Bell. Civ. 3, 39 §162 τὶς μετάνοια=something like remorse; 3, 77 §314 συγγνώμη τις=some kind of pardon).—So perh. δύο τινὰς τῶν μαθητῶν *several disciples, perhaps two* **Lk 7:18** (cp. Appian, Bell. Civ. 2, 59 §245 δύο τινάς=a few [ships], about two; Jos., Ant. 16, 274). But the expr. in **Ac 23:23** τινὰς δύο τῶν ἑκατονταρχῶν certainly means two, who simply cannot be more closely defined (s. W-S. §26, 1b; Rob. 742; Mlt-Turner 195).

ב. w. adjectives of quality and quantity to heighten the rhetorical emphasis φοβερά τις ἐκδοχὴ κρίσεως **Hb 10:27.** βραχύ τι *(only) a little* **2:7, 9** (Ps 8:6).

γ. of an indefinite quantity that is nevertheless not without importance, *some, considerable* χρόνον τινά (Diod. S. 13, 75, 6 μετά τινα χρόνον; Jos., Ant. 8, 398) **Ac 18:23; 1 Cor 16:7.** Cp. **Ro 1:11, 13.** μέρος τι **1 Cor 11:18.**

δ. τινές *several* (Appian, Bell. Civ. 2, 49 §202 ἱππεῖς τινες; Just., D. 50, 2 λόγους τινάς; Ath. 23, 1 τινὰς ... ἐνεργείας) ἡμέρας τινάς **Ac 9:19; 10:48; 15:36.** γυναῖκές τινες **Lk 8:2.** Cp. **Ac 15:2; 17:5f** al.—On its position in the sentence s. W-S. §26, 4; B-D-F §473, 1; Rob. 743.

❷ a ref. to someone of prominence, ***a person of importance*** τὶς εἶναι τις *to be a person of importance, to be somebody* (Eur., El. 939; Theocr. 11, 79; Herodas 6, 54; Epict. 3, 14, 2, Ench. 13; Lucian, Lexiph. 22, Adv. Indoct. 1; Tat. 16, 2 εἶναί τινες; PGM 13, 288 ἐγώ εἰμί τις) λέγων εἶναί τινα ἑαυτόν *claiming to be somebody* **Ac 5:36;** IEph 3:1 (so also τὶ; s. 1aβℶ above; antonym s.v. οὐδείς 2bβ).—DELG. M-M. EDNT.

Τίτιος, ου, ὁ (CIL III, 3053; 6010, 223; XII, 4141; Jos., Ant. 16, 270) ***Titius,*** a σεβόμενος τὸν θεόν (σέβω 1b) in Corinth, whose surname was Justus **Ac 18:7** (v.l. Τίτος; many mss. omit this half of the name entirely and have simply Ἰούστου).—EGoodspeed, JBL 69, '50, 382f identifies Titius Justus w. Gaius (Γάϊος 3; s. comm.).

τίτλος, ου, ὁ (Lat. loanw.=titulus: ins [Hahn 231, 10, w. lit.; Hatch 143f]; later pap; Jer 21:4 in Aq., Sym., Theod.; Mel., P. 95, 727) ***inscription, notice*** on the cross, which gave the reason for condemnation **J 19:19f** (on this custom s. Sueton., Calig. 32, Domit. 10; Cass. Dio 54, 8; also the letter of the churches at Lyons and Vienne: Eus., HE 5, 1, 44). P-FRegard, Le titre de la Croix d'après les Év.: RevArch 28, 1928, 95–105.—M-M.

Τίτος, ου, ὁ (Polyb.; Diod. S. 11, 51, 1; 15, 23, 1; 16, 40, 1 et al.; ins, pap; Jos., Ant. 14, 229f) ***Titus.***

❶ friend and colleague of Paul, mentioned in our lit. only in Paul's letters. As a Gentile Christian he accompanied Paul to a meeting at Jerusalem; Paul did not have him circumcised, though Judaizers demanded that he do so **Gal 2:1, 3.** Later he effected a reconciliation betw. Paul and the Corinthian church when the latter seemed lost to the apostle, and he arranged for a collection: **2 Cor 2:13; 7:6, 13f; 8:6, 16, 23; 12:18; subscr.—2 Ti 4:10** mentions a journey of Titus to Dalmatia. Acc. to **Tit 1:4** the apostle left him, his γνήσιον τέκνον, behind in Crete to organize the churches there (s. vs. 5); see also **title** and **subscr.** of **Tit** for the name. Τίτον καὶ τὸν Λουκᾶν AcPl Ha 11, 16 (Aa I, 116, 16f); AcPl Ant 13, 13 (Aa I, 237, 1).—AJülicher, RE XIX 1907, 798–800; CBarrett, MBlack Festschr. '69, 1–18. Lit. s.v. Τιμόθεος (Pölzl 103ff) and Ἰωάν(ν)ης 6.

❷ surnamed Justus **Ac 18:7 v.l.;** s. Τίτιος.—LGPN I. M-M.

τιτρώσκω 1 aor. ἔτρωσα LXX. Pass. fut. τρωθήσομαι LXX; aor. 2 sg. ἐτρώθης Is 57:10 Sym.; pf. τέτρωμαι 3 Km 22:34, ptc. τετρωμένος (Hom.+; ins, LXX, Philo; Jos., Bell. 2, 526, Ant. 7, 128) **to inflict a wound,** ***wound, injure, damage*** in imagery of damage to the inner life τετρωμένος κατὰ διάνοιαν *wounded in mind* (διάνοια 1) GPt 7:26 (cp. 2 Macc 3:16 τιτρώσκεσθαι τὴν διάνοιαν; Diod. S. 17, 112 τετρωμένος τὴν ψυχήν; Herodian 1, 8, 7; Philo).—DELG.

τοί (prop. ethical dat. of συ, L-S-J-M, s. also Denniston 537; Schwyzer I 602) enclitic particle (Hom.+; LXX; Jos., Ant. 15, 374; 16, 319; Just., A I, 4, 8 καὶ γάρ τοι) **marker of emphasis on the reliability of a statement,** ***let me tell you, surely,*** in our lit. only in the transition formula πέρας γέ τοι *and furthermore, besides* (πέρας 3) B 5:8; 10:2; 12:6; 15:6, 8; 16:3.—For μέν τοι s. μέντοι.—DELG s.v. το- 1.

τοιγαροῦν (on the form s. Schwyzer I 560; Denniston 114) (Soph., Hdt.+; PTebt 315, 14 [II AD]; PGiss 3, 7; Sb 6222, 12; LXX; En 102:9; GrBar 4:16; Philo, Virt. 202; Jos., Bell. 4, 168, Ant. 10, 10, C. Ap. 2, 178; Just., Mel.) **a particle introducing an inference,** ***for that very reason, then, therefore*** (in first position, as in most ancient writers, exc. Hippocrates and occasionally Lucian, s. Denniston 566–68) **1 Th 4:8;** 1 Cl 57:4, 6 (Pr 1:26, 31). In an exhortation (Achilles Tat. 7, 11, 3; Jos., C. Ap. 2, 201; GrBar 4:16; Just., D. 55, 3; 65, 7; 134, 2; Mel., P. 59, 428) **Hb 12:1** (here P^{46} has τοίγαρ).—M-M.

τοίνυν (Pind., Hdt.+) **a particle introducing an inference,** ***hence, so, well (then), indeed*** as the second word in its clause (the usual position, so Hdt., Demosth. et al. [s. Denniston 568–77 on the position and lively, conversational aspect of τ.]; POxy 902, 10; 1252 verso, 18; Wsd 1:11; Job 8:13; 36:14; En 101:1; TestAbr A 1 p. 77, 11 [Stone p. 2]; JosAs 6:5 [1:1, 7 al. cod. A]; ApcrEzk; Jos., Ant. 2, 67; 14, 32; Ar., Just., Ath.) **1 Cor 9:26; Js 2:24 v.l.;** Dg 3:2. Beginning its clause (only in later wr., e.g. Sext. Emp., Math. 8, 429; IG IV, 620, 13; POxy 940, 3; Is 3:10; 5:13; 27:4; 33:23; TestJob 41:5; Mel.) τ. ἀπόδοτε *well then, give back* **Lk 20:25** (w. impv.); **Hb 13:13** (w. hortatory subj.); 1 Cl 15:1 (w. hort. subj.)—M-M.

τοιόσδε, άδε, όνδε (Hom., Hdt. et al.; 2 Macc 11:27; 15:12; TestSol 22:2 B; Jos., Ant. 17, 142; 209) ***such as this, of this kind,*** referring to what follows and w. suggestion of unusual aspect **2 Pt 1:17.**—DELG s.v. τοῖος. M-M.

τοιοῦτος, αύτη, οῦτον (this form of the neut. is predom. in Attic wr.; also JosAs 6:7; 13:11; 1 Esdr 1:19; Jos., C. Ap. 1, 12; 2, 222; **Mt 18:5 v.l.; Ac 21:25** D; Just., A I, 12, 4; Tat. 15, 2) and **οῦτο** (PCairZen 379, 8; 482, 13 [III BC]; POsl 17, 9 [136 AD]; 1 Cl 43:1; Mel., HE 4, 26, 13) correlative adj. **pert. to being like some pers. or thing mentioned in a context,** ***of such a kind, such as this, like such*** (Hom.+).

ⓐ correlative οἷος . . . τοιοῦτος (X., Mem. 2, 6, 12; Lucian, Dial. Deor. 4, 4; Sir 49:14; Just., A II, 14, 2 τοιαῦτα, ὁποῖα) **1 Cor 15:48ab; 2 Cor 10:11b.** τοιούτους ὁποῖος (Jos., Ant. 7, 385) **Ac 26:29.**

ⓑ adj.**—α.** used w. a noun**—ℵ.** w. the art., mostly attributive (GrBar 7:5; Ar. 11, 2; Just., A I, 12, 4; Tat. 15, 2; Mel., HE 4, 26, 6; Ath. 7, 1) ἓν τῶν τοιούτων παιδίων *one child like this* (as indicated in vs. 36) **Mk 9:37.** τὸν τοιοῦτον ἄνθρωπον *such a man* **2 Cor 12:3** (cp. vs. 2). ἡ τοιαύτη παρθένος AcPl Ox 6, 15f (ἡ τοιαύτη αἰδὼς τῆς παρθένου Aa I 241, 15). τῆς τοιαύτης διακονίας IPhld 10:2 (cp. vs. 1). οἱ τοιοῦτοι δίκαιοι 2 Cl 6:9 (cp. vs. 8). Pred. αἱ δυνάμεις τοιαῦται *such are the miracles* **Mk 6:2.** ἡ γνῶσις τοιαύτη *the knowledge is of this kind* (as is described in what follows) B 19:1.

ℶ. without the article (TestAbr A 11 p. 89, 19 [Stone p. 26] ἐν τοιαύτῃ δόξῃ; JosAs 6:7; 13:11; GrBar 1:2; Ar. 13:1; Just., A I, 9, 5; Mel., P. 20, 137; Ath. 22, 1) ἐξουσίαν τοιαύτην *such power* **Mt 9:8.—18:5; Mk 4:33; J 9:16; Ac 16:24; 1 Cor 11:16; 2 Cor 3:4, 12; Hb 7:26; 13:16; Js 4:16.** AcPlCor 1:9 ἔστι γὰρ ἃ λέγουσιν . . . τοιαῦτα *what they say . . . is as follows*

ℷ. τοι. can have its mng. made clear by a rel. clause τοιαύτη πορνεία ἥτις οὐδὲ ἐν τοῖς ἔθνεσιν (sc. ἀκούεται) **1 Cor 5:1.** τοιοῦτος ἀρχιερεύς, ὅς **Hb 8:1** (Dio Chrys. 15 [32], 7 χορὸς τοιοῦτος . . . , ὅς). ἄνθρωποι τοιοῦτοι οἵτινες B 10:3–5.

β. τοιοῦτος ὤν (Just., A I, 43, 8; Ath. 29, 1) *since I am the sort of person* (who presumes to make an appeal) **Phlm 9** (foll. by ὡς=in my character as; Andoc., Alcibiades 16). τοιούτου σου ὄντος *since you* (Christ) *are so* (downcast) AcPl Ha 7, 31. ὁ πατὴρ τοιούτους ζητεῖ τοὺς προσκυνοῦντας αὐτόν *the Father seeks such people to worship him* **J 4:23** (double acc. as Vett. Val. 315, 20 τινὰς τοὺς τοιούτους; Jos., Ant. 12, 281). The pleonastic use of τοι. after a relative is due to Semitic infl.

(Ex 9:18, 24; 11:6) θλῖψις οἵα οὐ γέγονεν τοιαύτη *tribulation such as has never been seen* **Mk 13:19.**

ⓒ subst.—**α.** quite predom. w. the art. (B-D-F §274; Rob. 771)

א. of persons ὁ τοιοῦτος *such a person;* either in such a way that a definite individual with special characteristics is thought of, or that any bearer of certain definite qualities is meant (Just., D. 47, 2) **Ac 22:22; 1 Cor 5:5, 11; 2 Cor 2:6f; 10:11a; 12:2, 5; Gal 6:1; Tit 3:11.** Pl. οἱ τοιοῦτοι (Aeschyl., Thu. et al.; TestAsh 2:9; 4:5; ApcEsdr 1:18 p. 25, 12 Tdf.; Tat. 2, 2; Mel., HE 4, 26, 9; Ath. 34, 1) **Mt 19:14; Mk 10:14; Lk 18:16; Ro 16:18; 1 Cor 7:28; 16:16** al.

ב. of things τὰ τοιαῦτα *such* or *similar things, things like that* (X., Cyr. 1, 2, 2 a catalogue of vices concluding καὶ . . . τἆλλα τὰ τοιαῦτα ὡσαύτως; sim., Ael. Aristid. 37, 27 K.=2 p. 27 D.; Plut., Mor. 447a; GrBar 13:4; Just., D. 18, 3) **Ac 19:25; Ro 1:32; 2:2f; Gal 5:21; Eph 5:27.** ἐν τοῖς τοιούτοις *in such cases, under such circumstances* (X., Cyr. 5, 4, 17) **1 Cor 7:15.**

β. without the art. τοιαῦτα *such things* (Socrat., Ep. 14, 6 [p. 256 Malherbe]; TestNapht 9:1; GrBar 1:3; Ar. 8, 5; Just., D. 6, 1; Tat. 21, 1; Mel., P. 74, 544) **Lk 9:9; 13:2 v.l.** (for ταῦτα); **Hb 11:14.**—DELG s.v. τοῖος. M-M.

τοῖχος, ου, ὁ (Hom.+) ***wall,*** in denunciatory expression τοῖχε κεκονιαμένε *whitewashed wall* **Ac 23:3** (since RSmend, Ezech. 1880, Ezk 13:10 is usu. compared here).—DELG s.v. τεῖχος. M-M.

τοκετός, οῦ, ὁ (fr. τίκτω via τόκος; Aristot. et al.; BGU 665 II, 10 [I AD]; Sb 5873, 4; LXX; Jos., Ant. 1, 213) ***childbearing, giving birth*** IEph 19:1. In imagery of the tortures of martyrdom ὁ τοκετός μοι ἐπίκειται *the pains of birth are upon me* IRo 6:1.—DELG s.v. τίκτω.

τόκος, ου, ὁ (τίκτω; Hom. et al. in the sense 'offspring' etc.) ***interest*** on money loaned (Pind., Pla. et al.; ins, pap, LXX, Philo; Jos., C. Ap. 2, 208; Ath. 30, 3) **Mt 25:27; Lk 19:23** (PLond II, 218, 4 p. 15 [III BC] ἐδάνεισεν σὺν τόκῳ). τόκοι τόκων *compound interest* (Aristoph., Nub. 1156 al.) ApcPt 16:31.—JHerrmann, Zinssätze usw. [Greco-Egypt. pap], JJP 14, '62, 23–31. B. 800.—DELG s.v. τίκτω. M-M.

τόλμα, ης, ἡ (Ionic/Att. form of τόλμη; Pind., Hdt.+; Diod. S. 18, 25, 1; SIG 709, 25 [107 BC]; POxy 1119, 8; PFlor 382, 48; LXX; Jos., Bell. 4, 424, Ant. 14, 474, Vi. 222; SibOr 4, 154; Just., D. 79, 2; Tat. 14, 1) ***audacity*** 1 Cl 30:8 (w. θράσος [as Socrat., Ep. 14, 1=p. 252 Malherbe], αὐθάδεια).—DELG s.v. τόλμη. M-M. s.v. τολμάω. Sv.

τολμάω impf. ἐτόλμων; fut. τολμήσω; 1 aor. ἐτόλμησα; pf. inf. τετολμηκέναι (Just., D. 133) (s. τόλμα; Hom.+) **to show boldness or resolution in the face of danger, opposition, or a problem,** ***dare, bring oneself to (do someth.)***

ⓐ w. inf.—**α.** *dare, have the courage, be brave enough* ὑπὲρ τοῦ ἀγαθοῦ τάχα τις καὶ τολμᾷ ἀποθανεῖν **Ro 5:7** (on being willing to die for a good man cp. Ael. Aristid. 46 p. 346 D.; Vita Philonid. [s.v. τράχηλος]). Cp. **Phil 1:14.** Mostly used w. a neg. (TestAbr B 4 p. 109, 1 [Stone p. 66]; Jos., Ant. 20, 7 ἀντιλέγειν οὐκ ἐτόλμων; Just., A I, 19, 2 and D. 33, 1) οὐδὲ ἐτόλμησέν τις ἐπερωτῆσαι **Mt 22:46.** Cp. **Mk 12:34; Lk 20:40; J 21:12; Ac 5:13.** Μωϋσῆς οὐκ ἐτόλμα κατανοῆσαι *Moses did not venture to look at (it)* **7:32.**

β. *bring oneself, presume* (Theognis 1, 377 Zeus brings himself to include sinners and upright in the same fate; 'The Tragedy' in Simplicius In Epict. p. 95, 42 τολμῶ κατειπεῖν=I do not hesitate to say plainly; Himerius, Or. 20, 3 λέγειν τ.; 3 Macc 3:21; TestAbr B 6 p. 110, 12 [Stone p. 68]; TestJob 24, 7; Philo, Somn. 1, 54; Jos., C. Ap. 1, 318; Just., A I, 61, 11) τολμᾷ τις ὑμῶν κρίνεσθαι ἐπὶ τῶν ἀδίκων; *can any of you bring yourself to go to law before the unrighteous?* **1 Cor 6:1** (κρίνω 5aβ). W. a neg. (TestAbr B 4 p. 109, 1 [Stone p. 66]; GrBar 12:6; Just., A II, 3, 6 and D. 112, 4) οὐ τολμήσω τι λαλεῖν **Ro 15:18.** Cp. **2 Cor 10:12; Jd 9.**

ⓑ abs. *be courageous* (Job 15:12) ἐν ᾧ ἄν τις τολμᾷ, . . . τολμῶ κἀγώ *whatever anyone else dares to do, . . . I can bring myself (to do the same)* **2 Cor 11:21.** τολμῆσαι ἐπί τινα *show courage* or *boldness toward* or *against someone* (En 7:4) **10:2.** τολμήσας εἰσῆλθεν *he summoned up courage and went in* **Mk 15:43;** GJs 24:2 (cp. Plut., Camillus 140 [22, 6] τολμήσας παρέστη).—DELG s.v. τόλμη. B. 1149. M-M. TW.

τολμηρός, ά, όν (τόλμη; Eur., Thu. et al.; Sir 8:15; 19:3; JosAs 23:7 cod. A 17, 7 [p. 67, 5 Bat.]; Jos., Ant. 1, 113; 14, 165; Just.) ***bold, daring, audacious,*** adv. τολμηρῶς (Thu. 3, 74, 1; 83, 3; X. et al.; Mitt-Wilck. I/2, 461, 25 [III AD]). Comp. τολμηρότερος (Isocr. 14, 8 Bl. and oft.; Sir 19:2; Philo, Op. M. 170): its adverbs, **τολμηροτέρως Ro 15:15 v.l.** and **τολμηρότερον** (Thu. 4, 126, 4; Polyb. 1, 17, 7) **Ro 15:15,** both=***rather boldly.***—DELG s.v. τόλμη. TW.

τολμηροτέρως s. τολμηρός.—M-M.

τολμητής, οῦ, ὁ (τόλμη; Thu. 1, 70, 3; Plut.; Lucian; Philo, De Jos. 222; Jos., Bell. 3, 475) ***bold, audacious pers.*** τολμηταὶ αὐθάδεις **2 Pt 2:10** (on the semantic field cp. Reader, Polemo p. 296f).—DELG s.v. τόλμη. M-M. TW.

τομός, ή, όν (τέμνω; Soph., Pla.+) **pert. to having the capacity to cut efficiently,** ***cutting, sharp*** comp. τομώτερος (PSI 624, 1 [III BC]) in imagery of the word of God **Hb 4:12** (cp. Lucian, Tox. 11; Ps.-Phoc. 124 ὅπλον τοι λόγος ἀνδρὶ τομώτερόν ἐστι σιδήρου).—DELG s.v. τέμνω. M-M.

τόνος, ου, ὁ (τείνω 'stretch'; Aeschyl., Hdt. et al.; Philo; Jos., Bell. 6, 162) prim. 'stretching, tension', in our lit. only fig. ***force, lasting quality*** (Plut., Brut. 999 [34, 3] τῆς ὀργῆς) ὁ φόβος αὐτοῦ (the devil) τόνον οὐκ ἔχει=*fear of the devil puts one under no strain* Hm 12, 4, 7.—DELG s.v. τανυ- E.

τόξον, ου, τό (Hom.+; ins, pap, LXX; En; PsSol 17:33; TestAbr B 14 p. 118, 22 [Stone p. 84]; TestJud; SibOr 3, 730; Jos., Ant. 1, 103; Ar. 11, 1) ***the bow*** as an archer's weapon (Hecataeus: 264 fgm. 21, 203 Jac. [in Jos., C. Ap. 1, 203]; TestJud 3:3; 7:5; 9:3) **Rv 6:2** (AKerkeslager, JBL 112, '93, 116–21: the rider on the white horse, a negative image of false messianic kingship).—B. 1388. DELG. M-M.

τοξότης, ου, ὁ (Hom. et al.; ins, pap, JosAs, Joseph.) ***archer*** AcPl Ha 5, 6.—DELG s.v. τόξον.

τοπάζιον, ου, τό (Athenodorus [I BC]: 746 fgm. 4, 5 Jac. [in Clem. Alex., Protr. 4, 48, 5]; Diod. S. 3, 39, 5; Strabo 16, 4, 6; Ex 28:17; 36:17; Job 28:19; Ps 118:127; Ezk 28:13) ***topaz,*** a bright yellow, more or less transparent (Michel Psellus, in Lapidaires p. 204, ln. 7 λίθος διαφανής) precious stone, in ancient times oft. made into seals and gems; though perh. it is the more valuable golden-yellow chrysolith that is meant **Rv 21:20.**—For lit. see s.v. ἀμέθυστος.—DELG. M-M.

τοποθεσία, ας, ἡ (τόπος, θέσις [τίθημι]; Diod. S., Ptolem. et al.; pap) **an orderly arrangement in an area,** ***placement*** αἱ τοποθεσίαι αἱ ἀγγελικαί prob. refers to the celestial positioning of the angelic hosts *the angelic stations/ranks* ITr 5:2 (cp. the posting of angels in Rv; Vett. Val. 42, 12 of the arrangement of heavenly bodies).

τόπος, ου, ὁ (Aeschyl.+) prim. 'place, position, region'.

❶ an area of any size, gener. specified as a place of habitation—ⓐ inhabited geographical area: ***place,*** of a city, village, etc. (Manetho: 609 fgm. 10, 238 Jac.; in Jos., C. Ap. 1, 238; Diod. S. 1, 15, 6; 2, 13, 6; 13, 64, 7; Jos., C. Ap. 1, 86; 2, 34) οἱ ἄνδρες τοῦ τόπου ἐκείνου (cp. Gen 29:22) **Mt 14:35.** Cp. **Mk 6:11** (of the inhabitants); **Lk 4:37; 10:1** (w. πόλις as 2 Ch 34:6; Jos., C. Ap. 2, 115); **Ac 16:3; 27:2; Rv 18:17** (s. πλέω). ἐν παντὶ τόπῳ *everywhere* that people or Christians live (cp. Diod. S. 13, 22, 3 εἰς πάντα τόπον; Mal 1:11; TestDan 6:7; ParJer 5:32; Just., D. 41, 3, and on the exaggeration in epistolary style PLond III, 891, 9 p. 242 [IV AD, Christian] ἡ εὐφημία σου περιεκύκλωσεν τ. κόσμον ὅλον) **1 Cor 1:2; 2 Cor 2:14; 1 Th 1:8; 2 Th 3:16 v.l.;** MPol 19:1; AcPl Ha 6, 5 and15. Also κατὰ πάντα τόπον MPol ins ἐν παντὶ τόπῳ καὶ χρόνῳ D 14:3. This is perh. the place for τὸν τόπον καὶ τὸ ἔθνος **J 11:48** (the Sin. Syr. and Chrysost. vol. VIII 386e take τόπ. to mean Jerusalem [cp. 2 Macc 3:2, 12]; but s. 1b below). ἐν ποίῳ τόπῳ *where* AcPl Ha 6, 12; without ἐν Hv 1:7 Joly. εἰς ἕτερον τόπον *to another place* (Dio Chrys. 70 [20], 2; Plut., Mor. 108d) **Ac 12:17.** Cp. AFridrichsen, Kgl. Hum. Vetensk. Samf. i. Uppsala, Årsbok '43, 28–30.

ⓑ inhabited structure: ***space, place, building*** et al. (Diod. S. 20, 100, 4 τόποι=buildings; POslo 55, 10 [c. 200 AD]; 1 Km 24:23; 2 Ch 25:10) **Ac 4:31** (Stephan. Byz. s.v. Τρεμιθοῦς: the τόπος quakes at the παρουσία of Aphrodite). Esp. of a temple (2 Macc 5:17–20 [w. ἔθνος]; 10:7; 3 Macc 1:9ab al.; EpArist 81) perh. **J 11:48** (s. 1a above; the same problem arises concerning τόπος PLond 2710 recto, 6: HTR 29, '36, 40; 45f.—τ. of a temple Mitt-Wilck. I/2, 94, 20 [beg. II AD]; Jos., Ant. 16, 165); τόπος ἅγιος (cp. Is 60:13; 2 Macc 1:29; 2:18; 8:17) **Mt 24:15; Ac 6:13; 21:28b.**

ⓒ a portion of a larger area: ***place, location*** (Diod. S. 2, 7, 5 τόπος τῆς πόλεως=the place on which the city stands; Just., D. 40, 2 ὁ τ. τῆς Ἰερουσαλήμ) ἔρημος τόπος (ἔρημος 1a) **Mt 14:13;** cp. vs. **15; Mk 1:35; 6:31f, 35; Lk 4:42; 9:12;** GJs 17:3. Pl. **Mk 1:45.** πεδινός **Lk 6:17.** κρημνώδης Hv 1, 1, 3; s 6, 2, 6. καλός v 3, 1, 3b. τόπος τοῦ ἀγροῦ *a place in the country* 2, 1, 4; 3, 1, 3a; τοῦ σπηλαίου GJs 19:2 (cp. Just., D. 70, 1; 78, 6). Cp. Hv 2, 1, 1; s 6, 2, 4. On τόπος διθάλασσος **Ac 27:41** s. διθάλασσος. Cp. τραχεῖς τόποι *rocky places* vs. **29.** ὁ τόπος ὅπου (TestAbr B 10 p. 114, 13 [Stone p. 76]; ParJer 7:32; ApcMos 33; Just., D. 78, 8) *the place where* **Mt 28:6; Mk 16:6; J 4:20; 6:23; 10:40; 11:30; 19:20, 41.** ὁ τόπος ἔνθα GPt 13:56 (Just., A I, 19, 8; Mel., HE 4, 26, 14). ὁ τόπος ἐφ᾽ ᾧ ἕστηκας **Ac 7:33** (cp. Ex 3:5). The dat. for εἰς w. acc. (B-D-F §199) ποίῳ τόπῳ ἀπῆλθεν Hv 4, 3, 7. ἐν παντὶ τόπῳ *in every place* (in Jerusalem) 1 Cl 41:2. Combined w. a name εἰς τόπον λεγόμενον Γολγοθᾶ **Mt 27:33a.** ἐπὶ τὸν Γολγοθᾶν τόπον **Mk 15:22a.—Lk 23:33; J 19:13; Ac 27:8; Rv 16:16.** W. gen.: κρανίου τόπος **Mt 27:33b; Mk 15:22b; J 19:17** (s. κρανίον). τόπος τῆς καταπαύσεως **Ac 7:49;** B 16:2 (both Is 66:1; s. κατάπαυσις 1).—Pleonastic ἐν τόπῳ χωρίου Ῥωμαίων IRo insc. (s. τύπος 6c, end).—*(Definite) place, (particular) spot, scene* **Lk 10:32; 19:5; 22:40; J 5:13; 6:10.** ἐκεῖνον τὸν τόπον Papias (3:3) (Just., D. 3, 1 ἐκείνου τοῦ τόπου).

ⓓ pl. ***regions, districts*** (Diod. S. 4, 23, 2; 13, 109, 2; Artem. 2, 9 p. 92, 28; PHib 66, 2; PTebt 281, 12 al.; EpArist 22; Jos., C. Ap. 1, 9) ἄνυδροι τόποι **Mt 12:43; Lk 11:24.** οἱ ἀνατολικοὶ τόποι *the east* 1 Cl 25:1. κατὰ τόπους *in various regions* (κατά B 1a) **Mt 24:7; Mk 13:8; Lk 21:11.** εἰς τοὺς κατὰ τὴν Ἀσίαν τόπους **Ac 27:2** (Antig. Car. 172 εἰς τοὺς τόπους).

ⓔ an abode: ***place, room*** to live, stay, sit etc. (UPZ 146, 31; 37 [II BC]) **Rv 12:14.** ἔτι τόπος ἐστίν *there is still room* **Lk 14:22** (Epict. 2, 13, 10 ποῦ ἔτι τόπος; where is there still room?; Ath. 8, 4 τίς ἐστι τόπος;). οὐκ ἦν αὐτοῖς τόπος ἐν τῷ καταλύματι **2:7.** οὐκ ἔνι τ. ἀπόκρυφος *there was no hiding-place* GJs 22:3. ἔχειν τόπον *have (a) place* **Rv 12:6;** cp. IPhld 2:2; Hv 3, 5, 5; 3, 7, 5; 3, 9, 5; m 12, 5, 4ab. ἑτοιμάσαι τινὶ τόπον **J 14:2f** (cp. **Rv 12:6**). δὸς τούτῳ τόπον *make room for this person* **Lk 14:9a** (Epict 4, 1, 106 δὸς ἄλλοις τόπον=make room for others). ὁ ἔσχατος τόπος (ἔσχατος 1 and 3) vss. **9b** and **10** (on τόπος='a place to sit', cp. Jos., Ant. 12, 210 οἱ τ. τόπους κατὰ τὴν ἀξίαν διανέμοντες; Epict. 1, 25, 27; Paus. Attic. α, 128 τόπος of a seat in a theater; Diog. L. 7, 22 ὁ τῶν πτωχῶν τόπ.=the place where the poor people sat [in the auditorium where Zeno the Stoic taught]; Eunap. p. 21; IPergamon 618, s. Dssm., NB 95 [BS 267]). ὁ τόπος αὐτῶν μετὰ τῶν ἀγγέλων ἐστίν *their place is with the angels* Hs 9, 27, 3. On ὁ ἀναπληρῶν τὸν τόπον τοῦ ἰδιώτου **1 Cor 14:16** s. ἀναπληρόω 4 (for τόπος='position' s. TestAbr B 4 p. 108, 20 [Stone p. 64] ἕκαστος εἰς τὸν τόπον αὐτοῦ; Philo, Somn. 1, 238; Jos., Ant. 16, 190 ἀπολογουμένου τόπον λαμβάνων).

ⓕ the customary location of someth.: the ***place*** where someth. is found, or at least should or could be found; w. gen. of thing in question ἀπόστρεψον τὴν μάχαιράν σου εἰς τὸν τόπον αὐτῆς **Mt 26:52** (w. ref. to the sheath). ὁ τόπος τῶν ἥλων *the place where the nails had been* **J 20:25 v.l.** (Theodor. Prodr. 9, 174 'the mark' of scratch-wounds). ὁ τόπος αὐτῆς *its place,* of the lampstand's place **Rv 2:5.** Cp. **6:14.** τόπος οὐχ εὑρέθη αὐτοῖς *there was no longer any place for them* (Da 2:35 Theod.—Ps 131:5) **20:11;** cp. **12:8.** Non-literal use οὐκ ἂν δευτέρας (sc. διαθήκης) ἐζητεῖτο τόπος *there would have been no occasion sought for a second (covenant)* **Hb 8:7.** On τὸν τῆς ὑπακοῆς τόπον ἀναπληρώσαντες 1 Cl 63:1 s. ἀναπληρόω 3. ἀποκατασταθήσῃ εἰς τὸν τόπον σου (cod. A οἶκον) *you will be restored to your former circumstances* Hs 7:6.

ⓖ a transcendent site: esp. of the ***place*** to which one's final destiny brings one. Of the place of salvation (Tob 3:6 ὁ αἰώνιος τόπος; TestJob 49:2 τοῦ ὑψηλοῦ τόπου; JosAs 22:9 τῆς καταπαύσεως; ApcSed 16:5 ἀναψύξεως καὶ ἀναπαύσεως; Ath. 22, 7 οὐράνιον τόπον): 2 Cl 1:2. πορεύεσθαι εἰς τὸν ὀφειλόμενον τόπον τῆς δόξης 1 Cl 5:4. εἰς τὸν ὀφειλόμενον αὐτοῖς τόπον παρὰ τῷ κυρίῳ Pol 9:2. ὁ ἅγιος τόπος 1 Cl 5:7. Cp. 44:5; B 19:1.—ὁ ἴδιος τόπος can be neutral (PGM 4, 3123; Cyranides p. 120, 6), a place where one is destined to go IMg 5:1. But the expr. can also gain its specif. mng. fr. the context. Of a place of torment or evil (TestAbr A 13 p. 93, 12 [Stone p. 34; foll. by κολαστήριον]; TestAbr B 10 p. 114, 10 [Stone p. 76]; Iambl., Vi. Pyth. 30. 178 ὁ τῶν ἀσεβῶν τ. Proclus on Pla., Cratylus p. 72, 7 Pasqu.) **Ac 1:25b;** cp. Hs 9, 4, 7; 9, 5, 4; 9, 12, 4. W. gen. ὁ τόπος τῆς βασάνου **Lk 16:28.**

❷ a specific point of reference in a book, *place, passage* (Polyb. 12, 25f, 1; Περὶ ὕψους 9, 8 [=p. 18, 5 V.]; 1 Esdr 6:22 v.l.; Philo, De Jos. 151; Jos., Ant. 14, 114; Just., D. 112, 4; cp. Περὶ ὕψους 3, 5 [=p. 8, 6 V.]) **Lk 4:17.** Cp. 1 Cl 8:4; 29:3; 46:3.

❸ a position held in a group for discharge of some responsibility, *position, office* (Diod. S. 1, 75, 4 in a judicial body; 19, 3, 1 of a chiliarch [commander of 1,000 men]; Ps.-Callisth. 2, 1, 5 the τόπος of the priest-prophetess; ins [ΕΛΛΗΝΙΚΑ 7, '34, p. 179 ln. 50, 218 BC]; pap; Dssm., NB 95 [BS 267]) λαβεῖν τὸν τόπον τῆς διακονίας **Ac 1:25a.** For ἐκδίκει σου τὸν τόπον IPol 1:2 s. ἐκδικέω 3. τόπος μηδένα φυσιούτω *let high position inflate no one's ego* ISm 6:1. τοῖς ἱερεῦσιν ἴδιος ὁ τόπος προστέτακται *a special office has been assigned the priests* 1 Cl 40:5.—44:5. εἰς τὸν τόπον τοῦ Ζαχαρίου GJs 24:4.

❹ **a favorable circumstance for doing someth., *possibility, opportunity, chance*** (Just., D. 36, 2 ἐν τῷ ἁρμόζοντι τόπῳ *at the appropriate point* in the discussion; w. gen. Polyb. 1, 88, 2 τόπος ἐλέους; Heliod. 6, 13, 3 φυγῆς τόπος; 1 Macc 9:45) τόπον ἀπολογίας λαβεῖν *have an opportunity to defend oneself* **Ac 25:16** (cp. Jos., Ant. 16, 258 μήτ' ἀπολογίας μήτ' ἐλέγχου τόπον ἐχόντων). μετανοίας τόπον εὑρεῖν **Hb 12:17;** διδόναι (cp. Wsd 12:10) 1 Cl 7:5. In the latter pass. the persons to whom the opportunity is given are added in the dat. (cp. Plut., Mor. 62d; Mitt-Wilck. I/2, 14 III, 15 [I AD] βασιλεῖ τόπον διδόναι=give a king an opportunity; Sir 4:5). μηδὲ δίδοτε τόπον τῷ διαβόλῳ *do not give the devil a chance* to exert his influence **Eph 4:27.** δότε τόπον τῇ ὀργῇ *give the wrath (of God) an opportunity* to work out its purpose **Ro 12:19** (on ὀργῇ διδόναι τόπον cp. Plut., Mor. 462b; cp. also δὸς τόπον νόμῳ Sir 19:17. On **Ro 12:19** s. ESmothers, CBQ 6, '44, 205–15, w. reff. there; Goodsp., Probs. 152–54). τόπον ἔχειν *have opportunity* (to do the work of an apostle) **15:23.**

❺ idiom: ἐν τῷ τόπῳ οὗ ἐρρέθη αὐτοῖς …, ἐκεῖ κληθήσονται (=LXX Hos 2:1) is prob. to be rendered *instead of their being told …, there they shall be called* **Ro 9:26** (cp. Hos 2:1 בִּמְקוֹם אֲשֶׁר 'instead of' s. HWolff, Hosea [Hermeneia] '74, 27; Achmes 207, 17 ἐν τῷ τόπῳ ἐκείνῳ=instead of that).—DELG. M-M. EDNT. TW. Sv.

τοσοῦτος, αύτη, οῦτον (this form of the neut. is predom. in Attic Gr., also Appian, Bell. Civ. 3, 43 §177; LXX, GrBar; Jos., C. Ap. 1, 226; 2, 176; **Hb 7:22 v.l.; 12:1; Rv 21:16 v.l.;** 1 Cl 1:1; MPol 2:2; Hm 5, 1, 5; Just., Ath.) and **οῦτο** (Clearchus, fgm. 48 W.: Diod. S. 1, 58, 4; PCairZen 367, 38; PMich I [Zen] 28, 17 [III BC]; Num 15:5; 1 Macc 3:17; **Hb 7:22;** 1 Cl 45:7; Just., A I, 56, 2) correlative adj. (Hom.+) 'so great, so large, so far, so much, so strong' etc.

❶ **pert. to an indefinite high number of entities or events, *so many,*** pl.—ⓐ w. a noun (Just., D. 75, 4 ἐν τοσαύταις μορφαῖς) *so many* ἄρτοι τοσοῦτοι **Mt 15:33** (w. ὥστε foll.). ἔτη **Lk 15:29.** σημεῖα **J 12:37.** Cp. **21:11; 1 Cor 14:10** (s. τυγχάνω 2b); Hs 6, 4, 4.

ⓑ without a noun τοσοῦτοι *so many people* **J 6:9;** AcPl Ha 7, 21 (unless this goes under 2).

❷ **pert. to high degree of quantity, *so much, so great***

ⓐ w. a noun τοσοῦτος ὄχλος **Mt 15:33b.** ὁ τοσοῦτος πλοῦτος **Rv 18:17** (Erasmian rdg, and only here w. the art.; s. B-D-F §274; Rob. 771). τοσοῦτον μέλι *so great a quantity of honey* Hm 5, 1, 5. τοσαύτη ἔκρυσις Papias (3:2). Of space μῆκος **Rv 21:16 v.l.** Of time χρόνος (PLond I, 42, 23 p. 30 [168 BC]; POxy 1481, 2; ParJer 5:18; Jos., Bell. 1, 665; 2, 413; Dio Chrys. 74, 18b; Ath. 17, 3) *so long* **J 14:9; Hb 4:7.** τοσ. διαφορά so *great a difference* MPol 16:1. Referring back to ὅσα: τοσοῦτον βασανισμόν **Rv 18:7.** For **Hb 12:1** s. 3 below.

ⓑ without a noun, pl. τοσαῦτα of quantity *so much* (Socrat., Ep. 14, 6 [p. 256, 11 Malherbe]; Just., D. 77, 1 τοιαῦτα καὶ τοσαῦτα) Hv 2, 1, 3. ἡμαρτηκὼς τοσαῦτα *since I have sinned so many times* Hm 9:1. Some likewise understand quantitatively τοσαῦτο ἐπάθετε; *have you experienced so much?* **Gal 3:4** but on this and Hm 9:1 s. 3b.

❸ **pert. to high degree of quality or lack of it, *so great/strong, to such extent,*** etc.—ⓐ w. a noun and in a positive sense πίστις *faith as strong as this* **Mt 8:10; Lk 7:9.** ἔλεος 2 Cl 3:1. ζωή 14:5. χρηστότης 15:5. σπουδή MPol 7:2. τάχος 13:1. W. ὥστε foll. (Ps.-Callisth. 3, 26, 7 p. 127, 6; Just., D. 30, 3) τοσ. ἀπόνοια 1 Cl 46:7. W. ὡς foll. *as strong as* MPol 15:2; *so strong that* ApcPt 5:16 (Just., D. 132, 1). This is prob. the place for τοσοῦτον νέφος μαρτύρων *so great a cloud of witnesses* (the 'great' number being qualified, of course, by literary constraints) **Hb 12:1.**

ⓑ without a noun and in a negative sense, εἰς τοσοῦτο(ν) foll. by gen. and ὥστε *to such a degree of* (Andoc. 2, 7: εἰς τοσοῦτον ἦλθον τῆς δυσδαιμονίας …, ὥστε; Pla., Apol. 13, 25e; Clearchus, fgm. 48; Jos., Bell. 4, 317 εἰς τοσ. ἀσεβείας, ὥστε, C. Ap. 1, 226) 1 Cl 1:1; 45:7; MPol 2:2. τοσοῦτον *to the degree that, to such an extent that* (GrBar 1:3; 8:3; Just., D. 90, 4) τὰ βλέφαρα … τοσοῦτον ἐξοιδῆσαι ὡς *the eyelids (of Judas) became so swollen, that* Papias (3:2) (w. ὡς as Just., D. 121, 3). Perh. Hm 9:1 belongs here: *such serious sins* (s. 2b above). In satire τοσαῦτα ἐπάθετε; *have you had such remarkable experiences?* **Gal 3:4** (πάσχω 1; others put the pass. under 2b above).

❹ **pert. to a limited extent, *so much and no more*** τοσούτου (gen. of price) *for so and so much* **Ac 5:8ab.**

❺ **pert. to a correlative degree, *so much, as much*** τοσούτῳ w. the comp., corresp. to ὅσῳ *(by) so much* (greater, more, etc.) … *than* or *as* (X., Mem. 1, 3, 13; Ael. Aristid. 23, 55 K.=42 p. 786 D.; Just., D. 110, 4) **Hb 1:4; 10:25** (τοσούτῳ μᾶλλον ὅσῳ as Ael. Aristid. 33 p. 616 D.; 46 p. 345; cp. X., Mem. 1, 4, 10); *the more … the more* 1 Cl 41:4; 48:6. τοσοῦτον … ὅσον *as much … as* Papias (2:4) οὐ … τοσοῦτόν με ὠφελεῖν ὅσον *not the same (evidential) value as* (Just., D. 1, 3; Ath. 15, 2). καθ' ὅσον … κατὰ τοσοῦτο **Hb 7:20–22.** τοσούτῳ ἥδιον … ἐπειδή *all the more gladly … since* 1 Cl 62:3. τοσοῦτον.—DELG s.v. τόσος. M-M.

τότε (Hom.+) a correlative (s. ὅτε and ὁπότε) adv. of time, in the NT a special favorite of **Mt,** who uses it about 90 times (AMcNeile, Τότε in St. Matthew: JTS 12, 1911, 127f). In **Mk** 6 times, **Lk** 15 times, **Ac** 21 times, **J** 10 times. It is lacking in Eph, Phil, Phlm, 1 Ti, 2 Ti, Tit, Js, 1 Pt, 1, 2, and 3J, Jd, Rv.

❶ ***at that time***—ⓐ of the past *then* (Demetr.: 722 fgm. 1, 2 and 11 Jac.; Jos., Ant. 7, 317; 15, 354; Just., A I, 31, 2; D. 60, 1f) τότε ἐπληρώθη *then was fulfilled* **Mt 2:17; 27:9.** εἶχον τότε δέσμιον vs. **16.** Cp. **3:5.** (Opp. νῦν) **Gal 4:8, 29; Hb 12:26.** ἀπὸ τότε *from that time on* (PLond V, 1674, 21; 2 Esdr 5:16b; Ps 92:2) **Mt 4:17; 16:21; 26:16; Lk 16:16** (s. B-D-F §459, 3). Used as an adj. w. the art. preceding (Appian, Bell. Civ. 4, 30 §128 ἡ τότε τύχη; Lucian, Imag. 17; Jos., Ant. 14, 481) ὁ τότε κόσμος *the world at that time* **2 Pt 3:6** (PHamb 21, 9 ὁ τότε καιρός).

ⓑ of the fut. *then* (Just., A I, 52, 9, D. 50, 1; Socrat., Ep. 6, 10 [p. 238, 7 Malherbe]) τότε οἱ δίκαιοι ἐκλάμψουσιν **Mt 13:43.** (Opp. ἄρτι) **1 Cor 13:12ab.**

ⓒ of any time at all that fulfills certain conditions ὅταν ἀσθενῶ, τότε δυνατός εἰμι **2 Cor 12:10.**

❷ to introduce that which follows in time (not in accordance w. earlier Gr.) ***then, thereupon*** (B-D-F §459, 2) τότε Ἡρῴδης λάθρᾳ καλέσας τοὺς μάγους *then* (after he had received an answer fr. the council) *Herod secretly summoned the Magi* **Mt 2:7.** τότε (=after his baptism) ὁ Ἰησοῦς ἀνήχθη εἰς τὴν ἔρημον **4:1.** Cp. **2:16** (GJs 22:1); **3:13, 15; 4:5, 10f; 8:26; 12:22; 25:34–45** (five times); **26:65** and very oft.; **Lk 11:26; 14:21; 21:10; 24:45; Ac 1:12; 4:8;** B 8:1; GJs 22:3. καὶ τότε (Just., D. 78, 5; 88, 3) *and then* καὶ τότε ἐάν τις ὑμῖν εἴπῃ *and then if anyone says to you* **Mk 13:21.—Mt 7:23; 16:27; 24:10, 14, 30ab; Mk 13:26f; Lk 21:27; 1 Cor 4:5; Gal 6:4; 2 Th 2:8;** 2 Cl 16:3. τότε οὖν *(so) then* (TestJud 7:5; 9:7; TestIss 2:1; Just., D. 56, 19) **J 11:14; 19:1, 16; 20:8.** εὐθέως τότε *immediately thereafter* **Ac 17:14.**—W. correlatives: ὅτε (w. aor.) … τότε *when* (this or that happened) … *(then)* **Mt 13:26; 21:1; J 12:16;** B 5:9. Also ὡς (w. aor.) … τότε **J 7:10; 11:6.** ὅταν (w. aor. subj.) … τότε *when* (this or that happens) . . . *(then)* (Just., D. 110, 1; cp. Diod. S. 11, 40, 3 τότε . . . ὅταν [w. aor. subj.]=then . . . when) **Mt 24:16; 25:31; Mk 13:14; Lk 5:35; 21:20; J 8:28; 1 Cor 15:28, 54; 16:2; Col 3:4.** ὅταν (w. pres. subj.) . . . τότε *when* . . . *then* (Jos., Bell. 6, 287) ὅταν λέγωσιν . . . τότε **1 Th 5:3.** In an enumeration πρῶτον . . . , καὶ τότε *first* . . . , *and then* **Mt 5:24; 7:5; 12:29; Mk 3:27; Lk 6:42; J 2:10 v.l.** IEph 7:2.—It is put pleonastically (cp. Vett. Val. 211, 8) after μετά and the acc. μετὰ τὸ ψωμίον, τότε *after* (he took) *the piece of bread, (then)* **J 13:27.** Cp. Hv 2, 2, 4. Also after the ptc. διασωθέντες, τότε ἐπέγνωμεν **Ac 28:1.** Likew. pleonastically **6:11** D; **27:21;** Hs 6, 5, 4.—DELG. M-M.

τοὐναντίον s. ἐναντίον 2.

τοὔνομα s. ὄνομα 1a, end.

τοὐπίσω=τὸ ὀπίσω; s. ὀπίσω 1aα.

τουτέστιν s. εἰμί 2cα and on the spelling B-D-F §12, 3; 17; Rob. 207.—M-M.

τοῦτο s. οὗτος.

τράγος, ου, ὁ (Hom.+; ins, pap, LXX, Philo; Jos., Ant. 2, 35; Ar. 12, 7; Just.) ***he-goat*** named w. others as a sacrificial animal **Hb 9:12f, 19; 10:4;** B 2:5 (Is 1:11). Used esp. on the Day of Atonement 7:4 (prophetic saying of unknown origin), 6, 8, 10.—B. 165. DELG. M-M.

Τράλλεις, εων, αἱ (X., An. 1, 4, 8 al.; ins. It occurs mostly in the pl. form [X.; Diod. S. 14, 36, 3; Jos., Ant. 14, 245; OGI 441, 162], though the sing. Τράλλις, ιος [epigram in Agathias Hist. p. 102, 15; Stephan. Byz. s.v.; SibOr 3, 459; 5, 289] is not impossible) ***Tralles,*** a city in Caria (southwest Asia Minor), north of the Maeander River, ITr ins.—KHumann/WDorpfeld, MAI 18, 1893, 395ff; JWeiss, RE X 547; VSchultze, Altchristliche Städte und Landschaften II/2, 1926; GBean, Turkey beyond the Maeander '71, 208–11; Pauly-W. VI 2093–128; Kl. Pauly V 922; resident Jews, Schürer III 24, 167; PECS 931.

Τραλλιανός, οῦ, ὁ (Strabo 14, 1, 42; Appian, Mithr. 23; Polyaenus 7, 41; Jos., Ant. 14, 242; ins [OGI 498, 3, SIG index p. 156; IMagnMai index p. 204b]; correctly and predom. w. double λ) ***Trallian, from Tralles*** (s. Τράλλεις), of the ἀρχιερεύς Philip, under whom Polycarp suffered martyrdom MPol 21. S. also the title of ITr (Apollonius of Tyana wrote a letter Τραλλιανοῖς [no. 69]: Philostrat. I p. 364).

τράπεζα, ης, ἡ (Hom.+; ins, pap, LXX, TestSol, TestAbr, TestJob, Test12Patr, JosAs; SibOr 5, 470; EpArist; Philo; Joseph.; Ath., R. 4 p. 52, 21; loanw. in rabb.)

❶ **a structure or surface on which food or other things can be placed, *table*—**ⓐ of a cultic object: the table of showbread (cp. 1 Macc 1:22 τρ. τῆς προθέσεως; Ex 25:23–30; Jos., Bell. 5, 217) **Hb 9:2.** Of the τράπεζα τοῦ θεοῦ in the tabernacle, upon which Moses laid the twelve rods 1 Cl 43:2.

ⓑ specif. the *table* upon which a meal is spread out (Hom. et al.; Jos., Ant. 8, 239) **Mt 15:27; Mk 7:28; Lk 16:21; 22:21.** Of the heavenly table at which the Messiah's companions are to eat at the end of time vs. **30** (s. JJeremias, Zöllner u. Sünder, ZNW 30, '31, 293–300). Also in γενηθήτω ἡ τράπεζα αὐτῶν εἰς παγίδα it is prob. (cp. Jos., Ant. 6, 363) that this kind of table is meant **Ro 11:9** (Ps 68:23).—The contrast betw. τράπεζα κυρίου and τρ. δαιμονίων **1 Cor 10:21** is explained by the custom of eating a cult meal in the temple of divinities worshiped by polytheists (POxy 110 ἐρωτᾷ σε Χαιρήμων δειπνῆσαι εἰς κλείνην τοῦ κυρίου Σαράπιδος ἐν τῷ Σαραπείῳ αὔριον, ἥτις ἐστὶν ιε', ἀπὸ ὥρας θ' 'Chaeremon requests you to dine at the table of Sarapis in the Sarapeum on the morrow, the 15th, at the ninth hour'; 523; POslo 157 [all three II AD]; Jos., Ant. 18, 65. τράπεζα of the table of a divinity is found in such and similar connections Diod. S. 5, 46, 7 τρ. τοῦ θεοῦ; SIG 1106, 99 ἐπὶ τὴν τράπεζαν τὴν τοῦ θεοῦ; 1022, 2; 1038, 11; 1042, 20; LBW 395, 17 Σαράπιδι καὶ Ἴσιδι τράπεζαν; POxy 1755. Cp. Sb 8828, 4 [180–82 AD] ἐν ὀνίροις τὸ συμπόσιον ποιῆσαι τοῦ κυρίου Σεράπιδος=celebrate the meal with Lord Sarapis in dreams; s. also New Docs 1, 5–9; 2, 37; 3, 69.—Ltzm., Hdb. exc. on 1 Cor 10:21; HMischkowski, D. hl. Tische im Götterkultus d. Griech. u. Römer, diss. Königsberg 1917).

ⓒ the *table* on which the money changers display their coins (Pla., Ap. 17c; cp. PEleph 10, 2 [223/222 BC] the τραπεζῖται ἐν τοῖς ἱεροῖς) **Mt 21:12; Mk 11:15; J 2:15.** Hence simply *bank* (Lysias, Isocr., Demosth. et al.; EpArist; Jos., Ant. 12, 28; ins; PEleph 27, 23; POxy 98 al. in pap. The Engl. 'bank' is the money-lender's 'bench'; s. OED s.v. bank sb.[3]) διδόναι τὸ ἀργύριον ἐπὶ τράπεζαν *put the money in the bank* to bear interest **Lk 19:23.**—**Ac 6:2** may contain humorous wordplay, which mingles the idea of table service and accounting procedures: *serve as accountants* (on the banking terminology s. Field, Notes 113, referring to Plut., Caesar 721 [28, 4]; 739 [67, 1], but w. discount of meal service as a referent. In addition to Field's observations note the prob. wordplay relating to λόγος [for its commercial nuance s. λόγος 2a on the same verse; s. also Goodsp., Probs. 126f, w. reff. to pap]. For epigraphs s. RBogaert, Epigraphica III '76 index).—B. 352 (meal); 483; 778 (bank).

❷ **that which is upon a table, *a meal, food,*** metonymic ext. of 1 (Eur., Alc. 2; Hdt. 1, 162; Pla., Rep. 3, 404d; Lucian, Dial. Mort. 9, 2; Athen. 1, 25e) παραθεῖναι τράπεζαν *set food before* someone (Thu. 1, 130; Chariton 1, 13, 2; Aelian, VH 2, 17; Jos., Ant. 6, 338.—Ps 22:5 ἑτοιμάζειν τρ.) **Ac 16:34;** τράπ. κοινήν (κοινός 1a) Dg 5:7. ὁρίζειν τράπεζαν *order a meal* D 11:9. διακονεῖν τραπέζαις *wait on tables, serve meals* **Ac 6:2** (so ELohmeyer, JBL 56, '37, 231; 250f, but s. 1c above).—See GRichter, The Furniture of the Greeks, Etruscans, and Romans '66; Kl. Pauly III 1224f; BHHW III 1991–93.—DELG. M-M. TW. Sv.

τραπεζίτης, ου, ὁ (also -είτης; fr. τράπεζα; Lysias, Demosth.; ins, pap; EpArist 26=Jos., Ant. 12, 32; loanw. in rabb.) ***money changer, banker*** **Mt 25:27.** δόκιμος τραπεζίτης *an experienced money changer,* who accepts no counterfeit money; in imagery (on the subj. s. Philo, Spec. Leg. 4, 77) of Christians γίνεσθε δόκιμοι τραπεζῖται Agr 11a, cp. b (Cebes 31, 3 μηδὲ γίνεσθαι ὁμοίους τοῖς κακοῖς τραπεζίταις). AResch, Agrapha[2] 1906, 112–28; HVogels, BZ 8, 1910, 390; HSchoeps, Theol. u. Gesch. des Judenchristentums '49, 151–55; Unknown Sayings 89–93.—Cp. PEleph s.v. τράπεζα 1c. For epigraphs s. RBogaert, Epigraphica III '76 index.—New Docs 1, 138 no. 87. DELG s.v. τράπεζα. M-M. Spicq.

τραυλισμός, οῦ, ὁ (fr. τραυλός [via τραυλίζω] 'mispronouncing letters, lisping'; Hippocr.; [rdg. uncertain in Erotian 126, 4]; Plut., Mor. 53c of Aristotle's lisp) lit. 'lisping, stuttering', in a transferred sense ***irregular rumbling*** of sounds made by wooden vehicles on uneven roads ἤκουεν τῶν ἁμαξῶν τραυλισμόν (Paul) *heard the creaky rumbling of the wagons* AcPl Ha 2, 3.—DELG s.v. τραυλός.

τραῦμα, ατος, τό (fr. τιτρώσκω, cp. the Ionic/Doric τρῶμα; Aeschyl., Hdt. et al.; ins, pap, LXX; Jos., Bell. 1, 197, Ant. 4, 92 al.; Ath., R. 22 p. 75, 17) ***a wound*** **Lk 10:34;** IPol 2:1.—B.

304. Schmidt, Syn. III 297–302. DELG s.v. τιτρώσκω. M-M. S. also ἕλκος.

τραυματίζω (τραῦμα) 1 aor. ἐτραυμάτισα, pass. ἐτραυματίσθην; perf. pass. ptc. τετραυματισμένος (Aeschyl., Hdt. et al.; pap, LXX; JosAs 27:3 cod. A 29, 8 [p. 85, 10 Bat.]; Jos., C. Ap. 2, 243) ***to wound*** **Lk 20:12; Ac 19:16;** 1 Cl 16:5; B 5:2 (the last two Is 53:5).—DELG s.v. τιτρώσκω. M-M.

τραχηλίζω (τράχηλος) perf. pass. ptc. τετραχηλισμένος (Theophr., Teles et al. in a different mng. [twist the neck, etc.]; Philo, Cher. 78, Mos. 1, 297; Jos., Bell. 4, 375; PPetr II, 15 [1]a, 2); in its only occurrence in our lit. πάντα γυμνὰ καὶ τετραχηλισμένα τοῖς ὀφθαλμοῖς **Hb 4:13** it must certainly mean ***lay bear:*** *everything is open and laid bare to the eyes* (Hesychius explains τετραχηλισμένα with πεφανερωμένα, and as early as Oenomaus in Eus., PE 5, 29, 5 we have μισθοῦ τραχηλίζειν='reveal' or 'open for a price').—WWood, Exp. 9th ser., 3, 1925, 444–55; CSpicq, RB 58, '51, 484 n. 2; HMontefiore, The Epistle to the Hebrews '64, 89 ('everything is naked and prostrate before . . . him').—DELG s.v. τράχηλος. M-M.

τραχηλοκοπέω (τράχηλος, κόπτω) 1 aor. subj. τραχηλοκοπήσῃς, aor. pass. ἐτραχηλοκοπήθην; pf. τετραχηλοκόπημαι ***behead*** Καῖσαρ ἐκέλευσεν . . . Παῦλον τραχηλο[κοπηθῆναι] AcPl Ha 9, 16; s. also 9, 25 and 27; 10, 10–11; 11, 1.

τράχηλος, ου, ὁ (Eur., Hdt.+; ins, pap, LXX; TestSol, TestAbr; TestNapht 2:8; JosAs, ParJer; Jos., Ant. 3, 170 al.; Ath. 20, 1) ***neck, throat*** **Mt 18:6; Mk 9:42; Lk 17:2** (cp. Menand., fgm. 224 Kö. περὶ τὸν τρ. ἁλύσιον διδόναι). ἐπιπεσεῖν ἐπὶ τὸν τράχηλόν τινος *fall upon someone's neck, embrace someone* (ἐπιπίπτω 1b) **Lk 15:20; Ac 20:37.** ἐκρέμασεν ἀτὴν (for αὐτὴν) εἰς τὸν τράχηλον αὐτοῦ Ἄννα *Anna fell upon his neck* GJs 4:4 (s. κρεμάννυμι 1 and περιπλέκω).—In imagery: οἵτινες ὑπὲρ τῆς ψυχῆς μου τὸν ἑαυτῶν τράχηλον ὑπέθηκαν *who risked their necks for my life* **Ro 16:4** (cp. Vita Philonidis ed. Crönert [SBBerlAk 1900, 951] ὑπὲρ[?] τοῦ μάλιστ' ἀγαπωμένου παραβάλοι ἂν ἑτοίμως τὸν τράχηλον. S. on this Dssm., LO 94f [LAE 117f]. Endangering the τράχηλος Diog. L. 4, 11; s. Straub 47). On the other hand ὑποθεῖναι τὸν τράχηλον 1 Cl 63:1 *bow the neck* in obedience (cp. Epict. 4, 1, 77.—Sir 51:26). Also κάμπτειν τὸν τράχ. B 3:2 (Is 58:5). Opp. τὸν τράχ. σκληρύνειν 9:5 (Dt 10:16; PsSol 8:29). ἐπιθεῖναι ζυγὸν ἐπὶ τὸν τράχ. τινος **Ac 15:10** (cp. schol. on Appol. Rhod. 4, 1418 τὸ βάρος ἀπὸ τοῦ τραχήλου ἀποβαλέσθαι).—B. 232. DELG. M-M.

τραχύς, εῖα, ύ (prob. cognate w. θράσσω 'to trouble, disturb'; Hom.+; ins, pap, LXX, En, PsSol 8:17; EpArist, Philo; Jos., Bell. 4, 5, Ant. 7, 239 al.) ***rough, uneven,*** of a mountain (Herodian 6, 5, 5) Hs 9, 1, 7; 9, 22, 1. Of stones (Hom. et al.) 9, 6, 4; 9, 8, 6. τραχεῖς τόποι (schol. on Nicander, Ther. 143) **Ac 27:29.** Of a road (Hyperid., fgm. 70, 3 J. τραχεῖα ὁδός; Pla., Rep. 1, 328e ὁδὸς τραχεῖα; Cebes 15, 2; Jer 2:25; Bar 4:26; PsSol 8:17) Hm 6, 1, 3f. ἡ τραχεῖα (X., An. 4, 6, 12; Lucian, Rhet. Praec. 3; sc. ὁδός) *the rough road* pl. **Lk 3:5** (Is 40:4).—B. 1066. DELG. M-M.

Τραχωνῖτις, ιδος (Philo, Leg. ad Gai. 326; Joseph. index s.v. Τράχων) fem. of Τραχωνίτης, as Joseph. calls an inhabitant τοῦ Τράχωνος. The fem. is used abs. by Philo and Joseph. ἡ Τραχωνῖτις=***(the) Trachonitis.*** This is the district south of Damascus, also called ὁ Τράχων by Josephus. In the only place where the word occurs in our lit. it is used as an adj. ἡ Τρ. χώρα *the region of Trachonitis* Φιλίππου τετραρχοῦντος τῆς Ἰτουραίας καὶ Τραχωνίτιδος χώρας **Lk 3:1.**—GRindfleisch, Die Landschaft Haurān in röm. Zeit. u. in der Gegenwart: ZDPV 21, 1898, 1–46; Schürer I 337f; HGuthe, RE XX 7f; DSourdel, Les Cultes de Hauran à l' époque Romaine '52; Kl. Pauly I 839f; BHHW III 2017f.

τρεῖς, τρία gen. τριῶν, dat. τρισίν (Hom.+) ***three*** **Mt 12:40** (Jon 2:1); **Mk 8:2; Lk 1:56; J 2:19** al. τὰ τρία ταῦτα **1 Cor 13:13** (cp. Philo, Det. Pot. Ins. 169 τὰ ἑπτὰ ταῦτα and several times τρία ταῦτα: Leg. All. 1, 93; 3, 249, Mos. 1, 224). τρεῖς εἰσιν οἱ μαρτυροῦντες *there are three that bear witness* **1J 5:7** (cp. Alexis, fgm. 271 τρεῖς δ' εἰσὶν αἱ κεκτημέναι).—On ἐν τρισὶν ἡμέραις (ἐν 10a) and μετὰ τρεῖς ἡμέρας (μετά B 2a) s. WBauer, D. Leben Jesu im Zeitalter d. ntl. Apokryphen 1909, 253f. Both expressions together, evidently w. the same mng.: Sb 7696, 120f [250 AD]; on μετὰ τρ. ἡμ.='on the third day' s. Jos., Ant. 7, 280f; 8, 214 and 218.—For δύο ἢ τρεῖς s. δύο aa.—See s.v. πνεῦμα 8 and s. FGöbel, Formen u. Formeln der epischen Dreiheit in d. griech. Dichtung '35; FNötscher, Biblica 35, '54, 313–19; JBauer, Biblica 39, '58, 354–58; JJeremias, KGKuhn Festschr. '71, 221–29; RAC IV 269–310; BHHW I 354f.—B. 941ff. DELG. M-M. EDNT. TW. Sv.

Τρεῖς Ταβέρναι s. ταβέρναι.

τρέμω used only in the pres. and the impf. (Hom.+; PFay 124, 27; PGM 12, 248f; IDefixWünsch 4, 44; LXX, pseudepigr., Philo, Joseph.; Just., D. 30, 3; Mel., P. 24, 168 al.) but also fig. *be afraid, fear, stand in awe of* (Jos., Bell. 1, 341; 6, 395).

❶ **to shake involuntarily, *tremble, quiver*** (Mel., P. 98, 744f; τοῦ λαοῦ μὴ τρέμοντος ἔτρεμεν ἡ γῆ) **Lk 8:47.** W. φοβεῖσθαι (Da 5:19 Theod.; JosAs 23:16; Philo, Leg. All. 3, 54) **Mk 5:33.** In these passages physical shaking is prob. the prim. semantic component, whereas in the following there is stronger focus on the psychological aspect.

❷ **to feel intensely the impact of someth. transcendent, *tremble, be in awe.*** W. θαμβεῖν **Ac 9:6** t.r. (Erasmian rdg.) W. acc. *tremble at, stand in awe of* (trag. et al.; Herm. Wr. 1, 7; Just., D. 30, 3; Mel., P. 24, 168) τὰ λόγια 1 Cl 13:4 (Is 66:2). τοὺς λόγους B 19:4; D 3:8. δόξας οὐ τρέμουσιν βλασφημοῦντες *they are not afraid to blaspheme glorious angels* **2 Pt 2:10** (B-D-F §415; Rob. 1121f).—DELG. M-M.

τρέπω 1 aor. ἔτρεψα (Hom.+)—❶ act., ***to cause to tend toward a course of action, turn, direct*** τινὰ εἴς τι *turn* or *incline someone toward someth.* MPol 2:4 (TestJob 20:1; Ath. 22:3).

❷ mid.: fut. τρέψομαι (4 Macc 1:12; Tat. 3, 3); 1 aor. ἐτρεψάμην LXX; 2 aor. ἐτραπόμην (Ath. 6, 2); pass.: 2 aor. as mid. ἐτράπην LXX **to make a turn to do someth., *turn*** (Jos., C. Ap. 1, 25) w. indication of the place from which and of the goal (Socrat., Ep. 17, 2 [p. 264 Malherbe] οἱ νέοι εἰς ἀκρασίαν ἐτρέποντο; Appian, Bell. Civ. 2, 22 §83 ἐς ἁρπαγὰς ἐτράποντο=they turned to pillage; schol. on Nicander, Ther. 825 εἰς φυγὴν τρεπόμενοι; EpArist 245 τρέπεσθαι εἰς; likew. Jos., Ant. 18, 87; Just., D. 91, 3 εἰς τὴν εὐσέβειαν ἐτράπησαν) ἔνθεν εἰς βλασφημίαν τρέπονται *they turn from that* (i.e. fr. admiration) *to blasphemy* 2 Cl 13:3.—B. 666. DELG.

τρέφω fut. θρέψω; 1 aor. ἔθρεψα. Pass.: aor. ἐτράφην LXX; ptc. τραφείς; pf. ptc. τεθραμμένος (Hom.+).

❶ **to care for by providing food or nourishment, *feed, nourish, support*** animals (X., Mem. 2, 9, 2; Is 7:21; PsSol 5:9) or humans (PsSol 5:11; TestJob 10:3; Ar. 7, 1) w. acc.: **Mt 6:26; 25:37; Lk 12:24; Rv 12:6, 14** (pass.); B 10:11. Occasionally also of plants (Il. 18, 57) ἡ πτελέα ὕδωρ ἔχουσα τρέφει τὴν ἄμπελον Hs 2:8.—Of mothers' breasts that *nurse* or *nourish* (cp. Od. 12, 134; Hdt. 1, 136; PRyl 178, 5) **Lk 23:29** (abs.). ἐθρέψατε τὰς καρδίας ὑμῶν *you have fattened yourselves* by revelry **Js 5:5.** In imagery of Paul πόλλους θρέψει τῷ λόγῳ AcPl Ha 7, 6. In διὰ τὸ τρέφεσθαι αὐτῶν (i.e. the inhabitants of Tyre and Sidon) τὴν χώραν ἀπὸ τῆς βασιλικῆς, τρέφεσθαι can be either mid. or pass. *because their country supported itself* or *was supported* (by importing grain) *from the king's country* **Ac 12:20** (X., An. 7, 4, 11 has the mid. τρέφεσθαι ἐκ τῶν κωμῶν).

❷ **to care for children by bringing them up,** ***rear, bring up, train*** (Hom.+; 1 Macc 3:33; 11:39; Jos., Ant. 2, 209) τινά *someone* Hv 1, 1, 1. Pass. *grow up* (Diod. S. 4, 81, 1; Aelian, VH 12, 1 p. 117, 2 H.; Jos., C. Ap. 1, 141; Just., A I, 57, 1) Ναζαρά, οὗ ἦν τεθραμμένος **Lk 4:16** (s. ἀνατρέφω a). τραφέντα ἐν Ναζαρά AcPl Ha 8, 29.—CMoussy, Recherches sur τρέφω et al., '69. Schmidt, Syn. IV 98–105. DELG. M-M. Spicq. Sv.

τρέχω impf. ἔτρεχον; fut. δραμοῦμαι (LXX; TestJud 25:5); 2 aor. ἔδραμον (Hom.+) 'run'

❶ **to make rapid linear movement,** ***run, rush, advance*** lit. **Mk 5:6; J 20:2, 4;** GPt 3:6; GJs 4:4. δραμών w. finite verb foll. (Gen 24:28; Jos., Bell. 6, 254; 294) **Mt 27:48; Mk 15:36; Lk 15:20** (the father's rapid movement is contrary to the σεμνότης one would expect of a person in his position). Foll. by inf. of purpose **Mt 28:8.** The goal is indicated w. ἐπί and acc. (Alciphron 3, 17, 2; 3, 40, 3) ἐπὶ λῃστήν *advance against a robber* (to catch him) MPol 7:1 (cp. Sus 38 Theod.; Test Jud 3:1); ἐπὶ τὸ μνημεῖον **Lk 24:12** (cp. Gen 24:20). W. εἰς (TestAbr A 3 p. 80, 3f [Stone p. 8] δραμὼν εἰς τὸ φρέαρ): **Ac 19:28** D. τρ. εἰς πόλεμον *rush into battle* **Rv 9:9.** W. πρός (ParJer 9:31): GJs 12:2. Of foot-racing in a stadium **1 Cor 9:24ab.**—In the sense of *come on the run* GJs 8:3.

❷ **to make an effort to advance spiritually or intellectually,** ***exert oneself*** fig. ext. of 1: using the foot-races in the stadium as a basis (on the use of such figures in the Cynic-Stoic diatribe s. PWendland, Die urchristl. Literaturformen: Hdb. I 3, 1912 p. 357, 4) *exert oneself to the limit of one's powers in an attempt to go forward, strive to advance* **Ro 9:16** (the emphasis is entirely on the effort that the person makes; cp. Anth. Pal. 11, 56 Düb. μὴ τρέχε, μὴ κοπία); **1 Cor 9:24c, 26.** μήπως εἰς κενὸν τρέχω ἢ ἔδραμον **Gal 2:2** (πώς 2c). Cp. **Phil 2:16**=Pol 9:2. On τρ. τὸν ἀγῶνα **Hb 12:1** s. ἀγών 1. ἐτρέχετε καλῶς *you were making such fine progress* **Gal 5:7** (cp. Philo, Leg. All. 3, 48 καλὸν δρόμον κ. ἄριστον ἀγώνισμα; OdeSol 11:3 ἔδραμον ὁδὸν ἀληθείας).—VPfitzner, Paul and the Agon Motif '67; HFunke, Antisthenes bei Paulus: Her 98, '70, 459–71.

❸ **to proceed quickly and without restraint,** ***progress*** fig. ext. of 1 ἵνα ὁ λόγος τ. κυρίου τρέχῃ *that the word of the Lord might speed on* **2 Th 3:1** (cp. Ps 147:4).—JDerrett, Biblica 66, '85, 560–67.—B. 692. DELG. M-M. TW.

τρῆμα, ατος, τό (τετραίνω 'bore through'; Aristoph., Hippocr., Pla.+; PRyl 21 fgm. 3 II, 5 [I BC]; EpArist 61=Jos., Ant. 12, 66) ***opening, hole*** τρῆμα ῥαφίδος *eye of a needle* **Mt 19:24 v.l.** (for τρύπημα). **Mk 10:25 v.l.** (for τρυμάλια). Also τρῆμα βελόνης **Lk 18:25.** S. the lit. under κάμηλος, κάμιλος, τρυμαλιά.—DELG s.v. τετραίνω. M-M.

τριάκοντα (τρεῖς, -κοντα; s. Schwyzer I 593) indecl. (Hom.; Comic poet CGFP 366, 56 et al.) ***thirty*** **Mt 13:8, 23; Mk 4:8, 20** (a thirty-fold yield of grain on the Tauric peninsula: Strabo 7, 4, 6 p. 311. For the yield of wheat fr. good soil s. GDalman, Pj 22, 1926, 129–31); **Mt 26:15; 27:3, 5; Lk 3:23** (Porphyr., Vi. Plot. 4 ὢν ἐτῶν τρ.); **J 6:19;** Hv 4, 2, 1 (as numerical sign λ'); s 6, 4, 4. τρ. καὶ ὀκτώ *thirty-eight* **J 5:5.** τετρακόσια καὶ τρ. **Gal 3:17.** In Hs 9, 4, 3; 9, 5, 4; 9, 15, 4 the numerical sign λε' = τριάκοντα πεντε *thirty-five* (Just., A I, 34, 2; τριάκοντα ἕξ D. 132, 1).—DELG s.v. τρεῖς and διακόσιοι. M-M.

τριακόσιοι, αι, α (τρεῖς, -κοσιοι; s. Schwyzer I 593; Hom.+; ins, pap, LXX; TestAbr B 3 p. 107, 7 [Stone p. 62]; TestJob 15:4; GrBar; Jos., Bell. 1, 625, Ant. 11, 15; Just., D. 32, 4 τριακόσια πεντήκοντα ἔτη; Ath. 31, 1) ***three hundred*** **Mk 14:5; J 12:5;** B 9:8a (w. διαοκτώ Gen 14:14; Jos., Ant. 1, 178), 8b, 8c (in ref. to the τ in σταῦρος).—DELG s.v. τρεῖς and διακόσιοι.

τρίβολος, ου, ὁ (Alcaeus [600 BC] 100 Diehl [on this s. MTreu, Alkaios[2] '63, 169 n.]; Aristoph., Theophr. et al.; ins, pap, LXX; TestSol 12:2 [s. app.]; ApcMos 24; ApcrEzk P 1 vs. 5; Philo, Somn. 2, 161) of prickly weeds, esp. ***the thistle,*** which grows in Palestine in great abundance and infinite variety. Pl. Hs 9, 20, 3. W. ἄκανθαι (Gen 3:18; Hos 10:8; ApcMos 24; ApcrEzk) **Mt 7:16; Hb 6:8;** Hs 6, 2, 6f; 9, 1, 5; 9, 20, 1.—ILöw, Aram. Pflanzennamen 1881 §302, D. Flora der Juden IV '34, 660 (index); LFonck, Streifzüge durch die bibl. Flora 1900; FLundgreen, Die Pflanzen im NT: NKZ 28, 1917, 828ff; GDalman, Pj 22, 1926, 126ff (w. picture), Arbeit I 407, 2: blackberry bush; Zohary 159 (perh. centaurea iberica).—Kl. Pauly II 105; BHHW I 350f. DELG. M-M.

τριβολώδης, ες (τρίβολος, -ώδης) ***full of thistles*** Hs 6, 2, 6.

τρίβος, ου, ἡ (τρίβω 'rub'; Hom. Hymns, Hdt. et al.; ins: APF 1, 1901, p. 221, 21; PRainer 42, 14; LXX; Jos., Ant. 15, 347) **a defined track or route,** ***path***

ⓐ of a way that is familiar and well-worn *a beaten* (τρίβω) *path* Hm 6, 1, 3.

ⓑ *path* gener. **Mt 3:3; Mk 1:3; Lk 3:4** (all three Is 40:3; cp. also SibOr 3, 777).

ⓒ fig. of established ways of conduct τὰς τρίβους τῆς ζωῆς (cp. Pr 16:17; SibOr 3, 721) Hs 5, 6, 3.—DELG s.v. τρίβω. M-M.

τριετής, ες (τρεῖς, ἔτος; Hom., Od. 2, 106 and 13, 277 adv. τρίετες; Hdt., Pla., ins, pap; LXX τρίετες) ***of/for three years*** ἐγένετο τρ. ἡ παῖς *the child* (Mary) *was three years old* GJs 7:2.—DELG s.v. τρεῖς.

τριετία, ας, ἡ (τριέτης; Theophr. et al.; Plut., Lucian; Artem. 4, 1 p. 202, 9; OGI 669, 35; pap; Jos., Ant. 19, 351.—B-D-F §5, 3) **a period of three years,** ***three years*** **Ac 20:18** D, **31.**—M-M.

τρίζω (intr. Hom., Hdt. et al., likewise Am 2:13 Aq; Is 38:14 Sym. [fut. τρίσω]) orig. 'utter a shrill cry', of sounds made by birds (Hom. et al.), then of a variety of sounds including creaking of mobile objects, also of teeth that grind (Epicharmus, fgm. 21 Kaibel, Com. Gr. Fgm. p. 94, in Athen. 10, 411b), trans. in the only place where it occurs in our lit. ***gnash, grind*** τρίζειν τοὺς ὀδόντας *gnash* or *grind the teeth* (Ps.-Callisth. 3, 22, 13 [twice]; Cyranides p. 46, 5; TestSol 12:2) **Mk 9:18.** S. B-D-F §148, 1.—DELG. M-M.

τρίμηνος, ον (τρεῖς, μήν; Soph.et al.) ***of three months*** as subst. ἡ τρίμηνος (Hdt. 2, 124; Aeschin. 3, 70; PLond I, 18, 10 p. 23 [161 BC]; PSI 689, 5; 30. See B-D-F §241, 3: sc. περίοδος) or τὸ τρίμηνον (Polyb. 1, 38, 6; 5, 1, 12; Plut., Crass. 550 [12, 3]; Ptolem. 1, 8, 6.—Doubtful ἐν τριμήνῳ: SIG 527, 114 [perh. 220 BC]; 1023, 31; Jos., Ant. 3, 62; διὰ τριμήνου PLond II, 306, 22 p. 119 [II AD]; LXX) *(a period of) three months* τρίμηνον (acc.

in answer to the question, how long? 4 Km 24:8; 2 Ch 36:2.—B-D-F §161, 2; Rob. 469–71) *for three months* **Hb 11:23.**—DELG s.v. τρεῖς. M-M.

τρίς (adv.; on the formation Schwyzer I 597; Hom. et al.; Ael. Aristid. 30, 23 K.=10 p. 122 D.: ὦ τρὶς εὐδαίμονες; ins, LXX, Joseph.) ***three times, thrice*** **Mt 26:34, 75; Mk 14:30, 72; Lk 22:34, 61; J 13:38; 2 Cor 11:25ab; 12:8;** D 7:3; Hs 9, 6, 3 v.l.; MPol 12:1. ἐπὶ τρίς (CIG 1122, 9; PGM 36, 273= εἰς τρίς, found since Pind., Hdt., also Jos., Ant. 5, 348) *three times,* in both places where it occurs in our lit. prob.=*(yet) a third time* (PHolm 1, 18) **Ac 10:16; 11:10.**—DELG s.v. τρεῖς. M-M. TW.

τρίστεγον, ου, τό (τρεῖς, στέγη) **the third story of a building,** ***the third story,*** the second above ground level (Gen 6:16 Sym.—Neut. of τρίστεγος='of three stories' [Dionys. Hal. 3, 68; Jos., Bell. 5, 220; pap]) **Ac 20:9.**—M-M s.v. τρίστεγος.

τρισχίλιοι, αι, α (τρεῖς, χίλιοι; Hom. et al.; pap, LXX; En 7:2; TestJob; Jos., Bell. 2, 500, Vi. 213; 233; Just., A I, 31, 8) ***three thousand*** **Ac 2:41** (on the number of those converted cp. Iambl., Vi. Pyth. §29 [LDeubner, SBBerlAk '35, XIX p. 54].—In case the numbers in Ac 2:41 and 4:4 originally referred to the same event or account of it, then cp. Appian, Bell. Civ. 3, 42 §173: some, on the one hand, say χίλιοι, others τρισχίλιοι. διαφέρονται γὰρ περὶ τοῦ ἀριθμοῦ 'for they differ on the number'. Also 2, 70 §289f with the conclusion: 'so inexact are the reports of numbers' in the tradition; 2, 82 §345f).—DELG s.v. τρεῖς.

τρίτος, η, ον (τρεῖς; Hom.+)—❶ **third in a series,** ***third***

ⓐ used as adj., w. a noun that can oft. be supplied fr. the context ἕως τρίτου οὐρανοῦ **2 Cor 12:2** (GrBar 10:1; ApcSed 2:4; ApcMos 37.—IdeVuippens, Le Paradis terrestre au troisième ciel 1925. Also EPeterson, TLZ 52, 1927, 78–80. Further lit. s.v. οὐρανός 1e). τὸ τρίτον ζῷον **Rv 4:7.** Cp. **6:5ab; 8:10a; 11:14.** τρίτον γένος PtK 2 p. 15, 8 (s. γένος 3). τρίτου βαθμοῦ GJs 7:3. μίλιον τρ. 17:2. (ἐν) τῇ τρίτῃ ἡμέρᾳ (Appian, Liby. 122 §578; JosAs 29:8; AscIs 3:16; Just., D. 97, 1) **Mt 16:21; 17:23; 20:19; Lk 9:22; 24:7, 46; Ac 10:40.** τῇ ἡμέρᾳ τῇ τρίτῃ **Lk 18:33; J 2:1; 1 Cor 15:4.** (SMcCasland, The Scripture Basis of 'On the Third Day': JBL 48, 1929, 124–37; GLandes, JBL 86, '67, 446–50 [Jonah]. See s.v. τρεῖς). ἕως τρίτης ἡμέρας **Mt 27:64** (cp. TestAbr A 20 p. 103, 23 [Stone p. 54] ἕως τρίτης ἡμέρας). μετὰ τρίτην ἡμέραν *after three days* (Appian, Iber. 43 §177) **Ac 10:40** D. τρίτη ὥρα (=nine o'clock in the morning) **20:3** or ὥρα τρίτη **Mk 15:25** (AMahoney, CBQ 28, '66, 292–99); **Ac 2:15.** τρίτη ὥρα τῆς νυκτός (=nine o'clock at night, as TestAbr A 5 p. 82, 11 [Stone p. 12]) **Ac 23:23.** ἐν τῇ τρ. φυλακῇ **Lk 12:38.**—τρίτην ταύτην ἡμέραν (Lucian, Dial. Mort. 13, 3; Achilles Tat. 7, 11, 2; s. ἄγω 4) **Lk 24:21.** ἄλλος ἄγγελος τρίτος **Rv 14:9.**—The noun is supplied fr. the context (Diog. L. 2, 46 'Αριστοτέλης ἐν τρίτῳ [i.e., book] περὶ ποιητικῆς) **Mt 22:26; Mk 12:21; Lk 20:12, 31; Rv 16:4; 21:19.** τῇ τρίτῃ (sc. ἡμέρᾳ. Likew. τῇ τρίτῃ GDI p. 874, [n]50b, 3 [Chios about 600 BC]; Demosth. [I AD] in Aëtius 186, 16; Appian, Bell. Civ. 2, 88 §369; Arrian, Anab. 7, 11, 1. Cp. Jos., Vi. 229 εἰς τρίτην) **Lk 13:32** (looking toward the fut. after σήμερον and αὔριον=*the day after tomorrow;* cp. Epict. 4, 10, 31; 4, 12, 21; M. Ant. 4, 47.—Looking back at the past, the third day would = 'the day before yesterday'. Cp. Ps.-Lucian, Halc c. 3 ἑώρας τρίτην ἡμέραν ὅσος ἦν ὁ χειμών=the day before yesterday you experienced how severe the storm was); **Ac 27:19.** Sc. ἔτος GJs 7:1.

ⓑ used as adv. τὸ τρίτον *the third time* (Hom. et al.; PLips 33 II, 15; TestAbr A 13 p. 92, 18 [Stone p. 32]), τρίτον *a third time* (Aeschyl. et al.; Jos., Ant. 8, 371), both in the sense *for the third time* **Mk 14:41; Lk 23:22; J 21:17ab.** In the same sense ἐκ τρίτου (Pla., Tim. 54b; ParJer 7:8; Aelian, VH 14, 46) **Mt 26:44.** τρίτον τοῦτο *now for the third time, this is the third time* (Judg 16:15) **2 Cor 12:14; 13:1.** τοῦτο ἤδη τρίτον **J 21:14** (s. FNeirynck, ETL 64, '88, 431f). In enumerations (τὸ) τρίτον *in the third place* **1 Cor 12:28;** D 16:6 (cp. Pla., Rep. 2, 358c; Plut., Mor. 459d; Just., A I, 26, 1; Iambl., Vi. Pyth. 29, 165 πρῶτον . . . δεύτερον . . . τρίτον; 30, 171).

❷ as a subst. **a third part of someth.,** ***third, third part*** τὸ τρίτον (sc. μέρος; s. B-D-F §241, 7.—τὸ τρ. in this sense Diod. S. 17, 30, 3; Lucian, Tox. 46 τὸ τρ. τῆς ἀτιμίας; PFlor 4, 17; 19; Mitt-Wilck. I/2, 402 I, 18 τὸ νενομισμένον τρίτον=the third in accordance w. the law; Num 15:6, 7) *the third part, one-third* foll. by partitive gen. (Appian, Illyr. 26 §75 τὸ τρ. τούτων) **Rv 8:7–12; 9:15, 18; 12:4.**—DELG s.v. τρεῖς. M-M. EDNT. TW. Sv.

τρίχινος, η, ον (θρίξ; X., Pla.+; pap, LXX) *made of hair* σάκκος (oft. pap, e.g. PSI 427, 3 [III BC]; PHamb 10, 39) **Rv 6:12.**—DELG s.v. θρίξ. M-M.

τρόμος, ου, ὁ (τρέμω; Hom. et al.; PSI 135, 10; LXX; pseudepigr.; Philo, Leg. ad Gai. 267; Just., D. 67, 10) ***trembling, quivering*** fr. fear, w. ἔκστασις **Mk 16:8.** Mostly combined w. φόβος (as Gen 9:2; Ex 15:16; Dt 2:25; 11:25 al.; En 13:3; JosAs) μετὰ φόβου καὶ τρόμου (JosAs 16:7 A) **2 Cor 7:15; Eph 6:5; Phil 2:12** (s. κατεργάζομαι 2). ἐν φόβῳ καὶ ἐν τρόμῳ (cp. Is 19:16; Ps 2:1; JosAs 14:10; ApcSed 14:12) **1 Cor 2:3.** ὁ φόβος καὶ ὁ τρόμος ὑμῶν ἐπέπεσεν τοῖς κατοικοῦσιν αὐτήν 1 Cl 12:5 (cp. Ex 15:16; Jdth 2:28). τρόμος με ἔλαβεν Hv 3, 1, 5 (cp. Ex 15:15; Is 33:14; pl.: ApcMos 25 ἐν πολλοῖς τρόμοις).—B. 1153. DELG s.v. τρέμω. M-M.

τροπή, ῆς, ἡ (τρέπω; Hom. et al.) **the process of turning,** ***turn, turning, change*** (Pla., Plut. et al.; Jos. Ant. 10, 191; Just., D. 85, 5; Mel., P. 21, 147 ['reversal, destruction']; Ath. 22, 4). In our lit. the word occurs only in τροπῆς ἀποσκίασμα. *darkening caused by turning* **Js 1:17.** The context (s. φῶς 2) suggests imagery based on association of τρ. with astral phenomena, such as the 'solstice' (Hom. et al.; SIG 1264, 5; PHib 27, 120; 210 [III BC] ἡλίου τροπή; PRyl 27; Sb 358, 6; Dt 33:14; Wsd 7:18) or more gener. of the 'movements' of heavenly bodies fr. one place in the heavens or fr. one constellation to another (Pla., Tim. 39d; Aristot., HA 5, 9; Sext. Emp., Math. 5, 11; Philo, Agr. 51; Ath. 22, 7; Heath, Aristarchus 33 n. 3). In case the text is in proper order (but s. comm. ad loc.; Goodsp., Probs. 189f; vv.ll. include τροπὴ ἀποσκιάσματος, τροπῆς ἀποσκιάσματος), the more general sense (movements) is to be preferred to the more specialized (solstice), and the term τροπῆς ἀποσκίασμα (s. ἀποσκίασμα) means *darkening that has its basis in change.* That God, in contrast to all else, is unchangeable, was a truth often expressed in Hellenistic theol. (Herm. Wr. in Stob. I p. 277 Wachsm.=p. 432, 15 Sc. τί θεός; ἄτρεπτον ἀγαθόν. τί ἄνθρωπος; τρεπτὸν κακόν; Philo, Leg. All. 2, 89 πάντα τὰ ἄλλα τρέπεται, μόνος αὐτὸς [=θεός] ἄτρεπτός ἐστι; 33, Deus Imm. 22, Poster. Caini 19).—The transl. of τροπ. ἀποσκ. as 'shadow (=trace) of change', which has had some vogue fr. Oecumenius and Theophylact to HEwald et al., is lexically improbable.—DELG s.v. τρέπω C3. M-M. Sv.

τρόπος, ου ὁ (τρέπω; Pind., Hdt.+).—❶ **the manner in which someth. is done,** ***manner, way, kind, guise*** εἰς δούλου τρόπον κεῖσθαι *appear in the guise of* (=as) *a slave* (κεῖμαι 3c)

Hs 5, 5, 5; 5, 6, 1.—ἐν παντὶ τρόπῳ *in every way* (3 Macc 7:8 v.l.) **2 Th 3:16.** κατὰ πάντα τρόπον *in every way* or *respect* (X., An. 6, 6, 30 al.; Num 18:7; EpArist 215; Philo, Op. M. 10; SibOr 3, 430) **Ro 3:2;** IEph 2:2; ITr 2:3; ISm 10:1; IPol 3:2. μὴ . . . κατὰ μηδένα τρόπον *by no means, not . . . in any way (at all)* (SIG 799, 20 μηδὲ . . . κατὰ μηδένα τρόπον; 588, 44; PAmh 35, 28; 3 Macc 4:13b μὴ . . . κατὰ μηδένα τρ.; 4 Macc 4:24; 10:7; Just., D. 35, 7; cp. JosAs cod. A 23:1 [p. 75, 8 Bat.] οὐ . . . κατ' οὐδένα τρ.) **2 Th 2:3.** καθ' ὃν τρόπον *in the same way as* (POxy 237 VIII, 29 καθ' ὃν ἔδει τρόπον; CPR 5, 11; 9, 12; 10, 6; BGU 846, 12; 2 Macc 6:20; 4 Macc 14:17 v.l.) **Ac 15:11; 27:25.**—In the acc. (s. B-D-F §160; Johannessohn, Kasus 81f) τρόπον w. gen. *like* (Aeschyl., Hdt. et al.; Philo. Oft. w. animals: θηρίων τρόπον 2 Macc 5:27; 3 Macc 4:9; σκορπίου τρόπον 4 Macc 11:10) σητὸς τρόπον 1 Cl 39:5 (Job 4:19). τὸν ὅμοιον τρόπον τούτοις *in the same way* or *just as they* **Jd 7** (cp. Tat. 26, 2 κατὰ τὸν ὅμοιον τρόπον ἡμῖν). ὃν τρόπον *in the manner in which = (just) as* (X., Mem. 1, 2, 59, An. 6, 3, 1; Pla., Rep. 5, 466e; Diod. S. 3, 21, 1; SIG 976, 35; 849, 13f; PLips 41, 9; Gen 26:29; Ex 14:13; Dt 11:25 and very oft. in LXX; TestJob. 37:3; Jos., Ant. 3, 50, Vi. 412b; Just., A I, 4, 7; Tat. 35, 1) **Mt 23:37; Lk 13:34; Ac 7:28** (Ex 2:14); 1 Cl 4:10 (Ex 2:14); 2 Cl 9:4; corresponding to οὕτως (SIG 685, 51ff; Josh 10:1; 11:15; Is 10:11; 62:5; Ezk 12:11 al.; Just., A I, 7, 3, D. 94, 5; Mel., P. 42, 293) **Ac 1:11; 2 Ti 3:8;** 2 Cl 8:2; 12:4. τίνα τρόπον; *in what manner? how?* (Aristoph., Nub. 170; Pla., Prot. 322c; Jos., C. Ap. 1, 315; Just., A I, 32, 10) 1 Cl 24:4; 47:2 v.l. (Lat. quemadmodum).—In the dat. (B-D-F §198, 4; Rob. 487.—Pap. [Mayser II/2, p. 281]; Jos., Ant. 5, 339; Just., D. 10, 4; Tat. 17, 1) παντὶ τρόπῳ *in any and every way* (Aeschyl., Thu. et al.; X., Cyr. 2, 1, 13; Pla., Rep. 2, 368c; pap; 1 Macc 14:35; Jos., Ant. 17, 84; Just., D. 68, 2) **Phil 1:18.** ποίῳ τρόπῳ; (Aeschyl., Soph. et al.; TestJos 7:1; ApcrEzk [Epiph 70, 9]) Hv 1, 1, 7 (τόπῳ Joly). ποίοις τρόποις m 12, 3, 1.

❷ **the way in which a pers. behaves or lives, *ways, customs, kind of life*** (Pind., Hdt. et al; Michel 545, 7; pap, LXX; Jos., Ant. 12, 252; Tat. 21, 2; SibOr 4, 35; 'way of life, turn of mind, conduct, character') Hv 1, 1, 2. ἀφιλάργυρος ὁ τρόπος **Hb 13:5** (X., Cyr. 8, 3, 49 τρόπος φιλέταιρος). Also pl. (Aeschyl. et al.; Appian, Bell. Civ. 4, 95 §398; SIG 783, 11; IG XII/7, 408, 8; EpArist 144) ἔχειν τοὺς τρόπους κυρίου *have the ways that the Lord himself had* or *which the Lord requires of his own* D 11:8.—B. 656. DELG s.v. τρέπω C 2. M-M.

τροποφορέω (τρόπος, φορέω) 1 aor. ἐτροποφόρησα ***bear/put up with (someone's) manner, moods*** etc. (so Cicero, Ad Att. 13, 29, 2; schol. on Aristoph., Ran. 1479) w. acc. of pers. **Ac 13:18** (Dt 1:31 v.l., though τροφοφορεῖν stands in the text there, whereas in the Ac pass. it is a v.l. [Bruce, Acts ad loc.]—B-D-F §119, 1; Mlt-H. 390. Origen, In Matth. X, 14 p. 16, 16 Klostermann '35).—M-M.

τροφεύς, έως, ὁ (τρέφω; Aeschyl., Pla. et al.; OGI 148, 2 [II BC] al.; IGR III, 89, 14 [I AD] one who distributes free food to the people; Jos., Ant. 9, 127 tutor) ***nourisher,*** of God (Philo, Leg. All. 3, 177, Congr. Erud. Gr. 171; Herm. Wr. 16, 12 ὁ ἥλιος as σωτὴρ κ. τροφεύς; p. 390, 12 Sc. ὁ δημιουργός as πατὴρ κ. τροφεύς) Dg 9:6.—DELG s.v. τρέφω C 5.

τροφή, ῆς, ἡ (τρέφω) ***nourishment, food*** (so trag., Hdt., Hippocr., X., Pla. et al.; pap, LXX, pseudepigr., Philo; Jos., Vi. 200; 242; apolog. exc. Tat.).

ⓐ lit. **Mt 3:4** (on dietary note as rhetorical motif in narrative of a distinguished pers. s. Hermogenes, Progymnasmata 38 p. 15f); **6:25; 10:10** (s. HGrimme, BZ 23, '35, 254f; PTomson, Paul and the Jewish Law: CRINT III/1, '90, 125–31; on the topic of asceticism s. PvanderHorst, Chaeremon '87, 56 n. 1; 58 n. 21); **24:45** (for δοῦναι αὐτοῖς τ. τρ. ἐν καιρῷ cp. Ps 103:27 with v.l.); **Lk 12:23; Ac 14:17;** 1 Cl 20:4; B 10:4; Dg 9:6; Hv 3, 9, 3; D 13:1f. W. ποτόν 10:3. τροφὴν λαβεῖν *take nourishment* (Jos., C. Ap. 2, 230) **Ac 9:19;** AcPl Ha 1, 19; but *receive food* (TestJob 24:5) B 10:11; GJs 8:1; 13:2; 15:3. τροφῆς μεταλαμβάνειν (μεταλαμβάνω 1) **Ac 2:46; 27:33f;** προσλαμβάνεσθαι vs. **36;** κορεσθῆναι vs. **38.** Pl. (Diod. S. 15, 36, 1; Appian, Bell. Civ. 4, 136 §576; Aelian, VH 12, 37 p. 132, 28 ἀπορία τροφῶν; TestSol 2:2 D; Just., D. 88, 2; Ath. 31, 1) of a rather large supply of food **J 4:8.** τροφὴ φθορᾶς *perishable food* IRo 7:3. ἡ ἐφήμερος τροφή **Js 2:15** (s. ἐφήμερος).

ⓑ in imagery (Pythagorean saying: WienerStud 8, 1886 p. 277 no. 99 τ. ψυχὴν τρέφειν τῇ ἀϊδίῳ τροφῇ; Philo, Fuga 137 ἡ οὐράνιος τροφή) of spiritual nourishment ἡ στερεὰ τροφή *solid food* (opp. γάλα) **Hb 5:12, 14** (s. στερεός 1). ἡ χριστιανὴ τροφή (opp. the poisonous food of false teaching) ITr 6:1.—B. 329. DELG s.v. τρέφω C 2. M-M.

Τρόφιμος, ου, ὁ (IG III, 1026; 1062; 1095; 1119; 1144 al.; POxy 1160, 2) ***Trophimus*** a companion of Paul on his last journey to Jerusalem: T.'s home was in Ephesus **Ac 20:4; 21:29.—2 Ti 4:20.** For other ins relating to this name s. New Docs 3, 91–93: gener. used of pers. of servile status; Hemer, Acts 236f.—DELG s.v. τρέφω. LGPN I. M-M.

τροφός, οῦ, ἡ (Hom.+; ins, pap, LXX, Philo; Jos., C. Ap. 1, 122; SibOr 13, 43. In gener. as fem. = 'nurse', but also ὁ τρόφος Eur. et al. The masc. was ordinarily τροφεύς q.v.) ***nurse*** (X., Oec. 5, 17 [w. μήτηρ]; Ael. Aristid. 13 p. 163 D. [w. μήτηρ]; pap since III BC; s. also TestNapht 1:9), possibly ***mother*** (Lycophron 1284 Europa τροφὸς Σαρπηδόνος; Dionys. Byz. §2 μητέρα καὶ τροφόν of one and the same person; schol. on Pla. 112e of Phaedra in her relationship to Hippolytus [as stepmother]) **1 Th 2:7** (on Cynic background s. AMalherbe, NovTest 12, '70, 203–17; difft. KDonfried, NTS 31, '85, 338 and n. 18; New Docs 2, 8. SVilatte, AntCl 60, '91, 5–28).—DELG s.v. τρέφω C 3. M-M.

τροφοφορέω 1 aor. ἐτροφοφόρησα 'carry in one's arms', i.e. ***care for*** τινά *someone* (tenderly) **Ac 13:18 v.l.** (fr. Dt 1:31 [s. τροποφορέω]. Cp. 2 Macc 7:27 and Macarius, Hom. 46, 3). See Beginn. I/4, 149.—M-M.

τροχιά, ᾶς, ἡ (τροχός; as early as Philo Mech. 54, 41) ***wheel-track, course, way*** (Anth. Pal. 7, 478; 9, 418; Herodian Gr. I 301, 2; Pr 2:15; 4:11; 5:6, 21; Hesych.; Suda) τροχιὰς ὀρθὰς ποιεῖν *make straight paths* upon which one can advance quickly and in the right direction; in imagery of the moral life τροχιὰς ὀρθὰς ποιεῖτε τοῖς ποσὶν ὑμῶν **Hb 12:13** (Pr 4:26).—DELG s.v. τρέχω.

τροχός, οῦ, ὁ (τρέχω; Hom. et al.; pap, LXX, En; GrBar 9:3; Ps.-Phoc. 27 ὁ βίος τροχός Horst; astr. tt. Cat. Cod. Astr. IX/1 p. 150 ln. 35; 151 ln. 1 and 23; Philo; SibOr 2, 295; loanw. in rabb.) ***wheel,*** in our lit. only in the expr. ὁ τροχὸς τῆς γενέσεως **Js 3:6.** S. γένεσις 2b; Cat. Cod. Astr. IX/2 p. 176–79; also JStiglmayr, BZ 11, 1913, 49–52 (against Stiglmayr JSchäfers, ThGl 5, 1913, 836–39); VBurch, Exp. 8th ser., 16, 1918, 221ff; REisler, Orphischdionys. Mysteriengedanken in der christl. Antike: Vorträge der Bibl. Warburg II/2, 1925, 86–92; GerhKittel, Die Probleme des palästin. Spätjudentums u. das Urchristentum 1926, 141–68; GRendall, The Epistle of St. James and Judaic Christianity 1927, 59f; DRobertson, ET 39, 1928, 333; NMacnicol, ibid. 55, '43/44, 51f; WBieder, TZ 5, '49, 109f; Windisch,

Hdb.[2] exc. on Js 3:6; JMarty, L'épître de Jacques '35; Kl. Pauly IV 1460; V 1345f; BHHW III 2170–230, and comm. ad loc.—Or should the word be accented (ὁ) τρόχος (Soph., Hippocr. et al. On the difference betw. the words s. Trypho Alex. [I BC]: fgm. 11 AvVelsen [1853]; s. L-S-J-M s.v. τροχός; Diehl[3] accents the word as τρόχος in the passage Ps.-Phoc. 27 referred to above, but s. Horst p. 132 [w. reff.]), and should the transl. be the *course* or *round* of existence?—B. 725. DELG s.v. τρέχω. M-M. TW.

τρύβλιον, ου, τό (on the accent s. Tdf., Prol. 102) ***bowl, dish*** (Aristoph., Hippocr. et al.; Plut., Lucian; Aelian, VH 9, 37; LXX; TestAbr B 3 p. 107, 21 [Stone p. 62]; ApcEsdr 6:26 p. 32, 6 Tdf. εἰς τὸ τρύβλιον τοῦ ᾅδου εἰσῆλθον; EpArist 320; Jos., Ant. 3, 220; 12, 117; TestJos 6:2) ἐμβάπτειν μετά τινος τὴν χεῖρα ἐν τῷ τρυβλίῳ *dip one's hand into the bowl together with someone*=share one's meal w. someone **Mt 26:23;** cp. **Mk 14:20** (τρυβάλιον D).—DELG. M-M.

τρυγάω (cp. τρύγη 'grain crop') fut. τρυγήσω; 1 aor. ἐτρύγησα; aor. opt. pass. 3 sg. τρυγηθείη Job 15:33 (Hom. et al.; POxy 3313, 12f [II AD]; al. pap, LXX; JosAs 25:2) 'gather in' ripe fruit, esp. ***harvest (grapes)*** w. acc. of the fruit (POslo 21, 13 [71 AD]; Jos., Ant. 4, 227) **Lk 6:44; Rv 14:18** (in imagery, as in the foll. places). τὸν τῆς ἀναστάσεως καρπὸν τρυγήσουσι 2 Cl 19:3. Cp. also the textually uncertain (s. αἱρέω 1) pass. Dg 12:8.—W. acc. of that which bears the fruit *gather the fruit of* the vine (cp. X., Oec. 19, 19; Diod. S. 3, 62, 7; Lucian, Catap. 20 τὰς ἀμπέλους τρ.; Philostrat., Her. 1, 2) or the vineyard (s. ἄμπελος a) **Rv 14:19,** w. 'picking' done through the use of a sickle, δρέπανον (JosAs 25:2; cp. Procop. Soph., Ep. 11 χωρία τρ.).—DELG. M-M.

τρυγών, όνος, ἡ (τρύζω 'to murmur, coo'; Aristoph., Aristot., Theocr. et al.; Aelian, VH 1, 15; LXX; EpArist 145; Philo; Jos., Ant. 1, 184; 3, 230) ***small pigeon, turtledove,*** as a sacrificial animal of poor people **Lk 2:24** (Lev 12:8.—W. περιστερά Aëtius 42, 8; 20; 44, 22.—PGM 12, 31 τρυγόνα καὶ . . . νεοσσὰ δύο).—M-M. TW.

τρυμαλιά, ᾶς, ἡ (τρύω 'to rub away'; Sotades fgm. 1 Diehl=Coll. Alex. 1 p. 238 [in Plut., Mor. 11a, sexual connotation]; Aesop, Fab. 26 H. of the openings in a fisher's net; Judg 15:11 B; Jer 13:4; 16:16) ***hole*** τρυμαλιὰ ῥαφίδος *eye of a needle* **Mt 19:24 v.l.; Mk 10:25; Lk 18:25 v.l.**—See κάμηλος and κάμιλος.—On the eye of a needle as a symbol of the smallest thing imaginable s. JSepp, ZDPV 14, 1891, 30–34.—DELG s.v. τρύω. M-M.

τρῦπα (τρυπάω; Ps.-Herodian, Epim. p. 89 ἡ τοῦ μυὸς τρῦπα; Syntipas p. 55, 25; 27) or **τρύπη** (Anth. 14, 62, 2; Theognost., Canon. p. 24, 24; Ps.-Herodian, Epim. p. 136), **ης, ἡ** ***hole, opening,*** of the anus B 10:6 (on the subj. s. ἀφόδευσις).—DELG s.v. τρυπάω.

τρυπάω (s. τρῦπα) fut. τρυπήσω; 1 aor. ἐτρύπησα; pf. pass. ptc. masc. acc. τετρυπημένον Hg 1:6 (Hom. et al.; Hero Alex. I p. 4, 23; 36, 14; LXX; GrBar) ***make a hole in, bore through*** τί *someth.* τὸν οὐρανόν *the sky* Hm 11:18 (GrBar 3:7). τὸν λίθον 11:20.—B. 593. DELG.

τρύπη, ης, ἡ s. τρῦπα.

τρύπημα, ατος, τό (τρυπάω; Aristoph.; Aeneas Tact. 725 al.; Philo Mech. 57, 19; Hero Alex., Plut. et al.) **that which is bored, *a hole*** τρύπημα ῥαφίδος *eye of a needle* **Mt 19:24.**—DELG s.v. τρυπάω.

Τρύφαινα, ης, ἡ (fr. θρύπτω via τρυφ- + -αινα [cp. Buck, Reverse Index 289]) ***Tryphena*** ('Dainty'), a Christian acknowledged by Paul for her work in the Lord's service **Ro 16:12.** In the Gk. form this name in Lucian; Gk. ins from Cyprus: Κυπρ. I p. 50 no. 4, p. 91 no. 21; CIG 3092; as the name of an Israelite in a pap of 73 AD (in CPJ II, 421, 183, s. Schürer III 54), also BGU 1105, 2–5; 1119, 7; 1162, 16, esp. as the name of the daughter of Polemon of Pontus (SIG 798: 14, 17, 19; 799: 4, 29). Also AcPlTh 27ff (Aa I 255, 3ff). In its Lat. form CIL VI 15622–26; XII 3398; XIV 415; 734.—Mommsen, Ephemeris Epigraphica I 1872, 270ff; II 1875, 259ff; Lghtf., Phil 175f; Zahn, Einl.[3] I 299. S. Τρυφῶσα.—LGPN I. M-M.

τρυφάω (τρυφή) fut. 3 pl. τρυφήσουσιν Sir 14:4; 1 aor. ἐτρύφησα (Eur., Isocr.+; Kaibel 362, 5; PLond III, 973b, 13 p. 213 [III AD]; 2 Esdr 19:25; Is 66:11; Sir 14:4; TestJos 9:2; Philo; Jos., Ant. 4, 167; 7, 133; Mel., P. 47, 335) **to lead a life of self-indulgence, *live for pleasure, revel, carouse* Js 5:5;** Hs 6, 4, 1f; 4ab; 6, 5, 3–5.—Of animals *be contented, well fed* (Philo, Dec. 117) Hs 6, 1, 6; 6, 2, 6 (though the sheep here represent luxury-loving people). In bold imagery and in a good sense, of reveling in the doing of good Hs 6, 5, 7 (cp. τρυφή 3).—DELG s.v. θρύπτω III. M-M.

τρυφερός, ά, όν (Eur., Thu. et al.; BGU 1080, 18; LXX; TestGad 1:4 of Joseph, who was 'frail', i.e. not tough like his brothers; Philo, Somn. 2, 9; SibOr 3, 527) **pert. to being gentle and free from harshness, *delicate, gentle, subdued,*** of the Holy Spirit Hm 5, 1, 3; 5, 2, 6 (in these pass. in contrast to a spirit of bitterness). Of the ἄγγελος τῆς δικαιοσύνης 6, 2, 3. Of unmarried women s 9, 2, 5 (Chariton 2, 2, 2; cp. Sus 31, but there in ref. to a woman's voluptuousness).—DELG s.v. θρύπτω III.

τρυφή, ῆς, ἡ (θρύπτω; Eur., X., Pla.+; SIG 888, 124; LXX; OdeSol 11:16a, 24; Test12Patr; JosAs 16:8; ApcSed 11:11 p. 134, 27 Ja.; Mel., P. 18, 126)

❶ **engagement in a fast, self-indulgent lifestyle, *indulgence, reveling*** (Sextus 73; Philo, Spec. Leg. 2, 240, Somn. 1, 123; TestJos 3:4; TestBenj 6:3; Jos., Ant. 10, 193; 16, 301) **2 Pt 2:13** (cp. Cicero, Pro Caelio 47); Hs 6, 4, 4ab; 6, 5, 1; 3; 4; 5. τρυφὴ πονηρά Hm 8:3. ἄγγελος τρυφῆς Hs 6, 2, 1. Pl. (Jos., Vi. 284; ApcSed 11:11) Hm 6, 2, 5; 11:12; 12, 2, 1; s 6, 2, 2; 4; 6, 5, 6; 7c. AcPl Ha 2, 19 (s. πολῖτις).

❷ **a state of extraordinary ease and comfort, *luxury, splendor*** (Ps.-Lucian, Amor. 3 ἐσθὴς μέχρι ποδῶν τὴν τρυφὴν καθειμένη) **Lk 7:25.**

❸ **a state of intense satisfaction, *enjoyment, joy, delight,*** ext. of 1 in a good sense (cp. τρυφάω end) (Menand., Cith. fgm. 5, 2 J.; SEG VIII, 549, 28 bestowed by Isis; En 14:13; TestJud 25:2; JosAs 16:8; Philo, Cher. 12; Jos., C. Ap. 2, 228; Mel., P. 18, 126) οἵαν τρυφὴν ἔχει ἡ μέλλουσα ἐπαγγελία *what enjoyment the promise of the future brings* 2 Cl 10:4. παράδεισος τρυφῆς *a Paradise of delight* Dg 12:1 (Gen 3:23; OdeSol 11:24).—*Reveling* in the doing of good Hs 6, 5, 7b; ibid. a, the pl.—DELG s.v. θρύπτω. M-M.

Τρυφῶσα, ης, ἡ ***Tryphosa*** ('Luscious'), Christian recipient of a commendatory greeting **Ro 16:12.** The name is found in Gk. and Lat. ins (CIG II, 2819; 2839; 3348; IG III, 2880; IX/2, 766; XIV, 2246; LBW 710, 2f.—CIL VI, 4866; 15241; X, 2551 al.). She is mentioned together w. Τρύφαινα (q.v.) and hence is regarded by many (e.g. Lghtf., Phil p. 175, 7) as her sister.—LGPN I. M-M.

Τρῳάς, άδος, ἡ (also Τρωάς) ***Troas, (the) Troad,*** actually fem. of the noun Τρώς and the adj. Τρῳός; a city and region in the northwest corner of Asia Minor, near the site of ancient Troy. So since Hom. Hymns and trag.; the trag. connect it with γῆ, as does Hdt. 5, 26 ἐν τῇ Τρῳάδι γῇ. But Hdt. also uses the word 5, 122, 2 without any addition of the region in general, and the same is true of X.; Diod. S. 14, 38, 2 τὰς ἐν τῇ Τρῳάδι πόλεις; 14, 38, 3 several cities κατὰ τὴν Τρῳάδα; 17, 7, 10; 17, 17, 6 (cp. ἡ Ἰνδική Hdt. 3, 106, 2=Ἰνδικὴ χώρη 3, 98, 2). In a time when there were many cities named Ἀλεξάνδρεια the one located in the Troad was known as Ἀλεξάνδρεια [ἡ] Τρῳάς=the Trojan Alexandria (Polyb. 5, 111, 3; Strabo 13, 1, 1 p. 581; OGI 441, 165f [81 BC]). This city, as well as the region around it, was occasionally called Τρῳάς for short (Ath. 26, 2; Pauly-W. I 1396, 15f and 2d ser. VII/1, 383f).—In our lit. Τρῳάς has the article in Paul in **2 Cor 2:12** (B-D-F §261, 4) and prob. means the region, which the apostle soon left (vs. 13) for Macedonia. Elsewhere the article is almost always omitted, as is usually the case w. place-names (B-D-F §261, 1). In **Ac 20:6,** the only exception, the use of the art. can be justified as a glance backward at the preceding verse, where T. almost certainly means the city. In vs. **6** ἡ T.=Troas, which was just mentioned.—The other passages are: **Ac 16:8, 11; 2 Ti 4:13;** IPhld 11:2; ISm 12:1 and its terminal subscription; IPol 8:1.—Pauly-W. VII 525–84; Kl. Pauly V 975; PECS 407 (s.v. Ilion).

Τρωγύλλιον, ου, τό (Strabo, Ptolem. et al., in var. spellings; B-D-F §42, 3) ***Trogyllium*** a promontory and town south of Ephesus in Asia Minor. Acc. to **Ac 20:15 v.l.** ἐν Τρωγυλλίῳ (D has ἐν Τρωγυλίᾳ; another v.l. ἐν Τρωγυλίῳ) Paul stayed there one night.

τρώγω (Hom. et al.; TestJob 12:2; SIG 1171, 9; PGM 7, 177; Sb 5730, 5. Not found in LXX, EpArist, Philo or Joseph. B-D-F §101 s.v. ἐσθίειν; 169, 2; Rob. 351; JHaussleiter, Archiv für lat. Lexikographie 9, 1896, 300–302; GKilpatrick in: Studies and Documents 29, '67, 153) **to bite or chew food, *eat*** (audibly), of animals (Hom. et al. 'chew, nibble, munch') B 10:3.—Of human beings (Hdt. et al. and so in Mod. Gk.) τὶ *someth.* (Hdt. 1, 71, 3 σῦκα; Aristoph., Equ. 1077) B 7:8. ὁ τρώγων μου τὸν ἄρτον as a symbol of close comradeship (Polyb. 31, 23, 9 δύο τρώγομεν ἀδελφοί) **J 13:18** (s. Ps 40:10 ὁ ἐσθίων ἄρτους μου, which is the basis for this pass.). W. gen. (Athen. 8, 334b τῶν σύκων) Hs 5, 3, 7. Abs. B 10:2. W. πίνειν (Demosth. 19, 197; Plut., Mor. 613b; 716e) **Mt 24:38.** J uses it to offset any tendencies to 'spiritualize' the concept so that nothing physical remains in it, in what many hold to be the language of the Lord's Supper ὁ τρώγων τοῦτον τὸν ἄρτον **6:58.** ὁ τρώγων με vs. **57.** ὁ τρώγων μου τὴν σάρκα (w. πίνων μου τὸ αἷμα) vss. **54, 56.**—B. 327. DELG. M-M. TW.

τυγχάνω (Hom.+) impf. ἐτύγχανον; fut. τεύξομαι; 2 aor. ἔτυχον; 1 aor. mid. inf. τεύξασθαι LXX. Perf. (for Att. τετύχηκα, s. Phryn. p. 395 Lob.) τέτευχα (Ion. [Hdt. and Hippocr.; s. Kühner-Bl. II 556], then Aristot. et al.; OGI 194, 31 [42 BC]; pap [Mayser I/2[2] '38, 151f]; LXX [Thackeray §24 p. 287]; EpArist 121; Nachmanson 160, 1; Crönert 279; Schmid I 86; IV 40 and 600) **Hb 8:6 v.l.** or, as in the text, τέτυχα (Diod. S. 12, 17, 99; Aesop, Fab. 363 H. [removed by correction]; Jos., Bell. 7, 130 [removed by correction]; EpArist 180 συντέτυχε); s. B-D-F §101; W-S. §13, 2; Mlt-H. 262.

❶ **to experience some happening, *meet, attain, gain, find, experience*** w. gen. of pers. or thing that one meets, etc. (Hom. et al.; LXX; TestAbr A 19 p. 102, 9 [Stone p. 52]; GrBar 17:4; AssMos, apolog.) **Lk 20:35; Ac 24:2; 26:22; 27:3; 2 Ti 2:10** (Diod. S. 4, 48, 7 τετεύχασι τῆς σωτηρίας. With the v.l. σωτηρίαν in mss. FG cp. Solon 24, 2 D.[2] τυγχ. τι); **Hb 8:6; 11:35;** 1 Cl 61:2; 2 Cl 15:5; Dg 2:1; 9:6; IEph 10:1; IMg 1:3; ISm 9:2; 11:3; IPol 4:3; Hm 10, 1, 5; s 9, 26, 4.

❷ **to prove to be in the result, *happen, turn out,*** intr.

ⓐ *happen to be, find oneself* (X., Hell. 4, 3, 3; Tob 5:13 AB; TestJob 36:5; ApcMos 9; Just., D. 3, 2; Ath., R. p. 78, 14) ἐν σαρκὶ τυγχάνειν Dg 5:8; ἐπὶ γῆς 10:7. ἀφέντες ἡμιθανῆ τυγχάνοντα *they left him for half-dead, as indeed he was* **Lk 10:30 v.l.**

ⓑ εἰ τύχοι as a formula *if it should turn out that way, perhaps* (Cleanthes, fgm. 529 vArnim=Sext. Emp., Math. 9, 89; Dionys. Hal. 4, 19; Hero Alex. III p. 220, 13; Dio Chrys. 16 [33], 53; Philo [KReik, Der Opt. bei Polyb. u. Philo von Alex. 1907, 154]; Just., D. 27, 3; B-D-F §385, 2) **1 Cor 15:37** (cp. Plut., fgm. 104, ed. Sanbach, '67 πυροῦ τυχὸν ἢ κριθῆς=perhaps of wheat or barley); Dg 2:3. In τοσαῦτα εἰ τύχοι γένη φωνῶν εἰσιν **1 Cor 14:10,** εἰ τύχ. is prob. meant to limit τοσαῦτα (Heinrici: JWeiss) *there are probably ever so many different languages* (Goodsp.—Nicol. Dam.: 90 fgm. 130, 110 Jac. καθ' ἣν τύχοι πρόφασιν='under who knows what sort of pretext').

ⓒ τυχόν, actually the acc. absolute of the neut. of the aor. ptc. (B-D-F §424; Rob. 490) *if it turns out that way, perhaps, if possible* (X., An. 6, 1, 20; Ps.-Pla., Alcib. 2, 140a; 150c; Epict. 1, 11, 11; 2, 1, 1; 3, 21, 18 al.; letter [IV BC] in Dssm., LO 121 [LAE 151]; Just., D. 4, 7 τὸ τυχόν; SIG 1259, 8; SibOr 5, 236) **1 Cor 16:6; Lk 20:13** D; **Ac 12:15** D.

ⓓ ὁ τυχών the first one whom one happens to meet in the way (X., Pla. et al.; Philo, Op. M. 137), hence οὐχ ὁ τυχών *not the common* or *ordinary one* (Fgm. Com. Att. III 442 fgm. 178 Kock; Theophr., HP 8, 7, 2; Περὶ ὕψους 9 [of Moses]. Numerous other exx. fr. lit. in Wettstein on Ac 19:11. Ins fr. Ptolemaic times: BCH 22, 1898 p. 89 θόρυβον οὐ τὸν τυχόντα παρέχοντες; SIG 528, 10 [221/219 BC] ἀρωστίαις οὐ ταῖς τυχούσαις; BGU 36, 9; POxy 899, 14; 3 Macc 3:7; Jos., Ant. 2, 120; 6, 292) δυνάμεις οὐ τὰς τυχούσας *extraordinary miracles* **Ac 19:11.** Cp. **28:2;** 1 Cl 14:2.—B. 658. DELG. M-M. TW.

τυμπανίζω (τύμπανον 'drum, tambourine', e.g. Eur., Bacch. 156, Herac. 891) 1 aor. ptc. τυμπανίσας (ViAm 1 [p. 81, 11 Sch.]), pass. ἐτυμπανίσθην 'to torture with an instrument called τύμπανον' (so Aristoph., Plut. 476 et al.; 2 Macc 6:19, 28. S. L-S-J-M s.v. τύμπανον II 1 and ἀποτυμπανίζω.—AKeramopoulos, Ο Αποτυμπανισμος 1923), then ***torment, torture*** gener. (Aristot., Rhet. 2, 5; Plut., Mor. 60a; Lucian, Jupp. Tr. 19. The compound ἀποτυμπ. in the same sense Plut., Dio 28, 2; UPZ 119, 37 [156 BC]; 3 Macc 3:27; Jos., C. Ap. 1, 148) pass. **Hb 11:35.**—EOwen, JTS 30, 1929, 259–66.—DELG s.v. τύμπανον. M-M.

τυπικῶς (τύπος; Rufus [II AD] in Oribas. 8, 47, 11; schol. on Pind., O. 1, 118 v.l.) adv. of τυπικός (Plut., Mor. 442c) **pert. to serving as an example or model, *as an example/warning,*** in connection w. the typological interpr. of Scripture ταῦτα τυπικῶς συνέβαινεν ἐκείνοις **1 Cor 10:11.**—DELG s.v. τύπτω B. M-M. TW.

τύπος, ου, ὁ (Aeschyl., Hdt.+; ins in var. senses: New Docs 4, 41f; loanw. in rabb.).

❶ **a mark made as the result of a blow or pressure, *mark, trace*** (Posidon.: 169 fgm. 1 Jac.; Anth. Pal. 6, 57, 5 ὀδόντων; Athen. 13, 49, 585c τῶν πληγῶν; Diog. L. 7, 45; 50 of a seal-ring; ViJer 13 [p. 73, 10 Sch.]; Philo, Mos. 1, 119; Jos., Bell. 3, 420; PGM 4, 1429; 5, 307.—ὁ ἐκ τῆς αἰσθήσεως τ. ἐν διανοίᾳ γινόμενος Did., Gen. 217, 19) τῶν ἥλων **J 20:25ab** (v.l. τὸν τόπον).—This may be the place for οἱ τύποι τῶν λίθων Hs 9, 10, 1f (taking a stone out of the ground leaves a hole that bears the contours of the stone, but in effect the stone has made the impression; s. KLake, Apost. Fathers II, 1917; MDibelius, Hdb. But s. 4 below).

❷ **embodiment of characteristics or function of a model,** ***copy, image*** (cp. Artem. 2, 85 the children are τύπ. of their parents.—Cp. ὁ γὰρ ἥλιος ἐν τύπῳ θεοῦ ἐστιν Theoph. Ant. 2, 15 [p. 138, 8]) the master is a τύπος θεοῦ *image of God* to the slave B 19:7; D 4:11. The supervisor/bishop is τύπος τοῦ πατρός ITr 3:1; cp. IMg 6:1ab (in both instances here, τύπον is Zahn's conjecture, favored by Lghtf., for τόπον, which is unanimously read by Gk. and Lat. mss., and which can be retained, with Funk, Hilgenfeld, Krüger, Bihlmeyer).

❸ **an object formed to resemble some entity,** ***image, statue*** of any kind of material (Hdt. 3, 88,3 τύπ. λίθινος. Of images of the gods Herodian 5, 5, 6; Jos., Ant. 1, 311 τ. τύπους τῶν θεῶν; 15, 329; SibOr 3, 14) **Ac 7:43** (Am 5:26).

❹ **a kind, class, or thing that suggests a model or pattern,** ***form, figure, pattern*** (Aeschyl. et al.; Pla., Rep. 387c; 397c) ἐποίησεν ἡμᾶς ἄλλον τύπον *he has made us people of a different stamp* B 6:11. τύπος διδαχῆς *pattern of teaching* **Ro 6:17** (cp. διδαχή 2; Iambl., Vi. Pyth. 23, 105 τὸν τύπον τῆς διδασκαλίας.—The use of τύπος for the imperial 'rescripts' [e.g. OGI 521, 5; s. note 4, esp. the reff. for θεῖος τύπος] appears too late to merit serious consideration.—JKürzinger, Biblica 39, '58, 156–76; ELee, NTS 8, '61/62, 166–73 ['mold']). Of the *form (of expression)* (Dionys. Hal., Ad Pomp. 4, 2 Rad.; PLips 121, 28 [II AD]; POxy 1460, 12) γράψας ἐπιστολὴν ἔχουσαν τὸν τύπον τοῦτον (cp. EpArist 34 ἐπιστολὴ τὸν τύπον ἔχουσα τοῦτον) *somewhat as follows, after this manner, to this effect* (so numerous versions) **Ac 23:25,** but s. next.—On τοὺς τύπους τῶν λίθων ἀναπληροῦν Hs 9, 10, 1 s. ἀναπληρόω 3 and 1 above.

❺ **the content of a document,** ***text, content*** (Iambl., Vi. Pyth. 35, 259 τύπος τ. γεγραμμένων; 3 Macc 3:30; PFlor 278 II, 20 [III AD] τῷ αὐτῷ τύπῳ κ. χρόνῳ=of the same content and date) **Ac 23:25** (EpArist 34 ἐπιστολὴ τὸν τύπον ἔχουσα τοῦτον). Cp. POxy 3366, 28 (of a copy of a letter), 32 (the original). S. New Docs 1, 77f (with caution against confusing rhetorical practice in composition of speeches and the inclusion of letters whose value lay in their verbatim expression). For a difft. view s. 4 above; more ambivalently Hemer, Acts 347f.

❻ **an archetype serving as a model,** ***type, pattern, model*** (Pla., Rep. 379a περὶ θεολογίας)—ⓐ technically ***design, pattern*** (Diod. S. 14, 41, 4) **Ac 7:44; Hb 8:5** (cp. on both Ex 25:40).

ⓑ in the moral life ***example, pattern*** (OGI 383, 212 [I BC] τ. εὐσεβείας; SibOr 1, 380; Did., Gen. 125, 27; in a pejorative sense 4 Macc 6:19 ἀσεβείας τύπ.) τύπος γίνου τῶν πιστῶν **1 Ti 4:12.—Phil 3:17; 1 Th 1:7; 2 Th 3:9; Tit 2:7; 1 Pt 5:3;** IMg 6:2.—S. ESelwyn, 1 Pt '46, 298f.

ⓒ of the ***types*** given by God as an indication of the future, in the form of persons or things (cp. Philo, Op. M. 157; Iren. 1, 6, 4 [Harv. I 74, 3]); of Adam: τύπος τοῦ μέλλοντος (Ἀδάμ) *a type of the Adam to come* (i.e. of Christ) **Ro 5:14.** Cp. **1 Cor 10:6, 11 v.l.;** B 7:3, 7, 10f; 8:1; 12:2, 5f, 10; 13:5. χριστὸς Ἰησοῦς … ἑαυτὸν τύπον ἔδειξε *Jesus Christ showed himself as the prime exemplar of the resurrection* AcPlCor 2:6 (cp. Just., D. 40, 1 τύπος ἦν τοῦ χριστοῦ). Also of the pictorial *symbols* that Hermas sees, and their deeper *meaning* Hv 3, 11, 4. The vision serves εἰς τύπον τῆς θλίψεως τῆς ἐπερχομένης *as a symbol* or *foreshadowing of the tribulation to come* 4, 1, 1; cp. 4, 2, 5; 4, 3, 6. The two trees are to be εἰς τύπον τοῖς δούλοις τοῦ θεοῦ s 2:2a; cp. b.—ἐν τύπῳ χωρίου Ῥωμαίων IRo ins is a conjecture by Zahn for ἐν τόπῳ χ. Ῥ., which is read by all mss. and makes good sense.—AvBlumenthal, Τύπος u. παράδειγμα: Her 63, 1928, 391–414; LGoppelt, Typos. D. typolog. Deutung des AT im Neuen '39; RBultmann, TLZ 75, '50, cols. 205–12; AFridrichsen et al., The Root of the Vine (typology) '53; GLampe and KWoollcombe, Essays in Typology, '57; KOstmeyer, NTS 46, '00, 112–31.—New Docs 1, 77f; 4, 41. DELG s.v. τύπτω B. M-M. EDNT. TW. Spicq. Sv.

τύπτω impf. ἔτυπτον; 1 aor. 3 sg. ἔτυψεν GJs 13:1 (Hom.+.—Defective, s. B-D-F §101; Mlt-H. 262) **to inflict a blow,** ***strike, beat, wound***

ⓐ lit. τινά *someone* (Jos., Ant. 20, 206, Vi. 108; 233) **Mt 24:49; Lk 12:45; Ac 18:17; 21:32** (cp. 22:25; PLips 40, 21 ἐλευθέρους μὴ τύπτητε s. Taubenschlag, OpMin II 723); **Tit 1:11 v.l.** Pass. **Ac 23:3b.** τὸ στόμα τινός *strike someone on the mouth* **23:2.** τὸ πρόσωπόν τινος *strike someone in the face* (Hermippus Com. [V BC] 80) **Lk 22:64 v.l.;** αὐτοῦ τὴν κεφαλὴν καλάμῳ **Mk 15:19** (for the dat. cp. Diod. S. 15, 86, 2 ἀλλήλους τοῖς δόρασι; Quint. Smyrn. 1, 247). τινὰ ἐπὶ τὴν σιαγόνα *strike someone on the cheek* **Lk 6:29.** εἰς τὴν κεφαλήν τινος **Mt 27:30.** As a sign of contrition or sorrow (cp. Arrian, Anab. 7, 24, 3 τύπτεσθαι τὰ στήθη; ApcMos 42; Jos., Ant. 7, 252; Ath. 14, 2) ἔτυπτεν τὸ στῆθος ἑαυτοῦ **Lk 18:13.** τύπτοντες τὰ στήθη **23:48.** ἔτυψεν τὸ πρόσωπον αὐτοῦ GJs 13:1. τύπτω κατά τι *strike on someth.* (schol. on Nicander, Alexiph. 456): κατὰ ἕνα λίθον ἔτυπτεν *he struck on each individual stone* Hs 9, 6, 3. Pass. of an anvil IPol 3:1.

ⓑ fig. *strike, assault*—**α.** misfortunes designated as blows coming fr. God (Ex 7:27; 2 Km 24:17; Ezk 7:6; 2 Macc 3:39; EpArist 192) *strike* **Ac 23:3a.**

β. τύπ. τὴν συνείδησίν τινος *assault someone's conscience* **1 Cor 8:12** (Il. 19, 125 'sharp grief struck him to the depths of his mind'; Hdt. 3, 64, 1 Καμβύσεα ἔτυψε ἡ ἀληθείη τῶν λόγων 'the truth of the words hit Cambyses'; 1 Km 1:8).—B. 552f.—DELG. M-M. EDNT. TW. Cp. πατάσσω.

τυραννίς, ίδος, ἡ autocratic control of a state or a people, ***despotic rule, tyranny*** (so Archilochus [VII BC], Hdt. et al.; LXX, Philo; Jos., Bell. 4, 166, Ant. 1, 114, Vi. 260; SibOr 3, 202; Just., A I, 3, 2; Mel., P. 49, 354 al.; Ath. 30, 1) ἐπὶ τυραννίδι *in order to set up a tyranny* Dg 7:3.—HBerve, Die Tyrannis '67.—DELG s.v. τύραννος.

τύραννος, ου, ὁ (in the general sense 'absolute ruler', freq. of deities, without neg. connotation, Aeschyl. et al.; ins [e.g. IAndrosIsis, Kyme 3a]; but also, as indicated below, in the neg. sense used in our lit.) ***autocratic ruler, despot, tyrant*** (so Theognis, Hdt. +; ins, pap, LXX, TestSol; EpArist 289; Philo; Jos., Bell. 5, 439, C. Ap. 2, 241; apolog. exc. Ar.; loanw. in rabb.) MPol 2:4 v.l.(Mitt-Wilck, I/2, 20 II, 5=POxy 33: Appian, a political dissident, calls the Emperor Commodus (?) a τύραννος, though the emperor, ln. 6, wishes to be known as βασιλεύς). W. λῃστής and δυνάστης Ath., R. 19 p. 72, 25). W. βασιλεύς (Memnon [I BC/I AD]: 434 fgm. 1, 4, 6 Jac.; Wsd 12:14; Philo; Jos., Ant. 11, 287; 18, 169) **Ac 5:39** D.—DELG.

Τύραννος, ου, ὁ (lit.; Joseph. [index]; ins, pap) ***Tyrannus,*** an Ephesian in whose hall (s. σχολή) Paul lectured. Whether this otherw. unknown man was himself a teacher of philosophy or rhetoric, or whether he simply owned the house in which the hall was situated, we do not know (acc. to Diog. L. 9, 54 Protagoras held his lectures in Athens ἐν τῇ Εὐριπίδου οἰκίᾳ or acc. to others ἐν τῇ Μεγακλείδου) **Ac 19:9.**—Haenchen ad loc.; Hemer, Acts 234.—LGPN I. M-M.

τυρβάζω (τύρβη 'disorder, confusion'; Ps.-Hes, Soph. et al.) **to cause to be stirred up** mid. or pass. in act. sense ***trouble oneself, be troubled, be agitated*** περί τι *with* or *about someth.* (Aristoph., Pax 1007) περὶ πολλά **Lk 10:41 v.l.** (Nilus, Ep. 2, 258 μὴ ἄγαν τυρβάζου).—DELG s.v. τύρβη.

Τύριος, ου, ὁ (Hdt. et al.; Joseph. [index]; ins, LXX) ***the Tyrian*** (s. Τύρος; SibOr 4, 90) **Ac 12:20, 22** D.

Τύρος, ου, ἡ (Hdt. et al.; Joseph. [index], ins, LXX; SibOr 5, 455.—Heb. צֹר; Aram. טוּר) ***Tyre,*** a city in Phoenicia **Ac 21:3, 7.** Named w. Sidon **Mt 11:21f; 15:21; Mk 3:8; 7:24** (καί Σ. v.l.), **31; Lk 6:17; 10:13f.**—WFleming, The History of Tyre 1915; Kl. Pauly V 1027–29; PECS 944; OEANE V 247–50.

τυφλός, ή, όν (s. next entry; Hom.+) 'blind'—❶ **pert. to being unable to see, *blind,*** lit. (freq. in the canonical gospels)

ⓐ adj.—**α.** as attribute ἄνθρωπος τυφλός **J 9:1** (s. γενετή); τυφ. προσαίτης **Mk 10:46.**

β. as predicate **J 9:18, 24; Ac 13:11** (cp. blindness resulting fr. exposure to an apparition Hdt. 6, 117; Plut., Mor. 305c; s. Reader, Polemo 239); Dg 2:4 (almost word for word like Plut., Mor. 420b εἴδωλα κωφὰ κ. τυφλὰ κ. ἄψυχα). Mostly

ⓑ subst. **Mt 9:27f; 11:5; 20:30; Mk 8:22f** (LSzimonidesz, D. Heilung des Blinden von Bethsaida u. Buddhas Gleichn. von den Blindgeborenen u. dem Elefanten: NThT 24, '35, 233–59); **10:49, 51; Lk 7:21f; J 5:3; 10:21; 11:37** al. (on **Mt 11:5; Lk 7:22** s. also κωφός 2). On **Mt 15:14; Lk 6:39** s. ὁδηγέω 1 and cp. Sext. Emp., Πρὸς Μαθημ. I, 31 ὡς οὐδὲ ὁ τυφλὸς τὸν τυφλὸν ὁδηγεῖν (sc. δύναται). τυφλοὺς θεραπεύων AcPl Ha 8, 36.

❷ **pert. to being unable to understand, *incapable of comprehending, blind,*** of mental and spiritual blindness in imagery, fig. ext. of mng. 1 (since Pind.; Soph., Oed. R. 371; Lucian, Vit. Auct. 18 τῆς ψυχῆς τὸν ὀφθαλμόν; Ps 145:8; Philo; Jos., C. Ap. 2, 142 τυφλὸς τὸν νοῦν. ὀφθαλμοὶ τυφλῶν τὴν ψυχήν Orig., C. Cels. 2, 48, 38.).

ⓐ adj.—**α.** as attribute ὁδηγὸς τυφλός (cp. X., Mem. 1, 3, 4; Demetr. Phaler. [IV BC; ed. FWehrli '49], fgm. 121 οὐ μόνον τὸν πλοῦτον τυφλόν, ἀλλὰ καὶ τὴν ὁδηγοῦσαν αὐτὸν τύχην; Philo, Virt. 7; Just., D. 134, 1) **Mt 15:14; 23:16, 24.** Φαρισαῖε τυφλέ vs. **26.**

β. as a predicate **J 9:40f; 2 Pt 1:9; Rv 3:17.** τυφλοί εἰσιν τῇ καρδίᾳ αὐτῶν Ox 1 verso, 20f=GTh 28.

ⓑ subst. **Mt 23:17, 19; Ro 2:19** here metaphorically of those not converted to Mosaic way of life; B 14:7 (Is 42:7), 9 (Is 61:1), οὐαὶ τυφλοὶ μὴ ὁρῶντες Ox 840, 31.—SRoth, The Blind, the Lame, and the Poor '97 (Luke-Acts).—B. 322. DELG s.v. τύφομαι B. M-M. EDNT. TW.

τυφλόω (τυφλός) 1 aor. ἐτύφλωσα; pf. τετύφλωκα; aor. pass. 3 sg. ἐτυφλώθη, -θησαν LXX (Pind., Hdt. et al.; Ramsay, CB I/2, 386 no. 232, 15; PLond V, 1708, 84; LXX; TestSol 12:2 P; Test12Patr) **to deprive of sight, *to blind*** in our lit. only in imagery (Is 42:19) τετύφλωκεν αὐτῶν τοὺς ὀφθαλμούς (cp. TestDan 2:4) **J 12:40** (cp. Is 6:10).—**1J 2:11;** or fig. τυφ. τὰ νοήματα **2 Cor 4:4** (Pla., Phd. 99e μὴ τὴν ψυχὴν τυφλωθείην; Herm. Wr. 478, 32 Sc.; Philo, Ebr. 108 διάνοιαν τυφλωθείς; Jos., Ant. 8, 30; Test Sim 2:7 ὁ ἄρχων τῆς πλάνης ἐτύφλωσέ μου τὸν νοῦν).—DELG s.v. τύφομαι B. M-M. TW.

τῦφος, ους, τό (fr. τύφω, prim. 'make smoke') for the usual (cp. ζῆλος, beg.) **τῦφος, ου, ὁ a conviction that is not rooted in reality, *delusion, conceit, arrogance*** (so Pla. et al.; Philo Bybl. [c. 100 AD]: 790 fgm. 1 p. 805, 7 Jac. [in Eus., PE 1, 9, 26]; Dio Chrys. 4, 6; Vett. Val. 4, 28; 150, 5; 3 Macc 3:18; SibOr 8, 8; 111; Philo; Jos., Ant. 9, 922; Tat. 1, 2) of such as have exaggerated notions about their self-importance 1 Cl 13:1.—DELG s.v. τύφομαι. Sv.

τυφόω (τῦφος) 1 aor. pass. ἐτυφώθην; pf. pass. τετύφωμαι; 'becloud, delude', but only in a fig. sense and quite predom., in our lit. exclusively, in the pass. (Hippocr., Pla.) **τυφόομαι;** for our lit. the mngs. are surely

❶ ***be puffed up, conceited*** (Strabo 15, 1, 5; Plut., Mor. 59a; Aelian, VH 3, 28; Diog. L. 6, 7; 26 al.; Philo, Congr. Erud. Gr. 128; Jos., Vi. 53) τυφωθείς (cp. Sext. Emp., Pyrrh. 3, 193) **1 Ti 3:6.** Cp. **2 Ti 3:4.** The ancient versions also understand τετύφωται μηδὲν ἐπιστάμενος **1 Ti 6:4** in this sense, though this pass. may belong under mng. 2 or 3.

❷ ***be blinded, become foolish*** (Hippocr. et al.) pf. pass. in act. sense *be foolish, stupid* (Demosth. 9, 20; 19, 219 μαίνομαι καὶ τετύφωμαι; Polyb. 3, 81, 1 ἀγνοεῖ κ. τετύφωται; Dio Chrys. 30 [47], 18 ἢ ἐγὼ τετύφωμαι καὶ ἀνόητός εἰμι; Philo, Conf. Lingu. 106; Jos., C. Ap. 1, 15; 2, 255) **1 Ti 6:4** (s. 1).—DELG s.v. τύφομαι. M-M. Spicq.

❸ ***be mentally ill*** (cp. Demosth. 9, 20; Plut., Mor. 81f). AMalherbe (Medical Imagery in the Pastoral Letters: Paul and the Popular Philosophers '89, 123f, esp. n. 7) considers this mng. "quite likely" for **1 Ti 6:4.** Cp. VLeinieks, The City of Dionysos '96, 107–22.

τύφω (Eur., Hdt. et al.) **to give off smoke,** pass. ***smoke, smolder, glimmer*** (Philostrat., Vi. Apoll. 5, 17 p. 177, 30; Jos., Bell. 6, 257) of a wick **Mt 12:20** (s. the lit. s.v. κάλαμος 1).—DELG s.v. τύφομαι.

τυφωνικός, ή, όν ***like a whirlwind*** ἄνεμος τυφωνικός *a typhoon, hurricane* **Ac 27:14** (Etym. Mag. p. 755, 11 τῶν τυφωνικῶν καλουμένων πνευμάτων; schol. on Soph., Ant. 418 p. 239 P. τὸν τυφώνιον ἄνεμον; Eustath. in Il. 2, 782 p. 345, 43).—Rdm.[2] 28f.—Frisk s.v. τύφομαι. M-M.

τυχεῖν, τύχοι s. τυγχάνω.

τύχη, ης, ἡ (Hom. Hymns, Hdt.+; ins, pap, LXX; Jos., Bell. 4, 365, C. Ap. 2, 130; 227; Ath.) **the condition of happening without human intervention or control, *fortune,*** in our lit. only as v.l. in **Lk 10:31** D *by chance,* and in the expr. ὀμνύναι τὴν Καίσαρος τύχην *swear by the Fortune of Caesar* (cp. Cass. Dio 44, 6; 50; 57, 8; Jos., Ant. 16, 344. Very oft. in pap, from POxy 483, 21 [108 AD] on) MPol 9:2; 10:1.—On Τύχη and her cult s. UvonWilamowitz-Moellendorff, Der Glaube der Hellenen[2] '55, 298–305.—B. 1096. Schmidt, Syn. IV 364–76. DELG s.v. τυγχάνω. DDD s.v. Fortuna. Sv.

Τυχικός, οῦ, ὁ (ins, e.g. nine times in those fr. Magnesia; Hemer, Acts 236.—On the accent s. KLipsius, Gramm. Untersuchungen über die biblische Gräz. 1863, 30; Tdf., Proleg. 103) ***Tychicus,*** a man fr. the province of Asia who accompanied Paul on his journey to Jerusalem w. the collection **Ac 20:4.** In **Eph 6:21** he is called ὁ ἀγαπητὸς ἀδελφὸς καὶ πιστὸς διάκονος ἐν κυρίῳ, and in **Col 4:7** σύνδουλος is added to these. In both of these he is to report to the recipients of the letter concerning the apostle. In **2 Ti 4:12** he is sent to Ephesus. In **Tit 3:12** it is proposed to send him or Artemas to Titus in Crete. S. also **Eph subscr.; Col subscr.**—Cp. DELG s.v. τυγχάνω. LGPN I. M-M.

τυχόν adv. s. τυγχάνω 2c.

ὕαινα, ης, ἡ ***hyena*** (so Hdt. et al.; PAth 4, 12 [III AD]; Sir 13:18; Jer 12:9), named as an unclean animal whose flesh Israelites were not permitted to eat (but no specific prohibition in the OT) B 10:7 (for the extraordinary interpr. represented here s. Windisch ad loc; also Diod. S. 32, 12, 2, a report from mythological writers who maintain concerning the hyena ἄρρενας ἅμα καὶ θηλείας ὑπάρχειν καὶ παρ' ἐνιαυτὸν ἀλλήλους ὀχεύειν=are now male and then female and in alternate years have intercourse w. one another; Aesop, Fab. 242; 243 P.=405; 406 H.; Cyranides p. 74, 14–16; Horapollo 2, 69). OKeller, Antike Tierwelt 1909–13, I 152–57; NHenkel, Studien zum Physiologus im Mittelalter '76, 175 (reff.).—BHHW II 755. Pauly-W. Suppl. IV 1924, 761–68. DELG s.v. ὗς.

ὑακίνθινος, ίνη, ινον (ὑάκινθος; Hom.+; PSI 183, 5; LXX; JosAs 18:5 cod. A [p. 68, 1 Bat.] λίθος ὁ μέγας; Philo, Spec. Leg. 1, 94; Jos., Ant. 3, 165) ***hyacinth-colored,*** i.e. dark blue (dark red?) w. πύρινος **Rv 9:17** or violet τίς νήσει … τὸ ὑακίνθιον (cast lots to determine) *who will weave the hyacinth color* GJs 10:2 (foll. by κόκκινον and πορφύραν).—DELG s.v. ὑάκινθος. M-M.

ὑάκινθος, ου, ὁ (s. prec. entry; as early as Hom. as the name of a flower) ***the jacinth*** or ***hyacinth*** (Peripl. Eryth. 56 [gender undetermined]; Galen XIII 970; Ptolem. 7, 4, 1; Heliod. 2, 30, 3 [in him clearly fem]; Achilles Tat. 2, 11, 3 [gender undetermined]; the λίθος ἡλίου Cat. Cod. Astr. IX/2 p. 152, 18.—In the LXX; TestSol 21:2; JosAs 2:15 al. and in Philo and Joseph. [Ant. 3, 164] hyacinth-colored cloth is meant), a precious stone **Rv 21:20,** perh. blue in color (Michel Psellus, in Lapidaires p. 203, ln. 79f θαλαττόχρως 'sea-hued'), someth. like the sapphire (but s. vs. 19); on it s. OED s.v. hyacinth 1ab. It was often made into gems by the ancients (Pliny, NH 37, 9, 41f).—For lit. see s.v. ἀμέθυστος.—DELG. M-M.

ὑάλινος, η, ον (ὕαλος; since Corinna [VI BC] 36 Page [42 Diehl]; SIG 1106, 153; PPetr III, 42 H 7, 3 [III BC]; POxy 1740, 30) ***of glass,*** *transparent as glass* **Rv 4:6; 15:2ab.**—DELG s.v. ὕαλος. M-M.

ὕαλος, ου, ἡ (s. prec. entry; so since Hdt. 3, 24 [ὕελος]; Aristoph.; Pla.; PFay 134, 4), rarely **ὁ** (Theophr., Lapid. 49 [ὕελ.]; B-D-F §49, 1; Mlt-H. 67; 124.—Job 28:17 the gender cannot be determined)

❶ **some kind of crystalline stone,** ***crystal*** (Hdt. 3, 24 et al.) ὕαλ. καθαρός **Rv 21:18.** ὕαλ. διαυγής vs. **21** both with emphasis on transparency. If the stone is meant, the simile refers to its translucent quality, but in these two pass. ὕ. may also refer to

❷ **a translucent substance with a silicate base,** ***glass*** (Pla. et al.; w. χρυσίον; cp. Job 28:17) so NRSV and REB in both passages.—On ancient glass-making s. SGoldstein, 'Glass': ISBE II 475–77 (lit.). B. 620.—DELG. M-M.

ὑβρίζω fut. 3 sg. ὑβρίσει (TestBenj 5:4); 1 aor. ὕβρισα. Pass.: 1 fut. ὑβρισθήσομαι; 1 aor. ὑβρίσθην; pf. 3 sg. ὕβρισται (Mel.) (fr. ὕβρις, s. also ὑβριστής; Hom.+) in our lit. only trans. **to treat in an insolent or spiteful manner,** ***mistreat, scoff at, insult*** (Aristot., De Rhet. 2, 2 ἔστιν ὕβρις τὸ πράττειν καὶ λέγειν ἐφ' οἷς αἰσχύνη ἐστὶ τῷ πάσχοντι=insolence means to do and say things that bring shame to the victim; cp. Demosth. 21, 48 a humane pers. does not mistreat even slaves) τινά *someone* (oft. in pap [Mayser II/2 p. 303; reff. for the pass. also here]) *mistreat* **Mt 22:6** (w. ἀποκτείνω POxy 903, 5f [IV AD]); **Ac 14:5.** Pass. **Lk 18:32; 1 Th 2:2; Tit 1:11 v.l.;** Dg 5:15 (w. λοιδορεῖσθαι; cp. SIG 1109, 74; 76; 78 [178 AD]; TestBenj 5:4); Hs 6, 3, 4; *insult* (ParJer 5:20; Jos., Ant. 4, 187; Just., A I, 4, 9) w. words ἡμᾶς ὑβρίζεις **Lk 11:45;** by one's conduct *abuse, outrage someth.* τὴν σάρκα 2 Cl 14:4a. τὴν ἐκκλησίαν 14:4b (cp. Jos., Bell. 3, 371 [θεοῦ] τὸ δῶρον, Ant. 9, 257 τὸν θεόν; Theoph. Ant. 3, 30 [p. 268, 30]); *carry on presumptuously with* αὐτοὺς (χλευάζετε καὶ) ὑβρίζετε Dg 2:7.—DELG s.v. ὕβρις. M-M. TW.

ὕβρις, εως, ἡ (s. prec. and next entry; Hom.+)—❶ **the quality or state of being insolent,** ***insolence, arrogance,*** the act. sense (Appian, Basil. 5 §2 καθ' ὕβριν=out of arrogance; Pr 11:2; 29:23; Is 9:8; Philo, Spec. Leg. 3, 186; Jos., Ant. 6, 61; Tat., Ath.) ὕβρ. ὑπερηφάνων 1 Cl 59:3 (ὕβρ. w. ὑπερηφανία: Ael. Aristid. 28, 101 K.=49 p. 524 D.; Paroem. Gr.: Zenob. [II AD] 5, 44. Also ὑβριστικῶς κ. ὑπερηφάνως Diod. S. 16, 41, 2).

❷ **the experience of insolence,** ***shame, insult, mistreatment,*** the pass. sense (PEleph 1, 8 [311 BC] ἐφ' ὕβρει=for insult, for outrage; PMagd 24 verso; PsSol 2:26f; JosAs 28:14 Philonenko [Bat. p. 84, 7]; SibOr 3, 529; Philo, In Flacc. 58; Just.; Celsus 4, 46) ὕβριν ὑποφέρειν Hm 8:10. ὕβριν ποιεῖν τινι *do harm to someone* Hs 9, 11, 8 (JosAs 23:13). Pl. *mistreatment* (Polyb. 6, 8, 5; 10, 37, 8; 11, 5, 7; Sb 5235, 12 [I AD] ὕβρεις καὶ πληγάς; PLond II, 358, 8 p. 172 [II AD]; Sir 10:8; SibOr 4, 164.—'Chastisements' Theoph. Ant. 2, 25 [p. 162, 7]) **2 Cor 12:10.**

❸ **damage caused by use of force,** fig. ***hardship, disaster, damage*** caused by the elements (Pind., P. 1, 72 [140]; Anth. Pal. 7, 291, 4 δείσασα θαλάττης ὕβριν; Jos., Ant. 3, 133 τὴν ἀπὸ τῶν ὄμβρων ὕβριν) w. ζημία **Ac 27:10** (μετὰ ὕβ. as SIG 780, 18; 30; 3 Macc 3:25; JosAs 7:5; Jos., Ant. 1, 60), **21.** Of Judas' illness εἰς ὕβριν *to* (his) *shame* Papias (3:2).—DMacDowell, *Hybris* in Athens: Greece and Rome 2 ser. 23, '76, 14–31; NFisher, *Hybris* and Dishonour, pt. I: ibid., 177–93; pt. II, ibid., '79, 32–47; PMarshall, Hybrists not Gnostics in Corinth: SBLSP 23, '84, 275–87; DCohen, Sexuality, Violence, and the Athenian Law of *Hybris*: Greece and Rome 38, '91, 171–88; JHooker, The Original Meaning of ὕβρις: Archiv f. Begriffsgeschichte 19, '75, 125–37; s. lit. cited by CBrown, Mnemosyne 49, '96, 7 n. 13.—Schmidt, Syn. IV 273–80. DELG. M-M. TW. Sv.

ὑβριστής, οῦ, ὁ (ὑβρίζω; Hom.+; LXX; GrBar 16:4; Philo; Jos., Ant. 5, 339; SibOr 2, 259) ***a violent, insolent pers.*** **Ro 1:30** (w. ὑπερήφανος in a catalogue of vices in Ps.-Dicaearchus p. 143 Fuhr; Heraclid. Crit., Reisebilder 1, 14 p. 80, 2 Pf. The same juxtaposition of ὑπερήφανος and ὑβριστής in Diod. S. 5, 55, 6 and Aristot., Rhet. 1390b, 33 [II, 16, 1]); **1 Ti 1:13.**—DELG s.v. ὕβρις. M-M. TW.

ὑγεία (this spelling for the older ὑγίεια appears in pap fr. II AD: POxy 496, 10 [127 AD]; 497, 11; 715, 29; PTebt 298, 77; PAmh 132, 3; 18 [all II AD] and also in SIG 810, 15 [55 AD]; in favor of ὑγεῖα, Schwyzer I 194; PKatz TLZ 83, '58, 315.—EpArist 190; 237; 259; Test Napht 2:8; ParJer 7:7. Predom. in Philo; and s. Jos., Bell. 1, 647 codd. For the LXX s. Thackeray p. 63f.) 1 Cl 20:10.—Schweizer 101; Nachmanson 71; Crönert 34; Mayser I 92, 5; s. ὑγίεια.—DELG s.v. ὑγιής.

ὑγιαίνω (ὑγιής; Theognis, Hdt.+; ins, pap, LXX, TestSol; TestJob 35, 2; Test12Patr; Philo, Joseph.; Ath., R. 2 p. 49, 30)

❶ to be in good physical health, *be healthy,* lit. **Mt 8:13 v.l.; Lk 5:31** (Artem. 4, 22 οὐ τοῖς ὑγιαίνουσιν ἀλλὰ τοῖς κάμνουσιν δεῖ θεραπειῶν); **7:10; 15:27.** As a formula in an epistolary greeting (e.g. Ltzm., Griech. Papyri[2] [=Kl. T. 14] 1910 no. 1, 3 [=BGU 423]; 2, 3 [=BGU 846]; 8, 3 [=BGU 27]; 9, 4 [=BGU 38] and oft. in pap; cp. EpArist 41) **3J 2.**

❷ to be sound or free from error, *be correct,* fig. in the Pastoral Epistles w. ref. to Christian teaching: ὑγιαίνουσα διδασκαλία **1 Ti 1:10; 2 Ti 4:3; Tit 1:9; 2:1.** ὑγιαίνοντες λόγοι **1 Ti 6:3; 2 Ti 1:13.** ὑγιαίνειν (ἐν) τῇ πίστει **Tit 1:13; 2:2** (on its use w. the dat. cp. Jos., C. Ap. 1, 222). Cp. λόγος ὑγιής **Tit 2:8** (ὑγιής 2). Thus, in accord w. prevailing usage, Christian teaching is designated as *correct* instruction, since it is reasonable and appeals to sound intelligence (Plut., Mor. 2f αὗται γάρ εἰσιν ὑγιαίνουσαι περὶ θεῶν δόξαι καὶ ἀληθεῖς 'these are sound views about the gods and true'; Philo, Abr. 223 al. τοὺς ὑγιαίνοντας λόγους; Jos., C. Ap. 1, 222 οἱ ὑγιαίνοντες τῇ κρίσει [opp. ἀνόητοι]; Ath., R. 2 p. 49, 30 οὐχ ὑγιαινούσῃ κρίσει . . . χρωμένων. S. also ὑγιής 2).—MDibelius, Hdb. exc. on 1 Ti 1:10.—DELG s.v. ὑγιής. M-M. TW.

ὑγίεια, ας, ἡ (or Ion. ὑγιείη, Pind., Hdt.+; ins, pap, LXX; Philo, Sacr. Abel. 39, Aet. M. 116; Jos, Bell. 1, 647.—For the spelling ὑγεία in 1 Cl 20:10, s. ὑγεία) ***health*** 1 Cl 61:1; (w. ἀπόλαυσις) 20:10 v.l. (for ὑγείαν).—DELG s.v. ὑγιής. Sv.

ὑγιής, ές acc. ὑγιῆ (Hom.+; ins, pap, LXX; TestSol 18:20 A; TestIss 7:9; ApcEsdr 5:13 p. 30, 13 Tdf.; Philo, Joseph.)

❶ pert. to being physically well or sound, *healthy, sound.*

ⓐ of persons **Mt 15:31; Ac 4:10;** or of their individual members (SIG 1170, 26 ἡ χείρ) **Mt 12:13; Mk 3:5 v.l.; Lk 6:10 v.l.;** ὑγ. γίνεσθαι *get well* (SIG 1168, 47; 94; 102; 1169, 18 [IV BC]) **J 5:4, 6** (s. Artem. 3, 39: no one says to a healthy man 'ὑγιανεῖς'=you will get well), **9, 14.** ποιεῖν τινα ὑγιῆ *cure someone, restore someone to health* (X., Mem.4, 2, 7; Just., A I, 22, 6) **J 5:11, 15; 7:23.** ἴσθι ὑγιὴς ἀπό . . . *be healed* (and free) *from* . . . **Mk 5:34.** τὸ ὠτίον . . . ἐγένετο ὑγιές AcPl Ha 5, 35.

ⓑ of things *sound, undamaged* (Eur., Thu. et al.; ins, pap) of trees Hs 8, 1, 3f; 8, 3, 1. Of stones (SIG 972, 32; 101) 9, 8, 3 (comparative); 5; 7. ἔχοντες ὑγιῆ τὴν σάρκα (at the resurrection) AcPlCor 2:32.

❷ pert. to being uncorrupted or correct, fig. ext of 1: τηρεῖν ὑγιῆ i.e. τὴν σφραγῖδα *keep the seal* (=baptism) *unbroken* Hs 8, 6, 3.—λόγος ὑγιής *sound teaching* or *preaching* **Tit 2:8** (s. ὑγιαίνω 2 and cp. Musonius p. 6, 2 H.; Dio Chrys. 1, 49 ὑγ. λόγ.; Maximus Tyr. 16, 3f ἀλήθειάν γε καὶ ὑγιῆ λόγον; M. Ant. 8, 30 ὑγιὴς λόγος, also Epict. 1, 11, 28 ὑγιές ἐστι τὸ ὑπὸ τ. φιλοσόφων λεγόμενον; 1, 12, 5; 6; SIG 983, 5 γνώμην ὑγ.; Epict. 3, 9, 5 ὑγιῆ δόγματα; EpArist 250; Philo, Spec. Leg. 2, 164 ὑγ. δόξα; Jos., Ant. 9, 118 μηδὲν ὑγιὲς φρονεῖν; Just., D. 3, 3 ὡς οὐδὲν ὑγιὲς δρῶσιν).—ἀπόδος μοι ὑγιῆ τὴν χεῖρα μου GJs 20:2 v.l.—B. 300. DNP V "Hygieia", 777f. DELG. M-M. TW.

ὑγρός, ά, όν (Hom.+; ins, pap, LXX; SibOr 3, 144; Just.; Ath. 22, 4, R. 17 p. 68, 29) **pert. to being in a moist or yielding condition, *moist, pliant,*** of fresh wood ***green*** (so ὑγρότης Theophr., HP 5, 9, 7; 8; Philostrat., Ep. 55 ὑγρός of fresh roses) **Lk 23:31** (opp. ξηρός as Dio Chrys. 80 [30], 15 and oft. in Philo; Jos., Ant. 4, 267).—AJeremias, Hdb. der altoriental. Geisteskultur 1913, 263ff (cult of Tammuz).—B. 1074. Schmidt, Syn. II 335–58. DELG. M-M.

ὑδρία, ας, ἡ ***water jar*** (so Diocles Com. [V BC] 1; Aristoph., Eccl. 678, Vesp. 926; Athen. 5, 199d; 11, 462b; ins; POxy 502, 37; PSI 428, 89; Gen 24:14ff; TestSol 5:12; Jos., Ant. 8, 341) **J 2:6** (Synes., Ep. 126 p. 261 ὑδρία . . . κείσεται), **7; 4:28.**—B. 347. DELG s.v. ὕδωρ A 4. M-M.

ὑδροποτέω (ὕδωρ, πίνω; cp. οἰνοποτέω Pr 31:4; opp. οἴνῳ διαχρῆσθαι Hdt. 1, 71, 2; X., Cyr. 6, 2, 26; Pla., Rep. 8, 561c; Epict. 3, 13, 21, cp. 3, 14, 4; Aelian, VH 2, 38 μὴ ὁμιλεῖν οἴνῳ ἀλλὰ ὑδροποτεῖν; Lucian, Bis Accus. 16; Da 1:12) **to prefer water for drinking, *drink (only) water*** of an abstemious way of life μηκέτι ὑδροπότει, ἀλλὰ οἴνῳ ὀλίγῳ χρῶ **1 Ti 5:23.** The directive is apparently designed to counteract extreme asceticism and attendant criticism of Christians for aloofness to public life (cp. ὑδροπότης in the sense of 'spoilsport', as in our colloq. 'party-pooper', Anth. Pal. 11, 20).—DELG s.v. ὕδωρ and πίνω. M-M.

ὑδρωπικός, ή, όν ***suffering from dropsy, edema*** (Hippocr. et al. in medical [Hobart 24] and nonmedical [e.g. Περὶ ὕψους 3, 4; Ptolem., Apotel. 4, 9, 3; Proverbia Aesopi 95 P.; Diog. L. 4, 27; schol. on Nicander, Ther. 70 p. 10, 27] writers; on the usage s. HCadbury, JBL 45, 1926, 205; cp. ibid. 52, '33, 62f) ἄνθρωπός τις ἦν ὑδρωπικός **Lk 14:2.**—DELG s.v. ὕδωρ C. M-M.

ὕδωρ, ατος, τό (Hom.+; loanw. in rabb.) ***water*—❶** in a material sense, as an element Dg 8:2 (Ar. 5, 1f; Ath. 18, 3; s. στοιχεῖον 1). Of the ocean 1 Cl 33:3; pl. Hv 1, 3, 4 (cp. Ps 135:6, w. the sing. as v.l.; JosAs 12:3; Just., A I, 60, 6). The earth (before the Deluge) formed ἐξ ὕδατος καὶ δι' ὕδατος **2 Pt 3:5** (cp. HDiels, Doxographi Graeci 1879 p. 276, 12 [Θαλῆς] ἐξ ὕδατός φησι πάντα εἶναι καὶ εἰς ὕδωρ πάντα ἀναλύεσθαι; JChaine, Cosmogonie aquatique et conflagration finale d'après 2 Pt: RB 46, '37, 207–16. S. also Artem. 1, 77 p. 70, 6 al. ἐξ ὕδατος ἢ δι' ὕδατος). Of the waters of the Deluge **1 Pt 3:20; 2 Pt 3:6.** σίφων ὕδατος *a water-pump* Hm 11:18. κεράμιον ὕδατος *a water jar* (s. κεράμιον) **Mk 14:13; Lk 22:10.** ποτήριον ὕδατος (Just., A I, 65, 3; 66, 4; PGen 51, 9) *a cup of water* **Mk 9:41.** Water for washing **Mt 27:24; Lk 7:44; J 13:5.** Cp. Hs 9, 10, 3. Water fr. a well **J 4:7** (TestAbr A 3 p. 79f [Stone p. 7f] ὕδωρ ἀπὸ τοῦ φρέατος); fr. a spring **Js 3:12** (γλυκὺ ὕδωρ; s. γλυκύς, also Demetr.: 722 fgm. 4 Jac.; ParJer 9:18; Just., D. 86, 1; Herm. Wr. 13, 17); of a stream **Rv 16:12** (cp. ParJer 6:25 τοῦ ὕδατος τοῦ Ἰορδάνου; Just., D. 88, 3).—τὸ ὕδωρ specif.=the river **Mt 3:16; Mk 1:10;** =the pool **J 5:3f, 7;** =the lake **Lk 8:24,** pl. **Mt 8:32; 14:28f;** =the spring, etc. pl. **Rv 8:11ab;** cp. πηγαὶ (τῶν) ὑδάτων vs. **10; 14:7; 16:4** (Just. A I, 64, 1); =the mountain torrent pl. Hv 1, 1, 3; cp. GJs 18:3. Of waters gener., or not more exactly defined **Mt 17:15.** ὕδωρ τι **Ac 8:36a.** Cp. vs. **38f.** Pl. **Mk 9:22.** ὕδατα πολλά (Ps 28:3) **J 3:23; Rv 17:1;** ὕδατα ταῦτα GJs 3:2. φωνὴ ὑδάτων πολλῶν *the sound of many waters* (Ps 92:4) **Rv 1:15; 14:2; 19:6** (Mussies 82). χεόμενα ὕδατα *water that is poured out* Ox 840, 32f. γεμίσαι ὕδωρ *draw water* GJs 11:1 (cp. TestAbr A 3 p. 79, 34 [Stone p. 6]).—After Num 15:16ff of trial by water ὕδωρ τῆς ἐλέγξεως GJs 16:1. W. bread as that which is necessary to maintain life Hs 5, 3, 7 (cp. Am 8:11; JosAs 10:2; 4 [6] Esdr [POxy 1010]); AcPl Ha 4, 4. In contrast to wine **J 2:9** (ApcEsdr 4:27). W. blood **J 19:34** (s. αἷμα 1a). Christ came δι' ὕδατος καὶ αἵματος and ἐν τῷ ὕδατι καὶ ἐν τῷ αἵματι **1J 5:6abc;** cp. vs. **8** (s. διά A 1a, ἐν 5aβ and ἔρχομαι 1bα). Gener. of John's baptism by water (alone), opp. πνεῦμα **Mt 3:11; Mk 1:8; Lk 3:16; J 1:33 (26, 31); Ac 1:5; 11:16.** Of Christian baptism, the new birth ἐξ ὕδατος καὶ πνεύματος **J 3:5** (on the originality of the rdg. ὕδατος καί s. Hdb.[3] ad loc.; Bultmann 98, 2; cp.

Just., D. 138, 3 δι' ὕδατος καὶ πίστεως καὶ ξύλου), **8 v.l.** Cp. **Ac 10:47** AcPl Ha 3, 32. καθαρίσας τῷ λουτρῷ τοῦ ὕδατος ἐν ῥήματι **Eph 5:26.** λελουσμένοι τὸ σῶμα ὕδατι καθαρῷ **Hb 10:22** (καθαρός 1). Even the OT points to the water of baptism B 11:1ab, 8ab, which Christ has consecrated by his own baptism IEph 18:2. The symbolic language of Hermas makes many allusions to the baptismal water: δι' ὕδατος ἀναβαίνειν s 9, 16, 2. εἰς ὕδωρ καταβαίνειν m 4, 3, 1; s 9, 16, 6. The tower (=God's assembly, church) is built ἐπὶ ὑδάτων Hv 3, 2, 4; 3, 3, 5ab, ὅτι ἡ ζωὴ ὑμῶν διὰ ὕδατος ἐσώθη καὶ σωθήσεται 3, 3, 5c. Acc. to D 7:1, when at all poss., ὕδωρ ζῶν *running water* (ζάω 4) is to be used in baptizing. Cp. 7:2.

❷ **transcendent life-giving medium,** ***water,*** fig. ext. of 1, with the transition marked by **J 4:10f,** where (τὸ) ὕδωρ (τὸ) ζῶν (cp. JosAs 14:12; 1QH 8:7 and CD 6:4 [s. also 3:16]) is partly spring water and partly a symbol of the benefits conferred by Jesus (OCullmann, ThZ 4, '48, 367f.—For the imagery cp. Sir 15:3.—Cp. 1QH 8:4). Cp. **7:38; 4:14abc** (cp. Sir 24:21); IRo 7:2 (cp. OdeSol 11:6; Anacreontea 12, 7 p. 9 Preisendanz λάλον ὕδωρ). ὕδωρ (τῆς) ζωῆς *water of life* (s. Hdb. exc. on J 4:14; REisler, Orphisch-dionys. Mysteriengedanken in der christl. Antike: Vorträge der Bibl. Warburg II/2, 1925, 139ff; Herm. Wr. 1, 29 ἐτράφησαν ἐκ τοῦ ἀμβροσίου ὕδατος) **Rv 21:6** (the award granted a conquering hero; cp. Pind., I. 6, 74); **22:1, 17.** βεβάμμεθα ἐν ὕδασι ζωῆς Ox 840, 43f. ζωῆς πηγαὶ ὑδάτων *springs of living water* **Rv 7:17.**—SEitrem, Opferritus u. Voropfer der Griechen u. Römer 1915, 78ff, Beiträge z. griech. Religionsgesch. III 1920, 1ff; MNinck, Die Bed. des Wassers im Kult u. Leben der Alten 1921; AKing, Holy Water: A Short Account of the Use of Water for Ceremonial and Purificatory Purposes in Pagan, Jewish, and Christian Times 1926; TCanaan, Water and the 'Water of Life' in Palest. Superstition: JPOS 9, 1929, 57–69.—B. 35; BHHW III 2138–41 (lit.).—DELG. M-M. TW.

ὑετός, οῦ, ὁ (Hom.+; PPetr II, 49a, 13 [III BC]; LXX; ApcEsdr 2:28 p. 26, 23 Tdf.; Philo; Jos., Ant. 8, 106; 18, 285; SibOr 3, 690) ***rain*** **Ac 14:17; 28:2; Hb 6:7; Js 5:7 v.l., 18; Rv 11:6.**—B. 68. DELG s.v. ὕω. M-M.

υἱοθεσία, ας, ἡ (υἱός, θέσις 'placing'; Diod. S. 31, 27, 2 ed. Dind. X 31, 13; Diog. L. 4, 53. Oft. ins [SIG index; Dssm., NB 66f=BS 239; Rouffiac 47]; pap [PLips 28, 14; 17; 22 al.; POxy 1206, 8; 14 al., both IV AD; cp. Diod. S. 4, 39, 2 ποιεῖν θετὸν υἱόν; Preisigke, Fachwörter 1915; Jur. Pap., introd. to no. 10 p. 22]) ***adoption,*** lit. a legal t.t. of 'adoption' of children, in our lit., i.e. in Paul, only in a transferred sense of a transcendent filial relationship between God and humans (with the legal aspect, not gender specificity, as major semantic component)

ⓐ of the acceptance of the nation of Israel as son of God (cp. Ex 4:22; Is 1:2 al. where, however, the word υἱοθ. is lacking; it is found nowhere in the LXX) **Ro 9:4.**

ⓑ of those who believe in Christ and are accepted by God as God's children (Iren. 5, 12, 2 [Harv. II 351, 2]) with full rights τὴν υἱοθεσίαν ἀπολαβεῖν **Gal 4:5;** cp. **Eph 1:5.** ἡ δι' αὐτοῦ διδομένη υἱοθεσία AcPl Ha 2, 28 (s. app.). The Spirit, whom the converts receive, works as πνεῦμα υἱοθεσίας **Ro 8:15** (opp. πν. δουλείας=such a spirit as is possessed by a slave, not by the son of the house). The believers enter into full enjoyment of their υἱοθεσία only when the time of fulfillment releases them fr. the earthly body vs. **23.**—Harnack (s. παλιγγενεσία 2); TWhaling, Adoption: PTR 21, 1923, 223–35; AWentzel, Her 65, 1930, 167–76; ADieterich, Eine Mithrasliturgie 1903, 134–56; LMarshall, Challenge of NT Ethics '47, 258f; WRossell, JBL 71, '52, 233f; DTheron, EvQ 28, '56, 6–14; JScott, Adoption as Sons of God '92. S. Lampe s.v. υἱοθετέω.—New Docs 3, 17; 4, 173. DELG s.v. υἱός. M-M. TW. Sv.

υἱός, οῦ, ὁ (Hom.+; loanw. in rabb.) prim. 'son'—❶ **a male who is in a kinship relationship either biologically or by legal action,** ***son, offspring, descendant***

ⓐ the direct male issue of a person, ***son*** τέξεται υἱόν **Mt 1:21;** GJs 14:2 (cp. Mel., P. 8, 53 ὡς γὰρ υἱὸς τεχθείς). Cp. **Mt 1:23** (Is 7:14) and **25; 10:37** (w. θυγάτηρ); **Mk 12:6a; Lk 1:13, 31, 57; 11:11; 15:11** (on this JEngel, Die Parabel v. Verlorenen Sohn: ThGl 18, 1926, 54–64; MFrost, The Prodigal Son: Exp. 9th ser., 2, 1924, 56–60; EBuonaiuti, Religio 11, '35, 398–402); **Ac 7:29; Ro 9:9** (cp. Gen 18:10); **Gal 4:22** al. W. gen. **Mt 7:9; 20:20f; 21:37ab; Mk 6:3; 9:17; Lk 3:2; 4:22; 15:19; J 9:19f; Ac 13:21; 16:1; 23:16; Gal 4:30abc** (Gen 21:10abc); **Js 2:21;** AcPlCor 2:29. Also ἐγὼ Φαρισαῖός εἰμι υἱὸς Φαρισαίων **Ac 23:6** is prob. a ref. to direct descent. μονογενὴς υἱός (s. μονογενής 1) **Lk 7:12.** ὁ υἱὸς ὁ πρωτότοκος (πρωτότοκος 1) **2:7.**

ⓑ the immediate male offspring of an animal (Ps 28:1 υἱοὺς κριῶν; Sir 38:25. So Lat. filius: Columella 6, 37, 4) in our lit. only as ***foal*** ἐπὶ πῶλον υἱὸν ὑποζυγίου **Mt 21:5** (cp. Zech 9:9 πῶλον νέον).

ⓒ human offspring in an extended line of descent, ***descendant, son*** Ἰωσὴφ υἱὸς Δαυίδ **Mt 1:20** (cp. Jos., Ant. 11, 73); s. 2dα below. υἱοὶ Ἰσραήλ (Ἰσραήλ 1) **Mt 27:9; Lk 1:16; Ac 5:21; 7:23, 37; 9:15; 10:36; Ro 9:27; 2 Cor 3:7, 13; Hb 11:22** al.; AcPlCor 2:32. οἱ υἱοὶ Λευί (Num 26:57) **Hb 7:5.** υἱὸς Ἀβραάμ **Lk 19:9.** υἱοὶ Ἀδάμ 1 Cl 29:2 (Dt 32:8). υἱοι Ῥουβήλ GJs 6:3.

ⓓ one who is accepted or legally adopted as a son (Herodian 5, 7, 1; 4; 5; Jos, Ant. 2, 263; 20, 150) **Ac 7:21** (cp. Ex 2:10).—**J 19:26.**

❷ **a pers. related or closely associated as if by ties of sonship,** ***son,*** transf. sense of 1—ⓐ of a pupil, follower, or one who is otherw. a spiritual son (SIG 1169, 12 οἱ υἱοὶ τοῦ θεοῦ=the pupils and helpers [40] of Asclepius; sim. Maximus Tyr. 4, 2c; Just., D. 86, 6 οἱ υἱοὶ τῶν προφητῶν.—Some combination w. παῖδες is the favorite designation for those who are heirs of guild-secrets or who are to perpetuate a skill of some kind: Pla., Rep. 3, 407e, Leg. 6, 769b; Dionys. Hal., Comp. Verbi 22 p. 102, 4 Us./Rdm. ῥητόρων παῖδες; Lucian, Anach. 19, Dial. Mort. 11, 1 Χαλδαίων π.=dream-interpreters, Dips. 5 ἰατρῶν π., Amor. 49; Himerius, Or. 48 [=Or. 14], 13 σοφῶν π.): the 'sons' of the Pharisees **Mt 12:27; Lk 11:19.** Peter says Μᾶρκος ὁ υἱός μου **1 Pt 5:13** (perh. w. a component of endearment; s. Μᾶρκος). As a familiar form of address by a cherished mentor **Hb 12:5** (Pr 3:11; ParJer 5:28; 7:24). υἱοὶ καὶ θυγατέρες B 1:1.

ⓑ of the individual members of a large and coherent group (cp. the υἷες Ἀχαιῶν in Homer; also PsSol 2:3 οἱ υἱοὶ Ἰερουσαλήμ; Dio Chrys. 71 [21], 15; LXX) οἱ υἱοὶ τοῦ λαοῦ μου 1 Cl 8:3 (scripture quot. of unknown origin). υἱοὶ γένους Ἀβραάμ **Ac 13:26.** οἱ υἱοὶ τῶν ἀνθρώπων (Gen 11:5; Ps 11:2, 9; 44:3; TestLevi 3:10; TestZeb 9:7; GrBar 2:4) *the sons of men=humans* (cp. dγ below) **Mk 3:28; Eph 3:5;** 1 Cl 61:2 (of the earthly rulers in contrast to the heavenly king).

ⓒ of one whose identity is defined in terms of a relationship with a person or thing

α. of those who are bound to a personality by close, nonmaterial ties; it is this personality that has promoted the relationship and given it its character: ***son(s) of:*** those who believe are υἱοὶ Ἀβραάμ, because Abr. was the first whose relationship to

God was based on faith **Gal 3:7.** In a special sense the devout, believers, are sons of God, i.e., in the light of the social context, people of special status and privilege (cp. PsSol 17:27; Just., D, 124, 1; Dio Chrys. 58 [75], 8 ὁ τοῦ Διὸς ὄντως υἱός; Epict. 1, 9, 6; 1, 3, 2; 1, 19, 9; Sextus 58; 60; 135; 376a; Dt 14:1; Ps 28:1; 72:15; Is 43:6 [w. θυγατέρες μου]; 45:11; Wsd 2:18; 5:5; 12:21 al.; Jdth 9:4, 13; Esth 8:12q; 3 Macc 6:28; SibOr 3, 702) **Mt 5:45; Lk 6:35; Ro 8:14, 19** ('Redeemer figures' EFuchs, Die Freiheit des Glaubens, '49, 108; against him EHommel in ThViat 4, '52, 118, n. 26); **9:26** (Hos 2:1); **2 Cor 6:18** (w. θυγατέρες, s. Is 43:6 cited above); **Gal 3:26** (cp. PsSol 17:27); **4:6a, 7ab** (here the υἱός is the κληρονόμος and his opposite is the δοῦλος); **Hb 2:10** (JKögel, Der Sohn u. die Söhne: Eine exeget. Studie zu Hb 2:5–18, 1904); **12:5–8** (in vs. **8** opp. νόθος, q.v.); **Rv 21:7;** 2 Cl 1:4; B 4:9. Corresp. there are sons of the devil (on this subj. cp. Hdb. on J 8:44) υἱὲ διαβόλου **Ac 13:10.** οἱ υἱοὶ τοῦ πονηροῦ (masc.) **Mt 13:38b.** τοῦ υἱοῦ τοῦ ἐν Ἅιδου ApcPt Rainer. In υἱοί ἐστε τῶν φονευσάντων τοὺς προφήτας **Mt 23:31** this mng. is prob. to be combined w. sense 1c. The expr. υἱοὶ θεοῦ **Mt 5:9** looks to the future (s. Betz, SM ad loc.; cp. KKöhler, StKr 91, 1918, 189f). **Lk 20:36a** signifies a status akin to that of angels (Ps 88:7; θεῶν παῖδες as heavenly beings: Maximus Tyr. 11, 5a; 12a; 13, 6a.—Hierocles 3, 424 the ἄγγελοι are called θεῶν παῖδες; HWindisch, Friedensbringer-Gottessöhne: ZNW 24, 1925, 240–60, discounts connection w. angels and contends for the elevation of the ordinary followers of Jesus to the status of Alexander the Great in his role as an εἰρηνηποιός [cp. Plut., Mor. 329c]; for measured critique of this view s. Betz, SM 137–42.).

β. υἱός w. gen. of thing, to denote one who shares in it or who is worthy of it, or who stands in some other close relation to it, oft. made clear by the context; this constr. is prob. a Hebraism in the main, but would not appear barbaric (B-D-F §162, 6; Mlt-H. 441; Dssm., B p. 162–66 [BS 161–66]; PASA II 1884, no. 2 υἱὸς πόλεως [time of Nero; on this type of formulation SEG XXXIX, 1864]; IMagnMai 167, 5; 156, 12) οἱ υἱοὶ τοῦ αἰῶνος τούτου (αἰών 2a) **Lk 16:8a** (opp. οἱ υἱοί τοῦ φωτός vs. **8b**); **20:34.** τῆς ἀναστάσεως υἱοί (to Mediterranean publics the functional equivalent of ἀθάνατοι 'immortals'; cp. ἀνάστασις 2b) **20:36b.** υἱοὶ τῆς ἀνομίας (ἀνομία 1; cp. CD 6:15) Hv 3, 6, 1; ApcPt 1:3; τῆς ἀπειθείας (s. ἀπείθεια) **Eph 2:2; 5:6; Col 3:6;** τῆς ἀπωλείας ApcPt 1:2. ὁ υἱὸς τῆς ἀπωλείας of Judas the informer **J 17:12** (cp. similar expressions in Eur., Hec. 425; Menand., Dyscolus 88f: s. FDanker, NTS 7, '60/61, 94), of the end-time adversary **2 Th 2:3.** υἱοὶ τῆς βασιλείας (βασιλεία 1bη; s. SEG XXXIX, 1864 for related expressions) **Mt 8:12; 13:38a.** υἱοὶ βροντῆς **Mk 3:17** (s. Βοανηργές). υἱὸς γεέννης (s. γέεννα) **Mt 23:15;** τ. διαθήκης (PsSol 17:15) **Ac 3:25;** εἰρήνης **Lk 10:6.** υἱοὶ τοῦ νυμφῶνος (s. νυμφών) **Mt 9:15; Mk 2:19; Lk 5:34.** υἱὸς παρακλήσεως **Ac 4:36** (s. Βαρναβᾶς). υἱοὶ (τοῦ) φωτός (Hippol., Ref. 6, 47, 4 in gnostic speculation) **Lk 16:8b** (opp. υἱοὶ τοῦ αἰῶνος τούτου); **J 12:36.** υἱοὶ φωτός ἐστε καὶ υἱοὶ ἡμέρας **1 Th 5:5** (EBuonaiuti, 'Figli del giorno e della luce' [1 Th 5:5]: Rivista storico-critica delle Scienze teol. 6, 1910, 89–93).

ⓓ in various combinations as a designation of the Messiah and a self-designation of Jesus

α. υἱὸς Δαυίδ ***son of David*** of the Messiah (PsSol 17:21) **Mt 22:42–45; Mk 12:35–37; Lk 20:41–44;** B 12:10c. Specif. of Jesus as Messiah **Mt 1:1a; 9:27; 12:23; 15:22; 20:30f; 21:9, 15; Mk 10:47f; Lk 18:38f.**—WWrede, Jesus als Davidssohn: Vorträge u. Studien 1907, 147–77; WBousset, Kyrios Christos[2] 1921, 4, Rel.[3] 226f; ELohmeyer, Gottesknecht u. Davidssohn '45, esp. 68; 72; 77; 84; TNicklin, Gospel Gleanings '50, 251–56; WMichaelis, Die Davidsohnschaft Jesu usw., in D. histor. Jesus u. d. kerygm. Christus, ed. Ristow and Matthiae, '61, 317–30; LFisher, ECColwell Festschr. '68, 82–97.

β. ὁ υἱὸς τοῦ θεοῦ, υἱὸς θεοῦ ***(the) Son of God*** (for the phrase s. JosAs 6:2 al. Ἰωσὴφ ὁ υἱὸς τοῦ θεοῦ; there is no undisputed evidence of usage as messianic title in pre-Christian Judaism [s. Dalman, Worte 219–24, Eng. tr. 268–89; Bousset, Kyrios Christos[2] 53f; EHuntress, 'Son of God' in Jewish Writings Prior to the Christian Era: JBL 54, '35, 117–23]; cp. 4Q 246 col. 2, 1 [JFitzmyer, A Wandering Aramean '79, 90–93; JCollins, BRev IX/3, '93, 34–38, 57]. Among polytheists on the other hand, sons of the gods in a special sense [s. Just., A I, 21, 1f] are not only known to myth and legend, but definite historical personalities are also designated as such. Among them are famous wise men such as Pythagoras and Plato [HUsener, Das Weihnachtsfest[2] 1911, 71ff], and deified rulers, above all the Roman emperors since the time of Augustus [oft. in ins and pap: Dssm., B 166f=BS 166f, LO 294f=LAE 346f; Thieme 33]. According to Memnon [I BC/ I AD]: 434 fgm. 1, 1, 1 Jac., Clearchus [IV BC] carried his boasting so far as Διὸς υἱὸν ἑαυτὸν ἀνειπεῖν. Also, persons who were active at that time as prophets and wonder-workers laid claim to the title υἱὸς τοῦ θεοῦ, e.g. the Samaritan Dositheus in Origen, C. Cels. 6, 11; sim. an Indian wise man who calls himself Διὸς υἱός Arrian, Anab. 7, 2, 3; cp. Did., Gen. 213, 18 ὁ Ἀβρὰμ υἱὸς θεοῦ διὰ δικαιοσύνην. S. GWetter, 'Der Sohn Gottes' 1916; Hdb. exc. on J 1:34; s. also Clemen[2] 76ff; ENorden, Die Geburt des Kindes 1924, 75; 91f; 132; 156f; EKlostermann, Hdb. exc. on Mk 1:11 [4th ed. '50]; M-JLagrange, Les origines du dogme paulinien de la divinité de Christ: RB 45, '36, 5–33; HPreisker, Ntl. Zeitgesch. '37, 187–208; HBraun, ZTK 54, '57, 353–64; ANock, 'Son of God' in Paul. and Hellen. Thought: Gnomon 33, '61, 581–90 [=Essays on Religion and the Anc. World II, '72, 928–39]—originality in Paul's thought): Ps 2:7 is applied to Jesus υἱός μου εἶ σύ, ἐγὼ σήμερον γεγέννηκά σε **Lk 3:22** D; GEb 18, 37.—**Ac 13:33; Hb 1:5a; 5:5;** 1 Cl 36:4. Likew. Hos 11:1 (w. significant changes): **Mt 2:15,** and 2 Km 7:14: **Hb 1:5b.** The voice of God calls him ὁ υἱός μου ὁ ἀγαπητός (s. ἀγαπητός 1) at his baptism **Mt 3:17; Mk 1:11; Lk 3:22;** GEb 18, 37 and 39 and at the Transfiguration **Mt 17:5; Mk 9:7; Lk 9:35** (here ἐκλελεγμένος instead of ἀγαπ.); **2 Pt 1:17.** Cp. **J 1:34.** The angel at the Annunciation uses these expressions in referring to him: υἱὸς ὑψίστου **Lk 1:32;** GJs 11:3 and υἱὸς θεοῦ **Lk 1:35** (Ar. 15, 1 ὁ υἱὸς τοῦ θεοῦ τοῦ ὑψίστου. Cp. Just., A I, 23, 2 μόνος ἰδίως υἱὸς τῷ θεῷ γεγέννηται). The centurion refers to him at the crucifixion as υἱὸς θεοῦ **Mt 27:54; Mk 15:39;** GPt 11:45; cp. vs. 46 (CMann, ET 20, 1909, 563f; JPobee, The Cry of the Centurion, A Cry of Defeat: CFDMoule Festschr. '70, 91–102; EJohnson, JSNT 31, '87, 3–22 [an indefinite affirmation of Jesus]). The high priest asks εἰ σὺ εἶ ὁ Χριστὸς ὁ υἱὸς τοῦ θεοῦ **Mt 26:63** (DCatchpole, NTS 17, '71, 213–26). Passers-by ask him to show that he is God's Son **27:40;** sim. the devil **4:3, 6; Lk 4:3, 9.** On the other hand, evil spirits address him as the Son of God **Mt 8:29; Mk 3:11; 5:7; Lk 4:41; 8:28;** and disciples testify that he is **Mt 14:33; 16:16.** S. also **Mk 1:1** (s. SLegg, Ev. Sec. Marc. '35).—Jesus also refers to himself as Son of God, though rarely apart fr. the Fourth Gosp.: **Mt 28:19** (the Risen Lord in the trinitarian baptismal formula); **Mt 21:37f=Mk 12:6** (an allusion in the parable of the vinedressers).—**Mt 27:43; Mk 13:32; Rv 2:18.** The main pass. is the so-called Johannine verse in the synoptics **Mt 11:27=Lk 10:22** (s. PSchmiedel, PM 4, 1900,1–22; FBurkitt, JTS 12, 1911, 296f; HSchumacher, Die Selbstoffenbarung Jesu bei Mt 11:27 [Lk 10:22] 1912 [lit.]; Norden, Agn. Th. 277–308; JWeiss, Heinrici Festschr. 1914, 120–29,

Urchristentum 1917, 87ff; Bousset, Kyrios Christos[2] 1921, 45ff; EMeyer I 280ff; RBultmann, Gesch. d. synopt. Trad.[2] '31, 171f; MDibelius, Die Formgeschichte des Evangeliums[2] '33, 259; MRist, Is Mt 11:25–30 a Primitive Baptismal Hymn? JR 15, '35, 63–77; TArvedson, D. Mysterium Christi: E. Studie zu Mt 11:25–30, '37; WDavies, 'Knowledge' in the Dead Sea Scrolls and Mt 11:25–30, HTR 45, '53, 113–39; WGrundmann, Sohn Gottes, ZNW 47, '56, 113–33; JBieneck, Sohn Gottes als Christusbez. der Synopt. '51; PWinter, Mt 11:27 and Lk 10:22: NovT 1, '56, 112–48; JJocz, Judaica 13, '57, 129–42; OMichel/OBetz, Von Gott Gezeugt, Beih. ZNW [Jeremias Festschr.] 26, '60, 3–23 [Qumran]).—Apart fr. the synoptics, testimony to Jesus as the Son of God is found in many parts of our lit. Oft. in Paul: **Ro 1:3, 4, 9; 5:10; 8:3, 29, 32; 1 Cor 1:9; 15:28; 2 Cor 1:19; Gal 1:16; 2:20; 4:4; Eph 4:13; Col 1:13; 1 Th 1:10.** Cp. **Ac 9:20.** In **Hb: 1:2, 8; 4:14; 5:8; 6:6; 7:3, 28; 10:29.** In greatest frequency in John (cp. Herm. Wr. 1, 6 the Λόγος as υἱὸς θεοῦ. Likew. Philo, Agr. 51 πρωτόγονος υἱός, Conf. Lingu. 146 υἱὸς θεοῦ.—Theoph. Ant. 2, 1 [p. 154, 12] ὁ λόγος ὁ τοῦ θεοῦ, ὅς ἐστιν καὶ υἱὸς αὐτοῦ; Iren. 3, 12, 2 [Harv. II 55, 2]): **J 1:49; 3:16–18** (s. μονογενής 2), **35f; 5:19–26; 6:40; 8:35f; 10:36; 11:4, 27; 14:13; 17:1; 19:7; 20:31; 1J 1:3, 7; 2:22–24; 3:8, 23; 4:9f, 14f; 5:5, 9–13, 20; 2J 3, 9.**—B 5:9, 11; 7:2, 9; 12:8; 15:5; Dg 7:4; 9:2, 4; 10:2 (τὸν υἱὸν αὐτοῦ τὸν μονογενῆ; also ApcEsdr 6:16 p. 31, 22 Tdf.; ApcSed 9:1f); IMg 8:2; ISm 1:1; MPol 17:3; Hv 2, 2, 8; s 5, 2, 6 (ὁ υἱὸς αὐτοῦ ὁ ἀγαπητός); 8; 11; 5, 4, 1; 5, 5, 2; 3; 5; 5, 6, 1; 2; 4; 7 (on the Christology of the Shepherd s. Dibelius, Hdb. on Hs 5, also ALink and JvWalter [πνεῦμα 5cα]); s 8, 3, 2; 8, 11, 1. Cp. 9, 1, 1; 9, 12, 1ff.—In trinitarian formulas, in addition to **Mt 28:19,** also IMg 13:1; EpilMosq 5; D 7:1, 3.—The deceiver of the world appears w. signs and wonders ὡς υἱὸς θεοῦ D 16:4 (ApcEsdr 4:27 p. 28, 32 Tdf. ὁ λέγων· Ἐγώ εἰμι ὁ υἱὸς τοῦ θεοῦ [of Antichrist]).—EKühl, Das Selbstbewusstsein Jesu 1907, 16–44; GVos, The Self-disclosure of Jesus 1926.—EBurton, ICC Gal 1921, 404–17; TNicklin, Gospel Gleanings '50, 211–36; MHengel, The Son of God (tr. JBowden) '76; DJones, The Title υἱὸς θεοῦ in Acts: SBLSP 24, '85, 451–63.

γ. ὁ υἱὸς τοῦ ἀνθρώπου lit. 'the son of the man' (the pl. form οἱ υἱοὶ τῶν ἀνθρώπων appears freq. in the LXX to render בְּנֵי אָדָם = mortals, e.g. Gen 11:5; Ps 10:4; 11:2; cp. ὁ υἱὸς τῆς ἀπολείας **J 17:12** [s. 2cβ]) 'the human being, the human one, the man' in our lit. only as a byname in ref. to Jesus and in an exclusive sense ***the Human One, the Human Being,*** one intimately linked with humanity in its primary aspect of fragility yet transcending it, traditionally rendered 'the Son of Man.' The term is found predom. in the gospels, where it occurs in the synoptics about 70 times (about half as oft. if parallels are excluded), and in J 12 times (s. EKlostermann, Hdb. exc. on Mk 8:31). In every case the title is applied by Jesus to himself. Nowhere within a saying or narrative about him is it found in an address to him: **Mt 8:20; 9:6; 10:23; 11:19; 12:8, 32, 40; 13:37, 41; 16:13, 27f; 17:9, 12, 22; 18:10 [11] v.l.; 19:28; 20:18, 28; 24:27, 30, 37, 39, 44; 25:13 v.l., 31; 26:2, 24ab, 45, 64; Mk 2:10, 28; 8:31, 38; 9:9, 12, 31; 10:33, 45; 13:26; 14:21ab, 41, 62; Lk 5:24; 6:5, 22; 7:34; 9:22, 26, 44, 56 v.l., 58; 11:30; 12:8, 10, 40; 17:22, 24, 26, 30; 18:8, 31; 19:10; 21:27, 36; 22:22, 48, 69; 24:7.**—**John** (FGrosheide, Υἱὸς τ. ἀνθρ. in het Evang. naar Joh.: TSt 35, 1917, 242–48; HDieckmann, D. Sohn des Menschen im J: Scholastik 2, 1927, 229–47; HWindisch, ZNW 30, '31, 215–33; 31, '32, 199–204; WMichaelis, TLZ 85, '60, 561–78 [Jesus' earthly presence]) **1:51; 3:13, 14; 5:27** (BVawter, Ezekiel and John, CBQ 26, '64, 450–58); **6:27, 53, 62; 8:28; 9:35; 12:23, 34; 13:31.** Whether the component of fragility (suggested by OT usage in ref. to the brief span of human life and the ills to which it falls heir) or high status (suggested by traditions that appear dependent on Da 7:13, which refers to one 'like a human being'), or a blend of the two dominates a specific occurrence can be determined only by careful exegesis that in addition to extrabiblical traditions takes account of the total literary structure of the document in which it occurs. Much neglected in the discussion is the probability of prophetic association suggested by the form of address Ezk 2:1 al. (like the OT prophet [Ezk 3:4–11] Jesus encounters resistance).—On Israelite thought contemporary w. Jesus and alleged knowledge of a heavenly being looked upon as a 'Son of Man' or 'Man', who exercises Messianic functions such as judging the world (metaph., pictorial passages in En 46–48; 4 Esdr 13:3, 51f) s. Bousset, Rel.[3] 352–55; NMessel, D. Menschensohn in d. Bilderreden d. Hen. 1922; ESjöberg, Kenna 1 Henok och 4 Esra tanken på den lidande Människosonen? Sv. Ex. Årsb. 5, '40, 163–83, D. Menschensohn im äth. Hen. '46. This view is in some way connected w. Da 7:13; acc. to some it derives its real content fr. an eschatological tradition that ultimately goes back to Iran (WBousset, Hauptprobleme der Gnosis 1907, 160–223; Reitzenstein, Erlösungsmyst. 119ff, ZNW 20, 1921, 18–22, Mysterienrel.[3] 418ff; Clemen[2] 72ff; CKraeling, Anthropos and Son of Man: A Study in the Religious Syncretism of the Hellenistic Orient 1927); acc. to this tradition the First Man was deified; he will return in the last times and usher in the Kingdom of God.—Outside the gospels: **Ac 7:56** (v.l. τοῦ θεοῦ; GKilpatrick, TZ 21, '65, 209); **Rv 1:13; 14:14** (both after Da 7:13; sim. allusion to Da in Just., D. 31, 1). The quot. fr. Ps 8:5 in **Hb 2:6** prob. does not belong here, since there is no emphasis laid on υἱὸς ἀνθρώπου. In IEph 20:2 Jesus is described as υἱὸς ἀνθρώπου καὶ υἱὸς θεοῦ. Differently B 12:10 Ἰησοῦς, οὐχὶ υἱὸς ἀνθρώπου ἀλλὰ υἱὸς τοῦ θεοῦ *Jesus, not a man's son, but Son of God.*—HLietzmann, Der Menschensohn 1896; Dalman, Worte 191–219 (Eng. tr., 234–67); Wlh., Einl.[2] 123–30; PFiebig, Der Menschensohn 1901; NSchmidt, The Prophet of Nazareth 1905, 94–134, Recent Study of the Term 'Son of Man': JBL 45, 1926, 326–49; FTillmann, Der Menschensohn 1907; EKühl, Das Selbstbewusstsein Jesu 1907, 65ff; HHoltzmann, Das messianische Bewusstsein Jesu, 1907, 49–75 (lit.), Ntl. Theologie[2] I 1911, 313–35; FBard, D. Sohn d. Menschen 1908; HGottsched, D. Menschensohn 1908; EAbbott, 'The Son of Man', etc., 1910; EHertlein, Die Menschensohnfrage im letzten Stadium 1911, ZNW 19, 1920, 46–48; JMoffatt, The Theology of the Gospels 1912, 150–63; WBousset, Kyrios Christos[2] 1921, 5–22 (the titles of the works by Wernle and Althaus opposing his first edition [1913], as well as Bousset's answer, are found s.v. κύριος, end); DVölter, Jesus der Menschensohn 1914, Die Menschensohnfrage neu untersucht 1916; FSchulthess, ZNW 21, 1922, 247–50; Rtzst., Herr der Grösse 1919 (see also the works by the same author referred to above in this entry); EMeyer II 335ff; HGressmann, ZKG n.s. 4, 1922, 170ff, D. Messias 1929, 341ff; GDupont, Le Fils d'Homme 1924; APeake, The Messiah and the Son of Man 1924; MWagner, Der Menschensohn: NKZ 36, 1925, 245–78; Guillaume Baldensperger, Le Fils d'Homme: RHPR 5, 1925, 262–73; WBleibtreu, Jesu Selbstbez. als der Menschensohn: StKr 98/99, 1926, 164–211; AvGall, Βασιλεία τοῦ θεοῦ 1926; OProcksch, D. Menschensohn als Gottessohn: Christentum u. Wissensch. 3, 1927, 425–43; 473–81; CMontefiore, The Synoptic Gospels[2] 1927 I 64–80; ROtto, Reich Gottes u. Menschensohn '34, Eng. tr. The Kgdm. of God and the Son of Man, tr. Filson and Woolf[2] '43; EWechssler, Hellas im Ev. '36, 332ff; PParker, The Mng. of 'Son of Man': JBL 60, '41, 151–57; HSharman, Son of Man and Kingdom of God '43; JCampbell, The Origin and Mng. of the Term Son of Man: JTS 48, '47, 145–55; HRiesenfeld, Jésus Transfiguré '47, 307–13 (survey and lit.); TManson, ConNeot 11, '47, 138–46 (Son of Man=Jesus and his disciples in Mk 2:27f); GDuncan, Jesus, Son of Man '47, 135–53 (survey); JBowman, ET 59, '47/48, 283–88 (background); MBlack, ET 60, '48f, 11–15; 32–36; GKnight, Fr. Moses to Paul '49, 163–72 (survey); TNicklin, Gospel Gleanings '50, 237–50; TManson (Da, En and gospels), BJRL 32, '50, 171–93; TPreiss, Le Fils d'Homme: ÉThR 26/3, '51, Life in Christ, '54, 43–60; SMowinckel, He That Cometh, tr. Anderson, '54, 346–450; GIber, Überlieferungsgesch. Unters. z. Begriff des Menschensohnes im NT, diss. Heidelb. '53; ESjöberg, D. verborgene Menschensohn in den Ev. '55; WGrundmann, ZNW 47, '56, 113–33; HRiesenfeld, The Mythological Backgrd. of NT Christology, CHDodd Festschr. '56, 81–95; PhVielhauer, Gottesreich u. Menschensohn in d. Verk. Jesu, GDehn Festschr. '57, 51–79; ESidebottom, The Son of Man in J, ET 68, '57, 231–35; 280–83; AHiggins, Son of Man-*Forschung* since (Manson's) 'The Teaching of Jesus': NT Essays (TW Manson memorial vol.) '59, 119–35; HTödt, D. Menschensohn in d. synopt. Überl. '59 (tr. Barton '65); JMuilenburg, JBL 79, '60, 197–209 (Da, En); ESchweizer, JBL 79, '60, 119–29 and NTS 9, '63, 256–61; BvIersel, 'Der Sohn' in den synopt. Jesusworten, '61 (community?); MBlack, BJRL 45, '63, 305–18; FBorsch, ATR 45, '63, 174–90; AHiggins, Jesus and the Son of Man, '64; RFormesyn, NovT 8, '66, 1–35 (barnasha='I'); SSandmel, HSilver Festschr. '63, 355–67; JJeremias, Die älteste Schicht der Menschensohn-Logien, ZNW 58, '67, 159–72; GVermes, MBlack, Aram. Approach[3], '67, 310–30; BLindars, The New Look on the Son of Man: BJRL 63, '81, 437–62; WWalker, The Son of Man, Some Recent Developments CBQ 45, '83, 584–607; JDonahue, Recent Studies on the Origin of 'Son of Man' in the Gospels, CBQ 48, '86, 584–607; DBurkitt, The Nontitular Son of Man, A History and Critique: NTS 40, '94 504–21 (lit.); JEllington, BT 40, '89, 201–8; RGordon, Anthropos: DDD 108–13.—B. 105; DELG. M-M. EDNT. TW. Sv.

ὕλη, ης, ἡ (Hom.+)—❶ **a dense growth of trees,** ***forest*** (Hom.+; JosAs 24:16 al., Jos. Ant. 18, 357; 366) **Js 3:5.** The tendency to use hyperbole in diatribe (cp. the imagery that precedes: ship-tongue) suggests this mng. in preference to

❷ **the woody part of a tree,** ***wood, pile of wood, wood used for building,*** etc. (Hom. et al.; Jos., C. Ap. 1, 110) (cp. Sir 28:10; Ps.-Phoc. 144).

❸ **the stuff out of which a thing is made,** ***material, matter, stuff*** (Hom. et al.; Jos., C. Ap. 2, 191; Just., A I, 59, 1 al.; Tat. 37, 1; Mel., P. 38, 260; Ath. 19, 3) in our lit. only earthly, perishable, non-divine matter φθαρτὴ ὕλη (as Philo, Post. Cai. 165; Jos., Bell. 3, 372), fr. which idols are made (Maximus Tyr. 2, 3a; Just., A I, 9, 2) PtK 2 p. 14, 15; Dg 2:3. Humans, too, are made of such material 1 Cl 38:3 (Philo, Leg. All. 1, 83 ὕ. σωματική; Tat. 6, 2 σαρκική. Cp. Epict. 3, 7, 25 ἀνθρώπου ἡ ὕλη = τὰ σαρκίδια). W. connotation of that which is sinful, hostile to God (as in Philo and Gnostic lit.; Tat. 13, 2; 21, 4; Ath. 16, 3; 24, 4) IRo 6:2.—B. 46. DELG. M-M. Sv.

ὑμεῖς s. σύ.

Ὑμέναιος, ου, ὁ (esp. in mythol., also GDI 251, 5) ***Hymenaeus,*** handed over (w. Alexander) to Satan because of defection fr. the true faith **1 Ti 1:20.** Acc. to **2 Ti 2:17** his error and that of Philetus consisted in maintaining that the resurrection had already taken place (cp. AcPlTh 14 [Aa I 245, 5]; of the magician Menander: Just., A I, 26, 4 and Iren. 1, 23, 5 [Harv. I 195]).—DELG s.v. 2 ὑμήν. LGPN I. M-M.

ὑμέτερος, α, ον (cp. ὑμῶν; Hom. et al.; pap; LXX quite rarely; not at all in EpArist, Test12Patr and other pseudepigr., nor in Ar. or Mel. In Joseph., e.g. Ant. 16, 38; Just., Tat., Ath.) possessive adjectival pron. of the second pers. pl. 'your' (largely replaced by the gen. of the pers. pron.; B-D-F §285, 1; W-S. §22, 14; Rob. 288), in our lit. only 15 times: **pert. to persons addressed by a speaker or writer as possessors or recipients**

ⓐ ***belonging to*** or ***incumbent upon you*** etc.; **Lk 6:20; J 8:17** (ὑ. νόμος as Jos., Bell. 5, 402); **Ac 27:34; 2 Cor 8:8; Gal 6:13;** 1 Cl 47:7; 57:4 (Pr 1:26); MPol 13:3. ὁ καιρὸς ὁ ὑμέτερος *your time*=the time for you to act **J 7:6.** ὁ λόγος ὁ ὑμέτερος *your teaching* **15:20** (cp. Tat. 27, 2). Perh. **1 Cor 16:17** (s. b below).—Subst. τὸ ὑμέτερον (opp. τὸ ἀλλότριον) *your own property* **Lk 16:12.** τὶς τῶν ὑμετέρων *one of your own number* ISm 11:3.

ⓑ for the obj. gen. (Thu. 1, 69, 5 αἱ ὑμέτεραι ἐλπίδες. W-S. §22, 14b) τῷ ὑμετέρῳ ἐλέει *by the mercy shown to you* **Ro 11:31.** νὴ τὴν ὑμετέραν καύχησιν ἣν ἔχω *by the pride that I have in you = as surely as I may boast about you* **1 Cor 15:31.** Perh. (s. a above) τὸ ὑμέτερον ὑστέρημα *that which is lacking in you* **16:17.**—S. GKilpatrick s.v. ἐμός, end.—DELG s.v. ὑμεῖς. M-M.

ὑμνέω (ὕμνος) impf. ὕμνουν; fut. ὑμνήσω; 1 aor. ὕμνησα **to sing a song in a cultic setting,** esp. of praise and celebration

ⓐ trans. ***sing in praise to, sing in praise of*** (Hes., Hdt.+; ins; PGM 13, 628; 637; 21, 19; LXX, TestSol, ApcMos, ApcZeph, SibOr 5, 151; Just., D. 105, 1) *sing the praise of, sing a song of praise to* τινά *someone* God (Xenophanes [VI BC] 1, 13 Diehl[3] θεόν; X., Cyr. 8, 1, 23 θεόν; Dio Chrys. 80 [30], 26; Alciphron 4, 18, 16 Διόνυσον; SIG 662, 9–12 τοὺς θεοὺς ὕμνησεν; LXX; ApcMos 17 τὸν θεόν; ApcZeph; Philo, Leg. All. 2, 102 al.; Jos., Ant. 7, 80; 11, 80 τὸν θεόν; Just., D. 106, 1; Hippol., Ref. 9, 21, 3; Iren. 1, 2, 6 [Harv. I 23, 1] τὸν προπάτορα) **Ac 16:25; Hb 2:12** (Ps 21:23).

ⓑ intr. ***sing (a hymn)*** (Ps 64:14; 1 Macc 13:47; En 27:5; TestJob 14:2; TestJos 8:5a; Jos., Ant. 12, 349) ὑμνήσαντες *after they had sung the hymn* (of the second part of the Hallel [Pss 113–118 MT], sung at the close of the Passover meal) **Mt 26:30** (EBammel, JTS 24, '73, 189 [P[64]]).—DELG s.v. ὕμνος. M-M. TW.

ὕμνος, ου, ὁ (s. ὑμνέω; Hom.+) **a song with religious content,** ***hymn/song of praise*** esp. in honor of a deity (ὕμνος θεῶν Aeschyl., Cho. 475; Pla., Leg. 7, 801d; Athen. 14, 627f.—Pla., Rep. 10, 607a; Athen. 1, 22b; 14 p. 626b; Arrian, Anab. 4, 11, 2; SIG 449, 2 τοὺς ὕμνους τοῖς θεοῖς; 450, 4 θεῷ ὕμνον; 695, 29; OGI 56, 69; PGiss 99, 8 [II AD]; POxy 130, 21. On hymns of var. kinds s. Pla., Leg. 3, 700b; Menand. Rh. p. 333. S. Pauly-W. IX 1, 141f.—Ps 39:4; Is 42:10; 1 Macc 13:51; PsSol; TestAbr A 20 p. 103, 27 [Stone p. 54]; TestJob; Philo; Jos., Ant. 7, 305 [w. ᾠδαί] al.; TestLevi 3:8; TestGad 7:2; SibOr 3, 306; Just., A I, 13, 2; Hippol., Ref. 4, 49, 3 ὕμνους ἀναπέμπειν τῷ θεῷ; loanw. in rabb.) w. ψαλμοί (Jos., Ant. 12, 323), ᾠδαὶ πνευματικαί **Eph 5:19; Col 3:16** (Diod. S. 5, 46, 3 ὕμνοι μετ' ᾠδῆς in praise of the πράξεις of the gods and of their εὐεργεσίαι εἰς ἀνθρώπους; TestGad 7:2). ἀκούσασα τῶν ὕμνων αὐτῶν *you who heard (the angels') songs of praise* GJs 15:3 (ὕμνον pap).—JQuasten, Musik u. Gesang in d. Kulten der heidn. Antike u. christl. Frühzeit 1930; RMessenger, Christ. Hymns of the First Three Cent.: Papers of the Hymn Soc. 9, '42, 1–27; GSchille, Früchristliche Hymnen, '62; JKroll, Antike 2, 1926, 258ff, Gnomon 5, 1929,

30ff; D. christl. Hymnodik bis zu Klemens v. Alex.² '68; RDeichgräber, Gotteshymnus u. Christushymnus in der frühen Christenheit: Studien zur Umwelt des NT 5, '67, 188–214. S. ᾄδω, ᾠδή.—Pauly-W. IX/1, 140–83. DNP V 788–97. RAC, Lieferung 126, 915–46. DELG. M-M. TW.

ὑπάγω impf. ὑπῆγον (Hom.+, but predom. trans. [='bring under', etc.] in non-biblical Gk.; so also Ex 14:21; in NT gener. replaces ἀπέρχομαι). In our lit. (though not found at all in Ac, Paul, Hb; most frequently in John) used only intr. (so Hdt., Eur., Aristoph. et al.; oft. pap; JKalitsunakis, ByzZ 29, 1929, 228ff; also TestAbr B 6 p. 111, 1 [Stone p. 70]; TestJob 46, 5; JosAs 16:15; ParJer 7:11; ApcEsdr p. 25, 5 Tdf.; ApcSed 9:1) 'go away, withdraw, go' and only in the pres. (mostly in the impv.) and impf.—B-D-F §101 p. 43 under ἄγειν; 308: it tends more and more to mean simply 'go' in colloq. speech; so in Mod. Gk.

❶ **to leave soneone's presence,** ***go away*** (Epict. 3, 23, 12) ὕπαγε σατανᾶ *be gone, Satan!* **Mt 4:10;** combined w. ὀπίσω μου **ibid. v.l.; 16:23; Mk 8:33; Lk 4:8 v.l.** ὑπάγετε ἀπ' ἐμοῦ 2 Cl 4:5 (saying of Jesus, fr. an unknown source). μὴ καὶ ὑμεῖς θέλετε ὑπάγειν; *do you, too, want to go away* (fr. me)? **J 6:67.**—ὕπαγε *go (away)* (PGM 4, 348; 371; 36, 354), esp. *go home* (Epict. 3, 22, 108) **Mt 8:13; 19:21; 20:14; Mk 2:9 v.l.; 7:29; 10:52.** On ὕπαγε εἰς εἰρήνην **Mk 5:34** or ὑπάγετε ἐν εἰρήνῃ **Js 2:16** cp. εἰρήνη 2a. In other moods than the impv. in the general sense *go away* **J 18:8;** Hs 8, 2, 5; 9, 10, 4; *go away*=leave **Mk 6:33.** ὑπάγουσα λέγει *as she went she said* Hv 1, 4, 3. ἄφετε αὐτὸν ὑπάγειν *let him go* (prob.=*go home*) **J 11:44.** Naturally the boundary betw. *go away* and *go* (elsewhere) is not fixed; cp. e.g. οἱ ἐρχόμενοι καὶ οἱ ὑπάγοντες *people coming and going* **Mk 6:31.**

❷ **to be on the move, esp. in a certain direction,** ***go***—ⓐ in gener. (in a certain direction) w. the goal indicated by εἰς w. the acc. (Epict. 3, 22, 108; TestJob 46, 5; SEG VIII, 574, 19 [III AD]; PLond I, 131, 155 p. 174; 218 p. 176 [I AD]; al. in pap) **Mt 9:6; 20:4, 7; Mk 2:11; 11:2; 14:13; Lk 19:30; J 6:21; 7:3; 9:11; 11:31;** Hv 4, 1, 2; s 8, 3, 6; 9, 11, 6. Also in imagery of stones that go into a building = are used in its construction Hv 3, 5, 1 and 3; 3, 6, 2; s 9, 3, 3f. Fig. εἰς αἰχμαλωσίαν ὑπάγειν *go into captivity* **Rv 13:10;** εἰς ἀπώλειαν **17:8, 11** (ApcEsdr 1:11). ὑπάγετε εἰς τὴν πόλιν πρὸς τὸν δεῖνα **Mt 26:18;** cp. **Mk 5:19** (ὑπάγειν πρός τινα as PTebt 417, 4; 21). πρὸς Νέρωνα AcPl Ha 10, 15. ὑπάγειν μετά τινος (PTebt 422, 9 ὕπαγε μετὰ Μέλανος πρὸς Νεμεσᾶν) **Mt 5:41**=D 1:4; μετά τινος ἐπί τινα **Lk 12:58.** ἐκεῖ **J 11:8.** ποῦ (=ποῖ) **3:8;** cp. IPhld 7:1; **J 12:35.** ὅπου ἂν ὑπάγῃ **Rv 14:4** (cp. POxy 1477, 2 ὅπου ὑπάγω; TestLevi 13:3 ὅπου ὑπάγει). W. inf. of purpose ὑπάγω ἁλιεύειν **J 21:3** (the only pass. in the NT; s. M-EBoismard, RB 54, '47, 489; TestBenj ὑπάγειν αὐτὸν κρύψαι; TestAbr B 6 p. 111, 1 [Stone p. 70] ὑπάγω τηρῆσαι τὸν ἀδελφὸν Λὼτ ἀπὸ Σοδόμων).—The impv. ὕπαγε, ὑπάγετε is followed by another impv. in the NT almost always without a connective (Epict. 3, 21, 6; 22, 5; 23, 12 al.; Vi. Aesopi W 44 P. ὕπαγε, δός al.; ApcSed 9:1 ὕπαγε, λαβέ) ὕπαγε ἔλεγξον **Mt 18:15;** cp. **5:24; 8:4; 19:21; 21:28; 27:65; 28:10; Mk 1:44; 6:38; 10:21; 16:7; J 4:16; 9:7; Rv 10:8;** AcPl Ha 7, 32. W. the conjunction καί (PTebt 417, 5f [III AD] ὕπαγε καὶ εἴδε) ὑπάγετε καὶ ἐκχέετε **Rv 16:1;** cp. Hv 3, 1, 7; 4, 2, 5; s 8, 11, 1; 9, 10, 1. ὑπάγετε καὶ ζητήσατε GJs 21:2 (codd.; cp. πορευθέντες ἐξετάσατε Mt 2:8).—Abs. *go* (the context supplies the destination) ὑπάγετε **Mt 8:32;** cp. **13:44; Lk 10:3; J 15:16.** ἐν τῷ ὑπάγειν αὐτόν *as he was going* **Lk 8:42;** cp. **17:14.—J 12:11** (P⁶⁶ om. ὑπ.); Hv 3, 10, 2.

ⓑ used esp. of Christ and his *going* to the Father, characteristically of J. ὑπάγω πρὸς τὸν πέμψαντά με **J 7:33; 16:5a;** πρὸς τὸν πατέρα vss. **10, 17.** ἀπὸ θεοῦ ἐξῆλθεν καὶ πρὸς τὸν θεὸν ὑπάγει **13:3.** οἶδα πόθεν ἦλθον καὶ ποῦ ὑπάγω **8:14a;** cp. **b** (GWetter, E. gnost. Formel im vierten Ev.: ZNW 18, 1918, 49–63). ὅπου ἐγὼ ὑπάγω ὑμεῖς οὐ δύνασθε ἐλθεῖν vs. **21b, 22; 13:33;** cp. vs. **36b.** Abs. ἐγὼ ὑπάγω *I am taking my departure* **8:21a.** ὑπάγω καὶ ἔρχομαι *I am going away and returning again* **14:28.** S. in addition **13:36a; 14:4, 5; 16:5b; 1J 2:11.**

❸ as euphemism **to take the journey of death,** ***die*** ὁ υἱὸς τοῦ ἀνθρώπου ὑπάγει *the Human One is to go away*=he must die **Mt 26:24; Mk 14:21.**—B. 694. New Docs 4, 97; M-M. TW.

ὑπακοή, ῆς, ἡ (ὑπακούω; 2 Km 22:36; TestJud 17:3; Just., D. 131, 2; Ath. 3, 2; Iren. and pap fr. VI AD, e.g. PStras 40, 41; also Psellus p. 247, 18; 251, 35)

❶ **a state of being in compliance,** ***obedience*** (one listens and follows instructions)—ⓐ gener., the obedience which every slave owes his master εἰς ὑπακοήν= εἰς τὸ ὑπακούειν *to obey* **Ro 6:16a.**

ⓑ predom. of obedience to God and God's commands, abs. (opp. ἁμαρτία) **Ro 6:16b.** Cp. 1 Cl 9:3; 19:1. δι' ὑπακοῆς *obediently, in obedience* (toward God) 10:2, 7. Of Christ's obedience **Hb 5:8.**—W. subjective gen. of Christ's obedience to God **Ro 5:19** (opp. παρακοή); of human beings' obedience to the will of God as expressed in the gospel **Ro 15:18; 16:19;** of obedience to God's chosen representatives, the apostle and his emissaries **2 Cor 7:15; 10:6** (opp. παρακοή); **Phlm 21.**—W. the objective gen. ὑπ. τοῦ Χριστοῦ *obedience to Christ* **2 Cor 10:5; 1 Pt 1:2** (where Ἰησοῦ Χρ. goes w. ὑπακοήν). ὑπ. τῆς ἀληθείας vs. **22.** Perh. εἰς ὑπακοὴν πίστεως **Ro 1:5; 16:26** is to be taken in this sense *to promote obedience to the message of faith* (so DGarlington, 'The Obedience of Faith', A Pauline Phrase in Historical Context '91). But it may be better to render it more generally *with a view to (promoting) obedience which springs from faith* (so GParke-Taylor, ET 55, '44, 305f; gen. of source). On τέκνα ὑπακοῆς **1 Pt 1:14** s. τέκνον 6; on τὸν τῆς ὑπακοῆς τόπον ἀναπληροῦν 1 Cl 63:1 s. ἀναπληρόω 3.—OKuss, D. Begriff des Gehorsams im NT: ThGl 27, '35, 695–702; HvCampenhausen, Recht u. Gehors. in d. ältest. Kirche: ThBl 20, '41, 279–95; RAC IX 390–430.

❷ **reply made to a question,** ***answer*** (Pla, Soph. 217d) καὶ ὑπακοὴ ἠκούετο ἀπὸ τοῦ σταυροῦ ὅτι 'ναί' (soldiers heard a voice from heaven calling out, 'Did you proclaim to those who are asleep?') *and an answer was heard from the cross: Yes* GPt 10:42.—DELG s.v. ἀκούω. M-M. TW. Sv.

ὑπακούω impf. ὑπήκουον; fut. ὑπακούσομαι; 1 aor. ὑπήκουσα (s. ὑπακοή; Hom.+; ins, pap, LXX; TestSol 6:4 P; TestJob 4:8; Test12Patr; EpArist 44; Philo; Joseph., Ath. 15, 2) 'listen to'.

❶ **to follow instructions,** ***obey, follow, be subject to*** w. gen. of pers. (Hdt. 3, 101 al.; so predom. in pap and LXX; TestGad 8:3) B 9:1 (Ps 17:45 v.l.; the text has μοι). W. dat. of pers. (Thu., Aristoph. et al.; Philo, Mos. 1, 156; Jos., Ant. 13, 275; TestJud 1:4; 18:6 θεῷ; Ath. 15:2 αὐτῷ [God]; Iren. 3, 21, 2 [Harv. II 113, 2]; in pap and LXX the dat. is less freq. than the gen. B-D-F §173, 3; 187, 6; s. Rob. 507; 634): parents **Eph 6:1; Col 3:20;** masters **Eph 6:5; Col 3:22;** cp. **Ro 6:16;** husband (cp. Philemon Com. 132 K. ἀγαθῆς γυναικός ἐστιν μὴ κρείττον' εἶναι τἀνδρός, ἀλλ' ὑπήκοον; Jos., C. Ap. 2, 201) **1 Pt 3:6;** the ἐπίσκοπος IEph 20:2, cp. IMg 3:2 v.l. Funk (Sb 7835, 10 [I BC] in the charter of the cult-brotherhood of Zeus Hypsistos: ὑπακούειν πάντας τοῦ ἡγουμένου); Christ **Hb 5:9** (cp. Ael. Aristid. 50, 86 K.=26 p. 527 D.: τῷ θεῷ; EKamlah, Die Form der katalogischen Paränese im NT, '64 [moral exhortation]). The pers. is supplied fr. the context (cp. PTebt 24, 26; TestJob 4:8; EpArist 44; 2 Ch 24:19 v.l.) **Phil 2:12;** 1 Cl 7:6; 57:4 (Pr 1:24). ὑπακούσωμεν τῷ ὀνόματι αὐτοῦ 1 Cl 58:1 marks the transition to the next usage (w. things).—'To be in compliance' (Aesop, Fab. 179 H.), w. dat. of the thing to which one is obedient or which one embraces in full surrender (cp. Athen. 6, 247d ὑπ. δείπνῳ=accept the invitation Theoph. Ant. 2, 25 [p. 162, 4] τῇ πατρικῇ ἐντολῇ) ὑπακούειν τῇ πίστει **Ac 6:7;** τῷ εὐαγγελίῳ **Ro 10:16; 2 Th 1:8;** τῷ λόγῳ ἡμῶν **2 Th 3:14;** τῇ βουλήσει αὐτοῦ (=τοῦ θεοῦ) 1 Cl 9:1; 42:4 (Lat. tr.); τοῖς προστάγμασιν 2 Cl 19:3 (Aeschines 1, 49 and SIG 785, 18 τ. νόμοις; Demosth. 18, 204; Jos., Ant. 3, 207 τ. λεγομένοις; 5, 198); ταῖς ἐπιθυμίαις αὐτοῦ (=τοῦ θνητοῦ σώματος ὑμῶν) **Ro 6:12.** ὑπηκούσατε εἰς ὃν παρεδόθητε τύπον διδαχῆς vs. **17** (παραδίδωμι 1b, end).—MWolter, Ethos u. Identität in Paulinischen Gemeinden: NTS 43, '97, 439 n. 32 (lit. and pseudepigr. reff.).—Foll. by the inf. which shows what the obedience results in (Gen 39:10) Ἀβραὰμ ὑπήκουσεν ἐξελθεῖν *Abr. went out obediently* **Hb 11:8.**—Also of the enforced obedience of hostile spirits or powers ὑπακούουσιν αὐτῷ *they are forced to obey him* **Mk 1:27;** of the elements **Mt 8:27** (OBetz, ZNW 48, '57, 49–77, esp. 70–72); **Mk 4:41; Lk 8:25;** of a tree that must yield to a higher power **17:6** (cp. Hippocr., Epid. 3, 8; Galen VI 354 K., who speak of diseases that ὑπ.='must yield' to a remedy [dative]).

❷ **to grant one's request, *hear*** (of God Diod. S. 4, 34, 5 τοὺς ἀθανάτους ὑπακούσαντας; Vi. Aesopi I G 5 P. of Isis; Is 65:24; Jos., Ant. 14, 24.—X., Cyr. 8, 1, 18 of a judge who hears a plaintiff) 1 Cl 39:7 (Job 5:1).

❸ **to answer a knock at the door,** technically of the doorkeeper, whose duty it is to listen for the signals of those who wish to enter, and to admit them if they are entitled to do so: ***open*** or ***answer*** (the door) (Pla., Phd. 59e ὁ θυρωρός, ὅσπερ εἰώθει ὑπακούειν, Crito 43a; X., Symp. 1, 11; Theophr., Char. 4, 9; 28, 3; Lucian, Icar. 22 et al.) προσῆλθεν παιδίσκη ὑπακοῦσαι **Ac 12:13.**—M-M. TW.

ὑπαλείφω 1 aor. pass. ὑπηλείφθην (Aristoph., X. et al.) ***anoint*** fig. (a farmer desires some peace-ointment Aristoph., Ach. 1029 εἰρήνη τινά) ἐμὲ ἔδει ὑφ' ὑμῶν ὑπαλειφθῆναι πίστει *I needed to be anointed by you with faith* IEph 3:1 (s. Lightf. on the athletic metaphor and various applications to intellectual life).

ὕπανδρος, ον (ὑπό + ἀνήρ; Polyb. et al.; Cat. Cod. Astr. XIII 174, 9 al.,; LXX; lit. 'under the power of or subject to a man') **pert. to being legally bound to a man in marriage, *married*** ἡ ὕπανδρος γυνή *the married woman* (Polyb. 10, 26, 3; Aelian, NA 3, 42; Artem. 1, 78 p. 74, 6; Athen. 9, 388c; Heliod. 10, 22; Num 5:20, 29; Pr 6:24, 29; Sir 9:9; 41:23; TestAbr B 12 p. 116, 14 [Stone p. 80]; Test12Patr) **Ro 7:2.**—M-M.

ὑπαντάω impf. ὑπήντων; fut. 3 sg. ὑπαντήσεται LXX; 1 aor. ὑπήντησα (Pind., X. et al.; ins, pap, LXX, TestAbr A; JosAs 26:8) **to go to meet** τινί *someone*

ⓐ in a friendly sense ***meet*** (Appian, Bell. Civ. 4, 111 §406; 4, 134 §566; PStras 101, 4 [I BC] ἡμῖν; Tob 7:1 BA; TestAbr A 2 p. 78, 19 [Stone p. 4]; 16 p. 97, 19 [St. p. 42]; Philo, Det. Pot. Ins. 135; Jos., Vi. 49, Ant. 2, 279) **Mt 8:28; 28:9; Mk 5:2; Lk 8:27; 17:12 v.l.** (for ἀπ-); **J 4:51; 11:20, 30; 12:18; Ac 16:16** (freq. interchanged in NT mss. w. ἀπαντάω, q.v.); MPol 8:2; Hv 4, 2, 1.

ⓑ in a hostile sense ***encounter, oppose*** (X.; Appian, Illyr. 23 §68; 26 §75, Bell. Civ. 4, 115 §480; Jos., Bell. 1, 177, Ant. 7, 128; TestBenj 2:4) **Lk 14:31.**—S. ἀπαντάω.—DELG s.v. ἄντα 1. M-M. TW.

ὑπάντησις, εως, ἡ (ὑπαντάω) ***coming to meet*** (Ptolem., Apotel. 3, 11, 16; 32; 4, 9, 1; Appian, Bell. c. 4, 6 §22; Jos., Bell. 7, 100, Ant. 11, 327; SIG 798, 16; 23 [37 AD]) in our lit. only in the expr. εἰς ὑπάντησιν *to meet* τινί *someone,* and in a positive sense (Ps.-Callisth. p. 116, 23; PGiss 74, 6 [II AD] εἰς ὑπάντησιν Οὐλπιανῷ [acc. to the rdg. recommended by Preisigke, Wörterbuch s.v. and accepted by M-M.]; 1 Ch 14:8 A; Pr 7:15 v.l.) **Mt 8:34; J 12:13.** Also τινός (Jdth 2:6 S; 1 Macc 9:39 S) **Mt 25:1.**—NSvensson, BCH 50. '26, 527ff. DELG s.v. ἄντα 1. M-M. TW.

ὕπαρξις, εως, ἡ (ὑπάρχω; Aristot.+; Philo; Jos., Ant. 16, 48)

❶ **state or condition of existing or staying in existence, *existence, subsistence*** (Philodem, Piet. 114; Plut., Mor. 1067c et al.; Philo, Op. M. 170 θεοῦ) τὰ δοῦλα τ. ὑπάρξεως *things that ought to be at their service for their well-being* PtK 2 p. 14, 16.

❷ =τὰ ὑπάρχοντα **that which one has, *property, possession*** (Polyb. 2, 17, 11; Dionys. Hal. 5, 48; Diod. S. 20, 71, 1; Plut., Mor. 226c; Artem. 2, 24 p. 143, 11 Pack; POxy 707, 15; 1274, 14; BGU 195, 22; PAmh 80, 5 al.; 2 Ch 35:7; Ps 77:48; Pr 18:11; 19:14; Jer 9:9; TestLevi 17:9; TestZeb 8:6) **Hb 10:34;** Hs 1:5. Pl. *possessions, belongings* (w. κτήματα) **Ac 2:45.** (W. ἀγροί and οἰκήσεις) Hs 1:4.—DELG s.v. ἄρχω p. 121. M-M.

ὑπάρχω impf. ὑπῆρχον; fut. ὑπάρξω LXX; 1 aor. 3 sg. ὑπῆρξεν (Hom.+) the basic idea: come into being fr. an originating point and so take place; gener. 'inhere, be there'.

❶ **to really be there, *exist, be present, be at one's disposal*** (Pind., Aeschyl., Hdt.+) μηδενὸς αἰτίου ὑπάρχοντος *since there is no good reason* **Ac 19:40.** Cp. **27:21; 28:18;** *be* somewhere **4:34; 10:12; 17:27; Phil 3:20;** 1 Cl 61:2; EpilMosq 3 (TestAbr A p. 5, 23 [Stone p. 12] ἐν τῇ σκηνῇ; Just., A I, 29, 1 ἐν σώματι). ἀκούω σχίσματα ἐν ὑμῖν ὑπάρχειν *I hear that there are actually divisions among you* **1 Co 11:18.** εἷς Χριστὸς Ἰησοῦς καὶ ἄλλος οὐκ ὑπάρχει *there is only one Christ Jesus and no other* AcPl Ha 1, 18. σιγῆς ὑπαρχούσης 7, 25 (s. σιγή). W. dat. of pers. ὑπάρχει μοί τι *someth. is at my disposal, I have someth.* (X., An. 2, 2, 11; PMagd 9, 2 [III BC] ὑπάρχει ἐμοὶ Ἰσιεῖον; Sir 20:16; Jos., Ant. 7, 148) χρυσίον οὐχ ὑπάρχει μοι **Ac 3:6.** Cp. **4:37; 28:7; 2 Pt 1:8.** τὰ ὑπάρχοντά τινι *what belongs to someone, someone's property, possessions, means* (SIG 646, 25 [170 BC]; very oft. in pap since PHib 94, 2; 15; 95, 12 [III BC]; Tob 4:7; TestAbr A 8 p. 86, 7 [Stone p. 20]; Jos., Ant. 4, 261) **Lk 8:3; 12:15; Ac 4:32.** Subst. in the same sense τὰ ὑπάρχοντά τινος (SIG 611, 14; very oft. in pap since PHib 32, 5; 84, 9; PEleph 2, 3 [III BC]; Gen 31:18; Sir 41:1; Tob 1:20 BA; TestAbr A 4 p. 81, 28 [Stone p. 10]) **Mt 19:21; 24:47; 25:14; Lk 11:21; 12:33, 44; 14:33; 16:1; 19:8; 1 Cor 13:3; Hb 10:34.**

❷ **to be in a state or circumstance, *be*** as a widely used substitute in H. Gk. for εἶναι, but in some of the foll. pass. the sense 'be inherently (so)' or 'be really' cannot be excluded (s. 1; cp. IG XIV, 2014, 3 ἄνθρωπος ὑπάρχων='being mortal') (B-D-F §414, 1; s. Rob. 1121) w. a predicate noun (OGI 383, 48 [I BC] ὅπως οὗτος ... ὑπάρχῃ καθιδρυμένος; TestAbr A 4 p. 80, 26 [Stone p. 8] ἐνδοξότερος ὑπάρχει βασιλέων; ibid. B 2 p. 105, 9 [St. p. 58] ὑπῆρχεν ... γηραλέος πάνυ τῇ ἰδέᾳ; JosAs 7:11 cod. A [p. 48, 12 Bat.] εἰ θυγάτηρ ὑμῶν ἐστι καὶ παρθένος ὑπάρχει ... ; SibOr 3, 267, fgm. 1, 28; Ar. 13, 6; Just., A I, 4, 1; Tat. 60, 2) οὗτος ἄρχων τῆς συναγωγῆς ὑπῆρχεν **Lk 8:41.** ἐγὼ λειτουργὸς ὑπάρχω τοῦ θεοῦ *I am a minister of God* GJs 23:1. Cp. **Lk 9:48; Ac 7:55; 8:16; 16:3; 19:31** D (w. φίλος and dat., the standard form, s. ins Larfeld I 500); **36; 21:20; 1 Cor 7:26; 12:22; Js 2:15; 2 Pt 3:11;** 1 Cl 19:3 and oft.; MPol 6:2. Very freq. in the ptc. w. a predicate noun *who is, since he is,* etc. (TestSim 4:4 ἐλεήμων ὑπάρχων; Just., A II, 2, 10; Tat. 2, 2; Mel., P. 54, 396) οἱ Φαρισαῖοι φιλάργυροι ὑπάρχοντες **Lk 16:14.** Cp. **11:13** (v.l. ὄντες); **23:50; Ac 2:30; 3:2; 16:20, 37; 17:24, 29; 22:3; 27:12; Ro 4:19; 1 Cor 11:7; 2 Cor 8:17; 12:16; Gal 1:14; 2:14; 2 Pt 2:19;** 1 Cl 1:1; 11:1, 2; 25:2; B 5:10.—ὑπ. w. a prep.: ἐν (Jer 4:14; Philo, Leg. All. 1, 62; Jos., Ant. 7, 391; Just., D. 69, 7 ἐν λώβῃ τινὶ σώματος ὑπάρχων): οἱ ἐν ἱματισμῷ ἐνδόξῳ ὑπάρχοντες **Lk 7:25;** cp. **16:23; Ac 5:4; 14:9** D; **Phil 2:6;** 1 Cl 1:3; 32:2; 56:1. τοῦτο πρὸς τῆς ὑμετέρας σωτηρίας ὑπάρχει **Ac 27:34** (s. πρός 1).—Schmidt, Syn. II 538–41. DELG s.v. ἄρχω p. 121. M-M. Sv.

ὑπέβαλον s. ὑποβάλλω.

ὑπέδειξα s. ὑποδείκνυμι.

ὑπέθηκα s. ὑποτίθημι.

ὑπείκω (Hom. et al.) prim. 'withdraw, give way to', then by fig. extension **to yield to someone's authority,** ***yield, give way, submit*** (Hom. et al.; 4 Macc 6:35; TestSol 12:1 C; TestAbr A 9 p. 86, 30 [Stone p. 20]; Ath., R. 15 p. 66, 34 σῶμα . . . ταῖς τῆς ψυχῆς ἡνίαις ὑπεῖκον) w. dat. of pers. to whom one submits (Hom.; Pla., Leg. 4, 717d; Sextus 17; cp. Philo, Mos. 1, 156) **Hb 13:17.**—DELG s.v. εἴκω. M-M.

ὑπέλαβον s. ὑπολαμβάνω.

ὑπελείφθην s. ὑπολείπω.

ὑπέμεινα s. ὑπομένω.

ὑπεμνήσθην s. ὑπομιμνήσκω.

ὑπεναντίος, α, ον (Hes., Hdt. et al.) mostly ***opposed, contrary, hostile*** (Thu. 2, 2, 2; Pla., Tht. 176a; Demosth. 24, 108 al.; ins [e.g. ISmyrnaMcCabe 0421, 8], pap; Jos., C. Ap. 2, 180) τινί *against someone* **Col 2:14.** Subst. ὁ ὑπεναντίος *the opponent* (X.; Polyb. 1, 11, 14; Plut., Thes. 6 [13, 2]; ins; POxy 1151, 55; LXX; TestSol 8:10; predom. in pl.) οἱ ὑπεναντίοι *the adversaries* (X., Cyr. 1, 6, 38) of God **Hb 10:27** (cp. Is 26:11).—DELG s.v. ἄντα. M-M.

ὑπενεγκεῖν s. ὑποφέρω.

ὑπεξέρχομαι 2 aor. ὑπεξῆλθον ***go out quietly/secretly*** (Pla. et al.; Plut., Lucullus 502 [16, 7]; Lucian, Dial. Mar. 2, 4; Cass. Dio 38, 17; JosAs 24:11; Jos., Vi. 21, Ant. 14, 16) MPol 5:1a. W. the destination given (Hdt. 8, 36 ἐς Ἄμφισσαν) εἰς ἀγρίδιον 5:1b.

ὑπέπλευσα s. ὑποπλέω.

ὑπέρ (Hom.+) prep. w. gen. and acc. (lit. s.v. ἀνά, beg. In addition to this, for ὑπέρ: LWenger, Die Stellvertretung im Rechte der Papyri 1896; ARobertson, The Use of ὑπέρ in Business Documents in the Papyri: Exp. 8th ser., 28, 1919, 321–27). The loc. sense 'over, above' is not found in our lit. (not in the LXX either, but in JosAs 14:4; ApcEsdr 1:9; Just., Tat., Ath.) but does appear in nonliteral senses. The mss. oft. fluctuate between ὑπέρ and περί; see A3 below.

A. w. gen.—**❶ a marker indicating that an activity or event is in some entity's interest,** ***for, in behalf of, for the sake of someone/someth.***

ⓐ w. gen. of pers. or human collective—**α.** after words that express a request, prayer, etc. After the verbs δέομαι (q.v. b), εὔχομαι (q.v. 1), προσεύχομαι (q.v.), ἐντυγχάνω (q.v. 1a; cp. b), ὑπερεντυγχάνω (q.v.), λιτανεύω (q.v.) etc. After the nouns δέησις (q.v., end) and προσευχή (q.v. 1). S. also **1 Ti 2:1f.**

β. after words and expressions that denote working, caring, concerning oneself about. After the verbs ἀγρυπνέω (q.v. 2), ἀγωνίζομαι (q.v. 2b), μεριμνάω (q.v. 2), πρεσβεύω (q.v.) etc. After the nouns ζῆλος (q.v. 1), σπουδή (q.v. 2), ἔχειν πόνον (πόνος 1). ὑπὲρ ὑμῶν διάκονος **Col 1:7.**

γ. after expressions having to do w. sacrifice: ἁγιάζω (q.v. 2), ἁγνίζομαι (s. ἁγνίζω 3). τὸ πάσχα ἡμῶν ὑπὲρ ἡμῶν ἐτύθη Χριστός **1 Cor 5:7 v.l.** ἕως οὗ προσηνέχθη ὑπὲρ ἑνὸς ἑκάστου αὐτῶν ἡ προσφορά **Ac 21:26** (προσφέρω 2a).—**Eph 5:2; Hb 9:7.**

δ. gener. εἶναι ὑπέρ τινος *be for someone, be on someone's side* (PIand 16, 8 τὸ νόμιμον ὑπὲρ ἡμῶν ἐστιν.—Opp. εἶναι κατά τινος) **Mk 9:40; Lk 9:50; Ro 8:31.**—ἐπιτρέπεταί σοι ὑπὲρ σεαυτοῦ λέγειν **Ac 26:1 v.l.** (for περί). ἵνα μὴ εἷς ὑπὲρ τοῦ ἑνὸς φυσιοῦσθε κατὰ τοῦ ἑτέρου **1 Cor 4:6b.** Cp. **2 Cor 1:11ab; 5:20b** (δεόμεθα ὑπὲρ Χριστοῦ=*as helpers of Christ we beg you.* Also prob. is *we beg you by* or *in the name of* Christ [Apollon. Rhod. 3, 701 λίσσομ' ὑπὲρ μακάρων=by the gods, in imitation of Il. 22, 338.—Theaetetus, III BC: Anth. Pal. 7, 499, 2]). τοῦτο φρονεῖν ὑπὲρ πάντων ὑμῶν *to be thus minded in behalf of you all* **Phil 1:7** (perh. simply=*about;* s. 3 below); cp. **4:10** (think of me = care for, be interested in me).

ε. after expressions of suffering, dying, devoting oneself, etc. (JosAs 28:1 κύριος πολεμεῖ καθ' ἡμῶν ὑπὲρ Ἀσενεθ 'against us in behalf of Aseneth'; ApcEsdr 6:18 p. 31, 28 Tdf. δικάζεσθαι ὑπὲρ τοῦ γένους τῶν ἀνθρώπων) ἀποθνήσκειν ὑπέρ τινος *die for someone* or *someth.* (ἀποθνήσκω 1aα; also Jos., Ant. 13, 6) **J 11:50–52; 18:14; Ro 5:7ab.** τὴν ψυχὴν αὐτοῦ τίθησιν ὑπέρ τινος (cp. Jos., Bell. 2, 201; Sir 29:15; ApcSed 1:5; Ar. 15, 10; Mel., P. 103, 791) **J 10:11, 15; 13:37f; 15:13; 1J 3:16b.—Ro 16:4; 2 Cor 12:15; Eph 3:1, 13; Col 1:24a.**—So esp. of the death of Christ (already referred to at least in part in some of the passages already mentioned. S. also above 1aγ and below 1c) *for, in behalf of* humanity, the world, etc.: **Mk 14:24; Lk 22:19f; Ro 5:6, 8; 8:32; 14:15; 1 Cor 1:13** (where the hypothetical question μὴ Παῦλος ἐσταυρώθη ὑπὲρ ὑμῶν; was chosen for no other reason than its ref. to the redeeming death of Christ); **11:24; 15:3; Gal 2:20; 3:13; Eph 5:25; 1 Th 5:10** (v.l. περί); **1 Ti 2:6; Tit 2:14; Hb 2:9; 6:20; 1 Pt 2:21** (v.l. περί); **3:18a v.l.; 18b; 1J 3:16a;** MPol 17:2ab (Just., A I, 50, 1 ὑπὲρ ἡμῶν γενόμενος ἄνθρωπος).—AMetzinger, Die Substitutionstheorie u. das atl. Opfer, Biblica 21, '40, 159–87, 247–72, 353–77; EBlakeney, ET 55, '43/44, 306.

ⓑ w. gen. of thing, in which case it must be variously translated ὑπὲρ (τῶν) ἁμαρτιῶν *in order to atone for (the) sins* or *to remove* them **1 Cor 15:3; Gal 1:4; Hb 5:1b; 7:27; 9:7** (here ὑπὲρ . . . τῶν ἀγνοημάτων); **10:12;** B 7:3, 4 (prophetic saying of unknown origin), 5f.—ὑπὲρ τῆς τοῦ κόσμου ζωῆς *to bring life to the world* **J 6:51.** ὑπὲρ τῆς δόξης τοῦ θεοῦ *to reveal the glory of God* **11:4.** ὑπὲρ τοῦ ὀνόματος αὐτοῦ (cp. Sb 7681, 7 [312 AD] ὑπὲρ τοῦ ὀνόματός μου=in behalf of) *to spread his name* **Ro 1:5;** cp. **3J 7.** ὑπὲρ ἀληθείας θεοῦ=in order to show that God's promises are true **Ro 15:8.** ὑπὲρ τῆς ὑμῶν παρακλήσεως *in order to comfort you* **2 Cor 1:6ab.** Cp. **12:19.** ὑπὲρ τῆς πίστεως ὑμῶν *for the strengthening of your faith* **1 Th 3:2.**

ⓒ *in place of, instead of, in the name of* (Eur.; Polyb. 3, 67, 7; ApcEsdr 1:11 p. 25, 3 Tdf.; Jos., C. Ap. 2, 142; Just., D. 95, 2.—In pap very oft. ὑπὲρ αὐτοῦ to explain that the writer is writing 'as the representative of' an illiterate pers.; Dssm. LO 285, 2 [LAE 335, 4]; other exx. of pap in DWallace, Greek Grammar Beyond the Basics '96, 384–86) ἵνα ὑπὲρ σοῦ μοι διακονῇ **Phlm 13.** Somet. the mng. *in place of* merges w. *on behalf of, for the sake of* **Ro 9:3.** οἱ βαπτιζόμενοι ὑπὲρ τῶν νεκρῶν **1 Cor 15:29a** is debated; cp. **29b** (s. the lit. s.v. βαπτίζω 2c; also KBornhäuser, Die Furche 21, '34, 184–87; JWhite, JBL 116, '97, 487–99 [esp. 497f] favors a causal sense). εἷς ὑπὲρ πάντων ἀπέθανεν **2 Cor 5:14;** cp. **15ab, 21** (Eur., Alc. 701 κατθανεῖν ὑπέρ σου).

❷ **marker of the moving cause or reason,** ***because of, for the sake of, for*** (Diod. S. 10, 21, 2 τὴν ὑπὲρ τῶν ἁμαρτημάτων τιμωρίαν; schol. on Pind., O. 6, 154b [=OxfT 91]), w. verbs of suffering, giving the reason for it ὑπὲρ τοῦ ὀνόματος **Ac 5:41; 9:16; 21:13;** ὑπὲρ Χριστοῦ **Phil 1:29ab;** cp. **2 Th 1:5;** ὑπὲρ θεοῦ ἀποθνήσκω IRo 4:1. Likew. used w. nouns that denote suffering ὑπὲρ Χριστοῦ *for Christ's sake* **2 Cor 12:10.**—εὐχαριστεῖν ὑπέρ τινος *give thanks for someth.* **1 Cor 10:30; Eph 5:20;** D 9:2; 10:2 (cp. Sb 3926, 12 [I BC] τὸ κατεσκευασμένον ὑπὲρ [=in gratefulness for] τῆς ἡμετέρας σωτηρίας Ἰσιδεῖον; Just., A I, 65, 3). δοξάζειν τὸν θεὸν ὑπέρ τινος *praise God for someth.* **Ro 15:9.**—ὑπὲρ τούτου *with reference to someth.* (Synes., Ep. 67 p. 209c) **2 Cor 12:8.**—This is prob. the place for ὑπὲρ τῆς εὐδοκίας *with (God's) good pleasure in view* **Phil 2:13** (εὐδοκία 1).

❸ **marker of general content, whether of a discourse or mental activity,** ***about, concerning*** (about equivalent to περί [τινος], w. which it is freq. interchanged in the mss.; s. Kühner-G. I p. 487 [w. exx. fr. Hom., Pla. et al.]. Also quite common in Polyb., Diod. S., Dionys. Hal., Joseph., ins [e.g. ISardGauthier 2, 3 'write about'] and pap [Schmidt 396]; but Ath. differentiates between λόγος ὑπὲρ [in defense of] τῆς ἀληθείας and λόγος περὶ [about] τῆς ἀληθείας R 1 p. 48, 19; Mlt. 105; Rdm.[2] p. 140; Johannessohn, Präp 216–21; LDeubner, Bemerkungen z. Text der Vita Pyth. des Iamblichos: SBBerlAk '35, XIX 27; 71), oft. at the same time in the sense 'in the interest of' or 'in behalf of' οὗτός ἐστιν ὑπὲρ οὗ ἐγὼ εἶπον **J 1:30** (v.l. περί). Ἠσαΐας κράζει ὑπὲρ τοῦ Ἰσραήλ **Ro 9:27** (v.l. περί). Cp. **2 Cor 1:8** (v.l. περί); **5:12; 7:4, 14; 8:24; 9:2f; 12:5ab** (in all the passages in 2 Cor except the first dependent on καυχάομαι, καύχημα, καύχησις); **2 Th 1:4** (ἐγκαυχᾶσθαι). *With reference to* (Demosth. 21, 121) **2 Cor 8:23; 2 Th 2:1.** ἡ ἐλπὶς ἡμῶν βεβαία ὑπὲρ ὑμῶν *our hope with reference to you is unshaken* **2 Cor 1:7** (ἐλπὶς ὑ. τινος 'for someth.' Socrat., Ep. 6, 5 [p. 234, 28 Malherbe]).

B. w. acc. **marker of a degree beyond that of a compared scale of extent,** in the sense of excelling, surpassing, ***over and above, beyond, more than*** (so always PsSol; TestAbr A 4 p. 81, 29 [Stone p. 10] al.; TestJob 38:6 τὰ ὑπὲρ ἡμᾶς; JosAs 1:6 al.; Ath. 17, 1; 32, 1) κεφαλὴ ὑπὲρ πάντα *the supreme Head* **Eph 1:22** (Appian, Bell. Civ. 5, 74 §314 ὑπὲρ ἅπαντα). ὑπὲρ δύναμιν *beyond one's strength* **2 Cor 1:8;** cp. **8:3 v.l.** (OGI 767, 19f ὑπὲρ δύναμιν; Cyranides p. 63, 22 ὑπὲρ λόγον). Also ὑπὲρ ὃ δύνασθε **1 Cor 10:13.** μὴ ὑπὲρ ἃ γέγραπται *not* (to go) *beyond what is written* **1 Cor 4:6a** (s. WLütgert, Freiheitspredigt u. Schwarmgeister in Korinth 1908, 97ff; ASchlatter, Die korinth. Theologie 1914, 7ff; OLinton, StKr 102, 1930, 425–37; LBrun, ibid. 103, '31, 453–56; PWallis, TLZ 75, '50, 506–8; ALegault, NTS 18, '71/72, 227–31; PMarshall, Hybrists Not Gnostics in Corinth: SBLSP 23, 84, 275–87; on the prob. imagery of a school exercise in which children learn to stay between the lines, s. RTyler, CBQ 60, '98, 97–103; a public foundational document containing bylaws, JHanges, JBL 117, '98, 275–98 [pap and ins]). ὑπὲρ ἃ λέγω ποιήσεις *you will do even more than I ask* **Phlm 21.** ὑπέρ τι καὶ καθ' ὑπερβολὴν ὑπερευφραίνομαι *I feel an exceeding and overwhelming joy* B 1:2.—After an adj. in comp. or superl. for ἤ *than:* mostly so after the comp. (Judg 11:25 B; 15:2 B; 18:26 B; 3 Km 19:4; Ps 18:11; Hab 1:8) τομώτερος ὑπὲρ πᾶσαν μάχαιραν **Hb 4:12.** Cp. **Lk 16:8; J 12:43 v.l.;** MPol 18:2. In an unusually compressed statement: τοὺς ἀποστόλους ὄντας ὑπὲρ πᾶσαν ἁμαρτίαν ἀνομωτέρους *the apostles, who were more lawless than* (people who commit) *any and every sin* B 5:9; rarely after the superl. (TestAbr A 2 p. 78, 25 [Stone p. 4]) γλυκυτάτη ὑπὲρ τὸ μέλι Hm 5, 1, 6. Likew. after verbs that express the idea of comparison ἡσσώθητε (=ἐγένεσθε ἥσσονες) ὑπὲρ τὰς λοιπὰς ἐκκλησίας, *were you treated worse than the other churches?* **2 Cor 12:13.**—'More than' also takes on the sense *more exalted* or *excellent* or *glorious than;* as the timeless one (ἄχρονος), Christ is called ὁ ὑπὲρ καιρόν *the one who is exalted beyond time* IPol 3:2. ὑπὲρ θάνατον *exalted above death* ISm 3:2. οὐκ ἔστιν μαθητὴς ὑπὲρ τὸν διδάσκαλον *a disciple is not superior to his teacher* **Mt 10:24a; Lk 6:40.—Mt 10:24b; Ac 26:13; Phil 2:9.** οὐκέτι ὡς δοῦλον ἀλλὰ ὑπὲρ δοῦλον *no longer as a slave, but as someth. better than a slave* **Phlm 16.** τῷ δυναμένῳ ὑπὲρ πάντα ποιῆσαι *to (God) who is able to do greater things than all* (we can ask or imagine) **Eph 3:20.**—*More than* (PsSol 17:43; TestGad 7:1) ἀγαπᾶν ὑμᾶς ὑπὲρ τὴν ψυχήν μου (JosAs 13:11) B 1:4; cp. 4:6; 19:5; D 2:7. φιλεῖν **Mt 10:37ab.** ἀρέσει αὐτῷ ὑπὲρ μόσχον 1 Cl 52:2 (Ps 68:32). λάμπειν IEph 19:2. προκόπτειν **Gal 1:14.** στίλβειν Hs 9, 2, 2.

C. adv. use ***even more.*** The adv. use of ὑπέρ is, so far, almost unknown outside the NT (but s. L-S-J-M s.v. ὑπέρ E; Schwyzer II 518; Ursing 49 cites fr. an Aesop-ms. ὅπερ ἔτι ὑπὲρ ἀπεδέξατο, where all the other mss. have μᾶλλον [Phil 3:4 ἐγὼ μᾶλλον]. On the adv. use of other prepositions s. Kühner-G. I p. 526f). διάκονοι Χριστοῦ εἰσιν; ὑπὲρ ἐγώ *are they assistants of of Christ? I am so even more* (than they) **2 Cor 11:23** (W-H. accent ὕπερ; s. Mlt-Turner 250). Wallis (s. B above) classes **1 Cor 4:6** here.—RBieringer: The Four Gospels, Festschr. FNeirynck, ed. FvanSegbroeck et al. '92, I 219–48. On ὑπὲρ ἄγαν, ὑπὲρ ἐκεῖνα, ὑπὲρ ἐκπερισσοῦ, ὑπὲρ λίαν s. ὑπεράγαν, ὑπερέκεινα, ὑπερεκπερισσοῦ (-ῶς), ὑπερλίαν.—DELG. M-M. EDNT. TW.

ὑπεραγάλλομαι dep. ***rejoice/exult greatly*** ὑπεραγαλλόμενος *with the highest joy* IPhld 5:1.

ὑπεράγαν adv. (ὑπέρ + ἄγαν; Strabo 3, 2, 9; Aelian, NA 3, 38; Vett. Val. p. 63, 5; Diog. L. 3, 26; 2 Macc 10:34. Written separately as early as Eur., Med. 627.—B-D-F §116, 3) ***beyond measure*** 1 Cl 56:2.

ὑπεραγαπάω 1 aor. ὑπερηγάπησα (Demosth. 23, 196; Aristot., EN 9, 7, 1168a, 1; Cass. Dio 77, 22, 1; Herodian 4, 7, 4; Aristaen., Ep. 1, 19; 2, 16 σε; Eunap. p. 67; Jos., Ant. 1, 222; 12, 195) ***love most dearly*** τινά *someone* (Plut., Ages 616 [35, 2]; Ps.-Callisth. 2, 21, 2) B 5:8.

ὑπεραίρω aor. 3 sg. ὑπερῆρεν and ὑπερῆραν LXX. Pass.: fut. 3 sg. ὑπεραρθήσεται Ps 71:16; aor. 3 sg. ὑπερήρθη 2 Ch 32:23; pf. ptc. n. ὑπερηρμένον (Just., D. 91, 2) (Aeschyl., Pla. et al.; ins, pap, LXX, EpArist; Jos., C. Ap. 2, 223; Just., D. 91, 2 in var. mngs.) in our lit. only **ὑπεραίρομαι to have an undue sense of one's self-importance,** ***rise up, exalt oneself, be elated*** (Aristaen. 1, 17; Anth. Pal. 5, 299, 5; 2 Macc 5:23 [w. dat.]) ἐπὶ w. acc. **2 Th 2:4.** Abs. **2 Cor 12:7ab** (Byz. folksong in Theophanes Conf. [VIII AD], Chron. 283, 19ff deBoor [s. KKrumbacher, Byz. Lit.[2] 1897, 792] δὸς αὐτοῦ κατὰ κρανίου, ἵνα μὴ ὑπεραίρηται).—DELG s.v. 1 ἀείρω. M-M.

ὑπέρακμος, ον (Soranus, Hesych., Suda) fr. ἀκμή=highest point or prime of a person's development (ἀκ. in this sense in Pla., Rep. 5, 460e; Philo, Leg. All. 1, 10) in our lit. only **1 Cor 7:36.** Depending on one's understanding of this pass. (s. γαμίζω) the term may apply either to a woman or to a man.

❶ Understood temporally and as a status term applied to a woman: ***past one's prime, past marriageable age, past the bloom of youth*** (cp. Soranus p. 15, 8.—Diod. S. 32, 11, 1 speaks of the ἀκμὴ τῆς ἡλικίας of a woman and in 34 + 35 fgm. 2, 39 uses ἀκμή of the youthful bloom of a παρθένος.—Lycon [III BC], fgm. 27 Wehrli [in Diog. L. 5, 65], commiserates the father of a παρθένος who, because of the smallness of her dowry ἐκτρέχουσα [=goes beyond] τὸν ἀκμαῖον τῆς ἡλικίας καιρόν). So e.g. Tyndale, Phillips, KJV, Jerusalem Bible.

❷ Other interpreters focus on the ascensive force of ὑπέρ, 'exceedingly' (freq. found in compounds, as in ὑπέρκαλος 'exceedingly beautiful' and related terms Pollux 3, 71). In our pass., then, ὑπέρακμος means ***at one's sexual peak*** and may be applied to a woman (so, apparently, L-S-J-M 'sexually well developed') or to a man (cp. Diod. S. 36, 2, 3 ὁ ἔρως of a man in love ἤκμαζεν and became irresistible), ***with strong passions*** (REB and NRSV 'if his passions are strong').—Cp. DELG s.v. ἀκ- p. 44. M-M.

ὑπεράνω adv. (Aristot.+; ins, pap, LXX, TestAbr A) ***(high) above*** funct. as prep. w. gen. (B-D-F §215, 2; Rob. 646f) of place (Archimed. II 318, 6 Heib.; Eratosth. p. 46, 7; Ocellus Luc. c. 36 ὑπ. σελήνης; Diod. S. 20, 23, 1; schol. on Apollon. Rhod. 2, 160b; Ezk 43:15; TestAbr A 7 p. 83f [Stone p. 14f]; ViDa 21 [p. 79, 12 Sch.]; Jos., Ant. 3, 154) **Eph 4:10; Hb 9:5.**—Of rank, power, etc. (Lucian, Demon. 3; Dt 28:1; Philo, Conf. Lingu. 137; TestLevi 3:4) **Eph 1:21.**—M-M.

ὑπερασπίζω fut. ὑπερασπιῶ LXX, 3 sg. ὑπερασπίσει Pr 30:5 A (Polyb. 6, 39, 6 al.; Dionys. Hal. 6, 12, 2; ins; Gen 15:1; 4 Km 19:34; Pr 2:7; TestBenj 4:5; JosAs 28:10 [w. gen.]; also ch. 11 cod. A [p. 54, 15 Bat.]; Philo) lit. 'hold a shield over' (as protection, s. Polyb. and D. H. above) metaph. ***protect,*** αὐτούς **Js 1:27** P^{74}.—DELG s.v. ἀσπίς.

ὑπερασπισμός, οῦ, ὁ (Ps 17:36; see ὑπερασπίζω) ***protection*** 1 Cl 56:16.—B. -σις 1410.

ὑπερασπιστής, οῦ, ὁ (ὑπερασπίζω; LXX; PsSol 7:7; JosAs 12:11 [κύριος ὑπ' τῶν διωκομένων]; Philo, Ebr. 111; Lydus, Mag. 1, 46 p. 48, 22 W.; Hesych., Suda; Jos., Bell. 1, 627) ***protector*** 1 Cl 45:7.—DELG s.v. ἀσπίζω.

ὑπεραυξάνω (in trans. sense Andoc. et al.) intr. (Callisth. of Sybaris: 291 fgm. 5, 2 Jac. [Stob. 4, 36, 16=Ps.-Plut., Fluv. 6, 2]) ***grow wonderfully, increase abundantly*** fig., of faith **2 Th 1:3.**—DELG s.v. αὔξω. M-M. TW.

ὑπερβαίνω fut. ὑπερβήσομαι LXX; 2 aor. ὑπερέβην LXX; pf. 2 pl. ὑπερβεβήκατε 3 Macc 6:24 (Hom. et al.; ins, pap, LXX; TestAbr B 8 p. 113, 10 [Stone p. 74] al. ['surpass']; EpArist 122; Philo, Joseph.)

❶ **to go beyond a high point on a scale of linear extent,** lit. ***go beyond*** of the head of the risen Lord κεφαλὴν ὑπερβαίνουσαν τοὺς οὐρανούς *that reaches up above the heavens* GPt 10:40.

❷ in moral sense ('overstep, transgress, break' laws and commandments: Pind., Hdt.; Jos., Bell 4, 225) abs. **to transgress by going beyond proper limits in behavior, *trespass, sin*** (Il. 9, 501; Pla., Rep. 2, 366a) w. πλεονεκτεῖν τὸν ἀδελφόν **1 Th 4:6.**—M-M. TW.

ὑπερβαλλόντως (Pla., X.+; SIG 685, 36 [II BC]; PGM 4, 649; Job 15:11; TestSol [tit. cod. I p. 98*]; TestJob 41:4; Ath., R. 21 p. 75, 8) adv. of the pres. ptc. of ὑπερβάλλω: 'exceedingly, immeasurably', also comp. ***surpassingly, to a much greater degree*** (Philo, Plant. 126, Migr. Abr. 58) **2 Cor 11:23.**—M-M. TW.

ὑπερβάλλω 2 aor. 3 sg. ὑπερέβαλεν Sir 25:11 (Hom. et al.; ins, pap, LXX, JosAs, Just.; orig. 'to cast beyond' e.g. in a spear-throwing contest Il. 23, 637) **to attain a degree that extraordinarily exceeds a point on a scale of extent, *go beyond, surpass, outdo*** (Aeschyl., Pla., X.+; Philo, Mos. 2, 1; Jos., Ant. 2, 7; 8, 211) in an extraordinary constr. ἦν ὑπερβάλλων τὸ φῶς αὐτοῦ ὑπὲρ πάντα *it went far beyond them all as far as its light was concerned, it surpassed them all in light* IEph 19:2.—The ptc. ὑπερβάλλων, ουσα, ον *surpassing, extraordinary, outstanding* (Aeschyl., Hdt. et al.; Artem. 4, 72 ὑπερβάλλουσα εὐδαιμονία; 2 Macc 4:13; 7:42; 3 Macc 2:23; TestSol tit. rec. B p. 98*, 7; JosAs 23:2; EpArist 84; Philo; Jos., Ant. 4, 14; Just., D. 136, 2 τὸ ὑ. [subst.]) μέγεθος (Philo, Deus Imm. 116) **Eph 1:19.** πλοῦτος **2:7.** χάρις **2 Cor 9:14.** φιλανθρωπία Dg 9:2. δόξα **2 Cor 3:10.** δωρεαί (cp. Philo, Migr. Abr. 106) 1 Cl 19:2; 23:2. Used w. gen. of comparison (Alex. Aphr., An. Mant. p. 169, 17 Br. ὑπ. τούτων) ὑπερβάλλουσα τῆς γνώσεως ἀγάπη *a love that surpasses knowledge* **Eph 3:19.**—M-M. TW.

ὑπερβολή, ῆς, ἡ (ὑπερβάλλω; since Hdt. 8, 112, 4; ins, pap; TestSol 10:2 P; Ath.) **state of exceeding to an extraordinary degree a point on a scale of extent** (the context indicating whether in a good or a bad sense), ***excess, extraordinary quality/character*** w. gen. of thing (Diod. S. 4, 52, 2 εὐσεβείας ὑπερβολή; Epict. 4, 1, 17 ὑπ. τυραννίδος; Dio Chrys. 14 [31], 117; 123; Philo; Jos., Bell. 6, 373, Ant. 1, 234; 13, 244) ἡ ὑπ. τῆς δυνάμεως *the extraordinary (quality of the) power* **2 Cor 4:7.** ἡ ὑπ. τῶν ἀποκαλύψεων *the extraordinary revelations* **12:7.** ἡ ὑπ. τῆς ἀγαθότητος 2 Cl 13:4 (cp. Simplicius In Epict. p. 43, 9 Düb. ὑπ. τῆς θείας ἀγαθότητος; Ael. Aristid. 39 p. 743 D.: ὑπ. φαυλότητος).—καθ' ὑπερβολήν *to an extraordinary degree, beyond measure, utterly* (Soph., Oed. R. 1195; Isocr. 5, 11; Polyb. 3, 92, 10; Diod. S. 2, 16, 2; 17, 47; 19, 86, 3; PTebt 23, 4; 4, 25; PRein 7, 4 [all three II BC]; 4 Macc 3:18) w. verbs **2 Cor 1:8** (w. ὑπὲρ δύναμιν); **Gal 1:13;** B 1:2; w. an adj. καθ' ὑπ. ἁμαρτωλός *sinful in the extreme* **Ro 7:13;** w. a noun as a kind of adj. ἔτι καθ' ὑπερβολὴν ὁδὸν δείκνυμι *I will show* (you) *a far better way* **1 Cor 12:31;** in wordplay beside εἰς ὑπερβολήν (Diod. S. 14, 48, 2; Aelian, VH 12, 1; Vi. Aesopi III p. 309, 7 Ebh.), which means essentially the same thing *to excess,* etc. (Eur., Hipp. 939 al.; Lucian, Tox. 12; Diog. L. 2, 51), *beyond all measure and proportion* **2 Cor 4:17.** In an uncertain context AcPl Ha 4, 26.—DELG s.v. βάλλω. M-M. TW.

ὑπερδοξάζω (Suda) ***glory exceedingly, break out in rapturous praise*** abs. IPol 1:1.

ὑπερεγώ is the way Lachmann writes ὑπὲρ ἐγώ **2 Cor 11:23;** s. B-D-F §116, 3 on related forms; cp. ὑπέρ C.

ὑπερεῖδον 2 aor. of ὑπεροράω (q.v.).—M-M.

ὑπερέκεινα adv. (= ὑπέρ + ἐκεῖνα, cp. ἐπέκεινα. Thomas Mag. 155, 7 ἐπέκεινα ῥήτορες λέγουσιν . . . ὑπερέκεινα δὲ μόνοι οἱ σύρφακες [rabble].—B-D-F §116, 3; Rob. 171; 297) ***beyond*** used w. gen. τὰ ὑπερέκεινα ὑμῶν (sc. μέρη) *the lands that lie beyond you* **2 Cor 10:16** (B-D-F §184; Rob. 647).—DELG s.v. ἐκεῖ. M-M.

ὑπερεκπερισσοῦ adv. (elsewh. only Da 3:22 Complutensian and Aldine editions; TestJos 17:5.—B-D-F §12; 116, 3; Rob. 170f) ***quite beyond all measure*** (highest form of comparison imaginable) ὑπ. δεῖσθαι *pray as earnestly as possible* (to God) **1 Th 3:10.—5:13** (v.l. ὑπερεκπερισσῶς q.v.). W. gen. of comparison (B-D-F §185, 1; Rob. 647) ὑπ. ὧν (=τούτων ἅ) *infinitely more than* **Eph 3:20.**—Cp. DELG s.v. περί. M-M. TW.

ὑπερεκπερισσῶς adv. (s. prec. entry) ***beyond all measure, most highly*** w. ἡγέομαι (q.v. 2, end) **1 Th 5:13 v.l.** (for ὑπερεκπερισσοῦ, q.v.).—**Mk 7:37 v.l.;** 1 Cl 20:11.—TW.

ὑπερεκτείνω (Proclus, Theol. 59 p. 56, 35; Damasc., Princ. 284; Suda) ***stretch out beyond*** ὑπερεκτείνομεν ἑαυτούς *we are overextending ourselves* (beyond the limits set by God) **2 Cor 10:14.**—DELG s.v. τανυ- E.

ὑπερεκχύν(ν)ω (=ὑπερεκχέω; cp. ἐκχέω, beg.—For ὑπερεκχέω s. Diod. S. 11, 89, 4; Aelian, NA 12, 41; Artem. 2, 27; Jo 2:24; 4:13; Pr 5:16; Jos., Bell. 1, 407) ***pour out over,*** in our lit. only pass. (Hero Alex. I p. 26, 4; Philo, Ebr. 32) *overflow* ὑπερεκχυννόμενον **Lk 6:38.**—DELG s.v. χέω.

ὑπερεντυγχάνω (Clem. Alex., Paed. 1, 6, 47, 4 p. 118, 21f Stählin) **to intercede in behalf of another, *plead, intercede*** **Ro 8:26** (v.l. adds ὑπὲρ ἡμῶν, cp. a related construction involving ἐντυγχάνω w. κατά 'plead against' Ro 11:2)—M-M. TW.

ὑπερεπαινέω (Hdt., Aristoph. et al.) ***praise highly*** τὶ *someth.* (Aelian, VH 9, 30) IEph 6:2.—DELG s.v. αἶνος.

ὑπερευφραίνομαι (Arrian, Cyneg. 7, 2; Lucian, Icar. 2; Ps.-Lucian, Amor. 5; AcPlTh 7 [Aa I 241, 1]) ***rejoice exceedingly*** ἐπί τινι (Jos., Bell. 7, 14) B 1:2.—DELG s.v. φρήν.

ὑπερευχαριστέω (PTebt 12, 24 [118 BC]='am heartily grateful'; but ed. translates 'overjoyed'; Ar. Milne 261, 41; Eus., Martyr. Palaest. 11, 26) ***give heartiest thanks*** τινί *to someone*—B 5:3. DELG s.v. χάρις. M-M.

ὑπερέχω fut ὑπερέξω (Hom.+; ins, pap, LXX; En 24:3; TestJud 21:4; GrBar 10:3; ApcMos 38; Philo; Jos., Ant. 6, 25; Ath.)

❶ lit. **to be at a point higher than another on a scale of linear extent, *rise above, surpass, excel*** (Polyaenus 2, 2, 1) τὶ *someth* (3 Km 8:8; Jos., Ant. 1, 89) ἀνὴρ ὑψηλός, ὥστε τὸν πύργον ὑπερέχειν Hs 9, 6, 1.

❷ fig. **to be in a controlling position, *have power over, be in authority (over), be highly placed*** (οἱ ὑπερέχοντες='those in authority', 'superiors' Polyb. 28, 4, 9; 30, 4, 1 7; Herodian 4, 9, 2; Artem. 2, 9 p. 92, 17 H. [p. 109, 25 P.]; 2, 12 p. 102, 4 H. [p. 121, 21 P.]; PGM 4, 2169; of kings Wsd 6:5) βασιλεῖ ὡς ὑπερέχοντι **1 Pt 2:13.** ἐξουσίαι ὑπερέχουσαι *governing authorities* (Syntipas p. 127, 4) **Ro 13:1.** οἱ ὑπερέχοντες *those who are in high position* (cp. Epict. 3, 4, 3; Diog. L. 6, 78; Philo, Agr. 121) B 21:2, *those who are better off* (economically) Hv 3, 9, 5. λαὸς λαοῦ ὑπερέξει *one people shall rule over the other* B 13:2 (Gen 25:23).

❸ **to surpass in quality or value, *be better than, surpass, excel*—ⓐ** w. gen. (Ps.-X., Cyneg. 1, 11; Pla., Menex. 237d; Demosth. 23, 206; Diod. S. 17, 77, 3; PEdg 11 [=Sb 6717], 6 [257 BC]; Sir 33:7; Test Jud 21:4; GrBar 10:3; Ath. 6:2 [w. acc. 23:1]) ἀλλήλους ἡγούμενοι ὑπερέχοντας ἑαυτῶν *each one should consider the others better than himself* **Phil 2:3.** W. acc. (Eur., Hipp. 1365; X., Hell. 6, 1, 9; Da 5:11) of some angels who are greater than others ὑπερέχοντες αὐτούς Hv 3, 4, 2. ἡ εἰρήνη τοῦ θεοῦ ἡ ὑπερέχουσα πάντα νοῦν **Phil 4:7** (νοῦς 1b). Abs. ὑπερέχων *more excellent, superior* Hs 9, 28, 3; 4.

ⓑ The neut. of the pres. ptc. as subst. τὸ ὑπερέχον *the surpassing greatness* w. gen. τῆς γνώσεως *of personal acquaintance* (w. Christ; s. γνῶσις 1, end) **Phil 3:8.**—M-M. TW.

ὑπερηφανέω (ὑπερήφανος) 1 aor. ὑπερηφάνησα

❶ ***be proud, haughty,*** intr. (so Hom. and later wr. as Polyb. 6, 10, 8; BGU 48, 19 [III AD]; 2 Esdr 19:10; Jos., Bell. 3, 1, Ant. 4, 38) IEph 5:3.

❷ ***treat arrogantly/disdainfully, despise,*** trans. w. acc. (Polyb. 5, 33, 8; Lucian, Nigr. 31; POxy 1676, 16; PFlor 367, 12 [both III AD]; 4 Macc 5:21; Jos., Bell. 1, 344, Ant. 16, 194) δούλους IPol 4:3. τὰ δεσμά μου ISm 10:2.

ὑπερηφανία, ας, ἡ (Solon [cited Aristot., Ath. Pol. 5, 3], X., Pla. et al.; Alex. Ep. 14, 8 p. 204; LXX; En 5, 8; TestJob 15:8; Test12 Patr; EpArist 262; 269; Philo, Virt. 171; Jos., Ant. 1, 195; 16, 4; PGM 17a, 6; of the devil, the fallen angel ῥιφεὶς ἐπὶ γῆς διὰ τὴν ὑ. Did., Gen. 109, 6) **a state of undue sense of one's importance bordering on insolence, *arrogance, haughtiness, pride*** w. ἀλαζονεία 1 Cl 16:2. W. ἀλαζονεία and other vices 35:5; Hm 6, 2, 5; D 5:1. W. other vices (without ἀλαζ.) **Mk 7:22;** B 20:1; Hm 8:3; βδελυκτὴ ὑπ. 1 Cl 30:1. ὑπερηφανίαν μεγάλην ἐνδύσασθαι Hs 8, 9, 1.—DELG s.v. φαίνω. M-M. TW. Spicq.

ὑπερήφανος, ον (φαίνομαι) in our lit. only in an unfavorable sense (as Hes., Pla. et al.; Diod. S. 6, 7, 1–4 [Salmoneus was ἀσεβής as well as ὑπ. and was punished by Zeus, to whom he claimed to be superior by developing a machine that simulated claps of thunder; cp. 13, 21, 4 τοὺς ὑπερηφανοῦντας παρὰ θεοῖς μισουμένους; 20, 13, 3; 23, 12, 1; 24, 9, 2]; UPZ 144, 50 [164 BC, of Nemesis, whom Zeus threatens]; POxy 530, 28 [II AD]; LXX; PsSol 2:31; TestSol 5:3; JosAs 12:7; 2:1 cod. A [p. 40, 21 Bat.] and Pal. 364; EpArist; Jos., Ant. 4, 224; Tat. 3, 1) ***arrogant, haughty, proud*** **Lk 1:51** (on the διανοίᾳ καρδίας αὐτῶν s. διάνοια 2; PSchoonheim, NovT 8, '66, 235–46); **Ro 1:30** (w. ἀλαζών as Jos., Bell. 6, 172; in a list of vices as TestLevi 17:11; see also s.v. ὑβριστής); **2 Ti 3:2;** D 2:6. Opp. ταπεινός (after Pr 3:34; cp. EpArist 263; Diod. S. 13, 24, 6 Tyche ταπεινοῖ τοὺς ὑπερηφάνους; Cleobulus of Lindos in Stob. III p. 114, 3f H.; Xenophon of Ephesus 1, 2, 1 the god Eros is inexorable toward the ὑπ.) **Js 4:6; 1 Pt 5:5;** 1 Cl 30:2; cp. 59:3; IEph 5:3. ὑπ. αὐθάδεια 1 Cl 57:2. οὐδὲν ὑπερήφανον (cp. EpArist 170) 49:5.—B. 1146.—DELG s.v. φαίνω. M-M. TW. Spicq.

ὑπέρλαμπρος, ον ***exceedingly bright*** (of sound, Demosth. 18, 260. In the pap the word is used as an honorary title) of light (Aristoph., Nub. 571 ἀκτῖνες) χῶρος ὑπέρλαμπρος τῷ φωτί ApcPt 5:15 (cp. as omen in Or. Tiburt. 23).—DELG s.v. λάμπω.

ὑπερλίαν (Eustath. 1396, 42; 1184, 18) adv. (ὑπέρ + λίαν; B-D-F §12) ***exceedingly, beyond measure,*** as adj. οἱ ὑπερλίαν ἀπόστολοι the *super-apostles* **2 Cor 11:5; 12:11.** These are either the original apostles (so the older interpr., FBaur, Heinrici, HHoltzmann; KHoll, SBBerlAk 1921, 925; 936; EMeyer III 456; Rtzst., Mysterienrel.[3] 367ff; EKäsemann, ZNW 41, '42, 33–71) or, perh. w. more probability, the opponents of Paul in Corinth (OPfleiderer, Das Urchristentum[2] 1902, I 127 et al.; RBultmann, SymbOsl 9, '47, 23–30; WKümmel, Introd. to the NT, rev. ed. tr. HCKee, '73, 284–86).—M-M.

ὑπέρμαχος, ου, ὁ ***champion, defender*** (Archias [I BC]: Anth. Pal. 7, 147, 1; IKret I, xix 3, 29 [II BC]; LXX, Philo) of God

(2 Macc 14:34; Philo, Abr. 232; SibOr 3, 709) 1 Cl 45:7.—DELG s.v. μάχομαι.

ὑπερνικάω (Hippocr., Hebd. 50 [WRoscher 1913]; Menand., Monost. 299 Meineke [419 Jaekel] καλὸν τὸ νικᾶν, ὑπερνικᾶν δὲ σφαλερόν; Galen XIX 645 K.; Ps.-Libanius, Charact. Ep. p. 39, 24; Socrat., History of the Church 3, 21; Tactics of the Emperor Leo [MPG CVII 669–1120] 14, 25 νικᾷ, καὶ μὴ ὑπερνικᾷ=overcome, but no overkill; schol. on Eur., Hipp. 426 ὑπερνικάω as expl. for ἁμιλλάομαι; Hesych.; Ps 42:1 Sym.; Da 6:3 Theod.) as a heightened form of νικᾶν ***prevail completely*** ὑπερνικῶμεν *we are winning a most glorious victory* **Ro 8:37** (for the idea s. Epict. 1, 18, 22; Hermonax Delius [III or II BC] 2 p. 252 Coll.: νίκην κ. ὑπέρτερον εὖχος=victory and more than victory).—DELG s.v. νίκη. M-M. TW.

ὑπέρογκος, ον (X., Pla. et al.; LXX, Philo; Jos., Bell. 3, 471; TestAsh 2:8; 'of excessive size, puffed up, swollen') also ***haughty, pompous, bombastic*** (Plut., Mor. 1119b) of words (Arrian, Anab. 3, 10, 2; Aelian, fgm. 228; Ex 18:22, 26; cp. Himerius, Or. 69 [=Or. 22], 2 γλῶσσα ὑπέρογκος) λαλεῖν ὑπέρογκα **Jd 16** (cp. Da 11:36 Theod.); cp. **2 Pt 2:18.**—DELG s.v. 2 ὄγκος. M-M.

ὑπεροράω fut. ὑπερόψομαι; 2 aor. ὑπερεῖδον. Pass. fut. 3 sg. ὑπεροφθήσεται; pf. ptc. fem. ὑπερεωραμένη Na 3:11 (Hdt., Thu. et al.).

➊ **to disregard as not worthy of one's notice, *disdain, despise*** (Thu. et al.; Xen 1, 3, 4 Socrates disdains all human opinion in favor of divine guidance; PHamb 23, 36; LXX) w. acc. (since Hdt. 5, 69; Lev 26:37) τινά *someone* B 3:3 (cp. the pass. on which this is based, Is 58:7, where ὑπ. is also used, but is not trans.); D 15:2. τὸν κόσμον Dg 1.

➋ **to indulgently take no notice of, *overlook, disregard*** (Aristoxenus [300 BC], fgm. 89 Wehrli ['45]; Dionys. Hal. 5, 52, 2; δέομαι μὴ ὑπεριδεῖν με: PPetr II, 32, 1, 31; PRein 7, 26; PStras 98, 5 [all III/II BC]; Josh 1:5; Ps 9:22 al.; Philo, De Jos. 171; Jos., Bell. 2, 534, Ant. 6, 281; 14, 357) **Ac 17:30.**—Spicq.

ὑπεροχή, ῆς, ἡ gener. of a natural formation that protrudes 'projection, prominence', in our lit. only fig. (Pla.+; Polyb., Epict., Plut., ins, pap [ClPh 22, 1927, p. 245 no. 191, 11; PGM 1, 215]; LXX; TestSol 10:2; EpArist; Philo, Op. M. 109; Jos., Bell. 4, 171; Ath. 6, 1).

➊ **a state of excelling, *superiority, preeminence*** ἦλθον οὐ καθ' ὑπεροχὴν λόγου ἢ σοφίας *I have not come as a superior person* (κατά to denote kind and manner: κατά B 5bβ.—καθ' ὑπεροχήν: Aristot., HA 1, 1, 4) *in speech or* (human) *wisdom* (='to make it sound as if I were so wise' New Life Testament) **1 Cor 2:1** (cp. Eunap., Vi. Soph. p. 32 ὑπ. σοφίας; 50 λόγων ὑπ.). καθ' ὑπεροχὴν δοκοῦντες *being preeminent in reputation* 1 Cl 57:2 (s. Jos., Ant. 9, 3).

➋ **a state of high official rank, *authority*** of prominent officials οἱ ἐν ὑπεροχῇ ὄντες (Polyb. 5, 41, 3; IPergamon 252, 19f; PTebt 734, 24 [II BC]. Cp. 2 Macc 3:11; Jos., Ant. 9, 3) **1 Ti 2:2.**—B 1:2 v.l. (for ὑπερβολή).—DELG s.v. ἔχω. M-M. TW.

ὑπερπερισσεύω 1 aor. ὑπερεπερίσσευσα—➊ **to be very high on a scale of amount, *be in great excess*** intr. *be present in* (greater) *abundance* (Moschio, De Pass. Mulier., ed. FDewez 1793 p. 6, 13) **Ro 5:20.**

➋ **to cause someone to superabound in someth., *supply lavishly,*** trans. pass. w. act. sense ὑπερπερισσεύομαι τῇ χαρᾷ (on the dat. s. B-D-F §195, 2) *I am overflowing with joy* **2 Cor 7:4.**—DELG s.v. περί. TW.

ὑπερπερισσῶς adv. (B-D-F §12; 116, 3; Rob. 297) ***beyond all measure*** **Mk 7:37.**

ὑπερπλεονάζω 1 aor. ὑπερεπλεόνασα **to experience extraordinary abundance, *abound*** (Hero Alex. I p. 76, 14; Vett. Val. 85, 17; PsSol 5:16) **1 Ti 1:14.** Of a vessel that becomes too full ***run over, overflow*** Hm 5, 2, 5.—DELG s.v. πλείων. M-M. TW.

ὑπερσπουδάζω pf. ptc. ὑπερεσπουδακώς **to be very eager about some undertaking, *take great pains, be very eager*** (Menand., Sam. 219 S. [4 Kö.]; Lucian, Anach. 9; Philostrat., Vi. Apoll. 5, 26; Jos., Ant. 15, 69 ὑπερεσπουδακώς) ὑπερεσπουδακότα μανθάνειν *to learn* Dg 1.—DELG s.v. σπεύδω.

ὑπέρτατος, η, ον (Hom. et al.; SEG XLII, 846 p. 245; PStras 40, 41) superl. of ὑπέρ **pert. to the highest point on a scale of extent, *uppermost, loftiest, supreme*** (Aeschyl., Suppl. 672 of Zeus) God's ὑπερτάτη ὄψις 1 Cl 36:2. τῇ ὑπερτάτῃ (v.l. -τάτῳ adj. of two terminations) αὐτοῦ (i.e. God's) βουλήσει 40:3.—DELG s.v. ὑπέρ.

ὑπερτίθημι 2 aor. mid. ὑπερεθέμην (Pind., Hdt. as act. and mid. [the latter is quite predom. in ins, pap; Philo, Op. M. 156; Jos., Vi. 239; Just., D. 28, 2 and Tat. 35, 2 'postpone, defer']) mid. ***set aside, do away w.*** τὶ *someth.* (Appian, Illyr. 15 §45; cp. Pr 15:22) IMg 10:2.

ὑπερυψόω 1 aor. ὑπερύψωσα. Pass.: fut. 3 sg. ὑπερυψωθήσεται Da 11:12 v.l.; aor. 2 sg. ὑπερυψώθης Ps 96:9; pf. ptc. ὑπερυψωμένος LXX (Cat. Cod. Astr. XII p. 146, 31; cp. the astrological use of ὑψόω Neugebauer-Hoesen no. 81, 3 'the sun in exaltation [ὑψούμενος] in a male and northerly sign', sim. the noun ὕψωμα [s. p. 199 index]) **to raise to a high point of honor, *raise, exalt***

ⓐ act. *raise* τινά *someone to the loftiest height* (Synes., Ep. 79 p. 225a) **Phil 2:9** (cp. Ps 96:9, prob. the gods are astral deities; cp. Phil 2:10 ἐπουράνιοι).

ⓑ mid. *raise oneself, rise* 1 Cl 14:5 (=Ps 36:35).—DELG s.v. ὕψι. TW.

ὑπερφρονέω 1 aor. ὑπερεφρόνησα (Aeschyl., Hdt. et al.; 4 Macc; EpArist 122; Jos., Ant. 1, 194; Ath. 31, 2 'excel in intelligence') ***think too highly of oneself, be haughty*** (Ael. Aristid. 50, 19 K.=26 p. 507 D.) **Ro 12:3** (in wordplay w. φρονεῖν; cp. X., Mem. 4, 7, 6 παραφρονεῖν . . . φρονεῖν; Maximus Tyr. 18, 1c ἐσωφρόνει . . . ὑπερεφρόνει; Demetr. Phaler., fgm. 92 Wehrli ὑπερφρ. . . . καταφρ.).—DELG s.v. φρήν. M-M.

ὑπερῷον, ου, τό (cp. next entry; Hom.+; SEG II, 754; BGU 999 I, 6 [99 BC]; PFlor 285, 12; LXX; JosAs; Jos., Vi. 146 al. Really the neut. subst. of ὑπερῷος [q.v.], sc. οἴκημα [Philo, Mos. 2, 60]) ***upper story, room upstairs,*** also of the tower-like room (עֲלִיָּה) built on the flat roof of an oriental house **Ac 1:13** (here, too, a private house is meant [differently BThurston, ET 80, '68, 21f]; in JosAs Pharaoh's palace is in mind); **9:37, 39; 20:8;** 1 Cl 12:3.—FLuckhard, D. Privathaus im ptolem. u. röm. Ägypt. 1914, 72f.; comm. ad loc.—DELG s.v. ὑπερῴα. M-M.

ὑπερῷος, (α), ον (cp. prec. entry; Dionys. Hal., Plut. et al.; ins, pap; Ezk 42:5; Philo, Mos. 2, 60; Jos., Bell. 5, 221) **pert. to location in an upper area of a dwelling, *upstairs, in the upper story, under the roof*** δωμάτιον ὑπ. (s. δωμάτιον) MPol 7:1.—DELG s.v. ὑπερῴα.

ὑπέχω fut. inf. ὑφέξειν (Ath.); 2 aor. ὑπέσχον. Mid.: fut. 3 sg. ὑφέξεται PsSol (Hom.+; ins, pap, LXX [PsSol]) in our lit. only as a legal t.t. δίκην ὑπέχειν ***undergo punishment*** (Soph. et al. [δίκη 1]; PHal 1, 163 [III BC]; PFay 21, 25 [II AD] ὅπως τὴν προσήκουσαν δίκην ὑπόσχωσι; Mitt-Wilck. I/2, 469, 10; Jos., C. Ap. 2, 194, Ant. 1, 99; Ath. 3, 1) **Jd 7.** Also ὑπ. τιμωρίαν MPol 6:2 (Ath. 2, 1; cp. 2 Macc 4:48 ζημίαν ὑπ.; Theophyl. Sim., Ep. 68 ὑπ. κόλασιν).—M-M.

ὑπήκοος, ον (s. ὑπακούω; Aeschyl., Hdt.; ins, pap, LXX; EpArist 254; Philo, Joseph., Iren. Subst.: 'one who is in subjection' Just., D. 42, 3; Ath.) ***obedient*** **Phil 2:8.** W. dat. (X., Cyr. 2, 4, 22, Hell. 6, 1, 7; SIG 709, 13f; PPetr III, 53j, 10; PGM 5, 165 [the gen. is usual outside our lit.]; Pr 4:3; 13:1; Philo, Op. M. 72; τῇ ἐντολῇ Theoph. Ant. 2, 25 [p. 160, 12]) **Ac 7:39** (ὑπ. γενέσθαι as Jos., Ant.2, 48); 1 Cl 10:1; 13:3; 14:1; 60:4; 63:2. εἰς πάντα *in every respect* **2 Cor 2:9.**—B. 1328. DELG s.v. ἀκούω. M-M. TW. Sv.

ὑπήνεγκα s. ὑποφέρω.

ὑπηρεσία, ας, ἡ (fr. ὑπηρέτης, cp. ὑπηρετέω; orig. a 'body of rowers, ship's crew', then 'service' in gener.: Thu., Aristoph.+; Ael. Aristid. 28, 81 K.=49 p. 518 D.: ἡ τῷ θεῷ ὑπ.; Epict. 3, 24, 114: to God; ins, pap, LXX; TestJob 10:7; 15:1; ViDa 1 [p. 76, 13 Sch.]; SJCh 107, 7; Philo; Jos., Ant. 16, 184; Just., D. 131, 2; Tat. 17:3) ***service*** of Moses bringing judgment on Egypt 1 Cl 17:5; in satire: of earthenware used πρὸς τὴν ἀτιμοτάτην ὑπηρεσίαν *for the lowliest service* Dg 2:2.—DELG s.v. ὑπηρέτης.

ὑπηρετέω fut. 3 sg. ὑπηρετήσει Sir 39:4; aor. ὑπηρέτησα (cp. ὑπηρεσία; trag., Hdt.+; ins, pap, Wsd; Sir 39:4; TestAbr, TestJob; TestJos 14:3; JosAs 17:4; EpArist, Philo, Joseph., Just., Tat.; Ath. 37, 2) **to render service, *serve, be helpful*** w. dat. of pers. (Hyperid. 3, 39; PSI 502, 30 [257 BC]; JosAs 17:4; Just., A I, 17, 3) **Ac 24:23;** Hm 8:10; s 9, 10, 2. Δαυὶδ ὑπηρετήσας τῇ τοῦ θεοῦ βουλῇ **Ac 13:36** (Just., D, 125, 3; of obedience to God Aristaen., Ep. 1, 17 p. 148 H. ὑπ. θεῷ).—B 1:5. ἐν λόγῳ θεοῦ ὑπηρετεῖ μοι *he is of service to me in the word of God* IPhld 11:1. ὑπ. τί τινι *offer someth. (in helpfulness) to someone* (Epict. 4, 1, 37; Polyaenus 7, 23, 2; Lucian, Tim. 22; Jos., Ant. 14, 99) Dg 11:1. W. dat. of thing (PRev 22, 1 [258 BC]) ταῖς χρείαις μου **Ac 20:34** (cp. Jos., Ant. 13, 225; TestJob 11:1 τῇ διακονίᾳ; Just., D. 42, 3; Tat. 17, 3; on the motif s. JLambrecht, Paul's Farewell-Address at Miletus [Acts 20: 17–38]: Les Actes des Apôtres, ed. JKremer '78, 321 and 336). S. ὑπηρέτης.—DELG s.v. ὑπηρέτης. M-M. TW.

ὑπηρέτης, ου, ὁ (Aeschyl., Hdt.+; ins, pap, LXX; TestBenj 3:8; EpArist, Philo, Joseph., Just.; Tat. 4, 2; loanw. in rabb.; freq. as t.t. for a governmental or other official) **one who functions as a helper, freq. in a subordinate capacity, *helper, assistant*** (e.g. a physician's assistant: Hobart 88f; as adjutant: Arrian, Tact. 10, 4; 14, 4; the lictor beside the consul: Appian, Liby. 90 §424; the 20 senators with Pompey: Appian, Bell. Civ. 2, 18 §67; the priest's helpers: Diod. S. 1, 73, 3; the assistant to the ἡγούμενος of a cultic fellowship: Sb 7835, 11 [I BC]) Dg 7:2. John (Mark) as ὑπ. of Paul and Barnabas **Ac 13:5** (BHolmes, Luke's Description of John Mark: JBL 54, '35, 63–72; WHadorn, D. Gefährten u. Mitarbeiter des Pls: ASchlatter Festschr. 1922, 65–82; RTaylor, ET 54, '42/43, 136–38). Of the attendants of a board or court (Diod. S. 14, 5, 1f and Appian, Bell. Civ. 1, 31 §138 of attendants of the court; Diod. S. 17, 30, 4 παρέδωκε τοῖς ὑπηρέταις . . . ἀποκτεῖναι; Maximus Tyr. 3, 2b), of the Sanhedrin (Jos., Bell. 1, 655 παρέδωκεν τοῖς ὑπ. ἀνελεῖν, Ant. 4, 37 πέμψας ὑπ.; 16, 232) **Mt 5:25** (Ael. Aristid. 45 p. 68 D.: ὁ δικαστὴς παραδίδωσι τ. ὑπηρέταις 'deputies'); **26:58; Mk 14:54, 65; J 7:32, 45f; 18:3, 12, 22; 19:6; Ac 5:22, 26;** GJs 10:1; 15:2. W. δοῦλοι (as Pla., Polit. 289c [on this Collins 81–84, s. below]; Just., A I, 14, 1) **J 18:18.** Of a synagogue attendant (as prob. in the Roman-Jewish grave ins: RGarrucci, Dissertazioni archeologiche II 1865, p. 166 no. 22) **Lk 4:20** (ὑπ. as a title of cult officials: Thieme 33. Also Musaeus, fgm. 11 Diels [Paus. 10, 5, 6]: Pyrcon as Poseidon's ὑπηρέτης ἐς τὰ μαντεύματα; Dio Chrys. 19 [36], 33 ὑπ. τῶν τελετῶν; PLond 2710 recto, 11 [HTR 29, '36, p. 40; 50]). Of a king's retinue **J 18:36;** GJs 21:2; 23:1f. The apostles as assistants of Christ **Ac 26:16; 1 Cor 4:1** (Epict. 3, 22, 82 the Cynic as ὑπ. τοῦ Διός; Galen, Protr. 5 p. 12, 5 J.: Socr., Hom. et al. as ὑπ. τοῦ θεοῦ; Pythagorean saying: Wiener-Stud 8, 1886, p. 278 no. 105 τὸν εὐεργετοῦντά σε εἰς ψυχὴν ὡς ὑπηρέτην θεοῦ μετὰ θεὸν τίμα=one who has benefited you spiritually, esteem as God's helper after God; Sextus 319; Just., D. 57, 3). Believers gener. as θεοῦ ὑπηρέται (w. οἰκονόμοι [as 1 Cor 4:1] and πάρεδροι) IPol 6:1 (cp. PGM 59, 3; 5 and Jos., Bell. 2, 321, Ant. 3, 16).—Also w. objective gen. of that to which services are rendered (Appian, Bell. Civ. 3, 41 §169 τῆς πατρίδος ὑπ.; Wsd 6:4) ὑπηρέται τοῦ λόγου *ministers of the word* **Lk 1:2** (cp. the role of a scribe Sir 39:1–4; PMather, BR 30, '85, 28f). ἐκκλησίας θεοῦ ὑπηρέται *servants of God's assembly/church* ITr 2:3.—On the obscure οἱ τῶν ἐχθρῶν ὑπηρέται B 16:4 s. Windisch, Hdb. ad loc.—On the functions of the ὑπ. in Greco-Rom. Egypt, HKupiszewski and JModrzejewski, JJP XI and XII, '57/58, 141–66; JCollins, Diakonia '90, esp. 81–84, 173–75.—B. 1334. DELG. M-M. TW. Spicq. Sv.

ὑπισχνέομαι (cp. the collateral form ὑπέχομαι, s. L-S-J-M s.v. ὑπισχνέομαι) mid. dep. (Hom.+; ins, pap, LXX; ApcSed 16 p. 137, 8 Ja. [ὑπόσχομαι]; Philo; Jos., Ant. 11, 228, Vi. 111; SibOr 3, 769) 2 aor. ὑπεσχόμην ***promise*** w. dat., foll. by the aor. inf. Pol 5:2.—B. 1272. DELG.

ὕπνος, ου, ὁ (Hom.+) ***sleep*** lit. **Mt 1:24;** GJs 14:2 (a divine command in sleep, as e.g. ChronLind D, 68f; Diod. S. 1, 53, 9 Hephaestus κατ' ὕπνον; 5, 51, 4); **Lk 9:32; J 11:13;** καταφερόμενος ὕπνῳ βαθεῖ **Ac 20:9a** (Longus 1, 22, 3; =sopor altus Vergil, Aeneid 8, 27); cp. **9b;** sim. AcPl Ha 3, 26. Also in imagery (oft. Philo) ἐξ ὕπνου ἐγερθῆναι *wake from sleep,* i.e. bid farewell to the works of darkness **Ro 13:11** (for ἐξ ὕπνου cp. Appian, Liby. 21 §88).—DELG. M-M. TW.

ὑπνόω fut. ὑπνώσω LXX; 1 aor. ὕπνωσα intr. ***sleep, go to sleep*** (ὕπνος; Hippocr., Polyb. et al.; BGU 1141, 35 [14 BC]; LXX; En 100, 5; Test12Patr; JosAs 10:2; ParJer 5:2; Philo; Jos., Ant. 1, 208; Ath., R. 16 p. 68, 5 and 10) 1 Cl 26:2 (Ps 3:6).—DELG s.v. ὕπνος.

ὑπό (Hom.+; ins, pap, LXX, En, TestSol; TestAbr A; TestAbr B 14 p. 148, 20 [Stone p. 84 gen.]; TestJob, Test12Patr, JosAs, ParJer, GrBar [gen.], ApcEsdr [gen.], ApcSed [gen.], ApcMos [gen.], AscIs [gen.], EpArist, Philo, Joseph.; apolog. [in Ath. only gen.]) prep. w. gen. and acc., in our lit. not w. dat. (s. B-D-F §203; Rob. 634; for usage s. B-D-F §232; Rob. 633–36; w. dat. TestSol 13:6 C; Just., D. 126, 5; 132, 2).—Lit. s.v. ἀνά, beg.

A. w. gen. **marker of agency or cause, *by*** (in our lit. as well as the LXX no longer in a local sense)

ⓐ w. the pass. of a verb—**α.** w. gen. of pers. τὸ ῥηθὲν ὑπὸ κυρίου (cp. Gen 45:27; SIG 679, 85; Just., D. 44, 1 εἰρῆσθαι ὑπὸ τοῦ θεοῦ; τὰ εἰρημένα ὑπὸ τῶν προφητῶν) **Mt 1:22** (Jos., Ant. 8, 223 ὑπὸ τοῦ θεοῦ διὰ τ. προφήτου; Just., A I, 5,

4 διὰ Σωκράτους ὑπὸ λόγου); **2:15.** Cp. vs. **16; Mk 1:13; Lk 2:18; J 14:21; Ac 4:11; 1 Cor 1:11; 2 Cor 1:4; Gal 1:11; Eph 2:11; Phil 3:12; 1 Th 1:4;** 1 Cl 12:2; 2 Cl 1:2; Hm 4, 3, 6 and oft.; AcPlCor 2:7. Also w. the pass. in the sense 'allow oneself to be . . . by' **Mt 3:6, 13; Mk 1:5, 9.**

β. w. gen. of thing (cp. X., An. 1, 5, 5 ὑπὸ λιμοῦ ἀπολέσθαι; Diod. S. 5, 54, 3 ὑπὸ σεισμῶν διεφθάρησαν; Nicol. Dam.: 90 fgm. 22 p. 342, 17 Jac. ὑπὸ φαρμακῶν διαφθαρείς; Appian, Liby. 35 §147 ὑπὸ τοῦ χειμῶνος κατήγοντο, Bell. Civ. 4, 123 §515; Longus 2, 18 a nose smashed ὑπὸ πληγῆς τινος; Herm. Wr. 10, 4b; Tat. 8, 5 ὑπὸ βραχείας αὔρας νικηθείς; UPZ 42, 9 [162 BC]) καλύπτεσθαι ὑπὸ τῶν κυμάτων **Mt 8:24.** Cp. **11:7; 14:24; Lk 7:24; 8:14; Ac 27:41; Ro 3:21; 12:21; 1 Cor 10:29; 2 Cor 5:4; Col 2:18; Js 1:14; 3:4ab; 2 Pt 2:17; Jd 12; Rv 6:13;** Hm 10, 1, 4.

ⓑ w. verbs and verbal expressions that have a pass. sense πάσχειν ὑπό τινος (Mel., P. 75, 546ff; s. πάσχω 3aβ; 3b) **Mt 17:12; Mk 5:26; 1 Th 2:14ab.** ὑπὸ χειρὸς ἀνθρώπων παθεῖν B 5:5 (cp. Mel., P. 96, 737 ὑπὸ δεξιᾶς Ἰσραηλίτιδος). ἀπολέσθαι **1 Cor 10:9f** (Jos., Ant. 2, 300; cp. Sb 1209 Ἀπολλώνιος ἐτελεύτησεν ὑπὸ σκορπίου). ὑπομένειν ἀντιλογίαν **Hb 12:3.** τεσσεράκοντα παρὰ μίαν λαβεῖν **2 Cor 11:24.** ἃ . . . παρέλαβον ὑπὸ τῶν . . . ἀποστόλων *what I received from the apostles* AcPlCor 2:2; ὑπὸ τοῦ θεοῦ ἀναστάς *raised by God* Pol 9:2. γίνεσθαι ὑπό τινος *be done by someone* (s. γίνομαι 2a) **Lk 13:17; 23:8; Ac 20:3; 26:6; Eph 5:12.** Cp. **Ac 23:30 v.l.** The text of GJs 18:3 (not pap) is suspect. W. ὑπὸ γυναικός Hv 1, 2, 3 someth. like 'it was brought about' is to be supplied.

ⓒ w. nouns ἡ ἐπιτιμία ἡ ὑπὸ τῶν πλειόνων *the punishment at the hands of the majority* **2 Cor 2:6** (cp. X., Cyr. 3, 3, 2 ἡ ὑπὸ πάντων τιμή; SIG 1157, 10 διὰ τὰς εὐεργεσίας τὰς ὑπὸ τοῦ θεοῦ; Esth 1:20 ὁ νόμος ὁ ὑπὸ τοῦ βασιλέως).

ⓓ When used w. an act., ὑπό introduces the one through whose agency the action expressed by the verb becomes poss. (Hdt. 9, 98; Pla., Phlb. 66a ὑπ᾽ ἀγγέλων φράζειν='say through messengers'; cp. Herm. Wr. 9, 9 ὑπὸ δεισιδαιμονίας βλασφημεῖν; Just., D. 2, 6 ὑπὸ βλακείας ἤλπιζον αὐτίκα κατόψεσθαι τὸν θεόν=in my stupidity I thought that I would forthwith look upon God) ἀποκτεῖναι ὑπὸ τῶν θηρίων **Rv 6:8.** ὑπὸ ἀγγέλου βλέπεις *you see under the guidance of an angel* Hs 9, 1, 2b; cp. ibid. 2a and s. Mayser II/2, 511f; to the ref. there add PLeid XI, 1, col. 1, 15.

B. w. acc.—**❶ a position below an object or another position, *under,*** w. acc. of place *under, below*—ⓐ answering the question 'whither?' ἔρχεσθαι 1 Cl 16:17; Hs 8, 1, 1 (PsSol 18:7). εἰσέρχεσθαι ὑπὸ τὴν στέγην **Mt 8:8** (cp. Ar. 15, 7 ὑπὸ στέγην εἰσάγουσιν); **Lk 7:6.** συνάγειν 1 Cl 12:6. ἐπισυνάγειν **Mt 23:37; Lk 13:34.** τιθέναι **Mt 5:15; Mk 4:21ab; Lk 11:33.** κρύπτειν (cp. Job 20:12) 1 Cl 12:3. Also *(below) at* κάθου ὑπὸ τὸ ὑποπόδιόν μου **Js 2:3** (cp. ParJer 5:1 ἐκάθισεν ὑπὸ τὴν σκίαν; Just., D. 107, 3). ὑπὸ τοὺς πόδας *under the feet* (Hdt. 7, 88, 1) **1 Cor 15:25, 27; Eph 1:22.** ὁ θεὸς συντρίψει τὸν σατανᾶν ὑπὸ τοὺς πόδας ὑμῶν *God will crush Satan so that he will lie at your feet* **Ro 16:20.**

ⓑ in answer to the question 'where?' (Il. 5, 267; Ael. Aristid. 39 p. 734 D.: τὰ ὑπὸ τὸν ἥλιον; Maximus Tyr. 35, 5b) **Mk 4:32.** ὄντα ὑπὸ τὴν συκῆν **J 1:48.** Cp. **Ro 3:13** (Ps 13:3; 139:4); **1 Cor 10:1; Jd 6.** ὑπὸ τὸν οὐρανόν *under heaven*=on earth **Ac 4:12;** as adj. ὁ ὑπὸ τὸν οὐρανόν *(found) under heaven*=on earth (Demosth. 18, 270; UPZ 106, 14 [99 BC] τῶν ὑπὸ τὸν οὐρανὸν χωρῶν; Just., A II, 5, 2; cp. without the art. PsSol 2:32; TestAbr A 15 p. 96, 5 [Stone p. 40]) **2:5; Col 1:23;** Hm 12, 4, 2; ἡ ὑπὸ τὸν οὐρανόν (χώρα to be supplied; cp. Ex 17:14; Job 28:24) **Lk 17:24a;** cp. **b.** ὑπὸ ζυγὸν δοῦλοι (ζυγός 1) **1 Ti 6:1.**

❷ marker of that which is in a controlling position, *under, under the control of, under obligation* in ref. to power, rule, sovereignty, command, etc. w. acc. (OGI 56, 13 [237 BC] ὑπὸ τὴν βασιλείαν τασσόμενοι; PHib 44 [253 BC] et al. in pap; Just., D. 52, 4 εἶναι . . . ὑπὸ ἴδιον βασιλέα) ἄνθρωπος ὑπὸ ἐξουσίαν τασσόμενος (ἐξουσία 4) **Lk 7:8a;** cp. **Mt 8:9a;** Hs 1:3 (Vett. Val. 209, 35 ὑπὸ ἑτέρων ἐξουσίαν ὄντας). ἔχων ὑπ᾽ ἐμαυτὸν στρατιώτας (Polyb. 4, 87, 9 Μεγαλέαν ὑφ᾽ αὑτὸν εἶχεν) **Mt 8:9b; Lk 7:8b** (OGI 86, 11 [III BC] οἱ ὑπ᾽ αὐτὸν τεταγμένοι στρατιῶται). ὑπό τινα εἶναι *be under someone's power* (Thu. 6, 86, 4; PSI 417, 36 [III BC] ὑπὸ τὸν ὅρκον εἶναι) **Gal 3:25; 4:2;** ὑφ᾽ ἁμαρτίαν **Ro 3:9;** ὑπὸ νόμον **6:14, 15** (both opp. ὑπὸ χάριν); **1 Cor 9:20abcd; Gal 4:21; 5:18;** ὑπὸ κατάραν **3:10.** ὑπὸ νόμον ἐφρουρούμεθα vs. **23.** γενόμενος ὑπὸ νόμον **Gal 4:4** (γίνομαι 9d and Thu. 1, 110, 2 Αἴγυπτος ὑπὸ βασιλέα ἐγένετο). ὑπὸ τὰ στοιχεῖα τοῦ κόσμου ἤμεθα δεδουλωμένοι vs. **3.** συνέκλεισεν ἡ γραφὴ τὰ πάντα ὑπὸ ἁμαρτίαν **3:22** (s. συγκλείω 2). πεπραμένος ὑπὸ τὴν ἁμαρτίαν **Ro 7:14.** ταπεινώθητε ὑπὸ τὴν χεῖρα τοῦ θεοῦ **1 Pt 5:6** (s. ταπεινόω 3); cp. οὐκ ἔκλινας τὴν κεφαλήν σου ὑπὸ τὴν κραταιὰν χεῖραν GJs 15:4; τὸ αἷμά σου ὑπὸ τὴν χεῖράν μού ἐστιν 23:2. οἱ ὑπὸ νόμον *those who are under (the power of, obligation to) the law* **Gal 4:5** (Just., D. 45, 3 [w. art.]; cp. X., Cyr. 3, 3, 6 τινὰς τῶν ὑφ᾽ ἑαυτούς).

❸ marker of the approximate time of a period, *about* w. acc. (w. varying degrees of precision: in earlier Gk.: Aristoph et al.; PTebt 50, 18 [112 BC]; Jos., Ant. 14, 420. Rare in LXX and our lit.) ὑπὸ τὸν ὄρθρον *about daybreak* **Ac 5:21** (s. ὄρθρος).

❹ Special uses—ⓐ ὑφ᾽ ἕν *at one stroke* (Epict. 3, 22, 33; Wsd 12:9; Just., D. 65, 3 of topics treated 'collectively') B 4:4. ὑπὸ χεῖρα *continually* (see s.v. χείρ 3) Hv 3, 10, 7; 5, 5; m 4, 3, 6.

ⓑ ὑπὸ τὰ ἴχνη IEph 12:2 is translated *in the footsteps.* Can ὑπό mean this, someth. like Ezk 13:8 (ed. JZiegler '52 v.l.), where it stands for עַל? But if it = 'under', then τὰ ἴχνη would require a different interpretation. See ἴχνος 2. S. the grammarians: Kühner-Gerth II/1 521–26; Schwyzer II 522–23; Mayser II/2 509–15; Radermacher 114–19.—DELG. M-M.

ὑποβάλλω 2 aor. ὑπέβαλον (Hom.+ in various senses) ***instigate (secretly), suborn*** (Da 3:9 Theod. v.l.; TestSim 3:3; Just., D. 49, 4 [w. dat.]; Appian, Bell. Civ. 1, 74 §341 ὑπεβλήθησαν κατήγοροι;—ὑπόβλητος='secretly instigated' Jos., Bell. 5, 439) τινά *someone* **Ac 6:11;** MPol 17:2a. ταῦτα ὑποβαλλόντων Ἰουδαίων (they said) *this because the Judeans instigated them* 17:2b.—M-M.

ὑπογραμμός, οῦ, ὁ lit. 'model, pattern' to be copied in writing or drawing (2 Macc 2:28; cp. ὑπογράφειν Pla., Protag. 326d; also Just.), then **a model of behavior, *example*** (Ps.-Clem., Hom. 4, 16; cp. Pla., Leg. 4, 711b πάντα ὑπογράφειν τῷ πράττειν) of Paul ὑπομονῆς γενόμενος μέγιστος ὑπογραμμός 1 Cl 5:7. Mostly of Christ **1 Pt 2:21;** 1 Cl 16:17; 33:8; τοῦτον ἡμῖν τὸν ὑπογραμμὸν ἔθηκε δι᾽ ἑαυτοῦ Pol 8:2.—DELG s.v. γράφω. M-M.

ὑποδεής, ές (δέομαι)—**❶ pert. to being in a lower position, *inferior*** in gener. lit. (Hdt. et al., likew. IG IV²/1, 91, 3 [III AD]; pap, Joseph.) always in the comp. ὑποδεέστερος, α, ον, pl. οἱ ὑποδεέστεροι 'those who are inferior'; so also Dg 10:5.

❷ pert. to being responsive to authority, *subservient* in a transf. sense as sing. subst. τὸ ὑποδεές τινος *someone's subordination* (w. τὸ ταπεινόφρον) 1 Cl 19:1.—DELG s.v. ὑπό.

ὑπόδειγμα, ατος, τό (s. ὑποδείκνυμι; rejected by the Atticists in favor of παράδειγμα [Lob. on Phryn. p. 12]. It is found in X., Equ. 2, 2, b and Philo Mech. 69, 10, then fr. Polyb. on [exx. fr. lit. in FBleek, Hb II/1, 1836, 555]; Vett. Val.; IPriene 117, 57 [I BC]; OGI 383, 218; BGU 1141, 43 [I BC]; PFay 122, 16; LXX; EpArist 143; Philo, Joseph.)

❶ **an example of behavior used for purposes of moral instruction, *example, model, pattern*** (schol. on Nicander, Ther. 382=example; Polyb. 3, 17, 8; Sir 44:16) in a good sense as someth. that does or should spur one on to imitate it 1 Cl 5:1ab (τὰ γενναῖα ὑποδείγματα); 6:1 (ὑπόδειγμα κάλλιστον.—Jos., Bell. 6, 103 καλὸν ὑπόδειγμα; Philo, Rer. Div. Her. 256); 46:1; 55:1; 63:1. ὑπόδειγμα ἔδωκα ὑμῖν (cp. 2 Macc 6:28) **J 13:15.** W. gen. of thing (Sir 44:16; 2 Macc 6:31) **Js 5:10.**—In ἵνα μὴ ἐν τῷ αὐτῷ τις ὑποδείγματι πέσῃ τῆς ἀπειθείας **Hb 4:11,** ὑπόδειγμα refers not to an example of disobedience (as BGU 747 II, 13f [139 AD] ὑπόδιγμα τῆς ἀπειθίας), but to an example of falling into destruction as a result of disobedience.—A warning *example* (Cornutus 27 p. 51, 16; Vi. Aesopi W c. 95 πρὸς ὑπόδειγμα=as a warning example; Jos., Bell. 2, 397) Sodom and Gomorrah are ὑπόδειγμα μελλόντων ἀσεβεῖν *for the godless people of the future* **2 Pt 2:6** (εἰς τὸ δεῖγμα P^{72}). Of Judas μέγα … ἀσεβείας ὑπόδειγμα *a striking example of impiety* Papias (3:2).

❷ **an indication of someth. that appears at a subsequent time, *outline, sketch, symbol*** ὑπόδειγμα καὶ σκιά **Hb 8:5; 9:23** (Ezk 42:15; s. ELee, NTS 8, ’61/62, 167–69: ‘suggestion’; LHurst, JTS 34, ’83, 156–68).—PKatz, Biblica 33, ’52, 525.—DELG s.v. δείκνυμι. M-M. TW. Spicq.

ὑποδείκνυμι or ύω fut. ὑποδείξω; 1 aor. ὑπέδειξα. Pass.: 1 fut. 3 sg. ὑποδειχθήσεται Sir 14:12 v.l.; aor. 3 sg. ὑπεδείχθη Sir 3:23; 14:12; pf. ptc. n. pl. ὑποδεδειγμένα Esth 2:9 v.l. (Hdt., Thu.+) ‘show, indicate’.

❶ **to direct someone’s attention to someth., *indicate, point out,*** lit. τινί *to someone* ὑποδεικνύουσα αὐτοῖς ἐναλλάξ *as she pointed in the wrong direction* 1 Cl 12:4. Also of visions granted martyrs to whom the Lord has shown the eternal blessings that no earthly eye can behold, pass. MPol 2:3.

❷ **to give instruction or moral direction, *show, give direction, prove, set forth,*** fig. ext. of 1, τὶ *someth.* (TestJob 4:1; GrBar 1:8; Jos., Ant. 2, 21) B 1:8. Otherw. always w. dat. of pers. τινί *(to) someone:* foll. by a rel. clause (TestJob 1:4; Ath., R. 23 p. 77, 8) **Ac 9:16;** foll. by an inf. *warn* **Mt 3:7; Lk 3:7;** foll. by ὅτι (TestNapht 8:1; ApcMos 23; s. B-D-F §397, 4) **Ac 20:35** (πάντα=‘at every opportunity’); foll. by indirect question (TestJob 3:2) **Lk 6:47; 12:5.**—M-M.

ὑποδέχομαι mid. dep.; fut. 3 pl. ὑποδέξονται 4 Macc 13:17; 1 aor. ὑπεδεξάμην; pf. ὑποδέδεγμαι (Hom. et al.; ins [e.g. IG X/2, 255, 5; 17], pap, LXX; TestSol 16:2; TestAbr; Philo) **to receive hospitably, *receive, welcome, entertain as a guest*** τινά *someone* (POslo 55, 8 [c. 200 AD]; TestAbr 2 p. 78, 20 [Stone p. 4]; Jos., Ant. 1, 180 al.) **Lk 10:38; 19:6; Ac 17:7; Js 2:25;** ISm 10:1; AcPl Ant 13, 10 (=Aa I 237, 1). τινὰ εἰς τὴν οἰκίαν (Chion, Ep. 2 εἰς τὴν οἰκίαν ὑποδέχεσθαι αὐτόν) **Lk 10:38 v.l.** (s. οἰκία; RBorger TRu 52, ’87, 32f); cp. Hs 8, 10, 3; 9, 27, 2 (ὑπ. τινα εἰς as 1 Macc 16:15).—M-M.

ὑποδέω (Aristot. et al.; 2 Ch 28:15) predom. mid. in our lit. (aor. act. ὑπέδησα only LXX) and elsewh.: **ὑποδέομαι** (so Hdt., Aristoph. et al.) 1 aor. ὑπεδησάμην; pf. ptc. ὑποδεδεμένος ***tie/bind beneath, put on,*** of footwear (so the mid. since Alcaeus 21 Diehl[2] [318 L-P.]); w. acc. either of what is put on the foot (Hdt. et al.; ὑποδήματα X., Mem. 1, 6, 6; Pla., Gorg. 490e; PGM 4, 934; 2123 σάνδαλα; 7, 729 ὑποδήματα) ὑπόδησαι τὰ σανδάλιά σου **Ac 12:8;** cp. **Mk 6:9,** or of a part of the body that is covered (foot Thu. 3, 22, 2 τὸν ἀριστερὸν πόδα ὑποδεδεμένος; Lucian, Hist. Conscrib. 22; Aelian, VH 1, 18) τοὺς πόδας *put shoes on the feet* **Eph 6:15.**—DELG s.v. 1 δέω. M-M. TW.

ὑπόδημα, ατος, τό (ὑποδέω; Hom.+; ins, pap, LXX; PsSol 2:2; TestZeb; Jos., Bell. 6, 85; Just.) **a leather sole that is fastened to the foot by means of straps, *sandal.*** Pl. (τὰ) ὑποδήματα **Mt 3:11; 10:10; Mk 1:7; Lk 3:16; 10:4; 15:22; 22:35;** Hv 4, 2, 1 (on Mt 10:10; Lk 10:4 s. FSpitta, ZWT 55, 1913, 39–45; ibid. 166f; SKrauss, Αγγελος I 1925, 96–102; JKleist, The Gospel of St. Mark ’36, 257f). The sing. as a collective *footwear* (TestZeb 3:4f) **J 1:27.** W. gen. τῶν ποδῶν (cp. Ps.-Pla., Alc. 1, 128a ποδός) **Ac 13:25.** On holy ground τὸ ὑπόδημα τῶν ποδῶν must be taken off **7:33** (cp. Ex 3:5; Josh 5:15.—SIG 338, 25); s. JHeckenbach, De Nuditate Sacra 1911, 40ff; FPfister, ARW 9, 1906, 542; OWeinreich, Hessische Blätter für Volkskunde 10, 1911, 212f; Pauly-W. II 741–58; Kl. Pauly V 37f; BHHW III 1738.—B. 428. DELG s.v. 1 δέω. M-M. TW.

ὑπόδικος, ον (Aeschyl.+; ins, pap, GrBar 4:9; Philo; Jos., Vi. 74; Ath., R. 18 p. 70, 27; 21 p. 74, 20) **pert. to being liable to judgment/punishment, *answerable, accountable*** (Pla., Leg. 9, 871b et al.; ins; PFay 22, 9 [I BC] τῷ ἀδικουμένῳ) τῷ θεῷ **Ro 3:19.**—DELG s.v. δίκη. M-M. TW.

ὑπόδουλος, ον (Physiogn. II 345, 15; SibOr 12, 130) ***enslaved, subject as a slave*** γίνεσθαί τινι ὑπ. *become enslaved to someone* (Ps.-Clem., Hom. 8, 20) Hm 12, 5, 4: since the victims of the devil began as ‘slaves’ of God, the Shepherd contrasts their later condition by the intensive form ὑ.

ὑποδραμών s. ὑποτρέχω.

ὑποδύομαι 1 aor. ptc. pl. ὑποδύσαντες Jdth 6:13; pf. ὑποδέδυκα; plpf. ὑποδεδύκειν (Hom. et al.; Jos., Ant. 15, 282 al.) ***get under, take one’s place under*** ὑπό τι *(under) someth.* (Hdt. 1, 31): ὑπὸ τὰς γωνίας τοῦ λίθου *under the corners of the stone* Hs 9, 4, 1a. ἐκ τῶν πλευρῶν *along the sides* ibid. b.—DELG s.v. δύω.

ὑποζύγιον, ου, τό (Theognis, Hdt.+; ins, pap, LXX, Philo; Jos., Ant. 14, 471 al.; Ath. 31, 3) orig. ‘draught animal, beast of burden’ (lit. ‘under the yoke’) hence ‘pack animal’ (acc. to X., Oec. 18, 4 oxen, mules, horses) in our lit. ***donkey, ass*** (as schol. on Pla. 260c; PHib 34, 3; 5; 73, 9; s. Mayser II/1, 31; WBauer, JBL 72, ’53, 226) **Mt 21:5** (Zech 9:9); **2 Pt 2:16.**—DELG s.v. ζεύγνυμι III. M-M.

ὑποζώννυμι pres. ptc. ὑποζωννύς; aor. impv. ὑπόζωσον PsSol 17:22; pf. pass. ptc. fem. pl. ὑπεζωσμέναι 2 Macc 3:19 (Hdt. et al.; LXX; Jos., Bell. 2, 275, Vi. 293) ***undergird, brace,*** nautical t.t.: provide a ship w. ὑποζώματα (Pla., Rep. 616c; Athen. 5, 204a=funibus Horace, Odes 1, 14, 6; the technology is expressed in a joke Aristoph., Equ. 279), i.e. w. cables that go around the outside of the hull, and in the case of merchantmen, under it (s. Casson below), to give the ship greater firmness in a heavy sea (the verb has this mng. in Polyb. 27, 3, 3; IG I[2], 73, 9) **Ac 27:17.**—ABoeckh, Urkunden über das Seewesen des attischen Staates 1840, 134ff; TWoolsey, On an Expression in Ac 27:17, The American Biblical Repository 8, 1842, 405–12; JSmith, The Voyage and Shipwreck of St. Paul[4] 1880, 107ff; 204ff; Breusing 170–82; HBalmer, Die Romfahrt des Ap. Paulus 1905, 160–64;

ESchauroth, HSCP 22, 1911, 173–79; CVoigt, Die Romfahrt des Ap. Pls.: Hansa 53, 1916, 728f; FBrannigan, ThGl 25, '33, 182; HCadbury, Beginn. I/5, '33, 345–54; LCasson, Ships and Seamanship, etc., '71, 91f, 211; comm.—M-M.

ὑποκάτω adv. ***under, below*** (Pla. et al.; TestJob 27:3, 4, 5) in our lit. functions only as a prep. w. gen. (Pla.+; Ocellus Luc. c. 37 ὑ. σελήνης; ins, pap, LXX, En, TestSol; TestAbr A 16 p. 97, 13 [Stone p. 42]; TestIss 1:5; JosAs; Jos., Bell. 7, 289, Ant. 9, 12.—B-D-F §215, 2; 232, 1; Rob. 637) *under, below, down at* **Mt 22:44; Mk 6:11; 7:28; 12:36; Lk 8:16; J 1:50** (ὑπὸ τὴν συκῆν P[66]); **Hb 2:8** (Ps 8:7); **Rv 5:3, 13; 6:9; 12:1;** GJs 2:4.—M-M.

ὑποκάτωθεν adv. 'from below' (Pla., Leg. 6, 761b; Cyranides p. 61, 9; LXX; TestSol 11:7 C) funct. as prep. w. gen. (JosAs 2:20) ***(from) under*** ὑπ. τοῦ οὐρανοῦ 1 Cl 53:3 (Dt 9:14).

ὑπόκειμαι used as pass. of διατίθημι; dep. (Hom.+; w. a variety of mngs.)

❶ **to be in a position at a lower level than another position, *lie below,*** lit.—ⓐ *lie/be underneath* ὑπέκειτο αὐτοῖς πῦρ ApcPt 7:22.

ⓑ *lie below, be recessed* ἐν τῷ ὀφθαλμῷ *in the eye* **Lk 6:42** D.

❷ **to be exposed to someth. that threatens one's well-being, *be subject to, be exposed to,*** fig. (Philostrat., Vi. Apoll. 6, 41 p. 252, 11 τῷ φόβῳ; Jos., C. Ap. 1, 9) κινδύνῳ 1 Cl 41:1.

ὑποκρίνομαι 1 aor. mid. inf. ὑποκρίνασθαι 4 Macc 6:17; aor. mid.-pass. ὑπεκρίθην, B-D-F §78 (Hom. et al. mng. 'answer'=Attic ἀποκρ.; then in Attic 'play a part on the stage'; EpArist 219; Philo, Conf. Lingu. 48; Joseph.) ***pretend, make believe, dissemble*** (since Demosth.; Polyb.; LXX) foll. by the acc. and inf. (w. inf. foll.: Demosth. 31, 8; Polyb. 2, 49, 7; Appian, Hann. 16 §71; 4 Macc 6:15; Jos., Bell. 1, 520, Ant. 12, 216, Vi.36) **Lk 20:20** (B-D-F §157, 2; 397, 2; 406, 1; Rob. 481; 1036; 1038–40). Abs. of behavior, to pretend to be someth. that one is not *play a role, act a part, dissemble* (Epict. 2, 9, 20; Appian, Bell. Civ. 2, 10, §34; Polyaenus 8, 29; LXX) Hs 9, 19, 3.—DELG s.v. κρίνω. TW. Spicq.

ὑπόκρισις, εως, ἡ (ὑποκρίνομαι; Hdt.+='answer', then Attic 'playing a stage role') in our lit. only in a neg. sense **to create a public impression that is at odds with one's real purposes or motivations, *play-acting, pretense, outward show, dissembling*** (loanword in Engl. 'hypocrisy'; Polyb. 15, 17, 2; 35, 2, 13; Diod. S. 1, 76, 1; Appian, Hann. 19 §83, Syr. 61 §319, Mithrid. 14, 48; Ps.-Lucian, Amor. 3; Aesop 284 H.=166 H-H.; 2 Macc 6:25; Ps 4:6; Philo, Rer. Div. Her. 43, De Jos. 67; Jos., Bell. 1, 628, Ant. 16, 216; TestBenj 6:5; Hippol, Ref. 9, 11, 13; Did., Gen. 128, 18) **Mt 23:28; Mk 12:15; Lk 12:1; Gal 2:13; Js 5:12 v.l.** πᾶσαν ὑπόκρισιν; B 19:2; 20:1; 21:4; D 4:12; Hm 8:3. Pl. of the varied forms that pretentious piety assumes **1 Pt 2:1;** D 5:1.—ἐν ὑποκρίσει ψευδολόγων *misled by smooth talkers* **1 Ti 4:2.** ἐν ὑποκρίσει *insincerely* (schol. on Soph., El. 164 p. 111 Papag.) Pol 6:3; Hv 3, 6, 1; m 2:5; s 8, 6, 2. Also μεθ' ὑποκρίσεως 1 Cl 15:1. κατὰ μηδεμίαν ὑπόκρισιν *without any pretense at all* IMg 3:2 (κατὰ ὑπ. as schol. on Soph., Oed. Col. 1232 p. 451). ἄτερ ὑποκρίσεως *without pretense* Hs 9, 27, 2 (Leutzsch, Hermas p. 417 n. 338; p. 494 n. 432).—DELG s.v. κρίνω. M-M. TW. Spicq.

ὑποκριτής, οῦ, ὁ (ὑποκρίνω; Aristoph., X., Pla.+; ins; PEdg 71 [=Sb 6777], 44 mostly in the sense 'play-actor, role-player'; so also EpArist 219; Tat. 22, 1) in our lit. only metaph. ***actor,*** in the sense ***pretender, dissembler*** (Achilles Tat. 8, 8, 14; 8, 17, 3; Artem. 2, 44 p. 148, 3 in the marginal note of a ms.; Jos., Bell. 2, 587 ὑποκριτὴς φιλανθρωπίας; Did., Gen. 122, 9.—Job 15:34 Aquila and Theod. of the godless [=LXX ἀσεβής]; 20:5 Aquila [=LXX παράνομος]; 34:30 and 36:13 Theod.) **Mt 6:2, 5, 16** (in these three passages the dramatic aspect 'play-actor' is strongly felt); **7:5; 15:7; 16:3 v.l.; 22:18; 23:13–15, 23, 25, 27, 29; 24:51; Mk 7:6; Lk 6:42; 11:39** D; **12:56; 13:15;** Hs 8, 6, 5; 9, 18, 3; 9, 19, 2; D 2:6; 8:1f.—PJoüon, Ὑποκριτής dans l'Evang.: RSR 20, 1930, 312–17; DMatheson, ET 41, 1930, 333f; LMarshall, Challenge of NT Ethics '47, 60f; BZucchelli, ΥΠΟΚΡΙΤΗΣ, Origine e storia del termine '62; RBatey, Jesus and the Theatre: NTS 30, '84, 563–74; AStock, Jesus, Hypocrites, and Herodians: BTB 16, '86, 3–7 (theaters in many Palestinian localities).—DNP V 810–12. M-M.

ὑπολαμβάνω 2 aor. ὑπέλαβον; pf. ὑπείληφα (Just.), ptc. pl. ὑπειληφότες Wsd 17:2; pf. pass. impv. 3 sg. ὑπειλήφθω (Tat. 36, 1) (Hom.+; ins, pap, LXX, En; TestSol 1:4 L; TestAbr A, TestJob, Just., Tat.; Ath., R. 20 p. 73, 20)

❶ **to cause to ascend, *take up*** τινά *someone* (Jos., Ant. 11, 238) νεφέλη ὑπέλαβεν αὐτὸν ἀπὸ τῶν ὀφθαλμῶν αὐτῶν *a cloud took him up, out of their sight* **Ac 1:9.**

❷ **to take someone under one's care, *receive as a guest, support*** (X., An. 1, 1, 7; Diod. S. 19, 67, 1; Jos., C. Ap. 1, 247) **3J 8.**

❸ **to give an answer to what is said, *reply,*** abs. (lit. 'take up' on what is said; difft. from our colloq. 'take up on' in the sense of a favorable reply) (ὑπολαβὼν ἔφη etc.; Hdt. 7, 101; Thu. 3, 113, 3; Diod. S. 9, 25, 2; 37, 13, 1 al.; Aesop, Fab. 252 P.=Ch 181=H-H. 268 [difft. H. 225]; 4 Macc 8:13) ὑπολαβὼν ὁ Ἰησοῦς εἶπεν **Lk 10:30** (ὑπολαβὼν ὁ . . . εἶπεν as Diod. S. 17, 37, 6 ὁ βασιλεὺς ὑπολαβὼν εἶπε with direct quot.; Prodicus fgm. 2 [in X., Mem. 2, 1, 29]; Job 2:4; TestAbr A 5 p. 82, 30 [Stone p. 12]; 7 p. 83, 33f [Stone p. 14]; TestJob 37, 5 al. [w. ὅτι 36:4]; cp. Philostrat., Vi. Apoll. 1, 36 p. 38, 8; Jos., Ant. 7, 184).

❹ **to consider to be probable, *assume, think, believe, be of the opinion (that), suppose*** (X., Pla. et al.; ins, pap, LXX, En; Philo; Jos., C. Ap. 2, 162; 250; Just., A I, 33, 9; Tat. 36, 1) **Ac 2:15.** Foll. by ὅτι (Pla., Phd. 86b; Ps.-Callisth. 1, 46a, 9; En 106:6; EpArist 201; Philo, Rer. Div. Her. 300; Just., D. 138, 3) **Lk 7:43;** 1 Cl 35:9 (Ps 49:21); GPt 8:30.—W. inf. and acc. (Thu.) Papias (2:4) (Just., D. 47, 4; Ath., R. 20 p. 73:20).—M-M. TW.

ὑπολαμπάς, άδος, ἡ occurs as a **v.l.** at **Ac 20:8** where, instead of ἦσαν λαμπάδες ἱκαναὶ ἐν τῷ ὑπερῴῳ, D reads ἦσαν ὑπολαμπάδες κτλ. In its other occurrences, except JosAs below, the word refers to an opening such as ***window*** (L-S-J-M s.v.; cp. Phylarchus [III BC]: 81 fgm. 40 Jac.; ins fr. Delos: SIG[2] 588, 219 [II BC].—HSmith, ET 16, 1905, 478; Mlt-H. 328). This could be the mng. of the v.l., given the probability of a copyist's literary logic in preparing the auditor/reader for the fall of Eutychus, but s. JosAs 14:9 cod. A p. 59, 17 Bat. ὑπολαμπάδος καιομένης, where the sense is ***torch.***—DELG s.v. λάμπω. M-M.

ὑπόλειμμα (not ὑπόλιμμα, as W-H. spell it; see W-H. App. 154), **ατος, τό** (Hippocr., Aristot. et al.; PSI 860, 8 [III BC]; LXX) **a relatively small surviving group, *remnant*** **Ro 9:27** (v.l. κατάλειμμα.)—DELG s.v. λείπω. M-M.

ὑπολείπω 2 aor. subj. 1 pl. ὑπολίπωμεν 1 Km 14:36. Mid.: fut. ὑπολείψομαι LXX; aor. ὑπολιπόμην. Pass.: 1 fut. ὑπολειφθήσομαι; 1 aor. ὑπελείφθην; pf. ὑπολέλειμμαι LXX (Hom.+) ***leave remaining*** pass. *be left (remaining)* (Hom. et al.; Phlegon: 257 fgm. 36, 1, 4 Jac.; Philo, Aet. M. 99; Jos., Ant. 13,

111, C. Ap. 1, 314; Just., D. 56, 22) **Ro 11:3** (3 Km 19:10, 14); 1 Cl 14:4 (Pr 2:21).—M-M.

ὑπολήνιον, ου, τό (Demioprata [s. on this UKöhler, Her 23, 1888, 397–401], Pollux 10, 130; Geopon.; POxy 1735, 5; LXX.—The adj. OGI 383, 147) **a trough placed beneath the wine-press to hold the wine, *wine trough, vat* Mk 12:1.**—AWikenhauser, BZ 8, 1910, 273.—DELG s.v. ληνός. M-M.

ὑπόλιμμα s. ὑπόλειμμα.

ὑπολιμπάνω (cp. λιμπάνω, collateral form of λείπω; Dionys. Hal. 1, 23; Themist., Or. 10 p. 139 D.; ins; PHib 45, 13 [257 BC]; PSI 392, 4), a by-form of ὑπολείπω (on the by-form λιμπάνω s. Mayser 402) **to cause to remain subsequent to some temporal reference point, *leave, leave behind*** τινί τι *someth. for someone* **1 Pt 2:21** (ἀπολιμπάνω P^{72}).—DELG s.v. λείπω. M-M.

ὑπολύω (since Hom. in var. senses) lit. 'untie' then ***take off one's sandals/shoes*** (Aeschyl., Aristoph. et al.; LXX; Just., A I, 62, 2 and 4) w. acc. of the pers. whose sandals one takes off τινά (Pla., Symp. 213b; Plut., Pomp. 658 [73, 10]; Jos., Ant. 4, 256 ὑπ. αὐτὸν τὰ σάνδαλα; TestZeb 3:5) ὑπολύειν ἑαυτόν *take off one's own sandals* MPol 13:2.

ὑπομειδιάω 1 aor. ὑπεμειδίασα (Anacreontea 45, 14; Polyb. 18, 7, 6; Alciphron 4, 14, 6 al.; Cat. of the Gk. and Lat. pap in the JRyl. Libr. III '38 no. 478, 48; Philo, Abr. 151) ***smile a bit*** Hv 3, 8, 2.

ὑπομένω impf. ὑπέμενον; fut. ὑπομενῶ; 1 aor. ὑπέμεινα; pf. ptc. ὑπομεμενηκώς, inf. ὑπομεμενηκέναι (Just., D. 67, 6) (Hom.+; ins, pap, LXX; TestSol 11:6; TestJob; EpArist 175; Philo, Joseph., Just.; Tat. 11, 1; Mel., P. 69, 497; Ath. 35, 1)

❶ **to stay in a place beyond an expected point of time, *remain/stay (behind),*** while others go away ἐν w. dat. of place (Jos., Ant. 18, 328) **Lk 2:43.** ἐκεῖ **Ac 17:14.**

❷ **to maintain a belief or course of action in the face of opposition, *stand one's ground, hold out, endure*** (Il. et al.; remain instead of fleeing: Pla., Tht. 177b ἀνδρικῶς ὑπομεῖναι . . . ἀνάνδρως φεύγειν) in trouble, affliction, persecution (of Christ: ἐν τῷ νικᾶν καὶ ὑπομένειν Iren. 3, 19, 3 [Harv. II 104, 4]), abs. **Mt 10:22** (s. PJoüon, RSR 28, '38, 310f); **24:13; Mk 13:13** (all three times w. εἰς τέλος); **2 Ti 2:12** (TestJob 4:6 ἐὰν ὑπομείνῃς); **Js 5:11;** 1 Cl 35:3f; 45:8 (ἐν πεποιθήσει=full of confidence); 2 Cl 11:5 (ἐλπίσαντες=in joyful hope); IMg 9:2 (διὰ τοῦτο, ἵνα); MPol 2:2 (w. μέχρι and inf.); τοῖς ὑπομείνασιν vs. 3; D 16:5 (ἐν τῇ πίστει αὐτῶν=in their faith, i.e. endure the fiery trial). Hence of Christ simply = *submit to, suffer* B 5:1, 12 (in both cases w. εἰς τοῦτο=for this purpose); 14:4: IPol 3:2 (both w. δι' ἡμᾶς); Pol 1:2 (ὑπὲρ τῶν ἁμαρτιῶν ἡμῶν). κύριος ὑπέμεινεν παθεῖν B 5:5a; cp. 5b and 6; 2 Cl 1:2.—The purpose of the endurance is indicated by εἰς παιδείαν **Hb 12:7** (cp. Nicander in Anton. Lib. 28, 1 εἰς ἀλκήν).—The affliction under which one remains steadfast is expressed in var. ways: τῇ θλίψει *in tribulation* **Ro 12:12; 8:24 v.l.** (here perh. 'put up with', cp. Plut., Mor. 503b). By a ptc. (Jos., Ant. 12, 122) εἰ κολαφιζόμενοι ὑπομενεῖτε **1 Pt 2:20a;** cp. vs. **20b.** By acc. of thing (Hdt., Thu. et al.; ins, pap, LXX; TestJob 26:4; TestDan 5:13; Philo, Cher. 2; Jos., Ant. 3, 53; Just., A I, 39, 5 πάντα; Tat., Mel.; Orig., C. Cels. 8, 26, 5 πᾶν; Hippol., Ref. 10, 34, 3 πάθη; Did., Gen. 101, 13 κάματον) ταῦτα Dg 2:9. πάντα **1 Cor 13:7; 2 Ti 2:10;** ISm 4:2; 9:2; IPol 3:1; Dg 5:5; of Christ πάντα δι' ἡμᾶς Pol 8:1. σταυρόν **Hb 12:2.** τὰς βασάνους 2 Cl 17:7. δεινὰς κολάσεις MPol 2:4. τὸ πῦρ 13:3; cp. Dg 10:8. τὴν θλῖψιν Hv 2, 2, 7. τὴν ἐπήρειαν IMg 1:3. ἄθλησιν **Hb 10:32.** ἀντιλογίαν **12:3.** παιδείαν vs. **7 v.l.** πειρασμόν **Js 1:12;** cp. AcPl Ha 8, 22. τὴν ψῆφον τοῦ μαρτυρίου **Phlm subscr. v.l.**—W. cognate obj. ὑπομονήν Pol. 9:1.—In a weakened sense μηδὲν ἀηδὲς ὑπομείνατος *without experiencing anything unpleasant* Papias (2:9).—S. Leutzsch, Hermas 399 n. 185 for lit. on endurance of God's people.

❸ **to wait for with persistence, *wait for*** τινά *someone* (X., An. 4, 1, 21; Appian, Bell. Civ. 5, 81 §343; Sb 4369 II, 22; Ps 24:3, 5; 26:14 al.; Jos., Ant. 5, 121) 1 Cl 34:8; abs. 35:4. In a diff. sense Ox 840, 6, s. ἀπολαμβάνω 1.—PGoicoechea, De conceptu ὑπομονή apud s. Paulum, diss. Rome '65.—M-M. TW. Spicq.

ὑπομιμνήσκω fut. ὑπομνήσω; 1 aor. ὑπέμνησα, pass. ὑπεμνήσθην (also without iota subscript, Gignac II 277, 2a; Hom.+; ins, pap, LXX, TestSol 22:6; ApcEsdr 2:22 p. 26, 14 Tdf.; EpArist, Philo, Joseph.; Ath. 30, 3)

❶ **to put another in mind of someth.,** act.—ⓐ ***remind*** τινά *someone* τὶ of *someth.* (double acc. as Thu. 7, 64, 1; X., Cyr. 3, 3, 37; Pla., Philb. 67c al.; PFlor 189, 3 [III AD]; 4 Macc 18:14; TestLevi 9:6) **J 14:26.** Also τινὰ περί τινος (Pla., Phdr. 275d; PMich 100, 2 [III BC]; Jos., Ant. 14, 152) **2 Pt 1:12.** W. acc. of pers. and ὅτι foll. (Jos., Ant.6, 131) **Jd 5;** B 12:2. W. acc. of pers. and inf. foll. **Tit 3:1.** ἑαυτόν *oneself* 1 Cl 7:1.

ⓑ ***call to mind, bring up***—α. w. acc. τὶ *someth.* (Soph., Philoct. 1170; Hdt. 7, 171; Pla., Phdr. 241a al.; Mitt-Wilck. I/2, 238, 1 [II AD] ὑπομιμνήσκω τοῦτο; Wsd 18:22; Jos., Ant. 14, 384; Ath. 30, 3) ταῦτα **2 Ti 2:14;** 1 Cl 62:3. ὑπομνήσω αὐτοῦ τὰ ἔργα *I will* bring *up what he is doing* **3J 10.**

β. abs., foll. by acc. and inf. *remind someone that* 1 Cl 62:2.

❷ **to recollect for oneself,** pass. w. act. sense (Aeschyl. et al.) ***remember, think of*** τινός *someth.* (Lucian, Catapl. 4; Philo, Mos. 1, 193) **Lk 22:61.**—M-M.

ὑπόμνησις, εως, ἡ (ὑπομιμνήσκω; Eur., Thu. et al.; ins, pap, LXX)

❶ **the act of calling to someone's mind, *reminding*** (Thu., Pla., pap) Hv 3, 8, 9. ἐν ὑπ. *by a reminder,* i.e. as I remind you **2 Pt 1:13; 3:1.**

❷ **the act of remembering, *remembrance*** (X., Cyr. 3, 3, 38 ὑπόμνησίν τινος ἔχειν; Philo, Poster. Cai. 153; Jos., Ant. 4, 58) ὑπόμνησιν λαμβάνειν τινός *receive a remembrance of = remember someth.* **2 Ti 1:5.**—DELG s.v. μιμνήσκω. M-M. TW.

ὑπομονή, ῆς, ἡ (ὑπομένω)—❶ **the capacity to hold out or bear up in the face of difficulty, *patience, endurance, fortitude, steadfastness, perseverance*** (Ps.-Pla., Def. 412c; Aristot., Stoics [Stoic. IV 150 index; Musonius; Epict.—PBarth, D. Stoa[4] 1922, 119ff]; Polyb., Plut., LXX; PsSol 2:36; TestJob 1:5; TestJos; Philo; Jos., Ant. 3, 16 al.; Just.; beside καρτερία Orig., C. Cels. 7, 55, 6; καθ' ὑπομονὴν διὰ ἔργων ἀγαθῶν Theoph. Ant. 1, 14 [p. 90, 17]) esp. as they are shown in the enduring of toil and suffering **Lk 21:19; Rom 5:3f** (on the 'climax' form of the saying cp. Maximus Tyr. 16, 3b τὴν ἀρετὴν διδόασιν οἱ λόγοι, τοὺς δὲ λόγους ἡ ἄσκησις, τὴν δὲ ἄσκησιν ἡ ἀλήθεια, τὴν δὲ ἀλήθειαν ἡ σχολή); **15:4f; 2 Cor 6:4; 1 Th 1:3; 2 Th 1:4; 1 Ti 6:11; 2 Ti 3:10; Tit 2:2; Hb 10:36; Js 1:3f; 2 Pt 1:6ab; Rv 2:2f, 19;** 1 Cl 5:5, 7; B 2:2; IEph 3:1; Hm 8:9; D 5:2. πᾶσα ὑπ. *every kind of patience* **2 Cor 12:12; Col 1:11.** W. the subjective gen. ἡ ὑπ. Ἰώβ **Js 5:11** (ACarr, The Patience of Job [Js 5:11]: Exp. 8th ser., 6, 1913, 511–17); αὐτοῦ (i.e. Χριστοῦ) *the endurance that Christ showed* Pol 8:2. Differently ἡ ὑπ. τοῦ Χριστοῦ *a Christ-like fortitude,* i.e. a fortitude that comes fr. association w. Christ **2 Th 3:5** (OSchmitz, D. Christusgemeinschaft des Pls im Lichte seines Genetivbrauchs 1924, 139f); cp. IRo 10:3 (s.

also 2 below). W. the objective gen. ὑπ. ἔργου ἀγαθοῦ *perseverance in doing what is right* **Ro 2:7** (Polyb. 4, 51, 1 ὑπ. τοῦ πολέμου). ὑπ. τῶν παθημάτων *steadfast endurance of sufferings* **2 Cor 1:6** (Ps.-Pla., Def. 412c ὑπ. λύπης; Plut., Pelop. 278 [1, 8] ὑπ. θανάτου; Jos., Ant. 2, 7 πόνων ὑπ.). ὁ λόγος τῆς ὑπομονῆς μου (λόγος 1aβ) **Rv 3:10** (s. also 2 below). δι' ὑπομονῆς *with patience* or *fortitude* **Ro 8:25; Hb 12:1.** διὰ τῆς ὑπομονῆς *through his patient endurance* MPol 19:2 (Just., A I, 16, 3). ἐν ὑπομονῇ (PsSol 2:36; TestJos 10:2) **Lk 8:15** (LCerfaux, RB 64, '57, 481–91). ὑπομένειν πᾶσαν ὑπομονήν *practice endurance to the limit* Pol 9:1. ὧδέ ἐστιν ἡ ὑπ. τῶν ἁγίων *here is (an opportunity for) endurance on the part of the saints* (Weymouth) **Rv 13:10** (s. JSchmid, ZNW 43, '50/51, 112–28); cp. **14:12.** Text uncertain τὸν λόγον τῶν ὑ[πο]μονῶν AcPl Ha 6, 11f.—WMeikle, The Vocabulary of 'Patience' in the OT: Exp. 8th ser., 19, 1920, 219–25, The Voc. etc. in the NT: ibid. 304–13; CSpicq, Patientia: RSPT 19, 1930, 95–106; AFestugière, RSR 21, '31, 477–86; LMarshall, Challenge of NT Ethics '47, 91f.

❷ **the act or state of patient waiting for someone or someth.,** ***expectation*** (Ps 9:19; 61:6; 2 Esdr 10:2) **Rv 1:9** (on ὑπ. ἐν Ἰησοῦ s. IHeikel, StKr 106, '35, 317). Perh. (s. 1 above) **3:10** and **2 Th 3:5;** IRo 10:3 might also be classed here (so. Lightf.).—RAC IX 658–65. DDenton notes a close connection w. ἐλπίς: SJT 34, '81, 313–20. See ὑπομένω, end.—M-M.

ὑπομονητικός, ή, όν (ὑπομονή; Hippocr.+; Philo, Leg. All. 3, 88) **pert. to being able to hold up in the face of difficulty,** ***patient, showing endurance*** neut. subst. τὸ ὑπομονητικόν *fortitude* MPol 2:2.—DELG s.v. μένω.

ὑπονοέω impf. ὑπενόουν; fut. 3 sg. ὑπονοήσει Da 7:25 Theod.; 1 aor. ὑπενόησα (s. next entry; Eur., Hdt. et al.; pap, LXX; TestBenj 9:1; Philo, Joseph.; Just., D. 103, 3; 125, 1) **to form an opinion or conjecture on the basis of slight evidence,** ***suspect, suppose*** (Hdt. et al.; pap; Sir 23:21) w. acc. *someth.* (Hdt., Aristoph. et al.) **Ac 25:18** (w. attraction of the rel.; cp. PLond 1912, 97f ἐξ οὗ μείζονας ὑπονοίας ἀναγκασθήσομαι λαβεῖν). Foll. by acc. and inf. (B-D-F §397, 2; Rob. 1036.—Hdt. 9, 99 al.; Jos., Ant. 13, 315; Just.; PRyl 139, 14 [34 AD]) **13:25; 27:27;** cp. Hv 4, 1, 6.—DELG s.v. νόος. M-M. TW.

ὑπόνοια, ας, ἡ (ὑπονοέω; Thu. et al.; pap, LXX; EpArist 316; Philo; Jos., Bell. 1, 227; 631; Ath. 1, 4) **opinion or conjecture based on slight evidence,** ***suspicion, conjecture*** ὑπόνοιαι πονηραί *evil conjectures, false suspicions* **1 Ti 6:4** (Sir 3:24 ὑπόνοια πονηρά).—B. 1244. DELG s.v. νόος. M-M. TW.

ὑποπιάζω s. ὑπωπιάζω.

ὑποπίπτω 2 aor. ὑπέπεσον (Thu., Aristoph.+; ins, pap, LXX; TestJos 7:8; EpArist 214; Philo; Jos., Bell. 5, 382, Vi. 381; Just.)

❶ of pers., **to make the gesture of a suppliant by kneeling or prostrating oneself,** ***fall down before*** ἐὰν ὑποπέσῃς αὐτῷ καὶ δεηθῇς αὐτοῦ *if you fall down before (God) and petition (God)* AcPl Ha 9, 12.

❷ of things,**to be included within some classification,** ***fall under/within*** *someth.* ὑπό τι (Aristot.; Iambl., Vi. Pythag. 34 §241 ὑπὸ τὴν προειρημένην τάξιν) ὑπὸ τὴν διάνοιάν τινος *fall within someone's comprehension* (διάνοια 1) 1 Cl 35:2.

ὑποπλέω 1 aor. ὑπέπλευσα (Dio Chrys., Cass. Dio et al.) ***sail under the lee of*** an island, i.e. in such a way that the island protects the ship fr. the wind **Ac 27:4, 7.**—M-M.

ὑποπνέω 1 aor. ὑπέπνευσα (Aristot., Probl. 8, 6=blow underneath) ***blow gently*** ὑποπνεύσαντος νότου *when a moderate south(west) wind began to blow* **Ac 27:13.**

ὑποπόδιον, ου, τό (πούς; Chares [after 323 BC]: 125 fgm. 2 p. 658, 22 Jac. [in Athen. 12 p. 514f]; Lucian, Hist. Conscrib. 27; Athen. 5, 192e; ins; PTebt 45, 38 [113 BC]; CPR 22, 8; 27, 11 [both II AD]; LXX; loanw. in rabb.) ***footstool*** **Js 2:3.** Of the earth as God's footstool (after Is 66:1; cp. Philo, Conf. Lingu. 98) **Mt 5:35; Ac 7:49;** B 16:2. τιθέναι τινὰ ὑποπόδιον τῶν ποδῶν τινος *make someone a footstool for someone,* i.e. subject one pers. to another, so that the other can put a foot on the subject's neck (Ps 109:1) **Mt 22:44 v.l.; Mk 12:36 v.l.; Lk 20:43; Ac 2:35; Hb 1:13; 10:13;** 1 Cl 36:5; B 12:10.—DELG s.v. πούς. M-M.

ὑποπτεύω (cp. ὑφοράω: fut. ὑπόψομαι, 'look at fr. below, eye stealthily'; s. ὑποψία) 1 aor. ὑπώπτευσα, inf. pass. ὑποπτευθῆναι (Ath.) (trag., Thu. et al.; pap, LXX; En 101:5; Jos., Bell. 2, 617; 3, 367; Just., A II, 3, 3; Ath. 31, 2) ***suspect*** τινά *someone* (Soph., Hdt., Thu. et al.) foll. by acc. and inf. IPhld 7:2.—DELG s.v. ὄπωπα B 4.

ὑπορθόω (Sym.; Dositheus, Ars Gramm. 76, 1 p. 102) **to assist in standing upright,** ***support*** τινά *someone* GPt 10:39.—DELG s.v. ὀρθός.

ὑπόστασις, εως, ἡ (ὑφίστημι; Hippocr.+; Polyb. 4, 50, 10; 6, 55, 2; Diod. S. 16, 32, 3; 16, 33, 1; M. Ant. 10, 5; ins, pap, LXX; PsSol 15:5; 17:24; TestReub 2:7; TestZeb 2:4; Tat.; Ath. 21, 3; Iren. 5, 36, 1 [Harv. II 426, 1]; Hippol., Ref. 10, 17, 2; Did., Gen. 128, 11 in widely different meanings. See Dörrie 4 below.)

❶ **the essential or basic structure/nature of an entity,** ***substantial nature, essence, actual being, reality*** (underlying structure, oft. in contrast to what merely seems to be: Ps.-Aristot., De Mundo 4 p. 395a, 29f; Plut., Mor. 894b; Diog. L., Pyrrh. 9, 91; Artem. 3, 14; Ps 38:6; Wsd 16:21; TestReub 2:7; SJCh 78, 30; Philo, Aet. M. 88; 92; Jos., C. Ap. 1, 1; Tat. 6, 2; Ath. 21, 3; cp. the answer of a certain Secundus, who, when asked 'Quid fides?', answered: 'ignotae rei mira certitudo'=a marvelous certainty about someth. otherwise unknown [FPhGr I 516]; s. also Lexicon Sabbaiticum: Lexica Graeca Minora '65, 53)

ⓐ of the Son of God as χαρακτὴρ τῆς ὑποστάσεως αὐτοῦ *a(n) exact representation of (God's) real being* (i.e. as one who is in charge of the universe) **Hb 1:3.** Sim. of polytheists' deities, whose basic reality is someth. material like stone, metal etc. Dg 2:1.

ⓑ of things: among the meanings that can be authenticated for **Hb 11:1** a strong claim can be made for ***realization*** (Diod. S. 1, 3, 2 of the realization of a plan; Cornutus 9 p. 9, 3 of the realization of humanity; Jos., C. Ap. 1, 1 that of the Jewish people, both by a divine act; Tat. 5, 1 of God τοῦ παντὸς ἡ ὑπόστασις): ἔστιν πίστις ἐλπιζομένων ὑπ.=*in faith things hoped for become realized,* or *things hoped for take on* (but s. 3 and 4 below) *reality.* Conversely, 'without faith things hoped for would have no reality'. HKöster (s. bibliog. 4 below) argues for this sense also in **3:14,** but s. 2. Cp. the rendering 'substance' (e.g. KJV, REB).

❷ **a plan that one devises for action,** ***plan, project, undertaking, endeavor*** (Diod. Sic 15, 70, 2; 16, 32, 3; 16, 82, 6; 17, 69, 7; Ezk 19:5) ἐν τῇ ὑποστάσει ταύτῃ *in connection with this undertaking* i.e. the collection for Jerusalem **2 Cor 9:4.** The fact that meeting a financial obligation is the main theme (vss. 1–2) might well suggest association of ὑπ. with its use e.g. as a t.t. of expectation of rent due PTebt 61b, 194. To emphasize the importance of steadfast *commitment to professed obligation* (opp.

καρδία πονηρὰ ἀπιστίας ἐν τῷ ἀποστῆναι), the author of **Hb 3:14** uses ὑπ. in a way that invites an addressee to draw on the semantic component of obligation familiar in commercial usage of the term (s. PTebt above), an association that is invited by use of μέτοχος, a standard term for a business partner (PHib 109, 3; PCairZen 176, 102 [both III BC]), μέχρι τέλους (s.v. τέλος 2bβ), and βέβαιος (s. M-M s.v.). S. Köster 1b above for focus of ὑπ. on 'reality'.—Satirically, ἐν ταύτῃ τῇ ὑποστάσει τῆς καυχήσεως *in this boasting project of mine* **2 Cor 11:17.**

❸ The interp. ***situation, condition*** (Cicero, Ad Attic. 2, 3, 3 ὑπόστασιν nostram=our situation), also specif. ***frame of mind*** (Dio Cass. 49, 9; Themist., Or. 13 p. 178b; Jos., Ant. 18, 24 of determination in desperate circumstances; sim. Polyb. 6, 55, 2) has been suggested for some of the passages cited in 1 and 2 above: **2 Cor 9:4** (explained in a v.l. via the epexegetical gen. καυχήσεως); **11:17; Hb 3:14** (s. Dörrie [bibliog. 4 below], p. 39: the frame of mind described in **Hb 3:6**). The sense 'confidence', 'assurance' (based on LXX [Ruth 1:12; Ps 38:8; Ezk 19:5], where it renders תִּקְוָה etc.) favored by Melanchthon and Luther (also Tyndale, NRSV, but not KJV) for **Hb 11:1** has enjoyed much favor but must be eliminated, since examples of it cannot be found (s. Dörrie and Köster [4 below]). More prob. for **Hb 4:11** is

❹ **guarantee of ownership/entitlement, *title deed*** (Sb 9086 III, 1–11 [104 AD]; Spicq III 423 n. 14; cp. M-M s.v.) **Hb 11:1** (cp. 2 above for commercial use of ὕπ.).—ASchlatter, Der Glaube im NT[4] 1927, 614ff; MMathis, The Pauline πίστις-ὑπόστασις acc. to Hb 11:1, diss. Cath. Univ. of Amer., Washington, D.C. 1920, also Biblica 3, 1922, 79–87; RWitt, Hypostasis: 'Amicitiae Corolla' (RHarris Festschr.) '33, 319–43; MSchumpp, D. Glaubensbegriff des Hb: Divus Thomas 11, '34, 397–410; FErdin, D. Wort Hypostasis, diss. Freiburg '39; CArpe, Philologus 94, '41, 65–78; HDörrie, Ὑπόστασις, Wort- u. Bedeutungsgeschichte: NAWG 1955, no. 3, ZNW 46, '55, 196–202; HKöster, TW VIII 571–88 (Köster prefers *plan, project* [Vorhaben] for the passages in 2 Cor, and *reality* [Wirklichkeit] for all 3 occurrences in Hb, contrasting the reality of God with the transitory character of the visible world). S. also the lit. s.v. πίστις 2a.—DELG s.v. ἵστημι. M-M. EDNT. TW. Spicq. Sv.

ὑποστέλλω impf. ὑπέστελλον; 1 aor. mid. ὑπεστειλάμην (s. ὑποστολή; Pind. et al.; ins, pap, LXX, Philo, Joseph.)

❶ **to draw back or disappear from a position—ⓐ** act. (Pind. et al.; Philo, Leg. ad Gai. 71) ***draw back, withdraw*** (Polyb. 1, 21, 2 al.; Plut.) ἑαυτόν *draw (oneself) back* (Polyb. 1, 16, 10; 7, 17, 1 al.) ὑπέστελλεν καὶ ἀφώριζεν ἑαυτόν **Gal 2:12;** if ἑαυτόν does not go w. ὑπέστ., ὑποστέλλω is intr. here *draw back* (Polyb. 6, 40, 14; 10, 32, 3; Plut., Demetr. 912 [47, 6]; Philo, Spec. Leg. 1, 5).

ⓑ mid. ***draw back*** ἡ νεφέλη ὑπεστέλλετο τοῦ σπηλαίου *the cloud faded away from the cave* GJs 19:2. τὸ φῶς ἐκεῖνο ὑπεστέλλετο *that light faded out* ibid.

❷ **to be hesitant in regard to someth.,** mid.**—ⓐ *shrink back*** (Aelian, NA 7, 19; Philo, Mos. 1, 83; Jos., Vi. 215) **Hb 10:38** (Hab 2:4).

ⓑ ***shrink from, avoid*** implying fear (Demosth. et al.; Jos., Ant. 6, 86 ὑπ. φόβῳ εἰπεῖν) οὐ γὰρ ὑπεστειλάμην τοῦ μὴ ἀναγγεῖλαι *I did not shrink from proclaiming* **Ac 20:27.**

ⓒ ***be timid about, keep silent about,*** mid. τὶ *someth.* in fear (Demosth. 4, 51; Isocr. 8, 41; Diod. S. 13, 70, 3 Cyrus urges Lysander not to be timid about asking for money; Dio Chrys. 10 [11], 27 οὐδέν; Lucian, Deor. Conc. 2 οὐδέν; PCairZen 412, 24 [III BC]; BGU 1303, 10; Philo, Sacr. Abel. 35; Jos., Bell. 1, 387, Vi. 278 οὐδέν al.) οὐδὲν ὑπεστειλάμην τῶν συμφερόντων *I have kept silent about nothing that is profitable* **Ac 20:20.**—M-M. TW.

ὑποστολή, ῆς, ἡ (ὑποστέλλω) **the state of being timid, *hesitancy, timidity*** (Asclepiodot. Tact. [I BC] 10, 21 of holding a body of troops in reserve position.—Jos., Bell. 2, 277, Ant. 16, 112 of pers. who have no reservations about indulging themselves in baseness) οὐκ ἐσμὲν ὑποστολῆς *we do not belong to those who are timid,* in contrast to those who are earnestly committed **Hb 10:39.**—DELG s.v. στέλλω. M-M. TW.

ὑποστρέφω impf. ὑπέστρεφον; fut. ὑποστρέψω; 1 aor. ὑπέστρεψα; in our lit. only intr. (Hom.+; Thu.; pap, LXX; TestAbr B 12 p. 117, 2 and 5 [Stone p. 82] trans.; TestJob 7:9; TestZeb 4:6 v.l.; TestGad 1:5; ParJer, Philo, Joseph.; Just., D. 56, 22) ***turn back, return*** w. εἰς and acc. of place (PGiss 40 II, 8; Gen 8:9; ParJer 5:12; 8:8; Jos. Bell. 1, 229 εἰς Ἱεροσ.; Just., D. 56, 22 εἰς τὸν τόπον αὐτοῦ) **Lk 1:56; 2:45; 4:14** (cp. Jos., Bell. 1, 445); **8:39** (cp. Jos., Vi. 144 εἰς τὴν οἰκίαν); **Ac 8:25; 13:13; Gal 1:17;** GPt 14:58. εἰς τὰ ἴδια **Ac 21:6** (ἴδιος 4b). εἰς διαφθοράν *to corruption,* i.e. the grave **Ac 13:34.** διά w. gen. of place **20:3.** ἀπό w. gen. of place (Jos., Vi. 139) **Lk 4:1; 24:9** or a corresp. expr. (Jos., Vi. 329 ἀπὸ τ. πολιορκίας ὑπ.) ἀπὸ τῆς κοπῆς τῶν βασιλέων **Hb 7:1** (Gen 14:17). εἰς and ἀπό **Ac 1:12.** ἐκ w. gen. of place **Ac 12:25 v.l.** ἐκ τῆς ἁγίας ἐντολῆς *turn away* and go back to the former pattern of belief (s. ἐντολή 2bζ) **2 Pt 2:21** (cp. ἀνακάμπτω and ἐπιστρέφω). ἐπί τινα *to someone* Hm 4, 1, 7. Foll. by a final inf. **Lk 17:18.** Abs. *return* (Polyaenus 4, 2, 14; Lucian Bis Acc. 17; Josh 2:23; Jos., Ant. 11, 30) **Mk 14:40 v.l.; Lk 2:20, 43; 8:37, 40; Ac 8:28** al.—M-M. TW.

ὑποστρωννύω/ὑποστρώννυμι (cp. στρωννύω, beg.—The word occurs Hom. et al. [ὑποστορέννυμι, ὑποστόρνυμι]; LXX; JosAs 10:16 cod. A [p. 52, 20 Bat.]. In the form ὑποστρωννύω in Athen. 2, 48d; in the form ὑποστρώννυμι in Plut., Artox. 1022 [22, 10]) impf. ὑπεστρώννυον; 1 aor. ὑπέστρωσα; ***spread out underneath,*** τὶ *someth.* (PGM 5, 217 σινδόνα; 36, 151) ὑπεστρώννυον τὰ ἱμάτια ἐν τῇ ὁδῷ *they were spreading out their cloaks under him in the road* **Lk 19:36** (Jos., Ant. 9, 111 ἕκαστος ὑπεστρώννυεν αὐτῷ τὸ ἱμάτιον; 18, 204; Chariton 3, 2, 17; Aesop, Fab. 208 P.=378 H. ὑποστρώσας τὸ ἱμάτιον). σποδόν *spread out ashes underneath oneself = make one's bed in ashes* as a sign of repentance B 3:2 (Is 58:5; cp. JosAs 10:16 cod. A). Pass. κήρυκας ὑποστρωννύμενοι *those with trumpet-shells* (κῆρυξ 3) *under them*=those who were laid on trumpet-shells MPol 2:4. —DELG and Frisk s.v. στόρνυμι. M-M.

ὑποταγή, ῆς, ἡ (s. ταγή, and cp. 2 aor. of ὑποτάσσω; Dionys. Hal. 3, 66, 3 act. 'subjecting') in our lit. only pass. **the state of submissiveness, *subjection, subordination,*** as opposed to setting oneself up as controller (Plut., Mor. 142e) (Wsd 18:15 A; TestSol; ApcMos 10; Artem. 1, 73 p. 66, 14; Paradoxogr. p. 218, 7 Westermann ἐν ὑποταγῇ; Vett. Val. 106, 8; 11; 17; 24; 198, 28; BGU 96, 7 [III BC] τὸν ἐν ὑποταγῇ τυγχάνοντα. Cp. ἐν ὑπ. μένειν τοῦ θεοῦ Iren. 4, 38, 3 [Harv. II 196, 3]; Theoph. Ant 1, 6 [p. 70, 11]). ἡ ὑποταγὴ τῆς ὁμολογίας ὑμῶν εἰς τὸ εὐαγγέλιον **2 Cor 9:13** (ὁμολογία 1). ἐν πάσῃ ὑποταγῇ *subordinating herself in every respect* **1 Ti 2:11** (cp. cum omni subiectione Papias [1:3]); τέκνα ἔχειν ἐν ὑποταγῇ *keep children under control* **3:4.** ἐν μιᾷ ὑποταγῇ κατηρτισμένοι *made complete in unanimous subjection* IEph 2:2. εἴξαμεν τῇ ὑποταγῇ (dat. of manner) *we yielded in submission* **Gal 2:5.** The system of ordered relationships requires recognition of one's proper place in the structure. Since Paul is subordinate to the 'truth of the gospel' he cannot comply with some demands imposed by leaders in Jerusalem who have the obligation to recognize their place in the order of things.—Of the members of the body ὑποταγῇ μιᾷ χρῆται *they experience a mutual subjection* 1 Cl 37:5. ὁ κανὼν τῆς ὑποταγῆς *the established norm of obedience* (Kleist) 1:3.—DELG s.v. τάσσω. M-M. TW.

ὑποτάσσω 1 aor. ὑπέταξα. Pass.: 2 fut. ὑποταγήσομαι; 2 aor. ὑπετάγην; perf. ὑποτέταγμαι (Aristot., Polyb.+)

❶ **to cause to be in a submissive relationship, *to subject, to subordinate*—ⓐ** act., abs. **Ro 8:20b;** 1 Cl 2:1b. τινά *bring someone to subjection* (Herodian 7, 2, 9) IPol 2:1. τινί τινα or τι *someone* or *someth. to someone* (Epict. 4, 12, 12 of God ὑπ. τί τινι; cp. Da 11:39 Theod.; TestJud 21:2; ApcSed 6:2; SibOr fgm. 3, 12; Ar. [Milne 76, 49]; Menander Eph.: 783 fgm. 1, 119 Jac. [in Jos., C. Ap. 1, 119]; Just., A I, 49, 7, A II 5, 2.—Cp. ὑπέταξεν ἑαυτοῦ τῇ ἐξουσίᾳ τοὺς Πάρθους Hippol., Ref. 9, 16, 4) **1 Cor 15:27c, 28c; Phil 3:21; Hb 2:5, 8b;** Dg 10:2; Hm 12, 4, 2; AcPl Ha 8, 15. In the same sense ὑπ. τι ὑπὸ τοὺς πόδας τινός **1 Cor 15:27a; Eph 1:22;** also ὑποκάτω τῶν ποδῶν τινος **Hb 2:8a** (Ps 8:7). ὑποτάσσειν ἑαυτόν τινι *subject oneself to someone* (Plut., Mor. 142e to the husband; Simplicius In Epict. p. 33 Düb. to transcendent powers) Hs 9, 22, 3.

ⓑ pass.—**α.** *become subject* τινί to a pers. or a state of being (Iren. 5, 5, 2 [Harv. II 332, 11]) **Ro 8:20a; 1 Cor 15:28a; Hb 2:8c; 1 Pt 3:22;** Dg 7:2; Pol 2:1. Abs. (Diod. S. 1, 55, 10; Aristobulus in Eus., PE 8, 10, 10 [=p. 140 Holladay] πάνθ' ὑποτέτακται; Just., D. 85, 2 νικᾶται καὶ ὑποτάσσεται [Ath. 18, 2]; Iren. 1, 13, 4 [Harv. I 120, 7]) **1 Cor 15:27b.**

β. *subject oneself, be subjected* or *subordinated, obey* abs. (Jos., Bell. 4, 175) **Ro 13:5; 1 Cor 14:34** (cp. δουλεύετε ἀλλήλοις Gal 5:13); 1 Cl 2:1a; 57:2. Of submission involving recognition of an ordered structure, w. dat. of the entity to whom/which appropriate respect is shown (Palaeph. 38 p. 56, 15; 57, 2): toward a husband (s. Ps.-Callisth. 1, 22, 4 πρέπον ἐστὶ τὴν γυναῖκα τῷ ἀνδρὶ ὑποτάσσεσθαι, s. 1a above; cp. SEG 26, 1717, 26 [III/IV AD] in a love charm) **Eph 5:22 v.l.; Col 3:18; Tit 2:5; 1 Pt 3:1** (on an alleged impv. sense s. Schwyzer II 407), **5;** parents **Lk 2:51;** masters **Tit 2:9; 1 Pt 2:18;** B 19:7; D 4:11; secular authorities (1 Ch 29:24; Theoph. Ant. 1, 11 [p. 82, 14]) **Ro 13:1** (CMorrison, The Powers That Be—Ro 13:1–13, diss. Basel '56; EBarnikol, TU 77, '61, 65–133 [non-Pauline]); **Tit 3:1; 1 Pt 2:13;** 1 Cl 61:1; church officials 1 Cl 1:3; 57:1; IEph 2:2; IMg 2; 13:2; ITr 2:1f; 13:2; IPol 6:1; Pol 5:3; νεώτεροι ὑποτάγητε πρεσβυτέροις **1 Pt 5:5.** To God (Epict. 3, 24, 65 τ. θεῷ ὑποτεταγμένος; 4, 12, 11; Ps 61:2; 2 Macc 9:12) **1 Cor 15:28b; Hb 12:9; Js 4:7;** 1 Cl 20:1; IEph 5:3; to Christ **Eph 5:24.** To the will of God, the law, etc. **Ro 8:7; 10:3;** 1 Cl 34:5; Hm 12, 5, 1; τῇ ἐπιθυμίᾳ τῇ ἀγαθῇ 12, 2, 5.—Of submission in the sense of voluntary yielding in love **1 Cor 16:16; Eph 5:21; 1 Pt 5:5b v.l.;** 1 Cl 38:1.—The evil spirits must be subject to the disciples whom Jesus sends out **Lk 10:17, 20.** Likew. the prophetic spirits must be subject to the prophets in whom they dwell **1 Cor 14:32.**—HMerklein, Studien zu Jesus und Paulus (WUNT 105) '98, 405–37.

❷ **to add a document at the end of another document, *attach, append, subjoin*** (common in official documents, hence oft. ins, pap; also s. Jos., Vi. 364, Ant. 16, 161; Just., A I, 68, 4; Mel., HE 4, 26, 14) the letters of Ign. ὑποτεταγμέναι εἰσὶν τῇ ἐπιστολῇ ταύτῃ Pol 13:2.—M-M. EDNT. TW. Spicq.

ὑποτεταγμένως adv. fr. the pf. pass. ptc. of ὑποτάσσω ***submissively*** 1 Cl 37:2.

ὑποτίθημι fut. 2 sg. ὑποθήσεις Ex 26:12; 27:5; 1 aor. ὑπέθηκα; 2 aor. inf. ὑποθεῖναι; 2 aor. mid. impv. ὑπόθου (TestJob 23:7) (Hom. +).

❶ act.**to lay someth. down as expression of service, *lay down*** τὶ *someth.*—ⓐ in idiom *lay down, risk* τὸν τράχηλον (Lucian, Dem. 41 ὑπ. τὴν ψυχὴν ταῖς τῆς πατρίδος τύχαις; cp. Seneca, Ep. 47, 4; POxy 2722, 35 [commercial]) τὸν ἑαυτῶν τράχηλον ὑπέθηκαν *they put their own necks at risk (in my behalf)* or, in view of Paul's penchant for commercial imagery: *mortgaged their own necks* **Ro 16:4.**

ⓑ differently (somewhat as TestIss 5:3 ὑπ. τὸν νῶτον) *bow* in submission 1 Cl 63:1 (see s.v. τράχηλος for this pass. and Ro 16:4).

❷ mid. (Hom. et al.) aor. ὑπεθέμην (LXX) τινί τι **to provide instruction, *make known, teach*** *someth. to someone* (Pla., Hipp. Maj. 286b) ταῦτα ὑποτιθέμενος τοῖς ἀδελφοῖς **1 Ti 4:6.** This sense appears to fit the context better than *suggest* or *point out someth. to someone* (Hom.; Hdt. 1, 90; Pla., Charm. 155d; pap) or *enjoin, order someone (to do) someth.* (Hdt. 4, 134; Philo, Poster. Cai. 12; Jos., Bell. 2, 137, Ant. 1, 76).—M-M.

ὑποτρέχω 2 aor. ὑπέδραμον (Hom. et al.; PTebt 24, 67 [117 BC]; Jos., Ant. 7, 31; 326 al.) ***run*** or ***sail under the lee of,*** nautical t.t. (Plut., Mor. 243e ὅρμοις 'run in'. Also 'moor under' ἄκραν Heliod. 8, 16; ἄκρᾳ τινί Longus 3, 21) νησίον τι ὑπ. **Ac 27:16.**—M-M.

ὑποτύπωσις, εως, ἡ (τυπόομαι 'be stamped/marked'; Diog. L. 9, 78; Sext. Emp., Pyrrh. 2, 79; Pollux 7, 128; Philo, Abr. 71) **a pattern**

ⓐ as a model ***prototype*** **1 Ti 1:16** (as prime recipient of extraordinary mercy in view of his infamous past, Paul serves as a model for the certainty of availability of mercy to others).

ⓑ as a basis for behavioral comparison ***standard*** **2 Ti 1:13** (Philod., Mus. p. 77 Kemke [1884] ἀρετῶν; Synes., Dio 1 p. 38 Petav. ὁ λόγος [Δίωνος] ὑποτύπωσίς ἐστιν εὐδαίμονος βίου). ELee, NTS 8, '61/62, 171f proposes *outline* for both passages, w. reff.—DELG s.v. τύπτω. M-M. TW.

ὑπουργέω (ὑπουργός contr. form of ὑποεργός 'rendering service' [cp. ὑπουργία IMakedD 590, 4]) fut. 2 sg. ὑπουργήσεις (2 Km 9:10 Aq.) ***be helpful, assist*** (Aeschyl., Hdt. et al.; pap; TestDan 3, 4; Philo, Vi. Cont. 72; Jos., Ant. 3, 7) εἴς τι *in* or *at someth.* (Eunap., Vi. Soph. p. 108) MPol 13:1.—DELG s.v. ἔργον.

ὑποφέρω fut. ὑποίσω; aor. ὑπήνεγκα, inf. ὑπενεγκεῖν (Jos., Ant. 8, 213; on the aorist forms s. B-D-F § 81, 2), ὑπενέγκαι (Hs 7:6). (Hom.+) In our lit. as fig. ext. of 'bear or carry by being under' (s. example fr. X. in 2 below)

❶ **to bear up under trouble or difficulty, *submit to, endure*** τί *someth.* (Hippocr., X., Pla. et al.; Sb 5238, 22 [12 AD]; LXX; Tat. 21, 1 τιμωρίαν) Hv 3, 1, 9ab; 3, 2, 1. διωγμούς **2 Ti 3:11.** θλίψεις Hs 7:4–6. λύπας **1 Pt 2:19;** cp. Hm 10, 2, 6. πόνους 1 Cl 5:4 (cp. X., Hipparch, 1, 3; Pla., Tht. 173a; Isocr. 4, 64; 2 Macc 7:36). ὀργήν Hm 12, 4, 1 (cp. Pla., Leg. 9, 879c; Mi 7:9) κίνδυνον *incur danger* (Isocr. 3, 64) 1 Cl 14:2. ὕβριν *bear up under mistreatment* Hm 8:10. Abs. **1 Cor 10:13.**

❷ **to bear someth. for the benefit of another, *bear, bring, effect*** τὶ *someth.* in imagery of one who is under a burden (as e.g. an armor-bearer who is under the arms that he carries X., Cyr. 4, 5, 57) τὸ αἷμα τοῦ χριστοῦ ... παντὶ τῷ κόσμῳ μετανοίας χάριν ὑπήνεγκεν *the blood of Christ made the bounty of repentance available to all the world* 1 Cl 7:4 (v.l. ἐπήνεγκεν). (Here the blood of C. is viewed as capable of bearing a monumental burden of χάρις that benefits the entire world. As Lightf. points out, Soph., El. 834; X., Hell. 4, 7, 2 are not pertinent in establishing the questionable sense 'proffer'; nor is Plut., Publ. 109 [23], of a torch extended in symbolic gesture at a bier.)—M-M.

ὑποχθόνιος, (ία), ιον (χθόνιος 'in or under the earth') ***under the earth*** (Hes. et al.; Posidon.: 87 fgm. 47 Jac.) οἱ ὑποχθόνιοι *the powers under the earth* w. οἱ ἐπουράνιοι καὶ ἐπίγειοι (ἐπίγειος 1bβ) ITr 9:1.—DELG s.v. χθών.

ὑποχωρέω 1 aor. ὑπεχώρησα (Hom.+; ins, pap, LXX; TestAbr B 4 p. 108, 25 [Stone p. 64] ἐκ τοῦ σώματος; TestJob 27:2 [w. dat.]; GrBar 13:1f [ὑπό τινων]; Just., D. 9, 2)

❶ of persons (Hom. et al. in a military sense 'go back, retreat, withdraw', but also as Philo, Abr. 22 in a peaceful sense) **to withdraw from a location,** ***to go off, go away, retire,*** w. εἰς and acc. (Jos., Vi. 20; 246) εἰς πόλιν **Lk 9:10.** Used w. ἐν in the sense 'retire to a place and spend some time there' (cp. Kühner-G. I 541) ἦν ὑποχωρῶν ἐν ταῖς ἐρήμοις *he would steal away to (the) lonely places* **5:16.—Lk 20:20 v.l.**

❷ of things **to move from a position,** ***move away*** (Jos., Ant. 1, 91; 11, 240) of rolling movement ὁ λίθος ὑπεχώρησεν παρὰ μέρος GPt 9:37 corr. by Robinson (ἐπ'- cod., ἀπ'- Gebhardt, Blass; s. μέρος 1c, end).—DELG s.v. χώρα. M-M.

ὑποψία, ας, ἡ (ὑφοράω 'look at fr. below' cp. ὑποπτεύω; Hdt. et al.; CGFP 257, 69; pap; 2 Macc 4:34; Philo) ***suspicion*** διὰ τὴν ὑποψίαν τὴν πρὸς τὴν γυναῖκα *out of suspicion about his wife* AcPl Ha 4, 9.—Frisk s.v. ὄπωπα; cp. DELG. p. 811.

ὑπωπιάζω (on the v.l. ὑποπιάζειν s. W-S. §5, 19 note, end; Mlt-H. 75)('strike under the eye, give a black eye to' Aristot., Rhet. 3, 11, 15, 1413a, 20; TestSol 2:4 D [ὑποπ.]; Plut., Mor. 921f; Diog. L. 6, 89)

❶ **to blacken an eye,** ***give a black eye, strike in the face*** lit. τινά *someone,* of a woman who is driven to desperation and who the judge in the story thinks might in the end express herself physically ἵνα μὴ εἰς τέλος ἐρχομένη ὑπωπιάζῃ με *so that she might not finally come and blacken my eye* **Lk 18:5.** Hyperbole is stock-in-trade of popular storytelling. Some prefer to understand ὑπ. in this pass. in sense

❷ **to bring someone to submission by constant annoyance,** ***wear down,*** fig. ext. of 1 (s. L-S-J-M s.v. II, NRSV, REB, et al.). In this interp. ὑπ. in **Lk 18:5** has its meaning determined by εἰς τέλος. But in such case the denouement lacks punch, for the judge has already been worn down and wants nothing added to the κόπος that he has already endured. A more appropriate rendering for a fig. sense would be *browbeat.*—JDerrett, NTS 18, '71/72, 178–91 (esp. 189–91): a fig. expr. (common throughout Asia), *blacken my face = slander, besmirch* underlies ὑπ. here.

❸ **to put under strict discipline,** ***punish, treat roughly, torment,*** also fig. (cp. Aristoph., fgm. 541 πόλεις ὑπωπιασμέναι) **1 Cor 9:27** (of the apostle's self-imposed discipline. But the expr. is obviously taken fr. the language of prize-fighting vs. 26; on the virtue of self-control cp. X., Mem. 2, 1, 1; 5).—DELG s.v. ὄπωπα E. M-M. TW.

ὗς, ὑός, ἡ (Hom. et al.; ins, pap, LXX; En 89:41f; TestAsh 2:9 [bdg]; Jos., Ant. 13, 243 al.; Ar. 11, 4) **the female of the swine,** ***sow*** (ὁ ὗς is the boar) in a proverb ὗς λουσαμένη εἰς κυλισμὸν βορβόρου *a sow that has bathed herself, only to roll in the mud again* **2 Pt 2:22** (βόρβορος 2).—On **Lk 14:5 v.l.** see the editor's introd. to PBodm XIV '61, 18–19; EWiesenberg, HUCA 27, '56, 213–33 (swine).—DELG. M-M. OEANE IV 347f.

ὑσσός, οῦ, ὁ (Polyb. et al.; Dionys. Hal. 5, 46, 2 [as long as a spear of moderate length]; Strabo, Plut. et al.) ***javelin,*** Lat. 'pilum' **J 19:29 v.l.** S. ὕσσωπος.—DELG.

ὕσσωπος, ου, ἡ and **ὁ,** also **ὕσσωπον, τό** (in wr. outside our lit. [Nicander: II BC, Ther. 872; Alexiph. 603; Chaeremon 44, 6 al.; ins, pap] all three genders are quotable; for the LXX the masc. and fem. are certain; Philo, Vi. Cont. 73 excludes the neut. for that author; in Jos., Bell. 6, 201, Ant. 2, 312; 4, 80 the matter is not clear. In our lit. the neut. is certain only for Barnabas.—אֵזוֹב) ***the hyssop*** (acc. to Zohary, Plants 96f = the Origanum Syriacum, not the European Hyssopus), a small bush w. blue flowers and highly aromatic leaves; used in purificatory sacrifices (Ex 12:22; Lev 14:4; Num 19:6, 18.—SIG 1218, 16 [V BC], where the word is beyond doubt correctly restored, the hyssop serves to purify a house in which a corpse had lain; Chaeremon also mentions its purifying power) **Hb 9:19;** 1 Cl 18:7 (Ps 50:9); B 8:1, 6.—In **J 19:29** hyssop appears as a plant w. a long, firm stem or stalk, which creates some difficulty. The conjecture by JCamerarius († 1574), ὑσσῷ (=*javelin* [s. ὑσσός]: ὑσσῷ is actually found in mss. 476 and 1242, both antedating the conjecture) προπεριθέντες, has been accepted by many (e.g. Dalman, Jesus 187; Lagrange, JBernard; Field, Notes 106–8; M-M.; Goodsp., Probs. 115f; Mft.; NEB; w. reserve, Bultmann). Against the rdg. ὑσσός (not accepted by Weymouth, NAB [the margin suggests probability of 'symbolic' usage], NRSV, REB [marginal ref. to 'javelin']; 20th Century 'hyssop-stalk') it has been urged (by WBauer et al.) that the purifying effect of the hyssop (used acc. to Ex 12:22 specif. at the Passover) is the most important consideration here.—ILöw, Die Flora der Juden II 1924, 72f; 84–101, on J 19:29 esp. 99–101; LFonck, Streifzüge durch die biblische Flora 1900, 109; EbNestle, Zum Ysop bei Johannes, Josephus u. Philo: ZNW 14, 1913, 263–65; LBaldensperger and GCrowfoot, Hyssop: PEF 63, '31, 89–98; Metzger 253f; BHHW III 2197f.—DELG. M-M.

ὑστερέω fut. 3 sg. ὑστερήσει LXX; 1 aor. ὑστέρησα; pf. ὑστέρηκα. Pass.: fut. 2 sg. ὑστερηθήσει (ApcMos) 26; 1 aor. ὑστερήθην (fr. ὕστερος, s. three next entries; Eur., Hdt.+; ins, pap, LXX, PsSol 18:2; TestJob 9:5; ApcMos 26; Joseph.; Just., D. 82, 1)

❶ **to miss out on someth. through one's own fault,** ***to miss, fail to reach,*** act. (cp. 'come too late' Phlegon: 257 fgm. 36, 1, 3 Jac.) abs. **Hb 4:1.** ἀπό τινος *be excluded from someth.* (sim. constr. but difft sense Aesop, Fab. 97 P.=134 H. of a kid lagging behind the rest of the flock and pursued by a wolf ἔριφος ὑστερήσας ἀπὸ ποίμνης) **12:15.**

❷ **to be in short supply,** ***fail, give out, lack,*** act. (Socrat., Ep. 14, 9 [p. 258 Malherbe]; Diosc. 5, 75, 13 ὑστερούσης πολλάκις σποδοῦ; Is 51:14 [marginal note in the Cod. Marchal.] καὶ οὐ μὴ ὑστερήσῃ ὁ ἄρτος αὐτοῦ; PCairZen 311, 5 [250 BC] ἵνα μὴ ὑστερήσῃ τὸ μέλι; BGU 1074, 7 [III AD] μήτε ὑστερεῖν τι ὑμῖν) ὑστερήσαντος οἴνου **J 2:3.**—In a striking use w. acc. ἕν σε ὑστερεῖ (lit. 'one thing puts you later', 'laterizes you', i.e. jeopardizes your securing the inheritance) *in your case just one thing is missing* **Mk 10:21** (cp. the construction 4 below; acc. as Ps 22:1 οὐδέν με ὑστερήσει).

❸ **to be in need,** ***be needy, lack***—ⓐ act. w. gen. τινός *someth.* (Demosth. 19, 332 πολλῶν; Phalaris, Ep. 20 H.; PsSol 18:2; Jos., Bell. 2, 617, Ant. 2, 7; PEdg 45 [=Sb 6751], 5 [251/250 BC] ξύλων) **Lk 22:35.** Abs. *be in need, be poor* D 11:12.

ⓑ pass. in act. sense: ὑστερούμενοι **Hb 11:37** (TestJob 9:5) unless this belongs in 5 below. Subst. οἱ ὑστερούμενοι *those who are poor* or *needy* Hv 3, 9, 2; 4; 6; m 2:4. W. χῆραι s 9, 27, 2. W. widow(s) and orphan(s) Hm 8:10; s 5, 3, 7.

❹ **to be lower in status,** ***be less than, inferior to,*** act. w. gen. of comparison (Pla., Rep. 7, 539e ἐμπειρίᾳ τῶν ἄλλων) τινός *be inferior to someone* **2 Cor 11:5; 12:11.**—Abs. **1 Cor 12:24 v.l.** (s. under 5b).

❺ **to experience deficiency in someth. advantageous or desirable,** ***lack, be lacking, go without, come short of*****—ⓐ** act. τί ἔτι ὑστερῶ; *what do I still lack? in what respect do I still fall short?* **Mt 19:20** (cp. the construction in 2 above) (Phillips: 'What is still missing in my life?'; cp. Ps 38:5).

ⓑ pass. w. gen. of thing (Diod. S. 18, 71, 5; ApcMos 26; Jos., Ant. 15, 200) **Ro 3:23;** Dg 5:13 (opp. περισσεύειν); IEph 5:2. Also ἔν τινι **1 Cor 1:7.** Abs. (Sir 11:11) **Lk 15:14; 1 Cor 8:8** (opp. περισσ.); **2 Cor 11:9; Phil 4:12** (opp. περισσ.); B 10:3. Ptc. **1 Cor 12:24.**—DELG s.v. ὕστερος. M-M. TW. Spicq.

ὑστέρημα, ατος, τό (ὑστερέω; PTebt 786, 9 [II BC]; other pap Spicq, Lexique 1572 n. 2; LXX; TestBenj 11:5; Herm. Wr. 4, 9; PFredriksen, VigChr 33, '79, 287–90 [nag Hammadi])

❶ **the lack of what is needed or desirable, freq. in contrast to abundance,** ***need, want, deficiency*** (cp. Judg 18:10; 19:19; Ps 33:10; Achmes 111, 4) ἐκ τοῦ ὑστερήματος αὐτῆς πάντα τὸν βίον ἔβαλεν **Lk 21:4.**—**2 Cor 8:14ab** (opp. περίσσευμα in both instances; Eutecnius 4 p. 37, 17 opp. πλεονέκτημα). Oft. used w. ἀναπληρόω (q.v. 3) or προσαναπληρόω (q.v.) *supply a need:* ἀναπλ. αὐτοῦ τὸ ὑστ. *supply his need* 1 Cl 38:2. τὸ ὑστέρημά μου προσανεπλήρωσαν οἱ ἀδελφοί **2 Cor 11:9.** Also pl. πρ. τὰ ὑστερήματα τῶν ἁγίων **9:12.** To ἀναπλ. the ὑστέρημα of one person means *to make up for the person's absence, represent the person in the person's absence* **1 Cor 16:17; Phil 2:30** (λειτουργία 2). Also used w. ἀνταναπληρόω (q.v.) **Col 1:24.**

❷ **a defect that must be removed so that perfection can be attained,** ***lack, shortcoming*** as, in the pl. (Herm. Wr. 13, 1; TestBenj 11:5) τὸ ὑστερήματα τῆς πίστεως ὑμῶν **1 Th 3:10.** Of moral shortcomings 1 Cl 2:6 (w. παραπτώματα); Hv 3, 2, 2ab (w. ἁμαρτήματα).—DELG s.v. ὕστερος. TW. Spicq. Sv.

ὑστέρησις, εως, ἡ (ὑστερέω; Aq. Job 30:3; Aesop 106 P.=154 H./126 Ch./108 H-H.; Achmes 83, 13f; Cat. Cod. Astr. X 146, 20; 147, 2) **the condition of lacking that which is essential,** ***need, lack, poverty*** **Mk 12:44.** Pl. *deprivations* Hs 6, 3, 4.—καθ' ὑστέρησιν *because of need* or *want* (κατά II 5aδ) **Phil 4:11.**—DELG s.v. ὕστερος. TW. Spicq.

ὕστερος, α, ον (Hom.+; ins, pap, LXX; PsSol 2:28; Test12-Patr; AssMos fgm. f; Ar., Just., Tat.) in our lit. used as comp. and superl. (B-D-F §62; s. Rob. 294; 488; 662).

❶ **pert. to being subsequent in a series,** ***the second one,*** adj. comp. (1 Ch 29:29) ὁ ὕστερος (of two, as Aristot., Pol. 1312a, 4; Aristophon Com. [IV BC] 5), *the latter* **Mt 21:31 v.l.**

❷ **pert. to a point of time that is subsequent to another point of time—ⓐ** comp.: neut. ὕστερον as adv. (Hom. et al.) ***in the second place, later, then, thereafter*** (X., Mem. 2, 6, 7; Arrian, An. 7, 14, 10; GDI 1222, 4 [Arcadia] ὕστερον δὲ μή=later but no more; Pr 24:32; TestZeb 10:7; Jos., Bell. 7, 285, Ant. 1, 217; Just., A I, 46, 1, D. 105, 1; Tat. 31, 3) **Mt 4:2; 21:29, 32** (μεταμέλ. ὕστερον: Diod. S. 18, 47, 2 ὕστερον μετανοήσαντες ... ἀπέσχοντο=later they changed their minds and refrained; Hierocles 18 p. 460); **25:11; Mk 16:14; Lk 4:2 v.l.; J 13:36; Hb 12:11;** MPol 18:1; Papias (2:15).

ⓑ superl.—α. ὕστερος as adj. (PsSol 2:28 τὸ ὕστερον 'the end'; ὕστατος is not found in our lit.) ***last*** ἐν ὑστέροις καιροῖς *in the last times* **1 Ti 4:1** (possibly *in later,* i.e. *future, times:* Pla., Leg. 9, 865a ἐν ὑστέροις χρόνοις).

β. neut. ὕστερον as adv. ***finally*** (Theophrast., Char. 5, 10; Aelian, VH 9, 33; TestJos 3:8; Jos., Ant. 16, 315; Tat. 13, 1 εἰς ὕ.) **Mt 21:37; 26:60; Lk 20:32.** ὕστερον πάντων *last of all* **Mt 22:27; Lk 20:32 v.l.**—DELG. M-M. TW. Spicq.

ὑφαίνω 1 aor. 3 sg. ὕφανεν LXX, inf. ὑφᾶναι Ex 35:35; 37:21. Pass.: 1 aor. 3 sg. ὑφάνθη (Mel.); pf. ptc. ὑφασμένοι Lev 19:19; TestJob (s. next entry; Hom.+; ins; POxy 113, 9 [II AD]; 1414, 11; LXX; TestJob 25:7; Jos., C. Ap. 2, 242 al.; Mel., P. 20, 137) ***weave*** **Lk 12:27** D (text κοπιᾷ w. P^{45}, P^{75}, et al.).—B. 410. M-M.

ὑφαντός, ή, όν (Hom. et al.; PAmh 133, 15 [II AD]; Ex; Jos., Ant. 3, 57) ***woven*** **J 19:23.**—DELG s.v. ὑφαίνω. M-M.

ὑφίστημι 1 aor. 3 sg. ὑπέστησεν (Tat. 5, 1); 2 aor. ὑπέστην (LXX; TestJob 7:13); mid. fut. ὑποστήσομαι (Hom.+)

❶ **to hold out against or survive a powerful force,** ***resist, face, endure,*** w. acc. (Eur., Cycl. 199; Thu. 1, 144, 5; 7, 66, 2; Diod. S. 16, 51, 1 [τοὺς κινδύνους]; Jdth 6:3; Pr 13:8; TestJob 7:13; 26:1; Jos., Ant. 12, 282) τίς αὐτοῦ τὴν παρουσίαν ὑποστήσεται; Dg 7:6.

❷ **to become a reality,** ***take (structured) shape*** mid., of a thousand-year reign of Christ on earth: σωματικῶς τῆς Χριστοῦ βασιλείας ... ὑποστησομένης *the kingdom of Christ assuming physical presence/structure (on this earth)* Papias (2:12).—Sv.

ὑψηλός, ή, όν (Hom.+)—❶ **pert. to considerable extension upward,** ***tall, high,*** lit. ὄρος *a high mountain* (Epicurus in Diog. L. 10, 103; Diod. S. 14, 99, 1; Ezk 40:2; PsSol 11:4; TestLevi 2:5) **Mt 4:8; 17:1; Mk 9:2; Lk 4:5 v.l.; Rv 21:10.** τεῖχος (JosAs 2:17; cp. Jos., Ant. 20, 191) vs. **12** (in both places w. μέγα). ὑψηλὸν σπήλαιον *a lofty cave* B 11:4 (Is 33:16). Also of human or human-like figures *tall* (Dio Chrys. 71 [21], 1 νεανίσκος; Plut., Aemil. Paul. 264 [18, 3]; Jdth 16:6; on motif of tallness in lit. s. Leutzsch, Hermas 479f n. 194) Hs 8, 1, 2; 9, 3, 1; ὑψ. τῷ μεγέθει 9, 6, 1.—Comp. ὑψηλότερος w. gen. of comparison (Lucian, Nigrin. 25; En 26:3; TestAbr B) Hs 9, 2, 1. ὑψηλότερος τῶν οὐρανῶν γενόμενος *raised to greater heights than the heavens* **Hb 7:26** (DSilva, DLNT 360f). Moses stands on two shields ὑψηλότερος πάντων B 12:2.—μετὰ βραχίονος ὑψηλοῦ **Ac 13:17;** cp. 1 Cl 60:3 (s. βραχίων).—Subst. (PsSol 11:2 στῆθι, Ιερουσαλημ, ἐφ' ὑψηλοῦ; Appian, Liby. 130 §620 ἐφ' ὑψηλοῦ=on a high place, Bell. Civ. 3, 28 §110 τὰ ὑψηλά=the high places; likew. Diod. S. 20, 29, 9) τὰ ὑψηλά *the height(s)* (GrBar 4:10; Sb 6797, 33 [255/254 BC])=heaven ἐν ὑψηλοῖς *on high* (Ps 92:4; 112:5, cp. vs. 4) **Hb 1:3.**

❷ **pert. to being arrogant,** ***exalted, proud, haughty,*** fig. ext. of 1, subst. τὸ ἐν ἀνθρώποις ὑψηλόν *what is considered exalted among humans* **Lk 16:15.** ὑψηλὰ φρονεῖν *cherish proud thoughts, feel proud* (Quint. Smyrn. [IV AD] 2, 327) **Ro 11:20; 1 Ti 6:17 v.l.** (ὑψ. φρονεῖν='think lofty thoughts': Lucian, Herm. 5; Philo, Ebr. 128). τὰ ὑψηλὰ φρονεῖν *strive after things that are (too) high, be too ambitious,* prob. 'don't be a social climber' **Ro 12:16** (cp. Palaeph., Exc. Vat. p. 94, 6; 1 Km 2:3, and on the contrast ὑψ. ... ταπεινός: Περὶ ὕψους 43, 3). οἱ ὑψηλοί *the proud, the haughty, the high and mighty* (sing.: Philo, Mos. 1, 31) 1 Cl 59:3; B 19:6; D 3:9.

❸ **pert. to being of high quality,** ***noble, sublime*** the neut. of the comp. as adv. (Περὶ ὕψους 43, 3), ὀφείλομεν πλουσιώτερον καὶ ὑψηλότερον προσάγειν τῷ φόβῳ αὐτοῦ B 1:7, here either in a good sense, of richer and higher progress in the fear of God, or (more prob. in view of the thematic connection w. ch. 2 w. focus on appropriate sacrifice): *we ought to make a* *costlier and more sublime sacrifice in the fear of God*.—B. 852. DELG s.v. ὕψι 4. M-M.

ὑψηλόφθαλμος, ον (hapax leg.—ὑψηλοὶ ὀφθαλμοί in the lit. sense Physiogn. I 327, 2) ***lifting up the eyes***, perh. *in pride*, though the context calls rather for *in lust* or *wantonness* D 3:3 (s. Wengst, Didache p. 71 n. 16, w. ref. to TestIss 7:2; 1QS 1:6; CD 2:16; 2 Pt 2:14; v.l. in Apost. Const. 7 ῥιψόφθαλμος).—DELG s.v. ὕψι.

ὑψηλοφρονέω (ὑψηλόφρων 'haughty'; Pollux 9, 145; schol. on Pind., P. 2, 91; schol. on Eur., Hippol. 728; Phot. and Suda s.v. ὑψαυχεῖν; B-D-F §119, 5; Rob. 163 n.) ***be proud, haughty*** **Ro 11:20 v.l.; 1 Ti 6:17.**—DELG s.v. ὕψι and φρήν.

ὑψηλοφροσύνη, ης, ἡ (Physiogn. II 225, 6; Hesych. s.v. φυσίωσις; Leontius of Neap. [VII AD] 28 p. 61, 5; 10 HGelzer [1893]) ***pride, haughtiness*** Hm 8:3; s 9, 22, 3.—DELG s.v. ὕψι and φρήν.

ὑψηλόφρων, ον, gen. ονος (Eur., Pla.; Cass. Dio 72, 8, 3='high-minded, high-spirited') ***proud, haughty*** (so Pollux 9, 147; Eustath., Opuscula 23, 60 p. 209, 96; the adv. Pel.-Leg. 22, 31) Hs 8, 9, 1.—DELG s.v. ὕψι.

ὕψιστος, η, ον (Pind., Aeschyl.+; loanw. in rabb.) superl. of the adv. ὕψι; no positive in use

❶ **pert. to being the highest in a spatial sense, *highest*** (Diog. L. 8, 31 ὁ ὕψιστος τόπος, acc. to Pythagoras, is the place to which Hermes conducts pure souls) τὰ ὕψιστα *the highest heights*=heaven (Job 16:19; Ps 148:1; PsSol 18:10; JosAs 22:9=מְרוֹמִים; cp. 1QM 14, 14; 17, 8) ὡσαννὰ ἐν τοῖς ὑψίστοις *grant salvation*, (thou who art) *in the highest heaven* **Mt 21:9; Mk 11:10** (Goodsp., Probs. 34f). δόξα ἐν ὑψ. **Lk 2:14** (opp. ἐπὶ γῆς); **19:38** (w. ἐν οὐρανῷ, which means the same). ὁ ὕψιστος ἐν ὑψίστοις *the Most High in the highest (heaven)* 1 Cl 59:3 (cp. Is 57:15).

❷ **pert. to being the highest in status,** ὁ ὕψιστος ***the Most High*** of God, distinguished from lesser deities and other objects of cultic devotion (Ζεὺς ὕψιστος: Pind., N. 1, 60 [90]; 11, 2; Aeschyl., Eum. 28; CIG 498; 503; 1869 al.; Aristonous, in Coll. Alex. 1, 7 p. 163 [ACook, Zeus I/2, 1925, 876–89; CRoberts, TSkeat and ANock, The Gild of Zeus Hypsistos: HTR 29, '36, 39–88, Gk. text of Sb 7835 cited in this article was not reprinted in Nock, Essays: s. New Docs 1, 28]. θεὸς ὕψιστος: ins fr. Cyprus in BCH 20, 1896 p. 361; Sb 589 [II BC]; 1323, 1 [II AD]; OGI 378, 1 [I AD] θεῷ ἁγίῳ ὑψίστῳ; 755, 1f τοῦ ἁγιωτάτου [θεοῦ ὑψί]στου σωτῆρος; 756, 3–4 τοῦ ἁγιατάτου θεοῦ ὑψίστου: PGM 4, 1068 ἱερὸν φῶς τοῦ ὑψίστου θεοῦ; 5, 46; 12, 63; 71; New Docs 1, 25 no. 5. Isis as ὑψ. θεός: IAndrosIsis [Kyrene] 7 p. 129 Peek. Also simply Ὕψιστος CIG 499; 502. Other ins and pap New Docs 1, 25–28. On the syncretistic communities of the σεβόμενοι θεὸν ὕψιστον cp. ESchürer, SBBerlAk 1897, 200–225, History III 169; FCumont, Hypsistos: Suppl. à la Rev. de l'instruction publique en Belgique 1897, Pauly-W. s.v. Hypsistos; Kl. Pauly II 129f; APlassart, Mélanges Holleaux 1913, 201ff; Clemen² 58–60. Whether Israelite influence is present cannot be established, for the use of ὕψιστος pervades Gr-Rom. texts [s. lit. cited above and Nock, Essays I 414–43; s. also New Docs 1, 25–29], but 'God Most High' certainly has a firm place in Israelite experience, and OT usage [LXX] would account for its use in the NT, coupled w. semantic opportunity provided by polytheistic formulation. Examples of usage across cultural lines include: OGI 96, 5–7 [III/II BC]; APF 5, 1913, p. 163 [29 BC] θεῷ μεγάλῳ μεγάλῳ ὑψίστῳ; En, TestAbr, Test12Patr, JosAs; ApcEsdr 1, 2 p. 24, 5 Tdf.; ApcZeph; Philo, In Flacc. 46, Ad Gai. 278; 317; Jos., Ant. 16, 163; Ar. 15, 1; Just., D. 32, 3; 124, 1; the Jewish prayers for vengeance fr. Rheneia [Dssm., LO 352ff=LAE 416; SIG 1181, 1f]; CIJ I, 690, 727–30; SibOr 3, 519; 719; Ezek. Trag. 239 [in Eus., PE 9, 29, 14]; Philo Epicus: 729 fgm. 3, 2 Jac. [Eus., PE 9, 24]; ὁ μέγας καὶ ὑψ. θεός Hippol., Ref. 9, 15, 1; ANock, CRoberts, TSkeat, HTR 29, 36, 39–88). ὁ θεὸς ὁ ὕψ. (cp. Theoph. Ant. 2, 3 [p. 100, 1]) **Mk 5:7; Lk 8:28; Ac 16:17; Hb 7:1** (Gen 14:18). τὸν ὕψ. θεόν GJs 24:1. ὁ ὕψ. (TestAbr A 9 p. 87, 10 [Stone p. 22]; oft. Test12Patr; JosAs 8:10; ApcEsdr 1:2; Just., D. 32, 3. ἡ δύναμις τοῦ ὑ. Hippol., Ref. 6, 35, 7) **Ac 7:48;** 1 Cl 29:2 (Dt 32:8); 45:7; 52:3 (Ps 49:14). ὁ μόνος ὕψ. 59:3 (s. 1 above, end). Also without the art. (En 10:1; TestSim 2:5; TestLevi 8:15; Just., D. 124, 1 and 4; Mel., P. 98, 752 [w. art. Ps 17:14]) ὕψ. **Lk 1:35, 76.** υἱὸς ὑψίστου vs. **32** (of Christ; on the association of υἱὸς ὑψίστου and υἱὸς θεοῦ [vs. 34] cp. the Aramaic text 4QpsDan Aᵃ [=4Q 246], JFitzmyer, NTS 20, '73/74, 382–407 [esp. 391–94]); also GJs 11:3; in the pl. of humans (cp. Sir 4:10) **Lk 6:35.** πατὴρ ὕψ. IRo ins.—DNP V 821–23. DELG s.v. ὕψι. M-M. TW.

ὕψος, ους, τό (Aeschyl., Hdt.+; ins, pap, LXX, pseudepigr.; Philo; Jos., C. Ap. 2, 119 ὕψ., πλάτος al.; Just., D. 39, 5; Mel., P. [edd. and mss. fluctuate in use of the pl. ὕψη or ὕψηλα]) 'height'.

❶ **extent or distance upward, height**—ⓐ of dimension 1 Cl 49:4 (perh. sense b). W. other dimensions (τὸ μῆκος καὶ τὸ πλάτος) **Rv 21:16.** (πλάτος καὶ μῆκος καὶ βάθος) **Eph 3:18** (βάθος 1).—Pl. ἀναφέρεσθαι εἰς τὰ ὕψη IEph 9:1.

ⓑ of locale *height=high place* (SibOr 8, 235), mostly=*heaven* (Ps 17:17 ἐξ ὕψους; 101:20; TestJob 15:1 τῶν ἐν ὕψει; Just., D. 39, 5; Stephan. Byz. s.v. Λαοδίκεια: ἀφ' ὕψους ὁ θεός) **Lk 1:78** (ἀνατολή 3); **24:49; Eph 4:8** (Ps 67:19). τὰ ὕψη τῶν οὐρανῶν 1 Cl 36:2 (Diod. S. 4, 7, 4 ὕψος οὐράνιον; Aesop, Fab. 397b H. τὰ οὐράνια ὕψη).—τὰ ἐν ὕψεσι as someth. different from τὰ ἐν οὐρανοῖς Dg 7:2 (opp. τὰ ἐν βάθεσι).

❷ **a position of high status, *high position*** (of rank Herodian 1, 13, 6; 1 Macc 1:40; 10:24.—Of degree: Pla., Ep. 7, 351e ὕψος ἀμαθίας the 'height' of ignorance; Ps.-Aristot., De Mundo 6; Plut., Publ. 100 [6, 5]; Jos., Ant. 8, 126 ὕψος εὐδαιμονίας) **Js 1:9** (opp. ταπεινός and ταπείνωσις as TestAbr B 7 p. 111, 21 [Stone p. 70]) τὸν ποιοῦντα ταπεινοὺς εἰς ὕψος *who exalts the humble* (unless εἰς ὕψ. means 'upright', as Apollod. [II BC]: 244 fgm. 107d [=107e] Jac.) 1 Cl 59:3 (Job 5:11).

❸ **a lofty opinion of oneself, *pride, arrogance*** (PsSol 17:6) D 5:1. ὕψος δυνάμεως *arrogance in an influential position* B 20:1.—JKühn, Ὕψος '41.—DELG s.v. ὕψι. M-M. TW. Sv.

ὑψόω fut. ὑψώσω; 1 aor. ὕψωσα. Pass.: 1 fut. ὑψωθήσομαι; 1 aor. ὑψώθην; 1 pf. ptc. ὑψωμένος Jer 17:12 (fr. ὕψι 'on high', formed like its opposite ταπεινόω; since Hippocr.; also SIG 783, 45 [I BC]; PBrem 14, 7 [II AD]; LXX; pseudepigr.; Jos., Bell. 1, 146; 3, 171; Mel.)

❶ **to lift up spatially, *lift up, raise high*** τινά *or* τί *someone* or *someth.* (Batrach. 81; TestAbr A 9 p. 87, 14 [Stone p. 22]; 10, p. 87, 17 [St. p. 22]; JosAs 12:3; PGM 4, 2395; 2989f) Μωϋσῆς ὕψωσεν τὸν ὄφιν *Moses lifted up the serpent* by fastening it to a pole in the sight of all **J 3:14a.** In the same way Christ is lifted up on the cross vs. **14b** (Mel., P. 95, 727; cp. Artem. 4, 49 ὑψηλότατον εἶναι τὸν ἐσταυρωμένον; 1, 76 p. 69, 11; 2, 53; Ps.-Callisth. 2, 21, 26 ἔσεσθε περιφανεῖς κ. διάσημοι πᾶσιν ἀνθρώποις ἐπὶ τὸν σταυρὸν κρεμασθέντες [a play on words w. an ambiguous expr. which, by using the word 'outstanding', can mean social position as well as being lifted up on a cross before the eyes of all]); for J this 'lifting up' is not to be separated fr. the 'exaltation' into heaven, since the heavenly exaltation presupposes the earthly **8:28; 12:32** (ἐκ τῆς γῆς; CTorrey, JBL 51, '32, 320–22)—**12:34** (Hdb. on J 3:14; CLattey, Le verbe ὕψ. dans St. Jean: RSR 3, 1912, 597f; CLindeboom, 'Verhoogd worden' in Joh. 3:14: GereformTT 15, 1915, 491–98; MBlack, Aramaic Approach[3] 141; OCullmann, TZ 4, '48, 365f; WThüsing, Die Erhöhung und Verherrlichung Jesu im J, '60; JSchaberg, Daniel 7:12 and the NT Passion-Resurrection Predictions, NTS 31, '85, 208–22 [the Aramaic equivalent of ὑψωθῆναι is אזדקיף, meaning both 'to be exalted' and 'to be crucified or hanged', 217f]). τῇ δεξιᾷ τοῦ θεοῦ ὑψωθείς *exalted* (to heaven) *by the Power* (δεξιός 1b, end) *of God* **Ac 2:33.** Marking the transition to sense 2 are passages in which ἕως οὐρανοῦ ὑψωθῆναι is a metaphor for crowning w. the highest honors (cp. PsSol 1:5; ApcEsdr 4:32) **Mt 11:23; Lk 10:15.**

❷ **to cause enhancement in honor, fame, position, power, or fortune, *exalt*** fig. ext. of 1 (Polyb. 5, 26, 12 [opp. ταπεινοῦν]; Plut., Mor. 103e; LXX). God *exalts* τινά *someone* (TestJos 1:7; 18:1) ταπεινούς (cp. Ezk 21:31; EpArist 263) **Lk 1:52;** cp. **Js 4:10; 1 Pt 5:6.** Pass. (TestReub 6:5; SibOr 3, 582) **Mt 23:12b; Lk 14:11b; 18:14b; 2 Cor 11:7.**—τοῦτον (i.e. Christ) ὁ θεὸς ἀρχηγὸν ὕψωσεν *God has exalted him as leader* **Ac 5:31.** God τὸν λαὸν ὕψωσεν ἐν γῇ Αἰγύπτου *has made the people great* (in numbers and in power) *in Egypt* **13:17.**—ὑψοῦν ἑαυτόν *exalt oneself, consider oneself better* than others (TestJos 17:8; Hippol., Ref. 10, 14, 6; cp. ParJer 6:23 ὑψώθη ἡ καρδία ὑμῶν) **Mt 23:12a; Lk 14:11a; 18:14a;** B 19:3; D 3:9; Hm 11:12; s 9, 22, 3.—DELG s.v. ὕψι. M-M. TW.

ὕψωμα, ατος, τό (fr. ὕψι via ὑψόω; Plut., Mor. 782d; Sext. Emp., Math. 5, 33; 35; LXX; TestJob 41, 4; Philo, Praem. 2; Ps.-Phoc. 73; SibOr 8, 234; the mng. 'linear extension' ['height'] is not found in our lit.)

❶ as an astronomical term (cp. the t.t. 'exaltation' Plut., Mor. 149a; Ptolem., Apotel. 1, 20, 1ff; oft. Vett. Val.; PLond 110, 14; Cat. Cod. Astr. XII 102, 25. Neugebauer/Hoesen, glossary p. 199) **the space above the horizon, *the world above*** (which would be the domain of many transcendent forces) **Ro 8:39** (opp. βάθος, q.v. 1 and s. Rtzst., Poim. 80; WKnox, St. Paul and the Church of the Gentiles '39, 106f).—OGerhardt, D. Stern des Messias 1922, 15. ὁ θεὸς τῶν ὑψωμάτων GJs 6:2.

❷ **that which postures arrogantly, *arrogance,*** πᾶν ὕψωμα ἐπαιρόμενον *everything that rises up,* prob.=*all pride* (*every proud obstacle* NRSV) *that rises up against it* **2 Cor 10:5** (Euthym.: ὑψηλοφρονία. But Chrysost. MPG LXI, 545 explains it by using πύργωμα, which would mean someth. like 'towering fortress'; cp. PPetr III, 46, 3, 11 τοὺς ἐπαρθέντας τοίχους; TestJob 41:4 ἐποίησεν ἑαυτὸν ἀθρόως εἰς τὸ αὐτοῦ ὕψωμα 'self-aggrandizement').—DELG s.v. ὕψι. M-M. TW.

φαγεῖν, φάγομαι s. ἐσθίω.

φάγος (so accented by Hesychius [s.v. τρώκτης] and Eustath., Od. 1630, 15, though Herodian Gr. I 140, 4 prefers φαγός [s. PKatz, TLZ 83, '58, 316]), **ου, ὁ** (Zenob. Paroem. [II AD] 1, 73) ***glutton*** w. οἰνοπότης **Mt 11:19; Lk 7:34.**—S. ἐσθίω. DELG s.v. φαγεῖν. M-M.

φαιλόνης, ου, ὁ is to be spelled so (B-D-F §25) as against the great uncials and critical editions, which have φελόνης (PFay 347 [II AD]). This appears to be a Lat. loanw. (paenula; see Hahn p. 10, 8; EFraenkel, ZVS 42, 1909, 115, 1; ESchwyzer, MusHelv 3, '46, 50–52; but s. B. below), also in rabb. in var. spellings. Its original form was φαινόλας (Rhinthon [III BC], Com. Graec. fgm. 7 Kaibel [in Pollux 7, 61]) or φαινόλης (Epict. 4, 8, 34; Artem. 2, 3; 5, 29; Athen. 3, 97e; POxy 736, 4; 1737, 9; 15; PGiss 10, 21; PHamb 10, 19 [II BC]; Gignac I 100), also φαινόλιον (POxy 531, 14 [II AD]; 936, 18; 19). From these by metathesis (s. CLobeck, Pathologiae Sermonis Graeci Elementa I 1853, 514; W-S. §5, 18; B-D-F §32, 2; Mlt-H. 81; 106; 155) came φαιλόνης (which is still quotable at least in its dim. form φαιλόνιον [-ώνιον]: POxy 933, 30; PGiss 12, 4 [II AD]; BGU 816, 24 [III AD]; cp. Mod. Gk. φελόνι) ***cloak*** (POxy 531, 14 τὰ ἱμάτια τὰ λευκὰ τὰ δυνάμενα μετὰ τῶν πορφυρῶν φορεῖσθαι φαινολίων. Likew. Epict.; Athen., loc. cit. In view of these pass. the translation 'valise' is excluded; s. Field, Notes 217f, cited in M-M; also excluded is the interpretation in the direction of διφθέρα, the leather cover for papyrus rolls) **2 Ti 4:13** (on the subject-matter s. POxy 1489 [III AD] τὸ κιθώνιν [=χιτώνιον] ἐπιλέλησμαι παρὰ Τεκοῦσαν εἰς τὸν πυλῶνα. πέμψον μοι).—See B. 417, where φαινόλα is treated as the original fr. which Lat. paenula is borrowed, and not vice versa; s. also Mlt-H. 106.—Frisk. DELG s.v. φαίνω A. M-M.

φαίνω (Hom.+) fut. 3 pl. φανοῦσιν Da 12:3; 1 aor. ἔφανα (B-D-F §72; Mlt-H. 214f), subj. 3 sg. φάνῃ **Rv 8:12; 18:23;** 2 pf. πέφηνα (Tat.). Mid.: aor. subj. 3 sg. φάνηται (Just., A I, 7, 4). Pass.: impf. ἐφαινόμην; 2 fut. φανήσομαι (2 Macc 6:27; s. B-D-F §79; Mlt-H. 262; the older φανοῦμαι only in the LXX—quot. **1 Pt 4:18**); 2 aor. ἐφάνην; pf. 3 sg. πέφανται and inf. πέφανθαι (Just.)

❶ **to shine or to produce light, *shine*—ⓐ** as act., exc. for GJs 16:2 v.l. (s. deStrycker ad loc.), in our lit. only intr. *shine, give light, be bright* (Aristoph., Nub. 586 of the sun; Pla., Tim. 39b; Theocr. 2, 11 of the moon; Gen 1:15, 17; En 104:2; 2; TestJob 31:5 of stars; SibOr 5, 522; 8, 203) sun **Rv 1:16.** Sun and moon **21:23** (ApcMos 31); moon PtK 2 p. 14, 27; Dg 7:2. A lamp (1 Macc 4:50) **2 Pt 1:19;** in imagery **J 5:35** (in a comparison Theoph. Ant. 2, 13 [p. 134, 4]). Light **Rv 18:23** (φάνῃ modern edd.; φανῇ t.r.) in imagery **J 1:5; 1J 2:8.** Day and night *shine,* in so far as the sun, or moon and stars give their light **Rv 8:12** (text φάνῃ; v.l. φανῇ). φαίνοντος ἤδη τοῦ ὄρθρου AcPl Ha 4, 3 (s. ὄρθρος).—Of the brightness of a heavenly messenger AcPl Ha 3, 28; 31; 36.

ⓑ pass., in act. sense, of light and its sources *shine, flash* (Is 60:2) ἐφάνη φῶς μέγα ἐν τῷ σπηλαίῳ GJs 19:2 (JosAs 14:3 φῶς ἀνεκλάλητον) of stars, in imagery **Phil 2:15** (TestJob

31:5). Of lightning as a portent (X., Cyr. 1, 6, 1) **Mt 24:27.** Of light **Rv 18:23** (v.l. φανῇ). Of a star *appear* **Mt 2:7** (FBoll, ZNW 18, 1918, 45f); GJs 21:2 codd. Of the day (Appian, Iber. 35 §143 φαινομένης ἡμέρας) **Rv 8:12.**

❷ **to become visible,** ***appear,*** pass. φαίνομαι w. act./intr. sense—ⓐ *appear, be* or *become visible, be revealed* τότε ἐφάνη καὶ τὰ ζιζάνια **Mt 13:26** (cp. 2 Macc 1:33 τό ὕδωρ ἐφάνη). τά ἔργα τῶν ἀνθρώπων 2 Cl 16:3. τό σημεῖον τοῦ υἱοῦ τ. ἀνθρώπου **Mt 24:30.** Cp. D 16:6. ἀτμὶς φαινομένη (opp. ἀφανιζομένη) **Js 4:14.** Cp. Hv 3, 2, 6a. ὁ ἀσεβὴς ποῦ φανεῖται; *what will become of the godless man?* **1 Pt 4:18** (Pr 11:31). οὐδέποτε ἐφάνη οὕτως *nothing like this was ever seen* (=happened) **Mt 9:33.** τὸ φαινόμενον *that which is visible* (Philo, Rer. Div. Her. 270) IRo 3:3a. τὰ φαινόμενά σου εἰς πρόσωπον *whatever is visible before your face* (opp. τὰ ἀόρατα) IPol 2:2. φαινόμενα *things which appear* **Hb 11:3** (Ar. 1, 5 πάντων τῶν φαινομένων; Ath. 5, 2; cp. Sext. Emp., Hypotyp. 1, 138). Ign. explains: I will be a real believer ὅταν κόσμῳ μὴ φαίνωμαι *when I am no longer visibly present in the world* (because I have been devoured by the wild beasts) IRo 3:2. A play on words is meant to make this clear: Christ also, through the fact that he is ἐν πατρί and hence no longer visibly present in the world, μᾶλλον φαίνεται *is all the more plainly visible* as that which he really is, i.e. ὁ θεὸς ἡμῶν 3:3b. τὸ [τέλο]ς (or: τε[λο]ς) τῶν φαινο[μέ]νων (opp. ἀφανῶν) light of things seen Ox 1081, 29f (rev. rdg.; s. διέρχομαι 1bβ); ἡ πίστ[ις] εὑρ[ετ]έ[α] ἡ φαινομένη τοῦ ἀ.[. . . ι]κοῦ πατρός 32–34 (s. ἀπατρικός, but also ἀγέννητος, the preferred restoration being ἀγ[εννή]του on the basis of the Coptic).

ⓑ *make one's appearance, show oneself* (Diod. S. 4, 6, 5 θεὸν φαίνεσθαι παρ' ἀνθρώποις; 5, 2, 4 [divinity]; Chariton 5, 7, 10 φάνηθι, δαῖμον ἀγαθέ; Sb 8141, 24 [ins I BC] δαίμονος τοῦ ἀγαθοῦ υἱός . . . ἐφάνη; ParJer 7:20 θεὸς . . . ἐφάνη ἡμῖν διὰ τοῦ αἰέτου τούτου; SibOr 5, 152; Just., A I, 63, 10; ἐφάνη ὁ θεὸς . . . ἄλλως ἄλλοις Iren. 1, 10, 3 [Harv. I, 95, 9]; Did., Gen. 225, 13; τοῦ Ἰησοῦ . . . φαινομένου Just., D. 88, 8) Hv 1, 4, 3. Elijah (Jos., Ant. 8, 319) ἐφάνη *has made his appearance* (as forerunner of God's kingdom, Mal 3:22. Some people consider that Jesus is Elijah come again) **Lk 9:8.** ἕως ἐφάνη βρέφος *until the child (Jesus) appeared* (in ref. to his birth in a cave) GJs 19:2. Of the first advent of Jesus Christ, who comes from outside our world B 14:5; IMg 6:1; Dg 11:2; also w. dat. (X., Cyr. 1, 6, 43; Lucian, Dial. Deor. 20, 5; Ael. Aristid. 51, 25 K.=27 p. 540 D.: ἡ θεὸς ἐφάνη μοι) κόσμῳ 11:3. Of the risen Lord, w. dat. **Mk 16:9** (Just., D. 67, 7) τοῖς ἀποστόλοις. Of an angel, w. dat. (2 Macc 3:33; 10:29) **Mt 1:20** (GJs 14:2); **2:13, 19** (cp. Alcaeus L-P. [schol. on Nicander, Ther. 613 p. 48 Keil]: φανῆναι τὸν Ἀπόλλωνα καθ' ὕπνους; Jos., C. Ap. 1, 289 κατὰ τοὺς ὕπνους ἡ Ἶσις ἐφάνη τῷ Ἀ., Ant. 7, 147; 8, 196). ὅπως φανῶσιν τοῖς ἀνθρώποις *in order to be seen by people* **Mt 6:5;** w. ptc. to denote the role that one plays before people (Hyperid., fgm. 70, 1; Lucian, Dial. Deor. 4, 1; Ael. Aristid. 47 p. 428 D.) νηστεύοντες *as fasting* vs. **16;** cp. **18** (B-D-F § 414, 3).—Of the Antichrist φανήσεται ὡς υἱὸς θεοῦ *he will appear* (in the same way) *as a son of God* D 16:4.—Of earthly persons: ὅπου ἂν φανῇ ὁ ἐπίσκοπος, ἐκεῖ τὸ πλῆθος ἔστω ISm 8:2. Of participation in a meeting διὰ τί οὐκ ἐφάνης τῇ συνόδῳ ἡμῶν GJs 15:1. Παῦλος φανεὶς πᾶσι εἶπεν *Paul showed himself* (after his martyrdom) *to all and said* AcPl Ha 11, 5.

❸ **to become known,** ***be recognized, be apparent, be revealed,*** pass. φαίνομαι w. act./intr. sense—ⓐ w. predicate nom. εἰ ἦσαν, ἐφαίνοντο ἂν κλάδοι τοῦ σταυροῦ *if they* (the bogus teachers) *actually were* (God's planting), *they would appear as branches of the cross* ITr 11:2. οὐ φαίνονται *they are not apparent* Hs 3:2ab, 3ab. ἡ ἁμαρτία ἵνα φανῇ ἁμαρτία *in order that sin might be recognized as sin* **Ro 7:13.**

ⓑ *appear* to the eyes of the spirit, *be revealed* ὅπερ καὶ φανήσεται πρὸ προσώπου ἡμῶν, ἐξ ὧν ἀγαπῶμεν αὐτόν *which also will be revealed before our face by the fact that we love (the Lord)* IEph 15:3.

❹ **to be known by appearance as opposed to underlying reality,** ***appear as someth., appear to be someth.,*** pass. φαίνομαι w. act./intr. sense made more definite by a predicate nom. (X., Cyr. 1, 4, 19; Cebes 5, 1; Arrian, Anab. 4, 30, 4 πιστὸς ἐφαίνετο=he showed himself to be trustworthy; TestReub 5:7; Iren. 5, 1, 2 [Harv. II 315, 5]; Theoph. Ant. 3, 7 [p. 218, 5]) φαίνονται ὡραῖοι **Mt 23:27.** ἵνα ἡμεῖς δόκιμοι φανῶμεν **2 Cor 13:7.** W. dat. of pers. *appear to someone as someth.* (Lucian, Dial. Mort. 25, 1; TestAbr A 20 p. 103, 7 [Stone p. 54]) φαίνεσθε τοῖς ἀνθρώποις δίκαιοι **Mt 23:28** (cp. Pr 21:2). W. ἐνώπιόν τινος instead of the dat.: ἐφάνησαν ἐνώπιον αὐτῶν ὡσεὶ λῆρος τὰ ῥήματα ταῦτα **Lk 24:11.**—Foll. by ὡς *look as if* (TestJos 3:4) Hv 3, 2, 6b; s 9, 9, 7.

❺ **to make an impression on the mind,** ***have the appearance, seem,*** freq. w. focus on aspect of decision evoked by circumstance; pass. φαίνομαι w. act./intr. sense, w. dat. and inf. (Hom. et al.) οἱ τοιοῦτοι οὐκ εὐσυνείδητοί μοι εἶναι φαίνονται IMg 4. W. dat. and ptc. φαίνεσθέ μοι κατὰ ἀνθρώπους ζῶντες ITr 2:1. τί ὑμῖν φαίνεται; *how does it seem to you? what is your decision?* **Mk 14:64.** ἐάν σοι φανῇ *if it seems good to you* Hv 2, 3, 4 (acc. to CTurner, JTS 21, 1920, 198, a Latinism: si tibi videtur. Cp. POxy 811 [I AD] εἴ σοι φαίνεται). Without a dat. (Jos., C. Ap. 1, 12; Just., D. 91, 4) οὐδὲν φαίνεται κεκομμένον ἀπ' αὐτοῦ *nothing seems to have been cut from it* (the tree) or *apparently nothing has been cut from it* (cp. Aristoxenus, fgm. 83 φαίνεται Ὄλυμπος αὐξήσας μουσικήν=O. has apparently enriched music) Hs 8, 3, 1 (φαίνεται w. acc. and inf. Demetrius: 722 fgm. 5 Jac.).—B. 1045f.—DELG. M-M. EDNT. TW. Sv.

Φάλεκ (also Φαλέκ, Φαλέγ, Φάλεχ 1 Ch 1:25 B; Hebr. פֶּלֶג, in pause פָּלֶג, Gen 10:25 al.), **ὁ,** indecl. (in Joseph. Φάλεγος, ου [Ant. 1, 148]) ***Peleg,*** son of Eber and father of Reu (Gen 11:16–19; 1 Ch 1:25), in the genealogy of Jesus **Lk 3:35.**

φανεροποιέω 1 aor. ἐφανεροποίησα (Hephaestion Astr. [IV AD] 3, 37; s. Cat. Cod. Astr. V/3, 85 ln. 11; schol. on Aristoph., Eq. 1253; Joannes Sardianus, Comm. in Aphthonii Progymn. ed. HRabe 1928 p. 161, 23; pap since VI AD) ***reveal, make known*** τὶ *someth.* τὴν τοῦ κόσμου σύστασιν 1 Cl 60:1. Hs 4, 2 πᾶσι φανεροποιηθήσονται of the righteous in the world to come (v.l. φανερωθήσονται).—DELG s.v. φαίνω.

φανερός, ά, όν (φαίνομαι; Pind., Hdt.+; ins, pap, LXX; En 9:5; TestSol; TestAsh 2:3; ParJer 6:25; EpArist, Philo, Joseph., Ar., Just., Tat.)

❶ adj. **pert. to being evident so as to be readily known,** ***visible, clear, plainly to be seen, open, plain, evident, known*** τὰ φανερὰ ἔργα (opp. κρύφια) 2 Cl 16:3. Used w. εἶναι (Diod. S. 18, 55, 2 φανεροῦ ὄντος ὅτι=since it was clear that) οἱ καρποὶ φανεροὶ ἔσονται Hs 4:3; cp. 4:4. φ. ἔσονται οἱ δουλεύοντες τῷ θεῷ 4:2. φανερόν (-ά) ἐστιν **Ro 1:19** (ἐν αὐτοῖς; s. ἐν 8); **Gal 5:19; 1J 3:10** (ἐν τούτῳ *by this*); Hm 11:10; other passages w. dat. of pers. (TestSol 13:2 C) **1 Ti 4:15;** B 8:7 (opp. σκοτεινά). Without a copula, which is to be supplied: w. ὅτι (X., Mem. 3, 9, 2; Teles p. 12, 4; 7; TestAsh 2:3; Iren., 1, 4, 4 [Harv. I, 37, 8]) πᾶσιν φανερόν **Ac 4:16** (D has the copula and at the same time the comp.: φανερώτερόν ἐστιν *it is quite*

Φ

well known). φανερὸν τὸ δένδρον ἀπὸ τοῦ καρποῦ αὐτοῦ *the tree is known by its fruit* (cp. Mt 12:33) IEph 14:2 (Vi. Aesopi G, 3 P. φανερὸς ἀπὸ τῆς ὄψεως=clearly recognizable by its appearance).—Used w. γίνεσθαι (BGU 1141, 41 [14 BC]; Appian, Bell. Civ. 2, 46 §187 τοῦ κακοῦ φανεροῦ γενομένου; 1 Macc 15:9; 2 Macc 1:33; ParJer 6:25; Jos., Ant. 2, 270; 6, 238; Just., A 1, 63, 6) φανερὸν ἐγένετο τὸ ὄνομα αὐτοῦ **Mk 6:14.** Cp. **Lk 8:17a** (opp. κρυπτόν); **1 Cor 3:13; 11:19; 14:25;** Hs 9, 12, 3; w. dat. of pers. added (Ael. Aristid. 29, 24 K.=40 p. 758 D.: φανεροὶ πᾶσι γίγνεσθαι; Just., A I, 23, 1) **Ac 7:13.** ὥστε τοὺς δεσμούς μου φανεροὺς γενέσθαι ἐν ὅλῳ τῷ πραιτωρίῳ καὶ τοῖς λοιποῖς πᾶσιν **Phil 1:13.**—Used w. ποιεῖν (Hyperid. 4, 1; Menand., Epitr. 495 S. [319 Kö.]; IBM III, 482 A, 13f; POxy 928, 7; PTebt 333, 12; 2 Macc 12:41; Just., A II, 15, 2; Theoph. Ant. 2, 3 [p. 94, 13]) *make* (τι *someth.*) *known* (Jos., Ant. 12, 189; 204) 1 Cl 21:7; GJs 5:1. τινά *make someone known* as what he really is, *reveal the identity of someone* (Jos., Ant. 3, 73; Just., D. 8, 4) **Mt 12:16; Mk 3:12.**

❷ subst. τὸ φανερόν **that which is exposed to general view or knowledge,** ***(in) the open, public notice*** (Hyperid. 1, 13, 11 εἰς τὸ φ. φέρειν [cp. Just. A I, 15, 3 εἰς φανερὸν … φέρειν]; Polyb. 2, 46, 1; Just. A I, 17, 4 εἰς φανερὸν τιθέντων), εἰς φανερὸν ἐλθεῖν *come to light* **Mk 4:22; Lk 8:17b** (a proverb? Constant. Manasse 7, 34f H.: ἐστὶ σκότιον οὐδὲν ὅπερ εἰς φῶς οὐχ ἥκει, οὐκ ἔστι κρύφιον οὐδὲν ὃ μὴ πρὸς γνῶσιν φθάνει 'there is nothing in the dark that does not come into the light, and nothing hidden that does not become known'. εἰς φ. ἐλέγχειν Hippol., Ref. 8, 20, 4). ἐν τῷ φανερῷ (opp. ἐν τῷ κρυπτῷ as Ctesias: 688 fgm. 13, 12 p. 460 Jac.) **Mt 6:4 v.l., 6 v.l., 18 v.l.** (cp. Aeneas Tact. 426; Jos., Ant. 4, 34); preceded by an art. and used as an adj. ὁ ἐν τῷ φανερῷ Ἰουδαῖος *the Judean who is one outwardly* by reason of being circumcised **Ro 2:28a;** cp. **b.**—B. 1233. DELG s.v. φαίνω B. Schmidt, Syn. III 418–34. Cp. δῆλος. M-M. TW.

φανερόω fut. φανερώσω; 1 aor. ἐφανέρωσα; pf. πεφανέρωκα. Pass.: 1 fut. φανερωθήσομαι; 1 aor. ἐφανερώθην; perf. πεφανέρωμαι (cp. φανέρωσις; Hdt. 6, 122 [a late interpolation]; Dionys, Hal. 10, 37; Cass. Dio 59, 18; 77, 15; PGoodsp 15, 19 [IV AD]; Jer 40:6; TestSol; TestAbr B; JosAs 12:2; AscIs 3; 13; Philo; Jos., Ant. 20, 76; Just., Tat., Mel.)

❶ **to cause to become visible,** ***reveal, expose publicly*** (w. relatively more focus on the sensory aspect than on the cognitive as in 2 below. But distinctions are not always clear)

ⓐ of persons—**α.** act. of the Risen Lord **J 21:1a;** cp. **1b.**

β. pass. w. intr. sense *show* or *reveal oneself, be revealed, appear* τινί *to someone* Hs 2:1. ἡμᾶς φανερωθῆναι δεῖ ἔμπροσθεν τοῦ βήματος τοῦ Χριστοῦ **2 Cor 5:10.**—Esp. of Christ (Just., A I, 56, 1; Mel., P. 43, 302. Of the Logos φανερωθεὶς τοῖς ἀνθρώποις Iren. 3, 11, 8 [Harv. II 47, 8]) of his appearance in the world ἐφανερώθη ἐν σαρκί **1 Ti 3:16** (ALau, Manifest in Flesh, The Epiphany Christology of the Pastoral Epistles '96); cp. B 5:6; 6:7, 9, 14; 12:10. θεοῦ ἀνθρωπίνως φανερουμένου IEph 19:3.—**Hb 9:26; 1 Pt 1:20; 1J 1:2ab.** The purpose of the appearing is given by a ἵνα clause **1J 3:5, 8;** B 14:5; 2 Cl 14:2.—Of the appearing of the Risen Lord τοῖς μαθηταῖς **J 21:14;** cp. **Mk 16:12** (ἐν ἑτέρᾳ μορφῇ), **14.** Without a dat. B 15:9. Of the Second Advent **Col 3:4a; 1 Pt 5:4; 1J 2:28; 3:2b.**—ὑμεῖς σὺν αὐτῷ (i.e. Christ upon his return) φανερωθήσεσθε ἐν δόξῃ **Col 3:4b.** Of the Christian community ἡ ἐκκλησία πνευματικὴ οὖσα ἐφανερώθη ἐν τῇ σαρκὶ Χριστοῦ 2 Cl 14:3.

ⓑ of things, pass. w. intr. sense (Jos, Ant. 17, 194; Hippol., Ref. 9, 5, 1; Theoph. Ant. 2, 4 [p. 102, 22]) *become visible* or *known, be revealed* **Mk 4:22; 2 Cor 4:10f; Eph 5:13f; Rv 3:18.** Foll. by an indirect quest. **1J 3:2a.**

❷ **to cause to become known,** ***disclose, show, make known***

ⓐ of things—**α.** act. (PBrem 53, 26 [114 AD]; Hippol., Ref. 6, 47, 4) ἐφανέρωσεν τὴν δόξαν αὐτοῦ **J 2:11** (TestAbr B 14 p. 118, 18 [Stone p. 84] τὴν σαπρότητα; JosAs 12:2 τὰ ἀφανῆ; Jos., Vi. 231 φ. τὴν ὀργήν). ὁ θεὸς αὐτοῖς ἐφανέρωσεν *God has shown them* what can be known about God **Ro 1:19** (s. AKlöpper, ZWT 47, 1904, 169–80). Cp. **1 Cor 4:5; Tit 1:3;** 2 Cl 20:5; Dg 8:11 (w. ἀποκαλύπτειν); 9:1, 2b; 11:5; IRo 8:2. φανεροῦν τινι ἀποκάλυψιν *disclose a revelation to someone* Hv 3, 1, 2. κατὰ ἀποκάλυψιν φανεροῦν τινι *make known* or *show to someone in a revelation* MPol 22:3. ἐπὶ σοὶ … φανερώσει κύριος τὸ λύτρον *in connection with you the Lord will disclose salvation* GJs 7:2. τῷ θεῷ τὴν ὀσμὴν τῆς γνώσεως αὐτοῦ φανεροῦντι δι' ἡμῶν *to God who makes known through us the fragrance of the knowledge relating to him* (prob. Christ, but s. REB and NRSV of God) **2 Cor 2:14.** πάντα ὁ πατὴρ φανεροῖ περὶ τοῦ υἱοῦ Ἰησοῦ B 12:8. (ὁ κύριος) πεφανέρωκεν ἡμῖν διὰ τῶν προφητῶν ὅτι κτλ. 2:4.—*Make known* by word of mouth, *teach* ἐφανέρωσά σου τὸ ὄνομα τοῖς ἀνθρώποις **J 17:6** (though here the teaching is accompanied by a revelation that comes through a deed.—HHuber, D. Begriff der Offenbarung im Joh. ev. '34). ἐν παντὶ φανερώσαντες ἐν πᾶσιν εἰς ὑμᾶς *in every way we have made this* (i.e. τὴν γνῶσιν) *plain to you, in the sight of all men* **2 Cor 11:6.** Cp. **Col 4:4.**—*Disclose* τοὺς γάμους GJs 15:2, 4.

β. pass. w. intr. sense (Jos, Ant. 17, 194; Hippol., Ref. 9, 5, 1; Theoph. Ant. 2, 4 [p. 102, 22]) *become public knowledge, be disclosed, become known* **J 3:21; 9:3; Ro 16:26; 2 Cor 7:12; Col 1:26; 2 Ti 1:10; Hb 9:8; 1J 4:9; Rv 15:4;** B 7:7; IEph 19:2. Foll. by an indirect quest. **1J 3:2a.** Foll. by ὅτι Dg 9:2a. χωρὶς νόμου δικαιοσύνη θεοῦ πεφανέρωται *apart from law, the righteousness which is sent from God has been revealed* **Ro 3:21.**

ⓑ of persons—**α.** act. ἑαυτόν *show* or *reveal oneself:* of God (Philo, Leg. All. 3, 47) διὰ Ἰησοῦ IMg 8:2.—Of Christ φανέρωσον σεαυτὸν τῷ κόσμῳ **J 7:4.** Difft. ἐφανέρωσεν ἑαυτὸν εἶναι υἱὸν θεοῦ *he revealed that he was the Son of God* B 5:9.—*Expose* ἐὰν αὐτὴν φανερώσω τοῖς υἱοῖς Ἰσραήλ *if I expose (Mary) to the Israelites* GJs 14:1.

β. pass. w. intr. sense *be made known* ἵνα φανερωθῇ τῷ Ἰσραήλ **J 1:31.** θεῷ πεφανερώμεθα *we are well known to God* **2 Cor 5:11a,** cp. **11b; 11:6 v.l.** (for φανερώσαντες). W. ὅτι foll. *become known, be shown (that)* **3:3; 1J 2:19** (logically impersonal, as ἠκούσθη in Mk 2:1).—MBockmuehl, Das Verb φανερόω im NT: BZ 32, '88, 87–99.—DELG s.v. φαίνω. M-M. EDNT. TW.

φανερῶς adv. of φανερός (Aeschyl., Hdt. et al.; pap; 2 Macc 3:28; TestSol, Philo, Joseph., Just., Mel., HE 4, 26, 5)

❶ **in plain view,** ***openly, publicly*** **Mk 1:45.** (Opp. ἐν κρυπτῷ; cp. Jos., Ant. 5, 213 κρυπτῶς … φ.; TestJos 4:2) **J 7:10.** (Opp. λάθρᾳ, as Pla., Symp. 182d) IPhld 6:3; GMary 463 ln. 13f.

❷ **in sharp visual focus,** ***clearly, distinctly*** (Jos., Vi. 277) ἰδεῖν **Ac 10:3.**

❸ **in a readily understood manner,** ***clearly, plainly,*** δειχθῆναι Dg 11:2.—The neut. of the comp. as adv. φανερώτερον *(even) more plainly* λέγειν B 13:4 (Tat. 4, 3; Ath. 2, 2).—M-M.

φανέρωσις, εως, ἡ (cp. φανερόω; Aristot., De Plant. 2, 1; 9; Herm. Wr. 11, 1; Cat. Cod. Astr. VII 229, 23; 230, 20; VIII/1 p. 165, 6; Just., D. 49, 3 al.; ἡ τοῦ σωτῆρος φ. Hippol., Ref. 8,

10, 1; pap VIII AD) ***disclosure, announcement,*** w. objective gen. ἡ φαν. τῆς ἀληθείας *the open proclamation of the truth* **2 Cor 4:2.** The syntax of the gen. in ἡ φανέρωσις τοῦ πνεύματος **1 Cor 12:7** cannot be determined w. certainty. Whether the gen. is subj. or obj. the expr. means the same thing as χάρισμα.—DELG s.v. φαίνω. M-M. TW.

φανός, οῦ, ὁ (φάος 'light'; Aristoph., X.+; UPZ 5, 18 [163 BC]; 6, 15; loanw. in rabb.) **a portable light,** ***lamp*** orig.='torch' and later, to the great annoyance of the Atticists (Hesych. s.v.; Phryn. p. 59 Lob.; Athen. 15, 58 p. 699dff; Pollux 6, 103; 10, 116),=*lantern* (λυχνοῦχος); so **J 18:3** beside λαμπάς (q.v. 1).—DELG s.v. φάε C. Frisk s.v. φάος. M-M.

Φανουήλ, ὁ indecl. (פְּנוּאֵל; 1 Ch 4:4; 8:25 v.l.; cp. Gen 32:32, place name; Philo, Conf. Lingu. 129) ***Phanuel,*** father of Hanna(h)/Anna, a prophet **Lk 2:36.**—M-M.

φαντάζω (Aeschyl., Hdt.+; Sir 34:5; Wsd 6:16; TestSim 4:9) the act. 'make visible' but usu. in the pass. w. intr. sense ***become visible, appear*** (Philo), esp. of extraordinary phenomena (in nature, etc.; cp. Apollon. Rhod. 4, 1283; Περὶ ὕψους 15, 4; 7; PGM 7, 888) τὸ φανταζόμενον *sight, spectacle,* of a theophany (as Ps.-Aristot., Mirabilia 108 Athena; Herodian 8, 3, 9 of Apollo) **Hb 12:21.**—DELG s.v. φαίνω B 10. M-M. TW.

φαντασία, ας, ἡ (Aristot., Polyb. et al.; LXX, TestSol; TestReub 3:7; 5:7; Philo; Jos., Bell. 6, 69 al.; Just.; Tat. 14, 1; Ath. 27, 1f) ***pomp, pageantry*** (Polyb. 15, 25, 22; 16, 21, 1 μετὰ φαντασίας; Diod. S. 12, 83, 4; Vett. Val. 38, 26) ἐλθόντος τοῦ Ἀγρίππα μετὰ πολλῆς φαντασίας **Ac 25:23** (πολλὴ φ. as Pel.-Leg. 4, 7f; on the nature of such pomp s. BKinman, NTS 40, '94, 445 [lit]; s. also GWatson, ANRW 2/36/7, '94, 4765–4810 [philosophical aspect, fr. late Hellenism to early Neoplatonism]).—Rdm.[2] 12.—DELG s.v. φαίνω B 10. M-M. Sv.

φάντασμα, ατος, τό (Aeschyl., Pla. et al.; LXX; En 99:7; TestSol 8:9 C; Philo; Jos., Bell. 5, 381, Ant. 5, 21 3; Tat. 7:3) ***apparition,*** esp. ***ghost*** (Aeschyl. et al.; Pla., Phd. 81d, Tim. 71a; Dionys. Hal. 4, 62; Plut., Dio 2, 4; Lucian, Philops. 29; PGM 4, 2701; 7, 579 φυλακτήριον πρὸς δαίμονας, πρὸς πᾶσαν νόσον καὶ πάθος; Job 20:8 v.l.; Wsd 17:14; Jos., Ant. 1, 331; 333; Tat. 7, 3 s. Reader, Polemo 376) **Mt 14:26; Mk 6:49** (on these two pass. cp. Phlegon: 257 fgm. 36 II, 3 Jac.); **Lk 24:37** D.—FAltheim, ARW 27, 1929, 48.—DELG s.v. φαίνω B 10. M-M. TW. Sv.

φανῶ s. φαίνω.

φάραγξ, αγγος, ἡ *ravine* (so Alcman [VII BC] 3; Thu.; also LXX, En; TestSol 4:5; TestIss 1:5; AssMos fgm. f; SibOr 3, 682; EpArist 118; Jos., Bell. 1, 147; 6, 161) **Lk 3:5** (Is 40:4.—Cp. also Diod. S. 20, 36, 2 the laying out of the Appian Way in spite of heights and τόποι φαραγγώδεις), but also ***valley*** (e.g. Gen 26:17, 19; Josh 13:9; Ezk 34:13; so Vulg. Lk 3:5), but not a broad valley, for it can be filled.—B. 28. DELG. M-M.

Φαραώ, ὁ indecl. (פַּרְעֹה; Gen 12:15 al.; Ezek. Trag. 9 W. [Clem. Alex., Strom. 1, 155, 2]; TestSol, Test12Patr, JosAs, Philo; Jos., Bell. 5, 379; Mel., P. 11, 75 al.—As a rule Joseph. has Φαραώθης, ου [Ant. 2, 39]) ***Pharaoh,*** actually the title of Egyptian kings ('great house'; AGardiner, Egyptian Grammar[3] '57, 75), then a proper name; of the *Pharaoh* of the Exodus **Ac 7:10, 13, 21; Ro 9:17; Hb 11:24;** 1 Cl 4:10; 51:5; AcPl Ha 8, 11.—BHHW III 1445–47. M-M.

Φαρές, ὁ indecl. (פֶּרֶץ, פָּרֶץ; Gen 38:29; 1 Ch 2:4f; Ruth 4:18; Jos., Ant. 2, 178 Φάρεσος, ου) ***Perez,*** son of the patriarch Judah and of Tamar, twin brother of Zerah and father of Hezron; in the genealogy of Jesus **Mt 1:3ab; Lk 3:33.**

Φαρισαῖος, ου, ὁ (Hebr. הַפְּרוּשִׁים=Aram. פְּרִישַׁיָּא, the latter in Gk. transcription Φαρισαῖοι. The Semitic words mean 'the separated ones, separatists'. Acc. to ABaumarten [JBL 102, '83, 411–28], Φ.= 'specifiers', the party of accurate and specific observance of the law. On the sect of the Pharisees acc. to Josephus [Ant. 13, 288–98; on his views s. SMason, Flavius Josephus on the Pharisees '91] and the Mishnah s. Schürer II 381–403, where the pertinent passages are reproduced) ***Pharisee,*** though in our lit. it is rarely found in the sing. (**Mt 23:26; Lk 7:36b, 37, 39; 11:37f; 18:10f; Ac 5:34; 23:6b; 26:5; Phil 3:5**); as a rule in the pl. *Pharisees,* the organized followers of the experts in interpreting the scriptures (scribes). It was the purpose of the Pharisees to take the pattern of a pious Israelite as established by the scribes, and to put it into practice as nearly as possible. Some became followers of Jesus Christ and others opposed him and his followers. Mentioned w. Sadducees **Mt 3:7; 16:1, 6, 11f; Ac 23:6–8.** W. Herodians **Mk 3:6; 12:13;** cp. **8:15.** W. scribes **Mt 5:20; 12:38; 15:1; 23:2, 13, 15; Mk 2:16** (here οἱ γραμματεῖς τῶν Φ.; cp. Just., D. 51, 2; 102, 5); **7:5; Lk 5:21, 30; 6:7; 11:53; 15:2; J 8:3; Ac 23:9** (here γραμματεῖς τοῦ μέρους τῶν Φ.). W. scribes and elders GPt 8:28. As opponents of Jesus **Mt 9:11, 34; 12:2, 14, 24; 15:12; 22:15, 34, 41; Mk 7:1; 8:11, 15; 10:2; 12:13** al. W. chief priests **J 7:45; 11:47; 18:3** (UvonWahlde, NTS 42, '96, 506–22); a Pharisaic high priest Ox 840, 10. Their fasting **Mt 9:14; Mk 2:18** (**Lk 18:12**). Paul a Ph. **Ac 23:6b; 26:5** (κατὰ τὴν ἀκριβεστάτην αἵρεσιν τῆς ἡμετέρας θρησκείας ἔζησα Φαρισαῖος); **Phil 3:5.**—In addition to the lit. s.v. Σαδδουκαῖος that is pertinent here, s. also IElbogen, Die Religionsanschauung der Phar. 1904; Schürer II 404–14; IAbrahams, Studies in Pharisaism and the Gospels I 1917, II 1924; ARobertson, The Pharisees and Jesus 1920; EMeyer II 1921, 282ff; RHerford, The Pharisees 1924 (s. BEaston, Mr. Herford and the Phar.: ATR 7, 1925, 423–37); CMontefiore, The Synoptic Gospels[2] 1927 II 676a (index s.v. Pharisees); GMoore, Judaism in the First Centuries of the Christian Era I, II 1927; FBurkitt, Jesus and the 'Pharisees': JTS 28, 1927, 392–97; DRiddle, Jesus and the Ph. 1928; JoachJeremias, Jerus. zur Zeit Jesu,[3] '62, 279–303; LFinkelstein, The Ph.[2] '40, The Ph., The Sociol. Background of Their Faith, [3]'62; ILauterbach, The Ph. and Their Teach.: HUCA 6, 1929, 69–140; OHoltzmann, D. Prophet Mal u. d. Ursprung des Pharisäerbundes: ARW 29, '31, 1–21; LBaeck, Die Pharisäer '34; WFoerster, D. Ursprung des Pharisäismus: ZNW 34, '35, 35–51; TManson, BJRL '38, 144ff; SZeitlin, The Pharisees and the Gospels '38; idem, JQR '61; GAllon, Scripta Hild. VII '61; AFinkel, The Pharisees and the Teacher of Nazareth '64; ASalderini, Pharisees, Scribes and Sadducees in Palestinian Society '88; GStemberger, Pharisees, Sadducees, Essenes '95; on the rhetorical use of 'vituperatio' (vilification) in Mt and other ancient wr., s. the bibl. in LThuren, NTS 43, '97, 458 n. 45; Schürer II 381f (lit.).—EDNT. TW.

φαρμακεία, ας, ἡ (also -κία; X., Pla. et al.; Vett. Val., pap, LXX; En, AscIs; Philo, Spec. Leg. 3, 94; 98; Ar. 13, 7; Tat. 18, 1) ***sorcery, magic*** (φάρμακον; Polyb. 38, 16, 7; Ex 7:11, 22; 8:14; Is 47:9, 12; Wsd 12:4; 18:13; En 7:1; SibOr 5, 165) **Rv 18:23.** Pl. *magic arts* **9:21** (v.l. φαρμάκων). In a list of vices **Gal 5:20;** B 20:1 (AscIs 2:5 ἐπλήθυνεν [ἡ] φαρμακία καὶ ἡ μαγία καὶ ἡ μαντία ... καὶ ἡ πορνία ...); pl. D 5:1.—B. 1495. DELG s.v. φάρμακον. M-M.

φαρμακεύς, έως, ὁ (φάρμακον; Soph., Trach. 1140; Pla., Symp. 203d γόης καὶ φαρμ.; Philo, Det. Pot. Ins. 38 [otherw. φαρμακευτής, so also Just., A II, 6, 6]; Jos., Vi. 149f; Orig., C. Cels. 3, 46, 27. Whether poison is implied depends on the context) **maker of potions,** ***magician*** **Rv 21:8** t.r. (so Tdf. app., based on Erasmus' 2d ed. 1519; the 1st ed. 1516 has the correct rdg; s. RBorger, GGA 143; s. φάρμακος 2).—DELG s.v. φάρμακον.

φαρμακεύω fut. φαρμακεύσω; aor. ptc. φαρμακεύσας 2 Macc 10:13 (φαρμακεύς; Hdt., Pla. et al.; POxy 472, 1; 5 [II AD]; LXX; Philo, Det. Pot. Ins. 38) **to make potions,** ***practice magic*** D 2:2 (here mixing of poisons is not especially indicated; cp. Ps.-Phoc. 149 Horst p. 212f; Wengst, Didache p. 69 n. 8).—DELG s.v. φάρμακον.

φάρμακον, ου, τό (s. three prec. entries; Hom. et al.; ins, pap, LXX; TestAbr A, Test12Patr; Philo; Jos., Vi. 150). Prim. 'a drug', ordinarily contexts indicate whether salubrious or noxious.

❶ **a harmful drug,** ***poison*** (Hom. et al.; Jos., Ant. 16, 253; 17, 62; TestAbr A 17 p. 99, 28 [Stone p. 46]; TestJos 5:1; Hippol., Ref. 4, 30, 2) Hv 3, 9, 7a (w. φαρμακός); in imagery of the 'poisoned' heart, ibid. 7b. θανάσιμον φάρμ. (s. θανάσιμος) ITr 6:2. δηλητήριον φάρμ. *lethal poison* Papias (2:9).

❷ **a drug used as a controlling medium,** ***magic potion, charm*** (Hom.+; PSI 64, 20 [I BC]; 4 Km 9:22; TestReub 4:9; Jos., Ant. 15, 93; 19, 193; Hippol., Ref. 6, 39, 3) φαρμάκων **Rv 9:21** (v.l. φαρμακειῶν).

❸ **a healing remedy,** ***medicine, remedy, drug*** (Hom. et al.; SIG 1168, 40; 77; 119; PRyl 62, 22 [I BC]; PTebt 117, 22 [I BC]; PGM 5, 247; TestJos 2:7; Philo; Jos., Bell. 4, 573; Ar. 10, 5; Tat. 20, 1; λογικὸν φ. Orig., C. Cels. 5, 1, 11; Did., Gen. 72, 8) in trans. sense of *means of attaining someth.,* w. gen. of the thing desired (Eur., Phoen. 893 φ. σωτηρίας; likew. the teaching of Epicurus: CJensen, GGAbh III/5, '33, 81; Cleopatra ln. 45; 130 φ. τῆς ζωῆς; Sir 6:16), the Eucharist as φάρμακον ἀθανασίας *the medicine of* (i.e. *means of attaining*) *immortality* IEph 20:2 (φ. ἀθαν. Antiphanes Com. 86, 6; Diod. S. 1, 25, 6; Herm. Wr. 460, 13 Sc. The remedy, widely designated by the t.t. φ. ἀθαν., whose origin was credited to Isis, was prescribed for the most varied diseases. TSchermann, TQ 92, 1910, 6ff; Rtzst., Mysterienrel. 400).—TAllbutt, Greek Medicine in Rome 1921; other lit. OCD, s.v. 'Medicine'.—B. 310f. Schmidt, Syn. IV 106–16. DELG. M-M. Sv.

φάρμακος, ου, ὁ (LXX; other edd. ός; on the accent and differentiation fr. φαρμακός 'scapegoat' [Hipponax et al.] see L-S-J-M under both words, w. ref. to Herodian, Gr. I, 150; s. PKatz, TLZ 82, '57, 112, The Text of the Septuagint '73, 95; B-D-F §13; φάρ. is masc. Ex 7:11; fem. Mal 3:5; so also Orig., C. Cels. 5, 38, 38 w. μάγοι). In our lit. only masc.

❶ **one skilled in arcane uses of herbs or drugs,** prob. ***poisoner*** Hv 3, 9, 7ab, but w. implication of the role described in 2 next:

❷ **one who does extraordinary things through occult means,** ***sorcerer, magician*** (Ex 7:11; 9:11 al.; SibOr 3, 225) **Rv 21:8** (s. φαρμακεύς); **22:15.**—L-S-J-M s.v. fails to differentiate mng. in LXX pass. listed after a series of glosses.—For a vivid poetic description of a sorcerer's procedures s. Horace, Epodes 5.—DELG s.v. φάρμακον C. M-M.

φάσις, εως, ἡ (φημί; Pla.+; ins, pap, LXX, TestAbr, ParJer; Philo, Aet. M. 143) orig. 'information' concerning a crime, then gener. **information concerning a pers. or event,** ***report, announcement, news*** (TestAbr A 5 p. 82, 28 [Stone p. 12] al.; pap) ἀνέβη φάσις τῷ χιλιάρχῳ ὅτι **Ac 21:31** (ἀνέβη because it went up to the Tower Antonia).—DELG s.v. φημί II B. M-M.

φάσκω impf. ἔφασκον (Hom. et al.; ins, pap, LXX, Philo; Jos., Ant. 3, 305; 7, 250; Just., Tat.) **to state someth. w. confidence,** ***say, assert, claim*** foll. by acc. and inf. (PRyl 117, 19; Philo, Somn. 2, 291; Jos., C. Ap. 2, 145) **Ac 24:9; 25:19.** In an affirmation made concerning the speaker, after the nom. of the ptc. we have the inf. w. predicate nom. φάσκοντες εἶναι σοφοί **Ro 1:22;** after the acc. of the ptc., the inf. w. the predicate acc. τοὺς φάσκοντας εἶναι ἀποστόλους **Rv 2:2** t.r. (Erasmian rdg.).—DELG s.v. φημί II. M-M.

φάτνη, ης, ἡ (also πάθνη, s. Schwyzer I 269; cp. PLips 106, 8 [I AD]) ***manger, crib*** (so Hom.+; loanw. in rabb.) **Lk 13:15.** In the Infancy Narrative **Lk 2:7, 12, 16** (ἔβαλεν ἐν πάθνῃ βοῶν GJs 22:2; on Lk 2 as anticipation of Jesus' entombment s. JWinandy, NTS 43, '97, 140–46) φ. could perh. be a *stable* (Diod. S. 17, 95, 2 φ. is a place to keep horses, beside κατασκήνωσις, a place for humans to stay; Aelian, NA 16, 24 p. 402, 10 w. ὁδός) or even a *feeding-place* under the open sky, in contrast to κατάλυμα, a shelter where people stayed (s. HCadbury, JBL 45, 1926, 317–19; 52, '33, 61f) or other type of accommodation (s. κατάλυμα.—Manger: AvanVeldhuizen, NThSt 13, 1930, 175–78). Nicol. Dam.: 90 fgm. 3 p. 330, 15 Jac.—MDibelius, Jungfrauensohn u. Krippenkind '32, 59ff (Botschaft u. Geschichte I '53, 1–78).—BHHW II 1014. DELG. M-M. TW.

φάτνωμα, ατος, τό (Aristoph; LXX) ***coffer-work*** τὰ φατνώματα (παθν- pap) τοῦ ναοῦ ὠλόλυξαν *the ornamental panel on the ceiling of the temple broke into lamentation* GJs 24:3.—DELG s.v. φάτνη.

φαῦλος, η, ον (trag., Pre-Socr., Hdt.+; pap, LXX; TestSol 8:9; apolog. exc. Ar.) in Gk lit. ranging in mng. fr. 'easy, light, simple' to 'common, bad'.

❶ **pert. to being low-grade or morally substandard,** ***base*** (Soph., X., Pla. et al.; LXX; EpArist 142; Philo; Jos., Vi. 41, C. Ap. 1, 53; SibOr 3, 362 [w. ἄδικος]. πᾶς φ. ἀνόητός ἐστιν Orig., C. Cels. 3, 74, 3) πρᾶγμα **Js 3:16.** ἔργον 1 Cl 28:1 (cp. Just., D. 14, 3). οἱ φ. *those who are base* 36:6, i.e. those who do not reflect in their behavior the high status they could enjoy as pers. destined for 'deathless knowledge' (see 36:2; cp. Epict. 4, 1, 3; 5; 4, 5, 8; Philo; Jos., Bell. 2, 163 [opp. οἱ ἀγαθοί]; Just., A I, 16, 3; Iren. 4, 37, 2 [Harv. II 286, 1]. Sing.: Did., Gen. 161, 8). μηδὲν ἔχων λέγειν περὶ ἡμῶν φαῦλον *if he has nothing bad to say about us* **Tit 2:8** (cp. Plut., Mor. 717b οὐ φαύλως εἰπεῖν said of one who does not speak flippantly or without sufficient thought). πράσσειν τι ἀγαθὸν ἢ φαῦλον **Ro 9:11** (v.l. κακόν 1b [q.v.]. The contrast ἀγ. and φαῦλ. as Pla., Protag. 326e τῶν ἀγαθῶν πατέρων πολλοὶ υἱεῖς φαῦλοι γίγνονται 'many sons of respected fathers turn out to be worthless' noting the contrast between socially responsible parents and irresponsible children; Just. A I, 43, 2; A II, 9, 4; T. Kellis 22, 48; cp. Aeschin., Ctesiphon 174 opp. καλός); (τὰ) φαῦλα πράσσειν (Theoph. Ant. 1, 3 [p. 62, 22]) **J 3:20; 5:29** (Just., A I, 44, 5). κομίσασθαι … πρὸς ἃ ἔπραξεν, εἴτε ἀγαθὸν εἴτε φαῦλον **2 Cor 5:10** may refer to the performance of those under judgment: whether one has led a high-grade or a low-grade life, or more prob. (s. κομίζω 3) to be understood as

❷ **pert. to being relatively inferior in quality,** ***ordinary*** in ref. to the kinds of awards that are offered **2 Cor 5:10.** Yet, in this colloquially arranged sentence, the idea of the doing of good or bad (s. 1 above) certainly plays a part. (The phrase τὰ φαῦλα, τὰ ἀγαθά X., Symp. 4, 47 is formally but not conceptually sim. for X. thinks of temporal chastisements by deities, whereas Paul of awards intended for believers.)—DELG. M-M. TW.

φέγγος, ους, τό (Hom. Hymns+; ins, e.g. IAndrosIsis 39 [I BC]; LXX; TestJob 43:5; JosAs 14:9 φ. ἡλίου; GrBar; Ezek. Trag. 234 [Eus., PE 9, 29, 14] ἀπ᾽ οὐρανοῦ φ. 16; Philo; Jos., Ant. 2, 308; 11, 285; Tat. 20, 2) ***light, radiance,*** of the moon (Ps.-X., Cyneget. 5, 4; Philo, Somn. 1, 23) **Mt 24:29; Mk 13:24.** Of a λύχνος (Callim. 55, 3) **Lk 11:33 v.l.** (cp. TestJob 43:5 [w. λύχνος]). Of two heavenly beings πολὺ φέγγος ἔχοντες GPt 9:36.—DELG. Cp. φῶς.

φείδομαι mid. dep.; fut. φείσομαι; 1 aor. ἐφεισάμην (Hom.+).

➊ **to save fr. loss or discomfort, *spare*** (Hom.+) τινός *someone* or *someth.* **2 Cor 1:23.** ἐγὼ ὑμῶν φείδομαι *I would like to spare you* a great deal of trouble, by offering good advice **1 Cor 7:28.** φεῖσαί μου τῆς ψυχῆς ἀπὸ ῥομφαίας *spare my life* (by protecting me) *from the sword* B 5:13 (cp. Jer 13:14 οὐ φείσομαι ἀπὸ διαφθορᾶς αὐτῶν). Mostly w. a neg. *not spare* τινός (UPZ 146, 40 [II BC] μήτε θεῶν μήτε ἀνθρώπων φείδεσθαι) **Ac 20:29; Ro 8:32** (Lucian, Syr. D. 18 οὐδ᾽ . . . γυναικὸς ἐφείσατο, i.e. his own wife); **11:21ab; 2 Pt 2:4f;** IRo 1:2. οὐκ ἐφεισάμην αὐτοῦ *I did not spare him* from being put to death AcPt Ox 849, 17 (the Lat. vers. AcPt 26: Aa I 73, 22). Abs., but w. οὐδενός understood (Thu. 3, 59, 1; Pr 6:34; Jos., Ant. 14, 480) **2 Cor 13:2.**

➋ **to abstain from doing someth., *refrain*** (X., Cyr. 1, 6, 19; 35; Appian, Basil. 5 §1 πολέμου, Bell. Civ. 5, 120 §498; SIG 708, 36; Job 16:5; PsSol 5:14; TestAbr A; TestJob) w. inf. as obj., to be supplied **2 Cor 12:6** (τοῦ καυχᾶσθαι); ITr 3:3 (τοῦ γράφειν).—DELG. M-M.

φειδομένως (Plut., Alex. 679 [25, 7]; Cosmas and Damian 34, 70) adv. of the ptc. φειδόμενος **in a scanty or meager manner, *sparingly*** (cp. Theognis, fgm. 1, 931 φείδομαι=be miserly) σπείρειν **2 Cor 9:6a;** θερίζειν b.—DELG s.v. φείδομαι. M-M.

φελόνης s. φαιλόνης.—M-M.

φέρω (Hom.+) impf. ἔφερον; fut. οἴσω **J 21:18; Rv 21:26;** 1 aor. ἤνεγκα, ptc. ἐνέγκας; 2 aor. inf. ἐνεγκεῖν (B-D-F §81, 2); pf. ἐνήνοχα (LXX, JosAs). Pass.: 1 aor. ἠνέχθην **2 Pt 1:17, 21a,** 3 pl. ἐνέχθησαν Hs 8, 2, 1.

➊ **to bear or carry from one place to another,** w. focus on an act of transport—ⓐ lit.—α. ***carry, bear*** (Aristoph., Ra. [Frogs] 27 τὸ βάρος ὃ φέρεις; X., Mem. 3, 13, 6 φορτίον φέρειν; GrBar 12:1 κανίσκια 'baskets') ἐπέθηκαν αὐτῷ τὸν σταυρὸν φέρειν ὄπισθεν τοῦ Ἰησοῦ **Lk 23:26** (s. σταυρός 1).—In imagery drawn from Gen 2 οὗ ξύλον φέρων καὶ καρπὸν αἱρῶν *if you bear the tree* (of the word) *and pluck its fruit* Dg 12:8. For Papias (3:2) s. 3a.

β. ***bring with one, bring/take along*** (Diod. S. 6, 7, 8 γράμματα φέρων; GrBar 12:7 φέρετε ὃ ἠνέγκατε 'bring here what you have brought', for the nuance of φέρετε s. 2a; PTebt 418, 9; 421, 6; 8) φέρουσαι ἃ ἡτοίμασαν ἀρώματα **Lk 24:1.** Cp. **J 19:39.**

ⓑ fig.—α. ***carry a burden*** οὗτος τὰς ἁμαρτίας ἡμῶν φέρει 1 Cl 16:4 (Is 53:4).

β. ***bear a name*** τὸ ὄνομα τοῦ κυρίου *bear the name of the Lord,* i.e. of a Christian Pol 6:3 (cp. Just., D. 35, 6).

γ. ***bear/grant a favor*** χάριν τινὶ φέρειν (Il. 5, 211; Od. 5, 307; cp. Aeschyl., Ag. 421f; but not Andoc., De Reditu 9 'express gratitude') ἐλπίσατε ἐπὶ τὴν φερομένην ὑμῖν χάριν ἐν ἀποκαλύψει Ἰησοῦ Χριστοῦ hope for the favor that is being granted you in connection w. the revelation of Jesus Christ (i.e. when he is revealed) **1 Pt 1:13.**

➋ **to cause an entity to move from one position to another,** w. focus on the presentation or effecting of someth.—ⓐ a thing ***bring (on), produce*** (GrBar 12:7 φέρετε 'bring here' [what you have brought with you, s. 1aβ])

α. *bring (to), fetch* τὶ *someth.* **Mk 6:27, 28** (ἐπὶ πίνακι. On the bringing in of a head at a banquet cp. Diog. L. 9, 58: the presence of a severed head did not necessarily disturb the mood at a meal. Appian, Bell. Civ. 4, 20, §81 relates concerning Antony that he had the head of Cicero placed πρὸ τῆς τραπέζης); **Lk 13:7** D; **15:22 v.l.** for ἐξ-; **Ac 4:34, 37; 5:2; 2 Ti 4:13;** B 2:5; MPol 11:2; Hs 8, 1, 16 (w. double acc., of obj. and pred.); 9, 10, 1; δῶρα GJs 1:2; 5:1. Pass. **Mt 14:11a** (ἐπὶ πίνακι); Hv 3, 2, 7; 3, 5, 3; s 8, 2, 1ab; 9, 4, 7; 9, 6, 5–7; 9, 9, 4f. τινί τι (JosAs 16:1 φέρε δή μοι καὶ κηρίον μέλιτος; ApcMos 6) *someth. to someone* **Mt 14:18** (w.ὧδε); **Mk 12:15.** θυσίαν τῷ θεῷ 1 Cl 4:1 (s. Gen 4:3; cp. Just., A I, 24, 2 θυσίας). The acc. is supplied fr. the context **Mt 14:11b; J 2:8a.** The dat. and acc. are to be supplied οἱ δὲ ἤνεγκαν **Mk 12:16; J 2:8b.** φέρειν πρός τινα w. acc. of the thing to be supplied (X., Cyr. 8, 3, 47; Ex 32:2) Hs 8, 4, 3; 9, 10, 2. φ. τι εἰς (1 Km 31:12) **Rv 21:24, 26.** μή τις ἤνεγκεν αὐτῷ φαγεῖν; *do you suppose that anyone has brought him anything to eat?* **J 4:33.** S. φόρος.

β. Fig. *bring (about)* (Hom.+; Mitt-Wilck. I/2, 284, 11 [II BC] αἰσχύνην; PTebt 104, 30; POxy 497, 4; 1062, 14; Jos., Vi. 93, C. Ap. 1, 319; SibOr 3, 417; Just., A I, 27, 5 [βλάβην]) τὸ βάπτισμα τὸ φέρον ἄφεσιν *the baptism which brings (about) forgiveness* B 11:1.

ⓑ a living being, animal or human, ***lead, bring***—α. animals (TestAbr A 2 p. 79, 8 [Stone p. 6] ἵππους; ibid. B 2 p. 106, 21 [Stone p. 60] μόσχον) **Mk 11:2, 7** (πρός τινα); **Lk 15:23; Ac 14:13** (ἐπὶ τ. πυλῶνας); GJs 4:3.

β. people: *bring* or *lead* τινά *someone* ἀσθενεῖς **Ac 5:16.** κακούργους GPt 4:10. τινὰ ἐπὶ κλίνης (Jos., Ant. 17, 197) **Lk 5:18.** τινά τινι *someone to someone* **Mt 17:17** (w. ὧδε); **Mk 7:32; 8:22.** Also τινὰ πρός τινα **Mk 1:32; 2:3; 9:17, 19f.** φέρουσιν αὐτὸν ἐπὶ τὸν Γολγοθᾶν τόπον **15:22** (TestAbr A 11 p. 88, 27 [Stone p. 24] ἐπὶ τὴν ἀνατολήν). ἄλλος οἴσει (σε) ὅπου οὐ θέλεις **J 21:18.**

➌ **to cause to follow a certain course in direction or conduct, *move out of position, drive,*** the pass. can be variously rendered: ***be moved, be driven, let oneself be moved***

ⓐ lit., by wind and weather (Apollon. Rhod. 4, 1700; Chariton 3, 5, 1; Appian, Bell. Civ. 1, 62 §278 in spite of the storm Marius leaped into a boat and ἐπέτρεψε τῇ τύχῃ φέρειν let himself be driven away by fortune; Jer 18:14; PsSol 8:2 πυρὸς . . . φερομένου; TestNapht 6:5; Ar. 4, 2 ἄστρα . . . φερόμενα; Tat. 26, 1 τῆς νεὼς φερομένης) **Ac 27:15, 17.**—*Move, pass* (s. L-S-J-M s.v. φέρω B 1) φέρεσθαι δὲ δι᾽ αὐτοῦ . . . ἰχῶρας *foul discharges were emitted . . . through it* (Judas's penis) Papias (3:2).

ⓑ fig., of the Spirit of God, by whom people *are moved* (cp. Job 17:1 πνεύματι φερόμενος) ὑπὸ πνεύματος ἁγίου φερόμενοι **2 Pt 1:21b.** Cp. **Ac 15:29** D. τῇ πίστει φερόμενος ὁ Παῦλος AcPl Ha 5, 1. Of the impulse to do good Hs 6, 5, 7. Of the powers of evil (Ps.-Plut., Hom. 133 ὑπὸ ὀργῆς φερόμενοι; Jos., Bell. 6, 284; Ath. 25, 4) PtK 2 p. 14, 11; Dg 9:1; Hs 8, 9, 3.

ⓒ also of the wind itself (Ptolem., Apotel. 1, 11, 3 οἱ φερόμενοι ἄνεμοι; Diog. L. 10, 104 τ. πνεύματος πολλοῦ φερομένου; Quint. Smyrn. 3, 718) φέρεσθαι *rush* **Ac 2:2.**

ⓓ of various other entities: of fragrance φέρεσθαι ἐπί τινα *be borne* or *wafted to someone* (Dio Chrys. 66 [16], 6 'rush upon someone') ApcPt 5:16.—Of writings (Diog. L. 5, 86 φέρεται αὐτοῦ [i.e. Heraclid. Pont.] συγγράμματα κάλλιστα; Marinus, Vi. Procli 38; cp. Arrian, Anab. 7, 12, 6 λόγος ἐφέρετο Ἀλεξάνδρου=a saying of Alexander was circulated) οὗ (=τοῦ Εἰρηναίου) πολλὰ συγγράμματα φέρεται *of whom there are many writings in circulation* EpilMosq 2.—Of spiritual development ἐπὶ τὴν τελειότητα φερώμεθα *let us move on toward perfection* **Hb 6:1.**

❹ **to move an object to a particular point,** ***put, place*** φέρειν τὸν δάκτυλον, τὴν χεῖρα *put* or *reach out the finger, the hand* **J 20:27a** (ὧδε), vs. **27b.**

❺ **to cause to continue in a state or condition,** ***sustain,*** fig., of the Son of God φέρων τὰ πάντα τῷ ῥήματι τῆς δυνάμεως αὐτοῦ *who bears up the universe by his mighty word* **Hb 1:3** (cp. Plut., Lucull. 6, 3 φέρειν τὴν πόλιν; Num 11:14; Dt 1:9).

❻ **to afford passage to a place,** ***lead to,*** of a gate, *lead* somewhere (cp. Hdt. 2, 122; Thu. 3, 24, 1 τὴν ἐς Θήβας φέρουσαν ὁδόν; Ps.-Demosth. 47, 53 θύρα εἰς τὸν κῆπον φέρουσα; SIG 1118, 5; POxy 99, 7; 17 [I AD]; 69, 1 [II AD] θύρα φέρουσα εἰς ῥύμην) τὴν πύλην τὴν φέρουσαν εἰς τὴν πόλιν **Ac 12:10** (X., Hell. 7, 2, 7 αἱ εἰς τὴν πόλιν φέρουσαι πύλαι; Diog. L. 6, 78 παρὰ τῇ πύλῃ τῇ φερούσῃ εἰς τὸν Ἰσθμόν; Jos., Ant. 9, 146).—See Fitzmyer s.v. ἄγω.

❼ **to bring a thought or idea into circulation,** ***bring, utter, make*** a word, speech, announcement, charge, etc. (TestAbr B 6 p. 110, 8/Stone p. 68 [ParJer 7:8] φάσιν 'news'; Jos., Vi. 359, C. Ap. 1, 251; Just., A I, 54, 1 ἀπόδειξιν 'proof', A II, 12, 5 ἀπολογίαν), as a judicial expr. (cp. Demosth. 58, 22; Polyb. 1, 32, 4; PAmh 68, 62; 69; 72) κατηγορίαν **J 18:29.** Cp. **Ac 25:7 v.l., 18** (Field, Notes 140); **2 Pt 2:11.** Perh. this is the place for μᾶλλον ἑαυτῶν κατάγνωσιν φέρουσιν *rather they blame themselves* 1 Cl 51:2. διδαχήν **2J 10.** ὑποδείγματα *give* or *offer examples* 1 Cl 55:1 (Polyb. 18, 13, 7 τὰ παραδείγματα). τοῦτο φέρεται ἐν *this is brought out = this is recorded in* EpilMosq 4.—Of a divine proclamation, whether direct or indirect (Diod. S. 13, 97, 7 τ. ἱερῶν φερόντων νίκην; Just., D. 128, 2 τοῦ πατρὸς ὁμιλίας [of the Logos]) **2 Pt 1:17, 18, 21a.**

❽ **to demonstrate the reality of someth.,** ***establish*** θάνατον ἀνάγκη φέρεσθαι τοῦ διαθεμένου *the death of the one who made the will must be established* **Hb 9:16.**

❾ **to hold out in the face of difficulty,** ***bear patiently, endure, put up with*** (X., An. 3, 1, 23; Appian, Samn. 10 §13 παρρησίαν φ.=put up with candidness, Iber. 78 §337; Jos., Ant. 7, 372; 17, 342; AssMos fgm. j βλασφημίαν; Just., D. 18, 3 πάντα; Mel., HE 4, 26, 6 θανάτου τὸ γέρας) μαλακίαν 1 Cl 16:3 (Is 53:3). τὸν ὀνειδισμὸν αὐτοῦ (i.e. Ἰησοῦ) **Hb 13:13** (cp. Ezk 34:29). τὸ διαστελλόμενον **12:20.** εὐκλεῶς 1 Cl 45:5. Of God ἤνεγκεν ἐν πολλῇ μακροθυμίᾳ σκεύη ὀργῆς **Ro 9:22.** φῶς μέγα ... ὥστε τοὺς ὀφθαλμοὺς μὴ φέρειν *a light so bright that their eyes could not endure it* GJs 19:2.

❿ **to be productive,** ***bear, produce*** of a plant and its fruits, lit. and in imagery (Hom. et al.; Diod. S. 9, 11, 1; Aelian, VH 3, 18 p. 48, 20; Jo 2:22; Ezk 17:8; Jos., Ant. 4, 100) **Mt 7:18ab; Mk 4:8; J 12:24; 15:2abc, 4f, 8, 16;** Hs 2:3f, 8.—B. 707. DELG. Schmidt, Syn. III 167–93. M-M. EDNT. TW.

φεύγω fut. φεύξομαι; 2 aor. ἔφυγον; pf. πέφυγα LXX (Hom.)

❶ **to seek safety in flight,** ***flee,*** **Mt 8:33; 26:56; Mk 5:14; 14:50, 52** (mng. 2 is also poss.; cp. PTebt 48, 23f); **Lk 8:34; J 10:12, 13 v.l.; Ac 7:29;** GPt 13:57; AcPl Ha 4, 1; 9; 5, 8;12;17; ἀπό (X., Cyr. 7, 2, 4, Mem. 2, 6, 31; Arrian, Ind. 6, 5; Ex 4:3; 2 Km 19:10; PsSol 17:16; TestDan 5:1; JosAs 5:2 [ἀπὸ προσώπου]; Jos., Bell. 1, 474) **Mk 16:8; J 10:5; Js 4:7**=Hm 12, 4, 7; cp. 12, 5, 2; **Rv 9:6** (death will elude them); 1 Cl 4:10; 28:2; Hm 11:14; 12, 2, 4 (w. μακράν). ἐκ (Ael. Aristid. 30 p. 583 D.; Jos., Ant. 14, 177) **Ac 27:30.** εἰς (X., Mem. 1, 2, 24; Gen 14:10; Num 24:11; JosAs 28:7 εἰς τὴν ὕλην; Demetr.: 722 fgm. 1, 1 Jac.; Jos., Ant. 14, 418 εἰς τὰ ὄρη) **Mt 2:13; 10:23; 24:16; Mk 13:14; Lk 21:21** (cp. 1 Macc 2:28); **J 6:15 v.l.; Rv 12:6.** ἐπί w. acc. ἐπὶ τὰ ὄρη **Mt 24:16 v.l.** (X., Ages. 2, 11; JosAs 27:7 ἐπὶ τὴν ὕλην).—RBach, Die Aufforderungen zur Flucht und zum Kampf im alttestamentlichen Prophetenspruch '62.

❷ **to become safe from danger by eluding or avoiding it,** ***escape*** **Mk 14:52** (mng. 1 is also prob.); **Hb 12:25 v.l.** W. the acc. of that which one escapes (Artem. 1, 21; 4, 1 p. 200, 24; Jos., Vi. 94, Ant. 6, 344; Just., A I, 12, 11 ἄγνοιαν) ἔφυγον στόματα μαχαίρης **11:34.** τὸ αἰώνιον (πῦρ) MPol 2:3. Cp. 2 Cl 18:2. ἀπό **Mt 3:7; 23:33; Lk 3:7** (cp. Il. 20, 350).—*Guard against* w. acc. τὰς ἀπειλάς *the threats,* i.e. the punishments which they hold in prospect 1 Cl 58:1.

❸ **to keep from doing someth. by avoiding it because of its potential damage,** ***flee from, avoid, shun,*** fig. ext. of 1, and in a moral sense w. acc. of thing (Zaleucus in Stob. IV p. 125, 12 H. τ. ἀδικίαν; Cleobulus in Diog. L. 1, 92; Epict. 1, 7, 25; SIG 1268 I, 3 [III BC] ἄδικα φεῦγε; 4 Macc 8:19; Just., A I, 43, 3) φεύγετε τὴν πορνείαν (TestReub 5:5) **1 Cor 6:18.** In contrast to διώκειν **1 Ti 6:11** and **2 Ti 2:22** (beside διώκειν, φεύγειν τι may have the mng. 'run away from' as schol. on Nicander, Ther. 75).—1 Cl 30:1; 2 Cl 10:1; ITr 11:1; IPhld 2:1; 6:2; 7:2; ISm 7:2; IPol 5:1. Also ἀπό τινος (Sir 21:2 ἀπὸ ἁμαρτίας) **1 Cor 10:14;** B 4:1, 10; D 3:1; H 37, 3 v.l. (for ἀφέξῃ).

❹ **to cease being visible,** ***vanish, disappear*** (Ps.-Clem., Hom. 2, 28) πᾶσα νῆσος ἔφυγεν **Rv 16:20.** W. ἀπὸ τοῦ προσώπου τινός (as Ps 67:2; cp. also Dt 28:7; Josh 8:5; yet likew. as early as Ctesias: 688 fgm. 9, 1, 3 p. 454, 16 Jac. φυγεῖν ἀπὸ προσώπου Κύρου and schol. on Nicander, Ther. 377 in a free quot. from Herodas [8, 59] φεύγωμεν ἐκ προσώπου) **20:11.** Or does the writer focus on cessation from existence rather than on invisibility?—B. 698. DELG. M-M.

Φῆλιξ, ικος, ὁ (ins: Sb 4601, 3 [144 AD]; APF II 442 no. 56, 9 [II AD]; POxf 3, 1 [142 AD]; POxy 800 [153 AD]; Joseph. index; Just., A I, 29, 2f; on the accent B-D-F §13; Mlt-H. 57) Antonius ***Felix,*** a freedman of the House of the Claudians and brother of Pallas, the favorite of the Emperor Claudius. In 52/53 AD F. became procurator of Palestine. The year of his removal is in dispute (s. Schürer I, 465, 42; ESchwartz, NGG 1907, 284ff), but was in the neighborhood of 60. The infamous character of his administration helped to lay the ground for the revolt of 66–70 (per omnem saevitiam ac libidinem jus regium servili ingenio exercuit, 'he revelled in cruelty and lust, and wielded the power of a king with the mind of a slave': Tacitus, Hist. 5, 9). **Ac 23:24, 26; 24:3, 22, 24f, 27; 25:14.**—Zahn, Einl. II^3 647ff; Schürer I, 460ff; Pauly-W. I 2616–18; EMeyer III 47ff; BHHW I 469; Haenchen index.—On the question whether Pilate (s. Πιλᾶτος and Πόντιος), Felix, and Festus were procurators (s. ἐπίτροπος 1) or prefects (s. ἔπαρχος) see the Lat. ins from Caesarea discovered and first publ. by AFrova, Istituto Lombardo Rendiconti 95, '61 (see also Schürer I, 358 note 22, and 359), which officially refers to Pilate as prefect. A probability is that by the time of Felix and Festus this was officially changed to procurator. The terms were sometimes used interchangeably.—Hemer, Acts 171–73; HTajra, The Trial of St. Paul '89, 125–34.—M-M.

φήμη, ης, ἡ (Hom. et al.; LXX; TestSol 8:1 D; JosAs 1:9; Just.; Ath.) ***report, news*** ἐξῆλθεν ἡ φήμη αὕτη *the news of this was spread* (Jos., Bell. 2, 416; cp. Philo, Leg. ad Gai. 231) **Mt**

9:26. φ. περί τινος (Herodian 2, 1, 3; 2, 7, 5) **Lk 4:14.**—DELG s.v. φημί. M-M.

φημί 2 sg. φῄς (Just.), 3 sg. φησίν, 3 pl. φασίν **Ro 3:8; 2 Cor 10:10 v.l.;** 3 sg. of impf. and 2 aor. ἔφη (s. Kühner-Bl. II 210), 3 pl. ἔφασαν (Esth 10:31; Demetr.: 722 fgm. 5 Jac. [Eus., PE 9, 29, 16]); fut. φήσω (Just.); 1 aor. 3 sg. ἔφησεν 2 Macc 3:27 al. (Hom.+).

❶ **to state someth. orally or in writing, *say, affirm*** w. direct discourse—ⓐ w. interchange of first and third persons in dialogue Hv 2, 4, 1; 3, 2, 1; 3, 3, 1f and oft.

ⓑ introducing direct discourse—**α.** preceding it ὁ δέ φησιν· οὔ, μήποτε … **Mt 13:29.** Cp. **26:61; 27:11, 23; Mk 10:29; J 9:38; 18:29; Ac 7:2; 8:36; 10:30** al. Oft. w. dat. of the pers. addressed ἔφη αὐτῷ ὁ Ἰησοῦς· πάλιν γέγραπται … **Mt 4:7.** Cp. **13:28; 21:27; Mk 9:12; 14:29; Lk 7:44; Ac 26:32.** Also πρός τινα (TestAbr A 15 p. 96, 7 [Stone p. 40]) **Lk 22:70; Ac 10:28; 16:37; 26:1.**—Used w. a ptc. to denote the nature of the statement ἀποκριθεὶς ὁ ἑκατόνταρχος ἔφη· κύριε … **Mt 8:8.** Cp. **Lk 23:3, 40.**

β. inserted after the first word or words of the direct discourse (Oenomaus in Eus., PE 6, 7, 8 ἀγγελῶ, νὴ Δία, φήσει τις, …; TestJob 34:4; JosAs 24:8; Just., D. 1, 3) δός μοι, φησίν, ὧδε … **Mt 14:8.** ποίας; φησίν **19:18 v.l.** Cp. **Lk 7:40** (here φησίν stands at the close of a direct quot. consisting of only two words; cp. Just., D. 3, 7 οὐ γάρ, φημί); **Ac 2:38 v.l.; 23:35; 25:5, 22; 26:25.** ὡς ἔφην Papias (2:15) (ApcMos 42).

ⓒ without a subj., where it is self-evident ὅρα γάρ φησιν ποιήσεις πάντα *for see to it, (God) says* (Ex 25:40; Just., D. 126, 6; Mel., P. 12, 78; Ath. 32, 1), *you must make everything* **Hb 8:5.** But φησίν is also used impersonally, *it is said,* so that it can also go w. a plural subject that makes a statement (cp. Demosth. 23, 31; ViJer 8 [p. 72, 12 Sch.]; Epict., Enchir. 24, 2; Maximus Tyr. 5, 4a) αἱ ἐπιστολαὶ μέν, φησίν, βαρεῖαι **2 Cor 10:10** (the subject of this statement is the opposition to Paul in the Corinthian church; hence the v.l. φασίν). οὐ δεῖν, φησίν (i.e. gnostics) προφήταις χρῆσθαι AcPlCor 1:10. W. scripture quotations φησίν *it says* (φησίν abs. w. a quot. fr. Aratus: Synes., Prov. 2, 5 p. 125a) **1 Cor 6:16;** 1 Cl 30:2; 2 Cl 7:6; B 7:7.

ⓓ φησίν, in introducing scripture quot., can be pred. to a wide variety of subjects (cp. φησὶν ὁ λόγος Pla., Phil. 51c; Maximus Tyr. 22, 5b; Just., D. 93, 3) φησὶν ὁ ἅγιος λόγος 1 Cl 13:3. (τὸ πνεῦμα τὸ ἅγιον) 16:2. αὐτός (=ὁ κύριος) φησιν 16:15. ὁ θεός 33:5. ὁ ἐκλεκτὸς Δαυίδ 52:2.

❷ **to say someth. that provides a fuller explanation of a statement, *mean*** by one's statement (Artem. 1, 67 p. 62, 16 φημὶ δὲ ἐγώ=but I mean), w. acc. (Diod. S. 37, 29, 5 Κράσσον φημί; Syntipas p. 10, 12) τοῦτο **1 Cor 7:29;** cp. **10:15, 19.** Foll. by ὅτι **1 Cor 10:19** (Caecil. Calact., fgm. 103 p. 93, 18 ἀλλὰ τί φημι; ὅτι κτλ.); τοῦτο ὅτι **15:50.** Foll. by acc. and inf. (Synes., Kingship 15 p. 14c) **Ro 3:8;** Papias (3:2).—HFournier, Les verbes 'dire' en Grec ancien '46. B. 1257. DELG. M-M.

φημίζω 1 aor. pass. ἐφημίσθην; pf. inf. πεφημίσθαι (fr. φημί via φῆμις 'speech'; Hes. et al.; SibOr 3, 2; 406) **to cause a report to spread by word of mouth, *spread a report/rumor*** (Jos., Bell. 1, 450) pass. *be rumored, spread as a rumor* (Aeschyl. et al.; Plut., Mor. 264d οἱ τεθνάναι φημισθέντες='those reported to be dead'; PGiss 19, 4 [II AD]) **Mt 28:15 v.l.; Ac 13:43 v.l.** διὰ τὸ ἤδη πεφημίσθαι ἐν τῇ πόλει *because a rumor had already spread through the city* AcPl Ha 4, 17.—DELG s.v. φημί. M-M.

Φῆστος, ου, ὁ (PLond III, 904, 33 p. 126 [104 AD]; Josephus index) Porcius ***Festus,*** successor to Felix (s. Φῆλιξ) as procurator of Palestine. Neither the beginning nor the end (at his death) of his term of office can be determined with full certainty, though it is gener. assumed that he died in the early 60s. During his rule and w. his consent Paul went to the imperial court at Rome. **Ac 24:27; 25:1, 4, 9, 12–14, 22–24; 26:24f, 32.**—Schürer I, 467f; Zahn, Einl. II[3] 647ff; ESchwartz, NGG 1907, 294ff; UHolzmeister, Der hl. Pls vor dem Richterstuhle des Festus: ZKT 36, 1912, 489–511; 742–82; ESpringer, D. Prozess des Ap. Pls: PJ 217, 1929, 182–96: Taubenschlag, OpMin II, 721–26 (pap); RJewett, A Chronology of Paul's Life '79; RCassidy, Society and Politics in the Acts of the Apostles '87; Pauly-W. XXII, 200–227; BHHW I 479; Haenchen, index.—M-M.

φθάνω 1 aor. ἔφθασα; pf. 3 sg. ἔφθακεν SSol 2:12. (Hom.+) prim. 'come or do someth. first or before someone'.

❶ **to be beforehand in moving to a position, *come before, precede*** (exx. fr. the later period, incl. ins and pap, in Clark [s. below] 375f) w. acc. of the pers. whom one precedes (Diod. S. 15, 61, 4 τοὺς πολεμίους; Appian, Syr. 29 §142, Bell. Civ. 5, 30 §115; SIG 783, 35 [27 BC] φθάνοντες ἀλλήλους; Wsd 6:13; Jos., Ant. 7, 247) ἡμεῖς οὐ μὴ φθάσωμεν τοὺς κοιμηθέντας *we will by no means precede those who have fallen asleep* **1 Th 4:15.**

❷ **to get to or reach a position, *have just arrived,*** then simply ***arrive, reach*** (late and Mod. Gk.: Plut., Mor. 210e; 338a; Vett. Val. 137, 35; 174, 12 ἐπὶ ποῖον [ἀστέρα]; Herm. Wr. 9, 10; PParis 18, 14 [II AD] φθάσομεν εἰς Πελούσιον; PGM 3, 590; LXX [cp. Thackeray p. 288f]; TestAbr A 1 p. 77, 9 [Stone p. 2]; TestAbr B 2 p. 107, 3 al. [St. p. 62]; TestReub 5:7; TestNapht 6:9 ἐπὶ τ. γῆς [v.l. ἐπὶ τ. γῆν]; JosAs 26:5 AB; Philo, Op. M. 5, Leg. All. 3, 215 φθάσαι μέχρι θεοῦ, Conf. Lingu. 153, Mos. 1, 2.—JVogeser, Zur Sprache der griech. Heiligenlegenden, diss. Munich 1907, 46; JWittmann, Sprachl. Untersuchungen zu Cosmas Indicopleustes, diss. Munich 1913, 16) ἐπί τινα *come upon someone, overtake* perh. w. a suggestion of success (in an adverse sense, DDaube, The Sudden in Scripture, '64, 35f). ἄρα ἔφθασεν ἐφ' ὑμᾶς ἡ βασιλεία τοῦ θεοῦ **Mt 12:28; Lk 11:20** (KClark, JBL 59, '40, 367–83 ἐγγίζειν and φθ.; HMartin, ET 52, '40/41, 270–75). ἔφθασεν ἐπ' αὐτοὺς ἡ ὀργή **1 Th 2:16** (cp. Eccl 8:14a v.l.; TestLevi 6:11). ἄχρι ὑμῶν ἐφθάσαμεν **2 Cor 10:14** (SAndrews, SBLSP 36, '97, 479 n. 30: perh. an allusion to the military award 'corona militaris').

❸ **to come to or arrive at a particular state, *attain*** φθ. εἴς τι *come up to, reach, attain someth.* (BGU 522, 6) **Ro 9:31; Phil 3:16.**—B. 701f; 703. DELG. M-M. TW. Sv.

φθαρ- s. φθείρω.

φθαρτός, ή, όν (φθείρω) **subject to decay/destruction, *perishable*** (Aristot., Anal. 2, 22; Diod. S. 1, 6, 3 [γεννητὸς καὶ φθαρτός in contrast to ἀγέννητος and ἄφθαρτος; so also Just. D. 5, 4]; Plut., Mor. 106d; 717e; Sext. Emp., Math. 9, 141; TestAbr A 4 p. 81, 18 [Stone p. 10]; Philo, Leg. All. 2, 3, Cher. 5; 48 χρυσὸς καὶ ἄργυρος, οὐσίαι φθαρταί; 2 Macc 7:16; apolog. exc. Tat.) of pers. *mortal* ἄνθρωπος (Ps.-Callisth. 2, 22, 12; Philo, Somn. 1, 172) **Ro 1:23;** Hs 9, 23, 4. Of things στέφανος **1 Cor 9:25.** σπορά **1 Pt 1:23.** τὰ ἐνθάδε 2 Cl 6:6. ἀγῶνες *perishable contests,* i.e. *contests for a perishable prize* 7:1, 4. τὸ κατοικητήριον τῆς καρδίας φθαρτὸν καὶ ἀσθενές B 16:7. ὕλη (Wsd 9:15 σῶμα) Dg 2:3. σάρξ Hs 5, 7, 2 (Philo, Congr. Erud. Grat. 112).—Subst. οἱ φ. *the perishable* of humanity Dg 9:2. τὸ φ. (Wsd 14:8; Philo, Op. M. 82) τὸ φθαρτὸν τοῦτο *this perishable (nature)* **1 Cor 15:53f.** τὰ φθ. *perishable things* (Test Benj 6:2; Philo, Ebr. 209 [opp. τὰ ἄφθαρτα]; Just., A II, 7, 9; Ath. 15, 3) **1 Pt 1:18;** B 19:8; Dg 6:8.—DELG s.v. φθείρω. TW.

φθέγγομαι mid. dep. fut. φθέγξομαι LXX; 1 aor. ἐφθεγξάμην (Hom.+; SIG 1175, 6 ῥῆμα μοχθηρὸν φθ.; 23 [abs.]; PFlor 309, 10; LXX; TestJob 18:4; Just.; Tat. 1, 2) lit. 'produce a sound' (Iren. 1, 14, 7 [Harv. I, 142, 4]), then 'call out loudly' (Orig., C. Cels. 7, 55, 3), gener. ***speak, utter, proclaim*** τὶ *someth.*, w. focus on the act of utterance (Lucian, Nigrin. 3, 11; Iambl. Erot. 21; Sextus 356; Wsd 1:8 ἄδικα; TestDan 5:2 ἀλήθειαν; Philo; Jos., Bell. 2, 128, C. Ap. 2, 219) ὑπέρογκα *speak bombastically* **2 Pt 2:18.** Of an animal ἐν ἀνθρώπου φωνῇ vs. **16** (Alciphron 4, 19, 3 εἰ βοῦς μοι τὸ λεγόμενον φθέγξαιτο). Abs., of persons (opp. 'be silent'.—X., An. 6, 6, 28, Cyr. 7, 3, 11; Ael. Aristid. 30, 19 K.=10 p. 121 D.; TestJob 18:4) **Ac 4:18.**—DELG. M-M.

φθείρω fut. φθερῶ; 1 aor. ἔφθειρα. Pass.: 2 fut. φθαρήσομαι; 2 aor. ἐφθάρην; pf. ἔφθαρμαι, ptc. ἐφθαρμένος (Hom.+; ins, pap, LXX, TestJob 33:4; Test12Patr; ParJer 7:26; Philo, Ar., Just., Tat.) gener. 'destroy, ruin'

❶ **to cause harm to in a physical manner or in outward circumstances, *destroy, ruin, corrupt, spoil*—ⓐ** *ruin financially* τινά *someone,* so perh. **2 Cor 7:2** (s. 2a below).

ⓑ The expr. εἴ τις τὸν ναὸν τοῦ θεοῦ φθείρει **1 Cor 3:17** seems to be derived fr. the idea of the destruction of a house (X., Mem. 1, 5, 3 τὸν οἶκον τὸν ἑαυτοῦ φθείρειν. Oft in marriage contracts: Mitt-Wilck. I/2, 284, 11 [II BC]; PTebt 104, 29 [92 BC] et al.).

ⓒ *seduce* a virgin (Eur. et al.; Demetr.: 722 fgm. 1, 9 Jac.; Diod. S. 1, 23, 4; Jos., Ant. 4, 252; Just., A I, 9, 4) οὐδὲ Εὕα φθείρεται, ἀλλὰ παρθένος πιστεύεται *nor is Eve corrupted; instead, a virgin is trusted* Dg 12:8 (πιστεύω 1f).

ⓓ pass. *be ruined, be doomed to destruction* by earthly transitoriness or otherw. (Epict. 2, 5, 12 τὸ γενόμενον καὶ φθαρῆναι δεῖ; TestJob 33:4 ἡ δόξα αὐτοῦ [τοῦ κόσμου] φθαρήσεται; Just., A II, 11, 5 κάλλει τῷ ῥέοντι καὶ φθειρομένῳ) of cultic images Dg 2:4. Of a man bowed down by old age αὐτοῦ τὸ πνεῦμα τὸ ἤδη ἐφθαρμένον ἀπὸ τῶν προτέρων αὐτοῦ πράξεων *his spirit, which had already degenerated from its former condition* (s. πρᾶξις 6) Hv 3, 12, 2 (cp. Ocellus [II BC] c. 23 Harder [1926] φθείρονται ἐξ ἀλλήλων).

❷ **to cause deterioration of the inner life, *ruin, corrupt***

ⓐ *ruin* or *corrupt* τινά *someone,* by erroneous teaching or immorality, so perh. **2 Cor 7:2** (s. 1a above). ἥτις ἔφθειρεν τὴν γῆν (=τοὺς ἀνθρώπους; see γῆ 2) ἐν τῇ πορνείᾳ αὐτῆς **Rv 19:2.** Pass. (UPZ 20, 17 [163 BC]; TestJud 19:4 ἐν ἁμαρτίαις φθαρείς) τὸν παλαιὸν ἄνθρωπον τὸν φθειρόμενον κατὰ τὰς ἐπιθυμίας **Eph 4:22.** Cp. Hs 8, 9, 3 v.l.

ⓑ *ruin* or *corrupt* τὶ *someth.* by misleading tactics πίστιν θεοῦ ἐν κακῇ διδασκαλίᾳ IEph 16:2. The ἐκκλησία (opp. τηρεῖν) 2 Cl 14:3ab. On φθείρουσιν ἤθη χρηστὰ ὁμιλίαι κακαί **1 Cor 15:33** cp. ἦθος. Pass. *be led astray* (Jos., Bell. 4, 510) μήπως φθαρῇ τὰ νοήματα ὑμῶν ἀπὸ τῆς ἁπλότητος (νόημα 2) **2 Cor 11:3** (φθ. of the seduction of a virgin, s. 1c above).

❸ **to inflict punishment, *destroy*** in the sense 'punish w. eternal destruction' **1 Cor 3:17b** (='punish by destroying' as Jer 13:9). Pass. **2 Pt 2:12; Jd 10.** ἔφθαρται (w. ἀπώλετο) IPol 5:2.

❹ **break rules of a contest, *violate rules,*** ἀγῶνα φθείρειν t.t. (SIG 1076, 3) 2 Cl 7:4; cp. vs. 5 (here in imagery).—B. 758. DELG. M-M. TW.

φθινοπωρινός, ή, όν (φθινόπωρον, 'of late autumn' fr. φθίνω and ὀπώρα) ***belonging to late autumn*** (Aristot., HA 5, 11; Polyb. 4, 37, 2; Plut., Mor. 735b ὁ φθινοπωρινὸς ἀήρ, ἐν ᾧ φυλλοχοεῖ τὰ δένδρα; Aelian, NA 14, 26 p. 358, 24; PHib 27, 170 [III BC]). In **Jd 12** factious teachers are called δένδρα φθινοπωρινὰ ἄκαρπα *trees in late autumn, without fruit* (w. νεφέλαι ἄνυδροι). The point of the comparison is prob. that trees which have no fruit at the time of harvest (s. JMayor, φθινοπωρινός: Exp. 6th ser., 9, 1904, 98–104, The Ep. of St. Jude and 2 Pt 1907, 55–59) have not fulfilled the purpose for which they exist, any more than waterless clouds.—B. 1015. DELG s.v. φθίνω. M-M. EDNT.

φθόγγος, ου, ὁ (φθέγγομαι; Hom.+; PGM 7, 775; 778; Philo) **any clear or distinct sound**

ⓐ of musical instruments ***tone*** (Pla., Leg. 812d; Philostrat., Vi. Apoll. 5, 21 p. 181, 19.—Wsd 19:18) **1 Cor 14:7.**

ⓑ of the human ***voice*** (Hom. et al.) ἐξῆλθεν ὁ φθόγγος αὐτῶν **Ro 10:18** (cp. Ps 18:5).—DELG s.v. φθέγγομαι. M-M.

φθονέω (φθόνος) 1 aor. ἐφθόνησα (Hom.+; ins; PFlor 273, 5; Tob 4:7; 16; TestSol 1:2 A; Test12Patr, JosAs; GrBar 4:8; ApcEsdr 5:3 p. 29, 26 Tdf.; ApcMos 18; Philo; Just., A I, 31, 7 [φθονούμενος]; Tat. 1, 1) ***envy, be jealous*** τινί *(of) someone* (X., Mem. 3, 5, 16; Chares [IV BC] 1 [Anth. Lyr.[2] Diehl, suppl. '42]; Herodian 3, 2, 3; Jos., Vi. 230) ἀλλήλοις (Plut., Artox. 24, 7 v.l.) **Gal 5:26** (v.l. ἀλλήλους; the acc. as JosAs 24:2; Aesop 184, 1 H.=117P.//119 H-H.); w. inf. (Appian, Bell. Civ. 4, 95 §400 φθ. τινι w. inf.=begrudge someone [the chance to]; Jos., C. Ap. 2, 268) μὴ φθονήσωμεν ἑαυτοῖς τυχεῖν τοσούτων ἀγαθῶν *let us not begrudge each other the gaining of such benefits* 2 Cl 15:5 (ApcMos 18 τοῦτο … ἐφθόνησεν ὑμῖν; Jos., Ant. 4, 235 ἀγαθῶν φθονεῖν τινι; ApcEsdr 5:3 αὕτη τὸ γάλα ἐφθόνησεν τοῦ δοῦναι 'withhold').—φθ. τινι can also mean *dislike someone, be resentful toward someone* without the connotation of jealousy or a grudge (Appian, Bell. Civ. 1, 79 §360). Absol. **Js 4:2 v.l.**—DELG s.v. φθόνος. M-M. Sv.

φθόνος, ου, ὁ (Pind., Hdt. et al.; Demosth. 20, 165 opp. of φιλανθρωπία; Ael. Aristid. 29, 5 K.=40 p. 752 D.: φθ. as ἔσχατον τῶν ἀνθρωπίνων ἁμαρτημάτων; pap; ins freq. associated with 'evil eye' [s. Elliott s.v. βασκαίνω 1], reff. SEG XLI, 1526; LXX, pseudep.; Philo; Jos., Vi. 80; 122; Just.; Tat. 32, 3) ***envy, jealousy,*** w. ζῆλος (1 Macc 8:16; TestSim 4:5) 1 Cl 3:2; 4:7; 5:2. διὰ ζῆλος Δαυὶδ φθόνον ἔσχεν … ὑπὸ Σαοὺλ 1 Cl 4:13 *Saul envied David out of jealousy.* W. κακία (TestBenj 8:1) **Tit 3:3.** In catalogues of vices (in some of which κακία also occurs; s. also Herm. Wr. 13, 7) **Ro 1:29** (μεστοὺς φθόνου φόνου ἔριδος. The wordplay φθόν. φόν. as Eur., Tro. 766ff); **1 Ti 6:4** (w. ἔρις); φθόνοι **Gal 5:21** (v.l. + φόνοι); **1 Pt 2:1.** διὰ φθόνον *out of envy* (Anaximenes [IV BC]: 72 fgm. 33 Jac.; Philo, Mos. 1, 2; Jos., Vi. 204 ἐπιγνοὺς διὰ φθόνον ἀναιρεθῆναί με προστάξαι, C. Ap. 1, 222) **Mt 27:18; Mk 15:10; Phil 1:15** (w. ἔρις). On the difficult and perh. textually damaged pass. πρὸς φθόνον (Demosth. 20, 165) ἐπιποθεῖ τὸ πνεῦμα **Js 4:5** s. ἐπιποθέω; πρός 3f, and also FSpitta, Der Brief des Jk (=Zur Gesch. und Lit. des Urchristentums II) 1896, 118ff; PCorssen, GGA 1893, 596f; OKirn, StKr 77, 1904, 127ff; 593ff; CBruston, RTQR 11, 1907, 368–77; JFindlay, ET 37, 1926, 381f; AMeyer, D. Rätsel des Jk 1930, 258f; LJohnson, NovT 25, '83, 327–47 (Js 3:13–4:10; Gr-Rom. lit.)—B. 1139. DELG. M-M. Spicq. Sv.

φθορά, ᾶς, ἡ (Aeschyl., Hdt.+; ins, pap, LXX, En; PsSol 4:6; SibOr 2, 9; Philo; Jos., Ant. 18, 373; Mel., P. 49, 351; Ath., R. 16 p. 67, 24 al.)

❶ **breakdown of organic matter, *dissolution, deterioration, corruption,*** in the world of nature (Galen, In Hippocr. De Natura Hominis Comm. 45 p. 25, 6 Mewaldt γένεσις κ. φθορά=coming into being and passing away; 51 p. 28, 11 γένεσις κ. φθορὰ σώματος.—The cause of destruction is made clear by an addition. Cp. Plut., Artox. 1019 [16, 6] concerning Mithridates, who was allowed to decompose while he was still alive: εὐλαὶ κ. σκώληκες ὑπὸ φθορᾶς κ. σηπεδόνος ἀναζέουσιν=maggots and worms swarmed as a result of the destruction and putrefaction [of his body]) τροφὴ φθορᾶς *perishable food* IRo 7:3. ἅ ἐστιν πάντα εἰς φθορὰν τῇ ἀποχρήσει *all of which are meant for destruction by being consumed* **Col 2:22.** Of animals who are destined to be killed **2 Pt 2:12a** (X., Cyr. 7, 5, 64; Artem. 1, 78 p. 74, 27.—Schol. on Nicander, Ther. 795 explains κακόφθορα by saying that it designates animals τὰ ἐπὶ κακῇ φθορᾷ τεχθέντα=born to come to an evil end, i.e. destruction).—Of the *state of being perishable* (opp. ἀφθαρσία as Philo, Mos. 2, 194; Mel., Ath.) **1 Cor 15:42;** also concrete, *that which is perishable* vs. **50.** ἡ δουλεία τῆς φθορᾶς *slavery to decay* **Ro 8:21.** [ἀπ]ὸ φθορᾶς γεγ[ονός] *that which comes from the perishable* Ox 1081 13f (=Coptic SJCh 89, 11f; the restoration φθορᾶς pap ln. 12 also corresponds to the Coptic version; for the correct restoration of pap ln. 23 s. under διαφορά).

❷ **destruction of a fetus,** ***abortion*** (cp. SIG 1042, 7 [II/III AD] φθορά=miscarriage [which makes the mother unclean for 40 days] and φθόριον=a means of producing abortion) οὐ φονεύσεις ἐν φθορᾷ B 19:5; D 2:2.—On the topic of abortion s. Soranus, Gyn. 64f (procedures); Plut., Mor. 242c (διαφθείρω); SDickison, Abortion in Antiquity: Arethusa 6, '73, 159–66.

❸ **ruination of a pers. through an immoral act,** *seduction* of a young woman (Demetr.: 722 fgm. 1, 9 Jac.; Diod. S. 3, 59, 1; 5, 62, 1; Plut., Mor. 712c; Jos., Ant. 17, 309, C. Ap. 2, 202) w. μοιχεία (Philo, Det. Pot. Ins. 102) 2 Cl 6:4.

❹ **inward depravity,** ***depravity*** (Ex 18:18; Mi 2:10) ἡ ἐν τῷ κόσμῳ ἐν ἐπιθυμίᾳ φθορά *the depravity* that exists *in the world because of inordinate desire* (opp. θεία φύσις) **2 Pt 1:4.** δοῦλοι τῆς φθορᾶς **2:19.** Vs. **12b** (s. 5 below) scarcely belongs here.

❺ **total destruction of an entity,** ***destruction*** in the last days **Gal 6:8** (opp. ζωὴ αἰώνιος). ἐν τῇ φθορᾷ αὐτῶν καὶ φθαρήσονται *when they* (the dumb animals) *are destroyed* in the coming end of the world, *these* (the false teachers), *too, will be destroyed* (so BWeiss, Kühl, JMayor, Windisch, Knopf, Vrede) **2 Pt 2:12b.**—DELG s.v. θείρω. M-M. TW. Sv.

φθορεύς, έως, ὁ (φθορά) ***seducer*** (Plut., Mor. 18c; Epict. 2, 22, 28 [w. μοιχός]; 4 Macc 18:8; Philo, Decal. 168 [w. μοιχός]; Tat. 33, 3) this mng. is to be preferred for B 10:7 and prob. also for 20:2; D 5:2, where the word is oft. taken to mean *abortionist* (cp. φθορά 2).—D 16:3 it is *corrupter* gener.—DELG s.v. φθείρω B.

φθοριμαῖος, α, ον (also Eus.) ***destructive*** οἵτινες τήν τινων πίστιν ἀνατρέπουσιν φθοριμαίοις λόγοις *who upset the faith of some through destructive statements* AcPl Cor 1:2 (cp. 2 Ti 2:18).

φιάλη, ης, ἡ (Hom.+; ins, pap, LXX; TestSol 16:7; GrBar; ApcMos 33; EpArist; Jos., Ant. 3, 143; 272; Just., D. 22, 5 [s. Amos 6:6]; Ath. 15, 2; loanw. in rabb.) ***bowl,*** specif. a *bowl used in offerings* (Diod. S. 4, 49, 8) **Rv 5:8** (golden bowl as Ps.-Callisth. 2, 21, 16); **15:7; 16:1–4, 8, 10, 12, 17; 17:1; 21:9.**— B. 346. DELG. M-M.

φιλ- on the formation of terms w. φιλ- in the NT s. New Docs 2, 106.

φιλάγαθος, ον (Aristot., Magn. Mor. 2, 14, 1212b, 18 φιλάγαθος οὐ φίλαυτος; Polyb. 6, 53, 9; Plut., Mor. 140c, Rom. 30, 7; Vett. Val. 104, 7; ins; Mitt-Wilck. I/2, 20 II, 11 [II AD]; POxy 33 [II AD]; Cat. Cod. Astr. XII 178, 18; 183, 3; Wsd 7:22; EpArist; Philo, Mos. 2, 9; as subst. PByz 6, 72) ***loving what is good*** (in the Gr-Rom. world a characteristic of an esp. respected and responsible citizen) **Tit 1:8** (cp. the noun φιλαγαθία SB 8267, 44 w. ἀρετή; ISmyrnaMcCabe .0003, 5).—M-M. TW. Spicq.

Φιλαδέλφεια, ας, ἡ (so N.; other edd. Φιλαδελφία, Ign., MPol) ***Philadelphia,*** a city in Lydia (west central Asia Minor; this Philadelphia mentioned in Strabo 12, 8 p. 578; Ptolem. 5, 2, 17; Ael. Aristid. 26, 96 K. al.; ins) under Roman rule fr. 133 BC Significant as a seat of Hellenistic culture. The sixth letter of **Rv 1:11; 3:7** and one epistle of Ign., IPhld ins, are addressed to the Christian community there. MPol 19:1 mentions eleven martyrs fr. Phil. who were condemned together w. Polycarp in Smyrna.—An inhabitant of the city was called Φιλαδελφεύς title of IPhld (s. Hdb. z. NT on this).—Lghtf., The Apost. Fathers, Part II vol. II^2 1889, 237ff; KBuresch, Aus Lydien 1898; Ramsay, CB I/1, 196ff, Letters ch. 27f; VSchultze, Altchristl. Städte u. Landschaften II/2, 1926; Pauly-W. XIX, 2091–93; CHemer, The Letters to the Seven Churches of Asia in Their Local Setting '89 ('86), 153–77; Kl. Pauly IV, 733f; BHHW III, 1450f.—New Docs 3, 56 (lit.) M-M.

φιλαδελφία, ας, ἡ ***love of brother/sister*** (elsewh. in the lit. sense of love for blood brothers or sisters: Alexis Com. [IV BC] 334; Eratosth. [III BC], Cat. p. 12, 18; Plut., Περὶ φιλαδελφίας; Lucian, Dial. Deor. 26, 2; Babrius 47, 15; PLond V, 1708, 101; 4 Macc 13:23, 26; 14:1; Philo, Leg. ad Gai. 87; Jos., Ant. 4, 26) in our literature in the transf. sense of affection for a fellow-Christian (s. ἀδελφός 2a) **Ro 12:10; 1 Th 4:9; Hb 13:1; 2 Pt 1:7ab;** 1 Cl 48:1. ἀνυπόκριτος **1 Pt 1:22.** περιβόητος 1 Cl 47:5.—HSedlaczek, φιλαδελφία nach den Schriften des hl. Ap. Pls: TQ 76, 1894, 272–95; JKloppenberg, NTS 39, '93, 265–89 (1 Th 4:9–12).—M-M. TW. Sv.

φιλάδελφος, ον (for the prim. sense 'loving one's brother/sister' in ref. to siblings s. φιλαδελφία; Soph., X.+; on gravestones [Sb 6234; 6235; 6653]; 2 Macc 15:14; 4 Macc 13:21; 15:10; Philo, De Jos. 218) in our literature only in the transf. sense **having affection for an associate,** ***having brotherly love, having mutual affection*** (cp. Socrat., Ep. 28, 12=sociable; 2 Macc 15:14=loving one's compatriots) **1 Pt 3:8.**—New Docs 3, 87 (ins reff., incl. one fr. Bithynia: TAM IV, 111). M-M. TW.

φίλανδρος, ον (Aeschyl. et al., and esp. freq. in Plut. w. cognates) ***having affection/love for a husband*** (so Phalaris, Ep. 132 φ. καὶ σώφρων; Ep. 58 of Apollonius of Tyana [Philostrat. I 361, 30]; Plut., Mor. 142a φίλανδροι καὶ σώφρονες γυναῖκες; SIG 783, 39 [I BC]; SEG XLII, 1277, 4; 1211 A, 2 [superl.]; ins fr. Perg. in Dssm., LO 268 [LAE 314]; PCairMasp 310, 18; PLond V, 1711, 40; Philo, Exs. 139; Cat. Cod. Astr. XII 179, 9.—φιλανδρία: SEG XLII 1214, 11f; Jos., Ant. 18, 159.—Dibelius, Hdb. ad loc.) **Tit 2:4;** AcPl BMM verso 28 (text uncertain: φιλά]νδρων).—DELG s.v. ἀνήρ. New Docs 3, 42f (ins, reff.). M-M.

φιλανθρωπία, ας, ἡ (cp. next entry; X. [Mem. 4, 3, 7]; Pla. [Euthphr. 3d]+; ins, pap, LXX, TestAbr B 6 p. 110, 9 [Stone p. 68]; EpArist, Philo, Joseph.; Just.; Ath. 30, 2; Orig., C. Cels. 1, 67, 24) **affectionate concern for and interest in humanity,** ***(loving) kindness,*** of God (Musonius p. 90, 12 H.; Lucian, Bis Accus. 1, end; Philo, Cher. 99; Jos., Ant. 1, 24.—Contrast Aeschyl., who uses the adj. [Prom. 11 s. φιλάνθρωπος] in ref. to the crime of Prometheus, who, being an immortal, is without favor in heaven διὰ τὴν λίαν φιλότητα βροτῶν 'because of his excessive affection for mortals' 1231.—OWeinreich, ARW 18, 1915, 25; 50–52.—As a virtue of rulers: Diod. S. 34 + 35 fgm. 3 [w. χρηστότης]; OGI 139, 20; SIG 888, 101; Esth 8:121 [w. χρηστότης]; 3 Macc 3:15, 18; EpArist 265; 290; Ath. 30, 2; Did., Gen. 129, 27; associated w. εὐεργεσία Diod. S. 13, 27, 1.—PWendland, ZNW 5, 1904, 345, 2) and w. χρηστότης (Plut., Aristid. 27, 7 and oft. elsewh.; Philo, Spec. Leg. 2, 141; Jos., Ant. 10, 164) **Tit 3:4;** Dg 9:2. παρεῖχον οὐ τὴν τυχοῦσαν φ. *expressed no perfunctory kindness* (the context, with its detailed description of hospitality, accounts for the use of the qualifying ptc.; they may not be able to speak Greek [they are βάρβαροι] but they have the best of Hellenic manners; cp. ENorden, Die germanische Urgesch. in Tacitus' Germania[2] 1922 p. 137, 2; 138, 1) **Ac 28:2.**—Field, Notes 147f; 222f.—On the semantic development: SLorenz, De Progressu Notionis φιλανθρωπίας, diss. Leipzig 1914, w. further consideration by STrompdeRuiter, Mnemosyne n.s. 59, '32, 271–306.—CSpicq, La Philanthropie hellénistique (Tit 3:4): StTh 12, '58, 169–91; MvanVeldhuizen, Moses, A Model of Hellenistic Philanthropia: Reformed Review 38, '85, 215–24.—Larfeld I 500. DELG s.v. ἄνθρωπος. M-M. EDNT. TW. Spicq. Sv.

φιλάνθρωπος, ον (s. prec. and next entry; Aeschyl. [Prom. 11], Aristoph. [Pax 392 of Hermas], X., Pla. [of Eros]+; ins, pap, LXX; TestAbr B 2 p. 106, 3 [Stone p. 60]; JosAs; ApcMos 42; EpArist; Philo; Jos., Ant. 1, 200; Just.; Mel., HE 4, 26, 1; Ath.—Superl. φιλανθρωπότατοι Ath. 2, 1; 12, 3 [cp. sing. Pla., Symp. 189d]) **pert. to having a benevolent interest in humanity,** ***loving humanity, benevolent,*** of God (Pla., Symp. 189d, Leg. 4, 713d; Plut., Mor. 402a; Lucian, Prom. 6; Xenophon Eph. 5, 4, 10; Aelian, HA 9, 33; Philo; Weinreich [s. φιλανθρωπία]; JosAs cod. A 12:11; 13:1 [p. 56, 16; 17, 3 Bat.]; ApcMos 42; Just., D. 23, 2. Of the Wisdom of God Wsd 1:6; 7:23. Also of a ruler [EpArist 208; Ath. 1, 2; superl. 2, 1] 'humane' [Wendland, s. φιλανθρωπία; Thieme 38]) Dg 8:7. Of a virtue (TestAbr B 2 p. 106, 3 [Stone p. 60]; Just., D. 136, 2; cp. Ath. 12, 1 φιλάνθρωπον ... βίον) ἡ φιλόθεος καὶ φιλάνθρωπος ἀγάπη Agr 7 (w. φιλόθεος as Philo, Dec. 110).—DELG s.v. ἄνθρωπος. M-M s.v. φιλανθρωπία. Sv.

φιλανθρώπως adv. of φιλάνθρωπος (s. prec. two entries; Isocr., Demosth.+; ins, LXX, Philo, Joseph.) ***benevolently, kindly*** φιλανθρώπως χρῆσθαί (τινι) *treat someone in kindly fashion* (Isocr., Ep. 7, 6; Demosth. 19, 225; Aeschin. 3 [C. Ctes.], 57; Diod. S. 20, 17, 1; Plut., Aemil. 276 [39, 9], Alcib. 193 [4, 6], Mor. 88c; Cass. Dio 71, 14; 27; Jos., C. Ap. 1, 153, Ant. 12, 46; 14, 313 codd.; SIG 368, 4f [289/288 BC].—HCadbury, JBL 45, 1926, 202) **Ac 27:3.**—TW. Spicq.

φιλαργυρέω (φιλάργυρος; Epicurus; Alciphron 4, 15; Sext. Emp., Math. 11, 122; SIG 593, 12 [196/194 BC]; 2 Macc 10:20) ***love money, be avaricious*** 2 Cl 4:3.

φιλαργυρία, ας, ἡ (φιλάργυρος; Isocr. et al.; Polyb. 9, 25, 4; Diod. S. 7, 14, 5; Cebes 19, 5; Herodian 6, 9, 8; 4 Macc 1:26; TestJud 18:2; 19:1; AscIs 3:28; Philo; Jos., Bell. 2, 483; Tat.; Mel., P. 50, 366) ***love of money, avarice, miserliness*** w. other vices 2 Cl 6:4; Pol 2:2; 4:3; 6:1. As ῥίζα πάντων τῶν κακῶν *the root of all the evils* (Goodsp.) **1 Ti 6:10** or ἀρχὴ πάντων χαλεπῶν *the origin of all that is acrimonious* Pol 4:1 (cp. Hippocr., Ep. 17, 43 τούτων ἁπάντων αἰτίη ἡ φιλαργυρίη; Democritus in Gnomol. Vatican. 265 Sternbach [WienerStud 10, 1888, 231] Δημόκριτος τὴν φιλαργυρίαν ἔλεγε μητρόπολιν πάσης κακίας. Likew. Bion the Sophist in Stob., Eclog. III 417, 5 H.; Diog. L. 6, 50 μητρόπολιν πάντων τῶν κακῶν; Apollod. Com. 4 vol. III p. 280 Kock; also SibOr 2, 111; 8, 17).—JGeffcken, Kynika u. Verwandtes 1909, 38ff.—M-M. Spicq.

φιλάργυρος, ον (s. prec. two entries; Soph., X., Pla. et al.; Polyb. 9, 22, 8; 9, 25, 1; 9, 26, 11; Diod. S. 5, 27, 4; Epict.; Plut.; Cebes 34, 3; PPetr III, 53j, 14 [III BC]; 4 Macc 2:8; Philo; TestLevi 17:11) ***fond of money, avaricious*** **Lk 16:14; 2 Ti 3:2;** D 3:5. S. ἀφιλάργυρος.—M-M. Spicq.

φίλαυτος, ον (Aristot. [s. φιλάγαθος and s. the index of the Berlin ed. IV 818]; Musonius 86, 2 H.; Plut., Epict., Lucian, Sext. Emp.; Philo, Leg. All. 1, 49 φίλαυτος καὶ ἄθεος; Jos., Ant. 3, 190; Just.) ***loving oneself, selfish*** **2 Ti 3:2.**—M-M.

φιλέω impf. ἐφίλουν; fut. φιλήσω SSol 8:1; 1 aor. ἐφίλησα; pf. πεφίληκα (Hom.+; ins, pap, LXX, pseudepigr., Philo, Joseph.; Ar. 15, 4; Just., D. 27, 2 and 82, 4 [both φιλοῦντες—φ. is usual word in earlier Gk., but gradually loses ground to ἀγαπάω, esp. in the Koine— for ἀγαπῶντες Is 1:23]; Mel., P. 38, 266).

❶ **to have a special interest in someone or someth., freq. with focus on close association,** ***have affection for, like, consider someone a friend***

ⓐ w. acc. of pers.: relatives (X., Mem. 2, 7, 9) **Mt 10:37ab** (on this pass. TArvedson, SEÅ 5, '40, 74–82). Exceptional disciples IPol 2:1. Paul speaks of those who love him in (the) faith **Tit 3:15** (on the greeting here s. UWilcken, APF 6, 1920, 379; Sb 7253, 18–20 [296 AD] ἀσπάζομαι τοὺς φιλοῦντας ἡμᾶς κατ' ὄνομα). The world loves those who belong to it **J 15:19.** Jesus' disciples love him **J 16:27b; 21:15–17** (some think that here φ. seems to be = ἀγαπάω, q.v. 1aβ, w. the lit. there, pro and con, but a more intimate relationship may be implied; one can extend 'love' in general, but close friendship is limited; cp. Aristot., EN 8; Cass. Dio 44, 48; s. lit. φίλος 2b); so do all true Christians **1 Cor 16:22** (CSpicq, NovT 1, '56, 200–204). Christ also loves certain persons **Rv 3:19;** Lazarus (JLeal, VD 21, '41, 59–64) **J 11:3, 36;** the beloved disciple **20:2.** God loves the Son **5:20** and his disciples **16:27a** (φ. of the love of a deity, Simonides, fgm. 4, 12 οὓς ἂν οἱ θεοὶ φιλέωσιν [i.e. τ. ἀγαθούς]; Dio Chrys. 80 [30], 26; Biogr. p. 92; SibOr 3, 711). A directive to Christians: φιλεῖτε τοὺς μισοῦντας ὑμᾶς D 1, 3. θεὸς ... φιλούμενος και παρακαλούμενος ἀκούει *God heeds when called upon as a friend* (Ox 849, 25–27; cp. AcPt [Aa I 73, 26]).—SRoads, A Study of φιλεῖν and ἀγαπᾶν in the NT: Review and Expositor 10, 1913, 531–33; CHogg, Note on ἀγαπ. and φιλέω: ET 38, 1927, 379f; BWarfield, The Terminology of Love in the NT: PTR 16, 1918, 1–45; 153–203; FNormann, diss. Münster, '52; MPaeslack, Theologia Viatorum 5, '53, 51–142; MLattke, Einheit im Wort '75. S. the lit. s.v. ἀγάπη 1, end.

ⓑ w. acc. of thing (Hom. et al.; Wsd 8:2; ApcSed 11:4; AscIs 3:25; Just., Mel.) τὴν ψυχὴν αὐτοῦ **J 12:25** (Tyrtaeus 7, 18 Diehl[3] warns about φιλοψυχεῖν). Place of honor **Mt 23:6.—Lk 20:46; Rv 22:15** (cp. Pr 29:3).

ⓒ W. inf. foll. ***like*** or ***love to do*** *someth.*, hence *do someth. often* or *customarily* (Pind., N. 1, 12 [15]; Aeschyl., Sept. 619, Ag. 763; Soph., Aj. 989; Eur., Iph. T. 1198; Ps.-Eur., Rhes. 394; Hdt. 7, 10, 5; X., Hipparch. 7, 9; Pla., 7th Letter, 337b; Appian, Liby. 94 §442; Arrian, Anab. 3, 11, 2; Aelian, VH 14, 37; PGiss 84, 13; Is 56:10; Philo, Op. M. 103; Jos., Ant. 18, 60) φιλοῦσιν προσεύχεσθαι **Mt 6:5.** φιλοῦσιν καλεῖσθαι ῥαββί *they like to be called 'Rabbi'* **23:6f.**

❷ **to kiss as a special indication of affection,** ***kiss*** (Aeschyl., Ag. 1540; Hdt. 1, 134; X., Cyr. 1, 4, 27; Pla., Phdr. 256a; Aristot., Prob. 30, 1, 8; Plut., Mor. 139d, Alex. 667 [6, 8]; Lucian, Ver. Hist. 1, 8; PSI 26, 13; Gen 27:26f; 29:11 al.; TestBenj 1:2; JosAs

8:3ff) τινά *someone* **Mt 26:48; Mk 14:44; Lk 22:47;** GJs 7:2.—B. 1110; 1114.—RJoly, Le vocabulaire chrétien de l'amour est-il original? φιλεῖν et ἀγαπᾶν dans le grec antique '68. Schmidt, Syn. III 474–91. DELG s.v. φίλος. M-M. EDNT. TW. Spicq. Sv.

φίλη, ης, ἡ s. φίλος 2b.

φιλήδονος, ον pert. to having a special interest in pleasure, ***loving pleasure*** (so Polyb. 39, 1, 10; Plut., Mor. 6b; 766b; Epict. in Stob. no. 46 p. 474 Schenkl; Dio Chrys. 4, 115; M. Ant. 6, 51; Maximus Tyr. 24, 4f; Lucian, Herm. 16; Vett. Val. 7, 12; 9, 3; 40, 5; Philo, Agr. 88 al.; Just., A II, 1, 2; 12, 2) **2 Ti 3:4.**—DELG s.v. ἥδομαι and φίλος. M-M.

φίλημα, ατος, τό (Aeschyl.+; Pr 27:6; SSol 1:2; Philo, Div. Rer. Her. 40; Jos., Bell. 7, 391; Just., A I, 65, 2; Ath. 32, 3) ***a kiss*** (φιλέω 2) **Lk 22:48** (a basic betrayal of canons of friendship, cp. Aristot. EN 8; JDöller, Der Judaskuss: Korrespondenzblatt f. d. kath. Klerus Österreichs 1918; 127–29). φίλημά τινι διδόναι *give someone a kiss* (Nicophon Com. [V/IV BC] 8) **Lk 7:45.** The kiss w. which Christians give expression to their intimate fellowship (Ath. 32, 3 τὸ φ., μᾶλλον δὲ τὸ προσκύνημα 'the kiss, or rather the formal greeting'; here the qualification τὸ π. aims at thwarting charges of indecency) is called φίλημα ἅγιον: ἀσπάσασθε ἀλλήλους ἐν φιλήματι ἁγίῳ *greet one another w. a kiss of esteem* **Ro 16:16; 1 Cor 16:20; 2 Cor 13:12;** cp. **1 Th 5:26.** Also ἀσπάσασθε ἀλλήλους ἐν φιλήματι ἀγάπης *greet one another w. an affectionate kiss* **1 Pt 5:14** (Just., A I, 65, 2 [without ἐν]).—HAchelis, Das Christentum in den ersten drei Jahrhunderten I 1912, 292f; Windisch on 2 Cor 13:12; RSeeberg, Aus Rel. u. Gesch. I 1906, 118–22; AWünsche, Der Kuss in Bibel, Talmud u. Midrasch 1911; K-MHofmann, Philema Hagion '38; WLowrie, The Kiss of Peace, Theology Today 12, '55, 236–42; KThraede, JAC 11f, '68/69, 124–80; JEllington, Kissing in the Bible, Form and Meaning: BT 41, '90, 409–16; WKlassen, NTS 39, '93, 122–35.—B. 1114. DELG s.v. φίλος. M-M. TW.

Φιλήμων, ονος, ὁ a name freq. found, ***Philemon*** ('Affectionate-one'), a Christian, prob. at Colossae, a convert of Paul. Philemon's slave, Onesimus, ran away, met Paul, and was also won for Christianity by him. Paul sent him back to his master, and gave him a short letter, our Phlm., explaining the circumstances, **Phlm 1; subscr.**—Zahn, Einl.[3] I 312ff; Pölzl (Τιμόθεος, end) 293ff; MMitchell, John Chrysostom on Philemon, A Second Look: HTR 88, '95, 135–48. On the letter s. JKnox, Phlm among the Letters of Paul, a New View of Its Place and Importance '35 (2d ed. '59) and on this HGreeven, TLZ 79, '54, 373–78, also WRollins, JBL 78, '59, 277f; WDoty, Letters in Primitive Christianity '73; SWinter, NTS 33, '87, 1–15; JHElliott, Forum 3/4, '87, 39–48; WSchenk, Der Brief des Paulus an Philemon in der neureren Forschung ('45–'87) in ANRW 2/25/4, '87, 3135–55; WKümmel, Einleitung.[20] '80, 306–8, 572 lit. and comm.; ABD V 305–10.—DELG s.v. φίλος. New Docs 3 p. 91 no. 79. LGPN I. M-M.

Φίλητος, ου, ὁ (also Φιλητός; on the accent s. Kühner-Bl. I 329f; Tdf., Proleg. 103) (ins; POxy 72, 17 [90 AD]) ***Philetus*** ('Worthy-of-love'), an otherw. unknown dissident, mentioned w. Hymenaeus **2 Ti 2:17.**—DELG s.v. φίλος. M-M.

φιλία, ας, ἡ (Theognis, Hdt.+; ins, pap, LXX; TestSol 20:9; EpArist, Philo; Jos., Ant. 12, 414, C. Ap. 1, 109; 2, 207 al.; Just., D. 93, 4 φιλίαν ἢ ἀγάπην; 139, 4; Ath. 22, 1f) ***friendship, love*** foll. by the objective gen. (Thu. 1, 91, 1; Sir 27:18; Philo, Fuga 58 φ. θεοῦ) ἡ φιλία τοῦ κόσμου **Js 4:4** (there is also an αἰσχρὰ φ.: Biogr. p. 112), Pl. φιλίαι ἐθνικαί *friendships with polytheists* Hm 10, 1, 4 (φιλία can also = bond of friendship: Diod. S. 10, 4, 6 εἰς τὴν φιλίαν προσλαβέσθαι; 19, 73, 2). J-CFraisse, Philia, La notion d'amitiê dans la philosophie antique '74; LPizzolato, L' idea di amicizia nel mondo antico classico e cristiano '93; DKonstan, Friendship and the State, The Context of Cicero's 'De Amicitia': Hyperboreus 1, '94/95, 1–16, Greek Friendship: AJP 117, '96, 71–94, Friendship in the Classical World '97; JFitzgerald, Greco-Roman Perspectives on Friendship '96.—DNP IV 669–74. DELG s.v. φίλος. M-M. TW. Sv.

Φιλιππήσιος, ου, ὁ person from Philippi (s. Φίλιπποι), ***the Philippian*** this form (Stephan. Byz.: ὁ πολίτης Φιλιππεύς [CIG 1578, 13; cp. SIG 267a, 3f w. note 4], Φιλιππηνὸς δὲ παρὰ Πολυβίῳ.—WRamsay, On the Gk. Form of the Name Philippians: JTS 1, 1900, 115f; PCollart, Philippes '37, 303–5) is found **Phil 4:15** and in the titles of **Phil** and Pol (s. Iren. 3, 3, 4 [Harv. II, 14, 8]).—DELG s.v. ἵππος. M-M.

Φίλιπποι, ων, οἱ (s. prec. entry; Diod. S. 16, 3, 8; Appian, Bell. Civ. 4, 105 §438; Strabo 7 fgm. 34; 41; 43; Jos., Bell. 1, 242, Ant. 14, 301; 310f; ins) ***Philippi,*** a city in Macedonia, founded on the site of the older Κρηνῖδες by Philip of Macedonia (Diod. S. 16, 8, 6). Under Roman rule fr. about 167 BC. In **Ac 16:12** *Ph.* is called πρώτης τῆς μερίδος Μακεδονίας πόλις, κολωνία (s. μερίς 1). (On the history of Philippi: PCollart, Philippes, ville de Macédoine '37; LBormann, Philippi [NovT Suppl 78] '95; Pauly-W. XIX 2206–44; PLemerle, Philippes et la Macédoine orientale á l' époque Chretienne et Byzantine '45; Kl. Pauly IV, 742f; BHHW III 1453; PECS 704f). Here Paul founded the first congregation on European soil **16:12ff;** cp. **1 Th 2:2.** Ac also mentions Philippi **20:6,** where Paul touched at the city on his last journey to Jerusalem. ἐγράφη ἀπὸ Φ. (τῆς Μακεδονίας v.l.) **1** and **2 Cor subscr.** The author of AcPl Ha traces Paul's trip from Philippi to Corinth, where the apostle tells of his compulsory labor in Philippi AcPl Ha 6, 1–5. As a prisoner the apostle sent a letter to the Christians at Phil.: **Phil 1:1** (among the treatments of the circumstances under which this letter was written, esp. the place of its writing: PFeine, Die Abfassung des Philipper-briefes in Ephesus 1916; ADeissmann, Zur ephesin. Gefangenschaft des Ap. Pls: Anatolian Studies for Ramsay 1923, 121–27; WMichaelis, D. Datierung des Phil '33; Dibelius, Hdb. exc. on Phil, end; GDuncan, St. Paul's Ephesian Ministry 1930; JSchmid, Zeit u. Ort. d. paulin. Gefangenschaftsbriefe '31; TManson, BJRL 23, '39, 182–200; ELohmeyer, Phil 1930, 3; 41, 5; 43, 3; 47).—The name of the city also occurs in the letter of Polycarp to the congregation/church at Philippi (on this PHarrison, Polycarp's Two Epistles to the Philippians '36 [p. 337–51 lit.]; WKümmel, Einltg.[20] '80, 280–329; 501 [lit. and comm.]; ABD V 318–26), Pol ins.—S. also ESchweizer, Der 2 Th ein Phil.-brief: TZ 1, '45, 90–105.—DELG s.v. ἵππος. M-M.

Φίλιππος, ου, ὁ (freq. found in lit., ins, pap; occurring also in LXX and Joseph., Ath.) ***Philip*** ('Fond-of-horses') a common name in the Gr-Rom. world. In our lit.:

❶ the tetrarch, son of Herod the Great and Cleopatra of Jerusalem (s. Joseph., index Φίλιππος 6). He was tetrarch of Gaulanitis, Trachonitis, Auranitis, Batanea and Panias (so Joseph., if the indications he gives in var. passages may thus be brought together), and acc. to **Lk 3:1,** also Iturea (all small districts northeast of Palestine). He rebuilt Panias as Caesarea (Philippi) and Bethsaida as Julias. Joseph. praises his personality and administration (Ant. 18, 106f). He was married to Salome, the daughter of Herodias (s. Ἡρωδιάς and Σαλώμη, end). He died 33/34 AD, whereupon his territory was joined to the Rom. province of Syria, though only for a short time. **Mt 16:13; Mk 8:27.** Some think that this Philip is erroneously implied **Mt 14:3; Mk 6:17; Lk 3:19 v.l.;** s. 2 below.—Schürer I 336–40.

❷ The Philip mentioned **Mt 14:3** and **Mk 6:17** is associated by some scholars with a half-brother of Herod Antipas (s. Ἡρῳδιάς), but the identification is not otherwise attested.

❸ the apostle, one of the Twelve. In the lists of the Twelve (which is the only place where his name is mentioned in the synoptics and Ac), he is found in fifth place, after the two pairs of brothers Peter-Andrew, James-John **Mt 10:3; Mk 3:18; Lk 6:14; Ac 1:13.** He is given more prominence in **J,** where he is one of the first to be called, and comes fr. Bethsaida, the city of Simon and Andrew; cp. **1:43–46, 48; 6:5, 7; 12:21f; 14:8f.** Papias (2:4): one of the πρεσβύτεροι.—On the apostle and the evangelist (s. 4 below), who have oft. been confused, s. TZahn, Apostel u. Apostelschüler in der Provinz Asien: Forsch. VI 1900 p. 369b (index); EBishop, ATR 28, '46, 154–59 equates 3 and 4.

❹ one of the seven 'assistants' at Jerusalem **Ac 6:5; 21:8;** in the latter pass. also called the 'evangelist' (s. εὐαγγελιστής) to differentiate him fr. the apostle. **Ac 8:5–13** after the death of Stephen he worked in Samaria w. great success; vss. **26–39** he baptized a non-Israelite, the chamberlain of the Ethiopian Queen Candace (MvanWanroy, VD '40, 287–93; FBlanke, Kirchenfreund 84, '50, 145–49) and vs. **40** preached the gospel in all the cities fr. Ashdod to Caesarea. Later he lived in Caesarea w. his four unmarried daughters, who possessed the gift of prophecy 21:8f (s. LSwindler, Biblical Affirmations of Women '79); Papias (11:2).—Zahn (3 above); HWaitz, Die Quelle der Philippusgeschichten in der AG 8:5–40: ZNW 7, 1906, 340–55; AStrobel, ZNW 63, '72, 271–76.

❺ the Asiarch MPol 12:2, or high priest MPol 21, under whom Polycarp suffered martyrdom.—Pauly-W. XIX 2551f; 2266–2331; Suppl. II 158–62; Kl. Pauly IV 752f; BHHW III 1453f.—DELG s.v. ἵππος. M-M. EDNT.

φιλοδέσποτος, ον (δεσπότης; Theognis, Hdt. et al.; Diod. S. 17, 66, 5; Lucian; Aelian, NA 6, 62; Philo; Jos., Bell. 4, 175) ***loving one's master,*** the neut. subst. τὸ φιλοδέσποτον *love of their Master* (Lucian, Fug. 16; schol. on Aeschyl., Ag. 3; Philo, Praem. 89) in the Christian sense MPol 2:2.—DELG s.v. δεσπότης.

φιλόζωος, ον (φίλος + ζωή; w. or without iota subscr.; trag. et al.; Philo) ***loving life,*** also of plants *tenacious of life* (Theophr., HP 7, 13, 4; Nicander [II BC], Theriaca 68, Alexipharmaca 274; 591 OSchneider [1856]) Hs 8, 2, 7; 8, 6, 1.

φιλόθεος, ον (Aristot., Rhet. 2, 17, 6; Diod. S. 1, 95, 4; Lucian, Calumn. 14; Vett. Val. 17, 9; SEG XXXII, 501, 11 [I BC–I AD]; Philo, Agr. 88 al.; Just., D. 118, 3; Ath. 21, 2 [opp. ἄθεος]; Hippol., Ref. 9, 12, 10) **having special affection for God, *devout*** in a play on words w. φιλήδονος **2 Ti 3:4** (cp. Porphyr., Ad Marcellam 14 p. 283, 20f N. ἀδύνατον τὸν αὐτὸν φιλόθεόν τε εἶναι καὶ φιλήδονον; Pythagorean saying: WienerStud 8, 1886 p. 279 no. 110). ἀγάπη Agr 7 (w. φιλάνθρωπος, q.v.).—M-M. Sv.

Φιλόλογος, ου, ὁ ***Philologus,*** an otherw. unknown Christian, recipient of a greeting **Ro 16:15.** The name is found in Gk. and Lat. ins (exx. in Ltzm., Hdb. ad loc.), esp. of slaves and freedmen, given in some instances to indicate educational background (one who is 'fond of words', a 'scholar'), and also occurs in the 'familia' of the imperial house (CIL VI, 4116 al.).—HKuch, Φιλόλογος '65. LGPN I. M-M. Spicq.

Φιλομήλιον, ου, τό (Strabo 12, 8, 14; Ptolem. 5, 2, 25 al.) ***Philomelium,*** a city in Phrygia (central Asia Minor), not far fr. Antioch in Pisidia: MPol ins.—Pauly-W. XIX 2520–23; Kl. Pauly IV 769.

φιλονεικία, ας, ἡ (φιλόνεικος; also -νικία; Thu.+; ins, pap, LXX; TestSol 4:1 D [-νεικ-]; Tat. 23, 1; Mel., HE 4, 26, 6.—On the spelling B-D-F §23 and L-S-J-M s.v. φιλόνικος, end; PKatz, TLZ '36, 282; 83, '58, 315 and Kratylos 5, '60, 158; DGeorgacas, ClPh 76, '81, 156: φιλονεκία is the 'correct spelling')

❶ ***contentiousness*** (Pla. et al.; Diod. S. 13, 48, 2; 4 Macc 1:26; 8:26; Philo, Leg. ad Gai. 218) MPol 18:1.

❷ ***dispute, argument*** (Thu. 8, 76, 1; Diod. S. 3, 33, 3; M. Ant. 3, 4; Philo; Jos., Ant. 7, 182, C. Ap. 2, 243; 2 Macc 4:4) **Lk 22:24** ('emulation': Field, Notes 75f).—B. 1360. DELG s.v. νίκη. M-M.

φιλόνεικος, ον (also -νικος; on the spelling s. φιλονεικία; s. νεῖκος).

❶ ***quarrelsome, contentious*** (Pind., Pla., et al.; M. Ant. 5, 35; Ezk 3:7; Philo; Jos., C. Ap. 1, 160, Ant. 15, 166) **1 Cor 11:16.**

❷ in a favorable sense (X., Pla., Plut.; Philo, Det. Pot. Ins. 3, Aet. Min 104; Jos., Ant. 15, 156 al.) ***emulous,*** *(in) eager (rivalry)* φιλόν(ε)ικοι ἔστε καὶ ζηλωταὶ περὶ τῶν ἀνηκόντων εἰς σωτηρίαν 1 Cl 45:1.—DELG s.v. νίκη.

φιλοξενία, ας, ἡ (φιλόξενος; the idea highlighted Hom., Od. 6, 198–210, the word since Bacchylides 3, 16 Snell; Pla.; also -νικία; TestAbr A; SIG 859a, 4; PLond VI, 1917, 4; cp. Jos., Ant. 1, 250) ***hospitality*** **Ro 12:13;** Hm 8:10. Abraham's *hosp.* 1 Cl 10:7 (TestAbr A 17 p. 98, 27 [Stone p. 44]); Lot's 11:1. These two men are prob. thought of in **Hb 13:2.** Of Rahab 1 Cl 12:1. Of the Corinthian church 1:2. DRiddle, Early Christian Hospitality: JBL 57, '38, 141–54; on the hospitality theme relating to a godly pers., s. AHollis, ed., Callimachus 'Hecale' '90, 341–54, n. 1 (lit.).—DELG s.v. ξένος. M-M. TW. Spicq.

φιλόξενος, ον (s. prec. entry; Hom. et al.; Epict. 1, 28, 23; TestAbr A; Philo, Abr. 114; Jos., Vi. 142) ***hospitable*** **1 Pt 4:9;** 1 Cl 12:3 (Rahab); Hm 8:10. An overseer of Christians is to be *hosp.* **1 Ti 3:2** (w. κόσμιος as Epict. 1, 28, 23); **Tit 1:8;** cp. ἐπίσκοποι καὶ φιλόξενοι Hs 9, 27, 2.—DNP IV 793–97. DELG s.v. ξένος. M-M. TW. Spicq.

φιλοπονέω (X., Pla.+; pap; Sir prol. ln. 20) **to expend considerable effort, *exert oneself, devote oneself*** περί τι *in (to) someth.* (Isocr. 1, 46 τὸ περὶ τὴν ἀρετὴν φιλοπονεῖν; PLond I, 130, 5 p. 133 [I/II AD]) 2 Cl 19:1. The noun φιλοπονία appears in an ins fr. Beroia SEG XXVII, 261 B, 47 and 56.—DELG s.v. πένομαι.

φιλοπρωτεύω **to have a special interest in being in the leading position, *wish to be first, like to be leader,*** in our lit. with focus on controlling others (so far only in eccl. usage. But φιλόπρωτος in the same sense in Plut., Mor. 471d, Solon 95 [29, 5], Alcib. 192 [2, 1]; Artem. 2, 32. Also φιλοπρωτεία in Philod., Herculanensia Volumina coll. 2, vol. I 86, 6; VII 176, 16 [Philod., Rhet. II 159 fgm. 19 Sudh.]; Porphyr., Vi. Plot. 10, 53 Harder [=AKirchhoff, Plotini Op. I 1856 p. xxvii=Plotini Op. I 1954 p. 12 Bréhier]) **3J 9.**—DELG s.v. πρῶτος. M-M.

φίλος, η, ον (Hom.+; ins, pap, LXX, EpArist, Philo, Joseph., Test12Patr)

❶ **pert. to having a special interest in someone** (superl. φίλτατος PLond I, 130, 33 p. 134 [I/II AD]; JosAs cod. A 4, 7 and 10 [p. 44, 3 and 10 Bat.] and Pal. 364; Just., D. 8, 3; 141, 5; Tat. 2, 2; Ath., R. 8 p. 56, 31), both pass. ***beloved, dear,*** and act. ***loving, kindly disposed, devoted*** (both since Hom. [JHooker, Homeric φίλος: Glotta 65, '87, 44–65]) in the latter sense w. dat. of pers. (X., Cyr. 1, 6, 4; Dio Chrys. 52 [69], 4 θεοῖς) **Ac 19:31.**

❷ subst., **one who is on intimate terms or in close association w. another** (cp. Aristotle's definition: μία ψυχὴ δύο σώμασιν ἐνοικοῦσα 'one soul inhabiting two bodies' Diog. L. 5, 20)

ⓐ ὁ φίλος ***friend*** (male in sing., sometimes generic in pl.)

α. lit. **Lk 7:6; 11:5a; 16:9** (Plut., Mor. 175e ἀφ' ὧν … φίλον σεαυτῷ πεποίηκας); **23:12; Ac 16:39** D; **27:3.** The use **3J 15ab,** perh. also **Ac 27:3,** suggests a communal assoc. (on φίλοι=*Christians:* communication ['67] from HCadbury [who also compared **J 11:11; 15:14f**]; a society honors one of its associates ZPE 36, '79, 171–72, no. 29, 4 [170/71 AD]; on this s. New Docs 4, 17f); Hm 5, 2, 2 (on Ac and 3J s. Harnack, Mission[4] I 1923, 435f). φίλοι w. γείτονες **Lk 15:6** (s. γείτων); w. συγγενεῖς **21:16;** w. σύμβουλοι Hs 5, 2, 6 (Leutzsch, Hermas 471, 68). Opp. δοῦλοι (unknown comic poet vol. III fgm. 166 Kock; Chariton 7, 3, 2 δούλους οὐκ ἂν εἴποιμι τοὺς φίλους) **J 15:15** (ABöhlig, Vom 'Knecht' zum 'Sohn' '68, 63); cp. Hs 5, 2, 6; 11; 5, 4, 1; 5, 5, 3 (in Hermas we have the tetrad δεσπότης, υἱός, δοῦλος, φίλοι). On οἱ ἀναγκαῖοι φίλοι **Ac 10:24** s. ἀναγκαῖος 2 and Jos., Ant. 7, 350. φίλε as familiar address *friend* **Lk 11:5b; 14:10** (Just., D. 63, 1; pl. 27, 2). W. subjective gen. (TestAbr A 9 p. 87, 8 [Stone p. 22]; TestJob 39:4; JosAs 23:5; GrBar 15:2; Tat. 17, 1; Jos., C. Ap. 1, 109) **Lk 11:6, 8; 12:4; 14:12; 15:29; J 11:11; 15:13f** (s. EPeterson, Der Gottesfreund: ZKG n.s. 5, 1923, 161–202; MDibelius, J 15:13: Deissmann Festschr. 1927, 168–86; REgenter, Gottesfreundschaft 1928; HNeumark, D. Verwendung griech. u. jüd. Motive in den Ged. Philons über d. Stellung Gottes zu s. Freunden, diss. Würzb. '37; WGrundmann, NovT 3, '59, 62–69. Also AvHarnack, Die Terminologie der Wiedergeburt: TU 42, 1918, 97ff). Jesus is τελωνῶν φίλος καὶ ἁμαρτωλῶν **Mt 11:19; Lk 7:34.** Joseph of Arimathaea is ὁ φίλος Πιλάτου καὶ τοῦ κυρίου GPt 2:3. Rarely w. gen. of thing φίλος τοῦ κόσμου **Js 4:4.** Cp. 2 Cl 6:5.

β. in a special sense (Hdt. 1, 65=Galen, Protr. 9 p. 28, 26 J.: Lycurgus as φίλος of Zeus; Diod. S. 5, 7, 7 διὰ τὴν ὑπερβολὴν τῆς εὐσεβείας φίλον τῶν θεῶν ὀνομασθῆναι; Ael. Aristid. 27, 36 K.=16 p. 297 D.: θεῶν φίλοι; Maxim. Tyre 14, 6 φίλος θεοῦ as opposed to being δεισιδαίμων i.e. in a state of religious anxiety; JosAs 23:10 cod. A [p. 75, 4 Bat.; δοῦλος Philonenko] Jacob; SibOr 2, 245 Moses as ὁ μέγας φίλος Ὑψίστοιο; Just, D. 8, 1 χριστοῦ φίλοι [prophets]): on Abraham as φίλος (τοῦ) θεοῦ (TestAbr A 4 p. 81, 8 [Stone p. 10], B 4 p. 109, 1 [St. p. 66]) **Js 2:23;** 1 Cl 17:2; cp. 10:1 and s. Ἀβραάμ and MDibelius, exc. on Js 2:23. On ὁ φίλος τοῦ νυμφίου **J 3:29** s. νυμφίος (cp. Sappho, fgm. 124; Paus. Attic. [II AD] ζ, 3 [HErbse '50]). On φίλος τοῦ Καίσαρος **J 19:12** s. Καῖσαρ and EBammel, TLZ 77, '52, 205–10; New Docs 3, 87–89 (noting that it is questionable whether Pilate's fortunes were closely bound up with those of Sejanus after the latter's fall out of imperial favor, s. JLémonon, Pilate et le gouvernement de la Juée '81, esp. 275f).

ⓑ ἡ φίλη ***(woman) friend*** (X., Mem. 2, 1, 23; Jos., Ant. 9, 65 al.) pl. τὰς φίλας *her women friends* GPt 12:51. W. γείτονες **Lk 15:9** (s. γείτων).—GFuchs, D. Aussagen über d. Freundsch. im NT vergl. m. denen d. Aristot., diss. Leipzig 1914; FHauck, D. Freundschaft b. d. Griechen u. im NT: Festgabe f. TZahn 1928, 211–28. RAC VIII 418–24; DKonstan, JECS 4, '96, 87–113. S. ἑταῖρος.—MLandfester, Das griechische Nomen 'philos' und seine Ableitungen '66. DELG. M-M. TW. Spicq. Sv.

φιλοσοφία, ας, ἡ (Pla., Isocr. et al.; 4 Macc; EpArist 256; Philo; Jos., C. Ap. 1, 54, Ant. 18, 11 al.) ***philosophy,*** in our lit. only in one pass. and in a pejorative sense, w. κενὴ ἀπάτη, of erroneous teaching **Col 2:8** (perhaps in an unfavorable sense also in the Herm. wr. Κόρη Κόσμου in Stob. I p. 407 W.=494, 7 Sc.=Κόρη Κόσμου 68 [vol. IV p. 22, 9 Nock-Festugière]. In 4 Macc 5:11 the tyrant Antiochus terms the Hebrews' religion a φλύαρος φιλοσοφία).—GBornkamm, D. Haeresie des Kol: TLZ 73, '48, 11–20.—DELG s.v. σοφός. M-M. TW. Sv.

φιλόσοφος, ου, ὁ (as subst. X., Pla.+; ins, pap; Da 1:20; EpArist; Philo; Jos., C. Ap. 1, 176; apolog. exc. Mel.; loanw. in rabb.) ***philosopher*** of Epicureans and Stoics **Ac 17:18** (Jos., C. Ap. 2, 168 ἀπὸ τ. στοᾶς φιλόσοφοι). An ironical judgment on the nature philosophers τοὺς κενοὺς καὶ ληρώδεις λόγους τῶν ἀξιοπίστων φιλοσόφων Dg 8:2 (on unfavorable judgments concerning philosophers s. Cumont[3] '31, 171f; 303, 88). τοῦ Καίσαρος φιλοσόφων τε καὶ φίλων AcPlHa 11, 4 (sc. after cod. A of the MartPl Aa I 116, 5).—DELG s.v. σοφός. M-M.

φιλοστοργία, ας, ἡ (s. φιλόστοργος, cp. στοργή 'affection'; X.+; ins, pap [for both s. New Docs 2, 100–102; 3, 41f]; 2 Macc 6:20; 4 Macc 15:9; Jos., Ant. 8, 193 al.) ***heartfelt love, strong affection*** πρός τινα *for someone* (Polyb. 31, 25, 1 πρὸς ἀλλήλους; Plut., Mor. 962a; Lucian, Tyrannic. 1; Philo, Mos. 1, 150) of the deep affection of Christians for each other Dg 1.—DELG s.v. στέργω.

φιλόστοργος, ον (s. prec. entry; X.+; ins [e.g. SEG XLII, 1214, 12: II AD; cp. adv. ISmyrnaMcCabe 9, 6: 245/243 BC]; PMich 148 II, 9 [I AD]; for other ins and pap s. New Docs 3, 41f; 4 Macc 15:13; TestAbr A 1 p. 78, 4 [Stone p. 4]; JosAs 12:8; Philo; Jos., Ant. 7, 252 al.) ***loving dearly*** τῇ φιλαδελφίᾳ εἰς ἀλλήλους φιλόστοργοι *devoted to one another in brotherly love* **Ro 12:10.**—DELG s.v. στέργω. M-M. Spicq.

φιλότεκνος, ον (Eur., Hdt.+; ins: ZAly, Some Funerary Stelae fr. Kom Abou Bellou '49, p. 37 ln. 2 of a mother loving, or beloved by, her children; p. 23, ln. 1f of Heracles 'beloved by his children'; PMich 149, 18, 2 [II AD]; PCairMasp 20, 10; 4 Macc 15:4f; JosAs 12:8; Philo, Abr. 179) ***loving one's children,*** esp. of women (Aristoph. et al.) w. φίλανδρος (Plut., Mor. 769c; ins fr. Pergamon [Dssm., LO[4] 268=LAE 315] γυναικὶ φιλάνδρῳ καὶ φιλοτέκνῳ; Sb 330, 4) **Tit 2:4.** Of a father (SEG XXVIII, 1493, 6f [I/II AD]) in a reproachful sense (Synes., Ep. 1 p. 157d φιλότεκνος of an indulgent parent; Lucian, Tyrannic. 4 φ. ἐς ὑπερβολήν) φ. ὢν *because you are indulgent* Hv 1, 3, 1 (Leutzsch, Hermas 388, 91).—DELG s.v. τίκτω. New Docs 2 p. 64 ins no. 5, 28, cp. p. 101; 3 p. 42f (list of ins). M-M.

φιλοτιμέομαι dep. (s. next entry; Andoc., Pla.+; ins, pap, 4 Macc 1:35 v.l.[?]; Philo; Jos., Bell. 1, 206) special honor (τιμή) was accorded pers. who rendered exceptional service to the state or other institutions, and many wealthy pers. endeavored to outdo one another in philanthropic public service (cp. the billionaire Opramoas [IGR III, 739—II AD—tr. Danker, Benefactor 110–41], who prob. outdid all) ***have as one's ambition, consider it an honor, aspire,*** w. focus on idea of rendering service, w. inf. foll. (X., Mem. 2, 9, 3 al.; EpArist 79; Jos., Ant. 3, 207; 15, 330) **Ro 15:20; 2 Cor 5:9** (w. εὐάρεστος, q.v., a term freq. applied to philanthropists); **1 Th 4:11.** S. next entry.—DELG s.v. τιμή. M-M.

φιλοτιμία, ας, ἡ (φιλότιμος 'loving honor', s. prec. entry; trag., Hdt.+; ins, pap; Wsd 14:18; EpArist 227; Philo; Jos., Ant. 10, 25 περὶ τὸν θεόν; in a rhetorical ploy: of useless application to enumeration of data Ath., R. 18 p. 70, 16) ***generous zeal*** εἰς τὰ κωφὰ τὴν αὐτὴν ἐνδείκνυσθαι φιλοτιμίαν *show the same generous zeal to the mute (images)* Dg 3:5 (cp. SIG 457, 42f).—S. δείκνυμι. Larfeld I 501. DELG s.v. τιμή. Sv.

φιλόϋλος, ον (ὕλη 'material') ***loving material things*** (cp. Origen, fgm. in Luc. 71, l. 6 ed. MRauer 1930, p. 269 φιλοΰλων καὶ φιλοσωμάτων λόγοι πιθανοί) in imagery πῦρ φιλόϋλον *a fire that longs for material things* or *that desires to be fed w. material things* IRo 7:2 (ὕλη means 'material things' opposed to God 6:2, elsewh. = 'firewood' [ὕλη 2]).—DELG s.v. ὕλη.

φιλοφρόνως adv. of φιλόφρων (Soph., Hdt. et al.; ins; BGU 1009, 3 [II BC]; 2 Macc 3:9; 4 Macc 8:5; EpArist 173; Jos., Ant. 11, 340, C. Ap. 2, 210) ***in a friendly manner, hospitably*** **Ac 28:7** (Jos., Bell. 6, 115 φιλοφρόνως ἐδέξατο).—DELG s.v. φρήν II.

φιλόφρων, ον, gen. ονος (s. prec. entry; Pind., X. et al.; PGrenf I 30, 5 [II BC]) ***well-disposed, friendly, kind*** **1 Pt 3:8 v.l.**—DELG s.v. φρήν II.

Φίλων, ωνος, ὁ (a name freq. found; lit. [e.g. Diod. S. 16, 56, 3; 18, 7, 2; Tat. 34, 3], ins; PHib 45, 14 [257 BC]; BGU 1206, 6; 1207, 9 [both 28 BC]) ***Philo,*** fr. Cilicia IPhld 11:1 who, w. Rheus Agathopus, is in service to Ign., following him through Smyrna and Philadelphia, in order to overtake him at Troas (s. Hdb. on IPhld 11:1). ISm 10:1; 13:1.

φιμόω (φιμός 'muzzle'; Aristoph. et al.; LXX; TestJob 27:3; Joseph.) inf. φιμοῦν and less well attested φιμοῖν **1 Pt 2:15 v.l.** (W-H., App. 166, Introd. §410; B-D-F §91; W-S. §13, 25); fut. φιμώσω; 1 aor. ἐφίμωσα. Pass.: 1 aor. ἐφιμώθην; perf. impv. 2 sing. πεφίμωσο; 'tie shut' specif. of shutting a mouth w. a muzzle.

❶ ***muzzle,*** lit. οὐ φιμώσεις βοῦν ἀλοῶντα (Dt 25:4=Philo, De Virt. 145) **1 Cor 9:9 v.l.** (for κημώσεις); **1 Ti 5:18.**

❷ ***to silence, put to silence,*** fig. ext. of 1 (PGM 36, 164; IDefixAudollent 15, 24; 22, 42 by a spell) τινά *someone* **Mt 22:34; 1 Pt 2:15.** Pass. *be silenced* or *silent* (Lucian, Pereg. 15; Cyranides p. 64, 18; Jos., Bell. 1, 16; 438) ὁ δὲ ἐφιμώθη *but he was silent*=could say nothing **Mt 22:12** (RBauckham, JBL 115, '96, 486). In exorcisms (ERohde, Psyche[3] II 1903, 424) φιμώθητι καὶ ἔξελθε ἐξ (ἀπ') αὐτοῦ **Mk 1:25; Lk 4:35.** Addressed to the raging sea σιώπα, πεφίμωσο **Mk 4:39** (B-D-F §346; Rob. 908).—DELG s.v. φιμός. M-M.

φλαγελλόω (s. φραγέλλιον) = φραγελλόω **Mk 15:15** D.

φλέγω fut. 3 sg. φλέξει LXX, pass. φλεγήσεται (Ps 88:47 Sym.) (Hom.+; ins; PSI 28, 12; PGM 4, 1732; LXX; TestSol 1:10; En; Philo, Op. M. 58; SibOr 3, 761) 'burn', pass. 'be burned, burn'.

❶ **to be in flames,** ***burn*** (Alciphron 1, 2, 1; Aristobulus: Eus., PE 8, 10, 13ff [p. 220, 10ff Denis=p. 144, 96 Holladay]; Jos., Bell. 6, 272) of the mud in the nether world ApcPt 8:23.

❷ **to experience an intense emotion,** ***be on fire,*** fig. ext. of 1 (Chariton 8, 8, 7; Dio Chrys. 4, 52 φλεγόμενος ὑπὸ τ. φιλοτιμίας; Achilles Tat. 7, 3, 7; schol. on Nicander, Ther. 151; Anth. Pal. 16, 209 ὅλος φλέγομαι; Philo, Leg. All. 3, 224) ἐφλέγοντο ὑπὸ τῆς ὀργῆς *they were inflamed with anger* GPt 12:50.—B. 75. DELG.

Φλέγων, οντος, ὁ (a name freq. found among male slaves and freedpersons; s. Ltzm., Hdb. on Ro 16:14) ***Phlegon*** ('Blazer'), an otherw. unknown Christian, recipient of a greeting **Ro 16:14.**—DELG s.v. φλέγω. M-M.

φλέψ, φλεβός, ἡ (Hdt., Hippocr. et al.; PMich 149, 4, 35 [II AD]; Hos 13:15; Philo; Jos., Bell. 4, 462; gener. 'blood-vessel') ***vein*** MPol 2:2 (on the subj.-matter Jos., Bell. 2, 612).—DELG.

φλογίζω (fr. φλέγω via φλόξ) fut. 3 sg. φλογιεῖ Ps 96:3; aor. 3 sg. ἐφλόγισε LXX (Soph. et al.; LXX; PsSol 12:3; TestJob 16:3) ***set on fire*** in imagery, τὶ *someth.* **Js 3:6a.** Pass. aor. 3 sg. ἐφλογίσθη (Da 3:94 Theod.; Philostrat., Ep. 12 p. 230, 29 by love) **Js 3:6b.**—NMacnicol, ET 55, '43/44, 50–52.—DELG s.v. φλέγω. M-M.

φλόξ, φλογός, ἡ (φλέγω; Hom.+; SIG 1170, 24; PGM 4, 3073; LXX; En; TestSol 3:4; TestJos 2:2; JosAs 14:9, also cod. A 12:10 [p. 56, 7 Bat.] for ἄβυσσον; ApcEsdr 1:24 p. 25, 20 Tdf. [ἡ φλόγα codd.]; ApcSed 2:4; Philo; Jos., Bell. 6, 272, Ant. 13, 139; Ath. 22:7) ***flame*** **Lk 16:24.** φ. πυρός (Eur., Bacch. 8 al.; LXX; PsSol 15:4; JosAs 14:9; ViElijah 2 [p. 93, 11 Sch.]; πῦρ b) **Ac 7:30** (Ex 3:2); **Hb 1:7**=1 Cl 36:3 (s. LRadermacher, Lebende Flamme: WienerStud 49, '32, 115–18); **Rv 1:14; 2:18; 19:12** (for assoc. w. ancient views of the 'evil eye' s. PDuff, NTS 43, '97, 116–33). ἐν πυρὶ φλογός *in flaming fire* (Ex 3:2 B et al.; Sir 45:19; PsSol 12:4; the v.l. ἐν φλογὶ πυρός parallels the text of Is 66:15; cp. Ex 3:2; PKatz, ZNW 46, '55, 133–38) **2 Th 1:8.** μεγάλη φ. *a high flame* (Lucian, Tim. 6) MPol 15:1.—B. 72. DELG s.v. φλέγω. M-M.

φλυαρέω (φλύαρος; Hdt. et al.; PSI 434, 7; 9 [III BC]; Sb 2266, 12; Tat. 33, 1; Iren., Orig., Hippol., Theoph.) **to indulge in utterance that makes no sense,** ***talk nonsense (about), disparage*** (Isocr. 5, 79 w. βλασφημεῖν; X., Hell. 6, 3, 12; Philo, Somn. 2, 291) w. acc. of pers. (cp. the pass. Diog. L. 7, 173 τὸν Διόνυσον καὶ Ἡρακλέα φλυαρουμένους ὑπὸ τῶν ποιητῶν=Dionysus and Heracles, victims of poets' prattle) and dat. of thing λόγοις πονηροῖς φλυαρῶν ἡμᾶς *disparaging us w. outrageous statements* or *chattering maliciously about us* (=*bad-mouthing us*) **3J 10.**—DELG s.v. φλύαρος.

φλύαρος, ον (cp. φλύω 'to babble'; Menand., Perinth. 15 S.; Dionys. Hal., Comp. Verbi 26 of mediocre writers; Plut., Mor. 39a; 169e; 701a; Ps.-Pla., Axioch. 365e; 369a; Ps.-Lucian, Asin. 10; 4 Macc 5:11; Jos., Vi. 150) ***gossipy*** **1 Ti 5:13.**—Frisk s.v. φλυαρέω; cp. DELG s.v. φλύω. Spicq.

φοβερός, ά, όν (fr. φόβος, s. three next entries; Aeschyl. et al.) in our lit. only in the act sense (comp. φοβερώτερος [Just., D. 73, 6]; adv. φοβερῶς [TestAbr A 17 p. 99, 24=Stone p. 46]) ***causing fear, fearful, terrible, frightful*** (Hdt. et al.; BGU 428, 8 [II AD]; LXX; pseudepigr., Philo; Jos., Bell. 4, 510, Ant. 3, 56; 88; Just.) φοβερὰ ἐκδοχὴ κρίσεως **Hb 10:27** (cp. SibOr 3, 634 φοβ. δίκη). τὸ φανταζόμενον **12:21** (cp. Ezk. Trag. 125 [Eus., PE 9, 29, 11]). ἄκανθα B 7:11. ἐπιθυμία Hm 12, 1, 2. φοβερόν (sc. ἐστιν) τὸ ἐμπεσεῖν εἰς χεῖρας θεοῦ **Hb 10:31.**—DELG s.v. φέβομαι.

φοβέω (φέβομαι 'flee in terror'; Hom. et al.; Wsd 17:9; Jos., Ant. 14, 456), in our lit. only pass. **φοβέομαι** (Hom.+; OGI 669, 59; SIG 1268 II, 17; pap, LXX, pseudepigr., Philo, Joseph., Just.; Mel., P. 98, 746 al.; Ath. 20, 2; R. 21 p. 75, 1) impf. ἐφοβούμην; 1 fut. φοβηθήσομαι; 1 aor. ἐφοβήθην (Plut., Brut. 1002 [40, 9]; M. Ant. 9, 1, 7; Jer 40:9; Jos., C. Ap. 2, 277; s. B-D-F §79).

❶ **to be in an apprehensive state,** ***be afraid,*** the aor. oft. in the sense ***become frightened***—ⓐ intr., abs. (Iren. 1, 4, 2 [Harv. I 36, 4]) ἐφοβήθησαν σφόδρα *they were terribly frightened* (Ex

14:10; 1 Macc 12:52) **Mt 17:6; 27:54.** ἐπεστράφην φοβηθείς *I turned around in terror* Hv 4, 3, 7.—**Mt 9:8; 14:30; 25:25; Mk 5:33; Ac 16:38.** ἐφοβοῦντο γάρ *for they were afraid* **Mk 16:8** (Mk 16:9–20 is now rarely considered a part of the original gospel of Mk, though many scholars doubt that the gosp. really ended w. the words ἐφ. γάρ. The original ending may have been lost; among the possible reasons given are the accidental loss of the last page of Mark's own first copy [the same defect, at a very early stage, in the case of the 18th book of the Κεστοί of Jul. Africanus: WBauer, Orthodoxy etc. (Engl. tr. of 2d German ed. '64) '71, 159ff. S. also FKenyon, Papyrus Rolls and the Ending of St. Mk: JTS 40, '39, 56f; CRoberts, The Ancient Book and the Ending of St. Mk: ibid. 253–57] or by purposeful suppression, perh. because it may have deviated fr. the other accounts of the resurrection [for the purposeful omission of the end of a document cp. Athen. 4, 61, 166d on the 10th book of Theopompus' Philippica, ἀφ' ἧς τινες τὸ τελευταῖον μέρος χωρίσαντες, ἐν ᾧ ἐστιν τὰ περὶ τῶν δημαγωγῶν. S. also Diog. L. 7, 34: a report of Isidorus of Pergamum on the systematic mutilation of books in the library there by Athenodorus the Stoic].—Those who conclude that nothing ever came after ἐφ. γάρ must either assume that the evangelist was prevented fr. finishing his work [Zahn et al.], or indeed intended to close the book w. these words [s. γάρ 1a]. For a short sentence, composed of a verb + γάρ s. also Epict. 3, 9, 19; 4, 8, 4; Artem. 4, 64; 1, 33 p. 35, 6; Plotinus, Ennead 5, 5, a treatise ending in γάρ [PvanderHorst, JTS 23, '72, 121–24]; Musonius Rufus, Tr. XII; Oenomaus in Eus., PE 6, 7, 8; Libanius, Or. 53 p. 65, 20 F.; PMich 149 VI, 37 [II AD]. Among those favoring an ending w. γάρ: Wlh., Loisy, Lohmeyer ad loc.; ABauer, WienerStud 34, 1912, 306ff; LBrun, D. Auferst. Christi 1925, 10ff; OLinton, ThBl 8, 1929, 229–34; JCreed, JTS 31, 1930, 175–80; MGoguel, La foi à la résurr. de Jésus '33, 176ff; HMosbech, Mkevangeliets Slutning: SEÅ 5, '40, 56–73; WAllen, JTS 47, '46, 46–49 ['feel reverential awe']; ibid. 48, '47, 201–3. S. also EGoodspeed, Exp. 8th ser., 18, 1919, 155–60; reconstruction of the 'lost' ending, in Engl., by Goodsp. in his Introd. to the NT '37, 156; HProbyn, Exp. 9th ser., 4, 1925, 120–25; RKevin, JBL 45, 1926, 81–103; MEnslin, ibid. 46, 1927, 62–68; HCadbury, ibid. 344f; MRist, ATR 14, '32, 143–51; WKnox, HTR 35, '42, 13ff; EHelzle, Der Schluss des Mk, '59, diss. Tübingen; FDanker, CTM 38, '67, 26f; JLuzarraga, Biblica 50, '69, 497–510; KAland, MBlack Festschr., '69, 157–80, NTEntwürfe, '79, 246–83). φοβοῦμαι μᾶλλον *I am all the more fearful* IPhld 5:1. μὴ φοβηθῆτε *do not be afraid* **Mt 10:31 v.l.** (μή 1cεℵ). μὴ φοβοῦ, μὴ φοβεῖσθε *you must no longer be afraid, stop being afraid* (μή 1cγℵ) **Mt 10:31; 14:27; 17:7; Mk 5:36; Lk 1:13, 30; 2:10; 5:10; 8:50; 12:7** al. LKöhler, D. Offenbarungsformel 'Fürchte dich nicht!': SchTZ 36, 1919, 33ff.—W. acc. of inner obj. (B-D-F §153; Rob. 468; Pla., Prot. 360b; Ael. Aristid. 30 p. 586 D.: φοβοῦμαι φόβον; Did., Gen. 230, 1; on LXX usage s. Johannessohn, Kasus 73) ὁ φόβος ὃν δεῖ σε φοβηθῆναι *the fear which you must have* Hm 7:1c. ἐφοβήθησαν φόβον μέγαν (Jon 1:10; 1 Macc 10:8; TestAbr. B 13 p. 117, 17f [Stone p. 82]; JosAs 6:1) *they were very much afraid* **Mk 4:41; Lk 2:9.** If the nouns are to be taken in the pass. sense, this is also the place for τὸν φόβον αὐτῶν (objective gen.) μὴ φοβηθῆτε **1 Pt 3:14** (cp. Is 8:12) and μὴ φοβούμεναι μηδεμίαν πτόησιν vs. **6** (πτόησις 2); s. 1bγ below.—A recognizable Hellenic expr. (cp. ὁ ἀπὸ τῶν πολεμίων φόβος=fear in the face of the enemy), though encouraged by OT usage (Lev 26:2; Dt 1:29; Jer 1:8, 17; Jdth 5:23; 1 Macc 2:62; 8:12; En 106:4; Helbing 29; B-D-F §149; Rob. 577) φοβ. ἀπό τινος *be afraid of someone* **Mt 10:28a; Lk 12:4;** 1 Cl 56:11 (Job 5:22).—Foll. by gen. absol. 56:10. Foll. by μή and the aor. subj. to denote that which one fears (Thu. 1, 36, 1; Aesop, Fab. 317 H.=356a P.; Alex. Aphr. 31, II/2 p. 203, 20 τὸν Ἀπόλλω φοβεῖσθαι μή τι παρελθῇ τούτων ἄπρακτον=Apollo is concerned [almost as much as 'sees to it'] that nothing of this remains undone; Jos., Ant. 10, 8, Vi. 252) **Ac 23:10; 27:17;** ITr 5:1; Hs 9, 20, 2. Foll. by μήποτε (Phlegon: 257 fgm. 36, 2, 4 Jac. p. 1172, 30 φοβοῦμαι περὶ ὑμῶν, μήποτε; JosAs 7:3; ApcMos 16 al.): Hm 12, 5, 3. φοβηθῶμεν μήποτε δοκῇ τις **Hb 4:1;** μήπου (v.l. μήπως; ParJer 5:5) **Ac 27:29; 2 Cor 11:3; 12:20.** A notable feature is the prolepsis of the obj. (cp. Soph., Oed. R. 767; Thu. 4, 8, 7) φοβοῦμαι ὑμᾶς μήπως εἰκῇ κεκοπίακα εἰς ὑμᾶς *I am afraid my work with you may be wasted* **Gal 4:11** (B-D-F §476, 3; Rob. 423).—W. inf. foll. *be afraid to do* or *shrink from doing someth.* (B-D-F §392, 1b.—X., An. 1, 3, 17 al.; Gen 19:30; 26:7; ApcMos 10:18) **Mt 1:20; 2:22; Mk 9:32; Lk 9:45;** 2 Cl 5:1.—φοβεῖσθαι abs. in the sense *take care* (Just., D. 78, 4) πλέον φοβεῖσθαι *be more careful* than usually ITr 4:1.

ⓑ trans. *fear someone* or *someth.*—**α.** pers. τινά *someone* (X., An. 3, 2, 19 al.; PGM 4, 2171; Num 21:34; Dt 3:2; Jos., Ant. 13, 26; Just., D. 83, 1) μὴ φοβηθῆτε αὐτούς **Mt 10:26.** Ἡρῴδης ἐφοβεῖτο τὸν Ἰωάννην **Mt 6:20.** τοὺς Ἰουδαίους **J 9:22.—Gal 2:12;** 2 Cl 5:4b (saying of Jesus). God (Did., Gen. 64, 15; Theoph. Ant. 1, 14 [p. 92, 11]) **Mt 10:28b; Lk 12:5abc; 23:40;** 2 Cl 5:4c (saying of Jesus). The crowd **Mt 14:5; 21:26, 46; Mk 11:32; 12:12; Lk 20:19; 22:2; Ac 5:26** (foll. by μή). τὴν ἐξουσίαν (ἐξουσία 5a) **Ro 13:3.** The angel of repentance Hm 12, 4, 1; s 6, 2, 5. The Christian is to have no fear of the devil Hm 7:2a; 12, 4, 6f; 12, 5, 2.

β. animals (in imagery) μὴ φοβείσθωσαν τὰ ἀρνία τοὺς λύκους 2 Cl 5:4a (saying of Jesus, fr. an unknown source).

γ. things τὶ someth. (X., Hell. 4, 4, 8 al.; En 103:4; ApcEsdr 7:2 τὸν θάνατον; Just., D. 1, 5 κόλασιν; Ath., R. 21 p. 75, 1 οὐδέν; Jos., C. Ap. 1, 90; 2, 232) τὸ διάταγμα τοῦ βασιλέως **Hb 11:23.** τὸν θυμὸν τοῦ βασιλέως vs. **27.** τὴν κρίσιν 2 Cl 18:2. τὸν ὄντως θάνατον Dg 10:7. φοβοῦμαι τὴν ὑμῶν ἀγάπην, μὴ ... IRo 1:2. τὰ ὅπλα (in imagery) Hm 12, 2, 4.—**1 Pt 3:14** and **6** belong here if the nouns in them are to be taken in an act. sense; s. 1a above.—*Fear, avoid, shun* τὶ *someth.* (Ps.-Callisth. 1, 41, 9 Δαρεῖος τὸ ἅρμα φοβηθείς) τὴν πλάνην τῶν ἁμαρτωλῶν B 12:10. τὰ ἔργα τοῦ διαβόλου Hm 7:3ac.—AVStröm, Der Hirt des Hermas, Allegorie oder Wirklichkeit? Ntl. Sem. Uppsala 3, '36.

❷ **to have a profound measure of respect for, *(have) reverence, respect,*** w. special ref. to fear of offending—ⓐ God: *fear* (differently 1bα) in the sense *reverence* (Aeschyl., Suppl. 893 δαίμονας; Isocr. 1, 16 τοὺς μὲν θεοὺς φοβοῦ, τοὺς δὲ γονεῖς τίμα; Pla., Leg. 11, 927a; Lysias 9, 17; 32, 17; Plut., De Superstit. 2, 165b; LXX; PsSol 4:21; TestJob 43:9 [τὸν κύριον]; JosAs 2:5 [deities]; Philo, Migr. Abr. 21 [after Gen 42:18]. Cp. PTebt 59, 10 [II BC] φοβεῖσθαι καὶ σέβεσθαι τὸ ἱερόν) **Lk 1:50** (anticipates the οἱ φοβούμενοι in Ac: H-JKlauck, NTS 43, '97, 134–39); **18:2, 4** (was Ex 23:1–3 his motto: even God could not bribe him?); **Ac 10:35; 1 Pt 2:17; Rv 14:7; 19:5;** 1 Cl 21:7; 23:1; 28:1; 45:6; B 10:10f (τὸν κύριον); 19:2, 7; Hm 1:2; 7:1, 4f; s 5, 1, 5; 8, 11, 2; D 4:10. Also τὸ ὄνομα τοῦ θεοῦ (2 Esdr 11) **Rv 11:18.**—φοβούμενοι τὸν θεόν as a t.t.=σεβόμενοι τὸν θεόν (σέβω 1b; t.t. disputed by MWilcox, JSNT 13, '81, 102–22; cp. TFinn, CBQ 47, '85, 75–84; ILevinskaya, The Book of Acts in Its Diaspora Setting [BAFCS V] '96, 51–126; BWander, Gottesfürchtige und Sympathisanten [WUNT 104] '98, esp. 80–86; 180–203) **Ac 13:16, 26** (Just., D. 10, 4 al.; sing. **10:2, 22**).—τὸν κύριον (PsSol 2:33; 3:12 al.; JosAs 8:9) Christ: **Col**

3:22.—WAllen (s. 1a above) interprets **Mk 16:8** to mean reverence for the divine.

ⓑ pers. who command respect (Plut., Galba 1054 [3, 4]; Herodian 3, 13, 2; Lev 19:3 φοβ. πατέρα καὶ μητέρα; Jos., Ant. 19, 345): of a wife ἵνα φοβῆται τὸν ἄνδρα **Eph 5:33.** τὸν ἐπίσκοπον IEph 6:1.—RAC VIII 661–99; TRE XI 756–59; Schmidt, Syn. III 507–36. DELG s.v. φέβομαι II. M-M. EDNT. TW. Sv.

φόβητρον and **φόβηθρον** (φοβέω; different suffixes; s. B-D-F §35, 3; Mlt-H. 110; Thackeray 104), **ου, τό** (Hippocr., Morb. Sacr. 1 vol. VI p. 362 L.; Ps.-Pla., Axioch. 367a; Lucian, Alex. 25; Anth. Pal. 11, 189, 3 Düb.; Is 19:17) **someth. unusual that causes fear,** ***terrible sight/event, horror.*** Pl. φόβητρά τε καὶ σημεῖα ἔσται *there will be dreadful portents and signs* **Lk 21:11.**—DELG s.v. φέβομαι II.

φόβος, ου, ὁ (s. three prec. entries; Hom.+. In Hom. 'panic flight'; then in various senses).

❶ **intimidating entity,** the act. causative sense—ⓐ ***intimidation*** (Appian, Bell. Civ. 3, 27 §104 ἐς φ. τῆς βουλῆς=to intimidate the Senate) so prob. τὸν φόβον αὐτῶν μὴ φοβηθῆτε *do not be intimidated by their intimidation* (cp. REB et al.) **1 Pt 3:14** (Is 8:12; s. φοβέω 1bγ and cp. 2aα below).

ⓑ concretely, ***someth. terrible/awe-inspiring, a terror*** (Soph., Philoct. 1251; Polyb. 11, 30, 2; Appian, Bell. Civ. 2, 135 §565; SIG 442, 10 [III BC] οὐδένα οὔτε φόβον οὔτε κίνδυνον ὑποστελλόμενοι; Just., A II, 5, 4 διὰ φόβων καὶ τιμωριῶν ὧν ἐπέφερον) οἱ ἄρχοντες οὐκ εἰσὶν φόβος **Ro 13:3.** So perh. also εἰδότες οὖν τὸν φόβον τοῦ κυρίου *since we know what it is that causes fear of the Lord* **2 Cor 5:11** (i.e. the judgment to come, vs. 10; so Goodsp., REB et al.; ambiguously NRSV; s. also Field, Notes 183f); s. 2bα below.

❷ **the product of an intimidating/alarming force,** the pass. sense—ⓐ ***fear, alarm, fright***—α. gener. **2 Cor 7:11; 1 Pt 1:17** (mng. fear of the coming judge, unless ἐν φ. here means *reverently,* as ESelwyn, 1 Pt '46, 143); **Jd 23** (mng. the fear of defiling oneself); Dg 7:3. W. τρόμος (q.v.) **1 Cor 2:3; 2 Cor 7:15;** 1 Cl 12:5. Pl. *fears, apprehensions, feelings of anxiety* (as early as Thu. et al.; Diod. S. 16, 3, 1; 16, 42, 9 Ptolemy, Apotel. 2, 9, 5; Appian, Bell. Civ. 1, 16 §67; 3, 89 §368; SIG 326, 21 [307/306 BC]; Job 20:25; Wsd 18:17; Jos., Ant. 10, 24; 15, 44) ἔξωθεν μάχαι ἔσωθεν φόβοι **2 Cor 7:5.** παράγειν φόβους ἀνθρωπίνους *bring in fears of humans* 2 Cl 10:3.—W. obj. gen. of pers. (Diod. S. 10, 19, 6 ὁ τῶν Περσῶν φόβος), or of thing (Jos., C. Ap. 1, 259; Ath. 1, 1 φόβῳ δίκης; Did., Gen. 171, 14) causing fear ὁ φόβος τῶν Ἰουδαίων *the fear of the Judeans* **J 7:13; 19:38; 20:19.** φόβος θανάτου *fear of death* (Epict. 2, 1, 14; 2, 18, 30 et al.; TestAbr B 14 p. 118, 24 [Stone p. 84]; Philo, Omn. Prob. Lib. 111; Ath., R. 22 p. 75, 17; Orig., C. Cels. 1, 61, 37) **Hb 2:15.** τοῦ βασανισμοῦ **Rv 18:10, 15.** νόμου Dg 11:6.—ἀπὸ (τοῦ) φόβου (τινός) *because of, out of fear (of someone)* **Mt 14:26; 28:4; Lk 21:26;** Hm 11:14. Also διὰ τ. φόβον **Ac 26:14 v.l.** (Hyperid. 5, 5 διὰ τὸν φ.; Arrian, Anab. 5, 15, 6 διὰ τὸν φ.; Artem. 1, 1 p. 3, 23 διὰ φόβον; TestAbr B 14 p. 118, 24 [Stone p. 84]; Philo, Mos. 1, 164 διὰ φόβον τινός; Jos., Vi. 354 διὰ τὸν φόβον; Just., A II, 9, 1 διὰ φόβον). μετὰ φόβου *with* or *in fear* (Aeneas Tact. 1257; TestAbr A 16 p. 96, 22 [Stone p. 40]; GrBar 13:1) of the feeling that accompanies an action **Mt 28:8;** Dg 12:6; AcPl Ha 11, 12.—As subject (En 100:8): φόβος πίπτει ἐπί τινα *fear comes upon someone* **Ac 19:17 v.l.; Rv 11:11 v.l.** ἐπιπίπτει ἐπί τινα **Lk 1:12; Ac 19:17; Rv 11:11.** ἐστὶν ἐπί τινα **Ac 2:43b v.l.** γίνεται ἐπί τινα **Lk 1:65; Ac 5:5, 11** or γίνεταί τινι **Ac 2:43a.** λαμβάνει τινά (Jos., Vi. 148) **Lk 7:16;** Hv 5:4. πλησθῆναι φόβου **Lk 5:26.** φόβῳ συνέχεσθαι **8:37;** AcPl Ha 3, 33; 11, 16. φόβον ἔχειν **1 Ti 5:20;** Hm 7:2c; 12, 4, 7a; s 1:10. φοβεῖσθαι φόβον (μέγαν) **Mk 4:41; Lk 2:9;** cp. τὸν φόβον αὐτῶν μὴ φοβηθῆτε *do not fear what they fear* (NRSV; sim. et al.) **1 Pt 3:14** (but s. 1 above); Hm 7:1 (φοβέω 1a).

β. specif. of *slavish fear* (Diog. Cyn. in Diog. L. 6, 75 δούλου τὸ φοβεῖσθαι), which is not to characterize a Christian's relation to God οὐκ ἐλάβετε πνεῦμα δουλείας εἰς φόβον *you have not received a spirit of slavery, to cause you to fear* **Ro 8:15.** Cp. **1J 4:18abc** (opp. ἀγάπη; cp. κόλασις 2, end).

ⓑ ***reverence, respect***—α. toward God (Polyaenus 1, 16, 1; LXX; PsSol 6:5 al.; EpArist 159 ὁ περὶ θεοῦ φόβος; 189; cp. φόβος τὰ θεῖα τοῖσι σώφροσιν βροτῶν TGF, Adesp. no. 356 p. 906) and Christ, w. τρόμος **Phil 2:12** (s. τρόμος). W. ἀλήθεια 1 Cl 19:1; Pol 2:1. W. ἀγάπη 1 Cl 51:2. W. εὐλάβεια Pol 6:3. W. πίστις, εἰρήνη and other good things and virtues 1 Cl 64. W. ὑπομονή B 2:2. W. ἐλπίς: εἰς τὸν Ἰησοῦν 11:11. W. πίστις and ἐγκράτεια Hm 6, 1, 1. W. objective gen. φόβος (τοῦ) θεοῦ (PLond 1914, 12 φόβον θεοῦ ἔχοντες ἐν τῇ καρδίᾳ; Philo, Spec. Leg. 4, 199; TestLevi 13:7; TestNapht 2:9; Theoph. Ant. 1, 7 [p. 72, 26]) **Ro 3:18** (Ps 35:2); **2 Cor 7:1** (ἀγάπη P^{46}); 1 Cl 3:4; 21:6; cp. 8; B 4:11; 19:5; 20:2; Pol 4:2; Hm 10, 1, 6a; 12, 2, 4bc; D 4:9. φόβος (τοῦ) κυρίου (TestReub 4:1; TestSim 3:4) **Ac 9:31;** 1 Cl 22:1 (Ps 33:12); 57:5 (Pr 1:29); B 11:5 (Is 33:18 v.l.); Hm 7:4b; 8:9; 10, 1, 6b; 12, 2, 4a; 12, 3, 1. Some place here **2 Cor 5:11** (s. 1b above). φόβος Χριστοῦ **Eph 5:21.**—For **1 Pt 1:17** s. 2aα beg.

β. toward humans, *respect* that is due officials (cp. Byzantinische Papyri [Munich], ed. AHeisenberg/LWenger, 1914, no. 2, ln. 13 p. 43: ἔχοντες τὸν φόβον . . . τῆς ὑμετέρας ἐνδόξου ὑπεροχῆς=having respect for your esteemed authority) **Ro 13:7ab** (CCranfield, NTS 6, '60, 241–49: the ref. may be to God); fr. slave to master **1 Pt 2:18; Eph 6:5** (w. τρόμος); B 19:7=D 4:11 (w. αἰσχύνη); wife to husband **1 Pt 3:2** (cp. SEG XXXV, 1427, 5 [III AD]). Gener. **3:16** (w. πραΰτης).—WLütgert, Die Furcht Gottes: MKähler Festschr. 1905, SBerkelbach v.der Sprenkel, Vrees en Religie 1920, 165ff; RSander, Furcht u. Liebe im palästin. Judentum '35.—B. 1153. DELG s.v. φέβομαι I. M-M. EDNT. TW. Sv.

Φοίβη, ης, ἡ (freq. in mythology, but also e.g. SIG 805, 10 [c. 54 AD]; PFlor 50, 61 [III AD]) ***Phoebe,*** a Christian official, διάκονος τῆς ἐκκλησίας τῆς ἐν Κεγχρεαῖς (διάκονος 1), recommended by Paul to the Christian community for which **Ro 16:1** is intended. Cp. **Ro subscr.**—MGibson, Phoebe: ET 23, 1912, 281; EGoodspeed, HTR 44, '51, 55–57; RJewett, Paul, Phoebe and the Spanish Mission: The Social World of Formative Christianity and Judaism '88, 142–61; FGillman, Women Who Knew Paul '89.—On prominent women recognized in ins s. EForbis, AJP 111, '90, 493–507. DELG s.v. φοῖβος. M-M. TW.

Φοινίκη, ης, ἡ (Hom.+) ***Phoenicia,*** in NT times the name of the seacoast of central Syria, w. Tyre and Sidon as the most important cities **Ac 11:19; 15:3; 21:2.** HGuthe, RE XVIII 1906, 280–302 (lit.); SMoscati, D. Phøniker '66; Pauly-W. XVII '36, 350–80; Kl. Pauly IV 796–98; BHHW III 1464–68.

Φοινίκισσα s. Συροφοινίκισσα.

φοινικοῦς, ῆ, οῦν (uncontracted form φοινίκεος 'crimson' fr. φοῖνιξ 'purple, crimson' [s. L-S-J-M Φοῖνιξ B, 1]) so termed because the production of this color was first associated with the Phoenicians: **pert. to being of purple-red hue** (so X. et al.; SIG 1018, 4; Philo, Leg. All. 3, 57) subst. τὸ φοινικοῦν (w. χρῶμα or ἱμάτιον understood) ***purple(-red) color/garment*** 1 Cl 8:4 (Is 1:18). Because of the contrast with whiteness the highly prized darker hue must be meant here. S. πορφυροῦς.—DELG s.v. 1 φοῖνιξ.

I. φοῖνιξ/φοίνιξ, ικος, ὁ ('the date-palm'; its fruit JosAs 4:4)

❶ **the Phoenix dactylifera,** ***date-palm, palm tree*** (Hom. et al.; pap, LXX; En 24:4; TestNapht 5:4; EpArist 63; Demetr.: 722 fgm. 4 Jac.; Joseph.); at one time evidently a common tree in Palestine, since it is oft. depicted on coins; esp. common in Jericho (and still plentiful at the time of the Crusades), the 'city of palms' (Jos., Ant. 14, 54; 15, 96); τὰ βάϊα τῶν φοινίκων *the branches of palm-trees, the palm-branches* **J 12:13** (precisely stated; s. βάϊον and HBornhäuser, Sukka '35, 106f).—TFischer, Die Dattelpalme 1881; JTaglicht, Die Dattelpalme in Paläst.: AdSchwarz Festschr. 1917, 403–16; ILöw, Die Flora der Juden II 1924, 306–62; Zohary 60f; Pauly-W. XX 386–404; Kl. Pauly IV 801f; BHHW I 323f.

❷ **frond of the date-palm,** ***palm-branch, palm-leaf*** (Arist., Eth. Magn. 1, 34, 1196a, 36 ὁ λαβὼν τὸν φ. ἐν τοῖς ἀγῶσιν; 2 Macc 10:7; 14:4; Philo, Agr. 112, Deus Imm. 137 φ. τ. νίκης) φοίνικες ἐν τ. χερσὶν αὐτῶν **Rv 7:9.** στέφανοι ἐκ φοινίκων γεγονότες *wreaths made of palm-leaves* Hs 8, 2, 1.—DELG s.v. 3 φοῖνιξ. M-M.

II. φοῖνιξ/φοίνιξ, ικος, ὁ ***the phoenix,*** the fabulous bird of Egypt (since Hes., fgm. 171 Rzach[3]=fgm. 304 Merkelbach-West [Oxf. T.]; Hdt. 2, 73; Artem. 4, 47; Achilles Tat. 3, 25; PGM 5, 253; 12, 231; GrBar 6:10; 7:5; SibOr 8, 139; Celsus 4, 98; s. RKnopf, Hdb. exc. on 1 Cl 25) 1 Cl 25:2.—FSchöll, Vom Vogel Phönix 1890; FZimmermann, Die Phönixsage: ThGl 4, 1912, 202–23; THopfner, D. Tierkult der alten Ägypter: Denkschr. der Wiener Ak. 1914; JHubeaux/MLeroy, Le mythe du P. dans les litt. grecque et latine '39; RClark, Origin of the Phoenix: University of Birmingham Historical Journal 2, '49/50, 1ff; 105ff.; RvdBroek, The Myth of the Phoenix acc. to Class. and Early Christian Trad. '72. Roscher III/2, 3450–72: Phönix; Pauly-W. XX 414–23; Kl. Pauly IV 799f; DACL XIV 682–91; Lexikon der Ägyptologie IV 1030ff.—DELG s.v. 4 φοῖνιξ.

III. Φοῖνιξ, ικος, ὁ a seaport mentioned **Ac 27:12.** Two sites merit attention. The Phoinix mentioned Strabo 10, 4, 3 (475) lying in the territory of Lappa, some distance to the east fr. Loutro (s. 1), is not a serious contender; for, if correctly identified, it lacks a harbor.

❶ **Phoinix** (Ptolemy, Geogr. 3, 17, 3; Stadiasmus sive Periplus Maris Magni [a Byzantine version of a 3d cent. AD anonymous work] 328–29 [=GGM I 507f]) on the south coast of Crete near Loutro. On the protection offered to mariners by this harbor s. esp. Ogilvie, also Hemer, Acts 139 (lit.); but Warnecke discounts its value, given the size of the ship and the large number of crew and passengers (Ac 27:37), and favors

❷ **Phoinikous** (Ptolemy, Geogr. 3, 15, 3; Pausan. 4, 34, 12) on the southern coast of the area known as Messenia (Od. 21:15). According to Warnecke 28f (but without supporting grammatical references), the phrase λιμὴν τῆς Κρήτης means 'a harbor for Crete' (=a harbor suitable for trade to and fro fr. Crete). Paul's anxiety would stem from awareness of the type of weather conditions that would put mariners in peril on a trip from Crete to Messenian Phoinikous (cp. Hom., Od. 3, 291–98).—HBalmer, D. Romfahrt des Ap. Pls 1905, 319ff; Zahn, AG 1921, 825ff; ROgilvie, JTS n.s. 9, '58, 308–14; Warnecke, Romfahrt 19–36; Hemer, Acts 139–41; Pauly-W. XX 4335; Kl. Pauly 800; BHHW III 1464; Haenchen ad loc.; PECS 708.

φοιτάω aor. ptc. φοιτήσας (Hom. et al.; ins, pap; Jos., Ant. 3, 275, C. Ap. 2, 284; SibOr 4, 74; TestBenj 11:5) **to move from one position to another,** ***go back and forth, move about (regularly)*** of animals upon the earth 1 Cl 33:3 (Hdt. 1, 78 of horses at pasture; in a diff. sense the ref. to Papias [6] 'be an intimate of'; cp. φοιτητής Papias [7]).—DELG.

φονεύς, έως, ὁ (φόνος; Hom. et al.; BGU 1024 VIII, 11; PLips 37, 25; Wsd 12:5; Joseph.; Ar. 8, 2; Just.; Mel. 94, 718) ***murderer*** **Mt 22:7** (SvanTilborg, The Jewish Leaders in Mt, '72, 46–72); **Ac 7:52** (w. obj. gen., as Jos., Ant. 1, 57); **28:4; 1 Pt 4:15;** ApcPt 10, 25. In lists of vices **Rv 21:8; 22:15;** B 20:2; D 5:2 (the last two φονεῖς τέκνων). ἀνὴρ φ. **Ac 3:14.**—DELG s.v. θείνω; Frisk s.v. φόνος. M-M.

φονευτής, οῦ, ὁ (=φονεύς; LXX) ***executioner*** Ἡρῴδης . . . ἔπεμψεν αὐτοῦ τοὺς φονευτάς *Herod dispatched his executioners* GJs 22:1.

φονεύω fut. φονεύσω; 1 aor. ἐφόνευσα; pf. 3 sg. πεφόνευκεν Pr 7:26. Pass.: 1 fut. φονευθήσομαι; 1 aor. ἐφονεύθην (TestSol 1:3 D; GJs 23:3; AcPl Ha 1, 14); pf. 3 sg. πεφόνευται (Tob 2:3 S; GJs 24:3), ptc. πεφονευμένος (Judg 20:4 A; ApcMos 3) (cp. two prec. entries; Pind., Aeschyl., Hdt.+) ***murder, kill,*** abs. οὐ φονεύσεις *you shall not commit murder* (Ex 20:15) **Mt 5:21a** (cp. ibid. **b**); **19:18; Ro 13:9;** D 2:2a; also μὴ φονεύσῃς **Mk 10:19; Lk 18:20; Js 2:11a;** cp. **b** and **4:2** (where the conjecture φθονεῖτε, originated by Erasmus, has been favored by Calvin, Spitta, JMayor, Belser, Windisch, Dibelius, Hauck, Moffatt.—DeWette, Beyschlag, Meinertz et al. prefer to take φονεύω in a fig. sense [cp. PLond I, 113, 12d, 11f p. 227, c. 600 AD: ὁ χρεώστης ἐφόνευσέν με. A similar expr. as early as Herodas 6, 26 αὕτη μ' ἡ γυνή ποτε ἐκτρίψει=this woman will be the death of me yet], of anger; GRendall, The Ep. of St. James and Judaic Christianity 1927, 30f; 113 takes it literally, as do many before and after him, so e.g. NRSV, REB). τινά *someone* **Mt 23:31, 35; Js 5:6.** φ. τέκνον ἐν φθορᾷ B 19:5; D 2:2b (s. φθορά 2). Pass. *be put to death, die a violent death* 1 Cl 57:7 (Pr 1:32); GPt 2:5; 5:15; GJs 23:3; 24:2f; AcPl Ha1, 14.—DELG s.v. θείνω. M-M.

φόνος, ου, ὁ (Hom.+) ***murder, killing*** **Mk 15:7; Lk 23:19, 25** (cp. Sb 7992 [pap c. 200 AD] 22f κεκράτηται ἕνεκα φόνου); **Ac 9:1.** ἐν φόνῳ μαχαίρης (Ex 17:13; Dt 13:16; 20:13) *(by being murdered) with the sword* **Hb 11:37.** Anger as a cause D 3:2a. Pl. *bloody deeds* (Diod. S. 13, 48, 2; Ael. Aristid. 35, 7 K.=9 p. 100 D.; Lucian, Catapl. 27 al.; 2 Macc 4:3; Jos., C. Ap. 2, 269, Vi. 103; Mel., P. 50, 367) 3:2b. W. other sins **Mt 15:19; Mk 7:21; Rv 9:21.** In lists of vices (cp. Dio Chrys. 17 [34], 19 codd.; Hos 4:2; Mel., P. 50, 367; Ath., R. 23 p. 76, 12) **Ro 1:29** (sing. w. φθόνος.—A similar wordplay in Appian, Hann. 21 §93 φόνος τε καὶ πόνος); B 20:1 (sing.); D 5:1 (pl.).—B. 1455. Frisk. DELG s.v. θείνω. M-M.

φορά, ᾶς, ἡ (X., Pla.; ins, pap, TestSol, Philo; freq. in the sense 'being borne' or 'carried along', 'rapid motion' fr. φέρομαι) in our lit. only non-literally ***impulse, passion*** ἀτάκτοις φοραῖς φέρεσθαι *let oneself be carried away by disorderly urges* Dg 9:1.—DELG s.v. φέρω D.

φορέω (frequentative of φέρω) fut. φορέσω; 1 aor. ἐφόρεσα; pf. πεφόρηκα (B-D-F §70, 1; W-S. §13, 3) (Hom.+; ins, pap, LXX, TestSol, TestJob,Test12Patr, JosAs; GrBar 6:2; ApcEsdr [σάρκα]; Tat. 24:1; Mel., P. 105; 822 τὸν πατέρα).

❶ **to carry or bear habitually or for a considerable length of time,** ***bear*** (in contrast to φέρω) ***constantly/regularly,*** hence ***wear*** clothing (X., An. 7, 4, 4; Herm. Wr. 7, 2b; Jos., Ant. 3, 153 ἔνδυμα; 279; SIG 736, 117; POxy 531, 14; 15 [II AD]; 1300, 10; PGiss 47, 8 [armor]; Sir 11:5 διάδημα; EpArist; TestJob 25:7; Tat. 24, 1) **Mt 11:8; Js 2:3.** A wreath (Sir 40:4; TestBenj 4:1; GrBar 6:2) and a purple garment (Jos., Ant. 10, 235) **J 19:5** (ἔχων v.l.; SIG 1018, 1f φορείτω χλαμύδα καὶ στέφανον). Fetters 1 Cl 5:6. τὴν μάχαιραν **Ro 13:4** (cp. JosAs 29:2 ῥομφαίαν).

❷ **to identify habitually w. someth.,** ***bear,*** fig. ext. of 1: ὄνομα φορεῖν *bear a name* (Soph., fgm. 597, 2 TGF p. 274) Hs 9, 13, 2ac; 3abcd; 5; 9, 14, 5f; 9, 15, 2f; 9, 16, 3. δύναμιν 9, 13, 2b. πνεύματα 9, 15, 6; 9, 16, 1; 9, 17, 4. φορ. τὴν εἰκόνα τοῦ χοϊκοῦ *bear the image of the earthly person,* i.e. represent in one's own appearance **1 Cor 15:49a;** cp. **b.**—DELG s.v. φέρω D. M-M. TW.

φόρον, ου, τό s. Ἀππίου φόρον.—M-M.

φόρος, ου, ὁ (φέρω) **that which is brought in as payment to a state, with implication of dependent status,** ***tribute, tax*** (Hdt., Aristoph., et al.; ins, pap, LXX; TestJob 1:3 [n.pr.m.]), in our lit. in the expr. *pay taxes* or *tribute* φόρον (φόρους) δοῦναι (1 Macc 8:4, 7; cp. Just., A I, 17, 1 φόρους . . . φέρειν) **Lk 20:22; 23:2** (cp. Jos., Bell. 2, 403 Καίσαρι δεδώκατε τὸν φόρον); ἀποδοῦναι (Jos., Ant. 14, 203, C. Ap. 1, 119) **Ro 13:7** (φόρ. twice: *pay tribute to the one entitled to receive tribute*); τελεῖν (Jos., Ant. 5, 181; 12, 182; Tat. 4, 1) vs. **6** (φόρους).—B. 802; Pauly-W. VII 1–78; BHHW III, 1868f; RAC II 969–72.—DELG s.v. φέρω D. M-M. TW. Sv.

φορτίζω (φόρτος; mid. in Hes.; act. and pass. in Lucian, Navig. 45; Babrius 111, 3; Anth. Pal. 10, 5, 5; Ezk 16:33) pf. pass. ptc. πεφορτισμένος *to load/burden* τινά τι *someone with someth.*, more exactly *cause someone to carry someth.* (B-D-F §155, 7; Rob. 484) in imagery, of the burden of keeping the law φορτίζετε τοὺς ἀνθρώπους φορτία δυσβάστακτα **Lk 11:46.** Pass. οἱ κοπιῶντες καὶ πεφορτισμένοι *(you who are) weary and burdened* **Mt 11:28** (THaering, Mt 11:28–30: ASchlatter Festschr. 1922, 3–15).—Frisk s.v. φέρω B 10; DELG s.v. φόρτος. M-M. TW.

φορτίον, ου, τό (in form, a dim. of φόρτος; Hes.+; IG IV^2/1, 123, 6 [IV BC], pap, LXX; TestJob 18:7; Joseph.; Tat. 23, 1)

❶ **that which constitutes a load for transport,** ***load*** lit. φορτίον βαστάζειν (Teles p. 10 H.; Herm. Wr. 10, 8b) Hs 9, 2, 4. Of the *cargo* of a ship (Hes., X. et al.; Jos., Ant. 14, 377; POxy 1153, 9 [I AD]) **Ac 27:10** (v.l. φόρτος).

❷ **that which is carried and constitutes a burden,** ***burden,*** in imagery (Epict. 2, 9, 22; 4, 13, 16), of the oppressive burden of the law **Mt 23:4; Lk 11:46ab.** Cp. **Mt 11:30.** φορτίον βαστάζειν (Diog. L. 7, 170; Pythagorean in Stob., Flor. 85, 15 V 680 H.) **Gal 6:5** (one is to be concerned about one's own burden, rather than compare oneself complacently w. others [perh. gnomic fut. Burton, MT §69; Betz, Gal. 303f; cp. 2 Cor 5:10; DKuck, NTS 40, '94, 289–97, apocalyptic motif.]).—Frisk s.v. φέρω B 10. M-M. TW.

φόρτος, ου, ὁ (Hom. et al.; PLond II, 307, 2 p. 84 [II AD]; fr. φέρω of goods for transport) esp. ***the cargo*** of a ship (Lucian, Nav. 18, Ver. Hist. 1, 34; Achilles Tat. 3, 2, 9; Jos., C. Ap. 1, 63; SibOr 8, 348) **Ac 27:10 v.l.;** s. φορτίον 1.—Frisk s.v. φέρω B 10. DELG s.v. φόρτος.

Φορτουνᾶτος, ου, ὁ (also Φουρ-; Lat. Fortunatus. OGI 707, 5 Φορτουνᾶτος Σεβαστοῦ ἀπελεύθερος; APF 2, 1903, 571 no. 151, 5; Jos., Ant. 18, 247. S. Lghtf., The Apost. Fathers, Pt. I, vol. I, 1890 p. 29, 3; 62, 1, exx. fr. Lat. sources) ***Fortunatus.***

❶ an otherw. unknown Christian of Corinth who, w. his Christian fellow-townsmen Stephanas and Achaicus, was w. Paul in Ephesus when 1 Cor was written, **1 Cor 16:15 v.l., 17; subscr.**

❷ a member of the delegation sent by the Roman church to Corinth 1 Cl 65:1.—DDD 637. M-M.

φραγ- s. φράσσω.

φραγέλλιον, ου, τό (Lat. loanw.: flagellum [Horace, Sat. 1, 3, 119 horribile flagellum], consisting of a thong or thongs, freq. with metal tips to increase the severity of the punishment. In the form φλαγέλλιον PLond II, 191, 11 p. 265 [II AD]; CWessely, WienerStud 24, 1902 p. 150. Loanw. in rabb. B-D-F §5, 1b; 41, 2; Mlt-H. 103; 396; Hahn 261; 265. The spelling φραγέλλιον [so e.g. SEG XLII, 1240, 4] is found only in very late sources) ***whip, lash*** made of ropes (far less lethal than the penal 'flagellum', s. next entry) **J 2:15.**—DELG. M-M.

φραγελλόω (φραγγέλιον; in Christian usage [s. end of this entry]; but cp. TestBenj 2:3 and Aesop fr. the Cod. Paris. 1277: CRochefort, Notices et Extraits II [1789] 719 no. 19) 1 aor. ἐφραγέλλωσα (Lat. loanw.: flagello; s. φραγέλλιον) ***flog, scourge,*** a punishment inflicted on slaves and provincials after a sentence of death had been pronounced on them. So in the case of Jesus before the crucifixion (cp. Jos., Bell. 2, 306 οὓς μάστιξιν προαικισάμενος ἀνεσταύρωσεν [sc. Φλῶρος]; 5, 449; Lucian, Pisc. 2) **Mt 27:26; Mk 15:15** (Mommsen, Röm. Strafrecht 1899, 938f; 983f; RAC IX, 469–90; contrast the action Lk 23:16 παιδεύω; J 19:1 μαστιγόω). Performed after sentence to animal combat AcPl Ha 1, 30.—RGundry, Mark '93, 938f (reff.). DELG s.v. φραγέλλιον.

φραγμός, οῦ, ὁ (φράσσω; Soph., Hdt.+; BGU 1119, 32 [5 BC]; POxy 580; LXX, Philo)

❶ **a structure for enclosing an area,** ***fence, hedge,*** lit. (Theocr. 5, 108 the fence around the vineyard) περιέθηκεν φραγμόν (Is 5:2) **Mk 12:1;** w. dat. of the piece of ground enclosed **Mt 21:33.** ἄμπελος ἐν φραγμῷ τινι καταλειφθεῖσα *a vine that stands forsaken somewhere along the fence* Hs 9, 26, 4. Vagabonds and beggars frequent the hedges and fences around houses **Lk 14:23.**

❷ **a wall that separates,** ***partition,*** fig. ext. of 1, of the law, which separates circumcised from uncircumcised, Israelites from non-Israelites, and arouses enmity betw. them τὸ μεσότοιχον τοῦ φραγμοῦ **Eph 2:14** (s. μεσότοιχον and PFeine, Eph 2:14–16: StKr 72, 1899, 540–74; comm.).—DELG s.v. φράσσω. M-M.

φράζω fut.1 pl. φράσομεν; 1 aor. ἔφρασα, impv. φράσον (Hom. +) in our lit. only in the sense ***explain, interpret*** someth. mysterious (X., Oec. 16, 8; Cebes 33, 1; Herm. Wr. 380, 2 Sc. θεόν; Job 6:24 φράσατέ μοι) a parable **Mt 13:36 v.l.** (for διασάφησον); **15:15.**—DELG. M-M.

φράσσω 1 aor. ἔφραξα. Pass.: 2 fut. φραγήσομαι; 2 aor. ἐφράγην; pf. 3 sg. πέφρακται (Just.) (Hom. et al.; ins, pap, LXX; Jos., Bell. 3, 384; Just., D. 12, 2; 33, 1)

❶ **to close or keep from opening,** ***shut, close***—ⓐ lit. (Herodian 8, 1, 6; Lucian, Nigrin. 19 τὰ ὦτα κηρῷ φρ.) στόματα λεόντων *mouths of lions,* so that they can do no harm (cp. Da 6:17ff; vs. 23 Theod. ἐνέφραξεν τὰ στόματα τῶν λεόντων) **Hb 11:33.**

ⓑ fig. ext. of 1a: *close* or *stop* the mouth, so that the pers. must remain silent (Galen, Script. Min. I p. 73, 17 Marquardt; SibOr 8, 420 στόμα ἔφραξαν; 1 Macc 9:55 ἀπεφράγη τὸ στόμα αὐτοῦ) **Ro 3:19.** This sense may be the correct one for ἡ καύχησις αὕτη οὐ φραγήσεται *this boasting will not be silenced* **2 Cor 11:10.** But φράσσω also means

❷ **to cause someth. to cease,** ***block, bar*** (Thu. 4, 13, 4 φράξαι τοὺς ἔσπλους; Dio Chrys. 19 [36], 2 pass.); in that case **2 Cor 11:10** means *this boasting will not (let itself) be quashed* (permissive pass., Gildersleeve I §168).—DELG. M-M.

φρέαρ, ατος, τό (Hom. Hymns, Hdt. et al.; ins, pap, LXX; TestAbr A 3 p. 80, 1 and 4 [Stone p. 8]; Philo)

❶ **a construction consisting of a vertical shaft, covered with a stone, for water supply,** ***a well*** (Appian, Bell. Civ. 4, 107 §448; Arrian, Anab. 6, 18, 1; 6, 20, 4; Jos., Ant. 4, 283 οἱ φρέαρ ὀρύξαντες; Philo, Somn. 1, 8 [after Gen 26:32].—Contrast: πηγή . . . φρέαρ Paus. 1, 14; Philo, Poster. Cai. 153) **Lk 14:5** (Aesop, Fab. 9 P.=45a H.; 40 Ch.; 9 H-H. ἀλώπηξ πεσοῦσα εἰς φρέαρ); **J 4:11** (Gen 21:19 φρέαρ ὕδατος ζῶντος; 26:19), **12** (Hom. Hymns, Demeter 98f the motif of the divine wanderer who sits down near the city φρέατι, ὅθεν ὑδρεύοντο πολῖται). The wordplay πηγή . . . φρέαρ sets the stage for the saying in vss. 13f, and the shift to φρέαρ at vs. **11** is made to focus on the depth of the shaft (s. 2 below), which requires use of a bucket. In contrast, Jesus supplies water that 'wells up' vs. 14 (s. ἅλλομαι 2).

❷ **an opening that leads to the depths of the nether world,** ***pit, shaft*** (for the sense 'shaft' s. Hero Alex. I p. 32, 12; 15; s. also ἄβυσσος 2; cp. Ps 54:24 φρέαρ διαφθορᾶς) **Rv 9:1, 2abc.**—B. 44. DELG. M-M. Sv.

φρεναπατάω (in Christian usage; Hesych.; but s. φρεναπάτης) **mislead concerning the truth,** ***deceive*** ἑαυτόν *oneself* **Gal 6:3.**—DELG s.v. ἀπάτη. M-M.

φρεναπάτης, ου, ὁ (φρήν, ἀπάτη, cp. prec. entry; Herodian Gr. II 848, 27; PGrenf I, 1, 10 [II BC]=Coll. p. 178 ln. 18; s. UvWilamowitz, NGG 1896, 209 ff; PLond V, 1677, 22 [VI AD]) ***deceiver, misleader*** (w. ματαιολόγος) **Tit 1:10.**—Cp. DELG s.v. ἀπάτη. M-M.

φρήν, φρενός, ἡ pl. αἱ φρένες (mostly pl. and in various senses: Hom. et al.; ins, pap, LXX, TestSol, Philo) in our lit. only in one place and only in the pl. as **the process of careful consideration,** ***thinking, understanding*** (Hom. et al.; Plut., Mor. 116b φρένας ἔχειν; Herm. Wr. 13, 4; 5; Pr 7:7; 9:4 al.; Jos., Ant. 10, 114 ἀπολέσαντες τὰς φρένας Hippol., Ref. 4, 28, 6) **1 Cor 14:20ab.**—B. 1198. SSullivan, A Study of φρένες in Pindar and Bacchylides: Glotta 67, '89, 148–89, An Analysis of φρένες in the Gk. Lyric Poets (Excluding Pindar and Bacchylides): Glotta 66, '88, 26–62; s. also lit. cited by GMachemer, HSCP 95, '93, 121 n. 13.—DELG. M-M. TW. Sv.

φρίκη, ης, ἡ (Soph., Hdt.+; SIG 1239, 19; Am 1:11) **trembling caused by fear,** ***a shudder*** (Eur. et al.; Plut., Arat. 32, 2; Job 4:14; TestSol 18:19 P; Jos., Bell. 5, 565; 6, 123) Hv 3, 1, 5 (w. τρόμος, as in the Job pass., also Philo, Leg. ad Gai. 267).—DELG s.v. φρίξ. Sv.

φρίσσω 1 aor. ἔφριξα; pf. ptc. πεφρικώς (Hom. et al.; LXX; Joseph. [-ττ-]; TestSol 2:1; TestAbr [-ττ-]; ApcEsdr 7:7 p. 32, 19 Tdf. [θεὸς], ὃν πάντα φρίσσει; Just.) **to tremble fr. fear,** ***shudder*** (fr. φρίξ 'quivering, shuddering'; Hom. et al., w. acc. of pers. or thing that causes the fear), abs. (Da 7:15 Theod.; Philo, Det. Pot. Ins. 140) ὅλος ἤμην πεφρικώς Hv 1, 2, 1. Of hostile spirits (who shudder at exorcism: PGM 3, 227; 4, 2541f δαίμονες φρίσσουσί σε; 2829; 12, 118; Orph. Fgm. in Clem. Alex., Strom. 5, 125, 1; AcPh 132 [Aa II/2, 63, 12] φρίττοντες; Just., D. 49, 8; Ps.-Clem., Hom. 5, 5.—Of entities in general: Prayer of Manasseh [=Odes 12] 4; TestAbr A 9 p. 86, 30 [Stone p. 20]; 16 p. 96, 22f [St. p. 40]. On this subj. s. the commentaries w. further exx. [without the verb φρίσσω], esp. Dibelius, ad loc.; EPeterson, Εἷς Θεός 1926, 295–99.—Reff. and lit. on ὄνομα φρικτόν in SEitrem, Pap. Osloënses I 1925, 98) **Js 2:19.** In imagery of the earth B 11:2 (Jer 2:12).—DELG s.v. φρίξ. M-M.

φρονέω (s. φρήν) impf. ἐφρόνουν; fut. φρονήσω; 1 aor. ἐφρόνησα; pf. 1 pl. πεφρονήκαμεν (Ath. 10, 1) (Hom.+; ins, pap, LXX; TestJob 48:2; EpArist 236; Philo, Joseph., Ar., Just., Ath.)

❶ **to have an opinion with regard to someth.,** ***think, form/hold an opinion, judge*** ἐφρόνουν ὡς νήπιος *I thought like a child* **1 Cor 13:11** (schol. on Apollon. Rhod. 4, 868a νηπίου ὄντος καὶ νήπια φρονοῦντος). καθὼς φρονοῦσιν *as their opinion is* ISm 2. καλῶς καὶ ἀληθῶς φρονεῖς *your judgment is right and true* Hm 3:4 (εὖ φρ. Hippol., Ref. 10, 32, 4). ταῦτα φρονεῖν 9:12. ἃ φρονεῖς *the views that you hold* **Ac 28:22** (Just., D. 80, 2 ἕτερα λέγειν παρ' ἃ φρονῶ). πολλὰ φρονῶ ἐν θεῷ *many thoughts are mine when I take God's view of things* (so Kleist) ITr 4:1. φρονεῖν τι ὑπέρ τινος *think or feel in a certain way about someone* **Phil 1:7.** ὑπέρ τινος φρ. *think of someone* in the sense *be concerned about him* **4:10a;** cp. **10b.** φρ. περί τινος *think of* or *about someone* (Wsd 14:30; Just., D. 3, 7; Ath. 24, 1; περὶ τοῦ θεοῦ Theoph. Ant. 1, 1 [p. 58, 15]) 2 Cl 1:1a. φρ. τι περί τινος *think someth. concerning someone* (Isocr. 3, 60; Polyaenus 5, 2, 13; Lucian, Dial. Mort. 20, 5; Jos., Ant. 12, 125, C. Ap. 2, 168; Ar. 8, 1; Just., D. 48, 1) ISm 5:2. φρ. μικρὰ περί τινος *think little of someone* 2 Cl 1:2 (Philo, Spec. Leg. 2, 256 φρ. περὶ μοναρχίας τὰ ἄριστα); cp. 1:1b. On ἵνα ἀδελφὸς ἰδὼν ἀδελφὴν οὐδὲν φρονῇ περὶ αὐτῆς θηλυκόν 12:5a s. θηλυκός; cp. 12:5b. θεὸν δεσπότην φρ. *think of God as Master* Dg 3:2 (s. φρονίμως). οὐδὲν ἄλλο φρ. *think nothing different, not take a different view* **Gal 5:10** (Hdt. 7, 205, 3 ἄλλα φρ.; Jos., Bell. 5, 326 φρ. οὐδὲν ὑγιές). τοῦτο φρ. **Phil 3:15a;** τὶ ἑτέρως φρ. *think of* or *regard someth. differently* **15b;** τὸ αὐτὸ φρ. *think the same thing,* i.e. *be in agreement, live in harmony* (Hdt. 1, 60, 2; Dio Chrys. 17 [34], 20; Just., D. 65, 2 τὸ αὐτὸ φρ. . . . ἐμοί; OGI 669, 36.—Opp.: ἀνόμοια φρ. Iren. 1, Pr. 2 [Harv. I 4, 5f]) **2 Cor 13:11; Phil 2:2a; 3:16 v.l.; 4:2;** 2 Cl 17:3. τὸ αὐτὸ φρονεῖν ἐν ἀλλήλοις **Ro 15:5;** εἰς ἀλλήλους **12:16a.** Also τὰ αὐτὰ φρ. (Hdt. 5, 72, 2; Appian, Bell. Civ. 1, 65 §295 τὰ αὐτὰ ἐφρόνουν) Hs 9, 13, 7. τὸ ἓν φρ. **Phil 2:2b.**—*Cherish thoughts* μὴ ὑπερφρονεῖν παρ' ὃ δεῖ φρονεῖν *not to think more of oneself than one ought to think* **Ro 12:3a.** Cp. **1 Cor 4:6 v.l.** (cp. Diod. S. 27, 6, 2 τοὺς ὑπὲρ ἄνθρωπον φρονοῦντας). ὑψηλὰ φρονεῖν *be proud* **Ro 11:20; 1 Ti 6:17 v.l.**

❷ **to give careful consideration to someth.,** ***set one's mind on, be intent on,*** foll. by the acc. (Brutus, Ep. 14 τὰ σὰ φρ.)

ⓐ gener. ἀγαθὰ φρ. Hm 10, 3, 1. τὸ καλὸν φρ. Hs 5, 2, 7. τέλεια ISm 11:3. τὰ ὑψηλά **Ro 12:16b** (cp. 2 Macc 9:12). τὰ ἐπίγεια (Did., Gen. 50, 27; Theoph. Ant. 2, 17 [p. 142, 6]) **Phil 3:19.** τὰ ἐπὶ τῆς γῆς **Col 3:2** (opp. τὰ ἄνω; TestJob 48:2 τὰ τῆς γῆς φρ.).

ⓑ φρ. τά τινος *take someone's side, espouse someone's cause* (Diod. S. 13, 48, 4 and 7 ἐφρόνουν τὰ Λακεδαιμονίων; 13, 72, 1; 14, 32, 4; 20, 35, 2 and oft.; Appian, Liby. 70 §316, Bell. Civ. 3, 85, §351; Polyaenus 8, 14, 3 τὰ Ῥωμαίων φρ., cp. HAlmqvist, Plut. u. das NT '46, 56; Herodian 8, 6, 6; 1 Macc 10:20; Jos., Ant. 14, 450 οἱ τὰ Ἡρῴδου φρονοῦντες). τὰ τοῦ θεοῦ (opp. τὰ τῶν ἀνθρώπων) **Mt 16:23; Mk 8:33.** τὰ τῆς σαρκός (opp. τὰ τοῦ πνεύματος) **Ro 8:5.**

ⓒ of acknowledging the importance of someth. ὁ φρονῶν τὴν ἡμέραν κυρίῳ φρονεῖ *the one who is intent on the day* (i.e. a particular day rather than others) *in honor of the Lord* **Ro 14:6.** φρ. εἰς τὸ σωφρονεῖν **12:3b.**

❸ **to develop an attitude based on careful thought,** ***be minded/disposed*** τοῦτο φρονεῖτε ἐν ὑμῖν ὃ καὶ ἐν Χριστῷ Ἰησοῦ *let the same kind of thinking dominate you as dominated Christ Jesus* **Phil 2:5** (Christ went so far as to devoid himself of his divine status for the benefit of humanity; the opp. of φρονεῖν μέγα, 'to think presumptuously', s. Reader, Polemo 216f on the theme of hybris). Or, *have the same thoughts among yourselves as you have in your communion with Christ Jesus* (so CDodd, The Apost. Preaching '37, 106f).—B. 1198. DELG s.v. φρήν II. M-M. EDNT. TW. Sv.

φρόνημα, ατος, τό (fr. φρήν via φρονέω; Aeschyl., Hdt. et al.; Vett. Val. 109, 2; 2 Macc 7:21; 13:9; Philo, Joseph.; Hippol., Ref. 1, 2, 1 [philosophical: 'point of view']) **the faculty of fixing one's mind on someth.,** ***way of thinking, mind(-set),*** in our lit. (only Ro 8) w. focus on strong intention *aim, aspiration, striving* (φρονέω 2.—Diod. S. 11, 27, 2 of aspiration for control of the sea; Jos., Bell. 1, 204; 4, 358 φρόνημα ἐλευθερίου=striving for freedom, desire for independence.—διὰ φρονημάτων καὶ ἔργων ἀρετῆς Did., Gen. 195, 4) w. subjective gen. (Appian, Ital. 1) τῆς σαρκός **Ro 8:6a, 7.** τοῦ πνεύματος vss. **6b, 27.**—DELG s.v. φρήν II. M-M. TW.

φρόνησις, εως, ἡ (s. φρονέω; Soph., Isocr., Pla. et al.; OGI 332, 25; PSI 280; IDefixWünsch 1, 10 p. 6; LXX; En 98:3; TestSol; TestJob 37:8; 38:1; TestNapht 2:8; Philo, Jos., Just., Ath.)

❶ **the faculty of thoughtful planning,** ***way of thinking, (frame of) mind*** ἐπιστρέψαι ἀπειθεῖς ἐν φρονήσει (=εἰς φρόνησιν; but *with the thought, so that they have the thought* B-D-F §218) δικαίων **Lk 1:17.** W. νοῦς (Dio Chrys. 15 [32], 5) Hs 9, 17, 2ab, 4; 9, 18, 4. διέμειναν ἐν τῇ αὐτῇ φρονήσει 9, 29, 2. συγκεράσαι ὑμῶν τὴν φρόνησιν ἐπὶ τὸ αὐτό Hv 3, 9, 8 (s. συγκεράννυμι 2).

❷ **the ability to understand,** ***understanding, insight, intelligence*** (Isocr., Pla., Aristot.; OGI loc. cit.; PGM 5, 313; LXX; En 98:3 [w. ἐπιστήμη]; TestJob loc. cit.; EpArist 124; Just., D. 3, 3; Ath., R. 22 p. 75, 22; Theoph. Ant. 1, 3 [p. 62, 14] as an attribute of God) w. σοφία (Dio Chrys. 42 [59], 1; Synes., Ep. 103 p. 243d; Pr 10:23; 4 Macc 1:18; Philo, Praem. 81; Jos., Ant. 2, 87; 8, 171; Orig., C. Cels. 1, 31, 42) **Eph 1:8;** (opp.: the eyes alone) Dg 2:1.—DELG s.v. φρήν II 3. M-M. TW. Sv.

φρόνιμος, ον (cp. φρόνις 'prudence'; Soph., X., Pla. et al.; OGI 383, 106; PTebt 752, 7 [II BC]; LXX, pseudepigr., Philo; Jos., Ant. 9, 25; Tat. [s. below]) **pert. to understanding associated w. insight and wisdom,** ***sensible, thoughtful, prudent, wise*** **Mt 13:33** syr^{c} apparently rendering γυνὴ φρονίμη (s. Nestle[25] app.; RRiedinger, ZNW 51, '60, 154ff, cited by RBorger, GGA 143); **24:45; Lk 12:42** (both w. πιστός); **1 Cor 10:15.** Opp. μωρός **Mt 7:24; 25:2, 4, 8f; 1 Cor 4:10;** IEph 17:2. Opp. ἄφρων (as X., Mem. 2, 3, 1; Philo, Leg. All. 1, 86) **2 Cor 11:19;** 1 Cl 3:3. φρόνιμοι ὡς οἱ ὄφεις (cp. Gen 3:1.—'Wary'; cp. LKoehler, Kleine Lichter '45, 76–79) **Mt 10:16**=IPol 2:2. παρ' (v.l. ἐν) ἑαυτοῖς φρόνιμοι *wise in your own estimation = relying on your own wisdom* **Ro 11:25; 12:16** (cp. Pr 3:7); ἑαυτοῖς **11:25 v.l.** (without prep.; cp. Ps.-Demetr., El. c. 222 συνετὸς ἑαυτῷ). φρόνιμοι ἐν θεῷ (TestNapht 8:10 σοφοὶ ἐν θεῷ κ. φρόνιμοι) IMg 3:1; ἐν Χριστῷ **1 Cor 4:10.**—Comp. φρονιμώτερος *shrewder* (ApcMos 16; Philo; Jos., Bell. 5, 129; Tat. 7, 2; 16, 1) **Lk 16:8** εἰς τὴν γενεὰν τὴν ἑαυτῶν *in relation to their own generation.*—GKilpatrick, JTS 48, '47, 63f.—B. 1213. DELG s.v. φρήν II 2. M-M. TW.

φρονίμως adv. of φρόνιμος (Aristoph. et al.; X., Ages. 1, 17; PLond VI, 1927, 36; Eccl 7:11 Sym.; Philo; Jos., Ant. 19, 112) ***prudently, shrewdly*** **Lk 16:8.**—M-M.

φροντίζω (s. φροντίς) fut. 3 sg. φροντιεῖ Ps 39:18; aor. ἐφρόντισα LXX; pf. πεφρόντικα (Just.; Ath., R. 12 p. 61, 7) (Theognis, Hdt.+) **to give sustained thought to someth.,** ***think of, be intent on, be careful/concerned about*** foll. by gen. (X., Mem. 3, 11, 12; Polyb. 3, 12, 5; BGU 249, 20; 300, 4; Ps 39:18; 2 Macc 9:21; 11:15; EpArist 121; 245; Jos., Ant. 14, 312, Vi. 94; Just., D. 3, 2; Ath., R. 12 p. 61, 7) τῆς ἑνώσεως IPol 1:2. W. inf. foll. (ApcMos 40; Achilles Tat. 4, 9, 2; PRyl 78, 26) ἵνα φροντίζωσιν καλῶν ἔργων προΐστασθαι *in order that they might pay attention to engaging in good works* **Tit 3:8.**—DELG s.v. φρήν II 4. M-M. Spicq.

φροντίς, ίδος, ἡ (s. prec. entry; Pind., Hdt.+; ins, pap, LXX; EpArist 8; Philo; Jos., Ant. 5, 236; Ar. 11, 4; Just., D. 120, 6; Ath., R. 12 p. 61, 3 al.) ***reflection, thought*** w. ἐπίνοια Dg 5:3. In the sense ***care, concern*** foll. by εἰς=directed toward 1 Cl 63:4. Pl. (Dio Chrys. 80 [30], 14; Philostrat., Vi. Apoll. 8, 7 p. 304, 25; 316, 15; Jos., Ant. 2, 63) αἱ κεναὶ καὶ μάταιαι φροντίδες *empty and idle thoughts* or *cares* 1 Cl 7:2.—DELG s.v. φρήν II 4.

φροντιστής, οῦ, ὁ (s. φροντίζω; X., Pla. et al.; IG XIV, 715; 759; pap [oft. as a t.t. for 'guardian']; Philo, Somn. 2, 155) ***protector, guardian*** w. objective gen. (Jewish ins fr. Side in Pamphylia: JHS 28, 1908, 195f, no. 29 φρ. τῆς συναγωγῆς) σὺ αὐτῶν φρ. ἔσο IPol 4:1.—DELG s.v. φρήν II 4.

Φρόντων, ωνος, ὁ (Lat. Fronto. The Gk. form of the name in Jos., Bell. 6, 238; 242; OGI 533, 34; CIG II add. 2349k; III 5120; IV 9919; IPergamon 511; PGiss 59 II; POxy 1188) ***Fronto,*** member of the Ephesian congregation IEph 2:1.

φρουρά, ᾶς, ἡ (Aeschyl., Hdt. et al.; ins, pap, LXX; TestSol 18:43 P; Philo, Agr. 86 [=bodyguard]; Manetho 609 fgm. 8, 77 p. 85, 12 Jac. [Jos., C. Ap. 1, 77]; Jos., Ant. 7, 104; Mel., P. 15, 98; Ath. 6, 1)

❶ **the act or duty of guarding,** ***guard-duty, service as sentinel*** (Lucian, Ver. Hist. 2, 23) φυλάσσειν κατὰ φρουράν *stand guard as sentinel* GPt 9:35 (κατά B 5bβ).

❷ **site for detaining a pers. under guard,** ***prison*** (Aeschyl., Prom. 143; BGU 1074, 4 [II AD]) in imagery (Pla., Phdr. 62b; Aelian, HA 4, 41) Χριστιανοὶ κατέχονται ὡς ἐν φρουρᾷ τῷ κόσμῳ Dg 6:7 (apparently in allusion to Pla. above).—Frisk. DELG s.v. φρουρός. Sv.

φρουρέω (φρουρός 'a guard') impf. ἐφρούρουν; fut. φρουρήσω; aor. 3 sg. ἐφρούρησε Jdth 3:6. Pass.: impf. ἐφρουρούμην (Aeschyl., Hdt.+) in our lit. only trans.

❶ **to maintain a watch,** ***guard,*** lit. τὶ *someth.* (cp. Jdth 3: 6 φρ. τ. πόλεις=put garrisons in the cities; Jos., Bell. 3, 12) τὴν πόλιν Δαμασκηνῶν **2 Cor 11:32.** In this case the ref. is surely to the guarding of the city gates fr. within, as a control on all who went out (Jos., Vi. 53 τὰς ἐξόδους δὲ πάσας ἐφρούρει;

cp. Nicol. Dam.: 90 fgm. 130, 51 p. 400, 22 Jac.) rather than fr. the outside as was sometimes done, e.g. in sieges (Plut., Crassus 548 [9, 2]; Jos., Vi. 240); Zahn, NKZ 15, 1904, 34ff.

❷ **to hold in custody,** ***detain, confine*** (Plut., Ant. 954 [84, 4], Mor. 205f; Wsd 17:15; PGM 4, 2905; 3093) fig., pass.: of humankind before the coming of Jesus ὑπὸ νόμον ἐφρουρούμεθα *we were held under custody by the law* **Gal 3:23.** The terminology is consistent w. the Roman use of prisons principally for holding of prisoners until disposition of their cases.—In transf. sense ἡ ψυχὴ φρουρεῖται τῷ σώματι Dg 6:4.

❸ gener. **to provide security,** ***guard, protect, keep*** (Soph., Oed. R. 1479 δαίμων σε φρουρήσας τύχοι; Tat. 15, 3 τοῖς πνεύματι θεοῦ φρουρουμένοις Mel., P. 30, 205) the peace of God φρουρήσει τὰς καρδίας ὑμῶν **Phil 4:7** (w. weakened imagery of guarding, Straub 30). Pass. **1 Pt 1:5.**—DELG s.v. φρουρός. Frisk s.v. φρουρά. M-M.

φρυάσσω 1 aor. ἐφρύαξα; pf. mid. ptc. gen. πεφρυαγμένου 3 Macc 2:2 (the act. only Ps 2:1 and in the NT use of that passage. Elsewh. always φρυάσσομαι [since Callim., Hymn. 5, 2]; prim. in ref. to the utterance of spirited animals, such as the 'snorting' of a horse eager for the race Plut., Lyc. 53 [22, 1] or the 'crowing' of a cock Aelian, NA 7, 7) fig., of people ***be arrogant, haughty, insolent*** (Diod. S. 4, 74, 3; Anth. Pal. 4, 3, 27; 2 Macc 7:34 v.l.; 3 Macc 2:2; Philo, Cher. 66) **Ac 4:25** (Ps 2:1).—DELG s.v. φρυάσσομαι. M-M.

φρύγανον, ου, τό (φρύγω 'to roast or parch'; Hdt., Aristoph. et al.; ins, pap, LXX)

❶ ***bush, shrub*** (Theophr., HP 1, 3, 1 defines it as τὸ ἀπὸ ῥίζης πολυστέλεχες καὶ πολύκλαδον=from the root up full of stems and branches) B 7:8.

❷ in the pl., ***pieces of dry wood/brushwood*** esp. for making fires (cp. the use of the verb φρύγω for roasting or cooking.—X., An. 4, 3, 11 et al. Cp. Is 47:14; Philo, In Flacc. 68) **Ac 28:3.** W. ξύλα (Diod. S. 14, 90, 6; Plut., Mor. 525e) *kindling* MPol 13:1.—DELG s.v. φρύγω. M-M.

Φρυγία, ας, ἡ ***Phrygia*** (Hom. et al.; ins, Joseph., SibOr; Tat. 39, 3.—On the use of the art. s. B-D-F §261, 6; as adj., s. Hemer, Acts 112 and 283, JTS n.s. 27, '76, 122–26; also n.s. 28, '77, 99–101) a large district in Central Asia Minor, whose boundaries varied considerably fr. time to time: **Ac 2:10; 16:6; 18:23** (in the last two places w. ἡ Γαλατικὴ χώρα); **1 Ti subscr.** (s. Πακατιανός); MPol 4.—Ramsay, CB (other publications by Ramsay in Harnack, Mission[4] II 1924 p. 677, 3; WGasque, Sir William M. Ramsay '66, 86–91); JWeiss, RE X 557ff; VSchultze, Altchristl. Städte u. Landschaften II 1, 1922; AGoltze, Kleinasien[2] '57; Pauly-W. XX 781–891; Kl. Pauly IV 822–26; BHHW III 1468f; WSchepelern, D. Montanismus u. d. phrygischen Kulte 1929.—M-M.

Φρύξ, γός, ὁ (Hom. et al.; ins; Just., D. 119, 4; Tat. 1, 1) ***a Phrygian*** (s. Φρυγία) MPol 4.—DELG s.v. Φρυγία.

φυγαδεύω (fr. φεύγω via φυγάς, cp. φυγή) 1 aor. ἐφυγάδευσα; pass. ἐφυγαδεύθην

❶ **to cause to become a fugitive,** ***banish from the country,*** trans. (X. et al.; Diod. S. 5, 44, 7; ins, pap; TestGad 5:7; Philo, Congr. Erud. Gr. 171) ἐφυγάδευσεν δὲ Μωϋσῆν ἐν τῷ λόγῳ τούτῳ *and by this word he drove Moses from the country* **Ac 7:29 v.l.** Pass. (Jos., Bell. 1, 661; 4, 504 φυγαδευθείς, Ant. 12, 399) of Paul φυγαδευθείς *banished from the country* or *an exile* 1 Cl 5:6.

❷ **to be a fugitive,** ***live in exile*** intr. (Polyb. 10, 25, 1; SIG 175, 20 [IV BC]; 679, 84 [143 BC]; LXX) οὕτως καὶ ἐφυγάδευσεν Μωϋσῆς **Ac 7:29** D.—DELG s.v. φεύγω II B.

Φύγελος (also **Φύγελλος**), **ου, ὁ** (on the name and its spelling s. B-D-F §42, 3; W-S.§5, 26d; Mlt-H. 101; OBenndorf, Z. Ortskunde u. Stadtgeschichte v. Ephesus 1905, 74) ***Phygelus,*** an otherw. unknown Christian in Asia who, acc. to **2 Ti 1:15,** w. Hermogenes turned his back on Paul.—M-M.

φυγή, ῆς, ἡ (Hom.+; ins, pap, LXX, SibOr, Philo; Jos., Ant 18, 324; 20, 4; Just., A I, 21, 2 φυγὴ πόνων to avoid pain) ***flight*** **Mt 24:20; Mk 13:18 v.l.**—DELG s.v. φεύγω II A. M-M.

φυλακή, ῆς, ἡ (φύλαξ, cp. φυλάσσω; Hom.+; ins, pap, LXX, En, TestSol, TestJos; JosAs 4:14; AscIs 2:13; EpArist, Philo, Joseph., Just., D. 131, 6 φ. ἀπὸ κρούους; Ath., R. 18 p. 70, 9 ἁπάντων φυλακήν τε καὶ πρόνοιαν; loanw. in rabb.) 'watch, guard'.

❶ **the act of guarding,** ***guarding,*** in the expr. φυλάσσειν φυλακάς *keep watch, do guard duty* (X., An. 2, 6, 10; Pla., Leg. 6, 758d; Demosth. 7, 14; Plut., Mor. 198a; LXX.—B-D-F §153, 3) φυλ. φυλακὰς τῆς νυκτὸς ἐπὶ τὴν ποίμνην *keep watch over the flock at night* (s. φυλ. τῆς νυκτός 4 below) **Lk 2:8.**

❷ **the act of guarding embodied in a pers.,** ***guard, sentinel*** (Hom. et al.; OGI 229, 96; 99; PGiss 19, 16; Jos., Bell. 6, 131) **Ac 12:10** (the πρώτη and δευτέρα φ. as first and second sentinel, as Arrian, Anab. 3, 18, 6).

❸ **the place where guarding is done,** ***prison*** (in sg. and pl. Hdt., Thu. et al.; OGI 90, 13; 669, 17; pap, LXX; Jos., Vi. 178) οἶκος φυλακῆς B 14:7 (Is 42:7). Also simply φυλακή (TestJos 1:6) **Mt 14:10; 25:36, 39, 43f; Mk 6:27; Lk 22:33; Ac 5:19, 22** (on prison escapes s. the lit. cited RPervo, Profit w. Delight '87, 147 n. 15; s. also ἀνοίγω 1); **12:6, 17; 16:27, 39** D, **40; Hb 11:36.** The pl. of several prisons (Appian, Bell. Civ. 4, 17 §65) **Lk 21:12; Ac 22:4; 26:10; 2 Cor 6:5; 11:23;** Hv 3, 2, 1. βάλλειν τινὰ εἰς φυλακήν (βάλλω 2; cp. JosAs 4:14 ἐνέβαλεν αὐτὸν εἰς τὴν φ.) *throw someone into prison* **Mt 18:30** (s. PSchmidt, Die Gesch. Jesu II 1904, 326f); **Lk 12:58; Ac 16:23f, 37; Rv 2:10.** Pass. **Mt 5:25; Lk 23:25; J 3:24;** cp. **Lk 23:19.** παραδιδόναι εἰς φ. (Diod. S. 11, 40, 3 παρέδωκαν εἰς φ.; 12, 31, 2; 17, 32, 2; OGI 669, 15) **Ac 8:3;** cp. **Lk 21:12.** τίθεσθαι εἰς φ. (cp. PEleph 12, 2 [III BC]) **Ac 12:4.** ἐν (τῇ) φυλακῇ τίθεσθαι **Mt 14:3 v.l.; Ac 5:25;** ἀποτίθεσθαι **Mt 14:3;** δῆσαι **Mk 6:17;** κατακλείειν **Lk 3:20; Ac 26:10.** τηρεῖν pass. **12:5.** Of the nether world or its place of punishment (πνεῦμα 2 and 4c) **1 Pt 3:19** (BReicke, The Disobedient Spirits and Christian Baptism '46, 116f). It is in a φ. in the latter sense that Satan will be rendered harmless during the millennium **Rv 20:7.** The fallen city of Babylon becomes a φυλακή *haunt* for all kinds of unclean spirits and birds **18:2ab.**

❹ **one of the periods of time into which the night was divided,** ***a watch of the night*** (Hdt. 9, 51 al.; Diod. S. 14, 24, 4 δευτέρα φ.; Arrian, Anab. 6, 25, 5 φυλακὴ τῆς νυκτός; PPetr II, 45 II, 18 [246 BC] πρώτης φυλακῆς ἀρχομένης; LXX; Joseph.). Our lit. reflects the Rom. custom of dividing the time betw. 6 p.m. and 6 a.m. into four equal periods or *watches* (assigned pers. were responsible for security during each period) **Mt 14:25; Mk 6:48** (Diod. S. 19, 26, 1 περὶ δευτέραν φυλακήν; Jos., Ant. 18, 356 περὶ τετάρτην φυλακήν; for περί s. also the Freiburg pap 76, 7 [II BC]: UWilcken, Deissmann Festschr. 1927, 10ff ln. 9f περὶ πρώτην φυλακὴν τ. νυκτός). Cp. **Mt 24:43; Lk 12:38** (here perh. we are to think of only three night-watches, as among the Hebrews and Greeks [s. Jülicher, Gleichn. 168]: thus Diod, S. 19, 38, 3; Polyaenus 4, 8, 4; Jos., Bell. 5, 510). (Mk 13:35 uses the popular designations ὀψέ 2, μεσονύκτιον, ἀλεκτοροφωνία, πρωΐ; s. these entries.)—B. 1451. DELG s.v. φύλαξ. M-M. TW.

φυλακίζω (cp. φυλακή; Wsd 18:4; TestJos 2:3; Ar. [JTS 25, 1924, p. 74 ln. 23]; Achmes 84, 3; 87, 12) aor. pass inf. φυλακισθῆναι Wsd 18:4, ptc. pl. φυλακισθέντας (Ar.) ***take into custody, imprison*** **Ac 22:19;** 1 Cl 45:4. S. φυλακή 3.—DELG s.v. φύλαξ.

φυλακτήριον, ου, τό (φύλαξ, cp. φυλάσσω; Hdt.+; TestJob 47:11; Jos., Ant. 15, 249; Just., D. 46, 5; in var. senses) **leather prayer band and case containing scripture passages, sometimes used as an amulet, *prayer-band, prayer-case.*** One of the lit. senses of φ., which occurs only once in our lit., **Mt 23:5,** is 'safeguard, means of protection' (Demosth. 6, 24; Philo), esp. 'amulet', (Dioscor., Mat. Med. 5, 154; Plut., Mor. 377b al.; OGI 90, 45; PGM 1, 275; 3, 97; 127; 4, 86; 660; 708; 1071; 2506; 2510; 2694; 2705; 13, 796), but this sense is only one component of a more complex semantic phenomenon, where the referent reflects the Aramaic תְּפִלִּין, i.e. two black leather boxes containing scripture passages worn on the forehead and the left arm, in keeping with Mosaic instruction Ex 13:9, 16; Dt 6:8; 11:18, where the directives appear to be figurative. Discovery of such small boxes, some with compartments, at the caves of Murabbaat, further confirms literary evidence of the practice. In some circles the devices were viewed as amulets protecting against demonic influences, and this understanding is reflected in Goodspeed's rendering ('they wear wide Scripture texts as charms'), which avoids the ambiguous Eng. loanword 'phylacteries'.—Schürer II 479–81 (note 86 lit.; add YYadin, Tefillin fr. Qumran '69); MFriedländer, Der Antichrist 1901, 155ff; GKropatscheck, De Amuletorum apud Antiquos Usu, diss. Greifswald 1907; Billerb. IV 1928, 250–76; GLanger, Die jüd. Gebetsriemen '31; WKnox, St. Paul and the Church of the Gentiles '39, 209; GFox, JNES 1, '42, 373–77; Goodsp., Probs. 35f; CBonner, HTR 39, '46, 25–53 (esp. 35), Studies in Magical Amulets '50; JBowman, TU 73, '59, 523–38; JTigay, HTR 72, '79, 45–53; Pauly-W. I 467–76; Kl. Pauly IV 834; BHHW I 90f; RAC I 397–411 (lit.).—DELG s.v. φυλαξ 9. M-M. Sv.

φύλαξ, ακος, ὁ (s. prec. three entries and φυλάσσω; Hom.+; ins, pap, LXX, JosAs, GrBar, Philo; Jos., Ant. 7, 287 al.; Just.) ***guard, sentinel*** **Mt 27:65** D, **66** D; **Ac 5:23; 12:6, 19;** Dg 2:7; AcPl Ha 3, 25; 4, 4.—DELG. M-M.

φύλαρχος, ου, ὁ (X., Pla. et al.; ins, pap, LXX) 'ruler of a φυλή', ***head of a tribe*** (X., Cyr. 1, 2, 14; Plut., Crass. 555 [21, 1]; Jos., Ant. 17, 56) of the rulers of the 12 Hebrew tribes (Dt 31:28; 1 Esdr 7:8; EpArist 97; Jos., Ant. 3, 169) 1 Cl 43:2ab, 5.—Renehan '75, 201 (ins). DELG s.v. φῦλον.

φυλάσσω (-ττ- Ar. [Milne 76, 32]; s. Gignac I 152f) fut. φυλάξω; 1 aor. ἐφύλαξα; pf. πεφύλαχα. Pass.: 1 fut. 3 pl. φυλαχθήσονται (TestSol 13:8 C; JosAs 15:6); 1 aor. ἐφυλάχθην; pf. 3 sg. πεφύλακται Ezk 18:9, ptc. πεφυλαγμένος LXX (also PsSol 6:2; Just., D. 102, 4) (Hom.+).

❶ **to carry out sentinel functions, *watch, guard,*** act.

ⓐ φυλάσσειν φυλακάς **Lk 2:8** (s. also 2 below; φυλακή 1). φυλάσσειν κατὰ φρουράν GPt 9:35 (φρουρά 1).

ⓑ τινά *guard someone* to prevent the pers. fr. escaping (Plut., Mor. 181a) **Mk 15:25** D; **Ac 12:4; 28:16.** Pass. **Lk 8:29; Ac 23:35.**

ⓒ abs. *stand guard* (Hom. et al.) GPt 8:33.

❷ **to protect by taking careful measures, *guard, protect,*** act.—ⓐ φυλάσσειν φυλακάς **Lk 2:8** (s. also 1a above).

ⓑ w. acc. *someone* or *someth.* τινά *someone* (ChronLind D, 47 τούς ἀνθρώπους τούτους θεοὶ φυλάσσουσι; Ex 23:20; Pr 13:6; ParJer 6:10; ApcSed 7:11; ApcMos 7) **J 17:12** (w. τηρέω as Dio Chrys. 14 [31], 150); **2 Pt 2:5.** Of Joseph (in the sense of Mt 1:25) GJs 13:1; 14:2. τὶ *someth.* (Gen 3:24; TestJob 9:3 οἶκον; ParJer 3:11 τὰ σκεύη τῆς λειτουργίας ApcMos 28) αὐλήν **Lk 11:21.** τὸν πύργον (EpArist 102) Hs 9, 5, 1. πάντα τὰ στοιχεῖα Dg 7:2a. Clothes, to prevent them fr. being stolen **Ac 22:20.** τὴν ψυχὴν αὐτοῦ (εἰς ζωὴν αἰώνιον) φυλάσσειν *preserve his life* (for eternal life; cp. Jos., Ant. 3, 199 ἔλαιον φ. εἰς τ. λύχνους) **J 12:25.** τὴν παραθήκην *what has been entrusted* so that it is not lost or damaged **1 Ti 6:20; 2 Ti 1:14;** foll. by an indication of time (Aelian, VH 9, 21 ὦ Ζεῦ, ἐς τίνα με καιρὸν φυλάττεις;) εἰς ἐκείνην τὴν ἡμέραν vs. **12.** Cp. B 19:11; D 4:13. ἀκακίαν 1 Cl 14:5 (Ps 36:37). θνητὴν ἐπίνοιαν Dg 7:1. τὴν ἁγνείαν Hm 4, 1, 1. τὴν πίστιν κτλ. 6, 1, 1. ὡς ναὸν θεοῦ φυλάσσειν τὴν σάρκα 2 Cl 9:3. τινά w. a predicate acc. (Wsd 14:24) φυλάξαι ὑμᾶς ἀπταίστους **Jd 24.** τινὰ ἀπό τινος (X., Cyr. 1, 4, 7; Menand., Sam. 302f S. [87f Kö.]) **2 Th 3:3** (PGM 4, 2699 φύλαξόν με ἀπὸ παντὸς δαίμονος; 36, 177 ἀπὸ παντὸς πράγματος; Sir 22:26; Ps 140:9). ἑαυτὸν ἀπό τινος (Horapollo 2, 94; Herm. Wr. p. 434, 13 Sc.; TestReub 4:8; JosAs 7:6) **1J 5:21.** Of a cultic image χρήζων ἀνθρώπου τοῦ φυλάξαντος ἵνα μὴ κλαπῇ *needing a person to guard (it) so that it may not be stolen* Dg 2:2.

❸ **to be on one's guard against, *look out for, avoid*** mid. (Hom. et al.; LXX. Test12Patr; ParJer 2:5; Just.) w. acc. of pers. or thing avoided τινά (Aeschyl., Prom. 717; Appian, Bell. Civ. 2, 25 §96 τὸν Πομπήιον; 5, 8 §32: Ps.-Liban., Charact. Ep. p. 30, 12; Just., D. 82, 1) **2 Ti 4:15;** IEph 7:1; ITr 7:1. τὶ (Hdt., Aristot. et al.; Jos., Bell. 4, 572) **Ac 21:25;** ITr 2:3. Also ἀπό τινος (PLond IV, 1349, 35; Dt 23:10; TestSim 4:5; 5:3) **Lk 12:15;** Hm 5, 1, 7; s 5, 3, 6. Foll. by ἵνα μή (B-D-F §392, 1b; cp. Gen 31:29; Just., A I, 14, 1 μή) **2 Pt 3:17.**

❹ **to hold in reserve, *keep, reserve*** pass. (Diod. S. 1, 8, 7) τί τινι *someth. for someone* Dg 10:7.

❺ **to continue to keep a law or commandment from being broken—**ⓐ act. ***observe, follow*** (νόμον Soph., Trach. 616; Dio Chrys. 58 [75], 1; νόμους X., Hell. 1, 7, 29; Pla., Rep. 6, 484b, Pol. 292a. Cp. Aristoxenus, fgm. 18 p. 13, 31 τὰ ἤθη καὶ τὰ μαθήματα; OGI 669, 28; PTebt 407, 9; POxy 905, 9; PFay 124, 13; Wsd 6:4; Sir 21:11; 4 Macc 5:29; 15:10; Jos., C. Ap. 1, 60; TestJud 26:1; TestIss 5:1; Just., D. 11, 2 al.; Ath., R. 20 p. 73, 25) τὶ *someth.* **Mt 19:20; Lk 18:21; 1 Ti 5:21;** Hm 1:2a; 3:5ab; 4, 4, 3; 8:9; s 5, 3, 4. τὸν νόμον (ViEzk 17 [p. 76, 5 Sch.]; Just., D. 10, 4; Lucian, Jud. 5) **Ac 7:53; 21:24; Gal 6:13.** τὴν ἐντολήν Hm 1:2b; 2:7; 8:12a. τὰς ἐντολάς (Jos., Ant. 6, 336; TestZeb 5:1; TestBenj 10:3, 5; ApcEsdr 5:19; ApcMos 10; Ar. 15:3; Just., D. 46, 4) 2 Cl 8:4; B 4:11; Hv 5, 5, 7; m 2:7; 4, 2, 4ab; 4, 4, 4ab; 5, 2, 8; 12, 5, 1; s 5, 3, 2f al. Pass. Hm 12, 3, 4f; s 1:7. τὰ δικαιώματα τοῦ νόμου *the requirements of the law* **Ro 2:26** (ParJer 6:23 τὰ δικαιώματά μου). τὸν λόγον τοῦ θεοῦ **Lk 11:28.** τὰ ῥήματα (i.e. of Christ) **J 12:47** (cp. ApcMos 3 τὸ ῥῆμα). τὰ δόγματα **Ac 16:4.** φυλ. τὸ σάββατον *keep the Sabbath* B 15:2 (cp. Ex 31:16). τὴν Ἰουδαίων δεισιδαμονίαν φυλ. *practice Judean fanaticism/superstition* Dg 1. τά μέτρα τῶν τῆς ἡμέρας δρόμων φυλ. 7:2b (μέτρον 2a).

ⓑ OT infl. is prob. felt in the use of the mid. for the act. (s. B-D-F §316, 1) in sense a: *keep, observe, follow* (Lev 20:22; 26:3; Ps 118:5 al. But as early as Hesiod, Op. 263 ταῦτα φυλασσόμενοι=if you observe this; 765; Ocellus [II BC] c. 56 Harder φυλάττεσθαι τὸ . . . γίνεσθαι) ταῦτα πάντα **Mt 19:20 v.l.; Mk 10:20; Lk 18:21 v.l.**

❻ **to store up, *lay up for oneself,*** mid. (='look out for oneself') PtK 2 p. 15, 2.—B. 752. DELG s.v. φύλαξ. M-M. TW.

φυλή, ῆς, ἡ (φῦλον 'race, tribe, class'; Pind., Hdt.+).

❶ **a subgroup of a nation characterized by a distinctive blood line,** ***tribe,*** of the 12 tribes of Israel (Diod. S. 40, 3, 3 δώδεκα φυλαί of the 'Judeans'; LXX; TestAbr A; cp. AscIs 3:2 τὰς ἐννέα ἥμισυ θυλάς; TestBenj 9:2; Demetr.: 722 fgm. 6 Jac.; Jos., Ant. 11, 133) **Hb 7:13; Rv 7:4;** 1 Cl 43:2ab, 4; GJs 1:1; 6:3; AcPl Ha 8, 3. Certain tribes are mentioned by name: Ἀσήρ **Lk 2:36.** Βενιαμίν **Ac 13:21; Ro 11:1; Phil 3:5.** Ἰούδα **Rv 5:5;** cp. **Hb 7:14;** all the tribes **Rv 7:5–8** (except that, according to ancient trad., Manasseh takes the place of Dan, since the latter is the tribe fr. which, because of Gen 49:17, the Antichrist is alleged to come [WBousset, D. Antichrist 1895, 112ff; s. Iren. 5, 30, 2; other reff. Charles, ICC Rv I 208f]). Of Mary ἦν τῆς φυλῆς τοῦ Δαυίδ GJs 10:1b; cp. vs. 1a. αἱ δώδεκα φυλαὶ τοῦ Ἰσραήλ **Mt 19:28; Lk 22:30;** cp. **Rv 21:12;** B 8:3ab; πᾶσαι αἱ φ. τοῦ λαοῦ GJs 24:3; in imagery **Js 1:1;** Hs 9, 17, 1f.

❷ **a relatively large people group that forms a sociopolitical subgroup of the human race,** ***nation, people*** (X., Cyr. 1, 2, 5; Dionys. Hal. 2, 7) πᾶσαι αἱ φυλαὶ τῆς γῆς (Gen 12:3; 28:14; Ezk 20:32) **Mt 24:30; Rv 1:7;** 1 Cl 10:3 (Gen 12:3). W. synonymous expressions (TestAsh 7:6 χώρα, φυλή, γλῶσσα) πάντα τὰ ἔθνη, φυλὰς καὶ γλώσσας 2 Cl 17:4; cp. **Rv 5:9; 7:9; 11:9; 13:7; 14:6.**—B. 1317. DELG s.v. φῦλον. M-M. TW.

φύλλον, ου, τό (Hom. et al.; pap, LXX, En; TestSol [also PVindob 18, 37]; ApcSed 8:8; ApcMos 20) ***leaf*** 1 Cl 23:4 (scripture quot. of unknown origin). Collectively ***foliage*** B 11:6 (Ps 1:3). Elsewh. in our lit. (as prevailingly in Lucian) in the pl. (En 24:4; EpArist 70; Jos., Ant. 1, 44; 3, 174; TestLevi 9:12; ApcSed, ApcMos) **Mt 21:19; 24:32; Mk 11:13ab; 13:28; Rv 22:2;** B 11:8; Hs 3:1. ἀποβάλλειν τὰ φ. 3:3.—B. 525. DELG. M-M.

φυλλοροέω (φύλλον, ῥέω; Pherecrates Com. [V BC], fgm. 130, 10 Kock [in Athen. p. 269d]; Plut., Mor. 648d; 649cd; 723e; Epict. 1, 14, 3; 3, 24, 91. Predom. w. double ρ: φυλλορροέω [X.; Artem. 4, 57; Aristaen., Ep. 1, 10; Philo, Ebr. 9 al.]) ***shed leaves, lose foliage*** 1 Cl 23:4=2 Cl 11:3 (prophetic saying of unknown origin).

φύραμα, ατος, τό (fr. φυράω 'to mix substances')

❶ **that which is mixed/kneaded,** ***mixture/batch of dough*** (Aristot., Probl. 21, 18, 929a, 25; Plut., Mor. 693e; PTebt 401, 27 [I AD]; Num 15:20f) μικρὰ ζύμη ὅλον τὸ φύραμα ζυμοῖ **1 Cor 5:6; Gal 5:9** (ζύμη 1). On **Ro 11:16** cp. Num 15:20f. Metaph. (Philo, Sacr. Abel. 108): the Christians are to be νέον φύραμα *fresh dough* containing no leaven **1 Cor 5:7** (cp. Philo, Spec. Leg. 2, 158 φυράμαπα ἄζυμα; cp. the warning against toleration of fornicators in the congregation).

❷ **the dough-like mixture fr. which potters make their wares,** ***lump*** (Plut., Mor. 811c) **Ro 9:21.**—B. 360. DELG s.v. φύρω. M-M.

φυσικός, ή, όν (fr. φύω via φύσις; X.+; PLips 28, 18; EpArist 222 al.; TestDan 2:4; 3:4; Philo; Jos., Ant. 12, 99; Ar. 13:7; Just., D. 39, 1; Ath.; φυσικώτερον Tat. 21, 2) **pert. to being in accordance w. the basic order of things in nature**

ⓐ of human behavior ***natural*** (Dionys. Hal., Plut. et al. φυσικὴ χρῆσις) **Ro 1:26f.**

ⓑ of animals, whose natural destiny is to be the victims of predators ***in accordance with nature*** γεγεννημένα φυσικὰ εἰς ἅλωσιν καὶ φθοράν (mere) *creatures of instinct, born to be caught and killed* **2 Pt 2:12.**—DELG s.v. φύομαι C 6. M-M. Sv.

φυσικῶς adv. of φυσικός; comp. φυσικώτερον (Tat. 26, 3) (Aristot., Diod. S., Plut., Philo et al.) ***naturally, by instinct*** **Jd 10** (cp. Diog. L, 10, 137 φυσικῶς καὶ χωρὶς λόγου al.; X., Cyr. 2, 3, 9 μάχην ὁρῶ πάντας ἀνθρώπους φύσει ἐπισταμένους, ὥσπέρ γε καὶ τἆλλα ζῷα ἐπίσταταί τινα μάχην ἕκαστα οὐδὲ παρ' ἑνὸς ἄλλου μαθόντα ἢ παρὰ τῆς φύσεως 'I perceive that all human beings have a natural understanding of combat, just as other creatures severally understand some way of fighting, without having learned anything from another, but simply by instinct').

φυσιόω (a later substitute for φυσάω; it is largely limited to Christian lit. [but also in Philod., Mus. p. 26 JKemke 1884]) pass.: pf. ptc. πεφυσιωμένος; 1 aor. ἐφυσιώθην lit. 'blow up, inflate' fr. φῦσα (orig. 'pair of bellows', then var. 'wind, blast', etc.) fig. **to cause to have an exaggerated self-conception,** ***puff up, make proud*** τινά *someone* ITr 4:1. τόπος μηδένα φυσιούτω *let no one be puffed up because of* (high) *position* ISm 6:1. Of knowledge φυσιοῖ *it* (only) *puffs up* **1 Cor 8:1**=Dg 12:5.—Pass. in act. sense *become puffed up* or *conceited, put on airs* (TestLevi 14:7, 8 v.l.; schol. on Apollon. Rhod. 3, 368b of anger, that swells the heart; Hesych.; cp. Babrius 114 v.l. L-P. [=349 P.]) **1 Cor 4:18f; 5:2; 13:4;** IMg 12; ITr 7:1; IPol 4:3. εἰκῇ φυσιούμενος ὑπὸ τοῦ νοὸς τῆς σαρκὸς αὐτοῦ *groundlessly inflated by his fleshly mind* **Col 2:18.** ἵνα μὴ εἷς ὑπὲρ τοῦ ἑνὸς φυσιοῦσθε (perh. subjunctive; s. ἵνα 1c) κατὰ τοῦ ἑτέρου *in order that no one of you might be puffed up in favor of the one* (apostle and thus) *against the other* **1 Cor 4:6.**—B. 684. DELG s.v. φῦσα. M-M.

φύσις, εως, ἡ (φύω; Hom.+)—❶ **condition or circumstance as determined by birth,** ***natural endowment/condition, nature,*** esp. as inherited fr. one's ancestors, in contrast to status or characteristics that are acquired after birth (Isocr. 4, 105 φύσει πολίτης; Isaeus 6, 28 φύσει υἱός; Pla., Menex. 245d φύσει βάρβαροι, νόμῳ Ἕλληνες; Just., A I, 1, 1 Καίσαρος φύσει υἱῷ; SIG 720, 3; OGI 472, 4; 558, 6 al.; PFay 19, 11.—Theoph. Ant. 1, 13 [p. 86, 16]) ἡμεῖς φύσει Ἰουδαῖοι **Gal 2:15** (cp. Ptolemaeus, Περὶ Ἡρῴδου τ. βασιλέως: no. 199 Jac. [I AD] Ἰουδαῖοι . . . ἐξ ἀρχῆς φυσικοί; Jos., Ant. 7, 130; φύσει Λιμναίου IK XXXVII, 15, 3 of the birth daughter of L. in contrast to her adoptive relationship w. one named Arsas). ἡ ἐκ φύσεως ἀκροβυστία *the uncircumcision that is so by nature* (a ref. to non-Israelites, who lack the moral cultivation of those who are circumcised and yet 'observe the upright requirements of the law' [Ro 2:26]. Israelites who violate their responsibilities to God, despite their privileged position indicated by receipt of circumcision and special revelation, run the risk of placing themselves in the condition of the uncircumcised) **Ro 2:27.** ἤμεθα τέκνα φύσει ὀργῆς *we were, in our natural condition* (as descendants of Adam), *subject to (God's) wrath* **Eph 2:3** (the position of φύσει betw. the two words as Plut., Mor. 701a; DTurner, Grace Theological Journal 1, '80, 195–219). The Christians of Tralles have a blameless disposition οὐ κατὰ χρῆσιν, ἀλλὰ κατὰ φύσιν *not from habit, but by nature* ITr 1:1 (here the contrast is between perfunctory virtue and spontaneous or instinctive behavior; Pindar sim. extolled the virtues of athletes who, in contrast to those w. mere acquired learning, reflected their ancestral breeding for excellence: O. 7, 90–92; P. 10, 11–14; N. 3, 40–42; 6, 8–16). οἱ κατὰ φύσιν κλάδοι *the natural branches* **Ro 11:21, 24c.** ἡ κατὰ φύσιν ἀγριέλαιος *a tree which by nature is a wild olive* vs. **24a;** opp. παρὰ φύσιν *contrary to nature* vs. **24b;** s. lit. s.v. ἀγριέλαιος and ἐλαία 1. On κατὰ and παρὰ φύσιν s. MPohlenz, Die Stoa I '48, 488c.

❷ **the natural character of an entity,** ***natural characteristic/disposition*** (χρυσὸς . . . τὴν ἰδίαν φ. διαφυλάττει Iren. 1, 6,

2 [Harv. I 55, 2]; Hippol., Ref. 5, 8, 12) ἡ φύσις ἡ ἀνθρωπίνη *human nature* (Pla., Tht. 149b, Tim. 90c; Aristot. 1286b, 27; Epict. 2, 20, 18; Philo, Ebr. 166 al.; Aelian, VH 8, 11 τῶν ἀνθρώπων φύσις θνητή; TestJob 3:3 ἡ ἀνθρωπίνη φ.; Orig., C. Cels. 1, 52, 13; Just., A II, 6, 3 τῇ φύσει τῶν ἀνθρώπων) **Js 3:7b** (unless the sense should be *humankind,* s. 4 below). Euphemistically: παρθένος ἐγέννησεν, ἃ οὐ χωρεῖ ἡ φύσις αὐτῆς *while remaining a virgin, a virgin has had a child* or *a virgin has given birth, something that does not accord w. her natural condition (as a virgin)* GJs 19:3. τὸ ἀδύνατον τῆς ἡμετέρας φύσεως *the weakness of our nature* Dg 9:6. θείας κοινωνοὶ φύσεως *sharers in the divine nature* **2 Pt 1:4** (cp. ὅσοι φύσεως κοινωνοῦντες ἀνθρω[πίν]ης IReisenKN, p. 371, 46f; Jos., C. Ap. 1, 232 θείας μετεσχηκέναι φύσεως; Himerius, Or. 48 [=Or. 14], 26 of Dionysus: πρὶν εἰς θεῶν φύσιν ἐλθεῖν=before he attained to the nature of the gods; Ar. 13, 5 μία φ. τῶν θεῶν. Difft. AWolters, Calvin Theological Journal 25, '90, 28–44 'partners of the Deity').—Also specif. of sexual characteristics (Diod. S. 16, 26, 6 originally παρθένοι prophesied in Delphi διὰ τὸ τῆς φύσεως ἀδιάφθορον=because their sexuality was uncorrupted. φύσις of sex and its change Dicaearchus, fgm. 37 W.; ἑρμαφροδίτου φ. Iren. 1, 11, 5 [Harv. I 108, 8]. Obviously φ. also has the concrete mng. 'sex organ': Nicander, fgm. 107; Diod. S. 32, 10, 7 φ. ἄρρενος corresponding to φ. θηλείας following immediately; Anton. Lib. 41, 5; Phlegon: 257 fgm. 36, 2, 1 Jac.). In the context of Mary's virginal delivery ἐραυνήσω τὴν φύσιν αὐτῆς=*I will examine whether she remains a virgin* GJs 19:3b; 20:1 (where Tdf. with codd. reads ἔβαλε Σαλώμη τὸν δάκτυλον αὐτῆς εἰς τὴν φύσιν αὐτῆς [cp. J 20:25]). The hyena παρ' ἐνιαυτὸν ἀλλάσσει τὴν φύσιν *changes its nature every year,* fr. male to female and vice versa B 10:7 (s. ὕαινα). Polytheists worship τοῖς φύσει μὴ οὖσιν θεοῖς *beings that are by nature no gods at all* **Gal 4:8** (s. CLanger, Euhemeros u. die Theorie der φύσει u. θέσει θεοί: Αγγελος II 1926, 53–59; Mel., P. 8, 58 φύσει θεὸς ὢν καὶ ἄνθρωπος; Synes., Prov. 1, 9 p. 97c τοῖς φύσει θεοῖς; Diod. S. 3, 9, 1 differentiates between two kinds of gods: some αἰώνιον ἔχειν κ. ἄφθαρτον τὴν φύσιν, others θνητῆς φύσεως κεκοινωνηκέναι κ. δι' ἀρετὴν . . . τετευχέναι τιμῶν ἀθανάτων=some 'have an everlasting and incorruptible nature', others 'share mortal nature and then, because of their personal excellence, . . . attain immortal honors').—ὅταν ἔθνη φύσει τὰ τοῦ νόμου ποιῶσιν *when gentiles spontaneously* (i.e. without extraneous legal instruction; cp. the prophetic ideal Jer 31:32–34) *fulfill the demands of the (Mosaic) law* **Ro 2:14** (s. WMundle, Theol. Blätter 13, '34, 249–56 [the gentile as Christian under direction of the πνεῦμα]; difft. s. 3 below).

❸ **the regular or established order of things,** ***nature*** (Ar. 4, 2 κατὰ ἀπαραίτητον φύσεως ἀνάγκην=in accordance with the non-negotiable order of things; Ath. 3, 1 νόμῳ φύσεως) μετήλλαξαν τὴν φυσικὴν χρῆσιν εἰς τὴν παρὰ φύσιν *they exchanged the natural function for one contrary to nature* **Ro 1:26** (Diod. S. 32, 11, 1 παρὰ φύσιν ὁμιλία; Appian, Bell. Civ. 1, 109 §511; Athen. 13, 605d οἱ παρὰ φύσιν τῇ Ἀφροδίτῃ χρώμενοι=those who indulge in Aphrodite contrary to nature; TestNapht 3:4; Philo, Spec. Leg. 3, 39 ὁ παιδεραστὴς τὴν παρὰ φύσιν ἡδονὴν διώκει=a lover of boys pursues unnatural pleasure; Jos., C. Ap. 2, 273; Tat. 3:4; Ath. 26, 2; on φ. as definer of order s. JKube, ΤΕΧΝΗ und ΑΡΕΤΗ '69, esp. 44–46; on relation to κτίσις in Paul, s. OWischmeyer, ZTK 93, '96, 352–75). ὅταν ἔθνη φύσει τὰ τοῦ νόμου ποιῶσιν *when gentiles fulfil the law's demands by following the natural order* (of things) **Ro 2:14** (cp. Ltzm., Hdb., exc. on Ro 2:14–16; but s. 2 above). ἡ φύσις διδάσκει ὑμᾶς **1 Cor 11:14** (Epict. 1, 16, 9f; Plut., Mor. 478d; Synes., Calv. [Baldhead] 14 p. 78c φύσις as well as νόμος prescribes long hair for women, short hair for men.—Ltzm., Hdb. ad loc.). τὸ ὄνομα, ὃ κέκτησθε φύσει δικαίᾳ *the name which you bear because of a just natural order* IEph 1:1 (s. Hdb. ad loc.—τῇ φ. τὸ ἀγαθὸν ἀνώφορόν ἐστιν Did., Gen. 21, 5.—JKleist, transl. '46, 119 n. 2 suggests 'natural disposition').—RGrant, Miracle and Natural Law '52, 4–18.

❹ **an entity as a product of nature,** ***natural being, creature*** (X., Cyr. 6, 2, 29 πᾶσα φύσις=every creature; 3 Macc 3:29.—Diod. S. 2, 49, 4 plants are called φύσεις καρποφοροῦσαι; 3, 6, 2 θνητὴ φ.= a mortal creature. Ps.-Callisth. 1, 10, 1 ἀνθρωπίνη φ. = a human creature. It can also mean *species* [X. et al.; 4 Macc 1:20; Philo] and then at times disappear in translation: Ps.-Pla, Epin. 948d ἡ τῶν ἄστρων φύσις=the stars; X., Lac. 3, 4 ἡ τῶν θηλειῶν φύσις=the women; Aristot., Part. An. 1, 5 περὶ τῆς ζῳϊκῆς φ.=on animals) πᾶσα φύσις θηρίων κτλ. **Js 3:7a.** Also prob. ἡ φ. ἡ ἀνθρωπίνη *humankind* **3:7b;** s. 2 above.—Kl. Pauly IV 841–44 (lit.).—DELG s.v. φύομαι C 6. M-M. EDNT. TW. Sv.

φυσίωσις, εως, ἡ (φυσιόω; in non-biblical wr. as a medical t.t. and in Achmes 153, 6; otherw. a Christian word; Hesych.) lit. 'inflated/bloated condition', in our lit. ***swelled-headedness, pride, conceit*** **2 Cor 12:20.**

φυτεία, ας, ἡ (X., Theophr. et al.; pap [e.g. POxy 1778, 31], LXX; PsSol 14:4; GrBar 4:8; AscIs 4:3 and Jos., Ant. 3, 281 in the sense 'planting') **that which is planted,** ***a plant*** (Aelian, VH 3, 40; Athen. 5, 207d; OGI 606, 7; Philo, Op. M. 41) in imagery (PsSol 14:4) **Mt 15:13;** ITr 11:1; IPhld 3:1 (w. Ign. cp. Synes., Prov. 10 p. 100d of the truly good man: ἔστιν ἐπὶ γῆς φυτὸν οὐράνιον after Pla., Tim. 90a).—M-M.

φυτεύω impf. ἐφύτευον; 1 aor. ἐφύτευσα; pf. 3 pl. πεφύτευκαν Ezk 19:13. Pass.: 1 aor. ἐφυτεύθην: pf. πεφύτευμαι, ptc. πεφυτευμένος (Hom.+; ins, pap, LXX; pseudepigr.; Philo; Jos., Bell. 3, 516, Ant. 11, 50 ἀμπέλους; Just., D. 110, 4 φυτευθεῖσα . . . ἄμπελος) *to plant* τὶ *someth.* φυτείαν (q.v.; cp. SibOr 3, 397) **Mt 15:13;** a tree (since Od. 18, 359) Dg 12:3; cp. pass. 12:2, 4; **Lk 13:6** (foll. by ἔν τινι as X., Oec. 20, 3); B 11:6 (Ps 1:3; foll. by παρά τι); sticks Hs 8, 2, 6; 8ab; pass. 8, 2, 7; 8, 3, 8; 8, 4, 2. φυτεύθητι ἐν τῇ θαλάσσῃ *be planted in the sea* **Lk 17:6.** ἀμπελῶνα *a vineyard* (s. ἀμπελών) **Mt 21:33; Mk 12:1; Lk 20:9; 1 Cor 9:7;** cp. Hs 5, 5, 2; 5, 6, 2. εἰς μέρος τι τοῦ ἀγροῦ ἐφύτευσεν ἀμπελῶνα *he had a part of his field planted as a vineyard* 5, 2, 2. Abs. (X., Mem. 2, 1, 13) **Lk 17:28;** in imagery Dg 12:6 and of the apostle's work (w. ποτίζειν) **1 Cor 3:6–8** (Libanius, Or. 13, 52 vol. II p. 82, 2 F.: τὸ καλὸν ἐγὼ μὲν ἐφύτευσα, σὺ δὲ ἔθρεψας, αἱ δὲ πόλεις δρέπονται).—BHHW III 1441–43.—M-M.

φυτόν, οῦ, τό (φύω; Hom.+) ***a plant*** ApcPt 5:15.—B. 521; BHHW III 1441–43.

φύω (Hom.+) fut. 3 pl. φυήσουσι Is 37:32 (trans.); pf. (intr.) 3 pl. πεφύκασι (Tat. 8, 2), ptc., neut. πεφυκότα 1 Macc 4:38. Pass.: 2 aor. ἐφύην, ptc. φυείς, neut. φυέν (for earlier 2 aor. act. ἔφυν; 3 pl. ἔφυσαν [Ath. 22, 9]; ptc. φύς, φύν [Ath., R. 16 p. 68, 9 φύντας acc. pl.]; inf. φῦναι [TestSol]). The 2 aor. pass. forms appear in Hippocr. and later wr., incl. Joseph. (e.g. Ant. 17, 19; 18, 6; beside them φύς Ant. 1, 63; 4, 245; φῦναι 18, 43); CIG 8735.—B-D-F § 76, 2; W-S. §13, 11; Mlt-H. 264; Rob. 350. On the LXX s. Thackeray p. 235, 289f.—In our lit. the word has intr. aspect, even in the pres. act. (s. B-D-F §309, 2; Rob. 800; SibOr 8, 21) ***grow (up), come up*** lit. **Lk 8:6, 8.** In imagery ῥίζα πικρίας ἄνω φύουσα **Hb 12:15** (Dt 29:17).—DELG s.v. φύομαι. M-M.

φωλεός, οῦ, ὁ (Aristot. et al.; TestSol 6:4 D; Jos., Bell. 4, 507) **hole for animals, *den, lair, hole*** (Aristot., Plut., Lucian et al.; Herm. Wr. 406, 12 Sc.) of a fox-hole (Neptunianus [II AD] ed. WGemoll, Progr. Striegau 1884, 27) **Mt 8:20; Lk 9:58** (cp. Plut., Tib. Gr. 828 [9, 5] animals have φωλ., but those who are fighting for Italy are without shelter).—DELG. M-M.

φωνέω (φωνή) impf. ἐφώνουν; fut. φωνήσω; 1 aor. ἐφώνησα, pass. ἐφωνήθην (Hom.+; ins, pap [though not common in either]; LXX; En 14:8; TestSol 12:3 C; TestJob 27:4; GrBar, Philo, Joseph.)

❶ **to produce a voiced sound/tone, freq. w. ref. to intensity of tone—**ⓐ of animals (Aristot.; Anton. Lib. 7, 8; Is 38:14; Jer 17:11; Zeph 2:14) of a cock: ***crow*** (Aesop, Fab. 225 H.=268 H-H.; 323b H.=84 H-H. III) **Mt 26:34, 74f; Mk 14:30, 68 v.l., 72ab; Lk 22:34, 60f; J 13:38; 18:27.**

ⓑ of humans ***call/cry out, speak loudly, say with emphasis* Lk 8:8;** sim. [ἐφώ]νει ὁ ἔχων ὦ[τ]α τ[ῶν ἀ]περάντων [ἀ]κο[ύει]ν ἀκουέτω *(Jesus) cried out, 'Let one who has ears to hear the things that are without limits (or that never end) hear/listen'* Ox 1081, 5f (restoration based on the Coptic SJCh 89, 4, s. Borger, GGA 122). φ. (v.l. κράξαν) φωνῇ μεγάλῃ *in a loud voice* **Mk 1:26** (of an evil spirit in a pers.); **Lk 23:46; Ac 16:28; Rv 14:18** (w. dat. of the pers. for whom the call is meant; κραυγῇ μεγάλῃ **v.l.**). ἐφώνησεν λέγων **Lk 8:54; Ac 16:28; Rv 14:18** (of an angel issuing an order; s. PGM 13, 148). Also φωνήσας εἶπεν **Lk 16:24; 23:46.**

❷ **to use an attribution in speaking of a person, *address as*** ὑμεῖς φωνεῖτέ με: ὁ διδάσκαλος *you call me 'Teacher'* (nom. w. art. as voc.; s. B-D-F §143; 147, 3; Rob. 458; 466) **J 13:13.**

❸ **to call to oneself, *summon*** (Tob 5:9) τινά *someone* (Jos., Vi. 172, Ant. 6, 314) ὁ Ἰησοῦς ἐφώνησεν αὐτούς **Mt 20:32.** Cp. **27:47; Mk 3:31 v.l.** (for καλοῦντες); **9:35; 10:49ab; 15:35; J 1:48; 2:9; 4:16; 11:28a; 18:33; Ac 4:18** D; **9:41; 10:7.** τὸν Λάζαρον ἐφώνησεν ἐκ τοῦ μνημείου **J 12:17.**—τὰ πρόβατα φωνεῖ κατ' ὄνομα **10:3** (s. καλέω 1a). *Have* τινά *someone called* **Mk 10:49c; Lk 16:2; J 9:18, 24; 11:28b.** Pass. εἶπεν φωνηθῆναι αὐτῷ τοὺς δούλους *he said the slaves should be called into his presence* **Lk 19:15.** W. obj. omitted φωνήσαντες ἐπυνθάνοντο *they called* (someone) *and inquired* **Ac 10:18.**

❹ **to extend hospitality through invitation, *invite*** τινά *someone* **Lk 14:12.**—DELG s.v. φωνή. M-M. TW.

φωνή, ῆς, ἡ (s. prec. entry; Hom.+).—❶ **an auditory effect, *sound, tone, noise*** the source of which is added in the gen.: of musical instruments (Pla., Rep. 3, 397a ὀργάνων; Eur., Tro. 127 συρίγγων; Plut., Mor. 713c ψαλτηρίου καὶ αὐλοῦ; Aristoxenus, fgm. 6; Paus. Attic. α, 169; Ex 19:16, Is 18:3 and PsSol 8:1 σάλπιγγος; cp. ParJer 3:2; Is 24:8 κιθάρας; Aristobul. in Eus., PE 8, 10, 13=p. 144, 94f Holladay) σάλπιγγος **Mt 24:31 v.l.;** D 16:6. φωναὶ τῆς σάλπιγγος *blasts of the trumpet* **Rv 8:13b;** or of those who play them κιθαρῳδῶν **14:2d; 18:22a;** cp. **10:7.** Of the noise made by a millstone **18:22b.** Of a shout produced by a crowd of people φωνὴ ὄχλου πολλοῦ **19:1, 6a** (cp. Da 10:6 Theod.; also λαοῦ πολλοῦ PsSol 8:2). Of the sound caused by spoken words (Da 10:9; Just., D. 131, 2 μηδὲ μέχρι φωνῆς) ἡ φωνὴ τοῦ ἀσπασμοῦ σου **Lk 1:44.** φωνὴ ῥημάτων *sound of words* **Hb 12:19.** Cp. 1 Cl 27:7 (Ps 18:4). ἔσομαι φωνή *I will be just a meaningless sound* (in contrast to Ignatius functioning as a λόγος θεοῦ [=meaningful expression of God] if his adherents abstain from pleas in his behalf) IRo 2:1 (s. ἠχώ). Abs. of the sound made by a wail of sorrow (cp. TestJob 40:9; TestIss 1:4) **Mt 2:18** (Jer 38:15). μεγάλη φωνὴ ἐγένετο ἐν τ. οὐρανῷ GPt 9:35.—Of musical instruments it is said that they φωνὴν διδόναι *produce sound* (in ref. to mere sonant capability in contrast to distinguishable notes) **1 Cor 14:7f.**—In **Rv** we have ἀστραπαὶ καὶ φωναὶ καὶ βρονταί (cp. Ex 19:16) **4:5; 8:5; 11:19; 16:18** (are certain other sounds in nature thought of here in addition to thunder, as e.g. the roar of the storm? In Ex 19:16 φωναὶ κ. ἀστραπαί are surely thunder and lightning. But in Ex 9:23, 28; 1 Km 12:18 the mng. of φωναί remains unclear. Cp. also Esth 1:1d φωναί, βρονταί).—Freq. in imagery: of wind sound **J 3:8;** cp. **Ac 2:6.** Of thunderclap (1 Km 7:10; GrBar 6:13) **Rv 6:1; 14:2c; 19:6c.** Of roar of water (Ezk 1:24b) **1:15b; 14:2b; 19:6b.** Of whirring of wings (Ezk 1:24a) **9:9a.** Of the clatter of chariots **9:9 b** (cp. Ezk 3:13; 26:10).

❷ **the faculty of utterance, *voice*** (Tat. 15:3 προύχει τῶν θηρίων ὁ ἄνθρωπος κατὰ τὴν ἔναρθον φωνήν=humankind excels beasts in articulate utterance)

ⓐ gener. of sonant aspect: any form of speech or other utterance w. the voice can take place μετὰ φωνῆς μεγάλης **Lk 17:15;** ἐν φωνῇ μεγάλῃ **Rv 5:2; 14:7, 9;** mostly φωνῇ μεγάλῃ (TestAbr A 5 p. 82, 20f [Stone p. 12]; ParJer 2:2; Achilles Tat. 8, 1, 1; SibOr 3, 669; 5, 63) **Mt 27:46, 50; Mk 1:26; 5:7; 15:34; Lk 1:42 v.l.** (s. κραυγή 1b); **4:33; 8:28; 19:37; J 11:43; Ac 7:57, 60; 8:7; Rv 6:10; 7:2, 10** al.; IPhld 7:1a. μεγάλῃ τῇ φωνῇ (Diod. S. 1, 70, 5; 8, 23, 3; Lucian, Hist. Conscr. 1, Tim. 9; ParJer 9:8; Jos., Bell. 6, 188) **Ac 14:10 v.l. 26:24;** ἐν ἰσχυρᾷ φωνῇ **Rv 18:2.** ἐν φωνῇ μιᾷ IEph 4:2; μιᾷ φ. (Pla., Laws 1, 634e; Diod. S. 11, 9, 3; 11, 26, 6; 19, 81, 2; Ael. Aristid. 24, 4 K.=44 p. 825 D.; Lucian, Nigr. 14) ApcPt 5:19.—αἴρειν φωνήν (αἴρω 1b) **Lk 17:13;** πρός τινα **Ac 4:24.** ἐπαίρειν φωνήν (ParJer 9:14; s. ἐπαίρω 1) **Lk 11:27; Ac 2:14; 14:11; 22:22;** AcPl Ha 6, 33. ἀκούειν τῆς φωνῆς τινος *hear someone speaking* or *calling* (TestAbr B 3 p. 107, 10 [Stone p. 62]; TestJob 42:3; TestJos 9:4; ParJer 3:10) **J 5:25, 28; 10:3; Hb 3:7, 15; 4:7** (the last three Ps 94:7); w. a neg. and acc. (φωνήν) **Mt 12:19** (cp. Is 42:2); **J 5:37.** The same expr.=*listen to someone's speech* or *call, follow someone* (Gen 3:17) **10:16, 27; 18:37; Rv 3:20;** B 8:7; cp. 9:2 (s. Ex 15:26).—(ἡ) φωνὴ (τοῦ) νυμφίου (cp. Jer 25:10) **J 3:29** (cp. Arrian, Cyneg. 17, 1 the dogs χαίρουσιν τὴν φωνὴν τοῦ δεσπότου γνωρίζουσαι); **Rv 18:23.**

ⓑ *voice* as it varies from individual to individual or fr. one mood to another (X., An. 2, 6, 9; Gen 27:22; Tat. 5:2) ἐπιγνοῦσα τὴν φωνὴν τοῦ Πέτρου **Ac 12:14.** Cp. **J 10:4f** (s. Ael. Aristid. 46 p. 320, horses). ἤθελον ἀλλάξαι τὴν φωνήν μου **Gal 4:20** (ἀλλάσσω 1; φωνή=tone: Diod. S 8, 5, 4 πᾶσαν φωνήν=every variation in tone; Artem. 4, 56 p. 235, 15).

ⓒ that which the voice gives expression to: *call, cry, outcry, loud* or *solemn declaration* (Sb 7251, 21 [III/IV AD]=order, command) ὁ Ἰησοῦς ἀφεὶς φωνὴν μεγάλην **Mk 15:37.** φωνὴ ἐγένετο μία *a single outcry arose* **Ac 19:34** (cp. Jos., Vi. 133). Cp. **22:14; 24:21.** Pl. (Ael. Aristid. 52, 3 K.=28 p. 551 D.: ἦσαν φωναί; Jos., Vi. 231, Ant. 15, 52) φωναὶ μεγάλαι *loud cries* **Lk 23:23a;** cp. **23b.** ἐλάλησαν αἱ βρονταὶ τὰς ἑαυτῶν φωνάς *the thunders sounded forth their crashing peals* **Rv 10:3b.** θεοῦ φωνὴ (D φωναί) καὶ οὐκ ἀνθρώπου (this is) *the utterance of a god and not of a mere mortal* **Ac 12:22** (Just., D. 119, 6 τῇ φωνῇ τοῦ θεοῦ; cp. 21, 1 αἱ φωναὶ αὐτοῦ; Plut., Mor. 567f: a divine φωνή sounds forth fr. a φῶς μέγα that appears suddenly; Ael. Aristid. 45 p. 11 D.: Πυθίας φωνή; Epict. 3, 23, 20 ἰδοὺ φωναὶ φιλοσόφου; 3, 22, 50; Biogr. p. 454 people received sayings of Hippocr. ὡς θεοῦ φωνὰς κ. οὐκ ἀνθρωπίνου προελθούσας ἐκ στόματος). φωνὴ ἐνεχθεῖσα αὐτῷ *a* *declaration (was) borne to him* **2 Pt 1:17;** cp. vs. **18.** Also of sayings in scripture αἱ φωναὶ τῶν προφητῶν **Ac 13:27** (Ath. 9, 1; cp. Diod. S. 19, 1, 4 ἡ Σόλωνος φωνή; 20, 30, 2 τῆς τοῦ μάντεως [=τοῦ δαιμονίου] φωνῆς; Diog. L. 8, 14 sayings of Pythagoras). Of apostolic tradition τὰ παρὰ ζώσης φωνῆς καὶ μενούσης Papias (2:4) (s. ζάω, end; on Papias' 'living voice' s. ABaum, NTS 44, '98, 144–51).

ⓓ In accordance w. OT and Jewish usage gener. (s. Bousset, Rel.[3] 315. The Socratic δαιμόνιον [=ὁ θεός Ep. 1, 7] is called ἡ φωνή: Socrat., Ep. 1, 9 [p. 222, 34 Malherbe] τὸ δαιμόνιόν μοι, ἡ φωνή, γέγονεν, cp. Pla., Apol. 31d) 'the voice' oft. speaks, though the (heavenly) speaker neither appears nor is mentioned (cp. PGM 3, 119 ἐξορκίζω σε κατὰ τῆς ἑβραικῆς φωνῆς.—In most cases the divine voice is differentiated fr. the divinity: Theopompus [IV BC]: 115 fgm. 69 Jac. [in Diog. L. 1, 115] when Epimenides wishes to build τὸ τῶν Νυμφῶν ἱερόν: ῥαγῆναι φωνὴν ἐξ οὐρανοῦ "Ἐπιμενίδη, μὴ Νυμφῶν, ἀλλὰ Διός'=[when E. was building] a shrine for the Nymphs: a voice cried out from heaven, "Epimenides! Not for the Nymphs, but for Zeus!"; Plut., Mor. 355e; 775b; Oenomaus in Eus., PE 5, 28, 2 Lycurgus receives the laws ὑπὸ τῆς θεοῦ φωνῆς in Delphi; Artapanus; 726 fgm. 3, 21 Jac. [in Eus., PE 9, 27, 21]; Jos., Ant. 1, 185 φ. θεία παρῆν; 3, 90 φ. ὑψόθεν; cp. 2, 267) ἰδοὺ φωνὴ ἐκ τῶν οὐρανῶν λέγουσα (on the voice fr. heaven s. the lit. s.v. βαπτίζω 2a; also JKosnetter, D. Taufe Jesu '36, esp. 140–90, and FDölger, AC V/3, '36, 218–23) **Mt 3:17;** cp. **17:5.** ἦλθεν φ. (ἐκ) **Mk 9:7 v.l.; J 12:28; 30 v.l.** (TestAbr A 10 p. 88, 15 [Stone p. 24] al.; cp. Ps. Callisth, 1, 45, 2f ἦλθεν φωνὴ ἀπὸ τοῦ ἀδύτου the divine saying follows in direct discourse). ἐξῆλθεν φ. **Rv 16:17** (ἐκ); **19:5** (ἀπό τοῦ θρόνου). γίνεται (ἐγένετο) φ. (ἐκ: Plut., Agis et Cleom. 807 [28, 3]: φωνὴν ἐκ τοῦ ἱεροῦ γενέσθαι φράζουσαν; Ael. Aristid. 40, 22 K.=5 p. 62 D.: φωνῆς θείας γενομένης . . . ἐκ τοῦ μητρῴου [=temple of the Mother of the Gods]) **Mk 1:11; 9:7; Lk 3:22; 9:35f; J 12:30** (v.l. ἦλθεν; s. above); **Ac 10:13, 15** (both πρὸς αὐτόν); MPol 9:1a; GEb 18, 37 (verb of origin understood), cp. ibid. ln. 38; ἐγένετο φ. κυρίου **Ac 7:31** (cp. Jos., Vi. 259 ἐγένοντο φωναί). ἀπεκρίθη φ. ἐκ τ. οὐρανοῦ **11:9;** ἦχος φωνῆς μοι ἀπεκρίθη Hv 4, 1, 4. ἀκούειν φωνήν *hear a voice* (also w. such additions as λέγουσαν, ἐκ w. gen. of place, μεγάλην, gen. of the speaker) **Ac 9:4; 22:9; 26:14; Rv 6:6f; 9:13; 10:4, 8; 12:10; 14:2; 18:4;** MPol 9:1b; EpilMosq 4; φωνῆς w. the same mng. (w. corresp. additions) **Ac 9:7; 11:7; 22:7** (MMeyer, The Light and Voice on the Damascus Road: Forum 2, '86, 27–35 [Nag Hammadi pp. 30–32]); **Rv 11:12; 14:13; 16:1; 21:3;** GPt 10:41. Paul speaks διὰ φωνῆς πνεύματος ἁγίου AcPl Ha 11, 5.

ⓔ special cases: ἐπέστρεψα βλέπειν τὴν φωνὴν ἥτις ἐλάλει μετ' ἐμοῦ *I turned around to see* (to whom) *the voice that was speaking to me* (belonged) **Rv 1, 12** (cp. X., Hell. 5, 1, 22 σκεψόμενοι τίς ἡ κραυγή; Aesop 248b H.=141 P.=146 H-H. ἐπεστράφη πρὸς τὴν φ.). φ. βοῶντος ἐν τῇ ἐρήμῳ *(it is) the voice of one calling out in the wilderness* (Is 40:3; cp. En 9:2; Jos., Bell. 6, 301) **Mt 3:3; Mk 1:3; Lk 3:4.** Referring to Is 40:3, John the Baptist applies its words to himself **J 1:23** *the voice of one calling out in the wilderness* (Ael. Aristid. 49, 5 K.=25 p. 489 D.: φ. λέγοντός του 'τεθεράπευσαι'; Ps.-Pla., Axioch. 1 p. 364a φωνὴ βοῶντός του).—B 9:3.

❸ **a verbal code shared by a community to express ideas and feelings,** ***language*** (Aeschyl., Hdt. et al.; Cebes 33, 6; Aelian, VH 12, 48; Herodian 5, 3, 4; Diog. L. 8, 3; SEG VIII, 548, 17 [I BC]; PLond I, 77, 13 p. 232 [Christ. VIII AD]; PGM 12, 188 πᾶσα γλῶσσα κ. πᾶσα φωνή; Gen 11:1; Dt 28:49; 2 Macc 7:8, 21, 27; 4 Macc 12:7; Jos., C. Ap. 1, 1; 50; 73 al.; Just., A I, 31, 1; Tat. 37, 1; Mel., P. 29, 199) **1 Cor 14:10f; 2 Pt 2:16** (an animal w. ἀνθρώπου φ. as Appian, Bell. Civ. 4:4 §14 βοῦς φωνὴν ἀφῆκεν ἀνθρώπου; schol. on Appolon. Rhod. 2, 1146 ὁ κριὸς ἀνθρωπίνῃ χρησάμενος φωνῇ; sim. TestAbr A 3 p. 79, 19 [Stone p. 6]; sim. TestAbr B 3 p. 107, 10 [St. p. 62] a tree; ParJer 7:2 an eagle; Philo, Op. M. 156); Dg 5:1. ὁ λέων εἶπεν μιᾷ φωνῇ AcPlHa 5, 4 (on the probability that μια was misread for θεια s. the editor's note, p. 41, 4).—B. 1248; 1260. DELG. M-M. EDNT. TW. Sv.

φῶς, φωτός, τό (trag.+ [in Hom. φάος or φόως]; loanw. in rabb.) 'light'

❶ **light in contrast to darkness,** ***light***—ⓐ in the physical realm καθόλου τὸ φῶς μὴ βλέπειν (of Judas) Papias (3:2).—Opp. σκότος, as Job 18:18; En 104:8; PGM 5, 101; 7, 262; 13, 335; Theoph. Ant. 1, 2 (p. 60, 7) **2 Cor 4:6** (cp. Gen 1:3ff); **6:14.** Not present at night **J 11:10.** λευκὸς ὡς τὸ φ. **Mt 17:2.** νεφέλη φωτός a bright cloud vs. **5 v.l.** (TestAbr A 9 p. 87, 12 [Stone p. 22]). Of the light of the sun (φ. ἡλίου: Dio Chrys. 57 [74], 20 fr. Eur., Hippol. 617; Ael. Aristid. 45, 29 K.=8 p. 95 D; ApcZeph; Just., D. 128, 4; τὸ φ. τοῦ ἡλίου Theoph. Ant. 1, 2 [p. 60, 16]) **Rv 22:5b;** of a wondrous star IEph 19:2ab. Of lamp-light (Jer 25:10; Jos., Ant. 12, 319) **Lk 8:16; 11:33** (v.l. φέγγος); **J 5:35** (in imagery); **Rv 18:23; 22:5a.** Light fr. a transcendent source (Ael. Aristid. 49, 46 K.=p. 500, 17 D. ἐγένετο φῶς παρὰ τῆς Ἴσιδος; Marinus, Vi. Procli 23: a halo of light around Proclus' head moves the beholder to προσκύνησις): an angel **Ac 12:7; 2 Cor 11:14** (here ἄγγελος φωτός [cp. 1QS 3:20] is a messenger of the world of light in contrast to Satan); of Paul's conversion experience **Ac 9:3; 22:6** (both w. ἐκ τοῦ οὐρανοῦ, as X., Cyr. 4, 2, 15; Dio Chrys. 11 [12], 29), **9, 11; 26:13** (οὐρανόθεν); the heavenly city **Rv 21:24** (s. also bα below). ἐφάνη φῶς μέγα ἐν τῷ σπηλαίῳ *a bright light appeared in the cave* GJs 19:2, followed by φῶς ἐκεῖνο ὑπεστέλλετο *that light faded out.* ἦν τὸ ὄρος ἐκεῖνο διαφαίνων (pap=διαφαῖνον) αὐτῇ φ. *that mountain was shining a light for her* GJs 22:3.—In imagery: (εἰς φ. ἐλθεῖν='become apparent' Hippol., Ref. 4, 28, 4) ἐν τῷ φωτί *in the open, publicly* (φ. of 'the open' X., Ages. 9, 1.—Opp. ἐν τῇ σκοτίᾳ) **Mt 10:27; Lk 12:3** (Proverbia Aesopi 104 P.: ἅπερ ἐν νυκτὶ καλύπτεται, ταῦτα εἰς φῶς λαληθέντα . . . 'what is hidden in the night gets talked about in the light'). Of an evil-doer it is said: μισεῖ τὸ φῶς καὶ οὐκ ἔρχεται πρὸς τὸ φῶς **J 3:20** (cp. Eur., Iph. T. 1026 κλεπτῶν γὰρ ἡ νύξ, τῆς δ' ἀληθείας τὸ φῶς=the night's for thieves, the light's for truth; Plut., Mor. 82b, Contra Volupt. in Stob., Anthol. 3, 6, 33 vol. III 299 H.; Philo, De Jos. 68, Spec. Leg. 1, 319–23; TestNapht 2:10).

ⓑ in a transcendent sense—**α.** the passages in the central portion of 1a above show that light is the element and sphere of the divine (Ael. Aristid. 28, 114 K.=49 p. 528 D.: τοῦ θεοῦ φῶς; SibOr 3, 787 ἀθάνατον φ.; Tat. 13, 2 λόγος . . . ἐστὶ τὸ τοῦ θεοῦ φ.—Iren. 1, 4, 1 [Harv. I 32, 1]). God is called φῶς οἰκῶν ἀπρόσιτον **1 Ti 6:16** (Plut., Pericl. 173 [39, 2] the gods dwell in τὸν τόπον ἀσάλευτον φωτὶ καθαρωτάτῳ περιλαμπόμενον, Mor. 567f: the divine φωνή proceeds fr. a φῶς μέγα that suddenly shines forth), or it is said that God dwells ἐν τῷ φωτί **1J 1:7b.** In fact, God is described as light pure and simple ὁ θεὸς φῶς ἐστιν vs. **5** (Philo, Somn. 1, 75; cp. TestJob 4:1 εἶπεν τὸ φῶς; ParJer 6:12; Ath. 31, 3 πάντα δὲ φῶς αὐτὸν ὄντα.—OSchaefer, StKr 105, '33, 467–76). Cp. Dg 9:6. Likew. the Divine Redeemer (ParJer 9:14 τὸ φῶς τῶν αἰώνων πάντων) in the Fourth Gospel: **J 1:7–9** (FAuer, Wie ist J 1:9 zu verstehen?: ThGl 28, '36, 397–407); **12:35ab, 36ab** (for **1J 2:8** s. β; on divinity as light s. RCharles, The Book of Enoch 1912, 71f; GWetter, Phōs [ΦΩΣ] 1915. S. also MDibelius, Die Vorstellung v. göttl. Licht: Deutsche Literaturzeitung 36, 1915,

1469–83 and MNilsson, GGA 1916, 49ff; FDölger, Die Sonne der Gerechtigkeit 1918, Sol Salutis 1920; WBousset, Kyrios Christos 2, 1921, 173; 174, 2 and 3; HJonas, Gnosis u. spätantiker Geist I '34; Dodd 133–36; 183–87 al.; EGoodenough, By Light, Light: The Mystic Gospel of Hellenistic Judaism '35; RBultmann, Z. Gesch. der Lichtsymbolik im Altertum: Philol 97, '48, 1–36; 1QH 4:6; 18:29; BGU 597, 33 [I AD]). Jesus calls himself τὸ φῶς τοῦ κόσμου **J 8:12a; 9:5; 12:46;** cp. **3:19a** (Mel., P. 103, 795; Wetter, 'Ich bin das Licht der Welt': Beiträge zur Religionswissenschaft I/2, 1914, 171ff), and is called τὸ φῶς τῶν ἀνθρώπων **1:4** (Ael. Aristid. 45, 33 K.=8 p. 97 D.: Sarapis as κοινὸν ἅπασιν ἀνθρώποις φῶς; hymn to Anubis fr. Kios [IAndrosIsis, p. 139] 7: Isis as φῶς πᾶσι βροτοῖσι). His very being is light and life (ζωή 2aβ; s. JWeisengoff, CBQ 8, '46, 448–51) **1:4.** Cp. also vs. **5; 3:19b, 21; Lk 2:32** (Jesus is a φῶς εἰς ἀποκάλυψιν ἐθνῶν).—FDölger, Lumen Christi: AC V/1, '35, 1–43. The martyr καθαρὸν φῶς λαμβάνει *receives the pure light* of heaven IRo 6:2.

β. light, that illuminates the spirit and soul of humans (OdeSol 11:19 μεταβληθέντες ἀπὸ σκότους εἰς τὸ φῶς; JosAs 15:13 ἀναγαγεῖν με εἰς τὸ φῶς; Mel., P. 68, 491 ῥυσάμενος … ἐκ σκότους εἰς φῶς; Philosoph. Max. 499, 39 σωφροσύνη … ψυχῆς φῶς ἐστιν), is gener. the element in which the redeemed person lives, rich in blessings without and within (En 5:6 σωτηρία, φῶς ἀγαθόν; vs. 8 φ. καὶ χάρις; PsSol 3:12 ἡ ζωὴ αὐτῶν ἐν φωτὶ κυρίου): τότε ῥαγήσεται πρώϊμον τὸ φῶς σου *then your light will break out early in the morning* B 3:4 (Is 58:8; s. πρόϊμος, end). Of God δεῖξαι αὐτῷ (God's servant) φῶς 1 Cl 16:12 (Is 53:11); of Messianic salvation, the gospel, etc. (opp. σκοτία, σκότος) **Mt 4:16ab;** AcPl Ha 8, 32f (Is 9:1ab; cp. Lucian, Nigr. 4 ἔχαιρον ὥσπερ ἐκ ζοφεροῦ ἀέρος ἐς μέγα φῶς ἀναβλέπων 'I rejoiced, looking up as it were from a gloomy atmosphere into a bright light'); **Ac 26:18; Eph 5:13; Col 1:12; 1 Pt 2:9;** 1 Cl 36:2; 59:2; 2 Cl 1:4. τὸ φῶς τῆς ζωῆς (cp. 1QS 3:7) **J 8:12b.** τὸ φῶς τὸ ἀληθινόν (ParJer 9:3 φ. ἀληθινόν; cp. τὸ τῆς ἀληθείας φ. Did., Gen. 87, 23f; Orig., C. Cels. 5, 13, 20; saying of Pythagoreans: WienerStud 8, 1886 p. 280 no. 118 in contrast to σκότος; cp. TestJob 43:6 ὁ τοῦ σκότους καὶ οὐχὶ τοῦ φωτός [of Elihu]) **1J 2:8,** cp. **J 1:9** (s. α above). φῶς καταγγέλλειν **Ac 26:23.** To be filled w. Christian truth means ἐν τῷ φωτὶ περιπατεῖν **1J 1:7a,** εἶναι **2:9,** μένειν vs. **10.** Such persons are called υἱοὶ τοῦ φωτός **Lk 16:8; J 12:36c** (cp. 1QS 1:9 et passim); **1 Th 5:5;** τέκνα φωτός **Eph 5:8b** (ESelwyn, 1 Pt '46, 375–82; KKuhn, NTS 7, '61, 339: 1QS 3:20; 5:9, 10); τέκνα φωτὸς ἀληθείας IPhld 2:1 (Porphyr., Ep. ad Marcellam 20 φῶς τοῦ θεοῦ τῆς ἀληθείας; Simplicius p. 88, 3; 138, 30 Düb. τὸ τῆς ἀληθείας φῶς). They put on τὰ ὅπλα τοῦ φωτός **Ro 13:12,** travel the ὁδὸς τοῦ φωτός B 18:1; 19:1, 12, and produce the καρπὸς τοῦ φωτός **Eph 5:9.** The rdg. τ̣ο̣ [φω]ς Ox 1081, 29 is better restored after the Coptic SJCh as τέλος (q.v. 1).

γ. bearers or bringers of this kind of light (φῶς of persons: Od. 16, 23; Anacr. 51 Diehl [32 Page; 124 Bergk] φάος Ἑλλήνων; Pind., I. 2, 17; trag.; Biogr. p. 453 Hippocr. as ἀστήρ and φῶς of the healing art; TestJob 53:3 Job as φῶς τῶν τυφλῶν; SIG 1238, 2 [c. 160 AD] Φήγιλλα, τὸ φῶς τῆς οἰκίας) Is 49:6 φῶς ἐθνῶν is referred to Paul and Barnabas **Ac 13:47,** and to Christ B 14:8 (as Just., D. 65, 7); cp. 14:7 (Is 42:6) and cp. bα above. The Ἰουδαῖος considers himself a φῶς τῶν ἐν σκότει **Ro 2:19.** Jesus' disciples are τὸ φῶς τοῦ κόσμου **Mt 5:14;** cp. vs. **16.**—On Is 49:6 s. HOrlinsky, The 75th Anniv. Vol. of the JQR '67, 409–28.

δ. by metonymy, one who is illuminated or filled w. such light, or who stands in it **Eph 5:8a** (s. 1bβ above).—On the dualism of light and darkness, etc., s. Hebr. texts in the Dead Sea scrolls: KKuhn, ZTK 47, '50, 192–211; WBrownlee, Excerpts fr. the Transl. of the Dead Sea Manual of Discipline: BASOR no. 121, '51, 8–13; HPreisker, TLZ 77, '52, 673–78; CHowie, The Cosmic Struggle: Int 8, '54, 206–17.

❷ **that which gives/bears light,** ***torch, lamp, lantern,*** etc. (X., Hell. 5, 1, 8 φῶς ἔχειν; Musaeus vs. 224 of a λύχνος. Pl.: Plut., Ant. 927 [26, 6], Pelop. 284 [12, 3] al.; Lucian, Philops. 31) **Ac 16:29.** Fire, which furnishes both light and heat (X., Hell. 6, 2, 29; Cyr. 7, 5, 27; 1 Macc 12:29) **Mk 14:54** (GBuchanan, ET 68, '56, 27); **Lk 22:56.** Heavenly bodies (Manetho, Apotel. 6, 146 sun and moon δύο φῶτα; likew. Dio Chrys. 23 [40], 38; Ptolem., Apotel. 2, 13, 8; 3, 3, 3; 3, 5, 3 al. τὰ φ=constellations; Vett. Val. index II p. 384; PGM 13, 400; Ps 135:7; Jer 4:23): God is πατὴρ τῶν φώτων **Js 1:17** (TestAbr B 7 p. 111, 11 [Stone p. 70] φῶς καλούμενον πατὴρ τοῦ φωτός; cp. ApcMos 36; 38); the sun as τὸ φῶς τοῦ κόσμου τούτου **J 11:9** (Macrobius, Saturnal. 1, 23, 21 ἥλιε παντοκράτορ, … κόσμου φῶς; cp. Ps.-Demosth. 60, 24). Of the eye as an organ of light (Eur., Cycl. 633 φῶς Κύκλωπος; Ath. 32, 2) **Mt 6:23; Lk 11:35.**

❸ **that which is illuminated by light:** πᾶν τὸ φανερούμενον φῶς ἐστιν *everything that becomes visible is (=stands in the) light* **Eph 5:14.**—CMugler, Dictionnaire historique de la terminologie optique des Grecs '64.—B. 60. Cp. φέγγος; s. Schmidt, Syn. I 563–98. DELG s.v. φάε. Frisk s.v. φάος. New Docs 1, 98f. M-M. EDNT. TW. Spicq. Sv.

φωστήρ, ῆρος, ὁ (cp. φῶς)—❶ **light-giving body,** esp. of heavenly bodies, specif. *star* (Heliod. 2, 24, 6; Vett. Val. 104, 30; 105, 7; Herm. Wr. 496, 2 Sc. [the sun]; Anth. Pal. 15, 17, 3 [Christian]; T. Kellis 22, 17 PGM 13, 298; IDefixWünsch 5, 23; Gen 1:14, 16; Wsd 13:2; Sir 43:7; En; PsSol 18:10;. SibOr 3, 88; TestLevi 14:3; TestJud 25:2; Ar.; Tat. 12, 4; Mel., P. 83, 618; 97, 740) **Phil 2:15** (cp. Da 12:3; En 104:2 ὡσεὶ φωστῆρες τοῦ οὐρανοῦ ἀναλάμψετε).—In a fragmentary text: [φ]ωσ̣[τὴ]ρ ἀπεδίκνυεν (as would) *a star* (the Lord) *showed* (the way) (?) AcPl Ha 7. 35.

❷ **state of brightness or shining,** ***splendor, radiance*** (Anth. Pal. 11, 359, 7; 1 Esdr 8:76) **Rv 21:11.**—Cp. φέγγος, s. Schmidt, Syn. I 563–98. DELG s.v. φάε C. Frisk s.v. φάος. M-M. TW. Spicq.

φωσφόρος, ον (cp. φῶς, φέρω; as adj. 'bringing/giving light' Eur. et al.; pap, Philo) in our lit. only once and as subst. ὁ φ. prob. ***the morning star,*** the planet Venus (Eur., Ion 1157; Ps.-Pla., Tim. Locr. 96e; 97a; Plut., Mor. 430a; 601a; 889a al.; Cicero, Nat. Deor. 2, 20; Vett. Val. 236, 6; SibOr 5, 516; PRyl 524, 17; Neugebauer-Hoesen, glossary p. 200) fig. **2 Pt 1:19** (v.l. ἑωσφόρος). JBoehmer, ZNW 22, 1923, 228–33; FBoll, Sternglaube u. Sterndeutung 4 '31, 47f.—FDölger, AC V/1, '35, 1ff interprets the 'light-bearer' to mean the sun (this mng. of φ. in Nicetas Eugen. 1, 87; 3, 21; 5, 258 Hercher); cp. HWindisch ad loc.—M-M. TW. Spicq.

φωταγωγός, ον (cp. φῶς, ἄγω, and ἀγωγή 'carrying away'; so in Lucian et al.; PGM 5, 190; ApcSed 11:18 p. 135, 1 and 3 Ja.; φωταγωγία in Vett. Val. 301, 22; ApcSed 16:7 p. 137, 14 Ja.; PGM 4, 955; φωταγωγέω in Celsus 2, 71; TestAbr A 7 p. 84, 1f [Stone p. 16]; ParJer 5, 35; Mel., P. 72, 527 al.) ***light-bringing, light-giving*** ἄγγελοι φ. *light-bringing angels* who are set over the way of light B 18:1.—DELG s.v. φάε D.

φωτεινός, ή, όν (cp. φῶς; also -ινός as En 22:2.—X. et al.; pseudepigr.; Just., A I, 32, 13; Tat. 13, 1; also comp. φωτεινότερος Sir 17:31; 23:19; ApcSed 7:5; Just., D. 121, 2) ***shining, bright, radiant*** νεφέλη φ. a bright cloud indicating the presence of God **Mt 17:5;** GJs 19:2 (cp. X., Mem. 4, 3, 4 ἥλιος φ.). ApcPt 3:7 (cp. TestSol 12:3f C) of the radiant garments of angels.—Opp. σκοτεινός (X., Mem. 3, 10, 1; En 22:2) *illuminated, full of light* (Artem. 1, 64 βαλανεῖα φωτεινά; 2, 36) **Mt 6:22; Lk 11:34, 36ab.**—DELG s.v. φάε C. M-M. TW. Spicq.

φωτίζω fut. φωτίσω (**1 Cor 4:5; Rv 22:5**) and φωτιῶ (**Rv 22:5 v.l.;** TestLevi 4:3; s.Thackeray 228f); 1 aor. ἐφώτισα. Pass.: 1 fut. 3 sg. pl. φωτισθήσεται, -σονται; 1 aor. ἐφωτίσθην; pf. ptc. πεφωτισμένος (cp. φῶς; Aristot.+; ins, pap, LXX; En 5:8; Test12Patr; ParJer 9:3; Philo, Joseph., Just.; Mel., P. 35, 243 al.)

❶ intr. (Aristot.; Theophr.; Plut., Num. 4, 9; 8, 2; Sir 42:16; Philo, Dec. 49) **to function as a source of light,** ***to shine,*** of God (Ps 75:5) ἐπί τινα upon someone **Rv 22:5.**

❷ trans. **to cause to be illumined,** ***give light to, light (up), illuminate*** (Aristarch. Sam. [III BC] p. 358, 20 al.; Diod. S. 3, 48, 4 of the sun ἀκτῖσι τὸν κόσμον; Galen XIX p. 174 K.; PGM 3, 152; 4, 2345; IDefixWünsch 4, 14; 2 Esdr 19:12, 19 τὴν ὁδόν) τινά someone **Lk 11:36; Rv 22:5 v.l.;** τὴν πόλιν **Rv 21:23.** Pass. (Anaximander, Vorsokr. 12 A 1 [in Diog. L. 2, 1] ἀπὸ ἡλίου; Plut., Mor. 1120e; Diog. L. 7, 144 the whole earth ὑπ' αὐτοῦ [the sun] φωτίζεσθαι) **18:1.**

❸ trans. **to make known in reference to the inner life or transcendent matters and thus enlighten,** ***enlighten, give light to, shed light upon*** (φῶς 2; 3) fig. ext. of 2

ⓐ in imagery of the heavenly light that is granted the 'enlightened one' (cp. the prayer PGM 4, 990, that calls upon the μέγιστος θεός as τὸν τὰ πάντα φωτίζοντα καὶ διαυγάζοντα τῇ ἰδίᾳ δυνάμει τὸν σύμπαντα κόσμον; Herm. Wr. 1, 32 the inspired one prays to a deity for δύναμις and χάρις: ἵνα φωτίσω τοὺς ἐν ἀγνοίᾳ. S. also 13, 18; 19 τὸ πᾶν τὸ ἐν ἡμῖν σῷζε ζωή, φώτιζε φῶς, πνευμάτιζε θεέ; Philo, Fuga 139 and TestBenj 6:4 τ. ψυχήν; Sextus 97; ViHab 14 [p. 87, 6 Sch.].—GAnrich, Das antike Mysterienwesen 1894, 125f; GWobbermin, Religionsgesch. Studien 1896, 155ff; Rtzst., Mysterienrel. 3, 1927, 44; 264; 292); τὸ φῶς τὸ ἀληθινὸν (i.e. Christ, the heavenly Redeemer) φωτίζει πάντα ἄνθρωπον **J 1:9** (s. Hdb. ad loc. and s.v. φῶς 1bα.—For the combination w. φῶς: ParJer 9:3; Cleom. [II AD] 2, 4 p. 188, 18 τὸ φῶς τὸ φωτίζον αὐτόν; Proclus on Pla., Cratyl. p. 103, 28 Pasqu.); φωτίσαι πάντας τίς ἡ οἰκονομία τοῦ μυστηρίου *to enlighten everyone about God's private/mysterious plan* **Eph 3:9** (perh. in the sense 'instruct', cp. 4 Km 17:27f). God is implored to grant πεφωτισμένους τοὺς ὀφθαλμοὺς τῆς καρδίας *enlightened in the eyes of (your) heart = . . . your inward sight* **1:18** (φωτίζειν ὀφθαλμούς: 2 Esdr 9:8; Ps 18:9; Bar 1:12). The Roman Christian community is πεφωτισμένη ἐν θελήματι (i.e. of God) IRo ins (cp. Just., D. 122, 3 ἐθνῶν πεφωτισμένων). οἱ ἅπαξ φωτισθέντες **Hb 6:4;** cp. **10:32.**

ⓑ *bring to light, reveal* τὶ someth. (Polyb. 22, 5, 10; Epict. 1, 4, 31 τὴν ἀλήθειαν; Plut., Mor. 902c; Jos., Ant. 8, 143 the hidden mng. of a riddle; pass., Lucian, Calum. 32; Mel., P. 41, 285 τὸ εὐαγγέλιον) τὰ κρυπτὰ τοῦ σκότους *that which is hidden in the dark* **1 Cor 4:5.** φ. ζωὴν καὶ ἀφθαρσίαν διὰ τοῦ εὐαγγελίου *bring life and immortality to light through the gospel* **2 Ti 1:10.** Abs., foll. by indir. question φωτίσαι τίς ἡ οἰκονομία τοῦ μυστηρίου *to make clear what (God's) mysterious plan is* **Eph 3:9 v.l.**—DELG s.v. φάε C. M-M. EDNT. TW. Spicq. Sv.

φωτισμός, οῦ, ὁ, (φωτίζω; illumination in the physical sense: Strato of Lamps. [300 BC] fgm. 76 Wehrli '50; Petosiris, fgm. 12 ln. 178 τῆς σελήνης; Sext. Emp., Math. 10, 224 ἐξ ἡλίου; Plut., Mor. 929d; 931a; PMich 149, 3; 33 [II AD]; Ps 26:1; 43:4; 77:14; Job 3:9; Philo, Somn. 1, 53. Of daylight: ὁ φ. τοῦ περὶ ὑμᾶς ἀέρος Did., Gen. 23, 20) in our lit. only in imagery (TestLevi 14:4 τὸ φῶς τοῦ νόμου . . . εἰς φωτισμὸν παντὸς ἀνθρώπου; Just., A I, 61, 12 καλεῖται τοῦτο τὸ λουτρὸν φωτισμός [of baptism]) **illumination for the inner life**

ⓐ ***enlightenment, light*** εἰς τὸ μὴ αὐγάσαι τὸν φωτισμὸν τοῦ εὐαγγελίου τῆς δόξης τοῦ Χριστοῦ *so that they do not see the light of the gospel of the glory of Christ* **2 Cor 4:4** (s. αὐγάζω 1).

ⓑ ***bringing to light, revealing*** (φωτίζω 3b) πρὸς φωτισμὸν τῆς γνώσεως **2 Cor 4:6** (but for other interpretations s. the commentaries. S. also Herm. Wr. 10, 21 τὸ τῆς γνώσεως φῶς; 7, 2a).—DELG s.v. φάε C. M-M. TW. Sqicq.

χαίρω mid. by-form χαίρεται TestAbr s. below; impf. ἔχαιρον; fut. χαρήσομαι (B-D-F §77; Mlt-H. 264); 2 aor. pass. ἐχάρην (Hom.+).

❶ **to be in a state of happiness and well-being,** ***rejoice, be glad*** opp. κλαίειν **J 16:20; Ro 12:15ab** (Damasc., Vi. Isid. 284 χαρίεις πρὸς τοὺς χαρίεντας); **1 Cor 7:30ab;** Hv 3, 3, 2. Opp. λύπην ἔχειν **J 16:22.** W. ἀγαλλιᾶσθαι (Hab 3:18; TestJob 43:15; ParJer 6:20; cp. TestAbr A 11 p. 89, 17 [Stone p. 26]) **Mt 5:12; 1 Pt 4:13b;** cp. **Rv 19:7;** GJs 17:2. W. εὐφραίνεσθαι (Jo 2:23 al. in LXX) **Lk 15:32; Rv 11:10.** W. σκιρτᾶν **Lk 6:23.** W. acc. of inner obj. (B-D-F §153, 1; Rob. 477) χ. χαρὰν μεγάλην *be very glad* (Jon 4:6; JosAs 3:4 al.) **Mt 2:10.** τῇ χαρᾷ ᾗ (by attraction for ἥν) χαίρομεν **1 Th 3:9.** Also χαρᾷ χ., which prob. betrays the infl. of the OT (Is 66:10), **J 3:29** (B-D-F §198, 6; Rob. 531; 550). The ptc. is used w. other verbs *with joy, gladly* (Appian, Bell. Civ. 4, 40 §169 ἄπιθι χαίρων; 3 Km 8:66; Eutecnius 4 p. 43, 7 ἄπεισι χαίρουσα; Laud. Therap. 12 χαίρων ἐστέλλετο) ὑπεδέξατο αὐτὸν χαίρων **Lk 19:6;** cp. vs. **37; 15:5; Ac 5:41; 8:39.**—The obj. of or reason for the joy is denoted in var. ways: w. simple dat. τοῖς τὰ πολλὰ λέγουσιν*those who are (merely) garrulous* Papias (2:3) (Aristonous 1, 45 [p. 164 Coll. Alex.]; Just., A I, 5, 3 al.; Orig., C. Cels. 8, 69, 20; s. also below on **Ro 12:12**) or prep. χαίρειν ἐπί τινι *rejoice over someone* or *someth.* (Soph. et al.; X., Cyr. 8, 4, 12, Mem. 2, 6, 35; Pla., Leg. 5, 729d; Diod. S. 1, 25, 2; Plut., Mor. 87e; 1088e; BGU 531 I, 4 [I AD]; POxy 41, 17; Tob 13:15ab; Pr 2:14; 24:19; Bar 4:33; JosAs 4:4; Jos., Ant. 1, 294; 3, 32; Ar. 15, 7; Just., D. 28, 4; Iren. 1, 16, 3 [Harv I 163, 9]) **Mt 18:13; Lk 1:14; 13:17; Ac 15:31; Ro 16:19; 1 Cor 13:6; 16:17; 2 Cor 7:13; Rv 11:10;** Hs 5, 2, 5 and 11; 8, 1, 16; 8, 5, 1 and 6; Dg 11:5. Also διά w. acc. (Appian, Bell. Civ. 4, 102 §428;

EpArist 42) **J 3:29; 11:15** the ὅτι- clause gives the reason, and δι ὑμᾶς is *for your sakes = in your interest*; cp. **1 Th 3:9.** ἔν τινι (Soph., Trach. 1118; Pla., Rep. 10, 603c; En 104:13) Hs 1:11. ἐν τούτῳ *over that* **Phil 1:18a** (for other functions of ἐν s. below). περί τινος *in someth.* (Pla., Ep. 2, 310e.—περὶ πλοῦτον Did., Gen. 150, 8) 1 Cl 65:1. ἵνα μὴ λύπην σχῶ ἀφ᾽ ὧν ἔδει με χαίρειν (either ἀπὸ τούτων ἀφ᾽ ὧν or ἀπὸ τούτων οἷς) **2 Cor 2:3.** The reason or object is given by ὅτι (Lucian, Charon 17; Ex 4:31; Just., A II, 2, 7) **Lk 10:20b; J 11:15** (s. above); **14:28; 2 Cor 7:9, 16; Phil 4:10; 2J 4.** χ. ἐν τούτῳ ὅτι **Lk 10:20a.** χ. ὅταν **2 Cor 13:9.** χ. . . . γάρ **Phil 1:18b (19).** The reason or obj. is expressed by a ptc. (X., Cyr. 1, 5, 12; Pla., Rep. 5, 458a; Dio Chrys. 22 [39], 1 al.; PGM 4, 1212 χαίρεις τοὺς σοὺς σῴζων; 1611; Just., D. 114, 4): ἰδόντες τὸν ἀστέρα ἐχάρησαν **Mt 2:10;** cp. **Lk 23:8; J 20:20; Ac 11:23; Phil 2:28;** Hv 3, 12, 3. ἀκούσαντες ἐχάρησαν *they were delighted by what they heard* **Mk 14:11;** cp. **Ac 13:48;** Hv 3, 3, 2.—1 Cl 33:7; Dg 5:16. λαβόντες τὰ ἐδέμσματα ἐχάρησαν Hs 5, 2, 10. W. gen. and ptc. (as Just., D. 85, 6) 9, 11, 7. If χαίρειν is also in the ptc., καί comes betw. the two participles: χαίρων καὶ βλέπων *(and) it is with joy that I see* **Col 2:5.** ἐχάρην ἐρχομένων ἀδελφῶν καὶ μαρτυρούντων *I was glad when some fellow-Christians came and testified* **3J 3.**—τῇ ἐλπίδι χαίρ. **Ro 12:12** is not 'rejoice over the hope' (the dat. stands in this mng. X., Mem. 1, 5, 4; Theopompus [IV BC]: 115 fgm. 114 Jac.; Epict., App. D, 3 [p. 479 Sch.] ἀρετῇ χ.; Iambl., Vi. Pyth. 28, 137 οἷς ὁ θεὸς χ.; Pr 17:19), but rather *rejoice in hope* or *filled with hope* (B-D-F §196). τὸ ἐφ᾽ ὑμῖν χαίρω *as far as you are concerned, I am glad* **Ro 16:19 v.l.** In the majority of cases in our lit. ἐν does not introduce the cause of the joy (s. above): χαίρω ἐν τοῖς παθήμασιν *I rejoice in the midst of* (though *because of* is also poss.) *(the) suffering(s)* **Col 1:24** (the Engl. 'in' conveys both ideas). χαίρ. ἐν κυρίῳ **Phil 3:1; 4:4a, 10** (the imperatives in **3:1; 4:4ab** are transl. *good-bye* [so Hom. et al.] by Goodsp., s. Probs. 174f; this would class them under 2a below). Abs. **Lk 22:5; J 4:36; 8:56** (EbNestle, Abraham Rejoiced: ET 20, 1909, 477; JMoulton, 'Abraham Rejoiced': ibid. 523–28); **2 Cor 6:10; 7:7; 13:11; Phil 2:17f; 4:4b** (s. Goodsp. above); **1 Th 5:16; 1 Pt 4:13a;** cp. **13b;** GPt 6:23; Hv 3, 3, 3f; Hs 1:11; 5, 3, 3; GJs 16:3.—On the rare mid. χαιρόμενος (TestAbr A 11 p. 89, 21 [Stone p. 26] χαίρεται καὶ ἀγάλλεται) **Ac 3:8** D, s. Mlt. 161 w. note 1; B-D-F §307.

❷ in impv., **a formalized greeting wishing one well,** also in indicative, **to use such a greeting** (in effect, to express that one is on good terms w. the other, cp. Soph., Oed. R. 596 νῦν πᾶσι χαίρω=now I bid everyone good day)

ⓐ in spoken address, oft. on meeting people (Hom. et al.; also χαίροις TestAbr A 16 p. 97, 21 [Stone p. 42]; B 13 p. 117, 18 [82]; JosAs 8:2; GrBar 11:6f; loanw. in rabb.) χαῖρε, χαίρετε ***welcome, good day, hail (to you), I am glad to see you,*** somet. (e.g. Hermas)=*how do you do?* or simply *hello* **Mt 26:49; 27:29; 28:9** (here perh. specif. *good morning* [Lucian, Laps. inter Salutandum 1 τὸ ἑωθινὸν . . . χαίρειν; also scholia p. 234, 13 Rabe; Cass. Dio 69, 18; Nicetas Eugen. 2, 31 H.; so Goodsp., Probs. 45f; he translates Lk 1:28 and the 2J and H passages in the same way]); **Mk 15:18; Lk 1:28;** GJs 11:1 (Ps.-Callisth. 1, 4, 2 Nectanebos says to Olympia upon entering her room: χαίροις Μακεδόνων βασίλεια); **J 19:3** (on the sarcastic greeting as king cp. Diod. S. 34 + 35, fgm. 2, 8f [Eunus]); Hv 1, 1, 4; 1, 2, 2ab; 4, 2, 2ab. χαίρειν τινὶ λέγειν *greet someone, bid someone the time of day* (Epict. 3, 22, 64; pass.: χαίρειν αὐτοῖς ὑφ᾽ ἡμῶν λέγεσθαι Iren. 1, 16, 3 [Harv. I 162, 11]) **2J 10f.**—On the poss. sense *farewell, good-bye* for **Phil 3:1; 4:4** s. 1 above, end.

ⓑ elliptically at the beginning of a letter ***greetings*** (X., Cyr. 4, 5, 27; Theocr. 14, 1; Plut., Ages. 607 [21, 10]=Mor. 213a; Aelian, VH 1, 25; Jos., Vi. 217; 365; Mel., HE 4, 26, 13; pap [Mitt-Wilck. I/2, 477–82; HLietzmann, Griech. Pap.: Kl. T. 14^2, 1910; Witkowski, Epistulae; GMilligan, Selections fr. the Gk. Pap.[2] 1911]; LXX.—B-D-F §389; 480, 5; Rob. 944; 1093. GGerhard, Untersuchungen zur Gesch. des griech. Briefes, diss. Heidelb. 1903, Philol 64, 1905, 27–65; FZiemann, De Epistularum Graecarum Formulis Sollemnibus: Dissertationes Philologicae Halenses XVIII/4, 1911; PWendland, Die urchristl. Literaturformen[2, 3] 1912, 411–17 [suppl. 15: Formalien des Briefes]; WSchubart, Einführung in die Papyruskunde 1918; Dssm., LO 116ff=LAE 146ff [lit.]; FExler, The Form of the Ancient Gk. Letter 1923; ORoller, D. Formular d. paul. Briefe '33; RArcher, The Ep. Form in the NT: ET 63, '51f, 296–98; Pauly-W. III 836ff; VII 1192ff; Kl. Pauly II 324–27; BHHW I 272f) τοῖς ἀδελφοῖς . . . χαίρειν *greetings to the brethren* **Ac 15:23;** cp. **23:26; Js 1:1;** AcPlCor 1:1; 2:1. Ign. uses the common formula πλεῖστα χαίρειν (πολύς 3bα) IEph ins; IMg ins; ITr ins; IRo ins; ISm ins; IPol ins.—The introduction to B is unique: χαίρετε, υἱοὶ καὶ θυγατέρες, ἐν ὀνόματι κυρίου, ἐν εἰρήνῃ 1:1.—JLieu, 'Grace to you and Peace', The Apostolic Greeting: BJRL 68, '85, 161–78.—Schmidt, Syn. II 550–73. DELG. M-M. EDNT. TW.

χάλαζα, ης, ἡ (Hom. et al.; LXX, En, Philo) ***hail*** **Rv 8:7** (w. fire as Ex 9:23–28); **11:19** (lightning, thunder, and hail as a divine manifestation as GrBar 16:3; Jos, Ant. 6, 92; cp. SibOr 3, 691; also Cat. Cod. Astr. passim); **16:21ab** (for the extraordinary size cp. Diod. S. 19, 45, 2 χ. ἄπιστος τὸ μέγεθος, a single hailstone weighed a mina [approx. a half kilogram] or more. The hail caused houses to collapse and killed people: Jos., Ant. 2, 305; deadly hail on the wicked as Ctesias, Pers. 25); ***hailstone*** Hm 11:20. Hail puts a halt to Paul's animal combat AcPl Ha 5, 6 and tears off one of the proconsul's ears 5, 10f.—DELG. M-M.

χαλάω fut. χαλάσω; 1 aor. ἐχάλασα, pass. ἐχαλάσθην (Pind., Aeschyl. et al.; PLond I, 131*, 12 p. 189 [78 AD]; LXX, TestSol 10:22 C; TestJos 1:4; Philo; Jos., Bell. 1, 657; Just., D. 90, 4) ***let down*** τὶ *someth.* (Apollon. Rhod. 2, 1267; Jer 45:6) τὸν κράβαττον *let down the pallet* (through the roof) **Mk 2:4** (see s.v. στέγη). τὰ δίκτυα *let down the nets* into the water (cp. Alciphron 1, 1, 4) **Lk 5:4f.** As a nautical t.t. τὸ σκεῦος (q.v. 1) **Ac 27:17.** τὴν σκάφην εἰς τὴν θάλασσαν vs. **30** (χαλ. εἰς as PMich 124 verso, 23 [46/49 AD]; PFouad 18, 15; 19, 11 [both 53 AD]; Jos., Bell. 1, 657; TestJos 1:4). τινά *someone* (Jer 45:6; TestJos 1:4) ἐν σπυρίδι *in a hamper* **Ac 9:25;** pass. **2 Cor 11:33** (cp. the escape in Plut., Aemil. Paul. 268 [26, 2]).—DELG. M-M.

Χαλδαῖος, ου, ὁ (Hdt. et al., both as a name for an inhabitant of Χαλδαία and as a designation for astrologers and interpreters of dreams; TestSol 15:8; TestNapht, ParJer, SibOr, Philo, Joseph., Ar.; Just., A I, 53, 8; Tat.) ***Chaldean:*** γῆ Χαλδαίων (Jer 24:5) *land of the Chaldeans,* as the home of Abraham (Gen 11:28, 31; 15:7; in these passages: [ἡ] χώρα [τῶν] Χ.) **Ac 7:4.**—DEdzard, in Reallexikon der Assyriologie V 291–97. Pauly-W. III 2045–62; Kl. Pauly I 1123f; BHHW I 296f; RAC II 1006–21 (lit.).

χαλεπός, ή, όν (s. next entry; Hom.+; ins, pap, LXX, TestSol, Philo; Jos., Ant. 4, 1 βίος, 13, 422 νόσος; Just., D. 1, 5; Tat.; comp. χαλεπώτερα Just., A II, 2, 6) **pert. to being troublesome, *hard, difficult*** καιροὶ χ. *hard times, times of stress* **2 Ti 3:1.** Of words that are hard to bear and penetrate deeply (Hes., Works 332; Dio Chrys. 49 [66], 19) Hv 1, 4, 2 (w. σκληρός). Of pers. (Od. 1, 198; Chion, Ep. 15, 1f; SIG 780, 31; EpArist 289; Jos., Ant. 15, 98) *hard to deal with, violent, dangerous* **Mt**

8:28. Of animals (Pla., Pol. 274b; Ps.-X., Cyneg. 10, 23; Dio Chrys. 5, 5) B 4:5 (comp.). In the sense *bad, evil* (Cebes 6, 2 of the πόμα of Ἀπάτη) τὰ ἔργα τοῦ ἀγγέλου τῆς πονηρίας χ. ἐστι *the deeds of the angel of wickedness are evil* Hm 6, 2, 10.—Subst. τὰ χ. *(that which is) evil* (X., Mem. 2, 1, 23; POxy 1242, 36) MPol 11:1 (opp. τὰ δίκαια). ἀρχὴ πάντων χαλεπῶν φιλαργυρία *everything that is acrimonious begins with love of money* Pol 4:1 (cp. 1 Ti 6:10).—B. 651. DELG. M-M. Spicq.

χαλεπῶς adv. of χαλεπός; *grievously* (Hom.; Philo, Leg. ad Gai. 346) AcPl Ox 6, 17 (Aa I 241, 15).

χαλιναγωγέω (χαλινός, ἄγω) fut. χαλιναγωγήσω; 1 aor. ἐχαλιναγώγησα ('guide with a bit and bridle, hold in check' Rhet. Gr. I 425, 19 ἵππον) in our lit. only fig. ***bridle, hold in check*** (Lucian, Tyrannic. 4 τὰς τῶν ἡδονῶν ὀρέξεις, Salt. 70 πάθη; Poll. 1, 215) τὶ *someth.* γλῶσσαν **Js 1:26** (cp. Philo, Somn. 2, 165). τὸ σῶμα **3:2** (in extended imagery, s. vs. 3; cp. Ath., R. 15 p. 66, 34 [s. ὑπείκω]; also of the horse Philo, Op. M. 86). τὴν ἐπιθυμίαν Hm 12, 1, 1 (Leutzsch, Hermas 464 n. 279 reff.). ἑαυτὸν ἀπό τινος *restrain oneself from someth.* Pol 5:3.—DELG s.v. χαλινός. M-M.

χαλινός, οῦ, ὁ (Hom. et al.; PSI 543, 50; PCairZen 659, 11 [both III BC]; LXX; Jos., Ant. 18, 320; loanw. in rabb.) ***bit, bridle*** **Js 3:3** (cp. Theognis 551 ἵπποισ' ἔμβαλλε χαλινούς; Soph., Antig. 477; X., Res Equ. 6, 7 ἵνα τὸν χ. ὀρθῶς ἐμβάλῃ; Philo, Agr. 94; cp. the Plut. quot. s.v. πηδάλιον); **Rv 14:20.**—DELG. M-M.

χαλινόω (χαλινός; X. et al., lit. and fig.) in our lit. only fig. ***bridle, hold in check*** (Theophr. et al.; Ps.-Phoc. 57 ὀργήν) **Js 1:26 v.l.**

χάλιξ, ικος, ὁ (Thu., Aristoph. et al.; pap, LXX) **a small, sharp stone, *pebble*** ApcPt 15, 30.—DELG.

χαλκεύς, έως, ὁ (χαλκός; Hom. et al.; ins, pap, LXX) first 'coppersmith', then gener. ***(black)smith, metalworker*** (Aristot., Poet. 25 χαλκέας τοὺς τὸν σίδηρον ἐργαζομένους; Gen 4:22; 2 Ch 24:12 χαλκεῖς σιδήρου) Ἀλέξανδρος ὁ χαλκεύς *A. the metalworker* **2 Ti 4:14** (so Goodsp. et al.; that A. was a 'coppersmith' [NRSV, REB] cannot be proved; he could as well have been a goldsmith [cp. Od. 3, 432]); Hv 1, 3, 2. θέλις χαλκέα ἄγωμεν; *do you want us to get a blacksmith?* (to break the chains) AcPl Ha 3, 5. Making cult images Dg 2:3.—B. 606. DELG s.v. χαλκός. M-M. Spicq.

χαλκεύω (χαλκός) pf. pass. ptc. κεχαλκευμένος (Hom. et al.; 1 Km 13:20; Jos., Ant. 3, 172, C. Ap. 2, 242; Ar. 10, 1; Tat.; Ath. 15, 2) **to work at a forge, *forge,*** first bronze, then metal gener. (Jos., Bell. 7, 429 a golden lamp) Dg 2:2f.—DELG s.v. χαλκός.

χαλκηδών, όνος, ὁ *chalcedony,* a precious stone (λίθος ὁ χαλκηδόνιος: Les lapidaires Grecs ed. MCh-ERuelle 1898 pp. 175, 187, 191) **Rv 21:19.** The stones designated by this term in modern times (agate, onyx, carnelian, etc.) are known by other names in ancient writers. On the other hand Pliny (NH 37, 7, 92ff) calls a kind of emerald and of jasper Chalcedonian. It is uncertain what is meant by the term in Rv.—S. the lit. s.v. ἀμέθυστος.—BHHW I 362–65.

χαλκίον, ου, τό (χαλκός) **a container or object made of copper, brass, or bronze, *bronze vessel, kettle*** (Aristoph. in Pollux 10, 109; X., Oec. 8, 19; IG I², 393; UPZ 120, 7 [II BC]; PFay 95, 11 [II AD]; PTebt 406, 21; 1 Km 2:14; 1 Esdr 1:13) **Mk 7:4.**—B. 342. DELG s.v. χαλκός. M-M.

χαλκολίβανον, ου, τό (χαλκός, λείβω 'pour'; as a neut. in Suidas, Oecumenius) or **χαλκολίβανος, ου, ὁ** (so the Coptic version and Ausonius [in Salmasius, Exerc. ad Solin. p. 810a], perh. even fem.: FRehkopf, JJeremias Festschr. '70, 216; B-D-R §49, 1; 115, 1) an exceptionally fine type of metal or alloy. Since the word is found nowhere independent of Rv, the exact nature of this metal or alloy remains unknown. One must be content **Rv 1:15; 2:18** with some such rendering as ***fine brass/bronze*** (perh. it is someth. like 'electrum'. Suda defines it s.v. χαλκολίβ.: εἶδος ἠλέκτρου τιμιώτερον χρυσοῦ. ἔστι δὲ τὸ ἤλεκτρον ἀλλότυπον χρυσίον μεμιγμένον ὑελῷ καὶ λιθείᾳ 'a kind of electrum, more precious than gold. Now, electrum is an alternate form of gold, composed of a crystalline substance and fine stone' [on ἤλεκτρον cp. Ezk 1:27 and Pliny, NH 33, 4 where ἤλ. is a natural alloy of gold and silver]. S. also Jos., Ant. 7, 106: χαλκός, ὃν τοῦ χρυσοῦ κρείττον' ἔλεγον=the metal which is claimed to be superior to gold). The Old Latin versions transl. the word 'aurichalcum' or 'orichalcum' (cp. Vergil, Aen. 12, 87 and Servius' observation on it). The Syrian version and Arethas consider it to be a metal fr. Lebanon (=Libanon in Gk., Lat., et al.).—S. esp. CHemer, The Letters to the Seven Churches of Asia in Their Local Setting '86, 111–17: 'copper-zinc'. Also PDiergart, Philol 64, 1905, 150–53.

χαλκός, οῦ, ὁ (Hom.+; ins, pap, LXX; TestSol; EpArist 119; Philo; Just., A I, 60, 3; Ath. 26, 3)

❶ **a metal of various types, such as copper, brass, or bronze** (Jos., Ant. 8, 76 w. gold and silver) prob. ***brass, bronze*** **Rv 18:12.** As a material (w. others) for making cult images PtK 2 p. 14, 14; Dg 2:2 (in a comparison w. vessels for everyday use)

❷ **anything made of such metal:** (loanw. in rabb. in the sense 'kettle') a cult image of brass 2 Cl 1:6. χαλκὸς ἠχῶν *a noisy (brass) gong* **1 Cor 13:1** (s. ἠχέω; also HRiesenfeld, ConNeot 12, '48, 50–53; or 'acoustical vase' used in theaters, NTS 32, '86, 286–89). *Copper coin, small change* (Lucian, Syr. Dea 29 w. gold and silver money), also simply *money* (Epicharmus 111 Kaibel [in Pollux, who rejects this usage 9, 90]; Artem 5, 82; PHib 66, 4 [III BC]; PTebt 79, 8; Sb 4369 II, 26; EpJer 34) **Mt 10:9; Mk 6:8; 12:41.**—B. 611f. DELG. M-M.

χαλκοῦς, ῆ, οῦν (trag., X., Pla.+; ins, pap, LXX, TestSol; TestLevi 6:1; GrBar 3:7; Just., D. 94, 3. Contracted fr. χάλκεος, which is found Hom. et al.; ins, but rare in pap and LXX [Thackeray p. 173]; **Rv 9:20 v.l.** [B-D-F §45; Mlt-H. 121; 347]. Both forms in Joseph. [Schmidt, Joseph. 491f]) ***made of copper/brass/bronze*** w. χρυσοῦς, ἀργυροῦς **Rv 9:20.** Gates πύλη χαλκῆ (Diod. S. 2, 8, 7; 2, 9, 3; 17, 71, 6. Similarly Ps.-Aristot., De Mundo 6, 8 θύραις χαλκαῖς) B 11:4 (cp. Is 45:2). θε[οὶ χαλκοῖ] AcPl Ha 1, 18 (restoration suggested by the context). Of the bronze serpent of Moses B 12:6 (Num 21:9; Philo).—DELG s.v. χαλκός. M-M., -εος.

χαμαί adv.—❶ **located on the ground, *on the ground*** (Hom. et al.; pap; Jdth 12:15; 14:18; ParJer 9:9; Jos., Ant. 7, 133) Hv 4, 1, 9; s 2:3f (ῥίπτω 2); 9, 11, 7; *on the* (level) *ground* (in contrast to 'on the rock and the gate') 9, 14, 4.

❷ **pert. to location on the ground as objective of movement, *to/on the ground*** (for χαμᾶζε as early as Hom.; Dionys. Hal. 4, 56, 3; Plut., Marc. 304 [13, 7], Sulla 470 [28, 7]; Lucian, Dial. Mort. 20, 2; PLips 40 II, 22; III, 2; Job 1:20; TestSol 7:3; TestAbr; SibOr 3, 685; Jos., Ant. 20, 89; Mel., P. 26, 187 ἐδαφίσθη χαμαί; cp. 99, 763; loanw. in rabb.) **J 9:6; 18:6;** Hm

11:20; GJs 6:1. ἔρριψεν αὐτὸν χαμαί *he threw himself down* (on sackcloth) 13:1.—DELG. M-M.

Χανάαν, ἡ indecl. (also Χαναάν; כְּנַעַן; Gen 11:31 al.; Philo, Test12Patr, JosAs, Philo, Just.—In Joseph. Χαναναία, ας [Ant. 1, 186]) ***Canaan,*** in our lit. (i.e. Ac) the land west of the Jordan, where the patriarchs lived **Ac 7:11** (w. Egypt), which God gave to the Hebrews upon their escape fr. Egypt **13:19** (γῆ Χ.).—FStähelin, Der Name Kanaan: JWackernagel Festschr. 1923, 150–53; BHHW II 926; TLL, Suppl. 1, 371f.

Χαναναῖος, α, ον (כְּנַעֲנִי; Gen 12:6; 13:7 al. Cp. Philo, Joseph., Test12Patr.; SibOr 13, 56) **belonging to the land and people of Canaan, *Canaanite*** γυνὴ Χαναναία *a Canaanite woman* fr. the region of Tyre and Sidon **Mt 15:22** (the parall. Mk 7:26 has Συροφοινίκισσα, q.v.). Subst. γῆν Χαναναίων AcPl Ha 8, 14.—KBornhäuser, Pastoralblätter 67, 1925, 249–53; BHHW II 926–38; TLL, Suppl. 1, 372f.—M-M.

χαρά, ᾶς, ἡ (χαίρω; trag., Pla.+) 'joy'.—❶ **the experience of gladness**—ⓐ gener. **Gal 5:22.** Opp. λύπη (X., Hell. 7, 1, 32; Philo, Abr. 151; TestJud 25:4; JosAs 9:1; ApcMos 39) **J 16:20f; 2 Cor 2:3; Hb 12:11.** Opp. κατήφεια **Js 4:9.** W. ἀγαλλίασις **Lk 1:14;** 1 Cl 63:2; MPol 18:2. χαρὰ μεγάλη (Jon 4:6; Jos., Ant. 12, 91; Iren. 1, 2, 6 [Harv. I 22, 10]; s. χαίρω 1) **Mt 28:8; Lk 24:52; Ac 15:3.** τὸ τῆς χ. μέγεθος AcPl Ha 6, 9; πολλὴ χ. (BGU 1141, 3 [I BC] μετὰ πολλῆς χαρᾶς) **Ac 8:8; Phlm 7.** πᾶσα χ. (Sb 991, 6 μετὰ πάσης χαρᾶς) **Ro 15:13; Phil 2:29; Js 1:2.**—W. prep. ἀπὸ τῆς χαρᾶς (B-D-F §210, 1; Rob. 580) *for joy* **Lk 24:41; Ac 12:14;** ἀπὸ τῆς χαρᾶς αὐτοῦ *in his joy* **Mt 13:44.** ἐν χαρᾷ **Ro 15:32;** IEph ins; MPol 18:2. μετὰ χαρᾶς (X., Hiero 1, 25; Polyb. 21, 34, 12 v.l.; Diod. S. 16, 79, 4; Plut., Mor. 1095b; Jos., Ant. 8, 124; LXX; PsSol 8:16; Did., Gen. 215, 9) *with joy* **Mt 13:20; 28:8; Mk 4:16; Lk 8:13; 10:17; 24:52** (Jos., Ant. 11, 67 ὥδευον μετὰ χ. [to Jerus.]); **Phil 1:4; Col 1:11; Hb 10:34; 13:17;** 1 Cl 65:1; Hv 1, 3, 4 (w. ἐπαγγέλλω, so Joly, cp. 1 Cl 34:7 'great and glorious promises').—W. subjective gen. **J 15:11b** (cp. **11a** ἡ χ. ἡ ἐμή); **16:22** (Lycon [III BC] fgm. 20 Wehrli '52: τὴν ἀληθινὴν χαρὰν τῆς ψυχῆς τέλος ἔλεγεν εἶναι=he designated the true joy of the soul as the goal); **2 Cor 1:24; 7:13; 8:2.** W. gen. to denote the origin of the joy χ. τῆς πίστεως *joy that comes from faith* **Phil 1:25.** χ. πνεύματος ἁγίου **1 Th 1:6;** also χ. ἐν πνεύματι ἁγίῳ **Ro 14:17.**—Used w. verbs: χαρῆναι χαρὰν μεγάλην *be filled with intense joy* **Mt 2:10.** Cp. **1 Th 3:9** (χαίρω 1); χαρᾷ χαίρειν (χαίρω 1) **J 3:29a** (foll. by διά τι *at someth.*). ἀγαλλιᾶσθαι χαρᾷ **1 Pt 1:8** (Pol. 1:3). ἔχειν χαράν *have joy, feel pleased* **2 Cor 1:15 v.l.; Phlm 7; 3J 4;** difft. Hs 1:10 (*have joy* accompanying it). χαρὰν λαμβάνειν *experience joy* Hv 3, 13, 2 (Just.. D. 100, 5); GJs 12:2; 20:4 (codd.). χαρὰν ποιεῖν τινι *give someone joy* **Ac 15:3.** χαράν τινι παρέχειν 1 Cl 63:2. πληροῦν τινα χαρᾶς *fill someone with joy* (Jos., Bell. 3, 28) **Ro 15:13;** pass. πληροῦσθαι χαρᾶς (Diod. S. 3, 17, 3 τέκνα . . . πεπληρωμένα χαρᾶς; Περὶ ὕψους 7, 2 ψυχὴ πληροῦται χαρᾶς; EpArist 261; Philo, Mos. 1, 177; Jos., Ant 15, 421; Just., A I, 49, 5) **Ac 13:52; 2 Ti 1:4;** Dg 10:3. Also χαρᾶς ἐμπί(μ)πλασθαι (cp. Philo, Det. Pot. Ins. 123; Jos., Ant. 3, 99) MPol 12:1; χαρᾶς πλησθείς AcPl Ha 2, 15; perh. 8, 6f. χαρᾷ ὑπερπερισσεύεσθαι **2 Cor 7:4.** πᾶσαν χαρὰν ἡγεῖσθαι **Js 1:2** (ἡγέομαι 2). ἔσται χαρά σοι **Lk 1:14;** ἔσται σοι χ. GJs 20:3 (codd.); without the dat. *there will be joy* **Lk 15:7** (χ. ἐπί w. dat. as Jos., Ant. 7, 252); also γίνεται χαρά (Tob 11:18 S) vs. **10,** cp. **Ac 8:8;** AcPl Ha 6, 3. χαρᾶς εἶναι (qualitative gen.) *be pleasant* **Hb 12:11.** χαρὰ ὅτι *joy that* **J 16:21.**—Ign. provides χαρά w. adjectives to set it off: ἄμωμος IEph ins; IMg 7:1; αἰώνιος κ. παράμονος IPhld ins.—The Johannine lit. places emphasis on joy as brought to the highest degree (πληρόω 3) ἡ χαρὰ ἡ ἐμὴ πεπλήρωται **J 3:29b;** cp. **15:11b; 16:24; 17:13; 1J 1:4; 2J 12.** Cp. also the act. πληρώσατέ μου τὴν χαράν **Phil 2:2.**—As **v.l.** for χάρις **2 Cor 1:15.**

ⓑ metonymically, *a state of joyfulness* (Nicol. Dam.: 90 fgm. 52 p. 354, 3 Jac. οἱ ἀκούοντες ἐν χαρᾷ ἦσαν) εἴσελθε εἰς τὴν χαρὰν τοῦ κυρίου σου (GrBar 15:4.—Of God: δωρήσεται ζωὴν αἰώνιον, χ., εἰρήνην Theoph. Ant. 1, 14 [p. 92, 2]) **Mt 25:21, 23** (so BWeiss; Jülicher, Gleichn. 475; Zahn, JWeiss, OHoltzmann; but s. 2c). Of Christ ὃς ἀντὶ τῆς προκειμένης αὐτῷ χαρᾶς ὑπέμεινεν σταυρόν **Hb 12:2** (πρόκειμαι 2).

❷ **a pers. or thing that causes joy, *joy,*** metonymically

ⓐ of persons as a source of joy, **Phil 4:1** (EPeterson, Nuntius 4, '50, 27f); **1 Th 2:19f.**

ⓑ of an event that calls forth joy. An angelic message εὐαγγελίζομαι ὑμῖν χαρὰν μεγάλην **Lk 2:10.**

ⓒ of a festive dinner or banquet (s. Dalman, Worte 96; Billerb. I 879; 972) so perh. **Mt 25:21, 23** (but would this have been intelligible to Greeks? S. 1b).—EGulin, Die Freude im NT I (Jesus, early church, Paul) '32; II (John's gosp.) '36; Bultmann on J 17:13; PBernadicou, Joy in the Gospel of Lk, diss. Rome, '70.—B. 1102; TRE XI 584–86; RAC VIII 348–418.—DELG s.v. χαίρω I A 3. M-M. EDNT. TW. Spicq.

χάραγμα, ατος, τό (χαράσσω; Soph.+)—❶ **a mark that is engraved, etched, branded, cut, imprinted, *mark, stamp*** (Anth. Pal. 6, 63, 6; 7, 220, 2; Anacreontea 27, 2 Preisendanz πυρός brands on horses; BGU 453, 8; PGrenf II, 50a, 3 [both II AD, brands on animals]. For stamps on documents: CPR 4, 37; PLond II, 277, 20 p. 218 [23 AD]; Sb 5231, 11; 5247, 34; 5275, 11 [all I AD]. An impression on coins: Plut., Ages. 604 [15, 8], Lys. 442 [16, 4], Mor. 211b al.; POxy 144, 6) in **Rv** of the mark of the Antichrist, which his adherents bear on hand or forehead (for the subj.-matter s. 3 Macc 2:29; UvWilamowitz, Her 34, 1899, 634f; HLilliebjörn, Über relig. Signierung in d. Antike; mit e. Exkurs über Rv, diss. Upps. '33): **13:16; 14:9; 20:4.** τὸ χάρ. τοῦ θηρίου **15:2 v.l.; 16:2; 19:20.** τὸ χάρ. τοῦ ὀνόματος αὐτοῦ **14:11.** τὸ χάρ. τὸ ὄνομα τοῦ θηρίου ἢ τὸν ἀριθμὸν τοῦ ὀνόματος αὐτοῦ **13:17.**—Dssm., NB 68–75 (BS 240–47), LO 289f (LAE 341); JYsebaert, Gk. Baptismal Terminology, '62, esp. 196–204.

❷ **an object fashioned by artistic skill involving alteration of a medium, *thing formed, image*** in the representative arts χάρ. τέχνης *an image formed by art* **Ac 17:29** (CIG 6208 Φοῖβον χαράττειν; cp. Horace, Sat. I, 8, 1–3).—DELG s.v. χαράσσω II, 1. M-M. TW.

χαρακόω (χάραξ) 1 aor. ἐχαράκωσα; pf. pass. ptc. κεχαρακωμένος ***fence in (with stakes)*** (Aeschin. 3, 140; Plut., Cleom. 813 [20, 1]; POxy 729, 23 [II AD]; Jer 39:2) τί *someth.* a vineyard Hs 5, 2, 2f; 5, 4, 1. Pass. 5, 2, 5 (cp. Is 5:2, where the verb prob. means 'provide w. stakes [for individual vines]', a sense which is excluded for H by s 5, 5, 3 [s. συγκρατέω 2]).—DELG s.v. χαράσσω I.

χαρακτήρ, ῆρος, ὁ (fr. χαράσσω 'engrave' via χάραγμα; Aeschyl., Hdt.+; ins, pap, LXX; TestSol 11:6; TestSim 5:4 ['copy', of the Book of Enoch]; ApcSed 7:4; EpArist; Philo; Jos., Ant. 13, 322; Just.; Tat. 17, 2 [in the two last, of letters of the alphabet]; loanw. in rabb.).

❶ **a mark or impression placed on an object**—ⓐ of coinage ***impress, reproduction, representation*** (Eur., El. 559; Aristot., Pol. 1, 6, Oec. 2; Diod. S. 17, 66, 2; OGI 339, 45; in imagery Polyb. 18, 34, 7; Philo, Plant. 18) in imagery IMg 5:2ab.

ⓑ of a distinguishing mark ***trademark*** τὸ κεφαλοδέσμιον . . . χαρακτῆρα ἔχει βασιλικόν *the headpiece bears a royal trademark* (i.e. the logo of a manufacturer for the imperial establishment; s. deStrycker ad loc. and AJohnson, Roman Egypt to the Reign of Diocletian '36, 332–33; 626–27) GJs 2:2. S. 3 below.

❷ **someth. produced as a representation, *reproduction, representation,*** fig., of God ἄνθρωπον ἔπλασεν τῆς ἑαυτοῦ εἰκόνος χαρακτῆρα *(God) formed a human being as reproduction of his own identity/reality* (s. εἰκών 2) 1 Cl 33:4 (cp. OGI 383, 60 of a picture χ. μορφῆς ἐμῆς; 404, 25; Philo, Det. Pot. Ins. 83 calls the soul τύπον τινὰ καὶ χαρακτῆρα θείας δυνάμεως). Christ is χαρ. τῆς ὑποστάσεως αὐτοῦ *an exact representation of (God's) real being* **Hb 1:3** (ὑπόστασις 1a).

❸ **characteristic trait or manner, *distinctive mark*** (Hdt. et al.; Diod. S. 1, 91, 7; Dionys. Hal., Ad Pomp. 3, 16; 2 Macc 4:10) ἐν ἀποστολικῷ χαρακτῆρι *in apostolic fashion* of an epistolary greeting ITr ins; cp. 1b above.

❹ **an impression that is made, *outward aspect, outward appearance, form*** (ApcSed 7:4 ὁ δὲ ἥλιος καὶ Ἀδάμ, μίαν χαρακτῆρα ἦσαν perh. read without the comma: 'Now, the sun and Adam were alike in appearance', in contrast to Eve who was more brightly beautiful than the moon) εὐειδέσταται τῷ χαρακτῆρι *exceptionally beautiful in appearance* Hs 9, 9, 5.—JGeffcken, Character: ET 21, 1910, 426f; AKörte, Her 64, 1929, 69–86 (semantic history).—DELG s.v. χαράσσω II 4. M-M. TW. Sv.

χαράκωσις, εως, ἡ (χαρακόω; Lycurg. Or. §44 p. 153; Plut., Mar. 409 [7, 4]; Dt 20:20) ***fencing in*** (s. χαρακόω) a vineyard Hs 5, 2, 3.—DELG s.v. χαράσσω I.

χάραξ, ακος, ὁ (Thu., Aristoph.+; ins, pap, LXX) prim. 'pointed stake'

❶ **pointed stick/post used to fence in an area, *stake*** pl. of the stakes used in fencing a vineyard (s. χαρακόω and s. BGU 830, 5 [I AD]) Hs 5, 4, 1; 5, 5, 3 (the χάρακες are oft. the stakes which support vines and other plants: Thu. 3, 70, 4; Aristoph., Ach. 986, Vesp. 1291; Theophr., HP 2, 1, 2; Plut., Mor. 4c; Lucian, Philops. 11; BGU 1122, 17 [I BC]).

❷ **military installation involving use of stakes, *palisade, entrenchment*** (var. for offensive or defensive purposes: Philo Mech. 82, 34; Polyb. 1, 80, 11; 3, 45, 5; Plut., Aemil. 264 [17, 5], Marcell. 308 [18, 2], Sulla 462 [17, 5]; 469 [28, 3] al.; Arrian, Exp. Alex. 2, 19, 5 Roos; EpArist 139; Jos., Vi. 214, 395 al., Ant. 15, 112; 150 al.; SIG 363, 1 [297 BC]; Is 37:33; Ezk 4:2; 26:8; GWatson, The Roman Soldier '69 66–68, w. caution respecting description by Vegetius) *siege-work* **Lk 19:43** (Theophil. Com. [IV BC], fgm. 9 K. ἐν χάρακι καὶ παρεμβολῇ; for details of the siege s. Jos., BJ 5, 258–6, 442; on problems connected w. Luke's account s. JFitzmyer, ABD: Luke ad loc.).—DELG s.v. χαράσσω I. M-M.

χαρήσομαι s. χαίρω.

χαρίζομαι (χάρις; Hom.+) mid. dep.: fut. χαρίσομαι **Ro 8:32** (also Lucian, Dial. Mort. 9, 1; Jos., Ant. 2, 28; for Att. χαριοῦμαι); 1 aor. ἐχαρισάμην; pf. κεχάρισμαι. Pass., w. pass. sense: 1 fut. χαρισθήσομαι **Phlm 22;** 1 aor. ἐχαρίσθην **Ac 3:14; 1 Cor 2:12; Phil 1:29.**

❶ **to give freely as a favor, *give graciously*** (a common term in honorific documents lauding officials and civic-minded pers. for their beneficence, s. SIG index and indexes of other inscriptional corpora) of God (so Ael. Aristid. 39, 3 K.=18 p. 409 D.; Herm. Wr. 12, 12; 16, 5 and p. 462, 30; 490, 9; 35; 492, 11 Sc.; 3 Macc 5:11; EpArist 196; TestSim 4:6; Jos., Ant. 3, 87; 4, 317) θεὸν . . . τὰ ἐκεῖ θαυμάσια χαριζόμενον *God, who graciously bestows wonderful things from the world beyond* (as opposed to the finery of this world, which in contrast is 'shit'; s. δεινός and σκύβαλον) AcPl Ha 2, 23f. τινί τι *someth. to someone* (Appian, Bell. Civ. 1, 79 §360 χαρίζεσθαί τινι τὴν σωτηρίαν; Paus. 6, 18, 4 χαρίσασθαί μοι τήνδε ὦ βασιλεῦ τὴν χάριν; TestAbr A 3 p. 79, 30 [Stone p. 6] τὴν ἐπαγγελίαν) **Ro 8:32; Phil 2:9;** 2 Cl 1:4; Hs 9, 28, 6; D 10:3. This is also the place for **Gal 3:18** if τὴν κληρονομίαν is to be supplied fr. the context (but s. end of this sec.). τυφλοῖς ἐχαρίσατο βλέπειν *to the blind he granted the power of sight* **Lk 7:21** (v.l. τὸ βλέπειν; cp. Plut., Mor. 609a; 2 Macc 3:31, 33). ὁ χαρισάμενος ὑμῖν τοιοῦτον ἐπίσκοπον κεκτῆσθαι *the one who (by his favor) granted you to obtain such a bishop* IEph 1:3. Pass. **1 Cor 2:12.** ὑμῖν ἐχαρίσθη τὸ ὑπὲρ Χριστοῦ πάσχειν *you have (graciously) been granted the privilege of suffering for Christ* **Phil 1:29.**—χ. τινά τινι *give* or *grant someone to someone* (Semonides 7, 93f D.[3]: Zeus χαρίζεταί τινά τινι=Z. grants one [i.e., a good wife] to someone) κεχάρισταί σοι ὁ θεὸς πάντας τοὺς πλέοντας μετά σου *God has given you all those who are sailing with you,* i.e. at your request God has granted them safety fr. deadly danger **Ac 27:24.** The one who is 'given' escapes death or further imprisonment by being handed over to those who wish him freed ᾐτήσασθε ἄνδρα φονέα χαρισθῆναι ὑμῖν **Ac 3:14.** Cp. **Phlm 22** (Diod. S. 13, 59, 3 ἐχαρίσατο αὐτῷ τοὺς συγγενεῖς=he granted him his [captured] relatives [and set them free]; Plut., C. Gracch. 836 [4, 3] χ. τὸν 'Οκτάβιον τῇ μητρί; PFlor 61, 61 [I AD] cited s.v. ὄχλος 1a, end; Jos., Vi. 355.—On the 'giving' of Barabbas s. JMerkel, Die Begnadigung am Passahfeste: ZNW 6, 1905, 293–316). On the other hand, the giving of a man to those who wish him ill results in harm to him (cp. Jos., Vi. 53) οὐδείς με δύναται αὐτοῖς χαρίσασθαι **Ac 25:11;** cp. vs. **16** (without dat., which is easily supplied; the v.l. adds εἰς ἀπώλειαν to it). Ign. rejects every attempt of others to save his life, because he wishes to leave the world and be with God, and martyrdom opens the way for this: τὸν τοῦ θεοῦ θέλοντα εἶναι κόσμῳ μὴ χαρίσησθε *do not give to the world the one who wishes to belong to God* IRo 6:2.—W. only the dat. χ. τινι *show oneself to be gracious to someone* (Diod. S. 14, 11, 1; Appian, Bell. Civ. 2, 112 §467; SIG 354, 4f βουλόμενος χαρίζεσθαι τῷ δήμῳ; ApcEsdr 25:7 τοὺς δικαίους τί χαρίζεις; Jos., Ant. 17, 222; Eunap. p. 77 Boiss.) **Gal 3:18** (s. above; also Betz, Gal. ad loc.).

❷ **to cancel a sum of money that is owed, *cancel*** (Ps.-Aeschin., Ep. 12, 14; Philo, Spec. Leg. 2, 39 τὰ δάνεια) **Lk 7:42f.** This forms a transition to

❸ **to show oneself gracious by forgiving wrongdoing, *forgive, pardon*** (Dionys. Hal. 5, 4, 3; Jos., Ant. 6, 144 ἁμαρτήματα χαρίζεσθαι) w. dat. of pers. and acc. of thing (TestJob 43:1 αὐτοῖς . . . τὴν ἁμαρτίαν αὐτῶν) χαρισάμενος ἡμῖν πάντα τὰ παραπτώματα **Col 2:13;** cp. **2 Cor 2:10a; 12:13.** W. dat. of pers. alone **Eph 4:32ab; Col 3:13ab** (Plut., Mor. 488a χαίρειν τῷ χαρίζεσθαι μᾶλλον αὐτοῖς ἢ τῷ νικᾶν=to delight in doing them favors rather than getting the better of them). W. acc. of thing alone **2 Cor 2:10bc.** Abs. (cp. EpArist 215) *rather forgive* **2 Cor 2:7.**—B. 1174. DELG s.v. χάρις. M-M. EDNT. TW.

χάριν acc. of χάρις, used as a prep. (B-D-F §160; Rob. 488) and (B-D-F §216, 1; Rob. 647) w. the gen. (Hom.+; ins, pap, LXX; TestSol 20:2; TestAbr A; JosAs 16:1 cod. A [p. 63, 3 Bat.]; ApcMos 36; Just., Tat.); almost always after the word it governs; only in **1J 3:12** before it (a tendency in later Gk.: SIG index p. 619b; PTebt 44, 8 [114 BC]; 410, 4 [16 AD]; PGiss 98, 1 [II AD]. The LXX also has it predom. before: Johannessohn, Kasus 244, 3; likewise Ar., Tat.) ***for the sake of, on behalf of, on account of.***

ⓐ indicating the goal (cp. Hes., Works 709 μηδὲ ψεύδεσθαι γλώσσης χάριν=do not lie for the sake of talking; Just., D. 30, 1 χάριν τοῦ γνῶναι; Tat. 23, 2 χάριν τοῦ φονεύσαι) τῶν παραβάσεων χάριν *for the sake of transgressions,* i.e. to bring them about and into the open **Gal 3:19.** αἰσχροῦ κέρδους χ. **Tit 1:11.** Cp. **1 Ti 5:14; Jd 16;** 1 Cl 7:4. τούτου χάριν *for this purpose* (Appian, Bell. Civ. 4, 89 §375; Just., D. 1, 2) **Tit 1:5.** οὗ χάριν (Appian, Iber. 54 §230; Just., D. 2, 1; PFlor 99, 9 [I/II AD]) Dg 11:3. ὧν χάριν 1 Cl 55:6.

ⓑ indicating the reason (Tat. 7, 1 χάριν τῶν ἀνδραγαθημάτων) χάριν τίνος ἔσφαξεν αὐτόν; *for what reason (=why) did he kill him?* **1J 3:12.** οὗ χάριν *for this reason, therefore* (Philo, Op. M. 44) **Lk 7:47** (JDublin, οὗ χάριν [Lk 7:47]: ET 37, 1926, 525f). τίνος χάριν; *for what reason? why?* (Polyb. 2, 42, 1; 3, 9, 1; UPZ 5, 42; 6, 29; JosAs 16 cod. A [p. 63, 2f Bat.]; EpArist 254; Jos., C. Ap. 2, 263; Just., A II, 12, 5; Tat. 4, 1) 1 Cl 31:2.—The τούτου χάριν (X., Mem. 1, 2, 54; Plut., Mor. 146e; SIG 888, 70f; BGU 884, 14; 1 Macc 12:45; TestAbr A 13 p. 92, 10 [Stone p. 32]; Jos., Ant. 4, 197) of **Eph 3:1, 14** may be classed under a or b.—DELG s.v. χάρις. M-M.

χάρις, ιτος, ἡ (Hom.+) acc. quite predom. χάριν, but χάριτα **Ac 24:27; 25:9 v.l.; Jd 4** and pl. χάριτας **Ac 24:27 v.l.;** 1 Cl 23:1 (Eur., Hel. 1378; Hdt. 6, 41; X., Hell. 3, 5, 16; ins, pap; Zech 4:7; 6:14; EpArist 272, pl. 230.—B-D-F §47, 3; W-S. §9, 7; Mayser 271f; Thackeray 150; Helbing 40f; Mlt-H. 132.—It seems that χάρις is not always clearly differentiated in mng. fr. χαρά; Apollodorus [II BC]: 244 fgm. 90 Jac. says in the second book περὶ θεῶν: κληθῆναι δὲ αὐτὰς ἀπὸ μὲν τ. χαρᾶς Χάριτας· καὶ γὰρ πολλάκις . . . οἱ ποιηταὶ τ. χάριν χαρὰν καλοῦσιν 'the [deities] Charites are so called from χαρά [joy], for poets freq. equate χάρις with χαρά'. Cp. the wordplay AcPl Ha 8, 7 χαρᾶς καὶ χάριτος the house was filled with *gaiety and gratitude.*).

❶ **a winning quality or attractiveness that invites a favorable reaction, *graciousness, attractiveness, charm, winsomeness*** (Hom.+; Jos., Ant. 2, 231) of human form and appearance παῖς λίαν εὐειδὴς ἐν χάριτι *an exceptionally fine-looking and winsome youth* AcPl Ha 3, 13. Of speech (Demosth. 51, 9; Ps.-Demetr. [I AD], Eloc. §127; 133; 135 al.; Eccl 10:12; Sir 21:16; Jos., Ant. 18, 208) οἱ λόγοι τῆς χάριτος (gen. of quality) *the gracious words* **Lk 4:22.** ὁ λόγος ὑμῶν πάντοτε ἐν χάριτι *let your conversation always be winsome* **Col 4:6** (cp. Plut., Mor. 514f; s. also HAlmqvist, Plut. u. das NT '46, 121f; Epict. 3, 22, 90). τὸ πρόσωπον αὐτοῦ χάριτος ἐπληροῦτο MPol 12:1 can also be placed here in case χάρις means nothing more than graciousness (s. 4 below); prob. also GJs 7:3 (s. 3b).

❷ **a beneficent disposition toward someone, *favor, grace, gracious care/help, goodwill*** (almost a t.t. in the reciprocity-oriented world dominated by Hellenic influence [cp. e.g. OGI 669, 29] as well as by the Semitic sense of social obligation expressed in the term חֶסֶד [NGlueck, Das Wort ḥesed in alttestamentlichen Sprachgebrauche etc. 1927]. Of a different order and spirit is the subset of reciprocity known as Roman patronage, in which superiority of the donor over the client is clearly maintained)

ⓐ act., that which one grants to another, the action of one who volunteers to do someth. not otherwise obligatory χάρις θεοῦ ἦν ἐπ' αὐτό **Lk 2:40.** ἡ χάρις τοῦ θεοῦ (cp. τῇ τοῦ θεοῦ Κλαυδίου χάριτι OGI 669, 29) **Ac 11:2** D; **14:26.** τοῦ κυρίου **15:40.**—Esp. of the beneficent intention of God (cp. χ. in reference to God: Apollon. Rhod. 3, 1005 σοὶ θεόθεν χάρις ἔσσεται; Dio Chrys. 80 [30], 40 χ. τῶν θεῶν; Ael. Aristid. 13 p. 320 D.; 53 p. 620; Sextus 436b; likew. in LXX, Philo, Joseph.; SibOr 4, 46=189; 5, 330; Ezk. Trag. 162 [Eus., PE 9, 29, 12].—χ. to denote beneficent dispensations of the emperor: OGI 669, 44 [I AD]; BGU 19 I, 21 [II AD] χάρ. τοῦ θεοῦ Αὐτοκράτορος; 1085 II, 4) and of Christ, who give (undeserved) gifts to people; God: δικαιούμενοι δωρεὰν τῇ αὐτοῦ χάριτι **Ro 3:24.** Cp. **5:15a, 20f; 6:1; 11:5** (ἐκλογή 1), **6abc; Gal 1:15** (διά A 3e); **Eph 1:6f** (KKuhn, NTS 7, '61, 337 [reff. to Qumran lit.]); **2:5, 7, 8;** cp. Pol 1:3; **2 Th 1:12; 2:16; 2 Ti 1:9; Tit 2:11** (ἡ χάρ. τοῦ θεοῦ σωτήριος; s. Dibelius, Hdb. exc. after Tit 2:14); **3:7; Hb 2:9** (χωρίς 2aα); **4:16a** (DdeSilva, JBL 115, '96, 100–103); 1 Cl 50:3; ISm 9:2; IPol 7:3. ἐν χάρ[ιτι θεοῦ] AcPl Ha 7, 23 (restoration uncertain). κατὰ χάριν *as a favor, out of goodwill* (cp. Pla., Leg. 740c; schol. on Soph., Oed. Col. 1751 p. 468 Papag.) **Ro 4:4** (opp. κατὰ ὀφείλημα), **16.**—The beneficence or favor of Christ: διὰ τῆς χάριτος τοῦ κυρίου Ἰησοῦ πιστεύομεν σωθῆναι **Ac 15:11.** Cp. **Ro 5:15b; 2 Cor 8:9; 1 Ti 1:14;** IPhld 8:1. On **Ac 2:47** in this sense s. TAnderson, NTS 34, '88, 604–10.

ⓑ pass., that which one experiences fr. another (Arrian, Anab. Alex. 3, 26, 4) χάριν ἔχειν *have favor* **3J 4 v.l.** πρός τινα *with someone*=win his respect **Ac 2:47** (cp. 2a end; cp. Pind., O. 7, 89f χάριν καὶ ποτ' ἀστῶν καὶ ποτὶ ξείνων grant him respect in the presence of his townfolk as well as strangers); παρά τινι (Appian, Bell. Civ. 2, 89 §376) Hm 10, 3, 1, cp. 5, 1, 5. εὑρεῖν χάριν παρά τινι (Philo, Leg. All. 3, 77, end) **Lk 1:30;** Hs 5, 2, 10; ἐνώπιόν τινος **Ac 7:46;** GJs 11:2 (JosAs 15:14). ἐν τοῖς μέλλουσι μετανοεῖν *among those who are about to repent* Hm 12, 3, 3. Ἰησοῦς προέκοπτεν χάριτι παρὰ θεῷ καὶ ἀνθρώποις **Lk 2:52** (an indication of exceptional ἀρετή, cp. Pind. above). Cp. **Ac 4:33; 7:10** (ἐναντίον Φαραώ); **Hb 4:16b.**—ποία ὑμῖν χάρις ἐστίν; *what credit is that to you?* **Lk 6:32–34;** s. D 1:3; 2 Cl 13:4. Cp. **1 Cor 9:16 v.l.** In these passages the mng. comes close to *reward* (s. Wetter [5 below] 209ff w. reff.).—Also by metonymy *that which brings someone* (God's) *favor* or *wins a favorable response* fr. God **1 Pt 2:19, 20.**

ⓒ In Christian epistolary lit. fr. the time of Paul χάρις is found w. the sense (divine) *favor* in fixed formulas at the beginning and end of letters (Zahn on Gal 1:3; vDobschütz on 1 Th 1:1; ELohmeyer, ZNW 26, 1927, 158ff; APujol, De Salutat. Apost. 'Gratia vobis et pax': Verb. Dom. 12, '32, 38–40; 76–82; WFoerster, TW II '34, 409ff; Goodsp., Probs. 141f. S. also the lit. s.v. χαίρω 2b). At the beginning of a letter χάρις ὑμῖν καὶ εἰρήνη (sc. εἴη; New Docs 8, 127f) **Ro 1:7; 1 Cor 1:3; 2 Cor 1:2; Gal 1:3; Eph 1:2; Phil 1:2; Col 1:2; 1 Th 1:1; 2 Th 1:2; Phlm 3; Rv 1:4;** without ὑμῖν **Tit 1:4.** χάρις ὑμῖν καὶ εἰρήνη πληθυνθείη **1 Pt 1:2; 2 Pt 1:2;** 1 Cl ins. χάρις, ἔλεος, εἰρήνη **1 Ti 1:2; 2 Ti 1:2; 2J 3** (on the triplet cp. En 5:7 φῶς καὶ χάρις καὶ εἰρήνη).—At the end ἡ χάρις (τοῦ κυρίου ἡμῶν Ἰησοῦ Χριστοῦ etc.) μεθ' ὑμῶν (or μετὰ πάντων ὑμῶν etc.) **Ro 16:20, 23 (24) v.l.; 1 Cor 16:23; 2 Cor 13:13; Gal 6:18; Eph 6:24; Phil 4:23; Col 4:18; 1 Th 5:28; 2 Th 3:18; 1 Ti 6:21; 2 Ti 4:22; Tit 3:15; Phlm 25; Hb 13:25; Rv 22:21;** 1 Cl 65:2. ἔσται ἡ χάρις μετὰ πάντων τῶν φοβουμένων τὸν Κύριον GJs 25:2. ὁ κύριος τῆς δόξης καὶ πάσης χάριτος μετὰ τοῦ πνεύματος ὑμῶν B 21:9. χάρις ὑμῖν, ἔλεος, εἰρήνη, ὑπομονὴ διὰ παντός ISm 12:2. ἔρρωσθε ἐν χάριτι θεοῦ 13:2.

❸ **practical application of goodwill, *(a sign of) favor, gracious deed/gift, benefaction*—ⓐ** on the part of humans (X., Symp. 8, 36, Ages. 4, 3; Appian, Bell. Civ. 1, 49 §213; Dionys. Hal. 2, 15, 4) χάριν (-ιτα) καταθέσθαι τινί (κατατίθημι 2) **Ac 24:27; 25:9.** αἰτεῖσθαι χάριν **25:3** (in these passages from Ac χ. suggests *[political] favor,* someth. one does for another within a reciprocity system. Cp. Appian, Bell. Civ. 1, 108 §506 ἐς χάριν Σύλλα=as a favor to Sulla; ApcSed 8:1 οὐκ ἐποίησάς μοι χάριν=you did me no favor). ἵνα δευτέραν χάριν σχῆτε *that you might have a second proof of my goodwill* **2 Cor 1:15** (unless χάρις here means *delight* [so in poetry, Pind. et al., but also Pla., Isocr.; L-S-J-M s.v. χάρις IV; cp. also the quot. fr. Apollodorus at the beg. of the present entry, and the fact that χαρά is v.l. in 2 Cor 1:15]; in that case δευτέρα means *double;* but s. comm.). Of the collection for Jerusalem (cp. Appian, Bell. Civ. 3, 42 §173 χάριτας λαμβάνειν=receive gifts) **1 Cor 16:3; 2 Cor 8:4, 6f, 19** (DdeSilva, JBL 115, '96, 101). Cp. B 21:7.—**Eph 4:29** may suggest a demonstration of human favor (cp. Plut., Mor. 514e χάριν παρασκευάζοντες ἀλλήλοις), but a ref. to the means by which divine grace is mediated is not to be ruled out (s. b below).

ⓑ on the part of God and Christ; the context will show whether the emphasis is upon the *possession of divine favor* as a source of blessings for the believer, or upon a *store of favor* that is dispensed, or a *favored status* (i.e. standing in God's favor) that is brought about, or a *gracious deed* wrought by God in Christ, or a *gracious work* that grows fr. more to more (so in contrast to the old covenant Mel., P. 3, 16 al.). God is called ὁ θεὸς πάσης χάριτος **1 Pt 5:10,** i.e. God, who is noted for any conceivable benefit or favor; cp. B 21:9.—χάριν διδόναι τινί *show favor to someone* (Anacr. 110 Diehl; Appian, Ital. 5 §10): τὸν δόντα αὐτῷ τὴν χάριν GJs 14:2. ταπεινοῖς δίδωσι χάριν (Pr 3:34) **Js 4:6b; 1 Pt 5:5;** 1 Cl 30:2; without a dat. **Js 4:6a** (Menand., Epitr. 231 S. [55 Kö.]). Perh. καὶ ἔβαλλε κύριος . . . χάριν ἐπ' αὐτήν GJs 7:3 (but s. 1 above). The Logos is πλήρης χάριτος **J 1:14.** Those who belong to him receive of the fullness of his grace, χάριν ἀντὶ χάριτος vs. **16** (ἀντί 2). Cp. vs. **17.** τὴν χάριν ταύτην ἐν ᾗ ἑστήκαμεν *this favor (of God) we now enjoy* **Ro 5:2** (Goodsp.).—**5:17; 1 Cor 1:4; 2 Cor 4:15** (divine beneficence in conversion); cp. **Ac 11:23; 6:1; Gal 1:6** (*by Christ's gracious deed*); **2:21; 5:4; Col 1:6; 2 Ti 2:1; Hb 12:15; 13:9; 1 Pt 1:10, 13; 3:7** (συνκληρονόμοι χάριτος ζωῆς *fellow-heirs of the gift that spells life*; s. ζωή 2bα); **5:12; 2 Pt 3:18; Jd 4;** IPhld 11:1; ISm 6:2. Christians stand ὑπὸ χάριν *under God's gracious will* as expressed in their release from legal constraint **Ro 6:14f,** or they come ὑπὸ τὸν ζυγὸν τῆς χάριτος αὐτοῦ 1 Cl 16:17 (ζυγός 1). The proclamation of salvation is the message of divine beneficence τὸ εὐαγγέλιον τῆς χάριτος τοῦ θεοῦ **Ac 20:24** or ὁ λόγος τῆς χάριτος αὐτοῦ (=τοῦ κυρίου) **14:3; 20:32.** Even the gospel message can be called ἡ χάρις τοῦ θεοῦ **13:43;** cp. **18:27;** MPol 2:3. τὸ πνεῦμα τῆς χάριτος *the Spirit from* or *through whom (God's) favor is shown* **Hb 10:29** (AArgyle, Grace and the Covenant: ET 60, '48/49, 26f).—Pl. *benefits, favors* (Diod. S. 3, 2, 4; 3, 73, 6; Sb 8139, 4 [ins of I BC] of Isis; Jos., C. Ap. 2, 190) 1 Cl 23:1.—Nelson Glueck, Das Wort ḥesed etc. 1927, but s. FAndersen, 'Yahweh, the Kind and Sensitive God': God Who is Rich in Mercy, ed. PO'Brien/DPeterson '86.

❹ **exceptional effect produced by generosity,** ***favor.*** Of effects produced by divine beneficence which go beyond those associated with a specific Christian's status (ins μεγάλαι χάριτες τοῦ θεου: FCumont, Syria 7, 1926, 347ff), in the congregations of Macedonia **2 Cor 8:1** and Corinth **9:14;** cp. vs. **8;** in Rome AcPl Ha 7, 8. The Christian confessor is in full possession of divine grace ISm 11:1. Paul knows that through the χάρις of God he has been called to be an apostle, and that he has been fitted out w. the powers and capabilities requisite for this office fr. the same source: **Ro 1:5; 12:3; 15:15; 1 Cor 3:10; 15:10ab** (for the subject matter cp. Polyb. 12, 12b, 3 αὐτὸν [Alex. the Great] ὑπὸ τοῦ δαιμονίου τετευχέναι τούτων ὧν ἔτυχεν=whatever he has received he has received from what is divine. [For this reason he does not deserve any divine honors.]); **2 Cor 12:9; Gal 2:9; Eph 3:2, 7f; Phil 1:7.**—The χάρις of God manifests itself in various χαρίσματα: **Ro 12:6; Eph 4:7; 1 Pt 4:10.** This brings into view a number of passages in which χάρις is evidently to be understood in a very concrete sense. It is hardly to be differentiated fr. δύναμις (θεοῦ) or fr. γνῶσις or δόξα (q.v. 1b. On this subj. s. Wetter [5 below] p. 94ff; esp. 130ff; pap in the GLumbroso Festschr. 1925, 212ff: χάρις, δύναμις, πνεῦμα w. essentially the same mng.; PGM 4, 2438; 3165; Herm. Wr. 1, 32; Just., D. 87, 5 ἀπὸ χάριτος τῆς δυνάμεως τοῦ πνεύματος). οὐκ ἐν σοφίᾳ σαρκικῇ ἀλλ' ἐν χάριτι θεοῦ **2 Cor 1:12.** οὐκ ἐγὼ δὲ ἀλλὰ ἡ χάρις τοῦ θεοῦ σὺν ἐμοί **1 Cor 15:10c.** αὐξάνετε ἐν χάριτι καὶ γνώσει τοῦ κυρίου **2 Pt 3:18;** cp. 1 Cl 55:3; B 1:2 (τῆς δωρεᾶς πνευματικῆς χάρις). Stephen is said to be πλήρης χάριτος καὶ δυνάμεως **Ac 6:8.** Divine power fills the Christian confessor or martyr w. a radiant glow MPol 12:1 (but s. 1 above). As the typical quality of the age to come, contrasted w. the κόσμος D 10:6.

❺ **response to generosity or beneficence,** ***thanks, gratitude*** (a fundamental component in the Gr-Rom. reciprocity system; exx. fr. later times: Diod. S. 11, 71, 4 [χάριτες=proofs of gratitude]; Appian, Syr. 3, 12; 13. Cp. Wetter [below] p. 206f) χάριν ἔχειν τινί *be grateful to someone* (Eur., Hec. 767; X., An. 2, 5, 14; Pla., Phlb. 54d; Ath. 2, 1; PLips 104, 14 [I BC] χάριν σοι ἔχω) foll. by ὅτι (Epict. 3, 5, 10; Jos., C. Ap. 1, 270; 2, 49) **Lk 17:9** (ERiggenbach, NKZ 34, 1923, 439–43); mostly of gratitude to God or Christ; χάρις in our lit. as a whole, in the sense *gratitude,* refers to appropriate respone to the Deity for benefits conferred (Hom., Pind., Thu. et al.; ins, pap, LXX; Jos., Ant. 7, 208) χάριν ἔχω τῷ θεῷ (POxy 113, 13 [II AD] χάριν ἔχω θεοῖς πᾶσιν.—Epict. 4, 7, 9) **2 Ti 1:3;** foll. by ὅτι *because* **1 Ti 1:12** (Herm. Wr. 6, 4 κἀγὼ χάριν ἔχω τῷ θεῷ . . . , ὅτι; Jos., Ant. 4, 316); χάριν ἔχειν ἐπί τινι *be grateful for someth.* **Phlm 7 v.l.** (to humans). ἔχωμεν χάριν *let us be thankful* (to God) **Hb 12:28** (the reason for it is given by the preceding ptc. παραλαμβάνοντες). Elliptically (B-D-F §128, 6; cp. Rob. 1201f) χάρις (ἔστω) τῷ θεῷ (X., Oec. 8, 16 πολλὴ χάρις τοῖς θεοῖς; Epict. 4, 4, 7 χάρις τῷ θεῳ; BGU 843, 6 [I/II AD] χάρις τοῖς θεοῖς al. in pap since III BC.—Philo, Rer. Div. Her. 309) **Ro 7:25;** MPol 3:1. Foll. by ὅτι (X., An. 3, 3, 14 τοῖς θεοῖς χάρις ὅτι; PFay 124, 16 τοῖς θεοῖς ἐστιν χάρις ὅτι; Epict. 4, 5, 9) **Ro 6:17.** Foll. by ἐπί τινι *for someth.* (UPZ 108, 30 [99 BC]) **2 Cor 9:15.** The reason for the thanks is given in the ptc. agreeing w. τῷ θεῷ **2:14; 8:16; 1 Cor 15:57** (cp. Jos., Ant. 6, 145; Philo, Somn. 2, 213). *Thankfulness* (Appian, Bell. Civ. 3, 15 §51 πρός τινα=toward someone) χάριτι *in thankfulness* **10:30.** So prob. also ἐν τῇ χάριτι *in a thankful spirit* **Col 3:16** (Dibelius, Hdb. ad loc.). πλησθῆναι χαρᾶς καὶ χάριτος AcPl Ha 8, 7. S. εὐχαριστέω, end. Also PSchubert, Form and Function of the Pauline Thanksgivings '39.—OLoew, Χάρις, diss., Marburg 1908; GWetter, Charis 1913; AvHarnack, Sanftmut, Huld u. Demut in der alten Kirche: JKaftan Festschr. 1920, 113ff; NBonwetsch, Zur Geschichte des Begriffs Gnade in der alten Kirche: Harnack Festgabe 1921, 93–101; EBurton, Gal ICC 1921, 423f; WWhitley, The Doctrine of Grace '32; JMoffatt, Grace in the NT '31; RWinkler, D. Gnade im NT: ZST 10, '33, 642–80; RHomann, D. Gnade in d. syn. Ev.: ibid. 328–48; JWobbe, D. Charisgedanke b. Pls '32; RBultmann, Theologie des NT '48, 283–310 (Paul); HBoers, Ἀγάπη and Χάρις in Paul's Thought: CBQ 59, '97, 693–713; on 2 Cor 8: FDanker, Augsburg Comm. 2 Cor, 116–34; PRousselot, La Grâce d'après St. Jean et d'après St. Paul: SR 18, 1928, 87–108, Christent. u. Wissensch. 8, '32, 402–30; JMontgomery, Hebrew Hesed and Gk. Charis: HTR 32, '39, 97–102; Dodd 61f; TTorrance, The Doctrine of Grace in the Apost. Fathers, '48; JRenié, Studia Anselmiana 27f, '51,

340–50; CRSmith, The Bible Doctrine of Grace, '56; EFlack, The Concept of Grace in Bibl. Thought: Bibl. Studies in Memory of HAlleman, ed. Myers, '60, 137–54; DDoughty, NTS 19, '73, 163–80.—B. 1166. DELG. M-M. EDNT. TW. Spicq. Sv.

χάρισμα, ατος, τό (χαρίζομαι) **that which is freely and graciously given,** ***favor bestowed, gift*** (Sir 7:33 v.l.; 38:30 v.l.; Theod. Ps 30:22; TestSol; OdeSol 11:10; Philo, Leg. All. 3, 78 [twice]: γενέσεως δὲ οὐδὲν χάρισμα and δωρεὰ καὶ εὐεργεσία καὶ χάρισμα θεοῦ; SibOr 2, 54 θεοῦ χ.; Just., D. 82, 1; 88, 1.—Alciphron 3, 17, 4 [it is poss. that this comes fr. Attic comedy: Kock III p. 677]; BGU 1044, 4 [IV AD] of benefits bestowed. Other non-Jewish/Christian exx. of the word come fr. later times: BGU 551, 3; PLond I, 77, 24 p. 233; Sb 4789, 7; Achmes 4, 13; Nicetas Eugen. 6, 537f) in our lit. only of gifts of divine beneficence.

ⓐ gener., the earthly goods bestowed by God D 1:5. The privileges granted to the people of Israel **Ro 11:29.** The gracious gift of rescue fr. mortal danger **2 Cor 1:11.** The spiritual possession of the believer **Ro 1:11** (χάρισμα πνευματικόν); **1 Cor 1:7;** ISm ins; IPol 2:2. The gracious gift of redemption **Ro 5:15f;** IEph 17:2. τὸ χάρισμα τοῦ θεοῦ ζωὴ αἰώνιος **Ro 6:23.**

ⓑ of special gifts of a non-material sort, bestowed through God's generosity on individual Christians **1 Pt 4:10;** 1 Cl 38:1. Of the gift for carrying out special tasks, mediated by the laying on of hands **1 Ti 4:14; 2 Ti 1:6.** Of the power to be continent in sexual matters **1 Cor 7:7.** Of spiritual gifts in a special sense (Just., D. 82, 1 and Iren. 5, 6, 1 [Harv. II 334, 2] προφητικὰ χ.; Orig., C. Cels. 3, 46, 12; Hippol., Ref. 8, 19, 2) **Ro 12:6; 1 Cor 12:4, 9, 28, 30, 31.**—S. in addition to the lit. s.v. γλῶσσα 3 also GWetter, Charis 1913, 168–87; EBuonaiuti, I Carismi: Ricerche religiose 4, 1928 259–61; FGrau, Der ntliche Begriff Χάρισμα, diss. Tübingen '47; HHCharles, The Charismatic Life in the Apost. Church, diss. Edinburgh, '58; APiepkorn, CTM 42, '71, 369–89 (NT and Ap. Fathers); ENardoni, The Concept of Charism in Paul: CBQ 55, '93, 68–80; TRE VII 688–93.—DELG s.v. χάρις. M-M. EDNT. TW. Sv.

χαριτόω (χάρις) 1 aor. ἐχαρίτωσα; pf. pass. ptc. κεχαριτωμένος (Sir 18:17; Ps 17:26 Sym.; EpArist 225; TestJos 1:6; BGU 1026, XXIII, 24 [IV AD]; Cat. Cod. Astr. XII 162, 14; Rhet. Gr. I 429, 31; Achmes 2, 18) **to cause to be the recipient of a benefit,** ***bestow favor on, favor highly, bless,*** in our lit. only w. ref. to the divine χάρις (but Did., Gen. 162, 8 of Noah διὰ τῶν τῆς ἀρετῆς ἔργων χαριτώσας ἑαυτόν): ὁ κύριος ἐχαρίτωσεν αὐτοὺς ἐν πάσῃ πράξει αὐτῶν Hs 9, 24, 3. τῆς χάριτος αὐτοῦ (=τοῦ θεοῦ), ἧς ἐχαρίτωσεν ἡμᾶς ἐν τῷ ἠγαπημένῳ *God's great favor, with which he favored us through his beloved (Son)* **Eph 1:6.** Pass. (Libanius, Progymn. 12, 30, 12 vol. VIII p. 544, 10 F. χαριτούμενος=favored; cp. Geminus [I BC], Elem. Astronomiae [Manitius 1898] 8, 9 κεχαρισμένον εἶναι τοῖς θεοῖς) in the angel's greeting to Mary κεχαριτωμένη *one who has been favored* (by God) **Lk 1:28** (SLyonnet, Biblica 20, '39, 131–41; MCambe, RB 70, '63, 193–207; JNolland, Luke's Use of χάρις: NTS 32, '86, 614–20); GJs 11:1.—DELG s.v. χάρις. M-M. TW.

Χαρράν (Χαράν TestIss 1:5 Charles; Just., D. 58, 11; חָרָן. Gen 11:31f; 12:4f; 27:43; Philo; TestLevi 2:1), **ἡ** indecl. (Jos., Ant. 1, 152; 285* εἰς [τὴν] Χαρράν is surely acc. of Χαρρά) ***Haran,*** a place in Mesopotamia (=Κάρραι, Carrhae, famous for the defeat of Crassus that took place there in 53 BC), where Abraham lived for a time (Gen 11:31; Demetr.: 722 fgm. 1, 18 Jac.) **Ac 7:2, 4.**—BHHW II 647.

χάρτης, ου, ὁ (since the comic poet Plato [IV BC] in Pollux 7, 210; Theopompus [IV BC]: 115 fgm. 263 Jac. p. 592, 28 [in Περὶ ὕψους 43, 2] χάρται βυβλίων; ins, pap; Jer 43:23; TestSol; TestAbr A 12 p. 91, 3 [Stone p. 30]; ParJer; Jos., C. Ap. 1, 307; loanw. in rabb.) ***papyrus,*** mostly taken in the sense ***a sheet of paper*** (so Cebes 4, 3; Plut., Mor. 900b; Leo 1, 3 al.; Anth. Pal. 9, 401, 3; 174, 4; 6; Geopon. 13, 5, 4. Oft. pap; s. esp. PFlor 367, 7 χάρτας ἐπιστολικούς letter paper, stationery.—On the word s. GGlotz, Bull. Soc. Arch. Alex. 25, 1930, 83–96; Preis., Wörterb.). But in several pap (PCairZen 654, 46; 687, 7f; PColZen I, 4), it obviously means a(n unwritten) *papyrus roll* (APF 10, '32, 241; 11, '35, 286f; NLewis, L'industrie du Papyrus '34; Gnomon 12, '36, 48) **2J 12** (w. μέλαν; ParJer ἤνεγκε χάρτην καὶ μέλανα).—TBirt, Das antike Buchwesen 1882; KDziatzko, Untersuchungen über ausgewählte Kapitel des antiken Buchwesens 1900; VGardthausen, Das Buch im Altertum 1911; WSchubart, Das Buch bei den Griechen u. Römern[2] 1921, 34; Nestle/Dobschütz, Einführung in das griechische NT[4] 1923, 32f; 78; JČerný, Paper and Books in Ancient Egypt '52.—B. 1289. DELG. M-M.

χάσμα, ατος, τό (χάσκω 'yawn, gape'; Hes. et al.; Eur.; Hdt. 4, 85; Philo; Jos., Bell. 5, 566, Ant. 6, 27; 7, 242; 2 Km 18:17 χ. μέγα; En 18:11 χ. μέγα) ***chasm*** (lit. 'a yawning') of the unbridgeable space betw. Abraham and the place of torture **Lk 16:26** (Diog. L. 8, 31: acc. to Pythagoras the ψυχαὶ ἀκάθαρτοι cannot approach the ὕψιστος τόπος to which Hermes has brought the ψυχαὶ καθαραί; cp. 1 Esdr 7:10–15; on the topic of finality cp. 2 Cl 8:3; Pind. O. 2, 53–78).—DELG s.v. χαίνω II.

χεῖλος, ους, τό gen. pl. uncontracted χειλέων (**Hb 13:15** [fr. Hos 14:3]; B-D-F §48; Mlt-H. 139) 'lip'

❶ ***the lips,*** pl. (Hom.+; pap, LXX, PsSol; OdeSol 11:6; TestSol 18:20; TestIss 7:4; JosAs, Philo; Just., A I, 32, 8, D. 101, 3) as used in speaking **Mt 15:8; Mk 7:6;** 1 Cl 15:2; 2 Cl 3:5; cp. 4 (all Is 29:13); **Ro 3:13** (Ps 139:4); **Hb 13:15** (Hos 14:3); **1 Pt 3:10** (Ps 33:14); 1 Cl 15:5 (Ps 30:19); 18:15 (Ps 50:17); 22:3 (Ps 33:14). ἐν χείλεσιν ἑτέρων λαλήσω **1 Cor 14:21** (Is 28:11, but significantly different). In another sense, of a derisive gesture λαλεῖν ἐν χείλεσιν 1 Cl 16:16 (Ps 21:8). ἐπὶ τοῖς χείλεσιν ἔχειν τινά *have someone* (i.e. his name) *on the lips* and nothing more (Dio Chrys. 15 [32], 50 ἐπὶ τοῖς χείλεσι τὰς ψυχὰς ἔχειν) Hm 12, 4, 4; also ἐπὶ τὰ χείλη s 9, 21, 1.

❷ ***shore, bank,*** sing. (of a river: Hdt. 2, 94; Polyb. 3, 14, 6 al.; Diod. S. 3, 10, 2; 20, 75, 3; of rivers and marshes Aristot., HA 6, 16; a pond Jos., Bell. 3, 511) of the sea (TestAbr A 1 p. 78, 1 [Stone p. 4]; ApcEsdr 3:10 p. 27, 20 Tdf.; ApcSed 8:9 p. 133, 14 Ja.; Achilles Tat. 2, 18, 2) **Hb 11:12** (Gen 22:17). τοῦ Ἰορδάνου PEg[2] 66.—DELG. M-M.

χειμάζω (χεῖμα 'winter weather'; Aeschyl., Thu. et al.; ins, pap; Pr 26:10; En 101:5; Test12Patr)

❶ **expose to bad weather,** ***toss in a storm*** in our lit. of an actual storm that impedes navigation, and in the pass. (cp. Aeschyl., Prom. 840; Pla., Phlb. 29a; Diod. S. 3, 55, 8; 5, 58, 2 κεχειμασμένος ἰσχυρῶς κατὰ τὸν πλοῦν; Ael. Aristid. 44, 13 K.=17 p. 405 D.: χειμαζόμενος; En 101:5; TestNapht 6:5; Jos., Ant. 12, 130 al.) σφοδρῶς χειμαζομένων **Ac 27:18.** In imagery (Polystrat. p. 31; Epict., fgm. Stob. 47; Jos., Bell. 3, 195; TestJud 21:6) IPol 2:3.

❷ **to cause physical or psychological distress,** ***distress*** of a pregnancy ἴσως τὸ ἐν αὐτῇ χειμάζει αὐτήν *perhaps that which is in her is distressing her* GJs 17:2 (s. deStrycker p. 308).—DELG s.v. χεῖμα. M-M.

χείμαρος s. χίμαρος.

χείμαρρος/χειμάρρους, ου, ὁ (χεῖμα 'winter weather', ῥέω; since Hom. [χειμάρροος and χείμαρρος Il. 4, 452; 5, 88] predom. in the form χειμάρρους, which also prevails throughout the LXX [χείμαρρος w. certainty only Ps 123:4, but also EpArist 117; SibOr 13, 55; s. Thackeray 144; Helbing 34], as well as in Philo [Rer. Div. Her. 32] and in Joseph. [Ant. 6, 360; w. χείμαρρος 314]) **a stream of water that flows abundantly in the winter** (Suda defines it: ὁ ἐν τῷ χειμῶνι ῥέων ποταμός; Polyb. 4, 70, 7 and Artem. 2, 27 add ποταμός to χ.), ***winter torrent, ravine, wadi*** **J 18:1** (s. Κεδρών and Jos., Ant. 8, 17 τὸν χειμάρρουν Κεδρῶνα). ἐπέβλεψα ἐπὶ τὸν χείμαρρον τοῦ ποταμοῦ *I looked at the flow of the stream* GJs 18:3.—B. 42. DELG s.v. χεῖμα. M-M.

χειμερινός, ή, όν (Hdt. et al.; ins, pap, LXX, En 17:7; Philo) **pert. to winter, *winter*** καιροὶ χειμερινοί *winter seasons* 1 Cl 20:9 (Diod. S. 14, 100, 5; 15, 65, 2 χειμερινὴ ὥρα=winter season).—DELG s.v. χεῖμα.

χειμών, ῶνος, ὁ (Hom.+, in var. senses relating to inclement/bad weather; contexts usually qualify the specific character of such weather, for which a receptor language may have discrete terms)

➊ **stormy weather, *bad weather, storm*** (Hom. et al.; Sb 998 [16/17 AD]; LXX; En 101:4; Test12Patr; Joseph.) σήμερον χειμών *today* it will be *stormy (weather)* **Mt 16:3.** On the sea, *storm, bad weather:* χειμῶνος οὐκ ὀλίγου ἐπικειμένου *with some rather bad weather pressing upon them* (indicative of a low-pressure area) **Ac 27:20.** For this pass. many render *storm* (cp. Demosth. 18, 194; Diod. S. 11, 13, 1 χ. μέγας=a severe storm; TestNapht 6:9; Jos., Ant. 6, 91; 14, 377; fig.: Philo, Congr. Erud. Gr. 93 [opp. γαλήνη] and Tat. 6, 3 a 'squall' of stupidity); based, according to Warnecke, Romfahrt 41 (n. 10; s. also p. 46), on misconceptions relating to meteorological conditions and geographical data and without due accounting of the unlikely feat of sailing through a violent storm for two weeks (Ac 27:27; s. Romfahrt 41–54).

➋ **the season of bad weather, *winter*** (Hom., Hdt., Thu., Aristoph.+; ins, pap; SSol 2:11; En 2:2; TestZeb 6:8; Philo; Jos., Ant. 14, 376; Ar. 4, 2) **J 10:22** (short clause as Polyaenus 7, 44, 2 πόλεμος ἦν, exc. 36, 8). χειμῶνος *in winter* (Pla., Rep. 3, 415e; X., Mem. 3, 8, 9; Appian, Illyr. 24 §70; SIG 495, 104f; cp. ἐν χειμῶνι TestSol 10:7 C) **Mt 24:20; Mk 13:18.** πρὸ χειμῶνος *before winter* (sets in) **2 Ti 4:21.**—In imagery: χειμών ἐστί τινι Hs 3, 2; 4, 2; τῷ χειμῶνι τὰ δένδρα ἀποβάλλειν τὰ φύλλα *the trees shed their leaves in winter* 3:3.—B. 1013. DELG s.v. χεῖμα. M-M.

χείρ, χειρός, ἡ (Hom.+); on the acc. form χεῖραν **J 20:25 v.l.; 1 Pt 5:6 v.l.;** GJs 15:4 23:2 s. JPsichari, Essai sur le Grec de la Septante 1908, 164–70. Exx. fr. the pap in the Hdb. at J 20:25. Dual acc. τὼ χεῖρε only Tat. 22, 1. Dat. χειροῖν ApcPt Rainer 'hand'.

➊ lit. **Mt 12:10; Mk 3:1; Lk 6:6, 8; Ac 12:7; 20:34** al.; AcPlCor 2:35. πόδες καὶ χεῖρες **Mt 22:13;** cp. **Lk 24:39, 40; Ac 21:11a.** W. other parts of the body in sing. and pl. **Mt 5:(29), 30; 18:8ab, (9); J 11:44.** In the gen. w. the verbs ἅπτομαι **Mt 8:15;** ἐπιλαμβάνομαι (q.v. 1); κρατέω (q.v. 3b). In the acc. w. the verbs αἴρω (q.v. 1a); ἀπονίπτομαι (q.v.); βάλλω **J 20:25b;** δέω (q.v. 1b); δίδωμι (q.v. 2); ἐκπετάννυμι (q.v.); ἐκτείνω (q.v. 1); ἐπαίρω (q.v. 1); ἐπιβάλλω (q.v. 1b); ἐπισείω (q.v. 1); ἐπιτίθημι (q.v. 1aα; s. New Docs 4, 248 on laying on of hands; JCoppens, L'imposition des mains dans les Actes des Apôtres: Les Actes des Apôtres, ed. JKremer '79, 405–38); cp. ἐπίθεσις (τῶν) χειρῶν (s. ἐπίθεσις); κατασείω (q.v.); νίπτομαι (s. νίπτω 1bβ and the lit. s.v. βαπτίζω 1; also JDöller, Das rituelle Händewaschen bei den Juden: Theol.-prakt. Quartalschr. 64, 1911, 748–58); τίθημι (q.v. 1aβ); ποιεῖν: ὀπίσω τὰς χεῖρας (ὀπίσω 1aβ) and τὰς χ. ἐναλλάξ (s. ἐναλλάξ); προσφέρω (q.v. 1bβ).—In the instrumental dat. ἔγραψα τῇ ἐμῇ χειρί (cp. Chariton 8, 4, 6; BGU 326 II, 2 al. in pap.—χείρ=*handwriting* as early as Hyperides in Pollux 2, 152, also Philod., π. ποιημ. 4, 33; 6, 14 Jens.; PMagd 25, 2 [III BC]; Jos., Ant. 14, 52) **Gal 6:11; Phlm 19.** ὁ ἀσπασμὸς τῇ ἐμῇ χειρί (i.e. γέγραπται) **1 Cor 16:21; Col 4:18; 2 Th 3:17** (on the conclusion of a letter written in the sender's own handwriting, in pap letters as well as in the works of the Emperor Julian [Epistulae, Leges etc., ed. Bidez and Cumont 1922, nos. 9; 11], s. CBruns, Die Unterschriften in den röm. Rechtsurkunden: ABA 1876, 41–138; KDziatzko, entry Brief: Pauly-W. III 1899, 836ff; Dssm., LO 132f; 137f [LAE 166f; 171f]; s. also lit. s.v. χαίρω 2b). ἐννεύω τῇ χ. (s. ἐννεύω). κατασείω τῇ χ. (s. κατασείω 2). κρατέω τῇ χ. (κρατέω 3b). Pl. ταῖς χερσίν *with the hands* (Demetr. Phaler.: 228 fgm. 38, 28 Jac. [in Diog. L. 2, 13] ταῖς ἰδίαις χερσίν; Diod. S. 16, 33, 1 τ. ἰδίαις χ. 17, 17, 7 al.; Aesop, Fab. 272 P.=425 H.; Herm. Wr. 5, 2) **Lk 6:1; 1 Cor 4:12; Eph 4:28; 1 Th 4:11** (s. HPreisker, Das Ethos d. Arbeit im NT '36); Papias (3:3).—τὸ ἔργον τῶν χειρῶν τινος s. ἔργον 3 and **Rv 9:20.**—W. prepositions: the hand on or in which someth. lies or fr. which someth. comes or is taken: ἐν τῇ χειρί **Mt 3:12; Lk 3:17.** (ἔχειν τι) εἰς τὰς χεῖρας Hv 1, 2, 2. ἐπὶ τὴν χεῖρα **Rv 20:1.** ἐπὶ χειρῶν **Mt 4:6; Lk 4:11** (both Ps 90:12; s. end of this section). ἐκ (τῆς) χειρός (Diod. S. 2, 8, 6) **Rv 8:4; 10:10.** The hand by which someth. comes about: of deities θεοὶ οἱ διὰ χειρῶν γινόμενοι *gods that are made by hand* **Ac 19:26** (cp. Just., A I, 20, 5). Of an earthly temple οἰκοδομητὸς ναὸς διὰ χειρός B 16:7.—The *arm* may be meant (as Hes., Theog. 150; Hdt. 2, 121, 5 ἐν τῷ ὤμῳ τὴν χεῖρα; Herodas 5, 83 ἐν τῇσι χερσὶ τῇσ᾽ ἐμῇσι=in my arms; Paus. 6, 14, 7; Galen, De Usu Part. 2, 2 vol. I p. 67, 1 Helmreich; Longus 1, 4, 2 χεῖρες εἰς ὤμους γυμναί) in ἐπὶ χειρῶν ἀροῦσίν σε **Mt 4:6; Lk 4:11** (both Ps 90:12; but s. above). Whole for the part: *finger* **Lk 15:22.**

➋ **an acting agent, *hand (of)*,** fig. ext. of 1. In this sense the focus is on the person or thing as the source of an activity.

ⓐ The OT (but cp. Diod. S. 3, 65, 3 ταῖς τῶν γυναικῶν χερσί=by the women; Ael. Aristid. 45 p. 70 D.: μετὰ τῆς χειρὸς τῶν δικαίων; Philostrat., Vi. Apoll. 6, 29; Nicetas Eugen. 7, 165 χειρὶ βαρβάρων) has a tendency to speak of a person's activity as the work of one's hand; διὰ χειρός ([τῶν] χειρῶν) τινος (בְּיַד) *through* or *by someone* or *someone's activity, at the hand of* **Mk 6:2; Ac 2:23; 5:12; 7:25; 11:30; 14:3; 15:23; 19:11.** Also ἐν χειρί (PsSol 16:14 ἐν χειρὶ σαπρίας *by corruption*; cp. AscIs 2:5 ἐν χερσίν) **Gal 3:19.** Corresp. *the hands* can represent the one who is acting οὐδὲ ὑπὸ χειρῶν ἀνθρωπίνων θεραπεύεται *nor does God need to be served by humans* **Ac 17:25.**

ⓑ The hand of deity means divine power (Il. 15, 695; Ael. Aristid. 47, 42 K.=23 p. 455 D.: ἐν χερσὶ τοῦ θεοῦ; LXX; Aristobulus in Eus., PE 8, 10, 1; 7–9 [p. 138 Holladay]; Ezk. Trag. 239 in Eus., PE 9, 29, 14; SibOr 3, 672; 795.—Porphyr. in Eus., PE 4, 23, 6 ὁ θεὸς ὁ ἔχων ὑπὸ χεῖρα, sc. τ. δαίμονας; Ath. 33, 2 παραβαίνων τὴν χεῖρα τοῦ θεοῦ). S. New Docs 2, 44.

α. as Creator (Ath. 34, 1) **Ac 7:50** (Is 66:2). ποίησις χειρῶν αὐτοῦ 1 Cl 27:7 (Ps 18:2). τὰ ἔργα τῶν χειρῶν σου **Hb 1:10** (Ps 101:26; ApcEsdr 1:10 p. 25, 2 Tdf.); **2:7 v.l.** (Ps 8:7). Cp. B 5:10. In connection w. the account of creation the words ἄνθρωπον ταῖς ἱεραῖς χερσὶν ἔπλασεν 1 Cl 33:4 could be taken in the lit. sense.

β. as ruler, helper, worker of wonders, regulator of the universe: χεὶρ κυρίου ἦν μετ' αὐτοῦ **Lk 1:66; Ac 11:21** (TestAbr A 18 p. 100, 21 [Stone p. 48]).—**Lk 23:46** (Ps 30:6); **J 10:29; Ac 4:28** (w. βουλή, hence almost='will'; cp. Sir 25:26), 30; **1 Pt 5:6** (cp. Gen 16:9); 1 Cl 60:3. ὑπὸ τὴν κραταιὰν χεῖραν GJs 15:4.

γ. as punisher (PsSol 5:6 μὴν βαρύνῃς τὴν χεῖρά σου ἐφ' ἡμᾶς; schol. on Apollon. Rhod. 4, 1043a ἐν ταῖς χερσὶ τῶν θεῶν νέμεσις) χεὶρ κυρίου ἐπί σε (1 Km 12:15) **Ac 13:11.** ἐμπεσεῖν εἰς χεῖρας θεοῦ ζῶντος (s. ἐμπίπτω 2) **Hb 10:31.** Cp. 1 Cl 28:2.

δ. of the powerful hand of Christ or of an angel **J 3:35; 10:28; 13:3.** ἐκ χειρὸς ἀγγέλου GJs 8:1; 13:2; cp. ἀγγέλων 15:3.—σὺν χειρὶ ἀγγέλου *with the help of an angel* **Ac 7:35.**

ⓒ hostile power (Hom. et al.; LXX) παραδιδόναι τινὰ εἰς χεῖράς τινος *hand over to someone('s power)* (TestJob 20:3; ParJer 1:6; s. παραδίδωμι 1b; cp. PsSol 2:7 ἐγκαταλείπειν; Jos., Ant 6, 273.—B-D-F §217, 2) **Ac 21:11b;** pass. **Mt 17:22; 26:45; Mk 9:31; Lk 9:44; 24:7; Ac 28:17;** D 16:4. Also παραδιδ. τινὰ ἐν χειρί τινος 1 Cl 55:5. τὸ αἷμα σου ὑπὸ τὴν χεῖράν μού ἐστιν *your blood is in my power* GJs 23:2; escape, etc. ἐκ (τῆς) χειρός τινος *from someone's power* (UPZ 79, 18 [159 BC] ἐκπέφευγεν ἐκ τῆς χειρός μου; Gen 32:12; Ex 18:10; Jos., Vi. 83) **Lk 1:71, 74; J 10:39; Ac 12:11;** AcPl Ha 8, 10f; AcPlCor 1:8. ἐκ χειρὸς σιδήρου λύσει σε *he will free you from the power of the sword* 1 Cl 56:9 (Job 5:20; Mel., P. 67, 478). ἐκ τῶν χειρῶν ἡμῶν **Ac 24:6 (7) v.l.** (cp. X., An. 6, 3, 4; Lucian, Hermot. 9, end). ἐξέφυγον τὰς χεῖρας αὐτοῦ **2 Cor 11:33** (Diod. S. 18, 73, 4 τὰς τοῦ Σελεύκου χεῖρας διαφυγών). ὑπὸ χειρὸς ἀνθρώπων παθεῖν B 5:5. πίε τὸ ποτήριον . . . ἐν χεροῖν τοῦ υἱοῦ τοῦ ἐν Ἅιδου *drink the cup out of the hand of the son, who is in the nether world* ApcPtRainer 17f.

❸ distinctive prepositional combinations: ἐν χερσίν of someth. that one has ***in hand,*** w. which one is concerned at the moment (Hdt. 1, 35 τὸν γάμον ἐν χερσὶν ἔχοντος; Appian, Bell. Civ. 5, 81 §342 τὰ ἐν χερσίν; Ael. Aristid. 45 p. 74 D.; PPetr II, 9 [2], 4 [III BC] ἃ εἶχον ἐν ταῖς χερσίν; Jos., Bell. 43 165) ἐν χερσὶν ὁ ἀγών *the contest is our concern at present* 2 Cl 7:1. ὑπὸ χεῖρα ***continually*** (Ps.-Aristot., Mirabilia 52; Jos., Ant. 12, 185) Hv 3, 10, 7; 5:5; m 4, 3, 6 (B-D-F §232, 1.—In pap we have the mng. 'privately', 'little by little': PTebt 71, 15 [II BC]; Gnomon [=BGU V] prooem. 2f; PAmh 136, 17).—KGrayston, The Significance of 'Hand' in the NT: B Rigaux Festschr. '70, 479–87.—B. 237ff. DELG. M-M. EDNT. TW. Sv.

χειραγωγέω (χείρ, ἄγω; Diod. S. 13, 20, 4; Plut., Maximus Tyr., Lucian et al.; UPZ 110, 55 [164 BC]; Judg 16:26 A; Tob 11:16 S; Jos., Ant. 5, 315) ***take/lead by the hand*** (e.g. a pers. suddenly blinded by an arrow: Appian, Bell. Civ. 2, 60 §248; a blind pers. in general: Artem. 5, 20) **Ac 9:8.** Pass. **22:11;** GPt 10:40.—M-M. TW. Spicq.

χειραγωγός, οῦ, ὁ **one who leads another by the hand,** ***leader*** (Plut., Mor. 794d; 1063b; Artem. 1, 48; Ael. Aristid. 45 p. 60 D.; Maximus Tyr. 8, 7h [of God]; Longus 4, 24, 2; Herm. Wr. 7, 2a) **Ac 13:11.**—M-M. TW. Spicq.

χειρόγραφον, ου, τό (since Polyb. 30, 8, 4; SIG 742, 50f [85 BC]. Oft. in pap fr. II BC [e.g. PYadin 5a I, 9]; Tob) **a handwritten document, specif. a certificate of indebtedness,** ***account, record of debts*** (so plainly TestJob 11:11; Vi. Aesopi G 122 P.—Dssm., LO 281ff [LAE 332ff]) τὸ καθ' ἡμῶν χειρόγραφον *the account that stood against us* **Col 2:14** (s. GMegas, ZNW 27, 1928, 305–20; OBlanchette, CBQ 23, '61, 306–12: identifies the χ. with Christ; on these and other views RYates, Biblica 71, '90, 251).—DELG s.v. χείρ. M-M. TW. Spicq. Sv.

χειροποίητος, ον (Hdt.+; Diod. S. 13, 82, 5; 15, 93, 4; 17, 71, 7; Arrian, Anab. 4, 28, 3; PLond III, 854, 4 p. 205 [I AD]; LXX; Jos., Bell. 1, 419, Ant. 4, 55; SibOr 3, 606; 618, fgm. 3, 29; Jos., Bell. 1, 419; Ant. 4, 55; Just.) ***made by human hands*** of buildings, specif. temples (SibOr 14, 62 ναῶν χειροποιήτων; Philo, Mos. 2, 88 ἱερόν of the tabernacle) **Mk 14:58; Ac 7:48 v.l.; 17:24; Hb 9:11, 24.** Subst. (ViJer 7 [Sch. p. 10]; Philo, Mos. 2, 168; Just., A I, 58, 3; D. 35, 6) χειροποίητα *temples built by human hands* **Ac 7:48.** Of physical circumcision (as opposed to 'circumcision of the heart') τῆς λεγομένης περιτομῆς ἐν σαρκὶ χειροποιήτου *of the so-called circumcision, brought about in the flesh by human hands* **Eph 2:11.**—DELG s.v. χείρ. M-M. TW. Sv.

χειροτονέω (τείνω) 1 aor. ἐχειροτόνησα, pass. ἐχειροτονήθην (Aristoph., X., Pla. et al.; ins, pap; Philo, Somn. 2, 243, Spec. Leg. 1, 78; Jos., Vi. 341 al.; Just., D. 108, 2) lit. 'stretch out the hand' in voting

❶ **to elect or choose someone for definite offices or tasks,** ***choose*** (IG IV^2/1, 89, 18 [II/III AD] χ. ἱερέας; Jos, Ant. 13:45). Congregations *choose* a representative to accompany Paul on his journey to take the collection to Jerusalem **2 Cor 8:19** (IG II^2/1, 1260 χειροτονηθεὶς ὑπὸ τοῦ δήμου στρατηγός.—S. Windisch ad loc.; Betz, 2 Cor p. 74f). Congregations *choose* envoys to bring congratulations to the ἐκκλησία at Antioch IPhld 10:1; ISm 11:2; IPol 7:2. Congregations are to *elect* their own supervisors (ἐπίσκοποι) and ministers (διάκονοι) D 15:1.

❷ On the other hand, elders (πρεσβύτεροι) in Lycaonia and Pisidia were not chosen by the congregations, but it is said of Paul and Barnabas χειροτονήσαντες αὐτοῖς κατ' ἐκκλησίαν πρεσβυτέρους **Ac 14:23.** Cp. **Tit 1:9 v.l.** and **subscr.; 2 Ti subscr.** This does not involve a choice by the group; here the word means ***appoint, install,*** w. the apostles as subj. (Philo, Praem. 54 βασιλεὺς ὑπὸ θεοῦ χειροτονηθείς, De Jos. 248 Joseph βασιλέως ὕπαρχος ἐχειροτονεῖτο, Mos. 1, 198, In Flacc. 109; Jos., Ant. 6, 312 τὸν ὑπὸ τοῦ θεοῦ κεχειροτονημένον βασιλέα; 13, 45). JRoss, ET 63, '51f, 288f; ELohse, D. Ordination im Spätjudentum u. im NT, '51; MWarkentin, Ordination '82.—Kl. Pauly I 1142. New Docs 1, 123. DELG s.v. χείρ. M-M. TW. Sv.

χειροτονία, ας, ἡ (Thu. et al.; ins, pap, Philo; Jos., Bell. 4, 147, Ant. 3, 192 of choosing and electing; s. χειροτονέω) lit. 'stretch out the hand'; in our lit. only once and in the sense **the lifting up of the hand as a hostile or scornful gesture,** ***scornful gesture*** ἐὰν ἀφέλῃς ἀπὸ σοῦ χειροτονίαν *if you stop raising your hand* B 3:5 (Is 58:9).—DELG s.v. χείρ. M-M s.v. χειροτονέω. DNP II 1114. Sv.

χείρων, ον, gen. **ονος** (Hom. et al.; pap, LXX; JosAs 1:13; GrBar, Philo, Joseph.) pl. masc., fem. χείρους (Just., D. 1, 5; Ath. 31, 1) comp. of κακός, superl. χείριστος LXX; adv. χεῖρον (GrBar 4:16), χείριστα (2 Macc 5:23) ***worse, more severe*** σχίσμα **Mt 9:16; Mk 2:21.** τιμωρία **Hb 10:29** (Jos., Vi. 172; cp. PGM 2, 54). ἵνα μὴ χεῖρόν σοί τι γένηται *that nothing worse may happen to you* **J 5:14** (cp. Jos., Ant. 4, 142). W. gen. of comparison (1 Km 17:43; Wsd 15:18) γίνεται τὰ ἔσχατα χείρονα τῶν πρώτων **Mt 12:45; Lk 11:26; 2 Pt 2:20.** Cp. **Mt 27:64.**—Of a sick woman εἰς τὸ χεῖρον ἐλθεῖν **Mk 5:26.**—In the moral realm Hs 9, 17, 5; 9, 18, 1. W. gen. of comparison (LXX, JosAs; GrBar 4:16; Ar. 8, 2; Just., A II, 3, 3) ἀπίστου χείρων **1 Ti 5:8.** προκόπτειν ἐπὶ τὸ χεῖρον **2 Ti 3:13** (ἐπὶ τὸ χ. as X., Mem.

3, 5, 13; Pla., Rep. 381b; Diod. S. 15, 88, 4; Strabo 16, 2, 39; Artem. 1, 74 p. 67, 11; UPZ 110, 124 [164 BC]; Jos., Ant. 16, 207). Christians know nothing of an ἀπὸ τῶν κρειττόνων ἐπὶ τὰ χείρω μετάνοια MPol 11:1 (Maximus Tyr. 5, 3a εἰ εἰς τὸ χεῖρον ἐκ τοῦ βελτίστου, πονηρῶς [sic] μετέθετο=if [a man turns] to the worse from the best, then the change he makes is a bad one). Of a military detachment likened to wild beasts οἳ χείρους γίνονται *who* (simply) *become harsher* the more they are kindly treated IRo 5:1 (cp. Philo, Abr. 129).—DELG. M-M.

Χερούβ, τό (Ezk 28:16) and **ὁ** (Ex 25:19; 38:7: כְּרוּב) indecl. **the image of the winged creature that stood over the covenant box, *winged creature*** the pl. w. various endings Χερουβίν, -βείν (En 20:7; PGM 13, 255; 334), -βείμ, -βίμ (TestSol, TestAbrB; TestJob 50:2; ApcEsdr 2:26 p. 26, 20 Tdf. al.; ApcMos; SibOr 3, 1 τὰ Χερουβίμ; En 14:11 Χερουβὶν πύρινα; PGM 7, 634 ἐπὶ τὰ Χερουβίν; IDefixWünsch 3, 24 ἐπὶ τῶν Χερουβί; Ps 79:2 ἐπὶ τῶν Χερουβίν; En 20:7 Χερουβείν.—As sing. PGM 4, 3061 τοῦ Χερουβίν; 7, 264 ἐπὶ Χερουβίν), predom. neut. τά (Gen 3:24; Ex 25:18; 3 Km 6:27f; 8:7; 2 Ch 3:10, 13; Ezk 10:3, 8, 15; 11:22; 41:18, 20; En 14:11; ApcSed 2:26; ApcMos 19; Philo, Cher. 1; 25; 28, Fuga 100) more rarely masc. οἱ (Ex 25:19; 38:6f; Jos., Ant. 3, 137.—Elsewh. Joseph. writes Χερουβεῖς; indeed, he used the word as a masc., Ant. 7, 378 and as a fem. 8, 72f), of the two winged figures over the ark of the covenant Χερουβὶν δόξης **Hb 9:5.**—AJacoby, ARW 22, 1924, 257–65; PDhorme/LVincent, Les Chérubins: RB 35, 1926, 328–58; 481–95; TLL, Suppl. 1, 389–92.—BHHW I 298f. M-M. TW.

χερσόω (χέρσος 'dry land'; Hom. et al.) ***make dry and barren*** (BGU 195, 21 [II AD]) in our lit. (Hermas) only pass. **χερσόομαι** (Strabo 17, 1, 36; IGR IV, 147; PTebt 5, 94 [118 BC]; 61b, 30; 75, 40; LXX) 1 aor. ἐχερσώθην; pf. ptc. κεχερσωμένος *become barren* or *wild,* lit. of untended vineyards Hm 10, 1, 5. Fig. of Christians who are entangled w. the world 10, 1, 4 or who deny their Lord s 9, 26, 3.—DELG s.v. χέρσος.

χέω (Hom. et al.; ins, pap, LXX; TestLevi 18:5 [beg.]) fut. 3 sg. χεεῖ Mal 3:3. Pass.: fut. 3 sg. χυθήσεται Jon 2:2; aor. ptc. gen. χυθέντος (Mel., P. 30, 207); pf. 3 sg. κέχυται and ptc. κεχυμένος LXX; in its only occurrence in our lit. it stands in the mid. and pass. **χέομαι *pour out, gush forth*** (Philo, Spec. Leg. 4, 26; Jos., Ant. 8, 232; SibOr, fgm. 3, 33) ταῦτα τὰ χεόμενα ὕδατα of the waters of the pool of David in contrast to the waters of eternal life Ox 840, 32.—B. 577. DELG.

χήρα, ας, ἡ (Hom.+) **a woman whose husband has died, *widow*—ⓐ** of a widow as such (with and without γυνή)—γυνὴ χήρα (Hom. et al.; BGU 522, 7; POxy 1120, 12; Jos., Ant. 4, 240; 8, 320; LXX) *a widow* **Lk 4:26** (after 3 Km 17:9). Elsewh. ἡ χήρα alone, *widow* (Hom.; Soph., Aj. 653; Eur.+; ins, pap, LXX, TestJob; SibOr 3, 77; Philo; Jos., Ant. 16, 221; Ar. 15, 7; Just.); the idea of neediness is oft. associated with this word, and it is oft. joined w. orphans (ὀρφανός 1) **Mt 23:13 (14) v.l.; Mk 12:40, 42f** (HHaas, 'Das Scherflein d. Witwe' u. seine Entsprechung im Tripitaka 1922); **Lk 2:37; 4:25; 7:12; 18:3, 5; 20:47** (JRoth, The Blind, The Lame, and the Poor, diss. Vanderbilt '94, esp. 320ff); **21:2f; Ac 6:1** (cp. X., Oec. 7, 42f on elderly women losing esteem); **9:39, 41; 1 Cor 7:8; 1 Ti 5:4, 11** (on the relatively young age [ca. 30 years in the Hellenic world] s. bibl. and ins reff. SEG XLIII, 1331), **16a; Js 1:27;** 1 Cl 8:4 (Is 1:17); B 20:2; 1 Sm 6:2; IPol 4:1; Pol 6:1; Hv 2, 4, 3; m 8:10; s 1:8; 5, 3, 7; 9, 26, 2; 9, 27, 2; GJs 4:4. ἡ ὄντως χήρα *the real widow* (ὄντως b) **1 Ti 5:3b, 5, 16b.**—Metaph., in the proud words of the harlot of Babylon κάθημαι βασίλισσα καὶ χήρα οὐκ εἰμί **Rv 18:7** (cp. La 1:1).

ⓑ of a special class in the Christian communities, to which only widows meeting certain requirements could belong. One had to be ὄντως χήρα (s. 1 above) **1 Ti 5:3, 9;** ISm 13:1 (s. παρθένος a); Pol 4:3.—On widows in the churches s. LZscharnack, Der Dienst der Frau 1902, 100ff; ABludau, D. Versorgung der Witwen (1 Ti 5:3–16): Der kathol. Seelsorger 19, 1907, 165–67; 204–11; 255–60; 305–10; 350–53; ALudwig, Weibl. Kleriker: Theolog.-prakt. Monatsschrift 20, 1910, 548–57; 609–17; EvdGoltz, D. Dienst d. Frau in d. christl. Kirche[2] 1914; JViteau, L'institution des Diacres et des Veuves: Revue d' Hist. ecclés. 22, 1926, 513–36; AKalsbach, D. Altkirchl. Einrichtung d. Diakonissen 1926; JMüller-Bardoff, EFascher Festschr. '58, 113–33; L-MGünther, Witwen in der griechischen Antike, Zwischen Oikos und Polis: Historia 42, '93, 308–25; FSpencer, CBQ 56, '94, 715–34; RPrice, The Widow Traditions in Luke-Acts (SBLDS 155) '97.—S. also s.v. γυνή 1.—B. 131. DELG. M-M. EDNT. TW. Sv.

χηρεία, ας, ἡ (χήρα; Thu. et al.; ins, pap, LXX, Philo) ***widowhood*** GJs 2:1 v.l. (for χηροσύνη).—DELG s.v. χήρα.

χηρεύω (χήρα) fut. 3 sg. χηρεύσει (SibOr 2, 206); aor. 3 sg. ἐχήρευσε Jer 28:5 (Hom., Od. 9, 124; Isaeus, Demosth., LXX; TestJud 12:1f; SibOr, Philo) lit. 'be empty', then ***be a widow*** τοὺς χηρεύοντας τοῦ λαοῦ GJs 8:3.—DELG s.v. χήρα.

χηροσύνη (χήρα; Appolon. Rhod.; Manetho, Apotelesmatica) lit. a condition of deprivation or bereavement, then ***widowhood*** κόψομαι τὴν χηροσύνην μου *I will lament my widowhood* GJs 2:1.—DELG s.v. χήρα.

χθές (Hom. Hymns et al.; the real Attic form; PSI 184, 5 [III AD]; PLond III, 983, 2 p. 229 [IV AD]; Jos., Ant. 6, 126, C. Ap. 1, 7; TestNapht 1:4; Ath., Just.) ***yesterday***=ἐχθές (q.v.) **J 4:52 v.l.; Ac 7:28 v.l.** (Ex 2:14 v.l.); **Hb 13:8 v.l.** (of the past [s. ἐχθές] as Diod. S. 2, 5, 5; Jos., Ant. 18, 243; Celsus 6, 10).—B. 1000. DELG. M-M.

χιϛ′ s. χξϛ′.

χιλίαρχος, ου, ὁ and **χιλιάρχης, ου, ὁ** (χίλιοι, ἄρχω; Aeschyl., X.+; ins, pap, LXX; Jos., Ant. 7, 368; 12, 301; loanw. in rabb.) lit. 'leader of a thousand soldiers', then also=the Rom. tribunus militum, ***military tribune,*** the commander of a cohort=about 600 men (so since Polyb. 1, 23, 1; 6, 19, 1; 7ff; also Polyaenus 7, 17; Jos., Ant. 17, 215; ins, pap; s. Hahn 47; 116; 168; Mason 99), in this sense (roughly equivalent to major or colonel) **J 18:12; Ac 21:31–33, 37; 22:24, 26–29; 23:10, 15, 17–19, 22; 24:7, 22; 25:23;** 1 Cl 37:3.—Of high-ranking military officers gener. **Mk 6:21** (but s. EKlostermann, Hdb. ad loc.); **Rv 6:15; 19:18.**—χιλιάρχης (for ἑκατόναρχος, -χης) **vv.ll. Mt 8:5, 8, 13.** S. the lit. s.v. ἑκατοντάρχης.—DELG s.v. χίλιοι. M-M.

χιλιάς, άδος, ἡ (χίλιοι; Aeschyl., Hdt.+; LXX; TestSol 26:9 H; TestAbr, TestJob, JosAs; GrBar 4:10) **a group of a thousand, *a thousand*** pl. (En 10:17, 19; Jos., Ant. 6, 193) **Lk 14:31ab; Ac 4:4; 1 Cor 10:8; Rv 7:4–8; 11:13; 14:1, 3; 21:16;** 1 Cl 43:5. χίλιαι χιλιάδες 34:6 (Da 7:10). χιλιάδες χιλιάδων *thousands upon thousands* **Rv 5:11** (χιλιάδων also a loanw. in rabb.). In Rv the noun denoting what is counted may stand in the same case as χιλ. (so Theophanes Conf., Chron. 482, 14 deBoor λ′ χιλιάδες νομίσματα; 7, 17 πολλὰς μυριάδας μάρτυρας) instead of the gen. **7:4, 5a, 8c; 11:13;** cp. ἐπὶ σταδίων δώδεκα χιλιάδων **21:16** (ἐπὶ σταδίους δώδεκα χιλιάδων **v.l.**). The millennium χιλιάδα τινὰ . . . ἐτῶν ἔσεσθαι Papias (2:12).—DELG s.v. χίλιοι. M-M. TW.

χίλιοι, αι, α (Hom.+; ins, pap, LXX, Philo; Jos., Bell. 1, 317; Ant; Jos., Bell. 1, 317, Ant. 11, 15, Vi. 95 al.; TestJob 32:3; TestJud 4:1; 9:8; Just.; loanw. in rabb.) ***a thousand*** **2 Pt 3:8ab** (Ps 89:4); **Rv 11:3; 12:6; 14:20;** 1 Cl 34:6 (Da 7:10; s. χιλιάς); B 15:4 (Ps 89:4). The millennium **Rv 20:2–7** (Just., D. 80, 5; 81, 3; intertestamental views JBailey, JBL 53, '34, 170–87.—LGry, Le Millénarisme dans ses origines et son développement 1904; JSickenberger, Das Tausendjährige Reich in Apk: SMerkle Festschr. 1922, 300–316; AWikenhauser, D. Problem d. 1000jähr. Reiches in Apk: Röm. Quartalschr. 40, '32, 13–25, D. Herkunft der Idee des 1000j. R. in Apk: ibid. 45, '38, 1–24, also TQ 127, '47, 399–417; HBietenhard, D. 1000j. Reich '55).—DELG. EDNT. TW.

χιλιονταετηρίς, ίδος, ἡ (III AD; fr. χίλιοι, ἔτος + -ηρίς) ***period of the millennium*** Παπίας δὲ περὶ τὴν χ. σφάλλεται *Papias is in error about the 'millennium'* Papias (11:1).

χίμαρος, ου, ὁ (Aristoph., Theocr., ins, pap, LXX; TestZeb 4:9; EpArist 170; Philo, Jos.) ***male goat*** φέρετέ μοι . . . ρ' χιμάρους καὶ ἔσονται οἱ ρ' χίμαροι παντὶ τῷ λαῷ *bring me . . . 100 he-goats, and they will be for the whole people* GJs 4:3.—DELG s.v. χίμαιρα.

χιόνινος, η, ον (fr. χεῖμα 'frost' via χιών; Ptolem. Euerg. II: 234, 10 Jac.=Athen. 9, 17, 375d) ***snowy, snow-white*** ἔρια Hv 1, 2, 2 (s. ἔριον).—DELG s.v. χεῖμα.

Χίος, ου, ἡ (Hom. et al.; Jos., Ant. 16, 18; ins) ***Chios,*** an island (w. a city by the same name) in the Aegean Sea off the west coast of Asia Minor **Ac 20:15.**—Pauly-W. III 2286–98; BHHW I 299; TLL, Suppl. 1, 397–99.

χιτών, ῶνος, ὁ ([κιθών Mel.] Hom. +; ins, pap, LXX, Test12Patr, JosAs; ApcrEzk P 1 verso, 16; EpArist, Philo; Jos., Ant. 3, 159; 7, 171 [on a woman]; Mel., P. 19, 134; 20, 137.—On the origin of the word s. UWilcken, UPZ I p. 390, 1) ***tunic, shirt,*** a garment worn next to the skin, and by both sexes **Mt 10:10; Mk 6:9** (on the wearing of two χιτῶνες, one over the other s. Jos., Ant. 17, 136.—The Cynic w. two coats, stick, and knapsack: Diog. L. 6, 13.—Polyaenus 4, 14 criticizes τρίβωνα διπλοῦν and βακτηρίαν as signs of effeminacy); **Lk 3:11; 9:3; Jd 23;** Hs 9, 2, 4; 9, 11, 7. W. ἱμάτιον (q.v. 2) **Mt 5:40; Lk 6:29;** D 1:4 (on these three passages, which belong together, s. GKittel, Die Probleme des paläst. Spätjudentums u. d. Urchristentum 1926); **J 19:23ab** (see s.v. ἄραφος); **Ac 9:39.**—**Mk 14:63** the pl. prob. does not mean a number of shirts, but ***clothes*** gener. (the pl. has this mng. Vi. Aesopi W 21 P.; B-D-F §141, 8).—JBrown, JJS 25, '80, 7–15; Dalman, Arbeit V 208–20; BHHW II 962–65.—B. 419; 421. DELG. M-M. DNP II 1131–32.

χιών, όνος, ἡ (χεῖμα 'frost'; Hom. et al.; PGM 5, 19; 7, 382; LXX, En, TestSol; TestLevi 3:2; JosAs; ParJer 9:18; Jos., Ant. 13, 208) ***snow*** as symbol of perfect whiteness λευκὸς ὡς χιών **Mt 28:3; Mk 9:3 v.l.; Rv 1:14;** Hs 8, 2, 3. λευκότερος πάσης χιόνος AcPt 3, 8 (the same hyperbole as early as Il. 10, 437; Ps.-Demetr., De Eloc. 124; En 14:20; 106:2).—1 Cl 8:4 (Is 1:18); 18:7 (Ps 50:9).—B. 69. DELG s.v. χεῖμα. M-M.

χλαμύς, ύδος, ἡ (acc. to Pollux 10, 164 it occurs in Sappho [56 D.; 54 L-P.]; elsewh. Aristoph. et al.; X., An. 7, 4, 4; ins, pap; 2 Macc 12:35; Philo, Leg. ad Gai. 94; Jos., Ant 5, 33; loanw. in rabb.), 'a loose outer garment worn by men', then gener. **a military cloak, *mantle*** (red in color: χλ. κοκκίνη as PGM 4, 636f) worn by Roman soldiers **Mt 27:28, 31** (s. Appian, Bell. Civ. 2, 90 §377 [χλ. of the Roman soldier's cloak=2, 150 ἡ πορφύρα]; Philo, In Flacc. 37; Philostrat., Vi. Ap. 5, 38 p. 199, 30).—DELG. M-M. DNP II 1133.

χλευάζω (χλεύη) impf. ἐχλεύαζον; fut. 3 sg. χλευάσει (Pr 19:28 Aq Theod.; TestLevi 7:2); aor. 3 sg. ἐχλεύασε (Is 37:22 Sym.); aor. pass. impv. 3 pl. χλευασθήτωσαν (Pr 4:21 Theod.) (Aristoph., Demosth. et al.; late pap; TestLevi; Jos., Bell. 6, 365, C. Ap. 2, 137; Just., Tat.)

❶ **to engage in mockery, *mock, sneer, scoff*** (Philo, Sacr. Abel. 70; Jos., Ant. 7, 85; TestLevi 14:8) **Ac 2:13 v.l.** (for δια-); **17:32** (cp. Herm. Wr. 1, 29.—ASizoo, GereformTT 24, 1924, 289–97).

❷ **to make fun of maliciously, *mock, scoff at, sneer at,*** trans. τινά *someone* (so also Appian, Bell. Civ. 2, 153 §645; Lucian, Prom. in Verb. 33; LXX; TestLevi 7:2; Jos., Ant. 12, 170; Tat. 33, 2f; cp. Philo, Mos. 1, 29; Just., D. 137, 1 αὐτοῦ τοὺς μώλωπας; Tat. 22, 1 τὰς πανηγύρεις) 1 Cl 39:1. W. ὑβρίζειν (Plut., Artox. 1025 [27, 5]) Dg 2:7.—DELG s.v. χλεύη. New Docs 2, 104. M-M.

χλεύη, ης, ἡ (s. χλευάζω; the pl. as early as Hom. Hymns; the sing. in Dio Chrys. 14 [31], 31; Lucian et al.; POxy 904, 2 [V AD]; Sb 5763, 51; TestSol 4:11; TestJob 32:11; SibOr 4, 37; Philo; Jos., Bell. 4, 157, Ant. 7, 61; Tat. 30, 2) ***scorn, ridicule*** Dg 4:4.—DELG. M-M s.v. χλευάζω.

χλιαρός, ά, όν (χλιαίνω 'to warm'; Ion. χλιερός **Rv 3:16 v.l.**) ***lukewarm*** (since Hdt. 4, 181; Diod. S. 17, 50, 5; Synes., Ep. 114 p. 254d χ. ὕδωρ.—The unpleasant taste of χ. ὕδ. causes vomiting: Vi. Aesopi W 3 p. 81, 29; 35 P.), in imagery of the church at Laodicea, that is neither hot nor cold and hence is to be spit out **Rv 3:16.**—MRudwick and EGreen, ET 69, '58, 176–78; CHemer, The Letters to the Seven Churches in Their Local Settings '89 ('86), 178–209.—M-M. TW.

Χλόη, ης, ἡ (cp. next entry) ***Chloe*** (Semos of Delos [III BC]: 396 fgm. 23 Jac. [Χλ. as a surname of Demeter, DNP II 1134]; Longus 1, 6, 3ff; in Lat.: Horace, Odes 3, 9, 9; TLL, Suppl. 1, 401), an otherw. unknown woman who prob. lived in Corinth or Ephesus and may or may not have been a Christian. οἱ Χλόης *Chloe's people* (slaves or freedpersons) **1 Cor 1:11** (FHitchcock, JTS 25, 1924, 163–67).—DELG. M-M.

χλωρός, ά, ό (cp. χλόη 'a young green shoot or plant', but s. DELG s.v. χλωρός and Frisk s.v. χλόη on relationship of the two words) an adj. of color somewhat indeterminate in sense, but gener. as part of the spectrum lying betwen blue and yellow, with shade more closely defined through context.

❶ ***yellowish-green, (light) green*** of plants (Hom. et al.; ins, pap, LXX; En 5:1; TestGad 2:2; Philo) χλωρὸς χόρτος (PLond II, 287, 15 p. 202 [I AD] al.; Gen 1:30) **Mk 6:39; Rv 8:7.** Of branches or sticks *green, fresh* Hs 8, 1, 10–18; 8, 2, 2 v.l.; 4 al. Of vegetation 9, 1, 6f; 9, 21, 1; 9, 22, 1; 9, 24, 1; cp. 9, 21, 2 w. application to the doubters, who are neither green nor dry.—Subst. τὸ χλωρόν (oft. pap). πᾶν χλωρόν *everything that is green=every plant* (Gen 2:5; Dt 29:22) **Rv 9:4.**

❷ ***pale, greenish gray*** (cp. the relatively paler appearance of the dorsal side of a leaf compared to its ventral side) as the color of a pers. in sickness contrasted with appearance in health (Hippocr., Prognost. 2 p. 79, 18 Kühlew.; Thu. 2, 49, 5; Maximus Tyr. 20, 5b.—Of 'pale' fear Il. 7, 479; 10, 376), so the horse ridden by Death (χλ. of death Sappho, fgm. 2, 14 Diehl[2] [31, 14 L-P.]; Artem. 1, 77 p. 71, 27) ἵππος χλωρός **Rv 6:8** (see s.v.

πυρρός).—RGradwohl, D. Farben im AT, Beih. ZAW 83, '63, 27–33; EIrwin, Colour Terms in Greek Poetry '74, 31–78 (in Sappho: χλ. 'greener than grass'; s. HKing IJCT 2, '96, 376, 26 [lit.]).—B. 1058. Schmidt, Syn. III 51–54. M-M.

χνοῦς, χνοῦ, ὁ (Hom. [χνόος]+; LXX; SibOr 8, 15 v.l.) ***dust, chaff*** B 11:7 (Ps 1:4).—DELG s.v. χνόος.

χξς′ numerical sign for ἑξακόσιοι (=χ′) ἑξήκοντα (=ξ′) ἕξ (=ς′) ***six hundred sixty six*** **Rv 13:18 v.l.** This is the number of the beast, which is the number of a human being. On the numerological technique involved here s. ἀριθμός 1 and FDornseiff, Das Alphabet in Mystik u. Magie[2] 1926 §7; PFriesenhahn, Hellen. Wortzahlenmystik im NT '36. The constantly recurring attempts to solve this riddle are based somet. on the Gk., somet. on the Hebr. alphabet; they may yield a name taken fr. mythology (as early as Irenaeus 5, 30, 3 Ευανθας, Λατεινος, Τειταν, and many others: GHeinrici, Griech.-byz. Gesprächsbücher 1911, p. 60, 3) or fr. history (e.g. Nero Caesar, Ulpius [Trajan] or Domitian [EStauffer, ConNeot 11, '47, 237–41], or Jesus in a heretical disguise, CCecchelli: GFunacoli Festschr. '55, 23–31), the numerical value of whose letters is 666. On the other hand, some prefer to treat the number 666 purely as a number; they suspect a symbolic mng. (GA van den Bergh van Eysinga, ZNW 13, 1912, 293–306, NThT 4, 1915, 62–66; ELohmeyer in Hdb. exc. on Rv 13:18). Further, cod. C and the Armenian version have the rdg. χις′=616, which is preferred by RSchütz (s. below) and EHirsch, Studien z. 4. Ev. '36, 167; it was known to Irenaeus (5, 30, 1), who rejected it. Comm. report on the attempts at solution already made; esp. E-BAllo, L'Apocalypse de St. Jean[3] '33, exc. 34 p. 232–36; JdeZwaan, De Openbaring van Joh. 1925, 46ff; IBeckwith, Apocalypse 1919, 393–411; DAune, Rev (Word) ad loc. S. also ZNW: PCorssen 3, 1902, 238ff; 4, 1903, 264ff; 5, 1904, 86ff; EVischer 4, 1903, 167ff; 5, 1904, 84ff; CBruston 5, 1904, 258ff; CClemen 11, 1910, 204ff; WHadorn 19, 1919/20, 11–29.—SAgrell, Eranos 26, 1928, 35–45; GMenken, GereformTT 36, '36, 136–52; MGoemans, Studia Cath. 13, '37, 28–36; DvdBosch, 666 het getal eens menschen '40. In general s. LBrun, Die röm. Kaiser in Apk: ZNW 26, 1927, 128–51; RSchütz, D. Ofb. d. Joh. u. Kaiser Domitian '33; KHolzinger, SBWienAk, Phil.-hist. Kl. 216, 3, '36; ABertholet, D. Macht der Schrift im Glauben u. Aberglauben: ABA '49, esp. p. 30.

χοϊκός, ή, όν (Rhet. Gr. I 613, 4 γυμνοὶ τούτους τοῦ χοϊκοῦ βάρους; Hesych.; Suda) ***made of earth/dust*** (χοῦς), ***earthy*** ὁ πρῶτος ἄνθρωπος ἐκ γῆς χοϊκός **1 Cor 15:47** (cp. Gen 2:7 ἔπλασεν ὁ θεὸς τὸν ἄνθρωπον χοῦν ἀπὸ τῆς γῆς; SibOr 8, 445 of Adam, χοϊκῷ πλασθέντι; GNaass 252, 59.—Philo, Leg. All. 1, 31 differentiates the οὐράνιος fr. the γήϊνος ἄνθρωπος).—Vss. **48; 49.**—DELG s.v. χέω. M-M. TW.

χοῖνιξ, ικος, ἡ (Hom.+; ins, pap; Ezk 45:10f) **a dry measure, oft. used for grain, approximately equivalent to one quart or one liter, *quart.*** A χ. of grain was a daily ration for one pers. (Hdt. 7, 187; Diog. L. 8, 18 ἡ χοῖνιξ ἡμερήσιος τροφή; Athen. 3, 20, 98e) **Rv 6:6ab.**—FStolle, D. röm. Legionar u. sein Gepäck 1914 (the appendix has an explanation of Rv 6:6). In general on the subject of military rations GWatson, The Roman Soldier '69, 62–66.—DNP II 1136f. DELG. M-M.

χοιρίον, ου, τό (χοῖρος; Aristoph. et al.; PMagd 4, 8 [III BC]; Sb 5304, 1) dim. of χοῖρος, lit. 'a little swine, piglet', but also dim. only in form, ***swine,*** and so B 10:3.—DELG s.v. χοῖρος.

χοῖρος, ου, ὁ (Hom. et al.; ins, pap; Sym. Is 65:4 and 66:3) 'young swine' then ***swine*** gener. (so Epict. 4, 11, 29; Plut., Cicero 864 [7, 6]; BGU 92, 7 [II AD]; 649, 7 al. in pap; Jos., C. Ap. 2, 137; TestJud 2:5) **Mt 8:30–32; Mk 5:11–13, 16** (AHarnack, Zu Mk 5:11–13: ZNW 8, 1907, 162; OBauernfeind, Die Worte der Dämonen im Mt 1927); **Lk 8:32f; 15:15f.** W. dogs: as unclean animals Ox 840, 33 (JJeremias, ConNeot 11, '47, 105: fig.); in a proverb **Mt 7:6** (Theophyl. Sim., Ep. 20 τὰ δῶρα τοῖς χοίροις διένειμε; FPerles, ZNW 25, 1926, 163f; APerry, ET 46, '35, 381). The prohibition against eating pork, and its interpretation B 10:1, 3ab, 10.—On swine and adherents of Mosaic dietary law s. Billerb. I 448ff; 492f; KRengstorf, Rabb. Texte 1. Reihe III '33ff, p. 36f.—Kl. Pauly V 43–47; BHHW III 1748f.—B. 161. DELG. M-M.

χολάω (fr. χόλος via χολή; Aristoph. et al., var. 'be given to melancholy, be angry') ***be angry*** (Artem. 1, 4; Diog. L. 9, 66 al.; ins [Ramsay, CB I/2, 471 no. 312 of divine wrath]; 3 Macc 3:1 v.l.) τινί *at someone* **J 7:23** (w. ὅτι foll.).—DELG s.v. χόλος. M-M.

χολή, ῆς, ἡ (χόλος 'gall, bile'; since Archilochus [VII BC], fgm. 96; PGM 36, 284; LXX; TestSol 5:9; 13; TestJob 43:8; Test12Patr, ApcEsdr, Philo; Jos., Ant. 17, 173; Mel., P. 79, 574; loanw. in rabb. The equivalent χόλος Hom. et al. is used in both the lit. sense of 'gall, bile' and the fig. 'bitter anger'.)

➊ lit. **a substance w. an unpleasant taste, *someth. bitter, gall*** (PSI 1180, 103 [II AD], bile of a hyena; the LXX uses χολή to transl. (a) מְרֵרָה=gall Job 16:13; (b) מְרֹרָה=poison Job 20:14; (c) לַעֲנָה=wormwood Pr 5:4; La 3:15; (d) רֹאשׁ=poison Dt 29:17 [of an unspecified poisonous plant]; Ps 68:22) ἔδωκαν αὐτῷ πιεῖν οἶνον μετὰ χολῆς μεμιγμένον *they gave him a drink of wine mixed with bitters* (so Moffatt) **Mt 27:34** (fr. Ps 68:22 [?]; cp. Mk 15:23 wine laced w. myrrh).—B 7:3, 5; GPt 5:16 (s. ὄξος).—Zohary, Plants 186.

➋ fig. ext. of 1: the Semitic idiom χολὴ πικρίας ***gall of bitterness, bitter gall*** **Ac 8:23** (πικρία 1) in ref. to Simon Magus prob.=*bitter poison* and refers to his predicament in a state of sin (cp. Dt 29:17 ἐν χολῇ καὶ πικρίᾳ; on the theme 1QS 2:11–17), not to an emotional condition. (Sometimes cited in this connection, but of a difft. order is Biogr. p. 153 the tragedian Philocles ἐπεκαλεῖτο Χολὴ διὰ τό πικρόν.)—PKatz conjectures ἐν χολῇ for ἐνοχλῇ (s. ἐνοχλέω) **Hb 12:15** (ZNW 49, '58, 213–23) on the basis of Dt 29:17 (cp. P[46] ἐνχ[.]λη). In such case χολή refers to an emotional condition: ***wrath.***—B. 1134. DELG s.v. χόλος. M-M.

χονδρίζω (hapax leg., cp. ἐγκονδρίζω 'form into grains/groats', fr. ἔγκονδρος 'in grains', derived fr. χόνδρος 'groats of wheat or spelt') prob.=χονδρεύω **to make coarsely crushed grain, *make groats*** (Hesych.): εἰς τὸν ἀγρὸν ὅπου χονδρίζεις Hv 3, 1, 2 prob. means a field in which was located an apparatus for preparing groats, where Hermas works.—DELG s.v. χόνδρος.

χόος s. χοῦς.

Χοραζίν, ἡ (also -ειν) indecl. ***Chorazin,*** a place in Galilee, the location of which may have been the ruins of Kerâzeh, a half hour's walk northwest of Tell Hum (Menachoth 85a mentions a place כרזיים [Billerb. I 605] and Eus., Onom. 303, 174 Klosterm. mentions ruins of Chorazin) **Mt 11:21; Lk 10:13.**—CKopp, The Holy Places of the Gospels, tr. RWalls '63, 187–89. OEANE I 490f.

χορδή, ῆς, ἡ (Hom. et al.; PPetr III, 142, 22 [III BC]; Ps 150:4; Na 3:8; Jos., Ant. 7, 306; TestJob 46:7 al.) ***string*** (made of gut) pl. w. κιθάρα (Diod. S. 5, 75, 3 τῆς κιθάρας χορδάς; Dio Chrys.

16 [33], 57; Ael. Aristid. 28, 121 K.=49 p. 531 D.) IEph 4:1; IPhld 1:2.—DELG.

χορεύω (χορός) impf. ἐχόρευον; aor. ptc. fem. χορεύσασα GJs (trag. et al.; LXX, Philo; Jos., Ant. 17, 235; Mel., P. 80, 592) ***dance in chorus*** Hs 9, 11, 5 (Leutzsch, Hermas 488, n. 322). In front of angels GJs 15:3; cp. Coll. Alex. p. 198 no. 36, 19 for Isis.—B. 689. DELG s.v. χορός.

χορηγέω (χορηγός 'chorus leader') fut. χορηγήσω; 1 aor. ἐχορήγησα. Pass.: 1 fut. 3 sg. χορηγηθήσεται Jdth 12:2; pf. pl. κεχορηγημένοι Sir 44:6; orig. 'lead a chorus' or 'pay the expenses for training a chorus', then gener. **defray the expenses of someth., *provide, supply (in abundance)*** (Aristoph. et al.; esp. ins as t.t. for assumption of costs by public benefactors; for ins s. LBW II nos. 252–99; ABrinck, Inscriptiones Graecae ad Choregiam pertinentes, diss. Halle 1886, 216–44; LMigeotte, Chiron 23, '93, 267–90 [lit. on ins]) τὶ *someth.* (Diod. S. 19, 3, 1 ἅπαντα; TestJob 31:4; ApcSed 10:2; Jos., Bell. 1, 625; Ar. [JTS 25, 1924, 74, 16]) **2 Cor 9:10** (alternating w. ἐπιχορηγεῖν); **1 Pt 4:11** (ἧς by attraction for ἥν). τί τινι (Polyb. 22, 26, 2; OGI 437, 71; SIG 888, 77; PTebt 51, 9; Sir 1:10, 26; 1 Macc 14:10; EpArist 259; Philo, Mos. 1, 255; Jos., Ant. 7, 279; cp. εἴς τι TestSol 8:1 D) Dg 1; 3:4; 10:6; Hs 2:5, 8. ἐκ τῶν κόπων αὐτῶν παντὶ ἀνθρώπῳ ἐχορήγησαν *they provided for every one from (the fruits of) their labor* Hs 9, 24, 2.—AHilhorst, Filología Neotestamentaria 1, '88, 27–34.—DELG s.v. χορός and on -ηγός s.v. ἄγω. M-M. TW.

χορός, οῦ, ὁ (Hom. et al.; ins, pap, LXX; GrBar 10:5; Philo, Joseph.)

❶ **rhythmic movements to the accompaniment of music, *(choral) dance, dancing*** lit. ἤκουσεν συμφωνίας καὶ χορῶν **Lk 15:25.**

❷ **a company of dancers, *troop, band*** in imagery of heavenly bodies (Maximus Tyr. 16, 6d; Herm. Wr. 416, 13 Sc. χορὸς ἀστέρων; Himerius, Or. 21, 6 W.; Sib. Or. 8, 450) ἥλιός τε καὶ σελήνη ἀστέρων τε χοροί 1 Cl 20:3. Cp. IEph 19:2.

❸ **a group of singers, *chorus, choir*** (so prob. Sb 3913, 8 χ. τῶν ἀγγέλων; Jos., Ant. 7, 85. In this sense a χορός of the stars is mentioned: Mesomedes 3, 10; 10, 17; Philo, Mos. 2, 239; ANock, JTS 31, 1930, 310ff) in imagery, the Christian community is to become a harmonious choir IEph 4:2; cp. IRo 2:2.—DELG. M-M. DNP II 1141–44.

χορτάζω (χόρτος) 1 aor. ἐχόρτασα. Pass.: 1 fut. χορτασθήσομαι; 1 aor. ἐχορτάσθην (Hes.; pap, LXX; TestSol 9:2; TestJob, TestJud) 'to feed'

❶ **to fill w. food, *feed, fill*—ⓐ** of animals, pass. in act. sense πάντα τὰ ὄρνεα ἐχορτάσθησαν ἐκ τῶν σαρκῶν αὐτῶν *all the birds gorged themselves with their flesh* **Rv 19:21** (cp. TestJud 21:8).

ⓑ of humans τινά *someone* **Mt 15:33;** 1 Cl 59:4 (τοὺς πεινῶντας). τινά τινος *someone with someth.* **Mk 8:4** (cp. Ps 131:15). Pass. (Pamphilus [I BC/I AD] in Ael. Dion. χ, 14 ed. HErbse '50; Epict. 1, 9, 19; 3, 22, 66; TestJob 22:2; 25:10) **Mt 14:20; 15:37; Mk 6:42; 7:27; 8:8; Lk 6:21** (οἱ πεινῶντες νῦν); **9:17; J 6:26; Phil 4:12** (opp. πεινᾶν); **Js 2:16.** ἀπό τινος (Ps 103:13) **Lk 16:21.** ἔκ τινος **15:16.**

❷ **to experience inward satisfaction in someth., *be satisfied,*** fig. ext. of 1 pass. (Ps.-Callisth. 2, 22, 4 χορτάζεσθαι τῆς λύπης=find satisfaction in grief; Ps 16:15) *be satisfied* **Mt 5:6** (χ. is also used in connection w. drink that relieves thirst: schol. on Nicander, Alexiph. 225 χόρτασον αὐτὸν οἴνῳ).—DELG s.v. χόρτος. M-M.

χόρτασμα, ατος, τό (χορτάζω; Poly. et al.; pap, LXX, always of fodder for domesticated animals) ***food*** for humans, pl. (Diod. S. 19, 26, 2 χορτάσματα) **Ac 7:11.**—DELG s.v. χόρτος. M-M.

χόρτος, ου, ὁ (Hom. et al.; in var. senses) ***grass, hay*** (Hes. et al.; pap, LXX; ViDa 8 [p. 78, 2 Sch.]; ApcrEzk P 1 verso 5 ἀκάνθας ἀντὶ χ[όρτου]; Jos., Bell. 6, 153, Ant. 20, 85; Just.), in our lit. almost always of green grass standing in field or meadow **Mt 14:19** (v.l. has the pl.); **J 6:10.** τὸν χόρτον τῆς γῆς **Rv 9:4.** ὁ χλωρὸς χόρτος (χλωρός 1) **Mk 6:39; Rv 8:7.** Of wild grass in contrast to cultivated plants ὁ χόρτος τοῦ ἀγροῦ **Mt 6:30;** cp. **Lk 12:28; Js 1:10, 11; 1 Pt 1:24abc** (Is 40:6, 7.—ἄνθεα ποίης as early as Od. 9, 449; Zohary 172f). Of stalks of grain in their early, grass-like stages **Mt 13:26; Mk 4:28.**—**1 Cor 3:12** mentions χόρτος *hay* as a building material (of inferior quality, as Diod. S. 20, 65, 1 κάλαμος and χόρτος).—B. 519f. DELG. M-M.

Χουζᾶς, ᾶ, ὁ ***Chuza*** (=כּוּזָא; the name occurs in a Nabataean [Corpus Inscr. Semiticarum II 1, 227; F Burkitt, Exp. 5th ser., 9, 1899, 118–22] and in a Syrian [ELittmann, Zeitschr. für. Assyriologie 27, 1913, 397] ins), an ἐπίτροπος (q.v. 1 and 2) of Herod Antipas, and the husband of a follower and benefactor of Jesus named Joanna **Lk 8:3.**—TLL, Suppl. 1, 427. M-M.

χοῦς, χοός, acc. χοῦν, **ὁ** (Hdt.+; ins, pap, LXX; JosAs 13:5; ParJer, ApcMos; ViJer 4 [Sch. p. 10, 2]; SibOr 8, 15; Philo; Jos., C. Ap. 1, 192, Ant. 14, 64; B-D-F §52; W-S. §8, 11 n. 7; Mlt-H. 127; 142) ***soil, dust,*** of the dust of the road (Is 49:23) ἐκτινάξατε τὸν χοῦν τὸν ὑποκάτω τῶν ποδῶν ὑμῶν **Mk 6:11** (cp. Is 52:2 and s. ἐκτινάσσω 1). Of the dust that grief-stricken persons scatter upon their heads (Josh 7:6; La 2:10; ParJer 2:1–3; 4:7; 7:22; 9:11) ἔβαλον χοῦν ἐπὶ τὰς κεφαλὰς αὐτῶν **Rv 18:19.**—DELG s.v. χέω II. M-M. DNP II 1190–91.

χράομαι (χρή) mid. dep. pres. 2 sg. χρᾶσαι (B-D-F §87), ind. and subj. 3 sg. χρῆται IRo 9:1; **1 Ti 1:8** (B-D-F §88); impf. ἐχρώμην; fut. χρήσομαι LXX; 1 aor. ἐχρησάμην; pf. κέχρημαι (Mlt-H. 200) (Hom.+) 'use', a common multivalent term.

❶ ***make use of, employ*—ⓐ** w. dat. τινί *someth.* (Appian, Bell. Civ. 4, 102 §427f θαλάσσῃ; Wsd 2:6; 13:18; 4 Macc 9:2; GrBar 6:12; Demetr.: 722 fgm. 5 Jac.; Philo, Aet. M. 70; 71; Jos., Bell. 3, 341; Just., A I, 14, 2, D. 57, 2; Tat. 12, 5.—B-D-F §193, 5; Rob. 532f) βοηθείαις ἐχρῶντο **Ac 27:17** (s. βοήθεια 2).—**1 Cor 7:31 v.l.; 9:12, 15; 1 Ti 5:23** (οἶνος 1); 2 Cl 6:5; Dg 6:5; 12:3 (ᾗ μὴ καθαρῶς χρησάμενοι *not using it in purity*); ITr 6:1; IPhld 4; Hs 9, 16, 4 (of the use of a seal as PHib 72, 16 [III BC]). διαλέκτῳ *use a language* Dg 5:2. Of law (trag., Hdt. et al.; Jos., C. Ap. 2, 125) τοῖς νόμοις *live in accordance with the laws* (Jos., Ant. 16, 27; Ath. 1, 1) Hs 1:3f; cp. 6. ἐάν τις αὐτῷ (=τῷ νόμῳ) νομίμως χρῆται **1 Ti 1:8.** προφήταις χρῆσθαι *appeal to the prophets* AcPlCor 1:10. A dat. is to be supplied w. μᾶλλον χρῆσαι *make the most of, take advantage of* **1 Cor 7:21,** either τῇ δουλείᾳ (so the Peshitta, Chrysostom, Theodoret, and many modern interpreters and translators, among the latter, 20th Century, Goodsp., NRSV; s. also HBellen, AC 6, '63, 177–80) or τῇ ἐλευθερίᾳ (so Erasmus, Luther, Calvin, FGodet, Lghtf., Zahn, Moffatt, RSV, NRSV mg., REB); s. μᾶλλον 2a.—If μ. χ. is construed without an implied dat., the phrase can be understood in the sense *be all the more useful, work all the harder* (cp. Vi. Aesopi G 17 P. on the theme of dedication to a task) i.e. as a freedperson be as industrious as a slave. (On this subj.: TZahn, Sklaverei u.

Christentum in d. alten Welt [1879]: Skizzen aus dem Leben d. alten Kirche[2] 1898, 116–59; EvDobschütz, Sklaverei u. Christent.: RE[3] XVIII 423–33; XXIV 521; JvWalter, Die Sklaverei im NT 1914; FKiefl, Die Theorien des modernen Sozialismus über den Ursprung d. Christentums, Zugleich ein Komm. zu 1 Cor 7:21, 1915, esp. p. 56–109; JWeiss, Das Urchristentum 1917, 456–60; ASteinmann, Zur Geschichte der Auslegung v. 1 Cor 7:21: ThRev 16, 1918, 341–48; AJuncker, D. Ethik des Ap. Pls II 1919, 175–81; JKoopmans, De Servitute Antiqua et Rel. Christ., diss. Amsterdam 1920, 119ff; ELohmeyer, Soz. Fragen im Urchrist. 1921; FGrosheide, Exegetica [1 Cor 7:21]: GereformTT 24, 1924, 298–302; HGreeven [s.v. πλοῦτος 1]; MEnslin, The Ethics of Paul 1930, 205–10; WWestermann, Enslaved Persons Who Are Free, AJP 59, '38, 1–30; HGülzow, Christent. u. Sklaverei [to 300 AD], '69, 177–81; SBartchy, MALLON CHRESAI, '73=SBLDS 11, '85; TWiedmann, Greek and Roman Slavery '81; COsiek, Slavery in the Second Testament World: BTB 22, '92, 174–79 [lit.]; JHarril, The Manumission of Slaves in Early Christianity '95, esp. 68–128. On slavery in antiquity gener.: WWestermann, Pauly-W. Suppl. VI '35, 894–1068, The Slave Systems of Gk. and Rom. Antiquity, '55; WKristensen, De antieke opvatting van dienstbaarheid '34; MPohlenz, D. hellen. Mensch '47, 387–96; Kl. Pauly V 230–34; BHHW III 1814f; MFinley, Slavery in Classical Antiquity '60; KBradley, The Problem of Slavery in Classical Culture: ClPh 92, '97, 273–82 [lit.]; PGarnsey, Ideas of Slavery from Aristotle to Augustine '96.) τινὶ εἴς τι *use someth. for someth.* (Oenomaus in Eus., PE 5, 33, 14; Simplicius In Epict. p. 27, 52 Düb.; cp. Tat. 17, 4 πρὸς τὸ κακοποιεῖν) Hv 3, 2, 8. σὺ αὐτὸς χρᾶσαι ἐκ τῶν αὐτῶν λίθων *you yourself function as one from these same stones* 3, 6, 7 (s. app. in Whittaker and Joly; for lit. s. Leutzsch, Hermas 418 n. 355).—W. a double dat. (trag. et al.) σχοινίῳ χρώμενοι τῷ πνεύματι *using as a rope the Holy Spirit* IEph 9:1. W. double dat. of pers. (Jos., C. Ap. 1, 227; Just., D. 7, 1; Tat. 36, 1; Ath. 32, 1) of the Syrian ἐκκλησία, which ποιμένι τῷ θεῷ χρῆται *resorts to God as shepherd* IRo 9:1.

ⓑ w. acc. (X., Ages. 11, 11; Ps.-Aristot., Oecon. 2, 22, 1350a, 7 χρ. τὰ τέλη εἰς διοίκησιν τῆς πόλεως; Ael. Aristid. 13 p. 162 D.; SIG 1170, 27 ἄνηθον μετ' ἐλαίου χρ.; PTebt 273, 28 ὕδωρ χρ.; Wsd 7:14 v.l.; 2 Macc 4:19.—B-D-F §152, 4; Rob. 476) τὸν κόσμον **1 Cor 7:31** (cp. Simplicius In Epict. p. 29, 30 Düb. τὸ τοῖς μὴ ἐφ' ἡμῖν ὡς ἐφ' ἡμῖν οὖσι κεχρῆσθαι=to use that which is not in our power as if it were in our power; s. also MDibelius, Urchristentum u. Kultur 1928).

❷ ***act, proceed*** (Hdt. et al.; POxy 474, 38 et al.) w. dat. of characteristic shown (Aelian, VH 2, 15; Jos., Ant. 10, 25; Just., D. 79, 2; Tat. 40, 1; Mel., HE 4, 26, 13) τῇ ἐλαφρίᾳ **2 Cor 1:17.** πολλῇ παρρησίᾳ **3:12.** ὑποταγῇ 1 Cl 37:5.—W. adv. (PMagd 6, 12 [III BC] et al.) ἀποτόμως **2 Cor 13:10.**

❸ ***treat a person in a certain way,*** w. dat. of pers. and an adv. (X., Mem. 1, 2, 48 φίλοις καλῶς χρ.; OGI 51, 8 [III BC] τοῖς τεχνίταις φιλανθρώπως χρῆται; PPetr III, 115, 8 [III BC] πικρῶς σοι ἐχρήσατο; POxy 745, 6; Esth 2:9; TestJob 20:3 ὡς ἐβούλετο; Jos., Ant. 2, 315, C. Ap. 1, 153 φιλανθρώπως; Just., A I, 27, 1 αἰσχρῶς) φιλανθρώπως ὁ Ἰούλιος τῷ Παύλῳ χρησάμενος; cp. Hs 5, 2, 10.—DELG s.v. χράομαι p. 1274. M-M. EDNT.

χράω s. κίχρημι.

χρεία, ας, ἡ (χρή, cp. χράομαι; Aeschyl.+; ins, pap, LXX; TestSol 13:2; TestAbr A 4 p. 80, 33 [Stone p. 8]; TestJob; TestZeb 6:5; GrBar 4:9; EpArist, Philo, Joseph.; Ar. [JTS 25, 1924 p. 74 ln. 26; p. 76 ln. 45]; Just.; Ath. 13, 2, R. 12 p. 61, 7)

❶ **that which should happen or be supplied because it is needed, *need, what should be*** (as distinguished fr. personal need, s. 2a) χρεία ἐστί τινος *there is need of someth., someth. is needed* (Polyb. 3, 111, 10; 5, 109, 1; SIG 707, 16f; 736, 63; Sir 3:22; 11:9; Just., D. 12, 3) **Lk 10:42** (on the texts s. GKilpatrick in: Essays in Memory of GCH MacGregor '65, 192). Without gen. (Diod. S. 1, 19, 5 ὅσον ἂν ᾖ χρεία) ἐὰν ᾖ χρεία *if it is necessary* D 11:5 (cp. Just., A II, 9, 4). τίς ἔτι χρεία; foll. by acc. w. inf. **Hb 7:11.** χρείαν ἔχειν τινός *(have) need (of) someone* or *someth.* (Pla. et al.; ins, pap; Is 13:17; Wsd 13:16; Philo, Plant. 65; Jos., Ant. 8, 228; Ar. [Milne 76, 45]; Just., A I, 15, 15 [for χρῄζετε Mt 6:32 and Lk 12:30]; Ath. 13, 2) **Mt 6:8; 9:12; 21:3; 26:65; Mk 2:17; 11:3; 14:63; Lk 5:31; 9:11; 15:7; 19:31, 34; 22:71; J 13:29; 1 Cor 12:21ab, 24** (w. τιμῆς to be supplied); **1 Th 4:12; Hb 5:12b; 10:36; Rv 21:23; 22:5.** W. gen. of the articular inf. (and acc.) χρείαν ἔχετε τοῦ διδάσκειν ὑμᾶς τινα **Hb 5:12a** (B-D-F §400, 1; Rob. 1038f; 1061). W. inf. foll. (Da 3:16) ἐγὼ χρ. ἔχω ὑπὸ σοῦ βαπτισθῆναι **Mt 3:14.** Cp. **14:16; J 13:10; 1 Th 1:8; 4:9** (B-D-F §393, 5); **5:1.** W. ἵνα foll. **J 2:25; 16:30; 1J 2:27.**

❷ **that which is lacking and needed, *need, lack, want, difficulty***—ⓐ of livelihood (Diod. S. 3, 16, 2; Appian, Basil. 5 §2 ὑπὸ χρείας=from necessity) χρείαν ἔχειν *be in need, lack someth.* abs. (Diod. S. 17, 77, 2; SIG[2] 857, 12 εἰ χρείαν ἔχοι Διονύσιος) **Mk 2:25; Ac 2:45; 4:35; Eph 4:28; 1J 3:17;** D 1:5ab. οὐδὲν χρείαν ἔχειν *have no lack of anything* (s. οὐδείς 2bγ) **Rv 3:17** (v.l. οὐδενός). πληροῦν τὴν χρείαν τινός *supply someone's need(s)* (Thu. 1, 70, 7 ἐπλήρωσαν τὴν χρείαν) **Phil 4:19.** εἰς τὴν χρείαν τινὶ πέμψαι *send someth. to someone to supply his need(s)* vs. **16.** λειτουργὸς τῆς χρείας μου *the one whose service supplied my need* **2:25.** Pl. *needs, necessities* (Socrat., Ep. 1, 5 [p. 220 Malherbe] αἱ τῆς πατρίδος χρεῖαι; Geminus [c. 70 BC], Elementa Astronomiae 1, 21 [ed. CManitius 1898] αἱ τοῦ βίου χρεῖαι; Philo, Dec. 99; Jos., Bell. 6, 390, Ant. 13, 225) **Ac 20:34; 28:10** (for πρὸς τὰς χρείας [v.l. τὴν χρείαν] cp. Polyb. 1, 52, 7; EpArist 11; 258); **Ro 12:13.** αἱ ἀναγκαῖαι χρεῖαι (ἀναγκαῖος 1) **Tit 3:14.**

ⓑ in wider sense Πέτρῳ, ὃς πρὸς τὰς χρείας ἐποιεῖτο τὰς διδασκαλίας Papias (2:15).

❸ **the thing that is lacking and (therefore) necessary, *necessary thing*** (TestJob 10:3 λαβεῖν τὴν χρείαν) πρὸς οἰκοδομὴν τῆς χρείας (objective gen.) *such as will build up where it is necessary* **Eph 4:29** (difft. JFindlay, ET 46, '35, 429).

❹ **an activity that is needed, *office, duty, service*** (Polyb. 4, 87, 9; 10, 21, 1; Diod. S. 5, 11, 3; 15, 81, 1 and al. in H. Gk.; ins, pap; 2 Macc 8:9; Jos., Ant. 13, 65) **Ac 6:3.**—B. 638. DELG s.v. χρή. M-M. Sv.

χρεοφειλέτης and the less well attested form **χρεωφειλέτης** (due to assimilation, B-D-F §35, 2; 119, 2; Tdf., Prol. 89; W-H., App. 152; W-S. §16, n. 28 Mlt-H. 73; in the LXX and as v.l. in the NT we have the spelling χρεοφιλέτης), **ου, ὁ** (Hippocr., Ep. 17, 55; Aeneas Tact. 192; 516; Diod. S. 32, 26, 3; Dionys. Hal.; Plut., Caesar 713 [12, 2], Luc. 504 [20, 3]; Aesop, Fab. 11 H. [=5 P.; 10 Ch.; H-H. 5]; SIG 742, 53; CWessely, Studien z. Paläogr. u. Papyrusk. 20, 1921, 129, 4; Job 31:37; Pr 29:13) ***debtor*** **Lk 7:41** (on the parable: PJoüon, RSR 29, '40, 615–19; GPerrella, Div. Thomas Piac. 42, '40, 553–58); **16:5.**—DELG s.v. χρή 2. M-M.

χρεώστης, ου, ὁ (cp. the Attic form χρέως; Plut., Mor. 100c; Dio Chrys. 28 [45], 10; Lucian, Abdic. 15; Herodian 5, 1, 6; SIG 833, 9 [120 AD]; BGU 106, 4 [II AD]; 786 II, 6; POxy 487, 11 al. in pap; Philo; Jos., Ant. 3, 282) ***debtor*** χρεώστας θλίβειν *oppress debtors* Hm 8:10.—DELG s.v. χρή 2.

χρεωφειλέτης s. χρεοφειλέτης.

χρή impersonal (Hom. +) impf. ἐχρῆν (TestJob 37:6; Tat.; Ath., R. 14 p. 65, 10) **that which should be/happen,** ***it is necessary, it ought*** foll. by acc. and inf. **Js 3:10** (Just., D. 33, 3; B-D-F §358, 2; Rob. 319; Schmid 592).—B. 640. Schmidt, Syn. III 702–5. DELG. M-M. Cp. δεῖ.

χρῄζω (cp. χρή; Hom.+; esp. dramatists) ***(have) need (of)*** τινός (Hom. et al.; BGU 37, 7 [50 AD]; PFlor 138, 6 al.; Jos., Ant. 1, 285; Test Jud 14:7; SibOr 8, 390; Ar. 1, 5; Just., D. 19, 3; Tat. 11, 1) **Mt 6:32; Lk 11:8** (a generous response to a shameless petitioner KSnodgrass, SBL '97, 505–13; w. διδόναι as Jos, Ant. 12, 203; TestZeb 7:3); **12:30; Ro 16:2; 2 Cor 3:1;** B 2:4; Dg 2:2; ITr 4:2; 12:3; Hv 3, 10, 6. οὐδὲν οὐδενὸς χρῄζει *he needs nothing at all* 1 Cl 52:1. W. inf. foll. (Jos., Ant. 1, 246) Dg 4:1. ἡ μετάνοια αὐτῶν ταχινὴ χρῄζει (v.l. ὀφείλει) εἶναι *their repentance must forthwith begin* Hs 8, 9, 4. On ὅσον χρῄζει **Lk 11:8 v.l.** (for ὅσων), s. 1 Km 17:18; SIG 57, 40 (450 BC) and s. Jülicher, Gleichn. 272.—DELG s.v. χράομαι. M-M.

χρῆμα, ατος, τό (χράομαι)—❶ **wealth in gener.,** ***property, wealth, means*** pl. (Hom. +; ins, LXX, TestSol, Philo, Joseph.; Ath. 1:3f) οἱ τὰ χρήματα ἔχοντες (X., Mem. 1, 2, 45) **Mk 10:23; Lk 18:24.** χρήματα πολλὰ ἔχειν Hs 2:5; cp. **Mk 10:24 v.l.**

❷ **any kind of currency,** ***money***—ⓐ mostly pl. (Thu., X. et al.; pap; Job 27:17; TestJud 21:7; EpArist 85; Philo, Poster. Cai. 117; Jos., Bell. 1, 159; Just., A I, 14, 2; Ath. 29, 2) **Ac 8:18, 20; 24:26** (χρ. διδόναι τινί as Diod. S. 8, 31; Jos., Ant. 7, 393).

ⓑ more rarely sing. (Alcaeus 109 + 110, 30 D.[2] [117b, 30 L-P.]; Hdt. 3, 38; Diod. S. 13, 106, 9; 36, fgm. a; POxy 474, 41; PHerm 23, 7; Jos., Ant. 11, 56 [property, wealth]) of a definite sum of money **Ac 4:37.**—B. 634; 769. DELG. Frisk s.v. χρή. M-M. TW. Sv.

χρηματίζω (χρῆμα) fut. χρηματίσω (χρηματιῶ LXX); 1 aor. ἐχρημάτισα.; pf. inf. κεχρηματικέναι Job 40:8. Pass.: 1 aor. ἐχρηματίσθην; pf. κεχρημάτισμαι (Hdt. et al.; ins, pap, LXX, EpArist, Philo, Joseph.; Ath.).

❶ **impart a divine message,** ***make known a divine injunction/warning*** (of oracles, etc., Diod. S. 3, 6, 2; 15, 10, 2; Plut., Mor. 435c; Lucian, Ep. Sat. 2, 25; Ael. Aristid. 50, 5 K.=26 p. 503 D.; SIG 663, 13 [200 BC] ὁ θεός μοι ἐχρημάτισεν κατὰ τὸν ὕπνον; 1110, 8; PFay 137, 2; 4 [I AD]; PGiss 20, 18.—Jer 32:30; 37:2; Philo, Mos. 2, 238; Jos., Ant. 5, 42; 10, 13; 11, 327 ἐχρημάτισεν αὐτῷ κατὰ τοὺς ὕπνους ὁ θεὸς θαρρεῖν; Ath. 26, 2f).

ⓐ act. (Orig. C. Cels. 1, 60, 39; Did., Gen. 221, 1) **Hb 12:25.**

ⓑ pass.—**α.** χρηματίζομαι *I receive a warning* (B-D-F §312, 1) χρηματισθεὶς κατ᾽ ὄναρ **Mt 2:22** (Sb 6713, 4 [258 BC] τὸν Σάραπίμ μοι χρηματίζειν πλεονάκις ἐν τοῖς ὕπνοις); cp. **Hb 8:5.** περί τινος (Jos., Ant. 3, 212) **11:7** (BHeininger, NTS 44, '98, 115–32, w. ref. to En 65:1–12). Foll. by the inf., which expresses the warning given (B-D-F §392, 1d) **Mt 2:12;** GJs 21:4. ἐχρηματίσθη ὑπὸ ἀγγέλου μεταπέμψασθαί σε *he was directed by an angel to send for you* **Ac 10:22.** Cp. κεχρηματισμένος **Lk 2:26** D; sim. ὁ χρηματισθεὶς ὑπὸ τοῦ ἁγίου πνεύματος GJs 24:4 (cp. Vett. Val. 67, 5 ὑπὸ δαιμονίων χρηματισθήσονται).

β. χρηματίζεταί τι *someth. is revealed* or *prophesied* (UPZ 71, 3 [152 BC] τὰ παρὰ τ. θεῶν σοι χρηματίζεται) ἦν αὐτῷ κεχρηματισμένον ὑπὸ τοῦ πνεύματος **Lk 2:26** (B-D-F §407).

❷ **to take/bear a name/title** (as so and so), **to go under the name of,** act., but freq. rendered as pass. in Engl. tr.: ***be called/named, be identified as*** (Polyb. 5, 57, 2; Strabo 13, 1, 55; Plut., Ant. 941 [54, 9]; Philo, Deus Imm. 121, Leg. ad Gai. 346; Jos., Bell. 2, 488, Ant. 8, 157; 13, 318, C. Ap. 2, 30; SIG 1150, 4 Καικίλιος ὁ χρηματίζων Βούλων; POxy 268, 2 [58 AD]; 320; APF 4, 1908, 122 V, 15 and oft. in pap) μοιχαλὶς χρηματίσει *she will be called an adulteress* **Ro 7:3.** ἐγένετο . . . χρηματίσαι τοὺς μαθητὰς Χριστιανούς *it came to pass . . . that the disciples got the name Christians* **Ac 11:26.**—Mlt-H. 265 holds that 1 and 2 are two entirely distinct words; that 1 comes fr. an equivalent of χρησμός 'oracle', and 2 fr. χρήματα 'business'.—DELG s.v. χρῆμα. Frisk s.v. χρή. M-M. TW.

χρηματισμός, οῦ, ὁ (χρηματίζω; X., Pla. et al.; ins, pap, LXX; Philo, Vi. Cont. 17; Jos., Ant. 14, 231) ***a divine statement, answer*** (2 Macc 2:4; PGM 4, 2206.—Of a dream, Artem. 1, 2 p. 5, 20) **Ro 11:4;** 1 Cl 17:5.—New Docs 4, 176 no. 92. DELG s.v. χρῆμα. Frisk s.v. χρή. M-M (s. critique New Docs 1, 77). TW.

χρῆσαι s. χράομαι.

χρήσιμος, η, ον (χράομαι; Theognis [406] +) ***useful, beneficial, advantageous*** IEph 4:2. τινί *for someone* (PSI 400, 4 [III BC] σοὶ χρήσιμος) **Mt 20:28** D. ἐπί τι (Pla., Gorg. 480b, 481b, Leg. 7, 796a; Plut., Mar. 10, 10) ἐπ᾽ οὐδέν (PCairZen 225, 3 [253 BC] ἐπ᾽ οὐθὲν χρήσιμος) **2 Ti 2:14.** εἴς τι (X., Vect. 4, 42; Pla., Leg. 7, 796 D.; Ezk 15:4) **2 Ti 2:14 v.l.** (Tat. 19, 1); Hv 4, 3, 4.—Larfeld I 502. DELG s.v. χρησ- 4. Frisk s.v. χρή. M-M.

χρῆσις, εως, ἡ (χράομαι; since Pindar and Democritus 282; ins, pap, LXX)

❶ **the state of being used,** ***use, usage*** (TestNapht 2:4; EpArist 143; Philo, Op. M. 42; Jos., Ant. 4, 199, C. Ap. 2, 213; Ar.; Ath., R. 12 p. 61, 6 al.) Dg 2:2; 4:2; PtK 2 p. 14, 13; 15. οὐ κατὰ χρῆσιν, ἀλλὰ φύσιν *not by usage* or *habit, but by nature* ITr 1:1.

❷ **the state of being useful,** ***usefulness*** 1 Cl 37:4. τὴν χρῆσιν ἀπώλεσεν (the honey) *has lost its usefulness* Hm 5, 1, 5.

❸ **state of intimate involvement w. a pers.,** ***relations, function,*** esp. of sexual intercourse (X., Symp. 8, 28; Pla., Leg. 8, 841a; Isocr. 19, 11; Ps.-Lucian, Am. 25 παιδική; Plut., Mor. 905b ὀρέξεις παρὰ τὰς χρήσεις; POxy 272, 12 al.) ἡ φυσικὴ χρῆσις **Ro 1:26;** w. objective gen. τῆς θηλείας vs. **27.**—DELG s.v. χρησ- 4. Frisk s.v. χρή. M-M. DNP II 1151. Sv.

χρησμοδοτέω (χρησμός 'oracular response', δότης [δίδωμι] 'giver') 1 aor. pass. ptc. χρησμοδοτηθείς ***give an oracular response*** (Ps.-Callisth. p. 3, 13; 52, 9; 81, 14; Lucian, Alex. 43 Jacobitz v.l.; Pollux 1, 17; Etym. Mag. p. 814, 40; ins [IV AD]: Ramsay, Phrygia I /2 p. 566), pass. *be given* or *follow an oracular response* 1 Cl 55:1.—DELG s.v. χρησ- 1.

χρῆσον s. κίχρημι.

χρηστεύομαι mid. dep. fut. 2 sg. χρηστεύσῃ (PsSol); pass. 1 fut. χρηστευθήσομαι; 1 aor. ἐχρηστευσάμην (PsSol 9:6; otherw. only in Christian wr.) ***be kind, loving, merciful*** **1 Cor 13:4.** τινί *to someone* 1 Cl 14:3. ὡς χρηστεύεσθε, οὕτως χρηστευθήσεται ὑμῖν *as you show kindness, kindness will be shown to you* 13:2 (saying of Jesus; for the thought s. also L-S-J-M s.v. χρηστός II, 4).—Cp. DELG s.v. χρησ- 3. M-M. TW. Spicq.

χρηστολογία, ας, ἡ (χρηστός, λέγω; Eustath. p. 1437, 53 on Il. 23, 598; eccl. writers) ***smooth, plausible speech*** (Julius Capitolinus, Pertinax 13 χρηστολόγον eum appellantes qui bene loqueretur et male faceret=a χρηστολόγος is a bad person who makes a fine speech) **Ro 16:18.** JNorth, NTS 42, '96, 600–614.—M-M. TW.

χρηστός, ή, όν (χράομαι; trag., Hdt.+; ins, pap, LXX; En 32:1; TestSol; TestJob 13:6; TestBenj 3:7; Just.; Ath.; superl. Just. A I, 4, 1) gener. 'useful, beneficial'

❶ **pert. to that which causes no discomfort,** ***easy*** (PsSol 8:32 of divine judgments; Jos., Ant. 3, 98 of news) ὁ ζυγός μου is *easy to wear* **Mt 11:30** (metaph.).

❷ **pert. to meeting a relatively high standard of value,** ***fine*** οἶνος (Plut., Mor. 240d; 1073a; Hippiatr. II 66, 16; Abercius ins 16; cp. En 32:1 'fine' nard) **Lk 5:39** *the old is (just) fine = the old suits me fine* (the Greek is normal, and it is not necessary to assume an Aramaism, but s. μέγας 9:48 and B-D-F §245; v.l. has the comp. χρηστότερος [Philo, In Flacc. 109; Jos., Ant. 8, 213]).

❸ **pert. to being morally good and benevolent.** This mng. is in keeping w. the Israelite and Hellenic ideal of morality as exhibition of usefulness within the socio-political structure (s. κακός, πονηρός; EWelskopf, Soziale Typenbegriffe im alten Griechenland '68; KDover, Greek Popular Morality '74).

ⓐ ***reputable*** (Ath. 36, 1 βίος) ἤθη χρηστά **1 Cor 15:33** (s. ἦθος.—ἦθος χρηστόν also POxy 642; 1663, 11; EpArist 290; Philo, Det. Pot. Ins. 38 ἤθη χρηστὰ διαφθείρεται).

ⓑ ***kind, loving, benevolent*** (Jos., Ant. 6, 92 w. ἐπιεικής; 9, 133 w. δίκαιος; Herodian 4, 3, 3 and Philo, Leg. ad Gai. 67 w. φιλάνθρωπος; Cass. Dio 66, 18; ins in FCumont, Études syr. 1917 p. 323, 12; POxy 642)

α. of humans (Nicophon Com. [V/IV BC] 16; Ps.-Demosth. 59, 2; TestJob 13:6 λίαν μου χρηστοῦ ὄντος) 1 Cl 14:4 (Pr 2:21). εἴς τινα *to someone* (POxy 416, 2) **Eph 4:32.**

β. of God (Hdt. 8, 111; Sb 158, 1; LXX; PsSol 2:36 al.; Philo, Det. Pot. Ins. 46 al.; SibOr 1, 159) **1 Pt 2:3** (Ps 33:9), Χριστός P[72]; Dg 8:8. ἐπί τινα *to someone* **Lk 6:35.** ἐν τοῖς κτλ. *among those = to those, who* 1 Cl 60:1.

❹ subst. τὸ χρηστόν **the quality of beneficence,** ***kindness*** (Philo, Virt. 160; Jos., Ant. 8, 214; Just., A I, 4, 5 [w. wordplay on Χριστιανοί]; 15:13, and D. 96, 3 [Luke 6:35f]; difft. Ath. 20, 3 τί τὸ σεμνὸν ἢ χρηστὸν τῆς τοιαύτης ἱστορίας;) τοῦ θεοῦ **Ro 2:4.**—JZiegler, Dulcedo Dei '37; CSpicq, RB 54, '47, 321–24.—DELG s.v. χρησ-. Frisk s.v. χρή. M-M. TW. Spicq. Sv.

χρηστότης, ητος, ἡ (χρηστός; Eur., Isaeus+; ins, pap, LXX; OdeSol 11:15; ApcEsdr 2:21 p. 26, 13 Tdf. [acc. χρηστότητα]; Philo, Joseph.) gener. 'usefulness, helpfulness'

❶ **uprightness in one's relations with others,** ***uprightness***—ποιεῖν χρηστότητα *do what is good* (Ps 36:3 do טוֹב [37:3 MT]) **Ro 3:12** (cp. Ps 13:3). But this pass. belongs equally well in 2 below, for the reason cited in χρηστός 3.

❷ **the quality of being helpful or beneficial,** ***goodness, kindness, generosity*** (Ps.-Pla., Def. 412e χ. = ἦθους σπουδαιότης 'readily generous in disposition'; Aristot., De Virt. et Vit. 8 w. ἐπιείκεια [as Philo, Exs. 166] and εὐγνωμοσύνη; Plut., Demetr. 913 [50, 1] w. φιλανθρωπία [as Philo, Leg. ad Gai. 73]; SIG 761, 12 w. μεγαλοψυχία; Plut., Galba 1063 [22, 7], Mor. 88b; 90e w. μεγαλοφροσύνη.—BGU 372, 18; LXX; opp. πονηρία OdeSol 11:20).

ⓐ of humans (PsSol 5:13; w. other virtues Orig., C. Cels. 1, 67, 25) **2 Cor 6:6; Gal 5:22** (both w. μακροθυμία); **Col 3:12** (w. σπλάγχνα οἰκτιρμοῦ).

ⓑ of God (Ps 30:20; PsSol 5:18 al.; OdeSol; ApcEsdr 2:21; Philo, Migr. Abr. 122; Jos., Ant. 1, 96; 11, 144; Iren. 4, 20, 5 [Harv. II 217, 10]; Orig., C. Cels. 5, 12, 1) **Ro 2:4** (w. ἀνοχή and μακροθυμία); **9:23 v.l.** (for δόξης); **11:22c** (s. ἐπιμένω 2); **Tit 3:4** (w. φιλανθρωπία); 1 Cl 9:1 (w. ἔλεος); 2 Cl 15:5; 19:1; Dg 9:1, 2 (w. φιλανθρωπία and ἀγάπη), 6; 10:4; IMg 10:1; ISm 7:1. (Opp. ἀποτομία) **Ro 11:22ab.** χρηστότης ἐφ' ἡμᾶς (cp. PsSol 5:18 χ. σου ἐπὶ Ἰσρ.) **Eph 2:7.**—LStachowiak, Chrestotes: Studia Friburgensia, n.s. 17, '57 (Freiburg, Switzerland).—DELG s.v. χρησ- 3. Frisk s.v. χρή. M-M. EDNT. TW. Spicq. Sv.

χρῖσις, εως, ἡ (χρίω, cp. χρῖσμα; Aristot. et al.; ins, pap, LXX, Joseph.) ***smearing, anointing,*** but not appropriate in the context ἐν [συν]έσει χρεῖσις καὶ πίστει AcPl BMM verso 7f (s. HSanders, HTR 31, '38, 88 ad loc.).—DELG s.v. χρίω.

χρῖσμα, ατος, τό (χρίω; cp. χρῖσις, later also χρίσμα; X. et al.; PGM 7, 874; LXX; Philo, Mos. 2, 146; 152; Jos., Ant. 3, 197; Just., D. 86, 3, mostly=oil for anointing, unguent. On the accent B-D-F §13; Mlt-H. 57; Crönert 228, 3) ***anointing*** (so lit. Ex 29:7) **1J 2:20, 27ab,** usu. taken to mean anointing w. the Holy Spirit (difft. Rtzst., Mysterienrel.[3] 1927, 396f, who thinks of the 'formal equation of the baptismal proclamation w. the χρῖσμα').—DELG s.v. χρίω. M-M. EDNT. TW.

χριστέμπορος, ου, ὁ (Χριστός, ἔμπορος 'trader'; only in Christian wr.) **one who carries on a cheap trade in (the teachings of) Christ,** ***Christmonger*** D 12:5.—DELG s.v. χρίω. Sv.

Χριστιανισμός, οῦ, ὁ **the way of life and belief associated w. Christ,** ***the Christian Way, Christianity*** IRo 3:3; MPol 10:1. W. Ἰουδαϊσμός IMg 10:3ab; IPhld 6:1. κατὰ Χριστιανισμὸν ζῆν IMg 10:1.—DELG s.v. χρίω. DNP II 1153–64. Sv.

Χριστιανός, οῦ, ὁ (formed like Ἡρῳδιανοί [q.v.] or Καισαριανοί Epict. 1, 19, 19; s. TMommsen, Her 34, 1899, 151f; Dssm., LO 323 [LAE 377]; Hahn 263, 9; B-D-F §5, 2. On the Pompeian ins CIL IV 679, the reading of which is quite uncertain, s. VSchultze, ZKG 5, 1881, 125ff. On the spelling Χρηστιανός Ac 11:26; 26:28; 1 Pt 4:16 [all v.l.]; AcPl Ha 9, 19 [cp. Just., A I, 4, 5]; s. FBlass, Her 30, 1895, 465ff; Harnack, SBBerlAk 1915, 762; B-D-F §24; Mlt-H. 72) **one who is associated w. Christ,** ***Christ-partisan, Christian*** (so also Lucian, Alex. 25; 38, M. Peregr. 11; 12; 13; 16; Tacitus, Ann. 15, 44; Suetonius, Nero 16; Pliny the Younger, Ep. 10, 96, 1; 2; 3 al., also in Trajan's reply; ApcSed prol.; Ar., Just., Ath.; s. Hemer, Acts 177) **Ac 11:26; 26:28; 1 Pt 4:16** (JKnox, JBL 72, '53, 187–89); IEph 11:2; IMg 4; IRo 3:2; IPol 7:3; MPol 3; 10:1; 12:1, 2; D 12:4; PtK 2 p. 15, 8; τῶν Χρ. Dg 1:1. Without the art. 2:6, 10; 4:6; 5:1; 6:1–9. πολλοὺς Χρ. ActPl Ha 9, 19.—As an adj. χριστιανός, ή, όν: ἡ χριστιανὴ τροφή ITr 6:1.—For inscriptions s. esp. EGibson, The 'Christians for Christians' Inscriptions from Phrygia '78; New Docs 128–39.—RLipsius, Über den Ursprung u. ältesten Gebr. des Christennamens, Prog. Jena 1873; Zahn, Einl. II[3] 41ff; FKattenbusch, Das apostol. Symbol II 1900, 557ff; JDaniels, De Naam ΧΡΙΣΤΙΑΝΟΙ: De Studiën 76, 1907, 568–80; JLeCoultre, De l'étymologie du mot 'Chrétien': RTP 40, 1907, 188–96; AGercke, Der Christenname ein Scheltname: Festschr. z. Jahrhundertfeier d. Univers. Breslau 1911, 360ff; Harnack, Mission I[4] 1923, 424ff; EPeterson, Christianus: Miscellanea Giov. Mercati I '46, 355–72; EBickerman, HTR 42, '49, 109–24; JMoreau, La Nouvelle Clio 4, '50, 190–92; HMattingly, JTS 9, '58, 26–37 (cp. the term Augustiani); CSpicq, StTh 15, '61, 68–78 (cp. the adj. Ciceronianus=of or belonging to Cicero: Sen., Con. 7, 2, 12).—DELG s.v. χρίω. M-M. EDNT. TW. Sv.

χριστομαθία, ας, ἡ (only in Christian wr.) ***discipleship with Christ*** or ***teaching of Christ*** κατὰ χριστομαθίαν *in accordance with discipleship to Christ* or *with Christ's teaching* IPhld

8:2.—For words with the termination -μαθία s. Buck, Reverse Index 136.—DELG s.v. χρίω.

χριστόνομος, ον (only in Ign.) ***keeping the law of Christ*** IRo ins.—DELG s.v. χρίω.

Χριστός, οῦ (as an adj. in trag. and LXX; TestReub 6:8; Just., D. 141, 3 [the compound νεόχριστος=newly plastered: Diod. S., 38 and 39, fgm. 4, 3; Appian, Bell. Civ. 1. 74 §342]; in our lit. only as a noun; pl. Just., D. 86, 3.—CTorrey, Χριστός: Quantulacumque '37, 317–24), **ὁ.**

❶ **fulfiller of Israelite expectation of a deliverer,** ***the Anointed One, the Messiah, the Christ,*** appellative (cp. Ps 2:2; PsSol 17:32; 18:5, 7; TestSol 1:12 D; TestLevi 10:2; ParJer 9:19; Just. A I, 15, 7 al.; Mel., P. 102, 779 al.—ESellin, Die israel-jüd. Heilandserwartung 1909; EBurton, ICC Gal 1920, 395–99; AvGall, Βασιλεία τ. θεοῦ 1926; HGressmann, D. Messias 1929; PVolz, D. Eschatol. der jüd. Gemeinde im ntl. Zeitalter '34; Dalman, Worte 237–45; Bousset, Rel.[3] 227, Kyrios Christos[2] 1921, 3f; Billerb. I 6–11; MZobel, Gottes Gesalbter: D. Messias u. d. mess. Zeit in Talm. u. Midr. '38; J-JBrierre-Narbonne, Le Messie souffrant dans la littérature rabbinique '40; HRiesenfeld, Jésus Transfiguré '47, 54–65; 81–96; TNicklin, Gospel Gleanings '50, 265–67; WCvUnnik, NTS 8, '62, 101–16; MdeJonge, The Use of 'Anointed' in the Time of Jesus, NovT 8, '66; TRE XXII 630–35) ἐπυνθάνετο ποῦ ὁ Χριστὸς γεννᾶται *he inquired where the Messiah was to be born* **Mt 2:4.** Cp. **16:16, 20; 22:42; 23:8 v.l., 10; 24:5, 23; 26:63; Mk 1:34 v.l.; 8:29; 12:35; 13:21; 14:61; Lk 3:15; 4:41; 20:41; 22:67; 23:2, 35, 39; 24:26, 46; J 1:20, 25; 3:28; 4:29, 42 v.l.; 6:69 v.l.; 7:26f, 31, 41ab, 42; 9:22; 10:24; 11:27; 12:34** (WCvUnnik, NovT 3, '59, 174–79); **20:31; Ac 2:30 v.l., 31, 36; 9:22; 17:3; 18:5, 28; 26:23; 1J 2:22; 5:1** (OPiper, JBL 66, '47, 445). **J** translates Μεσσίας as Χριστός **1:41; 4:25.** ὁ Χριστὸς κυρίου **Lk 2:26;** cp. **9:20; Ac 3:18; 4:26** (Ps 2:2); **Rv 11:15; 12:10.**—Ἰησοῦς ὁ Χριστός *Jesus the Messiah* (Mel., P. 10, 68) **Ac 5:42 v.l.; 9:34** t.r.; **1 Cor 3:11 v.l.; 1J 5:6 v.l.;** 1 Cl 42:1b; IEph 18:2. [Ἰησοῦν] τὸν Χριστὸν [καὶ σωτῆρα] ἡμῶν *Jesus the Messiah, our Savior* AcPl Ha 8, 28f. ὁ Χριστὸς Ἰησοῦς **Ac 5:42; 19:4 v.l.** Ἰησοῦς ὁ λεγόμενος Χριστός *Jesus, the so-called Messiah* **Mt 27:17, 22.**—The transition to sense 2 is marked by certain passages in which Χριστός does not mean the Messiah in general (even when the ref. is to Jesus), but a very definite Messiah, Jesus, who now is called *Christ* not as a title but as a name (cp. Jos., Ant. 20, 200 Ἰησοῦ τοῦ λεγομένου Χριστοῦ; Just., D. 32, 1 ὁ ὑμέτερος λεγόμενος Χριστός. On the art. w. Χρ. s. B-D-F §260, 1; Rob. 760f) ἀκούσας τὰ ἔργα τοῦ Χριστοῦ **Mt 11:2;** cp. **Ac 8:5; 9:20 v.l.; Ro 9:3, 5; 1 Cor 1:6, 13, 17; 9:12; 10:4, 16; 2 Cor 2:12; 4:4; Gal 1:7; 6:2; Eph 2:5; 3:17; 5:14; Phil 1:15; Col 1:7; 2:17; 2 Th 3:5; 1 Ti 5:11; Hb 3:14; 9:28; 1 Pt 4:13; 2J 9; Rv 20:4** al.

❷ **the personal name ascribed to Jesus,** ***Christ,*** which many gentiles must have understood in this way (to them it seemed very much like Χρηστός [even in pronunciation—cp. Alex. of Lycopolis, III AD, C. Manich. 24 Brinkmann 1905 p. 34, 18f], a name that is found in lit. [Appian, Mithrid. 10 §32 Σωκράτης . . . , ὅτῳ Χρηστὸς ἐπώνυμον ἦν; 57 §232 Σωκράτη τὸν Χρηστόν; Diod. S. 17, 15, 2 Φωκίων ὁ Χρηστός; Chion, Ep. 4, 3; Philostrat., Vi. Soph. 2, 11, 2: a pupil of Herodes Att.; Memnon Hist., I BC/I AD: 434, fgm. 1, 4, 8; 1, 22, 5 Jac. as surname or epithet of a beneficent ruler], in ins [e.g. fr. Bithynia ed. FDörner '41 no. 31 a foundation by Chrestos for the Great Mother; Sb 8819, 5] and pap [Preisigke, Namenbuch]; cp. v.l. εἶδος τοῦ Χριστοῦ TestAsh 7:2f for ὕδωρ ἄχρηστον; s. also Suetonius, Claud. 25.—TLL, Suppl. 1, 407f; B-D-F §24 [lit.]; Rob. 192) Ἰησοῦς Χριστός **Mt 1:1, 18; Mk 1:1; J 1:17; 17:3; Ac 2:38; 3:6; 4:10; 8:12; 9:34** al. Very oft. in the epistles **Ro 1:4, 6, 8; 3:22; 5:15** (see s.v. Ἀδάμ); **1 Cor 2:2; Col 2:19 v.l.** (in effect negating the metaph. force of κεφαλή) etc.; **Hb 10:10; 13:8, 21; Js 1:1; 2:1; 1 Pt 1:1–3, 7; 2 Pt 1:1ab; 1J 1:3; 2:1; 3:23; 2J 7; Jd 1ab; Rv 1:1, 2, 5;** 1 Cl 21:6 (GrBar 4:15); AcPl Ha 8, 24; AcPlCor 2:4 (GrBar 4:15; Ar., Just.; Mel., P. 45, 322).—Χριστὸς Ἰησοῦς (SMcCasland, JBL 65, '46, 377–83) **Ac 24:24; Ro 3:24; 6:3, 11; 8:1f, 11 v.l.; 1 Cor 1:2, 4, 30** etc.; 1 Cl 32:4; 38:1; IEph 1:1; 11:1; 12:2; IMg ins.; ITr 9:2; IRo 1:1; 2:2; IPhld 10:1; 11:2; ISm 8:2; Pol 8:1 (s. Ltzm., Hdb. exc. on Ro 1:1); AcPl Ha (throughout, exc. 8, 24) ; AcPlCor, exc. 2:4 (Just., D. 35, 8; Mel., P. 6, 42).—Χριστός **Mk 9:41; Ro 5:6, 8; 6:4, 9; 8:10** etc.; **Col 3:16** λόγος τοῦ Χριστοῦ, perh.=*the story of Christ;* **Hb 3:6; 9:11; 1 Pt 2:21; 3:18;** AcPlCor 2:10 and 35; AcPl Ha 2, 30 and 33; 8, 9 and 18 (Ar. 15, 10; Just., A I, 4, 7; Mel., P. 65, 465).—On the combination of Χριστός w. κύριος s. κύριος (II) 2bγℶ. On the formula διὰ Χριστοῦ (Ἰησοῦ) s. διά A 4b; on ἐν Χριστῷ (Ἰησοῦ) s. ἐν 4c (also Goodsp, Probs. 146f); on σὺν Χριστῷ s. σύν 1bβ.—OSchmitz, D. Christusgemeinsch. des Pls im Lichte s. Genetivgebrauchs 1924.—SMowinckel, He that Cometh, tr. GAnderson '54; HRiesenfeld, The Mythological Background of NT Christology: CHDodd Festschr. '64, 81–95. θεὸς χριστός **Jd 5** P^{72}.—On the question of Jesus' Messianic consciousness s. the lit. s.v. Ἰησοῦς 3; υἱός 2, esp. d; also J-BFrey, Le conflit entre le Messianisme de Jésus et le Messianisme des Juifs de son temps: Biblica 14, '33, 133–49; 269–93; KGoetz, Hat sich Jesus selbst für den Messias gehalten u. ausgegeben? StKr 105, '33, 117–37; GBornkamm, Jesus von Naz. '56, 155–63 (Engl. transl. JRobinson '60, 169–78).—LCerfaux, Christ in the Theol. of St. Paul, tr. GWebb and AWalker, '59; JMorgenstern, VetusT 11, '61, 406–31; RFuller, The Foundations of NT Christology, '65; WThüsing, Per Christum in Deum, '65; HBraun, Qumran u. d. NT II '66, 75–84; DJones, The Title 'Christos' in Lk-Ac, CBQ 32, '70, 69–76; JKingsbury, Matthew: Structure, Christology, Kingdom '75; RAC II 1250–62; TRE XXII 617–35; TLL Suppl. 1, 409–15.—DELG s.v. χρίω. M-M. EDNT. TW. Sv.

χριστοφόρος, ον (φέρω) only in Christian wr. **pert. to being in movement and constantly identified as a follower of Christ,** subst. ὁ χρ. ***the Christ-bearer*** IEph 9:2 (s. Hdb. ad loc.).—Cp. TLL Suppl. 1, 415f. DELG s.v. χρίω.

χρίω fut. 2 sg. χρίσεις LXX; 1 aor. ἔχρισα; pf. κέκρικα LXX. Pass.: 1 fut. 2 sg. χρισθήσῃ (JosAs 15:4), 3 sg. χρισθήσεται Ex 30:32; 1 aor. ἐχρίσθην; pf. ptc. κεχρισμένος (Hom.+) ***anoint*** in our lit. only in a fig. sense of an anointing by God setting a pers. apart for special service under divine direction (cp. Hom. Hymn to Demeter 237 χρίεσκ' ἀμβροσίῃ: Demeter anoints Demophon; Apollon. Rhod. 4, 871). God anoints

ⓐ David: ἐν ἐλέει αἰωνίῳ ἔχρισα αὐτόν 1 Cl 18:1 (cp. Ps 88:21).

ⓑ Jesus, the Christ, for his work or mission **Ac 4:27** (cp. SibOr 5, 68; Just. A II, 6, 3, D. 8, 4; 49, 1. ἔχρισέν με **Lk 4:18;** cp. B 14:9 (both Is 61:1). αὐτὸν πνεύματι ἁγίῳ *him with holy spirit* **Ac 10:38** (cp. PsSol 17:42; the dat. as Dio Chrys. 66 [16], 10; Jos., Ant. 7, 357 ἐλαίῳ χ.). W. double acc. (after LXX) ἔχρισέν σε ἔλαιον ἀγαλλιάσεως **Hb 1:9** (Ps 44:8).

ⓒ the prophets: μετὰ τὸ χρισθῆναι αὐτοὺς ἐν πνεύματι ἁγίῳ Judaicon, ASyn. 172, 8.

ⓓ the apostles or, more probably, all Christians (at baptism or through the Spirit) **2 Cor 1:21.**—EncRelEth XII 509–16; Reallexikon der Vorgeschichte XI 1928, 191ff.—DELG. M-M. EDNT. TW.

χρόα, ας, ἡ (Aristoph. et al.) ***color*** (Pla. et al.; Diod. S. 5, 32, 2; Lucian, LXX; En 30:2; EpArist, Philo; Jos., Ant. 2, 273; Ath. 4, 2; cp. τὴν χροίαν Ath. 4, 2) Hs 9, 13, 5; 9, 17, 3f. τὰς χρόας ἀλλάσσειν (s. ἀλλάσσω 1 and cp. 2 Macc 3:16) 9, 4, 5b; 8. χρόαι ποικίλαι 9, 4, 5a.—DELG s.v. χρώς.

χρονίζω (χρόνος) fut. χρονίσω and Att. χρονιῶ **Hb 10:37 v.l.;** 1 Cl 23:5; LXX; aor. ἐχρόνισα LXX; pf. κεχρόνικα LXX (Aeschyl., Hdt. et al.; ins, pap, LXX; Jos., Ant. 16, 403)

❶ to continue in a state or place, *stay* (Hdt. 3, 61, 1) w. the place indicated by ἐν (somewhere) *stay for a long time* (Polyb. 33, 18, 6; Alex. Aphr., Mixt. 9 p. 223, 5 Br.; Pr 9:18a v.l.; Jos., Bell. 4, 465) ἐν τῷ ναῷ **Lk 1:21;** ὅπου χρονίζεις Hv 3, 1, 2 v.l. (Leutzsch, Hermas p. 403 n. 234).

❷ to extend a state or an activity beyond an expected time ⓐ abs. ***take time, linger, fail to come*** or ***stay away for a long time*** (Thu. 8, 16, 3; Maximus Tyr. 33, 6b; Da 9:19; Tob 10:4; Sir 14:12) χρονίζει μου ὁ κύριος **Mt 24:48.** Cp. **25:5; Hb 10:37** (Hab 2:3); 1 Cl 23:5 (Is 13:22). χρονίσαντος . . . αὐτοῦ ἐφοβήθησαν *when (Zacharias) delayed (coming out), they were afraid* GJs 24:2.

ⓑ w. inf. foll. ***delay, take a long time (in doing someth.)*** (Dt 23:22) **Mt 24:48 v.l.; Lk 12:45.**—DELG s.v. χρόνος. M-M. EDNT.

χρόνος, ου, ὁ (Hom.+)—**❶ an indefinite period of time during which some activity or event takes place, *time, period of time*** πολὺς χρόνος *a long time* (PGiss 4, 11; PStras 41, 39; ApcSed 13:5; Jos., C. Ap. 1, 278 Just., D. 7, 1) **Mt 25:19; J 5:6** (πολὺν ἤδη χ. as Jos., Ant. 8, 342; 19, 28). πλείων χρ. *a longer time* (Diod. S. 1, 4, 3; Dio Chrys. 78 [29], 15; SIG 421, 38; 548, 11; PPetr II, 9, 2, 3; Jos., Ant. 9, 228) **Ac 18:20.** ἱκανὸς χρόνος *considerable time, a long time* (ἱκανός 3b) **Lk 8:27; Ac 8:11; 14:3; 27:9;** Qua 2. μικρὸς χρ. (Is 54:7) **J 7:33; 12:35; Rv 6:11; 20:3;** IEph 5:1. ὀλίγος (Aristot., Phys. 218b, 15; SIG 709, 11; PPetr II, 40a, 14; Just., D. 2, 6; Ath. 7, 3) **Ac 14:28;** 2 Cl 19:3; Hs 7:6; AcPl Ha 9, 26 (restored after Aa I 112, 14). πόσος; **Mk 9:21** (ApcMos 31; Just., D. 32, 4). τοσοῦτος (Lucian, Dial. Deor. 1, 1; ParJer 5:18; Jos., Bell. 2, 413) **J 14:9** (τοσούτῳ χρόνῳ as Epict. 3, 23, 16); **Hb 4:7.** ὅσος **Mk 2:19; Ro 7:1; 1 Cor 7:39; Gal 4:1;** cp. Hs 6, 4, 1 (ὅσος 1b). ὁ πᾶς χρόνος *the whole time, all the time* (Appian, Bell. Civ. 2, 132 §553; Jos., Ant. 3, 201; Just., D. 4, 5) **Ac 20:18;** AcPlCor 2:4; cp. **Ac 1:21.** ἐν παντὶ χρόνῳ *at every time* D 14:3. χρόνον τινά *for a time, for a while* (Arrian, Anab. Alex. 6, 6, 5; Synes., Prov. 2, 3 p. 121d) **1 Cor 16:7;** Hs 7:2. τῷ χρόνῳ *in time* (Herodas 4, 33 χρόνῳ) 9, 26, 4. στιγμὴ χρόνου (s. στιγμή) **Lk 4:5.** τὸ πλήρωμα τοῦ χρόνου (πλήρωμα 5) **Gal 4:4** (cp. Pind., fgm. 134 Bowra=147 Schr. foll. by BSnell ἐν χρόνῳ δ' ἔγεντ' Ἀπόλλων). Certain special verbs are used w. χρόνος: διαγενέσθαι **Ac 27:9** (s. διαγίνομαι), διατρίβειν (q.v.) **Ac 14:3, 28,** πληρωθῆναι **7:23;** 1 Cl 25:2; Hs 6, 5, 2 (πληρόω 2). χρόνον ἐπέχω (q.v. 3) **Ac 19:22;** ἔχω (q.v. 7b) **J 5:6;** ποιέω (q.v. 5c) **Ac 15:33; 18:23;** βιόω (q.v.) **1 Pt 4:2.**—Pl. χρόνοι of a rather long period of time composed of several shorter ones (Diod. S. 1, 5, 1; 5, 9, 4; Ael. Aristid. 46 p. 312 D.; UPZ 42, 45 [162 BC]; JosAs 13:12; SibOr 3, 649; AcPlCor 2:10; Just. A I, 13, 3 al.; Tat. 1, 1; Iren. 1, 15, 4 [Harv. I 153, 1]; Hippol. Ref. 9, 10, 11; Did., Gen. 24, 9) χρόνοι αἰώνιοι (αἰώνιος 1) **Ro 16:25; 2 Ti 1:9; Tit 1:2.** ἀρχαῖοι χρ. Pol 1:2. χρόνοι ἱκανοί (ἱκανός 3b) **Lk 8:27 v.l.; 20:9; 23:8.** πολλοὶ χρόνοι (πολύς 2aα Yet χρόνοι could somet. = *years:* Diod. S. 4, 13, 3 ἐκ πολλῶν χρόνων=over a period of many years; 33, 5a μετὰ δέ τινας χρόνους=after a few years; Ps.-Callisth. 2, 33 ed. CMüller of the age of a child ἦν χρόνων ὡσεὶ δώδεκα; Mitt-Wilck. I/2, 129, 14 [346 AD]; Lex. Vindob. p. 19, 104 ἀφήλικες ἄνδρες μέχρι τῶν κε' χρόνων; Philip of Side: Anecdota Gr. Oxon. ed. JCramer IV 1837 p. 246 ἑκατὸν ἔτη . . . καὶ μετὰ ἄλλους ἑκατὸν χρόνους; Cyrill. Scyth. 45, 5; 108, 8 and oft. Frequently in later Byzantine writers, e.g. Constantin. Porphyr. ed. GMoravcsik '49 p. 332 [index]) **Lk 8:29;** 1 Cl 42:5; 44:3. (οἱ) χρ. τῆς ἀγνοίας **Ac 17:30.** ἀποκαταστάσεως πάντων **3:21.** οἱ νῦν χρ. 2 Cl 19:4. οἱ πρότεροι χρ. Hs 9, 20, 4. οἱ καθ' ἡμᾶς χρ. (Proclus In Pla., Tim. 40cd ἐν τοῖς κατ' αὐτὸν χρόνοις [FBoll, Sternglaube und Sterndeutung '66, 95]) MPol 16:2. εἰς τοὺς ἡμετέρους χρόνους Qua 2. ἐπ' ἐσχάτου τῶν χρ. **1 Pt 1:20.** χρόνοι w. καιροί (the same juxtaposition: Demosth., Ep. 2, 3; Straton of Lamps. [300 BC], fgm. 10 Wehrli '50; PLond I, 42, 23 p. 30 [168 BC]; PCairMasp 159, 36; 167, 45. Cp. Ael. Aristid. 46 p. 291 and 290 D.; Ath. 22, 4. On the difference betw. the two Demosth., Ep. 5, 6) **Ac 1:7; 1 Th 5:1;** GMary 463, 1 (s. καιρός, end).—Both sing. and pl. are very oft. governed by prepositions: by ἄχρι (q.v. 1aα); διά w. the gen. (διά A 2), w. the acc. (διά B 2a); ἐκ (MPol 22:3; s. ἐκ 5a); ἐν (Menand., Peric. 546 S. [=296 Kö.] ἐν τούτῳ τῷ χρόνῳ; CPR 13, 2; 23, 23; Jer 38:1) **Ac 1:6;** IEph 5:1; ἐπί w. dat. (ἐπί 18b) 2 Cl 19:4, w. acc. (ἐπί 18c); κατά w. acc. (κατά B 2); μετά w. acc. (μετά B 2); πρό (πρό 2).

❷ a point of time consisting of an occasion for some event or activity, *time, occasion* ὁ χρόνος τῆς ἐπαγγελίας *the time for the fulfillment of the promise* **Ac 7:17;** τῆς παροικίας **1 Pt 1:17;** τῆς πίστεως B 4:9; D 16:2; τῆς ἀπάτης καὶ τρυφῆς Hs 6, 5, 1; cp. 6, 4, 4. ὁ χρ. τοῦ φαινομένου ἀστέρος *the time when the star appeared* **Mt 2:7.** ἐπλήσθη ὁ χρ. τοῦ τεκεῖν αὐτήν **Lk 1:57** (πίμπλημι 1bβ.—Ps.-Callisth. 1, 12 τελεσθέντος τοῦ χρόνου τοῦ τεκεῖν). Cp. also **Mt 2:16; Lk 18:4; Ac 1:6; 13:18, Hb 5:12; 11:32; 1 Pt 4:3; Jd 18;** Dg 9:1, 6; Hs 5, 5, 3.

❸ a period during which someth. is delayed, *respite, delay* (Aeschyl., Pers. 692; Menand., Dyscolus 186; Diod. S. 10, 4, 3; Lucian, Syr. D. 20; Vi. Aesopi I c. 21 p. 278, 3 χρόνον ᾔτησε; Wsd 12:20; Jos., Bell. 4, 188 ἂν ἡμεῖς χρόνον δῶμεν, Vi. 370) ἔδωκα αὐτῇ χρόνον ἵνα μετανοήσῃ **Rv 2:21** (Diod. S. 17, 9, 2 διδοὺς μετανοίας χρόνον). χρόνος οὐκέτι ἔσται *there should be no more delay* **10:6** (cp. 9:20; Goodsp., Probs. 200f).—For the history of the word s. KDietecrich, RhM n.s. 59, 1904, 233ff.—GDelling, D. Zeitverständnis des NTs '40; OCullmann, Christus u. d. Zeit '46, Engl. transl. Christ and Time, FFilson '50, 3d ed. '64, esp. 49f; 51–55; JWilch, Time and Event (OT) '69.—B. 954. Schmidt, Syn. II 54–72. DELG. M-M. DNP II 1174f. ENDT. TW. Sv. Cp. αἰών.

χρονοτριβέω (τρίβω 'rub, wear out, waste'; Aristot., Rhet. 3, 3, 3, 1406a, 37; Plut., Mor. 225b and d; the mid. UPZ 39, 29; 40 II, 21 [both II BC].—Cp. Jos., Ant. 12, 368 χρ. ἐτρίβετο) **to experience a duration of time, *spend time, lose time,*** ἐν τῇ Ἀσίᾳ **Ac 20:16.**—M-M.

χρύσεος s. χρυσοῦς.—M-M.

χρυσίον, ου, τό (χρυσός; Hdt.+)—**❶ gold as raw material, *gold*** (the most highly prized metal in most of the ancient world; dim. of χρυσός) **1 Pt 1:7;** MPol 18:2. Refined in fire **Rv 3:18;** Hv 4, 3, 4ab. χρ. καθαρόν (Ex 25:11; 2 Ch 3:4, 8) *pure gold* **Rv 21:18** (cp. the 'golden dwellings in heaven' Pind., N. 10, 88; Luc., Ver. Hist. 2, 11 ἡ πόλις πᾶσα χρυσῆ) **21** (s. τίμιος 1a). Cp. **1 Cor 3:12** (Dio Chrys. 30 [47], 14 a house of real gold, cp. 62 [79], 1); **Hb 9:4.**

❷ object made of gold or adorned with gold—ⓐ ***gold ornaments, jewelry*** **1 Ti 2:9; 1 Pt 3:3** (pl., as Demosth. 27, 10; 13; Plut., Tim. 243 [15, 10], Artox. 1013 [5, 4]; Alciphron 4, 9, 4; GDI

4689, 22 [Messenia]; PMich 214, 32 [296 AD]). κεχρυσωμένη (ἐν) χρυσίῳ *adorned with golden jewelry* **Rv 17:4; 18:16.**

ⓑ ***coined gold*** (X., An. 1, 1, 9; Synes., Ep. 18 p. 174a; EpArist 319; TestJob 11:3; 44:5) ἀργύριον καὶ (or ἢ) χρυσίον *silver and gold = money* (ins, LXX; PsSol 17:33; Philo, Deus Imm. 169; Jos., Ant. 15, 5) **Ac 3:6; 20:33; 1 Pt 1:18.**—DELG s.v. χρυσός. M-M.

χρυσοδακτύλιος,ον (Hesych. s.v. χρυσοκόλλητος) ***with a gold ring / rings on one's finger(s)*** **Js 2:2** (cp. Epict. 1, 22, 18).—M-M.

χρυσόλιθος, ου, ὁ prob. **a yellowish precious stone, *yellow topaz, chrysolite*** (Diod. S. 2, 52, 3; PLond III, 928, 15 p. 191 [III AD]; Ex 28:20; 36:20; Ezk 28:13; Jos., Bell, 5, 234, Ant. 3, 168); the ancients (Pliny, NH 37, 42) applied the term to yellow quartz or yellow topaz; the greenish mineral associated with the loanword 'chrysolite' and known as 'olivine' suggests a more precise definition than the data warrant **Rv 21:20.**—Lit. s.v. ἀμέθυστος.—ISBE '88, IV 628f. M-M.

χρυσόπρασος, ου, ὁ a precious stone of golden-green color, *chrysoprase* (Pliny, NH 37, 77; 113 chrysoprasus; cp. TLL s.v. chrysoprasus. The Gk. word in Michael Psellus [XI AD] 23: Les lap. Gr. [s. χαλκηδών] p. 204; 208), highly translucent, but not readily identifiable by modern lapidary standards **Rv 21:20.**—Lit. s.v. ἀμέθυστος.

χρυσός, οῦ, ὁ (Hom.+; 'gold', both as a raw material and as a finished product)

❶ **gold as raw material, *gold.*** As an esp. precious material AcPl Ha 2, 24; w. frankincense and myrrh **Mt 2:11;** GJs 21:3. W. silver PtK 2 p. 14, 14 (TestJob 25:6; Ath. 15, 1), and precious stones **1 Cor 3:12; Rv 18:12;** AcPl Ha 1, 11 (JosAs 2:7). Refined in the furnace (w. silver) MPol 15:2. Of wreaths ὅμοιοι χρυσῷ *with appearance of gold* **Rv 9:7.**

❷ **objects made of gold or adorned with gold—**ⓐ ***gold ornaments*** **1 Ti 2:9 v.l.; Rv 17:4 v.l.; 18:16 v.l.** (s. χρυσίον).

ⓑ ***gold thing,*** of a cult image **Ac 17:29;** 2 Cl 1:6.

ⓒ ***coined gold, money*** (Demosth. 9, 42), w. ἄργυρος (q.v.) **Mt 10:9.** This may also be the mng. in **Js 5:3** and **Mt 23:16f,** though vessels of gold may be meant.—Pauly-W. VII 1555–78; Kl. Pauly II 841f; BHHW I 852f; RAC XI 895–930.—B. 610. DELG. M-M. EDNT. TW.

χρυσοῦς, ῆ, οῦν (χρυσός; trag., Attic wr.; ins, pap, LXX; En 99:7; TestSol; TestAbr B 10 p. 114, 26 [Stone p. 76]; TestJob, JosAs; GrBar 6:7; ApcMos 33; EpArist, Philo; Tat 19, 1. Contracted from χρύσεος: Hom. et al.; ins; Just., D. 20, 4; rare in pap and LXX [Thackeray p. 173]. Both forms in Joseph. [Schmidt 491]. Uncontracted forms are found in our lit. only as v.l. in Rv: χρυσέων 2:1, χρυσέους 4:4, χρυσέας 5:8); the acc. fem. sing. χρυσᾶν Rv 1:13 instead of v.l. χρυσῆν is formed on the analogy of ἀργυρᾶν (s. PGM 10, 26 χρυσᾶν ἢ ἀργυρᾶν and B-D-F §45; s. Mlt-H. 120f; Psaltes p. 187f) **made of/adorned with gold, *golden*** **2 Ti 2:20; Hb 9:4ab; Rv 1:12f, 20; 2:1; 4:4; 5:8; 8:3ab; 9:13, 20; 14:14; 15:6f; 17:4; 21:15;** Dg 2:7.—*Golden* in color or appearance Hv 4, 1, 10; 4, 3, 4 (Demetr.: 722 fgm. 1, 15 p. 669 Jac. 'goldpiece').—DELG s.v. χρυσός. M-M. s.v. -εος.

χρυσοχόος, ου, ὁ (Hom., Od. 3, 425; ins, pap, LXX) 'one who pours gold' (χρυσός + χέω; s. Buck, Reverse Index 178 for parallel formations) ***goldsmith*** AcPl Ha 1, 28 (PPetaus 69, 34; cp. Ac 19:24 Demetrius, an artisan in silver: ἀργυροκόπος).—DELG s.v. χέω II.

χρυσόω (χρυσός) fut. 2 sg. χρυσώσεις Ex 25:11; 26:37; aor. 3 sg. ἐχρύσωσεν LXX; perf. pass. ptc. κεχρυσωμένος Ex 26:32 (also TestAbr A 11 p. 89, 4 [Stone p. 26]; Jos., Vi. 66) (Hdt., Aristoph. et al.; SIG 996, 25; POxy 521, 2; 4; 8; LXX) **to make golden, *gild, adorn with gold,*** κεχρυσωμένη, w. (ἐν) χρυσίῳ pleonastically added (cp. Hdt. 2, 132; Ex 26:32; 2 Ch 3:8–10), and the further addition of precious stones and pearls, of the prostitute Babylon **Rv 17:4; 18:16.**—DELG s.v. χρυσός. M-M.

χρῶμα,ατος,τό (cp. χρώννυμι 'to tinge, color')—❶ **color as hue, *color*** (Eur., Hdt. et al.; pap, LXX; En 18:7; 98:2; TestSol 21:2; EpArist 97; Philo, Jos; loanw. in rabb.) Hv 4, 1, 10; 4, 3, 1. τῷ χρώματι *in color* Hs 6, 1, 5. In imagery, of the complete purity of faith among Roman Christians ἀποδιϋλισμένοι ἀπὸ παντὸς ἀλλοτρίου χρώματος *filtered clear of every alien color* IRo ins.

❷ **musical tone, *tone-color, key, mode*** (Pla., Plut. et al.; Philo, Congr. Erud. Gr. 76) of singing in unison χρῶμα θεοῦ λαβόντες ᾄδετε *get the key from God and sing* IEph 4:2 (cp. Lghtf. ad loc.).—B. 1050. DELG s.v. χρώς 3.

χρώς, χρωτός, ὁ (Hom. et al.; LXX; ApcrEzk P1 verso, 16) **surface of the body, *skin*** **Ac 19:12;** MPol 13:2.—B. 200.—DELG.

χωλός, ή, όν (Hom.+) ***lame, crippled*** (also of the hand: Eupolis Com. [V BC] 247; 343; Hippocr., Prorrh. 2, 1) ἀνὴρ χωλὸς ἐκ κοιλίας μητρὸς αὐτοῦ **Ac 3:2; 14:8.** Pl. almost always w. τυφλοί (Antig. Car. 112; SIG 1168, 36; Job 29:15; Jos., C. Ap. 2, 23) and in addition oft. w. those subject to other infirmities **Mt 11:5** (also in imagery, cp. Pla., Laws 1, 634a of ἀνδρεία; Plut., Cim. 489 [16, 10] of Hellas; s. κωφός 2); **15:30, 31; 21:14; Lk 7:22** (also in imagery; s. κωφός 2); **14:13, 21; J 5:3.**—παραλελυμένοι καὶ χωλοί **Ac 8:7**—*Deprived of one foot* **Mt 18:8; Mk 9:45.**—τὸ χωλόν *what is lame, the lame leg(s)* in imagery **Hb 12:13** (ἐκτρέπω 1).—SRoth, The Blind, the Lame, and the Poor, Character Types in Luke-Acts '97.—B. 318. DELG. M-M.

χώνευμα, ατος, τό (χωνεύω 'cast in a mold') **image made of cast metal, *cast image*** (Philo of Byzantium, Sept. Orbis Spect. 4, 1 [ed. RHercher 1858, placed after his Paris ed. of Aelian]; PLeid X, 21b; LXX) of cult images 1 Cl 53:2; B 14:3 (both Dt 9:12).—DELG s.v. χέω.

χωνευτός, ή, όν (χωνεύω 'melt, pour metal'; Polyb. 34, 9, 11; Diod. S. 5, 35, 4; Plut., Lucull. 517 [37, 5]; schol. on Nicander, Ther. 257; ApcEsdr 4:43 p. 29, 22 Tdf. χωνεύσω τὴν γῆν; Just., A I, 9, 2) **pert. to receiving shape or form through pouring of metal into a mold, *cast, poured*** (LXX; ViElisha 3 [p. 95, 5 Sch.]; Eupolem. [II BC]: 723 fgm. 2, 34, 7 Jac. p. 676 [in Eus., PE 9, 34, 9]; Jos., Ant. 8, 77) subst. τὸ χωνευτόν *an image made of cast metal* (Philo, Leg. All. 3, 36) B 12:6 (Dt 27:15).—DELG s.v. χέω.

χώρα, ας, ἡ (Hom.+) country, land.—❶ **(dry) land in contrast to the sea, *land*** (Isocr. 7, 1; Diod. S. 3, 40, 2; 20, 61, 4 [opp. θάλασσα]) **Ac 27:27.**

❷ **a portion of land area, *district, region, place*—**ⓐ gener. **Mk 6:55; Lk 2:8; 15:14f; Ac 13:49.** χώρα μακρά **Lk 15:13; 19:12.** ἡ χώρα ἐγγὺς τῆς ἐρήμου **J 11:54.** ἔξω τῆς χώρας *out of that region* **Mk 5:10.**

ⓑ The district is more definitely described ὁ κύριος τῆς χώρας ταύτης *the lord of this country* Hs 1:4a (TestJob 3:7). Sharper definiteness is brought about by a gen. of the ruler 1:4b;

of the inhabitants αὐτῶν (Jos., Ant. 5, 318; Just., A I, 53, 9) **Mt 2:12;** GJs 21:4 (cp. TestJob 41:2 ἑαυτῶν) **Ac 12:20;** 1 Cl 12:2, mentioned by name (Josh 5:12; 1 Ch 20:1; Is 7:18; EpArist 107; Just., A I, 34, 2) τῶν Γαδαρηνῶν **Mt 8:28;** cp. **Mk 5:1; Lk 8:26; Ac 10:39;** of the provincial name (1 Macc 8:3) ἡ χώρα τῆς Ἰουδαίας **Ac 26:20;** cp. ἐν χώρᾳ Βηθλεέμ GJs 18:1 (AscIs 3:1, 5); also by a geograph. adj. (Just., D. 79, 2 τῇ Αἰγυπτίᾳ χώρᾳ) ἡ Γαλατικὴ χώρα **Ac 16:6; 18:23;** cp. **Lk 3:1;** 1 Cl 25:3 and **Mk 1:5** (here we have ἡ Ἰουδαία χώρα [Jos., Ant. 11, 4] by metonymy for the inhabitants).

❸ **the open country in contrast to the city,** ***country*** (Isocr. et al.; Diod. S. 18, 18, 9 πόλιν κ. χώραν; Appian, Iber. 10 §39; PTebt 416, 11; EpArist 108f; SibOr 3, 707) εἰς Ἱεροσόλυμα ἐκ τῆς χώρας **J 11:55.** κατὰ χώρας καὶ πόλεις κηρύσσοντες 1 Cl 42:4 (cp. TestLevi 13:7). Those who were dispersed by the persecution at Jerusalem διεσπάρησαν κατὰ τὰς χώρας τῆς Ἰουδαίας κ. Σαμαρείας **Ac 8:1.** Cp. **11:2** D.

❹ **land used for farming,** ***field, cultivated land*** (X. et al.; Sir 43:3; TestAbr A 2 p. 78, 13 [Stone p. 4]; p. 79, 1 [St. p. 6]; Jos., Ant. 7, 191; prob. also Cat. Cod. Astr. IX/2 p. 135, 1) pl. **Lk 21:21; J 4:35; Js 5:4.** Sing. *land, farm* (Jos., Ant. 11, 249; 16, 250) **Lk 12:16.**—ἐν τῇ χώρᾳ B 7:8 refers to land which, though uncultivated, grows fruit-bearing bushes.

❺ **a place or position in which an entity is located,** ***place*** (Ps.-Tyrtaeus 9, 42 D.[3] πάντες … εἴκουσ' ἐκ χώρης=they all withdraw from the place [that the seasoned soldier claims for himself]; Just., A I, 13, 3 ἐν δευτέρᾳ χώρᾳ of Jesus Christ, 'in second place', i.e. after God the Father; idem, D. 127, 2 ἐν τῇ αὐτοῦ χώρᾳ of God, who remains stationary 'in his place', i.e. God need not 'come down' to see someth.; Ath., R. 20 p. 73, 18; s. χωρέω 2) ἐν χώρᾳ καὶ σκιᾷ θανάτου = ἐν χώρᾳ σκιᾶς θανάτου *in the land of the shadow of death* **Mt 4:16** (Is 9:1).—For the history of the word s. KDieterich, RhM n.s. 59, 1904, 226ff.—B. 1302; 1304f.—DELG. M-M.

Χωραζίν s. Χοραζίν.

χωρέω fut. χωρήσω; 1 aor. ἐχώρησα; pf. κεχώρηκα (Just., Tat., Ath.) (Hom.+)

❶ **to make movement from one place or position to another,** ***go, go out/away, reach*** (trag. et al.; pap)—ⓐ lit. (Just., A I, 19, 5 εἰς ἐκεῖνο χωρεῖν ἕκαστον ἐξ οὗπερ ἐγένετο) of food εἰς τὴν κοιλίαν χωρεῖ **Mt 15:17** (=εἰσπορεύεται Mk 7:19.—Aristot., Probl. 1, 55 the drink εἰς τὰς σάρκας χωρεῖ). τοιαύτη διὰ τῆς σαρκὸς αὐτοῦ καὶ ἐπὶ τῆς γῆς ἔκρυσις ἐχώρησεν *so strong was the discharge from his (Judas's) body that it affected an entire region* Papias (3:3). Of pers. εἰς τὸν ἴδιον τόπον μέλλει χωρεῖν IMg 5:1; cp. IEph 16:2. οὗ μέλλουσι χωρήσειν, τοῦτο *that, to which they are destined to go* Dg 8:2. εἴς τινα *to someone* (Appian, Bell. Civ. 3, 95 §395 χ. ἐς τὸν ἀδελφόν; 5, 29 §114) of Christ, who has gone to the Father IMg 7:2. ἔτι κάτω χώρει *go down still farther* **Mt 20:28** D. Of the head of a tall figure χωροῦσα μέχρι τοῦ οὐρανοῦ *it reached up to the sky* GPt 10:40 (like Eris: Il. 4, 443).

ⓑ fig., of a report (Pla., Ep. 7, 333a; 338b λόγος ἐχώρει) εἰς ἡμᾶς ἐχώρησεν *it has reached us* 1 Cl 47:7. εἰς μετάνοιαν χωρεῖν *come to repentance* **2 Pt 3:9** (cp. Appian, Bell. Civ. 5, 30 §115 ἐς ἀπόστασιν χ.=turned to revolt). εἴς τι ἀγαθὸν χωρεῖν *lead to some good* B 21:7 (Soph., El. 615 εἰς ἔργον; Aristoph., Ran. 641 ἐς τὸ δίκαιον).

❷ **to make an advance in movement,** ***be in motion, go forward, make progress*** (Pla., Cratyl. 19, 402a the saying of Heraclitus πάντα χωρεῖ καὶ οὐδὲν μένει; Hdt. 3, 42; 5, 89; 7, 10; 8, 68; Aristoph., Pax 472; 509, Nub. 907; Polyb. 10, 35, 4; 28, 15, 12; Dionys. Hal. 1, 64, 4; Plut., Galba 1057 [10, 1]; TestIss 1:11 v.l.; Jos., Ant. 12, 242; PTebt 27, 81 ἕκαστα χωρῆσαι κατὰ τὴν ἡμετέραν πρόθεσιν) ὁ λόγος ὁ ἐμὸς οὐ χωρεῖ ἐν ὑμῖν *my word makes no headway among you* **J 8:37** (Moffatt; cp. Weymouth. Eunap., Vi. Soph. p. 103 χωρεῖ λόγος). Or perh. (as in 1b above) *there is no place in you for my word* (NRSV; cp. Goodsp. and 20th Cent.; Field, Notes 94f, w. ref. to Alciphron, Ep. 3, 7; Bultmann; DTabachovitz, Till betydelsen av χωρεῖν Joh. 8:37: Eranos 31, '33, 71f.—Perh. also=χώραν ἔχειν Appian, Bell. Civ. 2, 70 §289 ὀλίγην ἐν αὐτοῖς χώραν ἔχειν; Alex. Aphr., Fat. 6 p. 169, 31 Br. χώραν ἐν αὐτοῖς ἔχει τὸ παρὰ φύσιν 'even that which is contrary to nature has room [to be practiced] among them'; Ath., R. 20 p. 73, 18 οὐδ' οὕτως ἕξει χώραν ἡ κατ' αὐτῆς κρίσις not even so would any judgment of [the soul] take place).

❸ **to have room for,** ***hold, contain***—ⓐ lit., of vessels that hold a certain quantity (Hdt. et al.; Diod. S. 13, 83, 3 of stone πίθοι: χ. ἀμφορεῖς χιλίους; 3 Km 7:24; 2 Ch 4:5 χ. μετρητάς; EpArist 76 χωροῦντες ὑπὲρ δύο μετρητάς; TestNapht 2:2) **J 2:6;** cp. Hs 9, 2, 1. In a hyperbolic expr. οὐδ' αὐτὸν τὸν κόσμον χωρῆσαι (v.l. χωρήσειν) τὰ γραφόμενα βιβλία **J 21:25** (Philo, Ebr. 32 οὐδὲ τῶν δωρεῶν ἱκανὸς οὐδεὶς χωρῆσαι τὸ ἄφθονον πλῆθος, ἴσως δὲ οὐδ' ὁ κόσμος 'no one, probably not even the world, is capable of containing the inexhaustible multitude of their gifts'. On this subj. cp. Pind., O. 2, 98–100, N. 4, 71f; s. also ELucius, Die Anfänge des Heiligenkults 1904, 200, 1; OWeinreich, Antike Heilungswunder 1909, 199–201). Of a space that *holds* people (Thu. 2, 17, 3; Diod. S. 13, 61, 6 μὴ δυναμένων χωρῆσαι τῶν τριήρων τὸν ὄχλον=be able to hold the crowd; Plut., Mor. 804b; of theater capacity PSI 186, 4 χωρήσει τὸ θέαδρον [sic]; Gen 13:6; Jos., Bell, 6, 131) without an obj. (cp. οὐ χάρτης χωρεῖ in late pap = the sheet of paper is not large enough) ὥστε μηκέτι χωρεῖν μηδὲ τὰ πρὸς τὴν θύραν *so that there was no longer any room, even around the door* **Mk 2:2.** Cp. Hm 5, 2, 5. Of God πάντα χωρῶν, μόνος δὲ ἀχώρητος ὤν *containing everything, but the only one uncontained* Hm 1:1; quite sim. PtK 2 p. 13, 24 (Mel., P. 5, 38 Χριστός, ὃς κεχώρηκεν τὰ πάντα).

ⓑ fig.—**α.** of open-heartedness, having a 'big heart' χωρήσατε ἡμᾶς *make room for us* in your hearts **2 Cor 7:2** (cp. 6:12; Field, Notes 184; PDuff, Apostolic Suffering and the Language of Procession in 2 Cor 4:7–10: BTB 21, '91, 158–65).

β. *grasp* in the mental sense, *accept, comprehend, understand* (Περὶ ὕψους 9, 9 τὴν τοῦ θεοῦ δύναμιν; Plut., Cato Min. 791 [64, 5] τὸ Κάτωνος φρόνημα χωρεῖν; Synes., Kingship 29 p. 31d φιλοσοφία has her abode παρὰ τῷ θεῷ … καὶ ὅταν αὐτὴν μὴ χωρῇ κατιοῦσαν ὁ χθόνιος χῶρος, μένει παρὰ τῷ πατρί=and if she comes down and the region of the earth cannot contain her, she remains with the Father; SIG 814, 11 [67 AD]; Mitt-Wilck. I/2, 238, 8; PGM 4, 729; Ps.-Phocyl. 89; Philo; Jos., C. Ap. 1, 225) τὸν λόγον **Mt 19:11.** Pass. Dg 12:7. W. acc. to be supplied **Mt 19:12ab**=ISm 6:1; cp. ITr 5:1.

γ. of a native condition *permit, allow for* ἃ οὐ χωρεῖ ἡ φύσις αὐτῆς=(Mary has had a child) *something that her present native (virginal) condition does not allow for* GJs 19:3 (s. φύσις 2). DELG s.v. χώρα. M-M. Sv.

Χωρήβ (חֹרֵב) indecl. (LXX; Just.; Mel., P. 85, 638; 88, 663; but, as it seems, not in Hellenistic Jewish lit.) ***Horeb,*** the mountain where the law was given ὄρος Χ. (as Ex 3:1; 33:6; Just., D. 67, 9) PtK 2 p, 15, 6.—BHHW II 748.

χωρίζω (χωρίς) fut. χωρίσω; 1 aor. ἐχώρισα. Pass.: 1 aor. ἐχωρίσθην; pf. ptc. κεχωρισμένος (Hdt.+).

❶ **to cause separation through use of space between, *divide, separate,*** act. τὶ *someth.* (opp. συζεύγνυμι) **Mt 19:6; Mk 10:9.** τινὰ ἀπό τινος (cp. Pla., Phd. 12, 67c; Diogenes, Ep. 39, 1 χ. τὴν ψυχὴν ἀπὸ τοῦ σώματος; IAndrosIsis, Kyme 12; Jos, Bell. 5, 525 pl.; pass.: Ath., R. 18 [p. 71, 11]; Wsd 1:3; Philo, Leg. All, 2, 96) **Ro 8:35, 39** (ApcMos 42 οὐδεὶς μὴ χωρίσῃ ἡμᾶς).

❷ **to separate by departing from someone, *separate, leave,*** pass., freq. in act. sense—ⓐ *separate (oneself)* (ApcSed 8:12 οὐ χωρίζομαι ἀπὸ τὸ γένος ἡμῶν), *be separated* of divorce (Isaeus 8, 36; Polyb. 31, 26 κεχωρίσθαι ἀπὸ τοῦ Λευκίου; Just., A II, 2, 4 and 6. Oft. in marriage contracts in the pap ἀπ᾽ ἀλλήλων χωρισθῆναι: PSI 166, 11 [II BC]; BGU 1101, 5; 1102, 8; 1103, 6 [all I BC] et al. See Dssm., NB 67 [BS 247]) ἀπό τινος **1 Cor 7:10.** Abs. vss. **11, 15ab.** JMurphy-O'Connor, The Divorced Woman in 1 Cor 7:10–11: JBL 100, '81, 601–6.

ⓑ *be taken away, take one's departure, go away* of stones that represent people Hs 9, 8, 1. Of people (JosAs 26:1; Jos., Vi. 215), w. ἀπό foll, **Ac 1:4; 18:2.** Foll. by ἐκ (Polyb. 3, 90, 2) **18:1.** Abs. **Phlm 15** (Polyb. 3, 94, 9; SIG 709, 10; 32 [w. εἰς foll.]; PTebt 50, 9 [II BC]; BGU 1204, 6 al. in pap; Jos., Bell. 1, 640 al.).

ⓒ In the case of κεχωρισμένος ἀπὸ τῶν ἁμαρτωλῶν **Hb 7:26** the mng. can include not only that Christ has been *separated from sinful humans* by being exalted to the heavenly world (s. what follows in the context of Hb 7:26), but also that because of his attributes (s. what precedes in the context: ὅσιος, ἄκακος, ἀμίαντος) he is *different* from sinful humans (for this mng. cp. Hdt. 1, 172; 2, 91; Epict. 2, 9, 2; 2, 10, 2; 4, 11, 1).—B. 845. DELG s.v. χώρα. M-M. Sv.

χωρίον, ου, τό (dim. of χώρα; Hdt.+)—❶ **a piece of land other than a populated area, *place, piece of land, field*** (Thu. et al.) **Mt 26:36; Mk 14:32; J 4:5; Ac 1:18f** (Diog. L. 2, 52: Xenophon χωρίον ἐπρίατο); **4:34, 37** D; **5:3, 8; 28:7;** MPol 7:1; Papias (3:3ab). Of paradise Dg 12:2.

❷ **a limited geographical area, *(a city and its) environs*** (Polyaenus 7, 24), i.e. the region around a city that is closely related to it economically and politically: χωρίον Ῥωμαίων IRo ins (this may correspond to what is called τὰ ὑπὸ Ῥωμαίοις in Appian, Hann. 29 §123).—DELG s.v. χώρα. M-M.

χωρίς adv. (Hom.+)—❶ used as an adv. (Hom.+; ins; POxy 1088, 41 [I AD]; Jos., Bell. 1, 586, Ant. 17, 308) **pert. to occurring separately or being separate, *separately, apart, by itself*** **J 20:7;** ITr 11:2; Hs 8, 1, 6–17; 8, 4, 4–6.

❷ in our lit. freq. used as prep. w. gen. (coming only after the word it governs οὗ χωρίς **Hb 12:14;** ITr 9:2; s. Kuhring 48f; B-D-F §216, 2; 487; Rob. 425; 647f) **pert. to the absence or lack of someth., *without, apart from, independent(ly of)*** (Pind.+; the most typical Hellenistic word for 'without', s. FSolmsen, Beiträge zur griech. Wortforschung1909, 115; B-D-F §216, 2; Johannessohn, Präp. 337; 339f; MMargolis, PHaupt Festschr, 1926, 84ff).

ⓐ w. gen. of pers.—**α.** *separated from someone, far from someone, without someone* (Vi. Hom. 2 χωρὶς πάντων=apart fr. everyone) ἦτε χωρὶς Χριστοῦ **Eph 2:12;** cp. ITr 9:1f. χωρὶς ἐμοῦ *apart from me* **J 15:5.** χ. τοῦ ἐπισκόπου ITr 7:2; IPhld 7:2; ISm 8:1f; cp. IMg 4 (cp. Alex. Ep. 25, 44f). For ITr 3:1 s. β. οὔτε γυνὴ χωρὶς ἀνδρὸς οὔτε ἀνὴρ χωρὶς γυναικός *neither (is) woman (anything) apart fr. man, nor man fr. woman* **1 Cor 11:11.** χωρὶς ἡμῶν ἐβασιλεύσατε *without us you have already become kings* **4:8.** Cp. **Hb 11:40.**—**Hb 2:9** the v.l. χωρὶς θεοῦ (for χάριτι θεοῦ) *apart fr. God, forsaken by God* (schol. on Apollon, Rhod. 23 275 χωρὶς τοῦ Διός) is considered the original rdg. by BWeiss (Der Hb in zeitgeschichtl, Beleuchtung; TU 35, 3, 1910 p. 12, 1), EKühl (Theol. der Gegenwart 6, 1912, 252), AvHarnack (Zwei alte dogm. Korrekturen im Hb: SBBerl-Ak 1929, 3ff=Studien I '31, 236–45), and HMontefiore (The Epistle to the Hebrews '64, 59); this opinion is in contrast to nearly all Gk. mss. beginning w. P^{46} and to most other interpreters (s. JKögel, BFCT VIII 5/6, 1904, 131–41 for an older defense of this view; s. also later comm.).

β. *without* or *apart from = apart fr. someone's activity* or *assistance* (Appian, Bell. Civ. 1, 65 §298 χωρὶς ὑμῶν; Dionys. Perieg.[?], De Avibus: JCramer, Anecd. Paris. I 1839 p. 33, 13 the phoenix comes into being πατρός τε καὶ μητρὸς χωρίς; Jos., Ant. 15, 226) χωρὶς αὐτοῦ ἐγένετο οὐδὲ ἕν **J 1:3** (cp. 1QS 11:11). πῶς ἀκούσωσιν χωρὶς κηρύσσοντος; *how are they to hear without someone to preach* to them? **Ro 10:14.**—Cp. ITr 3:1, of var. eccl. officials; IMg 9:2 of Christ.

γ. *besides, in addition to, except (for) someone* (ApcMos 38; Jos., Ant. 7, 352; Just., A II, 1, 2) χωρὶς γυναικῶν καὶ παιδίων *besides women and children* **Mt 14:21; 15:38.** χωρὶς τούτου μηδέν *nothing except him* (i.e. Christ) IEph 11:2.

ⓑ w. gen. of thing—**α.** *outside (of) someth.* χ. τοῦ σώματος **2 Cor 12:3.**

β. *without making use of someth., without expressing* or *practicing someth.* (Jos., Ant. 20, 41 χ. τῆς περιτομῆς τὸ θεῖον σέβειν; Ath. 15, 2 χωρὶς τέχνης) χωρὶς παραβολῆς οὐδὲν ἐλάλει **Mt 13:34; Mk 4:34.** χωρὶς θεμελίου **Lk 6:49.** χωρὶς γογγυσμῶν **Phil 2:14.** Cp. **1 Ti 2:8; 5:21.** χωρὶς τῆς σῆς γνώμης *without having obtained your consent* (Polyb. 3, 21, 1; 2; 7) **Phlm 14** (γ below is also poss.). χωρὶς πάσης ἀντιλογίας **Hb 7:7** (ἀντιλογία 1). χ. οἰκτιρμῶν *without pity* **10:28** (POxy 509, 19 χ. ὑπερθέσεως=without delay); cp. **7:20ab; 9:7, 18, 22.** Christ was tempted χ. ἁμαρτίας *without committing any sin* **4:15.** πίστις χ. τῶν ἔργων *faith that does not express itself in deeds* **Js 2:20, 26b,** cp. vs. **18.** χωρὶς τῆς ἀσφαλείας *without (making use of) the security* MPol 13:3.

γ. *without possessing someth., apart fr. the presence of someth.* (Ath. 19, 3 χωρὶς τῆς ὕλης ἢ τοῦ τεχνίτου) χ. νόμου ἁμαρτία νεκρά **Ro 7:8;** on ἐγὼ ἔζων χωρὶς νόμου ποτέ vs. **9** s. [ζάω] 2a. τὸ σῶμα χ. πνεύματος **Js 2:26a.** Χ. τῆς σῆς γνώμης *without your consent* (cp. POxy 719, 27) **Phlm 14** (though bβ above is also prob.). Cp. **Hb 11:6; 12:8, 14.**

δ. *without relation to* or *connection with someth., independent(ly) of someth.* χ. ἁμαρτίας *without any relation to sin,* i.e. not w. the purpose of atoning for it **Hb 9:28.** χ. ἔργων νόμου *without regard to the observance of the law* **Ro 3:28;** cp. vs. **21; 4:6.**

ε. *apart from* (Diod. S. 13, 54, 7 χ. τούτων; Appian, Iber. 20 §76 and 64, Illyr. 15 §42; PTebt 67, 16; POxy 724, 6; Lev 9:17; Num 17:14; EpArist 165; Jos., Ant. 7, 350; Ath., R. 10 p. 58, 29 χ. δὲ τούτων) χωρὶς τῶν παρεκτός **2 Cor 11:28** (s. παρεκτός 1).—DELG s.v. χώρα. M-M. EDNT.

χωρισμός, οῦ, ὁ (χωρίζω; Aristot. et al.; Diod. S. 2, 60, 1; in pap freq. of divorce [s. Preis. s.v.]; LXX) ***division*** (Tat. 13, 2 [soul fr. spirit]; Ath., R. 16 p. 67, 31 χ. ψυχῆς ἀπὸ τοῦ σώματος [so Pla., Phd. 67d, of death]; Hierocles, 24, p. 472 ὁ ἀπὸ θεοῦ χ.) of the situation in the early church οὐκ ἦν χ. αὐτοῖς *there was no division among them* **Ac 4:32 v.l.**—DELG s.v. χώρα. Sv.

I. χῶρος, οῦ, ὁ (Hom.+; ins, pap; 4 Macc 18:23 πατέρων χῶρος; SibOr 1, 51; Philo, Aet. M. 33; Jos., Bell. 5, 402; Just., D. 5, 3; Mel., P. 50, 360 εἰς τοὺς χώρους τῶν ἐπιθυμιῶν) **an undefined area or location,** ***place*** μέγιστος *a very large place* ApcPt 5:15. εὐσεβῶν (Lycurg., Or. §96 p. 160; Socrat., Ep. 27, 1; Ps.-Pla., Ax. 13 p. 371c; Ps.-Plut., Mor. 120b; Just., D. 5, 3; Eranos 13, 1913 p. 87: ins 9, 8.—Also χ. ἀσεβῶν: Ps.-Pla., Ax. 13, 371e; Lucian, Necyom. 12, Ver. Hist. 2, 23; Philo, Cher. 2, Fuga 131) 1 Cl 50:3.—DELG.

II. χῶρος, οῦ, ὁ (the northwest wind; cp. the equation of Ἰάπυξ [the NW, or NNW, wind] w. Chorus [=corus, caurus] in IGR I, 177=IG XIV, 1308, s. Hemer, Acts 140f [prob. mariners' patois]) ***northwest*** **Ac 27:12.**

ψάλλω fut. ψαλῶ (Aeschyl.+; ins, LXX; TestAbr A 20 p. 103, 26f [Stone p. 54]; TestJob 14:2, 4; Jos., Ant. 11, 67; 12, 349; Just.; Mel., P. 80, 588; Did.) in our lit., in accordance w. OT usage, **to sing songs of praise, with or without instrumental accompaniment,** ***sing, sing praise*** w. dat. of the one for whom the praise is intended τῷ ὀνόματί σου ψαλῶ **Ro 15:9** (Ps 17:50). ψαλλῶ σοι B 6:16 (Ps 107:4). τῷ κυρίῳ **Eph 5:19:** in this pass. a second dat. is added τῇ καρδίᾳ ὑμῶν *in* or *with your hearts*; here ψ. is found with ᾄδω (as Ps 26:6; 32:3; 56:8), and the question arises whether a contrast betw. the two words is intended. The original mng. of ψ. was 'pluck', 'play' (a stringed instrument); this persisted at least to the time of Lucian (cp. Par. 17). In the LXX ψ. freq. means 'sing', whether to the accompaniment of an instrument (Ps 32:2, 97:5 al.) or not, as is usually the case (Ps 7:18; 9:12; 107:4 al.). This focus on singing continued until ψ. in Mod. Gk. means 'sing' exclusively; cp. ψάλτης=singer, chanter, w. no ref. to instrumental accompaniment. Although the NT does not voice opposition to instrumental music, in view of Christian resistance to mystery cults, as well as Pharisaic aversion to musical instruments in worship (s. EWerner, art. 'Music', IDB 3, 466–69), it is likely that some such sense as *make melody* is best understood in this Eph pass. Those who favor 'play' (e.g. L-S-J-M; ASouter, Pocket Lexicon, 1920; JMoffatt, transl. 1913) may be relying too much on the earliest mng. of ψάλλω. ψ. τῷ πνεύματι and in contrast to that ψ. τῷ νοΐ *sing praise in spiritual ecstasy* and *in full possession of one's mental faculties* **1 Cor 14:15.** Abs. *sing praise* **Js 5:13.** WSmith, Musical Aspects of the NT, '62; HSeidel, TRE XXIII 441–46.—DELG. M-M. EDNT. TW. Sv.

ψαλμός, οῦ, ὁ (ψάλλω; Pind., Aeschyl. et al; ins; PGM 3, 290; LXX; TestSol D 1:11; TestJob 14:1; ApcEsdr 7:15 p. 33, 2 Tdf.; Jos., Ant. 6, 214; 7, 80; 9, 35; Just.; loanw. in rabb.) in our lit. only ***song of praise, psalm*** in accordance w. OT usage.

ⓐ of OT Psalms ἐν τῷ νόμῳ Μωϋσέως καὶ τ. προφήταις καὶ ψαλμοῖς **Lk 24:44.** ἐν βίβλῳ ψαλμῶν **20:42; Ac 1:20.** ἐν τῷ ψαλμῷ τῷ δευτέρῳ **13:33** (v.l. ἐν τῷ πρώτῳ ψ.). ψαλμῶν τε Δαουὶδ καὶ ᾠδῶν AcPl Ha 7, 11.

ⓑ of Christian songs of praise **1 Cor 14:26.** (ἐν) ψαλμοῖς (καὶ) ὕμνοις (καὶ) ᾠδαῖς πνευματικαῖς **Eph 5:19;** sim. **Col 3:16.**—For lit. see s.v. ὕμνος.—DELG s.v. ψάλλω. M-M. TW.

ψευδάδελφος, ου, ὁ one who pretends to be a fellow-believer, but whose claim is belied by conduct toward fellow-believers, ***false brother, false member.*** Paul applies the term to certain opponents **2 Cor 11:26; Gal 2:4.** Of such as masquerade in allegiance to the Lord and mislead unsophisticated members w. wrong beliefs Pol 6:3.—TW.

ψευδαπόστολος, ου, ὁ one who claims to be an apostle without the divine commission necessary for the work, ***false/spurious/bogus apostle*** (cp. Polyaenus 5, 33, 6 ψευδάγγελοι=false messengers) **2 Cor 11:13.** Just., D. 35, 3 has ψευδοαπόστολοι for ψευδοπροφῆται in citation of Mt 24:11, 24 (Mk 13:22).—S. lit. s.v. ψευδόμαρτυς. DELG s.v. ψεύδομαι B. TW.

ψευδής, ές (ψεύδομαι; Hom.+) **pert. to being contrary to the truth,** ***false, lying***—ⓐ of persons (Thu. 4, 27, 4 al.; Jos., Ant. 18, 299) **Ac 6:13** (cp. Pr 19:5, 9 μάρτυς ψ.; Mel., P. 79, 573); **Rv 2:2.** Also of the human spirit Hm 3:2. Subst. *liar* (Pla., Hipp. Min. 365d; 367a; Sir 34:4; AscIs 3:10) **Rv 21:8.**—JPilch, Lying and Deceit in the Letters to the Seven Chruches, Perspectives fr. Cultural Anthropology: BTB 22, '92, 126–35.

ⓑ of things λόγος (Phalaris, Ep. 130; Maximus Tyr. 27, 8d; IG I^2, 700 λόγοι ἄδικοι ψευδεῖς; En 98:15; Philo, Mut. Nom. 248; Jos., Ant. 13, 292; Just., D. 8, 3; Ath. 30, 3) D 2:5. ὅρκος ψευδής *a false oath* B 2:8 (Zech 8:17). ἃ ἐλάλησας ψευδῆ Hm 3, 5.—DELG s.v. ψεύδομαι B. M-M. TW.

ψευδοδιδασκαλία, ας, ἡ ***false/spurious teaching*** Pol 7:2. S. next entry.

ψευδοδιδάσκαλος, ου, ὁ ***false/bogus teacher, quack teacher,*** of someone in the Christian community who pretends to be a qualified instructor, but whose teaching is contrary to the generally accepted tradition (Just., D. 82, 1; s. the lit. s.v. ψευδόμαρτυς) **2 Pt 2:1.**—DELG s.v. ψεύδομαι. TW.

ψευδολόγος, ον (Aristoph. et al.; Aesop, Fab. 103 P.=136 H.//105 H-H.//112 Ch.; Just., A 2, 2, 11; Tat.—Jos., Ant. 8, 410; 17, 105 ψευδολογία; so also CPR I, 19, 15 [330 AD]) ***speaking falsely, lying;*** subst. (Polyb. 31, 22, 9; Strabo 2, 1, 9) *liars* **1 Ti 4:2** (they are esp. dangerous because they play a role [ἐν ὑποκρίσει] that puts their victims off the scent; like actors who play parts so well that their words have the ring of truth).—DELG s.v. ψεύδομαι. M-M. Spicq.

ψεύδομαι in our lit. only mid. (Hom.+); fut. ψεύσομαι; 1 aor. ἐψευσάμην; pf. 2 sg. ἔψευσμαι (Sus 55 LXX; Sus 59 Theod.). Pass.: aor. inf. ψευσθῆναι (Mel., P. 26, 183), ptc. ψευσθείς (Just., D. 134, 3); pf. ptc. ἐψευσμένος (Tat. 16, 1).

❶ **to tell a falsehood,** ***lie*** abs. (X., Mem. 2, 6, 36; Aristot., EN 2, 7; 4, 7 et al.; Pr 14:5; TestAbr B 13 p. 118, 3 [Stone p. 84]; TestJos 13:9; ApcSed 7:8; Philo, Leg. All. 3, 124; Just., D. 117, 4; Tat. 32, 1) **Mt 5:11; Hb 6:18** (θεόν is subj. acc.); **1J**

1:6; **Rv 3:9;** 1 Cl 27:2abc (Artem. 2, 69 p. 161, 15 ἀλλότριον θεῶν τὸ ψεύδεσθαι); Hm 3:2. As a formula of affirmation οὐ ψεύδομαι (Jos., Vi. 296; cp. Plut., Mor. 1059a) **Ro 9:1; 2 Cor 11:31; Gal 1:20; 1 Ti 2:7.** εἴς τινα *tell lies against someone,* i.e. to that person's detriment (Sus 55 LXX) **Col 3:9.** κατά τινος *against someth.* κατὰ τῆς ἀληθείας *against the truth* **Js 3:14** (cp. Bel 11 Theod.). The pers. who is harmed by the lie can be added in the dat. (Ps 17:45; 88:36; Josh 24:27; Jer 5:12; JosAs 24:6) οὐκ ἀνθρώποις ἀλλὰ τῷ θεῷ **Ac 5:4.** πάντα *in every particular* **14:19 v.l.** (Tat. 22, 2). τὶ *in any point* Papias (2:15).

❷ **to attempt to deceive by lying,** ***tell lies to, impose*** upon τινά *someone* (Eur., X. et al.; Plut., Alcib. 206 [26, 8], Marcell. 314 [27, 7]; Jos., Ant. 3, 273; 13, 25; PSI 232, 10) **Ac 5:3** (Appian, Liby. 27 §113 τίς σε δαίμων ἔβλαψε . . . ψεύσασθαι θεοὺς οὓς ὤμοσας;='what evil spirit beguiled you . . . to lie to the gods by whom you swore?'; Tat. 19, 3 ἑαυτόν); 1 Cl 15:4 (Ps 77:36, but w. αὐτῷ).—DELG. M-M. TW.

ψευδομαρτυρέω impf. ἐψευδομαρτύρουν; fut. ψευδομαρτυρήσω; 1 aor. ἐψευδομαρτύρησα (ψεῦδος + μάρτυς, s. next entry; X., Mem. 4, 4, 11; Pla., Rep. 9, 575b, Leg. 11, 939c; Aristot., Rhet. 1, 14, 6, 1365a, 12, Rhet. ad Alex. 16, 1432a, 6; Jos., Ant. 3, 92; 4, 219; Ar. 15, 4; Just.) ***bear false witness, give false testimony*** **Mt 19:18; Mk 10:19; Lk 18:20; Ro 13:9 v.l.;** GJs 15:4 (all fr. the decalogue Ex 20:16; Dt 5:20; cp. Philo, Dec. 138; 172); D 2:3. κατά τινος *against someone* (so in the two decalogue passages in the OT; also Vi. Aesopi G 99 P.; schol. on Soph. Aj. 238 p. 24 Papag. [1888]) **Mk 14:56f.**—DELG s.v. ψεύδομαι and μάρτυς. M-M. EDNT. TW.

ψευδομαρτυρία, ας, ἡ (s. prec. entry; Pla.; Attic orators; Plut.; Philo, Rer. Div. Her. 173) ***false witness*** **Mt 15:19; 26:59;** Pol 2:2; 4:3; Hm 8:5; D 5:1.—B. 1461. DELG s.v. ψεύδομαι and μάρτυς. M-M. TW.

ψευδόμαρτυς, υρος, ὁ (accented ψευδομάρτυς L-S-J-M, Mod. Gk. et al.) ***one who gives false testimony, a false witness*** (Pla., Gorg. 472b; Aristot., Rhet. ad Alex. 16, 1432a, 6; Heraclides 15; IG V/2, 357, 4; Sus 60f; Philo, Dec. 138; Tat. 25, 3; Mel., P. 93, 700) **Mt 26:60;** ApcPt 14:29. ψευδομάρτυρες τοῦ θεοῦ (objective gen.) *pers. who give false testimony about God* **1 Cor 15:15.**—On ψευδόμαρτυς and the other compounds of ψευδ(ο)- s. RReitzenstein, NGG 1916, 463ff, Her 52, 1917, 446ff; KHoll, ibid. 301ff; ADebrunner, Griech. Wortbildungslehre 1917, 37; PCorssen, Sokrates 6, 1918, 106–14; B-D-F §119, 5; Mlt-H. 280; 285; further lit. in the Indogerm. Jahrb. 5, 1918, 123f. CBarrett in BRigaux Festschr. '70, 377–96; ATrites, The NT Concept of Witness '77, 75f.—DELG s.v. ψεύδομαι and μάρτυς. TW. Sv.

ψευδοπροφήτης, ου, ὁ one who falsely claims to be a prophet of God or who prophesies falsely, ***false/bogus prophet*** (Zech 13:2; Jer 6:13 al.; TestJud; AscIs; Philo, Spec. Leg. 4, 51; Jos., Bell. 6, 285, Ant. 8, 236; 318; 10, 111; Just.. D. 7, 3; 69, 1; 82, 1; Zosimus: Hermet. IV p. 111, 2; Iren. 5, 28, 2 [Harv. II 401, 25f]; Orig., C. Cels. 3, 2, 15; Hippol., Ref. 9, 15, 3) **Mt 7:15; 24:11, 24; Mk 13:22; Lk 6:26; Ac 13:6; 2 Pt 2:1; 1J 4:1; Rv 16:13; 19:20; 20:10;** ApcPt 1:1; Hm 11:1f, 4, 7 (Leutzsch, Hermas 461 n. 237 [lit.]); D 11:5f, 8–10; 16:3.—Harnack, Die Lehre der Zwölf Apostel 1884, 119ff, Mission I[4] 1923, 332ff; 362ff; EFascher, Προφήτης 1927; JReiling, The Use of ΨΕΥΔΟΠΡΟΦΗΤΗΣ in the Septuagint, Philo and Josephus: NovT 13, 71, 147–56.—DELG s.v. ψεύδομαι and φημί. TW. Sv.

ψεῦδος, ους, τό (Hom.+; SIG 1268, 27; Mitt-Wilck. I/2, 110 A, 18 [110 BC]; LXX, En, Test12Patr; ParJer 4:5; EpArist; Philo; Jos., Vi. 336; Mel., HE 4, 26, 9; Ath., R. 1 p. 48, 4 al.) ***a lie, falsehood.*** Gener. (opp. ἀλήθεια, as Pla., Hippias Minor 370e; Plut., Mor. 16a; EpArist 206; Philo; TestDan 1:3; 2:1 al.) ἀποθέμενοι τὸ ψεῦδος λαλεῖτε ἀλήθειαν **Eph 4:25;** cp. D 5:2; B 20:2 (here the v.l. pl. ψεύδη). In a catalogue of vices Hm 8:5; cp. s 9, 15, 3 (personified). The sing. used collectively τὸ ψεῦδος *lies, lying* (opp. ἀληθές) m 3:3; but 3:5 pl. ψεύδη.—Of God (ἀληθινὸς καὶ) οὐδὲν παρ' αὐτῷ ψεῦδος 3:1. In contrast, lying is characteristic of the devil **J 8:44** (cp. Porphyr., Abst. 2, 42 of evil divinities: τὸ ψεῦδος τούτοις οἰκεῖον=lying is their habit). For this transcendently conceived contrast betw. ψεῦδος and ἀλήθεια cp. **2 Th 2:11 (12); 1J 2:21, 27.** It is said of polytheists that μετήλλαξαν τὴν ἀλήθειαν τοῦ θεοῦ ἐν τῷ ψεύδει (s. μεταλλάσσω and cp. for the use of ψεῦδος as abstract for concrete Jer 3:10; 13:25) **Ro 1:25.** But of the 144,000 sealed ones of Rv ἐν τῷ στόματι αὐτῶν οὐχ εὑρέθη ψεῦδος **14:5.** The Lawless One appears w. τέρατα ψεύδους *deceptive wonders* **2 Th 2:9.** ποιεῖν ψεῦδος *practice (the things that go with) falsehood* **Rv 21:27; 22:15.**—WLuther, 'Wahrheit u. Lüge' im ältesten Griechentum '35.—B. 1170. DELG. M-M. TW. Sv.

ψευδόχριστος, ου, ὁ one who, in lying fashion, gives himself out to be the Anointed One, ***a bogus Messiah*** (cp. Ψευδοφίλιππος Diod. S. 32, 15, 7; 32; fgm. 9a and b; Strabo 13, 4, 2; Ψευδονέρων Lucian, Adv. Indoct. 20; Ψευδομάριος Appian, Bell. Civ. 3, 2 §2) pl. **Mt 24:24; Mk 13:22** (both w. ψευδοπροφῆται). On the subj. s. Bousset, Rel.[3] 223f.—DELG s.v. ψεύδομαι and cp. χρίω.

ψευδώνυμος, ον (ψευδής, ὄνομα [on the lengthening of the vowel s. DELG s.v. ὄνομα]; Aeschyl. et al.; Plut., Mor. 479e; Aelian, NA 9, 18; Philo, Mos. 2, 171 of Greco-Roman deities; Kaibel 42, 4) **pert. to using a membership name falsely,** ***falsely bearing a name, falsely called*** of the γνῶσις of heterodox Christians **1 Ti 6:20.**—M-M. TW.

ψεῦσμα, ατος, τό (ψεύδομαι, cp. next entry; Pla. et al.; Plut., Lucian, Aq., Sym., Theod.; Jos., C. Ap. 2, 115 al., Ant. 16, 349) 'lie, falsehood' in our lit. in the sense **engagement in lying,** ***lying, untruthfulness, undependability*** (opp. ἡ ἀλήθεια, q.v. 1; Philo, Aet. M. 56) **Ro 3:7.**—Hm 3:5; 8:3; D 3:5.—DELG s.v. ψεύδομαι A. TW.

ψεύστης, ου, ὁ (ψεύδομαι, cp. prec. entry; Hom. et al.; LXX; Tat. 4, 1) ***liar*** **J 8:55; Ro 3:4** (Ps 115:2); **1J 2:4, 22; 4:20;** D 3:5. W. other sinners (SibOr 2, 257) **1 Ti 1:10; Tit 1:9 v.l.;** Hs 6, 5, 5. ψεύστην ποιεῖν τινα *make someone a liar* **1J 1:10; 5:10.** The devil as a liar **J 8:44** (s. ψεῦδος). The Cretans **Tit 1:12** (Ath. 30, 2=Call., Hymn. in Jovem 8, 8; cp. JHaft, ClJ 79, '84, 289–304, on Homeric treatment; s. ἀργός 2 and Κρής; a pejorative cliché, as Posidonius about Phoenicians Strabo 3, 5, 5; Livy 22, 6, 12 punica fides, a satirical comment about Carthaginian trustworthiness).—DELG s.v. ψεύδομαι. M-M. EDNT. TW.

ψηλαφάω (cp. ψάλλω and ἀφάω [=ἁφάω] 'feel, handle') fut. ψηλαφήσω LXX; 1 aor. ἐψηλάφησα; fut. pass. 3 sg. ψηλαφηθήσεται Na 3:1 (Hom. et al.; Polyb. 8, 18, 4; PLond IV, 1396, 4 [709/14 AD]; LXX; Jos., Ant. 13, 262 v.l.; Mel., P. 22, 151 al.) 'feel (about for), grope after'

❶ **to touch by feeling and handling,** ***touch, handle,*** τινά or τὶ *someone* or *someth.* (Gen 27:12; Judg 16:26 al.) ψηλαφήσατέ με **Lk 24:39;** 1Sm 3:2. Cp. **1J 1:1.** λίθον Hs 9, 6, 3. In οὐ προσεληλύθατε ψηλαφωμένῳ **Hb 12:18,** even if the v.l. ὄρει is dropped, the reference is to Mt. Sinai, where God gave a self-revelation according to the OT with manifestations that *could be felt* or *touched, were tangible* (ESelwyn, On ψηλ. in Hb 12:18: JTS 12, 1911, 133f).—In imagery (Polyb. 8, 18, 4) πάντα τόπον ἐψηλαφήσαμεν *we have touched upon every subject* 1 Cl 62:2.

❷ **to look for someth. in uncertain fashion,** ***to feel around for, grope for,*** in imagery of humans in their search for God (cp. Philo, Mut. Nom. 126 ψ. τὰ θεῖα) εἰ ἄρα γε ψηλαφήσειαν αὐτὸν καὶ εὕροιεν *if perhaps* (=in the hope that) *they might grope for him and find him* **Ac 17:27** (Norden, Agn. Th. 14–18; BGärtner, The Areopagus Speech '55, 161).—B. 1061. Cp. θιγγάνω: Schmidt, Syn. I 225–43. DELG. LfgrE s.v. ἀφάω. M-M. EDNT.

ψηφίζω (ψῆφος) 1 aor. ἐψήφισα; 1 fut. pass. 3 sg. ψηφισθήσεται (v.l. 3 Km 3:8 and 8:5) (Aeschyl., Hdt. et al.; ins, pap, LXX, Philo; Jos., Ant. 17, 43 al.; SibOr 13, 47.—B-D-F §310, 1)

❶ **to add up digits and calculate a total,** ***count (up), calculate, reckon*** (lit. 'w. pebbles') (PCairZen 328, 111 [248 BC]; Palaeph. 53 [AWestermann, Mythographi 1843 p. 311, 24] τὰς περιόδους τῶν ἡμερῶν; Plut.) τὴν δαπάνην **Lk 14:28.**

❷ **to probe a number for its meaning,** ***interpret, figure out*** τὸν ἀριθμὸν τοῦ θηρίου **Rv 13:18** See χξς' and ἀριθμός 1.—DELG s.v. ψῆφος. M-M. TW.

ψῆφος, ου, ἡ (Pind., Hdt.+; ins, pap, LXX, TestSol, Just.; Mel., P. 92, 689; Ath. 30, 2; loanw. in Aramaic ins [ZNW 20, 1921, 253]) 'pebble'

❶ **a pebble used in voting: a black one for conviction, a white one for acquittal,** ***voting-pebble,*** used in cases of injuries and in other circumstances (Plut., Mor. 186e, Alcib. 202 [22, 2] al.) καταφέρειν ψῆφον *cast a vote against* **Ac 26:10** (καταφέρω 2.—ψῆφον φέρειν: Philo, Deus Imm. 75; Jos., Ant, 2, 163; 10, 60 [both κατά τινος]). ἡ ψῆφος τ. μαρτυρίου *condemnation to martyrdom* **Phlm subscr.**

❷ **a pebble serving as an amulet,** ***amulet.*** This may well be the sense in which the ψῆφος λευκή (Paroem. Gr.: Diogenianus 6, 9; cp. Cyranides p. 12, 9 of beryl) w. the new name on it (s. Artem. 5, 26 τοῦ Σαράπιδος τὸ ὄνομα ἐγγεγραμμένον λεπίδι χαλχῇ περὶ τὸν τράχηλον δεδέσθαι ὥσπερ σκυτίδα; PGM 5, 449 of a wonder-working stone: ὄπισθε τ. λίθου τὸ ὄνομα) is to be taken **Rv 2:17ab** (WHeitmüller, 'Im Namen Jesu' 1903, 234; WRamsay, The White Stone and the 'Gladiatorial' Tessera: ET 16, 1905, 558–61); perh. as entrance pass, WReader, Stadt Gottes '71, 214.—DELG. M-M. TW.

ψιθυρισμός, οῦ, ὁ (ψιθυρίζω 'to whisper'; Menand., Mis. 140 S.; Plut.; Eccl 10:11, but in a neutral sense='hiss, whisper'; likew. Ps.-Lucian, Am. 15; Philopon., In Aristot., De Anima 263, 3; 403, 12; Etym. Mag. p. 818, 55) in our lit. only in a bad sense **derogatory information about someone that is offered in a tone of confidentiality,** ***(secret) gossip, tale-bearing*** (Philodem., De Ira p. 55 W.; GrBar 8, 5 [pl.]; 13, 4 [sing.], in the two last passages not far fr. καταλαλιά; Cat. Cod. Astr. VIII/1 p. 170, 8 [pl., near διαβολαί]), always w. καταλαλιά, in the sing. 1 Cl 30:3, pl. **2 Cor 12:20;** 1 Cl 35:5.—DELG s.v. ψιθυρίζω.

ψιθυριστής, οῦ, ὁ (ψιθυρίζω, s. prec. entry; in Athens an epithet of Hermes: [Ps.-]Demosth. 59, 39; Anecd. Gr. p. 317, 11 and Suda.—Cat. Cod. Astr. X 119, 17; 191, 6; XII 190, 24; Thom. Mag. 403, 7 ψίθυρος οὐ ψιθυριστής) ***rumormonger, tale-bearer*** **Ro 1:29.**—DELG s.v. ψιθυρίζω. M-M.

ψιλός, ή, όν (Hom. et al.; ins, pap, Philo; adverb ψιλῶς Just., D. 112, 1) ***bare,*** of land without vegetation (Aesop, Fab. 74 P.=128 H.=76 H-H.). A mountain is ψιλόν, βοτάνας μὴ ἔχον Hs 9, 1, 5; cp. 9, 19, 2 (Jos., Bell. 4, 452 ψιλὸν κ. ἄκαρπον ὄρος).—DELG.

ψίξ, χός, ἡ (ψίω, of infants 'feed on morsels or milk'; Plut., Aretaeus p. 142, 23; 167, 17; Herodian Gr. I 396, 22 al.; Rhet. Gr. I 646, 16) ***bit, crumb,*** esp. of bread **Mt 15:27** D; **Lk 16:21** D.—DELG s.v. ψίω.

ψιχίον, ου, τό (dim. of ψίξ [q.v.].—Achmes 46, 22) ***a very little bit, crumb*** pl. (Soranus: CMG IV p. 86, 10) **Mt 15:27; Mk 7:28: Lk 16:21 v.l.**—DELG s.v. ψίω. M-M.

ψοφοδεής, ές (ψόφος, δέος; Pla. et al.; Philo, Sacr. Abel. 32 p. 215 ln. 15) the lit. sense 'pert. to being easily frightened' transfers to ***timid, anxious*** the neut. as subst. τὸ ψοφοδεές *timidity, anxiety* (Plut., Comp. Nic. cum Crass. 566 [2, 4], Nic. 524 [2, 6]) Dg 4:1.—DELG s.v. ψόφος.

ψόφος, ου, ὁ (cp. prec. entry; Eur., Thu.+; ins fr. Palestine: JPeters and HThiersch, Painted Tombs in . . . Marissa 1905, 33, 4 [II BC]; PStras 100, 14 [II BC]; Mi 1:13; EpArist 91; Philo, Sacr. Abel. 69; Jos., Bell. 4, 108, Ant. 3, 81) ***noise, sound*** Hv 4, 3, 7 v.l. (s. νέφος).—Schmidt, Syn. III 312–17. DELG.

ψυγήσομαι s. ψύχω.

ψυχαγωγέω (ψυχή, ἄγω [ἀγωγή] 'conduct a soul'; in var. senses Pla., X. et al.; PHamb 91, 22 [167 BC]; PRyl 128, 12 [c. 30 AD]; Philo) in a bad sense (cp. the satirical comment about Socrates: Aristoph., Aves 1555) **to lead someone's soul astray,** ***attract, beguile*** τινά *someone* (Isoc. 2, 49; Lycurgus 33; Epict. 3, 21, 23) ὁ πλοῦτος ὁ ψυχαγωγῶν αὐτούς Hv 3, 6, 6.—DELG s.v. ψυχή.

ψυχή, ῆς, ἡ (Hom.+; 'life, soul') It is oft. impossible to draw hard and fast lines in the use of this multivalent word. Gen. it is used in ref. to dematerialized existence or being, but, apart fr. other data, the fact that ψ. is also a dog's name suggests that the primary component is not metaphysical, s. SLonsdale, Greece and Rome 26, '79, 146–59. Without ψ. a being, whether human or animal, consists merely of flesh and bones and without functioning capability. Speculations and views respecting the fortunes of ψ. and its relation to the body find varied expression in our lit.

❶ **life on earth in its animating aspect making bodily function possible—ⓐ** ***(breath of) life, life-principle, soul,*** of animals (Galen, Protr. 13 p. 42, 27 John; Gen 9:4) **Rv 8:9.** As a rule of human beings (Gen 35:18; 3 Km 17:21; ApcEsdr 5:13 λαμβάνει τὴν ψυχὴν the fetus in its sixth month) **Ac 20:10.** When it leaves the body death occurs **Lk 12:20** (cp. Jos., C. Ap. 1, 164; on the theme cp. Pind., I. 1, 67f). The soul is delivered up to death (the pass. in ref. to divine initiative), i.e. into a condition in which it no longer makes contact with the physical structure it inhabited 1 Cl 16:13 (Is 53:12), whereupon it leaves the realm of earth and lives on in Hades (Lucian, Dial. Mort. 17, 2; Jos., Ant. 6, 332) **Ac 2:27** (Ps 15:10), **31 v.l.** or some other place outside the earth **Rv 6:9; 20:4;** ApcPt 10:25 (GrBar 10:5 τὸ πεδίον . . . οὗπερ ἔρχονται αἱ ψυχαὶ τῶν δικαίων; ApcEsdr 7:3 ἀπέρχεται εἰς τὸν οὐρανόν; Himerius, Or. 8 [23]: his consecrated son [παῖς ἱερός 7] Rufinus, when he dies, leaves his σῶμα to the death-daemon, while his ψυχή goes into οὐρανός, to live w. the gods 23).—B 5:13 (s. Ps 21:21).

ⓑ the condition of being alive, ***earthly life, life*** itself (Diod. S. 1, 25, 6 δοῦναι τὴν ψυχήν=give life back [to the dead Horus]; 3,

26, 2; 14, 65, 2; 16, 78, 5; Jos., Ant. 18, 358 σωτηρία τῆς ψυχῆς; 14, 67; s. Reader, Polemo 354 [reff.]) ζητεῖν τὴν ψυχήν τινος **Mt 2:20** (cp. Ex 4:19); **Ro 11:3** (3 Km 19:10, 14). δοῦναι τὴν ψυχὴν ἑαυτοῦ (cp. Eur., Phoen. 998) **Mt 20:28; Mk 10:45;** John says for this τιθέναι τὴν ψυχὴν **J 10:11, 15, 17, (18); 13:37f; 15:13; 1J 3:16ab;** παραδιδόναι **Ac 15:26;** Hs 9, 28, 2. παραβολεύεσθαι τῇ ψυχῇ **Phil 2:30** (s. παραβολεύομαι). To love one's own life (JosAs 13:1 ἐγὼ ἀγαπῶ αὐτὸν ὑπὲρ τὴν ψυχήν μου) **Rv 12:11;** cp. B 1:4; 4:6; 19:5; D 2:7. Life as prolonged by nourishment **Mt 6:25ab; Lk 12:22f.** Cp. **14:26; Ac 20:24; 27:10, 22; 28:19 v.l.; Ro 16:4.** S. also 2e below.

ⓒ by metonymy, ***that which possesses life/soul*** (cp. 3 below) ψυχὴ ζῶσα (s. Gen 1:24) *a living creature* **Rv 16:3 v.l.** for ζωῆς. Cp. ἐγένετο Ἀδὰμ εἰς ψυχὴν ζῶσαν **1 Cor 15:45** (Gen 2:7. S. πνεῦμα 5f). ψυχὴ ζωῆς **Rv 16:3.**

❷ **seat and center of the inner human life in its many and varied aspects, *soul***—ⓐ of the desire for luxurious living (cp. the OT expressions Ps 106:9 [=ParJer 9:20, but in sense of d below]; Pr 25:25; Is 29:8; 32:6; Bar 2:18b; PsSol 4:17. But also X., Cyr. 8, 7, 4; ins in Ramsay, CB I/2, 477 no. 343, 5 the soul as the seat of enjoyment of the good things in life) of the rich man ἐρῶ τῇ ψυχῇ μου: ψυχή, ἀναπαύου, φάγε, πίε, εὐφραίνου **Lk 12:19** (cp. PsSol 5:12; Aelian, VH 1, 32 εὐφραίνειν τὴν ψυχήν; X., Cyr. 6, 2, 28 ἡ ψυχὴ ἀναπαύσεται.—The address to the ψυχή as PsSol 3, 1; Cyranides p. 41, 27). Cp. **Rv 18:14.**

ⓑ of evil desires (PsSol 4:13; Tat. 23, 2) 2 Cl 16:2; 17:7.

ⓒ of feelings and emotions (Anacr., fgm. 4 Diehl^2 [15 Page]; Diod. S. 8, 32, 3; JosAs 6:1; SibOr 3, 558; Just., D. 2, 4; Mel., P. 18, 124 al.) περίλυπός ἐστιν ἡ ψυχή μου (cp. Ps 41:6, 12; 42:5) **Mt 26:38; Mk 14:34.** ἡ ψυχή μου τετάρακται **J 12:27;** cp. **Ac 2:43** (s. 3 below).—**Lk 1:46; 2:35; J 10:24; Ac 14:2, 22; 15:24; Ro 2:9; 1 Th 2:8** (τὰς ἑαυτῶν ψυχάς *our hearts full of love*); **Hb 12:3; 2 Pt 2:8;** 1 Cl 16:12 (Is 53:11); 23:3 (scriptural quot. of unknown origin); B 3:1, 5b (s. on these two passages Is 58:3, 5, 10b); 19:3; Hm 4, 2, 2; 8:10; s 1:8; 7:4; D 3:9ab. ἐμεγαλύνθη ἡ ψυχή μου GJs 5:2; 19:2 (s. μεγαλύνω 1). αὔξειν τὴν ψυχὴν τοῦ Παύλου AcPl Ha 6, 10. It is also said of God in the anthropomorphic manner of expr. used by the OT ὁ ἀγαπητός μου εἰς ὃν εὐδόκησεν ἡ ψυχή μου **Mt 12:18** (cp. Is 42:1); cp. **Hb 10:38** (Hab 2:4).—One is to love God ἐν ὅλῃ τῇ ψυχῇ **Mt 22:37; Lk 10:27.** Also ἐξ ὅλης τῆς ψυχῆς (Dt 6:5; 10:12; 11:13) **Mk 12:30, 33 v.l.** (for ἰσχύος); **Lk 10:27 v.l.** (Epict. 2, 23, 42; 3, 22, 18; 4, 1, 131; M. Ant. 12, 29; Sextus 379.—X., Mem. 3, 11, 10 ὅλῃ τῇ ψυχῇ). ἐκ ψυχῆς *from the heart, gladly* (Jos., Ant. 17, 177.—The usual form is ἐκ τῆς ψυχῆς: X., An. 7, 7, 43, Apol. 18 al.; Theocr. 8, 35) **Eph 6:6; Col 3:23;** ἐκ ψυχῆς σου B 3:5a (Is 58:10a); 19:6. μιᾷ ψυχῇ *with one mind* (Dio Chrys. 19 [36], 30) **Phil 1:27;** cp. **Ac 4:32** (on the combination w. καρδία s. that word 1bη and EpArist 17); 2 Cl 12:3 (s. 1 Ch 12:39b; Diog. L. 5, 20 ἐρωτηθεὶς τί ἐστι φίλος, ἔφη: μία ψυχὴ δύο σώμασιν ἐνοικοῦσα).

ⓓ as the seat and center of life that transcends the earthly (Pla., Phd. 28, 80ab; Paus. 4, 32, 4 ἀθάνατός ἐστιν ἀνθρώπου ψ.; Just., A I, 44, 9 περὶ ἀθανασίας ψυχῆς; Ath. 27, 2 ἀθάνατος οὖσα. Opp. Tat. 13, 1, who argues the state of the ψ. before the final judgment and states that it is not immortal per se but experiences the fate of the body οὐκ ἔστιν ἀθάνατος). As such it can receive divine salvation σῴζου σὺ καὶ ἡ ψυχή σου *be saved, you and your soul* Agr 5 (Unknown Sayings 61–64). σῴζειν τὰς ψυχάς **Js 1:21.** ψυχὴν ἐκ θανάτου **5:20;** cp. B 19:10; Hs 6, 1, 1 (on death of the ψ. s. Achilles Tat. 7, 5, 3 τέθνηκας θάνατον διπλοῦν, ψυχῆς κ. σώματος). σωτηρία ψυχῶν **1 Pt 1:9.** περιποίησις ψυχῆς **Hb 10:39.** It can also be lost 2 Cl 15:1; B 20:1; Hs 9, 26, 3. Humans cannot injure it, but God can hand it over to destruction **Mt 10:28ab;** AcPl Ha 1, 4. ζημιωθῆναι τὴν ψυχήν (ζημιόω 1) **Mt 16:26a; Mk 8:36** (FGrant, Introd. to NT Thought, '50, 162); 2 Cl 6:2. There is nothing more precious than ψυχή in this sense **Mt 16:26b; Mk 8:37.** It stands in contrast to σῶμα, in so far as that is σάρξ (cp. Ar. 15, 7 οὐ κατὰ σάρκα . . . ἀλλὰ κατὰ ψυχήν; Tat. 15, 1 οὔτε . . . χωρὶς σώματος; Ath. 1, 4 τὰ σώματα καὶ τὰς ψυχάς; SIG 383, 42 [I BC]) Dg 6:1–9. The believer's soul knows God 2 Cl 17:1. One Christian expresses the hope that all is well w. another's soul **3J 2** (s. εὐοδόω). For the soul of the Christian is subject to temptations **1 Pt 2:11** and **2 Pt 2:14;** longs for rest **Mt 11:29** (ParJer 5:32 ὁ θεὸς . . . ἡ ἀνάπαυσις τῶν ψυχῶν); and must be purified **1 Pt 1:22** (cp. Jer 6:16). The soul must be entrusted to God **1 Pt 4:19;** cp. 1 Cl 27:1. Christ is its ποιμὴν καὶ ἐπίσκοπος (s. ἐπίσκοπος 1) **1 Pt 2:25;** its ἀρχιερεὺς καὶ προστάτης 1 Cl 61:3; its σωτήρ MPol 19:2. Apostles and congregational leaders are concerned about the souls of the believers **2 Cor 12:15; Hb 13:17.** The Christian hope is called the *anchor of the soul* **6:19.** Paul calls God as a witness against his soul; if he is lying, he will forfeit his salvation **2 Cor 1:23.**—Also *life* of this same eternal kind κτήσεσθε τὰς ψυχὰς ὑμῶν *you will gain (real) life for yourselves* **Lk 21:19.**

ⓔ Since the soul is the center of both the earthly (1a) and the transcendent (2d) life, pers. can find themselves facing the question concerning the wish to ensure it for themselves: ὃς ἐὰν θέλῃ τὴν ψυχὴν αὐτοῦ σῶσαι, ἀπολέσει αὐτήν· ὃς δ' ἂν ἀπολέσει τὴν ψυχὴν αὐτοῦ ἕνεκεν ἐμοῦ, σώσει αὐτήν **Mk 8:35.** Cp. **Mt 10:39; 16:25; Lk 9:24; 17:33; J 12:25.** The contrast betw. τὴν ψυχὴν εὑρεῖν and ἀπολέσαι is found in **Mt 10:39ab** (s. HGrimme, BZ 23, '35, 263f); **16:25b;** σῶσαι and ἀπολέσαι vs. **25a; Mk 8:35ab; Lk 9:24ab;** περιποιήσασθαι, ζῳογονῆσαι and ἀπολέσαι **17:33;** φιλεῖν and ἀπολλύναι **J 12:25a;** μισεῖν and φυλάσσειν vs. **25b.**

ⓕ On the combination of ψυχή and πνεῦμα in **1 Th 5:23; Hb 4:12** (Just., D. 6, 2; Tat. 15, 1 χρὴ . . . ζευγνύναι . . . τὴν ψυχὴν τῷ πνεύματι τῷ ἁγίῳ) s. πνεῦμα 3a, end.—A-JFestugière, L'idéal religieux des Grecs et l'Évangile '32, 212–17.—A unique combination is . . . σωμάτων, καὶ ψυχὰς ἀνθρώπων, *slaves and human lives* **Rv 18:13** (cp. Ezk 27:13; on the syntax s. Mussies 98).

ⓖ In var. Semitic languages the reflexive relationship is paraphrased with נֶפֶשׁ (Gr.-Rom. parallels in W-S. §22, 18b note 33); the corresp. use of ψυχή may be detected in certain passages in our lit., esp. in quots. fr. the OT and in places where OT modes of expr. have had considerable influence (B-D-F §283, 4; W-S. §22, 18b; Mlt. 87; 105 n. 2; Rob. 689; KHuber, Untersuchungen über d. Sprachcharakter des griech. Lev., diss. Zürich 1916, 67), e.g. **Mt 11:29; 26:38; Mk 10:45; 14:34; Lk 12:19; 14:26; J 10:24; 12:27; 2 Cor 1:23; 3J 2; Rv 18:14;** 1 Cl 16:11 (Is 53:10); B 3:1, 3 (Is 58:3, 5); 4:2; 17:1. Cp. also **2 Cor 12:15; Hb 13:17;** GJs 2:2; 13:2; 15:3 (on these last s. ταπεινόω 2b).

❸ **an entity w. personhood, *person*** ext. of 2 by metonymy (cp. 1c): πᾶσα ψυχή *everyone* (Epict. 1, 28, 4; Lev 7:27; 23:29 al.) **Ac 2:43; 3:23** (Lev 23:29); **Ro 2:9; 13:1; Jd 15;** 1 Cl 64; Hs 9, 18, 5.—Pl. *persons,* cp. our expression 'number of souls' (Pla. et al.; PTebt 56, 11 [II BC] σῶσαι ψυχὰς πολλάς; LXX) ψυχαὶ ὡσεὶ τρισχίλιαι **Ac 2:41;** cp. **7:14** (Ex 1:5); **27:37; 1 Pt 3:20.**—This may also be the place for ἔξεστιν ψυχὴν σῶσαι ἢ ἀποκτεῖναι; *is it permissible to rescue a person* (*a human life* is also poss.) *or must we let the person die?* **Mk 3:4; Lk 6:9.** Cp. **9:55 [56] v.l.**—EHatch, Essays in Bibl. Gk. 1889, 112–24;

ERohde, Psyche[9–10] 1925; JBöhme, D. Seele u. das Ich im homer. Epos 1929; EBurton, Spirit, Soul and Flesh 1918; FRüsche, Blut, Leben u. Seele 1930; MLichtenstein, D. Wort nefeš in d. Bibel 1920; WStaples, The 'Soul' in the OT: JSL 44, 1928, 145–76; FBarth, La notion Paulinienne de ψυχή: RTP 44, 1911, 316–36; ChGuignebert, RHPR 9, 1929, 428–50; NSnaith, Life after Death: Int 1, '47, 309–25; essays by OCullmann, HWolfson, WJaeger, HCadbury in Immortality and Resurrection, ed. KStendahl, '65, 9–53; GDautzenberg, Sein Leben Bewahren '66 (gospels); R Jewett, Paul's Anthropological Terms, '71, 334–57; also lit. cited GMachemer, HSCP 95, '93, 121, 13.—TJahn, Zum Wortfeld 'Seele-Geist' in der Sprache Homers (Zetemata 83) '81.—B. 1087. New Docs 4, 38f (trichotomy). DELG. M-M. EDNT. TW. Sv.

ψυχικός, ή, όν (ψυχή; in var. mngs. Diocles, Aristot. et al.; Ptolem., Apotel. 3, 14, 1 [opp. σωματικος]; SIG 656, 20 [166 BC]; 4 Macc 1:32; Philo; Jos., Bell. 1, 430; Just., D. 30, 1; Tat.; Ath. 23, 2 [Thales]) 'of the soul/life', in our lit. **pert. to the life of the natural world and whatever belongs to it, in contrast to the realm of experience whose central characteristic is πνεῦμα, *natural, unspiritual, worldly*** (cp. PGM 4, 524f and 510=Rtzst., Mysterienrel.[3] 175f lines 28 and 20, where the ἀνθρωπίνη ψυχικὴ δύναμις is contrasted w. the ἱερὸν πνεῦμα. On this s. πνευματικός 2aγ; also β and PGM 4, 725; Herm. Wr. 9, 9; Iambl., Myst. 6, 6 P.: the ἀνθρωπίνη ψυχή in contrast to the gods and to γνῶσις; Orig., C. Cels. 4, 57, 14).

ⓐ adj. ψυχικὸς ἄνθρωπος (Hippol., Ref. 5, 27, 3) *an unspiritual pers.*, one who merely functions bodily, without being touched by the Spirit of God **1 Cor 2:14.** σῶμα ψυχ. *a physical body* **15:44ab.** The wisdom that does not come fr. above is called ἐπίγειος, ψυχική (*unspiritual*), δαιμονιώδης **Js 3:15.**

ⓑ subst.—**α.** τὸ ψυχικόν *the physical* in contrast to τὸ πνευματικόν (cp. Iren. 1, 5, 1 [Harv. I 42, 1]) **1 Cor 15:46.**

β. Jd 19 calls the teachers of error ψυχικοί, πνεῦμα μὴ ἔχοντες *worldly* (lit. 'psychic') *people, who do not have the Spirit,* thereby taking over the terminology of gnostic (on 'psychic' and 'pneumatic' people in gnostic thinking s. AHilgenfeld, Die Ketzergeschichte des Urchristentums 1884, index) opponents, but applying to gnostics the epithets that they used of orthodox Christians.—DELG s.v. ψυχή. M-M. TW. Sv.

ψῦχος, ους, τό (cp. ψύχω 'make cool or cold'; Hom. et al.; SIG 969, 92; PTebt 278, 47; LXX; En 100:13; TestSol 18:18 LP. On the accent s. B-D-F §13; Mlt-H. 57) ***cold* J 18:18; Ac 28:2; 2 Cor 11:27** (w. γυμνότης).—Frisk s.v. ψυχή, but s. DELG s.v. ψυχή and ψυχρός, ψῦχος. M-M.

ψυχρός, ά, όν (cp. ψῦχος and ψύχω; Hom.+; ins, pap, LXX; En 14:13; TestSol 18:18 H [adv.]; Philo, Joseph.; Tat. 35, 1) 'cold'.

❶ **pert. to being physically cold, *cold,*** lit.—ⓐ adj. ὕδωρ (Hom. et al.; Sb 6941, 4; Pr 25:25; Philo; Jos., Ant. 7, 130) **Mt 10:42** D; D 7:2. Of courageous confessors' estimate of the intensity of fire set for them τὸ πῦρ ἦν αὐτοῖς ψυχρόν *the fire felt cold to them* MPol 2:3 (cp. 4 Macc 11:26).

ⓑ subst. τὸ ψυχρόν (i.e. ὕδωρ) *cold water* (Hdt. 2, 37 al.; SIG 1170, 30; SEG XLII 1506 [reff.]; s. New Docs 3, 144f; ψυχρὸν πίνειν Epict. 3, 12, 17; 3, 15, 3, Ench. 29, 2) **Mt 10:42.**

❷ fig. (trag., Hdt. et al.; Jos., Bell. 1, 357; 6, 16, C. Ap. 2, 255) **pert. to being without enthusiasm, *cool, cold*** (Neugebauer-Hoesen no. 95, 112 p. 32=PLond I, 98, 71 p. 130 [I/II AD]; Epict. 3, 15, 7; Lucian, Tim. 2 ψ. τὴν ὀργήν) **Rv 3:15ab, 16** (w. ζεστός and χλιαρός).—B. 1078f. DELG. M-M. TW.

ψύχω (cp. ψῦχος and ψυχρός; Hom.+; ins; PPetr II, 14 [3], 8 [III BC]; LXX) fut. 3 pl. ψύξουσιν Jer 8:2; 1 aor. ἔψυξα LXX; 2 fut. pass. ψυγήσομαι (Galen XI 388 K.—Lob., Phryn. p. 318; Moeris p. 421 P.) 'make cool/cold' (Philo, Leg. All. 1, 5) pass. 'become/grow cold' (Hdt. et al.; Philo, Cher. 88; Jos., Ant. 7, 343), of fire and flame ***go out, be extinguished*** (Pla., Critias 120b) fig. (cp. Jos., Bell. 5, 472 of hope) ψυγήσεται ἡ ἀγάπη **Mt 24:12.**—DELG. M-M.

ψωμίζω (ψωμός 'morsel') fut. ψωμιῶ LXX and 3 pl. ψωμίσουσιν Da 4:32 LXX; 1 aor. ἐψώμισα (Aristoph., Aristot. et al.; LXX; Mel. P. 79, 578)

❶ w. acc. of pers. (Antig. Car. 99; Num 11:4 τίς ἡμᾶς ψωμιεῖ κρέα; TestLevi 8:5 ἐψώμισέν με ἄρτον; Mel., P. 79, 578 τὸ στόμα τὸ ψωμίσαν σε ζωήν) **to cause someone to eat, *to feed* Ro 12:20** (Pr 25:21 v.l.); 1 Cl 55:2.

❷ w. acc. of thing (s. Num and TestLevi under 1 above) **to give away, prob. in installments, *give away, dole out*** πάντα τὰ ὑπάρχοντα **1 Cor 13:3** is either *give away all one's property bit* (cp. ψωμίον) *by bit, dole it out* (so w. double acc. Dt 32:13; Ps 79:6) or *divide in small pieces = fritter away* in the process of such charitable activity (but the text makes no mention of feeding 'the poor' as KJV; s. Goodsp., Probs. 163f).—DELG s.v. *ψήω. Frisk s.v. ψῆν. M-M.

ψωμίον, ου, τό (ψωμός 'morsel'; since PTebt 33, 14 [112 BC]; also PFay 119, 34; POxy 1071, 5 al. pap; M. Ant. 7, 3, 1; Diog. L. 6, 37) dim. of ψωμός (Hom. et al.; Epict. 1, 26, 16; 1, 27, 18; LXX) ***(small) piece/bit of bread* J 13:26ab,** 27, 30 (cp. Mod. Gk. γωμί 'bread').—PKretschmer, Brot u. Wein im Neugriech.: Glotta 15, 1926, 60ff.—B. 357. DELG s.v. *ψήω. Frisk s.v. ψῆν. M-M.

ψωριάω (ψώρα 'itch, mange') pf. ptc. ἐψωριακώς (Hippocr., Theophr. et al.) ***have a rough surface,*** of stones Hv 3, 2, 8; 3, 6, 2; s 9, 6, 4; 9, 8, 2; 9, 26, 3.—DELG s.v. *ψήω C 2. Frisk s.v. ψῆν.

ψώχω (Hesych.; Etym. Mag. p. 818, 44; as a mid. Nicander, Theriaca 629) **to rub someth. under pressure so as to make it smaller** (cp. ψώμιον), ***rub*** so as to thresh or separate the seed from its husk (Diosc., Mat. Med. 5, 159 pass.) ἤσθιον τοὺς στάχυας ψώχοντες ταῖς χερσίν **Lk 6:1.**—DELG s.v. *ψήω D. Frisk s.v. ψῆν. M-M.

Ω, ὦ, τό last (24th) letter of the Gk. alphabet, *o(mega)* in our lit. as symbol (in conjunction w. ἄλφα) of an entity that is in control of everything from beginning to end, *last, end, omega:* ἐγώ (εἰμι) τὸ ἄλφα καὶ τὸ ὦ **Rv 1:8; 21:6; 22:13;** cp. **1:11 v.l.** ἐγώ εἰμι τὸ Α καὶ τὸ Ω I am the A and the O̅ (='the A and the Z', i.e. 'the First and the Last').—S. the entry A; also EbNestle, Philol. 70, 1911, 155–57 and lit. cited EDNT s.v. Ἄλφα. The name ω μέγα does not appear until the Byzantine period, s. Theognostos, Canones 13, in Anecdota Graeca, ed. JCramer, II (1835–37).—DELG.

ὦ interjection (Hom.+)—**❶ marker of personal address *O, O . . . !*** (oft. before the voc., in accord w. the Koine and w. Semitic usage, but never used when calling upon God. See B-D-F §146; Rob. 463f; Mlt-Turner 33).

ⓐ mostly expressing emotion (at the beginning of a clause; Cornutus 14 p. 14, 9 ὦ πονηρέ, κτλ.; TestAbr B 10 p. 115, 3 [Stone p. 78] ὦ ταλαίπωρε ψυχή; ParJer 5:28 ὦ υἱέ μου; ApcEsdr 5:6; ApcSed 11:1ff; ApcMos 10; Just., D. 32, 1 ὦ ἄνθρωπε; Mel., P. 81, 596 ὦ Ἰσραὴλ παράνομε) ὦ γύναι **Mt 15:28;** within a statement Hv 1, 1, 7 (as TestAbr B 6 p. 110, 22 [Stone p. 68]; TestJob 24:9). Cp. **Lk 24:25; Ro 2:1, 3; 9:20; Gal 3:1; 1 Ti 6:20; Js 2:20.** ὦ ἀνόητοι 1 Cl 23:4. The nom. takes the place of the voc. (Maximus Tyr. 1, 10g; Philostrat., Ep. 37) **Mt 17:17; Mk 9:19; Lk 9:41; Ac 13:10.**

ⓑ without emotion (in accord w. Attic usage, also EpArist 1; 120; Ar. 2, 1; Just., A II, 1, 1; Mel., P. 32, 216; Tat. 14, 1) ὦ Θεόφιλε **Ac 1:1.** Cp. **18:14; 27:21.**

❷ an exclamatory utterance, *O, Oh, How . . . !* etc. (in this use it can also be written ὤ). In modern versions the term is frequently rendered in some functional equivalent, e.g. 'I stand amazed at' (so Phillips: **Ro 11:33**), or w. the punctuation mark (!) serving as a semantic component.

ⓐ w. the nom. (Aeschyl. et al.; Chariton 6, 6, 4; Is 6:5; TestAbr A 7 p. 84, 26 [Stone, p. 16] ὦ θαῦμα) ὦ βάθος πλούτου **Ro 11:33.**

ⓑ w. the gen. (Chariton 6, 2, 8; 10; 11; Galen: CMG V/9, 1 p. 387, 2 ὦ τῆς ἀσυνεσίας; Achilles Tat. 5, 11, 2; TestJob 21:3 ὦ τῆς ἀλαζονείας; Philo, Fuga 149 ὦ θαυμαστῆς δοκιμασίας; Jos., Bell. 4, 166, C. Ap. 1, 301 ὦ τῆς εὐχερείας; Ar. 9, 5 ὦ τῆς ἀνοίας; Just., A I, 9, 5 ὦ τῆς ἐμβροντησίας; Mel., P. 97, 738 ὢ φόνου καινοῦ, ὢ ἀδικίας καινῆς) ὢ τῆς ὑπερβαλλούσης φιλανθρωπίας τοῦ θεοῦ *O, the surpassing kindness of God to humanity!* Dg 9:2; cp. vs. 5abc. ὢ μεγάλης ἀγάπης, ὢ τελειότητος ἀνυπερβλήτου *What strong affection, what unexcelled maturity!* 1 Cl 53:5.—Johannessohn, Kasus 9–13. DELG. M-M.

ὤ s. ὦ 2.

Ὠβήδ for Ἰωβήδ (q.v.).

Ὤγ (עוֹג; Ὤγης Joseph.) indecl. ***Og,*** after Num 21:33 Amorite king of Bashan AcPl Ox 1602 (in AcPl Ha 8, 12 erroneously corrected to Γωγ by a copyist, s. Schubart's note, p. 57).—FBruce, BIOSCS 12, '79, 17–21.

ὧδε (Hom.+) adv. of ὅδε, in our lit. adv. of place (Hippocr. [Kühner-G. I p. 444, 3] et al.; Hdt. 1, 49; 5, 48; Pla., Protagoras 328d; Herodas 7, 113; 126; ins, pap, LXX; pseudepigr.; Ar. 17, 1; Ath. 13, 1).

❶ a position or point that is relatively near, *here*—ⓐ in the sense *to this place, hither* (as early as Od. 1, 182; also PSI 599, 3 [III BC]; POxy 295, 3; LXX; En 14:24 al.; TestAbr A 16 p. 96, 16 [Stone p. 40]; 98, 8 [St. p. 44]; TestAbr B 7 p. 111, 4 [St. p. 70], B 11 p. 115, 17 [St. p. 78]; ParJer 7:4; ApcEsdr 5:10 p. 30, 3 Tdf.; ApcSed 9:4.—B-D-F §103) ἦλθες ὧδε **Mt 8:29.** Cp. **14:18; 17:17; 22:12; Mk 11:3; Lk 9:41; 14:21; 19:27; J 6:25; 20:27; Ac 9:21; Rv 4:1; 11:12;** Hs 5, 1, 1; GJs 4:3. ἕως ὧδε *to this place, this far* (TestAbr A 18 p. 100, 16 [Stone p. 48]; Ar. 17, 1; cp. ἕως 3b) **Lk 23:5;** 1 Cl 20:7. ὧδε κἀκεῖ *here and there, hither and thither* Hm 5, 2, 7; s 9, 3, 1; cp. 6, 1, 6; 6, 2, 7.—Temporal sense: ὡς τοῦ σωτῆρος μέχρι ὧδε εἰρηκότος *inasmuch as the Savior has spoken up to this point* GMary 463, 4.

ⓑ in the sense *in this place* (Herodas 2, 98; 3, 96; SIG 985, 54; PHib 46, 15 [III BC]; PGrenf II, 36, 17 [95 BC]; BGU 1097, 11; 14; PFay 123, 10; LXX; TestAbr A 13 p. 92, 7 [Stone p. 32]; ParJer 3:16; Apion in Jos., C. Ap. 2, 10; B-D-F §103; Rob. 299; BKeil, Her 43, 1908 p. 553, 1) **Mt 12:6, 41f; 14:17; 16:28; 17:4ab; 20:6; 24:2; Mk 9:1, 5; 13:2; 16:6; Lk 9:33; 11:31f; 15:17; J 6:9; Ac 9:14;** Hs 9, 11, 1b. ὧδε=*here* on earth **Hb 13:14.** τὰ μὲν ὧδε . . . τὰ δὲ ἐκεῖ AcPl Ha 2, 23. καθίζειν ὧδε (cp. καθίζω 3) **Mk 14:32;** Hv 3, 1, 8. τὰ ὧδε **Col 4:9.** ὧδε . . . ἐκεῖ *here . . . there* (Plut., Mor. 34a; Celsus 2, 43) **Mk 13:21; Lk 17:21, 23; Js 2:3.** ὧδε . . . ὧδε **Mt 24:23** (Callim., Epigr. 282 Pf.; Herodas 4, 42 ὧδε καὶ ὧδε). Made more definite by a prepositional phrase ὧδε πρὸς ἡμᾶς **Mk 6:3.** Cp. **8:4; Lk 4:23.**

❷ a ref. to a present event, object, or cicumstance, *in this case, at this point, on this occasion, under these circumstances* (Herodas 5, 85; Crates, Ep. 6; Quint. Smyrn. 13, 5; PFay 117, 12 [108 AD]; PMeyer 22, 6) ὧδε λοιπόν (cp. Epict. 2, 12, 24) *in this case moreover* **1 Cor 4:2.** ὧδε ἡ σοφία ἐστίν (lit. *there is wisdom* [i.e. *someth. deep*] *here*) *this calls for discernment* **Rv 13:18;** cp. **17:9.** ὧδέ ἐστιν ἡ ὑπομονή *this calls for endurance* or *here is (an opportunity for) endurance* (s. ὑπομονή 1) **13:10; 14:12.** ὧδε . . . ἐκεῖ *in one case . . . in the other* **Hb 7:8.** λάχετέ μοι ὧδε *now, cast lots for me* GJs 10:2.—DELG s.v. 2 ὥς. M-M.

ᾠδή, ῆς, ἡ (ᾄδω; Hom. Hymns, Soph., Pla., X. et al.; of a rooster Aesop Fab. 110 H.; ins, LXX; ParJer 7:33) ***song,*** in our lit. only of sacred song, a song of praise to God (εἰς [τὸν] θεόν: Philo, Somn. 2, 34, Virt. 95; Jos., Ant. 7, 305) or to Christ **Rv 5:9; 14:3ab** (on ᾠ. καινή cp. Ps 143:9; on worship in heaven gener. EPeterson, Liturgisches Leben '34, 297–306.—Lucian, Zeux. 2 ἡ νέα ᾠ.). ᾄδουσιν τὴν ᾠδὴν Μωϋσέως καὶ τὴν ᾠδὴν τοῦ ἀρνίου **15:3** (cp. Ex 15:1 and on Ex 15 as a song in the liturgy of Judaism s. Elbogen[2] 23; 86; 113; 117; 136.—ᾄδ. ᾠδήν as Achilles Tat. 3, 15, 3 ὁ ἱερεὺς ᾖδεν ᾠδήν); ᾠδὴν ἁγίαν *holy song* GJs 6:3. ἐν ψαλμοῖς καὶ ὕμνοις καὶ ᾠδαῖς πνευματικαῖς **Eph 5:19;** cp. **Col 3:16** (on the hymn as a means of private edification cp. Hierocles 19 p. 460, where the examination of one's conscience at the close of day [Hierocles 27 p. 484 the golden verses of the Pythagoreans are to be read aloud morning and evening] is designated as ἐπικοίτιον ᾆσμα θεῷ=an evening hymn in the presence of God); AcPl Ha 7, 11 (s. ψαλμός).—Lit. s.v. ὕμνος. DELG s.v. ἀείδω. M-M. TW.

-ώδης suffix to adjectives indicating that something is 'like, full of'; cp. -ειδής (Schwyzer I, 418).—DOpdeHipt, Adjektive auf -ώδης in Corpus Hippocraticum '72; s. also Buck, Reverse Index 708–15 for list of words terminating in -ώδης.

ὠδίν, ῖνος, ἡ (as a nom. in Suda) **1 Th 5:3** (Is 37:3) for the usual form ὠδίς, ῖνος (s. next entry; Hom.+; SEG VIII, 802; Sb 4312, 4f; Coll. Alex. p. 198 no. 36, 11 [Isis], =IAndrosIsis p. 145; LXX; PsSol 3:9; TestJob 18:4; Philo; Jos., Ant. 2, 218.—B-D-F §46, 4; Mlt-H. 135) **experience of pains associated with childbirth**

ⓐ lit., ***birth-pain(s)*** **1 Th 5:3** (sing. as Pind., O. 6, 43 [73]; Plut., Thes. 9 [20, 5]; PsSol 3:9; TestJob 18:4).

ⓑ in imagery, ***great pain (as in giving birth)*** (Aeschyl. et al.; Himerius, Or. 10, 3; 18, 3; Ex 15:14; Heraclit. Sto. 39 p. 58, 9 ἐπειδὰν ἡ μεμυκυῖα γῆ τὰς κυοφορουμένας ἔνδον ὠδῖνας ἐκφήνῃ='when [after the winter's cold] the groaning earth gives birth in pain to what has been formed within her'; Philo)

α. ὠδῖνες τοῦ θανάτου **Ac 2:24** (on the sources of the text s. MWilcox, The Semitisms of Ac, '65, 46–48; s. also s.v. θάνατος 1bβ and λύω 4; RBratcher, BT 10, '59, 18–20: 'cords of death'). ὠδῖνες τοῦ ᾄδου Pol 1:2 (ᾄδης 1).

β. of the 'Messianic woes', the terrors and torments traditionally viewed as prelude to the coming of the Messianic Age (Billerb. I 950) are associated with the appearance of the Human One (Son of Man) at the end of history, as the *beginning of the (endtime) woes* ἀρχὴ ὠδίνων **Mt 24:8; Mk 13:8;** FBusch, Z. Verständnis der syn. Eschatol., Mk 13 neu unters. '38.—DELG s.v. ὠδίς. M-M. TW.

ὠδίνω fut. 3 pl. ὠδινήσουσιν Hab 3:10; aor. 3 sg. ὠδίνησεν LXX (s. prec. entry; Hom.+; Kaibel 321, 12; 1103, 2; UPZ 77 col. 2, 27 [160 BC]; LXX; Philo, Mos. 1, 280 al.; SibOr 5, 514; Just., D. 111, 2) **to experience pains associated with giving birth, *have birth-pains***

ⓐ lit. *to have birth-pains, be in labor* abs. **Rv 12:2** (cp. Is 66:7; Mi 4:10); Ro 8:22 v.l. As a voc. ἡ οὐκ ὠδίνουσα *you who have no birth-pains* **Gal 4:27;** 2 Cl 2:1, 2 (all three Is 54:1).

ⓑ in imagery, *be in labor = suffer greatly* (PGM 2, 92; Philo, Just.) τέκνα μου, οὓς πάλιν ὠδίνω **Gal 4:19** (the acc. as in the lit. sense 'bring forth in pain' trag.; Is 51:2).—DELG s.v. ὠδίς. M-M. TW.

ὠθέω impf. ὤθουν; fut. 2 sg. ὤσεις Is 30:22; aor. 2 sg. ὦσας Job 14:20, 3 pl. (?) ἔωσαν Jer 41:11 (v.l. ἔσωσαν), subj. 3 sg. ὤσῃ LXX. Pass.: aor. ptc. ὠσθείς Ps 117:13; pf. ptc. ὠσμένος Ps 61:4 (Hom. et al.; LXX; Philo, Aet. M. 136; Jos., Bell. 1, 250) ***push, shove*** τινά *someone* GPt 3:6.—B. 716. DELG.

ὠκεανός, οῦ, ὁ (Hom.+; ins; POslo 3, 14; TestAbr B 8 p. 112, 19 [Stone p. 72] ἐπὶ τὸν Ὠ. ποταμόν; Philo, Leg. ad Gai. 10; Jos., Bell. 2, 155, Ant. 1, 130; SibOr; Ath. 18, 3; loanw. in rabb.) ***ocean*** 1 Cl 20:8.—DELG.

ὠμόλινον, ου, τό (ὠμός, λίνον; since Cratinus Com. [V BC] 9 'towel'; Hippocr., Morb. 2, 47 vol. VII p. 70 L. 'raw flax'; PTebt 703, 100 [III BC]; Sir 40:4 'sackcloth') **a piece of cloth made of coarse linen for workers, *apron, towel*** (a barber's towel: Plut., Mor. 509a) Hs 8, 4, 1ab.—DELG s.v. ὠμός and λίνον.

ὦμος, ου, ὁ (Hom.+; ins, pap, LXX; TestSol; TestJob 7:1; TestZeb 9:4; JosAs 22 A cod. A [p. 73, 2 Bat.]; ParJer 5:7; AscIs 3:17; EpArist 151; Philo; Jos., Ant. 3, 170; 215; Just., D. 35, 2; Tat. 25, 1) ***shoulder*** **Mt 23:4** (in imagery); **Lk 15:5;** Hv 5:1; s 6, 2, 5; 9, 2, 4; 9, 9, 5; 9, 13, 8.—B. 235. DELG. M-M.

ὠνέομαι mid. dep. (Hes., Hdt.+; ins, pap, Test12Patr, Philo, Joseph.; Tat. 23, 1f) 1 aor. ὠνησάμην (Eupolis [V BC. But s. Kühner-Bl. II 577]; Plut., Nic. 529 [10, 2]; Paus. 3, 4, 4; Lucian, Herm. 81; ins [Schweizer 177; OGI 669, 31]; pap [UPZ 12, 16, 158 BC; POxy 1188, 19]; Jos., Ant. 2, 39. Beside it ἐωνησάμην and the Att. ἐπριάμην.—Crönert 283) ***buy*** τὶ παρά τινος *someth. from someone* w. gen. of price (Aristoxenus [IV BC], Fgm. 43 Wehrli ἑκατὸν μνῶν; Jos., Ant. 7, 332) **Ac 7:16** (cp. Jos., Ant. 1, 237).—B. 817. DELG. M-M.

ᾠόν, οῦ, τό (Hdt. et al.; ins, pap, LXX. On the spelling, as also in Joseph. and Ath., s. B-D-F §26; Mlt-H. 84) ***egg*** **Lk 11:12.**—B. 256. DELG. M-M.

ὥρα, ας, ἡ (Hom. [ὥρη]+; ins, pap, LXX; PsSol 18:10; TestSol, TestAbr, TestJob, Test12Patr, JosAs, ParJer, GrBar; ApcEsdr 3:4 p. 27, 9 Tdf.; ApcSed, ApcMos, EpArist, Philo, Joseph.; Ar. 15:10; Just.; Tat. 20, 2).

❶ **an undefined period of time in a day, *time of day*** ὀψὲ ἤδη οὔσης τῆς ὥρας *since it was already late in the day* or *since the hour was (already) late* **Mk 11:11 v.l.;** cp. MPol 7:1b (s. ὀψέ 1 and 2; Demosth. 21, 84; Polyb. 3, 83, 7 ὀψὲ τῆς ὥρας). ὀψίας οὔσης τῆς ὥρας **Mk 11:11** (ὄψιος 1). ὥρα πολλή *late hour* (Polyb. 5, 8, 3; Dionys. Hal. 2, 54; TestAbr A 14 p. 94, 24 [Stone p. 36]; Jos., Ant. 8, 118) **6:35ab.** ἡ ὥρα ἤδη παρῆλθεν **Mt 14:15** (παρέρχομαι 2).—**Mt 24:42 v.l., 44; Lk 12:39, 40; Rv 3:3;** D 16:1. W. ἡμέρα *day* and *time of day, hour* (ApcEsdr 3:4 p. 27, 9 Tdf.) **Mt 24:36, 50; 25:13; Mk 13:32; Lk 12:46.**

❷ **a period of time as division of a day, *hour*—**ⓐ beside year, month, and day **Rv 9:15;** the twelfth part of a day (=period of daylight) οὐχὶ δώδεκα ὧραί εἰσιν τῆς ἡμέρας; **J 11:9** (TestAbr B 7 p. 111, 24 [Stone p. 70]). μίαν ὥραν ἐποίησαν **Mt 20:12** (s. ποιέω 6); cp. **Lk 22:59; Ac 5:7; 19:34** (ἐπὶ ὥρας δύο CBurchard, ZNW 61, '70, 167f; TestBenj 3:7, Judah 3, 4); MPol 7:3. συνεψήφισα τὰς ὥρας *I counted the hours* Hv 3, 1, 4. One ὥρα in this world corresponds to a ὥρα thirty days in length in the place of punishment Hs 6, 4, 4. μίαν ὥραν *(not even) one hour* **Mt 26:40; Mk 14:37.** Such passages help us to understand how ὥρα can acquire the sense

ⓑ *a short period of time* μιᾷ ὥρᾳ (cp. TestJob 7:12; ApcMos 25 [both ἐν]) *in a single hour*=in an extraordinarily short time **Rv 18:10, 17, 19.** μίαν ὥραν *for a very short time* **17:12.** Likew. πρὸς ὥραν *for a while, for a moment* **J 5:35; 2 Cor 7:8; Gal 2:5** (s. on this pass. KLake, Gal 2:3–5: Exp. 7th ser., 1, 1906, 236–45; CWatkins, Der Kampf des Pls um Galatien 1913; BBacon, JBL 42, 1923, 69–80); **Phlm 15;** MPol 11:2. πρὸς καιρὸν ὥρας **1 Th 2:17.**

ⓒ as a temporal indicator, reckoned from the beginning of the day (6 hours or 6 a.m., our time) or the night (18 hours or 6 p.m.) (Plut. et al.; Appian, Mithrid. 19 §72 ἑβδόμης ὥρας=at the 7th hour or 1 p.m.; SIG 671A, 9 [162/160 BC] ὥρας δευτέρας; 736, 109 [92 BC] ἀπὸ τετάρτας ὥρας ἕως ἑβδόμας; Jos., Vi. 279 ἕκτη ὥ.; Mitt-Wilck. I/2, 1 II, 21 [246 BC] περὶ ὀγδόην ὥραν; PTebt 15, 2 [II BC]; Sb 5252, 20 [I AD] ἀφ' ὥρας ὀγδόης; EpArist 303 μέχρι μὲν ὥρας ἐνάτης) ἕως ὥρας δευτέρας *until the second hour* (=8 a.m.) Hs 9, 11, 7. ὥρα τρίτη *nine o'clock* (a.m.) **Mk 15:25** (Goodsp., Probs. 68f); **Ac 2:15** (τῆς ἡμέρας); περὶ τρίτην ὥραν *about nine o'clock* (Appian, Bell. Civ. 2, 45 §182 περὶ τρίτην ὥραν ἡμέρας) **Mt 20:3;** ἀπὸ τρίτης ὥρας τῆς νύκτος *by nine o'clock at night* (*=21 hours*, or simply *tonight*) **Ac 23:23** (TestAbr A 5 p. 82, 11 [Stone p. 12] περὶ ὥραν τρίτην τῆς νυκτός; cp. ibid. B 6 p. 109, 27 [St. p. 66]; Jos., Bell. 6, 68; 79 ἀπὸ ἐνάτης ὥ. τῆς νυκτὸς εἰς ἑβδόμην τῆς ἡμέρας). ἀπὸ ὥρας ε' (=πέμπτης) ἕως δεκάτης *from eleven o'clock in the* *morning until four in the afternoon* (=*16 hours*) **Ac 19:9 v.l.** περὶ ὥραν πέμπτην (PTebt 15, 2 [114 BC]; POxy 1114, 24 περὶ ὥ. τρίτην) *at eleven o'clock* (a.m.) Hv 3, 1, 2. ὥρα ἕκτη *twelve o'clock noon* **Mt 20:5; 27:45a; Mk 15:33a; Lk 23:44a; J 4:6** (ὥρα ὡς ἕκτη *about noon;* TestJos 8:1 ὥρα ὡσεὶ ἕκτη; ParJer 1:11 ἕκτην ὥραν τῆς νυκτός); **19:14** (ὥρα ὡς ἕκτη); **Ac 10:9.** ἐχθὲς ὥραν ἑβδόμην *yesterday at one o'clock in the afternoon* (=*13 hours*) **J 4:52b** (on the use of the acc. to express a point of time s. Hdb. ad loc.; Soph., Lex. I 44; B-D-F §161, 3; Rob. 470). ὥρᾳ ὀγδόῃ *at two o'clock in the afternoon* (=*14 hours*) MPol 21. ὥρα ἐνάτη *three in the afternoon* (=*15 hours*) **Mt 20:5; 27:45f; Mk 15:33b, 34; Lk 23:44b; Ac 3:1** (ἐπὶ τὴν ὥραν τῆς προσευχῆς τὴν ἐνάτην); **10:3** (ὡσεὶ περὶ ὥ. ἐνάτην τῆς ἡμέρας); ὥρας θ' AcPl Ha 11, 3; περὶ ὥραν ἐνάτην GJs 2:4; GPt 6:22 (TestAbr B 12 p. 117, 2 [Stone p. 82] κατὰ τὴν ἐνάτην ὥραν). ὥρα ὡς δεκάτη *about four in the afternoon* (=*16 hours*) **J 1:39.** ἑνδεκάτη ὥρα *five o'clock in the afternoon* (=*17 hours*) **Mt 20:**(6, without ὥρα), **9.** ἀπὸ τετάρτης ἡμέρας μέχρι ταύτης τῆς ὥρας ἤμην τὴν ἐνάτην προσευχόμενος *four days ago, reckoned from (=at) this very hour, I was praying at three o'clock in the afternoon* (=*15 hours*) **Ac 10:30** (echoing vs. **3,** but inelegantly phrased; s. comm. on the textual problems). ἐπύθετο τὴν ὥραν ἐν ᾗ . . . *he inquired at what time* . . . **J 4:52a;** cp. vs. **53** (cp. Ael. Arist. 50, 56 K.=26 p. 519 D.: . . . τὴν ὥραν αἰσθάνομαι . . . ἐκείνην, ἐν ᾗ . . . ; 47, 56 K.=23 p. 459 D.: ἀφυπνιζόμην κ. εὗρον ἐκείνην τὴν ὥραν οὖσαν, ᾗπερ . . .). ᾗ ἡμέρᾳ καὶ ὥρᾳ ἐμαρτύρησεν ὁ Πολύκαρπος *the very day and hour that* . . . EpilMosq 4.—Less definite are the indications of time in such expressions as ἄχρι τῆς ἄρτι ὥρας *up to the present moment* **1 Cor 4:11.** πᾶσαν ὥραν *hour after hour, every hour, constantly* (Ex 18:22; Lev 16:2; JosAs 15:7; Ar. [Milne 76, 34]; cp. TestJob 10:1 πάσας ὥρας) **15:30.** Also καθ' ὥραν (Strabo 15, 1, 55; Ps.-Clem., Hom. 3, 69) 2 Cl 12:1. αὐτῇ τῇ ὥρᾳ *at that very time, at once, instantly* (oft. pap, e.g. POxy 235, 7 [I AD]; Da 3:6, 15; TestAbr B 12 p. 116, 27 [Stone p. 80]; GrBar 14:1; 15:1; ApcMos 20) **Lk 2:38; 24:33; Ac 16:18; 22:13.**

❸ **a point of time as an occasion for an event, *time*** (BGU 1816, 12 [I BC] πρὸ ὥρας=before the right time) ἐν ἐκείνῃ τῇ ὥρᾳ **Mt 8:13; 10:19; 18:1** (v.l. ἡμέρᾳ); **26:55; Mk 13:11; Lk 7:21; Ac 16:33; Rv 11:13;** MPol 7:2a; GJs 20:2 (only pap). Likew. ἐν αὐτῇ τῇ ὥρᾳ **Lk 10:21; 12:12; 13:31; 20:19** (on both expressions s. JJeremias, ZNW 42, '49, 214–17). ἀπὸ τῆς ὥρας ἐκείνης *from that time on, at once* **Mt 9:22; 15:28; 17:18; J 19:27.** ὥρα ἐν ᾗ **J 5:28.** ὥρα ὅτε **4:21, 23; 5:25; 16:25** (cp. ApcMos 17 περὶ ὥραν ὅταν). ὥρα ἵνα **16:2, 32.** W. gen. of thing, the time for which has come (Diod. S. 13, 94, 1; Ael. Aristid. 51, 1 K.=27 p. 534 D.; PGM 1, 221 ἀνάγκης; JosAs 3:3 μεσημβρίας . . . καὶ ἀρίστου; ApcMos 42 [of Eve's request] ἐν τῇ ὥρᾳ τῆς τελευτῆς αὐτῆς; Jos., Ant. 7, 326 ὥ. ἀρίστου; SibOr 4, 56) ἡ ὥρα τοῦ θυμιάματος **Lk 1:10;** τοῦ δείπνου **14:17,** cp. MPol 7:1a; τοῦ πειρασμοῦ **Rv 3:10;** τῆς κρίσεως **14:7;** τῆς δοξολογίας αὐτοῦ GJs 13:1; τοῦ ἀσπασμοῦ 24:1; ἡ ὥρα αὐτῶν *the time for them* **J 16:4;** w. the gen. (of the Passover) to be supplied **Lk 22:14.** Also w. inf. (Hom. et al.; Lucian, Dial. Deor. 20, 1; Aelian, VH 1, 21) ἡ ὥρα θερίσαι *the time to reap* **Rv 14:15** (cp. Theopomp. [IV BC]: 115 fgm. 31 Jac. θερινὴ ὥ.; Paus. 2, 35, 4 ὥ. θέρους). Also acc. w. inf. (Gen 29:7) ὥρα (ἐστιν) ὑμᾶς ἐξ ὕπνου ἐγερθῆναι **Ro 13:11.**—W. gen. of pers. *the time of* or *for someone* to do or to suffer someth. (cp. Philo, Leg. ad Gai. 168 σὸς νῦν ὁ καιρός ἐστιν, ἐπέγειρε σαυτόν) of a woman who is to give birth (cp. GrBar 3:5 ἐν τῇ ὥρᾳ τοῦ τεκεῖν αὐτήν) ἡ ὥρα αὐτῆς **J 16:21** (v.l. ἡμέρα, s. ἡμέρα 3, beg.).—**Lk 22:53.** Esp. of Jesus, of whose ὥρα J speaks, as the time of his death (Diod. S. 15, 87, 6: the dying Epaminondas says ὥρα ἐστὶ τελευτᾶν. Cp. MPol 8:1 τοῦ ἐξιέναι) and of the glorification which is inextricably bound up w. it ἡ ὥρα αὐτοῦ **J 7:30; 8:20; 13:1** (foll. by ἵνα); cp. ἡ ὥρα μου **2:4** (s. Hdb. ad loc.). ἡ ὥρα ἵνα δοξασθῇ **12:23.** ἡ ὥρα αὕτη **12:27ab.** Also abs. ἐλήλυθεν ἡ ὥρα **17:1** (AGeorge, 'L'heure' de J 17, RB 61, '54, 392–97); cp. **Mt 26:45; Mk 14:35, 41.**—ἐσχάτη ὥρα *the last hour* in the present age of the world's existence **1J 2:18ab.**—CCowling, Mark's Use of ὥρα, Australian Biblical Review 5, '56, 153–60. EBickermann, Chronology of the Ancient World [2] '80, 13–16.—B. 954 and esp. 1001. DELG. M-M. EDNT. TW.

ὡραῖος, α, ον (ὥρα; Hes., Hdt.+)—❶ **pert. to an opportune point of time, *happening/coming at the right time, timely*** ὡς ὡραῖοι οἱ πόδες τῶν εὐαγγελιζομένων ἀγαθά *how timely is the arrival of those who who proclaim good news* (i.e. salvation) **Ro 10:15** (Is 52:7 cod. Q, margin [JZiegler '39 ad loc.]. See KBarth; RBultmann, TLZ 72, '47, 199). But the πόδες ὡραῖοι Sir 26:18 are without doubt *well-formed feet;* see 2 below. DHamm, Biblica 67, '86, 305–19, suggests a symbolic connection **Ac 3:2, 10.**

❷ **pert. to being attractive, *beautiful, fair, lovely, pleasant*** of persons and things, an angel GPt 13:55 (of Daniel ViDa 3 [p. 77, 5 Sch.] ὡ. ἐν χάριτι ὑψίστου). Trees (cp. Gen 2:9; En 24:5) B 11:10 (prophetic saying of uncertain origin). θύρα or πύλη **Ac 3:2, 10** (cp. GrBar prol. 2.—ESchürer, ZNW 7, 1906, 51–68; OHoltzmann, ibid. 9, 1908, 71–74; KLake: Beginn. I/5, '33, 479–86; Boffo, Iscrizioni p. 345f.—Of costly and artistic gates of polytheists' temples Diod. S. 5, 46, 6 θυρώματα τοῦ ναοῦ). Cp. **Mt 23:27.**—B. 1191. DELG. M-M.

ὥριμος, ον (Aristot. et al.; Diod. S. et al.; PTebt 54, 6 [I BC]; LXX) ***ripe*** σῖτος ὥριμος 1 Cl 56:15 (Job 5:26).—DELG s.v. ὥρα.

ὠρύομαι mid. dep. fut. 3 sg. ὠρύσεται Hos 11:10 (Pind., Hdt. et al.; LXX) ***to roar*** of lions (Apollon. Rhod. 4, 1339; Dio Chrys., Or. 77 + 78 §35; Judg 14:5; Ps 21:14; Jer 2:15; Philo, Somn. 1, 108.—What drives them to it is hunger: Hesych., ὠρυομένων of wolves and lions) **1 Pt 5:8.** καὶ γὰρ ὠρύετο πικρῶς καὶ ἐμβρ[ιμῶς] *for (the lion) roared fiercely and furiously* AcPl Ha 2, 7.—DELG. M-M.

ὡς (Hom.+; loanw. in rabb.) relative adv. of the relative pron. ὅς. It is used as

❶ **a comparative particle, marking the manner in which someth. proceeds, *as, like*—ⓐ** corresponding to οὕτως='so, in such a way': σωθήσεται, οὕτως ὡς διὰ πυρός *he will be saved,* (but only) *in such a way as* (one, in an attempt to save oneself, must go) *through fire* (and therefore suffer fr. burns) **1 Cor 3:15.** τὴν ἑαυτοῦ γυναῖκα οὕτως ἀγαπάτω ὡς ἑαυτόν **Eph 5:33;** cp. vs. **28.** ἡμέρα κυρίου ὡς κλέπτης οὕτως ἔρχεται **1 Th 5:2.** The word οὕτως can also be omitted ἀσφαλίσασθε ὡς οἴδατε *make it as secure as you know how = as you can* **Mt 27:65.** ὡς οὐκ οἶδεν αὐτός *(in such a way) as he himself does not know = he himself does not know how, without his knowing (just) how* **Mk 4:27.** ὡς ἀνῆκεν *(in such a way) as is fitting* **Col 3:18.** Cp. **4:4; Eph 6:20; Tit 1:5** (cp. Just., A I, 3, 1 ὡς πρέπον ἐστίν). ὡς πᾶσα γυνὴ γεννᾷ GJs 11:2; ὡς ἀπεκαλύφθη AcPlCor 1:8.

ⓑ special uses—α. in ellipses (TestAbr A 12 p. 90, 22 [Stone p. 28] θρόνος . . . ἐξαστράπτων ὡς πῦρ; TestJob 20:3 χρήσασθαι . . . ὡς ἐβούλετο; JosAs 12:7 πρὸς σὲ κατέφυγον ὡς παιδίον ἐπὶ τὸν πατέρα) ἐλάλουν ὡς νήπιος *I used to speak as a child (is accustomed to speak)* **1 Cor 13:11a;** cp. **bc; Mk 10:15; Eph 6:6a; Phil 2:22; Col 3:22.** ὡς τέκνα φωτὸς περιπατεῖτε *walk as (is appropriate for) children of light* **Eph 5:8;** cp. **6:6b.** ὡς ἐν ἡμέρᾳ *as (it is one's duty to walk) in the daylight* **Ro 13:13.** The Israelites went through the Red Sea ὡς διὰ ξηρᾶς γῆς *as (one travels) over dry land* **Hb 11:29.** οὐ λέγει ὡς ἐπὶ πολλῶν ἀλλ' ὡς ἐφ' ἑνός *he speaks not as one would of a plurality* (s. ἐπί 8), *but as of a single thing* **Gal 3:16.—Ro 15:15; 1 Pt 5:3.** Also referring back to οὕτως (GrBar 6:16 ὡς γὰρ τὰ δίστομα οὕτως καὶ ὁ ἀλέκτωρ μηνύει τοῖς ἐν τῷ κόσμῳ *like articulate beings the rooster informs earth's inhabitants*) οὕτως τρέχω ὡς οὐκ ἀδήλως *I run as (a person) with a fixed goal* **1 Cor 9:26a.** Cp. ibid. **b; Js 2:12.**

β. ὡς and the words that go w. it can be the subj. or obj., of a clause: γενηθήτω σοι ὡς θέλεις *let it be done (=it will be done) for you as you wish* **Mt 15:28.** Cp. **8:13; Lk 14:22 v.l.** (for ὅ; cp. ὡς τὸ θέλημά σου OdeSol 11:21). The predicate belonging to such a subj. is to be supplied in οὐχ ὡς ἐγὼ θέλω (γενηθήτω) **Mt 26:39a.**—ἐποίησεν ὡς προσέταξεν αὐτῷ ὁ ἄγγελος *he did as (=that which) the angel commanded him* (to do) **Mt 1:24;** cp. **26:19** (on the structure s. RPesch, BZ 10, '66, 220–45; 11, '67, 79–95; cp. the formula Job 42:9 and the contrasting negation Ex 1:17; s. also Ex 3:21f); **28:15.**—Practically equivalent to ὅ, which is a v.l. for it **Mk 14:72** (JBirdsall, NovT 2, '58, 272–75; cp. Lk 14:22 above).

γ. ἕκαστος ὡς *each one as* or *according to what* **Ro 12:3; 1 Cor 3:5; 7:17ab; Rv 22:12.** ὡς ἦν δυνατὸς ἕκαστος *each person interpreted them as best each could* Papias (2:16).

δ. in indirect questions (X., Cyr. 1, 5, 11 ἀπαίδευτοι ὡς χρὴ συμμάχοις χρῆσθαι) ἐξηγοῦντο ὡς ἐγνώσθη αὐτοῖς ἐν τῇ κλάσει τοῦ ἄρτου *they told how he had made himself known to them when they broke bread together* **Lk 24:35.** Cp. **Mk 12:26 v.l.** (for πῶς); **Lk 8:47; 23:55; Ac 10:38; 20:20; Ro 11:2; 2 Cor 7:15.**

❷ a conjunction marking a point of comparison, ***as.*** This 'as' can have a 'so' expressly corresponding to it or not, as the case may be; further, both sides of the comparison can be expressed in complete clauses, or one or even both may be abbreviated.

ⓐ ὡς is correlative w. οὕτως=*so.* οὕτως ... ὡς *(so, in such a way) ... as:* οὐδέποτε ἐλάλησεν οὕτως ἄνθρωπος ὡς οὗτος λαλεῖ ὁ ἄνθρωπος **J 7:46.** ὡς ... οὕτως **Ac 8:32** (Is 53:7); **23:11; Ro 5:15** (ὡς τὸ παράπτωμα, οὕτως καὶ τὸ χάρισμα, both halves to be completed), **18.** ὡς κοινωνοί ἐστε τῶν παθημάτων, οὕτως καὶ τῆς παρακλήσεως *as you are comrades in suffering, so (shall you be) in comfort as well* **2 Cor 1:7.** Cp. **7:14; 11:3 v.l.**—ὡς ... καί *as ... so* (Plut., Mor. 39e; Ath. 15, 2) **Mt 6:10; Ac 7:51; 2 Cor 13:2; Gal 1:9; Phil 1:20.**

ⓑ The clause beginning w. ὡς can easily be understood and supplied in many cases; when this occurs, the noun upon which the comparison depends can often stand alone, and in these cases ὡς acts as a particle denoting comparison. οἱ δίκαιοι ἐκλάμψουσιν ὡς ὁ ἥλιος *the righteous will shine out as the sun (shines)* **Mt 13:43.** ὡς ἐπὶ λῃστὴν ἐξήλθατε συλλαβεῖν με *as (one goes out) against a robber, (so) you have gone out to arrest me* **26:55** (Mel., P. 79, 574 ὡς ἐπὶ φόνιον λῄστην). γίνεσθε φρόνιμοι ὡς οἱ ὄφεις *be (as) wise as serpents (are)* **10:16b.** Cp. **Lk 12:27; 21:35; 22:31; J 15:6; 2 Ti 2:17; 1 Pt 5:8.**

ⓒ Semitic infl. is felt in the manner in which ὡς, combined w. a subst., takes the place of a subst. or an adj.

α. a substantive—**א.** as subj. (cp. Da 7:13 ὡς υἱὸς ἀνθρώπου ἤρχετο; cp. 10:16, 18) ἐνώπιον τοῦ θρόνου (ἦν) ὡς θάλασσα ὑαλίνη *before the throne there was something like a sea of glass* **Rv 4:6.** Cp. **8:8; 9:7a.** ἀφ' ἑνὸς ἐγενήθησαν ὡς ἡ ἄμμος *from one man they have come into being as the sand,* i.e. countless descendants **Hb 11:12.**

ב. as obj. (JosAs 17:6 εἶδεν 'Ασενὲθ ὡς ἅρμα πυρός) ᾄδουσιν ὡς ᾠδὴν καινήν *they were singing, as it were, a new song* **Rv 14:3.** ἤκουσα ὡς φωνήν *I heard what sounded like a shout* **19:1, 6abc;** cp. **6:1.**

β. as adjective, pred. (mostly εἶναι, γίνεσθαι ὡς; the latter also in rendering of כְּ to express the basic reality of something: GDelling, Jüd. Lehre u. Frömmigkeit '67, p. 58, on ParJer 9:7) ἐὰν μὴ γένησθε ὡς τὰ παιδία *if you do not become child-like* **Mt 18:3.** ὡς ἄγγελοί εἰσιν *they are similar to angels* **22:30.** πᾶσα σὰρξ ὡς χόρτος **1 Pt 1:24.** Cp. **Mk 6:34; 12:25; Lk 22:26ab; Ro 9:27** (Is 10:22); **29a** (Is 1:9a); **1 Cor 4:13; 7:7f, 29–31; 9:20f; 2 Pt 3:8ab** (Ps 89:4); **Rv 6:12ab** al. (cp. GrBar 14:1 ἐγένετο φωνὴ ὡς βροντή). Sim. also ποίησόν με ὡς ἕνα τῶν μισθίων σου *treat me like one of your day laborers* **Lk 15:19.**—The adj. or adjectival expr. for which this form stands may be used as an attribute πίστιν ὡς κόκκον σινάπεως *faith like a mustard seed*=faith no greater than a tiny mustard seed **Mt 17:20; Lk 17:6.** προφήτης ὡς εἷς τῶν προφητῶν **Mk 6:15.** Cp. **Ac 3:22; 7:37** (both Dt 18:15); **10:11; 11:5.** ἐγένετο ὡς εἷς τῶν φευγόντων AcPl Ha 5, 18. ἀρνίον ὡς ἐσφαγμένον *a lamb that appeared to have been slaughtered* **Rv 5:6.**—In expressions like τρίχας ὡς τρίχας γυναικῶν **9:8a** the second τρίχας can be omitted as self-evident (Ps 54:7 v.l.): ἡ φωνὴ ὡς σάλπιγγος **4:1;** cp. **1:10; 9:8b; 13:2a; 14:2c; 16:3.**

ⓓ other noteworthy uses—**α.** ὡς *as* can introduce an example ὡς καὶ 'Ηλίας ἐποίησεν **Lk 9:54 v.l.;** cp. **1 Pt 3:6;** or, in the combination ὡς γέγραπται, a scripture quotation **Mk 1:2 v.l.; 7:6; Lk 3:4; Ac 13:33;** cp. **Ro 9:25;** or even an authoritative human opinion **Ac 17:28; 22:5; 25:10;** or any other decisive reason **Mt 5:48; 6:12** (ὡς καί).

β. ὡς introduces short clauses: ὡς εἰώθει *as his custom was* **Mk 10:1.** Cp. Hs 5, 1, 2. ὡς λογίζομαι *as I think* **1 Pt 5:12.** ὡς ἐνομίζετο *as was supposed* **Lk 3:23** (Diog. L. 3, 2 ὡς 'Αθήνησιν ἦν λόγος [about Plato's origin]; TestAbr A 5 p. 82, 32 [Stone p. 12] ὡς ἐμοὶ δοκεῖ; Just., A I, 6, 2 ὡς ἐδιδάχθημεν). ὡς ἦν *as he was* **Mk 4:36.** ὡς ἔφην Papias (2:15) (ApcMos 42; cp. Just., A I, 21, 6 ὡς προέφημεν).

γ. The expr. οὕτως ἐστὶν ἡ βασιλεία τοῦ θεοῦ ὡς ἄνθρωπος βάλῃ τὸν σπόρον **Mk 4:26** may well exhibit colloquial syntax; but some think that ἄν (so one v.l. [=ἐάν, which is read by many mss.]) once stood before ἄνθρωπος and was lost inadvertently. S. the comm., e.g. EKlostermann, Hdb. z. NT[4] '50 ad loc.; s. also Jülicher, Gleichn. 539; B-D-F §380, 4; Mlt. 185 w. notes; Rdm.[2] 154; Rob. 928; 968.

❸ marker introducing the perspective from which a pers., thing, or activity is viewed or understood as to character, function, or role, ***as***

ⓐ w. focus on quality, circumstance, or role—**α.** *as* (JosAs 26:7 ἔγνω ... Λευὶς ... ταῦτα πάντα ὡς προφήτης; Just., A I, 7, 4 ἵνα ὡς ἄδικος κολάζηται) τί ἔτι κἀγὼ ὡς ἁμαρτωλὸς κρίνομαι; *why am I still being condemned as a sinner?* **Ro 3:7.** ὡς σοφὸς ἀρχιτέκτων **1 Cor 3:10.** ὡς ἀρτιγέννητα βρέφη *as newborn children* (in reference to desire for maternal milk) **1 Pt 2:2.** μή τις ὑμῶν πασχέτω ὡς φονεύς **4:15a;** cp. **b, 16.—1:14; 1 Cor 7:25; 2 Cor 6:4; Eph 5:1; Col 3:12; 1 Th 2:4, 7a.**—In the oblique cases, genitive (ApcSed 16:2 ὡς νέου αὐτοῦ ἐπαράβλεπον τὰ πταίσματα αὐτοῦ; Just., A I, 14, 4 ὑμέτερον ἔστω ὡς δυνατῶν βασιλέων): τιμίῳ αἵματι ὡς ἀμνοῦ ἀμώμου Χριστοῦ *with the precious blood of Christ, as of a lamb without blemish* **1 Pt 1:19.** δόξαν ὡς μονογενοῦς παρὰ πατρός *glory as of an only-begotten son, coming from the Father* **J 1:14.** Cp. **Hb 12:27.** Dative (Ath. 14, 2 θύουσιν ὡς θεοῖς; 28, 3 πιστεύειν ὡς μυθοποιῷ; Stephan. Byz. s.v. Κυνόσαργες:

Ἡρακλεῖ ὡς θεῷ θύων): λαλῆσαι ὑμῖν ὡς πνευματικοῖς **1 Cor 3:1a**; cp. **bc; 10:15; 2 Cor 6:13; Hb 12:5; 1 Pt 2:13f; 3:7ab; 2 Pt 1:19.** Accusative (JosAs 22:8 ἠγάπα αὐτὸν ὡς ἄνδρα προφήτην; Just., A I, 4, 4 τὸ ὄνομα ὡς ἔλεγχον λαμβάνετε; Tat. 27, 1 ὡς ἀθεωτάτους ἡμᾶς ἐκκηρύσσετε; Ath. 16, 4 οὐ προσκυνῶ αὐτὰ ὡς θεούς): οὐχ ὡς θεὸν ἐδόξασαν **Ro 1:21; 1 Cor 4:14; 8:7; Tit 1:7; Phlm 16; Hb 6:19; 11:9.** παρακαλῶ ὡς παροίκους καὶ παρεπιδήμους **1 Pt 2:11** (from the perspective of their conversion experience the recipients of the letter are compared to temporary residents and disenfranchised foreigners, cp. the imagery **1 Pt 1:19** above and s. παρεπίδημος and πάροικος 2).—This is prob. also the place for ὃ ἐὰν ποιῆτε, ἐργάζεσθε ὡς τῷ κυρίῳ *whatever you have to do, do it as work for the Lord* **Col 3:23.** Cp. **Eph 5:22.** εἴ τις λαλεῖ ὡς λόγια θεοῦ *if anyone preaches, (let the pers. do so) as if (engaged in proclaiming the) words of God* **1 Pt 4:11a;** cp. ibid. **b; 2 Cor 2:17bc; Eph 6:5, 7.**

β. ὡς w. ptc. gives the reason for an action *as one who, because* (X., Cyr. 7, 5, 13 κατεγέλων τῆς πολιορκίας ὡς ἔχοντες τὰ ἐπιτήδεια; Appian, Liby. 56 §244 μέμφεσθαι τοῖς θεοῖς ὡς ἐπιβουλεύουσι=as being hostile; Polyaenus 2, 1, 1; 3, 10, 3 ὡς ἔχων=just as if he had; TestAbr B 8 p. 112, 17 [Stone p. 72] ὡς αὐτῷ ὄντι φίλῳ μου *(do it for) him* [Abraham] *as a friend of mine;* TestJob 17:5 καθ' ἡμῶν ὡς τυραννούντων *against us as though we were tyrants;* ApcMos 23 ὡς νομίζοντες *on the assumption that (we would not be discovered);* Jos., Ant. 1, 251; Ath. 16, 1 ὁ δὲ κόσμος οὐχ ὡς δεομένου τοῦ θεοῦ γέγονεν; SIG 1168, 35); Paul says: I appealed to the Emperor οὐχ ὡς τοῦ ἔθνους μου ἔχων τι κατηγορεῖν *not that I had any charge to bring against my (own) people* **Ac 28:19** (PCairZen 44, 23 [257 BC] οὐχ ὡς μενῶν=not as if it were my purpose to remain there). ὡς foll. by the gen. abs. ὡς τὰ πάντα ἡμῖν τῆς θείας δυνάμεως αὐτοῦ δεδωρημένης *because his divine power has granted us everything* **2 Pt 1:3.** Cp. Dg. 5:16.—Only in isolated instances does ὡς show causal force when used w. a finite verb *for, seeing that* (PLeid 16, 1, 20; Lucian, Dial. Mort. 17, 2, end, Vit. Auct. 25; Aesop, Fab. 109 P.=148 H.; 111 H-H.: ὡς εὐθέως ἐξελεύσομαι=because; Tetrast. Iamb. 1, 6, 3; Nicetas Eugen. 6, 131 H. Cp. Herodas 10, 3: ὡς=because [with the copula 'is' to be supplied]) **Mt 6:12** (ὡς καί as **Mk 7:37 v.l.;** TestDan 3:1 v.l.; the parallel Lk 11:4 has γάρ). AcPlCor 1:6 ὡς οὖν ὁ κύριος ἠλέησεν ἡμᾶς *inasmuch as the Lord has shown us mercy (by permitting us).* So, more oft., καθώς (q.v. 3).

γ. ὡς before the predicate acc. or nom. w. certain verbs functions pleonastically and further contributes to the aspect of perspective ὡς προφήτην ἔχουσιν τὸν Ἰωάννην **Mt 21:26.** Cp. **Lk 16:1.** λογίζεσθαί τινα ὡς foll. by acc. *look upon someone as* **1 Cor 4:1; 2 Cor 10:2** (for this pass. s. also c below). Cp. **2 Th 3:15ab; Phil 2:7; Js 2:9.**

ⓑ w. focus on a conclusion existing only in someone's imagination or based solely on someone's assertion (PsSol 8:30; Jos., Bell. 3, 346; Just., A I, 27, 5; Mel., P. 58, 422) προσηνέγκατέ μοι τὸν ἄνθρωπον τοῦτον ὡς ἀποστρέφοντα τὸν λαόν, καὶ ἰδοὺ . . . *you have brought this fellow before me as one who* (as you claim) *is misleading the people, and now* . . . **Lk 23:14.** τί καυχᾶσαι ὡς μὴ λαβών; *why do you boast, as though you* (as you think) *had not received?* **1 Cor 4:7.** Cp. **Ac 3:12; 23:15, 20; 27:30.** ὡς μὴ ἐρχομένου μου *as though I were not coming* (acc. to their mistaken idea) **1 Cor 4:18.** ὡς μελλούσης τῆς πόλεως αἵρεσθαι *assuming that the city was being destroyed* AcPl Ha 5, 16.

ⓒ w. focus on what is objectively false or erroneous ἐπιστολὴ ὡς δι' ἡμῶν *a letter* (falsely) *alleged to be from us* **2 Th 2:2a** (Diod. S. 33, 5, 5 ἔπεμψαν ὡς παρὰ τῶν πρεσβευτῶν ἐπιστολήν they sent a letter which purported to come from the emissaries; Diog. L. 10:3 falsified ἐπιστολαὶ ὡς Ἐπικούρου; Just., A, II, 5, 5 ὡς ἀπ' αὐτοῦ σπορᾷ γενομένους υἱούς). τοὺς λογιζομένους ἡμᾶς ὡς κατὰ σάρκα περιπατοῦντας **2 Cor 10:2** (s. also aγ above). Cp. **11:17; 13:7.** Israel wishes to become righteous οὐκ ἐκ πίστεως ἀλλ' ὡς ἐξ ἔργων *not through faith but through deeds* (the latter way being objectively wrong) **Ro 9:32** (Rdm.[2] 26f). ὡς ἐκ παραδόσεως ἀγράφου εἰς αὐτὸν ἥκοντα *(other matters he recounts) as having reached him through unwritten tradition* (Eus. about Papias) Papias (2:11).

❹ conj., **marker of result in connection with indication of purpose**=ὥστε ***so that*** (trag., Hdt.+, though nearly always w. the inf.; so also POxy 1040, 11; PFlor 370, 10; Wsd 5:12; TestJob 39:7; ApcMos 38; Jos., Ant. 12, 229; Just., A I, 56, 2; Tat. 12, 2. W. the indic. X., Cyr. 5, 4, 11 οὕτω μοι ἐβοήθησας ὡς σέσῳσμαι; Philostrat., Vi. Apoll. 8, 7 p. 324, 25f; Jos., Bell. 3, 343; Ath. 15, 3; 22, 2) **Hb 3:11; 4:3** (both Ps 94:11). ὡς αὐτὸν καθόλου τὸ φῶς μὴ βλέπειν Papias (3:2) (s. φῶς 1a). ὡς πάντας ἄχθεσθαι (s. ἄχθομαι) AcPl Ha 4, 14. ὡς πάντας . . . ἀγαλλιᾶσθαι 6, 31 al.

❺ **marker of discourse content, *that, the fact that*** after verbs of knowing, saying (even introducing direct discourse: Maximus Tyr. 5:4f), hearing, etc.=ὅτι *that* (X., An. 1, 3, 5; Menand., Sam. 590 S. [245 Kö.]; Aeneas Tact. 402; 1342; PTebt 10, 6 [119 BC]; 1 Km 13:11; EpArist; Philo, Op. M. 9; Jos., Ant. 7, 39; 9, 162; 15, 249 al.; Just., A I, 60, 2; Tat. 39, 2; 41, 1; Ath. 30, 4.—ORiemann, RevPhilol n.s. 6, 1882, 73–75; HKallenberg, RhM n.s. 68, 1913, 465–76; B-D-F §396) ἀναγινώσκειν **Mk 12:26 v.l.** (for πῶς); **Lk 6:4** (w. πῶς as v.l.). μνησθῆναι **Lk 24:6** (D ὅσα); cp. **22:61** (=Lat. quomodo, as in ms. c of the Old Itala; cp. Plautus, Poen. 3, 1, 54–56). ἐπίστασθαι (Jos., Ant. 7, 372) **Ac 10:28; 20:18b v.l.** (for πῶς). εἰδέναι (MAI 37, 1912, 183 [= Kl. T. 110, 81, 10] ἴστε ὡς [131/132 AD]) **1 Th 2:11a.** μάρτυς ὡς **Ro 1:9; Phil 1:8; 1 Th 2:10.**—ὡς ὅτι s. ὅτι 5b.

❻ w. numerals, **a degree that approximates a point on a scale of extent, *about, approximately, nearly*** (Hdt., Thu. et al.; PAmh 72, 12; PTebt 381, 4 [VSchuman, ClW 28, '34/35, 95f: pap]; Jos., Ant. 6, 95; Ruth 1:4; 1 Km 14:2; TestJob 31:2; JosAs 1:6) ὡς δισχίλιοι **Mk 5:13.** Cp. **8:9; Lk 1:56; 8:42; J 1:39; 4:6; 6:10, 19; 19:14, 39; 21:8; Ac 4:4; 5:7, 36; 13:18, 20; 27:37 v.l.** (Hemer, Acts 149 n. 140); **Rv 8:1.**

❼ **a relatively high point on a scale involving exclamation, *how!*** (X., Cyr. 1, 3, 2 ὦ μῆτερ, ὡς καλός μοι ὁ πάππος! Himerius, Or. 54 [=Or. 15], 1 ὡς ἡδύ μοι τὸ θέατρον=how pleasant . . . ! Ps 8:2; 72:1; TestJob 7:12) ὡς ὡραῖοι οἱ πόδες τῶν εὐαγγελιζομένων ἀγαθά **Ro 10:15** (cp. Is 52:7). Cp. **11:33.** ὡς μεγάλη μοι ἡ σήμερον ἡμέρα GJs 19:2.

❽ **temporal conjunction** (B-D-F §455, 2; 3; Harnack, SBBerlAk 1908, 392).—ⓐ w. the aor. *when, after* (Hom., Hdt. et al.; Diod. S. 14, 80, 1; pap [POxy 1489, 4 al.]; LXX; TestAbr B 3 p. 107, 6 [Stone p. 62]; JosAs 3:2; ParJer 3:1; ApcMos 22; Jos., Bell. 1, 445b; Just., D. 2, 4; 3, 1) ὡς ἐπλήσθησαν αἱ ἡμέραι **Lk 1:23.** ὡς ἐγεύσατο ὁ ἀρχιτρίκλινος **J 2:9.—Lk 1:41, 44; 2:15, 39; 4:25; 5:4; 7:12; 15:25; 19:5; 22:66; 23:26; J 4:1, 40; 6:12, 16; 7:10; 11:6, 20, 29, 32f; 18:6; 19:33; 21:9; Ac 5:24; 10:7, 25; 13:29; 14:5; 16:10, 15; 17:13; 18:5; 19:21; 21:1, 12; 22:25; 27:1, 27; 28:4.** AcPl Ha 3, 20.

ⓑ w. pres. or impf. *while, when, as long as* (Menand., fgm. 538, 2 K. ὡς ὁδοιπορεῖς; Cyrill. Scyth. [VI AD] ed. ESchwartz '39 p. 143, 1; 207, 22 ὡς ἔτι εἰμί=as long as I live) ὡς ὑπάγεις μετὰ τοῦ ἀντιδίκου σου *while you are going with your opponent* **Lk 12:58.** ὡς ἐλάλει ἡμῖν, ὡς διήνοιγεν ἡμῖν τὰς γραφάς *while he was talking, while he was opening the scriptures to us* **24:32.**—**J 2:23; 8:7; 12:35f** (*as long as*; cp. ἕως 2a); **Ac 1:10; 7:23; 9:23; 10:17; 13:25; 19:9; 21:27; 25:14; Gal 6:10** (*as long as*); 2 Cl 8:1; 9:7; IRo 2:2; ISm 9:1 (all four *as long as*).—ὡς w. impf., and in the next clause the aor. ind. w. the same subject (Diod. S. 15, 45, 4 ὡς ἐθεώρουν . . . , συνεστήσαντο 'when [or 'as soon as'] they noticed . . . , they put together [a fleet]'; SIG 1169, 58 ὡς ἐνεκάθευδε, εἶδε 'while he was sleeping [or 'when he went to sleep'] [in the temple] he saw [a dream or vision]') **Mt 28:9 v.l.; J 20:11; Ac 8:36; 16:4; 22:11.**—*Since* (Soph., Oed. R. 115; Thu. 4, 90, 3) ὡς τοῦτο γέγονεν **Mk 9:21.**

ⓒ ὡς ἄν or ὡς ἐάν w. subjunctive of the time of an event in the future *when, as soon as.*

α. ὡς ἄν (Hyperid. 2, 43, 4; Herodas 5, 50; Lucian, Cronosolon 11; PHib 59, 1 [c. 245 BC] ὡς ἄν λάβῃς; UPZ 71, 18 [152 BC]; PTebt 26, 2. Cp. Witkowski 87; Gen 12:12; Josh 2:14; Is 8:21; Da 3:15 Theod.; Ath. 31, 3 [ἐάν Schwartz]) **Ro 15:24; 1 Cor 11:34; Phil 2:23.**

β. ὡς ἐάν (PFay 111, 16 [95/96 AD] ὡς ἐὰν βλέπῃς) 1 Cl 12:5f; Hv 3, 8, 9; 3, 13, 2.

ⓓ w. the superlative ὡς τάχιστα (a bookish usage; s. B-D-F §244, 1; Rob. 669) *as quickly as possible* **Ac 17:15** (s. ταχέως 1c).

❾ a final particle, expressing intention/purpose, *with a view to, in order to*—ⓐ w. subjunctive (Hom.+; TestAbr A 4 p. 80, 33 [Stone p. 8]; SibOr 3, 130; Synes., Hymni 3, 44 [NTerzaghi '39]) ὡς τελειώσω *in order that I might finish* **Ac 20:24 v.l.** (s. Mlt. 249).

ⓑ w. inf. (X.; Arrian [very oft.: ABoehner, De Arriani dicendi genere, diss. Erlangen 1885 p. 56]; PGen 28, 12 [II AD]; ZPE 8, '71, 177: letter of M. Ant. 57, cp. 44–46; 3 Macc 1:2; Joseph.; cp. the use of the opt. Just., D. 2, 3) **Lk 9:52.** ὡς τελειῶσαι **Ac 20:24.** ὡς ἔπος εἰπεῖν **Hb 7:9** (s. ἔπος).

ⓒ used w. prepositions to indicate the direction intended (Soph., Thu., X. [Kühner-G. I 472 note 1]; Polyb. 1, 29, 1; LRadermacher, Philol 60, 1901, 495f) πορεύεσθαι ὡς ἐπὶ τὴν θάλασσαν **Ac 17:14 v.l.**—WStählin, Symbolon, '58, 99–104. S. also ὡσάν, ὡσαύτως, ὡσεί 2, ὥσπερ b, ὡσπερεί, ὥστε 2b. DELG. M-M.

ὡς ἄν or ὡσάν **marker indicating perspective or point of view, with component of cautious statement, *as if, as it were, so to speak*** (B-D-F §453, 3; Rob. 974) Hs 9, 9, 7. W. the inf. ὡς ἂν ἐκφοβεῖν **2 Cor 10:9.**—On **1 Cor 12:2** s. B-D-R 367, 3; 453, 6; Ltzm., Hdb.; HConzelmann, Hermeneia comm.

ὡσαννά=Aram. הוֹשַׁע נָא=Hebr. הוֹשִׁיעָה נָּא (Hebr. Ps 118:25); on the spelling s. W-H., Introd. §408; Tdf., Prol. 107; indecl. **a shout of praise, *hosanna*** (lit.='help' or 'save, I pray', an appeal that became a liturgical formula; as a part of the Hallel [Ps 113–18 Hebr.] it was familiar to everyone in Israel. In the course of time an acclamation, abs. **Mk 11:9** (RGundry, Mark '93, 630); **J 12:13.** W. additions: τῷ υἱῷ Δαυίδ **Mt 21:9a, 15** (FCoggan, ET 52, '40/41, 76f; CWood, ibid. 357). τῷ θεῷ Δ. D 10:6. ἐν τοῖς ὑψίστοις **Mt 21:9b; Mk 11:10** (s. ὕψιστος 1).—W-S. p. xv; EKautzsch, Gramm. d. Bibl.-Aram. 1884, 173; Dalman, Gramm.[2] 1905, 249; Billerb. I 1922, 845ff; Zahn, Einl. I[3] 14; EbNestle, Philol. 68, 1909, 462; FSpitta, ZWT 52, 1910, 307–20; FBurkitt, JTS 17, 1916, 139–49; Elbogen[2] 138f; 219f; HBornhäuser, Sukka '35, 106f; EBishop, ET 53, '42, 212–14; Goodsp., Probs. 34f; EWerner, JBL 65, '46, 97–122; JKennard, Jr., JBL 67, '48, 171–76; ELohse, NovT 6, '63, 183–89.—M-M. EDNT. TW.

ὡσαύτως adv. of ὁ αὐτός (as one word [s. MReil, ByzZ 19, 1910, 507f] it is post-Homeric; ins, pap, LXX, TestLevi 17:7; TestAsh 2:3; ViIs 5; EpArist; Philo, Op. M. 54; Just.) **a marker of similarity that approximates identity, *(in) the same (way), similarly, likewise*** ἐποίησεν ὡσαύτως **Mt 20:5.** Cp. **21:30, 36; 25:17; Lk 13:3 v.l., 5; 1 Ti 5:25; Tit 2:6;** Hs 2:7; 5, 4, 2; 8, 4, 4; D 11:11; 13:2, 6. ὡσαύτως δὲ καί (Demetr.: 722 fgm. 1, 15 Jac.; Strabo 10, 3, 10) **Mk 14:31; Lk 20:31; Ro 8:26; 1 Ti 5:25 v.l.** The verb is to be supplied fr. the context (TestLevi 17:7) **Mk 12:21; Lk 22:20; 1 Cor 11:25; 1 Ti 2:9** (acc. to vs. 8 βούλομαι is to be supplied); **3:8** and **11** (sc. δεῖ εἶναι); **Tit 2:3** (λάλει εἶναι); 1 Cl 43:3.—See ὁμοίως. HLungvik, Eranos 62, '64, 37.—M-M.

ὡσεί (Hom. et al.)—**❶ marker denoting comparison, *as, like (something) like,*** lit. 'as if' (Hom.; Epicharmus [in CGFP 83,1 p. 55] et al.; PSI 343, 10 [256/255 BC]; PTebt 58, 26; LXX, En; TestSol 7:1; TestJob 30:2; Test12Patr;, JosAs; ApcEsdr 4:29 p. 29, 4 Tdf.; Mel., P. 48, 341) in the mss. oft. interchanged w. ὡς (B-D-F §453, 3; s. Rob. 968) πνεῦμα καταβαῖνον ὡσεὶ περιστεράν **Mt 3:16; Lk 3:22 v.l.; Mk 1:10 v.l.; J 1:32 v.l.;** GJs 8:1. Cp. **Mt 9:36; Ac 2:3; 6:15; 9:18 v.l.** (for ὡς); **16:9** D; **Ro 6:13; Ro 6:13; Hb 1:12** (Ps 101:27); **11:12 v.l.** (for ὡς ἡ); **Rv 1:14 v.l.;** B 6:6 (Ps 117:12); Hv 3, 1, 5ab; 4, 1, 6ab; s 6, 2, 5. γίνεσθαι ὡσεί **Mt 28:4 v.l.** (for ὡς); **Mk 9:26; Lk 22:44** (cp. Photius, Bibl. 94 p. 74b πίπτουσι παρὰ ὁδὸν ὡσεὶ νεκροί). εἶναι ὡσεί **Mt 28:3 v.l.** (for ὡς); Hs 3:1f. φαίνεσθαι ὡσεί τι *seem like someth.* **Lk 24:11.**

❷ marker denoting approximation w. numbers and measures ***about*** (X., Hell. 1, 2, 9; 2, 4, 25; PTebt 15, 2; 25 [114 BC]; Sb 5115, 4 [145 BC]; LXX; TestAbr A 17 p. 100, 3 [Stone p. 48]; GrBar; EpArist 13; Jos., Ant. 6, 247; 12, 292) ὡσεὶ πεντακισχίλιοι **Mt 14:21; Mk 6:44 v.l.; Lk 9:14a; J 6:10 v.l.** Cp. **Lk 9:14ab; J 19:39 v.l.; Ac 1:15; 2:41; 4:4 v.l.; 5:36 v.l.; 19:7.** ὡσεὶ μῆνας τρεῖς **Lk 1:56 v.l.** (for ὡς). μῆνει ὡσεὶ ἕξ GJs 5:2. Cp. **Lk 3:23** (Boffo, Iscrizioni 193 n. 23); **9:28; 22:59; Ac 19:34 v.l.** ὡσεὶ ὥρα ἕκτη (TestJos 8:1) **23:44; J 4:6 v.l.** (for ὡς); **19:14 v.l.** (for ὡς). Cp. **Ac 10:3.** ὡσεὶ στάδια δέκα Hv 4, 1, 2. Cp. 4, 2, 1. ὡσεὶ λίθου βολήν **Lk 22:41.**—M-M.

Ὡσηέ or Ὡσῆε (הוֹשֵׁעַ; Hos 1:1f; Philo, Mut. Nominum 121; Just.—In Joseph. the name is written: Ὡσῆος, ου, also Ὡσήης [Ant. 9, 277] and Ὡσῆς [278]), **ὁ** indecl. ***Hosea,*** one of the 'minor' prophets. Metonymically of his book (Caecilius Calactinus, fgm. 74 p. 56, 20: κεῖσθαι παρὰ τῷ Θουκυδίδῃ, i.e. 3, 13, 3) ἐν τῷ Ὡσηέ **Ro 9:25.**

ὠσί see οὖς.

ὥσπερ (Hom.+) gener. 'just (as)' **marker of similarity between events and states—ⓐ** in the protasis of a comparison, the apodosis of which begins w. οὕτως (καί) ***(just) as . . . , so*** (X., Mem. 1, 6, 14; Epict., Ench. 27; Dio Chrys. 17 [34], 44; 19 [36], 20; ParJer 7:26f; GrBar 4:16; ApcEsdr 1:14; 5:12; Just., D. 6, 2; Tat. 5, 2; POxy 1065, 6) **Mt 12:40; 13:40; 24:27, 37; Lk 17:24; J 5:21, 26; Ro 5:19, 21; Js 2:26;** Hv 3, 6, 6; 3, 11, 3; 4, 3, 4ab; m 10, 3, 3; s 3:3 al. Cp. ISm 8:2.—ὥσπερ . . . , ἵνα καί w. subjunctive (as a substitute for the impv.) **2 Cor 8:7.** In anacoluthon w. the apodosis to be supplied **Ro 5:12;** ὥσπερ γάρ *for it is just like* (Plut., Mor. 7c) **Mt 25:14.** Cp. IMg 5:2. In sim. sense

ⓑ connecting w. what goes before μὴ σαλπίσῃς ὥσπερ οἱ ὑποκριταὶ ποιοῦσιν **Mt 6:2.** Cp. **20:28; 25:32; Hb 9:25; Rv 10:3;** IEph 8:1; 21:2; IMg 4 (ὥσπερ καί, as PSI 486, 6 [258/257 BC]; PFay 106, 24; Just., D. 85, 3). ὥσπερ εἰσὶν θεοὶ πολλοί *just as indeed there are many gods* **1 Cor 8:5** (s. EvDobschütz, ZNW 24, 1925, 50). οὐχ ὥσπερ σύνταξιν τῶν κυριακῶν ποιούμενος λογίων (s. σύνταξις) Papias (2:15).—The ὥσπερ-clause is somet. shortened and needs to be supplemented (JosAs 28:8 τρέχοντες ὥσπερ ἔλαφοι; Just., D. 5, 6; Tat. 18, 2) μὴ βατταλογήσητε ὥσπερ οἱ ἐθνικοί (sc. βατταλογοῦσιν) **Mt 6:7.** Cp. **Ac 3:17; 11:15; 1 Th 5:3; Hb 4:10; 7:27;** Dg 5:3; IEph 8:2. Foll. by gen. abs. ἐγένετο ἦχος ὥσπερ φερομένης πνοῆς βιαίας **Ac 2:2** (Jos., Bell. 2, 556 ὥσπερ βαπτιζομένης νεώς). εἰμὶ ὥσπερ τις *I am like someone* (JosAs 14:9) **Lk 18:11.** ἔστω σοι ὥσπερ ὁ ἐθνικός *as far as you are concerned, let the pers. be as a gentile = treat the pers. as you would a gentile* **Mt 18:17.** γενόμενος ὥσπερ ἐξ ἀρχῆς καινὸς ἄνθρωπος *become, as it were, a new person from the beginning* Dg 2:1.—DELG s.v. 1 ὡς. M-M.

ὡσπερεί (Aeschyl., Pla. et al.; Diod. S. 5, 31, 4; 10, 3, 2; 17, 112, 5; Ps.-Lucian, Asin. 56; Ps 57:9 Sym.; En 5:2) **statement of comparison, with component of caution,** ***like, as though, as it were*** **1 Cor 4:13 v.l.** (for ὡς); **15:8.**—M-M.

ὥστε (Hom.+; B-D-F §391, 2; 3; Mayser II/1, 1926, 297ff)

❶ introducing independent clauses ***for this reason, therefore, so***—ⓐ foll. by the indic. (X., An. 1, 7, 7; 2, 2, 17 al.; Ar. 13, 6; Just., A I, 44, 8 and 11 al.; Tat. 9, 1) ὥστε ἔξεστιν τοῖς σάββασιν καλῶς ποιεῖν **Mt 12:12.** Cp. **19:6; 23:31; Mk 2:28; 10:8; Ro 7:4, 12; 13:2; 1 Cor 3:7; 7:38; 11:27; 14:22; 2 Cor 4:12; 5:16f; Gal 3:9, 24; 4:7, 16;** Hm 7:4.

ⓑ foll. by the impv. (X., Cyr. 1, 3, 18; Lucian, Dial. Deor. 6, 1; PLond I, 17, 38 p. 11 [162 BC; cp. UWilcken, GGA 1894, 721]; PEdg 26 [=Sb 6732], 19 [255 BC] ὥστε φρόντισον; Job 6:21; Wsd 6:25; 4 Macc 11:16; Just., D. 57, 3; 94, 4) ὥστε ἑδραῖοι γίνεσθε **1 Cor 15:58.** Cp. **10:12; 11:33; 14:39; Phil 2:12; 4:1; 1 Th 4:18; Js 1:19 v.l.; 1 Pt 4:19.** ὥστε μή w. impv. **1 Cor 3:21; 4:5.** The hortatory subjunctive can take the place of the impv. ὥστε ἑορτάζωμεν **1 Cor 5:8.** Cp. 2 Cl 4:3; 7:1, 3; 10:1; w. the neg. μή 11:5.

❷ introducing dependent clauses—ⓐ of the actual result ***so that***—**α.** foll. by the indic. (Soph., Demosth., X.; POxy 471, 89; 1672, 6 [I AD]; Jos., Ant. 12, 124) **Gal 2:13.** οὕτως . . . , ὥστε (Epict. 1, 11, 4; 4, 11, 19; Jos., Ant. 8, 206; Just., A I, 22, 4, D. 2, 4 al.; Tat. 19, 1) **J 3:16;** Qua 2.

β. foll. by the acc. w. inf. (Ps.-Callisth. 2, 4, 7; TestAbr A 17 p. 100, 4 [Stone p. 48]; TestJob 23:1; 24:7; BGU 27, 13; POxy 891, 12; Josh 10:14; EpArist 59; 64 al.; Demetr.: 722 fgm. 1, 5 al.; Jos., Ant. 12, 124; Just., D. 2, 4 al.; Tat. 19, 1) ὥστε τὸ πλοῖον καλύπτεσθαι **Mt 8:24.** Cp. **12:22; 13:2, 32, 54; 15:31; 24:24 v.l.; 27:14; Mk 2:12; 4:32, 37; 9:26; 15:5; Lk 5:7; Ac 1:19; 14:1** (οὕτως ὥστε); **15:39; Ro 7:6; 15:19; 1 Cor 5:1** (*of such a kind that,* cp. Diod. S. 11, 61, 3 ἄγνοια τοιαύτη ὥστε); **2 Cor 1:8; 2:7; 7:7; Phil 1:13; 1 Th 1:7; 2 Th 1:4; 2:4; Hb 13:6; 1 Pt 1:21;** 1 Cl 1:1: 11:2; B 4:2; ITr 1:1 (οὕτως . . . , ὥστε); MPol 2:2a; 12:3; Hv 3, 2, 6 (οὕτως . . . , ὥστε); 4, 1, 8 (οὕτω . . . , ὥστε); AcPl Ha 2, 6 and 11 (restored); 3, 33 al. ὥστε μή w. acc. and inf. **Mt 8:28; Mk 1:45; 2:2; 3:20; 1 Cor 1:7; 2 Cor 3:7; 1 Th 1:8;** MPol 2:2b; GJs 19:2; 21:2 (codd.).—W. the inf. alone (Aeschyl., Pers. 461; Soph., El. 393; Chariton 2, 2, 2; TestJob 21:1; Anth. Pal. 11, 144, 6; POxy 1279, 14; Gen 1:17; EpArist 95; 99; SibOr 5, 413; 475 [οὕτως . . . , ὥ]; Ath. 12, 3) **Mt 15:33; 24:24; Mk 3:10; Lk 12:1; Ac 5:15; 19:16; 1 Cor 13:2;** 1 Cl 45:7.

ⓑ of the intended result, scarcely to be distinguished in mng. fr. ἵνα (B-D-F §391, 3; Mlt. p. 207; 210; 249; Rdm.[2] p. 197; Rob. 990) *for the purpose of, with a view to, in order that* w. inf. foll. (X., Cyr. 3, 2, 16; Ps.-Lucian, Asin. 46; SIG 736, 114 οἱ κατεσταμένοι ὥστε γράψαι; UPZ 12, 15 [158 BC]; POxy 501, 14; Gen 9:15; Job 6:23; ApcMos 17; Jos., Ant. 19, 279) **Mt 10:1; 27:1; Lk 4:29; 9:52 v.l.; 20:20.**—DELG s.v. 1ὡς. M-M.

ὠτάριον, ου, τό dim. of οὖς, but equivalent to it in later Gk. **the outer ear,** ***ear*** (Lucillius [I AD]: Anth. Pal. 11, 75, 2 of the severed ear of a gladiator; Anaxandrides [IV BC] in Athen. 3, 95c of an animal's ear.—Elsewh., incl. pap, the word means 'handle') **Mk 14:47; J 18:10** (in both ὠτίον as v.l.).—DELG s.v. οὖς. M-M. TW.

ὠτίον, ου, τό dim. of οὖς (s. PJoüon, RSR 24, '34, 473f), but equivalent to it in late Gk.; **the outer ear,** ***ear*** (a human's or an animal's: Eratosth. p. 22, 22; Nicol. Dam.: 90 fgm. 119 Jac. ἀποτέμνει ὠ.; Anth. Pal. 11, 81, 3 [gladiator]; Epict. 1, 18, 18; Athen. 3, 95a; 107a; POxy 108 II, 17 [II BC]; LXX; Jos., Ant. 14, 366 v.l.; TestSol 18:21; ApcMos 26.—In pap it means mostly 'handle') **Mt 26:51; Mk 14:47 v.l.; Lk 22:51; J 18:10 v.l., 26;** B 9:1 (Ps 17:45); AcPl Ha 5, 11; 22, 35. S. οὖς 1 and ὠτάριον.—B. 226. DELG s.v. οὖς. M-M. TW.

ὠφέλεια, ας, ἡ (ὠφελέω; Soph., Hdt.+; ins, pap, LXX; TestSol prol. 3 C; EpArist, Philo; Jos., Ant. 4, 274; 12, 29 al.; Tat. 24, 1; Ath. 11, 3.—But beside it the spelling ὠφελία is attested as early as Attic Gk.; s. B-D-F §23; cp. B-D-R §23, 3; Mlt-H. 78) ***use, gain, advantage*** w. gen. (EpArist 241) τίς ἡ ὠφέλεια τῆς περιτομῆς; *what is the use/point of circumcision?* **Ro 3:1** (AFridrichsen, StKr 102, 1930, 291–94. Cp. Jos., C. Ap. 2, 143 μηδὲν ὠφεληθεὶς ὑπὸ τῆς περιτομῆς). ὠφελείας χάριν *for the sake of an advantage* (cp. Polyb. 3, 82, 8) **Jd 16.**—DELG s.v. 2 ὀφέλλω. M-M.

ὠφελέω (ὄφελος) fut. ὠφελήσω; 1 aor. ὠφέλησα. Pass.: 1 fut. ὠφεληθήσομαι; 1 aor. ὠφελήθην (Aeschyl., Hdt.+)

❶ to provide assistance, ***help, aid, benefit, be of use (to)***

ⓐ w. personal obj. in the acc. (X., Mem. 1, 2, 61 al.; Herm. Wr. 12, 8; Sb 4305, 10 [III BC]; POxy 1219, 12; Jos., Ant. 2, 282; Just., D. 92, 4; B-D-F §151, 1; Rob. 472) οὐκ ὠφέλησεν ὁ λόγος ἐκείνους **Hb 4:2** (cp. Plut., Mor. 5f). Cp. D 16:2. Mostly a second acc. is added τινά τι *someone in respect to someth.* (Soph. et al.; Hdt. 3, 126) τί ὑμᾶς ὠφελήσω; *how will I benefit you?* **1 Cor 14:6.** Cp. **Mk 8:36;** ISm 5:2. Χριστὸς ὑμᾶς οὐδὲν ὠφελήσει **Gal 5:2** (s. PSI 365, 19 [III BC] ὁ σῖτος οὐθὲν ὠφελεῖ ἡμᾶς). οὐδὲν γάρ σε ταῦτα ὠφελήσει *for it will profit you nothing* AcPl Ha 2, 22. οὐ γὰρ τὰ ἐκ τῶν βιβλίων τοσοῦτόν με ὠφελεῖν ὑπελάμβανον ὅσον *for, in my judgment, accounts derived from books were not worth as much as* Papias (2:4). Cp. B 4:9; IRo 6:1. Pass. *receive help, be benefited* (X., An. 5, 1, 12; EpArist 294; Philo; Jos., Ant. 2, 81 οὐδὲν ὠφελοῦντο) τί ὠφεληθήσεται ἄνθρωπος; *what good will it do one?* **Mt 16:26.** Cp. **Mk 5:26; Lk 9:25; 1 Cor 13:3;** Hv 2, 2, 2; s 9, 13, 2. ἔν τινι *by someth.* (cp. Ps 88:23) **Hb 13:9.** τὶ ἔκ τινος ὠφεληθῆναι *be benefited by someone* or *someth. in a certain respect* (X., Mem. 2, 4, 1 al.; Jer 2:11) **Mt 15:5; Mk 7:11** (Goodsp., Probs. 60–62; RBorger, TRu 52, '87, 25); Pol 13:2.

ⓑ w. personal obj. in the dat. (poets since Aeschyl.; prose wr. since Aristot., Rhetor. 1, 1; ins) οὐδέν μοι ὠφελήσει τὰ τερπνὰ τοῦ κόσμου *the joys* (but s. τερπνός) *of the world will not benefit me at all* IRo 6:1 v.l.

ⓒ abs., of a thing ὠφελεῖ *it is of value* **Ro 2:25.** W. a neg. **J 6:63** (Jos., Ant. 18, 127; cp. ApcSed 7:6 τί ὠφελοῦν τὰ κάλλη . . . ; Tat. 27, 3 τί δ' ἂν ὠφελήσειε λέξις Ἀττική . . . ;—LTondelli, Biblica 4, 1923, 320–27). οὐδὲν ὠφελεῖ **Mt 27:24** *nothing does any good, avails* (s. 2).

❷ **to be successful in accomplishing some objective, *accomplish,*** abs. of a pers. (ApcEsdr 6:23 p. 32, 2 Tdf.; Just., A I, 52, 9) οὐδὲν ὠφελεῖ *he is accomplishing nothing* **Mt 27:24** (s. 1c). Cp. **J 12:19.**—B. 1353f. Schmidt, Syn. IV 162–72. DELG s.v. 2 ὀφέλλω. M-M.

ὠφέλιμος, ον (ὠφελέω; Thu.+) ***useful, beneficial, advantageous*** τινί *for someone* or *for someth.* (Polyaenus 8 prooem.) **Tit 3:8;** Hv 3, 6, 7. Also πρός τι (Pla., Rep. 10, 607d) **1 Ti 4:8ab; 2 Tim 3:16.** Heightened ὑπεράγαν ὠφέλιμος 1 Cl 56:2.—The superl. (Artem. 5 p. 252, 13; Ps.-Lucian, Hipp. 6; Vi. Aesopi II p. 306, 12 Ebh.; Jos., Ant. 19, 206; PMich 149 XVIII, 20 [II AD]) subst. τὰ ὠφελιμώτατα *what is particulary helpful* 62:1 (Appian, Bell. Civ. 5, 44 §186 τὰ μάλιστα ὠφελιμώτατα).—DELG s.v. 2 ὀφέλλω. M-M.

ὤφθην s. ὁράω.